sky SPORTS

FOOTBALL YEARBOOK 2012-2013

EDITORS: GLENDA ROLLIN AND JACK ROLLIN

headline

First published in 2012
by HEADLINE PUBLISHING GROUP

1

Front cover photographs: (left) Gareth Bale (Tottenham Hotspur) – *Action Images/Andrew Couldridge*; (centre and background) Demba Ba (Newcastle) – *Stu Forster/Getty Images*; (right) Sergio Aguero (Manchester City) – *David Davies/PA Archive/Press Association Images*

Spine photograph: Andrea Barzagli (Italy) and Fernando Torres (Spain), Euro 2012 Final, July 2012 – *Action Images/Carl Recine Livepic*

Back cover photographs: (above) Philipp Lamm (Bayern Munich), Salomon Kalou (Chelsea) and Didier Drogba (Chelsea), Champion's League Final, May 2012 – *Martin Meissner/AP/Press Association Images*; (below) Steven Davis (Rangers) and James Forrest (Celtic) – *Action Images/Jason Cairnduff Livepic*

Cataloguing in Publication Data is available from the British Library

ISBN 978 0 7553 6355 1 (Hardback)
ISBN 978 0 7553 6356 8 (Trade paperback)

Typeset by Wearset Ltd, Boldon, Tyne and Wear

Printed and bound by
CPI Group (UK) Ltd, Croydon, CR0 4YY

Headline's policy is to use papers that are natural, renewable and recyclable products and made from wood grown in sustainable forests. The logging and manufacturing processes are expected to conform to the environmental regulations of the country of origin.

HEADLINE PUBLISHING GROUP
An Hachette UK Company
338 Euston Road
London NW1 3BH

www.headline.co.uk
www.hachette.co.uk

CONTENTS

Foreword by Graeme Souness 5
Introduction and Acknowledgements 6
Editorial 7
Daily Round-Up 2011–12 10
Cups and Ups and Downs Diary 35
Review of the Season 41

THE FA PREMIER LEAGUE AND FOOTBALL LEAGUE: THE CLUBS
The Clubs 46
English League Players Directory 418
English League Players – Index 560

ENGLISH CLUBS STATISTICS
English League Tables 2011–12 36
Football League Play-Offs 2011–12 38
Leading Goalscorers 2011–12 40
The FA Charity Shield Winners 1908–2011 45
The FA Community Shield 2011 45
Transfers 2011–12 570
The New Foreign Legion 2011–12 580
English League Honours 1888 to 2012 583
League Attendances since 1946–47 592
English League Attendances 2011–12 593

THE LEAGUE CUP AND OTHER FOOTBALL LEAGUE COMPETITIONS
League Cup Finalists 1961–2012 595
Carling Cup 2011–12 596
Johnstone's Paint Trophy 2011–12 603
Football League Competition Attendances 606

THE FA CUP
FA Cup Finals 1872–2012 607
FA Cup Attendances 1969–2012 609
The E.ON FA Cup 2011–12 (*preliminary and qualifying rounds*) 610
The E.ON FA Cup 2011–12 (*competition proper*) 614

SCOTTISH FOOTBALL
Review of the Scottish Season 2011–12 676
Scottish League Tables 2011–12 677
The Scottish Football League Clubs 678
Scottish League Play-Offs 2011–12 762
Scottish League Honours 1890 to 2012 763
Scottish League Attendances 2011–12 768
Scottish League Cup Finals 1946–2012 769
Scottish Communities League Cup 2011–12 770
League Challenge Finals 1991–2012 772
Ramsdens League Challenge Cup 2011–12 773
Scottish Cup Finals 1874–2012 775
William Hill Scottish Cup 2011–12 777

WELSH AND NORTHERN IRISH FOOTBALL
Welsh Football 2011–12 782
Northern Irish Football 2011–12 786

EUROPEAN FOOTBALL
European Football Review 2011–12 790
European Cup Finals 1956–1992 and UEFA Champions League Finals 1993–2012 791
UEFA Champions League 2011–12 792
European Cup-Winners' Cup Finals 1961–99 808
Inter-Cities Fairs Cup Finals 1958–71 808
UEFA Cup Finals 1972–97 809
UEFA Cup Finals 1998–2009 809
UEFA Europa League Finals 2010–12 809
UEFA Europa League 2011–12 810
UEFA Champions League 2012–13 – participating clubs 842
UEFA Europa League 2012–13 – participating clubs 842

Summary of Appearances (*British and Irish Clubs*) 844
FIFA Club World Cup 2011 845
World Club Championship 846
European Super Cup 2011 846

INTERNATIONAL FOOTBALL
International Directory 847
Euro 2012 Qualifying Competition 872
Euro 2012 Finals Review 891
Euro 2012 Final Competition 892
World Cup 2014 Qualifying Competition 895
World Cup 2014 Fixtures 897
Olympics 2012 898
The World Cup 1930–2010 899
European Football Championship (*formerly European Nations' Cup*) 899
British and Irish International Results 1872–2012 900
Other British and Irish International Matches 2011–12 922
International Appearances 1872–2012 924
British and Irish International Goalscorers since 1872 953
British & Irish International Managers 957
South America 958
Africa 960
North America 960
UEFA Under-21 Championship 2011–13 961
FIFA Under-20 World Cup 962
The NextGen Series Trophy 962
UEFA Under-19 Championship 2011–12 963
UEFA Under-17 Championship 2011–12 963
England Under-21 Results 1976–2012 964
England C 2011–12 966
British and Irish Under-21 Teams 2011–12 967
British Under-21 Appearances 1976–2012 969

NON-LEAGUE FOOTBALL
Blue Square Premier 2011–12 625
Blue Square North and South 2011–12 627
Blue Square Premier Clubs 628
FA Schools & Youth Games 2011–12 981
Schools Football 2011–12 984
University Football 2012 984
Women's Football 2011–12 985
Non-League Tables 2011–12 992
The FA Trophy 2011–12 993
The FA Vase 2011–12 995
The FA County Youth Cup 2011–12 998
The FA Youth Cup 2011–12 999
The FA Inter-League Cup 1002
The FA Sunday Cup 2011–12 1003
FA Premier Reserve League 2011–12 1004
The Central League 2011–12 1005
FA Academy Under-18 League 2011–12 1005
The Football Combination 2011–12 1005

INFORMATION AND RECORDS
Sky Sports Football Yearbook Honours 8
Football Awards 2012 9
Refereeing and the Laws of the Game 567
National List of Referees and Assistants for Season 2012–13 568
The Things They Said 581
Important Addresses 1006
Football Club Chaplaincy 1007
Obituaries 1008
The Football Records 1021
International Records 1031
Landmarks 1032
Ads 1033
The FA Barclays Premiership and Coca-Cola Football League Fixtures 2012–13 1034
Blue Square Premier Fixtures 2012–13 1044
The Scottish Premier League and Football League Fixtures 2012–13 1047
Other Fixtures 2012–13 1052
Stop Press 1054

FOREWORD

I've seen the great Sky revolution from both sides in my time in the business – from the manager's dug-out to the pundit's chair.

And what a long way we have come as I look back to a decade or so ago when I was on the other side of the fence, an old-school boss looking in on this new kid on the block.

Like a few others I was suspicious of the ever-growing media's ideas and intentions in those days. But it has not taken me long to realise how wrong that view is.

There simply can't be a better influence on the game than Sky. The coverage, the interest, the debate, the professionalism and the sheer love of the game. I have come across it all in my new line of work.

You just have to see the talent and technology around to know that football is in safe hands when it comes to Sky. It certainly changed my mind and my attitude.

This is an era of the greatest promotion our great old game has had. All of the fresh ways of looking at the game, all of the depth we go into, but – above all – the dedication we have to covering football professionally and properly.

There has been so much ground-breaking that it is hard to keep up, but it is all based on treating football with respect and giving the public a better and more interesting insight.

Personally I really enjoy the debate we have in the studio before and after games. Of course, we don't all share the same views – it would be pretty dull if we did. But I like the fact that we can go into things and say our piece and encourage discussion.

It is a privilege to be part of something so big and so committed to being the best. I always looked for professionalism in football as a player and a manager – and I have found that at Sky.

We do it right, we take it seriously.

Enjoy this year's Sky Sports Football Yearbook, and let's hope the season ahead is as good as the last.

Graeme Souness, Sky Sports

Graeme Souness

INTRODUCTION

The 43rd edition of the Yearbook, our tenth with sponsors Sky Sports, gives full coverage of the Euro 2012 competition with both the qualifying stages and the finals in Poland and Ukraine included. With the next major tournament now looking ahead to the World Cup 2014 in Brazil, there are results from around the world for the qualifying stages up to the time of going to press, plus the fixtures for the European countries starting their preliminaries during 2012–13.

While the game at the highest international level is well catered for in the new edition, both the Champions League and Europa League have their usual comprehensive details included with results, goalscorers, attendances and full-line ups for the qualifying rounds and also from the respective group stages onwards.

The Daily Round-up has carried on expanding as an informative, detailed log of the previous season's events, but it is not designed to pinpoint specific items at a glance. This is not its function, but to give extra weight to the concept, the concise feature entitled Cups and Ups and Downs Diary, that proved popular when introduced for last year's edition, can again be found at the end of the June entry for the Daily Round-up with dates of those events affecting cup finals, plus promotion and relegation issues.

The 2011–12 campaign arguably provided the most exciting climax to the race for the Premier League title. It proved a fitting end to the league's 20th season and also recorded a record number of 1,066 goals. There were plenty of high-scoring matches as well as a sprinkling of goalless draws; indeed a cross-section of everything that occurs in a season. All these facets are reproduced in the pages devoted to not only the Premier League, but the three Football League competitions, too, as well as all major allied cup competitions.

While transfer fees are invariably those reported at the time and rarely given as official figures, the edition reflects those listed at the time. For the new season, too, at least one club is likely to play at a new venue – Rotherham United. As for Newcastle United, though the ground remains the same, the name was changed to Sports Direct Arena, but is still referred to as St James' Park by the club's supporters.

The Players Directory and its accompanying A to Z index enables the reader to quickly find the club of any specific player. In the club-by-club pages that contain the line-ups of all league matches, appearances are split into starting line-ups and those who were brought in as substitutes. But in the Players Directory the totals show figures combined.

Throughout the book players sent off are designated thus ■, substitutes in the club pages are 12, 13 and 14 with 15 for the substitute goalkeeper. Squad numbers are not used.

In addition to competitions already mentioned there is full coverage of Scottish Premier League and Scottish League and cup competitions. There are also sections devoted to Welsh, Irish, Women's football, the Under-21s and various other youth levels affecting UEFA, schools, reserve team, academies, referees and the leading non-league competitions as well as the work of the chaplains at clubs. The chief tournaments outside the UK at club and national level are not forgotten. The International Directory itself features Europe in some depth as well as every FIFA country's international records for the previous year.

Naturally there are international appearances and goals scored by players for England, Scotland, Northern Ireland, Wales and the Republic. For easy reference, those players making appearances and scoring goals in the season covered are picked out in bold type.

The Editors would like to extend their appreciation to the publishers Headline for excellent support in the preparation of this edition, particularly Jonathan Taylor for photographic selection throughout the book. Thanks, too, to Tony Brown for sequences and instances of match results in the Records Section, Ian Nannestad for the obituaries and as ever thanks to John English for his conscientious proof reading.

ACKNOWLEDGEMENTS

In addition the Editors are also keen to thank the following individuals and organisations for their co-operation. David Barber at the Football Association, David C. Thomson (Scottish League), Dr Malcolm Brodie, Grahame Lloyd, Rev. Nigel Sands, Ken Goldman, Marshall Gillespie, Michael Joyce, Sean Creedon, Bob Bannister, Martin Cooper, Alan Platt and Emily Kitchin (Headline).

Special mention as well for the indefatigable, ebullient and loquacious Lorraine Jerram, for her generosity, clinical expertise, constant support, determined resilience, enduring patience, endearing sincerity, perspicacity and appreciation, not to forget her unfailing humour, stoicism, quick-wit, courtesy, quiet consideration and understated authority; the consummate professional.

Finally sincere thanks to John Anderson, Simon Dunnington, Geoff Turner, Brian Tait and the staff at Wearset for their much appreciated efforts in the production of the book throughout the year.

EDITORIAL

Even before the wheel was invented, things used to revolve in cycles. So, surely one day England must win another major international tournament. Or will they? It has been a while since 1966. Moreover, as far as Euro 2012 is concerned, the feeling pre-tournament was one with no great expectations of achieving anything startling. Roy Hodgson, the new man at the steering end, had had no real quality time to implement any new, even controversial or untried ideas, having to approach it with his well known sensible, unsensational attitude to the task for which he had been taken on.

After all, he was not in charge of the qualifying campaign and had managed a couple of single goal friendly wins in the run-up to the main event in Poland and the Ukraine. But once out there and England drawing their first group match with the much fancied and confident French team that had gone 21 matches unbeaten, the attitude at home changed dramatically. Suddenly "going all the way" replaced "getting to the quarter-finals". Sadly there was little substantial evidence for such a switch to confidence, apart from after losing the lead to Sweden and conceding two goals before pulling off a victory, the first ever against that country in a competitive match – burying memories of Swedes and Turnips.

The last group fixture was against Ukraine and the hitherto suspended Wayne Rooney was back. Yet while his header could be measured in inches rather than yards, it was enough to win the match; the locals, with far more chances, merely lacked a marksman. But it mattered little, because England were now in the last eight and finishing top of the group, able to avoid Spain and play Italy instead. The media was now convincing even the most doubting of Thomases that the heartache of 46 years was in danger of being bypassed.

Fortunately, the Italians' finishing was wretched. For England, aside of a well-organised defence, any midfield effectiveness was patchy; there were too many unforced errors in conceding possession and the frailty of the attack overexposed. The counter-attacking idea – where was that one? But as long as the match went on without Italy scoring, there was always a chance, though this came after a deadlocked extra time in the penalty shoot-out with the possibility of snatching victory from the jaws of mediocrity. Usually we don't do penalties and the wheel of misfortune again spun away from us.

As mentioned in last year's Editorial, penalties should remain a punishment not an equal opportunity. Players missing spot kicks are pilloried. You might just as well put them in the stocks. Tossing a coin would be kinder, but the only fair answer is playing on until a "proper" goal is scored. It is still possible to win a knock-out competition without scoring anything except in a shoot-out. How is this football?

Yet on this occasion England had been second best in the 120 minutes and the Italians deserved to go on. Interestingly enough, the media cleverly responded. Unleashing those quietly kept in the background during the era of erupting euphoria, this cunningly allowed for a re-evaluation of the situation. Moving the goalposts was a softening of the stance for those who had unreservedly championed the cause weeks beforehand.

Roy and co. returned from the Euro-"rovers" excursion with no time to lick wounds for the next battle rapidly approaches: qualifying for the World Cup 2014 in Brazil (now ranked 11th!). The last time England played there in a World Cup we lost to the USA, in the days when we still considered we had taught the funny foreigners how to play.

As far as Euro 2012 was concerned, it was sad to see that, even with five officials operating at matches, an obvious goal was missed; goalkeepers still cleared their lines outside the penalty area and a spot of GBH as the ball was running over the bye-line still flourished. A couple of penalties were harshly awarded, sound claims for others ignored. Goal-line technology is promised at last. Yet sadly racism among spectators was evident at times. Overall, the standard of football was encouraging.

Vicente Del Bosque, relaxed, if dictatorial, as the Spanish main-man, presides over a team of all the talents; instinctive, innovative and in control. How we must envy them.

But back at base camp, 20 years of the Premier League has attracted many of the best players in the world. Alas most of them are foreign. It supplied the highest number to countries in Euro 2012. Its existence is in no small measure courtesy of the income derived from television sponsorship. In 2011–12 the full England squad had in the season called upon the services of 35 different players. The Under-21s used four fewer. Whereas the seniors blooded seven uncapped at full level, the intermediates had 18 new boys. Their futures will be tested quite definitely in the months to come. Alas the Under-19s reached the semi-final of the UEFA tournament only to slip up on Greece.

Mercifully the World Cup qualifying group should hold few real terrors, but it will mean little enough. In the final analysis we need more of the F-word: flair, finesse, fluency and finish. Nothing short of this will do; the alternative is failure, yet again. It is a tall order. These are not the qualities for which we are renowned. Yet why create such fuss? We defeated Spain in a friendly match in November and FIFA ranks us fourth in the world! Power, of course, is the difference between being eccentric and just odd.

SKY SPORTS FOOTBALL YEARBOOK HONOURS

SKY SPORTS FOOTBALL YEARBOOK TEAM OF THE SEASON 2011–12

Joe Hart
(Manchester C)

Kyle Walker *(Tottenham H)* | Vincent Kompany *(Manchester C)* | Fabricio Coloccini *(Newcastle U)* | Leighton Baines *(Everton)*

Yohan Cabaye *(Newcastle U)* | Scott Parker *(Tottenham H)* | David Silva *(Manchester C)*

Yaya Toure
(Manchester C)

Sergio Aguero *(Manchester C)* | Robin Van Persie *(Arsenal)*

Manager:
Brendan Rodgers *(Swansea C)*

Substitutes:
Rio Ferdinand *(Manchester U)*
Ramires *(Chelsea)*
Wayne Rooney *(Manchester U))*

TWENTY YEARS OF THE PREMIER LEAGUE

Best: *Player* – Ryan Giggs (Manchester U)
Manager – Sir Alex Ferguson (Manchester U)
Team – Arsenal 2003–04
Season – 2011–12
Quote – Kevin Keegan "I will love it." 1996
Goal – Wayne Rooney, Manchester U v Manchester C, February 2011
Match – Manchester U 4 Manchester C, 3 September 2009
Save – Craig Gordon, Sunderland v Bolton W, December 2010
Celebration – Eric Cantona, Manchester U v Sunderland, December 1996

Public's team – Peter Schmeichel, Gary Neville, Ashley Cole, Steven Gerrard, Tony Adams, Nemanja Vidic, Cristiano Ronaldo, Paul Scholes, Alan Shearer, Thierry Henry, Ryan Giggs.

Experts' team – Peter Schmeichel, Gary Neville, Ashley Cole, Roy Keane, Rio Ferdinand, Tony Adams, Cristiano Ronaldo, Paul Scholes, Alan Shearer, Thierry Henry, Ryan Giggs.

EUROPEAN GOLDEN SHOE

The European Golden Shoe award is presented to the leading goalscorer in European League football. However, the determination of the winner comes from a points system which depends on the status of the country involved. The goals total is multiplied by either two, one and a half or just by one.

Thus for the unfortunate Aleksandrs Cekulajevs of the Estonian club Narva Trans, his 46 goals yielded him only 46 points, whereas Cristiano Ronaldo who also hit as many goals for Real Madrid is placed second with 92 points!

The first six places were as follows with Lionel Messi (Barcelona) top with 100 points from 50 goals and the outright winner for 2011–12.

Lionel Messi (Barcelona)	50	100
Cristiano Ronaldo (Real Madrid)	46	92
Robin Van Persie (Arsenal)	30	60
Klaas-Jan Huntelaar (Schalke)	29	58
Zlatan Ibrahimovic (AC Milan)	28	56
Wayne Rooney (Manchester United)	27	54

FOOTBALL AWARDS 2012

FOOTBALLER OF THE YEAR

The Football Writers' Association Sir Stanley Matthews Trophy for the Footballer of the Year was awarded to Robin Van Persie of Arsenal and Holland. Wayne Rooney (Manchester U) was runner-up, Paul Scholes (Manchester U) came third and Clint Dempsey (Fulham) was fourth.

Past Winners

1947–48 Stanley Matthews (Blackpool), 1948–49 Johnny Carey (Manchester U), 1949–50 Joe Mercer (Arsenal), 1950–51 Harry Johnston (Blackpool), 1951–52 Billy Wright (Wolverhampton W), 1952–53 Nat Lofthouse (Bolton W), 1953–54 Tom Finney (Preston NE), 1954–55 Don Revie (Manchester C), 1955–56 Bert Trautmann (Manchester C), 1956–57 Tom Finney (Preston NE), 1957–58 Danny Blanchflower (Tottenham H), 1958–59 Syd Owen (Luton T), 1959–60 Bill Slater (Wolverhampton W), 1960–61 Danny Blanchflower (Tottenham H), 1961–62 Jimmy Adamson (Burnley), 1962–63 Stanley Matthews (Stoke C), 1963–64 Bobby Moore (West Ham U), 1964–65 Bobby Collins (Leeds U), 1965–66 Bobby Charlton (Manchester U), 1966–67 Jackie Charlton (Leeds U), 1967–68 George Best (Manchester U), 1968–69 Dave Mackay (Derby Co) shared with Tony Book (Manchester C), 1969–70 Billy Bremner (Leeds U), 1970–71 Frank McLintock (Arsenal), 1971–72 Gordon Banks (Stoke C), 1972–73 Pat Jennings (Tottenham H), 1973–74 Ian Callaghan (Liverpool), 1974–75 Alan Mullery (Fulham), 1975–76 Kevin Keegan (Liverpool), 1976–77 Emlyn Hughes (Liverpool), 1977–78 Kenny Burns (Nottingham F), 1978–79 Kenny Dalglish (Liverpool), 1979–80 Terry McDermott (Liverpool), 1980–81 Frans Thijssen (Ipswich T), 1981–82 Steve Perryman (Tottenham H), 1982–83 Kenny Dalglish (Liverpool), 1983–84 Ian Rush (Liverpool), 1984–85 Neville Southall (Everton), 1985–86 Gary Lineker (Everton), 1986–87 Clive Allen (Tottenham H), 1987–88 John Barnes (Liverpool), 1988–89 Steve Nicol (Liverpool), 1989–90 John Barnes (Liverpool), 1990–91 Gordon Strachan (Leeds U), 1991–92 Gary Lineker (Tottenham H), 1992–93 Chris Waddle (Sheffield W), 1993–94 Alan Shearer (Blackburn R), 1994–95 Jurgen Klinsmann (Tottenham H), 1995–96 Eric Cantona (Manchester U), 1996–97 Gianfranco Zola (Chelsea), 1997–98 Dennis Bergkamp (Arsenal), 1998–99 David Ginola (Tottenham H), 1999–2000 Roy Keane (Manchester U), 2000–01 Teddy Sheringham (Manchester U), 2001–02 Robert Pires (Arsenal), 2002–03 Thierry Henry (Arsenal), 2003–04 Thierry Henry (Arsenal), 2004–05 Frank Lampard (Chelsea), 2005–06 Thierry Henry (Arsenal), 2006–07 Cristiano Ronaldo (Manchester U), 2007–08 Cristiano Ronaldo (Manchester U), 2008–09 Ryan Giggs (Manchester U), 2009–10 Wayne Rooney (Manchester U), 2010–11 Scott Parker (West Ham U), 2011–12 Robin Van Persie (Arsenal).

THE PFA AWARDS 2012

Player of the Year: Robin Van Persie, Arsenal and Holland.
Young Player of the Year: Kyle Walker, Tottenham H and England.
Merit Award: Graham Alexander, Preston NE.

OTHER AWARDS

EUROPEAN FOOTBALLER OF THE YEAR 2011

Lionel Messi, Barcelona and Argentina

WORLD PLAYER OF THE YEAR 2011

Lionel Messi, Barcelona and Argentina

WOMEN'S PLAYER OF THE YEAR 2011

Homare Sawa, INAC Kobe Leonessa and Japan

SCOTTISH PFA PLAYER OF THE YEAR AWARDS 2012

Player of the Year: Charlie Mulgrew, Celtic and Scotland.
Young Player of the Year: James Forrest, Celtic and Scotland.
First Division Player of the Year: Farid El Alagui, Falkirk.
Second Division Player of the Year: Jon Robertson, Cowdenbeath.
Third Division Player of the Year: Steven May, Alloa Ath.
Manager of the Year: Derek Adams, Ross Co.

SCOTTISH FOOTBALL WRITERS' ASSOCIATION 2012

Player of the Year: Charlie Mulgrew, Celtic and Scotland.
Young Player of the Year: James Forrest, Celtic and Scotland.
Manager of the Year: Neil Lennon, Celtic.

DAILY ROUND-UP 2011–12

JULY

MPs aim at football . . . Celtic already ahead . . . Aguero at £38m to MC . . . England WC 2014 opponents.

1 MPs are gunning for FIFA. England Ladies snatch late win over NZ. Tug-of-war tightens over Fabregas. Chelsea joins the Nasri queue. Tranmere's Jennings sought by Bayern!

2 More departures likely at Arsenal. Villas-Boas warns Chelsea over behaviour and Torres will get his old personal trainer back.

3 Government is concerned over Olympic Stadium row. Fenerbahce president arrested over match-fixing. Kevin Keen joins Steve Clarke as first team coach at Liverpool.

4 Tevez wants away for reasons of family; Man C will require £50m. Kraut kids bomb out England U17s despite fight back.

5 Hargreaves seeks club via YouTube. England Ladies take out Japan to reach last eight. Hamann is new Stockport boss. Rushden decides to call it a day.

6 Nasri's departure nears as Gervinho ex-ASEC Mimosas arrives. Adam goes to Liverpool for £8.5m. Stefan Savic £6m joins Clichy £7m at Man C. Earnshaw moves to Cardiff. Qatar 2022 may see three halves. England Ladies will play France.

7 Modric told to stay at Spurs. Fulham through ok in Faeroes draw. Twente roof collapse kills one injures 16. Sunderland makes it nine newcomers with Vaughan, Brown and O'Shea signings.

8 Man C Eastlands ground now called Etihad Stadium after £400m sponsorship. Santander becomes seventh club to file for creditor protection in Spain. Essien will miss start with injury. Wenger is anxious to retain Fabregas and Nasri. U-17 WC: Uruguay beats Brazil easily, Mexico edges Germany in semis. Copa America is well under way: ten games, 7 draws, 13 goals!

9 WC Ladies victims in shoot-out, too, as French put us out on the spot. Arsenal is keen on Downing.

10 Modric is unhappy with Spurs chairman. Qatar whistleblower admits lie. Hope Powell lashes into "cowards" at shoot-out.

11 Adebayor is no show for training. Chelsea bids £27m for Modric. Carry on Pearce as U-21 boss gets new deal. FIFA gives up on Qatar bribe probe.

12 Mystery over offer said to be by Corinthians for Tevez. Sneijder is being tracked by Man U.

13 Modric puts in transfer request. Downing may go to Liverpool for £20m. Wenger hits out at Xavi over Fabregas. Roger Johnson goes to Wolves for £7m. Ch Lge: Bangor beaten by HJK and Linfield also held initially by BATE. Women's WC Japan, USA win semis vice Sweden and France.

14 Baldini heads for Roma come October. Vieira retires. Sheffield FC rule book (actually pamphlet) c.1857 sells for £881,250 at Sotheby's. Carry on tinkering says PL. E Lge: Fulham put Crusaders to the sword. Follows helps Llanelli take lead over Tbilisi. Glentoran upset by Vorskla. Oh! Bohs against Olimpija, St Pat's edged by Shakhtyor, Dundee U concedes one in Wroclaw and TNS hit by Midtjylland.

15 "No offer" Corinthians up Tevez bid to £38m. FA appoints Roger Burden as vice-chairman. Darlo – Toon friendly sparks pitch invasion. Bribes stay on FIFA agenda.

16 Tevez fluffs pen so Argies lose to Uruguay in Copa shoot-out. Wanting away boys are Fabregas, Modric, Nasri and yes, Tevez.

17 Japs shoo Yanks in Women's WC shoot-out, Paraguay does same to Brazil in Copa and Peru and Venezuela are the others in last four vice Colombia and Chile respectively.

18 Sir Alex warns over Man C. Wenger will get "wonga." Bryan Robson under scrutiny over company avoiding FA rules re-ownership. Spurs snap up Coulibaly, 16, Ivory Coast. FL is puzzled over who owns which club.

19 Match-fixing appears rife. MPs continue investigation into how game is run. Theyab Awana (UAE) back heels penalty v Lebanon! Suarez double sends Uruguay to Copa final against ten-man Peru.

20 Corinthians scrap Tevez deal, but Aguero may join Man C. N'Zogbia wants away from Wigan. Chelsea lures Lukaku. Paraguay beats Venezuela on pens – of course.

21 Inter takes Tevez interest. Bin Hammam faces FIFA enquiry. Becks writes off Man C. Torres is unimpressive on tour. Better than Messi? Rooney aims to be. E Lge: Fulham ease through, Dundee U checks three goal lead and is out, Llanelli and TNS both ship five, Bohs and Glentoran depart, too, but St Pat's battle bravely on. FL will bench only five subs.

22 Tensions rise at Man C. Chelsea £7.9m capture Courtois heads on loan to Atletico Madrid and Blues may add Romeu to roster. Soccer boom in USA is boosted by Man U visit. Bin Hammam will go to court if banned.

23 SPL start sees Hearts hold McCoist's Rangers. Ramsdens Cup with non-league Deveronvale and Buckie Thistle in – and out; Stranraer gives Morton its usual kick start, this time eight goals! Life ban imposed on Bin Hammam by FIFA over bribes for votes. Peru takes third Copa spot over Venezuela.

24 Celtic wins at Hibs to open two pt lead over Rangers! Forlan double, Suarez solo lifts Uruguay's record 15th Copa title over Paraguay. Balotelli bother at Man C. Becks still seethes over failed WC bid. Welsh club Cardiff targets Scots skipper Miller from Turkish Bursa. Bin Hammam will fight ban.

25 Xavi, Messi and Ronaldo listed for top UEFA award – Rooney and Vidic from Man U were among the top ten nominated.

26 Man U eyes Sneijder again, Man C looks to Aguero. FIFA zooms in on Caribbean officials. Batista resigns as Argies coach. Shevchenko had better first season at Chelsea than Torres! Ch Lge: Rangers lose to Malmo at Ibrox.

27 Sergio Aguero arrives in Manchester. Farce of WC draw when competition already started in some areas. Birmingham owner has assets frozen. "Little Pea" suffers concussion. Ch Lge: Shamrock edged in Copenhagen. Barclays Asian Trophy pairs Villa – Chelsea final.

28 Aguero seals £38m move from Atletico Madrid. Migraine concerns over Chicharito. US fires coach Bradley. Brazil's WC plans under microscope. E Lge: Stoke takes slender lead over Hajduk; Fulham held in Split; Sligo holds Vorskla; Hearts draw at Paksi but St Pat's lose to Karpaty.

29 Man C wants to swap Tevez for Eto'o. Villa signs N'Zogbia. Klinsmann is US coach. WC draw is imminent and concerns over England group before it's made! Teixeira is anti-England but Pele is on our side. MPs are still out to get FA. C Cup: AFC Dons bow to Crawley. Arsenal leaves Fabregas out of tournament. England U-20s zero all with N Korea.

30 England gets Montenegro again, Ukraine, Poland, Moldova and San Marino – scorers of quickest goal conceded! Scots and Welsh in same group, Northern Ireland in with Russians and Republic will meet Germans. SPL: Rangers win at St J. Gerrard is to miss start. Scottish C Cup: Livi hits six against Arbroath's ten men, Airdrie gets five beating Stirling's nine. Ten sent off in 15 ties. End note: Bolton (The Trotters) lose reserve game at Fulham conceding seven goals, five scored by Trotta!

31 Wilshere injured as Arsenal held by Yankie Red Bulls. Redknapp dismisses top-four likelihood. Chelsea will offer more for Modric.

AUGUST

Street riots affect fixtures . . . Man U tipped for title . . . Mata man at Chelsea . . . Liverpool goes top!

1 Newcastle will let Barton go. Balotelli is restless. Liverpool owner seeks Ch Lge berth. Jim Jefferies sacked by Hearts. What's the Mata? Arsenal miss out on Valencia winger. England U-20s are goalless again with Argies. Spain wins U-19 title edging Czechs.

2 High-tech PL will happen and issues warning to FIFA over fixtures.

3 Fabregas and Tevez are given more time. Ch Lge: Rangers out as their nine lose to Malmo's ten. Goodwillie goes to Blackburn.

4 Eriksson says winter break essential for England team. Toon in a spin as Pardew warns players. Chelsea captures Oriol Romeu £4.7m from Barca. Mears follows Lee with broken leg at Bolton. E Lge: Fulham and Stoke do the "splits" with – Hajduk and RNK! Hearts send Paks packing. Sligo and St Pat's are out. England draws third goalless with Mexico in FIFA U-20 WC.

5 FLC starts: Blackpool wins at Hull – but no reports as some media at odds with PL and FL over rights. Wenger urges Fabregas to stay. Man C signs Costel Pantilimon 6ft 8in Romanian gk. Scholes signs off with goal as Man U hits Cosmos for six (76,000).

6 Quiet FL start: 84 goals, seven red cards. Leicester off to flier in ten a side at Coventry. Soton stamps on Leeds. No Brum start for City at Derby (27,210). Brighton scrapes 98th min winner at new venue against Donny (20,219). Chopra double (second was his 100th) as Ipswich downs Bristol C. L1: Colchester hits four at PNE; Sheff joy two: U at Oldham, W home to Rochdale. L2: New boys: AFC Dons edged out by Bristol R, Crawley's ten held at Vale. SPL; Severin (Dundee U) suffers triple fracture against St M. Fifers – ICT share six. SL1: Hamilton edges Ayr. SL2: Arbroath six against three Albion gks – two sent off! SL3: Annan high five; Gunn all four for Elgin.

7 FLC: Hammers grounded by late Miller strike for Cardiff. SPL: Ezaguirre breaks leg as Celtic wins at Aberdeen.

8 London riots lead to calling off Tuesday's C Cup games at Charlton, C Palace, West Ham and Bristol C, too. FIFA will charge ten Caribbean officials with corruption.

9 C Cup: Barnsley, Coventry, Derby, Doncaster, Forest, Hull and Portsmouth are FLC casualties but Burnley (Rodriguez 4) hits six against Burton after six shared in 90 mins; Bournemouth gets five, fours for winners Huddersfield, Leicester, MK Dons, Posh and Saints. England game with Holland called off. U-20s out as Nigeria scores – England fourth game no goals!

10 N Ireland puts four past Faeroes in Euro 2012 game. Friendlies: Republic held by Croatia, Wales lose to Aussies but Scots beat Danes. U-21: N Ireland repeats senior score v Faeroes, Scots beat Norway, but Wales loses to Hungary. Fabregas nears to Barca.

11 Spurs game off, Cheltenham and AFC Telford, too. Gordon Taylor calls for PFA members to set example. Jose Enrique on way £7m to Liverpool as Anfield lists £50m in moves. Mutu and Tamas banned for drinking by Romania.

12 Cheltenham on! Robbie Keane may go to LA Galaxy. Season over? Five Daily Telegraph pundits give Man U the nod. Stockport opens BSP with FGR draw.

13 PL back: punch-up in goalless Toon-Goners affair; "slapper" Gervinho red-carded (19th such PL debutant) in Barton clash, eight yellows. Ward is volley-good for Wolves at injury-hit Blackburn. King Kenny complains of no Richardson red by ref Dowd; scorer Suarez misses pen in Sunderland draw. Given to saving – Shay gets pt for Villa at Fulham (Hughes 400th PL game). Bolton four-play (Cahill special) silences newcomers QPR, but Canaries in better voice at Wigan leveller. FLC: Goals? 13 scored in ten games but at least one in each. Ref Taylor comes under fire for nine-man Leeds losing to ten-man Boro and home fans unhappy with hierarchy. Reading brings Leicester to earth. Soton hits club record 8th successive win at Barnsley. Brighton single coasts it at Pompey but Lawrence post-pen shot. Coventry edged out at Birmingham. One is enough for Hammers at Donny. Palace is up to Parr over Burnley. L1: Lester's 97th leveller for Chesterfield home to Stevenage. Sheff U sends Brentford packing. Buchanan's belt seals it on left-back bow for Tranmere at Orient. Charlton surprises Notts at Meadow Lane. L2: Macc old boy Barnett strikes them for Crawley. Cheltenham stuns Swindon. Rotherham four-play too much Argyle. Vet Westwood two mins – so it's Cobblers to Shots! Torquay cruel on old boss Buckle at Bristol R. NB: only nine of 72 FL teams 100%! SPL: Hooper injury mars Celtic five star at Dundee U. Rangers take care of ICT, but Motherwell stays top at St M. SL only four 100%! Div 1: Accies hit five over Ross and Raith wins at QoS; Div 2: Stirling on goal standard with five at Dumbarton. Div 3: Annan edges it at Peterhead. BSP: Promoted all lose relegated two draw. Reprieved Wrexham get 4306 for Camb U all square. WL: Bangor starts beating Llanelli.

14 Og from Young shot gives Man U the nod at WBA, but Ferdinand suffers hamstring injury. Chelsea has to settle for goalless at Stoke. SPL: Hibs concede four to Killie.

15 Debut double strike for Aguero (first PL since 2005) as Swans are pummelled by Man C (only home winners). Song Billong hit by ban for Barton clash. Fabregas unveiled at Barca. Robbie Keane moves to LA at £3.5m. Steve Kean hit by drink driving ban. Mikel's father is kidnapped in Nigeria. Walcott brought to book by going into print.

16 Ch Lge: Walcott gives Arsenal precious Udinese lead. UEFA looks at Etihad deal. FLC: Saints hit five at Ipswich, West Ham four at Watford and even Leeds get four. BBC misses two late Palace goals – so Coventry actually loses! L1: Charlton roll on at Colchester, Sheff U gives Walsall two goal start and wins. L2: AFC Dons win at Plymouth, Crawley moves to second behind leaders Rotherham, winners at Crewe. BSP: Grimsby crashes at Braintree!

17 Festival leaves Spurs seeking hotel for Hearts tie but change of such over Modric?. Chelsea aims for Porto pair. Fabregas debut as Barca sub as Super Cup ends with three red cards and Real losing and JM in trouble. Parker is target of QPR. Brighton put skids under Cardiff; Leicester loses again.

18 E Lge: Hearts sink to five-star Spurs, Stoke stuns Thun, Fulham four-play rattles Dnepr and Birmingham earns a goalless Madeira slice to Nacional, but Celtic fails to beat Sion and Rangers even lose to Maribor. Shamrock holds Partizan. Only a Mata of time as Chelsea seeks Valencia's forward? Malaysian Tony Fernandes buys QPR and chases signings. Man U aims to cut interest payments.

19 Nasri will figure for Arsenal as Wenger stays under pressure. De Gea needs to gain confidence. Cash-strapped Everton may not sign anyone.

20 Arsenal bows to Liverpool and suffers 56th PL red under Wenger. Chelsea scrapes late win over WBA after trailing to AVB relief. Ryan Taylor's 62nd min goal suits Toon at Sunderland in 145th derby, but ref Webb reckoned Larsson did "no arm" in 13th min. Big Eck gets Villa approval in win over Blackburn. Vorm turns to save Wigan pen show in Swans draw. Hit by virus but QPR gets the winning bug at Everton. FLC: Soton extends record winning streak to ten and eleventh at home in edging Millwall. Seven-up Posh (Tomlin 3) takes out Ipswich. Blackpool fight back (Kevin Phillips 2) robs Brighton of best start in 58 years, but Derby's fourth win and no goals is Rams best since five in 1905-06 openers as no-pts Donny loses. Steele two Reading pen saves give Barnsley win. Earnshaw hits 200th career goal as Cardiff draws at Burnley. Schmeichel red as Leicester chucks two goal lead in Forest draw in meeting of Sven and McClaren. L1: Baldock treble in new toppers MK Dons six-hit on Chesterfield. Brentford stings pointless O's five times. Bury ends Wycombe's 14-game run. Scunny holds up Charlton. Sheff U drops two pts at Tranmere, too. L2: Three more for Crawley goals and pts at Torquay. Rotherham held by Barnet. Gills lean on Argyle. Crewe are still chasing a pt after loss to Shrews. BSP: No 100% as Gateshead held by ten-man Kettering. FGR gets six at Atherton, Luton five at home to Southport. SPL: Away winners Dunfermline and St M are third and fourth respectively. SL1: Hamilton at Partick, Raith home to Morton both in draws, so no 100%. SL2: Cowden strikes five at Airdrie. SL3: Only Annan stays three out of three beating Alloa. No games in Spain due to strike.

21 Hairy at times, but stripy Man C clips Bolton for top points. De Laet for Norwich, even later hit for Stoke. Wolves maintain good start beating Fulham. SPL: Commons has pen saved and St J wins at Celtic first time in 13 years, so Rangers go top displacing Motherwell. L2: Oxford wins at Swindon.

22 Man U, second youngest under Sir Alex, makes Spurs first of season a loser. Liverpool eyes another Uruguayan. Fabregas scores for Barca in trophy game. Nasri set to move.

23 Ch Lge: Apoel, Bayern, Genk, Dinamo Zagreb and Villarreal through to group stage. C Cup: PL casualties: Sunderland aet at Brighton, Norwich hit by MK Dons foursome, QPR taken out by Rochdale and Swans at Shrewsbury. Cardiff hits five, Leicester and Forest four apiece. SC Cup: Fifers battle sees East dumping Dunfermline. Hibs get five against Berwick. BSP: Gateshead, Wrexham, York, Braintree and Barrow stay as pacemakers. Wilshere injured. Nasri is finally off to Man C in £23m deal. Eto'o hits jackpot – in Russia with Anzhi paying £340,000 a week. Zico will coach Iraq. Romelu Lukaku moves to Chelsea for £18m and chases Alvaro Pereira. Spurs may drop Olympic idea. JM says sorry to Real fans.

24 Ch Lge: Arsenal needs Szczesny pen save to boost win over Udinese and join Benfica, Viktoria Plzen, Lyon and BATE Borisov in group stage. But UEFA kicks out Fenerbahce from the competition and promotes Turkish runners-up Trabzonspor from the E Lge over match-fixing! C Cup: Shot-shy Shots burst ten-man West Ham bubbles; Blackburn scores three in four minutes against Sheff Wed, Macc gives Bolton a bit of a fright. SC Cup: Inverness CT bows to Ayr. Mata joins Chelsea for £27m. Now Italian players may strike.

25 E Lge: Birmingham, Stoke win well; Spurs held by Hearts and Fulham loses in Dnepr, but all four through to group stage. Ch Lge draw: Man C toughie group with Bayern, Villarreal and Napoli; Man U easier with Benfica, Basle and Otelul (who?); Chelsea ok perhaps with Valencia, Leverkusen and Genk while Arsenal find themselves pitted against Marseille, Olympiakos and Dortmund. Chelsea ups the ante with £40m bid for Modric. C Cup: Newcastle win after Scunny scare. Peter Jackson quits at Bradford. Italy players prepare for strike. Sir Alex ends BBC boycott.

26 Sir Alex blasts FA. Bolton turns down Cahill bid by Arsenal. Super Cup gives Fabregas another goal for Barca over Porto and his second gong in ten days. Parker aims for Spurs. Barton goes to QPR.

27 Liverpool top! First time in over two years; Adam even scores with right as Bolton is beaten. Chelsea (Drogba injury) checked by gutsy Norwich until gk red card and sub Mata' 101st min winner for AVB. Goalless Swans draw with winless Sunderland and goalless levels Villa-Wolves. Wigan's Di Santo claws two goals to defeat QPR. Late Everton pen stuns two-pen missing Blackburn! FLC: Posh punished at best start Brighton. Run-ended Saints cling to second place as Leicester gets lucky. Derby sequence halted by ex-brickie Austin's double cementing Burnley win. Donny gets first point after pen-missing (vet James saves) Hayter atones against Bristol C. Loanee Brady sparks Hull over Reading. L1: Top six all winners. MK Dons edge Stevenage with debutant MacDonald on target. Charlton from behind at Bury. Colchester 18 secs start on way to foursome over Oldham. Birthday boy Nichols, 18, is Exeter scorer beating Chesterfield. Orient stays pointless as Miller scores two on Carlisle bow. L2: Crawley loses ground at Cheltenham. Le Fondre-less Rotherham beats Gills. Southend hits two in seven mins on way to Port Vale victory. Ten Shots draw at Oxford. Morecambe keeps Northampton at bay. First pts for Crewe as Plymouth suffer club record-equalling sixth home league defeat. SPL: Motherwell regains head at Dunfermline. SL1: Morton wins at Dundee to level top as Accies held by Livingston. SL2: Dumbarton six (Prunty 4) at E Fife! SL3: Stranraer six at Montrose! BSP: Born again Wrexham leaps ahead of Gateshead, both away winners at Alfreton, Barrow. Moves: Le Fondre to Reading; Ulises Davila Chivas to Chelsea (5th signing), Luke Young, Villa to QPR. La Liga resumes.

28 It is Capital punishment! Manchester hits 13 against N London's two: Man U savages Arsenal 8-2 (Rooney 3), Man C whacks five at Spurs (Dzeko 4). West Ham gets revenge at Forest in four-play. Ronaldo gets hat trick in six-goal Real romp. Phil Parkinson appointed at Bradford C.

29 Arsenal backs Wenger who will now splash cash. Fabregas scores again in La Liga five-goal romp. BSP: Wrexham, Gateshead, Darlington leading the way – all ex-FL clubs.

30 Hargreaves joins Man C. Gunners fan Mertesacker joins Arsenal. Fulham grabs Bryan Ruiz for £10.6m from Twente. Newcastle pays £5m for Inter's Davide Santon. C Cup: O's, Saints and Shots into round three. JPT: Crawley loses at Southend, five ties need shoot-out. UEFA misers cut youth payment because of domestic fixture clashes with Euro games.

31 Window closes: Raul Meireles to Chelsea £11.5m; Arteta to Arsenal £10m; Crouch to Stoke C £10m, Dann to Blackburn £7m, Palacios to Stoke C £6m, Parker to Spurs £6m are top moves, Joe Cole loaned to Lille. Modric stays at Spurs. Foster snubs England. Bellamy goes to Liverpool.

SEPTEMBER

Good England Euro prospects? . . . Torres toils . . . Goal-line technology tests . . . No easy Ch lge rides.

1 Boy Jones might get England call against Bulgars guided by Matthaus. Under-21s hit six against Azer. Republic prepares for crucial week. Man U posts £110m profit. Blackburn axes Diouf. McClaren may quit Forest. Cost-cutting at Liverpool has worked.

2 Euro 2012: Sofia so good as Rooney twosome helps easy win in Bulgaria and Wales surprises Montenegro to give Speed a respite. But N Ireland loses at home to Serbia and the Republic gets the bird after goalless with Slovakia.

Eight out of eight and Germany qualifies already, hitting six against neighbours Austria. Dutch treat themselves to double figures (Van Persie 4 of 11). Ronaldo two in Portugal's four-play. Celtic back in Europe as it's Sion-ara as Swiss are declared forfeit for fielding ineligible players.

3 Euro 2012: Dutch ref Blom – bit of a "tulip" – awards Czechs equalizing pen but denies Scots one. L1: MK Dons, Sheff U stay in poll positions: Dons treble-up at Carlisle, Blades cut foursome over Bury. Huddersfield makes it 31 unbeaten in draw at ten-man Oldham. Scunny's Grant is scorer and red card man in Colchester draw. Lester breaks arm as Chesterfield holds Orient. L2: Crawley four-play hits Bristol R. No strike Plymouth still loses at Burton. Ex-gardener Hannah digs deep for Bradford leveller at Morecambe. Two off but Accrington holds Barnet. Gills miss a pen, Shrews get one. Rotherham slips up at Swindon. Southend chucks two goal lead as Northampton draws with ten men. BSP: Wrexham beats Kiddy, Gateshead defeats Alfreton and Mansfield wins at Darlo. But Lincoln loses at Braintree. FA Cup: Goal glut: Yate gets ten, nines for Maldon & Tiptree, Maidstone at Corinthian (Shaun Welford 5), Sholing, too. Biggleswade and Haringey share ten. WL: Unfancied Bala leads after win at Aberystwyth.

4 R Cup: Annan, Livi, Falkirk and Accies in semis now. Inter's Ch Lge boob over Forlan – he had already played in E Lge!

5 Capello reckons he is on a roll, but Speed ups Welsh threat. Scots upbeat ahead of Lithuania, but Worthingon worries over N Ireland attack. Trapattoni faces Russia challenge with confidence. Under-21s: England hits four against Israelis, Scots held by Bulgaria. Brazil beats Ghana at Fulham – of course. Leading Euro clubs want cut in international calendar. Cook is under pressure at Man C.

6 Euro 2012: Young one for England but old problems and Earnshaw misses levelling sitter for Wales. Fan dies after attack at Wembley. Scots scrape win, Irish defence gives it to Estonia but Republic keeps Russia out in draw. Italy, six-hit Spain and Holland qualify. U-21s: Wales loses in Montenegro, N Ireland home to Danes and Republic in Turkey.

7 Out comes the Capello chopper? Police bail six after killing. Is Becks for QPR? Black candidates may be mandatory for managerial shortlists. Penalty farce: Daggers beat O's 14-13 in JPT shootout – one kick saved!

8 King Kenny to Carroll defence over lifestyle. Pardew is on the defensive over transfers. Kean faces Rovers' fans ire. Man U sympathetic over Lokomotiv Yaroslavl ice hockey team wiped out in air crash. Montenegro sacks coach Kranjcar. Notts draw friendly away to Juve.

9 Cook calls time at Man C.

10 Manchester bound PL title? Sleek Silva service, Aguero treble for Man C, Tevez pen miss, then Man U five-star adds to record 20 PL goals start, Rooney's trio (7th like Sir Bobby), two from Little Pea, as Wigan and Bolton are respective losers, but Kevin Davies takes out Cleverley and eventually gets his 100th PL caution. Bit part entry for Torres as Chelsea wins at Sunderland. Stoke pens in Liverpool – Suarez off target – but K K is unhappy with ref Clattenburg. One goal enough for Arsenal but short of a convincing win as Swans flap around. Everton shares four goals with visiting Villa. Spurs find Adebayor repaying loan already at Wolves. FLC: Best start in 76 years Saints club record 12th home win as Lambert cuts down Forest with treble. Brighton keeps ahead despite vet James' heroics for Bristol C. Earnshaw erases Welsh miss as Cardiff ditch Donny. Hammers best of seven win over Pompey in ten-a-side. Middlesbrough registers finest opening for 18 years, winning at Burnley. Leicester held at Barnsley. First win for Coventry but crowd unhappy during Derby game. McLean does in ex-Posh mates for Hull. L1: Sheff U draws at ten-man Scunthorpe. Charlton adds ten-man Exeter scalp. Huddersfield makes it 32 undefeated. Rochdale four-play surprises Bury at Gigg Lane. Madine double helps Sheff W beating MK Dons McCormack brace does same for Leeds over Palace. Hartlepool seven unbeaten in best start at Carlisle. Chesterfield is on the mark at Bournemouth. L2: Carlton hat trick in Morecambe's six thrashing of Crawley. Grabban grabs twosome for Rotherham over Daggers, Morgan similarly for Shrews against Hereford. SPL: Rangers just win at ten-man Dundee U, but Celtic hits four against Motherwell. SL1: Morton new leaders after scoring four against Ayr as Accies lose at Q of S. SL2: Abroath clips best of seven goals at Dumbarton. SL3: Elgin goes top as Annan loses derby at Stranraer. BSP: Bad day for leaders: ten-man Wrexham downed at Barrow, Gateshead at Fleetwood. Vase: Anthony Shadran six goals for Bedlington nine-hitters; Plymouth Parkway scores eleven, Hanworth eight, Hillingdon seven and Stafford just edges Goodrich best of thirteen! La Liga: JM having turned down Anzhi offer sees Real win, as Barca is held by Sociedad.

11 Odemwingie goal is sufficient for WBA at Norwich, who loses Vaughan to Tamas elbow. Fulham and Blackburn divide points on offer. Wood threesome as Birmingham tames Millwall. SPL: Bottom of the table sees Hibs and Dons scoreless.

12 Torres is to face Villas-Boas after criticism in Spanish press. Man charged with Wembley death. Drug takers named. Gyan loaned to Al-Ain. Barton meets Newcastle again after QPR draw.

13 Ch Lge: Chelsea latish winners over Leverkusen; Arsenal pegged back late, too. Barca held in early, late AC Milan show. Shakhtar's nine beaten by Porto. Apoel surprises Zenit, Marseille wins at Olympiakos, BATE dividend draw at Plzen and Genk and Valencia are goalless. C Cup: PNE wins at Charlton, Palace edges Wigan. L1: Bad Sheffield day as Utd loses to Huddersfield, Wed concedes five at Stevenage. L2: Crawley beaten again by Swindon. Morecame held at Macc. Plymouth loses again at Barnet. Mansfield appoints CEO Carolyn Still, 29.

14 Ch Lge: Mancunians rescued as Giggs levels for Utd at Benfica (17 years since first) in changed side and Kolarov spares City blushes in Napoli draw. Trabzonspor shakes Inter, Otelul suffer Frei-ings at Basle. Real is away winner at Zagreb and Bayern does well at Villarreal. Cole sub as Lille and CSKA Moscow shares four goals. Ajax and Lyon are scoreless. King Kenny is happy after meeting ref supreme. Lennon attacker is jailed. Bardsley gets four-game ban.

15 E Lge: Three draws up: Spurs at PAOK, Stoke at Dynamo Kiev, Fulham home to Twente (Schwarzer og); Birmingham loses to Braga and Celtic at Atletico Madrid.

16 Sion wins second court battle. Becks interests PSG?

17 Double og, double agony as Gunners defence loses four in seven-goal game at first win Blackburn. New kids on a rock and roll as first winners Canaries and Swans plus Rangers take out Bolton, Baggies and Wolves respectively. Everton first home win beats one-shot Wigan. Unbeaten Toon shares it with undefeated Villa. FLC: 18 gls. Ten-man leaders Middlesbrough win at Palace go top, taking advantage of inactive Saints and first-time beaten Brighton at Leicester. Forde siesta? Keeper behind goal at kick-off, Hammers just fail to hit open goal in Millwall goalless. Forest's McClaren crisis as ten-men for 88 mins Derby wins there. Maynard pen is saved as Bristol C loses at Leeds. L1: Charlton edges Rochdale to stay ahead, Sheff U threesome over Cochester, pen-missing Huddersfield held at ten-man MK Dons. Hartlepool makes it eight no loss. First treble for Clarke helps Chesterfield against Carlisle. L2: Gills six-hit (all different scorers) floors Hereford, Plymouth crashes again at Southend. Morecambe stretches lead at Daggers as Rotherham shares six with Torquay. Shrews clip Vale. Seven no loss Shots win at Bristol R. SPL: Motherwell slumps to St J so they lose ground to winners Hearts over St M.

SL1: Morton hit buffers at Q of S (Smith 3), Accies held and four points separate first nine. SL2: Winners Arbroath, Cowdenbeath extend lead. SL3: Annan, Alloa, Stranraer keep up winning. BSP: Gateshead held by Cambridge but stay top as Wrexham hit by York, Luton goes second beating Lincoln. W L: TNS catch up with no-game Bala. FA Cup: Maidstone nine (Shaun Welford, Bapp Addae 3 each), Bradford PA eight, Dunstable seven and Deeping club record round reached. Messie treble-shooter and Fabregas' special as Barca hits eight. JM donates trophy to Sir Bobby Robson auction.

18 May the fours be . . . PL: Comedy as threesome Man U beats a Torres (yes) goal but the £50m man has miss of the century for Chelsea while Rooney trips over taking a pen. Mancini wants more players as Aguero double only gets Man C a four goal sharing point at Fulham. Spurs four-play crushes nine-finishing Liverpool. Black Cats scratch quartet of their own to sink Stoke. FLC: Saints shoot back top with four of their own against Birmingham; 13th home win, best start for 103 years. SPL: Rangers double Celtic's two to win derby. Plymouth sacks Reid, Carl Fletcher steps in. JM rages as ten-man Real loses to Levante. Bala loses unbeaten Welsh record to Llanelli.

19 Matthaus fired by Bulgaria after non-qualification for Euro. Redknapp aims to keep Modric happy. Wenger is on the attack. Ipswich beats Coventry. Man C plans youth academy site.

20 C Cup: Shrews shake Arsenal before losing, Owen at the double for Man U at Leeds, where fan trouble erupted, Wolves maul Lions five times, Palace upsets Boro, Forest pushes Toon to pens before losing odd goal in seven, Bolton surprises Villa, Orient just edged at Blackburn, late Burnley goal hits MK Dons and Stoke prevails in shootout with Spurs. Eight unbeaten Shots make fourth round history beating Rochdale. SC Cup: Struggling E Fife ousts Dons in shootout, Hibs do same to Motherwell, St M shakes St J, Killie hits Q of S for five and Dundee U wins at Airdrie. BSP: Luton goes top after draw at Bath as Gateshead loses, Wrexham only draws. Fleetwood fivers go fourth.

21 C Cup: Born-again Hargreaves scores on Man C debut as Brummies lose; Saints edge Preston to keep run going, Liverpool (with Gerrard) wins at Brighton, Cardiff needs pens to oust Leicester (one miss), as does Chelsea's ten against Fulham while Everton requires extra time for Baggies disposal. SC Cup: Rangers beaten at Falkirk in 93rd min by baby-Bairns (ten teens), Hearts lose shootout to Ayr but Celtic ok at Ross. Tevez gets reduced driving charge thanks to poor English.

22 Fourteen fans charged over Leeds-Man U. England Ladies hit Slovenia for four. Ranieri back at Inter.

23 Leeds deny Brighton in six-share. Hargreaves attacks Man U medico treatment, Sir Alex defends. Wilshere needs surgery. O'Driscoll given garden leave by Doncaster as Dean Saunders moves from Wrexham in his stead.

24 PL off day – four reds: Torres after scoring as Chelsea four-play swamps Swans; Wheater for Bolton – sent to bottom by Arsenal with skipper Van Persie double taking himself to 100 club goals (17th such Gunner); Olsson two yellows for Blackburn as Ba hat trick confirms Toon's best start for 17 years; double caution, too, for Gohouri as Wigan edged by Spurs. Man C second half ends Everton hopes but Moyes unhappy. De Gea starring Man U prevented from win by Crouch header for Stoke, but still make it 22 goals in first six games, best since Newcastle in 1994. Suarez scores, then throws wobbly as Liverpool needs og to hit Wolves. Foster saving Baggies draw with Fulham, ref Massey earning plaudits. FLC: 15 gls in ten games. Wasteful Saints draw at Burnley, Middlesbrough only unbeaten side held by Ipswich, so Derby makes progress beating Millwall. First win for Donny under new boss as Palace loses. Not pretty but Forest wins at Watford. L1: Charlton increases lead against Chesterfield as Sheff U loses to Wycombe (first goal in 531 mins). Hartlepool gets a pt at Bournemouth, Huddersfield (after two-goal lead) at home to Orient. L2: Crawley upsets Shots spoiling Man U cup-draw day, Morecambe loses to visiting Bristol R. Southend gets four at Rotherham. Shrewsbury's twosome beats Torquay. Burton's nine hit by Gills. Swindon foursome downs Barnet and Plymouth achieves first win against Macc. SPL: Rangers, Celtic, Motherwell all win, ICT and Dons stay in the toils. SL1: Morton edges Falkirk, Accies win at Dundee. SL2: Arbroath, Cowden and Sten stay on winning track. SL3: So do Annan, Alloa and Stranraer! BSP: Wrexham, Gateshead both win, bubbling Braintree four-play pushes them third. Spain: Ronaldo 3 in Real six; Messi 3 in Barca five. Cole scores first goal for Lille. Vase: Armthorpe hands out ten goals, Downton "happy" with nine.

25 PM Dave sees King of the Ogs Dunne (9th PL) give QPR pt against Villa. Cardiff and Leicester square it goalless. SPL: St J breaks Hearts.

26 Norwich beats Sunderland. Sir Alex swipes at TV power, but praises Man C for decision to lay wreath in Munich. Hawk-Eye will be tested at Soton. Blackburn is to play friendly in India.

27 Ch Lge: Manchester concerns: City loses to Bayern (Tevez refusing to come on), United scrapes draw with Basle after leading. Real impress against Ajax. Inter surprises CSKA Moscow. Lyon beats Dinamo Zagreb, Napoli twosome takes care of Villarreal. Lille holds Trabzonspor and one goal is sufficient for Benfica at Otelul. FLC: Brighton suffers Palace raid by old boy Murray. More woe for McClaren as Forest hit for five at Burnley. Hammers run over by Tractor Boys of Ipswich. L1: Charlton draws away at Milton Keynes. Preston turns tables on Wycombe. Carling calls it a day for its cup. BSP: Shaw treble restores Gateshead top, Braintree goes second beating Tamworth. SPL: Rangers beat Killie to keep up challenge.

28 Ch Lge: "UN" Eleven Arsenal edges Olympiakos with "Ox" boy the youngest English scorer, Chelsea hit by late Valencia pen leveller. Five goal Barca ignores the BATE and Messi bags two. AC Milan heads them on goal difference beating Plzen. Leverkusen twosome downs Genk, Marseille treble finishes Dortmund. Zenit surprises Porto, Shakhtar held by Apoel. FLC: Miller double grounds Saints, Boro draws again with Leicester but goes second. SPL: Hibs first home win over St J. Bramble arrested. Pearce does not want Capello job. Pleat sacked as Forest consultant. Tevez suspended by City. Mayor wants Spurs to accept stadium offer.

29 E Lge: Joy as Spurs recover to beat Shamrock, Stoke does the same over Besiktas, Birmingham wins in Maribor as does Fulham away to Odense, but Udinese holds Celtic. PL threats TV in Europe.

30 Shrimpers top after Shrews taming. Macc surprises Swindon. Aberdeen four-play (Vernon 3) stuns Dunfermline. Ten-man Morton hit by the Jags. Baby Mancini once did a "Tevez." No ground share for Merseyside giants.

OCTOBER

England qualifies but Rooney red . . . Republic play-off chance . . . Evra – Suarez in racist clash . . . Eriksson sacked at Leicester.

1 Off-colour Man U beats Norwich (Pilkington triple X misses costly) keeps one goal ahead of Man C foursome winners at under-fire Kean's Blackburn, but Aguero injury worry. Ref Atkinson's 15th red card flourish (4th of season) damages Everton's resistance (Howard stops Kuyt pen) in 216th derby with Liverpool much to Moyes rage. Two up in five mins Baggies brought level by fighting Black Cats. Ten unbeaten Newcastle edges Wolves but McCarthy riled over ref Halsey. Villa maintains run at Wigan expense. FLC: Five star Blackpool rakes Bristol C. Sven's anniversary at Leicester produces four-play to finish Derby. Saints back on top with four hit on Watford as Brighton loses at Ipswich and Boro draws for third game at Reading. Cardiff unhappy over no pen as vet Barmby scores Hull winner. Hammers seeking Tevez(!) share four goals at Palace. Gray posts 100th career goal as

Barnsley get first home win over Coventry. L1: Crucial success for Charlton at Sheff U. MK Dons go second as Notts are trussed up. First win for Orient ends Preston's seven on the trot. Huddersfield 36th undefeated in quartet at Brentford, but Hartlepool run ends home to Sheff W. Two-goal Grimes is Rochdale winner over Wycombe. L2: Crawley goes second as Plymouth loses and Morecambe held at Torquay. AFC Dons go fourth as Gills founder. Oxford clips Hereford while Vale shakes Rotherham. SPL: Rangers need just one to beat Hibs. Motherwell second again winning at Dundee U. SL1: Ross foursome beats Ayr. SL2: Arbroath draws with Cowden. E Fife is off bottom edging Forfar. SL3: Annan wins at Berwick, Nine-man Alloa loses five at Elgin so drawing Stranraer is second. W L: TNS resumes ahead odd goal in five over Aberystwyth. BSP: Hearn four in Grimsby five hit against Alfreton, Luton five, too. Gateshead held, Fleetwood catch them winning at a Braintree faced with ground downgrading. FA Cup; Woking dig deep at Wells with seven, Arlesey six hitters surprise Hampton & R B.

2 SW6 joy! Chelsea hits five at Bolton (Lampard 3), Fulham six-strikes at the Cottage against QPR (Johnson 3). It's Derby day joy for Spurs edging Arsenal. Swans poke two goals past Stoke. FLC: Late treble from Brummies flays Forest and McClaren quits. SPL: Ten Celts beaten by Hearts. W L: Bangor wins at Bala.

3 Chelsea seeks new home. Ancelotti weighs in on Wenger plight, but Arsenal and Spurs unite to deal with abusive fans. Quinn leaves Sunderland chair. Paul Hart could return to Forest in senior role. Bristol C sacks boss Millen. Running track will stay at Olympic venue.

4 Rodwell's red card scrubbed. Welbeck may get call up. Pub landlady wins first round in TV fight-rights. JPT: Serious Bender injury and Stanley game called to a halt. Huddersfield loses shoot-out to Bradford to query unbeaten run? BSP: Wrexham foursome floors Gateshead.

5 FA will no longer skirt the female idea. UEFA is to start two international games over six days from 2014. Sir Alex warns his "standing" away fans. JM gets two-game ban from Spanish FA. Tevez was wrongly accused? JPT: Brentford shocks Charlton.

6 Son Roo shrugs off Daddy arrest as Montenegro waits. Wales stay on watch to damage Swiss. Irish looks for second home win facing Estonia. Republic goes with high expectations to Andorra. U-21s: "Oxo" treble feeds England win in Iceland. Scots hit five in Luxembourg. Refs close ranks. MPs remain gunning for FA.

7 Euro 2012: England two ahead in Montenegro scrapes draw to qualify but Rooney sees red. Wales beats ten Swiss. N Ireland loses at home to Estonia, but Republic needs one point after win in Andorra to finish second and Scots boosted as Spain cashes in with win against ten Czechs. Greeks in trouble as flares and a petrol bomb cause hold-up in Croatia game refereed by Webb. WC: Argentina hits four against Chile, Uruguay similarly against Bolivia.

8 Euro 2012: Double-barrelled scorer (M-Smith) in Scots single shot win in Liechtenstein as prelude to Spanish main one. Roo ref Stark may save him a ban. U-21: Wales clip Montenegro. L1: Charlton held by Tranmere but best start since 1927-28. S Wed keeps unbeaten home record six out of six as Chesterfield loses. Huddersfield's 37th undefeated but Stevenage fluffed pen ruffles feathers. Orient first away win at Scunny, so Exeter bottoms out losing at Bury. Second outing Massey two goals (first 40 secs) gives Yeovil draw at Colchester. L2: Shrimpers net Crewe at Gresty Road. Crawley's lunchtime TV spots win at Northampton. AFC Dons upset Morecambe. Plymouth blows two-goal lead in Stanley draw on 125th anniversary. Ten-man Bradford edges Torquay. BSP: First win for Bath over Darlo. Table-topping Gateshead takes advantage of no-game Wrexham; one enough at Ebbsfleet. Braintree ships six at York. W L: Top three TNS, Llanelli and Bangor stay on winning track. Trophy: Seven little predators as Whitehawk hits seven at Soham. Needham goes to market, too, seven-up at Ramsgate.

9 L1: Notts are treble-sum for Hartlepool. BSP: Wrexham back top at Hayes.

10 U-21: England beats the Norwegians but Austrians hold Scots. Failed FA bid for 2018 cost £21m. Platini inspection of Poland is crucial. L1: Oldham singing in the rain over MK Dons. Worthington will stand down from N Ireland role.

11 Euro 2012: Play-off places: Four-leaf Shamrock? Republic gets handout against Armenia's ten to reach play-offs; Scots lose to Spain so Czechs come second. Germany's beating Belgium opens same door for Turkey edging Azers. Vidic pen miss costs Serbia in Slovenia so Estonia takes advantage. Danes put skids under new runners-up Portugal. Rest round-up: Italian treble hits N Ireland, but Wales win again in Bulgaria. Dutch suffer first defeat in Sweden. Greece finishes top of group at Georgia, denying Croatia. Penalty saves French against Bosnia, placed one and two in their section. U-21: Wales lose to Czechs, Republic hits four in Liechtenstein. Capello turns down Anzhi offer. Liverpool wants TV alone. Warner is in new bribe accusation. Olympic stadium deal scandal unfolds. WC: Argies lose to Venezuela.

12 Tevez faces Man C again. Chicharito gets five-year deal. Hammers withhold transfer money in FIFA row. More cash for Wenger to spend. MPs give FA four months to reform. JPT: Tranmere wins rearranged Stanley game. Sky Sports Victory Shield: England threesome beats N Ireland.

13 Ban-boy Rooney will be no groupie. Tevez becomes the lone trainer. Euro 2012- p-o: Turkey v Croatia, Estonia v Republic, Czechs v Montenegro, Bosnia v Portugal.

14 Capello wants Roo appeal. Chelsea seeks possible new site. Steve Cotterill is Forest manager. Leeds wins at Doncaster. Rotherham lets in five at Bristol R.

15 Man C are tops in foursome (27 in eight equals Arsenal 2009) over Villa as Man U draws at Liverpool after miss-hit free from Gerrard and "Little Pea" pops up with leveller. Space ace Mata is the Juan behind Chelsea ending its Everton hoodoo (Terry 350th PL game, 5th such at Bridge). Norwich 47 secs lead leads to Swans downing. Al Habsi saves pen but Wigan concedes as Bolton end six defeats. Late striking Stoke score with first on target as Fulham loses. Rangers and Rovers in draw as Blackburn bottoms out. FLC: Lambert rattles in 60th Saints goal in draw at Derby. Middlesbrough club record 11 no loss but another draw with Millwall. Hammers four-play blasts Blackpool. Cardiff rescues pt with pen against Ipswich. Forest goes down at Coventry. Sliding Brighton held by Hull. Burnley licked by Reading's flaky 99th winner. L1: Rhodes treble in 38th undefeated Huddersfield quartet at Exeter. Charlton run ends at Stevenage. MK Dons held by Bournemouth. Ten-man Walsall beats Preston. Notts nip to third at Chesterfield. L2: Crawley edges Shrewsbury to stay top as Southend draws with Morecambe. Seven undefeated as Oxford 94th min goal draws at Macc. Gills five grounds the Gulls. Free-fall Shots caught out at Barnet. SPL: Three down Hoops level at Killie (3 in 17 mins). St M hold Rangers at Ibrox. Motherwell goes second after win at Hibs. SL1: Winners Ross, Hamilton and Falkirk extend lead. SL2: Cowden goes top as Arbroath held. SL3: Progress for Stranraer at Peterhead, Clyde hits seven against E Stirling. BSP: Wrexham four v Stockport, Luton five against Gateshead sandwich Fleetwood. FA Cup: Goals! Gloucester seven, Salisbury six (Dan Fitchett 3), Southend Manor (Gary Patterson second 3 in successive ties), Stourbridge, Bishop's Stortford and Chelmsford all five (latter attracting 1065 at Lowestoft). Matt Rhead has trio for Corby, too. Redditch sacks player for hitting ref. Spain: Messi two (196 goals – 103 in last 100) so only Cesar Rodriguez 235 has more for Barca. Ronaldo 100th RM game (95 goals).

16 V P early (29 secs) and late (82 mins) cost equalizing Sunderland points at Arsenal. Shola Ameobi saves Toon record in Spurs draw. Black Country Baggies beat Wolves, first such top flight for 29 years. FLC: Ten-man Leicester loses at Birmingham. L1: 125th Steel City derby sees Owls bite back to draw with the Blades.

17 Evra accuses Suarez of racism. Foreign PL club owners want closed shop. Warner will step up attack on FIFA's alleged Zionism. Orient wants Mayor Boris axed from Olympic Stadium talk. Government will publish Hillsborough document.

18 Ch Lge: Roo (M U CL record 26 goals) rescues with two pens with Vidic red carded in win v Otelul. Aguero is "sub-stantial" winner for Man C against Villarreal. Lyon fed to Real four-play. Ajax cleans up in Zagreb, two-goals, too, for Benfica at Basle. Inter needs just one in Lille, but Bayern held in Napoli. CSKA takes three off Trabzonspor. FLC: Saints scrape another win to edge West Ham (32,150). Middlesbrough loses record at Forest. Posh turns tables on Cardiff in best of seven. Wrexham wins crucial game at Luton. Fleetwood nets four at Alfreton, Braintree clipped in best of nine goals at Kiddy. Gateshead ten-men lose to Southport. Blatter announces more FIFA reforms. Big Dunc Ferguson is new Everton youth coach. Rangers withdraw BBC co-operation. Plymouth gets council boost. Ghost internationals arranged for betting!

19 Ch Lge: Tor-Tor-Torres hits double in high-five for Chelsea against Genk. Arsenal leaves it until added time for winner in Marseille. Barca restricted to two against Viktoria, as are AC Milan over BATE. Porto held by group leaders Apoel, Shakhtar by Zenit. Leverkusen edges Valencia, but Olympiakos takes out Borussia. FLC: Leicester two better than Watford. L1: Sheff U back winning at PNE. Derek McInnes is Bristol C boss. Wales rises to 45th in FIFA rankings.

20 E Lge: Birmingham wins in Brugge, Spurs at home to Rubin, Stoke gets three in ten-a-side with Maccabi, but Celtic draws at Rennes and Fulham edged out in Krakow in ten-a-side finish in Krakow. Spotlight on Blatter as FIFA reforms enter. WC in Brazil 2014 will feature long hauls. Coach Pearce wants nucleus of Man U players including Rooney for GB.

21 FA will interview Suarez after allegations. Claridge, 45, is to play for Gosport. FIFA prepares to blow gaffe on bribe men.

22 Norwich's Ruddy good save prevents late Liverpool win. Sixth defeat recorded in a row for Wigan at Newcastle. Debt worried Bolton loses seventh home on the trot to Sunderland. Pen-missing WBA wins at ten-man Villa for first time in 32 years, but Long gets injury. Under cosh McCarthy sees Wolves claw back two goals in Swansea draw. FLC: Ten-man Soton nicks draw at Reading. Boro back winning as injury-hit Derby parades its youngest ever Mason Bennett at 15. Palace lifts to third at Ipswich. Leeds benefit 95th min goal downs ten-man Posh who criticise ref Stroud. Hull makes it eight no loss, Cardiff win eight-goal game, two better than Barnsley, though Miller is injury-hit. Forest stays on fire at Blackpool. L1: Charlton four-play erases ten-man Carlisle. Huddersfield's treble-shooter Rhodes aids 38th no-loss as Preston loses. Henderson hat trick stuns Leicester in Millwall's first win in 11. Sheff W keeps home record intact against Colchester. Notts held by the Bees, MK Dons by Scunny and Sheff U by ten-man Orient. L2: Crawley five at AFC Dons, Shots same at Dagenham. Shrimpers foursome grounds Gulls, Shrimps quarter hits Vale. Nine-man Gills go fifth edging Oxford. BSP: Newport holds Wrexham so Fleetwood creeps nearer top beating Bath. Trophy: Recall Chester? Some 1624 see them edge Ashton. Witton gets six. Dean Perrow four of Chasetown five, Ben Bradbury all three for Redbridge Leon Archer three of Chesham. John Frendo three for Hitchin. Claridge is Gosport winner! SPL: Motherwell held by Killie, Hibs wins at S M. SL1: Ross goes three points clear beating Hamilton, Falkirk held by Partick. SL2: Cowden three ahead, too, as Forfar loses. Vase: Erith, Enfield 1893 and Ellesmere hit six each. WL: TNS also three points ahead edging P Talbot. S Cup: Stranraer equals club record nine goals at Wigtown & B. Berwick stunned by Deveronvale four-play.

23 Balotelli fires home and away as Man C six stuns ten-man Man U – three in last five mins to end Old Trafford's 37 unbeaten run (City's 33 goals from nine best since 1894-95). Seven booked, two sent off for Chelsea losers at QPR. V Persie is sub hero with a couple for Arsenal (his first 200th PL Emirates in 100th game there) against Stoke. Injury time brings Everton victory at Fulham. V d V sees double as Spurs clip Blackburn. Birmingham wins at Bristol C. SPL: Rangers win at Hearts, Celtic at home to ten-man Aberdeen.

24 Leicester sacks Eriksson. Terry and Ferdinand quizzed over alleged racist moment. AVB is under spotlight over post-match comments. Brighton beached by the Hammers. Vermaelen is back.

25 C Cup: Shot in the arm for Man U at the Rec. Arsenal stiffs clip the Trotters, but Vermaelen injured again. Palace peaks progress at Saints expense. Mason strikes for Cardiff over Burnley. L1: W-P double for Charlton at Wycombe; Huddersfield draw extends streak at Scunny. Ten-man S Wed (ex-C U Madine) loses at Carlisle, so Sheff U moves closer beating MK Dons. L2: Crawley sees off Daggers, Southend treble hits Barnet; Shrews edge Stanley, Oxford fivers play off Plymouth. SC Cup: Falkirk shoots-out Dundee U, Killie beats E Fife, Ayr surprise St M. Tevez fined £792,000 and will sue Man C. O'Neill may return to Leicester. UEFA slow to respond to FA question over Rooney. FA comes under spotlight over agents' fees.

26 C Cup: All-change Man C still hits five at Wolves; Chelsea needs extra time to beat Everton, so does Blackburn against Newcastle in seven-goal affair. Suarez double strike finishes Stoke for Liverpool. FLC: Zigic makes it six wins on trot for Birmingham over Leeds. SC Cup: Celtic foursome ends Hibs interest. Real score another treble against Villarreal. FIFA probe net widens.

27 Chelsea fans want Bridge stay. PFA cuts Tevez fine. Man U chases £40m Gaitan. Sion may still play in Europa. England women: Fara Williams has pen saved in Dutch goalless treat.

28 King Kenny goes to war over Suarez situ. FA quizzes Terry. Man C will have to play Tevez or else! Bramble faces charges. Is King Kevin for Leicester? Plymouth deal could be on.

29 Chelsea hits 6000th League goal but three-goal Van-man Persie in top gear drives Arsenal to two-goal margin in eight-goal derby thriller. Second half masters Man C take ten-game total to record 42 in top flight as Wolves lose again. Man U needs just one at Everton. Suarez-inspired Liverpool defeats WBA. Holt 93rd min pens Blackburn to six-share draw with dodgy award at Norwich. Twice ahead Villa held at Sunderland. Winners Fulham leave Wigan without win since August. Swans end ten-man Bolton bid for a point. FLC: Saints post club record 16th straight home win to scupper Boro. Despite King's brace, Hammers trump Leicester. Reading holds Palace. Derby upsets Pompey. Forest revival ends with Hull visit. L1: Foursome Addicks which Hartlepool. Huddersfield hoists 41st unbeaten in the League after narrow win at Yeovil. Sheff W stays ahead of Sheff U by winning at Wycombe while the Blades are slicing up equal share of eight with Exeter. L2: Storming Southend adds Macc to scalps. Crawley finds Accrington a point taker. Morecambe celebrates 200th League game beating Gills. Shrews held goalless by AFC Dons. Cheltenham takes out Plymouth. Kee strikes treble as six-shooters Burton double Barnet trio. SPL: Title secure? Rangers go twelve ahead of game-in-hand Celtic held by Hibs, by beating ten-finishing Dons. Motherwell nine pts behind Ibrox men after win at ICT. SL1: Top four Ross, Falkirk, Livi and Jags all win. SL2: Arbroath levels with Cowden – losers at Brechin – by edging ten-man Sten. SL3: Lone game

Manchester City's David Silva celebrates his goal – and his team's fifth – in City's 6-1 thrashing of neighbours Manchester United at Old Trafford in October. (Reuters/Darren Staples)

sees QP win at Stranraer. S Cup: Annan beats Alloa, E Stirling keeps Buckie out. Elgin rattles in five against Fraserburgh and Inverurie goes loco beating ten-man Clach. W L: Bangor goes second beating Aberystwyth. FA Cup: Minnows Redbridge account for Ebbsfleet, FGR loses at Arlesey. E Thurrock creates club history beating Eastbourne. Wrexham edges York (2252). Cambridge gets six, Newport best of seven against Braintree. Fives for AFC Telford, Luton, Maidenhead, Stourbridge; Boyes gets all Barrow's four. La Liga: Messi hat trick in Barca five, too.

30 Bale duo aids Spurs over QPR. FLC: Cardiff frustrated in Leeds draw.

31 Ba-Ba-Ba leaves Stoke sheepish against Newcastle. Toure K may be hit by Man C fine over drug ban. Capello warns of Spanish dominance in Ch Lge. Gerrard injury likely to keep him out. E-H Diouf goes to Donny. Birmingham finances cause concern. Plymouth is out of administration.

NOVEMBER

England's 2000th goal . . . Republic qualifies for Euro 2012 . . . Record loss for Man C . . . Gary Speed commits suicide.

1 Ch Lge: Chelsea held in Genk, Arsenal goalless at home to Marseille. Messi treble posts his 202nd Barca goal in foursome over ten-man Viktoria as the Catalan team qualifies with AC Milan who drew away to BATE Borisov. Apoel surprises Porto with last gasp winner to top group with Zenit edging Shakhtar for second spot. Valencia still chases Leverkusen after beating them. Borussia gets first win over Olympiakos. FLC: Saints clip ten-man Posh to go further ahead as West Ham held up by vet James with Bristol C. Boro bounces back at Donny. Palace in goalless with Pompey, Brighton loses again, but Sven-less Leicester wins at Burnley. Harry R to have an op. Terry is under Police investigation. Tevez can apologise. Rooney is alone in Golden Ball shortlist. Gerrard out injured again. Chopra loses £2m in gambling.

2 Ch Lge: Man C three at Villarreal, Man U two at home to Otelul. Ronaldo hits 100th as Real keep another clean sheet in Lyon. Ajax four-play wipes out Dinamo. Benfica held by Basle. Gomez hat trick enables Bayern to just defeat Napoli in ten-a-side ending. Inter edges Lille while CSKA Moscow draws at Trabzon. Harry R recovers and Italy's Cassano will have small heart op. Ranger charged with assault. Rachubka gaffes give Blackpool high five at Leeds. Cardiff threesome shakes Derby.

3 E Lge: Birmingham fights back for Club Brugge draw, Stoke wins away to Maccabi, Fulham hits four against Wisla in fiery night at the Cottage, Celtic gets first win over Rennes but Spurs edged out by Rubin. Lee Clark declines Leicester approach.

4 FA will appeal Rooney ban. Liverpool rants at fixture congestion. Warnock calls for jail over Ferdinand abusers. Tim Gudgin, voice of BBC football scores, to retire at 82. Sky Sports Victory Shield: N Ireland edges the Scots.

5 Resilient Rangers push Man C to edgy win. Sir Alex gets og help from old boy Brown (and stand named after him) as Sunderland loses again to Man U as does boss Bruce. Newcastle confirms best start for 16 years in odd goal win over Everton. Lamps lights up Chelsea but dark days continue for Blackburn and manager Kean. Liverpool stalemate with Swans as each misses chance (Carroll and Gower). Rocking Robin V P again in focus as Arsenal threesome takes care of WBA. Capello watches as in-form Bent and Agbonlahor clip Canaries wings for Villa. FLC: Two ahead, then level, Saints four-play ends Coventry fight back and continues best opening in 90 years scoring in all 16 games. Hammers hit two against wasteful Hull. Bristol C first home win and Pearson scoring debut against Burnley. Middlesbrough (single), Cardiff (ending Palace's 619 min clean sheet), Blackpool (vet Phillips), win, too. Diouf double aids Donny and Ipswich. L1: Five-up Charlton allow PNE a couple of goals. Huddersfield equals Forest's 42-league unbeaten in Walsall draw. Sheff W drops first two home points against

Brentford. MK Dons defeat Rochdale but Sheff U loses at Stevenage. Wycombe recovers from 44 sec Notts Co to level. Gerrard, 38, saves two-goal Bishop's pen as Bury wins at Oldham. L2: Southend on the late flow beats Oxford to stay clear as Crawley is held at Hereford. Cheltenham goes third after win at Bradford. First win in ten for Rotherham as ten-man Shots fade. Shrews two-goal win at Dagenham. Morecambe draws at Plymouth. Swindon wins at Port Vale. Macc sub Mukendi off in record seven secs as they lose to Burton. It's Okay as O-K (Osei-Kuffour) first half treble helps Gills edge Cobblers best of seven. SPL: Rangers extend lead beating Dundee U; away-day ICT doubles Killie threesome in game of nine goals. SL1: Ross away, Falkirk home both winners. SL2: Chaplain has trio as Albion hit seven against ten-man Airdrie, but Cowden, Arbroath and Sten continue winning ways. SL3: Alloa takes Stranraer's second place. BSP: Fleetwood cuts Wrexham (held at York) lead by a pt. W L: TNS moves six ahead of Bangor (held by Afan Lido). Trophy: Chertsey edges Ashford T in 11-goal game of ten scorers. Marine, Uxbridge get five each. James Everitt strikes all four goals for Folkestone. Chester best gate: 1551. Ronaldo 12th RM hat trick out of seven goals takes him to 13 in La Liga.

6 Stoke's usual nil point after Euro but also ship five goals at – Bolton! Spurs make it 22 pts out of 24 on Modric's 100th game and Defoe's 99th goal overall as a sub! Wigan suffers eighth defeat on the trot at Wolves after seven no loss. Barca scrapes injury-time. FLC: Brighton back on track against Barnsley, Leeds make life difficult for Leicester and Birmingham edged out at Reading. SPL: Celtic overtakes Motherwell on the pitch and off it.

7 Wigan's Alcaraz accused of spitting incident, Suarez wants Evra apology. Hamann quits Stockport job. Kuszczak hits out at his Man U "slavery." Fog-off: St J and Dons.

8 Poppy bans rile England ahead of Spain game. Capello will miss son's wedding. Tevez goes AWOL again. Alcaraz accepts three-match ban. Jimmy Adamson, Burnley great, dies at 82. Ex-Juventus directors sent to jail for 2006 match-fixing. JPT: Grella hits four of Brentford six against Bournemouth. Bradford beats Sheff U in shoot-out. SL3: Annan, Alloa wins push them further ahead. Trophy replays: Six each for FA Cup bound Stourbridge and Weymouth.

9 HRH Wills and PM Dave get some Poppy way over FIFA. St James Park will become Sports Direct Arena. Even Gordon Taylor despairs of Tevez. Republic geared for big test. Chesterfield gets one goal better in seven against Tranmere in JPT.

10 U21s: England takes five off Iceland. Michael Appleton, WBA No.2 is Pompey's new boss and Steve Davis takes over from Dario Gradi at Crewe. SPL chief wants British Cup.

11 Euro 2012 p-o: RoI Irish foursome reel has Estonia spinning; Ronaldo off target as Portugal held in Bosnia; Czechs two ahead of Montenegro; Croatia hits Turkey for three. Friendly sees Scots edge Cyprus. Spain's Casillas on eve of 126th appearance as Capello prepares strange line-up. FA Cup: Cambridge and Wrexham share four. Tyneside Labour MPs to fight Toon name change. W Cup: Argies fail to beat Bolivia even with Messi about while Suarez foursome makes it cold comfort for Chile in Uruguay. Chelsea's AVB charged by FA.

12 Three shots, one goal youthful England too much for mighty Spain. Wales carries on good work in foursome win against Norway. FA Cup: Shocks at "Highbury" as ten-man Fleetwood smacks Wycombe, sub Watkins edges

Tottenham's Gareth Bale and Fulham's John Arne Riise tussle it out at Craven Cottage in November. Bale scored the opening goal in Spurs' 3-1 victory. (Action Images/Andrew Couldridge)

Northampton out for Luton. Glassboys Stourbridge mirrors nine-finishing Plymouth in six goal share. Maidenhead Mags (first goal against Lge opposition at York Road since 1871 campaign) scare Shots to earn replay; Daggers held by lowly Bath; Grimsby holds Vale goalless. BSP casualties to lower orders: Telford (at Chelmsford), Kettering (at Sutton – Watkins (another) on 100th outing. Chesterfield still seeks cup win over Lge team since 1997 as Torquay wins. Totton hits nine-man Bradford PA for eight (Stefan Brown 3 in 15 mins as sub). Highest gate: Sheff U (7,991) as Oxford U loses; Oxford C fails to beat Redbridge gk Adam Rafis 7hrs 30 mins cup clean sheet. Records tumble in MK Dons six-hit over Nantwich (furthest in 127 years) as teenagers – first Williams becomes the youngest goalscorer, then Galloway becomes the youngest player in FA Cup proper round. SL1: Ross opens six-pt lead beating Falkirk. SL2: Airdrie's Donnelly three in eight-goal share with Forfar. SL3: Four up Stranraer has gk sent off and Montrose levels! W L: Llanelli goes second after win at Newtown.

13 FA Cup: Charlton Addicks four at FC Halifax is their highest score in cup since 1972, Sheff W clips the Shrimps at Morecambe. Redknapp and Mandaric face fraud charges.

14 Cut-price Wembley but low gate predicted. Capello favours Becks for GB. England U21s lose to Belgium, but Republic beats Liechtenstein and Scots win in Holland! Gary Johnson leaves Northampton. Is Tevez serial AWOL? Brazil beats Egypt in a friendly.

15 England's 2,000th goal is a deflection but enough to beat Swedes first time in 43 years (48,876). Euro 2012: Republic held but marches on to finals with six-hitters Portugal, double Czechs and Croatia. U21s: Wales draw in Armenia, but N Ireland loses to Serbia. Record setting Casillas' 127th outing error as Spain held by Costa Rica. Barca boss wants PL shrink or breakaway. AVB denies FA charge. Leicester appoints Nigel Pearson manager as Hull makes Barmby caretaker.

16 Barking Blatter suggests handshakes to answer racism. Suarez is charged by FA over Evra incident. Spurs will use own resources for new ground. PL unimpressed by Barca shrinkage idea. Hiddink is to help Chelsea! Sky Sports Victory Shield sees Wales beat N Ireland.

17 The condemnation of Blatter increases. Fraud suspicions mount over Olympic Stadium. Capello goes cap-in-hand to plea for Rooney. Liverpool stays firmly behind Suarez. Police want Terry charged. Solskjaer sees Sir Alex job – eventually. Ojo, 14, moves from MK Dons to Liverpool. Everton ups Fellaini pay.

18 Record losses of £197.5m for Man C. Sorry, but Blatter will carry on. Sir Alex hits out at Poyet-supporting Suarez and Liverpool. Warnock wants black players to refuse international calls. Blackburn faces financial crisis. LA Galaxy and Becks may part after final.

19 Man C equals best PL start 11 wins, one draw (42 goals) in ending Newcastle's unbeaten run of eleven. Swans suffer first home loss choked by "Little Pea" and Sinclair miss as Man U stays second. Van Persie two more takes 2011 total to 31 goals as Arsenal wins at Norwich for Wenger's 200th away win. Stoke hit by fourth defeat in a row as QPR wins there. Fit again Long aides Albion against Bolton. Blackburn 68 secs lead, one via illegal corner and 98th min leveller in six-share at Wigan. Late pen gives Everton nod over Wolves. Westwood saves Sunderland in fifth Black Cats blank against Fulham. FLC: Soton (100th pt in 2011) make it 18 home wins in a row (20 all games) as Lambert trio (2 pens, one retaken, one not a pen) puts Brighton in place. Hammers keep on Saints tail at Coventry with 2000th away goal. Boro held by Blackpool so Cardiff moves upwards at Reading. Leeds edges it at Burnley. Hull under Barmby eye wins well at Derby. L1: Charlton get London derby win through W-P at Brentford. Huddersfield beats FL record with 43rd undefeated and with ten-men against Notts. MK Dons hit five at Colchester. Sheffield joy as Wed wins away, Utd at home. Simpson first half treble as Oldham strikes five against Chesterfield. L2: Winners Southend, Crawley, Cheltenham, Shrewsbury (seven at Northampton) and Burton control leader board. Torquay first win over Plymouth for 29 years. BSP: Wrexham, Fleetwood and Southport carry on winning, Luton draws at improving Cambridge. SPL: Rangers frustrated by St J in draw as Celtic wins at ICT. S Cup: "Gala" day for Airdrie in record 11 goals over Fairydean. Livi gets six at the "Meadow" E Fife, Morton five each – Culter does well to hold Partick. Vase: Dunston dozen digs out Blackhall CW (Stephen Goddard and Andrew Bulford 3 each), Bethnal Green seven – day outing at Felixstowe. Whitley Bay marches on. JM's 50th I/C Real sees victors at Valencia. German ref Rafati attempts suicide.

20 Chelsea has no case for the defence as old boy Johnson sentences them to defeat by Liverpool. FLC: Leicester takes shine off Crystal Palace. Bristol C ruins Millwall fun day. Becks and Galaxy wins MLS.

21 Spurs much two-good for Villa as Harry returns. Rovers ref Marriner gets weekend leave. SFO approached re-FIFA bribe allegations.

22 Ch Lge: Manchester gloom as City on brink after Napoli defeat and Utd held at home by Benfica after early og and gk gaffe. "Weak" Real hit Zagreb for six (first to score four in 20 mins and first with three after nine) Ajax almost there after draw at Lyon. Bayern in last 16 after Villarreal suffers fifth reverse. Inter will top group but fight for runners-up goes on after Lille wins at CSKA Moscow. Basle beats Otelul but has to do same v Man U. FLC: Birmingham late hits Burnley, Cardiff only draws at Coventry. FA Cup: Stourbridge stuns ten-man Plymouth. Grimsby outs Port Vale. AFC Dons win at Scunny. S Cup: Ayr wins at Montrose.

23 Ch Lge: VI (influential) Persie double rescues qualifying win for Arsenal against Dortmund, but Chelsea caught late in Leverkusen, so Valencia's seven-goal (Soldado 3 in 26 mins) dent of Genk forces crucial last game at the Bridge. Apoel becomes first Cypriot team to reach last 16 after holding Zenit in flare interrupted tie. Porto maintains hope after win at Shakhtar. Barca edges AC Milan in game of qualified already sides. Olympiakos menaces Marseille's chances. Plzen wins no-hopers game at BATE Borisov. FA Cup: D & R late shift Nurse runs Bath out; Daggers to face Walsall conquerors of Exeter. Women's international sees England defeat Serbia. Kean signs new Blackburn contract. England plans Brazil trip for 150th anniversary of FA. Pompey joint owner faces arrest warrant. First ever win for American Samoa best of three goals against Tonga after 30 defeats in 17 years.

24 PL nears goal-line technology? Becks mentioned for Olympics. Battersea site is still on for Chelsea. Colin Calderwood gets Brummie No.2 job.

25 Bannan is hit by drink-driving ban. AVB gets Roman backing. Van violence in Dresden means Dynamo cup next season. McLeod double beats Macc for Barnet. Sky Sports Victory Shield; England win in Scotland gives them title.

26 Roaring Sir Alex takes off over Flt Sgt lino John Flynn's flag for dodgy pen overruling ref Jones as ten-man Newcastle (gk Krul superb) snatches draw at Man U – last Toon win there 1972. Ten no loss Spurs best start since 1961 despite going behind at WBA (Adebayor seven goals in ten equals Klinsmann, Kanoute) and go third in 100th PL away win. Chelsea even hits three against Wolves. Vermaelen at both ends as Fulham manages draw at Arsenal (14 different nationalities!). Everton beats ten-man Bolton. Reliable sub Holt puts stop to QPR draw hope for Norwich. Stoke ends losing run defeating Blackburn. First win in ten as Wigan pen and late ones hit Sunderland at S of L. FLC: Soton fails to score first time in league as Bristol C gets third win in a row. Hammers cut Saints lead to two pts at Derby. Sub Mason's one enough for eight no loss Cardiff beating Forest. Middlesbrough has eighth draw at Posh. Barnsley wins at Leeds first time in 21 years. Blackpool held by

Birmingham. Murray misses pen so Palace goes 485 mins goalless in draw with Millwall. Hull loses two goal lead as Burnley claims 91st min winner. Ipswich concedes 91st and 93rd goals to Reading. L1: Sheff W moves nearer inactive Charlton edging ends Orient ten no loss run. MK Dons odd goal in seven goals clips Wycombe. Sheff U piles more hurt at Chesterfield. No win in 13 now for PNE at Bury. Notts stays in play-off bracket snipping Scunny. L2: Old boy Harrold stops Southend with Bristol R leveller, so Crawley moves one pt nearer winning at Rotherham. Cheltenham, Shrewsbury, Burton, eleven no loss Swindon all win. Gills draw. Plymouth scores four against Northampton. SPL: Five up Celtic cracks St M. SL1: Ross strides on at Livi. SL2: Cowden, Arbroath both held. SL3: Berwick gets five to Montrose three. S Cup: Partick, Forfar, Queen's Park win replays. BSP; Wrexham, Fleetwood draw, Southport and Luton are winners. Trophy: Guiseley hits seven (Gavin Rothery 3), Dave Harper trebles for Hampton & R. W L: Bangor does down at Newtown. 13th win for RM now six pts clear as Barca loses at Getafe; Ronaldo hits 106th goal overtaking his Brazilian namesake (104). Six Togo players die in bus crash.

27 Gary Speed commits suicide at 42. Hart saves Man C unbeaten run in all square at Liverpool. Sixth clean sheet for Vorm and Swansea in Villa draw. Pascali nods Killie into first win over Rangers in 17 years.

28 Huddersfield run shudders to halt at Charlton. Bruce teeters on knife-edge of departure. Jones and Flynn temporarily removed from PL list. QPR will only move locally.

29 C Cup: Aguero late gives Man C the nod at Arsenal; Cardiff two-good for Blackburn as are Liverpool at Chelsea. FLC: Saints come back to beat Hull and is first side to win 21-home-in-a-row since Liverpool 1971-72. Hammers fine win ends Boro home record. Leeds four-play easily overcomes ten-man Forest. Burnley hits four against Ipswich. Leicester goes sixth beating Blackpool. BSP: Fleetwood takes out Kettering, ten-man Southport loses to FGR and Grimsby humbles Stockport with seven strikes. Pompey chairman resigns, administration looms.

30 C Cup: Palace on overtime turns out Man U. Semi draw: Man C v Liverpool, Palace v Cardiff. Bruce is chopped, stakes high for Hughes or O'Neill. AVB is safe for three years at Chelsea. E Lge: Zigic pen miss puts Birmingham on brink after Braga defeat. Spurs leveller rightly ruled out as PAOK wins at WHL. Shamrock hit for four by Rubin. Aidy Boothroyd is new Northampton boss, Andy King No.2. Polish FA chief axed. BSP: Wrexham catches up with Fleetwood after beating Darlo.

DECEMBER

England draws France in Euro ... Eight game ban for Suarez, Terry faces court ... Man C, Man U out of Ch Lge ... Capello calls for foreigners ban.

1 Capello hoping against a pot boiler. E Lge: Fulham must beat Odense after loss at Twente. One point is sufficient for Stoke to qualify after draw with Dynamo Kiev.

2 Pot luck as England faces France, Sweden and Ukraine. WC 2022 will be played in winter. Hearts players await wages. Minute's applause for Speed will be universal for English football. FA Cup: Fleetwood earns Yeovil replay after two down. FLC: Palace held by Derby. SPL: Motherwell – Hibs called off at half-time for safety reasons.

3 PL goals oddity: five teams 19, nine scrape six. Five strikes Man C (12th home PL consecutive win) cages in Canaries. Man U seventh lone PL goal in a row (volley ball Jones) enough for three points at Villa. Spurs club record 6th PL win on the trot and equals best run 11 no loss in PL, but Bolton blown out by crazy Attwell red for Cahill. Krul saves Lamps pen but born again Chelsea (AVB relieved and talisman Drogba on target) ends Newcastle home record but Toon has both central defenders injured. Yakubu four-timer feeds on Blackburn scraps (see Landmarks) to peck Swans out. Four star Arsenal push Wigan back to bottom. QPR shares pts with WBA. FLC: Sharp's cutting edge for Donny gets them off bottom as top team Soton is beaten. Hammers even let Burnley (second win there in 50 years) defeat them. Boro gets a lift at Bristol C. Leeds celebrate against Millwall and Brighton is back in play-off mode edging Forest. Three up Barnsley almost let Posh in until late hit. FA Cup: Shock! – Brentford out? Yes, Welsh Wrexham! (Reserves fulfil W Cup fixture but lose!) Chelmsford Clarets toast replay with Macc. Tubbs treble in Crawley five over Redbridge. Stourbridge run ends with Stevenage. Sheff U (10,305) beats off plucky Torquay and Sheff W (10,162) edges Shots. Southend 17 overall unbeaten equals club record in Oldham draw. SPL: Rangers og and pen clip Dunfermline, winners ICT off foot at St M. SL1: Milne hat trick as Dundee has six at Accies. Ross foursome defeats Raith. SL2: Cowden, Arbroath both draw, Sten creeps nearer. SL3: E Stirling off bottom beating leaders Annan. BSP: York seven-up scatters Kettering. W Cup: Llanelli (Rhys Griffiths 3) wins at Bangor. TNS scores six, so do Aberystwyth, Bala and Prestatyn. Vase: Whitley Bay five goals beats Bridlington, Bethnal Green also lances the Bengal boys five times. Real's 14th win is one shy of record; Ronaldo's 49th goal in 49 games 2011. Barca has five goals. Job scene: O'Neill will be Sunderland boss.

4 O'Neill watches as Black Cats bagged by Wolves. Stoke achieves away day win at Everton – first since 1981. Ref Dean says sorry for not dismissing David Luiz at Newcastle. FLC: Miller single keeps Cardiff in tune over ten-man Birmingham. SPL: Celtic cuts Rangers lead to four points winning at Dundee U. FA Cup: Totton totters to Bristol R six-hit. Sutton loses to Notts. Havelange jumps IOC ship before bribes decision. Socrates, one-time Brazil ace, dies at 57.

5 Liverpool loses at Fulham and Suarez in a digital storm. Ex-Man U Wallwork in prison over car parts scam. Celtic cleared over IRA songs. Martin O'Neill starts at Stadium of Light.

6 Ch Lge: Improved Chelsea treble ends Valencia hopes and accompanies Leverkusen who draws at Genk. Arsenal loses to Olympiakos but already there as Greeks fail after Marseille upsets Borussia. Zenit gk Malafeev keeps them in, Porto out in draw. Shakhtar salvages some pride away to Apoel. Barca "reserves" foursome against BATE, AC Milan through, but surprised by Viktoria fight back. FLC: Palace beaten at reviving Barnsley. JPT: Oldham, Chesterfield will contest Northern final, Barnet and Swindon in the south. BSP: Wrexham makes Southport its latest casualty with Fleetwood inactive. SL: frozen pitches cause three off, but Stranraer wins south of Scotland battle at Annan. FBI involves itself in WC 2018 bid. Hartlepool sacks Wadsworth. Cahill cleared and Attwell career under review. Peter Ridsdale is Preston chairman.

7 Ch Lge: Mancunian gloom as winners Man C (Napoli victory at Villarreal) and losers Man U are both out after respective results over Bayern and Basle and heading for E Lge. Lille held by Trabzonspor so CSKA win at Inter pushes them on with the Italians. Real wins at Ajax and are joined by Lyon (six of seven in s-h) at Dinamo Zagreb! FLC: Hull revival goes on as Birmingham (and Barmby gets the job) as Birmingham loses again. Suarez is on another charge.

8 Rooney gets one free of his three as FA courts UEFA successfully, but Dalglish is unhappy over it. Vidic out for the season and joins eight on the injured list. UEFA will investigate Lyon affair.

9 Villas-Boas hits out at Neville comments. Statue unveiling at Emirates for Henry leaves him in tears. W L: Bangor back on top beating Bala.

10 Nani and Roo doubles lift Man U spirits against Wolves. Holt duo (51 goals in 98) as Norwich doubles says humbug to Newcastle's Ba pair before all-seat record 26,816. Arsenal celebrates 125th birthday with another V P goal over Everton. Vorm saves pen keeping clean sheet in win against Fulham. Moses leads Wigan out of the PL

bottom-three wilderness at WBA. Seventh home loss for Bolton as Villa edges it. Suarez atones for three misses to give Liverpool win over QPR. FLC: Soton gk gaffe and 93rd min leveller in Blackpool share of four goals. Hammers have two marched off as birthday boy Church parades a twosome for Reading. Cardiff has to settle for Millwall draw in eleven no loss run. It is a fourth home win for Boro after Brighton gk error. One is enough for Hull at Coventry. Two down at half-time Ipswich stuns Barnsley with five hits. James gaffe, too, as Derby's Ball ends home goal drought beating Bristol C. L1: Charlton held back in Walsall draw. Sheff W away, Sheff U home: both record wins. MK Dons also win at Tranmere. Huddersfield slips again this time to Bournemouth. Cellar clash sees Wycombe edge Chesterfield late on. L2: Southend 12 unbeaten run stopped at Cheltenham, so Crawley recaptures top spot beating Burton. Gills make it seven no loss at Macc. Shrews tamed at Shots. Swindon settles for draw at Bristol R. SPL: Status quo as Rangers, Celtic both win. SL1: Ross at Ayr off, Dundee squeezes win over QoS in ten a side. SL2: Cowden, Arbroath share goalless. Sten also draws with Airdrie. Two games off. SL3: Annan, Alloa and Stranraer (six-hitters over E Stirling). Two games off, too. Trophy: Shocks: Hinckley ousts Wrexham, Fleetwood sunk at Northwich, Mansfield beaten at Droylsden, Tamworth at Worksop and Hayes at Hampton & R. Hat tricks: Liam Enver-Marum (Ebbsfleet), Richard Jolly (Wealdstone) and Dan Fitchett (Salisbury). Chester continues to impress. W L: TNS held at Aberystwyth. La Liga top: Real 23 seconds lead, Ronaldo misses chances and Barca takes control (Puyol again not on losing side in 19 such clashes).

11 Spurs (after 11 wins, one draw) finish with ten men and defeat at Stoke as ref is blamed. O'Neill gets his usual first game boost as Black Cats catch Rovers who lose lead once more.

12 Brittle ten-man Man C bows to a Lamps pen shedding light on Chelsea revival.

13 FA Cup: Fleetwood gives old giant-killers Yeovil a taste of defeat, Salisbury prevails at Grimsby in overtime, Daggers unseat Saddlers in shoot-out, Southend's ten lose at Oldham. SPL: First away win for Dons at St J. Man U's Fletcher hit by serious illness.

14 E Lge: Already through ten-man Stoke loses to Besiktas, Wisla win and Fulham being held by a Fall of Odense, slip out. Top clubs will get Academy boost. Barnet will quit Underhill.

15 Spurs appear in four-leaf clover away to Shamrock but Rubin draw at PAOK costs them dearly. Birmingham edges Maribor but needed Braga to lose at Club Brugge. Celtic draws at Udinese when win was essential. Gerrard reported on way back to fitness. Balotelli is in training scrap with Richards. CWC: Silva breaks leg for Barca against Al Sadd. Sion finally ruled out of European tournament this season!

16 Ch Lge draw: Napoli v Chelsea; AC Milan v Arsenal; Lyon v Apoel; Leverkusen v Barca; Zenit v Benfica; CSKA Moscow v Real Madrid, Basle v Bayern, Marseille v Inter. E Lge (English) Porto v Man C, Ajax v Man U, Stoke C v Valencia. Suarez decision delayed. No Euro 2012 players will be in for Olympic GB. Bendtner and Cattermole arrested on car damage allegation. Keys and Gray to start after-dinner speaking act. Givet is given heart test after pulse race. Dyer is out for the season at QPR. Southend beaten by Bradford, Barnet draws with Cheltenham. W L: Llanelli top after win.

17 Cech makes a mess so Wigan gets a draw with Chelsea. Bolton suffers fifth successive defeat at Fulham. Anniversary day for Kean but another loss for Blackburn as Morrison hits 1000th PL goal of 2011 and Peter O has WBA winner. Stoke fourth successive win (Crough 99th Lge goal) at Wolves but fortunate to finish with ten men after ref Taylor leniency with Woodgate. Eighth clean- sheet for Swans in stalemate at Newcastle. Holt scores again for Norwich in level-pegging at Everton who end recent goal drought after 273 mins. FLC: Injury and suspension-hit Hammers blood Potts, 17 and edge Barnsley to level with inactive Soton. Two off in 12 mins as poorly disciplined Brighton loses to Burnley. Boro fight back leap frogs Cardiff in a cracker. Hull gets rare win over Millwall – first since 1987. Church services a Reading win at Leeds. In-form James makes it five games no goals for Forest at Bristol C. Andrews sorts out Ipswich against Derby. Sharp again Donny hero in beating Leicester. L1: Rhodes foursome salvages pt for Huddersfield in eight-goal thriller at Sheff W. Two ogs help Sheff U at Bournemouth. Charlton allows Oldham to draw. No-boss PNE ends MK Dons eight month home record. Bury saves pt against Brentford. Stevenage makes it eleven no loss clipping Tranmere. L2: Crawley held at Crewe but 15th unbeaten (Tubbs 15th goal, too) and ref Attwell in controversy again. Shrewsbury back to winning ways edging Macc. Swindon, Gills keep on winning trail. Nine straight defeats then ten-man D and R draw at Burton after brawl spat. Loanee Madjo treble shoots down Shots for Vale. Oxford first win in seven beats Northampton. BSP: Wrexham stays ahead, but Fleetwood, Southport and Luton win. SPL: Rangers just edges ICT, no-pay Hearts cracks Dunfermline. SL: 8 off; SL1: Dundee holds Ross, Falkirk hits five at QoS. SL2: Brechin wins at Airdrie. SL3: Three-tie at top as Stranraer clips Peterhead late on with Annan, Alloa also on 30 pts. Ronaldo threesome as ten-man Real has six at Seville. Basle may be out of Ch Lge giving Man U a chance.

18 Silva is the scoring difference in a classic as Man C defeats Arsenal. Under-fire Suarez is Liverpool's menace in win at Villa. Rooney strikes in 23 secs as Man U gets two at QPR. Spurs need only one against Sunderland. Saints squander in Pompey draw. Celtic moves four points nearer Rangers in catch-up at St J. Barca wins CWC taking four off Santos

19 Palace just beats Birmingham in dour affair. Tube strike may ko Boxing Day London games. Rotherham will move to New York Stadium (local foundry site). Scots will moot standing areas.

20 Suarez is savaged by eight-game ban. Bolton cellar win at Blackburn piles more grief on Kean. Wolves salvage pt against Norwich. BSP: Fleetwood level top after win at Hayes. Only one SL game survives as Peterhead pens in Berwick. Ibe, 16, is on way to Liverpool from Wycombe at £500,000.

21 Terry faces court over alleged racist remark. Albrighton hits 20,000th PL goal but Van Persie equals Henry's Arsenal record of 34 calendar goals as Gunners win at Villa. Man C takes three off Stoke. Giggs scores for 20th season as Man U goes nap hand at Fulham. Ba gets a double for Newcastle but WBA still wins. Osman wins it for Everton who go 11th against Swansea. Sunderland late show shakes QPR. Suarez in action as Liverpool is held at Wigan.

22 Chelsea gets a draw at Spurs thanks to Terry late clearance. Liverpool T-shirt defence of Suarez criticised all round and by PFA chief. Yaya Toure is African Player of Year. Heather Rabbatts becomes first women on FA board. Eusebio enters hospital. Barca hits nine in cup game. Arsenal calls off Boxing Day game but Chelsea will play Fulham.

23 Sir Alex puts boot in, too, over Suarez, but delay in announcing when the Uruguayan will start ban.

24 Chelsea reject idea of Terry-supporting T-shirts. Buddies beat nine-man Rangers and Celtic cuts Ibrox lead to one point beating Killie. SL3: Berwick fights back to draw but Annan sneaks back to top spot.

25 PL title challengers all confident ahead of the hectic holiday programme.

26 Man C draws blank at Baggies bargain boys, so five star Man U (Berbatov 3 and Lindegaard 7 plus hours no PL concede) catches them on pts against ten-man Wigan. Fulham holds Chelsea at the Bridge. Blackburn grateful for Adam og at Liverpool and rare pt. Newcastle inflicts another home defeat on Bolton. Stoke and Villa also blankety-blank. Lucky pen for Everton (ref Webb gaffe) stops Sunderland win. FLC: Saints (still to spend) look

better now three pts clear with twosome over Palace. Hammers (Cole 50th for them) held at Birmingham, so Boro (27,794) level with them beating Hull. Cardiff draws at Watford with og. Reading (in top six) defeats Brighton, but Matt Phillips hat trick gives it to Blackpool at Barnsley. Millwall (Jackett 100th win) edges Pompey. L1: Charlton leaves it very late at Yeovil, but Sheff W loses ground in injury-time loss at Walsall. MK Dons threesome hits Orient. Rhodes – naturally – (20th goal) is Huddersfield winner over Chesterfield. Stevenage best away day six at Colchester (worst home since 1956) now 12 undefeated. Trotta's treble lifts Wycombe over Exeter. PNE – Carlisle share six goals. Tranmere is off due to stand damage. L2: Nine no loss Gills end Crawley run in ten-a-side. Cheltenham, seven no loss, held goalless by Shrewsbury. Burton edges ten-man Northampton. Swindon loses away at Torquay after 15 no defeat. Plymouth clips Bristol R and levels at foot with Daggers and Cobblers. AFC Dons ten no win lose at Oxford. Shots off: lights fail losing with ten-men to Southend. BSP: one off: Wrexham wins at Telford but ten-man Fleetwood held by Southport. Luton hits struggling Kettering for five. SL1: Ross held at Falkirk, Dundee loses at home to Morton. SL2: 1 off, one abandoned. Cowden wins at Stenhousemuir. SL3: Alloa trebles it over Elgin. W L: TNS hits three at Newtown to go top.

27 Canaries tied up by double Bale as Spurs go marching on in third. No finish Arsenal held by Wolves as TH looks on and Attwell in another storm over Milijas red. Warnock blasts ref Probert over Swans goal in QPR draw. Og aids Sheff U over Notts. Blackburn reports £18.6m loss. WL: Bangor takes advantage as Llanelli loses to Neath.

28 SPL: Fierce Auld Firm derby edges Celtic way as Rangers lucky to finish with eleven as Hoops hit front. Motherwell is off for safety reasons. Suarez gets another one-match ban! Henry nears Arsenal return. Ancelotti may join PSG. Michael O'Neill appointed N Ireland boss. Neale Cooper returns as Hartlepool manager.

29 Capello wants foreigners banned. Ex-FIFA man Warner hits out at Blatter. Sion may sue FIFA, too. Ajax intruder banned and cup game to be replayed. Maradona fined by UAE for abusing rival.

30 Bellamy brace lifts Gerrard-inspired Liverpool against Newcastle. Bristol C completes double over faltering Saints (after 24 home unbeaten). Huddersfield held by Carlisle. Crawley, Cheltenham both win, but Gills lose to Daggers. Swiss FA takes 36 points off Sion after FIFA threats!

31 Man U odd starting line-up then involved in another five-goal affair – but Blackburn gets three of them! Drawing Spurs fail to hold lead at Swansea. V Persie breaks watching Henry record with 35th calendar goal enough to clip QPR. Chelsea hits the skids against three goal Villa after Drogba's 150th club goal equalling Osgood total. Stoke held by ten-man Wigan. Jackson arrival saves Norwich in 94th min draw against Fulham. Comeback boys Wolves level at cellar-dwelling Bolton. FLC: Early reverses at Derby cost Hammers, so Boro's pt against Posh gives them second place. Miller grinds a win for Cardiff at Forest (10 plus hours no goals or pts). Reading needs just one against Ipswich. Sub Vaz Te treble gives Tykes victory over slumping Leeds. Hull loses again at Burnley. Birmingham home alone in no FLC loss and three all round against Blackpool. L1: Ten-man Charlton loses at Orient. Good day for Sheffield: Utd home to Hartlepool and Wed away at Preston both have two-goal cushions. MK Dons stung by Brentford fight back three down in share of six. Stevenage goes 11 no Lge loss after win at Wycombe. L2: Southend whacks four at AFC Dons, Crewe hits five at Bristol R. Shrews lose at ten-finishing Bradford. Swindon poses more problems for Northampton. Burton achieves point at Morecambe. SL3: Stranraer goes top in S of Scotland derby with Annan.

JANUARY

Messi is Player of the Year . . . Chris Coleman gets Wales job . . . King Henry returns . . . quiet transfer scene.

1 Ding Ji Dong the City's dead as 93rd min winner (offside and four secs to spare!) jars brittle Man C in topsy-turvy New Year at Sunderland. Everton achieves 1002 (last of all-time PL teams) pts in win at WBA. Rooney fined £200,000 for being unfit to train and Gibson, Evans also culprits after family night out. BSP: Wrexham takes four off Telford. Even with ten men, Fleetwood gets six at Southport, Luton another five over Kettering.

2 Crouch hits 100th and 101st as Stoke brings Blackburn back to reality. Arsenal's ten lose it at Fulham, Wenger groans at ref and opposition players. Barton off as Norwich sneaks it at QPR. Clean sheet Swans get first PL away win at Villa. Chelsea leaves it late for win at Wolves, but scorer Lamps admits lucky to stay on. FLC: Lambert card proves costly as Brighton threesome finishes still ahead Soton. Hammers again level top on points edging Coventry. Cardiff (three in 24 mins) impresses against Reading, but Boro dives out at Blackpool. Hull suffers another blank day as Derby wins. Forest ends misery at Ipswich since beating them before! Leeds (95th min winner) is also grateful for Burnley down to ten men. L1: Charlton (surviving power cut), Sheff W both win, but Sheff U suffers ex-Owl McGovern and Zoko ko at Carlisle. Eleventh draw for Huddersfield at Notts. Orient wins ten-a-side finish to end Stevenage 11 game (13th overall) unbeaten run. First win in ten for Scunny at Hartlepool. L2: Crawley salvages a point at Oxford in dying seconds. Cheltenham holds off Port Vale successfully. Daggers snatch pt in Essex derby at Southend. Swindon makes it seven-in- a-row losses for AFC Dons. Shrewsbury held by the Cobblers (no win in 14), Burton turned over by the Hereford Bulls. Gills ten men still beat Shots. McLeod's 19th goal for Barnet puts pressure on Buckle at Bristol R. Nine no loss Stanley and four goals, too. SPL: Celtic away, Rangers at home each get three. One game is off at ICT. SL1: Ross off, but Falkirk and Dundee win away. SL2: Cowden foursome and Arbroath loss at Dumbarton. SL3: Alloa back on top with trio at E Stirling. W L: Bangor gets five, so does TNs, Llanelli loses. Gary Ablett, dies at 46.

3 Man C treble minus one red still three too much for Liverpool. Spurs do it by the minimum over Baggies. Born-again Sunderland hit four at Wigan. FLC: Bristol C wins again this time over Millwall. Liverpool remains unmoved over Suarez affair. McClaren may get Twente job back as Adriaanse axed. Bristol R sacks boss Buckle. Darlington enters administration (third in nine years) and have ten pts deducted. Leicester bids £2m for Donny's Sharp.

4 Newcastle turn the screw on Man U. Bolton survives freak Howard goal to win at Everton. Suarez apologises to all except Evra. Riot squads lined up for Mancunian cup game.

5 Glazers may need to find dollars for Sir Alex title retention. City will need to buy, too. McClaren has Twente nod. England will play in Norway. Bramble faces another charge.

6 FA Cup: Liverpool five-star show ends Oldham hopes after leading. L1: All Rhodes led to Huddersfield's win at Wycombe; striker hitting five of six. L2: Accrington marches on at Burton. Anfield is scene of racist abuse of Oldham player. Man U denies Rooney problem. Henry cleared for Arsenal loan return.

7 FA Cup: Swindon beats Wigan, 53 places above them. Macc Silkmen frighten the Bolton Trotters. MK Dons hold QPR (16 no such cup win. Wrexham earns draw at Brighton. Ref Lewis is no Friend for "Spiderman" Gutierrez booking 94th minute winner over Blackburn after Ben Arfa special. Hat tricks: Matty Phillips (Blackpool), Clint Dempsey (Fulham). Crawley takes out Bristol C. Saints youngsters beat Coventry (in 1987 replica cup kit). Ten-change Cardiff loses at WBA (also Cox treble). Stevenage gains revenge over Reading. Daggers hold Lions but police bill heavy. Tamworth and Salisbury are k'od at Everton (Moyes 300th win) and Sheff U respectively. L1: Carlisle foursome deflates Orient. L2: Southend moves nearer cup-tie Crawley beating Vale. Northampton

achieves first win after 13 tries. S Cup: Bell pen save stops Dundee beating Killie. Ten Sten men let in seven at Ross. Dundee U are six-hitters at Airdrie. Plucky Auchinleck restricts Hearts to one goal. St M held by Accies. SL3: Stranraer back on top at Montrose. BSP: Kettering faces winding-up and beaten at Telford.

8 FA Cup: City Kompany in the red pays United dividend; Mancunian tie sees City fight back just failing. Owls peck out the Hammers, Sunderland eases at Posh and Chelsea late flourish finishes Pompey. Warnock is axed at QPR. S Cup: Rangers, Celtic no problems with away days at Arbroath and Peterhead respectively.

9 FA Cup: King Henry back on the scoring throne in cameo winner, his 227th for Arsenal as Leeds loses. Cantona is up for Froggy President! Trading in Rangers shares suspended. Gary Johnson is back in seat at Yeovil with Skiverton assisting. Man C seeks defenders. Player of the Year: Messi (three in a row), Rooney even makes the team of the year.

10 Kompany gets four-match ban after appeal fails, Mancini unhappy. Mark Hughes is new QPR manager. Hull gives Barmby the job at last. Darlo on the brink may fold. C Cup: Advantage Palace edging Cardiff but Mackay complains over disallowed goal. Foursome from Sheff U strikes Yeovil. BSP: Fleetwood hits another four.

11 C Cup: Another defeat for Man C as Liverpool takes pen lead through Gerrard. PL: Spurs impressively add Everton to list of victims. Robbie Keane is likely Villa loanee. Ipswich moans over lineswoman as Zigic sneaks it for Birmingham.

12 Tevez move away is no nearer. New deal for Gerrard is finalized.

13 Chelsea nails Cahill for £7m. Spurs— West Ham feud over Olympic stadium continues. Bolton is £110m in debt. Avraam Grant is Partizan boss now. Wenger stays critical of TV scheduling.

14 Rooney spot off (4th miss in last 8 and 6 of 14 PL), but born-again legend Scholes sparks Man U to threesome over Bolton. Spurs concede 2000th PL goal to give Wolves a pt. No Torres goal but Lamps shows way against Sunderland (Essien Blues return for his 150th PL). Liverpool brings on Carroll late but no goals shared with Stoke – City no win there top flight for 49 years. Norwich uses headers away to defeat WBA. Everton earns draw at Villa in top's most frequent opponents – 194th and for the home side sixth share in last seven as Bent hits 98th PL goal. Yakubu off (first PL) but Rovers move out of bottom three beating Fulham. FLC: Ten-man Forest cut down by Saints but Cotterill unhappy with visiting bench. Pen writes off ten-man Pompey for Hammers. Cardiff held at Doncaster and Boro slips at home to Burnley. Sub Le Fondre helps Reading win at Watford. Minimum score for Hull winners against Posh – and one goal as usual for Palace level with Leeds. Nine-man Millwall crash to six-hit Birmingham. Coventry firmly bottom after Derby defeat. Gray double shifts Barnsley over Leicester. L1: Charlton ends Sheff W home record in crucial win but Sheff U has threesome at Bury. Lee gives Huddersfield success over Oldham. No Westley (now officially at PNE), but Stevenage still gets five at Rochdale. MK Dons frozen off. Walsall gk Walker makes 530th club appearance and clean sheet in Brentford draw. Point for Chesterfield but no in in 17 now. L2: Five-star Southend (three in last nine mins) shakes Northampton. Shots blanked again at Cheltenham. Crawley held goalless at Bristol R. Swindon early aids at Rotherham, but Oxford caught out by Crewe and Gills lose at Shrewsbury. Barnet's best of season at Accrington. SPL: Rangers win at St J, Celtic edges Dundee U; Skacel three as Hearts await wages again but strike St M with five. SL1: Dundee progresses against Livi as games-in-hand Ross is held away and Falkirk at home to Ayr. SL2: Cowden stretches lead to eight pts. SL3: Alloa overtakes Stranraer beating Annan. BSP: Wrexham alone overhauls inactive Fleetwood. Trophy: Barrow beaten at Wealdstone, Carshalton earns draw at Lincoln. Chester run ends at Ebbsfleet. York gets six at Salisbury.

15 V Persie early doors, but Swans close out Arsenal leveller in 45 secs to win. Newcastle puts QPR into last three.

16 One goal settles Man C at Wigan but Mancini in card waving row. Inter's Tevez bid turned down. Capello gazes at Swans. Darlo totters. Seven players snub GB.

17 FA Cup: No shocks in replays Henderson treble as Millwall hit Daggers for five, Liecester foursome over Forest, one goal QPR exits MK Dons and Bolton gets two over Macc. S Cup: St M wins at Accies, Dundee edged by Killie. Newcastle pays £10m for a Cisse.

18 FA Cup: Wolves bow to Brummies, Brighton needs shoot-out to beat Wrexham. JPT: Chesterfield takes lead over Oldham. S Cup: ICT upsets Dunfermline. Trophy: Carshalton knocks out Lincoln! Chris Coleman lined up for Wales job. JM likely to punish Pepe for stamping on Messi's hand as Real lose in cup. Becks will stay with LA. Mark McGhee is Bristol R boss.

19 Coleman is in place. Six Brighton players face charges. Only kids in as AZ cup replay beats Ajax. Newcastle will help Darlo.

20 Arsenal injury list broadens ahead of Man U clash. Eric Black appointed as Blackburn assistant manager. Pele discounts Messi!

21 No-goal Torres 15 hrs 19 mins taken off again in goalless deal at Norwich where no cards are issued! Dempsey second half treble ends Toon lead at Fulham in rare five for the Cottagers. Liverpool even loses at Bolton whose last treble against them was in 1950! WBA ends 30-year misery at Stoke. Sunderland continues upward taking out Swansea. Special K (Keane) (216 and 217th goals in 572nd game) chokes Wolves becomes seventh player to score for six PL clubs with double for Villa winners on McLeish's 53rd birthday. Blackburn pt at Everton but hand may have help homers. QPR puts Wigan to the sword. FLC: Hammers take advantage of Saints inactivity to go top two pens edging Forest. Boro has two sent off and loses to Coventry. Cardiff strikes late goal in disposing of Pompey in taxing times again. Davies two headers aids push for Brummies into promotion area. Hull prevents Reading (Russians moving in?) scoring at home and climbs above them. Henderson second treble in a week aids Millwall at Barnsley. Late effective Leeds ends Ipswich. Boss Saunders rails over no red shown as Donny loses at Bristol C. L1: Spooky: Jackson finishes Utd after Wed a week ago for Sheffield – axing Charlton! Two-adrift Huddersfield relies on Rhodes winner against Brentford. MK Dons draw at Notts. Stevenage settles for point at Scunny. Bournemouth six loss edge Tranmere. Westley bemoans unfit Preston losing to Orient. Chesterfield wins at Colchester – first win since September. Wycombe leaps above Rochdale in relegation mode. L2: Shrews ten-men beat Southend. Crawley draws at lowly Plymouth. AFC Dons get best of seven at Gills. Bristol R cheers new boss McGhee in win at Cheltenham. Nine hours 23 mins no goals Shots get a point against Stanley. One goal enough for Swindon over Macc but Di Canio sent to stand. Duberry hits hat trick- two ogs and one legit in Oxford's draw with Hereford. BSP: Wrexham batters sad Kettering, Fleetwood attracts 5658 at skint Darlo. Grimsby half a dozen goals, Luton has to share same at Southport. Vase: Whitley Bay makes it 29 wins consecutively in it as Chow scores in 13th consecutive round v ten-man South Park. Matthew Jukes trio as Tividale trash Binfield. West Auckland is in last 16 – first time. SPL: Celtic opens four-point gap over held Rangers. Dunfermline wins at Killie. SL1: Ross off but next four teams only draws. SL2: Cowden caught by lowly Forfar so Arbroath "sixers" make ground beating Albion. SL3: Alloa foursome floors Stranraer to extend lead to four points. Ernie Gregory, ex-West Ham goalkeeper dies at 90.

22 Balotelli faces ban after back-heel on Parker, then pens in Spurs at eleventh hour. Mancunian double as Man U wins at Arsenal.

23 Redknapp in the dock faces charges. Slipping Saints well beaten by Leicester. FA peruses Balotelli stamp. Ref Atkinson will officiate at Liverpool – Man U tie. John Coleman aims for Rochdale role. Training row at RM fuels rumours of JM departure.

24 C Cup: Cardiff emerges against ten-man Palace via shoot-out. L1: MK Dons lose at Stevenage but Sheff W beats Scunthorpe. L2: Another win for AFC Dons and Torquay. BSP: Wrexham lost in the Forest. Fleetwood go clear leaders beating Braintree. SPL: Motherwell defeats Dunfermline with ten players. Tevez strike costs him £9.3m in wages. Balotelli may quit England. John Coleman in at Rochdale.

25 C Cup: Draw not enough for creaking Man C at Liverpool. Financial fair-play menaces Chelsea and Man C. Real only draws with Barca and exits cup on JM 49th birthday. Gary Smith gets Stevenage job. Early doors play-offs pencilled in.

26 Redknapp will take his usual place for Spurs at Watford cup game. Platini pleads his case for not wanting to "kill the English."

27 FA Cup: V der V enables Spurs to win – just – and Everton edges Fulham. Anton Ferdinand receives death threat bullet in post ahead of Terry re-match. Evra prepares to face Liverpool crowd after Suarez affair. Chesterfield is off the bottom in win over Bournemouth. Wilshere is out injured again.

28 FA Cup: Brighton deflected og sufficient for win over Toon in poor affair. Crawley Red Devils add Hull to scalps. Og helps Stevenage to beat Notts. Diving pen issue settles unpleasant tie for Chelsea against QPR. Kuyt on a high as Liverpool brings Man U to earth. Birmingham foursome cuts out Sheff U, but Sheff W earns draw at Blackpool. Replay needed for Soton after Millwall leveller from Henderson's 100th career goal. Swans feel the Trotters tread. Norwich edges it at WBA. Stoke's 14th cup tie of season produces win at Derby. Beckford double ends Swindon run for Leicester. FLC: Pompey forgets fiscal worries with decisive win at Posh. Reading goes fourth beating Bristol C in only other match. L1: Yet again one goal Charlton wins it at Exeter. Rochdale revives in treble success over Bury. Rhodes makes a Huddersfield pt at Tranmere. Wycombe ships five at Brentford. Hartlepool sinks ten-man Carlisle with foursome. L2: Cheltenham hits the top at Macc. Shrewsbury ahead in derby at Hereford. Torquay keeps Northampton bottom with Vale giving Plymouth another defeat. Accrington best of seven goal win over Gills reprises only such score line for them since 1958. Barnet climbs to 17th as nine-man Crewe suffers. Shots goal drought ends after nine hours 36 mins with win at AFC Dons. Daggers move out of bottom two beating Rotherham. SPL: Rangers four-timer beats Hibs. Aberdeen leaps to sixth. SL1: 1 off. Ross goes five pts clear beating Livi. SL2: 3 off. Airdrie four hits Stirling. SL3: Alloa wins, Stranraer gets five. SC Cup: Killie extra time win at Ayr. BSP: Fleetwood, Wrexham, Luton all win. W Cup: TNS crashes four against Newport. Ronaldo's 24th goal as RM opens seven pt gap over Barca held at Villarreal, but JM may head PL way?

29 FA Cup: Two-down to Villa, Arsenal responds with threesome including double V P pens. Campbell earns Sunderland replay with Boro. SC Cup: Celtic clinches final spot with Killie by beating Falkirk.

30 Crawley loses Tubbs to Bournemouth. Pomey wages delay. Redknapp returns to trial.

31 Mancini blames himself for not preparing team at Everton as ex-Man U Gibson beats them. Man U catches them at the top with couple of pens over Stoke. Og rescues pt for Chelsea – Cole late off – at Swansea. Carroll celebrates year at Anfield with goal as Liverpool gets three at Wolves. Spurs steps out comfortable in third place as Wigan stays at the foot. FLC: Iron hammered by five-star best of season winners Ipswich. New boy Sharp sees Saints held by Cardiff. Zigic cracks four goals for Birmingham movers to fourth at Leeds. Sixth reverse on the trot for Forest home to Burnley. L1: Charlton scrapes a late draw against Bury, MK Dons and Sheff W also level. L2: Swindon sends Southend reeling at Roots Hall. SL3: Alloa opens seven-pt gap beating Peterhead. Transfer window closes including Kevin De Bruyne, Genk to Chelsea £7m, Roman Pavlyuchenko, Spurs to Lokomotiv Moscow £7.5m.

FEBRUARY

Capello resigns! . . . Redknapp cleared of charges . . . Rangers in administration! . . . Liverpool wins Carling Cup.

1 New Cisse is hit with QPR but Villa levels at two-down. Newcastle flattered in win at Blackburn. Bolton holds Arsenal. Late Baggies get a point at Fulham. Black Cats purred to another threesome against Norwich. FLC: Leicester and Boro share four goals. Barca held in away leg cup semi at Valencia. Simon Grayson sacked at Leeds. Over 70 fans die in stampede at Cairo at Al-Ahly – Al-Masry match.

2 Terry is likely to lose England armband. Redknapp claims he only lied to press, not the coppers. £5.5m Jelavic says only Everton offered to sign him!

3 Under pressure FA axes Terry as captain. Suarez is back for Liverpool. Weather predicted to cause fixture postponements.

4 Mancini gets his 50th Man C win in stop-start for snow during victory over Fulham. Goal of the season over 21 seconds as ten Arsenal players, ten passes and a V P finish (his three give 13th in 13 games) in seven-up over Blackburn – even Henry scores in last Emirates game. McClean tidies off ten-man Stoke for Sunderland – now eighth and best in-form PL. Norwich shoves Bolton in bottom trio as Wolves first win in ten gets over QPR (Cisse off). WBA joins the Trotters with worst home record as Swansea edges them. Wigan (Martinez 100th l/c) stays adrift but a point with Everton thanks to joke og. FLC: 2 off. Ten Hammers extend lead to four points clipping Millwall as Birmingham held goalless by ten-man Saints. The Phillips' boys stagger leading Cadiff with three in last 11 mins for Blackpool. Brighton's ten hit Leicester's nine finishers. Boro-Palace are goalless, too, and no wins in 2012. Ipswich hits 95th minute winner in five goal game at Coventry. Leeds beat nine-man Bristol C. Rodriguez solo stops Posh win at Burnley. L1: 8 off. Sheff W goes second beating Yeovil. Huddersfield and MK Dons share the points. Wycombe climbs out of drop zone against Tranmere. L2: 1 on! Two down Plymouth snatches pt off Southend (59 second opener). S Cup: 1 off. QoS and Ross earn replays at Aberdeen and St M. Motherwell crashes six past Morton. Hibs edge Killie. Celtic is away winner at ICT. SL only 3 Div £ on: Alloa extends lead to nine pts at Queen's Park, Stranraer levels at E Stirling but Annan held at Montrose. BSP: In only surviving game Fleetwood held by ten-man Tamworth but Vardy gets his 22nd goal of season. W L: TNS loses to Neath, Bangor (at new venue) beats Prestatyn. Forest's owner Nigel Doughty dies at 54.

5 Capello uses Italian TV interview to hit out at FA's Terry decision. Three down Man U fight back to earn draw at Chelsea with Rooney double pens (one unfair) and Cahill fortunate to stay on. Ba back and scoring for Newcastle (plus another Cisse!) in win over Villa. S Cup: Dundee U puts skids under Rangers at Ibrox, while St J earns replay with Hearts.

6 Capello faces wrath of FA but Terry has no intention of losing armband. Liverpool and Spurs in no goals; Suarez sub returns for a booking. Four injured in Brazil club game after gun shots.

Alex Oxlade-Chamberlain drives home his second goal as Arsenal go 5-1 up against Blackburn, on the way to an emphatic 7-1 win at the Emirates in February. (Action Images/Tony O'Brien)

7 FA Cup: Blackpool too good for Sheff W, Millwall lasts pace longer at Soton. FLC: Birmingham goes third beating Pompey. Tubbs scores for Bournemouth against Exeter, while his old club Crawley knocks Cheltenham off top and replaces them. JPT: Swindon beats Barnet and reaches final. SPL: Still no home win for Dunfermline held by Killie. Argentina steps up Falklands issue naming his First Division after cruiser General Belgrano sunk in 1982.

8 Capello resigns! Redknapp, not caught out, is out of court and free to take over? FA Cup: Sunderland prevails at Boro. SPL: Celtic foursome and four points ahead of Rangers after win at Hearts. AN Cup: Ivory Coast beats Mali and meets Zambia winners over Ghana in final.

9 Pearce is England caretaker. Polish roads are behind schedule for 2012 finals. Ajax board resigns. Cattermole and Bendtner charged with vandalising cars.

10 Redknapp appears keen for England. Shoal of matches likely to be called off. Villas-Boras wants referees punished for mistakes. Southend loses to Rotherham. TNS hits four against Prestatyn.

11 Suarez snubs Evra hand, scores consolation for Liverpool at Man U, raising temperature off field, as Rooney double in 500th club and country outing (213th goal) ensures home win. Goal King Henry the fourth strikes (PL outing and 176th PL goal in 259th such outing) ending second Arsenal domestic reign to win at Sunderland. Five-star Spurs win at Newcastle's expense best over Toon since seven in 1950. Chelsea slips up again at Everton – fans unhappy and owner at training sessions. Norwich has away day success at Swansea and Ruddy good late save. Pavel "Pog" off the mark – but Pulis claims red card not shown as Stoke edged at Fulham. Wigan after nine no PL win get bonus at Bolton. Three down £12m spending QPR just fail to level at Blackburn. FLC: 3 off, Ips-Boro abd. Soton cuts inactive Hammers lead beating Burnley. Cardiff slips up again at Leicester. Blackpool held by Pompey, but Hull treble hits Bristol C. Forest 649 min no-goal at home ends, but Watford gets the point, too. L1: 9 off. Sheff joy and despair as Utd threesome cracks Wycombe and Wed loses at Exeter. Hartlepool and Bournemouth are goalless. L2: 8 off. Shrewsbury loses at sixth-in-a-row winners Torquay. Bristol R achieves best of three goals against Morecambe, Hereford and Cheltenham share points. SPL: Rangers help themselves to four at Dunfermline, but Celtic's one over ICT keeps them ahead. Dundee U hits five at St J. SL1: Livi beats Partick, everyone else draws. SL2: Four each for Cowden against Stirling, Arbroath at Forfar, extending their leads. SL3: Alloa loses home record to Berwick. QP five blanks Montrose. BSP: 1 on! Stockport and Newport – are "County" sharers. Kettering and Darlo are still in trouble. W L: Top team Bangor wins at Llanelli. Vase: all 8 off. Barca falls further behind losing to Osasuna.

12 A sorry bunch as Suarez, Dalglish and Liverpool owners all apologize. ANC final: Drogba repeats penalty miss of a previous final and Zambia goes on to win a shoot-out against Ivory Coast. Man C resumes at the top, one enough at Villa. Wolves surrender, bludgeoned in the Black Country derby by five-striking Baggies (Peter O 3). Real shakes off stoic, ten-man Levante to open ten pt lead with Ronaldo getting three.

13 Tevez takes lead in "dog-days" comment to Mancini. Rangers enter administration as £50m tax bill emerges, Portsmouth may follow. McCarthy axed by Wolves. Southend is back on top at Gills. Paul Cook appointed Accrington manager with caretaker Leam Richardson now assistant.

14 Ch Lge: Barca takes lead at Leverkusen, Lyon just edges Apoel. E Lge: Away wins for Besiktas and Olympiakos. FLC: Controversy reigns at ten-man West Ham as Soton achieves a point. Cardiff beats Posh, Boro edges Forest and Birmingham and Hull settle for a pt. Blackpool wins at Donny. L1: Charlton holds off ten-ma MK Dons, Sheff W loses again to Stevenage, but Sheff U wins at Huddersfield. L2: Cheltenham loses to in-form Torquay who goes third. Swindon's treble hits Crawley. Shrewsbury and Oxford also prove winners. Rare win for Northampton. S Cup: Q of S, Ross both lose replays to Dons and St M, Hearts win at St J. Ten points deduction in

place for Rangers. Dennis Bergkamp wades into continental-mentality of Arsenal. Mourinho is in touch with old Chelsea players. FIFA warns over Argies "Belgrano" move. Alan Curbishley may be Wolves boss.

15 Ch Lge: Arsenal crashes to worst Euro defeat conceding four at AC Milan. Zenit accepts narrow lead against Benfica. S Cup: Ayr surprises Falkirk. Rangers' liquidation may scupper TV deal. Hiddink chased by Anzhi – and Chelsea? Ref Attwell demoted. Huddersfield surprise: Clark sacked.

16 E Lge: Manchester double away: Utd at Ajax, but Valencia injured, City at Porto where Balotelli suffers racist abuse. Stoke toppled by Mehmet screamer- for Valencia! Redknapp considers part-time England if required. Plastic pitches may return. Rangers "lost" £24m loan. Brazil's XV de Jau axes coach Nem after two days and FIFA man there Teixeira may quit after alleged scandal over payments. Head of security at FIFA also walks out.

17 St James' Park renamed Sports Direct Arena, though council will still use old version. AVB will wield axe at Chelsea. Porto denies racism. Pompey deducted ten points. Neil Warnock is appointed Leeds boss – in Monte Carlo! Reading goes third after beating Burnley.

18 FA Cup: Blanked again – Arsenal at Sunderland and rumours over Wenger out, Guardiola in. Chelsea scrapes draw with Birmingham. Foxes peck off the Canaries, Trotters trample Lions. Two in six mins (49 secs first) prove sufficient for Everton against Blackpool. FLC: Super Saints foursome ravages Rams. Cardiff gives four-on-the-spin Ipswich another win. Warnock's presence lifts Leeds successfully to recover two-goal deficit to Donny. Four goals for Palace – and first 2012 win – over Watford. Posh treble and first win in eight over Bristol C. Forest ends slump beating Coventry. Deducted ten points and ten-man Pompey loses at Barnsley. L1: Seven no loss Charlton levels at Tranmere equalling FL record for five consecutive draws against same team. Pen-missing Evans double hit helps Sheff U over PNE. Sheff W loses again to Morgan pen for Chesterfield. First win in six as MK Dons strike five against Oldham. Notts lose at Hartlepool and costs Martin Allen his job. Rock bottom Wycombe, despite Bull pen save, beaten at Walsall and six above them all win! L2: Southend keeps ahead of five-goal Cheltenham on goals scored only as Shrimpers edge Crewe and Robins hit ten-man Daggers. Swindon has seventh straight win in derby at Hereford. Shrewsbury wins at Barnet, but Torquay loses to first-win-in-six Bradford. Oxford draws at Bristol R. Plymouth stuns Stanley with foursome. SPL: Minus ten pts, now Killie adds to Rangers misery – but stays second! SL1: Falkirk makes ground as Ross held by cellar-dwellers Ayr. SL2: Cowden draws 1125 and game at Arbroath. SL3: Alloa loses again, but Stranraer, QP, Annan and Elgin all win. W L: TNS closes on inactive Bangor. BSP: Fleetwood, Wrexham, Luton and York remain winners at the top. Vase: Whitley Bay's 29 unbeaten run ends to West Auckland – but Herne Bay cheer 125th anniversary year with place in last eight.

19 FA Cup: Brighton bounced out in treble-og nightmare at six-scoring Liverpool – Albion's worst in cup since 1946. Spurs held goalless at Stevenage. Even with ten-man Stoke wins at Crawley. SPL: Celtic piles on the Rangers pressure with five at Hibs.

20 Villas-Boras wants to be backed. Wenger is also under fire. Quinn quits Sunderland. New bosses: Simon Grayson at Huddersfield, Keith Curle at Notts. Brentford foursome cracks Carlisle.

21 Ch Lge: Chelsea overtaken at Napoli, Real Madrid caught in late draw in Moscow. FLC: Even with ten-man Hammers hit four at Blackpool. Birmingham, Boro both win away. L1: Rochdale holds Charlton. MK Dons edge Bury, Walsall welcomes win at Scunny. L2: Swindon goes top beating Shrewsbury as Shots take out Southend and Cheltenham held by AFC Dons. BSP: Fleetwood sinks Ebbsfleet with six-salvo. Wrexham wins at Kiddy, but Luton loses at Barrow and Darlo concedes five. SPL: Dundee U foursome flays Killie. SL1: Dundee draws at Falkirk, Ross game off. SL2: Bottom Stirling holds top Cowden. SL3: QP fails to beat Berwick. Delap red card rescinded. Wolves want Reading manage. Olympic Stadium unfit for PL>

22 Ch Lge: Basle one up on Bayern, Marseille with Inter, too. E Lge: Quartet of goals enough for Man C against Porto. Hull and Brighton are goalless. Notts just beat Stevenage, Crawley held by Morecambe. York hit by Gateshead. SPL: Celtic beats Dunfermline, Motherwell just hold off Hibs. SL2: Doris Day at Arbroath; striker hits treble. Now the PM weighs in on racism situ. Pearce will go for youth. Pompey axes 30 staff and others defer wages.

23 E Lge: Man U scrapes through despite Ajax defeat. Stoke out after loss at Valencia. Pearce talks a good game. Samba signs for Anzhi in £12m deal. Tevez expects to be back soon. AVB is under fire at the Bridge. Leicester wins at Derby. Axe wielded at Rangers. Hammers Green card scrapped.

24 Wolves give Terry Connor stand-in role. Raymond Verheijen quits Wales coaching job.

25 Man C strolls (lucky 13th home win equalling 1957-58 – 67 goals in 26) to beat Blackburn. Chelsea's relief as old guard fashions usual win over Bolton. Newcastle chucks two-goal lead so TC starts Wolves leadership with a point. WBA make it back-to-back five-and-four goals ns their best for 76 years as Baggies hit Sunderland revival. Ten-man QPR hit by Fulham's Pavel "Pog." Wigan gets rare clean sheet but just a point with Villa. FLC: Lambert (19 goals) trio sends Soton back top at Watford as the Hammers fail to nail Palace. Five-in-a-row Reading away win at Boro consolidates third place. Blackpool bites back at Bristol C. Brummies 15-match run ends as "dexterous" Blackstock brace gives Forest victory. Nine-no-league-loss Brighton stops Ipswich revival. Coventry improves to edge Barnsley and no-dough Pompey holds Leeds. Millwall first win in seven at Burnley. £1m Barnett's goal saves point for Posh at Doncaster. L1: Charlton (26,546) two-good for Stevenage. Grayson boost as Huddersfield (Rhodes 30th) beats Exeter. One only and MK Dons win at Bournemouth (owner's wife alleged h-t pep talk). Carlisle has best of five win over Yeovil. Wycombe whacks five against Hartlepool! Oldham clips Tranmere (only one win in 17). L2: Swindon's ninth unbeaten League run sends them top, Cheltenham second as Southend falters again at Morecambe. Four goal Shots make it five consecutive wins as Barnet loses. AFC Dons fight back to share six at Crewe. "Poundland" Bradford (17,014) quid-only entry produces draw with Hereford. SPL: Celtic restricted to one goal in beating Motherwell. SL1: Ross held at Dundee, Falkirk cuts its lead to goal difference only! SL2: Cowden, Arbroath, Dumbarton are all winners. SL3: Alloa defeats Clyde while QP recovers to down Stranraer. W Cup: Airbus, Bala, Cefn and TNS reach semis. BSP: Fleetwood strides on as Wrexham loses at Stockport. Trophy: Cambridge rocked by Wealdstone's Jolly double. York wins at Grimsby, Luton beats Gateshead and Newport is successful at Northwich.

26 C Cup Final: Liverpool pushed to beat Cardiff in shoot-out. PL: Two-adrift Arsenal comes out fighting to crack five past ten-finishing Spurs. Giggs steals limelight and Man U win in dying moments at Norwich on 900th outing. Stoke twosome beats Swansea. L1: O'Grady says it for Wednesday over United in Sheffield derby. SPL: Rangers put worries aside with four at ICT.

27 Rangers hit by a fine! Independent body will check owners. Crawley is now fifth after loss at Shrewsbury.

28 Caretaker Pearce awaits his moment of truth. Bellamy is to skipper Wales in Speed tribute game. Lerner feeds Villa with £25m top-up. Lerner feeds Villa with £25m top-up. Tevez come back in reserve game. L1: W-P trio as Charlton hits four at Chesterfield; Huddersfield held at Stevenage. L2: Gills win nine-goal see-saw over Hereford with two in last two mins. SL2: Dumbarton continues winning run. SL3: QP moves to second at Montrose. England U-19s beat Czechs. W Lge Cup: Neath, TNS, Newtown and Afan Lido for semis.

29 England cracked at the death after recovering two goals against Holland. Pearce calls time. Michael O'Neill starts with N Ireland defeat to Norway. Useful draw recorded for Scots in Slovenia. Republic held by Czechs. Costa Rica spoils Wales' day. Messi strikes treble for Argies, France surprises Germany, Yanks win in Italy. Megson bounced out by Sheff W. Port Vale players not paid. U-21s: England foursome hits Belgians as does the Welsh quartet against Andorra. Dutch hold Scots. SL1: Ross back on top beating Ayr. SL2: Arbroath draws with Airdrie.

MARCH

Villas-Boas axed at Chelsea ... Muamba suffers heart attack ... Tevez in favour again ... Messi best paid.

1 Pompey teeters on the brink. FA will assemble managerial material. Becks for GB trial game. Last man fouler may escape red. FIFA investigates Bahrain (needing nine WC goals) beating Indonesia by ten! Is Jones boy for Wednesday? England Ladies beat Swiss.

2 Is England job likely to be held over until next season? Brazil delays concern FIFA. Birmingham and Coventry receive transfer bans. Dave Jones handed Sheff W role. Hull snatches last minute leveller at Blackpool.

3 Arsenal gives Liverpool a goal then V (I) P (first goals at Anfield) wins it at the death. Man C's 19th Man U equalling home win in a row and 14th first in season start since Newcastle 1906-07 as night owl Balotelli does his day job on Bolton (18 defeats in 26 always relegated). Chelsea loses at in-form WBA. Stoke leapfrogs Norwich. QPR gets a pt against Everton whose Moyes wants 20% all-round PL cut to help fans. Swansea doubles up at Wigan as Latics owner Whelan worries. Blackburn (27 no clean sheets worst since 1969) fights back as Villa gets 12th draw. FLC: Lambert scores one, Davis saves many as Saints win at Leeds in seventh lge no loss. Reading remains third after Millwall loses. Boro adds to Pompey's plight at Fratton. Derby end seven hour goal drought earning pt at Birmingham. Brighton goes ten no lge loss at Donny. L1: Charlton's club record 13th away win at Bournemouth. Sheff U finishes with nine men and defeat to Oldham. Sheff W held at Rochdale. Rhodes double for Huddersfield in six share with Bury. MK Dons draw at Hartlepool. Notts climbs over Exeter-drawing Stevenage by beating Carlisle. Chesterfield defeats free-falling Tranmere, Wycombe lets in four at Scunthorpe. L2: Oxford's early brace sees off Swindon despite ten-man. Northampton earns point at Cheltenham. Hereford ends ten-no-win at home against AFC Dons. Southend wins at 11 no win Burton. Crawley tumbles to Torquay. Daggers are out of bottom two edging Bradford. SPL: Celtic's 17 successive lge wins end at Aberdeen in a draw, but Rangers lose at Ibrox to Hearts. Motherwell victory at Dunfermline leaves them three pts away from second place. SL1: Ross nearer promotion as Dundee cuts Falkirk second place by winning at Livi. SL2: Cowden, Arbroath, Dumbarton all held. Stirling leaps Albion swapping bottom spot. SL3: Alloa pushes on at Annan, QP draws at Elgin, but Stranraer loses to Berwick. W L: Bangor slips up to Neath – TNS only a point away. Vase: West Auckland, Dunston, Herne Bay and Staveley reach semis.

4 AVB bites the dust at the Bridge, leaving Di Matteo in charge for the time being. The "Pog" pots three in Fulham's high five over Wolves. Newcastle digs a late leveller after Sunderland battled with ten men for 32 mins in nasty Tyne & Wear encounter. Man U keeps up its record of not losing to Spurs since 2001 over 26 games. Hammers move pt nearer Soton and dent Cardiff's ambitions. Parry axed by Tranmere and Ronnie Moore i/c until season end. Sky falls on Powerlines beaten 24-0 by Mamelodi Sundowns.

5 Chelsea clears out AVB assistants, will cull stars and seek top replacements. Newcastle is in profit. Fowler is planning come-back at Blackpool. FIFA wants truly GB for Olympics. Hereford removes Pitman and makes Richard O'Kelly manager. Now Rangers may lose titles! Ten-man Southend earns pt off Crawley by saving pen.

6 Ch Lge: Gallant Gunners just fall short with three-goal first half salvo against AC Milan, Benfica overturns Zenit advantage. FA Cup: Re-born Chelsea wins at Birmingham. FLC: Soton held late by Ipswich, Reading's one enough over Pompey, Boro a couple better than Barnsley, but Blackpool loses at improving Derby. Hull and Leeds share no goals, Donny wins at the Forest and Millwall hits Posh. L1: Charlton loses home record to Colchester, Sheff U missed out at Walsall, but Sheff W hits foursome over Bury. One is sufficient for Huddersfield against Hartlepool, but MK Dons beaten in ten-a-side by Yeovil. Wycombe relief as four goals double Orient's tally. L2: Swindon takes it out on Daggers with four-play, but Cheltenham loses at Morecambe, Shrewsbury held by Oxford but Torquay edges the Shots. Cobblers off the foot as Bristol R loses odd goal in five. BSP: Six-hit Alfreton surprises Stockport. Fleetwood held up until last min winner over Grimsby. SL1: Ross pushes nearer lift beating the Jags. SL:2: Cowden ends Dumbarton's run. SL3: Elgin levels pts with Stranraer after win over Annan. Rangers players refuse pay cuts. Italy's girls beat England's.

7 Ch Lge: Barca drinks in seven-up over Leverkusen with champagne Messi's record five goals. Apoel becomes first Cypriot team in last eight in Lyon shoot-out, but only starts with two native players! FA Cup: Spurs recover from fright to beat Stevenage. Hammers fail to beat Watford and Cardiff has to settle with a pt at Brighton. BSP: Wrexham beats Luton to stay in touch. England U-18s beat Poles. Pompey rescued for season by FL payment. Wolves' Johnson drunk at training. Deaths announced of Marquitos, Real Madrid, 78 and Smolarek, Poland, 54.

8 E Lge: Man(i)c depression: Utd lose at home to Bilbao, City in Lisbon on good night for Iberia as Atletico Madrid and Valencia also win. Protests over Newcastle ground name.

9 Rangers – no redundancies; pay cuts accepted, Blue Knights want to take over. Fleetwood picks off Kidderminster.

10 QPR robbed of goal 18" over the line 21st min and lose at Bolton. Ton-up birthday boy Drogba (22nd PL 100 club and first African, second such at Chelsea and 12th for one club) as ten-man Stoke are beaten. Spurs slip up again – third in a row for Harry – at Everton. Liverpool is also a three consecutive loser at Sunderland. Wolves suffer as well as Rovers (Hoilett twosome) achieve second away win. Weimann's first PL goal for Villa ousts Fulham – but only nine goals in six games. FLC: Talisman scorer Lallana double as first win over Tykes for 62 years sees Saints beat Barnsley as Hammers held by struggling Doncaster and eight-in-a-row Reading catch the Iron on pts beating Leicester. Brighton depresses Portsmouth even more. Palace eight no loss draws with ten-man at Burnley. Two ogs get Cardiff home at Bristol C spoiling David James 900th overall game. L1: On loan Forte treble fortifies Notts four-play to tip up top Charlton again. Sheff U and Sheff W win away and home respectively again Brentford and Bournemouth. Bottom club Rochdale draws with Huddersfield, MK Dons cast Exeter into last four. L2: Swindon just beats pen-missing Cheltenham, Sole fortress Shrewsbury (26 unbeaten at home equals club record) as Burton loses but Southend held by Accrington and Crawley surrender pt in last five minutes at Macc. Torquay held at home by Bristol R, but Oxford falls at Bradford. Northampton moves out of bottom two spots beating Shots. S Cup: Hibs win at Ayr, St M forces draw at Hearts. SL1: Ross goes 11 pts clear with game in hand as Falkirk only draws with Thistle. SL2: Cowden, Arbroath both win. SL3: Alloa hits E Stirling for five. Stranraer wins at Annan, Elgin slips at home to Peterhead. BSP: Wrexham stays in touch with Fleetwood after defeating Barrow. W L: TNS top after crucial win over Bangor. Trophy: Newport takes two goal lead over Wealdstone, York edges Luton.

11 Fortunes change as two-goal Rooney (Sir Alex wants 40 this season from him) aids Man U taking the lead beating ten-man WBA while Man C slips up again at Swansea. Wigan manages pt at Norwich. FLC: Leeds wins at ten-finishing Boro. S Cup: Celtic hits four against ten-man Dundee U. Aberdeen edges ten-man Motherwell.

12 Retrieving Arsenal does it again at Newcastle. Tevez may be brought back by Man C.

13 Ch Lge: Gomez foursome in Bayern seven-goal romp erases Basle first leg lead. Late drama sees Inter ousted by Marseille. PL: Gerrard triple wins Merseyside derby for Liverpool against Everton. FLC: Cardiff holed three times by Hull. Reading draws at Doncaster, Leciester beats Birmingham, Derby defeats ten-finishing Foresters – just. L1: Sheff U held at Colchester. L2: Shots draw at Crawley, Torquay wins at Rotherham. BSP: Wrexham five goal outing at Ebbsfleet as Fleetwood only draws at Mansfield. SL1: Ross held by Morton. Sixteen PL managers rate Spurs best to watch. Is Wenger for England?

14 Ch Lge: Chelsea turns on the style and substance in disposing of Napoli in extra time. Madrid is the Real deal, too, over CSKA. Sir Dave Richards falls out with FIFA after slip.

15 E Lge: Rui Patricio is Hart breaker as Man C goalie is foiled by last gasp header and gallant fight back ends in Sporting passage. Man U also ousted by defence errors in Bilbao. Other winners: Spain: Atletico Madrid, Valencia; Germany: Hannover, Schalke; Holland: AZ; Ukraine: Metalist Kharkiv. Abidal is to have liver transplant. Hearts wait on wonga. Merseyside police boss blamed fans for Hillsborough.

16 Messi is anxious to commit to Barca for life. Moyes hits out at fixture congestion ruining FA Cup calendar. FA Youth Cup semi-final: Chelsea takes lead at Man U.

17 FA Cup: Muamba collapses after heart attack, tie at Spurs abandoned. Everton moan over ref Marriner no pens and Mignolet earns Sunderland draw. PL: Swansea treble shakes Fulham at the Cottage while Wigan (204 days no win) and WBA finish all square. FLC: FL Player of Year Lambert trio (two late pens) overturns Millwall lead for Saints. On fire Reading (nine wins in ten) four-play at Barnsley takes them second as Hammers snatch 90th min leveller – third time in succession draw – at Leeds. Revived Birmingham gets three over Boro. Blackpool pushes Brighton out of p-o zone as only two points separate six teams! L1: Charlton held at Scunny as is Sheff U by Tranmere. Sheff W wins at Notts. Huddersfield needs og for draw at Colchester. MK Dons also in sharing at Chesterfield. Wycombe (Beavon 3) celebrate boss Waddock's 50th birthday with foursome at Bury. Symes hat trick gives Rochdale lift against Oldham. Westley first win for PNE at Exeter. Hartlepool five hours 20 mins no goal gets a pt against Stevenage. L2: Swindon suffers at seven-unbeaten Crewe but Torquay four at Burton costs Brewers' boss Peschisolido his job. Gary Rowett is caretaker. Southend 11th win over Hereford moves them third as Shrewsbury loses at Plymouth and Cheltenham at home to treble-shooting Gills. Crawley back to winning ways edging Vale as does Oxford against Rotherham. Daggers beat Macc but stay bottom. SPL: Rangers rattled again, losing at Dundee U so Motherwell beating Aberdeen levels them with inferior goal difference. SL1: Ross beats Raith to go 15 pts clear. SL2: Cowden, Arbroath both draw but Dumbarton crashes at home to E Fife. SL3: Alloa at Peterhead, QP at Berwick and Stranraer home to Montrose all win. W L: TNS regains lead winning at Neath. BSP: Fleetwood (six pt lead) succeeds at Telford but Wrexham has two games in hand.

18 FA Cup: Now it's another Tor-Tor-Torres revisited (ending 1,541 no-goal mins) as striker hits two of five for born-again Chelsea beating Leicester. Liverpool gets best of three goals with Stoke. PL:Man U underlines intention by five-star drubbing of ten-man Wolves. FLC: Burnley takes a pt at Cardiff. S Lge Cup final: Shock for Celtic as Van Tornhout seals it for Kilmarnock. SPL: No pay Hearts trump Hibs in Edinburgh derby. Riots end Athens derby. Darren Patterson becomes Rotherham caretaker.

19 Muamba shows improvement. Bobby Robson memorial vandalised. Rotherham sacks boss Scott. Messi is best paid at £27.5m, Becks £26.3m, Ronaldo only £24.3m! Brian Horton is in at Macclesfield.

20 Blackburn out of the drop zone beating Sunderland. FLC: Saints stay well ahead at Hull as Reading loses at Posh and Hammers draw yet again with Boro. Thus Brighton benefits up to fourth defeating Derby, but ten-man Birmingham slumps at struggling four-goal Pompey. Forest fires seven at Leeds! It was United's first seven at home. L1: More chipper Charlton beats Yeovil. Sheff U strikes five at ten-man Notts. Sheff W held by Walsall but Huddersfield wins at Chesterfield. Four goals for MK Dons ends Orient hopes. Wycombe is out of last four as they shove Exeter second from bottom. L2: Swindon goes seven pts clear beating nearest rivals Torquay. Crucial win for Shrews over Cheltenham going third as Southend loses to the Shots. Crawley wins at Gillingham, Oxford home to AFC Dons. BSP: Mansfield firms up on third spot with six at Alfreton as Luton is lost at the Forest. SL3: Queen's Park beats Clyde to take second place. Messi breaks Barca's scoring record of 232 set by Cesar Rodriguez with a hat trick taking his total to 234. Chelsea sacks Jacob Mellis for smoke bomb denotation and fines Billy Clifford for bringing it.

21 Sub Tevez timely makes Man C winner after Chelsea lead. QPR gives Liverpool two goal start and beats them. Spurs held to a draw again by Stoke. Arsenal wins again at Everton. Cardiff held by Coventry, Blackpool and Leicester share six goals. S Cup: Hearts win St M replay. Muamba defied death. Cardiff-Swansea denied Euro via Welsh Cup. Gibraltar edges nearer UEFA status.

22 UEFA will repay clubs for Euro 2012 players handsomely. Pulis let off driving ban. FA Youth Cup: Blackburn takes lead over Burnley.

23 Sir Alex in war of words repost against Man C. Rangers on brink of losing title to Celtic.

24 Tough top team tormentors Stoke leave Man C and its away day blues clinging precariously a pt ahead of Man U after Crouch volley good strike needs an equalizer of quality, too, from Ya Ya Toure. Set piece strugglers Spurs held goalless at Chelsea. Emotionally-charged Bolton is grateful for Wheater double to lift them over Blackburn in tear-filled atmosphere dedicated to improving Muamba. Wigan manages rare win at Liverpool. Double-helping Toffees surprise Swans getting sweet away win. Shock as two Englishmen score for Arsenal (first duo in 15 years – Gibbs also 17th different PL scorer) as threesome defeats Villa. QPR ten-man (6th PL red) fight back not enough at Sunderland. Two-goal Holt also so carded as Canaries peck out the Wolves. FLC: Double-hit Sharp cuts into old Doncaster mates as Saints win. Reading recovers from blip and takes out Blackpool. Boro held by ten-man Bristol C. Five draws in a row show Hammers' in a rut and needing fight-back at Burnley. Leicester's ten keeps Hull at bay. Coventry wins basement battle over Pompey. Derby ends Palace ten match unbeaten run. Brighton draws at woodwork-hitting Forest. Ten-man Barnsley's first win in eight sees off Posh. Pen save aids Leeds win at Millwall. L1: Rhodes breaks post-war Huddersfield scoring record with 35th goal beating leaders Charlton. Sheff W attracts 6196 at Orient and wins. First goal in five games provides Hartlepool a win at Yeovil. Wycombe snatches late pt off MK Dons. Carlisle shares pt at Colchester. L2: Torquay turns it around beating Vale. Ten-man Shrewsbury hangs on for win at Morecambe. Ex-Shrimper Harrold is yet again decider for Bristol R against Southend and Crawley maintains recent form beating Rotherham. Cheltenham and Oxford share no goals. Burton defeated at AFC Dons go 16 no-win and one goal over 770 mins. SPL: Motherwell loses chance to close gap on Rangers by losing at Killie. Still no home win for Dunfermline as Fifers draw with St M. SL1: Ross 17 pts clear at Partick as Dundee held. SL2: Cowden 7pts clear as Arbroath loses at Airdrie. SL3: Alloa four-play

conquerors QP, so Stranraer's quartet leaps over the Spiders beating E Stirling. BSP: Fleetwood (3106) silences Mansfied as Wrexham loses at home to FGR. W L: Slipping Bangor held by Llanelli. Vase: W Auckland draws at Herne Bay, Dunston holds slender lead over Staveley. Messi goal for Barca his 35th league beats Brazilian Ronaldo 96-97 – while Cristiano of that ilk gets two and levels for Real against Sociedad.

25 Newcastle win at West Bromwich puts them eight points ahead of Liverpool. Cardiff draws for 15th time at Birmingham after Marshall pen save. JPT final: Topsy-turvy as bottom Chesterfield defeats leaders Swindon. SPL: Title on hold as Rangers ten beats Celtic's nine men in another controversial Auld Firm derby. Bournemouth sacks boss Lee Bradbury – youth team boss Paul Groves is i/c.

26 Lucky Man U escapes pen claim as Fulham is just beaten, but winners are three points in front of Man C. Aguero injured, facing time out. Ranieri sacked by Inter. Euro U-17: England just beats ten-man Ukraine.

27 Ch Lge: "Finished" Chelsea wins Sporting contest in Lisbon. Real takes late three-goal lead away to Apoel. FA Cup: Spurs beat Bolton in replayed tie of emotion. Everton beats Sunderland in their replay. FLC: Hammers find winning formula at Peterborough. Off-foot Pompey beats Hull. Boro, Donny and Forest get away draws at Ipswich, Palace and Leicester. L1: Carlisle reduces MK Dons lead over them by defeating them. Walsall moves out of bottom four with win over Colchester. L2: Crawley success at Bradford ends in unsightly brawl; City three reds, visitors two. Shrewsbury game with Port Vale abandoned over fire in stand. Burton stops losing streak beating Gillingham. BSP: Wrexham four-play at Darlo cuts Fleetwood lead to six points with game to spare. Student jailed for Muamba racial abuse. Giggs writes off England's Euro 2012 bid.

28 Ch Lge: Robinho misses best chance for AC Milan as Barca draws. Bayern goes two-goals ahead at Marseille. L1: Chesterfield down to earth lets in four at Sheff U. FA Youth Cup: Blackburn clinches final place winning at Burnley. Euro U-17: Georgia beats England. Venables is technical director of Wembley FC!

29 E Lge: Bilbao turns it around late away to Schalke. Atletico, AZ and Sporting edge best-of-three goals lead over Hannover, Valencia and Metalist respectively. Sir Alex rages over Vieira suggestion over refs Man U favouritism. Allardyce hits out at some Hammers fans. Barca complains over Milan pitch. Bradford-Crawley charged. Torres next club Anzhi?

30 Improving Muamba is swamped by good wishes, but Villa's Petrov diagnosed with leutaemia. Is Man C in crisis? Aguero is out, Balotelli in another boss row, Dzeko off form. Wenger fined by UEFA criticises referees. Birmingham wins at Doncaster. Torquay succeeds at Barnet, Southend foursome over Cheltenham. FIFA brushes more under carpet over WC bids.

31 Blue Moon fading fast as Man C scrapes a draw with Sunderland and loses 100% home record but gets 8th home penalty. Torres breaks PL duck after 17 hours 15 mins as "fading" Chelsea four-play shakes Villa. Arsenal slips up at QPR (not unusual). Everton climbs over Liverpool after twosome against WBA. Early Dempsey puts Fulham on way to beating Norwich. One loss in eight Wigan's first home win since August as Stoke is defeated. Trailing Bolton finds extra bit in second half at Wolves (1 win in 17) in best of five goals as 19th min 60 secs applause rings out for Petrov (No 19). FLC: Sharp missed pen costs Soton at three-time scorers Blackpool. Hammer defensive horror (loss lead in 60 secs) as Reading hits four at Upton Park. Brighton stays two pts ahead of Boro after drawing with them. Sixteenth draw for Cardiff held by Millwall. Coventry finally wins away (last FL) and escapes last three. Seven-no-loss Watford downs Leeds. Ipswich – eight home no loss – edges Barnsley. Pompey nose-dives as Burnley stacks five (ex-Brickie Austin 3). Posh all but snuffs out Leicester play-off hopes. Forest revs in "Pole" position as Majewski cracks three at Palace. L1: Wagstaff 22nd birthday goal fires Charlton over Orient. Evans (of course) pens Hartlepool in for Sheff U. Sheff W (allegedly with Preston plans) beats Westley's North Enders. Carlisle has best of three goals over Huddersfield (Grayson first loss). Brentford boost at MK Dons. Chesterfield gets the bird as Scunny flies to four. Two down Rochdale hit three before Walsall levels. Wycombe unbeaten in six grabs pen equalizer at Stevenage. Bury first win in two months hits Tranmere. L2: Swindon has to settle for no goals with Bristol R as does Crawley (pen claiming) at Burton. Ex-Shots Morgan gets ten-man Shrewsbury a point to preserve home record against old team. Jolt for Oxford losing to Morecambe. Daggers make it ten pts from 12 with win at Vale. Kitson pen save as Northampton draws at Crewe.It's Four-time losers Hereford at Rotherham. SPL: Rangers hold up Celtic title hopes with win at Motherwell. SL1: Ross held by Raith just needs one more win. SL2: Leaders Cowden and Arbroath both lose. SL3: Alloa has a foursome at E Stirling in ten-a-side, Stranraer winners at Elgin move four points above QP losers to Peterhead. BSP: Wrexham drops further behind Fleetwood in draw at Cambridge. Brabin sacked at Luton. W Cup semis: Foursomes, too, for TNS and Cefn Druids also (first final for 108 years). Vase: Dunston and W Auckland reach final. England U-17s suffer four-goal defeat by Spain.

APRIL

Muamba recovering ... Manchester based title on knife edge ... More records for Messi ... Fleetwood bound for FL.

1 Spurs level on pts, now fourth behind on goal difference with Arsenal as Swans lose at WHL. Newcastle adds to red-carded Reina, sulky – Carroll – Liverpool's poor PL form (yet this fixture still mirrors the Gunners-Tottenham 114 PL goal clashes). Celtic nears title as St J is bowed. Crucial win for Hibs at ICT at the other end. R Cup final: Early Falkirk Bairns see off Hamilton Accies. Balotelli involved in another spat with Yaya Toure.

2 Two in five mins late on at Blackburn as Man U closes in on 13th title. Liverpool ownership gets itchy. Twenty percent of FL clubs in financial bother. Death announced of Giorgio Chinaglia ex-Swansea striker. Preston players are not guilty.

3 Ch Lge: Two-pen Messi equals Altafini's 14 Euro Cup goals 1962-63 and puts AC Milan away for Barca. Bayern completes axing of Marseille. FLC: Catching-up Birmingham wins at Burnley. L1: Two more goals for Rhodes as Huddersfield wins at Orient. L2: Swindon five points clear after defeating Barnet. Aldridge derides present Liverpool. Man C striking force concerns.

4 Ch Lge: "Down and out" Chelsea edges into semis against ten-man Benfica. Real five finishes off Apoel. Mancini is getting serially under pressure.

5 E Lge: Iberia rules ok? Bilbao, Sporting, Atletico and Valencia make last four. PFA chairman Carlisle wades in on divers. Westley virtually writes off his PNE players! Rangers' debt might rise to £134m! Terry has injured ribs.

6 Newcastle moves up to fifth in win at Swansea. FLC: Reading has super-sub Le Fondre's brace for shooting them top as Leeds ten loses, West Ham get four at Barnsley. Talisman Dobbie's duo gives Blackpool benefit at Watford, but Brighton loses at Burnley. L1: Wycombe's third in a row last minute goal draws Carlisle game. Exeter, also in the toils, loses at Scunthorpe. L2: One enough as Swindon wins at Morecambe, Torquay, too, beating Accrington (sixth such minimum). Shrews get three at plunging Macc. Crawley held by Crewe (4723 record). Nine men Southend is beaten at Bradford. Cheltenham stops rot over Barnet, but ten-man Oxford loses to Northampton. BSP: Now Wrexham slips up to visiting Alfreton.

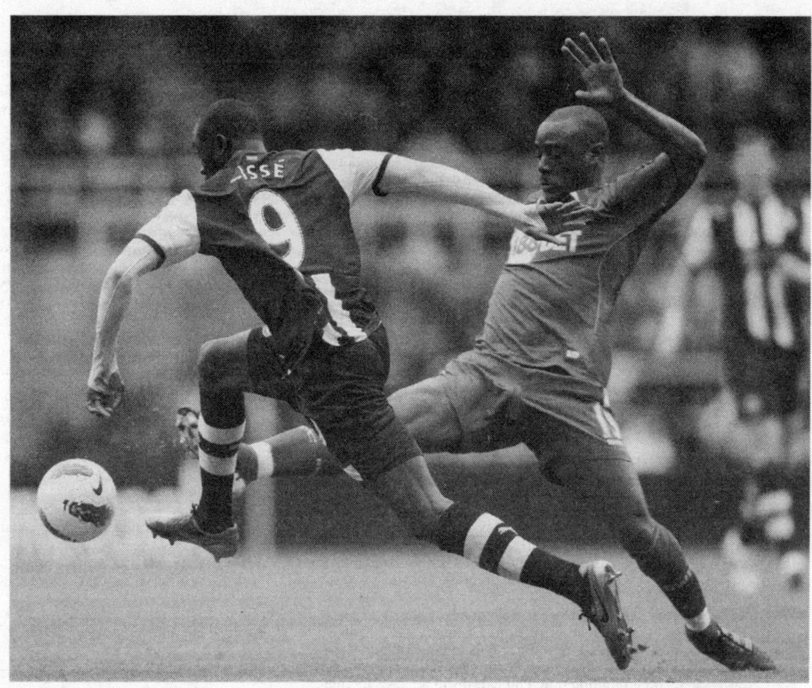

Newcastle United's Papiss Cisse powers past Bolton Wanderers' Nigel Reo-Coker in a Premier League clash in April. Cisse scored the second goal in Newcastle's 2-0 victory. (AP Photo/Scott Heppell)

7 Another goalless day for Spurs at Sunderland. Martinez is blunder-busted by officials as Chelsea sneaks 92nd minute off-side winner over Wigan. Jelavic double as Everton draws at Norwich in fine affair. Suarez has rescue pt for one PL win in nine Liverpool (28 season woodwork hits) against Villa. Dempsey double as Fulam treble floors Bolton. Stoke puts Wolves down deeper in Black Country meeting. Baggies bundle Blackburn towards exit, too. FLC: Saints caught late on by Pompey in south coast derby draw, but reclaim top spot. Best for weeks Cardiff wins at Boro. Another threesome pocketed for Birmingham against Palace. Four-goal Leicester rekindles play-off move, shoving Donny bottom. Bristol C win at Forest is first there since 1955! L1: Red-mist day as Charlton's nine beat Oldham's ten (11 yellows, too). Sheff U (Evans on 32 goals now) clips Bournemouth. Sheff W wins crucial Yorks derby at Huddersfield (boss Grayson unhappy). Walsall improves situ beating Chesterfield. MK Dons levelled by Preston at the death. Fifth straight win notched for Brentford. BSP: Fleetwood almost there winning at York. SPL: Six-hit Celtic celebrates title in style at Kilmarnock. SL1: Ross almost does it, too, one point to be sure after win at Livi. SL2: Arbroath wins at Cowden – black day for Blue Brazil! SL3: Alloa achieves promotion with eight goal rout of Elgin as Stranraer loses at Clyde. W L: TNS held by Llanelli. Messi notches 60th season goal from only 50 games!

8 Man C Blue Moon eclipsed by its fading stars as Arsenal snatch win that surely gives Man U – winners over ten-man QPR – their 13th PL title (20th overall). Balotelli sent off late faces City exit. But Rangers annoyed by officials' decisions.

9 Newcastle five-straight winners over Bolton slashes Spurs grip on fourth place to goal difference as one-win-in-eight Tottenham slip up to Norwich at WHL. That Dempsey pulls a leveller for Fulham in Chelsea derby. Everton maintains lead over Liverpool with foursome over Sunderland. Villa in 14th draw as Stoke equalizes. FLC: Lambert double (29th, 30th, 87th in three years) keeps Soton top at Palace. Two goals adrift Hammers rally to share six with Birmingham. Blackpool's ten men (Holloway unhappy over card) hold out drawing Barnsley. Draw No 17 for Cardiff against Watford. Boro loses at Hull (who end five defeats), but Leicester come back continues at Ipswich. Unpredictable Forest wins at Peterborough with ten men. Another defeat for ten-man Leeds as Derby wins there. L1: Charlton keeps the club-equalling pts total with a goal over Walsall. Sheff W nips above inactive Sheff U by beating Oldham. Huddersfield even loses at Bournemouth. MK Dons hoist century of goals in all games with three (2 pens) over Tranmere. Notts nip into play-off zone with on-loan Sam hat trick over Yeovil. Carlisle unbeaten in 17 but held at Scunny undefeated in ten. L2: Swindon (23rd clean sheet) extends lead over ten-man Torquay held at Oxford to seven points by beating Northampton. One goal is a win for Shrewsbury against Bradford. Crawley loses management team to Rotherham but still wins at Barnet, as Millers new boss Steve Evans sees them beat Cheltenham. Southend strengthens fifth spot against AFC Dons. Twelve unbeaten Crewe hits Bristol R. Chesterfield gets biggest season's win with four over Wycombe. Daggers fine win at Gills. Burton now no loss in four clips Morecambe. BSP: With Bath sinking to FGR, ten-man Kettering at Cambridge, Darlo's ten letting five in at Lincoln and Hayes losing at Luton, the relegation stakes seem set.

10 Liverpool has another goalie (Doni) sent off but sub Jones saves a pen and Carroll heads the injury-time winner in best of three goals at Blackburn. FLC: Reading cuts Saints lead to goal difference by winning at Brighton. Millwall

wins at Pompey. L1: Sheff U gets second place back with five goals at Rochdale. BSP: Wrexham's ten manage a point at Fleetwood (4994). SL1: Dundee held by QoS, so Ross is promoted!

11 Another twist? Man U loses at Wigan (Sir Alex unhappy with ref Dowd), Man C takes four-off WBA (Mancini still concedes title!). QPR slips out of danger zone beating Swansea. Arsenal puts ten-man Wolves firmly at the foot and heads for 15th consecutive Ch Lge season. Champions Ross win at Ayr. Crawley and Bradford fined. Ronaldo 3 (on 40 goals) as Real beats Atletico. Dortmund edges Bayern as Robben misses penalty to take six point Bundesliga lead. Police may ban Gillingham – Swindon match.

12 Comoli sacked at Liverpool. U-18s: England beat Scots, Wales draw with Republic.

13 Soton stunned by new leaders Reading thanks to sub Le Fondre's double. Bebe move to Man U under suspicion. BSP: Fleetwood held by Lincoln. Wilshere is doubt for Euro 2012. Trevor Francis suffers heart attack.

14 FA Cup: Semi-final specialists Liverpool comes back to beat Everton – twelfth s-f loss. PL: Martinez has a nap but Tevez wakes up as treble-shooter in Man C's six-hit at Norwich. Swansea inflicts Blackburn's fifth reverse in a row. Wolves manage a clean sheet and a point at Sunderland. WBA one goal strikes QPR's fifth away defeat in succession. FLC: West Ham best home for weeks with Vaz Te threesome in six-goal destruction of Brighton. Two down Birmingham rescues pt against Bristol C. Blackpool held goalless at Forest. Cardiff unbeaten in seven, wins at Barnsley. Two goals adrift Pompey recovers for best of seven goals to demote Doncaster, but Donny boss Saunders unhappy with refereeing. L1: Charlton earns promotion at Carlisle and Sheff U beating Orient moves closer to elevation as Sheff W only draws at Colchester. MK Dons top the season ton with three at Scunthorpe. Another slip-up for Huddersfield defeated at Preston. Notts in no goals draw at Brentford. Rochdale beats Exeter but both look vulnerable. L2: Swindon, Shrewsbury both win, Torquay, Crawley and Oxford all held at home. But seven-goal Bristol R (Richards 3) romp against Burton. Another hat trick for Wells as Bradford wins at Northampton. Crewe 13 undefeated now sharing four goals at Macc. S Cup s-f: Hibs early and late beats Aberdeen. SL1: Ross beat nearest rivals Dundee. SL2: Cowden extends lead as Arbroath and Sten both lose. SL3: Champions Alloa let in five at Berwick – Stranraer, Queen's Park and Elgin also beaten. BSP: Fleetwood's £10m investment pays off as Wrexham fails to beat Grimsby giving the Cod Army passage to FL. But Darlo, Kettering and Bath relegated. Piermario Morosini, 25, dies of heart attack in Serie B match. Muamba recovers at home now. Ronaldo hits 41st La Liga goal (53rd season) as Real equal club record 107 goals. Messi, too, gets 41st league strike.

15 FA Cup: semi-final: No-goal given to Chelsea – ref Atkinson poorly placed – but Blues go on to hit Spurs for five. PL: Man U foursome but diving (Sir Alex agrees) spoils it against Villa. S Cup s-f: Last gasp pen and Hearts beat Celtic for rare Edinburgh final – first since 1896.

16 Now Wigan wins at Arsenal and moves to 16th! No technology until 2013-14 – at least. Francis released from hospital. Muamba is still making more progress. Martin Allen goes back at Barnet in place of Sanchez. Diouf is in trouble after night club incident.

17 Ch Lge: Gomez late stuns Real as Bayern edges ahead. FLC: Reading promoted after minimum against Forest. Saints take out Posh. Green error stops Hammers winning at Bristol C. Birmingham held at Ipswich, Blackpool gets one to beat ten-man Leeds, Boro fails to beat Donny. Cardiff shoos the Rams. Pompey avoids drop for the moment beating Palace. Stevenage leaps over Carlisle. Shots deny Swindon a promotion point. Shrewsbury and Crawley keep on promotion trail. Phil Dowd will ref FA Cup final.

18 Ch Lge: Drogba goal beats Barcelona! Now Bebe in trouble breaking curfew in Turkey! England fans must prepare for Spartan conditions at Euro 2012. Reading takeover is under review. Gills police costs solved.

19 E Lge: Atletico doubles Valencia twosome; Sporting fights back to lead Bilbao. Mark Clattenburg is lone Brit ref at Olympics. NextGen League not for Man U as Arsenal, Chelsea, Liverpool, Man C and Spurs confirm.

20 Moyes weighs in on divers and even Sir Alex warns Young. Sheff U's Ched Evans jailed for five years convicted of rape. Mohsni hat trick as Southend beats relegation worried Barnet. BSP: Wrexham loses ground to Mansfield.

21 Chelsea (now 69 yellows), with thoughts on Barca, gets a goalless draw (first such in 39 years at Arsenal (Walcott injured). Newcastle hit "C" men make D-Day in Europe nearer beating Stoke with Cisse shades of Mick Quinn scoring rate. Taarabt finishes off Spurs (1 win in 9) for QPR then gets Rangers eighth red. Wigan's revival suffers the "Pog" at Fulham. Villa notches 15th draw and another no-goals affair with Sunderland. Two games in hand but Bolton (£100m debt) held by Swansea. Blackburn (with fans complaining over manager and owner) takes three points off Norwich. FLC: Soton (2922 travelling fans) 46 secs lead then fail to stop play-off chasing Boro winning. Roberts' first season red for Reading (one loss in 18) draw with Palace ensures title. Derby relegates Pompey and already doomed Donny sends Coventry the same way. Play-off spot taken for Birmingham in Brighton draw also for Blackpool beating Burnley. Bristol C is safe after win over Barnsley. L1: Charlton champions keep Wycombe sweating on demotion. Sheff U suffers loss on its debut at MK Dons (Smith first goal in 6 years). Sheff W maintains best home FL this season beating Carlisle. Stevenage ends Brentford's play-off hopes. Chesterfield delays drop but sends Rochdale down. Exeter four doubles equally concerned Walsall's score. Orient throws two-goal lead in Yeovil draw. L2: Beaten at Gillingham but Swindon still gains promotion. Daggers ok after draw with Crawley. Torquay's third no-win goes at AFC Dons. Accrington holds up Shrewsbury lift off in draw. Bradford out of danger but put no-win-in 2012 Macc in the mix. Northampton escapes in goalless at still threatened Hereford. Crewe 14 without loss edges Cheltenham. SPL: Dunfermline shares eight goals at St M. SL1: Bottom two both beaten as in SL2! Blue Brazil Cowden is champion! SL3: QP climbs over Stranraer (losers at Alloa) to second place. BSP: Cambridge sinks the Fleetwood, Luton leaps over Kiddy (8415). York ensures play-off winning at Braintree. Ronaldo's 42nd La Liga goal (54th in all) lifts out-passed and out possessed Real to win at Barca and go seven pts ahead with four left (400m tv) W L: TNS (1488) wins title in style hitting nearest rivals Bangor for five.

22 Twice two up Man U caught in eight goals share with Everton to open title race up again. Man C closes gap at the top and relegates Wolves at the same time. Albion becomes latest to win at Liverpool. PFA awards: Van Persie Player of the Year, Walker Young Player, Merit Award Alexander (PNE).

23 West Ham win at Leicester puts onus back on Saints. Mourinho sends Chelsea message. PL prepares for two sets of medals if it goes to the wire. Year transfer ban hits Rangers. GB Olympic draw will be kind. Senegal beats Oman in Olympic play-off in Coventry – of course!

24 Ch Lge: Chelsea's finest ten-man hour holding Barca and Torres scores the leveller after Terry is a jerk again. But Blues hit by injuries and suspensions for final; first time Messi lost three in a row but the Catalans had never overturned a semi deficit. Bolton heaps more pressure on Villa's boss. BSP: Luton held at Gateshead, Wrexham wins at Newport.

25 Ch Lge: Favourites unstuck again as Bayern prevails in shoot-out and Ronaldo misses one for Real! Ferdinand will not shake Terry's hand. Kaka is king of Twitter with 10m chirping. McLeish under fire has owner support. Italians beat Scots at U-21.

26 E Lge: Spanish final as Bilbao and Atletico win semis. Chelsea will chase Guardiola. Hands will be off for QPR-Chelsea says PL. Mancini writes off title chance till next season.

27 Monday's Derby-day in Manchester is awaited. Hawk-Eye lined up for St Mary's. Bombs explode in Ukraine's Dnepr. Offers pour in for Rangers. Spurs wanted Tevez.

28 May the fours! – Four-one up Swans have to share eight with Wolves, another Everton foursome banishes Fulham and can't-stop-winning Wigan whacks four against shaken Newcastle. Sunderland (ending 7 hrs 41 mins scoreless) divides four goals equally with Bolton (Davies K 2). Suarez treble includes a Becks-like 41 yard chip and dip at Norwich. Arsenal gets a draw at Stoke, but Villa (no win in 8, one in 14) is involved in another draw (16th) of no goals at WBA. FLC: Two ahead before Hammers had scored one against Hull, Saints go on to hit four over Coventry and secure PL status after seven-year absence. West Ham thus enters play-offs with Cardiff, unbeaten in ten, recovering to win at Palace, Birmingham even beating the Reading machine (second loss only in 19) and Blackpool earning a draw at Millwall. L1: Sheff W (no loss in 13) overtakes Sheff U with win at Brentford while the Blades just recover to hold Stevenage. Charlton falls short of 100 points as veteran Alexander (40) cracks 25-yard free kick in his 1,023rd match and last touch to force Preston draw. MK Dons win at already doomed Rochdale, but Exeter downed at Carlisle, Chesterfield edged at Yeovil and Wycombe leading with two minutes remaining still lose to Notts, all get relegated. Walsall earns safety draw with Huddersfield. L2: Swindon achieves title in style hitting five against Vale, Shrewsbury recaptures 1979 promotion for boss Turner beating Daggers and retaining unbeaten home record. Cheltenham makes a play-off place defeating Bradford, Southend surprises Oxford and Torquay drops two points to Crewe unbeaten in 15 now. Crawley crumples as menaced Hereford succeeds there and Barnet's four-play is too much for AFC Dons. But Macclesfield loses its 15 year FL association as Burton wins. SPL: Dunfermline wins at home hitting Dons for three. SL1: Ayr beats Dundee so Q of S is demoted losing to Raith. SL2: Airdrie keeps Stenhousemuir out of play-off spot beating E Fife. SL3: Queen's Park wins at Stranraer to leapfrog into second place. BSP: Luton wins at Fleetwood securing play-off spot as Kidderminster loses to in-form qualified, too, Mansfield. Wrexham hits five against Braintree, York clips FGR. Ronaldo strikes 43rd La Liga goal for Real.

29 Tor-Tor-Torres in tune with hat-trick in Chelsea's sextet over QPR; Spurs strengthen hold on fourth place beating Blackburn; Walker even scores with a free-kick! But RH now looks likely candidate for FA in reverse over HR. Celtic beats Rangers again. Hibs lose ten-a-side at St M.

30 Minimal scoring but maximum impact as Man C completes the double over Man U to lead PL on goal difference. SPL: Motherwell emphasises third place at Hearts.

MAY

Roy Hodgson becomes England manager ... Most exciting PL finale as Man C becomes champions ... Dalglish out at Liverpool ... Two cups for Chelsea.

1 Roy Hodgson appointed as England manager. Merseyside "og" day: Liverpool gives it to Fulham, Everton grateful for leveller at Stoke. SPL: Motherwell emphasises third place at Hearts. Previous month ended with five players on assault charges, another on drink-driving offence, more on implications in rape case and a manager querying owner's non-involvement! David Luiz and Cahill are battling for fitness.

2 Muambą returns to visit Bolton but Spurs foursome hits Wanderers situation. Cisse volley for Newcastle vanquishes Chelsea. SPL: Rangers strike five goals against Europe-chasing Dundee U. Cellar scene: Hibs wins at Aberdeen as Dunfermline is held. Real wins title – first in four years – Ronaldo also hits 44th La Liga goal and misses pen! BSP: Ten-man Mansfield holds York in play-off.

3 West Ham takes play-off lead at Cardiff. Luton, too, takes two against Wrexham. Celtic just edges St J. Capello warns Hodgson of things to come. Scudamore praises PL achievements over 20 years; Rooney goal last season is voted best strike. FWA awards: Van Persie Footballer of the Year, Rooney 2nd, Scholes 3rd, Dempsey 4th. Fans takeover at Darlo but face uncertain future. Fiorentina boss Guerini sacked for attacking his player! Rangers attract US man. Mansfield CEO Carolyn Still in street caution.

4 Hodgson appoints Ray Lewington as assistant. Blackpool takes Davies own goal to lead Birmingham in play-off. Now three Villa players are involved in brawl.

5 FA Cup final: Records tumble as Chelsea just beats Liverpool, lucky omen Ramires first goal, Drogba fourth in finals (8 in 8 Wembley games), Cole 7th winner's medal, Terry first skipper one-club four trophies, Di Matteo (first twice-scoring winner 1997 and 2000 then boss) third Italian manager in succession. Liverpool make a game of it when two down (always lose final when beating Everton in semis), Cech wonder save on the line – but correctly no goal as controversy reigns again! PL: Van Persie 29th, 30th goals (6th in PL of 30) yet Norwich salvages pt in Wenger's 900th i/c. L1: Sheff W snatches second promotion spot beating Wycombe (manager Jones no loss) as Sheff U consigned to play-offs in Exeter draw, while Stevenage beating Bury is able to join MK Dons and Huddersfield in them, despite Notts four against Colchester. Carlisle also loses out at Oldham. L2: Crawley second half winner at Accrington takes third automatic slot, Torquay loses at Hereford (still relegated) and joins play-off party with already there Southend (just-missing lift up), Cheltenham and Crewe 16th unbeaten managing necessary pt against Shots. Barnet is safe winning at Burton. SPL; Rangers are scoreless with Motherwell. SL1: Ross underlines its supremacy at three-goal QoS with five hits in incredible run of 34 games without defeat (just one in season, unbeaten at home, too). SL2: Airdrie in play-offs drawing at Cowden as Stenhousemuir loses to Forfar. SL3: Stranraer keeps losing run. Messi all four for Barca hits 50th La Liga goal, 72 in all, for team that lost only seven of 118 home games under Guardiola. Ronaldo scores his 45th of season. Previous World record for season: Archie Stark, Bethlehem Steel (USA), 70 goals, in 1924-25.

6 Okay YaYa? Toure de force double at Newcastle pushes Man C nearer the title, but Man U stays just goal difference away after beating Swansea, though the prospect of no trophies for the first time in seven years looms. Ten-man Spurs held as Villa equals PL and own 17th draw. Cisse goal boosts QPR over Stoke. Bolton discards two-goal lead as WBA equalises. Wolves and Everton go goalless together. Fulham edges Sunderland. SPL: Celtic loses at Dundee U.

7 Wigan's goal at Blackburn relegates Rovers and banishes their own fears. FLC p-o: Hammers complete whitewash of Cardiff Blues. BSP p-o: York prevails against ten-man Mansfield to meet Luton in final as Hatters just top Wrexham. SPL: Hibs finally dispel relegation worries with foursome in demoting Dunfermline. Wheater is out for nine months with ligament damage.

8 Liverpool four-play achieves revenge over Chelsea. Is Crewe's Powell sought by Man U? Barmby sacked by Hull. Cardiff thinks of becoming red. Rangers' bidder withdraws.

9 E Lge final: Atletico beats Athletic! FLC p-o: Blackpool four-share at Birmingham is enough. SL1 p-o: Ayr draws at Airdrie while Dumbarton takes slender lead over Arbroath. SL2 p-o: Elgin one goal ahead of Albion, Stranraer

two in front of QP. FA Youth Cup final second leg: Chelsea loses goal at Blackburn, but four at home was ample. Daily Telegraph says Man C spent £930m on chasing title.

10 Man U wins Reserve title beating Villa on pens. U-21s: ten-man N Ireland is beaten in Macedonia. Long-serving Pat Rice retires at Arsenal and Steve Bould is new No.2. Wolves appoint Stale Solbakken as manager. Gary Rowett handed Burton job. Cardiff will remain blue. Blackburn is not for sale.

11 Sir Alex tries mind games to unsettle Man C. L1 p-o: Sheff U in no goals with Stevenage.

12 L1 p-o: Rhodes hits 39th of season as Huddersfield has two-goal lead at MK Dons. L2 p-o: Crewe just shade Southend. Trophy final: York two-good for Newport. SL2 p-o: Dumbarton draw enough at Arbroath, Airdrie wins at Ayr in ten-a-side. SL3: Albion just edges Elgin, but Stranraer completes double over Spiders.

13 90 mins Man C seemingly out of it with QPR's ten men (Barton off at 1-1) leading 2-1 and Man U already awaiting the crown as winners at Sunderland. Then ironically in "Sir Alex time" Dzeko heads leveller and Aguero hits championship winner. Unbelievable! Rangers also survive the drop as Bolton is held at Stoke and goes down. Arsenal wins at gaffe-giving WBA to deprive Spurs – beating Fulham – of third place.

14 L1 p-o: Porter carries Sheff U into final to deprive Stevenage. Alex McLeish sacked by Villa. Arsenal wants to keep Van Persie. Tevez is in bother over "RIP Fergie" banner. Gary Neville joins Roy Hodgson coaching staff. Dalglish summoned to US for talks. Van Nistelrooy retires at 35.

15 L1 p-o: MK Dons win at Huddersfield but not enough to go on. Ferdinand is out of Euro selection. Allardyce will sue Kean over remarks. PL first for goal-line technology. Pennant jail time for drink-driving suspended. Cahill and David Luiz fit for Munich.

16 Dalglish joins dole queue. Hodgson picks his squad. Terry in but Gerrard is skipper. L2 p-o: Southend share four goals but Crewe reaches final. SL1 p-o: Dumbarton takes slender lead over Airdrie. SL2 p-o: Two-ahead Stranraer leaves Albion trailing. Euro U-17 final: Dutch beat Germans on penalties. Rangers lose appeal over fine and transfer embargo.

17 L2 p-o: Torquay batters Cheltenham but visitors still edge them. Liverpool chase new boss with Martinez first to be mentioned. Van Persie talks grind slowly. Capello is interested in Chelsea. Solskjaer is in Villa frame.

18 Bayern boss praises Chelsea's Di Matteo. Villa-Boas is latest in Liverpool sights. Norwich rejects Holt transfer request. Olympic final means Community Shield goes to Villa Park. Lineker rubbishes England Euro chance.

19 Ch Lge Final: Chelsea survives extra time and wins on penalties; Cech hero saving Robben's extra time spot kick (conceded by Drogba) then stopping two more in shoot-out leaving Drogba with equalising header to hit the winning penalty. Bayern must blame wasted chances. FLC play-off: Hammers back in PL after close contest with Birmingham. S Cup final: Hearts end 110 cup misery with five against ten-man Hibs in Edinburgh derby at Hampden.

20 BSP: York beats Luton (4th time this season) to regain FL status. SL2 p-o: Dumbarton ease over ten-man Airdrie to win promotion. SL3: Albion retains status beating Stranraer on penalties.

21 Now Drogba the Olympic torch-bearer! Giggs wants to play with Becks, but others decline. Capello bound for Liverpool? Torres recalled by Spain. Abidal recovers.

22 JM will stay with Real. Chelsea in Ch Lge means less "wonga" for Man C, Man U and Arsenal (who plans player axing). Hargreaves leaves Man C who increases season ticket prices but nine freeze them.

23 Barton gets 12-match ban. Bosingwa, Kalou to leave Chelsea, not Torres.

24 Carroll summoned up by England for Norway game. Martinez is in the Anfield frame. Ranieri may go to WBA. Muamba may play again.

25 Blatter wants alternative to shoot-out! Woken up at last? Gerrard will captain England. Butland replaces Norwich's Ruddy as a goalie choice. Darlington demoted to Northern League First Division and to share ground with Shildon. Chelsea chases Guardiola. Mancini jnr axed by Man C. MOTD continues after more "dosh" given. Suarez scores for Uruguay in Russia draw.

26 Young gives Hodgson a winning start in Norway. In short: Republic needs Long to beat Bosnia. Swiss hit treble Germans for five; Dutch even beaten by Bulgaria, but Spain defeats Serbia and Hulk gets two as Brazil hit Danes for three. L1 p-o final: Twenty-two pens including dozen successful in a row as Huddersfield beats Sheff U in shoot-out. Women's FA Cup final: Pens, too, settle it for Birmingham over Chelsea.

27 Sol Campbell warns travelling fans over Neo-Nazis at Euro 2012. FA is to copy small-sided games as in Spain and Germany for youngsters. Wales loses to Mexico in New York. Scotland slumps in Florida to USA. L2 p-o final: Crewe makes it against Cheltenham.

28 Injured Barry is out, Jagielka in for Euro 2012. Match-fixing hits Italian football again. Swansea pays £6.8m for to keep on loan Sigurdsson. Germans will take only three forwards to Euro. Danish U-21s beat Republic.

29 Italy's Balotelli says abuse will cause him to quit Euro 2012 game as UEFA informs refs to take players off the field if racism evident. Russian takeover of Reading completed. Rangers signing embargo lifted but SFA threatens S Cup entry. Brendan Rodgers is now Anfield favourite. Hulk may follow Hazard to Chelsea.

30 Limpard injury gives Henderson a chance. Brendan Rodgers is new Liverpool boss. Lambert moves out of Norwich – to Villa. Drogba is heading for Chinese takeaway. Powell set to change at Crewe'for Manchester (U). Holland, Spain and Sweden win friendly games

31 Parker is latest England doubt as injuries worry. Steve Clarke about to leave Anfield as Colin Pascoe becomes assistant manager to Rodgers. Scots U-21s draw in Bulgaria. Brazil, France and Germany also win friendly matches.

JUNE

Racist issues already affect Euro ... Holland shock departure ... England in last eight before penalties ... Master class Spain wins handsomely.

1 England expects – again. Russians beat Italy to add to its match-fixing scandals. Austrians edge Ukraine. Rodgers paraded as Liverpool boss.

2 Another one-nil for Roy H against Belgium (Hazard glimpse of £32m Chelsea's buy). Lineker changes tune boosting England. Dutch crash six past N Ireland. Ronaldo misses pen as Portugal bows to Turkey. Paul Lambert moves from Norwich to Villa.

3 Cahill out injured but no place for Ferdinand as Liverpool's Kelly (2 mins full England) moves in. Platini predicts Germany v Spain final. Brazil loses to Mexico (Giovani, Hernandez scoring!) in warm up. WC 2014: Argies take four off Ecuador, Venezuela holds Uruguay at the death. Chile wins in Bolivia. Kuyt flies to Fenerbahce for £1m. Bellamy is GB over-age player in Olympic. PL has 74 players in Euro 2012.

4 Unhappy people murmur over Ferdinand absence. GB delays squad. Republic held by Hungary and its U-21s draw with Italy. Only three German Euro players visit Auschwitz. Celtic No. 2 Thompson sacked on phone. Barton arrested after altercation.

5 French beat Estonia to make it 21 no loss. Sweden beats Serbia, Ukraine loses to Turkey. Terry misses training with injury. Euro will make £1b. Rodgers recalls Cole from Lille. Man U signs Shinji Kagawa £17m.
6 Players leaving pitch if racially abused will be booked – only refs can act. Chris Hughton appointed at Norwich.
7 Racist chants at Dutch training. Republic eases off training amid burnout concerns. Capello is on UEFA technical panel. WBA gives Steve Clarke first big job as boss. Chelsea will not have Battersea Power Station site. Super-Toon scout Carr, 67, gets eight year deal.
8 Euro 2012 off to bright start: Poles held by Greece in ten-a-side sparkler, sub gk Tyton (Szczesny red card) becomes first such to save Euro pen. Canny four-play by Russians beats Czechs in end to end affair. Strife rumours abound in Spanish training. Dutch fans need convincing over Van Persie. England team visits Death Camp. Assistant German coach Herr Flick ('Allo 'Allo) has to say sorry for "steel helmet" Gdansk gaffe. Ashley Cole misses training. Hull appoints Steve Bruce.
9 Danish slices into disappointing Dutch; Gomez header wins it for Germany against Portugal. Ukraine coach Blokhin fears the worst. UEFA threatens racist Russian fans.
10 Italy gives no-starting striker Spain a draw for its euros; Croatia treble leaves the Republic wondering. UEFA is to tackle missile throwing. WC 2014: Winners Chile away, Uruguay at home both climb to first and second spots over Argies (Messi 3) win friendly best of seven goals over Brazil. Di Matteo may be given Chelsea job.
11 Stoic England hold favourites France; Shevchenko (!) is Ukraine hero with double headers edging sorry Swedes.
12 Succeeding Czechs pay two early dividends before Greece makes a game of it in second half; trouble in town before Russia finds the Poles equal to demands.
13 Ronaldo has a rare off day but Varela switches foot to edge Portugal ahead of Denmark; Gomez double strikes for Germany put Dutch in danger despite Van Persie goal. Carroll likely to be England starter, Republic concerns before Spain. Redknapp parts from Spurs. PL gets massive 70 percent TV increase with Sky and BT at the helm. Di Matteo confirmed at Chelsea.
14 Croatia earns draw with Italy; Scintillating four-goal Spain completes record 859 Euro passes to bypass Republic and exit them..MPs question TV deal. The takeover of Rangers completed with Charles Green i/c. Michael Laudrup heads for Swansea.
15 Storm interrupts Donetsk game but France dampens Ukraine on resumption; Carroll heads ahead, Roy's team trails, but the W formation (Walcott, Welbeck) gives England first competitive win over Sweden. Rangers may not play in SPL as Dundee stands by to replace them! Laudrup is in at Swansea.
16 Greeks have a word for it: victory to eliminate Russia while Croatia axes host nation Poland. Swedish spy unhelpful against England. Soon-to-be wound-up Newco Rangers may play in a new SPL2 with no Scottish fixtures prepared yet, their place taken by "Club 12."
17 Ronaldo deprived of hat trick by post as otherwise wasteful Portugal puts final nail in Dutch coffin; Germany just gets better of Denmark for third win. Rooney raring to go, Shevchenko injured.
18 Compact but powder-puff Spain wants to walk the ball – then an arm/off-side – wins it over Croatia; Italy puts the Republic to rest.
19 Rooney hair-do(es) it for England, Ukraine wastes away chances but one was "a goal." France even loses to Sweden but will face Spain as England prepares for Italy. Smith consortium withdraws offer for newco Rangers.
20 After Platini dismissed goal-line cameras before England game, Blatter reacts positively after it. England prepares for shoot-out if necessary; Milner will target club colleague Balotelli! Roy pumps up Rooney factor. French dressing-room split. West Ham gets Diame for nothing.
21 Ace Ronaldo's header downloads Czechs and saves Portugal fritters. England players prepare for penalties. England Ladies hit Slovenia four times.
22 Decisive four goal Germans react quickly to Greek leveller. Jingoistic England is upbeat ahead of Italian clash.
23 Irritating, dismissive of forward-play, Spain (Xabi Alonso 100th cap, both goals) still beats France! Alan McDonald, record QPR Northern Ireland cap-holder, dies at 48.
24 Shoot-OUT! England suffers familiar exit against Italy who couldn't end our misery in 120 mins. Spurs intensify chase for boss.
25 Six SPL clubs are against allowing the newco Rangers in. Hodgson plans shake-up for Brazil. Arsenal may sign £13m Giroud – a French sub, to add to Podolski £11.9m. Barton fined and skipper's armband removed.
26 Spain plans to stop Ronaldo. Winter break on the agenda again. Villas-Boas is in line for Spurs. Lee Clark is new Birmingham C boss and John McGlynn takes over at Hearts.
27 Euro 2012: Scrappy, yellow card littered disappointment of a semi-final decided by penalties between two teams who knew too much of each other; Spain prevailed, Portugal's Ronaldo had an off target day and last in line didn't get to take a spot kick! Germans plan to halt Pirlo.
28 Balotelli heads and shoots Italy to deserved final place against below-par Germans who suffered first defeat after 15 successive competitive wins. Becks left out of GB!
29 Another club, St Mirren turns down newco Rangers place. Southgate calls for shrinks to cure penalty misses. Bale is out of GB through injury. Boring Spain may not be welcome final winners?
30 Spanish players defend "boring" play. Balotelli relishes final with Italy. Laurent Blanc parts with France.

JULY

1 Del (Boy) Bosque proves four-goal Spain are no trotters as they zip through Italy in a memorable classic display to win Euro 2012, third major title in succession.

CUPS AND UPS AND DOWNS DIARY

FEBRUARY

26 Carling Cup final: Liverpool 2 Cardiff C 2.
(Liverpool won 3-2 on penalties).

MARCH

18 Scottish Communities Cup final: Kilmarnock 1 Celtic 0.
25 Johnstone's Paint Trophy final: Chesterfield 2 Swindon Town 0.

APRIL

1 Ramsdens Cup final: Falkirk 1 Hamilton Academical 0.
7 Celtic Scottish Premier League Champions.
Alloa Athletic promoted to Scottish League Division 2.
10 Ross County promoted to Scottish Premier League.
14 Charlton Athletic promoted to Football League Championship.
Doncaster Rovers relegated to Football League One.
Fleetwood Town promoted to Football League Two as Blue Square Premier champions.
Darlington, Kettering Town and Bath City relegated from Blue Square Premier.
17 Reading promoted to Premier League.
21 Portsmouth and Coventry City relegated to Football League One.
Charlton Athletic Football League One Champions.
Swindon Town promoted to Football League One.
Rochdale relegated to Football League Two.
Cowdenbeath promoted to Scottish League Division 1.
The New Saints Welsh Premier League Champions.
22 Wolverhampton Wanderers relegated to Football League Championship.
28 Southampton promoted to Football League Championship.
Swindon Town Football League Two Champions.
Shrewsbury Town promoted to League One.
Chesterfield, Exeter City and Wycombe Wanderers relegated to Football League Two.
Macclesfield Town relegated to Blue Square Premier.
Queen of the South relegated to Scottish League Division 2.
Stirling Albion relegated to Scottish League Division 3.
Hayes & Yeading relegated from Blue Square Premier.
Welsh Premier League Cup final: Afan Lido 1 Newtown 1.
(Afan Lido won 4-3 on penalties).

MAY

5 FA Cup final: Chelsea 2 Liverpool 1.
Sheffield Wednesday promoted to Football League Championship.
Crawley Town promoted to Football League One.
Hereford United relegated to Blue Square Premier.
Welsh Cup final: The New Saints 2 Cefn Druids 0.
7 Blackburn Rovers relegated to Football League Championship.
Dunfermline Athletic relegated to Scottish League Division 1.
9 Europa League final: Atletico Madrid 3 Athletic Bilbao 0.
12 FA Trophy final: York City 2 Newport County 0.
Ayr United relegated to Scottish League Division 2.
13 Manchester City Premier League Champions.
Bolton Wanderers relegated to Football League Championship.
FA Vase final: Dunston UTS 2 West Auckland Town 0.
19 Champions League final: Bayern Munich 1 Chelsea 1.
(Chelsa won 4-3 on penalties).
Championship Play-off final; West Ham United 2 Birmingham C 1.
(West Ham United promoted to Premier League).
William Hill Scottish Cup final: Hearts 5 Hibernian 1.
20 Blue Square Play-off final: York City 2 Luton Town 1
(York City promoted to Football League Two).
Dumbarton promoted to Scottish League Division 1.
Albion Rovers retain Scottish League Division 2 status.
26 Football League One Play-off final: Huddersfield Town 0 Sheffield United 0.
(Huddersfield Town won 8-7 on penalties and promoted to Football League Championship).
Women's FA Cup final: Birmingham City 1 Chelsea 1.
(Birmingham City won 3-2 on penalties).

ENGLISH LEAGUE TABLES 2011–12

(P) *Promoted into division at end of 2010–11 season.* (R) *Relegated into division at end of 2010–11 season.*

BARCLAYS PREMIER LEAGUE 2011–12

		Total						Home					Away						
		P	*W*	*D*	*L*	*F*	*A*	*W*	*D*	*L*	*F*	*A*	*W*	*D*	*L*	*F*	*A*	*GD*	*Pts*
1	Manchester C	38	28	5	5	93	29	18	1	0	55	12	10	4	5	38	17	64	89
2	Manchester U	38	28	5	5	89	33	15	2	2	52	19	13	3	3	37	14	56	89
3	Arsenal	38	21	7	10	74	49	12	4	3	39	17	9	3	7	35	32	25	70
4	Tottenham H	38	20	9	9	66	41	13	3	3	39	17	7	6	6	27	24	25	69
5	Newcastle U	38	19	8	11	56	51	11	5	3	29	17	8	3	8	27	34	5	65
6	Chelsea	38	18	10	10	65	46	12	3	4	41	24	6	7	6	24	22	19	64
7	Everton	38	15	11	12	50	40	10	3	6	28	15	5	8	6	22	25	10	56
8	Liverpool	38	14	10	14	47	40	6	9	4	24	16	8	1	10	23	24	7	52
9	Fulham	38	14	10	14	48	51	10	5	4	36	26	4	5	10	12	25	–3	52
10	WBA	38	13	8	17	45	52	6	3	10	21	22	7	5	7	24	30	–7	47
11	Swansea C (P)	38	12	11	15	44	51	8	7	4	27	18	4	4	11	17	33	–7	47
12	Norwich C (P)	38	12	11	15	52	66	7	6	6	28	30	5	5	9	24	36	–14	47
13	Sunderland	38	11	12	15	45	46	7	7	5	26	17	4	5	10	19	29	–1	45
14	Stoke C	38	11	12	15	36	53	7	8	4	25	20	4	4	11	11	33	–17	45
15	Wigan Ath	38	11	10	17	42	62	5	7	7	22	27	6	3	10	20	35	–20	43
16	Aston Villa	38	7	17	14	37	53	4	7	8	20	25	3	10	6	17	28	–16	38
17	QPR (P)	38	10	7	21	43	66	7	5	7	24	25	3	2	14	19	41	–23	37
18	Bolton W	38	10	6	22	46	77	4	4	11	23	39	6	2	11	23	38	–31	36
19	Blackburn R	38	8	7	23	48	78	6	1	12	26	33	2	6	11	22	45	–30	31
20	Wolverhampton W	38	5	10	23	40	82	3	3	13	19	43	2	7	10	21	39	–42	25

NPOWER CHAMPIONSHIP 2011–12

		Total						Home					Away						
		P	*W*	*D*	*L*	*F*	*A*	*W*	*D*	*L*	*F*	*A*	*W*	*D*	*L*	*F*	*A*	*GD*	*Pts*
1	Reading	46	27	8	11	69	41	14	5	4	36	18	13	3	7	33	23	28	89
2	Southampton (P)	46	26	10	10	85	46	16	4	3	49	18	10	6	7	36	28	39	88
3	West Ham U¶ (R)	46	24	14	8	81	48	11	8	4	41	26	13	6	4	40	22	33	86
4	Birmingham C (R)	46	20	16	10	78	51	13	9	1	37	14	7	7	9	41	37	27	76
5	Blackpool (R)	46	20	15	11	79	59	13	7	3	42	21	7	8	8	37	38	20	75
6	Cardiff C	46	19	18	9	66	53	11	7	5	37	29	8	11	4	29	24	13	75
7	Middlesbrough	46	18	16	12	52	51	8	10	5	22	21	10	6	7	30	30	1	70
8	Hull C	46	19	11	16	47	44	12	4	7	28	22	7	7	9	19	22	3	68
9	Leicester C	46	18	12	16	66	55	11	6	6	36	22	7	6	10	30	33	11	66
10	Brighton & HA (P)	46	17	15	14	52	52	11	8	4	36	21	6	7	10	16	31	0	66
11	Watford	46	16	16	14	56	64	10	6	7	32	33	6	10	7	24	31	–8	64
12	Derby Co	46	18	10	18	50	58	11	4	8	28	23	7	6	10	22	35	–8	64
13	Burnley	46	17	11	18	61	58	7	9	7	33	27	10	2	11	28	31	3	62
14	Leeds U	46	17	10	19	65	68	9	3	11	34	41	8	7	8	31	27	–3	61
15	Ipswich T	46	17	10	19	69	77	11	3	9	39	32	6	7	10	30	45	–8	61
16	Millwall	46	15	12	19	55	57	7	7	9	27	30	8	5	10	28	27	–2	57
17	Crystal Palace	46	13	17	16	46	51	7	11	5	22	19	6	6	11	24	32	–5	56
18	Peterborough U (P)	46	13	11	22	67	77	10	3	10	41	38	3	8	12	26	39	–10	50
19	Nottingham F	46	14	8	24	48	63	6	5	12	21	32	8	3	12	27	31	–15	50
20	Bristol C	46	12	13	21	44	68	7	6	10	26	32	5	7	11	18	36	–24	49
21	Barnsley	46	13	9	24	49	74	9	4	10	31	37	4	5	14	18	37	–25	48
22	Portsmouth*	46	13	11	22	50	59	10	5	8	30	24	3	6	14	20	35	–9	40
23	Coventry C	46	9	13	24	41	65	8	7	8	28	26	1	6	16	13	39	–24	40
24	Doncaster R	46	8	12	26	43	80	4	8	11	22	35	4	4	15	21	45	–37	36

**Portsmouth deducted 10 points.* ¶*West Ham U promoted via play-offs.*

NPOWER LEAGUE 1 2011–12

		Total						*Home*					*Away*						
		P	*W*	*D*	*L*	*F*	*A*	*W*	*D*	*L*	*F*	*A*	*W*	*D*	*L*	*F*	*A*	*GD*	*Pts*
1	Charlton Ath	46	30	11	5	82	36	15	6	2	46	20	15	5	3	36	16	46	101
2	Sheffield W	46	28	9	9	81	48	17	4	2	48	19	11	5	7	33	29	33	93
3	Sheffield U (R)	46	27	9	10	92	51	16	4	3	54	27	11	5	7	38	24	41	90
4	Huddersfield T¶	46	21	18	7	79	47	14	6	3	35	19	7	12	4	44	28	32	81
5	Milton Keynes D	46	22	14	10	84	47	12	6	5	45	22	10	8	5	39	25	37	80
6	Stevenage	46	18	19	9	69	44	10	10	3	36	23	8	9	6	33	21	25	73
7	Notts Co	46	21	10	15	75	63	13	5	5	42	29	8	5	10	33	34	12	73
8	Carlisle U	46	18	15	13	65	66	12	7	4	41	30	6	8	9	24	36	–1	69
9	Brentford	46	18	13	15	63	52	10	6	7	36	24	8	7	8	27	28	11	67
10	Colchester U	46	13	20	13	61	66	8	11	4	38	33	5	9	9	23	33	–5	59
11	Bournemouth	46	15	13	18	48	52	9	5	9	23	23	6	8	9	25	29	–4	58
12	Tranmere R	46	14	14	18	49	53	9	11	3	27	16	5	3	15	22	37	–4	56
13	Hartlepool U	46	14	14	18	50	55	6	6	11	21	22	8	8	7	29	33	–5	56
14	Bury (P)	46	15	11	20	60	79	8	8	7	31	32	7	3	13	29	47	–19	56
15	Preston NE (R)	46	13	15	18	54	68	7	9	7	30	35	6	6	11	24	33	–14	54
16	Oldham Ath	46	14	12	20	50	66	9	5	9	26	26	5	7	11	24	40	–16	54
17	Yeovil T	46	14	12	20	59	80	10	3	10	34	41	4	9	10	25	39	–21	54
18	Scunthorpe U (R)	46	10	22	14	55	59	5	10	8	28	33	5	12	6	27	26	–4	52
19	Walsall	46	10	20	16	51	57	7	9	7	27	27	3	11	9	24	30	–6	50
20	Leyton O	46	13	11	22	48	75	6	6	11	23	34	7	5	11	25	41	–27	50
21	Wycombe W (P)	46	11	10	25	65	88	7	6	10	37	38	4	4	15	28	50	–23	43
22	Chesterfield (P)	46	10	12	24	56	81	7	6	10	26	33	3	6	14	30	48	–25	42
23	Exeter C	46	10	12	24	46	75	8	8	7	31	29	2	4	17	15	46	–29	42
24	Rochdale	46	8	14	24	47	81	6	8	9	30	39	2	6	15	17	42	–34	38

¶Huddersfield T promoted via play-offs.

NPOWER LEAGUE 2 2011–12

		Total						*Home*					*Away*						
		P	*W*	*D*	*L*	*F*	*A*	*W*	*D*	*L*	*F*	*A*	*W*	*D*	*L*	*F*	*A*	*GD*	*Pts*
1	Swindon T (R)	46	29	6	11	75	32	19	3	1	49	8	10	3	10	26	24	43	93
2	Shrewsbury T	46	26	10	10	66	41	18	5	0	37	12	8	5	10	29	29	25	88
3	Crawley T (P)	46	23	15	8	76	54	14	5	4	47	25	9	10	4	29	29	22	84
4	Southend U	46	25	8	13	77	48	12	6	5	36	18	13	2	8	41	30	29	83
5	Torquay U	46	23	12	11	63	50	12	8	3	36	23	11	4	8	27	27	13	81
6	Cheltenham T	46	23	8	15	66	50	13	5	5	32	16	10	3	10	34	34	16	77
7	Crewe Alex¶	46	20	12	14	67	59	11	6	6	38	28	9	6	8	29	31	8	72
8	Gillingham	46	20	10	16	79	62	13	4	6	44	27	7	6	10	35	35	17	70
9	Oxford U	46	17	17	12	59	48	10	9	4	36	24	7	8	8	23	24	11	68
10	Rotherham U	46	18	13	15	67	63	12	4	7	31	22	6	9	8	36	41	4	67
11	Aldershot T	46	19	9	18	54	52	11	5	7	26	19	8	4	11	28	33	2	66
12	Port Vale*	46	20	9	17	68	60	12	3	8	38	26	8	6	9	30	34	8	59
13	Bristol R (R)	46	15	12	19	60	70	10	6	7	37	29	5	6	12	23	41	–10	57
14	Accrington S	46	14	15	17	54	66	11	4	8	34	33	3	11	9	20	33	–12	57
15	Morecambe	46	14	14	18	63	57	6	6	11	31	29	8	8	7	32	28	6	56
16	AFC Wimbledon (P)	46	15	9	22	62	78	9	4	10	39	40	6	5	12	23	38	–16	54
17	Burton Alb	46	14	12	20	54	81	8	7	8	24	32	6	5	12	30	49	–27	54
18	Bradford C	46	12	14	20	54	59	8	9	6	34	27	4	5	14	20	32	–5	50
19	Dagenham & R (R)	46	14	8	24	50	72	9	3	11	31	35	5	5	13	19	37	–22	50
20	Northampton T	46	12	12	22	56	79	6	6	11	30	43	6	6	11	26	36	–23	48
21	Plymouth Arg (R)	46	10	16	20	47	64	6	9	8	23	26	4	7	12	24	38	–17	46
22	Barnet	46	12	10	24	52	79	6	6	11	29	39	6	4	13	23	40	–27	46
23	Hereford U	46	10	14	22	50	70	5	5	13	23	41	5	9	9	27	29	–20	44
24	Macclesfield T	46	8	13	25	39	64	5	11	7	25	26	3	2	18	14	38	–25	37

**Port Vale deducted 10 points. ¶Crewe Alex promoted via play-offs.*

FOOTBALL LEAGUE PLAY-OFFS 2011–12

CHAMPIONSHIP FIRST LEG

Thursday, 3 May 2012

Cardiff C (0) 0

West Ham U (2) 2 *(Collison 9, 41)* 23,029

Cardiff C: Marshall; Blake, Taylor, Gunnarsson, Hudson, Turner, Cowie (McPhail), Whittingham, Miller (Earnshaw), Mason, Lawrence.
West Ham U: Green; Demel (Faubert), Taylor, Nolan, Reid, Tomkins, O'Neil, Noble, Cole, Vaz Te (McCartney), Collison (Maynard).

Friday, 4 May 2012

Blackpool (1) 1 *(Davies 45 (og))*

Birmingham C (0) 0 13,832

Blackpool: Gilks; Eardley, Crainey, Ferguson, John Baptiste, Evatt, Angel, Dobbie (Phillips K), Taylor-Fletcher (Dicko), Ince, Phillips M.
Birmingham C: Doyle; Ramage, Murphy, Pablo, Davies, N'Daw, Burke, Mutch, King, Redmond (Spector), Elliott.

CHAMPIONSHIP SECOND LEG

Monday, 7 May 2012

West Ham U (2) 3 *(Nolan 15, Vaz Te 40, Maynard 90)*

Cardiff C (0) 0 34,682

West Ham U: Green; Demel, Taylor, Nolan (McCartney), Reid, Tomkins, O'Neil, Noble, Cole (Maynard), Vaz Te, Collison (Lansbury).
Cardiff C: Marshall; McNaughton (Blake), Taylor, Gunnarsson, Hudson, Turner, Whittingham, McPhail (Cowie), Miller (Kiss), Mason, Lawrence.

Wednesday, 9 May 2012

Birmingham C (0) 2 *(Zigic 64, Davies 73)*

Blackpool (1) 2 *(Dobbie 45, Phillips M 48)* 28,483

Birmingham C: Doyle; Ramage, Murphy, Pablo, Davies, Spector (N'Daw), Burke, Mutch, King, Zigic, Townsend (Redmond).
Blackpool: Gilks; Eardley, Crainey, Ferguson, John Baptiste, Evatt, Angel, Dobbie (Dicko), Taylor-Fletcher, Ince (Southern), Phillips M (Phillips K).

FINAL (at Wembley)

Saturday, 19 May 2012

Blackpool (0) 1 *(Ince 48)*

West Ham U (1) 2 *(Cole 35, Vaz Te 87)* 78,523

Blackpool: Gilks; Eardley, Crainey, Ferguson, John Baptiste, Evatt, Angel (Dicko), Dobbie (Bednar), Phillips K (Sylvestre), Ince, Phillips M.
West Ham U: Green; Demel (Faubert), Taylor, Nolan, Reid, Tomkins, O'Neil (McCartney), Noble, Cole, Vaz Te, Collison.
Referee: H. Webb (S. Yorkshire).

LEAGUE ONE FIRST LEG

Friday, 11 May 2012

Stevenage (0) 0

Sheffield U (0) 0 5802

Stevenage: Day; Lascelles (Myrie-Williams), Laird, Roberts, Ashton, Bostwick, Wilson, Byrom (Shroot), Agyemang, Reid (Mousinho), Freeman.
Sheffield U: Simonsen; Lowton, Hill, Doyle, Collins, Maguire, Williamson, McDonald (Ertl), Flynn (Cresswell), Porter, Quinn.

Saturday, 12 May 2012

Milton Keynes D (0) 0

Huddersfield T (1) 2 *(Rhodes 32, Hunt 73)* 11,893

Milton Keynes D: Martin; Chicksen, Lewington, Potter, MacKenzie, Williams S, Powell, Gleeson, Bowditch, MacDonald (Ibehre), Smith A (O'Shea).
Huddersfield T: Bennett; Hunt, Woods (Clarke T), Miller, Clarke P, Morrison, Johnson, Arfield (Higginbotham), Rhodes (Lee), Novak, Ward.

Crewe Alexandra's Lee Bell celebrates winning the npower Football League Two Play-Off Final. Crewe beat Cheltenham Town 2-0 to clinch their place in League One. (PA)

Huddersfield Town's goalkeeper Alex Smithies scores his spot kick to win the penalty shoot-out and secure his team's Championship status in the League One Play-Off Final at Wembley. The game against Sheffield United finished goalless after extra time, Huddersfield winning 8-7 on penalties. (PA)

LEAGUE ONE SECOND LEG

Monday, 14 May 2012

Sheffield U (0) 1 *(Porter 85)*

Stevenage (0) 0 21,182

Sheffield U: Simonsen; Lowton, Hill, Doyle, Collins, Maguire, Williamson, McDonald (Montgomery), Flynn, Porter, Quinn.
Stevenage: Day; Lascelles, Laird, Roberts, Ashton, Bostwick, Wilson, Byrom (Reid), Agyemang (Beardsley), Shroot (Mousinho), Freeman.

Tuesday, 15 May 2012

Huddersfield T (1) 1 *(Rhodes 18)*

Milton Keynes D (1) 2 *(Powell 39, Smith A 90)* 15,085

Huddersfield T: Bennett (Smithies); Hunt, Woods, Miller (Robinson), Clarke P, Morrison, Higginbotham (Clarke T), Johnson, Rhodes, Novak, Ward.
Milton Keynes D: Martin; Chicksen (Ibehre), Lewington, Potter, MacKenzie, Williams S, Powell, Gleeson, Bowditch (Chadwick), MacDonald (Smith A), O'Shea

FINAL (at Wembley)

Saturday, 26 May 2012

Huddersfield T (0) 0

Sheffield U (0) 0 52,100

Huddersfield T: Smithies; Hunt, Woods, Miller, Clarke P, Morrison, Higginbotham (Roberts), Johnson, Rhodes, Novak (Arfield), Ward (Lee).
Sheffield U: Simonsen; Lowton, Hill, Montgomery (Taylor), Collins, Maguire, Williamson, Doyle, Flynn (O'Halloran), Cresswell (Porter), Quinn.
aet; Huddersfield T won 8-7 on penalties: Miller saved; Williamson saved; Johnson missed; Collins scored; Lee saved; Lowton saved; Clarke P scored; Taylor hit post; Arfield scored; Porter scored; Rhodes scored; Quinn scored; Roberts scored; Maguire scored; Woods scored; Doyle scored; Hunt scored; O'Halloran scored; Morrison scored; Hill scored; Smithies scored; Simonsen missed.

LEAGUE TWO FIRST LEG

Saturday, 12 May 2012

Crewe Alex (0) 1 *(Dugdale 49)*

Southend U (0) 0 7221

Crewe Alex: Phillips; Tootle, Davis, Westwood, Martin C (Bodin), Dugdale, Mellor, Murphy (Bell), Powell, Leitch-Smith (Clayton), Moore.
Southend U: Belford; Clohessy, Gilbert, Mohsni, Barker, Phillips (Prosser), Grant, Timlin, Harris (Eastwood), Ferdinand (Leonard), Hall.

Sunday, 13 May 2012

Cheltenham T (1) 2 *(McGlashan 27, Burgess 50)*

Torquay U (0) 0 5273

Cheltenham T: Brown; Lowe, Jombati, Pack, Bennett, Elliott, McGlashan, Mohamed (Smikle), Spencer (Goulding), Burgess (Duffy), Summerfield.
Torquay U: Olejnik; Oastler, Nicholson, Mansell, Saah, Ellis, Lathrope (Rowe-Turner), O'Kane, Howe (Atieno), Morris, Jarvis.

LEAGUE TWO SECOND LEG

Wednesday, 16 May 2012

Southend U (0) 2 *(Harris 64, Barker 88)*

Crewe Alex (1) 2 *(Leitch-Smith 24, Clayton 86)* 8190

Southend U: Belford; Clohessy, Gilbert (Hills), Mohsni, Barker, Prosser, Grant, Timlin, Benyon (Harris), Eastwood, Hall.
Crewe Alex: Phillips; Tootle, Davis, Westwood, Artell, Dugdale, Bell, Mellor, Powell, Leitch-Smith (Clayton), Moore.

Thursday, 17 May 2012

Torquay U (0) 1 *(Atieno 85)*

Cheltenham T (0) 2 *(McGlashan 75, Pack 87)* 3606

Torquay U: Olejnik; Oastler, Nicholson, Mansell, Saah, Ellis, Lathrope (Atieno), O'Kane, Jarvis, Morris, Stevens (MacDonald).
Cheltenham T: Brown; Lowe, Jombati, Pack, Bennett, Elliott, McGlashan (Hooman), Mohamed, Spencer (Penn), Burgess (Goulding), Summerfield.

FINAL (AT WEMBLEY)

Sunday, 27 May 2012

Cheltenham T (0) 0

Crewe Alex (0) 2 *(Powell 15, Moore 82)* 24,029

Cheltenham T: Brown; Jombati, Garbutt, Pack (Penn), Bennett, Elliott, McGlashan, Mohamed, Burgess (Spencer), Goulding (Duffy), Summerfield.
Crewe Alex: Phillips; Tootle, Davis, Westwood, Artell, Dugdale, Mellor, Murphy, Powell (Clayton), Leitch-Smith (Martin C), Moore (Bell).

LEADING GOALSCORERS 2011–12

	League	Carling Cup	FA Cup	Other	Total
BARCLAYS PREMIERSHIP					
Only goals scored in the same division are included.					
Robin Van Persie *(Arsenal)*	30	0	2	5	37
Wayne Rooney *(Manchester U)*	27	0	2	5	34
Sergio Aguero *(Manchester C)*	23	1	1	5	30
Clint Dempsey *(Fulham)*	17	0	3	3	23
Emmanuel Adebayor *(Tottenham H)*	17	0	1	0	18
(On loan from Manchester C).					
Aiyegbeni Yakubu *(Blackburn R)*	17	1	0	0	18
Demba Ba *(Newcastle U)*	16	0	0	0	16
Grant Holt *(Norwich C)*	15	0	2	0	17
Edin Dzeko *(Manchester C)*	14	3	0	2	19
Mario Balotelli *(Manchester C)*	13	1	0	3	17
Papiss Cisse *(Newcastle U)*	13	0	0	0	13
Danny Graham *(Swansea C)*	12	0	2	0	14
Steven Fletcher *(Wolverhampton W)*	12	0	0	0	12
Highest overall total of players with 11 League games:					
Jermain Defoe *(Tottenham H)*	11	0	3	3	17
NPOWER FOOTBALL CHAMPIONSHIP					
Rickie Lambert *(Southampton)*	27	2	2	0	31
Ricardo Vaz Te *(West Ham U)*	20	0	2	0	22
(Includes 10 League and 2 FA Cup goals for Barnsley).					
Ross McCormack *(Leeds U)*	18	1	0	0	19
Marlon King *(Birmingham C)*	16	0	0	2	18
Charlie Austin *(Burnley)*	16	1	0	0	17
Kevin Phillips *(Blackpool)*	16	0	1	0	17
Matt Fryatt *(Hull C)*	16	0	0	0	16
Jay Rodriguez *(Burnley)*	15	5	1	0	21
Darius Henderson *(Millwall)*	15	0	4	0	19
David Nugent *(Leicester C)*	15	0	1	0	16
Marvin Emnes *(Middlesbrough)*	14	3	1	0	18
Carlton Cole *(West Ham U)*	14	1	0	0	15
Michael Chopra *(Ipswich T)*	14	0	0	0	14
Robert Snodgrass *(Leeds U)*	13	0	0	0	13
NPOWER FOOTBALL LEAGUE 1					
Jordan Rhodes *(Huddersfield T)*	35	2	0	2	39
Ched Evans *(Sheffield U)*	29	0	5	1	35
Bradley Wright-Phillips *(Charlton Ath)*	22	0	0	0	22
Stuart Beavon *(Wycombe W)*	21	1	0	3	25
Gary Madine *(Sheffield W)*	18	0	0	0	18
Andy Williams *(Yeovil T)*	16	0	1	0	17
Lee Miller *(Carlisle U)*	14	0	1	0	15
Jeff Hughes *(Notts Co)*	13	0	4	0	17
Lee Novak *(Huddersfield T)*	13	2	1	1	17
Francois Zoko *(Carlisle U)*	13	0	0	1	14
Lee Williamson *(Sheffield U)*	13	0	0	0	13
Anthony Wordsworth *(Colchester U)*	13	0	0	0	13
NPOWER FOOTBALL LEAGUE 2					
Izale McLeod *(Barnet)*	18	0	1	3	22
Lewis Grabban *(Rotherham U)*	18	0	3	0	21
Jack Midson *(AFC Wimbledon)*	18	1	1	0	20
Adebayo Akinfenwa *(Northampton T)*	18	0	0	0	18
Marc Richards *(Port Vale)*	17	0	0	0	17
Matt Harrold *(Bristol R)*	16	1	0	1	18
Kevin Ellison *(Morecambe)*	15	1	0	1	17
James Collins *(Shrewsbury T)*	14	2	0	0	16
Danny Hylton *(Aldershot T)*	13	2	0	1	16
Nick Powell *(Crewe Alex)*	14	0	0	1	15
Tyrone Barnett *(Crawley T)*	14	0	1	0	15
James Hanson *(Bradford C)*	13	0	1	0	14
Bilel Mohsni *(Southend U)*	13	0	0	0	13

Other matches consist of European games, J Paint Trophy, Community Shield and Football League play-offs. Players listed in order of League goals total.

REVIEW OF THE SEASON

Never sounds like a finite word but echoes of the past often reveal it as unbounded. But surely the last moments of the 2011–12 Premier League season will not be repeated? Manchester City won in overtime but the difference between their figures and runners-up Manchester United was on goals scored as otherwise they had identical records.

Such a gripping last day – and minutes – came after a season where the title was likely to stay in Manchester, but on which side? City started 14 unbeaten. United went eight before the incredible 6-1 defeat at Old Trafford to their neighbours. Sir Alex Ferguson's teams invariably respond positively to adversity and went another nine games undefeated.

Home and away defeats respectively against Blackburn Rovers and Newcastle United at the turn of the year was United's real wobble, while Roberto Mancini's team found the tides of March almost sweeping them aside including dropping their first two points at home as the gap went from five points to eight with United ahead. Yet City recovered and won their last six including the return with United who lost twice in the same period.

Manchester City used 24 different players, three of them with just one substitute appearance each. Only goalkeeper Joe Hart was ever-present. David Silva made the most appearances of the outfield players, missing two games and coming on three times from the bench. Gareth Barry and Sergio Aguero also made three substitute appearances each in missing just four times. Aguero, the title winner on the last day, was top scorer with 23, four behind Wayne Rooney at United.

The 20th Premier League season also produced a record 1,066 goals. The average per game at 2.81 was the best in the top flight for 35 years. Manchester United's 89 points was the highest by runners-up in the Premier. Only two outfield players Stephen Ward (Wolverhampton Wanderers) and Brede Hangeland (Fulham) completed 3,420 minutes without being replaced.

Of course the leading Premier League marksman was Robin Van Persie at Arsenal with 30. The Gunners finished third but 19 points adrift of the leading pair. A poor opening saw them lose four of their first seven including that amazing 8-2 reverse away to Manchester United. Inconsistency again was evident – two spells of eight without loss their most settled sequences – but they qualified for the Champions League for a 15th consecutive time.

One of the reverses at the start for Arsenal was against Tottenham Hotspur, who early on faced a rampant Manchester City before eleven unbeaten into December. But one win in nine to mid-April and losing 5-2 against Arsenal in late February did nothing to increase confidence. Even so, only a point separated them from their North London rivals and they scored in every home game; a first since 1961–62.

Newcastle might have improved on fifth place. An excellent undefeated beginning of eleven matches before six arrived without a win, followed by six victories in succession but it tailed off when they lost three of the last four. Just four points was the gap behind Spurs.

Defeated just once in the first eight games, Chelsea did not manage more than two other spells of six matches without loss. A change of manager with Andre Villas-Boas being replaced by Roberto Di Matteo was too late for better league results but produced two excellent ones in the FA Cup and outstandingly in the Champions League, the first London club so to do and the first outside the top five finishers.

Seventh was the highest for Everton all season and came after the last nine unbeaten matches and enabled them to finish a place in front of Merseyside rivals Liverpool and hoisted 1,000 PL points, the last of the seven all-present clubs so to do.

On the last day of the Premier League season and four minutes into injury time, Sergio Aguero scores Manchester City's third goal against QPR to complete a remarkable comeback and dramatically clinch the Premier League trophy. (Action Images/Carl Recine)

Liverpool's success came in the cups, with a League Cup win in March followed by an FA Cup run all the way to the final against Chelsea, having cast the Indian sign on Everton in semi-finals again. At no stage did Liverpool win more than two league games in a row. Fulham struggled for its first win. It came beating Queens Park Rangers 6-0 in the seventh. Eighth position in early March came after three successive wins. West Bromwich Albion held Manchester City to a goalless draw at The Hawthorns on Boxing Day to take ninth place; it proved their highest all season.

Swansea City would have been generally satisfied, with 14 clean sheets and several times squeezing into the top ten. Norwich City, too, had their moments. They were eighth in October and again in February, while their best run was seven with only one reverse. Sunderland had a new manager during the term with Martin O'Neill taking command. But they slipped away with no wins in the last eight, having started the season with one win in the first eight.

Stoke City gave a good account of themselves in Europe, but a bright August was not maintained. Four wins in a row to mid-December but then no victory in the last six of the season and only 36 goals overall. Yet escape artists personified were Wigan Athletic. Suffering eight defeats in a row to November, they won seven of their last nine and accounted for Manchester United and Arsenal in successive matches!

Aston Villa won only one of their last sixteen, equalled the Premier record of 17 draws and failed to score in 15 games and scored only 37 goals. Queens Park Rangers managed the feat of alternate wins and defeats in the last 11 matches; a first in the top flight. But it saved them from relegation.

Not so Bolton Wanderers, Blackburn Rovers and Wolverhampton Wanderers, the first time three Football League founders had foundered together. Three successive wins in March stimulated hopes of recovery, but there was only one other. For Blackburn Rovers it was their lowest points total since 1978–79. Surprisingly Wolves won the first two and drew the third game, easily their most productive in 2011–12. The last win was in February, none in the last 14.

Heading back in the Premier League after four years, Reading timed their gallop to perfection beating both of their chief Championship rivals Southampton and West Ham United in a run of six successive wins to mid-April. This was achieved after a slow August and just one off the bottom in September. Dropping just two points in ten games from the end of January, the Royals went top after beating the Saints on 13 April.

Southampton lost their way after scarcely being out of first place. They appeared to be running into form with a dozen unbeaten matches under their belt before missing a penalty at Blackpool and losing on 31 April. Problems appeared before eventually snatching the second automatic place. However, one of the problems of the clubs chasing the play-off zone was their tendency to draw matches. West Ham were guilty of this. The Hammers had five in a row while sitting in second place.

But they did vanquish their rivals in a play-off tale of two cities, seeing off first Cardiff and then Birmingham to return to the Premier League at the first time of asking. Still Birmingham City could have had few complaints, ten points behind the Hammers at the final analysis. Boxing Day had seen the onset of City's best sequence with 11 without loss and, allowing for drawn affairs, were undefeated in the last nine.

Blackpool were as low as 13th by the end of October. They had two spells of seven without loss until early in the New Year to cement their launch towards a play-off berth. Cardiff City squeaked into sixth place, courtesy of not losing any of the last ten, with six draws for a season's total of 18.

Middlesbrough missed out. Second in December and still fifth in mid-March, they, too, drew 16 matches. They also won only two of their last twelve fixtures. As to Hull City they were realistically still in for play-off contention until mid-March. But goals were scarce. Leicester City dispensed with Sven-Goran Eriksson but only twice throughout contrived to win twice in a row.

In contrast Brighton & Hove Albion, the leaders in September, went searching nine games for another win. They went twelve without loss from January but there were no successes in the last eight games. For Watford, beating

Wayne Rooney scores Manchester United's fourth goal as they thrash Arsenal 8-2 at Old Trafford in August. He completed a hat-trick including a penalty. (Action Images)

Blackpool's Thomas Ince troubles West Ham United's Gary O'Neil and Mark Noble in the Championship Play-Off Final at Wembley. But the Hammers won 2-1 to earn a return to the Premier League for 2012–13. (PA)

Middlesbrough on the last day of the season took the team to the highest position of eleventh. On 5 November they had been 21st – after losing at Middlesbrough!

Derby County were still fifth at the end of October but during the season they failed to score in sixteen matches. Seventh at the end of December, Burnley scraped only seven more wins, so heading for mid-table at best. Leeds back in the Championship, sailing along nicely in mid-season and fifth early December, yet subsequently no more than two wins in succession.

Ipswich Town were 21st on 31 January when they defeated West Ham United 5-1 and improved to finish mid-table. Only an undefeated flourish in the last seven helped Millwall who had been 21st in early February. Crystal Palace were third at the end of October then failed to score in five games. They pulled themselves together but no wins came in the last nine.

For Peterborough United, the second half of the season was undistinguished, five without defeat at the turn of the year the best for Posh. However at Nottingham Forest they went seven games without scoring and achieving just one point. In fact in 19 games they failed to score.

Bristol City only saved themselves from the drop with an unbeaten run of eight at the end of the campaign and Barnsley were fortunate to miss the danger zone after failing to score more than one goal in five of their last fifteen!

Portsmouth, Coventry City and Doncaster Rovers were the relegated trio. Portsmouth would just have avoided it without the ten-point deduction for going into administration. Nine goals without a win was their poorest period into March. Coventry were never out of the bottom three from the end of October and even seven undefeated to the beginning of March was not enough. Doncaster Rovers claimed only two goals and one point in their first seven outings, and overall had 15 games in which they failed to score once.

Apart from a March wobble of three matches and just one point, League One champions Charlton Athletic enjoyed a splendid season and topped a century of points in the process. The struggle for runners-up position was an all-Sheffield affair. Wednesday prevailed thanks to a superb run at the end of the season – 14 undefeated matches in which only three were drawn. City rivals United lost the services of their leading scorer for the last three matches and in the later play-offs.

As it was, Huddersfield Town emerged having en route broken Nottingham Forest's record of consecutive League matches without defeat. They needed to recover after losing their way a little in April, but took care of Milton Keynes Dons and Sheffield United in the play-offs, the latter only following a marathon of 22 penalties. MK Dons topped a century of goals in League and Cup games and were one of the early leaders in September.

Stevenage snared sixth place with four wins and a draw in the last five outings and, but for an enormous tally of 19 drawn matches, might well have obtained automatic promotion. For Notts County inconsistency was their undoing. Only one run of six without defeat offered any springboard towards the middle of March.

Carlisle United seemed to be heading for at least sixth place until they were let down with just one win in the last seven, while Brentford placed fourth in the opening games, faltered when they managed to win only one of the last five after five wins in succession. Colchester United topped the draw lists with no fewer than 20 of them. There was just one win in the last 13.

Bournemouth, bottom but one in September, raised themselves to eighth by early January but shortly afterwards lost five times on the trot. Tranmere Rovers looked in real danger when mid-season they won only one game in nineteen before sustaining a revival in March. Hartlepool United, third at the end of September, slipped to seventeenth by early January before heading towards mid-table.

A wretched run of 13 without a win and just six points was a concern for Bury into March before three wins in a row steadied them. Conversely Preston North End won seven from the middle of August before failing to win one of the next nine. There were only two wins in the last seventeen. Oldham Athletic had only three wins in the last 15 matches and never had more than two in a row.

Yeovil Town had held up the rest of the teams by 5 November, but rocketed up with ten wins in the second half of the season. Scunthorpe United steered themselves out of trouble with no defeats in ten to early April and were the draw champions with 22. Walsall came close to emulating them sharing the spoils 20 times, yet still had to draw with Huddersfield and win at MK Dons on the last day. Leyton Orient, too, were worried and won just one of their last eight again following a disappointing start.

So the unlucky foursome was Wycombe Wanderers, Chesterfield, Exeter City and Rochdale. Wycombe hovered around the relegation zone most of the season despite seven without defeat into April. Chesterfield's consolation was winning the Johnstone's Paint Trophy. They had gone 17 league games without winning to mid-January. Exeter scraped just two wins in the last 14 and Rochdale remained in the bottom four from late November.

Swindon Town became champions of League Two, ten wins in succession to the end of February really hitting all serious opposition. The only blow was losing the JPT. Shrewsbury Town and Crawley Town accompanied them on automatic promotion, Shrewsbury after nine without defeat into late April. However Crawley had poor spells between two sequences of 13 without loss.

Bottom in August, Crewe Alexandra came through for the final play-off success with the best run of any club over the last third of the season: 16 without loss and none in the play-offs. Cheltenham Town, their victims at Wembley, were still second in early March but were hampered by no wins in seven. Southend United, too, were at their best to the end of November and again when top in mid-February. But it was all change after beating Crewe. Torquay United lost to Cheltenham in the play-offs after a good second half of the season losing just five times.

Gillingham were erratic: no loss in the first four, none in the last quartet. In between there were better and poorer periods. Oxford United, fourth at the end of October, had no wins in the last seven. Rotherham United looked useful in September but went nine without a win shortly afterwards. Aldershot Town, too, were inconsistent, earning a club record six wins in a row after six without one.

Port Vale were hit with a ten-point deduction; eight undefeated to early March its high spot. Bristol Rovers shrugged off a unimpressive first half of the term and enjoyed occasional bursts of goal scoring – a seven and two fives.

Matters appeared to be looking up for Accrington Stanley with ten unbeaten to the end of January, but it was a false dawn. Morecambe led at the end of September, but again there were no sustained spells afterwards, while AFC Wimbledon, third in October, produced no further wins until January.

Burton Albion were fifth on Boxing Day before enduring 16 games without another win bonus. Bradford City won three in a row in December but hovered above the danger zone thereafter. Dagenham & Redbridge pulled off a Houdini act. Between the end of August and the middle of December they won just once, yet lost just one of the last ten.

Northampton Town were bottom on 3 March but won four of the next five to stay out of the drop zone. Plymouth Argyle as well snatched their first win at the end of September and remained bottom in January before picking up sufficient points, whereas Barnet had to win their last two games as they had gone 17 with just one win.

Back to the Conference arena went Hereford United and Macclesfield Town. Hereford had two spells of eight without a win and despite ending with two wins and two draws it was not enough. Macclesfield failed to win a match in 2012 with the final 23 yielding just seven points. So now York City are back in the Football League with new boys Fleetwood Town.

Reading's Adam Le Fondre negotiates Southampton goalkeeper Kelvin Davis to score his team's third goal in a top-of-the table 3-1 victory at St Mary's in April. Reading went on to win the Championship, Southampton claiming the other automatic promotion place. (PA)

THE FA CHARITY SHIELD WINNERS 1908–2011

1908	Manchester U v QPR	4-0 after 1-1 draw
1909	Newcastle U v Northampton T	2-0
1910	Brighton v Aston Villa	1-0
1911	Manchester U v Swindon T	8-4
1912	Blackburn R v QPR	2-1
1913	Professionals v Amateurs	7-2
1920	WBA v Tottenham H	2-0
1921	Tottenham H v Burnley	2-0
1922	Huddersfield T v Liverpool	1-0
1923	Professionals v Amateurs	2-0
1924	Professionals v Amateurs	3-1
1925	Amateurs v Professionals	6-1
1926	Amateurs v Professionals	6-3
1927	Cardiff C v Corinthians	2-1
1928	Everton v Blackburn R	2-1
1929	Professionals v Amateurs	3-0
1930	Arsenal v Sheffield W	2-1
1931	Arsenal v WBA	1-0
1932	Everton v Newcastle U	5-3
1933	Arsenal v Everton	3-0
1934	Arsenal v Manchester C	4-0
1935	Sheffield W v Arsenal	1-0
1936	Sunderland v Arsenal	2-1
1937	Manchester C v Sunderland	2-0
1938	Arsenal v Preston NE	2-1
1948	Arsenal v Manchester U	4-3
1949	Portsmouth v Wolverhampton W	1-1*
1950	World Cup Team v Canadian Touring Team	4-2
1951	Tottenham H v Newcastle U	2-1
1952	Manchester U v Newcastle U	4-2
1953	Arsenal v Blackpool	3-1
1954	Wolverhampton W v WBA	4-4*
1955	Chelsea v Newcastle U	3-0
1956	Manchester U v Manchester C	1-0
1957	Manchester U v Aston Villa	4-0
1958	Bolton W v Wolverhampton W	4-1
1959	Wolverhampton W v Nottingham F	3-1
1960	Burnley v Wolverhampton W	2-2*
1961	Tottenham H v FA XI	3-2
1962	Tottenham H v Ipswich T	5-1
1963	Everton v Manchester U	4-0
1964	Liverpool v West Ham U	2-2*
1965	Manchester U v Liverpool	2-2*
1966	Liverpool v Everton	1-0
1967	Manchester U v Tottenham H	3-3*
1968	Manchester C v WBA	6-1
1969	Leeds U v Manchester C	2-1
1970	Everton v Chelsea	2-1
1971	Leicester C v Liverpool	1-0
1972	Manchester C v Aston Villa	1-0
1973	Burnley v Manchester C	1-0
1974	Liverpool† v Leeds U	1-1
1975	Derby Co v West Ham U	2-0
1976	Liverpool v Southampton	1-0
1977	Liverpool v Manchester U	0-0*
1978	Nottingham F v Ipswich T	5-0
1979	Liverpool v Arsenal	3-1
1980	Liverpool v West Ham U	1-0
1981	Aston Villa v Tottenham H	2-2*
1982	Liverpool v Tottenham H	1-0
1983	Manchester U v Liverpool	2-0
1984	Everton v Liverpool	1-0
1985	Everton v Manchester U	2-0
1986	Everton v Liverpool	1-1*
1987	Everton v Coventry C	1-0
1988	Liverpool v Wimbledon	2-1
1989	Liverpool v Arsenal	1-0
1990	Liverpool v Manchester U	1-1*
1991	Arsenal v Tottenham H	0-0*
1992	Leeds U v Liverpool	4-3
1993	Manchester U† v Arsenal	1-1
1994	Manchester U v Blackburn R	2-0
1995	Everton v Blackburn R	1-0
1996	Manchester U v Newcastle U	4-0
1997	Manchester U† v Chelsea	1-1
1998	Arsenal v Manchester U	3-0
1999	Arsenal v Manchester U	2-1
2000	Chelsea v Manchester U	2-0
2001	Liverpool v Manchester U	2-1
2002	Arsenal v Liverpool	1-0
2003	Manchester U† v Arsenal	1-1
2004	Arsenal v Manchester U	3-1
2005	Chelsea v Arsenal	2-1
2006	Liverpool v Chelsea	2-1
2007	Manchester U† v Chelsea	1-1
2008	Manchester U† v Portsmouth	0-0
2009	Chelsea† v Manchester U	2-2
2010	Manchester U v Chelsea	3-1
2011	Manchester U v Manchester C	3-2

** Each club retained shield for six months.* *† Won on penalties.*

THE FA COMMUNITY SHIELD 2011

Manchester C (2) 2, Manchester U (0) 3

At Wembley Stadium, 7 August 2011, attendance 77,169

Manchester C: Hart; Richards, Kolarov (Clichy 73), De Jong, Lescott, Kompany, Silva, Toure Y, Balotelli (Barry 59), Dzeko, Milner (Johnson A 67).
Scorers: Lescott 38, Dzeko 45.

Manchester United: De Gea; Smalling, Evra (Rafael 71), Carrick (Jones 46), Ferdinand (Evans J 46), Vidic (Cleverley 46), Young, Anderson, Welbeck (Berbatov 89), Rooney, Nani.
Scorers: Smalling 52, Nani 58, 90.

Referee: P. Dowd (Staffordshire).

ACCRINGTON STANLEY FL Championship 2

FOUNDATION

Accrington Football Club, founder members of the Football League in 1888, were not connected with Accrington Stanley. In fact both clubs ran concurrently between 1891 when Stanley were formed and 1895 when Accrington FC folded. Actually Stanley Villa was the original name, those responsible for forming the club living in Stanley Street and using the Stanley Arms as their meeting place. They became Accrington Stanley in 1893. In 1894–95 they joined the Accrington & District League, playing at Moorhead Park. Subsequently they played in the North-East Lancashire Combination and the Lancashire Combination before becoming founder members of the Third Division (North) in 1921, two years after moving to Peel Park. In 1962 they resigned from the Football League, were wound up, re-formed in 1963, disbanded in 1966 only to restart as Accrington Stanley (1968), returning to the Lancashire Combination in 1970.

The Fraser Eagle Stadium, Livingstone Road, Accrington, Lancashire BB5 5BX.

Telephone: (0871) 434 1968.

Fax: (01254) 356 951.

Ticket Office: (01254) 356 950/336 954.

Website: www.accringtonstanley.co.uk

Email: info@accringtonstanley.co.uk

Ground Capacity: 5,057.

Record Attendance: 13,181 v Hull C, Division 3 (N), 28 September 1948 (at Peel Park); 4,368 v Colchester U, FA Cup 1st rd, 3 January 2004 (at Fraser Eagle Stadium – Crown Inn).

Pitch Measurements: 111yd × 72yd.

Chairman: Peter Marsden.

Chief Executive: Robert Heys.

Managing Director: David O'Neill.

Manager: Paul Cook.

Assistant Manager: Leam Richardson.

Physio: TBC.

Colours: All red.

Year Formed: 1891, reformed 1968.

Turned Professional: 1919.

Club Nickname: 'Reds'.

Previous Names: 1891, Stanley Villa; 1893, Accrington Stanley.

Grounds: 1891, Moorhead Park; 1897, Bell's Ground; 1919, Peel Park; 1970, Crown Inn.

First Football League Game: 27 August 1921, Division 3 (N), v Rochdale (a) L 3-6 – Tattersall; Newton, Baines, Crawshaw, Popplewell, Burkinshaw, Oxley, Makin, Green (1), Hosker (2), Hartles.

HONOURS

Football League – Division 3 (N): ***Runners-up*** 1954–55, 1957–58.

Conference: ***Champions*** 2005–06.

FA Cup: 4th rd 1927, 1937, 1959, 2010.

Football League Cup: never past 2nd rd.

Northern Premier League: ***Champions*** 2002–03.

Northern League – Division 1: ***Champions*** 1999–2000.

North-West Counties: ***Runners-up*** 1986–87.

Cheshire County League – Division 2: ***Champions*** 1980–81; ***Runners-up*** 1979–80.

Lancashire Combination: ***Champions*** 1973–74, 1977–78; ***Runners-up*** 1971–72, 1975–76.

Lancashire Combination Cup: ***Winners*** 1971–72, 1972–73, 1973–74, 1976–77.

sky SPORTS FACT FILE

After two games (one as a substitute) for Blackburn Rovers in 2011–12, Micah Evans, 18, was sent on loan six miles down the road to Accrington Stanley. He was given his Football League debut on 5 November and made it a scoring one after five minutes against Bristol Rovers.

Record League Victory: 8–0 v New Brighton, Division 3 (N), 17 March 1934 – Maidment; Armstrong (pen), Price, Dodds, Crawshaw, McCulloch, Wyper, Lennox (2), Cheetham (4), Leedham (1), Watson.

Record Cup Victory: 7–0 v Spennymoor U, FA Cup 2nd rd, 8 December 1938 – Tootill; Armstrong, Whittaker, Latham, Curran, Lee, Parry (2), Chadwick, Jepson (3), McLoughlin (2), Barclay.

Record Defeat: 9–1 v Lincoln C, Division 3 (N), 3 March 1951.

Most League Points (2 for a win): 61, Division 3 (N), 1954–55.

Most League Points (3 for a win): 73, FL 2, 2010–11.

Most League Goals: 96, Division 3 (N), 1954–55.

Highest League Scorer in Season: George Stewart, 35, Division 3 (N), 1955–56; George Hudson, 35, Division 4, 1960–61.

Most League Goals in Total Aggregate: George Stewart, 136, 1954–58.

Most League Goals in One Match: 5, Billy Harker v Gateshead, Division 3 (N), 16 November 1935; George Stewart v Gateshead, Division 3 (N), 27 November 1954.

Most Capped Player: Romuald Boco, 19 (42), Benin.

Most League Appearances: Jim Armstrong, 260, 1927–34.

Youngest League Player: Ian Gibson, 15 years 358 days, v Norwich C, 23 March 1959.

Record Transfer Fee Received: £250,000 (including sell-on from Blackpool 2001) for Brett Ormerod, March 1997.

Record Transfer Fee Paid: £85,000 to Swansea C for Ian Craney, January 2008.

Football League Record: 1921 Original Member of Division 3 (N); 1958–60 Division 3; 1960–62 Division 4; 2006– FL 2.

MANAGERS

William Cronshaw *c.*1894
John Haworth 1897–1910
Johnson Haworth *c.*1916
Sam Pilkingson 1919–24
(*Tommy Booth p-m 1923–24*)
Ernie Blackburn 1924–32
Amos Wade 1932–35
John Hacking 1935–49
Jimmy Porter 1949–51
Walter Crook 1951–53
Walter Galbraith 1953–58
George Eastham snr 1958–59
Harold Bodle 1959–60
James Harrower 1960–61
Harold Mather 1962–63
Jimmy Hinksman 1963–64
Terry Neville 1964–65
Ian Bryson 1965
Danny Parker 1965–66
Gerry Keenan
Gary Pierce
Dave Thornley
Phil Staley
Eric Whalley
Stan Allen 1995–96
Tony Greenwood 1996–98
Billy Rodaway 1998
Wayne Harrison 1998–99
John Coleman 1999–2012
Paul Cook February 2012–

LATEST SEQUENCES

Longest Sequence of League Wins: 7, 27.12.1954 – 5.2.1955.

Longest Sequence of League Defeats: 9, 8.3.1030 – 21.4.1930.

Longest Sequence of League Draws: 4, 10.9.1927 – 27.9.1927.

Longest Sequence of Unbeaten League Matches: 14, 15.3.2011 – 6.8.2011.

Longest Sequence Without a League Win: 18, 17.9.1938 – 31.12.1938.

Successive Scoring Runs: 22 from 14.11.1936.

Successive Non-scoring Runs: 5 from 15.3.1930.

TEN YEAR LEAGUE RECORD

		P	W	D	L	F	A	Pts	Pos
2002-03	U Pr	44	30	10	4	97	44	100	1
2003-04	Conf	42	15	13	14	68	61	58	10
2004-05	Conf	42	18	11	13	72	58	65	10
2005-06	Conf	42	28	7	7	76	45	91	1
2006-07	FL 2	46	13	11	22	70	81	50	20
2007-08	FL 2	46	16	3	27	49	83	51	17
2008-09	FL 2	46	13	11	22	42	59	50	16
2009-10	FL 2	46	18	7	21	62	74	61	15
2010-11	FL 2	46	18	19	9	73	55	73	5
2011-12	FL 2	46	14	15	17	54	66	57	14

DID YOU KNOW ?

Accrington Stanley were grateful to Billy Watkinson for his 23 League goals in 1951–52 that helped towards avoding relegation by one point. The former Liverpool forward originally with Prescot Cables made over 100 appearances at centre or on the wing before moving to Halifax Town.

ACCRINGTON STANLEY 2011–12 LEAGUE RECORD

Match No.	Date	Venue	Opponents	Result	H/T Score	Lg Pos.	Goalscorers	Attendance
1	Aug 6	A	Northampton T	D 0-0	0-0	—		4621
2	13	H	Southend U	L 1-2	1-1	19	Procter [40]	1491
3	16	H	Bradford C	W 1-0	0-0	—	Fletcher [77]	2652
4	20	A	Port Vale	L 1-4	0-4	18	Murphy [81]	4615
5	27	H	Burton Alb	W 2-1	0-1	15	Winnard [72], Fletcher [81]	1362
6	Sept 3	A	Barnet	D 0-0	0-0	15		2380
7	10	A	Gillingham	D 1-1	0-0	17	Craney [84]	4619
8	13	H	Rotherham U	D 1-1	0-1	—	Hessey [83]	1486
9	17	H	Crewe Alex	L 0-2	0-2	18		1503
10	24	A	Oxford U	D 1-1	0-1	19	Murphy [62]	6472
11	Oct 1	H	Aldershot T	W 3-2	1-2	18	Hessey [11], Coid [56], Barnett [88]	1438
12	8	A	Plymouth Arg	D 2-2	0-2	16	Long [56], Amond [67]	8013
13	15	H	Swindon T	L 0-2	0-1	18		1663
14	21	H	Cheltenham T	L 0-1	0-1	—		1641
15	25	A	Shrewsbury T	L 0-1	0-1	—		5076
16	29	A	Crawley T	D 1-1	1-0	19	Murphy [41]	2987
17	Nov 5	H	Bristol R	W 2-1	2-0	17	Evans [5], Long [30]	1643
18	19	A	Macclesfield T	D 1-1	0-1	18	Stockley [78]	1792
19	26	H	Dagenham & R	W 3-0	0-0	17	Lindfield [57], Amond 2 [83, 84]	1308
20	Dec 10	A	AFC Wimbledon	W 2-0	2-0	15	Amond [3], Lindfield [24]	4053
21	17	H	Torquay U	W 3-1	1-0	13	Hughes [13], Stockley [62], Long [89]	1404
22	26	A	Morecambe	W 2-1	1-0	12	Stockley [34], Hughes [75]	2569
23	30	A	Hereford U	D 1-1	0-1	—	Evans [72]	2057
24	Jan 2	H	Macclesfield T	W 4-0	2-0	11	Lindfield [13], Long [45], Evans [62], Procter [76]	1704
25	6	A	Burton Alb	W 2-0	1-0	—	McIntyre [31], Austin (og) [65]	2486
26	14	H	Barnet	L 0-3	0-2	10		1652
27	21	A	Aldershot T	D 0-0	0-0	10		2581
28	28	H	Gillingham	W 4-3	4-1	8	Smith 3 [1, 19, 45], Joyce [31]	1734
29	Feb 14	A	Rotherham U	L 0-1	0-1	—		2572
30	18	H	Plymouth Arg	L 0-4	0-2	10		2186
31	21	A	Crewe Alex	L 0-2	0-0	—		3179
32	25	A	Swindon T	L 0-2	0-2	14		7962
33	Mar 3	H	Port Vale	D 2-2	1-1	14	Amond [45], Hatfield [88]	2093
34	6	A	Bradford C	D 1-1	0-0	—	Hatfield [90]	9379
35	10	A	Southend U	D 2-2	1-0	12	Devitt [41], Amond [90]	5954
36	17	H	Northampton T	W 2-1	1-0	13	Devitt [42], Lindfield [87]	1803
37	20	H	Morecambe	D 1-1	1-0	—	Murphy [14]	1924
38	24	A	Dagenham & R	L 1-2	1-0	13	Grant [43]	1476
39	27	H	Oxford U	L 0-2	0-1	—		1408
40	31	H	AFC Wimbledon	W 2-1	1-1	13	Joyce [4], Hatfield [80]	1627
41	Apr 6	A	Torquay U	L 0-1	0-0	13		3934
42	9	H	Hereford U	W 2-1	0-0	12	Grant [47], Amond [85]	1749
43	14	A	Cheltenham T	L 1-4	0-1	12	Grant [76]	3217
44	21	H	Shrewsbury T	D 1-1	0-1	12	Hughes [78]	3275
45	28	A	Bristol R	L 1-5	1-3	13	McIntyre [38]	7073
46	May 5	H	Crawley T	L 0-1	0-0	14		2299

Final League Position: 14

GOALSCORERS

League (54): Amond 7, Lindfield 4, Long 4, Murphy 4, Evans 3, Grant 3, Hatfield 3, Hughes 3, Smith 3, Stockley 3, Devitt 2, Fletcher 2, Hessey 2, Joyce 2, McIntyre 2, Procter 2, Barnett 1, Coid 1, Craney 1, Winnard 1, own goal 1.
Carling Cup (0).
FA Cup (1): Joyce 1.
J Paint Trophy (3): Dunbavin 1, Lindfield 1, Procter 1.

Murdoch S 12 + 1	McIntyre K 44 + 1	Winnard D 30	Long K 24	Miller K 2	Procter A 25	Lindfield C 29 + 10	Barnett C 27 + 15	Guthrie K 6 + 7	Craney I 7 + 15	Joyce L 43	Taylor N 1 + 1	Murphy P 36 + 2	Hessey S 17	Fletcher W 10	Moult L 1 + 3	Burton A — + 1	Coid D 16 + 5	Amond P 37 + 5	Bender T — + 2	Dunbavin I 25	Hatfield W 4 + 13	Dobie L — + 4	Spray J 3	Hughes B 15 + 6	Evans M 14 + 9	Stockley J 5 + 4	Richardson L — + 1	Nsiala A 19	Smith M 4 + 2	Devitt J 15 + 1	Willis L 1 + 1	Nicholls L 9	Liddle M 12	Kiernan R 3	Grant R 8	Hopper R 1 + 3	Carver M 1 + 1	*Match No.*
1	2	3	4	5	6	7	8	9	10	11																												1
1	2■	3	4	5	6	7	8^2	9	10^1	11	12	13																										2
1		3	4		6	12	8	9^1	13	11	7^2	2	5	10																								3
1	2^2	3	4		6	12	8^1		13	11		5	7	9	10^3	14																						4
1	7	3	4		6	13	12		8^2	11			5	10	14		2^1	9^3																				5
1	2	3	4■		6		8■		12	11			5	10			7^2	9^1	13																			6
1	2	3	4		6	7			12	11		8	5	10^2	13			9^1																				7
1	2	3	4		6	7			12	11		8^1	5	10				9																				8
1	2	3	4		6	7^1		14	12	11		8^2	5	10	13			9^3																				9
1	2	3^1	4		6	14	13		8	11		7	5	10^3			12	9^2																				10
1	3		4		6	12	13	14	8	11		7	5	10^1			2^2	9^3																				11
1	3		4		6		12	10	8	11		2	5■	7^1				9																				12
	2	3	4		6^3		12	10^2	8	11		7	5					9^1		1	13	14																13
	2^3	3	4		6		10	14		11^2			5				13	9		1	7^1	12	8															14
	2	3	4		6^1	13	10			11		5					12	9^2		1	7^3	14	8															15
	2	3	4		6	12	8			11		5					7^2	9		1	13		10^1															16
15	2	3	5				8			11		6■					10	9^1		1^6				4	7	12												17
	2	3	5		6	9	10^2			11			4					13		1				8^1	7	12												18
	2	3	5		6	9^3	12			11			4					13		1		14		8^1	7	10^2												19
	2	3	5		6	7	12			11			4					9		1				8		10^1												20
	2	3	5		6	7	12			11■		4						10		1				8		9^1												21
	2	3	5		6	7^2	8^3					4					14	10		1				11	12	9^1	13											22
	2	3	5		6	7						11	4					10		1				8	12	9^1												23
	2	3	5		6	7	8					12	4^1				13	10^3		1				11^2	9	14												24
	2	3			6	7	13			11		4						9	12	1				8^2	10^3	14		5^1										25
	2	3			6	7^2	12		13	11		4						9		1				8^1	10			5										26
	3	6					12		13	11		4					2	9		1				8^1	7^2			5	10									27
	3	5					12		13	11		8					2	9^2		1				4^1	7			6	10									28
	3	6				13	12			11		4					2^1	9^2		1				8	7			5	10									29
	3	5				7	8^1			11		2						14		1				4	10^2			6	9^3	12	13							30
	3	4				7^2	10^1			11		6^3					2	9		1				13	12			5	14	8								31
	7	5^1				10	12			11		4					2	9						13^3				6^2	14	8		1	3					32
	3					7^1	8	13		11		6					2^2	9			14				12			5		10^3		1	4					33
	3					7^2	8^3	12		11		6					2	9			14				13			5		10^1		1	4					34
	3					7^2	8	14		11		6					2^1	9			13				12			5		10^3		1	4■					35
	3					12	8^1			11		4					2	9			13							5		7^2		1		6	10			36
	3					12	8		14	11		4^1					2	9^3			13							5		7^2		1		6	10			37
	3					9^2	8		14	11		4					2^1	13			12							5■		7		1		6^3	10			38
	3					2	8^2		14	11		6						9			12				7^1					4		1	5		10^3	13		39
	3					11	4		13	8		6						9^3		1	12				7^1					2^2			5		10	14		40
	3					7	8		12	11		5						9^1		1	14				13					6^2			4		10	2^3		41
	3					7	8^2		14	11		4						9		1	12			13				5		6^1			2		10^3			42
	14					2	13	10^3		11								12			8			4^2	7^1			5			6	1	3		9			43
	3					2	10	14		11		6						9		1	8^1			13	12			5		7^2			4^3					44
	3					2	8^1			11		6						9		1				12	7^2			5		10^3			4			14	13	45
	3					2	8^3			11		6						9		1	14			13	12			5		10^2			4				7^1	46

FA Cup
First Round Notts Co (a) 1-4

Carling Cup
First Round Scunthorpe U (h) 0-2

J Paint Trophy
First Round Carlisle U (h) 3-2
Second Round Tranmere R (h) 0-1

AFC WIMBLEDON FL Championship 2

FOUNDATION

While the history of AFC Wimbledon is straightforward since it was a new club formed in 2002, there were in effect two clubs operating for two years with Wimbledon connections. The other club was MK Dons, of course. In August 2001, the Football League had rejected the existing Wimbledon's application to move to Milton Keynes. In May 2002, they rejected local sites and were given permission to move by an independent commission set up by the Football League. AFC Wimbledon was founded in the summer of 2002 and held its first trials on Wimbledon Common. In subsequent years, there was considerable debate over the rightful home of the trophies obtained by the former Wimbledon football club. In October 2006, an agreement was reached between Milton Keynes Dons FC, its Supporters Association, the Wimbledon Independent Supporters Association and the Football Supporters Federation to transfer such trophies and honours to the London Borough of Merton.

The Cherry Red Records Fans' Stadium, Kingsmeadow, Jack Goodchild Way, 422a Kingston Road, Kingston-upon-Thames, Surrey KT1 3PB.

Telephone: (0208) 547 3528.

Fax: (0808) 2800 816.

Website: www.afcwimbledon.co.uk

Email: info@afcwimbledon.co.uk

Ground Capacity: 5,194 (1,265 seated).

Record Attendance: 4,722 v St Albans C, Blue Square Premier, 25 April 2009.

Chairman: Erik Samuelson.

Manager: Terry Brown.

Assistant Manager: Stuart Cash.

Coach: Simon Bassey.

Physio: Mike Rayner.

Club Nickname: "The Dons".

Colours: All blue with yellow trim.

Year Formed: 2002.

Turned Professional: 2002.

MANAGERS

Terry Eames 2002–04
Nicky English *(Caretaker)* 2004
Dave Anderson 2004–07
Terry Brown 2007–

sky SPORTS FACT FILE

While Kevin Cooper holds the overall record of goals for AFC Wimbledon it should be put on record that his total of 107 in all matches was remarkably achieved in 105 League and Cup games. In 2003–04 he racked up an incredible 66 which eclipsed the record of Eddie Reynolds.

First Football League Game: 6 August 2011, FL 2 v Bristol R (h) L 2-3 – Brown; Hatton, Gwillim (Bush), Porter (Minshull), Stuart (1), Johnson B, Moore L, Wellard, Jolley (Ademeno (1)), Midson, Yussuff.

Record League Victory: 9-0 v Slough T, Isthmian Premier League 31 March 2007.

Record Defeat: 5-0 v York C, Blue Square Premier, 7 April 2010.

Most League Points (3 for a win): 54, FL 2, 2011–12.

Most League Goals: 62, FL 2, 2011–12.

Highest League Scorer in Season: Jack Midson, 18, 2011–12.

Most League Goals in Total Aggregate: Kevin Cooper, 107, 2002–04.

Most League Appearances: Jack Midson, 46, 2011–12.

LATEST SEQUENCES

Inherited records from Wimbledon

Longest Sequence of League wins: 7, 9.4.1983 – 7.5.1983.

Longest Sequence of League Defeats: 11, 10.1.2004 – 27.3.2004.

Longest Sequence of League Draws: 4, 3.3.1984 – 17.3.1984.

Longest Sequence of Unbeaten League Matches: 22, 15.1.1983 – 14.5.1983.

Longest Sequence Without a League Win: 14, 23.2.1980 – 15.4.1980.

Successive Scoring Runs: 23 from 18.2.1984 – 22.9.1984.

Successive Non-scoring Runs: 7 from 7.2.2004 – 24.3.2004.

HONOURS

Blue Square Conference: ***Runners-up*** 2010–11.

Blue Square South: ***Champions*** 2008–09.

Isthmian League – Premier Division: ***Play-off Winners*** 2007–08. **Division 1:** ***Champions*** 2004–05.

Combined Counties League: ***Champions*** 2003–04.

Combined Counties League: ***Challenge Cup Winners*** 2004.

Surrey Senior Cup: ***Winners*** 2005; ***Runners-up*** 2006.

Supporters Direct Cup: ***Winners*** 2003, 2006, 2010; ***Runners-up*** 2005, 2007.

Phil Ledger Memorial Cup: ***Winners*** 2011.

Inherited records from Wimbledon
FA Premier League: best season: 6th, 1993–94.

Football League: Division 3 – ***Runners-up*** 1983–84; **Division 4 –** ***Champions*** 1982–83.

FA Cup: ***Winners*** 1988.

Football League Cup: ***Semi-final*** 1996–97, 1998–99.

League Group Cup: ***Runners-up*** 1982.

Amateur Cup: ***Winners*** 1963; ***Runners-up*** 1935, 1947.

European Competitions
Intertoto Cup: 1995.

TEN YEAR LEAGUE RECORD

		P	W	D	L	F	A	Pts	Pos
2002-03	CC	46	36	3	7	125	46	111	3
2003-04	CC	46	42	4	0	180	32	130	1
2004-05	Isth DI	42	29	10	3	91	33	97	1
2005-06	Isth PR	42	22	11	9	67	36	77	4
2006-07	Isth PR	42	21	15	6	76	37	75	5
2007-08	Isth PR	42	22	9	11	81	47	75	3
2008-09	BSS	42	26	10	6	86	36	88	1
2009-10	BSP	44	18	10	16	61	47	64	8
2010-11	BSP	46	27	9	10	83	47	90	2
2011-12	FL 2	46	15	9	22	62	78	54	16

DID YOU KNOW ?

On 10 January 2012, AFC Wimbledon broke the club's transfer record by signing striker Byrom Harrison from Stevenage. He had been the first top scorer for a promoted Football League club scoring fewer than ten goals, registering just eight of 62 goals in 2010–11.

AFC WIMBLEDON 2011–12 LEAGUE RECORD

Match No.	Date		Venue	Opponents	Result		H/T Score	Lg Pos.	Goalscorers	Attendance
1	Aug	6	H	Bristol R	L	2-3	1-2	—	Stuart [39], Ademeno [68]	4629
2		13	A	Dagenham & R	W	2-0	1-0	10	Moore, L (pen) [38], Yussuff [57]	2904
3		16	A	Plymouth Arg	W	2-0	0-0	—	Midson 2 [54, 60]	5900
4		20	H	Hereford U	D	1-1	1-1	7	Midson [25]	4239
5		27	A	Macclesfield T	L	0-4	0-2	14		1881
6	Sept	3	H	Port Vale	W	3-2	1-0	7	Midson [40], Gwillim [60], Jolley [90]	4404
7		10	A	Aldershot T	D	1-1	1-0	9	Porter [17]	4110
8		13	H	Northampton T	L	0-3	0-1	—		4271
9		17	H	Cheltenham T	W	4-1	2-0	12	Wellard [31], Elliott (og) [40], Midson [66], Yussuff [84]	3860
10		24	A	Bradford C	W	2-1	1-1	7	Midson [31], Jolley [57]	10,255
11	Oct	1	H	Gillingham	W	3-1	3-0	4	Jolley 2 [10, 12], Midson [22]	4606
12		8	A	Morecambe	W	2-1	1-1	3	Midson [35], Jolley [83]	2631
13		15	H	Crewe Alex	L	1-3	0-0	6	Jolley [60]	4604
14		22	H	Crawley T	L	2-5	2-2	9	Davis (og) [11], Midson [44]	4549
15		25	A	Torquay U	L	0-4	0-3	—		2353
16		29	A	Shrewsbury T	D	0-0	0-0	12		5861
17	Nov	5	H	Barnet	D	1-1	0-1	11	Moore, S [63]	4369
18		19	H	Swindon T	D	1-1	1-0	12	Hatton [6]	4581
19		26	A	Burton Alb	L	2-3	1-2	13	Moore, L [45], Webster (og) [82]	3282
20	Dec	10	H	Accrington S	L	0-2	0-2	17		4053
21		17	A	Rotherham U	L	0-1	0-0	17		3343
22		26	H	Oxford U	L	0-2	0-2	17		4547
23		31	H	Southend U	L	1-4	1-1	17	Midson [7]	4529
24	Jan	2	A	Swindon T	L	0-2	0-0	17		8374
25		14	A	Port Vale	W	2-1	1-1	16	Midson [41], Moore, L [77]	4326
26		21	A	Gillingham	W	4-3	0-1	15	Moore, L [60], Richards (og) [73], Midson 2 (1 pen) [80 (p), 89]	6236
27		24	H	Macclesfield T	W	2-1	0-0	—	Knott [60], Moore, S [88]	4000
28		28	H	Aldershot T	L	1-2	1-1	15	Moore, S [28]	4634
29	Feb	14	A	Northampton T	L	0-1	0-0	—		4072
30		18	H	Morecambe	D	1-1	0-0	17	Yussuff [75]	3964
31		21	A	Cheltenham T	D	0-0	0-0	—		2603
32		25	A	Crewe Alex	D	3-3	1-3	17	Knott [7], Moore, S [81], Jolley [90]	4240
33	Mar	3	A	Hereford U	L	1-2	0-2	17	Midson [68]	2147
34		6	H	Plymouth Arg	L	1-2	1-1	—	Midson [41]	4578
35		10	H	Dagenham & R	W	2-1	0-0	12	Midson [73], Djilali [86]	4243
36		13	H	Bradford C	W	3-1	1-1	—	Midson 2 (2 pens) [33, 75], Knott [54]	4064
37		17	A	Bristol R	L	0-1	0-1	15		5828
38		20	A	Oxford U	L	0-1	0-0	—		6366
39		24	H	Burton Alb	W	4-0	1-0	15	Moore, L [9], Moncur [75], Harrison [89], Moore, S [90]	3819
40		31	A	Accrington S	L	1-2	1-1	15	Moore, L [30]	1627
41	Apr	6	H	Rotherham U	L	1-2	0-1	17	Moore, L [65]	4387
42		9	A	Southend U	L	0-2	0-0	17		6962
43		14	A	Crawley T	D	1-1	0-0	17	Moore, S [77]	3768
44		21	H	Torquay U	W	2-0	0-0	16	Yussuff [79], Moncur [85]	4171
45		28	A	Barnet	L	0-4	0-1	17		4422
46	May	5	H	Shrewsbury T	W	3-1	0-0	16	Harrison [47], Moore, L 2 [55, 61]	3678

Final League Position: 16

GOALSCORERS

League (62): Midson 18 (3 pens), Moore, L 9 (1 pen), Jolley 7, Moore, S 6, Yussuff 4, Knott 3, Harrison 2, Moncur 2, Ademeno 1, Djilali 1, Gwillim 1, Hatton 1, Porter 1, Stuart 1, Wellard 1, own goals 4.
Carling Cup (2): Midson 1, Moore, L 1.
FA Cup (2): Midson 1, Moore, L 1.
J Paint Trophy (3): Yussuff 2, Hatton 1 (pen).

Brown S 44	Hatton S 41 + 3	Gwillim G 27	Porter M 11 + 4	Stuart J 33 + 1	Johnson B 14 + 4	Yussuff R 29 + 11	Wellard R 16 + 6	Jolley C 23 + 14	Midson J 43 + 3	Moore L 29 + 8	Ademeno C 5 + 10	Minshull L 13 + 5	Bush C 16 + 6	Moore S 40 + 1	Djilali K 4 + 8	McNaughton C 18	Jackson R 3 + 4	Kiernan B 1 + 8	Mulley J 3 + 7	Mitchel-King M 24	Franks F 3 + 1	Moncur G 20	Euell J 8 + 1	Harrison B 11 + 8	Knott B 14 + 6	Hoyte G 2 + 1	Prior J 2 + 1	Balkestein P 6	Turner J 2	Jones R 1	Johnson H — + 1	*Match No.*
1	2	3^{3}	4^{1}	5	6	7	8	9^{2}	10	11	12	13	14																			1
1	2	3	4^{1}	5	6	7^{3}	14	13	10	11	9^{2}	8		12																		2
1	2	3	14	5	6	7	12	13	10	11	9^{2}	4^{1}		8^{3}																		3
1	2	3		5	6	7	4	13	10	11	9^{2}	12		8^{1}																		4
1	2	3^{3}		5	6	7	13	9^{2}	10	11	12	8^{1}	14	4																		5
1	2	3	4^{3}	5	6	13	8	12	10	11^{1}		14		7	9^{2}																	6
1	2	3	4	5		12	8■	9^{2}	10	11^{3}				7^{1}	13	6	14															7
1	2	3^{2}	4^{1}	5				12	10	11^{3}	14	8	13	7	9	6																8
1	2	3	14	5		12	8^{1}	9	10	13		4^{3}		7	11^{2}	6																9
1	2	3		5		7		9	10	11^{1}		4		8		6		12														10
1	2	3^{1}	14	5	12	7		9	10	11^{2}		4^{3}		8		6			13													11
1	2		12	5		7		9	10	11^{2}		4^{1}	3	8		6	13															12
1	2			5	13	7	12	9	10	11^{3}	14	4^{1}	3^{2}	8		6																13
1	2		4	5			8	9^{2}	10		13	11^{1}	3	7		6		12														14
1	2		4	5	3		8	9^{1}	10	11^{3}	12		14	7		6^{2}			13													15
1	2		4	5	3	7^{2}	8		10		13			11	12	6			9^{1}													16
1	2		4	5	3^{1}	8^{2}		9	10	11^{3}	14			7	13	6			12													17
1	4				5	11	8	9^{1}	10			13	3	7		6	2^{2}		12													18
1	2			5	6	8	4		10	11^{1}	9^{2}	12	3	7			13															19
1	2	3	4^{1}	5			8^{3}		10	9^{2}	12			11		6	14	13	7													20
1	2	3		5		11^{2}	8		10	9		4					7^{1}	12	13	6^{3}	14											21
1	2	3^{3}		5		8	12		10	9		4^{2}	14	11			7^{1}		13	6												22
1	2			5	13	8	4^{3}	9■	10	11^{1}	14		3^{2}	7					12	6												23
1			4^{1}		5	10			13		9^{2}	8	3	7		6		12	11		2											24
1	12	3				14			10	13				7		6				5	2^{1}	4	8^{2}	9	11^{3}							25
1	2	3		14		12			10	11^{1}				7		6		13		5		4		9^{3}	8^{2}							26
1	2	3				12		13	10	11^{3}				7		6		14		5		4^{1}		9^{2}	8							27
1		3		5		12		13	10	11^{1}				7						6		4^{3}		9^{2}	8	2	14					28
1	14	3^{3}		5		12		13	10					7						6		4	8	9^{2}	11^{1}	2						29
1	2			5		11		13	10				3	7						6		4	8^{2}	9^{1}	12							30
1	2			5		11		9^{2}	10				3	7						6		4	8^{1}	13	12							31
1	2			5		11		14	10				3^{1}	7						6		4^{2}	9^{3}	13	8	12						32
1	2			5		12		11	10	14			3	7						6		4^{3}	13	9^{2}	8^{1}							33
1	2^{2}					8		11^{3}	10	13			3	7		6				5		4	9^{1}	14	12							34
1	2	3			12	8		9	10					7	13					5^{1}				11^{2}	4			6				35
1	2	3				11^{3}		14	10	12				7	13					5		4	9^{2}		8^{1}			6				36
1	2	3				11^{3}		12	10	14				7	13					5		4	9^{1}		8^{2}			6				37
1	2	3				11^{1}		13	10	9^{3}				7	12					5		4		14	8^{2}			6				38
1	2	3					12	9	10	11^{2}				7						5		4		13	8^{1}			6				39
1	2	3				7^{2}	8	9^{1}	10	11					13					5		4		12				6				40
	2	3			6^{1}	7^{3}	8	13	10	9			12		11^{2}					5		4			14				1			41
1	2			5		12		10	13	14			3	7						6		4^{3}		9	8^{1}		11^{2}					42
1	2	3		5				9	10	11				7						6		4		12			8^{1}					43
1	2			5		12		9	10^{2}	11^{3}			3	7				14		6		4		13	8^{1}							44
	2			5		7	8^{2}	10^{1}	12	14			3					4^{3}		6		11		9	13				1			45
1	14			5	6	8^{2}			10	11			3	7							4^{3}			9	12					2^{1}	13	46

FA Cup

First Round	Scunthorpe U	(h)	0-0
		(a)	1-0
Second Round	Bradford C	(a)	1-3

Carling Cup

Preliminary Round	Crawley T	(a)	2-3

J Paint Trophy

Second Round	Stevenage	(h)	2-2
Southern Quarter-Final	Swindon T	(a)	1-1

ALDERSHOT TOWN FL Championship 2

FOUNDATION

It was through the initiative of Councillor Jack White, a local newsagent, who immediately captured the interest of the Town Clerk D. Llewellyn Griffiths, that Aldershot Town was formed in 1926. Having established a limited liability company under the chairmanship of Norman Clinton, an Aldershot resident and chairman of the Hampshire County FA, they rented the Recreation Ground from the Aldershot Borough Council. Admitted to the Southern League for 1927–28, they were elected to the Football League in 1932 but were removed from the competition in March 1992 and their record expunged. Re-formed almost immediately as Aldershot Town Football Club.

The EBB Stadium at the Recreation Ground, High Street, Aldershot GU11 1TW.

Telephone: (01252) 320211.

Fax: (01252) 324347.

Ticket Office: (01252) 320211.

Website: enquiries@theshots.co.uk

Email: www.theshots.co.uk

Ground Capacity: 7,100.

Record Attendance: 19,138 v Carlisle U, FA Cup 4th rd (replay), 28 January 1970.

Pitch Measurements: 117yd × 74yd.

Chairman: Kris Machala.

Chief Operating Officer: Richard Low.

Manager: Dean Holdsworth.

Assistant Manager: Matt Bishop.

Physio: Nic Brink.

Colours: All red shirts with blue sleeves, red shorts with blue and white trim, red stockings with blue and white trim.

Year Formed: 1926.

Turned Professional: 1927.

Previous Names: 1926, Aldershot Town; c.1937 Aldershot; 1992, Aldershot Town.

Club Nickname: 'The Shots'.

Ground: 1927, Recreation Ground.

First Football League Game: 27 August 1932, Division 3 (S), v Southend U (h) L 1–2 – Robb; Wade, McDougall, Lawson, Spence, Middleton, Proud, White, Gamble, Douglas, Fishlock (1).

HONOURS

Football League: Best season: 8th, Division 3, 1973–74.

FA Cup: Best season: 5th rd, 1932–33, 5th rd replay, 1978–79.

Football League Cup: Best season: 4th rd, 2011–12.

Blue Square Premier League: *Champions* 2007–08.

Conference: ***Runners-up*** 2003–04.

Southern League: *Champions* 1929–30; *Runners-up* 1930–31.

Football Combination Division 2: *Champions* 1930–31.

Isthmian League Division 3: *Champions* 1992–93.

Isthmian First Division Champions: 1997–98.

Isthmian League Premier Division: *Champions* 2002–03.

Hampshire Senior Cup: *Winners* 1928, 1999, 2000, 2002, 2003, 2007.

Setanta Shield: ***Winners*** 2008.

sky SPORTS FACT FILE

On 20 September 2011, Aldershot Town reached the fourth round of the Carling Cup for the first time beating Rochdale 2-1. The Shots had previously beaten West Ham United of the Championship 2-1 at Upton Park and then Carlisle United at the Recreation Ground.

Record League Victory: 8–1 v Gateshead, Division 4, 13 September 1958 – Marshall; Henry, Jackson, Mundy, Price, Gough, Walters, Stepney (3), Lacey (3), Matthews (2), Tyrer.

Record Cup Victory: 7–0 v Chelmsford, FA Cup, 1st rd, 28 November 1931 – Robb; Twine, McDougall (1), Norman Wilson, Gardiner, Middleton (1), Blackbourne, Stevenson (1), Thom (3), Hopkins (1), Edgar. 7–0 v Newport (IW), FA Cup, 2nd rd, 8 December 1945 – Reynolds; Horton, Sheppard, Ray, White, Summerbee, Sinclair, Hold (1), Brooks (5), Fitzgerald, Hobbs (1). *N.B.* 11–1 v Kingstonian, FA Cup, 4th qual rd, 16 November 1929 – Mobbs; Thomas, McDougall, Norman Wilson, Gardiner, Middleton (2), Young (1), Common (1), Horton (2), Hopkins (3), Edgar (2).

Record Defeat: 1–10 v Southend U, Leyland Daf Cup, Pr rd, 6 November 1990.

Most League Points: (2 for a win): 57, Division 4, 1978–79.

Most League Points (3 for a win): 75, Division 4, 1983–84.

Most League Goals: 83, Division 4, 1963–64.

Highest League Scorer in Season: John Dungworth, 26, Division 4, 1978–79.

Most League Goals in Total Aggregate: Jack Howarth, 171, 1965–71 and 1972–77.

Most League Goals in One Match: 5, Charlie Mortimore v Leyton Orient, Division 3 (S), 25 February 1950.

Most Capped Player: Anthony Straker, 5, Grenada.

Most League Appearances: Murray Brodie, 461, 1970–83.

Youngest League Player: Clive Jackman, 16 years 135 days v Leyton Orient, 16 April 1953.

Record Transfer Fee Received: Reported £200,000 from Swansea C for Scott Donnelly, July 2010.

Record Transfer Fee Paid: £54,000 to Portsmouth for Colin Garwood, February 1980.

Football League Record: 1932 Elected to Division 3 (S); 1958–73 Division 4; 1973–76 Division 3; 1976–87 Division 4; 1987–89 Division 3; 1989–92 Division 4; 1992–93 Isthmian League Division 3; 1993–94 Isthmian League Division 2; 1994–98 Isthmian League Division 1; 1998–2003 Isthmian League Premier Division; 2003–08 Conference; 2008– FL 2.

MANAGERS

Angus Seed 1927–37
Bill McCracken 1937–49
Gordon Clark 1950–55
Harry Evans 1955–59
Dave Smith 1959–71
(GM from 1967)
Tommy McAnearney 1967–68
Jimmy Melia 1968–72
Tommy McAnearney 1972–81
Len Walker 1981–84
Ron Harris (GM) 1984–85
Len Walker 1985–91
Brian Talbot 1991
Ian McDonald 1991–92
Steve Wignall 1992–95
Steve Wigley 1995–97
George Borg 1997–2002
Terry Brown 2002–07
Gary Waddock 2007–09
Kevin Dillon 2009–11
Dean Holdsworth January 2011–

LATEST SEQUENCES

Longest Sequence of League Wins: 6, 28.1.2012 – 3.3.2012.

Longest Sequence of League Defeats: 9, 20.11.1965 – 5.2.1966.

Longest Sequence of League Draws: 6, 6.10.1962 – 27.10.1962.

Longest Sequence of Unbeaten League Matches: 13, 30.9.1978 – 26.12.1978.

Longest Sequence Without a League Win: 17, 10.10.1936 – 30.1.1937.

Successive Scoring Runs: 29 from 1.4.1961.

Successive Non-scoring Runs: 6 from 22.3.1988.

TEN YEAR LEAGUE RECORD

		P	W	D	L	F	A	Pts	Pos
2002-03	Isth PR	46	33	6	7	81	36	105	1
2003-04	Conf	42	20	10	12	80	67	70	5
2004-05	Conf	42	21	10	11	68	52	73	4
2005-06	Conf	42	16	6	20	61	74	54	13
2006-07	Conf	46	18	11	17	64	62	65	9
2007-08	B Sq Pr	46	31	8	7	82	48	101	1
2008-09	FL 2	46	14	12	20	59	80	54	15
2009-10	FL 2	46	20	12	14	69	56	72	6
2010-11	FL 2	46	14	19	13	54	54	61	14
2011-12	FL 2	46	19	9	18	54	52	66	11

DID YOU KNOW?

History repeated itself on 22 October 2011, when Aldershot Town won 5-2 at Dagenham & Redbridge. Their last visit to Victoria Road on 1 December 2009 had produced exactly the same score. Only left-back Anthony Straker played in both matches for the Shots.

ALDERSHOT TOWN 2011–12 LEAGUE RECORD

Match No.	Date	Venue	Opponents	Result	H/T Score	Lg Pos.	Goalscorers	Attendance
1	Aug 6	A	Bradford C	W 2-1	2-0	—	Hylton [18], Threlfall (og) [38]	10,205
2	13	H	Northampton T	L 0-1	0-1	12		2790
3	16	H	Torquay U	L 0-1	0-1	—		2236
4	20	A	Morecambe	L 0-2	0-1	20		1833
5	27	A	Oxford U	D 1-1	0-1	20	Guttridge [66]	6673
6	Sept 3	H	Cheltenham T	W 1-0	0-0	17	Hylton [72]	2755
7	10	H	AFC Wimbledon	D 1-1	0-1	18	Hylton [90]	4110
8	13	A	Hereford U	W 2-0	1-0	—	Rankine [19], Vincenti [82]	1599
9	17	A	Bristol R	W 1-0	1-0	11	Rodman [36]	5640
10	24	H	Crawley T	L 0-1	0-0	15		3276
11	Oct 1	A	Accrington S	L 2-3	2-1	17	Hylton 2 [7, 24]	1438
12	8	H	Macclesfield T	L 1-2	1-0	18	Hylton [41]	2341
13	15	A	Barnet	L 1-2	1-0	19	Hylton [27]	2015
14	22	A	Dagenham & R	W 5-2	4-1	15	McGlashan 2 [3, 90], Vincenti [6], Rankine (pen) [38], Guttridge [45]	1796
15	29	H	Crewe Alex	W 3-1	1-1	16	Hylton 2 [23, 62], McGlashan [48]	2552
16	Nov 1	H	Burton Alb	W 2-0	2-0	—	McGlashan [38], Guttridge [43]	3713
17	5	A	Rotherham U	L 0-2	0-2	15		3284
18	19	H	Gillingham	L 1-2	0-2	15	Davies [81]	3449
19	26	A	Swindon T	L 0-2	0-0	16		7526
20	Dec 10	H	Shrewsbury T	W 1-0	0-0	14	Guttridge [67]	2384
21	17	A	Port Vale	L 0-4	0-1	16		3714
22	31	H	Plymouth Arg	D 0-0	0-0	16		3886
23	Jan 2	A	Gillingham	L 0-1	0-0	16		5432
24	7	H	Oxford U	L 0-3	0-3	—		3194
25	14	A	Cheltenham T	L 0-2	0-1	17		3147
26	21	H	Accrington S	D 0-0	0-0	19		2581
27	28	A	AFC Wimbledon	W 2-1	1-1	18	Straker 2 [13, 70]	4634
28	Feb 14	H	Hereford U	W 1-0	0-0	—	Madjo [53]	1871
29	18	A	Macclesfield T	W 1-0	0-0	15	Morris [65]	1715
30	21	H	Southend U	W 2-0	1-0	—	Mekki [26], Payne, J (pen) [64]	2949
31	25	H	Barnet	W 4-1	3-0	13	Madjo 2 [6, 51], Hylton [17], Brown, T [30]	2511
32	Mar 3	H	Morecambe	W 1-0	1-0	12	Madjo [26]	2381
33	6	A	Torquay U	L 0-1	0-1	—		2277
34	10	A	Northampton T	L 1-3	0-2	13	Hylton [90]	5071
35	13	A	Crawley T	D 2-2	1-1	—	Morris [4], Vincenti [63]	3017
36	17	H	Bradford C	W 1-0	0-0	12	Risser [70]	2763
37	20	A	Southend U	W 1-0	0-0	—	Hylton [59]	4580
38	27	H	Bristol R	W 1-0	1-0	—	Vincenti [43]	2870
39	31	A	Shrewsbury T	D 1-1	0-0	10	Payne, J (pen) [51]	5588
40	Apr 6	H	Port Vale	L 1-2	0-1	11	Risser [86]	2747
41	9	A	Plymouth Arg	L 0-1	0-1	11		8677
42	14	H	Dagenham & R	D 1-1	0-0	11	Brown, T [86]	2393
43	17	H	Swindon T	W 2-1	1-0	—	Madjo [12], Hylton [58]	3562
44	21	A	Burton Alb	W 4-0	1-0	11	Vincenti [16], Risser [61], Madjo 2 [76, 82]	2255
45	28	H	Rotherham U	D 2-2	1-2	11	Vincenti [20], Madjo [56]	2578
46	May 5	A	Crewe Alex	D 2-2	2-1	11	Davis (og) [31], Molesley [45]	6919

Final League Position: 11

GOALSCORERS

League (54): Hylton 13, Madjo 8, Vincenti 6, Guttridge 4, McGlashan 4, Risser 3, Brown, T 2, Morris 2, Payne, J 2 (2 pens), Rankine 2 (1 pen), Straker 2, Davies 1, Mekki 1, Molesley 1, Rodman 1, own goals 2.
Carling Cup (6): Hylton 2, Rankine 2, Guttridge 1, own goal 1.
FA Cup (3): Guttridge 1, Rankine 1, Rodman 1.
J Paint Trophy (1): Hylton 1.

Young J 24 + 1	Herd B 45	Straker A 44	Collins J 21 + 4	Jones D 42	Brown A 6 + 5	McGlashan J 18 + 5	Vincenti P 33 + 9	Rankine M 21 + 1	Hylton D 43 + 1	Rodman A 15 + 3	Mekki A 16 + 9	Morris A 36 + 3	Guttridge L 24 + 1	Taylor J — + 3 / Sinclair R 1 + 3	Bubb B 1 + 8	Pulis A 1 + 4 / Molesley M 2 + 6	Worner R 22	Brown J 2 + 1 / Bergqvist D — + 2	Andrade B — + 1	Smith A 7 + 5	Davies S 3 + 5	Pearson G 1 + 4	Henry C 3 + 4	Doig C 2	Brown T 14 + 3	Bradley S 13 + 1	Collins C — + 1	Madjo G 15 + 5	Payne J 14 + 3	Payne S — + 1	Panther M — + 1	Murphy D 2 + 1	Connolly R 1 + 6	Risser W 8 + 8	Smith B 3 + 5	Roberts J 1 + 3	Doughty M 2 + 3	Match No.
1	2	3	4	5	6	7^{2}	8	9	10^{1}	11	12	13																										1
1	2	3	4	5	6	7^{3}	8^{2}	9	10	11^{1}			12	13	14																							2
1	2	3	4	5	6	7^{3}	10^{1}	9^{2}	11	12			8	13	14																							3
1	2	3	8^{2}	5	6		10^{1}	9	11	7^{3}	14		4	13	12																							4
1	2	3■	8	5		7^{2}	12	9^{1}	10	11^{3}		6	4		13	14																						5
	2		8	5	14	7	10^{1}	9	11^{2}		12	6	4			13^{3}	1	3																				6
	2	3	8^{3}	5		7^{2}	14	9	10	12	11^{1}	6	4		13		1																					7
	2	3	8	5		7^{1}	12	9	10	11		6	4				1																					8
	2	3	8	5	13	7^{1}	12	9	10	11		6	4^{2}				1																					9
	2		8^{2}	5		12	10^{1}	9	7	11		6	4		13		1	3																				10
	2	3	8	5	12	7^{2}		9	10	11^{3}		6^{1}	4		14		1		13																			11
	2	3	8	5	14	12	11^{2}	9^{3}	10	7^{1}		6	4				1			13																		12
	2	3	8	5		12	11^{1}	9	10	7^{2}		6	4				1			13																		13
		3			5	7	8	9	13			6	4		10^{2}	2	1	12		11^{1}																		14
	2	3	13	5		7^{1}	8^{2}	9	10^{3}			6	4			14	1			11	12																	15
	2	3	12	5		7^{1}	8	9	10^{3}			6	4^{2}			13	1			11	14																	16
	2	3	15	5		7^{1}	8	9	10^{G}			6	4		13		1■			11^{2}	12																	17
1	2	3	12	5	6	7^{3}	8^{1}	9	10	11^{2}	14		4								13																	18
1	2	3	8^{3}	5		7^{1}		9	10	11^{2}		6	4							12	14	13																19
1	2	3	8	5			14	13	9^{3}	11^{2}		6	4							7^{1}	10		12															20
1	2	3	8	5		13		9		11^{2}		6	4							7^{3}	10^{1}	12	14															21
	2	3	8			7^{1}	10^{3}		9	13		6	4				1			11^{2}		12	14	5														22
	2	3			12	7	6	9^{2}		11^{3}			4				1			13	8	10	14	5^{1}														23
	2	11	8			12	10^{1}		9^{3}			3	4				1			13		14	7^{2}		5	6												24
	2	3	8	5		7	10^{2}		9				4				1						11^{1}		6	13	12											25
	2	3	8	5			7		10		12		4^{2}				1						11^{1}		6			9	13									26
	2	3	8^{1}	5			11		10^{3}		7^{2}	12					1									6		9	4	13	14							27
	2	3		5			10^{2}		11		7	12					1									6		9^{3}	8			4^{1}	13	14				28
	2	3		5			10^{2}		11		7^{3}	4					1								14	6		9^{1}	8					12	13			29
	2	3		5			10^{2}		11		7^{3}	4					1								12	6		9^{1}	8					13	14			30
15	2	3		5			10		11		7^{1}	8					1^{G}								4	6		9^{2}					12			13		31
1	2	3		5			7		10^{1}		12	8													4■	6		9^{2}	11^{3}					13	14			32
1	2	3		5			14		10		7^{1}	8														6		9^{2}	11			4^{3}		12			13	33
1	2^{1}	3		5			7^{3}		10		12	4														6		9	11			14			8^{2}		13	34
1	2	3		5			12		10		7^{1}	4		14												6		13	8					9^{2}			11^{3}	35
1	2	3		5			14		11			4		13											12	6		9^{2}	8^{1}					10^{3}			7	36
1	2	3		5			10		9^{3}		7^{2}	8		13											4	6		12	11^{1}						14			37
1	2	3		5			11^{3}		10		7^{1}	8													4	6		9^{2}	13					14			12	38
1	2	3		5					10		7^{1}	4		11^{2}		14									6			12	8					9^{3}	13			39
1	2	3		5			14		10^{3}		7	4				12									6			9^{2}	8					13	11^{1}			40
1	2	3		5			8		10^{3}		7^{2}	4				13									6			14					12	9	11^{1}			41
1	2	3		5			8		10^{3}		7	4				14									6			12					13	9^{1}		11^{2}		42
1	2	3		5			8		11^{3}		7^{1}	4				13									6			9					12	10^{2}		14		43
1	2	3		5			8^{1}		11		14	4				7^{3}		12							6			9	13					10^{2}				44
1	2	3		5			8		11		12	6				7^{2}									6			10^{3}	4				14	9^{1}		13■		45
1	2	3		5			11		10		7^{3}	4^{1}				12		14							6				8				9^{2}	13				46

FA Cup

First Round	Maidenhead U	(a)	1-1
		(h)	2-0
Second Round	Sheffield W	(a)	0-1

Carling Cup

First Round	West Ham U	(a)	2-1
Second Round	Carlisle U	(h)	2-0
Third Round	Rochdale	(h)	2-1
Fourth Round	Manchester U	(h)	0-3

J Paint Trophy

Second Round	Oxford U	(h)	1-2

ARSENAL FA Premiership

FOUNDATION

Formed by workers at the Royal Arsenal, Woolwich in 1886, they began as Dial Square (name of one of the workshops), and included two former Nottingham Forest players, Fred Beardsley and Morris Bates. Beardsley wrote to his old club seeking help and they provided the new club with a full set of red jerseys and a ball. The club became known as the 'Woolwich Reds' although their official title soon after formation was Woolwich Arsenal.

Emirates Stadium, Highbury House, 75 Drayton Park, Islington, London N5 1BU.

Telephone: (020) 7619 5003.

Fax: (020) 7704 4001.

Ticket Office: (020) 7619 5000.

Website: www.arsenal.com

Email: contactafc@arsenal.com

Ground Capacity: 60,361.

Record Attendance: 73,295 v Sunderland, Div 1, 9 March 1935 (at Highbury); 73,707 v RC Lens, UEFA Champions League, 25 November 1998 (at Wembley); 60,162 v Manchester U, FA Premier League, 3 November 2007 (at Emirates).

Pitch Measurements: 105m × 68m.

Chairman: Peter Hill-Wood.

Acting Managing Director: Ken Friar OBE.

Manager: Arsène Wenger.

Assistant Manager: Steve Bould.

Physio: Colin Lewin.

Colours: Red shirts with white trim, white shorts, white stockings with red tops.

Year Formed: 1886.

Turned Professional: 1891.

Previous Names: 1886, Dial Square; 1886, Royal Arsenal; 1891, Woolwich Arsenal; 1914, Arsenal.

Club Nickname: 'Gunners'.

Grounds: 1886, Plumstead Common; 1887, Sportsman Ground; 1888, Manor Ground; 1890, Invicta Ground; 1893, Manor Ground; 1913, Highbury; 2006, Emirates Stadium.

HONOURS

FA Premier League: ***Champions*** 1997–98, 2001–02, 2003–04. ***Runners-up*** 1998–99, 1999–2000, 2000–01, 2002–03, 2004–05.

Football League – Division 1: ***Champions*** 1930–31, 1932–33, 1933–34, 1934–35, 1937–38, 1947–48, 1952–53, 1970–71, 1988–89, 1990–91; ***Runners-up*** 1925–26, 1931–32, 1972–73; **Division 2**: ***Runners-up*** 1903–04.

FA Cup: ***Winners*** 1930, 1936, 1950, 1971, 1979, 1993, 1998, 2002, 2003, 2005; ***Runners-up*** 1927, 1932, 1952, 1972, 1978, 1980, 2001.

Double performed: 1970–71, 1997–98, 2001–02.

Football League Cup: ***Winners*** 1987, 1993; ***Runners-up*** 1968, 1969, 1988, 2007, 2011.

European Competitions
European Cup: 1971–72, 1991–92. **UEFA Champions League:** 1998–99, 1999–2000, 2000–01, 2001–02, 2002–03, 2003–04, 2004–05, 2005–06 (*runners-up*), 2006–07, 2007–08 (*q-f*), 2008–09 (*s-f*), 2009–10, 2010–11, 2011–12. **Fairs Cup:** 1963–64, 1969–70 (*winners*), 1970–71. **UEFA Cup:** 1978–79, 1981–82, 1982–83, 1996–97, 1997–98, 1999–2000 (*runners-up*). **European Cup-Winners' Cup:** 1979–80 (*runners-up*), 1993–94 (*winners*), 1994–95 (*runners-up*). **Super Cup:** 1994 (*runners-up*).

sky SPORTS FACT FILE

On 24 September 2011, Robin Van Persie scored his 100th goal for Arsenal against Bolton Wanderers in his 238th match to become the 17th player to hit a century for the club. Seventy-one were scored with his left foot, twenty-three with the right and six with his head.

First Football League Game: 2 September 1893, Division 2, v Newcastle U (h) D 2–2 – Williams; Powell, Jeffrey; Devine, Buist, Howat; Gemmell, Henderson, Shaw (1), Elliott (1), Booth.

Record League Victory: 12–0 v Loughborough T, Division 2, 12 March 1900 – Orr; McNichol, Jackson; Moir, Dick (2), Anderson (1); Hunt, Cottrell (2), Main (2), Gaudie (3), Tennant (2).

Record Cup Victory: 11–1 v Darwen, FA Cup 3rd rd, 9 January 1932 – Moss; Parker, Hapgood; Jones, Roberts, John; Hulme (2), Jack (3), Lambert (2), James, Bastin (4).

Record Defeat: 0–8 v Loughborough T, Division 2, 12 December 1896.

Most League Points (2 for a win): 66, Division 1, 1930–31.

Most League Points (3 for a win): 90, FA Premier League, 2003–04.

Most League Goals: 127, Division 1, 1930–31.

Highest League Scorer in Season: Ted Drake, 42, 1934–35.

Most League Goals in Total Aggregate: Thierry Henry, 174, 1999–2007.

Most League Goals in One Match: 7, Ted Drake v Aston Villa, Division 1, 14 December 1935.

Most Capped Player: Thierry Henry, 81 (123), France.

Most League Appearances: David O'Leary, 558, 1975–93.

Youngest League Player: Jack Wilshere, 16 years 256 days v Blackburn R, 13 September 2008.

Record Transfer Fee Received: £25,000,000 from Manchester C for Emmanuel Adebayor, July 2009.

Record Transfer Fee Paid: £15,000,000 to Zenit for Andrei Arshavin, February 2009.

Football League Record: 1893 Elected to Division 2; 1904–13 Division 1; 1913–19 Division 2; 1919–92 Division 1; 1992– FA Premier League.

MANAGERS

Sam Hollis 1894–97
Tom Mitchell 1897–98
George Elcoat 1898–99
Harry Bradshaw 1899–1904
Phil Kelso 1904–08
George Morrell 1908–15
Leslie Knighton 1919–25
Herbert Chapman 1925–34
George Allison 1934–47
Tom Whittaker 1947–56
Jack Crayston 1956–58
George Swindin 1958–62
Billy Wright 1962–66
Bertie Mee 1966–76
Terry Neill 1976–83
Don Howe 1984–86
George Graham 1986–95
Bruce Rioch 1995–96
Arsène Wenger September 1996–

LATEST SEQUENCES

Longest Sequence of League Wins: 14, 10.2.2002 – 18.8.2002.

Longest Sequence of League Defeats: 7, 12.2.1977 – 12.3.1977.

Longest Sequence of League Draws: 6, 4.3.1961 – 1.4.1961.

Longest Sequence of Unbeaten League Matches: 49, 7.5.2003 – 24.10.2004.

Longest Sequence Without a League Win: 23, 28.9.1912 – 1.3.1913.

Successive Scoring Runs: 55 from 19.5.2001.

Successive Non-scoring Runs: 6 from 25.2.1987.

TEN YEAR LEAGUE RECORD

		P	W	D	L	F	A	Pts	Pos
2002-03	PR Lge	38	23	9	6	85	42	78	2
2003-04	PR Lge	38	26	12	0	73	26	90	1
2004-05	PR Lge	38	25	8	5	87	36	83	2
2005-06	PR Lge	38	20	7	11	68	31	67	4
2006-07	PR Lge	38	19	11	8	63	35	68	4
2007-08	PR Lge	38	24	11	3	74	31	83	3
2008-09	PR Lge	38	20	12	6	68	37	72	4
2009-10	PR Lge	38	23	6	9	83	41	75	3
2010-11	PR Lge	38	19	11	8	72	43	68	4
2011-12	PR Lge	38	21	7	10	74	49	70	3

DID YOU KNOW ?

On 28 September 2011, Arsenal fielded eleven different nationalities in their starting line-up against Olympiakos. They opened the scoring with Alex Oxlade-Chamberlain, at 18 years 44 days the youngest Englishman to score in the Champions League. Arsenal won 2-1.

ARSENAL 2011–12 LEAGUE RECORD

Match No.	*Date*	*Venue*	*Opponents*	*Result*		*H/T Score*	*Lg Pos.*	*Goalscorers*	*Attendance*
1	Aug 13	A	Newcastle U	D	0-0	0-0	—		46,894
2	20	H	Liverpool	L	0-2	0-0	14		60,090
3	28	A	Manchester U	L	2-8	1-3	17	Walcott ^{45}, Van Persie ^{74}	75,448
4	Sept 10	H	Swansea C	W	1-0	1-0	11	Arshavin ^{40}	60,087
5	17	A	Blackburn R	L	3-4	2-1	17	Gervinho ^{10}, Arteta ^{34}, Chamakh ^{85}	22,637
6	24	H	Bolton W	W	3-0	0-0	12	Van Persie 2 $^{46, 71}$, Song Billong ^{89}	59,727
7	Oct 2	A	Tottenham H	L	1-2	0-1	15	Ramsey ^{51}	36,274
8	16	H	Sunderland	W	2-1	1-1	10	Van Persie 2 $^{1, 82}$	60,078
9	23	H	Stoke C	W	3-1	1-1	7	Gervinho ^{27}, Van Persie 2 $^{73, 82}$	59,671
10	29	A	Chelsea	W	5-3	1-2	7	Van Persie 3 $^{36, 85, 90}$, Andre Santos ^{49}, Walcott ^{55}	41,801
11	Nov 5	H	WBA	W	3-0	2-0	7	Van Persie ^{22}, Vermaelen ^{39}, Arteta ^{74}	60,091
12	19	A	Norwich C	W	2-1	1-1	7	Van Persie 2 $^{26, 59}$	26,801
13	26	H	Fulham	D	1-1	0-0	7	Vermaelen ^{82}	60,043
14	Dec 3	A	Wigan Ath	W	4-0	2-0	5	Arteta ^{28}, Vermaelen ^{29}, Gervinho ^{61}, Van Persie ^{78}	19,280
15	10	H	Everton	W	1-0	0-0	4	Van Persie ^{70}	60,062
16	18	A	Manchester C	L	0-1	0-0	5		47,303
17	21	A	Aston Villa	W	2-1	1-0	—	Van Persie (pen) ^{17}, Benayoun ^{87}	35,818
18	27	H	Wolverhampton W	D	1-1	1-1	—	Gervinho ^{8}	59,686
19	31	H	QPR	W	1-0	0-0	4	Van Persie ^{60}	60,067
20	Jan 2	A	Fulham	L	1-2	1-0	—	Koscielny ^{21}	25,700
21	15	A	Swansea C	L	2-3	1-1	5	Van Persie ^{5}, Walcott ^{69}	20,409
22	22	H	Manchester U	L	1-2	0-1	5	Van Persie ^{71}	60,093
23	Feb 1	A	Bolton W	D	0-0	0-0	—		24,371
24	4	H	Blackburn R	W	7-1	3-1	6	Van Persie 3 $^{2, 38, 62}$, Oxlade-Chamberlain 2 $^{40, 54}$, Arteta ^{51}, Dann (og) ^{90}	59,643
25	11	A	Sunderland	W	2-1	0-0	4	Ramsey ^{75}, Henry ^{90}	40,312
26	26	H	Tottenham H	W	5-2	2-2	4	Sagna ^{40}, Van Persie ^{43}, Rosicky ^{51}, Walcott 2 $^{65, 68}$	60,106
27	Mar 3	A	Liverpool	W	2-1	1-1	4	Van Persie 2 $^{31, 90}$	44,922
28	12	H	Newcastle U	W	2-1	1-1	—	Van Persie ^{15}, Vermaelen ^{90}	60,095
29	21	A	Everton	W	1-0	1-0	—	Vermaelen ^{8}	30,330
30	24	H	Aston Villa	W	3-0	2-0	3	Gibbs ^{16}, Walcott ^{25}, Arteta ^{90}	60,108
31	31	A	QPR	L	1-2	1-1	3	Walcott ^{37}	18,033
32	Apr 8	H	Manchester C	W	1-0	0-0	4	Arteta ^{87}	60,096
33	11	A	Wolverhampton W	W	3-0	2-0	—	Van Persie (pen) ^{9}, Walcott ^{11}, Benayoun ^{69}	25,815
34	16	H	Wigan Ath	L	1-2	1-2	—	Vermaelen ^{21}	60,060
35	21	H	Chelsea	D	0-0	0-0	3		60,111
36	28	A	Stoke C	D	1-1	1-1	3	Van Persie ^{15}	27,502
37	May 5	H	Norwich C	D	3-3	1-2	3	Benayoun ^{2}, Van Persie 2 $^{72, 80}$	60,092
38	13	A	WBA	W	3-2	2-2	3	Benayoun ^{4}, Andre Santos ^{30}, Koscielny ^{54}	26,358

Final League Position: 3

GOALSCORERS

League (74): Van Persie 30 (2 pens), Walcott 8, Arteta 6, Vermaelen 6, Benayoun 4, Gervinho 4, Andre Santos 2, Koscielny 2, Oxlade-Chamberlain 2, Ramsey 2, Arshavin 1, Chamakh 1, Gibbs 1, Henry 1, Rosicky 1, Sagna 1, Song Billong 1, own goal 1.
Carling Cup (5): Arshavin 1, Benyoun 1, Gibbs 1, Park 1, Oxlade-Chamberlain 1.
FA Cup (4): Van Persie 2 (2 pens), Henry 1, Walcott 1.
Champions League (13): Van Persie 5 (1 pen), Walcott 2, Andre Santos 1, Benayoun 1, Koscielny 1, Oxlade-Chamberlain 1, Ramsey 1, Rosicky 1.

Szczesny W 38	Sagna B 20 + 1	Gibbs K 15 + 1	Song Billong A 34	Vermaelen T 28 + 1	Koscielny L 33	Rosicky T 19 + 9	Ramsey A 27 + 7	Gervinho 19 + 9	Van Persie R 37 + 1	Arshavin A 8 + 11	Walcott T 32 + 3	Frimpong E 3 + 3	Djourou J 14 + 4	Jenkinson C 5 + 4	Nasri S 1	Miquel I 1 + 3	Lansbury H — + 2	Bendtner N — + 1	Traore A 1	Coquelin F 6 + 4	Oxlade-Chamberlain A 6 + 10	Chamakh M 1 + 10	Arteta M 29	Mertesacker P 21	Benayoun Y 10 + 9	Andre Santos C 10 + 5	Diaby A — + 4	Squillaci S — + 1	Henry T — + 4	Yennaris N — + 1	Park C — + 1	*Match No.*
1	2	3	4	5	6	7²	8³	9■	10	11¹	12	13	14																			1
1	2			5	6¹		8		10	9²	7³	4■		3	11	12	13	14														2
1					6	11	8		10³	9	7²		5	2			14		3	4¹	12	13										3
1	2	3			6		8		10³	11¹	9	7²								13		14	4	5	12							4
1	2¹		4³		6		8	11	10	9²	13		12									14	7	5		3						5
1	2	3	4		6	13	8	11¹	10³	12	9											14	7²	5								6
1	2¹	3	4				8	11³	10	14	9²			12						6			7	5	13							7
1		3¹	4		6	7³		11²	10	13	9			2									8	5	14	12						8
1			4		6		8	11³	12	13	9²	14	2									10¹	7	5		3						9
1			4	14	6	13	8	9³	10		7²		2¹	12									11	5		3						10
1			4	5	6	12	8¹	9²	10	14	7³			2									11		13	3						11
1			4	6	2		8	9¹	10		7²		13										11	5	12	3						12
1			4	6			8¹	12	10	9³	7		2									14	11	5²		3	13					13
1			4¹	6	2		8	9³	10	12	7²									14			11	5	13	3						14
1			4	6¹	3	13	8	9²	10		7³	14	2			12							11	5								15
1			4	6	3		8	9	10	13	7²		2¹			12						14	11	5³								16
1				6	3	12	8³	9²	10	13	7	4¹								2			11	5	14							17
1			4²	6	3	8	13	9	10	12			2³									14	11	5	7¹							18
1			4	6¹	3	13	8	14	10	9²	7³		2							12			11	5								19
1			4		6	12	8³	9²	10		7¹		2■							3			11	5	13			14				20
1			4		6	12	8		10	9²	7		2			3					14			5³	11¹				13			21
1			4	6	3	7	8³		10	13	9		2¹								11²			5						12	14	22
1	2		4	6	3	13	8²		10		7										9¹		11	5					12			23
1	12		4³	6	2¹	11			10		7									3	9²		8	5	14				13			24
1	2		4	6	3	11	13		10	14	7³										9¹		8	5²					12			25
1	2	3¹	4	5	6	9		14	10		7²			12							13		8		11³							26
1	2	3	4	5	6	9		13	10		7										14		8¹		11²		12³					27
1	2	3	4	5	6	11²	13	12	10		7										9¹		8									28
1	2	3	4	5	6	9²	8	12	10		7¹		13										11									29
1	2	3¹	4	5		11	13	9²	10		7³		6								14		8			12						30
1	2	3²	4	5	6	9	8¹	12	10		7										13	14	11³									31
1	2	3¹	4	5	6	9	13		10		7³										14		8		11²	12						32
1	2²		4	5			8		10		9¹		6	13							12		7		11	3						33
1	2		4	5		7	12	14	10		9		6³								13		8¹		11²	3						34
1	2	3	4	5	6	11²	8	12	10		7¹										9³					14	13					35
1	2	3	4	5	6	7	8¹	9²	10													13			11³	14	12					36
1	2¹	3	4	5	6	7	8²	9	10											12	13	14			11³							37
1		13	4	5	6	7¹	14	9²	10		12			2						8					11	3³						38

FA Cup

Third Round	Leeds U	(h)	1-0
Fourth Round	Aston Villa	(h)	3-2
Fifth Round	Sunderland	(a)	0-2

Champions League

Play-Off Round	Udinese	(h)	1-0
		(a)	2-1
Group F	Borussia Dortmund	(a)	1-1
	Olympiakos	(h)	2-1
	Marseille	(a)	1-0
		(h)	0-0
	Borussia Dortmund	(h)	2-1
	Olympiakos	(a)	1-3
Knock-Out Round	AC Milan	(a)	0-4
		(h)	3-0

Carling Cup

Third Round	Shrewsbury T	(h)	3-1
Fourth Round	Bolton W	(h)	2-1
Quarter-Final	Manchester C	(h)	0-1

ASTON VILLA FA Premiership

FOUNDATION

Cricketing enthusiasts of Villa Cross Wesleyan Chapel, Aston, Birmingham decided to form a football club during the winter of 1874–75. Football clubs were few and far between in the Birmingham area and in their first game against Aston Brook St Mary's rugby team they played one half rugby and the other soccer. In 1876 they were joined by Scottish soccer enthusiast George Ramsay who was immediately appointed captain and went on to lead Aston Villa from obscurity to one of the country's top clubs in a period of less than ten years.

Villa Park, Birmingham B6 6HE.

Telephone: (0121) 327 2299.

Fax: (0121) 322 2107.

Ticket Office/Consumer Sales: (0800) 612 0970.

Website: www.avfc.co.uk

Email: postmaster@avfc.co.uk

Ground Capacity: 42,582.

Record Attendance: 76,588 v Derby Co, FA Cup 6th rd, 2 March 1946.

Pitch Measurements: 115yd × 75yd.

Chairman: Randolph Lerner.

Manager: Paul Lambert.

Assistant Manager: Ian Culverhouse.

Physio: Alan Smith.

Colours: Claret body, blue sleeve shirts, white shorts, sky blue stockings.

Year Formed: 1874.

Turned Professional: 1885.

Club Nickname: 'The Villans'.

Grounds: 1874, Wilson Road and Aston Park (also used Aston Lower Grounds for some matches); 1876, Wellington Road, Perry Barr; 1897, Villa Park.

First Football League Game: 8 September 1888, Football League, v Wolverhampton W (a) D 1–1 – Warner; Cox, Coulton; Yates, Harry Devey, Dawson; Albert Brown, Green (1), Allen, Garvey, Hodgetts.

Record League Victory: 12–2 v Accrington S, Division 1, 12 March 1892 – Warner; Evans, Cox; Harry Devey, Jimmy Cowan, Baird; Athersmith (1), Dickson (2), John Devey (4), Lewis Campbell (4), Hodgetts (1).

HONOURS

FA Premier League: *Runners-up* 1992–93.

Football League – Division 1: *Champions* 1893–94, 1895–96, 1896–97, 1898–99, 1899–1900, 1909–10, 1980–81; ***Runners-up*** 1888–89, 1902–03, 1907–08, 1910–11, 1912–13, 1913–14, 1930–31, 1932–33, 1989–90;
Division 2: ***Champions*** 1937–38, 1959–60; ***Runners-up*** 1974–75, 1987–88;
Division 3: ***Champions*** 1971–72.

FA Cup: ***Winners*** 1887, 1895, 1897, 1905, 1913, 1920, 1957; ***Runners-up*** 1892, 1924, 2000.

Double Performed: 1896–97.

Football League Cup: ***Winners*** 1961, 1975, 1977, 1994, 1996; ***Runners-up*** 1963, 1971, 2010.

European Competitions
European Cup: 1981–82 (*winners*), 1982–83. **UEFA Cup:** 1975–76, 1977–78, 1983–84, 1990–91, 1993–94, 1994–95, 1996–97, 1997–98, 1998–99, 2001–02, 2008–09.
Europa League: 2009–10, 2010–11.
World Club Championship: 1982.
Super Cup: 1982 (*winners*). **Intertoto Cup:** 2000, 2001 (*winners*), 2002, 2008 (*winners*).

sky SPORTS FACT FILE

In 1912–13 League champions Aston Villa defeated Sunderland 1-0 in the FA Cup. It was the first time the top two in the First Division had contested the final. Villa had scored 20 goals in their Cup run, conceding only one, but Charlie Wallace then missed a penalty in the final.

Record Cup Victory: 13–0 v Wednesbury Old Ath, FA Cup 1st rd, 30 October 1886 – Warner; Coulton, Simmonds; Yates, Robertson, Burton (2); Richard Davis (1), Albert Brown (3), Hunter (3), Loach (2), Hodgetts (2).

Record Defeat: 1–8 v Blackburn R, FA Cup 3rd rd, 16 February 1889.

Most League Points (2 for a win): 70, Division 3, 1971–72.

Most League Points (3 for a win): 78, Division 2, 1987–88.

Most League Goals: 128, Division 1, 1930–31.

Highest League Scorer in Season: 'Pongo' Waring, 49, Division 1, 1930–31.

Most League Goals in Total Aggregate: Harry Hampton, 215, 1904–15.

Most League Goals in One Match: 5, Harry Hampton v Sheffield W, Division 1, 5 October 1912; 5, Harold Halse v Derby Co, Division 1, 19 October 1912; 5, Len Capewell v Burnley, Division 1, 29 August 1925; 5, George Brown v Leicester C, Division 1, 2 January 1932; 5, Gerry Hitchens v Charlton Ath, Division 2, 18 November 1959.

Most Capped Player: Steve Staunton 64 (102), Republic of Ireland.

Most League Appearances: Charlie Aitken, 561, 1961–76.

Youngest League Player: Jimmy Brown, 15 years 349 days v Bolton W, 17 September 1969.

Record Transfer Fee Received: £24,000,000 from Manchester C for James Milner, August 2010.

Record Transfer Fee Paid: £19,000,000 to Sunderland for Darren Bent, January 2011.

Football League Record: 1888 Founder Member of the League; 1936–38 Division 2; 1938–59 Division 1; 1959–60 Division 2; 1960–67 Division 1; 1967–70 Division 2; 1970–72 Division 3; 1972–75 Division 2; 1975–87 Division 1; 1987–88 Division 2; 1988–92 Division 1; 1992– FA Premier League.

MANAGERS

George Ramsay 1884–1926
(*Secretary-Manager*)
W. J. Smith 1926–34
(*Secretary-Manager*)
Jimmy McMullan 1934–35
Jimmy Hogan 1936–44
Alex Massie 1945–50
George Martin 1950–53
Eric Houghton 1953–58
Joe Mercer 1958–64
Dick Taylor 1964–67
Tommy Cummings 1967–68
Tommy Docherty 1968–70
Vic Crowe 1970–74
Ron Saunders 1974–82
Tony Barton 1982–84
Graham Turner 1984–86
Billy McNeill 1986–87
Graham Taylor 1987–90
Dr Jozef Venglos 1990–91
Ron Atkinson 1991–94
Brian Little 1994–98
John Gregory 1998–2002
Graham Taylor OBE 2002–03
David O'Leary 2003–06
Martin O'Neill 2006–10
Gerard Houllier 2010–11
Alex McLeish 2011–12
Paul Lambert June 2012–

LATEST SEQUENCES

Longest Sequence of League Wins: 9, 15.10.1910 – 10.12.1910.

Longest Sequence of League Defeats: 11, 23.3.1963 – 4.5.1963.

Longest Sequence of League Draws: 6, 12.9.1981 – 10.10.1981.

Longest Sequence of Unbeaten League Matches: 15, 12.3.1949 – 27.8.1949.

Longest Sequence Without a League Win: 12, 27.12.1986 – 25.3.1987.

Successive Scoring Runs: 35 from 10.11.1895.

Successive Non-scoring Runs: 5 from 29.2.1992.

TEN YEAR LEAGUE RECORD

		P	W	D	L	F	A	Pts	Pos
2002-03	PR Lge	38	12	9	17	42	47	45	16
2003-04	PR Lge	38	15	11	12	48	44	56	6
2004-05	PR Lge	38	12	11	15	45	52	47	10
2005-06	PR Lge	38	10	12	16	42	55	42	16
2006-07	PR Lge	38	11	17	10	43	41	50	11
2007-08	PR Lge	38	16	12	10	71	51	60	6
2008-09	PR Lge	38	17	11	10	54	48	62	6
2009-10	PR Lge	38	17	13	8	52	39	64	6
2010-11	PR Lge	38	12	12	14	48	59	48	9
2011-12	PR Lge	38	7	17	14	37	53	38	16

DID YOU KNOW ?

Aston Villa still retain the Football League record of 51 consecutive matches without a draw. After sharing eight goals with Burnley on 8 November 1890, they did not share the points again until meeting Blackburn Rovers on 11 February 1893 when the game ended in a 2-2 draw.

ASTON VILLA 2011–12 LEAGUE RECORD

Match No.	Date	Venue	Opponents	Result		H/T Score	Lg Pos.	Goalscorers	Attendance
1	Aug 13	A	Fulham	D	0-0	0-0	—		25,700
2	20	H	Blackburn R	W	3-1	2-0	3	Agbonlahor [12], Heskey [25], Bent [67]	32,319
3	27	H	Wolverhampton W	D	0-0	0-0	7		30,776
4	Sept 10	A	Everton	D	2-2	0-1	8	Petrov [63], Agbonlahor [83]	32,736
5	17	H	Newcastle U	D	1-1	1-0	6	Agbonlahor [13]	34,248
6	25	A	QPR	D	1-1	0-0	8	Bannan (pen) [58]	16,707
7	Oct 1	H	Wigan Ath	W	2-0	1-0	7	Agbonlahor [36], Bent [62]	30,744
8	15	A	Manchester C	L	1-4	0-1	8	Warnock [65]	47,019
9	22	H	WBA	L	1-2	1-1	11	Bent (pen) [23]	34,152
10	29	A	Sunderland	D	2-2	1-1	9	Petrov [20], Dunne [85]	37,062
11	Nov 5	H	Norwich C	W	3-2	1-1	8	Bent 2 [30, 62], Agbonlahor [48]	35,290
12	21	A	Tottenham H	L	0-2	0-2	—		35,818
13	27	A	Swansea C	D	0-0	0-0	8		20,404
14	Dec 3	H	Manchester U	L	0-1	0-1	9		40,053
15	10	A	Bolton W	W	2-1	2-0	9	Albrighton [33], Petrov [39]	20,285
16	18	H	Liverpool	L	0-2	0-2	10		37,460
17	21	H	Arsenal	L	1-2	0-1	—	Albrighton [54]	35,818
18	26	A	Stoke C	D	0-0	0-0	12		27,739
19	31	A	Chelsea	W	3-1	1-1	9	Ireland [28], Petrov [83], Bent [86]	41,332
20	Jan 2	H	Swansea C	L	0-2	0-1	—		35,642
21	14	H	Everton	D	1-1	0-0	13	Bent [56]	31,853
22	21	A	Wolverhampton W	W	3-2	1-2	11	Bent (pen) [11], Keane 2 [51, 84]	27,084
23	Feb 1	H	QPR	D	2-2	1-2	—	Bent [45], N'Zogbia [79]	32,063
24	5	A	Newcastle U	L	1-2	1-1	13	Keane [45]	48,569
25	12	H	Manchester C	L	0-1	0-0	15		35,132
26	25	A	Wigan Ath	D	0-0	0-0	15		20,601
27	Mar 3	A	Blackburn R	D	1-1	1-0	15	N'Zogbia [24]	20,717
28	10	H	Fulham	W	1-0	0-0	15	Weimann [90]	32,372
29	24	A	Arsenal	L	0-3	0-2	15		60,108
30	31	H	Chelsea	L	2-4	0-1	15	Collins [77], Lichaj [80]	34,740
31	Apr 7	A	Liverpool	D	1-1	1-0	15	Herd [10]	44,321
32	9	H	Stoke C	D	1-1	1-0	—	Weimann [32]	30,100
33	15	A	Manchester U	L	0-4	0-2	15		75,138
34	21	H	Sunderland	D	0-0	0-0	15		32,557
35	24	H	Bolton W	L	1-2	0-0	—	Warnock [61]	32,263
36	28	A	WBA	D	0-0	0-0	15		25,984
37	May 6	H	Tottenham H	D	1-1	1-0	15	Clark [35]	36,008
38	13	A	Norwich C	L	0-2	0-2	16		26,803

Final League Position: 16

GOALSCORERS

League (37): Bent 9 (2 pens), Agbonlahor 5, Petrov 4, Keane 3, Albrighton 2, N'Zogbia 2, Warnock 2, Weimann 2, Bannan 1 (1 pen), Clark 1, Collins 1, Dunne 1, Herd 1, Heskey 1, Ireland 1, Lichaj 1.
Carling Cup (2): Delfouneso 1, Lichaj 1.
FA Cup (5): Agbonlahor 1, Albrighton 1, Bent 1, Clark 1, Dunne 1.

Given S 32	Young L 2	Warnock S 34 + 1	Collins J 31 + 1	Dunne R 28	Petrov S 26 + 1	Delph F 10 + 1	Agbonlahor G 32 + 1	Bent D 21 + 1	Heskey E 18 + 10	N'Zogbia C 24 + 6	Albrighton M 15 + 11	Clark C 13 + 2	Bannan B 10 + 18	Herd C 19	Hutton A 29 + 2	Ireland S 19 + 5	Delfouneso N 1 + 5	Weimann A 5 + 9	Cuellar C 17 + 1	Jenas J 1 + 2	Guzan B 6 + 1	Gardner G 5 + 9	Keane R 5 + 1	Baker N 6 + 2	Lichaj E 9 + 1	Carruthers S — + 3	Match No.
1	2	3	4	5	6^{2}	7	8	9	10	11^{1}	12	13															1
1	2^{2}	3	4	5	6	7	8^{1}	9	10^{3}	11	12	13	14														2
1		3	4	5	6	7^{2}	8	9	10	11^{1}	13		12	2													3
1		3	4	5	6	7^{3}	8	9	10^{1}	11^{2}	13		12		2	14											4
1		3	4	5	6^{2}	7	10	9^{3}		11	12		8^{1}		2	13	14										5
1		3	4	5	6	7	9			10^{2}	12		8^{1}		2	11		13									6
1		3	4	5	6	7	10^{3}	9^{2}	12	13			8		2	11^{1}		14									7
1		3		5	6	7^{3}	8	9	10^{2}	12	14	4	13		2	11^{1}											8
1		3	4	5	6		10	9	13	11^{2}	14		8^{3}	7■	2^{1}				12								9
1		3	4	5	6		8	9	10	11^{1}	12			7	2												10
1		3	4	5	6^{2}		8	9	10^{1}	11				7	2	13				12							11
1		3	4	5	6	13	11	9	10				12	8^{2}	7				2^{1}								12
1		3	4	5		6^{2}	8	9	10^{1}	11			13	7	2					12							13
1^{0}		3	4	5	12		10	9	13		11		6	7^{1}	2					8^{2}	15						14
		3	4	5	6		10	9^{1}	12	11	7			8	2						1						15
		3	4	5	6	8^{2}			10^{1}	11	7		12		2		9	13			1						16
		3		5	11		9			10	7^{2}	4	12		2■	8^{1}	13		6		1						17
		3	4	5	8		9		10^{1}	11	7	6					12		2		1						18
		3	4	5	6^{3}		9	13		11^{2}	7^{1}	8	14			10			2		1	12					19
		3	4	5	6		10	9		11	13	8^{3}	14		12	7^{2}			2^{1}		1						20
1		3^{1}	4	5	6		10	9			7	8			2	11							12				21
1		12	4	5	6		11^{1}	9			7	3	13		2			14				8^{2}	10^{3}				22
1		3		5	6			9		11		8^{1}	12		2	7			4				10				23
1		3		5	6			9	13	11^{2}		8^{3}	12		2	7^{1}			4			14	10				24
1			4	5^{3}	6			9	10^{1}	12	7^{2}				2	13			3			8	11	14			25
1		3	4				11	9^{3}	12	14	7^{1}		8		2	13			5			6^{2}	10				26
1		3	4		6		9			10^{2}	7^{3}		12	8^{1}	2	11		14	5			13					27
1		3	4		6^{3}		9			10^{1}	7		13	8^{2}	2	11		12	5			14					28
1		3	4		6		9		10^{2}		7			8^{1}	2^{3}	11		13	5			12			14		29
1		3	4				9		13		12		8	7^{1}		11		10^{2}				6		5	2		30
1		3	4				9		10^{1}				8^{3}	7^{2}	2	11		13				12		5	6	14	31
1		3^{1}	4				9		14	13			8^{2}	7^{3}	2	11		10				12		5	6		32
1			4				9		12	14		6^{1}	8		2	11^{2}		10^{3}				7		5	3	13	33
1			4^{1}				9^{2}		13	11^{3}	7		14	6	12	8		10	2					5	3		34
1		11					12		10^{1}	9	7^{2}		13	4^{3}	2		14	8	5					6	3		35
1		11		5			9		10	8^{1}		4^{2}		7	2				6			12			3	13	36
1		3	14	5					10^{3}	11		4		8	2^{1}	9	13	12^{2}	6						7		37
1		11^{3}	6	5			9		10			4	12	8^{1}		7			2^{2}			13		14	3		38

FA Cup

Third Round	Bristol R	(a)	3-1
Fourth Round	Arsenal	(a)	2-3

Carling Cup

Second Round	Hereford U	(h)	2-0
Third Round	Bolton W	(h)	0-2

BARNET — FL Championship 2

FOUNDATION

Barnet Football Club was formed in 1888 as an amateur organisation and they played at a ground in Queen's Road until they disbanded in 1901. A club known as Alston Works FC was then formed and they played at Totteridge Lane until changing to Barnet Alston FC in 1906. They moved to their present ground a year later, combining with The Avenue to form Barnet and Alston in 1912. The club progressed to senior amateur football by way of the Athenian and Isthmian Leagues, turning professional in 1965. It was as a Southern League and Conference club that they made their name.

Underhill Stadium, Barnet Lane, Barnet, Herts EN5 2DN.

Telephone: (020) 8441 6932.

Fax: (020) 8447 0655.

Ticket Office: (020) 8449 6325.

Website: www.barnetfc.com

Email: info@barnetfc.com

Ground Capacity: 5,345.

Record Attendance: 11,026 v Wycombe Wanderers, FA Amateur Cup 4th rd 1951–52.

Pitch Measurements: 100m × 64m.

Chairman: Anthony Kleanthous.

Group Finance Director: Andrew Adie.

Head Coach: Mark Robson.

Assistant Manager: Giuliano Grazioli.

Physio: James Peckitt.

Colours: All black with amber trim.

Year Formed: 1888.

Turned Professional: 1965.

Previous Name: 1906, Barnet Alston FC; 1919, Barnet.

Club Nickname: The Bees.

Grounds: 1888, Queen's Road; 1901, Totteridge Lane; 1907, Barnet Lane.

First Football League Game: 17 August 1991, Division 4, v Crewe Alex (h) L 4–7 – Phillips; Blackford, Cooper (Murphy), Horton, Bodley (Stein), Johnson, Showler, Carter (2), Bull (2), Lowe, Evans.

Record League Victory: 7–0 v Blackpool, Division 3, 11 November 2000 – Naisbitt; Stockley, Sawyers, Niven (Brown), Heald, Arber (1), Currie (3), Doolan, Richards (2) (McGleish), Cottee (1) (Riza), Toms.

HONOURS

Football League – Division 2: Best season: 24th, 1993–94.

FA Amateur Cup: ***Winners*** 1946.

FA Trophy: ***Runners-up*** 1972.

GM Vauxhall Conference: ***Winners*** 1990–91.

Conference: ***Winners*** 2004–05.

FA Cup: 4th rd, 2007, 2008.

League Cup: Best season: 3rd rd, 2006.

sky SPORTS FACT FILE

The Barnet club's official badge dates back to the 1950s and was designed by the then chairman Sidney Robert Price. Part of it depicts the Lancastrian red rose and the Yorkist white rose after the Battle of Barnet on 14 April 1471, during the English War of the Roses.

Record Cup Victory: 6–1 v Newport Co, FA Cup 1st rd, 21 November 1970 – McClelland; Lye, Jenkins, Ward, Embery, King, Powell (1), Ferry, Adams (1), Gray, George (3), (1 og).

Record Defeat: 1–9 v Peterborough U, Division 3, 5 September 1998.

Most League Points (3 for a win): 79, Division 3, 1992–93.

Most League Goals: 81, Division 4, 1991–92.

Highest League Scorer in Season: Dougie Freedman, 24, Division 3, 1994–95.

Most League Goals in Total Aggregate: Sean Devine, 47, 1995–99.

Most League Goals in One Match: 4, Dougie Freedman v Rochdale, Division 3, 13 September 1994; 4, Lee Hodges v Rochdale, Division 3, 8 April 1996.

Most Capped Player: Ken Charlery, 4, St Lucia.

Most League Appearances: Lee Harrison, 270, 1996–2002, 2006–09.

Youngest League Player: Kieran Adams, 17 years 71 days v Mansfield T, 31 December 1994.

Record Transfer Fee Received: £800,000 from Crystal Palace for Dougie Freedman, September 1995.

Record Transfer Fee Paid: £130,000 to Peterborough U for Greg Heald, August 1997.

Football League Record: 1991 Promoted to Division 4 from GMVC; 1991–92 Division 4; 1992–93 Division 3; 1993–94 Division 2; 1994–2001 Division 3; 2001–05 Conference; 2005– FL 2.

MANAGERS

Lester Finch
George Wheeler
Dexter Adams
Tommy Coleman
Gerry Ward
Gordon Ferry
Brian Kelly
Bill Meadows 1976–79
Barry Fry 1979–85
Roger Thompson 1985
Don McAllister 1985–86
Barry Fry 1986–93
Edwin Stein 1993
Gary Phillips (*Player-Manager*) 1993–94
Ray Clemence 1994–96
Alan Mullery (*Director of Football*) 1996–97
Terry Bullivant 1997
John Still 1997–2000
Tony Cottee 2000–01
John Still 2001–02
Peter Shreeves 2002–03
Martin Allen 2003–04
Paul Fairclough 2004–08
Ian Hendon 2008–10
Mark Stimson 2010–11
Martin Allen 2011
Lawrie Sanchez 2011–12
Mark Robson April 2012–

LATEST SEQUENCES

Longest Sequence of League Wins: 6, 28.8.1993 – 25.9.1999.

Longest Sequence of League Defeats: 11, 8.5.1993 – 2.10.1993.

Longest Sequence of League Draws: 4, 22.1.1994 – 12.2.1994.

Longest Sequence of Unbeaten League Matches: 12, 5.12.1992 – 2.3.1993.

Longest Sequence Without a League Win: 14, 24.4.1993 – 10.10.1993.

Successive Scoring Runs: 12 from 19.3.1995.

Successive Non-scoring Runs: 5 from 12.2.2000.

TEN YEAR LEAGUE RECORD

		P	*W*	*D*	*L*	*F*	*A*	*Pts*	*Pos*
2002-03	Conf	42	13	14	15	65	68	53	11
2003-04	Conf	42	19	14	9	60	48	71	4
2004-05	Conf	42	26	8	8	90	44	86	1
2005-06	FL 2	46	12	18	16	44	57	54	18
2006-07	FL 2	46	16	11	19	55	70	59	14
2007-08	FL 2	46	16	12	18	56	63	60	12
2008-09	FL 2	46	11	15	20	56	74	48	17
2009-10	FL 2	46	12	12	22	47	63	48	21
2010-11	FL 2	46	12	12	22	58	77	48	22
2011-12	FL 2	46	12	10	24	52	79	46	22

DID YOU KNOW ?

The prized amateur competition in the metropolis was the London Senior Cup. But it had eluded Barnet until 14 March 1938, when they defeated Leyton 4-0 in the final at Highbury attended by a crowd of 20,000. Their earlier victims had been the Casuals, Ilford and Leytonstone.

BARNET 2011–12 LEAGUE RECORD

Match No.	*Date*	*Venue*	*Opponents*	*Result*		*H/T Score*	*Lg Pos.*	*Goalscorers*	*Attendance*
1	Aug 6	A	Morecambe	W	1-0	0-0	—	Byrne [76]	1874
2	13	H	Port Vale	L	1-3	0-2	14	Price [63]	2260
3	16	H	Gillingham	D	2-2	0-1	—	McLeod 2 [61, 90]	2466
4	20	A	Rotherham U	D	2-2	1-0	15	Kamdjo [36], McLeod (pen) [63]	3546
5	27	A	Bradford C	L	2-4	1-1	17	McLeod 2 [15, 90]	9656
6	Sept 3	H	Accrington S	D	0-0	0-0	19		2380
7	10	A	Crewe Alex	L	1-3	0-1	22	McLeod [81]	3142
8	13	H	Plymouth Arg	W	2-0	1-0	—	McLeod [7], Leach [64]	1849
9	17	H	Oxford U	L	0-2	0-2	21		2812
10	24	A	Swindon T	L	0-4	0-3	21		7279
11	Oct 1	H	Northampton T	L	1-2	1-0	21	Holmes [17]	2304
12	8	A	Shrewsbury T	L	2-3	0-2	22	Holmes [69], Marshall [82]	5192
13	15	H	Aldershot T	W	2-1	0-1	21	Kabba (pen) [63], Holmes [79]	2015
14	22	A	Hereford U	L	0-1	0-0	23		2124
15	25	H	Southend U	L	0-3	0-2	—		2744
16	29	H	Burton Alb	L	3-6	1-2	23	McLeod [39], Holmes [55], Deering [88]	1745
17	Nov 5	A	AFC Wimbledon	D	1-1	1-0	23	McLeod [45]	4369
18	19	A	Bristol R	W	2-0	1-0	21	McLeod [19], Byrne [90]	5024
19	25	H	Macclesfield T	W	2-1	2-0	—	McLeod 2 (2 pens) [41, 45]	2200
20	Dec 9	A	Torquay U	L	0-1	0-0	—		2125
21	16	H	Cheltenham T	D	2-2	1-2	—	McLeod 2 (1 pen) [41, 60 (p)]	1775
22	26	A	Dagenham & R	L	0-3	0-2	20		2135
23	30	A	Crawley T	L	0-1	0-1	—		3008
24	Jan 2	H	Bristol R	W	2-0	0-0	20	McLeod [69], Kamdjo [80]	2537
25	14	A	Accrington S	W	3-0	2-0	20	Holmes [23], Hughes [45], Deering [54]	1652
26	21	A	Northampton T	W	2-1	0-1	18	Byrne [48], Holmes [69]	4561
27	28	H	Crewe Alex	W	2-0	1-0	17	McLeod (pen) [30], Hector [77]	2263
28	Feb 14	A	Plymouth Arg	D	0-0	0-0	—		5879
29	18	H	Shrewsbury T	L	1-2	0-1	18	McLeod [48]	2046
30	21	A	Oxford U	L	1-2	1-1	—	Hector [16]	5848
31	25	A	Aldershot T	L	1-4	0-3	18	Taylor [58]	2511
32	28	H	Bradford C	L	0-4	0-2	—		1509
33	Mar 3	H	Rotherham U	D	1-1	1-0	19	Byrne [7]	1765
34	6	A	Gillingham	L	1-3	1-0	—	Kamdjo [39]	3751
35	10	A	Port Vale	W	2-1	0-0	19	May [66], Yiadom [89]	5522
36	17	H	Morecambe	L	0-2	0-1	20		1536
37	20	H	Dagenham & R	D	2-2	1-1	—	McLeod [30], May [79]	1725
38	23	A	Macclesfield T	D	0-0	0-0	—		2123
39	30	H	Torquay U	L	0-1	0-0	—		2263
40	Apr 3	H	Swindon T	L	0-2	0-2	—		2211
41	6	A	Cheltenham T	L	0-2	0-0	22		3319
42	9	H	Crawley T	L	1-2	1-0	22	Holmes [15]	2099
43	13	H	Hereford U	D	1-1	1-1	—	May [31]	3189
44	20	A	Southend U	L	0-3	0-3	—		6451
45	28	H	AFC Wimbledon	W	4-0	1-0	22	Holmes [33], Deering [81], May [86], Hughes [90]	4422
46	May 5	A	Burton Alb	W	2-1	1-1	22	Byrne [6], Hughes [60]	3359

Final League Position: 22

GOALSCORERS

League (52): McLeod 18 (5 pens), Holmes 8, Byrne 5, May 4, Deering 3, Hughes 3, Kamdjo 3, Hector 2, Kabba 1 (1 pen), Leach 1, Marshall 1, Price 1, Taylor 1, Yiadom 1.
Carling Cup (3): Holmes 1, Hughes 1, Kabba 1.
FA Cup (3): Kamdjo 1, McLeod 1, Taylor 1.
J Paint Trophy (9): McLeod 3 (2 pens), Marshall 2, Holmes 1, Hughes 1, Kabba 1, Taylor 1.

Brill D 36	Senda D 19	Parkes J 11	Hughes M 44 + 1	Uddin A 9	Kamdjo C 41	Deering S 39 + 5	Byrne M 38 + 5	Price J 5	McLeod I 43 + 1	Marshall M 24 + 1	Holmes R 33 + 8	Taylor C 2 + 16	Fraser T 2 + 3	Geohaghon E — + 2	Vilhete M — + 3	Dennehy D 18 + 1	Kabba S 5 + 4	Leach D 9 + 1	Owusu L — + 5	Borrowdale G 11	O'Brien L 10	Hector M 26 + 1	Saville J 14 + 3	Downing P 25 + 1	N'Diaye A 2 + 4	Baseya C — + 2	McCallum G — + 2	Obita J 3 + 2	Hajrovic S 7 + 3	Yiadom A 1 + 6	Mustoe J 15 + 3	McGleish S 5 + 4	May B 9 + 2	Gambin L — + 1	*Match No.*
1	2	3	4	5	6	7	8^{3}	9	10^{2}	11^{1}	12	13	14																						1
1	2	3	4	5	6	13	8^{2}	9	10	11		12	7^{1}																						2
1	2	3	4^{1}	5	6	7^{3}	8	9^{2}	10	11	14	13	12																						3
1	2	3	4^{3}	5	6	7^{1}	8	9^{2}	10	11	12		14	13																					4
1	2	3	4	5	6		8	9^{2}	10	11	7^{1}			13	12																				5
1	2	3	4		6	7^{1}	8			11	10	12				5	9																		6
1	2	3	4^{3}		6	14	8		10	11	7	12				5^{2}	9^{1}	13																	7
1	2	3	4		6	12	8		10	11^{1}	7	9^{2}						5	13																8
1	2^{3}	3	4		6	13	8		10	11^{1}	7	9^{2}					12	5	14																9
1			4	5	6		8^{1}		10	11	12		2			3	9	7																	10
1		3	4^{2}	5	2	8	13		10^{3}	11	7^{1}	12					14	6		9															11
	2			5	4	7	8		10	11	9^{1}					12		6		3	1														12
	2^{2}		13		4	7	8^{1}		10	11	9^{3}	14				5	12	6		3	1														13
		3	4^{2}		6	7	12		10	11	9					5		8	13	2^{1}	1														14
			4^{2}		3	7	12		10	11^{1}	8^{3}				14	5■	9	6	13	2	1														15
			4	5	3	7	8		10	12	11						9^{2}	6^{1}	13	2	1														16
1	2		4		8	7			10	11	9^{1}					5	12			3		6													17
1	2		4		3	9	8		10^{2}	11						5^{1}						12	6	7	13										18
1	2		4		7	9	8		10^{2}	11^{1}												5	3	6		12	13								19
1	2		4		7	9	8^{3}		10^{2}	11^{1}	12					5				3				6		13	14								20
1	2		4		7	9	8		10	11										3		5		6											21
1	2		4			9	8^{1}		10	11^{2}	12	13								3		5		6	7										22
1	2		4^{2}		7	9	8^{1}		10	11	12	13								3		5		6											23
1	2		4		7	9			10	11	8^{1}	12										5	3	6											24
1			4		7	9			10	11	8					5						2	3	6											25
1			4		7	9	8		10^{1}		11^{2}	12				5						2	3	6	13										26
1			4		7^{1}	9	8		10		11^{2}	13				5						2	3^{3}	6				12	14						27
1			4		7	9	12		10		11					5							3	6				2^{1}	8						28
1			4^{2}		7^{1}	9	12		10		8					5							6^{3}	2				11	3	13	14				29
1			4		7^{2}	9	8		10		11					5^{1}						2	3^{3}	6				13	12		14				30
1			4			9^{1}	8		10			12										3	13	6	7			11	2^{2}		5				31
			4		7	9	8		10		11^{1}	12				5■					1	2	3^{2}	6							13				32
			4		5	11	8		10		7^{2}										1	2		6■					12	13	3	9^{1}			33
			4		6	11^{2}	8		10^{1}		7	12									1	5							2	13	3	9			34
			4		2	11	8				7^{2}	12									1	5		6						13	3	9^{1}	10		35
			4			9^{1}	8		10		11					5					1	2		6						12	3		7		36
1			4		7^{1}	12	8		10		11					5						2		6							3		9		37
1			4		2	11	8		10		7^{2}											5	12	6^{1}						13	3		9		38
1			4			7	8		10		11^{2}											5	6		12				2^{1}		3	13	9		39
1			4			11	8^{1}		10^{2}		12											2	6	5						7	3	13	9		40
1			4		2	7	8		10		11											5		6							3		9		41
1			4		2	9	8		10		11				12							5		6^{2}					7^{1}		3	13			42
1			4		7	9	8		10		11											5		6					2^{1}		3		12		43
1			4		2	7^{3}	8		10		11											5^{1}	12	6	14						3	13	9^{2}		44
1			4		2	7	8		10^{2}		11											5	6^{1}	12							3	9^{3}	13	14	45
1			4		2	7	8		12		11											5	6								3	10^{1}	9		46

FA Cup

First Round	Southport	(a)	2-1
Second Round	Milton Keynes D	(h)	1-3

Carling Cup

First Round	Portsmouth	(a)	1-0
Second Round	Burnley	(a)	2-3

J Paint Trophy

First Round	Colchester U	(a)	3-1
Second Round	Gillingham	(a)	3-1
Southern Quarter-Final	Cheltenham T	(a)	2-0
Southern Semi-Final	Brentford	(h)	0-0
Southern Final	Swindon T	(h)	1-1
		(a)	0-1

BARNSLEY FL Championship

FOUNDATION

Many clubs owe their inception to the Church and Barnsley are among them, for they were formed in 1887 by the Rev. T. T. Preedy, curate of Barnsley St Peter's, and went under that name until it was dropped in 1897 a year before being admitted to the Second Division of the Football League.

Oakwell Stadium, Grove Street, Barnsley, South Yorkshire S71 1ET.

Telephone: (01226) 211 211.

Fax: (01226) 211 444.

Ticket Office: (0871) 22 66 777.

Website: www.barnsleyfc.co.uk

Email: thereds@barnsleyfc.co.uk

Ground Capacity: 23,186.

Record Attendance: 40,255 v Stoke C, FA Cup 5th rd, 15 February 1936.

Pitch Measurements: 110yd × 73yd.

Owner: Patrick Cryne.

Director: Barry Taylor.

General Manager: Albert Donald Rowing.

Manager: Keith Hill. ***Assistant Manager:*** David Flitcroft.

Physio: Chris Burton.

Colours: Red shirts with white trim, white shorts, red stockings.

Year Formed: 1887.

Turned Professional: 1888.

Previous Name: 1887, Barnsley St Peter's; 1897, Barnsley.

Club Nickname: 'The Tykes', 'Reds' or 'Colliers'.

Ground: 1887, Oakwell.

First Football League Game: 1 September 1898, Division 2, v Lincoln C (a) L 0–1 – Fawcett; McArtney, Nixon; King, Burleigh, Porteous; Davis, Lees, Murray, McCullough, McGee.

Record League Victory: 9–0 v Loughborough T, Division 2, 28 January 1899 – Greaves; McArtney, Nixon; Porteous, Burleigh, Howard; Davis (4), Hepworth (1), Lees (1), McCullough (1), Jones (2). 9–0 v Accrington S, Division 3 (N), 3 February 1934 – Ellis; Cookson, Shotton; Harper, Henderson, Whitworth; Spence (2), Smith (1), Blight (4), Andrews (1), Ashton (1).

Record Cup Victory: 6–0 v Blackpool, FA Cup 1st rd replay, 20 January 1910 – Mearns; Downs, Ness; Glendinning, Boyle (1), Utley; Bartrop, Gadsby (1), Lillycrop (2), Tufnell (2), Forman. 6–0 v Peterborough U, League Cup 1st rd 2nd leg, 15 September 1981 – Horn; Joyce, Chambers, Glavin (2), Banks, McCarthy, Evans, Parker (2), Aylott (1), McHale, Barrowclough (1).

HONOURS

Football League – Division 1: ***Runners-up*** 1996–97;
Division 3 (N): ***Champions*** 1933–34, 1938–39, 1954–55; ***Runners-up*** 1953–54;
Division 3: ***Runners-up*** 1980–81;
Division 4: ***Runners-up*** 1967–68.

FA Cup: ***Winners*** 1912; ***Runners-up*** 1910.

Football League Cup: Best season: 5th rd, 1982.

sky SPORTS FACT FILE

Outside-left Bobby Morton played only one senior game for Barnsley on 9 April 1928 but scored their goal in a 1-1 draw with Nottingham Forest. Ex-Ashington and Bedlington United, he was signed by an impressed Forest and was later with Bradford (PA), Newark Town and Port Vale.

Record Defeat: 0–9 v Notts Co, Division 2, 19 November 1927.

Most League Points (2 for a win): 67, Division 3 (N), 1938–39.

Most League Points (3 for a win): 82, Division 1, 1999–2000.

Most League Goals: 118, Division 3 (N), 1933–34.

Highest League Scorer in Season: Cecil McCormack, 33, Division 2, 1950–51.

Most League Goals in Total Aggregate: Ernest Hine, 123, 1921–26 and 1934–38.

Most League Goals in One Match: 5, Frank Eaton v South Shields, Division 3 (N), 9 April 1927; 5, Peter Cunningham v Darlington, Division 3 (N), 4 February 1933; 5, Beau Asquith v Darlington, Division 3 (N), 12 November 1938; 5, Cecil McCormack v Luton T, Division 2, 9 September 1950.

Most Capped Player: Gerry Taggart, 35 (50), Northern Ireland.

Most League Appearances: Barry Murphy, 514, 1962–78.

Youngest League Player: Reuben Noble-Lazarus, 15 years 45 days v Ipswich T, 30 September 2008.

Record Transfer Fee Received: £4,500,000 from Blackburn R for Ashley Ward, December 1998.

Record Transfer Fee Paid: £1,500,000 to Partizan Belgrade for Georgi Hristov, July 1997.

Football League Record: 1898 Elected to Division 2; 1932–34 Division 3 (N); 1934–38 Division 2; 1938–39 Division 3 (N); 1946–53 Division 2; 1953–55 Division 3 (N); 1955–59 Division 2; 1959–65 Division 3; 1965–68 Division 4; 1968–72 Division 3; 1972–79 Division 4; 1979–81 Division 3; 1981–92 Division 2; 1992–97 Division 1; 1997–98 FA Premier League; 1998–2002 Division 1; 2002–04 Division 2; 2004–06 FL 1; 2006– FL C.

MANAGERS

Arthur Fairclough 1898–1901 (*Secretary-Manager*)
John McCartney 1901–04 (*Secretary-Manager*)
Arthur Fairclough 1904–12
John Hastie 1912–14
Percy Lewis 1914–19
Peter Sant 1919–26
John Commins 1926–29
Arthur Fairclough 1929–30
Brough Fletcher 1930–37
Angus Seed 1937–53
Tim Ward 1953–60
Johnny Steele 1960–71 (*continued as General Manager*)
John McSeveney 1971–72
Johnny Steele (*General Manager*) 1972–73
Jim Iley 1973–78
Allan Clarke 1978–80
Norman Hunter 1980–84
Bobby Collins 1984–85
Allan Clarke 1985–89
Mel Machin 1989–93
Viv Anderson 1993–94
Danny Wilson 1994–98
John Hendrie 1998–99
Dave Bassett 1999–2000
Nigel Spackman 2001
Steve Parkin 2001–02
Glyn Hodges 2002–03
Gudjon Thordarson 2003–04
Paul Hart 2004–05
Andy Ritchie 2005–06
Simon Davey 2007–10 (*caretaker from November 2006*)
Mark Robins 2009–11
Keith Hill June 2011–

LATEST SEQUENCES

Longest Sequence of League Wins: 10, 5.3.1955 – 23.4.1955.

Longest Sequence of League Defeats: 9, 14.3.1953 – 25.4.1953.

Longest Sequence of League Draws: 7, 28.3.1911 – 22.4.1911.

Longest Sequence of Unbeaten League Matches: 21, 1.1.1934 – 5.5.1934.

Longest Sequence Without a League Win: 26, 13.12.1952 – 26.8.1953.

Successive Scoring Runs: 44 from 2.10.1926.

Successive Non-scoring Runs: 6 from 7.10.1899.

TEN YEAR LEAGUE RECORD

		P	*W*	*D*	*L*	*F*	*A*	*Pts*	*Pos*
2002-03	Div 2	46	13	13	20	51	64	52	19
2003-04	Div 2	46	15	17	14	54	58	62	12
2004-05	FL 1	46	14	19	13	69	64	61	13
2005-06	FL 1	46	18	18	10	62	44	72	5
2006-07	FL C	46	15	5	26	53	85	50	20
2007-08	FL C	46	14	13	19	52	65	55	18
2008-09	FL C	46	13	13	20	45	58	52	20
2009-10	FL C	46	14	12	20	53	69	54	18
2010-11	FL C	46	14	14	18	55	66	56	17
2011-12	FL C	46	13	9	24	49	74	48	21

DID YOU KNOW ?

On 6 March 1954, Barnsley were due to play Carlisle United at Brunton Park. Unfortunately a fire at the ground forced the visiting players to change at the public baths. The team boarded a double-decker bus having changed into their kit. Journey's end: Barnsley won 4-2.

BARNSLEY 2011–12 LEAGUE RECORD

Match No.	*Date*	*Venue*	*Opponents*	*Result*	*H/T Score*	*Lg Pos.*	*Goalscorers*	*Attendance*
1	Aug 6	A	Nottingham F	D 0-0	0-0	—		22,951
2	13	H	Southampton	L 0-1	0-1	18		10,501
3	16	H	Middlesbrough	L 1-3	1-3	—	McManus (og)[4]	10,603
4	20	A	Reading	W 2-1	1-0	16	Foster[27], Done[68]	15,878
5	27	A	Millwall	D 0-0	0-0	16		10,033
6	Sept 10	H	Leicester C	D 1-1	1-0	16	Butterfield[38]	10,862
7	17	H	Watford	D 1-1	0-1	16	Gray[57]	9733
8	24	A	Birmingham C	D 1-1	1-0	17	Butterfield[33]	17,836
9	27	A	Derby Co	D 1-1	1-0	—	Butterfield[35]	23,454
10	Oct 1	H	Coventry C	W 2-0	1-0	16	Gray 2 (1 pen)[42 (p), 55]	9497
11	15	A	Portsmouth	L 0-2	0-0	18		11,261
12	18	H	Burnley	W 2-0	1-0	—	Butterfield[21], Vaz Te[81]	9692
13	22	A	Cardiff C	L 3-5	1-3	18	Drinkwater[36], McNulty[82], Vaz Te[86]	20,665
14	29	H	Bristol C	L 1-2	0-1	19	Davies[74]	8900
15	Nov 1	H	Hull C	W 2-1	0-0	—	Davies[48], Gray[59]	9869
16	6	A	Brighton & HA	L 0-2	0-1	19		19,841
17	19	H	Doncaster R	W 2-0	1-0	15	Davies 2[30, 64]	11,783
18	26	A	Leeds U	W 2-1	2-0	14	Vaz Te[27], Davies[43]	25,900
19	Dec 3	A	Peterborough U	W 4-3	2-0	13	O'Brien[17], Butterfield[45], Vaz Te[55], Davies[78]	8320
20	6	H	Crystal Palace	W 2-1	1-1	—	Vaz Te 2[1, 77]	9524
21	10	H	Ipswich T	L 3-5	2-0	12	Davies 2 (1 pen)[14 (p), 89], Vaz Te[39]	9107
22	17	A	West Ham U	L 0-1	0-1	13		34,749
23	26	H	Blackpool	L 1-3	1-1	16	Done[18]	11,776
24	31	H	Leeds U	W 4-1	1-0	13	Vaz Te 3[16, 51, 72], Davies[61]	17,499
25	Jan 2	A	Doncaster R	L 0-2	0-1	16		11,446
26	14	A	Leicester C	W 2-1	2-1	14	Gray 2[12, 34]	22,116
27	21	H	Millwall	L 1-3	0-2	14	McNulty[88]	9185
28	31	H	Derby Co	W 3-2	3-0	—	Done[11], Gray (pen)[23], Wiseman[30]	10,149
29	Feb 4	A	Watford	L 1-2	0-1	15	Golbourne[85]	11,306
30	14	A	Burnley	L 0-2	0-1	—		12,355
31	18	H	Portsmouth	W 2-0	0-0	14	O'Brien[76], Done[90]	9336
32	21	H	Birmingham C	L 1-3	1-2	—	Davies[19]	9558
33	25	A	Coventry C	L 0-1	0-0	14		13,928
34	Mar 3	H	Nottingham F	D 1-1	0-1	15	Davies[79]	10,550
35	6	A	Middlesbrough	L 0-2	0-0	—		14,745
36	10	A	Southampton	L 0-2	0-1	17		24,862
37	17	H	Reading	L 0-4	0-0	17		9381
38	20	A	Crystal Palace	L 0-1	0-0	—		11,853
39	24	H	Peterborough U	W 1-0	1-0	17	Cotterill[24]	9698
40	31	A	Ipswich T	L 0-1	0-0	18		20,053
41	Apr 6	H	West Ham U	L 0-4	0-3	—		11,151
42	9	A	Blackpool	D 1-1	0-0	18	Perkins[47]	13,525
43	14	H	Cardiff C	L 0-1	0-0	20		9122
44	17	A	Hull C	L 1-3	0-2	—	Gray[74]	16,604
45	21	A	Bristol C	L 0-2	0-1	21		18,562
46	28	H	Brighton & HA	D 0-0	0-0	21		10,151

Final League Position: 21

GOALSCORERS

League (49): Davies 11 (1 pen), Vaz Te 10, Gray 8 (2 pens), Butterfield 5, Done 4, McNulty 2, O'Brien 2, Cotterill 1, Drinkwater 1, Foster 1, Golbourne 1, Perkins 1, Wiseman 1, own goal 1.
Carling Cup (0).
FA Cup (2): Vaz Te 2.

Steele L 36	Wiseman S 34+9	McEveley J 25+4	Doyle N 16+5	Edwards R 17	Foster S 41	Butterfield J 24	Addison M 9+2	Davies C 33+7	Haynes D 4+8	Perkins D 31+2	O'Brien J 23+8	Vaz Te R 12+10	Preece D 1	McNulty J 43+1	Noble-Lazarus R 2+6	Done M 22+9	Hassell B 17+2	Gray A 25+7	Drinkwater D 16+1	Park C 1+2	Clark J 1+1	Digby P 2+2	Rose D 2+2	Ranger N 3+2	Dagnall C 4+5	Taylor A —+1	Tonge M 7+3	Smith K 10+2	Golbourne S 10+2	Cotterill D 6+5	Dawson S 9+3	Nouble F 5+1	Collins L 4+3	Stones J —+2	Button D 9	Higginbotham K 2+3	*Match No.*
1	2	3	4	5	6	7^{2}	8	9^{1}	10	11	12	13																									1
	2	3	4^{2}	5		7^{1}	8	9	10	11		13	1	6	12																						2
1	2	3	4^{1}	5	6	9	8^{3}	12	10	11	7^{2}				13	14																					3
1	2	3^{2}		5	6	7^{3}		9	10^{1}	11	14			13		8	4	12																			4
1	2	14		5	6	7^{1}			12	11^{2}	13			4		8	3	10	9^{3}																		5
1	12			5^{1}	6	7			13	11	4			3		9^{2}	2	10	8																		6
1		3	13		6	7				11	4	12		5			2	10	8^{2}	9^{1}																	7
1		3			6	7	13			11	4			5		9^{1}	2	10	8		12^{2}																8
1	13	3^{2}			6	4				11^{1}	8	7^{3}		5			2	10	9			12	14														9
1	12	3	4		6	7					8	11^{2}		5			2^{1}	10	9	13																	10
1	12	3	4		5	7		14			8^{3}	11^{2}		6			2^{1}	10	9	13																	11
1	2		4	5	6	7		9^{1}			8	12		3				10	11																		12
1	2	12	6	4^{1}	5	7		13		11^{3}	8^{2}	14		3				10	9																		13
1	2	3	4^{3}		5	7		12		14	8	13		6		11^{1}		10^{2}	9																		14
1	2	3	12		5	4^{2}		9^{3}		11	8	14		6		13		10	7^{1}																		15
1	2	3			5	7	4^{2}	9^{1}		11		12		6		13		10	8																		16
1		3			5	4		9	12	11	8	10^{1}		6		7	2																				17
1	14	3			5	4		9^{2}		11■	8	10^{1}		6		7^{3}	2		12					13													18
1	14	3^{2}			5	4		9	13		8	12		6		11^{1}	2		7					10^{3}													19
1	12				5	4^{3}	14	9	13	3	8	11		6			2		7^{1}					10^{2}													20
1	3				5	4		9	13	11	8^{3}	10^{1}		6		12	2		7^{2}					14													21
1	2	3		4		7	6	9	13	11	12	8^{1}		5										10^{2}													22
1	2	3		6		4		9	13	11	8^{1}	7^{2}		5		10		12																			23
1	2	3			5	8^{1}	4	9		11		12		6		10^{2}	7	13																			24
1	2	3			5		4^{2}	9		11		8		6	12	10^{1}	7	13																			25
1	14	3			5		4^{2}	13		11		7^{3}		6		12	2	10	8						9^{1}												26
1	14	3			5		4	9^{1}		11		7		6		13	2^{2}	10							8^{3}	12											27
1	2^{3}		12	5	6			9		11				3	13	8	14	10									4^{1}	7^{2}									28
1	2		14	5	6			9		11				3^{3}		8^{1}		10							12		4^{2}	7	13								29
1	2		14	4				9		11^{3}	12			3		8^{2}		10							13		5^{1}	6	7								30
1	2	12		4	5			9		11^{1}	8			6		14		10^{2}							13			7	3^{3}								31
1	2	3^{2}		5				9			12			6		11						4			10		14	8^{3}	13	7^{1}							32
1	2	3		4	5			9						6		12		14									10^{2}	8	11^{1}	13	7^{3}						33
1	2	3^{1}			6			9						5		10		12				4			13		8^{2}	7^{3}	11		14						34
1	2	12	4^{2}		6			9						5		8		10^{3}							11^{1}			13	3	14	7						35
1	2	3	4		5			9						6		11^{3}						12	13		14					7^{2}	8^{1}	10					36
1	2^{1}		4^{2}		5			9						6		11							7^{3}					8		14	13	10	3	12			37
	2		4		5			9^{2}						6		11		10									12		3		7	8^{1}	13		1		38
	2		4■		5			9^{1}						6		11		10										12	3	7	8				1		39
	2				5			9			14			6		11^{1}		10^{2}										4^{3}	3	7	8	13			1	12	40
	2				5			9^{3}		14	13			6				10										4^{2}	3^{1}	7	8		12		1	11	41
	2			6	5			13		11	8			3	9^{1}												4^{3}			12		10^{2}	7		1	14	42
	2		4		5			13		11	8			3	9^{1}			14									7^{2}			12		10^{3}	6		1		43
	2		4		5^{1}			9		11	8^{2}			3	14			10												7^{3}	12		6		1	13	44
	2		4^{1}		5			9^{3}		11^{2}	8			6	14			10									12				7		13		1	3	45
	2				5			9		11	8			6		13	12				4^{2}		10						3^{3}		7^{1}			14	1		46

FA Cup
Third Round Swansea C (h) 2-4

Carling Cup
First Round Morecambe (h) 0-2

BIRMINGHAM CITY FL Championship

FOUNDATION

In 1875, cricketing enthusiasts who were largely members of Trinity Church, Bordesley, determined to continue their sporting relationships throughout the year by forming a football club which they called Small Heath Alliance. For their earliest games played on waste land in Arthur Street, the team included three Edden brothers and two James brothers.

St Andrews Stadium, Birmingham B9 4RL.

Telephone: (0844) 557 1875.

Fax: (0844) 557 1975.

Ticket Office: (0844) 557 1875 (then option 2).

Website: www.bcfc.com

Email: reception@bcfc.com

Ground Capacity: 30,079.

Record Attendance: 66,844 v Everton, FA Cup 5th rd, 11 February 1939.

Pitch Measurements: 101m × 68m.

Chairman: Vico Hui.

Vice-chairman: Peter Pannu.

Manager: Lee Clark.

First-Team Coaches: Terry McDermott and Derek Fazackerley.

Head of Sports Science: Nick Davies.

Colours: Blue shirts with white trim, white shorts, blue stockings.

Year Formed: 1875.

Turned Professional: 1885.

Previous Names: 1875, Small Heath Alliance; 1888, dropped 'Alliance'; 1905, Birmingham; 1945, Birmingham City.

Club Nickname: 'Blues'.

Grounds: 1875, waste ground near Arthur St; 1877, Muntz St, Small Heath; 1906, St Andrews.

First Football League Game: 3 September 1892, Division 2, v Burslem Port Vale (h) W 5–1 – Charsley; Bayley, Speller; Ollis, Jenkyns, Devey; Hallam (1), Edwards (1), Short (1), Wheldon (2), Hands.

Record League Victory: 12–0 v Walsall T Swifts, Division 2, 17 December 1892 – Charsley; Bayley, Jones; Ollis, Jenkyns, Devey; Hallam (2), Walton (3), Mobley (3), Wheldon (2), Hands (2). 12–0 v Doncaster R, Division 2, 11 April 1903 – Dorrington; Goldie, Wassell; Beer, Dougherty (1), Howard; Athersmith, Leonard (4), McRoberts (1), Wilcox (4), Field (1), (1 og).

Record Cup Victory: 9–2 v Burton W, FA Cup 1st rd, 31 October 1885 – Hedges; Jones, Evetts (1); Fred James, Felton, Arthur James (1); Davenport (2), Stanley (4), Simms, Figures, Morris (1).

HONOURS

Football League – FL C: ***Runners-up*** 2006–07, 2008–09;
Division 2: ***Champions*** 1892–93, 1920–21, 1947–48, 1954–55, 1994–95; ***Runners-up*** 1893–94, 1900–01, 1902–03, 1971–72, 1984–85;
Division 3: ***Runners-up*** 1991–92.

FA Cup: ***Runners-up*** 1931, 1956.

Football League Cup: ***Winners*** 1963, 2011; ***Runners-up*** 2001.

Leyland Daf Cup: ***Winners*** 1991.

Auto Windscreens Shield: ***Winners*** 1995.

European Competitions
European Fairs Cup: 1955–58, 1958–60 (*runners-up*), 1960–61 (*runners-up*), 1961–62.
Europa League: 2011–12.

sky SPORTS FACT FILE

In 1925–26 Birmingham was to finish a modest 14th in the First Division. But they arranged a friendly with Spain's Real Madrid, who became the first foreign opposition to play at St Andrew's. It proved a milestone in several ways as the Blues ran out comfortable winners at 3-0.

Record Defeat: 1–9 v Sheffield W, Division 1, 13 December 1930. 1–9 v Blackburn R, Division 1, 5 January 1895.

Most League Points (2 for a win): 59, Division 2, 1947–48.

Most League Points (3 for a win): 89, Division 2, 1994–95.

Most League Goals: 103, Division 2, 1893–94 (only 28 games).

Highest League Scorer in Season: Joe Bradford, 29, Division 1, 1927–28.

Most League Goals in Total Aggregate: Joe Bradford, 249, 1920–35.

Most League Goals in One Match: 5, Walter Abbott v Darwen, Division 2, 26 November, 1898; 5, John McMillan v Blackpool, Division 2, 2 March 1901; 5, James Windridge v Glossop, Division 2, 23 January 1915.

Most Capped Player: Maik Taylor, 50 (88), Northern Ireland.

Most League Appearances: Frank Womack, 491, 1908–28.

Youngest League Player: Trevor Francis, 16 years 7 months v Cardiff C, 5 September 1970.

Record Transfer Fee Received: £6,800,000 from Liverpool for Jermaine Pennant, July 2006.

Record Transfer Fee Paid: £8,500,000 to Santos Laguna for Christian Benitez, July 2009.

Football League Record: 1892 Elected to Division 2; 1894–96 Division 1; 1896–1901 Division 2; 1901–02 Division 1; 1902–03 Division 2; 1903–08 Division 1; 1908–21 Division 2; 1921–39 Division 1; 1946–48 Division 2; 1948–50 Division 1; 1950–55 Division 2; 1955–65 Division 1; 1965–72 Division 2; 1972–79 Division 1; 1979–80 Division 2; 1980–84 Division 1; 1984–85 Division 2; 1985–86 Division 1; 1986–89 Division 2; 1989–92 Division 3; 1992–94 Division 1; 1994–95 Division 2; 1995–2002 Division 1; 2002–06 FA Premier League; 2006–07 FL C; 2007–08 FA Premier League; 2008–09 FL C; 2009–11 FA Premier League; 2011– FL C.

MANAGERS

Alfred Jones 1892–1908 (*Secretary-Manager*)
Alec Watson 1908–10
Bob McRoberts 1910–15
Frank Richards 1915–23
Billy Beer 1923–27
William Harvey 1927–28
Leslie Knighton 1928–33
George Liddell 1933–39
William Camkin and **Ted Goodier** were in charge during 1939–45
Harry Storer 1945–48
Bob Brocklebank 1949–54
Arthur Turner 1954–58
Pat Beasley 1959–60
Gil Merrick 1960–64
Joe Mallett 1964–65
Stan Cullis 1965–70
Fred Goodwin 1970–75
Willie Bell 1975–77
Sir Alf Ramsay 1977–78
Jim Smith 1978–82
Ron Saunders 1982–86
John Bond 1986–87
Garry Pendrey 1987–89
Dave Mackay 1989–91
Lou Macari 1991
Terry Cooper 1991–93
Barry Fry 1993–96
Trevor Francis 1996–2001
Steve Bruce 2001–07
Alex McLeish 2007–11
Chris Hughton 2011–12
Lee Clark June 2012–

LATEST SEQUENCES

Longest Sequence of League Wins: 13, 17.12.1892 – 16.9.1893.

Longest Sequence of League Defeats: 8, 28.9.1985 – 23.11.1985.

Longest Sequence of League Draws: 8, 18.9.1990 – 23.10.1990.

Longest Sequence of Unbeaten League Matches: 20, 3.9.1994 – 2.1.1995.

Longest Sequence Without a League Win: 17, 28.9.1985 – 18.1.1986.

Successive Scoring Runs: 24 from 24.9.1892.

Successive Non-scoring Runs: 6 from 1.10.1949.

TEN YEAR LEAGUE RECORD

		P	*W*	*D*	*L*	*F*	*A*	*Pts*	*Pos*
2002-03	PR Lge	38	13	9	16	41	49	48	13
2003-04	PR Lge	38	12	14	12	43	48	50	10
2004-05	PR Lge	38	11	12	15	40	46	45	12
2005-06	PR Lge	38	8	10	20	28	50	34	18
2006-07	FL C	46	26	8	12	67	42	86	2
2007-08	PR Lge	38	8	11	19	46	62	35	19
2008-09	FL C	46	23	14	9	54	37	83	2
2009-10	PR Lge	38	13	11	14	38	47	50	9
2010-11	PR Lge	38	8	15	15	37	58	39	18
2011-12	FL C	46	20	16	10	78	51	76	4

DID YOU KNOW ?

Billy Beer spent eight years as a Birmingham (Small Heath) midfield player and penalty taker until 1910 making 250 first team appearances. After retiring he became a sheep-farmer in Australia before returning and taking up a position as manager of Birmingham in the 1920s!

BIRMINGHAM CITY 2011–12 LEAGUE RECORD

Match No.	Date	Venue	Opponents	Result	H/T Score	Lg Pos.	Goalscorers	Attendance
1	Aug 6	A	Derby Co	L 1-2	1-2	—	Davies [19]	27,210
2	13	H	Coventry C	W 1-0	0-0	12	Fahey [73]	19,225
3	21	A	Middlesbrough	L 1-3	1-0	18	Rooney (pen) [36]	17,567
4	28	A	Watford	D 2-2	1-0	21	Rooney [39], Wood [88]	11,937
5	Sept 11	H	Millwall	W 3-0	1-0	12	Wood 3 [29, 62, 90]	17,901
6	18	A	Southampton	L 1-4	0-3	14	Wood [49]	22,155
7	24	H	Barnsley	D 1-1	0-1	16	Burke [86]	17,836
8	Oct 2	A	Nottingham F	W 3-1	0-1	17	Burke [75], Wood 2 [79, 88]	20,556
9	16	H	Leicester C	W 2-0	0-0	15	King (pen) [50], Wood [84]	17,102
10	23	A	Bristol C	W 2-0	1-0	11	Burke 2 [36, 90]	13,577
11	26	H	Leeds U	W 1-0	1-0	—	Zigic [35]	21,426
12	29	H	Brighton & HA	D 0-0	0-0	8		20,095
13	Nov 6	A	Reading	L 0-1	0-0	13		18,361
14	19	H	Peterborough U	D 1-1	1-0	13	King [22]	18,090
15	22	H	Burnley	W 2-1	1-0	—	Beausejour [2], Burke [90]	16,253
16	26	A	Blackpool	D 2-2	1-1	8	King [29], Zigic [87]	13,436
17	Dec 4	A	Cardiff C	L 0-1	0-0	14		22,010
18	7	A	Hull C	L 1-2	1-0	—	Wood [34]	17,438
19	10	H	Doncaster R	W 2-1	0-0	13	King 2 [62, 88]	17,369
20	19	A	Crystal Palace	L 0-1	0-0	—		12,057
21	26	H	West Ham U	D 1-1	0-1	15	Murphy [81]	20,214
22	31	H	Blackpool	W 3-0	1-0	12	Davies [45], King [52], Redmond [89]	19,995
23	Jan 2	A	Peterborough U	D 1-1	0-1	14	King (pen) [90]	11,167
24	11	H	Ipswich T	W 2-1	1-1	—	Zigic 2 [9, 90]	16,528
25	14	A	Millwall	W 6-0	1-0	7	Davies [18], King 2 [59, 83], Burke [74], Rooney [81], Redmond [90]	10,539
26	21	H	Watford	W 3-0	1-0	6	Davies 2 [35, 60], Burke [81]	18,681
27	31	A	Leeds U	W 4-1	1-1	—	Zigic 4 [31, 61, 64, 68]	19,628
28	Feb 4	H	Southampton	D 0-0	0-0	5		17,904
29	7	H	Portsmouth	W 1-0	0-0	—	Redmond [86]	16,930
30	14	H	Hull C	D 0-0	0-0	—		18,900
31	21	A	Barnsley	W 3-1	2-1	—	Edwards (og) [8], Fahey [27], Redmond [78]	9558
32	25	H	Nottingham F	L 1-2	0-1	5	Burke [55]	19,166
33	Mar 3	H	Derby Co	D 2-2	1-0	6	Huseklepp [19], King [57]	17,996
34	10	A	Coventry C	D 1-1	0-0	7	King [72]	22,240
35	13	A	Leicester C	L 1-3	1-1	—	Elliott (pen) [20]	21,092
36	17	H	Middlesbrough	W 3-0	1-0	4	Zigic [11], King [57], Fahey [60]	19,927
37	20	A	Portsmouth	L 1-4	1-0	—	Zigic [7]	12,186
38	25	H	Cardiff C	D 1-1	0-0	6	Huseklepp [68]	17,704
39	30	A	Doncaster R	W 3-1	1-1	—	Murphy [15], Burke [61], King [80]	8656
40	Apr 3	A	Burnley	W 3-1	1-0	—	King [11], Mutch [75], Murphy [88]	13,221
41	7	H	Crystal Palace	W 3-1	3-1	4	Burke [21], Fahey [22], Murphy [32]	21,932
42	9	A	West Ham U	D 3-3	3-1	4	Mutch [27], King [30], Burke [45]	31,045
43	14	H	Bristol C	D 2-2	1-2	4	King [44], Zigic [61]	23,230
44	17	A	Ipswich T	D 1-1	1-0	—	Burke [45]	16,503
45	21	A	Brighton & HA	D 1-1	0-0	5	Redmond [69]	20,594
46	28	H	Reading	W 2-0	1-0	4	Rooney [24], Elliott (pen) [75]	25,516

Final League Position: 4

GOALSCORERS

League (78): King 16 (2 pens), Burke 12, Zigic 11, Wood 9, Davies 5, Redmond 5, Fahey 4, Murphy 4, Rooney 4 (1 pen), Elliott 2 (2 pens), Huseklepp 2, Mutch 2, Beausejour 1, own goal 1.
Carling Cup (0).
FA Cup (6): Elliott 2, Rooney 2, Murphy 1, Redmond 1.
Europa League (11): King 2 (1 pen), Murphy 2, Wood 2, Beausejour 1, Burke 1, Elliott 1, Redmond 1, Rooney 1.
Play-Offs (2): Davies 1, Zigic 1.

Myhill B 42	Carr S 20	Ridgewell L 13 + 1	Caldwell S 43	Davies C 42	Gomis M 13 + 3	Burke C 45 + 1	Mutch J 18 + 3	Rooney A 6 + 12	Beausejour J 22	Fahey K 34 + 1	Wood C 13 + 10	Murphy D 30 + 3	Spector J 31	Redmond N 5 + 19	Jerome C — + 1	King M 37 + 3	Elliott W 15 + 14	Zigic N 20 + 15	Pablo 7 + 6	N'Daw G 17 + 2	Doyle C 4 + 1	Townsend A 11 + 4	Huseklepp E 4 + 7	Ramage P 14	Match No.
1	2	3	4	5	6	7	8	9	10	11^1	12														1
1	2	3	4	5	6	7	8	12	11	10	9^1														2
1	2		4	5		7		9	10	11	12	3	6^1	8											3
1	2	4		5		7		10^1	11		9	3	6	8	12										4
1	2	3	4	5	6^2	7		10^1	11		9		8			12	13								5
1	2	3	4	5	6	7		13	11		9		8^1			10^2	12								6
1	2	3	4	5^1		7			8		9^3	12	6^2	11		10	13	14							7
1		3	5		6	7			11	9	14	12	2^1			13	8^2	10^3	4						8
1	2	3	4		6	7			11^1	8	9^2					10	12	13	5						9
1	2	3	4	5	6	7			11	8	9^1	13				10^2		12							10
1	2	3	4	5		7			11	8	12		6			9^1		10							11
1	2	3	4	5		7		12	11	8	9^2		6			10^1		13							12
1	2	3	4	5		7				8	9		6	13		10^2	11^1	12							13
1	2		4	5		7			11^2	8	9^1	3	6			10	13	12							14
1	2		4	5		7			11^1	8	13	3	6	12		9^2		10							15
1	2		4	5		7			11^1	8	13	3	6			9	10^2	12							16
1	2		4	5■		7			11^2	8	14	3	6^3			9	13	10^1	12						17
1	2		4			7^3		14		8^2	9^1	3	6			10	11	12	5	13					18
1	2		4	5		7				13	9^3	3	6	12		10	11^1	14		8^2					19
1	2		4	5		7				8	14	3	6	10^3		9^1	13	12		11^2					20
1			4			7			11^2	8	9^1	3	2	13		10		12	5	6					21
1			4	5		7^1	13		11	8	14	3	2	12		9^3		10^2		6					22
1		14	4	5		7			11^1	8	13	3	2^3	12		9		10^2		6					23
1^6			4	5	6^2	7	13		11^1	8		3	2	12		9		10			15				24
1		3	4	5	12	7^3	6^1	13	11	8			2	14		9		10^2							25
1			4	5		7	6	12	11^3	8		3	2	14		9^1	13	10^2							26
1			4	5	6^2	7	8	12		11		3	2	13			9	10^1							27
1			4	5		7	8	10^1		11		3	2			9	12			6					28
1			4	5		7	8	10		11		3	2	13		9^2	12			6^1					29
1	2		4	5		7	8			10		3	6	12		9	11^1								30
1			4	5	6^1	7	8	12		10		3	2^3	13		9^2	11		14						31
1			4	5		7	6			8		3	2	13		9		10^1				11^2	12		32
1			4	5		7^2	8						2	13		9		12		6		11	10^1	3	33
1			4	5		7	13■			8			3			9^3	14	12		6^2		11	10^1	2	34
1			4	5		7				8			3^1			13	9	10^2	12	6		11	14	2^3	35
1			4	5		7				8		3				9^2	14	10	12	6		11^3	13	2^1	36
1			4	5		7		14		8^2		3■				9	12	10^3	13	6		11		2^1	37
1			4	5	13	7	8									9	11		2^2	6		12	10^1	3	38
1			4	5		7^2	8					3		14		9	12	10^3		6		11^1	13	2	39
1			4	5		7	8					3				9^2	11	10^1		6		12	13	2	40
1			4	5		7	6	14		8^2		3				9^3		10^1		13		11	12	2	41
1			4	5		7	8			10		3				9^2	11	12		6^1		13		2	42
			4	5	12	7	6			8^1		3		13		9		10^3			1	11^2	14	2	43
			4^1	5	6	7		14				3		13		9	8	10^3	12		1	11^2		2	44
				5	6^1	7	8					3		12		9^3	11	14	4		1	13	10^2	2	45
				5	8	13		12				3		7			9	10^1	4	6^2	1	11		2	46

FA Cup

Third Round	Wolverhampton W	(h)	0-0
		(a)	1-0
Fourth Round	Sheffield U	(a)	4-0
Fifth Round	Chelsea	(a)	1-1
		(h)	0-2

Carling Cup

Third Round	Manchester C	(a)	0-2

Play-Offs

Semi-Final	Blackpool	(a)	0-1
		(h)	2-2

Europa League

Play-Off Round	Nacional	(a)	0-0
		(h)	3-0
Group H	Braga	(h)	1-3
	Maribor	(a)	2-1
	Club Brugge	(a)	2-1
		(h)	2-2
	Braga	(a)	0-1
	Maribor	(h)	1-0

BLACKBURN ROVERS FL Championship

FOUNDATION

It was in 1875 that some public school old boys called a meeting at which the Blackburn Rovers club was formed and the colours blue and white adopted. The leading light was John Lewis, later to become a founder of the Lancashire FA, a famous referee who was in charge of two FA Cup finals, and a vice-president of both the FA and the Football League.

Ewood Park, Blackburn, Lancs BB2 4JF.

Telephone: (0871) 702 1875.

Fax: (01254) 671 042.

Ticket Office: (0871) 222 1444.

Website: www.rovers.co.uk

Email: enquiries@rovers.co.uk

Ground Capacity: 31,367.

Record Attendance: 62,522 v Bolton W, FA Cup 6th rd, 2 March 1929.

Pitch Measurements: 105m × 65.8m.

General Manager: Paul Agnew.

Manager: Steve Kean.

Assistant Manager: Eric Black.

Physio: Dave Fevre.

Colours: Blue and white halved shirts, white shorts, blue stockings.

Year Formed: 1875.

Turned Professional: 1880.

Club Nickname: Rovers.

HONOURS

FA Premier League: *Champions* 1994–95; *Runners-up* 1993–94.

Football League: Division 1: *Champions* 1911–12, 1913–14; *Runners-up* 2000–01; **Division 2:** ***Champions*** 1938–39; ***Runners-up*** 1957–58; **Division 3:** ***Champions*** 1974–75; ***Runners-up*** 1979–80.

FA Cup: ***Winners*** 1884, 1885, 1886, 1890, 1891, 1928; ***Runners-up*** 1882, 1960.

Football League Cup: ***Winners*** 2002.

Full Members' Cup: ***Winners*** 1987.

European Competitions
European Cup: 1995–96.
UEFA Cup: 1994–95, 1998–99, 2002–03, 2003–04, 2006–07, 2007–08.
Intertoto Cup: 2007.

Grounds: 1875, all matches played away; 1876, Oozehead Ground; 1877, Pleasington Cricket Ground; 1878, Alexandra Meadows; 1881, Leamington Road; 1890, Ewood Park.

First Football League Game: 15 September 1888, Football League, v Accrington (h) D 5–5 – Arthur; Beverley, James Southworth; Douglas, Almond, Forrest; Beresford (1), Walton, John Southworth (1), Fecitt (1), Townley (2).

Record League Victory: 9–0 v Middlesbrough, Division 2, 6 November 1954 – Elvy; Suart, Eckersley; Clayton, Kelly, Bell; Mooney (3), Crossan (2), Briggs, Quigley (3), Langton (1).

Record Cup Victory: 11–0 v Rossendale, FA Cup 1st rd, 13 October 1884 – Arthur; Hopwood, McIntyre; Forrest, Blenkhorn, Lofthouse; Sowerbutts (2), Jimmy Brown (1), Fecitt (4), Barton (3), Birtwistle (1).

sky SPORTS FACT FILE

The sole England international nicknamed "Jocky" was John Simpson, born in Pendleton but raised in Scotland. An outstanding winger for Falkirk with 115 League goals in under six seasons, he went to Blackburn Rovers in January 1911 and won eight full caps.

Record Defeat: 0–8 v Arsenal, Division 1, 25 February 1933.

Most League Points (2 for a win): 60, Division 3, 1974–75.

Most League Points (3 for a win): 91, Division 1, 2000–01.

Most League Goals: 114, Division 2, 1954–55.

Highest League Scorer in Season: Ted Harper, 43, Division 1, 1925–26.

Most League Goals in Total Aggregate: Simon Garner, 168, 1978–92.

Most League Goals in One Match: 7, Tommy Briggs v Bristol R, Division 2, 5 February 1955.

Most Capped Player: Henning Berg, 58 (100), Norway.

Most League Appearances: Derek Fazackerley, 596, 1970–86.

Youngest League Player: Harry Dennison, 16 years 155 days v Bristol C, 8 April 1911.

Record Transfer Fee Received: £18,000,000 from Manchester C for Roque Santa Cruz, June 2009.

Record Transfer Fee Paid: £7,500,000 to Manchester U for Andy Cole, December 2001.

Football League Record: 1888 Founder Member of the League; 1936–39 Division 2; 1946–48 Division 1; 1948–58 Division 2; 1958–66 Division 1; 1966–71 Division 2; 1971–75 Division 3; 1975–79 Division 2; 1979–80 Division 3; 1980–92 Division 2; 1992–99 FA Premier League; 1999–2001 Division 1; 2001–12 FA Premier League; 2012– FL C.

LATEST SEQUENCES

Longest Sequence of League Wins: 8, 1.3.1980 – 7.4.1980.

Longest Sequence of League Defeats: 7, 12.3.1966 – 16.4.1966.

Longest Sequence of League Draws: 5, 11.10.1975 – 1.11.1975.

Longest Sequence of Unbeaten League Matches: 23, 30.9.1987 – 27.3.1988.

Longest Sequence Without a League Win: 16, 11.11.1978 – 24.3.1979.

Successive Scoring Runs: 32 from 24.4.1954.

Successive Non-scoring Runs: 4 from 12.12.1908.

MANAGERS

Thomas Mitchell 1884–96
(*Secretary-Manager*)
J. Walmsley 1896–1903
((*Secretary-Manager*)
R. B. Middleton 1903–25
Jack Carr 1922–26
(*Team Manager under Middleton to 1925*)
Bob Crompton 1926–31
(*Hon. Team Manager*)
Arthur Barritt 1931–36
(*had been Secretary from 1927*)
Reg Taylor 1936–38
Bob Crompton 1938–41
Eddie Hapgood 1944–47
Will Scott 1947
Jack Bruton 1947–49
Jackie Bestall 1949–53
Johnny Carey 1953–58
Dally Duncan 1958–60
Jack Marshall 1960–67
Eddie Quigley 1967–70
Johnny Carey 1970–71
Ken Furphy 1971–73
Gordon Lee 1974–75
Jim Smith 1975–78
Jim Iley 1978
John Pickering 1978–79
Howard Kendall 1979–81
Bobby Saxton 1981–86
Don Mackay 1987–91
Kenny Dalglish 1991–95
Ray Harford 1995–96
Roy Hodgson 1997–98
Brian Kidd 1998–99
Graeme Souness 2000–04
Mark Hughes 2004–08
Paul Ince 2008
Sam Allardyce 2008–10
Steve Kean December 2010–

TEN YEAR LEAGUE RECORD

		P	W	D	L	F	A	Pts	Pos
2002-03	PR Lge	38	16	12	10	52	43	60	6
2003-04	PR Lge	38	12	8	18	51	59	44	15
2004-05	PR Lge	38	9	15	14	32	43	42	15
2005-06	PR Lge	38	19	6	13	51	42	63	6
2006-07	PR Lge	38	15	7	16	52	54	52	10
2007-08	PR Lge	38	15	13	10	50	48	58	7
2008-09	PR Lge	38	10	11	17	40	60	41	15
2009-10	PR Lge	38	13	11	14	41	55	50	10
2010-11	PR Lge	38	11	10	17	46	59	43	15
2011-12	PR Lge	38	8	7	23	48	78	31	19

DID YOU KNOW 

On 7 October 2011, Blackburn Rovers created history by becoming the first Premier League team to play in India. They defeated Pune 3-0 with two goals from Jason Roberts and one from Ruben Rochina. The match was completed in a downpour of torrential rain.

BLACKBURN ROVERS 2011–12 LEAGUE RECORD

Match No.	Date	Venue	Opponents	Result		H/T Score	Lg Pos.	Goalscorers	Attendance
1	Aug 13	H	Wolverhampton W	L	1-2	1-1	—	Formica [20]	21,996
2	20	A	Aston Villa	L	1-3	0-2	20	Pedersen [52]	32,319
3	27	H	Everton	L	0-1	0-0	19		22,826
4	Sept 11	A	Fulham	D	1-1	1-1	20	Rochina [32]	24,856
5	17	H	Arsenal	W	4-3	1-2	16	Yakubu 2 [25, 59], Song Billong (og) [50], Koscielny (og) [68]	22,637
6	24	A	Newcastle U	L	1-3	1-2	18	Hoilett [37]	46,236
7	Oct 1	H	Manchester C	L	0-4	0-0	19		24,760
8	15	A	QPR	D	1-1	1-1	20	Samba [24]	16,487
9	23	H	Tottenham H	L	1-2	1-1	20	Formica [28]	22,786
10	29	A	Norwich C	D	3-3	1-0	18	Hoilett [45], Yakubu [62], Samba [64]	26,440
11	Nov 5	H	Chelsea	L	0-1	0-0	19		21,985
12	19	A	Wigan Ath	D	3-3	1-2	19	Yakubu 2 (1 pen) [2, 90 (p)], Hoilett [59]	17,392
13	26	A	Stoke C	L	1-3	0-1	20	Rochina [86]	26,686
14	Dec 3	H	Swansea C	W	4-2	2-1	18	Yakubu 4 (1 pen) [20, 45, 57, 82 (p)]	23,080
15	11	A	Sunderland	L	1-2	1-0	19	Vukcevic [17]	39,863
16	17	H	WBA	L	1-2	0-0	19	Dann [72]	22,909
17	20	H	Bolton W	L	1-2	0-2	—	Yakubu [67]	25,570
18	26	A	Liverpool	D	1-1	1-0	20	Adam (og) [45]	44,441
19	31	A	Manchester U	W	3-2	1-0	19	Yakubu 2 (1 pen) [16 (p), 51], Hanley [80]	75,146
20	Jan 2	H	Stoke C	L	1-2	0-2	—	Goodwillie [69]	20,615
21	14	H	Fulham	W	3-1	1-0	17	Pedersen [45], Dunn [46], Formica [79]	18,003
22	21	A	Everton	D	1-1	0-1	18	Goodwillie [72]	32,464
23	Feb 1	H	Newcastle U	L	0-2	0-1	—		20,817
24	4	A	Arsenal	L	1-7	1-3	19	Pedersen [31]	59,643
25	11	H	QPR	W	3-2	3-0	17	Yakubu [15], N'Zonzi [23], Onuoha (og) [45]	20,252
26	25	A	Manchester C	L	0-3	0-1	18		46,782
27	Mar 3	H	Aston Villa	D	1-1	0-1	17	Dunn [85]	20,717
28	10	A	Wolverhampton W	W	2-0	1-0	16	Hoilett 2 [43, 69]	26,121
29	20	H	Sunderland	W	2-0	0-0	—	Hoilett [58], Yakubu [86]	20,056
30	24	A	Bolton W	L	1-2	0-2	16	N'Zonzi [56]	26,901
31	Apr 2	H	Manchester U	L	0-2	0-0	—		26,532
32	7	A	WBA	L	0-3	0-1	18		23,414
33	10	H	Liverpool	L	2-3	1-2	—	Yakubu 2 (1 pen) [36, 61 (p)]	23,571
34	14	A	Swansea C	L	0-3	0-2	19		18,985
35	21	H	Norwich C	W	2-0	1-0	18	Formica [41], Hoilett [49]	23,218
36	29	A	Tottenham H	L	0-2	0-1	19		35,798
37	May 7	H	Wigan Ath	L	0-1	0-0	—		26,144
38	13	A	Chelsea	L	1-2	0-2	19	Yakubu [60]	40,742

Final League Position: 19

GOALSCORERS

League (48): Yakubu 17 (4 pens), Hoilett 7, Formica 4, Pedersen 3, Dunn 2, Goodwillie 2, N'Zonzi 2, Rochina 2, Samba 2, Dann 1, Hanley 1, Vukcevic 1, own goals 4.
Carling Cup (10): Rochina 4, Givet 1, Goodwillie 1, Pedersen 1, Roberts 1 (pen), Vukcevic 1, Yakubu 1 (pen).
FA Cup (1): Goodwillie 1.

Robinson P 34	Salgado M 9	Olsson Martin 23 + 4	Dunn D 21 + 5	N'Zonzi S 31 + 1	Hanley G 19 + 4	Emerton B 2	Hoilett D 34	Roberts J 5 + 5	Formica M 25 + 9	Pedersen M 33	Rochina R 9 + 9	Goodwillie D 4 + 16	Blackman N — + 1	Nelsen R 1	Petrovic R 10 + 9	Givet G 21 + 1	Samba C 16	Dann S 27	Lowe J 30 + 2	Yakubu A 29 + 1	Vukcevic S 4 + 3	Grella V — + 1	Henley A 4 + 3	Bunn M 3	Morris J — + 2	Slew J — + 1	Modeste A 3 + 6	Orr B 10 + 2	Olsson Marcus 10 + 2	Kean J 1	Match No.
1	2	3	4	5	6	7¹	8	9	10³	11²	12	13	14																		1
1	2	3	4	7	6		8	9²	12	11¹		10		5	13																2
1	2	3	8¹	4		7	10	9³	12	11²		14			13	5	6														3
1	2	12	4²	8			7		11		9³	10			13	3	6¹	5	14												4
1	2¹	13		8			7		10³		11²				12	3	6	5	4	9	14										5
1	2	11▮		8			7	13	10²		12					3	4	5¹	6	9³		14									6
1				6			8		12	11		10¹			7	3	4	5	2	9											7
1	2	11		4			10	9¹				12			8	3	6	5	7												8
1		3		4			8	9³	10²	11	13	14				5	6		2	12	7¹										9
1		3	12	4			8³		10	11	7¹	13			14	5	6		2	9²											10
1		3	13	4	12		8		10	11	7²					5	6¹		2	9											11
1	2¹		8▮	4	6		10	14	13	11	7²					3³		5		9			12								12
1				4	6		8	12	10¹	11	7					3		5	2	9											13
1			4²				8	14	10	11	7¹				13	3	6	5	2	9³	12										14
1	2²	12³	8		13				10	11						3¹	6	5	4	9	7		14								15
1			8¹	4	13			12	10	3	7³	14					6	5	2	9	11²										16
1			8	4	5		7		10²	3	12	13					6		2	9	11¹										17
			8²	4	5		11¹		10	3		14			13		6		2	9³	12		7	1							18
				4	5				10²	3	7¹	13			11		6		2	9³			8	1	12	14					19
			8³	4	5				10	3	14	12			11¹	13	6		2	9			7²	1							20
1		3	8²	4	6		10		13	11		12			7¹	5			2	9▮											21
1		3	8¹	4			10		12	11		9²			7	5		6	2								13				22
1		3	8²	4			10		12	11	13				7¹	5		6	2								9				23
1		3	8²	4	13		10			11					7	5▮		6	2¹								9	12			24
1		3		7	6		8¹		10²	11		14						5	4	9³			12				13	2			25
1		3		12	5		6		10²	11	13				7¹			4		9								2	8		26
1		3	12	4	6		8		10²	11					7¹			5		9								2	13		27
1		3	12	4	6		8		10	11¹								5	2	9									7		28
1		3		4	6		8		10¹	11								5	2	9								12	7		29
1		3	12	4	6		8		10¹	11								5	2	9									7		30
1		3		4	6		10			11								5	2	9								7	8		31
1		3	8	4	6		10		13	11²								5	2¹	9							12▮	7			32
1		3	8²	4	6		7		10¹		12							5	13	9								2	11		33
1			8	4	6¹		10²		12	11		14						5	2	9³							13	7	3		34
1		12	8¹				7³		10	11					14	5		6	4	9²							13	2	3		35
1			8²				7		10	11		13				6		5	4	9¹							12	2	3		36
1		3	8¹				7			11		14			13	5²		6	4	9							10	2³	12		37
		3					8		10¹	11²	13	14				5		6	4	9³			2		12				7	1	38

FA Cup

Third Round	Newcastle U	(a)	1-2

Carling Cup

Second Round	Sheffield W	(h)	3-1
Third Round	Leyton Orient	(h)	3-2
Fourth Round	Newcastle U	(h)	4-3
Quarter-Final	Cardiff C	(a)	0-2

BLACKPOOL FL Championship

FOUNDATION

Old boys of St John's School, who had formed themselves into a football club, decided to establish a club bearing the name of their town and Blackpool FC came into being at a meeting at the Stanley Arms Hotel in the summer of 1887. In their first season playing at Raikes Hall Gardens, the club won both the Lancashire Junior Cup and the Fylde Cup.

Bloomfield Road, Seasiders Way, Blackpool FY1 6JJ.

Telephone: (0871) 6221 953.

Fax: (01253) 405 011.

Ticket Office: (0871) 6221 953.

Website: www.blackpoolfc.co.uk

Email: info@blackpoolfc.co.uk

Ground Capacity: 9,491.

Record Attendance: 38,098 v Wolverhampton W, Division 1, 17 September 1955.

Pitch Measurements: 110yd × 74yd.

Chairman: Karl Oyston.

Manager: Ian Holloway.

Assistant Manager: Steve Thompson.

Physio: Phil Horner.

Colours: Tangerine shirts with white trim, white shorts, tangerine stockings with white tops.

Year Formed: 1887.

Turned Professional: 1887.

Previous Name: 'South Shore' combined with Blackpool in 1899, twelve years after the latter had been formed on the breaking up of the old 'Blackpool St John's' club.

Club Nickname: 'The Seasiders'.

Grounds: 1887, Raikes Hall Gardens; 1897, Athletic Grounds; 1899, Raikes Hall Gardens; 1899, Bloomfield Road.

First Football League Game: 5 September 1896, Division 2, v Lincoln C (a) L 1–3 – Douglas; Parr, Bowman; Stuart, Stirzaker, Norris; Clarkin, Donnelly, Robert Parkinson, Mount (1), Jack Parkinson.

Record League Victory: 7–0 v Reading, Division 2, 10 November 1928 – Mercer; Gibson, Hamilton, Watson, Wilson, Grant, Ritchie, Oxberry (2), Hampson (5), Tufnell, Neal. 7–0 v Preston NE (away), Division 1, 1 May 1948 – Robinson; Shimwell, Crosland; Buchan, Hayward, Kelly; Hobson, Munro (1), McIntosh (5), McCall, Rickett (1). 7–0 v Sunderland, Division 1, 5 October 1957 – Farm; Armfield, Garrett, Kelly J, Gratrix, Kelly H, Matthews, Taylor (2), Charnley (2), Durie (2), Perry (1).

Record Cup Victory: 7–1 v Charlton Ath, League Cup 2nd rd, 25 September 1963 – Harvey; Armfield, Martin; Crawford, Gratrix, Cranston; Lea, Ball (1), Charnley (4), Durie (1), Oates (1).

HONOURS

Football League – Division 1: ***Runners-up*** 1955–56;
Division 2: ***Champions*** 1929–30; ***Runners-up*** 1936–37, 1969–70;
Division 4: ***Runners-up*** 1984–85.

FA Cup: ***Winners*** 1953; ***Runners-up*** 1948, 1951.

Football League Cup: Semi-final 1962.

Anglo-Italian Cup: ***Winners*** 1971; ***Runners-up*** 1972.

LDV Vans Trophy: ***Winners*** 2002, 2004.

sky SPORTS FACT FILE

The first Blackpool player to be awarded international honours was goalkeeper Fred Griffiths capped twice for Wales during 1899–1900, his only season with the club. In the First World War he enlisted in the Sherwood Foresters but sadly lost his life during the conflict.

Record Defeat: 1–10 v Small Heath, Division 2, 2 March 1901 and v Huddersfield T, Division 1, 13 December 1930.

Most League Points (2 for a win): 58, Division 2, 1929–30 and Division 2, 1967–68.

Most League Points (3 for a win): 86, Division 4, 1984–85.

Most League Goals: 98, Division 2, 1929–30.

Highest League Scorer in Season: Jimmy Hampson, 45, Division 2, 1929–30.

Most League Goals in Total Aggregate: Jimmy Hampson, 248, 1927–38.

Most League Goals in One Match: 5, Jimmy Hampson v Reading, Division 2, 10 November 1928; 5, Jimmy McIntosh v Preston NE, Division 1, 1 May 1948.

Most Capped Player: Jimmy Armfield, 43, England.

Most League Appearances: Jimmy Armfield, 568, 1952–71.

Youngest League Player: Matty Kay, 16 years 32 days v Scunthorpe U, 13 November 2005.

Record Transfer Fee Received: £1,750,000 from Southampton for Brett Ormerod, December 2001.

Record Transfer Fee Paid: £1,500,000 to Leicester C for D.J. Campbell, August 2010.

Football League Record: 1896 Elected to Division 2; 1899 Failed re-election; 1900 Re-elected; 1900–30 Division 2; 1930–33 Division 1; 1933–37 Division 2; 1937–67 Division 1; 1967–70 Division 2; 1970–71 Division 1; 1971–78 Division 2; 1978–81 Division 3; 1981–85 Division 4; 1985–90 Division 3; 1990–92 Division 4; 1992–2000 Division 2; 2000–01 Division 3; 2001–04 Division 2; 2004–07 FL 1; 2007–10 FL C; 2010–11 FA Premier League; 2011– FL C.

MANAGERS

Tom Barcroft 1903–33 (*Secretary-Manager*)
John Cox 1909–11
Bill Norman 1919–23
Maj. Frank Buckley 1923–27
Sid Beaumont 1927–28
Harry Evans 1928–33 (*Hon. Team Manager*)
Alex 'Sandy' Macfarlane 1933–35
Joe Smith 1935–58
Ronnie Suart 1958–67
Stan Mortensen 1967–69
Les Shannon 1969–70
Bob Stokoe 1970–72
Harry Potts 1972–76
Allan Brown 1976–78
Bob Stokoe 1978–79
Stan Ternent 1979–80
Alan Ball 1980–81
Allan Brown 1981–82
Sam Ellis 1982–89
Jimmy Mullen 1989–90
Graham Carr 1990
Bill Ayre 1990–94
Sam Allardyce 1994–96
Gary Megson 1996–97
Nigel Worthington 1997–99
Steve McMahon 2000–04
Colin Hendry 2004–05
Simon Grayson 2005–08
Ian Holloway May 2009–

LATEST SEQUENCES

Longest Sequence of League Wins: 9, 21.11.1936 – 1.1.1937.

Longest Sequence of League Defeats: 8, 26.11.1898 – 7.1.1899.

Longest Sequence of League Draws: 5, 4.12.1976 – 1.1.1977.

Longest Sequence of Unbeaten League Matches: 17, 6.4.1968 – 21.9.1968.

Longest Sequence Without a League Win: 19, 19.12.1970 – 24.4.1971.

Successive Scoring Runs: 33 from 23.2.1929.

Successive Non-scoring Runs: 5 from 12.4.1975.

TEN YEAR LEAGUE RECORD

		P	W	D	L	F	A	Pts	Pos
2002-03	Div 2	46	15	13	18	56	64	58	13
2003-04	Div 2	46	16	11	19	58	65	59	14
2004-05	FL 1	46	15	12	19	54	59	57	16
2005-06	FL 1	46	12	17	17	56	64	53	19
2006-07	FL 1	46	24	11	11	76	49	83	3
2007-08	FL C	46	12	18	16	59	64	54	19
2008-09	FL C	46	13	17	16	47	58	56	16
2009-10	FL C	46	19	13	14	74	58	70	6
2010-11	PR Lge	38	10	9	19	55	78	39	19
2011-12	FL C	46	20	15	11	79	59	75	5

DID YOU KNOW ?

Stanley Matthews had several deputies for his right-wing berth at Blackpool, but few emulated the one outing of 17-year-old Ken Booth on 6 October 1956 at Burnley. He scored once in a 2-2 draw (Jackie Mudie the other). He later played frequently for Bradford (PA), Workington and Southport.

BLACKPOOL 2011–12 LEAGUE RECORD

Match No.	Date	Venue	Opponents	Result		H/T Score	Lg Pos.	Goalscorers	Attendance
1	Aug 5	A	Hull C	W	1-0	0-0	—	Taylor-Fletcher [81]	18,907
2	14	H	Peterborough U	W	2-1	1-0	3	Phillips, K 2 [44, 48]	12,881
3	17	H	Derby Co	L	0-1	0-0	—		13,489
4	20	A	Brighton & HA	D	2-2	0-1	9	Phillips, K 2 [60, 90]	19,494
5	27	A	Crystal Palace	D	1-1	1-0	8	John-Baptiste [41]	14,776
6	Sept 10	H	Ipswich T	W	2-0	0-0	7	Taylor-Fletcher [49], Ferguson [60]	12,804
7	17	H	Cardiff C	D	1-1	0-0	7	Phillips, K [62]	12,798
8	24	A	Portsmouth	L	0-1	0-0	8		14,935
9	27	A	Coventry C	D	2-2	1-0	—	Taylor-Fletcher [18], Southern [90]	12,822
10	Oct 1	H	Bristol C	W	5-0	1-0	7	Taylor-Fletcher [37], Shelvey [66], Bogdanovic 2 [83, 90], Ormerod [89]	11,734
11	15	A	West Ham U	L	0-4	0-1	12		31,448
12	18	H	Doncaster R	W	2-1	0-1	—	Ince 2 [63, 90]	11,587
13	22	H	Nottingham F	L	1-2	1-1	12	Phillips, K [43]	13,520
14	29	A	Burnley	L	1-3	0-2	13	Shelvey [90]	15,614
15	Nov 2	A	Leeds U	W	5-0	3-0	—	Lua-Lua 2 [13, 65], Shelvey 3 (1 pen) [27 (p), 31, 78]	22,423
16	5	H	Millwall	W	1-0	0-0	5	Phillips, K [61]	12,455
17	19	A	Middlesbrough	D	2-2	1-1	7	Sylvestre [21], Shelvey [78]	18,128
18	26	H	Birmingham C	D	2-2	1-1	6	Crainey [31], Eardley [57]	13,436
19	29	A	Leicester C	L	0-2	0-1	—		21,578
20	Dec 3	H	Reading	W	1-0	0-0	7	McManaman [55]	11,656
21	10	A	Southampton	D	2-2	1-1	8	Basham [36], McManaman [49]	22,776
22	17	H	Watford	D	0-0	0-0	8		11,652
23	26	A	Barnsley	W	3-1	1-1	7	Phillips, M 3 (1 pen) [37, 67, 82 (p)]	11,776
24	31	A	Birmingham C	L	0-3	0-1	9		19,995
25	Jan 2	H	Middlesbrough	W	3-0	0-0	7	Phillips, M [50], Lua-Lua [57], Hines (og) [70]	13,449
26	14	A	Ipswich T	D	2-2	0-1	9	Grandin [65], Phillips, K [80]	16,497
27	21	H	Crystal Palace	W	2-1	0-1	7	Grandin [85], Basham [90]	12,053
28	31	H	Coventry C	W	2-1	0-0	—	Phillips, K [87], Taylor-Fletcher [90]	11,414
29	Feb 4	A	Cardiff C	W	3-1	0-0	4	Phillips, K [79], Phillips, M 2 [83, 90]	22,577
30	11	H	Portsmouth	D	1-1	0-1	5	Crainey [76]	12,545
31	14	A	Doncaster R	W	3-1	2-1	—	Taylor-Fletcher 2 [20, 34], Dicko [72]	8319
32	21	H	West Ham U	L	1-4	1-2	—	Phillips, K [45]	13,043
33	25	A	Bristol C	W	3-1	0-1	4	Ince 2 [55, 84], Phillips, K [87]	13,192
34	Mar 2	H	Hull C	D	1-1	1-0	—	Ince [27]	12,491
35	6	A	Derby Co	L	1-2	1-0	—	Ince [2]	26,320
36	10	A	Peterborough U	L	1-3	0-2	8	Dicko [80]	7540
37	17	H	Brighton & HA	W	3-1	2-1	5	Evatt [37], Phillips, K 2 [40, 80]	12,782
38	21	H	Leicester C	D	3-3	1-1	—	Phillips, K 2 [33, 90], Bednar [69]	12,485
39	24	A	Reading	L	1-3	1-2	7	Lua-Lua [41]	20,906
40	31	H	Southampton	W	3-0	2-0	5	Dobbie 2 (1 pen) [22 (p), 31], Evatt [52]	13,499
41	Apr 6	A	Watford	W	2-0	1-0	—	Dobbie 2 (1 pen) [25, 70 (p)]	16,314
42	9	H	Barnsley	D	1-1	0-0	5	Phillips, M [71]	13,525
43	14	A	Nottingham F	D	0-0	0-0	5		24,078
44	17	H	Leeds U	W	1-0	0-0	—	Angel [79]	14,134
45	21	H	Burnley	W	4-0	1-0	4	Dobbie [21], Taylor-Fletcher [47], Crainey [62], Dicko [80]	14,141
46	28	A	Millwall	D	2-2	1-1	5	Evatt [27], Dicko [71]	13,122

Final League Position: 5

GOALSCORERS

League (79): Phillips, K 16, Taylor-Fletcher 8, Phillips, M 7 (1 pen), Ince 6, Shelvey 6 (1 pen), Dobbie 5 (2 pens), Dicko 4, Lua-Lua 4, Crainey 3, Evatt 3, Basham 2, Bogdanovic 2, Grandin 2, McManaman 2, Angel 1, Bednar 1, Eardley 1, Ferguson 1, John-Baptiste 1, Ormerod 1, Southern 1, Sylvestre 1, own goal 1.
Carling Cup (0).
FA Cup (9): Phillips, M 4, LuaLua 2, Ince 1, Phillips, K 1 (pen), Sylvestre 1.
Play-Offs (4): Dobbie 1, Ince 1, Phillips, M 1, own goal 1.

Gilks M 42	John-Baptiste A 43	Crainey S 40 + 2	Ferguson B 40 + 2	Cathcart C 27	Evatt I 37 + 2	Southern K 24 + 1	Grandin E 4 + 3	Phillips K 20 + 18	Ormerod B 10 + 7	Taylor-Fletcher G 34 + 3	Clarke B 4 + 5	Sutherland C 2 + 5	Basham C 8 + 9	Phillips M 25 + 8	Hill M 4	Ince T 22 + 11	Eardley N 22 + 4	Sylvestre L 20 + 8	Bogdanovic D 1 + 7	Hurst J — + 2	Angel 10 + 5	Shelvey J 10	Lua-Lua L 18 + 11	McManaman C 9 + 5	Bruna G — + 1	Howard M 4	Wilson D 6	Fleck J 4 + 3	Bednar R 3 + 6	Dicko N 4 + 6	Dobbie S 5 + 2	Harris R 4 + 1	*Match No.*
1	2	3	4	5	6	7	8^3	9	10^1	11^2	12	13	14																				1
1	2	3	4	5	6	7	8^2	9^3	10^1	11	13	14		12																			2
1	2	3	4		6	7	8^2	9	10^1	11	12	14			5^3	13																	3
1	2	3	4		6	7		9	13	11	8^2	14	5^1	10^3			12																4
1	2	3	4	5	6	7		9	10^2	11	8^1					13		12															5
1	2		4^2	5	6	7		9	10	11^3	8^1			12	3			13	14														6
1	2	14	4	5^1	6	7		9	10	11	8^2			12	3^3					13													7
1	2	3	4	5	6	7		9		11^3				10^1		8^2		12	14	13													8
1	2	3	4	5	6^3	7		9		10^2		11		14			12		13		8^1												9
1	2	3	4	5	6	7		9^2	13	11^1		10^3				14			12			8											10
1	2	3	4		6	7		9^3	12	10					5	11^1			13			8^2	14										11
1	6	3	4	5		7		12	10^2	11						13	2		9^3			8^1		14									12
1	6	3	4	5	12			9		7		14				11^2	2^1					8		10^3	13								13
1	2	3	4	5	6	7		9^2	10^1							11^3			12			8	13	14									14
1	2	3	4	5	6	7^1										14		8	13		12	10	9^3	11^2									15
1	6	3	4	5		7^1		12					14				2	8^3			13	10	9^2	11									16
1	2	3	4	5	6	7		13		9^1	14			12				8^3				10		11^2									17
1	5	3	4		6					7^1				11^3		13	2	8			12	10	9^2	14									18
1	5^1	3	4		6			14		7			12	11			2	8^2				10	9^3	13									19
1		3	4	5	6			12		7			13	10			2	8^3			14		9^1	11^2									20
1		3	4	5	6			12		7			10^2	11^3		14	2	8					13	9^1									21
1		3	4	5	6			12		7	13		14	11			2	8^2					9^1	10^3									22
	2	3	4	5	6		12			7^3			14	11		13		8					9^1	10^2		1							23
	2	3	4■	5	6		11^2	14		9^3			12	7		13		8						10^1		1							24
	2	3		5	6			13					4	11		10	12	8^2			7^1		9^3	14		1							25
	5	3					14	13		12			7	11		10^3	2	8			4^2		9^1			1	6						26
1	2	3	4	5^1	6		13	14		9			12	11		10		8^2										7^3					27
1	2	3	4	5	6			12		7				11		10^3		8^1					9^2					13	14				28
1	6	3	4	5				12		9^3			7	11			14										2	8^1	13	10^2			29
1	2	3	4	5				13		12			7^3	11		10^1		14					8^2				6		9				30
1	5	3	4		6			13		9^2						12	2	8			14		10^1					7^3		11			31
1	2	3	4	5	6			12					7^1	11				8^2					9^3					10	14	13			32
1	2	3	4			14		9	12							11	5	8^1			7^3		13				6			10^2			33
1	5	3	4		13	7		9^3	8^2							11	2						14				6	12	10^1				34
1	5	3	4			7		9^3	8^1	13				12		11	2						14				6		10^2				35
1	2	3	4	5	6			12		7				11^3		10^2		8					9^1						13	14			36
1	5	3	4		6	8		9^3		7				11^1		10^2	2						14						13	12			37
1	5	3	4		6	8^1		9		7				11		10	2^2	12					14						13^3				38
1	2	3	4	5	6			9		11^2			7	13		14		8^1					10^3								12		39
1	5				6	4			12	9				11^2		10^3	2				7		14					13			8^1	3	40
1	5		12		6	4			14	9^1				11^2		10	2				7		13								8^3	3	41
1	5		12		6	4■								11		10	2	14			7^2		9^1							13	8^3	3	42
1	5	12	4		6				13	9				11		10^2	2				7		14								8^3	3^1	43
1	5	3	4		6					9^2				11		10^3	2	13			7		8^1							12		14	44
1	5	3	4		6			14		9^1				11^3		10	2	13			7									12	8^2		45
1	5	3			6	4		9^2					13	12		10	2	8^3					7^1							11	14		46

FA Cup

Third Round	Fleetwood T	(a)	5-1
Fourth Round	Sheffield W	(h)	1-1
		(a)	3-0
Fifth Round	Everton	(a)	0-2

Carling Cup

First Round	Sheffield W	(a)	0-0

Play-Offs

Semi-Final	Birmingham C	(h)	1-0
		(a)	2-2
Final *(at Wembley).*	West Ham U		1-2

BOLTON WANDERERS FL Championship

FOUNDATION

In 1874 boys of Christ Church Sunday School, Blackburn Street, led by their master Thomas Ogden, established a football club which went under the name of the school and whose president was vicar of Christ Church. Membership was 6d (two and a half pence). When their president began to lay down too many rules about the use of church premises, the club broke away and formed Bolton Wanderers in 1877, holding their earliest meetings at the Gladstone Hotel.

The Reebok Stadium, Burnden Way, Lostock, Bolton BL6 6JW.

Telephone: (0844) 871 2932. ***Fax:*** (01204) 673 773.

Ticket Office: (0844) 871 2932.

Website: www.bwfc.co.uk

Email: reception@bwfc.co.uk

Ground Capacity: 28,101.

Record Attendance: 69,912 v Manchester C, FA Cup 5th rd, 18 February 1933 (at Burnden Park); 28,353 v Leicester C, FA Premier League, 23 December 2003 (at The Reebok Stadium).

Pitch Measurements: 105m × 68m.

Chairman: Phil A. Gartside.

Vice Chairman: W. B. Warburton.

Manager: Owen Coyle.

Assistant Manager: Sandy Stewart.

Fitness Coaches: James Barrow and Mike Rawson.

Colours: White shirts with blue body trim, blue shorts, white stockings.

Year Formed: 1874.

Turned Professional: 1880.

Previous Name: 1874, Christ Church FC; 1877, Bolton Wanderers.

Club Nickname: 'The Trotters'.

Grounds: Park Recreation Ground and Cockle's Field before moving to Pike's Lane ground 1881; 1895, Burnden Park; 1997, Reebok Stadium.

First Football League Game: 8 September 1888, Football League, v Derby Co (h) L 3–6 – Harrison; Robinson, Mitchell; Roberts, Weir, Bullough, Davenport (2), Milne, Coupar, Barbour, Brogan (1).

Record League Victory: 8–0 v Barnsley, Division 2, 6 October 1934 – Jones; Smith, Finney; Goslin, Atkinson, George Taylor; George T. Taylor (2), Eastham, Milsom (1), Westwood (4), Cook, (1 og).

Record Cup Victory: 13–0 v Sheffield U, FA Cup 2nd rd, 1 February 1890 – Parkinson; Robinson (1), Jones; Bullough, Davenport, Roberts; Rushton, Brogan (3), Cassidy (5), McNee, Weir (4).

HONOURS

Football League – Division 1: ***Champions*** 1996–97;
Division 2: ***Champions*** 1908–09, 1977–78; ***Runners-up*** 1899–1900, 1904–05, 1910–11, 1934–35, 1992–93;
Division 3: ***Champions*** 1972–73.

FA Cup: ***Winners*** 1923, 1926, 1929, 1958; ***Runners-up*** 1894, 1904, 1953.

Football League Cup: ***Runners-up*** 1995, 2004.

Freight Rover Trophy: ***Runners-up*** 1986.

Sherpa Van Trophy: ***Winners*** 1989.

European Competitions
UEFA Cup: 2005–06, 2007–08.

sky SPORTS FACT FILE

Ted Vizard made an immediate impact during his first season with Bolton Wanderers at outside-left, helping them to win promotion in 1911 and being capped for Wales. Twenty-one years at Burnden Park, he survived the Great War and also became a successful League manager.

Record Defeat: 1–9 v Preston NE, FA Cup 2nd rd, 10 December 1887.

Most League Points (2 for a win): 61, Division 3, 1972–73.

Most League Points (3 for a win): 98, Division 1, 1996–97.

Most League Goals: 100, Division 1, 1996–97.

Highest League Scorer in Season: Joe Smith, 38, Division 1, 1920–21.

Most League Goals in Total Aggregate: Nat Lofthouse, 255, 1946–61.

Most League Goals in One Match: 5, Tony Caldwell v Walsall, Division 3, 10 September 1983.

Most Capped Player: Ricardo Gardner, 63 (109), Jamaica.

Most League Appearances: Eddie Hopkinson, 519, 1956–70.

Youngest League Player: Ray Parry, 15 years 267 days v Wolverhampton W, 13 October 1951.

Record Transfer Fee Received: £15,000,000 from Chelsea for Nicolas Anelka, January 2008.

Record Transfer Fee Paid: £8,200,000 to Toulouse for Johan Elmander, July 2008.

Football League Record: 1888 Founder Member of the League; 1899–1900 Division 2; 1900–03 Division 1; 1903–05 Division 2; 1905–08 Division 1; 1908–09 Division 2; 1909–10 Division 1; 1910–11 Division 2; 1911–33 Division 1; 1933–35 Division 2; 1935–64 Division 1; 1964–71 Division 2; 1971–73 Division 3; 1973–78 Division 2; 1978–80 Division 1; 1980–83 Division 2; 1983–87 Division 3; 1987–88 Division 4; 1988–92 Division 3; 1992–93 Division 2; 1993–95 Division 1; 1995–96 FA Premier League; 1996–97 Division 1; 1997–98 FA Premier League; 1998–2001 Division 1; 2001–12 FA Premier League; 2012– FL C.

LATEST SEQUENCES

Longest Sequence of League Wins: 11, 5.11.1904 – 2.1.1905.

Longest Sequence of League Defeats: 11, 7.4.1902 – 18.10.1902.

Longest Sequence of League Draws: 6, 25.1.1913 – 8.3.1913.

Longest Sequence of Unbeaten League Matches: 23, 13.10.1990 – 9.3.1991.

Longest Sequence Without a League Win: 26, 7.4.1902 – 10.1.1903.

Successive Scoring Runs: 24 from 22.11.1996.

Successive Non-scoring Runs: 5 from 3.1.1898.

MANAGERS

Tom Rawthorne 1874–85 (*Secretary*)
J. J. Bentley 1885–86 (*Secretary*)
W. G. Struthers 1886–87 (*Secretary*)
Fitzroy Norris 1887 (*Secretary*)
J. J. Bentley 1887–95 (*Secretary*)
Harry Downs 1895–96 (*Secretary*)
Frank Brettell 1896–98 (*Secretary*)
John Somerville 1898–1910
Will Settle 1910–15
Tom Mather 1915–19
Charles Foweraker 1919–44
Walter Rowley 1944–50
Bill Ridding 1951–68
Nat Lofthouse 1968–70
Jimmy McIlroy 1970
Jimmy Meadows 1971
Nat Lofthouse 1971 (*then Admin. Manager to 1972*)
Jimmy Armfield 1971–74
Ian Greaves 1974–80
Stan Anderson 1980–81
George Mulhall 1981–82
John McGovern 1982–85
Charlie Wright 1985
Phil Neal 1985–92
Bruce Rioch 1992–95
Roy McFarland 1995–96
Colin Todd 1996–99
McFarland and Todd joint managers 1995–96
Sam Allardyce 1999–2007
Sammy Lee 2007
Gary Megson 2007–09
Owen Coyle January 2010–

TEN YEAR LEAGUE RECORD

		P	W	D	L	F	A	Pts	Pos
2002-03	PR Lge	38	10	14	14	41	51	44	17
2003-04	PR Lge	38	14	11	13	48	56	53	8
2004-05	PR Lge	38	16	10	12	49	44	58	6
2005-06	PR Lge	38	15	11	12	49	41	56	8
2006-07	PR Lge	38	16	8	14	47	52	56	7
2007-08	PR Lge	38	9	10	19	36	54	37	16
2008-09	PR Lge	38	11	8	19	41	53	41	13
2009-10	PR Lge	38	10	9	19	42	67	39	14
2010-11	PR Lge	38	12	10	16	52	56	46	14
2011-12	PR Lge	38	10	6	22	46	77	36	18

DID YOU KNOW ?

Bolton Wanderers registered their 4000th goal in the top flight on 31 January 2009 against Tottenham Hotspur. Bolton won 3-2 but it was the first goal scored by Sebastien Puygrenier, a French-born defender on loan from Russia's Zenit St Petersburg, which was the landmark.

BOLTON WANDERERS 2011–12 LEAGUE RECORD

Match No.	Date	Venue	Opponents	Result	H/T Score	Lg Pos.	Goalscorers	Attendance
1	Aug 13	A	QPR	W 4-0	1-0	—	Cahill [45], Gabbidon (og) [67], Klasnic [70], Muamba [79]	15,195
2	21	H	Manchester C	L 2-3	1-2	7	Klasnic [39], Davies, K [63]	24,273
3	27	A	Liverpool	L 1-3	0-1	10	Klasnic [90]	44,725
4	Sept 10	H	Manchester U	L 0-5	0-3	13		25,944
5	17	H	Norwich C	L 1-2	0-2	19	Petrov (pen) [64]	21,223
6	24	A	Arsenal	L 0-3	0-0	20		59,727
7	Oct 2	H	Chelsea	L 1-5	0-4	20	Boyata [46]	24,657
8	15	A	Wigan Ath	W 3-1	2-1	18	Caldwell (og) [4], N'Gog [45], Eagles [90]	17,261
9	22	H	Sunderland	L 0-2	0-0	18		24,349
10	29	A	Swansea C	L 1-3	0-0	19	Graham (og) [73]	19,477
11	Nov 6	H	Stoke C	W 5-0	2-0	18	Davies, K [2], Eagles 2 [23, 73], Klasnic 2 [61, 81]	20,028
12	19	A	WBA	L 1-2	1-1	18	Klasnic (pen) [21]	26,221
13	26	H	Everton	L 0-2	0-0	18		24,058
14	Dec 3	A	Tottenham H	L 0-3	0-1	19		35,896
15	10	H	Aston Villa	L 1-2	0-2	20	Klasnic [55]	20,285
16	17	A	Fulham	L 0-2	0-2	20		25,643
17	20	A	Blackburn R	W 2-1	2-0	—	Davies, M [5], Reo-Coker [30]	25,570
18	26	H	Newcastle U	L 0-2	0-0	19		26,080
19	31	H	Wolverhampton W	D 1-1	1-0	20	Ricketts [22]	20,354
20	Jan 4	A	Everton	W 2-1	0-0	—	N'Gog [67], Cahill [78]	29,561
21	14	A	Manchester U	L 0-3	0-1	19		75,444
22	21	H	Liverpool	W 3-1	2-1	17	Davies, M [4], Reo-Coker [29], Steinsson [50]	26,854
23	Feb 1	H	Arsenal	D 0-0	0-0	—		24,371
24	4	A	Norwich C	L 0-2	0-0	18		26,358
25	11	H	Wigan Ath	L 1-2	0-1	19	Davies, M [67]	23,450
26	25	A	Chelsea	L 0-3	0-0	19		40,999
27	Mar 3	A	Manchester C	L 0-2	0-1	19		47,219
28	10	H	QPR	W 2-1	1-0	17	Pratley [37], Klasnic [86]	21,551
29	24	H	Blackburn R	W 2-1	2-0	17	Wheater 2 [28, 35]	26,901
30	31	A	Wolverhampton W	W 3-2	0-0	16	Petrov (pen) [63], Alonso [80], Davies, K [84]	25,215
31	Apr 7	H	Fulham	L 0-3	0-2	16		21,939
32	9	A	Newcastle U	L 0-2	0-0	—		52,264
33	21	H	Swansea C	D 1-1	1-1	19	Eagles [14]	25,401
34	24	A	Aston Villa	W 2-1	0-0	—	Petrov (pen) [62], N'Gog [63]	32,263
35	28	A	Sunderland	D 2-2	1-1	18	Davies, K 2 [26, 70]	40,768
36	May 2	H	Tottenham H	L 1-4	0-1	—	Reo-Coker [51]	22,349
37	6	H	WBA	D 2-2	1-0	18	Petrov (pen) [24], Jones (og) [72]	25,662
38	13	A	Stoke C	D 2-2	2-1	18	Davies, M [39], Davies, K [45]	27,789

Final League Position: 18

GOALSCORERS

League (46): Klasnic 8 (1 pen), Davies, K 6, Davies, M 4, Eagles 4, Petrov 4 (4 pens), N'Gog 3, Reo-Coker 3, Cahill 2, Wheater 2, Alonso 1, Boyata 1, Muamba 1, Pratley 1, Ricketts 1, Steinsson 1, own goals 4.
Carling Cup (5): Eagles 1, Kakuta 1, Muamba 1, Petrov 1, Tuncay 1.
FA Cup (9): Davies, K 2, Eagles 1, Klasnic 1, Miyaichi 1, N'Gog 1, Petrov 1, Pratley 1, Wheater 1.

Jaaskelainen J 18	Steinsson G 20 + 3	Robinson P 15 + 2	Muamba F 18 + 2	Cahill G 19	Knight Z 21 + 4	Eagles C 26 + 8	Reo-Coker N 37	Klasnic I 16 + 13	Davies K 21 + 10	Petrov M 30 + 1	Davies M 29 + 6	Pratley D 14 + 11	Blake R — + 1	Tuncay S 3 + 13	Boyata D 13 + 1	N'Gog D 24 + 9	Wheater D 24	Bogdan A 20	Gardner R 2 + 2	Kakuta G — + 4	Riley J 2 + 1	Alonso M 4 + 1	Ricketts S 20	Mears T 1	Sordell M — + 3	Miyaichi R 8 + 4	Ream T 13	Vela J — + 3	Lee C — + 2	*Match No.*
1	2	3	4	5	6	7^{1}	8^{2}	9^{3}	10	11	12	13	14																	1
1	2	3	4^{1}	5	6	7^{2}	8	9	10	11	12	13																		2
1	2	3	4^{1}	5	6	7^{2}	8	9	10^{3}	11	12	14		13																3
1		3		5	6	7^{1}	8	9^{3}	10^{2}	11	4	12		14	2	13														4
1		3		5	6	12	8	9■	10^{2}	11	14	4^{3}		7^{1}	2	13														5
1	2	3	4^{2}		6	7^{3}	8		12	10	14	11			13	9^{1}	5■													6
	2^{1}	3		5	12	13	8		10	11		4		14	6	9^{3}		1	7^{2}											7
1		3		5		7^{3}	4	12	10	11^{2}	14	8			2	9^{1}	6		13											8
1		3		5		7	8	13	10^{2}	11^{3}		4			2^{1}	9	6		12	14										9
1	2	12		5		7	8	13		10^{1}	11	4^{2}				9^{3}	6		3■	14										10
1		3	4	5	14	11	8^{2}	9^{1}	10		7	13		12			6				2^{3}									11
1		3	4^{3}	5		7^{1}	8	9	10^{2}	12	11					13	6			14	2									12
1	13	3	4^{1}	5	6	11	8^{2}	9	10^{3}		7	12		14			2■													13
1	12	3	4^{1}	5■	6	11	8	9^{3}	10^{2}		7	13			2	14														14
1		3		5	6	11		9^{2}	10		7	4		8^{1}	2	13				12										15
1	12		4	5	6	13	8	9	10^{3}		11	7^{2}			2^{1}	14						3								16
1	2	12	4	5	6		8	9^{3}		11	7	14		13		10^{2}						3^{1}								17
1		3	4^{1}	5	6	12	8	9^{3}	13	11	7			14	2	10^{2}														18
1	2		4	5	6		8	9^{1}	13	11	7			12		10^{2}							3							19
	2		4	5	6	9^{1}	8		13	11	7	12				10^{2}		1					3							20
	2		4^{2}		5	7^{1}	8			11^{3}	10	13		14		9	6	1			12		3							21
	2		4		5	7^{2}	8		12	11	10			13		9^{1}	6	1					3							22
	2		4		5	7	8^{3}		12	11^{2}	10	14		13		9^{1}	6	1					3							23
			4^{1}		5	7^{2}	8		12	11	10			13		9^{3}	6	1					3	2	14					24
	2				5	7^{2}	4	14	10^{3}	11^{1}	8			13		9	6	1					3			12				25
	2		4			13	8					11		7^{2}		9^{1}	6	1					3		12	10	5			26
	2		12		5		8				7	11^{1}				9	6	1					3			10	4			27
	2		14			12	8	13		11^{1}	7	4^{2}				9^{3}	5	1					3			10	6			28
	2						8	12		11	7	4				9^{1}	5	1					3			10	6			29
					14	13	4	10^{1}	12	11	7					9^{3}	6	1				2	3			8^{2}	5			30
						12	8	14	13	11	7	4^{1}				9^{3}	6	1				2	3			10^{2}	5			31
	2					9^{2}	8	14	10^{1}	11	7	4^{3}				12	6	1					3			13	5			32
	2					8	4	13	10^{2}	11	7^{3}					12	6	1					3			9^{1}	5	14		33
	2					10^{3}	4	13	12	11	7					9^{2}	6	1				14	3			8^{1}	5			34
						8^{1}	4^{3}	12	10	11	7				2	9^{2}	6	1					3			13	5	14		35
						8^{3}	4^{1}	12	10	11	7				2	9^{2}	6	1					3			14	5	13		36
					12	8	4	13	10	11^{3}	7				2	9^{2}	6^{1}	1					3				5		14	37
					6	8^{2}	4	9^{1}	10^{3}	11	7				2	12		1					3		14		5		13	38

FA Cup

Third Round	Macclesfield T	(a)	2-2
		(h)	2-0
Fourth Round	Swansea C	(h)	2-1
Fifth Round	Millwall	(a)	2-0
Quarter-Final	Tottenham H	(a)	1-3

Carling Cup

Second Round	Macclesfield T	(h)	2-1
Third Round	Aston Villa	(a)	2-0
Fourth Round	Arsenal	(a)	1-2

AFC BOURNEMOUTH FL Championship 1

FOUNDATION

There was a Bournemouth FC as early as 1875, but the present club arose out of the remnants of the Boscombe St John's club (formed 1890). The meeting at which Boscombe FC came into being was held at a house in Gladstone Road in 1899. They began by playing in the Boscombe and District Junior League.

Seward Stadium, Kings Park, Bournemouth, Dorset BH7 7AF.

Telephone: (0844) 576 1910.

Fax: (01202) 726 373.

Ticket Office: (0844) 576 1910.

Website: www.afcb.co.uk

Email: enquiries@afcb.co.uk

Ground Capacity: 10,375 (with temporary stand, 9,776 without).

Record Attendance: 28,799 v Manchester U, FA Cup 6th rd, 2 March 1957.

Pitch Measurements: 105m × 78m.

Chairmen: Eddie Mitchell and Maxim Demin.

Chief Executive: Neill Blake.

Manager: Paul Groves.

Assistant Manager: Shaun Brooks.

Physio: Steve Hard.

Colours: Red shirts with thin black vertical stripes, black shorts, black stockings.

Year Formed: 1899.

Turned Professional: 1910.

Previous Names: 1890, Boscombe St John's; 1899, Boscombe FC; 1923, Bournemouth & Boscombe Ath FC; 1971, AFC Bournemouth.

Club Nickname: 'Cherries'.

Grounds: 1899, Castlemain Road, Pokesdown; 1910, Dean Court.

First Football League Game: 25 August 1923, Division 3 (S), v Swindon T (a) L 1–3 – Heron; Wingham, Lamb; Butt, Charles Smith, Voisey; Miller, Lister (1), Davey, Simpson, Robinson.

Record League Victory: 7–0 v Swindon T, Division 3 (S), 22 September 1956 – Godwin; Cunningham, Keetley; Clayton, Crosland, Rushworth; Siddall (1), Norris (2), Arnott (1), Newsham (2), Cutler (1). 10–0 win v Northampton T at start of 1939–40 expunged from the records on outbreak of war.

Record Cup Victory: 11–0 v Margate, FA Cup 1st rd, 20 November 1971 – Davies; Machin (1), Kitchener, Benson, Jones, Powell, Cave (1), Boyer, MacDougall (9 incl. 1p), Miller, Scott (De Garis).

Record Defeat: 0–9 v Lincoln C, Division 3, 18 December 1982.

HONOURS

Football League:
Division 3: ***Champions*** 1986–87;
Division 3 (S): ***Runners-up*** 1947–48;
Division 4: ***Runners-up*** 1970–71.
FL 2: ***Runners-up*** 2009–10.

FA Cup: Best season: 6th rd, 1957.

Football League Cup: Best season: 4th rd, 1962, 1964.

Associate Members' Cup: ***Winners*** 1984.

Auto Windscreens Shield: ***Runners-up*** 1998.

sky SPORTS FACT FILE

Bournemouth completed a club record 33 League matches at home without defeat from 7 April 1962 until 19 October 1963. Fourteen of these games ended in draws, the team remained unbeaten at Dean Court throughout 1962–63 when finishing fifth in Division Three.

Most League Points (2 for a win): 62, Division 3, 1971–72.

Most League Points (3 for a win): 97, Division 3, 1986–87.

Most League Goals: 88, Division 3 (S), 1956–57.

Highest League Scorer in Season: Ted MacDougall, 42, 1970–71.

Most League Goals in Total Aggregate: Ron Eyre, 202, 1924–33.

Most League Goals in One Match: 4, Jack Russell v Clapton Orient, Division 3 (S), 7 January 1933; 4, Jack Russell v Bristol C, Division 3 (S), 28 January 1933; 4, Harry Mardon v Southend U, Division 3 (S), 1 January 1938; 4, Jack McDonald v Torquay U, Division 3 (S), 8 November 1947; 4, Ted MacDougall v Colchester U, 18 September 1970; 4, Brian Clark v Rotherham U, 10 October 1972; 4, Luther Blissett v Hull C, 29 November 1988; 4, James Hayter v Bury, Division 2, 21 October 2000.

Most Capped Player: Gerry Peyton, 7 (33), Republic of Ireland.

Most League Appearances: Steve Fletcher, 617, 1992–2007; 2008–12.

Youngest League Player: Jimmy White, 15 years 321 days v Brentford, 30 April 1958.

Record Transfer Fee Received: £800,000 from Everton for Joe Parkinson, March 1994; £800,000 from Ipswich T for Matt Holland, July 1997.

Record Transfer Fee Paid: £210,000 to Gillingham for Gavin Peacock, August 1989.

Football League Record: 1923 Elected to Division 3 (S) and remained a Third Division club for record number of years until 1970; 1970–71 Division 4; 1971–75 Division 3; 1975–82 Division 4; 1982–87 Division 3; 1987–90 Division 2; 1990–92 Division 3; 1992–2002 Division 2; 2002–03 Division 3; 2003–04 Division 2; 2004–08 FL 1; 2008–10 FL 2; 2010– FL 1.

MANAGERS

Vincent Kitcher 1914–23
(*Secretary-Manager*)
Harry Kinghorn 1923–25
Leslie Knighton 1925–28
Frank Richards 1928–30
Billy Birrell 1930–35
Bob Crompton 1935–36
Charlie Bell 1936–39
Harry Kinghorn 1939–47
Harry Lowe 1947–50
Jack Bruton 1950–56
Fred Cox 1956–58
Don Welsh 1958–61
Bill McGarry 1961–63
Reg Flewin 1963–65
Fred Cox 1965–70
John Bond 1970–73
Trevor Hartley 1974–75
John Benson 1975–78
Alec Stock 1979–80
David Webb 1980–82
Don Megson 1983
Harry Redknapp 1983–92
Tony Pulis 1992–94
Mel Machin 1994–2000
Sean O'Driscoll 2000–06
Kevin Bond 2006–08
Jimmy Quinn 2008
Eddie Howe 2008–11
Lee Bradbury 2011–12
Paul Groves March 2012–

LATEST SEQUENCES

Longest Sequence of League Wins: 7, 22.8.1970 – 23.9.1970.

Longest Sequence of League Defeats: 7, 13.8.1994 – 13.9.1994.

Longest Sequence of League Draws: 5, 25.4.2000 – 12.8.2000.

Longest Sequence of Unbeaten League Matches: 18, 6.3.1982 – 28.8.1982.

Longest Sequence Without a League Win: 14, 6.3.1974 – 27.4.1974.

Successive Scoring Runs: 31 from 28.10.2000.

Successive Non-scoring Runs: 6 from 1.2.1975.

TEN YEAR LEAGUE RECORD

		P	*W*	*D*	*L*	*F*	*A*	*Pts*	*Pos*
2002-03	Div 3	46	20	14	12	60	48	74	4
2003-04	Div 2	46	17	15	14	56	51	66	9
2004-05	FL 1	46	20	10	16	77	64	70	8
2005-06	FL 1	46	12	19	15	49	53	55	17
2006-07	FL 1	46	13	13	20	50	64	52	19
2007-08	FL 1	46	17	7	22	62	72	48*	21
2008-09	FL 2	46	17	12	17	59	51	46†	21
2009-10	FL 2	46	25	8	13	61	44	83	2
2010-11	FL 1	46	19	14	13	75	54	71	6
2011-12	FL 1	46	15	13	18	48	52	58	11

**10 pts deducted; †17 points deducted.*

DID YOU KNOW ?

Golden Goals are nothing new. In 1945–46 Bournemouth met Queens Park Rangers in a Third Division (South) Cup semi-final. No goals were scored in 90 minutes or three periods of extra time, so it was agreed on the first goal. Jack Kirkham did it for the Cherries after 136 minutes.

AFC BOURNEMOUTH 2011–12 LEAGUE RECORD

Match No.	*Date*	*Venue*	*Opponents*	*Result*	*H/T Score*	*Lg Pos.*	*Goalscorers*	*Attendance*
1	Aug 6	A	Charlton Ath	L 0-3	0-1	—		16,111
2	13	H	Sheffield W	W 2-0	1-0	11	Barrett [38], Arter [83]	6901
3	16	H	Stevenage	L 1-3	0-1	—	Arter [47]	5574
4	20	A	Carlisle U	L 1-2	0-0	20	Arter (pen) [61]	4422
5	27	H	Walsall	L 0-2	0-1	21		5092
6	Sept 3	A	Notts Co	L 1-3	0-1	21	Pugh [71]	5510
7	10	H	Chesterfield	L 0-3	0-1	23		4989
8	13	A	Leyton Orient	W 3-1	1-1	—	Arter (pen) [20], Thomas, W [74], Pugh [81]	3258
9	17	A	Exeter C	W 2-0	1-0	17	Thomas, W [38], Duffy (og) [90]	4593
10	24	H	Hartlepool U	L 1-2	1-1	18	Gregory [37]	5275
11	Oct 1	A	Tranmere R	D 0-0	0-0	20		4179
12	8	H	Rochdale	D 1-1	0-1	20	Symes (pen) [68]	5345
13	15	A	Milton Keynes D	D 2-2	0-1	20	Thomas, W 2 [61, 73]	8927
14	22	H	Bury	L 1-2	1-1	21	Pugh [41]	6122
15	25	A	Colchester U	D 1-1	1-0	—	Thomas, W [1]	3444
16	29	A	Preston NE	W 3-1	0-1	18	Thomas, W [48], Malone [57], Pugh [68]	10,185
17	Nov 5	H	Scunthorpe U	W 2-0	1-0	16	Malone [20], Thomas, W [73]	5478
18	19	A	Wycombe W	W 1-0	1-0	16	Pugh [23]	5350
19	26	H	Oldham Ath	D 0-0	0-0	15		5478
20	Dec 10	A	Huddersfield T	W 1-0	1-0	14	Arter [19]	13,930
21	17	H	Sheffield U	L 0-2	0-1	16		7260
22	26	A	Brentford	D 1-1	1-0	15	Sheringham [19]	6338
23	31	A	Yeovil T	W 3-1	2-0	13	Gregory [6], Fogden [26], Daniels [74]	5632
24	Jan 2	H	Wycombe W	W 2-0	1-0	10	Thomas, W [27], Symes [50]	7202
25	7	A	Walsall	D 2-2	0-2	—	Symes (pen) [62], Fletcher [90]	3658
26	14	H	Notts Co	W 2-1	1-1	9	Thomas, W [21], Fogden [83]	6529
27	21	H	Tranmere R	W 2-1	2-1	8	Thomas, W [18], Pugh [30]	5807
28	27	A	Chesterfield	L 0-1	0-0	—		6958
29	Feb 7	H	Exeter C	W 2-0	0-0	—	Tubbs [72], Malone [78]	5497
30	11	A	Hartlepool U	D 0-0	0-0	—		4548
31	14	H	Leyton Orient	L 1-2	1-1	—	Pugh [34]	5412
32	18	A	Rochdale	L 0-1	0-0	8		2499
33	25	H	Milton Keynes D	L 0-1	0-1	10		6419
34	Mar 3	H	Charlton Ath	L 0-1	0-0	12		8034
35	10	A	Sheffield W	L 0-3	0-3	12		19,416
36	17	H	Carlisle U	D 1-1	0-1	13	Addison [83]	5240
37	20	H	Brentford	W 1-0	1-0	—	Fogden [45]	4563
38	24	A	Oldham Ath	L 0-1	0-0	13		4459
39	27	A	Stevenage	D 2-2	2-2	—	Thomas, W [18], Malone [36]	2550
40	31	H	Yeovil T	D 0-0	0-0	12		6170
41	Apr 7	A	Sheffield U	L 1-2	0-1	13	Hines [67]	18,817
42	9	H	Huddersfield T	W 2-0	0-0	11	Malone [72], Pugh [82]	5500
43	14	A	Bury	L 0-1	0-1	12		2729
44	21	H	Colchester U	D 1-1	1-0	13	MacDonald [11]	5109
45	28	A	Scunthorpe U	D 1-1	1-0	14	McDermott [42]	4422
46	May 5	H	Preston NE	W 1-0	0-0	11	Daniels (pen) [51]	6267

Final League Position: 11

GOALSCORERS

League (48): Thomas, W 11, Pugh 8, Arter 5 (2 pens), Malone 5, Fogden 3, Symes 3 (2 pens), Daniels 2 (1 pen), Gregory 2, Addison 1, Barrett 1, Fletcher 1, Hines 1, MacDonald 1, McDermott 1, Sheringham 1, Tubbs 1, own goal 1.
Carling Cup (6): Taylor 2, Cooper 1, Feeney 1, Lovell 1, Pugh 1.
FA Cup (5): Arter 1, Malone 1, Purches 1, Zubar 1, own goal 1.
J Paint Trophy (7): Pugh 3, Stockley 2, MacDonald 1, own goal 1.

Flahavan D 44	Byrne N 9	Malone S 28 + 4	Cooper S 25 + 1	Barrett A 21	Baudry M 5 + 2	Gregory S 23 + 5	Arter H 28 + 6	Ings D 1	Pugh M 42	Feeney L 5	Taylor L 7 + 11	Molesley M 4 + 7	Fletcher S 2 + 18	Doble R 4 + 3	Cummings W 10 + 4	Lovell S 1 + 1 / Wakefield J — + 2	MacDonald S 22 + 3	Stockley J 1 + 9	Purches S 20 + 4	Thomas W 36	Carmichael J — + 1	Peters J 8	Zubar S 17 + 5	Symes M 7 + 8	Partington J 1 + 4	Fogden W 20 + 7	Sheringham C 2 + 4	Cook S 26	Francis S 29	Daniels C 20 + 1	Jalal S 2 + 1	Parsons A — + 1	McDermott D 10 + 4	Tubbs M 5 + 2	Strugnell D — + 1	Addison M 14	Hines Z 7 + 1	*Match No.*
1	2	3	4	5	6^1	7^2	8	9^3	10	11	12	13	14																									1
1	2	3	4	5	14	6^3	12		7	11	9^2	8^1	13	10																								2
1	2	3	4	5	13	6^1	12		7^3	11	9^2	8	14	10																								3
1	2	11	4		5		6			7	9^2	8	13	10^1	3	12																						4
1	2	3^3	4	5			8		7	11	9^1	13				10^2	6	12	14																			5
1	11		4	5			8		7		9^1	13	10^2		3		6	12	2																			6
1	11^2	3	4	5			8		7			12	14	10^3			6^1	13	2	9																		7
1	11	3	12	5	6	7^2	8		10			4^1	14	13					2	9^3																		8
1	7^3	3	4	5^2	6	11	8^1		10					12	13				2	9	14																	9
1		3	4		5	7	6		8				10^1		14			12	2^2	9		11^3	13															10
1		3^1	4	5		7	8		10					12	13				2	9^2		11	6															11
1			4^2	5		7^1	8		10						3				2	9		11^3	6	12	13	14												12
1			4^1	5		7	8		10						3				2	9^2		11^3	6	12	13	14												13
1				5		7	4^1		8				14		3				2	9		11	6	10^3	12^2	13												14
1		4		5		7			10						3				2	9^2		11	6	13		8^1	12											15
1		8		5		12	4		7				14		3				2^1	9^3		11		13		10^2		6										16
1		8		5			6		7			14			3				2^3	9^2		11		13		10^1	12	4										17
1		8		5			6		11						2				7	9^1				13		10^2	12	3	4									18
1		8		5		7	6		11				13							9^2						10^1	12	4	2	3								19
1		8^1	10	5		11	4^2		7										13	9^3				14		12		6	2	3								20
1			4^1	5		11			7		13	12												9		8^2	10	6	2	3								21
1						8			11		12	13					4^2		7				5			9	10^1	6	2	3								22
1^G				5^1		8	13		11								4^2		7				12	10		9		6	2	3	15							23
1						6	4		11^3		13				12				7	9			5	10^2		8^1			2	3		14						24
1						8^1	4^3		11		14		13		3				12	9			5	10^2		7		6	2									25
1				5^1			4^2		11				14				13		7	9			12	10^3		8		6	2	3								26
1						13	4^1		7				14				12		2^2	9			3	10^3		8		6	5	11								27
1						11			10				13				4^2		7^1	9			5	12		8		6	2	3								28
1		12				11^2			7				13				4		14	9			2					6	5	3			8^1	10^3				29
1		11^1				8	13		7				14				4^2			9^3			5					6	2	3			12	10				30
1		12					4		7^2				13				11			9			5					6	2	3			8^1	10				31
1		13					8		7				14				4		2^1	9			6						5	3			11^3	10^2	12			32
1		11					4										7	13		9			2			12			5	3			8^1	10^2		6		33
1		11^1					8										4	13		9						7^2		5	2	3			10	12		6		34
1		3^1				7											6	13		9^2						10		5	2	11			8	12		4		35
1		14	4^2				13		7								8	12		9						11^3		5	2	3			10^1			6		36
1		3	4						7		13						8	14		9^3			12^2			10		5	2				11^1			6		37
1		3	4^2				13		7		12						8	10^1								11		5	2							6	9	38
1		3	4			13	11^1		7		12						8			9								5	2							6	10^2	39
1		3	4			13	11^3		7								8^2			9						14		5	2				12			6	10^1	40
1		3	4				11^1		7^2		14						8			9						12		5	2				13			6	10^3	41
1		3	4^2			8^1			7		14						12			9					13	11		5	2							6	10^3	42
1		3	4						7		13									9					8^1	11		5	2	12						6	10^2	43
1		11	4^1			12			7								8			9			14					5	2	3^3			13			6	10^2	44
			4						7		10^2					12	8			9			5						2	3	1		11^1			6	13	45
			4						7		10^2		12			13	8			9			5						2	3	1		11^1			6		46

FA Cup

First Round	Gillingham	(h)	3-3
		(a)	2-3

Carling Cup

First Round	Dagenham & R	(h)	5-0
Second Round	WBA	(h)	1-4

J Paint Trophy

First Round	Hereford U	(h)	4-1
Second Round	Yeovil T	(h)	3-2
Southern Quarter-Final	Brentford	(a)	0-6

BRADFORD CITY FL Championship 2

FOUNDATION

Bradford was a rugby stronghold around the turn of the 20th century but after Manningham RFC held an archery contest to help them out of financial difficulties in 1903, they were persuaded to give up the handling code and turn to soccer. So they formed Bradford City and continued at Valley Parade. Recognising this as an opportunity to spread the dribbling code in this part of Yorkshire, the Football League immediately accepted the new club's first application for membership of the Second Division.

Coral Window Stadium, Valley Parade, Bradford, West Yorkshire BD8 7DY.

Telephone: (0871) 978 1911.

Fax: (01274) 773 356.

Ticket Office: (0871) 978 8000.

Website: www.bradfordcityfc.co.uk

Email: bradfordcityfc@compuserve.com

Ground Capacity: 25,136.

Record Attendance: 39,146 v Burnley, FA Cup 4th rd, 11 March 1911.

Pitch Measurements: 113yd × 70yd.

Joint Chairmen: Julian Rhodes and Mark Lawn.

Manager: Phil Parkinson.

Assistant Manager: Steve Parkin.

Head Physio: David Hanson.

Colours: Claret and amber striped shirts with claret sleeves, black shorts, black stockings.

Year Formed: 1903.

Turned Professional: 1903.

Club Nickname: 'The Bantams'.

Ground: 1903, Valley Parade.

First Football League Game: 1 September 1903, Division 2, v Grimsby T (a) L 0–2 – Seymour; Wilson, Halliday; Robinson, Millar, Farnall; Guy, Beckram, Forrest, McMillan, Graham.

Record League Victory: 11–1 v Rotherham U, Division 3 (N), 25 August 1928 – Sherlaw; Russell, Watson; Burkinshaw (1), Summers, Bauld; Harvey (2), Edmunds (3), White (3), Cairns, Scriven (2).

Record Cup Victory: 11–3 v Walker Celtic, FA Cup 1st rd (replay), 1 December 1937 – Parker; Rookes, McDermott; Murphy, Mackie, Moore; Bagley (1), Whittingham (1), Deakin (4 incl. 1p), Cooke (1), Bartholomew (4).

HONOURS

Football League –
Division 1: ***Runners-up*** 1998–99;
Division 2: ***Champions*** 1907–08;
Division 3: ***Champions*** 1984–85;
Division 3 (N): ***Champions*** 1928–29;
Division 4: ***Runners-up*** 1981–82.

FA Cup: ***Winners*** 1911.

Football League Cup: Best season: 5th rd, 1965, 1989.

European Competitions:
Intertoto Cup: 2000.

sky SPORTS FACT FILE

Bradford City managed to retain their hard-won Premier League status in 2000, but it was a close-run thing that went to the last match of the season. A goal by David Wetherall gave City a precious 1-0 win over Liverpool while Wimbledon were losing 2-0 at Southampton.

Record Defeat: 1–9 v Colchester U, Division 4, 30 December 1961.

Most League Points (2 for a win): 63, Division 3 (N), 1928–29.

Most League Points (3 for a win): 94, Division 3, 1984–85.

Most League Goals: 128, Division 3 (N), 1928–29.

Highest League Scorer in Season: David Layne, 34, Division 4, 1961–62.

Most League Goals in Total Aggregate: Bobby Campbell, 121, 1981–84, 1984–86.

Most League Goals in One Match: 7, Albert Whitehurst v Tranmere R, Division 3 (N), 6 March 1929.

Most Capped Player: Jamie Lawrence, 19 (24), Jamaica.

Most League Appearances: Cec Podd, 502, 1970–84.

Youngest League Player: Robert Cullingford, 16 years 141 days v Mansfield T, 22 April 1970.

Record Transfer Fee Received: £2,000,000 from Newcastle U for Des Hamilton, March 1997; £2,000,000 from Newcastle U for Andrew O'Brien, March 2001.

Record Transfer Fee Paid: £2,500,000 to Leeds U for David Hopkin, July 2000.

Football League Record: 1903 Elected to Division 2; 1908–22 Division 1; 1922–27 Division 2; 1927–29 Division 3 (N); 1929–37 Division 2; 1937–61 Division 3; 1961–69 Division 4; 1969–72 Division 3; 1972–77 Division 4; 1977–78 Division 3; 1978–82 Division 4; 1982–85 Division 3; 1985–90 Division 2; 1990–92 Division 3; 1992–96 Division 2; 1996–99 Division 1; 1999–2001 FA Premier League; 2001–04 Division 1; 2004–07 FL 1; 2007– FL 2.

LATEST SEQUENCES

Longest Sequence of League Wins: 10, 26.11.1983 – 3.2.1984.

Longest Sequence of League Defeats: 8, 21.1.1933 – 11.3.1933.

Longest Sequence of League Draws: 6, 30.1.1976 – 13.3.1976.

Longest Sequence of Unbeaten League Matches: 21, 11.1.1969 – 2.5.1969.

Longest Sequence Without a League Win: 16, 28.8.1948 – 20.11.1948.

Successive Scoring Runs: 30 from 26.12.1961.

Successive Non-scoring Runs: 7 from 18.4.1925.

MANAGERS

Robert Campbell 1903–05
Peter O'Rourke 1905–21
David Menzies 1921–26
Colin Veitch 1926–28
Peter O'Rourke 1928–30
Jack Peart 1930–35
Dick Ray 1935–37
Fred Westgarth 1938–43
Bob Sharp 1943–46
Jack Barker 1946–47
John Milburn 1947–48
David Steele 1948–52
Albert Harris 1952
Ivor Powell 1952–55
Peter Jackson 1955–61
Bob Brocklebank 1961–64
Bill Harris 1965–66
Willie Watson 1966–69
Grenville Hair 1967–68
Jimmy Wheeler 1968–71
Bryan Edwards 1971–75
Bobby Kennedy 1975–78
John Napier 1978
George Mulhall 1978–81
Roy McFarland 1981–82
Trevor Cherry 1982–87
Terry Dolan 1987–89
Terry Yorath 1989–90
John Docherty 1990–91
Frank Stapleton 1991–94
Lennie Lawrence 1994–95
Chris Kamara 1995–98
Paul Jewell 1998–2000
Chris Hutchings 2000
Jim Jefferies 2000–01
Nicky Law 2001–03
Bryan Robson 2003–04
Colin Todd 2004–07
Stuart McCall 2007–10
Peter Taylor 2010–11
Peter Jackson 2011
Phil Parkinson August 2011–

TEN YEAR LEAGUE RECORD

		P	*W*	*D*	*L*	*F*	*A*	*Pts*	*Pos*
2002-03	Div 1	46	14	10	22	51	73	52	19
2003-04	Div 1	46	10	6	30	38	69	36	23
2004-05	FL 1	46	17	14	15	64	62	65	11
2005-06	FL 1	46	14	19	13	51	49	61	11
2006-07	FL 1	46	11	14	21	47	65	47	22
2007-08	FL 2	46	17	11	18	63	61	62	10
2008-09	FL 2	46	18	13	15	66	55	67	9
2009-10	FL 2	46	16	14	16	59	62	62	14
2010-11	FL 2	46	15	7	24	43	68	52	18
2011-12	FL 2	46	12	14	20	54	59	50	18

DID YOU KNOW ?

On 13 August 2011, Ross Hannah made an immediate impact for Bradford City at Oxford United. Coming on as a second-half substitute he scored with his first touch in the 78th minute. He gave up his job as a landscape gardener to go full-time having been signed from Matlock Town.

BRADFORD CITY 2011–12 LEAGUE RECORD

Match No.	Date	Venue	Opponents	Result		H/T Score	Lg Pos.	Goalscorers	Attendance
1	Aug 6	H	Aldershot T	L	1-2	0-2	—	Hanson [90]	10,205
2	13	A	Oxford U	D	1-1	0-1	18	Hannah [78]	6523
3	16	A	Accrington S	L	0-1	0-0	—		2652
4	20	H	Dagenham & R	L	0-1	0-1	21		9594
5	27	H	Barnet	W	4-2	1-1	18	Hanson 2 [16, 54], Branston [49], Wells [90]	9656
6	Sept 3	A	Morecambe	D	1-1	0-0	21	Hannah [90]	4025
7	10	H	Bristol R	D	2-2	0-1	20	Flynn 2 (2 pens) [64, 90]	10,023
8	13	A	Port Vale	L	2-3	1-2	—	Devitt [24], Jones [50]	4769
9	17	A	Crawley T	L	1-3	1-0	22	Reid [12]	2479
10	24	H	AFC Wimbledon	L	1-2	1-1	22	Flynn (pen) [26]	10,255
11	Oct 1	A	Burton Alb	D	2-2	2-2	22	Reid [6], Hanson [16]	2925
12	8	H	Torquay U	W	1-0	1-0	21	Fagan [38]	11,738
13	15	A	Hereford U	L	0-2	0-0	22		2462
14	22	H	Northampton T	W	2-1	0-0	20	Fagan (pen) [64], Hanson [69]	9925
15	25	A	Macclesfield T	L	0-1	0-0	—		2373
16	29	A	Swindon T	D	0-0	0-0	21		7701
17	Nov 5	H	Cheltenham T	L	0-1	0-1	21		9645
18	19	H	Rotherham U	L	2-3	1-1	22	Mitchell [34], Flynn (pen) [90]	10,551
19	26	A	Gillingham	D	0-0	0-0	22		7074
20	Dec 10	H	Plymouth Arg	D	1-1	0-0	22	Hanson [86]	10,143
21	16	A	Southend U	W	1-0	0-0	—	Oliver [88]	5526
22	26	H	Crewe Alex	W	3-0	1-0	19	Wells [2], Hanson 2 [64, 84]	11,060
23	31	H	Shrewsbury T	W	3-1	2-0	19	Hanson [24], Wells [29], Fagan [49]	10,567
24	Jan 2	A	Rotherham U	L	0-3	0-0	18		5368
25	14	H	Morecambe	D	2-2	0-0	19	Ravenhill [60], Seip [89]	10,065
26	21	H	Burton Alb	D	1-1	1-0	20	Davies [43]	9744
27	28	A	Bristol R	L	1-2	0-1	20	Davies [72]	6164
28	Feb 14	H	Port Vale	D	1-1	0-1	—	Syers [90]	2149
29	18	A	Torquay U	W	2-1	2-1	19	Fagan [17], Reid [20]	2566
30	25	H	Hereford U	D	1-1	0-0	19	Syers [88]	17,014
31	28	A	Barnet	W	4-0	2-0	—	Fagan (pen) [17], Atkinson [37], Reid [58], Wells [88]	1509
32	Mar 3	A	Dagenham & R	L	0-1	0-0	18		3041
33	6	H	Accrington S	D	1-1	0-0	—	Wells [50]	9379
34	10	H	Oxford U	W	2-1	0-0	18	Fagan (pen) [57], Hanson [67]	10,059
35	13	A	AFC Wimbledon	L	1-3	1-1	—	Balkestein (og) [36]	4064
36	17	A	Aldershot T	L	0-1	0-0	18		2763
37	20	A	Crewe Alex	L	0-1	0-1	—		3556
38	24	H	Gillingham	D	2-2	0-1	19	Wells [71], Hanson [84]	9858
39	27	H	Crawley T	L	1-2	0-0	—	Dagnall [72]	9773
40	31	A	Plymouth Arg	L	0-1	0-1	20		6933
41	Apr 6	H	Southend U	W	2-0	1-0	19	Hanson [38], Fagan (pen) [54]	10,859
42	9	A	Shrewsbury T	L	0-1	0-1	21		6272
43	14	A	Northampton T	W	3-1	2-0	18	Wells 3 [11, 39, 54]	5060
44	21	H	Macclesfield T	W	1-0	0-0	18	Hanson [65]	10,106
45	28	A	Cheltenham T	L	1-3	1-0	18	Wells [8]	3930
46	May 5	H	Swindon T	D	0-0	0-0	18		11,576

Final League Position: 18

GOALSCORERS

League (54): Hanson 13, Wells 10, Fagan 7 (4 pens), Flynn 4 (4 pens), Reid 4, Davies 2, Hannah 2, Syers 2, Atkinson 1, Branston 1, Dagnall 1, Devitt 1, Jones 1, Mitchell 1, Oliver 1, Ravenhill 1, Seip 1, own goal 1.
Carling Cup (2): Compton 1, Flynn 1.
FA Cup (6): Wells 2, Fagan 1 (pen), Hannah 1, Hanson 1, own goal 1.
J Paint Trophy (3): Flynn 1, Oliver 1, own goal 1.

Hansen M 4	Moore L 16 + 1	Threlfall R 16 + 1	Flynn M 27 + 3	Branston G 15 + 1	Bullock L 14 + 5	Mitchell C 10 + 1	Syers D 8 + 10	Hanson J 36 + 3	Stewart M 5 + 7	Compton J 9 + 5 / Dagnall C 5 + 2	Wells N 18 + 15	Rodney N — + 5	Oliver L 39	Jones R 31 + 1	Bryan M 5 + 3	Hannah R 4 + 14 / Baker A — + 1	Jansson O 1	Duke M 18	Reid K 32 + 5	Devitt J 5 + 2	Hunt L — + 1	Fagan C 29 + 2	Davies A 26	Reed A 4	O'Brien L 3 + 6	Seip M 23	McLaughlin J 23	Williams S 1	Ravenhill R 25 + 1	Ramsden S 16 + 1	Taylor C 1 + 2	Kozluk R 17	Haworth A 2 + 1	Dean L — + 1	Smalley D 7 + 6	Atkinson W 6 + 6	Fry M 5 + 1	*Match No.*
1	2	3	4^{2}	5	6	7	8	9	10^{1}	11	12	13																										1
1	2	3	4	5		7		9^{1}	10^{2}	11		12	6	8^{3}	13	14																						2
1	2	3	4	5		7		9		11		12	6	13	8^{2}	10^{1}																						3
1	2	3	4	5		14		9^{1}	13	11		12	6	8^{3}	7^{2}	10																						4
	2	3	4	5		7		9	10^{1}	11	12		6	8			1																					5
	2	3	4	5		7^{1}		9	10^{3}	14			6	8		13		1	11^{2}	12																		6
	2^{3}	3	4	5		7^{1}		9	14	13			6	8		12		1	11^{2}	10																		7
	2	3	4	5		7		9		12	13		6	8				1	11^{1}	10^{2}																		8
	2	3^{1}	4	5		7		9					6	8		13		1	11	10^{3}	12^{2}	14																9
	2	3	4			7^{1}		9					6	8		13		1	11	10^{2}		12	5															10
	2	3	4					9		14			6	8^{1}		13		1	11^{3}			10^{2}	5	7	12													11
	2	3	4	12					10^{2}	7^{1}		14	6	8				1	11			9^{3}	5■		13													12
	2^{3}	3	4■						13				6	8	14			1	11	10^{2}		9		7^{1}	12	5												13
	2	3						9					6	4	7^{1}			1	11			10		8	12	5												14
	2	3^{1}	4					9					6	8^{3}	13			1	11	14		10		7^{2}	12	5												15
	12		7					9					6	8	2^{1}			1	11			10	4■		3	5												16
	2^{2}		4					9			13		6	8	7^{1}	12		1	11			10			3	5												17
			4			7^{1}		12		11^{3}	10		6			13			14			9^{2}			3	2	1	5	8									18
			4					9			12		6			10^{1}			11			8	3			5	1		7	2								19
			4					9		7	12		6						11			10^{1}	5			3	1		8	2								20
			4					9	12		10^{1}		6						11^{2}			7	5		13	3	1		8	2								21
							14	9	13	12	10^{2}		6	8^{3}					11^{1}			7	5			3	1		4	2								22
		14			13		8■	9		11^{2}	10^{1}		6	4		12^{3}						7	5			3	1			2								23
		3			14		8^{3}	9	13		10^{1}		6			12						7	5			2	1		4		11^{2}							24
								9	13		10		6^{1}	8								7	5			3	1		4		12	2^{3}	11^{2}	14				25
					6			9			10^{1}			8								7	5			3	1		4			2	11		12			26
					6^{3}		8	9			10^{2}								13			7	5			3	1		4		14	2■			12	11^{1}		27
								9^{1}			13		6	8		10^{2}			11				5			2	1		4	14					7	12	3^{3}	28
			7				12				13		6	8					11^{3}			9^{2}	5			3	1		4	2					10^{1}	14		29
			9^{1}		4		12				10^{3}			8		14			11				5			3	1		6			2			7^{2}	13		30
			9^{1}		14						13		6	8					11^{3}			10^{2}	5			3	1		4			2			7	12		31
					7						13		6	8^{2}					11			9^{3}	5				1		4			2	14		10^{1}	12	3	32
					8						9		6			12			11				5			3	1		4			2			10^{1}	7		33
					4		13	12			10^{3}		6	8		14			11			9^{2}	5			3	1					2				7^{1}		34
					4		8	9^{2}			10^{1}		6			13			11			7■	5			3^{3}	1					2				12	14	35
			8				14	9		10^{3}	12		6						11				5			3	1		4^{1}	2					13	7^{2}		36
					8^{2}		13	9		10	12		6						11				5				1		4	2					7^{1}		3	37
					8		12	9		10	13		6						11			7	5				1		4^{1}	2^{2}							3	38
			13		4		8	9		10	14		6						11			7	5				1		12^{2}			2^{1}					3^{3}	39
			11	5	6		7	13		9	14			8				1	12			10							4^{1}	2^{2}		3^{3}						40
			11	5	6		14	9		13	10^{3}			8^{2}				1	12			7							4^{1}	2		3						41
			11^{1}	5	6		14	9		12	10^{2}			8^{3}				1	13			7							4	2		3						42
			14	5	13			9			10^{1}		6	8^{2}				1	11^{3}			7							4	2		3			12			43
			12	5				9			10^{2}		6	8				1	11^{1}			7							4	2		3			13			44
				5^{2}	12		13	9			10		6	8^{1}				1	11										4	2		3			14	7^{3}		45
							8	9			10^{1}		6			12			11				5				1		4	2		3				7		46

FA Cup

First Round	Rochdale	(h)	1-0
Second Round	AFC Wimbledon	(h)	3-1
Third Round	Watford	(a)	2-4

Carling Cup

First Round	Leeds U	(a)	2-3

J Paint Trophy

First Round	Sheffield W	(h)	0-0
Second Round	Huddersfield T	(a)	2-2
Northern Quarter-Final	Sheffield U	(a)	1-1
Northern Semi-Final	Oldham Ath	(a)	0-2

BRENTFORD

FL Championship 1

FOUNDATION

Formed as a small amateur concern in 1889 they were very successful in local circles. They won the championship of the West London Alliance in 1893 and a year later the West Middlesex Junior Cup before carrying off the Senior Cup in 1895. After winning both the London Senior Amateur Cup and the Middlesex Senior Cup in 1898 they were admitted to the Second Division of the Southern League.

Griffin Park, Braemar Road, Brentford, Middlesex TW8 0NT.

Telephone: (0845) 3456 442.

Fax: (020) 8568 9940.

Ticket Office: (0845) 3456 442.

Website: www.brentfordfc.co.uk

Email: enquiries@brentfordfc.co.uk

Ground Capacity: 12,400.

Record Attendance: 38,678 v Leicester C, FA Cup 6th rd, 26 February 1949.

Pitch Measurements: 111yd × 74yd.

Chairman: Greg Dyke.

Chief Executive: Mark Devlin.

Manager: Uwe Rosler.

First Team Coaches: Alan Kernaghan and Peter Farrell.

Physio: Daryl Martin.

Colours: White shirts with red sleeves and black trim underneath, four separated red vertical stripes on body, black shorts, black stockings.

Year Formed: 1889.

Turned Professional: 1899.

Club Nickname: 'The Bees'.

Grounds: 1889, Clifden Road; 1891, Benns Fields, Little Ealing; 1895, Shotters Field; 1898, Cross Road, S. Ealing; 1900, Boston Park; 1904, Griffin Park.

First Football League Game: 28 August 1920, Division 3, v Exeter C (a) L 0–3 – Young; Hodson, Rosier, Jimmy Elliott, Levitt, Amos, Smith, Thompson, Spreadbury, Morley, Henery.

Record League Victory: 9–0 v Wrexham, Division 3, 15 October 1963 – Cakebread; Coote, Jones; Slater, Scott, Higginson; Summers (1), Brooks (2), McAdams (2), Ward (2), Hales (1), (1 og).

Record Cup Victory: 7–0 v Windsor & Eton (away), FA Cup 1st rd, 20 November 1982 – Roche; Rowe, Harris (Booker), McNichol (1), Whitehead, Hurlock (2), Kamara, Joseph (1), Mahoney (3), Bowles, Roberts. *N.B.* 8–0 v Uxbridge: Frail, Jock Watson, Caie, Bellingham, Parsonage (1), Jay, Atherton, Leigh (1), Bell (2), Buchanan (2), Underwood (2), FA Cup, 3rd Qual rd, 31 October 1903.

HONOURS

Football League – Division 1: Best season: 5th, 1935–36;
Division 2: ***Champions*** 1934–35, 1994–95; **Division 3:** ***Champions*** 1991–92, 1998–99;
Division 3 (S): ***Champions*** 1932–33, ***Runners-up*** 1929–30, 1957–58;
Division 4: ***Champions*** 1962–63;
FL 2: ***Champions*** 2008–09.

FA Cup: Best season: 6th rd, 1938, 1946, 1949, 1989.

Football League Cup: Best season: 4th rd, 1983, 2011.

Freight Rover Trophy: ***Runners-up*** 1985.

LDV Vans Trophy: ***Runners-up*** 2001.

Johnstone's Paint Trophy: ***Runners-up*** 2011.

sky SPORTS FACT FILE

In 1938–39 Brentford were able to field an entire forward line composed of full internationals: Dai Hopkins (Wales), Billy Scott (England), Dave McCulloch (Scotland), George Eastham (England) and Bobby Reid (Scotland). In May 1938 Arthur Bateman had also been England's 12th man.

Record Defeat: 0–7 v Swansea T, Division 3 (S), 8 November 1924; v Walsall, Division 3 (S), 19 January 1957; v Peterborough U, 24 November 2007.

Most League Points (2 for a win): 62, Division 3 (S), 1932–33 and Division 4, 1962–63.

Most League Points (3 for a win): 85, Division 2, 1994–95, Division 3, 1998–99 and FL 2, 2008–09.

Most League Goals: 98, Division 4, 1962–63.

Highest League Scorer in Season: Jack Holliday, 38, Division 3 (S), 1932–33.

Most League Goals in Total Aggregate: Jim Towers, 153, 1954–61.

Most League Goals in One Match: 5, Jack Holliday v Luton T, Division 3 (S), 28 January 1933; 5, Billy Scott v Barnsley, Division 2, 15 December 1934; 5, Peter McKennan v Bury, Division 2, 18 February 1949.

Most Capped Player: John Buttigieg, 22 (98), Malta.

Most League Appearances: Ken Coote, 514, 1949–64.

Youngest League Player: Danis Salman, 15 years 248 days v Watford, 15 November 1975.

Record Transfer Fee Received: £2,500,000 from Wimbledon for Hermann Hreidarsson, October 1999.

Record Transfer Fee Paid: £750,000 to Crystal Palace for Hermann Hreidarsson, September 1998.

Football League Record: 1920 Original Member of Division 3; 1921–33 Division 3 (S); 1933–35 Division 2; 1935–47 Division 1; 1947–54 Division 2; 1954–62 Division 3 (S); 1962–63 Division 4; 1963–66 Division 3; 1966–72 Division 4; 1972–73 Division 3; 1973–78 Division 4; 1978–92 Division 3; 1992–93 Division 1; 1993–98 Division 2; 1998–99 Division 3; 1999–04 Division 2; 2004–07 FL 1; 2007–09 FL 2; 2009– FL 1.

MANAGERS

Will Lewis 1900–03 (*Secretary-Manager*)
Dick Molyneux 1902–06
W. G. Brown 1906–08
Fred Halliday 1908–12, 1915–21, 1924–26 (*only Secretary to 1922*)
Ephraim Rhodes 1912–15
Archie Mitchell 1921–24
Harry Curtis 1926–49
Jackie Gibbons 1949–52
Jimmy Bain 1952–53
Tommy Lawton 1953
Bill Dodgin Snr 1953–57
Malcolm Macdonald 1957–65
Tommy Cavanagh 1965–66
Billy Gray 1966–67
Jimmy Sirrel 1967–69
Frank Blunstone 1969–73
Mike Everitt 1973–75
John Docherty 1975–76
Bill Dodgin Jnr 1976–80
Fred Callaghan 1980–84
Frank McLintock 1984–87
Steve Perryman 1987–90
Phil Holder 1990–93
David Webb 1993–97
Eddie May 1997
Micky Adams 1997–98
Ron Noades 1998–2000
Ray Lewington 2000–01
Steve Coppell 2001–02
Wally Downes 2002–04
Martin Allen 2004–06
Leroy Rosenior 2006
Scott Fitzgerald 2006–07
Terry Butcher 2007
Andy Scott 2007–11
Nicky Forster 2011
Uwe Rosler June 2011–

LATEST SEQUENCES

Longest Sequence of League Wins: 9, 30.4.1932 – 24.9.1932.

Longest Sequence of League Defeats: 9, 20.10.1928 – 25.12.1928.

Longest Sequence of League Draws: 5, 16.3.1957 – 6.4.1957.

Longest Sequence of Unbeaten League Matches: 26, 20.2.1999 – 16.10.1999.

Longest Sequence Without a League Win: 18, 9.9.2006 – 26.12.2006.

Successive Scoring Runs: 26 from 4.3.1963.

Successive Non-scoring Runs: 7 from 7.3.2000.

TEN YEAR LEAGUE RECORD

		P	W	D	L	F	A	Pts	Pos
2002-03	Div 2	46	14	12	20	47	56	54	16
2003-04	Div 2	46	14	11	21	52	69	53	17
2004-05	FL 1	46	22	9	15	57	60	75	4
2005-06	FL 1	46	20	16	10	72	52	76	3
2006-07	FL 1	46	8	13	25	40	79	37	24
2007-08	FL 2	46	17	8	21	52	70	59	14
2008-09	FL 2	46	23	16	7	65	36	85	1
2009-10	FL 1	46	14	20	12	55	52	62	9
2010-11	FL 1	46	17	10	19	55	62	61	11
2011-12	FL 1	46	18	13	15	63	52	67	9

DID YOU KNOW ?

On 8 November 2011, Brentford had their highest scoring cup result for 29 years when they defeated Bournemouth 6-0 in the Southern Section quarter-final of the Johnstone's Paint Trophy. Mike Grella scored four of the goals, Steve Saunders and Shaleum Logan the other two.

BRENTFORD 2011–12 LEAGUE RECORD

Match No.	Date	Venue	Opponents	Result	H/T Score	Lg Pos.	Goalscorers	Attendance
1	Aug 6	H	Yeovil T	W 2-0	1-0	—	Alexander (pen) 30, Logan 76	6278
2	13	A	Sheffield U	L 0-2	0-0	9		17,769
3	16	A	Exeter C	W 2-1	2-0	—	Dunne (og) 18, Donaldson 37	4344
4	20	H	Leyton Orient	W 5-0	1-0	4	McGinn 6, Legge 52, Saunders 2 54, 75, Bean 89	5399
5	27	H	Tranmere R	L 0-2	0-1	7		5381
6	Sept 3	A	Walsall	W 1-0	1-0	4	Donaldson 27	3972
7	10	A	Wycombe W	W 1-0	1-0	4	O'Connor (pen) 36	5045
8	13	H	Colchester U	D 1-1	0-0	—	Donaldson 56	4714
9	17	H	Preston NE	L 1-3	1-2	8	McGinn 21	6090
10	24	A	Oldham Ath	W 2-0	1-0	6	Douglas 38, Weston 73	3777
11	Oct 1	H	Huddersfield T	L 0-4	0-1	9		6101
12	8	A	Carlisle U	D 2-2	1-1	8	Clarkson 9, Diagouraga 88	4184
13	15	H	Scunthorpe U	D 0-0	0-0	8		4907
14	22	A	Notts Co	D 1-1	0-1	10	Donaldson 46	6735
15	25	H	Stevenage	L 0-1	0-0	—		4771
16	29	H	Chesterfield	W 2-1	1-1	8	Saunders 24, Bennett 82	4566
17	Nov 5	A	Sheffield W	D 0-0	0-0	9		18,107
18	19	H	Charlton Ath	L 0-1	0-0	9		8095
19	26	A	Rochdale	W 2-1	1-0	7	Alexander (pen) 11, Saunders 78	2466
20	Dec 10	H	Hartlepool U	W 2-1	0-0	6	McGinn 80, Alexander 85	6352
21	17	A	Bury	D 1-1	0-0	6	Alexander (pen) 61	4008
22	26	H	Bournemouth	D 1-1	0-1	7	Legge 90	6338
23	31	H	Milton Keynes D	D 3-3	0-3	7	Alexander 2 (1 pen) 65, 75 (p), Legge 90	5397
24	Jan 2	A	Charlton Ath	L 0-2	0-1	8		17,506
25	7	A	Tranmere R	D 2-2	2-1	—	Alexander 22, Donaldson 32	4432
26	14	H	Walsall	D 0-0	0-0	8		4867
27	21	A	Huddersfield T	L 2-3	2-2	9	Alexander 2 (1 pen) 21 (p), 29	14,405
28	28	H	Wycombe W	W 5-2	3-0	8	Alexander 3 10, 29, 81, Saunders 22, Diagouraga 73	5560
29	Feb 14	A	Colchester U	L 1-2	0-0	—	McGinn 57	2923
30	20	H	Carlisle U	W 4-0	3-0	—	Dean 28, Saunders 32, Berahino 2 41, 53	4292
31	25	A	Scunthorpe U	D 0-0	0-0	9		3844
32	Mar 3	A	Yeovil T	L 1-2	1-0	10	Saunders 25	3930
33	6	H	Exeter C	W 2-0	1-0	—	Berahino 2 41, 69	4124
34	10	H	Sheffield U	L 0-2	0-1	10		7414
35	17	A	Leyton Orient	L 0-2	0-2	10		4173
36	20	A	Bournemouth	L 0-1	0-1	—		4563
37	24	H	Rochdale	W 2-0	1-0	10	Diagouraga 32, Donaldson 85	4919
38	27	A	Preston NE	W 3-1	2-1	—	Logan 9, Donaldson 2 (1 pen) 22 (p), 53	9148
39	31	A	Milton Keynes D	W 2-1	2-0	9	Donaldson 12, Douglas 26	11,570
40	Apr 3	H	Oldham Ath	W 2-0	1-0	—	Bean 2, McGinn 67	4573
41	7	H	Bury	W 3-0	1-0	8	Saunders 2 44, 63, Logan 68	5192
42	9	A	Hartlepool U	D 0-0	0-0	8		4292
43	14	H	Notts Co	D 0-0	0-0	8		7079
44	21	A	Stevenage	L 1-2	0-0	9	Saunders 90	4256
45	28	H	Sheffield W	L 1-2	0-1	9	Donaldson (pen) 62	7381
46	May 5	A	Chesterfield	W 3-2	1-0	9	Legge 12, Diagouraga 59, Donaldson 80	5699

Final League Position: 9

GOALSCORERS

League (63): Alexander 12 (5 pens), Donaldson 11 (2 pens), Saunders 10, McGinn 5, Berahino 4, Diagouraga 4, Legge 4, Logan 3, Bean 2, Douglas 2, Bennett 1, Clarkson 1, Dean 1, O'Connor 1 (1 pen), Weston 1, own goal 1.
Carling Cup (0).
FA Cup (1): Saunders 1.
J Paint Trophy (12): Grella 4, Alexander 2, Adams 1, Diagouraga 1, Logan 1, O'Connor 1 (pen), Saunders 1, Thompson 1.

Lee R 37	Logan S 26 + 1	Woodman C 18	Douglas J 46	Eger M 13 + 3	Osborne K 22 + 3	McGinn N 27 + 10	Reeves J 7 + 1	Alexander G 20 + 4	Donaldson C 40 + 6	Weston M 11 + 15	Saunders S 29 + 8	MacDonald C — + 3	O'Connor K 9 + 5	Legge L 23 + 5	Forrester H 7 + 12	Bean M 22 + 10	Grella M 1 + 10	Thompson A 16 + 4	Wood S 3 + 2	Spillane M — + 1	Llera M 10 + 1	Adams B 6 + 1	Clarkson D 4	Diagouraga T 30 + 5	Bennett D 5	Dean H 23 + 3	Bidwell J 24	Oyeleke E 1	Moore S 9 + 1	Berahino S 5 + 3	Forshaw A 6 + 1	Balkestein P 2 + 3	German A — + 2	Morrison C 4 + 4	Norris L — + 1	Match No.
1	2	3	4	5	6	7[2]	8[3]	9	10	11[1]	12	13	14																							1
1	2	3	4		6	7[1]	8	9[3]	10[2]	11	12	13	14	5																						2
1	2	3	4		6	11[3]	8[1]	9	10	13	7[2]		12	5	14																					3
1		3	4		6	11	8[1]	9[2]	10	14	7[3]	13	2	5		12																				4
1		3	4	13	6	11	8[1]	9	10		7[3]		2	5[2]		12	14																			5
1		3	4	5	6			14	9[3]	11[2]			7		12	8		2	10[1]	13																6
1		3	4	5	6	12			10	11[1]			7[2]		14	8		2	9[3]		13															7
1			4		6	7	8[2]		9	10[3]			13			11	14	2	12		5	3[1]														8
1		3[2]	4		6	7	8[1]		10	9					13	11	12	2			5															9
1			4	5	13	7[3]			9	12			8[2]			11		2			6■	3	10[1]	14												10
1			8	5	6	7			9	12			4[1]		14	11[2]		2				3	10[3]	13												11
1		3	4	5[2]					13	12	14		7					2	11[1]		6	9[3]	10	8												12
1		3	8	5		7			9	11			12			13	14	2[2]			6		10[3]	4[1]												13
1		3	4		6	11[2]			10		12		2			8			13		5	9[1]		7												14
1	2	3[2]	4	12	5[1]	11			10	9[3]						8	14				6	13		7												15
1	2		4	14		11[2]		12	9	13	7[3]						10[1]				6	3		8	5											16
1		3	4	5		11[3]		9[2]	10	12	7[1]		2			13	14				6			8												17
1	2[1]	3	4			11[2]		9	10	13	7[3]			5		12	14				6			8												18
1	2	3	4	6		11[1]		9	10[2]	13	7[3]			5			12							8		14										19
1	2		4			11		9	10		7[1]			5		12								8		6	3									20
1	2		4			11[2]		9	12	13	7[1]			5		8								10		6	3									21
1	2[2]		4			11[1]		9	10	12	7			5		13	14							8[3]		6	3									22
1	2[3]		4	6				9	12	10[2]	7			5	13	8										14	3	11[1]								23
1		3	4	6		7		13	9	10[3]	14			5		11[2]								8	2[1]	12										24
1		3	4			13		9	10[3]		7[2]			5	11[1]	8	14							12	2	6										25
			4	5		14		9	10[2]	13	7			6	11[3]	8[1]								12	2		3		1							26
1			4	6		11[1]		9	12	13	7[3]			5	14	10[2]								8	2		3									27
1	2		4					9	10	12	7[1]			5		11								8		6	3									28
1	2		4			11[1]		9	12	10[3]	14			5		7[2]								8		6	3			13						29
1[6]	2[2]		4					9[1]	10		7			5		11		13						8		6	3		15	12						30
			4					13	10[2]		7[1]			5		11[3]		2						8		6	3		1	9	12	14				31
		3	4			11		9	10[2]		7[1]			5	13			2[3]								6			1	12	8	14				32
			4			11[1]		9[2]	13		12			5	14			2						8		6	3		1	10[3]	7					33
	2		4		14	12			10	13	7[1]			5										8		6[3]	3		1	9	11[2]					34
	2		4		14	11[2]			10					5[3]	12									8		6	3		1	9[1]	7		13			35
1	14		4		5	11[2]			10		13				9			2[3]						8[1]		6	3				7		12			36
1	2		4		5				10		7			13		8[2]								12		6	3			9[3]	11[1]			14		37
1	11		4		5	13			10		7[2]				9[1]			2						8		6	3							12		38
1	11[3]		4		5	12			10		7[2]			14	9[1]	13		2						8		6	3									39
1	2		4		5	13			10		7[3]				14	11[1]		12						8		6	3							9[2]		40
1	2		4[1]		5[3]	13			10		7			14		11		12						8		6	3							9[2]		41
1	9		4		5	11[1]			10[3]		7[2]					14		2						8		6	3					13		12		42
1	2		4		5	12			10		7			13		11[2]								8		6	3							9[1]		43
	2		4		5[2]				10		7			13	12			11[1]						8		6	3		1					9		44
	10[3]		11		5	12			9		7				2[1]	13								8		6	3		1			4[2]			14	45
	2		4				13		10		7[2]			5	9[1]			14						8		6	11[3]		1			3		12		46

FA Cup

First Round	Basingstoke T	(h)	1-0
Second Round	Wrexham	(h)	0-1

Carling Cup

First Round	Hereford U	(a)	0-1

J Paint Trophy

First Round	Milton Keynes D	(a)	3-3
Second Round	Charlton Ath	(a)	3-0
Southern Quarter-Final	Bournemouth	(h)	6-0
Southern Semi-Final	Barnet	(a)	0-0

BRIGHTON & HOVE ALBION FL Championship

FOUNDATION

A professional club Brighton United was formed in November 1897 at the Imperial Hotel, Queen's Road, but folded in March 1900 after less than two seasons in the Southern League at the County Ground. An amateur team Brighton & Hove Rangers was then formed by some prominent United supporters and after one season at Withdean, decided to turn semi-professional and play at the County Ground. Rangers were accepted into the Southern League but folded in June 1901. John Jackson, the former United manager, organised a meeting at the Seven Stars public house, Ship Street on 24 June 1901 at which a new third club Brighton & Hove United was formed. They took over Rangers' place in the Southern League and pitch at County Ground. The name was changed to Brighton & Hove Albion before a match was played because of objections by Hove FC.

American Express Community Stadium, Village Way, Falmer, Brighton BN1 9BL.

Telephone: (01273) 878 288.

Fax: (01273) 878 238.

Ticket Office: (0845) 496 1901 (128 Queen's Road).

Website: www.seagulls.co.uk

Email: seagulls@bhafc.co.uk

Ground Capacity: 22,374.

Record Attendance: 36,747 v Fulham, Division 2, 27 December 1958 (at Goldstone Ground); 8,691 v Leeds U, FL 1, 20 October 2007 (at Withdean).

Pitch Measurements: 115yd × 75yd.

Chairman: Tony Bloom.

Chief Executive: Paul Barber.

Manager: Gus Poyet.

Assistant Manager: Mauricio Taricco.

Physio: Nathan Ring.

Colours: Blue and white striped shirts, white sleeves with blue trim, white shorts, white stockings.

Year Formed: 1901.

Turned Professional: 1901.

Club Nickname: 'The Seagulls'.

Grounds: 1901, County Ground; 1902, Goldstone Ground; 1997, groundshare at Gillingham FC; 1999, Withdean Stadium; 2011, American Express Community Stadium.

First Football League Game: 28 August 1920, Division 3, v Southend U (a) L 0–2 – Hayes; Woodhouse, Little; Hall, Comber, Bentley; Longstaff, Ritchie, Doran, Rodgerson, March.

Record League Victory: 9–1 v Newport Co, Division 3 (S), 18 April 1951 – Ball; Tennant (1p), Mansell (1p); Willard, McCoy, Wilson; Reed, McNichol (4), Garbutt, Bennett (2), Keene (1). 9–1 v Southend U, Division 3, 27 November 1965 – Powney; Magill, Baxter; Leck, Gall, Turner; Gould (1), Collins (1), Livesey (2), Smith (3), Goodchild (2).

HONOURS

Football League – Division 1: Best season: 13th, 1981–82;
Division 2: ***Champions*** 2001–02;
Runners-up 1978–79;
FL 1: ***Champions*** 2010–11.
Division 3 (S): ***Champions*** 1957–58;
Runners-up 1953–54, 1955–56;
Division 3: ***Champions*** 2000–01;
Runners-up 1971–72, 1976–77, 1987–88;
Division 4: ***Champions*** 1964–65.

FA Cup: ***Runners-up*** 1983.

Football League Cup: Best season: 5th rd, 1979.

sky SPORTS FACT FILE

On 6 August 2011, Brighton & Hove Albion played their first match at the new Amex Stadium and defeated Doncaster Rovers 2-1. The Seagulls' final League game at the Goldstone Ground on 26 April 1997 was also against Rovers and Brighton won that too, with a Stuart Storer goal.

Record Cup Victory: 10–1 v Wisbech, FA Cup 1st rd, 13 November 1965 – Powney; Magill, Baxter; Collins (1), Gall, Turner; Gould, Smith (2), Livesey (3), Cassidy (2), Goodchild (1), (1 og).

Record Defeat: 0–9 v Middlesbrough, Division 2, 23 August 1958.

Most League Points (2 for a win): 65, Division 3 (S), 1955–56 and Division 3, 1971–72.

Most League Points (3 for a win): 95, FL 1, 2010–11.

Most League Goals: 112, Division 3 (S), 1955–56.

Highest League Scorer in Season: Peter Ward, 32, Division 3, 1976–77.

Most League Goals in Total Aggregate: Tommy Cook, 114, 1922–29.

Most League Goals in One Match: 5, Jack Doran v Northampton T, Division 3 (S), 5 November 1921; 5, Adrian Thorne v Watford, Division 3 (S), 30 April 1958.

Most Capped Player: Steve Penney, 17, Northern Ireland.

Most League Appearances: 'Tug' Wilson, 509, 1922–36.

Youngest League Player: Ian Chapman, 16 years 259 days v Birmingham C, 14 February 1987.

Record Transfer Fee Received: £1,500,000 from Tottenham H for Bobby Zamora, July 2003; £1,500,000 from Celtic for Adam Virgo, July 2005.

Record Transfer Fee Paid: £1,000,000 to Watford for Will Buckley, June 2011.

Football League Record: 1920 Original Member of Division 3; 1921–58 Division 3 (S); 1958–62 Division 2; 1962–63 Division 3; 1963–65 Division 4; 1965–72 Division 3; 1972–73 Division 2; 1973–77 Division 3; 1977–79 Division 2; 1979–83 Division 1; 1983–87 Division 2; 1987–88 Division 3; 1988–96 Division 2; 1996–2001 Division 3; 2001–02 Division 2; 2002–03 Division 1; 2003–04 Division 2; 2004–06 FL C; 2006–11 FL 1; 2011– FL C.

MANAGERS

John Jackson 1901–05
Frank Scott-Walford 1905–08
John Robson 1908–14
Charles Webb 1919–47
Tommy Cook 1947
Don Welsh 1947–51
Billy Lane 1951–61
George Curtis 1961–63
Archie Macaulay 1963–68
Fred Goodwin 1968–70
Pat Saward 1970–73
Brian Clough 1973–74
Peter Taylor 1974–76
Alan Mullery 1976–81
Mike Bailey 1981–82
Jimmy Melia 1982–83
Chris Cattlin 1983–86
Alan Mullery 1986–87
Barry Lloyd 1987–93
Liam Brady 1993–95
Jimmy Case 1995–96
Steve Gritt 1996–98
Brian Horton 1998–99
Jeff Wood 1999
Micky Adams 1999–2001
Peter Taylor 2001–02
Martin Hinshelwood 2002
Steve Coppell 2002–03
Mark McGhee 2003–06
Dean Wilkins 2006–08
Micky Adams 2008–09
Russell Slade 2009
Gus Poyet November 2009–

LATEST SEQUENCES

Longest Sequence of League Wins: 9, 2.10.1926 – 20.11.1926.

Longest Sequence of League Defeats: 12, 17.8.2002 – 26.10.2002.

Longest Sequence of League Draws: 6, 16.2.1980 – 15.3.1980.

Longest Sequence of Unbeaten League Matches: 16, 8.10.1930 – 28.1.1931.

Longest Sequence Without a League Win: 15, 21.10.1972 – 27.1.1973

Successive Scoring Runs: 31 from 4.2.1956.

Successive Non-scoring Runs: 6 from 8.11.1924.

TEN YEAR LEAGUE RECORD

		P	W	D	L	F	A	Pts	Pos
2002-03	Div 1	46	11	12	23	49	67	45	23
2003-04	Div 2	46	22	11	13	64	43	77	4
2004-05	FL C	46	13	12	21	40	65	51	20
2005-06	FL C	46	7	17	22	39	71	38	24
2006-07	FL 1	46	14	11	21	49	58	53	18
2007-08	FL 1	46	19	12	15	58	50	69	7
2008-09	FL 1	46	13	13	20	55	70	52	16
2009-10	FL 1	46	15	14	17	56	60	59	13
2010-11	FL 1	46	28	11	7	85	40	95	11
2011-12	FL C	46	17	15	14	52	52	66	10

DID YOU KNOW ?

Brighton & Hove Albion had three players serving in the 17th Battalion (Football) Middlesex Regiment in the Great War: centre-forward Billy Jones twice, signed from Birmingham, left-back George Beech twice a Seagull, too, and centre-half Billy Booth. All three survived it.

BRIGHTON & HOVE ALBION 2011–12 LEAGUE RECORD

Match No.	*Date*	*Venue*	*Opponents*	*Result*		*H/T Score*	*Lg Pos.*	*Goalscorers*	*Attendance*
1	Aug 6	H	Doncaster R	W	2-1	0-1	—	Buckley 2 [83, 90]	20,219
2	13	A	Portsmouth	W	1-0	1-0	4	Mackail-Smith [45]	16,496
3	17	A	Cardiff C	W	3-1	1-0	—	Barnes 2 (1 pen) [39, 63 (p)], Hoskins [87]	23,013
4	20	H	Blackpool	D	2-2	1-0	4	Mackail-Smith [29], Barnes [50]	19,494
5	27	H	Peterborough U	W	2-0	1-0	1	Noone [10], Harley [64]	19,656
6	Sept 10	A	Bristol C	W	1-0	0-0	1	Barnes [80]	13,911
7	17	A	Leicester C	L	0-1	0-0	3		24,128
8	23	H	Leeds U	D	3-3	0-2	—	Mackail-Smith 2 [47, 84], Barnes (pen) [60]	20,646
9	27	H	Crystal Palace	L	1-3	1-0	—	Mackail-Smith [7]	20,968
10	Oct 1	A	Ipswich T	L	1-3	0-0	5	Vicente [53]	19,793
11	15	H	Hull C	D	0-0	0-0	5		19,722
12	18	A	Millwall	D	1-1	0-0	—	Noone [61]	11,688
13	24	H	West Ham U	L	0-1	0-1	—		20,686
14	29	A	Birmingham C	D	0-0	0-0	10		20,095
15	Nov 1	A	Watford	L	0-1	0-0	—		11,818
16	6	H	Barnsley	W	2-0	1-0	10	Greer [44], Harley [57]	19,841
17	19	A	Southampton	L	0-3	0-0	12		31,812
18	26	H	Coventry C	W	2-1	2-1	11	Keogh (og) [7], Vincelot [37]	19,108
19	29	A	Derby Co	W	1-0	1-0	—	Mackail-Smith [13]	22,040
20	Dec 3	H	Nottingham F	W	1-0	0-0	6	Buckley [90]	20,358
21	10	A	Middlesbrough	L	0-1	0-1	7		16,594
22	17	H	Burnley	L	0-1	0-1	9		19,641
23	26	A	Reading	L	0-3	0-2	11		22,141
24	31	A	Coventry C	L	0-2	0-1	16		14,158
25	Jan 2	H	Southampton	W	3-0	0-0	13	Caskey [66], Sparrow 2 [76, 86]	20,773
26	14	H	Bristol C	W	2-0	1-0	12	Calderon [37], Buckley [73]	20,398
27	21	A	Peterborough U	W	2-1	1-0	10	Buckley 2 [32, 88]	9474
28	31	A	Crystal Palace	D	1-1	0-0	—	Barnes (pen) [74]	17,271
29	Feb 4	H	Leicester C	W	1-0	0-0	10	Buckley [90]	20,223
30	11	A	Leeds U	W	2-1	0-0	8	Mackail-Smith [77], Navarro [90]	23,171
31	14	H	Millwall	D	2-2	0-1	—	Vokes [52], LuaLua [88]	19,503
32	22	A	Hull C	D	0-0	0-0	—		17,769
33	25	H	Ipswich T	W	3-0	1-0	7	Mackail-Smith [20], Barnes 2 [65, 88]	20,490
34	Mar 3	A	Doncaster R	D	1-1	1-0	7	Mackail-Smith [20]	8964
35	7	H	Cardiff C	D	2-2	0-0	—	Barnes [72], Vokes [89]	18,786
36	10	H	Portsmouth	W	2-0	0-0	5	Vicente 2 [75, 90]	20,772
37	17	A	Blackpool	L	1-3	1-2	9	Mattock [7]	12,782
38	20	H	Derby Co	W	2-0	1-0	—	Calderon [10], Barnes [66]	18,412
39	24	A	Nottingham F	D	1-1	0-0	4	Vokes [63]	21,249
40	31	H	Middlesbrough	D	1-1	0-0	6	Calderon [73]	20,553
41	Apr 6	A	Burnley	L	0-1	0-1	—		13,516
42	10	H	Reading	L	0-1	0-1	—		20,610
43	14	A	West Ham U	L	0-6	0-3	8		32,339
44	17	H	Watford	D	2-2	0-2	—	Calderon [55], Buckley [79]	19,189
45	21	H	Birmingham C	D	1-1	0-0	9	Barnes [84]	20,594
46	28	A	Barnsley	D	0-0	0-0	10		10,151

Final League Position: 10

GOALSCORERS

League (52): Barnes 11 (3 pens), Mackail-Smith 9, Buckley 8, Calderon 4, Vicente 3, Vokes 3, Harley 2, Noone 2, Sparrow 2, Caskey 1, Greer 1, Hoskins 1, LuaLua 1, Mattock 1, Navarro 1, Vincelot 1, own goal 1.
Carling Cup (3): Barnes 2 (2 pens), Mackail-Smith 1.
FA Cup (4): Barnes 1, Forster-Caskey 1, LuaLua 1, own goal 1.

Ankergren C 19	Calderon I 30 + 2	Painter M 20	Bridcutt L 43	Dunk L 31	Greer G 42	Sparrow M 15 + 3	Dicker G 17 + 1	Barnes A 36 + 7	Mackail-Smith C 40 + 5	LuaLua K 11 + 16	Noone C 18 + 15	Buckley W 16 + 13	Vincelot R 10 + 5	Navarro A 24 + 9	Hoskins W 2 + 5	Harley R 13 + 3	Vicente R 11 + 6	Taricco M 9 + 2	Harper S 5	Jara G 4	Paynter B 6 + 4	El-Abd A 21 + 2	Caskey J 3 + 1	Brezovan P 20	Cook S 1	Hall G — + 1	Agdestein T — + 4	Vokes S 7 + 7	Mattock J 14 + 1	Jara G 10	Razak A 4 + 2	Assulin G 2 + 5	Gonzalez D 2	*Match No.*
1	2	3	4	5	6	7^{2}	8	9	10	11^{1}	12	13																						1
1	2	3	4^{2}	5	6		8	9	10		12	11^{1}	7	13																				2
1	2	3	4	5	6	7^{1}	8	9	10				11^{2}	12	13																			3
1	2	3	4	5	6		8^{2}	9	10	12	7^{1}		11	13																				4
1	2	3	4	5	6	13	8	9	10^{3}	14	11^{2}			12		7^{1}																		5
1	2	3	4	5	6		8	9	10	12	11^{1}	13				7^{2}																		6
1	2	3■	4	5	6		8^{2}	9	10	14	11^{1}	12		13		7^{3}																		7
1	2	3	4	5	6		8	9	10^{3}	7^{2}	11^{1}		14		13		12																	8
1		3	4	5	6		8	9	10	13	11^{2}		12			7^{3}	14	2^{1}																9
1	2	3	4		6		8^{3}	9	10		13		5	11^{1}	14	12	7^{2}																	10
1	2	3	4	5	6	7	8^{1}	9	10		12						11																	11
1	2	3	4	5	6	7		12	10	13	11				9^{1}	8^{2}																		12
		3	4	5	2	7^{2}	8^{3}	9^{1}	10		11	13			12	14			1	6														13
	2	3	4		5	7^{1}		9	11		10		8					13	1	6^{2}	12													14
	2	3	4^{1}		5	7^{3}		13	10	14	11		6			8^{2}		12	1		9													15
	2		4	5	6			12	10		11^{2}	13		8		7^{1}		3	1		9													16
	12	3	4	5	6	13		14	10		11			8^{2}		7^{1}		2■	1		9^{3}													17
1	2	3^{1}	4	5	6			13	10	14	11		12	8		7^{3}					9^{2}													18
1	2^{1}		4	5	6			9^{2}	10		13		3	8	11^{3}	7					14	12												19
1			4	5	6			7^{1}	10	12	11^{2}	13	14	8^{3}				3		2	9													20
1			4	5	6	7^{1}		13	10^{3}	9	11^{2}	12	8					3		2	14													21
1			4^{3}	5	2			11■	10	9^{2}	13	14	8■	12		7^{1}		3				6												22
1			4	5	6	8			10	9^{1}	12	11^{2}				7		3			13	2												23
1				5	6	8			10	13	11^{2}	12		4		7^{3}		3^{1}			9	2	14											24
			4		6■	7			10	9^{2}		11				13		3^{1}				2	5	1	8	12								25
	2		4	5		7		9	10^{1}			11	3	13	12							6	8^{2}	1										26
	2	3^{1}	4	5	6	7^{3}		9	10			11		13								12	8^{2}	1			14							27
	2		4	5	6	7^{1}		9	10^{2}			11		8								3		1			12	13						28
	2		4	5	6	7■		9	10^{3}			11		8^{2}			14					3^{1}		1				13	12					29
			4		5			9	14	7^{2}	12	11^{1}		8			13					6		1				10^{3}	3	2				30
	2		4^{3}	5	6			9	10^{2}	14	12			8										1			13	11	3	7^{1}				31
			4		5			9	10	7^{1}		12		8								6		1					3	2	11^{2}	13		32
			4		5			9	10^{2}	14		11^{1}		8								6		1				13	3	2	7^{3}	12		33
			4		5			9	10^{3}		12	11^{2}		8								6		1				14	3	2	7^{1}	13		34
			4		5			9	10^{2}		14	13		8								6		1				12	3	2	7^{1}	11^{3}		35
			4		5			7	13	14	10^{1}	11^{3}		8			12					6		1				9^{2}	3	2				36
	12		4		5			9	10^{3}		11^{1}	13		8			7^{2}					6		1				14	3	2■				37
	2		4	5	6			9	12	11^{2}	13			8			7^{3}							1				10^{1}	3		14			38
	2		4	5	6	12■		9		11^{1}				8			7^{2}							1			14	10^{3}	3		13			39
	2		4		5			9^{1}	12	13		11^{2}		8			7					6		1				10	3					40
	2				5		4	12	10		14	13		8			11					6		1				9^{2}	3^{3}	7^{1}				41
	2				5		4	9^{3}	10^{2}	12		11^{1}		8			7					6		1				13		3		14		42
	2	3	4		5		10	9^{2}	12	13	14			8			7^{3}					6		1								11^{1}		43
	2	3^{1}	4	5			8	9	10	7^{2}		11	12				13					6											1	44
	2		4	5			13	9	10		12	11		8^{2}			7					6		1					3^{1}					45
	2		4	5			8^{1}	9	10			11^{2}		12			7					6							3			13	1	46

FA Cup

Third Round	Wrexham	(h)	1-1
		(a)	1-1
Fourth Round	Newcastle U	(h)	1-0
Fifth Round	Liverpool	(a)	1-6

Carling Cup

First Round	Gillingham	(h)	1-0
Second Round	Sunderland	(h)	1-0
Third Round	Liverpool	(h)	1-2

BRISTOL CITY FL Championship

FOUNDATION

The name Bristol City came into being in 1897 when the Bristol South End club, formed three years earlier, decided to adopt professionalism and apply for admission to the Southern League after competing in the Western League. The historic meeting was held at the Albert Hall, Bedminster. Bristol City employed Sam Hollis from Woolwich Arsenal as manager and gave him £40 to buy players. In 1900 they merged with Bedminster, another leading Bristol club.

Ashton Gate Stadium, Bristol BS3 2EJ.

Telephone: (0117) 963 0600.

Fax: (0117) 9630 700.

Ticket Office: (0871) 222 6666 (option 1).

Website: www.bcfc.co.uk

Email: enquiries@bcfc.co.uk

Ground Capacity: 21,804.

Record Attendance: 43,335 v Preston NE, FA Cup 5th rd, 16 February 1935.

Pitch Measurements: 115yd × 75yd.

Chairman: Keith Dawe.

Chief Executive: Guy Price.

Manager: Derek McInnes.

Assistant Manager: Tony Docherty.

Physio: Michael McBride.

Colours: Red shirts with white trim, white shorts, red stockings.

Year Formed: 1894.

Turned Professional: 1897.

Previous Name: 1894, Bristol South End; 1897, Bristol City.

Club Nickname: 'Robins'.

Grounds: 1894, St John's Lane; 1904, Ashton Gate.

First Football League Game: 7 September 1901, Division 2, v Blackpool (a) W 2–0 – Moles; Tuft, Davies; Jones, McLean, Chambers; Bradbury, Connor, Boucher, O'Brien (2), Flynn.

Record League Victory: 9–0 v Aldershot, Division 3 (S), 28 December 1946 – Eddols; Morgan, Fox; Peacock, Roberts, Jones (1); Chilcott, Thomas, Clark (4 incl. 1p), Cyril Williams (1), Hargreaves (3).

Record Cup Victory: 11–0 v Chichester C, FA Cup 1st rd, 5 November 1960 – Cook; Collinson, Thresher; Connor, Alan Williams, Etheridge; Tait (1), Bobby Williams (1), Atyeo (5), Adrian Williams (3), Derrick, (1 og).

HONOURS

Football League –
Division 1: ***Runners-up*** 1906–07;
Division 2: ***Champions*** 1905–06;
Runners-up 1975–76, 1997–98;
FL 1: ***Runners-up*** 2006–07;
Division 3 (S): ***Champions*** 1922–23, 1926–27, 1954–55;
Runners-up 1937–38;
Division 3: ***Runners-up*** 1964–65, 1989–90.

FA Cup: ***Runners-up*** 1909.

Football League Cup: Semi-final 1971, 1989.

Welsh Cup: ***Winners*** 1934.

Anglo-Scottish Cup: ***Winners*** 1978.

Freight Rover Trophy: ***Winners*** 1986; ***Runners-up*** 1987.

Auto Windscreens Shield: ***Runners-up*** 2000.

LDV Vans Trophy: ***Winners*** 2003.

sky SPORTS FACT FILE

In recent years the Ashton Gate "anthem" has been adopted from The Wurzels' recording of "One for the Bristol City" which reached No. 66 in the charts in September 2007. But the original version by the group was first recorded in 1976 with "Cheddar Cheese" on the flipside.

Record Defeat: 0–9 v Coventry C, Division 3 (S), 28 April 1934.

Most League Points (2 for a win): 70, Division 3 (S), 1954–55.

Most League Points (3 for a win): 91, Division 3, 1989–90.

Most League Goals: 104, Division 3 (S), 1926–27.

Highest League Scorer in Season: Don Clark, 36, Division 3 (S), 1946–47.

Most League Goals in Total Aggregate: John Atyeo, 314, 1951–66.

Most League Goals in One Match: 6, Tommy 'Tot' Walsh v Gillingham, Division 3 (S), 15 January 1927.

Most Capped Player: Billy Wedlock, 26, England.

Most League Appearances: John Atyeo, 597, 1951–66.

Youngest League Player: Marvin Brown, 16 years 105 days v Bristol R, 17 October 1999.

Record Transfer Fee Received: £3,000,000 from Wolverhampton W for Ade Akinbiyi, September 1999.

Record Transfer Fee Paid: £2,250,000 to Crewe Alex for Nicky Maynard, August 2008.

Football League Record: 1901 Elected to Division 2; 1906–11 Division 1; 1911–22 Division 2; 1922–23 Division 3 (S); 1923–24 Division 2; 1924–27 Division 3 (S); 1927–32 Division 2; 1932–55 Division 3 (S); 1955–60 Division 2; 1960–65 Division 3; 1965–76 Division 2; 1976–80 Division 1; 1980–81 Division 2; 1981–82 Division 3; 1982–84 Division 4; 1984–90 Division 3; 1990–92 Division 2; 1992–95 Division 1; 1995–98 Division 2; 1998–99 Division 1; 1999–04 Division 2; 2004–07 FL 1; 2007– FL C.

MANAGERS

Sam Hollis 1897–99
Bob Campbell 1899–1901
Sam Hollis 1901–05
Harry Thickett 1905–10
Frank Bacon 1910–11
Sam Hollis 1911–13
George Hedley 1913–17
Jack Hamilton 1917–19
Joe Palmer 1919–21
Alex Raisbeck 1921–29
Joe Bradshaw 1929–32
Bob Hewison 1932–49
(*under suspension 1938–39*)
Bob Wright 1949–50
Pat Beasley 1950–58
Peter Doherty 1958–60
Fred Ford 1960–67
Alan Dicks 1967–80
Bobby Houghton 1980–82
Roy Hodgson 1982
Terry Cooper 1982–88
(*Director from 1983*)
Joe Jordan 1988–90
Jimmy Lumsden 1990–92
Denis Smith 1992–93
Russell Osman 1993–94
Joe Jordan 1994–97
John Ward 1997–98
Benny Lennartsson 1998–99
Tony Pulis 1999–2000
Tony Fawthrop 2000
Danny Wilson 2000–04
Brian Tinnion 2004–05
Gary Johnson 2005–10
Steve Coppell 2010
Keith Millen 2010–11
Derek McInnes October 2011–

LATEST SEQUENCES

Longest Sequence of League Wins: 14, 9.9.1905 – 2.12.1905.

Longest Sequence of League Defeats: 7, 3.10.1970 – 7.11.1970.

Longest Sequence of League Draws: 4, 6.11.1999 – 27.11.1999.

Longest Sequence of Unbeaten League Matches: 24, 9.9.1905 – 10.2.1906.

Longest Sequence Without a League Win: 15, 29.4.1933 – 4.11.1933.

Successive Scoring Runs: 25 from 26.12.1905.

Successive Non-scoring Runs: 6 from 10.9.1910.

TEN YEAR LEAGUE RECORD

		P	*W*	*D*	*L*	*F*	*A*	*Pts*	*Pos*
2002-03	Div 2	46	24	11	11	79	48	83	3
2003-04	Div 2	46	23	13	10	58	37	82	3
2004-05	FL 1	46	18	16	12	74	57	70	7
2005-06	FL 1	46	18	11	17	66	62	65	9
2006-07	FL 1	46	25	10	11	63	39	85	2
2007-08	FL C	46	20	14	12	54	53	74	4
2008-09	FL C	46	15	16	15	54	54	61	10
2009-10	FL C	46	15	18	13	56	65	63	10
2010-11	FL C	46	17	9	20	62	65	60	15
2011-12	FL C	46	12	13	21	44	68	49	20

DID YOU KNOW ?

Billy Coggins succeeded Frank Vallis in goal for Bristol City. He made his bow on Boxing Day 1925 at 24 after service with Victoria Albion and Bristol St George. He let in only nine goals in his first 15 matches, was ever-present in the 1926–27 promotion and later played for Everton.

BRISTOL CITY 2011–12 LEAGUE RECORD

Match No.	*Date*	*Venue*	*Opponents*	*Result*		*H/T Score*	*Lg Pos.*	*Goalscorers*	*Attendance*
1	Aug 6	H	Ipswich T	L	0-3	0-1	—		14,517
2	14	A	Cardiff C	L	1-3	0-3	24	Maynard [82]	22,639
3	17	A	Leicester C	W	2-1	1-0	—	Maynard 2 [5, 66]	20,794
4	20	H	Portsmouth	D	0-0	0-0	17		12,496
5	27	A	Doncaster R	D	1-1	1-0	17	Adomah [45]	7778
6	Sept 10	H	Brighton & HA	L	0-1	0-0	22		13,911
7	17	A	Leeds U	L	1-2	1-1	23	Kilkenny [11]	22,655
8	24	H	Hull C	D	1-1	0-0	23	Pitman [79]	12,254
9	27	H	Reading	L	2-3	1-0	—	Adomah [23], Pitman [59]	12,018
10	Oct 1	A	Blackpool	L	0-5	0-1	24		11,734
11	15	H	Peterborough U	L	1-2	0-0	24	Elliott [82]	13,115
12	18	A	Crystal Palace	L	0-1	0-0	—		11,869
13	23	H	Birmingham C	L	0-2	0-1	24		13,577
14	29	A	Barnsley	W	2-1	1-0	24	Adomah [14], Maynard [90]	8900
15	Nov 1	A	West Ham U	D	0-0	0-0	—		27,980
16	5	H	Burnley	W	3-1	1-0	22	Pearson [42], Pitman [61], Adomah [73]	12,187
17	20	A	Millwall	W	2-1	1-0	22	Maynard 2 [14, 63]	10,252
18	26	H	Southampton	W	2-0	0-0	22	Adomah [48], Maynard [84]	16,346
19	29	A	Watford	D	2-2	1-2	—	Elliott [44], Mariappa (og) [46]	12,418
20	Dec 3	H	Middlesbrough	L	0-1	0-0	20		14,467
21	10	A	Derby Co	L	1-2	0-0	21	Woolford [56]	23,906
22	17	H	Nottingham F	D	0-0	0-0	21		13,121
23	26	A	Coventry C	L	0-1	0-0	21		15,302
24	30	A	Southampton	W	1-0	0-0	—	Pearson [79]	30,328
25	Jan 3	H	Millwall	W	1-0	0-0	—	Maynard [90]	12,410
26	14	A	Brighton & HA	L	0-2	0-1	20		20,398
27	21	H	Doncaster R	W	2-1	2-0	19	Wood [26], Cisse [31]	14,951
28	28	A	Reading	L	0-1	0-0	—		17,825
29	Feb 4	H	Leeds U	L	0-3	0-1	20		15,257
30	11	A	Hull C	L	0-3	0-2	21		17,435
31	14	H	Crystal Palace	D	2-2	0-1	—	Pitman 2 [77, 90]	12,470
32	18	A	Peterborough U	L	0-3	0-1	20		7004
33	25	H	Blackpool	L	1-3	1-0	21	Stead [29]	13,192
34	Mar 3	A	Ipswich T	L	0-3	0-1	21		16,671
35	6	H	Leicester C	W	3-2	1-1	—	Cisse [45], Pitman [54], Stead [79]	12,033
36	10	H	Cardiff C	L	1-2	0-1	21	Stead [52]	12,495
37	17	A	Portsmouth	D	0-0	0-0	21		16,695
38	20	H	Watford	L	0-2	0-2	—		12,017
39	24	A	Middlesbrough	D	1-1	1-0	21	Ephraim [13]	15,275
40	31	H	Derby Co	D	1-1	0-1	22	Pitman [74]	12,794
41	Apr 7	A	Nottingham F	W	1-0	0-0	21	Wood (pen) [55]	22,851
42	9	H	Coventry C	W	3-1	0-1	20	Stead [47], Bolasie [82], Wood [90]	19,003
43	14	A	Birmingham C	D	2-2	2-1	21	Pearson [21], Stead [33]	23,230
44	17	H	West Ham U	D	1-1	1-1	—	Skuse [29]	16,669
45	21	H	Barnsley	W	2-0	1-0	19	Skuse [11], Stead (pen) [51]	18,562
46	28	A	Burnley	D	1-1	0-0	20	Taylor [81]	13,369

Final League Position: 20

GOALSCORERS

League (44): Maynard 8, Pitman 7, Stead 6 (1 pen), Adomah 5, Pearson 3, Wood 3 (1 pen), Cisse 2, Elliott 2, Skuse 2, Bolasie 1, Ephraim 1, Kilkenny 1, Taylor 1, Woolford 1, own goal 1.
Carling Cup (0).
FA Cup (0).

James D 36	Spence J 9 + 1	McAllister J 11 + 1	Fontaine L 26	Nyatanga L 28 + 1	Skuse C 36	Adomah A 39 + 6	Elliott M 28	Stead J 16 + 8	Maynard N 26 + 1	Campbell-Ryce J 12 + 5	Kilkenny N 32 + 9	Pitman B 12 + 23	Woolford M 11 + 14	Wilson J 14 + 7	Gerken D 10	Cisse K 26 + 6	Taylor R — + 7	McGivern R 26 + 5	Bolasie Y 7 + 16	Carey L 18 + 2	Stewart D 3	Clarkson D — + 4	Pearson S 28	Foster R 20	Wood C 12 + 7	McManus S 6	Davis S 2 + 1	Bryan J 1	Bikey A 7	Ephraim H 3 + 2	Edwards J 1 + 1	Keinan D — + 1	Match No.
1	2	3^{3}	4	5	6	7	8	9^{2}	10	11^{1}	12	13	14																				1
1	2	3^{1}		5	6	7^{3}	8	13	10	14	11	9^{2}	12	4																			2
	2	3^{1}		5	6	7^{3}	8		10	11	9^{2}		12	4	1	13	14																3
	2	3		5	6	7^{2}	8		10	11	9^{1}		13	4	1		12																4
1	2	3^{1}		5	6	9	7	14	10^{3}	11	8^{2}	13	12	4																			5
1	2^{3}			5	6^{2}	9	8	12	10	11^{1}	7	13	14	4				3															6
1	2^{3}			5	6	9^{2}	7	14	10	11	8^{1}	12		4				3	13														7
1				5	2	7^{3}	8	9^{1}	10^{2}	11	4	13		6			12	3	14														8
1				5		7^{1}	8		10	11	4	9		6			12	3		2													9
	12			5		7	8		10^{3}	11^{2}	4	9	13	6	1		14	3^{1}		2													10
1	2^{2}			5	3	7	8	13	10	12	11	9				4^{1}					6												11
1				5	2	9	8		10^{1}	11	7	12				4^{2}	13	3			6												12
1			6	5	2^{1}	7	8	9^{3}	10	11^{2}	4	14				13		12			3												13
1			6	5	2	9	8		10^{3}		7	14	11^{1}	13		4^{2}		3	12														14
1			6	5	2	9	8		10^{3}		7		11^{1}	13		4^{2}		3	12			14											15
1			6	5	2	7	8		10^{3}		4	12	14			13		3	11^{1}				9^{2}										16
1			6	5	2	9^{3}	7		10^{2}		8	13	12			4^{1}		3	14				11										17
1			6	5	2	9	7		10^{3}		8	14	12	13		4^{1}		3					11^{2}										18
1			6	5^{3}	2	9	7		10		8	13	12	14		4^{2}		3					11^{1}										19
1			6		2	9			10		8	13	11^{1}	5		4		3	12				7^{2}										20
1			6	12	2	9	7		10	14	8^{3}	13	11	5		4^{2}		3^{1}															21
1			6	5	2	9	8		10^{2}		4^{3}	12	11^{1}			13		3				14	7										22
1				5	2	9	7	12	10^{3}	14	8^{2}	13		6		4^{1}		3					11										23
1				5	8	9^{3}	7		10		12		13	6		4^{1}		3		2		14	11^{2}										24
1				5	6	7	8^{1}		10		4	9^{3}				12^{2}		3	14	2		13	11										25
1				5	4		7^{2}		10		8^{3}	14	11^{1}			13		3	12	6				2	9								26
1				5	2^{1}	9		13			8	12		14		4			7^{3}	6			11	3	10^{2}								27
1				5	4	10			13		14			12		8^{3}		3^{2}	7^{1}	6■			11	2	9								28
1			6		2	10		13		14	4^{1}			5■		8^{3}		12	7■				11	3	9^{2}								29
1			6	5	2	10	8			7^{2}		13				4^{1}		12					11	3	9								30
1			6		4^{1}	10	7				12	13						3	8^{2}				11	2	9	5							31
1			6			9	7				8^{3}	10		13		4^{1}		3	14				11	2	12	5^{2}							32
1	2		6			7		10			4	12							13	5			11	3	9^{1}		8^{2}						33
1			6	5		9^{2}		10			8^{1}	14				4			13	3			11	2	12		7^{3}						34
1		3	6			14		10^{1}			13	9^{2}				4				2			11	7	12	5		8^{3}					35
1		3^{3}	6			12		10				9	11^{2}			4			14	2^{1}			8	7		5	13						36
1		3^{3}	6			8^{2}		10				9^{1}	13			4		14		2			11	7	12	5							37
1		3	6■			8		10			12	9^{2}				4^{3}			14	2^{1}			11	7	13	5							38
						9		10^{3}			4^{2}				1	8		3■		5			11	2	14				6	7^{1}	12	13	39
		12			2^{3}	9		10			8	13			1	4^{1}			14	6			11	3					5	7^{2}			40
		3			8	12		10^{2}			13		11		1	4				6				2	9				5	7^{1}			41
			6		4	7^{3}		10^{1}			8	9■			1			3	14				11^{2}	2	12				5	13			42
			6		8	12		10^{1}			14		11^{3}		1	4^{2}				3			7	2	9				5	13			43
			6		8	13		10^{3}					12		1	4^{2}		3	7^{1}	14			11	2	9				5				44
			6		4^{1}	8^{3}		10			13		11		1			3	14	12			7	2	9^{2}				5				45
1^{6}		3	6		4	15						10	11				13	12	8^{2}	5			7		9^{1}						2		46

FA Cup
Third Round Crawley T (a) 0-1

Carling Cup
First Round Swindon T (h) 0-1

BRISTOL ROVERS FL Championship 2

FOUNDATION

Bristol Rovers were formed at a meeting in Stapleton Road, Eastville, in 1883. However, they first went under the name of the Black Arabs (wearing black shirts). Changing their name to Eastville Rovers in their second season in 1888–89, they won the Gloucestershire Senior Cup. Original members of the Bristol & District League in 1892, this eventually became the Western League and Eastville Rovers adopted professionalism in 1897.

The Memorial Stadium, Filton Avenue, Horfield, Bristol BS7 0BF.

Telephone: (0117) 909 6648.

Fax: (0117) 907 4312.

Ticket Office: (0117) 909 8848.

Website: www.bristolrovers.co.uk

Email: rodwesson@bristolrovers.co.uk; dave@bristolrovers.co.uk

Ground Capacity: 11,626.

Record Attendance: 38,472 v Preston NE, FA Cup 4th rd, 30 January 1960 (at Eastville); 9,464 v Liverpool, FA Cup 4th rd, 8 February 1992 (at Twerton Park); 12,011 v WBA, FA Cup 6th rd, 9 March 2008 (at Memorial Stadium).

Pitch Measurements: 110yd × 73yd 6in.

Chairman: Nick Higgs.

Manager: Mark McGhee.

Assistant Manager: Shaun North.

Physio: Phil Kite.

Colours: Blue and white quarters, white shorts, white stockings.

Year Formed: 1883.

Turned Professional: 1897.

Previous Names: 1883, Black Arabs; 1884, Eastville Rovers; 1897, Bristol Eastville Rovers; 1898, Bristol Rovers. ***Club Nickname:*** 'Pirates'.

Grounds: 1883, Purdown; Three Acres, Ashley Hill; Rudgeway, Fishponds; 1897, Eastville; 1986, Twerton Park; 1996, The Memorial Stadium.

First Football League Game: 28 August 1920, Division 3, v Millwall (a) L 0–2 – Stansfield; Bethune, Panes; Boxley, Kenny, Steele; Chance, Bird, Sims, Bell, Palmer.

Record League Victory: 7–0 v Brighton & HA, Division 3 (S), 29 November 1952 – Hoyle; Bamford, Fox; Pitt, Warren, Sampson; McIlvenny, Roost (2), Lambden (1), Bradford (1), Petherbridge (2), (1 og). 7–0 v Swansea T, Division 2, 2 October 1954 – Radford; Bamford, Watkins; Pitt, Muir, Anderson; Petherbridge, Bradford (2), Meyer, Roost (1), Hooper (2), (2 og). 7–0 v Shrewsbury T, Division 3, 21 March 1964 – Hall; Hillard, Gwyn Jones; Oldfield, Stone (1), Mabbutt; Jarman (2), Brown (1), Biggs (1p), Hamilton, Bobby Jones (2).

HONOURS

Football League – Division 2: Best season: 4th, 1994–95; **Division 3 (S):** ***Champions*** 1952–53; **Division 3:** ***Champions*** 1989–90; ***Runners-up*** 1973–74.

FA Cup: Best season: 6th rd, 1951, 1958, 2008.

Football League Cup: Best season: 5th rd, 1971, 1972.

Leyland Daf: ***Runners-up*** 1990.

Johnstone's Paint Trophy: ***Runners-up*** 2007.

sky SPORTS FACT FILE

Twenty years' service with Bristol Rovers, half-back and skipper Ray Warren's career spanned the Second World War. He made 453 League appearances, another 43 in wartime games though Rovers missed five seasons 1940–45. He also helped Bristol City ten times as a guest.

Record Cup Victory: 6–0 v Merthyr Tydfil, FA Cup 1st rd, 14 November 1987 – Martyn; Alexander (Dryden), Tanner, Hibbitt, Twentyman, Vaughan Jones, Holloway, Meacham (1), White (2), Penrice (3) (Reece), Purnell.

Record Defeat: 0–12 v Luton T, Division 3 (S), 13 April 1936.

Most League Points (2 for a win): 64, Division 3 (S), 1952–53.

Most League Points (3 for a win): 93, Division 3, 1989–90.

Most League Goals: 92, Division 3 (S), 1952–53.

Highest League Scorer in Season: Geoff Bradford, 33, Division 3 (S), 1952–53.

Most League Goals in Total Aggregate: Geoff Bradford, 242, 1949–64.

Most League Goals in One Match: 4, Sidney Leigh v Exeter C, Division 3 (S), 2 May 1921; 4, Jonah Wilcox v Bournemouth, Division 3 (S), 12 December 1925; 4, Bill Culley v QPR, Division 3 (S), 5 March 1927; 4, Frank Curran v Swindon T, Division 3 (S), 25 March 1939; 4, Vic Lambden v Aldershot, Division 3 (S), 29 March 1947; 4, George Petherbridge v Torquay U, Division 3 (S), 1 December 1951; 4, Vic Lambden v Colchester U, Division 3 (S), 14 May 1952; 4, Geoff Bradford v Rotherham U, Division 2, 14 March 1959; 4, Robin Stubbs v Gillingham, Division 2, 10 October 1970; 4, Alan Warboys v Brighton & HA, Division 3, 1 December 1973; 4, Jamie Cureton v Reading, Division 2, 16 January 1999.

Most Capped Player: Vitalijs Astafjevs, 31 (167), Latvia.

Most League Appearances: Stuart Taylor, 546, 1966–80.

Youngest League Player: Ronnie Dix, 15 years 173 days v Charlton Ath, 25 February 1928.

Record Transfer Fee Received: £2,100,000 from Fulham for Barry Hayles, November 1998; £2,100,000 from WBA for Jason Roberts, July 2000.

Record Transfer Fee Paid: £375,000 to QPR for Andy Tillson, November 1992.

Football League Record: 1920 Original Member of Division 3; 1921–53 Division 3 (S); 1953–62 Division 2; 1962–74 Division 3; 1974–81 Division 2; 1981–90 Division 3; 1990–92 Division 2. 1992–93 Division 1; 1993–2001 Division 2; 2001–04 Division 3; 2004–07 FL 2; 2007–11 FL 1; 2011– FL 2.

MANAGERS

Alfred Homer 1899–1920 (*continued as Secretary to 1928*)
Ben Hall 1920–21
Andy Wilson 1921–26
Joe Palmer 1926–29
Dave McLean 1929–30
Albert Prince-Cox 1930–36
Percy Smith 1936–37
Brough Fletcher 1938–49
Bert Tann 1950–68 (*continued as General Manager to 1972*)
Fred Ford 1968–69
Bill Dodgin Snr 1969–72
Don Megson 1972–77
Bobby Campbell 1978–79
Harold Jarman 1979–80
Terry Cooper 1980–81
Bobby Gould 1981–83
David Williams 1983–85
Bobby Gould 1985–87
Gerry Francis 1987–91
Martin Dobson 1991
Dennis Rofe 1992
Malcolm Allison 1992–93
John Ward 1993–96
Ian Holloway 1996–2001
Garry Thompson 2001
Gerry Francis 2001
Garry Thompson 2001–02
Ray Graydon 2002–04
Ian Atkins 2004–05
Paul Trollope 2005–10
Dave Penney 2011
Paul Buckle 2011
Mark McGhee January 2012–

LATEST SEQUENCES

Longest Sequence of League Wins: 12, 18.10.1952 – 17.1.1953.

Longest Sequence of League Defeats: 8, 26.10.2002 – 21.12.2002.

Longest Sequence of League Draws: 5, 1.11.1975 – 22.11.1975.

Longest Sequence of Unbeaten League Matches: 32, 7.4.1973 – 27.1.1974.

Longest Sequence Without a League Win: 20, 5.4.1980 – 1.11.1980.

Successive Scoring Runs: 26 from 26.3.1927.

Successive Non-scoring Runs: 6 from 14.10.1922.

TEN YEAR LEAGUE RECORD

		P	W	D	L	F	A	Pts	Pos
2002-03	Div 3	46	12	15	19	50	57	51	20
2003-04	Div 3	46	14	13	19	50	61	55	15
2004-05	FL 2	46	13	21	12	60	57	60	12
2005-06	FL 2	46	17	9	20	59	67	60	12
2006-07	FL 2	46	20	12	14	49	42	72	6
2007-08	FL 1	46	12	17	17	45	53	53	16
2008-09	FL 1	46	17	12	17	79	61	63	11
2009-10	FL 1	46	19	5	22	59	70	62	11
2010-11	FL 1	46	11	12	23	48	82	45	22
2011-12	FL 2	46	15	12	19	60	70	57	13

DID YOU KNOW?

The first Bristol Rovers player to score a hat trick on his League debut was centre-forward Joe Riley. On 2 January 1922, his treble came from a 4-1 win over Bournemouth. Snapped up by neighbours Bristol City a year later, he subsequently played for Bournemouth!

BRISTOL ROVERS 2011–12 LEAGUE RECORD

Match No.	Date	Venue	Opponents	Result		H/T Score	Lg Pos.	Goalscorers	Attendance
1	Aug 6	A	AFC Wimbledon	W	3-2	2-1	—	McGleish [17], Harrold [20], Virgo (pen) [85]	4629
2	13	H	Torquay U	L	1-2	0-2	11	Anthony [56]	8427
3	16	H	Northampton T	W	2-1	1-0	—	Osei-Kuffour [29], Harrold [75]	5812
4	20	A	Macclesfield T	D	0-0	0-0	9		1865
5	27	H	Hereford U	D	0-0	0-0	10		6342
6	Sept 3	A	Crawley T	L	1-4	0-2	14	Brown, L [80]	3693
7	10	A	Bradford C	D	2-2	1-0	15	Harrold [40], Richards [78]	10,023
8	13	H	Shrewsbury T	W	1-0	1-0	—	Zebroski [19]	5065
9	17	H	Aldershot T	L	0-1	0-1	16		5640
10	24	A	Morecambe	W	3-2	1-0	12	Bolger [27], McGleish [65], Anyinsah [72]	2583
11	Oct 1	H	Cheltenham T	L	1-3	0-2	15	Brown, L [65]	6108
12	8	A	Oxford U	L	0-3	0-1	17		9291
13	14	H	Rotherham U	W	5-2	3-1	—	McGleish 2 (1 pen) [10, 29 (p)], Bolger [32], Brown, L [58], Anyinsah [88]	5395
14	22	A	Burton Alb	L	1-2	1-2	14	Harrold [14]	3094
15	25	H	Port Vale	L	0-3	0-2	—		5444
16	29	H	Dagenham & R	W	2-0	0-0	15	Anyinsah [50], Harrold (pen) [90]	5475
17	Nov 5	A	Accrington S	L	1-2	0-2	16	Anyinsah [48]	1643
18	19	H	Barnet	L	0-2	0-1	17		5024
19	26	A	Southend U	D	1-1	0-0	18	Harrold [77]	6237
20	Dec 10	H	Swindon T	D	1-1	0-1	18	Woodards [88]	7726
21	17	A	Gillingham	L	1-4	0-2	18	Carayol [52]	7750
22	26	H	Plymouth Arg	L	2-3	2-0	18	Harrold 2 (1 pen) [30 (p), 32]	8090
23	31	H	Crewe Alex	L	2-5	1-4	19	Harrold [9], McGleish [48]	5037
24	Jan 2	A	Barnet	L	0-2	0-0	19		2537
25	10	A	Hereford U	W	2-1	1-0	—	Brown, L [9], McGleish [72]	2411
26	14	H	Crawley T	D	0-0	0-0	18		5082
27	21	A	Cheltenham T	W	2-0	0-0	17	Zebroski [60], Richards [63]	5288
28	28	H	Bradford C	W	2-1	1-0	16	Brown, L [6], Richards [55]	6164
29	Feb 11	H	Morecambe	W	2-1	0-0	—	Brown, L [57], McGleish (pen) [75]	5381
30	14	A	Shrewsbury T	L	0-1	0-0	—		4928
31	18	H	Oxford U	D	0-0	0-0	16		6512
32	25	A	Rotherham U	W	1-0	0-0	16	Dorman [90]	3937
33	Mar 3	H	Macclesfield T	D	0-0	0-0	16		5420
34	6	A	Northampton T	L	2-3	0-3	—	Stanley [66], Brown, L (pen) [86]	4028
35	10	A	Torquay U	D	2-2	1-0	16	Harrold [45], Zebroski [69]	3920
36	17	H	AFC Wimbledon	W	1-0	1-0	14	Carayol [11]	5828
37	20	A	Plymouth Arg	D	1-1	1-0	—	Harrold [14]	7531
38	24	H	Southend U	W	1-0	0-0	14	Harrold (pen) [86]	6258
39	27	A	Aldershot T	L	0-1	0-1	—		2870
40	31	A	Swindon T	D	0-0	0-0	14		9645
41	Apr 6	H	Gillingham	D	2-2	0-0	14	Richards [59], Carayol [80]	6160
42	9	A	Crewe Alex	L	0-3	0-2	15		4139
43	14	H	Burton Alb	W	7-1	1-0	14	Carayol [42], Richards 3 [46, 76, 81], Harrold 2 (1 pen) [61 (p), 75], Paterson [65]	5353
44	21	A	Port Vale	L	0-1	0-1	15		4066
45	28	H	Accrington S	W	5-1	3-1	12	Harrold 2 (1 pen) [11, 22 (p)], Dorman [29], Lund 2 [58, 78]	7073
46	May 5	A	Dagenham & R	L	0-4	0-1	13		2377

Final League Position: 13

GOALSCORERS

League (60): Harrold 16 (5 pens), Brown, L 7 (1 pen), McGleish 7 (2 pens), Richards 7, Anyinsah 4, Carayol 4, Zebroski 3, Bolger 2, Dorman 2, Lund 2, Anthony 1, Osei-Kuffour 1, Paterson 1, Stanley 1, Virgo 1 (1 pen), Woodards 1.
Carling Cup (3): Harrold 1, Richards 1, Zebroski 1.
FA Cup (10): McGleish 2 (1 pen), Richards 2, Carayol 2, Anthony 1, Anyinsah 1, Woodards 1, Zebroski 1.
J Paint Trophy (1): Harrold 1.

Bevan S 37	Smith M 8 + 12	Brown L 35 + 7	Virgo A 9	Anthony B 14 + 2	Stanley C 30 + 4	Anyinsah J 23 + 8	Gill M 32 + 1	Harrold M 35 + 5	McGleish S 14 + 13	Zebroski C 28 + 11	Lines C — + 1	Osei-Kuffour J 3 + 2	Carayol M 24 + 6	Brown W 4 + 8	Bolger C 38 + 1	Richards E 18 + 14	Campbell S 10 + 1	Woodards D 39	Sawyer G 23 + 1	Rendell S 4 + 1	Norburn O 1 + 4	Dorman A 20 + 5	McLaggon K — + 1	Cronin L — + 1	Poke M 8	Downes A 8	Paterson J 17	Parkes T 14	Lund M 9 + 4	Gough C 1	Harding M — + 1	*Match No.*
1	2	3	4	5	6	7^{3}	8	9	10^{2}	11^{1}	12	13	14																			1
1	2	3	4	5	6^{2}	7	8	9	10^{1}	14		12	11^{3}	13																		2
1		3	4	2	6	7^{1}	8	9	10^{2}	12		11		13	5																	3
1		3	4	2	6		8	9	10	7^{2}		11^{1}		12	5	13																4
1	2^{2}	3	4	5	6^{1}		8	9	10	7		11^{3}	14	13			12															5
1	12	3	4^{2}	5			8	9^{3}	13	10			11^{1}	6		14	7	2														6
1		3	4	12		13	8^{1}	9	10^{2}					7	5	11	6	2														7
1	12	3^{1}	4			14	8^{2}	9	13	10^{3}				7	5	11	6	2														8
1		3	4		12	8^{3}		9	14	10			13	7^{1}	5	11^{2}	6	2														9
1	13	3		6	12	7^{3}	8^{1}	9	10	11					5	14	4	2^{2}														10
1	12	3		4	6	8		13		10^{3}			11^{2}	14	5	9	7	2^{1}														11
1	12	3		2^{1}	6	8		13	10^{2}	11					5		7		4	9												12
1		3			6	12	8	11^{3}	10^{1}	14					5		7^{2}	2	4	9	13											13
1		3			6	13	8^{3}	9	10^{2}	14					5		7^{1}	2	4	11	12											14
1		3			6	12	8	9	10^{3}	14			13		5			2^{2}	4	11	7^{1}											15
1		3			6	7	8	9	10^{1}				11		5			2	4	12												16
1		3			6	7		9	10^{1}	12			11		5		8	2	4													17
1		3			12	7	8^{1}	9^{2}	13^{3}	10			11		5	14		2	6			4										18
1		3		5	6	7	8	13		10^{2}			11^{1}			12		2	4			9										19
1		3		5	6	7		9		10^{1}			11^{2}			12		2	4		13	8										20
1		3		5^{1}	6	7^{3}		13		10^{2}			11		12■	9		2	4		14	8										21
1		3		5	6	7^{2}		9	12	11^{1}						10		2	4			8	13									22
1^{G}		13		5^{1}	6	7^{2}		9	12	10			11		3			2	4			8		15								23
					6^{2}	13		9^{1}	12	10			11		5	7		2	3			8			1	4						24
		3			6	7			12	10					5	9		2	4^{1}			8			1	11						25
		11		13	6	7^{1}			12	10					5	9^{2}		2	3			8			1	4						26
		11			6	7^{1}			12	10					5	9		2	3			8			1	4						27
	7	3			6		11		12	10					5	9		2^{1}				8			1	4						28
		11			6	7^{1}	8	9^{2}	10						5	12		2							1		3	4	13			29
		11^{3}			6	7^{2}	8	9^{1}	13						5	10		2				14			1		3	4	12			30
		11				9^{2}	4		14	10^{3}			12		5	13		2				8^{1}			1		3	6	7			31
1		14				9^{3}	8	12		10^{1}			11^{2}		5	13		2				7					3	6	4			32
1	2^{2}	11			13		7	9		12			10		5			4				8^{1}					3		6			33
1	12	11			6	9^{2}	8			14			10		5	13		2^{1}									3	4	7^{3}			34
1					6	13^{3}	7	9^{2}		10			11^{1}		5	14		2				8					3	4	12			35
1	12	7^{1}			6		8	9		10			11^{2}		5	13		2									3	4				36
1	12	7^{1}			6		8	9		10			11^{2}		5			2				13					3	4				37
1		12			6		8^{3}	9		10^{1}			11		5	13		2				14					3	4	7^{2}			38
1	2	6^{2}						9		12			13		5	10^{1}		4	3			8					11		7			39
1	12	13					8	9		10^{3}			11^{1}		5			2	3^{2}			14					6	4	7			40
1	14				6		12	9		10^{2}			11		5	13		2^{3}	7								3^{1}	4	8			41
1	10^{1}					14	6	9		12					5	8		2	7^{3}			13				3		4	11^{2}			42
1	14	13					6	9					11^{2}	12	5	10		2^{3}	7			8					3^{1}	4				43
1	12	14					6	9		13			11^{1}		5	10^{2}		2	3			8					7^{3}	4■				44
1	2	12					6	9					11	14	5	10^{3}			7^{1}			8				4	3^{2}		13			45
		4^{2}					7	9					11	13	5	10^{3}		2	12			8				6	3^{1}			1	14	46

FA Cup

First Round	Corby T	(h)	3-1
Second Round	AFC Totton	(a)	6-1
Third Round	Aston Villa	(h)	1-3

Carling Cup

First Round	Watford	(h)	1-1
Second Round	Leyton Orient	(a)	2-3

J Paint Trophy

First Round	Wycombe W	(a)	1-3

BURNLEY FL Championship

FOUNDATION

On 18 May 1882 Burnley (Association) Football Club was still known as Burnley Rovers as members of that rugby club had decided on that date to play Association Football in the future. It was only a matter of days later that the members met again and decided to drop Rovers from the club's name.

Turf Moor, Harry Potts Way, Burnley, Lancashire BB10 4BX.

Telephone: (0871) 221 1882.

Fax: (01282) 700 014.

Ticket Office: (0871) 221 1914.

Website: www.burnleyfc.com

Email: info@burnleyfc.com

Ground Capacity: 22,610.

Record Attendance: 54,775 v Huddersfield T, FA Cup 3rd rd, 23 February 1924.

Pitch Measurements: 112yd × 70yd.

Chairmen: Mike Garlick and John Banaszkiewicz.

Manager: Eddie Howe.

Assistant Manager: Jason Tindall.

Head Physio: Alasdair Beattie.

Colours: Claret shirts with blue sleeves, white shorts, claret stockings.

Year Formed: 1882.

Turned Professional: 1883.

Previous Name: 1882, Burnley Rovers; 1882, Burnley.

Club Nickname: 'The Clarets'.

Grounds: 1882, Calder Vale; 1883, Turf Moor.

First Football League Game: 8 September 1888, Football League, v Preston NE (a) L 2–5 – Smith; Lang, Bury, Abrahams, Friel, Keenan, Brady, Tait, Poland (1), Gallocher (1), Yates.

Record League Victory: 9–0 v Darwen, Division 1, 9 January 1892 – Hillman; Walker, McFettridge, Lang, Matthews, Keenan, Nicol (3), Bowes, Espie (1), McLardie (3), Hill (2).

Record Cup Victory: 9–0 v Crystal Palace, FA Cup 2nd rd (replay), 10 February 1909 – Dawson; Barron, McLean; Cretney (2), Leake, Moffat; Morley, Ogden, Smith (3), Abbott (2), Smethams (1). 9–0 v New Brighton, FA Cup 4th rd, 26 January 1957 – Blacklaw; Angus, Winton; Seith, Adamson, Miller; Newlands (1), McIlroy (3), Lawson (3), Cheesebrough (1), Pilkington (1). 9–0 v Penrith, FA Cup 1st rd, 17 November 1984 – Hansbury; Miller, Hampton, Phelan, Overson (Kennedy), Hird (3 incl. 1p), Grewcock (1), Powell (2), Taylor (3), Biggins, Hutchison.

Record Defeat: 0–10 v Aston Villa, Division 1, 29 August 1925 and v Sheffield U, Division 1, 19 January 1929.

HONOURS

Football League – Division 1: ***Champions*** 1920–21, 1959–60; ***Runners-up*** 1919–20, 1961–62; **Division 2: *Champions*** 1897–98, 1972–73; ***Runners-up*** 1912–13, 1946–47, 1999–2000; **Division 3: *Champions*** 1981–82; **Division 4: *Champions*** 1991–92. Record 30 consecutive Division 1 games without defeat 1920–21.

FA Cup: *Winners* 1914; ***Runners-up*** 1947, 1962.

Football League Cup: Semi-final 1961, 1969, 1983, 2009.

Anglo-Scottish Cup: *Winners* 1979.

Sherpa Van Trophy: ***Runners-up*** 1988.

European Competitions
European Cup: 1960–61.
European Fairs Cup: 1966–67.

sky SPORTS FACT FILE

In 1885–86 in a dispute with the Football Association over the professional status of some of their players, Burnley fielded their reserves in an FA Cup tie against Darwen Old Wanderers and lost 11-0. Two years later at the same stage they managed some redress beating the Old Boys 4-0.

Most League Points (2 for a win): 62, Division 2, 1972–73.

Most League Points (3 for a win): 88, Division 2, 1999–2000.

Most League Goals: 102, Division 1, 1960–61.

Highest League Scorer in Season: George Beel, 35, Division 1, 1927–28.

Most League Goals in Total Aggregate: George Beel, 179, 1923–32.

Most League Goals in One Match: 6, Louis Page v Birmingham C, Division 1, 10 April 1926.

Most Capped Player: Jimmy McIlroy, 51 (55), Northern Ireland.

Most League Appearances: Jerry Dawson, 522, 1907–28.

Youngest League Player: Tommy Lawton, 16 years 174 days v Doncaster R, 28 March 1936.

Record Transfer Fee Received: £6,500,000 from Wolverhampton W for Steven Fletcher, June 2010.

Record Transfer Fee Paid: £3,000,000 to Hibernian for Steven Fletcher, June 2009.

Football League Record: 1888 Original Member of the Football League; 1897–98 Division 2; 1898–1900 Division 1; 1900–13 Division 2; 1913–30 Division 1; 1930–47 Division 2; 1947–71 Division 1; 1971–73 Division 2; 1973–76 Division 1; 1976–80 Division 2; 1980–82 Division 3; 1982–83 Division 2; 1983–85 Division 3; 1985–92 Division 4; 1992–94 Division 2; 1994–95 Division 1; 1995–2000 Division 2; 2000–04 Division 1; 2004–09 FL C; 2009–10 FA Premier League; 2010– FL C.

MANAGERS

Harry Bradshaw 1894–99 (*Secretary-Manager from 1897*)
Club Directors 1899–1900
J. Ernest Mangnall 1900–03 (*Secretary-Manager*)
Spen Whittaker 1903–10 (*Secretary-Manager*)
John Haworth 1910–24 (*Secretary-Manager*)
Albert Pickles 1925–31 (*Secretary-Manager*)
Tom Bromilow 1932–35
Selection Committee 1935–45
Cliff Britton 1945–48
Frank Hill 1948–54
Alan Brown 1954–57
Billy Dougall 1957–58
Harry Potts 1958–70 (*General Manager to 1972*)
Jimmy Adamson 1970–76
Joe Brown 1976–77
Harry Potts 1977–79
Brian Miller 1979–83
John Bond 1983–84
John Benson 1984–85
Martin Buchan 1985
Tommy Cavanagh 1985–86
Brian Miller 1986–89
Frank Casper 1989–91
Jimmy Mullen 1991–96
Adrian Heath 1996–97
Chris Waddle 1997–98
Stan Ternent 1998–2004
Steve Cotterill 2004–07
Owen Coyle 2007–10
Brian Laws 2010
Eddie Howe January 2011–

LATEST SEQUENCES

Longest Sequence of League Wins: 10, 16.11.1912 – 18.1.1913.

Longest Sequence of League Defeats: 8, 2.1.1995 – 25.2.1995.

Longest Sequence of League Draws: 6, 21.2.1931 – 28.3.1931.

Longest Sequence of Unbeaten League Matches: 30, 6.9.1920 – 25.3.1921.

Longest Sequence Without a League Win: 24, 16.4.1979 – 17.11.1979.

Successive Scoring Runs: 27 from 13.2.1926.

Successive Non-scoring Runs: 6 from 9.8.1997.

TEN YEAR LEAGUE RECORD

		P	W	D	L	F	A	Pts	Pos
2002-03	Div 1	46	15	10	21	65	89	55	16
2003-04	Div 1	46	13	14	19	60	77	53	19
2004-05	FL C	46	15	15	16	38	39	60	13
2005-06	FL C	46	14	12	20	46	54	54	17
2006-07	FL C	46	15	12	19	52	49	57	15
2007-08	FL C	46	16	14	16	60	67	62	13
2008-09	FL C	46	21	13	12	72	60	76	5
2009-10	PR Lge	38	8	6	24	42	82	30	18
2010-11	FL C	46	18	14	14	65	61	68	8
2011-12	FL C	46	17	11	18	61	58	62	13

DID YOU KNOW ?

Twelve goals were scored in a game involving Burnley on 28 March 1898 when Loughborough Town were beaten 9-3. Jimmy Ross had a hat trick in only 14 minutes and finished the game with five to his credit. Burnley won the Second Division championship that same season.

BURNLEY 2011–12 LEAGUE RECORD

Match No.	Date	Venue	Opponents	Result	H/T Score	Lg Pos.	Goalscorers	Attendance
1	Aug 6	H	Watford	D 2-2	0-1	—	Austin [77], Treacy [84]	14,617
2	13	A	Crystal Palace	L 0-2	0-1	19		13,167
3	20	H	Cardiff C	D 1-1	1-1	21	Austin [2]	13,428
4	27	A	Derby Co	W 2-1	0-0	15	Austin 2 [49, 74]	23,913
5	Sept 10	H	Middlesbrough	L 0-2	0-1	20		15,220
6	17	A	Peterborough U	L 1-2	1-2	21	Treacy [45]	7901
7	24	H	Southampton	D 1-1	0-0	21	Austin [53]	14,170
8	27	H	Nottingham F	W 5-1	4-0	—	Rodriguez 2 [5, 15], McCann [29], Wallace [44], Austin [71]	13,265
9	Oct 1	A	Millwall	W 1-0	1-0	14	Rodriguez [37]	10,460
10	15	H	Reading	L 0-1	0-0	16		13,664
11	18	A	Barnsley	L 0-2	0-1	—		9692
12	22	A	Coventry C	W 2-1	0-0	17	Wallace [73], Austin [90]	12,785
13	29	H	Blackpool	W 3-1	2-0	15	Austin [20], Wallace [29], Bartley [79]	15,614
14	Nov 1	H	Leicester C	L 1-3	1-1	—	Wallace [23]	13,286
15	5	A	Bristol C	L 1-3	0-1	18	Wallace [47]	12,187
16	19	H	Leeds U	L 1-2	1-0	21	Rodriguez [10]	17,226
17	22	A	Birmingham C	L 1-2	0-1	—	Bartley [49]	16,253
18	26	A	Hull C	W 3-2	0-1	16	Edgar 2 [78, 82], Rodriguez [90]	20,238
19	29	H	Ipswich T	W 4-0	2-0	—	Vokes [33], McCann 2 [45, 66], Rodriguez [77]	12,499
20	Dec 3	A	West Ham U	W 2-1	0-0	10	McCann [57], Vokes [75]	26,274
21	10	H	Portsmouth	L 0-1	0-0	15		13,411
22	17	A	Brighton & HA	W 1-0	1-0	11	Trippier [32]	19,641
23	26	H	Doncaster R	W 3-0	1-0	9	Rodriguez (pen) [37], Paterson [84], Hird (og) [90]	16,756
24	31	H	Hull C	W 1-0	1-0	7	Paterson [34]	15,071
25	Jan 2	A	Leeds U	L 1-2	0-0	10	Austin [69]	27,295
26	14	A	Middlesbrough	W 2-0	2-0	10	Rodriguez [6], Trippier [28]	17,001
27	21	H	Derby Co	D 0-0	0-0	12		14,302
28	31	A	Nottingham F	W 2-0	1-0	—	Rodriguez 2 [3, 64]	23,147
29	Feb 4	H	Peterborough U	D 1-1	0-1	11	Rodriguez [87]	13,258
30	11	A	Southampton	L 0-2	0-2	11		24,099
31	14	H	Barnsley	W 2-0	1-0	—	Rodriguez [3], Austin [63]	12,355
32	17	A	Reading	L 0-1	0-1	—		17,185
33	25	H	Millwall	L 1-3	0-2	11	Rodriguez (pen) [90]	13,000
34	Mar 3	A	Watford	L 2-3	1-0	12	Rodriguez [41], Nosworthy (og) [50]	11,612
35	10	H	Crystal Palace	D 1-1	1-0	13	Rodriguez (pen) [2]	13,216
36	18	A	Cardiff C	D 0-0	0-0	14		21,276
37	21	A	Ipswich T	L 0-1	0-0	—		16,564
38	24	H	West Ham U	D 2-2	2-0	16	Bartley [25], Paterson [36]	15,246
39	31	A	Portsmouth	W 5-1	1-1	16	Trippier [16], Ings [47], Austin 3 [74, 89, 90]	15,739
40	Apr 3	H	Birmingham C	L 1-3	0-1	—	Ings [74]	13,221
41	6	H	Brighton & HA	W 1-0	1-0	—	Austin [23]	13,516
42	9	A	Doncaster R	W 2-1	1-0	12	McQuoid [36], Austin (pen) [76]	8350
43	14	H	Coventry C	D 1-1	1-0	11	Austin [20]	13,398
44	17	A	Leicester C	D 0-0	0-0	—		19,806
45	21	A	Blackpool	L 0-4	0-1	12		14,141
46	28	H	Bristol C	D 1-1	0-0	13	Ings [76]	13,369

Final League Position: 13

GOALSCORERS

League (61): Austin 16 (1 pen), Rodriguez 15 (3 pens), Wallace 5, McCann 4, Bartley 3, Ings 3, Paterson 3, Trippier 3, Edgar 2, Treacy 2, Vokes 2, McQuoid 1, own goals 2.
Carling Cup (11): Rodriguez 5 (2 pens), Austin 1, Bikey 1, Elliott 1, McCann 1, Trippier 1, Wallace 1.
FA Cup (1): Rodriguez 1.

Grant L 42 + 1	Trippier K 46	Fox D 1	Bikey A 9 + 5	Mee B 29 + 2	McCann C 45 + 1	Elliott W 2 + 2	Marney D 29 + 8	Rodriguez J 36 + 1	Paterson M 9 + 5	Wallace R 41 + 3	Austin C 30 + 11	Treacy K 16 + 8	Easton B 17 + 4	Edgar D 44	Bartley M 25 + 14	Duff M 30 + 1	Hines Z — + 13	MacDonald A — + 5	Jensen B 4	Stanislas J 25 + 6	Vokes S 3 + 6	McQuoid J 9 + 8	Ings D 9 + 6	Lafferty D 5	Howieson C — + 2	Hewitt S — + 1	McCartan S — + 1	Jackson J — + 1	*Match No.*
1	2	3	4	5	6	7[2]	8	9	10[1]	11	12	13																	1
1	2		4	5	6	7		9		11	12	10[2]	3	8[1]	13■														2
1	2			5	6	13	8	9		11[3]	10[1]	7[2]	3			4	12	14											3
	2		13	5	6	12	8	9		11[1]	10[2]	7[3]	3	4				14	1										4
	2			5	6		8[2]	9		11	10[3]	7[1]	3	4	13		14		1	12									5
15	2			5	6		8[2]	9		11[1]	10	7	3	4	13				1[G]	12									6
1	2		4		6		12	9		11[2]	10[3]		3	5	8		13	14		7[1]									7
1	2		5		6		12	9		11	10[2]		3	4	8[3]		13	14		7[1]									8
1	2		4		6		12	9		11	10	13	5	3	8[1]					7[2]									9
1	2		5		6			9		11	10	12	3	4	8					7[1]									10
1	2		5		6			9		11[2]	10	12	3	4	8		13			7[1]									11
1	2		5[2]	13	6			9[3]		11	12	10[1]	3	4	8		14			7									12
1	2		12	5	6		14	9		11[3]	10	13	3[1]	4	8					7[2]									13
1	2		5	3	6			9		11[2]	10	12		4	8[3]	14	13			7[1]									14
1	2			3	6[2]		14	9		11	10	12	5	4	8[3]		13			7[1]									15
1	2				6			9			10[1]	7	3	4	8	5	13			11[2]	12								16
1	2		13		6[1]		12	9		11		7[2]	3	4	8	5					10								17
1	2		13	5	6			9		11[2]		10		4	8	3				7[1]	12								18
1	2			3	6		12	9[3]				7		4	8[1]	5	13	14		11	10[2]								19
1	2			3	6		10	9		12		7[1]		4	8	5				11[2]	13								20
1	2			3	6			9	12	11	13			4	8	5				7[1]	10[2]								21
1	2			3	6		8	9	10[2]	11	13			4	7[1]	5					12								22
1	2			3	6		8	9	10[3]	7	14		12	4	13	5[1]				11[2]									23
1	2			5	6		8	9	10[2]	11		7[1]	3	4	12						13								24
1	2■		12	5	6		8	9		11	10[2]		3	4						7[1]	13								25
1	2			3	6		8	9	10[2]	7	13			4	12	5				11[1]									26
1	2			3	6		8	9		11[1]	10	7[2]		4	13	5						12							27
1	2			3	6		8	9		12	10[3]	11[1]		4	13	5	14					7[2]							28
1	2			3[2]	6		8[3]	9		11	10	12		4	13	5	14					7[1]							29
1	2			3[3]	6		8[1]	9		7	10	11[2]		4	13	5	14					12							30
1	2[3]			3	6		8	9		11[1]	10[2]		14	4	12	5						7	13						31
1	2			3	6		8[3]	9	12	7	10[2]			4	14	5						11[1]	13						32
1	2			3	6[1]			9	12	7	10[3]	11[2]	14	4	8	5							13						33
1	2			3	6		8	9	14	11	10[2]		12	4		5[1]						7[3]	13						34
1	2			3	6		8	9[1]	10[3]	7[2]	13			4		5				14		12	11						35
1	2				6		8		10[2]	7	13			4	12	5				11[1]		14	9[3]	3					36
1	2			12	6		8[2]	9	14	13	10[3]			4	7	5				11				3[1]					37
1	2			3	6		8		10[3]	11	12			4	7[1]	5				14		13	9[2]						38
1	2			3[2]	6		8		10[1]	11	12			4	7	5				14		13	9[3]						39
1	2				6		8[1]			3	10			4	7	5				12		11[2]	9		13				40
1	2				6		12			3	10[2]			4	8[1]	5				11		7	9			13			41
1	2				6		8			3	10			4		5				11[1]		7	9				12		42
1	2				6		8[1]			3	10			4	12	5				11		7	9						43
1	2				6[2]		8			7	10			4	9	5				11[1]		12	13	3					44
1	2				6		8			7	10[2]			4	11[1]	5				9[3]		13	12	3				14	45
	2				12		6[1]	13		7[2]	10			4	8	5			1	11[3]			9	3	14				46

FA Cup

Third Round	Norwich C	(a)	1-4

Carling Cup

First Round	Burton Alb	(h)	6-3
Second Round	Barnet	(h)	3-2
Third Round	Milton Keynes D	(h)	2-1
Fourth Round	Cardiff C	(a)	0-1

BURTON ALBION FL Championship 2

FOUNDATION

Once upon a time there were three Football League clubs bearing the name Burton. Then there was none. In reality it had been two. Originally Burton Swifts and Burton Wanderers competed in it until 1901 when they amalgamated to form Burton United. This club disbanded in 1910. There was no senior club representing the town until 1924 when Burton Town, formerly known as Burton All Saints, played in the Birmingham & District League, subsequently joining the Midland League in 1935–36. When the Second World War broke out the club fielded a team in a truncated version of the Birmingham & District League taking over from the club's reserves. But it was not revived in peacetime. So it was not until a further decade that a club bearing the name of Burton reappeared. Founded in 1950 Burton Albion made progress from the Birmingham & District League, too, then into the Southern League and because of its geographical situation later had spells in the Northern Premier League. In April 2009 Burton Albion restored the name of the town to the Football League competition as champions of the Blue Square Premier League.

Pirelli Stadium, Princess Way, Burton-on-Trent, Staffordshire DE13 0AR.

Telephone: (01283) 565 938.

Fax: (01283) 523 199.

Ticket Office: (01283) 565 938.

Website: www.burtonalbionfc.co.uk

Email: bafc@burtonalbionfc.co.uk

Ground Capactiy: 6,350 (2,034 seated).

Record Attendance: 5,806 v Weymouth, Southern League Cup final 2nd leg 1964 (at Eton Park); 6,192 v Oxford U, Blue Square Premier, 17 April 2009 (at Pirelli Stadium).

Pitch Measurements: 110yd × 72yd.

Chairman: Ben Robinson.

Manager: Gary Rowett.

Assistant Manager: Kevin Summerfield.

Physio: James Rowland.

Colours: Yellow shirts with black insert, black shorts, black stockings.

Year Formed: 1950.

Turned Professional: 1950.

HONOURS

Conference: ***Champions*** 2008–09.

FA Cup: 4th rd 2011.

FA Trophy: ***Runners-up*** 1986–87.

Southern League – Premier Division: ***Runners-up*** 1999–2000, 2000–01; **Division 1 (N):** ***Runners-up*** 1971–72, 1973–74. **Shared Cup:** 2000.
Southern League Cup: ***Winners*** 1964, 1997, 2000; ***Runners-up*** 1989.

Northern Premier League: ***Champions*** 2001–02.
Northern Premier League Shield: 1983. **Challenge Cup:** ***Winners*** 1983; ***Runners-up*** 1987.
President's Cup: ***Runners-up*** 1983, 1986.

Birmingham Senior Cup: ***Winners*** 1954, 1997; ***Runners-up*** 1970, 1971, 1987.

Staffordshire Senior Cup: ***Winners*** 1956; ***Runners-up*** 1977.

Midland Floodlit Cup: ***Winners*** 1976; ***Runners-up*** 1973.

sky SPORTS FACT FILE

On 29 October 2011, Burton Albion won 6-3 away to Barnet. It was their highest away score in the Football League. The scoring sequence was 0-1, 0-2, 1-2, 2-2, 2-3, 2-4, 2-5, 3-5, 3-6 and £20,000 signing Billy Kee became the third Brewer to score a hat trick in the competition.

Club Nickname: Brewers.

Grounds: 1950, Eton Park; 2005, Pirelli Stadium.

First Football League Game: 8 August 2009, FL 2, v Shrewsbury T (a) L 1–3 – Redmond; Edworthy, Boertien, Austin, Branston, McGrath, Maghoma, Penn, Phillips (Stride), Walker, Shroot (Pearson) (1).

Record League Victory: 6-1 v Aldershot T, FL 2, 12 December 2009 – Krysiak; James, Boertien, Stride, Webster, McGrath, Jackson, Penn, Kabba (2), Pearson (3) (Harrad) (1), Gilroy (Maghoma).

Record Cup Victory: 12–1 v Coalville T, Birmingham Senior Cup, 6 September 1954.

Record Defeat: 0–10 v Barnet, Southern League, 7 February 1970.

Most League Points (3 for a win): 62, FL 2, 2009–10.

Most League Goals: 71, FL 2, 2009–10.

Highest League Scorer in Season: Shaun Harrad, 21, 2009–10.

Most League Goals in Total Aggregate: Shaun Harrad, 31, 2009–11.

Most League Goals in One Match: 3, Greg Pearson v Aldershot T, FL 2, 12 December 2009; 3, Shaun Harrad v Rotherham U, FL 2, 11 September 2010.

Most Capped Player: Jacques Maghoma, 3, DR Congo.

Most League Appearances: John McGrath, 117, 2009–12.

Youngest League Player: Tom Parkes, 18 years 8 days v Torquay U, 23 January 2010.

Record Transfer Fee Received: £130,000 from Crewe Alex for John Brayford, September 2008.

Record Transfer Fee Paid: £20,000 to Kidderminster H for Russell Penn, July 2009.

Football League Record: Promoted from Blue Square Premier 2008–09; 2009– FL 2.

MANAGERS

Reg Weston
Sammy Crooks 1957
Eddie Shimwell 1958
Bill Townsend 1959–62
Peter Taylor 1962–65
Richie Norman
Reg Gutteridge
Harold Bodle 1974–76
Ian Storey-Moore 1978–81
Neil Warnock 1981–86
Brian Fidler 1986–88
Vic Halom 1988
Bobby Hope 1988
Chris Wright 1988–89
Ken Blair 1989–90
Frank Upton (*caretaker*) 1990
Steve Powell 1990–91
Brian Fidler 1991–92
Brian Kenning 1992–94
John Barton 1994–98
Nigel Clough 1998–2009
Roy McFarland 2009
Paul Peschisolido 2009–12
Gary Rowett March 2012–

LATEST SEQUENCES

Longest Sequence of League Wins: 3, 4.10.2009 – 17.10.2009.

Longest Sequence of League Defeats: 8, 25.2.2012 – 24.3.2012.

Longest Sequence of League Draws: 6, 25.4.2011 – 16.8.2011.

Longest Sequence of Unbeaten League Matches: 10, 16.4.2011 – 20.8.2012.

Longest Sequence Without a League Win: 16, 31.12.2011 – 24.3.2012.

Successive Scoring Runs: 18 from 16.4.2011 – 8.10.2011.

Successive Non-scoring Runs: 5 from 25.2.2012 – 10.3.2012.

TEN YEAR LEAGUE RECORD

		P	*W*	*D*	*L*	*F*	*A*	*Pts*	*Pos*
2002-03	Conf	42	13	10	19	52	77	49	16
2003-04	Conf	42	15	7	20	57	59	51*	14
2004-05	Conf	42	13	11	18	50	66	50	16
2005-06	Conf	42	16	12	14	50	52	60	9
2006-07	Conf	46	22	9	15	52	47	75	6
2007-08	B Sq Pr	46	23	12	11	79	56	81	5
2008-09	B Sq Pr	46	27	7	12	81	52	88	1
2009-10	FL 2	46	17	11	18	71	71	62	13
2010-11	FL 2	46	12	15	19	56	70	51	19
2011-12	FL 2	46	14	12	20	54	81	54	17

**1 pt deducted.*

DID YOU KNOW ?

While the installation of Hawk-Eye or other similar goal-line technology seems as far away as ever, it is interesting to note that the architect for the new home for Burton Albion was one Jon Hawkeye. His ideas have been the inspiration for other grounds existing and planned.

BURTON ALBION 2011–12 LEAGUE RECORD

Match No.	Date	Venue	Opponents	Result		H/T Score	Lg Pos.	Goalscorers	Attendance
1	Aug 6	A	Torquay U	D	2-2	0-0	—	Richards 2 $^{49, 53}$	3142
2	13	H	Shrewsbury T	D	1-1	1-0	16	Zola ^{14}	2989
3	16	H	Port Vale	D	1-1	1-1	—	Webster ^{23}	3608
4	20	A	Southend U	W	1-0	1-0	11	Zola ^{30}	4794
5	27	A	Accrington S	L	1-2	1-0	16	Richards ^{39}	1362
6	Sept 3	H	Plymouth Arg	W	2-1	1-0	10	Richards ^{45}, Zola ^{57}	3042
7	10	A	Oxford U	D	2-2	0-1	10	Richards 2 (1 pen) $^{55 (p), 66}$	8043
8	13	H	Crewe Alex	W	1-0	1-0	—	Richards ^{34}	2246
9	17	H	Swindon T	W	2-0	1-0	4	Kee ^{21}, Maghoma ^{47}	3320
10	24	A	Gillingham	L	1-3	1-1	9	Kee ^{40}	4946
11	Oct 1	H	Bradford C	D	2-2	2-2	10	Kee ^{38}, Richards (pen) ^{45}	2925
12	8	A	Rotherham U	W	1-0	1-0	8	Richards ^{8}	3645
13	14	H	Cheltenham T	L	0-2	0-0	—		2701
14	22	H	Bristol R	W	2-1	2-1	8	Taylor ^{27}, Kee ^{35}	3094
15	29	A	Barnet	W	6-3	2-1	8	Kee 3 $^{7, 31, 62}$, Yussuf ^{74}, Dyer ^{84}, Zola ^{90}	1745
16	Nov 1	A	Aldershot T	L	0-2	0-2	—		3713
17	5	H	Macclesfield T	W	1-0	1-0	8	Kee ^{11}	2698
18	19	A	Hereford U	W	3-2	1-2	5	Zola ^{24}, Webster ^{89}, Kee ^{90}	2136
19	26	H	AFC Wimbledon	W	3-2	2-1	5	Kee 2 $^{14, 29}$, Bolder ^{62}	3282
20	Dec 10	A	Crawley T	L	0-3	0-1	5		3001
21	17	H	Dagenham & R	D	1-1	0-1	6	Zola ^{54}	2658
22	26	A	Northampton T	W	3-2	1-2	5	Taylor ^{2}, Palmer ^{61}, Richards (pen) ^{88}	5044
23	31	A	Morecambe	D	2-2	1-1	6	Kee ^{38}, Zola ^{53}	1810
24	Jan 2	H	Hereford U	L	0-2	0-1	7		3322
25	6	H	Accrington S	L	0-2	0-1	—		2486
26	14	A	Plymouth Arg	L	1-2	0-0	9	Zola ^{73}	6082
27	21	A	Bradford C	D	1-1	0-1	9	Palmer ^{85}	9744
28	29	H	Oxford U	D	1-1	1-0	11	Bolder ^{13}	3189
29	Feb 14	A	Crewe Alex	L	2-3	0-1	—	Driver ^{57}, Zola ^{90}	3157
30	18	H	Rotherham U	D	1-1	1-0	11	Zola ^{40}	3313
31	25	A	Cheltenham T	L	0-2	0-1	15		2945
32	28	A	Swindon T	L	0-2	0-0	—		7261
33	Mar 3	H	Southend U	L	0-2	0-0	15		2424
34	6	A	Port Vale	L	0-3	0-1	—		5197
35	10	A	Shrewsbury T	L	0-1	0-0	15		5840
36	17	H	Torquay U	L	1-4	0-2	17	Richards ^{69}	2397
37	20	H	Northampton T	L	0-1	0-0	—		2692
38	24	A	AFC Wimbledon	L	0-4	0-1	17		3819
39	27	H	Gillingham	W	1-0	0-0	—	Fish (og) ^{54}	1714
40	31	H	Crawley T	D	0-0	0-0	16		2572
41	Apr 6	A	Dagenham & R	D	1-1	0-0	16	Maghoma ^{48}	2035
42	9	H	Morecambe	W	3-2	2-1	16	Bolder ^{6}, Webster ^{39}, Palmer ^{87}	2329
43	14	A	Bristol R	L	1-7	0-1	16	Zola ^{54}	5353
44	21	H	Aldershot T	L	0-4	0-1	17		2255
45	28	A	Macclesfield T	W	2-0	0-0	16	Maghoma ^{81}, Zola ^{90}	2760
46	May 5	H	Barnet	L	1-2	1-1	17	Maghoma ^{27}	3359

Final League Position: 17

GOALSCORERS

League (54): Kee 12, Zola 12, Richards 11 (3 pens), Maghoma 4, Bolder 3, Palmer 3, Webster 3, Taylor 2, Driver 1, Dyer 1, Yussuf 1, own goal 1.
Carling Cup (3): Maghoma 1, Taylor 1, Zola 1.
FA Cup (1): Zola 1.
J Paint Trophy (1): Richards 1.

Atkins R 45	Corbett A 31 + 2	Webster A 33 + 2	Stanton N 22	Parkes T 4	McGrath J 28 + 3	Taylor C 23 + 8	Bolder A 41 + 3	Richards J 28 + 7	Zola C 34 + 2	Palmer C 16 + 18	Pearson G 6 + 6	Austin R 34 + 4	Phillips J 21 + 12	James T 29 + 1	Maghoma J 32 + 4	Yussuf A 2 + 15	Blanchett D 9 + 5	Moore D 1 + 3	Kee B 14 + 6	Banton J — + 1	Amankwaah K 8	Dyer J 16 + 1	Gurrieri A 6 + 7	Driver C 8	Lucas L 1	Ada P 5 + 4	Ainsworth L 4 + 3	Harriott M 3 + 1	Legzdins A 1	Clucas S 1 + 1	*Match No.*
1	2	3	4	5■	6	7	8	9^{2}	10^{1}	11^{3}	12	13	14																		1
1	2	3		5	12	7^{1}	4	9^{2}	10	11				6	8	13															2
1	2	3		5^{2}	6		8	9	10	11^{1}		13	12	4	7																3
1	2	3			6		8	9	10^{2}	11^{1}		4		5	7		12	13													4
1	2	3			6		8	9	10^{2}	11^{1}		5	12	4	7				13												5
1	2	3			6		8	9^{2}	10	12		5	11	4	7^{1}	13															6
1	2	3			6		8	9^{2}	10^{1}			4	11	5	7	13			12												7
1	2	3			6		8	9^{2}	10	11^{1}		4	7	5			12		13												8
1	2	3			6		8	9^{3}		13		4	11	5	7^{2}	14	12		10^{1}												9
1	2	3■			6		8	9		14		4■	11^{2}	5^{1}	7^{3}		13	12	10												10
1	2				6		8	9^{1}	10^{2}				11	5		13	3	4	7	12											11
1	2	14			6	7^{2}	8	9^{3}	12	13		4	11	5			3		10^{1}												12
1		13			6	7^{2}	8	9	10	14		4	11^{3}	5			3^{1}		12		2										13
1		3			6	7^{1}	8		10	13		4	11	5	12				9^{2}		2										14
1		3			6^{2}	7	8		10			4	11^{1}	5	12	14			9^{3}		2	13									15
1		3			13	7	8		10			4	11^{2}	5	14			12	9		2^{1}	6^{3}									16
1	2	3	4		6	7^{1}	8		10^{2}		13	5	12		11				9												17
1	2^{3}	3	4		6	7^{2}	8^{1}		10	12			13	5	11				9				14								18
1	12	3	4			7^{2}	8^{3}		10	6			14	5	11				9		2^{1}		13								19
1		3			12	14	8^{3}	13	10	6		4	11^{1}	5	9						2		7^{2}								20
1		3	4		6	7^{1}	8	9^{2}	10			5			11				12		2		13								21
1		3	4		6^{1}	7	8	13	10^{2}	12		5			11^{3}				9		2		14								22
1	2	3	4^{1}		6	7	13	14	10^{3}	8		5			11		12		9^{2}												23
1	2■	3			6^{2}	7^{3}	14	12	10	8		4		5	11				9^{1}				13								24
1					6	12	8	9	10^{3}	7^{1}		4	13	5	11^{2}	14	3							2							25
1					6^{2}	13	8	9	10	11^{1}		4		5	12		3						7	2							26
1			4	3	6^{3}	11^{2}	8	9^{1}	10	13		5			7	12							14	2							27
1	12	3^{1}	4		6		8		10^{3}	13		5			11	14							9^{2}	2	7						28
1			4		6^{2}	14	8	12	10	13		5			9^{3}		3					11	7^{1}	2							29
1			4		6	13	8		10	14		5			9^{3}		3		12			11^{2}	7^{1}	2							30
1			4		6	14	8	13		11		5					3^{1}		9^{3}			10	7^{2}	2		12■					31
1	2		4		6^{3}	7	8^{1}	9		10^{2}			13	5		12						11	14	3							32
1	2	3	4^{1}			7	6^{2}	9		13		12	11	5		10						8									33
1	2^{3}	3				14	6	9		13		4	11^{2}	5		12						8					7	10^{1}			34
1	2	3	4^{1}			7	13	9^{3}	10			12	11			14						8				5		6^{2}			35
1	2	3				11^{2}		12	10^{1}					5	9	13						8				6	7	4			36
	2	3				11^{3}		9^{1}		13	10^{2}	4	12	5	8							6					7	14	1		37
1	2	3					8	9		13	10^{3}	6	12	5	11	14											7^{1}			4^{2}	38
1	2	3	4				8	9^{2}			10^{1}	5	11		7							6				13	12				39
1	2	3	4				8	9			10^{1}	5	11		7							6					12				40
1	2	3	4				8	9^{2}	13		10^{3}	5	11		7							6^{1}				14	12				41
1	2	3^{1}	4			7^{2}	6	9^{3}	10	13	14	5	11		8											12					42
1	2		4			13	8	9^{3}	10^{2}	12	14	5	11		7		3									6^{1}					43
1	2	3	4^{1}				8		10		9^{2}	5	11	12	7	13						6									44
1	2					7^{2}	8		10	11	13		12	5^{1}	9^{3}	4						6				3				14	45
1	2		4			7^{1}	8^{2}		10	11	12		13	5	9							6				3					46

FA Cup
First Round Oldham Ath (a) 1-3

Carling Cup
First Round Burnley (a) 3-6

J Paint Trophy
First Round Sheffield U (h) 1-2

BURY FL Championship 1

FOUNDATION

A meeting at the Waggon & Horses Hotel, attended largely by members of Bury Wesleyans and Bury Unitarians football clubs, decided to form a new Bury club. This was officially formed at a subsequent gathering at the Old White Horse Hotel, Fleet Street, Bury on 24 April 1885.

Gigg Lane, Bury, Lancs BL9 9HR.

Telephone: (08445) 790009.

Fax: (0161) 764 5521.

Ticket Office: (08445) 790009.

Website: www.buryfc.co.uk

Email: info@buryfc.co.uk

Ground Capacity: 11,669.

Record Attendance: 35,000 v Bolton W, FA Cup 3rd rd, 9 January 1960.

Pitch Measurements: 112yd × 72yd.

Chairman: Brian Fenton.

Directors: Mark Catlin, Jeremy Rothwell, Margaret Ladkin.

Manager: Richie Barker.

Assistant Manager: Peter Shirtliff.

Physio: Tom Walsh.

Colours: Black and blue halved shirts, white shorts, black stockings.

Year Formed: 1885.

Turned Professional: 1885.

Club Nickname: 'Shakers'.

Ground: 1885, Gigg Lane.

First Football League Game: 1 September 1894, Division 2, v Manchester C (h) W 4–2 – Lowe; Gillespie, Davies; White, Clegg, Ross; Wylie, Barbour (2), Millar (1), Ostler (1), Plant.

Record League Victory: 8–0 v Tranmere R, Division 3, 10 January 1970 – Forrest; Tinney, Saile; Anderson, Turner, McDermott; Hince (1), Arrowsmith (1), Jones (4), Kerr (1), Grundy, (1 og).

Record Cup Victory: 12–1 v Stockton, FA Cup 1st rd (replay), 2 February 1897 – Montgomery; Darroch, Barbour; Hendry (1), Clegg, Ross (1); Wylie (3), Pangbourn, Millar (4), Henderson (2), Plant, (1 og).

Record Defeat: 0–10 v Blackburn R, FA Cup pr rd, 1 October 1887. 0–10 v West Ham U, Milk Cup 2nd rd 2nd leg, 25 October 1983.

Most League Points (2 for a win): 68, Division 3, 1960–61.

Most League Points (3 for a win): 84, Division 4, 1984–85 and Division 2, 1996–97.

HONOURS

Football League – Division 1: Best season: 4th, 1925–26;
Division 2: ***Champions*** 1894–95, 1996–97; ***Runners-up*** 1923–24;
Division 3: ***Champions*** 1960–61; ***Runners-up*** 1967–68;
FL 2: ***Runners-up*** 2010–11.

FA Cup: ***Winners*** 1900, 1903.

Football League Cup: Semi-final 1963.

sky SPORTS FACT FILE

Scots-born left-half George Ross, one of three Bury brothers (Jack and David, the others), was signed from Bury Unitarians at 16. He made a scoring debut against Everton on 26 February 1887, captained both FA Cup final teams and completed 366 League appearances.

Most League Goals: 108, Division 3, 1960–61.

Highest League Scorer in Season: Craig Madden, 35, Division 4, 1981–82.

Most League Goals in Total Aggregate: Craig Madden, 129, 1978–86.

Most League Goals in One Match: 5, Eddie Quigley v Millwall, Division 2, 15 February 1947; 5, Ray Pointer v Rotherham U, Division 2, 2 October 1965.

Most Capped Player: Bill Gorman, 11 (13), Republic of Ireland and (4), Northern Ireland.

Most League Appearances: Norman Bullock, 506, 1920–35.

Youngest League Player: Brian Williams, 16 years 133 days v Stockport Co, 18 March 1972.

Record Transfer Fee Received: £1,100,000 from Ipswich T for David Johnson, November 1997.

Record Transfer Fee Paid: £200,000 to Ipswich T for Chris Swailes, November 1997; £200,000 to Swindon T for Darren Bullock, February 1999.

Football League Record: 1894 Elected to Division 2; 1895–1912 Division 1; 1912–24 Division 2; 1924–29 Division 1; 1929–57 Division 2; 1957–61 Division 3; 1961–67 Division 2; 1967–68 Division 3; 1968–69 Division 2; 1969–71 Division 3; 1971–74 Division 4; 1974–80 Division 3; 1980–85 Division 4; 1985–96 Division 3; 1996–97 Division 2; 1997–99 Division 1; 1999–2002 Division 2; 2002–04 Division 3; 2004–11 FL 2; 2011– FL 1.

LATEST SEQUENCES

Longest Sequence of League Wins: 9, 26.9.1960 – 19.11.1960.

Longest Sequence of League Defeats: 8, 18.8.2001 – 25.9.2001.

Longest Sequence of League Draws: 6, 6.3.1999 – 3.4.1999.

Longest Sequence of Unbeaten League Matches: 18, 4.2.1961 – 29.4.1961.

Longest Sequence Without a League Win: 19, 1.4.1911 – 2.12.1911.

Successive Scoring Runs: 24 from 1.9.1894.

Successive Non-scoring Runs: 6 from 11.1.1969.

MANAGERS

T. Hargreaves 1887 (*Secretary-Manager*)
H. S. Hamer 1887–1907 (*Secretary-Manager*)
Archie Montgomery 1907–15
William Cameron 1919–23
James Hunter Thompson 1923–27
Percy Smith 1927–30
Arthur Paine 1930–34
Norman Bullock 1934–38
Charlie Dean 1938–44
Jim Porter 1944–45
Norman Bullock 1945–49
John McNeil 1950–53
Dave Russell 1953–61
Bob Stokoe 1961–65
Bert Head 1965–66
Les Shannon 1966–69
Jack Marshall 1969
Colin McDonald 1970
Les Hart 1970
Tommy McAnearney 1970–72
Alan Brown 1972–73
Bobby Smith 1973–77
Bob Stokoe 1977–78
David Hatton 1978–79
Dave Connor 1979–80
Jim Iley 1980–84
Martin Dobson 1984–89
Sam Ellis 1989–90
Mike Walsh 1990–95
Stan Ternent 1995–98
Neil Warnock 1998–99
Andy Preece 1999–2003
Graham Barrow 2003–05
Chris Casper 2005–08
Alan Knill 2008–11
Richie Barker April 2011–

TEN YEAR LEAGUE RECORD

		P	W	D	L	F	A	Pts	Pos
2002-03	Div 3	46	18	16	12	57	56	70	7
2003-04	Div 3	46	15	11	20	54	64	56	12
2004-05	FL 2	46	14	16	16	54	54	58	17
2005-06	FL 2	46	12	17	17	45	57	52*	19
2006-07	FL 2	46	13	11	22	46	61	50	21
2007-08	FL 2	46	16	11	19	58	61	59	13
2008-09	FL 2	46	21	15	10	63	43	78	4
2009-10	FL 2	46	19	12	15	54	59	69	9
2010-11	FL 2	46	23	12	11	82	50	81	2
2011-12	FL 1	46	15	11	20	60	79	56	14

**1 pt deducted.*

DID YOU KNOW ?

Though he spent ten successful years playing for Bury, Joe Leeming scored only twice in the FA Cup, but reserved his tally for the 1903 final against Derby County in the 6-0 triumph. He did achieve 18 in the League for the Shakers and later played for Brighton & Hove Albion.

BURY 2011–12 LEAGUE RECORD

Match No.	Date	Venue	Opponents	Result		H/T Score	Lg Pos.	Goalscorers	Attendance
1	Aug 6	A	Huddersfield T	D	1-1	0-0	—	Lowe 76	13,873
2	13	H	Carlisle U	L	0-2	0-0	21		3640
3	16	H	Sheffield W	W	2-1	2-0	—	Lowe 7, Mozika 41	5219
4	20	A	Wycombe W	W	2-0	1-0	6	Jones, M 24, Lowe 65	3259
5	27	H	Charlton Ath	L	1-2	1-0	13	Lowe 40	3084
6	Sept 3	A	Sheffield U	L	0-4	0-1	16		17,956
7	10	H	Rochdale	L	2-4	1-3	16	Jones, M 21, Bishop 63	4897
8	13	A	Chesterfield	L	0-1	0-0	—		5727
9	17	A	Hartlepool U	L	0-3	0-1	20		5343
10	24	H	Milton Keynes D	D	0-0	0-0	22		2378
11	Oct 1	A	Yeovil T	W	3-1	1-1	18	Coke 43, Amoo 67, Sweeney 85	3127
12	8	H	Exeter C	W	2-0	1-0	14	Bishop 14, Oakley (og) 48	2672
13	15	A	Leyton Orient	L	0-1	0-1	16		3943
14	22	A	Bournemouth	W	2-1	1-1	15	Coke 45, Bishop 53	6122
15	25	H	Notts Co	D	2-2	1-1	—	Bishop 5, Coke (pen) 55	2917
16	29	H	Stevenage	L	1-2	0-1	16	Bishop (pen) 78	2683
17	Nov 5	A	Oldham Ath	W	2-0	2-0	15	Bishop 2 22, 30	5149
18	19	A	Walsall	W	4-2	1-1	13	Sweeney 6, Jones, M 46, Schumacher 63, John-Lewis 87	4785
19	26	H	Preston NE	W	1-0	1-0	10	Amoo 15	4957
20	Dec 10	A	Colchester U	L	1-4	0-3	11	John-Lewis 90	3156
21	17	H	Brentford	D	1-1	0-0	12	John-Lewis 85	4008
22	26	A	Scunthorpe U	W	3-1	0-1	11	Sweeney 50, Bishop 69, Sodje 82	4569
23	30	A	Tranmere R	L	0-2	0-1	—		5253
24	Jan 2	H	Walsall	W	2-1	2-1	9	Sadler (og) 20, Sweeney 40	3095
25	14	H	Sheffield U	L	0-3	0-0	11		6970
26	21	H	Yeovil T	W	3-2	3-1	10	Schumacher 2 (1 pen) 8, 35 (p), Skarz 21	2527
27	28	A	Rochdale	L	0-3	0-2	11		5033
28	31	A	Charlton Ath	D	1-1	1-0	—	John-Lewis 42	13,264
29	Feb 14	H	Chesterfield	D	1-1	0-1	—	Schumacher 88	2266
30	18	A	Exeter C	L	2-3	1-3	14	Amoo 29, Eastham 90	4281
31	21	A	Milton Keynes D	L	1-2	1-2	—	Amoo 10	6405
32	25	H	Leyton Orient	D	1-1	0-1	14	Elford-Alliyu 68	2807
33	28	H	Hartlepool U	L	1-2	0-1	—	Worrall 79	2072
34	Mar 3	H	Huddersfield T	D	3-3	1-3	14	Schumacher 32, John-Lewis 70, Eastham 90	5988
35	6	A	Sheffield W	L	1-4	0-1	—	Schumacher 72	17,684
36	10	A	Carlisle U	L	1-4	1-1	16	Coke 23	4855
37	17	H	Wycombe W	L	1-4	1-2	19	Harrad 11	2479
38	20	H	Scunthorpe U	D	0-0	0-0	—		2351
39	24	A	Preston NE	D	1-1	0-0	19	Elford-Alliyu 90	10,735
40	31	H	Tranmere R	W	2-0	0-0	19	Sodje 67, Coke 72	3733
41	Apr 7	A	Brentford	L	0-3	0-1	19		5192
42	9	H	Colchester U	W	4-1	2-0	17	Grella 40, Harrad 43, Coke 56, Worrall 73	3119
43	14	H	Bournemouth	W	1-0	1-0	15	Grella 10	2729
44	21	A	Notts Co	W	4-2	1-0	12	Worrall 42, Grella 2 49, 67, Carrington 90	6732
45	28	H	Oldham Ath	D	0-0	0-0	12		5111
46	May 5	A	Stevenage	L	0-3	0-1	14		4781

Final League Position: 14

GOALSCORERS

League (60): Bishop 8 (1 pen), Coke 6 (1 pen), Schumacher 6 (1 pen), John-Lewis 5, Amoo 4, Grella 4, Lowe 4, Sweeney 4, Jones, M 3, Worrall 3, Eastham 2, Elford-Alliyu 2, Harrad 2, Sodje 2, Carrington 1, Mozika 1, Skarz 1, own goals 2.
Carling Cup (5): Lowe 3, Bishop 1, Jones, M 1.
FA Cup (0).
J Paint Trophy (0).

Belford C 23	Picken P 36 + 1	Skarz J 45	Hughes M 21 + 4	Sodje E 40 + 1	Sweeney P 41	Worrall D 29 + 12	Schumacher S 29 + 3	Cullen M 1 + 3	Lowe R 5	Jones M 24	Bishop A 33 + 7	Haworth A — + 6	Mozika D 3 + 1	John-Lewis L 8 + 20	Cregg P 5 + 2	Eastham A 22 + 3	Oyenuga K — + 1	Byrne S 10 + 4	Coke G 28 + 2	Harrad S 14 + 12	Carson T 8	Jones A 9 + 2	Amoo D 19 + 8	Carrington M 12 + 9	Doble R 3 + 2	Harrop M — + 5	Carson T 9	Elford-Alliyu L 4 + 9	Grella M 8 + 2	Clarke N 11	Bond J 6	*Match No.*
1	2	3	4	5	6	7	8	9¹	10³	11²	12	13	14																			1
1	2	3	4	5	6	7			9	11²	10¹	13	8	12																		2
1	2	3	4	5	6	7²			9	11	10¹		8	12	13																	3
1	2	3	4¹	5	6	7		13	9³	11²	10	14	8		12																	4
1	2¹	3		5	6	7			9	11²	10	13			8	4	12															5
1	2	3		5	6	7²				11	10	13				4		8¹	9	12												6
1	2	3		5	6	7		12		11³	10	14				4		13	9²	8¹												7
	2	3		5	6	7		12		11³	10			14		4		8¹	13	9²	1											8
	2	3			6²	7				11	10¹			12		4		13	8	9	1	5										9
	2	3		5	6	7				11²	12					4		8	10	9¹	1		13									10
	2²	3		5	6	12				11¹	10³					4		7	8	14	1	13	9									11
	2	3		5	6	12	13			11	10					4		7²	8		1		9¹									12
	2³	3	12	5	6		13			11	10					4¹		7²	8	14	1		9									13
	2	3	4	5	6		7			11	10			12					8	9¹	1											14
	2	3	4	5	6		7			11³	10¹			12				13	8	9²	1	14										15
1	2	3²	4	5	6		7			11	10			13				12	8	9¹												16
1	2	3	5		6		8			11¹	10			9▮		4		7		12												17
1	2	3		5	8	13	4			11	10³			12		6		7²		14			9¹									18
1	2	3		5	6¹	13	7			11	10²			12		4		8					9									19
1	2	3		5	8	12	4			11	10			13		6		9¹					7²									20
1	2	3▮		5	6	13	8			11²	10³			12		4				14			9	7¹								21
1	2		4	5	6	13	8			11³	10¹			12		3				14			9²	7								22
1	2³	3	6	5		7¹				11	10²			9	4	14				13			12	8								23
1	2	3	5		6	13	8			11²	10¹			12		4				14			9³	7								24
1	2	3	4	5	6	11²	8				10			13					12	14			9³	7¹								25
1	2	3		5	6	7³	11¹				10			14		4			8				13	12	9²							26
1	2	3		5	6²	7¹	8³				10			13		4			11				9	14	12							27
1	2	3	4	5	6	12²	8				13			11					7³				9	14	10¹							28
1	2	3	4	5	6	12	11				10³			13					8				7²	14	9¹							29
1	2	3	4	5	6¹	7²	11							10³		14			8				9		12	13						30
1	2²	3	4	5	6¹	12	11³							10		13			8▮				9	7		14						31
		3	2	5	6	13	8				10			11¹		4							9²	7			1	12				32
	2	3	4			7	6				10²			14		5			8¹				12	11³			1	9	13			33
	2	3	4		6	7	8				14			9³		5							12	11¹			1	13	10²			34
	2²	3	4	13	6	7³	8				10¹					5							9			14	1	11	12			35
	2¹	3		5	11▮	7									4²				8				12			13	1	9	10	6		36
		3	2²	5		7					13								8	9			12	4			1	11	10¹	6		37
		3		5		7					10				4²				8	9¹		2	12	11			1	13		6		38
		3		5		7	12				10				4¹				8	13		2³	9	11²			1	14		6		39
		3	13	5²	6³	7¹	11				10								8			2	9	14			1	12		4		40
		3		5	6¹	7	11				10			9²					8	13		2						12		4	1	41
	14	3	13	5	6¹	7²	11												8	9³		2		12					10	4	1	42
		3		5	6³	7²	11				12								8	9¹		2		13				14	10	4	1	43
		3	13	5	6²	7	11				12								8	9¹		2▮		14					10³	4	1	44
	2	3		5	6	7	11							13					8¹	9²						12		14	10³	4	1	45
		3		5	11	7	4							12					8²	9³		2		13				14	10¹	6	1	46

FA Cup
First Round Crawley T (h) 0-2

Carling Cup
First Round Coventry C (h) 3-1
Second Round Leicester C (h) 2-4

J Paint Trophy
First Round Crewe Alex (h) 0-0

CARDIFF CITY — FL Championship

FOUNDATION

Credit for the establishment of a first class professional football club in such a rugby stronghold as Cardiff is due to members of the Riverside club formed in 1899 out of a cricket club of that name. Cardiff became a city in 1905 and in 1908 the South Wales and Monmouthshire FA granted Riverside permission to call themselves Cardiff City. The club turned professional under that name in 1910.

Cardiff City Stadium, Leckwith Road, Cardiff CF11 8AZ.

Telephone: (0845) 365 1115. ***Fax:*** (0845) 365 1116.

Ticket Office: (0845) 345 1400.

Website: www.cardiffcityfc.co.uk

Email: club@cardiffcityfc.co.uk

Ground Capacity: 26,828.

Record Attendance: 57,893 v Arsenal, Division 1, 22 April 1953 (at Ninian Park); 26,055 v Leicester C, FL C Play-Off semi-final 2nd leg 12 May 2010 (at Cardiff City Stadium).

Ground Record Attendance: 62,634, Wales v England, 17 October 1959 (at Ninian Park).

Pitch Measurements: 110yd × 75yd.

Chairman: Dato Chan Tien Ghee.

Chief Executive: Alan Whiteley.

Manager: Malky Mackay.

Assistant Manager: David Kerslake.

Physio: Sean Connelly BHSc MCSP, SRP.

Colours: Red shirts, black shorts, red stockings.

Year Formed: 1899.

Turned Professional: 1910.

Previous Names: 1899, Riverside; 1902, Riverside Albion; 1908, Cardiff City.

Club Nickname: 'Bluebirds'.

Grounds: Riverside, Sophia Gardens, Old Park and Fir Gardens; 1910, Ninian Park; 2009, Cardiff City Stadium.

First Football League Game: 28 August 1920, Division 2, v Stockport Co (a) W 5–2 – Kneeshaw; Brittan, Leyton; Keenor (1), Smith, Hardy; Grimshaw (1), Gill (2), Cashmore, West, Evans (1).

Record League Victory: 9–2 v Thames, Division 3 (S), 6 February 1932 – Farquharson; Eric Morris, Roberts; Galbraith, Harris, Ronan; Emmerson (1), Keating (1), Jones (1), McCambridge (1), Robbins (5).

HONOURS

Football League Division 1: ***Runners-up*** 1923–24;
Division 2: *Runners-up* 1920–21, 1951–52, 1959–60;
Division 3 (S): *Champions* 1946–47;
Division 3: *Champions* 1992–93. ***Runners-up*** 1975–76, 1982–83, 2000–01;
Division 4: *Runners-up* 1987–88.

FA Cup: *Winners* 1927 (only occasion the Cup has been won by a club outside England); ***Runners-up*** 1925, 2008.

Football League Cup: *Runners-up* 2012.

Welsh Cup: *Winners* 22 times (joint record).

Charity Shield: Winners 1927.

European Competitions
European Cup-Winners' Cup: 1964–65, 1965–66, 1967–68 (*s-f*), 1968–69, 1969–70, 1970–71, 1971–72, 1973–74, 1974–75, 1976–77, 1977–78, 1988–89, 1992–93, 1993–94.

sky SPORTS FACT FILE

Kenny Miller, born in Scotland, made his League debut for Cardiff City against West Ham United on 7 August 2011 and scored the only goal at Upton Park. It was Cardiff's first win there in 15 attempts since 15 April 1950 when Arthur "Buller" Lever was their lone marksman, too.

Record Cup Victory: 8–0 v Enfield, FA Cup 1st rd, 28 November 1931 – Farquharson; Smith, Roberts; Harris (1), Galbraith, Ronan; Emmerson (2), Keating (3); O'Neill (2), Robbins, McCambridge.

Record Defeat: 2–11 v Sheffield U, Division 1, 1 January 1926.

Most League Points (2 for a win): 66, Division 3 (S), 1946–47.

Most League Points (3 for a win): 86, Division 3, 1982–83.

Most League Goals: 95, Division 3, 2000–01.

Highest League Scorer in Season: Robert Earnshaw, 31, Division 2, 2002–03.

Most League Goals in Total Aggregate: Len Davies, 128, 1920–31.

Most League Goals in One Match: 5, Hugh Ferguson v Burnley, Division 1, 1 September 1928; 5, Walter Robbins v Thames, Division 3 (S), 6 February 1932; 5, William Henderson v Northampton T, Division 3 (S), 22 April 1933.

Most Capped Player: Alf Sherwood, 39 (41), Wales.

Most League Appearances: Phil Dwyer, 471, 1972–85.

Youngest League Player: Bob Adams, 15 years 355 days v Southend U, 18 February 1933.

Record Transfer Fee Received: £5,000,000 from Sunderland for Michael Chopra, August 2006; £5,000,000 from Arsenal for Aaron Ramsey, June 2008; £5,000,000 from Birmingham C for Roger Johnson, June 2009.

Record Transfer Fee Paid: £3,000,000 to Sunderland for Michael Chopra, July 2009.

Football League Record: 1920 Elected to Division 2; 1921–29 Division 1; 1929–31 Division 2; 1931–47 Division 3 (S); 1947–52 Division 2; 1952–57 Division 1; 1957–60 Division 2; 1960–62 Division 1; 1962–75 Division 2; 1975–76 Division 3; 1976–82 Division 2; 1982–83 Division 3; 1983–85 Division 2; 1985–86 Division 3; 1986–88 Division 4; 1988–90 Division 3; 1990–92 Division 4; 1992–93 Division 3; 1993–95 Division 2; 1995–99 Division 3; 1999–2000 Division 2; 2000–01 Division 3; 2001–03 Division 2; 2003–04 Division 1; 2004– FL C.

MANAGERS

Davy McDougall 1910–11
Fred Stewart 1911–33
Bartley Wilson 1933–34
B. Watts-Jones 1934–37
Bill Jennings 1937–39
Cyril Spiers 1939–46
Billy McCandless 1946–48
Cyril Spiers 1948–54
Trevor Morris 1954–58
Bill Jones 1958–62
George Swindin 1962–64
Jimmy Scoular 1964–73
Frank O'Farrell 1973–74
Jimmy Andrews 1974–78
Richie Morgan 1978–81
Graham Williams 1981–82
Len Ashurst 1982–84
Jimmy Goodfellow 1984
Alan Durban 1984–86
Frank Burrows 1986–89
Len Ashurst 1989–91
Eddie May 1991–94
Terry Yorath 1994–95
Eddie May 1995
Kenny Hibbitt (*Chief Coach*) 1995
Phil Neal 1996
Russell Osman 1996–97
Kenny Hibbitt 1997–98
Frank Burrows 1998–2000
Billy Ayre 2000
Bobby Gould 2000
Alan Cork 2000–02
Lennie Lawrence 2002–05
Dave Jones 2005–11
Malky Mackay June 2011–

LATEST SEQUENCES

Longest Sequence of League Wins: 9, 26.10.1946 – 28.12.1946.

Longest Sequence of League Defeats: 7, 4.11.1933 – 25.12.1933.

Longest Sequence of League Draws: 6, 29.11.1980 – 17.1.1981.

Longest Sequence of Unbeaten League Matches: 21, 21.9.1946 – 1.3.1947.

Longest Sequence Without a League Win: 15, 21.11.1936 – 6.3.1937.

Successive Scoring Runs: 23 from 24.10.1992.

Successive Non-scoring Runs: 8 from 20.12.1952.

TEN YEAR LEAGUE RECORD

		P	W	D	L	F	A	Pts	Pos
2002-03	Div 2	46	23	12	11	68	43	81	6
2003-04	Div 1	46	17	14	15	68	58	65	13
2004-05	FL C	46	13	15	18	48	51	54	16
2005-06	FL C	46	16	12	18	58	59	60	11
2006-07	FL C	46	17	13	16	57	53	64	13
2007-08	FL C	46	16	16	14	59	55	64	12
2008-09	FL C	46	19	17	10	65	53	74	7
2009-10	FL C	46	22	10	14	73	54	76	4
2010-11	FL C	46	23	11	12	76	54	80	4
2011-12	FL C	46	19	18	9	66	53	75	6

DID YOU KNOW ?

Ken McDonald was born in Wales, played in Scotland, returned to score seven goals in eleven matches for Cardiff City in 1921, before being snapped up by Manchester United. He scored freely for several Yorkshire clubs, had a spell in Northern Ireland then settled in the north-east.

CARDIFF CITY 2011–12 LEAGUE RECORD

Match No.	Date	Venue	Opponents	Result		H/T Score	Lg Pos.	Goalscorers	Attendance
1	Aug 7	A	West Ham U	W	1-0	0-0	—	Miller [90]	25,680
2	14	H	Bristol C	W	3-1	3-0	1	Hudson [18], Conway [23], Earnshaw [36]	22,639
3	17	H	Brighton & HA	L	1-3	0-1	—	Whittingham (pen) [90]	23,013
4	20	A	Burnley	D	1-1	1-1	8	Earnshaw [40]	13,428
5	27	A	Portsmouth	D	1-1	0-0	7	Taylor [71]	14,354
6	Sept 10	H	Doncaster R	W	2-0	0-0	6	Gerrard [52], Earnshaw [75]	21,863
7	17	A	Blackpool	D	1-1	0-0	6	Cowie [49]	12,798
8	25	H	Leicester C	D	0-0	0-0	6		21,154
9	28	H	Southampton	W	2-1	0-0	—	Miller 2 [56, 63]	22,502
10	Oct 1	A	Hull C	L	1-2	0-1	9	Ralls [62]	18,305
11	15	H	Ipswich T	D	2-2	1-1	9	Gestede [19], Whittingham (pen) [72]	21,809
12	18	A	Peterborough U	L	3-4	1-2	—	Cowie [6], Whittingham [60], Gunnarsson [79]	6351
13	22	H	Barnsley	W	5-3	3-1	9	Miller [10], Mason [34], Gunnarsson 2 [38, 71], Cowie [60]	20,665
14	30	A	Leeds U	D	1-1	1-0	9	Mason [17]	20,270
15	Nov 2	A	Derby Co	W	3-0	1-0	—	Kiss [20], Kilbane (og) [62], Whittingham [73]	23,078
16	5	H	Crystal Palace	W	2-0	0-0	4	Miller [69], Whittingham [80]	22,032
17	19	A	Reading	W	2-1	1-0	4	Whittingham [2], Hudson [70]	20,361
18	22	A	Coventry C	D	1-1	0-0	—	Whittingham [48]	12,317
19	26	H	Nottingham F	W	1-0	0-0	3	Mason [70]	22,556
20	Dec 4	H	Birmingham C	W	1-0	0-0	3	Miller [68]	22,010
21	10	A	Millwall	D	0-0	0-0	3		11,314
22	17	H	Middlesbrough	L	2-3	2-1	5	Turner [23], Gunnarsson [44]	23,373
23	26	A	Watford	D	1-1	0-0	4	Mariappa (og) [80]	14,604
24	31	A	Nottingham F	W	1-0	0-0	4	Miller [59]	19,750
25	Jan 2	H	Reading	W	3-1	3-1	3	Mason [13], Gunnarsson [19], Miller [36]	23,655
26	14	A	Doncaster R	D	0-0	0-0	3		8834
27	21	H	Portsmouth	W	3-2	1-1	3	Miller [15], Hudson [69], Conway [90]	22,199
28	31	A	Southampton	D	1-1	1-0	—	Conway [36]	24,356
29	Feb 4	H	Blackpool	L	1-3	0-0	3	Mason [59]	22,577
30	11	A	Leicester C	L	1-2	0-1	4	Whittingham (pen) [77]	21,375
31	14	H	Peterborough U	W	3-1	3-0	—	Whittingham [34], Gestede [38], Vuckic [40]	21,342
32	18	A	Ipswich T	L	0-3	0-1	4		17,032
33	Mar 4	H	West Ham U	L	0-2	0-1	8		23,872
34	7	A	Brighton & HA	D	2-2	0-0	—	Mason [57], Whittingham [74]	18,786
35	10	A	Bristol C	W	2-1	1-0	6	McManus (og) [45], Cisse (og) [87]	12,495
36	13	H	Hull C	L	0-3	0-1	—		20,366
37	18	H	Burnley	D	0-0	0-0	8		21,276
38	21	H	Coventry C	D	2-2	1-0	—	McDonald (og) [18], Whittingham [83]	20,564
39	25	A	Birmingham C	D	1-1	0-0	8	Hudson [78]	17,704
40	31	H	Millwall	D	0-0	0-0	8		21,259
41	Apr 7	A	Middlesbrough	W	2-0	2-0	6	Turner [11], Mason [19]	17,564
42	9	H	Watford	D	1-1	1-0	6	Miller [45]	21,259
43	14	A	Barnsley	W	1-0	0-0	6	Lawrence [69]	9122
44	17	H	Derby Co	W	2-0	1-0	—	Mason [24], Hudson [63]	21,216
45	21	H	Leeds U	D	1-1	1-0	6	Mason [41]	25,109
46	28	A	Crystal Palace	W	2-1	0-1	6	Whittingham [53], Cowie [62]	15,510

Final League Position: 6

GOALSCORERS

League (66): Whittingham 12 (3 pens), Miller 10, Mason 9, Gunnarsson 5, Hudson 5, Cowie 4, Conway 3, Earnshaw 3, Gestede 2, Turner 2, Gerrard 1, Kiss 1, Lawrence 1, Ralls 1, Taylor 1, Vuckic 1, own goals 5.
Carling Cup (16): Cowie 3, Conway 2, Mason 2, Gerrard 1, Gestede 1, Gyepes 1, Jarvis 1, Miller 1, Parkin 1, Turner 1, Whittingham 1, own goal 1.
FA Cup (2): Earnshaw 1, Mason 1.
Play-Offs (0).

Marshall D 45	McNaughton K 41 + 1	Taylor A 42	Gunnarsson A 41 + 1	Hudson M 38 + 1	Gerrard A 18 + 2	Cowie D 43	Whittingham P 46	Miller K 41 + 2	Earnshaw R 8 + 11	Conway C 24 + 7	Gestede R 5 + 20	Mason J 23 + 16	Blake D 9 + 11	Kiss F 13 + 13	Naylor L 2	Taiwo S — + 1	Quinn P — + 1	Keinan D — + 1	Ralls J 5 + 5	Turner B 36 + 1	McPhail S 11 + 8	Heaton T 1 + 1	Vuckic H 2 + 3	Lawrence L 12 + 1	*Match No.*
1	2	3	4	5	6	7	8	9	10[1]	11[2]	12	13													1
1	2	3	4[1]	5	6	7	8	9	10[2]	11	13	12													2
1	2	3		5	6	7	8	9	10[1]	11	12	4													3
1	2	3		5	6	7	8	9	10[2]	11	13	4[1]	12												4
1	2	3		5	6	7	8	9[1]	10	11	12		4												5
1	2	3	12	5	6	7	8	9[3]	10	11[2]	14		4[1]	13											6
1	2	3	4	5	6	7	8	9[1]		11	12	13		10[2]											7
1	2		4	5[3]	6	7	8	9	12[2]	11[1]	13		14	10	3										8
1	2[1]		4	5	6	7	8	9				10[3]	3	11[2]		12	13	14							9
1	2		4	5	6	7	8	9[1]				10	3	11[2]					12	13					10
1	2	3	4	5		7	8		10[2]	11[1]	9	13		12						6					11
1	2	3	4	5		7	8		10[3]	14	9[1]	12		11[2]						6	13				12
1	2	3	4	5		7	10	9[1]	14	11[2]		12		13						6	8[3]				13
1	2	3	4	5		7	10	13		11[1]		9[2]		12						6	8				14
1[6]	2[1]	3	4	5		7	8	9		11[2]		13		10						6	12	15			15
	2	3	4[1]	5		7	8	9		11[2]		13		10					12	6		1			16
1	2	3	4	5	13	7	8	9		11[2]				10[1]						6	12				17
1	2[2]	3	4		5	7	8	9		11			13	10[1]						6	12				18
1	2	3	4		6	7	10	9		11[1]		12							13	5	8[2]				19
1	2		4[1]	13	5[2]	7	8	9		11		14		10[3]	3				12	6					20
1	2	3		5		7	8	9		11[2]	13	12		10[1]					4	6					21
1	2	3	4	5		7[2]	8	9		11[3]	13	14		12					10[1]	6					22
1	2[1]	3	4	5		7	8	9		14	13	10[3]	12	11[2]						6					23
1		3	4	5		7	8	9		12	10	11[1]	2							6					24
1		3	4	5	13	7	8	9[3]			12	11[1]	2						10	6[2]	14				25
1		3	4	5		7	8	9				10[2]	2	13					11[1]	6	12				26
1		3	4	5		7	8	9		11		10	2							6					27
1	2	3	4		5	7	10	9		11[1]	12			13						6	8[2]				28
1	2[2]	3	4		5	7	8	9[3]		11	14	12	13						10[1]	6					29
1	2	3	4[1]		5	7	8	9		11	13	14		12[3]						6			10[2]		30
1	2	3	4[1]		5	7[3]	8	9		14	10	13		12						6			11[2]		31
1	2	3	4		5[2]	7	8	9				10	13	11[1]						6			12		32
1	2	3	4	5		7	8	9			10[1]	11								6			12		33
1	2	3	4[1]	5		7	8	9				10		12						6				11	34
1	2[2]	3	4	5		7	8	9[3]				10	13	14						6			12	11[1]	35
1	2	3	4	5		7[1]	8	9[2]	13	12		10								6				11	36
1	2	3	4[3]	5		7[1]	8	9[2]	13	12		10								6	14			11	37
1	2	3	4	5		7	10		13		12	9								6	8[1]			11[2]	38
1	2	3	4	5		7[1]	10	13			12	9								6	8[2]			11	39
1	2	3	4	5			11	9[3]	14	13	12	10[2]								6	8[1]			7	40
1	14	3	4	5		7	10	9[1]			13[3]	12	2							6	8[2]			11	41
1	2	3	4	5		7	10	9	14	11[1]				13						6	8[2]			12[3]	42
1	2	3	4[2]	5		7[1]	8	9	14			10[3]	13							6	12			11	43
1	2	3	4	5			11	9[2]	13			10[3]	14						12	6	8[1]			7	44
1	2[2]	3	4	5			11	9[3]	13			10	14	12						6	8[1]			7	45
1	2[1]	3	4	5		7	8	9[2]	14		13	10[3]	12							6				11	46

FA Cup

Third Round	WBA	(a)	2-4

Carling Cup

First Round	Oxford U	(a)	3-1
Second Round	Huddersfield T	(h)	5-3
Third Round	Leicester C	(h)	2-2
Fourth Round	Burnley	(h)	1-0
Quarter-Final	Blackburn R	(h)	2-0
Semi-Final	Crystal Palace	(a)	0-1
		(h)	1-0
Final *(at Wembley).*	Liverpool		2-2

Play-Offs

Semi-Final	West Ham U	(h)	0-2
		(a)	0-3

CARLISLE UNITED FL Championship 1

FOUNDATION

Carlisle United came into being when members of Shaddongate United voted to change its name on 17 May 1904. The new club was admitted to the Second Division of the Lancashire Combination in 1905–06, winning promotion the following season. Devonshire Park was officially opened on 2 September 1905, when St Helens Town were the visitors. Despite defeat in a disappointing 3–2 start, a respectable mid-table position was achieved.

Brunton Park, Warwick Road, Carlisle CA1 1LL.

Telephone: (01228) 526 237.

Fax: (01228) 554 141.

Ticket Office: (0844) 371 1921.

Website: www.carlisleunited.co.uk

Email: enquiries@carlisleunited.co.uk

Ground Capacity: 16,981.

Record Attendance: 27,500 v Birmingham C, FA Cup 3rd rd, 5 January 1957 and v Middlesbrough, FA Cup 5th rd, 7 February 1970.

Pitch Measurements: 114yd × 74yd.

Chairman: Andrew Jenkins.

Manager: Greg Abbott.

Assistant Manager: Graham Kavanagh.

Physio: Neil Dalton.

Colours: Blue shirts with white and red trim, white shorts, white stockings.

Year Formed: 1904.

Turned Professional: 1921.

Previous Name: 1904, Shaddongate United; 1904, Carlisle United.

Club Nicknames: 'Cumbrians' or 'The Blues'.

Grounds: 1904, Milholme Bank; 1905, Devonshire Park; 1909, Brunton Park.

First Football League Game: 25 August 1928, Division 3 (N), v Accrington S (a) W 3–2 – Prout; Coulthard, Cook; Harrison, Ross, Pigg; Agar (1), Hutchison, McConnell (1), Ward (1), Watson.

Record League Victory: 8–0 v Hartlepool U, Division 3 (N), 1 September 1928 – Prout; Smiles, Cook; Robinson (1) Ross, Pigg; Agar (1), Hutchison (1), McConnell (4), Ward (1), Watson. 8–0 v Scunthorpe U, Division 3 (N), 25 December 1952 – MacLaren; Hill, Scott; Stokoe, Twentyman, Waters; Harrison (1), Whitehouse (5), Ashman (2), Duffett, Bond.

Record Cup Victory: 6–0 v Shepshed Dynamo, FA Cup 1st rd, 16 November 1996 – Caig; Hopper, Archdeacon (pen), Walling, Robinson, Pounewatchy, Peacock (1), Conway (1) (Jansen), Smart (McAlindon (1)), Hayward, Aspinall (Thorpe), (2 og).

HONOURS

Football League – Division 1: 22nd, 1974–75;
Division 3: ***Champions*** 1964–65, 1994–95; ***Runners-up*** 1981–82;
Division 4: ***Runners-up*** 1963–64;
FL 2: ***Champions*** 2005–06.

FA Cup: 6th rd 1975.

Football League Cup: Semi-final 1970.

Auto Windscreens Shield: ***Winners*** 1997; ***Runners-up*** 1995.

LDV Vans Trophy: ***Runners-up*** 2003, 2006.

Johnstone's Paint Trophy: ***Winners*** 2011; ***Runners-up*** 2010.

sky SPORTS FACT FILE

Three Carlisle United players each scored just one crucial goal in their only League outings: Stan Keen v Rotherham United, 16 September 1933 (1-0), George Gray v New Brighton, 15 November 1947 (2-1) and David Bell v Crystal Palace, 1 November 1958 (3-3).

Record Defeat: 1–11 v Hull C, Division 3 (N), 14 January 1939.

Most League Points (2 for a win): 62, Division 3 (N), 1950–51.

Most League Points (3 for a win): 91, Division 3, 1994–95.

Most League Goals: 113, Division 4, 1963–64.

Highest League Scorer in Season: Jimmy McConnell, 42, Division 3 (N), 1928–29.

Most League Goals in Total Aggregate: Jimmy McConnell, 126, 1928–32.

Most League Goals in One Match: 5, Hugh Mills v Halifax T, Division 3 (N), 11 September 1937; 5, Jim Whitehouse v Scunthorpe U, Division 3 (N), 25 December 1952.

Most Capped Player: Eric Welsh, 4, Northern Ireland.

Most League Appearances: Allan Ross, 466, 1963–79.

Youngest League Player: John Slaven, 16 years 162 days v Scunthorpe U, 16 March 2002.

Record Transfer Fee Received: £1,500,000 from Crystal Palace for Matt Jansen, February 1998.

Record Transfer Fee Paid: £140,000 to Blackburn R for Joe Garner, August 2007.

Football League Record: 1928 Elected to Division 3 (N); 1958–62 Division 4; 1962–63 Division 3; 1963–64 Division 4; 1964–65 Division 3; 1965–74 Division 2; 1974–75 Division 1; 1975–77 Division 2; 1977–82 Division 3; 1982–86 Division 2; 1986–87 Division 3; 1987–92 Division 4; 1992–95 Division 3; 1995–96 Division 2; 1996–97 Division 3; 1997–98 Division 2; 1998–04 Division 3; 2004–05 Conference; 2005–06 FL 2; 2006– FL 1.

LATEST SEQUENCES

Longest Sequence of League Wins: 7, 18.2.06 – 8.4.06.

Longest Sequence of League Defeats: 12, 27.9.2003 – 13.12.2003.

Longest Sequence of League Draws: 6, 11.2.1978 – 11.3.1978.

Longest Sequence of Unbeaten League Matches: 19, 1.10.1994 – 11.2.1995.

Longest Sequence Without a League Win: 14, 19.1.1935 – 19.4.1935.

Successive Scoring Runs: 26 from 23.8.1947.

Successive Non-scoring Runs: 5 from 24.8.1968.

MANAGERS

Harry Kirkbride 1904–05 (*Secretary-Manager*)
McCumiskey 1905–06 (*Secretary-Manager*)
Jack Houston 1906–08 (*Secretary-Manager*)
Bert Stansfield 1908–10
Jack Houston 1910–12
Davie Graham 1912–13
George Bristow 1913–30
Billy Hampson 1930–33
Bill Clarke 1933–35
Robert Kelly 1935–36
Fred Westgarth 1936–38
David Taylor 1938–40
Howard Harkness 1940–45
Bill Clark 1945–46 (*Secretary-Manager*)
Ivor Broadis 1946–49
Bill Shankly 1949–51
Fred Emery 1951–58
Andy Beattie 1958–60
Ivor Powell 1960–63
Alan Ashman 1963–67
Tim Ward 1967–68
Bob Stokoe 1968–70
Ian MacFarlane 1970–72
Alan Ashman 1972–75
Dick Young 1975–76
Bobby Moncur 1976–80
Martin Harvey 1980
Bob Stokoe 1980–85
Bryan 'Pop' Robson 1985
Bob Stokoe 1985–86
Harry Gregg 1986–87
Cliff Middlemass 1987–91
Aidan McCaffery 1991–92
David McCreery 1992–93
Mick Wadsworth (*Director of Coaching*) 1993–96
Mervyn Day 1996–97
David Wilkes and John Halpin (*Directors of Coaching*), and **Michael Knighton** 1997–99
Nigel Pearson 1998–99
Keith Mincher 1999
Martin Wilkinson 1999–2000
Ian Atkins 2000–01
Roddy Collins 2001–02; 2002–03
Paul Simpson 2003–06
Neil McDonald 2006–07
John Ward 2007–08
Greg Abbott December 2008–

TEN YEAR LEAGUE RECORD

		P	W	D	L	F	A	Pts	Pos
2002-03	Div 3	46	13	10	23	52	78	49	22
2003-04	Div 3	46	12	9	25	46	69	45	23
2004-05	Conf	42	20	13	9	74	37	73	3
2005-06	FL 2	46	25	11	10	84	42	86	1
2006-07	FL 1	46	19	11	16	54	55	68	8
2007-08	FL 1	46	23	11	12	64	46	80	4
2008-09	FL 1	46	12	14	20	56	69	50	20
2009-10	FL 1	46	15	13	18	63	66	58	14
2010-11	FL 1	46	16	11	19	60	62	59	12
2011-12	FL 1	46	18	15	13	65	66	69	8

DID YOU KNOW 

On three occasions Carlisle United have called upon services of just 20 players in League matches: in 1951–52 when seventh, ten seasons later when in fourth position and in 1964–65 in winning the Third Division championship, when only two were ever-present, Terry Caldwell and Stan Harland.

CARLISLE UNITED 2011–12 LEAGUE RECORD

Match No.	Date	Venue	Opponents	Result		H/T Score	Lg Pos.	Goalscorers	Attendance
1	Aug 6	H	Notts Co	L	0-3	0-3	—		5941
2	13	A	Bury	W	2-0	0-0	12	Berrett 68, Noble 90	3640
3	16	A	Rochdale	D	0-0	0-0	—		2671
4	20	H	Bournemouth	W	2-1	0-0	8	Taiwo 49, Byrne (og) 77	4422
5	27	A	Leyton Orient	W	2-1	0-0	6	Miller 2 68, 87	3524
6	Sept 3	H	Milton Keynes D	L	1-3	0-1	9	Miller 52	4919
7	10	H	Hartlepool U	L	1-2	0-2	12	Loy (pen) 74	4765
8	13	A	Tranmere R	W	2-1	2-0	—	Miller 3, Berrett (pen) 35	4219
9	17	A	Chesterfield	L	1-4	1-2	13	Miller 20	6445
10	24	H	Stevenage	W	1-0	1-0	10	Murphy 27	4063
11	Oct 1	A	Walsall	D	1-1	0-1	10	Robson 50	3831
12	8	H	Brentford	D	2-2	1-1	10	Clarkson (og) 63, Berrett 23	4184
13	15	A	Yeovil T	W	3-0	0-0	9	Noble 55, McGovern 65, Livesey 84	3673
14	22	A	Charlton Ath	L	0-4	0-3	11		16,741
15	25	H	Sheffield W	W	3-2	0-1	—	Miller 50, Loy 56, Noble 64	6058
16	29	H	Oldham Ath	D	3-3	1-3	9	Miller 45, Zoko 2 48, 90	4803
17	Nov 5	A	Exeter C	D	0-0	0-0	10		4245
18	19	A	Sheffield U	L	0-1	0-1	11		16,840
19	26	H	Colchester U	W	1-0	1-0	8	Thirlwell 22	4435
20	Dec 10	A	Scunthorpe U	W	2-1	0-1	7	Berrett 64, Zoko 90	3624
21	17	H	Wycombe W	D	2-2	1-2	7	Loy 2, Zoko 86	4414
22	26	A	Preston NE	D	3-3	2-2	8	Miller (pen) 20, Zoko 45, Berrett 62	17,518
23	30	A	Huddersfield T	D	1-1	1-1	—	Noble 8	13,962
24	Jan 2	H	Sheffield U	W	3-2	2-2	7	Zoko 2 2, 15, McGovern 71	7721
25	7	H	Leyton Orient	W	4-1	3-0	—	Zoko 1, Robson 30, Taiwo 37, Berrett 73	4964
26	21	H	Walsall	D	1-1	1-0	7	Miller 7	5051
27	28	A	Hartlepool U	L	0-4	0-2	7		5995
28	Feb 4	H	Chesterfield	W	2-1	0-1	—	Parker 75, Zoko 84	4313
29	14	H	Tranmere R	D	0-0	0-0	—		4152
30	20	A	Brentford	L	0-4	0-3	—		4292
31	25	H	Yeovil T	W	3-2	1-0	6	Miller (pen) 34, Madden 49, Zoko 90	4265
32	Mar 3	A	Notts Co	L	0-2	0-2	8		6451
33	6	H	Rochdale	W	2-1	0-0	—	McGovern 57, Zoko 76	3694
34	10	H	Bury	W	4-1	1-1	7	Noble 25, Cook 78, Miller 2 (1 pen) 88 (p), 90	4855
35	17	A	Bournemouth	D	1-1	1-0	7	Miller 4	5240
36	20	H	Preston NE	D	0-0	0-0	—		6925
37	24	A	Colchester U	D	1-1	0-0	6	Berrett 68	3672
38	27	A	Milton Keynes D	W	2-1	0-0	—	Cook 2 (1 pen) 83, 90 (p)	8608
39	31	H	Huddersfield T	W	2-1	0-0	6	Berrett 48, Miller 90	7530
40	Apr 6	A	Wycombe W	D	1-1	0-0	—	Basey (og) 62	4823
41	9	H	Scunthorpe U	D	0-0	0-0	7		6555
42	14	H	Charlton Ath	L	0-1	0-0	7		6625
43	17	A	Stevenage	L	0-1	0-0	—		3438
44	21	A	Sheffield W	L	1-2	0-1	8	Berrett 82	21,934
45	28	H	Exeter C	W	4-1	2-1	8	Zoko 2 34, 77, Cook 42, Noble 51	6029
46	May 5	A	Oldham Ath	L	1-2	0-0	8	Taiwo 68	5152

Final League Position: 8

GOALSCORERS

League (65): Miller 14 (3 pens), Zoko 13, Berrett 9 (1 pen), Noble 6, Cook 4 (1 pen), Loy 3 (1 pen), McGovern 3, Taiwo 3, Robson 2, Livesey 1, Madden 1, Murphy 1, Parker 1, Thirlwell 1, own goals 3.
Carling Cup (1): McGovern 1.
FA Cup (4): Berrett 1, Loy 1, Miller 1, Noble 1.
J Paint Trophy (2): McGovern 1, Zoko 1.

Collin A 46	Simek F 25	Robson M 25 + 2	Thirlwell P 25 + 1	Michalik L 33 + 3	Murphy P 38 + 2	Taiwo T 32 + 5	Berrett J 42	Curran C 2 + 10	Zoko F 34 + 11	McGovern J 40 + 5	Welsh A 4 + 17	Loy R 18 + 2	Noble L 32 + 8	Tavernier J 16	O'Halloran S 3	Miller L 33	Livesey D 26 + 2	Helan J — + 2	Ribeiro C 5	Madden P 6 + 12	Chantler C 10 + 2	Cook J 6 + 8	Parker B 5	Beck M — + 2	*Match No.*
1	2^3	3	4^1	5	6	7	8	9^2	10	11	12	13	14												1
1		3	4	5	6	7^2	8	12	10^3	11	13	9^1	14	2											2
1		3	4	5	6	7^2	8	13	10	11	12	9^1		2											3
1		3	4^2	5	6	7	8	9	10^1	11	13	12		2											4
1		3	4^2	5		7^1	8	14	12	11^3	10		13	2	6	9									5
1		3	4^2			7^1	8	12	13	11	10^3		14	2	6	9	5								6
1		3	4	5		7^1		14	10^2	12	13	11	8	2	6^3	9									7
1		3	4	5	6		8		10			11	7	2		9									8
1		3	4	5	6		8	12	10^3	13	14	11	7^2	2		9^1									9
1		11	4	5	6	14	8	13	10	12		9^2	7^3	2			3^1								10
1		11	4^3	5	6	14	8		12	13		10^2	7	2		9	3^1								11
1		3			6	7	8		12	4		10^1	11	2		9	5								12
1		3			6	7	8	14	12	4^2		10^1	11	2		9^3	5	13							13
1		3■		12	6	7	8	14	13	4		10^3	11^1	2		9^2	5								14
1				6	3	7	8			4		10	11	2		9	5								15
1		13		6	3	7^1	8		12	4		10	11	2		9	5^2								16
1		11	4	5	6^1				8^2	3		10	7	2		9	12	13							17
1		3	4^2	6	12		8	14	13	7		10^3	11			9	5^1		2						18
1		3	4	5	6		8		12	7		10	11^1			9			2						19
1		3	4	5	6		8		12	7		10^1	11			9			2						20
1	2	3	4^1	5	6	12	8		13	7		10^3	11^2			9				14					21
1	2	3	4	5	6		8		10^2	7		11^1	12			9				13					22
1		3	4	5	6		8		10	7			11			9			2						23
1		3	4	5	6	11^1	8		10	7						9			2	12					24
1	2	3	4	5	6	11^1	8^2		10	7						9				13	12				25
1	3		4	6		11^1	8		10	7						9	5				2	12			26
1	2		4^3	6		8^1			10	7			11			9■	5^2			12	14	13	3		27
1	2		4	6	5	9			10	7	13		11^1							12		8^2	3		28
1	2		4	5	6	11^1	8^2		10	7	13		14							12		9^3	3		29
1	2		4^1	5^2	6		9		10	7	12		8				13			11			3		30
1	2				6	4	8		10	7						9	5			11			3		31
1	2			5	6	4^1	8		10	7			13			9				11^2	3	12			32
1	2				6	7	8		10	4			12			9	5			11^1	3				33
1	2				6	7^1	8		10	4			11			9	5				3	12			34
1	2				6	7	8		10^1	4	12		11^2			9	5			13	3				35
1	2				6	7^2	8		10^1	4	12		11			9	5			13	3				36
1	2				6	11^2	8		10^1	4	12		7			9	5				3	13			37
1	2				6	11^1	8		10^2	4	12		7			9	5				3	13			38
1	2			12	6	7^2	8		10	4			11			9	5				3^1	13			39
1	2			12	6	7	8		10	4			11			9	5				3^1				40
1	2			6	3	7	8^1		10^2	4	12		11			9^3	5			14		13			41
1	2			6	3	7^2	8		10	4^3	14		11				5			12		9^1		13	42
1	2			6^3	3	7	8		10	4^1	12		11^2				5			13		9		14	43
1	2	12		4	6^1	7^2	8		10	13	14		11				5			3^3		9			44
1	2	3	13	6	14	12	8^1		10	4	7^2		11^3				5					9			45
1	2	3		6		12	8		10	4	7		11				5			9^1					46

FA Cup

First Round	Alfreton T	(a)	4-0
Second Round	Charlton Ath	(a)	0-2

Carling Cup

First Round	Oldham Ath	(a)	1-1
Second Round	Aldershot T	(a)	0-2

J Paint Trophy

First Round	Accrington S	(a)	2-3

CHARLTON ATHLETIC FL Championship

FOUNDATION

The club was formed on 9 June 1905, by a group of 14- and 15-year-old youths living in streets by the Thames in the area which now borders the Thames Barrier. The club's progress through local leagues was so rapid that after the First World War they joined the Kent League where they spent a season before turning professional and joining the Southern League in 1920. A year later they were elected to the Football League's Division 3 (South).

The Valley, Floyd Road, Charlton, London SE7 8BL.

Telephone: (020) 8333 4000.

Fax: (020) 8333 4001.

Ticket Office: (0871) 226 1905.

Website: www.cafc.co.uk

Email: info@cafc.co.uk

Ground Capacity: 27,111.

Record Attendance: 75,031 v Aston Villa, FA Cup 5th rd, 12 February 1938 (at The Valley).

Pitch Measurements: 101.5m × 65.8m.

Chairman: Michael Slater.

Chief Executive: Stephen Kavanagh.

Manager: Chris Powell.

Assistant Manager: Alex Dyer.

Head Physio: Erol Umut.

Colours: Red shirts with white trim, white shorts, white stockings with red tops.

Year Formed: 1905.

Turned Professional: 1920.

Club Nickname: 'Addicks'.

Grounds: 1906, Siemen's Meadow; 1907, Woolwich Common; 1909, Pound Park; 1913, Horn Lane; 1920, The Valley; 1923, Catford (The Mount); 1924, The Valley; 1985, Selhurst Park; 1991, Upton Park; 1992, The Valley.

First Football League Game: 27 August 1921, Division 3 (S), v Exeter C (h) W 1–0 – Hughes; Johnny Mitchell, Goodman; Dowling (1), Hampson, Dunn; Castle, Bailey, Halse, Green, Wilson.

Record League Victory: 8–1 v Middlesbrough, Division 1, 12 September 1953 – Bartram; Campbell, Ellis; Fenton, Ufton, Hammond; Hurst (2), O'Linn (2), Leary (1), Firmani (3), Kiernan.

Record Cup Victory: 7–0 v Burton A, FA Cup 3rd rd, 7 January 1956 – Bartram; Campbell, Townsend; Hewie, Ufton, Hammond; Hurst (1), Gauld (1), Leary (3), White, Kiernan (2).

Record Defeat: 1–11 v Aston Villa, Division 2, 14 November 1959.

HONOURS

Football League – FL 1 *Champions* 2011–12; **Division 1: *Champions*** 1999–2000; ***Runners-up*** 1936–37; **Division 2: *Runners-up*** 1935–36, 1985–86; **Division 3 (S): *Champions*** 1928–29, 1934–35.

FA Cup: *Winners* 1947; ***Runners-up*** 1946.

Football League Cup: Quarter-final 2007.

Full Members' Cup: ***Runners-up*** 1987.

sky SPORTS FACT FILE

In 1927–28 Charlton Athletic enjoyed their best start to a season when they remained unbeaten in their opening twelve matches in Division Three (South). Unusually half of these fixtures ended drawn. The club's finishing position of eleventh was its highest at the time in the League.

Most League Points (2 for a win): 61, Division 3 (S), 1934–35.

Most League Points (3 for a win): 101, FL 1, 2011–12.

Most League Goals: 107, Division 2, 1957–58.

Highest League Scorer in Season: Ralph Allen, 32, Division 3 (S), 1934–35.

Most League Goals in Total Aggregate: Stuart Leary, 153, 1953–62.

Most League Goals in One Match: 5, Wilson Lennox v Exeter C, Division 3 (S), 2 February 1929; 5, Eddie Firmani v Aston Villa, Division 1, 5 February 1955; 5, John Summers v Huddersfield T, Division 2, 21 December 1957; 5, John Summers v Portsmouth, Division 2, 1 October 1960.

Most Capped Player: Jonatan Johansson, 42 (105), Finland.

Most League Appearances: Sam Bartram, 579, 1934–56.

Youngest League Player: Jonjo Shelvey, 16 years 59 days v Burnley, 26 April 2008.

Record Transfer Fee Received: £16,500,000 from Tottenham H for Darren Bent, May 2007

Record Transfer Fee Paid: £5,380,000 to Ipswich T for Darren Bent, June 2005.

Football League Record: 1921 Elected to Division 3 (S); 1929–33 Division 2; 1933–35 Division 3 (S); 1935–36 Division 2; 1936–57 Division 1; 1957–72 Division 2; 1972–75 Division 3; 1975–80 Division 2; 1980–81 Division 3; 1981–86 Division 2; 1986–90 Division 1; 1990–92 Division 2; 1992–98 Division 1; 1998–99 FA Premier League; 1999–2000 Division 1; 2000–07 FA Premier League; 2007–09 FL C; 2009–12 FL 1; 2012– FL C.

MANAGERS

Walter Rayner 1920–25
Alex Macfarlane 1925–27
Albert Lindon 1928
Alex Macfarlane 1928–32
Albert Lindon 1932–33
Jimmy Seed 1933–56
Jimmy Trotter 1956–61
Frank Hill 1961–65
Bob Stokoe 1965–67
Eddie Firmani 1967–70
Theo Foley 1970–74
Andy Nelson 1974–79
Mike Bailey 1979–81
Alan Mullery 1981–82
Ken Craggs 1982
Lennie Lawrence 1982–91
Steve Gritt/Alan Curbishley 1991–95
Alan Curbishley 1995–2006
Iain Dowie 2006
Les Reed 2006
Alan Pardew 2006–08
Phil Parkinson 2008–10
Chris Powell January 2011–

LATEST SEQUENCES

Longest Sequence of League Wins: 12, 26.12.1999 – 7.3.2000.

Longest Sequence of League Defeats: 10, 11.4.1990 – 15.9.1990.

Longest Sequence of League Draws: 6, 13.12.1992 – 16.1.1993.

Longest Sequence of Unbeaten League Matches: 15, 4.10.1980 – 20.12.1980.

Longest Sequence Without a League Win: 18, 18.10.2008 – 17.1.2009.

Successive Scoring Runs: 25 from 26.12.1935.

Successive Non-scoring Runs: 5 from 6.9.1922.

TEN YEAR LEAGUE RECORD

		P	*W*	*D*	*L*	*F*	*A*	*Pts*	*Pos*
2002-03	PR Lge	38	14	7	17	45	56	49	12
2003-04	PR Lge	38	14	11	13	51	51	53	7
2004-05	PR Lge	38	12	10	16	42	58	46	11
2005-06	PR Lge	38	13	8	17	41	55	47	13
2006-07	PR Lge	38	8	10	20	34	60	34	19
2007-08	FL C	46	17	13	16	63	58	64	11
2008-09	FL C	46	8	15	23	52	74	39	24
2009-10	FL 1	46	23	15	8	71	48	84	4
2010-11	FL 1	46	15	14	17	62	66	59	13
2011-12	FL 1	46	30	11	5	82	36	101	1

DID YOU KNOW ?

When Charlton Athletic attained 101 points in winning the championship of League One in 2011–12, they not only established a club record but they also became just the tenth team in Football League history to achieve a century after York City hit three figures in 1983–84.

CHARLTON ATHLETIC 2011–12 LEAGUE RECORD

Match No.	Date	Venue	Opponents	Result		H/T Score	Lg Pos.	Goalscorers	Attendance
1	Aug 6	H	Bournemouth	W	3-0	1-0	—	Stephens 2 [23, 51], Jackson (pen) [77]	16,111
2	13	A	Notts Co	W	2-1	2-0	1	Wagstaff [35], Hayes [45]	6397
3	16	A	Colchester U	W	2-0	2-0	—	Wright-Phillips 2 [13, 28]	5094
4	20	H	Scunthorpe U	D	2-2	1-0	2	Jackson [20], Wright-Phillips [57]	15,505
5	27	A	Bury	W	2-1	0-1	2	Hayes [49], Jackson [64]	3084
6	Sept 5	H	Sheffield W	D	1-1	1-0	—	Wright-Phillips [3]	14,014
7	10	H	Exeter C	W	2-0	1-0	2	Wright-Phillips [43], Stephens [81]	14,290
8	17	A	Rochdale	W	3-2	2-0	1	Hollands 2 [20, 80], Wiggins [44]	2909
9	24	H	Chesterfield	W	3-1	2-0	1	Hayes [19], Jackson [29], Wright-Phillips [90]	22,151
10	27	A	Milton Keynes D	D	1-1	0-1	—	Kermorgant [75]	8114
11	Oct 1	A	Sheffield U	W	2-0	0-0	1	Kermorgant [65], Wright-Phillips [67]	20,743
12	8	H	Tranmere R	D	1-1	0-1	1	Jackson (pen) [80]	15,038
13	15	A	Stevenage	L	0-1	0-1	1		4724
14	22	H	Carlisle U	W	4-0	3-0	1	Kermorgant 2 [13, 37], Wright-Phillips [21], Hollands [48]	16,741
15	25	A	Wycombe W	W	2-1	2-0	—	Wright-Phillips 2 [6, 41]	5406
16	29	A	Hartlepool U	W	4-0	2-0	1	Wright-Phillips 2 [9, 37], Hollands [55], Wagstaff [84]	5333
17	Nov 5	H	Preston NE	W	5-2	4-0	1	Jackson 2 (1 pen) [16, 26 (p)], Morrison [22], Wright-Phillips [38], Hollands [69]	17,486
18	19	A	Brentford	W	1-0	0-0	1	Wright-Phillips [64]	8095
19	28	H	Huddersfield T	W	2-0	2-0	—	Kermorgant [23], Ephraim [41]	18,029
20	Dec 10	A	Walsall	D	1-1	1-1	1	Kermorgant [45]	4537
21	17	H	Oldham Ath	D	1-1	0-0	1	Russell [60]	19,564
22	26	A	Yeovil T	W	3-2	1-1	1	Hollands [16], Kermorgant [60], Green [90]	4977
23	31	A	Leyton Orient	L	0-1	0-1	1		5097
24	Jan 2	H	Brentford	W	2-0	1-0	1	Morrison [31], Green [90]	17,506
25	14	A	Sheffield W	W	1-0	1-0	1	Jackson [28]	26,759
26	21	H	Sheffield U	W	1-0	1-0	1	Jackson [21]	20,992
27	28	A	Exeter C	W	1-0	0-0	1	Green [55]	5439
28	31	H	Bury	D	1-1	0-1	—	Stephens [90]	13,264
29	Feb 14	H	Milton Keynes D	W	2-1	2-0	—	Jackson 2 (2 pens) [44, 45]	15,569
30	18	A	Tranmere R	D	1-1	0-1	1	Morrison [60]	4685
31	21	H	Rochdale	D	1-1	0-0	—	Kermorgant [56]	15,067
32	25	H	Stevenage	W	2-0	0-0	1	Morrison [49], Wright-Phillips [64]	26,546
33	28	A	Chesterfield	W	4-0	1-0	—	Wright-Phillips 3 [43, 56, 66], Jackson [58]	6405
34	Mar 3	A	Bournemouth	W	1-0	0-0	1	Kermorgant [90]	8034
35	6	H	Colchester U	L	0-2	0-1	—		13,650
36	10	H	Notts Co	L	2-4	0-4	1	Wright-Phillips [50], Wagstaff [55]	17,033
37	17	A	Scunthorpe U	D	1-1	1-1	1	Wright-Phillips [6]	4544
38	20	H	Yeovil T	W	3-0	1-0	—	N'Guessan [7], Wright-Phillips [60], Russell [90]	13,717
39	24	A	Huddersfield T	L	0-1	0-1	1		15,735
40	31	H	Leyton Orient	W	2-0	1-0	1	Wagstaff [7], N'Guessan [82]	17,425
41	Apr 7	A	Oldham Ath	W	1-0	0-0	1	Kermorgant [49]	3641
42	9	H	Walsall	W	1-0	1-0	1	N'Guessan [35]	15,253
43	14	A	Carlisle U	W	1-0	0-0	1	Wright-Phillips [76]	6625
44	21	H	Wycombe W	W	2-1	1-1	1	Kermorgant [14], Stephens [74]	18,539
45	28	A	Preston NE	D	2-2	2-0	1	Haynes [11], N'Guessan [35]	12,029
46	May 5	H	Hartlepool U	W	3-2	0-1	1	Hollands [70], Haynes [78], Kermorgant [81]	26,749

Final League Position: 1

GOALSCORERS

League (82): Wright-Phillips 22, Jackson 12 (5 pens), Kermorgant 12, Hollands 7, Stephens 5, Morrison 4, N'Guessan 4, Wagstaff 4, Green 3, Hayes 3, Haynes 2, Russell 2, Ephraim 1, Wiggins 1.
Carling Cup (2): Benson 1, Euell 1.
FA Cup (6): Euell 1, Hollands 1, Jackson 1, Morrison 1, Pritchard 1, Taylor 1.
J Paint Trophy (0).

Elliot R 4	Solly C 44	Wiggins R 45	Hollands D 43	Morrison M 45	Taylor M 38 + 3	Wagstaff S 19 + 15	Stephens D 28 + 2	Hayes P 12 + 7	Wright-Phillips B 41 + 1	Jackson J 35 + 1	Benson P — + 1	Pritchard B 10 + 10	Doherty G — + 3	Euell J — + 11	Hughes A 5 + 10	Green D 25 + 7	Hamer B 41	Cort L 10 + 5	Kermorgant Y 33 + 3	Evina C 2 + 1	Ephraim H 4 + 1	Russell D 8 + 3	Sullivan J 1 + 2	Clarke L 1 + 6	Haynes D 3 + 11	N'Guessan D 6 + 1	Cook L 3 + 1	*Match No.*
1	2	3	4	5	6	7^{2}	8	9^{1}	10^{3}	11	12	13	14															1
1	2	3	4	5	6	7^{3}	8	9^{1}	10^{2}	11			13	12	14													2
1	2	3	4	5	6	7	8^{1}	9^{2}	10^{3}	11				12	13	14												3
1	2	3	4	5	6	7^{1}	8	9^{2}	10^{3}	11			14	13		12												4
	2	3	4	5	6	7	8	9^{2}		11		12		13		10^{1}	1											5
	2	3	4	5	6	7	8	9^{1}	10	11				12			1											6
	2	3	4	5	6	7	8^{2}	9^{1}	10^{3}	11		14		12	13		1											7
	2	3	4	5	6	7	8^{1}	9^{2}	10^{3}	11				13	12		1	14										8
	2	3	4	5	6	7^{2}	8	9^{1}	10	11					13		1		12									9
	2	3	4	5	6	7^{1}	8	9^{2}	10^{3}	11					14	12	1		13									10
	2	3	4	5	6	7^{3}	8	9^{1}	10^{2}	11					14	13	1		12									11
	2	3	4	5	6	12	8		10	11						7^{1}	1		9									12
		3	4	5	6^{1}	12	8^{3}	14	10	11						7^{2}	1	2	9	13								13
	2	3	4^{2}	5	6	12		14	10^{3}	11				13	8	7^{1}	1		9									14
	2	3	4	5	6	12			10^{1}	11					8	7	1		9									15
	2	3	4^{3}	5	6	12		13	10	11				14	8	7^{1}	1		9^{2}									16
	2	3	4	5	6	13		12	10^{1}	11^{3}				14	8	7^{2}	1		9									17
	2	3	4	5	6	13			10	11^{1}					8	7^{2}	1		9		12							18
	2	3	4	5	6	13		14	10						12	7	1		9^{3}		11^{2}	8^{1}						19
	2	3	4	5	6	12			10							7^{1}	1		9		11	8						20
	2	3	4	5	6	12			10							7	1		9		11^{1}	8						21
	2	3	4	5	6				10^{2}						12	7	1	13	9		11^{1}	8						22
	2	3	4	5	6	7^{G}		13	10^{1}	11^{2}		12					1■		9			8	15					23
	2	3	4	5		12			10^{2}	11^{1}		8			14	7^{3}	1	6	9					13				24
	2	3	4	5	6				10^{2}	11		8^{3}				7^{1}	1	14	9			12		13				25
	2	3	4	5	6				10^{2}	11		8				7^{1}	1		9			12■			13			26
	2	3	4	5	6		13		10^{2}	11		8^{3}				7^{1}	1		9					12	14			27
	2	3	4^{2}	5	6		8			11		13				7	1		9					10^{1}	12			28
	2	3	4	5	6		8		10^{2}	11^{1}		13				7	1		9						12			29
	2	3	4	5	6		11		12			8				7	1		9						10^{1}			30
		2	4	5	6	12	8		10^{2}			11				7^{1}	1	14	9	3^{3}				13				31
	2	3	4	5	6		8		10^{2}	11^{1}		13				7	1		9						12			32
	2	3	4	5^{2}	6		8		10	11^{3}						7	1	13	9^{1}					12	14			33
	2	3	4	5	6		8		10^{1}	11^{2}						7	1^{G}		9			13	15		12			34
	2	3	4	5	6		8		10	11^{2}						7^{1}	1		9					13	12			35
	2	3	4	5	6	12	8		10	11							1		9						7^{1}			36
	2	3	4	5	6	7			10	11^{1}						12	1		9			8						37
	2	3	4	5		7			10							12	1	6	9			8				11^{1}		38
	2	3	4	5		7	12	9^{2}	10			13					1	6				8■				11^{1}		39
	2	3	4	5		7	8		10^{1}							13	1	6	9							12	11^{2}	40
	2	3	4■	5	13	7■	8					12					1	6	9							10^{1}	11^{2}	41
	2	3		5	14		4		10^{1}	11^{3}		8					1	6	9						12	7^{2}	13	42
	2	3		5	13	12	4		10^{2}	11		8					1	6	9							7^{1}		43
	2	3		5		7	4		10^{1}	11		8					1	6	9						12			44
	2		4		6	12		14		13		8				7^{2}		5		3			1		10	9^{3}	11^{1}	45
	2	3	4	5	6	7^{2}	8		10^{3}	11^{1}		13		14			1		9						12			46

FA Cup

First Round	FC Halifax T	(a)	4-0
Second Round	Carlisle U	(h)	2-0
Third Round	Fulham	(a)	0-4

Carling Cup

First Round	Reading	(h)	2-1
Second Round	Preston NE	(h)	0-2

J Paint Trophy

Second Round	Brentford	(h)	0-3

CHELSEA FA Premiership

FOUNDATION

Chelsea may never have existed but for the fact that Fulham rejected an offer to rent the Stamford Bridge ground from Mr H. A. Mears who had owned it since 1904. Fortunately he was determined to develop it as a football stadium rather than sell it to the Great Western Railway and got together with Frederick Parker, who persuaded Mears of the financial advantages of developing a major sporting venue. Chelsea FC was formed in 1905 and applications made to join both the Southern League and Football League. The latter competition was decided upon because of its comparatively meagre representation in the south of England.

Stamford Bridge, Fulham Road, London SW6 1HS.
Telephone: (0871) 984 1955.
Fax: (020) 7381 4831.
Ticket Office: (0871) 984 1905.
Website: www.chelseafc.com
Email: (see website).
Ground Capacity: 41,841.
Record Attendance: 82,905 v Arsenal, Division 1, 12 October 1935.
Pitch Measurements: 103m × 67m.
Chairman: Bruce Buck.
Chief Executive: Ron Gourlay.
Manager: Roberto Di Matteo.
Technical Director: Michael Emenalo.
Assistant First Team Coaches: Eddie Newton, Steve Holland.
Head Physio: Jason Palmer.
Colours: Reflex blue shirt, reflex blue shorts, white stockings with blue trim.
Year Formed: 1905.
Turned Professional: 1905.
Club Nickname: 'The Blues'.
Ground: 1905, Stamford Bridge.
First Football League Game: 2 September 1905, Division 2, v Stockport Co (a) L 0–1 – Foulke; Mackie, McEwan; Key, Harris, Miller; Moran, Jack Robertson, Copeland, Windridge, Kirwan.
Record League Victory: 8-0 v Wigan Ath, FA Premier League, 9 May 2010 – Cech; Ivanovic (Belletti), Ashley Cole (1), Ballack (Matic), Terry, Alex, Kalou (1) (Joe Cole), Lampard (pen), Anelka (2), Drogba (3, 1 pen), Malouda.

HONOURS

FA Premier League: *Champions* 2004–05, 2005–06, 2009–10. *Runners-up* 2003–04, 2006–07, 2007–08, 2010–11.

Football League – Division 1: *Champions* 1954–55; **Division 2:** *Champions* 1983–84, 1988–89; *Runners-up* 1906–07, 1911–12, 1929–30, 1962–63, 1976–77.

FA Cup: ***Winners*** 1970, 1997, 2000, 2007, 2009, 2010, 2012. ***Runners-up*** 1915, 1967, 1994, 2002.

Football League Cup: ***Winners*** 1965, 1998, 2005, 2007; ***Runners-up*** 1972, 2008.

Full Members' Cup: ***Winners*** 1986.

Zenith Data Systems Cup: ***Winners*** 1990.

European Competitions
Champions League: 1999–2000, 2003–04 (*s-f*), 2004–05 (*s-f*), 2005–06, 2006–07 (*s-f*), 2007–08 (*runners-up*), 2008–09 (*s-f*), 2009–10, 2010–11, 2011–12 (*winners*). **European Fairs Cup:** 1958–60, 1965–66, 1968–69. **European Cup-Winners' Cup:** 1970–71 (*winners*), 1971–72, 1994–95, 1997–98 (*winners*), 1998–99 (*s-f*). **UEFA Cup:** 2000–01, 2001–02, *2002–03*. **Super Cup:** 1998–99 (*winners*).

sky SPORTS FACT FILE

Chelsea headed the table of the highest average attendances in ten seasons during their Football League days. The first occasion was in 1907–08, only the third season of the club's existence and after winning promotion to the First Division. At 32,894 no other club averaged over 30,000.

Record Cup Victory: 13–0 v Jeunesse Hautcharage, ECWC, 1st rd 2nd leg, 29 September 1971 – Bonetti; Boyle, Harris (1), Hollins (1p), Webb (1), Hinton, Cooke, Baldwin (3), Osgood (5), Hudson (1), Houseman (1).

Record Defeat: 1–8 v Wolverhampton W, Division 1, 26 September 1953.

Most League Points (2 for a win): 57, Division 2, 1906–07.

Most League Points (3 for a win): 99, Division 2, 1988–89.

Most League Goals: 103, FA Premier League, 2009–10.

Highest League Scorer in Season: Jimmy Greaves, 41, 1960–61.

Most League Goals in Total Aggregate: Bobby Tambling, 164, 1958–70.

Most League Goals in One Match: 5, George Hilsdon v Glossop, Division 2, 1 September 1906; 5, Jimmy Greaves v Wolverhampton W, Division 1, 30 August 1958; 5, Jimmy Greaves v Preston NE, Division 1, 19 December 1959; 5, Jimmy Greaves v WBA, Division 1, 3 December 1960; 5, Bobby Tambling v Aston Villa, Division 1, 17 September 1966; 5, Gordon Durie v Walsall, Division 2, 4 February 1989.

Most Capped Player: Frank Lampard, 88 (90), England.

Most League Appearances: Ron Harris, 655, 1962–80.

Youngest League Player: Ian Hamilton, 16 years 138 days v Tottenham H, 18 March 1967.

Record Transfer Fee Received: £12,000,000 from Rangers for Tore Andre Flo, November 2000; £12,000,000 from Manchester C for Wayne Bridge, January 2009.

Record Transfer Fee Paid: £50,000,000 to Liverpool for Fernando Torres, January 2011.

Football League Record: 1905 Elected to Division 2; 1907–10 Division 1; 1910–12 Division 2; 1912–24 Division 1; 1924–30 Division 2; 1930–62 Division 1; 1962–63 Division 2; 1963–75 Division 1; 1975–77 Division 2; 1977–79 Division 1; 1979–84 Division 2; 1984–88 Division 1; 1988–89 Division 2; 1989–92 Division 1; 1992– FA Premier League.

MANAGERS

John Tait Robertson 1905–07
David Calderhead 1907–33
Leslie Knighton 1933–39
Billy Birrell 1939–52
Ted Drake 1952–61
Tommy Docherty 1961–67
Dave Sexton 1967–74
Ron Suart 1974–75
Eddie McCreadie 1975–77
Ken Shellito 1977–78
Danny Blanchflower 1978–79
Geoff Hurst 1979–81
John Neal 1981–85 (*Director to 1986*)
John Hollins 1985–88
Bobby Campbell 1988–91
Ian Porterfield 1991–93
David Webb 1993
Glenn Hoddle 1993–96
Ruud Gullit 1996–98
Gianluca Vialli 1998–2000
Claudio Ranieri 2000–04
Jose Mourinho 2004–07
Avram Grant 2007–08
Luiz Felipe Scolari 2008–09
Guus Hiddink 2009
Carlo Ancelotti 2009–2011
Andre Villas-Boas 2011–12
Roberto Di Matteo March 2012–

LATEST SEQUENCES

Longest Sequence of League Wins: 11, 25.4.2009 – 20.9.2009.

Longest Sequence of League Defeats: 7, 1.11.1952 – 20.12.1952.

Longest Sequence of League Draws: 6, 20.8.1969 – 13.9.1969.

Longest Sequence of Unbeaten League Matches: 40, 23.10.2004 – 29.10.2005.

Longest Sequence Without a League Win: 21, 3.11.1987 – 2.4.1988.

Successive Scoring Runs: 27 from 29.10.1988.

Successive Non-scoring Runs: 9 from 14.3.1981.

TEN YEAR LEAGUE RECORD

		P	*W*	*D*	*L*	*F*	*A*	*Pts*	*Pos*
2002-03	PR Lge	38	19	10	9	68	38	67	4
2003-04	PR Lge	38	24	7	7	67	30	79	2
2004-05	PR Lge	38	29	8	1	72	15	95	1
2005-06	PR Lge	38	29	4	5	72	22	91	1
2006-07	PR Lge	38	24	11	3	64	24	83	2
2007-08	PR Lge	38	25	10	3	65	26	85	2
2008-09	PR Lge	38	25	8	5	68	24	83	3
2009-10	PR Lge	38	27	5	6	103	32	86	1
2010-11	PR Lge	38	21	8	9	69	33	71	2
2011-12	PR Lge	38	18	10	10	65	46	64	6

DID YOU KNOW ?

In 1999–2000 Chelsea were involved in a club record 61 first class matches. In addition to the 38 Premier League games, there were 16 in the Champions League, six in the FA Cup and one League Cup tie. Nearest to being an ever-present was goalkeeper Ed de Goey missing one.

CHELSEA 2011–12 LEAGUE RECORD

Match No.	Date	Venue	Opponents	Result		H/T Score	Lg Pos.	Goalscorers	Attendance
1	Aug 14	A	Stoke C	D	0-0	0-0	—		27,421
2	20	H	WBA	W	2-1	0-1	5	Anelka [53], Malouda [83]	41,091
3	27	H	Norwich C	W	3-1	1-0	4	Bosingwa [6], Lampard (pen) [82], Mata [90]	41,765
4	Sept 10	A	Sunderland	W	2-1	1-0	3	Terry [18], Sturridge [51]	36,699
5	18	A	Manchester U	L	1-3	0-3	3	Torres [46]	75,455
6	24	H	Swansea C	W	4-1	2-0	3	Torres [29], Ramires 2 [36, 76], Drogba [90]	41,800
7	Oct 2	A	Bolton W	W	5-1	4-0	3	Sturridge 2 [2, 25], Lampard 3 [15, 27, 59]	24,657
8	15	H	Everton	W	3-1	2-0	3	Sturridge [31], Terry [45], Ramires [61]	41,789
9	23	A	QPR	L	0-1	0-1	3		18,050
10	29	H	Arsenal	L	3-5	2-1	3	Lampard [14], Terry [45], Mata [80]	41,801
11	Nov 5	A	Blackburn R	W	1-0	0-0	4	Lampard [51]	21,985
12	20	H	Liverpool	L	1-2	0-1	4	Sturridge [55]	41,820
13	26	H	Wolverhampton W	W	3-0	3-0	5	Terry [7], Sturridge [29], Mata [45]	41,648
14	Dec 3	A	Newcastle U	W	3-0	1-0	4	Drogba [38], Kalou [89], Sturridge [90]	52,305
15	12	H	Manchester C	W	2-1	1-1	—	Raul Meireles [34], Lampard (pen) [83]	41,730
16	17	A	Wigan Ath	D	1-1	0-0	4	Sturridge [59]	18,320
17	22	A	Tottenham H	D	1-1	1-1	—	Sturridge [23]	36,141
18	26	H	Fulham	D	1-1	0-0	4	Mata [47]	41,548
19	31	H	Aston Villa	L	1-3	1-1	5	Drogba (pen) [23]	41,332
20	Jan 2	A	Wolverhampton W	W	2-1	0-0	—	Ramires [54], Lampard [89]	27,289
21	14	H	Sunderland	W	1-0	1-0	4	Lampard [13]	41,696
22	21	A	Norwich C	D	0-0	0-0	4		26,792
23	31	A	Swansea C	D	1-1	0-1	—	Taylor (og) [90]	20,526
24	Feb 5	H	Manchester U	D	3-3	1-0	4	Evans (og) [36], Mata [46], Luiz [50]	41,668
25	11	A	Everton	L	0-2	0-1	5		33,924
26	25	H	Bolton W	W	3-0	0-0	5	Luiz [48], Drogba [61], Lampard [79]	40,999
27	Mar 3	A	WBA	L	0-1	0-0	5		24,838
28	10	H	Stoke C	W	1-0	0-0	5	Drogba [68]	40,945
29	21	A	Manchester C	L	1-2	0-0	—	Cahill [60]	46,324
30	24	H	Tottenham H	D	0-0	0-0	5		41,830
31	31	A	Aston Villa	W	4-2	1-0	5	Sturridge [9], Ivanovic 2 [51, 83], Torres [90]	34,740
32	Apr 7	H	Wigan Ath	W	2-1	0-0	5	Ivanovic [62], Mata [90]	40,651
33	9	A	Fulham	D	1-1	1-0	—	Lampard (pen) [45]	25,697
34	21	A	Arsenal	D	0-0	0-0	6		60,111
35	29	H	QPR	W	6-1	4-0	6	Sturridge [1], Terry [13], Torres 3 [19, 25, 64], Malouda [80]	41,675
36	May 2	H	Newcastle U	L	0-2	0-1	—		41,559
37	8	A	Liverpool	L	1-4	0-3	—	Ramires [50]	40,721
38	13	H	Blackburn R	W	2-1	2-0	6	Terry [31], Raul Meireles [34]	40,742

Final League Position: 6

GOALSCORERS

League (65): Lampard 11 (3 pens), Sturridge 11, Mata 6, Terry 6, Torres 6, Drogba 5 (1 pen), Ramires 5, Ivanovic 3, Luiz 2, Malouda 2, Raul Meireles 2, Anelka 1, Bosingwa 1, Cahill 1, Kalou 1, own goals 2.
Carling Cup (2): Kalou 1, Sturridge 1.
FA Cup (20): Mata 4 (1 pen), Ramires 4, Drogba 2, Lampard 2, Raul Meireles 2, Torres 2, Cahill 1, Kalou 1, Malouda 1, Sturridge 1.
Champions League (25): Drogba 6, Lampard 3 (2 pens), Ramires 3, Torres 3, Ivanovic 2, Kalou 2, Mata 2, Raul Meireles 2, David Luiz 1, Terry 1.

Cech P 34	Bosingwa J 24 + 3	Cole A 31 + 1	Mikel J 15 + 7	Terry J 31	Alex 3	Ramires 28 + 2	Lampard F 26 + 4	Torres F 20 + 12	Kalou S 7 + 5	Malouda F 11 + 15	Anelka N 3 + 6	Drogba D 16 + 8	Benayoun Y — + 1	Hilario 2	Ivanovic B 26 + 3	Mata J 29 + 5	Lukaku R 1 + 7	Sturridge D 28 + 2	Raul Meireles 23 + 5	Romeu O 11 + 5	McEachran J — + 2	Luiz D 18 + 2	Paulo Ferreira 3 + 3	Essien M 10 + 4	Cahill G 9 + 1	Bertrand R 6 + 1	Hutchinson S 1 + 1	Turnbull R 2	*Match No.*
1	2	3	4	5	6	7	8	9^{3}	10^{2}	11^{1}	12	13	14																1
	2	3	4	5	6^{3}	7	8	9^{2}	10^{1}	12	11	13		1	14														2
	2	3	4	5		7	8	9^{3}		11^{2}	12	10^{1}		1	6	13	14												3
1	2	3		5		4	8	13		12	9^{3}				6	7^{2}		10^{1}	11	14									4
1	2	3	14	5		4	8^{1}	9			12				6	7	13	10^{2}	11^{3}										5
1	2	3	4	5		8		9■		12	10^{2}	13			6	7^{1}			11^{3}		14								6
1	2^{1}	3	13	5		4^{2}	8				14	10			12	7^{3}		9	11			6							7
1	2	3	4^{2}	5		7^{1}	8			12	13	10			6	11^{3}		9		14									8
1	2■	3	4	5			8			14	13	10■			12	11^{2}		9^{1}	7^{3}			6							9
1	2	3	4^{3}	5		7^{2}	8	9		12					6	11	13	10^{1}	14										10
1		3	4	5	6	7^{3}	8	12		11^{1}					2	10^{2}		9	13	14									11
1		3	4^{1}	5		7^{2}	8	13		11		9^{3}			2	10		12	14			6							12
1	14	3		5		4	12	13				10^{3}			2^{2}	11		9	7^{1}	8		6							13
1		3		5		4	8^{1}	14	13			10^{3}			2	11^{2}		9	12	7		6							14
1	2	3	14	5		8	12			13		10			6	11^{2}		9^{3}	7^{1}	4									15
1	2	3	13	5			8		12	14		10			6	11^{2}		9^{3}	7	4^{1}									16
1	2	3	4^{2}	5		7		14				10^{3}			6^{1}	11		9	8	13			12						17
1	2^{3}	3		5			8^{1}	9		12		13				11		10^{2}	7	4		6	14						18
1	14	3		5		7	12	13				10				11		9^{2}	8	4^{1}		6	2^{3}						19
1	2	3		5		7	8	9								11^{1}			10	4	12	6							20
1	2	3		5		7	8^{1}	9		13						10^{2}			11	4		6		12					21
1	2	3		5		4	8^{1}	9^{2}		12						11	13	10	7^{3}			6		14					22
1	2	3■						9		11^{2}					5	10	13	8	7	4^{1}		6		12					23
1	3							9		11					2	10		8^{1}	7	12		6		4	5				24
1	2	3^{2}					8	9		12					5	11^{3}	13	10	7			6		4^{1}		14			25
1		3	14			7^{3}	8	12	13			9^{1}			2	11		10^{2}				6		4	5				26
1		3				7	8	13		12		10			2^{3}	11		9^{1}	14			6		4^{2}	5				27
1		3	4^{3}	6		7	8		9			10			2^{2}	12		14	11^{1}			13			5				28
1	12	3	4			7	8	9^{3}				14			2^{1}	10			11^{2}			6		13	5				29
1	2^{1}	3		5		7	8	13	14			10				11		9^{3}				12		4^{2}	6				30
1		3	4	5		13	8	9	10^{2}	14					2	11^{3}		7				6^{1}			12				31
1			13					12	14	11^{1}		10			2	9		8^{3}	7			6		4^{2}	5	3			32
1			4	5		7^{2}	8	9	10			13			2	12			11^{1}						6	3			33
1	2	14	12	5				9	10^{2}	11						13		8		7^{1}				4	6	3^{3}			34
1	6^{3}	3		5		13	8	9	7^{2}	12						11^{1}		10					2	4			14		35
1	2		4	5		7	14	9		11^{2}		13			6	12		10^{1}	8^{3}							3			36
				5		7		9		11					6		12	10^{1}		8			2	4		3		1	37
				5		7		14		11^{1}		13			6		9^{2}	10	8				12	4		3	2^{3}	1	38

FA Cup

Third Round	Portsmouth	(h)	4-0
Fourth Round	QPR	(a)	1-0
Fifth Round	Birmingham C	(h)	1-1
		(a)	2-0
Quarter-Final	Leicester C	(h)	5-2
Semi-Final *(at Wembley).*	Tottenham H		5-1
Final *(at Wembley).*	Liverpool		2-1

Carling Cup

Third Round	Fulham	(h)	0-0
Fourth Round	Everton	(a)	2-1
Quarter-Final	Liverpool	(h)	0-2

Champions League

Group E	Leverkusen	(h)	2-0
	Valencia	(a)	1-1
	Genk	(h)	5-0
		(a)	1-1
	Leverkusen	(a)	1-2
	Valencia	(h)	3-0
Knock-out Round	Napoli	(a)	1-3
		(h)	4-1
Quarter-Finals	Benfica	(a)	1-0
		(h)	2-1
Semi-Final	Barcelona	(h)	1-0
		(a)	2-2
Final *(at Munich).*	Bayern Munich		1-1

CHELTENHAM TOWN FL Championship 2

FOUNDATION

Although a scratch team representing Cheltenham played a match against Gloucester in 1884, the earliest recorded match for Cheltenham Town FC was a friendly against Dean Close School on 12 March 1892. The School won 4–3 and the match was played at Prestbury (half a mile from Whaddon Road). Cheltenham Town played Wednesday afternoon friendlies at a local cricket ground until entering the Mid Gloucester League. In those days the club played in deep red coloured shirts and were nicknamed 'the Rubies'. The club moved to Whaddon Lane for season 1901–02 and changed to red and white colours two years later.

The Abbey Business Stadium, Whaddon Road, Cheltenham, Gloucestershire GL52 5NA.

Telephone: (01242) 573 558.

Fax: (01242) 224 675.

Ticket Office: (01242) 573 558 (option 1).

Website: www.ctfc.com

Email: info@ctfc.com

Ground Capacity: 7,136.

Record Attendance: 10,389 v Blackpool, FA Cup 3rd rd, 13 January 1934 (at Cheltenham Athletic Ground); 8,326 v Reading, FA Cup 1st rd, 17 November 1956 (at Whaddon Road).

Pitch Measurements: 112yd × 72yd.

Chairman: Paul Baker.

Vice-chairman: Colin Farmer.

Manager: Mark Yates.

Assistant Manager: Neil Howarth.

Physio: Ian Weston.

Colours: All red with white trim.

Year Formed: 1892.

Turned Professional: 1932.

Club Nickname: 'The Robins'.

Grounds: Pre-1932, Agg-Gardner's Recreation Ground; Whaddon Lane; Carter's Lane; 1932, Whaddon Road.

First Football League Game: 7 August 1999, Division 3, v Rochdale (h) L 0–2 – Book; Griffin, Victory, Banks, Freeman, Brough (Howarth), Howells, Bloomer (Devaney), Grayson, Watkins (McAuley), Yates.

HONOURS

Football League: Best Season Division 3 2001–02 (4th).

FA Cup: Best season: 5th rd 2002.

Football League Cup: never past 2nd rd.

Football Conference: *Champions* 1998–99, *Runners-up* 1997–98.

Trophy: ***Winners*** 1997–98.

Southern League: ***Champions*** 1984–85; **Southern League Cup:** ***Winners*** 1957–58, ***runners-up*** 1968–69, 1984–85; **Southern League Merit Cup:** ***Winners*** 1984–85; **Southern League Championship Shield:** ***Winners*** 1985.

Gloucestershire Senior Cup: ***Winners*** 1998–99; **Gloucestershire Northern Senior Professional Cup:** ***Winners*** 30 times; **Midland Floodlit Cup:** ***Winners*** **1985–86, 1986–87, 1987–88; Mid Gloucester League:** ***Champions*** 1896–97; **Gloucester and District League:** ***Champions*** 1902–03, 1905–06; **Cheltenham League:** ***Champions*** 1910–11, 1913–14; **North Gloucestershire League:** ***Champions*** 1913–14; **Gloucestershire Northern Senior League:** ***Champions*** 1928–29, **1932–33; Gloucestershire Northern Senior Amateur Cup:** ***Winners*** 1929–30, 1930–31, 1932–33, 1933–34, 1934–35; **Leamington Hospital Cup:** ***Winners*** 1934–35.

sky SPORTS FACT FILE

Jack Bowles had his goalkeeping career launched with his local club Cheltenham Town in the pre-war Southern League. Short spells with Newport County and Accrington Stanley followed then a 14-year, 277 League appearances stint spanning the war years with Stockport County.

Record League Victory: 5–0 v Manfield T, FL 2, 6 May 2006 – Higgs; Gallinagh, Bell, McCann (1) (Connolly), Caines, Duff, Wilson, Bird (1p), Gillespie (1) (Spencer), Guinan (Odejayi (1)), Vincent (1).

Record Cup Victory: 12–0 v Chippenham R, FA Cup 3rd qual. rd, 2 November 1935 – Bowles; Whitehouse, Williams; Lang, Devonport (1), Partridge (2); Perkins, Hackett, Jones (4), Black (4), Griffiths (1).

Record Defeat: 1–8 v Crewe Alex, FL 2, 2 April 2011. *N.B.* 1–10 v Merthyr T, Southern League, 8 March 1952.

Most League Points (2 for a win): 60, Southern League Division 1, 1963–64.

Most League Points (3 for a win): 78, Division 3, 2001–02.

Most League Goals: 66, Division 3, 2001–02; 66, FL 2, 2011–12.

Highest League Scorer in Season: Julian Alsop, 20, Division 3, 2001–02.

Most League Goals in Total Aggregate: Julian Alsop, 39, 2000–03; 2009–10.

Most League Goals in One Match: 3, Martin Devaney v Plymouth Arg, Division 3, 23 September 2000; 3, Neil Grayson v Cardiff C, Division 3, 1 April 2001; 3, Damien Spencer v Hull C, Division 3, 23 August 2003; 3, Damien Spencer v Milton Keynes D, FL 1, 31 January 2009; 3, Michael Pook v Burton Alb, FL 2, 13 March 2010.

Most Capped Player: Grant McCann, 7 (39), Northern Ireland.

Most League Appearances: David Bird, 288, 2001–11.

Youngest League Player: Kyle Haynes, 17 years, 2 months, 26 days v Oldham Ath, FL 1, 24 March 2009.

Record Transfer Fee Received: £400,000 from Colchester U for Steve Gillespie, July 2008.

Record Transfer Fee Paid: £50,000 to West Ham U for Grant McCann, January 2003; £50,000 to Stoke C for Brian Wilson, March 2004.

Football League Record: 1999 Promoted to Division 3; 2002 Division 2; 2003–04 Division 3; 2004–06 FL 2; 2006–09 FL 1; 2009– FL 2.

MANAGERS

George Blackburn 1932–34
George Carr 1934–37
Jimmy Brain 1937–48
Cyril Dean 1948–50
George Summerbee 1950–52
William Raeside 1952–53
Arch Anderson 1953–58
Ron Lewin 1958–60
Peter Donnelly 1960–61
Tommy Cavanagh 1961
Arch Anderson 1961–65
Harold Fletcher 1965–66
Bob Etheridge 1966–73
Willie Penman 1973–74
Dennis Allen 1974–79
Terry Paine 1979
Alan Grundy 1979–82
Alan Wood 1982–83
John Murphy 1983–88
Jim Barron 1988–90
John Murphy 1990
Dave Lewis 1990–91
Ally Robertson 1991–92
Lindsay Parsons 1992–95
Chris Robinson 1995–97
Steve Cotterill 1997–2002
Graham Allner 2002–03
Bobby Gould 2003
John Ward 2003–07
Keith Downing 2007–08
Martin Allen 2008–09
Mark Yates December 2009–

LATEST SEQUENCES

Longest Sequence of League Wins: 5, 29.10.2011 – 10.12.2011.
Longest Sequence of League Defeats: 7, 27.1.2009 – 28.2.2009
Longest Sequence of League Draws: 5, 5.4.2003 – 21.4.2003.
Longest Sequence of Unbeaten League Matches: 16, 1.12.2001 – 12.3.2002.
Longest Sequence Without a League Win: 14, 20.12.2008 – 7.3.2009
Successive Scoring Runs: 17 from 16.2.2008.
Successive Non-scoring Runs: 5 from 10.3.2012 – 30.3.2012.

TEN YEAR LEAGUE RECORD

		P	*W*	*D*	*L*	*F*	*A*	*Pts*	*Pos*
2002-03	Div 2	46	10	18	18	53	68	48	21
2003-04	Div 3	46	14	14	18	57	71	56	14
2004-05	FL 2	46	16	12	18	51	54	60	14
2005-06	FL 2	46	19	15	12	65	53	72	5
2006-07	FL 1	46	15	9	22	49	61	54	17
2007-08	FL 1	46	13	12	21	42	64	51	19
2008-09	FL 1	46	9	12	25	51	91	39	23
2009-10	FL 2	46	10	18	18	54	71	48	22
2010-11	FL 2	46	13	13	20	56	77	52	17
2011-12	FL 2	46	23	8	15	66	50	77	6

DID YOU KNOW ?

Inside-forward Jim Black, the scorer of four goals in the record Cup victory for Cheltenham Town, was a Scot who played extensively in the Scottish League before coming south with Charlton Athletic then Burton Town and Aldershot. He joined Cheltenham in the 1935–36 season.

CHELTENHAM TOWN 2011–12 LEAGUE RECORD

Match No.	*Date*	*Venue*	*Opponents*	*Result*	*H/T Score*	*Lg Pos.*	*Goalscorers*	*Atten-dance*
1	Aug 6	A	Gillingham	L 0-1	0-1	—		5360
2	13	H	Swindon T	W 1-0	0-0	13	Elliott [48]	4402
3	16	H	Morecambe	L 1-2	0-0	—	Goulding [84]	2035
4	20	A	Northampton T	W 3-2	1-1	12	Duffy 2 (1 pen) [12 (p), 68], Low [80]	4114
5	27	H	Crawley T	W 3-1	3-0	6	Mohammed [22], Pack [31], Goulding [39]	2609
6	Sept 3	A	Aldershot T	L 0-1	0-0	11		2755
7	10	H	Macclesfield T	W 2-0	1-0	5	Goulding (pen) [34], Spencer [88]	2268
8	13	A	Torquay U	D 2-2	2-1	—	Low [4], Mohammed [45]	2018
9	17	A	AFC Wimbledon	L 1-4	0-2	13	Duffy [89]	3860
10	24	H	Hereford U	D 0-0	0-0	14		3011
11	Oct 1	A	Bristol R	W 3-1	2-0	11	Mohammed [36], Summerfield [43], Spencer [48]	6108
12	8	H	Dagenham & R	W 2-1	1-1	7	Bennett [40], Spencer [49]	2814
13	14	A	Burton Alb	W 2-0	0-0	—	Low [46], Spencer [64]	2701
14	21	A	Accrington S	W 1-0	1-0	—	Goulding [44]	1641
15	25	H	Crewe Alex	L 0-1	0-0	—		3089
16	29	H	Plymouth Arg	W 2-1	0-1	5	Duffy 2 (1 pen) [83 (p), 90]	4026
17	Nov 5	A	Bradford C	W 1-0	1-0	3	Mohammed [8]	9645
18	19	H	Port Vale	W 2-0	0-0	3	Duffy (pen) [55], Summerfield [69]	3165
19	26	A	Oxford U	W 3-1	1-0	3	Jombati [8], Spencer [56], Mohammed [86]	8037
20	Dec 10	H	Southend U	W 3-0	1-0	3	Spencer [20], Penn [52], Pack [80]	4304
21	16	A	Barnet	D 2-2	2-1	—	Mohammed [32], Duffy (pen) [44]	1775
22	26	H	Shrewsbury T	D 0-0	0-0	2		5004
23	30	H	Rotherham U	W 1-0	1-0	—	Pack [11]	3582
24	Jan 2	A	Port Vale	W 2-1	0-0	2	Bennett [63], Smikle [74]	4696
25	14	H	Aldershot T	W 2-0	1-0	2	Summerfield [10], Mohammed [90]	3147
26	21	H	Bristol R	L 0-2	0-0	3		5288
27	28	A	Macclesfield T	W 3-1	1-1	1	Jombati [37], Goulding [67], Garbutt [90]	1659
28	Feb 7	A	Crawley T	L 2-4	1-3	—	Garbutt [5], Duffy [75]	3871
29	11	A	Hereford U	D 1-1	0-1	—	Mohammed [49]	2607
30	14	H	Torquay U	L 0-1	0-1	—		3010
31	18	A	Dagenham & R	W 5-0	3-0	2	Summerfield [20], Elliott [22], Mohammed [42], Spencer [62], Spillane (og) [71]	1516
32	21	H	AFC Wimbledon	D 0-0	0-0	—		2603
33	25	H	Burton Alb	W 2-0	1-0	2	McGlashan 2 [5, 73]	2945
34	Mar 3	H	Northampton T	D 2-2	0-2	2	Duffy 2 (1 pen) [76 (p), 90]	3503
35	6	A	Morecambe	L 1-3	1-1	—	Duffy [13]	1207
36	10	A	Swindon T	L 0-1	0-1	4		10,659
37	17	H	Gillingham	L 0-3	0-1	5		3137
38	20	A	Shrewsbury T	L 0-2	0-1	—		5705
39	24	H	Oxford U	D 0-0	0-0	6		4365
40	30	A	Southend U	L 0-4	0-2	—		6525
41	Apr 6	H	Barnet	W 2-0	0-0	6	Mohammed [75], Spencer [88]	3319
42	9	A	Rotherham U	L 0-1	0-0	6		3066
43	14	H	Accrington S	W 4-1	1-0	6	Lowe [12], Burgess [56], Pack [62], Mohammed [90]	3217
44	21	A	Crewe Alex	L 0-1	0-1	6		5495
45	28	H	Bradford C	W 3-1	0-1	6	Spencer 2 [46, 63], Burgess [71]	3930
46	May 5	A	Plymouth Arg	W 2-1	1-0	6	MacLean [23], Pack [55]	8342

Final League Position: 6

GOALSCORERS

League (66): Duffy 11 (5 pens), Mohammed 11, Spencer 10, Goulding 5 (1 pen), Pack 5, Summerfield 4, Low 3, Bennett 2, Burgess 2, Elliott 2, Garbutt 2, Jombati 2, McGlashan 2, Lowe 1, MacLean 1, Penn 1, Smikle 1, own goal 1.
Carling Cup (1): Summerfield 1.
FA Cup (5): Duffy 2 (1 pen), Pack 1, Penn 1, Summerfield 1.
J Paint Trophy (5): Duffy 2, Goulding 1, Smikle 1, Spencer 1.
Play-Offs (4): McGlashan 2, Burgess 1, Pack 1.

Brown S 22	Lowe K 24 + 6	Andrew D 10	Pack M 43	Bennett A 44	Elliott S 38	Mohammed K 39 + 6	Low J 26 + 13	Spencer J 27 + 14	Goulding J 16 + 19	Summerfield L 37 + 4	Penn R 39 + 4	Duffy D 25 + 16	Smikle B 3 + 32	Graham B 1 + 6	Jombati S 33 + 3	Hooman H 1 + 1	Butland J 24	Garbutt L 34	Jackson M — + 1	Reid B — + 1	McGlashan J 10 + 6	Burgess B 6 + 1	MacLean S 3	Lewis T 1	*Match No.*
1	2	3	4	5	6	7	8^2	9^1	10	11^3	12	13	14												1
1	2	3	4	5	6	7^2	8	9■	12		11	10^1	13												2
1	2	3	4	5	6	7^2	8^1		10		11	9	13	12											3
1	2	3^3	4	5	6	7^2	12		10	11^1	8	9	13		14										4
1	2	3	4	5	6	7^3	8		10^1	13	11	9^2	12			14									5
1	2	3	4	5	6	7^1	8	12	10	14	11^2	9^3	13												6
	2	3		5	6	7^2	8	12	10^3	11	4	9^1	13		14		1								7
	2	3	4	5	6	7^2	8	9	10^1	12	11		13				1								8
	2	3	4	5	6	7^2	8^3	9^1	10		11	12	13		14		1								9
	2	3	4	5	6	7	8	9^2	12		11	10^1	13				1								10
	2		4	5	6	11^3	7	9^2	13	10	8^1	14	12		3		1								11
1			4	5	6	10^3	7	9^2	12	11	8^1	13	14		2			3							12
			4	5	6	10^1	7	9^3	13	11	8^2	14	12		2		1	3							13
	14		4	5	6	10^3	8	9^1	12	11	7^2		13		2		1	3							14
1			4	5	6	10^2	8^3	9	12	11	7^1	13	14		2			3							15
			4	5	6	11^1	7^2		10	8^3	13	9	14	12	2		1	3							16
			4	5	6	11^2	12	10^3	14	8	7	9^1	13		2		1	3							17
			4	5	6	10^2	12	7^3	14	8	11	9^1	13		2		1	3							18
			4	5	6	11^3	13	10		8	7^1	9^2	12		2		1	3	14						19
			4	5	6	10^3	7	9^2	13	11	8^1		12		2		1	3		14					20
1			4	5	6	11^2	7^1	10^3	14	8		9	12	13	2			3							21
1			4	5	6	11^2	12	10		8	7	9^1		13	2			3							22
1			4	5	6	13	7^2	9^3		11	8	12	14	10^1	2			3							23
1	14		4	5	6	10	7^1		12	11	8^2	9^3	13		2			3							24
1	5		4	6		10	14	7^1	12	11	8^2	9^3	13		2			3							25
1			4	5		10^3	6	7	13	11	8^2	9^1	14		2			3			12				26
1	6		4	5		9^3		13	10^2	8	12	14	11		2			3			7^1				27
1	6		4	5		9		13	10^3	11	8^2	14	12		2			3			7^1				28
1	5		4	6		11	14	10^3	12	8		9^1	13		2			3			7^2				29
1	6		4	5		10		7^2	13	11	8^3	9^1	14		2			3			12				30
1	14		4^2	5	6^3	9	7	12	10^1	11	8		13		2			3							31
	14		4	5	6	9	7^1	13	10^2	11	8^3	12			2		1	3							32
			4	5	6	13	8^2	9	10^1		11	12	14		2		1	3			7^3				33
			4	5	6	14	8^2	9	10^3	11^1	13	12			2		1	3			7				34
	5		4	6		10^3	13	14	12	11^2	8	9^1			2		1	3			7				35
	2		4	5	6	10^1		13	14	11	8^2	9		12	3		1				7^3				36
			4^1	5	6	10^2	13	12	14	11	8	9			2		1	3^3			7				37
	2		4^1	5	6	10^3	13	9		11	8	12			7		1	3^2			14				38
			4	5	6	13	14	12		7	8^3	9^2			2		1	3				10	11^1		39
	12		4	5	6	7	13	14		11	8^2	9^1			2■		1	3				10^3			40
	2			5	6	14	7^3	13		11	4	9^2					1	3			12	10	8^1		41
	2			4	6	10	13	5^3		11	8	14	12				1	3			7^2	9^1			42
	2		4	5	6	7		12		11	8^2	9^3	14				1	3			13	10^1			43
1	5		4		6	10^3		9		7	8^1	14	11^2		2			3			13	12			44
1	13		4	5	6	12	7^2	9^3		11	8^1	14			2			3				10			45
1	5		4					13	10	14			11	12	2	6		3^1			7		9^2	8^3	46

FA Cup

First Round	Tranmere R	(a)	1-0
Second Round	Luton T	(a)	4-2
Third Round	Tottenham H	(a)	0-3

Carling Cup

First Round	Milton Keynes D	(h)	1-4

J Paint Trophy

First Round	Torquay U	(h)	2-1
Second Round	Wycombe W	(a)	3-1
Southern Quarter-Final	Barnet	(h)	0-2

Play-Offs

Semi-Final	Torquay U	(h)	2-0
		(a)	2-1
Final *(at Wembley).*	Crewe Alex		0-2

CHESTERFIELD FL Championship 2

FOUNDATION

Chesterfield are fourth only to Stoke, Notts County and Nottingham Forest in age for they can trace their existence as far back as 1866, although it is fair to say that they were somewhat casual in the first few years of their history, playing only a few friendlies a year. However, their rules of 1871 are still in existence, showing an annual membership of 2s (10p), but it was not until 1891 that they won a trophy (the Barnes Cup) and followed this a year later by winning the Sheffield Cup, Barnes Cup and the Derbyshire Junior Cup.

b2net Stadium, 1866 Sheffield Road, Whittington Moor, Chesterfield S41 8NZ.

Telephone: (01246) 209 765.

Fax: (01246) 556 799.

Ticket Office: (01246) 488 232.

Website: www.chesterfield-fc.co.uk

Email: reception@chesterfield-fc.co.uk

Ground Capacity: 8,502.

Record Attendance: 30,968 v Newcastle U, Division 2, 7 April 1939 (at Saltergate).

Pitch Measurements: 111yd × 71yd.

Chairman: Barrie Hubbard.

Vice-chairman: David C. Jones.

Manager: John Sheridan.

Assistant Manager: Tommy Wright.

Physio: Jamie Hewitt.

Colours: Blue shirts with white trim, white shorts, white stockings.

Year Formed: 1866.

Turned Professional: 1891.

Previous Name: 1867, Chesterfield Town; 1919, Chesterfield.

Club Nicknames: 'Blues' or 'Spireites'.

Grounds: 1867, Drill Field; 1871, Recreation Ground, Saltergate; 2010, b2net Stadium.

First Football League Game: 2 September 1899, Division 2, v Sheffield W (a) L 1–5 – Hancock; Pilgrim, Fletcher; Ballantyne, Bell, Downie; Morley, Thacker, Gooing, Munday (1), Geary.

Record League Victory: 10–0 v Glossop NE, Division 2, 17 January 1903 – Clutterbuck; Thorpe, Lerper; Haig, Banner, Thacker; Tomlinson (2), Newton (1), Milward (3), Munday (2), Steel (2).

Record Cup Victory: 5–0 v Wath Ath (a), FA Cup 1st rd, 28 November 1925 – Birch; Saxby, Dennis; Wass, Abbott, Thompson; Fisher (1), Roseboom (1), Cookson (2), Whitfield (1), Hopkinson.

HONOURS

Football League – Division 2: Best season: 4th, 1946–47; **Division 3 (N):** ***Champions*** 1930–31, 1935–36; ***Runners-up*** 1933–34; **FL 2:** ***Champions*** 2010–11; **Division 4:** ***Champions*** 1969–70, 1984–85.

FA Cup: Semi-final 1997.

Football League Cup: Best season: 4th rd, 1965, 2007.

Johnstone's Paint Trophy: ***Winners*** 1981, 2012.

Anglo-Scottish Cup: ***Winners*** 1981.

sky SPORTS FACT FILE

In their 1969–70 Division Four championship-winning season, Chesterfield used only 19 players in League games including a sprinkling of substitute appearances from the bench. Surprisingly only one player, right-back Albert Holmes, was an ever-present during the season.

Record Defeat: 0–10 v Gillingham, Division 3, 5 September 1987.

Most League Points (2 for a win): 64, Division 4, 1969–70.

Most League Points (3 for a win): 91, Division 4, 1984–85.

Most League Goals: 102, Division 3 (N), 1930–31.

Highest League Scorer in Season: Jimmy Cookson, 44, Division 3 (N), 1925–26.

Most League Goals in Total Aggregate: Ernie Moss, 161, 1969–76, 1979–81 and 1984–86.

Most League Goals in One Match: 4, Jimmy Cookson v Accrington S, Division 3 (N), 16 January 1926; 4, Jimmy Cookson v Ashington, Division 3 (N), 1 May 1926; 4, Jimmy Cookson v Wigan Borough, Division 3 (N), 4 September 1926; 4, Tommy Lyon v Southampton, Division 2, 3 December 1938.

Most Capped Player: Walter McMillen, 4 (7), Northern Ireland; Mark Williams, 4 (30), Northern Ireland.

Most League Appearances: Dave Blakey, 613, 1948–67.

Youngest League Player: Dennis Thompson, 16 years 160 days v Notts Co, 26 December 1950.

Record Transfer Fee Received: £750,000 from Southampton for Kevin Davies, May 1997.

Record Transfer Fee Paid: £250,000 to Watford for Jason Lee, August 1998.

Football League Record: 1899 Elected to Division 2; 1909 failed re-election; 1921–31 Division 3 (N); 1931–33 Division 2; 1933–36 Division 3 (N); 1936–51 Division 2; 1951–58 Division 3 (N); 1958–61 Division 3; 1961–70 Division 4; 1970–83 Division 3; 1983–85 Division 4; 1985–89 Division 3; 1989–92 Division 4; 1992–95 Division 3; 1995–2000 Division 2; 2000–01 Division 3; 2001–04 Division 2; 2004–07 FL 1; 2007–11 FL 2; 2011–12 FL 1; 2012– FL 2.

MANAGERS

E. Russell Timmeus 1891–95 (*Secretary-Manager*)
Gilbert Gillies 1895–1901
E. F. Hind 1901–02
Jack Hoskin 1902–06
W. Furness 1906–07
George Swift 1907–10
G. H. Jones 1911–13
R. L. Weston 1913–17
T. Callaghan 1919
J. J. Caffrey 1920–22
Harry Hadley 1922
Harry Parkes 1922–27
Alec Campbell 1927
Ted Davison 1927–32
Bill Harvey 1932–38
Norman Bullock 1938–45
Bob Brocklebank 1945–48
Bobby Marshall 1948–52
Ted Davison 1952–58
Duggie Livingstone 1958–62
Tony McShane 1962–67
Jimmy McGuigan 1967–73
Joe Shaw 1973–76
Arthur Cox 1976–80
Frank Barlow 1980–83
John Duncan 1983–87
Kevin Randall 1987–88
Paul Hart 1988–91
Chris McMenemy 1991–93
John Duncan 1993–2000
Nicky Law 2000–01
Dave Rushbury 2002–03
Roy McFarland 2003–07
Lee Richardson 2007–09
John Sheridan June 2009–

LATEST SEQUENCES

Longest Sequence of League Wins: 10, 6.9.1933 – 4.11.1933.

Longest Sequence of League Defeats: 9, 22.10.1960 – 27.12.1960.

Longest Sequence of League Draws: 8, 26.11.2005 – 2.1.2006.

Longest Sequence of Unbeaten League Matches: 21, 26.12.1994 – 29.4.1995.

Longest Sequence Without a League Win: 18, 11.9.1999 – 3.1.2000.

Successive Scoring Runs: 46 from 25.12.1929.

Successive Non-scoring Runs: 7 from 23.9.1977.

TEN YEAR LEAGUE RECORD

		P	*W*	*D*	*L*	*F*	*A*	*Pts*	*Pos*
2002-03	Div 2	46	14	8	24	43	73	50	20
2003-04	Div 2	46	12	15	19	49	71	51	20
2004-05	FL 1	46	14	15	17	55	62	57	17
2005-06	FL 1	46	14	14	18	63	73	56	16
2006-07	FL 1	46	12	11	23	45	53	47	21
2007-08	FL 2	46	19	12	15	76	56	69	8
2008-09	FL 2	46	16	15	15	62	57	63	10
2009-10	FL 2	46	21	7	18	61	62	70	8
2010-11	FL 2	46	24	14	8	85	51	86	1
2011-12	FL 1	46	10	12	24	56	81	42	22

DID YOU KNOW ?

Four Chesterfield players made their only first team outings (except wartime matches) in the 1945–46 FA Cup: inside-left George Dooley, left-half Les Hobson, right-back Allen Pringle and right-winger Robert Sinclair. Pringle and Sinclair also played in the aborted 1939–40 campaign.

CHESTERFIELD 2011–12 LEAGUE RECORD

Match No.	Date	Venue	Opponents	Result		H/T Score	Lg Pos.	Goalscorers	Attendance
1	Aug 6	A	Tranmere R	L	0-1	0-0	—		5755
2	13	H	Stevenage	D	1-1	0-1	18	Lester [90]	5836
3	16	H	Preston NE	L	0-2	0-1	—		6706
4	20	A	Milton Keynes D	L	2-6	1-1	23	Boden 2 [37, 67]	7011
5	27	A	Exeter C	L	1-2	1-1	23	Whitaker (pen) [33]	4113
6	Sept 3	H	Leyton Orient	D	0-0	0-0	23		6197
7	10	A	Bournemouth	W	3-0	1-0	20	Mendy [33], Westcarr [59], Clarke [71]	4989
8	13	H	Bury	W	1-0	0-0	—	Clarke [66]	5727
9	17	H	Carlisle U	W	4-1	2-1	14	Clarke 3 [3, 26, 51], Westcarr [65]	6445
10	24	A	Charlton Ath	L	1-3	0-2	15	Whitaker (pen) [72]	22,151
11	Oct 1	H	Colchester U	L	0-1	0-1	16		6295
12	8	A	Sheffield W	L	1-3	0-1	19	Clarke [79]	24,514
13	15	H	Notts Co	L	1-3	0-2	22	Westcarr [52]	8342
14	22	H	Hartlepool U	L	2-3	1-2	22	Clarke [10], Holden [52]	5937
15	25	A	Rochdale	D	1-1	1-0	—	Westcarr [36]	2494
16	29	A	Brentford	L	1-2	1-1	22	Clarke [27]	4566
17	Nov 5	H	Yeovil T	D	2-2	1-1	22	Bowery 2 [4, 55]	5882
18	19	A	Oldham Ath	L	2-5	1-4	24	Westcarr [30], Clarke [87]	3699
19	26	H	Sheffield U	L	0-1	0-0	24		9259
20	Dec 10	A	Wycombe W	L	2-3	1-1	24	Morgan 2 [4, 54]	4320
21	17	H	Walsall	D	1-1	0-1	24	Lester [90]	6236
22	26	A	Huddersfield T	L	0-1	0-1	24		15,380
23	31	A	Scunthorpe U	D	2-2	0-1	24	Boden [48], Westcarr [70]	4456
24	Jan 2	H	Oldham Ath	D	1-1	1-1	24	Bowery [34]	6723
25	7	H	Exeter C	L	0-2	0-0	—		5856
26	14	A	Leyton Orient	D	1-1	0-1	24	Juan [69]	4174
27	21	A	Colchester U	W	2-1	2-1	24	Lester [6], Thompson [44]	3312
28	27	H	Bournemouth	W	1-0	0-0	—	Ridehalgh [55]	6958
29	Feb 4	A	Carlisle U	L	1-2	1-0	—	Talbot [16]	4313
30	14	A	Bury	D	1-1	1-0	—	Ajose [41]	2266
31	18	H	Sheffield W	W	1-0	0-0	22	Morgan (pen) [78]	9279
32	25	A	Notts Co	L	0-1	0-0	24		8257
33	28	H	Charlton Ath	L	0-4	0-1	—		6405
34	Mar 3	H	Tranmere R	W	1-0	0-0	22	Bowery [75]	5861
35	6	A	Preston NE	D	0-0	0-0	—		9264
36	10	A	Stevenage	D	2-2	2-0	23	Trotman [12], Bowery [22]	3534
37	17	H	Milton Keynes D	D	1-1	1-0	24	Talbot [4]	6444
38	20	H	Huddersfield T	L	0-2	0-2	—		6916
39	28	A	Sheffield U	L	1-4	1-1	—	Moussa [44]	20,159
40	31	H	Scunthorpe U	L	1-4	1-1	24	Westcarr [21]	6152
41	Apr 7	A	Walsall	L	2-3	1-2	24	Moussa [20], Randall [54]	4051
42	9	H	Wycombe W	W	4-0	1-0	23	Westcarr [29], Moussa [47], Mendy [52], Bowery [79]	5087
43	14	A	Hartlepool U	W	2-1	0-1	22	Whitaker [59], Bowery [69]	4004
44	21	H	Rochdale	W	2-1	0-0	22	Boden [81], Whitaker [86]	5954
45	28	A	Yeovil T	L	2-3	1-1	22	Bowery [8], Whitaker [69]	4563
46	May 5	H	Brentford	L	2-3	0-1	22	Moussa [69], Allott [90]	5699

Final League Position: 22

GOALSCORERS

League (56): Clarke 9, Bowery 8, Westcarr 8, Whitaker 5 (2 pens), Boden 4, Moussa 4, Lester 3, Morgan 3 (1 pen), Mendy 2, Talbot 2, Ajose 1, Allott 1, Holden 1, Juan 1, Randall 1, Ridehalgh 1, Thompson 1, Trotman 1.
Carling Cup (2): Whitaker 2 (1 pen).
FA Cup (1): Bowery 1.
J Paint Trophy (13): Bowery 3, Westcarr 3, Boden 1, Lester 1, Mendy 1, Morgan 1, Randall 1, Whitaker 1 (pen), own goal 1.

Lee T 35	Talbot D 43	Smith N 22 + 3	Randall M 10 + 6	Mattis D 6 + 1	Ford S 18	Morgan D 10 + 7	Allott M 36	Lester J 16 + 5	Bowery J 23 + 17	Whitaker D 23 + 7	Niven D 4 + 3	Holden D 9 + 5	Boden S 7 + 19	Downes A 8 + 1	Lowry J 2 + 4	Johnson L 11	Grounds J 13	Westcarr C 32 + 6	Mendy A 31 + 3	Clarke L 14	Fleming G 9 + 1	Clay C — + 5	Soderberg O 2	Trotman N 23	Obadeyi T 3 + 2	Griffiths S 3	Robertson G 11 + 1	Ridehalgh L 20	Hurst J 10	Davis D 9	Juan J 6 + 1	Thompson J 20	Ajose N 5 + 7	Darikwah T 2	Moussa F 10	*Match No.*
1	2	3	4^{2}	5	6^{3}	7^{1}	8	9	10	11	12	13	14																							1
1	10	3	13	5		7	8^{2}	9	12	11	6^{1}	2	14	4^{3}																						2
1	7	3		5		10^{1}	8	9^{3}	12	11	4^{2}	2	13	6	14																					3
1	2	3		5^{1}		13	8^{3}	9^{2}	10	11	4	12	7	6	14																					4
1	7	3			6^{2}	14	8^{3}	12	13	11		2	10^{1}			4	5	9																		5
1	2	3			6	13	8	9^{3}	14	11			12			4^{2}	5	10^{1}	7																	6
1	2	3	13		6^{1}		8		14	11		12				4^{2}	5	9	7	10^{3}																7
1^{G}	2	3	13		6^{1}		8					12	11			4^{2}	5	9	7	10	15															8
	2	3			6^{2}		8		14	11		13	12			4	5	9^{1}	7	10^{3}	1															9
	2	3			6	12	8			11			13			4^{1}	5	9^{2}	7	10	1															10
	2	3^{3}	12				8		14	11^{2}		5	13			4^{1}	6	9	7	10	1															11
	2		4			11	8^{2}		12	13		5		6			3	9^{1}	7	10	1															12
	2		4^{3}			11^{1}	8		13	12		5		6			3	9^{2}	7	10	1	14														13
	2	3^{1}	4^{2}			14	8^{3}			11		5		13			6	9	7	10	1	12														14
	8	2								11^{1}		5		6		4	3	9	7	10	1	12														15
	2	8							13	11^{1}		5		6		4^{2}	3	9	7	10	1	12														16
		3		5	2^{1}		8		11	12						4		9	7	10			1	6												17
	2	3		4^{1}			8		12								6	9	7	10			1	5	11											18
	2				6	14	8	13	10							4^{1}		12	7	9^{2}	1			5	11^{3}	3										19
1	2				6	10^{1}	8	12	13	4				5				11^{3}	7	9^{2}					14	3										20
1	2				6	10^{2}	8	9	12	4								11^{1}	7					5	13	3										21
1	2	6				10	8		11	4								12	7					5	9^{1}		3									22
1	2^{1}	3		14		11^{3}	8		10^{2}	4	13		12					9	7					5			6									23
1	2	11			6		8		10	4			12					9	7^{1}					5			3									24
1	2	14					8^{3}	9	10	4	12		13					11^{1}	7^{2}					5			6	3								25
1	7							12	10^{1}	11			9											5			6	3	2	4	8					26
1	7						8	9	12				10^{1}											5			3	11	2	4		6				27
1	7						8	9	12				10^{1}											5			3	11	6	4		2				28
1	7						8	9^{2}	13				10^{1}		14									5			3	11^{3}	6	4		2	12			29
1	7							9					12		4			13	11					5			6	3^{2}		8		2	10^{1}			30
1	7				2	12	8	9^{2}										13						5			3^{1}	11		4		6	10			31
1						10^{2}		9	12						11			7						5				3		4	8^{1}	6	13	2		32
1					6		8	9^{2}	10	13								7^{1}	12					5				3		4		2	11			33
1	2						8	9^{2}	10	11								13	12					5				3		4		6	7^{1}			34
1	2						8		10	11			12					7	4					5				3				6	9^{1}			35
1	7						8	12	10		4							9^{1}	11					5				3	2			6				36
1	7						8	9^{2}	10	11^{3}								13	12					5				3	2			6	14		4^{1}	37
1	7	3					8^{1}		10									9	11					5					2			6	12		4	38
1	7	3	14				8^{1}		10^{3}				13					9^{2}	11					5					2			6	12		4	39
1	7	14	13				8^{2}		10									9	11^{1}					5^{3}				3	2			4	12		6	40
1	7	11^{1}	8		6^{2}				10				14					9^{3}										3	2		13	5	12		4	41
1	2	13	8		6^{2}				10				12					9^{1}	11									3			7	5			4	42
1	2		7		6				10	13			12					9^{1}	11									3			8^{2}	5			4	43
1	2		7^{3}		6^{1}				10	13			14					9^{2}	11								12	3			8	5			4	44
1	2		7						10	12			13					9	11^{2}								6	3			8^{1}	5			4	45
1	7		6^{2}				8		10				13		12			9	11^{1}			14						3				5^{3}		2	4	46

FA Cup
First Round Torquay U (h) 1-3

Carling Cup
First Round Rochdale (a) 2-3

J Paint Trophy
Second Round Notts Co (a) 3-1

Northern Quarter-Final
Tranmere R (h) 4-3
Northern Semi-Final
Preston NE (a) 1-1
Northern Final Oldham Ath (h) 2-1
(a) 1-0
Final Swindon T 2-0
(at Wembley).

COLCHESTER UNITED FL Championship 1

FOUNDATION

Colchester United was formed in 1937 when a number of enthusiasts of the much older Colchester Town club decided to establish a professional concern as a limited liability company. The new club continued at Layer Road which had been the amateur club's home since 1909.

Weston Homes Community Stadium, United Way, Colchester, Essex CO4 5UP.

Telephone: (01206) 755 100.

Fax: (01206) 755 112.

Ticket Office: (0845) 437 9089.

Website: www.cu-fc.com

Email: caroline@colchesterunited.net

Ground Capacity: 10,000.

Record Attendance: 19,072 v Reading, FA Cup 1st rd, 27 November 1948 (at Layer Road); 10,064 v Norwich C, FL 1, 16 January 2010 (at Community Stadium).

Pitch Measurements: 106m × 68m.

Executive Chairman: Robbie Cowling.

Vice-chairman: Richard Cowling.

Manager: John Ward.

Assistant Manager: Joe Dunne.

Physio: Tony Flynn.

Colours: Royal blue and white striped shirts with white sleeves, royal blue shorts, white stockings.

Year Formed: 1937.

Turned Professional: 1937.

Club Nickname: 'The U's'.

Grounds: 1937, Layer Road; 2008, Weston Homes Community Stadium.

First Football League Game: 19 August 1950, Division 3 (S), v Gillingham (a) D 0–0 – Wright; Kettle, Allen; Bearryman, Stewart, Elder; Jones, Curry, Turner, McKim, Church.

Record League Victory: 9–1 v Bradford C, Division 4, 30 December 1961 – Ames; Millar, Fowler; Harris, Abrey, Ron Hunt; Foster, Bobby Hunt (4), King (4), Hill (1), Wright.

Record Cup Victory: 9-1 v Leamington, FA Cup 1st rd, 5 November 2005 – Davison; Stockley (Garcia), Duguid, Brown (1), Chilvers, Watson (1), Halford (1), Izzet (Danns) (2), Iwelumo (1) (Williams), Cureton (2), Yeates (1).

HONOURS

Football League – FL 1: *Runners-up* 2005–06;
Division 4: *Runners-up* 1961–62.

FA Cup: Best season: 6th rd, 1971.

Football League Cup: Best season: 5th rd, 1975.

Auto Windscreens Shield: *Runners-up* 1997.

GM Vauxhall Conference: *Winners* 1991–92.

FA Trophy: *Winners* 1992.

sky SPORTS FACT FILE

When Colchester United were elected to the Football League in 1950 they had many experienced players, several with outstanding war records: centre-forward Arthur Turner in the RAF, left-back John Moore in the Navy, while inside-forward Fred Cutting had won the Military Medal.

Record Defeat: 0–8 v Leyton Orient, Division 4, 15 October 1988.

Most League Points (2 for a win): 60, Division 4, 1973–74.

Most League Points (3 for a win): 81, Division 4, 1982–83.

Most League Goals: 104, Division 4, 1961–62.

Highest League Scorer in Season: Bobby Hunt, 38, Division 4, 1961–62.

Most League Goals in Total Aggregate: Martyn King, 130, 1956–64.

Most League Goals in One Match: 4, Bobby Hunt v Bradford C, Division 4, 30 December 1961; 4, Martyn King v Bradford C, Division 4, 30 December 1961; 4, Bobby Hunt v Doncaster R, Division 4, 30 April 1962.

Most Capped Player: Bela Balogh, 2 (9), Hungary.

Most League Appearances: Micky Cook, 613, 1969–84.

Youngest League Player: Lindsay Smith, 16 years 218 days v Grimsby T, 24 April 1971.

Record Transfer Fee Received: £2,500,000 from Reading for Greg Halford, January 2007.

Record Transfer Fee Paid: £400,000 to Cheltenham T for Steve Gillespie, July 2008.

Football League Record: 1950 Elected to Division 3 (S); 1958–61 Division 3; 1961–62 Division 4; 1962–65 Division 3; 1965–66 Division 4; 1966–68 Division 3; 1968–74 Division 4; 1974–76 Division 3, 1976–77 Division 4; 1977–81 Division 3; 1981–90 Division 4; 1990–92 GM Vauxhall Conference; 1992–98 Division 3; 1998–04 Division 2; 2004–06 FL 1; 2006–08 FL C; 2008– FL 1.

MANAGERS

Ted Fenton 1946–48
Jimmy Allen 1948–53
Jack Butler 1953–55
Benny Fenton 1955–63
Neil Franklin 1963–68
Dick Graham 1968–72
Jim Smith 1972–75
Bobby Roberts 1975–82
Allan Hunter 1982–83
Cyril Lea 1983–86
Mike Walker 1986–87
Roger Brown 1987–88
Jock Wallace 1989
Mick Mills 1990
Ian Atkins 1990–91
Roy McDonough 1991–94
George Burley 1994
Steve Wignall 1995–99
Mick Wadsworth 1999
Steve Whitton 1999–2003
Phil Parkinson 2003–06
Geraint Williams 2006–08
Paul Lambert 2008–09
Aidy Boothroyd 2009–10
John Ward May 2010–

LATEST SEQUENCES

Longest Sequence of League Wins: 7, 29.11.1968 – 1.2.1969.

Longest Sequence of League Defeats: 8, 9.10.1954 – 4.12.1954.

Longest Sequence of League Draws: 6, 21.3.1977 – 11.4.1977.

Longest Sequence of Unbeaten League Matches: 20, 22.12.1956 – 19.4.1957.

Longest Sequence Without a League Win: 20, 2.3.1968 – 31.8.1968.

Successive Scoring Runs: 24 from 15.9.1962.

Successive Non-scoring Runs: 5 from 7.4.1981.

TEN YEAR LEAGUE RECORD

		P	W	D	L	F	A	Pts	Pos
2002-03	Div 2	46	14	16	16	52	56	58	12
2003-04	Div 2	46	17	13	16	52	56	64	11
2004-05	FL 1	46	14	17	15	60	50	59	15
2005-06	FL 1	46	22	13	11	58	40	79	2
2006-07	FL C	46	20	9	17	70	56	69	10
2007-08	FL C	46	7	17	22	62	86	38	24
2008-09	FL 1	46	18	9	19	58	58	63	12
2009-10	FL 1	46	20	12	14	64	52	72	8
2010-11	FL 1	46	16	14	16	57	63	62	10
2011-12	FL 1	46	13	20	13	61	66	59	10

DID YOU KNOW ?

Alex Cheyne had won five Scottish international caps with Aberdeen before joining Chelsea. This inside-forward then had two seasons with Nimes before returning. He became a much-prized capture when he moved to Colchester United in their first ever League season 1937–38.

COLCHESTER UNITED 2011–12 LEAGUE RECORD

Match No.	*Date*	*Venue*	*Opponents*	*Result*		*H/T Score*	*Lg Pos.*	*Goalscorers*	*Attendance*
1	Aug 6	A	Preston NE	W	4-2	1-0	—	Wordsworth [12], Henderson 2 [49, 65], Odejayi [76]	11,451
2	13	H	Wycombe W	D	1-1	1-0	4	Vincent [24]	3902
3	16	H	Charlton Ath	L	0-2	0-2	—		5094
4	20	A	Huddersfield T	L	2-3	2-1	17	Odejayi [5], Antonio [27]	11,043
5	27	H	Oldham Ath	W	4-1	2-1	11	Wordsworth 2 (1 pen) [1, 45 (p)], Henderson [46], Heath [56]	3023
6	Sept 3	A	Scunthorpe U	D	1-1	0-1	13	Gillespie [74]	3700
7	10	H	Leyton Orient	D	1-1	1-0	13	Wordsworth [43]	4258
8	13	A	Brentford	D	1-1	0-0	—	Wordsworth [90]	4714
9	17	A	Sheffield U	L	0-3	0-2	15		15,783
10	24	H	Walsall	W	1-0	1-0	14	Wordsworth (pen) [33]	3103
11	Oct 1	A	Chesterfield	W	1-0	1-0	11	Antonio [30]	6295
12	8	H	Yeovil T	D	2-2	1-1	11	Bond [38], Antonio [54]	3521
13	15	A	Rochdale	D	2-2	2-1	12	Henderson [3], Odejayi [14]	2226
14	22	A	Sheffield W	L	0-2	0-0	13		17,634
15	25	H	Bournemouth	D	1-1	0-1	—	Zubar (og) [72]	3444
16	29	H	Notts Co	W	4-2	0-0	12	Wordsworth [49], Antonio [66], Henderson [71], Odejayi [74]	3585
17	Nov 5	A	Tranmere R	D	0-0	0-0	11		4312
18	19	H	Milton Keynes D	L	1-5	1-2	14	Heath [24]	4247
19	26	A	Carlisle U	L	0-1	0-1	14		4435
20	Dec 10	H	Bury	W	4-1	3-0	12	Duguid 2 [2, 31], Henderson [19], James [66]	3156
21	17	A	Hartlepool U	W	1-0	1-0	11	Wordsworth [36]	4029
22	26	H	Stevenage	L	1-6	0-2	13	Henderson [51]	5276
23	31	H	Exeter C	W	2-0	1-0	9	Wordsworth [16], Bond [62]	3667
24	Jan 2	A	Milton Keynes D	L	0-1	0-0	12		7892
25	14	H	Scunthorpe U	D	1-1	1-1	12	Gillespie (pen) [28]	3165
26	21	H	Chesterfield	L	1-2	1-2	15	Gillespie [32]	3312
27	28	A	Leyton Orient	W	1-0	1-0	12	Forbes (og) [28]	4659
28	Feb 14	H	Brentford	W	2-1	0-0	—	Gillespie 2 [83, 85]	2923
29	18	A	Yeovil T	L	2-3	1-0	12	Gillespie [19], Rowlands [90]	3442
30	25	H	Rochdale	D	0-0	0-0	12		3096
31	28	A	Oldham Ath	D	1-1	0-1	—	Wordsworth [81]	3956
32	Mar 3	H	Preston NE	W	3-0	1-0	11	Gillespie 2 (1 pen) [19, 52 (p)], Bond [90]	3333
33	6	A	Charlton Ath	W	2-0	1-0	—	Wordsworth [5], Gillespie [73]	13,650
34	10	A	Wycombe W	D	0-0	0-0	9		4838
35	13	H	Sheffield U	D	1-1	0-1	—	Gillespie [56]	4572
36	17	H	Huddersfield T	D	1-1	1-0	9	Gillespie [3]	3929
37	20	A	Stevenage	D	0-0	0-0	—		2419
38	24	H	Carlisle U	D	1-1	0-0	9	Rowlands [51]	3672
39	27	A	Walsall	L	1-3	1-2	—	Wordsworth [11]	3331
40	31	A	Exeter C	D	1-1	1-0	10	Duguid [6]	3889
41	Apr 6	H	Hartlepool U	D	1-1	0-1	—	Sears (pen) [81]	3921
42	9	A	Bury	L	1-4	0-2	10	Eastman [57]	3119
43	14	H	Sheffield W	D	1-1	1-0	10	Henderson [3]	6643
44	21	A	Bournemouth	D	1-1	0-1	10	Eastman [84]	5109
45	28	H	Tranmere R	W	4-2	1-0	10	Henderson [4], Eastman [46], Goodison (og) [66], Sears [84]	4061
46	May 5	A	Notts Co	L	1-4	0-3	10	Wordsworth [90]	8942

Final League Position: 10

GOALSCORERS

League (61): Wordsworth 13 (2 pens), Gillespie 11 (2 pens), Henderson 9, Antonio 4, Odejayi 4, Bond 3, Duguid 3, Eastman 3, Heath 2, Rowlands 2, Sears 2 (1 pen), James 1, Vincent 1, own goals 3.
Carling Cup (3): Gillespie 1 (pen), Henderson 1, Odejayi 1.
FA Cup (4): James 2, Bond 1, Coker 1.
J Paint Trophy (1): Baldwin 1.

Cousins M 10	Wilson B 46	Rose M 12 + 2	Izzet K 29 + 5	Okuonghae M 42	Heath M 22 + 4	O'Toole J 8 + 7	Wordsworth A 44	Odejayi K 33 + 10	Henderson I 45 + 1	Vincent A 5 + 4	James L 17 + 6	White J 21 + 5	Gillespie S 19 + 14	Antonio M 14 + 1	Coker B 15 + 5	Bond A 28 + 12	Duguid K 16 + 9	Baldwin P 4 + 1	Williams B 36	Eastman T 24 + 1	Thomas C — + 2	Massey G 2 + 1	Rowlands M 7 + 2	Sears F 5 + 6	Massey G 2 + 3	Hamilton B — + 1	Match No.
1	2	3	4	5	6	7	8^{2}	9	10	11^{1}	12	13															1
1	2	3	4	5	6	7	8^{2}	9	10	11^{1}	13		12														2
1	2	3	4^{1}	5	6	7	8	9	10		13		12	11^{2}													3
1	2	3	4^{2}	5^{3}	6	7	8	9	10			14		11^{1}	12	13											4
1	2		14	5	6	7^{2}	8	9^{1}	10		4		12	11^{3}	3	13											5
1	2^{2}			5	6	7^{1}	8	9	10		4		12	11^{3}	3	14	13										6
1	2		12		6	7^{1}	8^{2}	9	10		4			11^{3}	3	13	14	5									7
1	2		4^{1}	5	6	12■	8	9^{3}	10		7		13	11^{2}	3	14											8
1	2		4^{3}	5	6^{1}		8	9	10		11^{2}		13	14	3	7		12									9
	2		4	5	13		8	9^{1}	10^{2}					11	3	7	12	6	1								10
	2		4	5			8	9	10					11^{1}	3	7	12	6	1								11
	2		4	5			8^{1}	9	10				12	11	3	7		6	1								12
	2		4	5■	6^{2}	14	8	9	10^{1}			12		11^{3}	3	7	13		1								13
	2^{3}		4^{2}		5	13	8	9	10			14	12	11^{1}	3	7			1	6							14
	2		4^{1}	5	6		8	9	10^{2}	12	14		13	11^{3}	3	7			1								15
	2			6	5		4	9	8	12^{2}			10^{1}	11	3	7	13		1								16
	2		12	5	6		4	9	10	8^{1}				11	3	7			1								17
	2				5		8	9	10	11	4^{1}				3	7			1	6	12						18
	2		4	5	6		8	9	10^{3}	11^{1}	13	12			3	7^{2}			1		14						19
	2	3		5	6	13	8	9^{2}	10		4				12	7	11^{1}		1								20
	2	3	12	5	6		8	9	10		4^{1}					7	11		1								21
	2	3^{2}		5	6	8^{1}		9	10		4		12		13	7	11		1								22
	2			5	6^{1}		8		10		4	3	9		13	7	11^{2}		1	12							23
	2		13	5				8^{1}	10		4^{2}	3	9		12	7	11		1	6							24
	2			5		13	8	12^{2}	10		4^{1}	3	9			7	11		1	6							25
	2			5			8		10		4	3	9			7^{1}	11		1	6		12					26
	3		4	5			8	12	10		7	2					11		1	6		9^{1}					27
	2		4^{2}	5			8	14	10		11^{1}	3	12				7^{3}		1	6		9	13				28
	2			5			8	12	10^{1}			3	9			13	7		1	4			6	11^{2}			29
	2		4	5			8		10			3	9			12			1	6			7^{1}	11			30
	2		4^{2}	5	13		8	12	10			3	9			14			1	6^{3}			7	11^{1}			31
	2	14	4^{1}	5			8	11	10			3	9^{2}			12	13		1	6			7^{3}				32
	2		4	5			8	11	10			3	9^{2}			12	13		1	6			7^{1}				33
	2		4	5			8	11	10			3	9^{2}			12			1	6			7^{1}	13			34
	2		4	5			8	11	10^{1}			3	9			7	12		1	6							35
	2		4^{2}	5	13		8	11	10			3	9^{1}			7			1	6					12		36
	2		4^{2}	5			8	11	10			3	9			7^{1}			1	6				13	12		37
	2		4	5			8	13	10			3	9^{2}			12			1	6			7^{1}	14	11^{3}		38
	2			5	14		8	11	10	12		3	9			7^{2}			1	6^{3}				13	4^{1}		39
	2	6	4	5	3		8	9^{1}	10				12			7	11		1								40
	2	3	4	5			8^{3}	12	10^{1}				9^{2}				7		1	6			13	11	14		41
	2	3	4		5		8^{3}	9	13	12			14			7	11^{1}		1	6				10^{2}			42
	2		4^{1}	5		13	8	12	10^{2}			3	9			7	11		1	6							43
1	2	12	4^{2}	5			8	13	10		14	3	9^{3}			7	11^{1}			6							44
	2	11		5			8	9^{1}	10		4	3	12^{2}			7^{3}			1	6				13		14	45
	9	3^{1}		5		14	8	12	10		4^{3}	2				7^{2}	11		1	6				13			46

FA Cup
First Round Crewe Alex (a) 4-1
Second Round Swindon T (h) 0-1

Carling Cup
First Round Wycombe W (a) 3-3

J Paint Trophy
First Round Barnet (h) 1-3

COVENTRY CITY FL Championship 1

FOUNDATION

Workers at Singers' cycle factory formed a club in 1883. The first success of Singers' FC was to win the Birmingham Junior Cup in 1891 and this led in 1894 to their election to the Birmingham & District League. Four years later they changed their name to Coventry City and joined the Southern League in 1908 at which time they were playing in blue and white quarters.

The Ricoh Arena, Phoenix Way, Foleshill, Coventry CV6 6GE.

Telephone: (0844) 873 1883.

Fax: (0870) 421 1988.

Ticket Office: (0844) 873 1883 (option 1).

Website: www.ccfc.co.uk

Email: info@ccfc.co.uk

Ground Capacity: 32,609.

Record Attendance: 51,455 v Wolverhampton W, Division 2, 29 April 1967 (at Highfield Road); 31,407 v Chelsea, FA Cup 6th rd, 7 March 2009 (at Ricoh Arena).

Pitch Measurements: 110yd × 75yd.

Managing Director: Tim Fisher.

Vice-chairman: John Clarke OBE.

Manager: Andy Thorn.

Assistant Manager: Richard Shaw.

Physio: TBC.

Colours: Sky blue shirts with grey horizontal stripes, white shorts, sky blue stockings.

Year Formed: 1883.

Turned Professional: 1893.

Previous Name: 1883, Singers' FC; 1898, Coventry City.

Club Nickname: 'Sky Blues'.

Grounds: 1883, Binley Road; 1887, Stoke Road; 1899, Highfield Road; 2005, Ricoh Arena.

First Football League Game: 30 August 1919, Division 2, v Tottenham H (h) L 0–5 – Lindon; Roberts, Chaplin, Allan, Hawley, Clarke, Sheldon, Mercer, Sambrooke, Lowes, Gibson.

Record League Victory: 9–0 v Bristol C, Division 3 (S), 28 April 1934 – Pearson; Brown, Bisby; Perry, Davidson, Frith; White (2), Lauderdale, Bourton (5), Jones (2), Lake.

Record Cup Victory: 8–0 v Rushden & D, League Cup 2nd rd, 2 October 2002 – Debec; Caldwell, Quinn, Betts (1p), Konjic (Shaw), Davenport, Pipe, Safri (Stanford), Mills (2) (Bothroyd (2)), McSheffery (3), Partridge.

Record Defeat: 2–10 v Norwich C, Division 3 (S), 15 March 1930.

HONOURS

Football League – Division 1: Best season: 6th, 1969–70;
Division 2: ***Champions*** 1966–67;
Division 3: ***Champions*** 1963–64;
Division 3 (S): ***Champions*** 1935–36; ***Runners-up*** 1933–34;
Division 4: ***Runners-up*** 1958–59.

FA Cup: ***Winners*** 1987.

Football League Cup: Semi-final 1981, 1990.

European Competitions
European Fairs Cup: 1970–71.

sky SPORTS FACT FILE

Three seasons out of four in the late 1930s, Coventry City conceded just 45 goals. The first occasion was 1935–36 as champions of Division Three (South), again in 1937–38 when fourth in Division Two and in the following term fourth again and once more five points off promotion!

Most League Points (2 for a win): 60, Division 4, 1958–59 and Division 3, 1963–64.

Most League Points (3 for a win): 66, Division 1, 2001–02.

Most League Goals: 108, Division 3 (S), 1931–32.

Highest League Scorer in Season: Clarrie Bourton, 49, Division 3 (S), 1931–32.

Most League Goals in Total Aggregate: Clarrie Bourton, 171, 1931–37.

Most League Goals in One Match: 5, Clarrie Bourton v Bournemouth, Division 3 (S), 17 October 1931; 5, Arthur Bacon v Gillingham, Division 3 (S), 30 December 1933.

Most Capped Player: Magnus Hedman, 44 (58), Sweden.

Most League Appearances: Steve Ogrizovic, 507, 1984–2000.

Youngest League Player: Ben Mackey, 16 years 167 days v Ipswich T, 12 April 2003.

Record Transfer Fee Received: £13,000,000 from Internazionale for Robbie Keane, July 2000.

Record Transfer Fee Paid: £6,500,000 to Wolverhampton W for Robbie Keane, August 1999; £6,500,000 to Norwich C for Craig Bellamy, August 2000.

Football League Record: 1919 Elected to Division 2; 1925–26 Division 3 (N); 1926–36 Division 3 (S); 1936–52 Division 2; 1952–58 Division 3 (S); 1958–59 Division 4; 1959–64 Division 3; 1964–67 Division 2; 1967–92 Division 1; 1992–2001 FA Premier League; 2001–04 Division 1; 2004–12 FL C; 2012– FL 1.

LATEST SEQUENCES

Longest Sequence of League Wins: 6, 25.4.1964 – 5.9.1964.

Longest Sequence of League Defeats: 9, 30.8.1919 – 11.10.1919.

Longest Sequence of League Draws: 6, 1.11.2003 – 29.11.2003.

Longest Sequence of Unbeaten League Matches: 25, 26.11.1966 – 13.5.1967.

Longest Sequence Without a League Win: 19, 30.8.1919 – 20.12.1919.

Successive Scoring Runs: 25 from 10.9.1966.

Successive Non-scoring Runs: 11 from 11.10.1919.

MANAGERS

H. R. Buckle 1909–10
Robert Wallace 1910–13
(*Secretary-Manager*)
Frank Scott-Walford 1913–15
William Clayton 1917–19
H. Pollitt 1919–20
Albert Evans 1920–24
Jimmy Kerr 1924–28
James McIntyre 1928–31
Harry Storer 1931–45
Dick Bayliss 1945–47
Billy Frith 1947–48
Harry Storer 1948–53
Jack Fairbrother 1953–54
Charlie Elliott 1954–55
Jesse Carver 1955–56
George Raynor 1956
Harry Warren 1956–57
Billy Frith 1957–61
Jimmy Hill 1961–67
Noel Cantwell 1967–72
Bob Dennison 1972
Joe Mercer 1972–75
Gordon Milne 1972–81
Dave Sexton 1981–83
Bobby Gould 1983–84
Don Mackay 1985–86
George Curtis 1986–87
(*became Managing Director*)
John Sillett 1987–90
Terry Butcher 1990–92
Don Howe 1992
Bobby Gould 1992–93
(*Bobby Gould and Don Howe joint managers June 1992*)
Phil Neal 1993–95
Ron Atkinson 1995–96
(*became Director of Football*)
Gordon Strachan 1996–2001
Roland Nilsson 2001–02
Gary McAllister 2002–04
Eric Black 2004
Peter Reid 2004–05
Micky Adams 2005–07
Iain Dowie 2007–08
Chris Coleman 2008–10
Aidy Boothroyd 2010–11
Andy Thorn April 2011–

TEN YEAR LEAGUE RECORD

		P	W	D	L	F	A	Pts	Pos
2002-03	Div 1	46	12	14	20	46	62	50	20
2003-04	Div 1	46	17	14	15	67	54	65	12
2004-05	FL C	46	13	13	20	61	73	52	19
2005-06	FL C	46	16	15	15	62	65	63	8
2006-07	FL C	46	16	8	22	47	62	56	17
2007-08	FL C	46	14	11	21	52	64	53	21
2008-09	FL C	46	13	15	18	47	58	54	17
2009-10	FL C	46	13	15	18	47	64	54	19
2010-11	FL C	46	14	13	19	54	58	55	18
2011-12	FL C	46	9	13	24	41	65	40	23

DID YOU KNOW

Jimmy Loughlin did not score any FA Cup goals while with either Newcastle United or West Ham United, but struck a purple patch in the competition when joining Coventry City. In 1929–30 he scored six times in four consecutive matches including a narrow defeat against Sunderland.

COVENTRY CITY 2011–12 LEAGUE RECORD

Match No.	*Date*	*Venue*	*Opponents*	*Result*	*H/T Score*	*Lg Pos.*	*Goalscorers*	*Attendance*
1	Aug 6	H	Leicester C	L 0-1	0-0	—		21,102
2	13	A	Birmingham C	L 0-1	0-0	22		19,225
3	16	A	Crystal Palace	L 1-2	0-0	—	Jutkiewicz [48]	12,330
4	20	H	Watford	D 0-0	0-0	23		13,043
5	27	A	Middlesbrough	D 1-1	0-1	23	Jutkiewicz [76]	17,432
6	Sept 10	H	Derby Co	W 2-0	0-0	19	Jutkiewicz (pen) [59], Baker [79]	14,219
7	19	A	Ipswich T	L 0-3	0-2	—		15,650
8	24	H	Reading	D 1-1	1-1	22	McSheffrey [2]	12,309
9	27	H	Blackpool	D 2-2	0-1	—	Deegan [78], Jutkiewicz [83]	12,822
10	Oct 1	A	Barnsley	L 0-2	0-1	22		9497
11	15	H	Nottingham F	W 1-0	0-0	19	Jutkiewicz [57]	15,712
12	18	A	Leeds U	D 1-1	0-1	—	Wood [90]	21,528
13	22	H	Burnley	L 1-2	0-0	21	McDonald [59]	12,785
14	29	A	Doncaster R	D 1-1	1-0	22	Clingan [31]	8426
15	Nov 1	A	Millwall	L 0-3	0-0	—		9517
16	5	H	Southampton	L 2-4	0-2	23	Jutkiewicz [47], Platt [70]	15,621
17	19	H	West Ham U	L 1-2	1-0	23	Platt [33]	20,524
18	22	H	Cardiff C	D 1-1	0-0	—	Jutkiewicz [61]	12,317
19	26	A	Brighton & HA	L 1-2	1-2	23	Gardner [9]	19,108
20	Dec 3	A	Portsmouth	L 1-2	0-1	24	Jutkiewicz [54]	12,236
21	10	H	Hull C	L 0-1	0-0	24		12,652
22	17	A	Peterborough U	L 0-1	0-0	24		8062
23	26	H	Bristol C	W 1-0	0-0	24	Deegan [72]	15,302
24	31	H	Brighton & HA	W 2-0	1-0	23	McSheffrey [34], Jutkiewicz [54]	14,158
25	Jan 2	A	West Ham U	L 0-1	0-0	24		34,936
26	14	A	Derby Co	L 0-1	0-0	24		24,126
27	21	H	Middlesbrough	W 3-1	1-0	24	McSheffrey [36], Nimely-Tchuimeni [57], Bates (og) [64]	14,112
28	31	A	Blackpool	L 1-2	0-0	—	Thomas [59]	11,414
29	Feb 4	H	Ipswich T	L 2-3	2-1	24	Clingan (pen) [29], Deegan [45]	13,464
30	11	A	Reading	L 0-2	0-2	24		18,006
31	14	H	Leeds U	W 2-1	1-1	—	McSheffrey 2 (2 pens) [21, 90]	15,704
32	18	A	Nottingham F	L 0-2	0-0	23		21,588
33	25	H	Barnsley	W 1-0	0-0	22	Platt [90]	13,928
34	Mar 3	A	Leicester C	L 0-2	0-1	22		25,487
35	6	H	Crystal Palace	D 1-1	0-1	—	McDonald [80]	12,054
36	10	H	Birmingham C	D 1-1	0-0	22	McSheffrey [70]	22,240
37	17	A	Watford	D 0-0	0-0	22		12,563
38	21	A	Cardiff C	D 2-2	0-1	—	Clarke [69], Norwood [90]	20,564
39	24	H	Portsmouth	W 2-0	0-0	22	McSheffrey [55], Norwood [77]	15,809
40	31	A	Hull C	W 2-0	1-0	21	Cooper (og) [13], McDonald [86]	17,279
41	Apr 7	H	Peterborough U	D 2-2	2-1	22	McDonald [26], McSheffrey (pen) [45]	18,760
42	9	A	Bristol C	L 1-3	1-0	22	Stead (og) [33]	19,003
43	14	A	Burnley	D 1-1	0-1	22	Platt [67]	13,398
44	17	H	Millwall	L 0-1	0-0	—		13,974
45	21	H	Doncaster R	L 0-2	0-0	23		15,124
46	28	A	Southampton	L 0-4	0-2	23		32,363

Final League Position: 23

GOALSCORERS

League (41): Jutkiewicz 9 (1 pen), McSheffrey 8 (3 pens), McDonald 4, Platt 4, Deegan 3, Clingan 2 (1 pen), Norwood 2, Baker 1, Clarke 1, Gardner 1, Nimely-Tchuimeni 1, Thomas 1, Wood 1, own goals 3.
Carling Cup (1): O'Donovan 1.
FA Cup (1): McSheffrey 1.

Murphy J 46	Christie C 27 + 10	Hussey C 28 + 1	Clingan S 34 + 2	Keogh R 45	Cranie M 38	Bell D 19 + 9	Baker C 20 + 6	Jutkiewicz L 25	Bigirimana G 16 + 10	McSheffrey G 37 + 2	Wood R 12 + 5	O'Donovan R 6 + 5	Jeffers S — + 3	Thomas C 24 + 3	Ruffels J — + 1	Eastwood F — + 4	McDonald C 16 + 7	Dunn C — + 2	Cameron N 11 + 3	Platt C 23 + 10	Deegan G 19 + 5	McPake J 3 + 2	Willis J 1 + 2	Gardner G 4	Clarke J 17 + 2	Hreidarsson H 2	Nimely-Tchuimeni A 16 + 1	Norwood O 17 + 1	Roberts W — + 1	Henderson J — + 1	*Match No.*
1	2^{1}	3	4	5	6	7	8■	9	10	11^{2}	12	13																			1
1	2	3	4	5	6	7		9	8	11		10^{1}	12																		2
1	2	3	4	5	6			9	8	11^{1}		10		7	12																3
1	2	3	4	5	6	7	8	9	11			10^{1}				12															4
1	2	3	4	5	6	7^{1}	8	9	11			10		12																	5
1^{G}	2	3	4	5	6	7	8	9	11			12					10^{1}	15													6
1	2^{3}	3	4	5	6	7	8	9	11^{1}	12		13					10^{2}		14												7
1	2	3	4	5	6	7		9		11^{2}		13		8			10^{1}			12											8
1	13	3^{2}	4	2	6	7^{1}		9		11		10^{3}		8					5	14	12										9
1	12	3^{1}	4	2	6^{3}	14		9		11		10^{2}		8					5	13	7										10
1^{G}	2	3	4	5		7		9	13		6^{1}			8^{2}				15	12	10	11										11
1	2	3	4	5		7		9	13		6			8			12			10^{2}	11^{1}										12
1	2	3	4	5		7		9	11■		6	12		8			10^{1}														13
1	2	3^{1}	4	5		14	7^{3}	9		11^{2}				8			10		6		13	12									14
1			4	2		13	8^{3}	9		11^{2}	3			14			10		6	12	7^{1}	5									15
1	3		4	2		12		9		11				8			10^{3}		5	14	7^{1}	6^{2}	13								16
1	2^{2}	3	4	5	6		12	9	7	11^{1}	13			8						10											17
1	2	3^{2}	4	5	6		12	9	7	11^{1}	13			8						10											18
1	2^{1}	3	4	5	6		8	9	13		12			11^{2}			14			7^{3}				10							19
1	14		4	5	2		8	9	11	12	6^{3}						13		3	10^{2}				7^{1}							20
1	14			5	3		8	9	13	11^{2}	6^{3}			4			10^{1}		2	12				7							21
1	2	3		5		7^{1}		9	12	11	6			8						10				4							22
1	2^{3}	3^{1}		5		7	8	9	11^{2}	10	6			4					13		12	14									23
1	2			5	3	7	8	9	12	10	6			4							11^{1}										24
1		3		5	2	7^{1}	8	9^{2}	12	10	6		13	4							11										25
1	2		4	5	3		8			10				7		13				9^{2}	11	6^{1}			12						26
1	2		4	5	3	12				11				8		13				9^{2}	7^{1}					6	10				27
1	2		4	5	6	13				11	12			8^{2}						9	7					3	10^{1}				28
1			4	5	6	7^{2}				11	3									9	8		13		2^{1}		10	12			29
1	2		4^{2}	5	3	13	14			11	6^{1}									9	8^{3}				12		10	7			30
1	2			5	6		8			11										9	7				3		10	4			31
1	2			5	6	12	8^{1}			11						13				9	7^{2}				3		10	4			32
1	2			5	6	12	8^{1}			11										9	7				3		10	4			33
1	2		13	5	6	7^{1}	12			11^{3}							14			9	8^{2}				3		10	4			34
1	14		12	5	3		8			11							13		6	9^{2}	7^{1}				2^{3}		10	4			35
1			4	5	3		8^{2}			11				13			10^{1}		6	12					2		9	7			36
1	13		4	5	3					11							12		6	9	7				2^{2}		10^{1}	8			37
1		13	4	5	3^{2}					11				8^{3}			10^{1}		6	12	14				2		9	7			38
1	13	3^{2}	4	5	6				12	11				8^{1}						9					2		10	7			39
1	13	3^{2}	4	5	6				8	11							12			9					2		10^{1}	7			40
1		3	4	5	6				8^{2}	11							10			12	13				2		9^{1}	7			41
1	12	3^{1}	4	5	6				14	11							10^{2}			9	8^{3}				2		13	7			42
1	13	3	4	5	6	8^{2}			14	11							10			12					2^{1}		9^{3}	7			43
1		3	4	5	6	8^{1}	12			11							10			9					2			7			44
1		3		5■	6		12		8	11				4^{1}			10			9					2			7			45
1		3			5		8		11^{2}	9^{1}			13	4			10						6^{3}		2			7	12	14	46

FA Cup
Third Round Southampton (h) 1-2

Carling Cup
First Round Bury (a) 1-3

CRAWLEY TOWN — FL Championship 1

FOUNDATION

Formed in 1896, Crawley Town initially entered the West Sussex League before switching to the mid-Sussex League in 1901, winning the Second Division in its second season. The club remained at such level until 1951 when it became members of the Sussex County League and five years later moved to the Metropolitan League while remaining as an amateur club. It was not until 1962 that the club turned semi-professional and a year later, joined the Southern League. Many honours came the club's way, but the most successful run was achieved in 2010–11 when they reached the fifith round of the FA Cup and played before a crowd of 74,778 spectators at Old Trafford against Manchester United. Crawley Town spent 48 years at the Town Mead ground before a new site was occupied at Broadfield in 1997, ideally suited to access from the neighbouring motorway. History was also made on 9 April when the team won promotion to the Football League after beating Tamworth 3-0 to stretch their unbeaten League record to 26 games. They finished the season with a Conference record points total of 105 and at the same time, established another milestone for the longest unbeaten run, having extended it to 30 matches by the end of the season.

Broadfield Stadium, Winfield Way, Crawley, Sussex RH11 9RX.

Telephone: (01293) 410 000.

Fax: (01293) 410 002.

Website: www.crawleytownfc.com

Email: info@crawleytownfc.com

Ground Capacity: 4,996 (1,150 seated).

Record Attendance: 4,522 v Weymouth, Doc Martens Premier League, 6 March 2004.

Pitch Measurements: 110yd × 72yd.

Chairman: Victor Marley.

Chief Executive: Alan Williams.

Manager: Sean O'Driscoll.

Coach: Craig Brewster.

Head of Medical: Mark Stein.

Club Nickname: 'Red Devils'.

Colours: All red.

Year Formed: 1896.

MANAGERS

Managers have included:
Tom Jarvie
John Hollins
Colin Pates
Francis Vines
Simon Wormull
David Woozley
Steve Evans 2007–12
Sean O'Driscoll May 2012–

sky SPORTS FACT FILE

On 7 January 2012 when Crawley Town defeated Bristol City in a third round FA Cup tie with a goal from Matt Tubbs, it extended the team's clean sheets in the competition to five hours 32 minutes dating back to the previous season which began after conceding to Manchester United.

Turned Professional: 1962.

Grounds: Town Mead to 1997; Broadfield Stadium 1997.

First Football League Game: 6 August 2011, FL 2 v Port Vale (a) D 2-2 – Shearer; Hunt, Howell, Bulman, McFadzean (1), Dempster (Thomas), Simpson, Torres, Tubbs (Neilson), Barnett (1) (Wassmer), Smith.

Record League Victory: 5-2 v AFC Wimbledon, FL 2, 22 October 2011.

Record League Defeat: 6-0 v Morecambe, FL 2, 10 September 2011.

Most League Points (3 for a win): 84, FL 2, 2011–12.

Most League Goals: 76, FL 2, 2011–12.

Highest League Scorer in Season: Tyrone Barnett, 14, 2011–12.

Most League Appearances: Dannie Bulman, 41, 2011–12.

Football League Record: 2011–12 FL 2; 2012– FL 1.

LATEST SEQUENCES

Longest Sequence of League Wins: 7, 17.9.2011 – 25.10.2011.

Longest Sequence of League Defeats: 2, 10.9.2011 – 13.9.2011.

Longest Sequence of League Draws: 3, 2.1.2012 – 21.1.2012.

Longest Sequence of Unbeaten League Matches: 13, 17.9.2011 – 17.12.2011

Longest Sequence Without a League Win: 7, 14.2.2012 – 13.3.2012.

Successive Scoring Runs: 16 from 17.9.2011 – 2.1.2012.

Successive Non-scoring Runs: 2 from 10.9.2011 – 13.9.2011.

HONOURS

FA Cup: Best Season: 5th rd 2011, 2012.

Blue Square Premier: ***Champions*** 2010–11.

Southern League: ***Champions*** 2003–04.

Southern League Cup: ***Winners*** 2003, 2004.

Southern League Championship Trophy: ***Winners*** 2004, 2005.

Southern League Merit Cup: ***Winners*** 1971.

Sussex Professional Cup: ***Winners*** 1970.

Sussex Senior Cup: ***Winners*** 1990, 1991, 2003, 2005.

Sussex Intermediate Cup: ***Winners*** 1928.

Sussex Floodlit Cup: ***Winners*** 1991, 1992, 1993, 1999.

Southern Counties Floodlit League: ***Champions*** 1985–86.

Mid-Sussex Senior League: ***Champions*** 1902–03.

Montgomery Cup: ***Winners*** 1926.

Gilbert Rice Floodlit Cup: ***Winners*** 1980, 1984.

Roy Hayden Trophy: ***Winners*** 1991, 1992.

William Hill Senior Cup: ***Winners*** 1993.

Metropolitan League Challenge Cup: ***Winners*** 1959.

Highest Placed Amateur Award: 1961–62.

FA Ronnie Radford Award: 2011.

TEN YEAR LEAGUE RECORD

		P	*W*	*D*	*L*	*F*	*A*	*Pts*	*Pos*
2002-03	S PR	42	17	13	12	64	51	64	7
2003-04	S PR	42	25	9	8	77	43	84	1
2004-05	Conf	42	16	9	17	50	50	57	12
2005-06	Conf	42	12	11	19	48	55	44	17
2006-07	Conf	46	17	12	17	52	52	53	18
2007-08	BSP	46	19	9	18	73	67	60	15
2008-09	BSP	46	19	14	13	77	55	70	9
2009-10	BSP	44	19	9	16	50	57	66	7
2010-11	BSP	46	31	12	3	93	50	105	1
2011-12	FL 2	46	23	15	8	76	54	84	3

DID YOU KNOW ?

Matt Tubbs originally made his name playing for Salisbury City. At the time he was a part-time professional combining his football with work as a lifeguard at a leisure centre. Briefly with Bolton Wanderers then Bournemouth (later loaned to them) he progressed via Dorchester Town.

CRAWLEY TOWN 2011–12 LEAGUE RECORD

Match No.	Date	Venue	Opponents	Result	H/T Score	Lg Pos.	Goalscorers	Attendance
1	Aug 6	A	Port Vale	D 2-2	1-1	—	Barnett [39], McFadzean [51]	5889
2	13	H	Macclesfield T	W 2-0	0-0	5	Barnett [57], Thomas [75]	2389
3	16	H	Southend U	W 3-0	0-0	—	Howell [56], Tubbs 2 (1 pen) [68 (p), 70]	3220
4	20	A	Torquay U	W 3-1	2-0	1	Davies [4], Wassmer [44], Simpson [46]	2658
5	27	A	Cheltenham T	L 1-3	0-3	3	Tubbs (pen) [51]	2609
6	Sept 3	H	Bristol R	W 4-1	2-0	1	Barnett 2 [14, 84], Smith [28], Tubbs [74]	3693
7	10	A	Morecambe	L 0-6	0-2	4		2054
8	13	H	Swindon T	L 0-3	0-1	—		2790
9	17	H	Bradford C	W 3-1	0-1	5	Barnett 2 [54, 88], Drury [62]	2479
10	24	A	Aldershot T	W 1-0	0-0	4	Barnett [64]	3276
11	Oct 1	H	Plymouth Arg	W 2-0	1-0	2	Tubbs 2 [5, 61]	3175
12	8	A	Northampton T	W 1-0	1-0	2	Tubbs [23]	4803
13	15	H	Shrewsbury T	W 2-1	2-0	1	Torres [14], Howell [43]	3453
14	22	A	AFC Wimbledon	W 5-2	2-2	1	Bush (og) [3], Davis [9], Tubbs (pen) [54], Bulman 2 [59, 84]	4549
15	25	H	Dagenham & R	W 3-1	2-1	—	Tubbs (pen) [18], Torres [45], Pittman [85]	2862
16	29	H	Accrington S	D 1-1	0-1	2	Akpan [78]	2987
17	Nov 5	A	Hereford U	D 1-1	1-1	2	Drury [41]	2227
18	19	H	Oxford U	W 4-1	3-1	2	Barnett 2 [4, 14], Drury [45], Howell [52]	4042
19	26	A	Rotherham U	W 2-1	0-1	2	Barnett [48], Simpson [68]	3962
20	Dec 10	H	Burton Alb	W 3-0	1-0	1	Davis [22], Webster (og) [56], Tubbs [83]	3001
21	17	A	Crewe Alex	D 1-1	1-1	1	Tubbs [31]	3635
22	26	H	Gillingham	L 1-2	1-0	1	Tubbs (pen) [34]	4255
23	30	H	Barnet	W 1-0	1-0	—	Barnett [3]	3008
24	Jan 2	A	Oxford U	D 1-1	0-0	1	Barnett [90]	9004
25	14	A	Bristol R	D 0-0	0-0	3		5082
26	21	A	Plymouth Arg	D 1-1	1-0	2	Mills [45]	6417
27	Feb 7	H	Cheltenham T	W 4-2	3-1	—	Watt 2 [12, 64], Barnett 2 [14, 39]	3871
28	14	A	Swindon T	L 0-3	0-1	—		8311
29	22	H	Morecambe	D 1-1	0-1	—	Neilson [49]	2184
30	27	A	Shrewsbury T	L 1-2	1-1	—	Akinde [33]	5229
31	Mar 3	H	Torquay U	L 0-1	0-0	6		3361
32	5	A	Southend U	D 0-0	0-0	—		5439
33	10	A	Macclesfield T	D 2-2	1-0	6	Davis [37], McFadzean [47]	1802
34	13	H	Aldershot T	D 2-2	1-1	—	Alexander (pen) [33], Clarke, B [88]	3017
35	17	H	Port Vale	W 3-2	1-1	6	Torres [42], Alexander 2 [70, 83]	2375
36	20	A	Gillingham	W 1-0	0-0	—	Bulman [50]	5204
37	24	H	Rotherham U	W 3-0	1-0	4	Clarke, B [43], Alexander (pen) [53], Mills [67]	2766
38	27	A	Bradford C	W 2-1	0-0	—	Clarke, L [54], Alexander [76]	9773
39	31	A	Burton Alb	D 0-0	0-0	3		2572
40	Apr 6	H	Crewe Alex	D 1-1	0-1	4	Alexander (pen) [88]	4723
41	9	A	Barnet	W 2-1	0-1	4	Dempster [52], Davies [61]	2099
42	14	H	AFC Wimbledon	D 1-1	0-0	4	Alexander [81]	3768
43	17	H	Northampton T	W 3-1	3-0	—	Neilson [14], Clarke, B [22], Kitson (og) [39]	2861
44	21	A	Dagenham & R	D 1-1	1-1	3	Wassmer [18]	2456
45	28	H	Hereford U	L 0-3	0-0	3		4615
46	May 5	A	Accrington S	W 1-0	0-0	3	Neilson [67]	2299

Final League Position: 3

GOALSCORERS

League (76): Barnett 14, Tubbs 12 (5 pens), Alexander 7 (3 pens), Bulman 3, Clarke, B 3, Davis 3, Drury 3, Howell 3, Neilson 3, Torres 3, Davies 2, McFadzean 2, Mills 2, Simpson 2, Wassmer 2, Watt 2, Akinde 1, Akpan 1, Clarke, L 1, Dempster 1, Pittman 1, Smith 1, Thomas 1, own goals 3.
Carling Cup (3): Akpan 1, Torres 1, Tubbs 1.
FA Cup (9): Tubbs 5 (2 pens), Barnett 1, Drury 1, Doughty 1, McFadzean 1.
J Paint Trophy (0).

Shearer S 25	Hunt D 26 + 1	Howell D 36 + 1	Bulman D 41	McFadzean K 36 + 1	Dempster J 6 + 1	Simpson J 31 + 9	Torres S 37 + 1	Tubbs M 23 + 1	Barnett T 25 + 1	Smith B 3 + 2	Wassmer C 12 + 1	Neilson S 11 + 19	Thomas W 2 + 4	Akpan H 17 + 9	Davies S 17 + 3	Akinde J 7 + 18	Doughty M 2 + 14	Wilson G 2 + 2	Kuipers M 15	Griffiths S 6	Eastman T 6	Pittman J — + 4	Davis C 27 + 2	Drury A 13	Mills P 19 + 2	Watt S 6 + 8	Clarke B 16 + 1	Hawley K 1 + 3	Gilmartin R 6	Batt S — + 1	James L 6	Cummings W 6 + 3	Batt S 2 + 2	Alexander G 14	Clarke L 4	*Match No.*
1	2	3	4	5	6■	7	8	9^{2}	10^{3}	11^{1}	12	13	14																							1
1	2	3		5		7	8	9^{2}	10^{3}		6	13	12	4	11^{1}	14																				2
1	2	3		5		7	8	9^{2}	10^{3}	12	6	11^{1}	13	4		14																				3
1	2	3		5	14	7	8		10^{3}		6	13	9^{2}	4^{1}	11		12																			4
1	2	3	4	5		7		12	10		6		9^{3}	8^{1}	11^{2}		14	13																		5
	2	3		5	6	7^{1}	8	9	10^{3}	11^{2}	4		14	12			13		1																	6
	2		4			7	8^{2}	9	10	11^{1}	6	12					13	5	1	3																7
	2		4			7^{1}		9^{2}	10		6			8		13	11		1	3	5	12														8
1	2		4					9	10^{3}			11^{1}			7	14	13			3	6	12	5	8^{2}												9
1	2		4	14			8	9	10^{2}						11^{3}	13	12			3	6		5	7^{1}												10
1	2		4	11			8	9^{3}	10^{2}						12	13	14			3	6		5	7^{1}												11
1	2		4	11			8	9^{2}	10^{1}							12	13	14		3	6		5	7^{3}												12
1	2	3	4	11		14	8	9^{1}	10^{2}			13				12					6		5	7^{3}												13
1	2^{2}	3	4	6		11	8^{3}	9	10^{1}			14		13		12							5	7												14
1		3	4	6		2	8^{3}	9				11		14		10^{2}						13	5^{1}	7	12											15
1	14	3	4^{2}	6		2^{3}	8	9				11^{1}		13		10	12						5	7												16
1	2	3	4			11		9^{2}	13			12		8		10							5^{1}	7	6											17
1	2	3	4	5^{1}		11	8^{3}	9	10^{2}							13	14						12	7	6											18
1	2	3	4			11	8	9^{1}	10					13								12	5	7^{2}	6											19
1	2	3	4^{2}	6		11	8	9^{3}	10					13		14	12						5	7^{1}												20
1	2	3	4	6		11^{2}	8	9^{3}	10							13	14						5^{1}	7	12											21
1	2	3	7	6		12	8^{2}	9	10			13					11^{1}						5■		4											22
1		3	4^{1}	5		11	8	9^{3}	10	14		7^{2}		12			13	2							6											23
1	2	3		4		11	8		10			12		7^{1}		9^{2}	13						5		6											24
1	2	3	4	11^{2}		7	8^{1}	9	10			12		13									5		6											25
1	2	3	4	7			8	9	10			11		12									5^{1}		6											26
1	2	3	4	11		13	8		10														5		6	7^{2}	9^{1}	12								27
	2	3	4	11		13	8^{2}		10			14							1				5		6^{3}	9^{1}	7	12								28
		3	4	2		14	8^{1}					13		11^{3}		12							5		6	9	7	10^{2}	1							29
		3	4	5		11^{2}					2^{3}	12		8		10									6	7^{1}	9	14	1	13						30
		3	4	5^{3}		13	12					7^{1}		8^{2}		10									6	9	11		1		2	14				31
			4			11^{1}	8					12			10	13							5		6		7		1		2	3	9^{2}			32
		13	4	11			8^{2}								7								5		6		9^{1}		1		2	3	12	10		33
			4	6		14	8					13			7^{3}	12							5				11		1		2	3	9^{1}	10^{2}		34
		3	4	11		13	8								12				1				5^{2}		6	14	7^{3}				2^{1}			9	10	35
		3	4	5		2	8							11	7				1						6									10	9	36
		3	4	5		2	8^{1}							11	7				1						6	13	9^{2}					12	14	10^{3}		37
		3	4	5		2	8							11^{3}	7				1				13		6	12						14		10^{2}	9^{1}	38
		3	4	5	6	2	8					13		11	7^{2}				1							12	9^{1}							10		39
		3	4		5	11	8					14		6^{2}	7^{1}				1							12	13					2		10	9^{3}	40
		3	4		5	13	8■					14		11	12				1							9^{2}	7^{3}				6^{1}	2		10		41
		3	4		5	11					6	7		8■	2				1							12	9^{1}							10		42
		3	4	8		11					6	7^{2}			2	12			1				5			13	9^{1}							10		43
		3	4	8		11					6	7^{1}			2	12			1				5				9							10		44
		3^{1}	4	7		11	8				6	13			2^{3}	12			1				5			14	9^{2}							10		45
1	2		4	6		11	8					7				10							5									3		9		46

FA Cup

First Round	Bury	(a)	2-0
Second Round	Redbridge	(h)	5-0
Third Round	Bristol C	(h)	1-0
Fourth Round	Hull C	(a)	1-0
Fifth Round	Stoke C	(h)	0-2

Carling Cup

Preliminary Round	AFC Wimbledon	(h)	3-2
First Round	Crystal Palace	(a)	0-2

J Paint Trophy

First Round	Southend U	(a)	0-1

CREWE ALEXANDRA FL Championship 1

FOUNDATION

The first match played at Crewe was on 1 December 1877 against Basford, the leading North Staffordshire team of that time. During the club's history they have also played in a number of other leagues including the Football Alliance, Football Combination, Lancashire League, Manchester League, Central League and Lancashire Combination. Two former players, Aaron Scragg in 1899 and Jackie Pearson in 1911, had the distinction of refereeing FA Cup finals. Pearson was also capped for England against Ireland in 1892.

The Alexandra Stadium, Gresty Road, Crewe, Cheshire CW2 6EB.

Telephone: (01270) 213 014.

Fax: (01270) 216 320.

Ticket Office: (01270) 252 610.

Website: www.crewealex.net

Email: info@crewealex.net

Ground Capacity: 10,107.

Record Attendance: 20,000 v Tottenham H, FA Cup 4th rd, 30 January 1960.

Pitch Measurements: 112m × 74m.

Chairman: John Bowler.

Vice-chairman: David Rowlinson.

Manager: Steve Davis.

Assistant Manager: Neil Baker.

Physio: Rob Sharp.

Colours: Red shirts with white trim, white shorts, red stockings.

Year Formed: 1877. ***Turned Professional:*** 1893.

Club Nickname: 'Railwaymen'.

Ground: 1898, Gresty Road.

First Football League Game: 3 September 1892, Division 2, v Burton Swifts (a) L 1–7 – Hickton; Moore, Cope; Linnell, Johnson, Osborne; Bennett, Pearson (1), Bailey, Barnett, Roberts.

Record League Victory: 8–0 v Rotherham U, Division 3 (N), 1 October 1932 – Foster; Pringle, Dawson; Ward, Keenor (1), Turner (1); Gillespie, Swindells (1), McConnell (2), Deacon (2), Weale (1).

Record Cup Victory: 8–0 v Hartlepool U, Auto Windscreens Shield 1st rd, 17 October 1995 – Gayle; Collins (1), Booty, Westwood (Unsworth), Macauley (1), Whalley (1), Garvey (1), Murphy (1), Savage (1) (Rivers (1p)), Lennon, Edwards, (1 og). 8–0 v Doncaster R, LDV Vans Trophy 3rd rd, 10 November 2002 – Bankole; Wright, Walker, Foster, Tierney; Lunt (1), Brammer, Sorvel, Vaughan (1) (Bell); Ashton (3) (Miles), Jack (2) (Jones (1)).

HONOURS

Football League – Division 2: ***Runners-up*** 2002–03.

FA Cup: Semi-final 1888.

Football League Cup: never past 3rd round.

Welsh Cup: ***Winners*** 1936, 1937.

sky SPORTS FACT FILE

On 14 May 1927, Crewe Alexandra beat Manchester United 2-1 in the final of the Manchester Senior Challenge Cup. Their goals were scored by Harold Kay and Arthur Cooper, a native of Manchester himself and making his first appearance for the club.

Record Defeat: 2–13 v Tottenham H, FA Cup 4th rd replay, 3 February 1960.

Most League Points (2 for a win): 59, Division 4, 1962–63.

Most League Points (3 for a win): 86, Division 2, 2002–03.

Most League Goals: 95, Division 3 (N), 1931–32.

Highest League Scorer in Season: Terry Harkin, 35, Division 4, 1964–65.

Most League Goals in Total Aggregate: Bert Swindells, 126, 1928–37.

Most League Goals in One Match: 5, Tony Naylor v Colchester U, Division 3, 24 April 1993.

Most Capped Player: Clayton Ince, 38 (79), Trinidad & Tobago.

Most League Appearances: Tommy Lowry, 436, 1966–78.

Youngest League Player: Steve Walters, 16 years 119 days v Peterborough U, 6 May 1988.

Record Transfer Fee Received: £4,000,000 from Derby Co for Seth Johnson, May 1999 (including sell-on).

Record Transfer Fee Paid: £650,000 to Torquay U for Rodney Jack, June 1998.

Football League Record: 1892 Original Member of Division 2; 1896 Failed re-election; 1921 Re-entered Division (N); 1958–63 Division 4; 1963–64 Division 3; 1964–68 Division 4; 1968–69 Division 3; 1969–89 Division 4; 1989–91 Division 3; 1991–92 Division 4; 1992–94 Division 3; 1994–97 Division 2; 1997–2002 Division 1; 2002–03 Division 2; 2003–04 Division 1; 2004–06 FL C; 2006–09 FL 1; 2009–12 FL 2; 2012– FL 1.

LATEST SEQUENCES

Longest Sequence of League Wins: 7, 30.4.1994 – 3.9.1994.

Longest Sequence of League Defeats: 10, 16.4.1979 – 22.8.1979.

Longest Sequence of League Draws: 5, 31.8.1987 – 18.9.1987.

Longest Sequence of Unbeaten League Matches: 17, 25.3.1995 – 16.9.1995.

Longest Sequence Without a League Win: 30, 22.9.1956 – 6.4.1957.

Successive Scoring Runs: 26 from 7.4.1934.

Successive Non-scoring Runs: 9 from 6.11.1974.

MANAGERS

W. C. McNeill 1892–94 (*Secretary-Manager*)
J. G. Hall 1895–96 (*Secretary-Manager*)
R. Roberts (*1st team Secretary-Manager*) 1897
J. B. Blomerley 1898–1911 (*Secretary-Manager, continued as Hon. Secretary to 1925*)
Tom Bailey (*Secretary only*) 1925–38
George Lillycrop (*Trainer*) 1938–44
Frank Hill 1944–48
Arthur Turner 1948–51
Harry Catterick 1951–53
Ralph Ward 1953–55
Maurice Lindley 1956–57
Willie Cook 1957–58
Harry Ware 1958–60
Jimmy McGuigan 1960–64
Ernie Tagg 1964–71 (*continued as Secretary to 1972*)
Dennis Viollet 1971
Jimmy Melia 1972–74
Ernie Tagg 1974
Harry Gregg 1975–78
Warwick Rimmer 1978–79
Tony Waddington 1979–81
Arfon Griffiths 1981–82
Peter Morris 1982–83
Dario Gradi 1983–2007
Steve Holland 2007–08
Gudjon Thordarson 2008–09
Dario Gradi 2009–11
Steve Davis October 2011–

TEN YEAR LEAGUE RECORD

		P	W	D	L	F	A	Pts	Pos
2002-03	Div 2	46	25	11	10	76	40	86	2
2003-04	Div 1	46	14	11	21	57	66	53	18
2004-05	FL C	46	12	14	20	66	86	50	21
2005-06	FL C	46	9	15	22	57	86	42	22
2006-07	FL 1	46	17	9	20	66	72	60	13
2007-08	FL 1	46	12	14	20	47	65	50	20
2008-09	FL 1	46	12	10	24	59	82	46	22
2009-10	FL 2	46	15	10	21	68	73	55	18
2010-11	FL 2	46	18	11	17	87	65	65	10
2011-12	FL 2	46	20	12	14	67	59	72	7

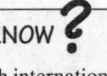

DID YOU KNOW

Legendary Welsh international centre-half Fred Keenor was never a prolific goalscorer in his career with Cardiff City and Crewe Alexandra, but had originally started as an inside-forward and actually played in the first schoolboy international for Wales occupying the right-wing berth.

CREWE ALEXANDRA 2011–12 LEAGUE RECORD

Match No.	Date	Venue	Opponents	Result	H/T Score	Lg Pos.	Goalscorers	Attendance
1	Aug 6	A	Swindon T	L 0-3	0-1	—		8249
2	13	H	Gillingham	L 1-2	0-2	23	Miller [74]	3401
3	16	H	Rotherham U	L 1-2	0-1	—	Moore [74]	3458
4	20	A	Shrewsbury T	L 0-2	0-1	24		5050
5	27	A	Plymouth Arg	W 1-0	1-0	22	Miller [42]	5720
6	Sept 3	H	Oxford U	W 3-1	2-0	20	Miller 2 [30, 37], Leitch-Smith [65]	3680
7	10	H	Barnet	W 3-1	1-0	16	Murphy [27], Miller [55], Dugdale [90]	3142
8	13	A	Burton Alb	L 0-1	0-1	—		2246
9	17	A	Accrington S	W 2-0	2-0	15	Leitch-Smith [11], Moore [14]	1503
10	24	H	Port Vale	D 1-1	0-0	16	Moore [72]	6613
11	Oct 1	A	Dagenham & R	L 1-2	0-0	19	Moore [75]	1725
12	8	H	Southend U	L 1-3	0-1	19	Davis [75]	3808
13	15	A	AFC Wimbledon	W 3-1	0-0	15	Powell [46], Dugdale [79], Leitch-Smith [88]	4604
14	22	H	Macclesfield T	L 0-1	0-1	16		3877
15	25	A	Cheltenham T	W 1-0	0-0	—	Davis (pen) [54]	3089
16	29	A	Aldershot T	L 1-3	1-1	17	Leitch-Smith [30]	2552
17	Nov 5	H	Torquay U	L 0-3	0-1	18		3521
18	19	A	Morecambe	W 2-1	0-0	16	Powell [79], Clayton [90]	2169
19	26	H	Hereford U	W 1-0	0-0	15	Powell [60]	3591
20	Dec 10	A	Northampton T	D 1-1	0-1	16	Moore [61]	4579
21	17	H	Crawley T	D 1-1	1-1	14	Fletcher [9]	3635
22	26	A	Bradford C	L 0-3	0-1	15		11,060
23	31	A	Bristol R	W 5-2	4-1	15	Leitch-Smith [2], Bolger (og) [27], Powell 2 [33, 90], Artell [45]	5037
24	Jan 2	H	Morecambe	L 0-1	0-1	15		3840
25	7	H	Plymouth Arg	W 3-2	2-0	—	Murphy 2 [20, 44], Westwood (pen) [53]	3707
26	14	A	Oxford U	W 1-0	0-0	13	Pearson [89]	7052
27	21	H	Dagenham & R	W 4-1	1-1	11	Pearson [41], Ogogo (og) [71], Dugdale [83], Powell [86]	3282
28	28	A	Barnet	L 0-2	0-1	12		2263
29	Feb 14	H	Burton Alb	W 3-2	1-0	—	Shelley [30], Westwood [55], Murphy [87]	3157
30	18	A	Southend U	L 0-1	0-0	12		5645
31	21	H	Accrington S	W 2-0	0-0	—	Clayton [81], Murphy [90]	3179
32	25	H	AFC Wimbledon	D 3-3	3-1	9	Moore [10], Powell [11], Pearson [31]	4240
33	28	A	Port Vale	D 1-1	0-0	—	Moore [80]	6356
34	Mar 3	H	Shrewsbury T	D 1-1	1-1	10	Powell [22]	5086
35	6	A	Rotherham U	D 1-1	1-0	—	Davis (pen) [16]	2447
36	10	A	Gillingham	W 4-3	1-0	9	Powell 2 [27, 53], Leitch-Smith [52], Clayton [90]	5428
37	17	H	Swindon T	W 2-0	1-0	9	Powell [29], Westwood [65]	4641
38	20	H	Bradford C	W 1-0	1-0	—	Davis (pen) [22]	3556
39	24	A	Hereford U	W 1-0	0-0	8	Murphy [79]	2326
40	31	H	Northampton T	D 1-1	1-0	8	Murphy [17]	4893
41	Apr 6	A	Crawley T	D 1-1	1-0	8	Moore [29]	4723
42	9	H	Bristol R	W 3-0	2-0	8	Leitch-Smith [2], Mellor [6], Davis (pen) [49]	4139
43	14	A	Macclesfield T	D 2-2	1-1	8	Powell 2 [40, 58]	3434
44	21	H	Cheltenham T	W 1-0	1-0	7	Artell [44]	5495
45	28	A	Torquay U	D 1-1	0-0	7	Powell [90]	3802
46	May 5	H	Aldershot T	D 2-2	1-2	7	Leitch-Smith [4], Murphy [76]	6919

Final League Position: 7

GOALSCORERS

League (67): Powell 14, Leitch-Smith 8, Moore 8, Murphy 8, Davis 5 (4 pens), Miller 5, Clayton 3, Dugdale 3, Pearson 3, Westwood 3 (1 pen), Artell 2, Fletcher 1, Mellor 1, Shelley 1, own goals 2.
Carling Cup (2): Artell 1, Miller 1.
FA Cup (1): Moore 1.
J Paint Trophy (2): Clayton 1, Powell 1.
Play-Offs (5): Clayton 1, Dugdale 1, Leitch-Smith 1, Moore 1, Powell 1.

Phillips S 46	Tootle M 36 + 1	Davis H 39 + 2	Westwood A 39 + 2	Artell D 31 + 1	Dugdale A 43	Bell L 22 + 8	Powell N 34 + 4	Miller S 26 + 7	Shelley D 12 + 14	Moore B 42	Leitch-Smith A 31 + 7	Clayton M 1 + 23	Martin C 26 + 3	Murphy L 39 + 3	Hughes C — + 4	Sarcevic A 1 + 5	Mellor K 6 + 6	Turton O — + 2	Lowry J 9 + 1	Fletcher W 3 + 3	Pearson G 8 + 1	Tunnicliffe J 2	Brown J 2 + 5	Bodin B 8	Match No.
1	2	3	4	5	6	7	8	9^{2}	10^{1}	11	12	13													1
1		3	4	5	6	7	8^{1}	9^{3}	12	11	13	14	2	10^{2}											2
1			4	5	6	7	13	9	10^{2}	11	8^{1}	12	2	3											3
1		3	4	5	6	7^{2}	12■	9		11^{1}	10	13	2	8											4
1		3^{3}	4	5	6	7		9^{2}	10		11^{1}	12	2	8	13	14									5
1	13	3	4	5	6	7		9	10^{3}		11^{1}		2^{2}	8	12		14								6
1	2	3	4		6	7		9	12	11	10^{1}		5	8											7
1	2	3			6	7^{2}		9	10^{1}	11	8	12	5	4	13										8
1	2	3	4		6	7		9^{1}	12	11^{3}	10^{2}		5	8		13	14								9
1	2	3	4		6	7^{1}		9	12	11^{2}	10		5	8			13								10
1	2	3	4		6		8^{1}	9		11	10		5	7	12										11
1	2	3	4		6	13	7	9^{1}		11^{2}	10	12	5	8											12
1	2	3	4		6	13	7^{3}	9^{1}		11	10^{2}	12	5	8				14							13
1	2	3	4		6		7^{1}	9		11	10		5	8		12									14
1	2	3		13	6	7	11^{2}	9^{1}	12	10			5	8		4									15
1	2	3	4		6	7^{1}	13	9	14	11	10^{2}		5	8^{3}		12									16
1	2	3	4		6	7^{2}	12	9		11	10^{1}		5	8		13									17
1	2	13		5	6	7	4^{2}	9^{1}		11	10	12	3	8											18
1	2	13		5	6	7	8^{3}	9	14	11	10^{2}		3						4^{1}	12					19
1	2			5	6	7	8	12		11	10^{2}	13	3						4	9^{1}					20
1	2		12	5	6	7	8^{2}	9■		11	13		3						4	10^{1}					21
1	2		12	5	6	8	7^{3}			11	13	9^{1}	3	14					4	10^{2}					22
1	2	3	4	5	6	7^{2}	9			11	10^{1}			13					8	12					23
1	2	3	4	5	6	7^{2}	9^{1}			11	10^{3}	12		13					8	14					24
1	2	3	4	5	6	7	9	12		11	10^{2}			8^{1}					13						25
1	2	3	4	5	6		9		10^{1}	11				8					7		12				26
1	2	3	4	5	6		7			11	12			8					10		9^{1}				27
1	2	3	4	5■	6■		7^{2}		14	11	13		12	8					10^{3}		9^{1}				28
1	2	3	4				10^{3}	9	7^{2}	11^{1}		13	5	8			14	12				6			29
1	2	11	4	5		12	7	9^{2}				13	3	8							10	6^{1}			30
1	2	3	4	5		7^{1}	11	9^{2}	12			13	6	8							10				31
1	2	3	4	5	6	12	9^{2}	14	7^{1}	11			13	8							10^{3}				32
1	2	3	4	5	6		9	12	7^{2}	11			13	8							10^{1}				33
1	2	3	4		6		7	9^{2}	12	11		13	5	8							10^{1}				34
1	2^{1}	3	4	5	6			9^{2}	13	11	14		7	8							10^{3}		12		35
1	2	3	4	5	6		9		7^{1}	11	10^{2}	13		8									12		36
1	2	3	4	5	6		9^{3}	14	7^{1}	11	10^{2}	13		8									12		37
1	2^{1}	3	4	5	6		9		7	11	10			8									12		38
1		3^{1}	4	5	6		9		14	11	10^{2}	13		8			12						2	7^{3}	39
1			4	5	6		9	13	12	11	10^{2}			8			7						3	2^{1}	40
1		3	4	5	6	12	9^{1}			11	10			8			2							7	41
1		3	4	5	6		9		12	11^{1}	10^{2}	13		8			2						14	7^{3}	42
1		3	4	5	6		9	12		11	10^{2}	13		8			2							7^{1}	43
1	2	3	4^{3}	5^{1}	6	14		9^{2}		11	10	13		8			12							7	44
1	2	3	4^{1}		6	12	9			11	10	13		8			5							7^{2}	45
1	2	3	4^{2}		6	13	9			11	10	12		8			5							7^{1}	46

FA Cup

First Round	Colchester U	(h)	1-4

Carling Cup

First Round	Preston NE	(a)	2-3

J Paint Trophy

First Round	Bury	(a)	0-0
Second Round	Macclesfield T	(h)	1-0
Northern Quarter-Final	Oldham Ath	(a)	1-3

Play-Offs

Semi-Final	Southend U	(h)	1-0
		(a)	2-2
Final *(at Wembley).*	Cheltenham T		2-0

CRYSTAL PALACE FL Championship

FOUNDATION

There was a Crystal Palace club as early as 1861 but the present organisation was born in 1905 after the formation of a club by the company that controlled the Crystal Palace (building) had been rejected by the FA, who did not like the idea of the Cup Final hosts running their own club. A separate company had to be formed and they had their home on the old Cup Final ground until 1915.

Selhurst Park Stadium, Whitehorse Lane, London SE25 6PU.

Telephone: (020) 8768 6000.

Fax: (020) 8771 5311.

Ticket Office: (0871) 200 0071.

Website: www.cpfc.co.uk

Email: info@cpfc.co.uk

Ground Capacity: 26,225.

Record Attendance: 51,482 v Burnley, Division 2, 11 May 1979 (at Selhurst Park).

Pitch Measurements: 110yd × 74yd.

Co-Chairmen: Steve Parish and Martin Long.

Chief Executive: Phil Alexander.

Manager: Dougie Freedman.

Assistant Manager: Lennie Lawrence.

Physio: Alex Manos.

Colours: Red and blue striped shirts, blue shorts, blue stockings.

Year Formed: 1905.

Turned Professional: 1905.

Club Nickname: 'The Eagles'.

Grounds: 1905, Crystal Palace; 1915, Herne Hill; 1918, The Nest; 1924, Selhurst Park.

First Football League Game: 28 August 1920, Division 3, v Merthyr T (a) L 1–2 – Alderson; Little, Rhodes; McCracken, Jones, Feebury; Bateman, Conner, Smith, Milligan (1), Whibley.

Record League Victory: 9–0 v Barrow, Division 4, 10 October 1959 – Rouse; Long, Noakes; Truett, Evans, McNichol; Gavin (1), Summersby (4 incl. 1p), Sexton, Byrne (2), Colfar (2).

Record Cup Victory: 8–0 v Southend U, Rumbelows League Cup 2nd rd (1st leg), 25 September 1990 – Martyn; Humphrey (Thompson (1)), Shaw, Pardew, Young, Thorn, McGoldrick, Thomas, Bright (3), Wright (3), Barber (Hodges (1)).

Record Defeat: 0–9 v Burnley, FA Cup 2nd rd replay, 10 February 1909; 0–9 v Liverpool, Division 1, 12 September 1990.

HONOURS

Football League –
Division 1: ***Champions*** 1993–94;
Division 2: ***Champions*** 1978–79; ***Runners-up*** 1968–69;
Division 3: ***Runners-up*** 1963–64;
Division 3 (S): ***Champions*** 1920–21; ***Runners-up*** 1928–29, 1930–31, 1938–39;
Division 4: ***Runners-up*** 1960–61.

FA Cup: ***Runners-up*** 1990.

Football League Cup: Semi-final 1993, 1995, 2001.

Zenith Data Systems Cup: ***Winners*** 1991.

European Competition Intertoto Cup: 1998.

sky SPORTS FACT FILE

Former Tottenham Hotspur forward George Payne had a useful goalscoring season for Crystal Palace in 1909–10 registering 25 goals in only 34 Southern League matches. Twenty-one of these came before Christmas. He scored 30 in 45 games plus one in the FA Cup in two seasons.

Most League Points (2 for a win): 64, Division 4, 1960–61.

Most League Points (3 for a win): 90, Division 1, 1993–94.

Most League Goals: 110, Division 4, 1960–61.

Highest League Scorer in Season: Peter Simpson, 46, Division 3 (S), 1930–31.

Most League Goals in Total Aggregate: Peter Simpson, 153, 1930–36.

Most League Goals in One Match: 6, Peter Simpson v Exeter C, Division 3 (S), 4 October 1930.

Most Capped Player: Aleksandrs Kolinko, 23 (86), Latvia.

Most League Appearances: Jim Cannon, 571, 1973–88.

Youngest League Player: John Bostock, 15 years 287 days v Watford, 29 October 2007.

Record Transfer Fee Received: £8,500,000 from Everton for Andy Johnson, May 2006.

Record Transfer Fee Paid: £2,750,000 to RC Strasbourg for Valerien Ismael, January 1998.

Football League Record: 1920 Original Members of Division 3; 1921–25 Division 2; 1925–58 Division 3 (S); 1958–61 Division 4; 1961–64 Division 3; 1964–69 Division 2; 1969–73 Division 1; 1973–74 Division 2; 1974–77 Division 3; 1977–79 Division 2; 1979–81 Division 1; 1981–89 Division 2; 1989–92 Division 1; 1992–93 FA Premier League; 1993–94 Division 1; 1994–95 FA Premier League; 1995–97 Division 1; 1997–98 FA Premier League; 1998–2004 Division 1; 2004–05 FA Premier League; 2005– FL C.

LATEST SEQUENCES

Longest Sequence of League Wins: 8, 9.2.1921 – 26.3.1921.

Longest Sequence of League Defeats: 8, 10.1.1998 – 14.3.1998.

Longest Sequence of League Draws: 5, 21.9.2002 – 19.10.2002.

Longest Sequence of Unbeaten League Matches: 18, 22.2.1969 – 13.8.1969.

Longest Sequence Without a League Win: 20, 3.3.1962 – 8.9.1962.

Successive Scoring Runs: 24 from 27.4.1929.

Successive Non-scoring Runs: 9 from 19.11.1994.

MANAGERS

John T. Robson 1905–07
Edmund Goodman 1907–25 (*Secretary 1905–1933*)
Alex Maley 1925–27
Fred Mavin 1927–30
Jack Tresadern 1930–35
Tom Bromilow 1935–36
R. S. Moyes 1936
Tom Bromilow 1936–39
George Irwin 1939–47
Jack Butler 1947–49
Ronnie Rooke 1949–50
Charlie Slade and Fred Dawes (*Joint Managers*) 1950–51
Laurie Scott 1951–54
Cyril Spiers 1954–58
George Smith 1958–60
Arthur Rowe 1960–62
Dick Graham 1962–66
Bert Head 1966–72 (*continued as General Manager to 1973*)
Malcolm Allison 1973–76
Terry Venables 1976–80
Ernie Walley 1980
Malcolm Allison 1980–81
Dario Gradi 1981
Steve Kember 1981–82
Alan Mullery 1982–84
Steve Coppell 1984–93
Alan Smith 1993–95
Steve Coppell (*Technical Director*) 1995–96
Dave Bassett 1996–97
Steve Coppell 1997–98
Attilio Lombardo 1998
Terry Venables (*Head Coach*) 1998–99
Steve Coppell 1999–2000
Alan Smith 2000–01
Steve Bruce 2001
Trevor Francis 2001–03
Steve Kember 2003
Iain Dowie 2003–06
Peter Taylor 2006–07
Neil Warnock 2007–10
Paul Hart 2010
George Burley 2010–11
Dougie Freedman January 2011–

TEN YEAR LEAGUE RECORD

		P	*W*	*D*	*L*	*F*	*A*	*Pts*	*Pos*
2002-03	Div 1	46	14	17	15	59	52	59	14
2003-04	Div 1	46	21	10	15	72	61	73	6
2004-05	PR Lge	38	7	12	19	41	62	33	18
2005-06	FL C	46	21	12	13	67	48	75	6
2006-07	FL C	46	18	11	17	59	51	65	12
2007-08	FL C	46	18	17	11	58	42	71	5
2008-09	FL C	46	15	12	19	52	55	57	15
2009-10	FL C	46	14	17	15	50	53	49*	21
2010-11	FL C	46	12	12	22	44	69	48	20
2011-12	FL C	46	13	17	16	46	51	56	17

** 10 pts deducted.*

DID YOU KNOW ?

In 1923–24 Crystal Palace had already sent Tottenham Hotspur packing in the FA Cup when they faced another First Division team Notts County. Three attempts between the two teams failed to produce a goal until a second visit to neutral Villa Park witnessed a 2-1 win for Palace.

CRYSTAL PALACE 2011–12 LEAGUE RECORD

Match No.	Date	Venue	Opponents	Result		H/T Score	Lg Pos.	Goalscorers	Attendance
1	Aug 6	A	Peterborough U	L	1-2	1-0	—	Scannell 33	11,604
2	13	H	Burnley	W	2-0	1-0	10	Parr 10, Garvan (pen) 67	13,167
3	16	H	Coventry C	W	2-1	0-0	—	Scannell 89, Easter 90	12,330
4	20	A	Hull C	W	1-0	1-0	5	Chester (og) 15	17,797
5	27	H	Blackpool	D	1-1	0-1	6	Murray 79	14,776
6	Sept 10	A	Leeds U	L	2-3	2-1	8	McCarthy 12, Scannell 21	23,916
7	17	H	Middlesbrough	L	0-1	0-0	12		15,198
8	24	A	Doncaster R	L	0-1	0-0	12		9362
9	27	A	Brighton & HA	W	3-1	0-1	—	Zaha 80, Ambrose 89, Murray 90	20,968
10	Oct 1	H	West Ham U	D	2-2	1-1	12	Ambrose 6, Murray 52	20,074
11	15	A	Watford	W	2-0	0-0	8	Zaha 66, Easter 90	12,559
12	18	H	Bristol C	W	1-0	0-0	—	Murray (pen) 81	11,869
13	22	A	Ipswich T	W	1-0	0-0	3	McCarthy 55	24,763
14	29	H	Reading	D	0-0	0-0	3		21,002
15	Nov 1	H	Portsmouth	D	0-0	0-0	—		12,933
16	5	A	Cardiff C	L	0-2	0-0	6		22,032
17	20	A	Leicester C	L	0-3	0-0	9		22,449
18	26	H	Millwall	D	0-0	0-0	10		15,150
19	Dec 2	H	Derby Co	D	1-1	1-0	—	Martin 15	14,338
20	6	A	Barnsley	L	1-2	1-1	—	Easter 33	9524
21	10	A	Nottingham F	W	1-0	0-0	11	Murray 56	21,405
22	19	H	Birmingham C	W	1-0	0-0	—	Dikgacoi 84	12,057
23	26	A	Southampton	L	0-2	0-1	10		31,524
24	31	A	Millwall	W	1-0	1-0	8	Easter 23	16,085
25	Jan 2	H	Leicester C	L	1-2	1-2	11	Parr 41	14,468
26	14	H	Leeds U	D	1-1	1-0	13	Martin 6	17,796
27	21	A	Blackpool	L	1-2	1-0	13	Garvan (pen) 27	12,053
28	31	H	Brighton & HA	D	1-1	0-0	—	Martin (pen) 64	17,271
29	Feb 4	A	Middlesbrough	D	0-0	0-0	14		15,725
30	14	A	Bristol C	D	2-2	1-0	—	Zaha 14, Ambrose (pen) 69	12,470
31	18	H	Watford	W	4-0	2-0	12	Zaha 22, Martin 2 38, 50, Dikgacoi 64	13,324
32	25	A	West Ham U	D	0-0	0-0	13		34,900
33	Mar 3	H	Peterborough U	W	1-0	0-0	13	Jedinak 76	18,559
34	6	A	Coventry C	D	1-1	1-0	—	Ambrose (pen) 40	12,054
35	10	A	Burnley	D	1-1	0-1	11	Ambrose (pen) 63	13,216
36	17	H	Hull C	D	0-0	0-0	13		13,324
37	20	H	Barnsley	W	1-0	0-0	—	Scannell 90	11,853
38	24	A	Derby Co	L	2-3	0-2	14	Martin 79, Ambrose 90	25,222
39	27	H	Doncaster R	D	1-1	0-0	—	Easter 57	13,401
40	31	H	Nottingham F	L	0-3	0-0	15		14,928
41	Apr 7	A	Birmingham C	L	1-3	1-3	16	Garvan 45	21,932
42	9	H	Southampton	L	0-2	0-1	16		18,753
43	14	H	Ipswich T	D	1-1	1-0	16	Martin 36	17,961
44	17	A	Portsmouth	L	1-2	0-1	—	Ambrose (pen) 71	14,847
45	21	A	Reading	D	2-2	1-1	17	Zaha 14, Murray 76	23,431
46	28	H	Cardiff C	L	1-2	1-0	17	Zaha 13	15,510

Final League Position: 17

GOALSCORERS

League (46): Ambrose 7 (4 pens), Martin 7 (1 pen), Murray 6 (1 pen), Zaha 6, Easter 5, Scannell 4, Garvan 3 (2 pens), Dikgacoi 2, McCarthy 2, Parr 2, Jedinak 1, own goal 1.
Carling Cup (11): Ambrose 3, Zaha 3, Andrew 1, Easter 1 (pen), Gardner 1, Murray 1, Williams 1.
FA Cup (0).

Speroni J 42	Ramage P 14 + 3	McGivern R 5	Davies A 1	McCarthy P 42 + 1	Wright D 22	Ambrose D 26 + 10	Dikgacoi K 24 + 3	Scannell S 27 + 10	Murray G 25 + 13	Parr J 35 + 4	Zaha W 34 + 7	Easter J 18 + 15	Garvan O 13 + 9	Tunchev A 9	Andrew C 2 + 4	Jedinak M 29 + 2	Williams J 5 + 9	Dorman A — + 1	Moxey D 20 + 4	Gardner A 25 + 3	Clyne N 28	Iversen S — + 3	Martin C 20 + 6	Keinan D 3	Pedroza A 1 + 3	O'Keefe S 13	Price L 4 + 1	Dumbuya M 2	McShane P 9 + 2	Parsons M 3 + 1	Egan J 1	Sekajja I 1	Cadogan K 1	De Silva K 2 + 4	Marrow A — + 1	Appiah K — + 4	*Match No.*
1	2	3^{3}	4	5	6	7	8	9^{1}	10^{2}	11	12	13	14																								1
1	2	3		5	6	7^{1}	12	9^{3}		8	13	10^{2}	11	4	14																						2
1	2	3^{3}		5	6^{2}		8^{1}	9		7	12	10	11	4		13	14																				3
1	2	3		5	6	13		9^{3}		8	7^{1}	10		4	14	11^{2}		12																			4
1		3^{1}		5	6^{3}	7^{2}		9	13	11	12	10	14	4		8			2																		5
1	2			5	6	13		9^{3}	12	11^{2}	10	8^{1}		4	14	7			3																		6
1	2			5	6^{3}	7^{1}		9	13	11^{2}	12	10		4		8	14		3																		7
1	2			5	6^{2}	7		9^{1}	10		11	12		4		8	13		3																		8
1	2^{1}			5	6^{2}	13		9	10	12	7			4		8	11^{3}		3	14																	9
1	13			5	6	7^{2}		12	10	2	9^{3}	14				8	11^{1}		3	4																	10
1	3			5	6		8^{1}	11^{3}	10	7^{2}	9	14		4		12				13	2																11
1	3^{1}			5	6	7^{2}	14	11^{3}	10	12	9					8	13			4	2																12
1				5	6		8^{1}	11^{2}	10	7	9	13				3	12			4	2																13
1				5	6	12		7^{1}	10	13	9					4	8^{2}		11	3	2																14
1				5	6	7^{2}	8	12	10	11^{1}	9	13							3	4	2																15
1				5	6^{3}		8^{1}	11^{2}	10		9	13				7	12		3	4	2	14															16
1				5	6		8^{2}	12	10	11^{1}	9					7			3	4	2		13														17
1				5		12		11	10^{2}		8	13	6			7			3	4	2		9^{1}														18
1	2			5		11			10	3	12		6		8^{2}	7							9^{1}	4	13												19
1	3			12	6	7	8		10^{3}		11	9^{2}								4	2	14	13	5^{1}													20
1				5	6		12	11^{2}	10	3	9	13				7				4	2					8^{1}											21
1	14			5		7^{2}	4	11^{3}	10	3		12			13	8				6	2		9^{1}														22
1	4^{1}			5			8	11	10^{3}	3	9	14	13							6	2		12			7^{2}											23
	14			5		7	6	12	13	3	11^{1}	10^{2}				8				4	2		9^{3}				1										24
	5					12		11^{2}	10^{3}	3	9	13	6			7					2		14	4		8^{1}	1										25
1				5	6	7	8	11▮	14	3	13	10^{3}								4			9^{2}					2^{1}	12								26
					11								6^{3}		9^{1}							14				10	1	2	5	3	4	7^{2}	8	12	13		27
1						12	6	11^{1}	13	3	7	10^{2}	14			8				4	2		9^{3}						5								28
1				5		7^{1}	6	12		3	11	10				8				4	2		9														29
1				5		7^{3}	6		12	3	11	10^{1}	13			8				4	2		9^{2}						14								30
1				5		7	6	13	12	3	11^{2}	10	14			8^{3}				4	2		9^{1}														31
1				5		7^{1}	6	12	13	3	11	10^{2}	14			8				4			9^{3}						2								32
1				5		7^{2}			12	3	11	10^{1}	6			8			13	4			9						2								33
1				5		7^{1}			12	3	11	10^{2}	6			8			13	4			9^{3}						2							14	34
1				5		7			10	3	11▮					8			12	4	2		9^{1}			6											35
1				5				12	10^{3}	11		14				8	7^{2}		3^{1}	4	2		9			6								13			36
1				5		7^{1}	6	11	10^{2}	3		12				8	13			4	2		9^{3}													14	37
1				5		7	6	11^{2}	10	3^{3}						8^{1}	12		13	4	2		9													14	38
1				5		13	6		14		11	10					7^{2}		3	12^{3}	2		9			8			4^{1}								39
1				5	6^{1}		8	11^{2}	10^{3}	4	9	14	7				12		3		2		13														40
1				5		7^{2}	6	12	14	11	9	10^{1}	4						3		2		13			8^{3}											41
1				5		13	6	11^{2}			10		12						7		2		9			8				3				4^{1}			42
1				5		7^{3}	6^{1}	11^{2}		14	10		12						3		2		9			8			4					13			43
1				5		13		14		11^{2}	10		6						3		2		9^{1}		7^{3}	8			4							12	44
1^{6}				5		7^{2}			10	11	9		6						3						13	8	15		4^{1}	12				2			45
				5		7^{2}		11^{1}	10	2	9		4						6						12	8	1			3				13			46

FA Cup

Third Round	Derby Co	(a)	0-1

Carling Cup

First Round	Crawley T	(h)	2-0
Second Round	Wigan Ath	(h)	2-1
Third Round	Middlesbrough	(h)	2-1
Fourth Round	Southampton	(h)	2-0
Quarter-Final	Manchester U	(a)	2-1
Semi-Final	Cardiff C	(h)	1-0
		(a)	0-1

DAGENHAM & REDBRIDGE FL Championship 2

FOUNDATION

The roots of Dagenham & Redbridge lie firmly in the Essex side of the Greater London area. Though formed only in 1992 their complex origins date back to the 19th century involving Ilford (founded 1881) and Leytonstone (1886) who merged in 1979 to form Leytonstone-Ilford. They and Walthamstow Avenue (1900) joined together in 1988 to become Redbridge Forest who in turn merged with Dagenham FC (1949) in 1992. Victoria Road has existed as a football ground since 1917. Initially used by Sterling Works, in the summer of 1955 Briggs Sports vacated the premises and Dagenham FC moved in and the pitch was enclosed.

The London Borough of Barking and Dagenham Stadium, Victoria Road, Dagenham, Essex RM10 7XL.

Telephone: (020) 8592 1549.

Fax: (020) 8593 7227.

Ticket Office: (020) 8592 1549 (extension 21).

Website: www.daggers.co.uk

Email: info@daggers.co.uk

Ground Capacity: 6,007.

Record Attendance: 4,791 v Shrewsbury T, FL 2, 2 May 2009.

Pitch Measurements: 100m × 64.5m.

Chairman: David J. Andrews.

Vice-chairman: David E. Ward.

Manager: John L. Still.

Assistant Manager: Terry W. Harris.

Physio: John Gowens.

Colours: Red shirts with blue sleeves and red trim, blue shorts, blue stockings.

Year Formed: 1992.

Turned Professional: 1992.

Club Nickname: The Daggers.

Ground: 1992, Victoria Road.

First Football League Game: 11 August 2007, FL 2 v Stockport Co (a) L 0–1 – Roberts; Foster, Griffiths, Rainford, Uddin, Boardman, Saunders (Strevens), Southam, Benson (Moore), Nurse, Sloma (Huke).

Record League Victory: 6–0 v Chester C, FL 2, 9 August 2008 – Roberts; Okuonghae, Griffiths, Arber, Uddin, Taiwo, Saunders (2), Green (1) (Southam), Benson (1) (Nurse), Strevens (1p) (Nwokeji (1)), Gain.

MANAGERS

John Still 1992–94
Dave Cusack 1994–95
Graham Carr 1995–96
Ted Hardy 1996–99
Garry Hill 1999–2004
John Still April 2004–

sky SPORTS FACT FILE

When Anwar Uddin was playing for Dagenham & Redbridge from 2004 he was the only player of Bangladesh origin in the Football League and the first British Asian to captain a team in it. The Whitechapel-born centre-half subsequently joined Barnet.

Record Cup Victory: 6–1 v Stowmarket T, FA Cup 2nd qual rd, 28 September 1992; 6–1 v Wealdstone (a), FA Cup 3rd qual rd, 12 October 1992.

Record Defeat: 0–9 v Hereford U, Conference, 27 February 2004.

Most League Points (3 for a win): 72, FL 2, 2009–10.

Most League Goals: 77, FL 2, 2008–09.

Highest League Scorer in Season: Paul Benson, 28, Conference, 2006–07.

Most League Goals in Total Aggregate: 40, Paul Benson, 2007–.

Most League Goals in One Match: 4, Paul Benson v Shrewsbury T, FL 2, 18 August 2009.

Most Capped Player: Jon Nurse, 6, Barbados.

Most League Appearances: Jon Nurse, 179, 2007–12.

Youngest League Player: Dominic Green, 18 years 93 days v Brentford, 2 October 2007.

Record Transfer Fee Received: £200,000 from Cardiff C for Solomon Taiwo, August 2009.

Record Transfer Fee Paid: £20,000 to Plymouth Arg for Damien McCrory, February 2010.

Football League Record: 2006–07 Promoted from Conference; 2007–10 FL 2; 2010–11 FL 1; 2011– FL 2.

LATEST SEQUENCES

Longest Sequence of League Wins: 5, 12.2.2008 – 1.3.2008.

Longest Sequence of League Defeats: 9, 8.10.2011 – 10.12.2011.

Longest Sequence of League Draws: 3, 21.9.2010 – 28.9.2010.

Longest Sequence of Unbeaten League Matches: 8, 17.3.2012 – 21.4.2012.

Longest Sequence Without a League Win: 10, 8.10.2011 – 17.12.2011.

Successive Scoring Runs: 16 from 12.4.2008.

Successive Non-scoring Runs: 3 from 12.1.2008.

HONOURS

FA Cup: Best season: 3rd rd, 2008, 2012.

Conference: ***Champions*** 2006–07. ***Runners-up*** 2001–02.

Isthmian League (Premier): ***Champions*** 1999–2000.

Essex Senior Cup: ***Winners*** 1997–98, 2000–01; ***Runners-up*** 2001–02.

AS DAGENHAM FC

FA Trophy: ***Winners*** 1979–80; ***Runners-up*** 1976–77.
Amateur Cup: ***Runners-up*** 1969–70, 1970–71.

AS ILFORD

FA Amateur Cup: ***Winners*** 1929, 1930. **Isthmian League:** ***Champions*** 1906–07, 1920–21, 1921–22.

AS LEYTONSTONE

FA Amateur Cup: ***Winners*** 1947, 1948, 1968.
Isthmian League: ***Champions*** 1918–19, 1937–38, 1938–39, 1946–47, 1947–48, 1949–50, 1950–51, 1951–52, 1965–66.

AS LEYTONSTONE/ILFORD

Isthmian League: ***Champions*** 1981–82, 1988–89.

AS WALTHAMSTOW AVENUE

FA Amateur Cup: ***Winners*** 1952, 1961. **Isthmian League:** ***Champions*** 1945–46, 1948–49, 1952–53, 1954–55.
Athenian League: ***Champions*** 1929–30, 1932–33, 1933–34, 1937–38, 1938–39.

AS REDBRIDGE FOREST

Isthmian League: ***Winners*** 1990–91.

TEN YEAR LEAGUE RECORD

		P	*W*	*D*	*L*	*F*	*A*	*Pts*	*Pos*
2002-03	Conf	42	21	9	12	71	59	72	5
2003-04	Conf	42	15	9	18	59	64	54	13
2004-05	Conf	42	19	8	15	68	60	65	11
2005-06	Conf	42	16	19	16	63	59	58	10
2006-07	Conf	46	28	11	7	93	48	95	1
2007-08	FL 2	46	13	10	23	49	70	49	20
2008-09	FL 2	46	19	11	16	77	53	68	8
2009-10	FL 2	46	20	12	14	69	58	72	7
2010-11	FL 1	46	12	11	23	52	70	47	21
2011-12	FL 2	46	14	8	24	50	72	50	19

DID YOU KNOW ?

On 7 September 2011, Dagenham & Redbridge won a marathon Johnstone's Paint Trophy penalty shootout 14-13 against neighbours Leyton Orient after a 1-1 draw. Only one shot was saved – the very last attempt – and this by on-loan goalkeeper James Shea.

DAGENHAM & REDBRIDGE 2011–12 LEAGUE RECORD

Match No.	Date	Venue	Opponents	Result		H/T Score	Lg Pos.	Goalscorers	Attendance
1	Aug 6	A	Macclesfield T	W	1-0	0-0	—	Elito [60]	1566
2	13	H	AFC Wimbledon	L	0-2	0-1	15		2904
3	16	H	Swindon T	W	1-0	0-0	—	Arber (pen) [70]	2063
4	20	A	Bradford C	W	1-0	1-0	5	Nurse [27]	9594
5	27	H	Torquay U	D	1-1	1-0	5	Williams [25]	2012
6	Sept 3	A	Hereford U	L	0-1	0-0	8		1885
7	10	A	Rotherham U	L	1-3	1-3	11	Doe [21]	3286
8	13	H	Oxford U	L	0-1	0-1	—		1921
9	17	H	Morecambe	L	1-2	0-0	19	Lee [73]	1728
10	24	A	Northampton T	L	1-2	0-1	20	Lee [90]	4274
11	Oct 1	H	Crewe Alex	W	2-1	0-0	20	Williams [76], Rose [90]	1725
12	8	A	Cheltenham T	L	1-2	1-1	20	Nurse [45]	2814
13	15	H	Plymouth Arg	L	2-3	0-1	20	Doe [58], Nurse [68]	2025
14	22	H	Aldershot T	L	2-5	1-4	21	Nurse [43], McCrory [80]	1796
15	25	A	Crawley T	L	1-3	1-2	—	Lee [9]	2862
16	29	A	Bristol R	L	0-2	0-0	22		5475
17	Nov 5	H	Shrewsbury T	L	0-2	0-1	22		1726
18	19	H	Southend U	L	2-3	1-2	23	Montano [13], Ogogo [49]	3259
19	26	A	Accrington S	L	0-3	0-0	23		1308
20	Dec 10	H	Port Vale	L	1-2	1-1	24	Woodall [23]	1682
21	17	A	Burton Alb	D	1-1	1-0	24	Spillane [26]	2658
22	26	H	Barnet	W	3-0	2-0	22	Montano 2 [14, 45], Woodall [63]	2135
23	30	H	Gillingham	W	2-1	1-1	—	Bingham [22], Woodall [65]	3120
24	Jan 2	A	Southend U	D	1-1	0-1	22	Woodall [87]	7564
25	14	H	Hereford U	L	0-1	0-1	22		1732
26	21	A	Crewe Alex	L	1-4	1-1	23	Woodall [17]	3282
27	24	A	Torquay U	L	0-1	0-1	—		2280
28	28	H	Rotherham U	W	3-2	0-1	22	Nurse [50], Bradley (og) [62], Doe [78]	1744
29	Feb 14	A	Oxford U	L	1-2	0-0	—	Arber [72]	5653
30	18	H	Cheltenham T	L	0-5	0-3	24		1516
31	25	A	Plymouth Arg	D	0-0	0-0	24		7804
32	28	A	Morecambe	W	2-1	1-1	—	Elito [13], Scott [71]	1246
33	Mar 3	H	Bradford C	W	1-0	0-0	22	Saunders [71]	3041
34	6	A	Swindon T	L	0-4	0-1	—		6839
35	10	A	AFC Wimbledon	L	1-2	0-0	24	Spillane [83]	4243
36	13	H	Northampton T	L	0-1	0-0	—		2164
37	17	H	Macclesfield T	W	2-0	1-0	24	Elito 2 [16, 90]	1446
38	20	A	Barnet	D	2-2	1-1	—	Spillane [25], Doe [72]	1725
39	24	H	Accrington S	W	2-1	0-1	21	Woodall [85], Doe [90]	1476
40	31	A	Port Vale	W	1-0	0-0	19	Spillane [65]	4127
41	Apr 6	H	Burton Alb	D	1-1	0-0	20	Woodall [88]	2035
42	9	A	Gillingham	W	2-1	1-0	19	Woodall [38], Green, Dominic [73]	5773
43	14	A	Aldershot T	D	1-1	0-0	19	Doe [60]	2393
44	21	H	Crawley T	D	1-1	1-1	19	Bingham [45]	2456
45	28	A	Shrewsbury T	L	0-1	0-1	20		9441
46	May 5	H	Bristol R	W	4-0	1-0	19	Woodall 3 [24, 54, 81], Green, Danny J [64]	2377

Final League Position: 19

GOALSCORERS

League (50): Woodall 11, Doe 6, Nurse 5, Elito 4, Spillane 4, Lee 3, Montano 3, Arber 2 (1 pen), Bingham 2, Williams 2, Green, Danny J 1, Green, Dominic 1, McCrory 1, Ogogo 1, Rose 1, Saunders 1, Scott 1, own goal 1.
Carling Cup (0).
FA Cup (5): Nurse 3, Woodall 2.
J Paint Trophy (2): McCrory 1, Williams 1.

Lewington C 41	Ogogo A 40	McCrory D 32+1	Howell L 10	Doe S 41	Arber M 32+1	Elito M 20+4	Lee O 15+1	Nurse J 36+3	Williams S 10	Tomlin G 15+2 / Akinde J 4+1	Shea J —+1	Reed J 1+6	Walsh P 4+4	Woodall B 26+13	Rose R 9+1	Green Danny J 4+4	Scannell D 7+7	Gain P 16+4	Bingham B 17+10	Ilesanmi F 17	Hewitt T 3+3	Maher K 8 / Wassmer C —+1	Green Dominic 8+8	Spillane M 29	Montano C 10	Scott J 12+8	Cunnington A 2+7	Geohaghon E 1+1	Abdullah A 4+1	Wearen E —+2	Saunders M 5	Hogan D —+1	Bond J 5	Reeves B 5	Edmans R —+3	Baudry M 11	Parker J 6+2	*Match No.*
1■	2	3	4	5	6	7[6]	8	9	10	11	15																											1
1	2[1]	3[2]	4	5	6	13	8	9	10	11		7[3]	12	14																								2
1		3	4	5	6	7[1]	8	9		10[2]		13		11	2	12																						3
1	2	3	4	5	6	7	8	9[1]	10	11[2]				13			12																					4
1	2	3	4[1]	5	6		8	9	10	11[2]				13		7[3]	14	12																				5
1	2	3	4[1]	5			8		10	9		13	6			7[2]	11	12																				6
1	2	3		5	12		8	13	10	11			6[1]				9	4	7[2]																			7
1	2			5	6		8	9	10	13				12			11[2]	4	7[1]	3																		8
1		13		5	6		8	9	10	11[2]			14	12	2[3]		7[1]	4		3																		9
1	2			5	6		8	9	10				13	7[1]		12	11[2]	4		3																		10
1		3		5	6		8	9	10[2]	7					2	13	11[1]	4			12																	11
1	2	3		5	6		8	9		11				12			7	4[2]	13		10[1]																	12
1	2	3■		5	6		8[1]	9		7				10[2]			12	11			13	4																13
1	2	3		5	4		14	9		11[3]				10[1]		7[2]	13	8			12	6																14
1	2	3		5■	4		7	9		11[1]			12				13	8[3]	14		10	6[2]																15
1	2	3			5		7[1]	9		11			4	12			13	8			10[2]	6																16
1	2	3		5■		11[2]		9						10[3]	6	7[1]	12	8	14	4			13															17
1	2	3						9					5	10[2]	7[1]			8		6			12	4	11	13												18
1	2	3		5				9		13				10[1]				8		6				4	11	12	7[2]											19
1	2			5		12		9		7[1]				10[2]				4		3				11		8	13	6										20
1	2■			6				13						9[1]	5			11	12	3		4		7	10[3]	8[2]	14											21
1				5				13						9	2			11[1]	12	3		6	7	4	10[3]	8[2]	14											22
1				4				9						10	2				8	3		6	7	5	11													23
1				4				9						10	2				8	3		6[1]	7	5	11			12										24
1	2			4				9[1]				12		10					6[2]	3			8	5	11				7	13								25
1	2			4				9						10[1]					6	3			7[2]	5	11		12		8	13								26
1	2			4	6			9				12							8[1]	3				5	11		10		7									27
1	2			5	6			9						10[2]					4	3				8	11	12	13		7[1]									28
1	2			5	6	13		9				14							4[1]	3			7[2]	11		10[3]	12				8							29
1■	7[2]			5	4	11[6]		9						8[1]	13					3				2		10	12				6	15						30
	7	3		5	6	12		9						10[1]										2		8					4		1	11[2]	13			31
	7	3		5	6	11[2]		9						12					13					2		8[1]					4		1	10				32
	7	3		5	6	11		9						12					13					2		10					4[2]		1	8[1]				33
	7	3		5	6	11[2]		9						12					4				13	2		10■							1	8[1]				34
	7	3		5	6	11[2]		9						10					4				12	2									1	8[1]	13			35
1	7	3	4		6	11[2]		9						10[1]									13	2											12	5	8	36
1	7	3	4[1]		6	11		9		10[2]				13					12					2												5	8	37
1	7	3		5	6	11		9		10[2]				13										2		12										4	8[1]	38
1	7	3		5	6	11		9[2]		10[3]				14					12					2		13										4	8[1]	39
1	2	3		5	6	11		9						10[2]					8			12		7		13										4[1]		40
1	2	3[3]		5	6	11				10[1]				9					14				8[2]	7		12										4	13	41
1	2	3		5	6	11[3]				14				9[2]					8				12	7		13										4	10[1]	42
1	2	3		5	6	11								10					8				9[1]	7												4	12	43
1	2	3		5	6	11								9					8				12	7		10[1]										4		44
1	2	3	6	5		11[2]								9[3]				12	8[1]				13	7		10			14							4		45
1	2	3	6[2]			11						13		9		12		14	8					5		10[3]										4	7[1]	46

FA Cup

First Round	Bath C	(h)	1-1
		(a)	3-1
Second Round	Walsall	(h)	1-1
		(a)	0-0
Third Round	Millwall	(h)	0-0
		(a)	0-5

Carling Cup

First Round	Bournemouth	(a)	0-5

J Paint Trophy

First Round	Leyton Orient	(a)	1-1
Second Round	Southend U	(h)	1-3

DERBY COUNTY FL Championship

FOUNDATION

Derby County was formed by members of the Derbyshire County Cricket Club in 1884, when football was booming in the area and the cricketers thought that a football club would help boost finances for the summer game. To begin with, they sported the cricket club's colours of amber, chocolate and pale blue, and went into the game at the top immediately entering the FA Cup.

Pride Park Stadium, Derby DE24 8XL.

Telephone: (0871) 472 1884.

Fax: (01332) 667 519.

Ticket Office: (0871) 472 1884.

Website: www.dcfc.co.uk

Email: derby.county@dcfc.co.uk

Ground Capacity: 33,597.

Record Attendance: 41,826 v Tottenham H, Division 1, 20 September 1969 (at Baseball Ground); 33,597, England v Mexico, 25 May 2001 (at Pride Park).

Pitch Measurements: 100.58m × 67.66m.

Chairman of GSC and Club Chairman: Andy Appleby.

President and Chief Executive: Tom Glick.

Manager: Nigel Clough.

Coaches: Gary Crosby, Andy Garner, Martin Taylor, Johnny Metgod.

Physio: Neil Sullivan.

Colours: White shirts with black trim, black shorts with white trim, white stockings with black trimz

Year Formed: 1884.

Turned Professional: 1884.

Club Nickname: 'The Rams'.

HONOURS

Football League – Division 1: ***Champions*** 1971–72, 1974–75; ***Runners-up*** 1895–96, 1929–30, 1935–36, 1995–96;
Division 2: *Champions* 1911–12, 1914–15, 1968–69, 1986–87; ***Runners-up*** 1925–26;
Division 3 (N): *Champions* 1956–57; ***Runners-up*** 1955–56.

FA Cup: *Winners* 1946; ***Runners-up*** 1898, 1899, 1903.

Football League Cup: Semi-final 1968, 2009.

Texaco Cup: *Winners* 1972.

European Competitions
European Cup: 1972–73, 1975–76.
UEFA Cup: 1974–75, 1976–77.
Anglo-Italian Cup: *Runners-up* 1993.

Grounds: 1884, Racecourse Ground; 1895, Baseball Ground; 1997, Pride Park.

First Football League Game: 8 September 1888, Football League, v Bolton W (a) W 6–3 – Marshall; Latham, Ferguson, Williamson; Monks, Walter Roulstone; Bakewell (2), Cooper (2), Higgins, Harry Plackett, Lol Plackett (2).

Record League Victory: 9–0 v Wolverhampton W, Division 1, 10 January 1891 – Bunyan; Archie Goodall, Roberts; Walker, Chalmers, Walter Roulstone (1); Bakewell, McLachlan, Johnny Goodall (1), Holmes (2), McMillan (5). 9–0 v Sheffield W, Division 1, 21 January 1899 – Fryer; Methven, Staley; Cox, Archie Goodall, May; Oakden (1), Bloomer (6), Boag, McDonald (1), Allen, (1 og).

Record Cup Victory: 12–0 v Finn Harps, UEFA Cup 1st rd 1st leg, 15 September 1976 – Moseley; Thomas, Nish, Rioch (1), McFarland, Todd (King), Macken, Gemmill, Hector (5), George (3), James (3).

sky SPORTS FACT FILE

The first season that Derby County recorded more than 100 goals was in 1955–56. On 7 April the Rams beat Accrington Stanley 6-2 with the recalled to the attack Alf Ackerman scoring four of the goals. His first successful strike proved to be the 100th. The season ended with them on 110.

Record Defeat: 2–11 v Everton, FA Cup 1st rd, 1889–90.

Most League Points (2 for a win): 63, Division 2, 1968–69 and Division 3 (N), 1955–56 and 1956–57.

Most League Points (3 for a win): 84, Division 3, 1985–86, Division 3, 1986–87 and FL C, 2006–07.

Most League Goals: 111, Division 3 (N), 1956–57.

Highest League Scorer in Season: Jack Bowers, 37, Division 1, 1930–31; Ray Straw, 37 Division 3 (N), 1956–57.

Most League Goals in Total Aggregate: Steve Bloomer, 292, 1892–1906 and 1910–14.

Most League Goals in One Match: 6, Steve Bloomer v Sheffield W, Division 1, 2 January 1899.

Most Capped Player: Deon Burton, 42 (59), Jamaica.

Most League Appearances: Kevin Hector, 486, 1966–78 and 1980–82.

Youngest League Player: Mason Bennett, 15 years 99 days v Middlesbrough 22 October 2011.

Record Transfer Fee Received: £7,000,000 rising to £9,000,000 for Seth Johnson from Leeds U, October 2001.

Record Transfer Fee Paid: £4,000,000 to Crewe Alex for Seth Johnson, May 1999 (including sell-on).

Football League Record: 1888 Founder Member of the Football League; 1907–12 Division 2; 1912–14 Division 1; 1914–15 Division 2; 1915–21 Division 1; 1921–26 Division 2; 1926–53 Division 1; 1953–55 Division 2; 1955–57 Division 3 (N); 1957–69 Division 2; 1969–80 Division 1; 1980–84 Division 2; 1984–86 Division 3; 1986–87 Division 2; 1987–91 Division 1; 1991–92 Division 2; 1992–96 Division 1; 1996–2002 FA Premier League; 2002–04 Division 1; 2004–07 FL C; 2007–08 FA Premier League; 2008– FL C.

MANAGERS

W. D. Clark 1896–1900
Harry Newbould 1900–06
Jimmy Methven 1906–22
Cecil Potter 1922–25
George Jobey 1925–41
Ted Magner 1944–46
Stuart McMillan 1946–53
Jack Barker 1953–55
Harry Storer 1955–62
Tim Ward 1962–67
Brian Clough 1967–73
Dave Mackay 1973–76
Colin Murphy 1977
Tommy Docherty 1977–79
Colin Addison 1979–82
Johnny Newman 1982
Peter Taylor 1982–84
Roy McFarland 1984
Arthur Cox 1984–93
Roy McFarland 1993–95
Jim Smith 1995–2001
Colin Todd 2001–02
John Gregory 2002–03
George Burley 2003–05
Phil Brown 2005–06
Billy Davies 2006–07
Paul Jewell 2007–08
Nigel Clough January 2009–

LATEST SEQUENCES

Longest Sequence of League Wins: 9, 15.3.1969 – 19.4.1969.

Longest Sequence of League Defeats: 8, 12.12.1987 – 10.2.1988.

Longest Sequence of League Draws: 6, 26.3.1927 – 18.4.1927.

Longest Sequence of Unbeaten League Matches: 22, 8.3.1969 – 20.9.1969.

Longest Sequence Without a League Win: 36, 22.9.2007 – 30.8.2008.

Successive Scoring Runs: 29 from 3.12.1960.

Successive Non-scoring Runs: 8 from 30.10.1920.

TEN YEAR LEAGUE RECORD

		P	W	D	L	F	A	Pts	Pos
2002-03	Div 1	46	15	7	24	55	74	52	18
2003-04	Div 1	46	13	13	20	53	67	52	20
2004-05	FL C	46	22	10	14	71	60	76	4
2005-06	FL C	46	10	20	16	53	67	50	20
2006-07	FL C	46	25	9	12	62	46	84	3
2007-08	PR Lge	38	1	8	29	20	89	11	20
2008-09	FL C	46	14	12	20	55	67	54	18
2009-10	FL C	46	15	11	20	53	63	56	14
2010-11	FL C	46	13	10	23	58	71	49	19
2011-12	FL C	46	18	10	18	50	58	64	12

DID YOU KNOW ?

Right-back Jimmy Methven was one of three Derby County players (plus Jack Fryer, John Boag) who played in three FA Cup finals: 1898, 1899 and 1903. A Scot, he was previously with Leith Athletic, Hearts and St Bernards. He made 511 League and Cup appearances for the Rams.

DERBY COUNTY 2011–12 LEAGUE RECORD

Match No.	*Date*	*Venue*	*Opponents*	*Result*		*H/T Score*	*Lg Pos.*	*Goalscorers*	*Attendance*
1	Aug 6	H	Birmingham C	W	2-1	2-1	—	Shackell [26], Davies, S [42]	27,210
2	13	A	Watford	W	1-0	0-0	5	Davies, S [51]	12,263
3	17	A	Blackpool	W	1-0	0-0	—	Bryson [69]	13,489
4	20	H	Doncaster R	W	3-0	1-0	2	Kilbane [6], Davies, S [46], Davies, B [62]	23,377
5	27	H	Burnley	L	1-2	0-0	3	Robinson [71]	23,913
6	Sept 10	A	Coventry C	L	0-2	0-0	5		14,219
7	17	A	Nottingham F	W	2-1	1-1	4	Ward [29], Hendrick [72]	27,356
8	24	H	Millwall	W	3-0	2-0	3	Bryson [24], Hendrick [39], Davies, S [65]	24,120
9	27	H	Barnsley	D	1-1	0-1	—	Davies, S (pen) [62]	23,454
10	Oct 1	A	Leicester C	L	0-4	0-2	3		22,496
11	15	H	Southampton	D	1-1	1-0	4	Robinson [3]	33,010
12	18	A	Reading	D	2-2	0-0	—	Robinson [59], Cywka [75]	15,704
13	22	A	Middlesbrough	L	0-2	0-1	6		17,407
14	29	H	Portsmouth	W	3-1	3-0	5	Bryson [3], Maguire [14], Ward [33]	24,148
15	Nov 2	H	Cardiff C	L	0-3	0-1	—		23,078
16	5	A	Peterborough U	L	2-3	2-1	8	Robinson 2 [28, 32]	9666
17	19	H	Hull C	L	0-2	0-2	10		30,391
18	26	A	West Ham U	L	1-3	1-1	15	Priskin [34]	27,864
19	29	H	Brighton & HA	L	0-1	0-1	—		22,040
20	Dec 2	A	Crystal Palace	D	1-1	0-1	—	McCarthy (og) [75]	14,338
21	10	H	Bristol C	W	2-1	0-0	14	Bryson [64], Ball [73]	23,906
22	17	A	Ipswich T	L	0-1	0-0	16		17,256
23	26	H	Leeds U	W	1-0	0-0	14	Ward [67]	33,010
24	31	H	West Ham U	W	2-1	2-1	11	Ball [2], Green [10]	28,067
25	Jan 2	A	Hull C	W	1-0	0-0	9	Robinson [46]	20,704
26	14	H	Coventry C	W	1-0	0-0	8	Ball [75]	24,126
27	21	A	Burnley	D	0-0	0-0	11		14,302
28	31	A	Barnsley	L	2-3	0-3	—	Ward [69], Carroll [90]	10,149
29	Feb 11	A	Millwall	D	0-0	0-0	13		10,069
30	14	H	Reading	L	0-1	0-0	—		22,567
31	18	A	Southampton	L	0-4	0-1	15		24,536
32	23	H	Leicester C	L	0-1	0-1	—		28,205
33	Mar 3	A	Birmingham C	D	2-2	0-1	16	Davies, B [61], Robinson [66]	17,996
34	6	H	Blackpool	W	2-1	0-1	—	Davies, S 2 [51, 75]	26,320
35	10	H	Watford	L	1-2	1-2	15	Davies, S [31]	23,130
36	13	H	Nottingham F	W	1-0	0-0	—	Buxton [90]	33,010
37	17	A	Doncaster R	W	2-1	1-0	11	Robinson [13], Roberts [55]	9791
38	20	A	Brighton & HA	L	0-2	0-1	—		18,412
39	24	H	Crystal Palace	W	3-2	2-0	12	Davies, S [6], Hendrick [29], Robinson (pen) [49]	25,222
40	31	A	Bristol C	D	1-1	1-0	13	Bryson [20]	12,794
41	Apr 7	H	Ipswich T	D	0-0	0-0	12		24,156
42	9	A	Leeds U	W	2-0	1-0	11	Bryson [32], Davies, S [66]	21,363
43	14	H	Middlesbrough	L	0-1	0-0	13		24,654
44	17	A	Cardiff C	L	0-2	0-1	—		21,216
45	21	A	Portsmouth	W	2-1	1-0	11	Buxton [41], Davies, S (pen) [78]	17,707
46	28	H	Peterborough U	D	1-1	1-0	12	Robinson [21]	27,354

Final League Position: 12

GOALSCORERS

League (50): Davies, S 11 (2 pens), Robinson 10 (1 pen), Bryson 6, Ward 4, Ball 3, Hendrick 3, Buxton 2, Davies, B 2, Carroll 1, Cywka 1, Green 1, Kilbane 1, Maguire 1, Priskin 1, Roberts 1, Shackell 1, own goal 1.
Carling Cup (2): Maguire 1, Robinson 1.
FA Cup (1): Robinson 1.

Fielding F 44	Brayford J 22 + 1	Kilbane K 7 + 2	Bailey J 17 + 5	Anderson R 5 + 3	Shackell J 46	Croft L 4 + 4	Bryson C 44	Davies S 20 + 6	Ward J 35 + 2	Davies B 30 + 5	O'Brien M 15 + 5	Robinson T 27 + 12	Hendrick J 38 + 4	Roberts G 39 + 2	Maguire C 2 + 5	Cywka T 3 + 5	Tyson N 13 + 10	Legzdins A 2 + 2	Doyle C 1 + 5	Ball C 11 + 12	Bennett M 2 + 7	Buxton J 12 + 9	Hughes W 1 + 2	Barker S 19 + 1	Green P 26 + 1	Priskin T 4 + 1	Noble R 1 + 1	Carroll T 8 + 4	Naylor T 8	Match No.
1	2	3	4^{3}	5^{1}	6	7	8	9	10^{2}	11	12	13	14																	1
1	2	3	4^{1}		6	7	8	9^{2}	10^{3}	11	5	13	12	14																2
1	2	3	4		6	12	8	9^{2}	10^{1}	11^{3}	5	13	7	14																3
1	2	3	4		6	12	8^{3}	9^{2}	10^{1}	11	5	13	7		14															4
1	2	3	4		6	13	8	9^{2}	10^{1}	11	5	12	7																	5
1	2	3			6	7^{1}	8	9^{2}	10	11	5	12	4		13															6
1■	2			13	6		8		10^{1}	11	5	9^{2}	4	3		7^{G}	12	15												7
	2			14	6^{3}		8	9^{1}	11^{2}	7	5	10	4	3	13	12		1												8
1	2			12	6		8	9	11	7	5	10^{2}	4	3^{1}		13														9
1	2				6	12	8	9^{1}	11^{2}	7	5	10	4	3					13											10
1				2	6		8	9^{1}	11	7	5	10	4	3		12														11
1				2	6		8		11^{1}	7	5	10	4	3		9^{2}			12	13										12
1		12			6^{1}	2	8		11	7	5	9^{2}	4	3	13	14					10^{3}									13
1		12		2	6		8		11	7	5^{1}	9^{3}	4	3	10^{2}				14		13									14
1		5		2^{1}	6		8		11	7			4	3	10^{2}	13				14	9^{3}	12								15
1					6		8		10^{3}	11	5	9^{1}	4	3					7^{2}	13	12	2	14							16
1	2				6		8		10	7	5	9^{1}	4^{3}	3	12	11^{2}								13	14					17
1	2^{2}		4		6		8		10^{3}	11	13		12	3					14					5^{1}	7	9				18
1			4		6		8		10	11^{2}			7	3						12	13			5	2	9^{1}				19
1			4^{2}		6		8		10	11^{1}	14		7	3						13	12			5	2	9^{3}				20
1			4^{3}		6		8		10	11^{2}	14		7	3						12	13			5	2	9^{1}				21
1	2^{2}		4^{1}		6		8		10	14		12	11^{3}	3			13			9				5	7					22
1	2		4		6		8		11		13	12		3			9^{1}			10^{2}				5	7					23
1	2		4		6		8		11^{2}	13		12		3			9^{1}			10^{3}		14		5	7					24
1	2		4		6		8		11^{3}	12		9^{2}		3						10^{1}		14		5	7	13				25
1	2		4		6		8		11			9		3						10^{1}		12		5	7					26
1	2		4^{1}		6		8		11			9^{2}	12	3						10^{3}		14		5	7		13			27
1	2				6		8		11				4	3			12			10				5			9^{1}	7		28
1			12		6		8		11^{3}				4	3			10^{2}		14	9		13		5	2			7^{1}		29
1			14		6		8^{1}	12	11			13	4	3			9			10^{2}				5	2			7^{3}		30
1	2^{1}		4^{3}		6			14	10			13	8	3			9^{2}			12				5	7			11		31
1					6		8^{2}	12	11			13	4	3			9			10^{1}				5	2			7		32
1					6		8	9^{2}		12		11	4	3			10^{1}			13		14		5	2			7^{3}		33
1					6		8	9^{2}		11		10	4	3			12					13		5	2			7^{1}		34
1			14		6		8	9		11^{2}		10	4^{3}				12			13		3		5	2			7^{1}		35
1					6		8	9^{2}		7		11	4	3			10			13		12		5^{1}	2					36
1					6		8	13		11		10^{2}	4	3			12			9^{1}		2			7				5	37
1			8^{2}		6			9^{1}		13		11	4	3			10^{3}			14		5			7			12	2	38
1					6		8	9^{1}		11		10^{2}	4	3			13			12		5			7				2	39
1					6		8	9		11		10^{1}	4	3			12					5			7				2	40
1					6		8		10^{1}	11		9	4	3			12					5			7				2	41
1					6		8^{3}	12	13	11		10^{2}	4	3			9^{1}					5			7			14	2	42
1					6		8	9	12	11^{1}		10^{2}	4^{3}	3			13					5			7			14	2	43
1	12		14		6		8	13	11^{2}			10^{3}	4	3			9					5			7				2^{1}	44
1^{G}	2				6		8	9	7			10^{1}	4	3			11^{2}	15			13	5	12							45
	2		14		6		8^{3}	9				10^{1}	4	3			11	1			12	5	7^{2}					13		46

FA Cup

Third Round	Crystal Palace	(h)	1-0
Fourth Round	Stoke C	(h)	0-2

Carling Cup

First Round	Shrewsbury T	(h)	2-3

DONCASTER ROVERS FL Championship 1

FOUNDATION

In 1879, Mr Albert Jenkins assembled a team to play a match against the Yorkshire Institution for the Deaf. The players remained together as Doncaster Rovers, joining the Midland Alliance in 1889 and the Midland Counties League in 1891.

Keepmoat Stadium, Stadium Way, Lakeside, Doncaster, South Yorkshire DN4 5JW.

Telephone: (01302) 764 664.

Fax: (01302) 363 525.

Ticket Office: (01302) 762 576.

Website: www.doncasterroversfc.co.uk

Email: info@doncasterroversfc.co.uk

Ground Capacity: 15,231.

Record Attendance: 37,149 v Hull C, Division 3 (N), 2 October 1948 (at Belle Vue); 15,001 v Leeds U, FL 1, 1 April 2008 (at Keepmoat Stadium).

Pitch Measurements: 100m × 70m.

Chairman: John Ryan.

Chief Executive: Gavin Baldwin.

Manager: Dean Saunders.

Assistant Manager: Brian Carey.

Fitness Coach: Mal Purchase.

Colours: Red and white hooped shirts, red sleeves with black trim, black shorts with red trim, black stockings with red tops.

Year Formed: 1879.

Turned Professional: 1885.

Club Nickname: 'Rovers'.

Grounds: 1880–1916, Intake Ground; 1920, Benetthorpe Ground; 1922, Low Pasture, Belle Vue; 2007, Keepmoat Stadium.

First Football League Game: 7 September 1901, Division 2, v Burslem Port Vale (h) D 3–3 – Eggett; Simpson, Layton; Longden, Jones, Wright, Langham, Murphy, Price, Goodson (2), Bailey (1).

Record League Victory: 10–0 v Darlington, Division 4, 25 January 1964: Potter; Raine, Meadows, Windross (1), White, Ripley (2), Robinson, Book (2), Hale (4), Jeffrey, Broadbent (1).

Record Cup Victory: 7–0 v Blyth Spartans, FA Cup 1st rd, 27 November 1937: Imrie; Shaw, Rodgers, McFarlane, Bycroft, Cyril Smith, Burton (1), Killourhy (4), Morgan (2), Malam, Dutton.

HONOURS

Football League: Best season 2007–08.
Division 3: ***Champions*** 2003–04;
Division 3 (N): ***Champions*** – 1934–35, 1946–47, 1949–50;
Runners-up 1937–38, 1938–39;
Division 4: ***Champions*** 1965–66, 1968–69; ***Runners-up*** 1983–84.

FA Cup: Best season 5th rd, 1952, 1954, 1955, 1956.

Football League Cup: Best season: 5th rd, 1976, 2006.

J Paint Trophy: ***Winners*** 2007.

Football Conference: ***Champions*** 2002–03

Sheffield County Cup: ***Winners*** 1891, 1912, 1936, 1938, 1956, 1968, 1976, 1986.

Midland Counties League: ***Champions*** 1897, 1899.

Conference Trophy: ***Winners*** 1999, 2000.

Sheffield & Hallamshire Senior Cup: ***Winners*** 2001, 2002.

sky SPORTS FACT FILE

Bert Tindall was discovered by Doncaster Rovers in wartime football. He made a scoring debut at outside-right in an 8-1 win at Hull City on 26 August 1944. Ranking third in both total number of League appearances (401) and goals (125), he later became more of a utility forward.

Record Defeat: 0–12 v Small Heath, Division 2, 11 April 1903.

Most League Points (2 for a win): 72, Division 3 (N), 1946–47.

Most League Points (3 for a win): 92, Division 3, 2003–04.

Most League Goals: 123, Division 3 (N), 1946–47.

Highest League Scorer in Season: Clarrie Jordan, 42, Division 3 (N), 1946–47.

Most League Goals in Total Aggregate: Tom Keetley, 180, 1923–29.

Most League Goals in One Match: 6, Tom Keetley v Ashington, Division 3 (N), 16 February 1929.

Most Capped Player: Len Graham, 14, Northern Ireland.

Most League Appearances: Fred Emery, 417, 1925–36.

Youngest League Player: Alick Jeffrey, 15 years 229 days v Fulham, 15 September 1954.

Record Transfer Fee Received: £2,000,000 from Reading for Matthew Mills, July 2009.

Record Transfer Fee Paid: £1,150,000 to Sheffield U for Billy Sharp, August 2010.

Football League Record: 1901 Elected to Division 2; 1903 Failed re-election; 1904 Re-elected; 1905 Failed re-election; 1923 Re-elected to Division 3 (N); 1935–37 Division 2; 1937–47 Division 3 (N); 1947–48 Division 2; 1948–50 Division 3 (N); 1950–58 Division 2; 1958–59 Division 3; 1959–66 Division 4; 1966–67 Division 3; 1967–69 Division 4; 1969–71 Division 3; 1971–81 Division 4; 1981–83 Division 3; 1983–84 Division 4; 1984–88 Division 3; 1988–92 Division 4; 1992–98 Division 3; 1998–2003 Conference; 2003–04 Division 3; 2004–08 FL 1; 2008–12 FL C; 2012– FL 1.

LATEST SEQUENCES

Longest Sequence of League Wins: 10, 22.1.1947 – 4.4.1947.

Longest Sequence of League Defeats: 9, 14.1.1905 – 1.4.1905.

Longest Sequence of League Draws: 4, 29.10.1932 – 19.11.1932.

Longest Sequence of Unbeaten League Matches: 20, 26.12.1968 – 12.4.1969.

Longest Sequence Without a League Win: 20, 9.8.1997 – 29.11.1997.

Successive Scoring Runs: 27 from 10.11.1934.

Successive Non-scoring Runs: 7 from 27.9.1947.

MANAGERS

Arthur Porter 1920–21
Harry Tufnell 1921–22
Arthur Porter 1922–23
Dick Ray 1923–27
David Menzies 1928–36
Fred Emery 1936–40
Bill Marsden 1944–46
Jackie Bestall 1946–49
Peter Doherty 1949–58
Jack Hodgson and Sid Bycroft (*Joint Managers*) 1958
Jack Crayston 1958–59 (*continued as Secretary-Manager to 1961*)
Jackie Bestall (*TM*) 1959–60
Norman Curtis 1960–61
Danny Malloy 1961–62
Oscar Hold 1962–64
Bill Leivers 1964–66
Keith Kettleborough 1966–67
George Raynor 1967–68
Lawrie McMenemy 1968–71
Maurice Setters 1971–74
Stan Anderson 1975–78
Billy Bremner 1978–85
Dave Cusack 1985–87
Dave Mackay 1987–89
Billy Bremner 1989–91
Steve Beaglehole 1991–93
Ian Atkins 1994
Sammy Chung 1994–96
Kerry Dixon (*Player-Manager*) 1996–97
Dave Cowling 1997
Mark Weaver 1997–98
Ian Snodin 1998–99
Steve Wignall 1999–2001
Dave Penney 2002–06
Sean O'Driscoll 2006–11
Dean Saunders September 2011–

TEN YEAR LEAGUE RECORD

		P	W	D	L	F	A	Pts	Pos
2002-03	Conf.	42	22	12	8	73	47	78	3
2003-04	Div 3	46	27	11	8	79	37	92	1
2004-05	FL 1	46	16	18	12	65	60	66	10
2005-06	FL 1	46	20	9	17	55	51	69	8
2006-07	FL 1	46	16	15	15	52	47	63	11
2007-08	FL 1	46	23	11	12	65	41	80	3
2008-09	FL C	46	17	7	22	42	53	58	14
2009-10	FL C	46	15	15	16	59	58	60	12
2010-11	FL C	46	11	15	20	55	81	48	21
2011-12	FL C	46	8	12	26	43	80	36	24

DID YOU KNOW?

On 11 January 1930, Doncaster Rovers were trailing 3-2 to Stoke City in a third round FA Cup tie when a snowstorm called a halt to proceedings in the 75th minute. Five days later in the replay Doncaster had a player sent off but still managed to win with a Fred Emery goal in 66 minutes.

DONCASTER ROVERS 2011–12 LEAGUE RECORD

Match No.	*Date*	*Venue*	*Opponents*	*Result*		*H/T Score*	*Lg Pos.*	*Goalscorers*	*Attendance*
1	Aug 6	A	Brighton & HA	L	1-2	1-0	—	Sharp ^{39}	20,219
2	13	H	West Ham U	L	0-1	0-1	21		11,344
3	16	H	Nottingham F	L	0-1	0-1	—		9464
4	20	A	Derby Co	L	0-3	0-1	24		23,377
5	27	H	Bristol C	D	1-1	0-1	24	Hayter ^{68}	7778
6	Sept 10	A	Cardiff C	L	0-2	0-0	24		21,863
7	17	A	Reading	L	0-2	0-0	24		15,124
8	24	H	Crystal Palace	W	1-0	0-0	24	Oster ^{65}	9362
9	27	H	Hull C	D	1-1	0-1	—	Gillett ^{58}	9786
10	Oct 1	A	Peterborough U	W	2-1	0-1	20	Stock ^{55}, Bennett ^{67}	8220
11	14	H	Leeds U	L	0-3	0-1	—		12,962
12	18	A	Blackpool	L	1-2	1-0	—	Sharp ^{27}	11,587
13	22	A	Portsmouth	L	1-3	1-1	23	Gillett ^{27}	12,779
14	29	H	Coventry C	D	1-1	0-1	23	Hayter ^{60}	8426
15	Nov 1	H	Middlesbrough	L	1-3	1-2	—	Sharp ^{14}	9792
16	5	A	Ipswich T	W	3-2	3-0	24	Diouf 2 $^{18, 39}$, Sharp ^{24}	17,184
17	19	A	Barnsley	L	0-2	0-1	24		11,783
18	26	H	Watford	D	0-0	0-0	24		8389
19	29	A	Millwall	L	2-3	1-2	—	Sharp 2 (1 pen) $^{40 (p), 86}$	9062
20	Dec 3	H	Southampton	W	1-0	0-0	23	Sharp ^{60}	9527
21	10	A	Birmingham C	L	1-2	0-0	23	Fortune ^{50}	17,369
22	17	H	Leicester C	W	2-1	0-1	23	Sharp 2 $^{63, 65}$	9461
23	26	A	Burnley	L	0-3	0-1	23		16,756
24	31	A	Watford	L	1-4	0-1	24	Sharp ^{47}	11,654
25	Jan 2	H	Barnsley	W	2-0	1-0	23	Hayter ^{14}, Bennett ^{89}	11,446
26	14	H	Cardiff C	D	0-0	0-0	23		8834
27	21	A	Bristol C	L	1-2	0-2	23	Diouf ^{75}	14,951
28	31	A	Hull C	D	0-0	0-0	—		19,187
29	Feb 14	H	Blackpool	L	1-3	1-2	—	Diouf (pen) ^{43}	8319
30	18	A	Leeds U	L	2-3	1-0	24	Bagayoko 2 $^{32, 54}$	21,181
31	25	H	Peterborough U	D	1-1	1-0	24	Barnes ^{45}	10,375
32	Mar 3	H	Brighton & HA	D	1-1	0-1	24	Diouf (pen) ^{79}	8964
33	6	A	Nottingham F	W	2-1	1-0	—	Piquionne ^{44}, Bennett ^{47}	18,521
34	10	A	West Ham U	D	1-1	0-1	23	Coppinger ^{73}	34,650
35	13	H	Reading	D	1-1	1-0	—	Bennett ^{27}	8287
36	17	H	Derby Co	L	1-2	0-1	23	Diouf ^{67}	9791
37	20	H	Millwall	L	0-3	0-2	—		7572
38	24	A	Southampton	L	0-2	0-0	23		30,209
39	27	A	Crystal Palace	D	1-1	0-0	—	Brown, C ^{76}	13,401
40	30	H	Birmingham C	L	1-3	1-1	—	Piquionne ^{4}	8656
41	Apr 7	A	Leicester C	L	0-4	0-1	24		22,054
42	9	H	Burnley	L	1-2	0-1	24	Brown, C ^{56}	8350
43	14	H	Portsmouth	L	3-4	2-0	24	Beye ^{3}, Robert ^{5}, Coppinger ^{67}	8196
44	17	A	Middlesbrough	D	0-0	0-0	—		14,967
45	21	A	Coventry C	W	2-0	0-0	24	Hayter (pen) ^{81}, Gillett ^{87}	15,124
46	28	H	Ipswich T	L	2-3	1-2	24	Robert ^{34}, Beye ^{90}	9764

Final League Position: 24

GOALSCORERS

League (43): Sharp 10 (1 pen), Diouf 6 (2 pens), Bennett 4, Hayter 4 (1 pen), Gillett 3, Bagayoko 2, Beye 2, Brown, C 2, Coppinger 2, Piquionne 2, Robert 2, Barnes 1, Fortune 1, Oster 1, Stock 1.
Carling Cup (4): Bennett 1, Brown, C 1 (pen), Hayter 1, Mason 1.
FA Cup (0).

Woods G 14	Dumbuya M 6+4	Spurr T 19	Friend G 24+3	Naylor R 13	Oster J 23+7	Coppinger J 31+7	Mason R 2+2	Hayter J 18+13	Sharp B 18+2	Gillett S 43+3	Barnes G 24+9	Bennett K 15+21	Hird S 23+8	Brown C 7+4	Baxendale J —+2	Keegan P 1+1	Brown R 1+2	Lalkovic M 1+5 / Robert F 7+6	Wilson M —+3	O'Connor J 24+4	Sullivan N 9	Martis S 14+1	Stock B 24+2	Parkin J 4+1 / Piquionne F 8	Kirkland C 1	Ilunga H 19	Chimbonda P 16	Diouf E 22	Ikeme C 15	Lockwood A 11+3	Beye H 22	Goulon H 5+1 / Husband J 2+1	Fortune M 5	Button D 7	Woods M 2+2	Bamogo H 4	Bagayoko M 2+3	Match No.
1	2	3	4	5	6	7^3	8^2	9	10^1	11	12	13	14																									1
1	2	3	4	5	6	7				8^3	10^2	11^1	14	9	12	13																						2
1	2	3	4		6	7				8	10^2	11^1	5	9	13		12																					3
1	2^3	3	4	5	6					11	10	12	14	9^2			7^1	8	13																			4
1	3	11	4	5^1	6			9		7	8^3	10	2^2				14	13		12																		5
1	7^3	3	4	5^1	6	10		9		8	13	11^2						12	14	2																		6
		3^2	4		6	10		9		7	8^3	11^1	13					12		2	1	5	14															7
			3	5	6	7^1		9	13	11								12		2	1	4	8	10^2														8
			3	5	6^2	11^3		9^1	12	7		14						13		2	1	4	8	10														9
			3	5	6^2	7		13	10^1	11		12								2	1	4	8	9														10
			4	5	6^2	7^1	12	14	10	11		13								2			8	9^3	1	3												11
			4		6	12			10	11	9^1	7	5								1		8			3	2											12
			4		6^2	14		12	10	7	9^3	11^1	5								1		8	13		3	2											13
	13		6	5		12	14	9		7	10^1	11^2									1	4	8^3			3	2											14
			6	5		12	7^1	9^2	10	11	14	13									1	4				3	2	8^3										15
			4	5		9		12	10^1	11										13	1	6	8			3	2	7^2										16
			3	5		7^2			10	8	13	14								2		4^1	6^3			11		9	1	12■								17
								14	10	7	12	13	5							2			6^3			3		11^1	1		4	8^2	9					18
						14			10	11	7	12	5						13	2			6^3			3			1		4^1	8^2	9					19
			13			7		14	10^3	11	12		5							2			6			3			1		4	8^1	9^2					20
			12			7^1			10	11	13	14	5							2			6			3			1		4	8^3	9^2					21
1						7		12	10	11	8		5							2			6			3					4		9^1					22
1						7		13	10	11^1	8^2	12	5							2			6			3		9^3			4	14						23
1						7		14	10	11^2	6	13	5							12						3	2^1	9^3			4	8■						24
			4^1			7		9	10	8		11	5							2			6			3				12				1				25
		3				7		9	10	11		12	5							2			6					8^1			4			1				26
		3			12	7^1		9^2	10	11^3		14	5							2			6					8		13	4■			1				27
		3			11			9		13		12	4							2		14	6					10^3		5				1	7^2	8^1		28
		3			8			9^3		13		12	4							2			6					11		5				1	7^2	10^1	14	29
		3^3						9^2		11	8		4					13		14			6				2	10		5				1		7^1	12	30
		3			12			14		11	8	10^2						13				4	6				2	7^3			5			1			9^1	31
		3				7^1		9^2		14	8	13						12				5	6^3				2	10	1		4					11		32
		3^2			14	7				8	6	11	13									5		10^1			2	9^3	1		4						12	33
		3			12	7				8	6	11	13									5^2					2	10	1		4						9^1	34
		3				7				8	6	11	5											10			2	9	1		4							35
		3			12	7^1		14		8	6^3	11	13									5^2		10			2	9	1		4							36
	13	3			12	7^2		9^1		8	6		5					14		2				10				11^3	1		4							37
					11^3	7^1				8	6^2	12		13				14						10		3	2	9	1	5	4							38
			14		11					8	12			13		6^2		7^1						10		3	2^3	9	1	5	4							39
	13		5		11^3	14				8	6			12				7						10^1		3		9	1	2	4^2							40
					11	7				8	6^3			12				14					13	10^1		3	2	9^2	1	5	4							41
1			3		14	13		9		8	12	11^2	4	10				7^3		2			6^1							5								42
1	14		3		11^2	7		12		8	6		13	9^3				10^1		2										5	4■							43
1			3		11	7				8		13	6	9				10^2		2		4^1								5		12						44
1			3		11	7^3		12		8		13	4	9^1				10^2		2										5		6			14			45
1			5		11^2	7		9		8		12	6^1					10		2											4	3			13			46

FA Cup

Third Round	Notts Co	(h)	0-2

Carling Cup

First Round	Tranmere R	(h)	3-0
Second Round	Leeds U	(h)	1-2

EVERTON — FA Premiership

FOUNDATION

St Domingo Church Sunday School formed a football club in 1878 which played at Stanley Park. Enthusiasm was so great that in November 1879 they decided to expand membership and changed the name to Everton, playing in black shirts with a scarlet sash and nicknamed the 'Black Watch'. After wearing several other colours, royal blue was adopted in 1901.

Goodison Park, Goodison Road, Liverpool L4 4EL.

Telephone: (0871) 663 1878.

Fax: (0151) 286 9112.

Ticket Office: (0871) 663 1878.

Website: www.evertonfc.com

Email: everton@evertonfc.com

Ground Capacity: 40,158.

Record Attendance: 78,299 v Liverpool, Division 1, 18 September 1948.

Pitch Measurements: 100.48m × 68m.

Chairman: Bill Kenwright CBE.

Chief Executive: Robert Elstone.

Manager: David Moyes.

Assistant Manager: Steve Round.

Fitness Coach: Dave Billows.

Colours: Blue shirts with white trim, white shorts, white stockings.

Year Formed: 1878.

Turned Professional: 1885.

Previous Name: 1878, St Domingo FC; 1879, Everton.

Club Nickname: 'The Toffees'.

Grounds: 1878, Stanley Park; 1882, Priory Road; 1884, Anfield Road; 1892, Goodison Park.

First Football League Game: 8 September 1888, Football League, v Accrington (h) W 2–1 – Smalley; Dick, Ross; Holt, Jones, Dobson; Fleming (2), Waugh, Lewis, Edgar Chadwick, Farmer.

Record League Victory: 9–1 v Manchester C, Division 1, 3 September 1906 – Scott; Balmer, Crelley; Booth, Taylor (1), Abbott (1); Sharp, Bolton (1), Young (4), Settle (2), George Wilson. 9–1 v Plymouth Arg, Division 2, 27 December 1930 – Coggins; Williams, Cresswell; McPherson, Griffiths, Thomson; Critchley, Dunn, Dean (4), Johnson (1), Stein (4).

HONOURS

Football League – Division 1: ***Champions*** 1890–91, 1914–15, 1927–28, 1931–32, 1938–39, 1962–63, 1969–70, 1984–85, 1986–87; ***Runners-up*** 1889–90, 1894–95, 1901–02, 1904–05, 1908–09, 1911–12, 1985–86; **Division 2:** ***Champions*** 1930–31; ***Runners-up*** 1953–54.

FA Cup: ***Winners*** 1906, 1933, 1966, 1984, 1995; ***Runners-up*** 1893, 1897, 1907, 1968, 1985, 1986, 1989, 2009.

Football League Cup: ***Runners-up*** 1977, 1984.

League Super Cup: ***Runners-up*** 1986.

Simod Cup: ***Runners-up*** 1989.

Zenith Data Systems Cup: ***Runners-up*** 1991.

European Competitions
European Cup: 1963–64, 1970–71.
European Cup-Winners' Cup: 1966–67, 1984–85 (*winners*), 1995–96.
European Fairs Cup: 1962–63, 1964–65, 1965–66.
Champions League: 2005–06.
UEFA Cup: 1975–76, 1978–79, 1979–80, 2005–06, 2007–08, 2008–09.
Europa League: 2009–10.

sky SPORTS FACT FILE

One of the quickest debutant goalscorers for Everton was Jackie Keeley. At the age of 21 he made his first appearance on Boxing Day 1957 away to Bolton Wanderers. He was replacing the injured George Kirby and found the target in three minutes. Everton won 5-1.

Record Cup Victory: 11–2 v Derby Co, FA Cup 1st rd, 18 January 1890 – Smalley; Hannah, Doyle (1); Kirkwood, Holt (1), Parry; Latta, Brady (3), Geary (3), Edgar Chadwick, Millward (3).

Record Defeat: 4–10 v Tottenham H, Division 1, 11 October 1958.

Most League Points (2 for a win): 66, Division 1, 1969–70.

Most League Points (3 for a win): 90, Division 1, 1984–85.

Most League Goals: 121, Division 2, 1930–31.

Highest League Scorer in Season: William Ralph 'Dixie' Dean, 60, Division 1, 1927–28 (All-time League record).

Most League Goals in Total Aggregate: William Ralph 'Dixie' Dean, 349, 1925–37.

Most League Goals in One Match: 6, Jack Southworth v WBA, Division 1, 30 December 1893.

Most Capped Player: Neville Southall, 92, Wales.

Most League Appearances: Neville Southall, 578, 1981–98.

Youngest League Player: James Vaughan, 16 years 271 days v Crystal Palace, 10 April 2005.

Record Transfer Fee Received: £25,000,000 rising to £29,000,000 from Manchester U for Wayne Rooney, August 2004.

Record Transfer Fee Paid: £15,000,000 to Standard Liege for Marouane Fellaini, September 2008.

Football League Record: 1888 Founder Member of the Football League; 1930–31 Division 2; 1931–51 Division 1; 1951–54 Division 2; 1954–92 Division 1; 1992– FA Premier League.

MANAGERS

W. E. Barclay 1888–89 *(Secretary-Manager)*
Dick Molyneux 1889–1901 *(Secretary-Manager)*
William C. Cuff 1901–18 *(Secretary-Manager)*
W. J. Sawyer 1918–19 *(Secretary-Manager)*
Thomas H. McIntosh 1919–35 *(Secretary-Manager)*
Theo Kelly 1936–48
Cliff Britton 1948–56
Ian Buchan 1956–58
Johnny Carey 1958–61
Harry Catterick 1961–73
Billy Bingham 1973–77
Gordon Lee 1977–81
Howard Kendall 1981–87
Colin Harvey 1987–90
Howard Kendall 1990–93
Mike Walker 1994
Joe Royle 1994–97
Howard Kendall 1997–98
Walter Smith 1998–2002
David Moyes March 2002–

LATEST SEQUENCES

Longest Sequence of League Wins: 12, 24.3.1894 – 13.10.1894.

Longest Sequence of League Defeats: 6, 26.12.1996 – 29.1.1997.

Longest Sequence of League Draws: 5, 4.5.1977 – 16.5.1977.

Longest Sequence of Unbeaten League Matches: 20, 29.4.1978 – 16.12.1978.

Longest Sequence Without a League Win: 14, 6.3.1937 – 4.9.1937.

Successive Scoring Runs: 40 from 15.3.1930.

Successive Non-scoring Runs: 6 from 3.3.1951.

TEN YEAR LEAGUE RECORD

		P	*W*	*D*	*L*	*F*	*A*	*Pts*	*Pos*
2002-03	PR Lge	38	17	8	13	48	49	59	7
2003-04	PR Lge	38	9	12	17	45	57	39	17
2004-05	PR Lge	38	18	7	13	45	46	61	4
2005-06	PR Lge	38	14	8	16	34	49	50	11
2006-07	PR Lge	38	15	13	10	52	36	58	6
2007-08	PR Lge	38	19	8	11	55	33	65	5
2008-09	PR Lge	38	17	12	9	55	37	63	5
2009-10	PR Lge	38	16	13	9	60	49	61	8
2010-11	PR Lge	38	13	15	10	51	45	54	7
2011-12	PR Lge	38	15	11	12	50	40	56	7

DID YOU KNOW ?

In a two-week period in February 1954, Everton scored 20 goals in three successive Second Division matches. On the 13th they won 6-2 at Derby County to start the trio off. Amazingly it was also the third time in history they had hit six away from home and all against Derby.

EVERTON 2011–12 LEAGUE RECORD

Match No.	*Date*	*Venue*	*Opponents*	*Result*		*H/T Score*	*Lg Pos.*	*Goalscorers*	*Attendance*
1	Aug 20	H	QPR	L	0-1	0-1	18		35,008
2	27	A	Blackburn R	W	1-0	0-0	11	Arteta (pen) [90]	22,826
3	Sept 10	H	Aston Villa	D	2-2	1-0	10	Osman [19], Baines (pen) [69]	32,736
4	17	H	Wigan Ath	W	3-1	1-1	7	Jagielka [33], Vellios [84], Drenthe [90]	31,576
5	24	A	Manchester C	L	0-2	0-0	10		47,293
6	Oct 1	H	Liverpool	L	0-2	0-0	13		39,510
7	15	A	Chelsea	L	1-3	0-2	15	Vellios [81]	41,789
8	23	A	Fulham	W	3-1	1-0	13	Drenthe [3], Saha [89], Rodwell [90]	25,646
9	29	H	Manchester U	L	0-1	0-1	16		35,494
10	Nov 5	A	Newcastle U	L	1-2	1-2	17	Rodwell [45]	50,671
11	19	H	Wolverhampton W	W	2-1	1-1	12	Jagielka [44], Baines (pen) [83]	33,953
12	26	A	Bolton W	W	2-0	0-0	9	Fellaini [49], Vellios [78]	24,058
13	Dec 4	H	Stoke C	L	0-1	0-1	10		33,219
14	10	A	Arsenal	L	0-1	0-0	12		60,062
15	17	H	Norwich C	D	1-1	0-1	14	Osman [81]	31,004
16	21	H	Swansea C	W	1-0	0-0	—	Osman [60]	32,004
17	26	A	Sunderland	D	1-1	0-1	10	Baines (pen) [51]	43,619
18	Jan 1	A	WBA	W	1-0	0-0	12	Anichebe [87]	23,038
19	4	H	Bolton W	L	1-2	0-0	—	Howard [63]	29,561
20	11	A	Tottenham H	L	0-2	0-1	—		36,132
21	14	A	Aston Villa	D	1-1	0-0	11	Anichebe [69]	31,853
22	21	H	Blackburn R	D	1-1	1-0	14	Cahill [24]	32,464
23	31	H	Manchester C	W	1-0	0-0	—	Gibson [60]	29,856
24	Feb 4	A	Wigan Ath	D	1-1	0-0	11	Anichebe [83]	18,340
25	11	H	Chelsea	W	2-0	1-0	10	Pienaar [5], Stracqualursi [71]	33,924
26	Mar 3	A	QPR	D	1-1	1-1	13	Drenthe [31]	18,033
27	10	H	Tottenham H	W	1-0	1-0	9	Jelavic [22]	34,992
28	13	A	Liverpool	L	0-3	0-1	—		44,921
29	21	H	Arsenal	L	0-1	0-1	—		30,330
30	24	A	Swansea C	W	2-0	0-0	9	Baines [59], Jelavic [76]	20,509
31	31	H	WBA	W	2-0	1-0	7	Osman [18], Anichebe [68]	32,051
32	Apr 7	A	Norwich C	D	2-2	1-1	7	Jelavic 2 [22, 61]	26,554
33	9	H	Sunderland	W	4-0	0-0	—	Gueye [52], Pienaar [75], Osman [76], Colback (og) [81]	32,249
34	22	A	Manchester U	D	4-4	1-1	7	Jelavic 2 [33, 83], Fellaini [67], Pienaar [85]	75,522
35	28	H	Fulham	W	4-0	3-0	7	Jelavic 2 (1 pen) [7 (p), 40], Fellaini [16], Cahill [60]	31,885
36	May 1	A	Stoke C	D	1-1	1-0	—	Crouch (og) [44]	26,500
37	6	A	Wolverhampton W	D	0-0	0-0	7		25,466
38	13	H	Newcastle U	W	3-1	2-0	7	Pienaar [16], Jelavic [27], Heitinga [65]	39,517

Final League Position: 7

GOALSCORERS

League (50): Jelavic 9 (1 pen), Osman 5, Anichebe 4, Baines 4 (3 pens), Pienaar 4, Drenthe 3, Fellaini 3, Vellios 3, Cahill 2, Jagielka 2, Rodwell 2, Arteta 1 (1 pen), Gibson 1, Gueye 1, Heitinga 1, Howard 1, Saha 1, Stracqualursi 1, own goals 2.

Carling Cup (6): Anichebe 1, Arteta 1, Fellaini 1, Neville 1, Saha 1, own goal 1.

FA Cup (10): Jelavic 2, Stracqualursi 2, Baines 1 (pen), Cahill 1, Drenthe 1, Fellaini 1, Heitinga 1, own goal 1.

Howard T 38	Neville P 24 + 3	Baines L 33	Heitinga J 29 + 1	Distin S 24 + 3	Jagielka P 29 + 1	Barkley R 2 + 4	Rodwell J 11 + 3	Beckford J 1 + 1	Cahill T 27 + 8	Osman L 28 + 2	Arteta M 1 + 1	Fellaini M 31 + 3	Saha L 15 + 3	Anichebe V 5 + 7	Bilyaletdinov D 7 + 3	Hibbert T 31 + 1	Coleman S 14 + 4	Drenthe R 10 + 11	Vellios A 2 + 11	Stracqualursi D 7 + 14	Gueye M 3 + 14	McFadden J 2 + 5	McAleny C — + 2	Donovan L 7	Duffy S 2 + 2	Gibson D 11	Baxter J — + 1	Pienaar S 14	Jelavic N 10 + 3	*Match No.*
1	2	3	4^{3}	5	6	7	8^{1}	9^{2}	10	11	12	13	14																	1
1	2	3	4^{3}	5	6	8^{1}		14	12	7^{2}	11	10		9	13															2
1		3		5	6	13	4		10^{3}	11		8			9^{1}	2	7^{2}	12	14											3
1		3		5	6		4		10^{3}	11		8			9^{1}	2	7^{2}	12	13	14										4
1	7^{2}	3		5	6		4		10^{1}	11		8	12			2	9^{3}	13	14											5
1	13	3		5	6		4■		10	11^{2}		8	9			2^{3}	7^{1}	12	14											6
1	13	3		5	6		4		10^{2}	11		8	9^{3}			2	7^{1}	12	14											7
1	8^{3}	3		5	6		4		13	7^{2}		10	12			2	14	11	9^{1}											8
1		3	5		6	12	4			11^{2}		8	9^{3}		10^{1}	2	7		13		14									9
1	8^{1}	3	5^{2}	12	6		4		13	11			9			2^{3}	7	10				14								10
1		3	5		6				10^{1}	11		4	9^{3}		13	2	7	8^{2}	12	14										11
1		3	5		6	13			10^{2}	11		4	9^{1}		8^{3}	2	7		12		14									12
1		3	5		6		12		10	11		4			8^{1}	2^{3}	7		9^{2}	13	14									13
1	4^{2}	3	5	12	6				10			8	9^{1}		11^{3}	2	7				13		14							14
1	4	3	5		6				10^{1}	11		8	9^{3}			2		13		12	7^{2}		14							15
1	4	3	5		6				14	11		8	9^{2}			2	7^{1}	10^{3}		13	12									16
1	8	3	4	5	6				10^{3}	11			9^{2}			2		7^{1}	13		12	14								17
1	8^{2}	3	4	5	6		7^{1}		10	11			9^{3}	14		2				13	12									18
1	8	3	4	5	6^{1}		12^{2}		13	11^{3}			9			2				7	14			10						19
1	2	3	6	5^{1}					11			8	9	10^{2}	4^{3}			13			14			7	12					20
1	2	3	6						10			8	9^{3}	12	13			11^{1}		14				7	5	4^{2}				21
1	2	3	6						10			8	9^{1}	11^{2}				12	13	14				7	5	4^{3}				22
1	2	3	6						10			8				5		11^{1}	13	9^{2}				7		4	12			23
1	12	3	6	5					10^{1}			8		14		2^{3}				9^{2}				11		4		7	13	24
1	2	3	6	5					10			8				13		12		9^{3}				7	14	4^{2}		11^{1}		25
1	4	3	6	5					10^{2}	13		8				2	14	7^{1}		9^{3}								11	12	26
1	2	3	6	5	14		12		10	8		4					7^{3}	11^{1}		13									9^{2}	27
1		3		5	6		4			14		8		10^{3}		2	7^{1}	13		9^{2}								11	12	28
1		3	6	5					10^{3}	8^{1}		4		13		2		11^{2}		14	12							7	9	29
1	7	3	14	5	6				10^{1}	8		12				2				13						4^{3}		11	9^{2}	30
1		3	5		6				10^{2}	7^{1}		8		13		2					12	14				4		11	9^{3}	31
1	8^{2}	3		5	6				10^{3}			13		14		2	12				7^{1}					4		11	9	32
1	3^{3}		5		6					8		4^{2}		13		2	14	12		9	7	10^{1}						11		33
1	3		4	5^{2}	6				13	7^{1}		10				2						12				8		11	9	34
1	3		4	5	6	13			12	7		10^{2}				2					14					8^{1}		11^{3}	9	35
1			6	5	3				4	7^{2}		8		10^{1}		2				14	12^{3}	13						11	9	36
1			6	5	3				4^{2}	7		8				2				12	13	10^{1}						11	9	37
1	8^{2}	3	6^{1}	12	5				13	7		10				2				14						4		11	9^{3}	38

FA Cup

Third Round	Tamworth	(h)	2-0
Fourth Round	Fulham	(h)	2-1
Fifth Round	Blackpool	(h)	2-0
Quarter-Final	Sunderland	(h)	1-1
		(a)	2-0
Semi-Final *(at Wembley).*	Liverpool		1-2

Carling Cup

Second Round	Sheffield U	(h)	3-1
Third Round	WBA	(h)	2-1
Fourth Round	Chelsea	(h)	1-2

EXETER CITY

FL Championship 2

FOUNDATION

Exeter City was formed in 1904 by the amalgamation of St Sidwell's United and Exeter United. The club first played in the East Devon League and then the Plymouth & District League. After an exhibition match between West Bromwich Albion and Woolwich Arsenal, which was held to test interest as Exeter was then a rugby stronghold, it was decided to form Exeter City. At a meeting at the Red Lion Hotel in 1908, the club turned professional.

St James Park, Stadium Way, Exeter EX4 6PX.

Telephone: (01392) 411 243.

Fax: (01392) 413 959.

Ticket Office: (01392) 411 243.

Website: www.exetercityfc.co.uk

Email: reception@exetercityfc.co.uk

Training Ground: (01395) 232784.

Ground Capacity: 8,830.

Record Attendance: 20,984 v Sunderland, FA Cup 6th rd (replay), 4 March 1931.

Pitch Measurements: 114yd × 73yd.

Chairman: Edward Chorlton OBE.

Vice-chairman: Julian Tagg.

Manager: Paul Tisdale.

First Team Coach: Rob Edwards.

Sports Medicine: Ian Andrews.

Colours: Red and white striped shirts, red sleeves, white shorts, white stockings.

Year Formed: 1904.

Turned Professional: 1908.

Club Nickname: 'The Grecians'.

Ground: 1904, St James Park.

First Football League Game: 28 August 1920, Division 3, v Brentford (h) W 3–0 – Pym; Coleburne, Feebury (1p); Crawshaw, Carrick, Mitton; Appleton, Makin, Wright (1), Vowles (1), Dockray.

Record League Victory: 8–1 v Coventry C, Division 3 (S), 4 December 1926 – Bailey; Pollard, Charlton; Pullen, Pool, Garrett; Purcell (2), McDevitt, Blackmore (2), Dent (2), Compton (2). 8–1 v Aldershot, Division 3 (S), 4 May 1935 – Chesters; Gray, Miller; Risdon, Webb, Angus; Jack Scott (1), Wrightson (1), Poulter (3), McArthur (1), Dryden (1), (1 og).

Record Cup Victory: 14–0 v Weymouth, FA Cup 1st qual rd, 3 October 1908 – Fletcher; Craig, Bulcock; Ambler, Chadwick, Wake; Parnell (1), Watson (1), McGuigan (4), Bell (6), Copestake (2).

HONOURS

Football League – Division 3: Best season: 8th, 1979–80;
Division 3 (S): ***Runners-up*** 1932–33;
Division 4: ***Champions*** 1989–90;
Runners-up 1976–77;
FL 2: ***Runners-up*** 2008–09.

FA Cup: est season: 6th rd replay, 1931, 6th rd 1981.

Football League Cup: never beyond 4th rd.

Division 3 (S) Cup: ***Winners*** 1934.

sky SPORTS FACT FILE

Seven times capped Welsh international centre-half Harry Hanford had a lengthy and distinguished career that ended in 1946–47 with Exeter City. He made 37 League appearances for the Grecians at the age of 39 and later returned there as trainer.

Record Defeat: 0–9 v Notts Co, Division 3 (S), 16 October 1948. 0–9 v Northampton T, Division 3 (S), 12 April 1958.

Most League Points (2 for a win): 62, Division 4, 1976–77.

Most League Points (3 for a win): 89, Division 4, 1989–90.

Most League Goals: 88, Division 3 (S), 1932–33.

Highest League Scorer in Season: Fred Whitlow, 33, Division 3 (S), 1932–33.

Most League Goals in Total Aggregate: Tony Kellow, 129, 1976–78, 1980–83, 1985–88.

Most League Goals in One Match: 4, Harold 'Jazzo' Kirk v Portsmouth, Division 3 (S), 3 March 1923; 4, Fred Dent v Bristol R, Division 3 (S), 5 November 1927; 4, Fred Whitlow v Watford, Division 3 (S), 29 October 1932.

Most Capped Player: Dermot Curtis, 1 (17), Eire.

Most League Appearances: Arnold Mitchell, 495, 1952–66.

Youngest League Player: Cliff Bastin, 16 years 31 days v Coventry C, 14 April 1928.

Record Transfer Fee Received: £500,000 from Manchester C for Martin Phillips, November 1995.

Record Transfer Fee Paid: £65,000 to Blackpool for Tony Kellow, March 1980.

Football League Record: 1920 Elected to Division 3; 1921–58 Division 3 (S); 1958–64 Division 4; 1964–66 Division 3; 1966–77 Division 4; 1977–84 Division 3; 1984–90 Division 4; 1990–92 Division 3; 1992–94 Division 2; 1994–2003 Division 3; 2003–08 Conference; 2008–09 FL 2; 2009–12 FL 1; 2012– FL 2.

LATEST SEQUENCES

Longest Sequence of League Wins: 7, 23.4.1977 – 20.8.1977.

Longest Sequence of League Defeats: 7, 14.1.1984 – 25.2.1984.

Longest Sequence of League Draws: 6, 13.9.1986 – 4.10.1986.

Longest Sequence of Unbeaten League Matches: 13, 23.8.1986 – 25.10.1986.

Longest Sequence Without a League Win: 18, 21.2.1995 – 19.8.1995.

Successive Scoring Runs: 22 from 15.9.1958.

Successive Non-scoring Runs: 6 from 24.11.1923.

MANAGERS

Arthur Chadwick 1910–22
Fred Mavin 1923–27
Dave Wilson 1928–29
Billy McDevitt 1929–35
Jack English 1935–39
George Roughton 1945–52
Norman Kirkman 1952–53
Norman Dodgin 1953–57
Bill Thompson 1957–58
Frank Broome 1958–60
Glen Wilson 1960–62
Cyril Spiers 1962–63
Jack Edwards 1963–65
Ellis Stuttard 1965–66
Jock Basford 1966–67
Frank Broome 1967–69
Johnny Newman 1969–76
Bobby Saxton 1977–79
Brian Godfrey 1979–83
Gerry Francis 1983–84
Jim Iley 1984–85
Colin Appleton 1985–87
Terry Cooper 1988–91
Alan Ball 1991–94
Terry Cooper 1994–95
Peter Fox 1995–2000
Noel Blake 2000–01
John Cornforth 2001–02
Neil McNab 2002–03
Gary Peters 2003
Eamonn Dolan 2003–04
Alex Inglethorpe 2004–06
Paul Tisdale June 2006–

TEN YEAR LEAGUE RECORD

		P	W	D	L	F	A	Pts	Pos
2002-03	Div 3	46	11	15	20	50	64	48	23
2003-04	Conf	42	19	12	11	71	51	69	6
2004-05	Conf	42	20	11	11	71	50	71	6
2005-06	Conf	42	18	9	15	65	48	63	7
2006-07	Conf	46	22	12	12	67	48	78	5
2007-08	B Sq Pr	46	22	17	7	83	58	83	4
2008-09	FL 2	46	22	13	11	65	50	79	2
2009-10	FL 1	46	11	18	17	48	60	51	18
2010-11	FL 1	46	20	10	16	66	73	70	8
2011-12	FL 1	46	10	12	24	46	75	42	23

DID YOU KNOW ?

Exeter City had their finest FA Cup success between the wars on 10 January 1931, when First Division Derby County were beaten at St James Park. Although City played most of the second half with ten players and for part of it with only nine owing to injuries, they survived to win 3-2.

EXETER CITY 2011–12 LEAGUE RECORD

Match No.	Date	Venue	Opponents	Result		H/T Score	Lg Pos.	Goalscorers	Attendance
1	Aug 6	A	Stevenage	D	0-0	0-0	—		3829
2	13	H	Milton Keynes D	L	0-2	0-1	22		4832
3	16	H	Brentford	L	1-2	0-2	—	Bauza (pen) [66]	4344
4	20	A	Preston NE	L	0-1	0-1	22		10,655
5	27	H	Chesterfield	W	2-1	1-1	19	Archibald-Henville [16], Nichols [82]	4113
6	Sept 3	A	Hartlepool U	L	0-2	0-1	20		5152
7	10	A	Charlton Ath	L	0-2	0-1	22		14,290
8	13	H	Notts Co	D	1-1	1-1	—	Sheehan (og) [8]	3474
9	17	H	Bournemouth	L	0-2	0-1	23		4593
10	24	A	Sheffield W	L	0-3	0-2	23		16,995
11	Oct 1	H	Oldham Ath	W	2-0	1-0	23	Nardiello [18], Bauza [49]	3753
12	8	A	Bury	L	0-2	0-1	24		2672
13	15	H	Huddersfield T	L	0-4	0-2	24		4244
14	22	H	Rochdale	W	3-1	1-1	23	Nardiello 2 (1 pen) [45, 56 (p)], Taylor [81]	3844
15	25	A	Walsall	W	2-1	1-1	—	Nardiello 2 [8, 78]	4003
16	29	A	Sheffield U	D	4-4	2-1	19	Nardiello [9], Noble [23], O'Flynn [82], Dunne [86]	17,052
17	Nov 5	H	Carlisle U	D	0-0	0-0	19		4245
18	19	A	Yeovil T	D	2-2	2-1	20	Taylor [4], O'Flynn (pen) [30]	5635
19	26	H	Tranmere R	W	3-0	1-0	17	Bennett [41], Coles [66], Logan [78]	4108
20	Dec 10	A	Leyton Orient	L	0-3	0-0	18		4291
21	17	H	Scunthorpe U	D	0-0	0-0	18		4470
22	26	A	Wycombe W	L	1-3	1-2	19	Coles [23]	4904
23	31	A	Colchester U	L	0-2	0-1	19		3667
24	Jan 2	H	Yeovil T	D	1-1	0-1	20	Logan [75]	5912
25	7	A	Chesterfield	W	2-0	0-0	—	Logan [78], Sercombe [87]	5856
26	14	H	Hartlepool U	D	0-0	0-0	18		4016
27	21	A	Oldham Ath	D	0-0	0-0	18		3587
28	28	H	Charlton Ath	L	0-1	0-0	19		5439
29	Feb 7	A	Bournemouth	L	0-2	0-0	—		5497
30	11	H	Sheffield W	W	2-1	0-0	—	Jones [68], Noble [84]	5555
31	14	A	Notts Co	L	1-2	1-2	—	Bennett [14]	4741
32	18	H	Bury	W	3-2	3-1	19	Archibald-Henville [5], Nardiello (pen) [9], Logan [41]	4281
33	25	A	Huddersfield T	L	0-2	0-1	19		14,105
34	Mar 3	H	Stevenage	D	1-1	1-0	20	Logan [16]	4437
35	6	A	Brentford	L	0-2	0-1	—		4124
36	10	A	Milton Keynes D	L	0-3	0-2	21		9016
37	17	H	Preston NE	L	1-2	0-1	23	Sercombe [65]	4741
38	20	H	Wycombe W	L	1-3	0-0	—	Dunne [66]	4121
39	24	A	Tranmere R	L	0-2	0-0	23		4786
40	31	H	Colchester U	D	1-1	0-1	23	Cureton [83]	3889
41	Apr 6	A	Scunthorpe U	L	0-1	0-0	—		4361
42	9	H	Leyton Orient	W	3-0	1-0	22	Taylor [4], Sercombe 2 [60, 63]	4142
43	14	A	Rochdale	L	2-3	1-0	23	Nardiello (pen) [28], Sercombe [62]	1930
44	21	H	Walsall	W	4-2	0-1	23	Nardiello [50], Gow 2 [69, 77], Sercombe [88]	4307
45	28	A	Carlisle U	L	1-4	1-2	23	Sercombe [35]	6029
46	May 5	H	Sheffield U	D	2-2	1-1	23	Gow [24], Bennett [90]	6045

Final League Position: 23

GOALSCORERS

League (46): Nardiello 9 (3 pens), Sercombe 7, Logan 5, Bennett 3, Gow 3, Taylor 3, Archibald-Henville 2, Bauza 2 (1 pen), Coles 2, Dunne 2, Noble 2, O'Flynn 2 (1 pen), Cureton 1, Jones 1, Nichols 1, own goal 1.
Carling Cup (3): Bauza 1, Nardiello 1 (pen), Shephard 1.
FA Cup (3): Frear 1, Logan 1, Noble 1.
J Paint Trophy (2): Dunne 1, Nardiello 1.

Krysiak A 38	Tully S 42 + 2	Golbourne S 26	Dunne J 44 + 1	Archibald-Henville T 45	Duffy R 22 + 6	Sercombe L 27 + 6	Noble D 42	Bignall N 3	Nardiello D 28 + 8	Shephard C 7 + 4	Logan R 11 + 17	Coles D 28 + 3	McNish C 2 + 3	Nichols T 2 + 5	Jones B 16 + 3	Bauza G 12 + 15	Vine R 4 + 1	Pidgeley L 8 + 2	Keohane J — + 4	Whichelow M 2	Taylor J 26 + 4	O'Flynn J 8 + 16	Bennett S 13 + 2	Oakley M 7	Frear E 5 + 5	Hackett C 5	Dawson A 2	O'Brien L 2 + 1	Cureton J 5 + 2	Fortune J 5	Baldwin P 9	Dalla Valle L 4 + 1	Ricketts R — + 1	Gow A 6 + 1	*Match No.*
1	2	3	4	5	6^{2}	7	8	9	10^{1}	11	12	13																							1
1	2	3	4	5	6	7	8	9		11^{2}			10^{1}	12	13																				2
1	2	3	4	5	6	7^{3}	8	9^{2}		11	10^{1}			13	14	12																			3
1	2■	11	4	5	6		8		10	7					3	9																			4
1	2	11	4	5	6		8		10	12	14	3^{3}		13	7^{1}		9^{2}																		5
	2	11	4	5	6^{1}		8		10	7^{3}	12	3		13	14		9^{2}	1																	6
	2	11	4	5	6		8		10■	12	13	3^{1}			7^{2}		9^{3}	1	14																7
	2		4	5	6		8			11	9^{1}	3		10^{2}	7		12	1	13																8
	2		4	5	6		8			11^{1}	14	3			7	12	9^{3}	1	13	10^{2}															9
1	2	11	4	5^{2}	3		8		10			6				12				9^{1}	7^{3}	13	14												10
1	2	3	4	5			8		10^{2}		13	6				9^{1}					11	12		7											11
1	2	11	4			6	8				12	5				9						10^{1}	3	7											12
1^{G}	2^{1}	3	4	5		12	8		10			6				9^{2}		15			11	13		7											13
1	2	3	4	5		12	8		10			6				9^{1}					11			7											14
1	2	3	4	5		9^{1}	8		10			6				12^{2}					11	13		7											15
1	2	3^{1}	4	5		8	9		10			6									11	12		7											16
1^{G}	2	3	4	5		8	9		10			6	12^{2}					15			11	13		7^{1}											17
1	2	11	4	5	3^{1}	7	8				13	6							14		10^{3}	9^{2}			12										18
1	2	3		5	4						9	6	12								10		8		11	7^{1}									19
1	2	3	13	5	4^{2}	8^{3}	9				12	6									10	14			11^{1}	7									20
1	2	3	4	5	13	11	8^{3}		14		12	6^{2}									10				9^{1}	7									21
1	2^{2}	3	4	5	13	11	8		12			6				9					10					7^{1}									22
1	14	3	4	5	2	8	11		12^{2}			6■				9^{3}					10	13				7^{1}									23
1	2	3	4	5	6	7	8		10^{2}		9					12					11^{1}				13										24
1	2	3	4	5	6^{1}	8	11		10^{2}		7	12				9						13													25
1	2	3	4	5	6	7^{1}	11		10		8^{2}	14				9^{3}					12	13													26
1	2	3	4	5	6		8		12		10^{2}					9^{1}					11	13	7												27
1	2	11	4	5	3^{2}		8		14		12	6				13					10^{3}	9^{1}	7												28
1	2		4	5	3^{2}		11		10		9^{1}	8			6	12					14	13	7^{3}												29
1	2		4	5	14	12	8		10^{2}			6^{3}			3	9^{1}					11	13	7												30
1	2^{1}		4	5	12	14	11^{3}		10		13	6			3	9^{2}						8	7												31
1			4	5	2	12	8^{1}		10		9^{3}	6			3	14					11^{2}	13	7												32
1			4	5		7^{2}	11		10		12	6			3	13					9		8				2^{1}								33
1	2		4^{3}	5		7^{1}	8		14		9^{2}	6				12					13		11					3	10						34
1	2		4	5		13	8■		12		9^{1}	6									11	14	3					7^{2}	10^{3}						35
1	2		4	5		8				12	13	6									11^{2}	9	7^{1}					14	10	3^{3}					36
1	2		4	5		8				14	12					13					11	9^{2}			3		7^{1}		10^{3}	6					37
	2		4	5		8			10		12					13		1			11^{1}				7					6^{2}	3	9			38
	2		4	5		8^{1}	7		10^{2}							14		1			12	9^{3}								6	3	11	13		39
1	14		4	5	2^{3}		8		10				7												12				13	6^{1}	3	9		11^{2}	40
1	2		4	5		7^{2}	8		13		12				3						11								10^{3}		6	9^{1}		14	41
1	2		4	5		7	8		10^{2}				14	13	3	12					11^{1}										6			9^{3}	42
1	2		4	5		7	8		10^{1}						3						11								13		6	12^{2}		9	43
	2		4	5		7	8		10					11^{1}	3			1							12						6			9	44
	2		4	5	13	7	8		10^{3}						3			1				14	11^{1}		12						6^{2}			9	45
1	2		4^{1}	5	13	7	8		10						3	14						11^{3}	12								6^{2}			9	46

FA Cup

First Round	Walsall	(h)	1-1
		(a)	2-3

Carling Cup

First Round	Yeovil T	(h)	2-0
Second Round	Liverpool	(h)	1-3

J Paint Trophy

First Round	Plymouth Arg	(h)	1-1
Second Round	Swindon T	(h)	1-2

FLEETWOOD TOWN FL Championship 2

FOUNDATION

Originally formed in 1908 as Fleetwood FC, it was liquidated in 1976. Re-formed as Fleetwood Town in 1977, it folded again in 1996. Once again, it was re-formed a year later as Fleetwood Wanderers, but a sponsorship deal saw the club's name immediately changed to Fleetwood Freeport through the local retail outlet centre. This sponsorship ended in 2002, but since then local energy businessman Andy Pilley took charge and the club has risen through the non-league pyramid until finally achieving Football League status in 2012 as Fleetwood Town.

Highbury Stadium, Park Avenue, Fleetwood, Lancs FY7 5TX.

MANAGER

Micky Mellon September 2008–

Telephone: (01253) 775 080.

Email: info@fleetwoodtownfc.com

Ground Capacity: 5,094.

Record attendance: (Before 1997) 6,150 v Rochdale, FA Cup 1st Rd, 13 November 1965; (Since 1997) 5,092 v Blackpool, FA Cup 3rd Rd, 7 January 2012.

Pitch Measurements: 115yd × 71yd.

Chairman: Andy Pilley.

Chief Executive: Steve Curwood.

Secretary: Steve Edwards.

Manager: Micky Mellon.

Assistant Manager: Craig Madden.

Physio: Ian Liversedge.

Colours: Red shirts with white sleeves, white shorts, red stockings.

sky SPORTS FACT FILE

Fleetwood Town enjoyed their best season in the FA Cup during 2011–12 defeating Mansfield Town, Wycombe Wanderers and Yeovil Town to reach the third round. The team also registered a 29-game unbeaten run in the Blue Square Premier League to attain promotion.

Year Formed: 1908 (re-formed 1997).

Club nicknames: The Trawlermen, The Cod Army.

Grounds: 1908, North Euston Hotel; 1934, Memorial Park (now Highbury Stadium).

Record League Victory: 13-0 v Oldham T, North West Counties Div 2, 5 December 1998.

Record Defeat: 0-7 v Billingham T, FA Cup 1st Qual rd, 2001-02, 15 September 2001.

Most League Appearances: Percy Ronson, 416, 1949-64.

Record Transfer Fee Received: £1,000,000 from Leicester C for Jamie Vardy, May 2012.

Record Transfer Fee Paid: £150,000 to Halifax T for Jamie Vardy, August 2011.

HONOURS

1908 Foundation

Lancashire Combination: Champions 1923–24. ***Runners-Up:*** 1933–34, 1934–35.

Northern Premier League Challenge Cup: ***Winners:*** 1971.

Lancashire Combination Cup: ***Winners:*** 1926, 1932, 1933, 1934. ***Runners-up:*** 1953, 1967.

1976 Foundation

Northern Premier League First Division: ***Champions:*** 1987–88.

North West Counties Football League First Division: ***Champions:*** 1983–84.

Northern Premier League Presiden's Cup: ***Winners:*** 1990.

FA Vase: ***Runners Cup:*** 1984–85.

Northern Premier League Challenge Cup: ***Runners-up:*** 1989.

1997 Foundation

FA Cup: 3rd rd 2011–12.

Conference: ***Champions:*** 2011–12.

Conference North: ***Runners-up and Play-off winners:*** 2009–10.

Northern Premier League Premier Division: ***Champions:*** 2007–08.

Northern Premier League First Division: ***Runners-up*** (promoted): 2005–06.

North West Counties Football League Premier Division: ***Champions:*** 2004–05.

North West Counties Football League First Divison: ***Champions:*** 1998–99.

Peter Swales Memorial Shield: ***Winners:*** 2008.

Northern Premier League Challenge Cup: ***Winners:*** 2007.

North West Counties Football League First Division Trophy: ***Winners:*** 1999.

Lancashire League West Division Reserve League: ***Winners:*** 2008–09.

TEN YEAR LEAGUE RECORD

		P	*W*	*D*	*L*	*F*	*A*	*Pts*	*Pos*
2002-03	NWC 1	42	17	9	16	73	70	60	10
2003-04	NWC 1	42	26	8	8	84	51	86	3
2004-05	NWC 1	42	31	6	5	107	42	99	1
2005-06	Uni 1	42	22	10	10	72	48	76	2
2006-07	Uni Pr	42	19	10	13	71	60	67	8
2007-08	Uni Pr	40	28	7	5	81	39	91	1
2008-09	Conf N	42	17	11	14	70	66	62	8
2009-10	Conf N	42	26	7	7	86	44	85	2
2010-11	Conf	46	22	12	12	68	42	78	5
2011-12	Conf	46	31	10	5	102	48	103	1

DID YOU KNOW?

On 17 May 2012 Leicester City paid a non-league record fee of £1m to obtain the signature of top scorer Jamie Vardy from Fleetwood Town. This versatile forward had started his career with Stocksbridge Park Steels and joined the Cod Army from FC Halifax Town in August 2011.

FULHAM FA Premiership

FOUNDATION

Churchgoers were responsible for the foundation of Fulham, which first saw the light of day as Fulham St Andrew's Church Sunday School FC in 1879. They won the West London Amateur Cup in 1887 and the championship of the West London League in its initial season of 1892–93. The name Fulham had been adopted in 1888.

Craven Cottage, Stevenage Road, London SW6 6HH.

Telephone: (0843) 208 1222.

Fax: (0870) 442 0236 (Motspur Park).

Ticket Line: (0843) 208 1234.

Website: www.fulhamfc.co.uk

Email: enquiries@fulhamfc.com

Ground Capacity: 26,600.

Record Attendance: 49,335 v Millwall, Division 2, 8 October 1938.

Pitch Measurements: 100m × 65m.

Chairman: Mohamed Al Fayed.

Chief Executive: Alistair Mackintosh.

Manager: Martin Jol.

Head Coach: Michael Lindeman.

Head of Sports Medicine and Exercise Science: Mark Taylor.

HONOURS

Football League –
Division 1: *Champions* 2000–01;
Division 2: *Champions* 1948–49, 1998–99; ***Runners-up*** 1958–59;
Division 3 (S): *Champions* 1931–32;
Division 3: *Runners-up* 1970–71, 1996–97.

FA Cup: *Runners-up* 1975.

Football League Cup: Best season: 5th rd, 1968, 1971, 2000, 2005.

European Competitions
UEFA Cup: 2002–03.
Intertoto Cup: 2002 (*winners*).
Europa League: 2009–10 (*runners-up*), 2011–12.

Colours: White shirts with black trim, black shorts, white stockings.

Year Formed: 1879.

Turned Professional: 1898.

Reformed: 1987.

Previous Name: 1879, Fulham St Andrew's; 1888, Fulham.

Club Nickname: 'Cottagers'.

Grounds: 1879, Star Road, Fulham; c.1883, Eel Brook Common, 1884, Lillie Road; 1885, Putney Lower Common; 1886, Ranelagh House, Fulham; 1888, Barn Elms, Castelnau; 1889, Purser's Cross (Roskell's Field), Parsons Green Lane; 1891, Eel Brook Common; 1891, Half Moon, Putney; 1895, Captain James Field, West Brompton; 1896, Craven Cottage.

First Football League Game: 3 September 1907, Division 2, v Hull C (h) L 0–1 – Skene; Ross, Lindsay; Collins, Morrison, Goldie; Dalrymple, Freeman, Bevan, Hubbard, Threlfall.

Record League Victory: 10–1 v Ipswich T, Division 1, 26 December 1963 – Macedo; Cohen, Langley; Mullery (1), Keetch, Robson (1); Key, Cook (1), Leggat (4), Haynes, Howfield (3).

Record Cup Victory: 7–0 v Swansea C, FA Cup 1st rd, 11 November 1995 – Lange; Jupp (1), Herrera, Barkus (Brooker (1)), Moore, Angus, Thomas (1), Morgan, Brazil (Hamill), Conroy (3) (Bolt), Cusack (1).

Record Defeat: 0–10 v Liverpool, League Cup 2nd rd 1st leg, 23 September 1986.

sky SPORTS FACT FILE

The week in which the Premier League restarted in August 2011 was a landmark one for Aaron Hughes. On the 10th he scored his first goal for Northern Ireland in 77 full appearances and four days later made his 400th Premier League outing for Fulham against Aston Villa.

Most League Points (2 for a win): 60, Division 2, 1958–59 and Division 3, 1970–71.

Most League Points (3 for a win): 101, Division 2, 1998–99. 101, Division 1, 2000–01.

Most League Goals: 111, Division 3 (S), 1931–32.

Highest League Scorer in Season: Frank Newton, 43, Division 3 (S), 1931–32.

Most League Goals in Total Aggregate: Gordon Davies, 159, 1978–84, 1986–91.

Most League Goals in One Match: 5, Fred Harrison v Stockport Co, Division 2, 5 September 1908; 5, Bedford Jezzard v Hull C, Division 2, 8 October 1955; 5, Jimmy Hill v Doncaster R, Division 2, 15 March 1958; 5, Steve Earle v Halifax T, Division 3, 16 September 1969.

Most Capped Player: Johnny Haynes, 56, England.

Most League Appearances: Johnny Haynes, 594, 1952–70.

Youngest League Player: Matthew Briggs, 16 years 65 days v Middlesbrough, 13 May 2007.

Record Transfer Fee Received: £11,500,000 from Manchester U for Louis Saha, January 2004.

Record Transfer Fee Paid: £11,500,000 to Lyon for Steve Marlet, August 2001.

Football League Record: 1907 Elected to Division 2; 1928–32 Division 3 (S); 1932–49 Division 2; 1949–52 Division 1; 1952–59 Division 2; 1959–68 Division 1; 1968–69 Division 2; 1969–71 Division 3; 1971–80 Division 2; 1980–82 Division 3; 1982–86 Division 2; 1986–92 Division 3; 1992–94 Division 2; 1994–97 Division 3; 1997–99 Division 2; 1999–2001 Division 1; 2001– FA Premier League.

LATEST SEQUENCES

Longest Sequence of League Wins: 12, 7.5.2000 – 18.10.2000.

Longest Sequence of League Defeats: 11, 2.12.1961 – 24.2.1962.

Longest Sequence of League Draws: 6, 14.10.1995 – 18.11.1995.

Longest Sequence of Unbeaten League Matches: 15, 26.1.1999 – 13.4.1999.

Longest Sequence Without a League Win: 15, 25.2.1950 – 23.8.1950.

Successive Scoring Runs: 26 from 28.3.1931.

Successive Non-scoring Runs: 6 from 21.8.1971.

MANAGERS

Harry Bradshaw 1904–09
Phil Kelso 1909–24
Andy Ducat 1924–26
Joe Bradshaw 1926–29
Ned Liddell 1929–31
Jim McIntyre 1931–34
Jimmy Hogan 1934–35
Jack Peart 1935–48
Frank Osborne 1948–64
(was Secretary-Manager or General Manager for most of this period and Team Manager 1953–56)
Bill Dodgin Snr 1949–53
Duggie Livingstone 1956–58
Bedford Jezzard 1958–64
(General Manager for last two months)
Vic Buckingham 1965–68
Bobby Robson 1968
Bill Dodgin Jnr 1968–72
Alec Stock 1972–76
Bobby Campbell 1976–80
Malcolm Macdonald 1980–84
Ray Harford 1984–96
Ray Lewington 1986–90
Alan Dicks 1990–91
Don Mackay 1991–94
Ian Branfoot 1994–96
(continued as General Manager)
Micky Adams 1996–97
Ray Wilkins 1997–98
Kevin Keegan 1998–99
(Chief Operating Officer)
Paul Bracewell 1999–2000
Jean Tigana 2000–03
Chris Coleman 2003–07
Lawrie Sanchez 2007
Roy Hodgson 2007–10
Mark Hughes 2010–11
Martin Jol June 2011–

TEN YEAR LEAGUE RECORD

		P	W	D	L	F	A	Pts	Pos
2002-03	PR Lge	38	13	9	16	41	50	48	14
2003-04	PR Lge	38	14	10	14	52	46	52	9
2004-05	PR Lge	38	12	8	18	52	60	44	13
2005-06	PR Lge	38	14	6	18	48	58	48	12
2006-07	PR Lge	38	8	15	15	38	60	39	16
2007-08	PR Lge	38	8	12	18	38	60	36	17
2008-09	PR Lge	38	14	11	13	39	34	53	7
2009-10	PR Lge	38	12	10	16	39	46	46	12
2010-11	PR Lge	38	11	16	11	49	43	49	8
2011-12	PR Lge	38	14	10	14	48	51	52	9

DID YOU KNOW ?

The first African player to turn out for Fulham was Hassan "Heggy" Hegazi, an amateur inside-forward who scored on his only appearance against Stockport County on 11 November 1911. Remaining an amateur, he played for Dulwich Hamlet and won his blue at Cambridge.

FULHAM 2011–12 LEAGUE RECORD

Match No.	*Date*	*Venue*	*Opponents*	*Result*	*H/T Score*	*Lg Pos.*	*Goalscorers*	*Attendance*
1	Aug 13	H	Aston Villa	D 0-0	0-0	—		25,700
2	21	A	Wolverhampton W	L 0-2	0-2	15		22,657
3	28	A	Newcastle U	L 1-2	0-0	16	Dempsey [88]	42,684
4	Sept 11	H	Blackburn R	D 1-1	1-1	18	Zamora [38]	24,856
5	18	H	Manchester C	D 2-2	0-1	18	Zamora [56], Kompany (og) [76]	24,750
6	24	A	WBA	D 0-0	0-0	17		23,835
7	Oct 2	H	QPR	W 6-0	3-0	12	Johnson, A 3 [2, 38, 59], Murphy (pen) [20], Dempsey [65], Zamora [74]	23,766
8	15	A	Stoke C	L 0-2	0-0	14		26,890
9	23	H	Everton	L 1-3	0-1	17	Ruiz [67]	25,646
10	29	A	Wigan Ath	W 2-0	1-0	15	Dempsey [41], Dembele [86]	15,796
11	Nov 6	H	Tottenham H	L 1-3	0-2	16	Kaboul (og) [57]	25,698
12	19	A	Sunderland	D 0-0	0-0	16		37,688
13	26	A	Arsenal	D 1-1	0-0	15	Vermaelen (og) [65]	60,043
14	Dec 5	H	Liverpool	W 1-0	0-0	—	Dempsey [85]	25,688
15	10	A	Swansea C	L 0-2	0-0	14		19,296
16	17	H	Bolton W	W 2-0	2-0	11	Dempsey [32], Ruiz [34]	25,643
17	21	H	Manchester U	L 0-5	0-3	—		25,700
18	26	A	Chelsea	D 1-1	0-0	13	Dempsey [56]	41,548
19	31	A	Norwich C	D 1-1	1-0	13	Sa [7]	26,406
20	Jan 2	H	Arsenal	W 2-1	0-1	—	Sidwell [85], Zamora [90]	25,700
21	14	A	Blackburn R	L 1-3	0-1	14	Duff [56]	18,003
22	21	H	Newcastle U	W 5-2	0-1	12	Murphy (pen) [52], Dempsey 3 [59, 65, 89], Zamora (pen) [68]	25,692
23	Feb 1	H	WBA	D 1-1	0-0	—	Dempsey [69]	25,689
24	4	A	Manchester C	L 0-3	0-2	14		46,963
25	11	H	Stoke C	W 2-1	2-0	12	Pogrebnyak [16], Sorensen (og) [28]	23,555
26	25	A	QPR	W 1-0	1-0	11	Pogrebnyak [7]	18,015
27	Mar 4	H	Wolverhampton W	W 5-0	2-0	8	Pogrebnyak 3 [36, 44, 61], Dempsey 2 [56, 83]	24,034
28	10	A	Aston Villa	L 0-1	0-0	10		32,372
29	17	H	Swansea C	L 0-3	0-1	—		25,690
30	26	A	Manchester U	L 0-1	0-1	—		75,570
31	31	H	Norwich C	W 2-1	2-0	10	Dempsey [2], Duff [13]	25,700
32	Apr 7	A	Bolton W	W 3-0	2-0	10	Dempsey 2 [30, 45], Diarra [80]	21,939
33	9	H	Chelsea	D 1-1	0-1	—	Dempsey [82]	25,697
34	21	H	Wigan Ath	W 2-1	0-0	9	Pogrebnyak [58], Senderos [89]	25,689
35	28	A	Everton	L 0-4	0-3	9		31,885
36	May 1	A	Liverpool	W 1-0	1-0	—	Skrtel (og) [5]	40,106
37	6	H	Sunderland	W 2-1	2-1	8	Dempsey [12], Dembele [35]	25,683
38	13	A	Tottenham H	L 0-2	0-1	9		36,256

Final League Position: 9

GOALSCORERS

League (48): Dempsey 17, Pogrebnyak 6, Zamora 5 (1 pen), Johnson, A 3, Dembele 2, Duff 2, Murphy 2 (2 pens), Ruiz 2, Diarra 1, Sa 1, Senderos 1, Sidwell 1, own goals 5.
Carling Cup (0).
FA Cup (5): Dempsey 3 (1 pen), Duff 1, Murphy 1 (pen).
Europa League (24): Johnson 8, Dempsey 3, Duff 3, Murphy 3 (3 pens), Sidwell 2, Zamora 2, Briggs 1, Frei 1, Hughes 1.

Schwarzer M 30	Hughes A 18 + 1	Riise J 35 + 1	Murphy D 33 + 3	Senderos P 21	Hangeland B 38	Duff D 23 + 5	Etuhu D 9 + 13	Johnson A 13 + 7	Zamora B 14 + 1	Dempsey C 37	Dembele M 33 + 3	Kasami P 3 + 4	Sidwell S 12 + 2	Baird C 13 + 6	Briggs M 1 + 1	Ruiz B 17 + 10	Kelly S 21 + 3	Grygera Z 5	Sa O 3 + 4	Gecov M — + 2	Davies S 3 + 3	Frei K 6 + 10	Stockdale D 8	Pogrebnyak P 12	Diarra M 8 + 3	Kacaniklic A 2 + 2	Trotta M — + 1	*Match No.*
1	2	3	4	5	6	7	8	9	10^1	11	12																	1
1	2	3	4	5	6	7	8^1	9		11	12	10^2	13															2
1	5		4		6	7		12		11	9	10^1	8	2	3													3
1	2^1	3^3	4	5	6	7		14	10	9	13		8			11^2	12											4
1		3	4		6	7^1			10	11	9^2	12	8	5		13	2											5
1		3	4^2		6		13			11	9	7^1	8	2		12		5	10									6
1		3	4^2		6		13	9^1	10	11	7^3		8	5		12		2	14									7
1	5	3	4^2		6	12	13	9^3	10	11	7^1		8	2					14									8
1	13	3	4^1		6			9	10	11	7		8	5		12		2^2										9
1		3	4^1		6	14	12	9	10^2	11	7^3		8	5		13		2										10
1		3	4^3		6	7^2	14		10	11	9		8	5		13	12	2^1										11
1	2		4	3	6	7^2	8	12	10^1	11^3	9			5	14	13												12
1		3	4	5	6		8	13	10^2	7	9	12		2		11^1												13
1		3	4^2	5	6		8	12	10^1	7	9					11	2			13								14
1		3		5	6		4	9		7	10^1					11	2		13		8^2	12						15
		3	4	5	6		8	9		7	10			2		11							1					16
		3	4	5	6		8	9	13	7^2	10			2^1		11	12						1					17
		3	4	5	6					7	10	12				11	2		9^1			8	1					18
		3	4^1	5	6	14	12			7	10		13			11	2		9^2			8^3	1					19
		3	4^1	5	6				10	7	9		8			11	2					12	1					20
		3^3	4	5	6	7		14	10	9	8^1					11	2				13	12^2	1					21
		3	4	5	6	7		12	10	9^3			8^1	13		11^2	2					14	1					22
		3	4	5	6	7				9			8			11	2				10		1					23
1		13	4	5^2	6	7	8^1			10	9^3			3		12	2			14	11							24
1	5	3	4^2		6	7	13			10	8			14		11^3	2				12			9^1				25
1	5	3	4^1		6	13	14	10^3		7	8			12		11^2	2							9				26
1	2	3	4^1	5	6	7^2		10		11	8										13	14		9^3	12			27
1		3	4^2	5	6	7		10^1		11	8					12	2							9	13			28
1		3	14	5	6	12		10^2		11	8					7^1	2					13		9	4^3			29
1	5	3	13		6	7				10	8					12	2					11^1		9	4^2			30
1	5	3	4^2		6	7	14			10	8					11^3	2							9^1	13	12		31
1	5	3			6	7^2	12			9	8					11^1	2					13			4	10^3	14	32
1	5	3	4^1		6	7	12			9	10						2		13			11^3			8^2	14		33
1	2	3	4^1	5	6	7				11	10											12		9	8			34
1	2	3	13	5^1	6	7	14			10	8			12								11		9^2	4^3			35
1	5	3	4		6	7	13			10	8^3			14			2					12		9^2		11^1		36
1	5	3	4^2		6	7				11	10			13			2					12		9^1	8			37
1	5	3	4^1		6	7					10	12					2					11		9	8			38

FA Cup

Third Round — Charlton Ath (h) 4-0

Fourth Round — Everton (a) 1-2

Carling Cup

Third Round — Chelsea (a) 0-0

Europa League

First Qualifying Round — NSI (h) 3-0, (a) 0-0

Second Qualifying Round — Crusaders (a) 3-1, (h) 4-0

Third Qualifying Round — Split (a) 0-0, (h) 2-0

Play-Off Round — Dnepr (h) 3-0, (a) 0-1

Group K — Twente (h) 1-1

Odense (a) 2-0

Wisla (a) 0-1

(h) 4-1

Twente (a) 0-1

Odense (h) 2-2

GILLINGHAM FL Championship 2

FOUNDATION

The success of the pioneering Royal Engineers of Chatham excited the interest of the residents of the Medway Towns and led to the formation of many clubs including Excelsior. After winning the Kent Junior Cup and the Chatham District League in 1893, Excelsior decided to go for bigger things and it was at a meeting in the Napier Arms, Brompton, in 1893 that New Brompton FC came into being, buying and developing the ground which is now Priestfield Stadium. They changed their name to Gillingham in 1913, when they also changed their strip from black and white stripes to predominantly blue.

MEMS Priestfield Stadium, Redfern Avenue, Gillingham, Kent ME7 4DD.

Telephone: (01634) 300 000.

Fax: (01634) 850 986.

Ticket Office: (01634) 300 000 (option 3).

Website: www.gillinghamfootballclub.com

Email: info@priestfield.com

Ground Capacity: 11,440.

Record Attendance: 23,002 v QPR, FA Cup 3rd rd, 10 January 1948.

Pitch Measurements: 110yd × 70yd.

Chairman: Paul D. P. Scally.

Vice-chairman: Michael Anderson.

Manager: Martin Allen.

Assistant Manager: John Schofield.

Physio: James Barker.

Colours: Red shirts with blue sleeves, white shorts, white stockings.

Year Formed: 1893.

Turned Professional: 1894.

Previous Name: 1893, New Brompton; 1913, Gillingham.

Club Nickname: 'The Gills'.

Ground: 1893, Priestfield Stadium.

First Football League Game: 28 August 1920, Division 3, v Southampton (h) D 1–1 – Branfield; Robertson, Sissons; Battiste, Baxter, Wigmore; Holt, Hall, Gilbey (1), Roe, Gore.

Record League Victory: 10–0 v Chesterfield, Division 3, 5 September 1987 – Kite; Haylock, Pearce, Shipley (2) (Lillis), West, Greenall (1), Pritchard (2), Shearer (2), Lovell, Elsey (2), David Smith (1).

Record Cup Victory: 10–1 v Gorleston, FA Cup 1st rd, 16 November 1957 – Brodie; Parry, Hannaway; Riggs, Boswell, Laing; Payne, Fletcher (2), Saunders (5), Morgan (1), Clark (2).

HONOURS

Football League – Division 1: 11th, 2002–03; **Division 3:** ***Runners-up*** 1995–96; **Division 4:** ***Champions*** 1963–64; ***Runners-up*** 1973–74.

FA Cup: Best season: 6th rd, 2000.

Football League Cup: Best season: 4th rd, 1964, 1997.

sky SPORTS FACT FILE

Inside-forward Tom Hall had played for both Sunderland and Newcastle United in his native north-east prior to the Great War and joined Gillingham on their election to the Third Division in 1920. He made 190 League appearances, scored 47 goals and later became their trainer.

Record Defeat: 2–9 v Nottingham F, Division 3 (S), 18 November 1950.

Most League Points (2 for a win): 62, Division 4, 1973–74.

Most League Points (3 for a win): 85, Division 2, 1999–2000.

Most League Goals: 90, Division 4, 1973–74.

Highest League Scorer in Season: Ernie Morgan, 31, Division 3 (S), 1954–55; Brian Yeo, 31, Division 4, 1973–74.

Most League Goals in Total Aggregate: Brian Yeo, 135, 1963–75.

Most League Goals in One Match: 6, Fred Cheesmur v Merthyr T, Division 3 (S), 26 April 1930.

Most Capped Player: Mamady Sidibe, 7 (14), Mali.

Most League Appearances: John Simpson, 571, 1957–72.

Youngest League Player: Luke Freeman, 15 years 247 days v Hartlepool U, 24 November 2007.

Record Transfer Fee Received: £1,500,000 from Manchester C for Robert Taylor, November 1999.

Record Transfer Fee Paid: £600,000 to Reading for Carl Asaba, August 1998.

Football League Record: 1920 Original Member of Division 3; 1921 Division 3 (S); 1938 Failed re-election; Southern League 1938–44; Kent League 1944–46; Southern League 1946–50; 1950 Re-elected to Division 3 (S); 1958–64 Division 4; 1964–71 Division 3; 1971–74 Division 4; 1974–89 Division 3; 1989–92 Division 4; 1992–96; Division 3; 1996–2000 Division 2; 2000–04 Division 1; 2004–05 FL C; 2005–08 FL 1; 2008–09 FL 2; 2009–10 FL 1; 2010– FL 2.

LATEST SEQUENCES

Longest Sequence of League Wins: 7, 18.12.1954 – 29.1.1955.

Longest Sequence of League Defeats: 10, 20.9.1988 – 5.11.1988.

Longest Sequence of League Draws: 5, 28.8.1993 – 18.9.1993.

Longest Sequence of Unbeaten League Matches: 20, 13.10.1973 – 10.2.1974.

Longest Sequence Without a League Win: 15, 1.4.1972 – 2.9.1972.

Successive Scoring Runs: 20 from 31.10.1959.

Successive Non-scoring Runs: 6 from 11.2.1961.

MANAGERS

W. Ironside Groombridge 1896–1906 *(Secretary-Manager)* *(previously Financial Secretary)*
Steve Smith 1906–08
W. I. Groombridge 1908–19 *(Secretary-Manager)*
George Collins 1919–20
John McMillan 1920–23
Harry Curtis 1923–26
Albert Hoskins 1926–29
Dick Hendrie 1929–31
Fred Mavin 1932–37
Alan Ure 1937–38
Bill Harvey 1938–39
Archie Clark 1939–58
Harry Barratt 1958–62
Freddie Cox 1962–65
Basil Hayward 1966–71
Andy Nelson 1971–74
Len Ashurst 1974–75
Gerry Summers 1975–81
Keith Peacock 1981–87
Paul Taylor 1988
Keith Burkinshaw 1988–89
Damien Richardson 1989–92
Glenn Roeder 1992–93
Mike Flanagan 1993–95
Neil Smillie 1995
Tony Pulis 1995–99
Peter Taylor 1999–2000
Andy Hessenthaler 2000–04
Stan Ternent 2004–05
Neale Cooper 2005
Ronnie Jepson 2005–07
Mark Stimson 2007–10
Andy Hessenthaler 2010–12
Martin Allen July 2012–

TEN YEAR LEAGUE RECORD

		P	*W*	*D*	*L*	*F*	*A*	*Pts*	*Pos*
2002-03	Div 1	46	16	14	16	56	65	62	11
2003-04	Div 1	46	14	9	23	48	67	51	21
2004-05	FL C	46	12	14	20	45	66	50	22
2005-06	FL 1	46	16	12	18	50	64	60	14
2006-07	FL 1	46	17	8	21	56	77	59	16
2007-08	FL 1	46	11	13	22	44	73	46	22
2008-09	FL 2	46	21	12	13	58	55	75	5
2009-10	FL 1	46	12	14	20	48	64	50	21
2010-11	FL 2	46	17	17	12	67	57	68	8
2011-12	FL 2	46	20	10	16	79	62	70	8

DID YOU KNOW ?

On their return to the Football League in 1950–51, Gillingham were involved in a match of thirteen goals. On 17 January they defeated Exeter City 9-4. Derek Lewis who scored a hat trick that day subsequently died of a brain haemorrhage in the summer of 1953 while with Preston North End.

GILLINGHAM 2011–12 LEAGUE RECORD

Match No.	Date	Venue	Opponents	Result	H/T Score	Lg Pos.	Goalscorers	Atten-dance
1	Aug 6	H	Cheltenham T	W 1-0	1-0	—	Montrose [26]	5360
2	13	A	Crewe Alex	W 2-1	2-0	2	Whelpdale [23], Spiller [25]	3401
3	16	A	Barnet	D 2-2	1-0	—	Spiller [6], Payne, J [73]	2466
4	20	H	Plymouth Arg	W 3-0	0-0	3	Kedwell 2 (2 pens) [74, 90], Rooney [86]	5053
5	27	A	Rotherham U	L 0-3	0-0	4		3740
6	Sept 3	H	Shrewsbury T	L 0-1	0-0	6		4869
7	10	H	Accrington S	D 1-1	0-0	8	Rooney (pen) [88]	4619
8	13	A	Southend U	L 0-1	0-0	—		4598
9	17	A	Hereford U	W 6-1	3-0	9	Nouble [19], Richards [24], Heath (og) [40], Jackman [49], Whelpdale [79], Payne, S [83]	1848
10	24	H	Burton Alb	W 3-1	1-1	6	Kedwell 2 [20, 50], Nouble [49]	4946
11	Oct 1	A	AFC Wimbledon	L 1-3	0-3	9	Lee, C [67]	4606
12	8	H	Port Vale	D 1-1	0-1	10	Kedwell (pen) [63]	4676
13	15	A	Torquay U	W 5-2	2-0	9	Osei-Kuffour 2 [6, 39], Rooney (pen) [56], Nouble [78], Whelpdale [89]	2582
14	22	H	Oxford U	W 1-0	1-0	5	Montrose [45]	5819
15	25	A	Swindon T	L 0-2	0-0	—		7787
16	29	A	Morecambe	L 1-2	0-1	10	Nouble (pen) [90]	2067
17	Nov 5	H	Northampton T	W 4-3	3-1	9	Osei-Kuffour 3 (1 pen) [11, 30, 45 (p)], Kedwell (pen) [90]	4704
18	19	A	Aldershot T	W 2-1	2-0	8	Nouble [7], Whelpdale [36]	3449
19	26	H	Bradford C	D 0-0	0-0	7		7074
20	Dec 10	A	Macclesfield T	D 0-0	0-0	7		1724
21	17	H	Bristol R	W 4-1	2-0	7	Montrose [8], Kedwell 2 (2 pens) [45, 73], Jackman [68]	7750
22	26	A	Crawley T	W 2-1	0-1	6	Osei-Kuffour 2 [50, 52]	4255
23	30	A	Dagenham & R	L 1-2	1-1	—	Kedwell [7]	3120
24	Jan 2	H	Aldershot T	W 1-0	0-0	6	Jackman [46]	5432
25	14	A	Shrewsbury T	L 0-2	0-1	7		4940
26	21	H	AFC Wimbledon	L 3-4	1-0	8	Tomlin 2 [4, 62], Osei-Kuffour [54]	6236
27	28	A	Accrington S	L 3-4	1-4	9	Jackman [7], Tomlin 2 [70, 85]	1734
28	Feb 13	H	Southend U	L 1-2	0-2	—	Tomlin [87]	4441
29	18	A	Port Vale	L 1-2	1-0	13	Whelpdale [45]	4027
30	21	H	Rotherham U	D 0-0	0-0	—		3248
31	25	H	Torquay U	W 2-0	0-0	10	King [51], Kedwell (pen) [90]	4865
32	28	H	Hereford U	W 5-4	1-2	—	Whelpdale [45], Kedwell [46], Lee, C 2 [81, 88], Tomlin [90]	3784
33	Mar 3	A	Plymouth Arg	W 1-0	1-0	8	Martin [23]	6382
34	6	H	Barnet	W 3-1	0-1	—	Oli [47], Obita [76], Lee, C [87]	3751
35	10	H	Crewe Alex	L 3-4	0-1	8	Payne, J [48], Whelpdale [67], Miller [73]	5428
36	17	A	Cheltenham T	W 3-0	1-0	8	Obita 2 [45, 54], Whelpdale [83]	3137
37	20	H	Crawley T	L 0-1	0-0	—		5204
38	24	A	Bradford C	D 2-2	1-0	9	Montrose [25], Ramsden (og) [56]	9858
39	27	A	Burton Alb	L 0-1	0-0	—		1714
40	31	H	Macclesfield T	W 2-0	0-0	9	Fish [51], Whelpdale [85]	4562
41	Apr 6	A	Bristol R	D 2-2	0-0	9	Whelpdale [56], Oli [90]	6160
42	9	H	Dagenham & R	L 1-2	0-1	9	Vine [58]	5773
43	14	A	Oxford U	D 0-0	0-0	9		7322
44	21	H	Swindon T	W 3-1	1-0	9	Kedwell [26], Whelpdale 2 (1 pen) [52, 90 (p)]	6390
45	28	A	Northampton T	D 1-1	0-1	9	Osei-Kuffour [54]	5832
46	May 5	H	Morecambe	W 2-0	1-0	8	Lee, C 2 [18, 76]	4382

Final League Position: 8

GOALSCORERS

League (79): Kedwell 12 (7 pens), Whelpdale 12 (1 pen), Osei-Kuffour 9 (1 pen), Lee, C 6, Tomlin 6, Nouble 5 (1 pen), Jackman 4, Montrose 4, Obita 3, Rooney 3 (2 pens), Oli 2, Payne, J 2, Spiller 2, Fish 1, King 1, Martin 1, Miller 1, Payne, S 1, Richards 1, Vine 1, own goals 2.
Carling Cup (0).
FA Cup (8): Kedwell 2, Weston 2, Jackman 1, Payne, J 1, Payne, S 1, Richards 1.
J Paint Trophy (1): Richards 1.

Flitney R 27	Fuller B 9	Martin J 32 + 3	Lee C 28 + 5	Lawrence M 24 + 2	Frampton A 27 + 1	Whelpdale C 34 + 5	Payne J 29 + 1	Kedwell D 37 + 3	Spiller D 6 + 9	Montrose L 28 + 9	Rooney L 11 + 6	Weston C 21 + 9	Payne S — + 12	Fish M 19 + 4	Oli D 4 + 19	Jackman D 36 + 4	Richards G 24	Nouble F 12 + 1	Osei-Kuffour J 26 + 4	Evans J 4 + 3	King S 8 + 1	Tomlin G 9 + 1	Gazzaniga P 19 + 1	Essam C 17 + 1	Lee O 5 + 3	Davies C — + 2	Obita J 5 + 1	Miller A 2 + 3	Vine R 3 + 6	Brown A — + 1	*Match No.*
1	2	3	4	5	6	7	8	9	10[1]	11[2]	12■	13																			1
1	2	3	4	5	6	7[1]	8[2]	9	10[3]	11		12	13	14																	2
1	2	3	4	5	6		8[2]	9	10[1]	11		7[3]		14	12	13															3
1	2	3	4	5	6		8	9	10[2]	11[1]	13	7[3]			12	14															4
1	2	3[3]	4	5	6		8[1]	9	10[2]	11	13	7			12	14															5
1	2	14	4	5	6	13	8[1]	9		11[3]	7	10[2]			12	3															6
1	2	3	4[1]	5		7[2]		9[3]	13	11	10		12		14	8	6														7
1	2	3	4	5[2]		7[1]		9	10[3]	13	11		14		12	8	6														8
1	2	3	4		5	7		9[3]		12	8		13		14	11[1]	6	10[2]													9
1			4	5	3	7		9[3]		12	11[1]		13	2	14	8	6	10[2]													10
1			4[3]	5[1]	3	7[2]		9		14	11	12		2		8	6	10	13												11
1		3	4[1]	5		12		9			11[3]	7	13	2	14		6	8	10[2]												12
1		3		5		7[2]				8	11	4	12	2			6	9	10[1]	13											13
1		3■	13	5	14	7[2]				8■	11[3]	4		2		12	6	9[1]	10												14
1			4	5		7		12			11	8[2]	13	2		3	6	9	10[1]												15
1			4	5		7		12			11[2]	8[1]	13	2		3	6	9	10												16
1		11	4[2]	5	3	7[3]		9			13	14		12		2	6[1]	10	8												17
1		2	4	5		7	8	9		12		13				3[2]	6	10[1]	11												18
1		3	2	5	4		8	9[1]		12		7	13				6	11[2]	10												19
1		3	2[1]	12	5	14	8	9		4		7[3]				11	6	13	10[2]												20
1		3	2[2]	12	5[1]	14	8	9		4		7[3]		13		11	6	10													21
1		2		5		7[3]	8	9			12■	4[2]		3[1]	13	11	6		10		14										22
1		2[1]		5	3	7	4	9[3]		12		11[2]	13		14	8	6		10												23
1		2■	12	5	3	7	4	9		8		11[1]				10	6														24
1			2	5	3	7[2]	8			4[1]	12	11	14		9[3]	10	6					13									25
1		3	2	5		13	8	9		4		12			14	11[2]	6		7[1]			10[3]									26
1[6]		3	2		5		7[1]	9		4		12				11	6		10			8	15								27
		2		5[1]	3[3]		12	9		4[2]		7				11	6		8	13		10	1	14							28
		12				7	8	9				4				3			11[1]	2	5	10	1	6							29
						7	8	9				4[1]				3			11	2	5	10	1	6	12						30
			12			7	8	9		13		4[1]				3			11[2]	2	5	10	1	6							31
			12			7[2]	8	9		13		4[3]				3			11	2[1]	5	10	1	6	14						32
		3■	2			7				8						11	6		9[3]		5[1]	10[2]	1		4	12	13	14			33
			2			7		9[1]	14	8					13	3	6[3]						1	5	4[2]	12	11	10			34
			2[2]			7	11	12	13■	8					10[3]	3				14	5		1	6	4[1]			9			35
						7	8	9						2	10[1]	3			12		5		1	6	4		11				36
		14				7	8	9						2	10[1]	3			13		5		1	6	4[2]		11[3]	12			37
		3			5	7	8			4				2	12	11			9[2]				1	6			10[1]		13		38
		3	13[3]		5	7	8[1]			4				2[2]	12	11			9				1	6			10		14		39
		3			5	7	8	9	13	4				2		11[2]			10[1]				1	6					12		40
		3			5	7	8	9	12	4[1]				2	14	11[3]							1	6				13	10[2]		41
		3[2]			5	7	8	9	12	4[1]				2	14	11			13				1	6					10[3]		42
		3			5	7		9	12[2]	4				2	13				11			8[1]	1	6	14				10[3]		43
		3	4[1]		5	7		9[3]	12	8		14		2		11			10[2]				1	6					13		44
		3	4[2]		5	7		9[3]		8		13		2	14	11			10[1]				1	6					12		45
		3	4		5		8[3]	9	12	7[1]				2		11			10[2]				1	6					13	14	46

FA Cup

First Round	Bournemouth	(a)	3-3
		(h)	3-2
Second Round	Leyton Orient	(a)	1-0
Third Round	Stoke C	(h)	1-3

Carling Cup

First Round	Brighton & HA	(a)	0-1

J Paint Trophy

Second Round	Barnet	(h)	1-3

HARTLEPOOL UNITED FL Championship 1

FOUNDATION

The inspiration for the launching of Hartlepool United was the West Hartlepool club which won the FA Amateur Cup in 1904–05. They had been in existence since 1881 and their cup success led in 1908 to the formation of the new professional concern which first joined the North-Eastern League. In those days they were Hartlepools United and won the Durham Senior Cup in their first two seasons.

Victoria Park, Clarence Road, Hartlepool TS24 8BZ.

Telephone: (01429) 272 584.

Fax: (01429) 863 007.

Ticket Office: (01429) 272 584 (option 2).

Website: www.hartlepoolunited.co.uk

Email: enquires@hartlepoolunited.co.uk

Ground Capacity: 7,630.

Record Attendance: 17,426 v Manchester U, FA Cup 3rd rd, 5 January 1957.

Pitch Measurements: 110yd × 74yd.

Chairman: Ken Hodcroft.

Chief Executive: Russ Green.

First Team Coach: Neale Cooper.

Physio: James Haycock.

Colours: Broad blue and white striped shirts with blue sleeves, blue shorts, white stockings.

Year Formed: 1908.

Turned Professional: 1908.

Previous Names: 1908, Hartlepools United; 1968, Hartlepool; 1977, Hartlepool United.

Club Nickname: 'The Pool'.

Ground: 1908, Victoria Park.

First Football League Game: 27 August 1921, Division 3 (N), v Wrexham (a) W 2–0 – Gill; Thomas, Crilly; Dougherty, Hopkins, Short; Kessler, Mulholland (1), Lister (1), Robertson, Donald.

Record League Victory: 10–1 v Barrow, Division 4, 4 April 1959 – Oakley; Cameron, Waugh; Johnson, Moore, Anderson; Scott (1), Langland (1), Smith (3), Clark (2), Luke (2), (1 og).

Record Cup Victory: 6–0 v North Shields, FA Cup 1st rd, 30 November 1946 – Heywood; Brown, Gregory; Spelman, Lambert, Jones; Price, Scott (2), Sloan (4), Moses, McMahon; 6–0 v Gainsborough Trinity (a), FA Cup 1st rd, 10 November 2007 – Budtz; McCunnie, Humphreys, Liddle (1) (Antwi), Nelson, Clark, Moore (1), Sweeney, Barker (2) (Monkhouse), Mackay (Porter 1), Brown (1).

Record Defeat: 1–10 v Wrexham, Division 4, 3 March 1962.

HONOURS

Football League –
FL 2: ***Runners-up*** 2006–07;
Division 3: ***Runners-up*** 2002–03;
Division 3 (N): ***Runners-up*** 1956–57.

FA Cup: Best season: 4th rd, 1955, 1978, 1989, 1993, 2005, 2009.

Football League Cup: Best season: 4th rd, 1975.

sky SPORTS FACT FILE

Centre-forward Jimmy Sloan had his first experience of senior football with Newcastle United in 1944–45 and 1945–46 and was signed by Hartlepool United at the start of the following season. The high point of his goalscoring for the club came with a four-timer in a record Cup victory.

Most League Points (2 for a win): 60, Division 4, 1967–68.

Most League Points (3 for a win): 88, FL 2, 2006–07.

Most League Goals: 90, Division 3 (N), 1956–57.

Highest League Scorer in Season: William Robinson, 28, Division 3 (N), 1927–28; Joe Allon, 28, Division 4, 1990–91.

Most League Goals in Total Aggregate: Ken Johnson, 98, 1949–64.

Most League Goals in One Match: 5, Harry Simmons v Wigan Borough, Division 3 (N), 1 January 1931; 5, Bobby Folland v Oldham Ath, Division 3 (N), 15 April 1961.

Most Capped Player: Ambrose Fogarty, 1 (11), Republic of Ireland.

Most League Appearances: Wattie Moore, 447, 1948–64.

Youngest League Player: David Foley, 16 years 105 days v Port Vale, 25 August 2003.

Record Transfer Fee Received: £750,000 from Ipswich T for Tommy Miller, July 2001.

Record Transfer Fee Paid: £75,000 to Northampton for Chris Freestone, March 1993; £75,000 to Notts Co for Gary Jones, March 1999; £75,000 to Mansfield T for Darrell Clarke, July 2001.

Football League Record: 1921 Original Member of Division 3 (N); 1958–68 Division 4; 1968–69 Division 3; 1969–91 Division 4; 1991–92 Division 3; 1992–94 Division 2; 1994–2003 Division 3; 2003–04 Division 2; 2004–06 FL 1; 2006–07 FL 2; 2007– FL 1.

LATEST SEQUENCES

Longest Sequence of League Wins: 9, 18.11.2006 – 1.1.2007.

Longest Sequence of League Defeats: 8, 27.1.1993 – 27.2.1993.

Longest Sequence of League Draws: 6, 30.4.2011 – 20.8.2011.

Longest Sequence of Unbeaten League Matches: 23, 18.11.2006 – 30.3.2007.

Longest Sequence Without a League Win: 18, 9.1.1993 – 3.4.1993.

Successive Scoring Runs: 27 from 18.11.2006.

Successive Non-scoring Runs: 11 from 9.1.1993.

MANAGERS

Alfred Priest 1908–12
Percy Humphreys 1912–13
Jack Manners 1913–20
Cecil Potter 1920–22
David Gordon 1922–24
Jack Manners 1924–27
Bill Norman 1927–31
Jack Carr 1932–35
(had been Player-Coach from 1931)
Jimmy Hamilton 1935–43
Fred Westgarth 1943–57
Ray Middleton 1957–59
Bill Robinson 1959–62
Allenby Chilton 1962–63
Bob Gurney 1963–64
Alvan Williams 1964–65
Geoff Twentyman 1965
Brian Clough 1965–67
Angus McLean 1967–70
John Simpson 1970–71
Len Ashurst 1971–74
Ken Hale 1974–76
Billy Horner 1976–83
Johnny Duncan 1983
Mike Docherty 1983
Billy Horner 1984–86
John Bird 1986–88
Bobby Moncur 1988–89
Cyril Knowles 1989–91
Alan Murray 1991–93
Viv Busby 1993
John MacPhail 1993–94
David McCreery 1994–95
Keith Houchen 1995–96
Mick Tait 1996–99
Chris Turner 1999–2002
Mike Newell 2002–03
Neale Cooper 2003–05
Martin Scott 2005–06
Danny Wilson 2006–08
Chris Turner 2008–10
Mick Wadsworth 2010–11
Neale Cooper December 2011–

TEN YEAR LEAGUE RECORD

		P	*W*	*D*	*L*	*F*	*A*	*Pts*	*Pos*
2002-03	Div 3	46	24	13	9	71	51	85	2
2003-04	Div 2	46	20	13	13	76	61	73	6
2004-05	FL 1	46	21	8	17	76	66	71	6
2005-06	FL 1	46	11	17	18	44	59	50	21
2006-07	FL 2	46	26	10	10	65	40	88	2
2007-08	FL 1	46	15	9	22	63	66	54	15
2008-09	FL 1	46	13	11	22	66	79	50	19
2009-10	FL 1	46	14	11	21	59	67	50*	20
2010-11	FL 1	46	15	12	19	47	65	57	16
2011-12	FL 1	46	14	14	18	50	55	56	13

**3 pts deducted.*

DID YOU KNOW

On 21 November 1936 the local derby against Darlington produced ten goals. Two down, Hartlepools United levelled but were 4-2 in arrears at half-time. They recovered the deficit but conceded a fifth 15 minutes from the end. Still in the 88th minute Johnny Wigham equalised.

HARTLEPOOL UNITED 2011–12 LEAGUE RECORD

Match No.	Date	Venue	Opponents	Result	H/T Score	Lg Pos.	Goalscorers	Attendance
1	Aug 6	A	Milton Keynes D	D 2-2	1-0	—	Boyd[20], Poole[85]	7287
2	13	H	Walsall	D 1-1	1-1	13	Nish[5]	5170
3	16	H	Huddersfield T	D 0-0	0-0	—		5506
4	20	A	Stevenage	D 2-2	2-0	16	Hartley[34], Boyd (pen)[41]	2831
5	27	A	Rochdale	W 3-1	1-1	12	Boyd[7], Poole 2[47, 87]	2600
6	Sept 3	H	Exeter C	W 2-0	1-0	6	Liddle[5], Luscombe[89]	5152
7	10	A	Carlisle U	W 2-1	2-0	6	Liddle[21], Boyd[41]	4765
8	17	H	Bury	W 3-0	1-0	5	Solano[33], Nish 2[51, 74]	5343
9	24	A	Bournemouth	W 2-1	1-1	3	Solano[42], Horwood[87]	5275
10	Oct 1	H	Sheffield W	L 0-1	0-1	7		6800
11	9	A	Notts Co	L 0-3	0-1	9		6172
12	15	H	Wycombe W	L 1-3	0-2	10	Boyd (pen)[89]	5421
13	22	A	Chesterfield	W 3-2	2-1	7	Murray[17], Poole 2[19, 48]	5937
14	25	H	Tranmere R	L 0-2	0-0	—		5200
15	29	H	Charlton Ath	L 0-4	0-2	13		5333
16	Nov 5	A	Leyton Orient	D 1-1	0-1	12	Austin (pen)[54]	4424
17	19	A	Scunthorpe U	W 2-0	1-0	10	Monkhouse[21], Sweeney[77]	3861
18	26	H	Yeovil T	L 0-1	0-1	11		4604
19	29	H	Preston NE	L 0-1	0-1	—		4156
20	Dec 10	A	Brentford	L 1-2	0-0	13	Collins[83]	6352
21	17	H	Colchester U	L 0-1	0-1	14		4029
22	26	A	Oldham Ath	W 1-0	1-0	12	Poole[7]	4459
23	31	A	Sheffield U	L 1-3	0-3	16	Hartley[90]	20,372
24	Jan 2	H	Scunthorpe U	L 1-2	0-1	17	Monkhouse[83]	5289
25	7	H	Rochdale	W 2-0	0-0	—	Brown[74], James[80]	4663
26	14	A	Exeter C	D 0-0	0-0	13		4016
27	21	A	Sheffield W	D 2-2	0-0	13	Hartley[47], Sweeney[87]	17,469
28	28	H	Carlisle U	W 4-0	2-0	10	James 2[6, 67], Sweeney[17], Nish[81]	5995
29	Feb 11	H	Bournemouth	D 0-0	0-0	—		4548
30	14	A	Preston NE	L 0-1	0-0	—		14,191
31	18	H	Notts Co	W 3-0	1-0	9	Sweeney 2[37, 53], Monkhouse[78]	4718
32	25	A	Wycombe W	L 0-5	0-3	11		4408
33	28	A	Bury	W 2-1	1-0	—	Humphreys[45], Boyd[74]	2072
34	Mar 3	H	Milton Keynes D	D 1-1	1-0	9	Poole[40]	4955
35	6	A	Huddersfield T	L 0-1	0-0	—		12,316
36	10	A	Walsall	D 0-0	0-0	11		3751
37	17	H	Stevenage	D 0-0	0-0	11		4484
38	20	H	Oldham Ath	L 0-1	0-1	—		4109
39	24	A	Yeovil T	W 1-0	0-0	11	Noble[65]	4033
40	31	H	Sheffield U	L 0-1	0-0	11		5825
41	Apr 6	A	Colchester U	D 1-1	1-0	—	Sweeney[17]	3921
42	9	H	Brentford	D 0-0	0-0	12		4292
43	14	H	Chesterfield	L 1-2	1-0	13	Liddle[37]	4004
44	21	A	Tranmere R	D 1-1	0-1	14	Sweeney[69]	4757
45	28	H	Leyton Orient	W 2-1	1-1	11	Sweeney[23], Noble[73]	4502
46	May 5	A	Charlton Ath	L 2-3	1-0	13	Hartley[31], Liddle[86]	26,749

Final League Position: 13

GOALSCORERS

League (50): Sweeney 8, Poole 7, Boyd 6 (2 pens), Hartley 4, Liddle 4, Nish 4, James 3, Monkhouse 3, Noble 2, Solano 2, Austin 1 (1 pen), Brown 1, Collins 1, Horwood 1, Humphreys 1, Luscombe 1, Murray 1.
Carling Cup (1): Sweeney 1.
FA Cup (0).
J Paint Trophy (0).

Flinders S 45	Austin N 46	Horwood E 38 + 3	Liddle G 37 + 2	Collins S 35 + 1	Hartley P 44	Solano N 11 + 3	Sweeney A 39	Nish C 12 + 7	Boyd A 13 + 20	Monkhouse A 39 + 6	Luscombe N 3 + 10	Murray P 44 + 1	Poole J 15 + 12	Humphreys R 19 + 10	Larkin C 2	Brown J 10 + 14	Haslam S 3 + 7	Wright S 10	Rafferty A 1	Baldwin J 14 + 3	James L 12 + 7	Hassan C — + 1	Adjei S — + 1	Rowbotham J 1	Hawkins L 1	Noble R 9	Richards J 1 + 1	Rutherford G — + 1	Holden D 2 + 1	*Match No.*
1	2	3	4	5	6	7^{1}	8	9^{3}	10^{2}	11	12	13	14																	1
1	2	3^{3}	4	5	6	7^{1}		9	10^{2}	11	12■	8	13	14																2
1	2	3		5	6			9^{2}	13	11		8^{3}	7^{1}	4	10	12	14													3
1	2	3		5	6			9	10^{1}	11		4	12^{2}	7	8^{3}	14	13													4
1	5	3	4		6			9^{1}	10^{2}	7		8	12	11		13	2													5
1	2		4		6	7^{1}	8^{3}	9^{2}	10	13	14	11	12	3				5												6
1	2		4	12	6	7^{3}	8	9	10^{2}	13	14	11		3^{1}				5												7
1	2		4	5	6	7^{3}	8	9	10^{2}	12		11^{1}	13	14				3												8
1	2	14	4	5	6	7^{3}	8	9	10^{1}	12		11^{2}	13	3																9
1	2	12	4	5	6	7	8	9	10^{2}	14		11^{1}	13	3^{3}																10
1	2	12	4	5	6	7^{3}	8	9	10^{2}	13		11	14	3^{1}																11
1	2	11	4	5	6		8^{1}	13	14	9	12	7^{3}	10^{2}					3												12
1	7	3	4	5	6			13		11^{3}	10^{1}	8	9^{2}	14		12		2												13
1	2	11	4	5	6				13	10	7	8^{2}	9			12		3^{1}												14
1	2	3	4^{1}	5	6			9	10^{2}	11	13	8	7			12														15
1	7	11^{2}	12	5	6		4			10	14	8■	9^{3}	3^{1}		13		2												16
	2	3	4		6	7^{1}	11		14	10		8^{2}	9^{3}	12			13	5	1											17
1	2	3	4		6	7^{2}	11		12	10	13	8^{3}	9^{1}	14				5												18
1	2	3	12		6	7^{1}	4		10^{3}	11	13	8^{2}	9	14				5												19
1	2	3	4^{3}	5	6	13	7		12	11	14	10^{2}	9			8^{1}														20
1	2	3	4	5		13	7		14	11		8^{2}	9^{3}			10^{1}				6	12									21
1	2	3	4	5	6		7			10		8	9^{1}							11	12									22
1	2	3	4	5^{3}	6		7		13	10		8^{2}		9		12				11^{1}	14									23
1	2	3	4		5	13	7		9^{2}	10	8^{1}			11		12					6									24
1	2	3	4	5	6		7			10		8^{1}		13		12				11	9^{2}									25
1	2	3	4	5	6		8					11				9^{1}	12			7^{2}	10	13								26
1	2	3	4	5	6		7			10		11^{1}		12		13	8^{2}				9									27
1	2	3^{1}	4	5	6		7	13		10		8^{3}				9^{2}	12			14	11									28
1	2	3	4	5	6		7	12		11		8				9					10^{1}									29
1	2	3	4	5	6		7	12		11		8^{1}				9^{2}	13				10									30
1	2	3	4^{1}	5	6		7		13	11		8^{3}		14		9^{2}	12				10									31
1	2	3		5	6		7	14	12	11		8^{2}				9^{3}	4^{1}			13	10									32
1	2	3		5	6		7		12	11		8		10		9^{1}				4										33
1	2	3		5	6		4		14	10		8	7^{1}	11^{2}		9^{3}				13			12							34
1	2	3		5	6		7	13	14	10		8^{3}	9^{1}	11^{2}		12				4										35
1	2	3			6		10		13	9		8		11		12				4				5^{2}	7^{1}					36
1	2	3	4	5	6		11		13	10		8	12	9^{2}						7^{1}										37
1	2	3	4	5	6		7		12	11		8^{2}	9^{1}													10	13			38
1	2	3	4	5	6^{1}		11		13	9		8		12						7						10^{2}				39
1	2	3	4	5	6■		7		13	11		8^{2}				12					9^{1}					10				40
1	2	3	4	5			7			11		8		9						6	12					10^{1}				41
1	2	3	4	5	6		7		13	11		8^{1}		9^{2}							12					10				42
1	2	3	4^{2}	5	6		7		12	11		8^{1}									9					10		13		43
1	2		4		6		7			11		8								5	9^{1}					10	3		12	44
1	2	3	4		6		7			9		8^{2}	13							5	12					10			11^{1}	45
1	2		4		6		7			11		8^{2}	13	3^{1}						5	12					10			9	46

FA Cup
First Round Stevenage (h) 0-1

Carling Cup
First Round Sheffield U (h) 1-1

J Paint Trophy
First Round Scunthorpe U (a) 0-2

HEREFORD UNITED Blue Square Premier

FOUNDATION

Two local teams RAOC and St Martins amalgamated in 1924 under the chairmanship of Dr E.W. Maples to form Hereford United and joined the Birmingham Combination. The first game at Edgar Street was against Atherstone Town on 24 August 1924, the visitors winning 3–2. The players used the Wellington Hotel as a changing room. They graduated to the Birmingham League four years later and the Southern League in 1939.

Athletic Ground, Edgar Street, Hereford HR4 9JU.

Telephone: (08442) 761 939.

Fax: (08442) 761 982.

Ticket Office: (08442) 761 939.

Website: www.herefordunited.co.uk

Email: club@herefordunited.co.uk

Ground Capacity: 7,149.

Record Attendance: 18,114 v Sheffield W, FA Cup 3rd rd, 4 January 1958.

Pitch Measurements: 100m × 72m.

Chairman: David Keyte.

Manager: Martin Foyle.

Assistant Manager: Andy Porter.

Physio: Ian Rodgerson.

Colours: White shirts with black trim, black shorts, white stockings.

Year Formed: 1924.

Turned Professional: 1924.

Club Nickname: 'United'.

Ground: 1924, Edgar Street.

First Football League Game: 12 August 1972, Division 4, v Colchester U (a) L 0-1 – Potter; Mallender, Naylor; Jones, McLaughlin, Tucker; Slattery, Hollett, Owen, Radford, Wallace.

Record League Victory: 6–0 v Burnley (away), Division 4, 24 January 1987 – Rose; Rodgerson, Devine, Halliday, Pejic, Dalziel, Harvey (1p), Wells, Phillips (3), Kearns (2), Spooner.

HONOURS

Football League – Division 2: 22nd, 1976–77; **Division 3:** ***Champions*** 1975–76; **Division 4:** ***Runners-up*** 1972–73.

FA Cup: Best season: 4th rd, 1972, 1974, 1977, 1982, 1990, 1992, 2008, 2011.

Football League Cup: Best season: 3rd rd, 1975.

Welsh Cup: ***Winners*** 1990.

Conference: ***Runners-up*** 2003–04, 2004–05.

sky SPORTS FACT FILE

Right-back John Layton played for Hereford United in their post-war Southern League days making a total of 549 appearances between 1946 and 1962. His son, also John, later both played and coached the club, originally combining football with his trade as a local bricklayer.

Record Cup Victory: 6–1 v QPR, FA Cup 2nd rd, 7 December 1957 – Sewell; Tomkins, Wade; Masters, Niblett, Horton (2p); Reg Bowen (1), Clayton (1), Fidler, Williams (1), Cyril Beech (1).

Record Defeat: 0–7 v Middlesbrough, Coca-Cola Cup 2nd rd, 1st leg, 18 September 1996.

Most League Points (2 for a win): 63, Division 3, 1975–76.

Most League Points (3 for a win): 88, FL 2, 2007–08.

Most League Goals: 86, Division 3, 1975–76.

Highest League Scorer in Season: Dixie McNeil, 35, 1975–76.

Most League Goals in Total Aggregate: Stewart Phillips, 93, 1980–88, 1990–91.

Most League Goals in One Match: 4, Dixie McNeil v Chester C, Division 3, 10 March 1976; 4, Steve White v Cambridge U, Division 3, 13 January 1996.

Most Capped Player: Trevor Benjamin, 2, Jamaica.

Most League Appearances: Mel Pejic, 412, 1980–92.

Youngest League Player: Stewart Phillips, 16 years 112 days v Swindon T, 22 April 1979.

Record Transfer Fee Received: £440,000 from QPR for Darren Peacock, December 1990.

Record Transfer Fee Paid: £80,000 to Walsall for Dean Smith, June 1994.

Football League Record: 1972 Elected to Division 4; 1973–76 Division 3; 1976–77 Division 2; 1977–78 Division 3; 1978–92 Division 4; 1992–97 Division 3; 1997–2006 Vauxhall Conference; 2006–08 FL 2; 2008–09 FL 1; 2009–12 FL 2; 2012– Blue Square Premier.

MANAGERS

Eric Keen 1939
George Tranter 1948–49
Alex Massie 1952
George Tranter 1953–55
Joe Wade 1956–62
Ray Daniels 1962–63
Bob Dennison 1963–67
John Charles 1967–71
Colin Addison 1971–74
John Sillett 1974–78
Mike Bailey 1978–79
Frank Lord 1979–82
Tommy Hughes 1982–83
Johnny Newman 1983–87
Ian Bowyer 1987–90
Colin Addison 1990–91
John Sillett 1991–92
Greg Downs 1992–94
John Layton 1994–95
Graham Turner 1995–2009
John Trewick 2009–10
Graham Turner 2010
Simon Davey 2010
Jamie Pitman 2010–12
Martin Foyle May 2012–

LATEST SEQUENCES

Longest Sequence of League Wins: 6, 2.4.1996 – 20.4.1996.

Longest Sequence of League Defeats: 8, 7.2.1987 – 18.3.1987.

Longest Sequence of League Draws: 6, 12.4.1975 – 23.8.1975.

Longest Sequence of Unbeaten League Matches: 14, 21.10.1972 – 17.1.1973.

Longest Sequence Without a League Win: 13, 19.11.1977 – 25.2.1978.

Successive Scoring Runs: 23 from 20.9.1975.

Successive Non-scoring Runs: 6 from 10.3.2007.

TEN YEAR LEAGUE RECORD

		P	*W*	*D*	*L*	*F*	*A*	*Pts*	*Pos*
2002-03	Conf	42	19	7	16	64	51	64	6
2003-04	Conf	42	28	7	7	103	44	91	2
2004-05	Conf	42	21	11	10	68	41	74	2
2005-06	Conf	42	22	14	6	59	33	80	2
2006-07	FL 2	46	14	13	19	45	53	55	16
2007-08	FL 2	46	26	10	10	72	41	88	3
2008-09	FL 1	46	9	7	30	42	79	34	24
2009-10	FL 2	46	17	8	21	54	65	59	16
2010-11	FL 2	46	12	17	17	50	66	50*	21
2011-12	FL 2	46	10	14	22	50	70	44	23

**3 points deducted.*

DID YOU KNOW 

History almost exactly repeated itself in consecutive seasons of the FA Cup for Hereford United. In 1970–71 they drew 2-2 with Northampton Town before winning the replay 2-1. The following season the two met again drawing goalless, before another 2-2 and a 2-1 victory.

HEREFORD UNITED 2011–12 LEAGUE RECORD

Match No.	Date	Venue	Opponents	Result	H/T Score	Lg Pos.	Goalscorers	Attendance
1	Aug 6	A	Southend U	L 0-1	0-1	—		5105
2	13	H	Morecambe	L 0-3	0-2	24		2045
3	16	H	Macclesfield T	L 0-4	0-0	—		1609
4	20	A	AFC Wimbledon	D 1-1	1-1	23	Facey [8]	4239
5	27	A	Bristol R	D 0-0	0-0	23		6342
6	Sept 3	H	Dagenham & R	W 1-0	0-0	23	Winnall [85]	1885
7	10	A	Shrewsbury T	L 1-3	0-1	23	Barkhuizen [73]	5684
8	13	H	Aldershot T	L 0-2	0-1	—		1599
9	17	H	Gillingham	L 1-6	0-3	23	Winnall [87]	1848
10	24	A	Cheltonham T	D 0-0	0-0	23		3011
11	Oct 1	H	Oxford U	L 0-1	0-1	23		2502
12	8	A	Swindon T	D 3-3	0-2	23	Barkhuizen [67], Arquin [76], Pell [90]	7456
13	15	H	Bradford C	W 2-0	0-0	23	Leslie [79], Barkhuizen [89]	2462
14	22	H	Barnet	W 1-0	0-0	22	Elder [66]	2124
15	25	A	Northampton T	W 3-1	2-0	—	Elder [13], Leslie [20], Pell [71]	3643
16	29	A	Torquay U	L 0-2	0-2	20		2459
17	Nov 5	H	Crawley T	D 1-1	1-1	19	Barkhuizen [9]	2227
18	19	H	Burton Alb	L 2-3	2-1	19	Purdie (pen) [19], Barkhuizen [34]	2136
19	26	A	Crewe Alex	L 0-1	0-0	20		3591
20	Dec 10	H	Rotherham U	L 2-3	2-2	21	Arquin [34], Facey [42]	1908
21	17	A	Plymouth Arg	D 1-1	0-0	21	Barkhuizen [67]	6531
22	26	H	Port Vale	L 1-2	0-0	21	Barkhuizen [55]	3097
23	30	H	Accrington S	D 1-1	1-0	—	Arquin [5]	2057
24	Jan 2	A	Burton Alb	W 2-0	1-0	21	Evans, W [23], Arquin [78]	3322
25	10	H	Bristol R	L 1-2	0-1	—	Facey [49]	2411
26	14	A	Dagenham & R	W 1-0	1-0	21	Arquin [39]	1732
27	21	A	Oxford U	D 2-2	1-1	7	Duberry 2 (2 ogs) [32, 86]	6630
28	28	H	Shrewsbury T	L 0-2	0-2	21		3515
29	Feb 11	H	Cheltenham T	D 1-1	1-0	—	Facey [12]	2607
30	14	A	Aldershot T	L 0-1	0-0	—		1871
31	18	H	Swindon T	L 1-2	0-1	22	Purdie [65]	3068
32	25	A	Bradford C	D 1-1	0-0	22	Anthony [82]	17,014
33	28	A	Gillingham	L 4-5	2-1	—	Purdie (pen) [4], Barkhuizen 2 [7, 70], Evans, W [80]	3784
34	Mar 3	H	AFC Wimbledon	W 2-1	2-0	21	Taylor [18], Barkhuizen [34]	2147
35	6	A	Macclesfield T	D 2-2	2-0	—	Evans, W 2 [1, 26]	1676
36	10	A	Morecambe	W 1-0	1-0	21	Taylor [27]	1653
37	17	H	Southend U	L 2-3	1-2	23	Arquin (pen) [45], Elder [88]	2456
38	20	A	Port Vale	L 0-1	0-0	—		3959
39	24	H	Crewe Alex	L 0-1	0-0	24		2326
40	31	A	Rotherham U	L 0-1	0-1	24		3237
41	Apr 6	H	Plymouth Arg	D 1-1	0-1	24	Barkhuizen [52]	4597
42	9	A	Accrington S	L 1-2	0-0	24	Evans, W [57]	1749
43	13	A	Barnet	D 1-1	1-1	—	Facey [11]	3189
44	21	H	Northampton T	D 0-0	0-0	23		2970
45	28	A	Crawley T	W 3-0	0-0	23	Colbeck [55], Arquin 2 [77, 83]	4615
46	May 5	H	Torquay U	W 3-2	3-0	23	Facey [11], Pell (pen) [36], Purdie [40]	5143

Final League Position: 23

GOALSCORERS

League (50): Barkhuizen 11, Arquin 8 (1 pen), Facey 6, Evans, W 5, Purdie 4 (2 pens), Elder 3, Pell 3 (1 pen), Leslie 2, Taylor 2, Winnall 2, Anthony 1, Colbeck 1, own goals 2.
Carling Cup (1): Arquin 1.
FA Cup (0).
J Paint Trophy (1): Barkhuizen 1.

Bartlett A 18	Purdie R 34	Heath J 15 + 2	Pell H 22 + 8	Green R 26 + 2	Stam S 21 + 3	Lunt K 24 + 1	McQuilkin J 3 + 4	Fleetwood S 4 + 1	Facey D 32 + 8	Colbeck J 19 + 9	Arquin Y 16 + 18	Townsend M 36 + 3	Featherstone N 36 + 2	Hoult R 2	Connor D 1	Clist S 27 + 1	Dalibard B 9 + 1	Williams D 3 + 2	Cornell D 25	Evans W 21 + 4	Barkhuizen T 32 + 6	Winnall S 5 + 3	Elder N 13 + 13	Leslie S 10	Todd A 4	Clucas S 3 + 14	Peniket R 4 + 3	Purkiss B 15	Taylor L 6 + 2	Anthony B 13 + 2	Chambers J 7	Baxendale J — + 1	*Match No.*
1	2	3	4	5	6	7	8	9^{1}	10	11	12																						1
1	8	3	4	2	6	7^{2}		9	10^{1}	11	12	5	13																				2
	7	3^{1}	4	2	6		13	9	10	11	12	5	8^{2}	1																			3
			4	5	6^{3}	13		9	10^{1}	11	12	8	7		1	2	3^{2}	14															4
		3	4	2		7		12	10^{1}		9	5	8			11		6	1														5
		3	4	5		7^{2}			10^{3}		9	6	8			11		2^{1}	1	12	13	14											6
		3	4	5		7^{1}			10	12	14	6	8			11^{2}			1	2^{3}	13	9											7
		3	13	5					10^{1}	11	9	6	8			7			1	2	4^{2}	12											8
	2	3	4	5					12		9^{1}		8			11			1	6	7	10											9
	2	3	13	5	6	7			10		12		8			11			1		4^{2}	9^{1}											10
	2	3	13		6	7	8		10^{3}		14	5	11						1		4^{1}	9^{2}	12										11
	2	3	12		6	10^{1}					13	5	8	1		11^{2}					4	14	9^{3}	7									12
	2	3	4		6				13		12	14	8			11^{1}			1		7		9^{2}	10^{3}	5								13
	2	3	4		6		12				13		8						1		7	9^{1}	10^{2}	11	5								14
	2		4	13	6						12	14	8			10	3		1		7^{3}		9^{1}	11	5^{2}								15
	4	12		2	6						13	14	8			11	3^{2}		1		9^{3}		10	7	5^{1}								16
	3	6	4	2					12			5	8			11			1		10		9	7^{1}									17
	2	3^{1}	4	5					14		13	6	8^{3}			11	12		1		7^{2}		9	10									18
	2		4	5					10		9	6	8			3			1		7		12	11^{1}									19
1	2		4	5					10		9	6	8			3					7		12	11^{1}									20
1	2		4						10	12	9^{2}	5▮	8			3	6				7^{3}		13	11^{1}		14							21
1	2		4	5					10	11	9		8^{1}			3	6				7		12										22
1	6		13	2	4				10^{1}	8	9^{2}	5				11	3				7		12										23
1		14		2	6				10^{2}	8	9^{3}	5				11	3			4	7^{1}		13			12							24
1	2				6				10^{3}	8	9^{1}	5				11	3▮			4	7^{2}		12			13	14						25
1	2		4		6				10	7^{2}	9	5	8			11^{1}				3	13					12							26
1	3		4	2	6^{1}				10^{2}	7	9	5	8							11	13					12							27
1	3		4	6					10^{1}	7	9^{3}	5	8							11^{2}	12		13				14	2					28
1	6			4					10^{2}	9		5	8^{3}			14	3^{1}			11	7					12		2	13				29
1	6			2						12	9	5▮	13			11				7	4^{3}		8^{1}			14		3	10^{2}				30
1	6		13	4		10			14	7^{1}			8			11				3^{2}			9^{3}					2	12	5			31
	6		13			11^{2}			10	12			8			3			1	4	7							2▮	9^{1}	5			32
	6					11			10	13		5				3		8^{1}	1	4	7					12			9^{2}	2			33
	8					11			10			5				3		13	1	4	7^{1}					12		2	9^{2}	6			34
	8					11			10^{2}	14		5				3			1	4	7^{1}		13			12		2	9^{3}	6			35
	3				14	11			10^{1}		12	5	8						1	4	7^{2}					13		2	9^{3}	6			36
	3^{1}			12		11			10	14	9^{2}	5	8						1	4^{3}	7		13					2		6			37
				3	4^{1}	11				10		5	8^{2}						1	13	7^{3}		9			6	14	2		12			38
				3	6^{3}	11	8		13	7		5							1	14	12		10^{2}			4^{1}	9	2					39
				2	6^{3}	11			10^{1}	4		5	8^{2}						1	12	7		13				9			14	3		40
					6	11			12	13		5	8						1	4	7^{3}		10^{1}			14	9^{2}			2	3		41
					6	11			12	14		5	8						1	4^{3}	7		10^{2}			13	9^{1}			2	3		42
1						11			10^{3}		12	5	8							4^{1}	7		14			9		3		6	2^{2}	13	43
1	9^{3}		12			11^{1}			10		13	5	8							4^{2}	7					14		2		6	3		44
1	6		7		13	11^{3}	14	9^{2}	10^{1}		12	5	8															2		4	3		45
1	7^{2}		4		13	11^{3}	14		10	9^{1}	12	5	8															2		6	3		46

FA Cup

First Round	Yeovil T	(h)	0-3

Carling Cup

First Round	Brentford	(h)	1-0
Second Round	Aston Villa	(a)	0-2

J Paint Trophy

First Round	Bournemouth	(a)	1-4

HUDDERSFIELD TOWN FL Championship

FOUNDATION

A meeting, attended largely by members of the Huddersfield & District FA, was held at the Imperial Hotel in 1906 to discuss the feasibility of establishing a football club in this rugby stronghold. However, it was not until a man with both the enthusiasm and the money to back the scheme came on the scene that real progress was made. This benefactor was Mr Hilton Crowther and it was at a meeting at the Albert Hotel in 1908 that the club formally came into existence with an investment of £2,000 and joined the North-Eastern League.

The Galpharm Stadium, Stadium Way, Leeds Road, Huddersfield HD1 6PX.

Telephone: (0870) 4444 677.

Fax: (01484) 484 101.

Ticket Office: (0870) 4444 552.

Website: www.htafc.com

Email: info@htafc.com

Ground Capacity: 24,554.

Record Attendance: 67,037 v Arsenal, FA Cup 6th rd, 27 February 1932 (at Leeds Road); 23,678 v Liverpool, FA Cup 3rd rd, 12 December 1999 (at Alfred McAlpine Stadium).

Pitch Measurements: 115yd × 76yd.

Chairman: Dean Hoyle.

Operations Director: Ann Hough.

Manager: Simon Grayson.

First Team Coaches: Ian Miller and Glynn Snodin.

Physios: Dave Buckby, Adam Hirst.

Colours: Blue and white striped shirts, white shorts, blue stockings.

Year Formed: 1908.

Turned Professional: 1908.

Club Nickname: 'The Terriers'.

Grounds: 1908, Leeds Road; 1994, The Alfred McAlpine Stadium (renamed the Galpharm Stadium 2004).

First Football League Game: 3 September 1910, Division 2, v Bradford PA (a) W 1–0 – Mutch; Taylor, Morris; Beaton, Hall, Bartlett; Blackburn, Wood, Hamilton (1), McCubbin, Jee.

Record League Victory: 10–1 v Blackpool, Division 1, 13 December 1930 – Turner; Goodall, Spencer; Redfern, Wilson, Campbell; Bob Kelly (1), McLean (4), Robson (3), Davies (1), Smailes (1).

Record Cup Victory: 7–0 v Lincoln U, FA Cup 1st rd, 16 November 1991 – Clarke; Trevitt, Charlton, Donovan (2), Mitchell, Doherty, O'Regan (1), Stapleton (1) (Wright), Roberts (2), Onuora (1), Barnett (Ireland). *N.B.* 11–0 v Heckmondwike (a), FA Cup pr rd, 18 September 1909 – Doggart; Roberts, Ewing; Hooton, Stevenson, Randall; Kenworthy (2), McCreadie (1), Foster (4), Stacey (4), Jee.

HONOURS

Football League – Division 1: ***Champions*** 1923–24, 1924–25, 1925–26; ***Runners-up*** 1926–27, 1927–28, 1933–34;
Division 2: ***Champions*** 1969–70; ***Runners-up*** 1919–20, 1952–53;
Division 4: ***Champions*** 1979–80.

FA Cup: ***Winners*** 1922; ***Runners-up*** 1920, 1928, 1930, 1938.

Football League Cup: Semi-final 1968.

Autoglass Trophy: ***Runners-up*** 1994.

sky SPORTS FACT FILE

On 19 November 2011, Huddersfield Town beat Notts County 2-1 in their 43rd unbeaten Football League match, a record for the competition. The club's previous best had been between January and October 1925 in the middle of the club's three successive championship titles.

Record Defeat: 1–10 v Manchester C, Division 2, 7 November 1987.

Most League Points (2 for a win): 66, Division 4, 1979–80.

Most League Points (3 for a win): 87, FL 1, 2010–11.

Most League Goals: 101, Division 4, 1979–80.

Highest League Scorer in Season: Sam Taylor, 35, Division 2, 1919–20; George Brown, 35, Division 1, 1925–26; Jordan Rhodes, 35, 2011–12.

Most League Goals in Total Aggregate: George Brown, 142, 1921–29; Jimmy Glazzard, 142, 1946–56.

Most League Goals in One Match: 5, Dave Mangnall v Derby Co, Division 1, 21 November 1931; 5, Alf Lythgoe v Blackburn R, Division 1, 13 April 1935.

Most Capped Player: Jimmy Nicholson, 31 (41), Northern Ireland.

Most League Appearances: Billy Smith, 520, 1914–34.

Youngest League Player: Denis Law, 16 years 303 days v Notts Co, 24 December 1956.

Record Transfer Fee Received: £2,750,000 from Ipswich T for Marcus Stewart, February 2000.

Record Transfer Fee Paid: £1,200,000 to Bristol R for Marcus Stewart, July 1996.

Football League Record: 1910 Elected to Division 2; 1920–52 Division 1; 1952–53 Division 2; 1953–56 Division 1; 1956–70 Division 2; 1970–72 Division 1; 1972–73 Division 2; 1973–75 Division 3; 1975–80 Division 4; 1980–83 Division 3; 1983–88 Division 2; 1988–92 Division 3; 1992–95 Division 2; 1995–2001 Division 1; 2001–03 Division 2; 2003–04 Division 3; 2004–12 FL 1; 2012– FL C.

MANAGERS

Fred Walker 1908–10
Richard Pudan 1910–12
Arthur Fairclough 1912–19
Ambrose Langley 1919–21
Herbert Chapman 1921–25
Cecil Potter 1925–26
Jack Chaplin 1926–29
Clem Stephenson 1929–42
Ted Magner 1942–43
David Steele 1943–47
George Stephenson 1947–52
Andy Beattie 1952–56
Bill Shankly 1956–59
Eddie Boot 1960–64
Tom Johnston 1964–68
Ian Greaves 1968–74
Bobby Collins 1974
Tom Johnston 1975–78
(had been General Manager since 1975)
Mike Buxton 1978–86
Steve Smith 1986–87
Malcolm Macdonald 1987–88
Eoin Hand 1988–92
Ian Ross 1992–93
Neil Warnock 1993–95
Brian Horton 1995–97
Peter Jackson 1997–99
Steve Bruce 1999–2000
Lou Macari 2000–02
Mick Wadsworth 2002–03
Peter Jackson 2003–07
Andy Ritchie 2007–08
Stan Ternent 2008
Lee Clark 2008–12
Simon Grayson February 2012–

LATEST SEQUENCES

Longest Sequence of League Wins: 11, 5.4.1920 – 4.9.1920.

Longest Sequence of League Defeats: 7, 8.10.1955 – 19.11.1955.

Longest Sequence of League Draws: 6, 3.3.1987 – 3.4.1987.

Longest Sequence of Unbeaten League Matches: 43, 1.1.2011 – 19.11.2011.

Longest Sequence Without a League Win: 22, 4.12.1971 – 29.4.1972.

Successive Scoring Runs: 27 from 12.3.2005.

Successive Non-scoring Runs: 7 from 22.1.1972.

TEN YEAR LEAGUE RECORD

		P	*W*	*D*	*L*	*F*	*A*	*Pts*	*Pos*
2002-03	Div 2	46	11	12	23	39	61	45	22
2003-04	Div 3	46	23	12	11	68	52	81	4
2004-05	FL 1	46	20	10	16	74	65	70	9
2005-06	FL 1	46	19	16	11	72	59	73	4
2006-07	FL 1	46	14	17	15	60	69	59	15
2007-08	FL 1	46	20	6	20	50	62	66	10
2008-09	FL 1	46	18	14	14	62	65	68	9
2009-10	FL 1	46	23	11	12	82	56	80	6
2010-11	FL 1	46	25	12	9	77	48	87	3
2011-12	FL 1	46	21	18	7	79	47	81	4

DID YOU KNOW 

On 17 December 2011, Andy Rhodes scored his fourth hat trick of the season with a four-timer in an eight-goal thriller at Sheffield Wednesday. Two goals down, Wednesday surged to a 4-2 lead in the 74th minute but Rhodes doubled his tally for Huddersfield Town with a leveller in 97 minutes.

HUDDERSFIELD TOWN 2011–12 LEAGUE RECORD

Match No.	*Date*	*Venue*	*Opponents*	*Result*		*H/T Score*	*Lg Pos.*	*Goalscorers*	*Attendance*
1	Aug 6	H	Bury	D	1-1	0-0	—	Roberts [65]	13,873
2	13	A	Rochdale	D	2-2	1-1	14	Novak [15], Ward [69]	5074
3	16	A	Hartlepool U	D	0-0	0-0	—		5506
4	20	H	Colchester U	W	3-2	1-2	11	Rhodes 2 [3, 59], Novak [64]	11,043
5	27	H	Wycombe W	W	3-0	0-0	8	Lee 2 [57, 71], Roberts [82]	11,953
6	Sept 3	A	Oldham Ath	D	1-1	1-1	7	Kay [16]	6213
7	10	H	Tranmere R	W	2-0	1-0	5	Roberts [24], Arfield [82]	12,013
8	13	A	Sheffield U	W	3-0	3-0	—	Novak 2 [20, 37], Gobern [40]	17,373
9	17	A	Milton Keynes D	D	1-1	1-0	3	Arfield [37]	8243
10	24	H	Leyton Orient	D	2-2	1-0	8	Lee [22], Hunt [57]	12,269
11	Oct 1	A	Brentford	W	4-0	1-0	5	Rhodes 2 [36, 76], Novak [70], Roberts [78]	6101
12	8	H	Stevenage	W	2-1	1-0	3	Roberts [44], Novak [76]	12,890
13	15	A	Exeter C	W	4-0	2-0	2	Lee [8], Rhodes 3 [26, 65, 89]	4244
14	22	H	Preston NE	W	3-1	2-0	2	Rhodes 3 [4, 42, 57]	16,804
15	25	A	Scunthorpe U	D	2-2	1-1	—	Miller [25], Rhodes [86]	5858
16	29	A	Yeovil T	W	1-0	0-0	2	Robinson [80]	3486
17	Nov 5	H	Walsall	D	1-1	0-0	2	Novak [67]	13,005
18	19	H	Notts Co	W	2-1	0-0	2	Rhodes 2 [46, 65]	13,227
19	28	A	Charlton Ath	L	0-2	0-2	—		18,029
20	Dec 10	H	Bournemouth	L	0-1	0-1	4		13,930
21	17	A	Sheffield W	D	4-4	2-2	4	Rhodes 4 [12, 16, 77, 90]	28,600
22	26	H	Chesterfield	W	1-0	1-0	4	Rhodes [34]	15,380
23	30	H	Carlisle U	D	1-1	1-1	—	Rhodes [38]	13,962
24	Jan 2	A	Notts Co	D	2-2	0-0	5	Roberts [52], Rhodes [58]	8914
25	6	A	Wycombe W	W	6-0	3-0	—	Gobern [10], Rhodes 5 [19, 25, 49, 58, 69]	4465
26	14	H	Oldham Ath	W	1-0	0-0	3	Lee [86]	15,229
27	21	H	Brentford	W	3-2	2-2	2	Lee [41], McCombe [45], Rhodes [50]	14,405
28	28	A	Tranmere R	D	1-1	0-0	2	Rhodes [49]	5851
29	Feb 4	H	Milton Keynes D	D	1-1	1-0	—	McCombe [45]	16,898
30	14	H	Sheffield U	L	0-1	0-1	—		17,320
31	25	H	Exeter C	W	2-0	1-0	4	McCombe [40], Rhodes [85]	14,105
32	28	A	Stevenage	D	2-2	0-0	—	Ward [50], Novak [55]	3059
33	Mar 3	A	Bury	D	3-3	3-1	4	Morrison [21], Rhodes 2 [25, 29]	5988
34	6	H	Hartlepool U	W	1-0	0-0	—	Lee [75]	12,316
35	10	H	Rochdale	D	2-2	1-1	4	Ward [45], Rhodes [48]	13,715
36	17	A	Colchester U	D	1-1	0-1	4	Okuonghae (og) [90]	3929
37	20	A	Chesterfield	W	2-0	2-0	—	Novak [23], Rhodes [27]	6916
38	24	H	Charlton Ath	W	1-0	1-0	4	Rhodes (pen) [14]	15,735
39	31	A	Carlisle U	L	1-2	0-0	4	Novak [80]	7530
40	Apr 3	A	Leyton Orient	W	3-1	2-1	—	Smith (og) [18], Rhodes 2 [45, 90]	3674
41	7	H	Sheffield W	L	0-2	0-0	4		18,646
42	9	A	Bournemouth	L	0-2	0-0	4		5500
43	14	A	Preston NE	L	0-1	0-0	5		11,267
44	21	H	Scunthorpe U	W	1-0	0-0	5	Novak [89]	13,086
45	28	A	Walsall	D	1-1	1-0	5	Novak [2]	4646
46	May 5	H	Yeovil T	W	2-0	1-0	4	Novak [45], Ward [72]	13,520

Final League Position: 4

GOALSCORERS

League (79): Rhodes 35 (1 pen), Novak 13, Lee 7, Roberts 6, Ward 4, McCombe 3, Arfield 2, Gobern 2, Hunt 1, Kay 1, Miller 1, Morrison 1, Robinson 1, own goals 2.
Carling Cup (7): Novak 2, Rhodes 2, Hunt 1, Roberts 1, Ward 1.
FA Cup (1): Novak 1.
J Paint Trophy (4): Clarke, P 1, McDermott 1, Miller 1 (pen), Novak 1.
Play-Offs (3): Rhodes 2, Hunt 1.

Bennett I 33	Woods C 23 + 3	Naysmith G 20 + 2	Robinson A 12 + 13	Clarke P 31	Kay A 25 + 3	Gobern O 19 + 2	McDermott D 6 + 3	Rhodes J 36 + 4	Ward D 31 + 8	Roberts G 28 + 11	Miller T 24 + 2	Novak L 29 + 12	Hunt J 43	McCombe J 20	Arfield S 24 + 11	Lee A 18 + 13	Johnson D 16 + 2	Cooper L 2 + 2	Parkin J 2 + 1	Bruce A 3	Clarke T 7 + 7	Cadamarteri D 6 + 9	Morrison S 19	Higginbotham K 3 + 1	Smithies A 13	Gudjonsson J 6 + 2	Arismendi D 7 + 2	Atkinson C — + 1	Match No.
1	2	3	4[1]	5	6	7	8[2]	9	10	11	12	13																	1
1		3		5		7	8[1]		12	11	4	9	2	6	10														2
1		3		5		7	13	12	10[1]	11	4	9[2]	2	6	8														3
1		3	4	5	14		8[2]	9[3]	12	11[1]	7	10	2	6	13														4
1		3	4		6		7[1]	9	11[3]	12	8	10[2]	2	5	14	13													5
1		3	4		6	7[2]	12		10	11[1]	8	9	2	5		13													6
1	3		4		6		8[3]	9[2]	11[1]	12	7	13	2	5	14	10													7
1	3		12		6	7		13	11			10[2]	2	5	4[1]	9	8												8
1	3		13		6	7[2]			11[1]	12		10	2	5	8	9	4												9
1	3				6	7		14	11[1]	12[2]		10[3]	2	5■	8	9	4	13											10
1	3[1]		14	5	6			9		11	7	13	2		8[3]	10[2]	4	12											11
1	3		12	5	6				13	11[2]	4	10	2		8[1]	9	7												12
1	3			5	6			9	13	11[1]	4	12	2		8	10[2]	7												13
1	3			5	6			9	13	11[2]	4	12	2		8	10[1]	7												14
1		3		5	6			9	13	11[2]	4	12	2		8	10[1]	7												15
1	3		14	5				9	11[1]	12	4	13	2		8	10[2]	7[3]	6											16
1	3			5				9		11	4	10	2		8		7	6											17
1	3		12	5	6			9[2]		11[1]	4	13	2		8	10■	7												18
1	3		13	5	6			9	12	11[2]	4[1]		2		8		7		10										19
1	3	12	8[3]	5				9	11	14		13	2[1]		7		4		10[2]	6									20
1		3		5		7	12	9	8[1]	11	4	10[2]	2						13	6									21
1		3[3]			6	7	8[1]	9		11	4	10[2]	2		12	13				5	14								22
1		3		5	6	7		9		11	4	10[1]	2		13	12						8[2]							23
1		3	4	5		7		9		11[1]			2		12	10					6	8							24
1		3		5		8		9	7[2]	11[1]	4	10	2	6							13	12							25
1		3	12	5		8[1]		9	11	7[2]	4	10[3]	2	6		13						14							26
1		3	13	5		8		9	7[3]	11[1]	4		2	6		10[2]					14	12							27
1		3	13			7		9	11[3]			10[1]	2	6		12[2]	4				14	8	5						28
1		3	12			7		9			4[1]		2	6	8							10	5	11					29
	12	3	4			8[1]		9	7	11[2]		14	2	6		10[3]						13	5		1				30
		3	4[1]			8		9	7	11[2]		14	2	6		10[3]						13	5		1	12			31
		3	14		12	8[1]			11			10	2	6		9[2]						7	5	13	1	4[3]			32
	12	3			8	13		9	11[2]	14		10[3]	2[1]	6	7								5		1	4			33
	3				8			9	11[3]	13		10[2]	2	6	7[1]	12	14						5		1	4			34
	3	12			8			9	11			10[3]	2[1]	6	7	14	13						5		1	4[2]			35
	3			5	8[2]			9	7	11[1]		10[3]	2		14	12							6		1	4	13		36
				5	8			9[3]	7	11		10[1]	2			12					3	14	6		1	4[2]	13		37
				5	8[2]			9	7	11[1]		10	2		14	13					3		6		1	12	4[3]		38
				5	8			9	7	11[1]		10	2		12	13					6		3		1		4[2]		39
	12			5	8			9	11			7[2]	2[1]		13	10[3]					3	14	6		1		4		40
	3			5	8			9	7	12		11[2]			13	10[3]					2	14	6		1		4[1]		41
	3		8	5	14			9	11[2]	13					7	12					2	10[1]	6		1		4[3]		42
1	3		8[3]	5				9	10[1]	11	13	12	2		7							14	6				4[2]		43
1	3		8[2]	5				9[3]	12	11		10	2		7						14		6				4[1]	13	44
1	3[1]			5		14			11[2]	13	4	10	2		7		8[3]				12		6	9					45
1	3		13	5				12	11		4	10[1]	2[3]		7		8[2]				14		6	9					46

FA Cup

First Round	Swindon T	(a)	1-4

Carling Cup

First Round	Port Vale	(a)	4-2
Second Round	Cardiff C	(a)	3-5

J Paint Trophy

First Round	Northampton T	(a)	2-1
Second Round	Bradford C	(h)	2-2

Play-Offs

Semi-Final	Milton Keynes D	(a)	2-0
		(h)	1-2
Final *(at Wembley).*	Sheffield U		0-0

HULL CITY FL Championship

FOUNDATION

The enthusiasts who formed Hull City in 1904 were brave men indeed. More than that, they were audacious for they immediately put the club on the map in this Rugby League fortress by obtaining a three-year agreement with the Hull Rugby League club to rent their ground! They had obtained quite a number of conversions to the dribbling code, before the Rugby League forbade the use of any of their club grounds by Association Football clubs. By that time, Hull City were well away, having entered the FA Cup in their initial season and the Football League, Second Division after only a year.

The Circle, The KC Stadium, Walton Street, Hull, East Yorkshire HU3 6HU.

Telephone: (01482) 504 600.

Fax: (01482) 304 882.

Ticket Office: (01482) 505 600.

Website: www.hullcityafc.net

Email: info@hulltigers.com

Ground Capacity: 25,404.

Record Attendance: 25,512 v Sunderland, FL C, 28 October 2007 (at KC Stadium); 55,019 v Manchester U, FA Cup 6th rd, 26 February 1949 (at Boothferry Park).

Pitch Measurements: 100.5m × 67.5m.

Chairman: Assem Allam.

Vice-chairman: Ehab Allam.

Manager: Steve Bruce.

Assistant Manager: Steve Agnew.

Physio: Liam McGarry.

Colours: Black and amber striped shirts, black shorts, amber stockings with black hoops.

Year Formed: 1904.

Turned Professional: 1905.

Club Nickname: 'The Tigers'.

Grounds: 1904, Boulevard Ground (Hull RFC); 1905, Anlaby Road (Hull CC); 1944, Boulevard Ground; 1946, Boothferry Park; 2002, Kingston Communications Stadium.

First Football League Game: 2 September 1905, Division 2, v Barnsley (h) W 4–1 – Spendiff; Langley, Jones; Martin, Robinson, Gordon (2); Rushton, Spence (1), Wilson (1), Howe, Raisbeck.

Record League Victory: 11–1 v Carlisle U, Division 3 (N), 14 January 1939 – Ellis; Woodhead, Dowen; Robinson (1), Blyth, Hardy; Hubbard (2), Richardson (2), Dickinson (2), Davies (2), Cunliffe (2).

Record Cup Victory: 8–2 v Stalybridge Celtic (a), FA Cup 1st rd, 26 November 1932 – Maddison; Goldsmith, Woodhead; Gardner, Hill (1), Denby; Forward (1), Duncan, McNaughton (1), Wainscoat (4), Sargeant (1).

HONOURS

FA Premier League: Best season 17th, 2008–09.

Football League – FL C: Best season 3rd, 2007–08;
FL 1: ***Runners-up*** 2004–05;
Division 3 (N): ***Champions*** 1932–33, 1948–49;
Division 3: ***Champions*** 1965–66;
Runners-up 1958–59, 2003–04;
Division 4: ***Runners-up*** 1982–83.

FA Cup: Semi-final 1930.

Football League Cup: Best season: 4th, 1974, 1976, 1978.

Associate Members' Cup: ***Runners-up*** 1984.

sky SPORTS FACT FILE

On 28 October 1905, Hull City lost 1-0 at home to Manchester United in their first season in Division Two. The same day they fielded a reserve team in an FA Cup tie against Denaby United and won 2-0 with a brace of goals from John Smith.

Record Defeat: 0–8 v Wolverhampton W, Division 2, 4 November 1911.

Most League Points (2 for a win): 69, Division 3, 1965–66.

Most League Points (3 for a win): 90, Division 4, 1982–83.

Most League Goals: 109, Division 3, 1965–66.

Highest League Scorer in Season: Bill McNaughton, 39, Division 3 (N), 1932–33.

Most League Goals in Total Aggregate: Chris Chilton, 193, 1960–71.

Most League Goals in One Match: 5, Ken McDonald v Bristol C, Division 2, 17 November 1928; 5, Simon 'Slim' Raleigh v Halifax T, Division 3 (N), 26 December 1930.

Most Capped Player: Theo Whitmore, 28 (105), Jamaica.

Most League Appearances: Andy Davidson, 520, 1952–67.

Youngest League Player: Matthew Edeson, 16 years 63 days v Fulham, 10 October 1992.

Record Transfer Fee Received: £3,000,000 from Wolverhampton W for Stephen Hunt, August 2010.

Record Transfer Fee Paid: £5,000,000 to Fulham for Jimmy Bullard, January 2009.

Football League Record: 1905 Elected to Division 2; 1930–33 Division 3 (N); 1933–36 Division 2; 1936–49 Division 3 (N); 1949–56 Division 2; 1956–58 Division 3 (N); 1958–59 Division 3; 1959–60 Division 2; 1960–66 Division 3; 1966–78 Division 2; 1978–81 Division 3; 1981–83 Division 4; 1983–85 Division 3; 1985–91 Division 2; 1991–92 Division 3; 1992–96 Division 2; 1996–2004 Division 3; 2004–05 FL 1; 2005–08 FL C; 2008–10 FA Premier League; 2010– FL C.

LATEST SEQUENCES

Longest Sequence of League Wins: 10, 23.2.1966 – 20.4.1966.

Longest Sequence of League Defeats: 8, 7.4.1934 – 8.9.1934.

Longest Sequence of League Draws: 5, 30.3.1929 – 15.4.1929.

Longest Sequence of Unbeaten League Matches: 19, 13.3.2001 – 22.9.2001.

Longest Sequence Without a League Win: 27, 27.3.1989 – 4.11.1989.

Successive Scoring Runs: 26 from 10.4.1990.

Successive Non-scoring Runs: 6 from 13.11.1920.

MANAGERS

James Ramster 1904–05 *(Secretary-Manager)*
Ambrose Langley 1905–13
Harry Chapman 1913–14
Fred Stringer 1914–16
David Menzies 1916–21
Percy Lewis 1921–23
Bill McCracken 1923–31
Haydn Green 1931–34
John Hill 1934–36
David Menzies 1936
Ernest Blackburn 1936–46
Major Frank Buckley 1946–48
Raich Carter 1948–51
Bob Jackson 1952–55
Bob Brocklebank 1955–61
Cliff Britton 1961–70 *(continued as General Manager to 1971)*
Terry Neill 1970–74
John Kaye 1974–77
Bobby Collins 1977–78
Ken Houghton 1978–79
Mike Smith 1979–82
Bobby Brown 1982
Colin Appleton 1982–84
Brian Horton 1984–88
Eddie Gray 1988–89
Colin Appleton 1989
Stan Ternent 1989–91
Terry Dolan 1991–97
Mark Hateley 1997–98
Warren Joyce 1998–2000
Brian Little 2000–02
Jan Molby 2002
Peter Taylor 2002–06
Phil Parkinson 2006
Phil Brown *(after caretaker role December 2006)* 2007–10
Ian Dowie *(consultant)* 2010
Nigel Pearson 2010–11
Nick Barmby 2011–12
Steve Bruce June 2012–

TEN YEAR LEAGUE RECORD

		P	W	D	L	F	A	Pts	Pos
2002-03	Div 3	46	14	17	15	58	53	59	13
2003-04	Div 3	46	25	13	8	82	44	88	2
2004-05	FL 1	46	26	8	12	80	53	86	2
2005-06	FL C	46	12	16	18	49	55	52	18
2006-07	FL C	46	13	10	23	51	67	49	21
2007-08	FL C	46	21	12	13	65	47	75	3
2008-09	PR Lge	38	8	11	19	39	64	35	17
2009-10	PR Lge	38	6	12	20	34	75	30	19
2010-11	FL C	46	16	17	13	52	51	65	11
2011-12	FL C	46	19	11	16	47	44	68	8

DID YOU KNOW 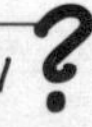

On 4 November 1911, Hull City were beaten 8-0 by Wolverhampton Wanderers with Billy Halligan scoring a hat trick. On 6 December 1913 there was a further game of eight goals between the two clubs. This time Hull won 7-1 with Halligan scoring four, having signed for the Tigers in May.

HULL CITY 2011–12 LEAGUE RECORD

Match No.	Date	Venue	Opponents	Result		H/T Score	Lg Pos.	Goalscorers	Attendance
1	Aug 5	H	Blackpool	L	0-1	0-0	—		18,907
2	13	A	Ipswich T	W	1-0	0-0	13	Fryatt 76	18,116
3	16	A	Leeds U	L	1-4	1-2	—	Lees (og) 21	22,363
4	20	H	Crystal Palace	L	0-1	0-1	19		17,797
5	27	H	Reading	W	1-0	0-0	13	Brady 73	17,295
6	Sept 10	A	Peterborough U	W	1-0	0-0	9	McLean 47	8685
7	17	H	Portsmouth	W	1-0	1-0	8	Koren 11	18,311
8	24	A	Bristol C	D	1-1	0-0	7	Koren 56	12,254
9	27	A	Doncaster R	D	1-1	1-0	—	Waghorn 25	9786
10	Oct 1	H	Cardiff C	W	2-1	1-0	6	Fryatt 39, Barmby 71	18,305
11	15	A	Brighton & HA	D	0-0	0-0	6		19,722
12	22	H	Watford	W	3-2	0-1	7	Fryatt 51, McLean 66, Koren 90	18,324
13	29	A	Nottingham F	W	1-0	0-0	6	McLean 74	22,841
14	Nov 1	A	Barnsley	L	1-2	0-0	—	Fryatt 79	9869
15	5	H	West Ham U	L	0-2	0-0	9		21,756
16	19	A	Derby Co	W	2-0	2-0	6	Fryatt 17, Stewart 23	30,391
17	26	H	Burnley	L	2-3	1-0	7	Fryatt 2 11, 55	20,238
18	29	A	Southampton	L	1-2	1-0	—	Koren 43	22,983
19	Dec 3	H	Leicester C	W	2-1	1-1	8	Fryatt (pen) 30, Koren 88	20,148
20	7	H	Birmingham C	W	2-1	0-1	—	Koren 47, McLean 67	17,438
21	10	A	Coventry C	W	1-0	0-0	5	Evans 60	12,652
22	17	H	Millwall	W	2-0	0-0	4	Smith (og) 54, Koren 80	17,841
23	26	A	Middlesbrough	L	0-1	0-0	5		27,794
24	31	A	Burnley	L	0-1	0-1	6		15,071
25	Jan 2	H	Derby Co	L	0-1	0-0	6		20,704
26	14	H	Peterborough U	W	1-0	1-0	6	Koren 27	18,074
27	21	A	Reading	W	1-0	0-0	5	Brady 66	17,556
28	31	H	Doncaster R	D	0-0	0-0	—		19,187
29	Feb 11	H	Bristol C	W	3-0	2-0	6	Hobbs 13, Koren 15, Fryatt 60	17,435
30	14	A	Birmingham C	D	0-0	0-0	—		18,900
31	22	H	Brighton & HA	D	0-0	0-0	—		17,769
32	Mar 2	A	Blackpool	D	1-1	0-1	—	Fryatt 90	12,491
33	6	H	Leeds U	D	0-0	0-0	—		22,676
34	10	H	Ipswich T	D	2-2	1-0	9	Brady 17, Koren 54	17,625
35	13	A	Cardiff C	W	3-0	1-0	—	McNaughton (og) 6, Chester 47, McLean 55	20,366
36	17	A	Crystal Palace	D	0-0	0-0	7		13,324
37	20	H	Southampton	L	0-2	0-1	—		18,066
38	24	A	Leicester C	L	1-2	1-2	9	Fryatt 8	23,759
39	27	A	Portsmouth	L	0-2	0-2	—		14,751
40	31	H	Coventry C	L	0-2	0-1	9		17,279
41	Apr 7	A	Millwall	L	0-2	0-1	10		12,372
42	9	H	Middlesbrough	W	2-1	0-1	10	King 58, Fryatt 88	19,613
43	14	A	Watford	D	1-1	1-1	10	Chester 4	11,596
44	17	H	Barnsley	W	3-1	2-0	—	Fryatt 3 37, 44, 83	16,604
45	21	H	Nottingham F	W	2-1	0-0	8	Gunter (og) 58, Fryatt (pen) 81	20,786
46	28	A	West Ham U	L	1-2	0-1	8	Evans 81	35,000

Final League Position: 8

GOALSCORERS

League (47): Fryatt 16 (2 pens), Koren 10, McLean 5, Brady 3, Chester 2, Evans 2, Barmby 1, Hobbs 1, King 1, Stewart 1, Waghorn 1, own goals 4.
Carling Cup (0).
FA Cup (3): Cairney 1, McLean 1, Stewart 1.

Gulacsi P 13 + 2	Rosenior L 44	Dudgeon J 17 + 7	McKenna P 37 + 4	Chester J 44	Hobbs J 40	Brady R 24 + 15	Koren R 41	Adebola D 2 + 8	Fryatt M 39 + 7	Cairney T 18 + 9	Barmby N — + 8	Simpson J — + 3	Evans C 38 + 5	McLean A 28 + 11	Dawson A 31 + 1	Basso A 12 + 1	Waghorn M 5	Pusic M 2	Harper J — + 1	Stewart C 26 + 5	Garcia R 6 + 4	McShane P 1	Mannone V 21	King J 8 + 10	Olofinjana S 1 + 2	Cullen M — + 4	Cooper L 7	Bradley S 1 + 1	*Match No.*
1	2	3	4^{2}	5	6	7	8	9^{1}	10	11	12	13																	1
1	2	3	4	5	6	7^{2}	8^{3}	14	10^{1}	11	12		9	13															2
1	2	7	4	5	6	9^{2}	8^{3}	13	10		14		11	12	3^{1}														3
	2	3	4^{1}	5	6	9^{2}	8	14	10	11^{3}	13		7	12		1													4
	2		4	5	6	7	8		10^{1}	11	12	13		9^{2}	3	1													5
	2	14	4	5	6	7	8^{1}		13	11^{3}			12	10^{2}	3	1	9												6
	2	3	4	5	6	7^{2}	8		12	11	13			10^{1}		1	9												7
	2	3	4	5	6	7	8^{2}		12	11			13	10^{1}		1	9												8
	2	3		5	6	7	8^{2}		10	11	13		4	12		1	9^{1}												9
15	2	3		5	6	7	8		10		12		4	13		1^{G}	9^{2}	11^{1}											10
	2	3	12	5	6	11^{2}	8		10	13			4^{1}	9		1		7											11
	2	3	13	5	6	7^{1}	8	12	10	11			4^{2}	9		1													12
	2	3	12	5	6	7^{2}	8	13	10	11^{1}			4	9^{3}		1			14										13
15	2	3	4	5	6	11^{1}	8	12	10	13			7^{2}	9		1^{G}													14
1	2	3	4	5	6	12	8	11^{1}	10				7	9															15
1	2	3	4^{2}	5	6	12	8		10	13			11	9						7^{1}									16
1	2	3	4	5	6	9^{2}	8	13	10				7		12					11^{1}									17
1	2	3		5	6	12■	8	13	10	11^{2}			4	9						7^{1}									18
1	2	12	4	5	6		8		10				7^{1}	9	3					11									19
1	2	12	4	5	6		8		10				7	9	3					11^{1}									20
1	2	12	4	5	6		8		10				7^{1}	9	3					11^{2}	13								21
1	2		4	5	6	12	8		10				7	9^{2}	3					11^{1}	13								22
1	2		4	5	6	12	8		10				7	9^{2}	3					11^{1}	13								23
1^{6}			4	5	6	12	8		10				7	9^{2}	3	15				11^{1}	13	2							24
	2		4^{2}	5	6	12	8		10	13			7	9^{1}	3	1				11									25
	2	13	4	5	6	12	8^{1}		10^{2}	14			7	9	3					11^{3}			1						26
	2^{3}	13	4	5	6	10^{2}	8		12				7	9	3					11^{1}			1	14					27
	2		4	5	6		8		10				7^{1}	9	3					11^{2}			1	12	13				28
	2		4	5	6	9^{3}	8^{2}		10	13			7^{1}	14	3					11			1	12					29
	2		4	5	6	11^{1}	8		10				7	9	3					12			1						30
	2		4	5	6	9^{1}	8		10	13			7^{2}	12	3					11			1						31
	2		4	5	6		8		10				12	9^{3}	3					11^{2}			1	13	7^{1}	14			32
	2		4	5	6		8		10	14			7^{3}	9^{1}	3					11^{2}			1	12		13			33
	2		4	5	6	9^{1}	8		10				7	12	3					11^{2}			1	13					34
	2	12	4	5	6		8		13				7	9	3					11^{1}			1	10^{2}					35
	2		4	5	6	14	8		13	12			7^{1}	9	3					11^{2}			1	10^{3}					36
	2		4^{2}	5	6	11^{3}	8^{1}		10	7			13	12	3					14			1	9					37
	2		4	5	6	12			10	8^{1}			7^{3}	14	3					11			1	9^{2}		13			38
	2	7	4	5	6	9			10^{2}			14	12	13	3^{1}					11			1	8^{3}					39
	2		4		6^{1}	8^{2}			10				7	9	3					11^{3}			1	13		14	5	12	40
	2^{2}		4			14			12	11			7	9^{3}	3					10^{1}	8		1	13			5	6	41
				5		9^{1}	8^{2}		10	11			7		3					12	2		1	4	13		6		42
	2			5		13	8		10	11			7		3					12	9^{2}		1	4^{1}			6		43
	2^{3}		13	5		14	8		10	11^{2}			7		3					9^{1}	4		1	12			6		44
	2		4	5		13	8^{1}		10				7		3					9^{2}	11		1	12			6		45
	2		4	5		13			10	8^{2}			7		3					12	11		1	9^{1}			6		46

FA Cup
Third Round Ipswich T (h) 3-1
Fourth Round Crawley T (h) 0-1

Carling Cup
First Round Macclesfield T (h) 0-2

IPSWICH TOWN FL Championship

FOUNDATION

Considering that Ipswich Town only reached the Football League in 1938, many people outside of East Anglia may be surprised to learn that this club was formed at a meeting held in the Town Hall as far back as 1878 when Mr T. C. Cobbold, MP, was voted president. Originally it was the Ipswich Association FC to distinguish it from the older Ipswich Football Club which played rugby. These two amalgamated in 1888 and the handling game was dropped in 1893.

Portman Road, Ipswich, Suffolk IP1 2DA.

Telephone: (01473) 400 500.

Fax: (01473) 400 040.

Ticket Office: (0844) 8011 555.

Website: www.itfc.co.uk

Email: enquiries@itfc.co.uk

Ground Capacity: 30,311.

Record Attendance: 38,010 v Leeds U, FA Cup 6th rd, 8 March 1975.

Pitch Measurements: 102.46m × 66m.

Chief Executive: Simon Clegg CBE.

Manager: Paul Jewell.

Assistant Manager: Chris Hutchings.

Physio: Matt Byard.

Colours: Blue shirts with white trim, white shorts, blue stockings.

Year Formed: 1878.

Turned Professional: 1936.

Previous Name: Ipswich Association FC; 1888, Ipswich Town.

Club Nicknames: 'Blues' or 'Town' or 'Tractor Boys'.

Grounds: 1878, Broom Hill and Brook's Hall; 1884, Portman Road.

First Football League Game: 27 August 1938, Division 3 (S), v Southend U (h) W 4–2 – Burns; Dale, Parry; Perrett, Fillingham, McLuckie; Williams, Davies (1), Jones (2), Alsop (1), Little.

Record League Victory: 7–0 v Portsmouth, Division 2, 7 November 1964 – Thorburn; Smith, McNeil; Baxter, Bolton, Thompson; Broadfoot (1), Hegan (2), Baker (1), Leadbetter, Brogan (3). 7–0 v Southampton, Division 1, 2 February 1974 – Sivell; Burley, Mills (1), Morris, Hunter, Beattie (1), Hamilton (2), Viljoen, Johnson, Whymark (2), Lambert (1) (Woods). 7–0 v WBA, Division 1, 6 November 1976 – Sivell; Burley, Mills, Talbot, Hunter, Beattie (1), Osborne, Wark (1), Mariner (1) (Bertschin), Whymark (4), Woods.

HONOURS

Football League – Division 1: ***Champions*** 1961–62; ***Runners-up*** 1980–81, 1981–82; **Division 2: *Champions*** 1960–61, 1967–68, 1991–92; **Division 3 (S): *Champions*** 1953–54, 1956–57.

FA Cup: *Winners* 1978.

Football League Cup: Semi-final 1982, 1985, 2001, 2011.

Texaco Cup: *Winners* 1973.

European Competitions
European Cup: 1962–63.
European Cup-Winners' Cup: 1978–79.
UEFA Cup: 1973–74, 1974–75, 1975–76, 1977–78, 1979–80, 1980–81 (*winners*), 1981–82, 1982–83, 2001–02, 2002–03.

sky SPORTS FACT FILE

The first Ipswich Town player to score more than three goals after the club joined the Football League was Fred Chadwick. He scored on his League debut, hit four goals against Street in an FA Cup tie, survived a Japanese POW camp after capture at Singapore and resumed playing.

Record Cup Victory: 10–0 v Floriana, European Cup prel. rd, 25 September 1962 – Bailey; Malcolm, Compton; Baxter, Laurel, Elsworthy (1); Stephenson, Moran (2), Crawford (5), Phillips (2), Blackwood.

Record Defeat: 1–10 v Fulham, Division 1, 26 December 1963.

Most League Points (2 for a win): 64, Division 3 (S), 1953–54 and 1955–56.

Most League Points (3 for a win): 87, Division 1, 1999–2000.

Most League Goals: 106, Division 3 (S), 1955–56.

Highest League Scorer in Season: Ted Phillips, 41, Division 3 (S), 1956–57.

Most League Goals in Total Aggregate: Ray Crawford, 204, 1958–63 and 1966–69.

Most League Goals in One Match: 5, Alan Brazil v Southampton, Division 1, 16 February 1981.

Most Capped Player: Allan Hunter, 47 (53), Northern Ireland.

Most League Appearances: Mick Mills, 591, 1966–82.

Youngest League Player: Jason Dozzell, 16 years 56 days v Coventry C, 4 February 1984.

Record Transfer Fee Received: £6,000,000 from Newcastle U for Kieron Dyer, July 1999; £6,000,000 from Arsenal for Richard Wright, July 2001.

Record Transfer Fee Paid: £5,000,000 to Sampdoria for Matteo Sereni, August 2001.

Football League Record: 1938 Elected to Division 3 (S); 1954–55 Division 2; 1955–57 Division 3 (S); 1957–61 Division 2; 1961–64 Division 1; 1964–68 Division 2; 1968–86 Division 1; 1986–92 Division 2; 1992–95 FA Premier League; 1995–2000 Division 1; 2000–02 FA Premier League; 2002–04 Division 1; 2004– FL C.

MANAGERS

Mick O'Brien 1936–37
Scott Duncan 1937–55
(continued as Secretary)
Alf Ramsey 1955–63
Jackie Milburn 1963–64
Bill McGarry 1964–68
Bobby Robson 1969–82
Bobby Ferguson 1982–87
Johnny Duncan 1987–90
John Lyall 1990–94
George Burley 1994–2002
Joe Royle 2002–06
Jim Magilton 2006–09
Roy Keane 2009–11
Paul Jewell January 2011–

LATEST SEQUENCES

Longest Sequence of League Wins: 8, 23.9.1953 – 31.10.1953.

Longest Sequence of League Defeats: 10, 4.9.1954 – 16.10.1954.

Longest Sequence of League Draws: 7, 10.11.1990 – 21.12.1990.

Longest Sequence of Unbeaten League Matches: 23, 8.12.1979 – 26.4.1980.

Longest Sequence Without a League Win: 21, 28.8.1963 – 14.12.1963.

Successive Scoring Runs: 31 from 7.3.2004.

Successive Non-scoring Runs: 7 from 28.2.1995.

TEN YEAR LEAGUE RECORD

		P	*W*	*D*	*L*	*F*	*A*	*Pts*	*Pos*
2002-03	Div 1	46	19	13	14	80	64	70	7
2003-04	Div 1	46	21	10	15	84	72	73	5
2004-05	FL C	46	24	13	9	85	56	85	3
2005-06	FL C	46	14	14	18	53	66	56	15
2006-07	FL C	46	18	8	20	64	59	62	14
2007-08	FL C	46	18	15	13	65	56	69	8
2008-09	FL C	46	17	15	14	62	53	66	9
2009-10	FL C	46	12	20	14	50	61	56	15
2010-11	FL C	46	18	8	20	62	68	62	13
2011-12	FL C	46	17	10	19	69	77	61	15

DID YOU KNOW ?

Winger Billy Reed was the first Ipswich Town player to receive full international honours while with the club. He was capped by Wales in 1954–55 against Yugoslavia and Scotland. As a lad he had won schoolboy honours and had also won recognition at amateur level for Wales.

IPSWICH TOWN 2011–12 LEAGUE RECORD

Match No.	*Date*	*Venue*	*Opponents*	*Result*		*H/T Score*	*Lg Pos.*	*Goalscorers*	*Attendance*
1	Aug 6	A	Bristol C	W	3-0	1-0	—	Chopra 2 [13, 60], Martin [51]	14,517
2	13	H	Hull C	L	0-1	0-0	9		18,116
3	16	H	Southampton	L	2-5	0-3	—	Andrews [56], Emmanuel-Thomas [61]	18,553
4	20	A	Peterborough U	L	1-7	1-4	20	Andrews [23]	7928
5	27	H	Leeds U	W	2-1	0-1	14	Scotland [77], Andrews [90]	19,758
6	Sept 10	A	Blackpool	L	0-2	0-0	18		12,804
7	19	H	Coventry C	W	3-0	2-0	—	Cranie (og) [7], Andrews [15], Scotland [67]	15,650
8	24	A	Middlesbrough	D	0-0	0-0	13		17,741
9	27	A	West Ham U	W	1-0	0-0	—	Bowyer [89]	27,709
10	Oct 1	H	Brighton & HA	W	3-1	0-0	10	Chopra 2 [59, 73], Sonko [70]	19,793
11	15	A	Cardiff C	D	2-2	1-1	10	Scotland [30], Chopra [51]	21,809
12	18	H	Portsmouth	W	1-0	0-0	—	Andrews [69]	17,297
13	22	H	Crystal Palace	L	0-1	0-0	8		24,763
14	29	A	Millwall	L	1-4	0-2	11	Bullard [66]	12,464
15	Nov 5	H	Doncaster R	L	2-3	0-3	15	Carson [53], Chopra [90]	17,184
16	19	A	Nottingham F	L	2-3	1-1	16	Collins 2 [25, 62]	21,143
17	26	H	Reading	L	2-3	0-0	18	Murphy, D [56], Carson [79]	17,154
18	29	A	Burnley	L	0-4	0-2	—		12,499
19	Dec 3	H	Watford	L	1-2	1-0	21	Andrews [45]	16,262
20	10	A	Barnsley	W	5-3	0-2	20	Andrews 2 [46, 49], Collins [66], Chopra [68], Scotland [83]	9107
21	17	H	Derby Co	W	1-0	0-0	19	Andrews [46]	17,256
22	26	A	Leicester C	D	1-1	1-0	19	Bowyer [4]	27,091
23	31	A	Reading	L	0-1	0-0	19		18,737
24	Jan 2	H	Nottingham F	L	1-3	0-2	19	Leadbitter (pen) [75]	18,964
25	11	A	Birmingham C	L	1-2	1-1	—	Martin [18]	16,528
26	14	H	Blackpool	D	2-2	1-0	19	Angel (og) [10], Smith [60]	16,497
27	21	A	Leeds U	L	1-3	1-0	21	Drury [34]	22,844
28	31	H	West Ham U	W	5-1	3-1	—	Chopra [3], Murphy, D [44], Martin (pen) [45], Emmanuel-Thomas 2 [64, 90]	22,185
29	Feb 4	A	Coventry C	W	3-2	1-2	19	Emmanuel-Thomas [22], Chopra 2 [64, 90]	13,464
30	14	A	Portsmouth	W	1-0	1-0	—	Chopra [13]	14,330
31	18	H	Cardiff C	W	3-0	1-0	16	Martin 2 [21, 73], Chopra [48]	17,032
32	25	A	Brighton & HA	L	0-3	0-1	16		20,490
33	Mar 3	H	Bristol C	W	3-0	1-0	14	Chopra [25], Smith [66], Drury [85]	16,671
34	6	A	Southampton	D	1-1	0-0	—	Scotland [85]	23,315
35	10	A	Hull C	D	2-2	0-1	16	Leadbitter 2 (1 pen) [67 (p), 70]	17,625
36	17	H	Peterborough U	W	3-2	1-1	15	Leadbitter [15], Murphy, D [77], Cresswell [85]	17,927
37	21	H	Burnley	W	1-0	0-0	—	Chopra [54]	16,564
38	24	A	Watford	L	1-2	1-0	15	Emmanuel-Thomas [18]	12,757
39	27	H	Middlesbrough	D	1-1	0-0	—	Leadbitter [74]	18,727
40	31	H	Barnsley	W	1-0	0-0	14	Murphy, D [48]	20,053
41	Apr 7	A	Derby Co	D	0-0	0-0	15		24,156
42	9	H	Leicester C	L	1-2	1-1	15	Scotland [43]	18,282
43	14	A	Crystal Palace	D	1-1	0-1	15	Scotland [59]	17,961
44	17	H	Birmingham C	D	1-1	0-1	—	Emmanuel-Thomas [75]	16,503
45	21	H	Millwall	L	0-3	0-1	15		18,947
46	28	A	Doncaster R	W	3-2	2-1	15	Smith [10], Stevenson [29], Scotland (pen) [79]	9764

Final League Position: 15

GOALSCORERS

League (69): Chopra 14, Andrews 9, Scotland 8 (1 pen), Emmanuel-Thomas 6, Leadbitter 5 (2 pens), Martin 5 (1 pen), Murphy, D 4, Collins 3, Smith 3, Bowyer 2, Carson 2, Drury 2, Bullard 1, Cresswell 1, Sonko 1, Stevenson 1, own goals 2.
Carling Cup (1): Emmanuel-Thomas 1.
FA Cup (1): Scotland 1.

Stockdale D 18	Kennedy M 6 + 1	Cresswell A 44	Ingimarsson I 6 + 2	Delaney D 26 + 3	Leadbitter G 32 + 2	Edwards C 45	Bowyer L 24 + 5	Emmanuel-Thomas J 28 + 14	Chopra M 39 + 6	Martin L 28 + 6	Smith T 24 + 2	Carson J 5 + 11	Ellington N 1 + 14	Andrews K 19 + 1	Scotland J 20 + 16	Ainsley J 1	Sonko I 20 + 2	Murphy D 31 + 2	Bullard J 12 + 9	Collins D 16	Wabara R 1 + 5	Healy C 1	Priskin T 1 + 1	Wright R 1	Lee-Barrett A 17 + 1	Drury A 20 + 1	McCarthy A 10	Hyam L 7 + 1	Stevenson R 3 + 8	Lawrence B — + 1	*Match No.*
1	2	3	4	5^{1}	6	7	8	9^{2}	10^{3}	11	12	13	14																		1
1	2^{1}	3		5	6	7	8^{3}	9^{2}	10	11	4	13	14	12																	2
1	2^{1}	3		5	6	7	8	12	9	13	4			11	10^{2}																3
1	13	3		5	6	7		9^{2}	10^{3}	11■	12■	8^{1}	14	4		2															4
1	2^{3}	3		5	6^{2}	7		11^{1}	10			12		8	14		4	9	13												5
1		3			7^{2}	2	8^{1}	12	10					4	13		5	9	11	6											6
1		3		12	6	2	8	14	10^{2}					4	9^{3}		5^{1}	13	7	11											7
1		3			6	2	8		10					4	9^{1}		5	12	7	11											8
1		3		13	6	2	11		10^{2}				12	8	9^{1}		5		7	4											9
1		3			6	2	8^{2}	13	10^{3}				12	11	9^{1}		5		7	4	14										10
1		3			6	2	8^{3}	13	9^{2}				12	11	10^{1}		5		7	4	14										11
1		3		14	6	2	8	13	9^{3}				12	11	10^{1}		5^{2}		7	4											12
1		3■	12	5^{1}	6	2	8	9	13				10^{3}	11	14				7^{2}	4											13
1	3		13		6	2^{3}	8^{1}	14	9					11	10		5^{2}		7	4	12										14
1		3	4		6			14	9	12		13		11					7^{2}	5	2	8^{1}	10^{3}								15
1		3	4		6	7	8^{1}	12	9^{3}	14		2	13		10^{2}				11	5											16
		3	4		6^{3}	2		9^{1}	10^{2}	12		7		11				8	13	5	14			1							17
	6^{3}	3	4			2	8^{2}	13	9			14		11	12			10^{1}	7	5					1						18
1		3				2	4		9^{1}	11			12	7	10		5	8		6											19
1		3				2	4		9^{3}	11^{1}		13	12	7	10		5	8^{2}		6	14										20
		3				2	4	12	9^{1}	11^{3}		14		7	10^{2}		5	8	13	6					1						21
		3		6		2	4	13	9^{2}	11			14	7^{1}	10^{3}		5	8	12						1						22
		3		4	6^{3}	2	8	7	9^{2}	11^{1}		13	12				5	10	14						1						23
		3	4	5	6	2	8^{1}	9	12	11^{3}		13	14					10^{2}							1	7					24
		3			6	2		8^{1}	13	11	4		12		10^{2}		5	9								7	1				25
		3				2		9		11	6	8^{2}			10^{1}		5		13				12			7	1	4			26
		3				2		8	12	11	6				10^{6}		5	9^{1}	13						15	7	1■	4^{2}			27
		3				2		9	10^{1}	11	6				12		5	8							1	7		4			28
		3				2		9	10	11	6						5	8							1	7		4			29
		3		5		2		9	10^{1}	11	6				12			8							1	7		4			30
		3		5	14	2		9^{3}	10^{1}	11^{2}	6				12			8	13						1	7		4			31
		3		5	12	2		9	10	11	6				13			8^{2}							1	7		4^{1}			32
		3		5	6^{3}	2	14	9^{1}	10^{2}	11	4				13			8								7	1		12		33
		3		5	6^{3}	2	14	9	10	11	4				12			8^{2}								7^{1}	1		13		34
		3		5	6^{3}	2	12	11	9	13	4				10			8^{2}								7^{1}	1		14		35
		3		5	6	2	12	9^{1}	10^{3}	11	4				14			8								7^{2}	1		13		36
		3		5	6■	2	7	9	10^{1}	11	4						12	8									1				37
		3		5		2	6^{1}	9	10^{2}	11^{3}	4	14						8								7	1	12	13		38
		3		5	6	2	7^{1}	9	10	11	4				13			8^{2}								12	1				39
		3		5	6	2		9^{2}	10^{1}	11	4				12			8							1	7			13		40
		3		5	6	2	13	9^{2}	10^{3}	11^{1}	4				12			8							1	7			14		41
		3		5	6	2	11	12	14	13	4	7^{1}			10			8^{3}							1				9^{2}		42
		3		5	6	2		9^{1}	12	11	4				10^{2}			8							1	7			13		43
		3		5	6	2		12	10	11	4				9^{1}			8							1	7					44
		3^{2}		5	6	2		9	10^{3}		4	14			12		13	8							1	7			11^{1}		45
				5		2		9^{3}	10^{2}	11	4				12		6	8^{1}	13						1	7			3	14	46

FA Cup
Third Round — Hull C — (a) — 1-3

Carling Cup
First Round — Northampton T — (h) — 1-2

LEEDS UNITED FL Championship

FOUNDATION

Immediately the Leeds City club (founded in 1904) was wound up by the FA in October 1919, following allegations of illegal payments to players, a meeting was called by a Leeds solicitor, Mr Alf Masser, at which Leeds United was formed. They joined the Midland League, playing their first game in that competition in November 1919. It was in this same month that the new club had discussions with the directors of a virtually bankrupt Huddersfield Town who wanted to move to Leeds in an amalgamation. But Huddersfield survived even that crisis.

Elland Road, Leeds, West Yorkshire LS11 0ES.

Telephone: (0871) 334 1919.

Fax: (0113) 367 6050.

Ticket Office: (0871) 334 1992.

Website: www.leedsunited.com

Email: reception@leedsunited.com

Ground Capacity: 39,457.

Record Attendance: 57,892 v Sunderland, FA Cup 5th rd (replay), 15 March 1967.

Pitch Measurements: 115yd × 76yd.

Chairman: Ken Bates.

Chief Executive: Shaun Harvey.

Manager: Neil Warnock.

Assistant Manager: Mick Jones.

Physio: Harvey Sharman.

Colours: White shirts, white shorts, white stockings with yellow trim.

Year Formed: 1919, as Leeds United after disbandment (by FA order) of Leeds City (formed in 1904).

Turned Professional: 1920.

Club Nickname: 'The Whites'.

Ground: 1919, Elland Road.

First Football League Game: 28 August 1920, Division 2, v Port Vale (a) L 0–2 – Down; Duffield, Tillotson; Musgrove, Baker, Walton; Mason, Goldthorpe, Thompson, Lyon, Best.

Record League Victory: 8–0 v Leicester C, Division 1, 7 April 1934 – Moore; George Milburn, Jack Milburn; Edwards, Hart, Copping; Mahon (2), Firth (2), Duggan (2), Furness (2), Cochrane.

HONOURS

Football League – Division 1: ***Champions*** 1968–69, 1973–74, 1991–92; ***Runners-up*** 1964–65, 1965–66, 1969–70, 1970–71, 1971–72; **Division 2:** ***Champions*** 1923–24, 1963–64, 1989–90; ***Runners-up*** 1927–28, 1931–32, 1955–56; **FL 1:** ***Runners-up*** 2009–10.

FA Cup: ***Winners*** 1972; ***Runners-up*** 1965, 1970, 1973.

Football League Cup: ***Winners*** 1968; ***Runners-up*** 1996.

European Competitions
European Cup: 1969–70, 1974–75 (*runners-up*).
Champions League: 1992–93, 2000–01 (*s-f*).
European Cup-Winners' Cup: 1972–73 (*runners-up*).
European Fairs Cup: 1965–66, 1966–67 (*runners-up*), 1967–68 (*winners*), 1968–69, 1970–71 (*winners*).
UEFA Cup: 1971–72, 1973–74, 1979–80, 1995–96, 1998–99, 1999–2000 (*s-f*), 2001–02, 2002–03.

sky SPORTS FACT FILE

When the South African Football Association was reinstated by FIFA in 1992, the first two players to be capped while with an English club were Lucas Radebe and Philemon Masinga from Leeds United on 4 September 1994 against Madagascar, Masinga scoring the only goal.

Record Cup Victory: 10–0 v Lyn (Oslo), European Cup 1st rd 1st leg, 17 September 1969 – Sprake; Reaney, Cooper, Bremner (2), Charlton, Hunter, Madeley, Clarke (2), Jones (3), Giles (2) (Bates), O'Grady (1).

Record Defeat: 1–8 v Stoke C, Division 1, 27 August 1934.

Most League Points (2 for a win): 67, Division 1, 1968–69.

Most League Points (3 for a win): 86, FL 1, 2009–10.

Most League Goals: 98, Division 2, 1927–28.

Highest League Scorer in Season: John Charles, 42, Division 2, 1953–54.

Most League Goals in Total Aggregate: Peter Lorimer, 168, 1965–79 and 1983–86.

Most League Goals in One Match: 5, Gordon Hodgson v Leicester C, Division 1, 1 October 1938.

Most Capped Player: Lucas Radebe, 58 (70), South Africa.

Most League Appearances: Jack Charlton, 629, 1953–73.

Youngest League Player: Peter Lorimer, 15 years 289 days v Southampton, 29 September 1962.

Record Transfer Fee Received: £30,000,000 from Manchester U for Rio Ferdinand, July 2002.

Record Transfer Fee Paid: £18,000,000 to West Ham United for Rio Ferdinand, November 2000.

Football League Record: 1920 Elected to Division 2; 1924–27 Division 1; 1927–28 Division 2; 1928–31 Division 1; 1931–32 Division 2; 1932–47 Division 1; 1947–56 Division 2; 1956–60 Division 1; 1960–64 Division 2; 1964–82 Division 1; 1982–90 Division 2; 1990–92 Division 1; 1992–2004 FA Premier League; 2004–07 FL C; 2007–10 FL 1; 2010– FL C.

MANAGERS

Dick Ray 1919–20
Arthur Fairclough 1920–27
Dick Ray 1927–35
Bill Hampson 1935–47
Willis Edwards 1947–48
Major Frank Buckley 1948–53
Raich Carter 1953–58
Bill Lambton 1958–59
Jack Taylor 1959–61
Don Revie OBE 1961–74
Brian Clough 1974
Jimmy Armfield 1974–78
Jock Stein CBE 1978
Jimmy Adamson 1978–80
Allan Clarke 1980–82
Eddie Gray MBE 1982–85
Billy Bremner 1985–88
Howard Wilkinson 1988–96
George Graham 1996–98
David O'Leary 1998–2002
Terry Venables 2002–03
Peter Reid 2003
Eddie Gray *(Caretaker)* 2003–04
Kevin Blackwell 2004–06
Dennis Wise 2006–08
Gary McAllister 2008
Simon Grayson 2008–12
Neil Warnock February 2012–

LATEST SEQUENCES

Longest Sequence of League Wins: 9, 26.9.1931 – 21.11.1931.

Longest Sequence of League Defeats: 6, 28.12.2003 – 7.2.2004.

Longest Sequence of League Draws: 5, 19.4.1997 – 9.8.1997.

Longest Sequence of Unbeaten League Matches: 34, 26.10.1968 – 26.8.1969.

Longest Sequence Without a League Win: 17, 1.2.1947 – 26.5.1947.

Successive Scoring Runs: 30 from 27.8.1927.

Successive Non-scoring Runs: 6 from 30.1.1982.

TEN YEAR LEAGUE RECORD

		P	*W*	*D*	*L*	*F*	*A*	*Pts*	*Pos*
2002-03	PR Lge	38	14	5	19	58	57	47	15
2003-04	PR Lge	38	8	9	21	40	79	33	19
2004-05	FL C	46	14	18	14	49	52	60	14
2005-06	FL C	46	21	15	10	57	38	78	5
2006-07	FL C	46	13	7	26	46	72	36*	24
2007-08	FL 1	46	27	10	9	72	38	76†	5
2008-09	FL 1	46	26	6	14	77	49	84	4
2009-10	FL 1	46	25	11	10	77	44	86	2
2010-11	FL C	46	19	15	12	81	70	72	7
2011-12	FL C	46	17	10	19	65	68	61	14

**10 pts deducted; †15 pts deducted.*

DID YOU KNOW ?

In addition to Peter Lorimer at only 15 making his debut for Leeds United against Southampton on 29 September 1962, Gary Sprake, Paul Reaney and Norman Hunter all played together for the first time. They were all still under the age of 20 at the time. The match ended 1-1.

LEEDS UNITED 2011–12 LEAGUE RECORD

Match No.	Date	Venue	Opponents	Result	H/T Score	Lg Pos.	Goalscorers	Attendance
1	Aug 6	A	Southampton	L 1-3	0-2	—	Gradel (pen) [90]	25,860
2	13	H	Middlesbrough	L 0-1	0-0	23		25,650
3	16	H	Hull C	W 4-1	2-1	—	McCormack [17], Lees [40], Snodgrass [47], Nunez [68]	22,363
4	21	A	West Ham U	D 2-2	0-1	13	McCormack [59], Clayton [90]	28,252
5	27	A	Ipswich T	L 1-2	1-0	19	McCormack [34]	19,758
6	Sept 10	H	Crystal Palace	W 3-2	1-2	13	McCormack 2 [8, 84], Becchio [71]	23,916
7	17	H	Bristol C	W 2-1	1-1	11	Clayton [3], McCormack [86]	22,655
8	23	A	Brighton & HA	D 3-3	2-0	—	Keogh [18], McCormack 2 [24, 90]	20,646
9	Oct 1	H	Portsmouth	W 1-0	1-0	11	Pugh [14]	22,476
10	14	A	Doncaster R	W 3-0	1-0	—	Pugh [20], McCormack [51], Lees [64]	12,962
11	18	H	Coventry C	D 1-1	1-0	—	O'Dea [26]	21,528
12	22	A	Peterborough U	W 3-2	1-1	5	Keogh [4], Clayton [54], O'Dea [90]	12,880
13	26	A	Birmingham C	L 0-1	0-1	—		21,426
14	30	H	Cardiff C	D 1-1	0-1	7	Snodgrass [73]	20,270
15	Nov 2	H	Blackpool	L 0-5	0-3	—		22,423
16	6	A	Leicester C	W 1-0	0-0	7	Clayton [69]	27,720
17	19	A	Burnley	W 2-1	0-1	5	Snodgrass 2 [76, 89]	17,226
18	26	H	Barnsley	L 1-2	0-2	5	McCormack [55]	25,900
19	29	A	Nottingham F	W 4-0	2-0	—	Snodgrass [20], Howson [45], Becchio [49], Clayton [66]	23,577
20	Dec 3	H	Millwall	W 2-0	0-0	5	Snodgrass 2 [62, 65]	27,161
21	10	A	Watford	D 1-1	0-1	6	Snodgrass (pen) [90]	13,573
22	17	H	Reading	L 0-1	0-1	6		23,162
23	26	A	Derby Co	L 0-1	0-0	8		33,010
24	31	A	Barnsley	L 1-4	0-1	10	Becchio [90]	17,499
25	Jan 2	H	Burnley	W 2-1	0-0	8	Easton (og) [88], McCormack [90]	27,295
26	14	A	Crystal Palace	D 1-1	0-1	11	Snodgrass [63]	17,796
27	21	H	Ipswich T	W 3-1	0-1	9	Snodgrass [74], McCormack [82], Becchio [90]	22,844
28	31	H	Birmingham C	L 1-4	1-1	—	McCormack [19]	19,628
29	Feb 4	A	Bristol C	W 3-0	1-0	9	Snodgrass [40], McCormack [79], Becchio [90]	15,257
30	11	H	Brighton & HA	L 1-2	0-0	10	Becchio [79]	23,171
31	14	A	Coventry C	L 1-2	1-1	—	McCormack [32]	15,704
32	18	H	Doncaster R	W 3-2	0-1	10	Townsend [55], Clayton [80], Becchio [90]	21,181
33	25	A	Portsmouth	D 0-0	0-0	10		17,571
34	Mar 3	H	Southampton	L 0-1	0-1	10		20,901
35	6	A	Hull C	D 0-0	0-0	—		22,676
36	11	A	Middlesbrough	W 2-0	2-0	10	Snodgrass [18], Becchio [27]	21,301
37	17	H	West Ham U	D 1-1	0-0	10	Becchio [83]	33,366
38	20	H	Nottingham F	L 3-7	1-2	—	Snodgrass (pen) [6], Becchio [53], Brown [55]	21,367
39	24	A	Millwall	W 1-0	0-0	10	McCormack [65]	14,309
40	31	H	Watford	L 0-2	0-1	10		21,766
41	Apr 6	A	Reading	L 0-2	0-0	—		22,775
42	9	H	Derby Co	L 0-2	0-1	14		21,363
43	14	H	Peterborough U	W 4-1	1-1	12	Paynter 2 [45, 73], McCormack 2 [47, 48]	19,469
44	17	A	Blackpool	L 0-1	0-0	—		14,134
45	21	A	Cardiff C	D 1-1	0-1	13	Becchio [73]	25,109
46	28	H	Leicester C	L 1-2	0-1	14	Webber [82]	25,664

Final League Position: 14

GOALSCORERS

League (65): McCormack 18, Snodgrass 13 (2 pens), Becchio 11, Clayton 6, Keogh 2, Lees 2, O'Dea 2, Paynter 2, Pugh 2, Brown 1, Gradel 1 (1 pen), Howson 1, Nunez 1, Townsend 1, Webber 1, own goal 1.
Carling Cup (5): Nunez 4, McCormack 1.
FA Cup (0).

Lonergan A 35	Connolly P 23 + 5	O'Dea D 35	Brown M 21 + 3	O'Brien A 2 + 2	Kisnorbo P 18 + 1	Clayton A 42 + 1	Howson J 19	Gradel M 4	McCormack R 42 + 3	Snodgrass R 42 + 1	Paynter B 2 + 3	Nunez R 6 + 13	Sam L 3 + 14	Lees T 41 + 1	Bromby L 7 + 3	Thompson Z 7 + 2	White A 35 + 1	Keogh A 17 + 5	Taylor C 2	Becchio L 25 + 16	Forssell M 1 + 14	Pugh D 31 + 3	Vayrynen M 2 + 8	Rachubka P 5 + 1	Cairns A — + 1	McCarthy A 6	Bruce A 8	Townsend A 5 + 1	Delph F 5	Smith A 3	Rogers R 1 + 3	Webber D 2 + 11	Robinson P 9 + 1	*Match No.*
1	2	3	4[1]	5	6	7	8	9	10[2]	11[3]	12	13	14																					1
1		3	4[1]		6	7	8■	9■	10[3]	11[2]		12	14	2	5	13																		2
1		3	4		6	7			10[2]	11		8[1]	12	2		13	5	9																3
1		3			6	7	4	9[2]	10[1]	11		12	13	2			5	8																4
1		5		12	6	8	4	7	10[1]	11[3]		14	13	2[2]			3■	9																5
1		5	8[3]		6		4		10	11		7[1]	14	2				9[2]	3	12	13													6
1		5			6■	7	4		10	11[3]		8[1]		2	13		3	9[2]		12	14													7
1		5				7	4		10	11[3]				2	6		3	9[1]		12	14	8[2]	13											8
1	2	5				7	6		10[3]	11[2]				4			3	9[1]		12	14	8	13											9
1[G]	2	5				8[2]	4		10[1]	11				6			3	9		12		7	13	15										10
	2	5				8	4		10[2]	11[3]				6			3	9[1]		13	12	7	14	1										11
	2	5				8	4		10[2]			13	12	6			3	9[3]		14		11	7[1]	1										12
	2	5				8[3]	4		10	11			13	6			3	9[1]		12		7[2]	14	1										13
	2	5[1]			12	8	4		10	11			14	6			3	9[2]		13		7[3]		1										14
	2				5	8[2]	4		10	11				6■			3	9[1]		12		7	13	1[G]	15									15
	2		14	5[1]	6	8	4		10[3]	11					12		3	9[2]		13		7				1								16
	2	6[3]			5	8	4		10[2]	11		13	7	14			3	9[1]		12						1								17
	2				5	8	4		10[3]	11		12	7[1]	6			3	13		9[2]		14				1								18
	2		8		5	7[1]	4		13	11[3]		14		6			3	12		9[2]		10				1								19
	2		8[2]		5	7	4[1]			11			12	6			3	13		10		9				1								20
	2				5	8			13	11			7[1]	6			3	9[2]		10		4	12			1								21
1	2		4[3]		5	8[1]			10[2]	11			12	6			3	13		9		7	14											22
1	12	6	4		5	8			10	11		14		2[1]			3[3]	13		9[2]		7												23
1	2	5	4		6	13			10			11					3	9[2]		12		7	8[1]											24
1		2			6[1]	8			14			10[3]	12			4	3			9[2]	13	7					5	11						25
1		5	4			8			10	12				6		2	3[1]			9[2]	13	7						11						26
1		5				8			10	7				6		2	13			12	9[2]	3						11[1]	4					27
1		5				8			10	7				6		2	3			9								11	4					28
1		5				8			10	7				6			3			9		11							4	2				29
1		5				8			10[2]	7		13		6			11[1]			9		3						12	4	2				30
1		5	12	13		8			10[3]	7		14		6			3			9		11							4[1]	2[2]				31
1		5	12			4			10	7				6			3			9	14	8[1]					2	11[2]			13[3]			32
1		5	8			4			10	7				6	12		3			9		11					2[1]							33
1	12	5	8[3]			4			10	7			14	2	6[1]		11[2]			9		3										13		34
1	2	5	8			4			10	7			12	6						9		3										11[1]		35
1	2	5	8			4[2]			10[1]	7				6			11			9[3]	14	13										12	3	36
1	2	5	8			4			10[2]	7				6			11[1]			9	12											13	3	37
1	2	5	8			4			10	7	13			6			11[1]			9[3]		14										12	3[2]	38
1	13	5	8			4			10[2]	7				2			11[1]			9							6					12	3	39
1	2■		8			4[2]			10	7		14		5			11[1]			9[3]	13						6					12	3	40
1			8						10[2]	7[1]				6	2	4■				9[3]	14	11					5				12	13	3	41
1	2	5	4■						10[3]	7	12	8[2]		6						9[1]		11									13	14	3	42
1		5				4			10	7	9[3]			6	2				3[2]	14		11									8[1]	12	13	43
1	14	5■				4[3]			10	7	9[1]			6	2					12	13	11										8[2]	3	44
1	12					4[3]			10[2]	7		14		6	2[1]	8				9		11					5					13	3	45
1	2		8			4			10	7				6		11[1]				9[2]	13	3					5					12		46

FA Cup

Third Round	Arsenal	(a)	0-1

Carling Cup

First Round	Bradford C	(h)	3-2
Second Round	Doncaster R	(a)	2-1
Third Round	Manchester U	(h)	0-3

LEICESTER CITY FL Championship

FOUNDATION

In 1884 a number of young footballers, who were mostly old boys of Wyggeston School, held a meeting at a house on the Roman Fosse Way and formed Leicester Fosse FC. They collected 9d (less than 4p) towards the cost of a ball, plus the same amount for membership. Their first professional, Harry Webb from Stafford Rangers, was signed in 1888 for 2s 6d (12p) per week, plus travelling expenses.

King Power Stadium, Filbert Way, Leicester LE2 7FL.

Telephone: (0844) 815 6000.

Fax: (0116) 229 4549.

Ticket Office: (0844) 815 5000.

Website: www.lcfc.co.uk

Email: customer.relations@lcfc.co.uk

Ground Capacity: 32,500 (all seated).

Record Attendance: 47,298 v Tottenham H, FA Cup 5th rd, 18 February 1928 (at Filbert Street); 32,148 v Manchester U, FA Premier League, 26 December 2003 (at Walkers Stadium).

Pitch Measurements: 110yd × 74yd.

Chairman: Vichai Raksriaksorn.

Chief Executive: Susan Whelan.

Manager: Nigel Pearson.

Assistant Managers: Craig Shakespeare and Steve Walsh.

Physio: Dave Rennie.

Colours: Blue shirts with white trim, white shorts, blue stockings with white trim.

Year Formed: 1884.

Turned Professional: 1888.

Previous Name: 1884, Leicester Fosse; 1919, Leicester City.

Club Nickname: 'Foxes'.

Grounds: 1884, Victoria Park; 1887, Belgrave Road; 1888, Victoria Park; 1891, Filbert Street; 2002, Walkers Stadium (now known as King Power Stadium from 2011).

First Football League Game: 1 September 1894, Division 2, v Grimsby T (a) L 3–4 – Thraves; Smith, Bailey; Seymour, Brown, Henrys; Hill, Hughes, McArthur (1), Skea (2), Priestman.

Record League Victory: 10–0 v Portsmouth, Division 1, 20 October 1928 – McLaren; Black, Brown; Findlay, Carr, Watson; Adcock, Hine (3), Chandler (6), Lochhead, Barry (1).

Record Cup Victory: 8–1 v Coventry C (a), League Cup 5th rd, 1 December 1964 – Banks; Sjoberg, Norman (2); Roberts, King, McDerment; Hodgson (2), Cross, Goodfellow, Gibson (1), Stringfellow (2), (1 og).

HONOURS

Football League – Division 1: ***Runners-up*** 1928–29, 2002–03; **Division 2:** ***Champions*** 1924–25, 1936–37, 1953–54, 1956–57, 1970–71, 1979–80; ***Runners-up*** 1907–08; **FL 1:** ***Champions*** 2008–09.

FA Cup: ***Runners-up*** 1949, 1961, 1963, 1969.

Football League Cup: ***Winners*** 1964, 1997, 2000; ***Runners-up*** 1965, 1999.

European Competitions
European Cup-Winners' Cup: 1961–62.
UEFA Cup: 1997–98, 2000–01.

sky SPORTS FACT FILE

On 9 August 2011, German youth cap Jeffrey Schlupp scored a second-half hat trick for Leicester City in a 4-1 Carling Cup win at Rotherham United. Loaned to Brentford in 2010–11 he was the first trio-scoring Foxes debutant since Bill Leitch, a Motherwell guest on 13 January 1945.

Record Defeat: 0–12 (as Leicester Fosse) v Nottingham F, Division 1, 21 April 1909.

Most League Points (2 for a win): 61, Division 2, 1956–57.

Most League Points (3 for a win): 96, FL 1, 2008–09.

Most League Goals: 109, Division 2, 1956–57.

Highest League Scorer in Season: Arthur Rowley, 44, Division 2, 1956–57.

Most League Goals in Total Aggregate: Arthur Chandler, 259, 1923–35.

Most League Goals in One Match: 6, John Duncan v Port Vale, Division 2, 25 December 1924; 6, Arthur Chandler v Portsmouth, Division 1, 20 October 1928.

Most Capped Player: John O'Neill, 39, Northern Ireland.

Most League Appearances: Adam Black, 528, 1920–35.

Youngest League Player: Dave Buchanan, 16 years 192 days v Oldham Ath, 1 January 1979.

Record Transfer Fee Received: £11,000,000 from Liverpool for Emile Heskey, March 2000.

Record Transfer Fee Paid: £5,000,000 to Wolverhampton W for Ade Akinbiyi, July 2000.

Football League Record: 1894 Elected to Division 2; 1908–09 Division 1; 1909–25 Division 2; 1925–35 Division 1; 1935–37 Division 2; 1937–39 Division 1; 1946–54 Division 2; 1954–55 Division 1; 1955–57 Division 2; 1957–69 Division 1; 1969–71 Division 2; 1971–78 Division 1; 1978–80 Division 2; 1980–81 Division 1; 1981–83 Division 2; 1983–87 Division 1; 1987–92 Division 2; 1992–94 Division 1; 1994–95 FA Premier League; 1995–96 Division 1; 1996–2002 FA Premier League; 2002–03 Division 1; 2003–04 FA Premier League; 2004–08 FL C; 2008–09 FL 1; 2009– FL C.

LATEST SEQUENCES

Longest Sequence of League Wins: 7, 28.2.1993 – 27.3.1993.

Longest Sequence of League Defeats: 8, 17.3.2001 – 28.4.2001.

Longest Sequence of League Draws: 6, 21.8.1976 – 18.9.1976.

Longest Sequence of Unbeaten League Matches: 23, 1.11.2008 – 7.3.2009.

Longest Sequence Without a League Win: 18, 12.4.1975 – 1.11.1975.

Successive Scoring Runs: 31 from 12.11.1932.

Successive Non-scoring Runs: 7 from 21.11.1987.

MANAGERS

Frank Gardner 1884–92
Ernest Marson 1892–94
J. Lee 1894–95
Henry Jackson 1895–97
William Clark 1897–98
George Johnson 1898–1912
Jack Bartlett 1912–14
Louis Ford 1914–15
Harry Linney 1915–19
Peter Hodge 1919–26
Willie Orr 1926–32
Peter Hodge 1932–34
Arthur Lochhead 1934–36
Frank Womack 1936–39
Tom Bromilow 1939–45
Tom Mather 1945–46
John Duncan 1946–49
Norman Bullock 1949–55
David Halliday 1955–58
Matt Gillies 1958–68
Frank O'Farrell 1968–71
Jimmy Bloomfield 1971–77
Frank McLintock 1977–78
Jock Wallace 1978–82
Gordon Milne 1982–86
Bryan Hamilton 1986–87
David Pleat 1987–91
Gordon Lee 1991
Brian Little 1991–94
Mark McGhee 1994–95
Martin O'Neill 1995–2000
Peter Taylor 2000–01
Dave Bassett 2001–02
Micky Adams 2002–04
Craig Levein 2004–06
Robert Kelly 2006–07
Martin Allen 2007
Gary Megson 2007
Ian Holloway 2007–08
Nigel Pearson 2008–10
Paulo Sousa 2010
Sven-Göran Eriksson 2010–11
Nigel Pearson November 2011–

TEN YEAR LEAGUE RECORD

		P	W	D	L	F	A	Pts	Pos
2002-03	Div 1	46	26	14	6	73	40	92	2
2003-04	PR Lge	38	6	15	17	48	65	33	18
2004-05	FL C	46	12	21	13	49	46	57	15
2005-06	FL C	46	13	15	18	51	59	54	16
2006-07	FL C	46	13	14	19	49	64	53	19
2007-08	FL C	46	12	16	18	42	45	52	22
2008-09	FL 1	46	27	15	4	84	39	96	1
2009-10	FL C	46	21	13	12	61	45	76	5
2010-11	FL C	46	19	10	17	76	71	67	10
2011-12	FL C	46	18	12	16	66	55	66	9

DID YOU KNOW ?

On 25 August 1923, two players who went on to have distinguished careers with Leicester City made their debut against Hull City in a 1-1 draw. Hugh Adcock at outside right made 434 League appearances, while centre-forward Arthur Chandler went on to record 259 League goals.

LEICESTER CITY 2011–12 LEAGUE RECORD

Match No.	*Date*	*Venue*	*Opponents*	*Result*		*H/T Score*	*Lg Pos.*	*Goalscorers*	*Attendance*
1	Aug 6	A	Coventry C	W	1-0	0-0	—	Peltier[52]	21,102
2	13	H	Reading	L	0-2	0-0	15		23,399
3	17	H	Bristol C	L	1-2	0-1	—	Nugent[56]	20,794
4	20	A	Nottingham F	D	2-2	2-0	15	Nugent[18], Gelson[21]	24,426
5	27	H	Southampton	W	3-2	3-1	10	Vassell[3], Wellens[22], Lambert (og)[45]	23,808
6	Sept 10	A	Barnsley	D	1-1	0-1	10	King[46]	10,862
7	17	H	Brighton & HA	W	1-0	0-0	9	Abe[46]	24,128
8	25	A	Cardiff C	D	0-0	0-0	9		21,154
9	28	A	Middlesbrough	D	0-0	0-0	—		16,883
10	Oct 1	H	Derby Co	W	4-0	2-0	8	Nugent[21], Vassell[44], Schlupp[88], Dyer[90]	22,496
11	16	A	Birmingham C	L	0-2	0-0	13		17,102
12	19	H	Watford	W	2-0	2-0	—	Nugent[19], Beckford[36]	20,304
13	22	H	Millwall	L	0-3	0-2	14		21,991
14	29	A	West Ham U	L	2-3	0-2	14	King 2[58, 74]	30,410
15	Nov 1	A	Burnley	W	3-1	1-1	—	Konchesky[20], Nugent[54], Gallagher (pen)[62]	13,286
16	6	H	Leeds U	L	0-1	0-0	12		27,720
17	20	H	Crystal Palace	W	3-0	0-0	8	Beckford[55], Gallagher 2[71, 74]	22,449
18	26	A	Portsmouth	D	1-1	0-0	9	Nugent[74]	14,391
19	29	H	Blackpool	W	2-0	1-0	—	King[35], Danns[82]	21,578
20	Dec 3	A	Hull C	L	1-2	1-1	9	Konchesky[41]	20,148
21	10	H	Peterborough U	D	1-1	0-0	9	Gallagher[56]	25,948
22	17	A	Doncaster R	L	1-2	1-0	10	Nugent[38]	9461
23	26	H	Ipswich T	D	1-1	0-1	12	Gallagher (pen)[69]	27,091
24	31	H	Portsmouth	D	1-1	1-1	14	Nugent[24]	25,356
25	Jan 2	A	Crystal Palace	W	2-1	2-1	12	Danns[19], Bamba[37]	14,468
26	14	H	Barnsley	L	1-2	1-2	15	Dyer[15]	22,116
27	23	A	Southampton	W	2-0	2-0	—	Nugent[15], Mills[26]	21,014
28	Feb 1	H	Middlesbrough	D	2-2	1-1	—	Nugent[7], Beckford[86]	20,512
29	4	A	Brighton & HA	L	0-1	0-0	13		20,223
30	11	H	Cardiff C	W	2-1	1-0	12	Gallagher 2 (1 pen)[41 (p), 71]	21,375
31	14	A	Watford	L	2-3	2-2	—	Nugent 2[11, 18]	11,800
32	23	A	Derby Co	W	1-0	1-0	—	Danns[16]	28,205
33	Mar 3	H	Coventry C	W	2-0	1-0	11	Nugent[11], Beckford[60]	25,487
34	6	A	Bristol C	L	2-3	1-1	—	Dyer[41], Danns[77]	12,033
35	10	A	Reading	L	1-3	0-1	12	Danns[90]	21,858
36	13	H	Birmingham C	W	3-1	1-1	—	Beckford 2[34, 90], Schlupp[80]	21,092
37	21	A	Blackpool	D	3-3	1-1	—	Beckford 2[38, 73], Nugent[54]	12,485
38	24	H	Hull C	W	2-1	2-1	11	Dyer[18], Marshall[19]	23,759
39	27	H	Nottingham F	D	0-0	0-0	—		23,412
40	31	A	Peterborough U	L	0-1	0-0	12		10,714
41	Apr 7	H	Doncaster R	W	4-0	1-0	9	Drinkwater[33], Peltier[47], Marshall[78], Gallagher[88]	22,054
42	9	A	Ipswich T	W	2-1	1-1	9	Marshall[45], Nugent[58]	18,282
43	14	A	Millwall	L	1-2	0-1	9	Drinkwater[82]	11,525
44	17	H	Burnley	D	0-0	0-0	—		19,806
45	23	H	West Ham U	L	1-2	1-1	—	Beckford[34]	23,172
46	28	A	Leeds U	W	2-1	1-0	9	Waghorn[39], Panayiotou[90]	25,664

Final League Position: 9

GOALSCORERS

League (66): Nugent 15, Beckford 9, Gallagher 8 (3 pens), Danns 5, Dyer 4, King 4, Marshall 3, Drinkwater 2, Konchesky 2, Peltier 2, Schlupp 2, Vassell 2, Abe 1, Bamba 1, Gelson 1, Mills 1, Panayiotou 1, Waghorn 1, Wellens 1, own goal 1.
Carling Cup (10): Schlupp 4, Dyer 2, Gallagher 2, Danns 1, Howard 1.
FA Cup (10): Beckford 6, Marshall 1, Nugent 1, St Ledger-Hall 1, own goal 1.

Schmeichel K 46	Peltier L 39 + 1	Konchesky P 42	Wellens R 39 + 2	Mills M 25	Bamba S 32 + 4	Abe Y 13 + 3	Danns N 22 + 7	Gelson 10 + 5	Nugent D 41 + 1	Vassell D 10 + 3	King A 24 + 6	Gallagher P 18 + 10	Pantsil J 4 + 2	Schlupp J 3 + 18	Waghorn M 1 + 3	St Ledger-Hall S 23 + 3	Dyer L 27 + 9	Weale C — + 1	Beckford J 33 + 6	Johnson M 3 + 4	Howard S 3 + 17	Tunchev A 2	Kennedy T 4 + 1	Moore L 2	Drinkwater D 13 + 6	Delfouneso N — + 4	Morgan W 15 + 2	Marshall B 12 + 4	Panayiotou H — + 1	Match No.
1	2¹	3	4	5	6	7	8	9	10²	11■	12	13																		1
1		3	4	5	6	7¹	8³	11	10		12	14	2	9²	13															2
1	2	3	4		6		12	7²	10		8	9			13	5	11¹													3
1■		3	4	5	6	13	8⁶	11	10¹	9	7²	12	2					15												4
1		3	4³	5	6	14	8	9	10¹	11	7²	13	2	12																5
1	13	3²	4	5	6		8	9		11	12	7¹	2				14		10³											6
1	2¹	3	4	5	6	7		9		11	8		12	13					10²											7
1	2	3	4	5	6	7		9²		11	8			12					10¹	13										8
1	2	3	8³	5	6	7	14	13		9	11			12					10¹	4²										9
1	2	3		5	6	7	8²	9	10¹	11³	4			12			13				14									10
1	2	3	13	5■	6	7²	4¹	9	10	11³	8		12						14											11
1	2	3	4		6	7¹		12	10³	13	8					5	14		9²	11										12
1	2	3	4		6	7¹		14	10	13	11					5	12		9²	8³										13
1	2	3	4		6	7			10	11¹	8					5	12²		9³	13	14									14
1	2	3	8	5	6²		4¹		10		11	7³		14		13				12	9									15
1	2	3	8	5	6		4¹		10		11	7³		14					13	12	9²									16
1	2³	3	4	5		14			10²		8	7		12		6	11		9¹		13									17
1	2	3	4	5			13		10		8	7¹				6	11		9²		12									18
1	2	3	4	5	6		13	14	10		8	7¹					11³		9²		12									19
1	2	3	4	5■	6		7¹	13	10²		8	12				14	11		9³											20
1	2	3	4		6		12		10³		8	7¹		14		5	11		9²		13									21
1	2	3	4		6				10		8	7				5	11¹		12		9									22
1	2	3	4³	5	6	7			10		12	8		14			11¹		9²		13									23
1	2	3	4²	5	6	7	13		10¹		9	11		8³			14		12											24
1				5	6	7	4		10²		11			9³			12		14		13■	2¹	3	8						25
1	2	3	7	5			4		10		8	9¹					11		12			6								26
1	2	3	8	5			4		10³			7¹				6	11		9²		14				12	13				27
1	2	3	8³	5			4		10			7²				6	11¹		9		14				12	13				28
1	2	3¹	8²	5			4■		10³							6	11		9■						7	14	12	13		29
1	2	3	4	5					10			7²				6	11¹		9		13				8			12		30
1	2¹	3	4	5			12		10			7				6	11³		9		14				8²		13			31
1	2¹	3	8		12		4		10							6	11		9²						14	13	5	7³		32
1	2	3■	8				4		10²					13		6	11		9³		14				12		5	7¹		33
1	2		8				4³		10			14		13		6	11		9²				3		12		5	7¹		34
1	2		8		12		4		10			14				6	11		9²		13		3¹		7³		5			35
1			8		2		4		10²			7¹		13		6	11		9				3				5	12		36
1	2	3	8¹		13		4		10³					14		6	11		9						7²		5	12		37
1	2	3			12		4■		10¹							6	11		9				13		7		5	8²		38
1	2	3			4				10¹					12		6	11²		9		13				7		5	8		39
1	2	3	12		4				10					13		6¹	11²		9						7		5	8		40
1	2	3	4¹		6				10		13	12		14			11²		9³						7		5	8		41
1	2	3	4		6				10		13	12					11²		9		14				7¹		5	8³		42
1	2³	3	8²		6				10		4	11¹					12		9		14				13		5	7		43
1	2	3	4		6				10			12		13			11¹		9²						7		5	8		44
1	2	3	8¹		6				10³		4²				14	13	12		9						7		5	11		45
1		3			4				13	12					10²	6	11³		9¹					2	7		5	8	14	46

FA Cup

Third Round	Nottingham F	(a)	0-0
		(h)	4-0
Fourth Round	Swindon T	(h)	2-0
Fifth Round	Norwich C	(a)	2-1
Quarter-Final	Chelsea	(a)	2-5

Carling Cup

First Round	Rotherham U	(a)	4-1
Second Round	Bury	(a)	4-2
Third Round	Cardiff C	(a)	2-2

LEYTON ORIENT FL Championship 1

FOUNDATION

There is some doubt about the foundation of Leyton Orient, and, indeed, some confusion with clubs like Leyton and Clapton over their early history. As regards the foundation, the most favoured version is that Leyton Orient was formed originally by members of Homerton Theological College who established Glyn Cricket Club in 1881 and then carried on through the following winter playing football. Eventually many employees of the Orient Shipping Line became involved and so the name Orient was chosen in 1888.

Matchroom Stadium, Brisbane Road, Leyton, London E10 5NF.

Telephone: (0871) 310 1881.

Fax: (0871) 310 1882.

Ticket Office: (0871) 310 1883.

Website: www.leytonorient.com

Email: info@leytonorient.net

Ground Capacity: 9,300.

Record Attendance: 34,345 v West Ham U, FA Cup 4th rd, 25 January 1964.

Pitch Measurements: 110yd × 76yd.

Chairman: Barry Hearn.

Chief Executive: Matthew Porter.

Manager: Russell Slade.

Assistant Manager: Kevin Nugent.

Physio: Dave Appanah.

Colours: Red shirts with white insert and striped sleeves, red shorts, red stockings.

Year Formed: 1881.

Turned Professional: 1903.

Previous Names: 1881, Glyn Cricket and Football Club; 1886, Eagle Football Club; 1888, Orient Football Club; 1898, Clapton Orient; 1946, Leyton Orient; 1966, Orient; 1987, Leyton Orient.

Club Nickname: 'The O's'.

Grounds: 1884, Glyn Road; 1896, Whittles Athletic Ground; 1900, Millfields Road; 1930, Lea Bridge Road; 1937, Brisbane Road.

First Football League Game: 2 September 1905, Division 2, v Leicester Fosse (a) L 1–2 – Butler; Holmes, Codling; Lamberton, Boden, Boyle; Kingaby (1), Wootten, Leigh, Evenson, Bourne.

Record League Victory: 8–0 v Crystal Palace, Division 3 (S), 12 November 1955 – Welton; Lee, Earl; Blizzard, Aldous, McKnight; White (1), Facey (3), Burgess (2), Heckman, Hartburn (2). 8–0 v Rochdale, Division 4, 20 October 1987 – Wells; Howard, Dickenson (1), Smalley (1), Day, Hull, Hales (2), Castle (Sussex), Shinners (2), Godfrey (Harvey), Comfort (2). 8–0 v Colchester U, Division 4, 15 October 1988 – Wells; Howard, Dickenson, Hales (1p), Day (1), Sitton (1), Baker (1), Ward, Hull (3), Juryeff, Comfort (1). 8–0 v Doncaster R, Division 3, 28 December 1997 – Hyde; Channing, Naylor, Smith (1p), Hicks, Clark, Ling, Roger Joseph, Griffiths (3) (Harris), Richards (2) (Baker (1)), Inglethorpe (1) (Simpson).

HONOURS

Football League – Division 1: 22nd, 1962–63;
Division 2: ***Runners-up*** 1961–62;
Division 3: ***Champions*** 1969–70;
Division 3 (S): ***Champions*** 1955–56;
Runners-up 1954–55.

FA Cup: Semi-final 1978.

Football League Cup: Best season: 5th rd, 1963.

sky SPORTS FACT FILE

Veteran goalkeeper Peter Shilton made his 1000th League appearance with Leyton Orient on 22 December 1996 at Brisbane Road against Brighton & Hove Albion. The match was screened live by *Sky Sports* and the 47-year-old kept a clean sheet in what proved to be a 2-0 win.

Record Cup Victory: 9–2 v Chester, League Cup 3rd rd, 15 October 1962 – Robertson; Charlton, Taylor; Gibbs, Bishop, Lea; Deeley (1), Waites (3), Dunmore (2), Graham (3), Wedge.

Record Defeat: 0–8 v Aston Villa, FA Cup 4th rd, 30 January 1929.

Most League Points (2 for a win): 66, Division 3 (S), 1955–56.

Most League Points (3 for a win): 81, FL 2, 2005–06.

Most League Goals: 106, Division 3 (S), 1955–56.

Highest League Scorer in Season: Tom Johnston, 35, Division 2, 1957–58.

Most League Goals in Total Aggregate: Tom Johnston, 121, 1956–58, 1959–61.

Most League Goals in One Match: 4, Wally Leigh v Bradford C, Division 2, 13 April 1906; 4, Albert Pape v Oldham Ath, Division 2, 1 September 1924; 4, Peter Kitchen v Millwall, Division 3, 21 April 1984.

Most Capped Players: Tunji Banjo, 7 (7), Nigeria; John Chiedozie, 7 (9), Nigeria; Tony Grealish, 7 (45), Republic of Ireland.

Most League Appearances: Peter Allen, 432, 1965–78.

Youngest League Player: Paul Went, 15 years 327 days v Preston NE, 4 September 1965.

Record Transfer Fee Received: £1,000,000 from Fulham for Gabriel Zakuani, July 2006.

Record Transfer Fee Paid: £175,000 to Wigan Ath for Paul Beesley, October 1989.

Football League Record: 1905 Elected to Division 2; 1929–56 Division 3 (S); 1956–62 Division 2; 1962–63 Division 1; 1963–66 Division 2; 1966–70 Division 3; 1970–82 Division 2; 1982–85 Division 3; 1985–89 Division 4; 1989–92 Division 3; 1992–95 Division 2; 1995–2004 Division 3; 2004–06 FL 2; 2006– FL 1.

LATEST SEQUENCES

Longest Sequence of League Wins: 10, 21.1.1956 – 30.3.1956.

Longest Sequence of League Defeats: 9, 1.4.1995 – 6.5.1995.

Longest Sequence of League Draws: 6, 30.11.1974 – 28.12.1974.

Longest Sequence of Unbeaten League Matches: 13, 30.10.1954 – 19.2.1955.

Longest Sequence Without a League Win: 23, 6.10.1962 – 13.4.1963.

Successive Scoring Runs: 24 from 3.5.2003.

Successive Non-scoring Runs: 8 from 19.11.1994.

MANAGERS

Sam Omerod 1905–06
Ike Ivenson 1906
Billy Holmes 1907–22
Peter Proudfoot 1922–29
Arthur Grimsdell 1929–30
Peter Proudfoot 1930–31
Jimmy Seed 1931–33
David Pratt 1933–34
Peter Proudfoot 1935–39
Tom Halsey 1939
Bill Wright 1939–45
Willie Hall 1945
Bill Wright 1945–46
Charlie Hewitt 1946–48
Neil McBain 1948–49
Alec Stock 1949–59
Les Gore 1959–61
Johnny Carey 1961–63
Benny Fenton 1963–64
Dave Sexton 1965
Dick Graham 1966–68
Jimmy Bloomfield 1968–71
George Petchey 1971–77
Jimmy Bloomfield 1977–81
Paul Went 1981
Ken Knighton 1981–83
Frank Clark 1983–91 *(Managing Director)*
Peter Eustace 1991–94
Chris Turner/John Sitton 1994–95
Pat Holland 1995–96
Tommy Taylor 1996–2001
Paul Brush 2001–03
Martin Ling 2003–09
Geraint Williams 2009–10
Russell Slade April 2010–

TEN YEAR LEAGUE RECORD

		P	W	D	L	F	A	Pts	Pos
2002-03	Div 3	46	14	11	21	51	61	53	18
2003-04	Div 3	46	13	14	19	48	65	53	19
2004-05	FL 2	46	16	15	15	65	67	63	11
2005-06	FL 2	46	22	15	9	67	51	81	3
2006-07	FL 1	46	12	15	19	61	77	51	20
2007-08	FL 1	46	16	12	18	49	63	60	14
2008-09	FL 1	46	15	11	20	45	57	56	14
2009-10	FL 1	46	13	12	21	53	63	51	17
2010-11	FL 1	46	19	13	14	71	62	70	7
2011-12	FL 1	46	13	11	22	48	75	50	20

DID YOU KNOW ?

Ex-Royal Engineer Bobby Turnbull, a Scot, joined Clapton Orient in 1927 having been with Arsenal (who converted him from full-back to centre-forward), Charlton Athletic and Chelsea. After leaving Orient this goalscorer played for Southend United, Chatham and Crystal Palace.

LEYTON ORIENT 2011–12 LEAGUE RECORD

Match No.	Date	Venue	Opponents	Result		H/T Score	Lg Pos.	Goalscorers	Attendance
1	Aug 6	A	Walsall	L	0-1	0-1	—		4753
2	13	H	Tranmere R	L	0-1	0-0	23		3658
3	16	H	Wycombe W	L	1-3	1-2	—	Cox 16	3503
4	20	A	Brentford	L	0-5	0-1	24		5399
5	27	H	Carlisle U	L	1-2	0-0	24	Smith, Jimmy 53	3524
6	Sept 3	A	Chesterfield	D	0-0	0-0	24		6197
7	10	A	Colchester U	D	1-1	0-1	24	Smith, Jimmy 90	4258
8	13	H	Bournemouth	L	1-3	1-1	—	Baudry (og) 23	3258
9	17	H	Oldham Ath	L	1-3	1-0	24	Porter 18	3699
10	24	A	Huddersfield T	D	2-2	0-1	24	Lisbie 85, Chorley 90	12,269
11	Oct 1	H	Preston NE	W	2-1	2-1	24	Cox 2 36, 45	4384
12	8	A	Scunthorpe U	W	3-2	0-1	23	Lisbie 2 46, 50, Cuthbert 67	4234
13	15	H	Bury	W	1-0	1-0	21	Cox 45	3943
14	22	H	Sheffield U	D	1-1	0-0	19	Lisbie 90	5928
15	25	A	Yeovil T	D	2-2	1-2	—	Mooney 2 (1 pen) 30, 87 (p)	3121
16	29	A	Rochdale	W	2-0	1-0	17	Smith, Jimmy 12, Mooney 65	2322
17	Nov 5	H	Hartlepool U	D	1-1	1-0	18	Cox 23	4424
18	19	H	Stevenage	D	0-0	0-0	17		4862
19	26	A	Sheffield W	L	0-1	0-1	18		18,355
20	Dec 10	H	Exeter C	W	3-0	0-0	17	Lisbie 2 (2 pens) 65, 87, Tehoue 75	4291
21	17	A	Notts Co	W	2-1	1-0	17	Dawson 44, Tehoue 85	5830
22	26	H	Milton Keynes D	L	0-3	0-1	17		4162
23	31	H	Charlton Ath	W	1-0	1-0	17	Spring 25	5097
24	Jan 2	A	Stevenage	W	1-0	1-0	15	Cook 15	5351
25	7	A	Carlisle U	L	1-4	0-3	—	Cureton 85	4964
26	14	H	Chesterfield	D	1-1	1-0	15	Mooney 42	4174
27	21	A	Preston NE	W	2-0	0-0	12	Laird 67, Smith, Jimmy 80	11,436
28	28	H	Colchester U	L	0-1	0-1	14		4659
29	Feb 14	A	Bournemouth	W	2-1	1-1	—	Lisbie 17, Smith, Jimmy 75	5412
30	18	H	Scunthorpe U	L	1-3	1-0	15	Tehoue 34	4055
31	25	A	Bury	D	1-1	1-0	15	Spring 27	2807
32	Mar 3	H	Walsall	D	1-1	1-0	16	Cox 34	4183
33	6	A	Wycombe W	L	2-4	0-4	—	Spring 46, Laird 74	3564
34	10	A	Tranmere R	L	0-2	0-2	17		6824
35	17	H	Brentford	W	2-0	2-0	15	Lisbie 29, Smith, Jimmy 45	4173
36	20	A	Milton Keynes D	L	1-4	1-2	—	Lisbie 13	6842
37	24	H	Sheffield W	L	0-1	0-0	18		6196
38	27	A	Oldham Ath	W	1-0	0-0	—	Mooney 70	4145
39	31	A	Charlton Ath	L	0-2	0-1	18		17,425
40	Apr 3	H	Huddersfield T	L	1-3	1-2	—	Spring 14	3674
41	6	H	Notts Co	L	0-3	0-0	—		4016
42	9	A	Exeter C	L	0-3	0-1	20		4142
43	14	A	Sheffield U	L	1-3	1-1	20	Lisbie 12	18,272
44	21	H	Yeovil T	D	2-2	1-0	19	Lisbie 2 23, 73	4888
45	28	A	Hartlepool U	L	1-2	1-1	20	Campbell-Ryce 34	4502
46	May 5	H	Rochdale	W	2-1	2-0	20	Cox 32, Odubajo 41	4110

Final League Position: 20

GOALSCORERS

League (48): Lisbie 12 (2 pens), Cox 7, Smith, Jimmy 6, Mooney 5 (1 pen), Spring 4, Tehoue 3, Laird 2, Campbell-Ryce 1, Chorley 1, Cook 1, Cureton 1, Cuthbert 1, Dawson 1, Odubajo 1, Porter 1, own goal 1.
Carling Cup (6): Mooney 2, Chorley 1 (pen), Cox 1, Dawson 1, Richardson 1.
FA Cup (3): Porter 1, Smith, Jimmy 1, Spring 1.
J Paint Trophy (1): Mooney 1.

Butcher L 23	Omozusi E 8 + 2	Daniels C 13	Chorley B 30 + 2	Cuthbert S 33	Smith Jimmy 35 + 3	Spring M 41	McSweeney L 28 + 1	Revell A 4 + 1	Cureton J 9 + 10	Cox D 35 + 3	Richardson M 1 + 2	Tehoue J 4 + 10	Porter G 9 + 25	Dawson S 20	Mooney D 28 + 9	Laird M 11 + 11	Button D 1	Forbes T 38 + 1	Alnwick B 6	Clarke T 10	Lisbie K 34 + 3	Odubajo M 1 + 2	Cestor M 1	Craig T 4 / Lobjoit B — + 1	Cook L 9	Chicksen A 3 / Obafemi A — + 1	Leacock D 15	Dickson R 9	Taiwo S 2 + 3	Stech M 2	Andrew C 2 + 8	Rachubka P 8	Ben Youssef S 6 + 3	Reed A 10 + 1	Campbell-Ryce J 7 + 1	Jones J 6	Smith Jamie — + 1	Match No.
1	2	3	4	5	6	7	8^{1}	9^{2}	10^{3}	11	12	13	14																									1
1	2	3	4	5	6^{2}	7^{1}		9	10^{3}	11	13		14	8	12																							2
1	2	3	4	5	6^{1}	7		9^{2}	10	11			13	8	12																							3
1	2	11	4	5	6			9^{1}	12	7	3^{2}			8	10	13																						4
	2	3	4	5	6		7^{2}	14	10^{3}	11		12		8	9^{1}	13	1																					5
1	2	3	4		6		14		10^{1}	11		12	13	8	9^{2}	7^{3}		5																				6
		3	4	2	6	7^{2}				11			12		9	13		5	1	8	10^{1}																	7
	12	3	4	2■	6	7^{2}				11			13		9^{1}			5	1	8	10																	8
	2	3	4		6	7^{1}				11			10		9			5	1	8		12																9
1	2		4			7	3			11			10	8	9^{1}	6		5			12																	10
1			4	5		7	3		12	11			10^{2}	8	13			6		2	9^{1}																	11
1		3		5		7	2		12	11^{1}				8	9			6		4	10																	12
1		3		5		7	2			11			12	8	9^{1}			6		4	10																	13
1	13	3■		5		7^{3}	2			11			14	8	9^{2}	12		6		4^{1}	10																	14
1				5	13	7	2		14	11			12	8	9	4^{1}		6			10^{3}		3^{2}															15
1				5	3	7^{2}	2		12	11			8^{3}	4	9	13		6			10^{1}	14																16
				5	3		2		10	11			7	8	9			6	1	4																		17
		3		5	4	7			12				11	8	9^{1}			6	1	2	10																	18
				5	4^{3}	7	8		14				13		9^{1}	12		6	1	2	10			3	11^{2}													19
1				5	8	7	2		10^{2}			13	12	4				6			9			3	11^{1}													20
1				5	8	7	2■		10^{1}			14	13	4	12			6			9^{3}			3	11^{2}													21
1			4	5	2	7^{1}			10^{2}			13	12	8	14			6			9^{3}			3	11													22
1			4	5	3	7	2			13		12		8	9^{1}			6			10				11^{2}													23
1			4■	5		7	3						13	8	9^{2}	10		6			12				11^{1}	2												24
1				5	12	7	2		14	13				8^{1}	9^{3}	4^{2}		6			10				11	3												25
1				5	4	8	2		14	7		13			9^{3}	12		6			10^{2}				11^{1}	3												26
1				5	4	7	2			11		12			9	8		6			10^{1}				3													27
1				5	8^{2}	7	2		12	11		14	13		9^{1}	4		6			10^{3}						3											28
1			13	5	8	7^{2}				11		9^{1}	12			4		6			10						2	3										29
1^{6}			15	5	8	7	2			11		9	12		13						10^{2}						6	3	4^{1}									30
			4	5	8	7				11		9^{1}	12					2			10						6	3		1								31
			4	5	8	7				11		9^{2}				13		2			10^{3}						6	3^{1}	12■	1	14							32
			4		8^{2}	7	2			11			13			6		5			10						3^{1}				9	1	12					33
			4		6^{2}	7	3						12		9	13		5													10	1	2	8	11^{1}			34
			4	5	6	7	3			9					12			2			10^{2}											1	13	8	11^{1}			35
			4	5	6^{1}	7	3			9					12	13		2			10^{3}										14	1		8	11^{2}			36
			4	5	8		3			10			12			13		2			9						6^{2}				14	1		7^{1}	11^{3}			37
			4		6	7							11^{2}		9^{1}			2			10						5	3■	13		12	1		8				38
			4	5^{1}	6	7				13			11^{3}		9^{2}			2			10						3				14	1	12	8				39
			4		6	7				11			10		9^{2}	8^{1}		2			12						5	3			13	1						40
			4		6^{1}	7				11^{2}			13		9			2			10						5	3	12					8		1		41
			4			7				11			12		9^{3}	6^{1}					10^{2}						5	3			13		2	8		1	14	42
			4			7^{3}				11			14		9^{2}			5			10						6	3■	8^{1}				2	13	12	1		43
			4		13	7	3			10								5			9						6				12		2	8^{1}	11^{2}	1		44
			4		6^{2}	7	3			10^{1}			12		13			5			9												2	8	11	1		45
			4		6	7	3			10								13			9^{3}	8^{2}		12		14	5						2		11^{1}	1		46

FA Cup

First Round	Bromley	(h)	3-0
Second Round	Gillingham	(h)	0-1

Carling Cup

First Round	Southend U	(a)	1-1
Second Round	Bristol R	(h)	3-2
Third Round	Blackburn R	(a)	2-3

J Paint Trophy

First Round	Dagenham & R	(h)	1-1

LIVERPOOL

FA Premiership

FOUNDATION

But for a dispute between Everton FC and their landlord at Anfield in 1892, there may never have been a Liverpool club. This dispute persuaded the majority of Evertonians to quit Anfield for Goodison Park, leaving the landlord, Mr John Houlding, to form a new club. He originally tried to retain the name 'Everton' but when this failed, he founded Liverpool Association FC on 15 March 1892.

Anfield Stadium, Anfield Road, Liverpool L4 0TH.

Telephone: (0151) 260 1433.

Fax: (0151) 260 8813.

Ticket Office: (0151) 260 8680.

Website: www.liverpoolfc.tv

Email: customercontact@liverpoolfc.tv or customerservices@liverpoolfc.tv

Ground Capacity: 45,522.

Record Attendance: 61,905 v Wolverhampton W, FA Cup 4th rd, 2 February 1952.

Pitch Measurements: 101m × 68m.

Chairman: Tom Werner.

Vice-Chairman: David Ginsberg.

Manager: Brendan Rodgers.

Assistant Manager: Colin Pascoe.

Physio: Rob Price.

Colours: All red with white trim.

Year Formed: 1892.

Turned Professional: 1892.

Club Nicknames: 'Reds' or 'Pool'.

Ground: 1892, Anfield.

First Football League Game: 2 September 1893, Division 2, v Middlesbrough Ironopolis (a) W 2–0 – McOwen; Hannah, McLean; Henderson, McQue (1), McBride; Gordon, McVean (1), Matt McQueen, Stott, Hugh McQueen.

HONOURS

FA Premier League: ***Runners-up*** 2001–02, 2008–09.
Football League – Division 1:
Champions 1900–01, 1905–06, 1921–22, 1922–23, 1946–47, 1963–64, 1965–66, 1972–73, 1975–76, 1976–77, 1978–79, 1979–80, 1981–82, 1982–83, 1983–84, 1985–86, 1987–88, 1989–90; ***Runners-up*** 1898–99, 1909–10, 1968–69, 1973–74, 1974–75, 1977–78, 1984–85, 1986–87, 1988–89, 1990–91;
Division 2: ***Champions*** 1893–94, 1895–96, 1904–05, 1961–62.

FA Cup: ***Winners*** 1965, 1974, 1986, 1989, 1992, 2001, 2006; ***Runners-up*** 1914, 1950, 1971, 1977, 1988, 1996, 2012.

Football League Cup: ***Winners*** 1981, 1982, 1983, 1984, 1995, 2001, 2003, 2012; ***Runners-up*** 1978, 1987, 2005.

League Super Cup: ***Winners*** 1986.

European Competitions: European Cup: 1964–65, 1966–67, 1973–74, 1976–77 (*winners*), 1977–78 (*winners*), 1978–79, 1979–80, 1980–81 (*winners*), 1981–82, 1982–83, 1983–84 (*winners*), 1984–85 (*runners-up*). **Champions League:** 2001–02, 2002–03, 2004–05 (*winners*), 2005–06, 2006–07 (*runners-up*), 2007–08 (*s-f*), 2008–09 (*q-f*), 2009–10. **European Cup-Winners' Cup:** 1965–66 (*runners-up*), 1971–72, 1974–75, 1992–93, 1996–97 (*s-f*). **European Fairs Cup:** 1967–68, 1968–69, 1969–70, 1970–71. **UEFA Cup:** 1972–73 (*winners*), 1975–76 (*winners*), 1991–92, 1995–96, 1997–98, 1998–99, 2000–01 (*winners*), 2002–03, 2003–04. **Europa League:** 2009–10, 2010–11. **Super Cup:** 1977 (*winners*), 1978, 1984, 2001 (*winners*), 2005 (*winners*). **World Club Championship:** 1981, 1984. **FIFA Club World Cup:** 2005.

Record League Victory: 10–1 v Rotherham T, Division 2, 18 February 1896 – Storer; Goldie, Wilkie; McCartney, McQue, Holmes; McVean (3), Ross (2), Allan (4), Becton (1), Bradshaw.

sky SPORTS FACT FILE

The only Merseyside derby debutant goalscorer for Liverpool was Bill White on 14 September 1901. It was to prove his only League goal for the club in half a dozen League appearances. Making the first of only two League outings that day against Everton was George Bowen.

Record Cup Victory: 11–0 v Stromsgodset Drammen, ECWC 1st rd 1st leg, 17 September 1974 – Clemence; Smith (1), Lindsay (1p), Thompson (2), Cormack (1), Hughes (1), Boersma (2), Hall, Heighway (1), Kennedy (1), Callaghan (1).

Record Defeat: 1–9 v Birmingham C, Division 2, 11 December 1954.

Most League Points (2 for a win): 68, Division 1, 1978–79.

Most League Points (3 for a win): 90, Division 1, 1987–88.

Most League Goals: 106, Division 2, 1895–96.

Highest League Scorer in Season: Roger Hunt, 41, Division 2, 1961–62.

Most League Goals in Total Aggregate: Roger Hunt, 245, 1959–69.

Most League Goals in One Match: 5, Andy McGuigan v Stoke C, Division 1, 4 January 1902; 5, John Evans v Bristol R, Division 2, 15 September 1954; 5, Ian Rush v Luton T, Division 1, 29 October 1983.

Most Capped Player: Steven Gerrard, 96, England.

Most League Appearances: Ian Callaghan, 640, 1960–78.

Youngest League Player: Jack Robinson, 16 years 250 days v Hull C, 9 May 2010.

MANAGERS

W. E. Barclay 1892–96
Tom Watson 1896–1915
David Ashworth 1920–23
Matt McQueen 1923–28
George Patterson 1928–36
(continued as Secretary)
George Kay 1936–51
Don Welsh 1951–56
Phil Taylor 1956–59
Bill Shankly 1959–74
Bob Paisley 1974–83
Joe Fagan 1983–85
Kenny Dalglish 1985–91
Graeme Souness 1991–94
Roy Evans 1994–98
(then Joint Manager)
Gerard Houllier 1998–2004
Rafael Benitez 2004–10
Roy Hodgson 2010–11
Kenny Dalglish 2011–12
Brendan Rodgers June 2012–

Record Transfer Fee Received: £50,000,000 from Chelsea for Fernando Torres, January 2011.

Record Transfer Fee Paid: £35,000,000 to Newcastle U for Andy Carroll, January 2011.

Football League Record: 1893 Elected to Division 2; 1894–95 Division 1; 1895–96 Division 2; 1896–1904 Division 1; 1904–05 Division 2; 1905–54 Division 1; 1954–62 Division 2; 1962–92 Division 1; 1992– FA Premier League.

LATEST SEQUENCES

Longest Sequence of League Wins: 12, 21.4.1990 – 6.10.1990.

Longest Sequence of League Defeats: 9, 29.4.1899 – 14.10.1899.

Longest Sequence of League Draws: 6, 19.2.1975 – 19.3.1975.

Longest Sequence of Unbeaten League Matches: 31, 4.5.1987 – 16.3.1988.

Longest Sequence Without a League Win: 14, 12.12.1953 – 20.3.1954.

Successive Scoring Runs: 29 from 27.4.1957.

Successive Non-scoring Runs: 5 from 22.12.1906.

TEN YEAR LEAGUE RECORD

		P	W	D	L	F	A	Pts	Pos
2002-03	PR Lge	38	18	10	10	61	41	64	5
2003-04	PR Lge	38	16	12	10	55	37	60	4
2004-05	PR Lge	38	17	7	14	52	41	58	5
2005-06	PR Lge	38	25	7	6	57	25	82	3
2006-07	PR Lge	38	20	8	10	57	27	68	3
2007-08	PR Lge	38	21	13	4	67	28	76	4
2008-09	PR Lge	38	25	11	2	77	27	86	2
2009-10	PR Lge	38	18	9	11	61	35	63	7
2010-11	PR Lge	38	17	7	14	59	44	58	6
2011-12	PR Lge	38	14	10	14	47	40	52	8

DID YOU KNOW?

The first Liverpool player to score a hat trick in an FA Cup tie was Sam Raybould against Southampton in the fourth round on 10 March 1906. He was also the first player to score more than 30 goals in a season for the club when he finished with 31 during 1902–03.

LIVERPOOL 2011–12 LEAGUE RECORD

Match No.	Date	Venue	Opponents	Result	H/T Score	Lg Pos.	Goalscorers	Attendance
1	Aug 13	H	Sunderland	D 1-1	1-0	—	Suarez [12]	45,018
2	20	A	Arsenal	W 2-0	0-0	4	Ramsey (og) [78], Suarez [90]	60,090
3	27	H	Bolton W	W 3-1	1-0	3	Henderson [15], Skrtel [52], Adam [53]	44,725
4	Sept 10	A	Stoke C	L 0-1	0-1	5		27,592
5	18	A	Tottenham H	L 0-4	0-1	8		36,129
6	24	H	Wolverhampton W	W 2-1	2-0	5	Johnson (og) [11], Suarez [38]	44,922
7	Oct 1	A	Everton	W 2-0	0-0	5	Carroll [71], Suarez [82]	39,510
8	15	H	Manchester U	D 1-1	0-0	5	Gerrard [68]	45,065
9	22	H	Norwich C	D 1-1	1-0	6	Bellamy [45]	44,931
10	29	A	WBA	W 2-0	2-0	6	Adam (pen) [9], Carroll [45]	25,522
11	Nov 5	H	Swansea C	D 0-0	0-0	6		45,013
12	20	A	Chelsea	W 2-1	1-0	6	Rodriguez [33], Johnson [87]	41,820
13	27	H	Manchester C	D 1-1	1-1	6	Lescott (og) [33]	45,071
14	Dec 5	A	Fulham	L 0-1	0-0	—		25,688
15	10	H	QPR	W 1-0	0-0	6	Suarez [47]	45,016
16	18	A	Aston Villa	W 2-0	2-0	6	Bellamy [11], Skrtel [15]	37,460
17	21	A	Wigan Ath	D 0-0	0-0	—		19,230
18	26	H	Blackburn R	D 1-1	0-1	6	Rodriguez [53]	44,441
19	30	H	Newcastle U	W 3-1	1-1	—	Bellamy 2 [29, 67], Gerrard [78]	44,372
20	Jan 3	A	Manchester C	L 0-3	0-2	—		47,131
21	14	H	Stoke C	D 0-0	0-0	7		44,691
22	21	A	Bolton W	L 1-3	1-2	7	Bellamy [37]	26,854
23	31	A	Wolverhampton W	W 3-0	0-0	—	Carroll [52], Bellamy [61], Kuyt [78]	27,447
24	Feb 6	H	Tottenham H	D 0-0	0-0	—		44,461
25	11	A	Manchester U	L 1-2	0-0	7	Suarez [80]	74,844
26	Mar 3	H	Arsenal	L 1-2	1-1	7	Koscielny (og) [23]	44,922
27	10	A	Sunderland	L 0-1	0-0	7		41,661
28	13	H	Everton	W 3-0	1-0	—	Gerrard 3 [34, 51, 90]	44,921
29	21	A	QPR	L 2-3	0-0	—	Coates [54], Kuyt [72]	18,033
30	24	H	Wigan Ath	L 1-2	0-1	7	Suarez [47]	44,431
31	Apr 1	A	Newcastle U	L 0-2	0-1	8		52,363
32	7	H	Aston Villa	D 1-1	0-1	8	Suarez [82]	44,321
33	10	A	Blackburn R	W 3-2	2-1	—	Rodriguez 2 [13, 16], Carroll [90]	23,571
34	22	H	WBA	L 0-1	0-0	8		43,660
35	28	A	Norwich C	W 3-0	2-0	8	Suarez 3 [24, 28, 82]	26,819
36	May 1	H	Fulham	L 0-1	0-1	—		40,106
37	8	H	Chelsea	W 4-1	3-0	—	Essien (og) [19], Henderson [25], Agger [28], Shelvey [61]	40,721
38	13	A	Swansea C	L 0-1	0-0	8		20,605

Final League Position: 8

GOALSCORERS

League (47): Suarez 11, Bellamy 6, Gerrard 5, Carroll 4, Rodriguez 4, Adam 2 (1 pen), Henderson 2, Kuyt 2, Skrtel 2, Agger 1, Coates 1, Johnson 1, Shelvey 1, own goals 5.
Carling Cup (14): Suarez 3, Bellamy 2, Gerrard 2 (2 pens), Kuyt 2, Rodriguez 2, Carroll 1, Kelly 1, Skrtel 1.
FA Cup (18): Carroll 4, Suarez 3, Downing 2, Gerrard 2 (1 pen), Agger 1, Bellamy 1, Kuyt 1, Shelvey 1, Skrtel 1, own goals 2.

Reina J 34	Flanagan J 5	Jose Enrique 33 + 2	Carragher J 19 + 2	Agger D 24 + 3	Adam C 27 + 1	Henderson J 31 + 6	Lucas 12	Carroll A 21 + 14	Suarez L 29 + 2	Downing S 28 + 8	Kuyt D 22 + 12	Raul Meireles — + 2	Kelly M 12	Skrtel M 33 + 1	Rodriguez M 10 + 2	Bellamy C 12 + 15	Johnson G 22 + 1	Coates S 4 + 3	Spearing J 15 + 1	Gerrard S 12 + 6	Shelvey J 8 + 5	Fabio Aurelio 1 + 1	Sterling R — + 3	Doni 4	Jones B — + 1	*Match No.*
1	2	3	4	5	6	7^{1}	8	9	10^{2}	11	12	13														1
1		3	4	5	6	7	8	9^{2}	13	11	10^{1}	12	2													2
1		3	4	5	6	7^{2}	8	13	10^{3}	11	9		2^{1}	12	14											3
1		3	2	5	6	7^{2}	8	12	9	11	10^{1}			4^{3}		13	14									4
1		3	2	5^{1}	6■	7	8	9	10^{3}	11^{2}				4■		14		12	13							5
1		3	4		6	7^{1}	8	9	10^{2}	11	12		2	5						13						6
1		3	4		6^{1}	14	8^{3}	9	10	11^{2}	7		2	5		13				12						7
1		3	4		6	12	8^{1}		9	11	7		2	5						10						8
1		3	4	14	6	12		13	9	11^{2}	7^{3}			5		10^{1}	2			8						9
1		3		4	6	7	8	9	10^{1}	11				5		12	2									10
1		3		4	6	7^{1}	8	9^{2}	10	11	12			5		13	2									11
1		3		5	6	12	8	14	10^{3}	13	7			4	11^{2}	9^{1}	2									12
1		3		5	6	7	8	12	9	11	10^{1}			4			2									13
1		3		5	6	7		9^{2}	10	13	12			4		11^{1}	2		8■							14
1		3		5	6	8			9	11^{2}	10			4	7^{1}	12	2				13					15
1		3	13	5	6	7		12	9^{1}	11	14			4		8^{3}	2				10^{2}					16
1		3		5	6	7		14	9^{3}	11	10^{1}			4	8^{2}	13	2				12					17
1		3		5	6^{1}	7		9	10	11				4	8^{2}	13	2			12						18
1		3		5	6^{1}	7		9		11	13			4		10^{2}	2		8	12						19
1		3		5	6^{1}	7		9		11	10^{2}			4	14	13	2		8^{3}	12						20
1		3	5		8	7^{2}		12		11^{1}	10			4		13	2	6		9						21
1		3		5	6^{2}	7		9		13	12			4	11^{1}	10	2			8						22
1		3	12	5^{1}	6^{2}	7		9			10^{3}			4		11	2		8		13	14				23
1				5	6			9	12	13	10^{1}		2	4		11^{2}	3		7	8						24
1		3		5	14	7		12	9	11^{2}	10^{3}			4		13	2		6^{1}	8						25
1		3	5		6	7		13	9	11^{1}	10		2	4		12			8^{2}							26
1		3			6^{1}	7^{3}		13	9	14	10		2	4		11^{2}		5	8	12						27
1		3	5			7^{1}		9	10	11	12		2	6					4	8						28
1		3	5		6^{2}	13		14	9^{3}	11	7		2^{1}	4				12	8	10						29
1	2	3	5			7^{1}		12	9	11^{2}	10^{3}			6					4	8	13		14			30
1■	2	3	5			13		9^{2}	10	12	14			6		11^{3}			4	8	7^{1}					31
	2	3^{3}	5	14		7		12	9	11^{2}	10			6		13				8	4^{1}			1		32
	2^{G}	13		12		7		9						6	11^{2}	10	3^{1}	5	4		8			1■	15	33
1		3		5		7		9	10	13	8^{1}			6	11^{2}	12	2		4^{3}		14					34
1		3	5	6		7			9^{2}	11	13					10	2	12		8^{1}	4					35
		14				7^{1}		9		12	10^{3}		2	6	11			5	4		8	3^{2}	13	1		36
1			5	3		7		9	10	11^{1}	12			6	8^{2}		2				4		13			37
			5	6		7		9	10	11^{1}	13		2		8^{2}	12	3				4			1		38

FA Cup

Third Round	Oldham Ath	(h)	5-1
Fourth Round	Manchester U	(h)	2-1
Fifth Round	Brighton & HA	(h)	6-1
Quarter-Final	Stoke C	(h)	2-1
Semi-Final *(at Wembley).*	Everton		2-1
Final *(at Wembley).*	Chelsea		1-2

Carling Cup

Second Round	Exeter C	(a)	3-1
Third Round	Brighton & HA	(a)	2-1
Fourth Round	Stoke C	(a)	2-1
Quarter-Final	Chelsea	(a)	2-0
Semi-Final	Manchester C	(a)	1-0
		(h)	2-2
Final *(at Wembley).*	Cardiff C		2-2

MACCLESFIELD TOWN Blue Square Premier

FOUNDATION

From the mid-19th century until 1874, Macclesfield Town FC played under rugby rules. In 1891 they moved to the Moss Rose ground and finished champions of the Manchester & District League in 1906 and 1908. By 1911, they had carried off the Cheshire Senior Cup five times. Macclesfield were founder members of the Cheshire County League in 1919.

Moss Rose Ground, London Road, Macclesfield, Cheshire SK11 7SP.

Telephone: (01625) 264 686.

Fax: (01625) 264 692.

Ticket Office: (01625) 264 686.

Website: www.mtfc.co.uk

Email: office@mtfc.co.uk

Ground Capacity: 6,141.

Record Attendance: 9,008 v Winsford U, Cheshire Senior Cup 2nd rd, 4 February 1948.

Pitch Measurements: 100m × 60m.

Chairman: Mike Rance.

Chief Executive: Jonathan Harris.

Manager: Steve King.

Physio: Nick Reid.

Colours: Blue shirts with white design, white shorts, blue stockings.

Year Formed: 1874.

Turned Professional: 1886.

Club Nickname: 'The Silkmen'.

Grounds: 1874, Rostron Field; 1891, Moss Rose.

First Football League Game: 9 August 1997, Division 3, v Torquay U (h) W 2–1 – Price; Tinson, Rose, Payne (Edey), Howarth, Sodje (1), Askey, Wood, Landon (1) (Power), Mason, Sorvel.

Record League Victory: 6–0 v Stockport Co, FL 1, 26 December 2005 – Fettis; Harsley, Sandwith, Morley, Swailes (Teague), Navarro, Whitaker (Miles (1)), Bullock (1), Parkin (2), Wijnhard (2) (Townson), McIntyre.

HONOURS

Football League – Division 3: ***Runners-up*** 1997–98.

FA Cup: Best season: 3rd rd, 1968, 1988, 2002, 2003, 2004, 2007, 2009, 2012.

Football League Cup: never past 2nd rd.

Vauxhall Conference: ***Champions*** 1994–95, 1996–97.

FA Trophy: ***Winners*** 1969–70, 1995–96; ***Runners-up*** 1988–89.

Bob Lord Trophy: ***Winners*** 1993–94; ***Runners-up*** 1995–96, 1996–97.

Vauxhall Conference Championship Shield: ***Winners*** 1996, 1997, 1998.

Northern Premier League: ***Winners*** 1968–69, 1969–70, 1986–87; ***Runners-up*** 1984–85.

Northern Premier League Challenge Cup: ***Winners*** 1986–87; ***Runners-up*** 1969–70, 1970–71, 1982–83.

Northern Premier League Presidents Cup: ***Winners*** 1986–87; ***Runners-up*** 1984–85.

Cheshire Senior Cup: ***Winners*** 20 times; ***Runners-up*** 11.

sky SPORTS FACT FILE

The first team to win promotion to the Football League and not lose a home League game was Macclesfield Town in 1997–98. As runners-up they dropped only four points and were the only team among the four top divisions to remain unbeaten on their own ground.

Record Cup Victory: 15–0 v Chester St Mary's, Cheshire Senior Cup 3rd rd, 6 February 1886; 15–0 v Barnton Rovers, Cheshire Senior Cup 1st rd, 12 November 1887.

Record Win: 15–0 v Chester St Marys, Cheshire Senior Cup 2nd rd, 16 February 1886.

Record Defeat: 1–13 v Tranmere R reserves, 3 May 1929.

Most League Points (3 for a win): 82, Division 3, 1997–98.

Most League Goals: 66, Division 3, 1999–2000.

Highest League Scorer in Season: Jon Parkin, 22, FL 2, 2004–05.

Most League Goals in Total Aggregate: Matt Tipton, 50, 2002–05; 2006–07; 2009–10.

Most League Goals in One Match: 3, Ricky Lambert v Luton T, Division 3, 24 November 2001; 3, Jonathan Parkin v Notts Co, FL 2, 25 January 2005; 3, Matt Tipton v Rochdale, FL 2, 19 February 2005.

Most Capped Player: George Abbey, 10 (18), Nigeria.

Most League Appearances: Darren Tinson, 263, 1997–2003.

Youngest League Player: Elliott Hewitt, 16 years 342 days v Hereford U, 7 May 2011.

Record Transfer Fee Received: £300,000 from Stockport Co for Rickie Lambert, April 2002.

Record Transfer Fee Paid: £40,000 to Bury for Danny Swailes, January 2005.

Football League Record: 1997 Promoted to Division 3; 1998–99 Division 2; 1999–2004 Division 3; 2004–12 FL 2; 2012– Blue Square Premier.

MANAGERS

Since 1967
Keith Goalen 1967–68
Frank Beaumont 1968–72
Billy Haydock 1972–74
Eddie Brown 1974
John Collins 1974
Willie Stevenson 1974
John Collins 1975–76
Tony Coleman 1976
John Barnes 1976
Brian Taylor 1976
Dave Connor 1976–78
Derek Partridge 1978
Phil Staley 1978–80
Jimmy Williams 1980–81
Brian Booth 1981–85
Neil Griffiths 1985–86
Roy Campbell 1986
Peter Wragg 1986–93
Sammy McIlroy 1993–2000
Peter Davenport 2000
Gil Prescott 2000–01
David Moss 2001–03
John Askey 2003–04
Brian Horton 2004–06
Paul Ince 2006–07
Ian Brightwell 2007–08
Keith Alexander 2008–10
Gary Simpson 2010–12
Steve King May 2012–

LATEST SEQUENCES

Longest Sequence of League Wins: 6, 25.1.2005 – 26.2.2005.

Longest Sequence of League Defeats: 8, 2.1.2012 – 21.2.2012.

Longest Sequence of League Draws: 5, 5.5.2007 – 1.9.2007.

Longest Sequence of Unbeaten League Matches: 8, 16.10.1999 – 27.11.1999.

Longest Sequence Without a League Win: 23, 2.1.2012 – Season's end.

Successive Scoring Runs: 14 from 11.10.2003.

Successive Non-scoring Runs: 5 from 18.12.1998.

TEN YEAR LEAGUE RECORD

		P	*W*	*D*	*L*	*F*	*A*	*Pts*	*Pos*
2002-03	Div 3	46	14	12	20	57	63	54	16
2003-04	Div 3	46	13	13	20	54	69	52	20
2004-05	FL 2	46	22	9	15	60	49	75	5
2005-06	FL 2	46	12	18	16	60	71	54	17
2006-07	FL 2	46	12	12	22	55	77	48	22
2007-08	FL 2	46	11	17	18	47	64	50	19
2008-09	FL 2	46	13	8	25	45	77	47	20
2009-10	FL 2	46	12	18	16	49	58	54	19
2010-11	FL 2	46	14	13	19	59	73	55	15
2011-12	FL 2	46	8	13	25	39	64	37	24

DID YOU KNOW ?

William Bromley-Davenport was a dashing amateur centre-forward briefly with Macclesfield Town in 1884. Eton, Oxford University, twice capped for England, he won the DSO in the Boer War, became Lord Lieutenant of Cheshire, was knighted in 1924 and served as the local MP.

MACCLESFIELD TOWN 2011–12 LEAGUE RECORD

Match No.	Date	Venue	Opponents	Result	H/T Score	Lg Pos.	Goalscorers	Attendance
1	Aug 6	H	Dagenham & R	L 0-1	0-0	—		1566
2	13	A	Crawley T	L 0-2	0-0	22		2389
3	16	A	Hereford U	W 4-0	0-0	—	Diagne [53], Draper [81], Tomlinson 2 [89, 90]	1609
4	20	H	Bristol R	D 0-0	0-0	16		1865
5	27	H	AFC Wimbledon	W 4-0	2-0	13	Brisley [3], Diagne [24], Sinclair [48], Mendy [87]	1881
6	Sept 3	A	Torquay U	L 0-3	0-0	16		2307
7	10	A	Cheltenham T	L 0-2	0-1	19		2268
8	13	H	Morecambe	D 1-1	1-1	—	Tomlinson [1]	1527
9	17	H	Northampton T	W 3-1	1-1	17	Tomlinson 2 [36, 84], Daniel [88]	2033
10	24	A	Plymouth Arg	L 0-2	0-1	18		6005
11	30	H	Swindon T	W 2-0	0-0	—	Donnelly [62], Draper [83]	2317
12	Oct 8	A	Aldershot T	W 2-1	0-1	12	Donnelly [53], Draper [73]	2341
13	15	H	Oxford U	D 1-1	0-0	12	Diagne [60]	2293
14	22	A	Crewe Alex	W 1-0	1-0	17	Draper [19]	3877
15	25	H	Bradford C	W 1-0	0-0	—	Chalmers (pen) [66]	2373
16	29	H	Southend U	L 0-2	0-1	11		2174
17	Nov 5	A	Burton Alb	L 0-1	0-1	13		2698
18	19	H	Accrington S	D 1-1	1-0	14	Brisley [20]	1792
19	25	A	Barnet	L 1-2	0-2	—	Hamshaw [61]	2200
20	Dec 10	H	Gillingham	D 0-0	0-0	13		1724
21	17	A	Shrewsbury T	L 0-1	0-0	15		4871
22	26	H	Rotherham U	D 0-0	0-0	14		3179
23	31	H	Port Vale	W 2-1	1-0	14	Tomlinson (og) [37], Donnelly [71]	4214
24	Jan 2	A	Accrington S	L 0-4	0-2	14		1704
25	14	H	Torquay U	L 1-2	0-0	15	Brisley [81]	1878
26	21	A	Swindon T	L 0-1	0-0	16		7639
27	24	A	AFC Wimbledon	L 1-2	0-0	—	Mattis [58]	4000
28	28	H	Cheltenham T	L 1-3	1-1	19	Marshall [30]	1659
29	Feb 14	A	Morecambe	L 0-1	0-0	—		1316
30	18	H	Aldershot T	L 0-1	0-0	20		1715
31	21	A	Northampton T	L 2-3	1-2	—	Donnelly [17], Tomlinson [85]	4529
32	25	A	Oxford U	D 1-1	1-1	20	Duberry (og) [9]	6189
33	28	H	Plymouth Arg	D 1-1	0-0	—	Donnelly [90]	1888
34	Mar 3	A	Bristol R	D 0-0	0-0	20		5420
35	6	H	Hereford U	D 2-2	0-2	—	Wedgbury [48], Hamshaw [79]	1676
36	10	H	Crawley T	D 2-2	0-1	20	Mukendi [85], Donnelly [90]	1802
37	17	A	Dagenham & R	L 0-2	0-1	21		1446
38	20	A	Rotherham U	L 2-4	0-1	—	Smith [65], Chalmers (pen) [73]	2505
39	23	H	Barnet	D 0-0	0-0	—		2123
40	31	A	Gillingham	L 0-2	0-0	23		4562
41	Apr 6	H	Shrewsbury T	L 1-3	0-1	23	Mendy [85]	3403
42	9	A	Port Vale	L 0-1	0-0	23		4246
43	14	H	Crewe Alex	D 2-2	1-1	23	Chalmers (pen) [17], Daniel [80]	3434
44	21	A	Bradford C	L 0-1	0-0	24		10,106
45	28	H	Burton Alb	L 0-2	0-0	24		2760
46	May 5	A	Southend U	L 0-2	0-1	24		9122

Final League Position: 24

GOALSCORERS

League (39): Donnelly 6, Tomlinson 6, Draper 4, Brisley 3, Chalmers 3 (3 pens), Diagne 3, Daniel 2, Hamshaw 2, Mendy 2, Marshall 1, Mattis 1, Mukendi 1, Sinclair 1, Smith 1, Wedgbury 1, own goals 2.
Carling Cup (3): Sinclair 3.
FA Cup (7): Tremarco 2, Daniel 1, Diagne 1, Donnelly 1, Hamshaw 1, Mendy 1.
J Paint Trophy (0).

Veiga J 35	Bateson J 17 + 4	Diagne T 40 + 1	Kay S 10 + 5	Brown N 37	Brisley S 29	Hamshaw M 30 + 8	Draper R 27 + 1	Fairhurst W 4 + 14	Tomlinson B 15 + 10	Wedgbury S 37 + 2	Sinclair E 4 + 1	Chalmers L 17 + 6	Tremarco C 35	Grant J — + 4	Hewitt E 17 + 4	Mendy A 23 + 5	Mukendi V 4 + 12	Daniel C 30 + 6	Donnelly G 28	Boden S 6 + 1	Roberts A 1 + 1	Gray D 2	Morgan P 2 + 1	Thomas M 2 + 4	Fisher T — + 1	Mills B 5 + 7	Bakare M — + 9	Mattis D 1	Marshall M 13 + 1	Futcher B 10	O'Donnell R 11	Connolly M 7	Smith M 6 + 2	Aley Z 1	*Match No.*
1	2	3	4^2	5	6	7	8	9^1	10	11	12	13																							1
1	2^3	4		5	6	13	8		10	11	9^2	7^1	3	12	14																				2
1		4	12	5	6	10^1	8		14	11	9^3	7^2	3		2	13																			3
1		10	4	5	6		8		12	11	9^1	7^2	3		2	13																			4
1		10	4	5	6^1		8^2		12	11	9^3	7	3	14	2	13																			5
1	2	9	4	5	6	14	8^2		10	11		7^3	3^1				12	13																	6
1	2	10	4^1	5	6	14	8			11		7^3	3^2				12	13	9																7
1		4	12	5	6		8		10	7			3		2			11^1	9																8
1		4		5	6	7^1	8	13	10^2	11^3		14	3		2			12	9																9
1		4		5	6	7	8	14	10^3	11^2		13	3^1		2			12	9																10
1		4	13	5	6	7^1	8		10	11		12	3		2				9^2																11
1	2	11		5	6		8		10^1	7		4	3	12					9																12
1	12	4	14	5	6		8		9	11		7^3	3		2^1	13				10^2															13
1		2	12	5	6	13	8		9^2	7^1		4	3					11^3		10	14														14
1		9	4^1	5	6	7^2	8			13		11	3		2		14	12		10^3															15
1		4		5	6	13				7		8	3^1	12	2		9	11^2		10															16
1		11^1		5	6	14	8	13		7		4^3	3		2		12■		9	10^2															17
1		4		5	6^2	12	8			7			3					11	9	10^1		2	13												18
1	12	4		5	6	10^3	8■	13		7			3^1					11	9	14		2^2													19
1	2	4		5	6	7		12		8			3				10^1	11	9																20
1	2	4^2		5	6	12	8	10		7			3				13	11	9^1																21
1	2	4		5	6	7	8	12		10			3^1					11	9																22
1	2	3		5	6	7^1	8			10					12	4		11	9																23
1		10			6^1			9^2	12	7			3		2	8		11					5	4	13										24
1	2	4		5	6	7^2		12		8^3			3		13	11		10	9^1							14									25
1		4		5■	6	7		10^1					3		2	8^3		11^2	9					14		12	13								26
1	12	11			6	7							3		2	8			9^3				5^1	13		10	14	4^2							27
1		5	4^1		6	7		12					3		2	8^2		10								9	13		11						28
1	2	5	4^2		6	7^1			14	12			3^3			8		10	9							13			11						29
1	2^1	6	4^3	5		7		14	13				3■		12	8		10								9^2			11						30
1	2	6	4^1						10	7						8	12	3	9										11	5					31
						7			10^2	8					2^3	4	12	3	9^1					14		13			11	5	1	6			32
						7^2		13	10^1	8						4	12	3	9					2			14		11	5	1	6^3			33
		4								8			3		10^1	6	13	11	9^2								12		7	5	1	2			34
		4		5		7		14		8			3^1			12	13	10	9										11^3	6^2	1	2			35
		6		5		7		12		8^2						4	10	3	9								13		11^1		1	2			36
		6		5		7^3			14	8^1		12	3^2			4		11	9								13				1	2	10		37
	2	6				7				8^2		12	3^1			4	13	11	9												1	5	10		38
	2	3		5		7			12			4^2				8	13	11	9^1											6	1		10		39
	2^1	3		5		7	13					4^2				8	10^3	11									14		12	6	1		9		40
		2^1		5		7	8									4		10						12		13			11^2	6	1		9	3	41
	13			5		7^2	4			8			3			6		11	9							12			2		1		10^1		42
1	2			5		7	10		13	8^1		4	3			6		12								9			11^2						43
1				5		7	10	14	12	8		4^3				6		11								9^2			3	2^1			13		44
1		13		5		7	4^2		10^1	8			3			2		11	9											6			12		45
1		6^3		5		7	10	14	9	8		4				2		11^1			3^2					13	12								46

FA Cup

First Round	East Thurrock U	(a)	3-0
Second Round	Chelmsford C	(a)	1-1
		(h)	1-0
Third Round	Bolton W	(h)	2-2
		(a)	0-2

Carling Cup

First Round	Hull C	(a)	2-0
Second Round	Bolton W	(a)	1-2

J Paint Trophy

Second Round	Crewe Alex	(a)	0-1

MANCHESTER CITY

FA Premiership

FOUNDATION

Manchester City was formed as a limited company in 1894 after their predecessors Ardwick had been forced into bankruptcy. However, many historians like to trace the club's lineage as far back as 1880 when St Mark's Church, West Gorton added a football section to their cricket club. They amalgamated with Gorton Athletic in 1884 as Gorton FC. Because of a change of ground they became Ardwick in 1887.

Etihad Stadium, Etihad Campus, Manchester M11 3FF.

Telephone: (0161) 444 1894.

Fax: (0161) 438 7999.

Ticket Office: (0161) 444 1894.

Website: www.mcfc.co.uk

Email: mcfc@mcfc.co.uk

Ground Capacity: 47,726.

Record Attendance: 84,569 v Stoke C, FA Cup 6th rd, 3 March 1934 (at Maine Road; British record for any game outside London or Glasgow); 47,370 v Tottenham H, FA Premier League, 5 May 2010 (at City of Manchester Stadium).

Pitch Measurements: 105m × 68m.

Chairman: Khaldoon Al Mubarak.

Chief Executive (temporary): John MacBeath.

Manager: Roberto Mancini.

Assistant Manager: Brian Kidd.

Fitness Coach: Ivan Carminati.

Colours: Sky blue shirts with white detail, white shorts with sky blue detail, white stockings with sky blue tops.

Year Formed: 1887 as Ardwick FC; 1894 as Manchester City.

Turned Professional: 1887 as Ardwick FC.

Previous Names: 1887, Ardwick FC (formed through the amalgamation of West Gorton and Gorton Athletic, the latter having been formed in 1880); 1894, Manchester City.

Club Nicknames: 'Blues' or 'The Citizens'.

Grounds: 1880, Clowes Street; 1881, Kirkmanshulme Cricket Ground; 1882, Queens Road; 1884, Pink Bank Lane; 1887, Hyde Road (1894–1923 as City); 1923, Maine Road; 2003, City of Manchester Stadium (now know as Etihad Stadium from 2011).

First Football League Game: 3 September 1892, Division 2, v Bootle (h) W 7–0 – Douglas; McVickers, Robson; Middleton, Russell, Hopkins; Davies (3), Morris (2), Angus (1), Weir (1), Milarvie.

Record League Victory: 10–1 v Huddersfield T, Division 2, 7 November 1987 – Nixon; Gidman, Hinchcliffe, Clements, Lake, Redmond, White (3), Stewart (3), Adcock (3), McNab (1), Simpson.

Record Cup Victory: 10–1 v Swindon T, FA Cup 4th rd, 29 January 1930 – Barber; Felton, McCloy; Barrass, Cowan, Heinemann; Toseland, Marshall (5), Tait (3), Johnson (1), Brook (1).

HONOURS

FA Premier League: ***Champions*** 2011–12.
Football League – Division 1: ***Champions*** 1936–37, 1967–68, 2001–02; ***Runners-up*** 1903–04, 1920–21, 1976–77, 1999–2000;
Division 2: ***Champions*** 1898–99, 1902–03, 1909–10, 1927–28, 1946–47, 1965–66; ***Runners-up*** 1895–96, 1950–51, 1988–89.

FA Cup: ***Winners*** 1904, 1934, 1956, 1969, 2011; ***Runners-up*** 1926, 1933, 1955, 1981.

Football League Cup: ***Winners*** 1970, 1976; ***Runners-up*** 1974.

Full Members Cup: ***Runners-up*** 1986.

European Competitions
Champions League: 2011–12.
European Cup: 1968–69.
European Cup-Winners' Cup: 1969–70 (*winners*), 1970–71.
UEFA Cup: 1972–73, 1976–77, 1977–78, 1978–79, 2003–04, 2008–09.
Europa League: 2010–11, 2011–12.

sky SPORTS FACT FILE

On 23 October 2011, Manchester City beat Manchester United 6-1 at Old Trafford. It was their best derby result since the same score there on 23 January 1926 when it saw two goals each from Frank Roberts and Billy Austin, one apiece from Tommy Johnson and George Hicks.

Record Defeat: 1–9 v Everton, Division 1, 3 September 1906.

Most League Points (2 for a win): 62, Division 2, 1946–47.

Most League Points (3 for a win): 99, Division 1, 2001–02.

Most League Goals: 108, Division 2, 1926–27, 108, Division 1, 2001–02.

Highest League Scorer in Season: Tommy Johnson, 38, Division 1, 1928–29.

Most League Goals in Total Aggregate: Tommy Johnson, 158, 1919–30.

Most League Goals in One Match: 5, Fred Williams v Darwen, Division 2, 18 February 1899; 5, Tom Browell v Burnley, Division 2, 24 October 1925; 5, Tom Johnson v Everton, Division 1, 15 September 1928; 5, George Smith v Newport Co, Division 2, 14 June 1947.

Most Capped Player: Colin Bell, 48, England.

Most League Appearances: Alan Oakes, 565, 1959–76.

Youngest League Player: Glyn Pardoe, 15 years 314 days v Birmingham C, 11 April 1962.

Record Transfer Fee Received: £21,000,000 from Chelsea for Shaun Wright-Phillips, July 2005.

Record Transfer Fee Paid: £38,000,000 to Atletico Madrid for Sergio Aguero, July 2011.

Football League Record: 1892 Ardwick elected founder member of Division 2; 1894 Newly-formed Manchester C elected to Division 2; Division 1 1899–1902, 1903–09, 1910–26, 1928–38, 1947–50, 1951–63, 1966–83, 1985–87, 1989–92; Division 2 1902–03, 1909–10, 1926–28, 1938–47, 1950–51, 1963–66, 1983–85, 1987–89; 1992–96 FA Premier League; 1996–98 Division 1; 1998–99 Division 2; 1999–2000 Division 1; 2000–01 FA Premier League; 2001–02 Division 1; 2002– FA Premier League.

LATEST SEQUENCES

Longest Sequence of League Wins: 9, 8.4.1912 – 28.9.1912.

Longest Sequence of League Defeats: 8, 23.8.1995 – 14.10.1995.

Longest Sequence of League Draws: 6, 5.4.1913 – 6.9.1913.

Longest Sequence of Unbeaten League Matches: 22, 16.11.1946 – 19.4.1947.

Longest Sequence Without a League Win: 17, 26.12.1979 – 7.4.1980.

Successive Scoring Runs: 44 from 3.10.1936.

Successive Non-scoring Runs: 6 from 30.1.1971.

MANAGERS

Joshua Parlby 1893–95
(Secretary-Manager)
Sam Omerod 1895–1902
Tom Maley 1902–06
Harry Newbould 1906–12
Ernest Magnall 1912–24
David Ashworth 1924–25
Peter Hodge 1926–32
Wilf Wild 1932–46
(continued as Secretary to 1950)
Sam Cowan 1946–47
John 'Jock' Thomson 1947–50
Leslie McDowall 1950–63
George Poyser 1963–65
Joe Mercer 1965–71
(continued as General Manager to 1972)
Malcolm Allison 1972–73
Johnny Hart 1973
Ron Saunders 1973–74
Tony Book 1974–79
Malcolm Allison 1979–80
John Bond 1980–83
John Benson 1983
Billy McNeill 1983–86
Jimmy Frizzell 1986–87
(continued as General Manager)
Mel Machin 1987–89
Howard Kendall 1989–90
Peter Reid 1990–93
Brian Horton 1993–95
Alan Ball 1995–96
Steve Coppell 1996
Frank Clark 1996–98
Joe Royle 1998–2001
Kevin Keegan 2001–05
Stuart Pearce 2005–07
Sven-Göran Eriksson 2007–08
Mark Hughes 2008–09
Roberto Mancini December 2009–

TEN YEAR LEAGUE RECORD

		P	W	D	L	F	A	Pts	Pos
2002-03	PR Lge	38	15	6	17	47	54	51	9
2003-04	PR Lge	38	9	14	15	55	54	41	16
2004-05	PR Lge	38	13	13	12	47	39	52	8
2005-06	PR Lge	38	13	4	21	43	48	43	15
2006-07	PR Lge	38	11	9	18	29	44	42	14
2007-08	PR Lge	38	15	10	13	45	53	55	9
2008-09	PR Lge	38	15	5	18	58	50	50	10
2009-10	PR Lge	38	18	13	7	73	45	67	5
2010-11	PR Lge	38	21	8	9	60	33	71	3
2011-12	PR Lge	38	28	5	5	93	29	89	1

DID YOU KNOW ?

In 2011–12, Manchester City recorded their highest average League attendance since the formation of the club. Their previous best figures were established in 1947–48 when, at the height of the post-war boom in crowds, the average home attendance at Maine Road was 42,725.

MANCHESTER CITY 2011–12 LEAGUE RECORD

Match No.	*Date*	*Venue*	*Opponents*	*Result*		*H/T Score*	*Lg Pos.*	*Goalscorers*	*Attendance*
1	Aug 15	H	Swansea C	W	4-0	0-0	—	Dzeko [57], Aguero 2 [68, 90], Silva [71]	46,802
2	21	A	Bolton W	W	3-2	2-1	1	Silva [26], Barry [37], Dzeko [47]	24,273
3	28	A	Tottenham H	W	5-1	2-0	2	Dzeko 4 [34, 41, 55, 90], Aguero [60]	36,150
4	Sept 10	H	Wigan Ath	W	3-0	1-0	2	Aguero 3 [13, 63, 69]	46,509
5	18	A	Fulham	D	2-2	1-0	2	Aguero 2 [18, 46]	24,750
6	24	H	Everton	W	2-0	0-0	2	Balotelli [68], Milner [89]	47,293
7	Oct 1	A	Blackburn R	W	4-0	0-0	2	Johnson, A [56], Balotelli [59], Nasri [73], Savic [87]	24,760
8	15	H	Aston Villa	W	4-1	1-0	1	Balotelli [28], Johnson, A [47], Kompany [52], Milner [71]	47,019
9	23	A	Manchester U	W	6-1	1-0	1	Balotelli 2 [22, 60], Aguero [69], Silva [88], Dzeko 2 [89, 90]	75,487
10	29	H	Wolverhampton W	W	3-1	0-0	1	Dzeko [52], Kolarov [67], Johnson, A [90]	47,142
11	Nov 5	A	QPR	W	3-2	1-1	1	Dzeko [43], Silva [52], Toure, Y [74]	18,076
12	19	H	Newcastle U	W	3-1	2-0	1	Balotelli (pen) [41], Richards [44], Aguero (pen) [72]	47,408
13	27	A	Liverpool	D	1-1	1-1	1	Kompany [31]	45,071
14	Dec 3	H	Norwich C	W	5-1	1-0	1	Aguero [32], Nasri [51], Toure, Y [68], Balotelli [88], Johnson, A [90]	47,201
15	12	A	Chelsea	L	1-2	1-1	—	Balotelli [2]	41,730
16	18	H	Arsenal	W	1-0	0-0	1	Silva [53]	47,303
17	21	H	Stoke C	W	3-0	2-0	—	Aguero 2 [29, 54], Johnson, A [36]	46,321
18	26	A	WBA	D	0-0	0-0	1		25,938
19	Jan 1	A	Sunderland	L	0-1	0-0	1		40,625
20	3	H	Liverpool	W	3-0	2-0	—	Aguero [10], Toure, Y [33], Milner (pen) [75]	47,131
21	16	A	Wigan Ath	W	1-0	1-0	—	Dzeko [22]	16,026
22	22	H	Tottenham H	W	3-2	0-0	1	Nasri [56], Lescott [59], Balotelli (pen) [90]	47,422
23	31	A	Everton	L	0-1	0-0	—		29,856
24	Feb 4	H	Fulham	W	3-0	2-0	1	Aguero (pen) [10], Baird (og) [30], Dzeko [72]	46,963
25	12	A	Aston Villa	W	1-0	0-0	1	Lescott [63]	35,132
26	25	H	Blackburn R	W	3-0	1-0	1	Balotelli [30], Aguero [52], Dzeko [81]	46,782
27	Mar 3	H	Bolton W	W	2-0	1-0	1	Steinsson (og) [23], Balotelli [69]	47,219
28	11	A	Swansea C	L	0-1	0-0	2		20,510
29	21	H	Chelsea	W	2-1	0-0	—	Aguero (pen) [78], Nasri [85]	46,324
30	24	A	Stoke C	D	1-1	0-0	1	Toure, Y [76]	27,535
31	31	H	Sunderland	D	3-3	1-2	2	Balotelli 2 (1 pen) [43 (p), 85], Kolarov [86]	47,007
32	Apr 8	A	Arsenal	L	0-1	0-0	2		60,096
33	11	H	WBA	W	4-0	1-0	—	Aguero 2 [6, 54], Tevez [61], Silva [64]	46,746
34	14	A	Norwich C	W	6-1	2-0	2	Tevez 3 [18, 73, 80], Aguero 2 [27, 75], Johnson, A [90]	26,812
35	22	A	Wolverhampton W	W	2-0	1-0	2	Aguero [27], Nasri [74]	24,576
36	30	H	Manchester U	W	1-0	1-0	—	Kompany [45]	47,259
37	May 6	A	Newcastle U	W	2-0	0-0	1	Toure, Y 2 [70, 89]	52,389
38	13	H	QPR	W	3-2	1-0	1	Zabaleta [39], Dzeko [89], Aguero [90]	48,000

Final League Position: 1

GOALSCORERS

League (93): Aguero 23 (3 pens), Dzeko 14, Balotelli 13 (3 pens), Johnson, A 6, Silva 6, Toure, Y 6, Nasri 5, Tevez 4, Kompany 3, Milner 3 (1 pen), Kolarov 2, Lescott 2, Barry 1, Richards 1, Savic 1, Zabaleta 1, own goals 2.
Carling Cup (10): Dzeko 3, Aguero 1, Balotelli 1, De Jong 1, Hargreaves 1, Johnson, A 1, Nasri 1, own goal 1.
FA Cup (2): Aguero 1, Kolarov 1.
Champions League (9): Toure, Y 3, Balotelli 2 (1 pen), Aguero 1, Kolarov 1, Silva 1, own goal 1.
Europa League (9): Aguero 4, Balotelli 1 (pen), Dzeko 1, Pizarro 1, Silva 1, own goal 1.
Community Shield (2): Dzeko 1, Lescott 1.

Hart J 38	Richards M 23 + 6	Clichy G 28	Kompany V 31	Lescott J 30 + 1	De Jong N 11 + 10	Barry G 31 + 3	Toure Y 31 + 1	Silva D 33 + 3	Dzeko E 16 + 14	Johnson A 10 + 16	Aguero S 31 + 3	Savic S 5 + 6	Milner J 17 + 9	Kolarov A 9 + 3	Tevez C 7 + 6	Zabaleta P 18 + 3	Nasri S 26 + 4	Balotelli M 14 + 9	Razak A — + 1	Toure K 8 + 6	Hargreaves O — + 1	Onuoha N — + 1	Pizarro D 1 + 4	Match No.
1	2	3	4	5	6^1	7	8	9^3	10	11^2	12	13	14											1
1	2		4	5		6	8	11^3	10^2	13	9^1		7	3	12	14								2
1	12	3	4	5		6	8	7	10		9^2	13				2^1	11							3
1	2	3	4	5			8^3	11		7	9^2		6		10^1		12	13	14					4
1	2	3	4	5		6	8	11^1	10	13	9^3				14	12	7^2							5
1	2	3	4	5		6	8	11	10^1		9^2	14	13				7^3	12						6
1			4	5			8	7	14	11^2	9^1	13	6	3		2	12	10^3						7
1	2^1	3	4	5	6	10	8^2	12		11^3			7					9		13	14			8
1	2	3	4	5		6	8	11	12		9^2		7^3	14			13	10^1						9
1	2		4■	5		6	8	7	10^1	12	9^3	14		3			11^2	13						10
1	2			5		4^2	8	11	10^3	12	9^1	6	7	3				13		14				11
1	2	3	4	5	6	14	8^3	12		13	9^2		11				7	10^1						12
1	2	3	4	5		6	8	10^3	13		9^2		7				11^1	12■		14				13
1	2	3	4		14	6	8	7	10^3	12	9^2						11^1	13		5				14
1		3■	4	5^3	13	6	8	7^2	14		9^1		11			2		10		12				15
1	2		4		14	6	8^2	7	13		9		12			3	11^3	10^1		5				16
1	2^1	3	4	5		6^3	8	10^2		11	9	12	14				7	13						17
1		3	4			12	8	7	14	13	9^2		6^3			2	11^1	10		5				18
1	14		4	5	6^1	10	8	13	9	11	12			3^3		2	7^2							19
1	2	3	4	13		6■	8	7^2	10	12	9^1		11							5				20
1		3		5	12	4		8^2	10	14	9^3	6	7			2	11^1					13		21
1	2	3		5		4		8	10^1		9	6	7				11	12						22
1	2	3	4	5^2	14	6^3		8	10	12	9		7^1	13			11							23
1	2			5	13	6		8	10	11^3	9^2	4	12	3			7^1						14	24
1	14		4	5	6	8		10^3	13	11^1	9^2		7	3		2	12							25
1			4	5	6		8^3	7	13	11^1	9		14	3		2		10^2					12	26
1		3	4	5		6	8		13	7			14			2^1	11^3	10		12			9^2	27
1	2	3			4^2	7^1	8	9^3	14	13	12	6					11	10		5				28
1	6	3			4^2	12	8	7^3	14		9				13	2	11	10^1		5				29
1	4	3				6^2	8	7^1	10	12			14		13	2^3	11	9		5				30
1	2^1		4		6		8	11^2	10	12			7^3	3	13			9		5			14	31
1		3	4	5		6	8^1				9^3		7	13	14	2	11^2	10■					12	32
1	2	3	4	5	6	8		7^3	13	12	9^2				10^1	14	11							33
1	14	3	4	5	8	6	12	7^2		13	9				10^3	2	11^1							34
1		3	4	5	12	6	8	7^1		13	9				10^2	2	11^3			14				35
1	13	3	4	5	12	6	8	7^2			9		14		10^1	2	11^3							36
1	14	3	4	5	12	6	8	7^3	13		9				10^2	2	11^1							37
1		3	4	5	12	6^2	8^1	7	13		9				10^3	2	11	14						38

FA Cup

Third Round	Manchester U	(h)	2-3

Carling Cup

Third Round	Birmingham C	(h)	2-0
Fourth Round	Wolverhampton W	(a)	5-2
Quarter-Final	Arsenal	(a)	1-0
Semi-Final	Liverpool	(h)	0-1
		(a)	2-2

Champions League

Group A	Napoli	(h)	1-1
	Bayern Munich	(a)	0-2
	Villarreal	(h)	2-1
		(a)	3-0
	Napoli	(a)	1-2
	Bayern Munich	(h)	2-0

Europa League

Second Round	Porto	(a)	2-1
		(h)	4-0
Third Round	Sporting Lisbon	(a)	0-1
		(h)	3-2

Community Shield

(at Wembley).	Manchester U	2-3

MANCHESTER UNITED FA Premiership

FOUNDATION

Manchester United was formed as comparatively recently as 1902 after their predecessors, Newton Heath, went bankrupt. However, it is usual to give the date of the club's foundation as 1878 when the dining room committee of the carriage and waggon works of the Lancashire and Yorkshire Railway Company formed Newton Heath L and YR Cricket and Football Club. They won the Manchester Cup in 1886 and as Newton Heath FC were admitted to the Second Division in 1892.

Old Trafford, Sir Matt Busby Way, Manchester M16 0RA.

Telephone: (0161) 868 8000.

Fax: (0161) 868 8804.

Ticket Office: (0161) 868 8000.

Website: www.manutd.com

Email: enquiries@manutd.co.uk

Ground Capacity: 75,769.

Record Attendance: 76,098 v Blackburn R, FA Premier League, 31 March 2007.

Ground Record Attendance: 76,962 Wolverhampton W v Grimsby T, FA Cup semi-final, 25 March 1939.

Pitch Measurements: 105m × 68m.

Co-Chairmen: Joel and Avram Glazer.

Chief Executive: David Gill.

Manager: Sir Alex Ferguson CBE.

Assistant Manager: Mike Phelan.

Fitness Coach: Tony Strudwick.

Colours: Red shirts with black chevron, white shorts with red side panels, black stockings.

Year Formed: 1878 as Newton Heath LYR; 1902, Manchester United.

Turned Professional: 1885.

Previous Name: 1880, Newton Heath; 1902, Manchester United.

Club Nickname: 'Red Devils'.

Grounds: 1880, North Road, Monsall Road; 1893, Bank Street; 1910, Old Trafford (played at Maine Road 1941–49).

HONOURS

FA Premier League: ***Champions*** 1992–93, 1993–94, 1995–96, 1996–97, 1998–99, 1999–2000, 2000–01, 2002–03, 2006–07, 2007–08, 2008–09, 2010–11; ***Runners-up*** 1994–95, 1997–98, 2005–06, 2009–10, 2011–12.

Football League – Division 1: ***Champions*** 1907–08, 1910–11, 1951–52, 1955–56, 1956–57, 1964–65, 1966–67; ***Runners-up*** 1946–47, 1947–48, 1948–49, 1950–51, 1958–59, 1963–64, 1967–68, 1979–80, 1987–88, 1991–92.
Division 2: ***Champions*** 1935–36, 1974–75; ***Runners-up*** 1896–97, 1905–06, 1924–25, 1937–38.

FA Cup: ***Winners*** 1909, 1948, 1963, 1977, 1983, 1985, 1990, 1994, 1996, 1999, 2004; ***Runners-up*** 1957, 1958, 1976, 1979, 1995, 2005, 2007.

Football League Cup: ***Winners*** 1992, 2006, 2009, 2010; ***Runners-up*** 1983, 1991, 1994, 2003.

European Competitions
European Cup: 1956–57 (*s-f*), 1957–58 (*s-f*), 1965–66 (*s-f*), 1967–68 (*winners*), 1968–69 (*s-f*).
Champions League: 1993–94, 1994–95, 1996–97 (*s-f*), 1997–98, 1998–99 (*winners*), 1999–2000, 2000–01, 2001–02 (*s-f*), 2002–03, 2003–04, 2004–05, 2005–06, 2006–07 (*s-f*), 2007–08 (*winners*), 2008–09 (*runners-up*), 2009–10, 2010–11 (*runners-up*), 2011–12.
European Cup-Winners' Cup: 1963–64, 1977–78, 1983–84, 1990–91 (*winners*). 1991–92. **Inter Cities Fairs Cup:** 1964–65. **UEFA Cup:** 1976–77, 1980–81, 1982–83, 1984–85, 1992–93, 1995–96.
Europa League: 2011–12. **Super Cup:** 1991 (*winners*), 1999, 2008. **World Club Championship:** 1968, 1999 (*winners*). **FIFA Club World Cup:** 2008 (*winners*).
NB: In 1958–59 FA refused permission to compete in European Cup.

sky SPORTS FACT FILE

The fastest goal scored by a Manchester United player was in a friendly match away to Bayern Munich on 8 August 1959. Within four seconds of the second-half restart, Albert Quixall scored from fully 48 yards after a tap pass from Dennis Viollet. United won 2-1.

First Football League Game: 3 September 1892, Division 1, v Blackburn R (a) L 3–4 – Warner; Clements, Brown; Perrins, Stewart, Erentz; Farman (1), Coupar (1), Donaldson (1), Carson, Mathieson.

Record League Victory (as Newton Heath): 10–1 v Wolverhampton W, Division 1, 15 October 1892 – Warner; Mitchell, Clements; Perrins, Stewart (3), Erentz; Farman (1), Hood (1), Donaldson (3), Carson (1), Hendry (1).

Record League Victory (as Manchester U): 9–0 v Ipswich T, FA Premier League, 4 March 1995 – Schmeichel; Keane (1) (Sharpe), Irwin, Bruce (Butt), Kanchelskis, Pallister, Cole (5), Ince (1), McClair, Hughes (2), Giggs.

Record Cup Victory: 10–0 v RSC Anderlecht, European Cup prel. rd 2nd leg, 26 September 1956 – Wood; Foulkes, Byrne; Colman, Jones, Edwards; Berry (1), Whelan (2), Taylor (3), Viollet (4), Pegg.

Record Defeat: 0–7 v Blackburn R, Division 1, 10 April 1926; 0–7 v Aston Villa, Division 1, 27 December 1930; 0–7 v Wolverhampton W, Division 2, 26 December 1931.

Most League Points (2 for a win): 64, Division 1, 1956–57.

Most League Points (3 for a win): 92, FA Premier League, 1993–94.

Most League Goals: 103, Division 1, 1956–57 and 1958–59.

Highest League Scorer in Season: Dennis Viollet, 32, 1959–60.

Most League Goals in Total Aggregate: Bobby Charlton, 199, 1956–73.

Most Capped Player: Bobby Charlton, 106, England.

Most League Appearances: Ryan Giggs, 638, 1991–.

Youngest League Player: Jeff Whitefoot, 16 years 105 days v Portsmouth, 15 April 1950.

Record Transfer Fee Received: £80,000,000 from Real Madrid for Cristiano Ronaldo, June 2009.

Record Transfer Fee Paid: £30,750,000 to Tottenham H for Dimitar Berbatov, September 2008.

Football League Record: 1892 Newton Heath elected to Division 1; 1894–1906 Division 2; 1906–22 Division 1; 1922–25 Division 2; 1925–31 Division 1; 1931–36 Division 2; 1936–37 Division 1; 1937–38 Division 2; 1938–74 Division 1; 1974–75 Division 2; 1975–92 Division 1; 1992– FA Premier League.

MANAGERS

J. Ernest Mangnall 1903–12
John Bentley 1912–14
John Robson 1914–21
(Secretary-Manager from 1916)
John Chapman 1921–26
Clarence Hilditch 1926–27
Herbert Bamlett 1927–31
Walter Crickmer 1931–32
Scott Duncan 1932–37
Walter Crickmer 1937–45
(Secretary-Manager)
Matt Busby 1945–69
(continued as General Manager then Director)
Wilf McGuinness 1969–70
Sir Matt Busby 1970–71
Frank O'Farrell 1971–72
Tommy Docherty 1972–77
Dave Sexton 1977–81
Ron Atkinson 1981–86
Sir Alex Ferguson November 1986–

LATEST SEQUENCES

Longest Sequence of League Wins: 14, 15.10.1904 – 3.1.1905.

Longest Sequence of League Defeats: 14, 26.4.1930 – 25.10.1930.

Longest Sequence of League Draws: 6, 30.10.1988 – 27.11.1988.

Longest Sequence of Unbeaten League Matches: 29, 26.12.1998 – 25.9.1999.

Longest Sequence Without a League Win: 16, 19.4.1930 – 25.10.1930.

Successive Scoring Runs: 36 from 3.12.2007.

Successive Non-scoring Runs: 5 from 22.2.1902.

TEN YEAR LEAGUE RECORD

		P	*W*	*D*	*L*	*F*	*A*	*Pts*	*Pos*
2002-03	PR Lge	38	25	8	5	74	34	83	1
2003-04	PR Lge	38	23	6	9	64	35	75	3
2004-05	PR Lge	38	22	11	5	58	26	77	3
2005-06	PR Lge	38	25	8	5	72	34	83	2
2006-07	PR Lge	38	28	5	5	83	27	89	1
2007-08	PR Lge	38	27	6	5	80	22	87	1
2008-09	PR Lge	38	28	6	4	68	24	90	1
2009-10	PR Lge	38	27	4	7	86	28	85	2
2010-11	PR Lge	38	23	11	4	78	37	80	1
2011-12	PR Lge	38	28	5	5	89	33	89	2

DID YOU KNOW ?

Manchester United have won more FA Cup matches than any other team in the history of the competition. On 8 January 2012, in a third round tie they defeated Manchester City 3-2 to record their 220th such victory. It was in their 407th match and represented a 54 per cent success rate overall.

MANCHESTER UNITED 2011–12 LEAGUE RECORD

Match No.	Date	Venue	Opponents	Result		H/T Score	Lg Pos.	Goalscorers	Attendance
1	Aug 14	A	WBA	W	2-1	1-1	—	Rooney [13], Reid (og) [81]	25,360
2	22	H	Tottenham H	W	3-0	0-0	—	Welbeck [61], Anderson [76], Rooney [87]	75,498
3	28	H	Arsenal	W	8-2	3-1	1	Welbeck [22], Young 2 [28, 90], Rooney 3 (1 pen) [41, 64, 82 (p)], Nani [67], Park [70]	75,448
4	Sept 10	A	Bolton W	W	5-0	3-0	1	Hernandez 2 [5, 58], Rooney 3 [20, 25, 68]	25,944
5	18	H	Chelsea	W	3-1	3-0	1	Smalling [8], Nani [37], Rooney [45]	75,455
6	24	A	Stoke C	D	1-1	1-0	1	Nani [27]	27,582
7	Oct 1	H	Norwich C	W	2-0	0-0	1	Anderson [68], Welbeck [87]	75,514
8	15	A	Liverpool	D	1-1	0-0	2	Hernandez [81]	45,065
9	23	H	Manchester C	L	1-6	0-1	2	Fletcher [81]	75,487
10	29	A	Everton	W	1-0	1-0	2	Hernandez [19]	35,494
11	Nov 5	H	Sunderland	W	1-0	1-0	2	Brown (og) [45]	75,570
12	19	A	Swansea C	W	1-0	1-0	2	Hernandez [11]	20,295
13	26	H	Newcastle U	D	1-1	0-0	2	Hernandez [49]	75,594
14	Dec 3	A	Aston Villa	W	1-0	1-0	2	Jones [20]	40,053
15	10	H	Wolverhampton W	W	4-1	2-0	2	Nani 2 [17, 56], Rooney 2 [27, 62]	75,627
16	18	A	QPR	W	2-0	1-0	2	Rooney [1], Carrick [56]	18,033
17	21	A	Fulham	W	5-0	3-0	—	Welbeck [5], Nani [28], Giggs [43], Rooney [88], Berbatov [90]	25,700
18	26	H	Wigan Ath	W	5-0	2-0	2	Park [8], Berbatov 3 (1 pen) [41, 58, 78 (p)], Valencia [75]	75,183
19	31	H	Blackburn R	L	2-3	0-1	2	Berbatov 2 [52, 62]	75,146
20	Jan 4	A	Newcastle U	L	0-3	0-1	—		52,299
21	14	H	Bolton W	W	3-0	1-0	2	Scholes [45], Welbeck [74], Carrick [83]	75,444
22	22	A	Arsenal	W	2-1	1-0	2	Valencia [45], Welbeck [81]	60,093
23	31	H	Stoke C	W	2-0	1-0	—	Hernandez (pen) [38], Berbatov (pen) [53]	74,719
24	Feb 5	A	Chelsea	D	3-3	0-1	2	Rooney 2 (2 pens) [58, 69], Hernandez [84]	41,668
25	11	H	Liverpool	W	2-1	0-0	2	Rooney 2 [47, 50]	74,844
26	26	A	Norwich C	W	2-1	1-0	2	Scholes [7], Giggs [90]	26,811
27	Mar 4	A	Tottenham H	W	3-1	1-0	2	Rooney [45], Young 2 [60, 69]	36,034
28	11	H	WBA	W	2-0	1-0	1	Rooney 2 (1 pen) [35, 71 (p)]	75,598
29	18	A	Wolverhampton W	W	5-0	3-0	—	Evans [21], Valencia [43], Welbeck [45], Hernandez 2 [56, 61]	27,494
30	26	H	Fulham	W	1-0	1-0	—	Rooney [42]	75,570
31	Apr 2	A	Blackburn R	W	2-0	0-0	—	Valencia [81], Young [86]	26,532
32	8	H	QPR	W	2-0	1-0	1	Rooney (pen) [15], Scholes [68]	75,505
33	11	A	Wigan Ath	L	0-1	0-0	—		18,115
34	15	H	Aston Villa	W	4-0	2-0	1	Rooney 2 (1 pen) [7 (p), 73], Welbeck [43], Nani [90]	75,138
35	22	H	Everton	D	4-4	1-1	1	Rooney 2 [41, 69], Welbeck [57], Nani [60]	75,522
36	30	A	Manchester C	L	0-1	0-1	—		47,259
37	May 6	H	Swansea C	W	2-0	2-0	2	Scholes [28], Young [41]	75,496
38	13	A	Sunderland	W	1-0	1-0	2	Rooney [20]	46,452

Final League Position: 2

GOALSCORERS

League (89): Rooney 27 (6 pens), Hernandez 10 (1 pen), Welbeck 9, Nani 8, Berbatov 7 (2 pens), Young 6, Scholes 4, Valencia 4, Anderson 2, Carrick 2, Giggs 2, Park 2, Evans 1, Fletcher 1, Jones 1, Smalling 1, own goals 2.
Carling Cup (7): Owen 3, Berbatov 1, Giggs 1, Macheda 1 (pen), Valencia 1.
FA Cup (4): Rooney 2, Park 1, Welbeck 1.
Champions League (11): Rooney 2 (2 pens), Welbeck 2, Berbatov 1, Fletcher 1, Giggs 1, Jones 1, Valencia 1, Young 1, own goal 1.
Europa League (6): Rooney 3 (1 pen), Hernandez 2, Young 1.
Community Shield (3): Nani 2, Smalling 1.

De Gea D 29	Smalling C 14 + 5	Fabio 2 + 3	Cleverley T 5 + 5	Ferdinand R 29 + 1	Vidic N 6	Young A 19 + 6	Anderson 8 + 2	Welbeck D 23 + 7	Rooney W 32 + 2	Nani 24 + 5	Evans J 28 + 1	Berbatov D 5 + 7	Jones P 25 + 4	Evra P 37	Giggs R 14 + 11	Park J 10 + 7	Hernandez J 18 + 10	Carrick M 27 + 3	Fletcher D 7 + 1	Valencia A 22 + 5	Owen M — + 1	Lindegaard A 8	Macheda F — + 3	Fryers E — + 2	Gibson D 1	Rafael 10 + 2	Keane W — + 1	Scholes P 14 + 3	Amos B 1	Pogba P — + 3	*Match No.*
1	2	3	4	5^{3}	6^{1}	7	8	9^{2}	10	11	12	13	14																		1
1	2		4^{1}			7^{2}	8	9^{3}	10	11	6		5	3	12	13	14														2
1	2		4			7	8^{3}	9^{1}	10	11^{2}	6		5	3	14	13	12														3
1	14		4^{1}	5		7^{3}	8		10	11	6^{2}		2	3	13		9	12													4
1	2^{2}					7	8^{1}		10	11	6	14	5	3			9^{3}	12	4	13											5
1				5		11^{2}	8	14		7		9^{3}	6	3	13		10^{1}		4	2	12										6
				14			8^{3}	13	10	11^{1}	6		5	3	12	7	9^{2}		4	2		1									7
1	2			5		7^{1}		9	12	13	6		4^{3}	3	10	11^{2}	14		8												8
1	2			5		11	8^{2}	9	10	7^{1}	6■		13	3			12		4												9
1			4^{1}		6			7^{2}	10	12	5	14	2	3		11	9^{3}		8	13											10
		14		5	6			8^{1}	10	7		12	2	3		11^{2}	9	13	4^{3}			1									11
1		12		5	6				10	7			2	3^{1}	11^{2}	8	9^{3}	4	13	14											12
1	13	2^{2}		5	6	11			10	7				3^{1}	8		9	4					12								13
	2			5^{2}	6	11^{3}		14	10	7			8	3	13		9^{1}	4		12		1									14
1	2			5		14		9^{2}	10	11^{3}	6		8	3^{1}				4		7			13	12							15
1	2			5		14		9^{1}	10^{2}	11^{3}	6		8	3	13		12	4		7											16
	2					12^{2}		9^{3}	10	11	6	14	5^{1}	3	8	13		4		7		1									17
									13	11^{3}	5^{1}	9		3	8^{2}	7	10	4		2		1	14	12	6						18
1							12	8		11		9	5	3		6	10^{1}	4		7						2^{2}	13				19
				5			14	12	10^{3}	11		9^{1}	6	3	8	7^{2}	13	4		2		1									20
				5				9^{3}	10	11^{2}	6			3	12	13	14	4		7		1				2		8^{1}			21
	5							9	10	11^{3}	6		2^{1}	3	8	13		4		7		1				12^{2}		14			22
	2			5							6	9		3		11	10^{1}	4		7								8	1	12	23
1				5		11^{1}		9^{3}	10		6			3	8	14	12	4		7						2^{2}		13			24
1				5				9	10		6			3	11			4		7						2		8			25
1	13			5		12		9		7	6		2	3	11^{2}		10^{1}	4										8			26
1				5		11		9	10	7^{2}	6		2	3	12	13		4										8^{1}			27
1			13	5		11		7^{2}	10		6		2	3			9	4										8^{1}		12	28
1	14	13		5				9	10		6^{3}			3^{2}			11	4^{1}		7						2		8		12	29
1	13			5^{2}		11		9^{1}	10^{3}		6			3	8		12	4		7						2		14			30
1				5		14		12	10		6		11^{2}	3	13		9^{1}	4		7						2		8^{3}			31
1			14	5		11^{1}		9	10		6		13	3	12			4		7						2^{2}		8^{3}			32
1			12	5		11^{1}		13	10^{3}	14	6		2	3	8		9^{2}	4		7											33
1			14	5		11^{1}		9	10^{2}	12	6	13		3				4		7						2		8^{3}			34
1				5				9	10	11	6		12	3			13	4		7^{2}						2		8^{1}			35
1	6			5		14		12	10	11^{3}			2	3	9	7^{1}		4		13								8^{2}			36
1	6		12	5^{3}		11			10^{2}			13	2	3			9	4		7						14		8^{1}			37
1				5		9^{1}			10	12	6		2	3	11			4		7								8			38

FA Cup

Third Round	Manchester C	(a)	3-2
Fourth Round	Liverpool	(a)	1-2

Champions League

Group C	Benfica	(a)	1-1
	Basle	(h)	3-3
	Otelul	(a)	2-0
		(h)	2-0
	Benfica	(h)	2-2
	Basle	(a)	1-2

Europa League

Second Round	Ajax	(a)	2-0
		(h)	1-2
Third Round	Athletic Bilbao	(h)	2-3
		(a)	1-2

Carling Cup

Third Round	Leeds U	(a)	3-0
Fourth Round	Aldershot T	(a)	3-0
Quarter-Final	Crystal Palace	(h)	1-2

Community Shield

	Manchester C	3-2

(at Wembley).

MIDDLESBROUGH FL Championship

FOUNDATION

A previous belief that Middlesbrough Football Club was founded at a tripe supper at the Corporation Hotel has proved to be erroneous. In fact, members of Middlesbrough Cricket Club were responsible for forming it at a meeting in the gymnasium of the Albert Park Hotel in 1875.

Riverside Stadium, Middlesbrough TS3 6RS.

Telephone: (0844) 499 6789.

Fax: (01642) 757 697.

Ticket Office: (0844) 499 1234.

Website: www.mfc.co.uk

Email: enquiries@mfc.co.uk

Ground Capacity: 35,100.

Record Attendance: 53,536 v Newcastle U, Division 1, 27 December 1949 (at Ayresome Park); 34,814 v Newcastle U, FA Premier League, 5 March 2003 (at Riverside Stadium).

Pitch Measurements: 105m × 68m.

Chairman: Steve Gibson.

Chief Executive: Neil Bausor.

Manager: Tony Mowbray.

Assistant Manager: Mark Venus.

Head of Medical: Chris Moseley.

Colours: Red shirts with white design and one white sleeve, white shorts with red trim, white stockings.

Year Formed: 1876; re-formed 1986.

Turned Professional: 1889; became amateur 1892, and professional again, 1899.

Club Nickname: 'Boro'.

Grounds: 1877, Old Archery Ground, Albert Park; 1879, Breckon Hill; 1882, Linthorpe Road Ground; 1903, Ayresome Park; 1995, Riverside Stadium.

First Football League Game: 2 September 1899, Division 2, v Lincoln C (a) L 0–3 – Smith; Shaw, Ramsey; Allport, McNally, McCracken; Wanless, Longstaffe, Gettins, Page, Pugh.

Record League Victory: 9–0 v Brighton & HA, Division 2, 23 August 1958 – Taylor; Bilcliff, Robinson; Harris (2p), Phillips, Walley; Day, McLean, Clough (5), Peacock (2), Holliday.

Record Cup Victory: 7–0 v Hereford U, Coca-Cola Cup 2nd rd, 1st leg, 18 September 1996 – Miller; Fleming (1), Branco (1), Whyte, Vickers, Whelan, Emerson (1), Mustoe, Stamp, Juninho, Ravanelli (4).

HONOURS

Football League – Division 1: ***Champions*** 1994–95; ***Runners-up*** 1997–98; **Division 2:** ***Champions*** 1926–27, 1928–29, 1973–74; ***Runners-up*** 1901–02, 1991–92; **Division 3:** ***Runners-up*** 1966–67, 1986–87.

FA Cup: ***Runners-up*** 1997.

Football League Cup: ***Winners*** 2004; ***Runners-up*** 1997, 1998.

Amateur Cup: ***Winners*** 1895, 1898.

Anglo-Scottish Cup: ***Winners*** 1976.

Zenith Data Systems Cup: ***Runners-up*** 1990.

European Competitions
UEFA Cup: 2004–05, 2005–06 (*runners-up*).

sky SPORTS FACT FILE

On 9 March 1938, Middlesbrough completed a fine home and away double over Manchester City, the then reigning League champions, with a 6-1 win at Maine Road, courtesy of four goals from Tom Cochrane and two from Mickey Fenton. At Ayresome Park the score had been 4-0.

Record Defeat: 0–9 v Blackburn R, Division 2, 6 November 1954.

Most League Points (2 for a win): 65, Division 2, 1973–74.

Most League Points (3 for a win): 94, Division 3, 1986–87.

Most League Goals: 122, Division 2, 1926–27.

Highest League Scorer in Season: George Camsell, 59, Division 2, 1926–27 (Second Division record).

Most League Goals in Total Aggregate: George Camsell, 325, 1925–39.

Most League Goals in One Match: 5, John Wilkie v Gainsborough T, Division 2, 2 March 1901; 5, Andy Wilson v Nottingham F, Division 1, 6 October 1923; 5, George Camsell v Manchester C, Division 2, 25 December 1926; 5, George Camsell v Aston Villa, Division 1, 9 September 1935; 5, Brian Clough v Brighton & HA, Division 2, 22 August 1958.

Most Capped Player: Wilf Mannion, 26, England.

Most League Appearances: Tim Williamson, 563, 1902–23.

Youngest League Player: Stephen Bell, 16 years 323 days v Southampton, 30 January 1982; Sam Lawrie, 16 years 323 days v Arsenal, 3 November 1951.

Record Transfer Fee Received: £12,000,000 from Atletico Madrid for Juninho, July 1997; £12,000,000 from Aston Villa for Stewart Downing, July 2009.

Record Transfer Fee Paid: £12,000,000 to Heerenveen for Afonso Alves, January 2008.

Football League Record: 1899 Elected to Division 2; 1902–24 Division 1; 1924–27 Division 2; 1927–28 Division 1; 1928–29 Division 2; 1929–54 Division 1; 1954–66 Division 2; 1966–67 Division 3; 1967–74 Division 2; 1974–82 Division 1; 1982–86 Division 2; 1986–87 Division 3; 1987–88 Division 2; 1988–89 Division 1; 1989–92 Division 2; 1992–93 FA Premier League; 1993–95 Division 1; 1995–97 FA Premier League; 1997–98 Division 1; 1998–2009 FA Premier League; 2009– FL C.

MANAGERS

John Robson 1899–1905
Alex Mackie 1905–06
Andy Aitken 1906–09
J. Gunter 1908–10
(Secretary-Manager)
Andy Walker 1910–11
Tom McIntosh 1911–19
Jimmy Howie 1920–23
Herbert Bamlett 1923–26
Peter McWilliam 1927–34
Wilf Gillow 1934–44
David Jack 1944–52
Walter Rowley 1952–54
Bob Dennison 1954–63
Raich Carter 1963–66
Stan Anderson 1966–73
Jack Charlton 1973–77
John Neal 1977–81
Bobby Murdoch 1981–82
Malcolm Allison 1982–84
Willie Maddren 1984–86
Bruce Rioch 1986–90
Colin Todd 1990–91
Lennie Lawrence 1991–94
Bryan Robson 1994–2001
Steve McClaren 2001–06
Gareth Southgate 2006–09
Gordon Strachan 2009–10
Tony Mowbray October 2010–

LATEST SEQUENCES

Longest Sequence of League Wins: 9, 16.2.1974 – 6.4.1974.

Longest Sequence of League Defeats: 8, 26.12.1995 – 17.2.1996.

Longest Sequence of League Draws: 8, 3.4.1971 – 1.5.1971.

Longest Sequence of Unbeaten League Matches: 24, 8.9.1973 – 19.1.1974.

Longest Sequence Without a League Win: 19, 3.10.1981 – 6.3.1982.

Successive Scoring Runs: 26 from 21.9.1946.

Successive Non-scoring Runs: 5 from 17.1.2009.

TEN YEAR LEAGUE RECORD

		P	W	D	L	F	A	Pts	Pos
2002-03	PR Lge	38	13	10	15	48	44	49	11
2003-04	PR Lge	38	13	9	16	44	52	48	11
2004-05	PR Lge	38	14	13	11	53	46	55	7
2005-06	PR Lge	38	12	9	17	48	58	45	14
2006-07	PR Lge	38	12	10	16	44	49	46	12
2007-08	PR Lge	38	10	12	16	43	53	42	13
2008-09	PR Lge	38	7	11	20	28	57	32	19
2009-10	FL C	46	16	14	16	58	50	62	11
2010-11	FL C	46	17	11	18	68	68	62	12
2011-12	FL C	46	18	16	12	52	51	70	7

DID YOU KNOW ?

In 1963, Middlesbrough defender Mel Nurse, the former Swansea Town and Welsh international centre-half, was detained by the police who suspected him of being one of the Great Train Robbers. He was quickly released when they realised the mistaken identity!

MIDDLESBROUGH 2011–12 LEAGUE RECORD

Match No.	Date	Venue	Opponents	Result	H/T Score	Lg Pos.	Goalscorers	Attendance
1	Aug 6	H	Portsmouth	D 2-2	1-0	—	Emnes 24, Williams, R 54	18,196
2	13	A	Leeds U	W 1-0	0-0	8	Emnes 67	25,650
3	16	A	Barnsley	W 3-1	3-1	—	McDonald 11, Robson 13, Emnes 44	10,603
4	21	H	Birmingham C	W 3-1	0-1	3	Robson 48, Haroun 69, Martin 72	17,567
5	27	H	Coventry C	D 1-1	1-0	4	Emnes 21	17,432
6	Sept 10	A	Burnley	W 2-0	1-0	3	Bailey 10, Bennett 49	15,220
7	17	A	Crystal Palace	W 1-0	0-0	2	Emnes 65	15,198
8	24	H	Ipswich T	D 0-0	0-0	2		17,741
9	28	H	Leicester C	D 0-0	0-0	—		16,883
10	Oct 1	A	Reading	D 0-0	0-0	2		17,418
11	15	H	Millwall	D 1-1	1-0	3	Robson 24	16,669
12	18	A	Nottingham F	L 0-2	0-1	—		20,630
13	22	H	Derby Co	W 2-0	1-0	2	Williams, R 45, Emnes 52	17,407
14	29	A	Southampton	L 0-3	0-2	4		26,630
15	Nov 1	A	Doncaster R	W 3-1	2-1	—	Robson 2 (1 pen) 30, 66 (p), Emnes 45	9792
16	5	H	Watford	W 1-0	1-0	3	McDonald 41	14,366
17	19	H	Blackpool	D 2-2	1-1	3	McDonald 2 15, 73	18,128
18	26	A	Peterborough U	D 1-1	0-0	4	Bates 54	10,013
19	29	H	West Ham U	L 0-2	0-1	—		18,457
20	Dec 3	A	Bristol C	W 1-0	0-0	4	Martin 90	14,467
21	10	H	Brighton & HA	W 1-0	1-0	4	McDonald 21	16,594
22	17	A	Cardiff C	W 3-2	1-2	3	Ogbeche 15, McDonald 60, Haroun 76	23,373
23	26	H	Hull C	W 1-0	0-0	3	Robson 87	27,794
24	31	H	Peterborough U	D 1-1	0-0	2	McDonald 51	18,899
25	Jan 2	A	Blackpool	L 0-3	0-0	4		13,449
26	14	H	Burnley	L 0-2	0-2	4		17,001
27	21	A	Coventry C	L 1-3	0-1	4	McDonald 66	14,112
28	Feb 1	A	Leicester C	D 2-2	1-1	—	McDonald 17, McMahon 79	20,512
29	4	H	Crystal Palace	D 0-0	0-0	6		15,725
30	14	H	Nottingham F	W 2-1	1-0	—	Emnes 45, Jutkiewicz 46	14,799
31	21	A	Millwall	W 3-1	2-1	—	Emnes 2 15, 38, Main 86	9286
32	25	H	Reading	L 0-2	0-1	8		17,314
33	Mar 3	A	Portsmouth	W 3-1	0-0	5	Robson (pen) 56, Bates 63, Emnes 83	16,770
34	6	H	Barnsley	W 2-0	0-0	—	Hines 60, Ogbeche 90	14,745
35	11	H	Leeds U	L 0-2	0-2	4		21,301
36	17	A	Birmingham C	L 0-3	0-1	6		19,927
37	20	A	West Ham U	D 1-1	0-0	—	Ogbeche 84	27,250
38	24	H	Bristol C	D 1-1	0-1	5	Martin 56	15,275
39	27	A	Ipswich T	D 1-1	0-0	—	Jutkiewicz 63	18,727
40	31	A	Brighton & HA	D 1-1	0-0	7	Emnes 61	20,553
41	Apr 7	H	Cardiff C	L 0-2	0-2	8		17,564
42	9	A	Hull C	L 1-2	1-0	8	Emnes 13	19,613
43	14	A	Derby Co	W 1-0	0-0	7	Main 80	24,654
44	17	H	Doncaster R	D 0-0	0-0	—		14,967
45	21	H	Southampton	W 2-1	1-1	7	Bailey 45, Zemmama 77	19,002
46	28	A	Watford	L 1-2	0-0	7	Emnes 85	14,022

Final League Position: 7

GOALSCORERS

League (52): Emnes 14, McDonald 9, Robson 7 (2 pens), Martin 3, Ogbeche 3, Bailey 2, Bates 2, Haroun 2, Jutkiewicz 2, Main 2, Williams, R 2, Bennett 1, Hines 1, McMahon 1, Zemmama 1.
Carling Cup (6): Emnes 3 (1 pen), Hines 1, Robson 1, Zemmama 1.
FA Cup (3): Emnes 1, Jutkiewicz 1, Robson 1.

Ikeme C 10	McMahon T 28 + 6	Hoyte J 39	Bailey N 37	Bates M 37	McManus S 21 + 3	Robson B 37	Williams R 34 + 1	Emnes M 37 + 5	McDonald S 31 + 2	Bennett J 40 + 1	Zemmama M 7 + 8	Arca J 22 + 8	Martin M — + 15	Hines S 20 + 3	Smallwood R 7 + 6	Haroun F 23 + 9	Thomson K 10 + 12	Nimely-Tchuimeni A — + 9	Steele J 34	Ogbeche B 5 + 12	Kink T — + 1	Reach A — + 1	Ripley C 1	Jutkiewicz L 17 + 2	Coyne D 1	Halliday A — + 1	Main C — + 12	Hammill A 8 + 2	Match No.
1	2	3	4	5	6	7	8	9[1]	10	11	12																		1
1	2■	7[1]	4	5	6	11[2]	8[3]	9	10	3		12	13	14															2
1		2[1]	4	5	6	7	8	9	10	3		11[2]		12	13														3
1	2		4	5	6	7	8	9	10[1]	3		11[2]	13			12													4
1	2	3[2]	4	5	6	7	8	9		11		10[1]	13			12													5
1	2	3	4	5	6[1]	7[2]	8	9[3]	10	11	14	13				12													6
1	2	3	4	5	13	7	8	9	10[1]	11■						6[2]	12												7
1	2	3[1]	4	5		7[2]	6	9	10	11						8	12	13											8
1	2	3[2]	4	5		7[3]	6	9	10[1]	11		14				8	13	12											9
1	2	3[2]	4	5	6	7	11	9	10[3]			13				8[1]	12	14											10
	2		4	5		7	6	9	10[3]	3		11[1]	14			13	8[2]	12	1										11
	2	3	4[2]		6	10		9		11[1]		13	14	5		7[3]	8	12	1										12
	2[3]	3	4		6		5	9[2]	10	11	7[1]	8	13						1	12	14								13
	2[3]	3	4	6		7	5	9	10[2]	11	14	8[1]				13		12	1										14
	2	3[1]	4[2]	5	6	7	8	9[3]	10	11	14	13				12			1										15
	2		4	5	6	7	8	9	10[2]	3	11[1]					12			1	13									16
	2		4	5	6	7	8[1]	9	10[2]	3	11[3]					14		12	1	13									17
	2		4	5	6	7	8	9[1]	10	3						11		12	1										18
	2		4[1]	5	6		8[2]	9	10	3	11[3]	13				7		14	1	12									19
	2	3	4	5	13		6[2]	9	10	11		8[1]	12			7			1										20
	2		4	5		7[3]	6	9[2]	10	3	11[1]	8	12				14		1	13									21
		2	4	5		7	6		10	3		8				11			1	9									22
		2	4	5		7	6		10	3	12	8[1]				11	13		1	9[2]									23
		2	4[1]	5		7	6	14	10	3	13	8[2]				11	12		1	9[3]									24
	2[1]	3		5		7	6	12	10	11				13	4[3]	8[2]			1	9		14							25
	13	2		5			6	9	10[3]	3	14	7[2]			4[1]	11	8						1	12					26
	13	2[3]		5	12	7	6[2]	9	10	3[1]		8■			14	11	4■								1				27
	3	2		5		7[1]	6	9[2]	10[3]				13	4		11	12		1					8		14			28
	3[3]	2		5			6	9[2]		11			12	4	14	7[1]	8		1					10			13		29
	13	2		5			6	10[2]		3		11		4	12	7[1]	8■		1					9[3]			14		30
	14	2		5		7[3]	6	10[2]		3		11		4	13	8[1]			1					9			12		31
		2		5		7	6	10[2]		3		8		4		11[1]			1	13				9			12		32
		2	8	5		7	6■	12		3		14		4		10[1]			1					9[2]			13	11[3]	33
		2		5		7		10		3		8[1]		6	4	13			1	14				9[2]			12	11[3]	34
		2	4	5		7■	8[3]	10		3				6			12[2]		1	13				9[1]			14	11	35
	2	3[1]	4	5						7		10[3]	12	6	14		8		1					9			13	11[2]	36
		2	4	5				10[1]		3	12		14	6	7[3]		8[2]		1	13				9				11	37
	13	2[2]	4[1]	5				14		3	7[3]		12	6			8		1	10				9				11	38
	12	2	4	5[1]		7		9[3]		3		8		6[2]	10		14		1					13				11	39
		2	4		5	7		10[1]	12	3		8		6	11				1	13				9[2]					40
		2	4[3]		5	7		12	10	3			13	6			8[1]		1	14				9				11[2]	41
	3	2	4		5	7[3]		9[2]	10			8[1]	14	6	11				1	13								12	42
	2	3	4		5	7		10[2]	8					6		11	13		1					9[1]			12		43
	3	2	4		5	7[2]		8[1]	10			11[3]		6			14		1					9			13	12	44
	3	2[1]	4		5	7[2]	13		10[3]	12	8			6		11			1					9			14		45
		2	4		5	7	8	10	12	3				6		11[1]			1					9[2]			13		46

FA Cup

Third Round	Shrewsbury T	(h)	1-0
Fourth Round	Sunderland	(a)	1-1
		(h)	1-2

Carling Cup

First Round	Walsall	(a)	3-0
Second Round	Peterborough U	(a)	2-0
Third Round	Crystal Palace	(a)	1-2

MILLWALL FL Championship

FOUNDATION

Formed in 1885 as Millwall Rovers by employees of Morton & Co, a jam and marmalade factory in West Ferry Road. The founders were predominantly Scotsmen. Their first headquarters was The Islanders pub in Tooke Street, Millwall. Their first trophy was the East End Cup in 1887.

The Den, Zampa Road, London SE16 3LN.

Telephone: (020) 7232 1222. ***Fax:*** (020) 7231 3663.

Ticket Office: (020) 7231 9999.

Website: www.millwallfc.co.uk

Email: questions@millwallplc.com

Ground Capacity: 19,734.

Record Attendance: 48,672 v Derby Co, FA Cup 5th rd, 20 February 1937 (at The Den, Cold Blow Lane); 20,093 v Arsenal, FA Cup 3rd rd, 10 January 1994 (at The Den, Bermondsey).

Pitch Measurements: 105m × 68m.

Chairman: John G Berylson.

Chief Executive: Andy Ambler.

Manager: Kenny Jackett.

Assistant Manager: Joe Gallen.

Physio: Bobby Bacic.

Colours: All blue with white detail on shirts.

Year Formed: 1885.

Turned Professional: 1893.

Previous Names: 1885, Millwall Rovers; 1889, Millwall Athletic; 1899, Millwall; 1985, Millwall Football & Athletic Company.

Club Nickname: 'The Lions'.

Grounds: 1885, Glengall Road, Millwall; 1886, Back of 'Lord Nelson'; 1890, East Ferry Road; 1901, North Greenwich; 1910, The Den, Cold Blow Lane; 1993, The Den, Bermondsey.

First Football League Game: 28 August 1920, Division 3, v Bristol R (h) W 2–0 – Lansdale; Fort, Hodge; Voisey (1), Riddell, McAlpine; Waterall, Travers, Broad (1), Sutherland, Dempsey.

Record League Victory: 9–1 v Torquay U, Division 3 (S), 29 August 1927 – Lansdale, Tilling, Hill, Amos, Bryant (3), Graham, Chance, Hawkins (3), Landells (1), Phillips (2), Black. 9–1 v Coventry C, Division 3 (S), 19 November 1927 – Lansdale, Fort, Hill, Amos, Collins (1), Graham, Chance, Landells (4), Cock (2), Phillips (2), Black.

Record Cup Victory: 7–0 v Gateshead, FA Cup 2nd rd, 12 December 1936 – Yuill; Ted Smith, Inns; Brolly, Hancock, Forsyth; Thomas (1), Mangnall (1), Ken Burditt (2), McCartney (2), Thorogood (1).

Record Defeat: 1–9 v Aston Villa, FA Cup 4th rd, 28 January 1946.

HONOURS

Football League – Division 1: Best season: 3rd, 1993–94; **Division 2:** ***Champions*** 1987–88, 2000–01; **Division 3 (S):** ***Champions*** 1927–28, 1937–38; ***Runners-up*** 1952–53; **Division 3:** ***Runners–up*** 1965–66, 1984–85; **Division 4:** ***Champions*** 1961–62; ***Runners-up*** 1964–65.

FA Cup: ***Runners-up*** 2004; Semi-final 1900, 1903, 1937 (first Division 3 side to reach semi-final).

Football League Cup: Best season: 5th rd, 1974, 1977, 1995.

Football League Trophy: ***Winners*** 1983.

Auto Windscreens Shield: ***Runners-up*** 1999.

European Competitions
UEFA Cup: 2004–05.

sky SPORTS FACT FILE

On 22 October 2011, Darius Henderson scored all three goals for Millwall at Leicester City. He had missed eleven months out of action with his previous club Sheffield United suffering from a hamstring injury. It was also Millwall's first win in eleven Championship matches.

Most League Points (2 for a win): 65, Division 3 (S), 1927–28 and Division 3, 1965–66.

Most League Points (3 for a win): 93, Division 2, 2000–01.

Most League Goals: 127, Division 3 (S), 1927–28.

Highest League Scorer in Season: Richard Parker, 37, Division 3 (S), 1926–27.

Most League Goals in Total Aggregate: Neil Harris, 124, 1995–2004; 2006–11.

Most League Goals in One Match: 5, Richard Parker v Norwich C, Division 3 (S), 28 August 1926.

Most Capped Player: Eamonn Dunphy, 22 (23), Republic of Ireland.

Most League Appearances: Barry Kitchener, 523, 1967–82.

Youngest League Player: Moses Ashikodi, 15 years 240 days v Brighton & HA, 22 February 2003.

Record Transfer Fee Received: £2,300,000 from Liverpool for Mark Kennedy, March 1995.

Record Transfer Fee Paid: £800,000 to Derby Co for Paul Goddard, December 1989.

Football League Record: 1920 Original Members of Division 3; 1921 Division 3 (S); 1928–34 Division 2; 1934–38 Division 3 (S); 1938–48 Division 2; 1948–58 Division 3 (S); 1958–62 Division 4; 1962–64 Division 3; 1964–65 Division 4; 1965–66 Division 3; 1966–75 Division 2; 1975–76 Division 3; 1976–79 Division 2; 1979–85 Division 3; 1985–88 Division 2; 1988–90 Division 1; 1990–92 Division 2; 1992–96 Division 1; 1996–2001 Division 2; 2001–04 Division 1; 2004–06 FL C; 2006–10 FL 1; 2010– FL C.

LATEST SEQUENCES

Longest Sequence of League Wins: 10, 10.3.1928 – 25.4.1928.

Longest Sequence of League Defeats: 11, 10.4.1929 – 16.9.1929.

Longest Sequence of League Draws: 5, 22.12.1973 – 12.1.1974.

Longest Sequence of Unbeaten League Matches: 19, 22.8.1959 – 31.10.1959.

Longest Sequence Without a League Win: 20, 26.12.1989 – 5.5.1990.

Successive Scoring Runs: 22 from 8.12.1923.

Successive Non-scoring Runs: 6 from 20.12.1947.

MANAGERS

F. B. Kidd 1894–99
(Hon. Treasurer/Manager)
E. R. Stopher 1899–1900
(Hon. Treasurer/Manager)
George Saunders 1900–11
(Hon. Treasurer/Manager)
Herbert Lipsham 1911–19
Robert Hunter 1919–33
Bill McCracken 1933–36
Charlie Hewitt 1936–40
Bill Voisey 1940–44
Jack Cock 1944–48
Charlie Hewitt 1948–56
Ron Gray 1956–57
Jimmy Seed 1958–59
Reg Smith 1959–61
Ron Gray 1961–63
Billy Gray 1963–66
Benny Fenton 1966–74
Gordon Jago 1974–77
George Petchey 1978–80
Peter Anderson 1980–82
George Graham 1982–86
John Docherty 1986–90
Bob Pearson 1990
Bruce Rioch 1990–92
Mick McCarthy 1992–96
Jimmy Nicholl 1996–97
John Docherty 1997
Billy Bonds 1997–98
Keith Stevens 1998–2000
(then Joint Manager)
(*plus* **Alan McLeary** 1999–2000)
Mark McGhee 2000–03
Dennis Wise 2003–05
Steve Claridge 2005
Colin Lee 2005
David Tuttle 2005–06
Nigel Spackman 2006
Willie Donachie 2006–07
Kenny Jackett November 2007–

TEN YEAR LEAGUE RECORD

		P	W	D	L	F	A	Pts	Pos
2002-03	Div 1	46	19	9	18	59	69	66	9
2003-04	Div 1	46	18	15	13	55	48	69	10
2004-05	FL C	46	18	12	16	51	45	66	10
2005-06	FL C	46	8	17	21	35	61	40	23
2006-07	FL 1	46	19	9	18	59	62	66	10
2007-08	FL 1	46	14	10	22	45	60	52	17
2008-09	FL 1	46	25	7	14	63	53	82	5
2009-10	FL 1	46	24	13	9	76	44	85	3
2010-11	FL C	46	18	13	15	62	48	67	9
2011-12	FL C	46	15	12	19	55	57	57	16

DID YOU KNOW ?

Centre-forward Dave Ridley made his only official first team appearance for Millwall in a first leg FA Cup tie at Northampton Town on 5 January 1946 and scored in the second half of a 2-2 draw. He had also scored in the first of four wartime regional matches against Queens Park Rangers.

MILLWALL 2011–12 LEAGUE RECORD

Match No.	*Date*	*Venue*	*Opponents*	*Result*	*H/T Score*	*Lg Pos.*	*Goalscorers*	*Attendance*
1	Aug 6	A	Reading	D 2-2	0-0	—	Henderson [49], Marquis [62]	18,531
2	13	H	Nottingham F	W 2-0	1-0	6	Henderson [7], Trotter [77]	12,010
3	17	H	Peterborough U	D 2-2	1-0	—	Trotter [32], Bouazza [55]	10,240
4	20	A	Southampton	L 0-1	0-1	10		23,333
5	27	H	Barnsley	D 0-0	0-0	11		10,033
6	Sept 11	A	Birmingham C	L 0-3	0-1	15		17,901
7	17	H	West Ham U	D 0-0	0-0	15		16,078
8	24	A	Derby Co	L 0-3	0-2	20		24,120
9	27	A	Watford	L 1-2	0-0	—	Feeney [68]	10,592
10	Oct 1	H	Burnley	L 0-1	0-1	23		10,460
11	15	A	Middlesbrough	D 1-1	0-1	21	Trotter [55]	16,669
12	18	H	Brighton & HA	D 1-1	0-0	—	Simpson [81]	11,688
13	22	A	Leicester C	W 3-0	2-0	20	Henderson 3 (1 pen) [36 (p), 45, 68]	21,991
14	29	H	Ipswich T	W 4-1	2-0	17	Simpson 2 [6, 75], Henderson [9], Feeney [73]	12,464
15	Nov 1	H	Coventry C	W 3-0	0-0	—	Henderson 2 [53, 69], Feeney [82]	9517
16	5	A	Blackpool	L 0-1	0-0	17		12,455
17	20	H	Bristol C	L 1-2	0-1	20	Simpson [57]	10,252
18	26	A	Crystal Palace	D 0-0	0-0	21		15,150
19	29	H	Doncaster R	W 3-2	2-1	—	Trotter 2 (1 pen) [25 (p), 42], Henderson [84]	9062
20	Dec 3	A	Leeds U	L 0-2	0-0	19		27,161
21	10	H	Cardiff C	D 0-0	0-0	19		11,314
22	17	A	Hull C	L 0-2	0-0	20		17,841
23	26	H	Portsmouth	W 1-0	0-0	20	N'Guessan [82]	11,002
24	31	H	Crystal Palace	L 0-1	0-1	20		16,085
25	Jan 3	A	Bristol C	L 0-1	0-0	—		12,410
26	14	H	Birmingham C	L 0-6	0-1	21		10,539
27	21	A	Barnsley	W 3-1	2-0	20	Henderson 3 (1 pen) [36 (p), 39, 75]	9185
28	31	H	Watford	L 0-2	0-1	—		9294
29	Feb 4	A	West Ham U	L 1-2	0-1	21	Trotter [66]	27,774
30	11	H	Derby Co	D 0-0	0-0	20		10,069
31	14	A	Brighton & HA	D 2-2	1-0	—	Keogh [23], Feeney [64]	19,503
32	21	H	Middlesbrough	L 1-3	1-2	—	Henderson [43]	9286
33	25	A	Burnley	W 3-1	2-0	19	Keogh [15], Wright [30], Kane [70]	13,000
34	Mar 3	H	Reading	L 1-2	1-1	19	Keogh [16]	11,271
35	6	A	Peterborough U	W 3-0	1-0	—	Bouazza [5], Keogh [70], Kane [89]	6392
36	10	A	Nottingham F	L 1-3	0-2	19	Henderson [64]	19,413
37	17	H	Southampton	L 2-3	2-1	19	Fonte (og) [23], Robinson [28]	12,144
38	20	A	Doncaster R	W 3-0	2-0	—	Keogh [8], Kane [13], Henderson [58]	7572
39	24	H	Leeds U	L 0-1	0-0	19		14,309
40	31	A	Cardiff C	D 0-0	0-0	20		21,259
41	Apr 7	H	Hull C	W 2-0	1-0	19	Kane [25], Keogh (pen) [81]	12,372
42	10	A	Portsmouth	W 1-0	1-0	—	Kane [37]	15,837
43	14	H	Leicester C	W 2-1	1-0	17	Kane [23], Keogh (pen) [55]	11,525
44	17	A	Coventry C	W 1-0	0-0	—	Lowry [66]	13,974
45	21	A	Ipswich T	W 3-0	1-0	16	Keogh 2 [3, 87], Trotter [63]	18,947
46	28	H	Blackpool	D 2-2	1-1	16	Keogh [12], Kane [83]	13,122

Final League Position: 16

GOALSCORERS

League (55): Henderson 15 (2 pens), Keogh 10 (2 pens), Kane 7, Trotter 7 (1 pen), Feeney 4, Simpson 4, Bouazza 2, Lowry 1, Marquis 1, N'Guessan 1, Robinson 1, Wright 1, own goal 1.
Carling Cup (3): Bouazza 1, Mkandawire 1, N'Guessan 1.
FA Cup (9): Henderson 4 (1 pen), Kane 2, Feeney 1, N'Guessan 1, Trotter 1.

Forde D 27	Dunne A 25 + 5	Craig T 21 + 2	Mkandawire T 10 + 3	Robinson P 41	Ward D 27 + 3	Henry J 24 + 15	Trotter L 33 + 2	Marquis J 7 + 10	Henderson D 25 + 6	Bouazza H 19 + 7	Barron S 18 + 2	Hackett C — + 3	Abdou N 35 + 5	N'Guessan D 6 + 9	McQuoid J 1 + 4	Mildenhall S 9 + 1	Stewart J 3 + 1	Feeney L 27 + 7	Simpson J 13 + 3	Howard B 11 + 1	Agyemang P 1 + 1	Smith J 30 + 3	Lowry S 22	Baker N 6	Wright J 16 + 2	Kane H 19 + 3	Mason R 3 + 2	Keogh A 17 + 1	Taylor M 10	Montgomery N — + 2	Batt S — + 4	*Match No.*
1	2	3	4	5	6	7^{2}	8	9^{3}	10	11^{1}	12	13	14																			1
1	2	3	4	5	6	7	8	9^{2}	10^{1}	11			13	12																		2
1	2	3	4	5	6	7	8	12	10^{2}	11			9^{1}		13																	3
	2	3	4	5	6	7	8^{1}	9^{2}	10	11^{3}		14	12		13	1																4
1	2	13	4	5	6	7^{1}		12	10	11			8		9		3^{2}															5
1	2	3	4	5	6	12	8	14	10	11^{2}				13				7^{1}	9^{3}													6
1	2		4^{3}	5	6	12	8	9		11^{1}			7	14			3	10^{2}	13													7
1	2			5	6	12	8	13		11^{1}			4	7			3	10	9^{2}													8
1	2	3		5	6	7	8	12		13			4^{1}	11^{2}				9		10												9
1			2	5	6	7^{2}	8	12		13	3			11				9	10^{1}	4												10
1			2	5	6		7		10		3^{2}		8					11	12	4	9^{1}	13										11
1	12		2	5	6		7		10^{2}		3^{1}		8					11	9	4	13											12
1	2			3	6	12	7		10				8	13				11^{1}	9^{2}	4		5										13
1	2		12	5	6	13	7		10				8	14				11^{3}	9^{1}	4^{2}		3										14
1	2		13	5	6	12	7		10^{3}				8	14				11	9^{2}	4^{1}		3										15
1	2		14	5	6	12	7		10				8^{2}		13			11	9^{1}	4^{3}		3										16
1^{6}	2			5	6	12	7		10^{2}				8	13		15		11	9	4^{1}		3										17
				5		12	8	9^{1}			11^{2}		4			1		7	10	13		2	3	6								18
					6	14	8	9^{1}	12	13	11^{2}		4			1		7^{3}	10			3	2	5								19
				5	14	13	8		10	12	11^{1}		4			1		7^{2}	9			2	6^{3}	3								20
				5		7	8		12	10^{2}			4	13		1		11	9^{1}			2	6	3								21
	4			5	13	7			9	14	11^{3}					1	12^{2}	10		8		2	6	3^{1}								22
	12			5			7	13	10^{2}	14			8	11		1		9		4^{3}		2	6	3^{1}								23
		3		5		13	8	9		7^{2}			4	11^{1}		1		10	12			2	6									24
	4	3		5			8	14	13	11			12			1		10				2^{3}	6		7^{1}	9^{2}						25
1	2■			5		14	7	13		8			4	11^{1}	12			10^{2}				3	6■			9^{3}						26
1		5			6	12	8		10	7^{1}	3		4					11				2				9						27
1		5			6		8	12	10		3	13	4					11				2				9^{2}	7^{1}					28
1	5				6		8		10		3^{1}		7					11^{2}				2	4			12	13	9				29
1	2			5		7^{2}	8		10		3							12				14	6		4^{3}	9^{1}	11	13				30
1	2			5			8		10^{2}		3							7				4	6		12	13	11^{1}	9				31
1	12			5		14	8		10		3^{1}		13					7^{3}				2	6		4^{2}	9		11				32
1	2	3		5		7			14	10^{2}	12		4					13					6		8^{1}	9^{3}		11				33
1	2	3		5		7^{3}				10^{1}			8	13				12					6		4	9^{2}	14	11				34
1	2	12		5	6	7				10^{1}	3											8			4	9		11				35
1	2			5	6	7	8^{1}		13	10	3^{3}		4									14			12	9^{2}		11				36
	2			5	6	7			10^{1}	11^{2}			8					13				3			4	12		9	1			37
		3		5	6	7^{1}			10				8					12				2			4^{2}	9		11	1	13		38
		3		5	6	7^{2}			10	12			8									2^{1}			4	9		11	1	13		39
		3		5	13	7			12				4					11				2	6		8^{2}	9^{1}		10	1			40
	13	3		5		7				11^{1}			8					12				2^{2}	6		4	9		10^{3}	1		14	41
		3		5		7					11		8									2	6		4	9		10	1			42
		3		5		7^{1}	12				11		8									2	6		4	9		10^{2}	1		13	43
	13	3			5^{2}	7	12				11		8									2	6		4^{1}	9		10	1			44
		3		5		7^{1}	11						8					12				2	6		4	9		10^{2}	1		13	45
		3		5		7	11						8									2	6		4^{1}	9		10	1		12	46

FA Cup

Third Round	Dagenham & R	(a)	0-0
		(h)	5-0
Fourth Round	Southampton	(h)	1-1
		(a)	3-2
Fifth Round	Bolton W	(h)	0-2

Carling Cup

First Round	Plymouth Arg	(a)	1-0
Second Round	Morecambe	(h)	2-0
Third Round	Wolverhampton W	(a)	0-5

MILTON KEYNES DONS FL Championship 1

FOUNDATION

In July 2004 Wimbledon became MK Dons and relocated to Milton Keynes. In 2007 it recognised itself as a new club with no connection to the old Wimbledon FC. In August of that year the replica trophies and other Wimbledon FC memorabilia were returned to the London Borough of Merton.

Stadiummk, Stadium Way West, Milton Keynes MK1 1ST.

Telephone: (01908) 622 922.

Fax: (01908) 622 933.

Ticket Office: (01908) 622 900.

Website: www.mkdons.com

Email: info@mkdons.com

Ground Capacity: 21,189.

Record Attendance: 8,306 v Tottenham H, League Cup 3rd rd, 25 October 2006 (at National Hockey Stadium); 17,717 v Leicester C, FL 1, 28 February 2009 (at Stadiummk).

Ground Record Attendance: 20,222, England U21 v Bulgaria U21, 16 November 2007.

Pitch Measurements: 105m × 68m.

Chairman: Pete Winkelman.

Manager: Karl Robinson.

Assistant Manager: Mick Harford.

Head of Sports Medicine: John Gorman.

Colours: White shirts with black sleeves, white shorts, white stockings with black tops.

Year Formed: 2004.

Turned Professional: 2004.

Grounds: 2003, The National Hockey Stadium; 2007, Stadiummk.

HONOURS

Football League – FL 2: *Champions* 2007–08.

Johnstone's Paint Trophy: *Winners* 2008.

sky SPORTS FACT FILE

On 12 November 2011, Milton Keynes Dons twice broke records in an FA Cup proper round in a 6-0 win over Nantwich Town. George Williams at 16 years, two months, five days became the youngest goalscorer, then Brendan Galloway at 15 years, seven months, 26 days became the youngest player.

Club Nickname: 'The Dons'.

Most League Points (3 for a win): 97, FL 2, 2007–08.

Most League Goals: 84, FL 1, 2011–12.

Highest League Scorer in Season: Izale McLeod, 21, 2006–07.

Most League Goals in Total Aggregate: Izale McLeod, 54, 2004–07.

Most Capped Player: Ali Gerba (29), Canada.

Most League Appearances: Dean Lewington, 347, 2004–12.

Youngest League Player: Brendon Galloway, 16 years 42 days v Rochdale, 28 April 2012.

Football League Record: 2004–06 FL 1; 2006–08 FL 2; 2008– FL 1.

MANAGERS

Stuart Murdock 2002–04
Danny Wilson 2004–06
Martin Allen 2006–07
Paul Ince 2007–08
Roberto Di Matteo 2008–09
Paul Ince 2009–10
Karl Robinson May 2010–

LATEST SEQUENCES

Longest Sequence of League Wins: 8, 7.9.2007 – 20.10.2007.

Longest Sequence of League Defeats: 4, 10.8.2004 – 28.8.2004.

Longest Sequence of League Draws: 4, 21.2.2009 – 10.3.2009.

Longest Sequence of Unbeaten League Matches: 18, 29.1.2008 – 3.5.2008.

Longest Sequence Without a League Win: 11, 13.3.2010 – 2.5.2010.

Successive Scoring Runs: 18 from 7.4.2007.

Successive Non-scoring Runs: 4, 17.12.2005–2.1.2006.

TEN YEAR LEAGUE RECORD

		P	W	D	L	F	A	Pts	Pos
2002-03*	Div 1	46	18	11	17	76	73	65	10
2003-04*	Div 1	46	8	5	33	41	89	29	24
2004-05	FL 1	46	12	15	19	54	68	51	20
2005-06	FL 1	46	12	14	20	45	66	50	22
2006-07	FL 2	46	25	9	12	76	58	84	4
2007-08	FL 2	46	29	10	7	82	37	97	1
2008-09	FL 1	46	26	9	11	83	47	87	3
2009-10	FL 1	46	17	9	20	60	68	60	12
2010-11	FL 1	46	23	8	15	67	60	77	5
2011-12	FL 1	46	22	14	10	84	47	80	5

**As Wimbledon.*

On 2 January 2012, when Milton Keynes Dons complete a double over Colchester United in winning 1-0, goalscorer Gary MacKenzie became the 19th different player to appear on the score sheet during the season. It was also their 69th goal in all games during the season for them.

MILTON KEYNES DONS FC 2011–12 LEAGUE RECORD

Match No.	Date	Venue	Opponents	Result		H/T Score	Lg Pos.	Goalscorers	Attendance
1	Aug 6	H	Hartlepool U	D	2-2	0-1	—	Chadwick [53], Ibehre [90]	7287
2	13	A	Exeter C	W	2-0	1-0	5	Ibehre [23], Bowditch [90]	4832
3	16	A	Yeovil T	W	1-0	1-0	—	Baldock, S [10]	3274
4	20	H	Chesterfield	W	6-2	1-1	1	Baldock, S 3 [12, 59, 72], Bowditch [61], Chadwick [70], O'Shea (pen) [86]	7011
5	27	H	Stevenage	W	1-0	0-0	1	MacDonald [51]	8128
6	Sept 3	A	Carlisle U	W	3-1	1-0	1	MacDonald [45], Bowditch [47], Lewington [62]	4919
7	10	A	Sheffield W	L	1-3	0-0	3	Balanta [77]	16,982
8	17	H	Huddersfield T	D	1-1	0-1	4	Lewington [65]	8243
9	24	A	Bury	D	0-0	0-0	9		2378
10	27	H	Charlton Ath	D	1-1	1-0	—	Williams, S (pen) [21]	8114
11	Oct 1	H	Notts Co	W	3-0	1-0	2	Balanta [11], Morrison [82], Powell [83]	7620
12	10	A	Oldham Ath	L	1-2	0-1	—	Morrison [85]	2408
13	15	H	Bournemouth	D	2-2	1-0	5	Balanta [42], Morrison [80]	8927
14	22	H	Scunthorpe U	D	0-0	0-0	6		10,554
15	25	A	Sheffield U	L	1-2	0-1	—	Gleeson [52]	16,367
16	29	A	Walsall	W	2-0	2-0	5	Lewington [35], Ibehre [45]	3712
17	Nov 5	H	Rochdale	W	3-1	3-1	4	Smith, Adam [17], MacDonald [22], Beevers [31]	7120
18	19	A	Colchester U	W	5-1	2-1	4	MacDonald 2 [38, 74], Flanagan [45], Gleeson [88], Ibehre [90]	4247
19	26	H	Wycombe W	W	4-3	1-0	4	Bowditch 2 [14, 55], Ibehre [66], Doumbe [71]	9701
20	Dec 10	A	Tranmere R	W	2-0	1-0	3	Ibehre [19], Williams, S [60]	4314
21	17	H	Preston NE	L	0-1	0-1	5		8009
22	26	A	Leyton Orient	W	3-0	1-0	3	Bowditch [37], Smith, Adam [57], MacDonald [63]	4162
23	31	A	Brentford	D	3-3	3-0	4	Potter [4], Balanta [6], MacDonald [41]	5397
24	Jan 2	H	Colchester U	W	1-0	0-0	4	MacKenzie [53]	7892
25	21	A	Notts Co	D	1-1	1-0	5	Flanagan [26]	6123
26	24	A	Stevenage	L	2-4	1-1	—	O'Shea [2], Flanagan [86]	3345
27	31	H	Sheffield W	D	1-1	1-1	—	Bywater (og) [17]	9776
28	Feb 4	A	Huddersfield T	D	1-1	0-1	—	Gleeson [62]	16,898
29	14	A	Charlton Ath	L	1-2	0-2	—	Bowditch [87]	15,569
30	18	H	Oldham Ath	W	5-0	1-0	5	Bowditch (pen) [9], Powell 2 [47, 66], Doumbe [69], Gleeson [78]	7817
31	21	H	Bury	W	2-1	2-1	—	Bowditch 2 (1 pen) [20, 45 (p)]	6405
32	25	A	Bournemouth	W	1-0	1-0	5	Doumbe [32]	6419
33	Mar 3	A	Hartlepool U	D	1-1	0-1	5	O'Shea [51]	4955
34	6	H	Yeovil T	L	0-1	0-1	—		6624
35	10	H	Exeter C	W	3-0	2-0	5	Doumbe [17], MacDonald [27], Ibehre [78]	9016
36	17	A	Chesterfield	D	1-1	0-1	5	O'Shea [56]	6444
37	20	H	Leyton Orient	W	4-1	2-1	—	MacDonald [3], Williams, S [23], Ibehre [80], Powell [84]	6842
38	24	A	Wycombe W	D	1-1	0-0	5	Powell [46]	5572
39	27	H	Carlisle U	L	1-2	0-0	—	Williams, S (pen) [80]	8608
40	31	H	Brentford	L	1-2	0-2	5	Williams, S (pen) [88]	11,570
41	Apr 7	A	Preston NE	D	1-1	1-0	5	Potter [27]	13,941
42	9	H	Tranmere R	W	3-0	2-0	5	Williams, S 2 (2 pens) [10, 74], Gleeson [42]	7355
43	14	A	Scunthorpe U	W	3-0	1-0	4	Bowditch [11], Powell [54], Williams, S [85]	4111
44	21	H	Sheffield U	W	1-0	1-0	4	Smith, Alan [16]	15,938
45	28	A	Rochdale	W	2-1	1-0	4	O'Shea [3], Bowditch [58]	2212
46	May 5	H	Walsall	L	0-1	0-1	5		10,607

Final League Position: 5

GOALSCORERS

League (84): Bowditch 12 (2 pens), MacDonald 9, Ibehre 8, Williams, S 8 (5 pens), Powell 6, Gleeson 5, O'Shea 5 (1 pen), Balanta 4, Baldock, S 4, Doumbe 4, Flanagan 3, Lewington 3, Morrison 3, Chadwick 2, Potter 2, Smith, Adam 2, Beevers 1, MacKenzie 1, Smith, Alan 1, own goal 1.
Carling Cup (9): Baldock, S 2, Chadwick 2, Powell 2, Balanta 1, Ibehre 1, Lewington 1.
FA Cup (10): Bowditch 3, Powell 2, Doumbe 1, MacDonald 1, O'Shea 1, Potter 1, Williams, G 1.
J Paint Trophy (3): Chadwick 1, MacDonald 1, own goal 1.
Play-Offs (2): Powell 1, Smith, Alan 1.

Martin D 46	Chicksen A 14 + 6	Lewington D 46	Potter D 40	MacKenzie G 26	Williams S 33 + 6	Powell D 22 + 21	Gleeson S 39	Baldock S 4	Chadwick L 34 + 8	Balanta A 10 + 10	Bowditch D 33 + 8	Ibehre J 23 + 16	O'Shea J 12 + 16	Smith Adam 17	MacDonald C 29 + 6	Beevers M 14	McNamee A — + 7	Guy L — + 1	Flanagan T 18 + 3	Morrison C 5 + 1	Doumbe S 19 + 1	Smith Alan 14 + 2	Tavernier J 7	Williams G — + 2	Slane P — + 5	Hall R — + 2	McLoughlin I — + 1	Galloway B 1	Match No.
1	2^{3}	3	4	5	6	7^{1}	8	9	10^{2}	11	12	13	14																1
1	2	3	4	5	6	13	8	9	10^{3}	11^{1}	12	7^{2}	14																2
1	13	3	4■	5	6	12	8	9		11^{2}	10^{1}	7		2															3
1	4	3		5	6^{1}	14	8	9^{2}	12	11^{3}	10	7	13	2															4
1	13	3	4	5	6	7^{1}	8		11		9		12	2	10^{2}														5
1	12	3	4	5			8		11		9	7		2^{1}	10^{2}	6	13												6
1		3	4	5	6	13	8^{1}		11^{3}	12	9	7■		2	10^{2}		14												7
1	12	3	4	5■	6	7^{3}	8		10^{2}		9			2^{1}		11	14	13											8
1	2	3	4		6	7^{2}	8		11^{1}	12	9	10^{3}					14		5	13									9
1	2	3	4		10	13	8		11	7^{1}	12					6			5	9^{2}									10
1	14	3	4	5	6	12			7^{2}	11^{1}	10					8	13			9^{3}	2								11
1		3	4	5	12	13	8		7	11^{1}	10^{2}					6	14			9	2^{3}								12
1		3	4	5		12	8		7^{2}	11	10^{1}			2	13	6				9									13
1		3	4	5		13	8		7	11^{2}	10^{1}	12		2	14	6				9^{3}									14
1		3	4		11^{1}	14	8		7	13	10^{3}	9^{2}		2■	12	6			5										15
1		3	4		13	7^{3}	8		11^{1}	12		9			10^{2}	6	14		5		2								16
1		3	4		14	7	8		11^{1}	13	12	9^{3}		2	10^{2}	6			5										17
1		3	4		14	7^{2}	8^{3}		11^{1}	13	12	9		2	10	6			5										18
1		3	4				8		11	12	9^{2}	7^{1}	13		10	6			5		2								19
1		3	8	5	4	14			11^{1}	13	9^{3}	7^{2}	12	2	10	6													20
1		3	4	5		13	8		11^{3}	12	9^{2}	7^{1}	14	2	10	6													21
1		3	4	5	13	12	8		11^{1}	14	9^{3}	7		2	10^{2}						6								22
1		3	6	5	12	13	8			11	9^{2}	7		2	10^{1}						4								23
1		3	4	5	6	12	8		11		9	7			10^{1}						2								24
1		3	4			12	8		11		9^{1}	7		2	10				6		5								25
1		3		5		13	8		11^{2}		9^{1}	7	6	2	10				12		4■								26
1	2^{1}	3		5	6	14	8		11		9	13	7^{3}		10^{2}				4			12							27
1		3	4	5	6	14	8		11^{3}		9^{2}	12	13		10							7^{1}	2						28
1		3	4	5■	6	13	8		7^{2}		9		14		10^{1}						12	11^{3}	2						29
1	14	3^{3}	4		6	11	8		10^{2}		9^{1}	7	13		12						5		2						30
1		3	4		6	7^{2}	8^{1}		14		9^{3}	12	13		10						5	11	2						31
1		3			6	7			13		9	12	8^{2}		10^{1}				4		5	11	2						32
1		3			6	7^{2}			10^{1}			9	11						5		4	8	2	12	13				33
1	2^{2}	3			6	11^{3}	8■		10^{1}		9	12	7								5	4		13	14				34
1		3	4		6	7^{1}			13		9^{2}	12	11		10^{3}				5		2	8			14				35
1		3	4		6	12			9^{2}			7^{1}	11		10				5		2	8				13			36
1	8	3	4		6	9^{3}			7^{1}		12	13	11^{2}		10				5		2				14				37
1		3	4		6	7	8		14		12	13	9^{1}		10^{3}				5		2	11^{2}							38
1		3	4		6	7	8		11^{3}		9	13	12		10^{2}				5		2^{1}	14							39
1		3	4		6	7	8					13	11^{1}		10				5			9	2^{2}			12			40
1	2	3	4	5	6	10	8		11^{1}			12	7^{3}		13							9^{2}			14				41
1	2	3	4	5^{7}	6	11	8		14		9^{1}	7^{3}	12		10				13										42
1^{6}	2	3	4	5	6	7	8				9^{1}	13	12		10							11^{2}					15		43
1	2	3	4	5	6	7■	8		12		9^{3}	13	14		10^{1}							11^{2}							44
1	2	3	7^{2}	5	6		8^{3}		10		12	9	4		13				14									11^{1}	45
1	2^{3}	3	4		6	7	8		14		9^{2}	12	13		10				5			11^{1}							46

FA Cup

First Round	Nantwich T	(h)	6-0
Second Round	Barnet	(a)	3-1
Third Round	QPR	(h)	1-1
		(a)	0-1

Carling Cup

First Round	Cheltenham T	(a)	4-1
Second Round	Norwich C	(a)	4-0
Third Round	Burnley	(a)	1-2

J Paint Trophy

First Round	Brentford	(h)	3-3

Play-Offs

Semi-Final	Huddersfield T	(h)	0-2
		(a)	2-1

MORECAMBE FL Championship 2

FOUNDATION

Several attempts to start a senior football club in a rugby stronghold finally succeeded on 7 May 1920 at the West View Hotel, Morecambe and a team competed in the Lancashire Combination for 1920–21. The club shared with a local cricket club at Woodhill Lane for the first season and a crowd of 3,000 watched the first game. The club moved to Roseberry Park, the name of which was changed to Christie Park after J.B. Christie who as President had purchased the ground.

Globe Arena, Christie Way, Westgate, Morecambe LA4 4TB.

Telephone: (01524) 411 797.

Fax: (01524) 832 230.

Ticket Office: (see website).

Website: www.morecambefc.com

Email: office@morecambefc.com

Ground Capacity: 6,402.

Record Attendance: 9,383 v Weymouth, FA Cup 3rd rd, 6 January 1962 (at Christie Park). 5,003 v Burnley, Lge Cup 2nd rd, 24 August 2010 (at Globe Arena).

Pitch Measurements: 110yd × 76yd.

Chairman: Peter McGuigan.

Chief Executive: Rod Taylor.

Player-Manager: Jim Bentley.

Assistant Manager: Ken McKenna.

Physio: Simon Farnworth.

Colours: Red shirts with black trim, white shorts, red stockings.

Year Formed: 1920.

Turned Professional: 1920.

Club Nickname: The Shrimps.

Grounds: 1920, Woodhill Lane; 1921, Christie Park; 2010, Globe Arena.

First Football League game: 11 August 2007, FL 2, v Barnet (h) D 0–0 – Lewis; Yates, Adams, Artell, Bentley, Stanley, Baker (Burns), Sorvel, Twiss (Newby), Curtis, Hunter (Thompson).

HONOURS

FA Cup: Best season: 3rd rd, 1962, 2001, 2003.

League Cup: Best season: 3rd rd, 2008.

Northern Premier League: *Runners-up* – 1994–95.

Presidents Cup: *Winners* – 1991–92.

FA Trophy: *Winners* 1973–74.

Lancs Senior Cup: *Winners* 1967–68.

Lancs Combination – *Champions* 1924–25, 1961–62, 1962–63, 1967–68.
Runners-up 1925–26.

Lancs Combination Cup: *Winners* 1926–27, 1945–46, 1964–65, 1966–67, 1967–68.
Runners-up 1923–24, 1924–25, 1962–63.

Lancs Junior Cup: *Winners* – 1927, 1928, 1962, 1963, 1969, 1986, 1987, 1994, 1996, 1999, 2004.

sky SPORTS FACT FILE

On 10 September 2011, Morecambe beat Crawley Town 6-0 for their record win in the Football League. It was also Crawley's heaviest defeat in the competition. Morecambe went to the top of the League Two table and Danny Carlton scored the club's second League hat trick.

Record League Victory: 6-0 v Crawley T, FL 2, 10 September 2011 – Roche; Reid, Wilson (pen), McCready, Haining (Parrish), Fenton (1), Drummond, McDonald, Price (Jevons), Carlton (3) (Alessandra), Ellison (1).

Record Cup Victory: 6–2 v Nelson (a), Lancashire Trophy, 27 January 2004.

Record Defeat: 2–7 v Port Vale, FL 2, 30 April 2011.

Most League Points (3 for a win): 73, FL 2, 2009–10.

Most League Goals: 73, FL 2, 2009–10.

Highest League Scorer in Season: Phil Jevons, 18, 2009–10.

Most League Goals in Total Aggregate: Stuart Drummond, 32, 2007–12.

Most League Goals in One Match: 3, Jon Newby v Rotherham U, FL 2, 29 March 2008.

Most Capped Player: None.

Most League Appearances: Stuart Drummond, 184, 2007–12.

Youngest League Player: James Spencer, 18 years 258 days v Gillingham, 28 August 2010.

Record Transfer Fee Received: undisclosed from Rushden & D for Justin Jackson, June 2000.

Record Transfer Fee Paid: undisclosed to Southport for Carl Baker, July 2007.

Football League Record: 2006–07 Promoted from Conference; 2007– FL 2.

MANAGERS

Jimmy Milne 1947–48
Albert Dainty 1955–56
Ken Horton 1956–61
Joe Dunn 1961–64
Geoff Twentyman 1964–65
Ken Waterhouse 1965–69
Ronnie Clayton 1969–70
Gerry Irving/Ronnie Mitchell 1970
Ken Waterhouse 1970–72
Dave Roberts 1972–75
Alan Spavin 1975–76
Johnny Johnson 1976–77
Tommy Ferber 1977–78
Mick Hogarth 1978–79
Don Curbage 1979–81
Jim Thompson 1981
Les Rigby 1981–84
Sean Gallagher 1984–85
Joe Wojciechowicz 1985–88
Eric Whalley 1988
Billy Wright 1988–89
Lawrie Milligan 1989
Bryan Griffiths 1989–93
Leighton James 1994
Jim Harvey 1994–2006
Sammy McIlroy 2006–11
Jim Bentley May 2011–

LATEST SEQUENCES

Longest Sequence of League Wins: 7, 31.10.2009 – 12.12.2009.

Longest Sequence of League Defeats: 4, 23.2.2008 – 12.3.2008.

Longest Sequence of League Draws: 4, 13.9.2008 – 4.10.2008.

Longest Sequence of Unbeaten League Matches: 12, 31.1.2009 – 21.3.2009.

Longest Sequence Without a League Win: 10, 5.4.2008 – 30.8.2008.

Successive Scoring Runs: 17 from 13.8.2011 – 19.11.2011.

Successive Non-scoring Runs: 3 from 26.11.2001 – 17.12.2011.

TEN YEAR LEAGUE RECORD

		P	*W*	*D*	*L*	*F*	*A*	*Pts*	*Pos*
2002-03	Conf	42	23	9	10	86	42	78	2
2003-04	Conf	42	20	7	15	66	66	67	7
2004-05	Conf	42	19	14	9	69	50	71	7
2005-06	Conf	42	22	8	12	68	41	74	5
2006-07	Conf	46	23	12	11	64	46	81	3
2007-08	FL 2	46	16	12	18	59	63	60	11
2008-09	FL 2	46	15	18	13	53	56	63	11
2009-10	FL 2	46	20	13	13	73	64	73	4
2010-11	FL 2	46	13	12	21	54	73	51	20
2011-12	FL 2	46	14	14	18	63	57	56	15

DID YOU KNOW?

On 29 October 2011, Morecambe celebrated their 200th Football League fixture by beating Gillingham 2-1. It was also the club's first home win in seven weeks and kept them in the third automatic promotion slot on goal difference from Oxford United.

MORECAMBE 2011–12 LEAGUE RECORD

Match No.	Date	Venue	Opponents	Result		H/T Score	Lg Pos.	Goalscorers	Attendance
1	Aug 6	H	Barnet	L	0-1	0-0	—		1874
2	13	A	Hereford U	W	3-0	2-0	8	Carlton 37, Jevons 45, Drummond 65	2045
3	16	A	Cheltenham T	W	2-1	0-0	—	Fenton 61, Ellison 90	2035
4	20	H	Aldershot T	W	2-0	1-0	4	Ellison 8, Alessandra 79	1833
5	27	A	Northampton T	W	2-0	2-0	2	Jevons 15, Wilson (pen) 25	4016
6	Sept 3	H	Bradford C	D	1-1	0-0	3	Reid 57	4025
7	10	H	Crawley T	W	6-0	2-0	1	Carlton 3 9, 62, 72, Fenton 22, Ellison 69, Wilson (pen) 84	2054
8	13	A	Macclesfield T	D	1-1	1-1	—	Carlton 16	1527
9	17	A	Dagenham & R	W	2-1	0-0	1	Carlton 47, Drummond 54	1728
10	24	H	Bristol R	L	2-3	0-1	1	Price 57, Ellison 63	2583
11	Oct 1	A	Torquay U	D	1-1	0-0	3	Ellison 82	2207
12	8	H	AFC Wimbledon	L	1-2	1-1	6	Drummond 20	2631
13	15	A	Southend U	D	1-1	0-0	7	Jevons 53	9782
14	22	A	Port Vale	W	4-0	2-0	4	Price 27, Alessandra 37, Wilson (pen) 87, Fleming 90	5004
15	25	H	Rotherham U	D	3-3	3-1	—	McDonald 3, Wilson 2 (2 pens) 28, 37	3012
16	29	H	Gillingham	W	2-1	1-0	3	Hunter 8, Ellison 68	2067
17	Nov 5	A	Plymouth Arg	D	1-1	0-1	5	Fenton 90	5409
18	19	H	Crewe Alex	L	1-2	0-0	6	Ellison 69	2169
19	26	A	Shrewsbury T	L	0-2	0-1	8		5623
20	Dec 10	H	Oxford U	D	0-0	0-0	8		1914
21	17	A	Swindon T	L	0-3	0-2	11		7116
22	26	H	Accrington S	L	1-2	0-1	13	Drummond 55	2569
23	31	H	Burton Alb	D	2-2	1-1	13	Alessandra 31, McDonald 68	1810
24	Jan 2	A	Crewe Alex	W	1-0	1-0	12	Ellison 28	3840
25	7	H	Northampton T	L	1-2	0-1	—	Ellison 81	1879
26	14	A	Bradford C	D	2-2	0-0	12	Davies (og) 86, Ellison 90	10,065
27	21	H	Torquay U	L	1-2	0-1	14	Jevons 88	1721
28	Feb 11	A	Bristol R	L	1-2	0-0	—	Ellison 88	5381
29	14	H	Macclesfield T	W	1-0	0-0	—	Carlton 56	1316
30	18	A	AFC Wimbledon	D	1-1	0-0	14	McDonald 52	3964
31	22	A	Crawley T	D	1-1	1-0	—	Fleming 21	2184
32	25	H	Southend U	W	1-0	0-0	12	Burrow 75	1971
33	28	H	Dagenham & R	L	1-2	1-1	—	Ellison 26	1246
34	Mar 3	A	Aldershot T	L	0-1	0-1	13		2381
35	6	H	Cheltenham T	W	3-1	1-1	—	Ellison 2 32, 55, Reid 48	1207
36	10	H	Hereford U	L	0-1	0-1	11		1653
37	17	A	Barnet	W	2-0	1-0	10	Ellison 42, Redshaw 63	1536
38	20	A	Accrington S	D	1-1	0-1	—	Carlton 70	1924
39	24	H	Shrewsbury T	L	0-1	0-0	12		2175
40	31	A	Oxford U	W	2-1	1-1	12	Curran 3, Drummond 74	7023
41	Apr 6	H	Swindon T	L	0-1	0-0	12		3011
42	9	A	Burton Alb	L	2-3	1-2	13	Burrow 45, Carlton 49	2329
43	14	H	Port Vale	D	0-0	0-0	13		2210
44	21	A	Rotherham U	L	2-3	1-1	14	Burrow 39, Redshaw (pen) 75	2876
45	28	H	Plymouth Arg	D	2-2	0-1	14	Burrow 51, Alessandra 70	2313
46	May 5	A	Gillingham	L	0-2	0-1	15		4382

Final League Position: 15

GOALSCORERS

League (63): Ellison 15, Carlton 9, Drummond 5, Wilson 5 (5 pens), Alessandra 4, Burrow 4, Jevons 4, Fenton 3, McDonald 3, Fleming 2, Price 2, Redshaw 2 (1 pen), Reid 2, Curran 1, Hunter 1, own goal 1.
Carling Cup (2): Carlton 1, Ellison 1.
FA Cup (1): Wilson 1 (pen).
J Paint Trophy (2): Ellison 1, Jevons 1.

Roche B 44	Haining W 36 + 4	Wilson L 30	Fleming A 11 + 6	McCready C 46	Fenton N 35	Reid I 26 + 10	Drummond S 36 + 2	Alessandra L 24 + 18	Jevons P 14 + 13	Hunter G 30 + 7	Carlton D 34 + 10	McDonald G 39 + 3	Ellison K 26 + 8	Parrish A 29 + 9	Parkinson D — + 3	Charnock K — + 4	Price J 12 + 6	Kettings C 2	Burrow J 14 + 5	McGinty S 4	Redshaw J 7 + 4	Cowperthwaite N 1 + 2	Mwasile J — + 6	Curran C 6 + 1	McGee J — + 1	Match No.
1	2	3	4[2]	5	6	7	8	9[1]	10	11	12	13														1
1	2	3		5	6	7	8	9[1]	10[2]		11	4	12	13												2
1	2	3		5	6	7	8	9[1]	10[2]		11	4	12	13												3
1	2	3		5	6	7	8	12	10[1]		9[2]	4	11[3]	13	14											4
1	2[1]	3		5	6	7	8	13	10[2]		9[3]	4	11	12		14										5
1		3		5	6	7	8	12	10[1]	13	9[2]	4	11	2												6
1	2[3]	3		5	6	7	8	13	12		9[2]	4	11	14			10[1]									7
1	2	3		5	6	7[3]	8	14		12	9	4[1]	11	13			10[2]									8
1	14	3		5	6[2]	7[3]	8	12		4	9		11	2		13	10[1]									9
1		3	12	5	6	7	8			4[1]	9		11	2			10									10
1	14	3	4[3]	5	6	12	8		13	7	9[1]		11	2			10[2]									11
1	13	3		5	6	7[1]	8	14	10[2]	4[3]		9	11	2			12									12
1	3	11	14	5	6		8	9[2]	10■	7[3]		4		2[1]		12	13									13
1	2	3	13	5	6	12	8	9[3]		7	11[2]	4			14		10[1]									14
1	2	3	13	5	6	14	8	9[3]		7[1]	11	4	12				10[2]									15
1	2[1]	3[2]		5		13	8	9		7	11	4	14	6		12	10[3]									16
1			12	5	4	7	8	10[2]	13	2[1]	9	6	11	3												17
1	2	3	4[2]	5	6		7	12	10	13	9[1]	8	11													18
1	2	3	4[2]	5	6	7	8	13	10[1]		12	9	11													19
1	6	3[2]		2	5	7	8	9	10[1]		12	4	11	13												20
1	2		4	3	6	7	8	10	12	13	9[3]	11[2]		5[1]			14									21
1	2	3	4	5	6	12	8[1]	9	14	7[2]	11	13					10[3]									22
1	5	11	4[1]	2	6	3	8	9	13		12	7					10[2]									23
1	13	3	14	5	6		12	9	10[1]	7	8[3]	4	11[2]	2												24
1		3		5	6			9	10[1]	7	8	4	11	2			12									25
1	5	11		2	6		8	9[3]	12	7[1]	10[2]	4	13	3			14									26
1	3	10		5	6		8	9[2]	12	7	13	4	11[3]	2[1]			14									27
	5	3[3]	4	6	2		8		10[2]	11	12	7	14				9[1]	1	13							28
	2	3		5	6		8	13	14	7[1]	10[3]	4	11	12				1	9[2]							29
1	2[1]	3	4[3]	5	6		8	14		13	10	7	11	12					9[2]							30
1		6	4	5	2	14		10[2]		11[3]	8	7	12	3			9[1]		13							31
1		3[2]	4[3]	5	6[1]	12	8	14		13	10	7	11	2					9							32
1	6[3]			5		13	8	14		7	10	4[1]	11	2					9[2]	3	12					33
1	6			5		7	4[1]	10[2]		8	14	12	11	2					9[3]	3	13					34
1	6			5		7		10[3]	12	8	14	4	11[1]	2					9	3[2]		13				35
1	6			5		7	14	10	13	8[2]	11	4		2					9[3]	3[1]	12					36
1	6			5		7	10	12		8	13	4	11[2]	2					9[3]		3[1]		14			37
1	6			5		7	10	12	13	8[2]	11	4		2					9		3[1]					38
1	6			5	2	7	4	9[1]	14	8	10[2]		11[3]	3					13					12		39
1	2			5	6	12	4	9[2]		13	8[3]	7	11[1]	3					14					10		40
1	2			5	6	14	7	9[1]			8[3]	4	11[2]	3					13		12			10		41
1	2			5	6[1]	7				8	12	4	13	3					9[2]		11[3]		14	10		42
1	4			5		2		13		8	11	6		3					9[2]		7[1]		12	10		43
1	6			5				12		8	11	4		2					9[1]		3[3]	7[2]	14	10	13	44
1	6			5		2		12		8	11[1]	4		3					9[2]		7		13	10		45
1	4[1]			5		2		10[3]		8	11	7		6	13				9		3[2]	12	14			46

FA Cup

First Round	Sheffield W	(h)	1-2

Carling Cup

First Round	Barnsley	(a)	2-0
Second Round	Millwall	(a)	0-2

J Paint Trophy

Second Round	Preston NE	(h)	2-2

NEWCASTLE UNITED — FA Premiership

FOUNDATION

In October 1882 a club called Stanley, which had been formed in 1881, changed its name to Newcastle East End to avoid confusion with two other local clubs, Stanley Nops and Stanley Albion. Shortly afterwards another club, Rosewood, merged with them. Newcastle West End had been formed in August 1882 and they played on a pitch which was part of the Town Moor. They moved to Brandling Park in 1885 and St James' Park 1886 (home of Newcastle Rangers). West End went out of existence after a bad run and the remaining committee men invited East End to move to St James' Park. They accepted and, at a meeting in Bath Lane Hall in 1892, changed their name to Newcastle United.

St James' Park, Newcastle-upon-Tyne NE1 4ST.
(Name changed to Sports Direct Arena)

Telephone: (0191) 201 8400.

Fax: (0191) 201 8600.

Ticket Office: (0844) 372 1892.

Website: www.nufc.co.uk

Email: admin@nufc.co.uk

Ground Capacity: 52,387.

Record Attendance: 68,386 v Chelsea, Division 1, 3 September 1930.

Pitch Measurements: 105m × 68m.

Managing Director: Derek Llambias.

Manager: Alan Pardew.

Assistant Manager: John Carver.

Physio: Derek Wright.

Colours: Black and white striped shirts, black shorts with white trim, black stockings with white trim.

Year Formed: 1881.

Turned Professional: 1889.

Previous Names: 1881, Stanley; 1882, Newcastle East End; 1892, Newcastle United.

Club Nickname: 'The Magpies'.

Grounds: 1881, South Byker; 1886, Chillingham Road, Heaton; 1892, St James' Park.

First Football League Game: 2 September 1893, Division 2, v Royal Arsenal (a) D 2–2 – Ramsay; Jeffery, Miller; Crielly, Graham, McKane; Bowman, Crate (1), Thompson, Sorley (1), Wallace. Graham not Crate scored according to some reports.

Record League Victory: 13–0 v Newport Co, Division 2, 5 October 1946 – Garbutt; Cowell, Graham; Harvey, Brennan, Wright; Milburn (2), Bentley (1), Wayman (4), Shackleton (6), Pearson.

HONOURS

FA Premier League: *Runners-up* 1995–96, 1996–97.

Football League – Division 1: *Champions* 1904–05, 1906–07, 1908–09, 1926–27, 1992–93;
Division 2: ***Champions*** 1964–65; ***Runners-up*** 1897–98, 1947–48;
FL C: ***Champions*** 2009–10.

FA Cup: ***Winners*** 1910, 1924, 1932, 1951, 1952, 1955; ***Runners-up*** 1905, 1906, 1908, 1911, 1974, 1998, 1999.

Football League Cup: *Runners-up* 1976.

Texaco Cup: ***Winners*** 1974, 1975.

European Competitions
Champions League: 1997–98, 2002–03, 2003–04. **European Fairs Cup:** 1968–69 (*winners*), 1969–70, 1970–71.
UEFA Cup: 1977–78, 1994–95, 1996–97, 1999–2000, 2003–04 (*s-f*), 2004–05, 2006–07.
European Cup Winners' Cup: 1998–99.
Anglo-Italian Cup: 1972–73 (*winners*).
Intertoto Cup: 2001 (*runners-up*), 2005, 2006 (*winners*).

sky SPORTS FACT FILE

Newcastle United have twice scored as many as seven goals to inflict defeats on Manchester United at Old Trafford. On 10 September 1927 they won 7-1, while on 13 September 1930 it finished 7-4 with Jackie Cape, who later joined Manchester United, scoring three times.

Record Cup Victory: 9–0 v Southport (at Hillsborough), FA Cup 4th rd, 1 February 1932 – McInroy; Nelson, Fairhurst; McKenzie, Davidson, Weaver (1); Boyd (1), Jimmy Richardson (3), Cape (2), McMenemy (1), Lang (1).

Record Defeat: 0–9 v Burton Wanderers, Division 2, 15 April 1895.

Most League Points (2 for a win): 57, Division 2, 1964–65.

Most League Points (3 for a win): 102, FL C, 2009–10.

Most League Goals: 98, Division 1, 1951–52.

Highest League Scorer in Season: Hughie Gallacher, 36, Division 1, 1926–27.

Most League Goals in Total Aggregate: Jackie Milburn, 177, 1946–57.

Most League Goals in One Match: 6, Len Shackleton v Newport Co, Division 2, 5 October 1946.

Most Capped Player: Shay Given, 82 (125), Republic of Ireland.

Most League Appearances: Jim Lawrence, 432, 1904–22.

Youngest League Player: Steve Watson, 16 years 223 days v Wolverhampton W, 10 November 1990.

Record Transfer Fee Received: £35,000,000 from Liverpool for Andy Carroll, January 2011.

Record Transfer Fee Paid: £16,000,000 to Real Madrid for Michael Owen, September 2005.

Football League Record: 1893 Elected to Division 2; 1898–1934 Division 1; 1934–48 Division 2; 1948–61 Division 1; 1961–65 Division 2; 1965–78 Division 1; 1978–84 Division 2; 1984–89 Division 1; 1989–92 Division 2; 1992–93 Division 1; 1993–2009 FA Premier League; 2009–10 FL C; 2010– FA Premier League.

MANAGERS

Frank Watt 1895–32
(Secretary-Manager)
Andy Cunningham 1930–35
Tom Mather 1935–39
Stan Seymour 1939–47
(Hon. Manager)
George Martin 1947–50
Stan Seymour 1950–54
(Hon. Manager)
Duggie Livingstone 1954–56
Stan Seymour 1956–58
(Hon. Manager)
Charlie Mitten 1958–61
Norman Smith 1961–62
Joe Harvey 1962–75
Gordon Lee 1975–77
Richard Dinnis 1977
Bill McGarry 1977–80
Arthur Cox 1980–84
Jack Charlton 1984
Willie McFaul 1985–88
Jim Smith 1988–91
Ossie Ardiles 1991–92
Kevin Keegan 1992–97
Kenny Dalglish 1997–98
Ruud Gullit 1998–99
Sir Bobby Robson 1999–2004
Graeme Souness 2004–06
Glenn Roeder 2006–07
Sam Allardyce 2007–08
Kevin Keegan 2008
Joe Kinnear 2008–09
Alan Shearer 2009
Chris Hughton 2009–10
Alan Pardew December 2010–

LATEST SEQUENCES

Longest Sequence of League Wins: 13, 25.4.1992 – 18.10.1992.

Longest Sequence of League Defeats: 10, 23.8.1977 – 15.10.1977.

Longest Sequence of League Draws: 4, 20.1.1990 – 24.2.1990.

Longest Sequence of Unbeaten League Matches: 17, 13.2.2010 – 2.5.2010.

Longest Sequence Without a League Win: 21, 14.1.1978 – 23.8.1978.

Successive Scoring Runs: 25 from 15.4.1939.

Successive Non-scoring Runs: 6 from 31.12.1938.

TEN YEAR LEAGUE RECORD

		P	*W*	*D*	*L*	*F*	*A*	*Pts*	*Pos*
2002-03	PR Lge	38	21	6	11	63	48	69	3
2003-04	PR Lge	38	13	17	8	52	40	56	5
2004-05	PR Lge	38	10	14	14	47	57	44	14
2005-06	PR Lge	38	17	7	14	47	42	58	7
2006-07	PR Lge	38	11	10	17	38	47	43	13
2007-08	PR Lge	38	11	10	17	45	65	43	12
2008-09	PR Lge	38	7	13	18	40	59	34	18
2009-10	FL C	46	30	12	4	90	35	102	1
2010-11	PR Lge	38	11	13	14	56	57	46	12
2011-12	PR Lge	38	19	8	11	56	51	65	5

DID YOU KNOW 

In October 1932, Newcastle United applied to take over the existing fixtures in the Scottish League of either Bo'ness or Armadale, both of whom had been expelled. United wanted to field their reserve team in the competition, but after some consideration the offer was declined.

NEWCASTLE UNITED 2011–12 LEAGUE RECORD

Match No.	*Date*	*Venue*	*Opponents*	*Result*		*H/T Score*	*Lg Pos.*	*Goalscorers*	*Attendance*
1	Aug 13	H	Arsenal	D	0-0	0-0	—		46,894
2	20	A	Sunderland	W	1-0	0-0	6	Taylor, R [62]	47,751
3	28	H	Fulham	W	2-1	0-0	6	Best 2 [48, 66]	42,684
4	Sept 12	A	QPR	D	0-0	0-0	—		16,211
5	17	A	Aston Villa	D	1-1	0-1	4	Best [57]	34,248
6	24	H	Blackburn R	W	3-1	2-1	4	Ba 3 [27, 30, 54]	46,236
7	Oct 1	A	Wolverhampton W	W	2-1	2-0	4	Ba [17], Gutierrez [38]	26,561
8	16	H	Tottenham H	D	2-2	0-1	4	Ba [48], Ameobi, Shola [86]	46,420
9	22	H	Wigan Ath	W	1-0	0-0	4	Cabaye [81]	48,321
10	31	A	Stoke C	W	3-1	2-0	—	Ba 3 (1 pen) [12, 40, 81 (p)]	26,564
11	Nov 5	H	Everton	W	2-1	2-1	3	Heitinga (og) [12], Taylor, R [29]	50,671
12	19	A	Manchester C	L	1-3	0-2	3	Gosling [89]	47,408
13	26	A	Manchester U	D	1-1	0-0	4	Ba (pen) [64]	75,594
14	Dec 3	H	Chelsea	L	0-3	0-1	6		52,305
15	10	A	Norwich C	L	2-4	1-1	7	Ba 2 [45, 71]	26,816
16	17	H	Swansea C	D	0-0	0-0	7		51,767
17	21	H	WBA	L	2-3	1-2	—	Ba 2 [34, 81]	51,060
18	26	A	Bolton W	W	2-0	0-0	7	Ben Arfa [69], Ba [71]	26,080
19	30	A	Liverpool	L	1-3	1-1	—	Agger (og) [25]	44,372
20	Jan 4	H	Manchester U	W	3-0	1-0	—	Ba [33], Cabaye [47], Jones (og) [90]	52,299
21	15	H	QPR	W	1-0	1-0	6	Best [37]	49,865
22	21	A	Fulham	L	2-5	1-0	6	Guthrie [43], Ben Arfa [85]	25,692
23	Feb 1	A	Blackburn R	W	2-0	1-0	—	Dann (og) [12], Obertan [90]	20,817
24	5	H	Aston Villa	W	2-1	1-1	5	Ba [30], Cisse [71]	48,569
25	11	A	Tottenham H	L	0-5	0-4	6		36,176
26	25	H	Wolverhampton W	D	2-2	2-0	6	Cisse [6], Gutierrez [18]	52,287
27	Mar 4	H	Sunderland	D	1-1	0-1	6	Ameobi, Shola [90]	52,388
28	12	A	Arsenal	L	1-2	1-1	—	Ben Arfa [14]	60,095
29	18	H	Norwich C	W	1-0	1-0	—	Cisse [11]	47,833
30	25	A	WBA	W	3-1	3-0	6	Cisse 2 [6, 34], Ben Arfa [12]	25,049
31	Apr 1	H	Liverpool	W	2-0	1-0	6	Cisse 2 [19, 59]	52,363
32	6	A	Swansea C	W	2-0	1-0	—	Cisse 2 [5, 69]	19,874
33	9	H	Bolton W	W	2-0	0-0	—	Ben Arfa [73], Cisse [83]	52,264
34	21	H	Stoke C	W	3-0	2-0	4	Cabaye 2 [14, 57], Cisse [18]	52,162
35	28	A	Wigan Ath	L	0-4	0-4	5		22,187
36	May 2	A	Chelsea	W	2-0	1-0	—	Cisse 2 [19, 90]	41,559
37	6	H	Manchester C	L	0-2	0-0	5		52,389
38	13	A	Everton	L	1-3	0-2	5	Hibbert (og) [73]	39,517

Final League Position: 5

GOALSCORERS

League (56): Ba 16 (2 pens), Cisse 13, Ben Arfa 5, Best 4, Cabaye 4, Ameobi, Shola 2, Gutierrez 2, Taylor, R 2, Gosling 1, Guthrie 1, Obertan 1, own goals 5.
Carling Cup (9): Lovenkrands 3 (2 pens), Ameobi, Sammy 1, Cabaye 1, Coloccini 1, Guthrie 1, Taylor, R 1, Simpson 1.
FA Cup (2): Ben Arfa 1, Gutierrez 1.

Krul T 38	Simpson D 35	Taylor R 23 + 8	Cabaye Y 34	Coloccini F 35	Taylor S 14	Barton J 2	Tiote C 24	Ameobi Shola 8 + 19	Ba D 32 + 2	Gutierrez J 37	Obertan G 18 + 5	Best L 16 + 2	Lovenkrands P 2 + 7	Williamson M 21 + 1	Gosling D 1 + 11	Vuckic H 2 + 2	Smith A — + 2	Marveaux S 1 + 6	Ameobi Sam 1 + 9	Ben Arfa H 16 + 10	Guthrie D 13 + 3	Santon D 19 + 5	Perch J 13 + 12	Ferguson S — + 7	Cisse P 13 + 1	Match No.
1	2	3	4^{3}	5	6	7	8	9^{2}	10^{1}	11	12	13	14													1
1	2	3	4^{1}	5	6	7	8	9		11	10^{2}			12	13											2
1	2	3	4	5	6		8		12	11	10	9^{2}	7^{1}			13^{3}	14									3
1	2	3	4	5	6		8	9^{1}	12	11	7^{3}	10^{2}						13	14							4
1	2	3	4	5	6		8	12	9^{2}	11^{3}	7	10^{1}						13	14							5
1	2	3	4	5	6		8		9^{1}	11^{2}	7	10						13		12						6
1	2	3	4^{2}	5	6		8		9^{1}	11	7^{3}	10	12					14			13					7
1	2^{3}	3	4	5	6		8	12	9^{2}	11	7	10^{1}								13		14				8
1	2	3	4	5	6		8	13	9^{2}	11	7^{3}	10^{1}						14		12						9
1	2	3	4^{1}	5	6				9	11	7	10^{2}			14				13		8^{3}		12			10
1	2	3	4^{1}	5	6				9	11		10^{3}			12			7^{2}	13	14	8					11
1	2	3	4^{3}	5	6				9	11			12		13				10^{2}	7^{1}	8		14			12
1	2	3	4	5	6				9	11■	7^{1}		14						12	10^{3}	8^{2}		13			13
1	2	3	4	5^{1}	6			13	9		7		11^{3}						14	10^{2}	8		12			14
1	5	3	4					10^{3}	9	11	7^{1}				8■		13		12			2^{2}	6	14		15
1	2		4	5			8^{3}	12	9	11	7^{2}	10^{1}				14			13			3	6			16
1	2	12		5			8	14	9	11	7^{3}	10^{2}				4				13		3^{1}	6			17
1	2	3	4^{3}	5			8	13	9	11	7^{2}	10^{1}		6						12			14			18
1	2	3^{1}	4	5			8		9	11	7^{3}			6		10^{2}			14	13		12				19
1	2	7	4^{2}	5			8	10^{1}	9^{3}	11	14	12		6								3	13			20
1	2	7^{3}	4^{1}	5				9		11		10^{2}		6	14					12	8	3	13			21
1	2	14	4^{2}	5				9		11		10^{3}		6	13					7	8^{1}	3	12			22
1	2	4^{3}		5				9		11	14	10^{2}	13	6						7^{1}	8	3	12			23
1	2	7^{2}		5				14	9^{3}	11	13	10^{1}		6							8	3	4		12	24
1	2			5					9	11	7^{1}		14	6	13						8^{3}	3	4	12	10^{2}	25
1	2	7^{1}	4	5			8^{3}	14	9	11				6						13	12	3			10^{2}	26
1	2	7^{3}	4	5			8	13	9	11			14	6						12		3^{1}			10^{2}	27
1	2		4	5			8^{3}	13	9	11	10^{2}			6						7	14	3^{1}	12			28
1	2		4	5				14	9	11				6	13					7^{1}	8^{2}	12	3		10^{3}	29
1	2		4	5^{1}				13	9	11				6						7^{2}	8	12	3	14	10^{3}	30
1	2		4				7	13	9	3				6	12					11^{3}	8^{1}	14	5		10^{2}	31
1	2	12	4^{3}				8^{1}		9^{2}	11				6	14					7		3	5	13	10	32
1	2	14	4	5				13	9^{2}	11				6						7^{3}		3	8^{1}	12	10	33
1	2^{3}		4^{1}	5			8	13	9	11				6	14					7		3	12		10^{2}	34
1	2^{2}	12	4^{3}	5			8		9	11				6						7^{1}		3	13	14	10	35
1		12	4	5			8^{1}	13	9^{2}	11	14			6						7^{3}		3	2		10	36
1		14	4	5			8^{3}	12	9	11				6						7^{2}		3	2^{1}	13	10	37
1		12	4	5			8^{3}	14	9	11				6				13		7		3^{2}	2^{1}		10	38

FA Cup

Third Round	Blackburn R	(h)	2-1
Fourth Round	Brighton & HA	(a)	0-1

Carling Cup

Second Round	Scunthorpe U	(a)	2-1
Third Round	Nottingham F	(a)	4-3
Fourth Round	Blackburn R	(a)	3-4

NORTHAMPTON TOWN FL Championship 2

FOUNDATION

Formed in 1897 by schoolteachers connected with the Northampton & District Elementary Schools' Association, they survived a financial crisis at the end of their first year when they were £675 in the red and became members of the Midland League – a fast move indeed for a new club. They achieved Southern League membership in 1901.

Sixfields Stadium, Upton Way, Northampton NN5 5QA.

Telephone: (01604) 683 700.

Fax: (01604) 751 613.

Ticket Office: (01604) 683 777.

Website: www.ntfc.co.uk

Email: gareth.willsher@ntfc.tv

Ground Capacity: 7,300.

Record Attendance: 24,523 v Fulham, Division 1, 23 April 1966 (at County Ground); 7,557 v Manchester C, Division 2, 26 September 1998 (at Sixfields Stadium).

Pitch Measurements: 116yd × 72yd.

Chairman: David Cardoza.

Manager: Aidy Boothroyd.

Assistant Manager: Andy King.

Physio: Stuart Barker.

Colours: Claret shirts, white shorts, white stockings.

Year Formed: 1897.

Turned Professional: 1901.

Grounds: 1897, County Ground; 1994, Sixfields Stadium.

Club Nickname: 'The Cobblers'.

First Football League Game: 28 August 1920, Division 3, v Grimsby T (a) L 0–2 – Thorpe; Sproston, Hewison; Jobey, Tomkins, Pease; Whitworth, Lockett, Thomas, Freeman, MacKechnie.

Record League Victory: 10–0 v Walsall, Division 3 (S), 5 November 1927 – Hammond; Watson, Jeffs; Allen, Brett, Odell; Daley, Smith (3), Loasby (3), Hoten (1), Wells (3).

Record Cup Victory: 10–0 v Sutton T, FA Cup prel rd, 7 December 1907 – Cooch; Drennan, Lloyd Davies, Tirrell (1), McCartney, Hickleton, Badenock (3), Platt (3), Lowe (1), Chapman (2), McDiarmid.

Record Defeat: 0–11 v Southampton, Southern League, 28 December 1901.

HONOURS

Football League – Division 1: 21st, 1965–66;
Division 2: ***Runners-up*** 1964–65;
Division 3: ***Champions*** 1962–63;
Division 3 (S): ***Runners-up*** 1927–28, 1949–50;
Division 4: ***Champions*** 1986–87; ***Runners-up*** 1975–76;
FL 2: ***Runners-up*** 2005–06.

FA Cup: Best season: 5th rd, 1934, 1950, 1970.

Football League Cup: Best season: 5th rd, 1965, 1967.

sky SPORTS FACT FILE

On 18 October 1902, Northampton Town became the first Southern League team to visit Fratton Park and beat Portsmouth. One goal from Len Benbow was enough to settle the match which owed much to the Cobblers' goalkeeper Fred Cook who joined Pompey three years later.

Most League Points (2 for a win): 68, Division 4, 1975–76.

Most League Points (3 for a win): 99, Division 4, 1986–87.

Most League Goals: 109, Division 3, 1962–63 and Division 3 (S), 1952–53.

Highest League Scorer in Season: Cliff Holton, 36, Division 3, 1961–62.

Most League Goals in Total Aggregate: Jack English, 135, 1947–60.

Most League Goals in One Match: 5, Ralph Hoten v Crystal Palace, Division 3 (S), 27 October 1928.

Most Capped Player: Edwin Lloyd Davies, 12 (16), Wales.

Most League Appearances: Tommy Fowler, 521, 1946–61.

Youngest League Player: Adrian Mann, 16 years 297 days v Bury, 5 May 1984.

Record Transfer Fee Received: £265,000 from Watford for Richard Hill, July 1987.

Record Transfer Fee Paid: £165,000 to Oldham Ath for Josh Low, July 2003.

Football League Record: 1920 Original Member of Division 3; 1921 Division 3 (S); 1958–61 Division 4; 1961–63 Division 3; 1963–65 Division 2; 1965–66 Division 1; 1966–67 Division 2; 1967–69 Division 3; 1969–76 Division 4; 1976–77 Division 3; 1977–87 Division 4; 1987–90 Division 3; 1990–92 Division 4; 1992–97 Division 3; 1997–99 Division 2; 1999–2000 Division 3; 2000–03 Division 2; 2003–04 Division 3; 2004–06 FL 2; 2006–09 FL 1; 2009– FL 2.

LATEST SEQUENCES

Longest Sequence of League Wins: 8, 27.8.1960 – 19.9.1960.

Longest Sequence of League Defeats: 8, 26.10.1935 – 21.12.1935.

Longest Sequence of League Draws: 6, 18.9.1983 – 15.10.1983.

Longest Sequence of Unbeaten League Matches: 21, 27.9.1986 – 6.2.1987.

Longest Sequence Without a League Win: 18, 26.3.1969 – 20.9.1969.

Successive Scoring Runs: 27 from 23.8.1986.

Successive Non-scoring Runs: 7 from 7.4.1939.

MANAGERS

Arthur Jones 1897–1907
(Secretary-Manager)
Herbert Chapman 1907–12
Walter Bull 1912–13
Fred Lessons 1913–19
Bob Hewison 1920–25
Jack Tresadern 1925–30
Jack English 1931–35
Syd Puddefoot 1935–37
Warney Cresswell 1937–39
Tom Smith 1939–49
Bob Dennison 1949–54
Dave Smith 1954–59
David Bowen 1959–67
Tony Marchi 1967–68
Ron Flowers 1968–69
Dave Bowen 1969–72
(continued as General Manager and Secretary 1972–85 when joined the board)
Billy Baxter 1972–73
Bill Dodgin Jnr 1973–76
Pat Crerand 1976–77
By committee 1977
Bill Dodgin Jnr 1977
John Petts 1977–78
Mike Keen 1978–79
Clive Walker 1979–80
Bill Dodgin Jnr 1980–82
Clive Walker 1982–84
Tony Barton 1984–85
Graham Carr 1985–90
Theo Foley 1990–92
Phil Chard 1992–93
John Barnwell 1993–94
Ian Atkins 1995–99
Kevin Wilson 1999–2001
Kevan Broadhurst 2001–03
Terry Fenwick 2003
Martin Wilkinson 2003
Colin Calderwood 2003–06
John Gorman 2006
Stuart Gray 2007–09
Ian Sampson 2009–11
Gary Johnson 2011
Aidy Boothroyd November 2011–

TEN YEAR LEAGUE RECORD

		P	W	D	L	F	A	Pts	Pos
2002-03	Div 2	46	10	9	27	40	79	39	24
2003-04	Div 3	46	22	9	15	58	51	75	6
2004-05	FL 2	46	20	12	14	62	51	72	7
2005-06	FL 2	46	22	17	7	63	37	83	2
2006-07	FL 1	46	15	14	17	48	51	59	14
2007-08	FL 1	46	17	15	14	60	55	66	9
2008-09	FL 1	46	12	13	21	61	65	49	21
2009-10	FL 2	46	18	13	15	62	53	67	11
2010-11	FL 2	46	11	19	16	63	71	52	16
2011-12	FL 2	46	12	12	22	56	79	48	20

DID YOU KNOW

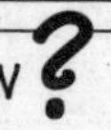

Stories behind the record Cup win of Northampton Town included amateur Harry Lowe being pitched in at the last moment for an injured player, soon-to-be-legendary manager Herbert Chapman scoring two and having three disallowed and the opponents missing from a penalty kick.

NORTHAMPTON TOWN 2011–12 LEAGUE RECORD

Match No.	Date	Venue	Opponents	Result		H/T Score	Lg Pos.	Goalscorers	Attendance
1	Aug 6	H	Accrington S	D	0-0	0-0	—		4621
2	13	A	Aldershot T	W	1-0	1-0	7	Westwood [2]	2790
3	16	A	Bristol R	L	1-2	0-1	—	Akinfenwa [64]	5812
4	20	H	Cheltenham T	L	2-3	1-1	17	Davies [39], Akinfenwa [51]	4114
5	27	H	Morecambe	L	0-2	0-2	19		4016
6	Sept 3	A	Southend U	D	2-2	0-1	22	Akinfenwa [60], Davies [65]	4805
7	10	H	Torquay U	D	0-0	0-0	21		4036
8	13	A	AFC Wimbledon	W	3-0	1-0	—	Akinfenwa (pen) [17], Jacobs 2 [73, 77]	4271
9	17	A	Macclesfield T	L	1-3	1-1	20	Jackson [44]	2033
10	24	H	Dagenham & R	W	2-1	1-0	17	Davies [17], Akinfenwa [60]	4274
11	Oct 1	A	Barnet	W	2-1	0-1	14	Davies [51], Tozer [89]	2304
12	8	H	Crawley T	L	0-1	0-1	15		4803
13	14	A	Port Vale	L	0-3	0-3	—		5082
14	22	A	Bradford C	L	1-2	0-0	17	Jacobs [58]	9925
15	25	H	Hereford U	L	1-3	0-2	—	Berahino [63]	3643
16	29	H	Rotherham U	D	1-1	1-1	18	Logan (og) [24]	4182
17	Nov 5	A	Gillingham	L	3-4	1-3	20	Berahino 2 [35, 60], Langmead [54]	4704
18	19	H	Shrewsbury T	L	2-7	0-3	20	Tozer [49], Akinfenwa [85]	5039
19	26	A	Plymouth Arg	L	1-4	0-4	21	Akinfenwa [90]	5762
20	Dec 10	H	Crewe Alex	D	1-1	1-0	20	Akinfenwa [16]	4579
21	17	A	Oxford U	L	0-2	0-0	22		7517
22	26	H	Burton Alb	L	2-3	2-1	23	Berahino [1], Jacobs (pen) [12]	5044
23	31	H	Swindon T	L	1-2	1-0	24	Jacobs (pen) [22]	4462
24	Jan 2	A	Shrewsbury T	D	1-1	1-1	23	Berahino [22]	6045
25	7	A	Morecambe	W	2-1	1-0	—	Johnson [21], Asante [52]	1879
26	14	H	Southend U	L	2-5	2-1	24	Johnson [10], Berahino [43]	5255
27	21	H	Barnet	L	1-2	1-0	24	Akinfenwa [10]	4561
28	28	A	Torquay U	L	0-1	0-0	24		2719
29	Feb 14	H	AFC Wimbledon	W	1-0	0-0	—	Guttridge [81]	4072
30	21	H	Macclesfield T	W	3-2	2-1	—	Jacobs [26], Guttridge [45], Akinfenwa [52]	4529
31	25	H	Port Vale	L	1-2	0-1	23	Akinfenwa [81]	5803
32	Mar 3	A	Cheltenham T	D	2-2	2-0	24	Tozer [20], Akinfenwa [35]	3503
33	6	H	Bristol R	W	3-2	3-0	—	Akinfenwa 2 [2, 10], Langmead [20]	4028
34	10	H	Aldershot T	W	3-1	2-0	22	Langmead [19], Akinfenwa 2 (1 pen) [40, 57 (p)]	5071
35	13	A	Dagenham & R	W	1-0	0-0	—	Silva [62]	2164
36	17	A	Accrington S	L	1-2	0-1	19	Williams [69]	1803
37	20	A	Burton Alb	W	1-0	0-0	—	Langmead [90]	2692
38	24	H	Plymouth Arg	D	0-0	0-0	18		6718
39	31	A	Crewe Alex	D	1-1	0-1	18	Akinfenwa [59]	4893
40	Apr 6	H	Oxford U	W	2-1	1-0	18	Guttridge [1], Williams [90]	6860
41	9	A	Swindon T	L	0-1	0-0	18		8745
42	14	H	Bradford C	L	1-3	0-2	20	Carlisle [53]	5060
43	17	A	Crawley T	L	1-3	0-3	—	Williams [65]	2861
44	21	A	Hereford U	D	0-0	0-0	20		2970
45	28	H	Gillingham	D	1-1	1-0	19	Wilson [41]	5832
46	May 5	A	Rotherham U	D	1-1	0-1	20	Akinfenwa [90]	4729

Final League Position: 20

GOALSCORERS

League (56): Akinfenwa 18 (2 pens), Berahino 6, Jacobs 6 (2 pens), Davies 4, Langmead 4, Guttridge 3, Tozer 3, Williams 3, Johnson 2, Asante 1, Carlisle 1, Jackson 1, Silva 1, Westwood 1, Wilson 1, own goal 1.
Carling Cup (2): Tozer 1, Turnbull 1.
FA Cup (0).
J Paint Trophy (1): Jacobs 1.

Walker S 21	Ofori-Twumasi N 4+1	Corker A 9+7	Turnbull P 9+5	Johnson J 43+2	Webster B 8+5	Davies A 15	Tozer B 42+3	Jacobs M 45+1	Akinfenwa A 33+6	Robinson J 15+17	Young L 20+10	Westwood A 14+3	Savage B 3+5	Langmead K 39+2	Thornton K —+2	McKoy N 5+4 / Duke M 9	Jackson M 5+1	Wedderburn N 1+1	Salihu L —+1	Kaziboni G —+3 / Charles A 5+4	Baldock G 4+1	Arthur C 5+2 / Kitson N 8	Holt A 5+4	Berahino S 14 / Wilson L 2+1	Niven D 4	Crowe J 11	Higgs S 3	Adams B 21+1	Harding B 19	Asante A 3+1	Hall F 2+1	Weale C 3	Gilligan R —+2	Guttridge L 19	Carlisle C 18	Williams B 8+10	Silva T 12+3	*Match No.*
1	2	3^3	4^1	5^2	6	7	8	9	10	11	12	13	14																									1
1	2	3	4^3	14	6	7	8	9		11^1	12	5	10^2	13																								2
1	2	3	4^2	12	6	7	8	9	14	11	13	5^1	10^3																									3
1	3			2^2	6	7	8	9	10	11^1	4		12	5	13																							4
1		3^1	4^2	2	6	7^3	8	12	10		11		9	5	14	13																						5
1			4^2	2	6	7	8	9^1	10	12	11	13		5		3■																						6
1		12	4	2	6^3	7^1	3	9	10	11^2	8	14	13	5																								7
1	12^2	13	4^1	2			3	9	10	14	7	6		5		8■	11^3																					8
1		12	4^1	2			3	8	10	11^3	7^2	6		5			9	13	14																			9
1		3	12	2		11	8	4	10^3	13	7^1	5		6			9^2			14																		10
1		3	14	2		7^3	8	9	10	13	11^1	5		6			12				4^2																	11
1		3^1		2			8	9	10	13	7^2	5	14	6			11				4^3	12																12
1		12		2			8	9		10	7	5^2		6		4^3	11				13	3^1	14															13
1				2			8	9		13	3^1	5^2	14	10		12					4	7^3	6	11														14
1			12	2			8^1	9		11^3	14	5		6		7^2					4	13	3	10														15
1				2			8	11	10		7^1	5		6								3	12	9	4													16
1			13	2			8	11	10	12	7	5		6								3^1		9	4^2													17
1						7	3	8	10	12		5^2		6		13						11^1		9	4	2												18
1		3	12	5		7	4	9	10	11		6													8^1	2												19
1		13		4		7	5	8	10	11^1				6■						12^2			3	9		2												20
1			8	4		7	5	11	10	12	13					6^1							3^2	9		2												21
		13		4■		7	5	8	12	11^2	10^1			6									3	9		2	1											22
		3		4		7^1	5	8	13	10^3	11			6		12				14				9		2^2	1											23
		13		4			5	11		14	7			6									12	9^2		2^1	1	3	8	10^3								24
				4			5	11		12	7			6									13	9^1		2		3	8	10^2	1							25
				4			5	11	12		7			6										9		2		3	8	10^1	1							26
				4			5	11	10		7^1			6										9		2^2		3	8	13		1	12					27
				10^2	6		14	11	13		7			5										9		2^3		3	8			1	12	4^1				28
				2	13			11	10^1	7^2				6														3	8		15	1^G		4	5	9	12	29
				2			12	11	10^1	13				6		1												3	8					4	5	9	7^2	30
				2			12	11	10	13				6		1												3	8					4	5	9^2	7^1	31
				2			7	11	10					6		1												3	8					4	5	9		32
				2	14		7	11^3	10^1	13				6		1												3	8					4^2	5	9	12	33
				2			7	11^2	10^1	14	13			6		1												3	8					4	5	12	9^3	34
				2	13		7	11	10^2					6		1												3	8					4	5	12	9^1	35
				2			7	11^2	10^1	13				6		1				14								3^3	8					4	5	12	9	36
				2			7	11			12			6		1				13								3	8					4	5	10^2	9^1	37
				2			7	11	12					6		1				3									8					4	5	10	9^1	38
				2			7	11	10^2	14				6						13		1						3	8					4^3	5	12	9^1	39
				2			7	11	10^3		12			6						14		1						3	8					4^2	5	13	9^1	40
				2	14		7	11	10^2		13			6						3		1						12	8^1					4	5	9^3		41
				2			7	9	10	11^2	13			6						3		1						8^1						4	5	12		42
				2^1			7	9	10^2	11^3				6				4				1		14				3						8	5	12	13	43
				2	13		7	11	10^2					6								1						3	8					4	5	12	9^1	44
				2			7	11	10^2					13						6		1		8^1				3						4	5	12	9	45
				2			7	11	10											6		1		8				3						4	5	12	9^1	46

FA Cup
First Round — Luton T — (a) — 0-1

Carling Cup
First Round — Ipswich T — (a) — 2-1
Second Round — Wolverhampton W — (h) — 0-4

J Paint Trophy
First Round — Huddersfield T — (h) — 1-2

NORWICH CITY — FA Premiership

FOUNDATION

Formed in 1902, largely through the initiative of two local schoolmasters who called a meeting at the Criterion Cafe, they were shocked by an FA Commission which in 1904 declared the club professional and ejected them from the FA Amateur Cup. However, this only served to strengthen their determination. New officials were appointed and a professional club established at a meeting in the Agricultural Hall in March 1905.

Carrow Road, Norwich NR1 1JE.

Telephone: (01603) 760 760.

Fax: (01603) 613 886.

Ticket Office: (0844) 826 1902.

Website: www.canaries.co.uk

Email: reception@ncfc-canaries.co.uk

Ground Capacity: 26,034.

Record Attendance: 25,037 v Sheffield W, FA Cup 5th rd, 16 February 1935 (at The Nest); 43,984 v Leicester C, FA Cup 6th rd, 30 March 1963 (at Carrow Road).

Pitch Measurements: 105m × 67m.

Chairman: Alan Bowkett.

Joint Majority Shareholders: Delia Smith and Michael Wynn Jones.

Manager: Chris Hughton.

First Team Coach: Colin Calderwood.

Physio: Neal Reynolds.

Colours: Yellow shirts with green trim, green shorts, yellow stockings.

Year Formed: 1902.

Turned Professional: 1905.

Club Nickname: 'The Canaries'.

Grounds: 1902, Newmarket Road; 1908, The Nest, Rosary Road; 1935, Carrow Road.

First Football League Game: 28 August 1920, Division 3, v Plymouth Arg (a) D 1–1 – Skermer; Gray, Gadsden; Wilkinson, Addy, Martin; Laxton, Kidger, Parker, Whitham (1), Dobson.

Record League Victory: 10–2 v Coventry C, Division 3 (S), 15 March 1930 – Jarvie; Hannah, Graham; Brown, O'Brien, Lochhead (1); Porter (1), Anderson, Hunt (5), Scott (2), Slicer (1).

Record Cup Victory: 8–0 v Sutton U, FA Cup 4th rd, 28 January 1989 – Gunn; Culverhouse, Bowen, Butterworth, Linighan, Townsend (Crook), Gordon, Fleck (3), Allen (4), Phelan, Putney (1).

HONOURS

FA Premier League: Best season: 3rd 1992–93.

Football League – Division 1: ***Champions*** 2003–04;
FL C: *Runners-up* 2010–11;
Division 2: *Champions* 1971–72, 1985–86;
FL 1: *Champions* 2009–10;
Division 3 (S): *Champions* 1933–34; ***Runners-up*** 1950–51;
Division 3: *Runners-up* 1959–60.

FA Cup: Semi-finals 1959, 1989, 1992.

Football League Cup: *Winners* 1962, 1985; ***Runners-up*** 1973, 1975.

European Competitions
UEFA Cup: 1993–94.

sky SPORTS FACT FILE

West Bromwich-born centre-forward Tommy Hunt had brief spells with both Birmingham and Wolverhampton Wanderers without managing to break into either of their first teams. It all changed when joining Norwich City where the goals flowed freely in League and Cup ties.

Record Defeat: 2–10 v Swindon T, Southern League, 5 September 1908.

Most League Points (2 for a win): 64, Division 3 (S), 1950–51.

Most League Points (3 for a win): 95, FL 1, 2009–10.

Most League Goals: 99, Division 3 (S), 1952–53.

Highest League Scorer in Season: Ralph Hunt, 31, Division 3 (S), 1955–56.

Most League Goals in Total Aggregate: Johnny Gavin, 122, 1945–54, 1955–58.

Most League Goals in One Match: 5, Tommy Hunt v Coventry C, Division 3 (S), 15 March 1930; 5, Roy Hollis v Walsall, Division 3 (S), 29 December 1951.

Most Capped Player: Mark Bowen, 35 (41), Wales.

Most League Appearances: Ron Ashman, 592, 1947–64.

Youngest League Player: Ryan Jarvis, 16 years 282 days v Walsall, 19 April 2003.

Record Transfer Fee Received: £7,250,000 from West Ham U for Dean Ashton, January 2006.

Record Transfer Fee Paid: £3,800,000 to Crewe Alex for Dean Ashton, January 2005 (including sell-on).

Football League Record: 1920 Original Member of Division 3; 1921 Division 3 (S): 1934–39 Division 2; 1946–58 Division 3 (S); 1958–60 Division 3; 1960–72 Division 2; 1972–74 Division 1; 1974–75 Division 2; 1975–81 Division 1; 1981–82 Division 2; 1982–85 Division 1; 1985–86 Division 2; 1986–92 Division 1; 1992–95 FA Premier League; 1995–2004 Division 1; 2004–05 FA Premier League; 2005–09 FL C; 2009–10 FL 1; 2010–11 FL C; 2011– FA Premier League.

LATEST SEQUENCES

Longest Sequence of League Wins: 10, 23.11.1985 – 25.1.1986.

Longest Sequence of League Defeats: 7, 1.4.1995 – 6.5.1995.

Longest Sequence of League Draws: 7, 15.1.1994 – 26.2.1994.

Longest Sequence of Unbeaten League Matches: 20, 31.8.1950 – 30.12.1950.

Longest Sequence Without a League Win: 25, 22.9.1956 – 23.2.1957.

Successive Scoring Runs: 25 from 31.8.1963.

Successive Non-scoring Runs: 5 from 21.2.1925.

MANAGERS

John Bowman 1905–07
James McEwen 1907–08
Arthur Turner 1909–10
Bert Stansfield 1910–15
Major Frank Buckley 1919–20
Charles O'Hagan 1920–21
Albert Gosnell 1921–26
Bert Stansfield 1926
Cecil Potter 1926–29
James Kerr 1929–33
Tom Parker 1933–37
Bob Young 1937–39
Jimmy Jewell 1939
Bob Young 1939–45
Duggie Lochhead 1945–46
Cyril Spiers 1946–47
Duggie Lochhead 1947–50
Norman Low 1950–55
Tom Parker 1955–57
Archie Macaulay 1957–61
Willie Reid 1961–62
George Swindin 1962
Ron Ashman 1962–66
Lol Morgan 1966–69
Ron Saunders 1969–73
John Bond 1973–80
Ken Brown 1980–87
Dave Stringer 1987–92
Mike Walker 1992–94
John Deehan 1994–95
Martin O'Neill 1995
Gary Megson 1995–96
Mike Walker 1996–98
Bruce Rioch 1998–2000
Bryan Hamilton 2000
Nigel Worthington 2000–06
Peter Grant 2006–07
Glenn Roeder 2007–09
Bryan Gunn 2009
Paul Lambert 2009–12
Chris Hughton June 2012–

TEN YEAR LEAGUE RECORD

		P	*W*	*D*	*L*	*F*	*A*	*Pts*	*Pos*
2002-03	Div 1	46	19	12	15	60	49	69	8
2003-04	Div 1	46	28	10	8	79	39	94	1
2004-05	PR Lge	38	7	12	19	42	77	33	19
2005-06	FL C	46	18	8	20	56	65	62	9
2006-07	FL C	46	16	9	21	56	71	57	16
2007-08	FL C	46	15	10	21	49	59	55	17
2008-09	FL C	46	12	10	24	57	70	46	22
2009-10	FL 1	46	29	8	9	89	47	95	1
2010-11	FL C	46	23	15	8	83	58	84	2
2011-12	PR Lge	38	12	11	15	52	66	47	12

DID YOU KNOW

Curtis "Tommy" Booth, an inside-forward signed from Newcastle United in 1920, had three seasons with Norwich City and became a successful coach in Germany (one of only two Brits at the time), France, Turkey, Holland and Egypt, until retiring to live permanently in Holland.

NORWICH CITY 2011–12 LEAGUE RECORD

Match No.	Date	Venue	Opponents	Result	H/T Score	Lg Pos.	Goalscorers	Attendance
1	Aug 13	A	Wigan Ath	D 1-1	1-1	—	Hoolahan [45]	17,454
2	21	H	Stoke C	D 1-1	1-0	10	De Laet [37]	26,272
3	27	A	Chelsea	L 1-3	0-1	14	Holt [63]	41,765
4	Sept 11	H	WBA	L 0-1	0-1	17		26,158
5	17	A	Bolton W	W 2-1	2-0	13	Pilkington [37], Johnson, B [42]	21,223
6	26	H	Sunderland	W 2-1	1-0	—	Barnett [31], Morison [48]	26,107
7	Oct 1	A	Manchester U	L 0-2	0-0	9		75,514
8	15	H	Swansea C	W 3-1	2-1	9	Pilkington 2 [1, 63], Martin, R [10]	26,567
9	22	A	Liverpool	D 1-1	0-1	8	Holt [60]	44,931
10	29	H	Blackburn R	D 3-3	0-1	8	Morison [53], Johnson, B [82], Holt (pen) [90]	26,440
11	Nov 5	A	Aston Villa	L 2-3	1-1	9	Pilkington [25], Morison [77]	35,290
12	19	H	Arsenal	L 1-2	1-1	11	Morison [16]	26,801
13	26	H	QPR	W 2-1	1-0	10	Martin, R [15], Holt [73]	26,781
14	Dec 3	A	Manchester C	L 1-5	0-1	11	Morison [81]	47,201
15	10	H	Newcastle U	W 4-2	1-1	10	Hoolahan [39], Holt 2 [59, 82], Morison [63]	26,816
16	17	A	Everton	D 1-1	1-0	9	Holt [28]	31,004
17	20	A	Wolverhampton W	D 2-2	1-1	—	Surman [12], Jackson [76]	27,067
18	27	H	Tottenham H	L 0-2	0-0	—		26,807
19	31	H	Fulham	D 1-1	0-1	10	Jackson [90]	26,406
20	Jan 2	A	QPR	W 2-1	1-1	—	Pilkington [42], Morison [83]	18,033
21	14	A	WBA	W 2-1	1-0	9	Surman [43], Morison [79]	22,474
22	21	H	Chelsea	D 0-0	0-0	9		26,792
23	Feb 1	A	Sunderland	L 0-3	0-2	—		34,476
24	4	H	Bolton W	W 2-0	0-0	9	Surman [70], Pilkington [85]	26,358
25	11	A	Swansea C	W 3-2	0-1	8	Holt 2 [47, 63], Pilkington [51]	19,927
26	26	H	Manchester U	L 1-2	0-1	8	Holt [83]	26,811
27	Mar 3	A	Stoke C	L 0-1	0-0	11		27,483
28	11	H	Wigan Ath	D 1-1	1-0	12	Hoolahan [10]	26,653
29	18	A	Newcastle U	L 0-1	0-1	—		47,833
30	24	H	Wolverhampton W	W 2-1	2-1	11	Holt 2 (1 pen) [26, 45 (p)]	26,752
31	31	A	Fulham	L 1-2	0-2	12	Wilbraham [77]	25,700
32	Apr 7	H	Everton	D 2-2	1-1	12	Howson [39], Holt [76]	26,554
33	9	A	Tottenham H	W 2-1	1-1	—	Pilkington [13], Bennett, E [66]	36,126
34	14	H	Manchester C	L 1-6	0-2	11	Surman [51]	26,812
35	21	A	Blackburn R	L 0-2	0-1	13		23,218
36	28	H	Liverpool	L 0-3	0-2	13		26,819
37	May 5	A	Arsenal	D 3-3	2-1	13	Hoolahan [12], Holt [27], Morison [85]	60,092
38	13	H	Aston Villa	W 2-0	2-0	12	Holt [8], Jackson [21]	26,803

Final League Position: 12

GOALSCORERS

League (52): Holt 15 (2 pens), Morison 9, Pilkington 8, Hoolahan 4, Surman 4, Jackson 3, Johnson, B 2, Martin, R 2, Barnett 1, Bennett, E 1, De Laet 1, Howson 1, Wilbraham 1.
Carling Cup (0).
FA Cup (7): Holt 2, Jackson 2, Hoolahan 1, Morison 1, Surman 1.

Ruddy J 37	Martin R 30 + 3	Tierney M 17	Crofts A 13 + 11	De Laet R 6	Whitbread Z 18	Surman A 21 + 4	Fox D 23 + 5	Morison S 22 + 12	Holt G 24 + 12	Hoolahan W 25 + 8	Barnett L 13 + 4	Bennett E 22 + 11	Pilkington A 23 + 7	Naughton K 29 + 3	Johnson B 25 + 3	Martin C 3 + 1	Ayala D 6 + 1	Jackson S 10 + 12	Rudd D 1 + 1	Vaughan J 1 + 4	Wilbraham A 2 + 9	Drury A 12	Lappin S 4	Ward E 12	Howson J 11	Bennett R 8	*Match No.*
1	2	3	4	5	6^{1}	7^{2}	8	9^{3}	10	11	12	13	14														1
1		3	4	5		13			10		6■	8^{2}	11^{1}	2	7	9^{3}	12	14									2
1■		11	4	5	6^{1}			13	10	7^{2}	2		12	3	8	9^{6}			15								3
		3	4	5		7^{1}		13	10^{2}	12	6	11		2	8	9^{3}			1	14							4
1	5	3	14				8	9^{1}	12	11^{3}	6	7	10^{2}	2	4					13							5
1	5	3	14				8	9^{2}	13	11	6	7^{3}	10^{1}	2	4					12							6
1	5	3	12				8^{2}	9		7^{3}	6	11^{1}	10	2	4	14		13									7
1	5	3	13				8	9^{1}	12	11^{2}	6	7	10	2	4												8
1	5	3	13				8	9	12	11	6	7^{1}	10^{2}	2	4												9
1	5	3	13				8^{2}	9	12	11	6	7^{1}	10^{3}	2	4			14									10
1	5	3	12				13	9	10	11^{3}	6	7^{2}	8	2	4^{1}			14									11
1	5	3	7				8^{1}	9	13	11^{2}	6	12	10^{3}	2	4			14									12
1	2	3	7	5^{1}		11		9	13	14	6		8^{2}	12	4			10^{3}									13
1	5	3	7			11	14	9	12	13	6	8^{1}	10^{2}	2	4^{3}												14
1	5	3	7		6^{2}	8^{1}	4	9	10	11^{3}	13			2	12			14									15
1	5	3	4		6	7	8	9^{2}	10	11^{1}				2	12						13						16
1	5	3	4		6	7	8^{1}	9	10^{2}	11^{3}		14		2	12			13									17
1	5		4^{3}	2^{1}	6	7	8	9	10	11	12	14	13									3^{2}					18
1	2				6	7	8^{1}	9^{2}	12	11		14	10^{3}	3	4		5	13									19
1	2				6		14	12	10^{3}	13		7	8		4		5	9				3^{1}	11^{2}				20
1	2		13		6	7	14	9	12	11			8^{3}	3	4^{2}		5	10^{1}									21
1	2		12		6	11^{3}	7^{1}	9^{2}	10			14	8	3	4		5	13									22
1	2		8		6	7		9	10^{3}	11^{1}		13	12	3	4^{2}		5				14						23
1	12				6^{2}	7	4	14	10	11		13	8	2			5^{1}	9^{3}				3					24
1	2					7	6	14	10	13	12	4^{2}	8	3				9^{3}				11^{1}		5			25
1					6	11	8		10	12		14	7^{3}	2	4^{2}			9^{1}			13	3		5			26
1	2				6	11	14		10			9	7^{1}	3	4^{3}			12			13			5	8^{2}		27
1			4^{2}		6	7^{3}	8	12	10^{1}	11		13	14	2				9				3		5			28
1	14				6	7	11	9	12	13		10	8^{3}	2								3^{2}		5	4^{1}		29
1	2				6	13	8	14	10■	11		7^{2}		12				9^{3}					3^{1}	5	4		30
1	2				6^{1}	7	8^{3}	9^{2}		10		14		3				12			13			5	11	4	31
1	2		14			7	11^{1}		9	10^{3}		8		13							12	3^{2}		6	4	5	32
1	2					13		12	9^{1}			7	11^{2}		4			14			10^{3}	3		6	8	5	33
1	2					12		14	9	13		7	11^{2}		4^{1}						10^{3}	3		6	8	5	34
1	2					7		12	10^{3}	11^{1}		8	13							9^{2}	14	3		6	4	5	35
1	12						11^{2}	9^{3}	14			7	10	2	8					13		3^{1}		6	4	5	36
1	5							12	10^{3}	11^{2}		7	13	2	4			9^{1}			14		3		8	6	37
1	5		14					12	10^{1}	11		7		2	4			9^{2}			13		3		8^{3}	6	38

FA Cup

Third Round	Burnley	(h)	4-1
Fourth Round	WBA	(a)	2-1
Fifth Round	Leicester C	(h)	1-2

Carling Cup

First Round	Milton Keynes D	(h)	0-4

NOTTINGHAM FOREST FL Championship

FOUNDATION

One of the oldest football clubs in the world, Nottingham Forest was formed at a meeting in the Clinton Arms in 1865. Known originally as the Forest Football Club, the game which first drew the founders together was 'shinney', a form of hockey. When they determined to change to football in 1865, one of their first moves was to buy a set of red caps to wear on the field.

The City Ground, Nottingham NG2 5FJ.

Telephone: (0115) 982 4444.

Fax: (0115) 982 4455.

Ticket Office: (0871) 226 1980.

Website: www.nottinghamforest.co.uk

Email: info@nottinghamforest.co.uk

Ground Capacity: 30,576.

Record Attendance: 49,946 v Manchester U, Division 1, 28 October 1967.

Pitch Measurements: 112yd × 76yd.

Chairman: Frank Clark.

Chief Executive: Mark Arthur.

Manager: TBC.

Assistant Manager: Rob Kelly.

Physios: Steve Devine, Andy Hunt.

Colours: Red shirt with white trim, white shorts, red stockings.

Year Formed: 1865.

Turned Professional: 1889.

Previous Name: Forest Football Club.

Club Nickname: 'Reds'.

Grounds: 1865, Forest Racecourse; 1879, The Meadows; 1880, Trent Bridge Cricket Ground; 1882, Parkside, Lenton; 1885, Gregory, Lenton; 1890, Town Ground; 1898, City Ground.

First Football League Game: 3 September 1892, Division 1, v Everton (a) D 2–2 – Brown; Earp, Scott; Hamilton, Albert Smith, McCracken; McCallum, 'Tich' Smith, Higgins (2), Pike, McInnes.

Record League Victory: 12–0 v Leicester Fosse, Division 1, 12 April 1909 – Iremonger; Dudley, Maltby; Hughes (1), Needham, Armstrong; Hooper (3), Marrison, West (3), Morris (2), Spouncer (3 incl. 1p).

Record Cup Victory: 14–0 v Clapton (away), FA Cup 1st rd, 17 January 1891 – Brown; Earp, Scott; Albert Smith, Russell, Jeacock; McCallum (2), 'Tich' Smith (1), Higgins (5), Lindley (4), Shaw (2).

Record Defeat: 1–9 v Blackburn R, Division 2, 10 April 1937.

Most League Points (2 for a win): 70, Division 3 (S), 1950–51.

HONOURS

Football League – Division 1: ***Champions*** 1977–78, 1997–98; ***Runners-up*** 1966–67, 1978–79, 1993–94; **FL 1:** ***Runners-up*** 2007–08; **Division 2:** ***Champions*** 1906–07, 1921–22; ***Runners-up*** 1956–57; **Division 3 (S):** ***Champions*** 1950–51.

FA Cup: ***Winners*** 1898, 1959; ***Runners-up*** 1991.

Football League Cup: ***Winners*** 1978, 1979, 1989, 1990; ***Runners-up*** 1980, 1992.

Anglo-Scottish Cup: ***Winners*** 1977.

Simod Cup: ***Winners*** 1989.

Zenith Data Systems Cup: ***Winners***: 1992.

European Competitions
European Cup: 1978–79 (*winners*), 1979–80 (*winners*), 1980–81.
European Fairs Cup: 1961–62, 1967–68. **UEFA Cup:** 1983–84, 1984–85, 1995–96. **Super Cup:** 1979 (*winners*), 1980.
World Club Championship: 1980.

sky SPORTS FACT FILE

John Brodie had four separate spells playing for Kilmarnock, a short stint at Burnley and in 1893–94 had a remarkable period with Nottingham Forest leading the attack and scoring eight goals in only 13 League and Cup games. Moreover Forest won all the games in which he scored.

Most League Points (3 for a win): 94, Division 1, 1997–98.

Most League Goals: 110, Division 3 (S), 1950–51.

Highest League Scorer in Season: Wally Ardron, 36, Division 3 (S), 1950–51.

Most League Goals in Total Aggregate: Grenville Morris, 199, 1898–1913.

Most League Goals in One Match: 4, Enoch West v Sunderland, Division 1, 9 November 1907; 4, Tommy Gibson v Burnley, Division 2, 25 January 1913; 4, Tom Peacock v Port Vale, Division 2, 23 December 1933; 4, Tom Peacock v Barnsley, Division 2, 9 November 1935; 4, Tom Peacock v Port Vale, Division 2, 23 November 1935; 4, Tom Peacock v Doncaster R, Division 2, 26 December 1935; 4, Tommy Capel v Gillingham, Division 3 (S), 18 November 1950; 4, Wally Ardron v Hull C, Division 2, 26 December 1952; 4, Tommy Wilson v Barnsley, Division 2, 9 February 1957; 4, Peter Withe v Ipswich T, Division 1, 4 October 1977; 4, Marlon Harewood v Stoke C, Division 1, 22 February 2003.

Most Capped Player: Stuart Pearce, 76 (78), England.

Most League Appearances: Bob McKinlay, 614, 1951–70.

Youngest League Player: Craig Westcarr, 16 years 257 days v Burnley, 13 October 2001.

Record Transfer Fee Received: £8,500,000 from Liverpool for Stan Collymore, June 1995.

Record Transfer Fee Paid: £3,500,000 to Celtic for Pierre van Hooijdonk, March 1997.

Football League Record: 1892 Elected to Division 1; 1906–07 Division 2; 1907–11 Division 1; 1911–22 Division 2; 1922–25 Division 1; 1925–49 Division 2; 1949–51 Division 3 (S); 1951–57 Division 2; 1957–72 Division 1; 1972–77 Division 2; 1977–92 Division 1; 1992–93 FA Premier League; 1993–94 Division 1; 1994–97 FA Premier League; 1997–98 Division 1; 1998–99 FA Premier League; 1999–2004 Division 1; 2004–05 FL C; 2005–08 FL 1; 2008– FL C.

MANAGERS

Harry Radford 1889–97
(Secretary-Manager)
Harry Haslam 1897–1909
(Secretary-Manager)
Fred Earp 1909–12
Bob Masters 1912–25
John Baynes 1925–29
Stan Hardy 1930–31
Noel Watson 1931–36
Harold Wightman 1936–39
Billy Walker 1939–60
Andy Beattie 1960–63
Johnny Carey 1963–68
Matt Gillies 1969–72
Dave Mackay 1972
Allan Brown 1973–75
Brian Clough 1975–93
Frank Clark 1993–96
Stuart Pearce 1996–97
Dave Bassett 1997–99
(previously General Manager)
Ron Atkinson 1999
David Platt 1999–2001
Paul Hart 2001–04
Joe Kinnear 2004
Gary Megson 2005–06
Colin Calderwood 2006–08
Billy Davies 2009–11
Steve McClaren 2011
Steve Cotterill 2011–12

LATEST SEQUENCES

Longest Sequence of League Wins: 7, 9.5.1979 – 1.9.1979.

Longest Sequence of League Defeats: 14, 21.3.1913 – 27.9.1913.

Longest Sequence of League Draws: 7, 29.4.1978 – 2.9.1978.

Longest Sequence of Unbeaten League Matches: 42, 26.11.1977 – 25.11.1978.

Longest Sequence Without a League Win: 19, 8.9.1998 – 16.1.1999.

Successive Scoring Runs: 22 from 28.3.1931.

Successive Non-scoring Runs: 7 from 13.12.2003.

TEN YEAR LEAGUE RECORD

		P	W	D	L	F	A	Pts	Pos
2002-03	Div 1	46	20	14	12	82	50	74	6
2003-04	Div 1	46	15	15	16	61	58	60	14
2004-05	FL C	46	9	17	20	42	66	44	23
2005-06	FL 1	46	19	12	15	67	52	69	7
2006-07	FL 1	46	23	13	10	65	41	82	4
2007-08	FL 1	46	22	16	8	64	32	82	2
2008-09	FL C	46	13	14	19	50	65	53	19
2009-10	FL C	46	22	13	11	65	40	79	3
2010-11	FL C	46	20	15	11	69	50	75	6
2011-12	FL C	46	14	8	24	48	63	50	19

DID YOU KNOW ?

On 2 January 2012, Nottingham Forest ended 10 hours 35 minutes without a win or a goal when they won 3-1 at Ipswich Town. Marcus Tudgay ended the drought and he had been their last scorer in the 90th minute on 19 November when Forest had also defeated Ipswich 3-2!

NOTTINGHAM FOREST 2011–12 LEAGUE RECORD

Match No.	Date	Venue	Opponents	Result		H/T Score	Lg Pos.	Goalscorers	Attendance
1	Aug 6	H	Barnsley	D	0-0	0-0	—		22,951
2	13	A	Millwall	L	0-2	0-1	20		12,010
3	16	A	Doncaster R	W	1-0	1-0	—	Gunter [31]	9464
4	20	H	Leicester C	D	2-2	0-2	12	McGugan (pen) [79], Boateng [90]	24,426
5	28	H	West Ham U	L	1-4	0-3	18	Findley [70]	21,379
6	Sept 10	A	Southampton	L	2-3	2-2	21	Derbyshire [7], Majewski [42]	24,784
7	17	H	Derby Co	L	1-2	1-1	22	Reid (pen) [5]	27,356
8	24	A	Watford	W	1-0	0-0	18	Miller [61]	11,437
9	27	A	Burnley	L	1-5	0-4	—	Miller [59]	13,265
10	Oct 2	H	Birmingham C	L	1-3	1-0	21	Miller [35]	20,556
11	15	A	Coventry C	L	0-1	0-0	23		15,712
12	18	H	Middlesbrough	W	2-0	1-0	—	Tudgay [35], McGugan [55]	20,630
13	22	A	Blackpool	W	2-1	1-1	19	Morgan [39], Majewski [76]	13,520
14	29	H	Hull C	L	0-1	0-0	20		22,841
15	Nov 1	H	Reading	W	1-0	0-0	—	Tudgay [75]	18,506
16	5	A	Portsmouth	L	0-3	0-1	20		14,207
17	19	H	Ipswich T	W	3-2	1-1	17	Findley [42], Lynch [84], Tudgay [90]	21,143
18	26	A	Cardiff C	L	0-1	0-0	20		22,556
19	29	H	Leeds U	L	0-4	0-2	—		23,577
20	Dec 3	A	Brighton & HA	L	0-1	0-0	22		20,358
21	10	H	Crystal Palace	L	0-1	0-0	22		21,405
22	17	A	Bristol C	D	0-0	0-0	22		13,121
23	26	H	Peterborough U	L	0-1	0-1	22		24,376
24	31	H	Cardiff C	L	0-1	0-0	22		19,750
25	Jan 2	A	Ipswich T	W	3-1	2-0	22	Tudgay 2 [5, 78], McCleary [26]	18,964
26	14	H	Southampton	L	0-3	0-1	22		20,221
27	21	A	West Ham U	L	1-2	0-1	22	McGugan [90]	31,718
28	31	H	Burnley	L	0-2	0-1	—		23,147
29	Feb 11	H	Watford	D	1-1	1-1	22	McCleary [19]	12,712
30	14	A	Middlesbrough	L	1-2	0-1	—	Lynch [66]	14,799
31	18	H	Coventry C	W	2-0	0-0	21	McCleary [74], Findley [86]	21,588
32	25	A	Birmingham C	W	2-1	1-0	20	Blackstock 2 [29, 63]	19,166
33	Mar 3	A	Barnsley	D	1-1	1-0	20	McCleary [33]	10,550
34	6	H	Doncaster R	L	1-2	0-1	—	Blackstock [63]	18,521
35	10	H	Millwall	W	3-1	2-0	20	McCleary [25], Higginbotham [38], Reid [80]	19,413
36	13	A	Derby Co	L	0-1	0-0	—		33,010
37	20	A	Leeds U	W	7-3	2-1	—	Guedioura [8], McCleary 4 [45, 56, 60, 71], Blackstock 2 [52, 81]	21,367
38	24	H	Brighton & HA	D	1-1	0-0	20	Lynch [90]	21,249
39	27	A	Leicester C	D	0-0	0-0	—		23,412
40	31	A	Crystal Palace	W	3-0	0-0	19	Majewski 3 [53, 72, 82]	14,928
41	Apr 7	H	Bristol C	L	0-1	0-0	20		22,851
42	9	A	Peterborough U	W	1-0	1-0	19	Blackstock [38]	11,631
43	14	H	Blackpool	D	0-0	0-0	19		24,078
44	17	A	Reading	L	0-1	0-0	—		22,899
45	21	A	Hull C	L	1-2	0-0	20	Majewski [90]	20,786
46	28	H	Portsmouth	W	2-0	0-0	19	Blackstock 2 [70, 89]	23,625

Final League Position: 19

GOALSCORERS

League (48): McCleary 9, Blackstock 8, Majewski 6, Tudgay 5, Findley 3, Lynch 3, McGugan 3 (1 pen), Miller 3, Reid 2 (1 pen), Boateng 1, Derbyshire 1, Guedioura 1, Gunter 1, Higginbotham 1, Morgan 1.
Carling Cup (10): Findley 3, McGugan 2 (1 pen), Derbyshire 1, Majewski 1, Miller 1, Morgan 1, Tudgay 1.
FA Cup (0).

Camp L 46	Gunter C 44+2	Cohen C 7	Chambers L 43	Morgan W 22	Boateng G 5	Anderson P 10+7	Greening J 24+7	McGoldrick D 3+6	McGugan L 27+8	Reid A 22+17	Garner J 1+1	Majewski R 23+5	Findley R 10+13	Tudgay M 24+10	Moloney B 3+5	Derbyshire M 7+8	Miller I 13+8	Lynch J 28+7	Moussi G 33+1	Hill C 5	Cunningham G 25+2	McCleary G 21+1	Blackstock D 16+6	Bamford P —+2	Harewood M 4	Lascelles J 1	Guedioura A 19	Elokobi G 8+4	Higginbotham D 5+1	Wootton S 7+6	*Match No.*
1	2	3	4	5	6	7	8	9^1	10	11^2	12	13																			1
1	2	3	4	5	6		8		7	11^2	9^1	13	10	12																	2
1	2	7	4	5			8	9^2		11^3		6	12		3	10^1	13	14													3
1	2	11	4	5	6		8	9^1	7			14	13		3^3	10^2	12														4
1	2	3	4	5	6^1		8		11^3	13		7^2	10			14	9	12													5
1	2	3	4	5			8^3	12	14	11		7				10	9^1	13	6^2												6
1	2	3^1	4	5			8^2		14	11^3		6	13			10	9	12	7												7
1	2		4	5			8		7^2	13			10^1	14		12	9^3	11	6	3											8
1	2^1		4	5			8		14	7^2		13	12			10^3	9	3	6	11											9
1	14		4	5			12		8			6^1	13	11		10	9^2	2	7	3^3											10
1	2		4	5			7^2		8	14		13	12	11^3		10^1	9		6	3											11
1	2		4	5			13		8^2			7^3	12	10		14	9^1	3	6	11											12
1	2		4	5			11^3		8	13		7		10	14	12^2	9^1	3	6■												13
1	2		4	5			11^2		8	13		6	12	10		14	9^1	7			3^3										14
1	2		4	5					8	12		6^1	9^2	10	13			7	11		3										15
1	2		4	5			11	13	8^1	12			9^3	10	14			7^2	6		3										16
1	2^1		4	5		12	7^2	14	8	13			9^3	10				3	6		11										17
1	2^1		4	5		12	11	14	8^2	13			9^3	10				7	6		3										18
1	13		4	5		7		14	8^3	11■			9^1	10			12	2	6		3^2										19
1	2		4	5		7^2	11	12				8		9	13				6		3	10^1									20
1	2		4	5^3		7^1	11		12	14		8^2		10					6		3	9	13								21
1	2		4			7	11		8			6		10	12			5^1			3		9								22
1	2		4			7^1	11		8	13		6^2		9^3		14			5		3	12	10								23
1	2		4				11^3		8	14			9^1	10		12^2		5	6		3	7		13							24
1	2		4		6		11		8	10^2				9		12			5		3	7^1		13							25
1	2		4■			12	11		8^1				13	10^3				5	6		3	7	14		9^2						26
1	2			5		12	11^2		8					10			14	6	4		3^1	7	13		9^3						27
1	2					7			10^1	14				12	3^3		9^2	5	4			8	13			6	11				28
1	2		4							14			12				9^1		6			11	13		10^2		7	3	5	8^3	29
1	2		4							14			12				9^1	13	6			11			10^2		8	3	5	7^3	30
1	2		4				14			11			13	10^2					6			9^3	12				8	3	5	7^1	31
1	2		4			13				11^3				9				12	6			7^2	10				8	3	5^1	14	32
1	2					12	8		14	11^1				9				5			13	7^3	10^2				4	3		6	33
1	2		4						14	12			9^3					5	6		13	11	10				8	3^2		7^1	34
1	2		4							11^2				9^1			13	14	6		3	7	10^3				8		5	12	35
1	2		4				12			11^3				9■			13	5	6		3	7	10^2				8^1			14	36
1	2		4						14	11		9^2					13	5	6^3		3	7	10^1				8			12	37
1	2		4						14	11		9^1		12			13	5	6		3^3	7^2	10				8				38
1	2		4							11^2		9^1		12				5	6		3		10				8		13	7	39
1	2		4							11^3		9		13				5	6		3	7^1	10^2				8	14		12	40
1	2		4							11		9		12				5	6^1		3	7	10				8				41
1	2		4						8^2	11^1		9		14				5			3	7■	10^3				6	12		13	42
1	2		4			7	13		8^2	11^1		9^3		14				5			3		10				6	12			43
1	2		4			7	13		8^2	12		9^3		14				5					10				6	3		11^1	44
1	2		4			7^2	13		6	11		10	12	9^1							5						8	3			45
1	2		4			12			8^2	11		9^1						5	13		3	7	10				6^3	14			46

FA Cup

Third Round	Leicester C	(h)	0-0
		(a)	0-4

Carling Cup

First Round	Notts Co	(h)	3-3
Second Round	Wycombe W	(a)	4-1
Third Round	Newcastle U	(h)	3-4

NOTTS COUNTY FL Championship 1

FOUNDATION

According to the official history of Notts County 'the true date of Notts' foundation has to be the meeting at the George Hotel on 7 December 1864'. However, there is documented evidence of continuous play from 1862, when club members played organised matches amongst themselves in The Park in Nottingham.

Meadow Lane Stadium, Meadow Lane, Nottingham NG2 3HJ.

Telephone: (0115) 952 9000.

Fax: (0115) 955 3994.

Ticket Office: (0115) 955 7204.

Website: www.nottscountyfc.co.uk

Email: office@nottscountyfc.co.uk

Ground Capacity: 20,300.

Record Attendance: 47,310 v York C, FA Cup 6th rd, 12 March 1955.

Pitch Measurements: 113yd × 72yd.

Executive Chairman: Ray Trew.

Chief Executive: James Rodwell.

Manager: Keith Curle.

Assistant Manager: Colin Lee.

Physio: John Wilson.

Colours: Black and white striped shirts, black shorts, black stockings.

HONOURS

Football League – Division 1: Best season: 3rd, 1890–91, 1900–01; **Division 2: *Champions*** 1896–97, 1913–14, 1922–23; ***Runners-up*** 1894–95, 1980–81; **Division 3 (S): *Champions*** 1930–31, 1949–50; ***Runners-up*** 1936–37; **Division 3: *Champions*** 1997–98; ***Runners-up*** 1972–73; **Division 4: *Champions*** 1970–71; ***Runners-up*** 1959–60; **FL 2: *Champions*** 2009–10.

FA Cup: *Winners* 1894; ***Runners-up*** 1891.

Football League Cup: Best season: 5th rd, 1964, 1973, 1976.

Anglo-Italian Cup: *Winners* 1995; ***Runners-up*** 1994.

Year Formed: 1862* (*see Foundation*). ***Turned Professional:*** 1885.

Club Nickname: 'Magpies'.

Grounds: 1862, The Park; 1864, The Meadows; 1877, Beeston Cricket Ground; 1880, Castle Ground; 1883, Trent Bridge; 1910, Meadow Lane.

First Football League Game: 15 September 1888, Football League, v Everton (a) L 1–2 – Holland; Guttridge, McLean; Brown, Warburton, Shelton; Hodder, Harker, Jardine, Albert Moore (1), Wardle.

Record League Victory: 11–1 v Newport Co, Division 3 (S), 15 January 1949 – Smith; Southwell, Purvis; Gannon, Baxter, Adamson; Houghton (1), Sewell (4), Lawton (4), Pimbley, Johnston (2).

Record Cup Victory: 15–0 v Rotherham T (at Trent Bridge), FA Cup 1st rd, 24 October 1885 – Sherwin; Snook, Henry Thomas Moore; Dobson (1), Emmett (1), Chapman; Gunn (1), Albert Moore (2), Jackson (3), Daft (2), Cursham (4), (1 og).

Record Defeat: 1–9 v Blackburn R, Division 1, 16 November 1889. 1–9 v Aston Villa, Division 1, 29 September 1888. 1–9 v Portsmouth, Division 2, 9 April 1927.

Most League Points (2 for a win): 69, Division 4, 1970–71.

sky SPORTS FACT FILE

In 1903 Juventus adopted the black and white kit design of Notts County. On 7 September 2011, the Italian club invited Notts to an inaugural match to open their new Juventus Arena. A near 41,000 capacity crowd saw Notts draw 1-1 with a Lee Hughes equaliser in the 87th minute.

Most League Points (3 for a win): 99, Division 3, 1997–98.

Most League Goals: 107, Division 4, 1959–60.

Highest League Scorer in Season: Tom Keetley, 39, Division 3 (S), 1930–31.

Most League Goals in Total Aggregate: Les Bradd, 125, 1967–78.

Most League Goals in One Match: 5, Robert Jardine v Burnley, Division 1, 27 October 1888; 5, Daniel Bruce v Port Vale, Division 2, 26 February 1895; 5, Bertie Mills v Barnsley, Division 2, 19 November 1927.

Most Capped Player: Kevin Wilson, 15 (42), Northern Ireland.

Most League Appearances: Albert Iremonger, 564, 1904–26.

Youngest League Player: Tony Bircumshaw, 16 years 54 days v Brentford, 3 April 1961.

Record Transfer Fee Received: £2,500,000 from Derby Co for Craig Short, September 1992.

Record Transfer Fee Paid: £800,000 to Manchester C for Kasper Schmeichel, July 2009.

Football League Record: 1888 Founder Member of the Football League; 1893–97 Division 2; 1897–1913 Division 1; 1913–14 Division 2; 1914–20 Division 1; 1920–23 Division 2; 1923–26 Division 1; 1926–30 Division 2; 1930–31 Division 3 (S); 1931–35 Division 2; 1935–50 Division 3 (S); 1950–58 Division 2; 1958–59 Division 3; 1959–60 Division 4; 1960–64 Division 3; 1964–71 Division 4; 1971–73 Division 3; 1973–81 Division 2; 1981–84 Division 1; 1984–85 Division 2; 1985–90 Division 3; 1990–91 Division 2; 1991–95 Division 1; 1995–97 Division 2; 1997–98 Division 3; 1998–2004 Division 2; 2004–10 FL 2; 2010– FL 1.

LATEST SEQUENCES

Longest Sequence of League Wins: 10, 3.12.1997 – 31.1.1998.

Longest Sequence of League Defeats: 7, 3.9.1983 – 16.10.1983.

Longest Sequence of League Draws: 6, 16.8.2008 – 20.9.2008.

Longest Sequence of Unbeaten League Matches: 19, 26.4.1930 – 6.12.1930.

Longest Sequence Without a League Win: 20, 3.12.1996 – 31.3.1997.

Successive Scoring Runs: 35 from 26.4.1930.

Successive Non-scoring Runs: 9 from 15.3.2011 – 16.4.2011.

MANAGERS

Edwin Browne 1883–93
Tom Featherstone 1893
Tom Harris 1893–1913
Albert Fisher 1913–27
Horace Henshall 1927–34
Charlie Jones 1934
David Pratt 1935
Percy Smith 1935–36
Jimmy McMullan 1936–37
Harry Parkes 1938–39
Tony Towers 1939–42
Frank Womack 1942–43
Major Frank Buckley 1944–46
Arthur Stollery 1946–49
Eric Houghton 1949–53
George Poyser 1953–57
Tommy Lawton 1957–58
Frank Hill 1958–61
Tim Coleman 1961–63
Eddie Lowe 1963–65
Tim Coleman 1965–66
Jack Burkitt 1966–67
Andy Beattie *(General Manager)* 1967
Billy Gray 1967–68
Jack Wheeler (*Caretaker Manager*) 1968–69
Jimmy Sirrel 1969–75
Ron Fenton 1975–77
Jimmy Sirrel 1978–82 *(continued as General Manager to 1984)*
Howard Wilkinson 1982–83
Larry Lloyd 1983–84
Richie Barker 1984–85
Jimmy Sirrel 1985–87
John Barnwell 1987–88
Neil Warnock 1989–93
Mick Walker 1993–94
Russell Slade 1994–95
Howard Kendall 1995
Colin Murphy 1995–96 *(General Manager)*
Steve Thompson 1995–96
Sam Allardyce 1997–99
Gary Brazil 1999–2000
Jocky Scott 2000–01
Gary Brazil 2001–02
Billy Dearden 2002–04
Gary Mills 2004
Ian Richardson 2004–05
Gudjon Thordarson 2005–06
Steve Thompson 2006–07
Ian McParland 2007–09
Hans Backe 2009
Steve Cotterill 2010
Craig Short 2010
Paul Ince 2010–11
Martin Allen 2011–12
Keith Curle February 2012–

TEN YEAR LEAGUE RECORD

		P	W	D	L	F	A	Pts	Pos
2002-03	Div 2	46	13	16	17	62	70	55	15
2003-04	Div 2	46	10	12	24	50	78	42	23
2004-05	FL 2	46	13	13	20	46	62	52	19
2005-06	FL 2	46	12	16	18	48	63	52	21
2006-07	FL 2	46	16	14	16	55	53	62	13
2007-08	FL 2	46	10	18	18	37	53	48	21
2008-09	FL 2	46	11	14	21	49	69	47	19
2009-10	FL 2	46	27	12	7	96	31	93	1
2010-11	FL 1	46	14	8	24	46	60	50	19
2011-12	FL 1	46	21	10	15	75	63	73	7

DID YOU KNOW

It is generally accepted that the first player to successfully use the offside trap to a defender's advantage was Herbert Morley at Notts County, helping them win promotion in 1914. Signed from Grimsby Town, this right-back was capped for England and retired during the First World War.

NOTTS COUNTY 2011–12 LEAGUE RECORD

Match No.	Date	Venue	Opponents	Result	H/T Score	Lg Pos.	Goalscorers	Attendance
1	Aug 6	A	Carlisle U	W 3-0	3-0	—	Hughes, J [13], Zoko (og) [32], Hughes, L [45]	5941
2	13	H	Charlton Ath	L 1-2	0-2	7	Montano [60]	6397
3	16	H	Tranmere R	W 3-2	0-1	—	Kelly [52], Pearce [60], Hughes, J (pen) [90]	4883
4	20	A	Sheffield W	L 1-2	1-0	9	Hughes, J (pen) [10]	16,979
5	27	A	Preston NE	L 0-2	0-0	15		10,759
6	Sept 3	H	Bournemouth	W 3-1	1-0	11	Hughes, L [1], Pearce [78], Montano [86]	5510
7	10	H	Walsall	W 2-1	1-0	9	Hughes, L [38], Montano [65]	6218
8	13	A	Exeter C	D 1-1	1-1	—	Burgess [16]	3474
9	17	A	Stevenage	W 2-0	1-0	7	Hughes, L [45], Burgess [50]	3434
10	24	H	Rochdale	W 2-0	1-0	4	Hughes, L [35], Sodje [90]	6199
11	Oct 1	A	Milton Keynes D	L 0-3	0-1	8		7620
12	9	H	Hartlepool U	W 3-0	1-0	6	Hawley 2 [29, 55], Montano [90]	6172
13	15	A	Chesterfield	W 3-1	2-0	4	Burgess [21], Judge [38], Talbot (og) [88]	8342
14	22	H	Brentford	D 1-1	1-0	4	Hughes, J (pen) [38]	6735
15	25	A	Bury	D 2-2	1-1	—	Hughes, J 2 (2 pens) [37, 80]	2917
16	29	A	Colchester U	L 2-4	0-0	6	Sodje [58], Heath (og) [90]	3585
17	Nov 5	H	Wycombe W	D 1-1	1-0	6	Burgess [1]	7664
18	19	A	Huddersfield T	L 1-2	0-0	6	Bishop [90]	13,227
19	26	H	Scunthorpe U	W 3-2	1-1	6.	Pearce [39], Hughes, J [65], Kelly [82]	6120
20	Dec 10	A	Yeovil T	L 0-1	0-0	8		3663
21	17	H	Leyton Orient	L 1-2	0-1	9	Hughes, L [86]	5830
22	27	A	Sheffield U	L 1-2	1-1	—	Judge [17]	20,538
23	31	A	Oldham Ath	L 2-3	2-1	10	Hughes, L [10], Bishop [39]	3623
24	Jan 2	H	Huddersfield T	D 2-2	0-0	11	Hughes, J (pen) [72], Hughes, L [84]	8914
25	14	A	Bournemouth	L 1-2	1-1	14	Bencherif [5]	6529
26	21	H	Milton Keynes D	D 1-1	0-1	14	Hughes, J (pen) [81]	6123
27	24	H	Preston NE	D 0-0	0-0	—		4901
28	31	A	Walsall	W 1-0	1-0	—	Hughes, L [3]	3647
29	Feb 14	H	Exeter C	W 2-1	2-1	—	Hughes, L [8], Hughes, J (pen) [28]	4741
30	18	A	Hartlepool U	L 0-3	0-1	11		4718
31	22	H	Stevenage	W 1-0	0-0	—	Hughes, J [90]	5733
32	25	H	Chesterfield	W 1-0	0-0	8	Forte [80]	8257
33	28	A	Rochdale	W 1-0	1-0	—	Bencherif [45]	2326
34	Mar 3	H	Carlisle U	W 2-0	2-0	6	Forte [33], Sheehan [38]	6451
35	6	A	Tranmere R	D 1-1	1-0	—	Stewart [5]	4565
36	10	A	Charlton Ath	W 4-2	4-0	6	Judge [16], Forte 3 [18, 35, 40]	17,033
37	17	H	Sheffield W	L 1-2	0-0	6	Sam [88]	12,410
38	20	H	Sheffield U	L 2-5	0-4	—	Judge [77], Kelly [90]	9468
39	24	A	Scunthorpe U	D 0-0	0-0	8		4619
40	31	H	Oldham Ath	W 1-0	0-0	7	Sheehan [89]	6326
41	Apr 6	A	Leyton Orient	W 3-0	0-0	—	Stewart [70], Hughes, J [76], Sam [90]	4016
42	9	H	Yeovil T	W 3-1	1-0	6	Sam 3 [37, 87, 90]	5852
43	14	A	Brentford	D 0-0	0-0	6		7079
44	21	H	Bury	L 2-4	0-1	7	Coke (og) [46], Edwards [79]	6732
45	28	A	Wycombe W	W 4-3	2-2	7	Bogdanovic [3], Judge 2 [40, 90], Adebola [89]	5947
46	May 5	H	Colchester U	W 4-1	3-0	7	Hughes, J [23], Bogdanovic [33], Judge [41], Freeman [51]	8942

Final League Position: 7

GOALSCORERS

League (75): Hughes, J 13 (8 pens), Hughes, L 10, Judge 7, Forte 5, Sam 5, Burgess 4, Montano 4, Kelly 3, Pearce 3, Bencherif 2, Bishop 2, Bogdanovic 2, Hawley 2, Sheehan 2, Sodje 2, Stewart 2, Adebola 1, Edwards 1, Freeman 1, own goals 4.
Carling Cup (3): Edwards 1, Hughes, L 1, Westcarr 1.
FA Cup (8): Hughes, J 4 (1 pen), Hawley 2, Judge 1, Sheehan 1.
J Paint Trophy (1): Hawley 1.

Nelson S 46	Kelly J 29 + 3	Sheehan A 39	Edwards M 27 + 3	Pearce K 25 + 2	Bencherif H 14 + 6	Bishop N 41	Ravenhill R 5	Hughes L 28 + 12	Hawley K 15 + 11	Hughes J 44 + 1	Westcarr C 2 + 2	Stirling J — + 8	Demontagnac I 2 + 15	Montano C 4 + 7	Judge A 40 + 3	Allen C 4 + 5	Mahon G 23 + 8	Burgess B 20 + 8	Harley J 11 + 3	Sodje S 7 + 9	Orenuga F — + 2	Hollis H 1	Freeman K 18 + 1	Chilvers L 16 + 1	Stewart D 16 + 1	Forte J 6 + 4	Montano C 1 + 3	Spicer J — + 1	Sam L 8 + 2	Adebola D 3 + 3	Yennaris N 2	Bogdanovic D 8	Harris L 1 + 1	Speiss F — + 1	*Match No.*
1	2	3	4	5	6	7	8	9^1	10^3	11^2	12	13	14																						1
1	2^3	3	4	5	6^1	7	8	12	10	11^2	9		14	13																					2
1	2^3	3	4	5		7	8^1	9	13	11	10	14		6^2	12																				3
1	2	3	4^3	5	6^2	7■		9	10	11	13	14		12	8^1																				4
1	2	3	4	5	6			9^1	10^3	11			14	12	13	7^2	8																		5
1	2	3	4	5		7		9^3	13	11		14		12	8^2		6	10^1																	6
1	2	3	4	5	12	7		9^2	13	11				10^3	8^1	14	6																		7
1	2	3	4	5		7		12	13	11				10^1	8^2		6	9																	8
1	2		4	5		7		9^3	14	11				13	12	8^1	6	10	3^2																9
1	2	3	4	5		7		9^2	13	11				12	8^3		6	10^1		14															10
1	2■	3	4	5		7		9	13	11		12		10^2	8^1		6^3			14															11
1	2	3	4	5^3		7		12	10	11				13	8^1		6	9^2		14															12
1	2	3	4	5		7		12	10^1	11			14		8		6^2	9^3		13															13
1	2	3	4	5		7		9	12	11					8^3		6^1	10^2		13	14														14
1	2	3	4	5	6^2	7		9	12	11		13			8^1			10^3		14															15
1	2	3^3	4			7	6^2	9	10	11		12			8^1	14				5	13														16
1	2	3	4	5			6	9^2	12	11		13^3			8	7^1		10		14															17
1	2	3	13	5		7		14	10^3	11^1			12		8		6	9		4^2															18
1	2	3	4	5		7		12	10^2	13			11^1		8		6	9^3		14															19
1	2	3		5		7^1			10	11			12		8^2	13	6	9		4															20
1	2^2	3	4			7		9	10	11			13		8	12	6^1			5															21
1	2	3		5^2		7		9	13	11			12■		8	4^1		10		6															22
1	2	3	4	5	6^2	7		9	10	11					8^1	13		12																	23
1	2^2	3		12	6	7		9	10	11					8			13		5^1		4													24
1					6	7		9	10^1	11			12		8^2			13	3				2	4	5										25
1				5	10	7		9		11			13		8		6^2	12	3^1				2		4										26
1		3				7		12	9^2	11			10^1		8		6	13					2	4	5										27
1		3			12	7		9^2							8		6	10^1	11				2	4	5	13									28
1				13	14	7		9^2		11					8^3		6	10	3				2	4^1	5		12								29
1		3				7		9^3		11					8^1		6	10^2		14			2	4	5	12	13								30
1		3		5		7		9		11					8^2		6						2	13	4	10^1	12								31
1			4		6^2	7		9^3		11					8		13	14	3				2	5		12	10^1								32
1	2		12		6	7		13■		11					10^3		8	9^2	3	5^1				4		14									33
1		3	5		6	7				11			13		8		12	9^1					2	4^3	14	10^2									34
1	2			5	6	7				11^1							12	9	3				8		4	10^2		13							35
1		3			12	7				11			13		8^2		6	14	10^1				2	4	5	9^3									36
1		3			14	7^3				11					8		6^2	13	10^1				2	4	5	9			12						37
1	14	3	4	5^3		7■		12		11					8			9^1					2			10^2			6	13					38
1	14	3	4					9		11			13		8								2	5					6^3		7^1	10^2	12		39
1	13	3	4		12			9		11					8^2		14						2	5					6		7^1	10^3			40
1	2	3			6^2			13		11					8		12		14					4	5				10			9^3	7^1		41
1	2	3				6		9^1		11					8^3		13		14					4	5				7	12		10^2			42
1	2^1	3				6				11			14		8				13				12	4	5				7^2	9^3		10			43
1		3^1	14			6		9		11					8				7				2	4^3	5				13	12		10^2			44
1		3	4			7^1		12		11			14		8		13						2^3		5				6	9		10^2			45
1^G		3	4			6^2		12		11					8		13						2		5				7	9^1		10		15	46

FA Cup

First Round	Accrington S	(h)	4-1
Second Round	Sutton U	(a)	2-0
Third Round	Doncaster R	(a)	2-0
Fourth Round	Stevenage	(a)	0-1

Carling Cup

First Round	Nottingham F	(a)	3-3

J Paint Trophy

Second Round	Chesterfield	(h)	1-3

OLDHAM ATHLETIC FL Championship 1

FOUNDATION

It was in 1895 that John Garland, the landlord of the Featherstall and Junction Hotel, decided to form a football club. As Pine Villa they played in the Oldham Junior League. In 1899 the local professional club, Oldham County, went out of existence and one of the liquidators persuaded Pine Villa to take over their ground at Sheepfoot Lane and change their name to Oldham Athletic.

Boundary Park, Furtherwood Road, Oldham OL1 2PA.

Telephone: (0161) 624 4972.

Fax: (0161) 627 5915.

Ticket Office: (0161) 785 5150.

Website: www.oldhamathletic.co.uk

Email: enquiries@oldhamathletic.co.uk

Ground Capacity: 13,624.

Record Attendance: 46,471 v Sheffield W, FA Cup 4th rd, 25 January 1930.

Pitch Measurements: 106yd × 72yd.

Chairman: Simon Corney.

Chief Executive: Neil Joy.

Manager: Paul Dickov.

Assistant Manager: Gerry Taggart.

Physio: Marc Czuczman.

Colours: Blue shirts with white sleeves, white shorts, white stockings.

Year Formed: 1895.

Turned Professional: 1899.

Previous Name: 1895, Pine Villa; 1899, Oldham Athletic.

Club Nickname: 'The Latics'.

Grounds: 1895, Sheepfoot Lane; 1900, Hudson Field; 1906, Sheepfoot Lane; 1907, Boundary Park.

First Football League Game: 9 September 1907, Division 2, v Stoke (a) W 3–1 – Hewitson; Hodson, Hamilton; Fay, Walders, Wilson; Ward, Billy Dodds (1), Newton (1), Hancock, Swarbrick (1).

Record League Victory: 11–0 v Southport, Division 4, 26 December 1962 – Bollands; Branagan, Marshall; McCall, Williams, Scott; Ledger (1), Johnstone, Lister (6), Colquhoun (1), Whitaker (3).

Record Cup Victory: 10–1 v Lytham, FA Cup 1st rd, 28 November 1925 – Gray; Wynne, Grundy; Adlam, Heaton, Naylor (1), Douglas, Pynegar (2), Ormston (2), Barnes (3), Watson (2).

Record Defeat: 4–13 v Tranmere R, Division 3 (N), 26 December 1935.

HONOURS

Football League – Division 1: *Runners-up* 1914–15;
Division 2: ***Champions*** 1990–91;
Runners-up 1909–10;
Division 3 (N): ***Champions*** 1952–53;
Division 2: ***Champions*** 1973–74;
Division 4: ***Runners-up*** 1962–63.

FA Cup: Semi-final 1913, 1990, 1994.

Football League Cup: ***Runners-up*** 1990.

sky SPORTS FACT FILE

Bert Lister holds the Football League Fourth Division record for the most goals in a match when he hit six against Southport on Boxing Day 1962. He also scored a fast 10 seconds goal against Chesterfield in an Oldham Athletic career of 95 goals in 152 League and Cup games.

Most League Points (2 for a win): 62, Division 3, 1973–74.

Most League Points (3 for a win): 88, Division 2, 1990–91.

Most League Goals: 95, Division 4, 1962–63.

Highest League Scorer in Season: Tom Davis, 33, Division 3 (N), 1936–37.

Most League Goals in Total Aggregate: Roger Palmer, 141, 1980–94.

Most League Goals in One Match: 7, Eric Gemmell v Chester, Division 3 (N), 19 January 1952.

Most Capped Player: Gunnar Halle, 24 (64), Norway.

Most League Appearances: Ian Wood, 525, 1966–80.

Youngest League Player: Wayne Harrison, 15 years 11 months v Notts Co, 27 October 1984.

Record Transfer Fee Received: £1,700,000 from Aston Villa for Earl Barrett, February 1992.

Record Transfer Fee Paid: £750,000 to Aston Villa for Ian Olney, June 1992.

Football League Record: 1907 Elected to Division 2; 1910–23 Division 1; 1923–35 Division 2; 1935–53 Division 3 (N); 1953–54 Division 2; 1954–58 Division 3 (N); 1958–63 Division 4; 1963–69 Division 3; 1969–71 Division 4; 1971–74 Division 3; 1974–91 Division 2; 1991–92 Division 1; 1992–94 FA Premier League; 1994–97 Division 1; 1997–2004 Division 2; 2004– FL 1.

MANAGERS

David Ashworth 1906–14
Herbert Bamlett 1914–21
Charlie Roberts 1921–22
David Ashworth 1923–24
Bob Mellor 1924–27
Andy Wilson 1927–32
Bob Mellor 1932–33
Jimmy McMullan 1933–34
Bob Mellor 1934–45
(continued as Secretary to 1953)
Frank Womack 1945–47
Billy Wootton 1947–50
George Hardwick 1950–56
Ted Goodier 1956–58
Norman Dodgin 1958–60
Danny McLennan 1960
Jack Rowley 1960–63
Les McDowall 1963–65
Gordon Hurst 1965–66
Jimmy McIlroy 1966–68
Jack Rowley 1968–69
Jimmy Frizzell 1970–82
Joe Royle 1982–94
Graeme Sharp 1994–97
Neil Warnock 1997–98
Andy Ritchie 1998–2001
Mick Wadsworth 2001–02
Iain Dowie 2002–03
Brian Talbot 2004–05
Ronnie Moore 2005–06
John Sheridan 2006–09
Joe Royle 2009
Dave Penney 2009–10
Paul Dickov June 2010–

LATEST SEQUENCES

Longest Sequence of League Wins: 10, 12.1.1974 – 12.3.1974.

Longest Sequence of League Defeats: 8, 15.12.1934 – 2.2.1935.

Longest Sequence of League Draws: 5, 26.12.1982 – 15.1.1983.

Longest Sequence of Unbeaten League Matches: 20, 1.5.1990 – 10.11.1990.

Longest Sequence Without a League Win: 17, 4.9.1920 – 18.12.1920.

Successive Scoring Runs: 25 from 15.1.1927.

Successive Non-scoring Runs: 6 from 4.2.1922.

TEN YEAR LEAGUE RECORD

		P	W	D	L	F	A	Pts	Pos
2002-03	Div 2	46	22	16	8	68	38	82	5
2003-04	Div 2	46	12	21	13	66	60	57	15
2004-05	FL 1	46	14	10	22	60	73	52	19
2005-06	FL 1	46	18	11	17	58	60	65	10
2006-07	FL 1	46	21	12	13	69	47	75	6
2007-08	FL 1	46	18	13	15	58	46	67	8
2008-09	FL 1	46	16	17	13	66	65	65	10
2009-10	FL 1	46	13	13	20	39	57	52	16
2010-11	FL 1	46	13	17	16	53	60	56	17
2011-12	FL 1	46	14	12	20	50	66	54	16

DID YOU KNOW 

Although amateur outside-right Harold Brown played only once in the Football League for Oldham Athletic, he scored and figured in a best of the season 6-1 win for the club against Chesterfield on 5 March 1932. He was a late replacement for regular choice Les Smalley.

OLDHAM ATHLETIC 2011–12 LEAGUE RECORD

Match No.	Date		Venue	Opponents	Result		H/T Score	Lg Pos.	Goalscorers	Attendance
1	Aug	6	H	Sheffield U	L	0-2	0-0	—		8032
2		13	A	Yeovil T	L	1-3	0-0	24	Reid (pen) 90	3237
3		16	A	Scunthorpe U	W	2-1	1-0	—	Mellor 16, Smith 82	4142
4		20	H	Rochdale	W	2-0	2-0	13	Reid (pen) 32, Clarke 45	5266
5		27	A	Colchester U	L	1-4	1-2	16	Reid (pen) 37	3023
6	Sept	3	H	Huddersfield T	D	1-1	1-1	15	Kuqi 6	6213
7		10	H	Stevenage	D	1-1	1-1	15	Kuqi 19	3402
8		13	A	Walsall	W	1-0	1-0	—	Taylor 29	3250
9		17	A	Leyton Orient	W	3-1	0-1	11	Kuqi 49, Reid 65, Smith 89	3699
10		24	H	Brentford	L	0-2	0-1	12		3777
11	Oct	1	A	Exeter C	L	0-2	0-1	13		3753
12		10	H	Milton Keynes D	W	2-1	1-0	—	Kuqi 43, Adeyemi 56	2408
13		15	A	Tranmere R	L	0-1	0-1	13		5117
14		22	H	Wycombe W	W	2-0	0-0	12	Wesolowski 59, Furman 80	3592
15		25	A	Preston NE	D	3-3	2-2	—	Kuqi 11, Wesolowski 2 44, 86	11,370
16		29	A	Carlisle U	D	3-3	3-1	14	Kuqi 2 (1 pen) 22 (p), 38, Adeyemi 33	4803
17	Nov	5	H	Bury	L	0-2	0-2	14		5149
18		19	H	Chesterfield	W	5-2	4-1	12	Lee 3, Simpson 3 12, 17, 33, Kuqi 58	3699
19		26	A	Bournemouth	D	0-0	0-0	13		5478
20	Dec	10	H	Sheffield W	L	0-2	0-0	16		7060
21		17	A	Charlton Ath	D	1-1	0-0	13	Morais 84	19,564
22		26	H	Hartlepool U	L	0-1	0-1	14		4459
23		31	H	Notts Co	W	3-2	1-2	14	Scapuzzi 27, Morais 70, Diamond 86	3623
24	Jan	2	A	Chesterfield	D	1-1	1-1	14	Smith 45	6723
25		14	A	Huddersfield T	L	0-1	0-0	16		15,229
26		21	H	Exeter C	D	0-0	0-0	16		3587
27	Feb	14	H	Walsall	W	2-1	2-0	—	Morais 2, Simpson 31	2583
28		18	A	Milton Keynes D	L	0-5	0-1	16		7817
29		25	H	Tranmere R	W	1-0	0-0	15	Kuqi (pen) 48	3866
30		28	H	Colchester U	D	1-1	1-0	—	Marsh-Brown 37	3956
31	Mar	3	A	Sheffield U	W	3-2	0-2	13	Cresswell (og) 65, Lee 69, Kuqi (pen) 90	17,267
32		6	H	Scunthorpe U	L	1-2	0-0	—	Morais 78	4376
33		10	H	Yeovil T	L	1-2	0-1	13	Diamond 55	4689
34		13	A	Stevenage	L	0-1	0-0	—		2453
35		17	A	Rochdale	L	2-3	1-1	17	Kuqi 21, Reid 74	4671
36		20	A	Hartlepool U	W	1-0	1-0	—	M'Voto 8	4109
37		24	H	Bournemouth	W	1-0	0-0	14	Taylor 52	4459
38		27	H	Leyton Orient	L	0-1	0-0	—		4145
39		31	A	Notts Co	L	0-1	0-0	14		6326
40	Apr	3	A	Brentford	L	0-2	0-1	—		4573
41		7	H	Charlton Ath	L	0-1	0-0	17		3641
42		9	A	Sheffield W	L	0-3	0-1	18		22,232
43		14	A	Wycombe W	D	2-2	1-1	18	Morais 14, Simpson (pen) 90	5109
44		21	H	Preston NE	D	1-1	0-0	18	Simpson 69	4824
45		28	A	Bury	D	0-0	0-0	18		5111
46	May	5	H	Carlisle U	W	2-1	0-0	16	Tarkowski 49, Tounkara 72	5152

Final League Position: 16

GOALSCORERS

League (50): Kuqi 11 (3 pens), Simpson 6 (1 pen), Morais 5, Reid 5 (3 pens), Smith 3, Wesolowski 3, Adeyemi 2, Diamond 2, Lee 2, Taylor 2, Clarke 1, Furman 1, M'Voto 1, Marsh-Brown 1, Mellor 1, Scapuzzi 1, Tarkowski 1, Tounkara 1, own goal 1.
Carling Cup (1): Reid 1 (pen).
FA Cup (6): Simpson 2, Furman 1, Kuqi 1 (pen), Taylor 1, Wesolowski 1.
J Paint Trophy (7): Kuqi 4, Adeyemi 1, Scapuzzi 1, Simpson 1.

Cisak A 38	Lee K 43	Black P 13	Furman D 21+2	Diamond Z 21+2	M'Voto J 35+1	Winchester C 9+3	Lund M 2+1	Reid R 17+3	Smith M 3+25	Taylor C 38	Parker J 7+6	Millar K 2+2	Wesolowski J 21	Morais F 23+13	Mellor D 19+2	Clarke N 16	Diallo B 12+3	Adeyemi T 33+3	Kuqi S 39+1	Simpson R 26+3	Scapuzzi L 8+2	Gerrard P —+1	Tarkowski J 13+3	Marsh-Brown K 5+6	Brown R 15	M'Changama Y 8+2	Bunn H 8+3	Hughes C —+4	Tounkara O 3+5	Bouzanis D 8+1	Belezika G —+1	Mancin A —+1	Match No.
1	2	3	4	5	6	7^1	8	9^2	10	11	12	13																					1
1	2	3^1		5	6		8	9	10	11	12		4	7																			2
1	2	3		5	6▮	7		9^2	13	11	10		4	12	8^1																		3
1	2	3		5		7		9^3	12	10	8^1	13	4	11^2		6	14																4
1	2	3^2		5		7		9	12	11			4	8	10^1	6	13																5
1	2			5	6		14	9^3	13	11			4	7^1	12		3▮	8	10^2														6
1	2			5^1	6	7		9^2	13	11			4			3		8	10	12													7
1	2				6			9	12	11			4		3	5		8	10^1	7													8
1	2			12	5			9^2	14	11			4	13	3^1	6		8	10	7^3													9
1	2			5	6			9	13	11			4^3	12		3^2	14	8	10	7^1													10
1	2			5				9	12	11			4	13		6	3	8	10^1	7^2													11
1	2		14	5	13			9^1		11			4	12	3^2	6		8	10	7^3													12
1	2		12		5				13	11			4	9	3	6		8^1	10	7^2													13
1	2		8		5				12	11			4	7^1	3	6			10	9													14
1	2		7		5				12	11			4		3	6		8	10^1	9													15
1	2		8		5					11			4^1	12	3	6		7	10	9													16
1▮	2		4	5					12	11					3	6^2		8^1	10	9	7^G	15										13	17
1	2	3	8^2	5	6				14	11			4	12				13	10	9^3	7^1												18
1	2	3	8	5	6				14	11^1			4	13				12	10	9^3	7^2												19
1	2	3	4	5	6^1				14		11^2			13				8^3	10	9	7		12										20
1			8	5					13	11	2		4	12	3	6		9^1	10		7^2												21
1			8	5					13	11	2		4^1	7	3	6		12	10		9^2												22
1	2	3	4	5	6					11	7			12				8	10		9^1												23
1	2	3	4	5					10^2	11	12			7^1		6		8	13	9^3	14												24
1	3		8	5	6				12	11	2^1		4					7	10		9												25
1	2	3			6				13	11	12		4^1	7				8	10^2	9^3	14		5										26
1	2	3			5					11	12			7				4	10^1	9			6	8									27
1	2	3^1		12	5				14	11	13			7				4^3	10	9			6	8^2									28
1	2				5	8				11				7^1	3			4	10	9			6	12									29
1	2				5	8			12					7	3			4	10	9			6	11^1									30
1	2				5	9^1		13		11				7^2	3			8	10				6	12	4								31
1	2				5			12	13	11^1				7	3^2			8	10				6	9▮	4								32
1	2			5		14		9	13	11^3				7	3			4	10^2				6		8^1	12							33
1	2			6^1	5			9^2	13	11				7				4	10				12		8	3							34
1	2				5	14		12		11					3^1			4	10				6▮		8	7^3	9^2	13					35
1	2				5			9		11					3			4	10						6	7	8						36
1	5				2			9^1		11							3	4	10	13					7	6	8^2		12				37
1^G	2				5			9^2		11							3	4	10	12			6	13		7	8^1			15			38
	2		8		5					11				12			3	4	10	7					6				9^1	1			39
	2		8		5					11^1				7^3			3	4	10^2	9					6	14	13		12	1			40
	2		8		5▮									7^3			3^2	4	10	11			12		6		9^1	14	13	1			41
	2		8											7^1			3	4	10^2	11			5^3	12	6		9		13	1	14		42
	2		4											7^2			3		10^1	11			5	12	6	8	13		9	1			43
	2		4		5									7			3		10^1	11				12	6	8	13		9^2	1			44
	2		4		5	12						7^2		13			3			9				11	6	8^1	10^3	14		1			45
			4		5	11						8^2		7	14		3		10^1				6		2		9^3	13	12	1			46

FA Cup

First Round	Burton Alb	(h)	3-1
Second Round	Southend U	(a)	1-1
		(h)	1-0
Third Round	Liverpool	(a)	1-5

Carling Cup

First Round	Carlisle U	(h)	1-1

J Paint Trophy

Second Round	Scunthorpe U	(a)	1-0
Northern Quarter-Final	Crewe Alex	(h)	3-1
Northern Semi-Final	Bradford C	(h)	2-0
Northern Final	Chesterfield	(a)	1-2
		(h)	0-1

OXFORD UNITED FL Championship 2

FOUNDATION

There had been an Oxford United club around the time of World War I but only in the Oxfordshire Thursday League and there is no connection with the modern club which began as Headington in 1893, adding 'United' a year later. Playing first on Quarry Fields and subsequently Wootten's Fields, they owe much to a Dr Hitchings for their early development.

The Kassam Stadium, Grenoble Road, Oxford OX4 4XP.

Telephone: (01865) 337 500.

Fax: (01865) 337 501.

Ticket Office: (01865) 337 533.

Website: www.oufc.co.uk

Email: admin@oufc.co.uk

Ground Capacity: 12,500.

Record Attendance: 22,730 v Preston NE, FA Cup 6th rd, 29 February 1964 (at Manor Ground); 12,243 v Leyton Orient, FL 2, 6 May 2006 (at The Kassam Stadium).

Pitch Measurements: 115yd × 71yd.

Chairman: Kelvin Thomas.

General Manager: Mick Brown.

Manager: Chris Wilder.

First Team Coach: Mickey Lewis.

Physios: Charlie Greig and Andy Lord.

Colours: Yellow shirts, blue shorts, blue stockings.

Year Formed: 1893.

Turned Professional: 1949.

Previous Names: 1893, Headington; 1894, Headington United; 1960, Oxford United.

Club Nickname: 'The U's'.

Grounds: 1893, Headington Quarry; 1894, Wootten's Fields; 1898, Sandy Lane Ground; 1902, Britannia Field; 1909, Sandy Lane; 1910, Quarry Recreation Ground; 1914, Sandy Lane; 1922, The Paddock Manor Road; 1925, Manor Ground; 2001, The Kassam Stadium.

First Football League Game: 18 August 1962, Division 4, v Barrow (a) L 2–3 – Medlock; Beavon, Quartermain; Ron Atkinson, Kyle, Jones; Knight, Graham Atkinson (1), Houghton (1), Cornwell, Colfar.

Record League Victory: 7–0 v Barrow, Division 4, 19 December 1964 – Fearnley; Beavon, Quartermain; Ron Atkinson (1), Kyle, Jones; Morris, Booth (3), Willey (1), Graham Atkinson (1), Harrington (1).

HONOURS

Football League – Division 1: Best season: 12th, 1997–98;
Division 2: ***Champions*** 1984–85;
Runners-up 1995–96;
Division 3: ***Champions*** 1967–68, 1983–84.

FA Cup: Best season: 6th rd, 1964 (shared record for 4th Division club).

Football League Cup: ***Winners*** 1986.

sky SPORTS FACT FILE

In 1983–84 Oxford United had a successful fourth round League Cup tie against Manchester United. They drew 1-1 at home and similarly after extra time at Old Trafford. The second replay also went into overtime but former Maths teacher Steve Biggins added their winner at 2-1.

Record Cup Victory: 9–1 v Dorchester T, FA Cup 1st rd, 11 November 1995 – Whitehead; Wood (2), Mike Ford (1), Smith, Elliott, Gilchrist, Rush (1), Massey (Murphy), Moody (3), Bobby Ford (1), Angel (Beauchamp (1)).

Record Defeat: 0–7 v Sunderland, Division 1, 19 September 1998.

Most League Points (2 for a win): 61, Division 4, 1964–65.

Most League Points (3 for a win): 95, Division 3, 1983–84.

Most League Goals: 91, Division 3, 1983–84.

Highest League Scorer in Season: John Aldridge, 30, Division 2, 1984–85.

Most League Goals in Total Aggregate: Graham Atkinson, 77, 1962–73.

Most League Goals in One Match: 4, Tony Jones v Newport Co, Division 4, 22 September 1962; 4, Arthur Longbottom v Darlington, Division 4, 26 October 1963; 4, Richard Hill v Walsall, Division 2, 26 December 1988; 4, John Durnin v Luton T, 14 November 1992.

Most Capped Player: Jim Magilton, 18 (52), Northern Ireland.

Most League Appearances: John Shuker, 478, 1962–77.

Youngest League Player: Jason Seacole, 16 years 149 days v Mansfield T, 7 September 1976.

Record Transfer Fee Received: £1,600,000 from Leicester C for Matt Elliott, January 1997.

Record Transfer Fee Paid: £475,000 to Aberdeen for Dean Windass, August 1998.

Football League Record: 1962 Elected to Division 4; 1965–68 Division 3; 1968–76 Division 2; 1976–84 Division 3; 1984–85 Division 2; 1985–88 Division 1; 1988–92 Division 2; 1992–94 Division 1; 1994–96 Division 2; 1996–99 Division 1; 1999–2001 Division 2; 2001–04 Division 3; 2004–06 FL2; 2006–10 Conference; 2010– FL 2.

MANAGERS

Harry Thompson 1949–58
(Player-Manager) 1949-51
Arthur Turner 1959–69
(continued as General Manager to 1972)
Ron Saunders 1969
Gerry Summers 1969–75
Mick Brown 1975–79
Bill Asprey 1979–80
Ian Greaves 1980–82
Jim Smith 1982–85
Maurice Evans 1985–88
Mark Lawrenson 1988
Brian Horton 1988–93
Denis Smith 1993–97
Malcolm Crosby 1997–98
Malcolm Shotton 1998–99
Micky Lewis 1999–2000
Denis Smith 2000
David Kemp 2000–01
Mark Wright 2001
Ian Atkins 2001–04
Graham Rix 2004
Ramon Diaz 2004–05
Brian Talbot 2005–2006
Darren Patterson 2006
Jim Smith 2006–07
Darren Patterson 2007–08
Chris Wilder December 2008–

LATEST SEQUENCES

Longest Sequence of League Wins: 6, 6.4.1985 – 24.4.1985.

Longest Sequence of League Defeats: 7, 4.5.1991 – 7.9.1991.

Longest Sequence of League Draws: 5, 7.10.1978 – 28.10.1978.

Longest Sequence of Unbeaten League Matches: 20, 17.3.1984 – 29.9.1984.

Longest Sequence Without a League Win: 27, 14.11.1987 – 27.8.1988.

Successive Scoring Runs: 17 from 10.9.1983.

Successive Non-scoring Runs: 6 from 26.3.1988.

TEN YEAR LEAGUE RECORD

		P	*W*	*D*	*L*	*F*	*A*	*Pts*	*Pos*
2002-03	Div 3	46	19	12	15	57	47	69	8
2003-04	Div 3	46	18	17	11	55	44	71	9
2004-05	FL 2	46	16	11	19	50	63	59	15
2005-06	FL 2	46	11	16	19	43	57	49	23
2006-07	Conf	46	22	15	9	66	33	81	2
2007-08	B Sq Pr	46	20	11	15	56	48	71	9
2008-09	B Sq Pr	46	24	10	12	72	51	77*	7
2009-10	B Sq Pr	44	25	11	8	64	31	86	3
2010-11	FL 2	46	17	12	17	58	60	63	12
2011-12	FL 2	46	17	17	12	59	48	68	9

** 5 points deducted.*

DID YOU KNOW ?

On 15 October 1969, Oxford United won for the first time on the ground of a First Division team. Nottingham Forest provided the venue in a League Cup tie which was decided in the 71st minute when Ken Skeen first headed, then followed up by successfully hitting in the rebound.

OXFORD UNITED 2011–12 LEAGUE RECORD

Match No.	*Date*	*Venue*	*Opponents*	*Result*		*H/T Score*	*Lg Pos.*	*Goalscorers*	*Attendance*
1	Aug 6	A	Rotherham U	L	0-1	0-0	—		4484
2	13	H	Bradford C	D	1-1	1-0	20	Heslop [29]	6523
3	16	H	Shrewsbury T	W	2-0	1-0	—	Heslop [8], Guy [52]	6102
4	21	A	Swindon T	W	2-1	2-1	8	Constable 2 [12, 43]	12,113
5	27	H	Aldershot T	D	1-1	1-0	9	Constable [21]	6673
6	Sept 3	A	Crewe Alex	L	1-3	0-2	13	Davis [77]	3680
7	10	H	Burton Alb	D	2-2	1-0	14	Potter [45], Leven [52]	8043
8	13	A	Dagenham & R	W	1-0	1-0	—	Hall, R [41]	1921
9	17	A	Barnet	W	2-0	2-0	7	Heslop [33], Davis [38]	2812
10	24	H	Accrington S	D	1-1	1-0	8	McLaren [35]	6472
11	Oct 1	A	Hereford U	W	1-0	1-0	6	Hall, R [32]	2502
12	8	H	Bristol R	W	3-0	1-0	5	Constable 2 [16, 84], Leven (pen) [52]	9291
13	15	A	Macclesfield T	D	1-1	0-0	3	Hall, R [90]	2293
14	22	A	Gillingham	L	0-1	0-1	7		5819
15	25	H	Plymouth Arg	W	5-1	1-0	—	Hall, R 2 [15, 67], Constable 2 [71, 90], Leven [77]	7802
16	29	H	Port Vale	W	2-1	1-0	4	Duberry [11], Leven [64]	8027
17	Nov 5	A	Southend U	L	1-2	0-1	7	Batt [62]	6157
18	19	A	Crawley T	L	1-4	1-3	9	Constable [30]	4042
19	26	H	Cheltenham T	L	1-3	0-1	9	Leven [82]	8037
20	Dec 10	A	Morecambe	D	0-0	0-0	10		1914
21	17	H	Northampton T	W	2-0	0-0	8	Craddock [50], Smalley [87]	7517
22	26	A	AFC Wimbledon	W	2-0	2-0	8	Constable [18], Hall, A [44]	4547
23	31	A	Torquay U	D	0-0	0-0	8		3043
24	Jan 2	H	Crawley T	D	1-1	0-0	8	Pittman [55]	9004
25	7	A	Aldershot T	W	3-0	3-0	—	Pittman [8], Duberry [38], Leven [45]	3194
26	14	H	Crewe Alex	L	0-1	0-0	6		7052
27	21	H	Hereford U	D	2-2	1-1	7	Pittman [12], Duberry [90]	6630
28	29	A	Burton Alb	D	1-1	0-1	7	Potter [59]	3189
29	Feb 14	H	Dagenham & R	W	2-1	0-0	—	Johnson [51], Constable [79]	5653
30	18	A	Bristol R	D	0-0	0-0	7		6512
31	21	H	Barnet	W	2-1	1-1	—	Rendell [43], Constable [56]	5848
32	25	H	Macclesfield T	D	1-1	1-1	7	Johnson [42]	6189
33	Mar 3	H	Swindon T	W	2-0	2-0	7	Hall, A [16], Johnson [18]	11,825
34	6	A	Shrewsbury T	D	2-2	2-0	—	Holmes 2 [1, 38]	5205
35	10	A	Bradford C	L	1-2	0-0	7	Hall, A [72]	10,059
36	17	H	Rotherham U	W	2-1	1-0	7	Rendell [45], Hall, A [52]	6756
37	20	H	AFC Wimbledon	W	1-0	0-0	—	Morgan [57]	6366
38	24	A	Cheltenham T	D	0-0	0-0	7		4365
39	27	A	Accrington S	W	2-0	1-0	—	Hall, A 2 [42, 73]	1408
40	31	H	Morecambe	L	1-2	1-1	6	Rendell [5]	7023
41	Apr 6	A	Northampton T	L	1-2	0-1	7	Montano [50]	6860
42	9	H	Torquay U	D	2-2	0-1	7	Chapman [59], Montano [68]	7867
43	14	H	Gillingham	D	0-0	0-0	7		7322
44	21	A	Plymouth Arg	D	1-1	1-1	8	Hall, A [36]	6668
45	28	H	Southend U	L	0-2	0-2	8		9356
46	May 5	A	Port Vale	L	0-3	0-1	9		5621

Final League Position: 9

GOALSCORERS

League (59): Constable 11, Hall, A 7, Leven 6 (1 pen), Hall, R 5, Duberry 3, Heslop 3, Johnson 3, Pittman 3, Rendell 3, Davis 2, Holmes 2, Montano 2, Potter 2, Batt 1, Chapman 1, Craddock 1, Guy 1, McLaren 1, Morgan 1, Smalley 1.
Carling Cup (1): Clist 1.
FA Cup (0).
J Paint Trophy (2): Hall, R 1, Smalley 1.

Clarke R 42	Batt D 34 + 6	Tonkin A 6 + 8	Payne J 2 + 4	Duberry M 36	Wright J 43	Whing A 36 + 5	Hall A 24 + 10	Constable J 32 + 8	Smalley D 7 + 15	Davis L 41 + 3	Potter A 21 + 4	Pittman J 6 + 9	Leven P 36 + 3	Heslop S 26 + 3	Guy L 8	McLaren P 16 + 2	Hall R 11 + 2	Worley H 6 + 4	Haworth A 2 + 2	Philliskirk D 2 + 2	Kinniburgh S — + 1	Franks J — + 1	Craddock T 6 + 3	Chapman A 10 + 4	Johnson O 8 + 9	Wilson M 3 + 3	Rendell S 15 + 3	Holmes L 5 + 2	Kerrouche M 1 + 3	Morgan D 10	Montano C 6 + 3	Brown W 2	Ripley C 1	Martinez D 1	Capaldi T 1	Match No.
1	2	3^{2}	4^{1}	5	6	7	8^{3}	9	10	11	12	13	14																							1
1			4	5	6	2	7^{2}	12	10	3	11^{1}	14	13	8^{3}	9																					2
1	13			5	6	2	7	9	10^{1}	3	14		12	8^{3}	11	4^{2}																				3
1	14			5	6	2	12	9	13	3	7^{3}		11	8^{1}	10^{2}	4																				4
1	13			5	6	2		9	10^{3}	3	12	14	7	8^{1}	11	4^{2}																				5
1	12		13	5	6	2^{1}	7		10	3	11	14		8^{2}	9^{3}	4																				6
1	12			5	6	2^{1}	13	9		3	11	14	7	8	10^{3}	4^{2}																				7
1	2		12	5	6			9^{2}	13	3	11		7	8^{1}		4^{3}	10	14																		8
1	2			5	6■	13		9^{3}	14	3	11		7	8^{1}		4^{2}	10		12																	9
1	2		12	5		7		9	14	3	11		6	8^{1}		4^{2}	10^{3}		13																	10
1	2			5	6	13	14	9^{2}	12	3	11		7	8^{3}		4^{1}	10																			11
1	2			5	6		13	10^{3}	14	3	12		7	8		4	9^{2}		11^{1}																	12
1	2			5	6		14	9	13	3	11		7	8^{2}		4^{3}	12		10^{1}																	13
1	2			5	6		14	12	10^{2}	3	11		7	8^{1}		4^{3}	9			13																14
1	2		13	5^{1}	6	12		10		3	11		7	8		4^{2}	9^{3}			14																15
1				5	6	2	12	10	13	3	11		7	8^{2}		4	9^{1}																			16
1	2				6	7		9	12	3^{2}	11		4	8		14		5^{3}		10^{1}	13															17
1	2^{2}				6	7		10	12	3			11	14		4^{3}	9	5		8^{1}		13														18
1	2				6	5		10	12	3■			7	8	11^{2}	4^{1}	9	13																		19
1	2	3			6	5	4	10					7	8^{2}	11^{1}		12						9	13												20
1	2	14			6	5	12	10	13	3	7^{2}		4	8			9^{1}						11^{3}													21
1	2	12			6	5	4	10	13	3	11^{2}		7	8									9^{1}													22
1	2	3		5	6		4	12	10^{1}		11	13	7	8									9^{2}													23
1	2			5	6	8	4	10		3	11^{2}	12	7	13									9^{1}													24
1	2			5	6	4	12	10^{3}	13	3	11	9^{2}	7	8^{1}									14													25
1	2	13		5	6	7^{1}		10	14	3	11	9^{3}	4	8^{2}		12																				26
1	2			5	6	7^{2}	13	10		3	11^{1}	9	4	8^{3}									14		12											27
1				5	6	2	7^{1}	10		3	11	9	4	8											12											28
1		14		5	6	2	7^{1}	10		3			4												9^{3}	8	11^{2}	12	13							29
1	7			5	6	2		10		3			4												13	8^{2}	11	12	9^{1}							30
1	2	13		5	6	7^{1}		10		3			4					14							8^{2}	12	9^{3}	11								31
1	2			5		7^{2}		10		3			4					6							8	13	9^{1}	11	12							32
1	2	3		5		6	4	10■		13		14												12	8^{3}	7^{1}	9	11^{2}								33
1	2	3		5	6	7	4			13														8^{1}	10^{2}		9	11	12							34
1	2■	3^{2}		5	6	7	4			13								14						8^{3}	12		9^{1}	11		10						35
1				5	6	2	7			3			4											8	10^{1}		9			11	12					36
1	12	14		5	6	2	7	13		3			4											8^{1}	10		9^{2}			11^{3}						37
1	2				6	7	8	10		3			4					5							12		9^{1}			11^{2}	13					38
1	2	13			6	12	7	10		3			4					5^{1}						8	9^{2}		14				11^{3}					39
1	2				6	5	7	12		3			4											8^{1}		13	9			10	11^{2}					40
1	2			5■	6	12	7	13		3		14	4^{1}											8			9^{2}			11	10^{3}					41
1	2				6	4	7	9^{1}		3								5						8	13		12			11	10^{2}					42
	2	14		5	6	4	7	13		3														8^{2}	12		9			11^{3}	10^{1}	1				43
				5	6	2	7	12^{3}		3			4	14										8	13		9^{1}			11	10^{2}	1				44
	2			5	6	4^{3}	7			3		10		8^{1}									13	12			9			11^{2}	14		1			45
	2			5	6	7^{3}	8			3^{1}		10	4										9^{2}	13	12		14							1	11	46

FA Cup

First Round	Sheffield U	(a)	0-3

Carling Cup

First Round	Cardiff C	(h)	1-3

J Paint Trophy

Second Round	Aldershot T	(a)	2-1
Southern Quarter-Final	Southend U	(h)	0-1

PETERBOROUGH UNITED FL Championship

FOUNDATION

The old Peterborough & Fletton club, founded in 1923, was suspended by the FA during season 1932–33 and disbanded. Local enthusiasts determined to carry on and in 1934 a new professional club, Peterborough United, was formed and entered the Midland League the following year. Peterborough's first success came in 1939–40, but from 1955–56 to 1959–60 they won five successive titles. During the 1958–59 season they were undefeated in the Midland League. They reached the third round of the FA Cup, won the Northamptonshire Senior Cup, the Maunsell Cup and were runners-up in the East Anglian Cup.

London Road Stadium, London Road, Peterborough PE2 8AL.

Telephone: (01733) 563 947. ***Fax:*** (01733) 344 140.

Ticket Office: (01733) 865 674.

Website: www.theposh.com

Email: info@theposh.com

Ground Capacity: 15,460.

Record Attendance: 30,096 v Swansea T, FA Cup 5th rd, 20 February 1965.

Pitch Measurements: 112yd × 71yd.

Chairman: Darragh MacAnthony.

Chief Executive: Bob Symns.

Manager: Darren Ferguson.

Assistant Manager: Kevin Russell.

Physio: Chris Burton.

Colours: Blue shirts with white design, white shorts, white stockings.

Year Formed: 1934.

Turned Professional: 1934.

Club Nickname: 'The Posh'.

Ground: 1934, London Road Stadium.

First Football League Game: 20 August 1960, Division 4, v Wrexham (h) W 3–0 – Walls; Stafford, Walker; Rayner, Rigby, Norris; Hails, Emery (1), Bly (1), Smith, McNamee (1).

Record League Victory: 9–1 v Barnet (a) Division 3, 5 September 1998 – Griemink; Hooper (1), Drury (Farell), Gill, Bodley, Edwards, Davies, Payne, Grazioli (5), Quinn (2) (Rowe), Houghton (Etherington) (1).

Record Cup Victory: 9–1 v Rushden T, FA Cup 1st qual rd, 6 October 1945 – Hilliard; Bryan, Parrott, Warner, Hobbs, Woods, Polhill (1), Fairchild, Laxton (6), Tasker (1), Rodgers (1); 9–1 v Kingstonian, FA Cup 1st rd, 25 November 1992. Match ordered to be replayed by FA. Peterborough won replay 1–0.

HONOURS

Football League – Division 1: Best season: 10th, 1992–93; **Division 2:** 1991–92 (play-offs); **FL 1:** ***Runners-up*** 2008–09; **FL 2:** ***Runners-up*** 2007–08; **Division 4:** ***Champions*** 1960–61, 1973–74.

FA Cup: Best season: 6th rd, 1965.

Football League Cup: Semi-final 1966.

sky SPORTS FACT FILE

Winger Tommy Rudkin had brief spells with Wolverhampton Wanderers and Lincoln City before signing for Peterborough United in 1939. When wartime service duties permitted, he starred in many matches for Posh and Arsenal paid £1,800 for him in 1946.

Record Defeat: 1–8 v Northampton T, FA Cup 2nd rd (2nd replay), 18 December 1946.

Most League Points (2 for a win): 66, Division 4, 1960–61.

Most League Points (3 for a win): 92, FL 2, 2007–08.

Most League Goals: 134, Division 4, 1960–61.

Highest League Scorer in Season: Terry Bly, 52, Division 4, 1960–61.

Most League Goals in Total Aggregate: Jim Hall, 122, 1967–75.

Most League Goals in One Match: 5, Guiliano Grazioli v Barnet, Division 3, 5 September 1998.

Most Capped Player: Craig Morgan, 19 (23), Wales.

Most League Appearances: Tommy Robson, 482, 1968–81.

Youngest League Player: Matthew Etherington, 15 years 262 days v Brentford, 3 May 1997.

Record Transfer Fee Received: £1,300,000 from Hull C for Aaron McLean, January 2011.

Record Transfer Fee Paid: £500,000 to Grimsby T for Ryan Bennett, January 2010.

Football League Record: 1960 Elected to Division 4; 1961–68 Division 3, when they were demoted for financial irregularities; 1968–74 Division 4; 1974–79 Division 3; 1979–91 Division 4; 1991–92 Division 3; 1992–94 Division 1; 1994–97 Division 2; 1997–2000 Division 3; 2000–04 Division 2; 2004–05 FL 1; 2005–08 FL 2; 2008–09 FL 1; 2009–10 FL C; 2010–11 FL 1; 2011– FL C.

LATEST SEQUENCES

Longest Sequence of League Wins: 9, 1.2.1992 – 14.3.1992.

Longest Sequence of League Defeats: 8, 12.1.2008 – 12.4.2008.

Longest Sequence of League Draws: 8, 18.12.1971 – 12.2.1972.

Longest Sequence of Unbeaten League Matches: 17, 17.12.1960 – 8.4.1961.

Longest Sequence Without a League Win: 17, 23.9.1978 – 30.12.1978.

Successive Scoring Runs: 33 from 20.9.1960.

Successive Non-scoring Runs: 6 from 13.8.2002.

MANAGERS

Jock Porter 1934–36
Fred Taylor 1936–37
Vic Poulter 1937–38
Sam Haden 1938–48
Jack Blood 1948–50
Bob Gurney 1950–52
Jack Fairbrother 1952–54
George Swindin 1954–58
Jimmy Hagan 1958–62
Jack Fairbrother 1962–64
Gordon Clark 1964–67
Norman Rigby 1967–69
Jim Iley 1969–72
Noel Cantwell 1972–77
John Barnwell 1977–78
Billy Hails 1978–79
Peter Morris 1979–82
Martin Wilkinson 1982–83
John Wile 1983–86
Noel Cantwell 1986–88 *(continued as General Manager)*
Mick Jones 1988–89
Mark Lawrenson 1989–90
Dave Booth 1990–91
Chris Turner 1991–92
Lil Fuccillo 1992–93
Chris Turner 1993–94
John Still 1994–95
Mick Halsall 1995–96
Barry Fry 1996–2005
Mark Wright 2005–06
Steve Bleasdale 2006
Keith Alexander 2006–07
Darren Ferguson 2007–09
Mark Cooper 2009–10
Jim Gannon 2010
Gary Johnson 2010–11
Darren Ferguson January 2011–

TEN YEAR LEAGUE RECORD

		P	*W*	*D*	*L*	*F*	*A*	*Pts*	*Pos*
2002-03	Div 2	46	14	16	16	51	54	58	11
2003-04	Div 2	46	12	16	18	58	58	52	18
2004-05	FL 1	46	9	12	25	49	73	39	23
2005-06	FL 2	46	17	11	18	57	49	62	9
2006-07	FL 2	46	18	11	17	70	61	65	10
2007-08	FL 2	46	28	8	10	84	43	92	2
2008-09	FL 1	46	26	11	9	78	54	89	2
2009-10	FL C	46	8	10	28	46	80	34	24
2010-11	FL 1	46	23	10	13	106	75	79	4
2011-12	FL C	46	13	11	22	67	77	50	18

DID YOU KNOW ?

In the close season before the start of 1966–67, Peterborough United had two players capped for Wales in South America. Goalkeeper Tony Millington played against Brazil and Chile (his sixth and seventh caps), centre-back Frank Rankmore won his one cap as a substitute against Chile.

PETERBOROUGH UNITED 2011–12 LEAGUE RECORD

Match No.	Date	Venue	Opponents	Result		H/T Score	Lg Pos.	Goalscorers	Attendance
1	Aug 6	H	Crystal Palace	W	2-1	0-1	—	McCann [58], Ball [73]	11,604
2	14	A	Blackpool	L	1-2	0-1	11	Boyd [82]	12,881
3	17	A	Millwall	D	2-2	0-1	—	Frecklington [72], Taylor [75]	10,240
4	20	H	Ipswich T	W	7-1	4-1	6	Taylor 2 [30, 40], Tomlin 3 [38, 42, 90], McCann 2 (1 pen) [48 (p), 56]	7928
5	27	A	Brighton & HA	L	0-2	0-1	9		19,656
6	Sept 10	H	Hull C	L	0-1	0-0	11		8685
7	17	H	Burnley	W	2-1	2-1	10	Sinclair 2 [3, 38]	7901
8	24	A	West Ham U	L	0-1	0-1	11		29,895
9	27	A	Portsmouth	W	3-2	2-1	—	Frecklington 2 [4, 21], Huseklepp (og) [90]	12,102
10	Oct 1	H	Doncaster R	L	1-2	1-0	13	McCann [19]	8220
11	15	A	Bristol C	W	2-1	0-0	11	Boyd [51], Tomlin [72]	13,115
12	18	H	Cardiff C	W	4-3	2-1	—	Boyd [21], McCann 2 (1 pen) [24, 87 (p)], Taylor [90]	6351
13	22	H	Leeds U	L	2-3	1-1	10	Zakuani [23], Little [88]	12,880
14	29	A	Watford	L	2-3	2-3	12	Frecklington [15], Sinclair [39]	15,031
15	Nov 1	A	Southampton	L	1-2	0-2	—	Sinclair [76]	21,350
16	5	H	Derby Co	W	3-2	1-2	11	Taylor [37], Rowe [51], McCann [90]	9666
17	19	A	Birmingham C	D	1-1	0-1	11	McCann [61]	18,090
18	26	H	Middlesbrough	D	1-1	0-0	12	Taylor [81]	10,013
19	29	A	Reading	L	2-3	1-1	—	Rowe [16], Sinclair [90]	15,907
20	Dec 3	H	Barnsley	L	3-4	0-2	16	Boyd [64], Bennett [68], Frecklington [70]	8320
21	10	A	Leicester C	D	1-1	0-0	17	Tomlin [71]	25,948
22	17	H	Coventry C	W	1-0	0-0	15	Sinclair [66]	8062
23	26	A	Nottingham F	W	1-0	1-0	13	Boyd [20]	24,376
24	31	A	Middlesbrough	D	1-1	0-0	15	Rowe [87]	18,899
25	Jan 2	H	Birmingham C	D	1-1	1-0	15	Sinclair [1]	11,167
26	14	A	Hull C	L	0-1	0-1	16		18,074
27	21	H	Brighton & HA	L	1-2	0-1	16	Ball [72]	9474
28	28	H	Portsmouth	L	0-3	0-2	—		7555
29	Feb 4	A	Burnley	D	1-1	1-0	18	Taylor [12]	13,258
30	14	A	Cardiff C	L	1-3	0-3	—	Taylor [90]	21,342
31	18	H	Bristol C	W	3-0	1-0	18	Tomlin 2 [7, 84], Ball [62]	7004
32	25	A	Doncaster R	D	1-1	0-1	18	Barnett [90]	10,375
33	Mar 3	A	Crystal Palace	L	0-1	0-0	18		18,559
34	6	H	Millwall	L	0-3	0-1	—		6392
35	10	H	Blackpool	W	3-1	2-0	18	Barnett [27], Taylor [43], Boyd [86]	7540
36	17	A	Ipswich T	L	2-3	1-1	18	Barnett [34], Sinclair [83]	17,927
37	20	H	Reading	W	3-1	2-1	—	Boyd [25], Barnett [34], Taylor [82]	6717
38	24	A	Barnsley	L	0-1	0-1	18		9698
39	27	H	West Ham U	L	0-2	0-0	—		13,517
40	31	H	Leicester C	W	1-0	0-0	17	Taylor [60]	10,714
41	Apr 7	A	Coventry C	D	2-2	1-2	17	Sinclair 2 [3, 76]	18,760
42	9	H	Nottingham F	L	0-1	0-1	17		11,631
43	14	A	Leeds U	L	1-4	1-1	18	Newell [38]	19,469
44	17	H	Southampton	L	1-3	0-2	—	Rowe [86]	9478
45	21	H	Watford	D	2-2	1-1	18	Tomlin (pen) [14], Taylor [54]	8725
46	28	A	Derby Co	D	1-1	0-1	18	Ball [82]	27,354

Final League Position: 18

GOALSCORERS

League (67): Taylor 12, Sinclair 10, McCann 8 (2 pens), Tomlin 8 (1 pen), Boyd 7, Frecklington 5, Ball 4, Barnett 4, Rowe 4, Bennett 1, Little 1, Newell 1, Zakuani 1, own goal 1.
Carling Cup (4): Ball 2, Boyd 1, Tomlin 1 (pen).
FA Cup (0).

Jones P 35	Little M 26 + 9	Basey G 2 + 1	Bennett R 32	Zakuani G 41	McCann G 38 + 3	Rowe T 40 + 3	Frecklington L 35 + 2	Ajose N 1 + 1	Tomlin L 31 + 6	Boyd G 45	Ball D 6 + 16	Tunnicliffe R 10 + 17	Wootton S 7 + 4	Alcock C 40 + 1	Taylor P 36 + 8	Gordon B — + 1	Sinclair E 21 + 14	Kearns D 5 + 15	Newell J 8 + 6	Kennedy T 8 + 2	Lewis J 11	Briggs M 5	Barnett T 12 + 1	Brisley S 11	Ntlhe K — + 2	Coulson C — + 1	*Match No.*
1	2	3	4	5	6	7	8^{2}	9^{1}	10	11	12	13															1
1	2	3^{1}	4		6^{2}	7	8		10	11	9^{3}	13	5	12	14												2
1	2	14	4		6	7^{2}	8^{3}		10	11	9^{1}	13	5	3	12												3
1	2^{1}		4		6	7	8^{2}		10	11		13	5	3	9	12											4
1	2		4	5	6	7	8		10	11^{1}	13	12		3	9^{2}												5
1	2		4	5^{2}	6	12	7^{1}		10	11		8	13	3	9^{3}		14										6
1	2		4	5	6	12	8^{3}		10^{1}	11^{2}		7	14	3	13		9										7
1	2		4	5	6	7	8^{3}		12^{2}	11		10^{1}		3	13		9	14									8
1	2		4	5	6	7^{2}	8^{3}			11		12	13	3	10^{1}		9		14								9
1	2		4	5	6	7	8^{2}			11		12		3	10^{1}		9	13									10
1	2		4	5	6^{2}	7	8		10^{1}	11	13	12		3			9										11
1	2		4	5	6	7	8^{1}		10	11		12		3^{2}	13		9										12
1	2		4	5	6	7	8^{3}		10■	11	14	12		3^{1}	13		9^{2}										13
1	2		4	5	6^{1}		8			11	12	7			10		9			3							14
1	2		4	5	6	7^{3}	8■			11	14	10^{1}			9^{2}		12	13		3							15
1	2		4	5	6	7				11	13	8^{2}			10		9^{1}	12		3							16
1	2^{1}		4	5	6^{3}	7^{2}	8		10	11		14		3	9		13			12							17
1			4	5	6	7^{2}	8^{1}		10	11		12		2	9		13			3							18
1			4	5	6	7			8	11				2	9		10			3							19
			4	5	6^{2}	7	14		8	11		12		2	9		10^{3}	13		3^{1}	1						20
			4	5	6^{1}	3	8^{2}		7	11		14		2	9^{3}		10	12	13		1						21
			4	5		3	8^{1}		10^{2}	11		6		2	12		9^{3}	7	14	13	1						22
			4	5		7			12	11			6	2	9		10^{1}	8^{2}	13	3	1						23
			4	5		7				11			6	2	9		10	8^{1}	12	3	1						24
	13		4	5		3				11		7	6	2	9		10^{2}	12	8^{1}		1						25
	2		4	5				14	10	11		7	13	3	12		9^{3}	6^{2}	8^{1}		1						26
	2		4	5	12	11^{2}			8		13	7	6^{1}	3	9		10^{3}		14		1						27
	14		4	5	6	3	8^{3}		10^{2}	11	12	13		2	9				7^{1}		1						28
	2		4	5	6	7	8^{1}		13	11	10^{2}	12		3	9						1						29
	12		4	5^{1}	6	7	8		13	11^{2}	10^{3}			3	9		14				1	2					30
1			4	5	6		7^{2}		8	11	10^{1}	13		2	9^{3}		12	14				3					31
1	2		4	5	6	14	8^{3}		10^{2}	11	9^{1}				7		13					3	12				32
1	2			5	6	8				11	13			7	9^{1}		12	4^{2}				3	10				33
1	2			5	6	7	12			11				4	8		9^{1}	13				3^{2}	10				34
1				5	6	3	8		7^{1}	11				2	9^{2}		13	12					10	4			35
1	13			5	6^{2}	3	8^{3}		7^{1}	11				2	9		14	12					10	4			36
1				5	6	3	8		7^{1}	11	12			2	9^{2}		13						10	4			37
1	12			5	6^{2}	2	8^{3}		7^{1}	11	13			3	9		14						10	4			38
1	12			5^{1}	6	3	8^{3}		7^{2}	11				2	9		13	14					10	4			39
1	2				6	3	8		7	11^{2}				5	9		12	13					10^{1}	4			40
1	12			5	6	3	8^{1}		7^{2}	11	13			2	9		10							4			41
1				5	6	3	8^{2}		14	11	12			2	9		10^{1}	13	7^{3}					4			42
1	12			5^{1}	6^{2}	3	8		13	11	14			2	9				7				10^{3}	4			43
1	13			5	12	3	8^{2}		7	11				2	9				4^{1}				10	6			44
1	2				12	3^{1}	8^{2}		7	11				5	9				6^{3}				10	4	13	14	45
1	2			5	6	3			8	11	14			4	9^{2}			12	7^{1}				10^{3}		13		46

FA Cup

Third Round	Sunderland	(h)	0-2

Carling Cup

First Round	Stevenage	(a)	4-3
Second Round	Middlesbrough	(h)	0-2

PLYMOUTH ARGYLE FL Championship 2

FOUNDATION

The club was formed in September 1886 as the Argyle Athletic Club by former public and private school pupils who wanted to continue playing the game. The meeting was held in a room above the Borough Arms (a coffee house), Bedford Street, Plymouth. It was common then to choose a local street/terrace as a club name and Argyle or Argyll was a fashionable name throughout the land due to Queen Victoria's great interest in Scotland.

Home Park, Plymouth, Devon PL2 3DQ.

Telephone: (01752) 562 561.

Fax: (01752) 606 167.

Ticket Office: (0845) 338 7232.

Website: www.pafc.co.uk

Email: argyle@pafc.co.uk

Ground Capacity: 21,118.

Record Attendance: 43,596 v Aston Villa, Division 2, 10 October 1936.

Pitch Measurements: 112yd × 73yd.

Chairman: James Brent.

Manager: Carl Fletcher.

Assistant Manager: Romain Larrieu.

Physio: Paul Atkinson.

HONOURS

Football League – Division 2: ***Champions*** 2003–04;
Division 3 (S): ***Champions*** 1929–30, 1951–52; ***Runners-up*** 1921–22, 1922–23, 1923–24, 1924–25, 1925–26, 1926–27 (record of six consecutive years);
Division 3: ***Champions*** 1958–59, 2001–02; ***Runners-up*** 1974–75, 1985–86.

FA Cup: Semi-final 1984.

Football League Cup: Semi-final 1965, 1974.

Colours: Dark green shirts with white design, white shorts, white stockings with green design.

Year Formed: 1886.

Turned Professional: 1903.

Previous Name: 1886, Argyle Athletic Club; 1903, Plymouth Argyle.

Club Nickname: 'The Pilgrims'.

Ground: 1886, Home Park.

First Football League Game: 28 August 1920, Division 3, v Norwich C (h) D 1–1 – Craig; Russell, Atterbury; Logan, Dickinson, Forbes; Kirkpatrick, Jack, Bowler, Heeps (1), Dixon.

Record League Victory: 8–1 v Millwall, Division 2, 16 January 1932 – Harper; Roberts, Titmuss; Mackay, Pullan, Reed; Grozier, Bowden (2), Vidler (3), Leslie (1), Black (1), (1 og). 8–1 v Hartlepool U (a), Division 2, 7 May 1994 – Nicholls; Patterson (Naylor), Hill, Burrows, Comyn, McCall (1), Barlow, Castle (1), Landon (3), Marshall (1), Dalton (2).

Record Cup Victory: 6–0 v Corby T, FA Cup 3rd rd, 22 January 1966 – Leiper; Book, Baird; Williams, Nelson, Newman; Jones (1), Jackson (1), Bickle (3), Piper (1), Jennings.

sky SPORTS FACT FILE

Plymouth Argyle helped out cash-strapped Newport County in February 1926 when they paid £1,500 for centre-half Fred McKenzie. A Scot, he became Argyle's penalty king and was in the promotion team in 1929–30 before returning to Newport in 1934.

Record Defeat: 0–9 v Stoke C, Division 2, 17 December 1960.

Most League Points (2 for a win): 68, Division 3 (S), 1929–30.

Most League Points (3 for a win): 102, Division 3, 2001–02.

Most League Goals: 107, Division 3 (S), 1925–26 and 1951–52.

Highest League Scorer in Season: Jack Cock, 32, Division 3 (S), 1926–27.

Most League Goals in Total Aggregate: Sammy Black, 180, 1924–38.

Most League Goals in One Match: 5, Wilf Carter v Charlton Ath, Division 2, 27 December 1960.

Most Capped Player: Moses Russell, 20 (23), Wales.

Most League Appearances: Kevin Hodges, 530, 1978–92.

Youngest League Player: Lee Phillips, 16 years 43 days v Gillingham, 29 October 1996.

Record Transfer Fee Received: £3,000,000 from Hull C for Peter Halmosi, July 2008.

Record Transfer Fee Paid: £500,000 to Cardiff C for Steve MacLean, January 2008; £500,000 to QPR for Simon Walton, August 2008.

Football League Record: 1920 Original Member of Division 3; 1921–30 Division 3 (S); 1930–50 Division 2; 1950–52 Division 3 (S); 1952–56 Division 2; 1956–58 Division 3 (S); 1958–59 Division 3; 1959–68 Division 2; 1968–75 Division 3; 1975–77 Division 2; 1977–86 Division 3; 1986–95 Division 2; 1995–96 Division 3; 1996–98 Division 2; 1998–2002 Division 3; 2002–04 Division 2; 2004–10 FL C; 2010–11 FL 1; 2011– FL 2.

MANAGERS

Frank Brettell 1903–05
Bob Jack 1905–06
Bill Fullerton 1906–07
Bob Jack 1910–38
Jack Tresadern 1938–47
Jimmy Rae 1948–55
Jack Rowley 1955–60
Neil Dougall 1961
Ellis Stuttard 1961–63
Andy Beattie 1963–64
Malcolm Allison 1964–65
Derek Ufton 1965–68
Billy Bingham 1968–70
Ellis Stuttard 1970–72
Tony Waiters 1972–77
Mike Kelly 1977–78
Malcolm Allison 1978–79
Bobby Saxton 1979–81
Bobby Moncur 1981–83
Johnny Hore 1983–84
Dave Smith 1984–88
Ken Brown 1988–90
David Kemp 1990–92
Peter Shilton 1992–95
Steve McCall 1995
Neil Warnock 1995–97
Mick Jones 1997–98
Kevin Hodges 1998–2000
Paul Sturrock 2000–04
Bobby Williamson 2004–05
Tony Pulis 2005–06
Ian Holloway 2006–07
Paul Sturrock 2007–09
Paul Mariner 2009–10
Peter Reid 2010–11
Carl Fletcher September 2011–

LATEST SEQUENCES

Longest Sequence of League Wins: 9, 8.3.1986 – 12.4.1986.

Longest Sequence of League Defeats: 9, 12.10.1963 – 7.12.1963.

Longest Sequence of League Draws: 5, 26.2.2000 – 14.3.2000.

Longest Sequence of Unbeaten League Matches: 22, 20.4.1929 – 21.12.1929.

Longest Sequence Without a League Win: 13, 27.4.1963 – 2.10.1963.

Successive Scoring Runs: 39 from 15.4.1939.

Successive Non-scoring Runs: 5 from 20.9.1947.

TEN YEAR LEAGUE RECORD

		P	*W*	*D*	*L*	*F*	*A*	*Pts*	*Pos*
2002-03	Div 2	46	17	14	15	63	52	65	8
2003-04	Div 2	46	26	12	8	85	41	90	1
2004-05	FL C	46	14	11	21	52	64	53	17
2005-06	FL C	46	13	17	16	39	46	56	14
2006-07	FL C	46	17	16	13	63	62	67	11
2007-08	FL C	46	17	13	16	60	50	64	10
2008-09	FL C	46	13	12	21	44	57	51	21
2009-10	FL C	46	11	8	27	43	68	41	23
2010-11	FL 1	46	15	7	24	51	74	42*	23
2011-12	FL 2	46	10	16	20	47	64	46	21

** 10 points deducted.*

DID YOU KNOW ?

Scottish international goalkeeper Bill Harper had sandwiched a four-year spell in the USA with five different clubs between two spells with Arsenal – winning a championship medal in 1930–31. He then joined Plymouth Argyle, returning to Highbury against them in an FA Cup tie in 1931–32.

PLYMOUTH ARGYLE 2011–12 LEAGUE RECORD

Match No.	Date	Venue	Opponents	Result		H/T Score	Lg Pos.	Goalscorers	Attendance
1	Aug 6	A	Shrewsbury T	D	1-1	0-0	—	Fletcher, C [90]	6421
2	13	H	Rotherham U	L	1-4	0-0	21	Atkinson [49]	6015
3	16	H	AFC Wimbledon	L	0-2	0-0	—		5900
4	20	A	Gillingham	L	0-3	0-0	22		5053
5	27	H	Crewe Alex	L	0-1	0-1	24		5720
6	Sept 3	A	Burton Alb	L	1-2	0-1	24	Atkinson [90]	3042
7	10	H	Port Vale	L	0-2	0-1	24		5018
8	13	A	Barnet	L	0-2	0-1	—		1849
9	17	A	Southend U	L	0-2	0-0	24		4984
10	24	H	Macclesfield T	W	2-0	1-0	24	Feeney [20], Williams [53]	6005
11	Oct 1	A	Crawley T	L	0-2	0-1	24		3175
12	8	H	Accrington S	D	2-2	2-0	24	Walton (pen) [27], Soukouna [45]	8013
13	15	A	Dagenham & R	W	3-2	1-0	24	Lecointe [20], Hourihane [52], Walton (pen) [90]	2025
14	22	H	Swindon T	L	0-1	0-0	24		6872
15	25	A	Oxford U	L	1-5	0-1	—	Walton (pen) [55]	7802
16	29	A	Cheltenham T	L	1-2	1-0	24	Elliott (og) [26]	4026
17	Nov 5	H	Morecambe	D	1-1	1-0	24	Walton [31]	5409
18	19	A	Torquay U	L	1-3	0-0	24	Atkinson [78]	3983
19	26	H	Northampton T	W	4-1	4-0	24	Walton (pen) [8], Chadwick [9], Hemmings [14], Atkinson [17]	5762
20	Dec 10	A	Bradford C	D	1-1	0-0	23	Sutherland [59]	10,143
21	17	H	Hereford U	D	1-1	0-0	23	Chadwick (pen) [81]	6531
22	26	A	Bristol R	W	3-2	0-2	24	Feeney [52], Chadwick [79], Hemmings [90]	8090
23	31	A	Aldershot T	D	0-0	0-0	23		3886
24	Jan 2	H	Torquay U	L	1-2	0-0	24	Young [72]	12,836
25	7	A	Crewe Alex	L	2-3	0-2	—	Walton (pen) [50], Lecointe [66]	3707
26	14	H	Burton Alb	W	2-1	0-0	23	Walton 2 (1 pen) [47, 89 (p)]	6082
27	21	H	Crawley T	D	1-1	0-1	22	Blanchard [90]	6417
28	28	A	Port Vale	L	0-1	0-0	23		4375
29	Feb 4	H	Southend U	D	2-2	0-2	—	Chadwick [86], MacDonald [88]	6328
30	14	H	Barnet	D	0-0	0-0	—		5879
31	18	A	Accrington S	W	4-0	2-0	21	MacDonald 2 [3, 24], Purse [72], Daley [90]	2186
32	25	H	Dagenham & R	D	0-0	0-0	21		7804
33	28	A	Macclesfield T	D	1-1	0-0	—	Hourihane [71]	1888
34	Mar 3	H	Gillingham	L	0-1	0-1	23		6382
35	6	A	AFC Wimbledon	W	2-1	1-1	—	Bhasera [1], Chadwick [49]	4578
36	10	A	Rotherham U	L	0-1	0-0	23		3475
37	17	H	Shrewsbury T	W	1-0	1-0	22	Wotton [21]	5931
38	20	H	Bristol R	D	1-1	0-1	—	Blanchard [84]	7531
39	24	A	Northampton T	D	0-0	0-0	22		6718
40	31	H	Bradford C	W	1-0	1-0	21	Tsoumou [4]	6933
41	Apr 6	A	Hereford U	D	1-1	1-0	21	Stam (og) [30]	4597
42	9	H	Aldershot T	W	1-0	1-0	20	MacDonald [14]	8677
43	14	A	Swindon T	L	0-1	0-0	21		10,422
44	21	H	Oxford U	D	1-1	1-1	21	Williams [2]	6668
45	28	A	Morecambe	D	2-2	1-0	21	Young [4], Purse [83]	2313
46	May 5	H	Cheltenham T	L	1-2	0-1	21	Tsoumou [54]	8342

Final League Position: 21

GOALSCORERS

League (47): Walton 8 (6 pens), Chadwick 5 (1 pen), Atkinson 4, MacDonald 4, Blanchard 2, Feeney 2, Hemmings 2, Hourihane 2, Lecointe 2, Purse 2, Tsoumou 2, Williams 2, Young 2, Bhasera 1, Daley 1, Fletcher, C 1, Soukouna 1, Sutherland 1, Wotton 1, own goals 2.
Carling Cup (0).
FA Cup (3): Bhasera 1, Feeney 1, Fletcher, C 1.
J Paint Trophy (1): Daley 1.

Cole J 37	Berry D 33 + 2	Gibson B 12 + 1	Fletcher C 8 + 1	Zubar S 4	Soukouna L 15 + 5	Daley L 14 + 4	Hourihane C 32 + 6	Feeney W 25 + 3	Hitchcock T 3 + 5	Williams R 27	Walton S 36 + 5	Vassell I — + 6	Atkinson W 20 + 2	Lecointe M 8 + 11	Larrieu R 8 + 2	Nelson C 16 + 1	King S 6	Griffiths J 4 + 5	Bhasera O 24 + 3	Sims J 3	Young L 21 + 7	Bignot P 14	Sutherland C 5 + 4	Blanchard M 28	Purse D 24	Chadwick N 19 + 3	Hemmings A 18 + 5	Wotton P 18	Lennox J 2 + 6	Tsoumou J 4 + 7	MacDonald A 15 + 3	Fletcher S — + 1	Fletcher S 2 + 3	Chenoweth O 1	*Match No.*
1	2	3	4	5	6	7	8	9	10[2]	11[1]	12	13																							1
1	2	3	4[1]	5	6	7	8	9	12		11		10																						2
1	2	3		5	6	7	8	9	10[1]		4		11	12																					3
	2	3■		5	6	7[1]	8	9			11		10	12	1	4																			4
	2		4		6	7[1]	8	9	13	3	11[2]		10	12	1	5																			5
1	2[1]	14	8		6	7			10[2]	3	11		9	12		4	5[3]	13																	6
	13		12		6■	7	8	9	14	3	4[1]		11	10[3]	1	2	5[2]																		7
		5	4			7[1]	8	9		3	6		10	12	1	2		11																	8
1	2	3	11■		6[2]	7[3]	8		14		13		10	12		4	5	9[1]																	9
1	2				6	7[1]	8	9		3	10		11			4	5	12																	10
1	2				6	7	8[1]	9	12	3	10		11[2]	14		4	5[3]	13																	11
1	2				6[1]	7	8			3	11		10	9		4	5	12																	12
1	2	5			6		8	9[1]		3	7	12	11	10		4																			13
1	2	5			6[2]		8	10[1]		3	11	12	7[3]	9		4		13	14																14
1	2	5			13					3	6	14	7[1]	9		4		8[3]	12	10[2]	11														15
1[6]	2	5	4				8				11	12			15	6		10■	3	9[1]	7														16
		5	11				8[2]	10			6		13	12	1	4			3	9[1]	7	2													17
		5				7[2]		9[1]			6	13	11	12	1	4			3		8	2	10												18
1	2					14	8				6[2]		7	12					3		13		10[3]	4	5	9[1]	11								19
1	2					13	8				6		7			12			3■				10[2]	4	5[1]	9	11								20
1	2						8	12		3	6[2]		7								13		10[1]	4	5■	9	11								21
1	2						8	10			6		7[1]						3		12	5		4		9	11								22
1	2				12		8[1]	10			6		7[2]						3		13	5		4		9	11								23
1	2						8	10			6								3		7	5	12	4		9[1]	11								24
1	2						8■	10			6		13	12					3		7[2]		9[1]	4	5		11								25
1					13			10			6			9[1]					3		7	2	12	4	5		11[2]	8							26
1					12			10[1]			8			9[3]					3		7[2]	2	13	4	5		11	6	14						27
1					12						8			9[2]					3		7[3]	2	13	4	5	10[1]	11	6	14						28
1							12				8[2]								3		7[1]	2		4	5	10	11	6	13	9[3]	14				29
1							8												3		7[1]	2		4	5	9	11	6		12	10				30
						14	8				12				1				3		7	2		4	5	9[2]	11[1]	6		13	10[3]				31
1						13	8			3											7[1]	2		4	5	9	11[2]	6		12	10				32
1						11[1]	8[2]			3	13										7	2		4	5	9	12	6			10				33
1	12						8			3	13										7	2[1]		4	5	9	11[2]	6[3]		14	10				34
1	2						13	12		3	8								11[2]		7			4	5	9		6			10[1]				35
1	2							12		3[2]	8								11		7[1]			4	5	9	14	6	13		10[3]				36
1	2						14	9[2]		3	8								11					4	5	10[1]		6[3]	7	12	13				37
1	2						8			3	6								11[2]		12			4	5		13		7[1]	9	10				38
1	2						8			3	7								11[1]		14			4	5	13	12	6		9[2]	10[3]				39
1	2									3	8								13					4	5	10[1]	11[2]	6		9	7	12			40
1	2						14	10[3]		3	8										13			4	5	9[1]	11	6			7[2]		12		41
	2						13	10[3]		3	8				1				11					4	5	9[1]		6		12	7[2]		14		42
1	2						14	9[2]		3	8[3]								11		7			4	5		12	6			10[1]		13		43
1	2						8	9[1]		3									11		7			4	5	13		6			12		10[2]		44
	2				6		8			3											7[1]			4	5	13	11		12		9[2]		10	1	45
1[6]	2				6		8	9		3[1]					15	5			11		7			4					13	12	10[2]				46

FA Cup
First Round Stourbridge (h) 3-3
(a) 0-2

Carling Cup
First Round Millwall (h) 0-1

J Paint Trophy
First Round Exeter C (a) 1-1

PORTSMOUTH FL Championship 1

FOUNDATION

At a meeting held in his High Street, Portsmouth offices in 1898, solicitor Alderman J. E. Pink and five other business and professional men agreed to buy some ground close to Goldsmith Avenue for £4,950 which they developed into Fratton Park in record breaking time. A team of professionals was signed up by manager Frank Brettell and entry to the Southern League obtained for the new club's September 1899 kick-off.

Fratton Park, Frogmore Road, Portsmouth, Hampshire PO4 8RA.

Telephone: (02392) 731 204.

Fax: (02392) 734 129.

Ticket Office: (0844) 847 1898.

Website: www.pompeyfc.co.uk

Email: info@pompeyfc.co.uk

Ground Capacity: 20,688.

Record Attendance: 51,385 v Derby Co, FA Cup 6th rd, 26 February 1949.

Pitch Measurements: 100m × 65m.

De Facto Owner: Deepak Chainrai.

Manager: Michael Appleton.

First Team Coach: Guy Whittingham.

Head of Sports Performance: Steve Allen.

Colours: Blue shirts with white trim, white shorts, red stockings.

Year Formed: 1898.

Turned Professional: 1898.

Club Nickname: 'Pompey'.

Ground: 1898, Fratton Park.

First Football League Game: 28 August 1920, Division 3, v Swansea T (h) W 3–0 – Robson; Probert, Potts; Abbott, Harwood, Turner; Thompson, Stringfellow (1), Reid (1), James (1), Beedie.

Record League Victory: 9–1 v Notts Co, Division 2, 9 April 1927 – McPhail; Clifford, Ted Smith; Reg Davies (1), Foxall, Moffat; Forward (1), Mackie (2), Haines (3), Watson, Cook (2).

Record Cup Victory: 7–0 v Stockport Co, FA Cup 3rd rd, 8 January 1949 – Butler; Rookes, Ferrier; Scoular, Flewin, Dickinson; Harris (3), Barlow, Clarke (2), Phillips (2), Froggatt.

Record Defeat: 0–10 v Leicester C, Division 1, 20 October 1928.

Most League Points (2 for a win): 65, Division 3, 1961–62.

HONOURS

Football League – Division 1: *Champions* 1948–49, 1949–50, 2002–03;
Division 2: ***Runners-up*** 1926–27, 1986–87;
Division 3 (S): ***Champions*** 1923–24;
Division 3: ***Champions*** 1961–62, 1982–83.

FA Cup: Winners 1939, 2008; ***Runners-up*** 1929, 1934, 2010.

Football League Cup: Best season: 5th rd, 1961, 1986, 1994, 2010.

European Competitions
UEFA Cup: 2008–09.

sky SPORTS FACT FILE

When Portsmouth won the FA Cup in 1939 beating Wolverhampton Wanderers at Wembley, they conceded only two goals during the run and were not involved in any replays. Their share of the gate was £5,380 and the players' total bonus for Cup matches amounted to £42.

Most League Points (3 for a win): 98, Division 1, 2002–03.

Most League Goals: 97, Division 1, 2002–03.

Highest League Scorer in Season: Guy Whittingham, 42, Division 1, 1992–93.

Most League Goals in Total Aggregate: Peter Harris, 194, 1946–60.

Most League Goals in One Match: 5, Alf Strange v Gillingham, Division 3, 27 January 1923; 5, Peter Harris v Aston Villa, Division 1, 3 September 1958.

Most Capped Player: Jimmy Dickinson, 48, England.

Most League Appearances: Jimmy Dickinson, 764, 1946–65.

Youngest League Player: Clive Green, 16 years 259 days v Wrexham, 21 August 1976.

Record Transfer Fee Received: £20,000,000 from Real Madrid for Lassana Diarra, January 2009.

Record Transfer Fee Paid: Reported fee of £11,000,000 to Liverpool for Peter Crouch, July 2008.

Football League Record: 1920 Original Member of Division 3; 1921 Division 3 (S); 1924–27 Division 2; 1927–59 Division 1; 1959–61 Division 2; 1961–62 Division 3; 1962–76 Division 2; 1976–78 Division 3; 1978–80 Division 4; 1980–83 Division 3; 1983–87 Division 2; 1987–88 Division 1; 1988–92 Division 2; 1992–2003 Division 1; 2003–10 FA Premier League; 2010–12 FL C; 2012– FL 1.

LATEST SEQUENCES

Longest Sequence of League Wins: 7, 17.8.2002 – 17.9.2002.

Longest Sequence of League Defeats: 9, 21.10.1975 – 6.12.1975.

Longest Sequence of League Draws: 5, 16.12.2000 – 13.1.2001.

Longest Sequence of Unbeaten League Matches: 15, 18.4.1924 – 18.10.1924.

Longest Sequence Without a League Win: 25, 29.11.1958 – 22.8.1959.

Successive Scoring Runs: 23 from 30.8.1930.

Successive Non-scoring Runs: 6 from 14.1.1939.

MANAGERS

Frank Brettell 1898–1901
Bob Blyth 1901–04
Richard Bonney 1905–08
Bob Brown 1911–20
John McCartney 1920–27
Jack Tinn 1927–47
Bob Jackson 1947–52
Eddie Lever 1952–58
Freddie Cox 1958–61
George Smith 1961–70
Ron Tindall 1970–73
(General Manager to 1974)
John Mortimore 1973–74
Ian St John 1974–77
Jimmy Dickinson 1977–79
Frank Burrows 1979–82
Bobby Campbell 1982–84
Alan Ball 1984–89
John Gregory 1989–90
Frank Burrows 1990–91
Jim Smith 1991–95
Terry Fenwick 1995–98
Alan Ball 1998–99
Tony Pulis 2000
Steve Claridge 2000–01
Graham Rix 2001–02
Harry Redknapp 2002–04
Velimir Zajec 2004–05
Alain Perrin 2005
Harry Redknapp 2005–08
Tony Adams 2008–09
Paul Hart 2009
Avram Grant 2009–10
Steve Cotterill 2010–11
Michael Appleton November 2011–

TEN YEAR LEAGUE RECORD

		P	W	D	L	F	A	Pts	Pos
2002-03	Div 1	46	29	11	6	97	45	98	1
2003-04	PR Lge	38	12	9	17	47	54	45	13
2004-05	PR Lge	38	10	9	19	43	59	39	16
2005-06	PR Lge	38	10	8	20	37	62	38	17
2006-07	PR Lge	38	14	12	12	45	42	54	9
2007-08	PR Lge	38	16	9	13	48	40	57	8
2008-09	PR Lge	38	10	11	17	38	57	41	14
2009-10	PR Lge	38	7	7	24	34	66	19*	20
2010-11	FL C	46	15	13	18	53	60	58	16
2011-12	FL C	46	13	11	22	50	59	40†	22

**9 pts deducted; †10 pts deducted.*

DID YOU KNOW ?

In 1902–03, the strength of the Portsmouth playing squad in the Southern League was such that they had nine full international players including the legendary C.B. (Charles) Fry. There were six England caps, two Scots and Matt Reilly who had represented Northern Ireland.

PORTSMOUTH 2011–12 LEAGUE RECORD

Match No.	*Date*	*Venue*	*Opponents*	*Result*		*H/T Score*	*Lg Pos.*	*Goalscorers*	*Attendance*
1	Aug 6	A	Middlesbrough	D	2-2	0-1	—	Norris [47], Varney [90]	18,196
2	13	H	Brighton & HA	L	0-1	0-1	16		16,496
3	16	H	Reading	W	1-0	0-0	—	Kitson [51]	13,438
4	20	A	Bristol C	D	0-0	0-0	11		12,496
5	27	H	Cardiff C	D	1-1	0-0	12	Kanu [80]	14,354
6	Sept 10	A	West Ham U	L	3-4	1-1	14	Varney [8], Norris [60], Halford (pen) [90]	33,465
7	17	A	Hull C	L	0-1	0-1	18		18,311
8	24	H	Blackpool	W	1-0	0-0	14	Huseklepp [90]	14,935
9	27	H	Peterborough U	L	2-3	1-2	—	Zakuani (og) [8], Mwaruwari [54]	12,102
10	Oct 1	A	Leeds U	L	0-1	0-1	19		22,476
11	15	H	Barnsley	W	2-0	0-0	7	Norris [61], Varney [62]	11,261
12	18	A	Ipswich T	L	0-1	0-0	—		17,297
13	22	H	Doncaster R	W	3-1	1-1	16	Varney 2 [3, 75], Kitson [68]	12,779
14	29	A	Derby Co	L	1-3	0-3	18	Pearce [79]	24,148
15	Nov 1	A	Crystal Palace	D	0-0	0-0	—		12,933
16	5	H	Nottingham F	W	3-0	1-0	16	Huseklepp 2 [45, 84], Kitson [76]	14,207
17	19	A	Watford	L	0-2	0-2	18		12,864
18	26	H	Leicester C	D	1-1	0-0	17	Norris [68]	14,391
19	Dec 3	H	Coventry C	W	2-1	1-0	18	Halford (pen) [20], Ward [59]	12,236
20	10	A	Burnley	W	1-0	0-0	16	Norris [90]	13,411
21	18	H	Southampton	D	1-1	0-0	17	Ward [84]	19,879
22	26	A	Millwall	L	0-1	0-0	17		11,002
23	31	A	Leicester C	D	1-1	1-1	18	Futacs [20]	25,356
24	Jan 2	H	Watford	W	2-0	0-0	17	Futacs [54], Mullins [87]	14,362
25	14	H	West Ham U	L	0-1	0-1	17		18,492
26	21	A	Cardiff C	L	2-3	1-1	17	Futacs [39], Halford [49]	22,199
27	28	A	Peterborough U	W	3-0	2-0	—	Huseklepp 2 [5, 79], Pearce [40]	7555
28	Feb 7	A	Birmingham C	L	0-1	0-0	—		16,930
29	11	A	Blackpool	D	1-1	1-0	17	Huseklepp [45]	12,545
30	14	H	Ipswich T	L	0-1	0-1	—		14,330
31	18	A	Barnsley	L	0-2	0-0	22		9336
32	25	H	Leeds U	D	0-0	0-0	23		17,571
33	Mar 3	H	Middlesbrough	L	1-3	0-0	23	Halford (pen) [66]	16,770
34	6	A	Reading	L	0-1	0-1	—		18,399
35	10	A	Brighton & HA	L	0-2	0-0	24		20,772
36	17	H	Bristol C	D	0-0	0-0	24		16,695
37	20	H	Birmingham C	W	4-1	0-1	—	Maguire [54], Norris [60], Etuhu [77], Futacs [90]	12,186
38	24	A	Coventry C	L	0-2	0-0	24		15,809
39	27	H	Hull C	W	2-0	2-0	—	Maguire [21], Ward [25]	14,751
40	31	H	Burnley	L	1-5	1-1	23	Norris [19]	15,739
41	Apr 7	A	Southampton	D	2-2	1-1	23	Maguire [36], Norris [90]	31,743
42	10	H	Millwall	L	0-1	0-1	—		15,837
43	14	A	Doncaster R	W	4-3	0-2	23	Halford 2 (2 pens) [59, 65], Kitson [89], Futacs [90]	8196
44	17	H	Crystal Palace	W	2-1	1-0	—	Allan [32], Halford [55]	14,847
45	21	H	Derby Co	L	1-2	0-1	22	Varney [74]	17,707
46	28	A	Nottingham F	L	0-2	0-0	22		23,625

Final League Position: 22

GOALSCORERS

League (50): Norris 8, Halford 7 (5 pens), Huseklepp 6, Varney 6, Futacs 5, Kitson 4, Maguire 3, Ward 3, Pearce 2, Allan 1, Etuhu 1, Kanu 1, Mullins 1, Mwaruwari 1, own goal 1.
Carling Cup (0).
FA Cup (0).

Ashdown J 21	Ben Haim T 33	Hreidarsson H 2	Mokoena A 15 + 3	Halford G 42	Ricardo Rocha 31 + 2	Ward J 38 + 6	Mullins H 34	Kitson D 22 + 11	Varney L 28 + 2	Norris D 39 + 1	Williams R — + 4	Kanu N 3 + 7	Dailly C — + 1	Lawrence L 23	Pearce J 43	Mwaruwari B 6 + 12	Huseklepp E 21 + 6	Futacs M 12 + 17	Riise B 2	Henderson S 25	Razak A 1 + 2	Mattock J 7	Thorne G 4	Webster A — + 3	Etuhu K 9 + 4	Thorne G 10	Allan S 15	Maguire C 10 + 1	Harris A 2 + 3	Scapuzzi L — + 2	Rekik K 8	*Match No.*
1	2	3^{1}	4	5	6^{2}	7	8^{3}	9	10	11	12	13	14																			1
1	2	3^{2}	4	5		11^{1}	6	12	10	8	13	9		7																		2
1	2		4	5		13	6	9	10	11		8^{1}		7^{2}	3	12																3
1	2		4	5			3	9	10	11		8^{1}		7^{2}	6	12	13															4
1	4		14	2		3	6^{3}	9	8^{2}	11		13		7	5	12	10^{1}															5
1	2		4	5		12	3		11	8				7■	6	9^{2}	10^{1}	13														6
1	2		4^{2}	5		7	3		11■	8	13	12			6	9^{3}	10^{1}	14														7
1	2		4^{1}	5	12	3	8			11^{2}		13		7	6	9	10															8
1	2			5		3	4			8		12		7	6	9^{2}	10	13	11^{1}													9
	2^{3}			5	13	3	4			8^{2}	14	12		7	6	9	10		11^{1}	1												10
	2			3	6	13	4	12	11	8				7	5	9^{1}	10^{2}			1												11
	3		14	2	6^{2}	11	4	9^{1}	10	8		13		7^{3}	5		12			1												12
	2			3	6	12	4	9^{2}	11	8				7	5		10^{1}	13		1												13
	2			3^{1}	6	12	4	9	11	8^{2}				7	5		10^{3}	13		1	14											14
	2		3		6	11	4	9	10	8				7^{1}	5		12			1												15
	2			3	6	12	4	9	11	8					5	13	10^{2}			1	7^{1}											16
	2^{1}			3	6	7	4	9	11	8^{2}					5	12	10			1	13											17
				2	6	11	4	9		8					5		10			1		3	7									18
				2	6	11	4^{1}	9	12	8					5	13	10^{2}			1		3	7									19
				2	6	7	8	9	11^{1}	10					5		12			1		3	4									20
				2	6	11	4^{2}	9		10				7^{1}	5		12	13		1		3	8									21
			12	2	6	11^{1}	4	9		8				7	5		10^{2}	13		1		3										22
			4	6		2	8	9		11				7	5			10		1		3										23
	2		4				6	9		11				7	5		10	8		1		3										24
	2		6^{1}	3^{2}		11	4^{3}	9		8■				7	5	14	12	10		1				13								25
	2			6		3	4	9						7	5	12	10^{2}	11		1				13	8^{1}							26
	3			2	6	11	4	12						7	5		10	9^{1}		1					8							27
	2			3	6	11	4	13						7	5	12	10	9^{1}		1					8^{2}							28
	2			3	6	11	4	12						7	5		10	9^{1}		1					8							29
	2			3^{3}	6	11	4	12						7^{1}	5	13	10	9		1				14	8^{2}							30
	2		3		6^{1}	11	4	8■							5	12	10	9		1						7						31
	3		2	8	6	11	4			12					5	13		9^{2}		1						7	10^{1}					32
	3			2	6	11	4	13	12	10					5			9^{2}		1						7^{1}	8					33
			2	3	6	11	4	12	10	8^{1}					5			13		1						7	9^{2}					34
1	2			3	6	11		13	10	8^{2}					5			9^{1}								7	4	12				35
1	2			3	6	11			10	8					5			12								7^{1}	4	9				36
1	2			3	6	11			10	8^{3}					5			13							12	7	4^{2}	9^{1}	14			37
1	2			3	6	11^{1}			10	8^{2}					5			12							13	7	4^{3}	9		14		38
1	2			3		11			10^{2}	8					5			13							12	7	4^{1}	9			6	39
1	2			6		11^{1}			10	8					5			12							13	7^{3}	4^{2}	9		14	3	40
1				7	6	2		12	10	8					5										11^{1}		4	9			3	41
1				2	6^{1}	11			10	8					5			12							7		4	9			3	42
1				7	6	2		12	10^{2}	8					5			14							11^{1}		4	9	13		3^{3}	43
1				7	6	2		11	10	8					5												4^{1}	9	12		3	44
1				7	6	2		9	10	8					5			12									4		11^{1}		3	45
1			6		5	2			11	10								12							8		4	9	7^{1}		3	46

FA Cup				**Carling Cup**			
Third Round	Chelsea	(a)	0-4	First Round	Barnet	(h)	0-1

PORT VALE FL Championship 2

FOUNDATION

Formed in 1876 as Port Vale, adopting the prefix 'Burslem' in 1884 upon moving to that part of the city. It was dropped in 1909.

Vale Park, Hamil Road, Burslem, Stoke-on-Trent ST6 1AW.

Telephone: (01782) 655 800.

Fax: (01782) 834 981.

Ticket Office: (01782) 655 832.

Website: www.port-vale.co.uk

Email: enquiries@port-vale.co.uk

Ground Capacity: 18,982.

Record Attendance: 22,993 v Stoke C, Division 2, 6 March 1920 (at Recreation Ground); 49,768 v Aston Villa, FA Cup 5th rd, 20 February 1960 (at Vale Park).

Pitch Measurements: 114yd × 75yd.

Administrators: Messrs Traynor, Young, Krasner & Currie.

Chief Executive: Perry Deakin.

Manager: Micky Adams.

Assistant Manager: Mark Grew.

Physio: Andrew Foster.

HONOURS

Football League – Division 2: *Runners-up* 1993–94; **Division 3 (N):** ***Champions*** 1929–30, 1953–54; ***Runners-up*** 1952–53; **Division 4:** ***Champions*** 1958–59.

FA Cup: Semi-final 1954, when in Division 3.

Football League Cup: Best season: 4th rd 2007.

Autoglass Trophy: Winners 1993.

Anglo-Italian Cup: ***Runners-up*** 1996.

LDV Vans Trophy: ***Winners*** 2001.

Colours: White shirts with black trim, black shorts with white trim, white stockings.

Year Formed: 1876.

Turned Professional: 1885.

Previous Names: 1876, Port Vale; 1884, Burslem Port Vale; 1909, Port Vale.

Club Nickname: 'Valiants'.

Grounds: 1876, Limekin Lane, Longport; 1881, Westport; 1884, Moorland Road, Burslem; 1886, Athletic Ground, Cobridge; 1913, Recreation Ground, Hanley; 1950, Vale Park.

First Football League Game: 3 September 1892, Division 2, v Small Heath (a) L 1–5 – Frail; Clutton, Elson; Farrington, McCrindle, Delves; Walker, Scarratt, Bliss (1), Jones. (Only 10 men).

Record League Victory: 9–1 v Chesterfield, Division 2, 24 September 1932 – Leckie; Shenton, Poyser; Sherlock, Round, Jones; McGrath, Mills, Littlewood (6), Kirkham (2), Morton (1).

Record Cup Victory: 7–1 v Irthlingborough, FA Cup 1st rd, 12 January 1907 – Matthews; Dunn, Hamilton; Eardley, Baddeley, Holyhead; Carter, Dodds (2), Beats, Mountford (2), Coxon (3).

Record Defeat: 0–10 v Sheffield U, Division 2, 10 December 1892. 0–10 v Notts Co, Division 2, 26 February 1895.

Most League Points (2 for a win): 69, Division 3 (N), 1953–54.

sky SPORTS FACT FILE

The first Port Vale player to score five goals in a Football League match was inside-left Frank Watkin on 22 February 1930 against Rotherham United in a 7-1 win. Previously with Congleton Town, Stoke City and Stoke St Peter's, it proved to be the high point of his career.

Most League Points (3 for a win): 89, Division 2, 1992–93.

Most League Goals: 110, Division 4, 1958–59.

Highest League Scorer in Season: Wilf Kirkham 38, Division 2, 1926–27.

Most League Goals in Total Aggregate: Wilf Kirkham, 154, 1923–29, 1931–33.

Most League Goals in One Match: 6, Stewart Littlewood v Chesterfield, Division 2, 24 September 1922.

Most Capped Player: Chris Birchall, 22 (39), Trinidad & Tobago.

Most League Appearances: Roy Sproson, 761, 1950–72.

Youngest League Player: Malcolm McKenzie, 15 years 347 days v Newport Co, 12 April 1966.

Record Transfer Fee Received: £2,000,000 from Wimbledon for Gareth Ainsworth, October 1998.

Record Transfer Fee Paid: £500,000 to Lincoln C for Gareth Ainsworth, September 1997.

Football League Record: 1892 Original Member of Division 2. Failed re-election in 1896; Re-elected 1898; Resigned 1907; Returned in Oct, 1919, when they took over the fixtures of Leeds City; 1929–30 Division 3 (N); 1930–36 Division 2; 1936–38 Division 3 (N); 1938–52 Division 3 (S); 1952–54 Division 3 (N); 1954–57 Division 2; 1957–58 Division 3 (S); 1958–59 Division 4; 1959–65 Division 3; 1965–70 Division 4; 1970–78 Division 3; 1978–83 Division 4; 1983–84 Division 3; 1984–86 Division 4; 1986–89 Division 3; 1989–94 Division 2; 1994–2000 Division 1; 2000–04 Division 2; 2004–08 FL 1; 2008– FL 2.

MANAGERS

Sam Gleaves 1896–1905
(Secretary-Manager)
Tom Clare 1905–11
A. S. Walker 1911–12
H. Myatt 1912–14
Tom Holford 1919–24
(continued as Trainer)
Joe Schofield 1924–30
Tom Morgan 1930–32
Tom Holford 1932–35
Warney Cresswell 1936–37
Tom Morgan 1937–38
Billy Frith 1945–46
Gordon Hodgson 1946–51
Ivor Powell 1951
Freddie Steele 1951–57
Norman Low 1957–62
Freddie Steele 1962–65
Jackie Mudie 1965–67
Sir Stanley Matthews
(General Manager) 1965–68
Gordon Lee 1968–74
Roy Sproson 1974–77
Colin Harper 1977
Bobby Smith 1977–78
Dennis Butler 1978–79
Alan Bloor 1979
John McGrath 1980–83
John Rudge 1983–99
Brian Horton 1999–2004
Martin Foyle 2004–07
Lee Sinnott 2007–08
Dean Glover 2008–09
Micky Adams 2009–10
Jim Gannon 2011
Micky Adams May 2011–

LATEST SEQUENCES

Longest Sequence of League Wins: 8, 8.4.1893 – 30.9.1893.

Longest Sequence of League Defeats: 9, 9.3.1957 – 20.4.1957.

Longest Sequence of League Draws: 6, 26.4.1981 – 12.9.1981.

Longest Sequence of Unbeaten League Matches: 19, 5.5.1969 – 8.11.1969.

Longest Sequence Without a League Win: 17, 7.12.1991 – 21.3.1992.

Successive Scoring Runs: 22 from 12.9.1992.

Successive Non-scoring Runs: 4 from 10.2.1896.

TEN YEAR LEAGUE RECORD

		P	*W*	*D*	*L*	*F*	*A*	*Pts*	*Pos*
2002-03	Div 2	46	14	11	21	54	70	53	17
2003-04	Div 2	46	21	10	15	73	63	73	7
2004-05	FL 1	46	17	5	24	49	59	56	18
2005-06	FL 1	46	16	12	18	49	54	60	13
2006-07	FL 1	46	18	6	22	64	65	60	12
2007-08	FL 1	46	9	11	26	47	81	38	23
2008-09	FL 2	46	13	9	24	44	66	48	18
2009-10	FL 2	46	17	17	12	61	50	68	10
2010-11	FL 2	46	17	14	15	54	49	65	11
2011-12	FL 2	46	20	9	17	68	60	59*	12

**10 pts deducted.*

DID YOU KNOW ?

Mick Hulligan burst onto the scene during the Second World War as a winger for Liverpool making his debut at 19 in December 1942. He was transferred to Port Vale in July 1948 with Stan Polk after ex-Liverpool favourite Gordon Hodgson signed them for the Potteries club.

PORT VALE 2011–12 LEAGUE RECORD

Match No.	Date	Venue	Opponents	Result		H/T Score	Lg Pos.	Goalscorers	Attendance
1	Aug 6	H	Crawley T	D	2-2	1-1	—	Richards [42], Dodds [90]	5889
2	13	A	Barnet	W	3-1	2-0	4	Rigg 2 [27, 57], Roberts [37]	2260
3	16	A	Burton Alb	D	1-1	1-1	—	Loft [40]	3608
4	20	H	Accrington S	W	4-1	4-0	6	Rigg 2 [19, 43], Roberts [23], Pope [37]	4615
5	27	H	Southend U	L	2-3	1-3	—	Loft 2 (1 pen) [25, 52 (p)]	4615
6	Sept 3	A	AFC Wimbledon	L	2-3	0-1	12	Dodds [46], Morsy [84]	4404
7	10	A	Plymouth Arg	W	2-0	1-0	7	Roberts 2 (1 pen) [26, 84 (p)]	5018
8	13	H	Bradford C	W	3-2	2-1	—	Taylor, R 2 [5, 39], Pope [90]	4769
9	17	H	Shrewsbury T	L	2-3	1-2	8	Williamson 2 [26, 81]	5541
10	24	A	Crewe Alex	D	1-1	0-0	11	Pope [74]	6613
11	Oct 1	H	Rotherham U	W	2-0	2-0	7	Richards 2 [18, 26]	4983
12	8	A	Gillingham	D	1-1	1-0	9	Richards [33]	4676
13	14	H	Northampton T	W	3-0	3-0	—	Pope [5], Griffith [19], McCombe [26]	5082
14	22	H	Morecambe	L	0-4	0-2	11		5004
15	25	A	Bristol R	W	3-0	2-0	—	Richards [19], Loft [37], Rigg [85]	5444
16	29	A	Oxford U	L	1-2	0-1	9	Richards [62]	8027
17	Nov 5	H	Swindon T	L	0-2	0-1	10		4961
18	19	A	Cheltenham T	L	0-2	0-0	13		3165
19	25	H	Torquay U	D	0-0	0-0	—		5168
20	Dec 10	A	Dagenham & R	W	2-1	1-1	12	Myrie-Williams [24], Madjo [65]	1682
21	17	H	Aldershot T	W	4-0	1-0	10	Madjo 3 [8, 48, 60], Rigg [83]	3714
22	26	A	Hereford U	W	2-1	0-0	9	Yates [78], Richards (pen) [84]	3097
23	31	A	Macclesfield T	L	1-2	0-1	9	Richards [61]	4214
24	Jan 2	H	Cheltenham T	L	1-2	0-0	13	Rigg [79]	4696
25	7	A	Southend U	L	0-3	0-2	—		5269
26	14	H	AFC Wimbledon	L	1-2	1-1	14	Richards [31]	4326
27	21	A	Rotherham U	W	1-0	0-0	12	Richards (pen) [57]	3189
28	28	H	Plymouth Arg	W	1-0	0-0	10	Pope [86]	4375
29	Feb 14	A	Bradford C	D	1-1	1-0	—	Dodds [39]	2149
30	18	H	Gillingham	W	2-1	0-1	8	Rigg [81], Richards (pen) [90]	4027
31	25	A	Northampton T	W	2-1	1-0	8	McCombe [4], Rigg [58]	5803
32	28	H	Crewe Alex	D	1-1	0-0	—	Artell (og) [49]	6356
33	Mar 3	A	Accrington S	D	2-2	1-1	9	McCombe [29], Shuker [56]	2093
34	6	H	Burton Alb	W	3-0	1-0	—	Richards [43], Dodds 2 [86, 88]	5197
35	10	H	Barnet	L	1-2	0-0	14	Richards [56]	5522
36	17	A	Crawley T	L	2-3	1-1	16	Richards [32], Dodds [58]	2375
37	20	H	Hereford U	W	1-0	0-0	—	Richards [86]	3959
38	24	A	Torquay U	L	1-2	1-0	16	McCombe [29]	3136
39	31	H	Dagenham & R	L	0-1	0-0	17		4127
40	Apr 6	A	Aldershot T	W	2-1	1-0	15	Dodds 2 [12, 74]	2747
41	9	H	Macclesfield T	W	1-0	0-0	14	Yates [82]	4246
42	14	A	Morecambe	D	0-0	0-0	15		2210
43	17	A	Shrewsbury T	L	0-1	0-0	—		7678
44	21	H	Bristol R	W	1-0	1-0	13	Richards [23]	4066
45	28	A	Swindon T	L	0-5	0-1	15		12,864
46	May 5	H	Oxford U	W	3-0	1-0	12	Richards [41], Rigg [69], Williamson [90]	5621

Final League Position: 12

GOALSCORERS

League (68): Richards 17 (3 pens), Rigg 10, Dodds 8, Pope 5, Loft 4 (1 pen), Madjo 4, McCombe 4, Roberts 4 (1 pen), Williamson 3, Taylor, R 2, Yates 2, Griffith 1, Morsy 1, Myrie-Williams 1, Shuker 1, own goal 1.
Carling Cup (2): Loft 1 (pen), Roberts 1.
FA Cup (0).
J Paint Trophy (1): Taylor, R 1.

Tomlinson S 38	Yates A 35 + 3	Green M 4	Griffith A 43	McCombe J 40	Collins L 15 + 1	Rigg S 33 + 9	Roberts G 9 + 2	Richards M 31 + 5	Pope T 34 + 7	Loft D 42 + 2	Taylor R 28 + 3	Haldane L — + 3	Dodds L 21 + 14	Owen G 21 + 3	McDonald C 23 + 7	Williamson B 12 + 23	Little A 2 + 5	Morsy S 11 + 15	Martin C 8	Kozluk R 4 + 2	Chilvers L 12	Lloyd R — + 2	Myrie-Williams J 6	Madjo G 5 + 1	James K — + 5	Roe P — + 2	Marshall P 10 + 5	Shuker C 12 + 4	Davis J 7 + 1	*Match No.*
1	2	3	4	5	6	7	8^1	9^2	10^3	11	12	13	14																	1
1	2		4	5	6	7^1	8^2		10	11			13	3	9	12														2
1	2		4	5	6	7^2	8^1		10^3	11	12		14	3	9	13														3
1	2		4	5	6	7^2	8^3		10^1	11		12	14	3	9	13														4
1	2		4	5	6	7^2	8^3		10	11		12	14	3	9^1	13														5
1	2		4	5			8^3	13	10		11		7	3	6^2	9^1	12	14												6
	2	3	4	5			8^2	9▮	10^3		11		12	6		14	7^1	13	1											7
	2	3	4	5			8^3		10	13	11^2		12	6		9	7^1	14	1											8
	2	3^2	4	5^1			8		10	13	11		7^3	6	12	9		14	1											9
1	14		4			12			10	11	3			7	5	9^2	13	8^1		2^3	6									10
1			4			12		9^2	10	7	11			3	5	8^1	13			2	6									11
1	2		4			13		9	10^2	7^3	11		14	3	5	8^1		12			6									12
1	14		4	5		8^2		9	10^1	7	11^3			6		12	13			2	3									13
1			4	5^1		8^2		9^3	10	7	11			6		13	14	12		2	3									14
1	2		4			8		9	10	7	11			5	6						3									15
1	2		4^3			8	13	9	10^1	7^2	11			6	5	12		14			3									16
1	2		4			8^1	12	9	10^3	7	3		14	6	5^2					13	11									17
1	2			5	3^1	8^2			10	7^3	11		9		12			4		13	6	14								18
1	2		4	5	3	13			10	8	11^1		12								6		7	9^2						19
1	2		4	5	3	13		12	10	8	11^3				14						6		7^2	9^1						20
1	2		4	5	3	14		13	10	8	11				12						6^1		7^3	9^2						21
1	2		4	5	3	13		14	10^2	8	11^1			6		12							7	9^3						22
1	2		4	5	3	14		12	10^3	8	11^2			6		13							7	9^1						23
1	2		4	5	3	12		9	10^3	8	11^1			6^2		13							7	14						24
	2		4^3	5	3^1	8		9	10	7			12	6^2	11▮			14	1						13					25
	2		4^2	5		8		9	10^1	3			12	6		11^3		7	1						14	13				26
1	2		4	5		8		9		7	3^2		12		6	10^1		11							13					27
1	2		4	5		8		9	13	7	3^2		12		6	10^1		11												28
1	2		4	5		8		9		3			7	12	6	10^1		11												29
1			4	5		8		9		2	3		7	12	6^1	10^3		11^2									13	14		30
1			4	5		10^3		9		2	3		7	13	6	14		12									11^1	8^2		31
1			4	6		10		9	14	2	3		7^3		5	13		12									11^1	8^2		32
1			4	5	12	10			9^3	2	3		7		6^1	14		13									11^2	8		33
1			4	5	6	10^1		9^2	13	2	3		7					12							14		11	8^3		34
1			4	5	6	10^1		9	14	2	3^3		7^2		12	13											11	8		35
1	14			5		10^3		9		2	3		7		6▮	13		8									11^1	4^2	12	36
1	2			5		10^2		9	12	3			7^1			13		11									8	4	6	37
1	2		4	5		10^2		9	13	3			7^3			14		11									12	8^1	6▮	38
1	2		4	5		8		9	12	3			7^3		6	10^2		11^1								14	13			39
1	2		4	5		8^1		9	10	3			7		6												11	12		40
1	2		4^1	5		8^3		9	10	3			7		6	14		12									11^2	13		41
1	2		4	5		11^2		9	10	3			7					12									8^1	13	6	42
	2		4^3	5		11		9	10^1	3			7			12			1						14		13	8^2	6	43
	2		4^1	5		11^3		9	10	3	14		7^2			13		12	1									8	6	44
	2		4^1	5		11		9	10^3	3			7		14	12			1								13	8^2	6	45
1	2^1		4	5		11^2		9	10^3	3			7		12	14						13						8	6	46

FA Cup
First Round Grimsby T (h) 0-0
(a) 0-1

Carling Cup
First Round Huddersfield T (h) 2-4

J Paint Trophy
First Round Tranmere R (a) 1-1

PRESTON NORTH END FL Championship 1

FOUNDATION

North End Cricket and Rugby Club, which was formed in 1863, indulged in most sports before taking up soccer in about 1879. In 1881 they decided to stick to football to the exclusion of other sports and even a 16–0 drubbing by Blackburn Rovers in an invitation game at Deepdale, a few weeks after taking this decision, did not deter them for they immediately became affiliated to the Lancashire FA.

Deepdale Stadium, Sir Tom Finney Way, Deepdale, Preston PR1 6RU.

Telephone: (0844) 856 1964.

Fax: (01772) 693 366.

Ticket Office: (0844) 856 1966.

Website: www.pne.com

Email: enquiries@pne.com

Ground Capacity: 23,408.

Record Attendance: 42,684 v Arsenal, Division 1, 23 April 1938.

Pitch Measurements: 110yd × 77yd.

Chairman: Peter Ridsdale.

Deputy Chairman: David Taylor.

Manager: Graham Westley.

Assistant Manager: John Dreyer.

Head Physio: Matthew Jackson.

Colours: White shirts, blue shorts, white stockings.

Year Formed: 1880.

Turned Professional: 1885.

Club Nicknames: 'The Lilywhites' or 'North End'.

Ground: 1881, Deepdale.

HONOURS

Football League – Division 1: ***Champions*** 1888–89 (first champions) 1889–90; ***Runners-up*** 1890–91, 1891–92, 1892–93, 1905–06, 1952–53, 1957–58;
Division 2: ***Champions*** 1903–04, 1912–13, 1950–51, 1999–2000; ***Runners-up*** 1914–15, 1933–34;
Division 3: ***Champions*** 1970–71, 1995–96;
Division 4: ***Runners-up*** 1986–87.

FA Cup: ***Winners*** 1889, 1938; ***Runners-up*** 1888, 1922, 1937, 1954, 1964.

Football League Cup: Best season: 4th rd, 2003.

Double Performed: 1888–89.

Football League Cup: Best season: 4th rd, 1963, 1966, 1972, 1981.

First Football League Game: 8 September 1888, Football League, v Burnley (h) W 5–2 – Trainer; Howarth, Holmes; Robertson, William Graham, Johnny Graham; Gordon (1), Jimmy Ross (2), Goodall, Dewhurst (2), Drummond.

Record League Victory: 10–0 v Stoke, Division 1, 14 September 1889 – Trainer; Howarth, Holmes; Kelso, Russell (1), Johnny Graham; Gordon, Jimmy Ross (2), Nick Ross (3), Thomson (2), Drummond (2).

Record Cup Victory: 26–0 v Hyde, FA Cup 1st rd, 15 October 1887 – Addision; Howarth, Nick Ross; Russell (1), Thomson (5), Johnny Graham (1); Gordon (5), Jimmy Ross (8), John Goodall (1), Dewhurst (3), Drummond (2).

Record Defeat: 0–7 v Blackpool, Division 1, 1 May 1948.

Most League Points (2 for a win): 61, Division 3, 1970–71.

Most League Points (3 for a win): 95, Division 2, 1999–2000.

Most League Goals: 100, Division 2, 1927–28 and Division 1, 1957–58.

sky SPORTS FACT FILE

The legendary Ross brothers, Nick and Jimmy, enjoyed distinguished careers with Preston North End in the 19th century. Nick played in the first Football League representative team and Jimmy scored over 250 goals, yet both died prematurely at the respective ages of 31 and 36.

Highest League Scorer in Season: Ted Harper, 37, Division 2, 1932–33.

Most League Goals in Total Aggregate: Tom Finney, 187, 1946–60.

Most League Goals in One Match: 4, Jimmy Ross v Stoke, Division 1, 6 October 1888; 4, Nick Ross v Derby Co, Division 1, 11 January 1890; 4, George Drummond v Notts Co, Division 1, 12 December 1891; 4, Frank Becton v Notts Co, Division 1, 31 March 1893; 4, George Harrison v Grimsby T, Division 2, 3 November 1928; 4, Alex Reid v Port Vale, Division 2, 23 February 1929; 4, James McClelland v Reading, Division 2, 6 September 1930; 4, Dick Rowley v Notts Co, Division 2, 16 April 1932; 4, Ted Harper v Burnley, Division 2, 29 August 1932; 4, Ted Harper v Lincoln C, Division 2, 11 March 1933; 4, Charlie Wayman v QPR, Division 2, 25 December 1950; 4, Alex Bruce v Colchester U, Division 3, 28 February 1978.

Most Capped Player: Tom Finney, 76, England.

Most League Appearances: Alan Kelly, 447, 1961–75.

Youngest League Player: Steve Doyle, 16 years 166 days v Tranmere R, 15 November 1974.

Record Transfer Fee Received: £6,000,000 from Portsmouth for David Nugent, August 2007.

Record Transfer Fee Paid: £1,500,000 to Manchester U for David Healy, December 2000.

Football League Record: 1888 Founder Member of League; 1901–04 Division 2; 1904–12 Division 1; 1912–13 Division 2; 1913–14 Division 1; 1914–15 Division 2; 1919–25 Division 1; 1925–34 Division 2; 1934–49 Division 1; 1949–51 Division 2; 1951–61 Division 1; 1961–70 Division 2; 1970–71 Division 3; 1971–74 Division 2; 1974–78 Division 3; 1978–81 Division 2; 1981–85 Division 3; 1985–87 Division 4; 1987–92 Division 3; 1992–93 Division 2; 1993–96 Division 3; 1996–2000 Division 2; 2000–04 Division 1; 2004–11 FL C; 2011– FL 1.

LATEST SEQUENCES

Longest Sequence of League Wins: 14, 25.12.1950 – 27.3.1951.

Longest Sequence of League Defeats: 8, 22.9.1984 – 27.10.1984.

Longest Sequence of League Draws: 6, 24.2.1979 – 20.3.1979.

Longest Sequence of Unbeaten League Matches: 23, 8.9.1888 – 14.9.1889.

Longest Sequence Without a League Win: 15, 14.4.1923 – 20.10.1923.

Successive Scoring Runs: 30 from 15.11.1952.

Successive Non-scoring Runs: 6 from 8.4.1897.

MANAGERS

Charlie Parker 1906–15
Vincent Hayes 1919–23
Jim Lawrence 1923–25
Frank Richards 1925–27
Alex Gibson 1927–31
Lincoln Hayes 1931–32
Run by committee 1932–36
Tommy Muirhead 1936–37
Run by committee 1937–49
Will Scott 1949–53
Scot Symon 1953–54
Frank Hill 1954–56
Cliff Britton 1956–61
Jimmy Milne 1961–68
Bobby Seith 1968–70
Alan Ball Snr 1970–73
Bobby Charlton 1973–75
Harry Catterick 1975–77
Nobby Stiles 1977–81
Tommy Docherty 1981
Gordon Lee 1981–83
Alan Kelly 1983–85
Tommy Booth 1985–86
Brian Kidd 1986
John McGrath 1986–90
Les Chapman 1990–92
Sam Allardyce 1992 (*Caretaker*)
John Beck 1992–94
Gary Peters 1994–98
David Moyes 1998–2002
Kelham O'Hanlon 2002 (*Caretaker*)
Craig Brown 2002–04
Billy Davies 2004–06
Paul Simpson 2006–07
Alan Irvine 2007–09
Darren Ferguson 2010
Phil Brown 2011
Graham Westley January 2012–

TEN YEAR LEAGUE RECORD

		P	*W*	*D*	*L*	*F*	*A*	*Pts*	*Pos*
2002-03	Div 1	46	16	13	17	68	70	61	12
2003-04	Div 1	46	15	14	17	69	71	59	15
2004-05	FL C	46	21	12	13	67	58	75	5
2005-06	FL C	46	20	20	6	59	30	80	4
2006-07	FL C	46	22	8	16	64	53	74	7
2007-08	FL C	46	15	11	20	50	56	56	15
2008-09	FL C	46	21	11	14	66	54	74	6
2009-10	FL C	46	13	15	18	58	73	54	17
2010-11	FL C	46	10	12	24	54	79	42	22
2011-12	FL 1	46	13	15	18	54	68	54	15

DID YOU KNOW ?

On 13 September 2011, in a League Cup tie at Charlton Athletic, Preston North End substitute Brandon Zibaka became the youngest to play for the club. He thus overtook substitute Doyle Middleton 16 years 121 days in the same competition at Stockport County on 9 August 2010.

PRESTON NORTH END 2011–12 LEAGUE RECORD

Match No.	Date	Venue	Opponents	Result	H/T Score	Lg Pos.	Goalscorers	Attendance
1	Aug 6	H	Colchester U	L 2-4	0-1	—	Mellor [60], Coutts [70]	11,451
2	13	A	Scunthorpe U	D 1-1	1-0	19	Hume [13]	4675
3	16	A	Chesterfield	W 2-0	1-0	—	Carlisle [17], Nicholson [70]	6706
4	20	H	Exeter C	W 1-0	1-0	5	Proctor [41]	10,655
5	27	H	Notts Co	W 2-0	0-0	4	McLean [83], Turner [86]	10,759
6	Sept 9	H	Yeovil T	W 4-3	1-1	—	Proctor [5], Nicholson [49], Mellor 2 [59, 70]	11,474
7	17	A	Brentford	W 3-1	2-1	6	Mellor 2 [10, 73], Hume [32]	6090
8	24	H	Tranmere R	W 2-1	1-0	5	Alexander (pen) [37], Mayor [71]	17,281
9	27	A	Wycombe W	W 4-3	2-3	—	Mellor 2 [7, 73], Hume 2 [9, 64]	3734
10	Oct 1	A	Leyton Orient	L 1-2	1-2	3	Coutts [2]	4384
11	15	A	Walsall	L 0-1	0-1	6		4834
12	19	H	Sheffield U	L 2-4	1-2	—	Carlisle [29], Hume [63]	11,520
13	22	A	Huddersfield T	L 1-3	0-2	9	Tsoumou [61]	16,804
14	25	H	Oldham Ath	D 3-3	2-2	—	Tsoumou [28], Proctor [32], Devine [64]	11,370
15	29	H	Bournemouth	L 1-3	1-0	11	Tsoumou [29]	10,185
16	Nov 5	A	Charlton Ath	L 2-5	0-4	13	Morgan [85], Daley [90]	17,486
17	19	H	Rochdale	L 0-1	0-0	15		10,456
18	26	A	Bury	L 0-1	0-1	16		4957
19	29	A	Hartlepool U	W 1-0	1-0	—	Mellor [22]	4156
20	Dec 10	H	Stevenage	D 0-0	0-0	10		9425
21	17	A	Milton Keynes D	W 1-0	1-0	10	Parry [7]	8009
22	26	H	Carlisle U	D 3-3	2-2	10	Hume [22], Parry (pen) [31], Douglas [90]	17,518
23	31	H	Sheffield W	L 0-2	0-2	11		15,904
24	Jan 2	A	Rochdale	D 1-1	1-1	13	Jervis [16]	4570
25	14	H	Wycombe W	W 3-2	1-1	10	Bunn [40], Jervis [58], Parry (pen) [62]	10,142
26	21	H	Leyton Orient	L 0-2	0-0	11		11,436
27	24	A	Notts Co	D 0-0	0-0	—		4901
28	28	A	Yeovil T	L 1-2	0-1	13	Carlisle [74]	4245
29	Feb 14	H	Hartlepool U	W 1-0	0-0	—	Mayor [76]	14,191
30	18	A	Sheffield U	L 1-2	1-1	13	Cummins [38]	17,579
31	25	H	Walsall	D 0-0	0-0	13		11,091
32	Mar 3	A	Colchester U	L 0-3	0-1	15		3333
33	6	H	Chesterfield	D 0-0	0-0	—		9264
34	10	H	Scunthorpe U	D 0-0	0-0	14		10,621
35	13	A	Tranmere R	L 1-2	1-1	—	Cummins [12]	4612
36	17	A	Exeter C	W 2-1	1-0	14	Hume 2 [12, 84]	4741
37	20	A	Carlisle U	D 0-0	0-0	—		6925
38	24	H	Bury	D 1-1	0-0	15	Aneke [68]	10,735
39	27	H	Brentford	L 1-3	1-2	—	Parry (pen) [42]	9148
40	31	A	Sheffield W	L 0-2	0-0	16		18,069
41	Apr 7	H	Milton Keynes D	D 1-1	0-1	16	Wright [90]	13,941
42	9	A	Stevenage	D 1-1	0-0	16	Hume [85]	3386
43	14	H	Huddersfield T	W 1-0	0-0	14	Robertson [54]	11,267
44	21	A	Oldham Ath	D 1-1	0-0	15	Holroyd [79]	4824
45	28	H	Charlton Ath	D 2-2	0-2	15	Hunt [57], Alexander [90]	12,029
46	May 5	A	Bournemouth	L 0-1	0-0	15		6267

Final League Position: 15

GOALSCORERS

League (54): Hume 9, Mellor 8, Parry 4 (3 pens), Carlisle 3, Proctor 3, Tsoumou 3, Alexander 2 (1 pen), Coutts 2, Cummins 2, Jervis 2, Mayor 2, Nicholson 2, Aneke 1, Bunn 1, Daley 1, Devine 1, Douglas 1, Holroyd 1, Hunt 1, McLean 1, Morgan 1, Robertson 1, Turner 1, Wright 1.
Carling Cup (6): Barton 1, Hume 1, Mayor 1, Mellor 1, Russell 1, own goal 1.
FA Cup (0).
J Paint Trophy (4): Barton 1, McCombe 1, McLean 1, Tsoumou 1.

Turner I 11	McLean B 15 + 1	Parry P 39 + 1	Alexander G 17 + 1	Carlisle C 20 / Cummins G 13 + 2	Morgan C 18 + 1	Nicholson B 22 + 8	Coutts P 41	Proctor J 24 + 7	Mellor N 15 + 2	Hume I 21 + 7	Mayor D 22 + 14	Devine D 13	Tsoumou J 5 + 11	Smith S 9 + 4	Clucas S — + 1	Middleton D 1 / Murphy R 1 + 4	McLaughlin C 10 + 7	Barton A 12 + 4 / Aneke C 3 + 4	Ashbee I 3 + 4	Arestidou A 7	Gray D 18 + 5	Daley K — + 8 / Brown A 4	Russell D 2	Stuckmann T 28	Clark L 2	Forte J 2 + 1 / Miller G 2 + 4	Doyle N 5	McCombe J 6 / Wright B 11 + 2	Douglas J — + 4	Jervis J 3 + 2 / Ehmer M 7 + 2	Bunn H 1	McAllister J 4 / Hayhurst W 1 + 1	Procter A 19	Holroyd C 14 + 6	Marrow A 3 + 1	Robertson C 17 + 1	Hunt N 15 + 2	*Match No.*
1	2	3	4	5	6^{1}	7	8	9	10	11	12																											1
1	2	3	4	5		7	8	9^{1}	10^{2}	11^{3}	12	6	13	14																								2
1	2	12	4	5		7	8	9^{2}	10	11^{3}	13	6		3^{1}	14																							3
1	2	3	4	5		7	8	9^{3}	10^{2}		12	6	13			11^{1}	14																					4
1	6	3	4^{3}	5		7	8	9	10^{2}	12	11^{1}		13				2	14																				5
1	6	3	4	5		7^{2}	8^{3}	9	10	11^{1}	12						2	14	13																			6
	6	3	4	5		7	8^{1}	9^{2}	10	11	13						2		12	1																		7
	6	3■	4	5		7	8	9^{1}	10	11^{3}	12^{2}						2		14	1	13																	8
	6		4	5		7	8	9^{2}	10	11^{1}	13			3			2		12	1																		9
	6	3^{3}	4^{2}	5		7	8	9^{1}	10	11	12		13	14						1	2																	10
1	6	3	7^{3}	5		11	8	9	10^{2}		12						2		4^{1}		14	13																11
1	6		4	5		7^{1}	8	9^{2}		10	11		13	3							2	12																12
1	2^{1}	3		5			8			10^{3}	11	6	9				12	7	4^{2}		14	13																13
1	12	3	4	5		13	8	10			11	6	9^{2}								2^{1}	14	7^{3}															14
1		3	4			12	8	10^{2}			11	6	9					5			2	13	7^{1}															15
	6^{1}	11	4		5	7	8				12		9	10^{2}			3			1	2	13																16
		3	4	5	6	14	8		12		11^{3}		9^{1}				2	13						1	7^{2}	10												17
		3			6	7	8	9	10										4^{2}		13	12		1		11^{1}	2	5										18
		3			6	7	8	9^{1}	10		11										2			1		12	4	5										19
		3^{2}	4^{1}		6				10	13	11		14	12			7^{3}	9			2			1			8	5										20
		11^{3}			6		8		10^{1}	9^{2}	7		13	3			14	12			2			1			4	5										21
		11^{1}			6		8			10^{2}	9		12				3	7			2			1			4	5	13									22
		11			6		8	9^{2}		10^{1}	7		12	3				4			2			1				5	13									23
		11^{3}		5	6		8	9^{1}			7^{2}			3			14	4			2	13		1					12	10								24
		11		5	6	7	8				12		13	3■			14	4^{1}			2			1						10^{2}	9^{3}							25
	2^{3}	11		5	6	12	8	9					13								14			1						7^{1}		3^{2}	4	10				26
		11^{1}		5	6	12	8	9										7			2			1						13		3	4	10^{2}				27
		11		5	6■		8	9						13				4^{1}			2^{2}			1						14		3^{3}	7	10	12			28
		11		10		7^{1}					12					13^{2}	14	8						1								3^{3}	4	9	2	5	6	29
		3		10^{2}		8^{1}										14	12	4^{3}				11		1					13				6	9	7	5	2	30
		3		10			8			14	12					13		7^{1}				4^{2}		1									6	9^{3}	11	5	2	31
		11		10			8	13		12				3^{1}		9^{2}						6		1		7							4			5	2	32
		3		10^{3}		14	8	9^{1}		12	11	6												1				13					4	7^{2}		5	2	33
		3		10		13	8^{2}	12		9^{1}	7	6												1									4	11		5	2	34
		3		10		8		12		9^{2}	7	6												1		14		13					4	11^{1}		5	2^{3}	35
		11		10^{2}		8				9^{3}	7^{1}	6												1		12		3		14			4	13		5	2	36
				10		11	8	14		9		6^{1}												1		7^{2}		3		12			4^{3}	13		5	2	37
		11		14		8^{1}	10		13	9^{3}		6						7						1				3					4	12^{2}		5	2	38
		11		10^{3}			8			9		6^{1}				14		7^{2}						1		13		3					4	12		5	2	39
		11		10^{1}	6		8			12								13				9^{2}		1				3		7			4^{3}	14		5	2	40
		11					8	12		9	7							14						1		13		3		6^{1}			4^{3}	10		5	2^{2}	41
		11					8	13		12	7							9^{2}			2			1				3		6			4	10^{1}		5		42
		11^{1}		13	12		8			9^{2}	7										2			1				3		6			4^{3}	10		5	14	43
				10^{1}	6		8	12			11^{3}							13			2			1				3		7			4^{2}	9		5	14	44
			14		6		8	9			11							13		1	2^{1}							3		4^{3}		12		10		5^{2}	7	45
				10	5	14	8	9^{3}			7									1					6^{2}			3		4		11^{1}		13		12	2	46

FA Cup

First Round	Southend U	(h)	0-0
		(a)	0-1

Carling Cup

First Round	Crewe Alex	(h)	3-2
Second Round	Charlton Ath	(a)	2-0
Third Round	Southampton	(a)	1-2

J Paint Trophy

Second Round	Morecambe	(a)	2-2
Northern Quarter-Final			
	Rochdale	(a)	1-1
Northern Semi-Final			
	Chesterfield	(h)	1-1

QUEENS PARK RANGERS FA Premiership

FOUNDATION

There is an element of doubt about the date of the foundation of this club, but it is believed that in either 1885 or 1886 it was formed through the amalgamation of Christchurch Rangers and St Jude's Institute FC. The leading light was George Wodehouse, whose family maintained a connection with the club until comparatively recent times. Most of the players came from the Queen's Park district so this name was adopted after a year as St Jude's Institute.

Loftus Road Stadium, South Africa Road, Shepherds Bush, London W12 7PJ.

Telephone: (020) 8743 0262.

Fax: (020) 8749 0994.

Ticket Office: (0844) 447 7007.

Website: www.qpr.co.uk

Email: iant@qpr.co.uk

Ground Capacity: 18,682.

Record Attendance: 41,097 v Leeds U, FA Cup 3rd rd, 9 January 1932 (at White City); 35,353 v Leeds U, Division 1, 27 April 1974 (at Loftus Road).

Pitch Measurements: 110yd × 73yd.

Chairman: Tony Fernandes.

Finance Director: Rebecca Caplehorn.

Manager: Mark Hughes.

Assistant Manager: Mark Bowen.

Physio: Nigel Cox.

HONOURS

Football League – Division 1: ***Runners-up*** 1975–76;
FL C: ***Champions*** 2010–11;
Division 2: ***Champions*** 1982–83; ***Runners-up*** 1967–68, 1972–73, 2003–04;
Division 3 (S): ***Champions*** 1947–48; ***Runners-up*** 1946–47;
Division 3: ***Champions*** 1966–67.

FA Cup: ***Runners-up*** 1982.

Football League Cup: ***Winners*** 1967; ***Runners-up*** 1986. (In 1966–67 won Division 3 and Football League Cup).

European Competitions
UEFA Cup: 1976–77, 1984–85.

Colours: Blue and white hooped shirts, white shorts, white stockings.

Year Formed: 1885* (*see Foundation*).

Turned Professional: 1898.

Previous Name: 1885, St Jude's; 1887, Queens Park Rangers. ***Club Nicknames:*** 'Rangers' or 'Rs'.

Grounds: 1885* (*see Foundation*), Welford's Fields; 1888–99, London Scottish Ground, Brondesbury, Home Farm, Kensal Rise Green, Gun Club Wormwood Scrubs, Kilburn Cricket Ground; 1899, Kensal Rise Athletic Ground; 1901, Latimer Road, Notting Hill; 1904, Agricultural Society, Park Royal; 1907, Park Royal Ground; 1917, Loftus Road; 1931, White City; 1933, Loftus Road; 1962, White City; 1963, Loftus Road.

First Football League Game: 28 August 1920, Division 3, v Watford (h) L 1–2 – Price; Blackman, Wingrove; McGovern, Grant, O'Brien; Faulkner, Birch (1), Smith, Gregory, Middlemiss.

Record League Victory: 9–2 v Tranmere R, Division 3, 3 December 1960 – Drinkwater; Woods, Ingham; Keen, Rutter, Angell; Lazarus (2), Bedford (2), Evans (2), Andrews (1), Clark (2).

Record Cup Victory: 8–1 v Bristol R (away), FA Cup 1st rd, 27 November 1937 – Gilfillan; Smith, Jefferson; Lowe, James, March; Cape, Mallett, Cheetham (3), Fitzgerald (3) Bott (2). 8–1 v Crewe Alex, Milk Cup 1st rd, 3 October 1983 – Hucker; Neill, Dawes, Waddock (1), McDonald (1), Fenwick, Micklewhite (1), Stewart (1), Allen (1), Stainrod (3), Gregory.

sky SPORTS FACT FILE

Wilf Heathcote was a prolific goalscorer for Queens Park Rangers during the Second World War with 88 goals in 97 games. He also did well in representative matches for the Combined Services, London District and the Army in which he was served as a Sergeant. Profession: School teacher.

Record Defeat: 1–8 v Mansfield T, Division 3, 15 March 1965. 1–8 v Manchester U, Division 1, 19 March 1969.

Most League Points (2 for a win): 67, Division 3, 1966–67.

Most League Points (3 for a win): 88, FL C, 2010–11.

Most League Goals: 111, Division 3, 1961–62.

Highest League Scorer in Season: George Goddard, 37, Division 3 (S), 1929–30.

Most League Goals in Total Aggregate: George Goddard, 172, 1926–34.

Most League Goals in One Match: 4, George Goddard v Merthyr T, Division 3 (S), 9 March 1929; 4, George Goddard v Swindon T, Division 3 (S), 12 April 1930; 4, George Goddard v Exeter C, Division 3 (S), 20 December 1930; 4, George Goddard v Watford, Division 3 (S), 19 September 1931; 4, Tom Cheetham v Aldershot, Division 3 (S), 14 September 1935; 4, Tom Cheetham v Aldershot, Division 3 (S), 12 November 1938.

Most Capped Player: Alan McDonald, 52, Northern Ireland.

Most League Appearances: Tony Ingham, 519, 1950–63.

Youngest League Player: Frank Sibley, 16 years 97 days v Bristol C, 10 March 1964.

Record Transfer Fee Received: £6,000,000 from Newcastle U for Les Ferdinand, June 1995.

Record Transfer Fee Paid: £3,500,000 to Instituto for Alejandro Faurlin, July 2009.

Football League Record: 1920 Original Members of Division 3; 1921–48 Division 3 (S); 1948–52 Division 2; 1952–58 Division 3 (S); 1958–67 Division 3; 1967–68 Division 2; 1968–69 Division 1; 1969–73 Division 2; 1973–79 Division 1; 1979–83 Division 2; 1983–92 Division 1; 1992–96 FA Premier League; 1996–2001 Division 1; 2001–04 Division 2; 2004–11 FL C; 2011– FA Premier League.

LATEST SEQUENCES

Longest Sequence of League Wins: 8, 7.11.1931 – 28.12.1931.

Longest Sequence of League Defeats: 9, 25.2.1969 – 5.4.1969.

Longest Sequence of League Draws: 6, 29.1.2000 – 5.3.2000.

Longest Sequence of Unbeaten League Matches: 20, 11.3.1972 – 23.9.1972.

Longest Sequence Without a League Win: 20, 7.12.1968 – 7.4.1969.

Successive Scoring Runs: 33 from 9.12.1961.

Successive Non-scoring Runs: 6 from 18.3.1939.

MANAGERS

James Cowan 1906–13
Jimmy Howie 1913–20
Ned Liddell 1920–24
Will Wood 1924–25
(had been Secretary since 1903)
Bob Hewison 1925–31
John Bowman 1931
Archie Mitchell 1931–33
Mick O'Brien 1933–35
Billy Birrell 1935–39
Ted Vizard 1939–44
Dave Mangnall 1944–52
Jack Taylor 1952–59
Alec Stock 1959–65
(General Manager to 1968)
Bill Dodgin Jnr 1968
Tommy Docherty 1968
Les Allen 1968–71
Gordon Jago 1971–74
Dave Sexton 1974–77
Frank Sibley 1977–78
Steve Burtenshaw 1978–79
Tommy Docherty 1979–80
Terry Venables 1980–84
Gordon Jago 1984
Alan Mullery 1984
Frank Sibley 1984–85
Jim Smith 1985–88
Trevor Francis 1988–89
Don Howe 1989–91
Gerry Francis 1991–94
Ray Wilkins 1994–96
Stewart Houston 1996–97
Ray Harford 1997–98
Gerry Francis 1998–2001
Ian Holloway 2001–06
Gary Waddock 2006
John Gregory 2006–07
Luigi Di Canio 2007–08
Iain Dowie 2008
Paulo Sousa 2008–09
Jim Magilton 2009
Paul Hart 2009–10
Neil Warnock 2010–12
Mark Hughes January 2012–

TEN YEAR LEAGUE RECORD

		P	W	D	L	F	A	Pts	Pos
2002-03	Div 2	46	24	11	11	69	45	83	4
2003-04	Div 2	46	22	17	7	80	45	83	2
2004-05	FL C	46	17	11	18	54	58	62	11
2005-06	FL C	46	12	14	20	50	65	50	21
2006-07	FL C	46	14	11	21	54	68	53	18
2007-08	FL C	46	14	16	16	60	66	58	14
2008-09	FL C	46	15	16	15	42	44	61	11
2009-10	FL C	46	14	15	17	58	65	57	13
2010-11	FL C	46	24	16	6	71	32	88	1
2011-12	PR Lge	38	10	7	21	43	66	37	17

DID YOU KNOW

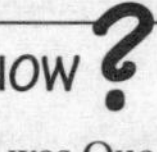

Frank Bedingfield was Queens Park Rangers' leading goalscorer in 1899–1900 with 21 Southern League and Cup goals. A short, stocky centre-forward, tragically to die at 27, he was previously with Yarmouth, Rushden and Aston Villa where he scored in his only first team game there.

QUEENS PARK RANGERS 2011–12 LEAGUE RECORD

Match No.	Date	Venue	Opponents	Result		H/T Score	Lg Pos.	Goalscorers	Attendance
1	Aug 13	H	Bolton W	L	0-4	0-1	—		15,195
2	20	A	Everton	W	1-0	1-0	9	Smith [31]	35,008
3	27	A	Wigan Ath	L	0-2	0-1	12		17,225
4	Sept 12	H	Newcastle U	D	0-0	0-0	—		16,211
5	17	A	Wolverhampton W	W	3-0	2-0	9	Barton [8], Faurlin [10], Campbell [87]	24,189
6	25	H	Aston Villa	D	1-1	0-0	9	Dunne (og) [90]	16,707
7	Oct 2	A	Fulham	L	0-6	0-3	11		23,766
8	15	H	Blackburn R	D	1-1	1-1	11	Helguson [16]	16,487
9	23	H	Chelsea	W	1-0	1-0	10	Helguson (pen) [10]	18,050
10	30	A	Tottenham H	L	1-3	0-2	12	Bothroyd [62]	36,147
11	Nov 5	H	Manchester C	L	2-3	1-1	11	Bothroyd [28], Helguson [69]	18,076
12	19	A	Stoke C	W	3-2	2-1	9	Helguson 2 [22, 54], Young [44]	27,618
13	26	A	Norwich C	L	1-2	0-1	11	Young [59]	26,781
14	Dec 3	H	WBA	D	1-1	1-0	12	Helguson [20]	17,290
15	10	A	Liverpool	L	0-1	0-0	13		45,016
16	18	H	Manchester U	L	0-2	0-1	15		18,033
17	21	H	Sunderland	L	2-3	0-1	—	Helguson [63], Mackie [67]	16,167
18	27	A	Swansea C	D	1-1	0-1	—	Mackie [58]	19,530
19	31	A	Arsenal	L	0-1	0-0	17		60,067
20	Jan 2	H	Norwich C	L	1-2	1-1	—	Barton [11]	18,033
21	15	A	Newcastle U	L	0-1	0-1	18		49,865
22	21	H	Wigan Ath	W	3-1	2-0	16	Helguson (pen) [33], Buzsaky [45], Smith [81]	16,002
23	Feb 1	A	Aston Villa	D	2-2	2-1	—	Cisse [12], Warnock (og) [29]	32,063
24	4	H	Wolverhampton W	L	1-2	1-0	16	Zamora [16]	17,351
25	11	A	Blackburn R	L	2-3	0-3	16	Mackie 2 [71, 90]	20,252
26	25	H	Fulham	L	0-1	0-1	17		18,015
27	Mar 3	H	Everton	D	1-1	1-1	16	Zamora [36]	18,033
28	10	A	Bolton W	L	1-2	0-1	18	Cisse [48]	21,551
29	21	H	Liverpool	W	3-2	0-0	—	Derry [77], Cisse [86], Mackie [90]	18,033
30	24	A	Sunderland	L	1-3	0-1	18	Taiwo [79]	37,128
31	31	H	Arsenal	W	2-1	1-1	18	Taarabt [22], Diakite [66]	18,033
32	Apr 8	A	Manchester U	L	0-2	0-1	17		75,505
33	11	H	Swansea C	W	3-0	1-0	—	Barton [45], Mackie [55], Buzsaky [67]	17,557
34	14	A	WBA	L	0-1	0-1	16		25,521
35	21	H	Tottenham H	W	1-0	1-0	16	Taarabt [24]	18,021
36	29	A	Chelsea	L	1-6	0-4	17	Cisse [84]	41,675
37	May 6	H	Stoke C	W	1-0	0-0	16	Cisse [89]	17,319
38	13	A	Manchester C	L	2-3	0-1	17	Cisse [48], Mackie [66]	48,000

Final League Position: 17

GOALSCORERS

League (43): Helguson 8 (2 pens), Mackie 7, Cisse 6, Barton 3, Bothroyd 2, Buzsaky 2, Smith 2, Taarabt 2, Young 2, Zamora 2, Campbell 1, Derry 1, Diakite 1, Faurlin 1, Taiwo 1, own goals 2.
Carling Cup (0).
FA Cup (2): Gabbidon 1, Helguson 1.

Kenny P 33	Dyer K 1	Hill C 19 + 3	Derry S 28 + 1	Hall F 11 + 3	Gabbidon D 15 + 2	Smith T 4 + 13	Taarabt A 24 + 3	Campbell D 2 + 9	Bothroyd J 12 + 9	Faurlin A 20	Orr B 2 + 4	Buzsaky A 10 + 8	Helguson H 13 + 3	Connolly M 5 + 1	Agyemang P 2	Ephraim H — + 2	Perone B 1	Harriman M — + 1	Andrade B — + 1	Young L 23	Traore A 18 + 5	Ferdinand A 31	Barton J 31	Wright-Phillips S 24 + 8	Puncheon J — + 2	Mackie J 24 + 7	Cerny R 5	Macheda F — + 3	Taiwo T 13 + 2	Onuoha N 16	Hulse R 1 + 1	Cisse D 7 + 1	Zamora B 14	Diakite S 9	*Match No.*
1	2^{1}	3	4	5	6	7^{2}	8^{3}	9	10	11	12	13	14																						1
1			4	5	6	7^{2}	8		12	11	2	10		3	9^{1}	13																			2
1			4	5^{1}	6	10^{3}	8		13	11		7^{2}		3	9		2	12	14																3
1			4		6		9	13	10^{2}	8				12						2	3^{1}	5	7	11^{3}	14										4
1			4	14	6^{3}	13	9^{2}	12	10^{1}	8										2	3	5	7	11											5
1			4^{2}	5		14	10	12	9^{1}	8			13							2	3■	6	7	11^{3}											6
1			4^{1}	5		13	10^{2}	12	9^{3}	11	2									3		6	8	7		14									7
1			4	5		13	12			11			9							2	3	6	8	7^{2}		10^{1}									8
1		3	4^{2}	5		12	10^{1}			11			9							2		6	8	7		13									9
1			4^{2}	5^{1}	12		10^{3}		13	11			9							2	3	6	8	7		14									10
1		14			6	13			10^{1}	11			9							2	3^{3}	5	4	7	12	8^{2}									11
1		3			6					8	12		9							2^{1}	11	5	4	7		10									12
		3^{1}	4^{2}		6	14			12	8		13	9							2	11	5		7^{3}		10	1								13
					6				10^{1}	11		12	9							2	3	5	4	7		8	1								14
		14			6	10^{2}		13	9	11	12									2	3	5^{1}	4	7		8^{3}	1								15
		14			6		12	13	10^{3}	11			9^{2}	5						2	3		4	7^{1}		8	1								16
1			4	13	6		12		14	11			9	5^{3}						2	3^{2}		8	7^{1}		10									17
1		6	4	5			10			11			9							2	3		8			7									18
					6	13	10	12	9^{1}	11	14			5						2	3^{3}		4	7		8^{2}	1								19
1		3	4		6		10^{3}	14		11			9^{2}							2		5	7■	12		8^{1}		13							20
1		3	4		6	12			10			8^{2}	9^{1}							2		5		7		11		13							21
1		3	13	5		12		10^{1}				8^{2}	9							2		6	4	7		11									22
1			4^{2}			12										13				2		5	8	7		11		14	3	6	9^{1}	10^{3}			23
1			4^{1}	13			11													2^{2}	12	5	8	7					3	6	14	9■	10^{3}		24
1				5^{2}	13		10					8^{1}									3	6	4	7		12			11	2			9		25
1		3					10					13									12	5	4	7^{2}		11			6^{1}	2			9	8■	26
1		5	4				10^{1}					11									3	6	8	7		12				2			9		27
1		5	4^{2}									12									3^{1}	6	11	7^{3}		14			13	2		9	10	8	28
1			4				11					14								2	3^{1}	6	7^{2}			13			12	5		9^{3}	10	8	29
1			4				7^{2}		14			12								2		6		13		11			3	5		9■	10^{3}	8^{1}	30
1		5	4				11															6	7	12		9			3	2			10^{1}	8	31
1		5	4■			12	10^{2}	14	9^{3}			11										6		13		7			3	2				8^{1}	32
1		5				14	10^{3}		13			4										6	7	12		11^{1}			3	2			9^{2}	8	33
1		5	4^{1}				10^{2}						13								14	6	7	12		11			3^{3}	2			9	8	34
1		5	4				10■					12										6	7			11			3	2			9	8^{1}	35
1		5	4									8^{1}									12	6	7	13		11			3	2		9	10^{2}		36
1		5	4^{2}				10		13			8^{1}										6	7	14		11			3	2		12	9^{3}		37
1		5	4						13												12	6	8■	7		11			3	2		9^{1}	10^{2}		38

FA Cup

Third Round	Milton Keynes D	(a)	1-1
		(h)	1-0
Fourth Round	Chelsea	(h)	0-1

Carling Cup

Second Round	Rochdale	(h)	0-2

READING FA Premiership

FOUNDATION

Reading was formed as far back as 1871 at a public meeting held at the Bridge Street Rooms. They first entered the FA Cup as early as 1877 when they amalgamated with the Reading Hornets. The club was further strengthened in 1889 when Earley FC joined them. They were the first winners of the Berks & Bucks Cup in 1878–79.

Madejski Stadium, Junction 11, M4, Reading, Berkshire RG2 0FL.

Telephone: (0118) 968 1100.

Fax: (0118) 968 1101.

Ticket Office: (0844) 249 1871.

Website: www.readingfc.co.uk

Email: customerservice@readingfc.co.uk

Ground Capacity: 24,082.

Record Attendance: 33,042 v Brentford, FA Cup 5th rd, 19 February 1927 (at Elm Park); 24,122 v Aston Villa, FA Premier League, 10 February 2007 (at Madejski Stadium).

Pitch Measurements: 105m × 68m.

Chairman: Sir John Madejski OBE, DL.

Chief Executive: Nigel Howe.

Director of Football: Nick Hammond.

Manager: Brian McDermott.

First Team Coach: Nigel Gibbs.

Physio: Luke Anthony.

Colours: Blue and white hooped shirts, blue shorts, blue stockings.

Year Formed: 1871.

Turned Professional: 1895.

Club Nickname: 'The Royals'.

Grounds: 1871, Reading Recreation; Reading Cricket Ground; 1882, Coley Park; 1889, Caversham Cricket Ground; 1896, Elm Park; 1998, Madejski Stadium.

First Football League Game: 28 August 1920, Division 3, v Newport Co (a) W 1–0 – Crawford; Smith, Horler; Christie, Mavin, Getgood; Spence, Weston, Yarnell, Bailey (1), Andrews.

Record League Victory: 10–2 v Crystal Palace, Division 3 (S), 4 September 1946 – Groves; Glidden, Gulliver; McKenna, Ratcliffe, Young; Chitty, Maurice Edelston (3), McPhee (4), Barney (1), Deverell (2).

Record Cup Victory: 6–0 v Leyton, FA Cup 2nd rd, 12 December 1925 – Duckworth; Eggo, McConnell; Wilson, Messer, Evans; Smith (2), Braithwaite (1), Davey (1), Tinsley, Robson (2).

HONOURS

FA Premier League: Best season: 8th 2006–07.

Football League – FL C: *Champions* 2005–06, 2011–12;
Division 1: ***Runners-up*** 1994–95;
Division 2: ***Champions*** 1993–94; ***Runners-up*** 2001–02;
Division 3: ***Champions*** 1985–86;
Division 3 (S): ***Champions*** 1925–26; ***Runners-up*** 1931–32, 1934–35, 1948–49, 1951–52;
Division 4: ***Champions*** 1978–79.

FA Cup: Semi-final 1927.

Football League Cup: Best season: 5th rd, 1996, 1998.

Simod Cup: ***Winners*** 1988.

sky SPORTS FACT FILE

On 18 September 1926, two Reading centre-forwards Hugh Davey and Frank Richardson were both on the injured list and the club was forced to play reserve centre-half Sid Helliwell as leader of the attack against Manchester City. He scored the only goal of the match.

Record Defeat: 0–18 v Preston NE, FA Cup 1st rd, 1893–94.

Most League Points (2 for a win): 65, Division 4, 1978–79.

Most League Points (3 for a win): 106, Championship, 2005–06.

Most League Goals: 112, Division 3 (S), 1951–52.

Highest League Scorer in Season: Ronnie Blackman, 39, Division 3 (S), 1951–52.

Most League Goals in Total Aggregate: Ronnie Blackman, 158, 1947–54.

Most League Goals in One Match: 6, Arthur Bacon v Stoke C, Division 2, 3 April 1931.

Most Capped Player: Kevin Doyle, 26 (50), Republic of Ireland.

Most League Appearances: Martin Hicks, 500, 1978–91.

Youngest League Player: Peter Castle, 16 years 49 days v Watford, 30 April 2003.

Record Transfer Fee Received: £6,500,000 from Wolverhampton W for Kevin Doyle, June 2009.

Record Transfer Fee Paid: Undisclosed to Nantes for Emerse Fae, August 2007.

Football League Record: 1920 Original Member of Division 3; 1921–26 Division 3 (S); 1926–31 Division 2; 1931–58 Division 3 (S); 1958–71 Division 3; 1971–76 Division 4; 1976–77 Division 3; 1977–79 Division 4; 1979–83 Division 3; 1983–84 Division 4; 1984–86 Division 3; 1986–88 Division 2; 1988–92 Division 3; 1992–94 Division 2; 1994–98 Division 1; 1998–2002 Division 2; 2002–04 Division 1; 2004–06 FL C; 2006–08 FA Premier League; 2008–12 FL C; 2012– FA Premier League.

MANAGERS

Thomas Sefton 1897–1901 *(Secretary-Manager)*
James Sharp 1901–02
Harry Matthews 1902–20
Harry Marshall 1920–22
Arthur Chadwick 1923–25
H. S. Bray 1925–26 *(Secretary only since 1922 and 1926–35)*
Andrew Wylie 1926–31
Joe Smith 1931–35
Billy Butler 1935–39
John Cochrane 1939
Joe Edelston 1939–47
Ted Drake 1947–52
Jack Smith 1952–55
Harry Johnston 1955–63
Roy Bentley 1963–69
Jack Mansell 1969–71
Charlie Hurley 1972–77
Maurice Evans 1977–84
Ian Branfoot 1984–89
Ian Porterfield 1989–91
Mark McGhee 1991–94
Jimmy Quinn/Mick Gooding 1994–97
Terry Bullivant 1997–98
Tommy Burns 1998–99
Alan Pardew 1999–2003
Steve Coppell 2003–09
Brendan Rodgers 2009
Brian McDermott December 2009–

LATEST SEQUENCES

Longest Sequence of League Wins: 13, 17.8.1985 – 19.10.1985.

Longest Sequence of League Defeats: 8, 29.12.2007 – 24.2.2008.

Longest Sequence of League Draws: 6, 23.3.2002 – 20.4.2002.

Longest Sequence of Unbeaten League Matches: 33, 9.8.2005 – 14.2.2006.

Longest Sequence Without a League Win: 14, 30.4.1927 – 29.10.1927.

Successive Scoring Runs: 32 from 1.10.1932.

Successive Non-scoring Runs: 6 from 13.4.1925.

TEN YEAR LEAGUE RECORD

		P	W	D	L	F	A	Pts	Pos
2002-03	Div 1	46	25	4	17	61	46	79	4
2003-04	Div 1	46	20	10	16	55	57	70	9
2004-05	FL C	46	19	13	14	51	44	70	7
2005-06	FL C	46	31	13	2	99	32	106	1
2006-07	PR Lge	38	16	7	15	52	47	55	8
2007-08	PR Lge	38	10	6	22	41	66	36	18
2008-09	FL C	46	21	14	11	72	40	77	4
2009-10	FL C	46	17	12	17	68	63	63	9
2010-11	FL C	46	20	17	9	77	51	77	5
2011-12	FL C	46	27	8	11	69	41	89	1

DID YOU KNOW ?

After beating Gillingham 4-0 on 17 April 1933, Reading remained unbeaten at Elm Park until after defeating Coventry City 4-1 on 4 January 1936, a run of 55 matches. The sequence encompassed two complete seasons in which the club finished third and second in the table.

READING 2011–12 LEAGUE RECORD

Match No.	*Date*	*Venue*	*Opponents*	*Result*	*H/T Score*	*Lg Pos.*	*Goalscorers*	*Attendance*
1	Aug 6	H	Millwall	D 2-2	0-0	—	Manset 2 [86, 89]	18,531
2	13	A	Leicester C	W 2-0	0-0	7	Hunt [64], Robson-Kanu [90]	23,399
3	16	A	Portsmouth	L 0-1	0-0	—		13,438
4	20	H	Barnsley	L 1-2	0-1	14	Robson-Kanu (pen) [74]	15,878
5	27	A	Hull C	L 0-1	0-0	20		17,295
6	Sept 10	H	Watford	L 0-2	0-1	23		17,128
7	17	H	Doncaster R	W 2-0	0-0	13	Church [52], Le Fondre [59]	15,124
8	24	A	Coventry C	D 1-1	1-1	15	Church [10]	12,309
9	27	A	Bristol C	W 3-2	0-1	—	McAnuff [72], Le Fondre [75], Manset [90]	12,018
10	Oct 1	H	Middlesbrough	D 0-0	0-0	15		17,418
11	15	A	Burnley	W 1-0	0-0	14	Karacan [90]	13,664
12	18	H	Derby Co	D 2-2	0-0	—	Le Fondre 2 [65, 77]	15,704
13	22	H	Southampton	D 1-1	0-0	15	Leigertwood [71]	21,889
14	29	A	Crystal Palace	D 0-0	0-0	16		21,002
15	Nov 1	A	Nottingham F	L 0-1	0-0	—		18,506
16	6	H	Birmingham C	W 1-0	0-0	14	Hunt [75]	18,361
17	19	H	Cardiff C	L 1-2	0-1	14	Kebe [77]	20,361
18	26	A	Ipswich T	W 3-2	0-0	13	Gorkss [76], Pearce [89], Hunt [90]	17,154
19	29	H	Peterborough U	W 3-2	1-1	—	Church [27], Le Fondre [78], Robson-Kanu [80]	15,907
20	Dec 3	A	Blackpool	L 0-1	0-0	11		11,656
21	10	H	West Ham U	W 3-0	0-0	10	Pearce [66], Church 2 [80, 86]	24,026
22	17	A	Leeds U	W 1-0	1-0	7	Church [2]	23,162
23	26	H	Brighton & HA	W 3-0	2-0	6	McAnuff 2 [17, 45], El-Abd (og) [90]	22,141
24	31	H	Ipswich T	W 1-0	0-0	5	Pearce [64]	18,737
25	Jan 2	A	Cardiff C	L 1-3	1-3	5	McAnuff [45]	23,655
26	14	A	Watford	W 2-1	1-1	5	Kebe [42], Le Fondre [85]	11,291
27	21	H	Hull C	L 0-1	0-0	8		17,556
28	28	H	Bristol C	W 1-0	0-0	—	Roberts [58]	17,825
29	Feb 11	H	Coventry C	W 2-0	2-0	7	Kebe [25], Roberts [43]	18,006
30	14	A	Derby Co	W 1-0	0-0	—	Hunt [61]	22,567
31	17	H	Burnley	W 1-0	1-0	—	Roberts [11]	17,185
32	25	A	Middlesbrough	W 2-0	1-0	3	Hunt [17], Harte [80]	17,314
33	Mar 3	A	Millwall	W 2-1	1-1	3	Robson-Kanu [45], Le Fondre [76]	11,271
34	6	H	Portsmouth	W 1-0	1-0	—	Hunt [24]	18,399
35	10	H	Leicester C	W 3-1	1-0	3	Leigertwood [15], Roberts [75], Church [89]	21,858
36	13	A	Doncaster R	D 1-1	0-1	—	Pearce [51]	8287
37	17	A	Barnsley	W 4-0	0-0	2	McAnuff [47], Karacan 2 [49, 65], Roberts [90]	9381
38	20	A	Peterborough U	L 1-3	1-2	—	Hunt [20]	6717
39	24	H	Blackpool	W 3-1	2-1	2	Harte [30], Pearce [35], Leigertwood [60]	20,906
40	31	A	West Ham U	W 4-2	2-1	2	Gorkss [44], Hunt [45], Harte (pen) [59], Leigertwood [84]	33,350
41	Apr 6	H	Leeds U	W 2-0	0-0	—	Le Fondre 2 [84, 90]	22,775
42	10	A	Brighton & HA	W 1-0	1-0	—	Harte [14]	20,610
43	13	A	Southampton	W 3-1	1-0	—	Roberts [19], Le Fondre 2 [72, 90]	31,892
44	17	H	Nottingham F	W 1-0	0-0	—	Leigertwood [81]	22,899
45	21	H	Crystal Palace	D 2-2	1-1	1	Gorkss [20], Le Fondre [53]	23,431
46	28	A	Birmingham C	L 0-2	0-1	1		25,516

Final League Position: 1

GOALSCORERS

League (69): Le Fondre 12, Hunt 8, Church 7, Roberts 6, Leigertwood 5, McAnuff 5, Pearce 5, Harte 4 (1 pen), Robson-Kanu 4 (1 pen), Gorkss 3, Karacan 3, Kebe 3, Manset 3, own goal 1.
Carling Cup (1): Morrison 1.
FA Cup (0).

Federici A 46	Griffin A 9	Harte I 30 + 2	Karacan J 36 + 1	Pearce A 46	Khumalo B 4	Kebe J 30 + 3	Leigertwood M 41	Long S 1	Hunt N 33 + 8	McAnuff J 40	Robson-Kanu H 19 + 17	Manset M 4 + 11	Gunnarsson B 1 + 4	Howard B — + 1	Church S 19 + 12	Gorkss K 42	Mills Joseph 13 + 2	Le Fondre A 17 + 15	Cummings S 32 + 2	Tabb J 10 + 9	Antonio M 2 + 4	Roberts J 17	Cywka T 1 + 3	Connolly M 6	Mullins H 6 + 1	Afobe B 1 + 2	*Match No.*
1	2	3	4[1]	5	6	7	8	9	10[2]	11	12	13															1
1	2	3	4	5	6	7	8		10	11	12	9[1]															2
1	2[2]	3	4[3]	5	6	7	8		10	11	12	9[1]	13	14													3
1		3	4	5	6	7	8		10[2]	11	9	12	2[1]		13												4
1	2[2]	3[3]	4	5		7	8		10	11	9[1]	12			13	6	14										5
1	2[1]		4[3]	5		7	8			11	12	9[2]			13	6	3	10	14								6
1				5		7[1]	8		10	11					9	6	3	12	2	4							7
1				5			4		9[1]	11	12	13			8	6	3	10[2]	2	7							8
1				5			4		8[2]	11	12	13			9[1]	6	3	10	2	7							9
1				5			4		13	11	8[1]	12			9[2]	6	3	10	2	7							10
1			13	5			4		12	11[1]	8	14			9[3]	6	3	10	2	7[2]							11
1			4	5		7[1]	8		13		11	12			9[2]	6	3	10	2								12
1		14	4	5		12	8			11[3]	7[1]	13			9[2]	6	3	10	2								13
1			4	5		13	8		12	11	7[2]				9[1]	6	3	10	2								14
1			4	5		13	8		12	11	7[1]	9[2]			14	6	3	10	2[3]								15
1			4	5		7[1]	8		13	11	12				9[2]	6	3	10	2								16
1			4	5		7	8		9	11	13	12				6	3	10[2]	2[1]								17
1		3	4[2]	5		7	8		10	11	13				9[1]	6		12	2								18
1		3	4[1]	5		7	8[3]		10	11	13				9[2]	6		12	2	14							19
1		3	4	5		7[1]	8				11	12			9[2]	6		10	2		13						20
1		3	4	5		7[2]	8		9[1]	11	13				12	6		10	2								21
1	2		4[1]	5			8			11	7				9	6		10[2]	3	12	13						22
1	2	14	4	5		7	8		12	11					9[2]	6[3]		10[1]	3		13						23
1	2		4[3]	5		7[2]	8		12	11	13				9	6		10[1]	3	14							24
1		3	4[1]	5		7	8		10	11	13				9[2]	6		12	2								25
1		3	4	5		7[2]			10		8				9[1]	6		12	2	11	13						26
1		3	4	5					10		8				9[1]	6		12	2	7	11						27
1	3		4	5					10	8					12	6			2	7	11[2]	9[1]	13				28
1		3	4	5		7[2]	8[3]		10[1]						12	6	11			14		9	13	2			29
1		3	4	5		7	8		10		11[1]					6	12					9		2			30
1		3	4	5		7	8		10	11[2]	13					6		12				9[1]		2			31
1		3	4	5		7	8		10	11						6						9		2			32
1		3	4	5			8		10[2]	11	7					6		13		12		9		2[1]			33
1		3	4	5			8		10	11[2]	7[1]					6		12	2			9	13				34
1		3	4	5			8		10	11	7				12	6			2			9[1]					35
1		3	4[2]	5			8		10	11	7[1]					6		13	2	12		9					36
1		3	4[2]	5		7[3]	8		10	11[1]	12				14	6				13		9			2		37
1		3	4	5		7	8		10	11					13	6		12				9[2]			2[1]		38
1		3	4	5		7	8		10	11					12	6			2							9[1]	39
1		3	4[1]	5		7[3]	8		10	11	13					6			2	12[2]		9				14	40
1		3	4[1]	5		7	8		10[2]	11	12[3]					6		13	2			9			14		41
1		3		5		7			10[2]	8			12		13	6			2			9	11[1]		4		42
1		3		5		7			10	8						6		12	2	11[1]		9[2]			4	13	43
1		3		5		7	8		10[1]	11						6		12	2			9			4		44
1		3		5			8[2]		10	11	7[1]		14			6		12	2	13		9[illegible]			4[3]		45
1		3		5			4[2]			8	7		13		9	6		10	12	11				2[1]			46

FA Cup
Third Round Stevenage (h) 0-1

Carling Cup
First Round Charlton Ath (a) 1-2

ROCHDALE FL Championship 2

FOUNDATION

Considering the love of rugby in their area, it is not surprising that Rochdale had difficulty in establishing an Association Football club. The earlier Rochdale Town club formed in 1900 went out of existence in 1907 when the present club was immediately established and joined the Manchester League, before graduating to the Lancashire Combination in 1908.

Spotland Stadium, Willbutts Lane, Rochdale OL11 5DS.

Telephone: (0844) 826 1907.

Fax: (01706) 648 466.

Ticket Office: (0844) 826 1907.

Website: www.rochdaleafc.co.uk

Email: office@rochdaleafc.co.uk

Ground Capacity: 9,223.

Record Attendance: 24,231 v Notts Co, FA Cup 2nd rd, 10 December 1949.

Pitch Measurements: 114yd × 76yd.

Chairman: Chris Dunphy.

Chief Executive: Colin Garlick.

Manager: John Coleman.

Assistant Manager: Jimmy Bell.

Physio: Andy Thorpe.

Colours: Black and blue striped shirts, white shorts, blue stockings with black tops.

Change Colours: Purple shirts with white sleeves and purple trim, purple shorts, purple stockings with white tops.

Year Formed: 1907.

Turned Professional: 1907.

Club Nickname: 'The Dale'.

Ground: 1907, St Clements Playing Fields (original name Spotland).

First Football League Game: 27 August 1921, Division 3 (N), v Accrington Stanley (h) W 6–3 – Crabtree; Nuttall, Sheehan; Hill, Farrer, Yarwood; Hoad, Sandiford, Dennison (2), Owens (3), Carney (1).

Record League Victory: 8–1 v Chesterfield, Division 3 (N), 18 December 1926 – Hill; Brown, Ward; Hillhouse, Parkes, Braidwood; Hughes, Bertram, Whitehurst (5), Schofield (2), Martin (1).

Record Cup Victory: 8–2 v Crook T, FA Cup 1st rd, 26 November 1927 – Moody; Hopkins, Ward; Braidwood, Parkes, Barker; Tompkinson, Clennell (3) Whitehurst (4), Hall, Martin (1).

HONOURS

Football League – Division 3: Best season: 9th, 1969–70; **Division 3 (N):** ***Runners-up*** 1923–24, 1926–27.

FA Cup: Best season: 5th rd, 1990, 2003.

Football League Cup: ***Runners-up*** 1962 (record for 4th Division club).

sky SPORTS FACT FILE

It was a red-letter day in more than one respect for inside-left Robert Schofield when he made his Rochdale debut on 18 December 1926. He had the distinction of scoring twice in a match which still stands as the club's record score. Moreover he came back to Spotland for a second spell.

Record Defeat: 1–9 v Tranmere R, Division 3 (N), 25 December 1931.

Most League Points (2 for a win): 62, Division 3 (N), 1923–24.

Most League Points (3 for a win): 82, FL 2, 2009–10.

Most League Goals: 105, Division 3 (N), 1926–27.

Highest League Scorer in Season: Albert Whitehurst, 44, Division 3 (N), 1926–27.

Most League Goals in Total Aggregate: Reg Jenkins, 119, 1964–73.

Most League Goals in One Match: 6, Tommy Tippett v Hartlepools U, Division 3 (N), 21 April 1930.

Most Capped Player: Leo Bertos, 6 (39), New Zealand.

Most League Appearances: Gary Jones, 379, 1998–2001; 2003–.

Youngest League Player: Zac Hughes, 16 years 105 days v Exeter C, 19 September 1987.

Record Transfer Fee Received: £400,000 from West Ham U for Stephen Bywater, August 1998.

Record Transfer Fee Paid: £150,000 to Stoke C for Paul Connor, March 2001.

Football League Record: 1921 Elected to Division 3 (N); 1958–59 Division 3; 1959–69 Division 4; 1969–74 Division 3; 1974–92 Division 4; 1992–2004 Division 3; 2004–10 FL 2; 2010–12 FL 1; 2012– FL 2.

LATEST SEQUENCES

Longest Sequence of League Wins: 8, 29.9.1969 – 3.11.1969.

Longest Sequence of League Defeats: 17, 14.11.1931 – 12.3.1932.

Longest Sequence of League Draws: 6, 17.8.1968 – 14.9.1968.

Longest Sequence of Unbeaten League Matches: 20, 15.9.1923 – 19.1.1924.

Longest Sequence Without a League Win: 28, 14.11.1931 – 29.8.1932.

Successive Scoring Runs: 29 from 8.1.1927.

Successive Non-scoring Runs: 9 from 14.3.1980.

MANAGERS

Billy Bradshaw 1920
Run by committee 1920–22
Tom Wilson 1922–23
Jack Peart 1923–30
Will Cameron 1930–31
Herbert Hopkinson 1932–34
Billy Smith 1934–35
Ernest Nixon 1935–37
Sam Jennings 1937–38
Ted Goodier 1938–52
Jack Warner 1952–53
Harry Catterick 1953–58
Jack Marshall 1958–60
Tony Collins 1960–68
Bob Stokoe 1967–68
Len Richley 1968–70
Dick Conner 1970–73
Walter Joyce 1973–76
Brian Green 1976–77
Mike Ferguson 1977–78
Doug Collins 1979
Bob Stokoe 1979–80
Peter Madden 1980–83
Jimmy Greenhoff 1983–84
Vic Halom 1984–86
Eddie Gray 1986–88
Danny Bergara 1988–89
Terry Dolan 1989–91
Dave Sutton 1991–94
Mick Docherty 1994–96
Graham Barrow 1996–99
Steve Parkin 1999–2001
John Hollins 2001–02
Paul Simpson 2002–03
Alan Buckley 2003
Steve Parkin 2003–06
Keith Hill 2007–11
(caretaker from December 2006)
Steve Eyre 2011
John Coleman January 2012–

TEN YEAR LEAGUE RECORD

		P	W	D	L	F	A	Pts	Pos
2002-03	Div 3	46	12	16	18	63	70	52	19
2003-04	Div 3	46	12	14	20	49	58	50	21
2004-05	FL 2	46	16	18	12	54	48	66	9
2005-06	FL 2	46	14	14	18	66	69	56	14
2006-07	FL 2	46	18	12	16	70	50	66	9
2007-08	FL 2	46	23	11	12	77	54	80	5
2008-09	FL 2	46	19	13	14	70	59	70	6
2009-10	FL 2	46	25	7	14	82	48	82	3
2010-11	FL 1	46	18	14	14	63	55	68	9
2011-12	FL 1	46	8	14	24	47	81	38	24

DID YOU KNOW ?

In 1919, Rochdale had two regular wartime "guest" players selected to play for Northern Ireland against Scotland in the Victory International. Shortly afterwards centre-forward Billy Halligan and centre-half Pat O'Donnell moved on to Preston North End and Dumbarton respectively.

ROCHDALE 2011–12 LEAGUE RECORD

Match No.	*Date*	*Venue*	*Opponents*	*Result*		*H/T Score*	*Lg Pos.*	*Goalscorers*	*Attendance*
1	Aug 6	A	Sheffield W	L	0-2	0-1	—		21,174
2	13	H	Huddersfield T	D	2-2	1-1	20	Akpa Akpro[43], Grimes[89]	5074
3	16	H	Carlisle U	D	0-0	0-0	—		2671
4	20	A	Oldham Ath	L	0-2	0-2	21		5266
5	27	H	Hartlepool U	L	1-3	1-1	22	Akpa Akpro[16]	2600
6	Sept 3	A	Stevenage	L	2-4	1-3	22	Jones[28], Ball[71]	3021
7	10	A	Bury	W	4-2	3-1	21	Grimes[5], Holness[10], Adams[18], Ball[47]	4897
8	13	H	Scunthorpe U	W	1-0	0-0	—	Kennedy[59]	2368
9	17	H	Charlton Ath	L	2-3	0-2	19	Grimes[57], Ball[60]	2909
10	24	A	Notts Co	L	0-2	0-1	23		6199
11	Oct 1	H	Wycombe W	W	2-1	1-1	17	Grimes 2[21, 66]	2266
12	8	A	Bournemouth	D	1-1	1-0	17	Jones (pen)[30]	5345
13	15	H	Colchester U	D	2-2	1-2	18	Holness[43], Jones[68]	2226
14	22	A	Exeter C	L	1-3	1-1	18	Eccleston[31]	3844
15	25	H	Chesterfield	D	1-1	0-1	—	Jones[74]	2494
16	29	H	Leyton Orient	L	0-2	0-1	21		2322
17	Nov 5	A	Milton Keynes D	L	1-3	1-3	21	Barry-Murphy[8]	7120
18	19	A	Preston NE	W	1-0	0-0	19	Adams[84]	10,456
19	26	H	Brentford	L	1-2	0-1	20	Holness[65]	2466
20	Dec 10	A	Sheffield U	L	0-3	0-1	22		15,892
21	17	H	Yeovil T	D	0-0	0-0	22		2692
22	31	A	Walsall	D	0-0	0-0	23		3907
23	Jan 2	H	Preston NE	D	1-1	1-1	23	Bogdanovic[25]	4570
24	7	A	Hartlepool U	L	0-2	0-0	—		4663
25	14	H	Stevenage	L	1-5	0-1	23	Ormerod[52]	2367
26	17	A	Tranmere R	D	0-0	0-0	—		4153
27	21	A	Wycombe W	L	0-3	0-1	23		4285
28	28	H	Bury	W	3-0	2-0	22	Akpa Akpro[15], Grimes 2[41, 55]	5033
29	Feb 14	A	Scunthorpe U	L	0-1	0-0	—		3409
30	18	H	Bournemouth	W	1-0	0-0	23	Jones (pen)[90]	2499
31	21	A	Charlton Ath	D	1-1	0-0	—	Adams[53]	15,067
32	25	A	Colchester U	D	0-0	0-0	23		3096
33	28	H	Notts Co	L	0-1	0-1	—		2326
34	Mar 3	H	Sheffield W	D	0-0	0-0	23		5361
35	6	A	Carlisle U	L	1-2	0-0	—	Kennedy[74]	3694
36	10	A	Huddersfield T	D	2-2	1-1	24	Tutte[45], Grimes[82]	13,715
37	17	H	Oldham Ath	W	3-2	1-1	22	Symes 3 (1 pen)[3, 47, 70 (p)]	4671
38	20	H	Tranmere R	L	0-2	0-1	—		2618
39	24	A	Brentford	L	0-2	0-1	22		4919
40	31	H	Walsall	D	3-3	0-2	22	Akpa Akpro 2[66, 90], Symes (pen)[82]	2516
41	Apr 7	A	Yeovil T	L	1-3	0-2	22	Grounds (og)[80]	3859
42	10	H	Sheffield U	L	2-5	1-4	—	Kennedy[3], Obadeyi[68]	5309
43	14	H	Exeter C	W	3-2	0-1	24	Adams[79], Thompson[81], Kennedy[88]	1930
44	21	A	Chesterfield	L	1-2	0-0	24	Akpa Akpro[73]	5954
45	28	H	Milton Keynes D	L	1-2	0-1	24	Akpa Akpro[85]	2212
46	May 5	A	Leyton Orient	L	1-2	0-2	24	Gray[75]	4110

Final League Position: 24

GOALSCORERS

League (47): Grimes 8, Akpa Akpro 7, Jones 5 (2 pens), Adams 4, Kennedy 4, Symes 4 (2 pens), Ball 3, Holness 3, Barry-Murphy 1, Bogdanovic 1, Eccleston 1, Gray 1, Obadeyi 1, Ormerod 1, Thompson 1, Tutte 1, own goal 1.
Carling Cup (6): Grimes 3, Akpa Akpro 1, Jones 1, own goal 1.
FA Cup (0).
J Paint Trophy (2): Ball 1, Bunn 1.

Kean J 14	Darby S 34 + 1	Widdowson J 30 + 2	Holness M 23 + 1	Trotman N 12	Tutte A 28 + 12	Kennedy J 38 + 6	Jones G 45	Akpa Akpro J 30 + 11	Grimes A 27 + 9	Adams N 30 + 11	O'Grady C — + 1	Thompson J 8 + 9	Marshall P — + 1	Balkestein P 12 + 1	Twaddle M 1 + 1	Lucas D 16	Barnes-Homer M 1 + 4	Ball D 12 + 2	Barry-Murphy B 17 + 5	Benali A — + 2	Eccleston N 3 + 2	Gray R 1 + 3	Jordan S 17 + 2	Holden D 20 + 1	Bunn H 5 + 1	Bergkamp R 2 + 1 / Byrme N 2 + 1	Edwards M 5 + 2	Kurucz P 11 / Minihan S 1	Bogdanovic D 5	Ormerod B 4 + 1 / Hackney S 1 + 1	Amankwaah K 15 + 1	Abadaki G — + 2	Long K 16	Symes M 14 + 1	Obadeyi T 3 + 3	Edwards P 1 + 2	McConville S 2 + 2	*Match No.*
1	2	3	4	5	6^{1}	7	8	9	10	11	12																											1
1	2	3	4	5	6	7^{1}	8	9	10	11		12																										2
1	2	3	4	5	6		8	9	10	11		7^{1}	12																									3
1	2	3	4	5■	6	14	8	9	10^{2}	11^{3}		7^{1}		12	13																							4
	2	3	4		6	7^{1}	8	9	10	11^{2}		12		5		1	13																					5
1	2	3	14	5	6	7^{1}	8	9	11^{2}	12				4^{3}			13	10																				6
1	2	3	4		6^{3}	13	8	9	10^{1}	11■				5			12	7^{2}	14																			7
1	2	3	4		6^{2}	7	8	9^{1}	10					5			12	11	13																			8
1	2	3	4		6	7^{1}	8	9	10	12				5				11																				9
1	13	3	2	5	6	7	8	9^{1}	10	12		14		4^{2}				11^{3}																				10
1	2		4	5	6	14	8	12	10^{3}	11^{2}		7^{1}		3				9	13																			11
1	2		4	3	6	13	8	7	10^{2}	11				5				9^{1}	12																			12
1	2		4	5	6		8	7	10	11				3			9^{1}			12																		13
1	2		4	3	6^{1}	12	8	9	10	11^{2}				5						13	7																	14
	2		4	5	6	13	8	9^{1}	10	12				3		1			11^{2}		7^{3}	14																15
1	2^{1}		4	5	6^{3}	7	8	13	10	11				3							9^{2}	14	12															16
	2		4		6^{3}	7^{1}	8	12	10	11^{2}						1			5		14		3	9	13													17
			4		13	7	6	12	10^{2}	11^{3}						1			5		14		3	2	8	9^{1}												18
			5		14	7	4	13	10	11^{3}						1		12	3				6	2	8^{2}	9^{1}												19
	2					7	4	12	10^{2}	11^{1}						1^{6}		9	6				3	5	8	13	15											20
		3	5		13	7	4	9^{2}	12	11								10^{1}					6	2	8		1											21
		3	6^{2}		13	7	4	12		11		9^{1}				1^{6}		10					5	2	8		15											22
	2	3			12	7	4	8^{1}	13	11		14						10^{2}					6	5				1	9^{3}									23
	2^{3}	3			14	7	4	13	12	11^{1}								8^{2}					6	5				1	9	10								24
		3■	5			7^{3}	4		12	11^{2}		8^{1}						13					6	2				1	9	10	14							25
	2					7	4	11											8				3	6				1	9^{1}	10	5	12						26
	2					7	4	11^{3}	12	13									8^{2}				3	6				1	9^{1}	10	5	14						27
	2	3			12	7	4	9	10^{1}	11^{2}									8									1		13	5		6					28
	2	3			13	7	4	9	10^{1}	11^{3}		14							8^{2}									1			5		6	12				29
	2	3				7	4	9^{1}	10	11^{2}		12							8				13					1			5		6					30
	2	3				7	10			11^{1}		12							8				4					1			5		6	9				31
	2	3			13	7	4		12	11^{2}									8				10^{1}	14				1			5^{3}		6	9				32
	2	3			13	7	4		10^{1}	11		12							8^{2}					5				1					6	9				33
	2	3			13	7	4	12		11^{1}		10^{2}				1			8					5									6	9				34
	2	3			13	7	4	10^{2}	12	11^{1}						1			8					5									6	9				35
	2	3			10	7	4		13	14						1			8^{2}				11^{3}	5^{1}									6	9		12		36
	2				8	7	4	12	10^{1}							1			14				3^{2}	5									6	9	11^{3}	13		37
					8	7	4	13	10^{2}	12						1							3	5			2						6	9	11^{1}			38
		14	6^{3}		11	7^{2}	4	10								1			8^{1}				3								5		2	9	13		12	39
		3			8	7	4	11	10^{1}	12						1										2^{2}					5		6	9	13			40
		3	2^{2}		8	7	4	10		11^{3}						1										12					5		6^{1}	9	13		14	41
		3			8	7	4	11								1								6		2					5			9	10			42
		13			8	4		10		11		12			3^{1}									6				2			5			9		1	7^{2}	43
	2	3			8	7	4	10	13	12		11^{2}															1				5		6				9^{1}	44
	2	3			8^{2}	7	4	10		14		11^{1}										12					1			13	5		6	9^{3}				45
	2	3			8	7	4	9		12												10		6			1			11^{1}	5							46

FA Cup

First Round	Bradford C	(a)	0-1

Carling Cup

First Round	Chesterfield	(h)	3-2
Second Round	QPR	(a)	2-0
Third Round	Aldershot T	(a)	1-2

J Paint Trophy

Second Round	Walsall	(h)	1-1
Northern Quarter-Final	Preston NE	(h)	1-1

ROTHERHAM UNITED FL Championship 2

FOUNDATION

Rotherham were formed in 1870 before becoming Town in the late 1880s. Thornhill United were founded in 1877 and changed their name to Rotherham County in 1905. The Town amalgamated with Rotherham County to form Rotherham United in 1925.

Don Valley Stadium, Worksop Road, Sheffield, South Yorkshire S9 3TL.
Club moving to new premises
New York Stadium, Rotherham.
Capacity: 12,021.

Telephone: (0844) 4140 737.

Fax: (0844) 4140 744.

Ticket Office: (0844) 4140 737.

Website: www.themillers.co.uk

Email: office@rotherhamunited.net

Ground Capacity: 25,000.

Record Attendance: 25,170 v Sheffield U, Division 2, 13 December 1952 (at Millmoor); 7,082 v Aldershot T, FL 2 Play-offs semi-final 2nd leg, 19 May 2010 (at Don Valley).

Pitch Measurements: 108yd × 72yd.

Chairman: Tony Stewart.

Manager: Steve Evans.

Assistant Manager: Paul Raynor.

Physio: Denis Circuit.

Colours: Red shirts with white design, white shorts, red stockings.

Year Formed: 1870. ***Turned Professional:*** 1905. ***Club Nickname:*** 'The Merry Millers'.

Previous Names: 1877, Thornhill United; 1905, Rotherham County; 1925, amalgamated with Rotherham Town under Rotherham United.

Grounds: 1870, Red House Ground; 1907, Millmoor; 2008, Don Valley Stadium.

First Football League Game: 2 September 1893, Division 2, Rotherham T v Lincoln C (a) D 1-1 – McKay; Thickett, Watson; Barr, Brown, Broadhead; Longden, Cutts, Leatherbarrow, McCormick, Pickering, (1 og). 30 August 1919, Division 2, Rotherham Co v Nottingham F (h) W 2–0 – Branston; Alton, Baines; Bailey, Coe, Stanton; Lee (1), Cawley (1), Glennon, Lees, Lamb.

Record League Victory: 8–0 v Oldham Ath, Division 3 (N), 26 May 1947 – Warnes; Selkirk, Ibbotson; Edwards, Horace Williams, Danny Williams; Wilson (2), Shaw (1), Ardron (3), Guest (1), Hainsworth (1).

Record Cup Victory: 6–0 v Spennymoor U, FA Cup 2nd rd, 17 December 1977 – McAlister; Forrest, Breckin, Womble, Stancliffe, Green, Finney, Phillips (3), Gwyther (2) (Smith), Goodfellow, Crawford (1). 6–0 v Wolverhampton W, FA Cup 1st rd, 16 November 1985 – O'Hanlon; Forrest, Dungworth, Gooding (1), Smith (1), Pickering, Birch (2), Emerson, Tynan (1), Simmons (1), Pugh. 6–0 v Kings Lynn, FA Cup 2nd rd, 6 December 1997 – Mimms; Clark, Hurst (Goodwin), Garner (1) (Hudson) (1), Warner (Bass), Richardson (1), Berry (1), Thompson, Druce (1), Glover (1), Roscoe.

Record Defeat: 1–11 v Bradford C, Division 3 (N), 25 August 1928.

HONOURS

Football League – Division 2: *Runners-up* 2000–01;
Division 3: ***Champions*** 1980–81; *Runners-up* 1999–2000;
Division 3 (N): ***Champions*** 1950–51; *Runners-up* 1946–47, 1947–48, 1948–49;
Division 4: ***Champions*** 1988–89; *Runners-up* 1991–92.

FA Cup: Best season: 5th rd, 1953, 1968.

Football League Cup: *Runners-up* 1961.

Auto Windscreens Shield: *Winners* 1996.

sky SPORTS FACT FILE

On 13 August 2011, Rotherham United defeated Plymouth Argyle 4-1. It was their first win at Home Park after 17 abortive trips since 1970 when they had won 3-0 with two goals from Neil Hague and one from David Lill, who was the Millers' match winner in the return win.

Most League Points (2 for a win): 71, Division 3 (N), 1950–51.

Most League Points (3 for a win): 91, Division 2, 2000–01.

Most League Goals: 114, Division 3 (N), 1946–47.

Highest League Scorer in Season: Wally Ardron, 38, Division 3 (N), 1946–47.

Most League Goals in Total Aggregate: Gladstone Guest, 130, 1946–56.

Most League Goals in One Match: 4, Roland Bastow v York C, Division 3 (N), 9 November 1935; 4, Roland Bastow v Rochdale, Division 3 (N), 7 March 1936; 4, Wally Ardron v Crewe Alex, Division 3 (N), 5 October 1946; 4, Wally Ardron v Carlisle U, Division 3 (N), 13 September 1947; 4, Wally Ardron v Hartlepools U, Division 3 (N), 13 October 1948; 4, Ian Wilson v Liverpool, Division 2, 2 May 1955; 4, Carl Gilbert v Swansea C, Division 3, 28 September 1971; 4, Carl Airey v Chester, Division 3, 31 August 1987; 4, Shaun Goater v Hartlepool U, Division 3, 9 April 1994; 4, Lee Glover v Hull C, Division 3, 28 December 1997; 4, Darren Byfield v Millwall, Division 1, 10 August 2002; 4, Adam Le Fondre v Cheltenham T, FL 2, 21 August 2010.

Most Capped Player: Shaun Goater, 14 (36), Bermuda.

Most League Appearances: Danny Williams, 459, 1946–62.

Youngest League Player: Kevin Eley, 16 years 72 days v Scunthorpe U, 15 May 1984.

Record Transfer Fee Received: £850,000 from Cardiff C for Alan Lee, August 2003.

Record Transfer Fee Paid: £150,000 to Millwall for Tony Towner, August 1980; £150,000 to Port Vale for Lee Glover, August 1996; £150,000 to Burnley for Alan Lee, September 2000; £150,000 to Reading for Martin Butler, September 2003. £150,000 to Crewe Alex for Tom Pope, June 2009; £150,000 to Burnley for John Mullin, October 2001.

Football League Record: 1893 Rotherham Town elected to Division 2; 1896 Failed re-election; 1919 Rotherham County elected to Division 2; 1923–51 Division 3 (N); 1951–68 Division 2; 1968–73 Division 3; 1973–75 Division 4; 1975–81 Division 3; 1981–83 Division 2; 1983–88 Division 3; 1988–89 Division 4; 1989–91 Division 3; 1991–92 Division 4; 1992–97 Division 2; 1997–2000 Division 3; 2000–01 Division 2; 2001–04 Division 1; 2004–05 FL C; 2005–07 FL 1; 2007– FL 2.

MANAGERS

Billy Heald 1925–29 *(Secretary only for several years)*
Stanley Davies 1929–30
Billy Heald 1930–33
Reg Freeman 1934–52
Andy Smailes 1952–58
Tom Johnston 1958–62
Danny Williams 1962–65
Jack Mansell 1965–67
Tommy Docherty 1967–68
Jimmy McAnearney 1968–73
Jimmy McGuigan 1973–79
Ian Porterfield 1979–81
Emlyn Hughes 1981–83
George Kerr 1983–85
Norman Hunter 1985–87
Dave Cusack 1987–88
Billy McEwan 1988–91
Phil Henson 1991–94
Archie Gemmill/John McGovern 1994–96
Danny Bergara 1996–97
Ronnie Moore 1997–2005
Mick Harford 2005
Alan Knill 2005–07
Mark Robins 2007–09
Ronnie Moore 2009–11
Andy Scott 2011–12
Steve Evans April 2012–

LATEST SEQUENCES

Longest Sequence of League Wins: 9, 2.2.1982 – 6.3.1982.

Longest Sequence of League Defeats: 8, 7.4.1956 – 18.8.1956.

Longest Sequence of League Draws: 6, 13.10.1969 – 22.11.1969.

Longest Sequence of Unbeaten League Matches: 18, 13.10.1969 – 7.2.1970.

Longest Sequence Without a League Win: 21, 9.5.2004 – 20.11.2004.

Successive Scoring Runs: 30 from 3.4.1954.

Successive Non-scoring Runs: 6 from 21.8.2004.

TEN YEAR LEAGUE RECORD

		P	*W*	*D*	*L*	*F*	*A*	*Pts*	*Pos*
2002-03	Div 1	46	15	14	17	62	62	59	15
2003-04	Div 1	46	13	15	18	53	61	54	17
2004-05	FL C	46	5	14	27	35	69	29	24
2005-06	FL 1	46	12	16	18	52	62	52	20
2006-07	FL 1	46	13	9	24	58	75	38	23
2007-08	FL 2	46	21	11	14	62	58	64*	9
2008-09	FL 2	46	21	12	13	60	46	58†	14
2009-10	FL 2	46	21	10	15	55	52	73	5
2010-11	FL 2	46	17	15	14	75	60	66	9
2011-12	FL 2	46	18	13	15	67	63	67	10

**10 pts deducted; †17 points deducted.*

DID YOU KNOW ?

Reg Freeman had had an interesting career as an amateur player before turning professional with Oldham Athletic. He was signed by Rotherham United as a full-back from Middlesbrough in August 1930, became manager and remained in that position with the club for 18 fine years.

ROTHERHAM UNITED 2011–12 LEAGUE RECORD

Match No.	Date	Venue	Opponents	Result	H/T Score	Lg Pos.	Goalscorers	Attendance
1	Aug 6	H	Oxford U	W 1-0	0-0	—	Grabban ^{48}	4484
2	13	A	Plymouth Arg	W 4-1	0-0	1	Evans 2 $^{52, 59}$, Le Fondre 2 $^{82, 87}$	6015
3	16	A	Crewe Alex	W 2-1	1-0	—	Le Fondre ^{15}, Pringle ^{72}	3458
4	20	H	Barnet	D 2-2	0-1	2	Brown ^{49}, Le Fondre ^{82}	3546
5	27	H	Gillingham	W 3-0	0-0	1	Harrison ^{53}, Grabban ^{63}, Evans ^{78}	3740
6	Sept 3	A	Swindon T	L 2-3	1-1	2	Revell 2 $^{21, 65}$	6304
7	10	H	Dagenham & R	W 3-1	3-1	2	Evans ^{8}, Grabban 2 $^{29, 38}$	3286
8	13	A	Accrington S	D 1-1	1-0	—	Cresswell ^{38}	1486
9	17	A	Torquay U	D 3-3	3-2	2	Grabban 2 $^{3, 34}$, Cresswell ^{9}	2330
10	24	H	Southend U	L 0-4	0-1	5		3433
11	Oct 1	A	Port Vale	L 0-2	0-2	8		4983
12	8	H	Burton Alb	L 0-1	0-1	11		3645
13	14	A	Bristol R	L 2-5	1-3	—	Taylor, J ^{37}, Schofield ^{53}	5395
14	22	H	Shrewsbury T	D 1-1	1-1	13	Grabban ^{22}	3561
15	25	A	Morecambe	D 3-3	1-3	—	Grabban (pen) ^{39}, Evans ^{58}, Revell ^{64}	3012
16	29	A	Northampton T	D 1-1	1-1	14	Evans ^{2}	4182
17	Nov 5	H	Aldershot T	W 2-0	2-0	14	Grabban ^{14}, Holroyd ^{41}	3284
18	19	A	Bradford C	W 3-2	1-1	11	Grabban (pen) ^{22}, Revell ^{51}, Marshall ^{57}	10,551
19	26	H	Crawley T	L 1-2	1-0	11	Williams ^{20}	3962
20	Dec 10	A	Hereford U	W 3-2	2-2	11	Mullins 2 $^{13, 65}$, Revell ^{23}	1908
21	17	H	AFC Wimbledon	W 1-0	0-0	9	Wood ^{78}	3343
22	26	A	Macclesfield T	D 0-0	0-0	11		3179
23	30	A	Cheltenham T	L 0-1	0-1	—		3582
24	Jan 2	H	Bradford C	W 3-0	0-0	10	Grabban 2 (1 pen) $^{63, 68 (p)}$, Williams ^{74}	5368
25	14	H	Swindon T	L 1-2	0-2	11	Revell ^{54}	4236
26	21	H	Port Vale	L 0-1	0-0	13		3189
27	28	A	Dagenham & R	L 2-3	1-0	13	Harrison ^{28}, Revell ^{63}	1744
28	Feb 10	A	Southend U	W 2-0	1-0	—	Harrad ^{9}, Revell ^{83}	4717
29	14	H	Accrington S	W 1-0	1-0	—	Harrad (pen) ^{28}	2572
30	18	A	Burton Alb	D 1-1	0-1	9	Harrad ^{55}	3313
31	21	A	Gillingham	D 0-0	0-0	—		3248
32	25	H	Bristol R	L 0-1	0-0	11		3937
33	Mar 3	A	Barnet	D 1-1	0-1	11	Pringle ^{50}	1765
34	6	H	Crewe Alex	D 1-1	0-1	—	Grabban ^{62}	2447
35	10	H	Plymouth Arg	W 1-0	0-0	10	Grabban (pen) ^{70}	3475
36	13	H	Torquay U	L 0-1	0-1	—		2538
37	17	A	Oxford U	L 1-2	0-1	11	Grabban (pen) ^{83}	6756
38	20	H	Macclesfield T	W 4-2	1-0	—	Bradley ^{37}, Pringle ^{57}, Revell ^{68}, Cadogan ^{77}	2505
39	24	A	Crawley T	L 0-3	0-1	10		2766
40	31	H	Hereford U	W 1-0	1-0	11	Grabban ^{43}	3237
41	Apr 6	A	AFC Wimbledon	W 2-1	1-0	10	Pringle ^{34}, Hoskins, S ^{83}	4387
42	9	H	Cheltenham T	W 1-0	0-0	10	Cresswell ^{90}	3066
43	14	A	Shrewsbury T	L 1-3	1-1	10	Cresswell ^{2}	5873
44	21	H	Morecambe	W 3-2	1-1	10	Grabban 2 $^{21, 90}$, Taylor, J ^{48}	2876
45	28	A	Aldershot T	D 2-2	2-1	10	Evans (pen) ^{11}, Hoskins, S ^{30}	2578
46	May 5	H	Northampton T	D 1-1	1-0	10	Revell ^{31}	4729

Final League Position: 10

GOALSCORERS

League (67): Grabban 18 (5 pens), Revell 10, Evans 7 (1 pen), Cresswell 4, Le Fondre 4, Pringle 4, Harrad 3 (1 pen), Harrison 2, Hoskins, S 2, Mullins 2, Taylor, J 2, Williams 2, Bradley 1, Brown 1, Cadogan 1, Holroyd 1, Marshall 1, Schofield 1, Wood 1.
Carling Cup (1): own goal 1.
FA Cup (3): Grabban 3 (2 pens).
*J Paint Trophy (1):*Revell 1.

Logan C 19	Tonge D 28 + 4	Newey T 15 + 5	Harrison D 35 + 6	Cresswell R 13 + 3	Brown T 4 + 2	Taylor J 38 + 1	Grabban L 39 + 4	Holroyd C 5 + 10	Le Fondre A 4	Schofield D 35 + 2	Evans G 29 + 3	Pringle B 14 + 7	Raynes M 31 + 2	Marshall M 8 + 7	Bradley M 18 + 3	Foster L 1 + 4	Revell A 40	Williams B 4 + 7	Mullins J 34 + 1	Warrington A 7	Harley J 11 + 1	Branston G 2	Wood S 24 + 2	Taylor R 20	Griffiths S 8	Naylor R 5	Cadogan K 7 + 6	Harrad S 6 + 2	Warne P — + 3	Hoskins S 2 + 6	Denton A — + 1	*Match No.*
1	2	3	4	5	6	7	8	9^{1}	10	11^{2}	12	13																				1
1	2	3	4	5		8	9^{1}	12	10	11	7		6																			2
1	2	3	4	5		8^{2}	9^{1}		10	11	7	12	6	13																		3
1	2^{1}	3	4		6		9^{2}	13	10^{3}	11	7	14	5	12	8																	4
1		3	4	5		8^{1}	9	10^{2}		11	7		6	2	12	13																5
1	13	3	4	5		14	10^{2}			11	7^{1}		6	2	8^{3}		9	12														6
1	2	3	4	5		8	9^{2}	13			7^{1}	12	6	11			10															7
1	2	3	4	5			9	12		11	7		6	8^{1}			10															8
1	2	3	4	5^{2}	13		9			11	7	12	6	8^{1}			10															9
1	2	3	4		6^{2}		9	12		11^{3}	7		5	8^{1}	14		10		13													10
1	12	3	4		5^{1}	8	9	13		11^{2}	7		6				10		2													11
	2	3	4			8	9			11^{2}	12	7^{1}	5	13			10		6	1												12
			4			8^{2}	9			11^{1}	7	13	6	12			10		2	1	3	5▪										13
	2	12	4			8^{2}	9	13		11	10		5	7^{1}					6	1	3											14
	2		4			8	9^{1}	12		11	7		5			13	10^{2}		6	1	3											15
1	2	14	4			8	9^{2}	13		11^{3}	7		5^{1}			12	10		6		3											16
1	2	12	4			8	9^{1}	11			7					6	10				3	5										17
1	2	14	4			8	9			11	7^{1}		13	12^{2}			10	6^{3}	5		3											18
1	2		4			5	9			11				12			10	8^{1}	6		3		7									19
1	2		4			6^{1}	9	14		11			13			12	10	8^{3}	5		3^{2}		7									20
1	2		4				9			11			6	12			10	8^{1}	5		3		7									21
1	2		4		12		9			11	7^{2}		6				10	13	5^{1}		3		8									22
1	2		4				9			11	7		6				10	12	5		3^{1}		8									23
	2		4^{1}			8	9	7^{2}		11			6				10	13	5		12		3	1								24
	2					4	9	8		11	7^{1}		5				10	12	6				3	1								25
	2	13	14			4	9			11			6	8^{1}			10	12	5				7^{3}	1	3^{2}							26
			4			8	9						5▪		2		10	12					11^{1}	1	3	6	7					27
			4			8	12								2		10		5				11	1	3	6	7^{1}	9				28
			4			8	12								2		10		5				11	1	3	6	7^{1}	9				29
			4	13		8	12								2		10		5				11	1	3	6^{2}	7^{1}	9				30
			4			8	7						6		2		10		5				11	1	3			9^{1}	12			31
			4			8	7								2		10		5	1			11		3	6	12	9^{1}				32
			4^{2}			8				12		13	6		2		10		5				11	1	3		7^{1}	9^{3}	14			33
			4			8	9			11^{1}		7	6		2		10		5				3	1				12				34
	14		4			8	9^{3}			11^{1}	12	7^{2}	6		2		10		5				3	1				13				35
			4^{1}	13		8	9			12	7	11	6^{2}		2		10		5				3	1								36
	14		4			8	9				7^{1}	11^{2}	6		2^{3}		10		5				3	1			12			13		37
			12			8				11	7^{2}	10	6		2		9^{1}		5				3	1			4			13		38
				14		8	13			11	7^{2}	9	6^{3}		2		10		5				3	1			4^{1}			12		39
				5		4	9			11	7^{1}	8			2		10		6				3	1			12					40
	2		12	5		4	9			11	7^{1}	8^{2}					10		6				3	1						13		41
	2			5		4	9			11	7^{1}	8					10^{2}		6				3	1			13			12		42
	2	3		5		4	9			11	7^{2}	8^{1}					10		6				12	1						13		43
	2	3	13	5▪		4	9			11^{1}	7^{2}	8^{3}			12		10		6	1							14					44
	2	3▪	13			4^{2}				11	7	8^{1}			5		9		6	1			12				14			10^{3}		45
	2^{1}		12			4	9			11		7^{3}	6		3		10		5					1					14	8^{2}	13	46

FA Cup

First Round	Barrow	(a)	2-1
Second Round	Shrewsbury T	(a)	1-2

Carling Cup

First Round	Leicester C	(h)	1-4

J Paint Trophy

Second Round	Sheffield U	(h)	1-2

SCUNTHORPE UNITED FL Championship 1

FOUNDATION

The year of foundation for Scunthorpe United has often been quoted as 1910, but the club can trace its history back to 1899 when Brumby Hall FC, who played on the Old Showground, consolidated their position by amalgamating with some other clubs and changing their name to Scunthorpe United. The year 1910 was when that club amalgamated with North Lindsey United as Scunthorpe and Lindsey United. The link is Mr W. T. Lockwood whose chairmanship covers both years.

Glanford Park, Jack Brownsword Way, Scunthorpe DN15 8TD.

Telephone: (0871) 221 1899.

Fax: (01724) 857 986.

Ticket Office: (0871) 221 1899 (option 1).

Website: www.scunthorpe-united.co.uk

Email: admin@scunthorpe-united.co.uk

Ground Capacity: 9,088.

Record Attendance: 23,935 v Portsmouth, FA Cup 4th rd, 30 January 1954 (at Old Showground); 9,077 v Manchester U, League Cup 3rd rd, 22 September 2010 (at Glanford Park).

Pitch Measurements: 112yd × 72yd.

Chairman: Steve Wharton.

Vice-chairman: Rex Garton.

Manager: Alan Knill.

Assistant Manager: Chris Brass.

Physio: Alex Dalton.

Colours: Claret shirts with light blue sleeves, white shorts, claret stockings.

Year Formed: 1899.

Turned Professional: 1912.

Previous Names: Amalgamated first with Brumby Hall then North Lindsey United to become Scunthorpe and Lindsey United, 1910; 1958, Scunthorpe United.

Club Nickname: 'The Iron'.

Grounds: 1899, Old Showground; 1988, Glanford Park.

First Football League Game: 19 August 1950, Division 3 (N), v Shrewsbury T (h) D 0–0 – Thompson; Barker, Brownsword; Allen, Taylor, McCormick; Mosby, Payne, Gorin, Rees, Boyes.

Record League Victory: 8–1 v Luton T, Division 3, 24 April 1965 – Sidebottom; Horstead, Hemstead; Smith, Neale, Lindsey; Bramley (1), Scott, Thomas (5), Mahy (1), Wilson (1). 8–1 v Torquay U (a), Division 3, 28 October 1995 – Samways; Housham, Wilson, Ford (1), Knill (1), Hope (Nicholson), Thornber, Bullimore (Walsh), McFarlane (4) (Young), Eyre (2), Paterson.

HONOURS

Football League – FL 1: ***Champions*** 2006–07; **FL 2: *Runners-up*** 2004–05; **Division 3 (N): *Champions*** 1957–58.

FA Cup: Best season: 5th rd, 1958, 1970.

Football League Cup: Best season: 4th rd, 2010.

Johnstone's Paint Trophy: ***Runners-up*** 2008–09.

sky SPORTS FACT FILE

In consecutive away matches in September 1951, Peter Platts, a 23-year-old local amateur centre-forward deputising for the regular choice Ray Powell, scored in each one, firstly at Darlington and then Lincoln City. They were Platts' only Football League appearances.

Record Cup Victory: 9–0 v Boston U, FA Cup 1st rd, 21 November 1953 – Malan; Hubbard, Brownsword; Sharpe, White, Bushby; Mosby (1), Haigh (3), Whitfield (2), Gregory (1), Mervyn Jones (2).

Record Defeat: 0–8 v Carlisle U, Division 3 (N), 25 December 1952.

Most League Points (2 for a win): 66, Division 3 (N), 1956–57, 1957–58.

Most League Points (3 for a win): 91, FL 1, 2006–07.

Most League Goals: 88, Division 3 (N), 1957–58.

Highest League Scorer in Season: Barrie Thomas, 31, Division 2, 1961–62.

Most League Goals in Total Aggregate: Steve Cammack, 110, 1979–81, 1981–86.

Most League Goals in One Match: 5, Barrie Thomas v Luton T, Division 3, 24 April 1965.

Most Capped Player: Grant McCann, 10 (39), Northern Ireland.

Most League Appearances: Jack Brownsword, 595, 1950–65.

Youngest League Player: Mike Farrell, 16 years 240 days v Workington, 8 November 1975.

Record Transfer Fee Received: £2,500,000 from Celtic for Gary Hooper, August 2010.

Record Transfer Fee Paid: £700,000 to Hibernian for Rob Jones, July 2009.

Football League Record: 1950 Elected to Division 3 (N); 1958–64 Division 2; 1964–68 Division 3; 1968–72 Division 4; 1972–73 Division 3; 1973–83 Division 4; 1983–84 Division 3; 1984–92 Division 4; 1992–99 Division 3; 1999–2000 Division 2; 2000–04 Division 3; 2004–05 FL 2; 2005–07 FL 1; 2007–08 FL C; 2008–09 FL 1; 2009–11 FL C; 2011– FL 1.

MANAGERS

Harry Allcock 1915–53
(Secretary-Manager)
Tom Crilly 1936–37
Bernard Harper 1946–48
Leslie Jones 1950–51
Bill Corkhill 1952–56
Ron Suart 1956–58
Tony McShane 1959
Bill Lambton 1959
Frank Soo 1959–60
Dick Duckworth 1960–64
Fred Goodwin 1964–66
Ron Ashman 1967–73
Ron Bradley 1973–74
Dick Rooks 1974–76
Ron Ashman 1976–81
John Duncan 1981–83
Allan Clarke 1983–84
Frank Barlow 1984–87
Mick Buxton 1987–91
Bill Green 1991–93
Richard Money 1993–94
David Moore 1994–96
Mick Buxton 1996–97
Brian Laws 1997–2004; 2004–06
Nigel Adkins 2006–10
Ian Baraclough 2010–11
Alan Knill March 2011–

LATEST SEQUENCES

Longest Sequence of League Wins: 7, 27.1.2007 – 3.3.2007.

Longest Sequence of League Defeats: 8, 29.11.1997 – 20.1.1998.

Longest Sequence of League Draws: 6, 2.1.1984 – 25.2.1984.

Longest Sequence of Unbeaten League Matches: 19, 22.12.2006 – 6.4.2007.

Longest Sequence Without a League Win: 14, 22.3.1975 – 6.9.1975.

Successive Scoring Runs: 24 from 13.1.2007.

Successive Non-scoring Runs: 7 from 19.4.1975.

TEN YEAR LEAGUE RECORD

		P	W	D	L	F	A	Pts	Pos
2002-03	Div 3	46	19	15	12	68	49	72	5
2003-04	Div 3	46	11	16	19	69	72	49	22
2004-05	FL 2	46	22	14	10	69	42	80	2
2005-06	FL 1	46	15	15	16	68	73	60	12
2006-07	FL 1	46	26	13	7	73	35	91	1
2007-08	FL C	46	11	13	22	46	69	46	23
2008-09	FL 1	46	22	10	14	82	63	76	6
2009-10	FL C	46	14	10	22	62	84	52	20
2010-11	FL C	46	12	6	28	43	87	42	24
2011-12	FL 1	46	10	22	14	55	59	52	18

DID YOU KNOW ?

As Scunthorpe and Lindsey United, the team achieved its first giant-killing act in the FA Cup when drawn against Hartlepools United on 30 November 1929. Scunthorpe's goal was scored by Arthur Smalley in his first of two spells with the club either side of three years at Blackpool.

SCUNTHORPE UNITED 2011–12 LEAGUE RECORD

Match No.	*Date*	*Venue*	*Opponents*	*Result*		*H/T Score*	*Lg Pos.*	*Goalscorers*	*Atten-dance*
1	Aug 6	A	Wycombe W	D	1-1	1-1	—	Nelson ^{40}	4451
2	13	H	Preston NE	D	1-1	0-1	15	Barcham ^{87}	4675
3	16	H	Oldham Ath	L	1-2	0-1	—	Dagnall ^{63}	4142
4	20	A	Charlton Ath	D	2-2	0-1	19	Grant 2 $^{73, 90}$	15,505
5	27	A	Sheffield W	L	2-3	0-2	20	Grant ^{67}, Duffy, M ^{85}	16,862
6	Sept 3	H	Colchester U	D	1-1	1-0	19	Grant ^{38}	3700
7	10	H	Sheffield U	D	1-1	1-0	17	Dagnall ^{45}	6047
8	13	A	Rochdale	L	0-1	0-0	—		2368
9	17	A	Walsall	D	2-2	0-1	21	Thompson ^{78}, Ryan ^{90}	3619
10	24	H	Yeovil T	W	2-1	1-1	16	Mozika 2 $^{44, 53}$	4086
11	Oct 1	A	Stevenage	W	2-1	1-0	15	Nolan ^{45}, O'Connor ^{90}	2957
12	8	H	Leyton Orient	L	2-3	1-0	16	Barcham 2 $^{31, 69}$	4234
13	15	A	Brentford	D	0-0	0-0	17		4907
14	22	A	Milton Keynes D	D	0-0	0-0	16		10,554
15	25	H	Huddersfield T	D	2-2	1-1	—	Norwood ^{10}, Dagnall ^{88}	5858
16	29	H	Tranmere R	W	4-2	2-2	15	Duffy, S ^{20}, Grant 2 (1 pen) $^{44, 67 (p)}$, Dagnall ^{52}	4282
17	Nov 5	A	Bournemouth	L	0-2	0-1	17		5478
18	19	H	Hartlepool U	L	0-2	0-1	18		3861
19	26	A	Notts Co	L	2-3	1-1	19	Barcham ^{44}, Grant ^{53}	6120
20	Dec 10	H	Carlisle U	L	1-2	1-0	20	Barcham ^{3}	3624
21	17	A	Exeter C	D	0-0	0-0	20		4470
22	26	H	Bury	L	1-3	1-0	22	Duffy, S ^{5}	4569
23	31	H	Chesterfield	D	2-2	1-0	20	Canavan ^{24}, Ryan ^{90}	4456
24	Jan 2	A	Hartlepool U	W	2-1	1-0	18	Togwell ^{32}, Thompson ^{74}	5289
25	14	A	Colchester U	D	1-1	1-1	19	Walker ^{8}	3165
26	21	H	Stevenage	D	1-1	0-0	19	Thompson ^{47}	3968
27	24	H	Sheffield W	L	1-3	0-2	—	Robertson ^{55}	5727
28	Feb 14	H	Rochdale	W	1-0	0-0	—	Thompson ^{64}	3409
29	18	A	Leyton Orient	W	3-1	0-1	20	Walker ^{61}, Barcham ^{85}, Parkin ^{89}	4055
30	21	H	Walsall	L	0-1	0-1	—		3455
31	25	H	Brentford	D	0-0	0-0	21		3844
32	29	A	Sheffield U	L	1-2	1-0	—	Duffy, M ^{31}	16,165
33	Mar 3	H	Wycombe W	W	4-1	2-0	18	Reid ^{5}, Barcham 2 $^{34, 47}$, Parkin ^{55}	3811
34	6	A	Oldham Ath	W	2-1	0-0	—	Mirfin ^{73}, Thompson ^{80}	4376
35	10	A	Preston NE	D	0-0	0-0	18		10,621
36	13	A	Yeovil T	D	2-2	0-1	—	Parkin 2 $^{53, 90}$	3767
37	17	H	Charlton Ath	D	1-1	1-1	18	Parkin (pen) ^{21}	4544
38	20	A	Bury	D	0-0	0-0	—		2351
39	24	H	Notts Co	D	0-0	0-0	17		4619
40	31	A	Chesterfield	W	4-1	1-1	17	Robertson 2 $^{28, 75}$, Walker ^{65}, Barcham ^{81}	6152
41	Apr 6	H	Exeter C	W	1-0	0-0	—	Parkin ^{76}	4361
42	9	A	Carlisle U	D	0-0	0-0	14		6555
43	14	H	Milton Keynes D	L	0-3	0-1	16		4111
44	21	A	Huddersfield T	L	0-1	0-0	17		13,086
45	28	H	Bournemouth	D	1-1	0-1	17	Thompson ^{79}	4422
46	May 5	A	Tranmere R	D	1-1	0-1	18	Thompson ^{61}	4952

Final League Position: 18

GOALSCORERS

League (55): Barcham 9, Grant 7 (1 pen), Thompson 7, Parkin 6 (1 pen), Dagnall 4, Robertson 3, Walker 3, Duffy, M 2, Duffy, S 2, Mozika 2, Ryan 2, Canavan 1, Mirfin 1, Nelson 1, Nolan 1, Norwood 1, O'Connor 1, Reid 1, Togwell 1.
Carling Cup (3): Dagnall 2 (1 pen), Barcham 1.
FA Cup (0).
J Paint Trophy (2): Grant 2.

Lillis J 6	Wright A 14+4	Nolan E 29+1	Togwell S 35+4	Nelson M 8+2	Reid P 36	Ryan J 20+4	O'Connor M 29+4	Dagnall C 19+4	Robertson J 12+7	Duffy M 27+10	Thompson G 19+20	Barcham A 37+4	Grant R 19+10	Canavan N 11+1	Norwood O 14+1	Collins M —+1	Mozika D 17+1	Johnstone S 12	Duffy S 18	Ajose N 2+5	Slocombe S 28	Byrne C 13+1	Palmer A —+1	Ribeiro C 10	Walker J 17+1	Jennings C —+4	Reckord J 17	Mirfin D 19	Parkin J 13+1	McAleny C 2+1	Gibbons R 3+1	Godden M —+1	*Match No.*
1	2	3	4	5	6	7	8	9	10^{1}	11	12																						1
1	2	3	4	5	6		8	9^{1}		11	7	10	12																				2
1	2	3	4	5	6		8	9		7	11^{1}	10	12																				3
1	2	3	4	5	6^{1}	13	8	9		7^{2}	14	11^{3}	10	12																			4
1	2	3	4^{2}	5		7^{1}		9		14	12	11^{3}	10	6	8	13																	5
1	2	3	4	5	6	7		9^{1}			12	11	10▮				8																6
	2	3	4		6	7^{1}		9		12	13	10▮			11^{2}		8	1	5														7
	2	3	4^{2}		6	7^{1}	13	9		12	14		10		11^{3}		8	1	5														8
		3	4		6	13	8	9		11	12		10		2^{1}		7^{2}	1	5														9
		3	4	13	6^{2}		8	9			11		10^{1}		2		7	1	5	12													10
	14	2	4	5			8	9^{3}			11	12	10^{2}		7^{1}		6	1	3	13													11
		3	4	5			8	9		12	7^{1}	11	13				6	1	2	10^{2}													12
	2▮		4		5		8	9^{2}		3^{1}	12	10	13		11		7	1	6														13
		3	4		6		8	9^{1}		7^{2}	12	11	10		2				5	13	1												14
		3	4		5		8	9		7^{1}	12	11	10		2				6		1												15
		3	4		5		8	9		12	7^{2}	11^{1}	10		2				6	13	1												16
		3	4	12	5^{1}		8	9		11	7^{2}		10		2				6	13	1												17
	2^{3}	3	4		6		8	9		13	12	11^{2}	10		14				5	7^{1}	1												18
		3					8	14	13	7^{1}	11^{2}	9^{3}	10	6	4▮			1	5			2	12										19
	2	3	4			12	8			7^{1}	11	10	9	6				1	5														20
	2	3	4			7^{2}	8	14	12	13	11^{1}	10	9^{3}	6				1	5														21
	2	3	4^{2}			7	8	12	10	14	13	11^{3}	9^{1}	6				1	5														22
	12		4			7	8	9^{3}	10		13	11	14	6	3^{2}			1	5			2^{1}											23
	12	3	2			7	8^{1}	13	10		11	9^{2}		6	4				5		1												24
		3	4		5		8		10^{1}		11	9		6							1			2	7	12							25
	2	3	4		5		8			7^{1}	11	10	12	6							1				9								26
	12	3	4		5		8^{2}		10	14	11	9^{3}	13	6							1			2^{1}	7								27
			4		6		8^{2}			9^{1}	11	12					13				1			2	7		3	5	10				28
			4		6		8			10^{1}	11	12									1			2	7		3	5	9				29
			4^{2}		6		8		13	10^{1}	11^{3}	12	14								1			2	7		3	5	9				30
			4		6		8		13	11	12	10^{1}									1			2	7		3	5	9^{2}				31
			4▮		6		8			11^{2}	12	10^{1}	14								1	13		2^{3}	7		3	5	9				32
					6		8▮		14	11^{1}	12	10^{2}	13				4				1			2	7		3	5	9^{3}				33
		13			6	7^{1}				11^{2}	12	10					4				1			2	8▮		3	5	9				34
		8			6	7^{1}				11	12	10					4				1			2			3	5	9				35
		8^{1}			6	7^{2}			14	11^{3}	12	10					4				1	2			13		3	5	9				36
					6				12	7	11^{1}	10					4				1	2			8		3	5	9				37
			13		6	12	14		8^{1}	11▮		10					4^{3}				1	2			7^{2}		3	5	9				38
					6	7	13		10^{1}			11					4				1	2			8^{2}		3	5	9	12			39
			12		6	11	13		9			10					4^{2}				1	2			7^{1}		3	5		8			40
			12		6	11			9^{2}			10					4^{1}				1	2			7		3	5	13	8			41
			4		6	11			10	12		8									1	2			7		3	5	9^{1}				42
			4		6	7			9▮	11^{2}		10									1	2			8^{1}	13	3	5			12		43
			4^{1}		6	7				11		10	9								1	2				12	3	5			8		44
		3	4^{1}		6	7				11	12	10	9								1	2						5			8		45
		3	12			7				8	11	10^{3}	9^{2}	6							1	2				13		5^{1}			4	14	46

FA Cup

First Round	AFC Wimbledon	(a)	0-0
		(h)	0-1

Carling Cup

First Round	Accrington S	(a)	2-0
Second Round	Newcastle U	(h)	1-2

J Paint Trophy

First Round	Hartlepool U	(h)	2-0
Second Round	Oldham Ath	(h)	0-1

SHEFFIELD UNITED FL Championship 1

FOUNDATION

In March 1889, Yorkshire County Cricket Club formed Sheffield United six days after an FA Cup semi-final between Preston North End and West Bromwich Albion had finally convinced Charles Stokes, a member of the cricket club, that the formation of a professional football club would prove successful at Bramall Lane. The United's first secretary, Mr J. B. Wostinholm, was also secretary of the cricket club.

Bramall Lane Ground, Cherry Street, Bramall Lane, Sheffield S2 4SU.

Telephone: (0871) 995 1899.

Fax: (0871) 663 2430.

Ticket Office: (0871) 995 1889.

Website: www.sufc.co.uk

Email: info@sufc.co.uk

Ground Capacity: 32,500.

Record Attendance: 68,287 v Leeds U, FA Cup 5th rd, 15 February 1936.

Pitch Measurements: 101.1m × 62.2m.

Chairman (Football Club): Chris Steer.

Chief Executive: Julian Winter.

Manager: Danny Wilson.

Assistant Manager: Frank Barlow.

Physio: Paul Teather.

Colours: Red and white striped shirts with red sleeves, black shorts, black stockings.

Year Formed: 1889.

Turned Professional: 1889.

Club Nickname: 'The Blades'.

Ground: 1889, Bramall Lane.

First Football League Game: 3 September 1892, Division 2, v Lincoln C (h) W 4–2 – Lilley; Witham, Cain; Howell, Hendry, Needham (1); Wallace, Dobson, Hammond (3), Davies, Drummond.

Record League Victory: 10–0 v Burslem Port Vale (a), Division 2, 10 December 1892 – Howlett; Witham, Lilley; Howell, Hendry, Needham; Drummond (1), Wallace (1), Hammond (4), Davies (2), Watson (2).

Record Cup Victory: 6–1 v Scarborough (a), FA Cup 1st qualifying rd, 5 October 1889 – Howlett; Stringer, Gilmartin, Mack, Hobson, Hudson, Galbraith (2), Robertson (1), Fraser (2), Duncan, Mosforth (1). 6–1 v Loughborough, FA Cup 4th qualifying rd, 6 December 1890. 6–1 v Lincoln C, League Cup, 22 August 2000 – Tracey; Uhlenbeek, Weber, Woodhouse (Ford), Murphy, Sandford, Devlin (pen), Ribeiro (Santos), Bent (3), Kelly (1) (Thompson), Jagielka, og (1).

HONOURS

Football League – FL C: ***Runners-up*** 2005–06;
Division 1: ***Champions*** 1897–98; ***Runners-up*** 1896–97, 1899–1900;
Division 2: ***Champions*** 1952–53; ***Runners-up*** 1892–93, 1938–39, 1960–61, 1970–71, 1989–90;
Division 3: ***Runners-up*** 1988–89;
Division 4: ***Champions*** 1981–82.

FA Cup: ***Winners*** 1899, 1902, 1915, 1925; ***Runners-up*** 1901, 1936.

Football League Cup: semi-final 2003.

sky SPORTS FACT FILE

Inside-forward Billy Gillespie was spotted playing against Sheffield United reserves and marked by the famous Ernest "Nudger" Needham who persuaded the club to sign him. Spending 20 years there spanning the Great War, he skippered the team and won 25 caps for Northern Ireland.

Record Defeat: 0–13 v Bolton W, FA Cup 2nd rd, 1 February 1890.

Most League Points (2 for a win): 60, Division 2, 1952–53.

Most League Points (3 for a win): 96, Division 4, 1981–82.

Most League Goals: 102, Division 1, 1925–26.

Highest League Scorer in Season: Jimmy Dunne, 41, Division 1, 1930–31.

Most League Goals in Total Aggregate: Harry Johnson, 205, 1919–30.

Most League Goals in One Match: 5, Harry Hammond v Bootle, Division 2, 26 November 1892; 5, Harry Johnson v West Ham U, Division 1, 26 December 1927.

Most Capped Player: Billy Gillespie, 25, Northern Ireland.

Most League Appearances: Joe Shaw, 629, 1948–66.

Youngest League Player: Steve Hawes, 17 years 47 days v WBA, 2 September 1995.

Record Transfer Fee Received: £4,000,000 from Everton for Phil Jagielka, July 2007.

Record Transfer Fee Paid: £4,000,000 to Everton for James Beattie, August 2007.

Football League Record: 1892 Elected to Division 2; 1893–1934 Division 1; 1934–39 Division 2; 1946–49 Division 1; 1949–53 Division 2; 1953–56 Division 1; 1956–61 Division 2; 1961–68 Division 1; 1968–71 Division 2; 1971–76 Division 1; 1976–79 Division 2; 1979–81 Division 3; 1981–82 Division 4; 1982–84 Division 3; 1984–88 Division 2; 1988–89 Division 3; 1989–90 Division 2; 1990–92 Division 1; 1992–94 FA Premier League; 1994–2004 Division 1; 2004–06 FL C; 2006–07 FA Premier League; 2007–11 FL C; 2011– FL 1.

MANAGERS

J. B. Wostinholm 1889–99 *(Secretary-Manager)*
John Nicholson 1899–1932
Ted Davison 1932–52
Reg Freeman 1952–55
Joe Mercer 1955–58
Johnny Harris 1959–68 *(continued as General Manager to 1970)*
Arthur Rowley 1968–69
Johnny Harris *(General Manager resumed Team Manager duties)* 1969–73
Ken Furphy 1973–75
Jimmy Sirrel 1975–77
Harry Haslam 1978–81
Martin Peters 1981
Ian Porterfield 1981–86
Billy McEwan 1986–88
Dave Bassett 1988–95
Howard Kendall 1995–97
Nigel Spackman 1997–98
Steve Bruce 1998–99
Adrian Heath 1999
Neil Warnock 1999–2007
Bryan Robson 2007–08
Kevin Blackwell 2008–10
Gary Speed 2010
Micky Adams 2010–11
Danny Wilson May 2011–

LATEST SEQUENCES

Longest Sequence of League Wins: 8, 14.9.1960 – 22.10.1960.

Longest Sequence of League Defeats: 7, 19.8.1975 – 20.9.1975.

Longest Sequence of League Draws: 6, 6.5.2001 – 8.9.2001.

Longest Sequence of Unbeaten League Matches: 22, 2.9.1899 – 13.1.1900.

Longest Sequence Without a League Win: 19, 27.9.1975 – 7.2.1976.

Successive Scoring Runs: 34 from 30.3.1956.

Successive Non-scoring Runs: 6 from 4.12.1993.

TEN YEAR LEAGUE RECORD

		P	W	D	L	F	A	Pts	Pos
2002-03	Div 1	46	23	11	12	72	52	80	3
2003-04	Div 1	46	20	11	15	65	56	71	8
2004-05	FL C	46	18	13	15	57	56	67	8
2005-06	FL C	46	26	12	8	76	46	90	2
2006-07	PR Lge	38	10	8	20	32	55	38	18
2007-08	FL C	46	17	15	14	56	51	66	9
2008-09	FL C	46	22	14	10	64	39	80	3
2009-10	FL C	46	17	14	15	62	55	65	8
2010-11	FL C	46	11	9	26	44	79	42	23
2011-12	FL 1	46	27	9	10	92	51	90	3

DID YOU KNOW ?

In 1903–04 Sheffield United could field an entire team of international players, ten of them representing England, the remaining one Northern Ireland. On 14 November against Liverpool in a 2-1 win there were eight English and one Irishman; two others were later capped for England.

SHEFFIELD UNITED 2011–12 LEAGUE RECORD

Match No.	Date	Venue	Opponents	Result	H/T Score	Lg Pos.	Goalscorers	Attendance
1	Aug 6	A	Oldham Ath	W 2-0	0-0	—	Maguire ^{48}, Cresswell ^{54}	8032
2	13	H	Brentford	W 2-0	0-0	2	Slew ^{49}, Cresswell ^{70}	17,769
3	16	H	Walsall	W 3-2	0-0	—	Lowton ^{59}, Williamson ^{68}, Cresswell (pen) ^{74}	16,443
4	20	A	Tranmere R	D 1-1	1-0	3	Montgomery ^{44}	6244
5	27	A	Yeovil T	W 1-0	1-0	3	Porter ^{41}	5001
6	Sept 3	H	Bury	W 4-0	1-0	2	Porter ^{43}, Mendez-Laing ^{47}, Lowton ^{71}, Tonne ^{84}	17,956
7	10	A	Scunthorpe U	D 1-1	0-1	1	Evans ^{72}	6047
8	13	H	Huddersfield T	L 0-3	0-3	—		17,373
9	17	H	Colchester U	W 3-0	2-0	2	Evans ^{3}, Porter ^{12}, Quinn ^{72}	15,783
10	24	A	Wycombe W	L 0-1	0-1	2		5506
11	Oct 1	H	Charlton Ath	L 0-2	0-0	6		20,743
12	16	H	Sheffield W	D 2-2	2-0	7	Quinn ^{11}, Evans ^{20}	28,136
13	19	A	Preston NE	W 4-2	2-1	—	Phillips 2 $^{4, 39}$, Williamson 2 $^{74, 87}$	11,520
14	22	A	Leyton Orient	D 1-1	0-0	5	Porter ^{84}	5928
15	25	H	Milton Keynes D	W 2-1	1-0	—	Cresswell ^{22}, Phillips ^{67}	16,367
16	29	H	Exeter C	D 4-4	1-2	4	Phillips 2 $^{45, 85}$, Clarke ^{65}, Lowton ^{70}	17,052
17	Nov 5	A	Stevenage	L 1-2	0-1	5	Evans ^{69}	4996
18	19	H	Carlisle U	W 1-0	1-0	5	Evans ^{21}	16,840
19	26	A	Chesterfield	W 1-0	0-0	5	Evans ^{82}	9259
20	Dec 10	H	Rochdale	W 3-0	1-0	5	Evans 2 $^{39, 64}$, Cresswell ^{57}	15,892
21	17	A	Bournemouth	W 2-0	1-0	3	Barrett (og) ^{5}, Cook (og) ^{77}	7260
22	27	H	Notts Co	W 2-1	1-1	—	Flynn ^{31}, Sheehan (og) ^{51}	20,538
23	31	H	Hartlepool U	W 3-1	3-0	2	Flynn ^{12}, Porter ^{34}, Evans ^{42}	20,372
24	Jan 2	A	Carlisle U	L 2-3	2-2	3	Evans 2 $^{7, 45}$	7721
25	10	H	Yeovil T	W 4-0	2-0	—	Cresswell ^{18}, Doyle ^{36}, Williamson 2 $^{48, 87}$	15,965
26	14	A	Bury	W 3-0	0-0	2	Cresswell ^{54}, Evans ^{62}, Williamson ^{81}	6970
27	21	A	Charlton Ath	L 0-1	0-1	3		20,992
28	Feb 11	H	Wycombe W	W 3-0	0-0	—	Hoskins ^{66}, Evans ^{73}, McDonald ^{90}	17,165
29	14	A	Huddersfield T	W 1-0	1-0	—	Collins ^{5}	17,320
30	18	H	Preston NE	W 2-1	1-1	2	Evans 2 $^{42, 83}$	17,579
31	26	A	Sheffield W	L 0-1	0-0	2		36,364
32	29	H	Scunthorpe U	W 2-1	0-1	—	Williamson ^{54}, Quinn ^{82}	16,165
33	Mar 3	H	Oldham Ath	L 2-3	2-0	2	Lowton ^{22}, Evans ^{38}	17,267
34	6	A	Walsall	L 2-3	0-0	—	Williamson ^{65}, Evans ^{76}	5003
35	10	A	Brentford	W 2-0	1-0	2	Evans 2 $^{6, 51}$	7414
36	13	A	Colchester U	D 1-1	1-0	—	Hoskins ^{32}	4572
37	17	H	Tranmere R	D 1-1	1-0	2	Evans ^{31}	17,444
38	20	A	Notts Co	W 5-2	4-0	—	Quinn ^{16}, Evans ^{22}, Lowton ^{27}, Collins ^{45}, Williamson ^{89}	9468
39	28	H	Chesterfield	W 4-1	1-1	—	Williamson ^{38}, Evans 3 (1 pen) $^{49 (p), 60, 63}$	20,159
40	31	A	Hartlepool U	W 1-0	0-0	2	Evans (pen) ^{79}	5825
41	Apr 7	H	Bournemouth	W 2-1	1-0	2	Evans ^{34}, Cresswell ^{50}	18,817
42	10	A	Rochdale	W 5-2	4-1	—	McDonald ^{5}, Evans 2 $^{22, 45}$, Williamson ^{25}, Doyle ^{57}	5309
43	14	H	Leyton Orient	W 3-1	1-1	2	Williamson ^{42}, Doyle ^{54}, Evans ^{83}	18,272
44	21	A	Milton Keynes D	L 0-1	0-1	2		15,938
45	28	H	Stevenage	D 2-2	0-1	3	Cresswell ^{63}, Lowton ^{85}	30,043
46	May 5	A	Exeter C	D 2-2	1-1	3	Williamson ^{44}, McDonald ^{47}	6045

Final League Position: 3

GOALSCORERS

League (92): Evans 29 (2 pens), Williamson 13, Cresswell 9 (1 pen), Lowton 6, Phillips 5, Porter 5, Quinn 4, Doyle 3, McDonald 3, Collins 2, Flynn 2, Hoskins 2, Clarke 1, Maguire 1, Mendez-Laing 1, Montgomery 1, Slew 1, Tonne 1, own goals 3.
Carling Cup (2): Cresswell 1, Quinn 1.
FA Cup (9): Evans 5, Flynn 1, Porter 1, own goals 2.
J Paint Trophy (5): Evans 1, McAllister 1, Phillips 1, Porter 1, Tonne 1.
Play-Offs (1): Porter 1.

Simonsen S 44	Lowton M 44	Lescinel J 22 + 3	Montgomery N 14 + 6	Collins N 42	Maguire H 44	Flynn R 12 + 14	Doyle M 39 + 4	Cresswell R 32 + 10	Porter C 18 + 16	Quinn S 43 + 2	Williamson L 31 + 9	Bogdanovic D — + 2	Mendez-Laing N 4 + 4	McDonald K 30 + 1	Slew J 3 + 1	McAllister D 3 + 1	Tonne E — + 2	Evans C 30 + 6	Williams M 14 + 5	Phillips M 5 + 1	Clarke B 5	Long G 2	Ertl J 2 + 5	Beattie J 2 + 16	Hoskins W 3 + 6	Taylor A 4	Hill M 11 + 1	Egan J 1	Hoskins W 1 + 2	O'Halloran M 1 + 6	*Match No.*
1	2	3	4	5	6	7¹	8	9	10²	11	12	13																			1
1	2	3	4	5	6			9		11	12	13	7¹	8	10²																2
1	2	3	4	5	6		12	9		11	13		7²	8¹	10																3
1	2	3	4	5	6		8	9	12	11²	7		13		10¹																4
1	2	3	4¹	5	6	7³	8	9	10²	11			14		13	12															5
1	2	3		5	6	12	8	9	10²	11³	14		7¹			4	13														6
1	2	3		5	6		8	9	10³	11	12		7²			4¹	13	14													7
1	2			5	6	7³	8	9	10²	11	4¹		14	13				12	3												8
1	2	14		5³	6	13	8	12	10	11²	7			4				9¹	3												9
1	2	12		5	6		8	13	10²	11	7³		14	4				9	3¹												10
1	2	3		5	6	13	8	12	10¹	11	7²			4				9													11
1	2		4	5	6			10	13	11	7¹			8				9²	3	12											12
1	2		4	5	6			13	10	11¹	12			8					3	7	9²										13
1	2		4	5	6		14		10	11	13³			8				12	3	7²	9¹										14
	2		4	5	6	14	12	10²		11				8¹				13	3	7	9³	1									15
	2		4	5	6		13	10¹	14	11				8²				12	3	7	9³	1									16
1	2	13	4	5	6		8	10³	14	11								12	3²	7	9¹										17
1	2		4	5	6	12	8	10	13	11	7¹							9²	3												18
1	2			5	6	12	4		10²	11	7¹					8		9	3				13								19
1	2	3	14	5	6	12	8	10²	13	11¹	7			4³				9													20
1	2	3		5	6		8	10²	13	11	7			4¹				9					12								21
1	2	3	14	5	6	7³	8	10²		11				4¹				9					12	13							22
1	2¹	3	14	5	6	11	8		10²		7			4³				9					12	13							23
1		3	2	5	6	7²	8³	12	10¹	11	13			4				9						14							24
1	2	3	14	5	6		8	10²	13	11	7³			4				9¹						12							25
1	2	3		5	6		8	10²	14	11¹	7			4				9³	12					13							26
1	2	3¹		5	6		8	10²	14	11	7³			4				9	13					12■							27
1	2	3		5	6	12	8	10²	14	11	7¹			4				9³							13						28
1	2	3		5	6	7	8	10¹	12	11				4				9²							13						29
1	2	3	12	5	6	7²	8	10³		11	13			4¹				9						14							30
1	2	3	4¹	5	6	12	8	10²		11³	7							9						14	13						31
1	2	3		5	4	11³	8	12		13	7							9					6¹	10²	14						32
1	2■	3¹			5■	8	6	10		11³	7							9					12	14	13	4²					33
1						8²	4	10¹	12	11	7							9					6	14	13	2³	3	5			34
1	2		12		6		4	13	10²	11	7							9	3						8¹		5				35
1	2				6		4	12	10²	11	7							9	3					13	8¹		5				36
1	2			5	6		4	13	10¹	11	7							9	12					14	8³		3²				37
1	2			5	6		4	10²		11	7			8¹				9³	12					13			3		14		38
1	2			6			4	10¹		11³	7			8				9²	3					13			5		12	14	39
1	2			5	6		4	10¹		11²	7			8				9	13								3			12	40
1	2			5	6	13	4	10¹		11²	7			8				9									3			12	41
1	2			5	6	12	4	10²	13	11	7¹			8				9³									3			14	42
1	2			5	6	13	4	10¹	12	11²	7			8				9³									3			14	43
1	2			5	6	13	4		10³	11²	7			8										14			3		9¹	12	44
1	2			5	6	12	4	13	10²	11¹	7			8										14		3³				9	45
1	2			5	6	11²	8	9¹	12	13	7³			4										10■		3	14				46

FA Cup

First Round	Oxford U	(h)	3-0
Second Round	Torquay U	(h)	3-2
Third Round	Salisbury C	(h)	3-1
Fourth Round	Birmingham C	(h)	0-4

Carling Cup

First Round	Hartlepool U	(a)	1-1
Second Round	Everton	(a)	1-3

J Paint Trophy

First Round	Burton Alb	(a)	2-1
Second Round	Rotherham U	(a)	2-1
Northern Quarter-Final	Bradford C	(h)	1-1

Play-Offs

Semi-Final	Stevenage	(a)	0-0
		(h)	1-0
Final *(at Wembley).*	Huddersfield T		0-0

SHEFFIELD WEDNESDAY FL Championship

FOUNDATION

Sheffield being one of the principal centres of early Association Football, this club was formed as long ago as 1867 by the Sheffield Wednesday Cricket Club (formed 1825) and their colours from the start were blue and white. The inaugural meeting was held at the Adelphi Hotel and the original committee included Charles Stokes who was subsequently a founder member of Sheffield United.

Hillsborough, Sheffield S6 1SW.

Telephone: (0871) 995 1867.

Fax: (0114) 221 2122.

Ticket Office: (0871) 900 1867.

Website: www.swfc.co.uk

Email: enquiries@swfc.co.uk

Ground Capacity: 39,812.

Record Attendance: 72,841 v Manchester C, FA Cup 5th rd, 17 February 1934.

Pitch Measurements: 110yd × 71yd.

Chairman: Milan Mandaric.

Vice-chairman: Paul Aldridge.

Manager: Dave Jones.

Assistant Manager: Terry Burton.

Head Physio: Paul Smith.

HONOURS

Football League – FL 1: ***Runners-up*** 2011–12; **Division 1:** ***Champions*** 1902–03, 1903–04, 1928–29, 1929–30; ***Runners-up*** 1960–61; **Division 2:** ***Champions*** 1899–1900, 1925–26, 1951–52, 1955–56, 1958–59; ***Runners-up*** 1949–50, 1983–84.

FA Cup: ***Winners*** 1896, 1907, 1935; ***Runners-up*** 1890, 1966, 1993.

Football League Cup: ***Winners*** 1991; ***Runners-up*** 1993.

European Competitions
European Fairs Cup: 1961–62, 1963–64. **UEFA Cup:** 1992–93. **Intertoto Cup:** 1995.

Colours: Blue and white striped shirts, black shorts, blue stockings.

Year Formed: 1867 (fifth oldest League club).

Turned Professional: 1887.

Previous Name: The Wednesday until 1929.

Club Nickname: 'The Owls'.

Grounds: 1867, Highfield; 1869, Myrtle Road; 1877, Sheaf House; 1887, Olive Grove; 1899, Owlerton (since 1912 known as Hillsborough). Some games were played at Endcliffe in the 1880s. Until 1895 Bramall Lane was used for some games.

First Football League Game: 3 September 1892, Division 1, v Notts Co (a) W 1–0 – Allan; Tom Brandon (1), Mumford; Hall, Betts, Harry Brandon; Spiksley, Brady, Davis, Bob Brown, Dunlop.

Record League Victory: 9–1 v Birmingham, Division 1, 13 December 1930 – Brown; Walker, Blenkinsop; Strange, Leach, Wilson; Hooper (3), Seed (2), Ball (2), Burgess (1), Rimmer (1).

Record Cup Victory: 12–0 v Halliwell, FA Cup 1st rd, 17 January 1891 – Smith; Thompson, Brayshaw; Harry Brandon (1), Betts, Cawley (2); Winterbottom, Mumford (2), Bob Brandon (1), Woolhouse (5), Ingram (1).

sky SPORTS FACT FILE

The legendary Sheffield Wednesday winger Fred Spiksley always laundered his own kit and was an immaculate off-field dresser. En route to Accrington in 1891 he was delayed and met a couple of Wednesday players. He stayed and went on to make 324 appearances and score 116 goals.

Record Defeat: 0–10 v Aston Villa, Division 1, 5 October 1912.

Most League Points (2 for a win): 62, Division 2, 1958–59.

Most League Points (3 for a win): 93, FL 1, 2011–12.

Most League Goals: 106, Division 2, 1958–59.

Highest League Scorer in Season: Derek Dooley, 46, Division 2, 1951–52.

Most League Goals in Total Aggregate: Andrew Wilson, 199, 1900–20.

Most League Goals in One Match: 6, Doug Hunt v Norwich C, Division 2, 19 November 1938.

Most Capped Player: Nigel Worthington, 50 (66), Northern Ireland.

Most League Appearances: Andrew Wilson, 501, 1900–20.

Youngest League Player: Peter Fox, 15 years 269 days v Orient, 31 March 1973.

Record Transfer Fee Received: £2,750,000 from Blackburn R for Paul Warhurst, September 1993.

Record Transfer Fee Paid: £4,500,000 to Celtic for Paolo Di Canio, August 1997.

Football League Record: 1892 Elected to Division 1; 1899–1900 Division 2; 1900–20 Division 1; 1920–26 Division 2; 1926–37 Division 1; 1937–50 Division 2; 1950–51 Division 1; 1951–52 Division 2; 1952–55 Division 1; 1955–56 Division 2; 1956–58 Division 1; 1958–59 Division 2; 1959–70 Division 1; 1970–75 Division 2; 1975–80 Division 3; 1980–84 Division 2; 1984–90 Division 1; 1990–91 Division 2; 1991–92 Division 1; 1992–2000 FA Premier League; 2000–03 Division 1; 2003–04 Division 2; 2004–05 FL 1; 2005–10 FL C; 2010–12 FL 1; 2012– FL C.

MANAGERS

Arthur Dickinson 1891–1920 *(Secretary-Manager)*
Robert Brown 1920–33
Billy Walker 1933–37
Jimmy McMullan 1937–42
Eric Taylor 1942–58 *(continued as General Manager to 1974)*
Harry Catterick 1958–61
Vic Buckingham 1961–64
Alan Brown 1964–68
Jack Marshall 1968–69
Danny Williams 1969–71
Derek Dooley 1971–73
Steve Burtenshaw 1974–75
Len Ashurst 1975–77
Jackie Charlton 1977–83
Howard Wilkinson 1983–88
Peter Eustace 1988–89
Ron Atkinson 1989–91
Trevor Francis 1991–95
David Pleat 1995–97
Ron Atkinson 1997–98
Danny Wilson 1998–2000
Peter Shreeves (Acting) 2000
Paul Jewell 2000–01
Peter Shreeves 2001
Terry Yorath 2001–02
Chris Turner 2002–04
Paul Sturrock 2004–06
Brian Laws 2006–09
Alan Irvine 2010–11
Gary Megson 2011–12
Dave Jones March 2012–

LATEST SEQUENCES

Longest Sequence of League Wins: 9, 23.4.1904 – 15.10.1904.

Longest Sequence of League Defeats: 8, 9.9.2000 – 17.10.2000.

Longest Sequence of League Draws: 7, 15.3.2008 – 14.4.2008.

Longest Sequence of Unbeaten League Matches: 19, 10.12.1960 – 8.4.1961.

Longest Sequence Without a League Win: 20, 11.1.1975 – 30.8.1975.

Successive Scoring Runs: 40 from 14.11.1959.

Successive Non-scoring Runs: 8 from 8.3.1975.

TEN YEAR LEAGUE RECORD

		P	*W*	*D*	*L*	*F*	*A*	*Pts*	*Pos*
2002-03	Div 1	46	10	16	20	56	73	46	22
2003-04	Div 2	46	13	14	19	48	64	53	16
2004-05	FL 1	46	19	15	12	77	59	72	5
2005-06	FL C	46	13	13	20	39	52	52	19
2006-07	FL C	46	20	11	15	70	66	71	9
2007-08	FL C	46	14	13	19	54	55	55	16
2008-09	FL C	46	16	13	17	51	58	61	12
2009-10	FL C	46	11	14	21	49	69	47	22
2010-11	FL 1	46	16	10	20	67	67	58	15
2011-12	FL 1	46	28	9	9	81	48	93	2

DID YOU KNOW ?

Tommy Crawshaw played in two winning Sheffield Wednesday FA Cup final teams eleven years apart. As an England centre-half with ten caps, he also won two First Division championship medals in 1903 and 1904 with the club and a Second Division title for them in 1900.

SHEFFIELD WEDNESDAY 2011–12 LEAGUE RECORD

Match No.	Date	Venue	Opponents	Result		H/T Score	Lg Pos.	Goalscorers	Attendance
1	Aug 6	H	Rochdale	W	2-0	1-0	—	Jones, R [16], Prutton [72]	21,174
2	13	A	Bournemouth	L	0-2	0-1	10		6901
3	16	A	Bury	L	1-2	0-2	—	Sedgwick [47]	5219
4	20	H	Notts Co	W	2-1	0-1	12	Bennett [53], Madine [68]	16,979
5	27	H	Scunthorpe U	W	3-2	2-0	9	Madine 2 [5, 70], Marshall [17]	16,862
6	Sept 5	A	Charlton Ath	D	1-1	0-1	—	Morrison [56]	14,014
7	10	H	Milton Keynes D	W	3-1	0-0	8	Madine 2 [54, 63], Palmer [89]	16,982
8	13	A	Stevenage	L	1-5	0-4	—	Madine [74]	4339
9	17	A	Yeovil T	W	3-2	1-2	9	McGoldrick [10], Bennett [53], Madine [72]	4445
10	24	H	Exeter C	W	3-0	2-0	7	O'Connor [40], Madine 2 (1 pen) [43, 75 (p)]	16,995
11	Oct 1	A	Hartlepool U	W	1-0	1-0	4	Johnson, R [33]	6800
12	8	H	Chesterfield	W	3-1	1-0	2	Buxton [17], Madine [59], Marshall [87]	24,514
13	16	A	Sheffield U	D	2-2	0-2	3	O'Grady [82], Madine [86]	28,136
14	22	H	Colchester U	W	2-0	0-0	3	Jones, R [59], Johnson, R [70]	17,634
15	25	A	Carlisle U	L	2-3	1-0	—	Marshall [35], Jones, R [88]	6058
16	29	A	Wycombe W	W	2-1	2-1	3	Semedo [23], Lowe [35]	6448
17	Nov 5	H	Brentford	D	0-0	0-0	3		18,107
18	19	A	Tranmere R	W	2-1	1-1	3	Lines [45], Lowe [80]	6652
19	26	H	Leyton Orient	W	1-0	1-0	2	Johnson, R [19]	18,355
20	Dec 10	A	Oldham Ath	W	2-0	0-0	2	Prutton [62], Lowe (pen) [84]	7060
21	17	H	Huddersfield T	D	4-4	2-2	2	Jones, R [26], Johnson, R [28], Marshall [63], O'Grady [74]	28,600
22	26	A	Walsall	L	1-2	0-0	2	Lowe [60]	8603
23	31	A	Preston NE	W	2-0	2-0	3	Batth [4], Marshall [42]	15,904
24	Jan 2	H	Tranmere R	W	2-1	2-0	2	Johnson, R [2], Lines [7]	24,254
25	14	H	Charlton Ath	L	0-1	0-1	4		26,759
26	21	H	Hartlepool U	D	2-2	0-0	4	Johnson, J [58], Madine [75]	17,469
27	24	A	Scunthorpe U	W	3-1	2-0	—	O'Grady 2 [1, 18], Johnson, J [47]	5727
28	31	A	Milton Keynes D	D	1-1	1-1	—	MacKenzie (og) [27]	9776
29	Feb 4	H	Yeovil T	W	2-1	0-1	—	Johnson, J [57], Johnson, R [80]	17,213
30	11	A	Exeter C	L	1-2	0-0	—	Johnson, J [65]	5555
31	14	H	Stevenage	L	0-1	0-1	—		16,185
32	18	A	Chesterfield	L	0-1	0-0	3		9279
33	26	H	Sheffield U	W	1-0	0-0	3	O'Grady [73]	36,364
34	Mar 3	A	Rochdale	D	0-0	0-0	3		5361
35	6	H	Bury	W	4-1	1-0	—	Antonio 2 [11, 58], Madine [61], Lowe [64]	17,684
36	10	H	Bournemouth	W	3-0	3-0	3	Batth [4], Addison (og) [9], Antonio [10]	19,416
37	17	A	Notts Co	W	2-1	0-0	3	Lowe [53], Madine [66]	12,410
38	20	H	Walsall	D	2-2	0-0	—	Lowe [60], Madine [90]	18,869
39	24	A	Leyton Orient	W	1-0	0-0	2	Johnson, R [49]	6196
40	31	H	Preston NE	W	2-0	0-0	3	Madine 2 [49, 64]	18,069
41	Apr 7	A	Huddersfield T	W	2-0	0-0	3	Llera [54], Ranger [72]	18,646
42	9	H	Oldham Ath	W	3-0	1-0	2	Madine [43], Llera [67], Lowe [80]	22,232
43	14	A	Colchester U	D	1-1	0-1	3	Llera [52]	6643
44	21	H	Carlisle U	W	2-1	1-0	3	Lines [26], Antonio [90]	21,934
45	28	A	Brentford	W	2-1	1-0	2	Treacy [38], Llera [66]	7381
46	May 5	H	Wycombe W	W	2-0	1-0	2	Antonio [25], Ranger [52]	38,082

Final League Position: 2

GOALSCORERS

League (81): Madine 18 (1 pen), Lowe 8 (1 pen), Johnson, R 7, Antonio 5, Marshall 5, O'Grady 5, Johnson, J 4, Jones, R 4, Llera 4, Lines 3, Batth 2, Bennett 2, Prutton 2, Ranger 2, Buxton 1, McGoldrick 1, Morrison 1, O'Connor 1, Palmer 1, Sedgwick 1, Semedo 1, Treacy 1, own goals 2.
Carling Cup (1): Morrison, C 1.
FA Cup (5): O'Grady 2, Lines 1, Lowe 1, Morrison, C 1.
J Paint Trophy (0).

Weaver N 8	Buxton L 36 + 1	Bennett J 16 + 5	Batth D 44	Jones R 32 + 1	Semedo J 46	Sedgwick C 5 + 5	Prutton D 19 + 6	Morrison C 7 + 12	Madine G 36 + 2	Palmer L 6 + 8	O'Connor J 11 + 7	Otsemobor J 8 + 3	Jones D 1 + 2	Lines C 37 + 4	O'Donnell R 6	O'Grady C 25 + 7	Johnson R 22 + 2	Uchechi D — + 1	Marshall B 22	Reynolds M 3	Lowe R 11 + 15	Johnson J 12 + 12	McGoldrick D 3 + 1	Bywater S 32	Tavernier J 6	Llera M 15 + 5	Watt S 2 + 2	Jones M 6 + 4	Beevers M 4 + 3	Bostock J 2 + 2	Antonio M 14	Ranger N 7 + 1	Treacy K 2 + 5	*Match No.*
1	2	3	4	5	6	7^{2}	8	9^{1}	10	11^{3}	12	13	14																					1
1	2	3^{3}	4	5	6^{2}	7^{1}	8	9	10	11	14	13		12																				2
	2	3	4	5^{1}	6	7	8^{3}		10			13		11	1	9^{2}	12	14																3
1	2	3	4		6	12	8	9	10^{2}		13			11^{1}			5		7															4
1	2	3	4	5	6		8	9^{2}	10	11^{1}	12			13					7															5
	2		4	5	6^{3}	7^{1}	8	13	10		14			11	1				9	3	12^{2}													6
	2	3	4	5	6		8	9^{2}	10	12	13			14	1				7^{3}			11^{1}												7
	2	3^{2}	4	5^{1}	6		8^{3}	9	10	11	12				1		13		7			14■												8
	2	12	4	5^{1}	6	13	8		10	14	7				1		3		11^{3}				9^{2}											9
	2		4	5	6				10^{2}	14	8			7		12	3		11^{3}		13		9^{1}	1										10
	2		4	5	6	14			10^{2}	13	8^{3}			7		12	3		11				9^{1}	1										11
	2	3	4	5	6	13			10^{3}		8^{1}			7		9^{2}			11			12	14	1										12
	2		4	5	6				10		7^{1}			8		9	3		11			12		1										13
	2		4	5	6				10	14	8^{1}			7		9^{2}	3		11^{3}		13	12		1										14
	2	3	4	5	6				10■		8^{1}			7		9^{2}			11		13	12		1										15
	2	13	4	5^{2}	6			12			8			7		9			11	3	10^{1}			1										16
	2		4	5	6^{3}			14		12	8^{2}			7^{1}		9			11	3	10	13		1										17
		13	4	5	2				10^{1}	7	6			8		9	3		11^{2}		12			1										18
			4		6		14	13		12	8^{1}			7		9^{3}	3		11		10^{2}			1	2	5								19
		13	4	5	6		7							8		9	3		11^{1}		12			1	2		10^{2}							20
		13	4	5	6		7							8		9	3		11^{2}		12			1	2		10^{1}							21
			4	5^{1}	6		7	13						8	1	9	3		11		10^{2}				2	12								22
1			4		6		13			12		2		8		9	3		11^{2}		10^{3}				7^{1}	5	14							23
1			4		6		14	10^{1}				2		8		9	3		11^{3}			13			7^{2}	5	12							24
1			4	5	6			14	10^{2}			2		8		9	3		11^{3}		12					13		7^{1}						25
1	7		4	5^{3}	6				10			2		8		9	3^{1}				13	12				14		11^{2}						26
			4		6			13	10^{2}	11		2	7^{1}	8		9						3^{3}		1		5		14	12					27
	2		4		6	7^{1}	8	14	10^{2}			3				9^{3}	11					13		1		5				12				28
	13		4		6		7	14	10^{1}			2^{2}				9^{3}	3				12	11		1		5				8				29
	2	3	4	13	6		7		10^{3}					12		9						11		1		5^{2}		14		8^{1}				30
	3		4	5	6		7^{2}	12	10^{1}			2		8		9						11		1				13						31
	2		4	5	6		7	14	13					8^{3}		9^{2}	3				10	11^{1}		1						12				32
	2		4	5	6		7^{2}		12					8		9	3				10^{1}			1		14		13			11^{3}			33
	2	3	4	5	6		7^{1}		10					8		9					12			1							11			34
	2	3	4	5	6		12		10^{2}					8		13					9^{1}			1				7			11			35
	2	3	4	5	6			12	10					8							9^{1}			1				7			11			36
	2	3	4	5^{1}	6		14		10					8		13					9^{2}			1		12		7^{3}			11			37
	2	3	4	5	6				10					8		13					9^{2}	12		1				7^{1}			11			38
	2			5	6				10^{3}					8		9^{1}	3				14	7^{2}		1		4					11	12	13	39
	2			5	6				10^{1}					8			3				12	7^{2}		1		4					11	9	13	40
	2		4		6	14			10					8			3^{1}					7^{2}		1		5			12		11^{3}	9	13	41
	2^{1}	3	4		6				10					8							14	7^{2}		1		5			12		11	9^{3}	13	42
	2		4		6				10					8		12						7		1		5			3		11	9^{1}		43
	2		4		6		13		10					8								7^{1}		1		5			3		11^{2}	9	12	44
	2		4		6				10				12	8		14						13		1		5			3^{1}		11^{2}	9	7^{3}	45
	2		4		6				10					8							13	12		1		5			3		11	9^{2}	7^{1}	46

FA Cup

First Round	Morecambe	(a)	2-1
Second Round	Aldershot T	(h)	1-0
Third Round	West Ham U	(h)	1-0
Fourth Round	Blackpool	(a)	1-1
		(h)	0-3

Carling Cup

First Round	Blackpool	(h)	0-0
Second Round	Blackburn R	(a)	1-3

J Paint Trophy

First Round	Bradford C	(a)	0-0

SHREWSBURY TOWN FL Championship 1

FOUNDATION

Shrewsbury School having provided a number of the early England and Wales international players it is not surprising that there was a Town club as early as 1876 which won the Birmingham Senior Cup in 1879. However, the present Shrewsbury Town club was formed in 1886 and won the Welsh FA Cup as early as 1891.

Greenhous Meadow, Oteley Road, Shrewsbury SY2 6ST.

Telephone: (01743) 289 177.

Fax: (01743) 246 942.

Ticket Office: (01743) 273 943.

Website: www.shrewsburytown.com

Email: info@shrewsburytown.co.uk

Ground Capacity: 10,000.

Record Attendance: 18,917 v Walsall, Division 3, 26 April 1961 (at Gay Meadow); 8,429 v Bury, FL 2 Play-off semi-final, 7 May 2009 (at ProStar Stadium).

Pitch Measurements: 115yd × 77yd.

Chairman: Roland Wycherley.

Manager: Graham Turner.

First Team Coach: John Trewick.

Physio: Chris Skitt.

Colours: All blue with yellow and red design.

Year Formed: 1886.

Turned Professional: 1896.

Club Nicknames: 'Town', 'Blues' or 'Salop'. The name 'Salop' is a colloquialism for the county of Shropshire. Since Shrewsbury is the only club in Shropshire, cries of 'Come on Salop' are frequently used!

Grounds: 1886, Old Racecourse Ground; 1889, Ambler's Field; 1893, Sutton Lane; 1895, Barracks Ground; 1910, Gay Meadow; 2007, New Meadow (re-named Greenhous Meadow 2010).

First Football League Game: 19 August 1950, Division 3 (N), v Scunthorpe U (a) D 0–0 – Egglestone; Fisher, Lewis; Wheatley, Depear, Robinson; Griffin, Hope, Jackson, Brown, Barker.

Record League Victory: 7–0 v Swindon T, Division 3 (S), 6 May 1955 – McBride; Bannister, Skeech; Wallace, Maloney, Candlin; Price, O'Donnell (1), Weigh (4), Russell, McCue (2); 7-0 v Gillingham, FL 2, 13 September 2008 – Daniels; Herd, Tierney, Davies (2), Jackson (1) (Langmead), Coughlan (1), Cansdell-Sherriff (1), Thornton, Hibbert (1) (Hindmarch), Holt (pen), McIntyre (Ashton).

Record Cup Victory: 11–2 v Marine, FA Cup 1st rd, 11 November 1995 – Edwards, Seabury (Dempsey (1)), Withe (1), Evans (1), Whiston (2), Scott (1), Woods, Stevens (1), Spink (3) (Anthrobus), Walton, Berkley, (1 og).

HONOURS

Football League – FL 2: ***Runners-up*** 2011–12; **Division 2:** Best season: 8th, 1983–84, 1984–85; **Division 3:** ***Champions*** 1978–79, 1993–94; **Division 4:** ***Runners-up*** 1974–75.

FA Cup: Best season: 6th rd, 1979, 1982.

Football League Cup: Semi-final 1961.

Welsh Cup: ***Winners*** 1891, 1938, 1977, 1979, 1984, 1985; ***Runners-up*** 1931, 1948, 1980.

Auto Windscreens Shield: ***Runners-up*** 1996.

sky SPORTS FACT FILE

In 1947–48, Shrewsbury Town had the assistance of left-back Eddie Hapgood, the former Arsenal and England captain. In an FA Cup tie that season against Stockport County the Shrewsbury goalkeeper Harry Rowley was injured, Hapgood took over, was unbeaten and earned a replay.

Record Defeat: 1–8 v Norwich C, Division 3 (S), 13 September 1952; 1–8 v Coventry C, Division 3, 22 October 1963.

Most League Points (2 for a win): 62, Division 4, 1974–75.

Most League Points (3 for a win): 88, FL 2, 2011–12.

Most League Goals: 101, Division 4, 1958–59.

Highest League Scorer in Season: Arthur Rowley, 38, Division 4, 1958–59.

Most League Goals in Total Aggregate: Arthur Rowley, 152, 1958–65 (thus completing his League record of 434 goals).

Most League Goals in One Match: 5, Alf Wood v Blackburn R, Division 3, 2 October 1971.

Most Capped Player: Jimmy McLaughlin, 5 (12), Northern Ireland; Bernard McNally, 5, Northern Ireland.

Most League Appearances: Mickey Brown, 418, 1986–91; 1992–94; 1996–2001.

Youngest League Player: Graham French, 16 years 177 days v Reading, 30 September 1961.

Record Transfer Fee Received: £600,000 from Manchester C for Joe Hart, May 2006.

Record Transfer Fee Paid: £170,000 to Nottingham F for Grant Holt, June 2008.

Football League Record: 1950 Elected to Division 3 (N); 1951–58 Division 3 (S); 1958–59 Division 4; 1959–74 Division 3; 1974–75 Division 4; 1975–79 Division 3; 1979–89 Division 2; 1989–94 Division 3; 1994–97 Division 2; 1997–2003 Division 3; 2003–04 Conference; 2004–12 FL 2; 2012– FL 1.

MANAGERS

W. Adams 1905–12
(Secretary-Manager)
A. Weston 1912–34
(Secretary-Manager)
Jack Roscamp 1934–35
Sam Ramsey 1935–36
Ted Bousted 1936–40
Leslie Knighton 1945–49
Harry Chapman 1949–50
Sammy Crooks 1950–54
Walter Rowley 1955–57
Harry Potts 1957–58
Johnny Spuhler 1958
Arthur Rowley 1958–68
Harry Gregg 1968–72
Maurice Evans 1972–73
Alan Durban 1974–78
Richie Barker 1978
Graham Turner 1978–84
Chic Bates 1984–87
Ian McNeill 1987–90
Asa Hartford 1990–91
John Bond 1991–93
Fred Davies 1994–97
(previously Caretaker-Manager 1993–94)
Jake King 1997–99
Kevin Ratcliffe 1999–2003
Jimmy Quinn 2003–04
Gary Peters 2004–08
Paul Simpson 2008–10
Graham Turner June 2010–

LATEST SEQUENCES

Longest Sequence of League Wins: 7, 28.10.1995 – 16.12.1995.

Longest Sequence of League Defeats: 11, 9.4.2003 – 14.8.2004.

Longest Sequence of League Draws: 6, 30.10.1963 – 14.12.1963.

Longest Sequence of Unbeaten League Matches: 16, 30.10.1993 – 26.2.1994.

Longest Sequence Without a League Win: 18, 8.3.2003 – 14.8.2004.

Successive Scoring Runs: 28 from 7.9.1960.

Successive Non-scoring Runs: 6 from 1.1.1991.

TEN YEAR LEAGUE RECORD

		P	*W*	*D*	*L*	*F*	*A*	*Pts*	*Pos*
2002-03	Div 3	46	9	14	23	62	92	41	24
2003-04	Conf.	42	20	14	8	67	42	74	3
2004-05	FL 2	46	11	16	19	48	53	49	21
2005-06	FL 2	46	16	13	17	55	55	61	10
2006-07	FL 2	46	18	17	11	68	46	71	7
2007-08	FL 2	46	12	14	20	56	65	50	18
2008-09	FL 2	46	17	18	11	61	44	69	7
2009-10	FL 2	46	17	12	17	55	54	63	12
2010-11	FL 2	46	22	13	11	72	49	79	4
2011-12	FL 2	46	26	10	10	66	41	88	2

On 15 October 1887 Shrewsbury Town made an encouraging start to their first FA Cup tie when they defeated Macclesfield 3-1. All three goals came from outside-right and team captain Harry Pearson. He also figured in Shrewsbury's successful Welsh Cup final win in 1891.

SHREWSBURY TOWN 2011–12 LEAGUE RECORD

Match No.	Date	Venue	Opponents	Result	H/T Score	Lg Pos.	Goalscorers	Attendance
1	Aug 6	H	Plymouth Arg	D 1-1	0-0	—	Collins [69]	6421
2	13	A	Burton Alb	D 1-1	0-1	17	Gornell [83]	2989
3	16	A	Oxford U	L 0-2	0-1	—		6102
4	20	H	Crewe Alex	W 2-0	1-0	14	McAllister, S [23], Wroe [90]	5050
5	27	H	Swindon T	W 2-1	0-1	11	Gornell [57], Morgan [71]	5323
6	Sept 3	A	Gillingham	W 1-0	0-0	5	Wroe (pen) [90]	4869
7	10	H	Hereford U	W 3-1	1-0	3	Morgan 2 [7, 79], Wright [48]	5684
8	13	A	Bristol R	L 0-1	0-1	—		5065
9	17	A	Port Vale	W 3-2	2-1	3	Morgan [3], Wright [14], Ainsworth [50]	5541
10	24	H	Torquay U	W 2-0	1-0	2	Collins 2 [6, 49]	5263
11	30	A	Southend U	L 0-3	0-1	—		6394
12	Oct 8	H	Barnet	W 3-2	2-0	4	Richards [31], Gornell [42], Ainsworth [90]	5192
13	15	A	Crawley T	L 1-2	0-2	5	Wright [72]	3453
14	22	A	Rotherham U	D 1-1	1-1	6	Cansdell-Sherriff [45]	3561
15	25	H	Accrington S	W 1-0	1-0	—	Bradshaw [28]	5076
16	29	H	AFC Wimbledon	D 0-0	0-0	6		5861
17	Nov 5	A	Dagenham & R	W 2-0	1-0	4	Gornell [6], Collins (pen) [90]	1726
18	19	A	Northampton T	W 7-2	3-0	4	Wright 2 [18, 40], Wildig [44], Morgan [82], Collins [88], Jacobson [89], Langmead (og) [90]	5039
19	26	H	Morecambe	W 2-0	1-0	4	Wroe (pen) [39], Wright [88]	5623
20	Dec 10	A	Aldershot T	L 0-1	0-0	4		2384
21	17	H	Macclesfield T	W 1-0	0-0	4	Cansdell-Sherriff [49]	4871
22	26	A	Cheltenham T	D 0-0	0-0	4		5004
23	31	A	Bradford C	L 1-3	0-2	4	Morgan [78]	10,567
24	Jan 2	H	Northampton T	D 1-1	1-1	5	Richards [34]	6045
25	14	H	Gillingham	W 2-0	1-0	5	Cansdell-Sherriff [30], Wright [87]	4940
26	21	H	Southend U	W 2-1	0-0	5	Collins (pen) [53], Grandison [82]	5601
27	28	A	Hereford U	W 2-0	2-0	4	Gornell [16], Collins [27]	3515
28	Feb 11	A	Torquay U	L 0-1	0-0	—		2592
29	14	H	Bristol R	W 1-0	0-0	—	Collins [86]	4928
30	18	A	Barnet	W 2-1	1-0	4	Kamdjo (og) [45], Collins [74]	2046
31	21	A	Swindon T	L 1-2	1-0	—	Richards [40]	7990
32	27	H	Crawley T	W 2-1	1-1	—	Wright [44], Morgan [74]	5229
33	Mar 3	A	Crewe Alex	D 1-1	1-1	4	Collins [5]	5086
34	6	H	Oxford U	D 2-2	0-2	—	Wright [54], Richards [90]	5205
35	10	H	Burton Alb	W 1-0	0-0	2	Sharps [51]	5840
36	17	A	Plymouth Arg	L 0-1	0-1	4		5931
37	20	H	Cheltenham T	W 2-0	1-0	—	Wroe [1], Gornell [57]	5705
38	24	A	Morecambe	W 1-0	0-0	3	Collins [68]	2175
39	31	H	Aldershot T	D 1-1	0-0	4	Morgan [78]	5588
40	Apr 6	A	Macclesfield T	W 3-1	1-0	3	Collins 2 [33, 86], Wright [83]	3403
41	9	H	Bradford C	W 1-0	1-0	3	Grandison [16]	6272
42	14	H	Rotherham U	W 3-1	1-1	2	Gornell 2 [45, 67], Wildig [48]	5873
43	17	H	Port Vale	W 1-0	0-0	—	Richards [55]	7678
44	21	A	Accrington S	D 1-1	1-0	2	Gornell [31]	3275
45	28	H	Dagenham & R	W 1-0	1-0	2	Collins [38]	9441
46	May 5	A	AFC Wimbledon	L 1-3	0-0	2	Cansdell-Sherriff [58]	3678

Final League Position: 2

GOALSCORERS

League (66): Collins 14 (2 pens), Wright 10, Gornell 9, Morgan 8, Richards 5, Cansdell-Sherriff 4, Wroe 4 (2 pens), Ainsworth 2, Grandison 2, Wildig 2, Bradshaw 1, Jacobson 1, McAllister, S 1, Sharps 1, own goals 2.
Carling Cup (7): Morgan 3, Collins 2, Wright 1, Wroe 1.
FA Cup (3): Gornell 1, Sharps 1, Wroe 1 (pen).
J Paint Trophy (1): own goal 1.

Smith B 11	Regan C 12 + 1	Cansdell-Sherriff S 35 + 2	Richards M 35 + 7	Sharps I 43	Hazell R 5 + 2	Ainsworth L 19 + 2	Wroe N 32 + 6	Collins J 32 + 10	Morgan M 26 + 16	Wright M 45 + 1	Taylor J 15 + 18	Gornell T 28 + 13	Grandison J 36 + 2	Jacobson J 37 + 2	McAllister S 14 + 3	Bradshaw T 5 + 3	Goldson C 2 + 2	Neal C 35	Wallace J 1 + 2	Hurst J 7	Wildig A 10 + 2	McAllister D 15	Sawyers R 2 + 5	McLaughlin C 4	*Match No.*
1	2	3	4	5	6	7^{1}	8	9	10^{2}	11	12	13													1
1	2	3	4	5	6	7	8	9^{2}	10	11^{1}	12	13													2
1	2^{3}	3	4	5	6	7	8	9^{2}	10	11^{1}	12	13	14												3
1		6	13	5		7^{2}	8	12	10	11		9^{1}	2	3	4										4
1		6		5	12	7	8		10	11		9	2	3^{1}	4										5
1		6		5		7	8		10	11		9	2	3	4										6
1		6	13	5	12	7^{1}	8	14	10^{3}	11^{2}		9▪	2	3	4										7
1		6		5		7	8	9^{1}	10	11	13		2	3^{2}	4	12									8
1		6^{1}	14		5	7^{3}	8	9^{2}	10	11			2	3	4	13	12								9
1			12		6	7	8	9^{3}	10^{2}	11		13	2	3	4^{1}	14	5								10
1		6	12			7	8	9^{2}	10	11	14	13	5	3	4^{1}		2^{3}								11
		6	4	5		7	8^{1}	13	10	11		9^{2}	2	3	12			1							12
		6	4	5		7^{1}	8	12	10	11	13	9^{2}	2	3				1							13
	2^{1}	12		5		7^{3}	8	13	10	11	14	9^{2}	6	3	4			1							14
		6	13	5		7	8		10^{2}	11^{1}	12		2	3	4	9^{3}	14	1							15
		6	12	5		7	8^{1}		10	11^{3}	14	13	2	3	4	9^{2}		1							16
		6	9	5		7^{2}		12		11	13	10^{1}	2	3	4			1	8						17
		6	8	5				12	10	11		9^{1}		3	4			1		2	7				18
		6	4	5		12	8	13	10	11		9^{2}		3				1		2	7^{1}				19
		6	4	5		7^{1}	8	13	10^{3}	11		9^{2}		3				1	14	2	12				20
		6	4	5			8	9	12	11	7			3		10^{1}		1		2					21
		6	4	5			8	9^{2}	12	7	11	13		3		10^{1}		1		2					22
		6	4	5			8	9^{2}	12	7	11^{3}	13		3		10^{1}		1	14	2					23
		3	8	5		7		13	10	11^{1}	12	9^{3}	6		4^{2}			1		2	14				24
		6	8	5				9^{1}	10	7	11	12	2	3				1				4			25
	12	6^{1}	8	5			14	9^{2}	10▪	7	11^{3}	13	2	3				1				4			26
	2		8	5				9		7	11	10	6	3				1				4			27
	2^{2}		7	5		12	8^{3}	9		13	14	10	6	3				1				4	11^{1}		28
	2		8	5			12	9		7	11	10^{2}	6	3				1				4^{1}	13		29
	2		8	5			12	9^{3}	13	7	11^{2}	10	6	3				1				4^{1}	14		30
	2	12	8	5				9	13	7	11^{3}	10^{2}	6	3^{1}				1				4	14		31
	2	6^{1}	8	5			14	9^{3}	13	7	11	10^{2}	12	3				1				4			32
	2		8	5				9	10	7	11^{1}		6					1				4	12	3	33
	2^{1}		8	5			12	9	10^{3}	7	11^{2}	14	6					1				4	13	3	34
			8	5				9^{2}	10	11	12	13	6	3				1				4	7^{1}	2	35
			8	5			12	9	10	7	11^{2}	13	6	3^{1}				1				4		2	36
		3	6	5			8	9	12	7	11	10^{1}	2					1				4			37
		3	6	5			8	9^{2}	13	7	11▪	10^{1}	2	12				1				4			38
		3	6	5			8	9	13	7		10^{2}	2^{3}	12	14			1			11^{1}	4▪			39
		6	4	5			8	9	12	11		10^{1}	2	3				1			7				40
		6	4	5			8	9	12	11		10^{1}	2	3				1			7				41
		6	4	5			8	9^{1}	12	11	13	10	2	3				1			7^{2}				42
		6	4	5			8	9	12	11	13	10^{1}	2	3				1			7^{2}				43
		6	4	5			8	9^{1}	12	11^{2}	13	10	2	3				1			7				44
		6	4	5			8	9	12	11	13	10^{1}	2	3				1			7^{2}				45
		6	4	5			8^{3}	9	12	11	13	10^{2}	2	3	14			1			7^{1}				46

FA Cup

First Round	Newport Co	(a)	1-0
Second Round	Rotherham U	(h)	2-1
Third Round	Tottenham H	(a)	0-3

Carling Cup

First Round	Derby Co	(a)	3-2
Second Round	Swansea C	(h)	3-1
Third Round	Arsenal	(a)	1-3

J Paint Trophy

First Round	Walsall	(a)	1-2

SOUTHAMPTON FA Premiership

FOUNDATION

The club was formed by members of the St Mary's Church of England Young Men's Association at a meeting of the Y.M.A. in November 1885 and it was named as such. For the sake of brevity this was usually shortened to St Mary's Y.M.A. The rector Canon Albert Basil Orme Wilberforce was elected president. The name was changed to plain St Mary's during 1887–88 and did not become Southampton St Mary's until 1894, the inaugural season in the Southern League.

St Mary's Stadium, Britannia Road, Southampton SO14 5FP.

Telephone: (0845) 688 9448.

Fax: (0845) 688 9445.

Ticket Office: (0845) 688 9288.

Website: www.saintsfc.co.uk

Email: sfc@saintsfc.co.uk

Ground Capacity: 32,689.

Record Attendance: 31,044 v Manchester U, Division 1, 8 October 1969 (at The Dell); 32,151 v Arsenal, FA Premier League, 29 December 2003 (at St Mary's).

Pitch Measurements: 112yd × 72yd.

Chairman: Nicola Cortese.

Manager: Nigel Adkins B.Sc (Hons).

Assistant Manager: Andy Crosby.

Sports Medicine and Science: Mo Gimpel.

Colours: White shirts with diagonal red stripe, white shorts, black stockings.

Year Formed: 1885.

Turned Professional: 1894.

Previous Names: 1885, St Mary's Young Men's Association; 1887–88, St Mary's; 1894–95 Southampton St Mary's; 1897, Southampton.

Club Nickname: 'The Saints'.

Grounds: 1885, 'The Common' (from 1887 also used the County Cricket Ground and Antelope Cricket Ground); 1889, Antelope Cricket Ground; 1896 The County Cricket Ground; 1898, The Dell; 2001, St Mary's.

First Football League Game: 28 August 1920, Division 3, v Gillingham (a) D 1–1 – Allen; Parker, Titmuss; Shelley, Campbell, Turner; Barratt, Dominy (1), Rawlings, Moore, Foxall.

Record League Victory: 9–3 v Wolverhampton W, Division 2, 18 September 1965 – Godfrey; Jones, Williams; Walker, Knapp, Huxford; Paine (2), O'Brien (1), Melia, Chivers (4), Sydenham (2).

Record Cup Victory: 7–1 v Ipswich T, FA Cup 3rd rd, 7 January 1961 – Reynolds; Davies, Traynor, Conner, Page, Huxford, Paine (1), O'Brien (3 incl. 1p), Reeves, Mulgrew (2), Penk (1).

HONOURS

Football League – FL C: ***Runners-up*** 2011–12; **Division 1:** ***Runners-up*** 1983–84; **Division 2:** ***Runners-up*** 1965–66, 1977–78;
Division 3 (S): ***Champions*** 1921–22;
Division 3: ***Champions*** 1959–60: ***Runners-up*** 1920–21.

FA Cup: ***Winners*** 1976; ***Runners-up*** 1900, 1902, 2003.

Football League Cup: ***Runners-up*** 1979.

Zenith Data Systems Cup: ***Runners-up*** 1992.

Johnstone's Paint Trophy: ***Winners*** 2009–10.

European Competitions
European Fairs Cup: 1969–70.
UEFA Cup: 1971–72, 1981–82, 1982–83, 1984–85, 2003–04.
European Cup-Winners' Cup: 1976–77.

sky SPORTS FACT FILE

An entry in *Saints: A complete history of Southampton Football Club* states that their first professional footballer in 1892 was Albert Edward Dollin, a versatile forward known as "Jack". It was later revealed that he had been paid £1 a week and also found employment locally.

Record Defeat: 0–8 v Tottenham H, Division 2, 28 March 1936; 0–8 v Everton, Division 1, 20 November 1971.

Most League Points (2 for a win): 61, Division 3 (S), 1921–22 and Division 3, 1959–60.

Most League Points (3 for a win): 92, FL 1, 2010–11.

Most League Goals: 112, Division 3 (S), 1957–58.

Highest League Scorer in Season: Derek Reeves, 39, Division 3, 1959–60.

Most League Goals in Total Aggregate: Mike Channon, 185, 1966–77, 1979–82.

Most League Goals in One Match: 5, Charlie Wayman v Leicester C, Division 2, 23 October 1948.

Most Capped Player: Peter Shilton, 49 (125), England.

Most League Appearances: Terry Paine, 713, 1956–74.

Youngest League Player: Theo Walcott, 16 years 143 days v Wolverhampton W, 6 August 2005.

Record Transfer Fee Received: Up to £10,000,000 from Arsenal for Theo Walcott, January 2006.

Record Transfer Fee Paid: £4,000,000 to Derby Co for Rory Delap, July 2001.

Football League Record: 1920 Original Member of Division 3; 1921–22 Division 3 (S); 1922–53 Division 2; 1953–58 Division 3 (S); 1958–60 Division 3; 1960–66 Division 2; 1966–74 Division 1; 1974–78 Division 2; 1978–92 Division 1; 1992–2005 FA Premier League; 2005–09 FL C; 2009–11 FL 1; 2011–12 FL C; 2012– FA Premier League.

LATEST SEQUENCES

Longest Sequence of League Wins: 10, 16.4.2011 – 20.8.2011.

Longest Sequence of League Defeats: 5, 16.8.1998 – 12.9.1998.

Longest Sequence of League Draws: 8, 29.8.2005 – 15.10.2005.

Longest Sequence of Unbeaten League Matches: 19, 5.9.1921 – 31.12.1921.

Longest Sequence Without a League Win: 20, 30.8.1969 – 27.12.1969.

Successive Scoring Runs: 28 from 10.2.2008.

Successive Non-scoring Runs: 5 from 1.9.1937.

MANAGERS

Cecil Knight 1894–95
(Secretary-Manager)
Charles Robson 1895–97
Er Arnfield 1897–1911
(Secretary-Manager)
(continued as Secretary)
George Swift 1911–12
Er Arnfield 1912–19
Jimmy McIntyre 1919–24
Arthur Chadwick 1925–31
George Kay 1931–36
George Gross 1936–37
Tom Parker 1937–43
J. R. Sarjantson stepped down from the board to act as Secretary-Manager 1943–47 with the next two listed being team Managers during this period
Arthur Dominy 1943–46
Bill Dodgin Snr 1946–49
Sid Cann 1949–51
George Roughton 1952–55
Ted Bates 1955–73
Lawrie McMenemy 1973–85
Chris Nicholl 1985–91
Ian Branfoot 1991–94
Alan Ball 1994–95
Dave Merrington 1995–96
Graeme Souness 1996–97
Dave Jones 1997–2000
Glenn Hoddle 2000–01
Stuart Gray 2001
Gordon Strachan 2001–04
Paul Sturrock 2004
Steve Wigley 2004
Harry Redknapp 2004–05
George Burley 2005–08
Nigel Pearson 2008
Jan Poortvliet 2008–09
Mark Wotte 2009
Alan Pardew 2009–10
Nigel Adkins September 2010–

TEN YEAR LEAGUE RECORD

		P	W	D	L	F	A	Pts	Pos
2002-03	PR Lge	38	13	13	12	43	46	52	8
2003-04	PR Lge	38	12	11	15	44	45	47	12
2004-05	PR Lge	38	6	14	18	45	66	32	20
2005-06	FL C	46	13	19	14	49	50	58	12
2006-07	FL C	46	21	12	13	77	53	75	6
2007-08	FL C	46	13	15	18	56	72	54	20
2008-09	FL C	46	10	15	21	46	69	45	23
2009-10	FL 1	46	23	14	9	85	47	73*	7
2010-11	FL 1	46	28	8	10	86	38	92	2
2011-12	FL C	46	26	10	10	85	46	88	2

**10 pts deducted.*

DID YOU KNOW 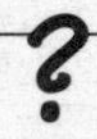

Three Southampton Academy graduates had an influential input for the third round FA Cup win at Coventry City on 7 January 2012. James Ward-Prowse, 17, scored the equalising goal from a pass by substitute Sam Hoskins, 18, while Aaron Martin, 22, won the tie at 2-1.

SOUTHAMPTON 2011–12 LEAGUE RECORD

Match No.	*Date*	*Venue*	*Opponents*	*Result*	*H/T Score*	*Lg Pos.*	*Goalscorers*	*Attendance*
1	Aug 6	H	Leeds U	W 3-1	2-0	—	Hammond [10], Lallana [25], Connolly [52]	25,860
2	13	A	Barnsley	W 1-0	1-0	2	Connolly [30]	10,501
3	16	A	Ipswich T	W 5-2	3-0	—	Lambert 2 [4, 11], Connolly [42], Lallana 2 [76, 90]	18,553
4	20	H	Millwall	W 1-0	1-0	1	Do Prado [18]	23,333
5	27	A	Leicester C	L 2-3	1-3	2	Harding [28], Connolly [53]	23,808
6	Sept 10	H	Nottingham F	W 3-2	2-2	2	Lambert 3 [8, 24, 82]	24,784
7	18	H	Birmingham C	W 4-1	3-0	1	Lambert (pen) [11], Do Prado [21], Lallana [34], Chaplow [78]	22,155
8	24	A	Burnley	D 1-1	0-0	1	Schneiderlin [80]	14,170
9	28	A	Cardiff C	L 1-2	0-0	—	De Ridder [90]	22,502
10	Oct 1	H	Watford	W 4-0	1-0	1	Lambert 2 (2 pens) [22, 55], Do Prado [70], Holmes [88]	23,574
11	15	A	Derby Co	D 1-1	0-1	1	Lambert [61]	33,010
12	18	H	West Ham U	W 1-0	1-0	—	Hooiveld [45]	32,152
13	22	A	Reading	D 1-1	0-0	1	De Ridder [80]	21,889
14	29	H	Middlesbrough	W 3-0	2-0	1	Do Prado 2 [15, 29], Connolly [80]	26,630
15	Nov 1	H	Peterborough U	W 2-1	2-0	—	Chaplow [14], Hooiveld [17]	21,350
16	5	A	Coventry C	W 4-2	2-0	1	Chaplow [34], Lallana [39], Do Prado [77], De Ridder [85]	15,621
17	19	H	Brighton & HA	W 3-0	0-0	1	Lambert 3 (2 pens) [49, 58 (p), 69 (p)]	31,812
18	26	A	Bristol C	L 0-2	0-0	1		16,346
19	29	H	Hull C	W 2-1	0-1	—	Do Prado [48], Lallana [55]	22,983
20	Dec 3	A	Doncaster R	L 0-1	0-0	1		9527
21	10	H	Blackpool	D 2-2	1-1	1	Lambert 2 [30, 90]	22,776
22	18	A	Portsmouth	D 1-1	0-0	1	Lambert [63]	19,879
23	26	H	Crystal Palace	W 2-0	1-0	1	Do Prado 2 [34, 77]	31,524
24	30	H	Bristol C	L 0-1	0-0	—		30,328
25	Jan 2	A	Brighton & HA	L 0-3	0-0	1		20,773
26	14	A	Nottingham F	W 3-0	1-0	1	Do Prado [27], Connolly [65], Schneiderlin [79]	20,221
27	23	H	Leicester C	L 0-2	0-2	—		21,014
28	31	H	Cardiff C	D 1-1	0-1	—	Lambert (pen) [57]	24,356
29	Feb 4	A	Birmingham C	D 0-0	0-0	2		17,904
30	11	H	Burnley	W 2-0	2-0	2	Lallana [8], Sharp [33]	24,099
31	14	A	West Ham U	D 1-1	0-1	—	Hooiveld [75]	32,875
32	18	H	Derby Co	W 4-0	1-0	1	Hooiveld [15], Martin [57], Lallana [65], Lee [75]	24,536
33	25	A	Watford	W 3-0	2-0	1	Lambert 3 (1 pen) [13, 21, 72 (p)]	13,424
34	Mar 3	A	Leeds U	W 1-0	1-0	1	Lambert [16]	20,901
35	6	H	Ipswich T	D 1-1	0-0	—	Lambert [74]	23,315
36	10	H	Barnsley	W 2-0	1-0	1	Lallana 2 [36, 54]	24,862
37	17	A	Millwall	W 3-2	1-2	1	Lambert 3 (2 pens) [16, 85 (p), 88 (p)]	12,144
38	20	A	Hull C	W 2-0	1-0	—	Hobbs (og) [14], Hooiveld [59]	18,066
39	24	H	Doncaster R	W 2-0	0-0	1	Sharp 2 [58, 75]	30,209
40	31	A	Blackpool	L 0-3	0-2	1		13,499
41	Apr 7	H	Portsmouth	D 2-2	1-1	1	Sharp 2 [27, 89]	31,743
42	9	A	Crystal Palace	W 2-0	1-0	1	Lambert 2 [39, 56]	18,753
43	13	H	Reading	L 1-3	0-1	—	Lambert [48]	31,892
44	17	A	Peterborough U	W 3-1	2-0	—	Hooiveld [5], Sharp 2 [10, 57]	9478
45	21	A	Middlesbrough	L 1-2	1-1	2	Sharp [1]	19,002
46	28	H	Coventry C	W 4-0	2-0	2	Sharp [16], Fonte [19], Hooiveld [59], Lallana [63]	32,363

Final League Position: 2

GOALSCORERS

League (85): Lambert 27 (9 pens), Lallana 11, Do Prado 10, Sharp 9, Hooiveld 7, Connolly 6, Chaplow 3, De Ridder 3, Schneiderlin 2, Fonte 1, Hammond 1, Harding 1, Holmes 1, Lee 1, Martin 1, own goal 1.
Carling Cup (9): Forte 2, Lambert 2, Chaplow 1, De Ridder 1, Do Prado 1, Hooiveld 1, Lallana 1.
FA Cup (5): Lambert 2, Lallana 1, Martin 1, Ward-Prowse 1.

Davis K 45	Richardson F 33 + 1	Harding D 12 + 8	Cork J 39 + 7	Martin A 7 + 3	Fonte J 42	Lallana A 41	Hammond D 31 + 12	Lambert R 42	Connolly D 17 + 9	Do Prado G 36 + 6	De Ridder S 5 + 27	Chaplow R 17 + 8	Schneiderlin M 29 + 13	Seaborne D 4	Fox D 37 + 4	Hooiveld J 39	Holmes L — + 6	Butterfield D 9 + 1	Barnard L — + 6	Bialkowski B 1	Forte J — + 1	Reeves B — + 2	Falque I 1	Puncheon J 4 + 4	Lee T 4 + 3	Sharp B 11 + 4	*Match No.*
1	2	3	4	5	6	7	8^3	9	10^1	11^2	12	13	14														1
1	2	3	4		6	7^3	8	9	10^2	11^1	13	12▪	14	5													2
1	2	3	4		6	7^3	8	9	10^2	11^1	14		12	5	13												3
1	2	3	4		6	7^2	8^1	9	10^3	11	14		12	5	13												4
1	2^1	3^3	4		6	7	8	9	10	11^2	13		12	5	14												5
1			2		6	7	8	9	10^2	11^1	13	12	4		5	3											6
1	2		4^2		6	7^3	8	9	10	11^1	14	12	13		3	5											7
1	2		4		6	7	8^2	9	10	11^1		12	13		3	5											8
1	2		8^2		6	7		9	10^1	11	12	13	4		3	5											9
1	2		4^2		6	7^3	8	9		11	10^1	12	13		3	5	14										10
1	2^2	14	8		6		13	9	10	7^3	12	11^1	4		3	5											11
1	2	12	13		6		8	9	10^2	7^3	14	11^1	4		3	5											12
1	2		4	12	6^1		8▪	9	10^2	7^3	13	11	14		3	5											13
1			4		6	7^2	8^3	9	12	10^1	14	11	13		3	5		2									14
1	2	3	14		6	7^2	8	9	13	10^1	12	11^3	4			5											15
1	2		8		6	7^2	12	9	14	10^3	13	11^1	4		3	5											16
1	2		4		6	7^2	8^1	9		10^3	13	11	12		3	5			14								17
1	2		4		6	7	8^3	9		10^2	13	11^1	12		3	5			14								18
1	2	3	4^1		6	7	8	9^2		10^3	12		11			5	14		13								19
1	2		4^2		6	7	8			10	9^1		11		3	5	12		13								20
	2	12	4		6	7	8^2	9		10	13		11		3^1	5				1							21
1	2	12	4		6	7	8	9		10			11		3^1	5											22
1	2		4		6	7	13	9	12	10	8^1		11^2		3	5											23
1	2^3		4	6		7^1	13	9	12	10	11		8^2		3	5	14										24
1	2	3^1	4	6		7^3	8	9▪	11	10^2					12	5					13	14					25
1		2^2	4	5		7^3	8		9	10^1			11		3	6	12	13				14					26
1	14	3	4	5			8^1		9	10	13		11		2	6^3	12						7^2				27
1	2		4	5	6	7	13	9	10^2				8		3									11^1	12		28
1	2		4^3	5	6	7	14	9	10^1	13			8		3▪									11^2		12	29
1	2		4		6	7	13	9^3	12	11^2			8		3	5									14	10^1	30
1	2^2		4		6	7	14	9	13	11^1			8		3	5								12		10^3	31
1		2	4	12	6	7		9				11^3	8		3	5^1								14	13	10^2	32
1			4		6	7^1	13	9^3	14			8^2	11		3	5		2						12	10		33
1	2	14	4		6		13	9		12		8	11		3^3	5								7^1	10^2		34
1	2	3	14		6	7^3	4	9		11^1	12		8			5									10^2	13	35
1	2		12		6	7^3	8	9^1	13	11			4		3	5									10^2	14	36
1	2		14		6	7^3	8^2	9		10	12	4^1	11		3	5										13	37
1	2	14	4		6	7	13	9		10^1	12		8		3^3	5								11^2			38
1			4		6	7^3	14	9^1			11^2	12	8		3	5		2	13							10	39
1			4		6	7				9^2	12	11^1	8		3	5		2	13							10	40
1	2	14	12		6	7	8	9		11^2	13		4^1		3	5										10^3	41
1		12	4		6	7	8	9^2		13	14	11^3			3^1	5		2								10	42
1			4		6	7	8^2	9		13	12	11^1			3	5		2								10	43
1			4	12	6	7	8	9		13		11			3	5^1		2								10^2	44
1			4		6	7	8	9		12		11^1	13		3	5		2^2								10	45
1			12		6	7^3	8^1	9		11	13		4		3	5		2						14		10^2	46

FA Cup

Third Round	Coventry C	(a)	2-1
Fourth Round	Millwall	(a)	1-1
		(h)	2-3

Carling Cup

First Round	Torquay U	(h)	4-1
Second Round	Swindon T	(a)	3-1
Third Round	Preston NE	(h)	2-1
Fourth Round	Crystal Palace	(a)	0-2

SOUTHEND UNITED FL Championship 2

FOUNDATION

The leading club in Southend around the turn of the 20th century was Southend Athletic, but they were an amateur concern. Southend United was a more ambitious professional club when they were founded in 1906, employing Bob Jack as secretary-manager and immediately joining the Second Division of the Southern League.

Roots Hall Stadium, Victoria Avenue, Southend-on-Sea, Essex SS2 6NQ.

Telephone: (01702) 304 050.

Fax: (01702) 304 124.

Ticket Office: (08444) 770 077.

Website: www.southendunited.co.uk

Email: info@southend-united.co.uk

Ground Capacity: 12,260.

Record Attendance: 22,862 v Tottenham H, FA Cup 3rd rd replay, 11 January 1936 (at Southend Stadium); 31,090 v Liverpool, FA Cup 3rd rd, 10 January 1979 (at Roots Hall).

Pitch Measurements: 110yd × 76yd.

Chairman: Ronald Martin.

Chief Executive: Gary Lockett.

Manager: Paul Sturrock.

Assistant Manager: Graham Coughlan.

Physio: Ben Clarkson.

Colours: Navy blue shirts with white collar, navy blue shorts, white stockings.

Year Formed: 1906.

Turned Professional: 1906.

Club Nicknames: 'The Blues' or 'The Shrimpers'.

Grounds: 1906, Roots Hall, Prittlewell; 1920, Kursaal; 1934, Southend Stadium; 1955, Roots Hall Football Ground.

First Football League Game: 28 August 1920, Division 3, v Brighton & HA (a) W 2–0 – Capper; Reid, Newton; Wileman, Henderson, Martin; Nicholls, Nuttall, Fairclough (2), Myers, Dorsett.

Record League Victory: 9–2 v Newport Co, Division 3 (S), 5 September 1936 – McKenzie; Nelson, Everest (1); Deacon, Turner, Carr; Bolan, Lane (1), Goddard (4), Dickinson (2), Oswald (1).

Record Cup Victory: 10–1 v Golders Green, FA Cup 1st rd, 24 November 1934 – Moore; Morfitt, Kelly; Mackay, Joe Wilson, Carr (1); Lane (1), Johnson (5), Cheesmuir (2), Deacon (1), Oswald. 10–1 v Brentwood, FA Cup 2nd rd, 7 December 1968 – Roberts; Bentley, Birks; McMillan (1) Beesley, Kurila; Clayton, Chisnall, Moore (4), Best (5), Hamilton. 10–1 v Aldershot, Leyland Daf Cup Prel rd, 6 November 1990 – Sansome; Austin, Powell, Cornwell, Prior (1), Tilson (3), Cawley, Butler, Ansah (1), Benjamin (1), Angell (4).

HONOURS

Football League – Division 1: Best season: 13th, 1994–95;
FL 1: ***Champions*** 2005–06;
Division 3: ***Runners-up*** 1990–91;
Division 4: ***Champions*** 1980–81;
Runners-up 1971–72, 1977–78.

FA Cup: Best season: old 3rd rd, 1921; 5th rd, 1926, 1952, 1976, 1993.

Football League Cup: Quarter final 2007.

LDV Vans Trophy: ***Runners-up*** 2004, 2005.

sky SPORTS FACT FILE

In 1910–11, Southend United were drawn at Enfield in an FA Cup fourth qualifying round tie. They arrived with only ten players but found one of their players, Louis Parke, in the crowd watching a relative playing for Enfield. He was press-ganged ten minutes late but helped out in a 3-3 draw.

Record Defeat: 1–9 v Brighton & HA, Division 3, 27 November 1965.

Most League Points (2 for a win): 67, Division 4, 1980–81.

Most League Points (3 for a win): 85, Division 3, 1990–91.

Most League Goals: 92, Division 3 (S), 1950–51.

Highest League Scorer in Season: Jim Shankly, 31, 1928–29; Sammy McCrory, 1957–58, both in Division 3 (S).

Most League Goals in Total Aggregate: Roy Hollis, 122, 1953–60.

Most League Goals in One Match: 5, Jim Shankly v Merthyr T, Division 3 (S), 1 March 1930.

Most Capped Player: George Mackenzie, 9, Eire.

Most League Appearances: Sandy Anderson, 452, 1950–63.

Youngest League Player: Phil O'Connor, 16 years 76 days v Lincoln C, 26 December 1969.

Record Transfer Fee Received: £4,200,000 from Nottingham F for Stan Collymore, June 1993.

Record Transfer Fee Paid: £750,000 to Crystal Palace for Stan Collymore, November 1992.

Football League Record: 1920 Original Member of Division 3; 1921–58 Division 3 (S); 1958–66 Division 3; 1966–72 Division 4; 1972–76 Division 3; 1976–78 Division 4; 1978–80 Division 3; 1980–81 Division 4; 1981–84 Division 3; 1984–87 Division 4; 1987–89 Division 3; 1989–90 Division 4; 1990–91 Division 3; 1991–92 Division 2; 1992–97 Division 1; 1997–98 Division 2; 1998–2004 Division 3; 2004–05 FL 2; 2005–06 FL 1; 2006–07 FL C; 2007–10 FL 1; 2010– FL 2.

MANAGERS

Bob Jack 1906–10
George Molyneux 1910–11
O. M. Howard 1911–12
Joe Bradshaw 1912–19
Ned Liddell 1919–20
Tom Mather 1920–21
Ted Birnie 1921–34
David Jack 1934–40
Harry Warren 1946–56
Eddie Perry 1956–60
Frank Broome 1960
Ted Fenton 1961–65
Alvan Williams 1965–67
Ernie Shepherd 1967–69
Geoff Hudson 1969–70
Arthur Rowley 1970–76
Dave Smith 1976–83
Peter Morris 1983–84
Bobby Moore 1984–86
Dave Webb 1986–87
Dick Bate 1987
Paul Clark 1987–88
Dave Webb *(General Manager)* 1988–92
Colin Murphy 1992–93
Barry Fry 1993
Peter Taylor 1993–95
Steve Thompson 1995
Ronnie Whelan 1995–97
Alvin Martin 1997–99
Alan Little 1999–2000
David Webb 2000–01
Rob Newman 2001–03
Steve Wignall 2003
Steve Tilson 2003–10
Paul Sturrock July 2010–

LATEST SEQUENCES

Longest Sequence of League Wins: 8, 29.8.2005 – 9.10.2005.

Longest Sequence of League Defeats: 6, 29.8.1987 – 19.9.1987.

Longest Sequence of League Draws: 6, 30.1.1982 – 19.2.1982.

Longest Sequence of Unbeaten League Matches: 16, 20.2.1932 – 29.8.1932.

Longest Sequence Without a League Win: 17, 31.12.1983 – 14.4.1984.

Successive Scoring Runs: 24 from 23.3.1929.

Successive Non-scoring Runs: 6 from 28.10.1933.

TEN YEAR LEAGUE RECORD

		P	W	D	L	F	A	Pts	Pos
2002-03	Div 3	46	17	3	26	47	59	54	17
2003-04	Div 3	46	14	12	20	51	63	54	17
2004-05	FL 2	46	22	12	12	65	46	78	4
2005-06	FL 1	46	23	13	10	72	43	82	1
2006-07	FL C	46	10	12	24	47	80	42	22
2007-08	FL 1	46	22	10	14	70	55	76	6
2008-09	FL 1	46	21	8	17	58	61	71	8
2009-10	FL 1	46	10	13	23	51	72	43	23
2010-11	FL 2	46	16	13	17	62	56	61	13
2011-12	FL 2	46	25	8	13	77	48	83	4

DID YOU KNOW 

On Boxing Day 1925, Bristol City's visit to Southend United produced a record crowd at the Kursaal of 13,438. On 28 January an FA Cup tie against Derby County had 14,225 and then on 20 February in the same competition against Nottingham Forest, it was raised to 18,153!

SOUTHEND UNITED 2011–12 LEAGUE RECORD

Match No.	Date	Venue	Opponents	Result		H/T Score	Lg Pos.	Goalscorers	Attendance
1	Aug 6	H	Hereford U	W	1-0	1-0	—	Mohsni [14]	5105
2	13	A	Accrington S	W	2-1	1-1	3	Dickinson (pen) [2], Hall [57]	1491
3	16	A	Crawley T	L	0-3	0-0	—		3220
4	20	H	Burton Alb	L	0-1	0-1	13		4794
5	27	A	Port Vale	W	3-2	3-1	7	Phillips [5], Dickinson [10], Leonard [29]	4615
6	Sept 3	H	Northampton T	D	2-2	1-0	9	Mohsni [27], Hall [59]	4805
7	10	A	Swindon T	L	0-2	0-1	12		6852
8	13	H	Gillingham	W	1-0	0-0	—	Phillips [87]	4598
9	17	H	Plymouth Arg	W	2-0	0-0	6	Dickinson (pen) [64], Gilbert [80]	4984
10	24	A	Rotherham U	W	4-0	1-0	3	Gilbert [10], Timlin 2 [47, 60], Harris [64]	3433
11	30	H	Shrewsbury T	W	3-0	1-0	—	Dickinson (pen) [27], Phillips [89], Harris (pen) [90]	6394
12	Oct 8	A	Crewe Alex	W	3-1	1-0	1	Ferdinand [37], Mohsni 2 [88, 90]	3808
13	15	H	Morecambe	D	1-1	0-0	2	Drummond (og) [83]	9782
14	22	H	Torquay U	W	4-1	0-0	2	Ferdinand 2 [47, 54], Dickinson [66], Phillips [71]	5425
15	25	A	Barnet	W	3-0	2-0	—	Hall [17], Mohsni [36], Harris [85]	2744
16	29	A	Macclesfield T	W	2-0	1-0	1	Hall [39], Ferdinand [62]	2174
17	Nov 5	H	Oxford U	W	2-1	1-0	1	Phillips [45], Hall [67]	6157
18	19	A	Dagenham & R	W	3-2	2-1	1	Ferdinand 2 [8, 64], Dickinson [33]	3259
19	26	H	Bristol R	D	1-1	0-0	1	Harris [66]	6237
20	Dec 10	A	Cheltenham T	L	0-3	0-1	2		4304
21	16	H	Bradford C	L	0-1	0-0	—		5526
22	31	A	AFC Wimbledon	W	4-1	1-1	3	Hall [30], Stuart (og) [51], Phillips [64], Harris [79]	4529
23	Jan 2	H	Dagenham & R	D	1-1	1-0	3	Timlin [37]	7564
24	7	H	Port Vale	W	3-0	2-0	—	Phillips [8], Dickinson [29], Owen (og) [55]	5269
25	14	A	Northampton T	W	5-2	1-2	1	Martin [41], Dickinson 2 (1 pen) [65 (p), 85], Mohsni 2 [81, 90]	5255
26	21	A	Shrewsbury T	L	1-2	0-0	1	Hall [66]	5601
27	31	H	Swindon T	L	1-4	1-3	—	Kalala [34]	5958
28	Feb 4	A	Plymouth Arg	D	2-2	2-0	—	Timlin [1], Martin [34]	6328
29	10	H	Rotherham U	L	0-2	0-1	—		4717
30	13	A	Gillingham	W	2-1	2-0	—	Dickinson [10], Martin (og) [31]	4441
31	18	H	Crewe Alex	W	1-0	0-0	1	Mohsni [74]	5645
32	21	A	Aldershot T	L	0-2	0-1	—		2949
33	25	A	Morecambe	L	0-1	0-0	3		1971
34	Mar 3	A	Burton Alb	W	2-0	0-0	3	Martin [60], Harris [75]	2424
35	5	H	Crawley T	D	0-0	0-0	—		5439
36	10	H	Accrington S	D	2-2	0-1	3	Prosser [65], Benyon [76]	5954
37	17	A	Hereford U	W	3-2	2-1	3	Harris [2], Benyon [33], Hall [57]	2456
38	20	H	Aldershot T	L	0-1	0-0	—		4580
39	24	A	Bristol R	L	0-1	0-0	5		6258
40	30	H	Cheltenham T	W	4-0	2-0	—	Ferdinand [29], Hall [39], Eastwood [51], Mohsni [67]	6525
41	Apr 6	A	Bradford C	L	0-2	0-1	5		10,859
42	9	H	AFC Wimbledon	W	2-0	0-0	5	Eastwood [70], Grant [90]	6962
43	14	A	Torquay U	D	0-0	0-0	5		3408
44	20	H	Barnet	W	3-0	3-0	—	Mohsni 3 [11, 25, 32]	6451
45	28	A	Oxford U	W	2-0	2-0	5	Hall [19], Mohsni [31]	9356
46	May 5	H	Macclesfield T	W	2-0	1-0	4	Gilbert [24], Harris [90]	9122

Final League Position: 4

GOALSCORERS

League (77): Mohsni 13, Dickinson 10 (4 pens), Hall 10, Harris 8 (1 pen), Ferdinand 7, Phillips 7, Timlin 4, Gilbert 3, Martin 3, Benyon 2, Eastwood 2, Grant 1, Kalala 1, Leonard 1, Prosser 1, own goals 4.
Carling Cup (1): Phillips 1.
FA Cup (2): Dickinson 1, Hall 1.
J Paint Trophy (6): Hall 3, Dickinson 1 (pen), Harris 1, Sturrock 1.
Play-Offs (2): Barker 1, Harris 1.

Morris G 24	Clohessy S 45	Prosser L 18+3	Kalala J 23+1	Barker C 42+1	Phillips M 38+1	Grant A 25+8	Johnson J 1+4	Harris N 21+12	Mohsni B 23+8	Hall R 35+8	Sawyer L 5+5	Ferdinand K 28+8	Dickinson L 28+2	Coughlan G 2+2	Leonard R 13+4	Gilbert P 29+2	Sturrock B 5+4	N'Diaye A —+1	Crawford H —+3	Timlin M 39	James-Lewis M —+1	Bentley D —+1	Daniels L 9	Benyon E 8+8	Martin D 11+6	Sampson J 5+4	Baldwin P 2	Belford C 13	Hills L 5+2	Flood A —+1	Dailly C 3	Eastwood F 6+1	*Match No.*
1	2	3	4	5	6	7²	8¹	9	10³	11	12	13	14																				1
1	2	3	4	5		7		12		11³	13	8	9²	6	10¹	14																	2
1	2	3	4	5		7	12	9	13	11³	14	8¹	10	6²																			3
1	2		4¹	5		7	13	9	6	11	12	8²	10	14		3³																	4
1	2	3		5	6	7		9³	12	13	11	8	10¹		4²		14																5
1	2	3		5	6	7	13		10	11		8			4¹		9²	12															6
1	2	3²	14	5	6	7			10¹	11		8			4³	13	9		12														7
1	2	12		5	6	7			10■	11		4				3	9¹			8													8
1	2			5	6	7		12		11		4²	10		13	3	9¹			8													9
1	2		4	5	6			9				8	10		7¹	3				11	12												10
1	2		4	5	6	12		9		13		8¹	10		7²	3				11													11
1	2		4¹	5	6	13		9	14	12		8²	10		7³	3				11													12
1	2		4¹	5	6	12		9	13	11			10		7²	3				8													13
1⁶	2	6	4¹		5			9		11		7	10²		12	3	13			8		15											14
	2			5	6	7	14	13	9²	11³		12	10		4	3				8¹			1										15
	2		4	5	6				10¹	11		7	9		12	3				8			1										16
	2			5	6	12		9²		11¹		7	10		4	3	13			8			1										17
	2		4	5	6				9	11		7	10			3				8			1										18
	2			5	6	12		9¹	7	11		4	10			3				8			1										19
	2		4¹	5	6	12			10	11		7	9		13	3²				8			1										20
	2	5			6	12		9		11	13	4¹	10		7²	3				8			1										21
	2	3	4	5³	6	7		9		11¹		13		14	8²		12			10			1										22
	2	3		5	6	7		13		11		12	10		4¹					8			1	9²									23
1	2		4	5	6					11			10			3				8				9	7								24
1	2		4	5	6				12	11			10			3				8				9²	7¹	13							25
1	2		4³	5	6²	7¹			13	12		14	10			3				8				9	11								26
1	2		4	5					12	11		7¹	10²			3				8					13	9	6						27
1	2		4	5				12	9	7			10			3				8					11¹		6						28
1	2		4¹	5		7		13	6	11			10²			3				8				9³	12	14							29
1	2	3	4	5	6				10	12		7	9²							8					11¹	13							30
1	2		4	5	6				10	12		7²	9			3				8				13	11¹								31
1	2		4²	5	6			13	10	12		7¹	9³			3				8				14	11								32
1	2	3	4¹	5	6	12			7²	11			10							8				13	14	9³							33
	2	13		5	6	7		9¹			4									8				12	11	10³		1	3²	14			34
	2	12		5■	6	7		10			4	14	13							8					11²	9¹		1	3³				35
	2	6			5	7		10³		12	4¹	14				3				8				13	11	9²		1					36
	2	3		5	6			10		11¹		7								8				9				1	12		4		37
	2			5³	6			12		11	7¹						10²			8				9	13	14		1	3		4		38
	2	3		5	6²	7		14	13	11										8				9³				1	12		4¹	10	39
	2	6		5		7		14	9²	11¹		4								8				13	12			1	3			10³	40
	2■	6		5	12	7		13	9	11		4²								8				14■				1	3¹			10³	41
		6²		13	5	7		12	8	11		2				3			14	4					9¹			1				10³	42
	2			5	6	7		9¹	10	11		4				3				8								1				12	43
	2			5	6	4³		9	10²	11		14				3			12	7					13			1				8¹	44
	2			5	6	7		9	10	11		4				3				8								1					45
	2			5	6	7		9	4	11						3				8				12				1				10¹	46

FA Cup

First Round	Preston NE	(a)	0-0
		(h)	1-0
Second Round	Oldham Ath	(h)	1-1
		(a)	0-1

Carling Cup

First Round	Leyton Orient	(h)	1-1

Play-Offs

Semi-Final	Crewe Alex	(a)	0-1
		(h)	2-2

J Paint Trophy

First Round	Crawley T	(h)	1-0
Second Round	Dagenham & R	(a)	3-1
Southern Quarter-Final	Oxford U	(a)	1-0
Southern Semi-Final	Swindon T	(h)	1-2

STEVENAGE FL Championship 1

FOUNDATION

There have been several clubs associated with the town of Stevenage. Stevenage Town was formed in 1884. They absorbed Stevenage Rangers in 1955 and later played at Broadhall Way. The club went into liquidation in 1968 and Stevenage Athletic was formed, but they, too, followed a similar path in 1976. Then Stevenage Borough was founded. The Broadhall Way pitch was dug up and remained unused for three years. Thus the new club started its life in the modest surrounds of the King George V playing fields with a roped-off ground in the Chiltern League. A change of competition followed to the Wallspan Southern Combination and by 1980 the club returned to the council-owned Broadhall Way when "Borough" was added to the name. Entry into the United Counties League was so successful the league and cup were won in the first season. On to the Isthmian League Division Two and the climb up the pyramid continued. In 1995–96 Stevenage Borough won the Conference but was denied a place in the Football League as the ground did not measure up to the competition's standards. Subsequent improvements changed this and the 7,100 capacity venue became one of the best appointed grounds in non-league football. After winning elevation to the Football League the club dropped Borough from its title.

Lamex Stadium, Broadhall Way, Stevenage, Herts SG2 8RH.

Telephone: (01438) 223223.

Fax: (01438) 743611.

Ticket Office: (0871) 855 1696.

Website: stevenagefc.com

Email: clivea@stevenagefc.com

Ground Capacity: 6,546.

Record Attendance: 6,489 v Kidderminster H, Conference, 25 January 1997.

Pitch Measurements: 110yd × 70yd.

Chairman: Phil Wallace.

Chief Executive: Bob Makin.

Manager: Gary Smith.

Assistant Manager: Mark Newson.

Sports Therapist: Paul Dando.

MANAGERS

Derek Montgomery 1976–83
Frank Cornwell 1983–87
John Bailey 1987–88
Brian Wilcox 1988–90
Paul Fairclough 1990–98
Richard Hill 1998–2000
Steve Wignall 2000
Paul Fairclough 2000–02
Wayne Turner 2002–03
Graham Westley 2003–06
Mark Stimson 2006–07
Peter Taylor 2007–08
Graham Westley 2008–12
Gary Smith January 2012–

sky SPORTS FACT FILE

On 29 January 2011, Stevenage were drawn at home to Reading in a fourth round FA Cup tie. Darius Charles equalised before the visitors won 2-1. On 7 January 2012, the two teams met this time at Reading in a third round encounter. This time Charles' goal was the game's winner.

Nickname: The Boro.

Previous Name: Stevenage Borough.

Grounds: 1976, King George V playing fields; 1980, Broadhall Way.

First Football League Game: 7 August 2010, FL 2, v Macclesfield T (h) D 2–2 – Day; Henry, Laird, Bostwick, Roberts, Foster, Wilson (Sinclair), Byrom, Griffin (1), Winn (Odubade), Vincenti (1) (Beardsley).

Colours: White shirts, red shorts, red stockings with white tops.

Year Formed: 1976.

Turned Professional: 1976.

Record Victory: 11–1 v British Timken Ath 1980–81.

Record Defeat: 0–7 v Southwick 1987–88.

Most League Points (3 for a win): 73, FL 1, 2011–12.

Most League Goals: 69, FL 1, 2011–12.

Highest League Scorer in Season: Byron Harrison, 8, 2010–11; Scott Laird, 8, 2011–12.

Most Goals in Total Aggregate: Scott Laird 12, 2010–12; Mark Roberts 12, 2010–12.

Most League Appearances: Chris Day, 90, 2010–12; Scott Laird, 90, 2010–12.

Record Transfer Fee Received: £260,000 from Peterborough U for George Boyd, January 2007.

Record Transfer Fee Paid: £20,000 to Hereford United for Richard Leadbetter, February 1999.

Football League Record: 2010–11 FL 2; 2011– FL 1.

HONOURS

Football League – FL 2: Best season: 6th 2010–11 promoted to FL 1.
FA Cup: Best season: 5th rd, 2012.
Blue Square Premier League: ***Champions*** 2009–10.

Conference: ***Champions*** 1995–96.

FA Trophy: ***Winners*** 2007, 2009; ***Runners-up*** 2002, 2010.

Herts Senior Cup: ***Winners*** 2009.

Isthmian League Premier Division: ***Champions*** 1993–94.

Isthmian League Division 1: ***Champions***: 1991–92.

Isthmian League Division 2 (N): ***Champions***: 1985–86, 1990–91.

United Counties League Division 1: ***Champions*** 1980–81.

United Counties League Cup: ***Winners*** 1981.

LATEST SEQUENCES

Longest Sequence of League Wins: 6, 12.3.2011 – 2.4.2011.

Longest Sequence of League Defeats: 4, 17.9.2011 – 8.10.2011.

Longest Sequence of League Draws: 5, 17.3.2012 – 31.3.2012.

Longest Sequence of Unbeaten League Matches: 11, 15.10.2011 – 31.12.2011.

Longest Sequence Without a League Win: 5, 13.11.2010 – 1.1.2011.

Successive Scoring Runs: 8 from 12.3.2011 – 16.4.2011.

Successive Non-scoring Runs: 8.2.2011 – 15.2.2011.

TEN YEAR LEAGUE RECORD

		P	*W*	*D*	*L*	*F*	*A*	*Pts*	*Pos*
2002-03	Con	42	14	10	18	61	55	52	12
2003-04	Conf	42	18	9	15	58	52	63	8
2004-05	Conf	42	22	6	14	65	52	72	5
2005-06	Conf	42	19	12	11	62	47	69	6
2006-07	Conf	46	20	10	16	76	66	70	8
2007-08	B Sq Pr	46	24	7	15	82	55	79	6
2008-09	B Sq Pr	46	23	12	11	73	54	81	5
2009-10	B Sq Pr	44	30	9	5	79	24	99	1
2010-11	FL 2	46	18	15	13	62	45	69	6
2011-12	FL 1	46	18	19	9	69	44	73	6

DID YOU KNOW ?

From December to March in 2008–09, Stevenage Borough improved markedly by completing 18 Conference matches without defeat. The team was narrowly beaten in the play-offs but won the Herts Senior Cup for the first time and also defeated York City in the Trophy final.

STEVENAGE 2011–12 LEAGUE RECORD

Match No.	Date	Venue	Opponents	Result		H/T Score	Lg Pos.	Goalscorers	Attendance
1	Aug 6	H	Exeter C	D	0-0	0-0	—		3829
2	13	A	Chesterfield	D	1-1	1-0	17	Charles [40]	5836
3	16	A	Bournemouth	W	3-1	1-0	—	Reid [43], Mousinho (pen) [65], Beardsley [90]	5574
4	20	H	Hartlepool U	D	2-2	0-2	10	Harrison [69], Laird [88]	2831
5	27	A	Milton Keynes D	L	0-1	0-0	14		8128
6	Sept 3	H	Rochdale	W	4-2	3-1	10	Reid [13], Beardsley 2 [30, 45], Trotman (og) [70]	3021
7	10	A	Oldham Ath	D	1-1	1-1	11	Roberts [4]	3402
8	13	H	Sheffield W	W	5-1	4-0	—	Reid [6], Mousinho [10], Bostwick [17], Wilson [38], Charles [67]	4339
9	17	H	Notts Co	L	0-2	0-1	12		3434
10	24	A	Carlisle U	L	0-1	0-1	13		4063
11	Oct 1	H	Scunthorpe U	L	1-2	0-1	14	Walker [90]	2957
12	8	A	Huddersfield T	L	1-2	0-1	15	Laird [67]	12,890
13	15	H	Charlton Ath	W	1-0	1-0	14	Long [11]	4724
14	22	H	Yeovil T	D	0-0	0-0	14		3036
15	25	A	Brentford	W	1-0	0-0	—	Beardsley [73]	4771
16	29	A	Bury	W	2-1	1-0	10	Harrison [38], Roberts [75]	2683
17	Nov 5	H	Sheffield U	W	2-1	1-0	7	Roberts [42], Laird [82]	4996
18	19	A	Leyton Orient	D	0-0	0-0	7		4862
19	26	H	Walsall	D	0-0	0-0	9		3140
20	Dec 10	A	Preston NE	D	0-0	0-0	9		9425
21	17	H	Tranmere R	W	2-1	1-0	8	Beardsley [38], Roberts [84]	3376
22	26	A	Colchester U	W	6-1	2-0	6	Shroot [9], Beardsley [25], Bostwick [64], Laird [71], Freeman [73], Byrom [82]	5276
23	31	A	Wycombe W	W	1-0	0-0	6	Wilson [82]	4942
24	Jan 2	H	Leyton Orient	L	0-1	0-1	6		5351
25	14	A	Rochdale	W	5-1	1-0	6	Freeman 2 [18, 58], Wilson 2 [46, 53], Byrom [66]	2367
26	21	A	Scunthorpe U	D	1-1	0-0	6	Charles [84]	3968
27	24	H	Milton Keynes D	W	4-2	1-1	—	Bostwick [25], Laird [65], Charles [68], MacKenzie (og) [88]	3345
28	Feb 14	A	Sheffield W	W	1-0	1-0	—	Laird [45]	16,185
29	22	A	Notts Co	L	0-1	0-0	—		5733
30	25	A	Charlton Ath	L	0-2	0-0	7		26,546
31	28	H	Huddersfield T	D	2-2	0-0	—	Bostwick [71], Shroot [88]	3059
32	Mar 3	A	Exeter C	D	1-1	0-1	7	Shroot [64]	4437
33	10	H	Chesterfield	D	2-2	0-2	8	Laird [76], Reid [77]	3534
34	13	H	Oldham Ath	W	1-0	0-0	—	Wilson [90]	2453
35	17	A	Hartlepool U	D	0-0	0-0	8		4484
36	20	H	Colchester U	D	0-0	0-0	—		2419
37	24	A	Walsall	D	1-1	0-1	7	Bostwick [60]	4786
38	27	H	Bournemouth	D	2-2	2-2	—	Freeman [38], Bostwick [45]	2550
39	31	H	Wycombe W	D	1-1	0-0	8	Bostwick [85]	3593
40	Apr 6	A	Tranmere R	L	0-3	0-2	—		8526
41	9	H	Preston NE	D	1-1	0-0	9	Roberts [90]	3386
42	14	A	Yeovil T	W	6-0	2-0	9	Freeman 2 [13, 88], Agyemang [44], Ashton [69], Lascelles [72], Roberts [82]	3610
43	17	H	Carlisle U	W	1-0	0-0	—	Mousinho [76]	3438
44	21	H	Brentford	W	2-1	0-0	6	Reid [52], Freeman [61]	4256
45	28	A	Sheffield U	D	2-2	1-0	6	Byrom [31], Laird [47]	30,043
46	May 5	H	Bury	W	3-0	1-0	6	Reid [24], Byrom (pen) [77], Beardsley [90]	4781

Final League Position: 6

GOALSCORERS

League (69): Laird 8, Beardsley 7, Bostwick 7, Freeman 7, Reid 6, Roberts 6, Wilson 5, Byrom 4 (1 pen), Charles 4, Mousinho 3 (1 pen), Shroot 3, Harrison 2, Agyemang 1, Ashton 1, Lascelles 1, Long 1, Walker 1, own goals 2.
Carling Cup (3): Beardsley 1, Bostwick 1, Long 1.
FA Cup (7): Beardsley 2, Byrom 1 (pen), Charles 1, Laird 1 (pen), Shroot 1, own goal 1.
J Paint Trophy (2): Roberts 1, Wilson 1.
Play-Offs (0).

Julian A 2 + 1	Henry R 32	Charles D 23 + 5	Roberts M 46	Ashton J 42 + 1	Edwards P 11 + 11	Wilson L 44 + 2	Bostwick M 43	Shroot R 11 + 14	Reid C 24 + 5	Laird S 46	Harrison B 10 + 8	Long S 18 + 12	Beardsley C 15 + 16	Day C 44	Mousinho J 14 + 5	Myrie-Williams J 3 + 14	Thalassitis M — + 3	May B 2 + 5	Byrom J 29 + 3	Walker J — + 5	Madjo G — + 1	Freeman L 22 + 4	Aneke C 2 + 4	Cowan D 2 + 6	Slew J 6 + 3	Agyemang P 10 + 3	Lascelles J 5 + 2	Match No.
1	2	3	4	5	6	7	8	9^{2}	10^{1}	11	12	13																1
1	2	11	4	5	6	7	8■	13		3	9^{1}	10^{2}	12															2
		3^{3}	4	5	6	2		12	10^{1}	11	9	8	14	1	7^{2}	13												3
		2^{2}	4	5	6	7	8	13		3	9	11^{1}	14	1	10^{3}	12												4
		4	7	5^{3}	6^{2}	2	8	11^{1}		3	9			1	10	12	13	14										5
	5	6^{1}	4		13	2	8		10^{3}	3			9	1	7			14	11^{2}	12								6
	2	3	4			7^{2}	5	12	10	11^{3}		14	9	1	6				8^{1}	13								7
	2	11	4	5	14	7	6		10^{3}	3		9^{2}		1	8^{1}	13				12								8
	2	6	4	5		7	8		10^{3}	3^{1}	14	9	12	1					11^{2}	13								9
	2		4	5^{2}	6^{3}	7	8	13	10	3		14		1	9	11^{1}					12							10
	6		4	5		2		13	10	3		11^{3}	12	1	7			9^{1}	8^{2}	14								11
	2	5	4	13	6	7	9^{2}		10^{3}	3	14	11^{1}	12	1	8													12
	6		4	5		2	7	13	10^{1}	3	9^{3}	11^{2}	12	1	8				14									13
	6		4	5		2	7	12	10	3	9^{2}	11^{1}	13	1	8													14
	2		6	5	14	12		7	10^{2}	3	13	11^{1}	9	1	4				8^{3}									15
	2		4	5	14	12	6	7	10^{1}	3	9^{2}		13	1	8				11^{3}									16
	2		4	5	14	7	6	13	10^{2}	3	12	11^{1}	9^{3}	1	8													17
	2	10^{2}	4	5	6	7	8	11^{1}		3		14	13	1					12			9^{3}						18
	2	12	4	5	13	7	6			3	9^{3}		14	1					8^{2}			11	10^{1}					19
		12	4	5	6^{3}	2	7	10		3	14		9^{1}	1					8			11^{2}	13					20
			4	5		2	6	12		3	9^{2}	7^{3}	10^{1}	1				13■				11	8	14				21
	2		4	5	12	7	6	8^{1}		3	14		9^{3}	1					11			13		10^{2}				22
	2		4	5	6	7	8			3	12	11^{2}	9^{1}	1								13	14	10^{3}				23
	2^{3}		4	5		7	6	11^{1}		3	9^{2}		10	1					8			12	14■	13				24
	2	10^{1}	4	5	12	7	6			3		13	9^{3}	1					8			11^{2}		14				25
	2	13	4	5	8^{1}	7	6	14		3			9^{2}	1					11			10^{3}		12				26
	2	10	4	5	14	7	6			3		13	9^{2}	1					8^{3}			11^{1}		12				27
	2	9^{1}	4	5	14	7	6			3		13	10^{3}	1				12	8			11^{2}						28
	2	10^{1}	4	5	14	7	6			3		13	9^{3}	1					8			11^{2}		12				29
	2	12	4	5^{3}		7	6			3		10^{2}	9^{1}	1		14			8			11	13					30
15	2	5	4			7	6	12	10^{2}	3		11^{1}		1^{6}		13		9	8									31
		3^{1}	4	5		2	6	7^{3}	10^{2}	11		14		1		12		13	8						9			32
		12	4	5		2	6	7^{1}	14	3			13	1					8			11^{3}			10	9^{2}		33
		7	4	5		2	6		10^{3}	3				1		14			8			11^{2}			9^{1}	12	13	34
		7	4	5		2	6	12	13	3				1		14			8			11^{1}			10^{2}	9^{3}		35
	2	11	4	5		7	6		13	3			12^{2}	1					8						10■	9^{1}		36
	2^{2}	3	4	5		7	6		10^{3}	11		13		1		12			8			14				9^{1}		37
	2	9^{3}	4	5		7	6		10^{1}	3		13		1		12	14		8			11^{2}						38
	2	10^{1}	4	5		7	6		13	3				1		9			8			11^{2}				12		39
	2^{3}		4	5		7	6		13	3				1		9^{1}			8			11			10^{2}	12	14	40
	2		4	5		7	6		10^{2}	3				1		14	13		8^{3}			11			12	9^{1}		41
			4	5		7^{2}	6^{3}		10^{1}	3		8		1	14	13						11			12	9	2	42
			4	5		7	6		10^{1}	3		8		1	13	14						11^{2}			12	9^{3}	2	43
			4	5		7	6		10^{2}	3		8^{1}	14	1	13				12			11				9^{3}	2	44
			4	5		7	6	10^{1}		3		14	13	1	12				8			11^{3}				9^{2}	2	45
			4	5		7	6	12	10^{1}	3			14	1	13				8^{2}			11				9^{3}	2	46

FA Cup

First Round	Hartlepool U	(a)	1-0
Second Round	Stourbridge	(a)	3-0
Third Round	Reading	(a)	1-0
Fourth Round	Notts Co	(h)	1-0
Fifth Round	Tottenham H	(h)	0-0
		(a)	1-3

Carling Cup

First Round	Peterborough U	(h)	3-4

J Paint Trophy

Second Round	AFC Wimbledon	(a)	2-2

Play-Offs

Semi-Final	Sheffield U	(h)	0-0
		(a)	0-1

STOKE CITY FA Premiership

FOUNDATION

The date of the formation of this club has long been in doubt. The year 1863 was claimed, but more recent research by local club historian Wade Martin has uncovered nothing earlier than 1868, when a couple of Old Carthusians, who were apprentices at the local works of the old North Staffordshire Railway Company, met with some others from that works, to form Stoke Ramblers. It should also be noted that the old Stoke club went bankrupt in 1908 when a new club was formed.

Britannia Stadium, Stanley Matthews Way, Stoke-on-Trent, Staffs ST4 4EG.

Telephone: (01782) 367 598.

Fax: (01782) 592 210.

Ticket Office: (0871) 663 2008.

Website: www.stokecityfc.com

Email: info@stokecityfc.com

Ground Capacity: 28,383.

Record Attendance: 51,380 v Arsenal, Division 1, 29 March 1937 (at Victoria Ground); 28,218 v Everton, Division 2, 5 January 2002 (at Britannia Stadium).

Pitch Measurements: 100m × 64m.

Chairman: Peter Coates.

Chief Executive: Tony Scholes.

Manager: Tony Pulis.

Assistant Manager: Dave Kemp.

Physio: Chris Banks.

Colours: Red and white striped shirts with red sleeves and shoulders, white shorts, white stockings.

Year Formed: 1863* (*see Foundation*).

Turned Professional: 1885.

Previous Names: 1868, Stoke Ramblers; 1870, Stoke; 1925, Stoke City.

Club Nickname: 'The Potters'.

Grounds: 1875, Sweeting's Field; 1878, Victoria Ground (previously known as the Athletic Club Ground); 1997, Britannia Stadium.

First Football League Game: 8 September 1888, Football League, v WBA (h) L 0–2 – Rowley; Clare, Underwood; Ramsey, Shutt, Smith; Sayer, McSkimming, Staton, Edge, Tunnicliffe.

Record League Victory: 10–3 v WBA, Division 1, 4 February 1937 – Doug Westland; Brigham, Harbot; Tutin, Turner (1p), Kirton; Matthews, Antonio (2), Freddie Steele (5), Jimmy Westland, Johnson (2).

Record Cup Victory: 7–1 v Burnley, FA Cup 2nd rd (replay), 20 February 1896 – Clawley; Clare, Eccles; Turner, Grewe, Robertson; Willie Maxwell, Dickson, Alan Maxwell (3), Hyslop (4), Schofield.

HONOURS

Football League – Division 1: Best season: 4th, 1935–36, 1946–47;
FL C: ***Runners-up*** 2007–08;
Division 2: ***Champions*** 1932–33, 1962–63, 1992–93;
Runners-up 1921–22;
Division 3 (N): ***Champions*** 1926–27.

FA Cup: ***Runners-up*** 2011.

Football League Cup: ***Winners*** 1972; ***Runners-up*** 1964.

Autoglass Trophy: ***Winners***: 1992.

Auto Windscreens Shield: ***Winners***: 2000.

European Competitions
UEFA Cup: 1972–73, 1974–75.
Europa League: 2011–12.

sky SPORTS FACT FILE

Prodigious scoring Freddie Steele amassed 220 goals in all matches from 1934 to 1949 in Stoke City colours and was an England international in pre-war days. Aside from his accomplishments on the field he was, in his heyday, a useful sprinter and hurdler competing in the Staffordshire area.

Record Defeat: 0–10 v Preston NE, Division 1, 14 September 1889.

Most League Points (2 for a win): 63, Division 3 (N), 1926–27.

Most League Points (3 for a win): 93, Division 2, 1992–93.

Most League Goals: 92, Division 3 (N), 1926–27.

Highest League Scorer in Season: Freddie Steele, 33, Division 1, 1936–37.

Most League Goals in Total Aggregate: Freddie Steele, 142, 1934–49.

Most League Goals in One Match: 7, Neville Coleman v Lincoln C, Division 2, 23 February 1957.

Most Capped Player: Gordon Banks, 36 (73), England.

Most League Appearances: Eric Skeels, 506, 1958–76.

Youngest League Player: Peter Bullock, 16 years 163 days v Swansea C, 19 April 1958.

Record Transfer Fee Received: £3,000,000 from Manchester U for Ritchie De Laat, January 2009; £3,000,000 from Hull C for Seyi Olofinjana, August 2009.

Record Transfer Fee Paid: £10,000,000 to Tottenham H for Peter Crouch, August 2011.

Football League Record: 1888 Founder Member of Football League; 1890 Not re-elected; 1891 Re-elected; relegated in 1907, and after one year in Division 2, resigned for financial reasons; 1919 re-elected to Division 2; 1922–23 Division 1; 1923–26 Division 2; 1926–27 Division 3 (N); 1927–33 Division 2; 1933–53 Division 1; 1953–63 Division 2; 1963–77 Division 1; 1977–79 Division 2; 1979–85 Division 1; 1985–90 Division 2; 1990–92 Division 3; 1992–93 Division 2; 1993–98 Division 1; 1998–2002 Division 2; 2002–04 Division 1; 2004–08 FL C; 2008– FA Premier League.

MANAGERS

Tom Slaney 1874–83
(Secretary-Manager)
Walter Cox 1883–84
(Secretary-Manager)
Harry Lockett 1884–90
Joseph Bradshaw 1890–92
Arthur Reeves 1892–95
William Rowley 1895–97
H. D. Austerberry 1897–1908
A. J. Barker 1908–14
Peter Hodge 1914–15
Joe Schofield 1915–19
Arthur Shallcross 1919–23
John 'Jock' Rutherford 1923
Tom Mather 1923–35
Bob McGrory 1935–52
Frank Taylor 1952–60
Tony Waddington 1960–77
George Eastham 1977–78
Alan A'Court 1978
Alan Durban 1978–81
Richie Barker 1981–83
Bill Asprey 1984–85
Mick Mills 1985–89
Alan Ball 1989–91
Lou Macari 1991–93
Joe Jordan 1993–94
Lou Macari 1994–97
Chic Bates 1997–98
Chris Kamara 1998
Brian Little 1998–99
Gary Megson 1999
Gudjon Thordarson 1999–2002
Steve Cotterill 2002
Tony Pulis 2002–05
Johan Boskamp 2005–06
Tony Pulis June 2006–

LATEST SEQUENCES

Longest Sequence of League Wins: 8, 30.3.1895 – 21.9.1895.

Longest Sequence of League Defeats: 11, 6.4.1985 – 17.8.1985.

Longest Sequence of League Draws: 5, 21.3.1987 – 11.4.1987.

Longest Sequence of Unbeaten League Matches: 25, 5.9.1992 – 20.2.1993.

Longest Sequence Without a League Win: 17, 22.4.1989 – 14.10.1989.

Successive Scoring Runs: 21 from 24.12.1921.

Successive Non-scoring Runs: 8 from 29.12.1984.

TEN YEAR LEAGUE RECORD

		P	*W*	*D*	*L*	*F*	*A*	*Pts*	*Pos*
2002-03	Div 1	46	12	14	20	45	69	50	21
2003-04	Div 1	46	18	12	16	58	55	66	11
2004-05	FL C	46	17	10	19	36	38	61	12
2005-06	FL C	46	17	7	22	54	63	58	13
2006-07	FL C	46	19	16	11	62	41	73	8
2007-08	FL C	46	21	16	9	69	55	79	2
2008-09	PR Lge	38	12	9	17	38	55	45	12
2009-10	PR Lge	38	11	14	13	34	48	47	11
2010-11	PR Lge	38	13	7	18	46	48	46	13
2011-12	PR Lge	38	11	12	15	36	53	45	14

DID YOU KNOW ?

On 4 December 1948, Stoke City played Blackpool and fielded a team composed entirely of players who only cost the signing-on fee of £10. The eleven included Frank Mountford, Neil Franklin and Freddie Steele. Blackpool had Stoke "local" Stanley Matthews in their side.

STOKE CITY 2011–12 LEAGUE RECORD

Match No.	*Date*	*Venue*	*Opponents*	*Result*	*H/T Score*	*Lg Pos.*	*Goalscorers*	*Attendance*
1	Aug 14	H	Chelsea	D 0-0	0-0	—		27,421
2	21	A	Norwich C	D 1-1	0-1	11	Jones [90]	26,272
3	28	A	WBA	W 1-0	0-0	9	Shotton [89]	22,909
4	Sept 10	H	Liverpool	W 1-0	1-0	4	Walters (pen) [21]	27,592
5	18	A	Sunderland	L 0-4	0-3	5		32,296
6	24	H	Manchester U	D 1-1	0-1	7	Crouch [52]	27,582
7	Oct 2	A	Swansea C	L 0-2	0-1	8		19,523
8	15	H	Fulham	W 2-0	0-0	7	Walters [80], Delap [87]	26,890
9	23	A	Arsenal	L 1-3	1-1	9	Crouch [34]	59,671
10	31	H	Newcastle U	L 1-3	0-2	—	Walters (pen) [75]	26,564
11	Nov 6	A	Bolton W	L 0-5	0-2	12		20,028
12	19	H	QPR	L 2-3	1-2	14	Walters [8], Shawcross [64]	27,618
13	26	H	Blackburn R	W 3-1	1-0	12	Delap [28], Whelan [58], Crouch [72]	26,686
14	Dec 4	A	Everton	W 1-0	1-0	8	Huth [15]	33,219
15	11	H	Tottenham H	W 2-1	2-0	8	Etherington 2 [13, 43]	27,529
16	17	A	Wolverhampton W	W 2-1	0-1	8	Doyle (og) [58], Crouch [70]	24,684
17	21	A	Manchester C	L 0-3	0-2	—		46,321
18	26	H	Aston Villa	D 0-0	0-0	8		27,739
19	31	H	Wigan Ath	D 2-2	0-1	8	Walters (pen) [77], Jerome [84]	26,595
20	Jan 2	A	Blackburn R	W 2-1	2-0	—	Crouch 2 [17, 45]	20,615
21	14	A	Liverpool	D 0-0	0-0	8		44,691
22	21	H	WBA	L 1-2	0-1	8	Jerome [86]	26,865
23	31	A	Manchester U	L 0-2	0-1	—		74,719
24	Feb 4	H	Sunderland	L 0-1	0-0	12		27,717
25	11	A	Fulham	L 1-2	0-2	13	Shawcross [78]	23,555
26	26	H	Swansea C	W 2-0	2-0	12	Upson [24], Crouch [39]	26,678
27	Mar 3	H	Norwich C	W 1-0	0-0	9	Etherington [72]	27,483
28	10	A	Chelsea	L 0-1	0-0	13		40,945
29	21	A	Tottenham H	D 1-1	0-0	—	Jerome [75]	35,172
30	24	H	Manchester C	D 1-1	0-0	12	Crouch [59]	27,535
31	31	A	Wigan Ath	L 0-2	0-0	13		19,786
32	Apr 7	H	Wolverhampton W	W 2-1	1-1	11	Huth [37], Crouch [61]	27,005
33	9	A	Aston Villa	D 1-1	0-1	—	Huth [71]	30,100
34	21	A	Newcastle U	L 0-3	0-2	14		52,162
35	28	H	Arsenal	D 1-1	1-1	14	Crouch [9]	27,502
36	May 1	H	Everton	D 1-1	0-1	—	Jerome [69]	26,500
37	6	A	QPR	L 0-1	0-0	14		17,319
38	13	H	Bolton W	D 2-2	1-2	14	Walters 2 (1 pen) [13, 77 (p)]	27,789

Final League Position: 14

GOALSCORERS

League (36): Crouch 10, Walters 7 (4 pens), Jerome 4, Etherington 3, Huth 3, Delap 2, Shawcross 2, Jones 1, Shotton 1, Upson 1, Whelan 1, own goal 1.
Carling Cup (1): Jones 1.
FA Cup (8): Crouch 2, Huth 2, Jerome 2, Walters 2 (1 pen).
Europa League (17): Jones 4, Crouch 2, Jerome 2, Walters 2 (1 pen), Fuller 1, Pugh 1, Shotton 1, Upson 1, Whelan 1, Whitehead 1, own goal 1.

Begovic A 22 + 1	Huth R 31 + 3	Wilson M 35	Whelan G 27 + 3	Shawcross R 36	Woodgate J 16 + 1	Pennant J 18 + 9	Delap R 18 + 8	Jones K 10 + 11	Walters J 38	Etherington M 30	Whitehead D 24 + 9	Pugh D — + 3	Shotton R 14 + 9	Wilkinson A 20 + 5	Upson M 10 + 4	Crouch P 31 + 1	Palacios W 9 + 9	Jerome C 7 + 16	Diao S 2 + 4	Higginbotham D 1 + 1	Sorensen T 16	Fuller R 3 + 10	*Match No.*
1	2	3	4	5	6	7	8^{2}	9^{3}	10	11^{1}	12	13	14										1
1	2	3	4	5	6^{2}	7^{1}		9	10	11	8	12	13										2
1	2	3^{1}	4	5	6	7^{3}		9	10	11^{2}	8	13	14	12									3
1	2^{1}	3		5		7	8^{3}	13	10	11^{2}	6			12	4	9	14						4
1	2	3		5	6	13	8^{3}	12	10	11^{2}	4					9	14	7^{1}					5
1	12	3	4	5	6	7^{3}	8^{2}		10	11	13			2^{1}		9		14					6
1	12	3^{1}	4	5	6	7^{3}	8^{2}		10		11		14	2		9		13					7
1		3	4	5		7^{1}	8		10	11^{2}	12			2	6	9			13				8
1		3	6	5			8^{3}	13	10	11^{1}	7			2	4	9^{2}		14	12				9
1	13	3^{2}	4	5^{1}	6	7	8	14	10	11^{3}				2	12	9							10
1	3		4^{3}		6	7^{2}	8	12	10		14			2^{1}	5	9		11		13			11
	4		14	5		7^{2}	8	12	10	11	6^{3}			2		9^{1}				3	1	13	12
	4	3	6	5		7^{1}	8	13	10	11	12			2		9^{2}					1		13
15	4	2	7	5	6^{1}				10	11^{2}	8		3	12	13	9					1^{6}		14
	2	3	4	5	6^{1}		12		10	11^{2}	8		7			9	13				1		15
	4	3	6^{2}	5	2^{1}	12			10	11^{3}	8		7			9	13				1	14	16
	2	3			4^{3}	13		9^{2}	10		8		7		5		6	11^{1}	14		1	12	17
	4	3		5	2^{2}	13	12	9	10	11	8		7				6^{1}				1		18
	4	3		5		7	8	14	10^{3}	11^{2}			12	2^{1}		9	6	13			1		19
	4	3	6^{2}	5	2		13		10	11^{1}	8^{3}		7			9		12	14		1		20
	4	3	6	5	2^{2}		7		10	11^{3}	12			13		9	8^{1}				1	14	21
	4	3	6	5	2^{1}	12	8^{3}		10	11			7^{2}	14		9		13			1		22
	4	3		5		7	14	9	8^{3}		11			2		10^{1}	6^{2}	12			1	13	23
	4■	3	6	5	13	7^{2}	8		11				14	2^{3}		10		9^{1}			1	12	24
		3	6	5		13		9^{2}	7	11^{1}			14	2^{3}	4	10	8				1	12	25
1		3	6	5			13		10	11^{1}	8		7^{3}	2	4	9^{2}	14	12					26
1	4	3	6	5		12		13	10^{2}	11	8		7	2^{1}		9^{3}		14					27
1	4	3^{2}		5				9^{3}	11		6		7	2	12		13	14	8^{1}			10■	28
1	4	3	12	5		7	14		10		13			2		9	6^{2}	11^{3}	8^{1}				29
1	4	3	6	5		12		14	10	11^{2}	8			2		9^{3}	13	7^{1}					30
1	4	3	6	5		7^{2}			10^{3}	11^{1}	8			2		9	14	12				13	31
1	4	3	6	5		7^{2}	14		10	11^{1}	8		2			9^{3}	13	12					32
1	4	3		5		12	7^{3}	9^{2}	10	11^{1}	8		2			13	6					14	33
1	4	3	8	5					10	11	12		2	7^{1}		9	6^{2}	13					34
1	4	3	6	5		7^{2}	14		10	11^{3}	8		2^{1}		12	9		13					35
1	2	3	12	5			8^{2}	9	7^{1}	11	6				4	10^{3}		14				13	36
	2	3^{1}	6	5			8	13	7		14		12		4	9		11^{2}			1	10^{3}	37
	3		6	5					7	11	8		13	2	4^{2}	9		12			1	10^{1}	38

FA Cup

Third Round	Gillingham	(a)	3-1
Fourth Round	Derby Co	(a)	2-0
Fifth Round	Crawley T	(a)	2-0
Quarter-Final	Liverpool	(a)	1-2

Carling Cup

Third Round	Tottenham H	(h)	0-0
Fourth Round	Liverpool	(h)	1-2

Europa League

Third Qualifying Round			
	Hajduk Split	(h)	1-0
		(a)	1-0
Play-Off Round	Thun	(a)	1-0
		(h)	4-1
Group E	Dynamo Kiev	(a)	1-1
	Besiktas	(h)	2-1
	Maccabi Tel Aviv	(h)	3-0
		(a)	2-1
	Dynamo Kiev	(h)	1-1
	Besiktas	(a)	1-3
Second Round	Valencia	(h)	0-1
		(a)	0-1

SUNDERLAND FA Premiership

FOUNDATION

A Scottish schoolmaster named James Allan, working at Hendon Board School, took the initiative in the foundation of Sunderland in 1879 when they were formed as The Sunderland and District Teachers' Association FC at a meeting in the Adults School, Norfolk Street. Due to financial difficulties, they quickly allowed members from outside the teaching profession and so became Sunderland AFC in October 1880.

Stadium of Light, Sunderland, Tyne and Wear SR5 1SU.

Telephone: (0871) 911 1200.

Fax: (0191) 551 5123.

Ticket Office: (0871) 911 1973.

Website: www.safc.com

Email: enquiries@safc.com

Ground Capacity: 49,000.

Record Attendance: 75,118 v Derby Co, FA Cup 6th rd replay, 8 March 1933 (at Roker Park); 48,353 v Liverpool, FA Premier League, 13 April 2002 (at Stadium of Light). (FA Premier League figure 46,062.)

Pitch Measurements: 105m × 68m.

Chairman: Ellis Short.

Chief Executive: Margaret Byrne.

Finance Director: Angela Lowes.

Manager: Martin O'Neill OBE.

First Team Coach: Steve Walford.

Physio: Dave Galley.

Colours: Red and white striped shirts, black shorts, black stockings with red tops.

Year Formed: 1879.

Turned Professional: 1886.

Previous Names: 1879, Sunderland and District Teachers AFC; 1880, Sunderland.

Club Nickname: Black Cats.

Grounds: 1879, Blue House Field, Hendon; 1882, Groves Field, Ashbrooke; 1883, Horatio Street; 1884, Abbs Field, Fulwell; 1886, Newcastle Road; 1898, Roker Park; 1997, Stadium of Light.

First Football League Game: 13 September 1890, Football League, v Burnley (h) L 2–3 – Kirtley; Porteous, Oliver; Wilson, Auld, Gibson; Spence (1), Miller, Campbell (1), Scott, Davy Hannah.

Record League Victory: 9–1 v Newcastle U (a), Division 1, 5 December 1908 – Roose; Forster, Melton; Daykin, Thomson, Low; Mordue (1), Hogg (3), Brown, Holley (3), Bridgett (2).

Record Cup Victory: 11–1 v Fairfield, FA Cup 1st rd, 2 February 1895 – Doig; McNeill, Johnston; Dunlop, McCreadie (1), Wilson; Gillespie (1), Millar (5), Campbell, Jimmy Hannah (3), Scott (1).

HONOURS

Football League: FL C: *Champions* 2004–05, 2006–07;
Division 1: ***Champions*** 1891–92, 1892–93, 1894–95, 1901–02, 1912–13, 1935–36, 1995–96, 1998–99;
Runners-up 1893–94, 1897–98, 1900–01, 1922–23, 1934–35;
Division 2: ***Champions*** 1975–76;
Runners-up 1963–64, 1979–80.
Division 3: ***Champions*** 1987–88.

FA Cup: ***Winners*** 1937, 1973;
Runners-up 1913, 1992.

Football League Cup:
Runners-up 1985.

European Competitions
European Cup-Winners' Cup: 1973–74.

sky SPORTS FACT FILE

Assistance from the law helped Sunderland on 4 September 1920, when they defeated Sheffield United 3-1. A shot from Barney Travers broke the goal net. The referee checked the damage and after consultation with the constable stationed behind the goal awarded the score.

Record Defeat: 0–8 v Sheff Wed, Division 1, 26 December 1911; 0–8 v West Ham U, Division 1, 19 October 1968; 0–8 v Watford, Division 1, 25 September 1982.

Most League Points (2 for a win): 61, Division 2, 1963–64.

Most League Points (3 for a win): 105, Division 1, 1998–99 (Football League Record).

Most League Goals: 109, Division 1, 1935–36.

Highest League Scorer in Season: Dave Halliday, 43, Division 1, 1928–29.

Most League Goals in Total Aggregate: Charlie Buchan, 209, 1911–25.

Most League Goals in One Match: 5, Charlie Buchan v Liverpool, Division 1, 7 December 1919; 5, Bobby Gurney v Bolton W, Division 1, 7 December 1935; 5, Dominic Sharkey v Norwich C, Division 2, 20 February 1962.

Most Capped Player: Charlie Hurley, 38 (40), Republic of Ireland.

Most League Appearances: Jim Montgomery, 537, 1962–77.

Youngest League Player: Derek Forster, 15 years 184 days v Leicester C, 22 August 1964.

Record Transfer Fee Received: £19,000,000 from Aston Villa for Darren Bent, January 2011.

Record Transfer Fee Paid: £13,250,000 to Rennes for Asamoah Gyan, August 2010.

Football League Record: 1890 Elected to Division 1; 1958–64 Division 2; 1964–70 Division 1; 1970–76 Division 2; 1976–77 Division 1; 1977–80 Division 2; 1980–85 Division 1; 1985–87 Division 2; 1987–88 Division 3; 1988–90 Division 2; 1990–91 Division 1; 1991–92 Division 2; 1992–96 Division 1; 1996–97 FA Premier League; 1997–99 Division 1; 1999–2003 FA Premier League; 2003–04 Division 1; 2004–05 FL C; 2005–06 FA Premier League; 2006–07 FL C; 2007– FA Premier League.

MANAGERS

Tom Watson 1888–96
Bob Campbell 1896–99
Alex Mackie 1899–1905
Bob Kyle 1905–28
Johnny Cochrane 1928–39
Bill Murray 1939–57
Alan Brown 1957–64
George Hardwick 1964–65
Ian McColl 1965–68
Alan Brown 1968–72
Bob Stokoe 1972–76
Jimmy Adamson 1976–78
Ken Knighton 1979–81
Alan Durban 1981–84
Len Ashurst 1984–85
Lawrie McMenemy 1985–87
Denis Smith 1987–91
Malcolm Crosby 1991–93
Terry Butcher 1993
Mick Buxton 1993–95
Peter Reid 1995–2002
Howard Wilkinson 2002–03
Mick McCarthy 2003–06
Niall Quinn 2006
Roy Keane 2006–08
Ricky Sbragia 2008–09
Steve Bruce 2009–11
Martin O'Neill December 2011–

LATEST SEQUENCES

Longest Sequence of League Wins: 13, 14.11.1891 – 2.4.1892.

Longest Sequence of League Defeats: 17, 18.1.2003 – 16.8.2003.

Longest Sequence of League Draws: 6, 26.3.1949 – 19.4.1949.

Longest Sequence of Unbeaten League Matches: 19, 3.5.1998 – 14.11.1998.

Longest Sequence Without a League Win: 22, 21.12.2002 – 16.8.2003.

Successive Scoring Runs: 29 from 8.11.1997.

Successive Non-scoring Runs: 10 from 27.11.1976.

TEN YEAR LEAGUE RECORD

		P	*W*	*D*	*L*	*F*	*A*	*Pts*	*Pos*
2002-03	PR Lge	38	4	7	27	21	65	19	20
2003-04	Div 1	46	22	13	11	62	45	79	3
2004-05	FL C	46	29	7	10	76	41	94	1
2005-06	PR Lge	38	3	6	29	26	69	15	20
2006-07	FL C	46	27	7	12	76	47	88	1
2007-08	PR Lge	38	11	6	21	36	59	39	15
2008-09	PR Lge	38	9	9	20	34	54	36	16
2009-10	PR Lge	38	11	11	16	48	56	44	13
2010-11	PR Lge	38	12	11	15	45	56	47	10
2011-12	PR Lge	38	11	12	15	45	46	45	13

DID YOU KNOW ?

Former grocer's boy and Doncaster Co-op Sports Club centre-forward Cliff Whitelum signed for Sunderland from Bentley Colliery in December 1938, made his debut at 19 and delivered the scoring goods in wartime football, topping the charts with over 100 goals in five seasons.

SUNDERLAND 2011–12 LEAGUE RECORD

Match No.	Date	Venue	Opponents	Result		H/T Score	Lg Pos.	Goalscorers	Attendance
1	Aug 13	A	Liverpool	D	1-1	0-1	—	Larsson 57	45,018
2	20	H	Newcastle U	L	0-1	0-0	13		47,751
3	27	A	Swansea C	D	0-0	0-0	13		19,938
4	Sept 10	H	Chelsea	L	1-2	0-1	16	Ji 90	36,699
5	18	H	Stoke C	W	4-0	3-0	12	Bramble 5, Woodgate (og) 11, Gardner 28, Larsson 59	32,296
6	26	A	Norwich C	L	1-2	0-1	—	Richardson 86	26,107
7	Oct 1	H	WBA	D	2-2	2-2	16	Bendtner 24, Elmohamady 26	34,815
8	16	A	Arsenal	L	1-2	1-1	17	Larsson 31	60,078
9	22	A	Bolton W	W	2-0	0-0	14	Sessegnon 82, Bendtner 90	24,349
10	29	H	Aston Villa	D	2-2	1-1	14	Wickham 38, Sessegnon 89	37,062
11	Nov 5	A	Manchester U	L	0-1	0-1	15		75,570
12	19	H	Fulham	D	0-0	0-0	16		37,688
13	26	H	Wigan Ath	L	1-2	1-1	16	Larsson 8	37,883
14	Dec 4	A	Wolverhampton W	L	1-2	0-0	17	Richardson 52	25,145
15	11	H	Blackburn R	W	2-1	0-1	16	Vaughan 84, Larsson 90	39,863
16	18	A	Tottenham H	L	0-1	0-0	16		36,021
17	21	A	QPR	W	3-2	1-0	—	Bendtner 19, Sessegnon 53, Brown 89	16,167
18	26	H	Everton	D	1-1	1-0	14	Colback 26	43,619
19	Jan 1	H	Manchester C	W	1-0	0-0	15	Ji 90	40,625
20	3	A	Wigan Ath	W	4-1	1-0	—	Gardner 45, McClean 55, Sessegnon 73, Vaughan 80	15,871
21	14	A	Chelsea	L	0-1	0-1	12		41,696
22	21	H	Swansea C	W	2-0	1-0	10	Sessegnon 14, Gardner 85	36,904
23	Feb 1	H	Norwich C	W	3-0	2-0	—	Campbell 21, Sessegnon 28, Ayala (og) 54	34,476
24	4	A	Stoke C	W	1-0	0-0	8	McClean 60	27,717
25	11	H	Arsenal	L	1-2	0-0	9	McClean 70	40,312
26	25	A	WBA	L	0-4	0-2	9		25,311
27	Mar 4	A	Newcastle U	D	1-1	1-0	12	Bendtner (pen) 24	52,388
28	10	H	Liverpool	W	1-0	0-0	8	Bendtner 56	41,661
29	20	A	Blackburn R	L	0-2	0-0	—		20,056
30	24	H	QPR	W	3-1	1-0	8	Bendtner 41, McClean 70, Sessegnon 76	37,128
31	31	A	Manchester C	D	3-3	2-1	9	Larsson 2 31, 55, Bendtner 45	47,007
32	Apr 7	H	Tottenham H	D	0-0	0-0	9		39,335
33	9	A	Everton	L	0-4	0-0	—		32,249
34	14	H	Wolverhampton W	D	0-0	0-0	9		37,476
35	21	A	Aston Villa	D	0-0	0-0	11		32,557
36	28	H	Bolton W	D	2-2	1-1	11	Bendtner 36, McClean 55	40,768
37	May 6	A	Fulham	L	1-2	1-2	11	Bardsley 34	25,683
38	13	H	Manchester U	L	0-1	0-1	13		46,452

Final League Position: 13

GOALSCORERS

League (45): Bendtner 8 (1 pen), Larsson 7, Sessegnon 7, McClean 5, Gardner 3, Ji 2, Richardson 2, Vaughan 2, Bardsley 1, Bramble 1, Brown 1, Campbell 1, Colback 1, Elmohamady 1, Wickham 1, own goals 2.
Carling Cup (0).
FA Cup (8): Bardsley 1, Campbell 1, Colback 1, Larsson 1, McClean 1, Richardson 1, Sessegnon 1, own goal 1.

Mignolet S 29	Bardsley P 29 + 2	Richardson K 26 + 3	Ferdinand A 3	Brown W 20	Cattermole L 23	Larsson S 32	Colback J 29 + 6	Gyan A 3	Sessegnon S 36	Elmohamady A 7 + 11	Ji D 2 + 17	Vaughan D 17 + 5	Gardner C 22 + 8	Wickham C 5 + 11	O'Shea J 29	Bramble T 8	Bendtner N 25 + 3	Turner M 23 + 1	Meyler D 1 + 6	Westwood K 8 + 1	Noble R — + 2	McClean J 20 + 3	Kilgallon M 9 + 1	Campbell F 6 + 6	Bridge W 3 + 5	Kyrgiakos S 2 + 1	Gordon C 1	Match No.
1	2	3	4	5	6	7[2]	8	9[1]	10	11	12	13																1
1	2■	3[1]	4	5	6	7[3]	8	9	10	11[2]	12		13	14														2
1	2	14	4	5	6[1]	7[3]	8	9[2]	10	13			11	12	3													3
1	2[1]	3		5	6[2]	7	11		10[3]	12	14		8	13		4	9											4
1		3		5		7[1]	12		10[2]	4	13	11	8	14	2	6	9[3]											5
1		3		5		7[1]			10[2]	4	13	11	8	12	2	6	9											6
1		3		5	6[1]	7	12		10	11[2]	13		8[3]		2		9	4	14									7
1		3		5	6[3]	9[1]	8		10[2]	7	12	11	14	13	2			4										8
1	12	3[1]		5		7	6		10			11		8	2		9	4										9
1[6]	12	3		5		7	6		10			11[2]		8	2[1]		9	4	13	15								10
	2	3		5	6	7	11[2]		10[3]	14	12			8[1]			9	4	13	1								11
	3	11		5	6		8[1]		10	7[2]	12				2		9	4		1	13							12
	3[1]	11		5	6[2]	7	8		10		14	13	12		2[3]		9	4		1								13
	2	3		5	6	7	8		10[2]	12	11[1]				4		9			1	13							14
	3	11		5		7	6[1]		10		12	8		9[2]	2	4				1		13						15
	3[2]	11		5		7	4[3]		10			8	14	9[1]	2	6	12			1		13						16
	3	11		5	6	7[2]	12		10			8[1]	13		2	4	9			1								17
	3[2]	11		5	6	7	12		10			8[3]	13		2	4[1]	9			1		14						18
1				5[1]	6	7	11		10	14	13	8[3]	4		2		9[2]					3	12					19
1		11[1]			6		7		10	13	14	8	4[2]		2		9		12			3[3]	5					20
1	2	3[3]			6	7			10			8[2]	13	14	5		9	12				11	4[1]					21
1	2	3		5	6	7[3]			10	14		8[2]	13	12	4		9[1]					11						22
1	2	3[2]				7	8		10[3]		12		4		5			6	14			11		9[1]	13			23
1	2	3				7	11		10	12			4		5			6	8[1]			9						24
1	2	3				7	8		10		12		4		5			6				11		9[1]				25
1	2	3[1]			6	7[3]	11[2]		10				8		5		13	4				9		12	14			26
1	2	3[3]			6	7[2]	13		10■				8		5		9[1]	4				11		12	14			27
1	2					7	8					12	4	13	5		10[2]	6				11		9[1]	3			28
1	2					7	13				12	8	4				10	6				11		9[1]	3[2]	5		29
1							7		10	14		8	4		2[1]		9[3]	6	13			11		12	3[2]	5		30
1	2				6[2]	7	3		10			13	8				9	4				11	5[1]			12		31
1	2[2]	13			6[1]	7	3		10			12	8				9	4				11	5					32
1	2[1]	12			6[2]	7	3		10		13	8[3]	9	14				4				11	5					33
1	2	3				7	4		10				8[1]				9	6				11	5	12				34
1	2					7	4		10				8■		3		9[1]	6				11	5	12				35
	3				6		8		10	12					2		9	4				11	5[2]	7[1]	13		1	36
1	2				6		8		10		9[1]		7		3		12	4				11	5[2]	13				37
1	3[2]						6		10	12		8[3]	7	14	2[1]	5		4				11		9	13			38

FA Cup

Third Round	Peterborough U	(a)	2-0
Fourth Round	Middlesbrough	(h)	1-1
		(a)	2-1
Fifth Round	Arsenal	(h)	2-0
Quarter-Final	Everton	(a)	1-1
		(h)	0-2

Carling Cup

Second Round	Brighton & HA	(a)	0-1

SWANSEA CITY FA Premiership

FOUNDATION

The earliest Association Football in Wales was played in the northern part of the country and no international took place in the south until 1894, when a local paper still thought it necessary to publish an outline of the rules and an illustration of the pitch markings. There had been an earlier Swansea club, but this has no connection with Swansea Town (now City) formed at a public meeting in June 1912.

Liberty Stadium, Morfa, Landore, Swansea SA1 2FA.

Telephone: (01792) 616 600.

Fax: (01792) 616 606.

Ticket Office: (0870) 040 0004.

Website: www.swanseacity.net

Email: info@swanseacityfc.co.uk

Ground Capacity: 20,520.

Record Attendance: 32,796 v Arsenal, FA Cup 4th rd, 17 February 1968 (at Vetch Field); 19,288 v Yeovil T, FL 1, 11 November 2005 (at Liberty Stadium).

Pitch Measurements: 115yd × 74yd.

Chairman: Huw Jenkins.

Vice-chairman: Leigh Dineen.

Manager: Michael Laudrup.

Assistant Manager: Erik Larsen.

Head Physio: Kate Rees.

Colours: All white.

Year Formed: 1912.

Turned Professional: 1912.

Previous Name: 1912, Swansea Town; 1970, Swansea City.

Club Nicknames: 'The Swans', 'The Jacks'.

Grounds: 1912, Vetch Field; 2005, Liberty Stadium.

First Football League Game: 28 August 1920, Division 3, v Portsmouth (a) L 0–3 – Crumley; Robson, Evans; Smith, Holdsworth, Williams; Hole, Ivor Jones, Edmundson, Rigsby, Spottiswood.

Record League Victory: 8–0 v Hartlepool U, Division 4, 1 April 1978 – Barber; Evans, Bartley, Lally (1) (Morris), May, Bruton, Kevin Moore, Robbie James (3 incl. 1p), Curtis (3), Toshack (1), Chappell.

Record Cup Victory: 12–0 v Sliema W (Malta), ECWC 1st rd 1st leg, 15 September 1982 – Davies; Marustik, Hadziabdic (1), Irwin (1), Kennedy, Rajkovic (1), Loveridge (2) (Leighton James), Robbie James, Charles (2), Stevenson (1), Latchford (1) (Walsh (3)).

Record Defeat: 0–8 v Liverpool, FA Cup 3rd rd, 9 January 1990; 0–8 v Monaco, ECWC, 1st rd 2nd leg, 1 October 1991.

HONOURS

Football League – Division 1: Best season: 6th, 1981–82; **FL 1:** ***Champions*** 2007–08; **Division 35(S):** ***Champions*** 1924–25, 1948–49; **Division 3:** ***Champions*** 1999–2000.

FA Cup: Semi-finals 1926, 1964.

Football League Cup: Best season: 4th rd, 1965, 1977, 2009, 2011.

Welsh Cup: ***Winners*** 11 times; ***Runners-up*** 8 times.

Autoglass Trophy: ***Winners*** 1994, 2006.

Football League Trophy: ***Winners*** 2006.

European Competitions
European Cup-Winners' Cup: 1961–62, 1966–67, 1981–82, 1982–83, 1983–84, 1989–90, 1991–92.

sky SPORTS FACT FILE

Swansea Town Welsh international Jack Fowler was signed from Plymouth Argyle for £1,250 in 1923. He went on to score 102 League goals for the club, reaching his century on 10 November 1928 against Tottenham Hotspur when he scored two of the four goals.

Most League Points (2 for a win): 62, Division 3 (S), 1948–49.

Most League Points (3 for a win): 92, FL 1, 2007–08.

Most League Goals: 90, Division 2, 1956–57.

Highest League Scorer in Season: Cyril Pearce, 35, Division 2, 1931–32.

Most League Goals in Total Aggregate: Ivor Allchurch, 166, 1949–58, 1965–68.

Most League Goals in One Match: 5, Jack Fowler v Charlton Ath, Division 3S, 27 December 1924.

Most Capped Player: Ivor Allchurch, 42 (68), Wales.

Most League Appearances: Wilfred Milne, 585, 1919–37.

Youngest League Player: Nigel Dalling, 15 years 289 days v Southport, 6 December 1974.

Record Transfer Fee Received: £2,000,000 from Wigan Ath for Jason Scotland, July 2009.

Record Transfer Fee Paid: £3,500,000 to Watford for Danny Graham, June 2011.

Football League Record: 1920 Original Member of Division 3; 1921–25 Division 3 (S); 1925–47 Division 2; 1947–49 Division 3 (S); 1949–65 Division 2; 1965–67 Division 3; 1967–70 Division 4; 1970–73 Division 3; 1973–78 Division 4; 1978–79 Division 3; 1979–81 Division 2; 1981–83 Division 1; 1983–84 Division 2; 1984–86 Division 3; 1986–88 Division 4; 1988–92 Division 3; 1992–96 Division 2; 1996–2000 Division 3; 2000–01 Division 2; 2001–04 Division 3; 2004–05 FL 2; 2005–08 FL 1; 2008–11 FL C; 2011– FA Premier League.

LATEST SEQUENCES

Longest Sequence of League Wins: 9, 27.11.1999 – 22.01.2000.

Longest Sequence of League Defeats: 9, 26.1.1991 – 19.3.1991.

Longest Sequence of League Draws: 8, 25.11.2008 – 28.12.2008.

Longest Sequence of Unbeaten League Matches: 19, 19.10.1970 – 9.3.1971.

Longest Sequence Without a League Win: 15, 25.3.1989 – 2.9.1989.

Successive Scoring Runs: 27 from 28.8.1947.

Successive Non-scoring Runs: 6 from 6.2.1996.

MANAGERS

Walter Whittaker 1912–14
William Bartlett 1914–15
Joe Bradshaw 1919–26
Jimmy Thomson 1927–31
Neil Harris 1934–39
Haydn Green 1939–47
Bill McCandless 1947–55
Ron Burgess 1955–58
Trevor Morris 1958–65
Glyn Davies 1965–66
Billy Lucas 1967–69
Roy Bentley 1969–72
Harry Gregg 1972–75
Harry Griffiths 1975–77
John Toshack 1978–83 *(resigned October re-appointed in December) 1983–84*
Colin Appleton 1984
John Bond 1984–85
Tommy Hutchison 1985–86
Terry Yorath 1986–89
Ian Evans 1989–90
Terry Yorath 1990–91
Frank Burrows 1991–95
Bobby Smith 1995
Kevin Cullis 1996
Jan Molby 1996–97
Micky Adams 1997
Alan Cork 1997–98
John Hollins 1998–2001
Colin Addison 2001–02
Nick Cusack 2002
Brian Flynn 2002–04
Kenny Jackett 2004–07
Roberto Martinez 2007–09
Paulo Sousa 2009–10
Brendan Rodgers 2010–12
Michael Laudrup June 2012–

TEN YEAR LEAGUE RECORD

		P	W	D	L	F	A	Pts	Pos
2002-03	Div 3	46	12	13	21	48	65	49	21
2003-04	Div 3	46	15	14	17	58	61	59	10
2004-05	FL 2	46	24	8	14	62	43	80	3
2005-06	FL 1	46	18	17	11	78	55	71	6
2006-07	FL 1	46	20	12	14	69	53	72	7
2007-08	FL 1	46	27	11	8	82	42	92	1
2008-09	FL C	46	16	20	10	63	50	68	8
2009-10	FL C	46	17	18	11	40	37	69	7
2010-11	FL C	46	24	8	14	69	42	80	3
2011-12	PR Lge	38	12	11	15	44	51	47	11

DID YOU KNOW ?

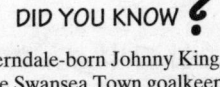

Ferndale-born Johnny King, the Swansea Town goalkeeper, made only one appearance for Wales but it was on the winning side on 22 October 1955 at Cardiff in a 2-1 win over England. It was during the Jack Kelsey era as Wales' first choice. King had won six schoolboy honours, too.

SWANSEA CITY 2011–12 LEAGUE RECORD

Match No.	*Date*	*Venue*	*Opponents*	*Result*	*H/T Score*	*Lg Pos.*	*Goalscorers*	*Attendance*
1	Aug 15	A	Manchester C	L 0-4	0-0	—		46,802
2	20	H	Wigan Ath	D 0-0	0-0	16		19,028
3	27	H	Sunderland	D 0-0	0-0	15		19,938
4	Sept 10	A	Arsenal	L 0-1	0-1	19		60,087
5	17	H	WBA	W 3-0	2-0	14	Sinclair (pen) [14], Lita [24], Dyer [49]	20,341
6	24	A	Chelsea	L 1-4	0-2	16	Williams [86]	41,800
7	Oct 2	H	Stoke C	W 2-0	1-0	10	Sinclair (pen) [9], Graham [85]	19,523
8	15	A	Norwich C	L 1-3	1-2	13	Graham [12]	26,567
9	22	A	Wolverhampton W	D 2-2	2-0	15	Graham [23], Allen [35]	25,216
10	29	H	Bolton W	W 3-1	0-0	10	Allen [49], Sinclair (pen) [57], Graham [90]	19,477
11	Nov 5	A	Liverpool	D 0-0	0-0	10		45,013
12	19	H	Manchester U	L 0-1	0-1	13		20,295
13	27	H	Aston Villa	D 0-0	0-0	13		20,404
14	Dec 3	A	Blackburn R	L 2-4	1-2	14	Lita [35], Moore [66]	23,080
15	10	H	Fulham	W 2-0	0-0	11	Sinclair [56], Graham [90]	19,296
16	17	A	Newcastle U	D 0-0	0-0	12		51,767
17	21	A	Everton	L 0-1	0-0	—		32,004
18	27	H	QPR	D 1-1	1-0	—	Graham [14]	19,530
19	31	H	Tottenham H	D 1-1	0-1	14	Sinclair [84]	20,393
20	Jan 2	A	Aston Villa	W 2-0	1-0	—	Dyer [4], Routledge [47]	35,642
21	15	H	Arsenal	W 3-2	1-1	10	Sinclair (pen) [16], Dyer [57], Graham [70]	20,409
22	21	A	Sunderland	L 0-2	0-1	13		36,904
23	31	H	Chelsea	D 1-1	1-0	—	Sinclair [39]	20,526
24	Feb 4	A	WBA	W 2-1	0-0	10	Sigurdsson [55], Graham [59]	24,274
25	11	H	Norwich C	L 2-3	1-0	11	Graham 2 (1 pen) [23, 87 (p)]	19,927
26	26	A	Stoke C	L 0-2	0-2	14		26,678
27	Mar 3	A	Wigan Ath	W 2-0	1-0	14	Sigurdsson 2 [45, 54]	19,001
28	11	H	Manchester C	W 1-0	0-0	11	Moore [83]	20,510
29	17	A	Fulham	W 3-0	1-0	—	Sigurdsson 2 [36, 66], Allen [77]	25,690
30	24	H	Everton	L 0-2	0-0	10		20,509
31	Apr 1	A	Tottenham H	L 1-3	0-1	11	Sigurdsson [59]	36,174
32	6	H	Newcastle U	L 0-2	0-1	—		19,874
33	11	A	QPR	L 0-3	0-1	—		17,557
34	14	H	Blackburn R	W 3-0	2-0	12	Sigurdsson [37], Dyer [43], Dann (og) [63]	18,985
35	21	A	Bolton W	D 1-1	1-1	12	Sinclair [6]	25,401
36	28	H	Wolverhampton W	D 4-4	4-2	12	Orlandi [1], Allen [4], Dyer [15], Graham [31]	19,408
37	May 6	A	Manchester U	L 0-2	0-2	12		75,496
38	13	H	Liverpool	W 1-0	0-0	11	Graham [86]	20,605

Final League Position: 11

GOALSCORERS

League (44): Graham 12 (1 pen), Sinclair 8 (4 pens), Sigurdsson 7, Dyer 5, Allen 4, Lita 2, Moore 2, Orlandi 1, Routledge 1, Williams 1, own goal 1.
Carling Cup (1): own goal 1.
FA Cup (5): Graham 2, Dyer 1, Moore 1, Rangel 1.

Vorm M 37	Rangel A 32 + 2	Tate A 1 + 4	Agustien K 7 + 6	Caulker S 26	Williams A 37	Britton L 35 + 1	Dobbie S 2 + 6	Dyer N 29 + 5	Graham D 32 + 4	Sinclair S 35 + 3	Routledge W 17 + 11	Allen J 31 + 5	Lita L 4 + 12	Taylor N 35 + 1	Gower M 14 + 6	Moore L 3 + 17	Monk G 14 + 2	Bessone F — + 1	Richards J 6 + 2	Orlandi A 2 + 1	Moras V — + 1	Sigurdsson G 17 + 1	McEachran J 1 + 3	Tremmel G 1	Match No.
1	2	3	4	5	6	7^{1}	8^{2}	9^{3}	10	11	12	13	14												1
1	2		4	5	6	8^{2}	12	10	9^{3}	11	7^{1}	13	14	3											2
1	2		4^{3}	5	6	8	13	9^{2}	10	11	7^{1}	14	12	3											3
1	2		4^{1}	5	6	7	13	9^{3}	10	11		8^{2}		3	12	14									4
1	2				6	4		10^{1}		11	12	8	9^{2}	3^{3}	7	13	5	14							5
1	2				6	4^{1}	14	10^{3}	13	11	12	8	9^{2}	3	7		5								6
1	2				6			9	10^{2}	11	7^{1}	4	13	3	8	12	5								7
1	2				6	8	12	10^{2}	9	11	7^{1}	4	13	3^{3}			5		14						8
1	2				6	7^{1}		10^{2}	9	11	13	4		3	8^{3}		5			12	14				9
1	2				6	7		10^{1}	9	11		4		3	8	12	5								10
1	2		13		6	7		9	10	12	11^{1}	4		3	8^{2}		5								11
1	2				6	4	13	9	10	11	7^{1}	12		3	8^{2}		5								12
1	2^{1}				6	7		9^{3}	10^{2}	11	14	4	13	3	8		5		12						13
1					6	7		10^{1}		11	12	4■	9	3	8^{2}	13	5		2						14
1			12	5	6	4		14	13	11	7^{3}		9^{2}	3	8	10^{1}			2						15
1			12	5	6	4		13	10	9^{2}	7	11		3	8^{1}				2						16
1	12		13	5	6	4^{3}			10	9	7	11	14	3^{1}	8^{2}				2						17
1	2^{2}		8	5	6	7		12	10	9	11^{1}	4				13			3						18
1	12		13		6		9	7	14	11		4		3	8^{2}	10^{3}	5		2^{1}						19
1	2		4	5	6	7		9^{2}	10	13	11	12		3						8^{1}					20
1	2		8^{1}	5	6	7		9^{2}	10^{3}	11	13	4	14	3								12			21
1	2			5	6	7^{2}		9	10	11	13	4		3								8^{1}	12		22
1	2		12	5	6	7		9	10	11^{2}		4		3		13						8^{1}			23
1	2			5	6	7		9^{1}	10	11	12	4		3								8			24
1	2			5	6	4		9^{2}	10	11^{3}	13		14	3	12							8	7^{1}		25
	2			5	6	7		9^{1}	10	11^{2}		4		3		13						8	12	1	26
1	2	12		5	6	7		9■	10^{2}	11		4		3		13						8^{1}			27
1	2			5	6	7			10^{1}	9	11^{2}	4		3		12	13					8			28
1	2	12		5		7			10^{3}	9	11	4		3^{1}	14	13	6					8^{2}			29
1	2			5	6	7			10^{2}	9^{3}	11^{1}	4	12	3		13						8	14		30
1	2				6	7		12	10^{2}	9	11^{1}	4^{3}		3	14	13	5					8			31
1	2			5	6	7		10^{1}	12	13	11	4		3		9^{2}						8			32
1	2	12		5	6	7^{3}		13	10	9	11^{2}	4		3^{1}		14						8			33
1	2^{3}			5	6	7^{1}		9	10^{2}	11		4	13	3	12		14					8			34
1	2			5	6	7		9^{1}	10^{2}	11		4	13	3		12						8			35
1				5	6	7		9	10^{2}	11		4		12		13	2			3^{1}		8			36
1	2	14		5^{3}	6	12		9^{2}	10	11		4		3	7^{1}	13						8			37
1	2			5	6	7		9^{1}	10	11	12	4		3	13							8^{2}			38

FA Cup

Third Round	Barnsley	(a)	4-2
Fourth Round	Bolton W	(a)	1-2

Carling Cup

Second Round	Shrewsbury T	(a)	1-3

SWINDON TOWN FL Championship 1

FOUNDATION

It is generally accepted that Swindon Town came into being in 1881, although there is no firm evidence that the club's founder, Rev. William Pitt, captain of the Spartans (an offshoot of a cricket club), changed his club's name to Swindon Town before 1883, when the Spartans amalgamated with St Mark's Young Men's Friendly Society.

The County Ground, County Road, Swindon, Wiltshire SN1 2ED.

Telephone: (0871) 876 1879.

Fax: (0844) 880 1112.

Ticket Office: (0871) 223 2300.

Website: www.swindontownfc.co.uk

Email: boxoffice@swindontownfc.co.uk

Ground Capacity: 14,700.

Record Attendance: 32,000 v Arsenal, FA Cup 3rd rd, 15 January 1972.

Pitch Measurements: 110yd × 75yd.

Chairman: Jeremy Wray (interim).

Chief Executive: Nicholas Watkins.

Manager: Paulo Di Canio.

Assistant Manager: Fabrizio Piccareta.

Physio: Paul Godfrey.

Colours: Red shirts with white inserts, red shorts with white inserts, red stockings with white inserts.

Year Formed: 1881* (*see Foundation*).

Turned Professional: 1894.

Club Nickname: 'Robins'.

Grounds: 1881, The Croft; 1896, County Ground.

First Football League Game: 28 August 1920, Division 3, v Luton T (h) W 9–1 – Nash; Kay, Macconachie; Langford, Hawley, Wareing; Jefferson (1), Fleming (4), Rogers, Batty (2), Davies (1), (1 og).

Record League Victory: 9–1 v Luton T, Division 3 (S), 28 August 1920 – Nash; Kay, Macconachie; Langford, Hawley, Wareing; Jefferson (1), Fleming (4), Rogers, Batty (2), Davies (1), (1 og).

Record Cup Victory: 10–1 v Farnham U Breweries (away), FA Cup 1st rd (replay), 28 November 1925 – Nash; Dickenson, Weston, Archer, Bew, Adey; Denyer (2), Wall (1), Richardson (4), Johnson (3), Davies.

HONOURS

Football League: FL 2: *Champions* 2011–12;
Division 2: *Champions* 1995–96;
Division 3: *Runners-up* 1962–63, 1968–69;
Division 4: *Champions* 1985–86 (with record 102 points).

FA Cup: Semi-finals 1910, 1912.

Football League Cup: *Winners* 1969.

Johnstone's Paint Trophy: *Runners-up* 2012.

Anglo-Italian Cup: *Winners* 1970.

sky SPORTS FACT FILE

In the years leading up to the Great War in 1914, Swindon Town featured prominently in the Southern League, winning the championship in 1911 and again in 1914. From 1907 to 1914 their lowest finishing position in the competition was fifth. Their first FA Cup venture was also 1907.

Record Defeat: 1–10 v Manchester C, FA Cup 4th rd (replay), 25 January 1930.

Most League Points (2 for a win): 64, Division 3, 1968–69.

Most League Points (3 for a win): 102, Division 4, 1985–86.

Most League Goals: 100, Division 3 (S), 1926–27.

Highest League Scorer in Season: Harry Morris, 47, Division 3 (S), 1926–27.

Most League Goals in Total Aggregate: Harry Morris, 216, 1926–33.

Most League Goals in One Match: 5, Harry Morris v QPR, Division 3 (S), 18 December 1926; 5, Harry Morris v Norwich C, Division 3 (S), 26 April 1930; 5, Keith East v Mansfield T, Division 3, 20 November 1965.

Most Capped Player: Rod Thomas, 30 (50), Wales.

Most League Appearances: John Trollope, 770, 1960–80.

Youngest League Player: Paul Rideout, 16 years 107 days v Hull C, 29 November 1980.

Record Transfer Fee Received: £1,500,000 from Manchester C for Kevin Horlock, January 1997; £1,500,000 from WBA for Simon Cox, July 2009.

Record Transfer Fee Paid: £800,000 to West Ham U for Joey Beauchamp, August 1994.

Football League Record: 1920 Original Member of Division 3; 1921–58 Division 3 (S); 1958–63 Division 3; 1963–65 Division 2; 1965–69 Division 3; 1969–74 Division 2; 1974–82 Division 3; 1982–86 Division 4; 1986–87 Division 3; 1987–92 Division 2; 1992–93 Division 1; 1993–94 FA Premier League; 1994–95 Division 1; 1995–96 Division 2; 1996–2000 Division 1; 2000–04 Division 2; 2004–06 FL 1; 2006–07 FL 2; 2007–11 FL 1; 2011–12 FL 2; 2012– FL 1.

MANAGERS

Sam Allen 1902–33
Ted Vizard 1933–39
Neil Harris 1939–41
Louis Page 1945–53
Maurice Lindley 1953–55
Bert Head 1956–65
Danny Williams 1965–69
Fred Ford 1969–71
Dave Mackay 1971–72
Les Allen 1972–74
Danny Williams 1974–78
Bobby Smith 1978–80
John Trollope 1980–83
Ken Beamish 1983–84
Lou Macari 1984–89
Ossie Ardiles 1989–91
Glenn Hoddle 1991–93
John Gorman 1993–94
Steve McMahon 1994–98
Jimmy Quinn 1998–2000
Colin Todd 2000
Andy King 2000–01
Roy Evans 2001
Andy King 2001–05
Iffy Onuora 2005–06
Dennis Wise 2006
Paul Sturrock 2006–07
Maurice Malpas 2008
Danny Wilson 2008–11
Paul Hart 2011
Paulo Di Canio May 2011–

LATEST SEQUENCES

Longest Sequence of League Wins: 10, 31.12.2011 – 28.2.2012

Longest Sequence of League Defeats: 8, 29.8.2005 – 8.10.2005.

Longest Sequence of League Draws: 6, 22.11.1991 – 28.12.1991.

Longest Sequence of Unbeaten League Matches: 22, 12.1.1986 – 23.8.86.

Longest Sequence Without a League Win: 19, 30.10.1999 – 4.3.2000.

Successive Scoring Runs: 31 from 17.4.1926.

Successive Non-scoring Runs: 5 from 16.11.1963.

TEN YEAR LEAGUE RECORD

		P	W	D	L	F	A	Pts	Pos
2002-03	Div 2	46	16	12	18	59	63	60	10
2003-04	Div 2	46	20	13	13	76	58	73	5
2004-05	FL 1	46	17	12	17	66	68	63	12
2005-06	FL 1	46	11	15	20	46	65	48	23
2006-07	FL 2	46	25	10	11	58	38	85	3
2007-08	FL 1	46	16	13	17	63	56	61	13
2008-09	FL 1	46	12	17	17	68	71	53	15
2009-10	FL 1	46	22	16	8	73	57	82	5
2010-11	FL 1	46	9	14	23	50	72	41	24
2011-12	FL 2	46	29	6	11	75	32	93	1

DID YOU KNOW ?

On 7 January 2012, Swindon Town defeated Premier League Wigan Athletic 2-1 at the County Ground in a third round FA Cup tie, the only top flight team to lose to a lower division one on the day. The winning goal came from a Matt Ritchie drive deflected off substitute Paul Benson.

SWINDON TOWN 2011–12 LEAGUE RECORD

Match No.	Date	Venue	Opponents	Result		H/T Score	Lg Pos.	Goalscorers	Attendance
1	Aug 6	H	Crewe Alex	W	3-0	1-0	—	Kennedy (pen) [45], Risser [63], Flint [77]	8249
2	13	A	Cheltenham T	L	0-1	0-0	9		4402
3	16	A	Dagenham & R	L	0-1	0-0	—		2063
4	21	H	Oxford U	L	1-2	1-2	19	Ritchie [20]	12,113
5	27	A	Shrewsbury T	L	1-2	1-0	21	Ritchie [25]	5323
6	Sept 3	H	Rotherham U	W	3-2	1-1	18	Ritchie [39], Connell 2 [69, 81]	6304
7	10	H	Southend U	W	2-0	1-0	13	Smith, J [38], Kerrouche [48]	6852
8	13	A	Crawley T	W	3-0	1-0	—	Connell [28], Kerrouche 2 [82, 85]	2790
9	17	A	Burton Alb	L	0-2	0-1	14		3320
10	24	H	Barnet	W	4-0	3-0	10	De Vita [11], Ritchie 2 [22, 65], Kerrouche [45]	7279
11	30	A	Macclesfield T	L	0-2	0-0	—		2317
12	Oct 8	H	Hereford U	D	3-3	2-0	13	De Vita [7], Kerrouche [40], Ferry [79]	7456
13	15	A	Accrington S	W	2-0	1-0	11	Jervis [39], Montano [58]	1663
14	22	A	Plymouth Arg	W	1-0	0-0	10	De Vita [82]	6872
15	25	H	Gillingham	W	2-0	0-0	—	Ritchie [80], Smith, J [90]	7787
16	29	H	Bradford C	D	0-0	0-0	7		7701
17	Nov 5	A	Port Vale	W	2-0	1-0	6	Magera [25], Kerrouche (pen) [49]	4961
18	19	A	AFC Wimbledon	D	1-1	0-1	7	Connell [73]	4581
19	26	H	Aldershot T	W	2-0	0-0	6	Jervis [52], Jones (og) [71]	7526
20	Dec 10	A	Bristol R	D	1-1	1-0	6	Caddis [37]	7726
21	17	H	Morecambe	W	3-0	2-0	5	Jervis [27], De Vita [45], Murray [76]	7116
22	26	A	Torquay U	L	0-1	0-1	7		4157
23	31	A	Northampton T	W	2-1	0-1	5	Connell [67], McCormack [90]	4462
24	Jan 2	H	AFC Wimbledon	W	2-0	0-0	4	Caddis [58], Connell [76]	8374
25	14	A	Rotherham U	W	2-1	2-0	4	Ritchie 2 [13, 20]	4236
26	21	H	Macclesfield T	W	1-0	0-0	4	Benson [76]	7639
27	31	A	Southend U	W	4-1	3-1	—	Ritchie [9], Smith, J [16], Devera [37], Bodin [55]	5958
28	Feb 14	H	Crawley T	W	3-0	1-0	—	Rooney [39], Bodin [53], Benson [68]	8311
29	18	A	Hereford U	W	2-1	1-0	3	Caddis (pen) [39], Benson [62]	3068
30	21	H	Shrewsbury T	W	2-1	0-1	—	Connell 2 [64, 76]	7990
31	25	H	Accrington S	W	2-0	2-0	1	Benson 2 [8, 29]	7962
32	28	H	Burton Alb	W	2-0	0-0	—	Murray [53], Benson [58]	7261
33	Mar 3	A	Oxford U	L	0-2	0-2	1		11,825
34	6	H	Dagenham & R	W	4-0	1-0	—	Bodin [22], Devera [59], Rooney [63], Benson [75]	6839
35	10	H	Cheltenham T	W	1-0	1-0	1	Benson [35]	10,659
36	17	A	Crewe Alex	L	0-2	0-1	1		4641
37	20	H	Torquay U	W	2-0	1-0	—	Connell [33], Risser [58]	8351
38	31	H	Bristol R	D	0-0	0-0	1		9645
39	Apr 3	A	Barnet	W	2-0	2-0	—	Murray [13], Risser [31]	2211
40	6	A	Morecambe	W	1-0	0-0	1	Benson [46]	3011
41	9	H	Northampton T	W	1-0	0-0	1	Holmes [52]	8745
42	14	H	Plymouth Arg	W	1-0	0-0	1	Connell [84]	10,422
43	17	A	Aldershot T	L	1-2	0-1	—	Caddis (pen) [53]	3562
44	21	A	Gillingham	L	1-3	0-1	1	McCormack [81]	6390
45	28	H	Port Vale	W	5-0	1-0	1	Ritchie [38], Benson 2 [51, 65], Flint [67], Connell [85]	12,864
46	May 5	A	Bradford C	D	0-0	0-0	1		11,576

Final League Position: 1

GOALSCORERS

League (75): Benson 11, Connell 11, Ritchie 10, Kerrouche 6 (1 pen), Caddis 4 (2 pens), De Vita 4, Bodin 3, Jervis 3, Murray 3, Risser 3, Smith, J 3, Devera 2, Flint 2, McCormack 2, Rooney 2, Ferry 1, Holmes 1, Kennedy 1 (1 pen), Magera 1, Montano 1, own goal 1.
Carling Cup (2): De Vita 1, Kerrouche 1.
FA Cup (7): Benson 1, Connell 1, De Vita 1, Ferry 1, Flint 1, Kerrouche 1, Ritchie 1.
J Paint Trophy (7): Jervis 2, Caddis 1, Connell 1, Flint 1, Murray 1, Risser 1.

Smith P 8	Caddis P 39	Kennedy C 18	Flint A 28 + 4	Devera J 28	Smith J 28 + 10	Ritchie M 40	Risser O 23 + 9	De Vita R 30 + 8	Bodin B 9 + 2	Timlin M 1	McCormack A 38 + 2	Connell A 13 + 19	Ferry S 36 + 8	Esajas E 2 + 4	Thompson N 2 + 3	Comazzi A 4	Kerrouche M 9 + 4	Clarke L 2	Gabilondo L 4 + 6	Smith C — + 1 / Magera L 7 + 5	Lanzano M 5 + 1	Abdullah A 1 + 5	Cibocchi A 11 + 7	Storey M — + 4	Jervis J 10 + 2	Ridehalgh L 9 + 2	Foderingham W 33	Montano C 3 + 1	Murray R 9 + 11	Benson P 20 + 2	Rooney L 13 + 7	Cox L 2 + 5	Boateng D 2	Tehoue J 1 + 2	Holmes L 7 + 3	McEveley J 8	Bostock J 3	Match No.
1	2	3	4	5	6[1]	7	8[3]	9	10[2]	11	12	13	14																									1
1	2	3	4	5		7[2]	8	9	10		11[1]	12	13	14	6[3]																							2
1	2	3	4			7	8	9[3]	10[2]		6	13		11	12	5[1]	14																					3
1	2	3	4	5	6	7		9[1]				14	8	11[3]			12[2]	10	13																			4
1	2	3	4	5	6	7		9[1]			13		8[2]	14				10[3]	11	12																		5
	2	3	4			7		9[3]			6	13	8[1]			5■	10			11[2]	1	12	14															6
	2	3		5	12	7	6[1]	9			4	11	8[2]				10[3]				1	13		14														7
	2	3		5	6	7		9[2]			4	11[1]	14				10				1	8[3]	12	13														8
	2	3		5	6	7		9[3]			4	11[1]	8[2]				10				1	13	14	12														9
1	2	3	13	5	6[3]	7		9[1]				11	8			4[2]	10			12		14																10
1[6]	2	3		5		7		9[2]			4		8			6	10[1]			11	15				12	13												11
	2			5	4[1]	7		9			6		8				10[2]			13	1	12	3[3]		11	14												12
	2		5		4[1]	7	12	9			6	13	8							14					11[3]	3	1	10[2]										13
	2		5		4[2]	7	13	9			6	14	8				12								11[3]	3	1	10[1]										14
	2		5		4	7	14	9			6[1]	13	8										12		11[3]	3	1	10[2]										15
	2		5		4	7		9[1]			6	13	8				10[2]								11	3	1	12										16
	2		4		6[2]	7	13				5	14	8				12		11[3]	9					10[1]	3	1											17
	2		4		14	7[2]	6[3]	9[1]			5	10	8	13					12						11	3	1											18
	2		5		4	7		9[2]			6		8						11[1]	14			13		10[3]	3	1		12									19
	2		5		4		14	9			6		8	13			10[1]		7[2]	11[3]			3		12		1											20
	2		5		4	7	13	9[3]			6		8[2]						14	11[1]					10	3	1		12									21
	2		5		4	7		9[2]			6	14	8						13	11[1]					10[3]	3	1		12									22
	2	3	14	5[3]	4[2]	7	8■	9			6	12	13							11[1]							1		10									23
	2	3[3]	5		4	7		9[2]			6	11	8						13				14				1		10[1]	12								24
	2	3[2]	6	5	14	7	4[3]	9	11[1]				8										13				1		12	10								25
	2		5	6	14	7	4	9[1]				11[2]	8[3]										3				1		13	10	12							26
	2	3		5	8	7	4[2]	14	12		6		13														1		10[1]	9	11[3]							27
	2			5	4	7		13	11[3]		6		8[1]										3				1		14	9	10[2]	12						28
	2				4[1]	7	12	13	11[3]		5	14											3				1			9	10[2]	8	6					29
	2				4[2]	7	14		11[1]		5	12	13										3				1			9	10	8	6[3]					30
	2	3		5		7	4	14			6	11[1]	8[2]														1		12	9	10[3]	13						31
	2			5	4[1]	7	12	14			6	11[2]	8										3				1		13	9	10[3]							32
	2			5	12[2]	7	4		14		6		8										3[1]				1		10[3]	9	11	13						33
	2[1]			5	12	7	4	9[2]	11[3]		6	14	8										3				1			10	13							34
				5	4[2]	7	6	14	11[1]		2		8										3				1			9	10[3]	13		12				35
		3[2]	6	5		7	4[3]				2		8														1		13	9	11[1]	14		10	12			36
			12	5	4	7[3]	6				2	10	8										3[1]				1			9[2]	14			13	11			37
			5	2	4	7[1]		14			6	9[2]	8														1		10[3]	13	12				11	3		38
			4	2	11[1]		6	7[3]			5	14	12		13												1		8	9	10[2]					3		39
			5	2			4	7			6	10[2]	8		14												1		13	9	11[1]				12[3]	3		40
			5	2	14		4[3]	12			6	13	8														1		10[2]	9	11[1]				7	3		41
	2		6	5	14		4[3]	7[2]				12	8														1		10[1]	9	13				11	3		42
	2	3	12	5[1]	8		4[3]	7[2]			6		14														1		10	9	11				13			43
1	2		5		13	7	4[2]				6	9[1]	8						14										12						11[3]	3	10	44
	2		5		12	7[3]	4[1]				6	13	8														1			9	14				11	3	10[2]	45
	6		5			7	4						8[2]		2[1]					12				13			1			9	14				11[3]	3	10	46

FA Cup

First Round	Huddersfield T	(h)	4-1
Second Round	Colchester U	(a)	1-0
Third Round	Wigan Ath	(h)	2-1
Fourth Round	Leicester C	(a)	0-2

Carling Cup

First Round	Bristol C	(a)	1-0
Second Round	Southampton	(h)	1-3

J Paint Trophy

Second Round	Exeter C	(a)	2-1
Southern Quarter-Final	AFC Wimbledon	(h)	1-1
Southern Semi-Final	Southend U	(a)	2-1
Southern Final	Barnet	(a)	1-1
		(h)	1-0
Final *(at Wembley).*	Chesterfield		0-2

TORQUAY UNITED FL Championship 2

FOUNDATION

The idea of establishing a Torquay club was agreed by old boys of Torquay College and Torbay College, while sitting in Princess Gardens listening to the band. A proper meeting was subsequently held at Tor Abbey Hotel at which officers were elected. This was on 1 May 1899 and the club's first competition was the Eastern League (later known as the East Devon League). As an amateur club it played at Teignmouth Road, Torquay Recreation Ground and Cricket Field Road before settling down for four years at Torquay Cricket Ground where the rugby club now plays. They became Torquay United in 1921 after merging with Babbacombe FC.

Plainmoor Ground, Torquay, Devon TQ1 3PS.

Telephone: (01803) 328 666.

Fax: (01803) 323 976.

Ticket Office: (01803) 328 666.

Website: www.torquayunited.com

Email: reception@torquayunited.com

Ground Capacity: 6,117.

Record Attendance: 21,908 v Huddersfield T, FA Cup 4th rd, 29 January 1955.

Pitch Measurements: 110yd × 74yd.

Chairman: Simon Baker.

Manager: Martin Ling.

First Team Coach: Shaun Taylor.

Physio: Damian Davey.

Colours: All yellow with blue inserts.

Year Formed: 1899.

Turned Professional: 1921.

Previous Name: 1910, Torquay Town; 1921, Torquay United.

Club Nickname: 'The Gulls'.

Grounds: 1899, Teignmouth Road; 1900, Torquay Recreation Ground; 1904, Cricket Field Road; 1906, Torquay Cricket Ground; 1910, Plainmoor Ground.

First Football League Game: 27 August 1927, Division 3 (S), v Exeter C (h) D 1–1 – Millsom; Cook, Smith; Wellock, Wragg, Connor, Mackey, Turner (1), Jones, McGovern, Thomson.

Record League Victory: 9–0 v Swindon T, Division 3 (S), 8 March 1952 – George Webber; Topping, Ralph Calland; Brown, Eric Webber, Towers; Shaw (1), Marchant (1), Tommy Northcott (2), Collins (3), Edds (2).

HONOURS

Football League – Division 3 (S): *Runners-up* 1956–57.

FA Cup: Best season: 4th rd, 1949, 1955, 1971, 1983, 1990, 2009, 2011.

Football League Cup: never past 3rd rd.

Sherpa Van Trophy: *Runners-up* 1989.

sky SPORTS FACT FILE

Free-scoring inside-left Albert Hutchinson played 320 League matches for Torquay United in the 1930s, was an ever-present in 1930–31 and 1931–32 and top scorer in 1934–35 and 1935–36. He subsequently switched to wing-half and even finished his career with them at left-back.

Record Cup Victory: 7–1 v Northampton T, FA Cup 1st rd, 14 November 1959 – Gill; Penford, Downs; Bettany, George Northcott, Rawson; Baxter, Cox, Tommy Northcott (1), Bond (3), Pym (3).

Record Defeat: 2–10 v Fulham, Division 3 (S), 7 September 1931; 2–10 v Luton T, Division 3 (S), 2 September 1933.

Most League Points (2 for a win): 60, Division 4, 1959–60.

Most League Points (3 for a win): 81, Division 3, 2003–04.

Most League Goals: 89, Division 3 (S), 1956–57.

Highest League Scorer in Season: Sammy Collins, 40, Division 3 (S), 1955–56.

Most League Goals in Total Aggregate: Sammy Collins, 204, 1948–58.

Most League Goals in One Match: 5, Robin Stubbs v Newport Co, Division 4, 19 October 1963.

Most Capped Player: Tony Bedeau, 4, Grenada.

Most League Appearances: Dennis Lewis, 443, 1947–59.

Youngest League Player: David Byng, 16 years 36 days v Walsall, 14 August 1993.

Record Transfer Fee Received: £650,000 from Crewe Alex for Rodney Jack, June 1998.

Record Transfer Fee Paid: £75,000 to Peterborough U for Leon Constantine, December 2004.

Football League Record: 1927 Elected to Division 3 (S); 1958–60 Division 4; 1960–62 Division 3; 1962–66 Division 4; 1966–72 Division 3; 1972–91 Division 4; 1991–2004 Division 3; 2004–05 FL 1; 2005–07 FL 2; 2007–09 Blue Square Pr; 2009– FL 2.

LATEST SEQUENCES

Longest Sequence of League Wins: 8, 24.1.1998 – 3.3.1998.

Longest Sequence of League Defeats: 8, 30.9.1995 – 18.11.1995.

Longest Sequence of League Draws: 8, 25.10.1969 – 13.12.1969.

Longest Sequence of Unbeaten League Matches: 15, 5.5.1990 – 3.11.1990.

Longest Sequence Without a League Win: 19, 23.9.2006 – 20.1.2007.

Successive Scoring Runs: 19 from 3.10.1953.

Successive Non-scoring Runs: 7 from 8.1.1972.

MANAGERS

Percy Mackrill 1927–29
A. H. Hoskins 1929 *(Secretary-Manager)*
Frank Womack 1929–32
Frank Brown 1932–38
Alf Steward 1938–40
Billy Butler 1945–46
Jack Butler 1946–47
John McNeil 1947–50
Bob John 1950
Alex Massie 1950–51
Eric Webber 1951–65
Frank O'Farrell 1965–68
Alan Brown 1969–71
Jack Edwards 1971–73
Malcolm Musgrove 1973–76
Frank O'Farrell 1976–77
Mike Green 1977–81
Frank O'Farrell 1981–82 *(continued as General Manager to 1983)*
Bruce Rioch 1982–84
Dave Webb 1984–85
John Sims 1985
Stuart Morgan 1985–87
Cyril Knowles 1987–89
Dave Smith 1989–91
John Impey 1991
Ivan Golac 1992
Paul Compton 1992–93
Don O'Riordan 1993–95
Eddie May 1995–96
Kevin Hodges *(Head Coach)* 1996–98
Wes Saunders 1998–2001
Roy McFarland 2001–02
Leroy Rosenior 2002–06
Ian Atkins 2006
John Cornforth 2006
Lubos Kubik 2006–07
Keith Curle 2007
Leroy Rosenior 2007
Paul Buckle 2007–11
Martin Ling June 2011–

TEN YEAR LEAGUE RECORD

		P	W	D	L	F	A	Pts	Pos
2002-03	Div 3	46	16	18	12	71	71	66	9
2003-04	Div 3	46	23	12	11	68	44	81	3
2004-05	FL 1	46	12	15	19	55	79	51	21
2005-06	FL 2	46	13	13	20	53	66	52	20
2006-07	FL 2	46	7	14	25	36	63	35	24
2007-08	B Sq Pr	46	26	8	12	83	57	86	3
2008-09	B Sq Pr	46	23	14	9	72	47	83	4
2009-10	FL 2	46	14	15	17	64	55	57	17
2010-11	FL 2	46	17	18	11	74	53	68*	7
2011-12	FL 2	46	23	12	11	63	50	81	5

** 1 point deducted.*

DID YOU KNOW ?

On 2 January 2012 Torquay United won 2-1 away to Plymouth Argyle at Home Park to complete the team's first League double over their Devonian neighbours since 1970–71, when they twice won 2-1, the victories being recorded on Boxing Day (at home) and at Easter (away).

TORQUAY UNITED 2011–12 LEAGUE RECORD

Match No.	*Date*	*Venue*	*Opponents*	*Result*	*H/T Score*	*Lg Pos.*	*Goalscorers*	*Attendance*
1	Aug 6	H	Burton Alb	D 2-2	0-0	—	Howe [59], Mansell [81]	3142
2	13	A	Bristol R	W 2-1	2-0	6	Atieno [11], Howe (pen) [15]	8427
3	16	A	Aldershot T	W 1-0	1-0	—	Mansell [36]	2236
4	20	H	Crawley T	L 1-3	0-2	10	Mansell [50]	2658
5	27	A	Dagenham & R	D 1-1	0-1	12	Howe (pen) [79]	2012
6	Sept 3	H	Macclesfield T	W 3-0	0-0	4	Saah [63], McPhee [75], O'Kane [90]	2307
7	10	A	Northampton T	D 0-0	0-0	6		4036
8	13	H	Cheltenham T	D 2-2	1-2	—	Bodin [6], Nicholson [71]	2018
9	17	H	Rotherham U	D 3-3	2-3	10	Bodin [11], Nicholson [42], Howe [47]	2330
10	24	A	Shrewsbury T	L 0-2	0-1	13		5263
11	Oct 1	H	Morecambe	D 1-1	0-0	13	Mansell [62]	2207
12	8	A	Bradford C	L 0-1	0-1	14		11,738
13	15	H	Gillingham	L 2-5	0-2	16	Robertson [47], Stevens [51]	2582
14	22	A	Southend U	L 1-4	0-0	18	Mansell [77]	5425
15	25	H	AFC Wimbledon	W 4-0	3-0	—	Stevens [32], O'Kane [43], Howe 2 [45, 56]	2353
16	29	H	Hereford U	W 2-0	2-0	13	Nicholson [40], Bodin [44]	2459
17	Nov 5	A	Crewe Alex	W 3-0	1-0	12	Howe [9], Mansell [53], Bodin [68]	3521
18	19	H	Plymouth Arg	W 3-1	0-0	10	O'Kane 2 [47, 49], Stevens [69]	3983
19	25	A	Port Vale	D 0-0	0-0	—		5168
20	Dec 9	H	Barnet	W 1-0	0-0	—	Nicholson [90]	2125
21	17	A	Accrington S	L 1-3	0-1	12	McPhee [90]	1404
22	26	H	Swindon T	W 1-0	1-0	10	Atieno [34]	4157
23	31	H	Oxford U	D 0-0	0-0	10		3043
24	Jan 2	A	Plymouth Arg	W 2-1	0-0	9	Bodin [58], Mansell [64]	12,836
25	14	A	Macclesfield T	W 2-1	0-0	8	Morris [52], Ellis [74]	1878
26	21	A	Morecambe	W 2-1	1-0	6	Ellis [17], Stevens [81]	1721
27	24	H	Dagenham & R	W 1-0	1-0	—	Mansell [40]	2280
28	28	H	Northampton T	W 1-0	0-0	5	Ellis [75]	2719
29	Feb 11	H	Shrewsbury T	W 1-0	0-0	—	Atieno [68]	2592
30	14	A	Cheltenham T	W 1-0	1-0	—	Morris [33]	3010
31	18	H	Bradford C	L 1-2	1-2	5	Stevens [12]	2560
32	25	A	Gillingham	L 0-2	0-0	6		4865
33	Mar 3	A	Crawley T	W 1-0	0-0	5	O'Kane [79]	3361
34	6	H	Aldershot T	W 1-0	1-0	—	Howe [7]	2277
35	10	H	Bristol R	D 2-2	0-1	5	Mansell 2 [72, 90]	3920
36	13	A	Rotherham U	W 1-0	1-0	—	Mansell [26]	2538
37	17	A	Burton Alb	W 4-1	2-0	2	Stevens [7], Mansell [36], Howe [82], Atieno [87]	2397
38	20	A	Swindon T	L 0-2	0-1	—		8351
39	24	H	Port Vale	W 2-1	0-1	2	Howe (pen) [71], Jarvis [74]	3136
40	30	A	Barnet	W 1-0	0-0	—	Stevens [49]	2263
41	Apr 6	H	Accrington S	W 1-0	0-0	2	Howe [73]	3934
42	9	A	Oxford U	D 2-2	1-0	2	Howe [17], Atieno [90]	7867
43	14	H	Southend U	D 0-0	0-0	3		3408
44	21	A	AFC Wimbledon	L 0-2	0-0	4		4171
45	28	H	Crewe Alex	D 1-1	0-0	4	Stevens [53]	3802
46	May 5	A	Hereford U	L 2-3	0-3	5	Jarvis [46], Atieno [63]	5143

Final League Position: 5

GOALSCORERS

League (63): Howe 12 (3 pens), Mansell 12, Stevens 8, Atieno 6, Bodin 5, O'Kane 5, Nicholson 4, Ellis 3, Jarvis 2, McPhee 2, Morris 2, Robertson 1, Saah 1.
Carling Cup (1): Mansell 1.
FA Cup (5): Howe 2, Stevens 2, Nicholson 1.
J Paint Trophy (1): Macklin 1.
Play-Offs (1): Atieno 1.

Olejnik R 46	Oastler J 45	Nicholson K 46	Mansell L 45	Robertson C 24 + 1	Saah B 35	Stevens D 38 + 3	O'Kane E 45	Howe R 36 + 3	Kee B 1 + 3	Morris I 33 + 4	Atieno T 17 + 26	Macklin L 1 + 3	McPhee C 6 + 20	Lathrope D 35 + 5	Ellis M 34 + 1	Bodin B 15 + 2	Leadbitter D — + 2	Halpin S — + 1	Rowe-Turner L — + 21	Yeoman A — + 1	MacDonald A 1 + 1	Jarvis R 3 + 11	*Match No.*
1	2	3	4	5	6	7	8	9	10^1	11^2	12	13											1
1	2	3	4	5	6	7^1	8	9	13	11	10^2		12										2
1	2	3	4	5	6	7^1	8	9^2	13	11	10		12										3
1	2^3	3	4	5	6	14	8	9	12	11^2	10		7^1	13									4
1		3	4	5	6	7^2	8	9		11	10^1		13		2	12							5
1	2	3	4	5	6	13	8			11^2	10	7^1	9^3	12	14								6
1	2	3	4	5	6		8	9^2		11	13		7^1	12		10							7
1	2	3	4	5	6		8	9		11^1	10^2		13	12		7							8
1	2	3	4	5	6		8	9			12		10^1	11		7							9
1	2	3	4	5	6		8	9■		12	14	13	11^2	7^1		10^3							10
1	2	3	4	5	6	13	8			9^2	10^1		12	11		7							11
1	2^1	3	4	5	6	11	8	9			10^3	13	14	7^2			12						12
1	2	3	4	5	6	11	8	9			10^1					7		12					13
1	7^1	3	4	2	6	11	8	9^3			12		14	13	5	10^2							14
1	2	3	4		6	11^1	8^3	9			12		13	7	5	10^2	14						15
1	2	3	4		6	11^1	8	9^2			13		12	7	5	10							16
1	2	3	4		6	11^2	8	9^1			12		13	7	5	10^3			14				17
1	2	3	4	12	6^1	11	8	9		13				7	5	10^2							18
1	2	3	4	5		11^1		9		10			13	8	6	7^2			12				19
1	2	3	4	5		11^2	8	9		12	13			10	6	7^1							20
1	2	3		5		11^2	8	9■		10^3	12		13	4	6	7^1			14				21
1	2	3	4	5		11^1	8			10	9^2		13	7	6				12				22
1	2	3	4	5		11^3	8			10^1	9^2		13	7	6	12			14				23
1	2	3	4	5		11^1	8				9		13	10	6	7^2			12				24
1	2	3	4	5		11^1	8			10	9			7	6				12				25
1	2	3	4	5		11	8	12		10	9^1			7	6								26
1	2^2	3	4	5		11	8	9^1		10	12			7	6				13				27
1	2	3	4	5		11	8	9^2		10^1	12		13	7	6								28
1	2	3	4		5	11^2	8			10	9^1		12	7	6				13				29
1	2	3	4		5	11^3	8	13		10	9		12^2	7^1	6				14				30
1	2	3	4		5	11	8	12		10	9^1		7^2		6					13			31
1	2■	3	4		5	11	8	9		10^1	12		13	7^2	6								32
1	2	3	4			11^1	8	9		10^2				7	6				13		5	12	33
1	2	3	4		5		8	9^2		10^3	12		14	7	6				13			11^1	34
1	2	3^1	4		5	11^2	8	9		10	14			7^3	6				12			13	35
1	2	3^3	4		5	11^1	8	9^2		10	13			7	6				14			12	36
1	2	3	4		5	11^2	8	9^1		10	13			7^3	6				14			12	37
1	2	3	4		5	11	8	9^3		10^2	12			7^1	6				14			13	38
1	2	3	4		5	11^2	8	9^3		10^1	13			7	6				14			12	39
1	2	3	4		5	11^3	8	9^2		12	13			7	6				14			10^1	40
1	2	3	4		5	11^2	8	9^3		10	13			7^1	6				14			12	41
1	2	3	4		5	11^2	8	9^1		10■	12			7	6							13	42
1	2	3	4		5	11^1	8	9			12			7	6				13			10^2	43
1	2	3	4		5	11^1	8	9		10^2	13			7	6							12	44
1	2	3	4		5	11^1	8	9^3		10^2	14			7	6				12			13	45
1	2	3	4		5	11^3	8	9^2		10	13			7^1	6						14	12	46

FA Cup

First Round	Chesterfield	(a)	3-1
Second Round	Sheffield U	(a)	2-3

Carling Cup

First Round	Southampton	(a)	1-4

J Paint Trophy

First Round	Cheltenham T	(a)	1-2

Play-Offs

Semi-Final	Cheltenham T	(a)	0-2
		(h)	1-2

TOTTENHAM HOTSPUR FA Premiership

FOUNDATION

The Hotspur Football Club was formed from an older cricket club in 1882. Most of the founders were old boys of St John's Presbyterian School and Tottenham Grammar School. The Casey brothers were well to the fore as the family provided the club's first goalposts (painted blue and white) and their first ball. They soon adopted the local YMCA as their meeting place, but after a couple of moves settled at the Red House, which is still their headquarters, although now known simply as 748 High Road.

White Hart Lane, Bill Nicholson Way, 748 High Road, Tottenham, London N17 0AP.

Telephone: (0844) 499 5000.

Fax: (020) 8365 5005.

Ticket Office: (0844) 844 0102.

Website: www.tottenhamhotspur.com

Email: website@tottenhamhotspur.com

Ground Capacity: 36,534.

Record Attendance: 75,038 v Sunderland, FA Cup 6th rd, 5 March 1938.

Pitch Measurements: 100m × 67m.

Executive Chairman: Daniel Levy.

Manager: Andre Villas-Boas.

First Team Coach: Luis Martins.

Head Physio: Geoff Scott.

Colours: White shirts with black and yellow trim, black shorts, white stockings.

Year Formed: 1882. ***Turned Professional:*** 1895.

Previous Name: 1882, Hotspur Football Club; 1884, Tottenham Hotspur.

Club Nickname: 'Spurs'.

Grounds: 1882, Tottenham Marshes; 1888, Northumberland Park; 1899, White Hart Lane.

HONOURS

Football League – Division 1: ***Champions*** 1950–51, 1960–61; ***Runners-up*** 1921–22, 1951–52, 1956–57, 1962–63;
Division 2: ***Champions*** 1919–20, 1949–50; ***Runners-up*** 1908–09, 1932–33.

FA Cup: ***Winners*** 1901 (as non-League club), 1921, 1961, 1962, 1967, 1981, 1982, 1991; ***Runners-up*** 1987.

Football League Cup: ***Winners*** 1971, 1973, 1999, 2008; ***Runners-up*** 1982, 2002, 2009.

European Competitions
European Cup: 1961–62.
Champions League: 2010–11.
European Cup-Winners' Cup: 1962–63 (*winners*), 1963–64, 1967–68, 1981–82, 1982–83, 1991–92.
UEFA Cup: 1971–72 (*winners*), 1972–73, 1973–74 (*runners-up*), 1983–84 (*winners*), 1984–85, 1999–2000, 2006–07, 2007–08, 2008–09. **Europa League:** 2011–12.
Intertoto Cup: 1995.

First Football League Game: 1 September 1908, Division 2, v Wolverhampton W (h) W 3–0 – Hewitson; Coquet, Burton; Morris (1), Danny Steel, Darnell; Walton, Woodward (2), Macfarlane, Bobby Steel, Middlemiss.

Record League Victory: 9–0 v Bristol R, Division 2, 22 October 1977 – Daines; Naylor, Holmes, Hoddle (1), McAllister, Perryman, Pratt, McNab, Moores (3), Lee (4), Taylor (1).

Record Cup Victory: 13–2 v Crewe Alex, FA Cup 4th rd (replay), 3 February 1960 – Brown; Hills, Henry; Blanchflower, Norman, Mackay; White, Harmer (1), Smith (4), Allen (5), Jones (3 incl. 1p).

sky SPORTS FACT FILE

Ben Ives was the pre-war chief scout for Tottenham Hotspur. Cwm Villa in Wales arranged a special trial in 1936 and from it Spurs signed four including Ronnie Burgess, a miner. In appreciation Ives bought fish and chips for all the players who had participated in the game.

Record Defeat: 0–8 v Cologne, UEFA Intertoto Cup, 22 July 1995.

Most League Points (2 for a win): 70, Division 2, 1919–20.

Most League Points (3 for a win): 77, Division 1, 1984–85.

Most League Goals: 115, Division 1, 1960–61.

Highest League Scorer in Season: Jimmy Greaves, 37, Division 1, 1962–63.

Most League Goals in Total Aggregate: Jimmy Greaves, 220, 1961–70.

Most League Goals in One Match: 5, Ted Harper v Reading, Division 2, 30 August 1930; 5, Alf Stokes v Birmingham C, Division 1, 18 September 1957; 5, Bobby Smith v Aston Villa, Division 1, 29 March 1958; 5, Jermain Defoe v Wigan Ath, FA Premier League, 22 November 2009.

Most Capped Player: Pat Jennings, 74 (119), Northern Ireland.

Most League Appearances: Steve Perryman, 655, 1969–86.

Youngest League Player: Ally Dick, 16 years 301 days v Manchester C, 20 February 1982.

Record Transfer Fee Received: £30,750,000 from Manchester U for Dimitar Berbatov, September 2008.

Record Transfer Fee Paid: £17,000,000 to Blackburn R for David Bentley, July 2008.

Football League Record: 1908 Elected to Division 2; 1909–15 Division 1; 1919–20 Division 2; 1920–28 Division 1; 1928–33 Division 2; 1933–35 Division 1; 1935–50 Division 2; 1950–77 Division 1; 1977–78 Division 2; 1978–92 Division 1; 1992– FA Premier League.

MANAGERS

Frank Brettell 1898–99
John Cameron 1899–1906
Fred Kirkham 1907–08
Peter McWilliam 1912–27
Billy Minter 1927–29
Percy Smith 1930–35
Jack Tresadern 1935–38
Peter McWilliam 1938–42
Arthur Turner 1942–46
Joe Hulme 1946–49
Arthur Rowe 1949–55
Jimmy Anderson 1955–58
Bill Nicholson 1958–74
Terry Neill 1974–76
Keith Burkinshaw 1976–84
Peter Shreeves 1984–86
David Pleat 1986–87
Terry Venables 1987–91
Peter Shreeves 1991–92
Doug Livermore 1992–93
Ossie Ardiles 1993–94
Gerry Francis 1994–97
Christian Gross *(Head Coach)* 1997–98
George Graham 1998–2001
Glenn Hoddle 2001–03
David Pleat (*Caretaker*) 2003–04
Jacques Santini 2004
Martin Jol 2004–07
Juande Ramos 2007–08
Harry Redknapp 2008–12
Andre Villas-Boas July 2012–

LATEST SEQUENCES

Longest Sequence of League Wins: 13, 23.4.1960 – 1.10.1960.

Longest Sequence of League Defeats: 7, 1.1.1994 – 27.2.1994.

Longest Sequence of League Draws: 6, 9.1.1999 – 27.2.1999.

Longest Sequence of Unbeaten League Matches: 22, 31.8.1949 – 31.12.1949.

Longest Sequence Without a League Win: 16, 29.12.1934 – 13.4.1935.

Successive Scoring Runs: 32 from 24.2.1962.

Successive Non-scoring Runs: 6 from 28.12.1985.

TEN YEAR LEAGUE RECORD

		P	*W*	*D*	*L*	*F*	*A*	*Pts*	*Pos*
2002-03	PR Lge	38	14	8	16	51	62	50	10
2003-04	PR Lge	38	13	6	19	47	57	45	14
2004-05	PR Lge	38	14	10	14	47	41	52	9
2005-06	PR Lge	38	18	11	9	53	38	65	5
2006-07	PR Lge	38	17	9	12	57	54	60	5
2007-08	PR Lge	38	11	13	14	66	61	46	11
2008-09	PR Lge	38	14	9	15	45	45	51	8
2009-10	PR Lge	38	21	7	10	67	41	70	4
2010-11	PR Lge	38	16	14	8	55	46	62	5
2011-12	PR Lge	38	20	9	9	66	41	69	4

DID YOU KNOW ?

When Tottenham Hotspur were attempting their 12th successive win from the start of 1960–61, they entertained Manchester City at White Hart Lane. Spurs were held to a 1-1 draw but the effort in going for victory was underlined by 39 shots at goal and 14 corner kicks as they laid siege.

TOTTENHAM HOTSPUR 2011–12 LEAGUE RECORD

Match No.	Date	Venue	Opponents	Result	H/T Score	Lg Pos.	Goalscorers	Attendance
1	Aug 22	A	Manchester U	L 0-3	0-0	—		75,498
2	28	H	Manchester C	L 1-5	0-2	20	Kaboul [68]	36,150
3	Sept 10	A	Wolverhampton W	W 2-0	0-0	14	Adebayor [67], Defoe [80]	25,274
4	18	H	Liverpool	W 4-0	1-0	11	Modric [7], Defoe [66], Adebayor 2 [68, 90]	36,129
5	24	A	Wigan Ath	W 2-1	2-0	6	Van der Vaart [3], Bale [23]	18,788
6	Oct 2	H	Arsenal	W 2-1	1-0	6	Van der Vaart [40], Walker [73]	36,274
7	16	A	Newcastle U	D 2-2	1-0	6	Van der Vaart (pen) [40], Defoe [68]	46,420
8	23	A	Blackburn R	W 2-1	1-1	5	Van der Vaart 2 [15, 53]	22,786
9	30	H	QPR	W 3-1	2-0	5	Bale 2 [20, 72], Van der Vaart [33]	36,147
10	Nov 6	A	Fulham	W 3-1	2-0	5	Baird (og) [10], Lennon [45], Defoe [90]	25,698
11	21	H	Aston Villa	W 2-0	2-0	—	Adebayor 2 [14, 40]	35,818
12	26	A	WBA	W 3-1	1-1	3	Adebayor 2 [25, 90], Defoe [81]	24,801
13	Dec 3	H	Bolton W	W 3-0	1-0	3	Bale [7], Lennon [50], Defoe [60]	35,896
14	11	A	Stoke C	L 1-2	0-2	3	Adebayor (pen) [62]	27,529
15	18	H	Sunderland	W 1-0	0-0	3	Pavlyuchenko [61]	36,021
16	22	H	Chelsea	D 1-1	1-1	—	Adebayor [8]	36,141
17	27	A	Norwich C	W 2-0	0-0	—	Bale 2 [55, 67]	26,807
18	31	A	Swansea C	D 1-1	1-0	3	Van der Vaart [44]	20,393
19	Jan 3	H	WBA	W 1-0	0-0	—	Defoe [63]	36,062
20	11	H	Everton	W 2-0	1-0	—	Lennon [35], Assou-Ekotto [63]	36,132
21	14	H	Wolverhampton W	D 1-1	0-1	3	Modric [51]	36,194
22	22	A	Manchester C	L 2-3	0-0	3	Defoe [60], Bale [65]	47,422
23	31	H	Wigan Ath	W 3-1	2-0	—	Bale 2 [29, 64], Modric [34]	35,801
24	Feb 6	A	Liverpool	D 0-0	0-0	—		44,461
25	11	H	Newcastle U	W 5-0	4-0	3	Assou-Ekotto [4], Saha 2 [6, 20], Kranjcar [34], Adebayor [64]	36,176
26	26	A	Arsenal	L 2-5	2-2	3	Saha [4], Adebayor (pen) [34]	60,106
27	Mar 4	H	Manchester U	L 1-3	0-1	3	Defoe [87]	36,034
28	10	A	Everton	L 0-1	0-1	3		34,992
29	21	H	Stoke C	D 1-1	0-0	—	Van der Vaart [90]	35,172
30	24	A	Chelsea	D 0-0	0-0	4		41,830
31	Apr 1	H	Swansea C	W 3-1	1-0	4	Van der Vaart [19], Adebayor 2 [73, 86]	36,174
32	7	A	Sunderland	D 0-0	0-0	3		39,335
33	9	H	Norwich C	L 1-2	1-1	—	Defoe [33]	36,126
34	21	A	QPR	L 0-1	0-1	5		18,021
35	29	H	Blackburn R	W 2-0	1-0	4	Van der Vaart [22], Walker [75]	35,798
36	May 2	A	Bolton W	W 4-1	1-0	—	Modric [37], Van der Vaart [60], Adebayor 2 [62, 69]	22,349
37	6	A	Aston Villa	D 1-1	0-1	4	Adebayor (pen) [62]	36,008
38	13	H	Fulham	W 2-0	1-0	4	Adebayor [2], Defoe [63]	36,256

Final League Position: 4

GOALSCORERS

League (66): Adebayor 17 (3 pens), Defoe 11, Van der Vaart 11 (1 pen), Bale 9, Modric 4, Lennon 3, Saha 3, Assou-Ekotto 2, Walker 2, Kaboul 1, Kranjcar 1, Pavlyuchenko 1, own goal 1.
Carling Cup (0).
FA Cup (11): Defoe 3, Bale 2, Adebayor 1 (pen), Giovani 1, Nelsen 1, Pavlyuchenko 1, Saha 1, Van der Vaart 1.
Europa League (14): Defoe 3, Pavlyuchenko 2, Bale 1, Giovani 1, Kane 1, Lennon 1, Livermore 1, Modric 1 (pen), Pienaar 1, Townsend 1, Van der Vaart 1.

Friedel B 38	Walker K 37	Assou-Ekotto B 34	Kaboul Y 33	Dawson M 6 + 1	Livermore J 7 + 17	Lennon A 19 + 4	Kranjcar N 9 + 3	Van der Vaart R 28 + 5	Defoe J 11 + 14	Bale G 36	Corluka V 1 + 2	Huddlestone T — + 2	Pavlyuchenko R — + 5	Modric L 36	Crouch P 1	King L 21	Parker S 28 + 1	Adebayor E 32 + 1	Giovani — + 7	Bassong S 1 + 4	Sandro 17 + 6	Rose D 3 + 8	Gallas W 15	Pienaar S — + 2	Lancaster C — + 1	Saha L 5 + 5	Nelsen R — + 5	Smith A — + 1	*Match No.*
1	2^{1}	3	4	5	6^{2}	7	8^{3}	9	10	11	12	13	14																1
1		3	4	5	14	7^{2}	8^{1}	9	13	11	2	12		6^{3}	10														2
1	2	3	5		12		7		10^{2}	11				4		6	8^{1}	9	13										3
1	2	3	5				7^{1}	12	10^{2}	11				4		6^{3}	8	9	13	14									4
1	2	3	5		13			10^{1}		11				4		6	8	9	12		7^{2}								5
1	2	3	5		13			7^{1}	10	11	14			4		6	8^{3}	9^{2}			12								6
1	2	3	5		7			9^{2}	13	11			14	4		6^{1}	8	10^{3}		12									7
1	2	3	5			7^{1}		9^{2}	13	11				4			8	10		6		12							8
1	2	3	5			7		10		11				4		6	8^{1}	9			12								9
1	2	3	5			7^{2}		9^{1}	12	11				4		6	8	10			13								10
1	2	3	5			7		9^{1}	12	11				4^{2}		6	8	10			13								11
1	2	3	5		12	7			9	11						6	8	10			4^{1}								12
1	2	3	5		13	7^{1}		12	10	11				4			8^{2}	9					6						13
1	2	3^{1}	5■			7^{2}		9^{3}	12	11				4			8	10	14	13			6						14
1	2	3			13	7^{1}		9^{3}					12	4		6	8	10			11^{2}	14	5						15
1	2	3						9^{1}		11			12	4		6	8	10			7		5						16
1	2	3^{1}	6		14		13	9^{2}		11				4			8^{3}	10			7	12	5						17
1	2	3	6		13			9^{1}	12	11				4			8^{2}	10			7		5						18
1	2	3	6		12^{2}		13	7	9	11				4				10		14	8^{1}		5^{3}						19
1	2	3	6	5	8	7^{1}		9		11			13	4				10^{2}						12					20
1	2	3^{2}	6	5		7^{1}		9	12	11				4			8	10				13							21
1	2	3	5		12	7^{2}		9^{1}	10	11				4		6	8							13					22
1	2^{2}	3	5		12		7	9^{1}		11				4		6	8	10^{3}			13				14				23
1	2	3		5	7		10^{2}			11				4		6	8	9^{1}				13				12			24
1	2	3		5		12	7		13	11^{1}				4		6^{3}	8	10								9^{2}	14		25
1	2	3	5	14			7^{1}	12		11				4		6^{3}	8■	10			13					9^{2}			26
1	2	3	5		11	7^{3}	13		12					4		6		10			8^{1}	14				9^{2}			27
1	2	3	5		14			13	10	11				4		6	8^{3}	9^{1}			7^{2}					12			28
1	2	3	5				7^{1}	10	12	11				4		6^{3}	8		13							9^{2}	14		29
1	2	3	5		13			9^{2}		11				4			8	10			7^{1}		6			12			30
1	2	3^{3}	5		13	12		9^{2}		11				4			8	10			7^{1}	14	6						31
1	2	3	6			12		9^{3}	14	11				4			8	10^{2}			7^{1}		5			13			32
1	2	3	5^{1}		8^{3}	7		14	10	11				4		6		13								9^{2}	12		33
1	2	3^{2}				12		9	10	11				4		6	8^{3}		14		7^{1}	13	5						34
1	2		6		14	7^{3}		9^{1}	13	11				4				10	12		8^{2}	3	5						35
1	2		6		12	7^{2}		9^{1}		11				4				10			8	3	5^{3}			13	14		36
1	2		6			7		9^{1}		11				4			12	10			8	3■	5						37
1	2^{1}		6^{3}		11	7		9^{2}	13	3				4				10			8		5				12	14	38

FA Cup

Third Round	Cheltenham T	(h)	3-0
Fourth Round	Watford	(a)	1-0
Fifth Round	Stevenage	(a)	0-0
		(h)	3-1
Quarter-Final	Bolton W	(h)	3-1
Semi-Final	Chelsea		1-5
(at Wembley).			

Carling Cup

Third Round	Stoke C	(a)	0-0

Europa League

Play-Off Round	Hearts	(a)	5-0
		(h)	0-0
Group A	PAOK Salonika	(a)	0-0
	Shamrock R	(h)	3-1
	Rubin	(h)	1-0
		(a)	0-1
	PAOK Salonika	(h)	1-2
	Shamrock R	(a)	4-0

TRANMERE ROVERS FL Championship 1

FOUNDATION

Formed in 1884 as Belmont they adopted their present title the following year and eventually joined their first league, the West Lancashire League, in 1889–90, the same year as their first success in the Wirral Challenge Cup. The club almost folded in 1899–1900 when all the players left en bloc to join a rival club, but they survived the crisis and went from strength to strength, winning the 'Combination' title in 1907–08 and the Lancashire Combination in 1913–14. They joined the Football League in 1921 from the Central League.

Prenton Park, Prenton Road West, Birkenhead, Merseyside CH42 9PY.

Telephone: (0871) 221 2001.

Fax: (0151) 609 0606.

Ticket Office: (0871) 221 2001.

Website: www.tranmererovers.co.uk

Email: info@tranmererovers.co.uk

Ground Capacity: 16,587.

Record Attendance: 24,424 v Stoke C, FA Cup 4th rd, 5 February 1972.

Pitch Measurements: 100yd × 70yd.

Chairman: Peter Johnson.

Chief Executive: Mick Horton.

Manager: Ronnie Moore.

First Team Coach: John McMahon.

Head of Youth/Centre of Excellence Manager: Shaun Garnett.

Physio: Gregg Blundell.

Colours: White shirts, white shorts, blue and white hooped stockings.

Year Formed: 1884.

Turned Professional: 1912.

Previous Name: 1884, Belmont AFC; 1885, Tranmere Rovers.

Club Nickname: 'The Rovers'.

Grounds: 1884, Steeles Field; 1887, Ravenshaws Field/Old Prenton Park; 1912, Prenton Park.

First Football League Game: 27 August 1921, Division 3 (N), v Crewe Alex (h) W 4–1 – Bradshaw; Grainger, Stuart (1); Campbell, Milnes (1), Heslop; Moreton, Groves (1), Hyam, Ford (1), Hughes.

Record League Victory: 13–4 v Oldham Ath, Division 3 (N), 26 December 1935 – Gray; Platt, Fairhurst; McLaren, Newton, Spencer; Eden, MacDonald (1), Bell (9), Woodward (2), Urmson (1).

HONOURS

Football League Division 1: Best season: 4th, 1992–93; **Division 3 (N):** ***Champions*** 1937–38; **Division 4:** ***Runners-up*** 1988–89.

FA Cup: Best season: 6th rd, 2000, 2001, 2004.

Football League Cup: ***Runners-up*** 2000.

Welsh Cup: ***Winners*** 1935; ***Runners-up*** 1934.

Leyland Daf Cup: ***Winners*** 1990; ***Runners-up*** 1991.

sky SPORTS FACT FILE

In 1975–76, Tranmere Rovers were the only team in the Football League to twice record the highest scores that season in the four divisions. They defeated Torquay United 7-1 and had a 6-0 victory over Workington. Both successes were achieved in the same month of October.

Record Cup Victory: 13–0 v Oswestry U, FA Cup 2nd prel rd, 10 October 1914 – Ashcroft; Stevenson, Bullough, Hancock, Taylor, Holden (1), Moreton (1), Cunningham (2), Smith (5), Leck (3), Gould (1).

Record Defeat: 1–9 v Tottenham H, FA Cup 3rd rd (replay), 14 January 1953.

Most League Points (2 for a win): 60, Division 4, 1964–65.

Most League Points (3 for a win): 80, Division 4, 1988–89; Division 3, 1989–90; Division 2, 2002–03.

Most League Goals: 111, Division 3 (N), 1930–31.

Highest League Scorer in Season: Bunny Bell, 35, Division 3 (N), 1933–34.

Most League Goals in Total Aggregate: Ian Muir, 142, 1985–95.

Most League Goals in One Match: 9, Bunny Bell v Oldham Ath, Division 3 (N), 26 December 1935.

Most Capped Player: John Aldridge, 30 (69), Republic of Ireland.

Most League Appearances: Harold Bell, 595, 1946–64 (incl. League record 401 consecutive appearances).

Youngest League Player: Iain Hume, 16 years 167 days v Swindon T, 15 April 2000.

Record Transfer Fee Received: £3,300,000 from Everton for Steve Simonsen, September 1998.

Record Transfer Fee Paid: £500,000 to Aston Villa for Shaun Teale, July 1995.

Football League Record: 1921 Original Member of Division 3 (N): 1938–39 Division 2; 1946–58 Division 3 (N); 1958–61 Division 3; 1961–67 Division 4; 1967–75 Division 3; 1975–76 Division 4; 1976–79 Division 3; 1979–89 Division 4; 1989–91 Division 3; 1991–92 Division 2; 1992–2001 Division 1; 2001–04 Division 2; 2004– FL 1.

MANAGERS

Bert Cooke 1912–35
Jackie Carr 1935–36
Jim Knowles 1936–39
Bill Ridding 1939–45
Ernie Blackburn 1946–55
Noel Kelly 1955–57
Peter Farrell 1957–60
Walter Galbraith 1961
Dave Russell 1961–69
Jackie Wright 1969–72
Ron Yeats 1972–75
John King 1975–80
Bryan Hamilton 1980–85
Frank Worthington 1985–87
Ronnie Moore 1987
John King 1987–96
John Aldridge 1996–2001
Dave Watson 2001–02
Ray Mathias 2002–03
Brian Little 2003–06
Ronnie Moore 2006–09
John Barnes 2009
Les Parry 2009–12
Ronnie Moore March 2012–

LATEST SEQUENCES

Longest Sequence of League Wins: 9, 9.2.1990 – 19.3.1990.

Longest Sequence of League Defeats: 8, 29.10.1938 – 17.12.1938.

Longest Sequence of League Draws: 5, 26.12.1997 – 31.1.1998.

Longest Sequence of Unbeaten League Matches: 18, 16.3.1970 – 4.9.1970.

Longest Sequence Without a League Win: 16, 8.11.1969 – 14.3.1970.

Successive Scoring Runs: 32 from 24.2.1934.

Successive Non-scoring Runs: 7 from 20.12.1997.

TEN YEAR LEAGUE RECORD

		P	*W*	*D*	*L*	*F*	*A*	*Pts*	*Pos*
2002-03	Div 2	46	23	11	12	66	57	80	7
2003-04	Div 2	46	17	16	13	59	56	67	8
2004-05	FL 1	46	22	13	11	73	55	79	3
2005-06	FL 1	46	13	15	18	50	52	54	18
2006-07	FL 1	46	18	13	15	58	53	67	9
2007-08	FL 1	46	18	11	17	52	47	65	11
2008-09	FL 1	46	21	11	14	62	49	74	7
2009-10	FL 1	46	14	9	23	45	72	51	19
2010-11	FL 1	46	15	11	20	53	60	56	17
2011-12	FL 1	46	14	14	18	49	53	56	12

DID YOU KNOW ?

On 13 August 2011, David Buchanan playing at left-back scored on his League debut for Tranmere Rovers at Leyton Orient. It was his first competitive goal in English football in a career started with Bury and later continued with Hamilton Academical where he also scored once.

TRANMERE ROVERS 2011–12 LEAGUE RECORD

Match No.	Date	Venue	Opponents	Result	H/T Score	Lg Pos.	Goalscorers	Attendance
1	Aug 6	H	Chesterfield	W 1-0	0-0	—	Weir[74]	5755
2	13	A	Leyton Orient	W 1-0	0-0	3	Buchanan[60]	3658
3	16	A	Notts Co	L 2-3	1-0	—	Welsh[10], Labadie[80]	4883
4	20	H	Sheffield U	D 1-1	0-1	7	Labadie[80]	6244
5	27	A	Brentford	W 2-0	1-0	5	Weir[28], Robinson[46]	5381
6	Sept 3	H	Yeovil T	D 0-0	0-0	5		5037
7	10	A	Huddersfield T	L 0-2	0-1	10		12,013
8	13	H	Carlisle U	L 1-2	0-2	—	Akins[51]	4219
9	17	H	Wycombe W	W 2-0	1-0	10	Showunmi[9], Taylor[60]	4297
10	24	A	Preston NE	L 1-2	0-1	11	Baxter[60]	17,281
11	Oct 1	H	Bournemouth	D 0-0	0-0	12		4179
12	8	A	Charlton Ath	D 1-1	1-0	12	McGurk[33]	15,038
13	15	H	Oldham Ath	W 1-0	1-0	11	Baxter[18]	5117
14	22	H	Walsall	W 2-1	0-0	8	Weir[59], Tiryaki[80]	4469
15	25	A	Hartlepool U	W 2-0	0-0	—	Akins 2[46, 66]	5200
16	29	A	Scunthorpe U	L 2-4	2-2	7	Tiryaki 2[4, 32]	4282
17	Nov 5	H	Colchester U	D 0-0	0-0	8		4312
18	19	H	Sheffield W	L 1-2	1-1	8	Baxter[38]	6652
19	26	A	Exeter C	L 0-3	0-1	12		4108
20	Dec 10	H	Milton Keynes D	L 0-2	0-1	15		4314
21	17	A	Stevenage	L 1-2	0-1	15	Labadie (pen)[90]	3376
22	30	H	Bury	W 2-0	1-0	—	Labadie[24], Taylor[90]	5253
23	Jan 2	A	Sheffield W	L 1-2	0-2	16	Goodison[82]	24,254
24	7	H	Brentford	D 2-2	1-2	—	Devaney[4], Dean (og)[55]	4432
25	14	A	Yeovil T	L 1-2	1-1	17	McGurk[9]	4083
26	17	H	Rochdale	D 0-0	0-0	—		4153
27	21	A	Bournemouth	L 1-2	1-2	17	Devaney[4]	5807
28	28	H	Huddersfield T	D 1-1	0-0	17	McGurk[51]	5851
29	Feb 4	A	Wycombe W	L 1-2	1-2	—	McGurk[5]	4398
30	14	A	Carlisle U	D 0-0	0-0	—		4152
31	18	H	Charlton Ath	D 1-1	1-0	17	Brunt[33]	4685
32	25	A	Oldham Ath	L 0-1	0-0	17		3866
33	Mar 3	A	Chesterfield	L 0-1	0-0	19		5861
34	6	H	Notts Co	D 1-1	0-1	—	Welsh[90]	4565
35	10	H	Leyton Orient	W 2-0	2-0	19	Robinson[35], Showunmi[45]	6824
36	13	H	Preston NE	W 2-1	1-1	—	Showunmi[15], Robinson[67]	4612
37	17	A	Sheffield U	D 1-1	0-1	16	Akins[54]	17,444
38	20	A	Rochdale	W 2-0	1-0	—	Wallace[28], Cassidy[82]	2618
39	24	H	Exeter C	W 2-0	0-0	12	Labadie[49], Cassidy[90]	4786
40	31	A	Bury	L 0-2	0-0	13		3733
41	Apr 6	H	Stevenage	W 3-0	2-0	—	Cassidy 2[2, 11], Akins[77]	8526
42	9	A	Milton Keynes D	L 0-3	0-2	13		7355
43	14	A	Walsall	W 1-0	0-0	11	Robinson[62]	3895
44	21	H	Hartlepool U	D 1-1	1-0	11	Welsh[40]	4757
45	28	A	Colchester U	L 2-4	0-1	13	Wallace[52], Cassidy[72]	4061
46	May 5	H	Scunthorpe U	D 1-1	1-0	12	McChrystal[27]	4952

Final League Position: 12

GOALSCORERS

League (49): Akins 5, Cassidy 5, Labadie 5 (1 pen), McGurk 4, Robinson 4, Baxter 3, Showunmi 3, Tiryaki 3, Weir 3, Welsh 3, Devaney 2, Taylor 2, Wallace 2, Brunt 1, Buchanan 1, Goodison 1, McChrystal 1, own goal 1.
Carling Cup (0).
FA Cup (0).
J Paint Trophy (5): Taylor 2, McGurk 1, Showunmi 1, Tiryaki 1.

Williams O 35	Kay M 4 + 2	Bakayogo Z 8 + 18	Weir R 29 + 10	Goodison I 41 + 2	McChrystal M 17 + 1	Devaney M 16 + 4	Welsh J 43 + 1	Tiryaki M 16 + 14	McGurk A 25 + 6	Robinson A 21 + 4	Akins L 36 + 8	Labadie J 9 + 18	Raven D 17	Buchanan D 41	Showunmi E 21 + 6	Taylor A 36 + 1	Power M 2 + 2	Donaldson R 1	Baxter J 14	Rachubka P 10	Holmes D 25 + 1	Elford-Alliyu L 2 + 2	Stockton C — + 1	Wallace J 18	Brunt R 11 + 4	Cassidy J 7 + 3	Coughlin A 1 + 1	Kirby J — + 1	Match No.
1	2	3	4	5	6	7[2]	8	9[1]	10	11	12	13																	1
1			4	5	6	7[2]	8		10	11[1]	13	12	2	3	9														2
1	12		4	5[1]	6	7[3]	8		10	11[2]	14	13	2■	3■	9														3
1	2	14	4	5	6	7[3]	8	12		11[2]	9[1]	13		3	10														4
1		14	4	5	6	7	8	9[1]		11[2]	10[3]	13	2	3	12														5
1		12	4	5		7[1]	8	9			13	6	2	3	10[2]	11													6
1		13	4	5			8	12	10[2]		9	14	2	3	11[1]	6	7[3]												7
1			4[1]	5			8	12	9		11	7	2	3	10	6													8
1		13	4	5			8	14	10[3]		7	12[2]	2	3	11	6		9[1]											9
1			4	5			8	12	10		11		2	3	9[1]	6			7										10
1		14	4[1]	5			8	13	10[3]		7	12	2	3	11[2]	6			9										11
1	13	12	4	5				14	10		7[2]	8	2	3	11[3]	6			9[1]										12
1			4	5			8	12	9[1]		7		2	3	11[2]	6	13		10										13
1		12	4	5			8	13	10[1]		7	14	2	3	11[2]	6			9[3]										14
1		12	4[3]	5			8	9[1]	11	13	7	14	2	3		6			10[2]										15
1		12	4	5			8	9	11[1]		7	13	2	3[2]		6			10■										16
1			4	5			8	9	11	10	7		2	3		6													17
1			4[3]	5		13	8	9[1]	12	11[2]	10	14	2	3		6			7										18
				5		13	8	12	7[1]	11	9[2]	4	2	3		6			10	1									19
	2		4[3]		5		8	13	12	11	7[1]	14		3	10[2]	6			9	1									20
	2[1]				5		8	14	10[2]	13	7	4		3	11	6			9[3]	1	12								21
		12	4[2]		5			9	11[1]		7	8		3		6	13		10	1	2								22
		11[3]	4[2]	14	5		12	9[1]	13		7	8		3		6			10	1	2								23
		3	12	13	5	11[3]	8	9	14		7	4[1]				6			10	1	2[2]								24
		3	4	5	6	12	8	9	10		7[1]					11				1	2								25
			4	5[1]	6	11	8				9[2]	12		3		10				1	2	7	13						26
			4[2]	5	6	11	8	9			12			3		13				1	2	10[1]		7					27
				5	6	11[2]	8	9	10[1]		7			3						1	2	12		4	13				28
1			12	5	6	11[1]	8	9[2]	10		7			3							2	14		4[3]	13				29
1			4	5[2]	13	7	8	12	10[3]		14			3		6					2			11	9[1]				30
1			4	5		11	8	13	10[1]		12			3		6					2			7	9[2]				31
1			4[3]	5		7	8		10	13		14		3	12	6					2			11[1]	9[2]				32
1		14	12	5		7[1]	4		10[3]	8				3	13	6					2			11	9[2]				33
1		13	4[2]	5			8			10	7[1]	14		3	12	6					2			11[3]	9				34
1		13	14	5			8			4[1]	7[3]	12		3	10[2]	6					2			11	9				35
1		12		5			4			8[1]	7			3	10	6					2			11	9				36
1		8[2]	13	5			4				7			3	10	6					2			11	9[1]	12			37
1		12		5			4			8	7			3	10[1]	6					2			11	9[2]	13			38
1		14		5			4			8[3]	7	12		3	10[2]	6					2			11[1]	9	13			39
1		12	14	5			4			11[3]	7	8[2]		3	13	6					2				9[1]	10			40
1				5			4			8	7			3	10[1]	6					2			11	12	9			41
1		3	10[2]	5			4			13	7			11	12	6					2			8		9[1]			42
1			13	5			4		12	8[2]	7			3	10[1]	6					2			11	14	9[3]			43
1■		3	12	5			4		10[1]	8	7					6					2			11		9[6]	15		44
		3	14	5	6	13	4	9	12	8[2]	7[1]										2			11[3]		10	1		45
1			12	5	6[1]	11	7	9[2]		8	13			3			4				2					10[3]		14	46

FA Cup
First Round Cheltenham T (h) 0-1

Carling Cup
First Round Doncaster R (a) 0-3

J Paint Trophy
First Round Port Vale (h) 1-1
Second Round Accrington S (a) 1-0
Northern Quarter-Final Chesterfield (a) 3-4

WALSALL FL Championship 1

FOUNDATION

Two of the leading clubs around Walsall in the 1880s were Walsall Swifts (formed 1877) and Walsall Town (formed 1879). The Swifts were winners of the Birmingham Senior Cup in 1881, while the Town reached the 4th round (5th round modern equivalent) of the FA Cup in 1883. These clubs amalgamated as Walsall Town Swifts in 1888, becoming simply Walsall in 1895.

Banks's Stadium, Bescot Crescent, Walsall WS1 4SA.

Telephone: (01922) 622 791. ***Fax:*** (01922) 613 202.

Ticket Office: (01922) 651 414/416.

Website: www.saddlers.co.uk

Email: info@walsallfc.co.uk

Ground Capacity: 11,300.

Record Attendance: 25,453 v Newcastle U, Division 2, 29 August 1961 (at Fellows Park); 11,049 v Rotherham U, Division 1, 9 May 2004 (at Bescot Stadium).

Pitch Measurements: 110yd × 73yd.

Chairman: Jeff Bonser.

Manager: Dean Smith.

Assistant Manager and Physio: Jon Whitney.

Colours: Red shirts with black trim, red shorts, red stockings with black tops.

Year Formed: 1888.

Turned Professional: 1888.

Previous Names: Walsall Swifts (founded 1877) and Walsall Town (founded 1879) amalgamated in 1888 as Walsall Town Swifts; 1895, Walsall.

Club Nickname: 'The Saddlers'.

Grounds: 1888, Fellows Park; 1990, Bescot Stadium.

First Football League Game: 3 September 1892, Division 2, v Darwen (h) L 1–2 – Hawkins; Withington, Pinches; Robinson, Whitrick, Forsyth; Marshall, Holmes, Turner, Gray (1), Pangbourn.

Record League Victory: 10–0 v Darwen, Division 2, 4 March 1899 – Tennent; Ted Peers (1), Davies; Hickinbotham, Jenkyns, Taggart; Dean (3), Vail (2), Aston (4), Martin, Griffin.

Record Cup Victory: 7–0 v Macclesfield T (a), FA Cup 2nd rd, 6 December 1997 – Walker; Evans, Marsh, Viveash (1), Ryder, Peron, Boli (2 incl. 1p) (Ricketts), Porter (2), Keates, Watson (Platt), Hodge (2 incl. 1p).

Record Defeat: 0–12 v Small Heath, 17 December 1892; 0–12 v Darwen, 26 December 1896, both Division 2.

Most League Points (2 for a win): 65, Division 4, 1959–60.

Most League Points (3 for a win): 89, FL 2, 2006–07.

Most League Goals: 102, Division 4, 1959–60.

Highest League Scorer in Season: Gilbert Alsop, 40, Division 3 (N), 1933–34 and 1934–35.

HONOURS

Football League – Division 2: ***Runners-up***, 1998–99; **FL 2:** ***Champions*** 2006–07; **Division 3:** ***Runners-up*** 1960–61, 1994–95; **Division 4:** ***Champions*** 1959–60; ***Runners-up*** 1979–80.

FA Cup: Best season: 5th rd, 1939, 1975, 1978, 1987, 2002, 2003 and last 16 1889.

Football League Cup: Semi-final 1984.

sky SPORTS FACT FILE

Walsall had a marathon four-match FA Cup tie with Brighton & Hove Albion in 1969–70. At Brighton it finished 1-1, as did the replay at Fellows Park. At Coventry there were no goals but two by Colin Taylor, in his third spell with the Saddlers, proved decisive at Fulham in a 2-1 win.

Most League Goals in Total Aggregate: Tony Richards, 184, 1954–63; Colin Taylor, 184, 1958–63, 1964–68, 1969–73.

Most League Goals in One Match: 5, Gilbert Alsop v Carlisle U, Division 3 (N), 2 February 1935; 5, Bill Evans v Mansfield T, Division 3 (N), 5 October 1935; 5, Johnny Devlin v Torquay U, Division 3 (S), 1 September 1949.

Most Capped Player: Mick Kearns, 15 (18), Republic of Ireland.

Most League Appearances: Colin Harrison, 467, 1964–82.

Youngest League Player: Geoff Morris, 16 years 218 days v Scunthorpe U, 14 September 1965.

Record Transfer Fee Received: £820,000 from Bolton W for Michael Ricketts, July 2000 (including sell-on).

Record Transfer Fee Paid: £175,000 to Birmingham C for Alan Buckley, June 1979.

Football League Record: 1892 Elected to Division 2; 1895 Failed re-election; 1896–1901 Division 2; 1901 Failed re-election; 1921 Original Member of Division 3 (N); 1927–31 Division 3 (S); 1931–36 Division 3 (N); 1936–58 Division 3 (S); 1958–60 Division 4; 1960–61 Division 3; 1961–63 Division 2; 1963–79 Division 3; 1979–80 Division 4; 1980–88 Division 3; 1988–89 Division 2; 1989–90 Division 3; 1990–92 Division 4; 1992–95 Division 3; 1995–99 Division 2; 1999–2000 Division 1; 2000–01 Division 2; 2001–04 Division 1; 2004–06 FL 1; 2006–07 FL 2; 2007– FL 1.

LATEST SEQUENCES

Longest Sequence of League Wins: 7, 10.10.1959 – 21.11.1959.

Longest Sequence of League Defeats: 15, 29.10.1988 – 4.2.1989.

Longest Sequence of League Draws: 5, 7.5.1988 – 17.9.1988.

Longest Sequence of Unbeaten League Matches: 21, 6.11.1979 – 22.3.1980.

Longest Sequence Without a League Win: 18, 15.10.1988 – 4.2.1989.

Successive Scoring Runs: 27 from 9.2.1928.

Successive Non-scoring Runs: 5 from 8.10.1927.

MANAGERS

H. Smallwood 1888–91 *(Secretary-Manager)*
A. G. Burton 1891–93
J. H. Robinson 1893–95
C. H. Ailso 1895–96 *(Secretary-Manager)*
A. E. Parsloe 1896–97 *(Secretary-Manager)*
L. Ford 1897–98 *(Secretary-Manager)*
G. Hughes 1898–99 *(Secretary-Manager)*
L. Ford 1899–1901 *(Secretary-Manager)*
J. E. Shutt 1908–13 *(Secretary-Manager)*
Haydn Price 1914–20
Joe Burchell 1920–26
David Ashworth 1926–27
Jack Torrance 1927–28
James Kerr 1928–29
Sid Scholey 1929–30
Peter O'Rourke 1930–32
Bill Slade 1932–34
Andy Wilson 1934–37
Tommy Lowes 1937–44
Harry Hibbs 1944–51
Tony McPhee 1951
Brough Fletcher 1952–53
Major Frank Buckley 1953–55
John Love 1955–57
Billy Moore 1957–64
Alf Wood 1964
Reg Shaw 1964–68
Dick Graham 1968
Ron Lewin 1968–69
Billy Moore 1969–72
John Smith 1972–73
Ronnie Allen 1973
Doug Fraser 1973–77
Dave Mackay 1977–78
Alan Ashman 1978
Frank Sibley 1979
Alan Buckley 1979–86
Neil Martin *(Joint Manager with Buckley)* 1981–82
Tommy Coakley 1986–88
John Barnwell 1989–90
Kenny Hibbitt 1990–94
Chris Nicholl 1994–97
Jan Sorensen 1997–98
Ray Graydon 1998–2002
Colin Lee 2002–04
Paul Merson 2004–06
Kevin Broadhurst 2006
Richard Money 2006–08
Jimmy Mullen 2008–09
Chris Hutchings 2009–10
Dean Smith January 2011–

TEN YEAR LEAGUE RECORD

		P	*W*	*D*	*L*	*F*	*A*	*Pts*	*Pos*
2002-03	Div 1	46	15	9	22	57	69	54	17
2003-04	Div 1	46	13	12	21	45	65	51	22
2004-05	FL 1	46	16	12	18	65	69	60	14
2005-06	FL 1	46	11	14	21	47	70	47	24
2006-07	FL 2	46	25	14	7	66	34	89	1
2007-08	FL 1	46	16	16	14	52	46	64	12
2008-09	FL 1	46	17	10	19	61	66	61	13
2009-10	FL 1	46	16	14	16	60	63	62	10
2010-11	FL 1	46	12	12	22	56	75	48	20
2011-12	FL 1	46	10	20	16	51	57	50	19

DID YOU KNOW?

Amazingly, Walsall went more than two and a half years without being involved in a drawn Football League match. Forty-four games were involved from 6 January 1894 to 7 September 1896. But before re-election in 1896 they had played Midland League football 1895–96!

WALSALL 2011–12 LEAGUE RECORD

Match No.	Date	Venue	Opponents	Result	H/T Score	Lg Pos.	Goalscorers	Attendance
1	Aug 6	H	Leyton Orient	W 1-0	1-0	—	Chambers [21]	4753
2	13	A	Hartlepool U	D 1-1	1-1	6	Macken (pen) [3]	5170
3	16	A	Sheffield U	L 2-3	0-0	—	Hurst [46], Grigg [51]	16,443
4	20	H	Yeovil T	D 1-1	1-1	14	Macken [19]	4247
5	27	A	Bournemouth	W 2-0	1-0	10	Jarvis 2 (1 pen) [15 (p), 55]	5092
6	Sept 3	H	Brentford	L 0-1	0-1	14		3972
7	10	A	Notts Co	L 1-2	0-1	14	Butler [61]	6218
8	13	H	Oldham Ath	L 0-1	0-1	—		3250
9	17	H	Scunthorpe U	D 2-2	1-0	16	Chambers [22], Grigg [83]	3619
10	24	A	Colchester U	L 0-1	0-1	17		3103
11	Oct 1	H	Carlisle U	D 1-1	1-0	19	Grigg [33]	3831
12	8	A	Wycombe W	D 1-1	0-0	18	Nicholls [81]	7097
13	15	H	Preston NE	W 1-0	1-0	15	Nicholls [10]	4834
14	22	A	Tranmere R	L 1-2	0-0	17	Butler [73]	4469
15	25	H	Exeter C	L 1-2	1-1	—	Nicholls [12]	4003
16	29	H	Milton Keynes D	L 0-2	0-2	20		3712
17	Nov 5	A	Huddersfield T	D 1-1	0-0	20	Paterson [78]	13,005
18	19	H	Bury	L 2-4	1-1	21	Macken (pen) [28], Bowerman [90]	4785
19	26	A	Stevenage	D 0-0	0-0	23		3140
20	Dec 10	H	Charlton Ath	D 1-1	1-1	21	Macken [36]	4537
21	17	A	Chesterfield	D 1-1	1-0	21	Nicholls [29]	6236
22	26	H	Sheffield W	W 2-1	0-0	18	Gnakpa [89], Smith [90]	8603
23	31	H	Rochdale	D 0-0	0-0	18		3907
24	Jan 2	A	Bury	L 1-2	1-2	19	Paterson [39]	3095
25	7	H	Bournemouth	D 2-2	2-0	—	Macken [15], Butler [44]	3658
26	14	A	Brentford	D 0-0	0-0	20		4867
27	21	A	Carlisle U	D 1-1	0-1	20	Nicholls (pen) [82]	5051
28	31	H	Notts Co	L 0-1	0-1	—		3647
29	Feb 14	A	Oldham Ath	L 1-2	0-2	—	Cuvelier [74]	2583
30	18	H	Wycombe W	W 2-0	0-0	21	Hurst [62], Bowerman [85]	3491
31	21	A	Scunthorpe U	W 1-0	1-0	—	Cuvelier [34]	3455
32	25	A	Preston NE	D 0-0	0-0	20		11,091
33	Mar 3	A	Leyton Orient	D 1-1	0-1	21	Lancashire [90]	4183
34	6	H	Sheffield U	W 3-2	0-0	—	Mantom [55], Macken [73], Nicholls [81]	5003
35	10	H	Hartlepool U	D 0-0	0-0	20		3751
36	17	A	Yeovil T	L 1-2	1-0	20	Mantom [44]	3705
37	20	A	Sheffield W	D 2-2	0-0	—	Macken [58], Paterson [73]	18,869
38	24	H	Stevenage	D 1-1	1-0	21	Butler [3]	4786
39	27	H	Colchester U	W 3-1	2-1	—	Ledesma [38], Sadler [44], Bowerman [73]	3331
40	31	A	Rochdale	D 3-3	2-0	20	Ledesma [25], Widdowson (og) [38], Butler [90]	2516
41	Apr 7	H	Chesterfield	W 3-2	2-1	18	Ledesma 2 [27, 33], Mantom [58]	4051
42	9	A	Charlton Ath	L 0-1	0-1	19		15,253
43	14	H	Tranmere R	L 0-1	0-0	19		3895
44	21	A	Exeter C	L 2-4	1-0	20	Nicholls [30], Cuvelier [55]	4307
45	28	H	Huddersfield T	D 1-1	0-1	19	Cuvelier [49]	4646
46	May 5	A	Milton Keynes D	W 1-0	1-0	19	Grigg [18]	10,607

Final League Position: 19

GOALSCORERS

League (51): Macken 7 (2 pens), Nicholls 7 (1 pen), Butler 5, Cuvelier 4, Grigg 4, Ledesma 4, Bowerman 3, Mantom 3, Paterson 3, Chambers 2, Hurst 2, Jarvis 2 (1 pen), Gnakpa 1, Lancashire 1, Sadler 1, Smith 1, own goal 1.
Carling Cup (0).
FA Cup (5): Bowerman 1, Gnakpa 1, Macken 1, Nicholls 1, Wilson 1.
J Paint Trophy (3): Hurst 1, Jarvis 1, Taundry 1.

Walker J 24	Westlake D 14 + 3	Sadler M 46	Butler A 42	Lancashire O 17 + 3	Taundry R 31 + 4	Gnakpa C 8 + 12	Chambers A 26 + 3	Grigg W 17 + 12	Macken J 33 + 4	Hurst K 30 + 4	Jarvis R 9 + 10	Nicholls A 32 + 13	Smith M 31 + 2	Peterlin A 20 + 6	Beevers L 28 + 7	Grof D 22 + 1	Martin D 4	Paterson J 24 + 10	Bowerman G 3 + 19	Wilson M 4	Halliday A 2 + 5	Cuvelier F 17 + 1	Mantom S 13	Ledesma E 9 + 1	Match No.
1	2	3	4	5	6	7	8	9^{1}	10^{3}	11^{2}	12	13	14												1
1	2	3	4■	5	6	7^{2}		9	10^{1}	11	13	12		8^{3}	14										2
1	2	3	4	5	6	7^{1}		9	10	11^{2}	13	12		8											3
1	2	3	4	5	6	7		9	10^{2}	11^{1}	13	12		8											4
	2	3	4		6	7^{1}	8	9		11	10^{2}	12	5		13	1									5
	2	3	4		6	12	8		10^{1}	11	9	7	5			1									6
	2^{3}	3	4		6	7^{1}	8	13	10	11	9^{2}	12	5		14	1									7
		3	4		6		8	9^{2}		11^{1}	10	13	5	14	2	1	7^{3}	12							8
1		3	4	5	6		8	12		14	7^{2}	13		11^{1}	2		9^{3}	10							9
1	13	3	4■	12	6		8	9^{2}	10^{3}	11	14		5		2			7^{1}							10
1		3		5	4		8	9		11^{1}	10^{3}	12	6	13	2^{2}			7	14						11
1	2	3	5			12	4	9^{3}		11^{1}	10^{2}	13	6	8			7	14							12
1	2	3	5		12	13	4	9^{1}		11^{2}		10	6	8			7■								13
1	2	3	5		12	14	4^{1}	9^{2}	13	11^{3}		10	6	8				7							14
1	2	3	5		4	12		13	10^{2}	11		9	6	8				7^{1}							15
1■		3	5		4	13			10^{1}	11^{2}		9	6	8	2			12		7					16
		3	5		4	11^{3}		13	10^{2}		14	9	6	8^{1}	2	1		12		7					17
		3		5		11^{1}	4	13	10^{2}		12	9^{3}	6		2	1		8	14	7					18
1		3		5	8		7	9^{1}	10^{3}		14	11	6		4				12	2^{2}	13				19
1		3■		5	4	12	8		10^{3}			9	6	14	2			11^{2}	13		7^{1}				20
1	2^{3}	3	5		4		7	12	10^{1}			11		8	6			9^{2}	14		13				21
1		3	5		4^{1}	13	7		10^{3}			11	6	8	2			9^{2}	12		14				22
1		3	5		4^{2}	13	7		10^{1}			11	6	8	2			9^{3}	12		14				23
1	2	3	5		12	13	7			14	6^{1}	9		11^{2}	4			10			8^{3}				24
1		3	5		4	13	7		10^{2}			11	6	8	2			9^{1}			12				25
1		3	5		4	12	7^{1}		10^{2}		13	11	6	8	2			9							26
1		3	5		4		7		10^{1}	14	13	9	6	8^{2}	2			11^{3}	12						27
1^{6}		3	5		4		7		10^{1}			9	6	8^{2}	2	15		11	12			13			28
		3	5	12	4^{2}		7	13			9^{3}	10	6^{1}		2	1		11	14			8			29
		3	6	5	2		7	9^{2}	13	11		10^{1}		14		1		8^{3}	12			4			30
		3	6	5	2		7	9^{2}	12	11		10^{1}		14	13	1		8				4^{3}			31
		3	6	5	2			9^{3}	10^{2}	11^{1}		14		8	13	1		7	12			4			32
		3	6	5	2			9^{1}	10	11^{3}		12		8^{2}	14	1		7	13			4			33
		3	6	5	2^{1}			14	10	11		13			12	1		7^{2}	9^{3}			4	8		34
		3	6	5^{1}			14	13	10^{3}	7		11	12		2	1			9^{2}			4	8		35
		3	6	5					10^{3}	11^{1}		7		13	2	1		12	14			4	8	9^{2}	36
	12	3	5						10^{1}	11		7	6		2	1		9^{2}	13			4	8		37
		3	5						10^{2}	11		9	6		2	1		7^{1}	13			4	8	12	38
		3	5						10^{1}	11		9	6		2	1		13	12			4	8	7^{2}	39
	2^{3}	3	5		13			12		11		10	6			1		14	9^{1}			4	8	7^{2}	40
		3	5				13		10^{1}	11^{2}		9	6		2	1		12				4	8	7	41
		3	5				14		10^{2}	11^{1}		9^{3}	6		2	1		12	13			4	8	7	42
		3	5						10	11^{1}		9^{2}	6		2■	1		12	13			4	8	7	43
	13	3	5	12	2^{3}			14	10^{2}	11^{1}		9	6■			1						4	8	7	44
1		3	6	5	7			12	10^{1}			9			2							4	8	11	45
1		3	5				4	9^{1}	12	13		7	6		2			10^{2}					8	11	46

FA Cup

First Round	Exeter C	(a)	1-1
		(h)	3-2
Second Round	Dagenham & R	(a)	1-1
		(h)	0-0

Carling Cup

First Round	Middlesbrough	(h)	0-3

J Paint Trophy

First Round	Shrewsbury T	(h)	2-1
Second Round	Rochdale	(a)	1-1

WATFORD FL Championship

FOUNDATION

The club was formed as Watford Rovers in 1881. The name was changed to West Herts in 1893 and then the name Watford was adopted after rival club Watford St Mary's was absorbed in 1898.

Vicarage Road Stadium, Vicarage Road, Watford, Herts WD18 0ER.

Telephone: (0844) 856 1881.

Fax: (01923) 496 001.

Ticket Office: (0844) 856 1881.

Website: www.watfordfc.com

Email: yourvoice@watfordfc.com

Ground Capacity: 19,920.

Record Attendance: 34,099 v Manchester U, FA Cup 4th rd (replay), 3 February 1969.

Pitch Measurements: 114 yd × 73yd.

Chairman: Raffaele Riva.

Manager: Gianfranco Zola.

Assistant Manager: Ian Woan.

First Team Coach: Tony Loughlan.

Head of Medicine: Dave Hart.

Colours: Yellow shirts with red and black trim, black shorts, yellow stockings.

Year Formed: 1881.

Turned Professional: 1897.

Previous Names: 1881, Watford Rovers; 1893, West Herts; 1898, Watford.

Club Nickname: 'The Hornets'.

Grounds: 1883, Vicarage Meadow, Rose and Crown Meadow; 1889, Colney Butts; 1890, Cassio Road; 1922, Vicarage Road.

First Football League Game: 28 August 1920, Division 3, v QPR (a) W 2–1 Williams; Horseman, Fred Gregory; Bacon, Toone, Wilkinson; Bassett, Ronald (1), Hoddinott, White (1), Waterall.

Record League Victory: 8–0 v Sunderland, Division 1, 25 September 1982 – Sherwood; Rice, Rostron, Taylor, Terry, Bolton, Callaghan (2), Blissett (4), Jenkins (2), Jackett, Barnes.

Record Cup Victory: 10–1 v Lowestoft T, FA Cup 1st rd, 27 November 1926 – Yates; Prior, Fletcher (1); Frank Smith, Bert Smith, Strain; Stephenson, Warner (3), Edmonds (3), Swan (1), Daniels (1), (1 og).

Record Defeat: 0–10 v Wolverhampton W, FA Cup 1st rd (replay), 24 January 1912.

HONOURS

Football League – Division 1: ***Runners-up*** 1982–83;
Division 2: ***Champions*** 1997–98;
Runners-up 1981–82;
Division 3: ***Champions*** 1968–69;
Runners-up 1978–79;
Division 4: ***Champions*** 1977–78.

FA Cup: ***Runners-up*** 1984, semi-finals 1970, 1984, 1987, 2003, 2007.

Football League Cup: Semi-final 1979, 2005.

European Competitions
UEFA Cup: 1983–84.

sky SPORTS FACT FILE

In 1931–32, Watford reached the sixth round of the FA Cup for the first time. They needed two cracks at Thames, one against Gainsborough Trinity, a replay, too, against Fulham, then accounted for Bristol City and Bradford Park Avenue before the run ended against Newcastle United.

Most League Points (2 for a win): 71, Division 4, 1977–78.

Most League Points (3 for a win): 88, Division 2, 1997–98.

Most League Goals: 92, Division 4, 1959–60.

Highest League Scorer in Season: Cliff Holton, 42, Division 4, 1959–60.

Most League Goals in Total Aggregate: Luther Blissett, 148, 1976–83, 1984–88, 1991–92.

Most League Goals in One Match: 5, Eddie Mummery v Newport Co, Division 3 (S), 5 January 1924.

Most Capped Players: John Barnes, 31 (79), England; Kenny Jackett, 31, Wales.

Most League Appearances: Luther Blissett, 415, 1976–83, 1984–88, 1991–92.

Youngest League Player: Keith Mercer, 16 years 125 days v Tranmere R, 16 February 1973.

Record Transfer Fee Received: £9,600,000 from Aston V for Ashley Young, January 2007.

Record Transfer Fee Paid: £3,250,000 to WBA for Nathan Ellington, August 2007.

Football League Record: 1920 Original Member of Division 3; 1921–58 Division 3 (S); 1958–60 Division 4; 1960–69 Division 3; 1969–72 Division 2; 1972–75 Division 3; 1975–78 Division 4; 1978–79 Division 3; 1979–82 Division 2; 1982–88 Division 1; 1988–92 Division 2; 1992–96 Division 1; 1996–98 Division 2; 1998–99 Division 1; 1999–2000 FA Premier League; 2000–04 Division 1; 2004–06 FL C; 2006–07 FA Premier League; 2007– FL C.

MANAGERS

John Goodall 1903–10
Harry Kent 1910–26
Fred Pagnam 1926–29
Neil McBain 1929–37
Bill Findlay 1938–47
Jack Bray 1947–48
Eddie Hapgood 1948–50
Ron Gray 1950–51
Haydn Green 1951–52
Len Goulden 1952–55
(General Manager to 1956)
Johnny Paton 1955–56
Neil McBain 1956–59
Ron Burgess 1959–63
Bill McGarry 1963–64
Ken Furphy 1964–71
George Kirby 1971–73
Mike Keen 1973–77
Graham Taylor 1977–87
Dave Bassett 1987–88
Steve Harrison 1988–90
Colin Lee 1990
Steve Perryman 1990–93
Glenn Roeder 1993–96
Kenny Jackett 1996–97
Graham Taylor 1997–2001
Gianluca Vialli 2001–02
Ray Lewington 2002–05
Adrian Boothroyd 2005–08
Brendan Rodgers 2008–09
Malky Mackay 2009–11
Sean Dyche 2011–12
Gianfranco Zola July 2012–

LATEST SEQUENCES

Longest Sequence of League Wins: 7, 28.8.2000 – 14.10.2000.

Longest Sequence of League Defeats: 9, 26.12.1972 – 27.2.1973.

Longest Sequence of League Draws: 7, 30.11.1996 – 27.1.1997.

Longest Sequence of Unbeaten League Matches: 22, 1.10.1996 – 1.3.1997.

Longest Sequence Without a League Win: 19, 27.11.1971 – 8.4.1972.

Successive Scoring Runs: 22 from 20.8.1985.

Successive Non-scoring Runs: 7 from 18.12.1971.

TEN YEAR LEAGUE RECORD

		P	W	D	L	F	A	Pts	Pos
2002-03	Div 1	46	17	9	20	54	70	60	13
2003-04	Div 1	46	15	12	19	54	68	57	16
2004-05	FL C	46	12	16	18	52	59	52	18
2005-06	FL C	46	22	15	9	77	53	81	3
2006-07	PR Lge	38	5	13	20	29	59	28	20
2007-08	FL C	46	18	16	12	62	56	70	6
2008-09	FL C	46	16	10	20	68	72	58	13
2009-10	FL C	46	14	12	20	61	68	54	16
2010-11	FL C	46	16	13	17	77	71	61	14
2011-12	FL C	46	16	16	14	56	64	64	11

DID YOU KNOW ?

Birmingham-born centre-forward Charlie Hare was signed by Watford from his local club Small Heath (Birmingham) in 1898. Previously with Woolwich Arsenal and Aston Villa, he produced a high rate of scoring for Watford with 35 goals in 55 League and Cup games.

WATFORD 2011–12 LEAGUE RECORD

Match No.	*Date*	*Venue*	*Opponents*	*Result*		*H/T Score*	*Lg Pos.*	*Goalscorers*	*Attendance*
1	Aug 6	A	Burnley	D	2-2	1-0	—	Forsyth [45], Yeates [70]	14,617
2	13	H	Derby Co	L	0-1	0-0	17		12,263
3	16	H	West Ham U	L	0-4	0-2	—		14,747
4	20	A	Coventry C	D	0-0	0-0	22		13,043
5	28	H	Birmingham C	D	2-2	0-1	22	Sordell [80], Taylor [90]	11,937
6	Sept 10	A	Reading	W	2-0	1-0	17	Yeates [12], Eustace [51]	17,128
7	17	A	Barnsley	D	1-1	1-0	17	Sordell [37]	9733
8	24	H	Nottingham F	L	0-1	0-0	19		11,437
9	27	H	Millwall	W	2-1	0-0	—	Dickinson [78], Forsyth [85]	10,592
10	Oct 1	A	Southampton	L	0-4	0-1	18		23,574
11	15	H	Crystal Palace	L	0-2	0-0	20		12,559
12	19	A	Leicester C	L	0-2	0-2	—		20,304
13	22	A	Hull C	L	2-3	1-0	22	Chester (og) [36], Iwelumo [56]	18,324
14	29	H	Peterborough U	W	3-2	3-2	21	Yeates [5], Sordell 2 (1 pen) [31 (p), 33]	15,031
15	Nov 1	H	Brighton & HA	W	1-0	0-0	—	Deeney [77]	11,818
16	5	A	Middlesbrough	L	0-1	0-1	21		14,366
17	19	H	Portsmouth	W	2-0	2-0	19	Kightly [2], Sordell [45]	12,864
18	26	A	Doncaster R	D	0-0	0-0	19		8389
19	29	H	Bristol C	D	2-2	2-1	—	Dickinson [25], Beattie [42]	12,418
20	Dec 3	A	Ipswich T	W	2-1	0-1	18	Sordell (pen) [70], Deeney [74]	16,262
21	10	H	Leeds U	D	1-1	1-0	18	Kightly [28]	13,573
22	17	A	Blackpool	D	0-0	0-0	18		11,652
23	26	H	Cardiff C	D	1-1	0-0	18	Buaben [62]	14,604
24	31	H	Doncaster R	W	4-1	1-0	17	Sordell 2 [44, 68], Eustace [84], Kightly [90]	11,654
25	Jan 2	A	Portsmouth	L	0-2	0-0	18		14,362
26	14	H	Reading	L	1-2	1-1	18	Cummings (og) [29]	11,291
27	21	A	Birmingham C	L	0-3	0-1	18		18,681
28	31	A	Millwall	W	2-0	1-0	—	Deeney [35], Garner [59]	9294
29	Feb 4	H	Barnsley	W	2-1	1-0	16	Eustace 2 [33, 68]	11,306
30	11	A	Nottingham F	D	1-1	1-1	16	Deeney [44]	12,712
31	14	H	Leicester C	W	3-2	2-2	—	Mariappa [5], Murray [33], Forsyth [80]	11,800
32	18	A	Crystal Palace	L	0-4	0-2	17		13,324
33	25	H	Southampton	L	0-3	0-2	17		13,424
34	Mar 3	H	Burnley	W	3-2	0-1	17	Nosworthy [54], Kacaniklic [72], Deeney [75]	11,612
35	7	A	West Ham U	D	1-1	0-0	—	Murray [68]	31,674
36	10	A	Derby Co	W	2-1	2-1	14	Murray [8], Deeney [15]	23,130
37	17	H	Coventry C	D	0-0	0-0	16		12,563
38	20	A	Bristol C	W	2-0	2-0	—	James (og) [15], Murray [20]	12,017
39	24	H	Ipswich T	W	2-1	0-1	13	Murray [71], Deeney [82]	12,757
40	31	A	Leeds U	W	2-0	1-0	11	Iwelumo 2 [5, 89]	21,766
41	Apr 6	H	Blackpool	L	0-2	0-1	—		16,314
42	9	A	Cardiff C	D	1-1	0-1	13	Nosworthy [82]	21,259
43	14	H	Hull C	D	1-1	1-1	14	Deeney [12]	11,596
44	17	A	Brighton & HA	D	2-2	2-0	—	Murray [6], Deeney (pen) [44]	19,189
45	21	A	Peterborough U	D	2-2	1-1	14	Deeney [26], Murray [48]	8725
46	28	H	Middlesbrough	W	2-1	0-0	11	Iwelumo [69], Deeney [88]	14,022

Final League Position: 11

GOALSCORERS

League (56): Deeney 11 (1 pen), Sordell 8 (2 pens), Murray 7, Eustace 4, Iwelumo 4, Forsyth 3, Kightly 3, Yeates 3, Dickinson 2, Nosworthy 2, Beattie 1, Buaben 1, Garner 1, Kacaniklic 1, Mariappa 1, Taylor 1, own goals 3.
Carling Cup (1): Sordell 1.
FA Cup (4): Forsyth 2, Deeney 1, Sordell 1.

Loach S 31	Doyley L 33	Dickinson C 38 + 1	Eustace J 34 + 5	Taylor M 20 + 2	Mariappa A 37 + 2	Yeates M 28 + 5	Jenkins R 4 + 5	Sordell M 25 + 1	Iwelumo C 21 + 18	Forsyth C 15 + 5	Deeney T 28 + 15	Massey G — + 3	Whichelow M — + 2	Walker J — + 1	Hogg J 40	Weimann A 3	Garner J 14 + 8	Murray S 17 + 1	Gilmartin R 2	Mirfin D 3 + 1	Kightly M 11 + 1	Buaben P 21 + 9	Hodson L 20	Nosworthy N 32	Beattie C 1 + 3	Bond J — + 1	Kacaniklic A 11 + 1	Kuszczak T 13	Trotta M 1	Bennett D 1 + 1	Assombalonga B 2 + 2	*Match No.*
1	2	3	4	5	6	7	8	9	10^{1}	11	12																					1
1	2	3	4	5	6	7	8	9	10^{1}	11^{2}	12	13																				2
1	2	3	4	5	6	7^{2}	8	9	10^{1}	11	13	12																				3
1	2	3	4	5	6	7^{1}	8	9		11	10^{2}		12	13																		4
1	2	3	4	5	6	7^{1}		9		11	12				8	10																5
1	2	3	4	5	6	7^{2}		9^{1}	14	11	13				8	10^{3}	12															6
1	2	3	4	5	6	7^{1}		9^{2}	13	11	12				8	10^{3}	14															7
1	2	3	4	5	6	7^{3}		9	13	11^{1}	12				8		10^{2}	14														8
	2	3	4	5	6	7^{1}		9^{2}	13	11	12				8		10		1													9
	2		4	5	6	7^{2}	12	9^{3}	14	11	13				8^{1}		10		1	3												10
1	2	3	4	5^{1}	6	13		9^{3}	14	11^{2}					8		10			12	7											11
1	2	3	4		6	13		14	9^{2}		11^{3}				8		10			5	7^{1}	12										12
1	2	3	4		6	7		9^{2}	10	12	11^{1}				8		13			5												13
1		3			6	7^{1}	13	9	10^{2}	11	12				8							4	2	5								14
1		3			6	7^{1}		9	10	11^{2}	13				8						12	4	2	5								15
1		3			6	7	13	9	10^{1}	14	11				8							4^{2}	2^{3}	5	12							16
1		3			6	7		9	10		12				8						11^{1}	4	2	5								17
1		3	4		6	7		9^{1}	10^{2}		13										11	8	2	5	12							18
1		3			6	7			10		12				8						11	4	2	5	9^{1}							19
1		3	12		6	7		9	10^{2}		13				8						11^{3}	4^{1}	2	5	14							20
1		3	12		6	7		9			10				8						11^{1}	4	2	5								21
1	3		12		6	7^{1}		9			10				8						11	4	2	5								22
1		3			6	7		9			10				8						11	4	2	5								23
1		3	12		6	7		9^{3}	13		10^{2}				8		14				11	4^{1}	2	5								24
1■		3	13		6	7^{2}		9	12		10^{1}				8						11	4^{6}	2	5		15						25
1		3	4		6	7^{2}	12	9	13	8^{1}	10											11	2	5								26
1		3	4		6	7	13	9	12		10				8^{2}							11^{1}	2	5								27
1	3		4		6				12		9				11		10^{2}	8				13	2	5			7^{1}					28
1	3		4		6						9				11		10	8				12	2	5			7^{1}					29
1	3		4		6	12			13		9				8		10	7^{2}					2	5			11^{1}					30
1	3■	14	4		6				10	12					8		9^{2}	7^{1}				13	2	5			11^{3}					31
1	3		4		6	13			10	11^{2}		12			8		9^{1}						2	5			7					32
	2	3	4		6	7^{3}			13		9				8		12					14		5			11^{2}	1	10^{1}			33
	3		4		6						10				11		9	7^{2}				8^{1}	2	5			12	1		13		34
	2	3	4	12	6				10		9				8			7^{2}				13					11	1		5^{1}		35
	2	3	4	14	6				12		9^{3}				8		10^{1}	7^{2}				13		5			11	1				36
	2	3	4		6	13			12		9				8			7						5			11^{2}	1			10^{1}	37
	2	3		5					10^{1}		9				8		12	7				4		6			11	1				38
	2	3	4	6					13		9				8^{1}		10^{2}	7				12		5			11	1				39
	2	3	4	5		7^{1}			10	12	9				8			11						6				1				40
	2	3	4	6		7^{1}			10		9				11			8^{2}				13		5				1			12	41
	2	3	4	6					13		9				11		12	8				10^{2}		5				1			7^{1}	42
	2	3	4	6^{1}	12■				13		9				11		10^{2}	8				7		5				1				43
	2	3	4	6					10^{1}		9				11		12	8				7^{2}		5				1			13	44
	2	3	4	6					10^{1}		9		12		11			8				7		5				1				45
1	2	3	4	6	13				10^{2}	12	9				11^{1}			8				7		5								46

FA Cup

Third Round	Bradford C	(h)	4-2
Fourth Round	Tottenham H	(h)	0-1

Carling Cup

First Round	Bristol R	(a)	1-1

WEST BROMWICH ALBION FA Premiership

FOUNDATION

There is a well known story that when employees of Salter's Spring Works in West Bromwich decided to form a football club, they had to send someone to the nearby Association Football stronghold of Wednesbury to purchase a football. A weekly subscription of 2d (less than 1p) was imposed and the name of the new club was West Bromwich Strollers.

The Hawthorns, West Bromwich, West Midlands B71 4LF.

Telephone: (0871) 271 1100.

Fax: (0871) 271 9861.

Ticket Office: (0871) 271 9780.

Website: www.wbafc.co.uk

Email: enquiries@wbafc.co.uk

Ground Capacity: 28,003.

Record Attendance: 64,815 v Arsenal, FA Cup 6th rd, 6 March 1937.

Pitch Measurements: 115yd × 74yd.

Chairman: Jeremy Peace.

Legal Director: Richard Garlick.

Head Coach: Steve Clarke.

Assistant Head Coach: Keith Downing.

Physio: Richie Rawlins.

Colours: Navy blue and white striped shirts, white shorts, white stockings.

Year Formed: 1878.

Turned Professional: 1885.

Previous Name: 1878, West Bromwich Strollers; 1881, West Bromwich Albion.

Club Nicknames: 'Throstles', 'Baggies', 'Albion'.

Grounds: 1878, Coopers Hill; 1879, Dartmouth Park; 1881, Bunns Field, Walsall Street; 1882, Four Acres (Dartmouth Cricket Club); 1885, Stoney Lane; 1900, The Hawthorns.

First Football League Game: 8 September 1888, Football League, v Stoke (a) W 2–0 – Roberts; Jack Horton, Green; Ezra Horton, Perry, Bayliss; Bassett, Woodhall (1), Hendry, Pearson, Wilson (1).

Record League Victory: 12–0 v Darwen, Division 1, 4 April 1892 – Reader; Jack Horton, McCulloch; Reynolds (2), Perry, Groves; Bassett (3), McLeod, Nicholls (1), Pearson (4), Geddes (1), (1 og).

Record Cup Victory: 10–1 v Chatham (away), FA Cup 3rd rd, 2 March 1889 – Roberts; Jack Horton, Green; Timmins (1), Charles Perry, Ezra Horton; Bassett (2), Walter Perry (1), Bayliss (2), Pearson, Wilson (3), (1 og).

HONOURS

Football League – Division 1: ***Champions*** 1919–20; ***Runners-up*** 1924–25, 1953–54, 2001–02, 2003–04.
FL C: ***Champions*** 2007–08; ***Runners-up*** 2009–10.
Division 2: ***Champions*** 1901–02, 1910–11; ***Runners-up*** 1930–31, 1948–49.

FA Cup: ***Winners*** 1888, 1892, 1931, 1954, 1968; ***Runners-up*** 1886, 1887, 1895, 1912, 1935.

Football League Cup: ***Winners*** 1966; ***Runners-up*** 1967, 1970.

European Competitions
European Cup-Winners' Cup: 1968–69.
European Fairs Cup: 1966–67.
UEFA Cup: 1978–79, 1979–80, 1981–82.

sky SPORTS FACT FILE

The Rev William Jordan was an amateur forward who scored a hat trick on his debut for West Bromwich Albion in a 5-0 win over Gainsborough Trinity on 16 February 1907. He actually doubled that score on his England amateur international bow with a six-timer against France.

Record Defeat: 3–10 v Stoke C, Division 1, 4 February 1937.

Most League Points (2 for a win): 60, Division 1, 1919–20.

Most League Points (3 for a win): 91, FL C, 2009–10.

Most League Goals: 105, Division 2, 1929–30.

Highest League Scorer in Season: William 'Ginger' Richardson, 39, Division 1, 1935–36.

Most League Goals in Total Aggregate: Tony Brown, 218, 1963–79.

Most League Goals in One Match: 6, Jimmy Cookson v Blackpool, Division 2, 17 September 1927.

Most Capped Player: Stuart Williams, 33 (43), Wales.

Most League Appearances: Tony Brown, 574, 1963–80.

Youngest League Player: Charlie Wilson, 16 years 73 days v Oldham Ath, 1 October 1921.

Record Transfer Fee Received: £8,000,000 from Aston Villa for Curtis Davies, July 2008.

Record Transfer Fee Paid: £4,700,000 to Mallorca for Borja Valero, August 2008.

Football League Record: 1888 Founder Member of Football League; 1901–02 Division 2; 1902–04 Division 1; 1904–11 Division 2; 1911–27 Division 1; 1927–31 Division 2; 1931–38 Division 1; 1938–49 Division 2; 1949–73 Division 1; 1973–76 Division 2; 1976–86 Division 1; 1986–91 Division 2; 1991–92 Division 3; 1992–93 Division 2; 1993–2002 Division 1; 2002–03 FA Premier League; 2003–04 Division 1; 2004–06 FA Premier League; 2006–08 FL C; 2008–09 FA Premier League; 2009–10 FL C; 2010– FA Premier League.

LATEST SEQUENCES

Longest Sequence of League Wins: 11, 5.4.1930 – 8.9.1930.

Longest Sequence of League Defeats: 11, 28.10.1995 – 26.12.1995.

Longest Sequence of League Draws: 5, 30.8.1999 – 3.10.1999.

Longest Sequence of Unbeaten League Matches: 17, 7.9.1957 – 7.12.1957.

Longest Sequence Without a League Win: 15, 16.10.2004 – 25.9.2004.

Successive Scoring Runs: 36 from 26.4.1958.

Successive Non-scoring Runs: 4 from 15.2.1913.

MANAGERS

Louis Ford 1890–92
(Secretary-Manager)
Henry Jackson 1892–94
(Secretary-Manager)
Edward Stephenson 1894–95
(Secretary-Manager)
Clement Keys 1895–96
(Secretary-Manager)
Frank Heaven 1896–1902
(Secretary-Manager)
Fred Everiss 1902–48
Jack Smith 1948–52
Jesse Carver 1952
Vic Buckingham 1953–59
Gordon Clark 1959–61
Archie Macaulay 1961–63
Jimmy Hagan 1963–67
Alan Ashman 1967–71
Don Howe 1971–75
Johnny Giles 1975–77
Ronnie Allen 1977
Ron Atkinson 1978–81
Ronnie Allen 1981–82
Ron Wylie 1982–84
Johnny Giles 1984–85
Nobby Stiles 1985–86
Ron Saunders 1986–87
Ron Atkinson 1987–88
Brian Talbot 1988–91
Bobby Gould 1991–92
Ossie Ardiles 1992–93
Keith Burkinshaw 1993–94
Alan Buckley 1994–97
Ray Harford 1997
Denis Smith 1997–1999
Brian Little 1999–2000
Gary Megson 2000–04
Bryan Robson 2004–06
Tony Mowbray 2006–09
Roberto Di Matteo 2009–11
Roy Hodgson 2011–12
Steve Clarke June 2012–

TEN YEAR LEAGUE RECORD

		P	W	D	L	F	A	Pts	Pos
2002-03	PR Lge	38	6	8	24	29	65	26	19
2003-04	Div 1	46	25	11	10	64	42	86	2
2004-05	PR Lge	38	6	16	16	36	61	34	17
2005-06	PR Lge	38	7	9	22	31	58	30	19
2006-07	FL C	46	22	10	14	81	55	76	4
2007-08	FL C	46	23	12	11	88	55	81	1
2008-09	PR Lge	38	8	8	22	36	67	32	20
2009-10	FL C	46	26	13	7	89	48	91	2
2010-11	PR Lge	38	12	11	15	56	71	47	11
2011-12	PR Lge	38	13	8	17	45	52	47	10

DID YOU KNOW 

On 22 October 2011, West Bromwich Albion won 2-1 at Aston Villa, seen by 34,152 spectators. It was the team's first success in a League match at Villa Park since 11 May 1979 when a goal by John Trewick settled it for the Baggies. The attendance that day had been 35,991.

WEST BROMWICH ALBION 2011–12 LEAGUE RECORD

Match No.	*Date*	*Venue*	*Opponents*	*Result*		*H/T Score*	*Lg Pos.*	*Goalscorers*	*Attendance*
1	Aug 14	H	Manchester U	L	1-2	1-1	—	Long ^{37}	25,360
2	20	A	Chelsea	L	1-2	1-0	19	Long ^{4}	41,091
3	28	H	Stoke C	L	0-1	0-0	18		22,909
4	Sept 11	A	Norwich C	W	1-0	1-0	12	Odemwingie ^{3}	26,158
5	17	A	Swansea C	L	0-3	0-2	20		20,341
6	24	H	Fulham	D	0-0	0-0	19		23,835
7	Oct 1	A	Sunderland	D	2-2	2-2	17	Morrison ^{4}, Long ^{5}	34,815
8	16	H	Wolverhampton W	W	2-0	1-0	12	Brunt ^{8}, Odemwingie ^{75}	24,872
9	22	A	Aston Villa	W	2-1	1-1	12	Olsson ^{45}, Scharner ^{57}	34,152
10	29	H	Liverpool	L	0-2	0-2	13		25,522
11	Nov 5	A	Arsenal	L	0-3	0-2	14		60,091
12	19	H	Bolton W	W	2-1	1-1	10	Thomas ^{16}, Long ^{56}	26,221
13	26	H	Tottenham H	L	1-3	1-1	14	Mulumbu ^{10}	24,801
14	Dec 3	A	QPR	D	1-1	0-1	13	Long ^{81}	17,290
15	10	H	Wigan Ath	L	1-2	1-1	15	Reid ^{33}	25,446
16	17	A	Blackburn R	W	2-1	0-0	13	Morrison ^{52}, Odemwingie ^{89}	22,909
17	21	A	Newcastle U	W	3-2	2-1	—	Odemwingie ^{20}, McAuley ^{44}, Scharner ^{85}	51,060
18	26	H	Manchester C	D	0-0	0-0	9		25,938
19	Jan 1	H	Everton	L	0-1	0-0	11		23,038
20	3	A	Tottenham H	L	0-1	0-0	—		36,062
21	14	H	Norwich C	L	1-2	0-1	15	Long (pen) ^{68}	22,474
22	21	A	Stoke C	W	2-1	1-0	15	Morrison ^{35}, Dorrans ^{90}	26,865
23	Feb 1	A	Fulham	D	1-1	0-0	—	Tchoyi ^{82}	25,689
24	4	H	Swansea C	L	1-2	0-0	15	Fortune ^{54}	24,274
25	12	A	Wolverhampton W	W	5-1	1-1	14	Odemwingie 3 $^{34, 77, 88}$, Olsson ^{64}, Andrews ^{85}	27,131
26	25	H	Sunderland	W	4-0	2-0	13	Odemwingie 2 $^{3, 48}$, Morrison ^{41}, Andrews ^{90}	25,311
27	Mar 3	H	Chelsea	W	1-0	0-0	10	McAuley ^{82}	24,838
28	11	A	Manchester U	L	0-2	0-1	14		75,598
29	17	A	Wigan Ath	D	1-1	0-0	—	Scharner ^{65}	21,379
30	25	H	Newcastle U	L	1-3	0-3	14	Long ^{52}	25,049
31	31	A	Everton	L	0-2	0-1	14		32,051
32	Apr 7	H	Blackburn R	W	3-0	1-0	13	Olsson, Martin (og) ^{7}, Fortune ^{69}, Ridgewell ^{85}	23,414
33	11	A	Manchester C	L	0-4	0-1	—		46,746
34	14	H	QPR	W	1-0	1-0	13	Dorrans ^{22}	25,521
35	22	A	Liverpool	W	1-0	0-0	10	Odemwingie ^{75}	43,660
36	28	H	Aston Villa	D	0-0	0-0	10		25,984
37	May 6	A	Bolton W	D	2-2	0-1	10	Brunt ^{75}, Morrison ^{90}	25,662
38	13	H	Arsenal	L	2-3	2-2	10	Long ^{11}, Dorrans ^{15}	26,358

Final League Position: 10

GOALSCORERS

League (45): Odemwingie 10, Long 8 (1 pen), Morrison 5, Dorrans 3, Scharner 3, Andrews 2, Brunt 2, Fortune 2, McAuley 2, Olsson 2, Mulumbu 1, Reid 1, Ridgewell 1, Tchoyi 1, Thomas 1, own goal 1.
Carling Cup (5): Fortune 2, Brunt 1 (pen), Cox 1, Thomas 1.
FA Cup (5): Cox 3, Fortune 1, Odemwingie 1.

Foster B 37	Reid S 21 + 1	Shorey N 22 + 3	Mulumbu Y 34 + 1	Tamas G 7 + 1	Olsson J 33	Brunt C 25 + 4	Scharner P 18 + 11	Long S 24 + 8	Tchoyi S 6 + 12	Morrison J 23 + 7	Jara G 1 + 3	Cox S 7 + 11	Odemwingie P 25 + 5	Dorrans G 16 + 15	Thomas J 26 + 3	Fortune M 12 + 5	Dawson C 6 + 2	McAuley G 32	Jones B 17 + 1	Gera Z 3	Thorne G 1 + 2	Ridgewell L 13	Andrews K 8 + 6	Fulop M 1	*Match No.*
1	2[1]	3	4	5	6	7	8	9[2]	10	11	12	13													1
1	2	3	4[2]	5	6	7	8	9	10[1]	11			12	13											2
1	2	3	4	5	6	7[1]	8	9	10[2]	11[3]				14	12	13									3
1	2	3	4	5	6	13	8	9[3]	14	12			10	11[1]	7[2]										4
1	2	3	4[2]		6	12	8[3]	9		11		14	10	13	7[1]		5								5
1	2	3	4		6	8		9	13	12			10	11[1]	7[2]			5							6
1	2	3	4[1]		6	8	12	9		11			10	7[2]	13			5							7
1	2	14	4		6	11	8	9	10[1]	13			12		7[2]			5	3[3]						8
1	2		4[2]		6	11	8	9[1]	12	13			10		7			5	3						9
1	2		4[2]		6	11	8[1]		10[3]	12		14	9	13	7			5	3						10
1	2		13		6	8			12	4		10[2]		11[3]	7			5	3	9[1]	14				11
1	2	3	4[2]		6	11		9		8		13		12	7[1]			5		10					12
1	2	3	4		6	11		9[2]	14	8		12	13		7[3]			5		10[1]					13
1	2	3	4[3]		6	10	14	9	13	8			12	11[2]	7[1]			5							14
1	2	3	4[1]		6	11	14	9	13	8[3]			10[2]	12	7			5							15
1	2	3	4		6	11	8[1]	9		7[2]			10[3]	12	13		14	5							16
1	2[1]	3	4[3]		6	11	8	9					10	13	7[2]			5	12		14				17
1		3	4[1]		6	11	8	9			13		10[2]	12	7			5	2						18
1		3				11[1]	4	9		8			10	12	7		6	5	2						19
1		3					4		14	13	12	10	9	11[2]	7[1]		6	5	2		8[3]				20
1		3	4				8[1]	12		7	2	10	9[2]	13	11[3]	14	6	5							21
1		3	4	2	6			12	13	8		10[2]		11	7[3]	9[1]	14	5							22
1	13	3	4	2	6				12	7[2]		8[1]	10	11		9		5							23
1	2	3	4[1]		6		12		14	8		13	10	11[2]	7[3]	9		5							24
1	2		4		6		11[1]			8		13	10[3]	14	7[2]	9		5				3	12		25
1	2	13	4[2]		3			14		8			10[3]	12	7[1]	9		5				6	11		26
1	2[1]		4	12	3	13		14		8			10		7[2]	9[3]		5				6	11		27
1		12	4	2	6■	8[2]	13	14		7			10			9[3]		5				3	11[1]		28
1		3	4[1]			10	11	9		8				13	7[2]			5	2			6	12		29
1			4[3]		3	13	14	12		8			10		7[2]	9		5	2			6	11[1]		30
1					3	11[3]	8[1]	9	7[2]			14	10	12		13		5	2			6	4		31
1			4		3	11[1]	13	14				12	10	7[2]		9[3]		5	2			6	8		32
1		3	4[1]		5		8	9	13			10		7[2]		12	6		2				11		33
1			4			8	14	12					10	11[2]	7[3]	9[1]	6	5	2			3	13		34
1			4		3	8	13	9				14	10[2]	11[3]	7[1]			5	2			6	12		35
1			4[2]		3	8		9[1]					10	11	7	12		5	2			6	13		36
1			4[2]		3	8	13	9		12		14		11[3]		10		5	2			6	7[1]		37
			4		3		14	9		7[1]		8[2]	13	11[3]		10		5	2			6	12	1	38

FA Cup
Third Round Cardiff C (h) 4-2
Fourth Round Norwich C (h) 1-2

Carling Cup
Second Round Bournemouth (a) 4-1
Third Round Everton (a) 1-2

WEST HAM UNITED FA Premiership

FOUNDATION

Thames Iron Works FC was formed by employees of this famous shipbuilding company in 1895 and entered the FA Cup in their initial season at Chatham and the London League in their second. The committee wanted to introduce professional players, so Thames Iron Works was wound up in June 1900 and relaunched a month later as West Ham United.

The Boleyn Ground, Upton Park, Green Street, London E13 9AZ.

Telephone: (0871) 222 2700.

Fax: (020) 8548 2758.

Ticket Office: (0871) 222 2700.

Website: www.whufc.co.uk

Email: yourcomments@westhamunited.co.uk

Ground Capacity: 35,303.

Record Attendance: 42,322 v Tottenham H, Division 1, 17 October 1970.

Pitch Measurements: 100.58m × 66.84m.

Joint Chairmen: David Sullivan and David Gold.

Vice-chairman: Karren Brady.

Manager: Sam Allardyce.

Assistant Manager: Neil McDonald.

Head of Sports Medicine: Andy Rolls.

Colours: Claret shirts with blue trim, white shorts, claret stockings.

Year Formed: 1895.

Turned Professional: 1900.

Previous Name: 1895, Thames Iron Works FC; 1900, West Ham United.

Club Nicknames: 'The Hammers', 'The Irons'.

Grounds: 1895, Memorial Recreation Ground, Canning Town; 1904, Boleyn Ground.

First Football League Game: 30 August 1919, Division 2, v Lincoln C (h) D 1–1 – Hufton; Cope, Lee; Lane, Fenwick, McCrae; David Smith, Moyes (1), Puddefoot, Morris, Bradshaw.

Record League Victory: 8–0 v Rotherham U, Division 2, 8 March 1958 – Gregory; Bond, Wright; Malcolm, Brown, Lansdowne; Grice, Smith (2), Keeble (2), Dick (4), Musgrove. 8–0 v Sunderland, Division 1, 19 October 1968 – Ferguson; Bonds, Charles; Peters, Stephenson, Moore (1); Redknapp, Boyce, Brooking (1), Hurst (6), Sissons.

HONOURS

Football League – Division 1: ***Runners-up*** 1992–93
Division 2: ***Champions*** 1957–58, 1980–81; ***Runners-up*** 1922–23, 1990–91.

FA Cup: ***Winners*** 1964, 1975, 1980; ***Runners-up*** 1923, 2006.

Football League Cup: ***Runners-up*** 1966, 1981.

European Competitions
European Cup-Winners' Cup: 1964–65 (*winners*), 1965–66, 1975–76 (*runners-up*), 1980–81.
UEFA Cup: 1999–2000; 2006–07.
Intertoto Cup: 1999 (*winners*).

sky SPORTS FACT FILE

Don Travis scored four times on his debut for West Ham United on 16 February 1946 in the transitional season of 1945–46 in a 7-0 win over Plymouth Argyle. Terry Woodgate scored the other three from the right wing. Travis at centre-forward scored seven times in six games.

Record Cup Victory: 10–0 v Bury, League Cup 2nd rd (2nd leg), 25 October 1983 – Parkes; Stewart (1), Walford, Bonds (Orr), Martin (1), Devonshire (2), Allen, Cottee (4), Swindlehurst, Brooking (2), Pike.

Record Defeat: 2–8 v Blackburn R, Division 1, 26 December 1963.

Most League Points (2 for a win): 66, Division 2, 1980–81.

Most League Points (3 for a win): 88, Division 1, 1992–93.

Most League Goals: 101, Division 2, 1957–58.

Highest League Scorer in Season: Vic Watson, 42, Division 1, 1929–30.

Most League Goals in Total Aggregate: Vic Watson, 298, 1920–35.

Most League Goals in One Match: 6, Vic Watson v Leeds U, Division 1, 9 February 1929; 6, Geoff Hurst v Sunderland, Division 1, 19 October 1968.

Most Capped Player: Bobby Moore, 108, England.

Most League Appearances: Billy Bonds, 663, 1967–88.

Youngest League Player: Billy Williams, 16 years 221 days v Blackpool, 6 May 1922.

Record Transfer Fee Received: £18,000,000 from Leeds U for Rio Ferdinand, November 2000.

Record Transfer Fee Paid: £7,500,000 to Liverpool for Craig Bellamy, July 2007.

Football League Record: 1919 Elected to Division 2; 1923–32 Division 1; 1932–58 Division 2; 1958–78 Division 1; 1978–81 Division 2; 1981–89 Division 1; 1989–91 Division 2; 1991–93 Division 1; 1993–2003 FA Premier League; 2003–04 Division 1; 2004–05 FL C; 2005–11 FA Premier League; 2011–12 FL C; 2012– FA Premier League.

MANAGERS

Syd King 1902–32
Charlie Paynter 1932–50
Ted Fenton 1950–61
Ron Greenwood 1961–74
(continued as General Manager to 1977)
John Lyall 1974–89
Lou Macari 1989–90
Billy Bonds 1990–94
Harry Redknapp 1994–2001
Glenn Roeder 2001–03
Alan Pardew 2003–06
Alan Curbishley 2006–08
Gianfranco Zola 2008–10
Avram Grant 2010–11
Sam Allardyce June 2011–

LATEST SEQUENCES

Longest Sequence of League Wins: 9, 19.10.1985 – 14.12.1985.

Longest Sequence of League Defeats: 9, 28.3.1932 – 29.8.1932.

Longest Sequence of League Draws: 5, 15.10.2003 – 1.11.2003.

Longest Sequence of Unbeaten League Matches: 27, 27.12.80 – 10.10.81.

Longest Sequence Without a League Win: 17, 31.1.1976 – 21.8.1976.

Successive Scoring Runs: 27 from 5.10.1957.

Successive Non-scoring Runs: 5 from 1.5.1971.

TEN YEAR LEAGUE RECORD

		P	W	D	L	F	A	Pts	Pos
2002-03	PR Lge	38	10	12	16	42	59	42	18
2003-04	Div 1	46	19	17	10	67	45	74	4
2004-05	FL C	46	21	10	15	66	56	73	6
2005-06	PR Lge	38	16	7	15	52	55	55	9
2006-07	PR Lge	38	12	5	21	35	59	41	15
2007-08	PR Lge	38	13	10	15	42	50	49	10
2008-09	PR Lge	38	14	9	15	42	45	51	9
2009-10	PR Lge	38	8	11	19	47	66	35	17
2010-11	PR Lge	38	7	12	19	43	70	33	20
2011-12	FL C	46	24	14	8	81	48	86	3

DID YOU KNOW ?

Stanley Bourne, a West Ham United full-back in the club's Southern League days, was the first professional player with a first-class team (apart from a goalkeeper) to wear spectacles when he was playing. In five seasons he also played left-half making 16 League and Cup appearances.

WEST HAM UNITED 2011–12 LEAGUE RECORD

Match No.	Date	Venue	Opponents	Result	H/T Score	Lg Pos.	Goalscorers	Attendance
1	Aug 7	H	Cardiff C	L 0-1	0-0	—		25,680
2	13	A	Doncaster R	W 1-0	1-0	14	Nolan [5]	11,344
3	16	A	Watford	W 4-0	2-0	—	Tomkins [3], O'Brien [45], Cole [71], Parker [90]	14,747
4	21	H	Leeds U	D 2-2	1-0	7	Cole [6], Kisnorbo (og) [62]	28,252
5	28	A	Nottingham F	W 4-1	3-0	—	Chambers (og) [21], Nolan [24], Cole [32], Reid [77]	21,379
6	Sept 10	H	Portsmouth	W 4-3	1-1	4	Taylor [9], Lansbury [53], Noble (pen) [72], Cole [76]	33,465
7	17	A	Millwall	D 0-0	0-0	5		16,078
8	24	H	Peterborough U	W 1-0	1-0	4	Noble (pen) [11]	29,895
9	27	H	Ipswich T	L 0-1	0-0	—		27,709
10	Oct 1	A	Crystal Palace	D 2-2	1-1	4	Nolan [16], Carew [80]	20,074
11	15	H	Blackpool	W 4-0	1-0	2	Carew [12], Baldock 2 [47, 51], Collison [55]	31,448
12	18	A	Southampton	L 0-1	0-1	—		32,152
13	24	A	Brighton & HA	W 1-0	1-0	—	Nolan [17]	20,686
14	29	H	Leicester C	W 3-2	2-0	2	Baldock 2 [21, 71], Faubert [22]	30,410
15	Nov 1	H	Bristol C	D 0-0	0-0	—		27,980
16	5	A	Hull C	W 2-0	0-0	2	Baldock [49], Collison [57]	21,756
17	19	A	Coventry C	W 2-1	0-1	2	Cole [69], Piquionne [75]	20,524
18	26	H	Derby Co	W 3-1	1-1	2	Cole [45], Nolan [64], Noble (pen) [74]	27,864
19	29	A	Middlesbrough	W 2-0	1-0	—	Piquionne [9], Cole [90]	18,457
20	Dec 3	H	Burnley	L 1-2	0-0	2	Nolan [52]	26,274
21	10	A	Reading	L 0-3	0-0	2		24,026
22	17	H	Barnsley	W 1-0	1-0	2	Diop [6]	34,749
23	26	A	Birmingham C	D 1-1	1-0	2	Cole [4]	20,214
24	31	A	Derby Co	L 1-2	1-2	3	Nouble [42]	28,067
25	Jan 2	H	Coventry C	W 1-0	0-0	2	Nolan [66]	34,936
26	14	A	Portsmouth	W 1-0	1-0	2	Noble (pen) [24]	18,492
27	21	H	Nottingham F	W 2-1	1-0	1	Noble 2 (2 pens) [45, 63]	31,718
28	31	A	Ipswich T	L 1-5	1-3	—	Collison [45]	22,185
29	Feb 4	H	Millwall	W 2-1	1-0	1	Cole [45], Reid [69]	27,774
30	14	H	Southampton	D 1-1	1-0	—	Noble (pen) [21]	32,875
31	21	A	Blackpool	W 4-1	2-1	—	Tomkins [28], Maynard [32], O'Neil [74], Vaz Te [90]	13,043
32	25	H	Crystal Palace	D 0-0	0-0	2		34,900
33	Mar 4	A	Cardiff C	W 2-0	1-0	2	Nolan [43], McCartney [77]	23,872
34	7	H	Watford	D 1-1	0-0	—	Vaz Te [87]	31,674
35	10	H	Doncaster R	D 1-1	1-0	2	Nolan [9]	34,650
36	17	A	Leeds U	D 1-1	0-0	3	Collins [90]	33,366
37	20	H	Middlesbrough	D 1-1	0-0	—	Bennett (og) [67]	27,250
38	24	A	Burnley	D 2-2	0-2	3	Nolan [68], Tomkins [70]	15,246
39	27	A	Peterborough U	W 2-0	0-0	—	Vaz Te [51], O'Neil [57]	13,517
40	31	H	Reading	L 2-4	1-2	3	Cole [8], Vaz Te [77]	33,350
41	Apr 6	A	Barnsley	W 4-0	3-0	—	Nolan [7], Maynard [23], Noble [35], Vaz Te [55]	11,151
42	9	H	Birmingham C	D 3-3	1-3	3	Vaz Te 2 (1 pen) [44, 89 (p)], Cole [70]	31,045
43	14	H	Brighton & HA	W 6-0	3-0	3	Vaz Te 3 [3, 8, 62], Nolan [11], Cole [64], Dicker (og) [78]	32,339
44	17	A	Bristol C	D 1-1	1-1	—	Tomkins [25]	16,669
45	23	A	Leicester C	W 2-1	1-1	—	Reid [39], Collison [58]	23,172
46	28	H	Hull C	W 2-1	1-0	3	Cole 2 [36, 49]	35,000

Final League Position: 3

GOALSCORERS

League (81): Cole 14, Nolan 12, Vaz Te 10 (1 pen), Noble 8 (7 pens), Baldock 5, Collison 4, Tomkins 4, Reid 3, Carew 2, Maynard 2, O'Neil 2, Piquionne 2, Collins 1, Diop 1, Faubert 1, Lansbury 1, McCartney 1, Nouble 1, O'Brien 1, Parker 1, Taylor 1, own goals 4.
Carling Cup (1): Stanislas 1.
FA Cup (0).
Play-Offs (7): Collison 2, Vaz Te 2, Cole 1, Maynard 1, Nolan 1.

Green R 42	Reid W 27 + 1	Ilunga H 4	Nolan K 42	Tomkins J 42 + 2	O'Brien J 27 + 5	Noble M 43 + 2	Parker S 4	Sears F 2 + 8	Piquionne F 8 + 12	Taylor M 26 + 2	Collison J 26 + 5	Cole C 28 + 12	Barrera P — + 1	Stanislas J — + 1	Faye A 25 + 4	Faubert J 28 + 6	Carew J 7 + 12	McCartney G 36 + 2	Lansbury H 13 + 9	Bentley D 2 + 3	Baldock S 10 + 13	Almunia M 4	Diop P 14 + 2	Demel G 7	Potts D 3	Nouble F 1 + 2	O'Neil G 9 + 7	Hall R — + 3	Vaz Te R 13 + 2	Maynard N 9 + 5	Collins D 4 + 7	Morrison R — + 1	*Match No.*
1	2	3	4	5	6	7^{1}	8	9^{3}	10^{2}	11	12	13	14																				1
1	2	3^{3}	4	5	6	7	8	13	10^{1}	11	9^{2}	12		14																			2
1	2	3	4	5^{1}	6	7	8		13	11	10^{3}	9^{2}			12	14																	3
1	2	3	4	5	6	7^{3}	8		14	11	10^{1}	9^{2}				12	13																4
1	2		4	5	3	8			12	11	10^{2}	9^{1}			13	7		6															5
1	2		4	5	6	8			13■	11		9^{2}				7^{1}		3	10	12													6
1	12		4	5^{1}	2	8				11^{2}		9			6	7		3	10^{3}	13	14												7
1	2		8	14	4	6				11^{3}		9^{1}			5	7^{2}	12	3	10	13													8
1			4	5	2	8^{3}					12	9^{2}			6	14	13	3	11^{1}	7	10												9
			4	5				14			10^{1}	9^{2}			6	2	13	3	11	7^{3}	12	1	8										10
	6		4	5^{1}		14		13		11^{2}	7				12	2	10^{3}	3			9	1	8										11
	5		4		14	13			12	11^{1}					6	2	10^{3}	3	7		9	1	8^{2}										12
	5		4		2	11		12	13		10				6	7^{3}	9^{2}	3			14	1	8^{1}										13
1	5		4	13	2	11		14	12		8				6^{2}	7	10^{1}	3			9^{3}												14
1	5^{1}		4	6	2	8		11^{3}	10			13			12	7		3			9^{2}		14										15
1			4	5		7		13	14		11	12			6	2	10^{1}	3			9^{3}		8^{2}										16
1			4	5	14	7			13		11	12			6	2	10^{1}	3			9^{3}		8^{2}										17
1			4	5	2	8			12	14	11	9^{2}			6	7^{3}	13	3			10^{1}												18
1			4	5	13	9			10^{1}	11		12			6	7		3					8	2^{2}									19
1			4	5	2^{2}	8			12	11^{1}	10	9			6	7	13	3															20
1			4	5	12■	11			10^{3}		9■	13			6	7	14	3					8^{2}	2^{1}									21
1			4	5		7		12	11			9				2^{2}	10^{1}	3	13				8		6								22
1			4	5	2	11		14	10^{1}			9^{2}				7^{3}	13	6	12				8		3								23
1	5			6	2	4			10^{2}			13							7		12		8^{3}		3	9	11^{1}	14					24
1	5		4	6	13	7					11	9^{2}				2		3			10^{1}		8			12							25
1	5		4	6	2	11					10	9				7^{1}		3	12				8										26
1	5		4	6		11			14		7	9^{3}				2		3	12		10^{2}		8^{1}					13					27
1	5		4	6		8^{1}				11^{2}	10	9^{3}				2		3	7		12					13		14					28
1	5		4■	6	11	8				12	10^{1}	9^{3}			2	7^{2}		3									13		14				29
1	5			4	2	11				3■	8^{1}	9^{2}			6	7		12									14		10^{3}	13			30
1■	5			4	2	11					8	14			6^{2}	7^{1}		3	12								13		9	10^{3}			31
1	5			4	2	8					11	12			6	7^{1}		3			14						13		9^{2}	10^{3}			32
1			4	5	2	11					8	12			6			3	7^{2}								13		9	10^{1}			33
1			4	5	2^{2}	8				11^{3}		9			6	7		3	14		12								13	10^{1}			34
1			4^{3}	5		11				3	8	9			6			2	7^{2}		12						13		10^{1}		14		35
1			4	7^{1}	2	8				11	9^{3}	13			6			3									12			10^{2}	5	14	36
1			4	8	2	7^{3}				11	12	9^{1}			6		13	3			14									10^{2}	5		37
1			4	5	2	8				11^{1}	10^{3}	9^{2}					14	3			12						7			13	6		38
1			4	5	2^{1}	8				11		9			6^{2}	12		3									7^{3}		10	14	13		39
1			4	5		8^{1}				11^{2}		9^{3}			6	2		3			13						7		10	14	12		40
1	5		4	6		8^{3}				11								3	13				14	2^{1}			7^{2}		9	10	12		41
1	2		4	5		8^{3}						9			6			3^{1}	13		14						7		11	10^{2}	12		42
1	5		4	6		8				3	12	9					14		11					2^{2}			7^{1}		10^{3}		13		43
1	5		4	6		8				11	13					14	12		7					2^{2}					9	10^{3}	3^{1}		44
1	5		4	6		8				3	10^{3}	9^{2}				12			14					2^{1}			7		11		13		45
1	5		4^{3}	6		8				3		9^{1}						14	11		12			2			7		10^{2}	13			46

FA Cup
Third Round Sheffield W (a) 0-1

Carling Cup
First Round Aldershot T (h) 1-2

Play-Offs
Semi-Final Cardiff C (a) 2-0
(h) 3-0
Final Blackpool 2-1
(at Wembley).

WIGAN ATHLETIC FA Premiership

FOUNDATION

Following the demise of Wigan Borough and their resignation from the Football League in 1931, a public meeting was called in Wigan at the Queen's Hall in May 1932 at which a new club, Wigan Athletic, was founded in the hope of carrying on in the Football League. With this in mind, they bought Springfield Park for £2,250, but failed to gain admission to the Football League until 46 years later.

The DW Stadium, Robin Park Complex, Newtown, Wigan, Lancashire WN5 0UZ.

Telephone: (01942) 774 000.

Fax: (01942) 770 477.

Ticket Office: (0871) 663 3552.

Website: www.wiganathletic.tv

Email: s.hayton@wiganathletic.com

Ground Capacity: 25,138.

Record Attendance: 27,526 v Hereford U, 12 December 1953 (at Springfield Park); 25,133 v Manchester U, FA Premier League, 11 May 2008 (at DW Stadium).

Pitch Measurements: 105m × 68m.

Chairman: David Whelan.

Chief Executive: Jonathan Jackson.

Manager: Roberto Martinez.

Assistant Manager: Graeme Jones.

Physios: Alex Cribley and Russell Hitchen.

Colours: Blue and white striped shirts with blue sleeves, blue shorts, white stockings.

Year Formed: 1932.

Turned Professional: 1932.

Club Nickname: 'The Latics'.

Grounds: 1932, Springfield Park; 1999, JJB Stadium (renamed the DW Stadium in 2009).

First Football League Game: 19 August 1978, Division 4, v Hereford U (a) D 0–0 – Brown; Hinnigan, Gore, Gillibrand, Ward, Davids, Corrigan, Purdie, Houghton, Wilkie, Wright.

Record League Victory: 7–1 v Scarborough, Division 3, 11 March 1997 – Lee Butler; John Butler, Sharp (Morgan), Greenall, McGibbon (Biggins (1)), Martinez (1), Diaz (2), Jones (Lancashire (1)), Lowe (2), Rogers, Kilford.

Record Cup Victory: 6–0 v Carlisle U (away), FA Cup 1st rd, 24 November 1934 – Caunce; Robinson, Talbot; Paterson, Watson, Tufnell; Armes (2), Robson (1), Roberts (2), Felton, Scott (1).

Record Defeat: 1–9 v Tottenham H, FA Premier League, 22 November 2009.

HONOURS

Football League – FL C: *Runners-up* 2004–05;
Division 2: ***Champions***, 2002–03;
Division 3: ***Champions***, 1996–97.

FA Cup: Best season: 6th rd, 1987.

Football League Cup: *Runners-up* 2006.

Freight Rover Trophy: ***Winners*** 1985.

Auto Windscreens Shield: *Winners* 1999.

sky SPORTS FACT FILE

In 1933–34, Wigan Athletic won all twenty-one home Cheshire League fixtures conceding only nine goals at Springfield Park. Of the 111 overall League goals, the left-wing pair of Teddy Felton and George Scott (the only ever-present) scored respectively 24 and 27 goals each.

Most League Points (2 for a win): 55, Division 4, 1978–79 and 1979–80.

Most League Points (3 for a win): 100, Division 2, 2002–03.

Most League Goals: 84, Division 3, 1996–97.

Highest League Scorer in Season: Graeme Jones, 31, Division 3, 1996–97.

Most League Goals in Total Aggregate: Andy Liddell, 70, 1998–2004.

Most League Goals in One Match: Not more than three goals by one player.

Most Capped Players: Kevin Kilbane, 22 (110), Republic of Ireland; Henri Camara, 22 (99), Senegal.

Most League Appearances: Kevin Langley, 317, 1981–86, 1990–94.

Youngest League Player: Steve Nugent, 16 years 132 days v Leyton Orient, 16 September 1989.

Record Transfer Fee Received: £15,250,000 from Manchester U for Antonio Valencia, June 2009.

Record Transfer Fee Paid: £6,000,000 to Newcastle U for Charles N'Zogbia, February 2009; £6,000,000 to Estudiantes for Mauro Boselli, August 2010.

Football League Record: 1978 Elected to Division 4; 1982–92 Division 3; 1992–93 Division 2; 1993–97 Division 3; 1997–2003 Division 2; 2003–04 Division 1; 2004–05 FL C; 2005– FA Premier League.

LATEST SEQUENCES

Longest Sequence of League Wins: 11, 2.11.2002 – 18.1.2003.

Longest Sequence of League Defeats: 8, 13.12.2006 – 30.1.2007.

Longest Sequence of League Draws: 6, 11.12.2001 – 5.1.2002.

Longest Sequence of Unbeaten League Matches: 25, 8.5.1999 – 3.1.2000.

Longest Sequence Without a League Win: 14, 9.5.1989 – 17.10.1989.

Successive Scoring Runs: 24 from 27.4.1996.

Successive Non-scoring Runs: 4 from 15.4.1995.

MANAGERS

Charlie Spencer 1932–37
Jimmy Milne 1946–47
Bob Pryde 1949–52
Ted Goodier 1952–54
Walter Crook 1954–55
Ron Suart 1955–56
Billy Cooke 1956
Sam Barkas 1957
Trevor Hitchen 1957–58
Malcolm Barrass 1958–59
Jimmy Shirley 1959
Pat Murphy 1959–60
Allenby Chilton 1960
Johnny Ball 1961–63
Allan Brown 1963–66
Alf Craig 1966–67
Harry Leyland 1967–68
Alan Saunders 1968
Ian McNeill 1968–70
Gordon Milne 1970–72
Les Rigby 1972–74
Brian Tiler 1974–76
Ian McNeill 1976–81
Larry Lloyd 1981–83
Harry McNally 1983–85
Bryan Hamilton 1985–86
Ray Mathias 1986–89
Bryan Hamilton 1989–93
Dave Philpotts 1993
Kenny Swain 1993–94
Graham Barrow 1994–95
John Deehan 1995–98
Ray Mathias 1998–99
John Benson 1999–2000
Bruce Rioch 2000–01
Steve Bruce 2001
Paul Jewell 2001–07
Chris Hutchings 2007
Steve Bruce 2007–09
Roberto Martinez June 2009–

TEN YEAR LEAGUE RECORD

		P	*W*	*D*	*L*	*F*	*A*	*Pts*	*Pos*
2002-03	Div 2	46	29	13	4	68	25	100	1
2003-04	Div 1	46	18	17	11	60	45	71	7
2004-05	FL C	46	25	12	9	79	35	87	2
2005-06	PR Lge	38	15	6	17	45	52	51	10
2006-07	PR Lge	38	10	8	20	37	59	38	17
2007-08	PR Lge	38	10	10	18	34	51	40	14
2008-09	PR Lge	38	12	9	17	34	45	45	11
2009-10	PR Lge	38	9	9	20	37	79	36	16
2010-11	PR Lge	38	9	15	14	40	61	42	16
2011-12	PR Lge	38	11	10	17	42	62	43	15

DID YOU KNOW ?

On 11 November 1981, Wigan Athletic, marshalled by Larry Lloyd, their centre back and player-manager, defeated Chelsea in a third round League Cup tie. Trailing from the 13th minute, the Latics hit back with three goals in eleven minutes to reach the fourth round for the first time.

WIGAN ATHLETIC 2011–12 LEAGUE RECORD

Match No.	Date	Venue	Opponents	Result	H/T Score	Lg Pos.	Goalscorers	Attendance
1	Aug 13	H	Norwich C	D 1-1	1-1	—	Watson (pen) [21]	17,454
2	20	A	Swansea C	D 0-0	0-0	12		19,028
3	27	H	QPR	W 2-0	1-0	8	Di Santo 2 [41, 66]	17,225
4	Sept 10	A	Manchester C	L 0-3	0-1	9		46,509
5	17	A	Everton	L 1-3	1-1	15	Di Santo [31]	31,576
6	24	H	Tottenham H	L 1-2	0-2	15	Diame [50]	18,788
7	Oct 1	A	Aston Villa	L 0-2	0-1	18		30,744
8	15	H	Bolton W	L 1-3	1-2	19	Diame [40]	17,261
9	22	A	Newcastle U	L 0-1	0-0	19		48,321
10	29	H	Fulham	L 0-2	0-1	20		15,796
11	Nov 6	A	Wolverhampton W	L 1-3	1-1	20	Watson [42]	23,536
12	19	H	Blackburn R	D 3-3	2-1	20	Gomez [7], Caldwell [31], Crusat [88]	17,392
13	26	A	Sunderland	W 2-1	1-1	19	Gomez (pen) [44], Di Santo [90]	37,883
14	Dec 3	H	Arsenal	L 0-4	0-2	20		19,280
15	10	A	WBA	W 2-1	1-1	18	Moses [37], Gomez (pen) [57]	25,446
16	17	H	Chelsea	D 1-1	0-0	18	Gomez [88]	18,320
17	21	H	Liverpool	D 0-0	0-0	—		19,230
18	26	A	Manchester U	L 0-5	0-2	18		75,183
19	31	A	Stoke C	D 2-2	1-0	18	Moses [45], Watson (pen) [87]	26,595
20	Jan 3	H	Sunderland	L 1-4	0-1	—	Rodallega [62]	15,871
21	16	H	Manchester C	L 0-1	0-1	—		16,026
22	21	A	QPR	L 1-3	0-2	20	Rodallega [66]	16,002
23	31	A	Tottenham H	L 1-3	0-2	—	McArthur [80]	35,801
24	Feb 4	H	Everton	D 1-1	0-0	20	Neville (og) [76]	18,340
25	11	A	Bolton W	W 2-1	1-0	20	Caldwell [43], McArthur [76]	23,450
26	25	H	Aston Villa	D 0-0	0-0	20		20,601
27	Mar 3	H	Swansea C	L 0-2	0-1	20		19,001
28	11	A	Norwich C	D 1-1	0-1	20	Moses [68]	26,653
29	17	H	WBA	D 1-1	0-0	—	McArthur [54]	21,379
30	24	A	Liverpool	W 2-1	1-0	19	Maloney (pen) [30], Caldwell [63]	44,431
31	31	H	Stoke C	W 2-0	0-0	19	Alcaraz [54], Moses [90]	19,786
32	Apr 7	A	Chelsea	L 1-2	0-0	19	Diame [82]	40,651
33	11	H	Manchester U	W 1-0	0-0	—	Maloney [50]	18,115
34	16	A	Arsenal	W 2-1	2-1	—	Di Santo [7], Gomez [8]	60,060
35	21	A	Fulham	L 1-2	0-0	17	Boyce [57]	25,689
36	28	H	Newcastle U	W 4-0	4-0	16	Moses 2 [13, 15], Maloney [36], Di Santo [45]	22,187
37	May 7	A	Blackburn R	W 1-0	0-0	—	Alcaraz [87]	26,144
38	13	H	Wolverhampton W	W 3-2	2-1	15	Di Santo [12], Boyce 2 [14, 79]	21,986

Final League Position: 15

GOALSCORERS

League (42): Di Santo 7, Moses 6, Gomez 5 (2 pens), Boyce 3, Caldwell 3, Diame 3, Maloney 3 (1 pen), McArthur 3, Watson 3 (2 pens), Alcaraz 2, Rodallega 2, Crusat 1, own goal 1.
Carling Cup (1): Watson 1.
FA Cup (1): McManaman 1.

Al-Habsi A 38	Boyce E 26	Figueroa M 37 + 1	McCarthy J 33	Caldwell G 36	Piscu 5	Gomez J 24 + 4	Watson B 14 + 7	Di Santo F 24 + 8	Moses V 36 + 2	Diame M 18 + 8	Sammon C 8 + 17	Rodallega H 11 + 12	Stam R 13 + 7	Alcaraz A 25	McArthur J 18 + 13	Crusat A 4 + 11	Van Aanholt P 3	Jones D 13 + 3	Maloney S 8 + 5	Gohouri S 8 + 2	McManaman C — + 2	Beausejour J 16	Match No.
1	2	3	4	5	6^3	7^1	8	9^2	10	11	12	13	14										1
1	2	3	4^2	5		7	8	9^3	10	11		14	12	6^1	13								2
1	2	3		5	6	7^3	8	9^2	11^1	4	13	10	14		12								3
1	2^1	3		5	6	14	8^2	9^3	10	4		7	12		11	13							4
1		3	4	5	6	7^1	8	9	11			10^2					2	12	13				5
1		6	4	5		10^1	8^2	9^3	11	7	14		12		13		3			2■			6
1	2	6	4^3	5			8	9	10	11^2	14		7^1		12		3		13				7
1	5	13	4^3	6			8^2	9	10	11		12		3				7	14	2^1			8
1	2	3		5			8^1		11	4	13	10		6	12	9^2		7					9
1	2^3	3		5			8	13	11	4^1		10	14	6	12	9^2		7					10
1	2	3					8^1	9	11	4	13	10^2		6	14	12		7^3		5			11
1		3	7	5		8^1			10	4	9^2	13	2^3		14	12		11		6			12
1		3	4	5		8		13	10	11	9^2		6^1		12			7		2			13
1		3	4	5		7^1		13	10	8^3	9^2		6		14	12		11		2			14
1		3	4	5		7		14	10	8	9^3		2^2	6^1	13			11		12			15
1		3	4	5		8		13	10	11	9^2	12	2	6				7^1					16
1		3	4	5		8^3	13	12	10	11	9^1	14	2	6				7^2					17
1		3	4	5		8^2		12	10^3	11^1	9■	14	2	6	13			7					18
1		3	4	5■		8^1	13		9	11		10	2	6				7^2		12			19
1		3	4			8	11^3		12	14	13	10	5^2	6		9^1		7		2			20
1		6	4	5		8^3	12	13	11			10	3	2	7^2	9^1					14		21
1	6^3	3	4	5		11^2	8		9		12	10	14		7^1	13				2			22
1	6	3	4	5		7^1	8^3	9^2	10		13		2		12	14						11	23
1	6	3	4	5		7^1		9^3	10			12	2^2		8	14		13				11	24
1	2	6	4	5		7^1		9^2	10			12		3	8			13				11	25
1	2	6	4^2	5		8^1		9	10^3	13		12		3	7	14						11	26
1	2	3^3	4	5		7		9	12	13	10^2	14		6	8^1							11	27
1	2	3	4^2	5		8^1			9	13		10		6	7				12			11	28
1	2	3^3	4^1	5				9	8	13				6	7	14			10^2		12	11	29
1	2	6	4	5			13	9^3	8^1		14			3	7	12			10			11^2	30
1	2	6	4	5		13	12	9^2	8		14			3	7				10^1			11^3	31
1	2	6	4	5			12	9^3	8	13	14			3	7^1				10			11^2	32
1	2	6	4	5				9^1	8	12	13			3	7				10^2			11	33
1	2	6	4	5		10^2		9^1	8	13	12			3	7							11	34
1	2	3	4^3	5		10^2	14	9^1	8		12			6	7				13			11	35
1	2	6	4	5		13		9^1	8^2		12			3	7				10			11	36
1	2	6	4	5				9^1	8		12			3	7				10			11	37
1	2	6	4	5	3	14		9^2	8^1			13			7	12			10^3			11	38

FA Cup
Third Round Swindon T (a) 1-2

Carling Cup
Second Round Crystal Palace (a) 1-2

WOLVERHAMPTON WANDERERS FL Championship

FOUNDATION

Enthusiasts of the game at St Luke's School, Blakenhall formed a club in 1877. In the same neighbourhood a cricket club called Blakenhall Wanderers had a football section. Several St Luke's footballers played cricket for them and shortly before the start of the 1879–80 season the two amalgamated and Wolverhampton Wanderers FC was brought into being.

Molineux Stadium, Waterloo Road, Wolverhampton WV1 4QR.

Telephone: (0871) 222 2220.

Fax: (01902) 687 006.

Ticket Office: (0871) 222 1877.

Website: wolves.co.uk

Email: info@wolves.co.uk

Ground Capacity: 28,565.

Record Attendance: 61,315 v Liverpool, FA Cup 5th rd, 11 February 1939.

Pitch Measurements: 110yd × 75yd.

Chairman: Steve Morgan OBE.

Chief Executive: Jez Moxey.

Manager: Stale Solbakken.

Assistant Manager: Terry Connor.

Physio: Phil Hayward.

Colours: Gold shirts with black trim, black shorts, gold stockings.

Year Formed: 1877* (*see Foundation*).

Turned Professional: 1888.

Previous Names: 1879, St Luke's combined with Wanderers Cricket Club to become Wolverhampton Wanderers (1923) Ltd. New limited companies followed in 1982 and 1986 (current).

Club Nickname: 'Wolves'.

HONOURS

Football League – Division 1: ***Champions*** 1953–54, 1957–58, 1958–59; ***Runners-up*** 1937–38, 1938–39, 1949–50, 1954–55, 1959–60; **Division 2:** ***Champions*** 1931–32, 1976–77; ***Runners-up*** 1966–67, 1982–83; **FL C:** ***Champions*** 2008–09; **Division 3 (N):** ***Champions*** 1923–24; **Division 3:** ***Champions*** 1988–89; **Division 4:** ***Champions*** 1987–88.

FA Cup: ***Winners*** 1893, 1908, 1949, 1960; ***Runners-up*** 1889, 1896, 1921, 1939.

Football League Cup: ***Winners*** 1974, 1980.

Texaco Cup: ***Winners*** 1971.

Sherpa Van Trophy: ***Winners*** 1988.

European Competitions
European Cup: 1958–59, 1959–60.
European Cup-Winners' Cup: 1960–61. **UEFA Cup:** 1971–72 (*runners-up*), 1973–74, 1974–75, 1980–81.

Grounds: 1877, Windmill Field; 1879, John Harper's Field; 1881, Dudley Road; 1889, Molineux.

First Football League Game: 8 September 1888, Football League, v Aston Villa (h) D 1–1 – Baynton; Baugh, Mason; Fletcher, Allen, Lowder; Hunter, Cooper, Anderson, White, Cannon, (1 og).

Record League Victory: 10–1 v Leicester C, Division 1, 15 April 1938 – Sidlow; Morris, Dowen; Galley, Cullis, Gardiner; Maguire (1), Horace Wright, Westcott (4), Jones (1), Dorsett (4).

Record Cup Victory: 14–0 v Crosswell's Brewery, FA Cup 2nd rd, 13 November 1886 – Ike Griffiths; Baugh, Mason; Pearson, Allen (1), Lowder; Hunter (4), Knight (2), Brodie (4), Bernie Griffiths (2), Wood. Plus one goal 'scrambled through'.

sky SPORTS FACT FILE

On 2 October 1948, Huddersfield Town were awarded a penalty after ten seconds against Wolverhampton Wanderers. They missed it. After twelve minutes Wolves led 4-0 and finished 7-1 winners. Jesse Pye scored two goals in eight minutes and completed a first half hat trick.

Record Defeat: 1–10 v Newton Heath, Division 1, 15 October 1892.

Most League Points (2 for a win): 64, Division 1, 1957–58.

Most League Points (3 for a win): 92, Division 3, 1988–89.

Most League Goals: 115, Division 2, 1931–32.

Highest League Scorer in Season: Dennis Westcott, 38, Division 1, 1946–47.

Most League Goals in Total Aggregate: Steve Bull, 250, 1986–99.

Most League Goals in One Match: 5, Joe Butcher v Accrington, Division 1, 19 November 1892; 5, Tom Phillipson v Barnsley, Division 2, 26 April 1926; 5, Tom Phillipson v Bradford C, Division 2, 25 December 1926; 5, Billy Hartill v Notts Co, Division 2, 12 October 1929; 5, Billy Hartill v Aston Villa, Division 1, 3 September 1934.

Most Capped Player: Billy Wright, 105, England (70 consecutive).

Most League Appearances: Derek Parkin, 501, 1967–82.

Youngest League Player: Jimmy Mullen, 16 years 43 days v Leeds U, 18 February 1939.

Record Transfer Fee Received: £6,000,000 from Coventry C for Robbie Keane, August 1999.

Record Transfer Fee Paid: £6,500,000 to Reading for Kevin Doyle, June 2009; £6,500,000 to Burnley for Steven Fletcher, June 2010.

Football League Record: 1888 Founder Member of Football League: 1906–23 Division 2; 1923–24 Division 3 (N); 1924–32 Division 2; 1932–65 Division 1; 1965–67 Division 2; 1967–76 Division 1; 1976–77 Division 2; 1977–82 Division 1; 1982–83 Division 2; 1983–84 Division 1; 1984–85 Division 2; 1985–86 Division 3; 1986–88 Division 4; 1988–89 Division 3; 1989–92 Division 2; 1992–2003 Division 1; 2003–04 FA Premier League; 2004–09 FL C; 2009–12 FA Premier League; 2012– FL C.

MANAGERS

George Worrall 1877–85
(Secretary-Manager)
John Addenbrooke 1885–1922
George Jobey 1922–24
Albert Hoskins 1924–26
(had been Secretary since 1922)
Fred Scotchbrook 1926–27
Major Frank Buckley 1927–44
Ted Vizard 1944–48
Stan Cullis 1948–64
Andy Beattie 1964–65
Ronnie Allen 1966–68
Bill McGarry 1968–76
Sammy Chung 1976–78
John Barnwell 1978–81
Ian Greaves 1982
Graham Hawkins 1982–84
Tommy Docherty 1984–85
Bill McGarry 1985
Sammy Chapman 1985–86
Brian Little 1986
Graham Turner 1986–94
Graham Taylor 1994–95
Mark McGhee 1995–98
Colin Lee 1998–2000
Dave Jones 2001–04
Glenn Hoddle 2004–06
Mick McCarthy 2006–12
Stale Solbakken July 2012–

LATEST SEQUENCES

Longest Sequence of League Wins: 8, 15.10.1988 – 26.11.1988.

Longest Sequence of League Defeats: 8, 5.12.1981 – 13.2.1982.

Longest Sequence of League Draws: 6, 22.4.1995 – 20.8.1995.

Longest Sequence of Unbeaten League Matches: 21, 15.1.2005 – 13.8.2005.

Longest Sequence Without a League Win: 19, 1.12.1984 – 6.4.1985.

Successive Scoring Runs: 41 from 20.12.1958.

Successive Non-scoring Runs: 7 from 2.2.1985.

TEN YEAR LEAGUE RECORD

		P	W	D	L	F	A	Pts	Pos
2002-03	Div 1	46	20	16	10	81	44	76	5
2003-04	PR Lge	38	7	12	19	38	77	33	20
2004-05	FL C	46	15	21	10	72	59	66	9
2005-06	FL C	46	16	19	11	50	42	67	7
2006-07	FL C	46	22	10	14	59	56	76	5
2007-08	FL C	46	18	16	12	53	48	70	7
2008-09	FL C	46	27	9	10	80	52	90	1
2009-10	PR Lge	38	9	11	18	32	56	38	15
2010-11	PR Lge	38	11	7	20	46	66	40	17
2011-12	PR Lge	38	5	10	23	40	82	25	20

DID YOU KNOW ?

Wolverhampton Wanderers opened 1962–63 in some style, remaining unbeaten in their first eleven League games. On 18 August they defeated Manchester City 8-1. In a quarter of an hour either side of the interval, they struck five times. Four of the eight goals were scored by Ted Farmer.

WOLVERHAMPTON WANDERERS 2011–12 LEAGUE RECORD

Match No.	*Date*	*Venue*	*Opponents*	*Result*		*H/T Score*	*Lg Pos.*	*Goalscorers*	*Atten-dance*
1	Aug 13	A	Blackburn R	W	2-1	1-1	—	Fletcher [22], Ward [47]	21,996
2	21	H	Fulham	W	2-0	2-0	2	Doyle [42], Jarvis [45]	22,657
3	27	A	Aston Villa	D	0-0	0-0	5		30,776
4	Sept 10	H	Tottenham H	L	0-2	0-0	7		25,274
5	17	H	QPR	L	0-3	0-2	10		24,189
6	24	A	Liverpool	L	1-2	0-2	11	Fletcher [49]	44,922
7	Oct 1	H	Newcastle U	L	1-2	0-2	14	Fletcher [88]	26,561
8	16	A	WBA	L	0-2	0-1	16		24,872
9	22	H	Swansea C	D	2-2	0-2	16	Doyle [84], O'Hara [86]	25,216
10	29	A	Manchester C	L	1-3	0-0	17	Hunt (pen) [75]	47,142
11	Nov 6	H	Wigan Ath	W	3-1	1-1	13	O'Hara [31], Edwards [55], Ward [66]	23,536
12	19	A	Everton	L	1-2	1-1	17	Hunt (pen) [37]	33,953
13	26	A	Chelsea	L	0-3	0-3	17		41,648
14	Dec 4	H	Sunderland	W	2-1	0-0	15	Fletcher 2 [73, 81]	25,145
15	10	A	Manchester U	L	1-4	0-2	17	Fletcher [47]	75,627
16	17	H	Stoke C	L	1-2	1-0	17	Hunt (pen) [17]	24,684
17	20	H	Norwich C	D	2-2	1-1	—	Ebanks-Blake [37], Zubar [82]	27,067
18	27	A	Arsenal	D	1-1	1-1	—	Fletcher [38]	59,686
19	31	A	Bolton W	D	1-1	0-1	16	Fletcher [49]	20,354
20	Jan 2	H	Chelsea	L	1-2	0-0	—	Ward [84]	27,289
21	14	A	Tottenham H	D	1-1	1-0	16	Fletcher [22]	36,194
22	21	H	Aston Villa	L	2-3	2-1	19	Kightly [21], Edwards [31]	27,084
23	31	H	Liverpool	L	0-3	0-0	—		27,447
24	Feb 4	A	QPR	W	2-1	0-1	17	Jarvis [46], Doyle [71]	17,351
25	12	H	WBA	L	1-5	1-1	18	Fletcher [45]	27,131
26	25	A	Newcastle U	D	2-2	0-2	16	Jarvis [50], Doyle [66]	52,287
27	Mar 4	A	Fulham	L	0-5	0-2	18		24,034
28	10	H	Blackburn R	L	0-2	0-1	19		26,121
29	18	H	Manchester U	L	0-5	0-3	—		27,494
30	24	A	Norwich C	L	1-2	1-2	20	Jarvis [25]	26,752
31	31	H	Bolton W	L	2-3	0-0	20	Kightly [53], Jarvis [88]	25,215
32	Apr 7	A	Stoke C	L	1-2	1-1	20	Kightly [26]	27,005
33	11	H	Arsenal	L	0-3	0-2	—		25,815
34	14	A	Sunderland	D	0-0	0-0	20		37,476
35	22	H	Manchester C	L	0-2	0-1	20		24,576
36	28	A	Swansea C	D	4-4	2-4	20	Fletcher [28], Jarvis 2 [33, 69], Edwards [54]	19,408
37	May 6	H	Everton	D	0-0	0-0	20		25,466
38	13	A	Wigan Ath	L	2-3	1-2	20	Jarvis [9], Fletcher [86]	21,986

Final League Position: 20

GOALSCORERS

League (40): Fletcher 12, Jarvis 8, Doyle 4, Edwards 3, Hunt 3 (3 pens), Kightly 3, Ward 3, O'Hara 2, Ebanks-Blake 1, Zubar 1.
Carling Cup (11): Ebanks-Blake 2, Milijas 2, Edwards 1, Elokobi 1, Guedioura 1, Hammill 1, O'Hara 1, Spray 1, Vokes 1.
FA Cup (0).

Hennessey W 34	Stearman R 28 + 2	Ward S 38	Henry K 30 + 1	Berra C 29 + 3	Johnson R 26 + 1	Jarvis M 31 + 6	O'Hara J 19	Doyle K 26 + 7	Fletcher S 26 + 6	Hunt S 16 + 8	Foley K 11 + 5	Elokobi G 3 + 6	Maierhofer S — + 1	Kightly M 14 + 4	Vokes S — + 4	Hammill A 3 + 6	Guedioura A 2 + 8	Edwards D 24 + 2	Doherty M — + 1	Milijas N 6 + 14	Ebanks-Blake S 8 + 15	Zubar R 14 + 1	Forde A 3 + 3	Craddock J 1	Frimpong E 5	Jonsson E 2 + 1	Bassong S 9	Davis D 6 + 1	Gorman J — + 1	De Vries D 4	Ikeme C — + 1	*Match No.*
1	2[1]	3	4	5	6	7[2]	8	9	10	11[3]	12	13	14																			1
1	2	3	4	5	6	7[2]	8	9	10[3]	11[1]	12	13		14																		2
1	2	3	4	5	6	7[1]	8	9	10[3]	11[2]	12	13			14																	3
1	2	3	4	5	6	13	8	9	10[3]	11[2]				7[1]	14	12																4
1	2	3	4	5	6	10[3]	8	9		14		11[1]		7[2]	12		13															5
1	2[1]	3	8	5	6	7	11	9	12	10[3]							14	4[2]	13													6
1	2	3	4[2]	5	6	7	8	9	10	11[1]						12	13															7
1	2	3	8	5	6	7[3]	10	9		13						11[2]	14			4[1]	12											8
1	2	3	4	5	6	7[1]	8	9							14	11[2]	13			12	10[3]											9
1	2	3	8	5	6	14	10	9		11[2]						12	7[3]	4[1]			13											10
1	2	3	8	5	6	12	11[2]	9		10							7[1]	4		13												11
1	2[1]	3	8	5	6	13	11	9	14	10		12						4[3]		7[2]												12
1		11	8	5	6	10			9[3]			3					14	7		4[1]	12	2[2]	13									13
1		3		5	14	7	8	9[2]	10	11[1]						13		4			12	2		6[3]								14
1		3	8	5	6	11	7[2]	9	10[3]	13								4[1]		12	14	2										15
1		3	8	5	6	7		9[2]	10	11[3]						14	13			4[1]	12	2										16
1		3	8	5	6	7		13	10	11[1]						12				4	9[2]	2										17
1	12	3	8	5	6	7		14	10	11[3]							13			9■		2[1]	4[2]									18
1	2	11	4	5	6	7		14	10[3]	8[2]	13	3[1]						12			9											19
1	2	3	8	5	6	12		9	13		14					11		10[3]					7[1]		4[2]							20
1		3	8	5	6	11[3]			10	12	2	14		7				9[2]		13					4[1]							21
1	13	3	8■	5	6	9			10		2[3]			7				11[2]		12	14				4[1]							22
1		3		5	6[1]	9			10	13	2			7[2]				11		14	12				4[3]	8						23
1	2[2]	3			6	9	11[3]	13	10		7							8		14	12				4[1]		5					24
1		3		12	6	11	8	7	10		2							4[2]		13	9						5[1]					25
1	6	3	8	5		10[2]	11[1]	9		13	7[3]			12				4		14		2										26
1	6	3	4[1]	5		9	8	10	13	14	7[3]			11[2]						12		2										27
1	5	3				11	7	9[3]	10					12				4[1]		13	14	2					6	8[2]				28
1	5	3				11		9[2]	10[3]		7			13				4			14	2■				12	6	8[1]				29
1	2	3			6	11		9[2]	10					7[3]				4		12	13					8[1]	5		14			30
1	2	3	13		6	11		12	10					7				4[3]		14	9[1]						5	8[2]				31
1	2	3	8[2]			11		12	10					7				4			9[1]	5					6	13				32
1	5	3	8	12		10		9[3]	14					7				4[2]		13		2					6■	11[1]				33
1	6	3	8	5		12			10		11[3]			7[2]				13			9	14	2[1]					4				34
	5	3	8	13		9		12	10[3]		2			7				11[1]			14						6[2]	4		1		35
	5	3	8	6		11[1]		9	10[2]	12	2			7				4			13									1		36
	5	3	8	6[1]				9	10[2]	11		12		7[3]				4			13	2	14							1		37
	5	3	8	6		7		10	13	11[1]								4			9[2]	2	12							1[6]	15	38

FA Cup

Third Round	Birmingham C	(a)	0-0
		(h)	0-1

Carling Cup

Second Round	Norwich C	(a)	4-0
Third Round	Millwall	(h)	5-0
Fourth Round	Manchester C	(h)	2-5

WYCOMBE WANDERERS FL Championship 2

FOUNDATION

In 1887 a group of young furniture trade workers called a meeting at the Steam Engine public house with the aim of forming a football club and entering junior football. It is thought that they were named after the famous FA Cup winners, The Wanderers, who had visited the town in 1877 for a tie with the original High Wycombe club. It is also possible that they played informally before their formation, although there is no proof of this.

Adams Park, Hillbottom Road, Sands, High Wycombe HP12 4HJ.

Telephone: (01494) 472 100. ***Fax:*** (01494) 527 633.

Ticket Office: (01494) 472 100.

Website: www.wwfc.com

Email: wwfc@wwfc.com

Ground Capacity: 10,000.

Record Attendance: 15,850 v St Albans C, FA Amateur Cup 4th rd, 25 February 1950 (at Loakes Park); 9,921 v Fulham, FA Cup 3rd rd, 9 January 2002 (at Adams Park).

Pitch Measurements: 115yd × 75yd.

Joint Chairmen: Ivor L. Beeks and Don Woodward.

Manager: Gary Waddock.

Assistant Manager: Richard Dobson.

Physio: Theo Farley.

Colours: Light blue and dark blue quartered shirts, dark blue shorts, light blue stockings.

Year Formed: 1887.

Turned Professional: 1974.

Club Nicknames: 'Chairboys' (after High Wycombe's tradition of furniture making), 'The Blues'.

Grounds: 1887, The Rye; 1893, Spring Meadow; 1895, Loakes Park; 1899, Daws Hill Park; 1901, Loakes Park; 1990, Adams Park.

First Football League Game: 14 August 1993, Division 3 v Carlisle U (a) D 2–2: Hyde; Cousins, Horton (Langford), Kerr, Crossley, Ryan, Carroll, Stapleton, Thompson, Scott, Guppy (1) (Hutchinson), (1 og).

Record League Victory: 5–0 v Burnley, Division 2, 15 April 1997 – Parkin; Cousins, Bell, Kavanagh, McCarthy, Forsyth, Carroll (2p) (Simpson), Scott (Farrell), Stallard (1), McGavin (1) (Read (1)), Brown. 5–0 v Northampton T, Division 2, 4 January 2003 – Talia; Senda, Ryan, Thomson, McCarthy, Johnson, Bulman, Simpson (1), Faulconbridge (Harris), Dixon (1) (Roberts 3), Brown (Currie).

Record Cup Victory: 5–0 v Hitchin T (a), FA Cup 2nd rd, 3 December 1994 – Hyde; Cousins, Brown, Crossley, Evans, Ryan (1), Carroll, Bell (1), Thompson, Garner (3) (Hemmings), Stapleton (Langford).

Record Defeat: 0–7 v Shrewsbury T, Johnstone's Paint Trophy, 7 October 2008.

HONOURS

Football League – Division 2: Best season: 6th, 1994–95.

FA Amateur Cup: ***Winners*** 1931.

FA Trophy: ***Winners*** 1991, 1993.

GM Vauxhall Conference: ***Winners*** 1992–93.

FA Cup: semi-final 2001.

Football League Cup: semi-final 2007.

sky SPORTS FACT FILE

On 9 August 2011, Jordan Ashley "F" Ibe made his debut for Wycombe Wanderers as a substitute in a League Cup tie. At 15 years 244 days he became the club's youngest first team player. On 29 October he became both their youngest player and goalscorer in a League game.

Most League Points (3 for a win): 80, FL 2, 2010-11.

Most League Goals: 72, FL 2, 2005–06.

Highest League Goalscorer in Season: Scott McGleish, 25, 2007–08.

Most League Goals in Total Aggregate: Nathan Tyson, 42, 2004–06.

Most League Goals in One Match: 3, Miquel Desouza v Bradford C, Division 2, 2 September 1995; 3, John Williams v Stockport Co, Division 2, 24 February 1996; 3, Mark Stallard v Walsall, Division 2, 21 October 1997; 3, Sean Devine v Reading, Division 2, 2 October 1999; 3, Sean Divine v Bury, Division 2, 26 February 2000; 3, Stuart Roberts v Northampton T, Division 2, 4 January 2003; 3, Nathan Tyson v Lincoln C, FL 2, 5 March 2005; 3, Nathan Tyson v Kidderminster H, FL 2, 2 April 2005; 3, Nathan Tyson v Stockport Co, FL 2, 10 September 2005; 3, Kevin Betsy v Mansfield T, FL 2, 24 September 2005; 3, Scott McGleish v Mansfield T, FL 2, 8 January 2008; 3, Stuart Roberts v Northampton T, Division 2, 4 January 2003.

Most Capped Player: Mark Rogers, 7, Canada.

Most League Appearances: Steve Brown, 371, 1994–2004.

Youngest League Player: Jordon Ibe, 15 years 311 days v Hartlepool U, 15 October 2011.

Record Transfer Fee Received: £600,000 from Nottingham F for Nathan Tyson, January 2006.

Record Transfer Fee Paid: £200,000 to Barnet for Sean Devine, 15 April 1999.

Football League Record: 1993 Promoted to Division 3 from GM Vauxhall Conference; 1993–94 Division 3; 1994–2004 Division 2; 2004–09 FL 2; 2009–10 FL 1; 2010–11 FL 2; 2011–12 FL 1; 2012– FL 2.

MANAGERS

First coach appointed 1951.
Prior to Brian Lee's appointment in 1969 the team was selected by a Match Committee which met every Monday evening.

James McCormack 1951–52
Sid Cann 1952–61
Graham Adams 1961–62
Don Welsh 1962–64
Barry Darvill 1964–68
Brian Lee 1969–76
Ted Powell 1976–77
John Reardon 1977–78
Andy Williams 1978–80
Mike Keen 1980–84
Paul Bence 1984–86
Alan Gane 1986–87
Peter Suddaby 1987–88
Jim Kelman 1988–90
Martin O'Neill 1990–95
Alan Smith 1995–96
John Gregory 1996–98
Neil Smillie 1998–99
Lawrie Sanchez 1999–2003
Tony Adams 2003–04
John Gorman 2004–06
Paul Lambert 2006–08
Peter Taylor 2008–09
Gary Waddock October 2009–

LATEST SEQUENCES

Longest Sequence of League Wins: 6, 19.8.2006 – 16.9.2006.

Longest Sequence of League Defeats: 6, 18.3.2006 – 17.4.2006.

Longest Sequence of League Draws: 5, 24.1.2004 – 21.2.2004.

Longest Sequence of Unbeaten League Matches: 21, 6.8.2005 – 10.12.2005.

Longest Sequence Without a League Win: 13, 16.8.2003 – 18.10.2003 and 10.1.2004 – 20.3.2004.

Successive Scoring Runs: 15 from 28.12.2004.

Successive Non-scoring Runs: 5 from 15.10.1996.

TEN YEAR LEAGUE RECORD

		P	W	D	L	F	A	Pts	Pos
2002-03	Div 2	46	13	13	20	59	66	52	18
2003-04	Div 2	46	6	19	21	50	75	37	24
2004-05	FL 2	46	17	14	15	58	52	65	10
2005-06	FL 2	46	18	17	11	72	56	71	6
2006-07	FL 2	46	16	14	16	52	47	62	12
2007-08	FL 2	46	22	12	12	56	42	78	7
2008-09	FL 2	46	20	18	8	54	33	78	3
2009-10	FL 1	46	10	15	21	56	76	45	22
2010-11	FL 2	46	22	14	10	69	50	80	3
2011-12	FL 1	46	11	10	25	65	88	43	21

DID YOU KNOW ?

On 24 September 2011, Wycombe Wanderers ended a 531-minute goal famine by inflicting upon Sheffield United their first away defeat of the season. This success also coincided with the Chairboys' manager Gary Waddock's 100th match in charge of the club.

WYCOMBE WANDERERS 2011–12 LEAGUE RECORD

Match No.	Date	Venue	Opponents	Result	H/T Score	Lg Pos.	Goalscorers	Attendance
1	Aug 6	H	Scunthorpe U	D 1-1	1-1	—	Tunnicliffe^{23}	4451
2	13	A	Colchester U	D 1-1	0-1	16	Rendell (pen)^{61}	3902
3	16	A	Leyton Orient	W 3-1	2-1	—	Strevens^{8}, Donnelly (pen)^{18}, Grant^{50}	3503
4	20	H	Bury	L 0-2	0-1	15		3259
5	27	A	Huddersfield T	L 0-3	0-0	17		11,953
6	Sept 10	H	Brentford	L 0-1	0-1	19		5045
7	13	A	Yeovil T	L 0-1	0-1	—		3134
8	17	A	Tranmere R	L 0-2	0-1	22		4297
9	24	H	Sheffield U	W 1-0	1-0	20	Beavon^{31}	5506
10	27	H	Preston NE	L 3-4	3-2	—	Ainsworth^{12}, Donnelly (pen)^{14}, Beavon^{27}	3734
11	Oct 1	A	Rochdale	L 1-2	1-1	22	Donnelly^{6}	2266
12	8	H	Walsall	D 1-1	0-0	22	Strevens^{49}	7097
13	15	A	Hartlepool U	W 3-1	2-0	19	Donnelly^{15}, Beavon^{36}, Collins (og)^{82}	5421
14	22	A	Oldham Ath	L 0-2	0-0	20		3592
15	25	H	Charlton Ath	L 1-2	0-2	—	Beavon^{63}	5406
16	29	H	Sheffield W	L 1-2	1-2	23	Ibe^{29}	6448
17	Nov 5	A	Notts Co	D 1-1	0-1	23	Grant^{90}	7664
18	19	H	Bournemouth	L 0-1	0-1	23		5350
19	26	A	Milton Keynes D	L 3-4	0-1	23	Beavon 2$^{51, 90}$, Trotta^{52}	9701
20	Dec 10	H	Chesterfield	W 3-2	1-1	23	McNamee^{31}, Trotta^{79}, Beavon^{90}	4320
21	17	A	Carlisle U	D 2-2	2-1	23	McNamee^{28}, Trotta^{36}	4414
22	26	H	Exeter C	W 3-1	2-1	20	Trotta 3$^{1, 40, 88}$	4904
23	31	H	Stevenage	L 0-1	0-0	21		4942
24	Jan 2	A	Bournemouth	L 0-2	0-1	22		7202
25	6	H	Huddersfield T	L 0-6	0-3	—		4465
26	14	A	Preston NE	L 2-3	1-1	22	Trotta 2$^{8, 89}$	10,142
27	21	H	Rochdale	W 3-0	1-0	22	Beavon 2$^{32, 73}$, Winfield^{75}	4285
28	28	A	Brentford	L 2-5	0-3	24	Winfield^{47}, Strevens^{76}	5560
29	Feb 4	H	Tranmere R	W 2-1	2-1	—	Whichelow^{23}, Ainsworth^{30}	4398
30	11	A	Sheffield U	L 0-3	0-0	—		17,165
31	14	H	Yeovil T	L 2-3	1-0	—	Beavon^{15}, Grant^{79}	3529
32	18	A	Walsall	L 0-2	0-0	24		3491
33	25	H	Hartlepool U	W 5-0	3-0	22	Hayes 2$^{5, 55}$, Doherty^{11}, Beavon 2$^{42, 71}$	4408
34	Mar 3	A	Scunthorpe U	L 1-4	0-2	24	McClure^{86}	3811
35	6	H	Leyton Orient	W 4-2	4-0	—	Beavon^{7}, Hayes^{26}, Bloomfield^{33}, Strevens^{39}	3564
36	10	H	Colchester U	D 0-0	0-0	22		4838
37	17	A	Bury	W 4-1	2-1	21	Beavon 3$^{4, 61, 70}$, Hayes^{12}	2479
38	20	A	Exeter C	W 3-1	0-0	—	Hayes 2$^{58, 70}$, Beavon^{63}	4121
39	24	H	Milton Keynes D	D 1-1	0-0	20	Beavon^{90}	5572
40	31	A	Stevenage	D 1-1	0-0	21	Basey (pen)^{90}	3593
41	Apr 6	H	Carlisle U	D 1-1	0-0	—	Lewis^{90}	4823
42	9	A	Chesterfield	L 0-4	0-1	21		5087
43	14	H	Oldham Ath	D 2-2	1-1	21	Beavon^{34}, Grant^{78}	5109
44	21	A	Charlton Ath	L 1-2	1-1	21	Beavon^{45}	18,539
45	28	H	Notts Co	L 3-4	2-2	21	Bloomfield^{1}, Basey (pen)^{17}, Beavon^{68}	5947
46	May 5	A	Sheffield W	L 0-2	0-1	21		38,082

Final League Position: 21

GOALSCORERS

League (65): Beavon 21, Trotta 8, Hayes 6, Donnelly 4 (2 pens), Grant 4, Strevens 4, Ainsworth 2, Basey 2 (2 pens), Bloomfield 2, McNamee 2, Winfield 2, Doherty 1, Ibe 1, Lewis 1, McClure 1, Rendell 1 (1 pen), Tunnicliffe 1, Whichelow 1, own goal 1.
Carling Cup (4): Beavon 1, Benyon 1 (pen), Donnelly 1, Grant 1.
FA Cup (0).
J Paint Trophy (4): Beavon 3, Betsy 1.

Bull N 46	Foster D 29	Sandell A 11	Halls J 5 + 2	Winfield D 25	Tunnicliffe J 16 + 1	Ainsworth G 16 + 16	Donnelly S 16 + 2	Rendell S 2 + 4	Strevens B 29 + 7	Grant J 22 + 8	Beavon S 40 + 3	Harris K 10 + 7	McCoy M 24 + 4	Benyon E 2 + 7	Harding B 3 + 4	Bloomfield M 24 + 7	Lewis S 38 + 3	Johnson L 24 + 3	Betsy K 1 + 2	Rowlands M 8 + 2	Basey G 29 + 3	Ibe J 2 + 5	Bignall N — + 1	Trotta M 8	McNamee A 11 + 4	Stewart A 4	Laing L 10 + 1	Kewley-Graham J — + 1	Harper J 5	Whichelow M 4	McClure M 3 + 9	Eastmond C 14	Doherty G 13	Hackett C 6 + 2	Hayes P 6	Dunne C — + 3	*Match No.*
1	2	3	4	5	6	7^{1}	8	9	10■	11^{2}	12	13																									1
1		3	4^{2}	5	6	7^{1}	8	9	10	11^{3}	14		2	12	13																						2
1	2	3	4	5	6	7^{1}	8^{3}		10	11	9^{2}			13	14	12																					3
1	2	3	4^{1}	5	6	7^{2}	8	14	10	11	9^{3}			13	12																						4
1		3			6	7^{2}	9^{1}		10^{3}	11	14		2	12	8		4	5	13																		5
1		3			6	13	8		10^{2}	11^{3}	9		2	12	4^{1}		7	5	14																		6
1	2	3			6		8	12	10^{1}	11		13		9		14	4^{3}	5	7^{2}																		7
1	2	3			6	7	8	14	10^{3}	11^{2}				9^{1}	13	12	4	5																			8
1	2	3	14		6		8^{2}		12	11^{3}	9	10^{1}			4	13	7	5																			9
1	2	3			6	7^{1}	8		12		9	10		13			11	5		4^{2}																	10
1	2	3^{1}			6	13	8			11^{2}	9	10	12	14			7^{3}	5		4																	11
1	2			5		7^{2}	8		12	14	9	10^{3}	13				11	6		4^{1}	3																12
1	2			5	12	7^{1}	8		10		9^{2}						11	6		4	3	13															13
1	2			5		7^{1}	8^{2}		10	12	9	13					11	6		4^{3}	3	14															14
1	2			5		13			10^{2}	11^{1}	9	7				8^{3}	4	6			3	14	12														15
1	2^{1}			5	6	7■				12	9	11					8			4	3	10															16
1	5						8		10^{2}	12	9	11	2				7^{1}	6		4	3	13															17
1	2				6		13	14	10^{3}	11	9	12				7^{2}	4	5			3	8^{1}															18
1	2^{2}			5	6		12			11^{3}	9	7	13				8			4^{1}	3	14		10													19
1				5			8^{1}			11	9		2			12	4	6			3			10	7												20
1				5						11^{2}	9	13	2			8	4	6		12	3			10^{1}	7												21
1	3			5		13				11^{1}	9	14	2			8	4	6		12				10^{3}	7^{2}												22
1	3		4	5^{2}		12				11	9		2			8		6			13			10	7^{1}												23
1	5				3	7^{2}					9	13	2^{1}			8	4	6			12			10	11												24
1	2		14		5	13				11	9		12			8	4	6^{1}			3			10^{3}	7^{2}												25
1	3					13			10	12	9	7	2^{2}			8	4				6^{1}			11		5											26
1	2			5		12			10	11^{1}	9^{2}	7				8	4				3						6	13									27
1	2			5		12			10	11	9					8	7^{1}				3						6		4								28
1				5		7^{1}			10		9^{3}					8	13	2			3				12		6		4	11^{2}	14						29
1	2			5					10^{3}		9					8	12	7^{2}			3				13		6		4	11^{1}	14						30
1				5		7^{1}			12	13	9					8	14	6			3				11^{2}		2		4^{3}	10							31
1	2			5		7^{2}			10^{3}	14	9						4				3				13		6		8	11^{1}	12						32
1									13		9^{2}		2			12	8				3				11		5				14	4^{1}	6	7	10^{3}		33
1						12			13				2			14	8^{2}				3				11		5^{3}				10	4	6	7^{1}	9		34
1	3			5		13			12		10		2			8	7										14				11^{1}	4^{3}	6		9^{2}		35
1	3			5					11		10		2			8	7															4	6		9		36
1	3^{1}			5					11		10^{2}		2			8	7				12										13	4	6	14	9^{3}		37
1				5^{1}		14			11^{3}		10		2			8	7	12			3											4	6	13	9^{2}		38
1						13			10		9		2				8				3				11^{1}		5				12	4	6	7^{2}			39
1						12			10		9		2			8	11^{1}				3					6					13	4	5	7^{2}			40
1									10		9		2			8^{1}	11				3				12	6^{2}					13	4	5	7			41
1						13			10		9		2^{3}			8	11	12			3					6^{1}					14	4	5	7^{2}			42
1				5^{1}					10	13	9		2			8	7	12			3				11^{2}							4	6				43
1	5								10	11	9		2			8	7	6			3^{1}											4				12	44
1						12			10^{1}	11^{2}	9		2			8	7	6			3											4	5			13	45
1						7					9		2			8	11				3^{1}						6				10	4	5			12	46

FA Cup

First Round	Fleetwood T	(a)	0-2

Carling Cup

First Round	Colchester U	(h)	3-3
Second Round	Nottingham F	(h)	1-4

J Paint Trophy

First Round	Bristol R	(h)	3-1
Second Round	Cheltenham T	(h)	1-3

YEOVIL TOWN FL Championship 1

FOUNDATION

One of the prime movers of Yeovil football was Ernest J. Sercombe. His association with the club began in 1895 as a playing member of Yeovil Casuals, of which team he became vice-captain and in his last season 1899–1900, he was chosen to play for Somerset against Devon. Upon the reorganisation of the club, he became secretary of the old Yeovil Town FC and with the amalgamation with Petters United in 1914, he continued to serve until his resignation in 1930.

Huish Park, Lufton Way, Yeovil, Somerset BA22 8YF.

Telephone: (01935) 423 662.

Fax: (01935) 473 956.

Ticket Office: (01935) 847 888.

Website: www.ytfc.net

Email: jcotton@ytfc.net

Ground Capacity: 9,665.

Record Attendance: 16,318 v Sunderland, FA Cup 4th rd, 29 January 1949 (at Huish); 9,527 v Leeds U, FL 1, 25 April 2008 (at Huish Park).

Pitch Measurements: 110m × 69m.

Chairman: John R. Fry.

Chief Executive: Martyn Starnes.

Manager: Gary Johnson.

Assistant Manager: Terry Skiverton.

Physio: Phil Cole.

Colours: Green and white hooped shirts with green sleeves and black trim, white shorts, white stockings.

Year Formed: 1895.

Turned Professional: 1921.

Previous Names: 1895, Yeovil Casuals; 1907, Yeovil Town; 1915, Yeovil & Petters United; 1946, Yeovil Town.

Club Nickname: 'Glovers'.

Grounds: 1895, Pen Mill Ground; 1921, Huish; 1990, Huish Park.

First Football League Game: 9 August 2003, Division 3 v Rochdale (a) W 3-1: Weale; Williams (Lindegaard), Crittenden, Lockwood, O'Brien, Pluck (Rodrigues), Gosling (El Kholti), Way, Jackson, Gall (2), Johnson (1).

Record League Victory: 6–1 v Oxford U, FL 2, 18 September 2004 – Weale; Rose, O'Brien, Way, Skiverton, Fontaine, Caceres (Tarachulski), Johnson, Jevons (3), Stoicers (2) (Mirza), Terry (Gall 1).

HONOURS

Football League – FL 2: ***Winners*** 2004–05.

Conference: *Champions* 2002–03.

FA Cup: 5th rd 1949.

League Cup: never past 2nd rd.

Southern League: ***Champions*** 1954–55, 1963–64, 1970–71; ***Runners-up***: 1923–24, 1931–32, 1934–35, 1969–70, 1972–73.

Southern League Cup: ***Winners*** 1948–49, 1954–55, 1960–61, 1965–66; ***Runners-up***: 1946–47, 1955–56.

Isthmian League: *Winners* 1987–88; ***Runners-up***: 1985–86, 1986–87, 1996–97.

AC Delco Cup: *Winners* 1987–88.

Bob Lord Trophy: *Winners* 1989–90.

FA Trophy: *Winners* 2002.

London Combination: ***Runners-up*** 1930–31, 1932–33.

sky SPORTS FACT FILE

In January 2004, Yeovil Town recorded "Yeovil True" ahead of the club's FA Cup tie with Liverpool. It was sold only in the town but 3,500 copies were snapped up in three days and the song went into the charts at No. 36. It was based on the Rolf Harris classic "Two Little Boys".

Record Cup Victory: 12–1 v Westbury United, FA Cup 1st qual rd, 1923–24.

Record Defeat: 0–8 v Manchester United, FA Cup 5th rd, 12 February 1949.

Most League Points (3 for a win): 83, FL 2, 2004–05.

Most League Goals: 90, FL 2, 2004–05.

Highest League Goalscorer in Season: Phil Jevons, 27, 2004–05.

Most League Goals in Total Aggregate: Phil Jevons, 42, 2004–06.

Most League Goals in One Match: 3, Phil Jevons v Oxford U, FL 2, 18 September 2004; 3, Phil Jevons v Chester C, FL 2, 30 October 2004; 3, Phil Jevons v Bristol R, FL 2, 12 February 2005; 3, Arron Davies v Chesterfield, FL 1, 4 March 2006.

Most Capped Players: Andrejs Stolcers, 1 (81), Latvia; Arron Davies, 1, Wales.

Most League Appearances: Terry Skiverton, 195, 2003–09.

Youngest League Player: TBC.

Record Transfer Fee Received: £1,200,000 from Nottingham F for Arron Davies and Chris Cohen, July 2007.

Record Transfer Fee Paid: £250,000 to Quilmes AC for Pablo Bastianini, August 2005.

Football League Record: 2003 Promoted to Division 3 from Conference; 2003–04 Division 3; 2004–05 FL 2; 2005– FL 1.

LATEST SEQUENCES

Longest Sequence of League Wins: 7, 7.12.2004 – 15.1.2005.

Longest Sequence of League Defeats: 5, 29.10.05 – 6.12.05.

Longest Sequence of Unbeaten League Matches: 7, 7.12.2004 – 15.1.2005.

Longest Sequence Without a League Win: 10, 17.9.2011 – 19.11.2011.

Successive Scoring Runs: 22 from 30.10.2004.

Successive Non-scoring Runs: 3 from 21.1.2006.

MANAGERS

Jack Gregory 1922–28
Tommy Lawes 1928–29
Dave Pratt 1929–33
Louis Page 1933–35
Dave Halliday 1935–38
Billy Kingdon 1938–46
Alec Stock 1946–49
George Patterson 1949–51
Harry Lowe 1951–53
Ike Clarke 1953–57
Norman Dodgin 1957
Jimmy Baldwin 1957–60
Basil Hayward 1960–64
Glyn Davies 1964–65
Joe McDonald 1965–67
Ron Saunders 1967–69
Mike Hughes 1969–72
Cecil Irwin 1972–75
Stan Harland 1975–81
Barry Lloyd 1978–81
Malcolm Allison 1981
Jimmy Giles 1981–83
Trevor Finnigan/Mike Hughes 1983
Steve Coles 1983–84
Ian McFarlane 1984
Gerry Gow 1984–87
Brian Hall 1987–90
Clive Whitehead 1990–91
Steve Rutter 1991–93
Brian Hall 1994–95
Graham Roberts 1995–98
Colin Lippiatt 1998–99
Steve Thompson 1999–2000
Dave Webb 2000
Gary Johnson 2001–05
Steve Thompson 2005–06
Russell Slade 2006–09
Terry Skiverton 2009–12
Gary Johnson January 2012–

TEN YEAR LEAGUE RECORD

		P	*W*	*D*	*L*	*F*	*A*	*Pts*	*Pos*
2002-03	Conf.	42	28	11	3	100	37	95	1
2003-04	Div 3	46	23	5	18	70	57	74	8
2004-05	FL 2	46	25	8	13	90	65	83	1
2005-06	FL 1	46	15	11	20	54	62	56	15
2006-07	FL 1	46	23	10	13	55	39	79	5
2007-08	FL 1	46	14	10	22	38	59	52	18
2008-09	FL 1	46	12	15	19	41	66	51	17
2009-10	FL 1	46	13	14	19	55	59	53	15
2010-11	FL 1	46	16	11	19	56	66	59	14
2011-12	FL 1	46	14	12	20	59	80	54	17

DID YOU KNOW ?

The first time Yeovil & Petters United met Football League opposition was in a fourth qualifying round of the FA Cup in 1924–25 against Bournemouth. A then record crowd of 5,500 saw Yeovil win 3-2 and in the next round the visit of Bristol Rovers saw the attendance bar raised to 6,600.

YEOVIL TOWN 2011–12 LEAGUE RECORD

Match No.	Date	Venue	Opponents	Result		H/T Score	Lg Pos.	Goalscorers	Attendance
1	Aug 6	A	Brentford	L	0-2	0-1	—		6278
2	13	H	Oldham Ath	W	3-1	0-0	8	Upson [49], Williams, A [74], Wotton (pen) [82]	3237
3	16	H	Milton Keynes D	L	0-1	0-1	—		3274
4	20	A	Walsall	D	1-1	1-1	18	Williams, G [42]	4247
5	27	H	Sheffield U	L	0-1	0-1	18		5001
6	Sept 3	A	Tranmere R	D	0-0	0-0	17		5037
7	9	A	Preston NE	L	3-4	1-1	—	Edgar [31], MacLean 2 (1 pen) [64, 81 (p)]	11,474
8	13	H	Wycombe W	W	1-0	1-0	—	Upson [8]	3134
9	17	H	Sheffield W	L	2-3	2-1	18	Agard 2 [28, 38]	4445
10	24	A	Scunthorpe U	L	1-2	1-1	19	Wotton (pen) [45]	4086
11	Oct 1	H	Bury	L	1-3	1-1	21	Agard [17]	3127
12	8	A	Colchester U	D	2-2	1-1	21	Massey 2 [1, 63]	3521
13	15	H	Carlisle U	L	0-3	0-0	23		3673
14	22	A	Stevenage	D	0-0	0-0	24		3036
15	25	H	Leyton Orient	D	2-2	2-1	—	Agard [37], N'Gala [41]	3121
16	29	H	Huddersfield T	L	0-1	0-0	24		3486
17	Nov 5	A	Chesterfield	D	2-2	1-1	24	Massey [29], Allott (og) [76]	5882
18	19	H	Exeter C	D	2-2	1-2	22	Upson [2], Blizzard [56]	5635
19	26	A	Hartlepool U	W	1-0	1-0	22	N'Gala [25]	4604
20	Dec 10	H	Notts Co	W	1-0	0-0	19	Williams, A [88]	3663
21	17	A	Rochdale	D	0-0	0-0	19		2692
22	26	H	Charlton Ath	L	2-3	1-1	21	Obika [8], Huntington [50]	4977
23	31	H	Bournemouth	L	1-3	0-2	22	Huntington [66]	5632
24	Jan 2	A	Exeter C	D	1-1	1-0	21	Williams, A [40]	5912
25	10	A	Sheffield U	L	0-4	0-2	—		15,965
26	14	H	Tranmere R	W	2-1	1-1	21	Edwards [19], Williams, A [90]	4083
27	21	A	Bury	L	2-3	1-3	21	Dickson [10], MacLean [87]	2527
28	28	H	Preston NE	W	2-1	1-0	18	Williams, A 2 [30, 62]	4245
29	Feb 4	A	Sheffield W	L	1-2	1-0	—	Obika [41]	17,213
30	14	A	Wycombe W	W	3-2	0-1	—	Williams, A 2 [59, 67], Agard [73]	3529
31	18	H	Colchester U	W	3-2	0-1	18	Parrett [55], D'Ath [70], Williams, A [72]	3442
32	25	A	Carlisle U	L	2-3	0-1	18	Obika [46], Blizzard [82]	4265
33	Mar 3	H	Brentford	W	2-1	0-1	17	Williams, A 2 [49, 87]	3930
34	6	A	Milton Keynes D	W	1-0	1-0	—	Williams, G [40]	6624
35	10	A	Oldham Ath	W	2-1	1-0	15	Williams, G [10], Williams, A [65]	4689
36	13	H	Scunthorpe U	D	2-2	1-0	—	Williams, G [30], Franks [68]	3767
37	17	H	Walsall	W	2-1	0-1	12	Williams, A 2 [63, 84]	3705
38	20	A	Charlton Ath	L	0-3	0-1	—		13,717
39	24	H	Hartlepool U	L	0-1	0-0	16		4033
40	31	A	Bournemouth	D	0-0	0-0	15		6170
41	Apr 7	H	Rochdale	W	3-1	2-0	14	Franks [7], Hinds [29], Woods [75]	3859
42	9	A	Notts Co	L	1-3	0-1	15	Franks [79]	5852
43	14	H	Stevenage	L	0-6	0-2	17		3610
44	21	A	Leyton Orient	D	2-2	0-1	16	Williams, A [82], Obika [90]	4888
45	28	H	Chesterfield	W	3-2	1-1	16	Blizzard [26], Agard [73], Williams, A [80]	4563
46	May 5	A	Huddersfield T	L	0-2	0-1	17		13,520

Final League Position: 17

GOALSCORERS

League (59): Williams, A 16, Agard 6, Obika 4, Williams, G 4, Blizzard 3, Franks 3, MacLean 3 (1 pen), Massey 3, Upson 3, Huntington 2, N'Gala 2, Wotton 2 (2 pens), D'Ath 1, Dickson 1, Edgar 1, Edwards 1, Hinds 1, Parrett 1, Woods 1, own goal 1.
Carling Cup (0).
FA Cup (5): Upson 2, Blizzard 1, Clifford 1, Williams, A 1.
J Paint Trophy (2): Ehmer 1, MacLean 1.

Steer J 12	Ayling L 44	Jones N 21 + 1	N'Gala B 24 + 7	Huntington P 37	Wotton P 22	Williams G 23 + 5	Upson E 40 + 1	MacLean S 14 + 6	Obika J 24 + 3	Ehmer M 24	Haynes-Brown C 1 + 9	Fallon R — + 5	Williams A 31 + 4	Gilbert K 3 + 5	Agard K 13 + 16	O'Brien A 8 + 5	Edgar A 5 + 5	Gibson B 1 + 4	Blizzard D 24 + 6	Massey G 8 + 8	Johnson O 5 + 1	Stech M 5	Morris J 3 + 2	Belson F 1	Purse D 5	Clifford C 6 + 1	Stewart G 1	Gilmartin R 8	Dickson R 5	Parrett D 9 + 1	Edwards J 4	Walker S 20	Youga K — + 1	Hinds R 15 + 1	D'Ath L 12 + 2	Franks J 13 + 1	Grounds J 13 + 1	Woods M 2 + 3	*Match No.*
1	2	3	4	5	6	7	8	9^{2}	10^{3}	11^{1}	12	13	14																										1
1	2	11		5	6	7^{3}	8	14	10^{1}	4		13	9	3^{2}	12																								2
1	2	11		5	6	7^{3}	8	9^{2}		4		13	10	3^{1}		12	14																						3
1	2		4^{1}	5	6	7	8		10	3	12	14	9^{3}			11^{2}	13																						4
1	2			5	6	7	8	9^{2}		4	3▮	13	10^{1}			11^{3}	12	14																					5
1	2	3		5	6	7	8	9		4				13	12	10^{2}	11^{1}																						6
1	2	3		5	6^{3}	7^{1}	8	9		4				13	12	10^{2}	11		14																				7
1	2	3		5	6		8	9		4				12	10^{1}	11^{2}	7^{3}		13	14																			8
1	2	3	12	5			8	9		4					10^{3}	11^{2}	7	14	6^{1}	13																			9
1	2	3^{3}		5	6		8	9		4	14				10	11^{2}	7^{1}	13		12																			10
1	2	3		5	6		8	9		4					10^{2}	11^{1}	14	7^{3}		13	12																		11
1	2	3	6	5	11		8	9		4					12					7	10^{1}																		12
	2	3^{2}	5		6		8	9^{3}		4	14				12		13			11	10^{1}	1		7▮															13
	2▮		3		6		8	9^{1}		4	14				7			13	12	11^{3}	10^{2}	1			5														14
		3	6		8		4			2	13			12	9				7^{2}	11	10^{1}	1			5														15
	2	3	4		6		8								9^{1}	12			7	11	10	1			5														16
		3^{1}	2		6		8			4			13	12	9	14			7^{2}	10		1			5	11^{3}													17
	2			5	6		8	14	13	3			9^{3}		10^{2}				7	12					4	11^{1}	1												18
	2		4	5	6		8	14	13	3			9^{2}		10^{3}				7	12						11^{1}		1											19
	2		4	5	6	12	8	14	9^{2}	3			13		10^{3}					7						11^{1}		1											20
	2			5	6	12	8		9^{3}	4			13	3▮		14			7	10^{2}						11^{1}		1											21
	2		4	5	6	7^{1}	8		10	3			9			12			11									1											22
	2		4	5		10		12	9	3			7		8^{2}				6	13						11^{1}		1											23
	2	3	4	5		11		9^{2}	10	6			7		13				8^{1}							12		1											24
	2	14	12	5	6^{1}	11^{3}	8	9^{2}	10	4			7							13								1	3										25
	2	3^{1}	4	5		12	8		10				9															1	11	6	7								26
	2	3^{1}	4	5		13	8	14	10				9																11^{3}	6^{2}	7	1	12						27
	2		4	5▮		7	8		10				9		12														3	6^{1}	11	1							28
	2		4			7	8		10		12		9																3	6^{1}	11	1		5					29
	2	3	4			7^{1}	8		10^{3}		14		9		12				13											11		1		5	6^{2}				30
	2	3	4			7	8		10				9		13▮				12											6^{1}		1		5	11^{2}				31
	2	3^{2}	4			7	6		10				9						12													1		5	8^{1}	11	13		32
	2	3^{2}	14	5		7	12		10				9						8											4^{1}		1		13		11^{3}	6		33
	2			5		7	8						9						11											4▮		1		6	10^{1}	12	3		34
	2		12	5		7	8		10				9						6^{1}													1		4		11	3		35
	2		14	5		7	8		10^{1}				9^{2}		13				6													1		4	12	11^{3}	3		36
	2			5		7	8		10^{2}				9						6^{1}											13		1		4		11	3	12	37
	2		13	5		7^{1}	8						9		14				6											10^{3}		1		4^{2}	12	11	3		38
	2		4	5			8		10				9		13				6^{1}				11									1			7^{2}		3	12	39
	2			5			8		10				9						6				3									1		4	7	11			40
	2			5			8						9^{2}		13				11				4^{1}									1		6	7	10	3	12	41
	2			5			8						9		13				11				12									1		6	7	10^{2}	3	4^{1}	42
	2		12	5^{1}		7^{2}			13		14		9						6													1		4	11	10	3^{3}	8▮	43
	2		8	5					10				9		12				6													1		4	7^{1}	11	3		44
	7		2	5					10^{1}				9		12				6													1		4	8	11	3		45
	2		4	5		12	8						9		10^{2}				6				13									1			11^{1}	7	3		46

FA Cup

First Round	Hereford U	(a)	3-0
Second Round	Fleetwood T	(a)	2-2
		(h)	0-2

Carling Cup

First Round	Exeter C	(a)	0-2

J Paint Trophy

Second Round	Bournemouth	(a)	2-3

YORK CITY FL Championship 2

FOUNDATION

Although there was a York City club formed in 1903 by a soccer enthusiast from Darlington, this has no connection with the modern club because it went out of existence during World War I. Unlike many others of that period who restarted in 1919, York City did not re-form until 1922 and the tendency now is to ignore the modern club's pre-1922 existence.

Bootham Crescent, York YO30 7AQ.

Telephone: (01904) 624 447.

Fax: (01904) 631 457.

Ticket Office: (01904) 624 447 (ext 2).

Email: enquiries@yorkcityfootballclub.co.uk

Ground Capacity: 9,496.

Record Attendance: 28,123 v Huddersfield T, FA Cup 6th rd, 5 March 1938.

Pitch Measurements: 115yd × 74yd.

Chairman: Jason McGill.

Manager: Gary Mills.

Assistant Manager: Darron Gee.

Physio: Jeff Miller.

Colours: Red shirts, navy shorts, navy stockings.

Year Formed: 1922.

Turned Professional: 1922.

Ltd Co.: 1922.

Club Nickname: 'Minstermen'.

Previous Grounds: 1922, Fulfordgate; 1932, Bootham Crescent.

First Football League Game: 31 August 1929, Division 3 (N), v Wigan Borough (a) W 2–0 – Farmery; Archibald, Johnson; Beck, Davis, Thompson; Evans, Gardner, Cowie (1), Smailes, Stockill (1).

Record League Victory: 9–1 v Southport, Division 3 (N), 2 February 1957 – Forgan; Phillips, Howe; Brown (1), Cairney, Mollatt; Hill, Bottom (4 incl. 1p), Wilkinson (2), Wragg (1), Fenton (1).

Record Cup Victory: 6–0 v South Shields (away), FA Cup 1st rd, 16 November 1968 – Widdowson; Baker (1p), Richardson; Carr, Jackson, Burrows; Taylor, Ross (3), MacDougall (2), Hodgson, Boyer.

Record Defeat: 0–12 v Chester, Division 3 (N), 1 February 1936.

Most League Points (2 for a win): 62, Division 4, 1964–65.

Most League Points (3 for a win): 101, Division 4, 1983–84.

HONOURS

Football League –Division 3: ***Promoted*** 1973–74 (3rd); **Division 4:** ***Champions*** 1983–84. 1992–93 *(play-offs)*.

FA Cup: ***Semi-finals*** 1955, *when in Division 3.*

Football League Cup: best season: 5th rd, 1962.

FA Trophy: ***Winners*** 2012; ***Runners-up*** 2009.

sky SPORTS FACT FILE

York City signed right-winger Joe Hulme from Stafford YMCA, his local club, in 1923. By February 1924 he had been snapped up by Blackburn Rovers for just £220 and went on to win nine full caps for England and extend his career with Huddersfield Town and then Arsenal.

Most League Goals: 96, Division 4, 1983–84.

Highest League Scorer in Season: Bill Fenton, 31, Division 3 (N), 1951–52; Arthur Bottom, 31, Division 3 (N), 1954–55 and 1955–56.

Most League Goals in Total Aggregate: Norman Wilkinson, 125, 1954–66.

Most League Goals in One Match: 5, Alf Patrick v Rotherham U, Division 3N, 20 November 1948.

Most Capped Player: Peter Scott, 7 (10), Northern Ireland.

Most League Appearances: Barry Jackson, 481, 1958–70.

Youngest League Player: Reg Stockill, 15 years 281 days v Wigan Borough, 31 August 1929.

Record Transfer Fee Received: £1,000,000 from Manchester U for Jonathan Greening, March 1998.

Record Transfer Fee Paid: £140,000 to Burnley for Adrian Randall, December 1995.

Football League Record: 1929 Elected to Division 3 (N); 1958–59 Division 4; 1959–60 Division 3; 1960–65 Division 4; 1965–66 Division 3; 1966–71 Division 4; 1971–74 Division 3; 1974–76 Division 2; 1976–77 Division 3; 1977–84 Division 4; 1984–88 Division 3; 1988–92 Division 4; 1992–93 Division 3; 1993–99 Division 2; 1999–04 Division 3; 2004–07 Conference; 2007–12 Blue Square Premier; 2012– FL 2.

MANAGERS

Bill Sherrington 1924–60
(was Secretary for most of this time but virtually Secretary-Manager for a long pre-war spell)
John Collier 1929–36
Tom Mitchell 1936–50
Dick Duckworth 1950–52
Charlie Spencer 1952–53
Jimmy McCormick 1953–54
Sam Bartram 1956–60
Tom Lockie 1960–67
Joe Shaw 1967–68
Tom Johnston 1968–75
Wilf McGuinness 1975–77
Charlie Wright 1977–80
Barry Lyons 1980–81
Denis Smith 1982–87
Bobby Saxton 1987–88
John Bird 1988–91
John Ward 1991–93
Alan Little 1993–99
Neil Thompson 1999–2000
Terry Dolan 2000–03
Chris Brass 2003–04
Billy McEwan 2005–07
Colin Walker 2007–08
Martin Foyle 2008–10
Gary Mills October 2010–

LATEST SEQUENCES

Longest Sequence of League Wins: 7, 31.10.1964 – 26.12.1964.

Longest Sequence of League Defeats: 8, 14.11.1966 – 31.12.1966.

Longest Sequence of League Draws: 6, 26.12.1992 – 22.1.1993.

Longest Sequence of Unbeaten League Matches: 21, 10.9.1973 – 12.1.1974.

Longest Sequence Without a League Win: 20, 17.1.2004 – continuing.

Successive Scoring Runs: 24 from 3.3.1984.

Successive Non-scoring Runs: 7 from 28.8.1972.

TEN YEAR LEAGUE RECORD

		P	W	D	L	F	A	Pts	Pos
2002-03	Div 3	46	17	15	14	52	53	66	10
2003-04	Div 3	46	10	14	22	35	66	44	24
2004-05	Conf	42	11	10	21	39	66	43	17
2005-06	Conf	42	17	12	13	63	48	63	8
2006-07	Conf	46	23	11	12	65	45	80	4
2007-08	BSP	46	17	11	18	71	74	62	14
2008-09	BSP	46	11	19	16	47	51	52	17
2009-10	BSP	44	22	12	10	62	35	78	5
2010-11	BSP	46	19	14	13	55	50	71	8
2011-12	BSP	46	23	14	9	81	45	83	4

DID YOU KNOW ?

Twice in a week in May 2012, York City defeated Luton Town at Wembley, initially winning the FA Trophy then regaining Football League status. It was the fourth time the teams had met in 2011–12, York again winning 3-0 at home and 2-1 away in the Blue Square Premier League.

ENGLISH LEAGUE PLAYERS DIRECTORY

Players listed represent those with their clubs during the 2011–12 season.

Players are listed alphabetically on pages 560–566.
The number alongside each player corresponds to the team number heading. (Abadaki, Godwin 69 = team 69 (Rochdale))

ACCRINGTON S (1)

AMOND, Padraig (F) **161** **44**
H: 5 11 W: 12 05 b.Carlow 15-4-88
Honours: Eire Under-21.
2006 Shamrock R 10 1
2007 Shamrock R 6 1
2007 *Kildare Co* 13 5 **13** **5**
2008 Shamrock R 26 9
2009 Shamrock R 20 4 **62** **15**
2010 Sligo R 27 17 **27** **17**
2010-11 Pacos 17 0 **17** **0**
2011-12 Accrington S 42 7 **42** **7**

BARNETT, Charlie (M) **118** **7**
H: 5 7 W: 11 07 b.Liverpool 19-9-88
Source: Scholar.
2006-07 Liverpool 0 0
2007-08 Liverpool 0 0
2008-09 Tranmere R 29 3
2009-10 Tranmere R 7 1 **36** **4**
2010-11 Accrington S 40 2
2011-12 Accrington S 42 1 **82** **3**

BURTON, Alan (M) **2** **0**
H: 6 0 W: 11 00 b.Blackpool 22-2-91
Source: Scholar.
2009-10 Accrington S 0 0
2010-11 Accrington S 1 0
2011-12 Accrington S 1 0 **2** **0**

CARVER, Marcus (F) **2** **0**
H: 5 11 W: 11 11 b.Blackburn 22-10-93
Source: Scholar.
2011-12 Accrington S 2 0 **2** **0**

COID, Danny (D) **294** **10**
H: 5 11 W: 11 07 b.Liverpool 3-10-81
Source: Trainee.
1998-99 Blackpool 1 0
1999-2000 Blackpool 21 1
2000-01 Blackpool 46 1
2001-02 Blackpool 27 3
2002-03 Blackpool 36 1
2003-04 Blackpool 35 3
2004-05 Blackpool 35 0
2005-06 Blackpool 13 0
2006-07 Blackpool 18 0
2007-08 Blackpool 13 0
2008-09 Blackpool 18 0
2009-10 Blackpool 1 0
2010-11 Blackpool 0 0 **264** **9**
2010-11 *Rotherham U* 9 0 **9** **0**
2011-12 Accrington S 21 1 **21** **1**

CRANEY, Ian (M) **176** **28**
H: 5 10 W: 12 00 b.Liverpool 21-7-82
Source: Runcorn, Altrincham.
2006-07 Accrington S 18 5
2006-07 Swansea C 27 0
2007-08 Swansea C 1 0 **28** **0**
2007-08 Accrington S 34 7
2008-09 Accrington S 2 1
2008-09 Huddersfield T 34 5
2009-10 Huddersfield T 0 0 **34** **5**
2009-10 *Morecambe* 16 2 **16** **2**
From Fleetwood T.
2010-11 Accrington S 22 7
From Fleetwood T.
2011-12 Accrington S 22 1 **98** **21**

DUNBAVIN, Ian (G) **223** **0**
H: 6 1 W: 12 10 b.Knowsley 27-5-80
Source: Trainee.
1998-99 Liverpool 0 0
1999-2000 Liverpool 0 0
1999-2000 Shrewsbury T 7 0
2000-01 Shrewsbury T 22 0
2001-02 Shrewsbury T 34 0
2002-03 Shrewsbury T 33 0
2003-04 Shrewsbury T 0 0 **96** **0**
From Halifax T.
2006-07 Accrington S 23 0
2007-08 Accrington S 23 0
2008-09 Accrington S 4 0
2009-10 Accrington S 27 0
2010-11 Accrington S 25 0
2011-12 Accrington S 25 0 **127** **0**

GUTHRIE, Kurtis (F) **13** **0**
H: 5 11 W: 11 00 b.Jersey 21-4-93
Source: Trinity.
2011-12 Accrington S 13 0 **13** **0**

HATFIELD, Will (M) **17** **3**
H: 5 8 W: 10 00 b.Liversedge 10-10-91
Source: Scholar.
2009-10 Leeds U 0 0
2010-11 Leeds U 0 0
2011-12 Leeds U 0 0
2011-12 Accrington S 17 3 **17** **3**

HESSEY, Sean (D) **284** **5**
H: 5 11 W: 12 08 b.Prescot 19-9-78
Source: Liverpool Trainee.
1997-98 Wigan Ath 0 0
1997-98 Leeds U 0 0
1997-98 Huddersfield T 1 0
1998-99 Huddersfield T 10 0 **11** **0**
1999-2000 Kilmarnock 11 0
2000-01 Kilmarnock 6 0
2001-02 Kilmarnock 15 0
2002-03 Kilmarnock 5 0
2003-04 Kilmarnock 7 1 **44** **1**
2003-04 Blackpool 6 0 **6** **0**
2004-05 Chester C 34 1
2005-06 Chester C 19 0
2006-07 Chester C 26 0
2007-08 Chester C 0 0 **79** **1**
2007-08 *Macclesfield T* 26 0
2008-09 Macclesfield T 33 0
2009-10 Macclesfield T 27 0 **86** **0**
2010-11 Accrington S 41 1
2011-12 Accrington S 17 2 **58** **3**

HOPPER, Ryan (M) **4** **0**
H: 5 11 W: 11 11 b.Manchester 13-11-93
Source: Scholar.
2011-12 Accrington S 4 0 **4** **0**

HUGHES, Bryan (M) **487** **55**
H: 5 10 W: 11 08 b.Liverpool 19-6-76
Source: Trainee. *Honours:* England Under-21.
1993-94 Wrexham 11 0
1994-95 Wrexham 38 9
1995-96 Wrexham 22 0
1996-97 Wrexham 23 3 **94** **12**
1996-97 Birmingham C 11 0
1997-98 Birmingham C 40 5
1998-99 Birmingham C 28 3
1999-2000 Birmingham C 45 10
2000-01 Birmingham C 45 4
2001-02 Birmingham C 31 7
2002-03 Birmingham C 22 2
2003-04 Birmingham C 26 3 **248** **34**
2004-05 Charlton Ath 17 1
2005-06 Charlton Ath 33 3
2006-07 Charlton Ath 24 1 **74** **5**
2007-08 Hull C 35 1
2008-09 Hull C 6 0
2009-10 Hull C 0 0 **41** **1**
2009-10 *Derby Co* 3 0 **3** **0**
2010-11 Burton Alb 1 0 **1** **0**
From Grimsby T.
2011 IBV 5 0 **5** **0**
2011-12 Accrington S 21 3 **21** **3**

JOYCE, Luke (M) **137** **6**
H: 5 11 W: 12 03 b.Bolton 9-7-87
Source: Scholar.
2005-06 Wigan Ath 0 0
2005-06 Carlisle U 0 0
2006-07 Carlisle U 16 1
2007-08 Carlisle U 3 1
2008-09 Carlisle U 7 0 **26** **2**
2009-10 Accrington S 41 1
2010-11 Accrington S 27 1
2011-12 Accrington S 43 2 **111** **4**

LINDFIELD, Craig (F) **106** **10**
H: 6 0 W: 10 05 b.Greasby 7-9-88
Source: Scholar. *Honours:* England Youth.
2006-07 Liverpool 0 0
2007-08 Liverpool 0 0
2007-08 *Notts Co* 3 1 **3** **1**
2007-08 *Chester C* 7 0 **7** **0**
2008-09 Liverpool 0 0
2008-09 *Bournemouth* 3 1 **3** **1**
2008-09 *Accrington S* 20 2
2009-10 Liverpool 0 0
2009-10 Macclesfield T 18 2 **18** **2**
2010-11 Accrington S 16 0
2011-12 Accrington S 39 4 **75** **6**

McINTYRE, Kevin (M) **315** **22**
H: 6 0 W: 11 10 b.Liverpool 23-12-77
Source: Trainee.
1996-97 Tranmere R 0 0
1997-98 Tranmere R 2 0
1998-99 Tranmere R 0 0
1999-2000 Tranmere R 0 0
2000-01 Tranmere R 0 0
2001-02 Tranmere R 0 0 **2** **0**
2004-05 Chester C 10 0 **10** **0**
2004-05 Macclesfield T 23 0
2005-06 Macclesfield T 44 5
2006-07 Macclesfield T 44 9
2007-08 Macclesfield T 23 2 **134** **16**
2007-08 Shrewsbury T 22 2
2008-09 Shrewsbury T 26 0
2009-10 Shrewsbury T 45 1
2010-11 Shrewsbury T 31 1 **124** **4**
2011-12 Accrington S 45 2 **45** **2**

MURDOCH, Sean (G) **70** **0**
H: 6 2 W: 11 09 b.Edinburgh 31-7-86
Honours: Scotland Youth.
2003-04 Dunfermline Ath 0 0
2004-05 Dunfermline Ath 0 0
2005-06 Dunfermline Ath 0 0
2005-06 *Forfar Ath* 13 0
2006-07 Dunfermline Ath 0 0
2006-07 *Forfar Ath* 17 0 **30** **0**
2006-07 *Hamilton A* 11 0
2007-08 Dunfermline Ath 5 0 **5** **0**
2008-09 Hamilton A 4 0
2009-10 Hamilton A 6 0
2010-11 Hamilton A 1 0 **22** **0**
2011-12 Accrington S 13 0 **13** **0**

MURPHY, Peter (D) **66** **4**
H: 6 0 W: 11 10 b.Liverpool 13-2-90
Source: Scholar.
2007-08 Accrington S 2 0
2008-09 Accrington S 3 0
2009-10 Accrington S 10 0
2010-11 Accrington S 13 0
2011-12 Accrington S 38 4 **66** **4**

RICHARDSON, Leam (D) **205** **2**
H: 5 7 W: 11 04 b.Leeds 19-11-79
Source: Trainee.
1997-98 Blackburn R 0 0
1998-99 Blackburn R 0 0
1999-2000 Blackburn R 0 0
2000-01 Bolton W 12 0
2001-02 Bolton W 1 0
2001-02 *Notts Co* 21 0 **21** **0**
2002-03 Bolton W 0 0 **13** **0**
2002-03 *Blackpool* 20 0
2003-04 Blackpool 28 0
2004-05 Blackpool 23 0 **71** **0**
2006-07 Accrington S 38 0
2007-08 Accrington S 37 1
2008-09 Accrington S 11 0
2009-10 Accrington S 2 0
2010-11 Accrington S 11 1
2011-12 Accrington S 1 0 **100** **2**

TAYLOR, Nat (F) **2 0**
H: 5 11 W: 11 00 b.Manchester 3-9-92
Source: Rossendale Coll.
2011-12 Accrington S 2 0 **2 0**

WILLIS, Liam (D) **2 0**
H: 6 0 W: 11 11 b.Liverpool 21-5-93
Source: Southport Youth, Wigan Scholar.
2011-12 Accrington S 2 0 **2 0**

WINNARD, Dean (D) **119 2**
H: 5 9 W: 10 04 b.Wigan 20-8-89
2006-07 Blackburn R 0 0
2007-08 Blackburn R 0 0
2008-09 Blackburn R 0 0
2009-10 Accrington S 44 0
2010-11 Accrington S 45 1
2011-12 Accrington S 30 1 **119 2**

AFC WIMBLEDON (2)

ADEMENO, Charlie (F) **19 1**
H: 5 10 W: 11 13 b.Milton Keynes 12-12-88
Source: Scholar.
2005-06 Southend U 1 0
2006-07 Southend U 1 0
2007-08 Southend U 0 0
2008-09 Southend U 2 0 **4 0**
From Crawley T, Grimsby T.
2011-12 AFC Wimbledon 15 1 **15 1**

BROWN, Sebastian (G) **44 0**
H: 6 2 W: 13 07 b. 24-11-89
Source: Scholar.
2008-09 Brentford 0 0
2009-10 Brentford 0 0
2011-12 AFC Wimbledon 44 0 **44 0**

BUSH, Chris (D) **22 0**
H: 6 3 W: 14 02 b.Leytonstone 12-6-92
Source: Brentford Scholar.
2011-12 AFC Wimbledon 22 0 **22 0**

DJILALI, Kieran (M) **58 4**
H: 6 3 W: 13 02 b.Lambeth 22-1-91
Source: Scholar.
2008-09 Crystal Palace 6 0
2009-10 Crystal Palace 8 1
2009-10 *Chesterfield* 8 1
2010-11 Crystal Palace 14 0 **28 1**
2010-11 *Chesterfield* 10 1 **18 2**
2011-12 AFC Wimbledon 12 1 **12 1**

FRANKS, Fraser (D) **4 0**
H: 6 0 W: 10 12 b.Hammersmith 22-11-90
Source: Scholar.
2009-10 Brentford 0 0
2011-12 AFC Wimbledon 4 0 **4 0**

GWILLIM, Gareth (M) **29 1**
H: 6 0 W: 12 06 b.Bromley 9-2-83
Source: Welling U.
2000-01 Crystal Palace 0 0
2001-02 Crystal Palace 0 0
From Ashford T, Farnborough T, Bishop's Stortford, Histon.
2010-11 Dagenham & R 2 0 **2 0**
2011-12 AFC Wimbledon 27 1 **27 1**

HARRISON, Byron (F) **57 12**
H: 6 3 W: 13 02 b.Wandsworth 15-6-87
Source: Havant & Waterlooville, Worthing, Boreham Wood, Harrow B, Ashford T, Carshalton Ath.
2010-11 Stevenage 20 8
2011-12 Stevenage 18 2 **38 10**
2011-12 AFC Wimbledon 19 2 **19 2**

HATTON, Sam (D) **44 1**
H: 5 11 W: 11 02 b.St Albans 7-2-88
Source: Stevenage.
2011-12 AFC Wimbledon 44 1 **44 1**

JACKSON, Ryan (M) **7 0**
H: 5 9 W: 10 03 b.Streatham 31-7-90
Source: Youth.
2011-12 AFC Wimbledon 7 0 **7 0**

JOHNSON, Brett (D) **54 0**
H: 6 1 W: 13 00 b.Hammersmith 15-8-85
Source: Ashford T, Aldershot T.
2005-06 Northampton T 6 0
2006-07 Northampton T 4 0
2007-08 Northampton T 16 0 **26 0**
2008-09 Brentford 10 0
2009-10 Brentford 0 0 **10 0**
2011-12 AFC Wimbledon 18 0 **18 0**

JOHNSON, Huw (F) **1 0**
b.Hammersmith 22-6-93
Source: Youth.
2011-12 AFC Wimbledon 1 0 **1 0**

JOLLEY, Christian (F) **37 7**
H: 6 0 W: 10 00 b.Fleet 12-5-88
Source: Kingstonian.
2011-12 AFC Wimbledon 37 7 **37 7**

JONES, Reece (M) **1 0**
H: 6 1 W: 11 09 b.Chessington 22-7-92
Source: Fulham Scholar. *Honours:* Wales Youth, Under-21.
2011-12 AFC Wimbledon 1 0 **1 0**

KIERNAN, Brendan (M) **9 0**
H: 5 9 W: 11 11 b.Lambeth 10-11-92
Source: Youth.
2011-12 AFC Wimbledon 9 0 **9 0**

McNAUGHTON, Callum (D) **18 0**
H: 6 2 W: 13 05 b.Harlow 25-10-91
Source: Scholar.
2010-11 West Ham U 0 0
2011-12 West Ham U 0 0
2011-12 AFC Wimbledon 18 0 **18 0**

MERRIFIELD, Frankie (M) **0 0**
2011-12 AFC Wimbledon 0 0

MIDSON, Jack (F) **76 26**
H: 5 8 W: 11 07 b.Stevenage 21-7-83
Source: Stevenage B, Chelmsford C (loan), Dagenham & R, Hemel Hempstead (loan), Bishop's Stortford, Histon.
2010-11 Oxford U 21 6 **21 6**
2010-11 *Southend U* 4 2 **4 2**
2010-11 *Barnet* 5 0 **5 0**
2011-12 AFC Wimbledon 46 18 **46 18**

MINSHULL, Lee (M) **18 0**
H: 6 2 W: 14 07 b.Chatham 11-11-85
Source: Sittingbourne, Lordswood, Ramsgate, Tonbridge Angels.
2011-12 AFC Wimbledon 18 0 **18 0**

MITCHEL-KING, Mat (D) **70 0**
H: 6 4 W: 13 00 b.Reading 12-9-83
Source: Cambridge C, Mildenhall T, Histon.
2009-10 Crewe Alex 32 0
2010-11 Crewe Alex 14 0 **46 0**
2011-12 AFC Wimbledon 24 0 **24 0**

MOORE, Luke (F) **37 9**
H: 5 11 W: 11 07 b.Gravesend 27-4-88
Source: Ebbsfleet U.
2011-12 AFC Wimbledon 37 9 **37 9**

MOORE, Sammy (M) **62 8**
H: 5 8 W: 9 00 b.Dover 7-9-87
Source: Scholar.
2006-07 Ipswich T 1 0
2007-08 Ipswich T 0 0
2007-08 *Brentford* 20 2 **20 2**
2008-09 Ipswich T 0 0 **1 0**
2011-12 AFC Wimbledon 41 6 **41 6**

MULLEY, James (M) **10 0**
H: 5 8 W: 10 00 b.Edgware 30-9-88
Source: Hayes & Yeading U, Chelmsford C.
2011-12 AFC Wimbledon 10 0 **10 0**

OSIFUWA, Adetayo (D) **0 0**
b.Ilford 15-8-92
Source: Southend Scholar, Maldon & Tiptree.
2011-12 AFC Wimbledon 0 0

PORTER, Max (M) **71 2**
H: 5 10 W: 12 04 b.Hornchurch 29-6-87
Source: Bishop's Stortford.
2007-08 Barnet 30 1
2008-09 Barnet 26 0 **56 1**
From Rushden & D.
2011-12 AFC Wimbledon 15 1 **15 1**

PRIOR, Jason (F) **3 0**
H: 6 1 W: 11 11 b.Portsmouth 20-12-88
Source: Bognor Regis T.
2011-12 AFC Wimbledon 3 0 **3 0**

STRUTTON, Charlie (F) **0 0**
Source: Chalfont St Peter.
2011-12 AFC Wimbledon 0 0

STUART, Jamie (D) **216 5**
H: 5 10 W: 12 06 b.Southwark 15-10-76
Source: Trainee. *Honours:* England Youth, Under-21.
1994-95 Charlton Ath 12 0
1995-96 Charlton Ath 27 2
1996-97 Charlton Ath 10 1
1997-98 Charlton Ath 1 0 **50 3**
1998-99 Millwall 35 0
1999-2000 Millwall 9 0
2000-01 Millwall 1 0
2001-02 Millwall 0 0 **45 0**
2001-02 Bury 24 1
2002-03 Bury 37 0 **61 1**
2003-04 Southend U 26 0
2004-05 Southend U 0 0
2005-06 Southend U 0 0
2006-07 Southend U 0 0
2007-08 Southend U 0 0
2008-09 Southend U 0 0 **26 0**
2011-12 AFC Wimbledon 34 1 **34 1**

THEOPHANOUS, Louie (F) **0 0**
b.Kennington
Source: Dagenham & R Youth.
2011-12 AFC Wimbledon 0 0

TURNER, Jack (G) **2 0**
H: 6 2 W: 13 07 b.Ashford 17-9-92
Source: Youth.
2011-12 AFC Wimbledon 2 0 **2 0**

WELLARD, Ricky (M) **22 1**
H: 5 11 W: 10 00 b.Hammersmith 9-5-88
Source: Ashford T.
2011-12 AFC Wimbledon 22 1 **22 1**

YUSSUFF, Rashid (M) **48 4**
H: 6 1 W: 10 07 b.Poplar 23-9-89
2007-08 Charlton Ath 0 0
2008-09 Charlton Ath 0 0
2009-10 Gillingham 8 0
2010-11 Gillingham 0 0 **8 0**
2011-12 AFC Wimbledon 40 4 **40 4**

ALDERSHOT T (3)

BERGQVIST, Doug (D) **3 0**
H: 6 0 W: 13 07 b.Stockholm 29-3-93
Source: Scholar.
2010-11 Aldershot T 1 0
2011-12 Aldershot T 2 0 **3 0**

BREIMYR, Henrik (D) **1 0**
H: 6 1 W: 12 02 b.Stavanger 20-7-93
Source: Scholar. *Honours:* Norway Youth.
2010-11 Aldershot T 0 0
2011-12 Aldershot T 0 0
2011-12 *Viking* 1 0 **1 0**

BUBB, Bradley (F) **9 0**
H: 5 7 W: 11 00 b.Harrow 30-5-88
Source: Hendon, QPR, Chalfont St Peter, Beaconsfield Sycob, Farnborough T.
Honours: Grenada 8 full caps.
2011-12 Aldershot T 9 0 **9 0**

CLEMENT, Jordan (G) **0 0**
H: 6 1 W: 12 08 b.Chertsey 12-6-93
Source: Scholar.
2009-10 Aldershot T 0 0
2010-11 Aldershot T 0 0
2011-12 Aldershot T 0 0

COLLINS, Jamie (M) **25 0**
H: 6 2 W: 12 02 b.Barking 28-9-84
Source: Watford Scholar, Havant & W'ville, Hampton & Richmond Bor, Newport Co.
2011-12 Aldershot T 25 0 **25 0**

CONNOLLY, Reece (F) **15 0**
H: 6 0 W: 11 09 b.Frimley 22-1-92
Source: Scholar.
2009-10 Aldershot T 3 0
2010-11 Aldershot T 5 0
2011-12 Aldershot T 7 0 **15 0**

DOIG, Chris (D) **246 5**
H: 6 2 W: 12 06 b.Dumfries 13-2-81
Source: Trainee. *Honours:* Scotland Schools, Youth, Under-21.
1997-98 Nottingham F 0 0
1998-99 Nottingham F 2 0
1999-2000 Nottingham F 11 0
2000-01 Nottingham F 15 0

2001-02	Nottingham F	8	1		
2002-03	Nottingham F	10	0		
2003-04	Nottingham F	10	0		
2003-04	*Northampton T*	9	0		
2004-05	Nottingham F	21	0	**77**	**1**
2005-06	Northampton T	38	2		
2006-07	Northampton T	39	0		
2007-08	Northampton T	15	1		
2008-09	Northampton T	28	1	**129**	**4**
2009-10	Central Coast M	26	0	**26**	**0**
2010-11	Pelita Jaya	12	0	**12**	**0**
2011-12	Aldershot T	2	0	**2**	**0**

HENRY, Charlie (M) 7 0
H: 5 5 W: 10 12 b.Stevenage 28-9-86
Source: Buntingford T, Arlesey T, Wycombe W, Grays Ath, Haverhill R, Cambridge C, Dorchester T, Havant & W'ville, Newport Co, Luton T.

2011-12	Aldershot T	7	0	**7**	**0**

On loan from Luton T.

HERD, Ben (D) 265 4
H: 5 9 W: 10 12 b.Welwyn 21-6-85
Source: Scholar.

2002-03	Watford	0	0		
2003-04	Watford	0	0		
2004-05	Watford	0	0		
2005-06	Shrewsbury T	46	2		
2006-07	Shrewsbury T	31	1		
2007-08	Shrewsbury T	45	0		
2008-09	Shrewsbury T	21	0	**143**	**3**
2009-10	Aldershot T	34	0		
2010-11	Aldershot T	43	1		
2011-12	Aldershot T	45	0	**122**	**1**

HYLTON, Danny (F) 127 26
H: 6 0 W: 11 13 b.Camden 25-2-89
Source: Youth.

2008-09	Aldershot T	29	5		
2009-10	Aldershot T	21	3		
2010-11	Aldershot T	33	5		
2011-12	Aldershot T	44	13	**127**	**26**

JONES, Darren (D) 142 5
H: 6 0 W: 14 12 b.Newport 28-8-83
Source: Scholar. *Honours:* Wales Schools, Youth.

2000-01	Bristol C	0	0		
2001-02	Bristol C	2	0		
2002-03	Bristol C	0	0		
2003-04	Bristol C	0	0	**2**	**0**
2003-04	*Cheltenham T*	14	1	**14**	**1**
From Forest Green R.					
2009-10	Hereford U	41	3	**41**	**3**
2010-11	Aldershot T	43	1		
2011-12	Aldershot T	42	0	**85**	**1**

MADJO, Guy (F) 85 27
H: 6 0 W: 13 05 b.Cameroon 1-6-84
Honours: Cameroon Under-23.

2005-06	Bristol C	5	0	**5**	**0**
From Forest GR, Staff R, Crawley on loan					
2007-08	*Cheltenham T*	5	0	**5**	**0**
2007-08	Shrewsbury T	15	3		
2008-09	Shrewsbury T	0	0	**15**	**3**
2008-09	Guangdong S C	18	10	**18**	**10**
2009-10	Bylis Ballsh	15	2	**15**	**2**
2011-12	Stevenage	1	0	**1**	**0**
2011-12	*Port Vale*	6	4	**6**	**4**
2011-12	Aldershot T	20	8	**20**	**8**

MEKKI, Adam (M) 33 1
H: 5 9 W: 11 00 b.Chester 24-12-91
Source: Scholar.

2009-10	Aldershot T	0	0		
2010-11	Aldershot T	8	0		
2011-12	Aldershot T	25	1	**33**	**1**

MORRIS, Aaron (D) 62 2
H: 6 1 W: 12 05 b.Cardiff 30-12-89
Source: Scholar. *Honours:* Wales Youth, Under-21.

2008-09	Cardiff C	0	0		
2009-10	Cardiff C	1	0	**1**	**0**
2010-11	Aldershot T	22	0		
2011-12	Aldershot T	39	2	**61**	**2**

PANTHER, Manny (F) 106 5
H: 6 0 W: 13 07 b.Glasgow 11-5-84

2001-02	St Johnstone	7	0		
2002-03	St Johnstone	4	0	**11**	**0**
2003-04	Partick T	8	0		
2004-05	Partick T	14	2	**22**	**2**
2004-05	*Brechin C*	8	1	**8**	**1**
From York C.					
2008-09	Exeter C	22	2		
2009-10	Exeter C	0	0	**22**	**2**
2009-10	*Morecambe*	19	0	**19**	**0**
2010-11	Aldershot T	23	0		
2011-12	Aldershot T	1	0	**24**	**0**

PAYNE, Josh (M) 70 5
H: 6 0 W: 11 09 b.Basingstoke 25-11-90
Source: Scholar.

2008-09	West Ham U	2	0		
2008-09	*Cheltenham T*	11	1	**11**	**1**
2009-10	West Ham U	0	0		
2009-10	*Colchester U*	3	0	**3**	**0**
2009-10	*Wycombe W*	3	1	**3**	**1**
2010-11	West Ham U	0	0	**2**	**0**
2010-11	Doncaster R	0	0		
2010-11	Oxford U	28	1		
2011-12	Oxford U	6	0	**34**	**1**
2011-12	Aldershot T	17	2	**17**	**2**

PULIS, Anthony (M) 46 1
H: 5 10 W: 10 10 b.Bristol 21-7-84
Source: Scholar. *Honours:* Wales Under-21.

2002-03	Portsmouth	0	0		
2003-04	Portsmouth	0	0		
2004-05	Portsmouth	0	0		
2004-05	Stoke C	0	0		
2004-05	*Torquay U*	3	0	**3**	**0**
2005-06	Stoke C	0	0		
2005-06	*Plymouth Arg*	5	0	**5**	**0**
2006-07	Stoke C	1	0		
2006-07	*Grimsby T*	9	0	**9**	**0**
2007-08	Stoke C	1	0		
2007-08	*Bristol R*	1	0	**1**	**0**
2008-09	Stoke C	0	0	**2**	**0**
2008-09	Southampton	0	0		
2009-10	Southampton	0	0		
2009-10	*Lincoln C*	7	0	**7**	**0**
2010-11	Southampton	0	0		
2010-11	*Stockport Co*	10	1	**10**	**1**
2010-11	*Barnet*	4	0	**4**	**0**
2011-12	Aldershot T	5	0	**5**	**0**

Transferred to Orlando City January 2012.

RANKINE, Michael (F) 46 3
H: 6 1 W: 14 12 b.Doncaster 15-1-85
Source: Doncaster R, Barrow.

2004-05	Scunthorpe U	21	1		
2005-06	Scunthorpe U	0	0	**21**	**1**
From Armthorpe W, Alfreton T, Rushden & D.					
2008-09	*Bournemouth*	3	0	**3**	**0**
From York C.					
2011-12	Aldershot T	22	2	**22**	**2**

RISSER, Wilko (F) 169 31
H: 6 3 W: 14 02 b.Windhoek 11-8-82
Source: Ramblers Windhoek, Wirges.
Honours: Namibia 14 full caps, 5 goals.

2004-05	Engers	14	2		
2005-06	Engers	20	3	**34**	**5**
2006-07	Eint Lahnstein	0	0		
2007-08	Schalke II	30	4	**30**	**4**
2008-09	Eint Trier	32	10		
2009-10	Eint Trier	30	9	**62**	**19**
2010-11	Elversberg	26	0	**26**	**0**
2011-12	Floriana	1	0	**1**	**0**
2011-12	Aldershot T	16	3	**16**	**3**

ROBERTS, Jordan (M) 4 0
H: 5 11 W: 12 13 b.Watford 5-1-94
Source: Scholar.

2011-12	Aldershot T	4	0	**4**	**0**

RODMAN, Alex (F) 57 15
H: 6 2 W: 12 08 b.Sutton Coldfield 15-2-87
Source: Leamington, Grantham T, Lincoln U, Gainsborough T, Tamworth.

2010-11	Tamworth	25	9	**25**	**9**
2010-11	Aldershot T	14	5		
2011-12	Aldershot T	18	1	**32**	**6**

SMITH, Adam (M) 82 3
H: 5 11 W: 12 00 b.Huddersfield 20-2-85
Source: Scholar.

2003-04	Chesterfield	3	0		
2004-05	Chesterfield	16	0		
2005-06	Chesterfield	26	3		
2006-07	Chesterfield	13	0		
2007-08	Chesterfield	8	0	**66**	**3**
2007-08	*Lincoln C*	4	0	**4**	**0**
From Gainsborough T, York C, Mansfield T.					
2011-12	Aldershot T	12	0	**12**	**0**

On loan from Mansfield T.

STRAKER, Anthony (D) 155 6
H: 5 9 W: 11 11 b.Ealing 23-9-88
Source: Crystal Palace Scholar. *Honours:* Grenada 5 full caps.

2008-09	Aldershot T	32	0		
2009-10	Aldershot T	37	2		
2010-11	Aldershot T	38	2		
2010-11	*Wycombe W*	4	0	**4**	**0**
2011-12	Aldershot T	44	2	**151**	**6**

VINCENTI, Peter (F) 70 13
H: 6 2 W: 11 13 b.St Peter 7-7-86
Source: St Peter.

2007-08	Millwall	0	0		
2010-11	Stevenage	5	1	**5**	**1**
2010-11	Aldershot T	23	6		
2011-12	Aldershot T	42	6	**65**	**12**

WORNER, Ross (G) 30 0
H: 6 1 W: 12 05 b.Hindhead 3-10-89
Source: Woking.

2010-11	Charlton Ath	8	0	**8**	**0**
2011-12	Aldershot T	22	0	**22**	**0**

YOUNG, Jamie (G) 140 0
H: 5 11 W: 13 00 b.Brisbane 25-8-85
Source: Scholar. *Honours:* England Youth, Under-20.

2003-04	Reading	1	0		
2004-05	Reading	0	0		
2005-06	Reading	0	0	**1**	**0**
2005-06	*Rushden & D*	20	0	**20**	**0**
2006-07	Wycombe W	19	0		
2007-08	Wycombe W	4	0		
2008-09	Wycombe W	15	0		
2009-10	Wycombe W	1	0	**39**	**0**
2009-10	Aldershot T	9	0		
2010-11	Aldershot T	46	0		
2011-12	Aldershot T	25	0	**80**	**0**

ARSENAL (4)

AFOBE, Benik (F) 31 5
H: 5 10 W: 11 00 b.Leyton 12-2-93
Source: Scholar. *Honours:* England Youth.

2009-10	Arsenal	0	0		
2010-11	Arsenal	0	0		
2010-11	*Huddersfield T*	28	5	**28**	**5**
2011-12	Arsenal	0	0		
2011-12	*Reading*	3	0	**3**	**0**

ALMUNIA, Manuel (G) 248 0
H: 6 3 W: 13 00 b.Pamplona 19-5-77

1996-97	Osasuna B	2	0		
1997-98	Osasuna B	31	0		
1998-99	Osasuna B	13	0	**46**	**0**
1999-2000	*Cartagena*	3	0	**3**	**0**
2000-01	Sabadell	25	0	**25**	**0**
2000-01	Celta Vigo	0	0		
2001-02	Celta Vigo	0	0		
2001-02	*Eibar*	35	0	**35**	**0**
2002-03	*Recreativo*	2	0	**2**	**0**
2003-04	*Albacete*	24	0	**24**	**0**
2004-05	Arsenal	10	0		
2005-06	Arsenal	0	0		
2006-07	Arsenal	1	0		
2007-08	Arsenal	29	0		
2008-09	Arsenal	32	0		
2009-10	Arsenal	29	0		
2010-11	Arsenal	8	0		
2011-12	Arsenal	0	0	**109**	**0**
2011-12	*West Ham U*	4	0	**4**	**0**

ANDRE SANTOS, Clarindo (D) 206 29
H: 5 10 W: 11 13 b.Sao Paulo 8-3-83
Honours: Brazil 22 full caps.

2004	Fiqueirense	30	2		
2005	*Flamengo*	24	0		
2006	*Flamengo*	0	0	**24**	**0**
2006	*Atletico Mineiro*	15	0	**15**	**0**
2007	Fiqueirense	31	6	**61**	**8**
2008	Corinthians	34	9		
2009	Corinthians	5	0	**39**	**9**
2009-10	Fenerbahce	27	5		
2010-11	Fenerbahce	25	5	**52**	**10**
2011-12	Arsenal	15	2	**15**	**2**

ANEKE, Chuks (M) 13 1
H: 6 3 W: 13 01 b.Newham 3-7-93
Source: Scholar. *Honours:* England Youth.

2010-11	Arsenal	0	0		
2011-12	Arsenal	0	0		

2011-12 *Stevenage* 6 0 **6 0**
2011-12 *Preston NE* 7 1 **7 1**

ANGHA, Martin (D) 0 0
H: 6 2 W: 12 10 b.Switzerland 22-1-94
Source: Zurich.
2010-11 Arsenal 0 0
2011-12 Arsenal 0 0

ANSAH, Zak (F) 0 0
H: 5 10 W: 11 00 b.Sidcup 4-5-94
Source: Scholar.
2010-11 Arsenal 0 0
2011-12 Arsenal 0 0

ARSHAVIN, Andrei (F) 346 77
H: 5 8 W: 9 11 b.St Petersburg 29-5-81
Honours: Russia 74 full caps, 17 goals.
1999 Zenit 0 0
2000 Zenit 10 0
2001 Zenit 29 4
2002 Zenit 30 4
2003 Zenit 27 5
2004 Zenit 28 6
2005 Zenit 29 9
2006 Zenit 28 7
2007 Zenit 30 10
2008 Zenit 27 6
2008-09 Arsenal 12 6
2009-10 Arsenal 30 10
2010-11 Arsenal 37 6
2011-12 Arsenal 19 1 **98 23**
2011-12 *Zenit* 10 3 **248 54**

ARTETA, Mikel (M) 340 51
H: 5 9 W: 10 08 b.San Sebastian 26-3-82
Honours: Spain Youth, Under-21.
1999-2000 Barcelona B 26 1
2000-01 Barcelona B 16 2 **42 3**
2000-01 Paris St Germain 6 1
2001-02 Paris St Germain 25 1 **31 2**
2002-03 Rangers 27 4
2003-04 Rangers 23 8 **50 12**
2004-05 Real Sociedad 14 1 **14 1**
2004-05 Everton 12 1
2005-06 Everton 29 1
2006-07 Everton 35 9
2007-08 Everton 28 1
2008-09 Everton 26 5
2009-10 Everton 13 6
2010-11 Everton 29 3
2011-12 Everton 2 1 **174 27**
2011-12 Arsenal 29 6 **29 6**

BARTLEY, Kyle (D) 59 1
H: 5 11 W: 11 00 b.Stockport 22-5-91
Source: Scholar.
2008-09 Arsenal 0 0
2009-10 Arsenal 0 0
2009-10 *Sheffield U* 14 0
2010-11 Arsenal 0 0
2010-11 *Sheffield U* 21 0 **35 0**
2010-11 *Rangers* 5 1
2011-12 Arsenal 0 0
2011-12 *Rangers* 19 0 **24 1**

BENDTNER, Nicklas (F) 169 41
H: 6 2 W: 13 00 b.Copenhagen 16-1-88
Source: Scholar. *Honours:* Denmark Youth, Under-21, 51 full caps, 20 goals.
2005-06 Arsenal 0 0
2006-07 Arsenal 0 0
2006-07 *Birmingham C* 42 11 **42 11**
2007-08 Arsenal 27 5
2008-09 Arsenal 31 9
2009-10 Arsenal 23 6
2010-11 Arsenal 17 2
2011-12 Arsenal 1 0 **99 22**
2011-12 *Sunderland* 28 8 **28 8**

BOATENG, Daniel (D) 2 0
H: 6 0 W: 12 04 b.Enfield 2-9-92
Source: Scholar.
2010-11 Arsenal 0 0
2011-12 Arsenal 0 0
2011-12 *Swindon T* 2 0 **2 0**

BOTHELO, Pedro (D) 127 6
H: 6 2 W: 13 00 b.Salvador 14-12-89
Source: Salamanca.
2007-08 Arsenal 0 0
2008-09 Arsenal 0 0
2008-09 *Salamanca* 36 0 **36 0**
2009-10 Arsenal 0 0
2009-10 *Celta Vigo* 27 1 **27 1**
2010-11 Arsenal 0 0
2010-11 *Cartagena* 39 4 **39 4**
2011-12 Arsenal 0 0
2011-12 *Rayo Vallecano* 11 1 **11 1**
2011-12 *Levante* 14 0 **14 0**

BRISLEN-HALL, George (D) 0 0
H: 5 7 W: 10 03 b.Harlow 24-12-92
Source: Scholar.
2011-12 Arsenal 0 0

CAMPBELL, Joel (F) 8 0
H: 5 10 W: 12 00 b.Costa Rica 26-6-92
Honours: Costa Rica Youth, 14 full caps, 6 goals.
2009-10 Saprissa 1 0
2010-11 Saprissa 2 0 **3 0**
2010-11 *Puntarenas* 5 0 **5 0**
2011-12 Arsenal 0 0
2011-12 *Lorient* 0 0

CHAMAKH, Marouane (F) 270 64
H: 6 1 W: 11 00 b.Tonnens 10-1-84
Honours: Morocco 61 full caps, 17 goals.
2002-03 Bordeaux 10 1
2003-04 Bordeaux 25 6
2004-05 Bordeaux 33 10
2005-06 Bordeaux 29 7
2006-07 Bordeaux 29 5
2007-08 Bordeaux 32 4
2008-09 Bordeaux 34 13
2009-10 Bordeaux 38 10 **230 56**
2010-11 Arsenal 29 7
2011-12 Arsenal 11 1 **40 8**

COQUELIN, Francis (M) 34 1
H: 5 10 W: 11 08 b.Laval 13-5-91
Source: Laval. *Honours:* France Under-21.
2008-09 Arsenal 0 0
2009-10 Arsenal 0 0
2010-11 Arsenal 0 0
2010-11 *Lorient* 24 1 **24 1**
2011-12 Arsenal 10 0 **10 0**

DENILSON (M) 138 6
H: 5 10 W: 10 10 b.Sao Paulo 16-2-88
Honours: Brazil Youth, Under-20.
2005 Sao Paulo 10 0
2006 Sao Paulo 2 0 **12 0**
2006-07 Arsenal 10 0
2007-08 Arsenal 13 0
2008-09 Arsenal 37 3
2009-10 Arsenal 20 3
2010-11 Arsenal 16 0
2011-12 Arsenal 0 0 **96 6**
2011-12 *Sao Paolo* 30 0 **30 0**

DIABY, Abou (M) 122 15
H: 6 2 W: 12 04 b.Paris 11-5-86
Honours: France Youth, Under-21, 15 full caps.
2004-05 Auxerre 5 0
2005-06 Auxerre 5 1 **10 1**
2005-06 Arsenal 12 1
2006-07 Arsenal 12 1
2007-08 Arsenal 15 1
2008-09 Arsenal 24 3
2009-10 Arsenal 29 6
2010-11 Arsenal 16 2
2011-12 Arsenal 4 0 **112 14**

DJOUROU, Johan (D) 99 1
H: 6 2 W: 12 05 b.Ivory Coast 18-1-87
Source: Scholar. *Honours:* Switzerland Youth, Under-20, Under-21, 32 full caps, 1 goal.
2004-05 Arsenal 0 0
2005-06 Arsenal 7 0
2006-07 Arsenal 21 0
2007-08 Arsenal 2 0
2007-08 *Birmingham C* 13 0 **13 0**
2008-09 Arsenal 15 0
2009-10 Arsenal 1 0
2010-11 Arsenal 22 1
2011-12 Arsenal 18 0 **86 1**

EASTMOND, Craig (D) 24 0
H: 6 0 W: 11 11 b.Wandsworth 9-12-90
Source: Scholar.
2009-10 Arsenal 4 0
2010-11 Arsenal 0 0
2010-11 *Millwall* 6 0 **6 0**
2011-12 Arsenal 0 0 **4 0**
2011-12 *Wycombe W* 14 0 **14 0**

EBECILIO, Kyle (M) 0 0
H: 5 11 W: 12 02 b.Rotterdam 17-2-94
Source: Feyenoord. *Honours:* Holland Youth.
2010-11 Arsenal 0 0
2011-12 Arsenal 0 0

EISFELD, Thomas (M) 0 0
b.Finsterwalde 18-1-93
Source: Borussia Dortmund.
2011-12 Arsenal 0 0

FABIANSKI, Lukasz (G) 80 0
H: 6 3 W: 13 01 b.Costrzyn nad Odra 18-4-85
Honours: Poland Under-21, 21 full caps.
2005-06 Legia 30 0
2006-07 Legia 23 0 **53 0**
2007-08 Arsenal 3 0
2008-09 Arsenal 6 0
2009-10 Arsenal 4 0
2010-11 Arsenal 14 0
2011-12 Arsenal 0 0 **27 0**

FRIMPONG, Emmanuel (M) 11 0
H: 5 11 W: 10 07 b.Ghana 10-1-92
Source: Scholar.
2008-09 Arsenal 0 0
2009-10 Arsenal 0 0
2010-11 Arsenal 0 0
2011-12 Arsenal 6 0 **6 0**
2011-12 *Wolverhampton W* 5 0 **5 0**

GALINDO, Samuel (M) 19 0
H: 6 3 W: 12 00 b.Bolivia 18-4-92
Source: Real America. *Honours:* Bolivia Youth, 2 full caps.
2010-11 Arsenal 0 0
2010-11 *Salamanca* 7 0 **7 0**
2011-12 Arsenal 0 0
2011-12 *Gimnastic* 12 0 **12 0**

GERVINHO (F) 215 55
H: 5 10 W: 10 10 b.Anyama 27-5-87
Honours: Ivory Coast 40 full caps, 8 goals.
2005-06 Beveren 32 6
2006-07 Beveren 29 8 **61 14**
2007-08 Le Mans 26 2
2008-09 Le Mans 33 7 **59 9**
2009-10 Lille 32 13
2010-11 Lille 35 15 **67 28**
2011-12 Arsenal 28 4 **28 4**

GIBBS, Kieran (M) 41 1
H: 5 10 W: 10 02 b.Lambeth 26-9-89
Source: Scholar. *Honours:* England Youth, Under-21, 2 full caps.
2007-08 Arsenal 0 0
2007-08 *Norwich C* 7 0 **7 0**
2008-09 Arsenal 8 0
2009-10 Arsenal 3 0
2010-11 Arsenal 7 0
2011-12 Arsenal 16 1 **34 1**

HAJROVIC, Sead (D) 10 0
H: 6 0 W: 12 08 b.Brugg 4-6-93
Source: Scholar.
2010-11 Arsenal 0 0
2011-12 Arsenal 0 0
2011-12 *Barnet* 10 0 **10 0**

HAYDEN, Isaac (D) 0 0
b.Chelmsford 22-3-95
Source: Scholar.
2011-12 Arsenal 0 0

HENDERSON, Conor (M) 0 0
H: 6 1 W: 11 13 b.Sidcup 8-9-91
Source: Scholar. *Honours:* Eire Youth, Under-21.
2008-09 Arsenal 0 0
2009-10 Arsenal 0 0
2010-11 Arsenal 0 0
2011-12 Arsenal 0 0

HENRY, Thierry (F) 496 249
H: 6 2 W: 13 05 b.Paris 17-8-77
Honours: France 123 full caps, 51 goals.
1994-95 Monaco 8 3
1995-96 Monaco 18 3
1996-97 Monaco 36 9
1997-98 Monaco 30 4
1998-99 Monaco 13 1 **105 20**
1998-99 Juventus 16 3 **16 3**
1999-2000 Arsenal 31 17
2000-01 Arsenal 35 17
2001-02 Arsenal 33 24
2002-03 Arsenal 37 24

2003-04 Arsenal 37 30
2004-05 Arsenal 32 25
2005-06 Arsenal 32 27
2006-07 Arsenal 17 10
2007-08 Barcelona 30 12
2008-09 Barcelona 29 19
2009-10 Barcelona 21 4 **80 35**
2010 NY Red Bulls 11 2
2011 NY Red Bulls 26 14 **37 16**
2011-12 Arsenal 4 1 **258 175**
On loan from New York Red Bulls.

HOYTE, Gavin (D) 41 0
H: 5 11 W: 11 00 b.Waltham Forest 6-6-90
Source: Scholar. *Honours:* England Youth, Under-20.
2007-08 Arsenal 0 0
2008-09 Arsenal 1 0
2008-09 *Watford* 7 0 **7 0**
2009-10 Arsenal 0 0
2009-10 *Brighton & HA* 18 0 **18 0**
2010-11 Arsenal 0 0
2010-11 *Lincoln C* 12 0 **12 0**
2011-12 Arsenal 0 0 **1 0**
2011-12 *AFC Wimbledon* 3 0 **3 0**

JENKINSON, Carl (D) 17 0
H: 6 1 W: 12 02 b.Harlow 8-2-92
Source: Scholar.
2010-11 Charlton Ath 8 0 **8 0**
2010-11 Arsenal 0 0
2011-12 Arsenal 9 0 **9 0**

KOSCIELNY, Laurent (D) 206 13
H: 6 1 W: 11 11 b.Tulle 10-9-85
Honours: France 4 full caps.
2004-05 Guingamp 11 0
2005-06 Guingamp 9 0
2006-07 Guingamp 21 0 **41 0**
2007-08 Tours 33 1
2008-09 Tours 34 5 **67 6**
2009-10 Lorient 35 3 **35 3**
2010-11 Arsenal 30 2
2011-12 Arsenal 33 2 **63 4**

LANSBURY, Henri (M) 101 14
H: 6 0 W: 13 06 b.Enfield 12-10-90
Source: Scholar. *Honours:* England Youth, Under-21.
2007-08 Arsenal 0 0
2008-09 Arsenal 0 0
2008-09 *Scunthorpe U* 16 4 **16 4**
2009-10 Arsenal 1 0
2009-10 *Watford* 37 5 **37 5**
2010-11 Arsenal 0 0
2010-11 *Norwich C* 23 4 **23 4**
2011-12 Arsenal 2 0 **3 0**
2011-12 *West Ham U* 22 1 **22 1**

MANNONE, Vito (G) 39 0
H: 6 0 W: 11 08 b.Milan 2-3-88
Source: Atalanta.
2005-06 Arsenal 0 0
2006-07 Arsenal 0 0
2006-07 *Barnsley* 2 0 **2 0**
2007-08 Arsenal 0 0
2008-09 Arsenal 1 0
2009-10 Arsenal 5 0
2010-11 Arsenal 0 0
2010-11 *Hull C* 10 0
2011-12 Arsenal 0 0 **6 0**
2011-12 *Hull C* 21 0 **31 0**

MARTINEZ, Damian (G) 1 0
H: 6 3 W: 13 05 b.Mar del Plata 2-9-92
Source: Independiente.
2010-11 Arsenal 0 0
2011-12 Arsenal 0 0
2011-12 *Oxford U* 1 0 **1 0**

McDERMOTT, Sean (G) 0 0
b.Kristiansand 30-5-93
Source: Scholar. *Honours:* Eire Youth.
2009-10 Arsenal 0 0
2010-11 Arsenal 0 0
2011-12 Arsenal 0 0
2011-12 *Leeds U* 0 0

MEADE, Jernade (M) 0 0
H: 5 8 W: 11 09 b.Luton 25-10-92
Source: Scholar.
2011-12 Arsenal 0 0

MERTESACKER, Per (D) 241 19
H: 6 6 W: 14 -02 b.Hannover 29-9-84
Honours: Germany Under-21, 81 full caps, 1 goal.
2003-04 Hannover 13 0
2004-05 Hannover 31 2
2005-06 Hannover 30 5 **74 7**
2006-07 Werder Bremen 25 2
2007-08 Werder Bremen 32 1
2008-09 Werder Bremen 23 2
2009-10 Werder Bremen 33 5
2010-11 Werder Bremen 29 2
2011-12 Werder Bremen 4 0 **146 12**
2011-12 Arsenal 21 0 **21 0**

MIQUEL, Ignasi (D) 4 0
H: 6 4 W: 13 05 b.Barcelona 28-9-92
Source: Scholar.
2009-10 Arsenal 0 0
2010-11 Arsenal 0 0
2011-12 Arsenal 4 0 **4 0**

MIYAICHI, Ryo (F) 12 0
H: 6 0 W: 11 02 b.Okazaki 14-12-92
Source: Chukyodai Chuyko High School.
Honours: Japan Youth, 1 full cap.
2010-11 Arsenal 0 0
2011-12 Arsenal 0 0
2011-12 *Bolton W* 12 0 **12 0**

MONTEIRO, Elton (D) 0 0
H: 6 3 W: 13 05 b.Sion 22-2-94
Source: Scholar.
2010-11 Arsenal 0 0
2011-12 Arsenal 0 0

MURPHY, Rhys (F) 10 0
H: 6 1 W: 11 13 b.Shoreham 6-11-90
Honours: England Youth. Eire Under-21.
2007-08 Arsenal 0 0
2008-09 Arsenal 0 0
2009-10 Arsenal 0 0
2009-10 *Brentford* 5 0 **5 0**
2010-11 Arsenal 0 0
2011-12 Arsenal 0 0
2011-12 *Preston NE* 5 0 **5 0**

NEITA, Nigel (F) 0 0
H: 5 11 W: 11 11 b.Southwark 23-12-93
Source: Scholar.
2011-12 Arsenal 0 0

OXLADE-CHAMBERLAIN, Alex (M) 52 11
H: 5 11 W: 11 00 b.Portsmouth 15-8-93
Source: Scholar. *Honours:* England Under-21, 5 full caps.
2009-10 Southampton 2 0
2010-11 Southampton 34 9 **36 9**
2011-12 Arsenal 16 2 **16 2**

OZYAKUP, Oguzhan (M) 0 0
H: 5 10 W: 11 00 b.Zaandam 23-9-92
Source: Scholar.
2009-10 Arsenal 0 0
2010-11 Arsenal 0 0
2011-12 Arsenal 0 0

PARK, Chu-Young (F) 161 48
H: 6 0 W: 11 11 b.Daegu 10-7-85
Honours: South Korea Youth, Under-23, 58 full caps, 24 goals.
2005 Seoul 19 12
2006 Seoul 26 7
2007 Seoul 11 2
2008 Seoul 13 2 **69 23**
2008-09 Monaco 31 5
2009-10 Monaco 27 8
2010-11 Monaco 33 12 **91 25**
2011-12 Arsenal 1 0 **1 0**

RAMSEY, Aaron (M) 95 8
H: 5 9 W: 10 07 b.Caerphilly 26-12-90
Source: School. *Honours:* Wales Youth, Under-21, 21 full caps, 5 goals.
2006-07 Cardiff C 1 0
2007-08 Cardiff C 15 1
2008-09 Arsenal 9 0
2009-10 Arsenal 18 3
2010-11 Arsenal 7 1
2010-11 *Nottingham F* 5 0 **5 0**
2010-11 *Cardiff C* 6 1 **22 2**
2011-12 Arsenal 34 2 **68 6**

REES, Josh (M) 0 0
H: 5 9 W: 11 00 b.Hemel Hempstead 4-10-93
Source: Scholar.
2011-12 Arsenal 0 0

ROSICKY, Tomas (M) 308 40
H: 5 10 W: 10 10 b.Prague 4-10-80
Honours: Czech Republic Under-21, 87 full caps, 20 goals.
1998-99 Sparta Prague 3 0
1999-2000 Sparta Prague 24 5
2000-01 Sparta Prague 14 3 **41 8**
2000-01 Borussia Dortmund 15 0
2001-02 Borussia Dortmund 30 5
2002-03 Borussia Dortmund 30 3
2003-04 Borussia Dortmund 19 2
2004-05 Borussia Dortmund 27 4
2005-06 Borussia Dortmund 28 5 **149 19**
2006-07 Arsenal 26 3
2007-08 Arsenal 18 6
2008-09 Arsenal 0 0
2009-10 Arsenal 25 3
2010-11 Arsenal 21 0
2011-12 Arsenal 28 1 **118 13**

SAGNA, Bakari (D) 240 3
H: 5 10 W: 11 05 b.Sens 14-2-83
Source: Auxerre B. *Honours:* France Under-21, 32 full caps.
2003-04 Auxerre 0 0
2004-05 Auxerre 26 0
2005-06 Auxerre 23 0
2006-07 Auxerre 38 0 **87 0**
2007-08 Arsenal 29 1
2008-09 Arsenal 35 0
2009-10 Arsenal 35 0
2010-11 Arsenal 33 1
2011-12 Arsenal 21 1 **153 3**

SHEA, James (G) 1 0
H: 5 11 W: 12 00 b.Islington 16-6-91
Source: Scholar.
2009-10 Arsenal 0 0
2010-11 Arsenal 0 0
2011-12 Arsenal 0 0
2011-12 *Dagenham & R* 1 0 **1 0**

SILVA, Wellington (M) 18 3
H: 5 6 W: 10 00 b.Rio de Janeiro 6-1-93
Source: Fluminense. *Honours:* Brazil Youth.
2010-11 Arsenal 0 0
2010-11 *Levante* 2 0 **2 0**
2011-12 Arsenal 0 0
2011-12 *Alcoyano* 16 3 **16 3**

SONG BILLONG, Alexandre (M) 150 7
H: 5 11 W: 12 04 b.Douala 9-9-87
Source: Bastia. *Honours:* France Youth, Cameroon Youth. Cameroon 33 full caps.
2005-06 Arsenal 5 0
2006-07 Arsenal 2 0
2006-07 *Charlton Ath* 12 0 **12 0**
2007-08 Arsenal 9 0
2008-09 Arsenal 31 1
2009-10 Arsenal 26 1
2010-11 Arsenal 31 4
2011-12 Arsenal 34 1 **138 7**

SQUILLACI, Sebastien (D) 323 22
H: 6 0 W: 11 13 b.Toulon 11-8-80
Honours: France 21 full caps.
1997-98 Toulon 6 0 **6 0**
1998-99 Monaco 0 0
1999-2000 Monaco 0 0
2000-01 Ajaccio 36 2
2001-02 Ajaccio 33 5 **69 7**
2002-03 Monaco 34 2
2003-04 Monaco 27 5
2004-05 Monaco 28 2
2005-06 Monaco 26 1 **115 10**
2006-07 Lyon 28 3
2007-08 Lyon 34 0 **62 3**
2008-09 Sevilla 32 0
2009-10 Sevilla 16 1 **48 1**
2010-11 Arsenal 22 1
2011-12 Arsenal 1 0 **23 1**

SZCZESNY, Wojciech (G) 81 0
H: 5 10 W: 11 11 b.Warsaw 18-4-90
Source: Scholar. *Honours:* Poland 11 full caps.
2007-08 Arsenal 0 0
2008-09 Arsenal 0 0
2009-10 Arsenal 0 0
2009-10 *Brentford* 28 0 **28 0**

2010-11 Arsenal 15 0
2011-12 Arsenal 38 0 **53 0**

TORAL HARPER, Jon-Miquel (M) 0 0
H: 6 3 W: 13 00 b.Reus 5-2-95
Source: Scholar.
2011-12 Arsenal 0 0

VAN PERSIE, Robin (F) 255 110
H: 6 0 W: 11 00 b.Rotterdam 6-8-83
Source: Excelsior. *Honours:* Holland Under-21, 68 full caps, 29 goals.
2001-02 Feyenoord 10 0
2002-03 Feyenoord 23 8
2003-04 Feyenoord 28 6 **61 14**
2004-05 Arsenal 26 5
2005-06 Arsenal 24 5
2006-07 Arsenal 22 11
2007-08 Arsenal 15 7
2008-09 Arsenal 28 11
2009-10 Arsenal 16 9
2010-11 Arsenal 25 18
2011-12 Arsenal 38 30 **194 96**

VELA, Carlos (F) 136 28
H: 5 9 W: 10 05 b.Cancun 1-3-89
Source: Guadalajara. *Honours:* Mexico Youth, Under-20, 35 full caps, 9 goals.
2005-06 Arsenal 0 0
2006-07 Arsenal 0 0
2006-07 *Salamanca* 31 8 **31 8**
2007-08 *Osasuna* 33 3 **33 3**
2007-08 Arsenal 0 0
2008-09 Arsenal 14 1
2009-10 Arsenal 11 1
2010-11 Arsenal 4 1
2010-11 *WBA* 8 2 **8 2**
2011-12 Arsenal 0 0 **29 3**
2011-12 *Real Sociedad* 35 12 **35 12**

VERMAELEN, Thomas (D) 179 22
H: 6 0 W: 11 11 b.Antwerp 14-11-85
Source: Ekeren, Antwerp. *Honours:* Belgium Under-21, 35 full caps, 1 goal.
2003-04 Ajax 1 0
2004-05 *RKC Waalwijk* 13 2 **13 2**
2005-06 Ajax 24 3
2006-07 Ajax 23 0
2007-08 Ajax 20 0
2008-09 Ajax 31 4 **99 7**
2009-10 Arsenal 33 7
2010-11 Arsenal 5 0
2011-12 Arsenal 29 6 **67 13**

WALCOTT, Theo (F) 170 30
H: 5 9 W: 11 01 b.Stanmore 16-3-89
Source: Scholar. *Honours:* England Youth, Under-21, B, 28 full caps, 4 goals.
2005-06 Southampton 21 4 **21 4**
2005-06 Arsenal 0 0
2006-07 Arsenal 16 0
2007-08 Arsenal 25 4
2008-09 Arsenal 22 2
2009-10 Arsenal 23 3
2010-11 Arsenal 28 9
2011-12 Arsenal 35 8 **149 26**

WATT, Sanchez (M) 50 3
H: 5 11 W: 12 00 b.Hackney 14-2-91
Source: Scholar. *Honours:* England Youth.
2008-09 Arsenal 0 0
2009-10 Arsenal 0 0
2009-10 *Southend U* 4 0 **4 0**
2009-10 *Leeds U* 6 0
2010-11 Arsenal 0 0
2010-11 *Leeds U* 22 1 **28 1**
2011-12 Arsenal 0 0
2011-12 *Sheffield W* 4 0 **4 0**
2011-12 *Crawley T* 14 2 **14 2**

WILSHERE, Jack (M) 51 2
H: 5 7 W: 11 03 b.Stevenage 1-1-92
Source: Scholar. *Honours:* England Youth, Under-21, 5 full caps.
2008-09 Arsenal 1 0
2009-10 Arsenal 1 0
2009-10 *Bolton W* 14 1 **14 1**
2010-11 Arsenal 35 1
2011-12 Arsenal 0 0 **37 1**

YENNARIS, Nico (D) 3 0
H: 5 7 W: 10 03 b.Leytonstone 23-5-93
Source: Scholar. *Honours:* England Youth.
2010-11 Arsenal 0 0
2011-12 Arsenal 1 0 **1 0**
2011-12 *Notts Co* 2 0 **2 0**

Scholars
Bellerin Hector; Bihmoutine Samir; Charles-Cook Reice Jordan; Fagan Zachari Freddy Casey; Glasgow Benjamin Luke; Gnabry Serge David; Jeffrey Anthony Lamar Malcolm; Olsson Mats Kristoffer; Roberts Philip James; Wynter Jordan James Cecil.

ASTON VILLA (5)

AGBONLAHOR, Gabriel (F) 225 53
H: 5 11 W: 12 05 b.Birmingham 13-10-86
Source: Scholar. *Honours:* England Under-20, Under-21, 3 full caps.
2005-06 Aston Villa 9 1
2005-06 *Watford* 2 0 **2 0**
2005-06 *Sheffield W* 8 0 **8 0**
2006-07 Aston Villa 38 9
2007-08 Aston Villa 37 11
2008-09 Aston Villa 36 11
2009-10 Aston Villa 36 13
2010-11 Aston Villa 26 3
2011-12 Aston Villa 33 5 **215 53**

ALBRIGHTON, Marc (M) 58 7
H: 6 2 W: 12 06 b.Tamworth 18-11-89
Source: Scholar. *Honours:* England Youth, Under-20, Under-21.
2008-09 Aston Villa 0 0
2009-10 Aston Villa 3 0
2010-11 Aston Villa 29 5
2011-12 Aston Villa 26 2 **58 7**

BAKER, Nathan (D) 36 0
H: 6 2 W: 11 11 b.Worcester 23-4-91
Source: Scholar. *Honours:* England Youth, Under-20, Under-21.
2008-09 Aston Villa 0 0
2009-10 Aston Villa 0 0
2009-10 *Lincoln C* 18 0 **18 0**
2010-11 Aston Villa 4 0
2011-12 Aston Villa 8 0 **12 0**
2011-12 *Millwall* 6 0 **6 0**

BANNAN, Barry (D) 77 3
H: 5 10 W: 10 08 b.Glasgow 1-12-89
Source: Scholar. *Honours:* Scotland Under-21, 11 full caps.
2008-09 Aston Villa 0 0
2008-09 *Derby Co* 10 1 **10 1**
2009-10 Aston Villa 0 0
2009-10 *Blackpool* 20 1 **20 1**
2010-11 Aston Villa 12 0
2010-11 *Leeds U* 7 0 **7 0**
2011-12 Aston Villa 28 1 **40 1**

BENT, Darren (F) 346 148
H: 5 11 W: 12 07 b.Wandsworth 6-2-84
Source: Scholar. *Honours:* England Youth, Under-21, 13 full caps, 4 goals.
2001-02 Ipswich T 5 1
2002-03 Ipswich T 35 12
2003-04 Ipswich T 37 16
2004-05 Ipswich T 45 20 **122 49**
2005-06 Charlton Ath 36 18
2006-07 Charlton Ath 32 13 **68 31**
2007-08 Tottenham H 27 6
2008-09 Tottenham H 33 12
2009-10 Tottenham H 0 0 **60 18**
2009-10 Sunderland 38 24
2010-11 Sunderland 20 8 **58 32**
2010-11 Aston Villa 16 9
2011-12 Aston Villa 22 9 **38 18**

BURKE, Graham (F) 0 0
H: 5 11 W: 11 11 b.Dublin 21-9-93
Source: Scholar. *Honours:* Eire Youth.
2010-11 Aston Villa 0 0
2011-12 Aston Villa 0 0

CAIRA, Reece (D) 0 0
b.Gosford 7-1-93
Source: Scholar.
2011-12 Aston Villa 0 0

CAMERON, Courtney (D) 0 0
b.Northampton 22-1-93
Source: Scholar.
2011-12 Aston Villa 0 0

CARRUTHERS, Samir (F) 3 0
H: 5 8 W: 11 00 b.Islington 4-4-93
Source: Scholar. *Honours:* Eire Youth.
2011-12 Aston Villa 3 0 **3 0**

CLARK, Ciaran (D) 35 4
H: 6 2 W: 12 00 b.Harrow 26-9-89
Source: Scholar. *Honours:* England Youth, Under-20. Eire 2 full caps.
2008-09 Aston Villa 0 0
2009-10 Aston Villa 1 0
2010-11 Aston Villa 19 3
2011-12 Aston Villa 15 1 **35 4**

COLLINS, James M (D) 211 10
H: 6 2 W: 14 05 b.Newport 23-8-83
Source: Scholar. *Honours:* Wales Youth, Under-21, 39 full caps, 2 goals.
2000-01 Cardiff C 3 0
2001-02 Cardiff C 7 1
2002-03 Cardiff C 2 0
2003-04 Cardiff C 20 1
2004-05 Cardiff C 34 1 **66 3**
2005-06 West Ham U 14 2
2006-07 West Ham U 16 0
2007-08 West Ham U 3 0
2008-09 West Ham U 18 0
2009-10 West Ham U 3 0 **54 2**
2009-10 Aston Villa 27 1
2010-11 Aston Villa 32 3
2011-12 Aston Villa 32 1 **91 5**

CUELLAR, Carlos (D) 290 12
H: 6 3 W: 13 03 b.Madrid 23-8-81
2000-01 Calahorra 27 0 **27 0**
2001-02 Numancia 23 1
2002-03 Numancia 39 3 **62 4**
2003-04 Osasuna 5 0
2004-05 Osasuna 14 0
2005-06 Osasuna 29 1
2006-07 Osasuna 23 1 **71 2**
2007-08 Rangers 36 4 **36 4**
2008-09 Aston Villa 28 0
2009-10 Aston Villa 36 2
2010-11 Aston Villa 12 0
2011-12 Aston Villa 18 0 **94 2**

DELFOUNESO, Nathan (F) 45 3
H: 6 1 W: 12 04 b.Birmingham 2-2-91
Source: Scholar. *Honours:* England Youth, Under-21.
2007-08 Aston Villa 0 0
2008-09 Aston Villa 4 0
2009-10 Aston Villa 9 1
2010-11 Aston Villa 11 1
2010-11 *Burnley* 11 1 **11 1**
2011-12 Aston Villa 6 0 **30 2**
2011-12 *Leicester C* 4 0 **4 0**

DELPH, Fabian (D) 75 6
H: 5 8 W: 11 00 b.Bradford 21-11-89
Source: Scholar. *Honours:* England Youth, Under-21.
2006-07 Leeds U 1 0
2007-08 Leeds U 1 0
2008-09 Leeds U 42 6
2009-10 Aston Villa 8 0
2010-11 Aston Villa 7 0
2011-12 Aston Villa 11 0 **26 0**
2011-12 *Leeds U* 5 0 **49 6**

DEVINE, Danny (M) 0 0
b.Dublin 8-5-93
Source: Scholar. *Honours:* Eire Yout, Northern Ireland Under-21.
2009-10 Aston Villa 0 0
2010-11 Aston Villa 0 0
2011-12 Aston Villa 0 0

DONACIEN, Janoi (D) 0 0
b.St Lucia
2011-12 Aston Villa 0 0

DRENNAN, Michael (F) 0 0
b.Kilkenny 2-2-94
Source: Scholar. *Honours:* Eire Youth.
2010-11 Aston Villa 0 0
2011-12 Aston Villa 0 0

DUNNE, Richard (D) 451 12
H: 6 2 W: 15 10 b.Dublin 21-9-79
Source: Trainee. *Honours:* Eire Schools, Youth, Under-21, B, 76 full caps, 8 goals.
1996-97 Everton 7 0
1997-98 Everton 3 0
1998-99 Everton 16 0
1999-2000 Everton 31 0
2000-01 Everton 3 0 **60 0**
2000-01 Manchester C 25 0
2001-02 Manchester C 43 1
2002-03 Manchester C 25 0

2003-04	Manchester C	29	0		
2004-05	Manchester C	35	2		
2005-06	Manchester C	32	3		
2006-07	Manchester C	38	1		
2007-08	Manchester C	36	0		
2008-09	Manchester C	31	1		
2009-10	Manchester C	2	0	**296**	**8**
2009-10	Aston Villa	35	3		
2010-11	Aston Villa	32	0		
2011-12	Aston Villa	28	1	**95**	**4**

GARDNER, Gary (M) **18** **1**
H: 6 2 W: 12 13 b.Solihull 29-6-92
Source: Scholar. *Honours:* England Youth, Under-20, Under-21.

2009-10	Aston Villa	0	0		
2010-11	Aston Villa	0	0		
2011-12	Aston Villa	14	0	**14**	**0**
2011-12	*Coventry C*	4	1	**4**	**1**

GIVEN, Shay (G) **460** **0**
H: 6 0 W: 13 03 b.Lifford 20-4-76
Source: Celtic. *Honours:* Eire Youth, Under-21, 125 full caps.

1994-95	Blackburn R	0	0		
1994-95	*Swindon T*	0	0		
1995-96	Blackburn R	0	0		
1995-96	*Swindon T*	5	0	**5**	**0**
1995-96	*Sunderland*	17	0	**17**	**0**
1996-97	Blackburn R	2	0	**2**	**0**
1997-98	Newcastle U	24	0		
1998-99	Newcastle U	31	0		
1999-2000	Newcastle U	14	0		
2000-01	Newcastle U	34	0		
2001-02	Newcastle U	38	0		
2002-03	Newcastle U	38	0		
2003-04	Newcastle U	38	0		
2004-05	Newcastle U	36	0		
2005-06	Newcastle U	38	0		
2006-07	Newcastle U	22	0		
2007-08	Newcastle U	19	0		
2008-09	Newcastle U	22	0	**354**	**0**
2008-09	Manchester C	15	0		
2009-10	Manchester C	35	0		
2010-11	Manchester C	0	0	**50**	**0**
2011-12	Aston Villa	32	0	**32**	**0**

GRAHAM, Jordan (M) **0** **0**
b.Coventry 5-3-95
Source: Scholar.

2011-12	Aston Villa	0	0		

GUZAN, Brad (G) **103** **0**
H: 6 4 W: 14 11 b.Chicago 9-9-84
Honours: USA 20 full caps.

2005	Chivas USA	24	0		
2006	Chivas USA	13	0		
2007	Chivas USA	27	0		
2008	Chivas USA	15	0	**79**	**0**
2008-09	Aston Villa	1	0		
2009-10	Aston Villa	0	0		
2010-11	Aston Villa	0	0		
2010-11	*Hull C*	16	0	**16**	**0**
2011-12	Aston Villa	7	0	**8**	**0**

HERD, Chris (M) **60** **7**
H: 5 9 W: 11 04 b.Perth 4-4-89
Source: Scholar. *Honours:* Australia Youth.

2007-08	Aston Villa	0	0		
2007-08	*Port Vale*	11	2	**11**	**2**
2007-08	*Wycombe W*	4	0	**4**	**0**
2008-09	Aston Villa	0	0		
2009-10	Aston Villa	0	0		
2009-10	*Lincoln C*	20	4	**20**	**4**
2010-11	Aston Villa	6	0		
2011-12	Aston Villa	19	1	**25**	**1**

HESKEY, Emile (F) **546** **117**
H: 6 2 W: 13 12 b.Leicester 11-1-78
Source: Trainee. *Honours:* England Youth, Under-21, B, 62 full caps, 7 goals.

1994-95	Leicester C	1	0		
1995-96	Leicester C	30	7		
1996-97	Leicester C	35	10		
1997-98	Leicester C	35	10		
1998-99	Leicester C	30	6		
1999-2000	Leicester C	23	7	**154**	**40**
1999-2000	Liverpool	12	3		
2000-01	Liverpool	36	14		
2001-02	Liverpool	35	9		
2002-03	Liverpool	32	6		
2003-04	Liverpool	35	7	**150**	**39**
2004-05	Birmingham C	34	10		
2005-06	Birmingham C	34	4	**68**	**14**
2006-07	Wigan Ath	34	8		
2007-08	Wigan Ath	28	4		
2008-09	Wigan Ath	20	3	**82**	**15**
2008-09	Aston Villa	14	2		
2009-10	Aston Villa	31	3		
2010-11	Aston Villa	19	3		
2011-12	Aston Villa	28	1	**92**	**9**

HUTTON, Alan (D) **175** **3**
H: 6 1 W: 11 05 b.Glasgow 30-11-84
Honours: Scotland Under-21, 23 full caps.

2004-05	Rangers	10	0		
2005-06	Rangers	19	0		
2006-07	Rangers	33	1		
2007-08	Rangers	20	0	**82**	**1**
2007-08	Tottenham H	14	0		
2008-09	Tottenham H	8	0		
2009-10	Tottenham H	8	0		
2009-10	*Sunderland*	11	0	**11**	**0**
2010-11	Tottenham H	21	2		
2011-12	Tottenham H	0	0	**51**	**2**
2011-12	Aston Villa	31	0	**31**	**0**

IRELAND, Stephen (F) **174** **17**
H: 5 8 W: 10 07 b.Cork 22-8-86
Source: Scholar. *Honours:* Eire Youth, Under-21, 6 full caps, 4 goals.

2005-06	Manchester C	24	0		
2006-07	Manchester C	24	1		
2007-08	Manchester C	33	4		
2008-09	Manchester C	35	9		
2009-10	Manchester C	22	2		
2010-11	Manchester C	0	0	**138**	**16**
2010-11	Aston Villa	10	0		
2010-11	*Newcastle U*	2	0	**2**	**0**
2011-12	Aston Villa	24	1	**34**	**1**

JOHNSON, Daniel (M) **0** **0**
H: 5 8 W: 10 07 b.Kingston, Jam 8-10-92
Source: Scholar.

2010-11	Aston Villa	0	0		
2011-12	Aston Villa	0	0		

KEANE, Robbie (F) **457** **167**
H: 5 9 W: 12 02 b.Dublin 8-7-80
Source: Trainee. *Honours:* Eire Youth, B, 120 full caps, 53 goals.

1997-98	Wolverhampton W	38	11		
1998-99	Wolverhampton W	33	11		
1999-2000	Wolverhampton W	2	2	**73**	**24**
1999-2000	Coventry C	31	12	**31**	**12**
2000-01	Internazionale	6	0	**6**	**0**
2000-01	Leeds U	18	9		
2001-02	Leeds U	25	3		
2002-03	Leeds U	3	1	**46**	**13**
2002-03	Tottenham H	29	13		
2003-04	Tottenham H	34	14		
2004-05	Tottenham H	35	11		
2005-06	Tottenham H	36	16		
2006-07	Tottenham H	27	11		
2007-08	Tottenham H	36	15		
2008-09	Liverpool	19	5	**19**	**5**
2008-09	Tottenham H	14	5		
2009-10	Tottenham H	20	6		
2009-10	*Celtic*	16	12	**16**	**12**
2010-11	Tottenham H	7	0	**238**	**91**
2010-11	*West Ham U*	9	2	**9**	**2**
2011-12	LA Galaxy	13	5	**13**	**5**

On loan from LA Galaxy.

2011-12	Aston Villa	6	3	**6**	**3**

LICHAJ, Eric (D) **46** **2**
H: 5 11 W: 12 07 b.Chicago 17-11-88
Source: Univ of North Carolina, Chicago Magic. *Honours:* USA 8 full caps.

2007-08	Aston Villa	0	0		
2008-09	Aston Villa	0	0		
2009-10	Aston Villa	0	0		
2009-10	*Lincoln C*	6	0	**6**	**0**
2009-10	*Leyton Orient*	9	1	**9**	**1**
2010-11	Aston Villa	5	0		
2010-11	*Leeds U*	16	0	**16**	**0**
2011-12	Aston Villa	10	1	**15**	**1**

MAKOUN, Jean II (M) **300** **28**
H: 5 8 W: 10 12 b.Yaounde 29-5-83
Honours: Cameroon 55 full caps, 3 goals.

2001-02	Lille B	20	9		
2002-03	Lille B	13	0	**33**	**9**
2002-03	Lille	10	0		
2003-04	Lille	32	1		
2004-05	Lille	33	0		
2005-06	Lille	31	5		
2006-07	Lille	33	1		
2007-08	Lille	26	2	**165**	**9**
2008-09	Lyon	35	6		
2009-10	Lyon	28	1		
2010-11	Lyon	13	1	**76**	**8**
2010-11	Aston Villa	7	0		
2011-12	Aston Villa	0	0	**7**	**0**
2011-12	*Olympiakos*	19	2	**19**	**2**

MARSHALL, Andy (G) **390** **0**
H: 6 3 W: 14 08 b.Bury St Edmunds 14-4-75
Source: Trainee. *Honours:* England Youth, Under-21.

1993-94	Norwich C	0	0		
1994-95	Norwich C	21	0		
1995-96	Norwich C	3	0		
1996-97	Norwich C	7	0		
1996-97	*Bournemouth*	11	0	**11**	**0**
1996-97	*Gillingham*	5	0	**5**	**0**
1997-98	Norwich C	42	0		
1998-99	Norwich C	37	0		
1999-2000	Norwich C	44	0		
2000-01	Norwich C	41	0	**195**	**0**
2001-02	Ipswich T	13	0		
2002-03	Ipswich T	40	0		
2003-04	Ipswich T	0	0	**53**	**0**
2003-04	Millwall	16	0		
2004-05	Millwall	22	0		
2005-06	Millwall	29	0	**67**	**0**
2006-07	Coventry C	41	0		
2007-08	Coventry C	16	0		
2008-09	Coventry C	2	0	**59**	**0**
2009-10	Aston Villa	0	0		
2010-11	Aston Villa	0	0		
2011-12	Aston Villa	0	0		

N'ZOGBIA, Charles (M) **230** **26**
H: 5 9 W: 11 00 b.Le Havre 28-5-86
Honours: France Youth, Under-21, 2 full caps, 1 goal.

2004-05	Newcastle U	14	0		
2005-06	Newcastle U	32	5		
2006-07	Newcastle U	22	0		
2007-08	Newcastle U	31	3		
2008-09	Newcastle U	18	1	**117**	**9**
2008-09	Wigan Ath	13	1		
2009-10	Wigan Ath	36	5		
2010-11	Wigan Ath	34	9	**83**	**15**
2011-12	Aston Villa	30	2	**30**	**2**

NELSON-ADDY, Ebby (M) **0** **0**
b.Milton Keynes 13-9-92
Source: Scholar.

2011-12	Aston Villa	0	0		

PETROV, Stilian (M) **451** **65**
H: 5 11 W: 11 09 b.Sofia 5-7-79
Source: FC Montana. *Honours:* Bulgaria 106 full caps, 8 goals.

1997-98	CSKA Sofia	10	0		
1998-99	CSKA Sofia	29	3	**39**	**3**
1999-2000	Celtic	29	1		
2000-01	Celtic	28	7		
2001-02	Celtic	27	6		
2002-03	Celtic	34	12		
2003-04	Celtic	35	6		
2004-05	Celtic	37	11		
2005-06	Celtic	37	10	**227**	**53**
2006-07	Aston Villa	30	2		
2007-08	Aston Villa	28	1		
2008-09	Aston Villa	36	1		
2009-10	Aston Villa	37	0		
2010-11	Aston Villa	27	1		
2011-12	Aston Villa	27	4	**185**	**9**

SERRANO, Juan Jose (M) **0** **0**
b.Lleida 30-11-93
Source: Scholar.

2010-11	Aston Villa	0	0		
2011-12	Aston Villa	0	0		

SIEGRIST, Benjamin (G) **0** **0**
H: 6 4 W: 13 05 b.Basle 31-1-92
Source: Scholar. *Honours:* Switzerland Youth.

2008-09	Aston Villa	0	0		
2009-10	Aston Villa	0	0		
2010-11	Aston Villa	0	0		
2011-12	Aston Villa	0	0		

STEVENS, Enda (D) **77** **0**
H: 6 0 W: 12 04 b.Dublin 9-7-90
Honours: Republic of Ireland Under-21.

2008	UCD	2	0	**2**	**0**
2009	St Patrick's Ath	30	0	**30**	**0**
2010	Shamrock R	18	0		
2011	Shamrock R	27	0	**45**	**0**
2011-12	Aston Villa	0	0		

STIEBER, Andras (M) 0 0
b.Zarvar 8-10-91
2010-11 Aston Villa 0 0
2011-12 Aston Villa 0 0

TAYLOR, Connor (F) 0 0
b.Coventry 5-9-92
Source: Scholar.
2011-12 Aston Villa 0 0

WARD, Charlie (D) 0 0
b.Reddtich 3-1-93
Source: Scholar.
2011-12 Aston Villa 0 0

WARNOCK, Stephen (D) 268 12
H: 5 7 W: 11 09 b.Ormskirk 12-12-81
Source: Trainee. *Honours:* England Schools, Youth, 2 full caps.
1998-99 Liverpool 0 0
1999-2000 Liverpool 0 0
2000-01 Liverpool 0 0
2001-02 Liverpool 0 0
2002-03 Liverpool 0 0
2002-03 *Bradford C* 12 1 **12 1**
2003-04 Liverpool 0 0
2003-04 *Coventry C* 44 3 **44 3**
2004-05 Liverpool 19 0
2005-06 Liverpool 20 1
2006-07 Liverpool 1 0 **40 1**
2006-07 Blackburn R 13 1
2007-08 Blackburn R 37 1
2008-09 Blackburn R 37 3
2009-10 Blackburn R 1 0 **88 5**
2009-10 Aston Villa 30 0
2010-11 Aston Villa 19 0
2011-12 Aston Villa 35 2 **84 2**

WEIMANN, Andreas (F) 36 6
H: 5 9 W: 11 09 b.Vienna 5-8-91
Source: Scholar. *Honours:* Austria Under-21.
2008-09 Aston Villa 0 0
2009-10 Aston Villa 0 0
2010-11 Aston Villa 1 0
2010-11 *Watford* 18 4
2011-12 Aston Villa 14 2 **15 2**
2011-12 *Watford* 3 0 **21 4**

WILLIAMS, Derrick (D) 0 0
H: 5 11 W: 11 11 b.Waterford 17-1-93
Source: Scholar. *Honours:* Eire Youth.
2009-10 Aston Villa 0 0
2010-11 Aston Villa 0 0
2011-12 Aston Villa 0 0

Scholars
Barrett Calum Alastair; Barton Joshua; Bateman Liam Vere; Eminoglu Umit; Hill Craig Dennis; Kinsella Lewis; Lewis Bradley; Melvin Malcolm Graham; Nelson Michael; Robinson Callum Jack; Stevenson Oliver; Ward Charlie; Watkins Bradley; Watkins Mason Bradley; Webb Joshua John; Williams Daniel Ashley.

BARNET (6)

BRILL, Dean (G) 183 0
H: 6 2 W: 14 05 b.Luton 2-12-85
Source: Scholar.
2003-04 Luton T 5 0
2004-05 Luton T 0 0
2005-06 Luton T 5 0
2006-07 Luton T 11 0
2006-07 *Gillingham* 8 0 **8 0**
2007-08 Luton T 37 0
2008-09 Luton T 23 0 **81 0**
2009-10 Oldham Ath 28 0
2010-11 Oldham Ath 30 0 **58 0**
2011-12 Barnet 36 0 **36 0**

BYRNE, Mark (M) 73 11
H: 5 9 W: 11 00 b.Dublin 9-11-88
Source: Crumlin U.
2006-07 Nottingham F 0 0
2007-08 Nottingham F 1 0
2008-09 Nottingham F 1 0
2009-10 Nottingham F 0 0
2010-11 Nottingham F 0 0 **2 0**
2010-11 *Barnet* 28 6
2011-12 Barnet 43 5 **71 11**

COX, Sam (D) 14 0
H: 5 7 W: 10 00 b.Edgware 10-10-90
Source: Scholar.
2009-10 Tottenham H 0 0
2009-10 *Cheltenham T* 1 0 **1 0**
2009-10 *Torquay U* 3 0 **3 0**
2010-11 Barnet 10 0
2011-12 Barnet 0 0 **10 0**

DEERING, Sam (M) 66 5
H: 5 5 W: 10 00 b.Stepney 26-2-91
Source: Oxford U Scholar.
2010-11 Oxford U 6 0 **6 0**
2010-11 *Barnet* 16 2
2011-12 Barnet 44 3 **60 5**

DENNEHY, Darren (D) 53 0
H: 6 3 W: 11 11 b.Tralee 21-9-88
Source: Scholar. *Honours:* Eire Under-21.
2005-06 Everton 0 0
2006-07 Everton 0 0
2007-08 Everton 0 0
2008-09 Cardiff C 0 0
2008-09 *Hereford U* 3 0
2009-10 Cardiff C 0 0
2009-10 *Hereford U* 7 0 **10 0**
2009-10 *Gillingham* 19 0 **19 0**
2010-11 Barnet 5 0
2011-12 Barnet 19 0 **24 0**

FRASER, Tom (M) 149 3
H: 5 10 W: 11 00 b.Brighton 5-12-87
Source: Bognor Regis T.
2006-07 Brighton & HA 28 1
2007-08 Brighton & HA 24 0
2008-09 Brighton & HA 27 1 **79 2**
2009-10 Port Vale 38 1
2010-11 Port Vale 12 0 **50 1**
2010-11 Barnet 15 0
2011-12 Barnet 5 0 **20 0**

GAMBIN, Luke (M) 1 0
Source: Scholar.
2011-12 Barnet 1 0 **1 0**

GEOHAGHON, Exodus (D) 51 2
H: 6 7 W: 11 11 b.Birmingham 27-2-85
Source: Sutton Coldfield T, Bromsgrove R, Redditch U, Kettering T, England C.
2009-10 Peterborough U 19 1
2010-11 Peterborough U 0 0 **19 1**
2010-11 *Rotherham U* 14 1 **14 1**
2010-11 *Shrewsbury T* 2 0 **2 0**
2010-11 *Port Vale* 12 0 **12 0**
2011-12 Barnet 2 0 **2 0**
2011-12 *Dagenham & R* 2 0 **2 0**

HOLMES, Ricky (M) 66 10
H: 6 2 W: 11 11 b.Southend 19-6-87
Source: Southend U, Chelmsford C.
2010-11 Barnet 25 2
2011-12 Barnet 41 8 **66 10**

HUGHES, Mark (M) 262 13
H: 5 10 W: 12 05 b.Dungannon 16-9-83
Source: Scholar. *Honours:* Northern Ireland Schools, Youth, Under-21, Under-23, 2 full caps.
2001-02 Tottenham H 0 0
2002-03 Tottenham H 0 0
2003-04 Tottenham H 0 0
2004-05 Tottenham H 0 0
2004-05 *Northampton T* 3 0 **3 0**
2004-05 *Oldham Ath* 27 0
2005-06 Oldham Ath 33 1
2006-07 Oldham Ath 0 0 **60 1**
From Thurrock.
2006-07 Chesterfield 2 1 **2 1**
From Stevenage B.
2007-08 Chester C 43 4
2008-09 Chester C 26 0 **69 4**
2008-09 Barnet 9 0
2009-10 Barnet 41 2
2010-11 Barnet 33 2
2011-12 Barnet 45 3 **128 7**

KABBA, Steven (F) 219 46
H: 5 10 W: 11 03 b.Lambeth 7-3-81
Source: Trainee.
1999-2000 Crystal Palace 1 0
2000-01 Crystal Palace 1 0
2001-02 Crystal Palace 4 0
2001-02 *Luton T* 3 0 **3 0**
2002-03 Crystal Palace 4 1 **10 1**
2002-03 *Grimsby T* 13 6 **13 6**
2002-03 Sheffield U 25 7
2003-04 Sheffield U 1 0
2004-05 Sheffield U 11 2
2005-06 Sheffield U 34 9
2006-07 Sheffield U 7 0 **78 18**
2006-07 Watford 11 0
2007-08 Watford 14 1
2008-09 Watford 0 0 **25 1**
2008-09 *Blackpool* 17 2 **17 2**
2008-09 *Oldham Ath* 8 0 **8 0**
2009-10 Brentford 10 0 **10 0**
2009-10 *Burton Alb* 23 6 **23 6**
2010-11 Barnet 23 11
2011-12 Barnet 9 1 **32 12**

KAMDJO, Clovis (D) 88 4
H: 5 11 W: 12 02 b.Cameroon 15-12-90
Source: Reading Youth. *Honours:* Cameroon Youth.
2009-10 Barnet 15 0
2010-11 Barnet 32 1
2011-12 Barnet 41 3 **88 4**

LEACH, Daniel (D) 37 2
H: 6 3 W: 12 10 b.Perth 5-1-86
Source: Queensland Academy, Brisbane Toro, Brisbane Strikers, Oregon State Univ, Portland Timbers.
2009-10 Barnet 13 0
2010-11 Barnet 14 1
2011-12 Barnet 10 1 **37 2**

MARSHALL, Mark (M) 98 7
H: 5 7 W: 10 07 b.Jamaica 9-5-86
Source: Carshalton Ath, Grays Ath, Eastleigh.
2008-09 Swindon T 12 0
2009-10 Swindon T 7 0 **19 0**
2009-10 *Hereford U* 8 0 **8 0**
2010-11 Barnet 46 6
2011-12 Barnet 25 1 **71 7**

McCALLUM, Gavin (M) 83 14
H: 5 9 W: 12 00 b.Toronto 24-8-87
Honours: Canada 1 full cap, 1 goal.
2005-06 Yeovil T 0 0
2006-07 Yeovil T 0 0
From Weymouth, Havant & W, Sutton U.
2009-10 Hereford U 27 8 **27 8**
2010-11 Lincoln C 36 3
2011-12 Lincoln C 18 3 **54 6**
2011-12 Barnet 2 0 **2 0**
On loan from Lincoln C.

McLEOD, Izale (F) 279 95
H: 6 1 W: 11 02 b.Birmingham 15-10-84
Source: Scholar. *Honours:* England Under-21.
2002-03 Derby Co 29 3
2003-04 Derby Co 10 1 **39 4**
2003-04 *Sheffield U* 7 0 **7 0**
2004-05 Milton Keynes D 43 16
2005-06 Milton Keynes D 39 17
2006-07 Milton Keynes D 34 21 **116 54**
2007-08 Charlton Ath 18 1
2007-08 *Colchester U* 2 0 **2 0**
2008-09 Charlton Ath 2 0
2008-09 *Millwall* 7 2 **7 2**
2009-10 Charlton Ath 11 2
2009-10 *Peterborough U* 4 0 **4 0**
2010-11 Charlton Ath 0 0 **31 3**
2010-11 Barnet 29 14
2011-12 Barnet 44 18 **73 32**

N'DIAYE, Alassane (M) 51 3
H: 6 4 W: 14 02 b.Montbeliard 25-2-90
Source: Scholar.
2008-09 Crystal Palace 0 0
2009-10 Crystal Palace 26 3
2010-11 Crystal Palace 12 0
2010-11 *Swindon T* 6 0 **6 0**
2011-12 Crystal Palace 0 0 **38 3**
2011-12 *Southend U* 1 0 **1 0**
2011-12 Barnet 6 0 **6 0**

O'BRIEN, Liam (G) 18 0
H: 6 1 W: 12 06 b.Ruislip 30-11-91
Source: Scholar. *Honours:* England Youth.
2008-09 Portsmouth 0 0
2009-10 Portsmouth 0 0
2010-11 Barnet 8 0
2011-12 Barnet 10 0 **18 0**

OWUSU, Lloyd (F) 410 120
H: 6 2 W: 14 00 b.Slough 12-12-76
Source: Slough T. *Honours:* Ghana 2 full caps.
1998-99 Brentford 46 22
1999-2000 Brentford 41 12

2000-01 Brentford 33 10
2001-02 Brentford 44 20
2002-03 Sheffield W 32 4
2003-04 Sheffield W 20 5 **52 9**
2003-04 Reading 16 4
2004-05 Reading 25 6 **41 10**
2005-06 Brentford 42 12
2006-07 Brentford 7 0 **213 76**
2007-08 Yeovil T 43 9
2008-09 Yeovil T 4 1 **47 10**
2008-09 Cheltenham T 22 7 **22 7**
2008-09 *Brighton & HA* 14 7 **14 7**
2009-10 Adelaide U 16 1 **16 1**
From Luton T.
2011-12 Paphos 0 0
2011-12 Barnet 5 0 **5 0**

PARKES, Jordan (D) **63 1**
H: 6 0 W: 12 00 b.Watford 26-7-89
Source: Scholar. *Honours:* England Youth, Under-20.
2006-07 Watford 0 0
2007-08 Watford 0 0
2007-08 *Brentford* 1 0 **1 0**
2007-08 *Barnet* 10 0
2008-09 Watford 1 0
2009-10 Watford 0 0 **1 0**
2010-11 Barnet 40 1
2011-12 Barnet 11 0 **61 1**

SAVILLE, Jack (D) **17 0**
H: 6 3 W: 12 00 b.Camberley 2-4-91
Source: Chelsea Scholar.
2009-10 Southampton 0 0
2010-11 Southampton 0 0
2011-12 Southampton 0 0
2011-12 Barnet 17 0 **17 0**

SENDA, Danny (D) **388 10**
H: 5 10 W: 10 02 b.Harrow 17-4-81
Source: Southampton Trainee. *Honours:* England Youth.
1998-99 Wycombe W 6 0
1999-2000 Wycombe W 27 1
2000-01 Wycombe W 31 2
2001-02 Wycombe W 43 0
2002-03 Wycombe W 41 2
2003-04 Wycombe W 40 0
2004-05 Wycombe W 44 4
2005-06 Wycombe W 44 0 **276 9**
2006-07 Millwall 36 0
2007-08 Millwall 40 1
2008-09 Millwall 0 0 **76 1**
2009-10 Inactive 0 0
2010-11 Torquay U 2 0 **2 0**
2010-11 Bristol R 15 0 **15 0**
2011-12 Barnet 19 0 **19 0**

TAYLOR, Charlie (F) **36 2**
H: 6 2 W: 11 13 b.Lewisham 28-12-85
Source: Charlton Ath, Crystal Palace, Nottingham F, Welling U, AFC Hornchurch, Fisher Ath, Margate, Dulwich Hamlet, Grays Ath, Sutton U.
2010-11 Barnet 18 1
2011-12 Barnet 18 1 **36 2**

UDDIN, Anwar (D) **122 3**
H: 5 11 W: 11 10 b.Whitechapel 1-11-81
Source: West Ham U Scholar.
2001-02 West Ham U 0 0
2001-02 Sheffield W 0 0
2002-03 Bristol R 18 1
2003-04 Bristol R 1 0
2004-05 Bristol R 0 0
2005-06 Bristol R 0 0
2006-07 Bristol R 0 0 **19 1**
2007-08 Dagenham & R 41 1
2008-09 Dagenham & R 17 0
2009-10 Dagenham & R 6 0 **64 1**
2010-11 Barnet 30 1
2011-12 Barnet 9 0 **39 1**

VILHETE, Mauro (M) **25 0**
H: 5 8 W: 11 09 b.Sintra 10-5-93
Source: Scholar.
2009-10 Barnet 2 0
2010-11 Barnet 20 0
2011-12 Barnet 3 0 **25 0**

YIADOM, Andy (M) **35 8**
H: 5 11 W: 11 11 b.Holloway 2-12-91
Source: Watford Scholar, Hayes & Yeading U, Braintree T.
2011-12 Braintree T 28 7 **28 7**
2011-12 Barnet 7 1 **7 1**

BARNSLEY (7)

BUTTERFIELD, Jacob (D) **90 8**
H: 5 10 W: 11 00 b.Bradford 10-6-90
Source: Scholar.
2007-08 Barnsley 3 0
2008-09 Barnsley 3 0
2009-10 Barnsley 20 1
2010-11 Barnsley 40 2
2011-12 Barnsley 24 5 **90 8**

CLARK, Jordan (F) **6 0**
H: 6 0 W: 11 07 b.Barnsley 22-9-93
Source: Scholar.
2010-11 Barnsley 4 0
2011-12 Barnsley 2 0 **6 0**

COLLINS, Lee (D) **165 4**
H: 6 1 W: 11 10 b.Telford 23-9-83
Source: Scholar. *Honours:* England Youth.
2006-07 Wolverhampton W 0 0
2007-08 Wolverhampton W 0 0
2007-08 *Hereford U* 16 0 **16 0**
2008-09 Wolverhampton W 0 0
2008-09 Port Vale 39 1
2009-10 Port Vale 45 1
2010-11 Port Vale 42 2
2011-12 Port Vale 16 0 **142 4**
2011-12 Barnsley 7 0 **7 0**

COTTERILL, David (F) **195 21**
H: 5 9 W: 11 02 b.Cardiff 4-12-87
Source: Scholar. *Honours:* Wales Youth, Under-21, 19 full caps, 1 goal.
2004-05 Bristol C 12 0
2005-06 Bristol C 45 7
2006-07 Bristol C 5 1 **62 8**
2006-07 Wigan Ath 16 1
2007-08 Wigan Ath 2 0 **18 1**
2007-08 *Sheffield U* 16 0
2008-09 Sheffield U 24 4
2009-10 Sheffield U 14 2 **54 6**
2009-10 Swansea C 21 3
2010-11 Swansea C 14 1
2010-11 *Portsmouth* 15 1 **15 1**
2011-12 Swansea C 0 0 **35 4**
2011-12 Barnsley 11 1 **11 1**

DAGNALL, Chris (F) **272 71**
H: 5 8 W: 12 03 b.Liverpool 15-4-86
Source: Scholar.
2003-04 Tranmere R 10 1
2004-05 Tranmere R 23 6
2005-06 Tranmere R 6 0 **39 7**
2005-06 Rochdale 21 3
2006-07 Rochdale 37 17
2007-08 Rochdale 14 7
2008-09 Rochdale 40 7
2009-10 Rochdale 45 20 **157 54**
2010-11 Scunthorpe U 37 5
2011-12 Scunthorpe U 23 4 **60 9**
2011-12 Barnsley 9 0 **9 0**
2011-12 *Bradford C* 7 1 **7 1**

DAVIES, Craig (F) **254 65**
H: 6 2 W: 13 05 b.Burton-on-Trent 9-1-86
Source: Manchester C. *Honours:* Wales Youth, Under-21, 5 full caps.
2004-05 Oxford U 28 6
2005-06 Oxford U 20 2 **48 8**
2005-06 Verona 0 0
2006-07 Wolverhampton W 23 0 **23 0**
2007-08 Oldham Ath 32 10
2008-09 Oldham Ath 12 0 **44 10**
2008-09 *Stockport Co* 9 5 **9 5**
2008-09 Brighton & HA 16 1
2009-10 Brighton & HA 5 0 **21 1**
2009-10 *Yeovil T* 4 0 **4 0**
2009-10 *Port Vale* 24 7 **24 7**
2010-11 Chesterfield 41 23 **41 23**
2011-12 Barnsley 40 11 **40 11**

DAWSON, Stephen (M) **277 13**
H: 5 9 W: 11 09 b.Dublin 4-12-85
Source: Scholar. *Honours:* Eire Under-21.
2003-04 Leicester C 0 0
2004-05 Leicester C 0 0
2005-06 Mansfield T 40 1
2006-07 Mansfield T 34 1
2007-08 Mansfield T 43 2 **117 4**
2008-09 Bury 43 2
2009-10 Bury 45 4 **88 6**
2010-11 Leyton Orient 40 2
2011-12 Leyton Orient 20 1 **60 3**
2011-12 Barnsley 12 0 **12 0**

DIGBY, Paul (M) **4 0**
H: 5 9 W: 10 00 b.Sheffield 2-2-95
Source: Scholar.
2011-12 Barnsley 4 0 **4 0**

DONE, Matt (M) **186 10**
H: 5 10 W: 10 04 b.Oswestry 22-6-88
Source: Scholar.
2005-06 Wrexham 6 0
2006-07 Wrexham 34 1
2007-08 Wrexham 26 0 **66 1**
2008-09 Hereford U 36 0
2009-10 Hereford U 20 0 **56 0**
2010-11 Rochdale 33 5 **33 5**
2011-12 Barnsley 31 4 **31 4**

DOYLE, Nathan (M) **157 2**
H: 5 11 W: 12 06 b.Derby 12-1-87
Source: Scholar. *Honours:* England Youth, Under-20.
2003-04 Derby Co 2 0
2004-05 Derby Co 3 0
2005-06 Derby Co 4 0
2005-06 *Notts Co* 12 0 **12 0**
2006-07 Derby Co 0 0 **9 0**
2006-07 *Bradford C* 28 0 **28 0**
2006-07 Hull C 1 0
2007-08 Hull C 1 0
2008-09 Hull C 3 0
2009-10 Hull C 0 0 **5 0**
2009-10 Barnsley 34 0
2010-11 Barnsley 43 2
2011-12 Barnsley 21 0 **98 2**
2011-12 *Preston NE* 5 0 **5 0**

EDWARDS, Rob (D) **205 5**
H: 6 1 W: 11 10 b.Telford 25-12-82
Source: Trainee. *Honours:* Wales Youth, 15 full caps.
1999-2000 Aston Villa 0 0
2000-01 Aston Villa 0 0
2001-02 Aston Villa 0 0
2002-03 Aston Villa 8 0
2003-04 Aston Villa 0 0 **8 0**
2003-04 *Crystal Palace* 7 1 **7 1**
2003-04 *Derby Co* 11 1 **11 1**
2004-05 Wolverhampton W 17 0
2005-06 Wolverhampton W 42 0
2006-07 Wolverhampton W 33 0
2007-08 Wolverhampton W 8 1 **100 1**
2008-09 Blackpool 36 2
2009-10 Blackpool 21 0
2010-11 Blackpool 2 0 **59 2**
2010-11 *Norwich C* 3 0 **3 0**
2011-12 Barnsley 17 0 **17 0**

FOSTER, Stephen (D) **430 23**
H: 6 0 W: 11 05 b.Warrington 10-9-80
Source: Trainee. *Honours:* England Schools.
1998-99 Crewe Alex 1 0
1999-2000 Crewe Alex 0 0
2000-01 Crewe Alex 30 0
2001-02 Crewe Alex 34 5
2002-03 Crewe Alex 35 4
2003-04 Crewe Alex 45 2
2004-05 Crewe Alex 34 1
2005-06 Crewe Alex 39 3 **218 15**
2006-07 Burnley 17 0
2007-08 Burnley 0 0 **17 0**
2007-08 Barnsley 41 1
2008-09 Barnsley 38 3
2009-10 Barnsley 42 2
2010-11 Barnsley 33 1
2011-12 Barnsley 41 1 **195 8**

GOLBOURNE, Scott (M) **179 4**
H: 5 8 W: 11 08 b.Bristol 29-2-88
Source: Scholar. *Honours:* England Youth.
2004-05 Bristol C 9 0
2005-06 Bristol C 5 0 **14 0**
2005-06 Reading 1 0
2006-07 Reading 0 0
2006-07 *Wycombe W* 34 1 **34 1**
2007-08 Reading 1 0
2007-08 *Bournemouth* 5 0 **5 0**
2008-09 Reading 0 0 **2 0**
2008-09 *Oldham Ath* 8 0 **8 0**
2009-10 Exeter C 34 0
2010-11 Exeter C 44 2
2011-12 Exeter C 26 0 **104 2**
2011-12 Barnsley 12 1 **12 1**

GRAY, Andy (F) 467 106
H: 6 1 W: 13 00 b.Harrogate 15-11-77
Source: Trainee. *Honours:* Scotland Youth, B, 2 full caps.

1995-96	Leeds U	15	0		
1996-97	Leeds U	7	0		
1997-98	Leeds U	0	0		
1997-98	*Bury*	6	1	**6**	**1**
1998-99	Leeds U	0	0	**22**	**0**
1998-99	Nottingham F	8	0		
1998-99	*Preston NE*	5	0	**5**	**0**
1998-99	*Oldham Ath*	4	0	**4**	**0**
1999-2000	Nottingham F	22	0		
2000-01	Nottingham F	18	0		
2001-02	Nottingham F	16	1	**64**	**1**
2002-03	Bradford C	44	15		
2003-04	Bradford C	33	5	**77**	**20**
2003-04	Sheffield U	14	9		
2004-05	Sheffield U	43	15		
2005-06	Sheffield U	1	1	**58**	**25**
2005-06	Sunderland	21	1	**21**	**1**
2005-06	Burnley	9	3		
2006-07	Burnley	35	14		
2007-08	Burnley	25	11	**69**	**28**
2007-08	Charlton Ath	16	2		
2008-09	Charlton Ath	27	7		
2009-10	Charlton Ath	2	0	**45**	**9**
2009-10	Barnsley	30	6		
2010-11	Barnsley	34	7		
2011-12	Barnsley	32	8	**96**	**21**

HASSELL, Bobby (D) 406 9
H: 5 10 W: 12 00 b.Derby 4-6-80
Source: Trainee.

1997-98	Mansfield T	9	0		
1998-99	Mansfield T	3	0		
1999-2000	Mansfield T	11	1		
2000-01	Mansfield T	40	1		
2001-02	Mansfield T	43	1		
2002-03	Mansfield T	20	0		
2003-04	Mansfield T	34	0	**160**	**3**
2004-05	Barnsley	39	0		
2005-06	Barnsley	28	2		
2006-07	Barnsley	39	2		
2007-08	Barnsley	20	0		
2008-09	Barnsley	40	0		
2009-10	Barnsley	24	1		
2010-11	Barnsley	37	1		
2011-12	Barnsley	19	0	**246**	**6**

LIDAKEVICIUS, Lukas (G) 0 0
H: 5 11 W: 11 05 b.Klaipeda 29-4-93
Source: Scholar.

2011-12	Barnsley	0	0		

McEVELEY, James (D) 210 7
H: 6 1 W: 13 03 b.Liverpool 11-2-85
Source: Trainee. *Honours:* England Under-20, Under-21. Scotland B, 3 full caps.

2002-03	Blackburn R	9	0		
2003-04	Blackburn R	0	0		
2003-04	*Burnley*	4	0	**4**	**0**
2004-05	Blackburn R	5	0		
2004-05	*Gillingham*	10	1	**10**	**1**
2005-06	Blackburn R	0	0		
2005-06	*Ipswich T*	19	1	**19**	**1**
2006-07	Blackburn R	4	0	**18**	**0**
2006-07	Derby Co	15	0		
2007-08	Derby Co	29	2		
2008-09	Derby Co	15	0		
2008-09	*Preston NE*	7	0	**7**	**0**
2008-09	*Charlton Ath*	6	0	**6**	**0**
2009-10	Derby Co	33	2	**92**	**4**
2010-11	Barnsley	17	1		
2011-12	Barnsley	29	0	**46**	**1**
2011-12	*Swindon T*	8	0	**8**	**0**

McNULTY, Jim (D) 137 5
H: 6 1 W: 12 00 b.Runcorn 13-2-85
Source: Wrexham Scholar, Caernarfon T. *Honours:* Scotland Youth.

2006-07	Macclesfield T	15	0		
2007-08	Macclesfield T	19	1	**34**	**1**
2007-08	Stockport Co	11	0		
2008-09	Stockport Co	26	1	**37**	**1**
2008-09	Brighton & HA	5	1		
2009-10	Brighton & HA	8	0		
2009-10	*Scunthorpe U*	3	0		
2010-11	Brighton & HA	0	0	**13**	**1**
2010-11	*Scunthorpe U*	6	0	**9**	**0**
2011-12	Barnsley	44	2	**44**	**2**

MILLER, Kern (D) 3 0
H: 5 9 W: 11 03 b.Skegness 2-9-91
Source: Scholar.

2008-09	Lincoln C	1	0		
2009-10	Lincoln C	0	0		
2010-11	Lincoln C	0	0	**1**	**0**
2010-11	Barnsley	0	0		
2011-12	Barnsley	0	0		
2011-12	*Accrington S*	2	0	**2**	**0**

NOBLE-LAZARUS, Reuben (F) 19 1
H: 5 11 W: 13 07 b.Huddersfield 16-8-93
Source: Youth.

2008-09	Barnsley	2	0		
2009-10	Barnsley	2	0		
2010-11	Barnsley	7	1		
2011-12	Barnsley	8	0	**19**	**1**

O'BRIEN, Jim (F) 152 8
H: 6 0 W: 11 11 b.Alexandria 28-9-87

2006-07	Celtic	0	0		
2006-07	*Dunfermline Ath*	13	1	**13**	**1**
2007-08	Celtic	1	0	**1**	**0**
2007-08	*Dundee U*	10	0	**10**	**0**
2008-09	Motherwell	29	1		
2009-10	Motherwell	35	3	**64**	**4**
2010-11	Barnsley	33	1		
2011-12	Barnsley	31	2	**64**	**3**

PERKINS, David (D) 205 13
H: 5 6 W: 11 06 b.Heysham 21-6-82

2006-07	Rochdale	18	0		
2007-08	Rochdale	40	4	**58**	**4**
2008-09	Colchester U	38	5		
2009-10	Colchester U	5	1		
2009-10	*Chesterfield*	13	1	**13**	**1**
2009-10	*Stockport Co*	22	0	**22**	**0**
2010-11	Colchester U	36	1	**79**	**7**
2011-12	Barnsley	33	1	**33**	**1**

PREECE, David (G) 261 0
H: 6 2 W: 11 11 b.Sunderland 26-8-76
Source: Sunderland Scholar.

1994-95	Sunderland	0	0		
1995-96	Sunderland	0	0		
1996-97	Sunderland	0	0		
1997-98	Darlington	45	0		
1998-99	Darlington	46	0	**91**	**0**
1999-2000	Aberdeen	10	0		
2000-01	Aberdeen	2	0		
2001-02	Aberdeen	8	0		
2002-03	Aberdeen	16	0		
2003-04	Aberdeen	36	0		
2004-05	Aberdeen	17	0	**89**	**0**
2005-06	Silkeborg	32	0		
2006-07	Silkeborg	23	0		
2007-08	Silkeborg	19	0	**74**	**0**
2008-09	Odense	0	0		
2009-10	Barnsley	6	0		
2010-11	Barnsley	0	0		
2011-12	Barnsley	1	0	**7**	**0**

ROSE, Danny (F) 5 0
H: 5 8 W: 9 00 b.Barnsley 10-12-93
Source: Scholar.

2010-11	Barnsley	1	0		
2011-12	Barnsley	4	0	**5**	**0**

STEELE, Luke (G) 186 0
H: 6 2 W: 12 00 b.Peterborough 24-9-84
Source: Scholar. *Honours:* England Youth, Under-20.

2001-02	Peterborough U	2	0	**2**	**0**
2001-02	Manchester U	0	0		
2002-03	Manchester U	0	0		
2003-04	Manchester U	0	0		
2004-05	Manchester U	0	0		
2004-05	*Coventry C*	32	0		
2005-06	Manchester U	0	0		
2006-07	WBA	0	0		
2006-07	*Coventry C*	5	0	**37**	**0**
2007-08	WBA	2	0	**2**	**0**
2007-08	*Barnsley*	14	0		
2008-09	Barnsley	10	0		
2009-10	Barnsley	39	0		
2010-11	Barnsley	46	0		
2011-12	Barnsley	36	0	**145**	**0**

STONES, John (D) 2 0
H: 6 2 W: 11 00 b.Barnsley 28-5-94
Source: Scholar.

2011-12	Barnsley	2	0	**2**	**0**

TAYLOR, Alistair (M) 4 0
H: 6 1 W: 10 06 b.Sheffield 13-9-91
Source: Scholar.

2009-10	Barnsley	1	0		
2010-11	Barnsley	2	0		
2011-12	Barnsley	1	0	**4**	**0**

THOMPSON, O'Neil (D) 55 1
H: 6 4 W: 13 00 b.Kingston 11-8-83
Source: Boys Town. *Honours:* Jamaica 21 full caps, 1 goal.

2007	Notodden	22	1		
2008	Notodden	14	0		
2009	Notodden	10	0	**46**	**1**
2009-10	Barnsley	1	0		
2009-10	*Burton Alb*	2	0	**2**	**0**
2010-11	Barnsley	0	0		
2010-11	*Hereford U*	6	0	**6**	**0**
2011-12	Barnsley	0	0	**1**	**0**

Transferred to Boys Town January 2011.

WISEMAN, Scott (D) 201 3
H: 6 0 W: 11 06 b.Hull 9-10-85
Source: Scholar. *Honours:* England Youth, Under-20.

2003-04	Hull C	2	0		
2004-05	Hull C	3	0		
2004-05	*Boston U*	2	0	**2**	**0**
2005-06	Hull C	11	0		
2006-07	Hull C	0	0	**16**	**0**
2006-07	*Rotherham U*	18	1	**18**	**1**
2006-07	*Darlington*	10	0		
2007-08	Darlington	7	0	**17**	**0**
2008-09	Rochdale	32	0		
2009-10	Rochdale	36	1		
2010-11	Rochdale	37	0	**105**	**1**
2011-12	Barnsley	43	1	**43**	**1**

BIRMINGHAM C (8)

ASANTE, Akwasi (F) 4 1
H: 5 7 W: 10 00 b.Amsterdam 22-9-92
Source: Scholar.

2010-11	Birmingham C	0	0		
2011-12	Birmingham C	0	0		
2011-12	*Northampton T*	4	1	**4**	**1**

BURKE, Chris (M) 243 38
H: 5 9 W: 10 10 b.Glasgow 2-12-83
Honours: Scotland Under-21, B, 2 full caps.

2001-02	Rangers	2	1		
2002-03	Rangers	0	0		
2003-04	Rangers	20	3		
2004-05	Rangers	12	0		
2005-06	Rangers	27	3		
2006-07	Rangers	22	2		
2007-08	Rangers	11	2		
2008-09	Rangers	1	0	**95**	**11**
2008-09	Cardiff C	14	1		
2009-10	Cardiff C	44	9		
2010-11	Cardiff C	44	5	**102**	**15**
2011-12	Birmingham C	46	12	**46**	**12**

BUTLAND, Jack (G) 24 0
H: 6 4 W: 12 00 b.Clevedon 10-3-93
Source: Scholar. *Honours:* England Youth, Under-20, Under-21.

2009-10	Birmingham C	0	0		
2010-11	Birmingham C	0	0		
2011-12	Birmingham C	0	0		
2011-12	*Cheltenham T*	24	0	**24**	**0**

CALDWELL, Steven (D) 289 11
H: 6 2 W: 13 12 b.Stirling 12-9-80
Source: Trainee. *Honours:* Scotland Youth, Under-21, B, 12 full caps.

1997-98	Newcastle U	0	0		
1998-99	Newcastle U	0	0		
1999-2000	Newcastle U	0	0		
2000-01	Newcastle U	9	0		
2001-02	Newcastle U	0	0		
2001-02	*Blackpool*	6	0	**6**	**0**
2001-02	*Bradford C*	9	0	**9**	**0**
2002-03	Newcastle U	14	1		
2003-04	Newcastle U	5	0	**28**	**1**
2003-04	*Leeds U*	13	1	**13**	**1**
2004-05	Sunderland	41	4		
2005-06	Sunderland	24	0		
2006-07	Sunderland	11	0	**76**	**4**
2006-07	Burnley	17	0		
2007-08	Burnley	29	2		
2008-09	Burnley	45	2		
2009-10	Burnley	13	1		

2010-11 Burnley 0 0 **104** **5**
2010-11 Wigan Ath 10 0 **10** **0**
2011-12 Birmingham C 43 0 **43** **0**

CARR, Stephen (D) **410** **8**
H: 5 9 W: 11 13 b.Dublin 29-8-76
Source: Trainee. *Honours:* Eire Schools, Youth, Under-21, 44 full caps.
1993-94 Tottenham H 1 0
1994-95 Tottenham H 0 0
1995-96 Tottenham H 0 0
1996-97 Tottenham H 26 0
1997-98 Tottenham H 38 0
1998-99 Tottenham H 37 0
1999-2000 Tottenham H 34 3
2000-01 Tottenham H 28 3
2001-02 Tottenham H 0 0
2002-03 Tottenham H 30 0
2003-04 Tottenham H 32 1 **226** **7**
2004-05 Newcastle U 26 1
2005-06 Newcastle U 19 0
2006-07 Newcastle U 23 0
2007-08 Newcastle U 10 0
2008-09 Newcastle U 0 0 **78** **1**
2008-09 Birmingham C 13 0
2009-10 Birmingham C 35 0
2010-11 Birmingham C 38 0
2011-12 Birmingham C 20 0 **106** **0**

DAVIES, Curtis (D) **230** **12**
H: 6 2 W: 11 13 b.Waltham Forest 15-3-85
Source: Scholar. *Honours:* England Under-21.
2003-04 Luton T 6 0
2004-05 Luton T 44 1
2005-06 Luton T 6 1 **56** **2**
2005-06 WBA 33 2
2006-07 WBA 32 0
2007-08 WBA 0 0 **65** **2**
2007-08 *Aston Villa* 12 1
2008-09 Aston Villa 35 1
2009-10 Aston Villa 2 1
2010-11 Aston Villa 0 0 **49** **3**
2010-11 *Leicester C* 12 0 **12** **0**
2010-11 Birmingham C 6 0
2011-12 Birmingham C 42 5 **48** **5**

DEAMAN, Jack (D) **0** **0**
b.Camden 18-5-93
Source: Wrexham Scholar.
2011-12 Birmingham C 0 0

DOYLE, Colin (G) **47** **0**
H: 6 5 W: 14 05 b.Cork 12-8-85
Honours: Eire Youth, Under-21, 1 full cap.
2004-05 Birmingham C 0 0
2004-05 *Chester C* 0 0
2004-05 *Nottingham F* 3 0 **3** **0**
2005-06 Birmingham C 0 0
2005-06 *Millwall* 14 0 **14** **0**
2006-07 Birmingham C 19 0
2007-08 Birmingham C 3 0
2008-09 Birmingham C 2 0
2009-10 Birmingham C 0 0
2010-11 Birmingham C 1 0
2011-12 Birmingham C 5 0 **30** **0**

ELLIOTT, Wade (M) **501** **52**
H: 5 10 W: 10 03 b.Eastleigh 14-12-78
Source: Bashley.
1999-2000 Bournemouth 12 3
2000-01 Bournemouth 36 9
2001-02 Bournemouth 46 8
2002-03 Bournemouth 44 4
2003-04 Bournemouth 39 3
2004-05 Bournemouth 43 4 **220** **31**
2005-06 Burnley 36 3
2006-07 Burnley 42 4
2007-08 Burnley 46 2
2008-09 Burnley 42 4
2009-10 Burnley 38 4
2010-11 Burnley 44 2
2011-12 Burnley 4 0 **252** **19**
2011-12 Birmingham C 29 2 **29** **2**

FAHEY, Keith (M) **256** **31**
H: 5 10 W: 12 07 b.Dublin 15-1-83
Source: Arsenal Trainee. *Honours:* Eire 15 full caps, 3 goals.
1999-2000 Aston Villa 0 0
2000-01 Aston Villa 0 0
2001-02 Aston Villa 0 0
2002-03 Aston Villa 0 0
2003 St Patrick's Ath 0 0
2004 St Patrick's Ath 33 5
2005 St Patrick's Ath 14 3
2005 Drogheda U 14 2
2006 Drogheda U 8 0 **22** **2**
2006 St Patrick's Ath 13 3
2007 St Patrick's Ath 32 1
2008 St Patrick's Ath 30 8 **122** **20**
2008-09 Birmingham C 19 4
2009-10 Birmingham C 34 0
2010-11 Birmingham C 24 1
2011-12 Birmingham C 35 4 **112** **9**

FOLAN, Caleb (F) **206** **34**
H: 6 2 W: 14 07 b.Leeds 26-10-82
Source: Trainee. *Honours:* Eire 7 full caps.
1999-2000 Leeds U 0 0
2000-01 Leeds U 0 0
2001-02 Leeds U 0 0
2001-02 *Rushden & D* 6 0 **6** **0**
2001-02 *Hull C* 1 0
2002-03 Leeds U 0 0
2002-03 Chesterfield 13 1
2003-04 Chesterfield 7 0
2004-05 Chesterfield 32 6
2005-06 Chesterfield 27 0
2006-07 Chesterfield 23 8 **102** **15**
2006-07 Wigan Ath 13 2
2007-08 Wigan Ath 2 0 **15** **2**
2007-08 Hull C 29 8
2008-09 Hull C 15 1
2009-10 Hull C 8 2
2009-10 *Middlesbrough* 1 0 **1** **0**
2010-11 Hull C 3 0 **56** **11**
2010-11 Colorado Rapids 26 6 **26** **6**
2011-12 Birmingham C 0 0

FOSTER, Ben (G) **179** **0**
H: 6 2 W: 12 08 b.Leamington Spa 3-4-83
Source: Racing Club Warwick. *Honours:* England 5 full caps.
2000-01 Stoke C 0 0
2001-02 Stoke C 0 0
2002-03 Stoke C 0 0
2003-04 Stoke C 0 0
2004-05 Stoke C 0 0
2004-05 *Kidderminster H* 2 0 **2** **0**
2004-05 *Wrexham* 17 0 **17** **0**
2005-06 Manchester U 0 0
2005-06 *Watford* 44 0
2006-07 Manchester U 0 0
2006-07 *Watford* 29 0 **73** **0**
2007-08 Manchester U 1 0
2008-09 Manchester U 2 0
2009-10 Manchester U 9 0 **12** **0**
2010-11 Birmingham C 38 0
2011-12 Birmingham C 0 0 **38** **0**
2011-12 *WBA* 37 0 **37** **0**

GNAHORE, Eddy (M) **0** **0**
b.Paris 14-11-93
Source: Scholar. *Honours:* France Youth.
2011-12 Birmingham C 0 0

GOMIS, Morgaro (M) **181** **8**
H: 5 9 W: 11 00 b.Le Blanc-Mesnil 14-7-85
Source: Windsor & E, Dagenham & R, Barnet, Lewes. *Honours:* Senegal 1 full cap.
2006-07 Cowdenbeath 15 2 **15** **2**
2006-07 Dundee U 12 0
2007-08 Dundee U 36 1
2008-09 Dundee U 37 0
2009-10 Dundee U 31 4
2010-11 Dundee U 34 1 **150** **6**
2011-12 Birmingham C 16 0 **16** **0**

HANCOX, Mitch (D) **0** **0**
H: 5 10 W: 11 03 b.Solihull 9-11-93
Source: Scholar.
2011-12 Birmingham C 0 0

HUBBINS, Luke (M) **0** **0**
b.Birmingham 11-9-91
Source: Scholar.
2010-11 Birmingham C 0 0
2011-12 Birmingham C 0 0

HUGHTON, Cian (D) **63** **6**
H: 5 8 W: 10 05 b.Enfield 25-1-89
Source: Tottenham H Scholar. *Honours:* Eire Under-21.
2007-08 Tottenham H 0 0
2008-09 Tottenham H 0 0
2009-10 Lincoln C 41 4
2010-11 Lincoln C 22 2 **63** **6**
2011-12 Birmingham C 0 0

JERVIS, Jake (F) **38** **7**
H: 6 3 W: 12 13 b.Birmingham 17-9-91
Source: Scholar.
2009-10 Birmingham C 0 0
2009-10 *Hereford U* 7 2
2010-11 Birmingham C 0 0
2010-11 *Notts Co* 10 0 **10** **0**
2010-11 *Hereford U* 4 0 **11** **2**
2011-12 Birmingham C 0 0
2011-12 *Swindon T* 12 3 **12** **3**
2011-12 *Preston NE* 5 2 **5** **2**

KERR, Fraser (D) **0** **0**
H: 6 3 W: 13 03 b.Motherwell 17-1-93
Source: Scholar.
2010-11 Birmingham C 0 0
2011-12 Birmingham C 0 0

KING, Marlon (F) **413** **136**
H: 5 10 W: 12 10 b.Dulwich 26-4-80
Source: Trainee. *Honours:* Jamaica 20 full caps, 12 goals.
1998-99 Barnet 22 6
1999-2000 Barnet 31 8 **53** **14**
2000-01 Gillingham 38 15
2001-02 Gillingham 42 17
2002-03 Gillingham 10 4
2003-04 Gillingham 11 4 **101** **40**
2003-04 Nottingham F 24 5
2004-05 Nottingham F 26 5
2004-05 *Leeds U* 9 0 **9** **0**
2005-06 Nottingham F 0 0 **50** **10**
2005-06 Watford 41 21
2006-07 Watford 13 4
2007-08 Watford 27 11 **81** **36**
2007-08 Wigan Ath 15 1
2008-09 Wigan Ath 0 0
2008-09 *Hull C* 20 5 **20** **5**
2008-09 *Middlesbrough* 13 2 **13** **2**
2009-10 Wigan Ath 3 0 **18** **1**
2010-11 Coventry C 28 12 **28** **12**
2011-12 Birmingham C 40 16 **40** **16**

MURPHY, David (D) **217** **11**
H: 6 1 W: 12 03 b.Hartlepool 1-3-84
Source: Scholar. *Honours:* England Youth.
2001-02 Middlesbrough 5 0
2002-03 Middlesbrough 8 0
2003-04 Middlesbrough 0 0 **13** **0**
2003-04 *Barnsley* 10 2 **10** **2**
2004-05 Hibernian 27 1
2005-06 Hibernian 30 1
2006-07 Hibernian 33 0
2007-08 Hibernian 17 2 **107** **4**
2007-08 Birmingham C 14 1
2008-09 Birmingham C 30 0
2009-10 Birmingham C 0 0
2010-11 Birmingham C 10 0
2011-12 Birmingham C 33 4 **87** **5**

MUTCH, Jordon (M) **67** **9**
H: 5 9 W: 10 03 b.Derby 2-12-91
Source: Scholar. *Honours:* England Youth, Under-21.
2007-08 Birmingham C 0 0
2008-09 Birmingham C 0 0
2009-10 Birmingham C 0 0
2009-10 *Hereford U* 3 0 **3** **0**
2009-10 *Doncaster R* 17 2 **17** **2**
2010-11 Birmingham C 3 0
2010-11 *Watford* 23 5 **23** **5**
2011-12 Birmingham C 21 2 **24** **2**

N'DAW, Guirane (M) **221** **8**
H: 6 2 W: 12 06 b.Rufisque 24-4-84
Honours: Senegal 43 full caps, 4 goals.
2001-02 Sochaux B 0 0
2002-03 Sochaux 1 0
2003-04 Sochaux 8 0
2004-05 Sochaux 16 0
2005-06 Sochaux 30 1
2006-07 Sochaux 37 1
2007-08 Sochaux 30 3 **122** **5**
2008-09 Nantes 32 3 **32** **3**
2009-10 *St Etienne* 34 0
2010-11 St Etienne 5 0 **39** **0**
2010-11 *Zaragoza* 9 0 **9** **0**
2011-12 Birmingham C 19 0 **19** **0**
On loan from St Etienne.

NTAMBWE, Brice (M) **0** **0**
b.Brussels 29-4-93
Source: Scholar.
2011-12 Birmingham C 0 0

PABLO (D) **253 12**
H: 6 3 W: 13 07 b.Madrigueras 3-8-81
Honours: Spain Under-21, 23 full caps.

Season	Club	Apps	Gls	Tot Apps	Tot Gls
2002-03	Albacete	38	1		
2003-04	Albacete	36	1	**74**	**2**
2004-05	Atletico Madrid	35	3		
2005-06	Atletico Madrid	35	2		
2006-07	Atletico Madrid	24	2		
2007-08	Atletico Madrid	34	1		
2008-09	Atletico Madrid	21	1		
2009-10	Atletico Madrid	7	0	**156**	**9**
2010-11	WBA	10	1	**10**	**1**
2011-12	Birmingham C	13	0	**13**	**0**

PACKWOOD, Will (M) **0 0**
b.Concord 21-5-93
Source: Scholar.

Season	Club	Apps	Gls	Tot Apps	Tot Gls
2011-12	Birmingham C	0	0		

REDMOND, Nathan (M) **24 5**
H: 5 8 W: 11 11 b.Birmingham 6-3-94
Source: Scholar. *Honours:* England Youth.

Season	Club	Apps	Gls	Tot Apps	Tot Gls
2011-12	Birmingham C	24	5	**24**	**5**

ROONEY, Adam (F) **176 62**
H: 5 10 W: 12 03 b.Dublin 21-4-87
Source: Scholar. *Honours:* Eire Youth, Under-21.

Season	Club	Apps	Gls	Tot Apps	Tot Gls
2005-06	Stoke C	5	4		
2006-07	Stoke C	10	0		
2006-07	*Yeovil T*	3	0	**3**	**0**
2007-08	Stoke C	0	0	**15**	**4**
2007-08	*Chesterfield*	22	7	**22**	**7**
2007-08	*Bury*	16	3	**16**	**3**
2008-09	Inverness CT	30	5		
2009-10	Inverness CT	35	24		
2010-11	Inverness CT	37	15	**102**	**44**
2011-12	Birmingham C	18	4	**18**	**4**

SAMMONS, Ashley (M) **0 0**
b.Solihull 10-11-91
Source: Scholar. *Honours:* England Youth.

Season	Club	Apps	Gls	Tot Apps	Tot Gls
2008-09	Birmingham C	0	0		
2009-10	Birmingham C	0	0		
2010-11	Birmingham C	0	0		
2011-12	Birmingham C	0	0		

SPECTOR, Jonathan (D) **155 1**
H: 6 0 W: 12 08 b.Chicago 1-3-86
Source: Chicago Sockers. *Honours:* USA Youth, 34 full caps.

Season	Club	Apps	Gls	Tot Apps	Tot Gls
2003-04	Manchester U	0	0		
2004-05	Manchester U	3	0		
2005-06	Manchester U	0	0	**3**	**0**
2005-06	*Charlton Ath*	20	0	**20**	**0**
2006-07	West Ham U	25	0		
2007-08	West Ham U	26	0		
2008-09	West Ham U	9	0		
2009-10	West Ham U	27	0		
2010-11	West Ham U	14	1	**101**	**1**
2011-12	Birmingham C	31	0	**31**	**0**

TAYLOR, Maik (G) **496 0**
H: 6 4 W: 14 02 b.Hildeshein 4-9-71
Source: Farnborough T. *Honours:* Northern Ireland Under-21, B, 88 full caps.

Season	Club	Apps	Gls	Tot Apps	Tot Gls
1995-96	Barnet	45	0		
1996-97	Barnet	25	0	**70**	**0**
1996-97	Southampton	18	0		
1997-98	Southampton	0	0	**18**	**0**
1997-98	Fulham	28	0		
1998-99	Fulham	46	0		
1999-2000	Fulham	46	0		
2000-01	Fulham	44	0		
2001-02	Fulham	1	0		
2002-03	Fulham	19	0		
2003-04	Fulham	0	0	**184**	**0**
2003-04	Birmingham C	34	0		
2004-05	Birmingham C	38	0		
2005-06	Birmingham C	34	0		
2006-07	Birmingham C	27	0		
2007-08	Birmingham C	34	0		
2008-09	Birmingham C	45	0		
2009-10	Birmingham C	2	0		
2010-11	Birmingham C	0	0		
2011-12	Birmingham C	0	0	**214**	**0**
2011-12	*Millwall*	10	0	**10**	**0**

VALLES, Enric (M) **4 0**
H: 6 2 W: 13 01 b.Barcelona 1-3-90

Season	Club	Apps	Gls	Tot Apps	Tot Gls
2008-09	NAC Breda	3	0		
2009-10	NAC Breda	1	0	**4**	**0**
2010-11	Birmingham C	0	0		
2011-12	Birmingham C	0	0		

ZIGIC, Nikola (F) **336 192**
H: 6 8 W: 14 02 b.Backa Topola 25-9-80
Honours: Serbia 57 full caps, 20 goals.

Season	Club	Apps	Gls	Tot Apps	Tot Gls
1998-99	Backa Topola	14	8		
1999-2000	Backa Topola	28	28		
2000-01	Backa Topola	30	30		
2001-02	Backa Topola	4	2	**76**	**68**
2001-02	Mornar Bar	23	15	**23**	**15**
2002-03	Kolubara	8	3	**8**	**3**
2002-03	Spartak Subotica	11	14	**11**	**14**
2003-04	Red Star Belgrade	28	19		
2004-05	Red Star Belgrade	25	15		
2005-06	Red Star Belgrade	23	11		
2006-07	Red Star Belgrade	3	2	**79**	**47**
2006-07	Santander	32	11		
2007-08	Valencia	15	1		
2008-09	Santander	19	13	**51**	**24**
2009-10	Valencia	13	4	**28**	**5**
2010-11	Birmingham C	25	5		
2011-12	Birmingham C	35	11	**60**	**16**

BLACKBURN R (9)

ALEY, Zach (M) **3 0**
b.Fazakerley 17-8-91
Source: Scholar.

Season	Club	Apps	Gls	Tot Apps	Tot Gls
2009-10	Blackburn R	0	0		
2010-11	Blackburn R	0	0		
2010-11	*Morecambe*	2	0	**2**	**0**
2011-12	Blackburn R	0	0		
2011-12	*Macclesfield T*	1	0	**1**	**0**

ANDERSON, Myles (D) **1 0**
b.Westminster 9-1-90
Source: Leyton Orient.

Season	Club	Apps	Gls	Tot Apps	Tot Gls
2010-11	Aberdeen	1	0	**1**	**0**
2011-12	Blackburn R	0	0		

BLACKMAN, Nick (F) **63 15**
H: 6 2 W: 11 08 b.Whitefield 11-11-89
Source: Scholar.

Season	Club	Apps	Gls	Tot Apps	Tot Gls
2006-07	Macclesfield T	1	0		
2007-08	Macclesfield T	11	1		
2008-09	Macclesfield T	0	0	**12**	**1**
2008-09	Blackburn R	0	0		
2008-09	*Blackpool*	5	1	**5**	**1**
2009-10	Blackburn R	0	0		
2009-10	*Oldham Ath*	12	1	**12**	**1**
2010-11	Blackburn R	0	0		
2010-11	*Motherwell*	18	10	**18**	**10**
2010-11	*Aberdeen*	15	2	**15**	**2**
2011-12	Blackburn R	1	0	**1**	**0**

BUNN, Mark (G) **131 0**
H: 6 0 W: 12 02 b.Southgate 16-11-84
Source: Scholar.

Season	Club	Apps	Gls	Tot Apps	Tot Gls
2004-05	Northampton T	0	0		
2005-06	Northampton T	0	0		
2006-07	Northampton T	42	0		
2007-08	Northampton T	45	0		
2008-09	Northampton T	3	0	**90**	**0**
2008-09	Blackburn R	0	0		
2008-09	*Leicester C*	3	0	**3**	**0**
2009-10	Blackburn R	0	0		
2009-10	*Sheffield U*	32	0	**32**	**0**
2010-11	Blackburn R	3	0		
2011-12	Blackburn R	3	0	**6**	**0**

COTTON, Robert (M) **0 0**
b.Rotherham 15-9-94
Source: Scholar.

Season	Club	Apps	Gls	Tot Apps	Tot Gls
2011-12	Blackburn R	0	0		

DANN, Scott (D) **183 13**
H: 6 2 W: 12 00 b.Liverpool 14-2-87
Source: Scholar. *Honours:* England Under-21.

Season	Club	Apps	Gls	Tot Apps	Tot Gls
2004-05	Walsall	1	0		
2005-06	Walsall	0	0		
2006-07	Walsall	30	4		
2007-08	Walsall	28	3	**59**	**7**
2007-08	Coventry C	16	0		
2008-09	Coventry C	31	3	**47**	**3**
2009-10	Birmingham C	30	0		
2010-11	Birmingham C	20	2		
2011-12	Birmingham C	0	0	**50**	**2**
2011-12	Blackburn R	27	1	**27**	**1**

DILO, Christopher (G) **0 0**
b.Paris 5-1-94
Source: Scholar.

Season	Club	Apps	Gls	Tot Apps	Tot Gls
2011-12	Blackburn R	0	0		

DUNN, David (M) **327 52**
H: 5 9 W: 12 03 b.Gt Harwood 27-12-79
Source: Trainee. *Honours:* England Youth, Under-21, 1 full cap.

Season	Club	Apps	Gls	Tot Apps	Tot Gls
1997-98	Blackburn R	0	0		
1998-99	Blackburn R	15	1		
1999-2000	Blackburn R	22	2		
2000-01	Blackburn R	42	12		
2001-02	Blackburn R	29	7		
2002-03	Blackburn R	28	8		
2003-04	Birmingham C	21	2		
2004-05	Birmingham C	11	2		
2005-06	Birmingham C	15	2		
2006-07	Birmingham C	11	1	**58**	**7**
2006-07	Blackburn R	11	0		
2007-08	Blackburn R	31	1		
2008-09	Blackburn R	15	1		
2009-10	Blackburn R	23	9		
2010-11	Blackburn R	27	2		
2011-12	Blackburn R	26	2	**269**	**45**

EDWARDS, Ryan (D) **0 0**
b.Liverpool 7-10-93
Source: Scholar.

Season	Club	Apps	Gls	Tot Apps	Tot Gls
2011-12	Blackburn R	0	0		

EMERTON, Brett (M) **433 40**
H: 6 1 W: 13 05 b.Bankstown 22-2-79
Honours: Australia Youth, Under-20, Under-23, 92 full caps, 19 goals.

Season	Club	Apps	Gls	Tot Apps	Tot Gls
1996-97	Sydney Olympic	18	2		
1997-98	Sydney Olympic	24	3		
1998-99	Sydney Olympic	21	2		
1999-2000	Sydney Olympic	31	9	**94**	**16**
2000-01	Feyenoord	28	2		
2001-02	Feyenoord	31	6		
2002-03	Feyenoord	33	3	**92**	**11**
2003-04	Blackburn R	37	2		
2004-05	Blackburn R	37	4		
2005-06	Blackburn R	30	1		
2006-07	Blackburn R	34	0		
2007-08	Blackburn R	33	1		
2008-09	Blackburn R	20	1		
2009-10	Blackburn R	24	0		
2010-11	Blackburn R	30	4		
2011-12	Blackburn R	2	0	**247**	**13**

Transferred to Sydney August 2011.

EVANS, Micah (F) **23 3**
b.Manchester 3-3-93
Source: Blackburn R Scholar.

Season	Club	Apps	Gls	Tot Apps	Tot Gls
2011-12	Blackburn R	0	0		
2011-12	*Accrington S*	23	3	**23**	**3**

FERNANDEZ, Hugo (D) **0 0**
b.Barcelona 13-1-94
Source: Scholar.

Season	Club	Apps	Gls	Tot Apps	Tot Gls
2011-12	Blackburn R	0	0		

FORMICA, Mauro (M) **109 21**
H: 5 9 W: 10 01 b.Rosario 4-4-88
Honours: Argentina Youth.

Season	Club	Apps	Gls	Tot Apps	Tot Gls
2007-08	Newell's Old Boys	4	0		
2008-09	Newell's Old Boys	19	7		
2009-10	Newell's Old Boys	36	8		
2010-11	Newell's Old Boys	16	2	**75**	**17**
2010-11	Blackburn R	0	0		
2011-12	Blackburn R	34	4	**34**	**4**

GIVET, Gael (D) **306 11**
H: 5 11 W: 11 11 b.Arles 9-10-81
Honours: France 13 full caps.

Season	Club	Apps	Gls	Tot Apps	Tot Gls
2000-01	Monaco	1	0		
2001-02	Monaco	23	2		
2002-03	Monaco	23	1		
2003-04	Monaco	33	2		
2004-05	Monaco	34	0		
2005-06	Monaco	32	2		
2006-07	Monaco	32	1	**178**	**8**
2007-08	Marseille	29	0		
2008-09	Marseille	0	0	**29**	**0**
2008-09	Blackburn R	14	0		
2009-10	Blackburn R	34	2		
2010-11	Blackburn R	29	1		
2011-12	Blackburn R	22	0	**99**	**3**

GOODWILLIE, David (F) **159 39**
H: 5 9 W: 11 02 b.Stirling 28-3-89
Honours: Scotland Youth, Under-21, 3 full caps, 1 goal.

Season	Club	Apps	Gls	Tot Apps	Tot Gls
2005-06	Dundee U	10	1		
2006-07	Dundee U	17	0		
2007-08	Dundee U	2	0		
2007-08	*Raith R*	23	9	**23**	**9**
2008-09	Dundee U	16	3		
2009-10	Dundee U	33	8		

2010-11 Dundee U 37 16
2011-12 Dundee U 1 0 **116 28**
2011-12 Blackburn R 20 2 **20 2**

GOULON, Herold (M) 47 0
H: 6 4 W: 14 07 b.Paris 12-6-88
Source: Soltaires Paris, Esperance Paris, Bourget. *Honours:* France Under-21.
2005-06 Lyon 0 0
2006-07 Middlesbrough 0 0
2007-08 Middlesbrough 0 0
2008-09 Le Mans 11 0
2009-10 Le Mans 26 0 **37 0**
2010-11 Blackburn R 4 0
2011-12 Blackburn R 0 0 **4 0**
2011-12 *Doncaster R* 6 0 **6 0**

GRELLA, Vince (M) 306 7
H: 6 0 W: 12 06 b.Melbourne 5-10-79
Honours: Australia Under-20, Under-23, 46 full caps.
1996-97 Canberra Cosmos 14 1 **14 1**
1997-98 Carlton SC 22 2
1998-99 Carlton SC 1 0 **23 2**
1998-99 Empoli 5 0
1999-2000 Empoli 0 0
1999-2000 Ternana 9 0
2000-01 Ternana 18 0 **27 0**
2001-02 Empoli 32 0
2002-03 Empoli 31 1
2003-04 Empoli 24 0
2004-05 Empoli 0 0 **92 1**
2004-05 Parma 23 0
2005-06 Parma 35 1
2006-07 Parma 26 1 **84 2**
2007-08 Torino 28 1 **28 1**
2008-09 Blackburn R 17 0
2009-10 Blackburn R 15 0
2010-11 Blackburn R 5 0
2011-12 Blackburn R 1 0 **38 0**

HANDS, Reece (M) 0 0
b.Rotherham 6-10-93
Source: Scholar.
2011-12 Blackburn R 0 0

HANLEY, Grant (D) 31 1
H: 6 2 W: 12 00 b.Dumfries 20-11-91
Source: Scholar. *Honours:* Scotland Youth, Under-21, 3 full caps.
2008-09 Blackburn R 0 0
2009-10 Blackburn R 1 0
2010-11 Blackburn R 7 0
2011-12 Blackburn R 23 1 **31 1**

HANLEY, Raheem (D) 0 0
H: 5 8 W: 11 00 b.Blackburn 24-3-94
Source: Manchester U Scholar.
2011-12 Blackburn R 0 0

HENLEY, Adam (D) 7 0
H: 5 10 W: 12 02 b.Knoxville 14-6-94
Source: Scholar. *Honours:* Wales Youth.
2011-12 Blackburn R 7 0 **7 0**

HOILETT, Junior (M) 114 19
H: 5 8 W: 11 00 b.Ottowa 5-6-90
Source: Scholar.
2007-08 Blackburn R 0 0
2007-08 *Paderborn* 12 1 **12 1**
2008-09 Blackburn R 0 0
2008-09 *St Pauli* 21 6 **21 6**
2009-10 Blackburn R 23 0
2010-11 Blackburn R 24 5
2011-12 Blackburn R 34 7 **81 12**

KEAN, Jake (G) 34 0
H: 6 4 W: 11 13 b.Derby 4-2-91
Source: Derby Co Scholar.
2010-11 Blackburn R 0 0
2010-11 *Hartlepool U* 19 0 **19 0**
2011-12 Blackburn R 1 0 **1 0**
2011-12 *Rochdale* 14 0 **14 0**

KNOWLES, James (M) 0 0
H: 5 9 W: 11 00 b.Lisburn 6-4-93
Source: Scholar. *Honours:* Northern Ireland Youth.
2009-10 Blackburn R 0 0
2010-11 Blackburn R 0 0
2011-12 Blackburn R 0 0

LENIHAN, Darragh (M) 0 0
b.Dublin 16-3-94
Source: Belvedere. *Honours:* Eire Youth.
2011-12 Blackburn R 0 0

LINGANZI, Amine (M) 6 0
H: 6 1 W: 10 00 b.Algiers 16-11-89
2008-09 St Etienne 3 0
2009-10 St Etienne 0 0 **3 0**
2009-10 Blackburn R 1 0
2010-11 Blackburn R 1 0
2010-11 *Preston NE* 1 0 **1 0**
2011-12 Blackburn R 0 0 **2 0**

LOWE, Jason (M) 40 2
H: 6 0 W: 12 08 b.Wigan 2-9-91
Source: Scholar. *Honours:* England Under-20, Under-21.
2009-10 Blackburn R 0 0
2010-11 Blackburn R 1 0
2010-11 *Oldham Ath* 7 2 **7 2**
2011-12 Blackburn R 32 0 **33 0**

MODESTE, Anthony (F) 140 36
H: 6 1 W: 11 07 b.Cannes 14-4-88
Honours: France Under-21.
2007-08 Nice 20 1
2008-09 Nice 22 2 **42 3**
2009-10 *Angers* 37 20 **37 20**
2010-11 Bordeaux 37 10
2011-12 Bordeaux 15 3 **52 13**
2011-12 Blackburn R 9 0 **9 0**
On loan from Bordeaux.

MOLINA, Hugo (D) 0 0
b.Spain 30-11-93
Source: Scholar.
2011-12 Blackburn R 0 0

MORRIS, Josh (M) 11 0
H: 5 9 W: 10 00 b.Preston 30-9-91
Source: Scholar. *Honours:* England Under-20.
2010-11 Blackburn R 4 0
2011-12 Blackburn R 2 0 **6 0**
2011-12 *Yeovil T* 5 0 **5 0**

N'ZONZI, Steven (M) 123 6
H: 6 3 W: 11 11 b.Paris 15-12-88
Honours: France Under-21.
2007-08 Amiens 3 0
2008-09 Amiens 34 1 **37 1**
2009-10 Blackburn R 33 2
2010-11 Blackburn R 21 1
2011-12 Blackburn R 32 2 **86 5**

O'CONNOR, Anthony (D) 0 0
b.Cork 25-10-92
Source: Scholar. *Honours:* Eire Youth.
2010-11 Blackburn R 0 0
2011-12 Blackburn R 0 0

O'SULLIVAN, John (M) 0 0
b.Birmingham 18-9-93
Source: Scholar. *Honours:* Eire Youth.
2011-12 Blackburn R 0 0

OLSSON, Marcus (M) 112 12
H: 5 11 W: 10 10 b.Gavle 17-5-88
Honours: Sweden Under-21, 2 full caps.
2008 Halmstad 21 2
2009 Halmstad 20 4
2010 Halmstad 30 4
2011 Halmstad 29 2 **100 12**
2011-12 Blackburn R 12 0 **12 0**

OLSSON, Martin (D) 88 3
H: 5 7 W: 12 12 b.Gavle 17-5-88
Source: Hogaborg. *Honours:* Sweden Under-21, 12 full caps, 4 goals.
2005-06 Blackburn R 0 0
2006-07 Blackburn R 0 0
2007-08 Blackburn R 2 0
2008-09 Blackburn R 9 0
2009-10 Blackburn R 21 1
2010-11 Blackburn R 29 2
2011-12 Blackburn R 27 0 **88 3**

ORR, Bradley (D) 284 13
H: 6 0 W: 11 11 b.Liverpool 1-11-82
Source: Scholar.
2001-02 Newcastle U 0 0
2002-03 Newcastle U 0 0
2003-04 Newcastle U 0 0
2003-04 *Burnley* 4 0 **4 0**
2004-05 Bristol C 37 0
2005-06 Bristol C 38 1
2006-07 Bristol C 35 4
2007-08 Bristol C 42 4
2008-09 Bristol C 38 1
2009-10 Bristol C 39 2 **229 12**
2010-11 QPR 33 1
2011-12 QPR 6 0 **39 1**
2011-12 Blackburn R 12 0 **12 0**

PAYNE, Tim (F) 0 0
b.New Zealand 10-1-94
Source: Waitakere U. *Honours:* New Zealand 3 full caps.
2011-12 Blackburn R 0 0

PEDERSEN, Morten (F) 423 79
H: 5 11 W: 11 00 b.Vadso 8-9-81
Honours: Norway Youth, Under-21, 73 full caps, 16 goals.
1997 Norlid 21 0
1998 Pola 20 4 **20 4**
1999 Norlid 19 0 **40 0**
2000 Tromso 10 3
2001 Tromso 26 5
2002 Tromso 23 18
2003 Tromso 26 8
2004 Tromso 18 7 **103 41**
2004-05 Blackburn R 19 4
2005-06 Blackburn R 34 9
2006-07 Blackburn R 36 6
2007-08 Blackburn R 37 4
2008-09 Blackburn R 33 1
2009-10 Blackburn R 33 3
2010-11 Blackburn R 35 4
2011-12 Blackburn R 33 3 **260 34**

PETROVIC, Radosav (M) 130 18
H: 6 4 W: 13 01 b.Ub 8-3-89
Honours: Serbia Under-21, 27 full caps, 1 goal.
2006-07 Jedinstvo Ub 16 0 **16 0**
2007-08 Radnicki 25 1 **25 1**
2008-09 Partizan Belgrade 21 1
2009-10 Partizan Belgrade 24 7
2010-11 Partizan Belgrade 25 9 **70 17**
2011-12 Blackburn R 19 0 **19 0**

PIVKOVSKI, Filip (M) 0 0
b.Sweden 31-1-94
Source: Scholar.
2010-11 Blackburn R 0 0
2011-12 Blackburn R 0 0

ROBINSON, Paul (G) 372 1
H: 6 1 W: 14 07 b.Beverley 15-10-79
Source: Trainee. *Honours:* England Under-21, 41 full caps.
1996-97 Leeds U 0 0
1997-98 Leeds U 0 0
1998-99 Leeds U 5 0
1999-2000 Leeds U 0 0
2000-01 Leeds U 16 0
2001-02 Leeds U 0 0
2002-03 Leeds U 38 0
2003-04 Leeds U 36 0 **95 0**
2003-04 Tottenham H 0 0
2004-05 Tottenham H 36 0
2005-06 Tottenham H 38 0
2006-07 Tottenham H 38 1
2007-08 Tottenham H 25 0 **137 1**
2008-09 Blackburn R 35 0
2009-10 Blackburn R 35 0
2010-11 Blackburn R 36 0
2011-12 Blackburn R 34 0 **140 0**

ROCHINA, Ruben (F) 35 4
H: 5 11 W: 11 00 b.Sagunto 23-3-91
Honours: Spain Youth.
2008-09 Barcelona B 10 2
2009-10 Barcelona B 3 0 **13 2**
2010-11 Blackburn R 4 0
2011-12 Blackburn R 18 2 **22 2**

SALGADO, Michel (D) 466 9
H: 5 9 W: 11 11 b.Pontevedra 22-10-75
Honours: Spain Youth, Under-20, Under-21, 53 full caps.
1992-93 Celta Vigo B 20 1
1993-94 Celta Vigo B 0 0 **20 1**
1994-95 Celta Vigo 14 0
1995-96 Celta Vigo 18 0
1996-97 Salamanque 36 1 **36 1**
1997-98 Celta Vigo 25 0
1998-99 Celta Vigo 35 3 **92 3**
1999-2000 Real Madrid 29 0
2000-01 Real Madrid 28 1
2001-02 Real Madrid 35 0
2002-03 Real Madrid 35 0
2003-04 Real Madrid 35 1
2004-05 Real Madrid 30 2
2005-06 Real Madrid 27 0
2006-07 Real Madrid 16 0

2007-08	Real Madrid	8	0		
2008-09	Real Madrid	9	0	**252**	**4**
2009-10	Blackburn R	21	0		
2010-11	Blackburn R	36	0		
2011-12	Blackburn R	9	0	**66**	**0**

SAMBA, Christopher (D) **215** **20**
H: 6 5 W: 13 03 b.Creteil 28-3-84
Source: Issy-les-Moulineaux, Rouen.
Honours: Congo 5 full caps.

2001-02	Sedan	1	0		
2002-03	Sedan	0	0		
2003-04	Sedan	3	0	**4**	**0**
2004-05	Hertha Berlin	0	0		
2004-05	Hertha Berlin II	16	3		
2005-06	Hertha Berlin	12	0		
2005-06	Hertha Berlin II	12	1		
2006-07	Hertha Berlin	8	0	**20**	**0**
2006-07	Hertha Berlin II	2	0	**30**	**4**
2006-07	Blackburn R	14	2		
2007-08	Blackburn R	33	2		
2008-09	Blackburn R	35	2		
2009-10	Blackburn R	30	4		
2010-11	Blackburn R	33	4		
2011-12	Blackburn R	16	2	**161**	**16**

Transferred to Anzhi February 2012.

SLEW, Jordan (F) **21** **3**
H: 6 3 W: 12 11 b.Sheffield 7-9-92
Source: Scholar.

2010-11	Sheffield U	7	2		
2011-12	Sheffield U	4	1	**11**	**3**
2011-12	Blackburn R	1	0	**1**	**0**
2011-12	*Stevenage*	9	0	**9**	**0**

USAI, Sebastian (G) **4** **0**
b.Brisbane 28-2-90
Source: Brisbane Strikers.

2010-11	N Queensland F	4	0	**4**	**0**
2011-12	Blackburn R	0	0		

VUKCEVIC, Simon (M) **164** **29**
H: 5 10 W: 12 02 b.Podgorica 29-1-86
Honours: Serbia Under-21, 5 full caps. Montenegro Under-21, 34 full caps, 2 goals.

2002-03	Partizan Belgrade	1	0		
2003-04	Partizan Belgrade	12	0		
2004-05	Partizan Belgrade	26	10		
2005-06	Partizan Belgrade	13	3	**52**	**13**
2006	Saturn Moscow O	24	0		
2007	Saturn Moscow O	4	1	**28**	**1**
2007-08	Sporting Lisbon	26	7		
2008-09	Sporting Lisbon	13	4		
2009-10	Sporting Lisbon	14	1		
2010-11	Sporting Lisbon	24	2	**77**	**14**
2011-12	Blackburn R	7	1	**7**	**1**

YAKUBU, Ayegbeni (F) **345** **135**
H: 6 0 W: 14 07 b.Benin City 22-11-82
Source: Julius Berger. *Honours:* Nigeria Under-21, Under-23, 57 full caps, 21 goals.

1999-2000	Gil Vicente	0	0		
1999-2000	Hapoel Kfar-Sava	23	6	**23**	**6**
2000-01	Maccabi Haifa	14	3		
2001-02	Maccabi Haifa	22	13	**36**	**16**
2002-03	Portsmouth	14	7		
2003-04	Portsmouth	37	16		
2004-05	Portsmouth	30	12	**81**	**35**
2005-06	Middlesbrough	34	13		
2006-07	Middlesbrough	37	12		
2007-08	Middlesbrough	2	0	**73**	**25**
2007-08	Everton	29	15		
2008-09	Everton	14	4		
2009-10	Everton	25	5		
2010-11	Everton	14	1		
2010-11	*Leicester C*	20	11	**20**	**11**
2011-12	Everton	0	0	**82**	**25**
2011-12	Blackburn R	30	17	**30**	**17**

Scholars
Beesley William; Boland Antonic James; Brown Thomas Hayden; Daly Kellen Joseph; Haley Curtis Oliver; Humphreys Ryan Christopher; Laverty Daniel Joseph; MacLaren Jamie; O'Connell Jack; Osawe Osayamen; Paul Thomas; Thompson Ryan Lewis; Urwin Matthew William; Ware Bradley Mason; Wylie Peter James John.

BLACKPOOL (10)

ADDAI, Alex (M) **0** **0**
b.Stepney
Source: Scholar.

2011-12	Blackpool	0	0		

ALMOND, Louis (F) **4** **0**
H: 5 11 W: 12 00 b.Blackburn 5-1-92
Source: Scholar.

2009-10	Blackpool	0	0		
2009-10	*Cheltenham T*	4	0	**4**	**0**
2010-11	Blackpool	0	0		
2011-12	Blackpool	0	0		

ANGEL (M) **155** **10**
H: 5 9 W: 11 13 b.Girona 31-1-86
Honours: Spain Youth, Under-21.

2006-07	Espanyol B	27	5	**27**	**5**
2006-07	Espanyol	7	0		
2007-08	Espanyol	28	2		
2008-09	Espanyol	15	0	**50**	**2**
2009-10	Rayo Vallecano	27	2	**27**	**2**
2010-11	Girona	36	0	**36**	**0**
2011-12	Blackpool	15	1	**15**	**1**

BARKHUIZEN, Tom (F) **38** **11**
H: 5 9 W: 11 00 b.Blackpool 4-7-93
Source: Scholar.

2011-12	Blackpool	0	0		
2011-12	*Hereford U*	38	11	**38**	**11**

BASHAM, Chris (M) **51** **3**
H: 5 11 W: 12 08 b.Hebburn 20-7-88
Source: Scholar.

2007-08	Bolton W	0	0		
2007-08	*Rochdale*	13	0	**13**	**0**
2008-09	Bolton W	11	1		
2009-10	Bolton W	8	0	**19**	**1**
2010-11	Blackpool	2	0		
2011-12	Blackpool	17	2	**19**	**2**

BEDNAR, Roman (F) **173** **49**
H: 6 3 W: 13 03 b.Prague 26-3-83
Honours: Czech Republic Under-21, 8 full caps, 1 goal.

2001-02	Mlada Boleslav	0	0		
2002-03	Mlada Boleslav	0	0		
2003-04	Mlada Boleslav	0	0		
2004-05	Mlada Boleslav	25	6	**25**	**6**
2004-05	Kaunas	0	0		
2005-06	Hearts	22	7		
2006-07	Hearts	18	4	**40**	**11**
2007-08	WBA	29	13		
2008-09	WBA	26	6		
2009-10	WBA	27	11		
2010-11	WBA	4	0		
2010-11	*Leicester C*	5	0	**5**	**0**
2010-11	*Ankaragucu*	8	1	**8**	**1**
2011-12	WBA	0	0	**86**	**30**
2011-12	Blackpool	9	1	**9**	**1**

BIGNOT, Paul (D) **35** **0**
H: 6 1 W: 12 03 b.Birmingham 14-2-86
Source: Newport Co.

2004-05	Crewe Alex	5	0		
2005-06	Crewe Alex	5	0		
2006-07	Crewe Alex	11	0	**21**	**0**
From Kidderminster H.					
2011-12	Blackpool	0	0		
2011-12	*Plymouth Arg*	14	0	**14**	**0**

BOGDANOVIC, Daniel (F) **100** **26**
H: 6 2 W: 11 02 b.Misurata 26-3-80
Source: Sliema W, Naxxar Lions, Valletta, Marsaxlokk, Cisco Roma, Lokomotiv Sofia. *Honours:* Malta 38 full caps, 1 goal.

2008-09	Barnsley	16	5		
2009-10	Barnsley	29	11	**45**	**16**
2010-11	Sheffield U	32	5		
2011-12	Sheffield U	2	0	**34**	**5**
2011-12	Blackpool	8	2	**8**	**2**
2011-12	*Rochdale*	5	1	**5**	**1**
2011-12	*Notts Co*	8	2	**8**	**2**

BRUNA, Gerardo (M) **1** **0**
H: 5 8 W: 10 02 b.Mendoza 29-1-91
Source: Real Madrid.

2007-08	Liverpool	0	0		
2008-09	Liverpool	0	0		
2009-10	Liverpool	0	0		
2010-11	Liverpool	0	0		
2011-12	Blackpool	1	0	**1**	**0**

CATHCART, Craig (D) **113** **4**
H: 6 2 W: 11 06 b.Belfast 6-2-89
Source: Scholar. *Honours:* Northern Ireland Youth, Under-21, 9 full caps.

2005-06	Manchester U	0	0		
2006-07	Manchester U	0	0		
2007-08	Manchester U	0	0		
2007-08	*Antwerp*	13	2	**13**	**2**
2008-09	Manchester U	0	0		
2008-09	*Plymouth Arg*	31	1	**31**	**1**
2009-10	Manchester U	0	0		
2009-10	*Watford*	12	0	**12**	**0**
2010-11	Blackpool	30	1		
2011-12	Blackpool	27	0	**57**	**1**

CRAINEY, Stephen (D) **269** **4**
H: 5 9 W: 9 11 b.Glasgow 22-6-81
Honours: Scotland B, Under-21, 12 full caps.

1999-2000	Celtic	9	0		
2000-01	Celtic	2	0		
2001-02	Celtic	15	0		
2002-03	Celtic	13	0		
2003-04	Celtic	2	0	**41**	**0**
2003-04	Southampton	5	0	**5**	**0**
2004-05	Leeds U	9	0		
2005-06	Leeds U	24	0		
2006-07	Leeds U	19	0	**52**	**0**
2007-08	Blackpool	40	1		
2008-09	Blackpool	17	0		
2009-10	Blackpool	41	0		
2010-11	Blackpool	31	0		
2011-12	Blackpool	42	3	**171**	**4**

DODD, Adam (D) **16** **2**
b.Kirkham 25-6-93
Source: Scholar.

2011-12	Blackpool	0	0		
2011-12	*Ayr U*	16	2	**16**	**2**

EARDLEY, Neal (M) **194** **12**
H: 5 11 W: 11 10 b.Llandudno 6-11-88
Source: Scholar. *Honours:* Wales Under-21, 16 full caps.

2005-06	Oldham Ath	1	0		
2006-07	Oldham Ath	36	2		
2007-08	Oldham Ath	42	6		
2008-09	Oldham Ath	34	2		
2009-10	Oldham Ath	0	0	**113**	**10**
2009-10	Blackpool	24	0		
2010-11	Blackpool	31	1		
2011-12	Blackpool	26	1	**81**	**2**

EASTHAM, Ashley (D) **55** **2**
H: 6 3 W: 12 06 b.Preston 22-3-91
Source: Scholar.

2009-10	Blackpool	1	0		
2009-10	*Cheltenham T*	20	0		
2010-11	Blackpool	0	0		
2010-11	*Cheltenham T*	9	0	**29**	**0**
2010-11	*Carlisle U*	0	0		
2011-12	Blackpool	0	0	**1**	**0**
2011-12	*Bury*	25	2	**25**	**2**

EVATT, Ian (D) **375** **18**
H: 6 3 W: 13 12 b.Coventry 19-11-81
Source: Trainee.

1998-99	Derby Co	0	0		
1999-2000	Derby Co	0	0		
2000-01	Derby Co	1	0		
2001-02	*Northampton T*	11	0	**11**	**0**
2001-02	Derby Co	3	0		
2002-03	Derby Co	30	0	**34**	**0**
2003-04	Chesterfield	43	5		
2004-05	Chesterfield	41	4	**84**	**9**
2005-06	QPR	27	0		
2006-07	QPR	0	0	**27**	**0**
2006-07	Blackpool	44	0		
2007-08	Blackpool	29	0		
2008-09	Blackpool	33	1		
2009-10	Blackpool	36	4		
2010-11	Blackpool	38	1		
2011-12	Blackpool	39	3	**219**	**9**

FERGUSON, Barry (M) **440** **48**
H: 5 7 W: 9 10 b.Hamilton 2-2-78
Source: Rangers SABC. *Honours:* Scotland Under-21, 45 full caps, 3 goals.

1994-95	Rangers	0	0		
1995-96	Rangers	0	0		
1996-97	Rangers	1	0		
1997-98	Rangers	7	0		
1998-99	Rangers	23	1		
1999-2000	Rangers	31	4		
2000-01	Rangers	30	2		
2001-02	Rangers	22	1		

2002-03	Rangers	36	16		
2003-04	Rangers	3	0		
2003-04	Blackburn R	15	1		
2004-05	Blackburn R	21	2	**36**	**3**
2004-05	Rangers	13	2		
2005-06	Rangers	32	5		
2006-07	Rangers	32	4		
2007-08	Rangers	38	7		
2008-09	Rangers	22	2	**290**	**44**
2009-10	Birmingham C	37	0		
2010-11	Birmingham C	35	0	**72**	**0**
2011-12	Blackpool	42	1	**42**	**1**

FLECK, John (M) **48 2**
H: 5 9 W: 11 05 b.Glasgow 24-8-91
Honours: Scotland Youth, Under-21.

2007-08	Rangers	1	0		
2008-09	Rangers	8	1		
2009-10	Rangers	15	1		
2010-11	Rangers	13	0		
2011-12	Rangers	4	0	**41**	**2**
2011-12	Blackpool	7	0	**7**	**0**

On loan from Rangers.

GILKS, Matthew (G) **271 0**
H: 6 3 W: 13 12 b.Rochdale 4-6-82
Source: Scholar.

2000-01	Rochdale	3	0		
2001-02	Rochdale	19	0		
2002-03	Rochdale	20	0		
2003-04	Rochdale	12	0		
2004-05	Rochdale	30	0		
2005-06	Rochdale	46	0		
2006-07	Rochdale	46	0	**176**	**0**
2007-08	Norwich C	0	0		
2008-09	Blackpool	5	0		
2008-09	*Shrewsbury T*	4	0	**4**	**0**
2009-10	Blackpool	26	0		
2010-11	Blackpool	18	0		
2011-12	Blackpool	42	0	**91**	**0**

GRANDIN, Elliot (F) **129 15**
H: 5 10 W: 10 07 b.Caen 17-10-87

2004-05	Caen	1	0		
2005-06	Caen	19	3		
2006-07	Caen	23	2		
2007-08	Caen	12	1	**55**	**6**
2007-08	Marseille	8	0		
2008-09	Marseille	8	2	**16**	**2**
2008-09	*Grenoble*	8	0	**8**	**0**
2009-10	CSKA Sofia	10	4		
2010-11	CSKA Sofia	1	0	**11**	**4**
2010-11	Blackpool	23	1		
2011-12	Blackpool	7	2	**30**	**3**
2011-12	*Nice*	9	0	**9**	**0**

HALSTEAD, Mark (G) **1 0**
H: 6 3 W: 14 00 b.Blackpool 1-9-90
Source: Scholar.

2009-10	Blackpool	0	0		
2010-11	Blackpool	1	0		
2011-12	Blackpool	0	0	**1**	**0**

HARRIS, Robert (D) **160 10**
H: 5 8 W: 10 00 b.Glasgow 28-8-87

2004-05	Clyde	1	0		
2005-06	Clyde	20	0		
2006-07	Clyde	24	0	**45**	**0**
2007-08	Queen of the S	26	2		
2008-09	Queen of the S	21	2		
2009-10	Queen of the S	32	4		
2010-11	Queen of the S	31	2	**110**	**10**
2011-12	Blackpool	5	0	**5**	**0**

HILL, Matt (D) **373 8**
H: 5 7 W: 12 06 b.Bristol 26-3-81
Source: Trainee.

1998-99	Bristol C	3	0		
1999-2000	Bristol C	14	0		
2000-01	Bristol C	34	0		
2001-02	Bristol C	40	1		
2002-03	Bristol C	42	3		
2003-04	Bristol C	42	2		
2004-05	Bristol C	23	0	**198**	**6**
2004-05	Preston NE	14	0		
2005-06	Preston NE	26	0		
2006-07	Preston NE	38	0		
2007-08	Preston NE	26	0		
2008-09	Preston NE	1	0	**105**	**0**
2008-09	Wolverhampton W	13	0		
2009-10	Wolverhampton W	2	0		
2009-10	*QPR*	16	0	**16**	**0**
2010-11	Wolverhampton W	0	0	**15**	**0**
2010-11	Barnsley	23	2	**23**	**2**
2011-12	Blackpool	4	0	**4**	**0**
2011-12	*Sheffield U*	12	0	**12**	**0**

HUSBAND, Stephen (M) **20 2**
H: 6 0 W: 12 13 b.Kelty 29-10-90

2006-07	Cowdenbeath	5	0	**5**	**0**
2007-08	Hearts	0	0		
2008-09	Hearts	0	0		
2009-10	Hearts	0	0		
2009-10	*Livingston*	7	0	**7**	**0**
2009-10	Blackpool	3	0		
2010-11	Blackpool	0	0		
2010-11	*Stockport Co*	5	2	**5**	**2**
2011-12	Blackpool	0	0	**3**	**0**

INCE, Thomas (F) **39 8**
H: 5 10 W: 10 05 b.Liverpool 30-1-92
Source: Scholar.

2009-10	Liverpool	0	0		
2010-11	Liverpool	0	0		
2010-11	*Notts Co*	6	2	**6**	**2**
2011-12	Blackpool	33	6	**33**	**6**

INCE, Tom (M) **0 0**
b.Stockport 30-1-92
Source: Liverpool.

2011-12	Blackpool	0	0		

JOHN-BAPTISTE, Alex (D) **301 12**
H: 6 0 W: 11 11 b.Sutton-in-Ashfield 31-1-86
Source: Scholar.

2002-03	Mansfield T	4	0		
2003-04	Mansfield T	17	0		
2004-05	Mansfield T	41	1		
2005-06	Mansfield T	41	1		
2006-07	Mansfield T	46	3		
2007-08	Mansfield T	25	0	**174**	**5**
2008-09	Blackpool	21	1		
2009-10	Blackpool	42	3		
2010-11	Blackpool	21	2		
2011-12	Blackpool	43	1	**127**	**7**

KETTINGS, Chris (G) **2 0**
H: 6 2 W: 12 04 b.Bolton 25-10-92
Source: Scholar. *Honours:* Scotland Youth.

2011-12	Blackpool	0	0		
2011-12	*Birmingham C*	0	0		
2011-12	*Morecambe*	2	0	**2**	**0**

LUA-LUA, Lomano (F) **304 58**
H: 5 8 W: 12 02 b.Kinshasa 28-12-80
Honours: DR Congo 28 full caps, 7 goals.

1998-99	Colchester U	13	1		
1999-2000	Colchester U	41	12		
2000-01	Colchester U	7	2	**61**	**15**
2000-01	Newcastle U	21	0		
2001-02	Newcastle U	20	3		
2002-03	Newcastle U	11	2		
2003-04	Newcastle U	7	0	**59**	**5**
2003-04	*Portsmouth*	15	4		
2004-05	Portsmouth	25	6		
2005-06	Portsmouth	25	7		
2006-07	Portsmouth	22	2	**87**	**19**
2007-08	Olympiakos	21	5		
2008-09	Al-Arabi	11	2	**11**	**2**
2009-10	Olympiakos	17	4	**38**	**9**
2010-11	Omonia	19	4	**19**	**4**
2011-12	Blackpool	29	4	**29**	**4**

ORMEROD, Brett (F) **411 90**
H: 5 11 W: 11 12 b.Blackburn 18-10-76
Source: Blackburn R Trainee, Accrington S.

1996-97	Blackpool	4	0		
1997-98	Blackpool	9	2		
1998-99	Blackpool	40	8		
1999-2000	Blackpool	13	5		
2000-01	Blackpool	41	17		
2001-02	Blackpool	21	13		
2001-02	Southampton	18	1		
2002-03	Southampton	31	5		
2003-04	Southampton	22	5		
2004-05	Southampton	9	0		
2004-05	*Leeds U*	6	0	**6**	**0**
2004-05	*Wigan Ath*	6	2	**6**	**2**
2005-06	Southampton	19	1	**99**	**12**
2005-06	Preston NE	15	4		
2006-07	Preston NE	29	8		
2007-08	Preston NE	18	1		
2007-08	*Nottingham F*	13	2	**13**	**2**
2008-09	Preston NE	0	0	**62**	**13**
2008-09	*Oldham Ath*	5	0	**5**	**0**
2008-09	Blackpool	15	2		
2009-10	Blackpool	36	11		
2010-11	Blackpool	19	1		
2011-12	Blackpool	17	1	**215**	**60**
2011-12	*Rochdale*	5	1	**5**	**1**

PHILLIPS, Kevin (F) **532 236**
H: 5 7 W: 11 00 b.Hitchin 25-7-73
Source: Baldock T. *Honours:* England B, 8 full caps.

1994-95	Watford	16	9		
1995-96	Watford	27	11		
1996-97	Watford	16	4	**59**	**24**
1997-98	Sunderland	43	29		
1998-99	Sunderland	26	23		
1999-2000	Sunderland	36	30		
2000-01	Sunderland	34	14		
2001-02	Sunderland	37	11		
2002-03	Sunderland	32	6	**208**	**113**
2003-04	Southampton	34	12		
2004-05	Southampton	30	10	**64**	**22**
2005-06	Aston Villa	23	4		
2006-07	Aston Villa	0	0	**23**	**4**
2006-07	WBA	36	16		
2007-08	WBA	35	22	**71**	**38**
2008-09	Birmingham C	36	14		
2009-10	Birmingham C	19	4		
2010-11	Birmingham C	14	1	**69**	**19**
2011-12	Blackpool	38	16	**38**	**16**

PHILLIPS, Matthew (M) **144 21**
H: 6 0 W: 12 10 b.Aylesbury 13-3-91
Source: Scholar. *Honours:* England Youth, Under-20. Scotland 1 full cap.

2007-08	Wycombe W	2	0		
2008-09	Wycombe W	37	3		
2009-10	Wycombe W	36	5		
2010-11	Wycombe W	3	0	**78**	**8**
2010-11	Blackpool	27	1		
2011-12	Blackpool	33	7	**60**	**8**
2011-12	*Sheffield U*	6	5	**6**	**5**

SOUTHERN, Keith (M) **330 25**
H: 5 10 W: 12 06 b.Gateshead 24-4-81
Source: Trainee.

1998-99	Everton	0	0		
1999-2000	Everton	0	0		
2000-01	Everton	0	0		
2001-02	Everton	0	0		
2002-03	Everton	0	0		
2002-03	Blackpool	38	1		
2003-04	Blackpool	28	2		
2004-05	Blackpool	27	6		
2005-06	Blackpool	42	2		
2006-07	Blackpool	39	5		
2007-08	Blackpool	30	3		
2008-09	Blackpool	35	3		
2009-10	Blackpool	45	2		
2010-11	Blackpool	21	0		
2011-12	Blackpool	25	1	**330**	**25**

SUTHERLAND, Craig (F) **16 1**
H: 6 0 W: 11 11 b.Edinburgh 17-12-88
Source: North Carolina Univ.

2011-12	Blackpool	7	0	**7**	**0**
2011-12	*Plymouth Arg*	9	1	**9**	**1**

SYLVESTRE, Ludovic (M) **157 16**
H: 6 0 W: 11 09 b.Le Blanc-Mesnil 5-2-84

2005-06	Barcelona B	20	0	**20**	**0**
2005-06	Barcelona	2	0	**2**	**0**
2006-07	Sparta Prague	19	0		
2007-08	Sparta Prague	6	0	**25**	**0**
2007-08	*Viktoria Plzen*	14	3	**14**	**3**
2008-09	Mlada Boleslav	29	4		
2009-10	Mlada Boleslav	27	7		
2010-11	Mlada Boleslav	4	1	**60**	**12**
2010-11	Blackpool	8	0		
2011-12	Blackpool	28	1	**36**	**1**

TAYLOR-FLETCHER, Gary (F) **368 80**
H: 6 0 W: 11 00 b.Widnes 4-6-81
Source: Northwich Vic. *Honours:* England Schools.

2000-01	Hull C	5	0	**5**	**0**
2001-02	Leyton Orient	9	0		
2002-03	Leyton Orient	12	1	**21**	**1**
2003-04	Lincoln C	42	16		
2004-05	Lincoln C	38	11	**80**	**27**
2005-06	Huddersfield T	43	10		
2006-07	Huddersfield T	39	11	**82**	**21**
2007-08	Blackpool	42	6		
2008-09	Blackpool	38	5		
2009-10	Blackpool	32	6		
2010-11	Blackpool	31	6		
2011-12	Blackpool	37	8	**180**	**31**

TOMSETT, Liam (M) **15 1**
b.Ulverston 1-11-92
Source: Scholar.
2011-12 Blackpool 0 0
2011-12 *Ayr U* 15 1 **15 1**

BOLTON W (11)

ALONSO, Marcus (D) **49 4**
H: 6 2 W: 13 05 b.Madrid 28-12-90
2008-09 RM Castilla 11 0
2009-10 RM Castilla 28 3 **39 3**
2009-10 Real Madrid 1 0 **1 0**
2010-11 Bolton W 4 0
2011-12 Bolton W 5 1 **9 1**

BENNETT, Rhys (D) **19 0**
b.Manchester 1-9-91
Source: Scholar. *Honours:* England Under-21.
2011-12 Bolton W 0 0
2011-12 *Falkirk* 19 0 **19 0**

BLAKE, Robbie (F) **571 145**
H: 5 9 W: 12 00 b.Middlesbrough 4-3-76
Source: Trainee.
1994-95 Darlington 9 0
1995-96 Darlington 29 11
1996-97 Darlington 30 10 **68 21**
1996-97 Bradford C 5 0
1997-98 Bradford C 34 8
1998-99 Bradford C 39 16
1999-2000 Bradford C 28 2
2000-01 Bradford C 21 4
2000-01 *Nottingham F* 11 1 **11 1**
2001-02 Bradford C 26 10 **153 40**
2001-02 Burnley 10 0
2002-03 Burnley 41 13
2003-04 Burnley 45 19
2004-05 Burnley 24 10
2004-05 Birmingham C 11 2 **11 2**
2005-06 Leeds U 41 11
2006-07 Leeds U 36 8 **77 19**
2007-08 Burnley 45 9
2008-09 Burnley 46 8
2009-10 Burnley 31 2 **242 61**
2010-11 Bolton W 8 1
2011-12 Bolton W 1 0 **9 1**

BLAKEMAN, Adam (D) **0 0**
b.Widnes 3-12-91
Source: Scholar.
2011-12 Bolton W 0 0

BOGDAN, Adam (G) **25 0**
H: 6 4 W: 14 02 b.Budapest 27-9-87
Source: Vasas. *Honours:* Hungary 7 full caps.
2007-08 Bolton W 0 0
2008-09 Bolton W 0 0
2009-10 Bolton W 0 0
2009-10 *Crewe Alex* 1 0 **1 0**
2010-11 Bolton W 4 0
2011-12 Bolton W 20 0 **24 0**

CONNOLLY, Mark (D) **8 0**
H: 6 1 W: 12 01 b.Monaghan 16-12-91
Source: Wolverhampton W Scholar. *Honours:* Eire Youth, Under-21.
2009-10 Bolton W 0 0
2009-10 *St Johnstone* 1 0 **1 0**
2010-11 Bolton W 0 0
2011-12 Bolton W 0 0
2011-12 *Macclesfield T* 7 0 **7 0**

DAVIES, Kevin (F) **584 112**
H: 6 0 W: 12 10 b.Sheffield 26-3-77
Source: Trainee. *Honours:* England Youth, Under-21, 1 full cap.
1993-94 Chesterfield 24 4
1994-95 Chesterfield 41 11
1995-96 Chesterfield 30 4
1996-97 Chesterfield 34 3 **129 22**
1996-97 Southampton 0 0
1997-98 Southampton 25 9
1998-99 Blackburn R 21 1
1999-2000 Blackburn R 2 0 **23 1**
1999-2000 Southampton 23 6
2000-01 Southampton 27 1
2001-02 Southampton 23 2
2002-03 Southampton 9 1 **107 19**
2002-03 *Millwall* 9 3 **9 3**
2003-04 Bolton W 38 9
2004-05 Bolton W 35 8
2005-06 Bolton W 37 7
2006-07 Bolton W 30 8
2007-08 Bolton W 32 3
2008-09 Bolton W 38 11
2009-10 Bolton W 37 7
2010-11 Bolton W 38 8
2011-12 Bolton W 31 6 **316 67**

DAVIES, Mark (M) **120 7**
H: 5 11 W: 11 08 b.Willenhall 18-2-88
Source: Scholar. *Honours:* England Youth.
2004-05 Wolverhampton W 0 0
2005-06 Wolverhampton W 20 1
2006-07 Wolverhampton W 7 0
2007-08 Wolverhampton W 0 0
2008-09 Wolverhampton W 0 0 **27 1**
2008-09 *Leicester C* 7 1 **7 1**
2008-09 Bolton W 10 0
2009-10 Bolton W 17 0
2010-11 Bolton W 24 1
2011-12 Bolton W 35 4 **86 5**

DAVIS, Sean (M) **278 16**
H: 5 10 W: 12 00 b.Clapham 20-9-79
Source: Trainee. *Honours:* England Under-21.
1996-97 Fulham 1 0
1997-98 Fulham 0 0
1998-99 Fulham 6 0
1999-2000 Fulham 26 0
2000-01 Fulham 40 6
2001-02 Fulham 30 0
2002-03 Fulham 28 3
2003-04 Fulham 24 5 **155 14**
2004-05 Tottenham H 15 0
2005-06 Tottenham H 0 0 **15 0**
2005-06 Portsmouth 17 1
2006-07 Portsmouth 31 0
2007-08 Portsmouth 22 0
2008-09 Portsmouth 32 1
2009-10 Portsmouth 0 0 **102 2**
2009-10 Bolton W 3 0
2010-11 Bolton W 0 0
2011-12 Bolton W 0 0 **3 0**
2011-12 *Bristol C* 3 0 **3 0**

EAGLES, Chris (M) **230 34**
H: 5 10 W: 11 07 b.Hemel Hempstead 19-11-85
Source: Trainee. *Honours:* England Youth.
2003-04 Manchester U 0 0
2004-05 Manchester U 0 0
2004-05 *Watford* 13 1
2005-06 Manchester U 0 0
2005-06 *Sheffield W* 25 3 **25 3**
2005-06 *Watford* 17 3 **30 4**
2006-07 Manchester U 2 1
2006-07 *NEC Nijmegen* 15 1 **15 1**
2007-08 Manchester U 4 0 **6 1**
2008-09 Burnley 43 8
2009-10 Burnley 34 2
2010-11 Burnley 43 11 **120 21**
2011-12 Bolton W 34 4 **34 4**

EAVES, Tom (M) **15 0**
H: 6 3 W: 13 07 b.Liverpool 14-1-92
Source: Scholar.
2009-10 Oldham Ath 15 0
2010-11 Bolton W 0 0
2010-11 *Oldham Ath* 0 0 **15 0**
2011-12 Bolton W 0 0

ECKERSLEY, Tom (D) **0 0**
b.Sale 6-12-91
Source: Scholar.
2011-12 Bolton W 0 0

FAZLIC, Dino (M) **0 0**
b.Bosnia 21-11-91
Source: Werder Bremen Youth.
2011-12 Bolton W 0 0

GARDNER, Ricardo (D) **346 20**
H: 5 9 W: 11 00 b.St Andrews 25-9-78
Source: Harbour View. *Honours:* Jamaica 109 full caps, 9 goals.
1998-99 Bolton W 30 2
1999-2000 Bolton W 29 5
2000-01 Bolton W 32 3
2001-02 Bolton W 31 3
2002-03 Bolton W 32 2
2003-04 Bolton W 22 0
2004-05 Bolton W 33 0
2005-06 Bolton W 30 0
2006-07 Bolton W 18 0
2007-08 Bolton W 26 0
2008-09 Bolton W 29 4
2009-10 Bolton W 21 1
2010-11 Bolton W 5 0
2010-11 *Preston NE* 4 0 **4 0**
2011-12 Bolton W 4 0 **342 20**

HOLDEN, Stuart (M) **115 17**
H: 5 10 W: 11 07 b.Aberdeen 1-8-85
Source: Clemson Tigers. *Honours:* USA 17 full caps, 2 goals.
2005-06 Sunderland 0 0
2006 Houston Dynamo 13 1
2007 Houston Dynamo 21 5
2008 Houston Dynamo 27 3
2009 Houston Dynamo 26 6 **87 15**
2009-10 Bolton W 2 0
2010-11 Bolton W 26 2
2011-12 Bolton W 0 0 **28 2**

JAASKELAINEN, Jussi (G) **592 0**
H: 6 3 W: 12 10 b.Vaasa 19-4-75
Honours: Finland Youth, Under-21, 56 full caps.
1992 MP 6 0
1993 MP 6 0
1994 MP 26 0
1995 MP 26 0 **64 0**
1996 VPS 27 0
1997 VPS 27 0 **54 0**
1997-98 Bolton W 0 0
1998-99 Bolton W 34 0
1999-2000 Bolton W 34 0
2000-01 Bolton W 27 0
2001-02 Bolton W 34 0
2002-03 Bolton W 38 0
2003-04 Bolton W 38 0
2004-05 Bolton W 36 0
2005-06 Bolton W 38 0
2006-07 Bolton W 38 0
2007-08 Bolton W 28 0
2008-09 Bolton W 38 0
2009-10 Bolton W 38 0
2010-11 Bolton W 35 0
2011-12 Bolton W 18 0 **474 0**

KLASNIC, Ivan (F) **353 101**
H: 6 1 W: 12 00 b.Hamburg 29-1-80
Honours: Croatia Under-21, 41 full caps, 12 goals.
1997-98 St Pauli 8 0
1998-99 St Pauli 24 8
1999-2000 St Pauli 32 8
2000-01 St Pauli 31 10 **95 26**
2001-02 Werder Bremen 23 1
2002-03 Werder Bremen 13 2
2003-04 Werder Bremen 29 13
2004-05 Werder Bremen 28 10
2005-06 Werder Bremen 30 15
2006-07 Werder Bremen 13 1
2007-08 Werder Bremen 16 7 **152 49**
2008-09 Nantes 28 6 **28 6**
2009-10 Bolton W 27 8
2010-11 Bolton W 22 4
2011-12 Bolton W 29 8 **78 20**

KNIGHT, Zat (D) **292 7**
H: 6 6 W: 15 02 b.Solihull 2-5-80
Source: Rushall Olympic. *Honours:* England Under-21, 2 full caps.
1998-99 Fulham 0 0
1999-2000 Fulham 0 0
1999-2000 *Peterborough U* 8 0 **8 0**
2000-01 Fulham 0 0
2001-02 Fulham 10 0
2002-03 Fulham 17 0
2003-04 Fulham 31 0
2004-05 Fulham 35 1
2005-06 Fulham 30 0
2006-07 Fulham 23 2
2007-08 Fulham 4 0 **150 3**
2007-08 Aston Villa 27 1
2008-09 Aston Villa 13 1
2009-10 Aston Villa 0 0 **40 2**
2009-10 Bolton W 35 1
2010-11 Bolton W 34 1
2011-12 Bolton W 25 0 **94 2**

LAINTON, Robert (G) **0 0**
H: 6 2 W: 12 06 b.Ashton-under-Lyne 12-10-89
Source: Scholar.
2009-10 Bolton W 0 0
2010-11 Bolton W 0 0
2011-12 Bolton W 0 0

LEE, Chung Yong (M) **118 17**
H: 5 11 W: 10 09 b.Seoul 2-7-88
Honours: South Korea 41 full caps, 5 goals.
2006 FC Seoul 2 0
2007 FC Seoul 15 3
2008 FC Seoul 20 5
2009 FC Seoul 14 2 **51 10**
2009-10 Bolton W 34 4
2010-11 Bolton W 31 3
2011-12 Bolton W 2 0 **67 7**

MEARS, Tyrone (D) **204 7**
H: 5 11 W: 11 10 b.Stockport 18-2-83
Source: Manchester C Juniors. *Honours:* Jamaica 1 full cap.
2000-01 Manchester C 0 0
2001-02 Manchester C 1 0 **1 0**
2002-03 Preston NE 22 1
2003-04 Preston NE 12 1
2004-05 Preston NE 4 0
2005-06 Preston NE 32 2 **70 4**
2006-07 West Ham U 5 0 **5 0**
2006-07 *Derby Co* 13 1
2007-08 Derby Co 25 1
2008-09 Derby Co 3 0 **41 2**
2008-09 *Marseille* 4 0 **4 0**
2009-10 Burnley 38 0
2010-11 Burnley 44 1
2011-12 Burnley 0 0 **82 1**
2011-12 Bolton W 1 0 **1 0**

MUAMBA, Fabrice (M) **201 5**
H: 6 1 W: 11 10 b.DR Congo 6-4-88
Source: Scholar. *Honours:* England Youth, Under-21.
2005-06 Arsenal 0 0
2006-07 Arsenal 0 0
2006-07 Birmingham C 34 0
2007-08 Birmingham C 37 2 **71 2**
2008-09 Bolton W 38 0
2009-10 Bolton W 36 1
2010-11 Bolton W 36 1
2011-12 Bolton W 20 1 **130 3**

N'GOG, David (F) **114 13**
H: 6 3 W: 12 04 b.Paris 1-4-89
Honours: France Youth, Under-21.
2006-07 Paris St Germain 4 0
2007-08 Paris St Germain 14 1 **18 1**
2008-09 Liverpool 14 2
2009-10 Liverpool 24 5
2010-11 Liverpool 25 2
2011-12 Liverpool 0 0 **63 9**
2011-12 Bolton W 33 3 **33 3**

O'HALLORAN, Michael (F) **7 0**
H: 6 2 W: 12 06 b.Glasgow 6-1-91
Source: Scholar. *Honours:* Scotland Under-21.
2009-10 Bolton W 0 0
2010-11 Bolton W 0 0
2011-12 Bolton W 0 0
2011-12 *Sheffield U* 7 0 **7 0**

OBADEYI, Temitope (F) **46 4**
H: 5 10 W: 11 09 b.Birmingham 29-10-89
Source: Coventry C. *Honours:* England Youth, Under-20.
2006-07 Bolton W 0 0
2007-08 Bolton W 0 0
2008-09 Bolton W 3 0
2009-10 Bolton W 0 0
2009-10 *Swindon T* 12 2 **12 2**
2009-10 *Rochdale* 11 1
2010-11 Bolton W 0 0
2010-11 *Shrewsbury T* 9 0 **9 0**
2011-12 Bolton W 0 0 **3 0**
2011-12 *Chesterfield* 5 0 **5 0**
2011-12 *Rochdale* 6 1 **17 2**

PETROV, Martin (F) **365 69**
H: 6 0 W: 12 02 b.Vzatza 15-1-79
Honours: Bulgaria 88 full caps, 19 goals.
1996-97 CSKA Sofia 3 0
1997-98 CSKA Sofia 4 0 **7 0**
1998-99 Servette 12 2
1999-2000 Servette 31 9
2000-01 Servette 32 11 **75 22**
2001-02 Wolfsburg 32 6
2002-03 Wolfsburg 26 2
2003-04 Wolfsburg 28 8
2004-05 Wolfsburg 30 12 **116 28**
2005-06 Atletico Madrid 36 1
2006-07 Atletico Madrid 13 2 **49 3**
2007-08 Manchester C 34 5
2008-09 Manchester C 9 0
2009-10 Manchester C 16 4 **59 9**
2010-11 Bolton W 28 3
2011-12 Bolton W 31 4 **59 7**

PRATLEY, Darren (M) **249 32**
H: 6 1 W: 10 12 b.Barking 22-4-85
Source: Scholar.
2001-02 Fulham 0 0
2002-03 Fulham 0 0
2003-04 Fulham 1 0
2004-05 Fulham 0 0
2004-05 *Brentford* 14 1
2005-06 Fulham 0 0 **1 0**
2005-06 *Brentford* 32 4 **46 5**
2006-07 Swansea C 28 1
2007-08 Swansea C 42 5
2008-09 Swansea C 37 4
2009-10 Swansea C 36 7
2010-11 Swansea C 34 9 **177 26**
2011-12 Bolton W 25 1 **25 1**

REAM, Tim (D) **172 7**
H: 6 1 W: 11 05 b.St Louis 5-10-87
Honours: USA 7 full caps.
2006 St Louis Billikens 19 0
2007 St Louis Billikens 19 0
2008 St Louis Billikens 22 0
2008 Chicago Fire 12 0
2009 Chicago Fire 7 0 **19 0**
2009 St Louis Billikens 22 6 **82 6**
2010 New York Red Bulls 30 1
2011 New York Red Bulls 28 0 **58 1**
2011-12 Bolton W 13 0 **13 0**

REO-COKER, Nigel (M) **317 21**
H: 5 8 W: 12 03 b.Southwark 14-5-84
Source: Scholar. *Honours:* England Youth, Under-20, Under-21.
2001-02 Wimbledon 1 0
2002-03 Wimbledon 32 2
2003-04 Wimbledon 25 4 **58 6**
2003-04 West Ham U 15 2
2004-05 West Ham U 39 3
2005-06 West Ham U 31 5
2006-07 West Ham U 35 1 **120 11**
2007-08 Aston Villa 36 0
2008-09 Aston Villa 26 1
2009-10 Aston Villa 10 0
2010-11 Aston Villa 30 0 **102 1**
2011-12 Bolton W 37 3 **37 3**

RICKETTS, Sam (D) **308 4**
H: 6 1 W: 12 01 b.Aylesbury 11-10-81
Source: Trainee. *Honours:* Wales 44 full caps.
1999-2000 Oxford U 0 0
2000-01 Oxford U 14 0
2001-02 Oxford U 29 1
2002-03 Oxford U 2 0 **45 1**
From Telford U
2004-05 Swansea C 42 0
2005-06 Swansea C 44 1 **86 1**
2006-07 Hull C 40 1
2007-08 Hull C 44 0
2008-09 Hull C 29 0
2009-10 Hull C 0 0 **113 1**
2009-10 Bolton W 27 0
2010-11 Bolton W 17 0
2011-12 Bolton W 20 1 **64 1**

RILEY, Joe (D) **3 0**
H: 6 0 W: 11 02 b.Salford 13-10-91
Source: Scholar.
2011-12 Bolton W 3 0 **3 0**

ROBINSON, Paul (D) **520 12**
H: 5 9 W: 11 12 b.Watford 14-12-78
Source: Trainee. *Honours:* England Under-21.
1996-97 Watford 12 0
1997-98 Watford 22 2
1998-99 Watford 29 0
1999-2000 Watford 32 0
2000-01 Watford 39 0
2001-02 Watford 38 3
2002-03 Watford 37 3
2003-04 Watford 10 0 **219 8**
2003-04 WBA 31 0
2004-05 WBA 30 1
2005-06 WBA 33 0
2006-07 WBA 42 2
2007-08 WBA 43 1
2008-09 WBA 35 0
2009-10 WBA 0 0 **214 4**
2009-10 *Bolton W* 25 0
2010-11 Bolton W 35 0
2011-12 Bolton W 17 0 **77 0**
2011-12 *Leeds U* 10 0 **10 0**

SAMPSON, Jack (F) **9 0**
b.Wigan 14-4-93
Source: Scholar. *Honours:* England Youth.
2010-11 Bolton W 0 0
2011-12 Bolton W 0 0
2011-12 *Southend U* 9 0 **9 0**

SORDELL, Marvin (F) **86 22**
H: 5 9 W: 12 06 b.Pinner 17-2-91
Source: Scholar. *Honours:* England Under-21.
2009-10 Watford 6 1
2009-10 *Tranmere R* 8 1 **8 1**
2010-11 Watford 43 12
2011-12 Watford 26 8 **75 21**
2011-12 Bolton W 3 0 **3 0**

STEINSSON, Gretar Rafn (D) **284 27**
H: 6 2 W: 12 04 b.Siglufjordur 9-1-82
Honours: Iceland 42 full caps, 4 goals.
1999 IA Akranes 0 0
2000 IA Akranes 13 0
2001 IA Akranes 18 6
2002 IA Akranes 17 2
2003 IA Akranes 11 2
2004 IA Akranes 17 2 **76 12**
2004-05 Young Boys 14 3
2005-06 Young Boys 7 0 **21 3**
2005-06 AZ 20 4
2006-07 AZ 25 1
2007-08 AZ 16 2 **61 7**
2007-08 Bolton W 16 0
2008-09 Bolton W 37 3
2009-10 Bolton W 27 0
2010-11 Bolton W 23 1
2011-12 Bolton W 23 1 **126 5**

VELA, Joshua (M) **3 0**
H: 5 11 W: 11 07 b.Salford 14-12-93
Source: Scholar.
2010-11 Bolton W 0 0
2011-12 Bolton W 3 0 **3 0**

WHEATER, David (D) **194 14**
H: 6 5 W: 12 12 b.Redcar 14-2-87
Source: Scholar. *Honours:* England Youth, Under-21.
2004-05 Middlesbrough 0 0
2005-06 Middlesbrough 6 0
2005-06 *Doncaster R* 7 1 **7 1**
2006-07 Middlesbrough 2 1
2006-07 *Wolverhampton W* 1 0 **1 0**
2006-07 *Darlington* 15 2 **15 2**
2007-08 Middlesbrough 34 3
2008-09 Middlesbrough 32 1
2009-10 Middlesbrough 42 1
2010-11 Middlesbrough 24 3 **140 9**
2010-11 Bolton W 7 0
2011-12 Bolton W 24 2 **31 2**

Scholars
Clough Zach Paul John; Colman Oliver John; Dennis Elliott Ben; Fielding Lewis; Hampson Benjamin Christopher; Kellett Andrew Paul; Lester Christopher James; Lynch Jay; Maher Niall Callum James Peter; Matthews Glenn William; McQuade Alexander Michael; Odelusi Oluwasanmi; Sievers Jan-Ole; Threlkeld Oscar George; Wolstenholme Dyllon Alan; Woodland Luke; Youngs Thomas Ronald.

BOURNEMOUTH (12)

ARTER, Harry (M) **57 6**
H: 5 9 W: 11 07 b.Sidcup 28-12-89
Source: Scholar.
2007-08 Charlton Ath 0 0
2008-09 Charlton Ath 0 0
From Woking.
2010-11 Bournemouth 18 0
2010-11 *Carlisle U* 5 1 **5 1**
From Woking.
2011-12 Bournemouth 34 5 **52 5**

BARRETT, Adam (D) **468 37**
H: 5 10 W: 12 00 b.Dagenham 29-11-79
Source: Leyton Orient Trainee.
1998-99 Plymouth Arg 1 0
1999-2000 Plymouth Arg 42 3
2000-01 Plymouth Arg 9 0 **52 3**
2000-01 Mansfield T 8 1

2001-02 Mansfield T 29 0 **37 1**
2002-03 Bristol R 45 1
2003-04 Bristol R 45 4 **90 5**
2004-05 Southend U 43 11
2005-06 Southend U 45 3
2006-07 Southend U 28 3
2007-08 Southend U 45 6
2008-09 Southend U 45 2
2009-10 Southend U 41 2 **247 27**
2010-11 Crystal Palace 7 0 **7 0**
2010-11 *Leyton Orient* 14 0 **14 0**
2011-12 Bournemouth 21 1 **21 1**

BAUDRY, Mathieu (D) 47 2
H: 6 2 W: 12 08 b.Le Havre 24-2-88
2007-08 Troyes 2 1
2008-09 Troyes 17 0
2009-10 Troyes 7 0 **26 1**
2010-11 Bournemouth 3 1
2011-12 Bournemouth 7 0 **10 1**
2011-12 *Dagenham & R* 11 0 **11 0**

BOWLES, Gary (D) 0 0
b.Yeovil 30-12-88
Source: Dorchester T.
2011-12 Bournemouth 0 0

CARMICHAEL, Josh (M) 1 0
H: 6 0 W: 12 06 b.Poole 27-9-94
Source: Youth.
2011-12 Bournemouth 1 0 **1 0**

COOK, Steve (D) 29 0
H: 6 1 W: 12 13 b.Hastings 19-4-91
Source: Scholar.
2008-09 Brighton & HA 2 0
2009-10 Brighton & HA 0 0
2010-11 Brighton & HA 0 0
2011-12 Brighton & HA 1 0 **3 0**
2011-12 Bournemouth 26 0 **26 0**

COOPER, Shaun (D) 237 1
H: 5 10 W: 10 05 b.Newport (IW) 5-10-83
Source: School.
2000-01 Portsmouth 0 0
2001-02 Portsmouth 7 0
2002-03 Portsmouth 0 0
2003-04 Portsmouth 0 0
2003-04 *Leyton Orient* 9 0 **9 0**
2004-05 Portsmouth 0 0
2004-05 *Kidderminster H* 10 0 **10 0**
2005-06 Portsmouth 0 0 **7 0**
2005-06 Bournemouth 35 0
2006-07 Bournemouth 33 0
2007-08 Bournemouth 38 1
2008-09 Bournemouth 37 0
2009-10 Bournemouth 6 0
2010-11 Bournemouth 36 0
2011-12 Bournemouth 26 0 **211 1**

CUMMINGS, Warren (D) 285 7
H: 5 9 W: 11 05 b.Aberdeen 15-10-80
Source: Trainee. *Honours:* Scotland Under-21, 1 full cap.
1999-2000 Chelsea 0 0
2000-01 Chelsea 0 0
2000-01 *Bournemouth* 10 1
2000-01 *WBA* 3 0
2001-02 Chelsea 0 0
2001-02 *WBA* 14 0 **17 0**
2002-03 Chelsea 0 0
2002-03 Bournemouth 20 0
2003-04 Bournemouth 42 2
2004-05 Bournemouth 30 2
2005-06 Bournemouth 0 0
2006-07 Bournemouth 31 0
2007-08 Bournemouth 32 2
2008-09 Bournemouth 32 0
2009-10 Bournemouth 34 0
2010-11 Bournemouth 14 0
2011-12 Bournemouth 14 0 **259 7**
2011-12 *Crawley T* 9 0 **9 0**

DANIELS, Charlie (M) 176 7
H: 6 1 W: 12 12 b.Harlow 7-9-86
Source: Scholar.
2005-06 Tottenham H 0 0
2006-07 Tottenham H 0 0
2006-07 *Chesterfield* 2 0 **2 0**
2007-08 Tottenham H 0 0
2007-08 *Leyton Orient* 31 2
2008-09 Tottenham H 0 0
2008-09 *Gillingham* 5 1 **5 1**
2008-09 Leyton Orient 21 2
2009-10 Leyton Orient 41 0
2010-11 Leyton Orient 42 0
2011-12 Leyton Orient 13 0 **148 4**
2011-12 Bournemouth 21 2 **21 2**

FLAHAVAN, Darryl (G) 355 0
H: 5 11 W: 12 05 b.Southampton 9-9-77
Source: Trainee.
From Woking.
2000-01 Southend U 29 0
2001-02 Southend U 41 0
2002-03 Southend U 41 0
2003-04 Southend U 37 0
2004-05 Southend U 28 0
2005-06 Southend U 43 0
2006-07 Southend U 46 0
2007-08 Southend U 26 0 **291 0**
2008-09 Crystal Palace 1 0
2008-09 *Leeds U* 0 0
2009-10 Crystal Palace 1 0
2009-10 *Oldham Ath* 18 0 **18 0**
2010-11 Crystal Palace 0 0 **2 0**
2011-12 Bournemouth 44 0 **44 0**

FLETCHER, Steve (F) 693 112
H: 6 2 W: 14 09 b.Hartlepool 26-7-72
Source: Trainee.
1990-91 Hartlepool U 14 2
1991-92 Hartlepool U 18 2 **32 4**
1992-93 Bournemouth 31 4
1993-94 Bournemouth 36 6
1994-95 Bournemouth 40 6
1995-96 Bournemouth 7 1
1996-97 Bournemouth 35 7
1997-98 Bournemouth 42 12
1998-99 Bournemouth 39 8
1999-2000 Bournemouth 36 7
2000-01 Bournemouth 45 9
2001-02 Bournemouth 2 0
2002-03 Bournemouth 35 5
2003-04 Bournemouth 41 9
2004-05 Bournemouth 36 9
2005-06 Bournemouth 27 4
2006-07 Bournemouth 41 1
2007-08 Chesterfield 38 5 **38 5**
From Crawley T.
2008-09 Bournemouth 21 4
2009-10 Bournemouth 45 4
2010-11 Bournemouth 38 6
2011-12 Bournemouth 20 1 **617 103**
2011-12 *Plymouth Arg* 6 0 **6 0**

FOGDEN, Wes (F) 30 3
H: 5 8 W: 10 04 b.Brighton 12-4-88
Source: Scholar.
2006-07 Brighton & HA 0 0
2007-08 Brighton & HA 3 0 **3 0**
From Dorchester T, Havant & W'ville.
2011-12 Bournemouth 27 3 **27 3**
On loan from Havant & W'ville.

FRANCIS, Simon (D) 309 6
H: 6 0 W: 12 06 b.Nottingham 16-2-85
Source: Scholar. *Honours:* England Youth, Under-20.
2002-03 Bradford C 25 1
2003-04 Bradford C 30 0 **55 1**
2003-04 Sheffield U 5 0
2004-05 Sheffield U 6 0
2005-06 Sheffield U 1 0 **12 0**
2005-06 *Grimsby T* 5 0 **5 0**
2005-06 *Tranmere R* 17 1 **17 1**
2006-07 Southend U 40 1
2007-08 Southend U 27 2
2008-09 Southend U 45 0
2009-10 Southend U 45 1 **157 4**
2010-11 Charlton Ath 34 0
2011-12 Charlton Ath 0 0 **34 0**
2011-12 Bournemouth 29 0 **29 0**

GARRY, Ryan (D) 78 3
H: 6 0 W: 11 05 b.Hornchurch 29-9-83
Source: Scholar. *Honours:* England Youth, Under-20.
2001-02 Arsenal 0 0
2002-03 Arsenal 1 0
2003-04 Arsenal 1 0
2004-05 Arsenal 0 0
2005-06 Arsenal 0 0
2006-07 Arsenal 0 0 **1 0**
2007-08 Bournemouth 8 0
2008-09 Bournemouth 25 0
2009-10 Bournemouth 34 1
2010-11 Bournemouth 10 2
2011-12 Bournemouth 0 0 **77 3**

GREGORY, Steven (D) 32 2
H: 6 1 W: 12 04 b.Haddenham 19-3-87
Source: Scholar.
2005-06 Wycombe W 1 0
2006-07 Wycombe W 3 0 **4 0**
From AFC Wimbledon, Hayes & Yeading U.
2011-12 Bournemouth 28 2 **28 2**

HESTER, Paddy (D) 0 0
b.Poole 3-1-93
Source: Youth.
2011-12 Bournemouth 0 0

JALAL, Shwan (G) 151 0
H: 6 2 W: 14 02 b.Baghdad 14-8-83
Source: Hastings T.
2001-02 Tottenham H 0 0
2002-03 Tottenham H 0 0
2003-04 Tottenham H 0 0
From Woking.
2006-07 *Sheffield W* 0 0
2006-07 Peterborough U 1 0
2007-08 Peterborough U 7 0
2007-08 *Morecambe* 12 0 **12 0**
2008-09 Peterborough U 0 0 **8 0**
2008-09 Bournemouth 41 0
2009-10 Bournemouth 44 0
2010-11 Bournemouth 43 0
2011-12 Bournemouth 3 0 **131 0**

LOVELL, Stephen (F) 261 65
H: 5 11 W: 11 08 b.Amersham 6-12-80
Source: Trainee.
1998-99 Bournemouth 7 0
1999-2000 Bournemouth 1 0
1999-2000 Portsmouth 3 0
1999-2000 *Exeter C* 5 1 **5 1**
2000-01 Portsmouth 9 1
2001-02 Portsmouth 20 2 **32 3**
2001-02 *Sheffield U* 5 1 **5 1**
2002-03 Dundee 28 11
2003-04 Dundee 21 5
2004-05 Dundee 33 12 **82 28**
2005-06 Aberdeen 27 8
2006-07 Aberdeen 27 9
2007-08 Aberdeen 22 3 **76 20**
2008-09 Falkirk 28 8 **28 8**
2009-10 Partick Th 16 3 **16 3**
2010-11 Bournemouth 7 1
2011-12 Bournemouth 2 0 **17 1**

MACDONALD, Shaun (M) 110 10
H: 6 1 W: 11 04 b.Swansea 17-6-88
Source: Scholar. *Honours:* Wales Youth, Under-21, 1 full cap.
2005-06 Swansea C 7 0
2006-07 Swansea C 8 0
2007-08 Swansea C 1 0
2008-09 Swansea C 5 0
2008-09 *Yeovil T* 4 2
2009-10 Swansea C 3 0
2009-10 *Yeovil T* 31 3
2010-11 Swansea C 0 0
2010-11 *Yeovil T* 26 4 **61 9**
2011-12 Swansea C 0 0 **24 0**
2011-12 Bournemouth 25 1 **25 1**

MALONE, Scott (D) 78 7
H: 6 2 W: 11 11 b.Rowley Regis 25-3-91
Source: Scholar. *Honours:* England Youth.
2008-09 Wolverhampton W 0 0
2008-09 *Ujpest* 7 1 **7 1**
2009-10 Wolverhampton W 0 0
2009-10 *Southend U* 17 0 **17 0**
2010-11 Wolverhampton W 0 0
2010-11 *Burton Alb* 22 1 **22 1**
2011-12 Wolverhampton W 0 0
2011-12 Bournemouth 32 5 **32 5**

McDERMOTT, Donal (F) 57 7
H: 6 6 W: 12 00 b.Co. Meath 19-10-89
Source: Scholar. *Honours:* Eire Youth.
2007-08 Manchester C 0 0
2008-09 Manchester C 0 0
2008-09 *Milton Keynes D* 1 0 **1 0**
2009-10 Manchester C 0 0
2009-10 *Chesterfield* 15 5 **15 5**
2009-10 *Scunthorpe U* 9 0 **9 0**
2010-11 Manchester C 0 0
2010-11 *Bournemouth* 9 1
2011-12 Huddersfield T 9 0 **9 0**
2011-12 Bournemouth 14 1 **23 2**

MOLESLEY, Mark (M) 60 6
H: 6 1 W: 12 07 b.Hillingdon 11-3-81
From Hayes, Cam C, Ald T, Steve B, Grays

2008-09 Bournemouth 29 4
2009-10 Bournemouth 10 1
2010-11 Bournemouth 2 0
2011-12 Bournemouth 11 0 **52 5**
2011-12 *Aldershot T* 8 1 **8 1**

PARSONS, Alex (F) 1 0
H: 5 11 W: 11 09 b.Worthing 7-9-92
Source: Youth.
2011-12 Bournemouth 1 0 **1 0**

PARTINGTON, Joe (M) 38 2
H: 5 11 W: 11 13 b.Portsmouth 1-4-90
Source: Scholar. *Honours:* Wales Youth, Under-21.
2007-08 Bournemouth 6 1
2008-09 Bournemouth 11 1
2009-10 Bournemouth 11 0
2010-11 Bournemouth 5 0
2011-12 Bournemouth 5 0 **38 2**

PUGH, Marc (M) 221 42
H: 5 11 W: 11 04 b.Bacup 2-4-87
Source: Scholar.
2005-06 Burnley 0 0
2005-06 Bury 6 1
2006-07 Bury 35 3 **41 4**
2007-08 Shrewsbury T 37 4
2008-09 Shrewsbury T 7 0 **44 4**
2008-09 *Luton T* 4 0 **4 0**
2008-09 *Hereford U* 9 1
2009-10 Hereford U 40 13 **49 14**
2010-11 Bournemouth 41 12
2011-12 Bournemouth 42 8 **83 20**

PURCHES, Stephen (D) 387 15
H: 5 11 W: 11 13 b.Ilford 14-1-80
1998-99 West Ham U 0 0
1999-2000 West Ham U 0 0
2000-01 Bournemouth 34 0
2001-02 Bournemouth 41 2
2002-03 Bournemouth 44 3
2003-04 Bournemouth 42 3
2004-05 Bournemouth 14 1
2005-06 Bournemouth 26 0
2006-07 Bournemouth 43 1
2007-08 Leyton Orient 37 1
2008-09 Leyton Orient 42 3
2009-10 Leyton Orient 31 1 **110 5**
2010-11 Bournemouth 9 0
2011-12 Bournemouth 24 0 **277 10**

SEABRIGHT, Jordan (G) 0 0
b. 1-5-94
Source: Youth.
2011-12 Bournemouth 0 0

SHERINGHAM, Charlie (F) 6 1
H: 6 1 W: 11 06 b.Chingford 17-4-88
2006-07 Crystal Palace 0 0
2007-08 Crystal Palace 0 0
From Ipswich T Scholar, LA Galaxy, C Palace Baltimore (loan), Cambridge C, Welling U, Bishop's Stortford, Histon (loan), Dartford.
2011-12 Bournemouth 6 1 **6 1**

STOCKLEY, Jayden (F) 25 3
H: 6 2 W: 12 07 b.Poole 10-10-93
Source: School.
2009-10 Bournemouth 2 0
2010-11 Bournemouth 4 0
2011-12 Bournemouth 10 0 **16 0**
2011-12 *Accrington S* 9 3 **9 3**

STRUGNELL, Dan (D) 1 0
H: 6 1 W: 12 08 b.Christchurch 30-6-92
Source: Youth.
2011-12 Bournemouth 1 0 **1 0**

SYMES, Michael (F) 201 48
H: 6 3 W: 12 04 b.Gt Yarmouth 31-10-83
Source: Scholar.
2001-02 Everton 0 0
2002-03 Everton 0 0
2003-04 Everton 0 0
2003-04 *Crewe Alex* 4 1 **4 1**
2004-05 Bradford C 12 2
2004-05 *Darlington* 0 0
2005-06 Bradford C 3 1
2005-06 *Stockport Co* 1 0 **1 0**
2006-07 Bradford C 0 0 **15 3**
2006-07 Shrewsbury T 33 9
2007-08 Shrewsbury T 21 3
2007-08 *Macclesfield T* 14 1 **14 1**
2008-09 Shrewsbury T 8 2 **62 14**
2008-09 *Bournemouth* 5 0
2008-09 *Accrington S* 7 1
2009-10 Accrington S 41 13 **48 14**
2010-11 Bournemouth 22 8
2011-12 Bournemouth 15 3 **42 11**
2011-12 *Rochdale* 15 4 **15 4**

TAYLOR, Lyle (F) 37 2
H: 6 2 W: 12 00 b.Greenwich 29-3-90
Source: Staines T.
2007-08 Millwall 0 0
From Concord R.
2008-09 Millwall 0 0
From Concord R.
2010-11 Bournemouth 11 0
From Concord R.
2011-12 Bournemouth 18 0 **29 0**
2011-12 *Hereford U* 8 2 **8 2**

THOMAS, Wesley (F) 111 33
H: 5 10 W: 11 00 b.Barking 23-1-87
Source: QPR Youth, Waltham Forest, Thurrock, Fisher Ath.
2008-09 Dagenham & R 5 0
2009-10 Dagenham & R 23 3 **28 3**
2010-11 Cheltenham T 41 18 **41 18**
2011-12 Crawley T 6 1 **6 1**
2011-12 Bournemouth 36 11 **36 11**

TUBBS, Matt (F) 39 14
H: 5 9 W: 11 00 b.Salisbury 15-7-84
Source: Bolton W Scholar.
On loan from Salisbury C.
2008-09 Bournemouth 8 1
2009-10 Bournemouth 0 0
2011-12 Crawley T 24 12 **24 12**
2011-12 Bournemouth 7 1 **15 2**

WAKEFIELD, Josh (M) 2 0
H: 5 11 W: 11 05 b.Frimley 6-11-93
Source: Youth.
2011-12 Bournemouth 2 0 **2 0**

ZUBAR, Stephane (D) 112 3
b.Guadeloupe 9-10-86
Honours: Guadeloupe 2 full caps.
2006-07 Caen 0 0
2006-07 *Pau* 10 0 **10 0**
2007-08 Caen 0 0
2007-08 *FC Brussels* 11 0 **11 0**
2008-09 Vaslui 10 0
2009-10 Vaslui 26 1 **36 1**
2010-11 Plymouth Arg 29 2
2011-12 Plymouth Arg 4 0 **33 2**
2011-12 Bournemouth 22 0 **22 0**

BRADFORD C (13)

BAKER, Adam (F) 1 0
b.Leeds 8-12-93
Source: Scholar.
2011-12 Bradford C 1 0 **1 0**

BRANSTON, Guy (D) 343 21
H: 6 1 W: 15 01 b.Leicester 9-1-79
Source: Trainee.
1997-98 Leicester C 0 0
1997-98 *Colchester U* 12 1
1998-99 Leicester C 0 0
1998-99 *Colchester U* 1 0 **13 1**
1998-99 *Plymouth Arg* 7 1 **7 1**
1999-2000 Leicester C 0 0
1999-2000 *Lincoln C* 4 0 **4 0**
1999-2000 Rotherham U 30 4
2000-01 Rotherham U 41 6
2001-02 Rotherham U 10 1
2002-03 Rotherham U 15 2
2003-04 Rotherham U 8 0
2003-04 *Wycombe W* 9 0 **9 0**
2003-04 *Peterborough U* 14 0
2004-05 Sheffield W 11 0 **11 0**
2004-05 *Peterborough U* 4 1
2004-05 Oldham Ath 7 1
2005-06 Oldham Ath 38 1 **45 2**
2006-07 Peterborough U 24 0
2007-08 Peterborough U 2 0 **44 1**
2007-08 *Rochdale* 4 0 **4 0**
2007-08 *Northampton T* 3 0 **3 0**
2007-08 Notts Co 1 0 **1 0**
2009-10 Burton Alb 19 0 **19 0**
From Kettering T.
2009-10 *Torquay U* 16 0
2010-11 Torquay U 45 2 **61 2**
2011-12 Bradford C 16 1 **16 1**
2011-12 *Rotherham U* 2 0 **106 13**

BULLOCK, Lee (M) 394 40
H: 6 0 W: 11 04 b.Stockton 22-5-81
Source: Trainee.
1999-2000 York C 24 0
2000-01 York C 33 3
2001-02 York C 40 8
2002-03 York C 39 6
2003-04 York C 35 7 **171 24**
2003-04 *Cardiff C* 11 3
2004-05 Cardiff C 21 3 **32 6**
2005-06 Hartlepool U 31 4
2006-07 Hartlepool U 25 1
2007-08 Hartlepool U 1 0 **57 5**
2007-08 *Mansfield T* 5 0 **5 0**
2007-08 *Bury* 8 0 **8 0**
2007-08 Bradford C 12 1
2008-09 Bradford C 23 3
2009-10 Bradford C 41 1
2010-11 Bradford C 26 0
2011-12 Bradford C 19 0 **121 5**

BURNS, Andrew (D) 0 0
b.Liverpool 2-7-93
Source: Bolton W Scholar.
2011-12 Bradford C 0 0

COMPTON, Jack (M) 51 3
H: 5 8 W: 10 07 b.Torquay 2-9-88
Source: West Bromwich Albion Scholar.
2008-09 Brighton & HA 0 0
From Havant & W'vlle, Weston-Super-Mare.
2010-11 Falkirk 24 3
2011-12 Falkirk 13 0 **37 3**
2011-12 Bradford C 14 0 **14 0**
On loan to Bradford C.

DALEY, Omar (M) 151 16
H: 5 10 W: 11 03 b.Kingston, Jamaica 25-4-81
Source: Portmore U. *Honours:* Jamaica Under-20, 65 full caps, 7 goals.
2003-04 Reading 6 0 **6 0**
2004-05 Preston NE 14 0 **14 0**
From Charleston B, Portmore U.
2006-07 Bradford C 14 2
2007-08 Bradford C 41 4
2008-09 Bradford C 28 3
2009-10 Bradford C 14 1
2010-11 Bradford C 26 5
2010-11 *Rotherham U* 8 1 **8 1**
2011-12 Bradford C 0 0 **123 15**

DEAN, Luke (F) 3 0
H: 5 9 W: 11 00 b.Cleckheaton 14-5-91
Source: Scholar.
2009-10 Bradford C 1 0
2010-11 Bradford C 1 0
2011-12 Bradford C 1 0 **3 0**

DUKE, Matt (G) 85 0
H: 6 5 W: 13 04 b.Sheffield 16-7-77
Source: Alfreton T.
1999-2000 Sheffield U 0 0
2000-01 Sheffield U 0 0
2001-02 Sheffield U 0 0
2004-05 Hull C 2 0
2005-06 Hull C 2 0
2005-06 *Stockport Co* 3 0 **3 0**
2005-06 *Wycombe W* 5 0 **5 0**
2006-07 Hull C 1 0
2007-08 Hull C 3 0
2008-09 Hull C 10 0
2009-10 Hull C 11 0
2010-11 Hull C 21 0 **50 0**
2011-12 Bradford C 18 0 **18 0**
2011-12 *Northampton T* 9 0 **9 0**

FAGAN, Craig (F) 280 46
H: 5 11 W: 11 11 b.Birmingham 11-12-82
Source: Scholar.
2001-02 Birmingham C 0 0
2002-03 Birmingham C 1 0
2002-03 *Bristol C* 6 1 **6 1**
2003-04 Birmingham C 0 0 **1 0**
2003-04 Colchester U 37 9
2004-05 Colchester U 26 8 **63 17**
2004-05 Hull C 12 4
2005-06 Hull C 41 5
2006-07 Hull C 27 6
2006-07 Derby Co 17 1
2007-08 Derby Co 22 0 **39 1**
2007-08 *Hull C* 8 0
2008-09 Hull C 22 3
2009-10 Hull C 25 2

2010-11	Hull C	5	0	**140**	**20**
2011-12	Bradford C	31	7	**31**	**7**

FLYNN, Michael (M) 285 38
H: 5 10 W: 13 04 b.Newport 17-10-80
Source: Barry T.

2002-03	Wigan Ath	17	1		
2003-04	Wigan Ath	8	0		
2004-05	Wigan Ath	13	1	**38**	**2**
2004-05	*Blackpool*	6	0		
2004-05	Gillingham	16	3		
2005-06	Gillingham	36	6		
2006-07	Gillingham	45	10	**97**	**19**
2007-08	Blackpool	28	3	**34**	**3**
2008-09	*Darlington*	0	0		
2008-09	Huddersfield T	25	4	**25**	**4**
2009-10	Bradford C	42	6		
2010-11	Bradford C	19	0		
2011-12	Bradford C	30	4	**91**	**10**

FRY, Matt (D) 42 1
H: 6 1 W: 12 02 b.Longfield 26-9-90
Source: Scholar.

2009-10	West Ham U	0	0		
2009-10	*Gillingham*	11	0	**11**	**0**
2010-11	West Ham U	0	0		
2010-11	*Charlton Ath*	25	1	**25**	**1**
2011-12	West Ham U	0	0		
2011-12	Bradford C	6	0	**6**	**0**

HANNAH, Ross (F) 18 2
H: 5 9 W: 11 11 b.Sheffield 14-5-86
Source: Gainsborough T, Stocksbridge PS, Belper T, Matlock T.

2011-12	Bradford C	18	2	**18**	**2**

HANSON, James (F) 109 31
H: 6 4 W: 12 04 b.Bradford 9-11-87
Source: Eccleshill U, Guiseley.

2009-10	Bradford C	34	12		
2010-11	Bradford C	36	6		
2011-12	Bradford C	39	13	**109**	**31**

HUNT, Lewis (D) 229 4
H: 5 11 W: 12 09 b.Birmingham 25-8-82
Source: Scholar.

2000-01	Derby Co	0	0		
2001-02	Derby Co	0	0		
2002-03	Derby Co	10	0		
2003-04	Derby Co	1	0	**11**	**0**
2003-04	*Southend U*	26	0		
2004-05	Southend U	31	0		
2005-06	Southend U	30	0		
2006-07	Southend U	35	2		
2007-08	Southend U	24	0	**146**	**2**
2008-09	Wycombe W	20	1		
2009-10	Wycombe W	27	0	**47**	**1**
2010-11	Bradford C	24	1		
2011-12	Bradford C	1	0	**25**	**1**

JONES, Richie (M) 151 9
H: 6 0 W: 11 00 b.Manchester 26-9-86
Source: Scholar. *Honours:* England Youth.

2004-05	Manchester U	0	0		
2005-06	Manchester U	0	0		
2006-07	Manchester U	0	0		
2006-07	*Colchester U*	6	0	**6**	**0**
2006-07	*Barnsley*	4	0	**4**	**0**
2007-08	Manchester U	0	0		
2007-08	*Yeovil T*	9	0	**9**	**0**
2008-09	Hartlepool U	36	3		
2009-10	Hartlepool U	33	4	**69**	**7**
2010-11	Oldham Ath	31	1	**31**	**1**
2011-12	Bradford C	32	1	**32**	**1**

KOZLUK, Rob (D) 350 3
H: 5 8 W: 10 02 b.Mansfield 5-8-77
Source: Trainee. *Honours:* England Under-21.

1995-96	Derby Co	0	0		
1996-97	Derby Co	0	0		
1997-98	Derby Co	9	0		
1998-99	Derby Co	7	0	**16**	**0**
1998-99	Sheffield U	10	0		
1999-2000	Sheffield U	39	0		
2000-01	Sheffield U	27	0		
2000-01	*Huddersfield T*	14	0	**14**	**0**
2001-02	Sheffield U	8	0		
2002-03	Sheffield U	32	1		
2003-04	Sheffield U	42	1		
2004-05	Sheffield U	9	0		
2004-05	*Preston NE*	1	0	**1**	**0**
2005-06	Sheffield U	27	0		
2006-07	Sheffield U	19	0		
2007-08	Barnsley	24	0		
2008-09	Barnsley	37	0		
2009-10	Barnsley	14	0	**75**	**0**
2010-11	Sheffield U	8	1	**221**	**3**
2011-12	Port Vale	6	0	**6**	**0**
2011-12	Bradford C	17	0	**17**	**0**

LACEY, Patrick (M) 0 0
b.Liverpool 16-3-93
Source: Sheffield W Scholar.

2011-12	Bradford C	0	0		

McLAUGHLIN, Jon (G) 56 0
H: 6 2 W: 13 00 b.Edinburgh 9-9-87
Source: Harrogate T.

2008-09	Bradford C	1	0		
2009-10	Bradford C	7	0		
2010-11	Bradford C	25	0		
2011-12	Bradford C	23	0	**56**	**0**

MITCHELL, Chris (D) 64 3
H: 5 9 W: 10 10 b.Stirling 21-7-88
Honours: Scotland Under-21.

2007-08	Falkirk	5	0		
2008-09	Falkirk	9	0		
2009-10	Falkirk	8	1		
2009-10	*Ayr U*	14	1	**14**	**1**
2010-11	Falkirk	17	0	**39**	**1**
2011-12	Bradford C	11	1	**11**	**1**

OLIVER, Luke (D) 126 4
H: 6 6 W: 14 05 b.Acton 1-5-84
Source: Brook House.

2002-03	Wycombe W	2	0		
2003-04	Wycombe W	2	0		
From Woking					
2005-06	Yeovil T	3	0	**3**	**0**
From Stevenage B.					
2008-09	Wycombe W	8	0		
2009-10	Wycombe W	23	0	**35**	**0**
2009-10	*Bradford C*	7	2		
2010-11	Bradford C	42	1		
2011-12	Bradford C	39	1	**88**	**4**

OVERSON, Dean (D) 0 0
b.Stoke 16-6-93
Source: Burnley Scholar.

2011-12	Bradford C	0	0		

RAMSDEN, Simon (D) 231 7
H: 6 0 W: 12 06 b.Bishop Auckland 17-12-81
Source: Scholar.

2000-01	Sunderland	0	0		
2001-02	Sunderland	0	0		
2002-03	Sunderland	0	0		
2002-03	*Notts Co*	32	0	**32**	**0**
2003-04	Sunderland	0	0		
2004-05	Grimsby T	25	0		
2005-06	Grimsby T	12	0	**37**	**0**
2005-06	Rochdale	15	1		
2006-07	Rochdale	34	3		
2007-08	Rochdale	35	2		
2008-09	Rochdale	28	0	**112**	**6**
2009-10	Bradford C	31	1		
2010-11	Bradford C	2	0		
2011-12	Bradford C	17	0	**50**	**1**

RAVENHILL, Ricky (M) 311 21
H: 5 10 W: 11 02 b.Doncaster 16-1-81
Source: Barnsley Trainee.

2003-04	Doncaster R	36	3		
2004-05	Doncaster R	35	3		
2005-06	Doncaster R	27	3	**98**	**9**
2006-07	Chester C	3	0	**3**	**0**
2006-07	Grimsby T	17	2	**17**	**2**
2006-07	Darlington	15	1		
2007-08	Darlington	35	3		
2008-09	Darlington	38	2	**88**	**6**
2008-09	Notts Co	0	0		
2009-10	Notts Co	40	3		
2010-11	Notts Co	34	0		
2011-12	Notts Co	5	0	**79**	**3**
2011-12	Bradford C	26	1	**26**	**1**

REID, Kyel (M) 139 12
H: 5 10 W: 12 05 b.Deptford 26-11-87
Source: Scholar. *Honours:* England Youth.

2004-05	West Ham U	0	0		
2005-06	West Ham U	2	0		
2006-07	West Ham U	0	0		
2006-07	*Barnsley*	26	2	**26**	**2**
2007-08	West Ham U	1	0		
2007-08	*Crystal Palace*	2	0	**2**	**0**
2008-09	West Ham U	0	0	**3**	**0**
2008-09	*Blackpool*	7	0	**7**	**0**
2008-09	*Wolverhampton W*	8	1	**8**	**1**
2009-10	Sheffield U	7	0	**7**	**0**
2009-10	*Charlton Ath*	17	4		
2010-11	Charlton Ath	32	1	**49**	**5**
2011-12	Bradford C	37	4	**37**	**4**

RODNEY, Nialle (F) 11 0
H: 6 1 W: 11 11 b.Nottingham 28-2-91
Source: Scholar.

2008-09	Nottingham F	0	0		
2009-10	Nottingham F	0	0		
2010-11	Nottingham F	3	0	**3**	**0**
2010-11	*Burton Alb*	3	0	**3**	**0**
2011-12	Bradford C	5	0	**5**	**0**

ROWE, Dominic (F) 2 0
H: 5 6 W: 10 07 b.Leeds 23-4-93
Source: Scholar.

2010-11	Bradford C	2	0		
2011-12	Bradford C	0	0	**2**	**0**

SEIP, Marcel (D) 292 11
H: 6 0 W: 11 03 b.Winschoten 5-4-82
Honours: Holland Under-21.

1999-2000	Veendam	9	0		
2000-01	Veendam	18	0	**27**	**0**
2001-02	Heerenveen	0	0		
2002-03	Heerenveen	6	0		
2003-04	Heerenveen	31	1		
2004-05	Heerenveen	30	1		
2005-06	Heerenveen	28	0	**95**	**2**
2006-07	Plymouth Arg	37	2		
2007-08	Plymouth Arg	34	1		
2008-09	Plymouth Arg	41	3		
2009-10	Plymouth Arg	5	0		
2009-10	*Blackpool*	7	2	**7**	**2**
2009-10	*Sheffield U*	6	0	**6**	**0**
2010-11	Plymouth Arg	17	0	**134**	**6**
2010-11	*Charlton Ath*	0	0		
2011-12	Bradford C	23	1	**23**	**1**

STEPHENSON, Darren (F) 1 0
b.Jamaica 6-3-93
Source: Scholar.

2010-11	Bradford C	1	0		
2011-12	Bradford C	0	0	**1**	**0**

STEWART, Mark (F) 132 26
H: 5 7 W: 10 07 b.Glasgow 22-6-88

2004-05	Partick Th	2	0		
2005-06	Partick Th	0	0	**2**	**0**
2006-07	Falkirk	18	0		
2007-08	Falkirk	5	0		
2007-08	*Stranraer*	8	6	**8**	**6**
2008-09	Falkirk	20	2		
2009-10	Falkirk	19	2		
2010-11	Falkirk	35	15	**97**	**19**
2011-12	Bradford C	12	0	**12**	**0**
2011-12	*Hamilton A*	13	1	**13**	**1**

SYERS, Dave (M) 55 10
H: 6 0 W: 11 07 b.Leeds 30-11-87
Source: Ossett Alb, Farsley C, Harrogate T.

2010-11	Bradford C	37	8		
2011-12	Bradford C	18	2	**55**	**10**

THRELFALL, Robbie (D) 72 2
H: 5 11 W: 11 00 b.Liverpool 25-11-88
Source: Scholar. *Honours:* England Youth.

2006-07	Liverpool	0	0		
2007-08	Liverpool	0	0		
2007-08	*Hereford U*	9	0		
2008-09	Liverpool	0	0		
2008-09	*Hereford U*	3	0	**12**	**0**
2008-09	*Stockport Co*	2	0	**2**	**0**
2009-10	Liverpool	0	0		
2009-10	*Northampton T*	4	0	**4**	**0**
2009-10	*Bradford C*	17	2		
2010-11	Bradford C	20	0		
2011-12	Bradford C	17	0	**54**	**2**

WELLS, Nahki (F) 36 10
H: 5 7 W: 11 00 b.Bermuda 1-6-90
Source: Dandy T Hornets, Bermuda Hogges. *Honours:* Bermuda 6 full caps.

2010-11	Carlisle U	3	0	**3**	**0**
2011-12	Bradford C	33	10	**33**	**10**

WILLIAMS, Steve (D) 77 9
H: 6 4 W: 13 06 b.Preston 24-4-87
Source: Charnock Richard, Chorley, Bamber Bridge, Hyde U, Fleetwood T, Bamber Bridge.

2009-10	Bradford C	39	4		
2010-11	Bradford C	28	3		
2011-12	Bradford C	1	0	**68**	**7**
2011-12	*Inverness CT*	9	2	**9**	**2**

BRENTFORD (14)

ALEXANDER, Gary (F) **483 145**
H: 6 0 W: 13 04 b.Lambeth 15-8-79
Source: Trainee.

1998-99	West Ham U	0	0		
1999-2000	West Ham U	0	0		
1999-2000	*Exeter C*	37	16	**37**	**16**
2000-01	Swindon T	37	7	**37**	**7**
2001-02	Hull C	43	17		
2002-03	Hull C	25	6	**68**	**23**
2002-03	Leyton Orient	17	2		
2003-04	Leyton Orient	44	15		
2004-05	Leyton Orient	28	9		
2005-06	Leyton Orient	46	14		
2006-07	Leyton Orient	44	12	**179**	**52**
2007-08	Millwall	36	7		
2008-09	Millwall	35	11		
2009-10	Millwall	15	1	**86**	**19**
2010-11	Brentford	38	9		
2011-12	Brentford	24	12	**62**	**21**
2011-12	*Crawley T*	14	7	**14**	**7**

BALKESTEIN, Pim (D) **87 2**
H: 6 3 W: 12 00 b.Gouda 29-4-87
Source: Heerenveen.

2008-09	Ipswich T	20	0		
2009-10	Ipswich T	9	0	**29**	**0**
2009-10	*Brentford*	14	1		
2010-11	Brentford	20	1		
2011-12	Brentford	5	0	**39**	**2**
2011-12	*Rochdale*	13	0	**13**	**0**
2011-12	*AFC Wimbledon*	6	0	**6**	**0**

BEAN, Marcus (M) **263 19**
H: 5 11 W: 11 06 b.Hammersmith 2-11-84
Source: Scholar.

2002-03	QPR	7	0		
2003-04	QPR	31	1		
2004-05	QPR	20	1		
2004-05	*Swansea C*	8	0		
2005-06	QPR	9	0	**67**	**2**
2005-06	*Swansea C*	9	1	**17**	**1**
2005-06	Blackpool	17	1		
2006-07	Blackpool	6	0		
2007-08	Blackpool	0	0	**23**	**1**
2007-08	*Rotherham U*	12	1	**12**	**1**
2008-09	Brentford	44	9		
2009-10	Brentford	31	0		
2010-11	Brentford	37	3		
2011-12	Brentford	32	2	**144**	**14**

BELLAMY, Liam (M) **0 0**
b.Wanstead 16-10-91
Source: Charlton Ath Scholar, Welling U.

2011-12	Brentford	0	0		

BLAKE, Ryan (D) **1 0**
H: 5 10 W: 10 10 b.Weybridge 8-12-91
Source: Scholar. *Honours:* Northern Ireland Youth, Under-21.

2009-10	Brentford	1	0		
2010-11	Brentford	0	0		
2011-12	Brentford	0	0	**1**	**0**

DIAGOURAGA, Toumani (M) **208 9**
H: 6 2 W: 11 05 b.Paris 10-6-87
Source: Scholar.

2004-05	Watford	0	0		
2005-06	Watford	1	0		
2005-06	*Swindon T*	8	0	**8**	**0**
2006-07	Watford	0	0		
2006-07	*Rotherham U*	7	0	**7**	**0**
2007-08	Watford	0	0	**1**	**0**
2007-08	*Hereford U*	41	2		
2008-09	Hereford U	45	2	**86**	**4**
2009-10	Peterborough U	19	0	**19**	**0**
2009-10	*Brentford*	20	0		
2010-11	Brentford	32	1		
2011-12	Brentford	35	4	**87**	**5**

DONALDSON, Clayton (F) **182 63**
H: 6 1 W: 11 07 b.Bradford 7-2-84
Source: Scholar.

2002-03	Hull C	2	0		
2003-04	Hull C	0	0		
2004-05	Hull C	0	0	**2**	**0**

From York C

2007-08	Hibernian	17	5	**17**	**5**
2008-09	Crewe Alex	37	6		
2009-10	Crewe Alex	37	13		
2010-11	Crewe Alex	43	28	**117**	**47**
2011-12	Brentford	46	11	**46**	**11**

DOUGLAS, Jonathan (M) **319 18**
H: 5 11 W: 11 11 b.Monaghan 22-11-81
Source: Trainee. *Honours:* Eire Under-21, 8 full caps.

1999-2000	Blackburn R	0	0		
2000-01	Blackburn R	0	0		
2001-02	Blackburn R	0	0		
2002-03	Blackburn R	1	0		
2002-03	*Chesterfield*	7	1	**7**	**1**
2003-04	Blackpool	16	3	**16**	**3**
2003-04	Blackburn R	14	1		
2004-05	Blackburn R	1	0		
2004-05	*Gillingham*	10	0	**10**	**0**
2005-06	Blackburn R	0	0		
2005-06	*Leeds U*	40	5		
2006-07	Blackburn R	0	0	**16**	**1**
2006-07	Leeds U	35	1		
2007-08	Leeds U	24	3		
2008-09	Leeds U	43	1	**142**	**10**
2009-10	Swindon T	43	0		
2010-11	Swindon T	39	1	**82**	**1**
2011-12	Brentford	46	2	**46**	**2**

EGER, Marcel (D) **178 9**
H: 6 3 W: 13 05 b.Nuremberg 23-3-83
Source: Nuremberg II.

2003-04	Feucht	26	1	**26**	**1**
2004-05	St Pauli	19	1		
2005-06	St Pauli	12	1		
2006-07	St Pauli	34	0		
2007-08	St Pauli	28	4		
2008-09	St Pauli	28	1		
2009-10	St Pauli	3	0		
2009-10	St Pauli II	5	0	**5**	**0**
2010-11	St Pauli	7	1	**131**	**8**
2011-12	Brentford	16	0	**16**	**0**

EKIM, Josh (M) **0 0**
b.Tottenham 17-11-91
Source: Tottenham H Scholar, Trabzonspor.

2011-12	Brentford	0	0		

FORRESTER, Harry (F) **26 0**
H: 5 9 W: 11 03 b.Milton Keynes 2-1-91
Source: Watford Scholar.

2007-08	Aston Villa	0	0		
2008-09	Aston Villa	0	0		
2009-10	Aston Villa	0	0		
2010-11	Aston Villa	0	0		
2010-11	*Kilmarnock*	7	0	**7**	**0**
2011-12	Brentford	19	0	**19**	**0**

GERMAN, Antonio (F) **31 2**
H: 5 10 W: 12 03 b.Wembley 26-12-91
Source: Scholar.

2008-09	QPR	3	0		
2009-10	QPR	13	2		
2009-10	*Aldershot T*	3	0	**3**	**0**
2010-11	QPR	2	0		
2010-11	*Southend U*	4	0	**4**	**0**
2010-11	*Yeovil T*	4	0	**4**	**0**
2011-12	QPR	0	0	**18**	**2**

From Stockport Co, Bromley.

2011-12	Brentford	2	0	**2**	**0**

GOUNET, Antoine (G) **0 0**
b.France 16-10-88
Source: Tours.

2011-12	Brentford	0	0		

GRIFFITHS, Sam (D) **0 0**
b.Bilston 2-11-92
Source: Wolverhampton W Scholar.

2011-12	Brentford	0	0		

KAMAU, Michael (D) **0 0**
b.Slough 22-1-93
Source: Fulham Scholar.

2011-12	Brentford	0	0		

LEE, Richard (G) **151 0**
H: 6 0 W: 12 06 b.Oxford 5-10-82
Source: Scholar. *Honours:* England Under-20.

2000-01	Watford	0	0		
2001-02	Watford	0	0		
2002-03	Watford	4	0		
2003-04	Watford	0	0		
2004-05	Watford	33	0		
2005-06	Watford	0	0		
2005-06	*Blackburn R*	0	0		
2006-07	Watford	10	0		
2007-08	Watford	35	0		
2008-09	Watford	10	0		
2009-10	Watford	0	0	**92**	**0**
2010-11	Brentford	22	0		
2011-12	Brentford	37	0	**59**	**0**

LEGGE, Leon (D) **87 9**
H: 6 1 W: 11 02 b.Bexhill 1-7-85
Source: Eastbourne UA, Hailsham T, Lewes, Tonbridge Angels.

2009-10	Brentford	29	2		
2010-11	Brentford	30	3		
2011-12	Brentford	28	4	**87**	**9**

LOGAN, Shaleum (D) **77 5**
H: 6 1 W: 12 07 b.Wythenshawe 29-1-88
Source: Scholar.

2006-07	Manchester C	0	0		
2007-08	Manchester C	0	0		
2007-08	*Grimsby T*	5	2	**5**	**2**
2007-08	*Scunthorpe U*	4	0	**4**	**0**
2007-08	*Stockport Co*	7	0	**7**	**0**
2008-09	Manchester C	1	0		
2009-10	Manchester C	0	0		
2009-10	*Tranmere R*	33	0	**33**	**0**
2010-11	Manchester C	0	0	**1**	**0**
2011-12	Brentford	27	3	**27**	**3**

McGINN, Niall (M) **138 19**
H: 6 0 W: 13 01 b.Dungannon 20-7-87
Honours: Northern Ireland Under-23, B, 18 full caps.

2005-06	Dungannon Swifts	1	0		
2006-07	Dungannon Swifts	23	0		
2007-08	Dungannon Swifts	18	4	**42**	**4**
2008	Derry C	31	6	**31**	**6**
2009-10	Celtic	14	2		
2010-11	Celtic	14	2	**28**	**4**

On loan from Celtic

2011-12	Brentford	37	5	**37**	**5**

On loan from Celtic.

MOORE, Simon (G) **21 0**
H: 6 3 W: 12 02 b.Sandown 19-5-90
Source: Farnborough T.

2009-10	Brentford	1	0		
2010-11	Brentford	10	0		
2011-12	Brentford	10	0	**21**	**0**

NORRIS, Luke (F) **1 0**
H: 6 1 W: 13 05 b. 3-6-93
Source: Hitchin T.

2011-12	Brentford	1	0	**1**	**0**

O'CONNOR, Kevin (F) **399 32**
H: 5 11 W: 12 00 b.Blackburn 24-2-82
Source: Trainee. *Honours:* Eire Youth, Under-21.

1999-2000	Brentford	6	0		
2000-01	Brentford	11	1		
2001-02	Brentford	25	0		
2002-03	Brentford	45	5		
2003-04	Brentford	43	1		
2004-05	Brentford	37	2		
2005-06	Brentford	30	7		
2006-07	Brentford	39	6		
2007-08	Brentford	37	3		
2008-09	Brentford	28	0		
2009-10	Brentford	43	4		
2010-11	Brentford	41	2		
2011-12	Brentford	14	1	**399**	**32**

OSBORNE, Karleigh (D) **161 6**
H: 6 2 W: 12 04 b.Southall 19-3-88
Source: Scholar.

2004-05	Brentford	1	0		
2005-06	Brentford	1	0		
2006-07	Brentford	21	0		
2007-08	Brentford	29	1		
2008-09	Brentford	23	4		
2009-10	Brentford	19	0		
2010-11	Brentford	42	1		
2011-12	Brentford	25	0	**161**	**6**

OYELEKE, Emmanuel (M) **1 0**
H: 5 9 W: 11 11 b.Wandsworth 24-12-92
Source: Scholar.

2011-12	Brentford	1	0	**1**	**0**

PIERRE, Aaron (D) **0 0**
b.Southall 17-2-93
Source: Fulham Scholar.

2011-12	Brentford	0	0		

REEVES, Jake (M) **9 0**
H: 5 8 W: 11 11 b.Lewisham 30-6-93
Source: Scholar.

2010-11	Brentford	1	0		
2011-12	Brentford	8	0	**9**	**0**

SAUNDERS, Sam (M) 146 27
H: 5 6 W: 11 04 b.Erith 29-8-83
Source: Welling U, Hastings T, Ashford T, Carshalton Ath.
2007-08 Dagenham & R 22 0
2008-09 Dagenham & R 40 14 **62 14**
2009-10 Brentford 26 1
2010-11 Brentford 21 2
2011-12 Brentford 37 10 **84 13**

WESTON, Myles (M) 181 15
H: 5 11 W: 12 05 b.Lewisham 12-3-88
Source: Scholar.
2006-07 Charlton Ath 0 0
2006-07 *Notts Co* 4 0
2007-08 Notts Co 25 0
2008-09 Notts Co 44 3 **73 3**
2009-10 Brentford 40 8
2010-11 Brentford 42 3
2011-12 Brentford 26 1 **108 12**

WOOD, Sam (M) 134 5
H: 6 0 W: 11 05 b.Sidcup 9-8-86
Source: Cray W, Bromley.
2008-09 Brentford 40 1
2009-10 Brentford 43 2
2010-11 Brentford 20 1
2011-12 Brentford 5 0 **108 4**
2011-12 *Rotherham U* 26 1 **26 1**

WOODMAN, Craig (D) 300 6
H: 5 9 W: 10 11 b.Tiverton 22-12-82
Source: Trainee.
1999-2000 Bristol C 0 0
2000-01 Bristol C 2 0
2001-02 Bristol C 6 0
2002-03 Bristol C 10 0
2003-04 Bristol C 21 0
2004-05 Bristol C 3 0
2004-05 *Mansfield T* 8 1 **8 1**
2004-05 *Torquay U* 22 1
2005-06 Bristol C 37 1
2005-06 *Torquay U* 2 0 **24 1**
2006-07 Bristol C 11 0 **90 1**
2007-08 Wycombe W 29 0
2008-09 Wycombe W 46 1
2009-10 Wycombe W 44 1 **119 2**
2010-11 Brentford 41 1
2011-12 Brentford 18 0 **59 1**

BRIGHTON & HA (15)

AGDESTEIN, Torbjorn (F) 4 0
H: 6 0 W: 12 10 b.Norway 18-9-91
Source: Stord.
2010-11 Brighton & HA 0 0
2011-12 Brighton & HA 4 0 **4 0**

ANKERGREN, Casper (G) 269 0
H: 6 3 W: 14 07 b.Koge 9-11-79
Source: Koge. *Honours:* Denmark Youth, Under-21.
2001-02 Brondby 1 0
2002-03 Brondby 16 0
2003-04 Brondby 1 0
2004-05 Brondby 32 0
2005-06 Brondby 18 0
2006-07 Brondby 18 0 **86 0**
2006-07 Leeds U 14 0
2007-08 Leeds U 43 0
2008-09 Leeds U 33 0
2009-10 Leeds U 29 0 **119 0**
2010-11 Brighton & HA 45 0
2011-12 Brighton & HA 19 0 **64 0**

BARKER, George (F) 0 0
H: 5 8 W: 11 02 b.Portsmouth 26-9-91
Source: Scholar.
2010-11 Brighton & HA 0 0
2011-12 Brighton & HA 0 0

BARNES, Ashley (F) 121 35
H: 6 0 W: 12 00 b.Bath 30-10-89
Source: Paulton R.
2006-07 Plymouth Arg 0 0
2007-08 Plymouth Arg 0 0
2008-09 Plymouth Arg 15 1
2009-10 Plymouth Arg 7 1 **22 2**
2009-10 *Torquay U* 6 0 **6 0**
2009-10 *Brighton & HA* 8 4
2010-11 Brighton & HA 42 18
2011-12 Brighton & HA 43 11 **93 33**

BERGKAMP, Rowland (F) 57 8
H: 6 4 W: 13 03 b.Amsterdam 3-4-91
Honours: Holland Under-21.
2009-10 Excelsior 26 3
2010-11 Excelsior 28 5 **54 8**
2011-12 Brighton & HA 0 0
2011-12 *Rochdale* 3 0 **3 0**

BREZOVAN, Peter (G) 135 0
H: 6 6 W: 14 13 b.Bratislava 9-12-79
Source: PS Bratislava, Vinohrady, Devin, Slovan Breclav, Zigma Olomouc. *Honours:* Slovakia U-21.
2002-03 Brno 10 0
2003-04 Brno 2 0
2004-05 Inter Bratislava 8 0 **8 0**
2005-06 Brno 7 0 **19 0**
2006-07 Swindon T 14 0
2007-08 Swindon T 31 0
2008-09 Swindon T 21 0 **66 0**
2009-10 Brighton & HA 20 0
2010-11 Brighton & HA 2 0
2011-12 Brighton & HA 20 0 **42 0**

BRIDCUTT, Liam (M) 110 2
H: 5 9 W: 11 07 b.Reading 8-5-89
Source: Scholar.
2007-08 Chelsea 0 0
2007-08 *Yeovil T* 9 0 **9 0**
2008-09 Chelsea 0 0
2008-09 *Watford* 6 0 **6 0**
2009-10 Chelsea 0 0
2009-10 *Stockport Co* 15 0 **15 0**
2010-11 Chelsea 0 0
2010-11 Brighton & HA 37 2
2011-12 Brighton & HA 43 0 **80 2**

BUCKLEY, Will (F) 127 26
H: 6 0 W: 13 00 b.Oldham 12-8-88
Source: Curzon Ashton.
2007-08 Rochdale 7 0
2008-09 Rochdale 37 10
2009-10 Rochdale 15 3 **59 13**
2009-10 Watford 6 1
2010-11 Watford 33 4 **39 5**
2011-12 Brighton & HA 29 8 **29 8**

CALDERON, Inigo (D) 300 20
H: 5 10 W: 12 02 b.Vitoria 4-1-82
2002-03 Alaves B 35 1
2003-04 Alaves B 33 0 **68 1**
2004-05 Alicante 25 0
2005-06 Alicante 31 4
2006-07 Alicante 28 1 **84 5**
2007-08 Alaves 20 0
2008-09 Alaves 33 2 **53 2**
2009-10 Brighton & HA 19 1
2010-11 Brighton & HA 44 7
2011-12 Brighton & HA 32 4 **95 12**

DICKENSON, Ben (F) 0 0
b.Ferndown 9-8-93
Source: Christchurch, Dorchester T.
2011-12 Brighton & HA 0 0

DICKER, Gary (M) 238 11
H: 6 0 W: 12 00 b.Dublin 31-7-86
Honours: Eire Under-21.
2004 UCD 9 1
2005 UCD 31 2
2006 UCD 28 2 **68 5**
2006-07 Birmingham C 0 0
2007-08 Stockport Co 30 0
2008-09 Stockport Co 25 0 **55 0**
2008-09 *Brighton & HA* 9 1
2009-10 Brighton & HA 42 2
2010-11 Brighton & HA 46 3
2011-12 Brighton & HA 18 0 **115 6**

DUNK, Lewis (D) 37 0
H: 6 3 W: 12 02 b.Brighton 1-12-91
Source: Scholar.
2009-10 Brighton & HA 1 0
2010-11 Brighton & HA 5 0
2011-12 Brighton & HA 31 0 **37 0**

EAST, Daniel (G) 0 0
b.Northwich 18-3-93
Source: Wolverhampton W Scholar.
2011-12 Brighton & HA 0 0

EL-ABD, Adam (D) 259 4
H: 5 10 W: 13 05 b.Brighton 11-9-84
Source: Scholar. *Honours:* Egypt 1 full cap.
2003-04 Brighton & HA 11 0
2004-05 Brighton & HA 16 0
2005-06 Brighton & HA 29 0
2006-07 Brighton & HA 42 1
2007-08 Brighton & HA 35 1
2008-09 Brighton & HA 31 0
2009-10 Brighton & HA 35 1
2010-11 Brighton & HA 37 1
2011-12 Brighton & HA 23 0 **259 4**

ELPHICK, Tommy (M) 153 7
H: 5 11 W: 11 07 b.Brighton 7-9-87
Source: Scholar.
2005-06 Brighton & HA 1 0
2006-07 Brighton & HA 3 0
2007-08 Brighton & HA 39 2
2008-09 Brighton & HA 39 1
2009-10 Brighton & HA 44 3
2010-11 Brighton & HA 27 1
2011-12 Brighton & HA 0 0 **153 7**

FORSTER-CASKEY, Jake (M) 5 1
H: 5 10 W: 10 00 b.Southend 25-4-94
Source: Scholar. *Honours:* England Youth.
2009-10 Brighton & HA 1 0
2010-11 Brighton & HA 0 0
2011-12 Brighton & HA 4 1 **5 1**

GONZALEZ, David (G) 254 0
H: 6 4 W: 13 01 b.Medellin 20-7-82
Honours: Colombia 2 full caps.
2001 At Nacional 0 0
2002 Independiente 21 0
2003 Independiente 38 0
2004 Independiente 46 0
2005 Independiente 22 0 **127 0**
2006 Dep Cali 35 0
2007 Dep Cali 22 0 **57 0**
2007-08 Rize 24 0 **24 0**
2009 Huracan 30 0 **30 0**
2009-10 Manchester C 0 0
2010-11 Manchester C 0 0
2010-11 *Leeds U* 0 0
2010-11 *Aberdeen* 0 0
2011-12 Manchester C 0 0
2011-12 Brighton & HA 2 0 **2 0**
2011-12 *Aberdeen* 14 0 **14 0**

GOODWIN, Shamir (M) 0 0
Source: Scholar.
2011-12 Brighton & HA 0 0

GREER, Gordon (D) 291 8
H: 6 2 W: 12 05 b.Glasgow 14-12-80
Source: Port Glasgow. *Honours:* Scotland B.
2000-01 Clyde 30 0 **30 0**
2000-01 Blackburn R 0 0
2001-02 Blackburn R 0 0
2002-03 Blackburn R 0 0
2002-03 *Stockport Co* 5 1 **5 1**
2003-04 Kilmarnock 25 0
2004-05 Kilmarnock 22 1
2005-06 Kilmarnock 27 2
2006-07 Kilmarnock 33 0 **107 3**
2007-08 Doncaster R 11 1
2008-09 Doncaster R 1 0 **12 1**
2008-09 *Swindon T* 19 1
2009-10 Swindon T 44 1 **63 2**
2010-11 Brighton & HA 32 0
2011-12 Brighton & HA 42 1 **74 1**

HALL, Grant (D) 1 0
H: 5 9 W: 11 02 b.Brighton 29-10-91
Source: Lewes.
2009-10 Brighton & HA 0 0
2010-11 Brighton & HA 0 0
2011-12 Brighton & HA 1 0 **1 0**

HARLEY, Ryan (M) 135 26
H: 5 11 W: 11 00 b.Bristol 22-1-85
Source: Scholar.
2004-05 Bristol C 2 0
2005-06 Bristol C 0 0 **2 0**
2008-09 Exeter C 31 4
2009-10 Exeter C 44 10
2010-11 Exeter C 21 6
2010-11 Swansea C 0 0
2010-11 *Exeter C* 21 4 **117 24**
2011-12 Swansea C 0 0
2011-12 Brighton & HA 16 2 **16 2**

HOSKINS, Will (F) 207 52
H: 5 11 W: 11 02 b.Nottingham 6-5-86
Source: Scholar. *Honours:* England Youth, Under-20.
2003-04 Rotherham U 4 2
2004-05 Rotherham U 22 2
2005-06 Rotherham U 23 4

2006-07 Rotherham U 24 15
2006-07 Watford 9 0
2007-08 Watford 1 0
2007-08 *Millwall* 10 2 **10 2**
2007-08 *Nottingham F* 2 0 **2 0**
2008-09 Watford 32 4
2009-10 Watford 18 3 **60 7**
2010-11 Bristol R 43 17 **43 17**
2011-12 Brighton & HA 7 1 **7 1**
2011-12 *Sheffield U* 12 2 **12 2**
2011-12 *Rotherham U* 0 0 **73 23**

KASIM, Yaser (M) 1 0
H: 5 11 W: 11 07 b.Bagdad 10-5-91
Source: Tottenham H Scholar.
2010-11 Brighton & HA 1 0
2011-12 Brighton & HA 0 0 **1 0**

LUALUA, Kazenga (F) 61 5
H: 5 11 W: 12 00 b.Kinshasa 10-12-90
Source: Scholar.
2007-08 Newcastle U 2 0
2008-09 Newcastle U 3 0
2008-09 *Doncaster R* 4 0 **4 0**
2009-10 Newcastle U 1 0
2009-10 *Brighton & HA* 11 0
2010-11 Newcastle U 2 0
2010-11 *Brighton & HA* 11 4
2011-12 Newcastle U 0 0 **8 0**
2011-12 Brighton & HA 27 1 **49 5**

MACKAIL-SMITH, Craig (F) 230 89
H: 6 3 W: 12 04 b.Watford 25-2-84
Source: Dagenham & R. *Honours:* Scotland 7 full caps, 1 goal.
2006-07 Peterborough U 15 8
2007-08 Peterborough U 36 12
2008-09 Peterborough U 46 23
2009-10 Peterborough U 43 10
2010-11 Peterborough U 45 27 **185 80**
2011-12 Brighton & HA 45 9 **45 9**

NAVARRO, Alan (M) 283 10
H: 5 10 W: 11 07 b.Liverpool 31-5-81
Source: Trainee.
1998-99 Liverpool 0 0
1999-2000 Liverpool 0 0
2000-01 Liverpool 0 0
2000-01 *Crewe Alex* 8 1
2001-02 Liverpool 0 0
2001-02 *Crewe Alex* 7 0 **15 1**
2001-02 Tranmere R 21 1
2002-03 Tranmere R 5 0
2003-04 Tranmere R 19 0
2004-05 Tranmere R 0 0
2004-05 *Chester C* 3 0 **3 0**
2004-05 *Macclesfield T* 11 1
2005-06 Tranmere R 0 0 **45 1**
From Accrington S.
2005-06 Macclesfield T 27 0
2006-07 Macclesfield T 32 2 **70 3**
2007-08 Milton Keynes D 39 3
2008-09 Milton Keynes D 38 1 **77 4**
2009-10 Brighton & HA 36 0
2010-11 Brighton & HA 4 0
2011-12 Brighton & HA 33 1 **73 1**

NOONE, Craig (M) 118 11
H: 6 3 W: 12 07 b.Kirkby 17-11-87
Source: Skelmersdale U, Burscough, Southport.
2008-09 Plymouth Arg 21 1
2009-10 Plymouth Arg 17 1
2009-10 *Exeter C* 7 2 **7 2**
2010-11 Plymouth Arg 17 3 **55 5**
2010-11 Brighton & HA 23 2
2011-12 Brighton & HA 33 2 **56 4**

PAINTER, Marcos (D) 158 1
H: 5 11 W: 12 04 b.Solihull 17-8-86
Source: Scholar. *Honours:* Eire Youth, Under-21.
2005-06 Birmingham C 4 0
2006-07 Birmingham C 1 0 **5 0**
2006-07 Swansea C 23 0
2007-08 Swansea C 30 0
2008-09 Swansea C 11 0
2009-10 Swansea C 4 0 **68 0**
2009-10 *Brighton & HA* 19 0
2010-11 Brighton & HA 46 1
2011-12 Brighton & HA 20 0 **85 1**

POKE, Michael (G) 41 0
H: 6 1 W: 13 12 b.Staines 21-11-85
Source: Trainee.
2003-04 Southampton 0 0
2004-05 Southampton 0 0
2005-06 Southampton 0 0
2005-06 *Oldham Ath* 0 0
2005-06 *Northampton T* 0 0
2006-07 Southampton 0 0
2007-08 Southampton 4 0
2008-09 Southampton 0 0
2009-10 Southampton 0 0 **4 0**
2009-10 *Torquay U* 29 0 **29 0**
2010-11 Brighton & HA 0 0
2011-12 Brighton & HA 0 0
2011-12 *Bristol R* 8 0 **8 0**

REDWOOD, Leon (M) 0 0
b. 23-9-91
Source: Scholar.
2010-11 Brighton & HA 0 0
2011-12 Brighton & HA 0 0

RODGERS, Anton (M) 0 0
b.Reading 26-1-93
Source: Chelsea Scholar.
2011-12 Brighton & HA 0 0

SAMPAYO, Ben (D) 0 0
b.Dagenham 10-12-92
Source: Chelsea Scholar.
2011-12 Brighton & HA 0 0

SANDAZA, Fran (F) 53 13
H: 6 2 W: 12 08 b.Toledo 30-11-84
Source: Toledo, Valencia, Onda, Puzol.
2008-09 Dundee U 31 10
2009-10 Dundee U 7 1 **38 11**
2010-11 Brighton & HA 15 2
2011-12 Brighton & HA 0 0 **15 2**

SIMMONDS, Ryan (M) 0 0
b.Sutton Coldfield 30-10-91
Source: Aston Villa Schools.
2010-11 Brighton & HA 0 0
2011-12 Brighton & HA 0 0

SPARROW, Matt (M) 383 43
H: 5 11 W: 10 06 b.Wembley 3-10-81
Source: Scholar.
1999-2000 Scunthorpe U 11 0
2000-01 Scunthorpe U 11 4
2001-02 Scunthorpe U 24 1
2002-03 Scunthorpe U 42 9
2003-04 Scunthorpe U 38 3
2004-05 Scunthorpe U 44 5
2005-06 Scunthorpe U 39 5
2006-07 Scunthorpe U 29 4
2007-08 Scunthorpe U 32 1
2008-09 Scunthorpe U 36 4
2009-10 Scunthorpe U 30 1 **336 37**
2010-11 Brighton & HA 29 4
2011-12 Brighton & HA 18 2 **47 6**

STRONG, Jamie (D) 0 0
b.Worthing 10-9-92
Source: Scholar.
2011-12 Brighton & HA 0 0

TARICCO, Mauricio (D) 304 6
H: 5 8 W: 11 07 b.Buenos Aires 10-3-73
Honours: Argentina Under-23.
1993-94 Argentinos Juniors 21 0 **21 0**
1994-95 Ipswich T 0 0
1995-96 Ipswich T 39 0
1996-97 Ipswich T 41 3
1997-98 Ipswich T 41 0
1998-99 Ipswich T 16 1 **137 4**
1998-99 Tottenham H 13 0
1999-2000 Tottenham H 29 0
2000-01 Tottenham H 5 0
2001-02 Tottenham H 30 0
2002-03 Tottenham H 21 1
2003-04 Tottenham H 32 1
2004-05 Tottenham H 0 0 **130 2**
2004-05 West Ham U 1 0
2005-06 West Ham U 0 0
2006-07 West Ham U 0 0
2007-08 West Ham U 0 0
2008-09 West Ham U 0 0 **1 0**
2010-11 Brighton & HA 4 0
2011-12 Brighton & HA 11 0 **15 0**

VICENTE, Rodriguez (M) 313 48
H: 5 9 W: 11 05 b.Valencia 16-7-81
Honours: Spain Youth, Under-21, 38 full caps, 3 goals.
1997-98 Levante 3 1
1998-99 Levante 16 1
1999-2000 Levante 35 7 **54 9**
2000-01 Valencia 33 5
2001-02 Valencia 31 1
2002-03 Valencia 28 1
2003-04 Valencia 33 12
2004-05 Valencia 12 3
2005-06 Valencia 21 3
2006-07 Valencia 16 4
2007-08 Valencia 17 0
2008-09 Valencia 27 6
2009-10 Valencia 11 0
2010-11 Valencia 13 1 **242 36**
2011-12 Brighton & HA 17 3 **17 3**

VINCELOT, Romain (M) 136 15
H: 5 9 W: 11 02 b.Poitiers 29-10-85
2004-05 Chamois Niortais 3 0 **3 0**
2005-06 Chemois Niortais 28 1
2006-07 Chemois Niortais 9 0
2007-08 Chemois Niortais 6 0 **43 1**
2008-09 Gueugnon 20 0 **20 0**
2009-10 Dagenham & R 9 1
2010-11 Dagenham & R 46 12 **55 13**
2011-12 Brighton & HA 15 1 **15 1**

WALKER, Mitch (G) 1 0
H: 6 2 W: 13 00 b.St Albans 24-9-91
Source: Scholar.
2009-10 Brighton & HA 1 0
2010-11 Brighton & HA 0 0
2011-12 Brighton & HA 0 0 **1 0**

BRISTOL C (16)

ADOMAH, Albert (F) 203 29
H: 6 1 W: 11 08 b.Lambeth 13-12-87
Source: Harrow Borough. *Honours:* Ghana 2 full caps.
2007-08 Barnet 22 5
2008-09 Barnet 45 9
2009-10 Barnet 45 5 **112 19**
2010-11 Bristol C 46 5
2011-12 Bristol C 45 5 **91 10**

ANDREWS, Zac (D) 0 0
b.Bristol
Source: Scholar.
2011-12 Bristol C 0 0

BOLASIE, Yannick (M) 116 14
H: 6 2 W: 13 02 b.DR Congo 24-5-89
2008-09 Plymouth Arg 0 0
2008-09 *Barnet* 20 3
2009-10 Plymouth Arg 16 1
2009-10 *Barnet* 22 2 **42 5**
2010-11 Plymouth Arg 35 7 **51 8**
2011-12 Bristol C 23 1 **23 1**

BRYAN, Joe (D) 1 0
H: 5 7 W: 11 05 b.Bristol 17-9-93
Source: Scholar.
2011-12 Bristol C 1 0 **1 0**

CAMPBELL-RYCE, Jamal (M) 291 19
H: 5 7 W: 12 03 b.Lambeth 6-4-83
Source: Scholar. *Honours:* Jamaica 20 full caps.
2002-03 Charlton Ath 1 0
2002-03 *Leyton Orient* 17 2
2003-04 Charlton Ath 2 0
2003-04 *Wimbledon* 4 0 **4 0**
2004-05 Charlton Ath 0 0 **3 0**
2004-05 *Chesterfield* 14 0 **14 0**
2004-05 Rotherham U 24 0
2005-06 Rotherham U 7 0 **31 0**
2005-06 *Southend U* 13 0
2005-06 *Colchester U* 4 0 **4 0**
2006-07 Southend U 43 2
2007-08 Southend U 2 0 **58 2**
2007-08 Barnsley 37 3
2008-09 Barnsley 40 9
2009-10 Barnsley 13 0 **90 12**
2009-10 Bristol C 14 0
2010-11 Bristol C 31 2
2011-12 Bristol C 17 0 **62 2**
2011-12 *Leyton Orient* 8 1 **25 3**

CAREY, Lewis (G) 0 0
b.Tunbridge Wells 2-6-93
Source: Scholar.
2011-12 Bristol C 0 0

CAREY, Louis (D) 564 12
H: 5 10 W: 11 00 b.Bristol 20-1-77
Source: Trainee. *Honours:* Scotland Under-21.
1995-96 Bristol C 23 0

1996-97 Bristol C 42 0
1997-98 Bristol C 38 0
1998-99 Bristol C 41 0
1999-2000 Bristol C 22 0
2000-01 Bristol C 46 3
2001-02 Bristol C 35 0
2002-03 Bristol C 24 1
2003-04 Bristol C 41 1
2004-05 Coventry C 23 0 **23 0**
2004-05 Bristol C 14 0
2005-06 Bristol C 38 3
2006-07 Bristol C 38 2
2007-08 Bristol C 33 0
2008-09 Bristol C 28 0
2009-10 Bristol C 37 2
2010-11 Bristol C 21 0
2011-12 Bristol C 20 0 **541 12**

CISSE, Kalifa (M) 184 9
H: 6 2 W: 12 11 b.Dreux 1-9-84
Source: Toulouse. *Honours:* Mali 5 full caps.
2004-05 Estoril 6 0 **6 0**
2005-06 Boavista 15 0
2006-07 Boavista 27 0 **42 0**
2007-08 Reading 22 1
2008-09 Reading 36 5
2009-10 Reading 17 1 **75 7**
2010-11 Bristol C 29 0
2011-12 Bristol C 32 2 **61 2**

CLARKSON, David (F) 289 61
H: 5 10 W: 10 03 b.Airdrie 10-9-85
Honours: Scotland Under 21, B, 2 full caps, 1 goal.
2002-03 Motherwell 19 3
2003-04 Motherwell 38 12
2004-05 Motherwell 35 3
2005-06 Motherwell 32 4
2006-07 Motherwell 29 2
2007-08 Motherwell 35 12
2008-09 Motherwell 33 13 **221 49**
2009-10 Bristol C 26 4
2010-11 Bristol C 34 7
2011-12 Bristol C 4 0 **64 11**
2011-12 *Brentford* 4 1 **4 1**

EDWARDS, Joe (D) 8 1
H: 5 8 W: 11 07 b.Gloucester 31-10-90
Source: Scholar.
2009-10 Bristol C 0 0
2010-11 Bristol C 2 0
2011-12 Bristol C 2 0 **4 0**
2011-12 *Yeovil T* 4 1 **4 1**

ELLIOTT, Marvin (M) 330 22
H: 6 0 W: 12 02 b.Wandsworth 15-9-84
Source: Scholar. *Honours:* Jamaica 1 full cap.
2001-02 Millwall 0 0
2002-03 Millwall 1 0
2003-04 Millwall 21 0
2004-05 Millwall 41 1
2005-06 Millwall 39 2
2006-07 Millwall 42 0 **144 3**
2007-08 Bristol C 45 5
2008-09 Bristol C 28 3
2009-10 Bristol C 39 1
2010-11 Bristol C 46 8
2011-12 Bristol C 28 2 **186 19**

FONTAINE, Liam (D) 244 5
H: 5 11 W: 11 09 b.Beckenham 7-1-86
Source: Trainee. *Honours:* England Youth, Under-20.
2003-04 Fulham 0 0
2004-05 Fulham 1 0
2004-05 *Yeovil T* 15 0
2005-06 Fulham 0 0 **1 0**
2005-06 *Yeovil T* 10 0 **25 0**
2005-06 *Bristol C* 15 0
2006-07 Bristol C 30 0
2007-08 Bristol C 38 1
2008-09 Bristol C 42 2
2009-10 Bristol C 36 2
2010-11 Bristol C 31 0
2011-12 Bristol C 26 0 **218 5**

FOSTER, Ricky (D) 269 8
H: 5 9 W: 12 00 b.Aberdeen 31-7-85
Honours: Scotland Under-21.
2002-03 Aberdeen 2 0
2003-04 Aberdeen 18 1
2004-05 Aberdeen 25 1
2005-06 Aberdeen 25 1
2006-07 Aberdeen 37 3
2007-08 Aberdeen 33 1
2008-09 Aberdeen 34 0
2009-10 Aberdeen 37 0
2010-11 Aberdeen 1 0
2010-11 *Rangers* 15 0 **15 0**
2011-12 Aberdeen 22 1 **234 8**
2011-12 Bristol C 20 0 **20 0**

GERKEN, Dean (G) 166 0
H: 6 3 W: 12 08 b.Southend 22-5-85
Source: Scholar.
2003-04 Colchester U 1 0
2004-05 Colchester U 13 0
2005-06 Colchester U 7 0
2006-07 Colchester U 27 0
2007-08 Colchester U 40 0
2008-09 Colchester U 21 0 **109 0**
2008-09 *Darlington* 7 0 **7 0**
2009-10 Bristol C 39 0
2010-11 Bristol C 1 0
2011-12 Bristol C 10 0 **50 0**

HOLLOWAY, Aaron (M) 0 0
H: 6 2 W: 13 01 b.Cardiff 21-2-93
Source: Scholar. *Honours:* Wales Youth.
2011-12 Bristol C 0 0

JACKSON, Marlon (F) 47 2
H: 5 11 W: 11 12 b.Bristol 6-12-90
Source: Scholar.
2009-10 Bristol C 0 0
2009-10 *Hereford U* 5 0 **5 0**
2009-10 *Aldershot T* 22 1
2010-11 Bristol C 4 0
2010-11 *Aldershot T* 9 0 **31 1**
2011-12 Bristol C 0 0 **4 0**
2011-12 *Northampton T* 6 1 **6 1**
2011-12 *Cheltenham T* 1 0 **1 0**

JAMES, David (G) 769 0
H: 6 5 W: 15 07 b.Welwyn 1-8-70
Source: Trainee. *Honours:* England Youth, Under-21, B, 53 full caps.
1988-89 Watford 0 0
1989-90 Watford 0 0
1990-91 Watford 46 0
1991-92 Watford 43 0 **89 0**
1992-93 Liverpool 29 0
1993-94 Liverpool 14 0
1994-95 Liverpool 42 0
1995-96 Liverpool 38 0
1996-97 Liverpool 38 0
1997-98 Liverpool 27 0
1998-99 Liverpool 26 0 **214 0**
1999-2000 Aston Villa 29 0
2000-01 Aston Villa 38 0 **67 0**
2001-02 West Ham U 26 0
2002-03 West Ham U 38 0
2003-04 West Ham U 27 0 **91 0**
2003-04 Manchester C 17 0
2004-05 Manchester C 38 0
2005-06 Manchester C 38 0 **93 0**
2006-07 Portsmouth 38 0
2007-08 Portsmouth 35 0
2008-09 Portsmouth 36 0
2009-10 Portsmouth 25 0 **134 0**
2010-11 Bristol C 45 0
2011-12 Bristol C 36 0 **81 0**

JOHNSON, Lee (M) 308 25
H: 5 6 W: 10 07 b.Newmarket 7-6-81
Source: Trainee.
1998-99 Watford 0 0
1999-2000 Watford 0 0
2000-01 Brighton & HA 0 0
2000-01 Brentford 0 0
2001-02 Brentford 0 0
2003-04 Yeovil T 45 5
2004-05 Yeovil T 44 7
2005-06 Yeovil T 26 2 **115 14**
2005-06 Hearts 4 0 **4 0**
2006-07 Bristol C 42 5
2007-08 Bristol C 40 1
2008-09 Bristol C 44 3
2009-10 Bristol C 28 1
2009-10 *Derby Co* 4 0 **4 0**
2010-11 Bristol C 20 1
2011-12 Bristol C 0 0 **174 11**
2011-12 *Chesterfield* 11 0 **11 0**
Transferred to Kilmarnock February 2012.

KILKENNY, Neil (M) 232 14
H: 5 8 W: 10 08 b.Enfield 19-12-85
Source: Arsenal Trainee. *Honours:* England Youth, Under-20, Australia Under-23, 14 full caps.
2003-04 Birmingham C 0 0
2004-05 Birmingham C 0 0
2004-05 *Oldham Ath* 27 4
2005-06 Birmingham C 18 0
2006-07 Birmingham C 8 0
2007-08 Birmingham C 0 0 **26 0**
2007-08 *Oldham Ath* 20 1 **47 5**
2007-08 Leeds U 16 1
2008-09 Leeds U 30 4
2009-10 Leeds U 35 2
2010-11 Leeds U 37 1 **118 8**
2011-12 Bristol C 41 1 **41 1**

McALLISTER, Jamie (D) 438 4
H: 5 10 W: 11 00 b.Glasgow 26-4-78
Honours: Scotland 1 full cap.
1995-96 Q of S 2 0
1996-97 Q of S 6 0
1997-98 Q of S 15 0
1998-99 Q of S 27 0 **50 0**
1999-2000 Aberdeen 34 0
2000-01 Aberdeen 25 0
2001-02 Aberdeen 29 0
2002-03 Aberdeen 29 0 **117 0**
2003-04 Livingston 34 1 **34 1**
2004-05 Hearts 30 0
2005-06 Hearts 17 0 **47 0**
2006-07 Bristol C 31 1
2007-08 Bristol C 41 0
2008-09 Bristol C 35 1
2009-10 Bristol C 33 0
2010-11 Bristol C 34 1
2011-12 Bristol C 12 0 **186 3**
2011-12 *Preston NE* 4 0 **4 0**

MUGGERIDGE, Henry (D) 0 0
b.Tunbridge Wells 22-7-93
Source: Scholar.
2011-12 Bristol C 0 0

NYATANGA, Lewin (D) 214 8
H: 6 2 W: 12 08 b.Burton 18-8-88
Source: Scholar. *Honours:* Wales Under-21, 34 full caps.
2005-06 Derby Co 24 1
2006-07 Derby Co 7 1
2006-07 *Sunderland* 11 0 **11 0**
2006-07 *Barnsley* 10 1
2007-08 Derby Co 2 1
2007-08 *Barnsley* 41 1 **51 2**
2008-09 Derby Co 30 1 **63 4**
2009-10 Bristol C 37 1
2010-11 Bristol C 20 1
2010-11 *Peterborough U* 3 0 **3 0**
2011-12 Bristol C 29 0 **86 2**

PEARSON, Stephen (M) 280 24
H: 6 0 W: 11 01 b.Lanark 2-10-82
Honours: Scotland Under-21, B, 10 full caps.
2000-01 Motherwell 6 0
2001-02 Motherwell 27 2
2002-03 Motherwell 29 6
2003-04 Motherwell 18 4 **80 12**
2003-04 Celtic 17 3
2004-05 Celtic 8 0
2005-06 Celtic 18 2
2006-07 Celtic 13 1 **56 6**
2006-07 Derby Co 9 0
2007-08 Derby Co 24 0
2007-08 *Stoke C* 4 0 **4 0**
2008-09 Derby Co 12 1
2009-10 Derby Co 37 1
2010-11 Derby Co 30 1
2011-12 Derby Co 0 0 **112 3**
2011-12 Bristol C 28 3 **28 3**

PITMAN, Brett (F) 248 78
H: 6 0 W: 11 00 b.Jersey 31-1-88
Source: St Pauls (Jersey).
2005-06 Bournemouth 19 1
2006-07 Bournemouth 29 5
2007-08 Bournemouth 39 6
2008-09 Bournemouth 39 17
2009-10 Bournemouth 46 26
2010-11 Bournemouth 2 3 **174 58**
2010-11 Bristol C 39 13
2011-12 Bristol C 35 7 **74 20**

REID, Bobby (M) 2 0
H: 5 7 W: 10 10 b.Bristol 1-3-93
Source: Scholar.
2010-11 Bristol C 1 0
2011-12 Bristol C 0 0 **1 0**
2011-12 *Cheltenham T* 1 0 **1 0**

RIBEIRO, Christian (D) 38 0
H: 5 11 W: 12 02 b.Neath 14-12-89
Source: Scholar. *Honours:* Wales Youth, Under-21, 2 full caps.
2006-07 Bristol C 0 0
2007-08 Bristol C 0 0
2008-09 Bristol C 0 0
2009-10 Bristol C 5 0
2009-10 *Stockport Co* 7 0 **7 0**
2009-10 *Colchester U* 2 0 **2 0**
2010-11 Bristol C 9 0
2011-12 Bristol C 0 0 **14 0**
2011-12 *Carlisle U* 5 0 **5 0**
2011-12 *Scunthorpe U* 10 0 **10 0**

SKUSE, Cole (M) 254 9
H: 6 1 W: 11 05 b.Bristol 29-3-86
Source: Scholar.
2004-05 Bristol C 7 0
2005-06 Bristol C 38 2
2006-07 Bristol C 42 0
2007-08 Bristol C 25 0
2008-09 Bristol C 33 2
2009-10 Bristol C 43 2
2010-11 Bristol C 30 1
2011-12 Bristol C 36 2 **254 9**

STEAD, Jon (F) 326 79
H: 6 3 W: 13 03 b.Huddersfield 7-4-83
Source: Scholar. *Honours:* England Under-21.
2001-02 Huddersfield T 0 0
2002-03 Huddersfield T 42 6
2003-04 Huddersfield T 26 16 **68 22**
2003-04 Blackburn R 13 6
2004-05 Blackburn R 29 2 **42 8**
2005-06 Sunderland 30 1
2006-07 Sunderland 5 1 **35 2**
2006-07 *Derby Co* 17 3 **17 3**
2006-07 Sheffield U 14 5
2007-08 Sheffield U 24 3
2008-09 Sheffield U 1 0 **39 8**
2008-09 Ipswich T 39 12
2009-10 Ipswich T 22 6
2009-10 *Coventry C* 10 2 **10 2**
2010-11 Ipswich T 3 1 **64 19**
2010-11 Bristol C 27 9
2011-12 Bristol C 24 6 **51 15**

STEWART, Damion (D) 215 13
H: 6 3 W: 13 10 b.Jamaica 18-8-80
Source: Harbour View. *Honours:* Jamaica 56 full caps, 3 goals.
2005-06 Bradford C 23 1 **23 1**
2006-07 QPR 45 1
2007-08 QPR 39 5
2008-09 QPR 37 2
2009-10 QPR 30 1 **151 9**
2010-11 Bristol C 21 1
2011-12 Bristol C 3 0 **24 1**
2011-12 *Notts Co* 17 2 **17 2**

TAYLOR, Ryan (F) 146 22
H: 6 2 W: 10 10 b.Rotherham 4-5-88
Source: Scholar.
2005-06 Rotherham U 1 0
2006-07 Rotherham U 10 0
2007-08 Rotherham U 35 6
2008-09 Rotherham U 33 4
2009-10 Rotherham U 19 0
2009-10 *Exeter C* 7 0 **7 0**
2010-11 Rotherham U 34 11 **132 21**
2011-12 Bristol C 7 1 **7 1**

WILSON, James (D) 52 0
H: 6 2 W: 11 05 b.Chepstow 26-2-89
Source: Scholar. *Honours:* Wales Youth, Under-21.
2005-06 Bristol C 0 0
2006-07 Bristol C 0 0
2007-08 Bristol C 0 0
2008-09 Bristol C 2 0
2008-09 *Brentford* 14 0
2009-10 Bristol C 0 0
2009-10 *Brentford* 13 0 **27 0**
2010-11 Bristol C 2 0
2011-12 Bristol C 21 0 **25 0**

WOOLFORD, Martyn (M) 143 16
H: 6 0 W: 11 09 b.Castleford 13-10-85
Source: Glasshoughton W, Frickley Ath, York C.
2008-09 Scunthorpe U 39 4
2009-10 Scunthorpe U 40 5
2010-11 Scunthorpe U 24 6 **103 15**
2010-11 Bristol C 15 0
2011-12 Bristol C 25 1 **40 1**

BRISTOL R (17)

ANTHONY, Byron (D) 178 8
H: 6 1 W: 11 02 b.Newport 20-9-84
Source: Scholar. *Honours:* Wales Youth, Under-21.
2003-04 Cardiff C 0 0
2004-05 Cardiff C 0 0
2005-06 Cardiff C 0 0
2006-07 Bristol R 23 0
2007-08 Bristol R 20 1
2008-09 Bristol R 30 2
2009-10 Bristol R 37 0
2010-11 Bristol R 37 3
2011-12 Bristol R 16 1 **163 7**
2011-12 *Hereford U* 15 1 **15 1**

ANYINSAH, Joe (M) 144 23
H: 5 8 W: 11 00 b.Bristol 8-10-84
Source: Scholar.
2001-02 Bristol C 0 0
2002-03 Bristol C 0 0
2003-04 Bristol C 0 0
2004-05 Bristol C 7 0 **7 0**
2005-06 Preston NE 3 0
2005-06 *Bury* 3 0 **3 0**
2006-07 Preston NE 3 0
2007-08 Preston NE 0 0
2007-08 *Carlisle U* 12 3
2007-08 *Crewe Alex* 8 0 **8 0**
2008-09 Preston NE 0 0 **6 0**
2008-09 *Brighton & HA* 11 0 **11 0**
2008-09 Carlisle U 19 4
2009-10 Carlisle U 28 9
2010-11 Carlisle U 0 0 **59 16**
2010-11 Charlton Ath 19 3 **19 3**
2011-12 Bristol R 31 4 **31 4**

BEVAN, Scott (G) 149 0
H: 6 6 W: 15 10 b.Southampton 16-9-79
Source: Trainee.
1997-98 Southampton 0 0
1998-99 Southampton 0 0
1999 *Ayr U* 0 0
1999-2000 Southampton 0 0
2000-01 Southampton 0 0
2001-02 Southampton 0 0
2001-02 *Stoke C* 0 0
2002-03 Southampton 0 0
2002-03 *Huddersfield T* 30 0 **30 0**
2003-04 Southampton 0 0
2003-04 *Wycombe W* 5 0 **5 0**
2003-04 Wimbledon 10 0 **10 0**
2004-05 Milton Keynes D 7 0
2005-06 Milton Keynes D 0 0 **7 0**
From Kidderminster H.
2007-08 Shrewsbury T 5 0 **5 0**
2009-10 Torquay U 18 0
2010-11 Torquay U 37 0 **55 0**
2011-12 Bristol R 37 0 **37 0**

BOATENG, Michael (D) 0 0
b.Peckham 17-8-91
Source: Carshalton Ath.
2011-12 Bristol R 0 0

BROWN, Lee (M) 43 7
H: 6 0 W: 12 06 b.Bromley 10-8-90
Source: Scholar.
2008-09 QPR 0 0
2009-10 QPR 1 0
2010-11 QPR 0 0 **1 0**
2011-12 Bristol R 42 7 **42 7**

BROWN, Wayne (M) 78 13
H: 5 9 W: 12 05 b.Kingston 6-8-88
Source: Scholar.
2006-07 Fulham 0 0
2007-08 Fulham 0 0
2007-08 *Brentford* 11 1 **11 1**
2008-09 Fulham 1 0
2009 *TPS Turku* 25 9 **25 9**
2009-10 Fulham 0 0 **1 0**
2009-10 *Bristol R* 4 0
2010-11 Bristol R 25 3
2011-12 Bristol R 12 0 **41 3**

CAMPBELL, Stuart (M) 482 14
H: 5 10 W: 10 08 b.Corby 9-12-77
Source: Trainee. *Honours:* Scotland Under-21.
1996-97 Leicester C 10 0
1997-98 Leicester C 11 0
1998-99 Leicester C 12 0
1999-2000 Leicester C 4 0
1999-2000 *Birmingham C* 2 0 **2 0**
2000-01 Leicester C 0 0 **37 0**
2000-01 *Grimsby T* 38 2
2001-02 Grimsby T 33 3
2002-03 Grimsby T 45 6
2003-04 Grimsby T 39 1 **155 12**
2004-05 Bristol R 25 0
2005-06 Bristol R 38 1
2006-07 Bristol R 41 1
2007-08 Bristol R 46 0
2008-09 Bristol R 44 0
2009-10 Bristol R 46 0
2010-11 Bristol R 37 0
2011-12 Bristol R 11 0 **288 2**
Transferred to Tampa Bay Rowdies December 2011.

CARAYOL, Mustapha (F) 83 13
H: 5 10 W: 11 11 b.Gambia 10-6-89
Source: Scholar.
2007-08 Milton Keynes D 0 0
2009-10 Torquay U 20 6 **20 6**
2010-11 Lincoln C 33 3 **33 3**
2011-12 Bristol R 30 4 **30 4**

CLARKE, Ollie (M) 1 0
H: 5 11 W: 11 11 b.Bristol 29-6-92
2009-10 Bristol R 0 0
2010-11 Bristol R 1 0
2011-12 Bristol R 0 0 **1 0**

CLOUGH, Charlie (M) 2 0
H: 6 2 W: 12 08 b.Taunton 4-9-90
Source: Scholar. *Honours:* Wales Youth.
2010-11 Bristol R 2 0
2011-12 Bristol R 0 0 **2 0**

CRONIN, Lance (G) 9 0
H: 6 1 W: 12 00 b.Brighton 11-9-85
Source: Scholar. *Honours:* England Youth.
2002-03 Crystal Palace 0 0
2003-04 Crystal Palace 0 0
2004-05 Crystal Palace 0 0
2004-05 *Wycombe W* 1 0 **1 0**
2005-06 Crystal Palace 0 0
2005-06 Oldham Ath 0 0
From Ebbsfleet U.
2010-11 Gillingham 7 0 **7 0**
From Ebbsfleet U.
2011-12 Bristol R 1 0 **1 0**

GILL, Matthew (M) 308 16
H: 5 11 W: 11 10 b.Cambridge 8-11-80
Source: Trainee.
1997-98 Peterborough U 2 0
1998-99 Peterborough U 26 0
1999-2000 Peterborough U 20 1
2000-01 Peterborough U 17 1
2001-02 Peterborough U 12 2
2002-03 Peterborough U 41 1
2003-04 Peterborough U 33 0
2004-05 Notts Co 43 0
2005-06 Notts Co 14 0 **57 0**
2008-09 Exeter C 43 9 **43 9**
2009-10 Norwich C 8 0
2010-11 Norwich C 4 0 **12 0**
2010-11 *Peterborough U* 4 0 **155 5**
2010-11 *Walsall* 8 2 **8 2**
2011-12 Bristol R 33 0 **33 0**

GODDARD, Jordan (M) 0 0
b.Wolverhampton 9-9-93
Source: Scholar.
2011-12 Bristol R 0 0

HARDING, Mitch (F) 1 0
b.Weston-Super-Mare 27-1-94
Source: Scholar.
2011-12 Bristol R 1 0 **1 0**

HARRISON, Ellis (F) 1 0
b.Newport 1-2-94
Source: Scholar.
2010-11 Bristol R 1 0
2011-12 Bristol R 0 0 **1 0**

HARROLD, Matt (F) **291 57**
H: 6 1 W: 11 10 b.Leyton 25-7-84
Source: Harlow T.

2003-04	Brentford	13	2		
2004-05	Brentford	19	0	**32**	**2**
2004-05	*Grimsby T*	6	2	**6**	**2**
2005-06	Yeovil T	42	9		
2006-07	Yeovil T	5	0	**47**	**9**
2006-07	Southend U	36	3		
2007-08	Southend U	16	0		
2008-09	Southend U	0	0	**52**	**3**
2008-09	Wycombe W	37	9		
2009-10	Wycombe W	36	8	**73**	**17**
2010-11	Shrewsbury T	41	8	**41**	**8**
2011-12	Bristol R	40	16	**40**	**16**

JEFFERIES, Darren (M) **0 0**
H: 6 0 W: 11 09 b.Swindon 25-10-93
Source: Scholar.

2010-11	Bristol R	0	0		
2011-12	Bristol R	0	0		

McGLEISH, Scott (F) **692 208**
H: 5 9 W: 11 09 b.Barnet 10-2-74
Source: Edgware T.

1994-95	Charlton Ath	6	0	**6**	**0**
1994-95	*Leyton Orient*	6	1		
1995-96	Peterborough U	12	0		
1995-96	*Colchester U*	15	6		
1996-97	Peterborough U	1	0	**13**	**0**
1996-97	*Cambridge U*	10	7	**10**	**7**
1996-97	Leyton Orient	28	7		
1997-98	Leyton Orient	8	0		
1997-98	Barnet	37	13		
1998-99	Barnet	36	8		
1999-2000	Barnet	42	10		
2000-01	Barnet	19	5		
2000-01	Colchester U	21	5		
2001-02	Colchester U	46	15		
2002-03	Colchester U	43	8		
2003-04	Colchester U	34	10	**159**	**44**
2004-05	Northampton T	44	13		
2005-06	Northampton T	42	17		
2006-07	Northampton T	25	12		
2006-07	Wycombe W	14	5		
2007-08	Wycombe W	46	25		
2008-09	Wycombe W	15	3	**75**	**33**
2008-09	*Northampton T*	9	1	**120**	**43**
2008-09	*Leyton Orient*	16	6		
2009-10	Leyton Orient	42	12		
2010-11	Leyton Orient	39	12	**139**	**38**
2011-12	Bristol R	27	7	**27**	**7**
2011-12	*Barnet*	9	0	**143**	**36**

McLAGGON, Kane (F) **8 1**
H: 6 2 W: 12 05 b.Barry 21-9-90
Source: Scholar. *Honours:* Wales Youth.

2007-08	Southampton	0	0		
2008-09	Southampton	7	1		
2009-10	Southampton	0	0	**7**	**1**
From Salisbury C.					
2011-12	Bristol R	1	0	**1**	**0**

PATERSON, Jim (M) **310 12**
H: 5 11 W: 12 13 b.Airdrie 25-9-79
Source: Dundee U BC. *Honours:* Scotland Under-21.

1998-99	Dundee U	15	0		
1999-2000	Dundee U	8	1		
2000-01	Dundee U	6	1		
2001-02	Dundee U	27	2		
2002-03	Dundee U	33	1		
2003-04	Dundee U	16	0	**105**	**5**
2004-05	Motherwell	35	3		
2005-06	Motherwell	19	1		
2006-07	Motherwell	34	1		
2007-08	Motherwell	20	0	**108**	**5**
2007-08	Plymouth Arg	8	1		
2008-09	Plymouth Arg	17	0		
2009-10	Plymouth Arg	12	0		
2009-10	*Aberdeen*	7	0	**7**	**0**
2010-11	Plymouth Arg	28	0	**65**	**1**
2011	Shamrock R	8	0	**8**	**0**
2011-12	Bristol R	17	1	**17**	**1**

POWELL, Lamar (F) **1 0**
H: 5 7 W: 11 00 b.Bristol 3-9-93
Source: Scholar.

2010-11	Bristol R	1	0		
2011-12	Bristol R	0	0	**1**	**0**

REECE, Charlie (M) **30 0**
H: 5 11 W: 11 03 b.Birmingham 8-9-88
Source: Scholar.

2007-08	Bristol R	1	0		
2008-09	Bristol R	1	0		
2009-10	Bristol R	14	0		
2010-11	Bristol R	14	0		
2011-12	Bristol R	0	0	**30**	**0**

RICHARDS, Eliot (M) **50 8**
H: 5 9 W: 11 09 b.New Tredegar 1-9-91
Source: Scholar. *Honours:* Wales Youth.

2009-10	Bristol R	5	0		
2010-11	Bristol R	13	1		
2011-12	Bristol R	32	7	**50**	**8**

SAWYER, Gary (D) **158 5**
H: 6 0 W: 11 08 b.Bideford 5-7-85
Source: Scholar.

2004-05	Plymouth Arg	0	0		
2005-06	Plymouth Arg	0	0		
2006-07	Plymouth Arg	22	0		
2007-08	Plymouth Arg	31	1		
2008-09	Plymouth Arg	13	3		
2009-10	Plymouth Arg	29	1	**95**	**5**
2009-10	*Bristol C*	2	0	**2**	**0**
2010-11	Bristol R	37	0		
2011-12	Bristol R	24	0	**61**	**0**

SMITH, Michael (D) **195 16**
H: 5 11 W: 11 02 b.Ballyclare 4-9-88
Honours: Northern Ireland Under-23.

2005-06	Ballyclare Comrades	1	0		
2006-07	Ballyclare Comrades	25	2		
2007-08	Ballyclare Comrades	39	1		
2008-09	Ballyclare Comrades	27	7	**92**	**10**
2008-09	Ballymena U	12	1		
2009-10	Ballymena U	37	2		
2010-11	Ballymena U	34	3	**83**	**6**
2011-12	Bristol R	20	0	**20**	**0**

STANLEY, Craig (M) **200 16**
H: 5 8 W: 10 08 b.Bedworth 3-3-83
Source: Scholar.

2002-03	Walsall	0	0		
2003-04	Walsall	0	0		
2003-04	*Raith R*	20	1	**20**	**1**
From Hereford U.					
2007-08	Morecambe	41	2		
2008-09	Morecambe	24	5		
2009-10	Morecambe	40	4		
2010-11	Morecambe	22	2	**127**	**13**
2010-11	*Torquay U*	19	1	**19**	**1**
2011-12	Bristol R	34	1	**34**	**1**

VIRGO, Adam (D) **246 21**
H: 6 2 W: 13 12 b.Brighton 25-1-83
Source: Juniors. *Honours:* Scotland B.

2000-01	Brighton & HA	6	0		
2001-02	Brighton & HA	6	0		
2002-03	Brighton & HA	3	0		
2002-03	*Exeter C*	9	0	**9**	**0**
2003-04	Brighton & HA	22	1		
2004-05	Brighton & HA	36	8		
2005-06	Celtic	10	0		
2006-07	Celtic	0	0	**10**	**0**
2006-07	Coventry C	15	1		
2007-08	Coventry C	0	0	**15**	**1**
2007-08	Colchester U	36	1	**36**	**1**
2008-09	Brighton & HA	36	3		
2009-10	Brighton & HA	25	1	**134**	**13**
2010-11	Yeovil T	33	5	**33**	**5**
2011-12	Bristol R	9	1	**9**	**1**

WOODARDS, Danny (D) **189 2**
H: 5 11 W: 11 01 b.Forest Gate 7-10-83
Source: Trainee.

2003-04	Chelsea	0	0		
2004-05	Chelsea	0	0		
2005-06	Chelsea	0	0		
From Exeter C.					
2006-07	Crewe Alex	11	0		
2007-08	Crewe Alex	36	0		
2008-09	Crewe Alex	37	0	**84**	**0**
2009-10	Milton Keynes D	29	0		
2010-11	Milton Keynes D	37	1	**66**	**1**
2011-12	Bristol R	39	1	**39**	**1**

ZEBROSKI, Chris (F) **190 35**
H: 6 1 W: 11 08 b.Swindon 29-10-86
Source: Cirencester T, Scholar.

2005-06	Plymouth Arg	4	0		
2006-07	Plymouth Arg	0	0	**4**	**0**
2006-07	Millwall	25	3		
2007-08	Millwall	0	0	**25**	**3**
2008-09	Wycombe W	33	7		
2009-10	Wycombe W	15	2	**48**	**9**
2009-10	Torquay U	30	6		
2010-11	Torquay U	44	14	**74**	**20**
2011-12	Bristol R	39	3	**39**	**3**

BURNLEY (18)

ANDERSON, Tom (D) **0 0**
b.Burnley 2-9-93
Source: Scholar.

2011-12	Burnley	0	0		

AUSTIN, Charlie (F) **99 47**
H: 6 2 W: 13 03 b.Hungerford 5-7-89
Source: Poole T.

2009-10	Swindon T	33	19		
2010-11	Swindon T	21	12	**54**	**31**
2010-11	Burnley	4	0		
2011-12	Burnley	41	16	**45**	**16**

BARTLEY, Marvyn (M) **157 6**
H: 6 1 W: 12 04 b.Reading 4-7-86
Source: Hampton & Richmond B.

2007-08	Bournemouth	20	1		
2008-09	Bournemouth	33	1		
2009-10	Bournemouth	34	0		
2010-11	Bournemouth	26	1	**113**	**3**
2010-11	Burnley	5	0		
2011-12	Burnley	39	3	**44**	**3**

BIKEY, Andre (D) **166 10**
H: 6 0 W: 12 08 b.Douala 8-1-85
Source: Espanyol, Marco. *Honours:* Cameroon 25 full caps, 1 goal.

2003-04	Pacos de Ferreira	2	0	**2**	**0**
2004-05	Dep Aves	0	0		
2005	Shinnik	11	1	**11**	**1**
2005	Loko Moscow	9	0		
2006	Loko Moscow	5	0	**14**	**0**
2006-07	Reading	15	0		
2007-08	Reading	22	3		
2008-09	Reading	25	3		
2009-10	Reading	0	0	**62**	**6**
2009-10	Burnley	28	1		
2010-11	Burnley	28	2		
2011-12	Burnley	14	0	**70**	**3**
2011-12	*Bristol C*	7	0	**7**	**0**

CARLISLE, Clarke (D) **434 30**
H: 6 2 W: 14 11 b.Preston 14-10-79
Source: Trainee. *Honours:* England Under-21.

1997-98	Blackpool	11	2		
1998-99	Blackpool	39	1		
1999-2000	Blackpool	43	4	**93**	**7**
2000-01	QPR	27	3		
2001-02	QPR	0	0		
2002-03	QPR	36	2		
2003-04	QPR	33	1	**96**	**6**
2004-05	Leeds U	35	4	**35**	**4**
2005-06	Watford	32	3		
2006-07	Watford	4	0		
2006-07	*Luton T*	5	0	**5**	**0**
2007-08	Watford	0	0	**36**	**3**
2007-08	Burnley	33	2		
2008-09	Burnley	36	3		
2009-10	Burnley	27	0		
2010-11	Burnley	35	1		
2011-12	Burnley	0	0	**131**	**6**
2011-12	*Preston NE*	20	3	**20**	**3**
2011-12	*Northampton T*	18	1	**18**	**1**

COLEMAN, Alex (D) **0 0**
b.Bury 17-12-93
Source: Scholar.

2011-12	Burnley	0	0		

CONLAN, Luke (D) **0 0**
b.Portaferry 31-10-94
Source: Scholar.

2011-12	Burnley	0	0		

DUFF, Michael (D) **433 17**
H: 6 1 W: 11 08 b.Belfast 11-1-78
Source: Trainee. *Honours:* Northern Ireland 24 full caps.

1999-2000	Cheltenham T	31	2		
2000-01	Cheltenham T	39	5		
2001-02	Cheltenham T	45	3		
2002-03	Cheltenham T	44	2		
2003-04	Cheltenham T	42	0	**201**	**12**
2004-05	Burnley	42	0		
2005-06	Burnley	41	0		
2006-07	Burnley	44	2		
2007-08	Burnley	8	1		
2008-09	Burnley	27	1		

2009-10 Burnley 11 0
2010-11 Burnley 28 1
2011-12 Burnley 31 0 **232 5**

EASTON, Brian (D) 147 3
H: 6 0 W: 12 00 b.Glasgow 5-3-88
Honours: Scotland Under-21, B.
2006-07 Hamilton A 31 1
2007-08 Hamilton A 36 0
2008-09 Hamilton A 35 1
2009-10 Burnley 0 0
2009-10 *Hamilton A* 12 0 **114 2**
2010-11 Burnley 12 1
2011-12 Burnley 21 0 **33 1**

EDGAR, David (D) 79 5
H: 6 2 W: 12 13 b.Ontario 19-5-87
Source: Scholar. *Honours:* Canada Youth, Under-20, 10 full caps.
2005-06 Newcastle U 0 0
2006-07 Newcastle U 3 1
2007-08 Newcastle U 5 0
2008-09 Newcastle U 11 1
2009-10 Newcastle U 0 0 **19 2**
2009-10 Burnley 4 0
2009-10 *Swansea C* 5 1 **5 1**
2010-11 Burnley 7 0
2011-12 Burnley 44 2 **55 2**

ERRINGTON, Jack (D) 0 0
b.Wallsend 9-12-94
Source: Scholar.
2011-12 Burnley 0 0

EVANS, Adam (F) 0 0
b.Dublin 3-5-94
Source: Scholar.
2011-12 Burnley 0 0

FLETCHER, Wes (F) 31 5
H: 5 11 W: 12 06 b.Ormskirk 28-2-91
Source: Scholar.
2009-10 Burnley 0 0
2009-10 *Grimsby T* 6 1 **6 1**
2010-11 Burnley 0 0
2010-11 *Stockport Co* 9 1 **9 1**
2011-12 Burnley 0 0
2011-12 *Accrington S* 10 2 **10 2**
2011-12 *Crewe Alex* 6 1 **6 1**

GRANT, Lee (G) 295 0
H: 6 3 W: 13 01 b.Hemel Hempstead 27-1-83
Source: Scholar. *Honours:* England Youth, Under-21.
2000-01 Derby Co 0 0
2001-02 Derby Co 0 0
2002-03 Derby Co 29 0
2003-04 Derby Co 36 0
2004-05 Derby Co 2 0
2005-06 Derby Co 0 0
2005-06 *Burnley* 1 0
2005-06 *Oldham Ath* 16 0 **16 0**
2006-07 Derby Co 7 0 **74 0**
2007-08 Sheffield W 44 0
2008-09 Sheffield W 46 0
2009-10 Sheffield W 46 0 **136 0**
2010-11 Burnley 25 0
2011-12 Burnley 43 0 **69 0**

HARVEY, Alex-Ray (M) 0 0
H: 5 7 W: 10 09 b.Burnley 4-4-90
Source: Scholar.
2009-10 Burnley 0 0
2010-11 Burnley 0 0
2011-12 Burnley 0 0

HEWITT, Steven (M) 1 0
H: 5 7 W: 11 00 b.Manchester 5-12-93
Source: Scholar.
2011-12 Burnley 1 0 **1 0**

HINES, Zavon (F) 50 3
H: 5 10 W: 10 07 b.Jamaica 27-12-88
Source: Scholar. *Honours:* England Under-21.
2007-08 West Ham U 0 0
2007-08 *Coventry C* 7 1 **7 1**
2008-09 West Ham U 0 0
2009-10 West Ham U 13 1
2010-11 West Ham U 9 0 **22 1**
2011-12 Burnley 13 0 **13 0**
2011-12 *Bournemouth* 8 1 **8 1**

HOWIESON, Cameron (M) 2 0
H: 5 9 W: 11 00 b.Dunedin 22-12-94
Source: Scholar. *Honours:* New Zealand 2 full caps.
2011-12 Burnley 2 0 **2 0**

INGS, Danny (F) 42 10
H: 5 10 W: 11 07 b.Winchester 16-3-92
Source: Youth.
2009-10 Bournemouth 0 0
2010-11 Bournemouth 26 7
2011-12 Bournemouth 1 0 **27 7**
2011-12 Burnley 15 3 **15 3**

JACKSON, Joe (F) 1 0
H: 5 11 W: 10 07 b.Barrow 3-2-93
Source: Scholar.
2011-12 Burnley 1 0 **1 0**

JENSEN, Brian (G) 317 0
H: 6 1 W: 12 04 b.Copenhagen 8-6-75
Source: Hvidovre, B93.
1997-98 AZ 0 0
1998-99 AZ 1 0 **1 0**
1999-2000 WBA 12 0
2000-01 WBA 33 0
2001-02 WBA 1 0
2002-03 WBA 0 0 **46 0**
2003-04 Burnley 46 0
2004-05 Burnley 27 0
2005-06 Burnley 39 0
2006-07 Burnley 31 0
2007-08 Burnley 19 0
2008-09 Burnley 45 0
2009-10 Burnley 38 0
2010-11 Burnley 21 0
2011-12 Burnley 4 0 **270 0**

KNOWLES, Dominic (F) 0 0
H: 5 9 W: 11 05 b.Accrington 13-2-92
Source: Scholar.
2010-11 Burnley 0 0
2011-12 Burnley 0 0

LAFFERTY, Danny (D) 65 8
H: 6 0 W: 12 08 b.Derry 1-4-89
Honours: Northern Ireland Youth, Under-21, B, 1 full cap.
2009-10 Celtic 0 0
2009-10 *Ayr U* 14 1 **14 1**
2010 Derry C 12 0
2011 Derry C 34 7 **46 7**
2011-12 Burnley 5 0 **5 0**

LAZAAR, Mehdi (F) 0 0
b.Liege 9-3-93
Source: Scholar. *Honours:* Belgium Youth.
2011-12 Burnley 0 0

LONG, Kevin (D) 71 4
H: 6 3 W: 13 01 b.Cork 18-8-90
2009 Cork City 16 0 **16 0**
2009-10 Burnley 0 0
2010-11 Burnley 0 0
2010-11 *Accrington S* 15 0
2011-12 Burnley 0 0
2011-12 *Accrington S* 24 4 **39 4**
2011-12 *Rochdale* 16 0 **16 0**

LOVE, Archie (M) 0 0
b.Manchester 12-1-93
Source: Scholar.
2011-12 Burnley 0 0

LYNCH, Chris (D) 10 0
H: 6 3 W: 15 06 b.Blackburn 31-1-91
Source: Scholar.
2009-10 Burnley 0 0
2009-10 *Chester C* 10 0 **10 0**
2010-11 Burnley 0 0
2011-12 Burnley 0 0

LYNCH, David (M) 0 0
b.Blackburn 5-7-93
Source: Scholar.
2011-12 Burnley 0 0

MACDONALD, Alex (F) 49 6
H: 5 7 W: 11 04 b.Warrington 14-4-90
Source: Scholar. *Honours:* Scotland Youth, Under-21.
2007-08 Burnley 2 0
2008-09 Burnley 3 0
2009-10 Burnley 0 0
2009-10 *Falkirk* 11 1 **11 1**
2010-11 Burnley 0 0
2010-11 *Inverness CT* 10 1 **10 1**
2011-12 Burnley 5 0 **10 0**
2011-12 *Plymouth Arg* 18 4 **18 4**

MARNEY, Dean (M) 233 14
H: 5 10 W: 11 09 b.Barking 31-1-84
Source: Scholar. *Honours:* England Under-21.
2002-03 Tottenham H 0 0
2002-03 *Swindon T* 9 0 **9 0**
2003-04 Tottenham H 3 0
2003-04 *QPR* 2 0 **2 0**
2004-05 Tottenham H 5 2
2004-05 *Gillingham* 3 0 **3 0**
2005-06 Tottenham H 0 0 **8 2**
2005-06 *Norwich C* 13 0 **13 0**
2006-07 Hull C 37 2
2007-08 Hull C 41 6
2008-09 Hull C 31 0
2009-10 Hull C 16 1 **125 9**
2009-10 Burnley 0 0
2010-11 Burnley 36 3
2011-12 Burnley 37 0 **73 3**

McCANN, Chris (M) 197 23
H: 6 1 W: 11 11 b.Dublin 21-7-87
Source: Scholar. *Honours:* Eire Youth.
2005-06 Burnley 23 2
2006-07 Burnley 38 5
2007-08 Burnley 35 5
2008-09 Burnley 44 6
2009-10 Burnley 7 0
2010-11 Burnley 4 1
2011-12 Burnley 46 4 **197 23**

McCARTAN, Shay (M) 1 0
H: 5 10 W: 11 09 b.Newry 18-5-94
Source: Scholar.
2011-12 Burnley 1 0 **1 0**

McKEE, Joe (M) 3 0
H: 5 11 W: 10 05 b.Linlithgow 30-10-92
Source: Scholar. *Honours:* Scotland Youth.
2009-10 Livingston 1 0 **1 0**
2009-10 Burnley 0 0
2010-11 Burnley 0 0
2011-12 Burnley 0 0
2011-12 *St Mirren* 2 0 **2 0**

MEE, Ben (D) 46 0
H: 5 11 W: 11 09 b.Sale 21-9-89
Source: Scholar. *Honours:* England Youth, Under-20, Under-21.
2007-08 Manchester C 0 0
2008-09 Manchester C 0 0
2009-10 Manchester C 0 0
2010-11 Manchester C 0 0
2010-11 *Leicester C* 15 0 **15 0**
2011-12 Manchester C 0 0
2011-12 Burnley 31 0 **31 0**

PATERSON, Martin (F) 161 41
H: 5 9 W: 10 11 b.Tunstall 13-5-87
Source: Scholar. *Honours:* Northern Ireland Youth, Under-21,13 full caps.
2004-05 Stoke C 3 0
2005-06 Stoke C 3 0
2006-07 Stoke C 9 1 **15 1**
2006-07 *Grimsby T* 15 6 **15 6**
2007-08 Scunthorpe U 40 13 **40 13**
2008-09 Burnley 43 12
2009-10 Burnley 23 4
2010-11 Burnley 11 2
2011-12 Burnley 14 3 **91 21**

RODRIGUEZ, Jay (F) 122 35
H: 6 0 W: 12 00 b.Burnley 29-7-89
Source: Scholar. *Honours:* England Under-21.
2007-08 Burnley 1 0
2007-08 Stirling Alb 11 3 **11 3**
2008-09 Burnley 25 2
2009-10 Burnley 0 0
2009-10 *Barnsley* 6 1 **6 1**
2010-11 Burnley 42 14
2011-12 Burnley 37 15 **105 31**

STANISLAS, Junior (M) 79 7
H: 6 0 W: 12 00 b.Kidbrooke 26-11-89
Source: Scholar. *Honours:* England Youth, Under-21.
2007-08 West Ham U 0 0
2008-09 West Ham U 9 2
2008-09 *Southend U* 6 1 **6 1**
2009-10 West Ham U 26 3

2010-11 West Ham U 6 1
2011-12 West Ham U 1 0 **42 6**
2011-12 Burnley 31 0 **31 0**

STEWART, Jon (G) 4 0
H: 6 2 W: 13 01 b.Hayes 13-3-89
Source: Swindon T Scholar, Weymouth.
2008-09 Portsmouth 0 0
2009-10 Portsmouth 0 0
2010-11 Bournemouth 4 0
2011-12 Bournemouth 0 0 **4 0**
2011-12 Burnley 0 0

TREACY, Keith (M) 118 13
H: 6 0 W: 13 02 b.Dublin 13-9-88
Source: Scholar. *Honours:* Eire Youth, Under-21, 6 full caps.
2005-06 Blackburn R 0 0
2006-07 Blackburn R 0 0
2006-07 *Stockport Co* 4 0 **4 0**
2007-08 Blackburn R 0 0
2008-09 Blackburn R 12 0
2009-10 Blackburn R 0 0 **12 0**
2009-10 *Sheffield U* 16 1 **16 1**
2009-10 Preston NE 17 2
2010-11 Preston NE 38 7 **55 9**
2011-12 Burnley 24 2 **24 2**
2011-12 *Sheffield W* 7 1 **7 1**

TRIPPIER, Keiran (D) 88 5
H: 5 10 W: 11 00 b.Bury 19-9-90
Source: Scholar. *Honours:* England Youth, Under-20, Under-21.
2007-08 Manchester C 0 0
2008-09 Manchester C 0 0
2009-10 Manchester C 0 0
2009-10 *Barnsley* 3 0
2010-11 Manchester C 0 0
2010-11 *Barnsley* 39 2 **42 2**
2011-12 Manchester C 0 0
2011-12 Burnley 46 3 **46 3**

WALLACE, Ross (M) 254 29
H: 5 6 W: 9 12 b.Dundee 23-5-85
Source: Celtic S Form. *Honours:* Scotland Youth, Under-21, B, 1 full cap.
2001-02 Celtic 0 0
2002-03 Celtic 0 0
2003-04 Celtic 8 1
2004-05 Celtic 16 0
2005-06 Celtic 11 0
2006-07 Celtic 2 0 **37 1**
2006-07 Sunderland 32 6
2007-08 Sunderland 21 2
2008-09 Sunderland 0 0 **53 8**
2008-09 Preston NE 39 5
2009-10 Preston NE 41 7 **80 12**
2010-11 Burnley 40 3
2011-12 Burnley 44 5 **84 8**

WILLIAMS, Aryn (D) 0 0
b.Perth 28-10-93
Source: Scholar.
2011-12 Burnley 0 0

WILSON, Ross (M) 0 0
b.Silsden 16-3-93
Source: Scholar.
2011-12 Burnley 0 0

YADOLAHI, Neil (D) 0 0
b.Dublin 19-6-93
Source: Scholar.
2011-12 Burnley 0 0

BURTON ALB (19)

ADA, Patrick (D) 70 1
H: 6 0 W: 13 05 b.Yaounde 14-1-85
Source: Redbridge, Barnet, St Albans C, Exeter C, Histon.
2009-10 Crewe Alex 18 0
2010-11 Crewe Alex 40 1 **58 1**
2011-12 Kilmarnock 3 0 **3 0**
2011-12 Burton Alb 9 0 **9 0**

AUSTIN, Ryan (D) 80 2
H: 6 2 W: 12 09 b.Stoke 15-11-84
Source: Crew Alex Scholar.
2009-10 Burton Alb 18 2
2010-11 Burton Alb 24 0
2011-12 Burton Alb 38 0 **80 2**

BLANCHETT, Danny (D) 73 1
H: 5 11 W: 11 12 b.Wembley 12-3-88
Source: Northwood, Hendon, Harrow Borough, Cambridge C.
2006-07 Peterborough U 3 1
2007-08 Peterborough U 1 0
2008-09 Peterborough U 3 0
2009-10 Peterborough U 0 0 **7 1**
2009-10 *Hereford U* 13 0 **13 0**
2010-11 Crewe Alex 39 0 **39 0**
2011-12 Burton Alb 14 0 **14 0**

BOLDER, Adam (M) 373 20
H: 5 9 W: 10 08 b.Hull 25-10-80
Source: Trainee.
1998-99 Hull C 1 0
1999-2000 Hull C 19 0 **20 0**
1999-2000 Derby Co 0 0
2000-01 Derby Co 2 0
2001-02 Derby Co 11 0
2002-03 Derby Co 45 6
2003-04 Derby Co 24 1
2004-05 Derby Co 36 2
2005-06 Derby Co 35 2
2006-07 Derby Co 13 0 **166 11**
2006-07 QPR 16 0
2007-08 QPR 24 2
2007-08 *Sheffield W* 13 2 **13 2**
2008-09 QPR 0 0 **40 2**
2008-09 Millwall 28 0
2009-10 Millwall 11 0 **39 0**
2009-10 *Bradford C* 14 1 **14 1**
2010-11 Burton Alb 37 1
2011-12 Burton Alb 44 3 **81 4**

CORBETT, Andy (F) 115 2
H: 6 0 W: 11 07 b.Worcester 20-2-82
2000-01 Kidderminster H 6 0
2001-02 Kidderminster H 2 0 **8 0**
From Solihull B, Nuneaton B.
2009-10 Burton Alb 34 1
From Solihull B, Nuneaton B.
2010-11 Burton Alb 40 1
From Solihull B, Nuneaton B.
2011-12 Burton Alb 33 0 **107 2**

DYER, Jack (M) 22 1
H: 5 9 W: 11 00 b.Sutton Coldfield 11-12-91
Source: Aston Villa Scholar.
2010-11 Burton Alb 5 0
2011-12 Burton Alb 17 1 **22 1**

GURRIERI, Andres (M) 55 2
H: 5 6 W: 10 05 b.Winterthur 3-7-89
2007-08 Ternana 0 0
2008-09 Ternana 6 0
2008-09 *Colligiana* 16 2 **16 2**
2009-10 Ternana 0 0 **6 0**
2010-11 Sud America 20 0 **20 0**
2011-12 Burton Alb 13 0 **13 0**

JAMES, Tony (D) 105 1
H: 5 10 W: 13 06 b.Abergavenny 9-10-78
Source: WBA Scholar, Hereford U, Weymouth.
2009-10 Burton Alb 42 1
2010-11 Burton Alb 27 0
2010-11 *Hereford U* 6 0 **6 0**
2011-12 Burton Alb 30 0 **99 1**

KEE, Billy (F) 101 30
H: 5 9 W: 11 04 b.Loughborough 1-12-90
Honours: Northern Ireland Youth, Under-21.
2009-10 Leicester C 0 0
2009-10 *Accrington S* 37 9 **37 9**
2010-11 Torquay U 40 9
2011-12 Torquay U 4 0 **44 9**
2011-12 Burton Alb 20 12 **20 12**

MAGHOMA, Jacques (M) 112 11
H: 5 9 W: 11 06 b.Lubumbashi 23-10-87
Source: Scholar. *Honours:* DR Congo 3 full caps, 2 goals.
2005-06 Tottenham H 0 0
2006-07 Tottenham H 0 0
2007-08 Tottenham H 0 0
2008-09 Tottenham H 0 0
2009-10 Burton Alb 35 3
2010-11 Burton Alb 41 4
2011-12 Burton Alb 36 4 **112 11**

McGRATH, John (M) 158 4
H: 5 10 W: 10 04 b.Limerick 27-3-80
Source: Belvedere. *Honours:* Eire Under-21.
1999-2000 Aston Villa 0 0
2000-01 Aston Villa 3 0
2001-02 Aston Villa 0 0
2002-03 Aston Villa 0 0 **3 0**
2003-04 Doncaster R 11 0
2004-05 Doncaster R 0 0 **11 0**
2004-05 *Shrewsbury T* 8 0 **8 0**
2004-05 Kidderminster H 19 0 **19 0**
From Weymouth, Tamworth.
2005-06 Limerick 0 0
2009-10 Burton Alb 45 1
2010-11 Burton Alb 41 3
2011-12 Burton Alb 31 0 **117 4**

MOORE, Darren (D) 595 31
H: 6 2 W: 15 07 b.Birmingham 22-4-74
Source: Trainee. *Honours:* Jamaica 3 full caps.
1991-92 Torquay U 5 1
1992-93 Torquay U 31 2
1993-94 Torquay U 37 2
1994-95 Torquay U 30 3 **103 8**
1995-96 Doncaster R 35 2
1996-97 Doncaster R 41 5 **76 7**
1997-98 Bradford C 18 0
1998-99 Bradford C 44 3
1999-2000 Bradford C 0 0 **62 3**
1999-2000 Portsmouth 25 1
2000-01 Portsmouth 32 1
2001-02 Portsmouth 2 0 **59 2**
2001-02 WBA 32 2
2002-03 WBA 29 2
2003-04 WBA 22 2
2004-05 WBA 16 0
2005-06 WBA 5 0 **104 6**
2005-06 Derby Co 14 1
2006-07 Derby Co 35 2
2007-08 Derby Co 31 0 **80 3**
2008-09 Barnsley 38 1
2009-10 Barnsley 35 1 **73 2**
2010-11 Burton Alb 34 0
2011-12 Burton Alb 4 0 **38 0**

MUNN, Bradley (M) 0 0
b.Nottingham 28-6-93
Source: Scholar.
2011-12 Burton Alb 0 0

PALMER, Chris (D) 207 14
H: 5 7 W: 11 00 b.Derby 16-10-83
Source: Scholar.
2003-04 Derby Co 0 0
2004-05 Notts Co 25 4
2005-06 Notts Co 29 1 **54 5**
2006-07 Wycombe W 32 0
2007-08 Wycombe W 1 0 **33 0**
2007-08 *Darlington* 4 0 **4 0**
2008-09 Walsall 44 1 **44 1**
2009-10 Gillingham 20 1
2010-11 Gillingham 18 4 **38 5**
2011-12 Burton Alb 34 3 **34 3**

PEARSON, Greg (F) 128 23
H: 6 0 W: 12 00 b.Birmingham 3-4-85
Source: Trainee.
2003-04 West Ham U 0 0
2004-05 West Ham U 0 0
2004-05 *Lincoln C* 3 0 **3 0**
2005-06 Rushden & D 22 1 **22 1**
From Bishop's Stortford.
2009-10 Burton Alb 42 14
From Bishop's Stortford.
2010-11 Burton Alb 35 5
From Bishop's Stortford.
2011-12 Burton Alb 12 0 **89 19**
2011-12 *Aldershot T* 5 0 **5 0**
2011-12 *Crewe Alex* 9 3 **9 3**

PHILLIPS, Jimmy (M) 80 1
H: 5 7 W: 10 00 b.Stoke 20-9-89
Source: Scholar.
2008-09 Stoke C 0 0
2009-10 Burton Alb 24 1
2010-11 Burton Alb 23 0
2011-12 Burton Alb 33 0 **80 1**

POOLE, Kevin (G) 313 0
H: 5 10 W: 12 11 b.Bromsgrove 21-7-63
Source: Apprentice.
1981-82 Aston Villa 0 0
1982-83 Aston Villa 0 0
1983-84 Aston Villa 0 0
1984-85 Aston Villa 7 0
1984-85 *Northampton T* 3 0 **3 0**
1985-86 Aston Villa 11 0
1986-87 Aston Villa 10 0 **28 0**
1987-88 Middlesbrough 1 0
1988-89 Middlesbrough 12 0

1989-90 Middlesbrough 21 0
1990-91 Middlesbrough 0 0 **34 0**
1990-91 *Hartlepool U* 12 0 **12 0**
1991-92 Leicester C 42 0
1992-93 Leicester C 19 0
1993-94 Leicester C 14 0
1994-95 Leicester C 36 0
1995-96 Leicester C 45 0
1996-97 Leicester C 7 0 **163 0**
1997-98 Birmingham C 1 0
1998-99 Birmingham C 36 0
1999-2000 Birmingham C 18 0
2000-01 Birmingham C 1 0
2001-02 Birmingham C 0 0 **56 0**
2001-02 Bolton W 3 0
2002-03 Bolton W 0 0
2003-04 Bolton W 0 0
2004-05 Bolton W 2 0 **5 0**
2005-06 Derby Co 6 0 **6 0**
2009-10 Burton Alb 6 0
2010-11 Burton Alb 0 0
2011-12 Burton Alb 0 0 **6 0**

RAMSEY-DICKSON, Kristian (D) 0 0
b.Birmingham 23-8-89
Source: Continental Star.
2011-12 Burton Alb 0 0

RICHARDS, Justin (F) 156 36
H: 5 11 W: 11 00 b.Sandwell 16-10-80
Source: Trainee.
1998-99 WBA 1 0
1999-2000 WBA 0 0
2000-01 WBA 0 0 **1 0**
2000-01 Bristol R 7 0
2001-02 Bristol R 1 0
2002-03 Bristol R 8 0 **16 0**
2002-03 *Colchester U* 2 0 **2 0**
From Stevenage B, Woking.
2006-07 Peterborough U 13 1 **13 1**
2006-07 *Boston U* 3 0 **3 0**
From Kidderminster H.
2009-10 Cheltenham T 44 15 **44 15**
2010-11 Port Vale 42 9 **42 9**
2011-12 Burton Alb 35 11 **35 11**

STANTON, Nathan (D) 421 0
H: 5 9 W: 12 06 b.Nottingham 6-5-81
Source: Trainee. *Honours:* England Youth.
1997-98 Scunthorpe U 1 0
1998-99 Scunthorpe U 4 0
1999-2000 Scunthorpe U 34 0
2000-01 Scunthorpe U 38 0
2001-02 Scunthorpe U 42 0
2002-03 Scunthorpe U 42 0
2003-04 Scunthorpe U 33 0
2004-05 Scunthorpe U 21 0
2005-06 Scunthorpe U 22 0 **237 0**
2006-07 Rochdale 35 0
2007-08 Rochdale 27 0
2008-09 Rochdale 39 0
2009-10 Rochdale 38 0 **139 0**
2010-11 Burton Alb 23 0
2011-12 Burton Alb 22 0 **45 0**

TAYLOR, Cleveland (M) 326 26
H: 5 8 W: 10 07 b.Leicester 9-9-83
Source: Scholar. *Honours:* Jamaica Youth.
2001-02 Bolton W 0 0
2002-03 Bolton W 0 0
2002-03 *Exeter C* 3 0 **3 0**
2003-04 Bolton W 0 0
2003-04 Scunthorpe U 20 3
2004-05 Scunthorpe U 44 6
2005-06 Scunthorpe U 45 3
2006-07 Scunthorpe U 45 3
2007-08 Scunthorpe U 20 0 **174 15**
2007-08 Carlisle U 18 0
2008-09 Carlisle U 42 3
2009-10 Carlisle U 1 0 **61 3**
2009-10 Brentford 12 1 **12 1**
2009-10 *Burton Alb* 24 4
2010-11 St Johnstone 21 1 **21 1**
2011-12 Burton Alb 31 2 **55 6**

WEBSTER, Aaron (D) 101 18
H: 6 1 W: 12 00 b.Burton-on-Trent 19-12-80
Source: Youth.
2009-10 Burton Alb 24 4
2010-11 Burton Alb 42 11
2011-12 Burton Alb 35 3 **101 18**

WREN, James (G) 0 0
b.Birmingham 26-6-93
Source: Walsall Scholar.
2011-12 Burton Alb 0 0

YUSSUF, Abdi (F) 17 1
H: 6 1 W: 11 13 b.Zanzibar 3-10-92
Source: Scholar.
2010-11 Leicester C 0 0
2011-12 Burton Alb 17 1 **17 1**

ZOLA, Calvin (F) 242 57
H: 6 3 W: 14 06 b.Kinshasa 31-12-84
Source: Scholar.
2001-02 Newcastle U 0 0
2002-03 Newcastle U 0 0
2003-04 Newcastle U 0 0
2003-04 *Oldham Ath* 25 5 **25 5**
2004-05 Tranmere R 15 2
2005-06 Tranmere R 22 4
2006-07 Tranmere R 29 5
2007-08 Tranmere R 30 5 **96 16**
2008-09 Crewe Alex 27 5
2009-10 Crewe Alex 34 15
2010-11 Crewe Alex 6 1 **67 21**
2010-11 *Burton Alb* 18 3
2011-12 Burton Alb 36 12 **54 15**

BURY (20)

BELFORD, Cameron (G) 84 0
H: 6 1 W: 11 10 b.Nuneaton 16-10-88
Source: Coventry C Scholar.
2007-08 Bury 1 0
2008-09 Bury 1 0
2009-10 Bury 7 0
2010-11 Bury 39 0
2011-12 Bury 23 0 **71 0**
2011-12 *Southend U* 13 0 **13 0**

BISHOP, Andy (F) 268 75
H: 6 0 W: 10 10 b.Cannock 19-10-82
Source: Scholar.
2002-03 Walsall 0 0
2002-03 *Kidderminster H* 29 5
2003-04 *Kidderminster H* 11 2 **40 7**
2003-04 *Rochdale* 10 1 **10 1**
2003-04 *Yeovil T* 5 2 **5 2**
From York C.
2006-07 Bury 43 15
2007-08 Bury 44 19
2008-09 Bury 42 16
2009-10 Bury 25 3
2010-11 Bury 19 4
2011-12 Bury 40 8 **213 65**

BRANAGAN, Richie (G) 2 0
H: 5 11 W: 12 10 b.Gravesend 20-10-91
Source: Bolton W. *Honours:* Eire Under-21.
2010-11 Bury 2 0
2011-12 Bury 0 0 **2 0**

CARRINGTON, Mark (M) 94 9
H: 6 0 W: 11 00 b.Warrington 4-5-87
Source: Scholar.
2006-07 Crewe Alex 3 0
2007-08 Crewe Alex 9 0
2008-09 Crewe Alex 17 2 **29 2**
2009-10 Milton Keynes D 20 4
2010-11 Milton Keynes D 12 2 **32 6**
2010-11 Hamilton A 12 0 **12 0**
2011-12 Bury 21 1 **21 1**

CARSON, Trevor (G) 52 0
H: 6 0 W: 14 11 b.Downpatrick 5-3-88
Source: Scholar. *Honours:* Northern Ireland Youth, Under-21, B.
2004-05 Sunderland 0 0
2005-06 Sunderland 0 0
2006-07 Sunderland 0 0
2007-08 Sunderland 0 0
2008-09 Sunderland 0 0
2008-09 *Chesterfield* 18 0 **18 0**
2009-10 Sunderland 0 0
2010-11 Sunderland 0 0
2010-11 *Lincoln C* 16 0 **16 0**
2010-11 *Brentford* 1 0 **1 0**
2011-12 Sunderland 0 0
2011-12 *Hull C* 0 0
2011-12 Bury 17 0 **17 0**

CREGG, Patrick (M) 152 8
H: 5 9 W: 10 04 b.Dublin 21-2-86
Source: Scholar. *Honours:* Eire Youth, Under-21.
2002-03 Arsenal 0 0
2003-04 Arsenal 0 0
2004-05 Arsenal 0 0
2005-06 Falkirk 16 0
2006-07 Falkirk 32 3
2007-08 Falkirk 36 4
2008-09 Falkirk 23 0 **107 7**
2009-10 Hibernian 15 1 **15 1**
2010-11 Morton 1 0 **1 0**
2010-11 St Mirren 22 0 **22 0**
2011-12 Bury 7 0 **7 0**

FUTCHER, Ben (D) 322 21
H: 6 7 W: 12 05 b.Manchester 20-2-81
Source: Trainee.
1999-2000 Oldham Ath 5 0
2000-01 Oldham Ath 5 0
2001-02 Oldham Ath 0 0 **10 0**
From Stalybridge C, Doncaster R
2002-03 Lincoln C 43 8
2003-04 Lincoln C 43 2
2004-05 Lincoln C 35 3 **121 13**
2005-06 Boston U 14 0 **14 0**
2005-06 Grimsby T 15 2
2006-07 Grimsby T 4 0 **19 2**
2006-07 Peterborough U 25 3 **25 3**
2007-08 Bury 40 0
2008-09 Bury 34 2
2009-10 Bury 32 0
2010-11 Bury 11 1
2010-11 *Oxford U* 6 0 **6 0**
2011-12 Bury 0 0 **117 3**
2011-12 *Macclesfield T* 10 0 **10 0**

GRELLA, Mike (F) 67 9
H: 5 11 W: 12 02 b.New York 23-1-87
Source: Duke University. *Honours:* USA Youth.
2008-09 Leeds U 11 0
2009-10 Leeds U 17 1
2010-11 Leeds U 1 0
2010-11 *Carlisle U* 10 3 **10 3**
2010-11 *Swindon T* 7 1 **7 1**
2011-12 Leeds U 0 0 **29 1**
2011-12 Brentford 11 0 **11 0**
2011-12 Bury 10 4 **10 4**

HARRAD, Shaun (F) 143 43
H: 5 10 W: 12 04 b.Nottingham 11-12-84
Source: Scholar.
2002-03 Notts Co 5 0
2003-04 Notts Co 8 0
2004-05 Notts Co 16 1 **29 1**
2009-10 Burton Alb 42 21
2010-11 Burton Alb 20 10 **62 31**
2010-11 Northampton T 18 6
2011-12 Northampton T 0 0 **18 6**
2011-12 Bury 26 2 **26 2**
2011-12 *Rotherham U* 8 3 **8 3**

HARROP, Max (M) 8 0
H: 5 8 W: 10 00 b.Oldham 30-6-93
Source: Scholar.
2010-11 Bury 3 0
2011-12 Bury 5 0 **8 0**

HAWORTH, Andrew (M) 60 3
H: 5 11 W: 11 10 b.Lancaster 28-11-88
Source: Scholar.
2007-08 Blackburn R 0 0
2008-09 Blackburn R 0 0
2009-10 Blackburn R 0 0
2009-10 *Rochdale* 7 0 **7 0**
2010-11 Bury 40 3
2011-12 Bury 6 0 **46 3**
2011-12 *Oxford U* 4 0 **4 0**
2011-12 *Bradford C* 3 0 **3 0**

HUDSON, Danny (F) 0 0
b.Manchester 12-9-92
Source: Scholar.
2011-12 Bury 0 0

HUGHES, Mark (D) 178 10
H: 6 1 W: 13 03 b.Liverpool 9-12-86
Source: Scholar.
2004-05 Everton 0 0
2005-06 Everton 0 0
2005-06 *Stockport Co* 3 1 **3 1**
2006-07 Everton 1 0 **1 0**
2006-07 Northampton T 17 2
2007-08 Northampton T 35 1

2008-09	Northampton T	41	1	**93**	**4**
2009-10	Walsall	26	1	**26**	**1**
2010-11	N Queensland Fury	30	4	**30**	**4**
2011-12	Bury	25	0	**25**	**0**

JOHN-LEWIS, Lemell (M) 139 15
H: 5 10 W: 11 10 b.Hammersmith 17-5-89
Source: Scholar.

2006-07	Lincoln C	0	0		
2007-08	Lincoln C	21	3		
2008-09	Lincoln C	27	4		
2009-10	Lincoln C	24	1	**72**	**8**
2010-11	Bury	39	2		
2011-12	Bury	28	5	**67**	**7**

JONES, Andrai (D) 12 0
H: 5 11 W: 10 10 b.Liverpool 1-1-92
Source: Scholar.

2010-11	Bury	1	0		
2011-12	Bury	11	0	**12**	**0**

McCARTHY, Luke (M) 1 0
H: 5 9 W: 10 10 b.Bolton 7-7-93
Source: Scholar.

2010-11	Bury	1	0		
2011-12	Bury	0	0	**1**	**0**

PICKEN, Phil (D) 237 2
H: 5 9 W: 10 07 b.Droylsden 12-11-85
Source: Scholar.

2004-05	Manchester U	0	0		
2005-06	Manchester U	0	0		
2005-06	*Chesterfield*	32	1		
2006-07	Chesterfield	39	1		
2007-08	Chesterfield	37	0		
2008-09	Chesterfield	11	0		
2008-09	*Notts Co*	22	0	**22**	**0**
2009-10	Chesterfield	21	0	**140**	**2**
2010-11	Bury	38	0		
2011-12	Bury	37	0	**75**	**0**

ROTHWELL, Zach (M) 0 0
H: 6 1 W: 11 07 b.Bury 16-7-92
Source: Scholar.

2010-11	Bury	0	0		
2011-12	Bury	0	0		

SCHUMACHER, Steven (M) 269 35
H: 5 10 W: 11 00 b.Liverpool 30-4-84
Source: Scholar. *Honours:* England Youth.

2000-01	Everton	0	0		
2001-02	Everton	0	0		
2002-03	Everton	0	0		
2003-04	Everton	0	0		
2003-04	*Carlisle U*	4	0	**4**	**0**
2004-05	Bradford C	43	6		
2005-06	Bradford C	30	1		
2006-07	Bradford C	44	6	**117**	**13**
2007-08	Crewe Alex	26	1		
2008-09	Crewe Alex	15	2		
2009-10	Crewe Alex	32	4	**73**	**7**
2010-11	Bury	43	9		
2011-12	Bury	32	6	**75**	**15**

SKARZ, Joe (D) 186 3
H: 5 10 W: 11 04 b.Huddersfield 13-7-89
Source: Scholar.

2006-07	Huddersfield T	17	0		
2007-08	Huddersfield T	27	0		
2008-09	Huddersfield T	9	1		
2008-09	*Hartlepool U*	7	0	**7**	**0**
2009-10	Huddersfield T	15	0	**68**	**1**
2009-10	*Shrewsbury T*	20	0	**20**	**0**
2010-11	Bury	46	1		
2011-12	Bury	45	1	**91**	**2**

SODJE, Efe (D) 512 34
H: 6 1 W: 12 00 b.Greenwich 5-10-72
Source: Delta Steel Pioneer, Stevenage Bor. *Honours:* Nigeria 9 full caps, 1 goal.

1997-98	Macclesfield T	41	3		
1998-99	Macclesfield T	42	3	**83**	**6**
1999-2000	Luton T	9	0	**9**	**0**
1999-2000	Colchester U	3	0	**3**	**0**
2000-01	Crewe Alex	32	0		
2001-02	Crewe Alex	36	2		
2002-03	Crewe Alex	30	1	**98**	**3**
2003-04	Huddersfield T	39	4		
2004-05	Huddersfield T	28	1	**67**	**5**
2004-05	Yeovil T	6	2		
2005-06	Yeovil T	19	1	**25**	**3**
2005-06	Southend U	13	1		
2006-07	Southend U	24	1	**37**	**2**
2007-08	Gillingham	13	0	**13**	**0**
2007-08	*Bury*	16	1		
2008-09	Bury	41	7		
2009-10	Bury	39	2		
2010-11	Bury	40	3		
2011-12	Bury	41	2	**177**	**15**

SWEENEY, Peter (M) 232 15
H: 6 0 W: 12 11 b.Glasgow 25-9-84
Source: Scholar. *Honours:* Scotland Youth, Under-21, B.

2001-02	Millwall	1	0		
2002-03	Millwall	5	1		
2003-04	Millwall	29	2		
2004-05	Millwall	24	2	**59**	**5**
2005-06	Stoke C	17	1		
2006-07	Stoke C	13	1		
2006-07	*Yeovil T*	8	0	**8**	**0**
2007-08	Stoke C	5	0	**35**	**2**
2007-08	*Walsall*	7	0	**7**	**0**
2007-08	Leeds U	9	0		
2008-09	Leeds U	0	0	**9**	**0**
2008-09	*Grimsby T*	8	0		
2009-10	Grimsby T	40	4	**48**	**4**
2010-11	Bury	25	0		
2011-12	Bury	41	4	**66**	**4**

WILLIAMS, Tony (G) 263 0
H: 6 2 W: 13 09 b.Maesteg 20-9-77
Source: Trainee. *Honours:* Wales Youth, Under-21.

1996-97	Blackburn R	0	0		
1997-98	Blackburn R	0	0		
1997-98	*QPR*	0	0		
1998-99	Blackburn R	0	0		
1998-99	*Macclesfield T*	4	0		
1998-99	*Huddersfield T*	0	0		
1998-99	*Bristol R*	9	0	**9**	**0**
1999-2000	Blackburn R	0	0		
1999-2000	*Gillingham*	2	0	**2**	**0**
1999-2000	*Macclesfield T*	11	0	**15**	**0**
2000-01	Hartlepool U	41	0		
2001-02	Hartlepool U	43	0		
2002-03	Hartlepool U	46	0		
2003-04	Hartlepool U	1	0	**131**	**0**
2003-04	*Swansea C*	0	0		
2003-04	*Stockport Co*	15	0	**15**	**0**
2004-05	Grimsby T	46	0	**46**	**0**
2005-06	Carlisle U	11	0		
2005-06	*Bury*	3	0		
2006-07	Carlisle U	0	0	**11**	**0**
2006-07	*Wrexham*	9	0		
2007-08	Wrexham	22	0		
2008-09	Wrexham	0	0		
2009-10	Wrexham	0	0	**31**	**0**
From Neath.					
2011-12	Bury	0	0	**3**	**0**

WORRALL, David (M) 135 9
H: 6 0 W: 11 03 b.Manchester 12-6-90
Source: Scholar.

2006-07	Bury	1	0		
2007-08	Bury	0	0		
2007-08	WBA	0	0		
2008-09	*Accrington S*	4	0	**4**	**0**
2008-09	*Shrewsbury T*	9	0	**9**	**0**
2009-10	WBA	0	0		
2009-10	Bury	40	4		
2010-11	Bury	40	2		
2011-12	Bury	41	3	**122**	**9**

CARDIFF C (21)

BLAKE, Darcy (M) 97 0
H: 5 10 W: 12 05 b.New Tredegar 13-12-88
Source: Scholar. *Honours:* Wales Youth, Under-21, 9 full caps, 1 goal.

2005-06	Cardiff C	1	0		
2006-07	Cardiff C	10	0		
2007-08	Cardiff C	8	0		
2008-09	Cardiff C	7	0		
2009-10	Cardiff C	18	0		
2009-10	*Plymouth Arg*	7	0	**7**	**0**
2010-11	Cardiff C	26	0		
2011-12	Cardiff C	20	0	**90**	**0**

CONWAY, Craig (M) 228 23
H: 5 7 W: 10 07 b.Irvine 2-5-85
Honours: Scotland 3 full caps.

2002-03	Ayr U	1	0		
2003-04	Ayr U	6	0		
2004-05	Ayr U	23	3		
2005-06	Ayr U	31	4	**61**	**7**
2006-07	Dundee U	30	0		
2007-08	Dundee U	15	1		
2008-09	Dundee U	36	5		
2009-10	Dundee U	33	4		
2010-11	Dundee U	22	3	**136**	**13**
2011-12	Cardiff C	31	3	**31**	**3**

COWIE, Don (M) 356 42
H: 5 5 W: 8 05 b.Inverness 15-2-83
Honours: Scotland 10 full caps.

2000-01	Ross Co	1	0		
2001-02	Ross Co	18	0		
2002-03	Ross Co	30	1		
2003-04	Ross Co	23	0		
2004-05	Ross Co	34	5		
2005-06	Ross Co	32	4		
2006-07	Ross Co	28	7	**166**	**17**
2007-08	Inverness CT	37	9		
2008-09	Inverness CT	22	3	**59**	**12**
2008-09	Watford	10	3		
2009-10	Watford	41	2		
2010-11	Watford	37	4	**88**	**9**
2011-12	Cardiff C	43	4	**43**	**4**

EARNSHAW, Robert (F) 408 165
H: 5 6 W: 9 09 b.Mulfulira 6-4-81
Source: Trainee. *Honours:* Wales Youth, Under-21, 58 full caps, 16 goals.

1997-98	Cardiff C	5	0		
1998-99	Cardiff C	5	1		
1998-99	*Middlesbrough*	0	0		
1999-2000	Cardiff C	6	1		
1999-2000	*Morton*	3	2	**3**	**2**
2000-01	Cardiff C	36	19		
2001-02	Cardiff C	30	11		
2002-03	Cardiff C	46	31		
2003-04	Cardiff C	46	21		
2004-05	Cardiff C	4	1		
2004-05	WBA	31	11		
2005-06	WBA	12	1	**43**	**12**
2005-06	Norwich C	15	8		
2006-07	Norwich C	30	19	**45**	**27**
2007-08	Derby Co	22	1	**22**	**1**
2008-09	Nottingham F	32	12		
2009-10	Nottingham F	32	15		
2010-11	Nottingham F	34	8	**98**	**35**
2011-12	Cardiff C	19	3	**197**	**88**

EVANS, Alex (D) 0 0
b.Treharris 17-9-92
Source: Scholar. *Honours:* Wales Youth, Under-21.

2011-12	Cardiff C	0	0		

FARAH, Ibrahim (M) 0 0
b.Cardiff 24-1-92
Source: Scholar.

2011-12	Cardiff C	0	0		

GERRARD, Anthony (D) 263 15
H: 6 2 W: 13 07 b.Huyton 6-2-86
Source: Scholar. *Honours:* Eire Youth.

2004-05	Everton	0	0		
2004-05	*Walsall*	8	0		
2005-06	Walsall	34	0		
2006-07	Walsall	35	1		
2007-08	Walsall	44	3		
2008-09	Walsall	42	3	**163**	**7**
2009-10	Cardiff C	39	2		
2010-11	Cardiff C	0	0		
2010-11	*Hull C*	41	5	**41**	**5**
2011-12	Cardiff C	20	1	**59**	**3**

GESTEDE, Rudy (F) 66 10
H: 6 4 W: 13 07 b.Nancy 10-10-88
Honours: France Youth.

2008-09	Metz	5	0		
2009-10	*Cannes*	22	4	**22**	**4**
2010-11	Metz	11	3	**16**	**3**
2010-11	Metz B	3	1	**3**	**1**
2011-12	Cardiff C	25	2	**25**	**2**

GUNNARSSON, Aron (M) 165 11
H: 5 9 W: 11 00 b.Akureyri 22-9-89
Honours: Iceland Under-21, 27 full caps.

2007-08	AZ	1	0	**1**	**0**
2008-09	Coventry C	40	1		
2009-10	Coventry C	40	1		
2010-11	Coventry C	42	4	**122**	**6**
2011-12	Cardiff C	42	5	**42**	**5**

HARRIS, Kedeem (M) 19 0
H: 5 9 W: 10 08 b.Westminster 8-6-93
Source: Scholar.

2009-10	Wycombe W	2	0		
2010-11	Wycombe W	0	0		
2011-12	Wycombe W	17	0	**19**	**0**
2011-12	Cardiff C	0	0		

HEATON, Tom (G) **92 0**
H: 6 1 W: 13 12 b.Chester 15-4-86
Source: Trainee. *Honours:* England Youth, Under-21.

2003-04	Manchester U	0	0		
2004-05	Manchester U	0	0		
2005-06	Manchester U	0	0		
2005-06	*Swindon T*	14	0	**14**	**0**
2006-07	Manchester U	0	0		
2007-08	Manchester U	0	0		
2008-09	Manchester U	0	0		
2008-09	*Cardiff C*	21	0		
2009-10	Manchester U	0	0		
2009-10	*Rochdale*	12	0	**12**	**0**
2009-10	*Wycombe W*	16	0	**16**	**0**
2010-11	Cardiff C	27	0		
2011-12	Cardiff C	2	0	**50**	**0**

HUDSON, Mark (D) **284 17**
H: 6 1 W: 12 01 b.Guildford 30-3-82
Source: Trainee.

1998-99	Fulham	0	0		
1999-2000	Fulham	0	0		
2000-01	Fulham	0	0		
2001-02	Fulham	0	0		
2002-03	Fulham	0	0		
2003-04	Fulham	0	0		
2003-04	*Oldham Ath*	15	0	**15**	**0**
2003-04	*Crystal Palace*	14	0		
2004-05	Crystal Palace	7	1		
2005-06	Crystal Palace	15	0		
2006-07	Crystal Palace	39	4		
2007-08	Crystal Palace	45	2	**120**	**7**
2008-09	Charlton Ath	43	3	**43**	**3**
2009-10	Cardiff C	27	2		
2010-11	Cardiff C	40	0		
2011-12	Cardiff C	39	5	**106**	**7**

JARVIS, Nathaniel (F) **6 0**
H: 6 0 W: 12 06 b.Cardiff 20-10-91
Source: Scholar.

2010-11	Cardiff C	0	0		
2010-11	*Southend U*	6	0	**6**	**0**
2011-12	Cardiff C	0	0		

KEINAN, Dekel (D) **209 13**
H: 6 0 W: 11 09 b.Rosh Hanikra 15-9-84
Honours: Israel 17 full caps.

2002-03	Maccabi Haifa	7	0		
2003-04	Maccabi Haifa	13	0		
2004-05	Maccabi Haifa	1	0		
2004-05	Hapoel Bnei Sakhnin	23	3	**23**	**3**
2005-06	Maccabi Haifa	1	0		
2005-06	Maccabi Netanya	21	2	**21**	**2**
2006-07	Maccabi Haifa	28	0		
2007-08	Maccabi Haifa	24	2		
2008-09	Maccabi Haifa	28	3		
2009-10	Maccabi Haifa	34	1	**136**	**6**
2010-11	Blackpool	6	0	**6**	**0**
2010-11	Cardiff C	18	2		
2011-12	Cardiff C	1	0	**19**	**2**
2011-12	*Crystal Palace*	3	0	**3**	**0**
2011-12	*Bristol C*	1	0	**1**	**0**

KISS, Filip (M) **81 11**
H: 6 1 W: 11 11 b.Dunajska 13-10-90
Honours: Slovakia Youth, Under-21.

2009-10	Petrzalka	25	4	**25**	**4**
2010-11	Slovan Bratislava	29	6		
2011-12	Slovan Bratislava	1	0	**30**	**6**
2011-12	Cardiff C	26	1	**26**	**1**

On loan from Slovan Bratislava July 2011.

MARSHALL, David (G) **228 0**
H: 6 3 W: 13 04 b.Glasgow 5-3-85
Source: Celtic Youth. *Honours:* Scotland Youth, Under-21, B, 5 full caps.

2003-04	Celtic	11	0		
2004-05	Celtic	18	0		
2005-06	Celtic	4	0		
2006-07	Celtic	2	0	**35**	**0**
2006-07	Norwich C	2	0		
2007-08	Norwich C	46	0		
2008-09	Norwich C	46	0	**94**	**0**
2008-09	Cardiff C	0	0		
2009-10	Cardiff C	43	0		
2010-11	Cardiff C	11	0		
2011-12	Cardiff C	45	0	**99**	**0**

MASON, Joe (F) **92 19**
H: 5 9 W: 11 11 b.Plymouth 13-5-91
Honours: Eire Youth, Under-21.

2009-10	Plymouth Arg	19	3		
2010-11	Plymouth Arg	34	7	**53**	**10**
2011-12	Cardiff C	39	9	**39**	**9**

McNAUGHTON, Kevin (D) **398 4**
H: 5 10 W: 10 06 b.Dundee 28-8-82
Honours: Scotland Under-21, 4 full caps.

1999-2000	Aberdeen	0	0		
2000-01	Aberdeen	33	0		
2001-02	Aberdeen	34	0		
2002-03	Aberdeen	22	1		
2003-04	Aberdeen	17	0		
2004-05	Aberdeen	35	2		
2005-06	Aberdeen	34	0	**175**	**3**
2006-07	Cardiff C	42	0		
2007-08	Cardiff C	35	1		
2008-09	Cardiff C	39	0		
2009-10	Cardiff C	21	0		
2010-11	Cardiff C	44	0		
2011-12	Cardiff C	42	0	**223**	**1**

McPHAIL, Stephen (M) **351 10**
H: 5 8 W: 11 04 b.Westminster 9-12-79
Source: Trainee. *Honours:* Eire Youth, B, Under-21, 10 full caps, 1 goal.

1996-97	Leeds U	0	0		
1997-98	Leeds U	4	0		
1998-99	Leeds U	17	0		
1999-2000	Leeds U	24	2		
2000-01	Leeds U	7	0		
2001-02	Leeds U	1	0		
2001-02	*Millwall*	3	0	**3**	**0**
2002-03	Leeds U	13	0		
2003-04	Leeds U	12	1	**78**	**3**
2003-04	*Nottingham F*	14	0	**14**	**0**
2004-05	Barnsley	36	2		
2005-06	Barnsley	34	2	**70**	**4**
2006-07	Cardiff C	43	0		
2007-08	Cardiff C	43	3		
2008-09	Cardiff C	32	0		
2009-10	Cardiff C	21	0		
2010-11	Cardiff C	28	0		
2011-12	Cardiff C	19	0	**186**	**3**

MEADES, Jonathan (M) **0 0**
H: 6 1 W: 13 00 b.Cardiff 2-3-92
Source: Scholar.

2010-11	Cardiff C	0	0		
2011-12	Cardiff C	0	0		

MILLER, Kenny (F) **444 144**
H: 5 10 W: 10 09 b.Edinburgh 23-12-79
Source: Hutchison Vale. *Honours:* Scotland Under-21, B, 60 full caps, 16 goals.

1996-97	Hibernian	0	0		
1997-98	Hibernian	7	0		
1998-99	Hibernian	7	1		
1999-2000	Hibernian	31	11	**45**	**12**
2000-01	Rangers	27	8		
2001-02	Rangers	3	0		
2001-02	Wolverhampton W	20	2		
2002-03	Wolverhampton W	43	19		
2003-04	Wolverhampton W	25	2		
2004-05	Wolverhampton W	44	19		
2005-06	Wolverhampton W	35	10	**167**	**52**
2006-07	Celtic	31	4		
2007-08	Celtic	2	0	**33**	**4**
2007-08	Derby Co	30	4	**30**	**4**
2008-09	Rangers	30	10		
2009-10	Rangers	33	18		
2010-11	Rangers	18	21	**111**	**57**
2010-11	Bursa	15	5	**15**	**5**
2011-12	Cardiff C	43	10	**43**	**10**

NAYLOR, Lee (D) **422 12**
H: 5 9 W: 11 03 b.Walsall 19-3-80
Source: Trainee. *Honours:* England Youth, Under-21.

1997-98	Wolverhampton W	16	0		
1998-99	Wolverhampton W	23	1		
1999-2000	Wolverhampton W	30	2		
2000-01	Wolverhampton W	46	1		
2001-02	Wolverhampton W	27	0		
2002-03	Wolverhampton W	32	1		
2003-04	Wolverhampton W	38	0		
2004-05	Wolverhampton W	38	1		
2005-06	Wolverhampton W	40	1		
2006-07	Wolverhampton W	3	0	**293**	**7**
2006-07	Celtic	32	0		
2007-08	Celtic	33	1		
2008-09	Celtic	23	1		
2009-10	Celtic	12	1	**100**	**3**
2010-11	Cardiff C	27	2		
2011-12	Cardiff C	2	0	**29**	**2**

PARISH, Elliot (G) **9 0**
H: 6 2 W: 13 00 b.Towcester 20-5-90
Source: Scholar. *Honours:* England Youth, Under-20.

2008-09	Aston Villa	0	0		
2009-10	Aston Villa	0	0		
2010-11	Aston Villa	0	0		
2010-11	*Lincoln C*	9	0	**9**	**0**
2011-12	Aston Villa	0	0		
2011-12	Cardiff C	0	0		

PARKIN, Jon (F) **366 95**
H: 6 4 W: 13 07 b.Barnsley 30-12-81
Source: Scholarship.

1998-99	Barnsley	2	0		
1999-2000	Barnsley	0	0		
2000-01	Barnsley	4	0		
2001-02	Barnsley	4	0	**10**	**0**
2001-02	*Hartlepool U*	1	0	**1**	**0**
2001-02	York C	18	2		
2002-03	York C	41	10		
2003-04	York C	15	2	**74**	**14**
2003-04	Macclesfield T	12	1		
2004-05	Macclesfield T	42	22		
2005-06	Macclesfield T	11	7	**65**	**30**
2005-06	Hull C	18	5		
2006-07	Hull C	29	6	**47**	**11**
2006-07	*Stoke C*	6	3		
2007-08	Stoke C	29	2		
2008-09	Stoke C	0	0	**35**	**5**
2008-09	Preston NE	39	11		
2009-10	Preston NE	43	10		
2010-11	Preston NE	19	7	**101**	**28**
2010-11	Cardiff C	11	1		
2011-12	Cardiff C	0	0	**11**	**1**
2011-12	*Doncaster R*	5	0	**5**	**0**
2011-12	*Huddersfield T*	3	0	**3**	**0**
2011-12	*Scunthorpe U*	14	6	**14**	**6**

QUINN, Paul (D) **207 4**
H: 6 0 W: 11 04 b.Wishaw 21-7-85
Honours: Scotland Under-21.

2002-03	Motherwell	4	0		
2003-04	Motherwell	26	0		
2004-05	Motherwell	23	0		
2005-06	Motherwell	18	0		
2006-07	Motherwell	26	0		
2007-08	Motherwell	31	2		
2008-09	Motherwell	33	1	**161**	**3**
2009-10	Cardiff C	22	0		
2010-11	Cardiff C	23	1		
2011-12	Cardiff C	1	0	**46**	**1**

RALLS, Joe (M) **10 1**
H: 5 10 W: 11 00 b.Farnborough 13-10-93
Source: Scholar. *Honours:* England Youth.

2011-12	Cardiff C	10	1	**10**	**1**

SANTIAGO, Jordan (G) **0 0**
H: 6 1 W: 12 02 b.Calgary 3-4-91
Source: Scholar.

2010-11	Cardiff C	0	0		
2011-12	Cardiff C	0	0		

TAIWO, Soloman (M) **86 4**
H: 6 1 W: 13 02 b.Lagos 29-4-85
Source: Sutton U.

2007-08	Dagenham & R	10	0		
2008-09	Dagenham & R	40	4		
2009-10	Dagenham & R	4	0		
2009-10	Cardiff C	8	0		
2010-11	Cardiff C	0	0		
2010-11	*Dagenham & R*	18	0	**72**	**4**
2011-12	Cardiff C	1	0	**9**	**0**
2011-12	*Leyton Orient*	5	0	**5**	**0**

TAYLOR, Andrew (D) **210 5**
H: 5 10 W: 11 04 b.Hartlepool 1-8-86
Source: Trainee. *Honours:* England Youth, Under-20, Under-21.

2003-04	Middlesbrough	0	0		
2004-05	Middlesbrough	0	0		
2005-06	Middlesbrough	13	0		
2005-06	*Bradford C*	24	0	**24**	**0**
2006-07	Middlesbrough	34	0		
2007-08	Middlesbrough	19	0		
2008-09	Middlesbrough	26	0		
2009-10	Middlesbrough	12	0		
2010-11	Middlesbrough	21	3	**125**	**3**
2010-11	*Watford*	19	1	**19**	**1**
2011-12	Cardiff C	42	1	**42**	**1**

TURNER, Ben (D) **118 6**
H: 6 4 W: 14 04 b.Birmingham 21-1-88
Source: Scholar. *Honours:* England Youth.

2005-06	Coventry C	1	0		

2006-07 Coventry C 1 0
2006-07 *Peterborough U* 8 0 **8 0**
2006-07 *Oldham Ath* 1 0 **1 0**
2007-08 Coventry C 19 0
2008-09 Coventry C 24 0
2009-10 Coventry C 13 0
2010-11 Coventry C 14 4 **72 4**
2011-12 Cardiff C 37 2 **37 2**

WHARTON, Theo (M) 0 0
b.Cwmbran 15-11-94
Source: Scholar. *Honours:* Wales Youth.
2011-12 Cardiff C 0 0

WHITTINGHAM, Peter (M) 299 56
H: 5 10 W: 9 13 b.Nuneaton 8-9-84
Source: Trainee. *Honours:* England Youth, Under-20, Under-21.
2002-03 Aston Villa 4 0
2003-04 Aston Villa 32 0
2004-05 Aston Villa 13 1
2004-05 *Burnley* 7 0 **7 0**
2005-06 Aston Villa 4 0
2005-06 *Derby Co* 11 0 **11 0**
2006-07 Aston Villa 3 0 **56 1**
2006-07 Cardiff C 19 4
2007-08 Cardiff C 41 5
2008-09 Cardiff C 33 3
2009-10 Cardiff C 41 20
2010-11 Cardiff C 45 11
2011-12 Cardiff C 46 12 **225 55**

WILDIG, Aaron (M) 28 3
H: 5 9 W: 11 02 b.Hereford 15-4-92
Source: Scholar. *Honours:* Wales Youth.
2009-10 Cardiff C 11 1
2010-11 Cardiff C 2 0
2010-11 *Hamilton A* 3 0 **3 0**
2011-12 Cardiff C 0 0 **13 1**
2011-12 *Shrewsbury T* 12 2 **12 2**

CARLISLE U (22)

BECK, Mark (F) 2 0
H: 6 5 W: 12 08 b.Sunderland 2-2-94
Source: Scholar.
2011-12 Carlisle U 2 0 **2 0**

BERRETT, James (M) 123 21
H: 5 10 W: 10 13 b.Halifax 13-1-89
Source: Scholar. *Honours:* Eire Youth, Under-21.
2006-07 Huddersfield T 2 0
2007-08 Huddersfield T 15 1
2008-09 Huddersfield T 9 1
2009-10 Huddersfield T 9 0 **35 2**
2010-11 Carlisle U 46 10
2011-12 Carlisle U 42 9 **88 19**

CHANTLER, Chris (M) 12 0
H: 5 8 W: 11 00 b.Cheadle Hulme 16-12-90
Source: Scholar.
2009-10 Manchester C 0 0
2010-11 Manchester C 0 0
2011-12 Manchester C 0 0
2011-12 Carlisle U 12 0 **12 0**

COLLIN, Adam (G) 121 0
H: 6 2 W: 12 00 b.Penrith 9-12-84
Source: Trainee.
2003-04 Newcastle U 0 0
2003-04 *Oldham Ath* 0 0
From Workington.
2009-10 Carlisle U 29 0
2010-11 Carlisle U 46 0
2011-12 Carlisle U 46 0 **121 0**

CURRAN, Craig (F) 161 23
H: 5 9 W: 11 09 b.Liverpool 23-9-89
Source: Scholar.
2006-07 Tranmere R 4 4
2007-08 Tranmere R 35 2
2008-09 Tranmere R 15 3
2009-10 Tranmere R 43 5 **97 14**
2010-11 Carlisle U 45 8
2011-12 Carlisle U 12 0 **57 8**
2011-12 *Morecambe* 7 1 **7 1**

GILLESPIE, Mark (G) 1 0
H: 6 3 W: 13 07 b.Newcastle 27-3-92
Source: Scholar.
2009-10 Carlisle U 1 0
2010-11 Carlisle U 0 0
2011-12 Carlisle U 0 0 **1 0**

KAVANAGH, Graham (M) 537 76
H: 5 10 W: 13 03 b.Dublin 2-12-73
Source: Home Farm. *Honours:* Eire Schools, Youth, Under-21, B, 16 full caps, 1 goal.
1991-92 Middlesbrough 0 0
1992-93 Middlesbrough 10 0
1993-94 Middlesbrough 11 2
1993-94 *Darlington* 5 0 **5 0**
1994-95 Middlesbrough 7 0
1995-96 Middlesbrough 7 1
1996-97 Middlesbrough 0 0 **35 3**
1996-97 Stoke C 38 4
1997-98 Stoke C 44 5
1998-99 Stoke C 36 11
1999-2000 Stoke C 45 7
2000-01 Stoke C 43 8 **206 35**
2001-02 Cardiff C 43 13
2002-03 Cardiff C 44 5
2003-04 Cardiff C 27 7
2004-05 Cardiff C 28 3 **142 28**
2004-05 Wigan Ath 11 0
2005-06 Wigan Ath 35 0
2006-07 Wigan Ath 2 0 **48 0**
2006-07 Sunderland 14 1
2007-08 Sunderland 0 0
2007-08 *Sheffield W* 23 2 **23 2**
2008-09 Sunderland 0 0 **14 1**
2008-09 Carlisle U 34 5
2009-10 Carlisle U 29 2
2010-11 Carlisle U 1 0
2011-12 Carlisle U 0 0 **64 7**

LIVESEY, Danny (D) 242 14
H: 6 3 W: 13 01 b.Salford 31-12-84
Source: Trainee.
2002-03 Bolton W 2 0
2003-04 Bolton W 0 0
2003-04 *Notts Co* 11 0 **11 0**
2003-04 *Rochdale* 13 0 **13 0**
2004-05 Bolton W 0 0 **2 0**
2004-05 *Blackpool* 1 0 **1 0**
2005-06 Carlisle U 36 4
2006-07 Carlisle U 31 1
2007-08 Carlisle U 45 6
2008-09 Carlisle U 27 0
2009-10 Carlisle U 38 2
2010-11 Carlisle U 10 0
2011-12 Carlisle U 28 1 **215 14**

LOY, Rory (F) 65 7
H: 5 10 W: 10 07 b.Dumfries 19-3-88
Honours: Scotland Under-21.
2008-09 Rangers 1 0
2008-09 *Dunfermline Ath* 18 3 **18 3**
2009-10 Rangers 0 0
2009-10 *St Mirren* 8 0 **8 0**
2010-11 Rangers 1 0 **2 0**
2010-11 Carlisle U 17 1
2011-12 Carlisle U 20 3 **37 4**

MADDEN, Patrick (F) 98 21
H: 6 0 W: 11 13 b.Dublin 4-3-90
Honours: Eire Youth, Under-21.
2008 Bohemians 18 4
2009 Bohemians 2 0
2009 Shelbourne 13 6 **13 6**
2010 Bohemians 34 10 **54 14**
2010-11 Carlisle U 13 0
2011-12 Carlisle U 18 1 **31 1**

McGOVERN, John-Paul (M) 310 21
H: 5 10 W: 12 02 b.Glasgow 3-10-80
Source: Celtic BC.
2001-02 Celtic 0 0
2002-03 Celtic 0 0
2002-03 *Sheffield U* 15 1 **15 1**
2003-04 Celtic 0 0
2004-05 Sheffield W 46 6
2005-06 Sheffield W 7 0 **53 6**
2006-07 Milton Keynes D 44 3
2007-08 Milton Keynes D 3 0 **47 3**
2007-08 Swindon T 41 2
2008-09 Swindon T 26 2
2009-10 Swindon T 45 1
2010-11 Swindon T 38 3 **150 8**
2011-12 Carlisle U 45 3 **45 3**

McKENNA, Ben (M) 15 0
b.Burnley 16-1-93
Source: Scholar. *Honours:* Northern Ireland Youth.
2010-11 Carlisle U 1 0
2011-12 Carlisle U 0 0 **1 0**
2011-12 *Annan Ath* 14 0 **14 0**

MICHALIK, Lubomir (D) 155 7
H: 6 4 W: 13 00 b.Cadca 13-8-83
Source: Cadca, Martin. *Honours:* Slovakia 7 full caps, 2 goals.
2005-06 Senec 8 1
2006-07 Senec 12 1 **20 2**
2006-07 *Leeds U* 7 1
2006-07 Bolton W 4 1
2007-08 Bolton W 7 0 **11 1**
2007-08 Leeds U 17 0
2008-09 Leeds U 19 0
2009-10 Leeds U 13 1
2010-11 Leeds U 0 0 **56 2**
2010-11 Carlisle U 32 2
2011-12 Carlisle U 36 0 **68 2**

MILLER, Lee (F) 353 98
H: 6 0 W: 11 07 b.Lanark 18-5-83
Source: Form S. *Honours:* Scotland 3 full caps.
2000-01 Falkirk 0 0
2001-02 Falkirk 27 11
2002-03 Falkirk 34 17 **61 28**
2003-04 Bristol C 42 8
2004-05 Bristol C 7 0 **49 8**
2004-05 Hearts 18 8 **18 8**
2005-06 Dundee U 34 8
2006-07 Dundee U 3 0 **37 8**
2006-07 Aberdeen 32 4
2007-08 Aberdeen 36 12
2008-09 Aberdeen 34 10
2009-10 Aberdeen 18 3 **120 29**
2009-10 Middlesbrough 10 0
2010-11 Middlesbrough 1 0
2010-11 *Notts Co* 6 2 **6 2**
2010-11 *Scunthorpe U* 18 1 **18 1**
2011-12 Middlesbrough 0 0 **11 0**
2011-12 Carlisle U 33 14 **33 14**

MURPHY, Peter (M) 374 15
H: 5 10 W: 12 10 b.Dublin 27-10-80
Source: Trainee. *Honours:* Eire Youth, Under-21, 1 full cap.
1998-99 Blackburn R 0 0
1999-2000 Blackburn R 0 0
2000-01 Blackburn R 0 0
2000-01 *Halifax T* 21 1 **21 1**
2001-02 Blackburn R 0 0
2001-02 Carlisle U 40 0
2002-03 Carlisle U 40 2
2003-04 Carlisle U 35 1
2004-05 Carlisle U 0 0
2005-06 Carlisle U 44 2
2006-07 Carlisle U 40 2
2007-08 Carlisle U 36 3
2008-09 Carlisle U 28 0
2009-10 Carlisle U 16 0
2010-11 Carlisle U 34 3
2011-12 Carlisle U 40 1 **353 14**

NOBLE, Liam (M) 61 9
H: 5 9 W: 10 05 b.Newcastle 8-5-91
Source: Scholar.
2009-10 Sunderland 0 0
2010-11 Sunderland 0 0
2010-11 *Carlisle U* 21 3
2011-12 Sunderland 0 0
2011-12 Carlisle U 40 6 **61 9**

O'HALLORAN, Stephen (D) 28 0
H: 6 0 W: 11 07 b.Cork 29-11-87
Source: Scholar. *Honours:* Eire Under-21, 2 full caps.
2005-06 Aston Villa 0 0
2006-07 Aston Villa 0 0
2006-07 *Wycombe W* 11 0 **11 0**
2007-08 Aston Villa 0 0
2007-08 *Southampton* 1 0 **1 0**
2008-09 Aston Villa 0 0
2008-09 *Swansea C* 2 0 **2 0**
2009-10 Aston Villa 0 0
2010-11 Coventry C 11 0 **11 0**
2011-12 Carlisle U 3 0 **3 0**

ROBSON, Matty (D) 243 17
H: 5 10 W: 11 02 b.Spennymoor 23-1-85
Source: Scholar.
2002-03 Hartlepool U 0 0
2003-04 Hartlepool U 23 1
2004-05 Hartlepool U 27 2
2005-06 Hartlepool U 19 1
2006-07 Hartlepool U 20 2
2007-08 Hartlepool U 17 1
2008-09 Hartlepool U 29 2 **135 9**
2009-10 Carlisle U 39 4

2010-11 Carlisle U 42 2
2011-12 Carlisle U 27 2 **108 8**

SIMEK, Frankie (D) 203 2
H: 6 0 W: 11 06 b.St Louis 13-10-84
Source: Trainee. *Honours:* USA 5 full caps.
2002-03 Arsenal 0 0
2003-04 Arsenal 0 0
2004-05 Arsenal 0 0
2004-05 *QPR* 5 0 **5 0**
2004-05 *Bournemouth* 8 0 **8 0**
2005-06 Sheffield W 43 1
2006-07 Sheffield W 41 1
2007-08 Sheffield W 17 0
2008-09 Sheffield W 6 0
2009-10 Sheffield W 12 0 **119 2**
2010-11 Carlisle U 46 0
2011-12 Carlisle U 25 0 **71 0**

SWINGLEHURST, Steven (D) 0 0
b.Carlisle 23-10-92
Source: Scholar.
2011-12 Carlisle U 0 0

TAIWO, Tom (M) 122 6
H: 5 8 W: 10 07 b.Pudsey 27-2-90
Source: Scholar.
2007-08 Chelsea 0 0
2008-09 Chelsea 0 0
2008-09 *Port Vale* 4 0 **4 0**
2009-10 Chelsea 0 0
2009-10 Carlisle U 35 1
2010-11 Carlisle U 46 2
2011-12 Carlisle U 37 3 **118 6**

THIRLWELL, Paul (M) 294 8
H: 5 11 W: 12 08 b.Washington 13-2-79
Source: Trainee. *Honours:* England Under-21.
1996-97 Sunderland 0 0
1997-98 Sunderland 0 0
1998-99 Sunderland 2 0
1999-2000 Sunderland 8 0
1999-2000 *Swindon T* 12 0 **12 0**
2000-01 Sunderland 5 0
2001-02 Sunderland 14 0
2002-03 Sunderland 19 0
2003-04 Sunderland 29 0 **77 0**
2004-05 Sheffield U 30 1 **30 1**
2005-06 Derby Co 21 0
2006-07 Derby Co 0 0 **21 0**
2006-07 Carlisle U 30 0
2007-08 Carlisle U 13 0
2008-09 Carlisle U 34 4
2009-10 Carlisle U 28 1
2010-11 Carlisle U 23 1
2011-12 Carlisle U 26 1 **154 7**

WELSH, Andy (M) 294 14
H: 5 8 W: 10 03 b.Manchester 24-11-83
Source: Scholar. *Honours:* Scotland Youth.
2001-02 Stockport Co 15 0
2002-03 Stockport Co 13 2
2002-03 *Macclesfield T* 6 2 **6 2**
2003-04 Stockport Co 34 1
2004-05 Stockport Co 13 0 **75 3**
2004-05 Sunderland 7 1
2005-06 Sunderland 14 0
2005-06 *Leicester C* 10 1
2006-07 Sunderland 0 0 **21 1**
2006-07 *Leicester C* 7 0 **17 1**
2007 Toronto Lynx 20 1 **20 1**
2007-08 Blackpool 21 0
2008-09 Blackpool 0 0 **21 0**
2008-09 Yeovil T 37 0
2009-10 Yeovil T 42 2
2010-11 Yeovil T 34 4 **113 6**
2011-12 Carlisle U 21 0 **21 0**

ZOKO, Francois (F) 313 53
H: 6 0 W: 11 05 b.Daloa 13-9-83
2001-02 Nancy 24 3
2002-03 Nancy 28 2
2003-04 Nancy 19 3 **71 8**
2004-05 Laval 27 7
2005-06 Laval 33 2 **60 9**
2006-07 Mons 23 4
2007-08 Mons 32 8 **55 12**
2008-09 Hacettepe 27 1 **27 1**
2009-10 Ostend 11 4 **11 4**
2010-11 Carlisle U 44 6
2011-12 Carlisle U 45 13 **89 19**

CHARLTON ATH (23)

ALONSO, Mikel (M) 220 7
H: 5 10 W: 11 12 b.Tolosa 16-5-80
2000-01 Real Sociedad 1 0
2001-02 Real Sociedad B 34 2 **34 2**
2001-02 Real Sociedad 1 0
2002-03 Real Sociedad 9 1
2003-04 Real Sociedad 2 0
2003-04 *Numancia* 10 1 **10 1**
2004-05 Real Sociedad 35 0
2005-06 Real Sociedad 37 0
2006-07 Real Sociedad 18 0 **103 1**
2007-08 Bolton W 7 0 **7 0**
2008-09 Tenerife 11 0
2009-10 Tenerife 28 1
2010-11 Tenerife 27 2 **66 3**
2011-12 Charlton Ath 0 0

BOVER, Ruben (M) 0 0
H: 5 7 W: 10 05 b.Mallorca 24-6-92
Source: Kidderminster H, Halesowen T.
2011-12 Charlton Ath 0 0

CLARKE, Leon (F) 234 53
H: 6 2 W: 14 02 b.Birmingham 10-2-85
Source: Scholar.
2003-04 Wolverhampton W 0 0
2003-04 *Kidderminster H* 4 0 **4 0**
2004-05 Wolverhampton W 28 7
2005-06 Wolverhampton W 24 1
2005-06 *QPR* 1 0
2005-06 *Plymouth Arg* 5 0 **5 0**
2006-07 Wolverhampton W 22 5 **74 13**
2006-07 Sheffield W 10 1
2006-07 *Oldham Ath* 5 3 **5 3**
2007-08 Sheffield W 8 3
2007-08 *Southend U* 16 8 **16 8**
2008-09 Sheffield W 29 8
2009-10 Sheffield W 36 6 **83 18**
2010-11 QPR 13 0 **14 0**
2010-11 *Preston NE* 6 1 **6 1**
2011-12 Swindon T 2 0 **2 0**
2011-12 *Chesterfield* 14 9 **14 9**
2011-12 Charlton Ath 7 0 **7 0**
2011-12 *Crawley T* 4 1 **4 1**

CORT, Leon (D) 363 36
H: 6 3 W: 13 01 b.Bermondsey 11-9-79
Source: Dulwich H. *Honours:* Guyana 6 full caps, 1 goal.
1997-98 Millwall 0 0
1998-99 Millwall 0 0
1999-2000 Millwall 0 0
2000-01 Millwall 0 0
2001-02 Southend U 45 4
2002-03 Southend U 46 6
2003-04 Southend U 46 1 **137 11**
2004-05 Hull C 44 6
2005-06 Hull C 42 4 **86 10**
2006-07 Crystal Palace 37 7
2007-08 Crystal Palace 12 0 **49 7**
2007-08 Stoke C 33 8
2008-09 Stoke C 11 0
2009-10 Stoke C 0 0 **44 8**
2009-10 Burnley 15 0
2010-11 Burnley 4 0
2010-11 *Preston NE* 13 0 **13 0**
2011-12 Burnley 0 0 **19 0**
2011-12 Charlton Ath 15 0 **15 0**

COUSINS, Jordan (D) 0 0
b.Greenwich 6-3-94
Source: Scholar. *Honours:* England Youth.
2011-12 Charlton Ath 0 0

DOHERTY, Gary (D) 390 28
H: 6 3 W: 13 13 b.Co. Donegal 31-1-80
Source: Trainee. *Honours:* Eire Youth, Under-20, Under-21, 34 full caps, 4 goals.
1997-98 Luton T 10 0
1998-99 Luton T 20 6
1999-2000 Luton T 40 6 **70 12**
1999-2000 Tottenham H 2 0
2000-01 Tottenham H 22 3
2001-02 Tottenham H 7 0
2002-03 Tottenham H 15 1
2003-04 Tottenham H 17 0
2004-05 Tottenham H 1 0 **64 4**
2004-05 Norwich C 20 2
2005-06 Norwich C 42 1
2006-07 Norwich C 34 0
2007-08 Norwich C 34 0
2008-09 Norwich C 34 3
2009-10 Norwich C 38 5 **202 11**
2010-11 Charlton Ath 38 0
2011-12 Charlton Ath 3 0 **41 0**
2011-12 *Wycombe W* 13 1 **13 1**

EUELL, Jason (F) 427 87
H: 5 11 W: 11 13 b.Lambeth 6-2-77
Source: Trainee. *Honours:* England Youth, Under-21, Jamaica 3 full caps, 1 goal.
1995-96 Wimbledon 9 2
1996-97 Wimbledon 7 2
1997-98 Wimbledon 19 4
1998-99 Wimbledon 33 10
1999-2000 Wimbledon 37 4
2000-01 Wimbledon 36 19 **141 41**
2001-02 Charlton Ath 36 11
2002-03 Charlton Ath 36 10
2003-04 Charlton Ath 31 10
2004-05 Charlton Ath 26 2
2005-06 Charlton Ath 10 1
2006-07 Charlton Ath 0 0
2006-07 Middlesbrough 17 0
2007-08 Middlesbrough 0 0 **17 0**
2007-08 Southampton 38 3
2008-09 Southampton 24 2 **62 5**
2009-10 Blackpool 33 4
2010-11 Blackpool 3 0 **36 4**
2010-11 *Doncaster R* 12 3 **12 3**
2011-12 Charlton Ath 11 0 **150 34**
2011-12 *AFC Wimbledon* 9 0 **9 0**

EVINA, Cedric (D) 30 2
H: 5 11 W: 12 08 b.Cameroon 16-11-91
Source: Scholar.
2009-10 Arsenal 0 0
2010-11 Arsenal 0 0
2010-11 Oldham Ath 27 2 **27 2**
2011-12 Charlton Ath 3 0 **3 0**

GOUGH, Conor (G) 1 0
H: 6 5 W: 14 00 b.Ilford 9-8-93
Source: Scholar.
2011-12 Charlton Ath 0 0
2011-12 *Bristol R* 1 0 **1 0**

GREEN, Danny (M) 119 27
H: 5 11 W: 12 00 b.Harlow 9-7-88
Source: Bishop's Stortford.
2006-07 Northampton T 0 0
2007-08 Nottingham F 0 0
From Bishop's Stortford.
2009-10 Dagenham & R 46 13
2010-11 Dagenham & R 41 11 **87 24**
2011-12 Charlton Ath 32 3 **32 3**

HAMER, Ben (G) 134 0
H: 5 11 W: 12 04 b.Chard 20-11-87
Source: Crawley T.
2006-07 Reading 0 0
2007-08 Reading 0 0
2007-08 *Brentford* 20 0
2008-09 Reading 0 0
2008-09 *Brentford* 45 0
2009-10 Reading 0 0
2010-11 Reading 0 0
2010-11 *Brentford* 10 0 **75 0**
2010-11 *Exeter C* 18 0 **18 0**
2011-12 Charlton Ath 41 0 **41 0**

HARRIOTT, Callum (M) 3 0
H: 5 5 W: 10 05 b.Norbury 4-3-94
Source: Scholar.
2010-11 Charlton Ath 3 0
2011-12 Charlton Ath 0 0 **3 0**

HAYES, Paul (F) 362 85
H: 6 0 W: 12 12 b.Dagenham 20-9-83
Source: Norwich C Scholar.
2002-03 Scunthorpe U 18 8
2003-04 Scunthorpe U 35 2
2004-05 Scunthorpe U 46 18
2005-06 Barnsley 45 6
2006-07 Barnsley 30 5
2006-07 *Huddersfield T* 4 1 **4 1**
2007-08 Scunthorpe U 40 8
2008-09 Scunthorpe U 44 17
2009-10 Scunthorpe U 45 9 **228 62**
2010-11 Preston NE 23 2 **23 2**
2010-11 *Barnsley* 7 0 **82 11**
2011-12 Charlton Ath 19 3 **19 3**
2011-12 *Wycombe W* 6 6 **6 6**

HAYNES, Danny (F) 216 35
H: 5 11 W: 12 04 b.Peckham 19-1-88
Source: Scholar. *Honours:* England Youth.
2005-06 Ipswich T 19 3

2006-07	Ipswich T	31	7		
2006-07	*Millwall*	5	2	**5**	**2**
2007-08	Ipswich T	40	7		
2008-09	Ipswich T	24	0	**114**	**17**
2009-10	Bristol C	38	7		
2010-11	Bristol C	13	1	**51**	**8**
2010-11	Barnsley	20	6		
2011-12	Barnsley	12	0	**32**	**6**
2011-12	Charlton Ath	14	2	**14**	**2**

HOLLANDS, Danny (M) 246 32
H: 6 0 W: 11 11 b.Ashford (Middlesex) 6-11-85
Source: Trainee.

2003-04	Chelsea	0	0		
2004-05	Chelsea	0	0		
2005-06	Chelsea	0	0		
2005-06	*Torquay U*	10	1	**10**	**1**
2006-07	Bournemouth	33	1		
2007-08	Bournemouth	37	4		
2008-09	Bournemouth	42	6		
2009-10	Bournemouth	39	6		
2010-11	Bournemouth	42	7	**193**	**24**
2011-12	Charlton Ath	43	7	**43**	**7**

HUGHES, Andy (M) 531 39
H: 5 11 W: 12 01 b.Stockport 2-1-78
Source: Trainee.

1995-96	Oldham Ath	15	1		
1996-97	Oldham Ath	8	0		
1997-98	Oldham Ath	10	0	**33**	**1**
1997-98	Notts Co	15	2		
1998-99	Notts Co	30	3		
1999-2000	Notts Co	35	7		
2000-01	Notts Co	30	5	**110**	**17**
2001-02	Reading	39	6		
2002-03	Reading	43	9		
2003-04	Reading	43	3		
2004-05	Reading	41	0	**166**	**18**
2005-06	Norwich C	36	2		
2006-07	Norwich C	36	0	**72**	**2**
2007-08	Leeds U	40	1		
2008-09	Leeds U	27	0		
2009-10	Leeds U	39	0		
2010-11	Leeds U	10	0	**116**	**1**
2010-11	Scunthorpe U	19	0	**19**	**0**
2011-12	Charlton Ath	15	0	**15**	**0**

JACKSON, Johnnie (M) 268 44
H: 6 1 W: 12 00 b.Camden 15-8-82
Source: Trainee. *Honours:* England Youth, Under-20.

1999-2000	Tottenham H	0	0		
2000-01	Tottenham H	0	0		
2001-02	Tottenham H	0	0		
2002-03	Tottenham H	0	0		
2002-03	*Swindon T*	13	1	**13**	**1**
2002-03	*Colchester U*	8	0		
2003-04	Tottenham H	11	1		
2003-04	*Coventry C*	5	2	**5**	**2**
2004-05	Tottenham H	8	0		
2004-05	*Watford*	15	0	**15**	**0**
2005-06	Tottenham H	1	0	**20**	**1**
2005-06	*Derby Co*	6	0	**6**	**0**
2006-07	Colchester U	32	2		
2007-08	Colchester U	46	7		
2008-09	Colchester U	29	4		
2009-10	Colchester U	0	0	**115**	**13**
2009-10	Notts Co	24	2	**24**	**2**
2009-10	*Charlton Ath*	4	0		
2010-11	Charlton Ath	30	13		
2011-12	Charlton Ath	36	12	**70**	**25**

KERMORGANT, Yann (F) 236 59
H: 6 0 W: 13 03 b.Vannes 8-11-81
Source: Vannes.

2004-05	Chatellerault	29	14	**29**	**14**
2005-06	Grenoble	26	6		
2006-07	Grenoble	32	10	**58**	**16**
2007-08	Reims	33	4		
2008-09	Reims	34	9	**67**	**13**
2009-10	Leicester C	20	1		
2010-11	Leicester C	0	0	**20**	**1**
2010-11	*Arles-Avignon*	26	3	**26**	**3**
2011-12	Charlton Ath	36	12	**36**	**12**

MAMBO, Yado (D) 0 0
H: 6 3 W: 13 01 b.Kilburn 22-10-91
Source: Scholar.

2009-10	Charlton Ath	0	0		
2010-11	Charlton Ath	0	0		
2011-12	Charlton Ath	0	0		

MORRISON, Michael (D) 134 9
H: 6 0 W: 12 00 b.Bury St Edmunds 3-3-88
Source: Cambridge U.

2008-09	Leicester C	35	3		
2009-10	Leicester C	31	2		
2010-11	Leicester C	11	0	**77**	**5**
2010-11	Sheffield W	12	0	**12**	**0**
2011-12	Charlton Ath	45	4	**45**	**4**

OSBORNE, Harry (D) 0 0
b.Greenwich 3-3-94
Source: Scholar.

2011-12	Charlton Ath	0	0		

POPE, Nick (G) 0 0
H: 6 3 W: 11 13 b.Cambridge 19-4-92
Source: Bury T.

2011-12	Charlton Ath	0	0		

POPO, Tosan (F) 0 0
H: 5 8 W: 11 00 b.Brentwood 26-9-92
Source: Scholar.

2011-12	Charlton Ath	0	0		

POYET, Diego (M) 0 0
b. 8-4-95
Source: Scholar.

2011-12	Charlton Ath	0	0		

PRITCHARD, Bradley (M) 20 0
H: 6 1 W: 14 02 b.Zimbabwe 19-12-85
Source: Nuneaton Bor, Tamworth, Hayes & Yeading U.

2011-12	Charlton Ath	20	0	**20**	**0**

SMITH, Michael (F) 6 3
H: 6 4 W: 11 02 b.Wallsend 17-10-91
Source: Darlington.

2011-12	Charlton Ath	0	0		
2011-12	*Accrington S*	6	3	**6**	**3**

SOLLY, Chris (D) 68 1
H: 5 8 W: 10 07 b.Rochester 20-1-91
Source: Scholar.

2008-09	Charlton Ath	1	0		
2009-10	Charlton Ath	9	0		
2010-11	Charlton Ath	14	1		
2011-12	Charlton Ath	44	0	**68**	**1**

STEPHENS, Dale (M) 111 18
H: 5 7 W: 11 04 b.Bolton 12-6-89
Source: Scholar.

2006-07	Bury	3	0		
2007-08	Bury	6	1	**9**	**1**
2008-09	Oldham Ath	0	0		
2009-10	Oldham Ath	26	2		
2009-10	*Rochdale*	6	1	**6**	**1**
2010-11	Oldham Ath	34	9	**60**	**11**
2010-11	*Southampton*	6	0	**6**	**0**
2011-12	Charlton Ath	30	5	**30**	**5**

SULLIVAN, John (G) 33 0
H: 5 10 W: 11 04 b.Brighton 8-3-88
Source: Scholar.

2005-06	Brighton & HA	0	0		
2006-07	Brighton & HA	0	0		
2007-08	Brighton & HA	0	0		
2008-09	Brighton & HA	13	0	**13**	**0**
2009-10	Millwall	0	0		
2010-11	Millwall	0	0		
2010-11	*Yeovil T*	13	0	**13**	**0**
2010-11	*Charlton Ath*	4	0		
2011-12	Charlton Ath	3	0	**7**	**0**

TAYLOR, Matthew (D) 146 9
H: 6 0 W: 12 04 b.Chorley 30-1-82
Source: Burscough, Rossendale U, Matlock T, Hucknall T, Guiseley, Team Bath.

2008-09	Exeter C	31	2		
2009-10	Exeter C	46	5		
2010-11	Exeter C	28	2	**105**	**9**
2011-12	Charlton Ath	41	0	**41**	**0**

WAGSTAFF, Scott (M) 113 16
H: 5 10 W: 10 03 b.Maidstone 31-3-90
Source: Scholar.

2007-08	Charlton Ath	2	0		
2008-09	Charlton Ath	2	0		
2008-09	*Bournemouth*	5	0	**5**	**0**
2009-10	Charlton Ath	30	4		
2010-11	Charlton Ath	40	8		
2011-12	Charlton Ath	34	4	**108**	**16**

WARREN, Freddie (M) 0 0
b.Barking 2-11-92
Source: Scholar.

2011-12	Charlton Ath	0	0		

WIGGINS, Rhoys (D) 113 3
H: 5 8 W: 11 05 b.Uxbridge 4-11-87
Source: Scholar. *Honours:* Wales Youth, Under-21.

2006-07	Crystal Palace	0	0		
2007-08	Crystal Palace	0	0		
2008-09	Crystal Palace	1	0	**1**	**0**
2008-09	*Bournemouth*	13	0		
2009-10	Norwich C	0	0		
2009-10	*Bournemouth*	19	0		
2010-11	Bournemouth	35	2	**67**	**2**
2011-12	Charlton Ath	45	1	**45**	**1**

WRIGHT-PHILLIPS, Bradley (F) 238 72
H: 5 10 W: 10 07 b.Lewisham 12-3-85
Source: Scholar. *Honours:* England Youth, Under-20.

2002-03	Manchester C	0	0		
2003-04	Manchester C	0	0		
2004-05	Manchester C	14	1		
2005-06	Manchester C	18	1	**32**	**2**
2006-07	Southampton	39	8		
2007-08	Southampton	39	8		
2008-09	Southampton	33	6	**111**	**22**
2009-10	Plymouth Arg	15	4		
2010-11	Plymouth Arg	17	13	**32**	**17**
2010-11	Charlton Ath	21	9		
2011-12	Charlton Ath	42	22	**63**	**31**

CHELSEA (24)

AFFANE, Amin (M) 0 0
b.Gothenburg 21-1-94
Source: Scholar.

2011-12	Chelsea	0	0		

ALEX (D) 233 30
H: 6 2 W: 14 00 b.Niteroi 17-6-82
Honours: Brazil 17 full caps.

2002	Santos	25	3		
2003	Santos	34	9		
2004	Santos	4	0	**63**	**12**
2004-05	PSV Eindhoven	27	3		
2005-06	PSV Eindhoven	28	2		
2006-07	PSV Eindhoven	29	6	**84**	**11**
2007-08	Chelsea	28	2		
2008-09	Chelsea	24	2		
2009-10	Chelsea	16	1		
2010-11	Chelsea	15	2		
2011-12	Chelsea	3	0	**86**	**7**

Transferred to Paris St Germain January 2012.

ANELKA, Nicolas (F) 459 150
H: 6 1 W: 13 03 b.Versailles 14-3-79
Honours: France Youth, Under-21, 69 full caps, 14 goals.

1995-96	Paris St Germain	2	0		
1996-97	Paris St Germain	8	1		
1996-97	Arsenal	4	0		
1997-98	Arsenal	26	6		
1998-99	Arsenal	35	17	**65**	**23**
1999-2000	Real Madrid	19	2	**19**	**2**
2000-01	Paris St Germain	27	8		
2001-02	Paris St Germain	12	2	**49**	**11**
2001-02	Liverpool	20	4	**20**	**4**
2002-03	Manchester C	38	14		
2003-04	Manchester C	32	16		
2004-05	Manchester C	19	7	**89**	**37**
2004-05	Fenerbahce	14	4		
2005-06	Fenerbahce	25	10	**39**	**14**
2006-07	Bolton W	35	11		
2007-08	Bolton W	18	10	**53**	**21**
2007-08	Chelsea	14	1		
2008-09	Chelsea	37	19		
2009-10	Chelsea	33	11		
2010-11	Chelsea	32	6		
2011-12	Chelsea	9	1	**125**	**38**

Transferred to Shanghai Shenhua January 2012.

ASHTON, James (D) 0 0
b.Gravesend 2-10-92
Source: Scholar.

2010-11	Chelsea	0	0		
2011-12	Chelsea	0	0		

BAMFORD, Patrick (F) 2 0
H: 6 1 W: 11 02 b.Newark 5-9-93
Source: Scholar. *Honours:* England Youth.

2010-11	Nottingham F	0	0		
2011-12	Nottingham F	2	0	**2**	**0**
2011-12	Chelsea	0	0		

BENAYOUN, Yossi (M) **403 112**

H: 5 10 W: 11 00 b.Beer Sheva 6-6-80

Honours: Israel 88 full caps, 24 goals.

1997-98	Hapoel Beer Sheva	25	15	**25**	**15**
1998-99	Maccabi Haifa	29	16		
1999-2000	Maccabi Haifa	38	19		
2000-01	Maccabi Haifa	37	13		
2001-02	Maccabi Haifa	26	7	**130**	**55**
2002-03	Santander	31	4		
2003-04	Santander	35	7		
2004-05	Santander	0	0	**66**	**11**
2005-06	West Ham U	34	5		
2006-07	West Ham U	29	3	**63**	**8**
2007-08	Liverpool	30	4		
2008-09	Liverpool	32	8		
2009-10	Liverpool	30	6	**92**	**18**
2010-11	Chelsea	7	1		
2011-12	Chelsea	1	0	**8**	**1**
2011-12	*Arsenal*	19	4	**19**	**4**

BERTRAND, Ryan (D) **153 1**

H: 5 10 W: 11 00 b.Southwark 5-8-89

Source: Scholar. *Honours:* England Youth, Under-21.

2006-07	Chelsea	0	0		
2006-07	*Bournemouth*	5	0	**5**	**0**
2007-08	Chelsea	0	0		
2007-08	*Oldham Ath*	21	0	**21**	**0**
2007-08	*Norwich C*	18	0		
2008-09	Chelsea	0	0		
2008-09	*Norwich C*	38	0	**56**	**0**
2009-10	Chelsea	0	0		
2009-10	*Reading*	44	1	**44**	**1**
2010-11	Chelsea	1	0		
2010-11	*Nottingham F*	19	0	**19**	**0**
2011-12	Chelsea	7	0	**8**	**0**

BLACKMAN, Jamal (G) **0 0**

b.Croydon 27-10-93

Source: Scholar. *Honours:* England Youth.

2011-12	Chelsea	0	0		

BOSINGWA, Jose (D) **248 6**

H: 6 0 W: 12 08 b.Kinshasa 24-8-82

Honours: Portugal Under-21, 24 full caps.

2000-01	Freamunde	11	0	**11**	**0**
2001-02	Boavista	15	0		
2002-03	Boavista	26	0	**41**	**0**
2003-04	Porto	13	1		
2004-05	Porto	25	1		
2005-06	Porto	21	0		
2006-07	Porto	25	0		
2007-08	Porto	23	1	**107**	**3**
2008-09	Chelsea	34	2		
2009-10	Chelsea	8	0		
2010-11	Chelsea	20	0		
2011-12	Chelsea	27	1	**89**	**3**

BRUMA, Jeffrey (D) **37 4**

H: 6 1 W: 12 00 b.Rotterdam 13-11-91

Source: Feyenoord. *Honours:* Holland Under-21, 4 full caps.

2009-10	Chelsea	2	0		
2010-11	Chelsea	2	0		
2010-11	*Leicester C*	11	2	**11**	**2**
2011-12	Chelsea	0	0	**4**	**0**
2011-12	*Hamburg*	22	2	**22**	**2**

CAHILL, Gary (D) **211 18**

H: 6 2 W: 12 06 b.Dronfield 19-12-85

Source: Trainee. *Honours:* England Youth, Under-20, Under-21, 9 full caps, 2 goals.

2003-04	Aston Villa	0	0		
2004-05	Aston Villa	0	0		
2004-05	*Burnley*	27	1	**27**	**1**
2005-06	Aston Villa	7	1		
2006-07	Aston Villa	20	0		
2007-08	Aston Villa	1	0	**28**	**1**
2007-08	*Sheffield U*	16	2	**16**	**2**
2007-08	Bolton W	13	0		
2008-09	Bolton W	33	3		
2009-10	Bolton W	29	5		
2010-11	Bolton W	36	3		
2011-12	Bolton W	19	2	**130**	**13**
2011-12	Chelsea	10	1	**10**	**1**

CECH, Petr (G) **384 0**

H: 6 5 W: 14 07 b.Plzen 20-5-82

Honours: Czech Republic Youth, Under-20, Under-21, 94 full caps.

1998-99	Viktoria Plzen	0	0		
1999-2000	Chmel	1	0		
2000-01	Chmel	26	0	**27**	**0**
2001-02	Sparta Prague	26	0	**26**	**0**
2002-03	Rennes	37	0		
2003-04	Rennes	38	0	**75**	**0**
2004-05	Chelsea	35	0		
2005-06	Chelsea	34	0		
2006-07	Chelsea	20	0		
2007-08	Chelsea	26	0		
2008-09	Chelsea	35	0		
2009-10	Chelsea	34	0		
2010-11	Chelsea	38	0		
2011-12	Chelsea	34	0	**256**	**0**

CHALOBAH, Nathaniel (D) **0 0**

H: 6 1 W: 11 11 b.Sierra Leone 12-12-94

Source: Scholar. *Honours:* England Youth.

2010-11	Chelsea	0	0		
2011-12	Chelsea	0	0		

CLIFFORD, Billy (M) **0 0**

b.Slough 18-10-92

Source: Scholar.

2010-11	Chelsea	0	0		
2011-12	Chelsea	0	0		

CLIFFORD, Conor (M) **23 0**

H: 5 8 W: 10 08 b.Dublin 1-10-91

Source: Scholar. *Honours:* Eire Youth, Under-21.

2008-09	Chelsea	0	0		
2009-10	Chelsea	0	0		
2010-11	Chelsea	0	0		
2010-11	*Plymouth Arg*	7	0	**7**	**0**
2010-11	*Notts Co*	9	0	**9**	**0**
2011-12	Chelsea	0	0		
2011-12	*Yeovil T*	7	0	**7**	**0**

COLE, Ashley (D) **351 15**

H: 5 8 W: 10 05 b.Stepney 20-12-80

Source: Trainee. *Honours:* England Schools, Youth, Under-21, B, 98 full caps, 1 goal.

1998-99	Arsenal	0	0		
1999-2000	Arsenal	1	0		
1999-2000	*Crystal Palace*	14	1	**14**	**1**
2000-01	Arsenal	17	3		
2001-02	Arsenal	29	2		
2002-03	Arsenal	31	1		
2003-04	Arsenal	32	0		
2004-05	Arsenal	35	2		
2005-06	Arsenal	11	0		
2006-07	Arsenal	0	0	**156**	**8**
2006-07	Chelsea	23	0		
2007-08	Chelsea	27	1		
2008-09	Chelsea	34	1		
2009-10	Chelsea	27	4		
2010-11	Chelsea	38	0		
2011-12	Chelsea	32	0	**181**	**6**

COURTOIS, Thibaut (G) **78 0**

b.Bree 11-5-92

Honours: Belgium 2 full caps.

2008-09	Genk	1	0		
2009-10	Genk	0	0		
2010-11	Genk	40	0	**41**	**0**
2011-12	Chelsea	0	0		
2011-12	*Atletico Madrid*	37	0	**37**	**0**

DAVILA, Ulises (M) **35 3**

b.Guadalajara 13-4-91

Honours: Mexico Youth.

2008-09	Tapatio	18	3	**18**	**3**
2009-10	Guadalajara	7	0		
2010-11	Guadalajara	8	0	**15**	**0**
2011-12	Chelsea	0	0		
2011-12	*Vitesse*	2	0	**2**	**0**

DE BRUYNE, Kevin (M) **79 14**

H: 5 11 W: 12 00 b.Ghent 28-6-91

Honours: Belgium Youth, 2 full caps.

2008-09	Genk	2	0		
2009-10	Genk	30	3		
2010-11	Genk	32	5		
2011-12	Genk	15	6	**79**	**14**
2011-12	Chelsea	0	0		

DEEN-CONTEH, Aziz (D) **0 0**

b.Sierra Leone 14-1-93

Source: Scholar. *Honours:* England Youth.

2010-11	Chelsea	0	0		
2011-12	Chelsea	0	0		

DELAC, Matej (G) **39 0**

b.Bosnia 20-8-92

Source: Vitesse.

2009-10	Inter Zapresic	38	0	**38**	**0**
2010-11	Chelsea	0	0		
2011-12	Chelsea	0	0		
2011-12	*Dynamo Ceske*	1	0	**1**	**0**

DROGBA, Didier (F) **370 149**

H: 6 2 W: 14 05 b.Abidjan 11-3-78

Honours: Ivory Coast 86 full caps, 55 goals.

1998-99	Le Mans	2	0		
1999-2000	Le Mans	30	6		
2000-01	Le Mans	11	0		
2001-02	Le Mans	21	5	**64**	**11**
2001-02	Guingamp	11	3		
2002-03	Guingamp	34	17	**45**	**20**
2003-04	Marseille	35	18	**35**	**18**
2004-05	Chelsea	26	10		
2005-06	Chelsea	29	12		
2006-07	Chelsea	36	20		
2007-08	Chelsea	19	8		
2008-09	Chelsea	24	5		
2009-10	Chelsea	32	29		
2010-11	Chelsea	36	11		
2011-12	Chelsea	24	5	**226**	**100**

ESSIEN, Michael (M) **300 35**

H: 5 10 W: 13 06 b.Accra 3-12-82

Source: Liberty Accra. *Honours:* Ghana 52 full caps, 9 goals.

2000-01	Bastia	13	1		
2001-02	Bastia	24	4		
2002-03	Bastia	29	6	**66**	**11**
2003-04	Lyon	34	3		
2004-05	Lyon	37	4	**71**	**7**
2005-06	Chelsea	31	2		
2006-07	Chelsea	33	2		
2007-08	Chelsea	27	6		
2008-09	Chelsea	11	1		
2009-10	Chelsea	14	3		
2010-11	Chelsea	33	3		
2011-12	Chelsea	14	0	**163**	**17**

FERUZ, Islam (F) **0 0**

b.Somalia 10-9-95

Source: Celtic. *Honours:* Scotland Youth, Under-21.

2011-12	Chelsea	0	0		

GORDON, Ben (D) **36 0**

H: 5 11 W: 12 06 b.Bradford 2-3-91

Source: Scholar. *Honours:* England Under-20.

2008-09	Chelsea	0	0		
2009-10	Chelsea	0	0		
2009-10	*Tranmere R*	4	0	**4**	**0**
2010-11	Chelsea	0	0		
2010-11	*Scunthorpe U*	14	0	**14**	**0**
2011-12	Chelsea	0	0		
2011-12	*Peterborough U*	1	0	**1**	**0**
2011-12	*Kilmarnock*	17	0	**17**	**0**

HILARIO (G) **253 2**

H: 6 2 W: 13 05 b.San Pedro da Cova 21-10-75

Honours: Portugal Under-21, B, 1 full cap.

1994-95	Naval	27	0	**27**	**0**
1995-96	Academica	33	2		
1996-97	Porto	18	0		
1997-98	Porto	3	0		
1998-99	Amadora	27	0	**27**	**0**
1999-2000	Porto	19	0		
2000-01	Porto	0	0		
2001-02	Varzim	24	0	**24**	**0**
2002-03	Porto	0	0	**40**	**0**
2002-03	Academica	10	0	**43**	**2**
2003-04	Nacional	29	0		
2004-05	Nacional	32	0		
2005-06	Nacional	11	0	**72**	**0**
2006-07	Chelsea	11	0		
2007-08	Chelsea	3	0		
2008-09	Chelsea	1	0		
2009-10	Chelsea	3	0		
2010-11	Chelsea	0	0		
2011-12	Chelsea	2	0	**20**	**0**

HUTCHINSON, Sam (M) **5 0**

H: 6 0 W: 11 07 b.Windsor 3-8-89

Source: Scholar. *Honours:* England Youth.

2006-07	Chelsea	1	0		
2007-08	Chelsea	0	0		
2008-09	Chelsea	0	0		
2009-10	Chelsea	2	0		
2010-11	Chelsea	0	0		
2011-12	Chelsea	2	0	**5**	**0**

INCE, Rohan (D) **0 0**

b.Whitechapel 8-11-92

Source: Scholar.

2010-11	Chelsea	0	0		
2011-12	Chelsea	0	0		

IVANOVIC, Branislav (M) 235 20
H: 6 0 W: 12 04 b.Sremska Mitreovica 22-2-84
Honours: Serbia Under-21, 51 full caps, 6 goals.

2002-03	Sremska	19	2	**19**	**2**
2003-04	OFK Belgrade	13	0		
2004-05	OFK Belgrade	27	2		
2005-06	OFK Belgrade	15	3	**55**	**5**
2006	Lokomotiv Moscow	28	2		
2007	Lokomotiv Moscow	26	3	**54**	**5**
2007-08	Chelsea	0	0		
2008-09	Chelsea	16	0		
2009-10	Chelsea	28	1		
2010-11	Chelsea	34	4		
2011-12	Chelsea	29	3	**107**	**8**

KAKUTA, Gael (F) 31 5
H: 5 8 W: 10 03 b.Lille 21-6-91
Source: Lens. *Honours:* Chelsea Scholar. France Youth, Under-21.

2008-09	Chelsea	0	0		
2009-10	Chelsea	1	0		
2010-11	Chelsea	5	0		
2010-11	*Fulham*	7	1	**7**	**1**
2011-12	Chelsea	0	0	**6**	**0**
2011-12	*Bolton W*	4	0	**4**	**0**
2011-12	*Dijon*	14	4	**14**	**4**

KALAS, Tomas (D) 5 0
H: 6 0 W: 12 00 b.Olomouc 15-5-93
Source: Sigma Olomouc. *Honours:* Czech Republic Under-21.

2009-10	Sigma Olomouc	1	0		
2010-11	Chelsea	0	0		
2010-11	*Sigma Olomouc*	4	0	**5**	**0**
2011-12	Chelsea	0	0		

KALOU, Salomon (F) 234 75
H: 6 0 W: 12 02 b.Oume 5-8-85
Source: Oume, ASEC Abidjan. *Honours:* Ivory Coast 49 full caps, 18 goals.

2003-04	Excelsior	11	4	**11**	**4**
2003-04	Feyenoord	2	0		
2004-05	Feyenoord	31	20		
2005-06	Feyenoord	34	15	**67**	**35**
2006-07	Chelsea	33	7		
2007-08	Chelsea	30	7		
2008-09	Chelsea	27	6		
2009-10	Chelsea	23	5		
2010-11	Chelsea	31	10		
2011-12	Chelsea	12	1	**156**	**36**

KANE, Todd (D) 0 0
b.Huntingdon 17-9-93
Source: Scholar. *Honours:* England Youth.

2011-12	Chelsea	0	0		

LALKOVIC, Milan (F) 8 0
b.Kosice 9-12-92
Source: Scholar. *Honours:* Slovakia Youth, Under-21.

2010-11	Chelsea	0	0		
2011-12	Chelsea	0	0		
2011-12	*Doncaster R*	6	0	**6**	**0**
2011-12	*Den Haag*	2	0	**2**	**0**

LAMPARD, Frank (M) 531 151
H: 6 0 W: 14 02 b.Romford 20-6-78
Source: Trainee. *Honours:* England Youth, Under-21, B, 90 full caps, 23 goals.

1994-95	West Ham U	0	0		
1995-96	West Ham U	2	0		
1995-96	*Swansea C*	9	1	**9**	**1**
1996-97	West Ham U	13	0		
1997-98	West Ham U	31	5		
1998-99	West Ham U	38	5		
1999-2000	West Ham U	34	7		
2000-01	West Ham U	30	7	**148**	**24**
2001-02	Chelsea	37	5		
2002-03	Chelsea	38	6		
2003-04	Chelsea	38	10		
2004-05	Chelsea	38	13		
2005-06	Chelsea	35	16		
2006-07	Chelsea	37	11		
2007-08	Chelsea	24	10		
2008-09	Chelsea	37	12		
2009-10	Chelsea	36	22		
2010-11	Chelsea	24	10		
2011-12	Chelsea	30	11	**374**	**126**

LUIZ, David (D) 140 9
H: 6 2 W: 13 03 b.Sao Paulo 22-4-87
Honours: Brazil Youth, 11 full caps.

2005	Vitoria	0	0		
2006	Vitoria	26	1	**26**	**1**
2006-07	Benfica	10	0		
2007-08	Benfica	8	0		
2008-09	Benfica	19	2		
2009-10	Benfica	29	2		
2010-11	Benfica	16	0	**82**	**4**
2010-11	Chelsea	12	2		
2011-12	Chelsea	20	2	**32**	**4**

LUKAKU, Romelu (F) 81 33
H: 6 3 W: 13 00 b.Antwerp 13-5-93
Honours: Belgium Under-21, 15 full caps, 2 goals.

2008-09	Anderlecht	1	0		
2009-10	Anderlecht	33	15		
2010-11	Anderlecht	37	16		
2011-12	Anderlecht	2	2	**73**	**33**
2011-12	Chelsea	8	0	**8**	**0**

MALOUDA, Florent (M) 438 80
H: 6 0 W: 11 06 b.Guyane 13-6-80
Honours: France 80 full caps, 9 goals.

1996-97	Chateauroux	2	0		
1997-98	Chateauroux	1	0		
1998-99	Chateauroux	28	3		
1999-2000	Chateauroux	28	2	**59**	**5**
2000-01	Guingamp	23	1		
2001-02	Guingamp	32	4		
2002-03	Guingamp	37	10	**92**	**15**
2003-04	Lyon	35	4		
2004-05	Lyon	37	5		
2005-06	Lyon	31	6		
2006-07	Lyon	35	10	**138**	**25**
2007-08	Chelsea	21	2		
2008-09	Chelsea	31	6		
2009-10	Chelsea	33	12		
2010-11	Chelsea	38	13		
2011-12	Chelsea	26	2	**149**	**35**

MATA, Juan (M) 202 49
H: 5 7 W: 11 00 b.Ocon de Villafranca 28-4-88
Honours: Spain Youth, Under-21, 19 full caps, 6 goals.

2006-07	Real Madrid B	39	10	**39**	**10**
2007-08	Valencia	24	5		
2008-09	Valencia	37	11		
2009-10	Valencia	35	9		
2010-11	Valencia	33	8	**129**	**33**
2011-12	Chelsea	34	6	**34**	**6**

McEACHRAN, Josh (D) 15 0
H: 5 10 W: 10 03 b.Oxford 1-3-93
Source: Scholar. *Honours:* England Under-21.

2010-11	Chelsea	9	0		
2011-12	Chelsea	2	0	**11**	**0**
2011-12	*Swansea C*	4	0	**4**	**0**

MIKEL, John Obi (M) 166 1
H: 6 0 W: 13 05 b.Plateau State 22-4-87
Source: Plateau U. *Honours:* Nigeria Youth, 37 full caps, 2 goals.

2005	Lyn	6	1	**6**	**1**
2006-07	Chelsea	22	0		
2007-08	Chelsea	29	0		
2008-09	Chelsea	34	0		
2009-10	Chelsea	25	0		
2010-11	Chelsea	28	0		
2011-12	Chelsea	22	0	**160**	**0**

MITROVIC, Marko (F) 0 0
b.Malmo 27-6-92
Source: Malmo.

2009-10	Chelsea	0	0		
2010-11	Chelsea	0	0		
2011-12	Chelsea	0	0		

NKUMU, Archange (M) 0 0
b.Tottenham 5-11-93
Source: Scholar.

2011-12	Chelsea	0	0		

OMERUO, Kenneth (D) 0 0
H: 6 1 W: 12 00 b.Nigeria 17-10-93
Source: Standard Liege Youth. *Honours:* Nigeria Youth.

2011-12	Chelsea	0	0		

PAPPOE, Daniel (D) 0 0
b.Accra 30-12-93
Source: Scholar.

2011-12	Chelsea	0	0		

PAULO FERREIRA (D) 304 4
H: 6 0 W: 11 13 b.Cascais 18-1-79
Honours: Portugal Under-21, 62 full caps.

1997-98	Estoril	1	0		
1998-99	Estoril	16	0		
1999-2000	Estoril	18	2	**35**	**2**
2000-01	Vitoria Setubal	34	2		
2001-02	Vitoria Setubal	34	0	**68**	**2**
2002-03	Porto	30	0		
2003-04	Porto	32	0	**62**	**0**
2004-05	Chelsea	29	0		
2005-06	Chelsea	21	0		
2006-07	Chelsea	24	0		
2007-08	Chelsea	18	0		
2008-09	Chelsea	7	0		
2009-10	Chelsea	13	0		
2010-11	Chelsea	21	0		
2011-12	Chelsea	6	0	**139**	**0**

PHILLIP, Adam (F) 3 0
H: 5 10 W: 11 00 b.Carshalton 19-6-91
Source: Scholar.

2009-10	Chelsea	0	0		
2010-11	Chelsea	0	0		
2010-11	*Yeovil T*	3	0	**3**	**0**
2011-12	Chelsea	0	0		

PIAZON, Lucas (M) 0 0
b.Curitiba 20-1-94
Source: Scholar.

2011-12	Chelsea	0	0		

PIREZ, Jhon (F) 0 0
b.Montevideo 20-2-93
Source: Scholar. *Honours:* Uruguay Youth.

2011-12	Chelsea	0	0		

RAMIRES (M) 160 24
H: 5 11 W: 10 03 b.Rio de Janeiro 24-3-87
Honours: Brazil 27 full caps, 2 goals.

2006	Joinville	14	3	**14**	**3**
2007	Cruzeiro	32	3		
2008	Cruzeiro	25	6		
2009	Cruzeiro	4	1	**61**	**10**
2009-10	Benfica	26	4	**26**	**4**
2010-11	Chelsea	29	2		
2011-12	Chelsea	30	5	**59**	**7**

RAUL MEIRELES (M) 271 23
H: 5 10 W: 10 12 b.Oporto 17-3-83
Honours: Portugal Under-21, 61 full caps, 8 goals.

2001-02	Aves	16	0		
2002-03	Aves	26	1	**42**	**1**
2003-04	Boavista	29	0	**29**	**0**
2004-05	Porto	13	0		
2005-06	Porto	18	2		
2006-07	Porto	25	3		
2007-08	Porto	28	4		
2008-09	Porto	28	4		
2009-10	Porto	25	2	**137**	**15**
2010-11	Liverpool	33	5		
2011-12	Liverpool	2	0	**35**	**5**
2011-12	Chelsea	28	2	**28**	**2**

ROMEU, Oriol (M) 66 1
H: 6 0 W: 12 06 b.Ulldecona 24-9-91
Honours: Spain Youth, Under-21.

2008-09	Barcelona B	5	0		
2009-10	Barcelona B	26	0		
2010-11	Barcelona B	18	1	**49**	**1**
2010-11	Barcelona	1	0	**1**	**0**
2011-12	Chelsea	16	0	**16**	**0**

SAVILLE, George (M) 0 0
b.Camberley 1-6-93
Source: Scholar.

2010-11	Chelsea	0	0		
2011-12	Chelsea	0	0		

STURRIDGE, Daniel (F) 89 25
H: 6 2 W: 12 00 b.Birmingham 1-9-89
Source: Scholar. *Honours:* England Youth, Under-21, 2 full caps.

2006-07	Manchester C	2	0		
2007-08	Manchester C	3	1		
2008-09	Manchester C	16	4		
2009-10	Manchester C	0	0	**21**	**5**
2009-10	Chelsea	13	1		
2010-11	Chelsea	13	0		
2010-11	*Bolton W*	12	8	**12**	**8**
2011-12	Chelsea	30	11	**56**	**12**

TAYLOR, Rhys (G) 64 0
H: 6 2 W: 12 08 b.Neath 7-4-90
Honours: Wales Under-21.

2007-08	Chelsea	0	0		
2008-09	Chelsea	0	0		
2009-10	Chelsea	0	0		
2010-11	Chelsea	0	0		
2010-11	*Crewe Alex*	44	0	**44**	**0**

2011-12	Chelsea	0	0		
2011-12	*Rotherham U*	20	0	**20**	**0**

TERRY, John (D) **379 28**
H: 6 1 W: 14 02 b.Barking 7-12-80
Source: Trainee. *Honours:* England Under-21, 77 full caps, 6 goals.

1997-98	Chelsea	0	0		
1998-99	Chelsea	2	0		
1999-2000	Chelsea	4	0		
1999-2000	*Nottingham F*	6	0	**6**	**0**
2000-01	Chelsea	22	1		
2001-02	Chelsea	33	1		
2002-03	Chelsea	20	3		
2003-04	Chelsea	33	2		
2004-05	Chelsea	36	3		
2005-06	Chelsea	36	4		
2006-07	Chelsea	28	1		
2007-08	Chelsea	23	1		
2008-09	Chelsea	35	1		
2009-10	Chelsea	37	2		
2010-11	Chelsea	33	3		
2011-12	Chelsea	31	6	**373**	**28**

TORRES, Fernando (F) **322 147**
H: 5 9 W: 12 03 b.Madrid 20-3-84
Honours: Spain 98 full caps, 31 goals.

2002-03	Atletico Madrid	29	13		
2003-04	Atletico Madrid	35	19		
2004-05	Atletico Madrid	38	16		
2005-06	Atletico Madrid	36	13		
2006-07	Atletico Madrid	36	14	**174**	**75**
2007-08	Liverpool	33	24		
2008-09	Liverpool	24	14		
2009-10	Liverpool	22	18		
2010-11	Liverpool	23	9	**102**	**65**
2010-11	Chelsea	14	1		
2011-12	Chelsea	32	6	**46**	**7**

TURNBULL, Ross (G) **95 0**
H: 6 4 W: 15 00 b.Bishop Auckland 4-1-85
Source: Trainee. *Honours:* England Youth, Under-20.

2002-03	Middlesbrough	0	0		
2003-04	Middlesbrough	0	0		
2003-04	*Darlington*	1	0	**1**	**0**
2003-04	*Barnsley*	3	0		
2004-05	Middlesbrough	0	0		
2004-05	*Bradford C*	2	0	**2**	**0**
2004-05	*Barnsley*	23	0	**26**	**0**
2005-06	Middlesbrough	2	0		
2005-06	*Crewe Alex*	29	0	**29**	**0**
2006-07	Middlesbrough	0	0		
2007-08	Middlesbrough	3	0		
2007-08	*Cardiff C*	6	0	**6**	**0**
2008-09	Middlesbrough	22	0		
2009-10	Middlesbrough	0	0	**27**	**0**
2009-10	Chelsea	2	0		
2010-11	Chelsea	0	0		
2011-12	Chelsea	2	0	**4**	**0**

VAN AANHOLT, Patrick (D) **53 1**
H: 5 9 W: 10 08 b.Den Bosch 3-7-88
Honours: Holland Youth, Under-21.

2007-08	Chelsea	0	0		
2008-09	Chelsea	0	0		
2009-10	Chelsea	2	0		
2009-10	*Coventry C*	20	0	**20**	**0**
2009-10	*Newcastle U*	7	0	**7**	**0**
2010-11	Chelsea	0	0		
2010-11	*Leicester C*	12	1	**12**	**1**
2011-12	Chelsea	0	0	**2**	**0**
2011-12	*Wigan Ath*	3	0	**3**	**0**
2011-12	*Vitesse*	9	0	**9**	**0**

WALKER, Sam (G) **48 0**
H: 6 5 W: 14 00 b.Gravesend 2-10-91
Source: Scholar.

2009-10	Chelsea	0	0		
2010-11	Chelsea	0	0		
2010-11	*Barnet*	7	0	**7**	**0**
2011-12	Chelsea	0	0		
2011-12	*Northampton T*	21	0	**21**	**0**
2011-12	*Yeovil T*	20	0	**20**	**0**

Scholars
Ake Nathan Benjamin; Baker Lewis Renard; Bangura Samuel; Davey Alex James; Figueira Walter; Gordon Alastair; Howard Tom; Nditi Adam Eric Richard; Nortey Nii Nortei; Osmanovic Anjur; Seremba Ismail; Swift John David.

CHELTENHAM T (25)

ANDREW, Danny (D) **65 4**
H: 5 11 W: 11 06 b.Holbeach 23-12-90

2009-10	Peterborough U	2	0	**2**	**0**
2009-10	*Cheltenham T*	10	0		
2010-11	Cheltenham T	43	4		
2011-12	Cheltenham T	10	0	**63**	**4**

BENNETT, Alan (D) **145 5**
H: 6 2 W: 12 08 b.Cork 4-10-81
Honours: Eire Under-21, B, 2 full caps.

2006-07	Reading	0	0		
2007-08	Reading	0	0		
2007-08	*Southampton*	10	0	**10**	**0**
2007-08	*Brentford*	11	1		
2008-09	Reading	0	0		
2008-09	*Brentford*	44	1		
2009-10	Brentford	13	0	**68**	**2**
2009-10	*Wycombe W*	6	1		
2010-11	Wycombe W	17	0	**23**	**1**
2011-12	Cheltenham T	44	2	**44**	**2**

BROWN, Scott P (G) **161 0**
H: 6 2 W: 13 01 b.Wolverhampton 26-4-85
Source: Wolverhampton W Trainee. From Welshpool T

2003-04	Bristol C	0	0		
2004-05	Cheltenham T	0	0		
2005-06	Cheltenham T	1	0		
2006-07	Cheltenham T	11	0		
2007-08	Cheltenham T	0	0		
2008-09	Cheltenham T	35	0		
2009-10	Cheltenham T	46	0		
2010-11	Cheltenham T	46	0		
2011-12	Cheltenham T	22	0	**161**	**0**

DUFFY, Darryl (F) **259 72**
H: 5 11 W: 12 01 b.Glasgow 16-4-84
Honours: Scotland Under-21, B.

2003-04	Rangers	1	0	**1**	**0**
2003-04	*Brechin C*	8	3	**8**	**3**
2004-05	Falkirk	35	17		
2005-06	Falkirk	21	9	**56**	**26**
2005-06	Hull C	15	3		
2006-07	Hull C	9	0	**24**	**3**
2006-07	*Hartlepool U*	10	5	**10**	**5**
2006-07	*Swansea C*	8	5		
2007-08	Swansea C	20	1	**28**	**6**
2008-09	Bristol R	43	13		
2009-10	Bristol R	30	4		
2009-10	*Carlisle U*	8	1	**8**	**1**
2010-11	Bristol R	3	0	**76**	**17**
2010-11	*Hibernian*	7	0	**7**	**0**
2011-12	Cheltenham T	41	11	**41**	**11**

ELLIOTT, Steve (D) **398 20**
H: 6 1 W: 14 00 b.Derby 29-10-78
Source: Trainee. *Honours:* England Under-21.

1996-97	Derby Co	0	0		
1997-98	Derby Co	3	0		
1998-99	Derby Co	11	0		
1999-2000	Derby Co	20	0		
2000-01	Derby Co	6	0		
2001-02	Derby Co	6	0		
2002-03	Derby Co	23	1		
2003-04	Derby Co	4	0	**73**	**1**
2003-04	Blackpool	28	0	**28**	**0**
2004-05	Bristol R	41	2		
2005-06	Bristol R	45	2		
2006-07	Bristol R	39	5		
2007-08	Bristol R	33	3		
2008-09	Bristol R	39	3		
2009-10	Bristol R	21	1	**218**	**16**
2010-11	Cheltenham T	41	1		
2011-12	Cheltenham T	38	2	**79**	**3**

GOULDING, Jeff (F) **118 19**
H: 6 2 W: 11 11 b.Sutton 13-5-84
Source: Croydon, Egham T, Aldershot T, Hayes, Yeading, Fisher Ath.

2008-09	Bournemouth	27	3		
2009-10	Bournemouth	17	1	**44**	**4**
2010-11	Cheltenham T	39	10		
2011-12	Cheltenham T	35	5	**74**	**15**

GRAHAM, Bagasan (M) **7 0**
b.Plaistow 6-10-92
Source: QPR Scholar.

2011-12	Cheltenham T	7	0	**7**	**0**

HOOMAN, Harry (D) **4 0**
H: 5 11 W: 12 06 b.Worcester 27-4-91
Source: Scholar.

2009-10	Shrewsbury T	2	0		
2010-11	Shrewsbury T	0	0	**2**	**0**
2011-12	Cheltenham T	2	0	**2**	**0**

JOMBATI, Sido (D) **36 2**
H: 6 0 W: 11 11 b.Lisbon 20-8-87
Source: Exeter C, Weymouth, Basingstoke T, Bath C.

2011-12	Cheltenham T	36	2	**36**	**2**

LEWIS, Theo (F) **40 0**
H: 5 10 W: 10 12 b.Oxford 10-8-91
Source: Scholar.

2008-09	Cheltenham T	2	0		
2009-10	Cheltenham T	15	0		
2010-11	Cheltenham T	22	0		
2011-12	Cheltenham T	1	0	**40**	**0**

LOW, Josh (M) **397 42**
H: 6 2 W: 14 03 b.Bristol 15-2-79
Source: Trainee. *Honours:* Wales Youth, Under-21.

1995-96	Bristol R	1	0		
1996-97	Bristol R	3	0		
1997-98	Bristol R	10	0		
1998-99	Bristol R	8	0	**22**	**0**
1999-2000	Leyton Orient	5	1	**5**	**1**
1999-2000	Cardiff C	17	2		
2000-01	Cardiff C	36	4		
2001-02	Cardiff C	22	0		
2002-03	Cardiff C	0	0	**75**	**6**
2002-03	Oldham Ath	21	3	**21**	**3**
2003-04	Northampton T	33	3		
2004-05	Northampton T	34	7		
2005-06	Northampton T	35	5	**102**	**15**
2006-07	Leicester C	16	0	**16**	**0**
2006-07	Peterborough U	19	1		
2007-08	Peterborough U	15	2		
2008-09	Peterborough U	0	0	**34**	**3**
2008-09	Cheltenham T	14	0		
2009-10	Cheltenham T	39	4		
2010-11	Cheltenham T	30	7		
2011-12	Cheltenham T	39	3	**122**	**14**

LOWE, Keith (D) **164 7**
H: 6 2 W: 13 03 b.Wolverhampton 13-9-85
Source: Scholar.

2004-05	Wolverhampton W	11	0		
2005-06	Wolverhampton W	3	0		
2005-06	*Burnley*	16	0	**16**	**0**
2005-06	*QPR*	1	0	**1**	**0**
2005-06	*Swansea C*	4	0	**4**	**0**
2006-07	Wolverhampton W	0	0		
2006-07	*Brighton & HA*	0	0		
2006-07	*Cheltenham T*	16	1		
2007-08	Wolverhampton W	0	0		
2007-08	*Port Vale*	28	3	**28**	**3**
2008-09	Wolverhampton W	0	0	**14**	**0**
2009-10	Hereford U	19	1	**19**	**1**
2010-11	Cheltenham T	36	1		
2011-12	Cheltenham T	30	1	**82**	**3**

McGLASHAN, Jermaine (M) **77 7**
H: 5 7 W: 10 00 b.Croydon 14-4-88
Source: Ashford T (Middlesex).

2010-11	Aldershot T	38	1		
2011-12	Aldershot T	23	4	**61**	**5**
2011-12	Cheltenham T	16	2	**16**	**2**

MOHAMMED, Kaid (F) **163 43**
H: 5 11 W: 12 06 b.Cardiff 23-7-84
Source: Carmarthen T.

2003-04	Cwmbran T	29	3		
2004-05	Cwmbran T	15	2		
2004-05	Llanelli	3	1		
2005-06	Carmarthen T	14	4		
2005-06	Cwmbran T	11	7	**55**	**12**
2006-07	Llanelli	5	0	**8**	**1**
2006-07	Carmarthen T	30	15	**44**	**19**
2007-08	Swindon T	11	0	**11**	**0**

From Forest Green R, Bath C, AFC Wimbledon.

2011-12	Cheltenham T	45	11	**45**	**11**

MOORE, Ethan (F) **0 0**
b.Gloucester 6-3-93
Source: Aston Villa Scholar.

2011-12	Cheltenham T	0	0		

PACK, Marlon (M) **107 8**
H: 6 2 W: 11 09 b.Portsmouth 25-3-91
Source: Scholar.

2008-09	Portsmouth	0	0		

2009-10 Portsmouth 0 0
2009-10 *Wycombe W* 8 0 **8 0**
2009-10 *Dagenham & R* 17 1 **17 1**
2010-11 Portsmouth 1 0 **1 0**
2010-11 *Cheltenham T* 38 2
2011-12 Cheltenham T 43 5 **81 7**

PENN, Russ (M) 124 8
H: 5 11 W: 12 13 b.Dudley 8-11-85
Source: Scunthorpe U, Kidderminster H.
Honours: England C.
2009-10 Burton Alb 40 4
2010-11 Burton Alb 41 3 **81 7**
2011-12 Cheltenham T 43 1 **43 1**

SMIKLE, Brian (M) 81 5
H: 5 11 W: 11 09 b.Tipton 3-11-85
Source: Scholar.
From Kidderminster H.
2005-06 WBA 0 0
2010-11 Cheltenham T 46 4
2011-12 Cheltenham T 35 1 **81 5**

SUMMERFIELD, Luke (M) 142 9
H: 6 0 W: 11 00 b.Ivybridge 6-12-87
Source: Scholar.
2004-05 Plymouth Arg 1 0
2005-06 Plymouth Arg 0 0
2006-07 Plymouth Arg 23 1
2006-07 *Bournemouth* 8 1 **8 1**
2007-08 Plymouth Arg 7 0
2008-09 Plymouth Arg 29 2
2009-10 Plymouth Arg 12 0
2009-10 *Leyton Orient* 14 0 **14 0**
2010-11 Plymouth Arg 7 1 **79 4**
2011-12 Cheltenham T 41 4 **41 4**

CHESTERFIELD (26)

ALLOTT, Mark (M) 579 52
H: 5 11 W: 11 07 b.Middleton 3-10-77
Source: Trainee.
1995-96 Oldham Ath 0 0
1996-97 Oldham Ath 5 1
1997-98 Oldham Ath 22 2
1998-99 Oldham Ath 41 7
1999-2000 Oldham Ath 32 10
2000-01 Oldham Ath 39 7
2001-02 Oldham Ath 15 4
2001-02 Chesterfield 21 4
2002-03 Chesterfield 33 0
2003-04 Chesterfield 40 2
2004-05 Chesterfield 45 2
2005-06 Chesterfield 43 3
2006-07 Chesterfield 39 0
2007-08 Oldham Ath 42 4
2008-09 Oldham Ath 45 3 **241 38**
2009-10 Chesterfield 45 2
2010-11 Chesterfield 36 0
2011-12 Chesterfield 36 1 **338 14**

BODEN, Scott (F) 102 15
H: 5 11 W: 11 00 b.Sheffield 19-12-89
Source: IFK Marlehamn.
2008-09 Chesterfield 11 2
2009-10 Chesterfield 35 6
2010-11 Chesterfield 23 3
2011-12 Chesterfield 26 4 **95 15**
2011-12 *Macclesfield T* 7 0 **7 0**

BOWERY, Jordan (F) 80 9
H: 6 1 W: 12 00 b.Nottingham 2-7-91
Source: Scholar.
2008-09 Chesterfield 3 0
2009-10 Chesterfield 10 0
2010-11 Chesterfield 27 1
2011-12 Chesterfield 40 8 **80 9**

CLAY, Craig (M) 8 1
H: 5 11 W: 11 07 b.Nottingham 5-5-92
Source: Scholar.
2010-11 Chesterfield 3 1
2011-12 Chesterfield 5 0 **8 1**

DARIKWA, Tendayi (M) 2 0
H: 6 2 W: 12 02 b.Nottingham 13-12-91
Source: Scholar.
2010-11 Chesterfield 0 0
2011-12 Chesterfield 2 0 **2 0**

DOWNES, Aaron (D) 182 10
H: 6 2 W: 13 02 b.Mudgee 15-5-85
Honours: Australia Youth, Under-20, Under-21, Under-23.
2004-05 Chesterfield 9 2
2005-06 Chesterfield 22 0
2006-07 Chesterfield 45 3
2007-08 Chesterfield 40 2
2008-09 Chesterfield 42 2
2009-10 Chesterfield 7 1
2010-11 Chesterfield 0 0
2011-12 Chesterfield 9 0 **174 10**
2011-12 *Bristol R* 8 0 **8 0**

FLEMING, Greg (G) 105 0
H: 5 11 W: 12 09 b.Dunfermline 27-9-86
Source: Livingston. *Honours:* Scotland Under-21.
2006-07 Gretna 2 0
2007-08 Gretna 28 0 **30 0**
2008-09 Oldham Ath 18 0
2009-10 Oldham Ath 0 0
2009-10 *Dunfermline Ath* 26 0 **26 0**
2010-11 Oldham Ath 0 0 **18 0**
2010-11 Galway U 21 0 **21 0**
2011-12 Chesterfield 10 0 **10 0**

FORD, Simon (D) 271 11
H: 6 1 W: 12 04 b.Lincoln 17-11-81
Source: Charlton Ath Scholar. *Honours:* Jamaica 3 full caps.
2001-02 Grimsby T 13 1
2002-03 Grimsby T 39 2
2003-04 Grimsby T 26 1 **78 4**
2004-05 Kilmarnock 18 1
2005-06 Kilmarnock 32 2
2006-07 Kilmarnock 16 0
2007-08 Kilmarnock 28 1
2008-09 Kilmarnock 27 1
2009-10 Kilmarnock 23 1 **144 6**
2010-11 Chesterfield 31 1
2011-12 Chesterfield 18 0 **49 1**

GRAY, Dan (M) 69 1
H: 6 0 W: 11 00 b.Mansfield 23-11-89
Source: Scholar.
2008-09 Chesterfield 25 0
2009-10 Chesterfield 19 0
2010-11 Chesterfield 2 0
2010-11 *Macclesfield T* 21 1
2011-12 Chesterfield 0 0 **46 0**
2011-12 *Macclesfield T* 2 0 **23 1**

HOLDEN, Dean (D) 340 20
H: 6 1 W: 12 04 b.Swinton 15-9-79
Source: Trainee. *Honours:* England Youth.
1997-98 Bolton W 0 0
1998-99 Bolton W 0 0
1999-2000 Bolton W 12 0
2000-01 Bolton W 1 1 **13 1**
2001 *Valur* 7 0 **7 0**
2001-02 *Oldham Ath* 23 2
2002-03 Oldham Ath 6 2
2003-04 Oldham Ath 39 4
2004-05 Oldham Ath 40 2 **108 10**
2005-06 Peterborough U 35 3
2006-07 Peterborough U 21 1 **56 4**
2006-07 Falkirk 9 1
2007-08 Falkirk 20 0
2008-09 Falkirk 19 1 **48 2**
2009-10 Shrewsbury T 37 0
2010-11 Shrewsbury T 13 0 **50 0**
2010-11 *Rotherham U* 6 0 **6 0**
2010-11 Chesterfield 17 2
2011-12 Chesterfield 14 1 **31 3**
2011-12 *Rochdale* 21 0 **21 0**

JUAN, Jimmy (M) 126 11
H: 6 2 W: 11 11 b.Valence 10-6-83
2003-04 Monaco 1 0
2004-05 Monaco 4 0 **5 0**
2004-05 Ipswich T 0 0
2005-06 *Ipswich T* 34 5 **34 5**
2006-07 Grenoble Foot 24 2
2007-08 Grenoble Foot 0 0
2008-09 *Chateauroux* 19 1 **19 1**
2009-10 Grenoble Foot 18 1
2010-11 Grenoble Foot 19 1 **61 4**
2011-12 Chesterfield 7 1 **7 1**

LEE, Tommy (G) 225 0
H: 6 2 W: 12 00 b.Keighley 3-1-86
Source: Scholar.
2005-06 Manchester U 0 0
2005-06 *Macclesfield T* 11 0
2006-07 Macclesfield T 34 0
2007-08 Macclesfield T 18 0 **63 0**
2007-08 *Rochdale* 11 0 **11 0**
2008-09 Chesterfield 28 0
2009-10 Chesterfield 42 0
2010-11 Chesterfield 46 0
2011-12 Chesterfield 35 0 **151 0**

LESTER, Jack (F) 526 137
H: 5 9 W: 12 08 b.Sheffield 8-10-75
Source: Trainee. *Honours:* England Schools.
1994-95 Grimsby T 7 0
1995-96 Grimsby T 5 0
1996-97 Grimsby T 22 5
1996-97 *Doncaster R* 11 1 **11 1**
1997-98 Grimsby T 40 4
1998-99 Grimsby T 33 4
1999-2000 Grimsby T 26 4 **133 17**
1999-2000 Nottingham F 15 2
2000-01 Nottingham F 19 7
2001-02 Nottingham F 32 5
2002-03 Nottingham F 33 7
2003-04 Sheffield U 32 12
2004-05 Sheffield U 12 0 **44 12**
2004-05 Nottingham F 3 1
2005-06 Nottingham F 38 5
2006-07 Nottingham F 35 6 **175 33**
2007-08 Chesterfield 36 23
2008-09 Chesterfield 37 20
2009-10 Chesterfield 29 11
2010-11 Chesterfield 40 17
2011-12 Chesterfield 21 3 **163 74**

LOWRY, Jamie (D) 124 11
H: 6 0 W: 12 00 b.Newquay 18-3-87
Source: Scholar.
2006-07 Chesterfield 8 0
2007-08 Chesterfield 42 6
2008-09 Chesterfield 42 0
2009-10 Chesterfield 13 5
2010-11 Chesterfield 3 0
2011-12 Chesterfield 6 0 **114 11**
2011-12 *Crewe Alex* 10 0 **10 0**

MENDY, Alex (M) 241 26
H: 6 3 W: 13 00 b.Paris 14-12-83
Source: Versailles.
2003-04 Marila 19 0
2004-05 Marila 25 4
2005-06 Marila 13 2 **57 6**
2005-06 SIAD 14 3
2006-07 SIAD 22 5
2007-08 SIAD 4 0 **40 8**
2007-08 Mlada 24 1
2008-09 Mlada 27 1
2009-10 Mlada 29 2
2010-11 Mlada 30 6 **110 10**
2011-12 Chesterfield 34 2 **34 2**

MORGAN, Dean (M) 305 36
H: 5 11 W: 13 00 b.Enfield 3-10-83
Source: Scholar.
2000-01 Colchester U 4 0
2001-02 Colchester U 30 0
2002-03 Colchester U 37 6
2003-04 Colchester U 0 0 **71 6**
2003-04 Reading 13 1
2004-05 Reading 18 2 **31 3**
2005-06 Luton T 36 6
2006-07 Luton T 36 4
2007-08 Luton T 16 1
2007-08 *Southend U* 8 0 **8 0**
2007-08 *Crewe Alex* 9 1 **9 1**
2008-09 Luton T 0 0
2008-09 *Leyton Orient* 32 5 **32 5**
2009-10 Luton T 0 0 **88 11**
2009-10 Milton Keynes D 9 1 **9 1**
2009-10 *Aldershot T* 9 4 **9 4**
2010-11 Chesterfield 21 1
2011-12 Chesterfield 17 3 **38 4**
2011-12 *Oxford U* 10 1 **10 1**

NEEDHAM, Matthew (D) 0 0
b.Sheffield 11-10-92
Source: Scholar.
2011-12 Chesterfield 0 0

NIVEN, Derek (M) 302 18
H: 5 11 W: 12 05 b.Falkirk 12-12-83
Source: Stenhousemuir.
2000-01 Raith R 1 0 **1 0**
2001-02 Bolton W 0 0
2002-03 Bolton W 0 0
2003-04 Bolton W 0 0
2003-04 Chesterfield 22 1
2004-05 Chesterfield 38 1
2005-06 Chesterfield 42 5
2006-07 Chesterfield 45 3
2007-08 Chesterfield 38 3
2008-09 Chesterfield 31 2
2009-10 Chesterfield 39 2
2010-11 Chesterfield 35 1

2011-12 Chesterfield 7 0 **297 18**
2011-12 *Northampton T* 4 0 **4 0**

RANDALL, Mark (M) 54 2
H: 6 0 W: 12 12 b.Milton Keynes 28-9-89
Source: Scholar. *Honours:* England Youth.
2006-07 Arsenal 0 0
2007-08 Arsenal 1 0
2007-08 *Burnley* 10 0 **10 0**
2008-09 Arsenal 1 0
2009-10 Arsenal 0 0
2009-10 *Milton Keynes D* 16 0 **16 0**
2010-11 Arsenal 0 0 **2 0**
2010-11 *Rotherham U* 10 1 **10 1**
2011-12 Chesterfield 16 1 **16 1**

ROBERTSON, Gregor (D) 205 4
H: 6 0 W: 12 04 b.Edinburgh 19-1-84
Honours: Scotland Under-21.
2000-01 Nottingham F 0 0
2001-02 Nottingham F 0 0
2002-03 Nottingham F 0 0
2003-04 Nottingham F 16 0
2004-05 Nottingham F 20 0 **36 0**
2005-06 Rotherham U 35 1
2006-07 Rotherham U 18 0 **53 1**
2007-08 Chesterfield 35 1
2008-09 Chesterfield 38 2
2009-10 Chesterfield 10 0
2010-11 Chesterfield 21 0
2011-12 Chesterfield 12 0 **116 3**

SMITH, Nathan (D) 139 1
H: 5 11 W: 12 00 b.Enfield 11-1-87
Source: Potters Bar T. *Honours:* Jamaica 1 full cap.
2007-08 Yeovil T 7 0
2008-09 Yeovil T 33 1
2009-10 Yeovil T 34 0
2010-11 Yeovil T 40 0 **114 1**
2011-12 Chesterfield 25 0 **25 0**

TALBOT, Drew (F) 215 21
H: 5 10 W: 11 00 b.Barnsley 19-7-86
Source: Dodworth Colliery.
2003-04 Sheffield W 0 0
2004-05 Sheffield W 21 4
2005-06 Sheffield W 0 0
2006-07 Sheffield W 8 0 **29 4**
2006-07 *Scunthorpe U* 3 1 **3 1**
2006-07 Luton T 15 3
2007-08 Luton T 27 0
2008-09 Luton T 7 0 **49 3**
2008-09 *Chesterfield* 17 2
2009-10 Chesterfield 30 6
2010-11 Chesterfield 44 3
2011-12 Chesterfield 43 2 **134 13**

THOMPSON, Josh (D) 59 5
H: 6 4 W: 12 00 b.Bolton 25-2-91
Source: Scholar. *Honours:* England Youth.
2008-09 Stockport Co 9 0 **9 0**
2009-10 Celtic 18 3 **18 3**
On loan from Celtic.
2010-11 Rochdale 12 1 **12 1**
On loan from Celtic.
2011-12 Chesterfield 20 1 **20 1**
On loan from Celtic.

TROTMAN, Neal (D) 119 6
H: 6 3 W: 13 08 b.Manchester 11-3-87
Source: Burnley Scholar.
2006-07 Oldham Ath 1 0
2007-08 Oldham Ath 17 1
2007-08 Preston NE 3 0
2008-09 Preston NE 0 0
2008-09 *Colchester U* 6 0 **6 0**
2009-10 Preston NE 0 0
2009-10 *Southampton* 18 2 **18 2**
2009-10 *Huddersfield T* 21 2 **21 2**
2010-11 Preston NE 0 0 **3 0**
2010-11 *Oldham Ath* 18 0 **36 1**
2011-12 Rochdale 12 0 **12 0**
2011-12 Chesterfield 23 1 **23 1**

WATKISS, Ben (M) 0 0
b.Derby 12-1-93
Source: Scholar.
2011-12 Chesterfield 0 0

WESTCARR, Craig (F) 158 31
H: 5 11 W: 11 04 b.Nottingham 29-1-85
Source: Scholar. *Honours:* England Youth.
2001-02 Nottingham F 8 0
2002-03 Nottingham F 11 1
2003-04 Nottingham F 3 0
2004-05 Nottingham F 1 0 **23 1**
2004-05 *Lincoln C* 6 1 **6 1**
2004-05 *Milton Keynes D* 4 0 **4 0**
From Cambridge U, Kettering T.
2009-10 Notts Co 42 9
From Cambridge U, Kettering T.
2010-11 Notts Co 41 12
From Cambridge U, Kettering T.
2011-12 Notts Co 4 0 **87 21**
2011-12 Chesterfield 38 8 **38 8**

WHITAKER, Danny (M) 413 65
H: 5 10 W: 11 00 b.Wilmslow 14-11-80
Source: Wilmslow Sports.
2000-01 Macclesfield T 0 0
2001-02 Macclesfield T 16 2
2002-03 Macclesfield T 41 10
2003-04 Macclesfield T 36 5
2004-05 Macclesfield T 36 2
2005-06 Macclesfield T 42 4 **171 23**
2006-07 Port Vale 45 7
2007-08 Port Vale 41 7 **86 14**
2008-09 Oldham Ath 39 6
2009-10 Oldham Ath 41 2 **80 8**
2010-11 Chesterfield 46 15
2011-12 Chesterfield 30 5 **76 20**

COLCHESTER U (27)

ALDRED, Tom (D) 12 0
H: 6 2 W: 13 02 b.Bolton 11-9-90
Source: Scholar.
2008-09 Carlisle U 0 0
2009-10 Carlisle U 5 0 **5 0**
2010-11 Watford 0 0
2010-11 *Stockport Co* 7 0 **7 0**
2011-12 Watford 0 0
2011-12 Colchester U 0 0
2011-12 *Torquay U* 0 0

BENDER, Tom (M) 3 0
H: 6 3 W: 12 00 b.Harlow 19-1-93
Source: Scholar. *Honours:* Wales Youth, Under-21.
2009-10 Colchester U 1 0
2010-11 Colchester U 0 0
2011-12 Colchester U 0 0 **1 0**
2011-12 *Accrington S* 2 0 **2 0**

BOND, Andy (M) 83 10
H: 5 10 W: 11 07 b.Wigan 16-3-86
Source: Crewe Alex Scholar, Barrow.
2010-11 Colchester U 43 7
2011-12 Colchester U 40 3 **83 10**

COKER, Ben (D) 40 0
H: 5 11 W: 11 09 b.Hatfield 17-6-89
Source: Bury T.
2010-11 Colchester U 20 0
2011-12 Colchester U 20 0 **40 0**

COUSINS, Mark (G) 35 0
H: 6 2 W: 12 02 b.Chelmsford 9-1-87
Source: Scholar.
2005-06 Colchester U 0 0
2006-07 Colchester U 0 0
2007-08 Colchester U 2 0
2008-09 Colchester U 9 0
2009-10 Colchester U 0 0
2010-11 Colchester U 14 0
2011-12 Colchester U 10 0 **35 0**

DUGUID, Karl (M) 517 47
H: 5 11 W: 11 06 b.Letchworth 21-3-78
Source: Trainee.
1995-96 Colchester U 16 1
1996-97 Colchester U 20 3
1997-98 Colchester U 21 3
1998-99 Colchester U 33 4
1999-2000 Colchester U 41 12
2000-01 Colchester U 41 5
2001-02 Colchester U 41 4
2002-03 Colchester U 27 3
2003-04 Colchester U 30 2
2004-05 Colchester U 0 0
2005-06 Colchester U 35 0
2006-07 Colchester U 43 5
2007-08 Colchester U 37 0
2008-09 Plymouth Arg 39 1
2009-10 Plymouth Arg 42 1
2010-11 Plymouth Arg 26 0 **107 2**
2011-12 Colchester U 25 3 **410 45**

EASTMAN, Tom (D) 41 3
H: 6 3 W: 13 12 b.Clacton 21-10-91
Source: Scholar.
2009-10 Ipswich T 1 0
2010-11 Ipswich T 9 0 **10 0**
2011-12 Colchester U 25 3 **25 3**
2011-12 *Crawley T* 6 0 **6 0**

GILBEY, Alex (M) 0 0
b.Dagenham
Source: Scholar.
2011-12 Colchester U 0 0

GILLESPIE, Steven (F) 196 55
H: 5 9 W: 11 02 b.Liverpool 4-6-84
Source: Liverpool Scholar.
2004-05 Bristol C 8 0
2004-05 *Cheltenham T* 12 5
2005-06 Bristol C 4 1 **12 1**
2005-06 Cheltenham T 14 5
2006-07 Cheltenham T 23 5
2007-08 Cheltenham T 37 14 **86 29**
2008-09 Colchester U 17 4
2009-10 Colchester U 30 1
2010-11 Colchester U 18 9
2011-12 Colchester U 33 11 **98 25**

HAMILTON, Bradley (D) 1 0
H: 6 0 W: 10 00 b.Newham 30-8-92
Source: Scholar.
2011-12 Colchester U 1 0 **1 0**

HEATH, Matt (D) 243 16
H: 6 4 W: 13 13 b.Leicester 1-11-81
Source: Scholar.
2000-01 Leicester C 0 0
2001-02 Leicester C 5 0
2002-03 Leicester C 11 3
2003-04 Leicester C 13 0
2003-04 *Stockport Co* 8 0 **8 0**
2004-05 Leicester C 22 3 **51 6**
2005-06 Coventry C 25 1
2006-07 Coventry C 7 0 **32 1**
2006-07 Leeds U 26 3
2007-08 Leeds U 26 1 **52 4**
2007-08 *Colchester U* 5 0
2008-09 Colchester U 14 0
2008-09 *Brighton & HA* 6 1 **6 1**
2009-10 Colchester U 18 0
2009-10 *Southend U* 4 0 **4 0**
2010-11 Colchester U 27 2
2011-12 Colchester U 26 2 **90 4**

HENDERSON, Ian (F) 228 29
H: 5 10 W: 11 06 b.Thetford 25-1-85
Source: Scholar. *Honours:* England Youth, Under-20.
2002-03 Norwich C 20 1
2003-04 Norwich C 19 4
2004-05 Norwich C 3 0
2005-06 Norwich C 24 1
2006-07 Norwich C 2 0 **68 6**
2006-07 *Rotherham U* 18 1 **18 1**
2007-08 Northampton T 23 0
2008-09 Northampton T 3 0 **26 0**
2008-09 Luton T 19 1 **19 1**
2009-10 Colchester U 13 2
2009-10 *Ankaragucu* 2 0 **2 0**
2010-11 Colchester U 36 10
2011-12 Colchester U 46 9 **95 21**

IZZET, Kem (M) 411 18
H: 5 7 W: 10 05 b.Mile End 29-9-80
Source: Trainee.
1998-99 Charlton Ath 0 0
1999-2000 Charlton Ath 0 0
2000-01 Charlton Ath 0 0
2000-01 Colchester U 6 1
2001-02 Colchester U 40 3
2002-03 Colchester U 45 8
2003-04 Colchester U 44 3
2004-05 Colchester U 4 0
2005-06 Colchester U 33 0
2006-07 Colchester U 45 1
2007-08 Colchester U 39 1
2008-09 Colchester U 43 1
2009-10 Colchester U 37 0
2010-11 Colchester U 41 0
2011-12 Colchester U 34 0 **411 18**

JAMES, Lloyd (M) 128 3
H: 5 11 W: 11 01 b.Bristol 16-2-88
Source: Scholar. *Honours:* Wales Youth, Under-21.
2005-06 Southampton 0 0
2006-07 Southampton 0 0

2007-08 Southampton 0 0
2008-09 Southampton 41 0
2009-10 Southampton 30 2 **71 2**
2010-11 Colchester U 28 0
2011-12 Colchester U 23 1 **51 1**
2011-12 *Crawley T* 6 0 **6 0**

LADAPO, Freddie (F) 0 0
b.Romford 1-2-93
Source: Scholar.
2011-12 Colchester U 0 0

O'TOOLE, John (M) 123 13
H: 6 2 W: 13 07 b.Harrow 30-9-88
Honours: Eire Under-21.
2007-08 Watford 35 3
2008-09 Watford 22 7
2008-09 *Sheffield U* 9 1 **9 1**
2009-10 Watford 0 0 **57 10**
2009-10 Colchester U 31 2
2010-11 Colchester U 11 0
2011-12 Colchester U 15 0 **57 2**

ODEJAYI, Kayode (F) 347 52
H: 6 2 W: 12 02 b.Ibadon 21-2-82
Source: Scholar. *Honours:* Nigeria 1 full cap.
1999-2000 Bristol C 3 0
2000-01 Bristol C 3 0
2001-02 Bristol C 0 0
2002-03 Bristol C 0 0 **6 0**
2003-04 Cheltenham T 30 5
2004-05 Cheltenham T 32 1
2005-06 Cheltenham T 41 11
2006-07 Cheltenham T 45 13 **148 30**
2007-08 Barnsley 39 3
2008-09 Barnsley 28 1
2008-09 *Scunthorpe U* 6 1 **6 1**
2009-10 Barnsley 5 0 **72 4**
2009-10 Colchester U 28 9
2010-11 Colchester U 44 4
2011-12 Colchester U 43 4 **115 17**

OKUONGHAE, Magnus (D) 177 5
H: 6 3 W: 13 04 b.Nigeria 16-2-86
Source: Scholar.
2003-04 Rushden & D 1 0
2004-05 Rushden & D 0 0
2005-06 Rushden & D 21 1
2006-07 Rushden & D 0 0 **22 1**
2007-08 Dagenham & R 10 0
2008-09 Dagenham & R 45 2 **55 2**
2009-10 Colchester U 44 0
2010-11 Colchester U 14 2
2011-12 Colchester U 42 0 **100 2**

PENTNEY, Carl (G) 1 0
H: 6 0 W: 12 00 b.Colchester 3-2-89
2007-08 Leicester C 0 0
2008-09 Leicester C 1 0
2009-10 Leicester C 0 0 **1 0**
2010-11 Colchester U 0 0
2011-12 Colchester U 0 0

ROSE, Michael (D) 224 13
H: 5 11 W: 12 04 b.Salford 28-7-82
Source: Trainee.
1999-2000 Manchester U 0 0
2000-01 Manchester U 0 0
2001-02 Manchester U 0 0
From Hereford U
2004-05 Yeovil T 40 1
2005-06 Yeovil T 1 0 **41 1**
2005-06 *Cheltenham T* 3 0 **3 0**
2005-06 *Scunthorpe U* 15 0 **15 0**
2006-07 Stockport Co 25 3
2007-08 Stockport Co 28 3
2008-09 Stockport Co 27 0
2009-10 Stockport Co 24 2 **104 8**
2009-10 *Norwich C* 12 1 **12 1**
2010-11 Swindon T 35 3 **35 3**
2010-11 Colchester U 0 0
2011-12 Colchester U 14 0 **14 0**

ROWLANDS, Martin (M) 367 55
H: 5 9 W: 10 10 b.Hammersmith 8-2-79
Source: Farnborough T. *Honours:* Eire Under-21, 5 full caps.
1998-99 Brentford 36 4
1999-2000 Brentford 40 6
2000-01 Brentford 32 2
2001-02 Brentford 23 7
2002-03 Brentford 18 1 **149 20**
2003-04 QPR 42 10
2004-05 QPR 35 3
2005-06 QPR 14 2
2006-07 QPR 29 10
2007-08 QPR 44 6
2008-09 QPR 24 2
2009-10 QPR 6 0
2010-11 QPR 4 0
2010-11 *Millwall* 1 0 **1 0**
2011-12 QPR 0 0 **198 33**
2011-12 *Wycombe W* 10 0 **10 0**
2011-12 Colchester U 9 2 **9 2**

SANDERSON, Jordan (M) 1 0
H: 6 0 W: 11 02 b.Chingford 7-8-93
Source: Scholar.
2010-11 Colchester U 1 0
2011-12 Colchester U 0 0 **1 0**

VINCENT, Ashley (M) 181 18
H: 5 10 W: 11 08 b.Oldbury 26-5-85
Source: Wolverhampton W Scholar.
2004-05 Cheltenham T 26 1
2005-06 Cheltenham T 13 2
2006-07 Cheltenham T 5 0
2007-08 Cheltenham T 37 2
2008-09 Cheltenham T 29 3 **110 8**
2008-09 Colchester U 6 1
2009-10 Colchester U 19 3
2010-11 Colchester U 37 5
2011-12 Colchester U 9 1 **71 10**

WHITE, John (D) 210 0
H: 6 0 W: 12 01 b.Maldon 26-7-86
Source: Scholar.
2004-05 Colchester U 20 0
2005-06 Colchester U 35 0
2006-07 Colchester U 16 0
2007-08 Colchester U 21 0
2008-09 Colchester U 26 0
2009-10 Colchester U 39 0
2009-10 *Southend U* 5 0 **5 0**
2010-11 Colchester U 22 0
2011-12 Colchester U 26 0 **205 0**

WILLIAMS, Ben (G) 295 0
H: 6 0 W: 13 01 b.Manchester 27-8-82
Source: Scholar. *Honours:* England Schools.
2001-02 Manchester U 0 0
2002-03 Manchester U 0 0
2002-03 *Coventry C* 0 0
2002-03 *Chesterfield* 14 0 **14 0**
2003-04 Manchester U 0 0
2003-04 *Crewe Alex* 10 0
2004-05 Crewe Alex 23 0
2005-06 Crewe Alex 17 0
2006-07 Crewe Alex 39 0
2007-08 Crewe Alex 46 0 **135 0**
2008-09 Carlisle U 31 0 **31 0**
2009-10 Colchester U 46 0
2010-11 Colchester U 33 0
2011-12 Colchester U 36 0 **115 0**

WILSON, Brian (D) 263 16
H: 5 10 W: 11 00 b.Manchester 9-5-83
Source: Scholar.
2001-02 Stoke C 1 0
2002-03 Stoke C 3 0
2003-04 Stoke C 2 0 **6 0**
2003-04 Cheltenham T 14 0
2004-05 Cheltenham T 43 3
2005-06 Cheltenham T 43 9
2006-07 Cheltenham T 25 2 **125 14**
2006-07 Bristol C 19 0
2007-08 Bristol C 18 1
2008-09 Bristol C 20 0
2009-10 Bristol C 3 0 **60 1**
2010-11 Colchester U 26 1
2011-12 Colchester U 46 0 **72 1**

WORDSWORTH, Anthony (M) 153 32
H: 6 1 W: 12 00 b.Camden 3-1-89
Source: Scholar.
2007-08 Colchester U 3 0
2008-09 Colchester U 30 3
2009-10 Colchester U 41 11
2010-11 Colchester U 35 5
2011-12 Colchester U 44 13 **153 32**

COVENTRY C (28)

BAKER, Carl (M) 164 24
H: 6 2 W: 12 06 b.Prescot 26-12-82
Source: Southport.
2007-08 Morecambe 42 10 **42 10**
2008-09 Stockport Co 22 3
2009-10 Stockport Co 20 9 **42 12**
2009-10 Coventry C 22 0
2010-11 Coventry C 32 1
2011-12 Coventry C 26 1 **80 2**

BELL, David (M) 308 22
H: 5 10 W: 11 05 b.Wellingborough 21-4-84
Source: Trainee. *Honours:* Eire Youth, Under-21.
2001-02 Rushden & D 0 0
2002-03 Rushden & D 30 3
2003-04 Rushden & D 37 1
2004-05 Rushden & D 40 3
2005-06 Rushden & D 14 3 **121 10**
2005-06 Luton T 9 0
2006-07 Luton T 34 3
2007-08 Luton T 32 4 **75 7**
2007-08 *Leicester C* 6 0 **6 0**
2008-09 Norwich C 19 0 **19 0**
2008-09 Coventry C 9 1
2009-10 Coventry C 28 2
2010-11 Coventry C 22 2
2011-12 Coventry C 28 0 **87 5**

BIGIRIMANA, Gael (M) 26 0
H: 5 9 W: 11 09 b.Burundi 22-10-93
Source: Scholar.
2011-12 Coventry C 26 0 **26 0**

BURGE, Lee (G) 0 0
b.Hereford 9-1-93
Source: Scholar.
2011-12 Coventry C 0 0

CAMERON, Nathan (D) 39 0
H: 6 2 W: 12 04 b.Birmingham 21-11-91
Source: Scholar.
2009-10 Coventry C 0 0
2010-11 Coventry C 25 0
2011-12 Coventry C 14 0 **39 0**

CHRISTIE, Cyrus (D) 37 0
H: 6 2 W: 12 03 b.Coventry 30-9-92
Source: Scholar.
2011-12 Coventry C 37 0 **37 0**

CLARKE, Jordan (D) 52 2
H: 6 0 W: 11 02 b.Coventry 19-11-91
Source: Scholar. *Honours:* England Youth.
2009-10 Coventry C 12 0
2010-11 Coventry C 21 1
2011-12 Coventry C 19 1 **52 2**

CLINGAN, Sammy (M) 259 17
H: 5 11 W: 11 06 b.Belfast 13-1-84
Source: Scholar. *Honours:* Northern Ireland Schools, Youth, Under-21, Under-23, 33 full caps.
2001-02 Wolverhampton W 0 0
2002-03 Wolverhampton W 0 0
2003-04 Wolverhampton W 0 0
2004-05 Wolverhampton W 0 0
2004-05 *Chesterfield* 15 2
2005-06 Wolverhampton W 0 0
2005-06 *Chesterfield* 21 1 **36 3**
2005-06 Nottingham F 15 0
2006-07 Nottingham F 28 0
2007-08 Nottingham F 42 1 **85 1**
2008-09 Norwich C 40 6
2009-10 Norwich C 0 0 **40 6**
2009-10 Coventry C 34 5
2010-11 Coventry C 28 0
2011-12 Coventry C 36 2 **98 7**

CRANIE, Martin (D) 172 1
H: 6 1 W: 12 09 b.Yeovil 23-9-86
Source: Scholar. *Honours:* England Youth, Under-20, Under-21.
2003-04 Southampton 1 0
2004-05 Southampton 3 0
2004-05 *Bournemouth* 3 0 **3 0**
2005-06 Southampton 11 0
2006-07 Southampton 1 0 **16 0**
2006-07 *Yeovil T* 12 0 **12 0**
2007-08 Portsmouth 2 0
2007-08 *QPR* 6 0 **6 0**
2008-09 Portsmouth 0 0
2008-09 *Charlton Ath* 19 0 **19 0**
2009-10 Portsmouth 0 0 **2 0**
2009-10 Coventry C 40 1
2010-11 Coventry C 36 0
2011-12 Coventry C 38 0 **114 1**

DEEGAN, Gary (M) 142 17
H: 5 9 W: 11 11 b.Dublin 28-9-87
2005-06 Shelbourne 0 0
2006 *Kilkenny City* 18 4 **18 4**
2007 Longford Town 30 3 **30 3**

2008 Galway U 17 0 **17 0**
2008 Bohemians 12 3 **12 3**
2009 Bohemains 23 2 **23 2**
2009-10 Coventry C 17 2
2010-11 Coventry C 1 0
2011-12 Coventry C 24 3 **42 5**

DUNN, Chris (G) 100 0
H: 6 5 W: 13 11 b.Brentwood 23-10-87
Source: Scholar.
2006-07 Northampton T 0 0
2007-08 Northampton T 1 0
2008-09 Northampton T 29 0
2009-10 Northampton T 29 0
2010-11 Northampton T 39 0 **98 0**
2011-12 Coventry C 2 0 **2 0**

EASTWOOD, Freddy (F) 266 75
H: 5 11 W: 12 04 b.Epsom 29-10-83
Source: West Ham U Trainee, Grays Ath.
Honours: Wales 11 full caps, 4 goals.
2004-05 Southend U 33 19
2005-06 Southend U 40 23
2006-07 Southend U 42 11
2007-08 Wolverhampton W31 3 **31 3**
2008-09 Coventry C 46 4
2009-10 Coventry C 36 8
2010-11 Coventry C 27 5
2011-12 Coventry C 4 0 **113 17**
2011-12 *Southend U* 7 2 **122 55**

HENDERSON, Joe (D) 1 0
H: 6 1 W: 12 00 b.Banbury 2-11-93
Source: Scholar.
2011-12 Coventry C 1 0 **1 0**

HREIDARSSON, Hermann (D) 507 26
H: 6 3 W: 12 12 b.Reykjavik 11-7-74
Honours: Iceland Under-21, 89 full caps, 5 goals.
1993 IBV 2 0
1994 IBV 18 2
1995 IBV 18 1
1996 IBV 17 2
1997 IBV 11 0 **66 5**
1997-98 Crystal Palace 30 2
1998-99 Crystal Palace 7 0 **37 2**
1998-99 Brentford 33 4
1999-2000 Brentford 8 2 **41 6**
1999-2000 Wimbledon 24 1
2000-01 Wimbledon 1 0 **25 1**
2000-01 Ipswich T 36 1
2001-02 Ipswich T 38 1
2002-03 Ipswich T 28 0 **102 2**
2002-03 Charlton Ath 0 0
2003-04 Charlton Ath 33 2
2004-05 Charlton Ath 34 1
2005-06 Charlton Ath 34 0
2006-07 Charlton Ath 31 0 **132 3**
2007-08 Portsmouth 32 3
2008-09 Portsmouth 23 2
2009-10 Portsmouth 17 1
2010-11 Portsmouth 28 1
2011-12 Portsmouth 2 0 **102 7**
2011-12 Coventry C 2 0 **2 0**

HUSSEY, Chris (D) 48 0
H: 5 10 W: 10 03 b.Hammersmith 2-1-89
Source: AFC Wimbledon.
2009-10 Coventry C 8 0
2010-11 Coventry C 11 0
2010-11 *Crewe Alex* 0 0
2011-12 Coventry C 29 0 **48 0**

IRELAND, Daniel (G) 1 0
H: 6 2 W: 13 00 b.Sydney 30-9-90
Source: Academy.
2007-08 Coventry C 0 0
2008-09 Coventry C 0 0
2009-10 Coventry C 0 0
2010-11 Coventry C 1 0
2011-12 Coventry C 0 0 **1 0**

JEFFERS, Shaun (F) 29 1
H: 6 1 W: 11 03 b.Bedford 14-4-92
Source: Scholar.
2009-10 Coventry C 4 0
2010-11 Coventry C 0 0
2010-11 *Cheltenham T* 22 1 **22 1**
2011-12 Coventry C 3 0 **7 0**

KEOGH, Richard (D) 233 9
H: 6 0 W: 11 02 b.Harlow 11-8-86
Source: Scholar. *Honours:* Eire Under-21.
2004-05 Stoke C 0 0
2005-06 Bristol C 9 1
2005-06 *Wycombe W* 3 0 **3 0**
2006-07 Bristol C 31 2
2007-08 Bristol C 0 0 **40 3**
2007-08 *Huddersfield T* 9 1 **9 1**
2007-08 *Carlisle U* 7 0
2007-08 *Cheltenham T* 10 0 **10 0**
2008-09 Carlisle U 32 1
2009-10 Carlisle U 41 3 **80 4**
2010-11 Coventry C 46 1
2011-12 Coventry C 45 0 **91 1**

McDONALD, Cody (F) 88 33
H: 5 10 W: 11 03 b.Witham 30-5-86
Source: Dartford.
2008-09 Norwich C 7 1
2009-10 Norwich C 17 3
2010-11 Norwich C 0 0
2010-11 *Gillingham* 41 25 **41 25**
2011-12 Norwich C 0 0 **24 4**
2011-12 Coventry C 23 4 **23 4**

McPAKE, James (D) 161 10
H: 6 2 W: 12 08 b.Airdrie 2-6-84
Honours: Northern Ireland 1 full cap.
2003-04 Livingston 1 0
2004-05 Livingston 15 2
2005-06 Livingston 15 0
2005-06 *Morton* 11 2 **11 2**
2006-07 Livingston 33 3
2007-08 Livingston 19 0
2008-09 Livingston 18 2 **101 7**
2008-09 Coventry C 4 0
2009-10 Coventry C 17 1
2010-11 Coventry C 12 0
2011-12 Coventry C 5 0 **38 1**
2011-12 *Hibernian* 11 0 **11 0**

McSHEFFREY, Gary (F) 340 88
H: 5 8 W: 10 06 b.Coventry 13-8-82
Source: Trainee. *Honours:* England Youth, Under-20.
1998-99 Coventry C 1 0
1999-2000 Coventry C 3 0
2000-01 Coventry C 0 0
2001-02 *Stockport Co* 5 1 **5 1**
2001-02 Coventry C 8 1
2002-03 Coventry C 29 4
2003-04 Coventry C 19 11
2003-04 *Luton T* 18 9
2004-05 Coventry C 37 12
2004-05 *Luton T* 5 1 **23 10**
2005-06 Coventry C 43 15
2006-07 Coventry C 3 1
2006-07 Birmingham C 40 13
2007-08 Birmingham C 32 3
2008-09 Birmingham C 6 0
2008-09 *Nottingham F* 4 0 **4 0**
2009-10 Birmingham C 5 0 **83 16**
2009-10 *Leeds U* 10 1 **10 1**
2010-11 Coventry C 33 8
2011-12 Coventry C 39 8 **215 60**

MURPHY, Joe (G) 354 0
H: 6 2 W: 13 06 b.Dublin 21-8-81
Source: Trainee. *Honours:* Eire Youth, Under-21, 2 full caps.
1999-2000 Tranmere R 21 0
2000-01 Tranmere R 20 0
2001-02 Tranmere R 22 0 **63 0**
2002-03 WBA 2 0
2003-04 WBA 3 0
2004-05 WBA 0 0 **5 0**
2004-05 *Walsall* 25 0
2005-06 Sunderland 0 0
2005-06 *Walsall* 14 0 **39 0**
2006-07 Scunthorpe U 45 0
2007-08 Scunthorpe U 45 0
2008-09 Scunthorpe U 42 0
2009-10 Scunthorpe U 40 0
2010-11 Scunthorpe U 29 0 **201 0**
2011-12 Coventry C 46 0 **46 0**

O'DONOVAN, Roy (F) 160 43
H: 5 10 W: 11 07 b.Cork 10-8-85
Source: Scholar. *Honours:* Eire Under-21, B.
2002-03 Coventry C 0 0
2003-04 Coventry C 0 0
2004-05 Coventry C 0 0
2005 Cork C 26 6
2006 Cork C 29 11
2007 Cork C 19 14 **74 31**
2007-08 Sunderland 17 0
2008-09 Sunderland 0 0
2008-09 *Dundee U* 11 1 **11 1**
2008-09 *Blackpool* 12 0 **12 0**
2009-10 Sunderland 0 0 **17 0**
2009-10 *Southend U* 4 1 **4 1**
2009-10 *Hartlepool U* 15 9 **15 9**
2010-11 Coventry C 2 0
2011-12 Coventry C 11 0 **13 0**
2011-12 *Hibernian* 14 1 **14 1**

PLATT, Clive (F) 551 102
H: 6 4 W: 12 07 b.Wolverhampton 27-10-77
Source: Trainee.
1995-96 Walsall 4 2
1996-97 Walsall 1 0
1997-98 Walsall 20 1
1998-99 Walsall 7 1
1999-2000 Walsall 0 0 **32 4**
1999-2000 Rochdale 41 9
2000-01 Rochdale 43 8
2001-02 Rochdale 43 7
2002-03 Rochdale 42 6 **169 30**
2003-04 Notts Co 19 3 **19 3**
2003-04 Peterborough U 18 2
2004-05 Peterborough U 19 4 **37 6**
2004-05 Milton Keynes D 20 3
2005-06 Milton Keynes D 40 6
2006-07 Milton Keynes D 42 18 **102 27**
2007-08 Colchester U 41 8
2008-09 Colchester U 43 10
2009-10 Colchester U 41 7 **125 25**
2010-11 Coventry C 34 3
2011-12 Coventry C 33 4 **67 7**

ROBERTS, Will (M) 1 0
H: 5 9 W: 11 07 b.Rhyl 24-4-94
Source: Scholar.
2011-12 Coventry C 1 0 **1 0**

RUFFELS, Joshua (M) 1 0
H: 5 10 W: 11 11 b.Oxford 23-10-93
Source: Scholar.
2011-12 Coventry C 1 0 **1 0**

THOMAS, Conor (M) 27 1
H: 6 1 W: 11 05 b.Coventry 29-10-93
Source: Scholar. *Honours:* England Youth.
2010-11 *Liverpool* 0 0
2010-11 Coventry C 0 0
2011-12 Coventry C 27 1 **27 1**

WILLIS, Jordan (D) 3 0
H: 5 11 W: 11 00 b.Coventry 24-8-94
Source: Scholar. *Honours:* England Youth.
2011-12 Coventry C 3 0 **3 0**

WILSON, Callum (M) 1 0
H: 5 11 W: 10 06 b.Coventry 27-2-92
Source: Scholar.
2009-10 Coventry C 0 0
2010-11 Coventry C 1 0
2011-12 Coventry C 0 0 **1 0**

WOOD, Richard (D) 252 12
H: 6 3 W: 12 13 b.Ossett 5-7-85
Source: Scholar.
2002-03 Sheffield W 3 1
2003-04 Sheffield W 12 0
2004-05 Sheffield W 34 1
2005-06 Sheffield W 30 1
2006-07 Sheffield W 12 0
2007-08 Sheffield W 27 2
2008-09 Sheffield W 42 0
2009-10 Sheffield W 11 2 **171 7**
2009-10 Coventry C 24 3
2010-11 Coventry C 40 1
2011-12 Coventry C 17 1 **81 5**

CRAWLEY T (29)

AKINDE, John (F) 88 12
H: 6 2 W: 10 01 b.Camberwell 8-7-89
Source: Ebbsfleet U.
2008-09 Bristol C 7 1
2008-09 *Wycombe W* 11 7
2009-10 Bristol C 7 0
2009-10 *Wycombe W* 6 1 **17 8**
2009-10 *Brentford* 2 0 **2 0**
2010-11 Bristol C 2 0 **16 1**
2010-11 *Bristol R* 14 0 **14 0**
2010-11 *Dagenham & R* 9 2
2011-12 Crawley T 25 1 **25 1**
2011-12 *Dagenham & R* 5 0 **14 2**

AKPAN, Hope (M) **28 1**
H: 6 0 W: 10 08 b.Liverpool 14-8-91
Source: Scholar.
2007-08 Everton 0 0
2008-09 Everton 0 0
2009-10 Everton 0 0
2010-11 Everton 0 0
2010-11 *Hull C* 2 0 **2 0**
2011-12 Crawley T 26 1 **26 1**

BRODIE, Richard (F) **0 0**
H: 6 2 W: 13 00 b.Gateshead 8-7-87
Source: Whickham, Newcastle Benfield, York C.
2011-12 Crawley T 0 0

BULMAN, Dannie (M) **248 17**
H: 5 9 W: 11 12 b.Ashford 24-1-79
Source: Ashford T.
1998-99 Wycombe W 11 1
1999-2000 Wycombe W 29 1
2000-01 Wycombe W 36 4
2001-02 Wycombe W 46 5
2002-03 Wycombe W 42 3
2003-04 Wycombe W 38 0 **202 14**
From Stevenage, Crawley T.
2010-11 Oxford U 5 0 **5 0**
2011-12 Crawley T 41 3 **41 3**

CLARKE, Billy (F) **145 26**
H: 5 7 W: 10 01 b.Cork 13-12-87
Source: Scholar. *Honours:* Eire Youth, Under-21.
2004-05 Ipswich T 0 0
2005-06 Ipswich T 2 0
2005-06 *Colchester U* 6 0 **6 0**
2006-07 Ipswich T 27 3
2007-08 Ipswich T 20 0
2007-08 *Falkirk* 8 1 **8 1**
2008-09 Ipswich T 0 0 **49 3**
2008-09 *Darlington* 20 8 **20 8**
2008-09 *Northampton T* 5 3 **5 3**
2008-09 *Brentford* 8 6 **8 6**
2009-10 Blackpool 18 1
2010-11 Blackpool 0 0
2011-12 Blackpool 9 0 **27 1**
2011-12 *Sheffield U* 5 1 **5 1**
2011-12 Crawley T 17 3 **17 3**

DAVIES, Scott (M) **107 20**
H: 5 11 W: 12 00 b.Aylesbury 10-3-88
Source: Scholar. *Honours:* Eire Under-21.
2006-07 Reading 0 0
2007-08 Reading 0 0
2008-09 Reading 0 0
2008-09 *Aldershot T* 41 13
2009-10 Reading 4 0
2009-10 *Wycombe W* 15 3
2009-10 *Yeovil T* 4 0 **4 0**
2010-11 Reading 0 0 **4 0**
2010-11 *Wycombe W* 8 1 **23 4**
2010-11 *Bristol R* 7 0 **7 0**
2011-12 Crawley T 20 2 **20 2**
2011-12 *Aldershot T* 8 1 **49 14**

DAVIS, Claude (D) **223 7**
H: 6 3 W: 14 04 b.Kingston, Jam 6-3-79
Source: Portmore U. *Honours:* Jamaica 67 full caps, 2 goals.
2003-04 Preston NE 22 1
2004-05 Preston NE 32 0
2005-06 Preston NE 40 3 **94 4**
2006-07 Sheffield U 21 0 **21 0**
2007-08 Derby Co 19 0
2008-09 Derby Co 8 0
2008-09 *Crystal Palace* 7 0
2009-10 Derby Co 0 0 **27 0**
2009-10 Crystal Palace 21 0
2010-11 Crystal Palace 24 0
2011-12 Crystal Palace 0 0 **52 0**
2011-12 Crawley T 29 3 **29 3**

DAY, Jamie (M) **110 5**
H: 5 9 W: 10 07 b.Wycombe 7-5-86
Source: Scholar.
2003-04 Peterborough U 0 0
2004-05 Peterborough U 1 0
2005-06 Peterborough U 25 1
2006-07 Peterborough U 24 1
2007-08 Peterborough U 42 3
2008-09 Peterborough U 5 0
2009-10 Peterborough U 5 0 **102 5**
From Rushden & D.
2009-10 *Dagenham & R* 8 0 **8 0**
2011-12 Crawley T 0 0
2011-12 *Aldershot T* 0 0

DEMPSTER, John (D) **79 5**
H: 6 1 W: 11 07 b.Kettering 1-4-83
Source: Trainee. *Honours:* Scotland Youth, Under-21.
2001-02 Rushden & D 2 0
2002-03 Rushden & D 16 1
2003-04 Rushden & D 19 0
2004-05 Rushden & D 15 0
2005-06 Rushden & D 14 3 **66 4**
2005-06 Oxford U 6 0
2006-07 Oxford U 0 0
2007-08 Oxford U 0 0
2008-09 Oxford U 0 0
2009-10 Oxford U 0 0 **6 0**
2011-12 Crawley T 7 1 **7 1**

EVANS, Daniel (F) **0 0**
b.Peterborough 24-11-93
Source: Peterborough U Scholar.
2011-12 Crawley T 0 0

HOWELL, Dean (D) **66 4**
H: 6 1 W: 12 05 b.Burton-on-Trent 29-11-80
Source: Trainee.
1999-2000 Notts Co 1 0 **1 0**
2000-01 Crewe Alex 1 0 **1 0**
2000-01 *Rochdale* 3 0 **3 0**
From Southport, Morecambe, Halifax T
2005-06 Colchester U 4 0 **4 0**
From Halifax, Weymouth, Grays, Rushden
2008-09 Aldershot T 14 0
2008-09 *Bury* 3 0 **3 0**
2009-10 Aldershot T 3 1
2010-11 Aldershot T 0 0 **17 1**
2011-12 Crawley T 37 3 **37 3**

HUNT, David (M) **243 11**
H: 5 11 W: 11 09 b.Dulwich 10-9-82
Source: Scholar.
2002-03 Crystal Palace 2 0 **2 0**
2003-04 Leyton Orient 38 1
2004-05 Leyton Orient 27 0 **65 1**
2004-05 Northampton T 4 0
2005-06 Northampton T 40 3
2006-07 Northampton T 29 0 **73 3**
2007-08 Shrewsbury T 27 2
2008-09 Shrewsbury T 2 0 **29 2**
2008-09 Brentford 20 2
2009-10 Brentford 24 3
2010-11 Brentford 3 0 **47 5**
2011-12 Crawley T 27 0 **27 0**

KUIPERS, Michels (G) **281 0**
H: 6 2 W: 14 03 b.Amsterdam 26-6-74
Source: SDW Amsterdam.
1998-99 Bristol R 1 0
1999-2000 Bristol R 0 0 **1 0**
2000-01 Brighton & HA 34 0
2001-02 Brighton & HA 39 0
2002-03 Brighton & HA 21 0
2003-04 Brighton & HA 10 0
2003-04 *Hull C* 3 0 **3 0**
2004-05 Brighton & HA 30 0
2005-06 Brighton & HA 5 0
2005-06 *Boston U* 15 0 **15 0**
2006-07 Brighton & HA 14 0
2007-08 Brighton & HA 46 0
2008-09 Brighton & HA 28 0
2009-10 Brighton & HA 20 0
2010-11 Brighton & HA 0 0 **247 0**
2011-12 Crawley T 15 0 **15 0**

McFADZEAN, Kyle (D) **37 2**
H: 6 1 W: 13 04 b.Sheffield 20-2-87
Source: Scholar.
2004-05 Sheffield U 0 0
2005-06 Sheffield U 0 0
2006-07 Sheffield U 0 0
2007-08 Sheffield U 0 0
2008-09 Sheffield U 0 0
2011-12 Crawley T 37 2 **37 2**

MILLS, Pablo (D) **245 6**
H: 5 9 W: 11 04 b.Birmingham 27-5-84
Source: Trainee. *Honours:* England Youth.
2002-03 Derby Co 16 0
2003-04 Derby Co 19 0
2004-05 Derby Co 22 0
2005-06 Derby Co 1 0 **58 0**
2005-06 *Milton Keynes D* 16 1 **16 1**
2005-06 *Walsall* 14 0 **14 0**
2006-07 Rotherham U 31 1
2007-08 Rotherham U 33 1
2008-09 Rotherham U 35 1
2009-10 Rotherham U 37 0 **136 3**
2011-12 Crawley T 21 2 **21 2**

NAPPER, Byron (M) **0 0**
b.Chichester 26-2-92
Source: Youth.
2011-12 Crawley T 0 0

NEILSON, Scott (M) **54 4**
H: 6 0 W: 12 10 b.Enfield 15-5-87
Source: Cambridge C.
2009-10 Bradford C 23 1
2010-11 Bradford C 1 0 **24 1**
2011-12 Crawley T 30 3 **30 3**

SHEARER, Scott (G) **255 0**
H: 6 3 W: 12 00 b.Glasgow 15-2-81
Source: Tower Hearts. *Honours:* Scotland B.
2000-01 Albion R 3 0
2001-02 Albion R 10 0
2002-03 Albion R 36 0 **49 0**
2003-04 Coventry C 30 0
2004-05 Coventry C 8 0 **38 0**
2004-05 *Rushden & D* 13 0 **13 0**
2005-06 Bristol R 45 0
2006-07 Bristol R 2 0 **47 0**
2006-07 *Shrewsbury T* 20 0 **20 0**
2007-08 Wycombe W 5 0
2008-09 Wycombe W 29 0
2009-10 Wycombe W 29 0
2010-11 Wycombe W 0 0 **63 0**
2011-12 Crawley T 25 0 **25 0**

SIMPSON, Josh (M) **78 5**
H: 5 10 W: 12 02 b.Cambridge 6-3-87
Source: Cambridge C, Cambridge U, Histon.
2009-10 Peterborough U 21 2
2010-11 Peterborough U 0 0 **21 2**
2010-11 *Southend U* 17 1 **17 1**
2011-12 Crawley T 40 2 **40 2**

SMITH, Ben (M) **138 12**
H: 5 9 W: 11 09 b.Chelmsford 23-11-78
Source: Arsenal.
1996-97 Reading 1 0 **1 0**
From Yeovil T.
2001-02 Southend U 1 0 **1 0**
From Hereford U.
2004-05 Shrewsbury T 12 3
From Weymouth.
2005-06 Shrewsbury T 12 1 **24 4**
2006-07 Hereford U 18 1
2007-08 Hereford U 44 5
2008-09 Hereford U 37 1 **99 7**
2011-12 Crawley T 5 1 **5 1**
2011-12 *Aldershot T* 8 0 **8 0**

TORRES, Sergio (M) **156 11**
H: 6 2 W: 12 04 b.Mar del Plata 8-11-83
Source: Basingstoke T.
2005-06 Wycombe W 24 1
2006-07 Wycombe W 20 0
2007-08 Wycombe W 42 5 **86 6**
2008-09 Peterborough U 15 1
2009-10 Peterborough U 9 0
2009-10 *Lincoln C* 8 1 **8 1**
2010-11 Peterborough U 0 0 **24 1**
2011-12 Crawley T 38 3 **38 3**

WASSMER, Charlie (D) **14 2**
H: 5 9 W: 11 00 b.Hammersmith 21-3-91
Source: Hayes & Yeading U.
2011-12 Crawley T 13 2 **13 2**
2011-12 *Dagenham & R* 1 0 **1 0**

WICKHAM, Aaron (M) **0 0**
b.Camden 11-12-93
Source: Peterborough U Scholar.
2011-12 Crawley T 0 0

WILSON, Glenn (D) **4 0**
H: 6 1 W: 12 08 b.Lewisham 16-3-86
Source: Scholar.
2005-06 Crystal Palace 0 0
From Rushden & D.
2011-12 Crawley T 4 0 **4 0**

CREWE ALEX (30)

ARTELL, Dave (D) **372 32**
H: 6 3 W: 14 01 b.Rotherham 22-11-80
Source: Trainee.
1999-2000 Rotherham U 1 0

2000-01 Rotherham U 36 4
2001-02 Rotherham U 0 0
2002-03 Rotherham U 0 0 **37 4**
2002-03 *Shrewsbury T* 28 1 **28 1**
2003-04 Mansfield T 26 3
2004-05 Mansfield T 19 2 **45 5**
2005-06 Chester C 37 2
2006-07 Chester C 43 1 **80 3**
2007-08 Morecambe 36 3
2008-09 Morecambe 37 3
2009-10 Morecambe 37 7 **110 13**
2010-11 Crewe Alex 40 4
2011-12 Crewe Alex 32 2 **72 6**

BELL, Lee (M) 235 8
H: 5 11 W: 12 04 b.Alsager 26-1-83
Source: Scholar.
2000-01 Crewe Alex 0 0
2001-02 Crewe Alex 0 0
2002-03 Crewe Alex 17 1
2003-04 Crewe Alex 3 0
2004-05 Crewe Alex 17 0
2005-06 Crewe Alex 17 2
2006-07 Crewe Alex 0 0
2007-08 Mansfield T 23 1 **23 1**
2008-09 Macclesfield T 41 1
2009-10 Macclesfield T 42 2 **83 3**
2010-11 Crewe Alex 45 1
2011-12 Crewe Alex 30 0 **129 4**

BROWN, Jordan (D) 10 0
H: 5 10 W: 12 00 b.Benfleet 11-10-91
Source: Scholar.
2010-11 West Ham U 0 0
2011-12 West Ham U 0 0
2011-12 *Aldershot T* 3 0 **3 0**
2011-12 Crewe Alex 7 0 **7 0**

CLAYTON, Harry (F) 0 0
b.Crewe 15-2-93
Source: Scholar.
2011-12 Crewe Alex 0 0

CLAYTON, Max (F) 26 3
H: 5 9 W: 11 00 b.Crewe 9-8-94
Source: Scholar. *Honours:* England Youth.
2010-11 Crewe Alex 2 0
2011-12 Crewe Alex 24 3 **26 3**

DANIELS, Brendon (M) 0 0
b.Stoke 24-9-93
Source: Scholar.
2011-12 Crewe Alex 0 0

DAVIS, Harry (D) 43 5
H: 6 2 W: 12 04 b.Burnley 24-9-91
Source: Scholar.
2009-10 Crewe Alex 1 0
2010-11 Crewe Alex 1 0
2011-12 Crewe Alex 41 5 **43 5**

DUGDALE, Adam (D) 65 4
H: 6 3 W: 12 07 b.Liverpool 12-9-87
Source: Scholar.
2006-07 Crewe Alex 0 0
2006-07 *Accrington S* 2 0 **2 0**
From Southport, Droylsden, Montagnee, Barrow, AFC Telford U.
2010-11 Crewe Alex 20 1
From Southport, Droylsden, Montagnee, Barrow, AFC Telford U.
2011-12 Crewe Alex 43 3 **63 4**

GARRATT, Ben (G) 0 0
b.Market Drayton 25-4-94
Source: Scholar. *Honours:* England Youth.
2011-12 Crewe Alex 0 0

GUTHRIE, Jon (D) 0 0
Source: Pewsey Vale.
2011-12 Crewe Alex 0 0

HUGHES, Caspar (M) 5 0
H: 5 7 W: 10 00 b.Crewe 9-6-93
Source: Scholar.
2010-11 Crewe Alex 1 0
2011-12 Crewe Alex 4 0 **5 0**

KORAL, Michael (F) 0 0
b.Manchester 6-10-92
Source: Scholar.
2011-12 Crewe Alex 0 0

LEITCH-SMITH, AJ (F) 73 18
H: 5 11 W: 12 04 b.Crewe 6-3-90
Source: Scholar.
2008-09 Crewe Alex 0 0
2009 *IBV* 18 5 **18 5**
2009-10 Crewe Alex 1 0
2010-11 Crewe Alex 16 5
2011-12 Crewe Alex 38 8 **55 13**

MARTIN, Alan (G) 22 0
H: 6 0 W: 11 11 b.Glasgow 1-1-89
Source: Motherwell. *Honours:* Scotland Youth, Under-21.
2007-08 Leeds U 0 0
2008-09 Leeds U 0 0
2009-10 Leeds U 0 0
2009-10 *Accrington S* 7 0 **7 0**
2010-11 Leeds U 0 0
2010-11 Ayr U 15 0 **15 0**
2011-12 Crewe Alex 0 0

MARTIN, Carl (D) 35 1
H: 5 8 W: 10 07 b.Camden 24-10-86
Source: Wealdstone.
2009-10 Crewe Alex 6 1
2010-11 Crewe Alex 0 0
2011-12 Crewe Alex 29 0 **35 1**

MELLOR, Kelvin (D) 13 1
H: 5 10 W: 11 09 b.Copenhagen 25-1-91
Source: Nantwich T.
2007-08 Crewe Alex 0 0
2008-09 Crewe Alex 0 0
2009-10 Crewe Alex 0 0
2010-11 Crewe Alex 1 0
2011-12 Crewe Alex 12 1 **13 1**

MILLER, Shaun (F) 163 38
H: 5 10 W: 11 08 b.Alsager 25-9-87
Source: Scholar.
2006-07 Crewe Alex 7 3
2007-08 Crewe Alex 15 1
2008-09 Crewe Alex 33 4
2009-10 Crewe Alex 33 7
2010-11 Crewe Alex 42 18
2011-12 Crewe Alex 33 5 **163 38**

MOORE, Byron (M) 181 23
H: 6 0 W: 10 06 b.Stoke 24-8-88
Source: Scholar.
2006-07 Crewe Alex 0 0
2007-08 Crewe Alex 33 3
2008-09 Crewe Alex 36 3
2009-10 Crewe Alex 32 3
2010-11 Crewe Alex 38 6
2011-12 Crewe Alex 42 8 **181 23**

MURPHY, Luke (M) 122 15
H: 6 1 W: 11 05 b.Alsager 21-10-89
Source: Scholar.
2008-09 Crewe Alex 9 1
2009-10 Crewe Alex 32 3
2010-11 Crewe Alex 39 3
2011-12 Crewe Alex 42 8 **122 15**

OSWELL, Jason (F) 0 0
b.Northwich 7-10-92
Source: Scholar.
2011-12 Crewe Alex 0 0

PHILLIPS, Steve (G) 481 0
H: 6 1 W: 11 10 b.Bath 6-5-78
Source: Paulton R.
1996-97 Bristol C 0 0
1997-98 Bristol C 0 0
1998-99 Bristol C 15 0
1999-2000 Bristol C 21 0
2000-01 Bristol C 42 0
2001-02 Bristol C 22 0
2002-03 Bristol C 46 0
2003-04 Bristol C 46 0
2004-05 Bristol C 46 0
2005-06 Bristol C 19 0 **257 0**
2006-07 Bristol R 44 0
2007-08 Bristol R 46 0
2008-09 Bristol R 46 0
2009-10 Bristol R 0 0 **136 0**
2009-10 *Shrewsbury T* 11 0 **11 0**
2009-10 *Crewe Alex* 28 0
2010-11 Crewe Alex 3 0
2011-12 Crewe Alex 46 0 **77 0**

POWELL, Nick (F) 55 14
H: 6 0 W: 10 05 b.Crewe 23-3-94
Source: Scholar. *Honours:* England Youth.
2010-11 Crewe Alex 17 0
2011-12 Crewe Alex 38 14 **55 14**

RAY, George (D) 0 0
b.Warrington 13-10-93
Source: Scholar.
2011-12 Crewe Alex 0 0

SARCEVIC, Antoni (M) 12 1
H: 5 10 W: 11 00 b. 13-3-92
Source: Woodley Sports.
2009-10 Crewe Alex 0 0
2010-11 Crewe Alex 6 1
2011-12 Crewe Alex 6 0 **12 1**

SHELLEY, Danny (D) 73 8
H: 5 9 W: 10 08 b.Stoke 29-12-90
Source: Scholar.
2008-09 Crewe Alex 3 0
2009-10 Crewe Alex 19 1
2010-11 Crewe Alex 25 6
2011-12 Crewe Alex 26 1 **73 8**

TING, Daniel (D) 0 0
b.Chester 1-12-92
Source: Scholar.
2011-12 Crewe Alex 0 0

TOOTLE, Matt (D) 104 1
H: 5 9 W: 11 00 b.Widnes 11-10-90
Source: Scholar.
2009-10 Crewe Alex 28 1
2010-11 Crewe Alex 39 0
2011-12 Crewe Alex 37 0 **104 1**

TURTON, Oliver (D) 3 0
H: 5 11 W: 11 11 b.Manchester 6-12-92
Source: Scholar.
2010-11 Crewe Alex 1 0
2011-12 Crewe Alex 2 0 **3 0**

WESTWOOD, Ashley (M) 125 14
H: 5 10 W: 11 00 b.Nantwich 1-4-90
Source: Scholar.
2008-09 Crewe Alex 2 0
2009-10 Crewe Alex 36 6
2010-11 Crewe Alex 46 5
2011-12 Crewe Alex 41 3 **125 14**

WHITE, Andrew (D) 0 0
b.Chester 8-10-92
Source: Scholar.
2011-12 Crewe Alex 0 0

CRYSTAL PALACE (31)

AMBROSE, Darren (M) 298 55
H: 6 0 W: 11 00 b.Harlow 29-2-84
Source: Scholar. *Honours:* England Youth, Under-20, Under-21.
2001-02 Ipswich T 1 0
2002-03 Ipswich T 29 8
2002-03 Newcastle U 1 0
2003-04 Newcastle U 24 2
2004-05 Newcastle U 12 3 **37 5**
2005-06 Charlton Ath 28 3
2006-07 Charlton Ath 26 3
2007-08 Charlton Ath 37 7
2008-09 Charlton Ath 21 0 **112 13**
2008-09 *Ipswich T* 9 0 **39 8**
2009-10 Crystal Palace 46 15
2010-11 Crystal Palace 28 7
2011-12 Crystal Palace 36 7 **110 29**

ANDREW, Calvin (F) 151 9
H: 6 0 W: 12 11 b.Luton 19-12-86
Source: Scholar.
2004-05 Luton T 8 0
2005-06 Luton T 1 1
2005-06 *Grimsby T* 8 1 **8 1**
2005-06 *Bristol C* 3 0 **3 0**
2006-07 Luton T 7 1
2007-08 Luton T 39 2 **55 4**
2008-09 Crystal Palace 7 0
2008-09 *Brighton & HA* 9 2 **9 2**
2009-10 Crystal Palace 27 1
2010-11 Crystal Palace 13 0
2010-11 *Millwall* 3 0 **3 0**
2010-11 *Swindon T* 10 1 **10 1**
2011-12 Crystal Palace 6 0 **53 1**
2011-12 *Leyton Orient* 10 0 **10 0**

APPIAH, Kwesi (F) 4 0
H: 5 11 W: 12 08 b.Thamesmead 12-8-90
Source: Margate, Ebbsfleet U.
2008-09 Peterborough U 0 0
From Brackley T, Thurrock, Margate.
2011-12 Crystal Palace 4 0 **4 0**

CADOGAN, Kieron (M) 36 3
H: 6 4 W: 12 07 b.Tooting 3-8-90
Source: Scholar.
2007-08 Crystal Palace 0 0

2008-09 Crystal Palace 4 1
2009-10 Crystal Palace 0 0
2009-10 *Burton Alb* 2 0 **2 0**
2010-11 Crystal Palace 16 1
2011-12 Crystal Palace 1 0 **21 2**
2011-12 *Rotherham U* 13 1 **13 1**

CAPRICE, Jake (M) 0 0
b.Lambeth 11-11-92
Source: Scholar.
2011-12 Crystal Palace 0 0

CHAMBERS, Michael (D) 0 0
Source: Dulwich Hamlet.
2011-12 Crystal Palace 0 0

CLYNE, Nathaniel (D) 122 1
H: 5 9 W: 10 07 b.Stockwell 5-4-91
Source: Scholar. *Honours:* England Youth, Under-21.
2008-09 Crystal Palace 26 0
2009-10 Crystal Palace 22 1
2010-11 Crystal Palace 46 0
2011-12 Crystal Palace 28 0 **122 1**

DE SILVA, Kyle (F) 6 0
H: 5 10 W: 11 05 b.Croydon 29-11-93
Source: Scholar.
2010-11 Crystal Palace 0 0
2011-12 Crystal Palace 6 0 **6 0**

DIKGACOI, Kagisho (M) 143 11
H: 5 11 W: 12 10 b.Brandfort 24-11-84
Honours: South Africa 41 full caps, 2 goals.
2004-05 Bloemfontein YT 10 0 **10 0**
2005-06 Lamontville GA 9 0
2006-07 Lamontville GA 25 0
2007-08 Lamontville GA 23 4
2008-09 Lamontville GA 23 4 **80 8**
2009-10 Fulham 12 0
2010-11 Fulham 1 0 **13 0**
2010-11 *Crystal Palace* 13 1
2011-12 Crystal Palace 27 2 **40 3**

DORMAN, Andy (M) 246 39
H: 6 0 W: 10 10 b.Chester 1-5-82
Honours: Wales 3 full caps.
2004 New England Rev 20 2
2005 New England Rev 30 2
2006 New England Rev 32 6
2007 New England Rev 30 7 **112 17**
2007-08 St Mirren 18 3
2008-09 St Mirren 36 10
2009-10 St Mirren 34 6 **88 19**
2010-11 Crystal Palace 20 1
2011-12 Crystal Palace 1 0 **21 1**
2011-12 *Bristol R* 25 2 **25 2**

EASTER, Jermaine (F) 302 72
H: 5 9 W: 12 02 b.Cardiff 15-1-82
Source: Trainee. *Honours:* Wales Youth, 10 full caps.
2000-01 Wolverhampton W 0 0
2000-01 Hartlepool U 4 0
2001-02 Hartlepool U 12 2
2002-03 Hartlepool U 8 0
2003-04 Hartlepool U 3 0 **27 2**
2003-04 *Cambridge U* 15 2
2004-05 Cambridge U 24 6 **39 8**
2004-05 Boston U 9 3 **9 3**
2005-06 Stockport Co 19 8 **19 8**
2005-06 Wycombe W 15 2
2006-07 Wycombe W 38 17
2007-08 Wycombe W 6 2 **59 21**
2007-08 Plymouth Arg 32 6
2008-09 Plymouth Arg 4 0 **36 6**
2008-09 *Millwall* 5 1 **5 1**
2008-09 *Colchester U* 5 2 **5 2**
2009-10 Milton Keynes D 36 14
2010-11 Milton Keynes D 14 0 **50 14**
2010-11 *Swansea C* 6 1 **6 1**
2010-11 Crystal Palace 14 1
2011-12 Crystal Palace 33 5 **47 6**

FENWICK, Bayan (F) 0 0
b. 16-11-93
Source: Lewes.
2011-12 Crystal Palace 0 0

GARDNER, Anthony (D) 243 7
H: 6 3 W: 14 00 b.Stone 19-9-80
Source: Trainee. *Honours:* England Under-21, 1 full cap.
1998-99 Port Vale 15 1
1999-2000 Port Vale 26 3 **41 4**
1999-2000 Tottenham H 0 0
2000-01 Tottenham H 8 0
2001-02 Tottenham H 15 0
2002-03 Tottenham H 12 1
2003-04 Tottenham H 33 0
2004-05 Tottenham H 17 0
2005-06 Tottenham H 17 0
2006-07 Tottenham H 8 0
2007-08 *Everton* 0 0
2007-08 Tottenham H 4 1 **114 2**
2008-09 Hull C 6 0
2009-10 Hull C 24 0
2010-11 Hull C 2 0 **32 0**
2010-11 *Crystal Palace* 28 1
2011-12 Crystal Palace 28 0 **56 1**

GARVAN, Owen (M) 212 19
H: 6 0 W: 10 07 b.Dublin 29-1-88
Source: Scholar. *Honours:* Eire Youth, Under-21.
2005-06 Ipswich T 32 3
2006-07 Ipswich T 27 1
2007-08 Ipswich T 43 2
2008-09 Ipswich T 37 7
2009-10 Ipswich T 25 0 **164 13**
2010-11 Crystal Palace 26 3
2011-12 Crystal Palace 22 3 **48 6**

HILLS, Lee (D) 57 1
H: 5 10 W: 11 11 b.Croydon 13-4-90
Source: Scholar. *Honours:* England Youth.
2007-08 Crystal Palace 12 1
2008-09 Crystal Palace 14 0
2008-09 *Colchester U* 2 0 **2 0**
2009-10 Crystal Palace 19 0
2009-10 *Oldham Ath* 3 0 **3 0**
2010-11 Crystal Palace 0 0
2011-12 Crystal Palace 0 0 **45 1**
2011-12 *Southend U* 7 0 **7 0**

HOLLAND, Jack (D) 0 0
H: 6 3 W: 12 02 b.West Wickham 1-3-92
Source: Scholar.
2010-11 Crystal Palace 0 0
2011-12 Crystal Palace 0 0

HOLNESS, Charlie (D) 0 0
H: 5 11 W: 13 01 b.Lewisham 9-2-92
Source: Scholar.
2010-11 Crystal Palace 0 0
2011-12 Crystal Palace 0 0

IVERSEN, Steffen (F) 364 125
H: 6 1 W: 12 07 b.Oslo 10-11-76
Honours: Norway 79 full caps, 21 goals.
1996 Rosenborg 25 10
1996-97 Tottenham H 16 6
1997-98 Tottenham H 13 0
1998-99 Tottenham H 27 8
1999-2000 Tottenham H 36 14
2000-01 Tottenham H 14 2
2001-02 Tottenham H 18 4
2002-03 Tottenham H 19 1 **143 35**
2003-04 Wolverhampton W 16 4 **16 4**
2004 Valerenga 11 4
2005 Valerenga 21 7 **32 11**
2006 Rosenborg 24 17
2007 Rosenborg 23 13
2008 Rosenborg 22 10
2009 Rosenborg 29 9
2010 Rosenborg 30 14 **153 73**
2010-11 Crystal Palace 17 2
2011-12 Crystal Palace 3 0 **20 2**
Transferred to Rosenborg February 2012.

JEDINAK, Mile (M) 224 30
H: 6 2 W: 13 12 b.Sydney 3-8-84
Honours: Australia Youth, 33 full caps, 3 goals.
2000-01 Sydney U 3 0
2001-02 Sydney U 7 1
2002-03 Sydney U 18 2
2003-04 Varteks 0 0
2004-05 Sydney U 24 3
2005-06 Sydney U 30 6 **82 12**
2006-07 Central Coast M 8 0
2007-08 Central Coast M 22 2
2008-09 Central Coast M 15 6 **45 8**
2008-09 Genclerbirligi 15 1
2009-10 Genclerbirligi 2 0
2009-10 Antalya 28 5 **28 5**
2010-11 Genclerbirligi 21 3 **38 4**
2011-12 Crystal Palace 31 1 **31 1**

KING, Tom (G) 0 0
b.Plymouth 9-3-95
Source: Scholar.
2011-12 Crystal Palace 0 0

MARROW, Alex (M) 58 1
H: 6 1 W: 13 00 b.Tyldesley 21-1-90
Source: Ashton Ath.
2007-08 Blackburn R 0 0
2008-09 Blackburn R 0 0
2009-10 Blackburn R 0 0
2009-10 *Oldham Ath* 32 1 **32 1**
2010-11 Blackburn R 0 0
2010-11 Crystal Palace 21 0
2011-12 Crystal Palace 1 0 **22 0**
2011-12 *Preston NE* 4 0 **4 0**

McCARTHY, Patrick (D) 252 11
H: 6 2 W: 13 07 b.Dublin 31-5-83
Source: Scholar. *Honours:* Eire Youth, B, Under-21.
2000-01 Manchester C 0 0
2001-02 Manchester C 0 0
2002-03 Manchester C 0 0
2002-03 *Boston U* 12 0 **12 0**
2002-03 *Notts Co* 6 0 **6 0**
2003-04 Manchester C 0 0
2004-05 Manchester C 0 0
2004-05 Leicester C 12 0
2005-06 Leicester C 38 2
2006-07 Leicester C 22 1 **72 3**
2007-08 Charlton Ath 29 2 **29 2**
2008-09 Crystal Palace 27 3
2009-10 Crystal Palace 20 0
2010-11 Crystal Palace 43 1
2011-12 Crystal Palace 43 2 **133 6**

MOXEY, Dean (D) 136 7
H: 6 2 W: 11 00 b.Exeter 14-1-86
Source: Scholar.
2008-09 Exeter C 43 4 **43 4**
2009-10 Derby Co 30 0
2010-11 Derby Co 22 2 **52 2**
2010-11 Crystal Palace 17 1
2011-12 Crystal Palace 24 0 **41 1**

MURRAY, Glenn (F) 248 91
H: 6 1 W: 12 12 b.Maryport 25-9-83
Source: Wilmington Hammerheads, Workington.
2005-06 Carlisle U 26 3
2006-07 Carlisle U 1 0 **27 3**
2006-07 *Stockport Co* 11 3 **11 3**
2006-07 Rochdale 31 16
2007-08 Rochdale 23 9 **54 25**
2007-08 Brighton & HA 21 9
2008-09 Brighton & HA 23 11
2009-10 Brighton & HA 32 12
2010-11 Brighton & HA 42 22 **118 54**
2011-12 Crystal Palace 38 6 **38 6**

O'KEEFE, Stuart (M) 27 0
H: 5 8 W: 10 00 b.Eye 4-3-91
Source: Ipswich T Scholar.
2008-09 Southend U 3 0
2009-10 Southend U 7 0
2010-11 Southend U 0 0 **10 0**
2010-11 Crystal Palace 4 0
2011-12 Crystal Palace 13 0 **17 0**

PARR, Jonathan (M) 160 10
H: 6 0 W: 11 11 b.Oslo 21-10-88
Honours: Norway Under-21, 6 full caps.
2006 Lyn 11 0 **11 0**
2007 Aalesund 19 1
2008 Aalesund 24 4
2009 Aalesund 27 2
2010 Aalesund 25 0
2011 Aalesund 15 1 **110 8**
2011-12 Crystal Palace 39 2 **39 2**

PARSONS, Matthew (D) 14 0
H: 5 10 W: 11 09 b.Catford 23-12-91
Source: Scholar.
2010-11 Crystal Palace 2 0
2010-11 *Barnet* 8 0 **8 0**
2011-12 Crystal Palace 4 0 **6 0**

PEDROZA, Antonio (F) 17 3
H: 5 7 W: 10 07 b.Chester 20-2-91
2010-11 Jaguares 13 3 **13 3**
2011-12 Crystal Palace 4 0 **4 0**

PINNEY, Nathaniel (F) 2 0
H: 6 0 W: 12 05 b.South Norwood 16-11-90
Source: Scholar.
2008-09 Crystal Palace 1 0
2009-10 Crystal Palace 0 0
2010-11 Crystal Palace 0 0
2010-11 *Dagenham & R* 1 0 **1 0**
2011-12 Crystal Palace 0 0 **1 0**

PRICE, Lewis (G) **102 0**
H: 6 3 W: 13 05 b.Bournemouth 19-7-84
Source: Southampton Academy. *Honours:* Wales Youth, Under-21, 9 full caps.

2002-03	Ipswich T	0	0		
2003-04	Ipswich T	1	0		
2004-05	Ipswich T	8	0		
2004-05	*Cambridge U*	6	0	**6**	**0**
2005-06	Ipswich T	25	0		
2006-07	Ipswich T	34	0	**68**	**0**
2007-08	Derby Co	6	0		
2008-09	Derby Co	0	0		
2008-09	*Milton Keynes D*	2	0	**2**	**0**
2008-09	*Luton T*	1	0	**1**	**0**
2009-10	Derby Co	0	0	**6**	**0**
2009-10	*Brentford*	13	0	**13**	**0**
2010-11	Crystal Palace	1	0		
2011-12	Crystal Palace	5	0	**6**	**0**

SCANNELL, Sean (F) **130 12**
H: 5 9 W: 11 07 b.Croydon 19-9-90
Source: Scholar. *Honours:* Eire Youth, Under-21.

2007-08	Crystal Palace	23	2		
2008-09	Crystal Palace	25	2		
2009-10	Crystal Palace	26	2		
2010-11	Crystal Palace	19	2		
2011-12	Crystal Palace	37	4	**130**	**12**

SEKAJJA, Ibra (F) **2 1**
H: 5 11 W: 11 00 b.Uganda 31-10-92
Source: Scholar.

2010-11	Crystal Palace	1	1		
2011-12	Crystal Palace	1	0	**2**	**1**

SPERONI, Julian (G) **332 0**
H: 6 0 W: 11 00 b.Buenos Aires 18-5-79
Honours: Argentina Under-20, Under-21.

1999-2000	Platense	2	0		
2000-01	Platense	0	0	**2**	**0**
2001-02	Dundee	17	0		
2002-03	Dundee	38	0		
2003-04	Dundee	37	0	**92**	**0**
2004-05	Crystal Palace	6	0		
2005-06	Crystal Palace	4	0		
2006-07	Crystal Palace	5	0		
2007-08	Crystal Palace	46	0		
2008-09	Crystal Palace	45	0		
2009-10	Crystal Palace	45	0		
2010-11	Crystal Palace	45	0		
2011-12	Crystal Palace	42	0	**238**	**0**

TAYLOR, Quade (M) **0 0**
b.Tooting 11-12-93
Source: Dulwich H.

2010-11	Crystal Palace	0	0
2011-12	Crystal Palace	0	0

WILLIAMS, Jon (M) **14 0**
H: 5 6 W: 10 00 b.Tunbridge Wells 9-10-93
Source: Scholar. *Honours:* Wales Youth, Under-21.

2010-11	Crystal Palace	0	0		
2011-12	Crystal Palace	14	0	**14**	**0**

WRIGHT, David (D) **431 8**
H: 5 11 W: 11 01 b.Warrington 1-5-80
Source: Trainee. *Honours:* England Youth.

1997-98	Crewe Alex	3	0		
1998-99	Crewe Alex	20	1		
1999-2000	Crewe Alex	45	0		
2000-01	Crewe Alex	42	0		
2001-02	Crewe Alex	30	0		
2002-03	Crewe Alex	31	1		
2003-04	Crewe Alex	40	1	**211**	**3**
2004-05	Wigan Ath	31	0		
2005-06	Wigan Ath	2	0		
2005-06	*Norwich C*	5	0	**5**	**0**
2006-07	Wigan Ath	12	0	**45**	**0**
2006-07	Ipswich T	19	1		
2007-08	Ipswich T	41	2		
2008-09	Ipswich T	34	1		
2009-10	Ipswich T	26	1	**120**	**5**
2010-11	Crystal Palace	28	0		
2011-12	Crystal Palace	22	0	**50**	**0**

WYNTER, Alex (M) **0 0**
H: 6 0 W: 13 04 b.Camberwell 15-9-93
Source: Scholar.

2009-10	Crystal Palace	0	0
2010-11	Crystal Palace	0	0
2011-12	Crystal Palace	0	0

ZAHA, Wilfred (F) **83 7**
H: 5 11 W: 10 05 b.Ivory Coast 10-11-92
Source: Scholar. *Honours:* England Under-21.

2009-10	Crystal Palace	1	0		
2010-11	Crystal Palace	41	1		
2011-12	Crystal Palace	41	6	**83**	**7**

DAGENHAM & R (32)

ARBER, Mark (D) **485 36**
H: 6 1 W: 11 09 b.Johannesburg 9-10-77
Source: Trainee.

1995-96	Tottenham H	0	0		
1996-97	Tottenham H	0	0		
1997-98	Tottenham H	0	0		
1998-99	Tottenham H	0	0		
1998-99	Barnet	35	2		
1999-2000	Barnet	45	6		
2000-01	Barnet	45	7		
2001-02	Barnet	0	0	**125**	**15**
2002-03	Peterborough U	25	2		
2003-04	Peterborough U	44	3		
2004-05	Oldham Ath	14	1	**14**	**1**
2004-05	Peterborough U	21	0		
2005-06	Peterborough U	46	2		
2006-07	Peterborough U	34	1		
2007-08	Peterborough U	0	0	**170**	**8**
2007-08	*Dagenham & R*	16	1		
2008-09	Dagenham & R	42	3		
2009-10	Dagenham & R	41	4		
2010-11	Dagenham & R	44	2		
2011-12	Dagenham & R	33	2	**176**	**12**

BATES, Jon-Jo (M) **0 0**
b.Hammersmith 29-3-91
Source: Bedfont T.

2010-11	Dagenham & R	0	0
2011-12	Dagenham & R	0	0

BINGHAM, Billy (D) **35 2**
H: 5 11 W: 11 02 b.Welling 15-7-90
Source: Crystal Palace.

2008-09	Dagenham & R	0	0		
2009-10	Dagenham & R	2	0		
2010-11	Dagenham & R	6	0		
2011-12	Dagenham & R	27	2	**35**	**2**

CUNNINGTON, Adam (F) **21 5**
b.Leighton Buzzard 7-10-87
Source: Solihull Moors, Kettering T.

2011-12	Kettering T	12	5	**12**	**5**

On loan from Kettering T.

2011-12	Dagenham & R	9	0	**9**	**0**

On loan from Kettering T.

DENNIS, Louis (F) **0 0**
b.Hendon
Source: Youth.

2011-12	Dagenham & R	0	0

DOE, Scott (D) **121 6**
H: 6 0 W: 11 06 b.Reading 6-11-88
Source: Swindon T Scholar, Weymouth.

2009-10	Dagenham & R	42	0		
2010-11	Dagenham & R	38	0		
2011-12	Dagenham & R	41	6	**121**	**6**

EDMANS, Rob (F) **3 0**
H: 6 5 W: 12 08 b.Greenwich 25-1-87
Source: Witham T, Chelmsford C.

2011-12	Dagenham & R	3	0	**3**	**0**

ELITO, Medy (M) **67 10**
H: 6 2 W: 13 00 b.Kinshasa 20-3-90
Source: Scholar. *Honours:* England Youth.

2007-08	Colchester U	11	1		
2008-09	Colchester U	5	0		
2009-10	Colchester U	3	0		
2009-10	*Cheltenham T*	12	3		
2010-11	Colchester U	0	0	**19**	**1**
2010-11	*Dagenham & R*	10	2		
2010-11	*Cheltenham T*	2	0	**14**	**3**
2011-12	Dagenham & R	24	4	**34**	**6**

GAIN, Peter (M) **447 34**
H: 5 9 W: 11 07 b.Hammersmith 11-11-76
Source: Trainee.

1995-96	Tottenham H	0	0		
1996-97	Tottenham H	0	0		
1997-98	Tottenham H	0	0		
1998-99	Tottenham H	0	0		
1998-99	Lincoln C	4	0		
1999-2000	Lincoln C	32	2		
2000-01	Lincoln C	24	5		
2001-02	Lincoln C	42	2		
2002-03	Lincoln C	43	5		
2003-04	Lincoln C	42	7		
2004-05	Lincoln C	40	0	**227**	**21**
2005-06	Peterborough U	37	3		
2006-07	Peterborough U	34	6		
2007-08	Peterborough U	0	0	**71**	**9**
2007-08	Dagenham & R	18	1		
2008-09	Dagenham & R	31	0		
2009-10	Dagenham & R	43	3		
2010-11	Dagenham & R	37	0		
2011-12	Dagenham & R	20	0	**149**	**4**

GAYLE, Dwight (F) **0 0**
b.Walthamstow 20-10-89
Source: Stansted.

2011-12	Dagenham & R	0	0

GAYLE, Ian (D) **0 0**
b.Welling 23-10-92
Source: Youth.

2011-12	Dagenham & R	0	0

GREEN, Danny J (M) **11 1**
H: 6 0 W: 12 06 b.Harlow 4-8-90
Source: Billericay T.

2010-11	Dagenham & R	3	0		
2011-12	Dagenham & R	8	1	**11**	**1**

GREEN, Dominic (F) **67 6**
H: 5 6 W: 11 02 b.Newham 5-7-89
Source: Scholar.

2007-08	Dagenham & R	12	0		
2008-09	Dagenham & R	2	1		
2008-09	Peterborough U	16	1		
2009-10	Peterborough U	11	1		
2009-10	*Chesterfield*	10	2	**10**	**2**
2010-11	Peterborough U	0	0	**27**	**2**
2011-12	Dagenham & R	16	1	**30**	**2**

HOGAN, Dave (G) **2 0**
H: 6 0 W: 13 10 b.Harlow 31-5-89
Source: Scholar.

2008-09	Dagenham & R	1	0		
2009-10	Dagenham & R	0	0		
2011-12	Dagenham & R	1	0	**2**	**0**

HOWELL, Luke (D) **89 2**
H: 5 10 W: 10 05 b.Heathfield 5-1-87
Source: Scholar.

2006-07	Gillingham	1	0	**1**	**0**
2007-08	Milton Keynes D	8	0		
2008-09	Milton Keynes D	15	1		
2009-10	Milton Keynes D	29	0		
2010-11	Milton Keynes D	1	0	**53**	**1**
2010-11	Lincoln C	25	1	**25**	**1**
2011-12	Dagenham & R	10	0	**10**	**0**

ILESANMI, Femi (D) **42 0**
H: 6 1 W: 11 13 b.Southwark 18-4-91
Source: QPR Scholar, Ashford T (M'sex).

2010-11	Dagenham & R	25	0		
2011-12	Dagenham & R	17	0	**42**	**0**

LEWINGTON, Chris (G) **44 0**
H: 6 1 W: 12 00 b.Sidcup 23-8-88
Source: Erith & B, Dulwich H, Fisher Ath, Sittingbourne, Leatherhead.

2009-10	Dagenham & R	0	0		
2010-11	Dagenham & R	3	0		
2011-12	Dagenham & R	41	0	**44**	**0**

MAHER, Kevin (M) **488 23**
H: 6 0 W: 12 13 b.Ilford 17-10-76
Source: Trainee. *Honours:* Eire Under-21.

1995-96	Tottenham H	0	0		
1996-97	Tottenham H	0	0		
1997-98	Tottenham H	0	0		
1997-98	Southend U	18	1		
1998-99	Southend U	34	4		
1999-2000	Southend U	24	0		
2000-01	Southend U	41	2		
2001-02	Southend U	36	5		
2002-03	Southend U	42	2		
2003-04	Southend U	42	1		
2004-05	Southend U	42	1		
2005-06	Southend U	44	1		
2006-07	Southend U	41	5		
2007-08	Southend U	19	0	**383**	**22**
2007-08	*Gillingham*	7	0		
2008-09	Oldham Ath	28	1	**28**	**1**
2009-10	Gillingham	26	0		
2010-11	Gillingham	36	0	**69**	**0**
2011-12	Dagenham & R	8	0	**8**	**0**

McCRORY, Damien (M) **103 1**
H: 6 2 W: 12 10 b.Limerick 22-2-90
Honours: Eire Youth.

2008-09	Plymouth Arg	0	0		
2008-09	*Port Vale*	12	0		
2009-10	Plymouth Arg	0	0		
2009-10	*Port Vale*	5	0	**17**	**0**
2009-10	*Grimsby T*	10	0	**10**	**0**
2009-10	Dagenham & R	20	0		
2010-11	Dagenham & R	23	0		
2011-12	Dagenham & R	33	1	**76**	**1**

NURSE, Jon (M) **179 27**
H: 5 9 W: 12 04 b.Barbados 1-3-81
Source: Stevenage B. *Honours:* Barbados 4 full caps.

2007-08	Dagenham & R	30	1		
2008-09	Dagenham & R	34	4		
2009-10	Dagenham & R	38	7		
2010-11	Dagenham & R	38	10		
2011-12	Dagenham & R	39	5	**179**	**27**

OGOGO, Abu (D) **112 5**
H: 5 8 W: 10 02 b.Epsom 3-11-89
Source: Scholar.

2007-08	Arsenal	0	0		
2008-09	Arsenal	0	0		
2008-09	*Barnet*	9	1	**9**	**1**
2009-10	Dagenham & R	30	2		
2010-11	Dagenham & R	33	1		
2011-12	Dagenham & R	40	1	**103**	**4**

OSBORN, Alex (F) **0 0**
b.Walthamstow 29-7-93
Source: Grays Ath.

2010-11	Dagenham & R	0	0		
2011-12	Dagenham & R	0	0		

REED, Jake (F) **7 0**
H: 5 9 W: 11 07 b.Great Yarmouth 13-5-91
Source: Great Yarmouth T.

2011-12	Dagenham & R	7	0	**7**	**0**

REYNOLDS, Duran-Rhys (D) **0 0**
b.Skegness 27-9-91
Source: Southend U Scholar.

2010-11	Dagenham & R	0	0		
2011-12	Dagenham & R	0	0		

ROSE, Richard (D) **242 5**
H: 6 0 W: 12 04 b.Tonbridge 8-9-82
Source: Trainee.

2000-01	Gillingham	4	0		
2001-02	Gillingham	3	0		
2002-03	Gillingham	2	0		
2002-03	*Bristol R*	9	0	**9**	**0**
2003-04	Gillingham	17	0		
2004-05	Gillingham	18	0		
2005-06	Gillingham	14	0	**58**	**0**
2006-07	Hereford U	33	1		
2007-08	Hereford U	31	1		
2008-09	Hereford U	42	0		
2009-10	Hereford U	25	0		
2010-11	Hereford U	34	2	**165**	**4**
2011-12	Dagenham & R	10	1	**10**	**1**

SAUNDERS, Matthew (M) **23 4**
H: 5 11 W: 11 05 b.Chertsey 12-9-89
Source: Scholar.

2008-09	Fulham	0	0		
2009-10	Fulham	0	0		
2009-10	*Lincoln C*	18	3	**18**	**3**
2010-11	Fulham	0	0		
2011-12	Fulham	0	0		
2011-12	Dagenham & R	5	1	**5**	**1**

SCANNELL, Damian (M) **89 4**
H: 5 10 W: 11 07 b.Croydon 28-4-85
Source: Eastleigh.

2007-08	Southend U	9	0		
2008-09	Southend U	19	1		
2008-09	*Brentford*	2	0	**2**	**0**
2009-10	Southend U	25	1	**53**	**2**
2010-11	Dagenham & R	20	2		
2011-12	Dagenham & R	14	0	**34**	**2**

SCOTT, Josh (F) **76 12**
H: 6 1 W: 12 00 b.Camden 10-5-85
Source: Hayes, Hayes & Yeading U.

2009-10	Dagenham & R	40	10		
2010-11	Dagenham & R	16	1		
2011-12	Dagenham & R	20	1	**76**	**12**

SPILLANE, Michael (M) **119 9**
H: 5 9 W: 11 10 b.Jersey 23-3-89
Source: Scholar. *Honours:* Eire Youth, Under-21.

2005-06	Norwich C	2	0		
2006-07	Norwich C	5	0		
2007-08	Norwich C	6	0		
2008-09	Norwich C	0	0		
2008-09	*Luton T*	39	3	**39**	**3**
2009-10	Norwich C	13	1	**26**	**1**
2010-11	Brentford	24	1		
2011-12	Brentford	1	0	**25**	**1**
2011-12	Dagenham & R	29	4	**29**	**4**

TOMLIN, Gavin (F) **147 26**
H: 6 0 W: 12 02 b.Gillingham 13-1-83
Source: Staines T, Yeading.

2006-07	Brentford	12	0		
2007-08	Brentford	0	0	**12**	**0**

From Fisher Ath.

2008-09	Yeovil T	42	7		
2009-10	Yeovil T	35	7	**77**	**14**
2010-11	Dagenham & R	19	2		
2010-11	*Torquay U*	12	4	**12**	**4**
2011-12	Dagenham & R	17	0	**36**	**2**
2011-12	*Gillingham*	10	6	**10**	**6**

WALSH, Phil (F) **33 3**
H: 6 3 W: 13 04 b.Hartlepool 4-2-84
Source: Dorchester T.

2009-10	Dagenham & R	9	0		
2010-11	Dagenham & R	3	0		
2010-11	*Barnet*	9	3	**9**	**3**
2010-11	*Cheltenham T*	4	0	**4**	**0**
2011-12	Dagenham & R	8	0	**20**	**0**

WILKINSON, Luke (D) **0 0**
H: 6 2 W: 11 09 b.Wells 2-12-92
Source: Bristol C Scholar.

2009-10	Portsmouth	0	0		
2010-11	Dagenham & R	0	0		
2011-12	Dagenham & R	0	0		

WILLIAMS, Sam (F) **115 14**
H: 5 11 W: 10 08 b.Greenwich 9-6-87
Source: Scholar.

2004-05	Aston Villa	0	0		
2005-06	Aston Villa	0	0		
2005-06	*Wrexham*	15	2	**15**	**2**
2006-07	Aston Villa	0	0		
2006-07	*Brighton & HA*	3	1	**3**	**1**
2007-08	Aston Villa	0	0		
2008-09	Aston Villa	0	0		
2008-09	*Colchester U*	1	0	**1**	**0**
2008-09	*Walsall*	5	1	**5**	**1**
2008-09	*Brentford*	11	2	**11**	**2**
2009-10	Yeovil T	34	4		
2010-11	Yeovil T	36	2	**70**	**6**
2011-12	Dagenham & R	10	2	**10**	**2**

WOODALL, Brian (F) **39 11**
H: 5 10 W: 11 09 b.Bielefeld 28-12-87
Source: SC Herford, Hinckley U, Gresley R, Atherstone T, Coventry Sphinx, Gresley.

2011-12	Dagenham & R	39	11	**39**	**11**

WOOTTON, Lee (M) **0 0**
H: 5 7 W: 10 05 b.Hackney 23-8-92
Source: Youth.

2010-11	Dagenham & R	0	0		
2011-12	Dagenham & R	0	0		

DERBY CO (33)

ADDISON, Miles (D) **90 4**
H: 6 2 W: 13 03 b.Newham 7-1-89
Source: Scholar. *Honours:* England Under-21.

2005-06	Derby Co	2	0		
2006-07	Derby Co	0	0		
2007-08	Derby Co	1	0		
2008-09	Derby Co	28	1		
2009-10	Derby Co	13	2		
2010-11	Derby Co	21	0		
2011-12	Derby Co	0	0	**65**	**3**
2011-12	*Barnsley*	11	0	**11**	**0**
2011-12	*Bournemouth*	14	1	**14**	**1**

ANDERSON, Russell (D) **327 19**
H: 5 11 W: 10 09 b.Aberdeen 25-10-78
Source: Dyce J. *Honours:* Scotland Under-21, 11 full caps.

1996-97	Aberdeen	14	0		
1997-98	Aberdeen	26	0		
1998-99	Aberdeen	16	0		
1999-2000	Aberdeen	34	1		
2000-01	Aberdeen	0	0		
2001-02	Aberdeen	24	1		
2002-03	Aberdeen	33	2		
2003-04	Aberdeen	25	5		
2004-05	Aberdeen	31	1		
2005-06	Aberdeen	36	6		
2006-07	Aberdeen	35	2	**274**	**18**
2007-08	Sunderland	1	0		
2007-08	*Plymouth Arg*	14	0	**14**	**0**
2008-09	Sunderland	0	0		
2008-09	*Burnley*	4	0	**4**	**0**
2009-10	Sunderland	0	0	**1**	**0**
2009-10	Derby Co	15	1		
2010-11	Derby Co	11	0		
2011-12	Derby Co	8	0	**34**	**1**

Transferred to Aberdeen January 2012.

ATKINS, Ross (G) **46 0**
H: 6 0 W: 13 00 b.Derby 3-11-89
Source: Scholar.

2008-09	Derby Co	0	0		
2009-10	Derby Co	0	0		
2010-11	Derby Co	1	0		
2011-12	Derby Co	0	0	**1**	**0**
2011-12	*Burton Alb*	45	0	**45**	**0**

BAILEY, James (M) **104 1**
H: 6 0 W: 12 05 b.Bollington 18-9-88
Source: Scholar.

2006-07	Crewe Alex	0	0		
2007-08	Crewe Alex	1	0		
2008-09	Crewe Alex	24	0		
2009-10	Crewe Alex	21	0	**46**	**0**
2010-11	Derby Co	36	1		
2011-12	Derby Co	22	0	**58**	**1**

BALL, Callum (F) **29 3**
H: 6 1 W: 10 03 b.Leicester 8-10-92
Source: Scholar.

2009-10	Derby Co	1	0		
2010-11	Derby Co	5	0		
2011-12	Derby Co	23	3	**29**	**3**

BARKER, Shaun (D) **355 18**
H: 6 2 W: 12 08 b.Nottingham 19-9-82
Source: Scholar.

2002-03	Rotherham U	11	0		
2003-04	Rotherham U	36	2		
2004-05	Rotherham U	33	2		
2005-06	Rotherham U	43	3	**123**	**7**
2006-07	Blackpool	45	3		
2007-08	Blackpool	46	2		
2008-09	Blackpool	43	0	**134**	**5**
2009-10	Derby Co	35	5		
2010-11	Derby Co	43	1		
2011-12	Derby Co	20	0	**98**	**6**

BENNETT, Mason (F) **9 0**
H: 5 10 W: 10 02 b.Shirebrook 15-7-96
Source: Scholar.

2011-12	Derby Co	9	0	**9**	**0**

BRAYFORD, John (D) **150 3**
H: 5 8 W: 11 02 b.Stoke 29-12-87
Source: Burton Alb.

2008-09	Crewe Alex	36	2		
2009-10	Crewe Alex	45	0	**81**	**2**
2010-11	Derby Co	46	1		
2011-12	Derby Co	23	0	**69**	**1**

BRYSON, Craig (M) **257 26**
H: 5 7 W: 10 00 b.Rutherglen 6-11-86
Honours: Scotland Under-21, 1 full cap.

2003-04	Clyde	0	0		
2004-05	Clyde	28	3		
2005-06	Clyde	33	2		
2006-07	Clyde	34	3	**95**	**8**
2007-08	Kilmarnock	19	4		
2008-09	Kilmarnock	33	2		
2009-10	Kilmarnock	33	4		
2010-11	Kilmarnock	33	2	**118**	**12**
2011-12	Derby Co	44	6	**44**	**6**

BUXTON, Jake (D) **192 8**
H: 6 1 W: 13 05 b.Sutton-in-Ashfield 4-3-85
Source: Scholar.

2002-03	Mansfield T	3	0		
2003-04	Mansfield T	9	1		
2004-05	Mansfield T	30	1		
2005-06	Mansfield T	39	0		
2006-07	Mansfield T	30	1		
2007-08	Mansfield T	40	2		
2008-09	Mansfield T	0	0	**151**	**5**

From Burton Alb.

2008-09 Derby Co 0 0
2009-10 Derby Co 19 1
2010-11 Derby Co 1 0
2011-12 Derby Co 21 2 **41 3**

COLE, Aaron (M) 0 0
b.Burton -on-Trent 10-9-92
Source: Scholar.
2011-12 Derby Co 0 0

CONNOLLY, Ryan (M) 10 0
H: 5 10 W: 10 04 b.Castlebar 13-1-92
Source: Scholar. *Honours:* Eire Youth.
2009-10 Derby Co 1 0
2010-11 Derby Co 0 0
2011-12 Derby Co 0 0 **1 0**
2011-12 *Ayr U* 9 0 **9 0**

CROFT, Lee (F) 199 14
H: 5 11 W: 13 00 b.Wigan 21-6-85
Source: Scholar. *Honours:* England Youth, Under-20.
2002-03 Manchester C 0 0
2003-04 Manchester C 0 0
2004-05 Manchester C 7 0
2004-05 *Oldham Ath* 12 0 **12 0**
2005-06 Manchester C 21 1 **28 1**
2006-07 Norwich C 36 3
2007-08 Norwich C 41 1
2008-09 Norwich C 41 5 **118 9**
2009-10 Derby Co 19 1
2010-11 Derby Co 0 0
2010-11 *Huddersfield T* 3 0 **3 0**
2011-12 Derby Co 8 0 **27 1**
2011-12 *St Johnstone* 11 3 **11 3**

DAVIES, Ben (M) 328 62
H: 5 7 W: 12 03 b.Birmingham 27-5-81
Source: Walsall trainee.
2000-01 Kidderminster H 3 0
2001-02 Kidderminster H 9 0 **12 0**
2004-05 Chester C 44 2
2005-06 Chester C 45 7 **89 9**
2006-07 Shrewsbury T 43 12
2007-08 Shrewsbury T 27 6
2008-09 Shrewsbury T 42 12 **112 30**
2009-10 Notts Co 45 15
2010-11 Notts Co 22 5 **67 20**
2010-11 Derby Co 13 1
2011-12 Derby Co 35 2 **48 3**

DAVIES, Steve (F) 143 25
H: 6 0 W: 12 00 b.Liverpool 29-12-87
Source: Scholar.
2005-06 Tranmere R 22 2
2006-07 Tranmere R 28 1
2007-08 Tranmere R 10 2 **60 5**
2008-09 Derby Co 19 3
2009-10 Derby Co 18 1
2010-11 Derby Co 20 5
2011-12 Derby Co 26 11 **83 20**

DEENEY, Saul (G) 52 0
H: 6 0 W: 12 13 b.Londonderry 12-3-83
Source: Scholar. *Honours:* Eire Youth, Under-21.
2000-01 Notts Co 0 0
2001-02 Notts Co 0 0
2002-03 Notts Co 7 0
2003-04 Notts Co 3 0
2004-05 Notts Co 32 0
2005-06 Notts Co 0 0
2006-07 Notts Co 7 0
2007-08 Notts Co 0 0
2008-09 Notts Co 0 0 **49 0**
2009-10 Derby Co 3 0
2010-11 Derby Co 0 0
2011-12 Derby Co 0 0 **3 0**

DOYLE, Conor (F) 20 0
H: 6 2 W: 12 04 b.Mckinney 13-10-91
Source: Creighton Univ. *Honours:* Eire Under-21.
2010-11 Derby Co 14 0
2011-12 Derby Co 6 0 **20 0**

FIELDING, Frank (G) 149 0
H: 5 11 W: 12 00 b.Blackburn 4-4-88
Source: Scholar. *Honours:* England Youth, Under-21.
2006-07 Blackburn R 0 0
2007-08 Blackburn R 0 0
2007-08 *Wycombe W* 36 0 **36 0**
2008-09 Blackburn R 0 0
2008-09 *Northampton T* 12 0 **12 0**
2008-09 *Rochdale* 23 0
2009-10 Blackburn R 0 0
2009-10 *Rochdale* 18 0 **41 0**
2010-11 Blackburn R 0 0
2010-11 Derby Co 16 0
2011-12 Derby Co 44 0 **60 0**

GREEN, Paul (M) 323 33
H: 5 9 W: 10 02 b.Pontefract 10-4-83
Source: Scholar. *Honours:* Eire 12 full caps, 1 goal.
2003-04 Doncaster R 43 8
2004-05 Doncaster R 42 7
2005-06 Doncaster R 34 3
2006-07 Doncaster R 41 2
2007-08 Doncaster R 38 5 **198 25**
2008-09 Derby Co 29 3
2009-10 Derby Co 33 2
2010-11 Derby Co 36 2
2011-12 Derby Co 27 1 **125 8**

HENDRICK, Jeff (M) 46 3
H: 6 1 W: 11 11 b.Dublin 31-1-92
Source: Scholar. *Honours:* Eire Youth, Under-21.
2010-11 Derby Co 4 0
2011-12 Derby Co 42 3 **46 3**

HUGHES, Will (M) 3 0
H: 6 1 W: 11 08 b.Weybridge 7-4-95
Source: Scholar. *Honours:* England Youth.
2011-12 Derby Co 3 0 **3 0**

JONES, Chris (D) 0 0
b.Derby 24-11-92
Source: Scholar.
2011-12 Derby Co 0 0

LEGZDINS, Adam (G) 57 0
H: 6 1 W: 14 02 b.Penkridge 28-11-86
Source: Scholar.
2006-07 Birmingham C 0 0
2007-08 Birmingham C 0 0
2008-09 Crewe Alex 0 0
2009-10 Crewe Alex 6 0 **6 0**
2010-11 Burton Alb 46 0
2011-12 Derby Co 4 0 **4 0**
2011-12 *Burton Alb* 1 0 **47 0**

MAGUIRE, Chris (F) 163 24
H: 5 7 W: 10 05 b.Bellshill 16-1-89
Honours: Scotland Under-21, 2 full caps.
2005-06 Aberdeen 1 0
2006-07 Aberdeen 19 1
2007-08 Aberdeen 28 4
2008-09 Aberdeen 31 3
2009-10 Aberdeen 17 1
2009-10 *Kilmarnock* 14 4 **14 4**
2010-11 Aberdeen 35 7 **131 16**
2011-12 Derby Co 7 1 **7 1**
2011-12 *Portsmouth* 11 3 **11 3**

MORCH, Mats (G) 0 0
b.Mandal
2010-11 Derby Co 0 0
2011-12 Derby Co 0 0

NAYLOR, Tom (D) 8 0
H: 5 11 W: 11 05 b.Sutton-in-Ashfield 28-6-91
Source: Mansfield T.
2011-12 Derby Co 8 0 **8 0**

O'BRIEN, Mark (D) 23 0
H: 5 11 W: 12 02 b.Dublin 20-11-92
Source: Cherry Orchard. *Honours:* Eire Youth.
2008-09 Derby Co 1 0
2009-10 Derby Co 0 0
2010-11 Derby Co 2 0
2011-12 Derby Co 20 0 **23 0**

ROBERTS, Gareth (D) 504 22
H: 5 8 W: 11 12 b.Wrexham 6-2-78
Source: Trainee. *Honours:* Wales Under-21, B, 9 full caps.
1995-96 Liverpool 0 0
1996-97 Liverpool 0 0
1997-98 Liverpool 0 0
1998-99 Liverpool 0 0
1998-99 Panionios 15 0 **15 0**
1999-2000 Tranmere R 37 1
2000-01 Tranmere R 34 0
2001-02 Tranmere R 45 2
2002-03 Tranmere R 37 4
2003-04 Tranmere R 44 1
2004-05 Tranmere R 40 3
2005-06 Tranmere R 44 2 **281 13**
2006-07 Doncaster R 30 1
2007-08 Doncaster R 37 3
2008-09 Doncaster R 32 1
2009-10 Doncaster R 42 3 **141 8**
2010-11 Derby Co 26 0
2011-12 Derby Co 41 1 **67 1**

ROBINSON, Theo (F) 170 48
H: 5 9 W: 10 03 b.Birmingham 22-1-89
Source: Scholar.
2005-06 Watford 1 0
2006-07 Watford 1 0
2007-08 Watford 0 0
2007-08 *Hereford U* 43 13 **43 13**
2008-09 Watford 3 0 **5 0**
2008-09 *Southend U* 21 7 **21 7**
2009-10 Huddersfield T 37 13
2010-11 Huddersfield T 1 0 **38 13**
2010-11 Millwall 11 3 **11 3**
2010-11 *Derby Co* 13 2
2011-12 Derby Co 39 10 **52 12**

SEVERN, James (G) 1 0
H: 6 4 W: 14 11 b.Nottingham 10-10-91
Source: Scholar.
2010-11 Derby Co 1 0
2011-12 Derby Co 0 0 **1 0**

SHACKELL, Jason (D) 256 8
H: 6 4 W: 13 06 b.Stevenage 27-9-83
Source: Scholar.
2002-03 Norwich C 2 0
2003-04 Norwich C 6 0
2004-05 Norwich C 11 0
2005-06 Norwich C 17 0
2006-07 Norwich C 43 3
2007-08 Norwich C 39 0
2008-09 Norwich C 15 0 **133 3**
2008-09 Wolverhampton W 12 0
2009-10 Wolverhampton W 0 0 **12 0**
2009-10 *Doncaster R* 21 1 **21 1**
2010-11 Barnsley 44 3
2011-12 Barnsley 0 0 **44 3**
2011-12 Derby Co 46 1 **46 1**

TYSON, Nathan (F) 337 80
H: 5 10 W: 10 02 b.Reading 4-5-82
Source: Trainee. *Honours:* England Under-20.
1999-2000 Reading 1 0
2000-01 Reading 0 0
2001-02 Reading 1 0
2001-02 *Swansea C* 11 1 **11 1**
2001-02 *Cheltenham T* 8 1 **8 1**
2002-03 Reading 23 1
2003-04 Reading 8 0 **33 1**
2003-04 Wycombe W 21 9
2004-05 Wycombe W 42 22
2005-06 Wycombe W 15 11 **78 42**
2005-06 Nottingham F 28 10
2006-07 Nottingham F 24 7
2007-08 Nottingham F 34 9
2008-09 Nottingham F 35 5
2009-10 Nottingham F 33 2
2010-11 Nottingham F 30 2 **184 35**
2011-12 Derby Co 23 0 **23 0**

WARD, Jamie (M) 214 57
H: 5 5 W: 9 04 b.Birmingham 12-5-86
Source: Scholar. *Honours:* Northern Ireland Youth, Under-21, 1 full cap.
2003-04 Aston Villa 0 0
2004-05 Aston Villa 0 0
2005-06 Aston Villa 0 0
2005-06 *Stockport Co* 9 1 **9 1**
2006-07 Torquay U 25 9 **25 9**
2006-07 Chesterfield 9 3
2007-08 Chesterfield 35 12
2008-09 Chesterfield 23 14 **67 29**
2008-09 Sheffield U 16 2
2009-10 Sheffield U 28 7
2010-11 Sheffield U 19 0 **63 9**
2010-11 Derby Co 13 5
2011-12 Derby Co 37 4 **50 9**

WITHAM, Alex (M) 0 0
b.Harrow 14-9-92
Source: Scholar.
2011-12 Derby Co 0 0

DONCASTER R (34)

BAGAYOKO, Mamadou (F) 335 92
H: 6 3 W: 12 06 b.Paris 21-5-79
Honours: Mali 31 full caps, 4 goals.

1997-98	Dunkerque	3	0		
1998-99	Dunkerque	4	0	**7**	**0**
1998-99	Sens	34	29	**34**	**29**
1999-2000	Strasbourg B	10	3		
1999-2000	Strasbourg	11	0		
2000-01	Strasbourg B	13	3	**23**	**6**
2000-01	Strasbourg	16	0		
2001-02	Strasbourg	21	2		
2002-03	Strasbourg	17	2	**65**	**4**
2003-04	Ajaccio	34	8	**34**	**8**
2004-05	Nantes	30	7		
2005-06	*Nice*	32	5		
2006-07	*Al-Wahda*	29	13	**29**	**13**
2007-08	Nantes	21	10		
2008-09	Nantes	26	7	**77**	**24**
2009-10	Nice	23	1		
2010-11	Nice	5	0	**60**	**6**
2011-12	PAS Giannina	1	0	**1**	**0**
2011-12	Doncaster R	5	2	**5**	**2**

BAMOGO, Habib (F) 317 63
H: 5 9 W: 11 05 b.Paris 8-5-82
Honours: Burkina Faso 28 full caps, 8 goals.

1998-99	Clairefontaine	0	0		
1999-2000	Montpellier B	1	0		
2000-01	Montpellier B	25	10		
2001-02	Montpellier B	8	7	**34**	**17**
2001-02	Montpellier	20	2		
2002-03	Montpellier	33	4		
2003-04	Montpellier	38	16	**91**	**22**
2004-05	Marseille	30	5		
2005-06	*Nantes*	31	4	**31**	**4**
2006-07	Marseille	15	3	**45**	**8**
2006-07	*Celta Vigo*	15	2	**15**	**2**
2007-08	Nice	35	2		
2008-09	Nice	34	7		
2009-10	Nice	13	0		
2010-11	Nice	11	1	**93**	**10**
2011-12	Panaitolikos	4	0	**4**	**0**
2011-12	Doncaster R	4	0	**4**	**0**

BARNES, Giles (M) 138 11
H: 6 0 W: 12 10 b.Barking 5-8-88
Source: Scholar. *Honours:* England Youth.

2005-06	Derby Co	19	1		
2006-07	Derby Co	39	8		
2007-08	Derby Co	21	1		
2008-09	Derby Co	3	0		
2008-09	*Fulham*	0	0		
2009-10	Derby Co	0	0	**82**	**10**
2009-10	WBA	9	0		
2010-11	WBA	14	0	**23**	**0**
2011-12	Doncaster R	33	1	**33**	**1**

BAXENDALE, James (M) 3 0
H: 5 8 W: 10 03 b.Thorne 16-9-92
Source: Leeds U Scholar.

2011-12	Doncaster R	2	0	**2**	**0**
2011-12	*Hereford U*	1	0	**1**	**0**

BENNETT, Kyle (F) 68 6
H: 5 5 W: 9 08 b.Telford 9-9-90
Source: Scholar. *Honours:* England Youth.

2007-08	Wolverhampton W	0	0		
2008-09	Wolverhampton W	0	0		
2009-10	Wolverhampton W	0	0		
2010-11	Bury	32	2	**32**	**2**
2011-12	Doncaster R	36	4	**36**	**4**

BEYE, Habib (D) 345 13
H: 6 0 W: 12 06 b.Paris 19-10-77
Honours: Senegal 45 full caps, 1 goal.

1997-98	Paris St Germain	0	0		
1998-99	Strasbourg	23	0		
1999-2000	Strasbourg	33	1		
2000-01	Strasbourg	31	3		
2001-02	Strasbourg	20	3		
2002-03	Strasbourg	26	1		
2003-04	Strasbourg	1	0	**134**	**8**
2003-04	Marseille	22	0		
2004-05	Marseille	37	1		
2005-06	Marseille	29	1		
2006-07	Marseille	36	0		
2007-08	Marseille	4	0	**128**	**2**
2007-08	Newcastle U	29	1		
2008-09	Newcastle U	23	0	**52**	**1**
2009-10	Aston Villa	6	0		
2010-11	Aston Villa	3	0		
2011-12	Aston Villa	0	0	**9**	**0**
2011-12	Doncaster R	22	2	**22**	**2**

BOUHBENNA, Rachid (D) 0 0
b.Algeria 29-6-91
Source: Sedan.

2011-12	Doncaster R	0	0		

BROWN, Chris (F) 236 41
H: 6 3 W: 13 01 b.Doncaster 11-12-84
Source: Trainee. *Honours:* England Youth.

2002-03	Sunderland	0	0		
2003-04	Sunderland	0	0		
2003-04	*Doncaster R*	22	10		
2004-05	Sunderland	37	5		
2005-06	Sunderland	13	1		
2005-06	*Hull C*	13	1	**13**	**1**
2006-07	Sunderland	16	3	**66**	**9**
2006-07	Norwich C	4	0		
2007-08	Norwich C	14	1	**18**	**1**
2007-08	Preston NE	17	5		
2008-09	Preston NE	30	6		
2009-10	Preston NE	43	6		
2010-11	Preston NE	16	1	**106**	**18**
2011-12	Doncaster R	11	2	**33**	**12**

CHAMBERS, James (D) 288 0
H: 5 10 W: 11 11 b.West Bromwich 20-11-80
Source: Trainee. *Honours:* England Youth.

1998-99	WBA	0	0		
1999-2000	WBA	12	0		
2000-01	WBA	31	0		
2001-02	WBA	5	0		
2002-03	WBA	8	0		
2003-04	WBA	17	0		
2004-05	WBA	0	0	**73**	**0**
2004-05	Watford	40	0		
2005-06	Watford	38	0		
2006-07	Watford	12	0	**90**	**0**
2006-07	*Cardiff C*	7	0	**7**	**0**
2007-08	Leicester C	24	0	**24**	**0**
2008-09	Doncaster R	37	0		
2009-10	Doncaster R	43	0		
2010-11	Doncaster R	7	0		
2011-12	Doncaster R	0	0	**87**	**0**
2011-12	*Hereford U*	7	0	**7**	**0**

CHIMBONDA, Pascal (D) 320 15
H: 5 10 W: 11 05 b.Les Abymes 21-2-79
Source: Port Louis. *Honours:* Guadeloupe 3 full caps, France 1 full cap.

1999-2000	Le Havre	2	0		
2000-01	Le Havre	32	1		
2001-02	Le Havre	27	2		
2002-03	Le Havre	24	2	**85**	**5**
2003-04	Bastia	31	1		
2004-05	Bastia	36	3	**67**	**4**
2005-06	Wigan Ath	37	2		
2006-07	Wigan Ath	1	0	**38**	**2**
2006-07	Tottenham H	33	1		
2007-08	Tottenham H	32	2		
2008-09	Sunderland	13	0	**13**	**0**
2008-09	Tottenham H	3	0	**68**	**3**
2009-10	Blackburn R	24	1		
2010-11	Blackburn R	6	0	**30**	**1**
2010-11	QPR	3	0	**3**	**0**
2011-12	Doncaster R	16	0	**16**	**0**

COPPINGER, James (F) 362 40
H: 5 7 W: 10 03 b.Middlesbrough 10-1-81
Source: Darlington Trainee. *Honours:* England Youth.

1997-98	Newcastle U	0	0		
1998-99	Newcastle U	0	0		
1999-2000	Newcastle U	0	0		
1999-2000	*Hartlepool U*	10	3		
2000-01	Newcastle U	1	0		
2001-02	Newcastle U	0	0	**1**	**0**
2001-02	*Hartlepool U*	14	2	**24**	**5**
2002-03	Exeter C	43	5		
2003-04	Exeter C	0	0	**43**	**5**
2004-05	Doncaster R	31	0		
2005-06	Doncaster R	36	5		
2006-07	Doncaster R	39	4		
2007-08	Doncaster R	39	3		
2008-09	Doncaster R	32	5		
2009-10	Doncaster R	39	4		
2010-11	Doncaster R	40	7		
2011-12	Doncaster R	38	2	**294**	**30**

DIOUF, El Hadji (F) 377 54
H: 5 11 W: 11 11 b.Dakar 15-1-81
Honours: Senegal 57 full caps, 16 goals.

1998-99	Sochaux	15	0	**15**	**0**
1999-2000	Rennes	28	1	**28**	**1**
2000-01	Lens	28	8		
2001-02	Lens	26	10	**54**	**18**
2002-03	Liverpool	29	3		
2003-04	Liverpool	26	0		
2004-05	Liverpool	0	0	**55**	**3**
2004-05	*Bolton W*	27	9		
2005-06	Bolton W	20	3		
2006-07	Bolton W	33	5		
2007-08	Bolton W	34	4	**114**	**21**
2008-09	Sunderland	14	0	**14**	**0**
2008-09	Blackburn R	14	1		
2009-10	Blackburn R	26	3		
2010-11	Blackburn R	20	0		
2010-11	*Rangers*	15	1	**15**	**1**
2011-12	Blackburn R	0	0	**60**	**4**
2011-12	Doncaster R	22	6	**22**	**6**

DUMBUYA, Mustapha (D) 38 0
H: 5 7 W: 11 00 b.Sierra Leone 7-8-87
Source: Potters Bar T.

2009-10	Doncaster R	3	0		
2010-11	Doncaster R	23	0		
2011-12	Doncaster R	10	0	**36**	**0**
2011-12	*Crystal Palace*	2	0	**2**	**0**

FRIEND, George (D) 99 3
H: 6 2 W: 13 01 b.Barnstaple 19-10-87

2008-09	Exeter C	4	0		
2008-09	Wolverhampton W	6	0		
2009-10	Wolverhampton W	1	0	**7**	**0**
2009-10	*Millwall*	6	0	**6**	**0**
2009-10	*Southend U*	6	1	**6**	**1**
2009-10	*Scunthorpe U*	4	0	**4**	**0**
2009-10	*Exeter C*	13	1	**17**	**1**
2010-11	Doncaster R	32	1		
2011-12	Doncaster R	27	0	**59**	**1**

GILLETT, Simon (M) 154 6
H: 5 6 W: 11 07 b.Oxford 6-11-85
Source: Trainee.

2003-04	Southampton	0	0		
2004-05	Southampton	0	0		
2005-06	Southampton	0	0		
2005-06	*Walsall*	2	0	**2**	**0**
2006-07	Southampton	0	0		
2006-07	*Blackpool*	31	1	**31**	**1**
2006-07	*Bournemouth*	7	1	**7**	**1**
2007-08	Southampton	2	0		
2007-08	*Yeovil T*	4	0	**4**	**0**
2008-09	Southampton	27	0		
2009-10	Southampton	2	0	**31**	**0**
2009-10	*Doncaster R*	11	0		
2010-11	Doncaster R	22	1		
2011-12	Doncaster R	46	3	**79**	**4**

HAYTER, James (F) 520 127
H: 5 9 W: 10 13 b.Sandown 9-4-79
Source: Trainee.

1996-97	Bournemouth	2	0		
1997-98	Bournemouth	5	0		
1998-99	Bournemouth	20	2		
1999-2000	Bournemouth	31	2		
2000-01	Bournemouth	40	11		
2001-02	Bournemouth	44	7		
2002-03	Bournemouth	45	9		
2003-04	Bournemouth	44	14		
2004-05	Bournemouth	39	19		
2005-06	Bournemouth	46	20		
2006-07	Bournemouth	42	10	**358**	**94**
2007-08	Doncaster R	34	7		
2008-09	Doncaster R	27	4		
2009-10	Doncaster R	38	9		
2010-11	Doncaster R	32	9		
2011-12	Doncaster R	31	4	**162**	**33**

HIRD, Samuel (D) 162 1
H: 5 7 W: 10 12 b.Askern 7-9-87
Source: Scholar.

2005-06	Leeds U	0	0		
2006-07	Leeds U	0	0		
2006-07	*Doncaster R*	5	0		
2007-08	Doncaster R	4	0		
2007-08	*Grimsby T*	17	0	**17**	**0**
2008-09	Doncaster R	37	1		
2009-10	Doncaster R	36	0		
2010-11	Doncaster R	32	0		
2011-12	Doncaster R	31	0	**145**	**1**

HUSBAND, James (D) 3 0
H: 5 10 W: 10 00 b.Leeds 3-1-94
Source: Scholar.

2011-12	Doncaster R	3	0	**3**	**0**

KEEGAN, Paul (M) **173 12**
H: 5 11 W: 11 05 b.Dublin 5-7-84
Source: Home Farm. *Honours:* Eire Youth, Under-21.

2000-01	Leeds U	0	0		
2001-02	Leeds U	0	0		
2002-03	Leeds U	0	0		
2003-04	Leeds U	0	0		
2003-04	*Scunthorpe U*	2	0	**2**	**0**
2004-05	Leeds U	0	0		
2005	Drogheda	11	0		
2006	Drogheda	25	4		
2007	Drogheda	30	1		
2008	Drogheda	27	1	**93**	**6**
2009	Bohemians	34	2		
2010	Bohemians	32	4	**66**	**6**
2010-11	Doncaster R	10	0		
2011-12	Doncaster R	2	0	**12**	**0**

LOCKWOOD, Adam (D) **233 15**
H: 6 0 W: 12 07 b.Wakefield 26-10-81
Source: Reading Trainee.

2003-04	Yeovil T	43	4		
2004-05	Yeovil T	10	0		
2005-06	Yeovil T	20	0	**73**	**4**
2005-06	*Torquay U*	9	3	**9**	**3**
2006-07	Doncaster R	44	2		
2007-08	Doncaster R	39	3		
2008-09	Doncaster R	22	0		
2009-10	Doncaster R	16	2		
2010-11	Doncaster R	16	1		
2011-12	Doncaster R	14	0	**151**	**8**

MARTIS, Shelton (D) **207 7**
H: 6 0 W: 11 11 b.Willemstad 29-11-82
Honours: Netherlands Antilles 1 full cap.

2002-03	Excelsior	12	0		
2003-04	Excelsior	10	0	**22**	**0**
2004-05	Eindhoven	32	0	**32**	**0**
2005-06	Darlington	40	2		
2006-07	Darlington	2	0	**42**	**2**
2006-07	Hibernian	26	0	**26**	**0**
2007-08	WBA	2	0		
2007-08	*Scunthorpe U*	3	0	**3**	**0**
2008-09	WBA	7	0		
2008-09	*Doncaster R*	5	1		
2009-10	WBA	13	2	**22**	**2**
2009-10	Doncaster R	14	1		
2010-11	Doncaster R	26	1		
2011-12	Doncaster R	15	0	**60**	**3**

McMAHON, Sam (F) **0 0**
b.Tyldesley 9-2-94
Source: Glasgow Rangers Youth.

2011-12	Doncaster R	0	0		

O'CONNOR, James (D) **270 5**
H: 5 10 W: 12 05 b.Birmingham 20-11-84
Source: Scholar.

2003-04	Aston Villa	0	0		
2004-05	Aston Villa	0	0		
2004-05	*Port Vale*	13	0	**13**	**0**
2004-05	Bournemouth	6	0		
2005-06	Bournemouth	39	1	**45**	**1**
2006-07	Doncaster R	40	1		
2007-08	Doncaster R	40	0		
2008-09	Doncaster R	32	1		
2009-10	Doncaster R	38	0		
2010-11	Doncaster R	34	2		
2011-12	Doncaster R	28	0	**212**	**4**

OSTER, John (M) **392 24**
H: 5 9 W: 10 08 b.Boston 8-12-78
Source: Trainee. *Honours:* Wales Youth, Under-21, B, 13 full caps.

1996-97	Grimsby T	24	3		
1997-98	Everton	31	1		
1998-99	Everton	9	0	**40**	**1**
1999-2000	Sunderland	10	0		
2000-01	Sunderland	8	0		
2001-02	Sunderland	0	0		
2001-02	*Barnsley*	2	0	**2**	**0**
2002-03	Sunderland	3	0		
2002-03	*Grimsby T*	17	6	**41**	**9**
2003-04	Sunderland	38	5		
2004-05	Sunderland	9	0	**68**	**5**
2004-05	*Leeds U*	8	1	**8**	**1**
2004-05	Burnley	15	1	**15**	**1**
2005-06	Reading	33	1		
2006-07	Reading	25	1		
2007-08	Reading	18	0	**76**	**2**
2008-09	Crystal Palace	31	3	**31**	**3**
2009-10	Doncaster R	40	1		
2010-11	Doncaster R	41	0		
2011-12	Doncaster R	30	1	**111**	**2**

RADFORD, Oscar (D) **0 0**
b.Rotherham 15-9-92
Source: Sheffield U Youth, Ferencvaros.

2011-12	Doncaster R	0	0		

ROBERT, Fabien (F) **51 4**
H: 5 8 W: 10 07 b.Hennebont 6-1-89
Honours: France Youth.

2007-08	Lorient	11	0		
2008-09	Lorient	11	1	**22**	**1**
2009-10	*Boulogne*	16	1	**16**	**1**
2011-12	Doncaster R	13	2	**13**	**2**

On loan from Lorient.

SPURR, Tommy (D) **211 5**
H: 6 1 W: 11 05 b.Leeds 13-9-87
Source: Scholar.

2005-06	Sheffield W	2	0		
2006-07	Sheffield W	36	0		
2007-08	Sheffield W	41	2		
2008-09	Sheffield W	41	2		
2009-10	Sheffield W	46	1		
2010-11	Sheffield W	26	0	**192**	**5**
2011-12	Doncaster R	19	0	**19**	**0**

STOCK, Brian (M) **343 34**
H: 5 11 W: 11 02 b.Winchester 24-12-81
Source: Trainee. *Honours:* Wales Under-21, 3 full caps.

1999-2000	Bournemouth	5	0		
2000-01	Bournemouth	1	0		
2001-02	Bournemouth	26	2		
2002-03	Bournemouth	27	2		
2003-04	Bournemouth	19	3		
2004-05	Bournemouth	41	6		
2005-06	Bournemouth	26	3	**145**	**16**
2005-06	Preston NE	6	1		
2006-07	Preston NE	2	0	**8**	**1**
2006-07	Doncaster R	36	3		
2007-08	Doncaster R	40	5		
2008-09	Doncaster R	36	6		
2009-10	Doncaster R	15	0		
2010-11	Doncaster R	37	2		
2011-12	Doncaster R	26	1	**190**	**17**

SULLIVAN, Neil (G) **538 0**
H: 6 2 W: 12 00 b.Sutton 24-2-70
Source: Trainee. *Honours:* Scotland 28 full caps.

1988-89	Wimbledon	0	0		
1989-90	Wimbledon	0	0		
1990-91	Wimbledon	1	0		
1991-92	Wimbledon	1	0		
1991-92	*Crystal Palace*	1	0	**1**	**0**
1992-93	Wimbledon	1	0		
1993-94	Wimbledon	2	0		
1994-95	Wimbledon	11	0		
1995-96	Wimbledon	16	0		
1996-97	Wimbledon	36	0		
1997-98	Wimbledon	38	0		
1998-99	Wimbledon	38	0		
1999-2000	Wimbledon	37	0	**181**	**0**
2000-01	Tottenham H	35	0		
2001-02	Tottenham H	29	0		
2002-03	Tottenham H	0	0	**64**	**0**
2003-04	Chelsea	4	0	**4**	**0**
2004-05	Leeds U	46	0		
2005-06	Leeds U	42	0		
2006-07	Leeds U	7	0	**95**	**0**
2006-07	*Doncaster R*	16	0		
2007-08	Doncaster R	46	0		
2008-09	Doncaster R	46	0		
2009-10	Doncaster R	45	0		
2010-11	Doncaster R	31	0		
2011-12	Doncaster R	9	0	**193**	**0**

WOODS, Gary (G) **31 0**
H: 6 1 W: 11 00 b.Kettering 1-10-90
Source: Manchester U Scholar.

2008-09	Doncaster R	1	0		
2009-10	Doncaster R	0	0		
2010-11	Doncaster R	16	0		
2011-12	Doncaster R	14	0	**31**	**0**

WOODS, Martin (M) **152 11**
H: 5 11 W: 11 13 b.Airdrie 1-1-86
Source: Trainee. *Honours:* Scotland Youth, Under-21.

2002-03	Leeds U	0	0		
2003-04	Leeds U	0	0		
2004-05	Leeds U	1	0	**1**	**0**
2004-05	*Hartlepool U*	6	0	**6**	**0**
2005-06	Sunderland	7	0	**7**	**0**
2006-07	Rotherham U	36	4	**36**	**4**
2007-08	Doncaster R	15	0		
2007-08	*Yeovil T*	3	0	**3**	**0**
2008-09	Doncaster R	41	2		
2009-10	Doncaster R	24	4		
2010-11	Doncaster R	15	1		
2011-12	Doncaster R	4	0	**99**	**7**

EVERTON (35)

ANICHEBE, Victor (F) **104 11**
H: 6 1 W: 13 00 b.Nigeria 23-4-88
Source: Scholar. *Honours:* Nigeria Under-23, 10 full caps, 1 goal.

2005-06	Everton	2	1		
2006-07	Everton	19	3		
2007-08	Everton	27	1		
2008-09	Everton	17	1		
2009-10	Everton	11	1		
2010-11	Everton	16	0		
2011-12	Everton	12	4	**104**	**11**

BAINES, Leighton (D) **306 15**
H: 5 8 W: 11 00 b.Liverpool 11-12-84
Source: Trainee. *Honours:* England Under-21, 8 full caps.

2002-03	Wigan Ath	6	0		
2003-04	Wigan Ath	26	0		
2004-05	Wigan Ath	41	1		
2005-06	Wigan Ath	37	0		
2006-07	Wigan Ath	35	3		
2007-08	Wigan Ath	0	0	**145**	**4**
2007-08	Everton	22	0		
2008-09	Everton	31	1		
2009-10	Everton	37	1		
2010-11	Everton	38	5		
2011-12	Everton	33	4	**161**	**11**

BARKLEY, Ross (M) **6 0**
H: 6 2 W: 12 00 b.Liverpool 5-12-93
Source: Scholar. *Honours:* England Youth, Under-21.

2010-11	Everton	0	0		
2011-12	Everton	6	0	**6**	**0**

BAXTER, Jose (F) **21 3**
H: 5 10 W: 11 07 b.Bootle 7-2-92
Source: Academy. *Honours:* England Youth.

2008-09	Everton	3	0		
2009-10	Everton	2	0		
2010-11	Everton	1	0		
2011-12	Everton	1	0	**7**	**0**
2011-12	*Tranmere R*	14	3	**14**	**3**

BIDWELL, Jake (D) **24 0**
H: 6 0 W: 11 00 b.Southport 21-3-93
Source: Scholar. *Honours:* England Youth.

2009-10	Everton	0	0		
2010-11	Everton	0	0		
2011-12	Everton	0	0		
2011-12	*Brentford*	24	0	**24**	**0**

BILYALETDINOV, Diniyar (F) **209 39**
H: 6 1 W: 11 11 b.Moscow 27-2-85
Honours: Russia 41 full caps, 5 goals.

2003	Lok Moscow	0	0		
2004	Lok Moscow	25	5		
2004	*Neftekhlmik*	0	0		
2005	Lok Moscow	29	8		
2006	Lok Moscow	29	3		
2007	Lok Moscow	28	3		
2008	Lok Moscow	26	9		
2009	Lok Moscow	13	3	**150**	**31**
2009-10	Everton	23	6		
2010-11	Everton	26	2		
2011-12	Everton	10	0	**59**	**8**

Transferred to Spartak Moscow January 2012.

BROWNING, Tyias (D) **0 0**
b.Liverpool 27-5-94
Source: Scholar.

2011-12	Everton	0	0		

CAHILL, Tim (M) **443 108**
H: 5 10 W: 10 12 b.Sydney 6-12-79
Source: Sydney U. *Honours:* Western Samoa Youth, Australia Under-23, 56 full caps, 24 goals.

1997-98	Millwall	1	0		
1998-99	Millwall	36	6		
1999-2000	Millwall	45	12		
2000-01	Millwall	41	9		
2001-02	Millwall	43	13		
2002-03	Millwall	11	3		
2003-04	Millwall	40	9	**217**	**52**

2004-05	Everton	33	11		
2005-06	Everton	32	6		
2006-07	Everton	18	5		
2007-08	Everton	18	7		
2008-09	Everton	30	8		
2009-10	Everton	33	8		
2010-11	Everton	27	9		
2011-12	Everton	35	2	**226**	**56**

COLEMAN, Seamus (D) **64** **5**
H: 6 4 W: 10 07 b.Donegal 11-10-88
Source: Sligo R. *Honours:* Eire Under-21, Under-23, 4 full caps.

2008-09	Everton	0	0		
2009-10	Everton	3	0		
2009-10	*Blackpool*	9	1	**9**	**1**
2010-11	Everton	34	4		
2011-12	Everton	18	0	**55**	**4**

DAVIES, Adam (G) **0** **0**
b.Rinteln 17-7-92
Source: Scholar.

2009-10	Everton	0	0		
2010-11	Everton	0	0		
2011-12	Everton	0	0		

DIER, Eric (D) **0** **0**
b.Cheltenham 15-1-94
Source: Sporting Lisbon Youth. *Honours:* England Youth.

2011-12	Everton	0	0		

On loan from Sporting Lisbon.

DISTIN, Sylvain (D) **464** **11**
H: 6 3 W: 14 06 b.Bagnolet 16-12-77

1998-99	Tours	26	3	**26**	**3**
1999-2000	Gueugnon	33	1	**33**	**1**
2000-01	Paris St Germain	28	0	**28**	**0**
2001-02	Newcastle U	28	0	**28**	**0**
2002-03	Manchester C	34	0		
2003-04	Manchester C	38	2		
2004-05	Manchester C	38	1		
2005-06	Manchester C	31	0		
2006-07	Manchester C	37	2	**178**	**5**
2007-08	Portsmouth	36	0		
2008-09	Portsmouth	38	0		
2009-10	Portsmouth	3	0	**77**	**0**
2009-10	Everton	29	0		
2010-11	Everton	38	2		
2011-12	Everton	27	0	**94**	**2**

DONOVAN, Landon (F) **313** **127**
H: 5 8 W: 11 05 b.Ontario 4-3-82
Honours: USA 142 full caps, 49 goals.

1999	Bradenton Academics	0	0		
1999-2000	Leverkusen II	20	6		
2000-01	Leverkusen II	8	3	**28**	**9**
2001	San Jose E	22	7		
2002	San Jose E	20	7		
2003	San Jose E	22	12		
2004	San Jose E	23	6	**87**	**32**
2004-05	Leverkusen	7	0	**7**	**0**
2005	LA Galaxy	22	12		
2006	LA Galaxy	24	13		
2007	LA Galaxy	25	8		
2008	LA Galaxy	25	20		
2008-09	Bayern Munich	6	0	**6**	**0**
2009	LA Galaxy	25	12		
2009-10	Everton	10	2		
2010	LA Galaxy	24	7		
2011	LA Galaxy	23	12	**168**	**84**
2011-12	Everton	7	0	**17**	**2**

On loan from LA Galaxy.

DRENTHE, Roysten (M) **110** **9**
H: 5 6 W: 10 07 b.Rotterdam 8-4-87
Honours: Holland Under-21, B, 1 full cap.

2005-06	Feyenoord	3	0		
2006-07	Feyenoord	26	0	**29**	**0**
2007-08	Real Madrid	18	2		
2008-09	Real Madrid	20	0		
2009-10	Real Madrid	8	0	**46**	**2**
2010-11	*Hercules*	14	4	**14**	**4**
2011-12	Everton	21	3	**21**	**3**

DUFFY, Shane (D) **23** **2**
H: 6 4 W: 12 00 b.Derry 1-1-92
Source: Scholar. *Honours:* Northern Ireland Under-21, Eire Under-21.

2008-09	Everton	0	0		
2009-10	Everton	0	0		
2010-11	Everton	0	0		
2010-11	*Burnley*	1	0	**1**	**0**
2011-12	Everton	4	0	**4**	**0**
2011-12	*Scunthorpe U*	18	2	**18**	**2**

FELLAINI, Marouane (M) **169** **20**
H: 6 4 W: 13 05 b.Brussels 22-11-87
Honours: Belgium 35 full caps, 5 goals.

2006-07	Standard Liege	29	0		
2007-08	Standard Liege	30	6		
2008-09	Standard Liege	3	0	**62**	**6**
2008-09	Everton	30	8		
2009-10	Everton	23	2		
2010-11	Everton	20	1		
2011-12	Everton	34	3	**107**	**14**

FORRESTER, Anton (F) **0** **0**
b.Liverpool 11-2-94
Source: Scholar.

2010-11	Everton	0	0		
2011-12	Everton	0	0		

FORSHAW, Adam (M) **8** **0**
H: 6 1 W: 11 02 b.Liverpool 8-10-91
Source: Scholar.

2009-10	Everton	0	0		
2010-11	Everton	1	0		
2011-12	Everton	0	0	**1**	**0**
2011-12	*Brentford*	7	0	**7**	**0**

GARBUTT, Luke (D) **34** **2**
H: 5 10 W: 11 07 b.Harrogate 21-5-93
Source: Scholar. *Honours:* England Youth.

2010-11	Everton	0	0		
2011-12	Everton	0	0		
2011-12	*Cheltenham T*	34	2	**34**	**2**

GIBSON, Darron (M) **63** **5**
H: 6 0 W: 12 04 b.Derry 25-10-87
Source: Scholar. *Honours:* Eire Youth, Under-21, 19 full caps, 1 goal.

2005-06	Manchester U	0	0		
2006-07	Manchester U	0	0		
2007-08	Manchester U	0	0		
2007-08	*Wolverhampton W*	21	1	**21**	**1**
2008-09	Manchester U	3	1		
2009-10	Manchester U	15	2		
2010-11	Manchester U	12	0		
2011-12	Manchester U	1	0	**31**	**3**
2011-12	Everton	11	1	**11**	**1**

GUEYE, Magaye (F) **49** **10**
H: 5 10 W: 11 07 b.Paris 6-7-90
Honours: France Youth, Under-21.

2008-09	Strasbourg	3	0		
2009-10	Strasbourg	24	9	**27**	**9**
2010-11	Everton	5	0		
2011-12	Everton	17	1	**22**	**1**

HAHNEMANN, Marcus (G) **394** **0**
H: 6 3 W: 13 03 b.Seattle 15-6-72
Honours: USA 9 full caps.

1997	Colorado Rapids	25	0		
1998	Colorado Rapids	28	0		
1999	Colorado Rapids	13	0	**66**	**0**
1999-2000	Fulham	0	0		
2000-01	Fulham	2	0		
2001-02	Fulham	0	0	**2**	**0**
2001-02	*Rochdale*	5	0	**5**	**0**
2001-02	*Reading*	6	0		
2002-03	Reading	41	0		
2003-04	Reading	36	0		
2004-05	Reading	46	0		
2005-06	Reading	45	0		
2006-07	Reading	38	0		
2007-08	Reading	38	0		
2008-09	Reading	32	0		
2009-10	Reading	0	0	**282**	**0**
2009-10	Wolverhampton W	25	0		
2010-11	Wolverhampton W	14	0		
2011-12	Wolverhampton W	0	0	**39**	**0**
2011-12	Everton	0	0		

HAMMAR, Johan (D) **0** **0**
b.Malmo 22-2-94
Source: Scholar.

2010-11	Everton	0	0		
2011-12	Everton	0	0		

HEITINGA, Johnny (D) **267** **10**
H: 5 11 W: 11 05 b.Alphen aan den Rijn 15-11-83
Honours: Holland 80 full caps, 7 goals.

2000-01	Ajax	0	0		
2001-02	Ajax	15	0		
2002-03	Ajax	1	0		
2003-04	Ajax	26	3		
2004-05	Ajax	26	1		
2005-06	Ajax	19	1		
2006-07	Ajax	32	0		
2007-08	Ajax	33	0	**152**	**5**
2008-09	Atletico Madrid	27	3	**27**	**3**
2009-10	Everton	31	0		
2010-11	Everton	27	1		
2011-12	Everton	30	1	**88**	**2**

HIBBERT, Tony (D) **253** **0**
H: 5 9 W: 11 05 b.Liverpool 20-2-81
Source: Trainee.

1998-99	Everton	0	0		
1999-2000	Everton	0	0		
2000-01	Everton	3	0		
2001-02	Everton	10	0		
2002-03	Everton	24	0		
2003-04	Everton	25	0		
2004-05	Everton	36	0		
2005-06	Everton	29	0		
2006-07	Everton	13	0		
2007-08	Everton	24	0		
2008-09	Everton	17	0		
2009-10	Everton	20	0		
2010-11	Everton	20	0		
2011-12	Everton	32	0	**253**	**0**

HOPE, Hallam (F) **0** **0**
b.Manchester 17-3-94
Source: Scholar. *Honours:* England Youth.

2010-11	Everton	0	0		
2011-12	Everton	0	0		

HOWARD, Tim (G) **354** **1**
H: 6 3 W: 14 12 b.North Brunswick 6-3-79
Honours: USA Under-21, Under-23, 77 full caps.

1998	NY/NJ MetrStars	1	0		
1999	NY/NJ MetrStars	9	0		
2000	NY/NJ MetrStars	9	0		
2001	NY/NJ MetrStars	26	0		
2002	NY/NJ MetrStars	27	0		
2003	NY/NJ MetrStars	13	0	**85**	**0**
2003-04	Manchester U	32	0		
2004-05	Manchester U	12	0		
2005-06	Manchester U	1	0		
2006-07	Manchester U	0	0	**45**	**0**
2006-07	Everton	36	0		
2007-08	Everton	36	0		
2008-09	Everton	38	0		
2009-10	Everton	38	0		
2010-11	Everton	38	0		
2011-12	Everton	38	1	**224**	**1**

JAGIELKA, Phil (D) **397** **22**
H: 6 0 W: 13 01 b.Manchester 17-8-82
Source: Scholar. *Honours:* England Youth, Under-20, Under-21, B, 12 full caps.

1999-2000	Sheffield U	1	0		
2000-01	Sheffield U	15	0		
2001-02	Sheffield U	23	3		
2002-03	Sheffield U	42	0		
2003-04	Sheffield U	43	3		
2004-05	Sheffield U	46	0		
2005-06	Sheffield U	46	8		
2006-07	Sheffield U	38	4	**254**	**18**
2007-08	Everton	34	1		
2008-09	Everton	34	0		
2009-10	Everton	12	0		
2010-11	Everton	33	1		
2011-12	Everton	30	2	**143**	**4**

JELAVIC, Nikica (F) **186** **72**
H: 6 2 W: 13 12 b.Capljina 27-8-85
Honours: Croatia Youth, 22 full caps, 3 goals.

2002-03	Hajduk Split	2	0		
2003-04	Hajduk Split	2	0		
2004-05	Hajduk Split	0	0		
2005-06	Hajduk Split	9	0		
2006-07	Hajduk Split	22	5	**35**	**5**
2007-08	Waregem	23	3	**23**	**3**
2008-09	Rapid Vienna	34	7		
2009-10	Rapid Vienna	33	17		
2010-11	Rapid Vienna	3	1	**70**	**25**
2010-11	Rangers	23	16		
2011-12	Rangers	22	14	**45**	**30**
2011-12	Everton	13	9	**13**	**9**

KELLY, Sam (M) **0** **0**
b.Huntingdon 21-10-93
Source: Norwich C Scholar.

2011-12	Everton	0	0		

LUNDSTRAM, John (M) **0** **0**
b.Liverpool 18-2-94
Source: Scholar. *Honours:* England Youth.

2011-12	Everton	0	0		

McALENY, Conor (F) **5 0**

H: 5 10 W: 12 05 b.Liverpool 12-8-92

Source: Scholar.

2009-10	Everton	0	0		
2010-11	Everton	0	0		
2011-12	Everton	2	0	**2**	**0**
2011-12	*Scunthorpe U*	3	0	**3**	**0**

McFADDEN, James (M) **261 50**

H: 6 0 W: 12 11 b.Glasgow 14-4-83

Honours: Scotland Under-21, B, 48 full caps, 15 goals.

2000-01	Motherwell	6	0		
2001-02	Motherwell	24	10		
2002-03	Motherwell	30	13		
2003-04	Motherwell	3	3	**63**	**26**
2003-04	Everton	23	0		
2004-05	Everton	23	1		
2005-06	Everton	32	6		
2006-07	Everton	19	2		
2007-08	Everton	12	2		
2007-08	Birmingham C	12	4		
2008-09	Birmingham C	30	4		
2009-10	Birmingham C	36	5		
2010-11	Birmingham C	4	0	**82**	**13**
2011-12	Everton	7	0	**116**	**11**

MUCHA, Jan (G) **127 0**

H: 6 2 W: 12 00 b.Bela nad Cirochou 5-12-82

Honours: Slovakia 33 full caps.

2002-03	Zilina	8	0		
2003-04	Zilina	12	0		
2004-05	Zilina	12	0	**32**	**0**
2005-06	Legia	0	0		
2006-07	Legia	7	0		
2007-08	Legia	29	0		
2008-09	Legia	29	0		
2009-10	Legia	30	0	**95**	**0**
2010-11	Everton	0	0		
2011-12	Everton	0	0		

NEVILLE, Phil (M) **487 9**

H: 5 11 W: 12 00 b.Bury 21-1-77

Source: Trainee. *Honours:* England Schools, Youth, B, Under-21, 59 full caps.

1994-95	Manchester U	2	0		
1995-96	Manchester U	24	0		
1996-97	Manchester U	18	0		
1997-98	Manchester U	30	1		
1998-99	Manchester U	28	0		
1999-2000	Manchester U	29	0		
2000-01	Manchester U	29	1		
2001-02	Manchester U	28	2		
2002-03	Manchester U	25	1		
2003-04	Manchester U	31	0		
2004-05	Manchester U	19	0	**263**	**5**
2005-06	Everton	34	0		
2006-07	Everton	35	1		
2007-08	Everton	37	2		
2008-09	Everton	37	0		
2009-10	Everton	23	0		
2010-11	Everton	31	1		
2011-12	Everton	27	0	**224**	**4**

NSIALA, Aristote (D) **29 0**

H: 6 4 W: 14 09 b.DR Congo 25-3-92

Source: Scholar.

2009-10	Everton	0	0		
2010-11	Everton	0	0		
2010-11	*Macclesfield T*	10	0	**10**	**0**
2011-12	Everton	0	0		
2011-12	*Accrington S*	19	0	**19**	**0**

ORENUGA, Femi (M) **2 0**

H: 5 6 W: 13 00 b.Lewisham 18-3-93

Source: Scholar.

2009-10	Everton	0	0		
2010-11	Everton	0	0		
2011-12	Everton	0	0		
2011-12	*Notts Co*	2	0	**2**	**0**

OSMAN, Leon (F) **277 38**

H: 5 8 W: 10 09 b.Billinge 17-5-81

Source: Trainee. *Honours:* England Schools, Youth.

1998-99	Everton	0	0		
1999-2000	Everton	0	0		
2000-01	Everton	0	0		
2001-02	Everton	0	0		
2002-03	Everton	2	0		
2002-03	*Carlisle U*	12	1	**12**	**1**
2003-04	Everton	4	1		
2003-04	*Derby Co*	17	3	**17**	**3**
2004-05	Everton	29	6		
2005-06	Everton	35	3		
2006-07	Everton	34	3		
2007-08	Everton	28	4		
2008-09	Everton	34	6		
2009-10	Everton	26	2		
2010-11	Everton	26	4		
2011-12	Everton	30	5	**248**	**34**

ROBERTS, Connor (G) **0 0**

b.Wrexham 8-12-92

Source: Scholar. *Honours:* Wales Youth.

2009-10	Everton	0	0		
2010-11	Everton	0	0		
2011-12	Everton	0	0		

RODWELL, Jack (D) **85 4**

H: 6 2 W: 12 08 b.Southport 11-3-91

Source: Scholar. *Honours:* England Youth, Under-21, 2 full caps.

2007-08	Everton	2	0		
2008-09	Everton	19	0		
2009-10	Everton	26	2		
2010-11	Everton	24	0		
2011-12	Everton	14	2	**85**	**4**

SANTOS, Francisco (M) **0 0**

b.Guinea-Bissau 18-1-92

Source: Benfica Youth.

2011-12	Everton	0	0		

SILVA, Joao (F) **58 20**

H: 6 2 W: 12 08 b.Vila das Aves 21-5-90

Honours: Portugal Youth, Under-21.

2009-10	Aves	30	13	**30**	**13**
2010-11	Everton	0	0		
2010-11	*Leiria*	12	4	**12**	**4**
2011-12	Everton	0	0		
2011-12	*Vitoria Setubal*	16	3	**16**	**3**

SPRINGTHORPE, Mason (D) **0 0**

b.Shrewsbury 1-11-94

Source: Scholar.

2011-12	Everton	0	0		

STRACQUALURSI, Denis (F) **56 22**

H: 6 3 W: 13 05 b.Rafaela 20-10-87

2010-11	Tigre	35	21	**35**	**21**
2011-12	Everton	21	1	**21**	**1**

On loan from Tigre.

TAUDUL, Mateusz (G) **0 0**

b.Bialystok 12-11-94

Source: Scholar.

2011-12	Everton	0	0		

VELLIOS, Apostolos (F) **38 7**

H: 6 3 W: 12 06 b.Salonika 8-1-92

Honours: Greece Youth.

2008-09	Iraklis	1	0		
2009-10	Iraklis	9	2		
2010-11	Iraklis	12	2	**22**	**4**
2010-11	Everton	3	0		
2011-12	Everton	13	3	**16**	**3**

WALLACE, James (M) **35 3**

H: 5 11 W: 12 08 b.Fazackerly 19-12-91

Source: Scholar. *Honours:* England Youth, Under-20.

2008-09	Everton	0	0		
2009-10	Everton	0	0		
2010-11	Everton	0	0		
2010-11	*Stockport Co*	14	1	**14**	**1**
2010-11	*Bury*	0	0		
2011-12	Everton	0	0		
2011-12	*Shrewsbury T*	3	0	**3**	**0**
2011-12	*Stevenage*	0	0		
2011-12	*Tranmere R*	18	2	**18**	**2**

YOBO, Joseph (D) **360 12**

H: 6 1 W: 13 00 b.Kano 6-9-80

Source: Mechelen. *Honours:* Nigeria B, 87 full caps, 7 goals.

1998-99	Standard Liege	0	0		
1999-2000	Standard Liege	18	0		
2000-01	Standard Liege	30	2	**48**	**2**
2001-02	Marseille	23	0	**23**	**0**
2002-03	Everton	24	0		
2003-04	Everton	28	2		
2004-05	Everton	27	0		
2005-06	Everton	29	1		
2006-07	Everton	38	2		
2007-08	Everton	30	1		
2008-09	Everton	27	1		
2009-10	Everton	17	1		
2010-11	Everton	0	0		
2010-11	*Fenerbahce*	30	1		
2011-12	Everton	0	0	**220**	**8**
2011-12	*Fenerbahce*	39	1	**69**	**2**

Scholars

Grant Conor James; Johns Jasper Nathaniel; Long Christopher; Molyneux Tom; Pennington Matthew; Touray Ibou Omar; Waring George Philip.

EXETER C (36)

ARCHIBALD-HENVILLE, Troy (D) **115 3**

H: 6 2 W: 13 03 b.Newham 4-11-88

Source: Scholar.

2007-08	Tottenham H	0	0		
2008-09	Tottenham H	0	0		
2008-09	*Norwich C*	0	0		
2008-09	*Exeter C*	19	0		
2009-10	Tottenham H	0	0		
2009-10	Exeter C	15	0		
2010-11	Exeter C	36	1		
2011-12	Exeter C	45	2	**115**	**3**

BAUZA, Guillem (F) **98 17**

H: 5 11 W: 12 01 b.Palma de Mallorca 25-10-84

Source: Mallorca, Espanyol.

2007-08	Swansea C	28	7		
2008-09	Swansea C	15	2		
2009-10	Swansea C	6	0	**49**	**9**
2010-11	Hereford U	12	2	**12**	**2**
2010-11	Northampton T	10	4	**10**	**4**
2011-12	Exeter C	27	2	**27**	**2**

BENNETT, Scott (D) **16 3**

H: 5 10 W: 12 10 b.Newquay 30-11-90

Source: Scholar.

2008-09	Exeter C	0	0		
2009-10	Exeter C	0	0		
2010-11	Exeter C	1	0		
2011-12	Exeter C	15	3	**16**	**3**

COLES, Danny (D) **315 10**

H: 6 1 W: 11 05 b.Bristol 31-10-81

Source: Scholarship.

1999-2000	Bristol C	1	0		
2000-01	Bristol C	2	0		
2001-02	Bristol C	23	0		
2002-03	Bristol C	39	2		
2003-04	Bristol C	45	2		
2004-05	Bristol C	38	1	**148**	**5**
2005-06	Hull C	9	0		
2006-07	Hull C	21	0		
2007-08	Hull C	1	0	**31**	**0**
2007-08	*Hartlepool U*	3	0	**3**	**0**
2007-08	Bristol R	24	1		
2008-09	Bristol R	5	1		
2009-10	Bristol R	36	1		
2010-11	Bristol R	37	0	**102**	**3**
2011-12	Exeter C	31	2	**31**	**2**

DAWSON, Aaron (M) **2 0**

H: 5 10 W: 10 10 b.Exmouth 24-3-92

Source: Scholar.

2010-11	Exeter C	0	0		
2011-12	Exeter C	2	0	**2**	**0**

DUFFY, Richard (D) **222 5**

H: 5 9 W: 10 03 b.Swansea 30-8-85

Source: Scholar. *Honours:* Wales Youth, Under-21, 13 full caps.

2002-03	Swansea C	0	0		
2003-04	Swansea C	18	1		
2003-04	Portsmouth	1	0		
2004-05	Portsmouth	0	0		
2004-05	*Burnley*	7	1	**7**	**1**
2004-05	*Coventry C*	14	0		
2005-06	Portsmouth	0	0		
2005-06	*Coventry C*	32	0		
2006-07	Portsmouth	0	0		
2006-07	*Coventry C*	13	0		
2006-07	*Swansea C*	11	0	**29**	**1**
2007-08	Portsmouth	0	0		
2007-08	*Coventry C*	2	0	**61**	**0**
2008-09	Portsmouth	0	0	**1**	**0**
2008-09	Millwall	12	0	**12**	**0**
2009-10	Exeter C	42	1		
2010-11	Exeter C	42	2		
2011-12	Exeter C	28	0	**112**	**3**

DUNNE, James (M) **110 6**

H: 5 11 W: 10 12 b.Bromley 18-9-89

Source: Scholar.

2007-08	Arsenal	0	0		

2008-09 Arsenal 0 0
2008-09 *Nottingham F* 0 0
2009-10 Exeter C 23 3
2010-11 Exeter C 42 1
2011-12 Exeter C 45 2 **110 6**

EDWARDS, Rob (D) 565 15
H: 6 0 W: 12 02 b.Kendal 1-4-73
Source: Trainee. *Honours:* Wales Youth, Under-21, B, 4 full caps.
1989-90 Carlisle U 12 0
1990-91 Carlisle U 36 5 **48 5**
1990-91 Bristol C 0 0
1991-92 Bristol C 20 1
1992-93 Bristol C 18 0
1993-94 Bristol C 38 2
1994-95 Bristol C 30 0
1995-96 Bristol C 19 0
1996-97 Bristol C 31 0
1997-98 Bristol C 37 2
1998-99 Bristol C 23 0 **216 5**
1999-2000 Preston NE 41 2
2000-01 Preston NE 42 0
2001-02 Preston NE 36 2
2002-03 Preston NE 26 0
2003-04 Preston NE 24 0 **169 4**
2004-05 Blackpool 26 1
2005-06 Blackpool 32 0 **58 1**
2008-09 Exeter C 44 0
2009-10 Exeter C 21 0
2010-11 Exeter C 9 0
2011-12 Exeter C 0 0 **74 0**

FORTUNE, Jon (D) 224 9
H: 6 2 W: 12 12 b.Islington 23-8-80
Source: Trainee.
1998-99 Charlton Ath 0 0
1999-2000 Charlton Ath 0 0
1999-2000 *Mansfield T* 4 0
2000-01 Charlton Ath 0 0
2000-01 *Mansfield T* 14 0 **18 0**
2001-02 Charlton Ath 19 0
2002-03 Charlton Ath 26 1
2003-04 Charlton Ath 28 2
2004-05 Charlton Ath 31 2
2005-06 Charlton Ath 11 0
2006-07 Charlton Ath 8 0
2006-07 *Stoke C* 14 1 **14 1**
2007-08 Charlton Ath 26 2
2008-09 Charlton Ath 17 0
2009-10 Charlton Ath 0 0
2009-10 Sheffield U 5 1
2010-11 Sheffield U 0 0 **5 1**
2010-11 Charlton Ath 16 0
2011-12 Charlton Ath 0 0 **182 7**
2011-12 Exeter C 5 0 **5 0**

FREAR, Elliott (F) 10 0
H: 5 8 W: 10 01 b.Exeter 11-9-90
Source: Scholar.
2009-10 Exeter C 0 0
2010-11 Exeter C 0 0
2011-12 Exeter C 10 0 **10 0**

GOSLING, Jake (M) 0 0
b.Newquay 11-8-93
Source: Scholar.
2011-12 Exeter C 0 0

GOW, Alan (M) 257 53
H: 6 0 W: 11 00 b.Clydebank 9-10-82
Honours: Scotland B.
2000-01 Clydebank 3 0
2001-02 Clydebank 5 0 **8 0**
2002-03 Airdrie U 27 5
2003-04 Airdrie U 32 12
2004-05 Airdrie U 26 9 **85 26**
2005-06 Falkirk 34 6
2006-07 Falkirk 36 7 **70 13**
2007-08 Rangers 0 0
On loan from Rangers.
2008-09 Blackpool 17 5 **17 5**
2008-09 Norwich C 13 0 **13 0**
2009-10 Plymouth Arg 14 2 **14 2**
2009-10 *Hibernian* 7 0 **7 0**
2010-11 Motherwell 15 1 **15 1**
2010-11 Notts Co 16 1 **16 1**
2010-11 East Bengal 5 2 **5 2**
2011-12 Exeter C 7 3 **7 3**

INGHAM, Roger (D) 0 0
b.Crediton 1-12-92
Source: Scholar.
2011-12 Exeter C 0 0

JONES, Billy (D) 203 9
H: 6 1 W: 11 05 b.Chatham 26-3-83
Source: Trainee.
2000-01 Leyton Orient 1 0
2001-02 Leyton Orient 16 0
2002-03 Leyton Orient 24 0
2003-04 Leyton Orient 31 0
2004-05 Leyton Orient 0 0 **72 0**
2004-05 Kidderminster H 12 0
2005-06 Kidderminster H 0 0
2006-07 Kidderminster H 0 0 **12 0**
2007-08 Crewe Alex 22 0
2008-09 Crewe Alex 38 6
2009-10 Crewe Alex 11 2 **71 8**
2010-11 Exeter C 29 0
2011-12 Exeter C 19 1 **48 1**

KEANE, Kallum (D) 0 0
b.Nottingham 23-11-91
Source: Derby Co, Exeter C Scholar.
2011-12 Exeter C 0 0

KEOHANE, Jimmy (M) 4 0
H: 5 11 W: 11 05 b.Wexford 22-1-91
Source: Wexford.
2010-11 Bristol C 0 0
2011-12 Bristol C 0 0
2011-12 Exeter C 4 0 **4 0**

KRYSIAK, Artur (G) 93 0
H: 6 1 W: 12 00 b.Lodz 11-8-89
Source: LKS Lodz. *Honours:* Poland Youth.
2006-07 Birmingham C 0 0
2007-08 *Gretna* 4 0 **4 0**
2007-08 Birmingham C 0 0
2008-09 Birmingham C 0 0
2008-09 *Motherwell* 1 0 **1 0**
2008-09 *Swansea C* 2 0 **2 0**
2009-10 Birmingham C 0 0
2009-10 *Burton Alb* 38 0 **38 0**
2010-11 Exeter C 10 0
2011-12 Exeter C 38 0 **48 0**

LOGAN, Richard (F) 287 57
H: 6 1 W: 12 05 b.Bury St Edmunds 4-1-82
Source: Trainee. *Honours:* England Youth.
1998-99 Ipswich T 2 0
1999-2000 Ipswich T 1 0
2000-01 Ipswich T 0 0
2000-01 *Cambridge U* 5 1 **5 1**
2001-02 Ipswich T 0 0
2001-02 *Torquay U* 16 4 **16 4**
2002-03 Ipswich T 0 0 **3 0**
2002-03 Boston U 27 10
2003-04 Boston U 8 0 **35 10**
2003-04 Peterborough U 29 7
2004-05 Peterborough U 26 4
2004-05 *Shrewsbury T* 5 1 **5 1**
2005-06 Peterborough U 28 4 **83 15**
2005-06 *Lincoln C* 8 2 **8 2**
From Weymouth.
2008-09 Exeter C 30 4
2009-10 Exeter C 34 4
2010-11 Exeter C 40 11
2011-12 Exeter C 28 5 **132 24**

McNISH, Callum (M) 6 0
H: 6 2 W: 12 06 b.Oxford 25-5-92
Source: Scholar.
2008-09 Southampton 0 0
2009-10 Southampton 1 0
2010-11 Southampton 0 0 **1 0**
2011-12 Exeter C 5 0 **5 0**

NARDIELLO, Daniel (F) 224 56
H: 5 11 W: 11 04 b.Coventry 22-10-82
Source: Trainee. *Honours:* Wales 3 full caps.
1999-2000 Manchester U 0 0
2000-01 Manchester U 0 0
2001-02 Manchester U 0 0
2002-03 Manchester U 0 0
2003-04 Manchester U 0 0
2003-04 *Swansea C* 4 0 **4 0**
2003-04 *Barnsley* 16 7
2004-05 Manchester U 0 0
2004-05 *Barnsley* 28 7
2005-06 Barnsley 34 5
2006-07 Barnsley 30 9
2007-08 QPR 8 0 **8 0**
2007-08 *Barnsley* 11 2 **119 30**
2008-09 Blackpool 2 0
2008-09 *Hartlepool U* 12 3 **12 3**
2009-10 Blackpool 5 0 **7 0**
2009-10 *Bury* 6 4 **6 4**
2009-10 *Oldham Ath* 2 0 **2 0**
2010-11 Exeter C 30 10
2011-12 Exeter C 36 9 **66 19**

NICHOLS, Tom (F) 8 1
H: 5 10 W: 10 10 b.Wellington 1-9-93
Source: Scholar.
2010-11 Exeter C 1 0
2011-12 Exeter C 7 1 **8 1**

NOBLE, David (M) 240 15
H: 6 0 W: 12 04 b.Hitchin 2-2-82
Source: Scholar. *Honours:* England Youth, Under-20. Scotland Under-21, B.
2000-01 Arsenal 0 0
2001-02 Arsenal 0 0
2001-02 *Watford* 15 1 **15 1**
2002-03 Arsenal 0 0
2002-03 West Ham U 0 0
2003-04 West Ham U 3 0 **3 0**
2003-04 Boston U 14 2
2004-05 Boston U 32 3
2005-06 Boston U 11 0 **57 5**
2005-06 Bristol C 24 1
2006-07 Bristol C 26 3
2007-08 Bristol C 26 2
2008-09 Bristol C 9 1 **85 7**
2008-09 *Yeovil T* 2 0 **2 0**
2009-10 Exeter C 0 0
2010-11 Exeter C 36 0
2011-12 Exeter C 42 2 **78 2**

O'BRIEN, Luke (D) 134 2
H: 5 9 W: 12 01 b.Halifax 11-9-88
Source: Scholar.
2007-08 Bradford C 2 0
2008-09 Bradford C 35 1
2009-10 Bradford C 43 1
2010-11 Bradford C 42 0
2011-12 Bradford C 9 0 **131 2**
2011-12 Exeter C 3 0 **3 0**

O'FLYNN, John (F) 283 105
H: 5 11 W: 11 11 b.Cobh 11-7-82
Source: Scholar, Cork C. *Honours:* Eire Under-21.
2001-02 Peterborough U 0 0
2002-03 Cork C 27 15
2003 Cork C 23 15
2004 Cork C 28 12
2005 Cork C 21 11
2006 Cork C 15 6
2007 Cork C 25 5
2008 Cork C 19 4 **158 68**
2008-09 Barnet 34 17
2009-10 Barnet 36 12 **70 29**
2010-11 Exeter C 31 6
2011-12 Exeter C 24 2 **55 8**

PIDGELEY, Lenny (G) 132 0
H: 6 4 W: 14 09 b.Twickenham 7-2-84
Source: Scholar. *Honours:* England Under-20.
2003-04 Chelsea 0 0
2003-04 *Watford* 27 0 **27 0**
2004-05 Chelsea 1 0
2005-06 Chelsea 1 0 **2 0**
2005-06 *Millwall* 0 0
2006-07 Millwall 42 0
2007-08 Millwall 13 0
2008-09 Millwall 0 0 **55 0**
2009-10 Carlisle U 17 0 **17 0**
From Woking.
2010-11 Bradford C 21 0 **21 0**
From Woking.
2011-12 Exeter C 10 0 **10 0**

RICKETTS, Rohan (M) 165 9
H: 5 10 W: 11 07 b.Clapham 22-12-82
Source: Scholar. *Honours:* England Youth, Under-20.
2001-02 Arsenal 0 0
2002-03 Tottenham H 0 0
2003-04 Tottenham H 24 1
2004-05 Tottenham H 6 0 **30 1**
2004-05 *Coventry C* 6 0 **6 0**
2004-05 *Wolverhampton W* 7 1
2005-06 Wolverhampton W 25 0
2006-07 Wolverhampton W 19 0 **51 1**
2006-07 *QPR* 2 0 **2 0**
2007-08 Barnsley 10 0 **10 0**
2008 Toronto 27 4
2009 Toronto 12 0 **39 4**
2009-10 Diosgyori 1 0 **1 0**
2010-11 Dacia 4 0 **4 0**
2010-11 Wilhelmshaven 12 1 **12 1**
2011 Shamrock R 9 2 **9 2**
2011-12 Exeter C 1 0 **1 0**

SERCOMBE, Liam (M) 132 13
H: 5 10 W: 10 10 b.Exeter 25-4-90
Source: Scholar.
2008-09 Exeter C 29 2
2009-10 Exeter C 28 1
2010-11 Exeter C 42 3
2011-12 Exeter C 33 7 **132 13**

SHEPHARD, Chris (M) 13 0
H: 6 3 W: 13 03 b.Exeter 25-12-88
Source: Scholar.
2008-09 Exeter C 2 0
2009-10 Exeter C 0 0
2010-11 Exeter C 0 0
2011-12 Exeter C 11 0 **13 0**

TISDALE, Paul (M) 1 0
H: 5 9 W: 11 13 b.Valletta 14-1-73
Source: Out of retirement.
2010-11 Exeter C 1 0
2011-12 Exeter C 0 0 **1 0**

TULLY, Steve (D) 267 5
H: 5 8 W: 11 02 b.Paignton 10-2-80
Source: Trainee.
1997-98 Torquay U 9 0
1998-99 Torquay U 37 2
1999-2000 Torquay U 13 0
2000-01 Torquay U 29 1
2001-02 Torquay U 18 0 **106 3**
From Weymouth.
2008-09 Exeter C 36 0
2009-10 Exeter C 38 1
2010-11 Exeter C 43 1
2011-12 Exeter C 44 0 **161 2**

FULHAM (37)

ALTMAN, Omri (M) 0 0
H: 5 10 W: 11 11 b.Tel Aviv 23-3-94
Source: Scholar. *Honours:* Israel Youth.
2011-12 Fulham 0 0

ARTHURWORREY, Stephen (D) 0 0
H: 6 4 W: 13 12 b.Hackney 15-10-94
Source: Scholar.
2011-12 Fulham 0 0

BAIRD, Chris (D) 194 5
H: 5 10 W: 11 11 b.Ballymoney 25-2-82
Source: Scholar. *Honours:* Northern Ireland Youth, Under-21, 56 full caps.
2000-01 Southampton 0 0
2001-02 Southampton 0 0
2002-03 Southampton 3 0
2003-04 Southampton 4 0
2003-04 *Walsall* 10 0 **10 0**
2003-04 *Watford* 8 0 **8 0**
2004-05 Southampton 0 0
2005-06 Southampton 17 0
2006-07 Southampton 44 3 **68 3**
2007-08 Fulham 18 0
2008-09 Fulham 10 0
2009-10 Fulham 32 0
2010-11 Fulham 29 2
2011-12 Fulham 19 0 **108 2**

BANYA, Charlie (M) 0 0
b.Tulse Hill 18-9-93
Source: Scholar.
2011-12 Fulham 0 0

BARROILHET, Richard (F) 0 0
H: 6 2 W: 11 13 b.Westminster 29-8-92
Source: Academy.
2010-11 Fulham 0 0
2011-12 Fulham 0 0

BETTINELLI, Marcus (G) 0 0
b.Camberwell 24-5-92
Source: Scholar.
2010-11 Fulham 0 0
2011-12 Fulham 0 0

BRIGGS, Matthew (D) 12 0
H: 6 1 W: 11 12 b.Wandsworth 6-3-91
Source: School. *Honours:* England Youth, Under-20, Under-21.
2006-07 Fulham 1 0
2007-08 Fulham 0 0
2008-09 Fulham 0 0
2009-10 Fulham 0 0
2009-10 *Leyton Orient* 1 0 **1 0**
2010-11 Fulham 3 0
2011-12 Fulham 2 0 **6 0**
2011-12 *Peterborough U* 5 0 **5 0**

BRISTER, Alex (M) 0 0
b.Epsom 19-12-93
Source: Scholar.
2011-12 Fulham 0 0

BURN, Dan (D) 4 0
H: 6 6 W: 13 00 b.Blyth 1-5-92
Source: Scholar.
2009-10 Darlington 4 0 **4 0**
2010-11 Fulham 0 0
2011-12 Fulham 0 0

COSGROVE, Jonathan (F) 0 0
b.Newtonabbey 12-1-93
Source: Scholar.
2010-11 Fulham 0 0
2011-12 Fulham 0 0

DALLA VALLE, Lauri (F) 33 5
H: 5 9 W: 11 03 b.Joensuu 14-9-91
Honours: Finland Youth, Under-21.
2007 JIPPO 8 0 **8 0**
2008-09 Liverpool 0 0
2009-10 Liverpool 0 0
2010-11 Fulham 0 0
2010-11 *Bournemouth* 8 2 **8 2**
2011-12 Fulham 0 0
2011-12 *Dundee U* 12 3 **12 3**
2011-12 *Exeter C* 5 0 **5 0**

DAVIES, Simon (M) 368 33
H: 5 10 W: 11 07 b.Haverfordwest 23-10-79
Source: Trainee. *Honours:* Wales Youth, Under-21, B, 58 full caps, 6 goals.
1997-98 Peterborough U 6 0
1998-99 Peterborough U 43 4
1999-2000 Peterborough U 16 2 **65 6**
1999-2000 Tottenham H 3 0
2000-01 Tottenham H 13 2
2001-02 Tottenham H 31 4
2002-03 Tottenham H 36 5
2003-04 Tottenham H 17 2
2004-05 Tottenham H 21 0 **121 13**
2005-06 Everton 30 1
2006-07 Everton 15 0 **45 1**
2006-07 Fulham 14 2
2007-08 Fulham 37 5
2008-09 Fulham 33 2
2009-10 Fulham 17 0
2010-11 Fulham 30 4
2011-12 Fulham 6 0 **137 13**

DELLA-VERDE, Lyle (M) 0 0
b.Leeds 9-1-95
Source: Scholar.
2011-12 Fulham 0 0

DEMBELE, Moussa (F) 231 39
H: 5 9 W: 10 01 b.Wilrijk 17-7-87
Honours: Belgium 39 full caps, 5 goals.
2003-04 Beerschot 1 0
2004-05 Beerschot 19 1 **20 1**
2005-06 Willem II 33 9 **33 9**
2006-07 AZ 33 6
2007-08 AZ 33 4
2008-09 AZ 23 10
2009-10 AZ 29 4 **118 24**
2010-11 Fulham 24 3
2011-12 Fulham 36 2 **60 5**

DEMPSEY, Clint (M) 261 76
H: 6 1 W: 12 02 b.Nacogdoches 9-3-83
Source: Furman Univ. *Honours:* USA Under-21, 86 full caps, 26 goals.
2004 New England Rev 24 7
2005 New England Rev 30 11
2006 New England Rev 23 8 **77 26**
2006-07 Fulham 10 1
2007-08 Fulham 36 6
2008-09 Fulham 35 7
2009-10 Fulham 29 7
2010-11 Fulham 37 12
2011-12 Fulham 37 17 **184 50**

DIARRA, Mahamadou (M) 347 27
H: 6 0 W: 11 13 b.Bamako 18-5-81
Honours: Mali 64 full caps, 6 goals.
1996 CSK Bamako 0 0
1997 CSK Bamako 24 6
1998 CSK Bamako 0 0 **24 6**
1998-99 OFI Crete 21 2 **21 2**
1999-2000 Vitesse 16 2
2000-01 Vitesse 29 4
2001-02 Vitesse 24 3 **69 9**
2002-03 Lyon 25 0
2003-04 Lyon 28 1
2004-05 Lyon 36 2
2005-06 Lyon 32 3
2006-07 Lyon 2 0 **123 6**
2006-07 Real Madrid 33 3
2007-08 Real Madrid 30 0
2008-09 Real Madrid 9 0
2009-10 Real Madrid 15 0
2010-11 Real Madrid 3 0 **90 3**
2010-11 Monaco 9 0 **9 0**
2011-12 Fulham 11 1 **11 1**

DONEGAN, Tom (M) 0 0
b.Huyton 15-9-92
Source: Everton Scholar.
2011-12 Fulham 0 0

DUFF, Damien (F) 418 58
H: 5 9 W: 12 06 b.Ballyboden 2-3-79
Source: Lourdes Celtic. *Honours:* Eire Schools, Youth, Under-20, B, 100 full caps, 8 goals.
1995-96 Blackburn R 0 0
1996-97 Blackburn R 1 0
1997-98 Blackburn R 26 4
1998-99 Blackburn R 28 1
1999-2000 Blackburn R 39 5
2000-01 Blackburn R 32 1
2001-02 Blackburn R 32 7
2002-03 Blackburn R 26 9 **184 27**
2003-04 Chelsea 23 5
2004-05 Chelsea 30 6
2005-06 Chelsea 28 3 **81 14**
2006-07 Newcastle U 22 1
2007-08 Newcastle U 16 0
2008-09 Newcastle U 30 3
2009-10 Newcastle U 1 1 **69 5**
2009-10 Fulham 32 6
2010-11 Fulham 24 4
2011-12 Fulham 28 2 **84 12**

ETHERIDGE, Neil (G) 0 0
H: 6 3 W: 14 00 b.Enfield 7-2-90
Source: Scholar. *Honours:* England Youth, Philippines 26 full caps.
2008-09 Fulham 0 0
2009-10 Fulham 0 0
2010-11 Fulham 0 0
2011-12 Fulham 0 0

ETUHU, Dickson (M) 319 27
H: 6 2 W: 13 04 b.Kano 8-6-82
Source: Scholar. *Honours:* Nigeria 20 full caps.
1999-2000 Manchester C 0 0
2000-01 Manchester C 0 0
2001-02 Manchester C 12 0 **12 0**
2001-02 Preston NE 16 3
2002-03 Preston NE 39 6
2003-04 Preston NE 31 3
2004-05 Preston NE 35 3
2005-06 Preston NE 13 2 **134 17**
2005-06 Norwich C 19 0
2006-07 Norwich C 43 6 **62 6**
2007-08 Sunderland 20 1
2008-09 Sunderland 0 0 **20 1**
2008-09 Fulham 21 1
2009-10 Fulham 20 0
2010-11 Fulham 28 2
2011-12 Fulham 22 0 **91 3**

FREI, Kerim (M) 16 0
H: 5 7 W: 10 05 b.Feldkirch 19-11-93
Source: Scholar. *Honours:* Switzerland Youth, Under-21.
2010-11 Fulham 0 0
2011-12 Fulham 16 0 **16 0**

GAMEIRO, Corey (F) 0 0
b.Wollongong 7-2-93
Source: Academy.
2010-11 Fulham 0 0
2011-12 Fulham 0 0

GECOV, Marcel (M) 81 3
H: 5 11 W: 11 00 b.Prague 1-1-88
Honours: Czech Republic Youth, Under-21, 1 full cap.
2005-06 Slavia Prague 0 0
2006-07 Slavia Prague 0 0
2006-07 *Kladno* 8 0
2007-08 *Kladno* 9 1 **17 1**
2007-08 Slovan Liberec 4 0
2008-09 Slovan Liberec 12 0

2009-10 Slovan Liberec 21 1
2010-11 Slovan Liberec 25 1 **62 2**
2011-12 Fulham 2 0 **2 0**

GRIMMER, Jack (M) 4 0
H: 6 0 W: 12 06 b.Aberdeen 25-1-94
Honours: Scotland Youth.
2009-10 Aberdeen 2 0
2010-11 Aberdeen 2 0
2011-12 Aberdeen 0 0 **4 0**
2011-12 Fulham 0 0

GRYGERA, Zdenek (D) 309 17
H: 6 1 W: 12 04 b.Prilepy u Holesova 14-5-80
Honours: Czech Republic 65 full caps, 2 goals.
1997-98 Zlin 20 1 **20 1**
1998-99 Drnovice 25 0
1999-2000 Drnovice 29 3 **54 3**
2000-01 Sparta Prague 15 0
2001-02 Sparta Prague 21 1
2002-03 Sparta Prague 29 1 **65 2**
2003-04 Ajax 20 0
2004-05 Ajax 18 4
2005-06 Ajax 18 1
2006-07 Ajax 22 3 **78 8**
2007-08 Juventus 24 1
2008-09 Juventus 31 2
2009-10 Juventus 19 0
2010-11 Juventus 13 0 **87 3**
2011-12 Fulham 5 0 **5 0**

HALLICHE, Rafik (D) 79 1
H: 6 2 W: 12 02 b.Algiers 2-9-86
Honours: Algeria Under-23, 21 full caps, 1 goal.
2006-07 Hussein Dey 28 1
2007-08 Hussein Dey 16 0 **44 1**
2007-08 Benfica 0 0
2007-08 *Nacional* 3 0
2008-09 *Nacional* 15 0
2009-10 *Nacional* 16 0 **34 0**
2010-11 Fulham 1 0
2011-12 Fulham 0 0 **1 0**

HANGELAND, Brede (D) 336 17
H: 6 4 W: 13 05 b.Houston 20-6-81
Honours: Norway Under-21, 75 full caps, 1 goal.
2000 Vidar 0 0
2001 Viking 22 0
2002 Viking 26 2
2003 Viking 26 1
2004 Viking 14 3
2005 Viking 26 0 **114 6**
2005-06 FC Copenhagen 13 1
2006-07 FC Copenhagen 32 0
2007-08 FC Copenhagen 18 2 **63 3**
2007-08 Fulham 15 0
2008-09 Fulham 37 1
2009-10 Fulham 32 1
2010-11 Fulham 37 6
2011-12 Fulham 38 0 **159 8**

HARRIS, Courtney (M) 0 0
b.Hammersmith 7-9-91
Source: Scholar.
2010-11 Fulham 0 0
2011-12 Fulham 0 0

HOESEN, Danny (F) 40 15
H: 6 1 W: 12 00 b.Kerkrade 15-1-91
Honours: Holland Youth.
2008-09 Fortuna Sittard 1 0
2008-09 Fulham 0 0
2009-10 Fulham 0 0
2009-10 *HJK Helsinki* 11 2 **11 2**
2010-11 Fulham 0 0
2011-12 Fulham 0 0
2011-12 *Fortuna Sittard* 28 13 **29 13**

HUGHES, Aaron (D) 418 5
H: 6 0 W: 11 02 b.Cookstown 8-11-79
Source: Trainee. *Honours:* Northern Ireland Youth, B, 80 full caps, 1 goal.
1996-97 Newcastle U 0 0
1997-98 Newcastle U 4 0
1998-99 Newcastle U 14 0
1999-2000 Newcastle U 27 2
2000-01 Newcastle U 35 0
2001-02 Newcastle U 34 0
2002-03 Newcastle U 35 1
2003-04 Newcastle U 34 0
2004-05 Newcastle U 22 1 **205 4**
2005-06 Aston Villa 35 0
2006-07 Aston Villa 19 0 **54 0**
2007-08 Fulham 30 0
2008-09 Fulham 38 0
2009-10 Fulham 34 0
2010-11 Fulham 38 1
2011-12 Fulham 19 0 **159 1**

JOHNSON, Andy (F) 370 112
H: 5 7 W: 10 09 b.Bedford 10-2-81
Source: Trainee. *Honours:* England Youth, Under-20, 8 full caps.
1997-98 Birmingham C 0 0
1998-99 Birmingham C 4 0
1999-2000 Birmingham C 22 1
2000-01 Birmingham C 34 4
2001-02 Birmingham C 23 3 **83 8**
2002-03 Crystal Palace 28 11
2003-04 Crystal Palace 42 27
2004-05 Crystal Palace 37 21
2005-06 Crystal Palace 33 15 **140 74**
2006-07 Everton 32 11
2007-08 Everton 29 6 **61 17**
2008-09 Fulham 31 7
2009-10 Fulham 8 0
2010-11 Fulham 27 3
2011-12 Fulham 20 3 **86 13**

JORENEN, Jesse (G) 0 0
b.Helsinki 21-3-93
Source: Scholar.
2010-11 Fulham 0 0
2011-12 Fulham 0 0

KACANIKLIC, Alex (M) 16 1
H: 5 11 W: 10 05 b.Helsingborg 13-8-91
Source: Scholar.
2008-09 Liverpool 0 0
2009-10 Liverpool 0 0
2010-11 Fulham 0 0
2011-12 Fulham 4 0 **4 0**
2011-12 *Watford* 12 1 **12 1**

KASAMI, Pajtim (M) 31 2
H: 6 2 W: 11 00 b.Macedonia 2-6-92
Honours: Switzerland Youth, Under-21.
2009-10 Bellinzona 10 2 **10 2**
2010-11 Palermo 14 0 **14 0**
2011-12 Fulham 7 0 **7 0**

KAVANAGH, Sean (D) 0 0
b.Dublin 20-1-94
Source: Scholar. *Honours:* Eire Youth.
2011-12 Fulham 0 0

KELLY, Stephen (D) 194 2
H: 6 0 W: 12 04 b.Dublin 6-9-83
Source: Juniors. *Honours:* Eire Youth, Under-21, 29 full caps.
2000-01 Tottenham H 0 0
2001-02 Tottenham H 0 0
2002-03 Tottenham H 0 0
2002-03 *Southend U* 10 0 **10 0**
2002-03 *QPR* 7 0 **7 0**
2003-04 Tottenham H 11 0
2003-04 *Watford* 13 0 **13 0**
2004-05 Tottenham H 17 2
2005-06 Tottenham H 9 0 **37 2**
2006-07 Birmingham C 36 0
2007-08 Birmingham C 38 0
2008-09 Birmingham C 5 0
2008-09 *Stoke C* 6 0 **6 0**
2009-10 Birmingham C 0 0 **79 0**
2009-10 Fulham 8 0
2010-11 Fulham 10 0
2011-12 Fulham 24 0 **42 0**

MINKWITZ, Ronny (M) 0 0
b.Duisburg 9-12-93
Source: Scholar.
2010-11 Fulham 0 0
2011-12 Fulham 0 0

MURPHY, Danny (M) 567 78
H: 5 10 W: 11 09 b.Chester 18-3-77
Source: Trainee. *Honours:* England Schools, Youth, Under-21, 9 full caps, 1 goal.
1993-94 Crewe Alex 12 2
1994-95 Crewe Alex 35 5
1995-96 Crewe Alex 42 10
1996-97 Crewe Alex 45 10
1997-98 Liverpool 16 0
1998-99 Liverpool 1 0
1998-99 *Crewe Alex* 16 1 **150 28**
1999-2000 Liverpool 23 3
2000-01 Liverpool 27 4
2001-02 Liverpool 36 6
2002-03 Liverpool 36 7
2003-04 Liverpool 31 5 **170 25**
2004-05 Charlton Ath 38 3
2005-06 Charlton Ath 18 4 **56 7**
2005-06 Tottenham H 10 0
2006-07 Tottenham H 12 1
2007-08 Tottenham H 0 0 **22 1**
2007-08 Fulham 33 5
2008-09 Fulham 38 5
2009-10 Fulham 25 5
2010-11 Fulham 37 0
2011-12 Fulham 36 2 **169 17**

NA BANGNA, Buomesca (M) 0 0
b.Guinea-Bissau 6-5-93
Source: Chelsea Scholar.
2011-12 Fulham 0 0

O'REILLY, Daniel (D) 0 0
H: 5 10 W: 11 13 b.Dublin 11-4-95
Source: Scholar.
2011-12 Fulham 0 0

OBERSCHMIDT, Max (G) 0 0
b.Germany 25-1-95
Source: Scholar.
2011-12 Fulham 0 0

PENIKET, Richard (F) 7 0
b.Stourbridge 4-3-93
Source: Scholar. *Honours:* Wales Youth.
2010-11 Fulham 0 0
2011-12 Fulham 0 0
2011-12 *Hereford U* 7 0 **7 0**

POGREBNYAK, Pavel (F) 257 83
H: 6 2 W: 14 05 b.Moscow 8-11-83
Honours: Russia 33 full caps, 8 goals.
2002 Spartak Moscow 2 0
2003 *Baltika* 40 15 **40 15**
2004 Spartak Moscow 16 2 **18 2**
2004 *Khimki* 12 6 **12 6**
2005 *Shinnik* 23 4 **23 4**
2006 Tomsk 26 13 **26 13**
2007 Zenit 24 11
2008 Zenit 19 6
2009 Zenit 15 5 **58 22**
2009-10 Stuttgart 28 6
2010-11 Stuttgart 26 8
2011-12 Stuttgart 14 1 **68 15**
2011-12 Fulham 12 6 **12 6**

PRITCHARD, Josh (M) 0 0
H: 5 9 W: 11 02 b.Stockport 23-9-92
Source: Scholar.
2011-12 Fulham 0 0

RIISE, Bjorn Helge (M) 164 13
H: 5 10 W: 11 11 b.Alesund 21-6-83
Honours: Norway Under-21, 31 full caps, 1 goal.
2002 *Viking* 0 0
2002-03 Standard Liege 9 0
2003-04 Standard Liege 8 0 **17 0**
2004-05 *FC Brussels* 31 2 **31 2**
2005 Lillestrom 13 0
2006 Lillestrom 25 1
2007 Lillestrom 24 3
2008 Lillestrom 9 0
2009 Lillestrom 15 6 **86 10**
2009-10 Fulham 12 0
2010-11 Fulham 3 0
2010-11 *Sheffield U* 13 1 **13 1**
2011-12 Fulham 0 0 **15 0**
2011-12 *Portsmouth* 2 0 **2 0**

RIISE, John Arne (M) 438 37
H: 6 1 W: 14 00 b.Molde 24-9-80
Honours: Norway Youth, Under-21, 103 full caps, 14 goals.
1997 Aalesund 8 1
1998 Aalesund 17 4 **25 5**
1998-99 Monaco 7 0
1999-2000 Monaco 21 1
2000-01 Monaco 16 3 **44 4**
2001-02 Liverpool 38 7
2002-03 Liverpool 37 6
2003-04 Liverpool 28 0
2004-05 Liverpool 37 6
2005-06 Liverpool 32 1
2006-07 Liverpool 33 1
2007-08 Liverpool 29 0 **234 21**
2008-09 Roma 31 2
2009-10 Roma 36 5
2010-11 Roma 32 0 **99 7**
2011-12 Fulham 36 0 **36 0**

RUIZ, Bryan (M) **236 84**
H: 6 2 W: 12 04 b.Alajuela 18-8-85
Honours: Costa Rica 46 full caps, 9 goals.
2004-05 Alajuelense 31 13
2005-06 Alajuelense 35 8 **66 21**
2006-07 Gent 15 3
2007-08 Gent 31 11
2008-09 Gent 32 12 **78 26**
2009-10 Twente 34 24
2010-11 Twente 27 9
2011-12 Twente 4 2 **65 35**
2011-12 Fulham 27 2 **27 2**

SA, Orlando (F) **61 13**
H: 6 2 W: 13 05 b.Barcelos 26-5-88
Honours: Portugal Under-21, 1 full cap.
2007-08 Braga 0 0
2007-08 *Maria da Fonte* 26 6 **26 6**
2008-09 Braga 10 3 **10 3**
2009-10 Porto 2 0
2010-11 Porto 0 0 **2 0**
2010-11 *Nacional* 16 3 **16 3**
2011-12 Fulham 7 1 **7 1**

SALCIDO, Carlos (D) **319 10**
H: 5 8 W: 11 00 b.Ocotlan 2-4-80
Honours: Mexico 103 full caps, 9 goals.
2000-01 Gallos 0 0
2001-02 Guadalajara 1 0
2002-03 Tapatio 42 4 **42 4**
2003-04 Guadalajara 35 1
2004-05 Guadalajara 31 1
2005-06 Guadalajara 29 0 **96 2**
2006-07 PSV Eindhoven 33 1
2007-08 PSV Eindhoven 33 0
2008-09 PSV Eindhoven 28 2
2009-10 PSV Eindhoven 27 0 **121 3**
2010-11 Fulham 23 0
2011-12 Fulham 0 0 **23 0**
2011-12 *Tigres Leon* 37 1 **37 1**

SCHWARZER, Mark (G) **580 0**
H: 6 4 W: 14 07 b.Sydney 6-10-72
Honours: Australia Youth, Under-20, Under-23, 97 full caps.
1990-91 Marconi Stallions 1 0
1991-92 Marconi Stallions 9 0
1992-93 Marconi Stallions 23 0
1993-94 Marconi Stallions 25 0 **58 0**
1994-95 Dynamo Dresden 2 0 **2 0**
1995-96 Kaiserslautern 4 0
1996-97 Kaiserslautern 0 0 **4 0**
1996-97 Bradford C 13 0 **13 0**
1996-97 Middlesbrough 7 0
1997-98 Middlesbrough 35 0
1998-99 Middlesbrough 34 0
1999-2000 Middlesbrough 37 0
2000-01 Middlesbrough 31 0
2001-02 Middlesbrough 21 0
2002-03 Middlesbrough 38 0
2003-04 Middlesbrough 36 0
2004-05 Middlesbrough 31 0
2005-06 Middlesbrough 27 0
2006-07 Middlesbrough 36 0
2007-08 Middlesbrough 34 0 **367 0**
2008-09 Fulham 38 0
2009-10 Fulham 37 0
2010-11 Fulham 31 0
2011-12 Fulham 30 0 **136 0**

SENDEROS, Philippe (D) **130 8**
H: 6 1 W: 13 10 b.Geneva 14-2-85
Honours: Switzerland Youth, Under-20, Under-21, 47 full caps, 5 goals.
2001-02 Servette 3 0
2002-03 Servette 23 3 **26 3**
2003-04 Arsenal 0 0
2004-05 Arsenal 13 0
2005-06 Arsenal 20 2
2006-07 Arsenal 14 0
2007-08 Arsenal 17 2
2008-09 Arsenal 0 0
2008-09 *AC Milan* 14 0 **14 0**
2009-10 Arsenal 0 0 **64 4**
2009-10 *Everton* 2 0 **2 0**
2010-11 Fulham 3 0
2011-12 Fulham 21 1 **24 1**

SIDWELL, Steve (M) **296 44**
H: 5 10 W: 11 00 b.Wandsworth 14-12-82
Source: Scholar. *Honours:* England Under-20, Under-21.
2001-02 Arsenal 0 0
2001-02 *Brentford* 30 4 **30 4**
2002-03 Arsenal 0 0
2002-03 *Brighton & HA* 12 5 **12 5**
2002-03 Reading 13 2
2003-04 Reading 43 8
2004-05 Reading 44 5
2005-06 Reading 33 10
2006-07 Reading 35 4 **168 29**
2007-08 Chelsea 15 0 **15 0**
2008-09 Aston Villa 16 3
2009-10 Aston Villa 25 0
2010-11 Aston Villa 4 0 **45 3**
2010-11 Fulham 12 2
2011-12 Fulham 14 1 **26 3**

SMITH, Alex (D) **0 0**
H: 5 9 W: 8 09 b.Clapham 31-10-91
Source: Scholar.
2009-10 Fulham 0 0
2010-11 Fulham 0 0
2011-12 Fulham 0 0

SOMOGYI, Csaba (G) **70 0**
H: 6 3 W: 13 05 b.Hungary 7-4-85
2003-04 Gyor 2 0
2004-05 Gyor 0 0
2005-06 Gyor 1 0
2006-07 Gyor 0 0
2006-07 *Integral-DAC* 5 0
2007-08 Gyor 0 0 **3 0**
2008-09 Integral-DAC 13 0 **18 0**
2009-10 Heviz 6 0 **6 0**
2009-10 Rakospalotai 14 0
2010-11 Rakospalotai 29 0 **43 0**
2011-12 Fulham 0 0

STOCKDALE, David (G) **119 0**
H: 6 3 W: 13 04 b.Leeds 20-9-85
Source: Scholar.
2002-03 York C 1 0
2003-04 York C 0 0 **1 0**
2006-07 Darlington 6 0
2007-08 Darlington 41 0 **47 0**
2008-09 Fulham 0 0
2008-09 *Rotherham U* 8 0 **8 0**
2008-09 *Leicester C* 8 0 **8 0**
2009-10 Fulham 1 0
2009-10 *Plymouth Arg* 21 0 **21 0**
2010-11 Fulham 7 0
2011-12 Fulham 8 0 **16 0**
2011-12 *Ipswich T* 18 0 **18 0**

TANKOVIC, Muamer (F) **0 0**
b.Norrkoping 22-2-95
Source: Scholar.
2011-12 Fulham 0 0

TROTTA, Marcello (F) **10 8**
H: 6 1 W: 12 12 b.Caserta 29-9-92
Source: Napoli. *Honours:* Italy Youth.
2009-10 Fulham 0 0
2010-11 Fulham 0 0
2011-12 Fulham 1 0 **1 0**
2011-12 *Wycombe W* 8 8 **8 8**
2011-12 *Watford* 1 0 **1 0**

VIGEN CHRISTENSEN, Lasse (M) **0 0**
H: 5 10 W: 12 00 b.Esbjerg 15-8-94
Source: Midtjylland. *Honours:* Denmark Youth.
2011-12 Fulham 0 0

WILLIAMS, Ryan (F) **4 0**
H: 5 11 W: 12 00 b.Perth 28-10-93
Source: Scholar.
2011-12 Portsmouth 4 0 **4 0**
2011-12 Fulham 0 0

WOODROW, Cauley (F) **0 0**
b.Hemel Hempstead 2-12-94
Source: Scholar.
2011-12 Fulham 0 0

Scholars
Passley Josh; Richards Tom Oliver; Tieku Derek.

GILLINGHAM (38)

BIRCHALL, Adam (F) **152 25**
H: 5 7 W: 10 09 b.Maidstone 2-12-84
Source: Trainee. *Honours:* Wales Under-21.
2002-03 Arsenal 0 0
2003-04 Arsenal 0 0
2004-05 Arsenal 0 0
2004-05 *Wycombe W* 12 4 **12 4**
2005-06 Mansfield T 31 2
2006-07 Mansfield T 5 0 **36 2**
2006-07 Barnet 23 6
2007-08 Barnet 42 11
2008-09 Barnet 39 2 **104 19**
From Dover Ath.
2011-12 Gillingham 0 0

BROWN, Alex (M) **1 0**
b.S Woodham Ferrers 30-9-92
Source: Scholar.
2011-12 Gillingham 1 0 **1 0**

BRUNT, Thomas (M) **0 0**
b.Chatham 5-1-93
Source: Scholar.
2011-12 Gillingham 0 0

CARTER, Joe (D) **0 0**
b.Buckhurst Hill 20-11-92
Source: Charlton Ath Scholar.
2011-12 Gillingham 0 0

DAVIES, Callum (D) **3 0**
H: 6 1 W: 11 11 b.Sittingbourne 8-2-93
Source: Scholar.
2010-11 Gillingham 1 0
2011-12 Gillingham 2 0 **3 0**

ESSAM, Connor (D) **18 0**
H: 6 0 W: 12 00 b.Sheerness 9-7-92
Source: Scholar.
2010-11 Gillingham 0 0
2011-12 Gillingham 18 0 **18 0**

EVANS, Jack (D) **7 0**
H: 5 10 W: 11 05 b.Gravesend 19-3-93
Source: Scholar.
2011-12 Gillingham 7 0 **7 0**

FISH, Matt (D) **23 1**
b.Croydon 5-1-89
Source: Crystal Palace Scholar, Dover Ath.
2011-12 Gillingham 23 1 **23 1**

FLITNEY, Ross (G) **80 0**
H: 6 3 W: 12 07 b.Hitchin 1-6-84
Source: Scholar.
2003-04 Fulham 0 0
2003-04 *Brighton & HA* 3 0 **3 0**
2004-05 Fulham 0 0
2004-05 *Doncaster R* 0 0
2005-06 Barnet 35 0
2006-07 Barnet 15 0 **50 0**
From Grays Ath, Croydon Ath, Dover Ath.
2011-12 Gillingham 27 0 **27 0**

FRAMPTON, Andrew (D) **302 8**
H: 5 11 W: 10 10 b.Wimbledon 3-9-79
Source: Trainee.
1998-99 Crystal Palace 6 0
1999-2000 Crystal Palace 9 0
2000-01 Crystal Palace 10 0
2001-02 Crystal Palace 2 0
2002-03 Crystal Palace 1 0 **28 0**
2002-03 Brentford 15 0
2003-04 Brentford 16 0
2004-05 Brentford 35 0
2005-06 Brentford 36 3
2006-07 Brentford 32 1 **134 4**
2007-08 Millwall 30 1
2008-09 Millwall 37 1
2009-10 Millwall 21 2
2010-11 Millwall 0 0 **88 4**
2010-11 *Leyton Orient* 1 0 **1 0**
2010-11 *Swindon T* 23 0 **23 0**
2011-12 Gillingham 28 0 **28 0**

FULLER, Barry (D) **149 1**
H: 5 10 W: 11 10 b.Ashford 25-9-84
Source: Scholar.
2004-05 Charlton Ath 0 0
2005-06 Charlton Ath 0 0
2005-06 *Barnet* 15 1 **15 1**
From Stevenage B.
2007-08 Gillingham 10 0
2008-09 Gillingham 37 0
2009-10 Gillingham 36 0
2010-11 Gillingham 42 0
2011-12 Gillingham 9 0 **134 0**

GAZZANIGA, Paulo (G) **20 0**
H: 6 5 W: 14 02 b.Santa Fe 2-1-92
Source: Valencia Youth.
2011-12 Gillingham 20 0 **20 0**

HAWKES, Darren (G) **0 0**
b.Ashford 24-6-93
Source: Scholar.

2011-12	Gillingham	0	0		

JACKMAN, Danny (D) **301 20**
H: 5 4 W: 10 00 b.Worcester 3-1-83
Source: Scholar.

2000-01	Aston Villa	0	0		
2001-02	Aston Villa	0	0		
2001-02	*Cambridge U*	7	1	**7**	**1**
2002-03	Aston Villa	0	0		
2003-04	Aston Villa	0	0		
2003-04	Stockport Co	27	2		
2004-05	Stockport Co	33	2	**60**	**4**
2005-06	Gillingham	42	0		
2006-07	Gillingham	31	1		
2007-08	Northampton T	39	1		
2008-09	Northampton T	43	8		
2009-10	Northampton T	0	0	**82**	**9**
2009-10	Gillingham	22	0		
2010-11	Gillingham	17	1		
2011-12	Gillingham	40	4	**152**	**6**

KEDWELL, Danny (F) **40 12**
H: 5 11 W: 12 13 b.Gillingham 3-8-83
Source: Chatham T, Tonbridge Angels, Fisher Ath, Lordswood, Maidstone U, Herne Bay, Welling U, Grays Ath, AFC Wimbledon.

2011-12	Gillingham	40	12	**40**	**12**

KING, Simon (D) **183 5**
H: 6 0 W: 13 00 b.Oxford 11-4-83
Source: Scholar.

2000-01	Oxford U	2	0		
2001-02	Oxford U	2	0		
2002-03	Oxford U	0	0		
2003-04	Oxford U	0	0		
2004-05	Oxford U	0	0	**4**	**0**
2005-06	Barnet	32	0		
2006-07	Barnet	43	2	**75**	**2**
2007-08	Gillingham	42	0		
2008-09	Gillingham	43	2		
2009-10	Gillingham	0	0		
2010-11	Gillingham	4	0		
2011-12	Gillingham	9	1	**98**	**3**
2011-12	*Plymouth Arg*	6	0	**6**	**0**

LAWRENCE, Matt (D) **552 6**
H: 6 1 W: 12 12 b.Northampton 19-6-74
Source: Grays Ath. *Honours:* England Schools.

1995-96	Wycombe W	3	0		
1996-97	Wycombe W	13	1		
1996-97	Fulham	15	0		
1997-98	Fulham	43	0		
1998-99	Fulham	1	0	**59**	**0**
1998-99	Wycombe W	34	2		
1999-2000	Wycombe W	29	2	**79**	**5**
1999-2000	Millwall	9	0		
2000-01	Millwall	45	0		
2001-02	Millwall	26	0		
2002-03	Millwall	33	0		
2003-04	Millwall	36	0		
2004-05	Millwall	44	0		
2005-06	Millwall	31	0	**224**	**0**
2006-07	Crystal Palace	34	0		
2007-08	Crystal Palace	37	1		
2008-09	Crystal Palace	32	0		
2009-10	Crystal Palace	18	0	**121**	**1**
2010-11	Gillingham	43	0		
2011-12	Gillingham	26	0	**69**	**0**

LEE, Charlie (M) **195 21**
H: 5 11 W: 11 07 b.Whitechapel 5-1-87
Source: Scholar.

2005-06	Tottenham H	0	0		
2006-07	Tottenham H	0	0		
2006-07	*Millwall*	5	0	**5**	**0**
2007-08	Peterborough U	42	6		
2008-09	Peterborough U	44	5		
2009-10	Peterborough U	33	2		
2010-11	Peterborough U	34	1	**153**	**14**
2010-11	*Gillingham*	4	1		
2011-12	Gillingham	33	6	**37**	**7**

MARTIN, Joe (M) **74 2**
H: 6 0 W: 12 13 b.Dagenham 29-11-88
Source: Scholar. *Honours:* England Youth.

2005-06	Tottenham H	0	0		
2006-07	Tottenham H	0	0		
2007-08	Tottenham H	0	0		
2007-08	*Blackpool*	1	0		
2008-09	Blackpool	15	0		
2009-10	Blackpool	6	0	**22**	**0**
2010-11	Gillingham	17	1		
2011-12	Gillingham	35	1	**52**	**2**

MILLER, Ashley (F) **6 1**
H: 5 7 W: 10 03 b.Dover 8-6-94
Source: Scholar.

2010-11	Gillingham	1	0		
2011-12	Gillingham	5	1	**6**	**1**

MONTROSE, Lewis (M) **104 8**
H: 6 0 W: 12 00 b.Manchester 17-11-88
Source: Scholar.

2006-07	Wigan Ath	0	0		
2007-08	Wigan Ath	0	0		
2008-09	Wigan Ath	0	0		
2008-09	*Cheltenham T*	5	0	**5**	**0**
2008-09	*Chesterfield*	12	0	**12**	**0**
2009-10	Wycombe W	14	0		
2010-11	Wycombe W	36	4	**50**	**4**
2011-12	Gillingham	37	4	**37**	**4**

OLI, Dennis (M) **161 15**
H: 6 0 W: 12 00 b.Newham 28-1-84

2001-02	QPR	2	0		
2002-03	QPR	18	0		
2003-04	QPR	3	0	**23**	**0**
2004-05	Swansea C	1	0	**1**	**0**
2004-05	Cambridge U	4	1	**4**	**1**

From Grays Ath.

2007-08	Gillingham	22	4		
2008-09	Gillingham	31	4		
2009-10	Gillingham	36	3		
2010-11	Gillingham	21	1		
2011-12	Gillingham	23	2	**133**	**14**

OSEI-KUFFOUR, Jo (F) **402 96**
H: 5 8 W: 11 11 b.Edmonton 17-11-81
Source: Scholar.

2000-01	Arsenal	0	0		
2001-02	Arsenal	0	0		
2001-02	*Swindon T*	11	2	**11**	**2**
2002-03	Torquay U	30	5		
2003-04	Torquay U	41	10		
2004-05	Torquay U	34	6		
2005-06	Torquay U	43	8	**148**	**29**
2006-07	Brentford	39	12	**39**	**12**
2007-08	Bournemouth	42	12		
2008-09	Bournemouth	2	0	**44**	**12**
2008-09	Bristol R	41	11		
2009-10	Bristol R	42	14		
2010-11	Bristol R	42	6		
2011-12	Bristol R	5	1	**130**	**32**
2011-12	Gillingham	30	9	**30**	**9**

PAYNE, Jack (M) **82 3**
H: 5 9 W: 9 02 b.Gravesend 5-12-91
Source: Scholar.

2008-09	Gillingham	2	0		
2009-10	Gillingham	19	0		
2010-11	Gillingham	31	1		
2011-12	Gillingham	30	2	**82**	**3**

PAYNE, Stefan (F) **29 1**
H: 5 10 W: 11 07 b.Lambeth 10-8-91
Source: Sutton U.

2009-10	Fulham	0	0		
2010-11	Gillingham	16	0		
2011-12	Gillingham	12	1	**28**	**1**
2011-12	*Aldershot T*	1	0	**1**	**0**

RANCE, Dean (M) **0 0**
H: 5 11 W: 11 02 b.Maidstone 24-9-91
Source: Scholar.

2010-11	Gillingham	0	0		
2011-12	Gillingham	0	0		

RICHARDS, Garry (D) **147 6**
H: 6 3 W: 13 00 b.Romford 11-6-86
Source: Scholar.

2005-06	Colchester U	15	0		
2006-07	Colchester U	5	1	**20**	**1**
2006-07	*Brentford*	10	1	**10**	**1**
2007-08	Southend U	10	0	**10**	**0**
2007-08	Gillingham	14	1		
2008-09	Gillingham	36	2		
2009-10	Gillingham	16	0		
2010-11	Gillingham	17	0		
2011-12	Gillingham	24	1	**107**	**4**

SPILLER, Danny (M) **192 11**
H: 5 8 W: 11 00 b.Maidstone 10-10-81
Source: Trainee.

2000-01	Gillingham	0	0		
2001-02	Gillingham	1	0		
2002-03	Gillingham	10	0		
2003-04	Gillingham	39	6		
2004-05	Gillingham	22	0		
2005-06	Gillingham	32	0		
2006-07	Gillingham	25	0		
2007-08	Millwall	6	1		
2008-09	Millwall	2	0	**8**	**1**
2009-10	Dagenham & R	10	0	**10**	**0**
2010-11	Gillingham	30	2		
2011-12	Gillingham	15	2	**174**	**10**

WESTON, Curtis (M) **192 17**
H: 5 11 W: 11 09 b.Greenwich 24-1-87
Source: Scholar.

2003-04	Millwall	1	0		
2004-05	Millwall	3	0		
2005-06	Millwall	0	0	**4**	**0**
2006-07	Swindon T	27	1	**27**	**1**
2007-08	Leeds U	7	1		
2007-08	*Scunthorpe U*	7	0	**7**	**0**
2008-09	Leeds U	0	0	**7**	**1**
2008-09	Gillingham	45	5		
2009-10	Gillingham	39	6		
2010-11	Gillingham	33	4		
2011-12	Gillingham	30	0	**147**	**15**

WHELPDALE, Chris (M) **168 27**
H: 6 0 W: 12 08 b.Harold Wood 27-1-87
Source: Billericay T.

2007-08	Peterborough U	35	3		
2008-09	Peterborough U	39	7		
2009-10	Peterborough U	29	1		
2010-11	Peterborough U	22	1	**125**	**12**
2010-11	*Gillingham*	4	3		
2011-12	Gillingham	39	12	**43**	**15**

HARTLEPOOL U (39)

AUSTIN, Neil (D) **319 11**
H: 5 10 W: 11 09 b.Barnsley 26-4-83
Source: Trainee. *Honours:* England Youth, Under-20.

1999-2000	Barnsley	0	0		
2000-01	Barnsley	0	0		
2001-02	Barnsley	0	0		
2002-03	Barnsley	34	0		
2003-04	Barnsley	37	0		
2004-05	Barnsley	15	0		
2005-06	Barnsley	38	0		
2006-07	Barnsley	24	0	**148**	**0**
2007-08	Darlington	29	2		
2008-09	Darlington	33	3	**62**	**5**
2009-10	Hartlepool U	39	3		
2010-11	Hartlepool U	24	2		
2011-12	Hartlepool U	46	1	**109**	**6**

BALDWIN, Jack (D) **17 0**
H: 6 1 W: 11 00 b.Barking 30-6-93
Source: Faversham T.

2011-12	Hartlepool U	17	0	**17**	**0**

BOYD, Adam (F) **346 97**
H: 5 9 W: 10 12 b.Hartlepool 25-5-82
Source: Scholarship.

1999-2000	Hartlepool U	4	1		
2000-01	Hartlepool U	5	0		
2001-02	Hartlepool U	29	9		
2002-03	Hartlepool U	22	5		
2003-04	Hartlepool U	18	12		
2003-04	*Boston U*	14	4	**14**	**4**
2004-05	Hartlepool U	45	22		
2005-06	Hartlepool U	21	4		
2006-07	Luton T	19	1	**19**	**1**
2007-08	Leyton Orient	44	14		
2008-09	Leyton Orient	33	9	**77**	**23**
2009-10	Hartlepool U	40	7		
2010-11	Hartlepool U	19	3		
2011-12	Hartlepool U	33	6	**236**	**69**

BROWN, James (F) **175 29**
H: 5 11 W: 11 00 b.Cramlington 3-1-87
Source: Cramlington Jun.

2004-05	Hartlepool U	0	0		
2005-06	Hartlepool U	4	1		
2006-07	Hartlepool U	36	6		
2007-08	Hartlepool U	35	10		
2008-09	Hartlepool U	18	6		
2009-10	Hartlepool U	32	4		
2010-11	Hartlepool U	26	1		
2011-12	Hartlepool U	24	1	**175**	**29**

COLLINS, Sam (D) **453 19**
H: 6 2 W: 14 03 b.Pontefract 5-6-77
Source: Trainee.

1994-95	Huddersfield T	0	0		
1995-96	Huddersfield T	0	0		
1996-97	Huddersfield T	4	0		

1997-98 Huddersfield T 10 0
1998-99 Huddersfield T 23 0 **37 0**
1999-2000 Bury 19 0
2000-01 Bury 34 2
2001-02 Bury 29 0 **82 2**
2002-03 Port Vale 44 5
2003-04 Port Vale 43 4
2004-05 Port Vale 33 2
2005-06 Port Vale 15 0 **135 11**
2005-06 Hull C 17 0
2006-07 Hull C 6 0
2007-08 Hull C 0 0 **23 0**
2007-08 *Swindon T* 4 0 **4 0**
2007-08 Hartlepool U 10 2
2008-09 Hartlepool U 40 1
2009-10 Hartlepool U 44 0
2010-11 Hartlepool U 42 2
2011-12 Hartlepool U 36 1 **172 6**

FLINDERS, Scott (G) 169 1
H: 6 4 W: 13 00 b.Rotherham 12-6-86
Source: Scholar. *Honours:* England Youth, Under-20.
2004-05 Barnsley 11 0
2005-06 Barnsley 3 0 **14 0**
2006-07 Crystal Palace 8 0
2006-07 *Gillingham* 9 0 **9 0**
2006-07 *Brighton & HA* 12 0 **12 0**
2007-08 Crystal Palace 0 0
2007-08 *Yeovil T* 9 0 **9 0**
2008-09 Crystal Palace 0 0 **8 0**
2009-10 Hartlepool U 46 0
2010-11 Hartlepool U 26 1
2011-12 Hartlepool U 45 0 **117 1**

HARTLEY, Peter (D) 135 8
H: 6 0 W: 12 06 b.Hartlepool 3-4-88
Source: Scholar.
2006-07 Sunderland 1 0
2007-08 Sunderland 0 0
2007-08 *Chesterfield* 12 0 **12 0**
2008-09 Sunderland 0 0 **1 0**
2009-10 Hartlepool U 38 2
2010-11 Hartlepool U 40 2
2011-12 Hartlepool U 44 4 **122 8**

HASLAM, Steven (M) 251 3
H: 5 11 W: 10 10 b.Sheffield 6-9-79
Source: Trainee. *Honours:* England Schools, Youth.
1996-97 Sheffield W 0 0
1997-98 Sheffield W 0 0
1998-99 Sheffield W 2 0
1999-2000 Sheffield W 23 0
2000-01 Sheffield W 27 1
2001-02 Sheffield W 41 0
2002-03 Sheffield W 26 1
2003-04 Sheffield W 25 0 **144 2**
2004-05 Northampton T 3 0
2005-06 Northampton T 0 0
2006-07 Northampton T 0 0 **3 0**
From Halifax T.
2007-08 Bury 37 1
2008-09 Bury 13 0 **50 1**
2009-10 Hartlepool U 15 0
2010-11 Hartlepool U 29 0
2011-12 Hartlepool U 10 0 **54 0**

HASSAN, Callum (F) 1 0
H: 6 4 W: 14 02 b.Southwark 23-1-93
Source: Scholar.
2011-12 Hartlepool U 1 0 **1 0**

HAWKINS, Lewis (M) 1 0
H: 5 10 W: 12 04 b.Middlesbrough 15-6-93
Source: Scholar.
2011-12 Hartlepool U 1 0 **1 0**

HOLDEN, Darren (D) 4 0
H: 5 11 W: 11 00 b.Krugersdorp 27-8-93
Source: Scholar.
2010-11 Hartlepool U 1 0
2011-12 Hartlepool U 3 0 **4 0**

HORWOOD, Evan (D) 207 4
H: 6 0 W: 10 06 b.Billingham 10-3-86
Source: Scholar.
2004-05 Sheffield U 0 0
2004-05 *Stockport Co* 10 0 **10 0**
2005-06 Sheffield U 0 0
2005-06 *Scunthorpe U* 0 0
2005-06 *Chester C* 1 0 **1 0**
2006-07 Sheffield U 0 0
2006-07 *Darlington* 20 0 **20 0**
2007-08 Sheffield U 0 0
2007-08 Gretna 15 1 **15 1**
2007-08 Carlisle U 19 0
2008-09 Carlisle U 24 0
2009-10 Carlisle U 32 0 **75 0**
2010-11 Hartlepool U 45 2
2011-12 Hartlepool U 41 1 **86 3**

HUMPHREYS, Richie (M) 546 44
H: 5 11 W: 12 07 b.Sheffield 30-11-77
Source: Trainee. *Honours:* England Youth, Under-21.
1995-96 Sheffield W 5 0
1996-97 Sheffield W 29 3
1997-98 Sheffield W 7 0
1998-99 Sheffield W 19 1
1999-2000 Sheffield W 0 0
1999-2000 *Scunthorpe U* 6 2 **6 2**
1999-2000 *Cardiff C* 9 2 **9 2**
2000-01 Sheffield W 7 0 **67 4**
2000-01 Cambridge U 7 3 **7 3**
2001-02 Hartlepool U 46 5
2002-03 Hartlepool U 46 11
2003-04 Hartlepool U 46 3
2004-05 Hartlepool U 46 3
2005-06 Hartlepool U 46 2
2006-07 Hartlepool U 38 3
2006-07 *Port Vale* 7 0 **7 0**
2007-08 Hartlepool U 45 3
2008-09 Hartlepool U 45 0
2009-10 Hartlepool U 38 0
2010-11 Hartlepool U 25 2
2011-12 Hartlepool U 29 1 **450 33**

JAMES, Luke (M) 19 3
H: 6 0 W: 12 08 b.Amble 4-11-94
Source: Scholar.
2011-12 Hartlepool U 19 3 **19 3**

JOHNSON, Paul (D) 1 0
H: 6 0 W: 12 11 b.Sunderland 5-4-92
Source: Scholar.
2010-11 Hartlepool U 1 0
2011-12 Hartlepool U 0 0 **1 0**

LARKIN, Colin (F) 316 49
H: 5 9 W: 11 07 b.Dundalk 27-4-82
Source: Trainee.
1998-99 Wolverhampton W 0 0
1999-2000 Wolverhampton W 1 0
2000-01 Wolverhampton W 2 0
2001-02 Wolverhampton W 0 0 **3 0**
2001-02 *Kidderminster H* 33 6 **33 6**
2002-03 Mansfield T 22 7
2003-04 Mansfield T 37 7
2004-05 Mansfield T 33 11 **92 25**
2005-06 Chesterfield 41 7
2006-07 Chesterfield 39 4 **80 11**
2007-08 Northampton T 33 2
2008-09 Northampton T 21 1
2009-10 Northampton T 0 0 **54 3**
2009-10 Hartlepool U 22 1
2010-11 Hartlepool U 30 3
2011-12 Hartlepool U 2 0 **54 4**

LIDDLE, Gary (D) 247 18
H: 6 1 W: 12 06 b.Middlesbrough 15-6-86
Source: Trainee. *Honours:* England Youth.
2003-04 Middlesbrough 0 0
2004-05 Middlesbrough 0 0
2005-06 Middlesbrough 0 0
2006-07 Hartlepool U 42 3
2007-08 Hartlepool U 41 2
2008-09 Hartlepool U 43 0
2009-10 Hartlepool U 40 3
2010-11 Hartlepool U 42 6
2011-12 Hartlepool U 39 4 **247 18**

LUSCOMBE, Nathan (M) 13 1
H: 5 8 W: 11 07 b.Gateshead 6-11-89
Source: Scholar.
2008-09 Sunderland 0 0
2009-10 Sunderland 0 0
2010-11 Sunderland 0 0
2011-12 Hartlepool U 13 1 **13 1**

MELLISH, Jordan (D) 0 0
b.South Shields 22-1-93
Source: Scholar.
2011-12 Hartlepool U 0 0

MONKHOUSE, Andy (M) 365 47
H: 6 1 W: 11 06 b.Leeds 23-10-80
Source: Trainee.
1998-99 Rotherham U 5 1
1999-2000 Rotherham U 0 0
2000-01 Rotherham U 12 0
2001-02 Rotherham U 38 2
2002-03 Rotherham U 20 0
2003-04 Rotherham U 27 3
2004-05 Rotherham U 14 2
2005-06 Rotherham U 12 1 **128 9**
2006-07 Swindon T 10 2 **10 2**
2006-07 Hartlepool U 26 7
2007-08 Hartlepool U 25 2
2008-09 Hartlepool U 44 6
2009-10 Hartlepool U 43 11
2010-11 Hartlepool U 44 7
2011-12 Hartlepool U 45 3 **227 36**

MURRAY, Paul (M) 480 31
H: 5 9 W: 10 08 b.Carlisle 31-8-76
Source: Trainee. *Honours:* England Youth, Under-21, B.
1993-94 Carlisle U 8 0
1994-95 Carlisle U 5 0
1995-96 Carlisle U 28 1
1995-96 QPR 1 0
1996-97 QPR 32 5
1997-98 QPR 32 1
1997-98 QPR 0 0
1998-99 QPR 39 1
1999-2000 QPR 30 0
2000-01 QPR 6 0 **140 7**
2001-02 Southampton 1 0 **1 0**
2001-02 Oldham Ath 24 5
2002-03 Oldham Ath 30 1
2003-04 Oldham Ath 41 9 **95 15**
2004-05 Beira Mar 17 2
2005-06 Beira Mar 0 0 **17 2**
2006-07 Carlisle U 14 1 **55 2**
2007-08 Gretna 32 1 **32 1**
2008-09 Shrewsbury T 32 2
2009-10 Shrewsbury T 27 0 **59 2**
2010-11 Hartlepool U 36 1
2011-12 Hartlepool U 45 1 **81 2**

NISH, Colin (F) 322 78
H: 6 3 W: 11 07 b.Edinburgh 7-3-81
1998-99 Dunfermline Ath 2 0
1999-2000 Dunfermline Ath 2 0
1999-2000 *Alloa Ath* 13 5
2000-01 Dunfermline Ath 4 0
2000-01 *Alloa Ath* 10 3 **23 8**
2001-02 Dunfermline Ath 14 0
2002-03 Dunfermline Ath 0 0 **22 0**
2002-03 *Clyde* 15 5 **15 5**
2003-04 Kilmarnock 30 9
2004-05 Kilmarnock 26 4
2005-06 Kilmarnock 34 7
2006-07 Kilmarnock 33 13
2007-08 Kilmarnock 22 7 **145 40**
2007-08 Hibernian 15 4
2008-09 Hibernian 31 7
2009-10 Hibernian 32 9
2010-11 Hibernian 20 1 **98 21**
2011-12 Hartlepool U 19 4 **19 4**

POOLE, James (F) 39 8
H: 5 11 W: 12 05 b.Stockport 20-3-90
Source: Scholar.
2008-09 Manchester C 0 0
2009-10 Manchester C 0 0
2009-10 *Bury* 9 0 **9 0**
2010-11 Manchester C 0 0
2010-11 *Hartlepool U* 3 1
2011-12 Hartlepool U 27 7 **30 8**

RAFFERTY, Andy (G) 2 0
H: 6 6 W: 13 07 b.Sidcup 27-5-88
Source: Guisborough T.
2010-11 Hartlepool U 1 0
2011-12 Hartlepool U 1 0 **2 0**

RICHARDS, Jordan (M) 2 0
H: 5 9 W: 11 05 b.Sunderland 25-4-93
Source: Scholar.
2011-12 Hartlepool U 2 0 **2 0**

ROWBOTHAM, Josh (M) 2 0
H: 5 11 W: 11 00 b.Stockton 7-1-94
Source: Scholar.
2010-11 Hartlepool U 1 0
2011-12 Hartlepool U 1 0 **2 0**

RUTHERFORD, Greg (M) 1 0
H: 5 10 W: 12 06 b.North Shields 17-5-94
Source: Scholar.
2011-12 Hartlepool U 1 0 **1 0**

SOLANO, Nolberto (M) 494 100
H: 5 8 W: 10 07 b.Callao 12-12-74
Honours: Peru 95 full caps, 20 goals.
1994-95 Sporting Cristal 38 12

1995-96 Sporting Cristal 26 13
1996-97 Sporting Cristal 11 7 **75 32**
1997-98 Boca Juniors 32 5 **32 5**
1998-99 Newcastle U 29 6
1999-2000 Newcastle U 30 3
2000-01 Newcastle U 33 6
2001-02 Newcastle U 37 7
2002-03 Newcastle U 31 7
2003-04 Newcastle U 12 0
2003-04 Aston Villa 10 0
2004-05 Aston Villa 36 8
2005-06 Aston Villa 3 0 **49 8**
2005-06 Newcastle U 29 6
2006-07 Newcastle U 28 2
2007-08 Newcastle U 1 0 **230 37**
2007-08 West Ham U 23 4 **23 4**
2008-09 Larissa 17 2 **17 2**
2009 Universitario 32 10 **32 10**
2009-10 Leicester C 11 0 **11 0**
2010-11 Hull C 11 0 **11 0**
2011-12 Hartlepool U 14 2 **14 2**

SWEENEY, Anthony (M) 332 51
H: 6 0 W: 11 07 b.Stockton 5-9-83
Source: Scholar.
2001-02 Hartlepool U 2 0
2002-03 Hartlepool U 4 0
2003-04 Hartlepool U 11 1
2004-05 Hartlepool U 44 13
2005-06 Hartlepool U 35 5
2006-07 Hartlepool U 35 4
2007-08 Hartlepool U 36 4
2008-09 Hartlepool U 44 5
2009-10 Hartlepool U 42 2
2010-11 Hartlepool U 40 9
2011-12 Hartlepool U 39 8 **332 51**

WRIGHT, Stephen (D) 221 2
H: 6 0 W: 12 06 b.Liverpool 8-2-80
Source: Trainee. *Honours:* England Youth, Under-21.
1997-98 Liverpool 0 0
1998-99 Liverpool 0 0
1999-2000 Liverpool 0 0
1999-2000 *Crewe Alex* 23 0 **23 0**
2000-01 Liverpool 2 0
2001-02 Liverpool 12 0 **14 0**
2002-03 Sunderland 26 0
2003-04 Sunderland 22 1
2004-05 Sunderland 39 1
2005-06 Sunderland 2 0
2006-07 Sunderland 3 0
2007-08 Sunderland 0 0 **92 2**
2007-08 *Stoke C* 16 0 **16 0**
2008-09 Coventry C 17 0
2009-10 Coventry C 38 0
2010-11 Coventry C 0 0 **55 0**
2010-11 Brentford 11 0 **11 0**
2011-12 Hartlepool U 10 0 **10 0**

HEREFORD U (40)

ARQUIN, Yoann (F) 125 25
H: 6 2 W: 13 05 b.Le Havre 15-4-88
2006-07 Nancy B 10 0 **10 0**
2007-08 Nantes B 17 1 **17 1**
2008-09 Quimper 24 9 **24 9**
2009-10 Paris St Germain B 29 5 **29 5**
2010-11 Red Star 93 11 2 **11 2**
2011-12 Hereford U 34 8 **34 8**

BARTLETT, Adam (G) 110 0
H: 6 0 W: 11 11 b.Newcastle-upon-Tyne 27-2-86
Source: Blyth Spartans, Kidderminster H, Cambridge U (loan). *Honours:* England C.
From Kidderminster H.
2009-10 Hereford U 46 0
From Kidderminster H.
2010-11 Hereford U 46 0
From Kidderminster H.
2011-12 Hereford U 18 0 **110 0**

CANHAM, Sean (F) 40 5
H: 6 1 W: 13 01 b.Exeter 26-9-84
Source: Exeter City Scholar, Team Bath.
2008-09 Notts Co 23 3
2009-10 Notts Co 1 0 **24 3**
2010-11 Hereford U 16 2
2011-12 Hereford U 0 0 **16 2**

CLIST, Simon (D) 147 9
H: 5 9 W: 11 09 b.Shaftesbury 13-6-81
Source: Tottenham H Trainee.
1999-2000 Bristol C 9 0
2000-01 Bristol C 38 4
2001-02 Bristol C 20 1
2002-03 Bristol C 3 1
2002-03 *Torquay U* 11 2 **11 2**
2003-04 Bristol C 1 0 **71 6**
2005-06 Barnet 14 0 **14 0**
From Forest Green R.
2010-11 Oxford U 23 1
From Forest Green R.
2011-12 Oxford U 0 0 **23 1**
2011-12 Hereford U 28 0 **28 0**

CLUCAS, Sam (M) 17 0
H: 5 10 W: 11 09 b.Lincoln 20-8-90
Source: Nettleham, Lincoln C.
2011-12 Hereford U 17 0 **17 0**

COLBECK, Joe (M) 214 17
H: 5 10 W: 10 12 b.Bradford 29-11-86
Source: Scholar.
2004-05 Bradford C 0 0
2005-06 Bradford C 11 0
2006-07 Bradford C 32 0
2007-08 Bradford C 33 6
2007-08 *Darlington* 6 2 **6 2**
2008-09 Bradford C 28 2
2009-10 Bradford C 5 0 **109 8**
2009-10 Oldham Ath 27 1 **27 1**
2010-11 Hereford U 44 5
2011-12 Hereford U 28 1 **72 6**

CONNOR, Dan (G) 153 0
H: 6 2 W: 13 04 b.Dublin 31-1-81
Source: Trainee.
1997-98 Peterborough U 0 0
1998-99 Peterborough U 2 0
1999-2000 Peterborough U 1 0
2000-01 Peterborough U 0 0
2001-02 Peterborough U 1 0
2002-03 Peterborough U 4 0 **8 0**
2003 Waterford U 0 0
2004 Waterford 29 0 **29 0**
2005 Drogheda U 29 0
2006 Drogheda U 30 0
2007 Drogheda U 22 0
2008 Drogheda U 1 0 **82 0**
2009 Cork C 28 0 **28 0**
2010 St Patrick's Ath 5 0 **5 0**
2010-11 Hereford U 0 0
2011-12 Hereford U 1 0 **1 0**

DALIBARD, Benoit (D) 29 1
H: 6 2 W: 12 08 b.Landemeau 26-3-91
2009-10 Guingamp 12 0
2010-11 Guingamp 7 1 **19 1**
2011-12 Hereford U 10 0 **10 0**

ELDER, Nathan (F) 111 17
H: 6 1 W: 13 12 b.Hornchurch 5-4-85
Source: Billericay T.
2006-07 Brighton & HA 13 1
2007-08 Brighton & HA 9 1 **22 2**
2007-08 Brentford 17 4
2008-09 Brentford 27 6 **44 10**
2009-10 Shrewsbury T 19 2
2010-11 Shrewsbury T 0 0 **19 2**
2011-12 Hereford U 26 3 **26 3**
On loan from Hayes & Yeading U.

EVANS, Will (M) 25 5
H: 6 2 W: 11 11 b.Cricklade 19-10-91
Source: Scholar.
2010-11 Swindon T 0 0
2011-12 Swindon T 0 0
2011-12 Hereford U 25 5 **25 5**

FACEY, Delroy (F) 408 69
H: 6 0 W: 15 02 b.Huddersfield 22-4-80
Source: Trainee.
1996-97 Huddersfield T 3 0
1997-98 Huddersfield T 3 0
1998-99 Huddersfield T 20 3
1999-2000 Huddersfield T 2 0
2000-01 Huddersfield T 34 10
2001-02 Huddersfield T 13 2
2002-03 Huddersfield T 0 0
2002-03 *Bradford C* 6 1 **6 1**
2002-03 Bolton W 9 1
2003-04 Bolton W 1 0 **10 1**
2003-04 *Burnley* 14 5 **14 5**
2003-04 WBA 9 0 **9 0**
2004-05 Hull C 21 4 **21 4**
2004-05 *Huddersfield T* 4 0 **79 15**
2004-05 Oldham Ath 6 0
2005-06 Oldham Ath 3 0 **9 0**
2005-06 Tranmere R 37 8 **37 8**
2006-07 Rotherham U 40 10 **40 10**
2007-08 Gillingham 32 3 **32 3**
2007-08 *Wycombe W* 6 1 **6 1**
2008-09 Notts Co 45 9
2009-10 Notts Co 18 2 **63 11**
2009-10 *Lincoln C* 10 1
2010-11 Lincoln C 32 3 **42 4**
2011-12 Hereford U 40 6 **40 6**

FEATHERSTONE, Nicky (F) 81 1
H: 5 6 W: 11 02 b.Goole 22-9-88
Source: Scholar.
2006-07 Hull C 2 0
2007-08 Hull C 6 0
2008-09 Hull C 0 0
2009-10 Hull C 0 0
2009-10 *Grimsby T* 8 0 **8 0**
2010-11 Hull C 0 0 **8 0**
2010-11 Hereford U 27 1
2011-12 Hereford U 38 0 **65 1**

FLEETWOOD, Stuart (F) 139 27
H: 5 10 W: 12 07 b.Chepstow 23-4-86
Source: Scholar. *Honours:* Wales Youth, Under-21.
2003-04 Cardiff C 2 0
2004-05 Cardiff C 6 0
2005-06 Cardiff C 0 0 **8 0**
2006-07 Hereford U 27 3
2006-07 *Accrington S* 3 0 **3 0**
2008-09 Charlton Ath 0 0
From Forest Green R.
2008-09 *Cheltenham T* 6 2 **6 2**
2008-09 *Brighton & HA* 11 1 **11 1**
2008-09 *Exeter C* 9 3
2009-10 Charlton Ath 0 0
2009-10 *Exeter C* 27 4 **36 7**
2010-11 Hereford U 43 14
2011-12 Hereford U 5 0 **75 17**

GREEN, Ryan (D) 206 2
H: 5 7 W: 10 10 b.Cardiff 20-10-80
Source: Danes Court. *Honours:* Wales Youth, Under-21, 2 full caps.
1997-98 Wolverhampton W 0 0
1998-99 Wolverhampton W 1 0
1999-2000 Wolverhampton W 0 0
2000-01 Wolverhampton W 7 0
2000-01 *Torquay U* 10 0 **10 0**
2001-02 Wolverhampton W 0 0 **8 0**
2001-02 Millwall 13 0 **13 0**
2002-03 Cardiff C 0 0
2002-03 Sheffield W 4 0 **4 0**
From Hereford U.
2006-07 Bristol R 33 0
2007-08 Bristol R 12 0
2008-09 Bristol R 26 0 **71 0**
2009-10 Hereford U 31 1
2010-11 Hereford U 41 1
2011-12 Hereford U 28 0 **100 2**

HANFORD, Daniel (G) 0 0
b.Swansea 6-3-91
Source: Rochdale Scholar, Glenn Hoddle Acad.
2011-12 Hereford U 0 0

HEATH, Joe (D) 57 0
H: 5 11 W: 11 11 b.Birkenhead 4-10-88
2005-06 Nottingham F 0 0
2006-07 Nottingham F 0 0
2007-08 Nottingham F 0 0
2008-09 Nottingham F 10 0
2009-10 Nottingham F 0 0 **10 0**
2009-10 *Lincoln C* 4 0 **4 0**
2010-11 Exeter C 0 0
2010-11 *Hereford U* 26 0
2011-12 Hereford U 17 0 **43 0**

HOULT, Russell (G) 435 0
H: 6 3 W: 14 09 b.Ashby 22-11-72
Source: Trainee.
1990-91 Leicester C 0 0
1991-92 Leicester C 0 0
1991-92 *Lincoln C* 2 0
1991-92 *Blackpool* 0 0
1992-93 Leicester C 10 0
1993-94 Leicester C 0 0
1993-94 *Bolton W* 4 0 **4 0**
1994-95 Leicester C 0 0 **10 0**
1994-95 *Lincoln C* 15 0 **17 0**
1994-95 *Derby Co* 15 0

1995-96	Derby Co	41	0		
1996-97	Derby Co	32	0		
1997-98	Derby Co	2	0		
1998-99	Derby Co	23	0		
1999-2000	Derby Co	10	0	**123**	**0**
1999-2000	Portsmouth	18	0		
2000-01	Portsmouth	22	0	**40**	**0**
2000-01	WBA	13	0		
2001-02	WBA	45	0		
2002-03	WBA	37	0		
2003-04	WBA	44	0		
2004-05	WBA	36	0		
2005-06	WBA	1	0		
2005-06	*Nottingham F*	8	0	**8**	**0**
2006-07	WBA	14	0	**190**	**0**
2006-07	Stoke C	0	0		
2007-08	Stoke C	1	0	**1**	**0**
2007-08	*Notts Co*	14	0		
2008-09	Notts Co	16	0		
2009-10	Notts Co	4	0	**34**	**0**
2009-10	*Darlington*	6	0	**6**	**0**
2010-11	Hereford U	0	0		
2011-12	Hereford U	2	0	**2**	**0**

KOVACS, Janos (D) **141** **8**
H: 6 4 W: 14 10 b.Budapest 11-9-85
Source: MTK. *Honours:* Hungary Under-20.

2005-06	Chesterfield	9	0		
2006-07	Chesterfield	7	0		
2007-08	Chesterfield	41	2	**57**	**2**
2008-09	Lincoln C	45	3		
2009-10	Lincoln C	14	1	**59**	**4**
2010-11	Hereford U	25	2		
2011-12	Hereford U	0	0	**25**	**2**

LUNT, Kenny (M) **540** **36**
H: 5 10 W: 10 05 b.Runcorn 20-11-79
Source: Trainee. *Honours:* England Schools, Youth.

1997-98	Crewe Alex	41	2		
1998-99	Crewe Alex	18	1		
1999-2000	Crewe Alex	43	3		
2000-01	Crewe Alex	46	1		
2001-02	Crewe Alex	45	5		
2002-03	Crewe Alex	46	7		
2003-04	Crewe Alex	45	7		
2004-05	Crewe Alex	46	5		
2005-06	Crewe Alex	43	4		
2006-07	Sheffield W	37	0		
2007-08	Sheffield W	4	0		
2007-08	*Crewe Alex*	14	0		
2008-09	Sheffield W	0	0	**41**	**0**
2008-09	*Crewe Alex*	3	0	**390**	**35**
2009-10	Hereford U	42	1		
2010-11	Hereford U	42	0		
2011-12	Hereford U	25	0	**109**	**1**

McQUILKIN, James (F) **73** **5**
H: 5 8 W: 11 10 b.Tipton 9-1-89
Source: WBA Scholar. *Honours:* Northern Ireland Youth, Under-21.

2007-08	Zlin	4	0		
2008-09	Zlin	2	0	**6**	**0**
2009-10	Hereford U	22	2		
2010-11	Hereford U	38	3		
2011-12	Hereford U	7	0	**67**	**5**

PELL, Harry (M) **47** **3**
H: 6 4 W: 13 05 b.Tilbury 21-10-91
Source: Charlton Ath Scholar.

2010-11	Bristol R	10	0	**10**	**0**
2010-11	*Hereford U*	7	0		
2011-12	Hereford U	30	3	**37**	**3**

PURDIE, Rob (M) **182** **19**
H: 5 9 W: 11 06 b.Leicester 28-9-82
Source: Leicester C.

2006-07	Hereford U	44	6		
2007-08	Darlington	39	0		
2008-09	Darlington	40	6	**79**	**6**
2009-10	Oldham Ath	0	0		
2010-11	Oldham Ath	0	0		
2010-11	Hereford U	25	3		
2011-12	Hereford U	34	4	**103**	**13**

PURKISS, Ben (D) **38** **0**
H: 6 2 W: 11 00 b.Sheffield 1-4-84

2001-02	Sheffield U	0	0		
2002-03	Sheffield U	0	0		
From Gainsborough T, York C.					
2010-11	Oxford U	23	0		
From Gainsborough T, York C.					
2011-12	Oxford U	0	0	**23**	**0**
2011-12	Hereford U	15	0	**15**	**0**

STAM, Stefan (D) **152** **2**
H: 6 2 W: 13 02 b.Amersfoort 14-9-79
Honours: Holland Under-21.

2004-05	Oldham Ath	13	0		
2005-06	Oldham Ath	13	0		
2006-07	Oldham Ath	22	1		
2007-08	Oldham Ath	36	0		
2008-09	Oldham Ath	13	0	**97**	**1**
2009-10	Yeovil T	18	1		
2010-11	Yeovil T	3	0	**21**	**1**
2010-11	*Hereford U*	10	0		
2011-12	Hereford U	24	0	**34**	**0**

TODD, Andy (D) **340** **11**
H: 5 11 W: 13 04 b.Derby 21-9-74
Source: Trainee.

1991-92	Middlesbrough	0	0		
1992-93	Middlesbrough	0	0		
1993-94	Middlesbrough	3	0		
1994-95	Middlesbrough	5	0	**8**	**0**
1994-95	*Swindon T*	13	0	**13**	**0**
1995-96	Bolton W	12	2		
1996-97	Bolton W	15	0		
1997-98	Bolton W	25	0		
1998-99	Bolton W	20	0		
1999-2000	Bolton W	12	0	**84**	**2**
1999-2000	Charlton Ath	12	0		
2000-01	Charlton Ath	23	1		
2001-02	Charlton Ath	5	0	**40**	**1**
2001-02	*Grimsby T*	12	3	**12**	**3**
2002-03	Blackburn R	12	1		
2003-04	Blackburn R	19	0		
2003-04	*Burnley*	7	0	**7**	**0**
2004-05	Blackburn R	26	1		
2005-06	Blackburn R	22	2		
2006-07	Blackburn R	9	0	**88**	**4**
2007-08	Derby Co	19	1		
2008-09	Derby Co	11	0	**30**	**1**
2008-09	*Northampton T*	7	0	**7**	**0**
2009-10	Perth Glory	25	0		
2010-11	Perth Glory	16	0	**41**	**0**
2010-11	Oldham Ath	6	0	**6**	**0**
2011-12	Hereford U	4	0	**4**	**0**

TOWNSEND, Michael (D) **229** **7**
H: 6 1 W: 13 12 b.Walsall 17-5-86
Source: Wolverhampton W scholar.

2004-05	Cheltenham T	0	0		
2005-06	Cheltenham T	31	0		
2006-07	Cheltenham T	30	1		
2007-08	Cheltenham T	13	1		
2008-09	Cheltenham T	26	1		
2008-09	*Barnet*	13	0	**13**	**0**
2009-10	Cheltenham T	34	3	**134**	**6**
2010-11	Hereford U	43	1		
2011-12	Hereford U	39	0	**82**	**1**

WEIR, Tyler (D) **7** **0**
H: 5 10 W: 11 10 b.Hereford 21-12-90
Source: Youth.

2009-10	Hereford U	3	0		
2010-11	Hereford U	4	0		
2011-12	Hereford U	0	0	**7**	**0**

WILLIAMS, Danny (D) **36** **0**
H: 5 9 W: 9 13 b.Sheffield 2-3-81
Source: Trainee.

1999-2000	Chesterfield	5	0		
2000-01	Chesterfield	2	0		
2001-02	Chesterfield	24	0	**31**	**0**
From Hereford U, Stevenage B, Forest R, Rushden & D, Northwich Vic, Montegnee, AFC Telford U.					
2011-12	Hereford U	5	0	**5**	**0**

HUDDERSFIELD T (41)

ALLINSON, Lloyd (G) **0** **0**
H: 6 2 W: 13 00 b.Rothwell 7-9-93
Source: Scholar.

2010-11	Huddersfield T	0	0		
2011-12	Huddersfield T	0	0		

ARFIELD, Scott (M) **183** **19**
H: 5 10 W: 10 01 b.Livingston 1-11-88
Honours: Scotland Under-21, B.

2007-08	Falkirk	35	3		
2008-09	Falkirk	37	7		
2009-10	Falkirk	36	3	**108**	**13**
2010-11	Huddersfield T	40	4		
2011-12	Huddersfield T	35	2	**75**	**6**

ATKINSON, Chris (M) **3** **0**
H: 6 1 W: 11 13 b. 13-2-92
Source: Scholar.

2010-11	Huddersfield T	2	0		
2011-12	Huddersfield T	1	0	**3**	**0**

BENNETT, Ian (G) **447** **0**
H: 6 0 W: 12 10 b.Worksop 10-10-71
Source: Newcastle U Trainee.

1991-92	Peterborough U	7	0		
1992-93	Peterborough U	46	0		
1993-94	Peterborough U	19	0	**72**	**0**
1993-94	Birmingham C	22	0		
1994-95	Birmingham C	46	0		
1995-96	Birmingham C	24	0		
1996-97	Birmingham C	40	0		
1997-98	Birmingham C	45	0		
1998-99	Birmingham C	10	0		
1999-2000	Birmingham C	21	0		
2000-01	Birmingham C	45	0		
2001-02	Birmingham C	18	0		
2002-03	Birmingham C	10	0		
2003-04	Birmingham C	6	0		
2004-05	Birmingham C	0	0	**287**	**0**
2004-05	*Sheffield U*	5	0		
2004-05	*Coventry C*	6	0	**6**	**0**
2005-06	Leeds U	4	0		
2006-07	Leeds U	0	0	**4**	**0**
2006-07	Sheffield U	2	0		
2007-08	Sheffield U	7	0		
2008-09	Sheffield U	2	0		
2009-10	Sheffield U	5	0	**21**	**0**
2010-11	Huddersfield T	24	0		
2011-12	Huddersfield T	33	0	**57**	**0**

CADAMARTERI, Danny (F) **324** **35**
H: 5 7 W: 13 05 b.Cleckheaton 12-10-79
Source: Trainee. *Honours:* England Youth, Under-21.

1996-97	Everton	1	0		
1997-98	Everton	26	4		
1998-99	Everton	30	4		
1999-2000	Everton	17	1		
1999-2000	*Fulham*	5	1	**5**	**1**
2000-01	Everton	16	4		
2001-02	Everton	3	0	**93**	**13**
2001-02	Bradford C	14	2		
2002-03	Bradford C	20	0		
2003-04	Bradford C	18	3		
2004-05	Leeds U	0	0		
2004-05	Sheffield U	21	1	**21**	**1**
2005-06	Bradford C	39	2		
2006-07	Bradford C	0	0	**91**	**7**
2006-07	*Doncaster R*	6	1	**6**	**1**
2006-07	Leicester C	9	0	**9**	**0**
2007-08	Huddersfield T	12	3		
2008-09	Huddersfield T	32	2		
2009-10	Huddersfield T	0	0		
2009-10	Dundee U	21	4		
2010-11	Dundee U	8	0	**29**	**4**
2010-11	Huddersfield T	11	3		
2011-12	Huddersfield T	15	0	**70**	**8**

CHIPPENDALE, Aiden (M) **6** **0**
H: 5 8 W: 10 10 b.Bradford 24-5-92
Source: Scholar.

2010-11	Huddersfield T	1	0		
2011-12	Huddersfield T	0	0	**1**	**0**
2011-12	*Inverness CT*	5	0	**5**	**0**

CLARKE, Nathan (D) **309** **9**
H: 6 2 W: 12 00 b.Halifax 30-11-83
Source: Scholar.

2001-02	Huddersfield T	36	1		
2002-03	Huddersfield T	3	0		
2003-04	Huddersfield T	26	1		
2004-05	Huddersfield T	37	0		
2005-06	Huddersfield T	46	0		
2006-07	Huddersfield T	16	0		
2007-08	Huddersfield T	44	2		
2008-09	Huddersfield T	38	3		
2009-10	Huddersfield T	17	1		
2010-11	Huddersfield T	1	0		
2010-11	*Colchester U*	18	0	**18**	**0**
2011-12	Huddersfield T	0	0	**264**	**8**
2011-12	*Oldham Ath*	16	1	**16**	**1**
2011-12	*Bury*	11	0	**11**	**0**

CLARKE, Peter (D) **376** **34**
H: 6 0 W: 12 00 b.Southport 3-1-82
Source: Trainee. *Honours:* England Schools, Youth, Under-20, Under-21.

1998-99	Everton	0	0		
1999-2000	Everton	0	0		
2000-01	Everton	1	0		

2001-02 Everton 7 0
2002-03 Everton 0 0
2002-03 *Blackpool* 16 3
2002-03 *Port Vale* 13 1 **13 1**
2003-04 Everton 1 0
2003-04 *Coventry C* 5 0 **5 0**
2004-05 Everton 0 0 **9 0**
2004-05 Blackpool 38 5
2005-06 Blackpool 46 6 **100 14**
2006-07 Southend U 38 2
2007-08 Southend U 45 4
2008-09 Southend U 43 4 **126 10**
2009-10 Huddersfield T 46 5
2010-11 Huddersfield T 46 4
2011-12 Huddersfield T 31 0 **123 9**

CLARKE, Tom (D) **112 3**
H: 6 0 W: 11 02 b.Sowerby Bridge 21-12-87
Source: Scholar. *Honours:* England Youth.
2004-05 Huddersfield T 12 0
2005-06 Huddersfield T 17 1
2006-07 Huddersfield T 9 0
2007-08 Huddersfield T 3 0
2008-09 Huddersfield T 15 1
2008-09 *Bradford C* 6 0 **6 0**
2009-10 Huddersfield T 21 0
2010-11 Huddersfield T 5 1
2011-12 Huddersfield T 14 0 **96 3**
2011-12 *Leyton Orient* 10 0 **10 0**

COLGAN, Nick (G) **283 0**
H: 6 1 W: 12 00 b.Drogheda 19-9-73
Source: Drogheda. *Honours:* Eire Schools, Youth, Under-21, B, 9 full caps.
1992-93 Chelsea 0 0
1993-94 Chelsea 0 0
1993-94 *Crewe Alex* 0 0
1994-95 Chelsea 0 0
1994-95 *Grimsby T* 0 0
1995-96 Chelsea 0 0
1995-96 *Millwall* 0 0
1996-97 Chelsea 1 0
1997-98 Chelsea 0 0 **1 0**
1997-98 *Brentford* 5 0 **5 0**
1997-98 *Reading* 5 0 **5 0**
1998-99 Bournemouth 0 0
1999-2000 Hibernian 24 0
2000-01 Hibernian 37 0
2001-02 Hibernian 30 0
2002-03 Hibernian 30 0
2003-04 Hibernian 0 0 **121 0**
2003-04 *Stockport Co* 15 0 **15 0**
2004-05 Barnsley 13 0
2005-06 Barnsley 43 0
2006-07 Barnsley 44 0
2007-08 Barnsley 1 0 **101 0**
2007-08 Ipswich T 0 0
2008-09 Sunderland 0 0
2009-10 Grimsby T 35 0 **35 0**
2011-12 Huddersfield T 0 0

CROOKS, Matt (M) **0 0**
b.Leeds 20-1-94
Source: Scholar.
2011-12 Huddersfield T 0 0

FIELD, Adam (D) **0 0**
b.Huddersfield 3-11-92
Source: Scholar.
2011-12 Huddersfield T 0 0

GOBERN, Oscar (M) **44 3**
H: 5 11 W: 10 10 b.Birmingham 26-1-91
Source: Scholar. *Honours:* England Youth.
2008-09 Southampton 6 0
2009-10 Southampton 4 0
2009-10 *Milton Keynes D* 2 0 **2 0**
2010-11 Southampton 11 1 **21 1**
2011-12 Huddersfield T 21 2 **21 2**

GUDJONSSON, Joey (M) **303 30**
H: 5 9 W: 12 04 b.Akranes 25-5-80
Honours: Iceland Youth, Under-21, 34 full caps, 1 goal.
1998-99 Genk 5 0 **5 0**
1999-2000 MVV 19 5 **19 5**
2000-01 RKC 31 4 **31 4**
2001-02 Betis 11 0 **11 0**
2002-03 Aston Villa 11 2 **11 2**
2003-04 Wolverhampton W 11 0 **11 0**
2004-05 Leicester C 35 2
2005-06 Leicester C 42 8 **77 10**
2006-07 AZ 5 0 **5 0**
2006-07 Burnley 11 0
2007-08 Burnley 28 1
2008-09 Burnley 39 6
2009-10 Burnley 10 0 **88 7**
2010-11 Huddersfield T 37 2
2011-12 Huddersfield T 8 0 **45 2**

HIGGINBOTHAM, Kallum (F) **140 14**
H: 5 11 W: 10 10 b.Manchester 15-6-89
2007-08 Rochdale 33 3
2008-09 Rochdale 7 1
2008-09 *Accrington S* 12 0 **12 0**
2009-10 Rochdale 29 3 **69 7**
2010-11 Falkirk 30 2
2011-12 Falkirk 20 5 **50 7**
2011-12 Huddersfield T 4 0 **4 0**
2011-12 *Barnsley* 5 0 **5 0**

HUNT, Jack (D) **82 2**
H: 5 9 W: 11 02 b.Rothwell 6-12-90
Source: Scholar.
2009-10 Huddersfield T 0 0
2010-11 Huddersfield T 19 1
2010-11 *Chesterfield* 20 0 **20 0**
2011-12 Huddersfield T 43 1 **62 2**

KAY, Antony (D) **351 38**
H: 5 11 W: 11 08 b.Barnsley 21-10-82
Source: Trainee. *Honours:* England Youth.
1999-2000 Barnsley 0 0
2000-01 Barnsley 7 0
2001-02 Barnsley 1 0
2002-03 Barnsley 16 0
2003-04 Barnsley 43 3
2004-05 Barnsley 39 6
2005-06 Barnsley 36 1
2006-07 Barnsley 32 1 **174 11**
2007-08 Tranmere R 38 6
2008-09 Tranmere R 44 11 **82 17**
2009-10 Huddersfield T 40 6
2010-11 Huddersfield T 27 3
2011-12 Huddersfield T 28 1 **95 10**

LEE, Alan (F) **460 101**
H: 6 2 W: 13 09 b.Galway 21-8-78
Source: Trainee. *Honours:* Eire Under-21, 10 full caps.
1995-96 Aston Villa 0 0
1996-97 Aston Villa 0 0
1997-98 Aston Villa 0 0
1998-99 Aston Villa 0 0
1998-99 *Torquay U* 7 2 **7 2**
1998-99 *Port Vale* 11 2 **11 2**
1999-2000 Burnley 15 0
2000-01 Burnley 0 0 **15 0**
2000-01 Rotherham U 31 13
2001-02 Rotherham U 38 9
2002-03 Rotherham U 41 15
2003-04 Rotherham U 1 0 **111 37**
2003-04 Cardiff C 23 3
2004-05 Cardiff C 38 5
2005-06 Cardiff C 25 2 **86 10**
2005-06 Ipswich T 14 4
2006-07 Ipswich T 41 16
2007-08 Ipswich T 45 11
2008-09 Ipswich T 3 0 **103 31**
2008-09 Crystal Palace 16 3
2008-09 *Norwich C* 7 2 **7 2**
2009-10 Crystal Palace 42 6
2010-11 Crystal Palace 3 1 **61 10**
2010-11 Huddersfield T 28 0
2011-12 Huddersfield T 31 7 **59 7**

McCOMBE, Jamie (D) **329 25**
H: 6 5 W: 12 05 b.Scunthorpe 1-1-83
Source: Scholar.
2001-02 Scunthorpe U 17 0
2002-03 Scunthorpe U 31 1
2003-04 Scunthorpe U 15 0 **63 1**
2003-04 Lincoln C 8 0
2004-05 Lincoln C 41 3
2005-06 Lincoln C 38 4 **87 7**
2006-07 Bristol C 41 4
2007-08 Bristol C 34 3
2008-09 Bristol C 28 1
2009-10 Bristol C 16 1 **119 9**
2010-11 Huddersfield T 34 5
2011-12 Huddersfield T 20 3 **54 8**
2011-12 *Preston NE* 6 0 **6 0**

MILLER, Tommy (M) **443 89**
H: 6 0 W: 11 07 b.Shotton 8-1-79
Source: Trainee.
1997-98 Hartlepool U 13 1
1998-99 Hartlepool U 34 4
1999-2000 Hartlepool U 44 14
2000-01 Hartlepool U 46 16
2001-02 Hartlepool U 0 0 **137 35**
2001-02 Ipswich T 8 0
2002-03 Ipswich T 30 6
2003-04 Ipswich T 34 11
2004-05 Ipswich T 45 13
2005-06 Sunderland 29 3
2006-07 Sunderland 4 0 **33 3**
2006-07 *Preston NE* 7 0 **7 0**
2007-08 Ipswich T 37 5
2008-09 Ipswich T 32 5 **186 40**
2009-10 Sheffield W 20 1
2010-11 Sheffield W 34 9 **54 10**
2011-12 Huddersfield T 26 1 **26 1**

NAYSMITH, Gary (D) **346 9**
H: 5 9 W: 12 01 b.Edinburgh 16-11-78
Source: Whitehill Welfare Colts. *Honours:* Scotland Schools, Under-21, B, 46 full caps, 1 goal.
1995-96 Hearts 1 0
1996-97 Hearts 10 0
1997-98 Hearts 16 2
1998-99 Hearts 26 0
1999-2000 Hearts 35 1
2000-01 Hearts 9 0 **97 3**
2000-01 Everton 20 2
2001-02 Everton 24 0
2002-03 Everton 28 1
2003-04 Everton 29 2
2004-05 Everton 11 0
2005-06 Everton 7 0
2006-07 Everton 15 1 **134 6**
2007-08 Sheffield U 38 0
2008-09 Sheffield U 39 0
2009-10 Sheffield U 2 0 **79 0**
2010-11 Huddersfield T 14 0
2011-12 Huddersfield T 22 0 **36 0**

NOVAK, Lee (F) **109 30**
H: 6 0 W: 12 04 b.Newcastle 28-9-88
Source: Gateshead.
2008-09 Huddersfield T 0 0
2009-10 Huddersfield T 37 12
2010-11 Huddersfield T 31 5
2011-12 Huddersfield T 41 13 **109 30**

PEARSON, Greg (D) **0 0**
b.Sowerby Bridge 25-12-92
Source: Scholar.
2011-12 Huddersfield T 0 0

RHODES, Jordan (F) **151 80**
H: 6 1 W: 11 03 b.Oldham 5-2-90
Source: Academy. *Honours:* Scotland Under-21, 1 full cap.
2007-08 Ipswich T 8 1
2008-09 Ipswich T 2 0 **10 1**
2008-09 *Rochdale* 5 2 **5 2**
2008-09 *Brentford* 14 7 **14 7**
2009-10 Huddersfield T 45 19
2010-11 Huddersfield T 37 16
2011-12 Huddersfield T 40 35 **122 70**

RIDEHALGH, Liam (D) **51 1**
H: 5 10 W: 11 05 b.Halifax 20-4-91
Source: Scholar.
2009-10 Huddersfield T 0 0
2010-11 Huddersfield T 20 0
2011-12 Huddersfield T 0 0 **20 0**
2011-12 *Swindon T* 11 0 **11 0**
2011-12 *Chesterfield* 20 1 **20 1**

ROBERTS, Gary (F) **234 42**
H: 5 10 W: 11 09 b.Chester 18-3-84
Source: Denbigh T, Bangor C.
2006-07 Accrington S 14 8 **14 8**
2006-07 Ipswich T 33 2
2007-08 Ipswich T 21 1 **54 3**
2007-08 *Crewe Alex* 4 0 **4 0**
2008-09 Huddersfield T 43 9
2009-10 Huddersfield T 43 7
2010-11 Huddersfield T 37 9
2011-12 Huddersfield T 39 6 **162 31**

ROBINSON, Anton (M) **131 11**
H: 5 9 W: 10 03 b.Harrow 17-2-86
Source: Millwall Scholar.
2004-05 Millwall 0 0
2005-06 Millwall 0 0
From Ex C, Eastb B, Fish A, Weymouth.
2008-09 Bournemouth 17 1
2009-10 Bournemouth 44 4
2010-11 Bournemouth 45 5 **106 10**
2011-12 Huddersfield T 25 1 **25 1**

SMITHIES, Alex (G) **110 0**
H: 6 1 W: 10 01 b.Huddersfield 25-3-90
Source: Scholar. *Honours:* England Youth.

2006-07	Huddersfield T	0	0		
2007-08	Huddersfield T	2	0		
2008-09	Huddersfield T	27	0		
2009-10	Huddersfield T	46	0		
2010-11	Huddersfield T	22	0		
2011-12	Huddersfield T	13	0	**110**	**0**

SPENCER, James (F) **73 18**
H: 6 1 W: 13 00 b.Leeds 13-12-91
Source: Scholar.

2008-09	Huddersfield T	0	0		
2009-10	Huddersfield T	0	0		
2010-11	Huddersfield T	0	0		
2010-11	*Morecambe*	32	8	**32**	**8**
2011-12	Huddersfield T	0	0		
2011-12	*Cheltenham T*	41	10	**41**	**10**

THOMAS, Simon (G) **20 0**
b.Victoria 12-4-90

2008-09	Whitecaps Res	13	0		
2009-10	Vancouver W'caps	1	0	**1**	**0**
2009-10	*Whitecaps Res*	6	0	**19**	**0**
2011-12	Huddersfield T	0	0		

WALLACE, Murray (D) **19 2**
H: 6 2 W: 11 07 b.Glasgow 10-1-93

2011-12	Falkirk	19	2	**19**	**2**
2011-12	Huddersfield T	0	0		

WARD, Danny (M) **81 14**
H: 5 11 W: 12 05 b.Bradford 11-12-91
Source: Leeds U.

2008-09	Bolton W	0	0		
2009-10	Bolton W	2	0		
2009-10	*Swindon T*	28	7	**28**	**7**
2010-11	Bolton W	0	0	**2**	**0**
2010-11	*Coventry C*	5	0	**5**	**0**
2010-11	*Huddersfield T*	7	3		
2011-12	Huddersfield T	39	4	**46**	**7**

WOODS, Calum (D) **154 10**
H: 5 11 W: 11 07 b.Liverpool 5-2-87
Source: Liverpool Scholar. *Honours:* England Youth.

2006-07	Dunfermline Ath	12	0		
2007-08	Dunfermline Ath	25	0		
2008-09	Dunfermline Ath	30	5		
2009-10	Dunfermline Ath	29	2		
2010-11	Dunfermline Ath	32	3	**128**	**10**
2011-12	Huddersfield T	26	0	**26**	**0**

HULL C (42)

ADEBOLA, Dele (F) **612 132**
H: 6 3 W: 12 08 b.Lagos 23-6-75
Source: Trainee.

1992-93	Crewe Alex	6	0		
1993-94	Crewe Alex	0	0		
1994-95	Crewe Alex	30	8		
1995-96	Crewe Alex	29	8		
1996-97	Crewe Alex	32	16		
1997-98	Crewe Alex	27	7	**124**	**39**
1997-98	Birmingham C	17	7		
1998-99	Birmingham C	39	13		
1999-2000	Birmingham C	42	5		
2000-01	Birmingham C	31	6		
2001-02	Birmingham C	0	0	**129**	**31**
2001-02	*Oldham Ath*	5	0	**5**	**0**
2002-03	Crystal Palace	39	5	**39**	**5**
2003-04	Coventry C	28	2		
2003-04	*Burnley*	3	1	**3**	**1**
2004-05	Coventry C	25	5		
2004-05	*Bradford C*	15	3	**15**	**3**
2005-06	Coventry C	44	12		
2006-07	Coventry C	40	8		
2007-08	Coventry C	26	4	**163**	**31**
2007-08	Bristol C	17	6		
2008-09	Bristol C	39	10	**56**	**16**
2009-10	Nottingham F	33	3		
2010-11	Nottingham F	29	2	**62**	**5**
2011-12	Hull C	10	0	**10**	**0**
2011-12	*Notts Co*	6	1	**6**	**1**

ATKINSON, Will (M) **95 12**
H: 5 10 W: 10 07 b.Beverley 14-10-88
Source: Scholar.

2006-07	Hull C	0	0		
2007-08	Hull C	0	0		
2007-08	*Port Vale*	4	0	**4**	**0**
2007-08	*Mansfield T*	12	0	**12**	**0**
2008-09	Hull C	0	0		
2009-10	Hull C	2	1		
2009-10	*Rochdale*	15	3		
2010-11	Hull C	4	0		
2010-11	*Rotherham U*	3	1	**3**	**1**
2010-11	*Rochdale*	21	2	**36**	**5**
2011-12	Hull C	0	0	**6**	**1**
2011-12	*Plymouth Arg*	22	4	**22**	**4**
2011-12	*Bradford C*	12	1	**12**	**1**

BARMBY, Nick (F) **488 79**
H: 5 7 W: 11 03 b.Hull 11-2-74
Source: Trainee. *Honours:* England Schools, Youth, Under-21, B, 23 full caps, 4 goals.

1991-92	Tottenham H	0	0		
1992-93	Tottenham H	22	6		
1993-94	Tottenham H	27	5		
1994-95	Tottenham H	38	9	**87**	**20**
1995-96	Middlesbrough	32	7		
1996-97	Middlesbrough	10	1	**42**	**8**
1996-97	Everton	25	4		
1997-98	Everton	30	2		
1998-99	Everton	24	3		
1999-2000	Everton	37	9	**116**	**18**
2000-01	Liverpool	26	2		
2001-02	Liverpool	6	0	**32**	**2**
2002-03	Leeds U	19	4		
2003-04	*Nottingham F*	6	1	**6**	**1**
2003-04	Leeds U	6	0	**25**	**4**
2004-05	Hull C	39	9		
2005-06	Hull C	26	5		
2006-07	Hull C	20	4		
2007-08	Hull C	15	1		
2008-09	Hull C	21	1		
2009-10	Hull C	20	0		
2010-11	Hull C	31	5		
2011-12	Hull C	8	1	**180**	**26**

BASSO, Adriano (G) **178 0**
H: 6 1 W: 11 07 b.Jundiai 18-4-75
Source: Ponte Preta, Atletico Paranaense, St Albans C, Woking.

2005-06	Bristol C	29	0		
2006-07	Bristol C	45	0		
2007-08	Bristol C	44	0		
2008-09	Bristol C	43	0		
2009-10	Bristol C	4	0	**165**	**0**
2010-11	Flamengo	0	0		
2010-11	Wolverhampton W	0	0		
2011-12	Hull C	13	0	**13**	**0**

BRADLEY, Sonny (D) **16 0**
H: 6 0 W: 11 05 b.Hedon 14-6-92
Source: Scholar.

2011-12	Hull C	2	0	**2**	**0**
2011-12	*Aldershot T*	14	0	**14**	**0**

CAIRNEY, Tom (M) **60 2**
H: 6 0 W: 11 05 b.Nottingham 20-1-91
Source: Scholar. *Honours:* Scotland Youth, Under-21.

2009-10	Hull C	11	1		
2010-11	Hull C	22	1		
2011-12	Hull C	27	0	**60**	**2**

CHESTER, James (D) **91 5**
H: 5 11 W: 11 04 b.Warrington 23-1-89
Source: Scholar.

2007-08	Manchester U	0	0		
2008-09	Manchester U	0	0		
2008-09	*Peterborough U*	5	0	**5**	**0**
2009-10	Manchester U	0	0		
2009-10	*Plymouth Arg*	3	0	**3**	**0**
2010-11	Manchester U	0	0		
2010-11	*Carlisle U*	18	2	**18**	**2**
2010-11	Hull C	21	1		
2011-12	Hull C	44	2	**65**	**3**

COOPER, Liam (D) **21 1**
H: 6 2 W: 13 07 b.Hull 30-8-91
Source: Scholar. *Honours:* Scotland Youth.

2008-09	Hull C	0	0		
2009-10	Hull C	2	0		
2010-11	Hull C	2	0		
2010-11	*Carlisle U*	6	1	**6**	**1**
2011-12	Hull C	7	0	**11**	**0**
2011-12	*Huddersfield T*	4	0	**4**	**0**

CULLEN, Mark (F) **32 1**
H: 5 9 W: 11 11 b.Ashington 24-4-92
Source: Scholar.

2009-10	Hull C	3	1		
2010-11	Hull C	17	0		
2010-11	*Bradford C*	4	0	**4**	**0**
2011-12	Hull C	4	0	**24**	**1**
2011-12	*Bury*	4	0	**4**	**0**

DAWSON, Andy (D) **484 16**
H: 5 9 W: 11 02 b.Leyburn 20-10-78
Source: Trainee.

1995-96	Nottingham F	0	0		
1996-97	Nottingham F	0	0		
1997-98	Nottingham F	0	0		
1998-99	Nottingham F	0	0		
1998-99	Scunthorpe U	24	0		
1999-2000	Scunthorpe U	43	2		
2000-01	Scunthorpe U	41	4		
2001-02	Scunthorpe U	44	0		
2002-03	Scunthorpe U	43	2	**195**	**8**
2003-04	Hull C	33	3		
2004-05	Hull C	34	0		
2005-06	Hull C	18	0		
2006-07	Hull C	38	2		
2007-08	Hull C	29	1		
2008-09	Hull C	25	1		
2009-10	Hull C	35	1		
2010-11	Hull C	45	0		
2011-12	Hull C	32	0	**289**	**8**

DEVITT, Jamie (F) **69 11**
H: 5 10 W: 10 05 b.Dublin 6-7-90
Source: Cherry Orchard BC, Hull C Scholar. *Honours:* Eire Youth, Under-21.

2007-08	Hull C	0	0		
2008-09	Hull C	0	0		
2009-10	Hull C	0	0		
2009-10	*Darlington*	6	1	**6**	**1**
2009-10	*Shrewsbury T*	9	2	**9**	**2**
2009-10	*Grimsby T*	15	5	**15**	**5**
2010-11	Hull C	16	0		
2011-12	Hull C	0	0	**16**	**0**
2011-12	*Bradford C*	7	1	**7**	**1**
2011-12	*Accrington S*	16	2	**16**	**2**

DILLON, Kealan (F) **0 0**
b.Mullingar 21-2-94
Source: Scholar. *Honours:* Eire Youth.

2010-11	Derby Co	0	0		
2011-12	Derby Co	0	0		
2011-12	Hull C	0	0		

DUDGEON, Joe (D) **26 0**
H: 5 9 W: 11 02 b.Leeds 26-11-90
Source: Scholar. *Honours:* Northern Ireland Under-21.

2009-10	Manchester U	0	0		
2010-11	Manchester U	0	0		
2010-11	*Carlisle U*	2	0	**2**	**0**
2011-12	Hull C	24	0	**24**	**0**

EAST, Danny (D) **0 0**
b.Hessle 26-12-91
Source: Scholar.

2011-12	Hull C	0	0		

EMERTON, Danny (M) **0 0**
H: 5 10 W: 11 02 b.Beverley 27-9-91
Source: Scholar.

2010-11	Hull C	0	0		
2011-12	Hull C	0	0		

EVANS, Corry (M) **62 5**
H: 5 8 W: 10 12 b.Belfast 30-7-90
Source: Scholar. *Honours:* Northern Ireland Under-21, B, 16 full caps, 1 goal.

2007-08	Manchester U	0	0		
2008-09	Manchester U	0	0		
2009-10	Manchester U	0	0		
2010-11	Manchester U	0	0		
2010-11	*Carlisle U*	1	0	**1**	**0**
2010-11	*Hull C*	18	3		
2011-12	Hull C	43	2	**61**	**5**

FRYATT, Matty (F) **316 104**
H: 5 10 W: 11 00 b.Nuneaton 5-3-86
Source: Scholar. *Honours:* England Youth.

2002-03	Walsall	0	0		
2003-04	Walsall	11	1		
2003-04	*Carlisle U*	10	1	**10**	**1**
2004-05	Walsall	36	15		
2005-06	Walsall	23	11	**70**	**27**
2005-06	Leicester C	19	6		
2006-07	Leicester C	32	3		
2007-08	Leicester C	30	2		
2008-09	Leicester C	46	27		
2009-10	Leicester C	29	11		
2010-11	Leicester C	12	2	**168**	**51**
2010-11	Hull C	22	9		
2011-12	Hull C	46	16	**68**	**25**

GARCIA, Richard (F) **230 28**
H: 5 11 W: 12 01 b.Perth 4-9-81
Source: Trainee. *Honours:* Australia Under-23, 13 full caps.

1998-99	West Ham U	0	0		
1999-2000	West Ham U	0	0		
2000-01	West Ham U	0	0		
2000-01	*Leyton Orient*	18	4	**18**	**4**
2001-02	West Ham U	8	0		
2002-03	West Ham U	0	0		
2003-04	West Ham U	7	0		
2004-05	West Ham U	1	0	**16**	**0**
2004-05	Colchester U	24	4		
2005-06	Colchester U	22	5		
2006-07	Colchester U	36	7	**82**	**16**
2007-08	Hull C	38	5		
2008-09	Hull C	23	1		
2009-10	Hull C	18	0		
2010-11	Hull C	25	2		
2011-12	Hull C	10	0	**114**	**8**

GHILAS, Kamel (F) **208 54**
H: 5 10 W: 11 00 b.Marseille 9-3-84
Honours: Algeria 16 full caps, 3 goals.

2003-04	Cannes	18	0		
2004-05	Cannes	31	7		
2005-06	Cannes	35	13	**84**	**20**
2006-07	Guimaraes	29	12		
2007-08	Guimaraes	30	6	**59**	**18**
2008-09	Celta Vigo	33	13	**33**	**13**
2009-10	Hull C	13	1		
2010-11	Hull C	0	0		
2010-11	*Arles-Avignon*	19	2	**19**	**2**
2011-12	Hull C	0	0	**13**	**1**

HARPER, James (M) **383 30**
H: 5 10 W: 11 02 b.Chelmsford 9-11-80
Source: Trainee.

1999-2000	Arsenal	0	0		
2000-01	Arsenal	0	0		
2000-01	*Cardiff C*	3	0	**3**	**0**
2000-01	Reading	12	1		
2001-02	Reading	26	1		
2002-03	Reading	36	2		
2003-04	Reading	39	1		
2004-05	Reading	41	3		
2005-06	Reading	45	7		
2006-07	Reading	38	3		
2007-08	Reading	38	6		
2008-09	Reading	34	1		
2009-10	Reading	3	0	**312**	**25**
2009-10	Sheffield U	34	4	**34**	**4**
2010-11	Hull C	28	1		
2011-12	Hull C	1	0	**29**	**1**
2011-12	*Wycombe W*	5	0	**5**	**0**

HOBBS, Jack (D) **179 3**
H: 6 3 W: 13 05 b.Portsmouth 18-8-88
Source: Scholar. *Honours:* England Youth.

2004-05	Lincoln C	1	0	**1**	**0**
2005-06	Liverpool	0	0		
2006-07	Liverpool	0	0		
2007-08	Liverpool	2	0		
2007-08	*Scunthorpe U*	9	1	**9**	**1**
2008-09	Liverpool	0	0	**2**	**0**
2008-09	Leicester C	44	1		
2009-10	Leicester C	44	0		
2010-11	Leicester C	26	0	**114**	**1**
2010-11	*Hull C*	13	0		
2011-12	Hull C	40	1	**53**	**1**

HOLOHAN, Gavan (M) **0 0**
b.Dublin 15-12-91
Source: Scholar.

2010-11	Hull C	0	0		
2011-12	Hull C	0	0		

KILBANE, Kevin (M) **530 37**
H: 6 1 W: 13 05 b.Preston 1-2-77
Source: Trainee. *Honours:* Eire Under-21, 110 full caps, 8 goals.

1993-94	Preston NE	0	0		
1994-95	Preston NE	0	0		
1995-96	Preston NE	11	1		
1996-97	Preston NE	36	2	**47**	**3**
1997-98	WBA	43	4		
1998-99	WBA	44	6		
1999-2000	WBA	19	5	**106**	**15**
1999-2000	Sunderland	20	1		
2000-01	Sunderland	30	4		
2001-02	Sunderland	28	2		
2002-03	Sunderland	30	1		
2003-04	Sunderland	5	0	**113**	**8**
2003-04	Everton	30	3		
2004-05	Everton	38	1		
2005-06	Everton	34	0		
2006-07	Everton	2	0	**104**	**4**
2006-07	Wigan Ath	31	1		
2007-08	Wigan Ath	35	1		
2008-09	Wigan Ath	10	0	**76**	**2**
2008-09	Hull C	16	0		
2009-10	Hull C	21	1		
2010-11	Hull C	14	1		
2010-11	*Huddersfield T*	24	2	**24**	**2**
2011-12	Hull C	0	0	**51**	**2**
2011-12	*Derby Co*	9	1	**9**	**1**

KOREN, Robert (M) **423 85**
H: 5 10 W: 11 03 b.Ljubljana 20-9-80
Honours: Slovenia Under-21, 61 full caps, 5 goals.

1999-2000	Dravograd	31	2		
2000-01	Dravograd	31	9	**62**	**11**
2001-02	Publikum	31	5		
2002-03	Publikum	32	12		
2003-04	Publikum	15	5	**78**	**22**
2004	Lillestrom	23	1		
2005	Lillestrom	26	8		
2006	Lillestrom	26	10	**75**	**19**
2006-07	WBA	18	1		
2007-08	WBA	40	9		
2008-09	WBA	35	1		
2009-10	WBA	34	5	**127**	**16**
2010-11	Hull C	40	7		
2011-12	Hull C	41	10	**81**	**17**

MAINWARING, Matty (M) **32 1**
H: 5 11 W: 12 02 b.Salford 28-3-90
Source: Preston NE Scholar.

2008-09	Stockport Co	21	1		
2009-10	Stockport Co	0	0		
2010-11	Stockport Co	11	0	**32**	**1**
2011-12	Hull C	0	0		

McKENNA, Paul (M) **530 33**
H: 5 7 W: 11 12 b.Eccleston 20-10-77
Source: Trainee.

1995-96	Preston NE	0	0		
1996-97	Preston NE	5	1		
1997-98	Preston NE	5	0		
1998-99	Preston NE	36	0		
1999-2000	Preston NE	24	2		
2000-01	Preston NE	44	5		
2001-02	Preston NE	38	4		
2002-03	Preston NE	41	3		
2003-04	Preston NE	39	6		
2004-05	Preston NE	39	3		
2005-06	Preston NE	41	2		
2006-07	Preston NE	33	2		
2007-08	Preston NE	33	0		
2008-09	Preston NE	44	2	**422**	**30**
2009-10	Nottingham F	35	1		
2010-11	Nottingham F	32	2	**67**	**3**
2011-12	Hull C	41	0	**41**	**0**

McLEAN, Aaron (F) **259 81**
H: 5 9 W: 10 10 b.Hammersmith 25-5-83
Source: Trainee.

1999-2000	Leyton Orient	3	0		
2000-01	Leyton Orient	2	1		
2001-02	Leyton Orient	27	1		
2002-03	Leyton Orient	8	0	**40**	**2**

From Aldershot T, Grays Ath.

2006-07	Peterborough U	16	7		
2007-08	Peterborough U	45	29		
2008-09	Peterborough U	42	18		
2009-10	Peterborough U	35	7		
2010-11	Peterborough U	19	10	**157**	**71**
2010-11	Hull C	23	3		
2011-12	Hull C	39	5	**62**	**8**

McSHANE, Paul (D) **183 8**
H: 6 0 W: 11 05 b.Wicklow 6-1-86
Source: Trainee. *Honours:* Eire Youth, Under-21, 27 full caps.

2002-03	Manchester U	0	0		
2003-04	Manchester U	0	0		
2004-05	Manchester U	0	0		
2004-05	*Walsall*	4	1	**4**	**1**
2005-06	Manchester U	0	0		
2005-06	*Brighton & HA*	38	3	**38**	**3**
2006-07	WBA	32	2	**32**	**2**
2007-08	Sunderland	21	0		
2008-09	Sunderland	3	0		
2008-09	*Hull C*	17	1		
2009-10	Sunderland	0	0	**24**	**0**
2009-10	Hull C	27	0		
2010-11	Hull C	19	0		
2010-11	*Barnsley*	10	1	**10**	**1**
2011-12	Hull C	1	0	**64**	**1**
2011-12	*Crystal Palace*	11	0	**11**	**0**

OLOFINJANA, Seyi (M) **248 36**
H: 6 4 W: 11 10 b.Lagos 30-6-80
Source: Kwara United Ilorin. *Honours:* Nigeria 44 full caps.

2003	Brann	25	9		
2004	Brann	9	2	**34**	**11**
2004-05	Wolverhampton W	42	5		
2005-06	Wolverhampton W	13	0		
2006-07	Wolverhampton W	44	8		
2007-08	Wolverhampton W	36	3	**135**	**16**
2008-09	Stoke C	18	2		
2009-10	Stoke C	0	0	**18**	**2**
2009-10	Hull C	19	1		
2010-11	Hull C	0	0		
2010-11	*Cardiff C*	39	6	**39**	**6**
2011-12	Hull C	3	0	**22**	**1**

OXLEY, Mark (G) **3 0**
H: 5 11 W: 11 05 b.Aston 2-6-90
Source: Rotherham U Scholar. *Honours:* England Youth.

2008-09	Hull C	0	0		
2009-10	Hull C	0	0		
2009-10	*Grimsby T*	3	0	**3**	**0**
2010-11	Hull C	0	0		
2011-12	Hull C	0	0		

PEET, Robert (G) **0 0**
H: 6 2 W: 12 01 b.Melton Mowbray 11-10-92
Source: Grimsby T Scholar.

2011-12	Hull C	0	0		

PUSIC, Martin (F) **89 19**
H: 6 0 W: 11 11 b.Vienna 24-10-87
Source: First Vienna. *Honours:* Austria Youth.

2007-08	Schwadorf	25	4	**25**	**4**
2008-09	Admira	24	7		
2009-10	Admira	23	4	**47**	**11**
2010-11	Altach	15	4	**15**	**4**
2011-12	Hull C	2	0	**2**	**0**

Transferred to Valerenga March 2012.

ROSENIOR, Liam (D) **274 3**
H: 5 10 W: 11 05 b.Wandsworth 9-7-84
Source: Scholar. *Honours:* England Youth, Under-20, Under-21.

2001-02	Bristol C	1	0		
2002-03	Bristol C	21	2		
2003-04	Bristol C	0	0	**22**	**2**
2003-04	Fulham	0	0		
2003-04	*Torquay U*	10	0	**10**	**0**
2004-05	Fulham	17	0		
2005-06	Fulham	24	0		
2006-07	Fulham	38	0		
2007-08	Fulham	0	0	**79**	**0**
2007-08	Reading	17	0		
2008-09	Reading	42	0		
2009-10	Reading	5	0		
2009-10	*Ipswich T*	29	1	**29**	**1**
2010-11	Reading	0	0	**64**	**0**
2010-11	Hull C	26	0		
2011-12	Hull C	44	0	**70**	**0**

SIMPSON, Jay (F) **144 29**
H: 5 11 W: 13 04 b.Enfield 1-12-88
Source: Scholar. *Honours:* England Youth.

2007-08	Arsenal	0	0		
2007-08	*Millwall*	41	6		
2008-09	Arsenal	0	0		
2008-09	*WBA*	13	1	**13**	**1**
2009-10	Arsenal	0	0		
2009-10	*QPR*	39	12	**39**	**12**
2010-11	Hull C	32	6		
2011-12	Hull C	3	0	**35**	**6**
2011-12	*Millwall*	16	4	**57**	**10**

STEWART, Cameron (M) **50 1**
H: 5 8 W: 11 05 b.Manchester 8-4-91
Source: Scholar. *Honours:* England Youth.

2009-10	Manchester U	0	0		
2010-11	Manchester U	0	0		
2010-11	*Yeovil T*	5	0	**5**	**0**
2010-11	Hull C	14	0		
2011-12	Hull C	31	1	**45**	**1**

TOWNSEND, Conor (D) **0 0**
b.Hessle 4-3-93
Source: Scholar.

2011-12	Hull C	0	0		

IPSWICH T (43)

AINSLEY, Jack (D) **2 0**
H: 5 11 W: 11 00 b.Ipswich 17-9-90
Source: Scholar.
2009-10 Ipswich T 0 0
2010-11 Ipswich T 1 0
2011-12 Ipswich T 1 0 **2 0**

BOWYER, Lee (M) **489 68**
H: 5 9 W: 10 12 b.Canning Town 3-1-77
Source: Trainee. *Honours:* England Youth, Under-21, 1 full cap.
1993-94 Charlton Ath 0 0
1994-95 Charlton Ath 5 0
1995-96 Charlton Ath 41 8 **46 8**
1996-97 Leeds U 32 4
1997-98 Leeds U 25 3
1998-99 Leeds U 35 9
1999-2000 Leeds U 33 5
2000-01 Leeds U 38 9
2001-02 Leeds U 25 5
2002-03 Leeds U 15 3 **203 38**
2002-03 West Ham U 10 0
2003-04 Newcastle U 24 2
2004-05 Newcastle U 27 3
2005-06 Newcastle U 28 1 **79 6**
2006-07 West Ham U 20 0
2007-08 West Ham U 15 4
2008-09 West Ham U 6 0 **51 4**
2008-09 *Birmingham C* 17 1
2009-10 Birmingham C 35 5
2010-11 Birmingham C 29 4 **81 10**
2011-12 Ipswich T 29 2 **29 2**

BULLARD, Jimmy (M) **310 40**
H: 5 10 W: 11 05 b.Newham 23-10-78
Source: Corinthian, Dartford, Gravesend & N.
1998-99 West Ham U 0 0
1999-2000 West Ham U 0 0
2000-01 West Ham U 0 0
2001-02 Peterborough U 40 8
2002-03 Peterborough U 26 3 **66 11**
2002-03 Wigan Ath 17 1
2003-04 Wigan Ath 46 2
2004-05 Wigan Ath 46 3
2005-06 Wigan Ath 36 4 **145 10**
2005-06 Fulham 0 0
2006-07 Fulham 4 2
2007-08 Fulham 17 2
2008-09 Fulham 18 2 **39 6**
2008-09 Hull C 1 0
2009-10 Hull C 14 5
2010-11 Hull C 8 2
2010-11 *Ipswich T* 16 5
2011-12 Hull C 0 0 **23 7**
2011-12 Ipswich T 21 1 **37 6**

BURKE, Cormac (M) **0 0**
b.Derry 11-8-93
Source: Scholar. *Honours:* Northern Ireland Youth.
2011-12 Ipswich T 0 0

CARSON, Josh (M) **25 5**
H: 5 9 W: 11 00 b.Ballymena 3-6-93
Source: Scholar. *Honours:* Northern Ireland Youth, Under-21, 3 full caps.
2010-11 Ipswich T 9 3
2011-12 Ipswich T 16 2 **25 5**

CHOPRA, Michael (F) **296 101**
H: 5 9 W: 10 10 b.Newcastle 23-12-83
Source: Scholar. *Honours:* England Youth, Under-20, Under-21.
2000-01 Newcastle U 0 0
2001-02 Newcastle U 0 0
2002-03 Newcastle U 1 0
2002-03 *Watford* 5 5 **5 5**
2003-04 Newcastle U 6 0
2003-04 *Nottingham F* 5 0 **5 0**
2004-05 Newcastle U 1 0
2004-05 *Barnsley* 39 17 **39 17**
2005-06 Newcastle U 13 1 **21 1**
2006-07 Cardiff C 42 22
2007-08 Sunderland 33 6
2008-09 Sunderland 6 2 **39 8**
2008-09 *Cardiff C* 27 9
2009-10 Cardiff C 41 16
2010-11 Cardiff C 32 9 **142 56**
2011-12 Ipswich T 45 14 **45 14**

CRESSWELL, Aaron (D) **114 6**
H: 5 7 W: 10 05 b.Liverpool 15-12-89
Source: Scholar.
2008-09 Tranmere R 13 1
2009-10 Tranmere R 14 0
2010-11 Tranmere R 43 4 **70 5**
2011-12 Ipswich T 44 1 **44 1**

CROPPER, Cody (G) **0 0**
b.Atlanta 16-2-93
Honours: From Scholar.
2011-12 Ipswich T 0 0

DELANEY, Damien (D) **404 10**
H: 6 3 W: 14 00 b.Cork 20-7-81
Source: Cork C. *Honours:* Eire 5 full caps.
2000-01 Leicester C 5 0
2001-02 Leicester C 3 0
2001-02 *Stockport Co* 12 1 **12 1**
2001-02 *Huddersfield T* 2 0 **2 0**
2002-03 Leicester C 0 0 **8 0**
2002-03 *Mansfield T* 7 0 **7 0**
2002-03 Hull C 30 1
2003-04 Hull C 46 2
2004-05 Hull C 43 1
2005-06 Hull C 46 0
2006-07 Hull C 37 1
2007-08 Hull C 22 0 **224 5**
2007-08 QPR 17 1
2008-09 QPR 37 1
2009-10 QPR 0 0 **54 2**
2009-10 Ipswich T 36 0
2010-11 Ipswich T 32 2
2011-12 Ipswich T 29 0 **97 2**

DRURY, Andy (M) **69 11**
H: 5 11 W: 12 06 b.Sittingbourne 28-11-83
Source: Sittingbourne, Ebbsfleet U, Lewes, Stevenage Bor, Luton T.
2010-11 Luton T 23 6 **23 6**
2010-11 Ipswich T 12 0
2011-12 Ipswich T 21 2 **33 2**
2011-12 *Crawley T* 13 3 **13 3**

EDWARDS, Carlos (M) **408 41**
H: 5 8 W: 11 02 b.Port of Spain 24-10-78
Source: Defence Force. *Honours:* Trinidad & Tobago 82 full caps, 4 goals.
2000-01 Wrexham 36 4
2001-02 Wrexham 26 5
2002-03 Wrexham 44 8
2003-04 Wrexham 42 5
2004-05 Wrexham 18 1 **166 23**
2005-06 Luton T 42 2
2006-07 Luton T 26 6 **68 8**
2006-07 Sunderland 15 5
2007-08 Sunderland 13 0
2008-09 Sunderland 22 0
2008-09 *Wolverhampton W* 6 0 **6 0**
2009-10 Sunderland 0 0 **50 5**
2009-10 Ipswich T 28 2
2010-11 Ipswich T 45 3
2011-12 Ipswich T 45 0 **118 5**

ELLINGTON, Nathan (F) **439 122**
H: 5 10 W: 13 01 b.Bradford 2-7-81
Source: Walton & Hersham.
1998-99 Bristol R 10 1
1999-2000 Bristol R 37 4
2000-01 Bristol R 42 15
2001-02 Bristol R 27 15 **116 35**
2001-02 Wigan Ath 3 2
2002-03 Wigan Ath 42 15
2003-04 Wigan Ath 44 18
2004-05 Wigan Ath 45 24 **134 59**
2005-06 WBA 31 5
2006-07 WBA 34 9
2007-08 WBA 3 0 **68 14**
2007-08 Watford 34 4
2008-09 Watford 0 0
2008-09 *Derby Co* 27 3 **27 3**
2009-10 Watford 17 1
2009-10 *Xanthi* 10 4 **10 4**
2010-11 Watford 0 0 **51 5**
2010-11 *Preston NE* 18 2 **18 2**
2011-12 Ipswich T 15 0 **15 0**

EMMANUEL-THOMAS, Jay (M) **82 14**
H: 5 9 W: 11 05 b.Forest Gate 27-12-90
Source: Scholar. *Honours:* England Youth.
2008-09 Arsenal 0 0
2009-10 Arsenal 0 0
2009-10 *Blackpool* 11 1 **11 1**
2009-10 *Doncaster R* 14 5 **14 5**
2010-11 Arsenal 1 0 **1 0**
2010-11 *Cardiff C* 14 2 **14 2**
2011-12 Ipswich T 42 6 **42 6**

GRIFFITHS, Jamie (M) **9 0**
H: 5 11 W: 9 13 b.Sudbury 4-1-92
Source: Scholar.
2010-11 Ipswich T 0 0
2011-12 Ipswich T 0 0
2011-12 *Plymouth Arg* 9 0 **9 0**

HEALY, Colin (M) **186 10**
H: 6 1 W: 12 13 b.Cork 14-3-80
Source: Wilton U. *Honours:* Eire Youth, Under-21, 13 full caps, 1 goal.
1998-99 Celtic 3 0
1999-2000 Celtic 10 1
2000-01 Celtic 11 0
2001-02 Celtic 4 0
2001-02 *Coventry C* 17 2 **17 2**
2002-03 Celtic 0 0 **28 1**
2003-04 Sunderland 20 0
2004-05 Sunderland 0 0 **20 0**
2005-06 Livingston 10 2 **10 2**
2006-07 Barnsley 8 0 **8 0**
2006-07 *Bradford C* 2 0 **2 0**
2007 Cork C 18 0
2008 Cork C 24 0
2009 Cork C 20 2 **62 2**
2009-10 Ipswich T 3 0
2009-10 *Falkirk* 19 1 **19 1**
2010-11 Ipswich T 16 2
2011-12 Ipswich T 1 0 **20 2**
Transferred to Cork City January 2012.

HYAM, Luke (M) **18 0**
H: 5 10 W: 11 05 b.Ipswich 24-10-91
Source: Scholar.
2010-11 Ipswich T 10 0
2011-12 Ipswich T 8 0 **18 0**

INGIMARSSON, Ivar (D) **485 34**
H: 6 0 W: 12 07 b.Reykjavik 20-8-77
Honours: Iceland Youth, Under-21, 30 full caps.
1995 Valur 12 0
1996 Valur 17 2
1997 Valur 16 3 **45 5**
1998 IBV 18 1
1999 IBV 18 4 **36 5**
1999-2000 Torquay U 4 1 **4 1**
1999-2000 Brentford 25 1
2000-01 Brentford 42 3
2001-02 Brentford 46 6 **113 10**
2002-03 Wolverhampton W13 2
2002-03 *Brighton & HA* 15 0 **15 0**
2003-04 Wolverhampton W0 0 **13 2**
2003-04 Reading 25 1
2004-05 Reading 44 3
2005-06 Reading 46 2
2006-07 Reading 38 2
2007-08 Reading 34 2
2008-09 Reading 26 1
2009-10 Reading 25 0
2010-11 Reading 13 0 **251 11**
2011-12 Ipswich T 8 0 **8 0**

KENNEDY, Mark (D) **466 32**
H: 5 11 W: 11 09 b.Dublin 15-5-76
Source: Belvedere, Trainee. *Honours:* Eire Schools, Youth, Under-21, 34 full caps, 3 goals.
1992-93 Millwall 1 0
1993-94 Millwall 12 4
1994-95 Millwall 30 5 **43 9**
1994-95 Liverpool 6 0
1995-96 Liverpool 4 0
1996-97 Liverpool 5 0
1997-98 Liverpool 1 0 **16 0**
1997-98 *QPR* 8 2 **8 2**
1997-98 Wimbledon 4 0
1998-99 Wimbledon 17 0 **21 0**
1999-2000 Manchester C 41 8
2000-01 Manchester C 25 0 **66 8**
2001-02 Wolverhampton W35 5
2002-03 Wolverhampton W31 3
2003-04 Wolverhampton W31 2
2004-05 Wolverhampton W30 0
2005-06 Wolverhampton W40 2 **167 12**
2006-07 Crystal Palace 38 1
2007-08 Crystal Palace 8 0 **46 1**
2008-09 Cardiff C 36 0
2009-10 Cardiff C 30 0 **66 0**
2010-11 Ipswich T 26 0
2011-12 Ipswich T 7 0 **33 0**

LAWRENCE, Byron (M) 1 0
H: 5 7 W: 10 03 b.Cambridge 12-3-96
Source: Schoolboy.

2011-12	Ipswich T	1	0	**1**	**0**

LEADBITTER, Grant (M) 232 25
H: 5 9 W: 11 06 b.Chester-le-Street 7-1-86
Source: Trainee. *Honours:* FA Schools, England Youth, Under-20, Under-21.

2002-03	Sunderland	0	0		
2003-04	Sunderland	0	0		
2004-05	Sunderland	0	0		
2005-06	Sunderland	12	0		
2005-06	*Rotherham U*	5	1	**5**	**1**
2006-07	Sunderland	44	7		
2007-08	Sunderland	31	2		
2008-09	Sunderland	23	2		
2009-10	Sunderland	1	0	**111**	**11**
2009-10	Ipswich T	38	3		
2010-11	Ipswich T	44	5		
2011-12	Ipswich T	34	5	**116**	**13**

LEE-BARRETT, Arran (G) 93 0
H: 6 2 W: 14 01 b.Ipswich 28-2-84
Source: Norwich C Scholar.

2002-03	Cardiff C	0	0		
2003-04	Cardiff C	0	0		
2004-05	Cardiff C	0	0		
2005-06	Cardiff C	0	0		
From Weymouth					
2006-07	Coventry C	0	0		
2007-08	Hartlepool U	18	0		
2008-09	Hartlepool U	37	0		
2009-10	Hartlepool U	0	0	**55**	**0**
2009-10	Ipswich T	13	0		
2010-11	Ipswich T	7	0		
2011-12	Ipswich T	18	0	**38**	**0**

MARTIN, Lee (M) 138 12
H: 5 10 W: 10 03 b.Taunton 9-2-87
Source: Scholar. *Honours:* England Youth.

2004-05	Manchester U	0	0		
2005-06	Manchester U	0	0		
2006-07	Manchester U	0	0		
2006-07	*Rangers*	7	0	**7**	**0**
2006-07	*Stoke C*	13	1	**13**	**1**
2007-08	Manchester U	0	0		
2007-08	*Plymouth Arg*	12	2	**12**	**2**
2007-08	*Sheffield U*	6	0	**6**	**0**
2008-09	Manchester U	1	0		
2008-09	*Nottingham F*	13	1	**13**	**1**
2009-10	Manchester U	0	0	**1**	**0**
2009-10	Ipswich T	16	1		
2010-11	Ipswich T	16	0		
2010-11	*Charlton Ath*	20	2	**20**	**2**
2011-12	Ipswich T	34	5	**66**	**6**

MURPHY, Daryl (F) 183 27
H: 6 2 W: 13 12 b.Waterford 15-3-83
Honours: Eire Youth, Under-21, 9 full caps.

2000-01	Luton T	0	0		
2001-02	Luton T	0	0		
2005-06	Sunderland	18	1		
2005-06	*Sheffield W*	4	0	**4**	**0**
2006-07	Sunderland	38	10		
2007-08	Sunderland	28	3		
2008-09	Sunderland	23	0		
2009-10	Sunderland	3	0	**110**	**14**
2009-10	*Ipswich T*	18	6		
2010-11	Celtic	18	3	**18**	**3**
2011-12	Ipswich T	33	4	**51**	**10**

MURRAY, Ronan (F) 35 4
H: 5 7 W: 11 00 b.Mayo 12-9-91
Source: Scholar. *Honours:* Eire Under-21.

2010-11	Ipswich T	8	0		
2010-11	*Torquay U*	7	1	**7**	**1**
2011-12	Ipswich T	0	0	**8**	**0**
2011-12	*Swindon T*	20	3	**20**	**3**

PETERS, Jaime (M) 124 5
H: 5 7 W: 10 12 b.Ontario 4-5-87
Source: Kaiserslautern. *Honours:* Canada Youth, Under-20, Under-23, 26 full caps, 1 goal.

2005-06	Ipswich T	13	0		
2006-07	Ipswich T	23	2		
2007-08	Ipswich T	5	0		
2007-08	*Yeovil T*	14	1	**14**	**1**
2008-09	Ipswich T	3	0		
2008-09	*Gillingham*	3	0	**3**	**0**
2009-10	Ipswich T	32	1		
2010-11	Ipswich T	23	1		
2011-12	Ipswich T	0	0	**99**	**4**
2011-12	*Bournemouth*	8	0	**8**	**0**

PRISKIN, Tamas (F) 212 49
H: 6 2 W: 13 03 b.Komarno 27-9-86
Honours: Hungary Under-21, 39 full caps, 11 goals.

2002-03	Gyor	3	0		
2003-04	Gyor	17	5		
2004-05	Gyor	23	8		
2005-06	Gyor	25	11	**68**	**24**
2006-07	Watford	16	2		
2007-08	Watford	14	1		
2007-08	*Preston NE*	5	2	**5**	**2**
2008-09	Watford	36	12		
2009-10	Watford	0	0	**66**	**15**
2009-10	Ipswich T	17	1		
2009-10	*QPR*	13	1	**13**	**1**
2010-11	Ipswich T	32	4		
2010-11	*Swansea C*	4	1	**4**	**1**
2011-12	Ipswich T	2	0	**51**	**5**
2011-12	*Derby Co*	5	1	**5**	**1**

Transferred to Alania January 2012.

SCOTLAND, Jason (F) 313 104
H: 5 8 W: 11 10 b.Morvant 18-2-79
Source: San Juan Jabloteh, Defence Force. *Honours:* Trinidad & Tobago 41 full caps, 8 goals.

2003-04	Dundee U	21	4		
2004-05	Dundee U	29	3	**50**	**7**
2005-06	St Johnstone	31	15		
2006-07	St Johnstone	35	18	**66**	**33**
2007-08	Swansea C	45	24		
2008-09	Swansea C	45	21		
2009-10	Swansea C	0	0	**90**	**45**
2009-10	Wigan Ath	32	1		
2010-11	Wigan Ath	0	0	**32**	**1**
2010-11	Ipswich T	39	10		
2011-12	Ipswich T	36	8	**75**	**18**

SMITH, Tommy (D) 78 6
H: 6 2 W: 12 02 b.Macclesfield 31-3-90
Source: Scholar. *Honours:* England Youth. New Zealand 14 full caps, 1 goal.

2007-08	Ipswich T	0	0		
2008-09	Ipswich T	2	0		
2009-10	Ipswich T	14	0		
2009-10	*Brentford*	8	0	**8**	**0**
2010-11	Ipswich T	22	3		
2010-11	*Colchester U*	6	0	**6**	**0**
2011-12	Ipswich T	26	3	**64**	**6**

SONKO, Ibrahima (D) 275 18
H: 6 3 W: 13 07 b.Bignola 22-1-81
Source: St Etienne, Grenoble. *Honours:* Senegal Under-21, 5 full caps, 1 goal.

2002-03	Brentford	37	5		
2003-04	Brentford	43	3	**80**	**8**
2004-05	Reading	39	1		
2005-06	Reading	46	3		
2006-07	Reading	23	1		
2007-08	Reading	16	0		
2008-09	Reading	3	3	**127**	**8**
2008-09	Stoke C	14	0		
2009-10	Stoke C	0	0		
2009-10	*Hull C*	9	0	**9**	**0**
2010-11	Stoke C	0	0	**14**	**0**
2010-11	*Portsmouth*	23	1	**23**	**1**
2011-12	Ipswich T	22	1	**22**	**1**

STEVENSON, Ryan (M) 253 44
H: 5 11 W: 12 07 b.Ayr 24-8-84
Source: Chelsea Scholar.

2001-02	Chelsea	0	0		
2002-03	St Johnstone	14	0		
2003-04	St Johnstone	12	0		
2004-05	St Johnstone	10	0		
2005-06	St Johnstone	35	5		
2006-07	St Johnstone	2	0	**73**	**5**
2006-07	*Ayr U*	24	2		
2007-08	Ayr U	33	15		
2008-09	Ayr U	34	10		
2009-10	Ayr U	17	2	**108**	**29**
2009-10	Hearts	11	0		
2010-11	Hearts	31	7		
2011-12	Hearts	19	2	**61**	**9**
2011-12	Ipswich T	11	1	**11**	**1**

WHIGHT, Joe (D) 0 0
H: 5 10 W: 11 00 b.Ipswich 6-1-94
Source: Scholar.

2011-12	Ipswich T	0	0		

WRIGHT, Richard (G) 380 0
H: 6 2 W: 14 04 b.Ipswich 5-11-77
Source: Trainee. *Honours:* England Schools, Youth, Under-21, 2 full caps.

1994-95	Ipswich T	3	0		
1995-96	Ipswich T	23	0		
1996-97	Ipswich T	40	0		
1997-98	Ipswich T	46	0		
1998-99	Ipswich T	46	0		
1999-2000	Ipswich T	46	0		
2000-01	Ipswich T	36	0		
2001-02	Arsenal	12	0	**12**	**0**
2002-03	Everton	33	0		
2003-04	Everton	4	0		
2004-05	Everton	7	0		
2005-06	Everton	15	0		
2006-07	Everton	1	0	**60**	**0**
2007-08	West Ham U	0	0		
2007-08	*Southampton*	7	0	**7**	**0**
2008-09	Ipswich T	46	0		
2009-10	Ipswich T	12	0		
2010-11	Ipswich T	0	0		
2010-11	Sheffield U	2	0	**2**	**0**
2011-12	Ipswich T	1	0	**299**	**0**

LEEDS U (44)

BECCHIO, Luciano (F) 264 92
H: 6 2 W: 13 05 b.Cordoba 28-12-83
Source: Boca Juniors.

2003-04	Mallorca B	0	0		
2004-05	Mallorca B	0	0		
2004-05	*Murcia*	16	3	**16**	**3**
2005-06	Terrassa	24	2	**24**	**2**
2006-07	Barcelona Athletic	10	0	**10**	**0**
2006-07	*Merida*	12	5		
2007-08	Merida	38	22	**50**	**27**
2008-09	Leeds U	45	15		
2009-10	Leeds U	37	15		
2010-11	Leeds U	41	19		
2011-12	Leeds U	41	11	**164**	**60**

BROMBY, Leigh (D) 329 12
H: 5 11 W: 11 06 b.Dewsbury 2-6-80
Honours: England Schools.

1998-99	Sheffield W	0	0		
1999-2000	Sheffield W	0	0		
1999-2000	*Mansfield T*	10	1	**10**	**1**
2000-01	Sheffield W	18	0		
2001-02	Sheffield W	26	1		
2002-03	Sheffield W	27	0		
2002-03	*Norwich C*	5	0	**5**	**0**
2003-04	Sheffield W	29	1	**100**	**2**
2004-05	Sheffield U	46	5		
2005-06	Sheffield U	35	1		
2006-07	Sheffield U	17	0		
2007-08	Sheffield U	11	0		
2007-08	Watford	16	1		
2008-09	Watford	22	0	**38**	**1**
2008-09	*Sheffield U*	12	1	**121**	**7**
2009-10	Leeds U	32	1		
2010-11	Leeds U	13	0		
2011-12	Leeds U	10	0	**55**	**1**

BROWN, Michael (M) 468 37
H: 5 9 W: 12 04 b.Hartlepool 25-1-77
Source: Trainee. *Honours:* England Under-21.

1994-95	Manchester C	0	0		
1995-96	Manchester C	21	0		
1996-97	Manchester C	11	0		
1996-97	*Hartlepool U*	6	1	**6**	**1**
1997-98	Manchester C	26	0		
1998-99	Manchester C	31	2		
1999-2000	Manchester C	0	0	**89**	**2**
1999-2000	*Portsmouth*	4	0		
1999-2000	Sheffield U	24	3		
2000-01	Sheffield U	36	1		
2001-02	Sheffield U	36	5		
2002-03	Sheffield U	40	16		
2003-04	Sheffield U	15	2	**151**	**27**
2003-04	Tottenham H	17	1		
2004-05	Tottenham H	24	1		
2005-06	Tottenham H	9	0	**50**	**2**
2005-06	Fulham	7	0		
2006-07	Fulham	34	0	**41**	**0**
2007-08	Wigan Ath	31	0		
2008-09	Wigan Ath	25	0		
2009-10	Wigan Ath	2	0	**58**	**0**
2009-10	Portsmouth	24	2		
2010-11	Portsmouth	21	2	**49**	**4**
2011-12	Leeds U	24	1	**24**	**1**

BRUCE, Alex (D) 185 3
H: 6 0 W: 11 06 b.Norwich 28-9-84
Source: Trainee. *Honours:* Eire B, Under-21, 2 full caps.

2002-03	Blackburn R	0	0		
2003-04	Blackburn R	0	0		
2004-05	Blackburn R	0	0		
2004-05	*Oldham Ath*	12	0	**12**	**0**
2004-05	Birmingham C	0	0		
2004-05	*Sheffield W*	6	0	**6**	**0**
2005-06	Birmingham C	6	0	**6**	**0**
2005-06	*Tranmere R*	11	0	**11**	**0**
2006-07	Ipswich T	41	0		
2007-08	Ipswich T	36	0		
2008-09	Ipswich T	25	1		
2009-10	Ipswich T	13	1		
2009-10	*Leicester C*	3	0	**3**	**0**
2010-11	Ipswich T	0	0	**115**	**2**
2010-11	Leeds U	21	1		
2011-12	Leeds U	8	0	**29**	**1**
2011-12	*Huddersfield T*	3	0	**3**	**0**

CAIRNS, Alex (G) 1 0
H: 6 0 W: 11 05 b.Doncaster 4-1-93
Source: Scholar.

2011-12	Leeds U	1	0	**1**	**0**

CLAYTON, Adam (M) 88 8
H: 5 9 W: 11 11 b.Manchester 14-1-89
Source: Scholar. *Honours:* England Under-20.

2007-08	Manchester C	0	0		
2008-09	Manchester C	0	0		
2009-10	Manchester C	0	0		
2009-10	*Carlisle U*	28	1	**28**	**1**
2010-11	Leeds U	4	0		
2010-11	*Peterborough U*	7	0	**7**	**0**
2010-11	*Milton Keynes D*	6	1	**6**	**1**
2011-12	Leeds U	43	6	**47**	**6**

CONNOLLY, Paul (D) 288 2
H: 6 0 W: 11 09 b.Liverpool 29-9-83
Source: Scholar.

2000-01	Plymouth Arg	1	0		
2001-02	Plymouth Arg	0	0		
2002-03	Plymouth Arg	2	0		
2003-04	Plymouth Arg	29	0		
2004-05	Plymouth Arg	19	0		
2005-06	Plymouth Arg	31	0		
2006-07	Plymouth Arg	38	0		
2007-08	Plymouth Arg	42	1	**162**	**1**
2008-09	Derby Co	40	1		
2009-10	Derby Co	21	0	**61**	**1**
2009-10	*Sheffield U*	7	0	**7**	**0**
2010-11	Leeds U	30	0		
2011-12	Leeds U	28	0	**58**	**0**

FORSSELL, Mikael (F) 278 66
H: 5 10 W: 10 10 b.Steinfurt 15-3-81
Honours: Finland Youth, Under-20, Under-21, 81 full caps, 26 goals.

1997	HJK Helsinki	1	0		
1998	HJK Helsinki	16	1	**17**	**1**
1998-99	Chelsea	10	1		
1999-2000	Chelsea	0	0		
1999-2000	*Crystal Palace*	13	3		
2000-01	Chelsea	0	0		
2000-01	*Crystal Palace*	39	13	**52**	**16**
2001-02	Chelsea	22	4		
2002-03	*M'gladbach*	16	7	**16**	**7**
2002-03	Chelsea	0	0		
2003-04	Chelsea	0	0		
2003-04	*Birmingham C*	32	17		
2004-05	Chelsea	1	0	**33**	**5**
2004-05	*Birmingham C*	4	0		
2005-06	Birmingham C	27	3		
2006-07	Birmingham C	8	1		
2007-08	Birmingham C	30	9	**101**	**30**
2008-09	Hannover	30	7		
2009-10	Hannover	2	0		
2010-11	Hannover	12	0	**44**	**7**
2011-12	Leeds U	15	0	**15**	**0**

GRADEL, Max (M) 138 35
H: 5 8 W: 12 03 b.Ivory Coast 30-9-87
Honours: Ivory Coast 1 full cap.

2005-06	Leicester C	0	0		
2006-07	Leicester C	0	0		
2007-08	Leicester C	0	0		
2007-08	*Bournemouth*	34	9	**34**	**9**
2008-09	Leicester C	27	1		
2009-10	Leicester C	0	0	**27**	**1**
2009-10	Leeds U	32	6		
2010-11	Leeds U	41	18		
2011-12	Leeds U	4	1	**77**	**25**

Transferred to St Etienne August 2011.

KISNORBO, Patrick (D) 290 14
H: 6 1 W: 11 11 b.Melbourne 24-3-81
Honours: Australia Schools, Under-20, Under-23, 18 full caps, 1 goal.

2000-01	South Melbourne	25	0		
2001-02	South Melbourne	23	2		
2002-03	South Melbourne	19	1	**67**	**3**
2003-04	Hearts	31	0		
2004-05	Hearts	17	1	**48**	**1**
2005-06	Leicester C	37	1		
2006-07	Leicester C	40	5		
2007-08	Leicester C	41	3		
2008-09	Leicester C	8	0	**126**	**9**
2009-10	Leeds U	29	1		
2010-11	Leeds U	1	0		
2011-12	Leeds U	19	0	**49**	**1**

LEES, Tom (D) 126 6
H: 6 1 W: 12 04 b.Warwick 28-11-90

2008-09	Leeds U	0	0		
2009-10	Leeds U	0	0		
2009-10	*Accrington S*	39	0	**39**	**0**
2010-11	Leeds U	0	0		
2010-11	*Bury*	45	4	**45**	**4**
2011-12	Leeds U	42	2	**42**	**2**

LONERGAN, Andrew (G) 248 1
H: 6 4 W: 13 02 b.Preston 19-10-83
Source: Scholar. *Honours:* Eire Youth, England Youth, Under-20.

2000-01	Preston NE	1	0		
2001-02	Preston NE	0	0		
2002-03	Preston NE	0	0		
2002-03	*Darlington*	2	0	**2**	**0**
2003-04	Preston NE	8	0		
2004-05	Preston NE	23	1		
2005-06	Preston NE	0	0		
2005-06	*Wycombe W*	2	0	**2**	**0**
2006-07	Preston NE	13	0		
2006-07	*Swindon T*	1	0	**1**	**0**
2007-08	Preston NE	43	0		
2008-09	Preston NE	46	0		
2009-10	Preston NE	45	0		
2010-11	Preston NE	29	0	**208**	**1**
2011-12	Leeds U	35	0	**35**	**0**

McCANN, Joe (M) 0 0
b.Leeds 11-10-92
Source: Scholar. *Honours:* England Youth.

2009-10	Leeds U	0	0		
2010-11	Leeds U	0	0		
2011-12	Leeds U	0	0		

McCORMACK, Ross (F) 218 62
H: 5 9 W: 11 00 b.Glasgow 18-8-86
Honours: Scotland Youth, Under-21, B, 7 full caps, 1 goal.

2003-04	Rangers	2	1		
2004-05	Rangers	1	0		
2005-06	Rangers	8	1	**11**	**2**
2005-06	Doncaster R	19	4	**19**	**4**
2006-07	Motherwell	12	2		
2007-08	Motherwell	36	9	**48**	**11**
2008-09	Cardiff C	38	21		
2009-10	Cardiff C	34	4		
2010-11	Cardiff C	2	0	**74**	**25**
2010-11	Leeds U	21	2		
2011-12	Leeds U	45	18	**66**	**20**

NUNEZ, Ramon (M) 180 31
H: 5 7 W: 10 00 b.Tegucigalpa 14-11-85
Honours: Honduras 44 full caps, 5 goals.

2004	Dallas	8	0		
2005	Dallas	21	5		
2006	Dallas	25	6		
2007	Dallas	13	3	**67**	**14**
2007	Chivas	8	0	**8**	**0**
2007-08	Olimpia	34	3		
2008-09	Olimpia	11	5	**45**	**8**
2008-09	Puebla	20	5	**20**	**5**
2009-10	Cruz Azul	11	0	**11**	**0**
2010-11	Leeds U	2	0		
2010-11	*Scunthorpe U*	8	3	**8**	**3**
2011-12	Leeds U	19	1	**21**	**1**

O'BRIEN, Andy (D) 393 12
H: 6 2 W: 11 13 b.Harrogate 29-6-79
Source: Trainee. *Honours:* England Youth, Under-21, Eire Under-21, 26 full caps, 1 goal.

1996-97	Bradford C	22	2		
1997-98	Bradford C	26	0		
1998-99	Bradford C	31	0		
1999-2000	Bradford C	36	1		
2000-01	Bradford C	18	0	**133**	**3**
2000-01	Newcastle U	9	1		
2001-02	Newcastle U	34	2		
2002-03	Newcastle U	26	0		
2003-04	Newcastle U	28	1		
2004-05	Newcastle U	23	2	**120**	**6**
2005-06	Portsmouth	29	0		
2006-07	Portsmouth	3	0		
2007-08	Portsmouth	0	0	**32**	**0**
2007-08	Bolton W	32	0		
2008-09	Bolton W	34	1		
2009-10	Bolton W	6	0		
2010-11	Bolton W	2	0	**74**	**1**
2010-11	Leeds U	30	2		
2011-12	Leeds U	4	0	**34**	**2**

O'DEA, Darren (D) 112 6
H: 6 1 W: 13 01 b.Dublin 4-2-87
Honours: Eire Under-21, 14 full caps.

2006-07	Celtic	14	2		
2007-08	Celtic	6	0		
2008-09	Celtic	10	1		
2009-10	Celtic	19	1	**49**	**4**
2009-10	*Reading*	8	0	**8**	**0**
2010-11	*Ipswich T*	20	0		
2011-12	*Ipswich T*	0	0	**20**	**0**
2011-12	Leeds U	35	2	**35**	**2**

PARKER, Ben (D) 96 1
H: 5 11 W: 11 06 b.Pontefract 8-11-87
Source: Scholar. *Honours:* England Youth.

2004-05	Leeds U	0	0		
2005-06	Leeds U	0	0		
2006-07	Leeds U	0	0		
2006-07	*Bradford C*	39	0	**39**	**0**
2007-08	Leeds U	9	0		
2007-08	*Darlington*	13	0	**13**	**0**
2008-09	Leeds U	24	0		
2009-10	Leeds U	4	0		
2010-11	Leeds U	2	0		
2011-12	Leeds U	0	0	**39**	**0**
2011-12	*Carlisle U*	5	1	**5**	**1**

PAYNE, Sanchez (M) 0 0
b.Leeds 31-1-93
Source: Scholar.

2010-11	Leeds U	0	0		
2011-12	Leeds U	0	0		

PAYNTER, Billy (F) 347 85
H: 6 1 W: 14 01 b.Liverpool 13-7-84
Source: Schoolboy.

2000-01	Port Vale	1	0		
2001-02	Port Vale	7	0		
2002-03	Port Vale	31	5		
2003-04	Port Vale	44	13		
2004-05	Port Vale	45	10		
2005-06	Port Vale	16	2	**144**	**30**
2005-06	Hull C	22	3	**22**	**3**
2006-07	Southend U	9	0		
2006-07	*Bradford C*	15	4	**15**	**4**
2007-08	Southend U	0	0	**9**	**0**
2007-08	Swindon T	36	8		
2008-09	Swindon T	42	11		
2009-10	Swindon T	42	26	**120**	**45**
2010-11	Leeds U	22	1		
2011-12	Leeds U	5	2	**27**	**3**
2011-12	*Brighton & HA*	10	0	**10**	**0**

PEARCE, Jason (D) 205 9
H: 5 11 W: 12 00 b.Hillingdon 6-12-87
Source: Scholar.

2006-07	Portsmouth	0	0		
2007-08	Bournemouth	33	1		
2008-09	Bournemouth	44	2		
2009-10	Bournemouth	39	1		
2010-11	Bournemouth	46	3	**162**	**7**
2011-12	Portsmouth	43	2	**43**	**2**
2011-12	Leeds U	0	0		

PUGH, Danny (M) 209 12
H: 6 0 W: 12 10 b.Cheadle Hulme 19-10-82
Source: Scholar.

2000-01	Manchester U	0	0		
2001-02	Manchester U	0	0		
2002-03	Manchester U	1	0		
2003-04	Manchester U	0	0	**1**	**0**
2004-05	Leeds U	38	5		
2005-06	Leeds U	12	0		
2006-07	Preston NE	45	4		
2007-08	Preston NE	7	0		
2007-08	Stoke C	30	0		
2008-09	Stoke C	17	0		
2009-10	Stoke C	7	1		
2010-11	Stoke C	10	0		
2010-11	*Preston NE*	5	0	**57**	**4**
2011-12	Stoke C	3	0	**67**	**1**
2011-12	Leeds U	34	2	**84**	**7**

RACHUBKA, Paul (G) 253 0

H: 6 1 W: 13 05 b.San Luis Opispo 21-5-81

Source: Trainee. *Honours:* England Youth, Under-20.

Season	Club				
1999-2000	Manchester U	0	0		
2000-01	Manchester U	1	0		
2001-02	Manchester U	0	0	**1**	**0**
2001-02	*Oldham Ath*	16	0	**16**	**0**
2001-02	Charlton Ath	0	0		
2002-03	Charlton Ath	0	0		
2003-04	Charlton Ath	0	0		
2003-04	*Huddersfield T*	13	0		
2004-05	Charlton Ath	0	0		
2004-05	*Milton Keynes D*	4	0	**4**	**0**
2004-05	*Northampton T*	10	0	**10**	**0**
2004-05	Huddersfield T	29	0		
2005-06	Huddersfield T	34	0		
2006-07	Huddersfield T	0	0	**76**	**0**
2006-07	*Peterborough U*	4	0	**4**	**0**
2006-07	*Blackpool*	8	0		
2007-08	Blackpool	46	0		
2008-09	Blackpool	42	0		
2009-10	Blackpool	20	0		
2010-11	Blackpool	2	0	**118**	**0**
2011-12	Leeds U	6	0	**6**	**0**
2011-12	*Tranmere R*	10	0	**10**	**0**
2011-12	*Leyton Orient*	8	0	**8**	**0**

ROGERS, Robbie (F) 135 20

H: 5 10 W: 12 13 b.Los Angeles 12-5-87

Honours: USA Youth, Under-23, 18 full caps, 2 goals.

Season	Club				
2005	Orange County BS	3	0	**3**	**0**
2006	Maryland Terrapins	22	7	**22**	**7**
2006-07	Heerenveen	0	0		
2007	Columbus Crew	10	3		
2008	Columbus Crew	27	6		
2009	Columbus Crew	22	1		
2010	Columbus Crew	20	1		
2011	Columbus Crew	27	2	**106**	**13**
2011-12	Leeds U	4	0	**4**	**0**

SAM, Lloyd (F) 180 13

H: 5 10 W: 11 00 b.Leeds 27-9-84

Source: Scholar. *Honours:* England Youth, Under-20.

Season	Club				
2002-03	Charlton Ath	0	0		
2003-04	Charlton Ath	0	0		
2003-04	*Leyton Orient*	10	0	**10**	**0**
2004-05	Charlton Ath	1	0		
2005-06	Charlton Ath	2	0		
2006-07	Charlton Ath	7	0		
2006-07	*Sheffield W*	4	0	**4**	**0**
2006-07	*Southend U*	2	0	**2**	**0**
2007-08	Charlton Ath	28	2		
2008-09	Charlton Ath	38	0		
2009-10	Charlton Ath	43	4	**119**	**6**
2010-11	Leeds U	18	2		
2011-12	Leeds U	17	0	**35**	**2**
2011-12	*Notts Co*	10	5	**10**	**5**

SNODGRASS, Robert (M) 259 55

H: 6 0 W: 12 02 b.Glasgow 7-9-87

Honours: Scotland Youth, Under-21, 5 full caps, 1 goal.

Season	Club				
2003-04	Livingston	0	0		
2004-05	Livingston	17	2		
2005-06	Livingston	27	4		
2006-07	Livingston	6	0		
2006-07	*Stirling A*	12	5	**12**	**5**
2007-08	Livingston	31	9	**81**	**15**
2008-09	Leeds U	42	9		
2009-10	Leeds U	44	7		
2010-11	Leeds U	37	6		
2011-12	Leeds U	43	13	**166**	**35**

SOMMA, Davide (F) 103 23

H: 6 1 W: 12 13 b.Johannesburg 26-3-85

Honours: South Africa 3 full caps, 1 goal.

Season	Club				
2005-06	Pro Vasto	20	2		
2006-07	Pro Vasto	19	0	**39**	**2**
2007-08	Olbia	15	1	**15**	**1**
2008	San Jose Eq	3	0	**3**	**0**
2009-10	Leeds U	0	0		
2009-10	*Chesterfield*	3	0	**3**	**0**
2009-10	*Lincoln C*	14	9	**14**	**9**
2010-11	Leeds U	29	11		
2011-12	Leeds U	0	0	**29**	**11**

TAYLOR, Charlie (D) 5 0

H: 5 9 W: 11 00 b.York 18-9-93

Source: Scholar. *Honours:* England Youth.

Season	Club				
2011-12	Leeds U	2	0	**2**	**0**
2011-12	*Bradford C*	3	0	**3**	**0**

THOMPSON, Zac (M) 9 0

H: 5 10 W: 11 00 b.Billinge 5-1-93

Source: Everton Scholar.

Season	Club				
2010-11	Leeds U	0	0		
2011-12	Leeds U	9	0	**9**	**0**

TURNER, Lewis (M) 0 0

b.Garforth 3-9-92

Source: Scholar.

Season	Club				
2011-12	Leeds U	0	0		

TURNER, Nathan (D) 0 0

b.Garforth 3-9-92

Source: Scholar.

Season	Club				
2011-12	Leeds U	0	0		

VAYRYNEN, Mika (M) 263 45

H: 5 11 W: 12 02 b.Eskilstuna 28-12-81

Honours: Finland 56 full caps, 5 goals.

Season	Club				
1999-2000	Lahti	15	1		
2000-01	Lahti	21	10	**36**	**11**
2001-02	Jokerit	30	4	**30**	**4**
2001-02	Heerenveen	18	0		
2002-03	Heerenveen	22	4		
2003-04	Heerenveen	32	5		
2004-05	Heerenveen	29	8		
2005-06	PSV Eindhoven	11	2		
2006-07	PSV Eindhoven	17	0		
2007-08	PSV Eindhoven	1	0		
2008-09	PSV Eindhoven	0	0	**29**	**2**
2008-09	Heerenveen	17	1		
2009-10	Heerenveen	10	1		
2010-11	Heerenveen	30	9	**158**	**28**
2011-12	Leeds U	10	0	**10**	**0**

WEBBER, Danny (F) 228 46

H: 5 10 W: 11 04 b.Manchester 28-12-81

Source: Trainee. *Honours:* England Youth, Under-20.

Season	Club				
1998-99	Manchester U	0	0		
1999-2000	Manchester U	0	0		
2000-01	Manchester U	0	0		
2001-02	Manchester U	0	0		
2001-02	*Port Vale*	4	0	**4**	**0**
2001-02	*Watford*	5	2		
2002-03	Manchester U	0	0		
2002-03	*Watford*	12	2		
2003-04	Watford	27	5		
2004-05	Watford	28	12	**72**	**21**
2004-05	*Sheffield U*	7	3		
2005-06	Sheffield U	35	10		
2006-07	Sheffield U	22	3		
2007-08	Sheffield U	14	3		
2008-09	Sheffield U	36	4		
2009-10	Sheffield U	0	0	**114**	**23**
2009-10	Portsmouth	17	1		
2010-11	Portsmouth	8	0		
2011-12	Portsmouth	0	0	**25**	**1**
2011-12	Leeds U	13	1	**13**	**1**

WHITE, Aidan (D) 75 4

H: 5 7 W: 10 00 b.Otley 10-10-91

Source: Scholar. *Honours:* England Youth. Eire Under-21.

Season	Club				
2008-09	Leeds U	5	0		
2009-10	Leeds U	8	0		
2010-11	Leeds U	2	0		
2010-11	*Oldham Ath*	24	4	**24**	**4**
2011-12	Leeds U	36	0	**51**	**0**

LEICESTER C (45)

ABE, Yuki (M) 386 52

H: 5 9 W: 12 02 b.Ichikawa 6-9-81

Honours: Japan 53 full caps, 3 goals.

Season	Club				
1998	JEF United	1	0		
1999	JEF United	30	1		
2000	JEF United	25	0		
2001	JEF United	17	3		
2002	JEF United	24	1		
2003	JEF United	27	3		
2004	JEF United	24	5		
2005	JEF United	33	12		
2006	JEF United	33	11	**214**	**36**
2007	Urawa	33	3		
2008	Urawa	33	6		
2009	Urawa	34	2		
2010	Urawa	20	3	**120**	**14**
2010-11	Leicester C	36	1		
2011-12	Leicester C	16	1	**52**	**2**

Transferred to Urawa Red Diamonds January 2012.

BAMBA, Souleymane (D) 167 7

H: 6 3 W: 14 02 b.Ivry-sur-Seine 13-1-85

Honours: Ivory Coast 18 full caps, 2 goals.

Season	Club				
2004-05	Paris St Germain	1	0		
2005-06	Paris St Germain	0	0	**1**	**0**
2006-07	Dunfermline Ath	23	0		
2007-08	Dunfermline Ath	15	0		
2008-09	Dunfermline Ath	1	0	**39**	**0**
2008-09	Hibernian	29	0		
2009-10	Hibernian	30	2		
2010-11	Hibernian	16	2	**75**	**4**
2010-11	Leicester C	16	2		
2011-12	Leicester C	36	1	**52**	**3**

BECKFORD, Jermaine (F) 221 97

H: 6 2 W: 13 02 b.Ealing 9-12-83

Source: Wealdstone.

Season	Club				
2005-06	Leeds U	5	0		
2006-07	Leeds U	5	0		
2006-07	*Carlisle U*	4	1	**4**	**1**
2006-07	*Scunthorpe U*	18	8	**18**	**8**
2007-08	Leeds U	40	20		
2008-09	Leeds U	34	26		
2009-10	Leeds U	42	25	**126**	**71**
2010-11	Everton	32	8		
2011-12	Everton	2	0	**34**	**8**
2011-12	Leicester C	39	9	**39**	**9**

BOLGER, Cian (D) 45 2

H: 6 4 W: 12 05 b.Co. Kildare 12-3-92

Source: Scholar.

Season	Club				
2009-10	Leicester C	0	0		
2010-11	Leicester C	0	0		
2010-11	*Bristol R*	6	0		
2011-12	Leicester C	0	0		
2011-12	*Bristol R*	39	2	**45**	**2**

BYRNE, Shane (M) 14 0

H: 5 10 W: 12 02 b.Dublin 25-4-93

Source: Scholar. *Honours:* Eire Youth.

Season	Club				
2010-11	Leicester C	0	0		
2011-12	Leicester C	0	0		
2011-12	*Bury*	14	0	**14**	**0**

CAIN, Michael (M) 0 0

b. 4-12-94

Source: Luton T Youth.

Season	Club				
2011-12	Leicester C	0	0		

CHAMBERLAIN, Elliott (F) 0 0

b.Bermuda 29-4-92

Source: Scholar. *Honours:* Wales Youth, Under-21.

Season	Club				
2009-10	Leicester C	0	0		
2010-11	Leicester C	0	0		
2011-12	Leicester C	0	0		

DANNS, Neil (M) 260 48

H: 5 10 W: 10 12 b.Liverpool 23-11-82

Source: Scholar.

Season	Club				
2000-01	Blackburn R	0	0		
2001-02	Blackburn R	0	0		
2002-03	Blackburn R	2	0		
2003-04	Blackpool	12	2	**12**	**2**
2003-04	Blackburn R	1	0		
2003-04	*Hartlepool U*	9	1	**9**	**1**
2004-05	Blackburn R	0	0	**3**	**0**
2004-05	Colchester U	32	11		
2005-06	Colchester U	41	8	**73**	**19**
2006-07	Birmingham C	29	3		
2007-08	Birmingham C	2	0	**31**	**3**
2007-08	Crystal Palace	4	0		
2008-09	Crystal Palace	20	2		
2009-10	Crystal Palace	42	8		
2010-11	Crystal Palace	37	8	**103**	**18**
2011-12	Leicester C	29	5	**29**	**5**

DRINKWATER, Daniel (M) 90 5

H: 5 10 W: 11 00 b.Manchester 5-3-90

Source: Scholar. *Honours:* England Youth.

Season	Club				
2008-09	Manchester U	0	0		
2009-10	Manchester U	0	0		
2009-10	*Huddersfield T*	33	2	**33**	**2**
2010-11	Manchester U	0	0		
2010-11	*Cardiff C*	9	0	**9**	**0**
2010-11	*Watford*	12	0	**12**	**0**
2011-12	Manchester U	0	0		
2011-12	*Barnsley*	17	1	**17**	**1**
2011-12	Leicester C	19	2	**19**	**2**

DYER, Lloyd (M) 289 39

H: 5 8 W: 10 03 b.Birmingham 13-9-82

Source: Aston Villa Juniors.

Season	Club				
2001-02	WBA	0	0		
2002-03	WBA	0	0		
2003-04	WBA	17	2		

2003-04	*Kidderminster H*	7	1	**7**	**1**
2004-05	WBA	4	0		
2004-05	*Coventry C*	6	0	**6**	**0**
2005-06	WBA	0	0	**21**	**2**
2005-06	*QPR*	15	0	**15**	**0**
2005-06	Millwall	6	0	**6**	**0**
2006-07	Milton Keynes D	41	5		
2007-08	Milton Keynes D	45	11	**86**	**16**
2008-09	Leicester C	44	10		
2009-10	Leicester C	33	3		
2010-11	Leicester C	35	3		
2011-12	Leicester C	36	4	**148**	**20**

GALLAGHER, Paul (F) 274 56
H: 6 1 W: 11 00 b.Glasgow 9-8-84
Source: Trainee. *Honours:* Scotland Under-21, B, 1 full cap.

2002-03	Blackburn R	1	0		
2003-04	Blackburn R	26	3		
2004-05	Blackburn R	16	2		
2005-06	Blackburn R	1	0		
2005-06	*Stoke C*	37	11		
2006-07	Blackburn R	16	1		
2007-08	Blackburn R	0	0		
2007-08	*Preston NE*	19	1	**19**	**1**
2007-08	*Stoke C*	7	0	**44**	**11**
2008-09	Blackburn R	0	0		
2008-09	*Plymouth Arg*	40	13	**40**	**13**
2009-10	Blackburn R	1	0	**61**	**6**
2009-10	Leicester C	41	7		
2010-11	Leicester C	41	10		
2011-12	Leicester C	28	8	**110**	**25**

GELSON (M) 219 7
H: 6 0 W: 11 03 b.Cape Verde Isl 2-9-86
Honours: Switzerland Under-21, 37 full caps, 2 goals.

2002-03	Sion	6	0		
2003-04	Sion	28	0		
2004-05	Sion	9	0		
2005-06	Sion	22	0		
2006-07	Sion	34	1	**99**	**1**
2007-08	Manchester C	26	2		
2008-09	Manchester C	17	1	**43**	**3**
2009-10	St Etienne	33	0		
2010-11	St Etienne	0	0	**33**	**0**
2010-11	*Chievo*	29	2	**29**	**2**
2011-12	Leicester C	15	1	**15**	**1**

On loan from St Etienne.

HOPPER, Tom (F) 0 0
b.Boston 14-12-93
Source: Scholar. *Honours:* England Youth.

2011-12	Leicester C	0	0		

HOWARD, Steve (F) 650 185
H: 6 3 W: 15 00 b.Durham 10-5-76
Source: Tow Law T. *Honours:* Scotland B.

1995-96	Hartlepool U	39	7		
1996-97	Hartlepool U	32	8		
1997-98	Hartlepool U	43	7		
1998-99	Hartlepool U	28	5	**142**	**27**
1998-99	Northampton T	12	0		
1999-2000	Northampton T	41	10		
2000-01	Northampton T	33	8	**86**	**18**
2000-01	Luton T	12	3		
2001-02	Luton T	42	24		
2002-03	Luton T	41	22		
2003-04	Luton T	34	14		
2004-05	Luton T	40	18		
2005-06	Luton T	43	14	**212**	**95**
2006-07	Derby Co	43	16		
2007-08	Derby Co	20	1	**63**	**17**
2007-08	Leicester C	21	6		
2008-09	Leicester C	41	13		
2009-10	Leicester C	36	5		
2010-11	Leicester C	29	4		
2011-12	Leicester C	20	0	**147**	**28**

JONES, Joe (D) 0 0
Source: Scholar.

2011-12	Leicester C	0	0		

KENNEDY, Tom (D) 311 14
H: 5 10 W: 11 01 b.Bury 24-6-85
Source: Scholar.

2002-03	Bury	0	0		
2003-04	Bury	27	0		
2004-05	Bury	46	1		
2005-06	Bury	33	4		
2006-07	Bury	37	0	**143**	**5**
2007-08	Rochdale	43	2		
2008-09	Rochdale	45	4		
2009-10	Rochdale	44	3		
2010-11	Leicester C	1	0		
2010-11	*Rochdale*	6	0	**138**	**9**
2010-11	*Peterborough U*	14	0		
2011-12	Leicester C	5	0	**6**	**0**
2011-12	*Peterborough U*	10	0	**24**	**0**

KING, Andy (M) 174 38
H: 6 0 W: 11 10 b.Barnstaple 29-10-88
Source: Scholar. *Honours:* Wales Youth, Under-21, 12 full caps, 1 goal.

2007-08	Leicester C	11	1		
2008-09	Leicester C	45	9		
2009-10	Leicester C	43	9		
2010-11	Leicester C	45	15		
2011-12	Leicester C	30	4	**174**	**38**

KONCHESKY, Paul (D) 389 11
H: 5 10 W: 11 07 b.Barking 15-5-81
Source: Trainee. *Honours:* England Youth, Under-20, Under-21, 2 full caps.

1997-98	Charlton Ath	3	0		
1998-99	Charlton Ath	2	0		
1999-2000	Charlton Ath	8	0		
2000-01	Charlton Ath	23	0		
2001-02	Charlton Ath	34	1		
2002-03	Charlton Ath	30	3		
2003-04	Charlton Ath	21	0		
2003-04	*Tottenham H*	12	0	**12**	**0**
2004-05	Charlton Ath	28	1	**149**	**5**
2005-06	West Ham U	37	1		
2006-07	West Ham U	22	0	**59**	**1**
2007-08	Fulham	33	0		
2008-09	Fulham	36	1		
2009-10	Fulham	27	1		
2010-11	Fulham	1	0	**97**	**2**
2010-11	Liverpool	15	0	**15**	**0**
2010-11	*Nottingham F*	15	1	**15**	**1**
2011-12	Leicester C	42	2	**42**	**2**

LANE, Patrick (G) 0 0
b.California 7-8-88
Source: Cercle Brugge.

2011-12	Leicester C	0	0		

LARRAURI, Pier (F) 0 0
H: 5 9 W: 11 12 b.Siena 26-3-94
Honours: Italy Youth.

2011-12	Leicester C	0	0		

LOGAN, Conrad (G) 134 0
H: 6 2 W: 14 00 b.Letterkenny 18-4-86
Source: Scholar. *Honours:* Eire Youth.

2003-04	Leicester C	0	0		
2004-05	Leicester C	0	0		
2005-06	Leicester C	0	0		
2005-06	*Boston U*	13	0	**13**	**0**
2006-07	Leicester C	18	0		
2007-08	Leicester C	0	0		
2007-08	*Stockport Co*	34	0		
2008-09	Leicester C	0	0		
2008-09	*Luton T*	22	0	**22**	**0**
2008-09	*Stockport Co*	7	0	**41**	**0**
2009-10	Leicester C	2	0		
2010-11	Leicester C	3	0		
2010-11	*Bristol R*	16	0	**16**	**0**
2011-12	Leicester C	0	0	**23**	**0**
2011-12	*Rotherham U*	19	0	**19**	**0**

MADUAKO, Jideofo (M) 0 0
Source: Scholar.

2011-12	Leicester C	0	0		

MARSHALL, Ben (F) 112 18
H: 5 11 W: 11 13 b.Salford 29-3-91
Source: Crewe Alex Scholar.

2009-10	Stoke C	0	0		
2009-10	*Northampton T*	15	2	**15**	**2**
2009-10	*Cheltenham T*	6	2	**6**	**2**
2009-10	*Carlisle U*	20	3		
2010-11	Stoke C	0	0		
2010-11	*Carlisle U*	33	3	**53**	**6**
2011-12	Stoke C	0	0		
2011-12	*Sheffield W*	22	5	**22**	**5**
2011-12	Leicester C	16	3	**16**	**3**

MILLS, Matthew (D) 192 11
H: 6 3 W: 12 12 b.Swindon 14-7-86
Source: Scholar. *Honours:* England Youth.

2004-05	Southampton	0	0		
2004-05	*Coventry C*	4	0	**4**	**0**
2004-05	*Bournemouth*	12	3	**12**	**3**
2005-06	Southampton	4	0	**4**	**0**
2005-06	Manchester C	1	0		
2006-07	Manchester C	1	0		
2006-07	*Colchester U*	9	0	**9**	**0**
2007-08	Manchester C	0	0	**2**	**0**
2007-08	*Doncaster R*	34	3		
2008-09	Doncaster R	41	0		
2009-10	Doncaster R	0	0	**75**	**3**
2009-10	Reading	23	2		
2010-11	Reading	38	2	**61**	**4**
2011-12	Leicester C	25	1	**25**	**1**

MOORE, Liam (D) 19 0
H: 6 1 W: 13 08 b.Loughborough 31-1-93
Source: Scholar.

2011-12	Leicester C	2	0	**2**	**0**
2011-12	*Bradford C*	17	0	**17**	**0**

MORGAN, Wes (D) 374 13
H: 6 2 W: 14 00 b.Nottingham 21-1-84
Source: Dunkirk.

2002-03	Nottingham F	0	0		
2002-03	*Kidderminster H*	5	1	**5**	**1**
2003-04	Nottingham F	32	2		
2004-05	Nottingham F	43	1		
2005-06	Nottingham F	43	2		
2006-07	Nottingham F	38	0		
2007-08	Nottingham F	42	1		
2008-09	Nottingham F	42	1		
2009-10	Nottingham F	44	3		
2010-11	Nottingham F	46	1		
2011-12	Nottingham F	22	1	**352**	**12**
2011-12	Leicester C	17	0	**17**	**0**

MOUSSA, Franck (M) 131 14
H: 5 8 W: 10 08 b.Brussels 24-7-89
Source: Scholar.

2005-06	Southend U	1	0		
2006-07	Southend U	4	0		
2007-08	Southend U	16	0		
2008-09	Southend U	26	2		
2008-09	*Wycombe W*	9	0	**9**	**0**
2009-10	Southend U	43	5	**90**	**7**
2010-11	Leicester C	8	1		
2010-11	*Doncaster R*	14	2	**14**	**2**
2011-12	Leicester C	0	0	**8**	**1**
2011-12	*Chesterfield*	10	4	**10**	**4**

NORBURN, Oliver (M) 5 0
b.Leicester 26-10-92
Source: Scholar.

2011-12	Leicester C	0	0		
2011-12	*Bristol R*	5	0	**5**	**0**

NUGENT, Dave (F) 332 88
H: 5 11 W: 12 13 b.Liverpool 2-5-85
Source: Scholar. *Honours:* England Youth, Under-20, Under-21, 1 full cap, 1 goal.

2001-02	Bury	5	0		
2002-03	Bury	31	4		
2003-04	Bury	26	3		
2004-05	Bury	26	11	**88**	**18**
2004-05	Preston NE	18	8		
2005-06	Preston NE	32	10		
2006-07	Preston NE	44	15	**94**	**33**
2007-08	Portsmouth	15	0		
2008-09	Portsmouth	16	3		
2009-10	Portsmouth	3	0		
2009-10	*Burnley*	30	6	**30**	**6**
2010-11	Portsmouth	44	13	**78**	**16**
2011-12	Leicester C	42	15	**42**	**15**

OAKLEY, Matthew (M) 461 33
H: 5 10 W: 12 06 b.Peterborough 17-8-77
Source: Trainee. *Honours:* England Under-21.

1994-95	Southampton	1	0		
1995-96	Southampton	10	0		
1996-97	Southampton	28	3		
1997-98	Southampton	33	1		
1998-99	Southampton	22	2		
1999-2000	Southampton	31	3		
2000-01	Southampton	35	1		
2001-02	Southampton	27	1		
2002-03	Southampton	31	0		
2003-04	Southampton	7	0		
2004-05	Southampton	7	1		
2005-06	Southampton	29	2	**261**	**14**
2006-07	Derby Co	37	6		
2007-08	Derby Co	19	3	**56**	**9**
2007-08	Leicester C	20	0		
2008-09	Leicester C	45	8		
2009-10	Leicester C	38	0		
2010-11	Leicester C	34	2		
2011-12	Leicester C	0	0	**137**	**10**
2011-12	*Exeter C*	7	0	**7**	**0**

PANAYIOTOU, Harry (F) 1 1
b.Leicester 28-10-94
Source: Scholar.

2011-12	Leicester C	1	1	**1**	**1**

PANTSIL, John (D) 229 5
H: 5 10 W: 12 08 b.Berekum 15-6-81
Source: Liberty Professionals, Berkum Arsenals. *Honours:* Ghana Youth, Under-20, 72 full caps.

2000-01	Liberty Pros	10	0	**10**	**0**
2001-02	Berekum Arsenal	12	1	**12**	**1**
2001-02	Widzew Lodz	19	1	**19**	**1**
2002-03	Maccabi Tel Aviv	17	0		
2003-04	Maccabi Tel Aviv	22	0		
2004-05	Maccabi Tel Aviv	7	0	**46**	**0**
2004-05	Hapoel Tel Aviv	15	1		
2005-06	Hapoel Tel Aviv	27	2	**42**	**3**
2006-07	West Ham U	5	0		
2007-08	West Ham U	14	0	**19**	**0**
2008-09	Fulham	37	0		
2009-10	Fulham	22	0		
2010-11	Fulham	16	0	**75**	**0**
2011-12	Leicester C	6	0	**6**	**0**

PARKES, Tom (D) 46 1
H: 6 3 W: 12 05 b.Sutton-in-Ashfield 15-1-92
Source: Scholar.

2008-09	Leicester C	0	0		
2009-10	Leicester C	0	0		
2009-10	*Burton Alb*	22	1		
2010-11	Leicester C	0	0		
2010-11	*Yeovil T*	1	0	**1**	**0**
2010-11	*Burton Alb*	5	0		
2011-12	Leicester C	0	0		
2011-12	*Burton Alb*	4	0	**31**	**1**
2011-12	*Bristol R*	14	0	**14**	**0**

PELTIER, Lee (D) 196 4
H: 5 10 W: 12 00 b.Liverpool 11-12-86
Source: Scholar.

2004-05	Liverpool	0	0		
2005-06	Liverpool	0	0		
2006-07	Liverpool	0	0		
2006-07	*Hull C*	7	0	**7**	**0**
2007-08	Liverpool	0	0		
2007-08	Yeovil T	34	0		
2008-09	Yeovil T	35	1	**69**	**1**
2009-10	Huddersfield T	42	0		
2010-11	Huddersfield T	38	1	**80**	**1**
2011-12	Leicester C	40	2	**40**	**2**

SCHLUPP, Jeffrey (M) 30 8
H: 5 8 W: 11 00 b.Hamburg 23-12-92
Source: Scholar. *Honours:* Ghana 1 full cap.

2010-11	Leicester C	0	0		
2010-11	*Brentford*	9	6	**9**	**6**
2011-12	Leicester C	21	2	**21**	**2**

SCHMEICHEL, Kasper (G) 205 0
H: 6 1 W: 13 00 b.Copenhagen 5-11-86
Source: Scholar. *Honours:* Denmark Youth, Under-20, Under-21.

2003-04	Manchester C	0	0		
2004-05	Manchester C	0	0		
2005-06	Manchester C	0	0		
2005-06	*Darlington*	4	0	**4**	**0**
2005-06	*Bury*	15	0		
2006-07	Manchester C	0	0		
2006-07	*Falkirk*	15	0	**15**	**0**
2006-07	*Bury*	14	0	**29**	**0**
2007-08	Manchester C	7	0		
2007-08	*Cardiff C*	14	0	**14**	**0**
2007-08	*Coventry C*	9	0	**9**	**0**
2008-09	Manchester C	1	0		
2009-10	Manchester C	0	0	**8**	**0**
2009-10	Notts Co	43	0	**43**	**0**
2010-11	Leeds U	37	0	**37**	**0**
2011-12	Leicester C	46	0	**46**	**0**

SMITH, Adam (G) 0 0
H: 5 11 W: 11 00 b.Sunderland 23-11-92
Source: Scholar.

2010-11	Leicester C	0	0		
2011-12	Leicester C	0	0		
2011-12	*Chesterfield*	0	0		
2011-12	*Bristol R*	0	0		

ST LEDGER-HALL, Sean (D) 305 13
H: 6 0 W: 11 09 b.Solihull 28-12-84
Source: Scholar. *Honours:* Eire 30 full caps, 3 goals.

2002-03	Peterborough U	1	0		
2003-04	Peterborough U	2	0		
2004-05	Peterborough U	33	0		
2005-06	Peterborough U	43	1	**79**	**1**
2006-07	Preston NE	41	1		
2007-08	Preston NE	37	1		
2008-09	Preston NE	46	5		
2009-10	Preston NE	30	2		
2009-10	*Middlesbrough*	15	2	**15**	**2**
2010-11	Preston NE	31	1	**185**	**10**
2011-12	Leicester C	26	0	**26**	**0**

TAFT, George (D) 0 0
H: 5 9 W: 11 09 b.Leicester 29-7-93
Source: Scholar. *Honours:* England Youth.

2010-11	Leicester C	0	0		
2011-12	Leicester C	0	0		

TUNCHEV, Aleksandar (D) 246 25
H: 6 2 W: 13 03 b.Pazardzhik 10-7-81
Honours: Bulgaria 26 full caps, 1 goal.

1998-99	Pazardzhik	6	0		
1999-2000	Pazardzhik	14	2		
1999-2000	Iskar	15	1	**15**	**1**
2000-01	Pazardzhik	18	3	**38**	**5**
2001-02	Belasitsa	30	3	**30**	**3**
2002-03	Lokomotiv Plovdiv	1	0		
2003-04	Lokomotiv Plovdiv	25	1		
2004-05	Lokomotiv Plovdiv	28	1		
2005-06	Lokomotiv Plovdiv	11	2	**65**	**4**
2005-06	CSKA Sofia	10	1		
2006-07	CSKA Sofia	27	7		
2007-08	CSKA Sofia	26	3	**63**	**11**
2008-09	Leicester C	20	1		
2009-10	Leicester C	2	0		
2010-11	Leicester C	2	0		
2011-12	Leicester C	2	0	**26**	**1**
2011-12	*Crystal Palace*	9	0	**9**	**0**

UCHECHI, Danny (F) 1 0
H: 6 0 W: 12 02 b.Abia State 14-9-89
Source: Charlton Ath Scholar, West Ham U, FC Dender. *Honours:* Nigeria Youth, Under-23.

2010-11	Leicester C	0	0		
2011-12	Leicester C	0	0		
2011-12	*Sheffield W*	1	0	**1**	**0**

On loan from FC Dender; transferred to Aberdeen January 2012.

VASSELL, Darius (F) 331 62
H: 5 9 W: 13 00 b.Birmingham 13-6-80
Source: Trainee. *Honours:* England Youth, Under-21, 22 full caps, 6 goals.

1998-99	Aston Villa	6	0		
1999-2000	Aston Villa	11	0		
2000-01	Aston Villa	23	4		
2001-02	Aston Villa	36	12		
2002-03	Aston Villa	33	8		
2003-04	Aston Villa	32	9		
2004-05	Aston Villa	21	2	**162**	**35**
2005-06	Manchester C	36	8		
2006-07	Manchester C	32	3		
2007-08	Manchester C	27	6		
2008-09	Manchester C	8	0	**103**	**17**
2009-10	Ankaragucu	22	4	**22**	**4**
2010-11	Leicester C	31	4		
2011-12	Leicester C	13	2	**44**	**6**

WAGHORN, Martyn (F) 95 19
H: 5 9 W: 13 01 b.South Shields 23-1-90
Source: Scholar. *Honours:* England Youth, Under-21.

2007-08	Sunderland	3	0		
2008-09	Sunderland	1	0		
2008-09	*Charlton Ath*	7	1	**7**	**1**
2009-10	Sunderland	0	0		
2009-10	*Leicester C*	43	12		
2010-11	Sunderland	2	0	**6**	**0**
2010-11	Leicester C	30	4		
2011-12	Leicester C	4	1	**77**	**17**
2011-12	*Hull C*	5	1	**5**	**1**

WEALE, Chris (G) 197 1
H: 6 2 W: 13 03 b.Chard 9-2-82
Source: Juniors.

2003-04	Yeovil T	35	0		
2004-05	Yeovil T	38	0		
2005-06	Yeovil T	25	0		
2006-07	Bristol C	1	0		
2007-08	Hereford U	1	0		
2007-08	Bristol C	3	0		
2008-09	Bristol C	5	0	**9**	**0**
2008-09	*Hereford U*	1	0	**2**	**0**
2008-09	*Yeovil T*	10	1	**108**	**1**
2009-10	Leicester C	45	0		
2010-11	Leicester C	29	0		
2011-12	Leicester C	1	0	**75**	**0**
2011-12	*Northampton T*	3	0	**3**	**0**

WELLENS, Richard (M) 486 37
H: 5 9 W: 11 06 b.Manchester 26-3-80
Source: Trainee. *Honours:* England Youth.

1996-97	Manchester U	0	0		
1997-98	Manchester U	0	0		
1998-99	Manchester U	0	0		
1999-2000	Manchester U	0	0		
1999-2000	Blackpool	8	0		
2000-01	Blackpool	36	8		
2001-02	Blackpool	36	1		
2002-03	Blackpool	39	1		
2003-04	Blackpool	41	3		
2004-05	Blackpool	28	3	**188**	**16**
2005-06	Oldham Ath	45	4		
2006-07	Oldham Ath	42	4	**87**	**8**
2007-08	Doncaster R	45	6		
2008-09	Doncaster R	39	3	**84**	**9**
2009-10	Leicester C	41	1		
2010-11	Leicester C	45	2		
2011-12	Leicester C	41	1	**127**	**4**

LEYTON ORIENT (46)

BEN YOUSSEF, Syam (D) 9 0
H: 6 2 W: 12 13 b.Marseille 31-3-89
Source: Bastia, Esperance.

2011-12	Leyton Orient	9	0	**9**	**0**

BUTCHER, Lee (G) 32 0
H: 6 1 W: 12 02 b.Waltham Forest 11-10-88
Source: Tottenham H.

2010-11	Leyton Orient	9	0		
2011-12	Leyton Orient	23	0	**32**	**0**

CESTOR, Mike (D) 3 0
H: 5 10 W: 12 04 b.Paris 30-4-92
Source: Youth.

2010-11	Leyton Orient	2	0		
2011-12	Leyton Orient	1	0	**3**	**0**

CHORLEY, Ben (D) 333 13
H: 6 3 W: 13 02 b.Sidcup 30-9-82
Source: Scholar.

2001-02	Arsenal	0	0		
2002-03	Arsenal	0	0		
2002-03	*Brentford*	2	0	**2**	**0**
2002-03	Wimbledon	10	0		
2003-04	Wimbledon	35	2	**45**	**2**
2004-05	Milton Keynes D	41	2		
2005-06	Milton Keynes D	26	0		
2006-07	Milton Keynes D	13	1	**80**	**3**
2006-07	*Gillingham*	27	1	**27**	**1**
2007-08	Tranmere R	31	1		
2008-09	Tranmere R	45	1	**76**	**2**
2009-10	Leyton Orient	42	1		
2010-11	Leyton Orient	29	3		
2011-12	Leyton Orient	32	1	**103**	**5**

COX, Dean (M) 229 34
H: 5 4 W: 9 08 b.Cuckfield 12-8-87
Source: Scholar.

2005-06	Brighton & HA	1	0		
2006-07	Brighton & HA	42	6		
2007-08	Brighton & HA	42	6		
2008-09	Brighton & HA	40	4		
2009-10	Brighton & HA	21	0	**146**	**16**
2010-11	Leyton Orient	45	11		
2011-12	Leyton Orient	38	7	**83**	**18**

CURETON, Jamie (F) 597 205
H: 5 8 W: 10 07 b.Bristol 28-8-75
Source: Trainee. *Honours:* England Youth.

1992-93	Norwich C	0	0		
1993-94	Norwich C	0	0		
1994-95	Norwich C	17	4		
1995-96	Norwich C	12	2		
1995-96	*Bournemouth*	5	0	**5**	**0**
1996-97	Norwich C	0	0		
1996-97	Bristol R	38	11		
1997-98	Bristol R	43	13		
1998-99	Bristol R	46	25		
1999-2000	Bristol R	46	22		
2000-01	Bristol R	1	1	**174**	**72**
2000-01	Reading	43	26		
2001-02	Reading	38	15		
2002-03	Reading	27	9	**108**	**50**

From Busan Icons.

2003-04	QPR	13	2		
2004-05	QPR	30	4	**43**	**6**
2005-06	Swindon T	30	7	**30**	**7**
2005-06	*Colchester U*	8	4		
2006-07	Colchester U	44	23	**52**	**27**

2007-08	Norwich C	41	12		
2008-09	Norwich C	22	2		
2008-09	*Barnsley*	8	2	**8**	**2**
2009-10	Norwich C	6	2	**98**	**22**
2009-10	*Shrewsbury T*	12	0	**12**	**0**
2010-11	Exeter C	41	17		
2011-12	Leyton Orient	19	1	**19**	**1**
2011-12	*Exeter C*	7	1	**48**	**18**

CUTHBERT, Scott (D) 146 7

H: 6 2 W: 14 00 b.Alexandria 15-6-87

Honours: Scotland Youth, Under-21, B.

2004-05	Celtic	0	0		
2005-06	Celtic	0	0		
2006-07	Celtic	0	0		
2006-07	*Livingston*	4	1	**4**	**1**
2007-08	Celtic	0	0		
2008-09	Celtic	0	0		
2008-09	*St Mirren*	29	0	**29**	**0**
2009-10	Swindon T	39	3		
2010-11	Swindon T	41	2	**80**	**5**
2011-12	Leyton Orient	33	1	**33**	**1**

FORBES, Terrell (D) 425 3

H: 5 11 W: 12 07 b.Southwark 17-8-81

Source: Trainee.

1999-2000	West Ham U	0	0		
1999-2000	*Bournemouth*	3	0	**3**	**0**
2000-01	West Ham U	0	0		
2001-02	QPR	43	0		
2002-03	QPR	38	0		
2003-04	QPR	30	0		
2004-05	QPR	3	0	**114**	**0**
2004-05	Grimsby T	33	0	**33**	**0**
2005-06	Oldham Ath	39	0	**39**	**0**
2006-07	Yeovil T	46	0		
2007-08	Yeovil T	41	0		
2008-09	Yeovil T	38	0		
2009-10	Yeovil T	38	1	**163**	**1**
2010-11	Leyton Orient	34	2		
2011-12	Leyton Orient	39	0	**73**	**2**

JONES, Jamie (G) 97 0

H: 6 2 W: 14 05 b.Kirkby 18-2-89

Source: Scholar.

2007-08	Everton	0	0		
2008-09	Leyton Orient	20	0		
2009-10	Leyton Orient	36	0		
2010-11	Leyton Orient	35	0		
2011-12	Leyton Orient	6	0	**97**	**0**

LAIRD, Marc (M) 123 10

H: 6 1 W: 10 07 b.Edinburgh 23-1-86

Source: Trainee.

2003-04	Manchester C	0	0		
2004-05	Manchester C	0	0		
2005-06	Manchester C	0	0		
2006-07	Manchester C	0	0		
2006-07	*Northampton T*	6	0	**6**	**0**
2007-08	Manchester C	0	0		
2007-08	*Port Vale*	7	1	**7**	**1**
2007-08	Millwall	17	1		
2008-09	Millwall	38	5		
2009-10	Millwall	20	0		
2010-11	Millwall	1	0	**76**	**6**
2010-11	*Brentford*	4	1	**4**	**1**
2010-11	*Walsall*	8	0	**8**	**0**
2011-12	Leyton Orient	22	2	**22**	**2**

LEACOCK, Dean (D) 154 1

H: 6 2 W: 12 04 b.Croydon 10-6-84

Source: Trainee. *Honours:* England Youth, Under-20.

2002-03	Fulham	0	0		
2003-04	Fulham	4	0		
2004-05	Fulham	0	0		
2004-05	*Coventry C*	13	0	**13**	**0**
2005-06	Fulham	5	0		
2006-07	Fulham	0	0	**9**	**0**
2006-07	Derby Co	38	0		
2007-08	Derby Co	26	0		
2008-09	Derby Co	11	0		
2009-10	Derby Co	17	0		
2010-11	Derby Co	25	1		
2011-12	Derby Co	0	0	**117**	**1**
2011-12	Leyton Orient	15	0	**15**	**0**

LISBIE, Kevin (F) 360 74

H: 5 10 W: 11 06 b.Hackney 17-10-78

Source: Trainee. *Honours:* England Youth. Jamaica 10 full caps, 2 goals.

1996-97	Charlton Ath	25	1		
1997-98	Charlton Ath	17	1		
1998-99	Charlton Ath	1	0		
1998-99	*Gillingham*	7	4	**7**	**4**
1999-2000	Charlton Ath	0	0		
1999-2000	*Reading*	2	0	**2**	**0**
2000-01	Charlton Ath	18	0		
2000-01	*QPR*	2	0	**2**	**0**
2001-02	Charlton Ath	22	5		
2002-03	Charlton Ath	32	4		
2003-04	Charlton Ath	9	4		
2004-05	Charlton Ath	17	1		
2005-06	Charlton Ath	6	0		
2005-06	*Norwich C*	6	1	**6**	**1**
2005-06	*Derby Co*	7	1	**7**	**1**
2006-07	Charlton Ath	8	0	**155**	**16**
2007-08	Colchester U	42	17		
2008-09	Ipswich T	41	6		
2009-10	Ipswich T	0	0		
2009-10	*Colchester U*	41	13	**83**	**30**
2010-11	Ipswich T	0	0		
2010-11	*Millwall*	20	4	**20**	**4**
2011-12	Ipswich T	0	0	**41**	**6**
2011-12	Leyton Orient	37	12	**37**	**12**

LOBJOIT, Billy (F) 1 0

H: 5 9 W: 11 05 b.Edgware 3-9-93

Source: Scholar.

2011-12	Leyton Orient	1	0	**1**	**0**

LOVELOCK, Thomas (G) 0 0

b.Harlow 14-5-93

Source: Scholar.

2011-12	Leyton Orient	0	0		

McSWEENEY, Leon (F) 171 13

H: 5 10 W: 10 11 b.Cork 19-2-83

Source: Cork C.

2001-02	Leicester C	0	0		
2002-03	Leicester C	0	0		

From Scarborough, Hucknall T, Hednesford T, Ilkeston T.

2007	Cork C	18	5	**18**	**5**
2007-08	Stockport Co	11	1		
2008-09	Stockport Co	36	4	**47**	**5**
2009-10	Hartlepool U	31	1		
2010-11	Hartlepool U	46	2	**77**	**3**
2011-12	Leyton Orient	29	0	**29**	**0**

MOONEY, David (F) 217 65

H: 6 2 W: 12 06 b.Dublin 30-10-84

Source: Shamrock R, Longford T. *Honours:* Eire Under-23.

2005	Longford T	13	4		
2005	Shamrock R	14	2	**14**	**2**
2006	Longford T	21	3		
2007	Longford T	32	19	**66**	**26**
2008	Cork City	22	15	**22**	**15**
2008-09	Reading	0	0		
2008-09	*Stockport Co*	2	0	**2**	**0**
2008-09	*Norwich C*	9	3	**9**	**3**
2009-10	Reading	0	0		
2009-10	*Charlton Ath*	28	5	**28**	**5**
2010-11	Reading	0	0		
2010-11	*Colchester U*	39	9	**39**	**9**
2011-12	Leyton Orient	37	5	**37**	**5**

OBAFEMI, Affy (F) 1 0

H: 6 2 W: 13 02 b.London 25-11-94

Source: Scholar.

2011-12	Leyton Orient	1	0	**1**	**0**

ODUBAJO, Moses (M) 3 1

H: 5 9 W: 11 05 b.Greenwich 28-7-93

Source: Scholar.

2011-12	Leyton Orient	3	1	**3**	**1**

OMOZUSI, Elliot (D) 88 0

H: 5 11 W: 12 09 b.Hackney 15-12-88

Source: Scholar. *Honours:* England Youth.

2005-06	Fulham	0	0		
2006-07	Fulham	0	0		
2007-08	Fulham	8	0		
2008-09	Fulham	0	0		
2008-09	*Norwich C*	21	0	**21**	**0**
2009-10	Fulham	0	0	**8**	**0**
2009-10	*Charlton Ath*	9	0	**9**	**0**
2010-11	Leyton Orient	40	0		
2011-12	Leyton Orient	10	0	**50**	**0**

PORTER, George (F) 35 1

H: 5 10 b.Sidcup 27-6-92

Source: Cray W.

2010-11	Leyton Orient	1	0		
2011-12	Leyton Orient	34	1	**35**	**1**

SMITH, Jamie (M) 11 0

H: 5 6 W: 10 07 b.Leytonstone 16-9-89

Source: Leytonstone.

2009-10	Brighton & HA	2	0		
2010-11	Brighton & HA	8	0		
2011-12	Brighton & HA	0	0	**10**	**0**
2011-12	Leyton Orient	1	0	**1**	**0**

SMITH, Jimmy (M) 176 21

H: 6 0 W: 10 03 b.Newham 7-1-87

Source: Scholar. *Honours:* England Youth.

2004-05	Chelsea	0	0		
2005-06	Chelsea	1	0		
2006-07	Chelsea	0	0		
2006-07	*QPR*	29	6	**29**	**6**
2007-08	Chelsea	0	0		
2007-08	*Norwich C*	9	0	**9**	**0**
2008-09	Chelsea	0	0	**1**	**0**
2008-09	*Sheffield W*	12	0	**12**	**0**
2008-09	*Leyton Orient*	16	0		
2009-10	Leyton Orient	40	2		
2010-11	Leyton Orient	31	7		
2011-12	Leyton Orient	38	6	**125**	**15**

SPRING, Matthew (M) 482 53

H: 5 11 W: 12 05 b.Harlow 17-11-79

Source: Trainee.

1997-98	Luton T	12	0		
1998-99	Luton T	45	3		
1999-2000	Luton T	45	6		
2000-01	Luton T	41	4		
2001-02	Luton T	42	6		
2002-03	Luton T	41	5		
2003-04	Luton T	24	1		
2004-05	Leeds U	13	1		
2005-06	Leeds U	0	0	**13**	**1**
2005-06	Watford	39	8		
2006-07	Watford	6	0	**45**	**8**
2006-07	Luton T	14	1		
2007-08	Luton T	44	9		
2008-09	Luton T	0	0	**308**	**35**
2008-09	*Sheffield U*	11	1	**11**	**1**
2008-09	Charlton Ath	13	2		
2009-10	Charlton Ath	12	0	**25**	**2**
2010-11	Leyton Orient	39	2		
2011-12	Leyton Orient	41	4	**80**	**6**

TEHOUE, Jonathan (F) 159 37

H: 5 8 W: 11 06 b.Paris 3-5-84

2003-04	Bastia	7	0	**7**	**0**
2004-05	Apoel	0	0		
2005-06	Virton	13	4	**13**	**4**
2006-07	FC Brussels	19	5	**19**	**5**
2007-08	Kasimpasa	15	6	**15**	**6**
2008-09	Konya	38	9	**38**	**9**
2009-10	Alfortville	2	1	**2**	**1**
2009-10	Leyton Orient	16	2		
2010-11	Leyton Orient	32	7		
2011-12	Leyton Orient	14	3	**62**	**12**
2011-12	*Swindon T*	3	0	**3**	**0**

LIVERPOOL (47)

ADAM, Charlie (M) 217 52

H: 6 1 W: 12 00 b.Dundee 10-12-85

Honours: Scotland Under-21, B, 16 full caps.

2004-05	Rangers	1	0		
2004-05	*Ross Co*	10	2	**10**	**2**
2005-06	Rangers	1	0		
2005-06	*St Mirren*	29	5	**29**	**5**
2006-07	Rangers	32	11		
2007-08	Rangers	16	2		
2008-09	Rangers	9	0	**59**	**13**
2008-09	Blackpool	13	2		
2009-10	Blackpool	43	16		
2010-11	Blackpool	35	12	**91**	**30**
2011-12	Liverpool	28	2	**28**	**2**

ADORJAN, Krisztian (F) 0 0

b.Budapest 19-1-93

Source: Scholar.

2010-11	Liverpool	0	0		
2011-12	Liverpool	0	0		

AGGER, Daniel (D) 154 9

H: 6 2 W: 12 06 b.Hvidovre 12-12-84

Honours: Denmark Youth, Under-20, Under-21, 49 full caps, 6 goals.

2004-05	Brondby	26	5		
2005-06	Brondby	8	0	**34**	**5**
2005-06	Liverpool	4	0		
2006-07	Liverpool	27	2		
2007-08	Liverpool	5	0		
2008-09	Liverpool	18	1		
2009-10	Liverpool	23	0		
2010-11	Liverpool	16	0		
2011-12	Liverpool	27	1	**120**	**4**

AMOO, David (F) **37 5**
H: 5 10 W: 12 03 b.Southwark 23-4-91
Source: Millwall.

2007-08	Liverpool	0	0		
2008-09	Liverpool	0	0		
2009-10	Liverpool	0	0		
2010-11	Liverpool	0	0		
2010-11	*Milton Keynes D*	3	0	**3**	**0**
2010-11	*Hull C*	7	1	**7**	**1**
2011-12	Liverpool	0	0		
2011-12	*Bury*	27	4	**27**	**4**

AQUILANI, Alberto (M) **206 17**
H: 6 0 W: 12 03 b.Rome 7-7-84
Honours: Italy 11 full caps, 2 goals.

2002-03	Roma	1	0		
2003-04	*Triestina*	31	4	**31**	**4**
2004-05	Roma	29	0		
2005-06	Roma	24	3		
2006-07	Roma	13	1		
2007-08	Roma	21	3		
2008-09	Roma	14	2	**102**	**9**
2009-10	Liverpool	18	1		
2010-11	Liverpool	0	0		
2010-11	*Juventus*	33	2	**33**	**2**
2011-12	Liverpool	0	0	**18**	**1**
2011-12	*AC Milan*	22	1	**22**	**1**

BAIO, Yalany (D) **0 0**
b.Guinea-Bissau 10-10-94
Source: Scholar.

2011-12	Liverpool	0	0

BANTON, Jason (F) **1 0**
b.Tottenham 15-12-92
Source: Scholar.

2009-10	Blackburn R	0	0		
2010-11	Blackburn R	0	0		
2010-11	Liverpool	0	0		
2011-12	Liverpool	0	0		
2011-12	*Burton Alb*	1	0	**1**	**0**

BELFORD, Tyrell (G) **0 0**
b.Nuneaton 6-5-94
Source: Scholar.

2011-12	Liverpool	0	0

BELLAMY, Craig (F) **403 129**
H: 5 9 W: 10 12 b.Cardiff 13-7-79
Source: Trainee. *Honours:* Wales Schools, Youth, Under-21, 69 full caps, 19 goals.

1996-97	Norwich C	3	0		
1997-98	Norwich C	36	13		
1998-99	Norwich C	40	17		
1999-2000	Norwich C	4	2		
2000-01	Norwich C	1	0	**84**	**32**
2000-01	Coventry C	34	6	**34**	**6**
2001-02	Newcastle U	27	9		
2002-03	Newcastle U	29	7		
2003-04	Newcastle U	16	4		
2004-05	Newcastle U	21	7	**93**	**27**
2004-05	*Celtic*	12	7	**12**	**7**
2005-06	Blackburn R	27	13	**27**	**13**
2006-07	Liverpool	27	7		
2007-08	West Ham U	8	2		
2008-09	West Ham U	16	5	**24**	**7**
2008-09	Manchester C	8	3		
2009-10	Manchester C	32	10		
2010-11	Manchester C	0	0		
2010-11	*Cardiff C*	35	11	**35**	**11**
2011-12	Manchester C	0	0	**40**	**13**
2011-12	Liverpool	27	6	**54**	**13**

BIJEV, Villyan (F) **0 0**
b.Fresno 3-1-93
Source: California Odyssey.

2011-12	Liverpool	0	0

CARRAGHER, Jamie (D) **484 3**
H: 5 9 W: 12 01 b.Liverpool 28-1-78
Source: Trainee. *Honours:* England Youth, Under-21, B, 38 full caps.

1995-96	Liverpool	0	0		
1996-97	Liverpool	2	1		
1997-98	Liverpool	20	0		
1998-99	Liverpool	34	1		
1999-2000	Liverpool	36	0		
2000-01	Liverpool	34	0		
2001-02	Liverpool	33	0		
2002-03	Liverpool	35	0		
2003-04	Liverpool	22	0		
2004-05	Liverpool	38	0		
2005-06	Liverpool	36	0		
2006-07	Liverpool	35	1		
2007-08	Liverpool	35	0		
2008-09	Liverpool	38	0		
2009-10	Liverpool	37	0		
2010-11	Liverpool	28	0		
2011-12	Liverpool	21	0	**484**	**3**

CARROLL, Andy (F) **133 38**
H: 6 4 W: 11 00 b.Gateshead 6-1-89
Source: Scholar. *Honours:* England Youth, Under-21, 7 full caps, 2 goals.

2006-07	Newcastle U	4	0		
2007-08	Newcastle U	4	0		
2007-08	*Preston NE*	11	1	**11**	**1**
2008-09	Newcastle U	14	3		
2009-10	Newcastle U	39	17		
2010-11	Newcastle U	19	11	**80**	**31**
2010-11	Liverpool	7	2		
2011-12	Liverpool	35	4	**42**	**6**

COADY, Conor (D) **0 0**
H: 6 1 W: 11 05 b.Liverpool 25-2-93
Source: Scholar. *Honours:* England Youth.

2010-11	Liverpool	0	0
2011-12	Liverpool	0	0

COATES, Sebastian (D) **62 5**
H: 6 5 W: 13 12 b.Montevideo 7-10-90
Honours: Uruguay Youth, 9 full caps, 1 goal.

2008-09	Nacional	6	1		
2009-10	Nacional	21	2		
2010-11	Nacional	27	1		
2011-12	Nacional	1	0	**55**	**4**
2011-12	Liverpool	7	1	**7**	**1**

COLE, Joe (M) **360 43**
H: 5 9 W: 11 09 b.Camden 8-11-81
Source: Trainee. *Honours:* England Schools, Youth, Under-21, B, 56 full caps, 10 goals.

1998-99	West Ham U	8	0		
1999-2000	West Ham U	22	1		
2000-01	West Ham U	30	5		
2001-02	West Ham U	30	0		
2002-03	West Ham U	36	4	**126**	**10**
2003-04	Chelsea	35	1		
2004-05	Chelsea	28	8		
2005-06	Chelsea	34	7		
2006-07	Chelsea	13	0		
2007-08	Chelsea	33	7		
2008-09	Chelsea	14	2		
2009-10	Chelsea	26	2	**183**	**27**
2010-11	Liverpool	20	2		
2011-12	Liverpool	0	0	**20**	**2**
2011-12	*Lille*	31	4	**31**	**4**

DARBY, Stephen (D) **71 0**
H: 5 9 W: 10 00 b.Liverpool 6-10-88
Source: Scholar. *Honours:* England Youth.

2006-07	Liverpool	0	0		
2007-08	Liverpool	0	0		
2008-09	Liverpool	0	0		
2009-10	Liverpool	1	0		
2009-10	*Swindon T*	12	0	**12**	**0**
2010-11	Liverpool	0	0		
2010-11	*Notts Co*	23	0	**23**	**0**
2011-12	Liverpool	0	0	**1**	**0**
2011-12	*Rochdale*	35	0	**35**	**0**

DONI (G) **238 0**
H: 6 4 W: 14 02 b.Sao Paulo 22-10-79
Honours: Brazil 10 full caps.

2001	Corinthians	9	0		
2002	Corinthians	24	0		
2003	Corinthians	26	0	**59**	**0**
2004	Santos	0	0		
2004	Cruzeiro	6	0	**6**	**0**
2005	Juventude	20	0	**20**	**0**
2005-06	Roma	28	0		
2006-07	Roma	32	0		
2007-08	Roma	37	0		
2008-09	Roma	29	0		
2009-10	Roma	7	0		
2010-11	Roma	16	0	**149**	**0**
2011-12	Liverpool	4	0	**4**	**0**

DOWNING, Stewart (M) **287 29**
H: 5 11 W: 10 04 b.Middlesbrough 22-7-84
Source: Scholar. *Honours:* England Youth, Under-21, B, 34 full caps.

2001-02	Middlesbrough	3	0		
2002-03	Middlesbrough	2	0		
2003-04	Middlesbrough	20	0		
2003-04	*Sunderland*	7	3	**7**	**3**
2004-05	Middlesbrough	35	5		
2005-06	Middlesbrough	12	1		
2006-07	Middlesbrough	34	2		
2007-08	Middlesbrough	38	9		
2008-09	Middlesbrough	37	0	**181**	**17**
2009-10	Aston Villa	25	2		
2010-11	Aston Villa	38	7	**63**	**9**
2011-12	Liverpool	36	0	**36**	**0**

DUNN, Jack (M) **0 0**
b.Liverpool 19-11-94
Source: Scholar. *Honours:* England Youth.

2011-12	Liverpool	0	0

ECCLESTON, Nathan (F) **39 5**
H: 5 10 W: 12 00 b.Manchester 30-12-90
Source: Scholar.

2007-08	Liverpool	0	0		
2008-09	Liverpool	0	0		
2009-10	Liverpool	1	0		
2009-10	*Huddersfield T*	11	1	**11**	**1**
2010-11	Liverpool	1	0		
2010-11	*Charlton Ath*	21	3	**21**	**3**
2011-12	Liverpool	0	0	**2**	**0**
2011-12	*Rochdale*	5	1	**5**	**1**

EMILSSON, Kristjan (M) **0 0**
b.Sweden 26-4-93
Source: Scholar.

2009-10	Liverpool	0	0
2010-11	Liverpool	0	0
2011-12	Liverpool	0	0

FABIO AURELIO (M) **235 17**
H: 5 10 W: 11 11 b.Sao Carlos 24-9-79
Honours: Brazil Youth, Under-20, Under-21.

1997	Sao Paulo	15	1		
1998	Sao Paulo	11	1		
1998	Santos	0	0		
1999	Sao Paulo	23	1		
2000	Sao Paulo	4	0	**53**	**3**
2000-01	Valencia	7	0		
2001-02	Valencia	15	1		
2002-03	Valencia	26	8		
2003-04	Valencia	2	0		
2004-05	Valencia	21	0		
2005-06	Valencia	24	2	**95**	**11**
2006-07	Liverpool	17	0		
2007-08	Liverpool	16	1		
2008-09	Liverpool	24	2		
2009-10	Liverpool	14	0		
2010-11	Liverpool	14	0		
2011-12	Liverpool	2	0	**87**	**3**

FERNANDEZ, Jesus (F) **0 0**
H: 5 9 W: 11 00 b.Cadiz 19-11-93
Source: Scholar.

2011-12	Liverpool	0	0

FLANAGAN, John (D) **12 0**
H: 5 11 W: 12 06 b.Liverpool 1-1-93
Source: Scholar. *Honours:* England Youth, Under-21.

2010-11	Liverpool	7	0		
2011-12	Liverpool	5	0	**12**	**0**

GERRARD, Steven (M) **405 89**
H: 6 0 W: 12 05 b.Huyton 30-5-80
Source: Trainee. *Honours:* England Youth, Under-21, 96 full caps, 19 goals.

1997-98	Liverpool	0	0		
1998-99	Liverpool	12	0		
1999-2000	Liverpool	29	1		
2000-01	Liverpool	33	7		
2001-02	Liverpool	28	3		
2002-03	Liverpool	34	5		
2003-04	Liverpool	34	4		
2004-05	Liverpool	30	7		
2005-06	Liverpool	32	10		
2006-07	Liverpool	36	7		
2007-08	Liverpool	34	11		
2008-09	Liverpool	31	16		
2009-10	Liverpool	33	9		
2010-11	Liverpool	21	4		
2011-12	Liverpool	18	5	**405**	**89**

GULACSI, Peter (G) **50 0**
H: 6 3 W: 13 01 b.Budapest 6-5-90
Source: MTK. *Honours:* Hungary Youth, Under-21.

2007-08	Liverpool	0	0		
2008-09	Liverpool	0	0		
2008-09	*Hereford U*	18	0	**18**	**0**
2009-10	Liverpool	0	0		
2009-10	*Tranmere R*	5	0		
2010-11	Liverpool	0	0		
2010-11	*Tranmere R*	12	0	**17**	**0**
2011-12	Liverpool	0	0		
2011-12	*Hull C*	15	0	**15**	**0**

HANSEN, Martin (G) **4 0**
H: 6 2 W: 12 07 b.Glostrup 15-6-90
Source: Brondby. *Honours:* Denmark Under-21.
2007-08 Liverpool 0 0
2008-09 Liverpool 0 0
2009-10 Liverpool 0 0
2010-11 Liverpool 0 0
2011-12 Liverpool 0 0
2011-12 *Bradford C* 4 0 **4 0**
Transferred to Viborg January 2012.

HENDERSON, Jordan (M) **118 7**
H: 6 0 W: 10 07 b.Sunderland 17-6-90
Source: Scholar. *Honours:* England Youth, Under-20, Under-21, 5 full caps.
2008-09 Sunderland 1 0
2008-09 *Coventry C* 10 1 **10 1**
2009-10 Sunderland 33 1
2010-11 Sunderland 37 3 **71 4**
2011-12 Liverpool 37 2 **37 2**

IBE, Jordan (F) **7 1**
H: 5 9 W: 11 00 b.Southwark 8-12-95
Source: Schoolboy.
2011-12 Wycombe W 7 1 **7 1**
2011-12 Liverpool 0 0

JOHNSON, Glen (D) **225 13**
H: 6 0 W: 13 04 b.Greenwich 23-8-84
Source: Scholar. *Honours:* England Youth, Under-20, Under-21, 40 full caps, 1 goal.
2001-02 West Ham U 0 0
2002-03 West Ham U 15 0 **15 0**
2002-03 *Millwall* 8 0 **8 0**
2003-04 Chelsea 19 3
2004-05 Chelsea 17 0
2005-06 Chelsea 4 0
2006-07 Chelsea 0 0
2006-07 *Portsmouth* 26 0
2007-08 Chelsea 2 0 **42 3**
2007-08 Portsmouth 29 1
2008-09 Portsmouth 29 3
2009-10 Portsmouth 0 0 **84 4**
2009-10 Liverpool 25 3
2010-11 Liverpool 28 2
2011-12 Liverpool 23 1 **76 6**

JONES, Brad (G) **101 0**
H: 6 3 W: 12 01 b.Armidale 19-3-82
Source: Trainee. *Honours:* Australia Under-20, Under-23, 3 full caps.
1998-99 Middlesbrough 0 0
1999-2000 Middlesbrough 0 0
2000-01 Middlesbrough 0 0
2001-02 Middlesbrough 0 0
2002 Shelbourne 2 0 **2 0**
2002-03 Middlesbrough 0 0
2002-03 *Stockport Co* 1 0 **1 0**
2003-04 Middlesbrough 1 0
2003-04 *Blackpool* 5 0
2003-04 *Rotherham U* 0 0
2004-05 Middlesbrough 5 0
2004-05 *Blackpool* 12 0 **17 0**
2005-06 Middlesbrough 9 0
2006-07 Middlesbrough 2 0
2006-07 *Sheffield W* 15 0 **15 0**
2007-08 Middlesbrough 1 0
2008-09 Middlesbrough 16 0
2009-10 Middlesbrough 24 0 **58 0**
2010-11 Liverpool 0 0
2010-11 *Derby Co* 7 0 **7 0**
2011-12 Liverpool 1 0 **1 0**

JOSE ENRIQUE (D) **210 2**
H: 6 0 W: 12 00 b.Valencia 23-1-86
Honours: Spain Under-21.
2004-05 Levante 19 1 **19 1**
2005-06 Valencia 0 0
2005-06 *Celta Vigo* 14 0 **14 0**
2006-07 Villarreal 23 0 **23 0**
2007-08 Newcastle U 23 0
2008-09 Newcastle U 26 0
2009-10 Newcastle U 34 1
2010-11 Newcastle U 36 0 **119 1**
2011-12 Liverpool 35 0 **35 0**

KELLY, Martin (D) **31 1**
H: 6 3 W: 12 02 b.Bolton 27-4-90
Source: Scholar. *Honours:* England Youth, Under-20, Under-21, 1 full cap.
2007-08 Liverpool 0 0
2008-09 Liverpool 0 0
2008-09 *Huddersfield T* 7 1 **7 1**
2009-10 Liverpool 1 0
2010-11 Liverpool 11 0
2011-12 Liverpool 12 0 **24 0**

KUYT, Dirk (F) **469 173**
H: 6 0 W: 12 02 b.Katwijk 22-7-80
Source: Quick Boys. *Honours:* Holland 90 full caps, 24 goals.
1998-99 Utrecht 28 5
1999-2000 Utrecht 32 6
2000-01 Utrecht 32 13
2001-02 Utrecht 34 7
2002-03 Utrecht 34 20 **160 51**
2003-04 Feyenoord 34 20
2004-05 Feyenoord 34 29
2005-06 Feyenoord 33 22 **101 71**
2006-07 Liverpool 34 12
2007-08 Liverpool 32 3
2008-09 Liverpool 38 12
2009-10 Liverpool 37 9
2010-11 Liverpool 33 13
2011-12 Liverpool 34 2 **208 51**

LUCAS (M) **156 5**
H: 5 10 W: 11 09 b.Dourados 9-1-87
Honours: Brazil Under-20, 20 full caps.
2005 Gremio 3 0
2006 Gremio 30 4 **33 4**
2007-08 Liverpool 18 0
2008-09 Liverpool 25 1
2009-10 Liverpool 35 0
2010-11 Liverpool 33 0
2011-12 Liverpool 12 0 **123 1**

LUSSEY, Jordan (M) **0 0**
b.Ormskirk 2-11-94
Source: Scholar. *Honours:* England Youth.
2011-12 Liverpool 0 0

McGIVERON, Matthew (D) **0 0**
b.Chester 3-9-92
Source: Scholar.
2011-12 Liverpool 0 0

McLAUGHLIN, Ryan (D) **0 0**
b.Belfast 30-9-94
Source: Scholar. *Honours:* Northern Ireland Youth.
2011-12 Liverpool 0 0

MERSIN, Yusuf (G) **0 0**
b.Greenwich 23-9-94
Source: Scholar.
2011-12 Liverpool 0 0

MORGAN, Adam (F) **0 0**
b.Liverpool 21-4-94
Source: Scholar. *Honours:* England Youth.
2011-12 Liverpool 0 0

NACHO (M) **0 0**
b.Spain 16-12-93
2011-12 Liverpool 0 0

NGOO, Michael (F) **0 0**
b.Walthamstow 23-10-92
Source: Southend U Scholar. *Honours:* England Youth, Under-20.
2009-10 Liverpool 0 0
2010-11 Liverpool 0 0
2011-12 Liverpool 0 0

PACHECO, Daniel (F) **22 2**
H: 5 6 W: 10 07 b.Malaga 5-1-91
Honours: Spain Youth, Under-21.
2007-08 Liverpool 0 0
2008-09 Liverpool 0 0
2009-10 Liverpool 4 0
2010-11 Liverpool 1 0
2010-11 *Norwich C* 6 2 **6 2**
2011-12 Liverpool 0 0 **5 0**
2011-12 *Rayo Vallecano* 11 0 **11 0**

PELOSI, Marc (D) **0 0**
b.Bad Sackingen 17-6-94
Source: DeAnza Force.
2011-12 Liverpool 0 0

PETERSSON, Kristoffer (M) **0 0**
b.Gothenburg 28-11-94
Source: Scholar.
2011-12 Liverpool 0 0

REINA, Jose (G) **423 0**
H: 6 2 W: 14 06 b.Madrid 31-8-82
Honours: Spain Youth, Under-21, 25 full caps.
1999-2000 Barcelona B 30 0 **30 0**
2000-01 Barcelona 19 0
2001-02 Barcelona 11 0 **30 0**
2002-03 Villarreal 33 0
2003-04 Villarreal 38 0
2004-05 Villarreal 38 0 **109 0**
2005-06 Liverpool 33 0
2006-07 Liverpool 35 0
2007-08 Liverpool 38 0
2008-09 Liverpool 38 0
2009-10 Liverpool 38 0
2010-11 Liverpool 38 0
2011-12 Liverpool 34 0 **254 0**

ROBERTS, Michael (M) **0 0**
b.Liverpool 5-12-91
2008-09 Liverpool 0 0
2009-10 Liverpool 0 0
2010-11 Liverpool 0 0
2011-12 Liverpool 0 0

ROBINSON, Jack (D) **3 0**
H: 5 11 W: 10 08 b.Warrington 1-9-93
Source: Scholar. *Honours:* England Youth.
2009-10 Liverpool 1 0
2010-11 Liverpool 2 0
2011-12 Liverpool 0 0 **3 0**

RODDAN, Craig (M) **0 0**
b.Kirkby 22-4-93
Source: Scholar.
2011-12 Liverpool 0 0

RODRIGUEZ, Maxi (M) **346 92**
H: 5 11 W: 12 06 b.Rosario 2-1-81
Honours: Argentina 41 full caps, 12 goals.
1999-2000 Newell's Old Boys 6 0
2000-01 Newell's Old Boys 18 5
2001-02 Newell's Old Boys 33 15 **57 20**
2002-03 Espanyol 37 7
2003-04 Espanyol 37 4
2004-05 Espanyol 37 15 **111 26**
2005-06 Atletico Madrid 29 10
2006-07 Atletico Madrid 10 5
2007-08 Atletico Madrid 35 8
2008-09 Atletico Madrid 33 6
2009-10 Atletico Madrid 14 2 **121 31**
2009-10 Liverpool 17 1
2010-11 Liverpool 28 10
2011-12 Liverpool 12 4 **57 15**

SAMA, Stephen (D) **0 0**
b.Cameroon 5-3-93
Source: Scholar.
2009-10 Liverpool 0 0
2010-11 Liverpool 0 0
2011-12 Liverpool 0 0

SHELVEY, Jonjo (M) **80 14**
H: 6 1 W: 11 02 b.Romford 27-2-92
Source: Scholar. *Honours:* England Youth, Under-21.
2007-08 Charlton Ath 2 0
2008-09 Charlton Ath 16 3
2009-10 Charlton Ath 24 4 **42 7**
2010-11 Liverpool 15 0
2011-12 Liverpool 13 1 **28 1**
2011-12 *Blackpool* 10 6 **10 6**

SILVA, Toni (M) **15 1**
H: 6 0 W: 11 09 b.Guinea-Bissau 15-9-93
Honours: Portugal Youth.
2010-11 Liverpool 0 0
2011-12 Liverpool 0 0
2011-12 *Northampton T* 15 1 **15 1**

SKRTEL, Martin (D) **235 8**
H: 6 3 W: 12 10 b.Handlova 15-12-84
Honours: Slovakia 53 full caps, 5 goals.
2002-03 Trencin 1 0
2003-04 Trencin 34 0 **35 0**
2004 Zenit 7 0
2005 Zenit 18 1
2006 Zenit 26 1
2007 Zenit 23 1 **74 3**
2007-08 Liverpool 14 0
2008-09 Liverpool 21 0
2009-10 Liverpool 19 1
2010-11 Liverpool 38 2
2011-12 Liverpool 34 2 **126 5**

SMITH, Bradley (D) **0 0**
b.New South Wales 9-4-94
Source: Scholar.
2011-12 Liverpool 0 0

SOKOLIK, Jakub (D) **0 0**
H: 5 6 b.Ostrava 28-8-93
Source: Scholar.

2010-11	Liverpool	0	0		
2011-12	Liverpool	0	0		

SPEARING, Jay (M) **37 1**
H: 5 6 W: 11 01 b.Wallasey 25-11-88
Source: Scholar.

2006-07	Liverpool	0	0		
2007-08	Liverpool	0	0		
2008-09	Liverpool	0	0		
2009-10	Liverpool	3	0		
2009-10	*Leicester C*	7	1	**7**	**1**
2010-11	Liverpool	11	0		
2011-12	Liverpool	16	0	**30**	**0**

STEPHENS, James (G) **0 0**
b.Wotton-under-Edge 24-8-93
Source: Scholar.

2010-11	Liverpool	0	0		
2011-12	Liverpool	0	0		

STERLING, Raheem (F) **3 0**
H: 5 7 W: 10 00 b.Kingston 8-12-94
Source: Scholar.

2011-12	Liverpool	3	0	**3**	**0**

SUAREZ, Luis (F) **210 116**
H: 5 11 W: 12 10 b.Salto 24-1-87
Honours: Uruguay 56 full caps, 27 goals.

2005-06	Nacional	27	10	**27**	**10**
2006-07	Groningen	29	10	**29**	**10**
2007-08	Ajax	33	17		
2008-09	Ajax	31	22		
2009-10	Ajax	33	35		
2010-11	Ajax	13	7	**110**	**81**
2010-11	Liverpool	13	4		
2011-12	Liverpool	31	11	**44**	**15**

SUSO (M) **20 7**
H: 5 8 W: 10 12 b.Cadiz 19-11-93

2010-11	Cadiz B	20	7	**20**	**7**
2010-11	Liverpool	0	0		
2011-12	Liverpool	0	0		

TEIXEIRA, Joao Carlos (M) **0 0**
b.Braga 18-1-93
Source: Sporting Lisbon Youth. *Honours:* Portugal Youth.

2011-12	Liverpool	0	0		

WARD, Danny (G) **0 0**
b.Wrexham 22-6-93
Source: Wrexham. *Honours:* Wales Youth.

2011-12	Liverpool	0	0		

WILSON, Danny (D) **22 1**
H: 6 2 W: 12 06 b.Livingston 27-12-91
Honours: Scotland Youth, Under-21, 5 full caps, 1 goal.

2009-10	Rangers	14	1	**14**	**1**
2010-11	Liverpool	2	0		
2011-12	Liverpool	0	0	**2**	**0**
2011-12	*Blackpool*	6	0	**6**	**0**

WISDOM, Andre (D) **0 0**
H: 6 1 W: 12 04 b.Leeds 9-5-93
Source: Scholar. *Honours:* England Youth, Under-21.

2009-10	Liverpool	0	0		
2010-11	Liverpool	0	0		
2011-12	Liverpool	0	0		

Scholars
Gainford Sam; Mukendi Henoc John; Quirk Nathan; Wilson Michael.

MACCLESFIELD T (48)

BAKARE, Michael (M) **9 0**
H: 6 0 W: 11 11 b.Hackney 1-12-86
Source: Leyton, Welling U, Thurrock, Bishop's Stortford, Chelmsford C.

2011-12	Macclesfield T	9	0	**9**	**0**

BATESON, Jonathan (D) **54 0**
H: 6 1 W: 12 04 b.Preston 20-9-89
Source: Scholar.

2008-09	Blackburn R	0	0		
2009-10	Blackburn R	0	0		
2009-10	Bradford C	21	0	**21**	**0**
2010-11	Accrington S	12	0	**12**	**0**
2011-12	Macclesfield T	21	0	**21**	**0**

BOLTON, James (D) **0 0**
b.Stone
Source: Scholar.

2011-12	Macclesfield T	0	0		

BROWN, Nat (D) **319 20**
H: 6 2 W: 12 05 b.Sheffield 15-6-81
Source: Trainee.

1999-2000	Huddersfield T	0	0		
2000-01	Huddersfield T	0	0		
2001-02	Huddersfield T	0	0		
2002-03	Huddersfield T	38	0		
2003-04	Huddersfield T	21	0		
2004-05	Huddersfield T	17	0	**76**	**0**
2005-06	Lincoln C	39	7		
2006-07	Lincoln C	28	1		
2007-08	Lincoln C	27	0	**94**	**8**
From Wrexham.					
2008-09	Macclesfield T	30	6		
2009-10	Macclesfield T	38	4		
2010-11	Macclesfield T	44	2		
2011-12	Macclesfield T	37	0	**149**	**12**

CHALMERS, Lewis (M) **99 6**
H: 6 0 W: 12 04 b.Manchester 4-2-86
Source: Altrincham.

2008-09	Aldershot T	23	1		
2009-10	Aldershot T	23	0	**46**	**1**
2010-11	Macclesfield T	30	2		
2011-12	Macclesfield T	23	3	**53**	**5**

COLLIS, Steve (G) **88 0**
H: 6 3 W: 12 05 b.Harrow 18-3-81
Source: Barnet Juniors.

1999-2000	Barnet	0	0		
2000-01	Nottingham F	0	0		
2001-02	Nottingham F	0	0		
2003-04	Yeovil T	11	0		
2004-05	Yeovil T	9	0		
2005-06	Yeovil T	23	0	**43**	**0**
2006-07	Southend U	1	0		
2007-08	Southend U	20	0	**21**	**0**
2008-09	Crewe Alex	18	0		
2009-10	Crewe Alex	1	0	**19**	**0**
2009-10	Bristol C	0	0		
2009-10	*Torquay U*	1	0	**1**	**0**
2010-11	Peterborough U	0	0		
2010-11	*Northampton T*	4	0	**4**	**0**
2011-12	Macclesfield T	0	0		

CUDWORTH, Jack (G) **0 0**
b.Preston 11-9-90
Source: Preston NE Scholar, Welshpool, Rhyl.

2010-11	Macclesfield T	0	0		
2011-12	Macclesfield T	0	0		

DANIEL, Colin (M) **139 14**
H: 5 11 W: 11 06 b.Eastwood 15-2-88
Source: Eastwood T.

2006-07	Crewe Alex	0	0		
2007-08	Crewe Alex	1	0		
2008-09	Crewe Alex	13	1	**14**	**1**
2008-09	*Macclesfield T*	8	0		
2009-10	Macclesfield T	38	3		
2010-11	Macclesfield T	43	8		
2011-12	Macclesfield T	36	2	**125**	**13**

DANIELS, Greg (M) **0 0**
b.Salford 21-1-93
Source: Scholar.

2011-12	Macclesfield T	0	0		

DIAGNE, Tony (D) **81 5**
H: 6 2 W: 11 11 b.Mantes-la-Jolie 17-9-90
Source: Scholar.

2008-09	Nottingham F	0	0		
2009-10	Nottingham F	0	0		
2010-11	Aubervilliers	20	1	**20**	**1**
2010-11	Macclesfield T	20	1		
2011-12	Macclesfield T	41	3	**61**	**4**

DRAPER, Ross (M) **97 10**
H: 6 3 W: 15 05 b.Wolverhampton 20-10-88
Source: Shrewsbury T, Stafford R, Hednesford T.

2009-10	Macclesfield T	29	1		
2010-11	Macclesfield T	40	5		
2011-12	Macclesfield T	28	4	**97**	**10**

FAIRHURST, Waide (F) **58 9**
H: 5 10 W: 10 07 b.Sheffield 7-5-89
Source: Scholar.

2008-09	Doncaster R	3	0		
2009-10	Doncaster R	6	2		
2009-10	*Shrewsbury T*	10	4	**10**	**4**
2010-11	Doncaster R	2	0	**11**	**2**
2010-11	*Southend U*	3	0	**3**	**0**
2010-11	*Hereford U*	16	3	**16**	**3**
2011-12	Macclesfield T	18	0	**18**	**0**

FISHER, Tom (F) **29 1**
H: 5 10 W: 11 07 b.Wythenshawe 28-6-92
Source: Scholar.

2008-09	Stockport Co	1	0		
2009-10	Stockport Co	1	0		
2010-11	Stockport Co	26	1	**28**	**1**
2011-12	Macclesfield T	1	0	**1**	**0**

GRANT, John (F) **82 10**
H: 5 11 W: 10 08 b.Manchester 9-8-81
Source: Trainee.

1999-2000	Crewe Alex	4	0		
2000-01	Crewe Alex	2	0		
2001-02	Crewe Alex	1	0	**7**	**0**
2001-02	*Rushden & D*	0	0		
From Here U, Telfd U					
2004-05	Shrewsbury T	19	2	**19**	**2**
From Halifax T.					
2008-09	Aldershot T	35	5		
2009-10	Aldershot T	17	3	**52**	**8**
From Barrow.					
2011-12	Macclesfield T	4	0	**4**	**0**

HAMSHAW, Matt (M) **325 20**
H: 5 10 W: 11 08 b.Rotherham 1-1-82
Source: Trainee. *Honours:* England Youth, Under-20.

1998-99	Sheffield W	0	0		
1999-2000	Sheffield W	0	0		
2000-01	Sheffield W	18	0		
2001-02	Sheffield W	21	0		
2002-03	Sheffield W	15	1		
2003-04	Sheffield W	0	0		
2004-05	Sheffield W	20	1	**74**	**2**
2005-06	Stockport Co	39	5	**39**	**5**
2006-07	Mansfield T	40	4		
2007-08	Mansfield T	45	2	**85**	**6**
2008-09	Notts Co	41	3		
2009-10	Notts Co	20	0	**61**	**3**
2010-11	Macclesfield T	28	2		
2011-12	Macclesfield T	38	2	**66**	**4**

HEWITT, Elliott (D) **22 0**
H: 5 11 W: 11 11 b.Rhyl 30-5-94
Source: Scholar.

2010-11	Macclesfield T	1	0		
2011-12	Macclesfield T	21	0	**22**	**0**

KAY, Scott (M) **15 0**
H: 5 10 W: 12 02 b.Denton 18-9-89
Source: Scholar.

2007-08	Manchester C	0	0		
2008-09	Manchester C	0	0		
2009-10	Manchester C	0	0		
2010-11	Manchester C	0	0		
2011-12	Macclesfield T	15	0	**15**	**0**

LANE, Jack (D) **0 0**
b.Winsford 26-3-93
Source: Scholar.

2011-12	Macclesfield T	0	0		

MATTIS, Dwayne (M) **291 23**
H: 6 1 W: 11 12 b.Huddersfield 31-7-81
Source: Trainee. *Honours:* Eire Youth, Under-21.

1998-99	Huddersfield T	2	0		
1999-2000	Huddersfield T	0	0		
2000-01	Huddersfield T	0	0		
2001-02	Huddersfield T	29	1		
2002-03	Huddersfield T	33	1		
2003-04	Huddersfield T	5	0	**69**	**2**
2004-05	Bury	39	5		
2005-06	Bury	36	5		
2006-07	Bury	22	1	**97**	**11**
2006-07	Barnsley	3	0		
2007-08	Barnsley	1	0	**4**	**0**
2007-08	*Walsall*	4	0		
2008-09	Walsall	37	4		
2009-10	Walsall	34	2	**75**	**6**
2010-11	Chesterfield	38	3		
2011-12	Chesterfield	7	0	**45**	**3**
2011-12	Macclesfield T	1	1	**1**	**1**

MENDY, Arnaud (F) **42 3**
H: 6 3 W: 13 10 b.Evreux 10-2-90
Source: Rouen. *Honours:* Guinea-Bissau 1 full cap.

2008-09	Derby Co	0	0		
2009-10	Derby Co	1	0		

2009-10	*Grimsby T*	1	0	**1**	**0**
2010-11	Derby Co	0	0	**1**	**0**
2010-11	*Tranmere R*	12	1	**12**	**1**
2011-12	Macclesfield T	28	2	**28**	**2**

MILLS, Andy (G) **0 0**
Source: Scholar.

2011-12	Macclesfield T	0	0		

MILLS, Ben (F) **12 0**
H: 6 2 W: 12 00 b.Stoke 23-3-89
Source: Stone Dominoes, Newcastle T, Leek T, Alfreton T, Stafford R, Nantwich T.

2011-12	Macclesfield T	12	0	**12**	**0**

MORGAN, Paul (D) **338 3**
H: 6 0 W: 11 05 b.Belfast 23-10-78
Source: Trainee. *Honours:* Northern Ireland Under-21.

1997-98	Preston NE	0	0		
1998-99	Preston NE	0	0		
1999-2000	Preston NE	0	0		
2000-01	Preston NE	0	0		
2001-02	Lincoln C	34	1		
2002-03	Lincoln C	45	0		
2003-04	Lincoln C	41	0		
2004-05	Lincoln C	39	0		
2005-06	Lincoln C	20	0		
2006-07	Lincoln C	33	1	**212**	**2**
2007-08	Bury	20	0		
2008-09	Bury	0	0	**20**	**0**
2008-09	*Macclesfield T*	39	1		
2009-10	Macclesfield T	36	0		
2010-11	Macclesfield T	28	0		
2011-12	Macclesfield T	3	0	**106**	**1**

MUKENDI, Vinny (F) **47 3**
H: 6 2 W: 12 00 b.Manchester 12-3-92
Source: Scholar.

2008-09	Macclesfield T	1	0		
2009-10	Macclesfield T	9	1		
2010-11	Macclesfield T	21	1		
2011-12	Macclesfield T	16	1	**47**	**3**

ROBERTS, Adam (M) **4 0**
H: 5 9 W: 10 07 b.Manchester 30-12-91
Source: Scholar.

2010-11	Macclesfield T	2	0		
2011-12	Macclesfield T	2	0	**4**	**0**

THOMAS, Michael (M) **10 0**
H: 6 1 W: 11 00 b.Manchester 12-8-92
Source: Scholar.

2009-10	Macclesfield T	4	0		
2010-11	Macclesfield T	0	0		
2011-12	Macclesfield T	6	0	**10**	**0**

TOMLINSON, Ben (F) **25 6**
H: 5 11 W: 11 11 b.Dinnington 31-10-89
Source: Worksop T.

2011-12	Macclesfield T	25	6	**25**	**6**

TREMARCO, Carl (D) **153 1**
H: 5 8 W: 11 11 b.Liverpool 11-10-85
Source: Scholar.

2003-04	Tranmere R	0	0		
2004-05	Tranmere R	3	0		
2005-06	Tranmere R	18	1		
2006-07	Tranmere R	23	0		
2007-08	Tranmere R	8	0	**52**	**1**
2007-08	Wrexham	10	0	**10**	**0**
2008-09	*Darlington*	2	0	**2**	**0**
2009-10	Macclesfield T	29	0		
2010-11	Macclesfield T	25	0		
2011-12	Macclesfield T	35	0	**89**	**0**

VEIGA, Jose Manuel (G) **358 0**
H: 6 2 W: 12 13 b.Lisbon 18-12-76
Source: Benfica. *Honours:* Cape Verde full caps.

1996-97	Alverca	14	0		
1997-98	Alverca	33	0	**47**	**0**
1998-99	Levante	38	0		
1999-2000	Levante	40	0		
2000-01	Levante	30	0		
2001-02	Levante	22	0	**130**	**0**
2001-02	Valladolid	0	0		
2002-03	Amadora	33	0		
2003-04	Amadora	28	0		
2004-05	Amadora	31	0	**92**	**0**
2005-06	Olhanense	2	0	**2**	**0**
From Tamworth, Atherstone T.					
2008-09	Hereford U	1	0		
2009-10	Hereford U	0	0	**1**	**0**
2009-10	Macclesfield T	5	0		
2010-11	Macclesfield T	46	0		
2011-12	Macclesfield T	35	0	**86**	**0**

WEDGBURY, Sam (M) **68 3**
H: 6 0 W: 12 08 b.Oldbury 26-2-89
Source: Scholar.

2006-07	Sheffield U	0	0		
2007-08	Sheffield U	0	0		
2008-09	Sheffield U	0	0		
2009-10	Sheffield U	0	0		
2009-10	*Ferencvaros*	6	1	**6**	**1**
2010-11	Macclesfield T	23	1		
2011-12	Macclesfield T	39	1	**62**	**2**

MANCHESTER C (49)

ABU, Mohammed (M) **0 0**
b.Ghana 14-11-91
Source: SC Accra. *Honours:* Ghana 4 full caps.

2010-11	Manchester C	0	0		
2011-12	Manchester C	0	0		

ADEBAYOR, Emmanuel (F) **307 116**
H: 6 4 W: 11 08 b.Lome 26-2-84
Source: Lome. *Honours:* Togo 42 full caps, 18 goals.

2001-02	Metz	10	2		
2002-03	Metz	34	13	**44**	**15**
2003-04	Monaco	31	8		
2004-05	Monaco	34	9		
2005-06	Monaco	13	1	**78**	**18**
2005-06	Arsenal	13	4		
2006-07	Arsenal	29	8		
2007-08	Arsenal	36	24		
2008-09	Arsenal	26	10	**104**	**46**
2009-10	Manchester C	26	14		
2010-11	Manchester C	8	1		
2010-11	*Real Madrid*	14	5	**14**	**5**
2011-12	Manchester C	0	0	**34**	**15**
2011-12	*Tottenham H*	33	17	**33**	**17**

AGUERO, Sergio (F) **263 120**
H: 5 8 W: 11 09 b.Buenos Aires 2-6-88
Honours: Argentina Youth, Under-23, 36 full caps, 15 goals.

2002-03	Independiente	1	0		
2003-04	Independiente	5	0		
2004-05	Independiente	12	5		
2005-06	Independiente	36	18	**54**	**23**
2006-07	Atletico Madrid	38	6		
2007-08	Atletico Madrid	37	19		
2008-09	Atletico Madrid	37	17		
2009-10	Atletico Madrid	31	12		
2010-11	Atletico Madrid	32	20	**175**	**74**
2011-12	Manchester C	34	23	**34**	**23**

ASSULIN, Gai (M) **74 13**
b.Nahariya 9-4-91
Honours: Israel Under-21, 1 full cap.

2007-08	Barcelona B	22	10		
2008-09	Barcelona B	20	1		
2009-10	Barcelona B	25	2	**67**	**13**
2009-10	Barcelona	0	0		
2010-11	Manchester C	0	0		
2011-12	Manchester C	0	0		
2011-12	*Brighton & HA*	7	0	**7**	**0**

BALOTELLI, Mario (F) **101 39**
H: 6 2 W: 13 08 b.Palermo 12-8-90
Honours: Italy Under-21, 13 full caps, 2 goals.

2005-06	Lumezzane	2	0	**2**	**0**
2006-07	Internazionale	0	0		
2007-08	Internazionale	11	3		
2008-09	Internazionale	22	8		
2009-10	Internazionale	26	9	**59**	**20**
2010-11	Manchester C	17	6		
2011-12	Manchester C	23	13	**40**	**19**

BARRY, Gareth (M) **466 46**
H: 5 11 W: 12 06 b.Hastings 23-2-81
Source: Trainee. *Honours:* England Youth, B, Under-21, 53 full caps, 3 goals.

1997-98	Aston Villa	2	0		
1998-99	Aston Villa	32	2		
1999-2000	Aston Villa	30	1		
2000-01	Aston Villa	30	0		
2001-02	Aston Villa	20	0		
2002-03	Aston Villa	35	3		
2003-04	Aston Villa	36	3		
2004-05	Aston Villa	34	7		
2005-06	Aston Villa	36	3		
2006-07	Aston Villa	35	8		
2007-08	Aston Villa	37	9		
2008-09	Aston Villa	38	5	**365**	**41**
2009-10	Manchester C	34	2		
2010-11	Manchester C	33	2		
2011-12	Manchester C	34	1	**101**	**5**

BENALI, Ahmed (M) **2 0**
b.Manchester 7-2-92
Source: Scholar.

2008-09	Manchester C	0	0		
2009-10	Manchester C	0	0		
2010-11	Manchester C	0	0		
2011-12	Manchester C	0	0		
2011-12	*Rochdale*	2	0	**2**	**0**

BOYATA, Dedryck (M) **24 1**
H: 6 2 W: 12 00 b.Brussels 8-9-90
Source: Scholar. *Honours:* Belgium Under-21, 1 full cap.

2008-09	Manchester C	0	0		
2009-10	Manchester C	3	0		
2010-11	Manchester C	7	0		
2011-12	Manchester C	0	0	**10**	**0**
2011-12	*Bolton W*	14	1	**14**	**1**

BRIDGE, Wayne (D) **316 3**
H: 5 10 W: 12 13 b.Southampton 5-8-80
Source: Trainee. *Honours:* England Youth, Under-21, 36 full caps, 1 goal.

1997-98	Southampton	0	0		
1998-99	Southampton	23	0		
1999-2000	Southampton	19	1		
2000-01	Southampton	38	0		
2001-02	Southampton	38	0		
2002-03	Southampton	34	1	**152**	**2**
2003-04	Chelsea	33	1		
2004-05	Chelsea	15	0		
2005-06	Chelsea	0	0		
2005-06	*Fulham*	12	0	**12**	**0**
2006-07	Chelsea	22	0		
2007-08	Chelsea	11	0		
2008-09	Chelsea	6	0	**87**	**1**
2008-09	Manchester C	16	0		
2009-10	Manchester C	23	0		
2010-11	Manchester C	3	0		
2010-11	*West Ham U*	15	0	**15**	**0**
2011-12	Manchester C	0	0	**42**	**0**
2011-12	*Sunderland*	8	0	**8**	**0**

BUNN, Harry (F) **18 1**
H: 5 9 W: 11 10 b.Oldham 25-11-92
Source: Scholar.

2010-11	Manchester C	0	0		
2011-12	Manchester C	0	0		
2011-12	*Rochdale*	6	0	**6**	**0**
2011-12	*Preston NE*	1	1	**1**	**1**
2011-12	*Oldham Ath*	11	0	**11**	**0**

CLICHY, Gael (D) **215 1**
H: 5 9 W: 10 04 b.Toulouse 26-7-85
Source: Cannes. *Honours:* France Under-21, B, 15 full caps.

2003-04	Arsenal	12	0		
2004-05	Arsenal	15	0		
2005-06	Arsenal	7	0		
2006-07	Arsenal	27	0		
2007-08	Arsenal	38	0		
2008-09	Arsenal	31	1		
2009-10	Arsenal	24	0		
2010-11	Arsenal	33	0	**187**	**1**
2011-12	Manchester C	28	0	**28**	**0**

CUNNINGHAM, Greg (D) **42 0**
H: 6 0 W: 11 00 b.Galway 31-1-91
Source: Scholar. *Honours:* Eire Youth, Under-21, 3 full caps.

2008-09	Manchester C	0	0		
2009-10	Manchester C	2	0		
2010-11	Manchester C	0	0		
2010-11	*Leicester C*	13	0	**13**	**0**
2011-12	Manchester C	0	0	**2**	**0**
2011-12	*Nottingham F*	27	0	**27**	**0**

DE JONG, Nigel (D) **265 12**
H: 5 8 W: 11 05 b.Amsterdam 30-11-84
Honours: Holland 63 full caps, 1 goal.

2002-03	Ajax	17	0		
2003-04	Ajax	32	1		
2004-05	Ajax	31	5		
2005-06	Hamburg	12	1		
2005-06	Ajax	16	2	**96**	**8**
2006-07	Hamburg	18	1		
2007-08	Hamburg	29	1		
2008-09	Hamburg	7	0	**66**	**3**
2008-09	Manchester C	16	0		
2009-10	Manchester C	34	0		
2010-11	Manchester C	32	1		
2011-12	Manchester C	21	0	**103**	**1**

DRURY, Adam (M) 0 0
b.Grimsby 21-9-93
Source: Scholar.
2010-11 Manchester C 0 0
2011-12 Manchester C 0 0

DZEKO, Edin (F) 227 105
H: 6 3 W: 12 08 b.Doboj 17-3-86
Honours: Bosnia Youth, Under-21, 44 full caps, 21 goals.
2004-05 Zeljeznicar 13 1 **13 1**
2005-06 Usti nad Labem 15 6 **15 6**
2005-06 Teplice 13 3
2006-07 Teplice 30 13 **43 16**
2007-08 Wolfsburg 28 8
2008-09 Wolfsburg 32 26
2009-10 Wolfsburg 34 22
2010-11 Wolfsburg 17 10 **111 66**
2010-11 Manchester C 15 2
2011-12 Manchester C 30 14 **45 16**

ELABDELLAOUI, Omar (M) 0 0
b.Norway 5-12-91
Source: Scholar.
2009-10 Manchester C 0 0
2010-11 Manchester C 0 0
2011-12 Manchester C 0 0

GUIDETTI, John (F) 13 4
H: 5 11 W: 12 06 b.Stockholm 15-4-92
Source: Scholar. *Honours:* Sweden Youth, Under-21, 1 full cap.
2009-10 Manchester C 0 0
2009-10 *Brommapojkana* 8 3 **8 3**
2010-11 Manchester C 0 0
2010-11 *Burnley* 5 1 **5 1**
2011-12 Manchester C 0 0

HARGREAVES, Owen (M) 173 7
H: 5 11 W: 11 07 b.Calgary 20-1-81
Source: Calgary Foothills. *Honours:* England Under-21, B, 42 full caps.
2000-01 Bayern Munich 14 0
2001-02 Bayern Munich 29 0
2002-03 Bayern Munich 25 1
2003-04 Bayern Munich 25 2
2004-05 Bayern Munich 27 1
2005-06 Bayern Munich 16 1
2006-07 Bayern Munich 9 0 **145 5**
2007-08 Manchester U 23 2
2008-09 Manchester U 2 0
2009-10 Manchester U 1 0
2010-11 Manchester U 1 0 **27 2**
2011-12 Manchester C 1 0 **1 0**

HART, Joe (G) 225 0
H: 6 3 W: 13 03 b.Shrewsbury 19-4-87
Source: Scholar. *Honours:* England Youth, Under-21, 22 full caps.
2004-05 Shrewsbury T 6 0
2005-06 Shrewsbury T 46 0 **52 0**
2006-07 Manchester C 1 0
2006-07 *Tranmere R* 6 0 **6 0**
2006-07 *Blackpool* 5 0 **5 0**
2007-08 Manchester C 26 0
2008-09 Manchester C 23 0
2009-10 Manchester C 0 0
2009-10 *Birmingham C* 36 0 **36 0**
2010-11 Manchester C 38 0
2011-12 Manchester C 38 0 **126 0**

HELAN, Jeremy (M) 2 0
b.Paris 9-5-92
Source: Rennes. *Honours:* France Youth.
2009-10 Manchester C 0 0
2010-11 Manchester C 0 0
2011-12 Manchester C 0 0
2011-12 *Carlisle U* 2 0 **2 0**

HENSHALL, Alex (M) 0 0
b.Swindon 15-2-94
Source: Scholar.
2010-11 Manchester C 0 0
2011-12 Manchester C 0 0

HUWS, Emyr (M) 0 0
b.Llanelli 30-9-93
Source: Scholar. *Honours:* Wales Youth.
2010-11 Manchester C 0 0
2011-12 Manchester C 0 0

IBRAHIM, Abdisalam (M) 20 1
H: 6 0 W: 11 02 b.Somalia 4-5-91
Source: Scholar. *Honours:* Norway Youth, Under-21.
2008-09 Manchester C 0 0
2009-10 Manchester C 1 0
2010-11 Manchester C 0 0
2010-11 *Scunthorpe U* 11 0 **11 0**
2011-12 Manchester C 0 0 **1 0**
2011-12 *NEC Nijmegen* 8 1 **8 1**

JOHANSEN, Eirik (G) 0 0
H: 6 4 W: 14 00 b.Tonsberg 12-7-92
Honours: Norway Youth.
2010-11 Manchester C 0 0
2011-12 Manchester C 0 0

JOHNSON, Adam (M) 186 29
H: 5 8 W: 10 00 b.Sunderland 14-7-87
Source: Scholar. *Honours:* England Youth, Under-21, 11 full caps, 2 goals.
2004-05 Middlesbrough 0 0
2005-06 Middlesbrough 13 1
2006-07 Middlesbrough 12 0
2006-07 *Leeds U* 5 0 **5 0**
2007-08 Middlesbrough 19 1
2007-08 *Watford* 12 5 **12 5**
2008-09 Middlesbrough 26 0
2009-10 Middlesbrough 26 11 **96 13**
2009-10 Manchester C 16 1
2010-11 Manchester C 31 4
2011-12 Manchester C 26 6 **73 11**

JOHNSON, Michael (M) 44 2
H: 6 1 W: 12 07 b.Urmston 3-3-88
Source: Scholar. *Honours:* England Youth, Under-21.
2005-06 Manchester C 0 0
2006-07 Manchester C 10 0
2007-08 Manchester C 23 2
2008-09 Manchester C 3 0
2009-10 Manchester C 1 0
2010-11 Manchester C 0 0
2011-12 Manchester C 0 0 **37 2**
2011-12 *Leicester C* 7 0 **7 0**

KENNEDY, Kieran (D) 0 0
b.Urmston 23-9-93
Source: Scholar. *Honours:* England Youth.
2011-12 Manchester C 0 0

KOLAROV, Aleksandar (D) 200 16
H: 6 2 W: 13 05 b.Belgrade 10-11-85
Honours: Serbia 32 full caps.
2004-05 Cukaricki 27 2
2005-06 Cukaricki 17 0 **44 2**
2005-06 OFK Belgrade 11 1
2006-07 OFK Belgrade 27 4 **38 5**
2007-08 Lazio 24 1
2008-09 Lazio 25 2
2009-10 Lazio 33 3 **82 6**
2010-11 Manchester C 24 1
2011-12 Manchester C 12 2 **36 3**

KOMPANY, Vincent (D) 217 11
H: 6 3 W: 13 05 b.Brussels 10-4-86
Honours: Belgium 47 full caps, 2 goals.
2004-05 Anderlecht 29 2
2005-06 Anderlecht 32 2 **61 4**
2006-07 Hamburg 6 0
2007-08 Hamburg 22 1
2008-09 Hamburg 1 0 **29 1**
2008-09 Manchester C 34 1
2009-10 Manchester C 25 2
2010-11 Manchester C 37 0
2011-12 Manchester C 31 3 **127 6**

LAWLOR, Ian (G) 0 0
b.Dublin 27-10-94
Source: Scholar. *Honours:* Eire Youth.
2011-12 Manchester C 0 0

LESCOTT, Jolean (D) 396 33
H: 6 2 W: 13 00 b.Birmingham 16-8-82
Source: Trainee. *Honours:* England Youth, Under-20, Under-21, B, 20 full caps, 1 goal.
1999-2000 Wolverhampton W 0 0
2000-01 Wolverhampton W 37 2
2001-02 Wolverhampton W 44 5
2002-03 Wolverhampton W 44 1
2003-04 Wolverhampton W 0 0
2004-05 Wolverhampton W 41 4
2005-06 Wolverhampton W 46 1 **212 13**
2006-07 Everton 38 2
2007-08 Everton 38 8
2008-09 Everton 36 4
2009-10 Everton 1 0 **113 14**
2009-10 Manchester C 18 1
2010-11 Manchester C 22 3
2011-12 Manchester C 31 2 **71 6**

MANCINI, Andrea (M) 8 0
b.Genoa 13-9-92
Source: Bologna Youth.
2011-12 *Oldham Ath* 1 0 **1 0**
From Internazionale, Bologna.
2011-12 Manchester C 0 0
2011-12 *Fano* 7 0 **7 0**

McGIVERN, Ryan (D) 69 1
H: 5 10 W: 11 07 b.Newry 8-1-90
Source: Scholar. *Honours:* Northern Ireland Youth, Under-21, B, 16 full caps.
2007-08 Manchester C 0 0
2008-09 Manchester C 0 0
2008-09 *Morecambe* 5 1 **5 1**
2009-10 Manchester C 0 0
2009-10 *Leicester C* 12 0 **12 0**
2010-11 Manchester C 1 0
2010-11 *Walsall* 15 0 **15 0**
2011-12 Manchester C 0 0 **1 0**
2011-12 *Crystal Palace* 5 0 **5 0**
2011-12 *Bristol C* 31 0 **31 0**

MEPPEN-WALTERS, Courtney (D) 0 0
b.Bury 2-8-94
Source: Scholar. *Honours:* England Youth.
2011-12 Manchester C 0 0

MILNER, James (M) 306 28
H: 5 9 W: 11 00 b.Leeds 4-1-86
Source: Trainee. *Honours:* FA Schools, Youth, England Under-20, Under-21, 30 full caps.
2002-03 Leeds U 18 2
2003-04 Leeds U 30 3 **48 5**
2003-04 *Swindon T* 6 2 **6 2**
2004-05 Newcastle U 25 1
2005-06 Newcastle U 3 0
2005-06 *Aston Villa* 27 1
2006-07 Newcastle U 35 3
2007-08 Newcastle U 29 2
2008-09 Newcastle U 2 0 **94 6**
2008-09 Aston Villa 36 3
2009-10 Aston Villa 36 7
2010-11 Aston Villa 1 1 **100 12**
2010-11 Manchester C 32 0
2011-12 Manchester C 26 3 **58 3**

NASRI, Samir (M) 237 34
H: 5 9 W: 11 11 b.Marseille 26-6-87
Honours: France Youth, Under-21, 35 full caps, 4 goals.
2004-05 Marseille 24 1
2005-06 Marseille 30 1
2006-07 Marseille 37 3
2007-08 Marseille 30 6 **121 11**
2008-09 Arsenal 29 6
2009-10 Arsenal 26 2
2010-11 Arsenal 30 10
2011-12 Arsenal 1 0 **86 18**
2011-12 Manchester C 30 5 **30 5**

NIMELY-TCHUIMENI, Alex (F) 27 1
H: 5 11 W: 11 03 b.Monrovia 11-5-91
Source: Mighty Barolle, Cotonsport Garoua, Manchester C Scholar. *Honours:* Liberia Youth. England Under-20.
2008-09 Manchester C 0 0
2009-10 Manchester C 1 0
2010-11 Manchester C 0 0
2011-12 Manchester C 0 0 **1 0**
2011-12 *Middlesbrough* 9 0 **9 0**
2011-12 *Coventry C* 17 1 **17 1**

NUHU, Razak (D) 23 0
b.Ghana 14-4-91
2011-12 Manchester C 0 0
2011-12 *Stromsgodset* 23 0 **23 0**

PANTILIMON, Costel (G) 102 0
H: 6 5 W: 15 02 b.Bacau 1-2-87
Honours: Romania Youth, Under-21, 14 full caps.
2005-06 Aerostar Bacau 9 0 **9 0**
2006-07 Poli Timisoara 8 0
2007-08 Poli Timisoara 5 0 **13 0**
2008-09 Timisoara 31 0
2009-10 Timisoara 21 0
2010-11 Timisoara 28 0 **80 0**
2011-12 Manchester C 0 0
On loan from Timisoara.

PIZARRO, David (M) 350 28
H: 5 7 W: 10 03 b.Valparaiso 11-9-79
Honours: Chile 36 full caps, 3 goals.
1997 Santiago Wanderers 18 0

1998	Santiago Wanderers	23	3		
1999	Santiago Wanderers	0	0	**41**	**3**
1999-2000	Udinese	5	0		
2000-01	Udinese	4	0		
2001	*Univ de Chile*	6	1	**6**	**1**
2001-02	Udinese	31	2		
2002-03	Udinese	33	7		
2003-04	Udinese	19	3		
2004-05	Udinese	34	2	**126**	**14**
2005-06	Internazionale	24	1	**24**	**1**
2006-07	Roma	32	1		
2007-08	Roma	31	3		
2008-09	Roma	25	2		
2009-10	Roma	31	2		
2010-11	Roma	22	1		
2011-12	Roma	7	0	**148**	**9**
2011-12	Manchester C	5	0	**5**	**0**

PLUMMER, Ellis (D) **0 0**

b.Denton 2-9-94

Source: Scholar.

2011-12	Manchester C	0	0		

RAZAK, Abdul (M) **11 0**

H: 5 10 W: 11 02 b.Abidjan 11-11-92

Source: Scholar.

2010-11	Manchester C	1	0		
2011-12	Manchester C	1	0	**2**	**0**
2011-12	*Portsmouth*	3	0	**3**	**0**
2011-12	*Brighton & HA*	6	0	**6**	**0**

REKIK, Karim (D) **8 0**

H: 6 0 W: 12 00 b.Den Haag 2-12-94

Source: Scholar. *Honours:* Holland Youth.

2011-12	Manchester C	0	0		
2011-12	*Portsmouth*	8	0	**8**	**0**

RICHARDS, Micah (D) **170 7**

H: 5 11 W: 13 00 b.Birmingham 24-6-88

Source: Scholar. *Honours:* England Youth, Under-21, 13 full caps, 1 goal.

2005-06	Manchester C	13	0		
2006-07	Manchester C	28	1		
2007-08	Manchester C	25	0		
2008-09	Manchester C	34	1		
2009-10	Manchester C	23	3		
2010-11	Manchester C	18	1		
2011-12	Manchester C	29	1	**170**	**7**

ROBINSON, Bradley (M) **0 0**

b.Ashton-under-Lyne 24-5-93

Source: Scholar.

2011-12	Manchester C	0	0		

ROMAN OLLE, Joan Angel (F) **0 0**

H: 5 7 W: 10 10 b.Barcelona 18-5-93

Source: Espanyol.

2011-12	Manchester C	0	0		

RUSNAK, Albert (M) **0 0**

b.Kosice 7-7-94

Source: Scholar.

2011-12	Manchester C	0	0		

SANTA CRUZ, Roque (F) **282 67**

H: 6 2 W: 13 12 b.Asuncion 16-8-81

Honours: Paraguay Under-20, 89 full caps, 25 goals.

1998-99	Olimpia	9	3	**9**	**3**
1999-2000	Bayern Munich	28	5		
2000-01	Bayern Munich	19	5		
2001-02	Bayern Munich	22	5		
2002-03	Bayern Munich	14	5		
2003-04	Bayern Munich	28	5		
2004-05	Bayern Munich	4	0		
2005-06	Bayern Munich	13	4		
2006-07	Bayern Munich	26	2	**154**	**31**
2007-08	Blackburn R	37	19		
2008-09	Blackburn R	20	4		
2009-10	Blackburn R	0	0		
2009-10	Manchester C	19	3		
2010-11	Manchester C	1	0		
2010-11	*Blackburn R*	9	0	**66**	**23**
2011-12	Manchester C	0	0	**20**	**3**
2011-12	*Betis*	33	7	**33**	**7**

SAVIC, Stefan (D) **58 3**

H: 6 1 W: 11 07 b.Belgrade 8-9-91

Honours: Montenegro Youth, Under-21, 14 full caps, 2 goals.

2008-09	BSK Borca	3	0		
2009-10	BSK Borca	21	1		
2010-11	BSK Borca	3	0	**27**	**1**
2010-11	Partizan Belgrade	20	1	**20**	**1**
2011-12	Manchester C	11	1	**11**	**1**

SCAPUZZI, Luca (F) **41 1**

H: 6 0 W: 11 11 b.Milan 15-4-91

2009-10	Portogruaro	22	0		
2010-11	Portogruaro	7	0	**29**	**0**
2011-12	Manchester C	0	0		
2011-12	*Oldham Ath*	10	1	**10**	**1**
2011-12	*Portsmouth*	2	0	**2**	**0**

SILVA, David (F) **273 40**

H: 5 7 W: 10 07 b.Arguineguin 8-1-86

Honours: Spain 64 full caps, 18 goals.

2003-04	Mestalla	14	1	**14**	**1**
2004-05	Eibar	35	5	**35**	**5**
2005-06	Celta Vigo	34	3	**34**	**3**
2006-07	Valencia	36	5		
2007-08	Valencia	34	4		
2008-09	Valencia	19	4		
2009-10	Valencia	30	8	**119**	**21**
2010-11	Manchester C	35	4		
2011-12	Manchester C	36	6	**71**	**10**

SUAREZ, Denis (M) **0 0**

b.Tui 6-1-94

Source: Celta Vigo Youth.

2011-12	Manchester C	0	0		

SWAN, George (D) **0 0**

b.Normanton 12-9-94

Source: Scholar.

2011-12	Manchester C	0	0		

TAYLOR, Stuart (G) **68 0**

H: 6 5 W: 13 07 b.Romford 28-11-80

Source: Trainee. *Honours:* FA Schools, England Youth, Under-21.

1998-99	Arsenal	0	0		
1999-2000	Arsenal	0	0		
1999-2000	*Bristol R*	4	0	**4**	**0**
2000-01	Arsenal	0	0		
2000-01	*Crystal Palace*	10	0	**10**	**0**
2000-01	*Peterborough U*	6	0	**6**	**0**
2001-02	Arsenal	10	0		
2002-03	Arsenal	8	0		
2003-04	Arsenal	0	0		
2004-05	Arsenal	0	0	**18**	**0**
2004-05	*Leicester C*	10	0	**10**	**0**
2005-06	Aston Villa	2	0		
2006-07	Aston Villa	6	0		
2007-08	Aston Villa	4	0		
2008-09	Aston Villa	0	0		
2008-09	*Cardiff C*	8	0	**8**	**0**
2009-10	Aston Villa	0	0	**12**	**0**
2009-10	Manchester C	0	0		
2010-11	Manchester C	0	0		
2011-12	Manchester C	0	0		

TEVEZ, Carlos (F) **272 119**

H: 5 8 W: 11 11 b.Buenos Aires 5-2-84

Source: All Boys. *Honours:* Argentina Youth, Under-20, Under-23, 59 full caps, 13 goals.

2001-02	Boca Juniors	11	1		
2002-03	Boca Juniors	32	11		
2003-04	Boca Juniors	23	12		
2004-05	Boca Juniors	9	2	**75**	**26**
2005	Corinthians	29	20	**29**	**20**
2006-07	West Ham U	26	7	**26**	**7**
2007-08	Manchester U	34	14		
2008-09	Manchester U	29	5		
2009-10	Manchester U	0	0	**63**	**19**
2009-10	Manchester C	35	23		
2010-11	Manchester C	31	20		
2011-12	Manchester C	13	4	**79**	**47**

TOURE, Kolo (D) **292 11**

H: 5 10 W: 13 08 b.Sokuora Bouake 19-3-81

Source: ASEC Mimosas. *Honours:* Ivory Coast 98 full caps, 6 goals.

2001-02	Arsenal	0	0		
2002-03	Arsenal	26	2		
2003-04	Arsenal	37	1		
2004-05	Arsenal	35	0		
2005-06	Arsenal	33	0		
2006-07	Arsenal	35	3		
2007-08	Arsenal	30	2		
2008-09	Arsenal	29	1		
2009-10	Arsenal	0	0	**225**	**9**
2009-10	Manchester C	31	1		
2010-11	Manchester C	22	1		
2011-12	Manchester C	14	0	**67**	**2**

TOURE, Yaya (M) **291 32**

H: 6 3 W: 14 02 b.Sokoura Bouake 13-5-83

Honours: Ivory Coast 67 full caps, 10 goals.

2001-02	Beveren	28	0		
2002-03	Beveren	30	3		
2003-04	Beveren	12	0	**70**	**3**
2003-04	Metalurgs Donetsk	11	1		
2004-05	Metalurgs Donetsk	22	2	**33**	**3**
2005-06	Olympiakos	20	3	**20**	**3**
2006-07	Monaco	27	5	**27**	**5**
2007-08	Barcelona	26	1		
2008-09	Barcelona	25	2		
2009-10	Barcelona	23	1	**74**	**4**
2010-11	Manchester C	35	8		
2011-12	Manchester C	32	6	**67**	**14**

WABARA, Reece (D) **7 0**

H: 6 0 W: 12 06 b.Birmingham 28-12-91

Honours: England Under-20.

2008-09	Manchester C	0	0		
2009-10	Manchester C	0	0		
2010-11	Manchester C	1	0		
2011-12	Manchester C	0	0	**1**	**0**
2011-12	*Ipswich T*	6	0	**6**	**0**

WEISS, Vladimir (M) **65 2**

H: 5 9 W: 10 10 b.Bratislava 30-11-89

Source: Scholar. *Honours:* Slovakia Under-21, 24 full caps, 2 goals.

2007-08	Manchester C	0	0		
2008-09	Manchester C	1	0		
2009-10	Manchester C	0	0		
2009-10	*Bolton W*	13	0	**13**	**0**
2010-11	Manchester C	0	0		
2010-11	*Rangers*	23	0	**23**	**0**
2011-12	Manchester C	0	0	**1**	**0**
2011-12	*Espanyol*	28	2	**28**	**2**

ZABALETA, Pablo (D) **249 15**

H: 5 8 W: 10 12 b.Buenos Aires 16-1-85

Honours: Argentina Youth, Under-23, 24 full caps.

2002-03	San Lorenzo	11	0		
2003-04	San Lorenzo	27	3		
2004-05	San Lorenzo	28	5	**66**	**8**
2005-06	Espanyol	27	2		
2006-07	Espanyol	21	0		
2007-08	Espanyol	32	1	**80**	**3**
2008-09	Manchester C	29	1		
2009-10	Manchester C	27	0		
2010-11	Manchester C	26	2		
2011-12	Manchester C	21	1	**103**	**4**

Scholars

Cole Devante; El-Fitouri Sadik; Evans George; Facey Shay; Glendon George; Hutton Louis Jack; Leigh Greg; Mayifuila Jordy Hiwula.

MANCHESTER U (50)

AMOS, Ben (G) **18 0**

H: 6 1 W: 13 00 b.Macclesfield 10-4-90

Source: Scholar. *Honours:* England Youth, Under-21.

2007-08	Manchester U	0	0		
2008-09	Manchester U	0	0		
2009-10	Manchester U	0	0		
2009-10	*Peterborough U*	1	0	**1**	**0**
2010-11	Manchester U	0	0		
2010-11	*Oldham Ath*	16	0	**16**	**0**
2011-12	Manchester U	1	0	**1**	**0**

ANDERSON (M) **106 7**

H: 5 8 W: 10 07 b.Porto Alegre 13-4-88

Honours: Brazil Youth, Under-23, 8 full caps.

2004-05	Gremio	5	1	**5**	**1**
2005-06	Porto	3	0		
2006-07	Porto	15	2	**18**	**2**
2007-08	Manchester U	24	0		
2008-09	Manchester U	17	0		
2009-10	Manchester U	14	1		
2010-11	Manchester U	18	1		
2011-12	Manchester U	10	2	**83**	**4**

BEBE (F) **32 4**

H: 6 3 W: 11 11 b.Agualva-cacem 12-7-90

Honours: Portugal Under-21.

2009-10	Amadora	26	4	**26**	**4**
2010-11	Guimaraes	0	0		
2010-11	Manchester U	2	0		
2011-12	Manchester U	0	0	**2**	**0**
2011-12	*Besiktas*	4	0	**4**	**0**

BERBATOV, Dimitar (F) **382 169**

H: 6 2 W: 12 06 b.Blagoevgrad 30-1-81

Honours: Bulgaria Under-21, 78 full caps, 48 goals.

1998-99	CSKA Sofia	11	3		

1999-2000	CSKA Sofia	27	14		
2000-01	CSKA Sofia	12	8	**50**	**25**
2000-01	Leverkusen	6	0		
2001-02	Leverkusen	24	8		
2002-03	Leverkusen	24	4		
2003-04	Leverkusen	33	16		
2004-05	Leverkusen	33	20		
2005-06	Leverkusen	34	21	**154**	**69**
2006-07	Tottenham H	33	12		
2007-08	Tottenham H	36	15		
2008-09	Tottenham H	1	0	**70**	**27**
2008-09	Manchester U	31	9		
2009-10	Manchester U	33	12		
2010-11	Manchester U	32	20		
2011-12	Manchester U	12	7	**108**	**48**

BRADY, Robert (F) **39** **3**
H: 5 9 W: 10 12 b.Belfast 14-1-92
Source: Scholar. *Honours:* Eire Youth, Under-21.

2008-09	Manchester U	0	0		
2009-10	Manchester U	0	0		
2010-11	Manchester U	0	0		
2011-12	Manchester U	0	0		
2011-12	*Hull C*	39	3	**39**	**3**

BROWN, Reece (D) **21** **0**
H: 6 2 W: 13 02 b.Manchester 1-11-91
Honours: England Under-20.

2010-11	*Bradford C*	3	0	**3**	**0**
2010-11	Manchester U	0	0		
2011-12	Manchester U	0	0		
2011-12	*Doncaster R*	3	0	**3**	**0**
2011-12	*Oldham Ath*	15	0	**15**	**0**

CARRICK, Michael (M) **388** **24**
H: 6 1 W: 11 10 b.Wallsend 28-7-81
Source: Trainee. *Honours:* England Youth, Under-21, B, 22 full caps.

1998-99	West Ham U	0	0		
1999-2000	West Ham U	8	1		
1999-2000	*Swindon T*	6	2	**6**	**2**
1999-2000	*Birmingham C*	2	0	**2**	**0**
2000-01	West Ham U	33	1		
2001-02	West Ham U	30	2		
2002-03	West Ham U	30	1		
2003-04	West Ham U	35	1		
2004-05	West Ham U	0	0	**136**	**6**
2004-05	Tottenham H	29	0		
2005-06	Tottenham H	35	2	**64**	**2**
2006-07	Manchester U	33	3		
2007-08	Manchester U	31	2		
2008-09	Manchester U	28	4		
2009-10	Manchester U	30	3		
2010-11	Manchester U	28	0		
2011-12	Manchester U	30	2	**180**	**14**

CLEVERLEY, Tom (M) **83** **16**
H: 5 9 W: 10 07 b.Basingstoke 12-8-89
Source: Scholar. *Honours:* England Youth, Under-20, Under-21.

2007-08	Manchester U	0	0		
2008-09	Manchester U	0	0		
2008-09	*Leicester C*	15	2	**15**	**2**
2009-10	Manchester U	0	0		
2009-10	*Watford*	33	11	**33**	**11**
2010-11	Manchester U	0	0		
2010-11	*Wigan Ath*	25	3	**25**	**3**
2011-12	Manchester U	10	0	**10**	**0**

COFIE, John (F) **0** **0**
b.Aboso 21-1-93
Source: Scholar.

2010-11	Manchester U	0	0		
2011-12	Manchester U	0	0		

COLE, Larnell (M) **0** **0**
b.Manchester 9-3-93
Source: Scholar. *Honours:* England Youth.

2011-12	Manchester U	0	0		

DAEHLI, Mats (M) **0** **0**
b.Oslo 2-3-95
Source: Scholar.

2011-12	Manchester U	0	0		

DE GEA, David (G) **86** **0**
H: 6 3 W: 12 13 b.Madrid 7-11-90
Honours: Spain Youth, Under-21.

2009-10	Atletico Madrid	19	0		
2010-11	Atletico Madrid	38	0	**57**	**0**
2011-12	Manchester U	29	0	**29**	**0**

DE LAET, Ritchie (D) **42** **1**
H: 6 1 W: 12 02 b.Antwerp 28-11-88
Source: Antwerp. *Honours:* Belgium Under-21, 2 full caps.

2007-08	Stoke C	0	0		
2008-09	Stoke C	0	0		
2008-09	Manchester U	1	0		
2009-10	Manchester U	2	0		
2010-11	Manchester U	0	0		
2010-11	*Sheffield U*	6	0	**6**	**0**
2010-11	*Preston NE*	5	0	**5**	**0**
2010-11	*Portsmouth*	22	0	**22**	**0**
2011-12	Manchester U	0	0	**3**	**0**
2011-12	*Norwich C*	6	1	**6**	**1**

EKANGAMENE, Charni (M) **0** **0**
b.Antwerp 16-2-94
Source: Scholar. *Honours:* Belgium Youth.

2011-12	Manchester U	0	0		

EVANS, Jonny (D) **124** **4**
H: 6 2 W: 12 02 b.Belfast 3-1-88
Source: Scholar. *Honours:* Northern Ireland Schools, Youth, Under-21, 29 full caps, 1 goal.

2004-05	Manchester U	0	0		
2005-06	Manchester U	0	0		
2006-07	Manchester U	0	0		
2006-07	*Antwerp*	14	2	**14**	**2**
2006-07	*Sunderland*	18	1		
2007-08	Manchester U	0	0		
2007-08	*Sunderland*	15	0	**33**	**1**
2008-09	Manchester U	17	0		
2009-10	Manchester U	18	0		
2010-11	Manchester U	13	0		
2011-12	Manchester U	29	1	**77**	**1**

EVRA, Patrice (D) **392** **7**
H: 5 8 W: 11 10 b.Dakar 15-5-81
Honours: France 42 full caps.

1998-99	Marsala	24	3	**24**	**3**
1999-2000	Monza	3	0	**3**	**0**
2000-01	Nice	5	0		
2001-02	Nice	34	1	**39**	**1**
2002-03	Monaco	36	1		
2003-04	Monaco	33	0		
2004-05	Monaco	36	0		
2005-06	Monaco	15	0	**120**	**1**
2005-06	Manchester U	11	0		
2006-07	Manchester U	24	1		
2007-08	Manchester U	33	0		
2008-09	Manchester U	28	0		
2009-10	Manchester U	38	0		
2010-11	Manchester U	35	1		
2011-12	Manchester U	37	0	**206**	**2**

FABIO (M) **21** **1**
H: 5 8 W: 10 03 b.Rio de Janeiro 9-7-90
Source: Fluminense. *Honours:* Brazil 2 full caps.

2008-09	Manchester U	0	0		
2009-10	Manchester U	5	0		
2010-11	Manchester U	11	1		
2011-12	Manchester U	5	0	**21**	**1**

FERDINAND, Rio (D) **461** **10**
H: 6 2 W: 13 12 b.Peckham 7-11-78
Source: Trainee. *Honours:* England Youth, Under-21, B, 81 full caps, 3 goals.

1995-96	West Ham U	1	0		
1996-97	West Ham U	15	2		
1996-97	*Bournemouth*	10	0	**10**	**0**
1997-98	West Ham U	35	0		
1998-99	West Ham U	31	0		
1999-2000	West Ham U	33	0		
2000-01	West Ham U	12	0	**127**	**2**
2000-01	Leeds U	23	2		
2001-02	Leeds U	31	0	**54**	**2**
2002-03	Manchester U	28	0		
2003-04	Manchester U	20	0		
2004-05	Manchester U	31	0		
2005-06	Manchester U	37	3		
2006-07	Manchester U	33	1		
2007-08	Manchester U	35	2		
2008-09	Manchester U	24	0		
2009-10	Manchester U	13	0		
2010-11	Manchester U	19	0		
2011-12	Manchester U	30	0	**270**	**6**

FLETCHER, Darren (M) **197** **17**
H: 6 0 W: 11 09 b.Edinburgh 1-2-84
Source: Scholar. *Honours:* Scotland Under-21, B, 58 full caps, 5 goals.

2000-01	Manchester U	0	0		
2001-02	Manchester U	0	0		
2002-03	Manchester U	0	0		
2003-04	Manchester U	22	0		
2004-05	Manchester U	18	3		
2005-06	Manchester U	27	1		
2006-07	Manchester U	24	3		
2007-08	Manchester U	16	0		
2008-09	Manchester U	26	3		
2009-10	Manchester U	30	4		
2010-11	Manchester U	26	2		
2011-12	Manchester U	8	1	**197**	**17**

FORNASIER, Michele (D) **0** **0**
b.Vittorio Veneto 22-8-93
Source: Scholar.

2010-11	Manchester U	0	0		
2011-12	Manchester U	0	0		

FRYERS, Zeki (D) **2** **0**
H: 6 0 W: 12 00 b.Manchester 9-9-92
Source: Scholar. *Honours:* England Youth.

2011-12	Manchester U	2	0	**2**	**0**

GIGGS, Ryan (F) **638** **112**
H: 5 11 W: 11 02 b.Cardiff 29-11-73
Source: School. *Honours:* England Schools, Wales Youth, Under-21, 64 full caps, 12 goals.

1990-91	Manchester U	2	1		
1991-92	Manchester U	38	4		
1992-93	Manchester U	41	9		
1993-94	Manchester U	38	13		
1994-95	Manchester U	29	1		
1995-96	Manchester U	33	11		
1996-97	Manchester U	26	3		
1997-98	Manchester U	29	8		
1998-99	Manchester U	24	3		
1999-2000	Manchester U	30	6		
2000-01	Manchester U	31	5		
2001-02	Manchester U	25	7		
2002-03	Manchester U	36	8		
2003-04	Manchester U	33	7		
2004-05	Manchester U	32	5		
2005-06	Manchester U	27	3		
2006-07	Manchester U	30	4		
2007-08	Manchester U	31	3		
2008-09	Manchester U	28	2		
2009-10	Manchester U	25	5		
2010-11	Manchester U	25	2		
2011-12	Manchester U	25	2	**638**	**112**

GIVERIN, Luke (D) **0** **0**
b.Salford 4-2-93
Source: Scholar.

2011-12	Manchester U	0	0		

HERNANDEZ, Javier (F) **162** **60**
H: 5 8 W: 9 11 b.Guadalajara 1-6-88
Honours: Mexico Youth, 37 full caps, 25 goals.

2005-06	Tapatio	11	0		
2006-07	Tapatio	12	3		
2006-07	Guadalajara	7	1		
2007-08	Guadalajara	5	0		
2007-08	Tapatio	15	6		
2008-09	Tapatio	7	2	**45**	**11**
2008-09	Guadalajara	22	4		
2009-10	Guadalajara	28	21	**62**	**26**
2010-11	Manchester U	27	13		
2011-12	Manchester U	28	10	**55**	**23**

JAMES, Matthew (M) **28** **2**
H: 6 0 W: 11 12 b.Bacup 22-7-91
Source: Scholar. *Honours:* England Youth, Under-20.

2007-08	Manchester U	0	0		
2008-09	Manchester U	0	0		
2009-10	Manchester U	0	0		
2009-10	*Preston NE*	18	2		
2010-11	Manchester U	0	0		
2010-11	*Preston NE*	10	0	**28**	**2**
2011-12	Manchester U	0	0		

JANUZAJ, Adrian (M) **0** **0**
b.Brussels 5-2-95
Source: Scholar.

2011-12	Manchester U	0	0		

JOHNSTONE, Samuel (G) **12** **0**
H: 6 0 W: 12 10 b.Preston 25-3-93
Source: Scholar. *Honours:* England Youth.

2009-10	Manchester U	0	0		
2010-11	Manchester U	0	0		
2011-12	Manchester U	0	0		
2011-12	*Scunthorpe U*	12	0	**12**	**0**

JONES, Phil (D) **64 1**
H: 5 11 W: 11 02 b.Preston 21-2-92
Source: Scholar. *Honours:* England Youth, Under-21, 5 full caps.
2009-10 Blackburn R 9 0
2010-11 Blackburn R 26 0 **35 0**
2011-12 Manchester U 29 1 **29 1**

KEANE, Michael (D) **0 0**
b.Stockport 11-1-93
Source: Scholar. *Honours:* Eire Youth, England Youth.
2011-12 Manchester U 0 0

KEANE, Will (F) **1 0**
H: 6 2 W: 11 05 b.Stockport 11-1-93
Source: Scholar. *Honours:* England Youth, Under-21.
2009-10 Manchester U 0 0
2010-11 Manchester U 0 0
2011-12 Manchester U 1 0 **1 0**

KING, Josh (F) **28 1**
H: 5 11 W: 11 09 b.Oslo 15-1-92
Source: Scholar. *Honours:* Norway Youth, Under-21.
2008-09 Manchester U 0 0
2009-10 Manchester U 0 0
2010-11 Manchester U 0 0
2010-11 *Preston NE* 8 0 **8 0**
2011-12 Manchester U 0 0
2011-12 *Moenchengladbach* 2 0 **2 0**
2011-12 *Hull C* 18 1 **18 1**

KUSZCZAK, Tomasz (G) **76 0**
H: 6 3 W: 13 03 b.Krosno Odrzansia 20-3-82
Source: Uerdingen. *Honours:* Poland Youth, Under-21, 10 full caps.
2001-02 Hertha Berlin 0 0
2002-03 Hertha Berlin 0 0
2003-04 Hertha Berlin 0 0
2004-05 WBA 3 0
2005-06 WBA 28 0
2006-07 WBA 0 0 **31 0**
2006-07 *Manchester U* 6 0
2007-08 Manchester U 9 0
2008-09 Manchester U 4 0
2009-10 Manchester U 8 0
2010-11 Manchester U 5 0
2011-12 Manchester U 0 0 **32 0**
2011-12 *Watford* 13 0 **13 0**

LINDEGAARD, Anders (G) **80 0**
H: 6 4 W: 12 08 b.Odense 13-4-84
Honours: Denmark Youth, 5 full caps.
2003-04 Odense 0 0
2004-05 Odense 0 0
2005-06 Odense 0 0
2006-07 Odense 1 0
2007-08 Odense 1 0
2008-09 *Kolding* 10 0 **10 0**
2009 *Aalesund* 26 0
2009 Odense 4 0 **6 0**
2010 Aalesund 30 0 **56 0**
2010-11 Manchester U 0 0
2011-12 Manchester U 8 0 **8 0**

LINGARD, Jesse (M) **0 0**
b.Warrington 15-12-92
Source: Scholar.
2011-12 Manchester U 0 0

MACHEDA, Federico (F) **36 4**
H: 6 0 W: 11 13 b.Rome 22-8-91
Source: Scholar. *Honours:* Italy Under-21.
2008-09 Manchester U 4 2
2009-10 Manchester U 5 1
2010-11 Manchester U 7 1
2010-11 *Sampdoria* 14 0 **14 0**
2011-12 Manchester U 3 0 **19 4**
2011-12 *QPR* 3 0 **3 0**

McGINTY, Sean (D) **4 0**
b.Maidstone 11-8-93
Source: Scholar. *Honours:* Eire Youth.
2010-11 Manchester U 0 0
2011-12 Manchester U 0 0
2011-12 *Morecambe* 4 0 **4 0**

NANI (M) **182 34**
H: 5 9 W: 10 04 b.Cape Verde 17-11-86
Honours: Portugal Under-21, 59 full caps, 13 goals.
2005-06 Sporting Lisbon 29 4
2006-07 Sporting Lisbon 29 5 **58 9**
2007-08 Manchester U 26 3
2008-09 Manchester U 13 1
2009-10 Manchester U 23 4
2010-11 Manchester U 33 9
2011-12 Manchester U 29 8 **124 25**

NORWOOD, Oliver (M) **39 3**
H: 5 11 W: 11 13 b.Burnley 12-4-91
Source: Scholar. *Honours:* Northern Ireland Youth, Under-21, 6 full caps.
2009-10 Manchester U 0 0
2010-11 Manchester U 0 0
2010-11 *Carlisle U* 6 0 **6 0**
2011-12 Manchester U 0 0
2011-12 *Scunthorpe U* 15 1 **15 1**
2011-12 *Coventry C* 18 2 **18 2**

OWEN, Michael (F) **354 162**
H: 5 8 W: 10 12 b.Chester 14-12-79
Source: Trainee. *Honours:* England Schools, Youth, Under-21, B, 89 full caps, 40 goals.
1996-97 Liverpool 2 1
1997-98 Liverpool 36 18
1998-99 Liverpool 30 18
1999-2000 Liverpool 27 11
2000-01 Liverpool 28 16
2001-02 Liverpool 29 19
2002-03 Liverpool 35 19
2003-04 Liverpool 29 16 **216 118**
2004-05 Real Madrid 36 13 **36 13**
2005-06 Newcastle U 11 7
2006-07 Newcastle U 3 0
2007-08 Newcastle U 29 11
2008-09 Newcastle U 28 8
2009-10 Newcastle U 0 0 **71 26**
2009-10 Manchester U 19 3
2010-11 Manchester U 11 2
2011-12 Manchester U 1 0 **31 5**

PARK, Ji-Sung (M) **273 43**
H: 5 9 W: 11 06 b.Seoul 25-2-81
Honours: South Korea 101 full caps, 13 goals.
2000 Kyoto Purple S 13 1
2001 Kyoto Purple S 38 3
2002 Kyoto Purple S 25 7 **76 11**
2002-03 PSV Eindhoven 8 0
2003-04 PSV Eindhoven 28 6
2004-05 PSV Eindhoven 28 7 **64 13**
2005-06 Manchester U 33 1
2006-07 Manchester U 14 5
2007-08 Manchester U 12 1
2008-09 Manchester U 25 2
2009-10 Manchester U 17 3
2010-11 Manchester U 15 5
2011-12 Manchester U 17 2 **133 19**

PETRUCCI, Davide (M) **0 0**
b.Rome 5-10-91
Source: Scholar.
2008-09 Manchester U 0 0
2009-10 Manchester U 0 0
2010-11 Manchester U 0 0
2011-12 Manchester U 0 0

POGBA, Paul (M) **3 0**
H: 6 1 W: 12 08 b.Lagny-sur-Marne 15-3-93
Source: Scholar. *Honours:* France Youth.
2009-10 Manchester U 0 0
2010-11 Manchester U 0 0
2011-12 Manchester U 3 0 **3 0**

RAFAEL (D) **52 2**
H: 5 8 W: 10 03 b.Rio de Janeiro 9-7-90
Source: Fluminense. *Honours:* Brazil Youth, 2 full caps.
2008-09 Manchester U 16 1
2009-10 Manchester U 8 1
2010-11 Manchester U 16 0
2011-12 Manchester U 12 0 **52 2**

ROONEY, Wayne (F) **318 144**
H: 5 10 W: 12 13 b.Liverpool 24-10-85
Source: Scholar. *Honours:* FA Schools, England Youth, 76 full caps, 29 goals.
2002-03 Everton 33 6
2003-04 Everton 34 9 **67 15**
2004-05 Manchester U 29 11
2005-06 Manchester U 36 16
2006-07 Manchester U 35 14
2007-08 Manchester U 27 12
2008-09 Manchester U 30 12
2009-10 Manchester U 32 26
2010-11 Manchester U 28 11
2011-12 Manchester U 34 27 **251 129**

SCHOLES, Paul (M) **483 106**
H: 5 7 W: 11 00 b.Salford 16-11-74
Source: Trainee. *Honours:* England Youth, 66 full caps, 14 goals.
1992-93 Manchester U 0 0
1993-94 Manchester U 0 0
1994-95 Manchester U 17 5
1995-96 Manchester U 26 10
1996-97 Manchester U 24 3
1997-98 Manchester U 31 8
1998-99 Manchester U 31 6
1999-2000 Manchester U 31 9
2000-01 Manchester U 32 6
2001-02 Manchester U 35 8
2002-03 Manchester U 33 14
2003-04 Manchester U 28 9
2004-05 Manchester U 33 9
2005-06 Manchester U 20 2
2006-07 Manchester U 30 6
2007-08 Manchester U 24 1
2008-09 Manchester U 21 2
2009-10 Manchester U 28 3
2010-11 Manchester U 22 1
2011-12 Manchester U 17 4 **483 106**

SMALLING, Chris (D) **48 1**
H: 6 4 W: 14 02 b.Greenwich 22-11-89
Source: Maidstone U. *Honours:* England Youth, Under-21, 3 full caps.
2008-09 Fulham 1 0
2009-10 Fulham 12 0 **13 0**
2010-11 Manchester U 16 0
2011-12 Manchester U 19 1 **35 1**

THORPE, Tom (D) **0 0**
H: 6 0 W: 14 00 b.Manchester 13-1-93
Source: Scholar. *Honours:* England Youth.
2010-11 Manchester U 0 0
2011-12 Manchester U 0 0

TUNNICLIFFE, Ryan (M) **27 0**
H: 6 0 W: 14 02 b.Bury 30-12-92
Source: Scholar.
2009-10 Manchester U 0 0
2010-11 Manchester U 0 0
2011-12 Manchester U 0 0
2011-12 *Peterborough U* 27 0 **27 0**

VALENCIA, Antonio (M) **244 28**
H: 5 10 W: 12 04 b.Lago Agrio 5-8-85
Honours: Ecuador Under-21, Under-23, 52 full caps, 6 goals.
2002 El Nacional 1 0
2003 El Nacional 26 2
2004 El Nacional 42 5
2005 El Nacional 14 4 **83 11**
2005-06 Villarreal 2 0 **2 0**
2005-06 *Recreativo* 4 0 **4 0**
2006-07 Wigan Ath 22 1
2007-08 Wigan Ath 31 3
2008-09 Wigan Ath 31 3 **84 7**
2009-10 Manchester U 34 5
2010-11 Manchester U 10 1
2011-12 Manchester U 27 4 **71 10**

VAN VELZEN, Gyliano (F) **0 0**
b.Amsterdam 14-4-94
Source: Scholar.
2010-11 Manchester U 0 0
2011-12 Manchester U 0 0

VERMIJL, Marnick (D) **0 0**
H: 5 11 W: 11 12 b.Overpelt 13-1-92
Honours: Belgium Youth.
2010-11 Manchester U 0 0
2011-12 Manchester U 0 0

VESELI, Frederic (D) **0 0**
H: 6 0 W: 12 08 b.Kosovo 20-11-92
Source: Scholar. *Honours:* Switzerland Youth.
2009-10 Manchester C 0 0
2010-11 Manchester C 0 0
2011-12 Manchester C 0 0
2011-12 Manchester U 0 0

VIDIC, Nemanja (D) **301 36**
H: 6 1 W: 13 02 b.Uzice 21-10-81
Honours: Serbia 56 full caps, 2 goals.
2000-01 Subotica 27 6 **27 6**
2001-02 Red Star Belgrade 22 2
2002-03 Red Star Belgrade 26 5
2003-04 Red Star Belgrade 20 5 **68 12**
2004 Spartak Moscow 12 2
2005 Spartak Moscow 27 2 **39 4**
2005-06 Manchester U 11 0
2006-07 Manchester U 25 3

2007-08 Manchester U 32 1
2008-09 Manchester U 34 4
2009-10 Manchester U 24 1
2010-11 Manchester U 35 5
2011-12 Manchester U 6 0 **167 14**

WELBECK, Danny (F) 72 18
H: 6 1 W: 11 07 b.Manchester 26-11-90
Source: Scholar. *Honours:* England Youth, Under-21, 9 full caps, 2 goals.
2007-08 Manchester U 0 0
2008-09 Manchester U 3 1
2009-10 Manchester U 5 0
2009-10 *Preston NE* 8 2 **8 2**
2010-11 Manchester U 0 0
2010-11 *Sunderland* 26 6 **26 6**
2011-12 Manchester U 30 9 **38 10**

WOOTTON, Scott (D) 31 1
H: 6 2 W: 13 00 b.Birkenhead 12-9-91
Source: Scholar.
2009-10 Manchester U 0 0
2010-11 Manchester U 0 0
2010-11 *Tranmere R* 7 1 **7 1**
2011-12 Manchester U 0 0
2011-12 *Peterborough U* 11 0 **11 0**
2011-12 *Nottingham F* 13 0 **13 0**

YOUNG, Ashley (M) 280 55
H: 5 10 W: 10 03 b.Stevenage 9-7-85
Source: Juniors. *Honours:* England Under-21, 25 full caps, 6 goals.
2002-03 Watford 0 0
2003-04 Watford 5 3
2004-05 Watford 34 0
2005-06 Watford 39 13
2006-07 Watford 20 3 **98 19**
2006-07 Aston Villa 13 2
2007-08 Aston Villa 37 9
2008-09 Aston Villa 36 7
2009-10 Aston Villa 37 5
2010-11 Aston Villa 34 7 **157 30**
2011-12 Manchester U 25 6 **25 6**

Scholars
Barmby Jack; Blackett Tyler Nathan; Byrne Sam John; Coll Joseph Aloysious; Dalley Declan Michael; Gollini Pierluigi; Gorre Kenji Joel; Grimshaw Liam David; Hendrie Luke John; Lawrence Thomas Morris; Love Donald Alistair; McCullough Luke; McNair Patrick James Coleman; Pearson Benjamin David; Rothwell Joseph Matthew; Rowley Louis James; Rudge Jack James; Sutherland Jonathan David; Weir James Michael; Wilkinson Matthew Gary.

MIDDLESBROUGH (51)

ARCA, Julio (M) 352 25
H: 5 9 W: 11 13 b.Quilmes 31-1-81
Honours: Argentina Youth, Under-21.
1999-2000 Argentinos Jun 19 0
2000-01 Argentinos Jun 17 1 **36 1**
2000-01 Sunderland 27 2
2001-02 Sunderland 22 1
2002-03 Sunderland 13 0
2003-04 Sunderland 31 4
2004-05 Sunderland 40 9
2005-06 Sunderland 24 1 **157 17**
2006-07 Middlesbrough 21 2
2007-08 Middlesbrough 24 2
2008-09 Middlesbrough 18 0
2009-10 Middlesbrough 34 0
2010-11 Middlesbrough 32 3
2011-12 Middlesbrough 30 0 **159 7**

ATKINSON, David (D) 0 0
b.Shildon 27-4-93
Source: Scholar. *Honours:* England Youth.
2010-11 Middlesbrough 0 0
2011-12 Middlesbrough 0 0

BAILEY, Nicky (M) 292 48
H: 5 10 W: 12 06 b.Hammersmith 10-6-84
Source: Sutton U.
2005-06 Barnet 45 7
2006-07 Barnet 44 5 **89 12**
2007-08 Southend U 44 9
2008-09 Southend U 1 0 **45 9**
2008-09 Charlton Ath 43 13
2009-10 Charlton Ath 44 12 **87 25**
2010-11 Middlesbrough 34 0
2011-12 Middlesbrough 37 2 **71 2**

BATES, Matthew (D) 113 6
H: 5 10 W: 12 03 b.Stockton 10-12-86
Source: Scholar. *Honours:* England Youth, Under-20.
2003-04 Middlesbrough 0 0
2004-05 Middlesbrough 2 0
2004-05 *Darlington* 4 0 **4 0**
2005-06 Middlesbrough 16 0
2006-07 Middlesbrough 1 0
2006-07 *Ipswich T* 2 0 **2 0**
2007-08 Middlesbrough 0 0
2007-08 *Norwich C* 3 0 **3 0**
2008-09 Middlesbrough 17 1
2009-10 Middlesbrough 0 0
2010-11 Middlesbrough 31 3
2011-12 Middlesbrough 37 2 **104 6**

BENNETT, Joe (D) 85 1
H: 5 10 W: 10 04 b.Rochdale 28-3-90
Source: Scholar. *Honours:* England Under-20, Under-21.
2008-09 Middlesbrough 1 0
2009-10 Middlesbrough 12 0
2010-11 Middlesbrough 31 0
2011-12 Middlesbrough 41 1 **85 1**

BROBBEL, Ryan (M) 0 0
b.Hartlepool 5-3-93
Source: Scholar. *Honours:* Northern Ireland Youth.
2011-12 Middlesbrough 0 0

COYNE, Danny (G) 441 0
H: 6 0 W: 13 00 b.Prestatyn 27-8-73
Source: Trainee. *Honours:* Wales Schools, Youth, Under-21, B, 16 full caps.
1991-92 Tranmere R 0 0
1992-93 Tranmere R 1 0
1993-94 Tranmere R 5 0
1994-95 Tranmere R 5 0
1995-96 Tranmere R 46 0
1996-97 Tranmere R 21 0
1997-98 Tranmere R 16 0
1998-99 Tranmere R 17 0
1999-2000 Grimsby T 44 0
2000-01 Grimsby T 46 0
2001-02 Grimsby T 45 0
2002-03 Grimsby T 46 0 **181 0**
2003-04 Leicester C 4 0 **4 0**
2004-05 Burnley 20 0
2005-06 Burnley 8 0
2006-07 Burnley 12 0 **40 0**
2007-08 Tranmere R 41 0
2008-09 Tranmere R 39 0 **191 0**
2009-10 Middlesbrough 23 0
2010-11 Middlesbrough 1 0
2011-12 Middlesbrough 1 0 **25 0**

DOBIE, Luke (M) 4 0
b.Ormskirk 7-10-92
Source: Everton Scholar.
2011-12 Middlesbrough 0 0
2011-12 *Accrington S* 4 0 **4 0**

DOLAN, Matthew (M) 0 0
b.Hartlepool 11-2-93
Source: Scholar.
2010-11 Middlesbrough 0 0
2011-12 Middlesbrough 0 0

EDWARDS, Curtis (M) 0 0
b.Middlesbrough 12-1-94
Source: Scholar.
2011-12 Middlesbrough 0 0

EMNES, Marvin (M) 156 29
H: 5 11 W: 10 06 b.Rotterdam 27-5-88
Honours: Holland Under-21.
2005-06 Sparta Rotterdam 11 1
2006-07 Sparta Rotterdam 16 0
2007-08 Sparta Rotterdam 29 8 **56 9**
2008-09 Middlesbrough 15 0
2009-10 Middlesbrough 16 1
2010-11 Middlesbrough 23 3
2010-11 *Swansea C* 4 2 **4 2**
2011-12 Middlesbrough 42 14 **96 18**

FOWLER, Jake (M) 0 0
b.Sunderland 22-9-93
Source: Scholar. *Honours:* England Youth.
2011-12 Middlesbrough 0 0

FRANKS, Jonathan (F) 43 6
H: 5 9 W: 11 03 b.Stockton 8-4-90
Source: Scholar. *Honours:* England Youth.
2007-08 Middlesbrough 0 0
2008-09 Middlesbrough 1 0
2009-10 Middlesbrough 23 3
2010-11 Middlesbrough 4 0
2011-12 Middlesbrough 0 0 **28 3**
2011-12 *Oxford U* 1 0 **1 0**
2011-12 *Yeovil T* 14 3 **14 3**

GIBSON, Ben (D) 14 0
H: 6 1 W: 12 04 b.Nunthorpe 15-1-93
Source: Scholar. *Honours:* England Youth.
2010-11 Middlesbrough 1 0
2011-12 Middlesbrough 0 0 **1 0**
2011-12 *Plymouth Arg* 13 0 **13 0**

GROUNDS, Jonathan (D) 76 4
H: 6 1 W: 13 10 b.Thornaby 2-2-88
Source: Scholar.
2007-08 Middlesbrough 5 0
2008-09 Middlesbrough 2 0
2008-09 *Norwich C* 16 3 **16 3**
2009-10 Middlesbrough 20 0
2010-11 Middlesbrough 6 1
2011-12 Middlesbrough 0 0 **33 1**
2011-12 *Chesterfield* 13 0 **13 0**
2011-12 *Yeovil T* 14 0 **14 0**

HALLIDAY, Andrew (M) 64 16
H: 5 8 W: 10 07 b.Glasgow 11-10-91
2008-09 Livingston 12 1
2009-10 Livingston 32 14 **44 15**
2010-11 Middlesbrough 12 1
2011-12 Middlesbrough 1 0 **13 1**
2011-12 *Walsall* 7 0 **7 0**

HAROUN, Faris (M) 227 41
H: 6 2 W: 13 00 b.Brussels 22-9-85
Honours: Belgium 6 full caps.
2003-04 Genk 12 3
2004-05 Genk 23 4
2005-06 Genk 20 0
2006-07 Genk 21 5
2007-08 Genk 28 4 **104 16**
2008-09 Beerschot 31 8
2009-10 Beerschot 31 10
2010-11 Beerschot 29 5 **91 23**
2011-12 Middlesbrough 32 2 **32 2**

HINES, Seb (D) 45 2
H: 6 1 W: 12 02 b.Wetherby 29-5-88
Source: Scholar. *Honours:* England Youth.
2005-06 Middlesbrough 0 0
2006-07 Middlesbrough 0 0
2007-08 Middlesbrough 1 0
2008-09 Middlesbrough 1 0
2008-09 *Derby Co* 0 0
2008-09 *Oldham Ath* 4 0 **4 0**
2009-10 Middlesbrough 2 0
2010-11 Middlesbrough 14 1
2011-12 Middlesbrough 23 1 **41 2**

HOYTE, Justin (D) 169 3
H: 5 11 W: 11 00 b.Waltham Forest 20-11-84
Source: Scholar. *Honours:* England Youth, Under-20, Under-21.
2002-03 Arsenal 1 0
2003-04 Arsenal 1 0
2004-05 Arsenal 5 0
2005-06 Arsenal 0 0
2005-06 *Sunderland* 27 1 **27 1**
2006-07 Arsenal 22 1
2007-08 Arsenal 5 0 **34 1**
2008-09 Middlesbrough 22 0
2009-10 Middlesbrough 30 1
2010-11 Middlesbrough 17 0
2011-12 Middlesbrough 39 0 **108 1**

JACKSON, Adam (D) 0 0
b.Darlington 18-5-94
Source: Scholar. *Honours:* England Youth.
2011-12 Middlesbrough 0 0

JUTKIEWICZ, Lucas (F) 168 37
H: 6 1 W: 12 11 b.Southampton 20-3-89
Source: Scholar.
2005-06 Swindon T 5 0
2006-07 Swindon T 33 5 **38 5**
2006-07 Everton 0 0
2007-08 Everton 0 0
2007-08 *Plymouth Arg* 3 0 **3 0**
2008-09 Everton 1 0
2008-09 *Huddersfield T* 7 0 **7 0**
2009-10 Everton 0 0 **1 0**
2009-10 *Motherwell* 33 12 **33 12**
2010-11 Coventry C 42 9

2011-12 Coventry C 25 9 **67 18**
2011-12 Middlesbrough 19 2 **19 2**

KINK, Tarmo (F) 189 135
H: 6 0 W: 11 09 b.Tallinn 6-10-85
Honours: Estonia 63 full caps, 5 goals.
2001 Real Tallinn 9 30
2002 *Viimsi* 6 31 **6 31**
2002 *Trans* 24 4 **24 4**
2003 Real Tallinn 6 16 **15 46**
2003 Spartak Moscow 2 0
2004 Spartak Moscow 0 0
2005 Spartak Moscow 0 0
2006 Spartak Moscow 0 0 **2 0**
2006 Levadia 16 3
2007 Levadia 31 16
2008 Levadia 33 16 **80 35**
2008-09 Gyor 12 3
2009-10 Gyor 28 12 **40 15**
2010-11 Middlesbrough 21 4
2011-12 Middlesbrough 1 0 **22 4**
Transferred to Karpaty Lvov February 2012.

MAIN, Curtis (F) 57 7
H: 5 9 W: 12 02 b.South Shields 20-6-92
Source: Scholar.
2007-08 Darlington 1 0
2008-09 Darlington 18 2
2009-10 Darlington 26 3
2010-11 Darlington 0 0 **45 5**
2011-12 Middlesbrough 12 2 **12 2**

MARTIN, Malaury (M) 37 3
H: 5 10 W: 11 07 b.Nice 25-8-88
Honours: France Youth, Under-21.
2005-06 Monaco 1 0
2006-07 Monaco 0 0
2007-08 Monaco 7 0
2008-09 *Nimes* 14 0 **14 0**
2009-10 Monaco 0 0 **8 0**
2010-11 Blackpool 0 0
2011-12 Middlesbrough 15 3 **15 3**

McDONALD, Scott (F) 308 121
H: 5 7 W: 12 07 b.Melbourne 21-8-83
Honours: Australia Youth, Under-20, Under-23, 25 full caps.
1998-99 Eastern Pride 3 0 **3 0**
1999-2000 Southampton 0 0
2000-01 Southampton 0 0
2001-02 Southampton 2 0
2002-03 Southampton 0 0 **2 0**
2002-03 *Huddersfield T* 13 1 **13 1**
2002-03 Bournemouth 7 1 **7 1**
2003-04 Wimbledon 2 0 **2 0**
2003-04 Motherwell 15 2
2004-05 Motherwell 27 15
2005-06 Motherwell 35 11
2006-07 Motherwell 32 15 **109 43**
2007-08 Celtic 36 25
2008-09 Celtic 34 16
2009-10 Celtic 18 10 **88 51**
2009-10 Middlesbrough 13 4
2010-11 Middlesbrough 38 12
2011-12 Middlesbrough 33 9 **84 25**

McMAHON, Tony (D) 136 4
H: 5 10 W: 11 04 b.Bishop Auckland 24-3-86
Source: Scholar. *Honours:* England Youth.
2003-04 Middlesbrough 0 0
2004-05 Middlesbrough 13 0
2005-06 Middlesbrough 3 0
2006-07 Middlesbrough 0 0
2007-08 Middlesbrough 1 0
2007-08 *Blackpool* 2 0 **2 0**
2008-09 Middlesbrough 13 0
2008-09 *Sheffield W* 15 1 **15 1**
2009-10 Middlesbrough 21 0
2010-11 Middlesbrough 34 2
2011-12 Middlesbrough 34 1 **119 3**

McMANUS, Stephen (D) 220 19
H: 6 2 W: 13 00 b.Lanark 10-9-82
Honours: Scotland 26 full caps, 2 goals.
2003-04 Celtic 5 0
2004-05 Celtic 2 0
2005-06 Celtic 36 7
2006-07 Celtic 31 2
2007-08 Celtic 37 4
2008-09 Celtic 31 4
2009-10 Celtic 8 0 **150 17**
2009-10 Middlesbrough 16 1
2010-11 Middlesbrough 24 1
2011-12 Middlesbrough 24 0 **64 2**
2011-12 *Bristol C* 6 0 **6 0**

OGBECHE, Bart (F) 240 44
H: 5 9 W: 11 00 b.Ogoja 1-10-84
Honours: Nigeria 11 full caps, 3 goals.
2000-01 Paris St Germain B 5 1
2001-02 Paris St Germain B 6 6 **11 7**
2001-02 Paris St Germain 21 4
2002-03 Paris St Germain 18 1
2003-04 Paris St Germain 13 0
2003-04 *Bastia* 15 2 **15 2**
2004-05 Paris St Germain 6 3 **58 8**
2004-05 *Mets* 12 1 **12 1**
2005-06 Al-Jazira 16 5 **16 5**
2006-07 Dep Alaves 29 5 **29 5**
2007-08 Valladolid 19 2
2008-09 Valladolid 16 1 **35 3**
2009-10 Cadiz 28 9 **28 9**
2010-11 Kavala 19 1 **19 1**
2011-12 Middlesbrough 17 3 **17 3**

OLIVER, Kyle (D) 0 0
b.Ashington 18-4-92
Source: Scholar.
2011-12 Middlesbrough 0 0

PARK, Cameron (M) 7 0
H: 5 10 W: 11 02 b.Marske 6-7-92
Source: Scholar. *Honours:* Scotland Youth.
2010-11 Middlesbrough 4 0
2011-12 Middlesbrough 0 0 **4 0**
2011-12 *Barnsley* 3 0 **3 0**

PILATOS, Bruno (D) 0 0
b.Angola 30-3-93
Source: Scholar. *Honours:* England Youth.
2010-11 Middlesbrough 0 0
2011-12 Middlesbrough 0 0

REACH, Adam (M) 2 1
H: 6 1 W: 11 07 b.Gateshead 3-2-93
Source: Scholar. *Honours:* England Youth.
2010-11 Middlesbrough 1 1
2011-12 Middlesbrough 1 0 **2 1**

RIPLEY, Connor (G) 3 0
H: 5 11 W: 11 13 b.Middlesbrough 13-2-93
Source: Scholar. *Honours:* England Youth.
2010-11 Middlesbrough 1 0
2011-12 Middlesbrough 1 0 **2 0**
2011-12 *Oxford U* 1 0 **1 0**

ROBSON, Barry (M) 429 82
H: 5 11 W: 12 00 b.Inverurie 7-11-78
Honours: Scotland B, 17 full caps.
1997-98 Inverness CT 23 3
1998-99 Inverness CT 16 0
1999-2000 Inverness CT 4 0
1999-2000 *Forfar Ath* 25 9 **25 9**
2000-01 Inverness CT 34 5
2001-02 Inverness CT 24 2
2002-03 Inverness CT 34 10 **135 20**
2003-04 Dundee U 28 3
2004-05 Dundee U 36 6
2005-06 Dundee U 31 1
2006-07 Dundee U 29 11
2007-08 Dundee U 21 11 **145 32**
2007-08 Celtic 15 2
2008-09 Celtic 12 1
2009-10 Celtic 10 1 **37 4**
2009-10 Middlesbrough 18 5
2010-11 Middlesbrough 32 5
2011-12 Middlesbrough 37 7 **87 17**

SMALLWOOD, Richard (M) 26 1
H: 5 11 W: 11 05 b.Redcar 29-12-90
Source: Scholar. *Honours:* England Youth.
2008-09 Middlesbrough 0 0
2009-10 Middlesbrough 0 0
2010-11 Middlesbrough 13 1
2011-12 Middlesbrough 13 0 **26 1**

STEELE, Jason (G) 82 0
H: 6 2 W: 12 07 b.Newton Aycliffe 18-8-90
Source: Scholar. *Honours:* England Youth, Under-21.
2007-08 Middlesbrough 0 0
2008-09 Middlesbrough 0 0
2009-10 Middlesbrough 0 0
2009-10 *Northampton T* 13 0 **13 0**
2010-11 Middlesbrough 35 0
2011-12 Middlesbrough 34 0 **69 0**

THOMSON, Kevin (M) 192 4
H: 6 2 W: 11 05 b.Edinburgh 14-10-84
Honours: Scotland 3 full caps.
2003-04 Hibernian 23 1
2004-05 Hibernian 3 0
2005-06 Hibernian 31 0
2006-07 Hibernian 23 1 **80 2**
2006-07 Rangers 9 0
2007-08 Rangers 26 1
2008-09 Rangers 11 1
2009-10 Rangers 25 0 **71 2**
2010-11 Middlesbrough 19 0
2011-12 Middlesbrough 22 0 **41 0**

WELDON, Paul (D) 0 0
b.Sunderland 27-11-91
Source: Scholar.
2010-11 Middlesbrough 0 0
2011-12 Middlesbrough 0 0

WILLIAMS, Luke (F) 10 0
H: 6 1 W: 11 08 b.Middlesbrough 11-6-93
Source: Scholar. *Honours:* England Youth.
2009-10 Middlesbrough 4 0
2010-11 Middlesbrough 6 0
2011-12 Middlesbrough 0 0 **10 0**

WILLIAMS, Rhys (M) 96 5
H: 6 2 W: 11 05 b.Perth 14-7-88
Source: Scholar. *Honours:* Wales Under-21. Australia 9 full caps.
2006-07 Middlesbrough 0 0
2007-08 Middlesbrough 0 0
2008-09 Middlesbrough 0 0
2008-09 *Burnley* 17 0 **17 0**
2009-10 Middlesbrough 32 2
2010-11 Middlesbrough 12 1
2011-12 Middlesbrough 35 2 **79 5**

WYKE, Charlie (F) 0 0
b.Middlesbrough 6-12-92
Source: Scholar.
2011-12 Middlesbrough 0 0

ZEMMAMA, Merouane (M) 124 14
H: 5 8 W: 10 05 b.Rabat 7-10-83
Source: Chabab Tabriquet. *Honours:* Morocco 7 full caps, 1 goal.
2003-04 Raja 23 2
2004-05 *Qatar SC* 0 0
2005-06 Raja 0 0 **23 2**
2006-07 Hibernian 23 2
2007-08 Hibernian 28 6
2008-09 Hibernian 1 0
2008-09 *Al-Sha'ab* 0 0
2009-10 Hibernian 21 2
2010-11 Hibernian 4 0 **77 10**
2010-11 Middlesbrough 9 1
2011-12 Middlesbrough 15 1 **24 2**

MILLWALL (52)

ABDOU, Nadjim (M) 290 8
H: 5 10 W: 11 02 b.Martigues 13-7-84
Honours: Comoros 4 full caps.
2002-03 Martigues 26 1 **26 1**
2003-04 Sedan 17 0
2004-05 Sedan 32 2
2005-06 Sedan 14 0
2006-07 Sedan 17 0 **80 2**
2007-08 Plymouth Arg 31 1 **31 1**
2008-09 Millwall 36 3
2009-10 Millwall 43 1
2010-11 Millwall 34 0
2011-12 Millwall 40 0 **153 4**

BARRON, Scott (D) 125 2
H: 5 9 W: 9 08 b.Preston 2-9-85
Source: Scholar.
2003-04 Ipswich T 0 0
2004-05 Ipswich T 0 0
2005-06 Ipswich T 15 0
2006-07 Ipswich T 0 0 **15 0**
2006-07 *Wrexham* 3 0 **3 0**
2007-08 Millwall 12 0
2008-09 Millwall 14 0
2009-10 Millwall 23 0
2010-11 Millwall 38 2
2011-12 Millwall 20 0 **107 2**

BATT, Shaun (M) 75 7
H: 6 3 W: 12 08 b.Harlow 22-2-87
Source: Stevenage B, Dagenham & R, Fisher Ath.
2008-09 Peterborough U 30 2
2009-10 Peterborough U 20 2 **50 4**
2009-10 *Millwall* 16 3
2010-11 Millwall 0 0

2011-12	Millwall	4	0	**20**	**3**
2011-12	*Crawley T*	5	0	**5**	**0**

BOUAZZA, Hameur (M) 223 22
H: 5 10 W: 12 01 b.Evry 22-2-85
Source: Scholar. *Honours:* Algeria 19 full caps, 3 goals.

2003-04	Watford	9	1		
2004-05	Watford	28	1		
2005-06	Watford	14	1		
2005-06	*Swindon T*	13	2	**13**	**2**
2006-07	Watford	32	6	**83**	**9**
2007-08	Fulham	20	1		
2008-09	Fulham	0	0	**20**	**1**
2008-09	*Charlton Ath*	25	4	**25**	**4**
2008-09	*Birmingham C*	16	1	**16**	**1**
2009-10	Sivas	0	0		
2009-10	Blackpool	19	1	**19**	**1**
2010-11	Arles-Avignon	9	1	**9**	**1**
2010-11	Millwall	12	1		
2011-12	Millwall	26	2	**38**	**3**

CRAIG, Tony (D) 236 7
H: 6 0 W: 10 03 b.Greenwich 20-4-85
Source: Scholar.

2002-03	Millwall	2	1		
2003-04	Millwall	9	0		
2004-05	Millwall	10	0		
2004-05	*Wycombe W*	14	0	**14**	**0**
2005-06	Millwall	28	0		
2006-07	Millwall	30	1		
2007-08	Crystal Palace	13	0	**13**	**0**
2007-08	*Millwall*	5	1		
2008-09	Millwall	44	2		
2009-10	Millwall	30	2		
2010-11	Millwall	24	0		
2011-12	Millwall	23	0	**205**	**7**
2011-12	*Leyton Orient*	4	0	**4**	**0**

DUNNE, Alan (D) 248 14
H: 5 10 W: 10 13 b.Dublin 23-8-82
Source: Trainee.

1999-2000	Millwall	0	0		
2000-01	Millwall	0	0		
2001-02	Millwall	1	0		
2002-03	Millwall	4	0		
2003-04	Millwall	8	0		
2004-05	Millwall	19	3		
2005-06	Millwall	40	0		
2006-07	Millwall	32	6		
2007-08	Millwall	19	3		
2008-09	Millwall	24	0		
2009-10	Millwall	32	2		
2010-11	Millwall	39	0		
2011-12	Millwall	30	0	**248**	**14**

FEENEY, Liam (M) 144 16
H: 5 10 W: 12 02 b.Hammersmith 21-1-87
Source: Salisbury C.
On loan from Salisbury C.

2008-09	Southend U	1	0	**1**	**0**
2008-09	Bournemouth	14	3		
2009-10	Bournemouth	44	5		
2010-11	Bournemouth	46	4		
2011-12	Bournemouth	5	0	**109**	**12**
2011-12	Millwall	34	4	**34**	**4**

FORDE, David (G) 261 0
H: 6 3 W: 13 06 b.Galway 20-12-79
Source: Barry T. *Honours:* Eire 2 full caps.

2001-02	West Ham U	0	0		
2002-03	West Ham U	0	0		
2003-04	West Ham U	0	0		
2004	Derry C	11	0		
2005	Derry C	33	0		
2006	Derry C	29	0	**73**	**0**
2006-07	Cardiff C	7	0		
2007-08	Cardiff C	0	0	**7**	**0**
2007-08	*Luton T*	5	0	**5**	**0**
2007-08	*Bournemouth*	11	0	**11**	**0**
2008-09	Millwall	46	0		
2009-10	Millwall	46	0		
2010-11	Millwall	46	0		
2011-12	Millwall	27	0	**165**	**0**

GALLAGHER, Jake (M) 0 0
b.Leatherhead 6-1-93
Source: Scholar.

2011-12	Millwall	0	0		

HACKETT, Chris (M) 260 14
H: 6 0 W: 12 08 b.Oxford 1-3-83
Source: Scholarship.

1999-2000	Oxford U	2	0		
2000-01	Oxford U	16	2		
2001-02	Oxford U	15	0		
2002-03	Oxford U	12	0		
2003-04	Oxford U	22	1		
2004-05	Oxford U	37	4		
2005-06	Oxford U	21	2	**125**	**9**
2005-06	Hearts	2	0	**2**	**0**
2006-07	Millwall	33	3		
2007-08	Millwall	6	0		
2008-09	Millwall	22	0		
2009-10	Millwall	40	2		
2010-11	Millwall	16	0		
2011-12	Millwall	3	0	**120**	**5**
2011-12	*Exeter C*	5	0	**5**	**0**
2011-12	*Wycombe W*	8	0	**8**	**0**

HENDERSON, Darius (F) 331 91
H: 6 3 W: 14 03 b.Sutton 7-9-81
Source: Trainee.

1999-2000	Reading	6	0		
2000-01	Reading	4	0		
2001-02	Reading	38	7		
2002-03	Reading	22	4		
2003-04	Reading	1	0	**71**	**11**
2003-04	*Brighton & HA*	10	2	**10**	**2**
2003-04	Gillingham	4	0		
2004-05	Gillingham	32	9	**36**	**9**
2004-05	*Swindon T*	6	5	**6**	**5**
2005-06	Watford	30	14		
2006-07	Watford	35	3		
2007-08	Watford	40	12	**105**	**29**
2008-09	Sheffield U	32	6		
2009-10	Sheffield U	32	12		
2010-11	Sheffield U	8	2	**72**	**20**
2011-12	Millwall	31	15	**31**	**15**

HENRY, James (M) 131 17
H: 6 1 W: 11 11 b.Reading 10-6-89
Source: Scholar. *Honours:* England Youth.

2006-07	Reading	0	0		
2006-07	*Nottingham F*	1	0	**1**	**0**
2007-08	Reading	0	0		
2007-08	*Bournemouth*	11	4	**11**	**4**
2007-08	*Norwich C*	3	0	**3**	**0**
2008-09	Reading	7	0		
2008-09	*Millwall*	16	3		
2009-10	Reading	3	0	**10**	**0**
2009-10	*Millwall*	9	5		
2010-11	Millwall	42	5		
2011-12	Millwall	39	0	**106**	**13**

KEOGH, Andy (F) 283 57
H: 6 0 W: 11 00 b.Dublin 16-5-86
Source: Scholar. *Honours:* Eire Youth, B, Under-21, 22 full caps, 1 goal.

2003-04	Leeds U	0	0		
2004-05	Leeds U	0	0		
2004-05	*Bury*	4	2	**4**	**2**
2004-05	Scunthorpe U	25	3		
2005-06	Scunthorpe U	45	11		
2006-07	Scunthorpe U	28	7	**98**	**21**
2006-07	Wolverhampton W	17	5		
2007-08	Wolverhampton W	43	8		
2008-09	Wolverhampton W	42	5		
2009-10	Wolverhampton W	13	1		
2010-11	Wolverhampton W	1	0		
2010-11	*Cardiff C*	16	2	**16**	**2**
2010-11	*Bristol C*	9	1	**9**	**1**
2011-12	Wolverhampton W	0	0	**116**	**19**
2011-12	*Leeds U*	22	2	**22**	**2**
2011-12	Millwall	18	10	**18**	**10**

LOWRY, Shane (D) 63 1
H: 6 1 W: 13 01 b.Perth 12-6-89
Source: Scholar. *Honours:* Eire Under-21.

2007-08	Aston Villa	0	0		
2008-09	Aston Villa	0	0		
2009-10	Aston Villa	0	0		
2009-10	*Plymouth Arg*	13	0	**13**	**0**
2009-10	*Leeds U*	11	0	**11**	**0**
2010-11	Aston Villa	0	0		
2010-11	*Sheffield U*	17	0	**17**	**0**
2011-12	Aston Villa	0	0		
2011-12	Millwall	22	1	**22**	**1**

MARQUIS, John (F) 29 5
H: 6 1 W: 11 03 b.Lewisham 16-5-92
Source: Scholar.

2009-10	Millwall	1	0		
2010-11	Millwall	11	4		
2011-12	Millwall	17	1	**29**	**5**

McLAREN, Connor (D) 0 0
b.Kennington 19-11-92
Source: Scholar.

2011-12	Millwall	0	0		

McQUOID, Josh (F) 102 12
H: 5 9 W: 10 10 b.Southampton 15-12-89
Source: Scholar. *Honours:* Northern Ireland Under-21, B, 5 full caps.

2006-07	Bournemouth	2	0		
2007-08	Bournemouth	5	0		
2008-09	Bournemouth	16	0		
2009-10	Bournemouth	29	1		
2010-11	Bournemouth	17	9	**69**	**10**
2010-11	Millwall	11	1		
2011-12	Millwall	5	0	**16**	**1**
2011-12	*Burnley*	17	1	**17**	**1**

MILDENHALL, Steve (G) 324 1
H: 6 4 W: 14 01 b.Swindon 13-5-78
Source: Trainee.

1996-97	Swindon T	1	0		
1997-98	Swindon T	4	0		
1998-99	Swindon T	0	0		
1999-2000	Swindon T	5	0		
2000-01	Swindon T	23	0	**33**	**0**
2001-02	Notts Co	26	0		
2002-03	Notts Co	21	0		
2003-04	Notts Co	28	0		
2004-05	Notts Co	1	0	**76**	**0**
2004-05	Oldham Ath	6	0	**6**	**0**
2005-06	Grimsby T	46	1	**46**	**1**
2006-07	Yeovil T	46	0		
2007-08	Yeovil T	29	0	**75**	**0**
2008-09	Southend U	34	0		
2009-10	Southend U	44	0		
2010-11	Southend U	0	0	**78**	**0**
2010-11	Millwall	0	0		
2011-12	Millwall	10	0	**10**	**0**

MKANDAWIRE, Tamika (D) 201 18
H: 6 1 W: 12 03 b.Malawi 28-5-83
Source: Scholar.

2002-03	WBA	0	0		
2003-04	WBA	0	0		
2006-07	Hereford U	39	2	**39**	**2**
2007-08	Leyton Orient	35	3		
2008-09	Leyton Orient	36	5		
2009-10	Leyton Orient	43	7	**114**	**15**
2010-11	Millwall	35	1		
2011-12	Millwall	13	0	**48**	**1**

N'GUESSAN, Dany (M) 177 29
H: 6 0 W: 12 13 b.Paris 11-8-87
Source: Auxerre, Rangers.

2006-07	Boston U	23	5	**23**	**5**
2006-07	Lincoln C	9	0		
2007-08	Lincoln C	37	7		
2008-09	Lincoln C	45	8	**91**	**15**
2009-10	Leicester C	27	3		
2010-11	Leicester C	5	0	**32**	**3**
2010-11	*Scunthorpe U*	3	1	**3**	**1**
2010-11	*Southampton*	6	0	**6**	**0**
2011-12	Millwall	15	1	**15**	**1**
2011-12	*Charlton Ath*	7	4	**7**	**4**

O'BRIEN, Aiden (F) 0 0
b.Islington 4-10-93
Source: Scholar. *Honours:* Eire Youth.

2010-11	Millwall	0	0		
2011-12	Millwall	0	0		

RACON, Therry (M) 134 10
H: 5 10 W: 10 02 b.Paris 1-5-84

2004-05	Lorient	28	3	**28**	**3**
2005-06	Guingamp	0	0		
2006-07	Guingamp	0	0		
2007-08	Charlton Ath	4	0		
2007-08	*Brighton & HA*	8	0	**8**	**0**
2008-09	Charlton Ath	19	3		
2009-10	Charlton Ath	36	1		
2010-11	Charlton Ath	39	3		
2011-12	Charlton Ath	0	0	**98**	**7**
2011-12	Millwall	0	0		

ROBINSON, Paul (D) 288 16
H: 6 1 W: 11 09 b.Barnet 7-1-82
Source: Scholar.

2000-01	Millwall	0	0		
2001-02	Millwall	0	0		
2002-03	Millwall	14	0		
2003-04	Millwall	9	0		
2004-05	Millwall	0	0		
2004-05	*Torquay U*	12	0	**12**	**0**
2005-06	Millwall	32	0		
2006-07	Millwall	38	3		
2007-08	Millwall	45	3		
2008-09	Millwall	26	2		
2009-10	Millwall	34	4		

2010-11 Millwall 37 3
2011-12 Millwall 41 1 **276 16**

SMITH, Jack (D) 236 12
H: 5 11 W: 11 05 b.Hemel Hempstead 14-10-83
Source: Scholar.
2001-02 Watford 0 0
2002-03 Watford 1 0
2003-04 Watford 17 2
2004-05 Watford 7 0 **25 2**
2005-06 Swindon T 38 0
2006-07 Swindon T 41 3
2007-08 Swindon T 21 1
2008-09 Swindon T 38 5 **138 9**
2009-10 Millwall 31 0
2010-11 Millwall 9 1
2011-12 Millwall 33 0 **73 1**

SOWAH, Lennard (D) 30 0
H: 6 1 W: 11 00 b.Hamburg 23-2-92
Source: St Pauli, Arsenal, Portsmouth Scholar. *Honours:* Germany Youth.
2009-10 Portsmouth 5 0 **5 0**
2010-11 Hamburg 0 0
2010-11 Hamburg II 25 0 **25 0**
2011-12 Millwall 0 0
On loan from Hamburg.

STEWART, Jordan (D) 286 11
H: 6 0 W: 12 09 b.Birmingham 3-3-82
Source: Trainee. *Honours:* England Youth, Under-21.
1999-2000 Leicester C 1 0
1999-2000 *Bristol R* 4 0 **4 0**
2000-01 Leicester C 0 0
2001-02 Leicester C 12 0
2002-03 Leicester C 37 4
2003-04 Leicester C 25 1
2004-05 Leicester C 35 1 **110 6**
2005-06 Watford 35 0
2006-07 Watford 31 0
2007-08 Watford 39 2 **105 2**
2008-09 Derby Co 26 2 **26 2**
2009-10 Sheffield U 23 0 **23 0**
2010-11 Xanthi 14 1 **14 1**
2011-12 Millwall 4 0 **4 0**

TROTTER, Liam (M) 142 20
H: 6 2 W: 12 02 b.Ipswich 24-8-88
Source: Scholar.
2005-06 Ipswich T 1 0
2006-07 Ipswich T 0 0
2006-07 *Millwall* 2 0
2007-08 Ipswich T 7 1
2008-09 Ipswich T 3 1
2008-09 *Grimsby T* 15 2 **15 2**
2008-09 *Scunthorpe U* 12 1 **12 1**
2009-10 Ipswich T 12 0 **23 2**
2009-10 *Millwall* 20 1
2010-11 Millwall 35 7
2011-12 Millwall 35 7 **92 15**

WARD, Darren (D) 426 14
H: 6 3 W: 11 04 b.Harrow 13-9-78
Source: Trainee.
1995-96 Watford 1 0
1996-97 Watford 7 0
1997-98 Watford 0 0
1998-99 Watford 1 0
1999-2000 Watford 9 1
1999-2000 *QPR* 14 0 **14 0**
2000-01 Watford 40 1
2001-02 Watford 1 0
2001-02 Millwall 14 0
2002-03 Millwall 39 1
2003-04 Millwall 46 3
2004-05 Millwall 43 0
2005-06 Crystal Palace 43 5
2006-07 Crystal Palace 20 0 **63 5**
2007-08 Wolverhampton W 30 0
2008-09 Wolverhampton W 1 0
2008-09 *Watford* 9 1 **68 3**
2008-09 *Charlton Ath* 16 0 **16 0**
2009-10 Wolverhampton W 0 0 **31 0**
2009-10 Millwall 31 1
2010-11 Millwall 31 1
2011-12 Millwall 30 0 **234 6**

WRIGHT, Josh (M) 133 2
H: 6 1 W: 11 07 b.Bethnal Green 6-11-89
Source: Scholar. *Honours:* England Youth.
2007-08 Charlton Ath 0 0
2007-08 *Barnet* 32 1 **32 1**
2008-09 Charlton Ath 2 0 **2 0**
2008-09 *Brentford* 5 0 **5 0**
2008-09 *Gillingham* 5 0 **5 0**
2009-10 Scunthorpe U 35 0
2010-11 Scunthorpe U 36 0 **71 0**
2011-12 Millwall 18 1 **18 1**

MILTON KEYNES D (53)

BALDOCK, George (M) 8 0
H: 5 9 W: 10 07 b.Buckingham 26-1-93
Source: Youth.
2009-10 Milton Keynes D 1 0
2010-11 Milton Keynes D 2 0
2011-12 Milton Keynes D 0 0 **3 0**
2011-12 *Northampton T* 5 0 **5 0**

BOWDITCH, Dean (F) 233 52
H: 5 11 W: 11 05 b.Bishops Stortford 15-6-86
Source: Trainee. *Honours:* FA Schools, England Youth.
2002-03 Ipswich T 5 0
2003-04 Ipswich T 16 4
2004-05 Ipswich T 21 3
2004-05 *Burnley* 10 1 **10 1**
2005-06 Ipswich T 21 0
2005-06 *Wycombe W* 11 1 **11 1**
2006-07 Ipswich T 9 1
2006-07 *Brighton & HA* 3 1
2007-08 Ipswich T 0 0
2007-08 *Northampton T* 10 2 **10 2**
2007-08 *Brighton & HA* 5 0 **8 1**
2008-09 Ipswich T 1 0 **73 8**
2008-09 *Brentford* 9 2 **9 2**
2009-10 Yeovil T 30 10
2010-11 Yeovil T 41 15 **71 25**
2011-12 Milton Keynes D 41 12 **41 12**

CHADWICK, Luke (M) 326 26
H: 5 11 W: 11 08 b.Cambridge 18-11-80
Source: Trainee. *Honours:* England Youth, Under-21.
1998-99 Manchester U 0 0
1999-2000 Manchester U 0 0
2000-01 Manchester U 16 2
2001-02 Manchester U 8 0
2002-03 Manchester U 1 0
2002-03 *Reading* 15 1 **15 1**
2003-04 Manchester U 0 0 **25 2**
2003-04 *Burnley* 36 5 **36 5**
2004-05 West Ham U 32 1
2005-06 West Ham U 0 0 **32 1**
2005-06 Stoke C 36 2
2006-07 Stoke C 15 3 **51 5**
2006-07 Norwich C 4 1
2007-08 Norwich C 13 1
2008-09 Norwich C 0 0 **17 2**
2008-09 Milton Keynes D 24 6
2009-10 Milton Keynes D 40 2
2010-11 Milton Keynes D 44 0
2011-12 Milton Keynes D 42 2 **150 10**

CHICKSEN, Adam (D) 44 0
H: 5 8 W: 11 09 b.Milton Keynes 27-9-91
Source: Scholar.
2008-09 Milton Keynes D 1 0
2009-10 Milton Keynes D 6 0
2010-11 Milton Keynes D 14 0
2011-12 Milton Keynes D 20 0 **41 0**
2011-12 *Leyton Orient* 3 0 **3 0**

COLLINS, Charlie (F) 4 0
H: 6 0 W: 11 11 b.Hammersmith 22-11-91
Source: Scholar. *Honours:* Eire Youth.
2009-10 Milton Keynes D 2 0
2010-11 Milton Keynes D 1 0
2011-12 Milton Keynes D 0 0 **3 0**
2011-12 *Aldershot T* 1 0 **1 0**

DOUMBE, Stephen (D) 276 16
H: 6 1 W: 12 05 b.Paris 28-10-79
Source: Paris St Germain. *Honours:* France Youth.
2001-02 Hibernian 0 0
2002-03 Hibernian 12 0
2003-04 Hibernian 33 2 **45 2**
2004-05 Plymouth Arg 26 2
2005-06 Plymouth Arg 43 1
2006-07 Plymouth Arg 29 0
2007-08 Plymouth Arg 12 0
2008-09 Plymouth Arg 24 1 **134 4**
2009-10 Milton Keynes D 33 1
2010-11 Milton Keynes D 44 5
2011-12 Milton Keynes D 20 4 **97 10**

FLANAGAN, Tom (D) 24 3
H: 6 2 W: 11 05 b.Hammersmith 21-10-91
Source: Scholar.
2009-10 Milton Keynes D 1 0
2010-11 Milton Keynes D 2 0
2011-12 Milton Keynes D 21 3 **24 3**

GALLOWAY, Brendon (M) 1 0
H: 6 2 W: 13 10 b.Zimbabwe 17-3-96
Source: Schoolboy.
2011-12 Milton Keynes D 1 0 **1 0**

GLEESON, Stephen (M) 157 11
H: 6 2 W: 11 00 b.Dublin 3-8-88
Source: Scholar. *Honours:* Eire Youth, Under-21, 2 full caps.
2006-07 Wolverhampton W 3 0
2006-07 *Stockport Co* 14 2
2007-08 Wolverhampton W 0 0
2007-08 *Hereford U* 4 0 **4 0**
2007-08 *Stockport Co* 6 0
2008-09 Wolverhampton W 0 0 **3 0**
2008-09 *Stockport Co* 21 2 **41 4**
2008-09 *Milton Keynes D* 5 0
2009-10 Milton Keynes D 29 0
2010-11 Milton Keynes D 36 2
2011-12 Milton Keynes D 39 5 **109 7**

GUY, Lewis (F) 206 24
H: 5 10 W: 10 07 b.Penrith 27-8-85
Source: Trainee. *Honours:* England Youth, Under-20.
2002-03 Newcastle U 0 0
2003-04 Newcastle U 0 0
2004-05 Newcastle U 0 0
2004-05 Doncaster R 9 3
2005-06 Doncaster R 31 3
2006-07 Doncaster R 36 4
2007-08 Doncaster R 29 6
2008-09 Doncaster R 29 2
2008-09 *Hartlepool U* 4 0 **4 0**
2009-10 Doncaster R 13 0 **147 18**
2009-10 *Oldham Ath* 12 3 **12 3**
2010-11 Milton Keynes D 34 2
2011-12 Milton Keynes D 1 0 **35 2**
2011-12 *Oxford U* 8 1 **8 1**

IBEHRE, Jabo (F) 363 63
H: 6 2 W: 13 13 b.Islington 28-1-83
Source: Trainee.
1999-2000 Leyton Orient 3 0
2000-01 Leyton Orient 5 2
2001-02 Leyton Orient 28 4
2002-03 Leyton Orient 25 5
2003-04 Leyton Orient 35 4
2004-05 Leyton Orient 19 2
2005-06 Leyton Orient 33 8
2006-07 Leyton Orient 30 4
2007-08 Leyton Orient 31 7 **209 36**
2008-09 Walsall 39 10 **39 10**
2009-10 Milton Keynes D 10 1
2009-10 *Southend U* 4 0 **4 0**
2009-10 *Stockport Co* 20 5 **20 5**
2010-11 Milton Keynes D 42 3
2011-12 Milton Keynes D 39 8 **91 12**

LEWINGTON, Dean (D) 376 14
H: 5 11 W: 11 07 b.Kingston 18-5-84
Source: Scholar.
2002-03 Wimbledon 1 0
2003-04 Wimbledon 28 1 **29 1**
2004-05 Milton Keynes D 43 2
2005-06 Milton Keynes D 44 1
2006-07 Milton Keynes D 45 1
2007-08 Milton Keynes D 45 0
2008-09 Milton Keynes D 40 2
2009-10 Milton Keynes D 42 1
2010-11 Milton Keynes D 42 3
2011-12 Milton Keynes D 46 3 **347 13**

MACDONALD, Charlie (F) 196 54
H: 5 8 W: 12 10 b.Southwark 13-2-81
Source: Trainee.
1998-99 Charlton Ath 0 0
1999-2000 Charlton Ath 3 0
2000-01 Charlton Ath 3 0
2000-01 *Cheltenham T* 8 2 **8 2**
2001-02 Charlton Ath 2 1 **8 1**
2001-02 *Torquay U* 5 0 **5 0**
2001-02 *Colchester U* 4 1 **4 1**
From Margate, Stevenage, Crawley T, Gravesend & N.
2007-08 Southend U 25 1 **25 1**
2008-09 Brentford 38 16
2009-10 Brentford 40 15

2010-11	Brentford	30	9		
2011-12	Brentford	3	0	**111**	**40**
2011-12	Milton Keynes D	35	9	**35**	**9**

MACKENZIE, Gary (D) **152 5**
H: 6 3 W: 13 01 b.Lanark 15-10-85

2003-04	Rangers	2	0		
2004-05	Rangers	0	0		
2005-06	Rangers	0	0	**2**	**0**
2006-07	Dundee	21	0		
2007-08	Dundee	33	1		
2008-09	Dundee	19	0		
2009-10	Dundee	25	1	**98**	**2**
2010-11	Milton Keynes D	26	2		
2011-12	Milton Keynes D	26	1	**52**	**3**

MARTIN, David E (G) **146 0**
H: 6 1 W: 13 04 b.Romford 22-1-86
Source: Scholar. *Honours:* England Youth, Under-20.

2003-04	Wimbledon	2	0	**2**	**0**
2004-05	Milton Keynes D	15	0		
2005-06	Milton Keynes D	0	0		
2005-06	Liverpool	0	0		
2006-07	Liverpool	0	0		
2006-07	*Accrington S*	10	0	**10**	**0**
2007-08	Liverpool	0	0		
2008-09	Liverpool	0	0		
2008-09	*Leicester C*	25	0	**25**	**0**
2009-10	Liverpool	0	0		
2009-10	*Tranmere R*	3	0	**3**	**0**
2009-10	*Leeds U*	0	0		
2009-10	*Derby Co*	2	0	**2**	**0**
2010-11	Milton Keynes D	43	0		
2011-12	Milton Keynes D	46	0	**104**	**0**

McLOUGHLIN, Ian (G) **6 0**
H: 6 3 W: 13 08 b.Dublin 9-8-91
Source: St Francis. *Honours:* Eire Under-21.

2008-09	Ipswich T	0	0		
2009-10	Ipswich T	0	0		
2010-11	Ipswich T	0	0		
2010-11	*Stockport Co*	5	0	**5**	**0**
2011-12	Milton Keynes D	1	0	**1**	**0**

MILTON, Harry (M) **0 0**
b.Romford 27-4-93
Source: Scholar.

2011-12	Milton Keynes D	0	0		

O'SHEA, Jay (M) **116 21**
H: 5 9 W: 12 00 b.Dun Laoghaire 10-8-88
Honours: Eire Under-21.

2007	Bray Wanderers	27	4	**27**	**4**
2008	Galway United	29	8		
2009	Galway United	19	3	**48**	**11**
2009-10	Birmingham C	1	0		
2009-10	*Middlesbrough*	2	0	**2**	**0**
2010-11	Birmingham C	0	0	**1**	**0**
2010-11	*Stevenage*	5	0	**5**	**0**
2010-11	*Port Vale*	5	1	**5**	**1**
2011-12	Milton Keynes D	28	5	**28**	**5**

POTTER, Darren (M) **204 10**
H: 6 0 W: 10 08 b.Liverpool 21-12-84
Source: Scholar. *Honours:* Eire Youth, B, Under-21, 5 full caps.

2001-02	Liverpool	0	0		
2002-03	Liverpool	0	0		
2003-04	Liverpool	0	0		
2004-05	Liverpool	2	0		
2005-06	Liverpool	0	0		
2005-06	*Southampton*	10	0	**10**	**0**
2006-07	Liverpool	0	0	**2**	**0**
2006-07	Wolverhampton W	38	0		
2007-08	Wolverhampton W	18	0		
2008-09	Wolverhampton W	0	0	**56**	**0**
2008-09	*Sheffield W*	17	2		
2009-10	Sheffield W	46	3		
2010-11	Sheffield W	33	3	**96**	**8**
2011-12	Milton Keynes D	40	2	**40**	**2**

POWELL, Daniel (F) **81 17**
H: 5 11 W: 13 03 b.Luton 12-3-91
Source: Scholar.

2008-09	Milton Keynes D	7	1		
2009-10	Milton Keynes D	2	1		
2010-11	Milton Keynes D	29	9		
2011-12	Milton Keynes D	43	6	**81**	**17**

SLANE, Paul (M) **8 0**
H: 5 8 W: 10 01 b.Glasgow 25-11-91
Honours: Scotland Youth.

2009-10	Motherwell	3	0	**3**	**0**
2010-11	Celtic	0	0		
2011-12	Celtic	0	0		
2011-12	Milton Keynes D	5	0	**5**	**0**

On loan from Celtic.

WILLIAMS, George (F) **2 0**
H: 5 10 W: 12 04 b.Milton Keynes 7-9-95
Source: Scholar. *Honours:* Wales Youth.

2011-12	Milton Keynes D	2	0	**2**	**0**

WILLIAMS, Shaun (M) **122 31**
H: 5 9 W: 11 11 b.Dublin 19-10-86
Honours: Eire Under-23.

2007	Drogheda U	0	0		
2007	*Dundalk*	19	9	**19**	**9**
2008	Drogheda U	4	0		
2008	*Finn Harps*	14	2	**14**	**2**
2009	Drogheda U	1	0	**5**	**0**
2009	Sporting Fingal	13	7		
2010	Sporting Fingal	32	5	**45**	**12**
2011-12	Milton Keynes D	39	8	**39**	**8**

MORECAMBE (54)

ALESSANDRA, Lewis (F) **109 12**
H: 5 9 W: 11 07 b.Heywood 8-2-89
Source: Scholar.

2007-08	Oldham Ath	15	2		
2008-09	Oldham Ath	32	5		
2009-10	Oldham Ath	1	0		
2010-11	Oldham Ath	19	1	**67**	**8**
2011-12	Morecambe	42	4	**42**	**4**

BENTLEY, Jim (D) **124 13**
H: 6 1 W: 13 00 b.Liverpool 11-6-76
Source: Trainee.

1993-94	Manchester C	0	0		
1994-95	Manchester C	0	0		
1995-96	Manchester C	0	0		
1996-97	Manchester C	0	0		
1997-98	Manchester C	0	0		
1998-99	Manchester C	0	0		
2007-08	Morecambe	43	6		
2008-09	Morecambe	45	3		
2009-10	Morecambe	28	3		
2010-11	Morecambe	8	1		
2011-12	Morecambe	0	0	**124**	**13**

BREEN, Sean (F) **0 0**
b.Birkenhead 26-10-93
Source: Youth.

2011-12	Morecambe	0	0		

BURROW, Jordan (F) **19 4**
H: 6 1 W: 11 13 b.Sheffield 12-9-92
Source: Chesterfield Scholar.

2011-12	Morecambe	19	4	**19**	**4**

CARLTON, Danny (F) **138 21**
H: 5 11 W: 12 04 b.Leeds 22-12-83
Source: Morecambe.

2007-08	Carlisle U	31	0		
2008-09	Carlisle U	12	3	**43**	**3**
2008-09	*Morecambe*	8	2		
2008-09	*Darlington*	17	4	**17**	**4**
2009-10	Bury	7	0		
2010-11	Bury	3	0	**10**	**0**
2010-11	Morecambe	16	3		
2011-12	Morecambe	44	9	**68**	**14**

CHARNOCK, Kieran (D) **99 1**
H: 6 1 W: 13 07 b.Preston 3-8-84
Source: Scholar.

2002-03	Wigan Ath	0	0		

From Southport, Northwich Vic.

2007-08	Peterborough U	10	0		
2008-09	Peterborough U	2	0	**12**	**0**
2008-09	*Accrington S*	34	0	**34**	**0**
2009-10	Torquay U	24	0		
2010-11	Torquay U	4	0	**28**	**0**
2010-11	Morecambe	21	1		
2011-12	Morecambe	4	0	**25**	**1**

COWPERTHWAITE, Niall (D) **10 1**
H: 5 11 W: 11 00 b.Barrow 28-1-92
Source: Youth.

2010-11	Morecambe	7	1		
2011-12	Morecambe	3	0	**10**	**1**

CULSHAW, Joe (D) **0 0**
b.Corwen 3-7-93
Source: Wrexham Scholar.

2011-12	Morecambe	0	0		

DRUMMOND, Stuart (M) **338 51**
H: 6 2 W: 13 08 b.Preston 11-12-75
Source: Morecambe.

2004-05	Chester C	45	6		
2005-06	Chester C	42	6	**87**	**12**
2006-07	Shrewsbury T	44	4		
2007-08	Shrewsbury T	23	3	**67**	**7**
2007-08	Morecambe	18	2		
2008-09	Morecambe	44	10		
2009-10	Morecambe	43	9		
2010-11	Morecambe	41	6		
2011-12	Morecambe	38	5	**184**	**32**

ELLISON, Kevin (M) **335 63**
H: 6 0 W: 12 00 b.Liverpool 23-2-79
Source: Altrincham.

2000-01	Leicester C	1	0		
2001-02	Leicester C	0	0	**1**	**0**
2001-02	Stockport Co	11	0		
2002-03	Stockport Co	23	1		
2003-04	Stockport Co	14	1	**48**	**2**
2003-04	*Lincoln C*	11	0	**11**	**0**
2004-05	Chester C	24	9		
2004-05	Hull C	16	1		
2005-06	Hull C	23	1	**39**	**2**
2006-07	Tranmere R	34	4	**34**	**4**
2007-08	Chester C	36	11		
2008-09	Chester C	39	8	**99**	**28**
2008-09	Rotherham U	0	0		
2009-10	Rotherham U	39	8		
2010-11	Rotherham U	23	3	**62**	**11**
2010-11	*Bradford C*	7	1	**7**	**1**
2011-12	Morecambe	34	15	**34**	**15**

FENTON, Nick (D) **486 26**
H: 6 0 W: 10 02 b.Preston 23-11-79
Source: Trainee. *Honours:* England Youth.

1996-97	Manchester C	0	0		
1997-98	Manchester C	0	0		
1998-99	Manchester C	15	0		
1999-2000	Manchester C	0	0		
1999-2000	*Notts Co*	13	1		
1999-2000	*Bournemouth*	8	0		
2000-01	Manchester C	0	0	**15**	**0**
2000-01	*Bournemouth*	5	0	**13**	**0**
2000-01	Notts Co	30	2		
2001-02	Notts Co	42	3		
2002-03	Notts Co	40	3		
2003-04	Notts Co	43	1	**168**	**10**
2004-05	Doncaster R	38	1		
2005-06	Doncaster R	25	2		
2006-07	Doncaster R	0	0	**63**	**3**
2006-07	Grimsby T	38	4		
2007-08	Grimsby T	42	2	**80**	**6**
2008-09	Rotherham U	45	1		
2009-10	Rotherham U	35	0		
2010-11	Rotherham U	32	3	**112**	**4**
2011-12	Morecambe	35	3	**35**	**3**

FLEMING, Andy (M) **53 4**
H: 6 1 W: 12 00 b.Liverpool 18-2-89
Source: Scholar.

2006-07	Wrexham	2	0		
2007-08	Wrexham	4	0	**6**	**0**
2010-11	Morecambe	30	2		
2011-12	Morecambe	17	2	**47**	**4**

HAINING, Will (D) **287 14**
H: 6 0 W: 11 02 b.Glasgow 2-10-82
Source: Scholar.

2001-02	Oldham Ath	4	0		
2002-03	Oldham Ath	26	2		
2003-04	Oldham Ath	31	2		
2004-05	Oldham Ath	35	5		
2005-06	Oldham Ath	15	0		
2006-07	Oldham Ath	44	2	**155**	**11**
2007-08	St Mirren	29	1		
2008-09	St Mirren	19	0	**48**	**1**
2009-10	Morecambe	32	1		
2010-11	Morecambe	12	1		
2011-12	Morecambe	40	0	**84**	**2**

HUNTER, Garry (M) **168 6**
H: 5 7 W: 10 03 b.Morecambe 1-1-85
Source: Scholar.

2007-08	Morecambe	38	1		
2008-09	Morecambe	29	1		
2009-10	Morecambe	31	2		
2010-11	Morecambe	33	1		
2011-12	Morecambe	37	1	**168**	**6**

JEVONS, Phil (F) **378 115**
H: 5 11 W: 12 00 b.Liverpool 1-8-79
Source: Trainee.

1996-97	Everton	0	0		

1997-98 Everton 0 0
1998-99 Everton 1 0
1999-2000 Everton 3 0
2000-01 Everton 4 0 **8 0**
2001-02 Grimsby T 31 6
2002-03 Grimsby T 3 0
2002-03 *Hull C* 24 3 **24 3**
2003-04 Grimsby T 29 12 **63 18**
2004-05 Yeovil T 46 27
2005-06 Yeovil T 38 15 **84 42**
2006-07 Bristol C 41 11
2007-08 Bristol C 2 0 **43 11**
2007-08 Huddersfield T 21 7
2008-09 Huddersfield T 23 2
2008-09 *Bury* 7 2 **7 2**
2009-10 Huddersfield T 0 0 **44 9**
2009-10 *Morecambe* 40 18
2010-11 Morecambe 38 8
2011-12 Morecambe 27 4 **105 30**

McCREADY, Chris (D) 261 7
H: 6 1 W: 12 05 b.Ellesmere Port 5-9-81
Source: Scholar.
2000-01 Crewe Alex 0 0
2001-02 Crewe Alex 1 0
2002-03 Crewe Alex 8 0
2003-04 Crewe Alex 22 0
2004-05 Crewe Alex 20 0
2005-06 Crewe Alex 25 0
2006-07 Tranmere R 42 1
2007-08 Crewe Alex 34 1
2008-09 Crewe Alex 5 1 **115 2**
2009-10 Northampton T 14 0 **14 0**
2009-10 *Tranmere R* 8 0 **50 1**
2010-11 Morecambe 36 4
2011-12 Morecambe 46 0 **82 4**

McDONALD, Gary (F) 303 33
H: 6 0 W: 11 06 b.Irvine 10-4-82
Honours: Scotland B.
1999-2000 Kilmarnock 0 0
2000-01 Kilmarnock 0 0
2001-02 Kilmarnock 6 0
2002-03 Kilmarnock 12 2
2003-04 Kilmarnock 23 3
2004-05 Kilmarnock 38 3
2005-06 Kilmarnock 27 3 **106 11**
2006-07 Oldham Ath 43 7
2007-08 Oldham Ath 35 4 **78 11**
2008-09 Aberdeen 28 5
2009-10 Aberdeen 24 3 **52 8**
2010-11 Hamilton A 25 0 **25 0**
2011-12 Morecambe 42 3 **42 3**

McGEE, Joe (M) 1 0
H: 5 11 W: 10 12 b.Liverpool 6-3-93
Source: Youth.
2011-12 Morecambe 1 0 **1 0**

MWASILIE, Joe (M) 6 0
H: 5 8 W: 10 01 b.Zambia 7-6-93
Source: Youth.
2011-12 Morecambe 6 0 **6 0**

PARKINSON, Dan (M) 3 0
H: 5 11 W: 11 02 b.Preston 2-11-92
Source: Youth.
2011-12 Morecambe 3 0 **3 0**

PARRISH, Andy (D) 170 1
H: 6 0 W: 11 00 b.Bolton 22-6-88
Source: Scholar.
2005-06 Bury 8 0
2006-07 Bury 9 0
2007-08 Bury 26 1 **43 1**
2008-09 Morecambe 13 0
2009-10 Morecambe 35 0
2010-11 Morecambe 41 0
2011-12 Morecambe 38 0 **127 0**

PRICE, Jason (M) 460 72
H: 6 2 W: 11 05 b.Pontypridd 12-4-77
Source: Aberaman Ath. *Honours:* Wales Under-21.
1995-96 Swansea C 0 0
1996-97 Swansea C 2 0
1997-98 Swansea C 34 3
1998-99 Swansea C 28 4
1999-2000 Swansea C 39 6
2000-01 Swansea C 41 4 **144 17**
2001-02 Brentford 15 1 **15 1**
2001-02 Tranmere R 24 7
2002-03 Tranmere R 25 4 **49 11**
2003-04 Hull C 33 9
2004-05 Hull C 27 2
2005-06 Hull C 15 2 **75 13**
2005-06 Doncaster R 11 4
2006-07 Doncaster R 31 6
2007-08 Doncaster R 29 7
2008-09 Doncaster R 22 0 **93 17**
2008-09 *Millwall* 8 3
2009-10 Millwall 15 1 **23 4**
2009-10 *Oldham Ath* 7 1 **7 1**
2009-10 *Carlisle U* 9 4
2010-11 Carlisle U 3 0 **12 4**
2010-11 *Bradford C* 10 1 **10 1**
2010-11 *Walsall* 5 0 **5 0**
2010-11 *Hereford U* 4 0 **4 0**
2011-12 Barnet 5 1 **5 1**
2011-12 Morecambe 18 2 **18 2**

REDSHAW, Jack (F) 13 2
H: 5 6 W: 10 00 b.Salford 20-11-90
Source: Scholar.
2009-10 Manchester C 0 0
2010-11 Rochdale 2 0 **2 0**
2011-12 Morecambe 11 2 **11 2**
From Salford C, Altrincham.

REID, Izak (M) 181 7
H: 5 5 W: 10 05 b.Stafford 8-7-87
Source: Scholar.
2006-07 Macclesfield T 8 0
2007-08 Macclesfield T 25 2
2008-09 Macclesfield T 38 2
2009-10 Macclesfield T 37 0
2010-11 Macclesfield T 37 1 **145 5**
2011-12 Morecambe 36 2 **36 2**

ROCHE, Barry (G) 313 0
H: 6 5 W: 14 08 b.Dublin 6-4-82
Source: Trainee.
1999-2000 Nottingham F 0 0
2000-01 Nottingham F 2 0
2001-02 Nottingham F 0 0
2002-03 Nottingham F 1 0
2003-04 Nottingham F 8 0
2004-05 Nottingham F 2 0 **13 0**
2005-06 Chesterfield 41 0
2006-07 Chesterfield 40 0
2007-08 Chesterfield 45 0 **126 0**
2008-09 Morecambe 46 0
2009-10 Morecambe 42 0
2010-11 Morecambe 42 0
2011-12 Morecambe 44 0 **174 0**

ROUTLEDGE, Shaun (G) 0 0
b.Whitehaven 30-12-92
Source: Oldham Ath Scholar.
2011-12 Morecambe 0 0

WILSON, Laurence (D) 239 16
H: 5 10 W: 10 09 b.Huyton 10-10-86
Source: Scholar. *Honours:* England Youth.
2004-05 Everton 0 0
2005-06 Everton 0 0
2005-06 *Mansfield T* 15 1 **15 1**
2006-07 Chester C 41 1
2007-08 Chester C 40 2
2008-09 Chester C 34 1 **115 4**
2009-10 Morecambe 41 3
2010-11 Morecambe 38 3
2011-12 Morecambe 30 5 **109 11**

NEWCASTLE U (55)

ABEID, Mehdi (M) 19 3
H: 6 1 W: 12 08 b.Paris 6-8-92
Honours: France Youth, Algeria Under-23.
2008-09 Lens B 0 0
2009-10 Lens B 8 0
2010-11 Lens B 11 3 **19 3**
2011-12 Newcastle U 0 0

ADJEI, Samuel (F) 1 0
H: 6 1 W: 12 00 b.Eksjo 18-1-92
Source: Jonkoping.
2008-09 Newcastle U 0 0
2009-10 Newcastle U 0 0
2010-11 Newcastle U 0 0
2011-12 Newcastle U 0 0
2011-12 *Hartlepool U* 1 0 **1 0**

AIREY, Philip (F) 1 0
H: 5 11 W: 10 05 b.Newcastle 14-11-91
Source: Scholar.
2009-10 Newcastle U 0 0
2010-11 Newcastle U 0 0
2011-12 Newcastle U 0 0
2011-12 *Hibernian* 1 0 **1 0**

ALNWICK, Jak (G) 0 0
b.Hexham 17-6-93
Source: Scholar. *Honours:* England Youth.
2010-11 Newcastle U 0 0
2011-12 Newcastle U 0 0

AMEOBI, Sam (F) 11 0
H: 6 3 W: 10 04 b.Newcastle 1-5-92
Source: Scholar. *Honours:* England Under-21.
2010-11 Newcastle U 1 0
2011-12 Newcastle U 10 0 **11 0**

AMEOBI, Shola (F) 269 50
H: 6 3 W: 11 13 b.Zaria 12-10-81
Source: Trainee. *Honours:* England Under-21.
1998-99 Newcastle U 0 0
1999-2000 Newcastle U 0 0
2000-01 Newcastle U 20 2
2001-02 Newcastle U 15 0
2002-03 Newcastle U 28 5
2003-04 Newcastle U 26 7
2004-05 Newcastle U 31 2
2005-06 Newcastle U 30 9
2006-07 Newcastle U 12 3
2007-08 Newcastle U 6 0
2007-08 *Stoke C* 6 0 **6 0**
2008-09 Newcastle U 22 4
2009-10 Newcastle U 18 10
2010-11 Newcastle U 28 6
2011-12 Newcastle U 27 2 **263 50**

BA, Demba (F) 181 90
H: 6 2 W: 12 13 b.Sevres 25-5-85
Honours: Senegal 15 full caps, 4 goals.
2005-06 Rouen 26 22 **26 22**
2006-07 Mouscron 10 8
2007-08 Mouscron 2 0 **12 8**
2007-08 Hoffenheim 30 12
2008-09 Hoffenheim 33 14
2009-10 Hoffenheim 17 5
2010-11 Hoffenheim 17 6 **97 37**
2010-11 West Ham U 12 7 **12 7**
2011-12 Newcastle U 34 16 **34 16**

BEN ARFA, Hatem (M) 189 31
H: 5 8 W: 10 08 b.Clamart 7-3-87
Honours: France Youth, Under-21, 13 full caps, 2 goals.
2003-04 Lyon B 3 2
2004-05 Lyon B 10 3
2004-05 Lyon 9 0
2005-06 Lyon 12 0
2005-06 Lyon B 10 1
2006-07 Lyon B 9 3 **32 9**
2006-07 Lyon 13 1
2007-08 Lyon 30 6 **64 7**
2008-09 Marseille 33 6
2009-10 Marseille 29 3
2010-11 Marseille 1 0 **63 9**
2010-11 Newcastle U 4 1
2011-12 Newcastle U 26 5 **30 6**

BEST, Leon (F) 197 48
H: 6 1 W: 13 03 b.Nottingham 19-9-86
Source: Scholar. *Honours:* Eire Youth, Under-21, 7 full caps.
2004-05 Southampton 3 0
2004-05 *QPR* 5 0 **5 0**
2005-06 Southampton 3 0
2005-06 *Sheffield W* 13 2 **13 2**
2006-07 Southampton 9 4 **15 4**
2006-07 *Bournemouth* 15 3 **15 3**
2006-07 *Yeovil T* 15 10 **15 10**
2007-08 Coventry C 34 8
2008-09 Coventry C 31 2
2009-10 Coventry C 27 9 **92 19**
2009-10 Newcastle U 13 0
2010-11 Newcastle U 11 6
2011-12 Newcastle U 18 4 **42 10**

CABAYE, Yohan (M) 225 35
H: 5 9 W: 11 05 b.Tourcoing 14-1-86
Honours: France Youth, Under-21, 16 full caps, 1 goal.
2004-05 Lille 6 0
2005-06 Lille 27 1
2006-07 Lille 22 3
2007-08 Lille 36 7
2008-09 Lille 32 5
2009-10 Lille 32 13
2010-11 Lille 36 2 **191 31**
2011-12 Newcastle U 34 4 **34 4**

CAMPBELL, Adam (F) **0 0**
b.North Shields 1-1-95
Source: Wallsend BC. *Honours:* England Youth.

Season	Club	Apps	Gls	Total Apps	Total Gls
2011-12	Newcastle U	0	0		

CISSE, Papiss (F) **256 126**
H: 6 0 W: 11 07 b.Dakar 3-6-85
Honours: Senegal 17 full caps, 10 goals.

Season	Club	Apps	Gls	Total Apps	Total Gls
2003-04	AS Douanes	26	23	**26**	**23**
2004-05	Metz B	10	3		
2005-06	Metz B	3	0	**13**	**3**
2005-06	Metz	1	0		
2005-06	*Cherbourg*	28	11	**28**	**11**
2006-07	Metz	32	12		
2007-08	Metz	9	0		
2007-08	*Chateauroux*	15	4	**15**	**4**
2008-09	Metz	37	15		
2009-10	Metz	16	8	**95**	**35**
2009-10	Freiburg	16	6		
2010-11	Freiburg	32	22		
2011-12	Freiburg	17	9	**65**	**37**
2011-12	Newcastle U	14	13	**14**	**13**

COLOCCINI, Fabricio (D) **359 20**
H: 6 0 W: 12 04 b.Cordoba 22-1-82
Honours: Argentina 34 full caps, 1 goal.

Season	Club	Apps	Gls	Total Apps	Total Gls
1998-99	Boca Juniors	1	1		
1999-2000	Boca Juniors	1	0	**2**	**1**
1999-2000	AC Milan	0	0		
2000-01	AC Milan	0	0		
2000-01	San Lorenzo	19	3	**19**	**3**
2001-02	Alaves	33	6	**33**	**6**
2002-03	Atletico Madrid	27	0	**27**	**0**
2003-04	Villarreal	31	1	**31**	**1**
2004-05	AC Milan	1	0	**1**	**0**
2004-05	La Coruna	15	1		
2005-06	La Coruna	26	0		
2006-07	La Coruna	26	0		
2007-08	La Coruna	38	4	**105**	**5**
2008-09	Newcastle U	34	0		
2009-10	Newcastle U	37	2		
2010-11	Newcastle U	35	2		
2011-12	Newcastle U	35	0	**141**	**4**

DONALDSON, Ryan (F) **15 0**
H: 5 9 W: 11 00 b.Newcastle 1-5-91
Source: Scholar. *Honours:* England Youth.

Season	Club	Apps	Gls	Total Apps	Total Gls
2008-09	Newcastle U	0	0		
2009-10	Newcastle U	2	0		
2010-11	Newcastle U	0	0		
2010-11	*Hartlepool U*	12	0	**12**	**0**
2011-12	Newcastle U	0	0	**2**	**0**
2011-12	*Tranmere R*	1	0	**1**	**0**

DUMMETT, Paul (D) **0 0**
H: 5 10 W: 10 02 b.Newcastle 26-9-91
Source: Scholar. *Honours:* Wales Under-21.

Season	Club	Apps	Gls	Total Apps	Total Gls
2010-11	Newcastle U	0	0		
2011-12	Newcastle U	0	0		

EDMUNDSSON, Joan (F) **49 10**
b.Faeroes 26-7-91
Honours: Faeroes Under-21, 13 full caps, 1 goal.

Season	Club	Apps	Gls	Total Apps	Total Gls
2008	B68	24	4		
2009	B68	25	6	**49**	**10**
2009-10	Newcastle U	0	0		
2010-11	Newcastle U	0	0		
2011-12	Newcastle U	0	0		

ELLIOT, Rob (G) **107 0**
H: 6 3 W: 14 10 b.Chatham 30-4-86
Source: Scholar.

Season	Club	Apps	Gls	Total Apps	Total Gls
2004-05	Charlton Ath	0	0		
2004-05	*Notts Co*	4	0	**4**	**0**
2005-06	Charlton Ath	0	0		
2006-07	Charlton Ath	0	0		
2006-07	*Accrington S*	7	0	**7**	**0**
2007-08	Charlton Ath	1	0		
2008-09	Charlton Ath	23	0		
2009-10	Charlton Ath	33	0		
2010-11	Charlton Ath	35	0		
2011-12	Charlton Ath	4	0	**96**	**0**
2011-12	Newcastle U	0	0		

FERGUSON, Shane (D) **14 0**
H: 5 9 W: 10 01 b.Limavady 12-7-91
Source: Scholar. *Honours:* Northern Ireland Under-21, B, 3 full caps.

Season	Club	Apps	Gls	Total Apps	Total Gls
2008-09	Newcastle U	0	0		
2009-10	Newcastle U	0	0		
2010-11	Newcastle U	7	0		
2011-12	Newcastle U	7	0	**14**	**0**

FOLAN, Stephen (M) **0 0**
H: 6 1 W: 12 01 b.Galway 14-1-92
Source: Scholar.

Season	Club	Apps	Gls	Total Apps	Total Gls
2010-11	Newcastle U	0	0		
2011-12	Newcastle U	0	0		

FORSTER, Fraser (G) **117 0**
H: 6 0 W: 12 00 b.Hexham 17-3-88
Source: Scholar.

Season	Club	Apps	Gls	Total Apps	Total Gls
2007-08	Newcastle U	0	0		
2008-09	Newcastle U	0	0		
2008-09	*Stockport Co*	6	0	**6**	**0**
2009-10	Newcastle U	0	0		
2009-10	*Bristol R*	4	0	**4**	**0**
2009-10	*Norwich C*	38	0	**38**	**0**
2010-11	Newcastle U	0	0		
2010-11	*Celtic*	36	0		
2011-12	Newcastle U	0	0		
2011-12	*Celtic*	33	0	**69**	**0**

Transferred to Celtic June 2012.

GOSLING, Dan (M) **57 7**
H: 6 0 W: 11 00 b.Brixham 2-2-90
Source: Scholar. *Honours:* England Youth, Under-21.

Season	Club	Apps	Gls	Total Apps	Total Gls
2006-07	Plymouth Arg	12	2		
2007-08	Plymouth Arg	10	0	**22**	**2**
2007-08	Everton	0	0		
2008-09	Everton	11	2		
2009-10	Everton	11	2	**22**	**4**
2010-11	Newcastle U	1	0		
2011-12	Newcastle U	12	1	**13**	**1**

GUTHRIE, Danny (M) **130 7**
H: 5 9 W: 11 06 b.Shrewsbury 18-4-87
Source: Scholar. *Honours:* England Schools, Youth.

Season	Club	Apps	Gls	Total Apps	Total Gls
2004-05	Liverpool	0	0		
2005-06	Liverpool	0	0		
2006-07	Liverpool	3	0		
2006-07	*Southampton*	10	0	**10**	**0**
2007-08	Liverpool	0	0	**3**	**0**
2007-08	*Bolton W*	25	0	**25**	**0**
2008-09	Newcastle U	24	2		
2009-10	Newcastle U	38	4		
2010-11	Newcastle U	14	0		
2011-12	Newcastle U	16	1	**92**	**7**

GUTIERREZ, Jonas (M) **335 15**
H: 6 0 W: 11 07 b.Buenos Aires 5-7-82
Honours: Argentina 22 full caps, 1 goal.

Season	Club	Apps	Gls	Total Apps	Total Gls
2001-02	Velez Sarsfield	17	0		
2002-03	Velez Sarsfield	21	1		
2003-04	Velez Sarsfield	27	0		
2004-05	Velez Sarsfield	33	0	**98**	**1**
2005-06	Mallorca	30	2		
2006-07	Mallorca	36	3		
2007-08	Mallorca	30	0	**96**	**5**
2008-09	Newcastle U	30	0		
2009-10	Newcastle U	37	4		
2010-11	Newcastle U	37	3		
2011-12	Newcastle U	37	2	**141**	**9**

HARPER, Steve (G) **196 0**
H: 6 2 W: 13 10 b.Easington 14-3-75
Source: Seaham Red Star.

Season	Club	Apps	Gls	Total Apps	Total Gls
1993-94	Newcastle U	0	0		
1994-95	Newcastle U	0	0		
1995-96	Newcastle U	0	0		
1995-96	*Bradford C*	1	0	**1**	**0**
1996-97	Newcastle U	0	0		
1996-97	*Stockport Co*	0	0		
1997-98	Newcastle U	0	0		
1997-98	*Hartlepool U*	15	0	**15**	**0**
1997-98	*Huddersfield T*	24	0	**24**	**0**
1998-99	Newcastle U	8	0		
1999-2000	Newcastle U	18	0		
2000-01	Newcastle U	5	0		
2001-02	Newcastle U	0	0		
2002-03	Newcastle U	0	0		
2003-04	Newcastle U	0	0		
2004-05	Newcastle U	2	0		
2005-06	Newcastle U	0	0		
2006-07	Newcastle U	18	0		
2007-08	Newcastle U	21	0		
2008-09	Newcastle U	16	0		
2009-10	Newcastle U	45	0		
2010-11	Newcastle U	18	0		
2011-12	Newcastle U	0	0	**151**	**0**
2011-12	*Brighton & HA*	5	0	**5**	**0**

HENDERSON, Jeff (D) **0 0**
H: 6 1 W: 12 01 b.Ashington 19-12-91
Source: Scholar.

Season	Club	Apps	Gls	Total Apps	Total Gls
2010-11	Newcastle U	0	0		
2011-12	Newcastle U	0	0		

INMAN, Bradden (M) **0 0**
H: 5 9 W: 11 03 b.Adelaide 10-12-91
Source: Scholar. *Honours:* Scotland Youth, Under-21.

Season	Club	Apps	Gls	Total Apps	Total Gls
2009-10	Newcastle U	0	0		
2010-11	Newcastle U	0	0		
2011-12	Newcastle U	0	0		

KADAR, Tamas (D) **15 0**
H: 6 0 W: 12 10 b.Veszprem 14-3-90
Honours: Hungary Youth, Under-21, 4 full caps.

Season	Club	Apps	Gls	Total Apps	Total Gls
2007-08	Newcastle U	0	0		
2008-09	Newcastle U	0	0		
2009-10	Newcastle U	13	0		
2010-11	Newcastle U	0	0		
2010-11	*Huddersfield T*	2	0	**2**	**0**
2011-12	Newcastle U	0	0	**13**	**0**

KRUL, Tim (G) **93 0**
H: 6 2 W: 11 08 b.Den Haag 3-4-88
Source: Academy. *Honours:* Holland Youth, Under-21, 3 full caps.

Season	Club	Apps	Gls	Total Apps	Total Gls
2005-06	Newcastle U	0	0		
2006-07	Newcastle U	0	0		
2007-08	*Falkirk*	22	0	**22**	**0**
2007-08	Newcastle U	0	0		
2008-09	Newcastle U	0	0		
2008-09	*Carlisle U*	9	0	**9**	**0**
2009-10	Newcastle U	3	0		
2010-11	Newcastle U	21	0		
2011-12	Newcastle U	38	0	**62**	**0**

LOVENKRANDS, Peter (F) **283 73**
H: 5 11 W: 11 02 b.Copenhagen 29-1-80
Honours: Denmark Youth, 22 full caps, 1 goal.

Season	Club	Apps	Gls	Total Apps	Total Gls
1998-99	AB Copenhagen	18	2		
1999-2000	AB Copenhagen	14	5	**32**	**7**
2000-01	Rangers	8	0		
2001-02	Rangers	18	2		
2002-03	Rangers	28	9		
2003-04	Rangers	25	8		
2004-05	Rangers	17	3		
2005-06	Rangers	33	14	**129**	**36**
2006-07	Schalke	24	6		
2007-08	Schalke	20	0	**44**	**6**
2008-09	Schalke B	3	2	**3**	**2**
2008-09	Newcastle U	12	3		
2009-10	Newcastle U	29	13		
2010-11	Newcastle U	25	6		
2011-12	Newcastle U	9	0	**75**	**22**

MARVEAUX, Sylvain (M) **109 16**
H: 5 8 W: 10 05 b.Vannes 15-4-86
Honours: France Under-21.

Season	Club	Apps	Gls	Total Apps	Total Gls
2006-07	Rennes	28	5		
2007-08	Rennes	24	0		
2008-09	Rennes	5	0		
2009-10	Rennes	35	10		
2010-11	Rennes	10	1	**102**	**16**
2011-12	Newcastle U	7	0	**7**	**0**

McDERMOTT, Greg (M) **0 0**
H: 5 10 W: 10 00 b.Liverpool 18-10-91
Source: Scholar.

Season	Club	Apps	Gls	Total Apps	Total Gls
2010-11	Newcastle U	0	0		
2011-12	Newcastle U	0	0		

MIELE, Brandon (M) **0 0**
b.Dublin 28-8-94
Source: Scholar.

Season	Club	Apps	Gls	Total Apps	Total Gls
2011-12	Newcastle U	0	0		

MOYO, Yven (M) **0 0**
b.Orleans 15-3-92
Source: Sochaux. *Honours:* Congo 2 full caps.

Season	Club	Apps	Gls	Total Apps	Total Gls
2010-11	Newcastle U	0	0		
2011-12	Newcastle U	0	0		

NEWTON, Conor (M) **0 0**
H: 5 11 W: 11 00 b.Whickham 17-10-91
Source: Scholar.

Season	Club	Apps	Gls	Total Apps	Total Gls
2010-11	Newcastle U	0	0		
2011-12	Newcastle U	0	0		

NZUZI, Patrick (D) **0 0**
b.Congo DR 24-10-92
Source: Scholar.

Season	Club	Apps	Gls	Total Apps	Total Gls
2011-12	Newcastle U	0	0		

OBERTAN, Gabriel (F) 106 5
H: 6 1 W: 12 06 b.Paris 26-2-89
Honours: France Youth, Under-21.

2006-07	Bordeaux	17	1		
2007-08	Bordeaux	26	2		
2008-09	Bordeaux	11	0	**54**	**3**
2008-09	*Lorient*	15	1	**15**	**1**
2009-10	Manchester U	7	0		
2010-11	Manchester U	7	0	**14**	**0**
2011-12	Newcastle U	23	1	**23**	**1**

PERCH, James (D) 228 12
H: 5 11 W: 11 05 b.Mansfield 29-9-85
Source: Scholar.

2002-03	Nottingham F	0	0		
2003-04	Nottingham F	0	0		
2004-05	Nottingham F	22	0		
2005-06	Nottingham F	38	3		
2006-07	Nottingham F	46	5		
2007-08	Nottingham F	30	0		
2008-09	Nottingham F	37	3		
2009-10	Nottingham F	17	1	**190**	**12**
2010-11	Newcastle U	13	0		
2011-12	Newcastle U	25	0	**38**	**0**

RANGER, Nile (F) 62 4
H: 6 2 W: 13 03 b.Wood Green 11-4-91
Source: Southampton Scholar. *Honours:* England Youth.

2008-09	Newcastle U	0	0		
2009-10	Newcastle U	25	2		
2010-11	Newcastle U	24	0		
2011-12	Newcastle U	0	0	**49**	**2**
2011-12	*Barnsley*	5	0	**5**	**0**
2011-12	*Sheffield W*	8	2	**8**	**2**

RICHARDSON, Michael (M) 3 0
b.Newcastle 17-3-92
Source: Walker Central.

2010-11	Newcastle U	0	0		
2011-12	Newcastle U	0	0		
2011-12	*Leyton Orient*	3	0	**3**	**0**

SANTON, Davide (D) 75 0
H: 6 2 W: 13 00 b.Portomaggiore 2-1-91
Honours: Italy Youth, Under-21, 7 full caps.

2008-09	Internazionale	16	0		
2009-10	Internazionale	12	0		
2010-11	Internazionale	12	0	**40**	**0**
2010-11	*Cesena*	11	0	**11**	**0**
2011-12	Newcastle U	24	0	**24**	**0**

SIMPSON, Danny (D) 141 1
H: 5 9 W: 11 05 b.Eccles 4-1-87
Source: Scholar.

2005-06	Manchester U	0	0		
2006-07	Manchester U	0	0		
2006-07	*Sunderland*	14	0	**14**	**0**
2007-08	Manchester U	3	0		
2007-08	*Ipswich T*	8	0	**8**	**0**
2008-09	Manchester U	0	0		
2008-09	*Blackburn R*	12	0	**12**	**0**
2009-10	Manchester U	0	0	**3**	**0**
2009-10	Newcastle U	39	1		
2010-11	Newcastle U	30	0		
2011-12	Newcastle U	35	0	**104**	**1**

SMITH, Alan (F) 333 46
H: 5 10 W: 12 04 b.Rothwell 28-10-80
Source: Trainee. *Honours:* England Youth, Under-21, B, 19 full caps, 1 goal.

1997-98	Leeds U	0	0		
1998-99	Leeds U	22	7		
1999-2000	Leeds U	26	4		
2000-01	Leeds U	33	11		
2001-02	Leeds U	23	4		
2002-03	Leeds U	33	3		
2003-04	Leeds U	35	9	**172**	**38**
2004-05	Manchester U	31	6		
2005-06	Manchester U	21	1		
2006-07	Manchester U	9	0	**61**	**7**
2007-08	Newcastle U	33	0		
2008-09	Newcastle U	6	0		
2009-10	Newcastle U	32	0		
2010-11	Newcastle U	11	0		
2011-12	Newcastle U	2	0	**84**	**0**
2011-12	*Milton Keynes D*	16	1	**16**	**1**

SMITH, Jamie (D) 0 0
b.Liverpool 21-1-94
Source: Scholar.

2011-12	Newcastle U	0	0		

SODERBERG, Ole (G) 2 0
H: 6 4 W: 14 07 b.Norrkoping 20-7-90
Source: BK Hacken. *Honours:* Sweden Youth.

2007-08	Newcastle U	0	0		
2008-09	Newcastle U	0	0		
2009-10	Newcastle U	0	0		
2010-11	Newcastle U	0	0		
2011-12	Newcastle U	0	0		
2011-12	*Chesterfield*	2	0	**2**	**0**

Transferred to Molde March 2012.

STREETE, Remie (D) 0 0
b.Boldon 2-11-94
Source: Scholar.

2011-12	Newcastle U	0	0		

TAVERNIER, James (D) 29 0
H: 5 9 W: 11 00 b.Bradford 31-10-91
Source: Scholar.

2009-10	Newcastle U	0	0		
2010-11	Newcastle U	0	0		
2011-12	Newcastle U	0	0		
2011-12	*Carlisle U*	16	0	**16**	**0**
2011-12	*Sheffield W*	6	0	**6**	**0**
2011-12	*Milton Keynes D*	7	0	**7**	**0**

TAYLOR, Ryan (M) 231 26
H: 5 8 W: 10 04 b.Liverpool 19-8-84
Source: Scholar. *Honours:* England Youth, Under-21.

2001-02	Tranmere R	0	0		
2002-03	Tranmere R	25	1		
2003-04	Tranmere R	30	5		
2004-05	Tranmere R	43	8	**98**	**14**
2005-06	Wigan Ath	11	0		
2006-07	Wigan Ath	16	1		
2007-08	Wigan Ath	17	3		
2008-09	Wigan Ath	12	2	**56**	**6**
2008-09	Newcastle U	10	0		
2009-10	Newcastle U	31	4		
2010-11	Newcastle U	5	0		
2011-12	Newcastle U	31	2	**77**	**6**

TAYLOR, Steven (D) 166 11
H: 6 2 W: 13 01 b.Greenwich 23-1-86
Source: Trainee. *Honours:* FA Schools, Youth, England Under-20, Under-21, B.

2002-03	Newcastle U	0	0		
2003-04	Newcastle U	1	0		
2003-04	*Wycombe W*	6	0	**6**	**0**
2004-05	Newcastle U	13	0		
2005-06	Newcastle U	12	0		
2006-07	Newcastle U	27	2		
2007-08	Newcastle U	31	1		
2008-09	Newcastle U	27	4		
2009-10	Newcastle U	21	1		
2010-11	Newcastle U	14	3		
2011-12	Newcastle U	14	0	**160**	**11**

TIOTE, Cheik (M) 138 4
H: 5 11 W: 12 06 b.Yamoussoukro 21-6-86
Honours: Ivory Coast 31 full caps.

2005-06	Anderlecht	2	0		
2006-07	Anderlecht	2	0	**4**	**0**
2007-08	Roda JC	26	2	**26**	**2**
2008-09	Twente	28	0		
2009-10	Twente	28	1		
2010-11	Twente	2	0	**58**	**1**
2010-11	Newcastle U	26	1		
2011-12	Newcastle U	24	0	**50**	**1**

VUCKIC, Haris (F) 16 1
H: 6 2 W: 12 02 b.Ljubljana 21-8-92
Source: Scholar. *Honours:* Slovenia Youth, 1 full cap.

2007-08	Domzale	1	0		
2008-09	Domzale	4	0	**5**	**0**
2009-10	Newcastle U	2	0		
2010-11	Newcastle U	0	0		
2011-12	Newcastle U	4	0	**6**	**0**
2011-12	*Cardiff C*	5	1	**5**	**1**

WILLIAMSON, Mike (D) 245 13
H: 6 4 W: 13 03 b.Stoke 8-11-83
Source: Trainee.

2001-02	Torquay U	3	0		
2001-02	Southampton	0	0		
2002-03	Southampton	0	0		
2003-04	Southampton	0	0		
2003-04	*Torquay U*	11	0	**14**	**0**
2003-04	*Doncaster R*	0	0		
2004-05	Southampton	0	0		
2004-05	*Wycombe W*	37	2		
2005-06	Wycombe W	39	5		
2006-07	Wycombe W	33	1		
2007-08	Wycombe W	12	0		
2008-09	Wycombe W	22	3	**143**	**11**
2008-09	Watford	17	1		
2009-10	Watford	4	1	**21**	**2**
2009-10	Portsmouth	0	0		
2009-10	Newcastle U	16	0		
2010-11	Newcastle U	29	0		
2011-12	Newcastle U	22	0	**67**	**0**

XISCO (F) 128 34
H: 6 0 W: 13 03 b.Palma 26-6-86
Honours: Spain Under-21.

2004-05	La Coruna	7	2		
2005-06	La Coruna	12	1		
2006-07	*Vecindario*	27	13	**27**	**13**
2007-08	La Coruna	25	9		
2008-09	Newcastle U	5	1		
2009-10	Newcastle U	2	0		
2009-10	*Santander*	23	3	**23**	**3**
2010-11	Newcastle U	2	0		
2010-11	*La Coruna*	9	2		
2011-12	Newcastle U	0	0	**9**	**1**
2011-12	*La Coruna*	16	3	**69**	**17**

Scholars
Aird Lewis Leigh; Desmond Lee; Grant Aidan Ryan; Hooper Jonathan; Kitchen Alexander Joel; Knight Dennis Peter; Logan Steven John; Lopez Esteban; Maddison Marcus Harley; Mitchell Jonathan Philip; Nicholson Alex Jack; Riley Michael Liam; Turton William John.

NORTHAMPTON T (56)

AKINFENWA, Adebayo (F) 310 103
H: 5 11 W: 13 07 b.Nigeria 10-5-82

2001	Atlantas	19	4		
2002	Atlantas	4	1	**23**	**5**

From Barry T

2003-04	Boston U	3	0	**3**	**0**
2003-04	Leyton Orient	1	0	**1**	**0**
2003-04	Rushden & D	0	0		
2003-04	Doncaster R	9	4	**9**	**4**
2004-05	Torquay U	37	14	**37**	**14**
2005-06	Swansea C	34	9		
2006-07	Swansea C	25	5		
2007-08	Swansea C	0	0	**59**	**14**
2007-08	Millwall	7	0	**7**	**0**
2007-08	Northampton T	15	7		
2008-09	Northampton T	33	13		
2009-10	Northampton T	40	17		
2010-11	Gillingham	44	11	**44**	**11**
2011-12	Northampton T	39	18	**127**	**55**

ARTHUR, Chris (M) 7 0
H: 5 10 W: 12 02 b.Enfield 25-1-90
Source: QPR, Bishop's Stortford, Havant & W'ville.

2011-12	Northampton T	7	0	**7**	**0**

CHARLES, Anthony (D) 181 11
H: 6 1 W: 12 07 b.Isleworth 11-3-81
Source: Brook House.

1999-2000	Crewe Alex	0	0		

From Brookhouse

2000-01	Crewe Alex	0	0		

From Hayes, Aldershot T, Farnborough T

2004-05	Barnet	0	0		
2005-06	Barnet	40	0		
2006-07	Barnet	17	0	**57**	**0**
2008-09	Aldershot T	41	2		
2009-10	Aldershot T	33	4		
2010-11	Aldershot T	41	5	**115**	**11**
2011-12	Northampton T	9	0	**9**	**0**

CORKER, Ashley (D) 16 0
H: 5 11 W: 11 11 b.Marske 18-9-90
Source: Middlesbrough Scholar, Horden CW.

2011-12	Northampton T	16	0	**16**	**0**

CROWE, Jason (D) 383 23
H: 5 9 W: 10 09 b.Sidcup 30-9-78
Source: Trainee. *Honours:* England Schools, Youth.

1995-96	Arsenal	0	0		
1996-97	Arsenal	0	0		
1997-98	Arsenal	0	0		
1998-99	Arsenal	0	0		
1998-99	*Crystal Palace*	8	0	**8**	**0**
1999-2000	Portsmouth	25	0		
2000-01	Portsmouth	23	0		
2000-01	*Brentford*	9	0	**9**	**0**
2001-02	Portsmouth	22	1		

2002-03 Portsmouth 16 4 **86 5**
2003-04 Grimsby T 32 0
2004-05 Grimsby T 37 4 **69 4**
2005-06 Northampton T 41 2
2006-07 Northampton T 43 3
2007-08 Northampton T 44 4
2008-09 Northampton T 43 5
2009-10 Leeds U 17 0
2010-11 Leeds U 0 0 **17 0**
2010-11 Leyton Orient 12 0 **12 0**
2011-12 Northampton T 11 0 **182 14**

DAVIES, Arron (M) 191 28
H: 5 9 W: 11 00 b.Cardiff 22-6-84
Source: Trainee. *Honours:* Wales Under-21, 1 full cap.
2002-03 Southampton 0 0
2003-04 Southampton 0 0
2003-04 *Barnsley* 4 0 **4 0**
2004-05 Southampton 0 0
2004-05 Yeovil T 23 8
2005-06 Yeovil T 39 8
2006-07 Yeovil T 39 6
2007-08 Nottingham F 19 1
2008-09 Nottingham F 13 0
2009-10 Nottingham F 0 0 **32 1**
2009-10 *Brighton & HA* 7 0 **7 0**
2009-10 Yeovil T 10 0 **111 22**
2010-11 Peterborough U 22 1 **22 1**
2011-12 Northampton T 15 4 **15 4**

GILLIGAN, Ryan (M) 187 20
H: 5 10 W: 11 07 b.Swindon 18-1-87
Source: Watford Scholar.
2005-06 Northampton T 23 4
2006-07 Northampton T 24 0
2007-08 Northampton T 38 4
2008-09 Northampton T 31 3
2009-10 Northampton T 42 8
2010-11 Northampton T 22 1
2010-11 *Torquay U* 5 0 **5 0**
2011-12 Northampton T 2 0 **182 20**

GUTTRIDGE, Luke (M) 372 44
H: 5 6 W: 9 07 b.Barnstaple 27-3-82
Source: Trainee.
1999-2000 Torquay U 1 0
2000-01 Torquay U 0 0 **1 0**
2000-01 Cambridge U 1 1
2001-02 Cambridge U 29 2
2002-03 Cambridge U 43 3
2003-04 Cambridge U 46 11
2004-05 Cambridge U 17 0 **136 17**
2004-05 Southend U 5 0
2005-06 Southend U 41 5
2006-07 Southend U 17 0 **63 5**
2006-07 Leyton Orient 17 1 **17 1**
2007-08 Colchester U 14 0 **14 0**
2008-09 Northampton T 25 2
2009-10 Northampton T 31 4
2010-11 Aldershot T 41 8
2011-12 Aldershot T 25 4 **66 12**
2011-12 Northampton T 19 3 **75 9**

HALL, Freddy (G) 14 0
H: 6 2 W: 12 02 b.Bermuda 3-3-85
Source: South Florida Bulls, Quinnipiac Univ. *Honours:* Bermuda 4 full caps.
2010-11 Bermuda Hogges 11 0 **11 0**
2011-12 Northampton T 3 0 **3 0**

HARDING, Ben (M) 174 12
H: 5 10 W: 11 02 b.Carshalton 6-9-84
Source: Scholar.
2001-02 Wimbledon 0 0
2002-03 Wimbledon 0 0
2003-04 Wimbledon 15 0 **15 0**
2004-05 Milton Keynes D 26 4
2005-06 Milton Keynes D 10 2
2006-07 Milton Keynes D 0 0 **36 6**
2008-09 Aldershot T 29 3
2009-10 Aldershot T 33 1
2010-11 Aldershot T 35 2 **97 6**
2011-12 Wycombe W 7 0 **7 0**
2011-12 Northampton T 19 0 **19 0**

HIGGS, Shane (G) 275 0
H: 6 3 W: 14 06 b.Oxford 13-5-77
Source: Trainee.
1994-95 Bristol R 0 0
1995-96 Bristol R 0 0
1996-97 Bristol R 2 0
1997-98 Bristol R 8 0 **10 0**
From Worcester C.
1999-2000 Cheltenham T 0 0
2000-01 Cheltenham T 1 0
2001-02 Cheltenham T 1 0
2002-03 Cheltenham T 10 0
2003-04 Cheltenham T 42 0
2004-05 Cheltenham T 46 0
2005-06 Cheltenham T 45 0
2006-07 Cheltenham T 36 0
2007-08 Cheltenham T 46 0
2008-09 Cheltenham T 10 0 **237 0**
2008-09 *Wolverhampton W* 0 0
2009-10 Leeds U 19 0
2010-11 Leeds U 6 0 **25 0**
2011-12 Northampton T 3 0 **3 0**

HOLT, Andy (M) 483 37
H: 6 1 W: 12 07 b.Stockport 21-5-78
Source: Trainee.
1996-97 Oldham Ath 1 0
1997-98 Oldham Ath 14 1
1998-99 Oldham Ath 43 5
1999-2000 Oldham Ath 46 3
2000-01 Oldham Ath 20 1 **124 10**
2000-01 *Hull C* 10 2
2001-02 Hull C 30 0
2002-03 Hull C 6 0
2002-03 *Barnsley* 7 0 **7 0**
2002-03 *Shrewsbury T* 9 0 **9 0**
2003-04 Hull C 25 1 **71 3**
2004-05 Wrexham 45 6
2005-06 Wrexham 36 3 **81 9**
2006-07 Northampton T 35 2
2007-08 Northampton T 36 2
2008-09 Northampton T 41 2
2009-10 Northampton T 31 3
2010-11 Northampton T 39 6
2011-12 Northampton T 9 0 **191 15**

JACOBS, Michael (M) 87 11
H: 5 9 W: 11 08 b.Rothwell 23-3-92
Source: Scholar.
2009-10 Northampton T 0 0
2010-11 Northampton T 41 5
2011-12 Northampton T 46 6 **87 11**

JOHNSON, John (D) 124 14
H: 6 0 W: 12 00 b.Middlesbrough 16-9-88
Source: Scholar.
2007-08 Middlesbrough 0 0
2008-09 Middlesbrough 1 0
2008-09 *Tranmere R* 4 0 **4 0**
2009-10 Middlesbrough 0 0 **1 0**
2009-10 *Northampton T* 36 5
2010-11 Northampton T 38 7
2011-12 Northampton T 45 2 **119 14**

KAZIBONI, Greg (M) 5 0
H: 5 9 W: 11 00 b.Uganda 16-5-92
Source: Gregory Celtic.
2010-11 Northampton T 2 0
2011-12 Northampton T 3 0 **5 0**

KITSON, Neal (G) 8 0
H: 6 1 W: 12 13 b.New York 4-1-86
Source: Dowling GL, St John's Red Storm, Newark IE, Rochester Rhinos.
2011-12 Northampton T 8 0 **8 0**

LANGMEAD, Kelvin (D) 326 28
H: 6 1 W: 12 00 b.Coventry 23-3-85
Source: Scholar.
2003-04 Preston NE 0 0
2003-04 *Carlisle U* 11 1 **11 1**
2004-05 Preston NE 1 0 **1 0**
2004-05 *Kidderminster H* 10 1 **10 1**
2004-05 Shrewsbury T 28 3
2005-06 Shrewsbury T 42 9
2006-07 Shrewsbury T 45 3
2007-08 Shrewsbury T 39 1
2008-09 Shrewsbury T 33 0
2009-10 Shrewsbury T 44 3 **231 19**
2010-11 Peterborough U 32 3
2011-12 Peterborough U 0 0 **32 3**
2011-12 Northampton T 41 4 **41 4**

McKOY, Nick (M) 37 0
H: 6 0 W: 12 06 b.Newham 3-9-86
Source: Scholar.
2003-04 Wimbledon 3 0 **3 0**
2004-05 Milton Keynes D 0 0
2005-06 Milton Keynes D 16 0 **16 0**
2006-07 Cardiff C 0 0
2006-07 *Torquay U* 4 0 **4 0**
From Potters Bar T.
2008-09 St Johnstone 5 0 **5 0**
From Enfield T, Grays Ath, Sutton U, Kettering T.
2011-12 Northampton T 9 0 **9 0**

OFORI-TWUMASI, Nana (D) 35 2
H: 5 8 W: 11 09 b.Accra 15-5-90
Source: Scholar. *Honours:* England Under-20.
2007-08 Chelsea 0 0
2008-09 Chelsea 0 0
2009-10 Chelsea 0 0
2009-10 *Dagenham & R* 8 2 **8 2**
2010-11 Peterborough U 11 0 **11 0**
2010-11 *Northampton T* 11 0
2011-12 Northampton T 5 0 **16 0**

OSMAN, Abdul (M) 122 8
H: 6 0 W: 11 00 b.Accra 27-2-87
Source: Hampton & Richmond B, Maidenhead U.
2007-08 Gretna 18 1 **18 1**
2008-09 Northampton T 36 2
2009-10 Northampton T 30 2
2010-11 Northampton T 38 3
2011-12 Northampton T 0 0 **104 7**

PURCELL, Tadhg (F) 106 27
H: 5 11 W: 11 08 b.Dublin 9-2-85
Source: UCD, Kilkenny City.
2007 Shamrock R 28 12
2008 Shamrock R 28 4
2009 Shamrock R 24 2 **80 18**
2009-10 Darlington 22 9 **22 9**
2010-11 Northampton T 4 0
2011-12 Northampton T 0 0 **4 0**

ROBINSON, Jake (F) 252 35
H: 5 7 W: 10 10 b.Brighton 23-10-86
Source: Scholar.
2003-04 Brighton & HA 9 0
2004-05 Brighton & HA 10 1
2005-06 Brighton & HA 27 1
2006-07 Brighton & HA 38 6
2007-08 Brighton & HA 34 4
2008-09 Brighton & HA 5 1 **123 13**
2008-09 *Aldershot T* 19 4 **19 4**
2009-10 Shrewsbury T 34 3
2010-11 Shrewsbury T 22 8 **56 11**
2010-11 *Torquay U* 22 7 **22 7**
2011-12 Northampton T 32 0 **32 0**

SALIHU, Lumbardh (F) 1 0
H: 5 9 W: 12 00 b.Kosovo 18-11-92
Source: Wienerberg.
2011-12 Northampton T 1 0 **1 0**

SAVAGE, Bas (F) 208 25
H: 6 3 W: 13 08 b.Wandsworth 7-1-82
Source: Walton & Hersham.
2001-02 Reading 1 0
2002-03 Reading 0 0
2003-04 Reading 15 0
2004-05 Reading 0 0 **16 0**
2004-05 *Wycombe W* 4 0 **4 0**
2004-05 *Bury* 5 0 **5 0**
2005-06 Bristol C 23 1 **23 1**
2006-07 Gillingham 14 1 **14 1**
2006-07 Brighton & HA 15 6
2007-08 Brighton & HA 21 3 **36 9**
2007-08 Millwall 11 2 **11 2**
2008-09 Tranmere R 42 9
2009-10 Tranmere R 13 0 **55 9**
2010-11 Dagenham & R 36 3 **36 3**
2011-12 Northampton T 8 0 **8 0**

SNEDKER, Dean (G) 0 0
H: 6 0 W: 11 13 b. 17-11-94
Source: Scholar.
2011-12 Northampton T 0 0

THORNTON, Kevin (M) 100 9
H: 5 7 W: 11 00 b.Drogheda 9-7-86
Source: Scholar. *Honours:* Eire Youth.
2003-04 Coventry C 0 0
2004-05 Coventry C 0 0
2005-06 Coventry C 16 0
2006-07 Coventry C 11 1
2007-08 Coventry C 19 1
2008-09 Coventry C 4 0 **50 2**
2008-09 *Brighton & HA* 12 0 **12 0**
From Nuneaton T.
2009-10 Northampton T 11 1
2010-11 Northampton T 25 6
2011-12 Northampton T 2 0 **38 7**

TOZER, Ben (D) 79 6
H: 6 1 W: 12 11 b.Plymouth 1-3-90
Source: Scholar.
2007-08 Swindon T 2 0 **2 0**
2007-08 Newcastle U 0 0
2008-09 Newcastle U 0 0

2009-10 Newcastle U 1 0
2010-11 Newcastle U 0 0 **1 0**
2010-11 *Northampton T* 31 3
2011-12 Northampton T 45 3 **76 6**

TURNBULL, Paul (M) 139 6
H: 6 0 W: 12 07 b.Handforth 23-1-89
Source: Scholar.
2004-05 Stockport Co 1 0
2005-06 Stockport Co 0 0
2006-07 Stockport Co 0 0
2007-08 Stockport Co 19 0
2008-09 Stockport Co 34 1
2009-10 Stockport Co 30 0
2010-11 Stockport Co 41 5 **125 6**
2011-12 Northampton T 14 0 **14 0**

WEBSTER, Byron (D) 58 4
H: 6 5 W: 12 07 b.Sherburn-in-Elmet 31-3-87
Source: York C, Harrogate T, Whitby T.
2007-08 Siad Most 23 4
2008-09 Siad Most 0 0 **23 4**
2009-10 Doncaster R 5 0
2010-11 Doncaster R 7 0 **12 0**
2010-11 *Hereford U* 2 0 **2 0**
2010-11 *Northampton T* 8 0
2011-12 Northampton T 13 0 **21 0**

WEDDERBURN, Nathanial (M) 45 0
H: 6 1 W: 13 05 b.Wolverhampton 30-6-91
Source: Scholar. *Honours:* England Youth.
2008-09 Stoke C 0 0
2008-09 *Notts Co* 9 0 **9 0**
2009-10 Stoke C 0 0
2009-10 *Hereford U* 3 0 **3 0**
2010-11 Northampton T 31 0
2011-12 Northampton T 2 0 **33 0**

WESTWOOD, Ashley M (D) 302 22
H: 6 0 W: 12 09 b.Bridgnorth 31-8-76
Source: Trainee. *Honours:* England Youth.
1994-95 Manchester U 0 0
1995-96 Crewe Alex 33 4
1996-97 Crewe Alex 44 2
1997-98 Crewe Alex 21 3
1998-99 Bradford C 19 2
1999-2000 Bradford C 5 0
2000-01 Bradford C 0 0 **24 2**
2000-01 Sheffield W 33 2
2001-02 Sheffield W 26 1
2002-03 Sheffield W 23 2 **82 5**
2003-04 Northampton T 9 0
2004-05 Northampton T 19 2
2005-06 Northampton T 3 0
2006-07 Chester C 21 3
2006-07 *Swindon T* 9 0 **9 0**
2007-08 Chester C 0 0 **21 3**
2007-08 *Port Vale* 12 0 **12 0**
From Stevenage B, Wrexham, Kettering T.
2010-11 Crewe Alex 8 0 **106 9**
From Stevenage B, Wrexham, Kettering T.
2011-12 Northampton T 17 1 **48 3**

WILSON, Lewis (F) 3 1
H: 5 10 W: 11 13 b.Milton Keynes 19-2-93
Source: Rushden & D, Newport Pagnell T.
2011-12 Northampton T 3 1 **3 1**

YOUNG, Lewis (M) 56 0
H: 5 10 W: 11 02 b.Stevenage 27-9-89
Source: Scholar.
2008-09 Watford 1 0
2009-10 Watford 0 0 **1 0**
2009-10 *Hereford U* 6 0 **6 0**
2010-11 Burton Alb 19 0 **19 0**
2011-12 Northampton T 30 0 **30 0**

NORWICH C (57)

ADEYEMI, Tom (M) 81 7
H: 6 1 W: 12 04 b.Milton Keynes 24-10-91
Source: Scholar.
2008-09 Norwich C 0 0
2009-10 Norwich C 11 0
2010-11 Norwich C 0 0
2010-11 *Bradford C* 34 5 **34 5**
2011-12 Norwich C 0 0 **11 0**
2011-12 *Oldham Ath* 36 2 **36 2**

AYALA, Daniel (M) 41 1
H: 6 3 W: 13 03 b.Sevilla 7-11-90
Honours: Spain Under-21.
2007-08 Liverpool 0 0
2008-09 Liverpool 0 0
2009-10 Liverpool 5 0
2010-11 Liverpool 0 0 **5 0**
2010-11 *Hull C* 12 1 **12 1**
2010-11 *Derby Co* 17 0 **17 0**
2011-12 Norwich C 7 0 **7 0**

BALL, Matt (M) 0 0
H: 5 10 W: 10 10 b.Welwyn GC 26-3-93
Source: Scholar. *Honours:* Northern Ireland Youth.
2011-12 Norwich C 0 0
2011-12 *Macclesfield T* 0 0

BARNETT, Leon (D) 166 8
H: 6 0 W: 12 04 b.Stevenage 30-11-85
Source: Scholar.
2003-04 Luton T 0 0
2004-05 Luton T 0 0
2005-06 Luton T 20 0
2006-07 Luton T 39 3 **59 3**
2007-08 WBA 32 3
2008-09 WBA 11 0
2009-10 WBA 2 0
2009-10 *Coventry C* 20 0 **20 0**
2010-11 WBA 0 0 **45 3**
2010-11 Norwich C 25 1
2011-12 Norwich C 17 1 **42 2**

BENNETT, Elliott (M) 196 19
H: 5 9 W: 10 11 b.Telford 18-12-88
Source: Scholar.
2006-07 Wolverhampton W 0 0
2007-08 Wolverhampton W 0 0
2007-08 *Crewe Alex* 9 1 **9 1**
2007-08 *Bury* 19 1
2008-09 Wolverhampton W 0 0
2008-09 *Bury* 46 3 **65 4**
2009-10 Wolverhampton W 0 0
2009-10 *Brighton & HA* 43 7
2010-11 Brighton & HA 46 6 **89 13**
2011-12 Norwich C 33 1 **33 1**

BENNETT, Ryan (M) 199 12
H: 6 2 W: 11 00 b.Thurrock 6-3-90
Source: Scholar. *Honours:* England Youth.
2006-07 Grimsby T 5 0
2007-08 Grimsby T 40 1
2008-09 Grimsby T 45 5
2009-10 Grimsby T 13 0 **103 6**
2009-10 Peterborough U 22 1
2010-11 Peterborough U 34 4
2011-12 Peterborough U 32 1 **88 6**
2011-12 Norwich C 8 0 **8 0**

CROFTS, Andrew (D) 295 30
H: 5 10 W: 12 09 b.Chatham 29-5-84
Source: Trainee. *Honours:* Wales Youth, Under-21, 23 full caps.
2000-01 Gillingham 1 0
2001-02 Gillingham 0 0
2002-03 Gillingham 0 0
2003-04 Gillingham 8 0
2004-05 Gillingham 27 2
2005-06 Gillingham 45 2
2006-07 Gillingham 43 8
2007-08 Gillingham 41 5
2008-09 Gillingham 9 0 **174 17**
2008-09 *Peterborough U* 9 0 **9 0**
2009-10 Brighton & HA 44 5 **44 5**
2010-11 Norwich C 44 8
2011-12 Norwich C 24 0 **68 8**

DAWKIN, Josh (M) 0 0
H: 5 9 W: 10 12 b.St Ives 16-1-92
Source: Scholar. *Honours:* Wales Youth.
2009-10 Norwich C 0 0
2010-11 Norwich C 0 0
2011-12 Norwich C 0 0

DRURY, Adam (D) 474 6
H: 5 10 W: 11 09 b.Cambridge 29-8-78
Source: Trainee.
1995-96 Peterborough U 1 0
1996-97 Peterborough U 5 1
1997-98 Peterborough U 31 0
1998-99 Peterborough U 40 0
1999-2000 Peterborough U 42 1
2000-01 Peterborough U 29 0 **148 2**
2000-01 Norwich C 6 0
2001-02 Norwich C 35 0
2002-03 Norwich C 45 2
2003-04 Norwich C 42 0
2004-05 Norwich C 33 1
2005-06 Norwich C 39 0
2006-07 Norwich C 39 0
2007-08 Norwich C 9 0
2008-09 Norwich C 11 0
2009-10 Norwich C 35 0
2010-11 Norwich C 20 1
2011-12 Norwich C 12 0 **326 4**

FOX, David (M) 176 11
H: 5 9 W: 11 08 b.Leek 13-12-83
Source: Scholar. *Honours:* England Youth, Under-20.
2000-01 Manchester U 0 0
2001-02 Manchester U 0 0
2002-03 Manchester U 0 0
2003-04 Manchester U 0 0
2004-05 Manchester U 0 0
2004-05 *Shrewsbury T* 4 1 **4 1**
2005-06 Manchester U 0 0
2005-06 Blackpool 7 1
2006-07 Blackpool 37 4
2007-08 Blackpool 28 1
2008-09 Blackpool 22 0 **94 6**
2009-10 Colchester U 18 3 **18 3**
2010-11 Norwich C 32 1
2011-12 Norwich C 28 0 **60 1**

FRANCOMB, George (D) 29 0
H: 5 11 W: 11 07 b.Hackney 8-9-91
Source: Scholar.
2009-10 Norwich C 2 0
2010-11 Norwich C 0 0
2010-11 *Barnet* 13 0 **13 0**
2011-12 Norwich C 0 0 **2 0**
2011-12 *Hibernian* 14 0 **14 0**

HOLT, Grant (F) 368 139
H: 6 1 W: 14 02 b.Carlisle 12-4-81
Source: Workington.
1999-2000 Halifax T 4 0
2000-01 Halifax T 2 0 **6 0**
From Sengkang,Barrow
2002-03 Sheffield W 7 1
2003-04 Sheffield W 17 2 **24 3**
2003-04 Rochdale 14 4
2004-05 Rochdale 40 17
2005-06 Rochdale 21 14 **75 35**
2005-06 Nottingham F 19 4
2006-07 Nottingham F 45 14
2007-08 Nottingham F 32 3 **96 21**
2007-08 *Blackpool* 4 0 **4 0**
2008-09 Shrewsbury T 43 20 **43 20**
2009-10 Norwich C 39 24
2010-11 Norwich C 45 21
2011-12 Norwich C 36 15 **120 60**

HOOLAHAN, Wes (M) 349 49
H: 5 6 W: 10 03 b.Dublin 10-8-83
Honours: Eire Under-21, 1 full cap.
2001-02 Shelbourne 20 3
2002-03 Shelbourne 23 0
2004 Shelbourne 31 2
2005 Shelbourne 29 4 **103 9**
2005-06 Livingston 16 0 **16 0**
2006-07 Blackpool 42 8
2007-08 Blackpool 45 5 **87 13**
2008-09 Norwich C 32 2
2009-10 Norwich C 37 11
2010-11 Norwich C 41 10
2011-12 Norwich C 33 4 **143 27**

HOWSON, Jonathan (M) 196 24
H: 5 11 W: 12 01 b.Morley 21-5-88
Source: Scholar. *Honours:* England Under-21.
2006-07 Leeds U 9 1
2007-08 Leeds U 26 3
2008-09 Leeds U 40 4
2009-10 Leeds U 45 4
2010-11 Leeds U 46 10
2011-12 Leeds U 19 1 **185 23**
2011-12 Norwich C 11 1 **11 1**

JACKSON, Simeon (M) 178 56
H: 5 10 W: 10 12 b.Kingston, Jamaica 28-3-87
Source: Scholar. *Honours:* Canada Youth, 28 full caps, 6 goals.
2004-05 Rushden & D 3 0
2005-06 Rushden & D 14 5
2006-07 Rushden & D 0 0
2007-08 Rushden & D 0 0 **17 5**
2007-08 Gillingham 18 4
2008-09 Gillingham 41 17
2009-10 Gillingham 42 14 **101 35**
2010-11 Norwich C 38 13
2011-12 Norwich C 22 3 **60 16**

JOHNSON, Brad (M) **209** **29**
H: 6 0 W: 12 10 b.Hackney 28-4-87
Source: Cambridge U Juniors.

2004-05	Cambridge U	1	0	**1**	**0**
2005-06	Northampton T	3	0		
2006-07	Northampton T	27	5		
2007-08	Northampton T	23	2	**53**	**7**
2007-08	Leeds U	21	3		
2008-09	Leeds U	15	1		
2008-09	*Brighton & HA*	10	4	**10**	**4**
2009-10	Leeds U	36	7		
2010-11	Leeds U	45	5	**117**	**16**
2011-12	Norwich C	28	2	**28**	**2**

LAPPIN, Simon (M) **275** **13**
H: 5 11 W: 9 06 b.Glasgow 25-1-83
Honours: Scotland Under-21.

2001-02	St Mirren	1	0		
2002-03	St Mirren	34	0		
2003-04	St Mirren	24	4		
2004-05	St Mirren	34	1		
2005-06	St Mirren	35	3		
2006-07	St Mirren	24	1	**152**	**9**
2006-07	Norwich C	14	1		
2007-08	*Motherwell*	14	2	**14**	**2**
2007-08	Norwich C	15	1		
2008-09	Norwich C	5	0		
2009-10	Norwich C	44	0		
2010-11	Norwich C	27	0		
2011-12	Norwich C	4	0	**109**	**2**

MARTIN, Chris (F) **167** **43**
H: 6 2 W: 12 06 b.Beccles 4-11-88
Source: Scholar. *Honours:* England Youth.

2006-07	Norwich C	18	4		
2007-08	Norwich C	7	0		
2008-09	Norwich C	0	0		
2008-09	*Luton T*	40	11	**40**	**11**
2009-10	Norwich C	42	17		
2010-11	Norwich C	30	4		
2011-12	Norwich C	4	0	**101**	**25**
2011-12	*Crystal Palace*	26	7	**26**	**7**

MARTIN, Russell (M) **277** **13**
H: 6 0 W: 11 08 b.Brighton 4-1-86
Source: Lewes. *Honours:* Scotland 3 full caps.

2004-05	Wycombe W	7	0		
2005-06	Wycombe W	23	3		
2006-07	Wycombe W	42	2		
2007-08	Wycombe W	44	0	**116**	**5**
2008-09	Peterborough U	46	1		
2009-10	Peterborough U	10	0	**56**	**1**
2009-10	Norwich C	26	0		
2010-11	Norwich C	46	5		
2011-12	Norwich C	33	2	**105**	**7**

MORISON, Steven (F) **140** **47**
H: 6 2 W: 13 07 b.Enfield 29-8-83
Source: Scholar. *Honours:* Wales 15 full caps, 1 goal.

2001-02	Northampton T	1	0		
2002-03	Northampton T	13	1		
2003-04	Northampton T	5	1		
2004-05	Northampton T	4	1	**23**	**3**
From Stevenage B.					
2008-09	Millwall	0	0		
2009-10	Millwall	43	20		
2010-11	Millwall	40	15	**83**	**35**
2011-12	Norwich C	34	9	**34**	**9**

PILKINGTON, Anthony (M) **197** **43**
H: 5 11 W: 12 00 b.Blackburn 3-11-87
Source: Atherton Collieries. *Honours:* Eire Under-21.

2006-07	Stockport Co	24	5		
2007-08	Stockport Co	29	6		
2008-09	Stockport Co	24	5	**77**	**16**
2008-09	Huddersfield T	16	2		
2009-10	Huddersfield T	43	7		
2010-11	Huddersfield T	31	10	**90**	**19**
2011-12	Norwich C	30	8	**30**	**8**

RUDD, Declan (G) **10** **0**
H: 6 3 W: 12 06 b.Diss 16-1-91
Source: Scholar. *Honours:* England Youth, Under-20.

2008-09	Norwich C	0	0		
2009-10	Norwich C	7	0		
2010-11	Norwich C	1	0		
2011-12	Norwich C	2	0	**10**	**0**

RUDDY, John (G) **216** **0**
H: 6 3 W: 12 07 b.St Ives 24-10-86
Source: Scholar. *Honours:* England Youth.

2003-04	Cambridge U	1	0		
2004-05	Cambridge U	38	0	**39**	**0**
2005-06	Everton	1	0		
2005-06	*Walsall*	5	0	**5**	**0**
2005-06	*Rushden & D*	3	0	**3**	**0**
2005-06	*Chester C*	4	0	**4**	**0**
2006-07	Everton	0	0		
2006-07	*Stockport Co*	11	0		
2006-07	*Wrexham*	5	0	**5**	**0**
2006-07	*Bristol C*	1	0	**1**	**0**
2007-08	Everton	0	0		
2007-08	*Stockport Co*	12	0	**23**	**0**
2008-09	Everton	0	0		
2008-09	*Crewe Alex*	19	0	**19**	**0**
2009-10	Everton	0	0	**1**	**0**
2009-10	*Motherwell*	34	0	**34**	**0**
2010-11	Norwich C	45	0		
2011-12	Norwich C	37	0	**82**	**0**

SMITH, Korey (M) **79** **4**
H: 5 9 W: 11 01 b.Hatfield 31-1-91
Source: Scholar.

2008-09	Norwich C	2	0		
2009-10	Norwich C	37	4		
2010-11	Norwich C	28	0		
2011-12	Norwich C	0	0	**67**	**4**
2011-12	*Barnsley*	12	0	**12**	**0**

STEER, Jed (G) **12** **0**
H: 6 2 W: 14 00 b.Norwich 23-9-92
Source: Scholar.

2009-10	Norwich C	0	0		
2010-11	Norwich C	0	0		
2011-12	Norwich C	0	0		
2011-12	*Yeovil T*	12	0	**12**	**0**

SURMAN, Andrew (M) **225** **30**
H: 5 10 W: 11 06 b.Johannesburg 20-8-86
Source: Trainee. *Honours:* England Under-21.

2003-04	Southampton	0	0		
2004-05	Southampton	0	0		
2004-05	*Walsall*	14	2	**14**	**2**
2005-06	Southampton	12	2		
2005-06	*Bournemouth*	24	6	**24**	**6**
2006-07	Southampton	37	4		
2007-08	Southampton	40	2		
2008-09	Southampton	44	7		
2009-10	Southampton	0	0	**133**	**15**
2009-10	Wolverhampton W	7	0	**7**	**0**
2010-11	Norwich C	22	3		
2011-12	Norwich C	25	4	**47**	**7**

TIERNEY, Marc (D) **229** **2**
H: 5 11 W: 11 04 b.Prestwich 23-8-85
Source: Trainee.

2003-04	Oldham Ath	2	0		
2004-05	Oldham Ath	11	0		
2005-06	Oldham Ath	19	0		
2006-07	Oldham Ath	5	0	**37**	**0**
2006-07	Shrewsbury T	18	0		
2007-08	Shrewsbury T	43	1		
2008-09	Shrewsbury T	18	0	**79**	**1**
2008-09	Colchester U	26	1		
2009-10	Colchester U	41	0		
2010-11	Colchester U	13	0	**80**	**1**
2010-11	Norwich C	16	0		
2011-12	Norwich C	17	0	**33**	**0**

VAUGHAN, James (F) **84** **16**
H: 5 11 W: 13 00 b.Birmingham 14-7-88
Source: Scholar. *Honours:* England Youth, Under-21.

2004-05	Everton	2	1		
2005-06	Everton	1	0		
2006-07	Everton	14	4		
2007-08	Everton	8	1		
2008-09	Everton	13	0		
2009-10	Everton	8	1		
2009-10	*Derby Co*	2	0	**2**	**0**
2010-11	Everton	1	0	**47**	**7**
2010-11	*Crystal Palace*	30	9	**30**	**9**
2011-12	Norwich C	5	0	**5**	**0**

WARD, Elliot (D) **212** **17**
H: 6 2 W: 13 00 b.Harrow 19-1-85
Source: Scholar.

2001-02	West Ham U	0	0		
2002-03	West Ham U	0	0		
2003-04	West Ham U	0	0		
2004-05	West Ham U	11	0		
2004-05	*Bristol R*	3	0	**3**	**0**
2005-06	West Ham U	4	0	**15**	**0**
2005-06	*Plymouth Arg*	16	1	**16**	**1**
2006-07	Coventry C	39	3		
2007-08	Coventry C	37	6		
2008-09	Coventry C	33	5		
2009-10	Coventry C	8	0	**117**	**14**
2009-10	*Doncaster R*	6	1	**6**	**1**
2009-10	*Preston NE*	4	0	**4**	**0**
2010-11	Norwich C	39	1		
2011-12	Norwich C	12	0	**51**	**1**

WHITBREAD, Zak (D) **144** **4**
H: 6 2 W: 12 07 b.Houston 4-3-84
Honours: USA Under-23.

2002-03	Liverpool	0	0		
2003-04	Liverpool	0	0		
2004-05	Liverpool	0	0		
2005-06	Liverpool	0	0		
2005-06	*Millwall*	25	0		
2006-07	Millwall	14	0		
2007-08	Millwall	23	3		
2008-09	Millwall	38	0		
2009-10	Millwall	0	0	**100**	**3**
2009-10	Norwich C	4	0		
2010-11	Norwich C	22	1		
2011-12	Norwich C	18	0	**44**	**1**

WILBRAHAM, Aaron (F) **399** **91**
H: 6 3 W: 12 04 b.Knutsford 21-10-79
Source: Trainee.

1997-98	Stockport Co	7	1		
1998-99	Stockport Co	26	0		
1999-2000	Stockport Co	26	4		
2000-01	Stockport Co	36	12		
2001-02	Stockport Co	21	3		
2002-03	Stockport Co	15	7		
2003-04	Stockport Co	41	8	**172**	**35**
2004-05	Hull C	19	2	**19**	**2**
2004-05	*Oldham Ath*	4	2	**4**	**2**
2005-06	Milton Keynes D	31	4		
2005-06	*Bradford C*	5	1	**5**	**1**
2006-07	Milton Keynes D	32	7		
2007-08	Milton Keynes D	35	10		
2008-09	Milton Keynes D	33	16		
2009-10	Milton Keynes D	35	10		
2010-11	Milton Keynes D	10	2	**176**	**49**
2010-11	Norwich C	12	1		
2011-12	Norwich C	11	1	**23**	**2**

Scholars
Barker Harry Darius; Callan-McFadden Kyle; Carroll Rian Conor; Clunan Michael Edward; Hall-Johnson Reece; Matthews Remi Luke; McGeehan Cameron Alexander; Murphy Jacob Kai; Murphy Joshua; Peacock Joe; St Louis Dominic; Toffolo Harry.

NOTTINGHAM F (58)

ANDERSON, Paul (M) **147** **16**
H: 5 9 W: 10 04 b.Leicester 23-7-88
Source: Scholar. *Honours:* England Youth.

2005-06	Hull C	0	0		
2005-06	Liverpool	0	0		
2006-07	Liverpool	0	0		
2007-08	Liverpool	0	0		
2007-08	*Swansea C*	31	7	**31**	**7**
2008-09	Liverpool	0	0		
2008-09	*Nottingham F*	26	2		
2009-10	Nottingham F	37	4		
2010-11	Nottingham F	36	3		
2011-12	Nottingham F	17	0	**116**	**9**

BLACKSTOCK, Dexter (F) **245** **68**
H: 6 2 W: 13 00 b.Oxford 20-5-86
Source: Scholar. *Honours:* England Youth, Under-20, Under-21.

2004-05	Southampton	9	1		
2004-05	*Plymouth Arg*	14	4	**14**	**4**
2005-06	Southampton	19	3	**28**	**4**
2005-06	*Derby Co*	9	3	**9**	**3**
2006-07	QPR	39	13		
2007-08	QPR	35	6		
2008-09	QPR	36	11	**110**	**30**
2008-09	*Nottingham F*	6	2		
2009-10	Nottingham F	39	12		
2010-11	Nottingham F	17	5		
2011-12	Nottingham F	22	8	**84**	**27**

BLAKE, Jack (M) **0** **0**
b.Scotland 22-9-94
Honours: Scotland Youth.

2011-12	Nottingham F	0	0		

BOATENG, George (M) **485** **21**
H: 5 9 W: 12 06 b.Nkawkaw 5-9-75
Honours: Holland Under-21, 4 full caps.

1994-95	Excelsior	9	0	**9**	**0**
1995-96	Feyenoord	24	1		
1996-97	Feyenoord	26	0		

1997-98 Feyenoord 18 0 **68 1**
1997-98 Coventry C 14 1
1998-99 Coventry C 33 4 **47 5**
1999-2000 Aston Villa 33 2
2000-01 Aston Villa 33 1
2001-02 Aston Villa 37 1 **103 4**
2002-03 Middlesbrough 28 0
2003-04 Middlesbrough 35 0
2004-05 Middlesbrough 25 3
2005-06 Middlesbrough 26 2
2006-07 Middlesbrough 35 1
2007-08 Middlesbrough 33 1 **182 7**
2008-09 Hull C 23 0
2009-10 Hull C 29 1 **52 1**
2010-11 Xanthi 19 2 **19 2**
2011-12 Nottingham F 5 1 **5 1**

CAMP, Lee (G) 317 0
H: 5 11 W: 11 11 b.Derby 22-8-84
Source: Scholar. *Honours:* England Youth, Under-20, Under-21. Northern Ireland 8 full caps.
2002-03 Derby Co 1 0
2003-04 Derby Co 0 0
2003-04 *QPR* 12 0
2004-05 Derby Co 45 0
2005-06 Derby Co 40 0
2006-07 Derby Co 3 0 **89 0**
2006-07 *Norwich C* 3 0 **3 0**
2006-07 *QPR* 11 0
2007-08 QPR 46 0
2008-09 QPR 4 0 **73 0**
2008-09 *Nottingham F* 15 0
2009-10 Nottingham F 45 0
2010-11 Nottingham F 46 0
2011-12 Nottingham F 46 0 **152 0**

CHAMBERS, Luke (D) 329 18
H: 6 1 W: 11 13 b.Kettering 29-8-85
Source: Scholar.
2002-03 Northampton T 1 0
2003-04 Northampton T 24 0
2004-05 Northampton T 27 0
2005-06 Northampton T 43 0
2006-07 Northampton T 29 1 **124 1**
2006-07 Nottingham F 14 0
2007-08 Nottingham F 42 6
2008-09 Nottingham F 39 2
2009-10 Nottingham F 23 3
2010-11 Nottingham F 44 6
2011-12 Nottingham F 43 0 **205 17**

COHEN, Chris (M) 267 16
H: 5 11 W: 10 11 b.Norwich 5-3-87
Source: Scholar. *Honours:* England Youth.
2003-04 West Ham U 7 0
2004-05 West Ham U 11 0
2005-06 West Ham U 0 0 **18 0**
2005-06 *Yeovil T* 30 1
2006-07 Yeovil T 44 6 **74 7**
2007-08 Nottingham F 41 2
2008-09 Nottingham F 41 2
2009-10 Nottingham F 44 3
2010-11 Nottingham F 42 2
2011-12 Nottingham F 7 0 **175 9**

DARLOW, Karl (G) 1 0
H: 6 1 W: 12 05 b.Northampton 8-10-90
Source: Scholar.
2009-10 Nottingham F 0 0
2010-11 Nottingham F 1 0
2011-12 Nottingham F 0 0 **1 0**

DERBYSHIRE, Matt (F) 145 32
H: 5 10 W: 11 01 b.Gt Harwood 14-4-86
Source: Gt Harwood T. *Honours:* England Under-21.
2003-04 Blackburn R 0 0
2004-05 Blackburn R 1 0
2005-06 Blackburn R 0 0
2005-06 *Plymouth Arg* 12 0 **12 0**
2005-06 *Wrexham* 16 10 **16 10**
2006-07 Blackburn R 22 5
2007-08 Blackburn R 23 3
2008-09 Blackburn R 17 2 **63 10**
2008-09 *Olympiakos* 7 5
2009-10 Olympiakos 19 6
2010-11 Olympiakos 0 0 **26 11**
2010-11 Birmingham C 13 0 **13 0**
2011-12 Nottingham F 15 1 **15 1**
On loan from Olympiakos.

FINDLEY, Robbie (F) 147 49
H: 5 9 W: 11 11 b.Phoenix 4-8-85
Source: Oregon State Beavers. *Honours:* USA 11 full caps.
2005 Boulder Rapids 9 10
2006 Boulder Rapids 8 5 **17 15**
2007 LA Galaxy 9 2 **9 2**
2007 Real Salt Lake 16 6
2008 Real Salt Lake 29 6
2009 Real Salt Lake 27 12
2010 Real Salt Lake 24 5 **96 29**
2010-11 Nottingham F 2 0
2011-12 Nottingham F 23 3 **25 3**

FREEMAN, Kieron (D) 19 1
H: 5 10 W: 12 05 b.Nottingham 21-3-92
Source: Scholar. *Honours:* Wales Youth.
2010-11 Nottingham F 0 0
2011-12 Nottingham F 0 0
2011-12 *Notts Co* 19 1 **19 1**

GREENING, Jonathan (M) 398 14
H: 5 11 W: 11 00 b.Scarborough 2-1-79
Source: Trainee. *Honours:* England Youth, Under-21.
1996-97 York C 5 0
1997-98 York C 20 2 **25 2**
1997-98 Manchester U 0 0
1998-99 Manchester U 3 0
1999-2000 Manchester U 4 0
2000-01 Manchester U 7 0 **14 0**
2001-02 Middlesbrough 36 1
2002-03 Middlesbrough 38 2
2003-04 Middlesbrough 25 1 **99 4**
2004-05 WBA 34 0
2005-06 WBA 38 2
2006-07 WBA 42 2
2007-08 WBA 46 1
2008-09 WBA 34 2
2009-10 WBA 2 0 **196 7**
2009-10 *Fulham* 23 1
2010-11 Fulham 10 0 **33 1**
2011-12 Nottingham F 31 0 **31 0**

GUNTER, Chris (D) 174 2
H: 5 11 W: 11 02 b.Newport 21-7-89
Source: Scholar. *Honours:* Wales Youth, Under-21, 37 full caps.
2006-07 Cardiff C 15 0
2007-08 Cardiff C 13 0 **28 0**
2007-08 Tottenham H 2 0
2008-09 Tottenham H 3 0 **5 0**
2008-09 *Nottingham F* 8 0
2009-10 Nottingham F 44 1
2010-11 Nottingham F 43 0
2011-12 Nottingham F 46 1 **141 2**

HAREWOOD, Marlon (F) 419 122
H: 6 1 W: 13 07 b.Hampstead 25-8-79
Source: Trainee.
1996-97 Nottingham F 0 0
1997-98 Nottingham F 1 0
1998-99 Nottingham F 23 1
1998-99 *Ipswich T* 6 1 **6 1**
1999-2000 Nottingham F 34 4
2000-01 Nottingham F 33 3
2001-02 Nottingham F 28 11
2002-03 Nottingham F 44 20
2003-04 Nottingham F 19 12
2003-04 West Ham U 28 13
2004-05 West Ham U 45 17
2005-06 West Ham U 37 14
2006-07 West Ham U 32 3 **142 47**
2007-08 Aston Villa 23 5
2008-09 Aston Villa 6 0
2008-09 *Wolverhampton W* 5 0 **5 0**
2009-10 Aston Villa 0 0 **29 5**
2009-10 *Newcastle U* 15 5 **15 5**
2010-11 Blackpool 16 5 **16 5**
2010-11 *Barnsley* 10 4 **10 4**
2011 Guangzhou 10 4 **10 4**
2011-12 Nottingham F 4 0 **186 51**

LASCELLES, Jamaal (D) 8 1
H: 6 2 W: 13 01 b.Derby 11-11-93
Source: Scholar. *Honours:* England Youth.
2010-11 Nottingham F 0 0
2011-12 Nottingham F 1 0 **1 0**
2011-12 *Stevenage* 7 1 **7 1**

LYNCH, Joel (D) 159 5
H: 6 1 W: 12 10 b.Eastbourne 3-10-87
Source: Scholar. *Honours:* England Youth.
2005-06 Brighton & HA 16 1
2006-07 Brighton & HA 39 0
2007-08 Brighton & HA 22 1
2008-09 Brighton & HA 2 0 **79 2**
2008-09 *Nottingham F* 23 0
2009-10 Nottingham F 10 0
2010-11 Nottingham F 12 0
2011-12 Nottingham F 35 3 **80 3**

MAJEWSKI, Radoslaw (M) 160 16
H: 5 7 W: 10 06 b.Pruszkow 15-12-86
Source: Znicz Pruszkow. *Honours:* Poland 9 full caps.
2006-07 Groclin 14 0
2007-08 Groclin 28 4 **42 4**
2008-09 Polonia Warsaw 29 1 **29 1**
2009-10 Nottingham F 35 3
2010-11 Nottingham F 26 2
2011-12 Nottingham F 28 6 **89 11**

McGOLDRICK, David (F) 170 29
H: 6 1 W: 11 10 b.Nottingham 29-11-87
Source: Schoolboy.
2003-04 Notts Co 4 0
2004-05 Notts Co 0 0
2005-06 Southampton 1 0
2005-06 *Notts Co* 6 0 **10 0**
2006-07 Southampton 9 0
2006-07 *Bournemouth* 12 6 **12 6**
2007-08 Southampton 8 0
2007-08 *Port Vale* 17 2 **17 2**
2008-09 Southampton 46 12 **64 12**
2009-10 Nottingham F 33 3
2010-11 Nottingham F 21 5
2011-12 Nottingham F 9 0 **63 8**
2011-12 *Sheffield W* 4 1 **4 1**

McGUGAN, Lewis (M) 172 32
H: 5 9 W: 11 06 b.Long Eaton 25-10-88
Source: Scholar.
2006-07 Nottingham F 13 2
2007-08 Nottingham F 33 6
2008-09 Nottingham F 33 5
2009-10 Nottingham F 18 3
2010-11 Nottingham F 40 13
2011-12 Nottingham F 35 3 **172 32**

MEADOWS, Danny (M) 0 0
b.Grantham 26-9-92
Source: Scholar.
2011-12 Nottingham F 0 0

MILLER, Ishmael (F) 120 18
H: 6 3 W: 14 00 b.Manchester 5-3-87
Source: Scholar.
2005-06 Manchester C 1 0
2006-07 Manchester C 16 0
2007-08 Manchester C 0 0 **17 0**
2007-08 WBA 34 9
2008-09 WBA 15 3
2009-10 WBA 15 2
2010-11 WBA 6 0 **70 14**
2010-11 *QPR* 12 1 **12 1**
2011-12 Nottingham F 21 3 **21 3**

MOLONEY, Brendan (M) 59 2
H: 6 1 W: 11 12 b.Killarney 18-1-89
Source: Scholar. *Honours:* Eire Under-21.
2005-06 Nottingham F 0 0
2006-07 Nottingham F 1 0
2007-08 Nottingham F 2 0
2007-08 *Chesterfield* 9 1 **9 1**
2008-09 Nottingham F 12 0
2009-10 Nottingham F 0 0
2009-10 *Notts Co* 18 1 **18 1**
2009-10 *Scunthorpe U* 3 0 **3 0**
2010-11 Nottingham F 6 0
2011-12 Nottingham F 8 0 **29 0**

MORGAN, David (M) 0 0
b.Northern Ireland 4-7-94
Source: Scholar.
2011-12 Nottingham F 0 0

MOUSSI, Guy (M) 198 5
H: 6 1 W: 12 11 b.Paris 23-1-85
2004-05 Angers 15 1
2005-06 Angers 9 0
2006-07 Angers 32 0
2007-08 Angers 35 1 **91 2**
2008-09 Nottingham F 15 0
2009-10 Nottingham F 27 3
2010-11 Nottingham F 31 0
2011-12 Nottingham F 34 0 **107 3**

OSBORN, Ben (D) 0 0
b.Derby 5-8-94
Source: Scholar.
2011-12 Nottingham F 0 0

REGAN, Matthew (D) 0 0
b.Liverpool 22-2-94
Source: Liverpool Scholar.
2011-12 Nottingham F 0 0

REID, Andy (M) 329 37
H: 5 9 W: 12 08 b.Dublin 29-7-82
Source: Trainee. *Honours:* Eire Youth, Under-21, 27 full caps, 4 goals.
1999-2000 Nottingham F 0 0
2000-01 Nottingham F 14 2
2001-02 Nottingham F 29 0
2002-03 Nottingham F 30 1
2003-04 Nottingham F 46 13
2004-05 Nottingham F 25 5
2004-05 Tottenham H 13 1
2005-06 Tottenham H 13 0 **26 1**
2006-07 Charlton Ath 16 2
2007-08 Charlton Ath 22 5 **38 7**
2007-08 Sunderland 13 1
2008-09 Sunderland 32 1
2009-10 Sunderland 21 2
2010-11 Sunderland 2 0 **68 4**
2010-11 *Sheffield U* 9 2 **9 2**
2010-11 Blackpool 5 0 **5 0**
2011-12 Nottingham F 39 2 **183 23**

SMITH, Paul (G) 232 0
H: 6 3 W: 14 00 b.Epsom 17-12-79
Source: Walton & Hersham.
1998-99 Charlton Ath 0 0
1998-99 *Brentford* 0 0
1999-2000 Charlton Ath 0 0
From Carshalton Ath.
2000-01 Brentford 2 0
2001-02 Brentford 18 0
2002-03 Brentford 43 0
2003-04 Brentford 24 0 **87 0**
2003-04 Southampton 0 0
2004-05 Southampton 6 0
2005-06 Southampton 9 0 **15 0**
2006-07 Nottingham F 45 0
2007-08 Nottingham F 46 0
2008-09 Nottingham F 28 0
2009-10 Nottingham F 1 0
2010-11 Nottingham F 0 0
2010-11 *Middlesbrough* 10 0 **10 0**
2011-12 Nottingham F 0 0 **120 0**

TUDGAY, Marcus (F) 343 78
H: 5 10 W: 12 04 b.Shoreham 3-2-83
Source: Trainee.
2002-03 Derby Co 8 0
2003-04 Derby Co 29 6
2004-05 Derby Co 34 9
2005-06 Derby Co 21 2 **92 17**
2005-06 Sheffield W 18 5
2006-07 Sheffield W 40 11
2007-08 Sheffield W 35 7
2008-09 Sheffield W 42 14
2009-10 Sheffield W 43 10
2010-11 Sheffield W 17 2 **195 49**
2010-11 Nottingham F 22 7
2011-12 Nottingham F 34 5 **56 12**

NOTTS CO (59)

ALLEN, Charlie (M) 9 0
H: 6 0 W: 11 10 b.Slough 24-3-92
Source: Brentford Scholar, Billericay T, Dagenham & R.
2011-12 Notts Co 9 0 **9 0**

BENCHERIF, Hamza (D) 92 19
H: 5 9 W: 12 03 b.Paris 9-2-88
Source: Scholar.
2006-07 Nottingham F 0 0
2007-08 *Lincoln C* 12 1 **12 1**
2008-09 Nottingham F 0 0
2009-10 Macclesfield T 19 5
2010-11 Macclesfield T 41 11 **60 16**
2011-12 Notts Co 20 2 **20 2**

BISHOP, Neil (M) 210 7
H: 6 1 W: 12 10 b.Stockton 7-8-81
Source: Billingham T, Gateshead, Spennymoor U, Whitby T, Scarborough, York C.
2007-08 Barnet 39 2
2008-09 Barnet 44 1 **83 3**
2009-10 Notts Co 43 1
2010-11 Notts Co 43 1
2011-12 Notts Co 41 2 **127 4**

BURCH, Rob (G) 115 0
H: 6 2 W: 12 13 b.Yeovil 8-10-83
Source: Trainee. *Honours:* England Under-20.
2002-03 Tottenham H 0 0
2003-04 Tottenham H 0 0
2004-05 Tottenham H 0 0
2004-05 *West Ham U* 0 0
2005-06 Tottenham H 0 0
2005-06 *Bristol C* 0 0
2006-07 Tottenham H 0 0
2006-07 *Barnet* 6 0 **6 0**
2007-08 Sheffield W 2 0 **2 0**
2008-09 Lincoln C 46 0
2009-10 Lincoln C 46 0 **92 0**
2010-11 Notts Co 15 0
2011-12 Notts Co 0 0 **15 0**

BURGESS, Ben (F) 346 91
H: 6 3 W: 14 04 b.Buxton 9-11-81
Source: Trainee. *Honours:* Eire Youth, Under-21.
1998-99 Blackburn R 0 0
1999-2000 Blackburn R 2 0
2000-01 Blackburn R 0 0
2000-01 Northern Spirit 27 16 **27 16**
2001-02 Blackburn R 0 0 **2 0**
2001-02 *Brentford* 43 17 **43 17**
2002-03 Stockport Co 19 4 **19 4**
2002-03 *Oldham Ath* 7 0 **7 0**
2002-03 Hull C 7 4
2003-04 Hull C 44 18
2004-05 Hull C 2 0
2005-06 Hull C 14 2
2006-07 Hull C 3 0 **70 24**
2006-07 Blackpool 27 2
2007-08 Blackpool 35 9
2008-09 Blackpool 29 6
2009-10 Blackpool 35 6 **126 23**
2010-11 Notts Co 17 1
2011-12 Notts Co 28 4 **45 5**
2011-12 *Cheltenham T* 7 2 **7 2**

CHILVERS, Liam (D) 276 6
H: 6 2 W: 12 03 b.Chelmsford 6-11-81
Source: Scholar.
2000-01 Arsenal 0 0
2000-01 *Northampton T* 7 0 **7 0**
2001-02 Arsenal 0 0
2001-02 *Notts Co* 9 1
2002-03 Arsenal 0 0
2002-03 *Colchester U* 6 0
2003-04 Arsenal 0 0
2003-04 *Colchester U* 32 0
2004-05 Colchester U 41 1
2005-06 Colchester U 34 2 **113 3**
2006-07 Preston NE 45 2
2007-08 Preston NE 28 0
2008-09 Preston NE 1 0
2009-10 Preston NE 23 0 **97 2**
2010-11 Notts Co 21 0
2011-12 Notts Co 17 0 **47 1**
2011-12 *Port Vale* 12 0 **12 0**

DEMONTAGNAC, Ishmel (F) 126 14
H: 5 10 W: 11 05 b.Newham 15-6-88
Source: Charlton Ath Scholar. *Honours:* England Youth.
2005-06 Walsall 24 2
2006-07 Walsall 19 1
2007-08 Walsall 30 3
2008-09 Walsall 10 3
2009-10 Walsall 0 0 **83 9**
2009-10 Blackpool 8 0
2009-10 *Chesterfield* 10 3 **10 3**
2010-11 Blackpool 1 0 **9 0**
2010-11 *Stockport Co* 7 2 **7 2**
2011-12 Notts Co 17 0 **17 0**

EDWARDS, Mike (D) 485 27
H: 6 0 W: 12 10 b.Hessle 25-4-80
Source: Trainee.
1997-98 Hull C 21 0
1998-99 Hull C 30 0
1999-2000 Hull C 40 1
2000-01 Hull C 42 4
2001-02 Hull C 39 1
2002-03 Hull C 6 0 **178 6**
2002-03 Colchester U 5 0 **5 0**
2003-04 Grimsby T 33 1 **33 1**
2004-05 Notts Co 9 0
2005-06 Notts Co 46 7
2006-07 Notts Co 45 3
2007-08 Notts Co 19 1
2008-09 Notts Co 43 2
2009-10 Notts Co 40 5
2010-11 Notts Co 37 1
2011-12 Notts Co 30 1 **269 20**

HARLEY, Jon (D) 397 14
H: 5 8 W: 10 03 b.Maidstone 26-9-79
Source: Trainee. *Honours:* England Under-21.
1996-97 Chelsea 0 0
1997-98 Chelsea 3 0
1998-99 Chelsea 0 0
1999-2000 Chelsea 17 2
2000-01 Chelsea 10 0 **30 2**
2000-01 *Wimbledon* 6 2 **6 2**
2001-02 Fulham 10 0
2002-03 Fulham 11 1
2002-03 *Sheffield U* 9 1
2003-04 Fulham 4 0 **25 1**
2003-04 *Sheffield U* 5 0
2003-04 *West Ham U* 15 1 **15 1**
2004-05 Sheffield U 44 2
2005-06 Sheffield U 4 0 **62 3**
2005-06 Burnley 41 2
2006-07 Burnley 45 1
2007-08 Burnley 33 0 **119 3**
2008-09 Watford 37 1
2009-10 Watford 38 1 **75 2**
2010-11 Notts Co 39 0
2011-12 Notts Co 14 0 **53 0**
2011-12 *Rotherham U* 12 0 **12 0**

HAWLEY, Karl (F) 237 53
H: 5 8 W: 12 02 b.Walsall 6-12-81
Source: Scholar.
2000-01 Walsall 0 0
2001-02 Walsall 1 0
2002-03 Walsall 0 0
2002-03 *Raith R* 17 7
2003-04 Walsall 0 0 **1 0**
2003-04 *Raith R* 11 2 **28 9**
2004-05 Carlisle U 0 0
2005-06 Carlisle U 46 22
2006-07 Carlisle U 32 12 **78 34**
2007-08 Preston NE 25 3
2008-09 Preston NE 5 0 **30 3**
2008-09 *Northampton T* 11 2 **11 2**
2008-09 *Colchester U* 4 0 **4 0**
2009-10 Notts Co 31 3
2010-11 Notts Co 24 0
2011-12 Notts Co 26 2 **81 5**
2011-12 *Crawley T* 4 0 **4 0**

HOLLIS, Haydn (D) 1 0
H: 6 4 W: 13 01 b.Selston 14-10-92
Source: Scholar.
2011-12 Notts Co 1 0 **1 0**

HUGHES, Jeff (D) 304 51
H: 6 1 W: 11 00 b.Larne 29-5-85
Source: Larne Tech Old Boys. *Honours:* Northern Ireland Under-21, 2 full caps.
2003-04 Larne 21 1
2004-05 Larne 29 0 **50 1**
2005-06 Lincoln C 22 2
2006-07 Lincoln C 41 6 **63 8**
2007-08 Crystal Palace 10 0 **10 0**
2007-08 *Peterborough U* 7 1 **7 1**
2008-09 Bristol R 43 6
2009-10 Bristol R 44 12
2010-11 Bristol R 42 10 **129 28**
2011-12 Notts Co 45 13 **45 13**

HUGHES, Lee (F) 421 183
H: 5 10 W: 12 00 b.Smethwick 22-5-76
Source: Kidderminster H.
1997-98 WBA 37 14
1998-99 WBA 42 31
1999-2000 WBA 36 12
2000-01 WBA 41 21
2001-02 Coventry C 38 14
2002-03 Coventry C 4 1 **42 15**
2002-03 WBA 23 0
2003-04 WBA 32 11 **211 89**
2007-08 Oldham Ath 18 7
2008-09 Oldham Ath 37 18 **55 25**
2008-09 *Blackpool* 3 1 **3 1**
2009-10 Notts Co 39 30
2010-11 Notts Co 31 13
2011-12 Notts Co 40 10 **110 53**

HUNT, Stephen (D) 152 7
H: 6 2 W: 13 00 b.Southampton 11-11-84
Source: Southampton Scholar.
2004-05 Colchester U 20 1
2005-06 Colchester U 2 0 **22 1**

2006-07	Notts Co	32	1		
2007-08	Notts Co	37	2		
2008-09	Notts Co	11	0		
2009-10	Notts Co	32	1		
2010-11	Notts Co	4	0		
2010-11	*Lincoln C*	14	2	**14**	**2**
2011-12	Notts Co	0	0	**116**	**4**

JUDGE, Alan (F) 116 15
H: 5 6 W: 11 03 b.Dublin 11-11-88
Honours: Eire Under-21.

2006-07	Blackburn R	0	0		
2007-08	Blackburn R	0	0		
2008-09	Blackburn R	0	0		
2008-09	*Plymouth Arg*	17	2		
2009-10	Blackburn R	0	0		
2009-10	*Plymouth Arg*	37	5	**54**	**7**
2010-11	Blackburn R	0	0		
2010-11	Notts Co	19	1		
2011-12	Notts Co	43	7	**62**	**8**

KELLY, Julian (D) 69 4
H: 5 8 W: 11 04 b.Enfield 6-9-89
Source: Arsenal Scholar.

2008-09	Reading	7	0		
2009-10	Reading	0	0		
2009-10	*Wycombe W*	9	1	**9**	**1**
2010-11	Reading	0	0	**7**	**0**
2010-11	*Lincoln C*	21	0	**21**	**0**
2011-12	Notts Co	32	3	**32**	**3**

MAHON, Gavin (M) 430 19
H: 5 11 W: 13 07 b.Birmingham 2-1-77
Source: Trainee.

1995-96	Wolverhampton W	0	0		
1996-97	Hereford U	11	1		
1997-98	Hereford U	0	0		
1998-99	Hereford U	0	0	**11**	**1**
1998-99	Brentford	29	4		
1999-2000	Brentford	37	3		
2000-01	Brentford	40	1		
2001-02	Brentford	35	0	**141**	**8**
2001-02	Watford	6	0		
2002-03	Watford	17	0		
2003-04	Watford	32	2		
2004-05	Watford	43	0		
2005-06	Watford	38	3		
2006-07	Watford	34	1		
2007-08	Watford	19	0	**189**	**6**
2007-08	QPR	16	1		
2008-09	QPR	35	2		
2009-10	QPR	7	1		
2010-11	QPR	0	0	**58**	**4**
2010-11	*Crystal Palace*	0	0		
2011-12	Notts Co	31	0	**31**	**0**

MITCHELL, Liam (G) 0 0
b.Nottingham 18-9-92
Source: Scholar.

2011-12	Notts Co	0	0		

NELSON, Stuart (G) 225 0
H: 6 1 W: 12 12 b.Stroud 17-9-81
Source: Doncaster R, Hucknall T.

2003-04	Brentford	9	0		
2004-05	Brentford	43	0		
2005-06	Brentford	45	0		
2006-07	Brentford	19	0	**116**	**0**
2007-08	Leyton Orient	30	0	**30**	**0**
2008-09	Norwich C	0	0		
2010-11	Notts Co	33	0		
2011-12	Notts Co	46	0	**79**	**0**

NICHOLAS, George (M) 1 0
H: 6 3 W: 11 07 b.Watford 19-12-92
Source: Scholar.

2010-11	Notts Co	1	0		
2011-12	Notts Co	0	0	**1**	**0**

PEARCE, Krystian (D) 116 5
H: 6 1 W: 13 05 b.Birmingham 5-1-90
Source: Scholar. *Honours:* England Youth.

2006-07	Birmingham C	0	0		
2007-08	Birmingham C	0	0		
2007-08	*Port Vale*	12	0	**12**	**0**
2007-08	*Notts Co*	8	1		
2008-09	Birmingham C	0	0		
2008-09	*Scunthorpe U*	39	0	**39**	**0**
2009-10	Birmingham C	0	0		
2009-10	*Peterborough U*	2	0	**2**	**0**
2009-10	Huddersfield T	1	0	**1**	**0**
2010-11	Notts Co	27	1		
2011-12	Notts Co	27	3	**62**	**5**

SHEEHAN, Alan (D) 147 8
H: 5 11 W: 11 02 b.Athlone 14-9-86
Source: Scholar. *Honours:* Eire Youth, Under-21.

2004-05	Leicester C	1	0		
2005-06	Leicester C	2	0		
2006-07	Leicester C	0	0		
2006-07	*Mansfield T*	10	0	**10**	**0**
2007-08	Leicester C	20	1	**23**	**1**
2007-08	*Leeds U*	10	1		
2008-09	Leeds U	11	1		
2008-09	*Crewe Alex*	3	0	**3**	**0**
2009-10	Leeds U	0	0		
2009-10	*Oldham Ath*	8	1	**8**	**1**
2009-10	*Swindon T*	22	1		
2010-11	Leeds U	0	0	**21**	**2**
2010-11	Swindon T	21	1	**43**	**2**
2011-12	Notts Co	39	2	**39**	**2**

SODJE, Sam (D) 180 21
H: 6 0 W: 12 00 b.Greenwich 29-5-79
Source: Stevenage B, Margate. *Honours:* Nigeria 5 full caps.

2004-05	Brentford	40	7		
2005-06	Brentford	43	5	**83**	**12**
2006-07	Reading	3	0		
2006-07	*WBA*	7	1	**7**	**1**
2007-08	Reading	0	0		
2007-08	*Charlton Ath*	27	2		
2008-09	Reading	0	0		
2008-09	*Watford*	1	0	**1**	**0**
2008-09	*Leeds U*	5	0	**5**	**0**
2009-10	Reading	0	0	**3**	**0**
2009-10	Charlton Ath	27	4	**54**	**6**
2010-11	Notts Co	11	0		
2011-12	Notts Co	16	2	**27**	**2**

SPEISS, Fabien (G) 1 0
H: 6 2 W: 12 11 b.Germany 30-11-93
Source: Scholar.

2011-12	Notts Co	1	0	**1**	**0**

SPICER, John (M) 195 14
H: 5 11 W: 11 07 b.Romford 13-9-83
Source: Scholar. *Honours:* England Schools, Youth, Under-20.

2001-02	Arsenal	0	0		
2002-03	Arsenal	0	0		
2003-04	Arsenal	0	0		
2004-05	Arsenal	0	0		
2004-05	Bournemouth	39	6		
2005-06	Bournemouth	4	0	**43**	**6**
2005-06	Burnley	34	3		
2006-07	Burnley	11	1		
2007-08	Burnley	24	0	**69**	**4**
2008-09	Doncaster R	30	1		
2009-10	Doncaster R	20	0	**50**	**1**
2009-10	*Leyton Orient*	9	1	**9**	**1**
2010-11	Notts Co	23	2		
2011-12	Notts Co	1	0	**24**	**2**

STIRLING, Jude (D) 161 5
H: 6 2 W: 11 12 b.Enfield 29-6-82
Source: Trainee.

1999-2000	Luton T	0	0		
2000-01	Luton T	9	0		
2001-02	Luton T	1	0	**10**	**0**
From Tamworth.					
2005-06	Oxford U	10	0	**10**	**0**
From Stevenage B, Hornchurch, Tamworth					
2005-06	Lincoln C	6	0	**6**	**0**
2006-07	Peterborough U	22	0	**22**	**0**
2006-07	Milton Keynes D	16	1		
2007-08	Milton Keynes D	34	2		
2008-09	Milton Keynes D	32	2		
2009-10	Milton Keynes D	9	0		
2009-10	*Grimsby T*	4	0	**4**	**0**
2010-11	Milton Keynes D	4	0	**95**	**5**
2010-11	*Barnet*	6	0	**6**	**0**
2011-12	Notts Co	8	0	**8**	**0**

THOMPSON, Curtis (M) 0 0
b.Nottingham 2-9-93
Source: Scholar.

2011-12	Notts Co	0	0		

WAITE, Tyrell (F) 0 0
b.Derby 1-7-94
Source: Ilkeston.

2011-12	Notts Co	0	0		

WHITELEY, Lewis (M) 0 0
b.Nottingham 17-1-93
Source: Scholar.

2011-12	Notts Co	0	0		

WHOLEY, Jake (D) 1 0
H: 5 10 W: 12 04 b.Nottingham 1-12-93
Source: Scholar.

2010-11	Notts Co	1	0		
2011-12	Notts Co	0	0	**1**	**0**

OLDHAM ATH (60)

BELEZIKA, Glenn (D) 1 0
H: 5 11 W: 13 01 b.Camden 24-12-94
Source: Stalybridge C.

2011-12	Oldham Ath	1	0	**1**	**0**

BEMBO-LITA, Djenny (F) 3 0
H: 5 10 W: 11 05 b.Kinshasa 9-11-91
Source: Scholar.

2009-10	Oldham Ath	0	0		
2010-11	Oldham Ath	3	0		
2011-12	Oldham Ath	0	0	**3**	**0**

BLACK, Paul (D) 60 1
H: 6 0 W: 12 10 b.Middleton 18-5-90
Source: Scholar.

2007-08	Oldham Ath	2	0		
2008-09	Oldham Ath	3	0		
2009-10	Oldham Ath	13	1		
2010-11	Oldham Ath	29	0		
2011-12	Oldham Ath	13	0	**60**	**1**

BOUZANIS, Dean (G) 23 0
H: 6 1 W: 13 06 b.Sydney 2-10-90
Source: St George Saints, Sydney, Melbourne Vic.

2007-08	Liverpool	0	0		
2008-09	Liverpool	0	0		
2009-10	Liverpool	0	0		
2009-10	*Accrington S*	14	0	**14**	**0**
2010-11	Liverpool	0	0		
2011-12	Oldham Ath	9	0	**9**	**0**

BROOKE, Ryan (F) 29 2
H: 6 1 W: 11 07 b.Congleton 4-10-90
Source: Scholar.

2008-09	Oldham Ath	1	1		
2009-10	Oldham Ath	15	1		
2010-11	Oldham Ath	13	0		
2011-12	Oldham Ath	0	0	**29**	**2**

BURNS, Ryan (M) 1 0
H: 6 1 W: 10 07 b.Belfast 8-9-92
Source: Scholar.

2010-11	Oldham Ath	1	0		
2011-12	Oldham Ath	0	0	**1**	**0**

CARR, Matthew (D) 0 0
b.Bury 23-12-92
Source: Scholar.

2011-12	Oldham Ath	0	0		

CISAK, Aleksander (G) 59 0
H: 6 3 W: 14 11 b.Krakow 19-5-89
Source: Scholar. *Honours:* Australia Under-20.

2006-07	Leicester C	0	0		
2007-08	Leicester C	0	0		
2008-09	Leicester C	0	0		
2009-10	Leicester C	0	0		
2010-11	Accrington S	21	0	**21**	**0**
2011-12	Oldham Ath	38	0	**38**	**0**

DIALLO, Bradley (D) 15 0
H: 6 0 W: 12 00 b.Paris 20-7-90
Source: Marseille Youth.

2011-12	Oldham Ath	15	0	**15**	**0**

DIAMOND, Zander (D) 227 18
H: 6 2 W: 11 07 b.Alexandria 3-12-85
Honours: Scotland Under-21.

2003-04	Aberdeen	19	2		
2004-05	Aberdeen	29	3		
2005-06	Aberdeen	33	0		
2006-07	Aberdeen	21	0		
2007-08	Aberdeen	26	3		
2008-09	Aberdeen	28	4		
2009-10	Aberdeen	16	3		
2010-11	Aberdeen	32	1	**204**	**16**
2011-12	Oldham Ath	23	2	**23**	**2**

FURMAN, Dean (M) 136 10
H: 6 0 W: 11 08 b.Cape Town 22-6-88
Source: Chelsea Scholar.

2007-08	Rangers	1	0	**1**	**0**
2008-09	*Bradford C*	32	4	**32**	**4**
2009-10	Oldham Ath	38	0		

2010-11	Oldham Ath	42	5		
2011-12	Oldham Ath	23	1	**103**	**6**

GERRARD, Paul (G) 321 0
H: 6 2 W: 13 11 b.Heywood 22-1-73
Source: Trainee. *Honours:* England Under-21.

1991-92	Oldham Ath	0	0		
1992-93	Oldham Ath	25	0		
1993-94	Oldham Ath	16	0		
1994-95	Oldham Ath	42	0		
1995-96	Oldham Ath	36	0		
1996-97	Everton	5	0		
1997-98	Everton	4	0		
1998-99	Everton	0	0		
1998-99	*Oxford U*	16	0	**16**	**0**
1999-2000	Everton	34	0		
2000-01	Everton	32	0		
2001-02	Everton	13	0		
2002-03	Everton	2	0		
2002-03	*Ipswich T*	5	0	**5**	**0**
2003-04	Everton	0	0	**90**	**0**
2003-04	*Sheffield U*	16	0		
2003-04	*Nottingham F*	8	0		
2004-05	Nottingham F	42	0		
2005-06	Nottingham F	22	0		
2006-07	Nottingham F	0	0	**72**	**0**
2006-07	Sheffield U	2	0		
2007-08	*Blackpool*	0	0		
2007-08	Sheffield U	0	0	**18**	**0**
2008-09	Stockport Co	0	0		
2009-10	Stockport Co	0	0		
2010-11	Oldham Ath	0	0		
2011-12	Oldham Ath	1	0	**120**	**0**

HUGHES, Connor (M) 4 0
H: 5 11 W: 12 10 b.Bolton 6-5-93
Source: Scholar.

2011-12	Oldham Ath	4	0	**4**	**0**

KUQI, Shefki (F) 556 156
H: 6 2 W: 13 13 b.Vushtrri 10-11-76
Source: Trepka, Miki. *Honours:* Albania 8 full caps, 1 goal, Finland 62 full caps, 8 goals.

1995	MP	24	3		
1996	MP	26	7	**50**	**10**
1997	HJK Helsinki	25	6		
1998	HJK Helsinki	22	1		
1999	HJK Helsinki	25	11	**72**	**18**
2000	Jokerit	33	19	**33**	**19**
From Jokerit					
2000-01	Stockport Co	17	6		
2001-02	Stockport Co	18	5	**35**	**11**
2001-02	Sheffield W	17	6		
2002-03	Sheffield W	40	8		
2003-04	Sheffield W	7	5	**64**	**19**
2003-04	Ipswich T	36	11		
2004-05	Ipswich T	43	19		
2005-06	Blackburn R	33	7		
2006-07	Blackburn R	1	0	**34**	**7**
2006-07	Crystal Palace	35	7		
2007-08	Crystal Palace	8	0		
2007-08	*Fulham*	10	0	**10**	**0**
2007-08	*Ipswich T*	4	0	**83**	**30**
2008-09	Crystal Palace	35	10	**78**	**17**
2009-10	Koblenz	17	7	**17**	**7**
2009-10	Swansea C	20	5		
2010-11	Swansea C	2	0	**22**	**5**
2010-11	*Derby Co*	12	2	**12**	**2**
2010-11	Newcastle U	6	0	**6**	**0**
2011-12	Oldham Ath	40	11	**40**	**11**

LEE, Kieran (D) 125 5
H: 6 1 W: 12 00 b.Stalybridge 22-6-88
Source: Scholar.

2006-07	Manchester U	1	0		
2007-08	Manchester U	0	0	**1**	**0**
2007-08	*QPR*	7	0	**7**	**0**
2008-09	Oldham Ath	7	0		
2009-10	Oldham Ath	24	1		
2010-11	Oldham Ath	43	2		
2011-12	Oldham Ath	43	2	**117**	**5**

M'CHANGAMA, Youssouf (M) 44 4
H: 5 9 W: 11 00 b.Marseille 29-8-90
Honours: Comoros 5 full caps.

2009-10	Sedan B	10	2	**10**	**2**
2010-11	Troyes B	24	2	**24**	**2**
2011-12	Oldham Ath	10	0	**10**	**0**

M'VOTO, Jean-Yves (D) 80 4
H: 6 4 W: 14 00 b.Paris 6-9-88
Source: Paris St Germain. *Honours:* France Youth.

2007-08	Sunderland	0	0		
2008-09	Sunderland	0	0		
2009-10	Sunderland	0	0		
2009-10	*Southend U*	17	1	**17**	**1**
2010-11	Sunderland	0	0		
2010-11	*Oldham Ath*	27	2		
2011-12	Oldham Ath	36	1	**63**	**3**

MARSH-BROWN, Keanu (F) 40 3
H: 5 11 W: 12 04 b.Hammersmith 10-8-92
Source: Scholar.

2009-10	Fulham	0	0		
2010-11	Fulham	0	0		
2010-11	*Milton Keynes D*	17	2	**17**	**2**
2010-11	*Dundee U*	1	0		
2011-12	Fulham	0	0		
2011-12	Oldham Ath	11	1	**11**	**1**
2011-12	*Dundee U*	11	0	**12**	**0**

McGRATH, Philip (M) 1 0
H: 5 9 W: 10 01 b.Banbridge 7-4-92
Source: Scholar. *Honours:* Northern Ireland Youth.

2009-10	Oldham Ath	0	0		
2010-11	Oldham Ath	1	0		
2011-12	Oldham Ath	0	0	**1**	**0**

MELLOR, David (D) 21 1
H: 5 9 W: 11 09 b.Oldham 10-7-93
Source: Scholar.

2011-12	Oldham Ath	21	1	**21**	**1**

MILLAR, Kirk (M) 16 0
H: 5 9 W: 10 07 b.Belfast 7-7-92
Source: Scholar. *Honours:* Northern Ireland Under-21.

2008-09	Linfield	1	0	**1**	**0**
2009-10	Oldham Ath	6	0		
2010-11	Oldham Ath	5	0		
2011-12	Oldham Ath	4	0	**15**	**0**

MORAIS, Filipe (M) 169 16
H: 5 9 W: 11 10 b.Lisbon 21-11-85
Source: Trainee. *Honours:* Portugal Youth, Under-21.

2003-04	Chelsea	0	0		
2004-05	Chelsea	0	0		
2005-06	Chelsea	0	0		
2005-06	*Milton Keynes D*	13	0	**13**	**0**
2006-07	Millwall	12	1	**12**	**1**
2006-07	*St Johnstone*	13	1		
2007-08	Hibernian	28	1		
2008-09	Hibernian	2	0	**30**	**1**
2008-09	Inverness CT	12	3	**12**	**3**
2009-10	St Johnstone	30	2	**43**	**3**
2010-11	Oldham Ath	23	3		
2011-12	Oldham Ath	36	5	**59**	**8**

PARKER, Josh (F) 30 0
H: 5 11 W: 12 00 b.Slough 1-12-90
Source: Scholar.

2009-10	QPR	4	0		
2010-11	QPR	1	0	**5**	**0**
2010-11	*Northampton T*	3	0	**3**	**0**
2010-11	*Wycombe W*	1	0	**1**	**0**
2011-12	Oldham Ath	13	0	**13**	**0**
2011-12	*Dagenham & R*	8	0	**8**	**0**

REID, Reuben (F) 152 32
H: 6 0 W: 12 02 b.Bristol 26-7-88
Source: Millfield School.

2005-06	Plymouth Arg	1	0		
2006-07	Plymouth Arg	6	0		
2006-07	*Rochdale*	2	0	**2**	**0**
2006-07	*Torquay U*	7	2	**7**	**2**
2007-08	Plymouth Arg	0	0	**7**	**0**
2007-08	*Wycombe W*	11	1	**11**	**1**
2007-08	Brentford	10	1	**10**	**1**
2008-09	Rotherham U	41	18	**41**	**18**
2009-10	WBA	4	0		
2009-10	*Peterborough U*	13	0	**13**	**0**
2010-11	WBA	0	0	**4**	**0**
2010-11	*Walsall*	18	3	**18**	**3**
2010-11	Oldham Ath	19	2		
2011-12	Oldham Ath	20	5	**39**	**7**

SIMPSON, Robbie (F) 130 14
H: 6 1 W: 11 11 b.Poole 15-3-85
Source: Cambridge U.

2007-08	Coventry C	28	1		
2008-09	Coventry C	33	3	**61**	**4**
2009-10	Huddersfield T	13	0		
2010-11	Huddersfield T	0	0		
2010-11	*Brentford*	27	4	**27**	**4**
2011-12	Huddersfield T	0	0	**13**	**0**
2011-12	Oldham Ath	29	6	**29**	**6**

SMITH, Matt (F) 36 4
H: 6 6 W: 14 00 b.Birmingham 7-6-89
Source: Cheltenham T Scholar, Redditch U, Droylsden, Solihull Moors.

2011-12	Oldham Ath	28	3	**28**	**3**
2011-12	*Macclesfield T*	8	1	**8**	**1**

TARKOWSKI, James (D) 25 1
H: 6 1 W: 12 10 b.Manchester 19-11-92
Source: Scholar.

2010-11	Oldham Ath	9	0		
2011-12	Oldham Ath	16	1	**25**	**1**

TAYLOR, Chris (M) 254 33
H: 5 11 W: 11 00 b.Oldham 20-12-86
Source: Scholar.

2005-06	Oldham Ath	14	0		
2006-07	Oldham Ath	44	4		
2007-08	Oldham Ath	42	5		
2008-09	Oldham Ath	42	10		
2009-10	Oldham Ath	32	1		
2010-11	Oldham Ath	42	11		
2011-12	Oldham Ath	38	2	**254**	**33**

WESOLOWSKI, James (M) 140 9
H: 5 8 W: 11 11 b.Sydney 25-8-87
Source: Scholar. *Honours:* Australia Youth, Under-20.

2004-05	Leicester C	0	0		
2005-06	Leicester C	5	0		
2006-07	Leicester C	19	0		
2007-08	Leicester C	22	0		
2008-09	Leicester C	0	0		
2008-09	*Dundee U*	8	0	**8**	**0**
2008-09	*Cheltenham T*	4	0	**4**	**0**
2009-10	Leicester C	0	0	**46**	**0**
2009-10	*Hamilton A*	29	4	**29**	**4**
2010-11	Peterborough U	32	2	**32**	**2**
2011-12	Oldham Ath	21	3	**21**	**3**

WINCHESTER, Carl (D) 18 1
H: 5 10 W: 11 08 b.Belfast 12-4-93
Source: Scholar. *Honours:* Northern Ireland Under-21, 1 full cap.

2010-11	Oldham Ath	6	1		
2011-12	Oldham Ath	12	0	**18**	**1**

OXFORD U (61)

BATT, Damian (D) 90 1
H: 5 10 W: 11 06 b.Hoddesdon 16-9-84
Source: Norwich C Trainee.

2005-06	Barnet	22	0	**22**	**0**
From St Albans C, Stevenage, Woking, Fisher Ath, Grays Ath.					
2010-11	Oxford U	28	0		
2011-12	Oxford U	40	1	**68**	**1**

BROWN, Wayne (G) 282 0
H: 6 0 W: 13 11 b.Southampton 14-1-77
Source: Supersport U.

1993-94	Bristol C	1	0		
1994-95	Bristol C	0	0		
1995-96	Bristol C	0	0	**1**	**0**
From Weston-S-Mare					
1996-97	Chester C	2	0		
1997-98	Chester C	13	0		
1998-99	Chester C	23	0		
1999-2000	Chester C	46	0		
2000-01	Chester C	0	0		
2001-02	Chester C	0	0		
2004-05	Chester C	23	0		
2005-06	Chester C	0	0	**107**	**0**
2006-07	Hereford U	39	0		
2007-08	Hereford U	44	0	**83**	**0**
2008-09	Bury	35	0		
2009-10	Bury	41	0	**76**	**0**
2010-11	Supersport U	13	0	**13**	**0**
2011-12	Oxford U	2	0	**2**	**0**

CAPALDI, Tony (D) 225 12
H: 6 0 W: 11 08 b.Porsgrunn 12-8-81
Source: Trainee. *Honours:* Northern Ireland Youth, Under-21, 22 full caps.

1999-2000	Birmingham C	0	0		
2000-01	Birmingham C	0	0		
2001-02	Birmingham C	0	0		
2002-03	Birmingham C	0	0		
2002-03	Plymouth Arg	1	0		
2003-04	Plymouth Arg	33	7		
2004-05	Plymouth Arg	35	2		
2005-06	Plymouth Arg	41	3		
2006-07	Plymouth Arg	31	0	**141**	**12**

2007-08	Cardiff C	44	0		
2008-09	Cardiff C	3	0		
2009-10	Cardiff C	15	0	**62**	**0**
2009-10	*Leeds U*	3	0	**3**	**0**
2010-11	Morecambe	18	0	**18**	**0**
2011-12	Oxford U	1	0	**1**	**0**

CHAPMAN, Adam (M) 14 1
H: 5 10 W: 11 00 b.Doncaster 29-11-89
Source: Scholar. *Honours:* Northern Ireland Under-21.

2008-09	Sheffield U	0	0		
2009-10	Sheffield U	0	0		
2010-11	Oxford U	0	0		
2011-12	Oxford U	14	1	**14**	**1**

CLARKE, Ryan (G) 162 0
H: 6 3 W: 13 00 b.Bristol 30-4-82
Source: Scholar.

2001-02	Bristol R	1	0		
2002-03	Bristol R	2	0		
2003-04	Bristol R	2	0		
2004-05	Bristol R	18	0	**23**	**0**
2004-05	*Southend U*	1	0	**1**	**0**
2004-05	*Kidderminster H*	6	0	**6**	**0**
From Salisbury C.					
2009-10	Oxford U	44	0		
2010-11	Oxford U	46	0		
2011-12	Oxford U	42	0	**132**	**0**

CONSTABLE, James (F) 121 33
H: 6 2 W: 12 12 b.Malmesbury 4-10-84
Source: Chippenham T.

2005-06	Walsall	17	3		
2006-07	Walsall	6	0	**23**	**3**
From Kidderminster H.					
2007-08	Shrewsbury T	14	4	**14**	**4**
2010-11	Oxford U	44	15		
2011-12	Oxford U	40	11	**84**	**26**

CRADDOCK, Tom (F) 130 48
H: 5 11 W: 11 10 b.Durham 14-10-86
Source: Scholar.

2005-06	Middlesbrough	1	0		
2006-07	Middlesbrough	0	0		
2006-07	*Wrexham*	1	1	**1**	**1**
2007-08	Middlesbrough	3	0		
2007-08	*Hartlepool U*	4	0	**4**	**0**
2008-09	Middlesbrough	0	0	**4**	**0**
2008-09	Luton T	27	10		
2009-10	Luton T	46	22	**73**	**32**
2010-11	Oxford U	39	14		
2011-12	Oxford U	9	1	**48**	**15**

DAVIS, Liam (M) 141 10
H: 5 9 W: 11 07 b.Wandsworth 23-11-86
Source: Scholar.

2005-06	Coventry C	2	0		
2006-07	Coventry C	3	0		
2006-07	*Peterborough U*	7	0	**7**	**0**
2007-08	Coventry C	6	0	**11**	**0**
2008-09	Northampton T	29	4		
2009-10	Northampton T	17	2		
2010-11	Northampton T	33	2	**79**	**8**
2011-12	Oxford U	44	2	**44**	**2**

DUBERRY, Michael (D) 398 10
H: 6 1 W: 13 10 b.Enfield 14-10-75
Source: Trainee. *Honours:* England Under-21.

1993-94	Chelsea	1	0		
1994-95	Chelsea	0	0		
1995-96	Chelsea	22	0		
1995-96	*Bournemouth*	7	0	**7**	**0**
1996-97	Chelsea	15	1		
1997-98	Chelsea	23	0		
1998-99	Chelsea	25	0	**86**	**1**
1999-2000	Leeds U	13	1		
2000-01	Leeds U	5	0		
2001-02	Leeds U	3	0		
2002-03	Leeds U	14	0		
2003-04	Leeds U	19	3		
2004-05	Leeds U	4	0	**58**	**4**
2004-05	Stoke C	25	0		
2005-06	Stoke C	41	1		
2006-07	Stoke C	29	0	**95**	**1**
2006-07	Reading	8	0		
2007-08	Reading	13	0		
2008-09	Reading	27	0	**48**	**0**
2009-10	Wycombe W	18	0	**18**	**0**
2009-10	St Johnstone	17	1		
2010-11	St Johnstone	33	0	**50**	**1**
2011-12	Oxford U	36	3	**36**	**3**

FLETCHER, Matthew (F) 0 0
H: 6 0 W: 12 00 b.Sydney 12-5-92
Source: Scholar.

2009-10	Sunderland	0	0		
2010-11	Sunderland	0	0		
2011-12	Oxford U	0	0		

HALL, Asa (M) 177 29
H: 6 2 W: 11 09 b.Sandwell 29-11-86
Source: Scholar. *Honours:* England Youth, Under-20.

2004-05	Birmingham C	0	0		
2005-06	Birmingham C	0	0		
2005-06	*Boston U*	12	0	**12**	**0**
2006-07	Birmingham C	0	0		
2007-08	Birmingham C	0	0		
2007-08	*Shrewsbury T*	15	3	**15**	**3**
2008-09	Luton T	42	10		
2009-10	Luton T	33	5	**75**	**15**
2010-11	Oxford U	41	4		
2011-12	Oxford U	34	7	**75**	**11**

HESLOP, Simon (M) 76 6
H: 5 11 W: 11 00 b.York 1-5-87
Source: Scholar.

2005-06	Barnsley	0	0		
2006-07	Barnsley	1	0		
2007-08	Barnsley	0	0		
2008-09	Barnsley	0	0		
2008-09	*Grimsby T*	8	0	**8**	**0**
2009-10	Barnsley	0	0	**1**	**0**
2010-11	Oxford U	38	3		
2011-12	Oxford U	29	3	**67**	**6**

JOHNSON, Oli (F) 101 17
H: 5 11 W: 12 04 b.Wakefield 6-11-87
Source: Nostell MW.

2008-09	Stockport Co	24	6		
2009-10	Stockport Co	16	1	**40**	**7**
2009-10	Norwich C	17	4		
2010-11	Norwich C	4	0		
2010-11	*Yeovil T*	17	3		
2011-12	Norwich C	0	0	**21**	**4**
2011-12	*Yeovil T*	6	0	**23**	**3**
2011-12	Oxford U	17	3	**17**	**3**

KINNIBURGH, Steve (D) 18 0
H: 6 0 W: 11 00 b.Glasgow 13-6-89

2007-08	Rangers	0	0		
2008-09	Rangers	0	0		
2008-09	*Queen of the S*	2	0	**2**	**0**
2008-09	*St Johnstone*	0	0		
2010-11	Partick Th	4	0	**4**	**0**
2010-11	Oxford U	11	0		
2011-12	Oxford U	1	0	**12**	**0**

LEVEN, Peter (M) 257 39
H: 5 11 W: 12 13 b.Glasgow 27-9-83
Source: Rangers.

2004-05	Kilmarnock	32	4		
2005-06	Kilmarnock	6	0		
2006-07	Kilmarnock	27	1	**65**	**5**
2007-08	Chesterfield	42	6	**42**	**6**
2008-09	Milton Keynes D	40	10		
2009-10	Milton Keynes D	31	4		
2010-11	Milton Keynes D	40	8	**111**	**22**
2011-12	Oxford U	39	6	**39**	**6**

McLAREN, Paul (M) 540 26
H: 6 0 W: 13 04 b.High Wycombe 17-11-76
Source: Trainee.

1993-94	Luton T	1	0		
1994-95	Luton T	0	0		
1995-96	Luton T	12	1		
1996-97	Luton T	24	0		
1997-98	Luton T	43	0		
1998-99	Luton T	23	0		
1999-2000	Luton T	29	1		
2000-01	Luton T	35	2	**167**	**4**
2001-02	Sheffield W	35	2		
2002-03	Sheffield W	36	4		
2003-04	Sheffield W	25	2	**96**	**8**
2004-05	Rotherham U	33	1		
2005-06	Rotherham U	39	3	**72**	**4**
2006-07	Tranmere R	42	1		
2007-08	Tranmere R	43	4		
2008-09	Bradford C	34	3	**34**	**3**
2009-10	Tranmere R	38	0		
2010-11	Tranmere R	6	0	**129**	**5**
2010-11	Oxford U	24	1		
2011-12	Oxford U	18	1	**42**	**2**

PITTMAN, Jon-Paul (F) 108 19
H: 5 9 W: 11 00 b.Oklahoma City 24-10-86
Source: Scholar.

2005-06	Nottingham F	0	0		
2005-06	*Hartlepool U*	3	0	**3**	**0**
2006-07	*Bury*	9	1	**9**	**1**
2006-07	Doncaster R	0	0		
From Crawley T.					
2008-09	Wycombe W	17	3		
2009-10	Wycombe W	41	7		
2010-11	Wycombe W	19	4	**77**	**14**
2011-12	Oxford U	15	3	**15**	**3**
2011-12	*Crawley T*	4	1	**4**	**1**

POTTER, Alfie (M) 65 4
H: 5 7 W: 9 06 b.Islington 9-1-89
Source: Millwall.

2007-08	Peterborough U	2	0	**2**	**0**
From Kettering T.					
2010-11	Oxford U	38	2		
From Kettering T.					
2011-12	Oxford U	25	2	**63**	**4**

SMALLEY, Deane (M) 171 23
H: 6 0 W: 11 10 b.Chadderton 5-9-88
Source: Scholar.

2006-07	Oldham Ath	2	0		
2007-08	Oldham Ath	37	2		
2008-09	Oldham Ath	34	5		
2009-10	Oldham Ath	29	3		
2010-11	Oldham Ath	3	0	**105**	**10**
2010-11	*Rochdale*	3	0	**3**	**0**
2010-11	*Chesterfield*	28	12	**28**	**12**
2011-12	Oxford U	22	1	**22**	**1**
2011-12	*Bradford C*	13	0	**13**	**0**

TONKIN, Anthony (D) 170 0
H: 5 11 W: 12 02 b.Newlyn 17-1-80
Source: Yeovil T.

2002-03	Stockport Co	24	0		
2003-04	Stockport Co	0	0	**24**	**0**
2003-04	Crewe Alex	26	0		
2004-05	Crewe Alex	35	0		
2005-06	Crewe Alex	27	0	**88**	**0**
2006-07	Yeovil T	5	0	**5**	**0**
From Forest Green R, Cambridge U.					
2010-11	Oxford U	39	0		
2011-12	Oxford U	14	0	**53**	**0**

WHING, Andrew (D) 285 4
H: 6 0 W: 12 00 b.Birmingham 20-9-84
Source: Scholar.

2002-03	Coventry C	14	0		
2003-04	Coventry C	28	1		
2004-05	Coventry C	16	1		
2005-06	Coventry C	32	0		
2006-07	Coventry C	16	0	**106**	**2**
2006-07	*Brighton & HA*	12	0		
2007-08	Brighton & HA	42	0		
2008-09	Brighton & HA	40	0		
2009-10	Brighton & HA	9	0		
2009-10	*Chesterfield*	11	0	**11**	**0**
2010-11	Brighton & HA	0	0	**103**	**0**
2010-11	Leyton Orient	24	2	**24**	**2**
2011-12	Oxford U	41	0	**41**	**0**

WILSON, Mark (M) 235 10
H: 5 10 W: 12 07 b.Scunthorpe 9-2-79
Source: Trainee. *Honours:* England Schools, Youth, Under-21.

1995-96	Manchester U	0	0		
1996-97	Manchester U	0	0		
1997-98	Manchester U	0	0		
1997-98	*Wrexham*	13	4	**13**	**4**
1998-99	Manchester U	0	0		
1999-2000	Manchester U	3	0		
2000-01	Manchester U	0	0	**3**	**0**
2001-02	Middlesbrough	10	0		
2002-03	Middlesbrough	6	0		
2002-03	*Stoke C*	4	0	**4**	**0**
2003-04	Middlesbrough	0	0		
2003-04	*Swansea C*	12	2	**12**	**2**
2003-04	*Sheffield W*	3	0	**3**	**0**
2004-05	Middlesbrough	0	0	**16**	**0**
2004-05	*Doncaster R*	3	0		
2004-05	*Livingston*	5	0	**5**	**0**
2005	Dallas	8	0		
2006	Dallas	12	1	**20**	**1**
2006-07	Doncaster R	22	1		
2007-08	Doncaster R	31	1		
2008-09	Doncaster R	22	1		
2008-09	*Tranmere R*	5	0	**5**	**0**
2009-10	Doncaster R	35	0		
2010-11	Doncaster R	28	0		
2011-12	Doncaster R	3	0	**144**	**3**
2011-12	*Walsall*	4	0	**4**	**0**
2011-12	Oxford U	6	0	**6**	**0**

WOODLEY, Aaron (F) **0** **0**

b.Abingdon 13-10-92

Source: Scholar.

2010-11	Oxford U	0	0		
2011-12	Oxford U	0	0		

WORLEY, Harry (D) **97** **2**

H: 6 3 W: 13 00 b.Warrington 25-11-88

Source: Scholar.

2005-06	Chelsea	0	0		
2006-07	Chelsea	0	0		
2006-07	*Doncaster R*	10	0	**10**	**0**
2007-08	Chelsea	0	0		
2007-08	*Carlisle U*	1	0	**1**	**0**
2007-08	Leicester C	2	0		
2008-09	Leicester C	0	0		
2008-09	*Luton T*	8	0	**8**	**0**
2009-10	Leicester C	0	0	**2**	**0**
2009-10	*Crewe Alex*	23	1	**23**	**1**
2010-11	Oxford U	43	1		
2011-12	Oxford U	10	0	**53**	**1**

WRIGHT, Jake (D) **85** **0**

H: 5 10 W: 11 07 b.Keighley 11-3-86

Source: Scholar.

2005-06	Bradford C	1	0	**1**	**0**

From Halifax T, Crawley T.

2009-10	Brighton & HA	6	0	**6**	**0**
2010-11	Oxford U	35	0		
2011-12	Oxford U	43	0	**78**	**0**

PETERBOROUGH U (62)

AJOSE, Nicholas (F) **49** **14**

H: 5 8 W: 11 00 b.Bury 7-10-91

Source: Scholar.

2009-10	Manchester U	0	0		
2010-11	Manchester U	0	0		
2010-11	*Bury*	28	13	**28**	**13**
2011-12	Peterborough U	2	0	**2**	**0**
2011-12	*Scunthorpe U*	7	0	**7**	**0**
2011-12	*Chesterfield*	12	1	**12**	**1**

ALCOCK, Craig (D) **148** **3**

H: 5 8 W: 11 00 b.Cornwall 8-12-87

Source: Youth.

2006-07	Yeovil T	1	0		
2007-08	Yeovil T	8	0		
2008-09	Yeovil T	30	1		
2009-10	Yeovil T	42	1		
2010-11	Yeovil T	26	1	**107**	**3**
2011-12	Peterborough U	41	0	**41**	**0**

BALL, David (F) **73** **14**

H: 6 0 W: 11 08 b.Whitefield 14-12-89

Source: Scholar.

2007-08	Manchester C	0	0		
2008-09	Manchester C	0	0		
2009-10	Manchester C	0	0		
2010-11	Manchester C	0	0		
2010-11	*Swindon T*	18	2	**18**	**2**
2010-11	Peterborough U	19	5		
2011-12	Peterborough U	22	4	**41**	**9**
2011-12	*Rochdale*	14	3	**14**	**3**

BARNETT, Tyrone (F) **84** **31**

H: 6 3 W: 13 05 b.Stevenage 28-10-85

Source: Rushall Olympic, AFC Telford U, Willenhall T, Hednesford T.

2010-11	Macclesfield T	45	13	**45**	**13**
2011-12	Crawley T	26	14	**26**	**14**
2011-12	Peterborough U	13	4	**13**	**4**

BOYD, George (M) **238** **59**

H: 5 10 W: 11 07 b.Chatham 2-10-85

Source: Stevenage B. *Honours:* Scotland B.

2006-07	Peterborough U	20	6		
2007-08	Peterborough U	46	12		
2008-09	Peterborough U	46	9		
2009-10	Peterborough U	32	9		
2009-10	*Nottingham F*	6	1	**6**	**1**
2010-11	Peterborough U	43	15		
2011-12	Peterborough U	45	7	**232**	**58**

BREEZE, Matthew (M) **0** **0**

b.Worcester 6-2-93

Source: Scholar.

2010-11	Peterborough U	0	0		
2011-12	Peterborough U	0	0		

BRISLEY, Shaun (M) **135** **6**

H: 6 2 W: 12 02 b.Macclesfield 6-5-90

Source: Scholar.

2007-08	Macclesfield T	10	2		
2008-09	Macclesfield T	38	0		
2009-10	Macclesfield T	33	1		
2010-11	Macclesfield T	14	0		
2011-12	Macclesfield T	29	3	**124**	**6**
2011-12	Peterborough U	11	0	**11**	**0**

COULSON, Charlie (M) **1** **0**

b.Kettering 11-1-96

Source: Schoolboy.

2011-12	Peterborough U	1	0	**1**	**0**

DAY, Joe (G) **0** **0**

b.Brighton 13-8-90

Source: Rushden & D.

2011-12	Peterborough U	0	0		

FRECKLINGTON, Lee (M) **212** **29**

H: 5 8 W: 11 00 b.Lincoln 8-9-85

Source: Scholar. *Honours:* Eire B.

2003-04	Lincoln C	0	0		
2004-05	Lincoln C	3	0		
2005-06	Lincoln C	18	2		
2006-07	Lincoln C	42	8		
2007-08	Lincoln C	34	4		
2008-09	Lincoln C	27	7	**124**	**21**
2008-09	Peterborough U	7	0		
2009-10	Peterborough U	35	2		
2010-11	Peterborough U	9	1		
2011-12	Peterborough U	37	5	**88**	**8**

GRANT, Peter (D) **0** **0**

b.Scotland

Source: Scholar.

2011-12	Peterborough U	0	0		

GRIFFITHS, Scott (D) **164** **1**

H: 5 9 W: 11 08 b.Westminster 27-11-85

Source: Aveley.

2007-08	Dagenham & R	41	0		
2008-09	Dagenham & R	44	0		
2009-10	Dagenham & R	13	1	**98**	**1**
2009-10	Peterborough U	20	0		
2010-11	Peterborough U	0	0		
2010-11	*Chesterfield*	29	0		
2011-12	Peterborough U	0	0	**20**	**0**
2011-12	*Crawley T*	6	0	**6**	**0**
2011-12	*Chesterfield*	3	0	**32**	**0**
2011-12	*Rotherham U*	8	0	**8**	**0**

HIBBERT, Dave (F) **160** **34**

H: 6 2 W: 12 00 b.Eccleshall 28-1-86

Source: Scholar.

2004-05	Port Vale	9	2	**9**	**2**
2005-06	Preston NE	10	0		
2006-07	Preston NE	0	0	**10**	**0**
2006-07	*Rotherham U*	21	2	**21**	**2**
2006-07	*Bradford C*	8	0	**8**	**0**
2007-08	Shrewsbury T	44	12		
2008-09	Shrewsbury T	23	3		
2009-10	Shrewsbury T	38	14	**105**	**29**
2010-11	Peterborough U	7	1		
2011-12	Peterborough U	0	0	**7**	**1**

JONES, Paul (G) **126** **0**

H: 6 3 W: 13 00 b.Maidstone 28-6-86

Source: Leyton Orient Scholar.

2008-09	Exeter C	46	0		
2009-10	Exeter C	26	0		
2010-11	Exeter C	18	0	**90**	**0**
2010-11	*Peterborough U*	1	0		
2011-12	Peterborough U	35	0	**36**	**0**

KEARNS, Daniel (M) **69** **9**

H: 5 10 W: 12 00 b.Belfast 26-8-91

Source: West Ham U. *Honours:* Northern Ireland Youth, Eire Youth, Under-21, Under-23.

2010	Dundalk	12	0		
2011	Dundalk	37	9	**49**	**9**
2011-12	Peterborough U	20	0	**20**	**0**

LEWIS, Joe (G) **191** **0**

H: 6 5 W: 12 10 b.Bungay 6-10-87

Source: Scholar. *Honours:* England Youth, Under-21.

2004-05	Norwich C	0	0		
2005-06	Norwich C	0	0		
2006-07	Norwich C	0	0		
2006-07	*Stockport Co*	5	0	**5**	**0**
2007-08	Norwich C	0	0		
2007-08	*Morecambe*	19	0	**19**	**0**
2007-08	Peterborough U	22	0		
2008-09	Peterborough U	46	0		
2009-10	Peterborough U	43	0		
2010-11	Peterborough U	45	0		
2011-12	Peterborough U	11	0	**167**	**0**

LITTLE, Mark (D) **144** **1**

H: 6 1 W: 12 10 b.Worcester 20-8-88

Source: Scholar. *Honours:* England Youth.

2005-06	Wolverhampton W	0	0		
2006-07	Wolverhampton W	26	0		
2007-08	Wolverhampton W	1	0		
2007-08	*Northampton T*	17	0		
2008-09	Wolverhampton W	0	0		
2008-09	*Northampton T*	9	0	**26**	**0**
2009-10	Wolverhampton W	0	0	**27**	**0**
2009-10	*Chesterfield*	12	0	**12**	**0**
2009-10	*Peterborough U*	9	0		
2010-11	Peterborough U	35	0		
2011-12	Peterborough U	35	1	**79**	**1**

McCANN, Grant (M) **418** **73**

H: 5 10 W: 11 00 b.Belfast 14-4-80

Source: Trainee. *Honours:* Northern Ireland Youth, Under-21, 39 full caps, 4 goals.

1998-99	West Ham U	0	0		
1999-2000	West Ham U	0	0		
2000-01	West Ham U	1	0		
2000-01	*Notts Co*	2	0	**2**	**0**
2000-01	*Cheltenham T*	30	3		
2001-02	West Ham U	3	0		
2002-03	West Ham U	0	0	**4**	**0**
2002-03	Cheltenham T	27	6		
2003-04	Cheltenham T	43	8		
2004-05	Cheltenham T	39	4		
2005-06	Cheltenham T	39	8		
2006-07	Cheltenham T	15	5	**193**	**34**
2006-07	Barnsley	22	1		
2007-08	Barnsley	19	3	**41**	**4**
2007-08	Scunthorpe U	14	1		
2008-09	Scunthorpe U	43	9		
2009-10	Scunthorpe U	42	8	**99**	**18**
2010-11	Peterborough U	38	9		
2011-12	Peterborough U	41	8	**79**	**17**

MILLS, Danny (F) **5** **0**

H: 6 4 W: 13 02 b.Croydon 27-11-91

Source: Crawley T.

2009-10	Peterborough U	3	0		
2009-10	*Torquay U*	2	0	**2**	**0**
2010-11	Peterborough U	0	0		
2011-12	Peterborough U	0	0	**3**	**0**

NEWELL, Joe (M) **16** **1**

H: 5 11 W: 11 02 b.Tamworth 15-3-93

Source: Scholar.

2010-11	Peterborough U	2	0		
2011-12	Peterborough U	14	1	**16**	**1**

NTLHE, Kgosietsile (D) **2** **0**

H: 5 9 W: 10 05 b.Pretoria 21-2-94

Source: Scholar.

2010-11	Peterborough U	0	0		
2011-12	Peterborough U	2	0	**2**	**0**

RALPH, Nathan (D) **0** **0**

b.Dunmow 14-2-93

Source: Scholar.

2011-12	Peterborough U	0	0		

ROWE, Tommy (M) **182** **24**

H: 5 11 W: 12 11 b.Manchester 1-5-89

Source: Scholar.

2006-07	Stockport Co	4	0		
2007-08	Stockport Co	24	6		
2008-09	Stockport Co	44	7	**72**	**13**
2008-09	Peterborough U	0	0		
2009-10	Peterborough U	32	2		
2010-11	Peterborough U	35	5		
2011-12	Peterborough U	43	4	**110**	**11**

SAGE, James (D) **0** **0**

2011-12	Peterborough U	0	0		

SINCLAIR, Emile (F) **149** **25**

H: 6 0 W: 11 04 b.Leeds 29-12-87

Source: Scholar.

2007-08	Nottingham F	12	1		
2007-08	*Brentford*	4	0	**4**	**0**
2008-09	Nottingham F	3	0	**15**	**1**
2008-09	*Macclesfield T*	17	1		
2009-10	Macclesfield T	42	7		
2010-11	Macclesfield T	31	5		
2011-12	Macclesfield T	5	1	**95**	**14**
2011-12	Peterborough U	35	10	**35**	**10**

TAYLOR, Paul (F) **58** **12**

H: 5 11 W: 11 02 b.Liverpool 4-11-87

Source: Vauxhall M.

on loan from Vauxhall M.

2008-09	*Chester C*	9	0	**9**	**0**
2009-10	Montegnee	1	0	**1**	**0**

2009-10 *Charleoi* 3 0 **3 0**
2010-11 Anderlecht 0 0
2010-11 Peterborough U 1 0
2011-12 Peterborough U 44 12 **45 12**

TOMLIN, Lee (F) 74 16
H: 5 11 W: 11 09 b.Leicester 12-1-89
Source: Leicester C, Rushden & D.
2010-11 Peterborough U 37 8
2011-12 Peterborough U 37 8 **74 16**

ZAKUANI, Gaby (D) 247 7
H: 6 1 W: 12 13 b.DR Congo 31-5-86
Source: Scholar. *Honours:* DR Congo 1 full cap.
2002-03 Leyton Orient 1 0
2003-04 Leyton Orient 10 2
2004-05 Leyton Orient 33 0
2005-06 Leyton Orient 43 1 **87 3**
2006-07 Fulham 0 0
2006-07 *Stoke C* 9 0
2007-08 Fulham 0 0
2007-08 *Stoke C* 19 0 **28 0**
2008-09 Fulham 0 0
2008-09 Peterborough U 32 1
2009-10 Peterborough U 29 0
2010-11 Peterborough U 30 2
2011-12 Peterborough U 41 1 **132 4**

PLYMOUTH ARG (63)

BERRY, Durrell (D) 35 0
H: 5 11 W: 11 11 b.Derby 27-5-92
Source: Aston Villa.
2010-11 Aston Villa 0 0
2011-12 Plymouth Arg 35 0 **35 0**

BHASERA, Onismor (D) 181 4
H: 5 9 W: 11 13 b.Mutare 7-12-86
Honours: Zimbabwe 16 full caps.
2004 Harare U 0 0
2004-05 Tembisa Classic 14 0 **14 0**
2005-06 Maritzburg U 27 0
2006-07 Maritzburg U 26 1 **53 1**
2007-08 Kaizer Chiefs 26 1
2008-09 Kaizer Chiefs 25 0 **51 1**
2009-10 Plymouth Arg 7 0
2010-11 Plymouth Arg 29 1
2011-12 Plymouth Arg 27 1 **63 2**

BLANCHARD, Maximo (D) 144 4
H: 5 11 W: 11 13 b.Alencon 27-9-86
2006-07 Laval 4 0
2007-08 Laval 22 0 **26 0**
2008-09 Entente 35 1 **35 1**
2009-10 Moulins 35 1 **35 1**
2010-11 Tranmere R 20 0 **20 0**
2011-12 Plymouth Arg 28 2 **28 2**

CHADWICK, Nick (F) 159 25
H: 6 0 W: 12 08 b.Market Drayton 26-10-82
Source: Scholar.
1999-2000 Everton 0 0
2000-01 Everton 0 0
2001-02 Everton 9 3
2002-03 Everton 1 0
2002-03 *Derby Co* 6 0 **6 0**
2003-04 Everton 3 0
2003-04 *Millwall* 15 4 **15 4**
2004-05 Everton 1 0 **14 3**
2004-05 Plymouth Arg 15 1
2005-06 Plymouth Arg 37 5
2006-07 Plymouth Arg 16 2
2007-08 Plymouth Arg 9 2
2008-09 Plymouth Arg 0 0
2008-09 Hereford U 10 1 **10 1**
2008-09 Shrewsbury T 15 2 **15 2**
From Chester C, Barrow.
2011-12 Stockport 0 0
2011-12 Plymouth Arg 22 5 **99 15**

CHENOWETH, Ollie (G) 1 0
H: 6 1 W: 11 09 b.Liskeard 17-2-92
Source: Scholar.
2010-11 Plymouth Arg 0 0
2011-12 Plymouth Arg 1 0 **1 0**

COLE, Jake (G) 130 0
H: 6 2 W: 13 00 b.Hammersmith 11-9-85
Source: Scholar.
2005-06 QPR 3 0
2006-07 QPR 3 0
2007-08 QPR 0 0
2008-09 QPR 0 0 **6 0**
2008-09 *Barnet* 10 0
2009-10 Barnet 46 0
2010-11 Barnet 31 0 **87 0**
2011-12 Plymouth Arg 37 0 **37 0**

DALEY, Luke (F) 31 1
H: 5 11 W: 11 00 b.Northampton 10-11-89
Source: Scholar.
2007-08 Norwich C 0 0
2008-09 Norwich C 3 0
2009-10 Norwich C 7 0
2010-11 Norwich C 1 0 **11 0**
2010-11 *Stevenage* 2 0 **2 0**
2011-12 Plymouth Arg 18 1 **18 1**

FEENEY, Warren (F) 321 72
H: 5 8 W: 12 04 b.Belfast 17-1-81
Source: Trainee. *Honours:* Northern Ireland Schools, Youth, Under-21, 46 full caps, 5 goals.
1997-98 Leeds U 0 0
1998-99 Leeds U 0 0
1999-2000 Leeds U 0 0
2000-01 Leeds U 0 0
2000-01 *Bournemouth* 10 4
2001-02 Bournemouth 37 13
2002-03 Bournemouth 21 7
2003-04 Bournemouth 40 12 **108 36**
2004-05 Stockport Co 31 15 **31 15**
2004-05 Luton T 6 0
2005-06 Luton T 42 6
2006-07 Luton T 29 2 **77 8**
2006-07 *Cardiff C* 6 0
2007-08 Cardiff C 5 0
2007-08 *Swansea C* 10 5 **10 5**
2008-09 *Dundee U* 23 6 **23 6**
2008-09 Cardiff C 0 0
2009-10 Cardiff C 9 0 **20 0**
2009-10 *Sheffield W* 1 0 **1 0**
2010-11 Oldham Ath 23 0 **23 0**
2011-12 Plymouth Arg 28 2 **28 2**

FLETCHER, Carl (M) 414 34
H: 5 10 W: 11 07 b.Camberley 7-4-80
Source: Trainee. *Honours:* Wales 36 full caps, 1 goal.
1997-98 Bournemouth 1 0
1998-99 Bournemouth 1 0
1999-2000 Bournemouth 25 3
2000-01 Bournemouth 43 6
2001-02 Bournemouth 35 5
2002-03 Bournemouth 42 1
2003-04 Bournemouth 40 2
2004-05 Bournemouth 6 2 **193 19**
2004-05 West Ham U 32 2
2005-06 West Ham U 12 1 **44 3**
2005-06 *Watford* 3 0 **3 0**
2006-07 Crystal Palace 37 3
2007-08 Crystal Palace 28 1
2008-09 Crystal Palace 3 0 **68 4**
2008-09 *Nottingham F* 5 0 **5 0**
2008-09 *Plymouth Arg* 13 1
2009-10 Plymouth Arg 41 4
2010-11 Plymouth Arg 38 2
2011-12 Plymouth Arg 9 1 **101 8**

HARPER-PENMAN, Ged (M) 2 0
H: 5 7 W: 11 00 b.Bideford 2-2-94
Source: Scholar.
2010-11 Plymouth Arg 2 0
2011-12 Plymouth Arg 0 0 **2 0**

HOURIHANE, Conor (M) 38 2
H: 5 11 W: 9 11 b.Cork 2-2-91
Source: Scholar. *Honours:* Eire Under-21.
2008-09 Sunderland 0 0
2009-10 Sunderland 0 0
2010-11 Ipswich T 0 0
2011-12 Plymouth Arg 38 2 **38 2**

JOHNSON, Damien (M) 313 9
H: 5 9 W: 11 09 b.Lisburn 18-11-78
Source: Trainee. *Honours:* Northern Ireland Youth, Under-21, 56 full caps.
1995-96 Blackburn R 0 0
1996-97 Blackburn R 0 0
1997-98 Blackburn R 0 0
1997-98 *Nottingham F* 6 0 **6 0**
1998-99 Blackburn R 21 1
1999-2000 Blackburn R 16 1
2000-01 Blackburn R 16 0
2001-02 Blackburn R 7 1 **60 3**
2001-02 Birmingham C 8 1
2002-03 Birmingham C 30 1
2003-04 Birmingham C 35 1
2004-05 Birmingham C 36 0
2005-06 Birmingham C 31 0
2006-07 Birmingham C 26 1
2007-08 Birmingham C 17 0
2008-09 Birmingham C 9 0
2009-10 Birmingham C 1 0 **193 4**
2009-10 Plymouth Arg 20 2
2010-11 Plymouth Arg 0 0
2010-11 *Huddersfield T* 16 0
2011-12 Plymouth Arg 0 0 **20 2**
2011-12 *Huddersfield T* 18 0 **34 0**

LARRIEU, Romain (G) 312 0
H: 6 4 W: 13 01 b.Mont-de-Marsan 31-8-76
Source: Montpellier, ASOA Valence.
Honours: France Youth.
2000-01 Plymouth Arg 15 0
2001-02 Plymouth Arg 45 0
2002-03 Plymouth Arg 43 0
2003-04 Plymouth Arg 6 0
2004-05 Plymouth Arg 23 0
2005-06 Plymouth Arg 45 0
2006-07 Plymouth Arg 6 0
2006-07 *Gillingham* 14 0 **14 0**
2007-08 Plymouth Arg 15 0
2007-08 *Yeovil T* 6 0 **6 0**
2008-09 Plymouth Arg 41 0
2009-10 Plymouth Arg 25 0
2010-11 Plymouth Arg 18 0
2011-12 Plymouth Arg 10 0 **292 0**

LECOINTE, Matt (F) 19 2
H: 5 10 W: 10 07 b.Plymouth 28-10-94
Source: Scholar. *Honours:* England Youth.
2011-12 Plymouth Arg 19 2 **19 2**

LENNOX, Joe (M) 8 0
H: 5 7 W: 11 00 b.Bristol 22-11-91
Source: Scholar.
2010-11 Bristol C 0 0
2011-12 Bristol C 0 0
2011-12 Plymouth Arg 8 0 **8 0**

NELSON, Curtis (D) 52 0
H: 6 0 W: 11 07 b.Newcastle-u-Lyme 21-5-93
Source: Scholar. *Honours:* England Youth.
2010-11 Plymouth Arg 35 0
2011-12 Plymouth Arg 17 0 **52 0**

PURSE, Darren (D) 518 32
H: 6 2 W: 12 08 b.Stepney 14-2-77
Source: Trainee. *Honours:* England Under-21.
1993-94 Leyton Orient 5 0
1994-95 Leyton Orient 38 3
1995-96 Leyton Orient 12 0 **55 3**
1996-97 Oxford U 31 1
1997-98 Oxford U 28 4 **59 5**
1997-98 Birmingham C 8 0
1998-99 Birmingham C 20 0
1999-2000 Birmingham C 38 2
2000-01 Birmingham C 37 3
2001-02 Birmingham C 36 3
2002-03 Birmingham C 20 1
2003-04 Birmingham C 9 0 **168 9**
2004-05 WBA 22 0 **22 0**
2005-06 Cardiff C 39 5
2006-07 Cardiff C 31 4
2007-08 Cardiff C 18 1
2008-09 Cardiff C 23 0 **111 10**
2009-10 Sheffield W 39 2
2010-11 Sheffield W 22 0 **61 2**
2010-11 Millwall 13 1
2011-12 Millwall 0 0 **13 1**
2011-12 *Yeovil T* 5 0 **5 0**
2011-12 Plymouth Arg 24 2 **24 2**

RICHARDS, Jamie (D) 0 0
b.Newton Abbot 24-6-94
Source: Scholar.
2011-12 Plymouth Arg 0 0

SIMS, Jared (F) 3 0
H: 5 9 W: 10 05 b.Truro 16-10-93
Source: Scholar.
2011-12 Plymouth Arg 3 0 **3 0**

SOUKOUNA, Ladjie (D) 20 1
H: 6 3 W: 12 08 b.Paris 15-12-90
Source: Creteil.
2011-12 Plymouth Arg 20 1 **20 1**

VASSELL, Isaac (F) 6 0
H: 5 7 W: 11 02 b.Newquay 9-9-93
Source: Scholar.
2011-12 Plymouth Arg 6 0 **6 0**

WALTON, Simon (M) **167 16**
H: 6 1 W: 13 05 b.Sherburn-in-Elmet 13-9-87
Source: Scholar. *Honours:* England Youth.

Season	Club				
2004-05	Leeds U	30	3		
2005-06	Leeds U	4	0	**34**	**3**
2006-07	Charlton Ath	0	0		
2006-07	*Ipswich T*	19	3	**19**	**3**
2006-07	*Cardiff C*	6	0	**6**	**0**
2007-08	QPR	5	0	**5**	**0**
2007-08	*Hull C*	10	0	**10**	**0**
2008-09	Plymouth Arg	13	0		
2008-09	*Blackpool*	1	0	**1**	**0**
2009-10	Plymouth Arg	0	0		
2009-10	*Crewe Alex*	31	1	**31**	**1**
2010-11	Plymouth Arg	7	1		
2010-11	*Sheffield U*	0	0		
2011-12	Plymouth Arg	41	8	**61**	**9**

WILLIAMS, Robbie (D) **210 15**
H: 5 10 W: 11 13 b.Pontefract 2-10-84
Source: Scholar.

Season	Club				
2002-03	Barnsley	8	0		
2003-04	Barnsley	4	1		
2004-05	Barnsley	17	1		
2005-06	Barnsley	22	2		
2006-07	Barnsley	15	0		
2006-07	*Blackpool*	9	4	**9**	**4**
2007-08	Barnsley	0	0	**66**	**4**
2007-08	Huddersfield T	25	2		
2008-09	Huddersfield T	35	0		
2009-10	Huddersfield T	17	2	**77**	**4**
2010-11	Stockport Co	22	1	**22**	**1**
2010-11	Rochdale	9	0	**9**	**0**
2011-12	Plymouth Arg	27	2	**27**	**2**

WOTTON, Paul (D) **518 59**
H: 5 11 W: 12 00 b.Plymouth 17-8-77
Source: Trainee.

Season	Club				
1994-95	Plymouth Arg	7	0		
1995-96	Plymouth Arg	1	0		
1996-97	Plymouth Arg	9	1		
1997-98	Plymouth Arg	34	1		
1998-99	Plymouth Arg	36	1		
1999-2000	Plymouth Arg	23	0		
2000-01	Plymouth Arg	42	4		
2001-02	Plymouth Arg	46	5		
2002-03	Plymouth Arg	43	8		
2003-04	Plymouth Arg	38	9		
2004-05	Plymouth Arg	40	12		
2005-06	Plymouth Arg	45	8		
2006-07	Plymouth Arg	22	4		
2007-08	Plymouth Arg	8	1		
2008-09	Southampton	29	0		
2009-10	Southampton	26	0		
2010-11	Southampton	2	0	**57**	**0**
2010-11	*Oxford U*	4	0	**4**	**0**
2010-11	Yeovil T	23	2		
2011-12	Yeovil T	22	2	**45**	**4**
2011-12	Plymouth Arg	18	1	**412**	**55**

YOUNG, Luke (M) **33 2**
H: 5 8 W: 11 05 b.Ivybridge 22-2-93
Source: Scholar.

Season	Club				
2010-11	Plymouth Arg	5	0		
2011-12	Plymouth Arg	28	2	**33**	**2**

PORT VALE (64)

BURGE, Ryan (M) **8 0**
H: 5 10 W: 10 03 b.Cheltenham 12-10-88
Source: Scholar.

Season	Club				
2005-06	Birmingham C	0	0		
2006-07	Birmingham C	0	0		
2007-08	Birmingham C	0	0		
2008-09	Barnet	2	0	**2**	**0**
From Jerez Industrial.					
2010-11	Doncaster R	1	0	**1**	**0**
2010-11	*Oxford U*	5	0	**5**	**0**
From Jerez Industrial.					
2011-12	Port Vale	0	0		

DAVIS, Joe (D) **9 0**
H: 6 0 W: 11 07 b.Burnley 10-11-93
Source: Scholar.

Season	Club				
2010-11	Port Vale	1	0		
2011-12	Port Vale	8	0	**9**	**0**

DODDS, Louis (M) **209 39**
H: 5 10 W: 12 04 b.Sheffield 8-10-86
Source: Scholar.

Season	Club				
2005-06	Leicester C	0	0		
2006-07	Leicester C	0	0		
2006-07	*Rochdale*	12	2	**12**	**2**
2007-08	Leicester C	0	0		
2007-08	*Lincoln C*	41	9	**41**	**9**
2008-09	Port Vale	44	7		
2009-10	Port Vale	44	6		
2010-11	Port Vale	33	7		
2011-12	Port Vale	35	8	**156**	**28**

GREEN, Mike (D) **4 0**
H: 6 0 W: 12 00 b. 12-5-89
Source: Eastleigh, AFC Totton, Eastleigh.

Season	Club				
2011-12	Port Vale	4	0	**4**	**0**

GRIFFITH, Anthony (M) **171 2**
H: 6 0 W: 12 00 b.Huddersfield 28-10-86
Source: Glasshoughton W.

Season	Club				
2005-06	Doncaster R	4	0		
2005-06	*Oxford U*	0	0		
2006-07	Doncaster R	2	0		
2006-07	*Darlington*	4	0	**4**	**0**
2007-08	Doncaster R	0	0	**6**	**0**
2007-08	Port Vale	0	0		
2008-09	Port Vale	38	0		
2009-10	Port Vale	40	0		
2010-11	Port Vale	40	1		
2011-12	Port Vale	43	1	**161**	**2**

HALDANE, Lewis (F) **210 18**
H: 6 0 W: 11 03 b.Trowbridge 13-3-85
Source: Scholar. *Honours:* Wales Under-21.

Season	Club				
2003-04	Bristol R	27	5		
2004-05	Bristol R	13	0		
2005-06	Bristol R	30	3		
2006-07	Bristol R	45	6		
2007-08	Bristol R	32	1		
2008-09	Bristol R	0	0	**147**	**15**
2009-10	Port Vale	37	3		
2010-11	Port Vale	23	0		
2011-12	Port Vale	3	0	**63**	**3**

JAMES, Kingsley (D) **5 0**
H: 6 1 W: 11 09 b.Rotherham 17-2-92
Source: Scholar.

Season	Club				
2010-11	Sheffield U	0	0		
2011-12	Port Vale	5	0	**5**	**0**

JOHNSON, Sam (G) **0 0**
b.Newcastle-under-Lyme 1-12-92
Source: Scholar.

Season	Club				
2011-12	Port Vale	0	0		

LITTLE, Andrew (M) **23 6**
H: 6 0 W: 12 00 b.Enniskillen 12-5-89
Honours: Northern Ireland Youth, Under-21, B, 8 full caps.

Season	Club				
2008-09	Rangers	0	0		
2009-10	Rangers	6	1		
2010-11	Rangers	0	0		
2011-12	Rangers	10	5	**16**	**6**
2011-12	Port Vale	7	0	**7**	**0**

On loan from Rangers.

LLOYD, Ryan (M) **3 0**
H: 5 10 W: 10 03 b.Newcastle-u-Lyme 1-2-94
Source: Scholar.

Season	Club				
2010-11	Port Vale	1	0		
2011-12	Port Vale	2	0	**3**	**0**

LOFT, Doug (M) **155 10**
H: 6 0 W: 12 01 b.Maidstone 25-12-86
Source: Hastings U.

Season	Club				
2005-06	Brighton & HA	3	1		
2006-07	Brighton & HA	11	1		
2007-08	Brighton & HA	13	0		
2008-09	Brighton & HA	12	0	**39**	**2**
2008-09	*Dagenham & R*	11	0	**11**	**0**
2009-10	Port Vale	32	3		
2010-11	Port Vale	29	1		
2011-12	Port Vale	44	4	**105**	**8**

MARSHALL, Paul (M) **58 2**
H: 6 1 W: 12 03 b.Manchester 9-7-89
Source: Scholar. *Honours:* England Under-20.

Season	Club				
2007-08	Manchester C	0	0		
2008-09	Manchester C	0	0		
2008-09	*Blackpool*	2	0	**2**	**0**
2008-09	*Port Vale*	13	1		
2009-10	Manchester C	0	0		
2009-10	*Aberdeen*	9	0	**9**	**0**
2010-11	Walsall	18	1	**18**	**1**
2011-12	Rochdale	1	0	**1**	**0**
2011-12	Port Vale	15	0	**28**	**1**

MARTIN, Chris (G) **74 0**
H: 6 0 W: 13 05 b.Mansfield 21-7-90
Source: Scholar.

Season	Club				
2007-08	Port Vale	2	0		
2008-09	Port Vale	11	0		
2009-10	Port Vale	39	0		
2010-11	Port Vale	14	0		
2011-12	Port Vale	8	0	**74**	**0**

McCOMBE, John (D) **194 13**
H: 6 2 W: 13 00 b.Pontefract 7-5-85
Source: Scholar.

Season	Club				
2002-03	Huddersfield T	1	0		
2003-04	Huddersfield T	0	0		
2004-05	Huddersfield T	5	0		
2005-06	Huddersfield T	1	0		
2005-06	*Torquay U*	0	0		
2006-07	Huddersfield T	7	0	**14**	**0**
2007-08	Hereford U	27	0	**27**	**0**
2008-09	Port Vale	31	2		
2009-10	Port Vale	40	3		
2010-11	Port Vale	42	4		
2011-12	Port Vale	40	4	**153**	**13**

McDONALD, Clayton (D) **74 1**
H: 6 6 W: 16 05 b.Liverpool 26-12-88
Source: Scholar.

Season	Club				
2007-08	Manchester C	0	0		
2008-09	Manchester C	0	0		
2008-09	*Macclesfield T*	2	0	**2**	**0**
2008-09	*Chesterfield*	2	0	**2**	**0**
2009-10	Manchester C	0	0		
2009-10	Walsall	26	1		
2010-11	Walsall	14	0	**40**	**1**
2011-12	Port Vale	30	0	**30**	**0**

MORSY, Sam (M) **43 2**
H: 5 9 W: 12 06 b.Wolverhampton 10-9-91
Source: Scholar.

Season	Club				
2009-10	Port Vale	1	0		
2010-11	Port Vale	16	1		
2011-12	Port Vale	26	1	**43**	**2**

OWEN, Gareth (D) **253 2**
H: 6 1 W: 11 07 b.Cheadle 21-9-82
Source: Scholar. *Honours:* Wales Youth.

Season	Club				
2001-02	Stoke C	0	0		
2002-03	Stoke C	0	0		
2003-04	Stoke C	3	0		
2003-04	*Oldham Ath*	15	1		
2004-05	Stoke C	2	0	**5**	**0**
2004-05	*Torquay U*	5	0	**5**	**0**
2004-05	*Oldham Ath*	9	0		
2005-06	Oldham Ath	17	0		
2006-07	Oldham Ath	0	0	**41**	**1**
2006-07	*Stockport Co*	39	0		
2007-08	Stockport Co	36	0		
2008-09	Stockport Co	8	0	**83**	**0**
2008-09	*Yeovil T*	7	0	**7**	**0**
2008-09	Port Vale	12	0		
2009-10	Port Vale	40	0		
2010-11	Port Vale	36	1		
2011-12	Port Vale	24	0	**112**	**1**

POPE, Tom (F) **163 29**
H: 6 3 W: 11 03 b.Stoke 27-8-85
Source: Biddulph Vic.

Season	Club				
2005-06	Crewe Alex	0	0		
2006-07	Crewe Alex	4	0		
2007-08	Crewe Alex	26	7		
2008-09	Crewe Alex	26	10	**56**	**17**
2009-10	Rotherham U	35	3		
2010-11	Rotherham U	18	1	**53**	**4**
2010-11	*Port Vale*	13	3		
2011-12	Port Vale	41	5	**54**	**8**

RAGLAN, Charlie (D) **0 0**
H: 6 0 W: 11 13 b.Wythenshawe 28-4-93
Source: Scholar.

Season	Club				
2011-12	Port Vale	0	0		

RICHARDS, Marc (F) **339 105**
H: 6 2 W: 12 06 b.Wolverhampton 8-7-82
Source: Trainee. *Honours:* England Youth, Under-20.

Season	Club				
1999-2000	Blackburn R	0	0		
2000-01	Blackburn R	0	0		
2001-02	Blackburn R	0	0		
2001-02	*Crewe Alex*	4	0	**4**	**0**
2001-02	*Oldham Ath*	5	0	**5**	**0**
2001-02	*Halifax T*	5	0	**5**	**0**
2002-03	Blackburn R	0	0		
2002-03	*Swansea C*	17	7	**17**	**7**
2003-04	Northampton T	41	8		
2004-05	Northampton T	12	2		
2004-05	*Rochdale*	5	2	**5**	**2**

2005-06	Northampton T	0	0	**53**	**10**
2005-06	Barnsley	38	12		
2006-07	Barnsley	31	6	**69**	**18**
2007-08	Port Vale	29	5		
2008-09	Port Vale	30	10		
2009-10	Port Vale	46	20		
2010-11	Port Vale	40	16		
2011-12	Port Vale	36	17	**181**	**68**

RIGG, Sean (F) **150 18**
H: 5 9 W: 12 01 b.Bristol 1-10-88
Source: Forest Green R.

2006-07	Bristol R	18	1		
2007-08	Bristol R	31	1		
2008-09	Bristol R	8	0		
2009-10	Bristol R	0	0	**57**	**2**
2009-10	*Port Vale*	26	3		
2010-11	Port Vale	25	3		
2011-12	Port Vale	42	10	**93**	**16**

ROBERTS, Gary (M) **211 22**
H: 5 8 W: 10 05 b.Chester 4-2-87
Source: Scholar. *Honours:* England Youth.

2003-04	Crewe Alex	2	0		
2004-05	Crewe Alex	2	0		
2005-06	Crewe Alex	33	2		
2006-07	Crewe Alex	43	3		
2007-08	Crewe Alex	42	6		
2008-09	Crewe Alex	0	0	**122**	**11**
2008-09	Yeovil T	30	2		
2009-10	Yeovil T	0	0	**30**	**2**
2009-10	Rotherham U	13	3	**13**	**3**
2010-11	Port Vale	35	2		
2011-12	Port Vale	11	4	**46**	**6**

ROE, Phil (D) **2 0**
H: 5 10 W: 12 06 b.Chelmsford 7-10-91
Source: Scholar.

2010-11	Sheffield U	0	0		
2011-12	Sheffield U	0	0		
2011-12	Port Vale	2	0	**2**	**0**

SHUKER, Chris (M) **313 37**
H: 5 5 W: 9 03 b.Liverpool 9-5-82
Source: Scholarship.

1999-2000	Manchester C	0	0		
2000-01	Manchester C	0	0		
2000-01	*Macclesfield T*	9	1	**9**	**1**
2001-02	Manchester C	2	0		
2002-03	Manchester C	3	0		
2002-03	*Walsall*	5	0	**5**	**0**
2003-04	Manchester C	0	0	**5**	**0**
2003-04	*Rochdale*	14	1	**14**	**1**
2003-04	*Hartlepool U*	14	1	**14**	**1**
2003-04	Barnsley	9	0		
2004-05	Barnsley	45	7		
2005-06	Barnsley	46	10	**100**	**17**
2006-07	Tranmere R	46	6		
2007-08	Tranmere R	23	3		
2008-09	Tranmere R	28	3		
2009-10	Tranmere R	26	2	**123**	**14**
2010-11	Morecambe	27	2		
2011-12	Morecambe	0	0	**27**	**2**
2011-12	Port Vale	16	1	**16**	**1**

TAYLOR, Rob (D) **126 14**
H: 6 0 W: 12 08 b.Shrewsbury 16-1-85
Source: Ludlow T, Stourport Swifts, Solihull B, Redditch U, Nuneaton B.

2008-09	Port Vale	20	3		
2009-10	Port Vale	39	8		
2010-11	Port Vale	36	1		
2011-12	Port Vale	31	2	**126**	**14**

TOMLINSON, Stuart (G) **94 0**
H: 6 1 W: 11 02 b.Ellesmere Port 10-5-85
Source: Scholar.

2002-03	Crewe Alex	1	0		
2003-04	Crewe Alex	1	0		
2004-05	Crewe Alex	0	0		
2005-06	Crewe Alex	2	0		
2006-07	Crewe Alex	7	0		
2007-08	Crewe Alex	0	0		
2008-09	Crewe Alex	9	0		
2009-10	Crewe Alex	0	0	**20**	**0**
From Barrow.					
2010-11	Port Vale	36	0		
From Barrow.					
2011-12	Port Vale	38	0	**74**	**0**

WILLIAMSON, Ben (F) **51 11**
H: 5 11 W: 11 13 b.Lambeth 25-12-88
Source: Worthing.

2010-11	Jerez Industrial	12	8	**12**	**8**
2010-11	Bournemouth	4	0		
2011-12	Bournemouth	0	0	**4**	**0**
2011-12	Port Vale	35	3	**35**	**3**

On loan from Hyde.

YATES, Adam (D) **192 2**
H: 5 10 W: 10 07 b.Stoke 28-5-83
Source: Scholar.

2000-01	Crewe Alex	0	0		
2001-02	Crewe Alex	0	0		
2002-03	Crewe Alex	0	0		
2003-04	Crewe Alex	0	0		
2004-05	Crewe Alex	0	0		
2005-06	Crewe Alex	0	0		
2006-07	Crewe Alex	0	0		
2007-08	Morecambe	44	0		
2008-09	Morecambe	32	0	**76**	**0**
2009-10	Port Vale	32	0		
2010-11	Port Vale	46	0		
2011-12	Port Vale	38	2	**116**	**2**

PORTSMOUTH (65)

ANTELMI, Patrick (F) **0 0**
b.Sydney 15-3-94
Source: Scholar.

2011-12	Portsmouth	0	0		

ASHDOWN, Jamie (G) **145 0**
H: 6 1 W: 13 05 b.Reading 30-11-80
Source: Scholar.

1999-2000	Reading	0	0		
2000-01	Reading	1	0		
2001-02	Reading	1	0		
2001-02	*Arsenal*	0	0		
2002-03	Reading	1	0		
2002-03	*Bournemouth*	2	0	**2**	**0**
2003-04	Reading	10	0	**13**	**0**
2003-04	*Rushden & D*	19	0	**19**	**0**
2004-05	Portsmouth	16	0		
2005-06	Portsmouth	17	0		
2006-07	Portsmouth	0	0		
2006-07	*Norwich C*	2	0	**2**	**0**
2007-08	Portsmouth	3	0		
2008-09	Portsmouth	0	0		
2009-10	Portsmouth	6	0		
2010-11	Portsmouth	46	0		
2011-12	Portsmouth	21	0	**109**	**0**

BEN HAIM, Tal (D) **264 3**
H: 5 11 W: 11 09 b.Rishon Le Zion 31-3-82
Source: Maccabi Tel Aviv. *Honours:* Israel Under-21, 67 full caps, 1 goal.

2000-01	Maccabi Tel Aviv	1	0		
2001-02	Maccabi Tel Aviv	29	1		
2002-03	Maccabi Tel Aviv	30	0		
2003-04	Maccabi Tel Aviv	26	1	**86**	**2**
2004-05	Bolton W	21	1		
2005-06	Bolton W	35	0		
2006-07	Bolton W	32	0	**88**	**1**
2007-08	Chelsea	13	0	**13**	**0**
2008-09	Manchester C	9	0		
2008-09	*Sunderland*	5	0	**5**	**0**
2009-10	Manchester C	0	0	**9**	**0**
2009-10	Portsmouth	22	0		
2010-11	Portsmouth	0	0		
2010-11	*West Ham U*	8	0	**8**	**0**
2011-12	Portsmouth	33	0	**55**	**0**

ETUHU, Kelvin (F) **47 4**
H: 5 11 W: 11 02 b.Kano 30-5-88
Source: Scholar.

2005-06	Manchester C	0	0		
2006-07	Manchester C	0	0		
2006-07	*Rochdale*	4	2	**4**	**2**
2007-08	Manchester C	6	1		
2007-08	*Leicester C*	4	0	**4**	**0**
2008-09	Manchester C	4	0		
2009-10	Manchester C	0	0		
2009-10	*Cardiff C*	16	0	**16**	**0**
2010-11	Manchester C	0	0	**10**	**1**
2011-12	Kavala	0	0		
2011-12	Portsmouth	13	1	**13**	**1**

FUTACS, Marko (F) **77 13**
H: 6 5 W: 14 00 b.Budapest 22-2-90
Honours: Hungary Youth, Under-21.

2008-09	Nancy B	12	3	**12**	**3**
2009-10	Werder Bremen II	13	3	**13**	**3**
2010-11	*Ingolstadt*	23	2	**23**	**2**
2011-12	Portsmouth	29	5	**29**	**5**

GRANT, Alex (D) **0 0**
b.Perth 23-1-94
Source: Scholar.

2011-12	Portsmouth	0	0		

HALFORD, Greg (D) **296 36**
H: 6 4 W: 12 10 b.Chelmsford 8-12-84
Source: Scholar. *Honours:* England Youth, Under-20.

2002-03	Colchester U	1	0		
2003-04	Colchester U	18	4		
2004-05	Colchester U	44	4		
2005-06	Colchester U	45	7		
2006-07	Colchester U	28	3	**136**	**18**
2006-07	Reading	3	0	**3**	**0**
2007-08	Sunderland	8	0		
2007-08	*Charlton Ath*	16	2	**16**	**2**
2008-09	Sunderland	0	0		
2008-09	*Sheffield U*	41	4	**41**	**4**
2009-10	Sunderland	0	0	**8**	**0**
2009-10	Wolverhampton W	15	0		
2010-11	Wolverhampton W	2	0	**17**	**0**
2010-11	*Portsmouth*	33	5		
2011-12	Portsmouth	42	7	**75**	**12**

HARRIS, Ashley (M) **5 0**
H: 5 8 W: 10 00 b.Waterlooville 9-12-93
Source: Scholar.

2011-12	Portsmouth	5	0	**5**	**0**

HENDERSON, Stephen (G) **71 0**
H: 6 3 W: 11 00 b.Dublin 2-5-88
Source: Scholar. *Honours:* Eire Under-21.

2005-06	Aston Villa	0	0		
2006-07	Aston Villa	0	0		
2007-08	Bristol C	1	0		
2008-09	Bristol C	1	0		
2009-10	Bristol C	3	0		
2009-10	*Aldershot T*	8	0	**8**	**0**
2010-11	Bristol C	0	0	**5**	**0**
2010-11	*Yeovil T*	33	0	**33**	**0**
2011-12	Portsmouth	25	0	**25**	**0**
2011-12	*West Ham U*	0	0		

HIGGINS, Andrew (M) **0 0**
b.Perth 21-9-93
Source: Scholar.

2011-12	Portsmouth	0	0		

HUSEKLEPP, Erik (F) **212 48**
H: 6 2 W: 14 00 b.Sandvika 5-9-84
Honours: Norway Under-21, 29 full caps, 7 goals.

2004	Fyllingen	25	8		
2005	Fyllingen	17	1	**42**	**9**
2005	Brann	9	1		
2006	Brann	11	0		
2007	Brann	22	1		
2008	Brann	18	2		
2009	Brann	30	15		
2010	Brann	28	10	**118**	**29**
2010-11	Bari	14	2	**14**	**2**
2011-12	Portsmouth	27	6	**27**	**6**
2011-12	*Birmingham C*	11	2	**11**	**2**

KANU, Nwankwo (F) **441 98**
H: 6 5 W: 12 08 b.Owerri 1-8-76
Honours: Nigeria 86 full caps, 13 goals.

1991-92	Federation Works	30	9	**30**	**9**
1992-93	Iwanyanwu	30	6	**30**	**6**
1993-94	Ajax	6	2		
1994-95	Ajax	18	10		
1995-96	Ajax	30	13	**54**	**25**
1996-97	Internazionale	0	0		
1997-98	Internazionale	11	1		
1998-99	Internazionale	1	0	**12**	**1**
1998-99	Arsenal	12	6		
1999-2000	Arsenal	31	12		
2000-01	Arsenal	27	3		
2001-02	Arsenal	23	3		
2002-03	Arsenal	16	5		
2003-04	Arsenal	10	1	**119**	**30**
2004-05	WBA	28	2		
2005-06	WBA	25	5	**53**	**7**
2006-07	Portsmouth	36	10		
2007-08	Portsmouth	25	4		
2008-09	Portsmouth	17	1		
2009-10	Portsmouth	23	2		
2010-11	Portsmouth	32	2		
2011-12	Portsmouth	10	1	**143**	**20**

KITSON, Dave (F) **355 114**
H: 6 3 W: 12 07 b.Hitchin 21-1-80
Source: Arlesey.

2000-01	Cambridge U	8	1		
2001-02	Cambridge U	33	9		
2002-03	Cambridge U	44	20		
2003-04	Cambridge U	17	10	**102**	**40**
2003-04	Reading	17	5		
2004-05	Reading	37	19		

2005-06 Reading 34 18
2006-07 Reading 13 2
2007-08 Reading 34 10
2008-09 Stoke C 16 0
2008-09 *Reading* 10 2 **145 56**
2009-10 Stoke C 18 3
2009-10 *Middlesbrough* 6 3 **6 3**
2010-11 Stoke C 0 0 **34 3**
2010-11 Portsmouth 35 8
2011-12 Portsmouth 33 4 **68 12**

LAWRENCE, Liam (M) 389 75
H: 5 11 W: 12 06 b.Retford 14-12-81
Source: Trainee. *Honours:* Eire 15 full caps, 2 goals.
1999-2000 Mansfield T 2 0
2000-01 Mansfield T 18 4
2001-02 Mansfield T 32 2
2002-03 Mansfield T 43 10
2003-04 Mansfield T 41 18 **136 34**
2004-05 Sunderland 32 7
2005-06 Sunderland 29 3
2006-07 Sunderland 12 0 **73 10**
2006-07 Stoke C 27 5
2007-08 Stoke C 41 14
2008-09 Stoke C 20 3
2009-10 Stoke C 25 1
2010-11 Stoke C 0 0 **113 23**
2010-11 Portsmouth 31 7
2011-12 Portsmouth 23 0 **54 7**
2011-12 *Cardiff C* 13 1 **13 1**

MAGRI, Sam (D) 0 0
b.Portsmouth 30-3-94
Source: Scholar. *Honours:* England Youth.
2010-11 Portsmouth 0 0
2011-12 Portsmouth 0 0

MOKOENA, Aaron (D) 257 4
H: 6 2 W: 14 00 b.Johannesburg 25-11-80
Honours: South Africa 106 full caps, 1 goal.
2000-01 Ajax 0 0
2000-01 Antwerp 6 0
2001-02 Antwerp 13 1
2002-03 Antwerp 29 1 **48 2**
2003-04 Genk 18 0
2004-05 Genk 12 0 **30 0**
2004-05 Blackburn R 16 0
2005-06 Blackburn R 22 0
2006-07 Blackburn R 27 0
2007-08 Blackburn R 18 0
2008-09 Blackburn R 18 0
2009-10 Blackburn R 0 0 **101 0**
2009-10 Portsmouth 23 0
2010-11 Portsmouth 37 2
2011-12 Portsmouth 18 0 **78 2**

MULLINS, Hayden (D) 523 25
H: 5 11 W: 11 12 b.Reading 27-3-79
Source: Trainee. *Honours:* England Under-21.
1996-97 Crystal Palace 0 0
1997-98 Crystal Palace 0 0
1998-99 Crystal Palace 40 5
1999-2000 Crystal Palace 45 10
2000-01 Crystal Palace 41 1
2001-02 Crystal Palace 43 0
2002-03 Crystal Palace 43 2
2003-04 Crystal Palace 10 0 **222 18**
2003-04 West Ham U 27 0
2004-05 West Ham U 37 1
2005-06 West Ham U 35 0
2006-07 West Ham U 30 2
2007-08 West Ham U 34 0
2008-09 West Ham U 17 1 **180 4**
2008-09 Portsmouth 17 0
2009-10 Portsmouth 18 0
2010-11 Portsmouth 45 2
2011-12 Portsmouth 34 1 **114 3**
2011-12 *Reading* 7 0 **7 0**

MWARUWARI, Benjamin (F) 279 67
H: 6 2 W: 12 03 b.Harare 13-8-78
Honours: Zimbabwe 31 full caps, 8 goals.
1999-2000 Jomo Cosmos 15 7
2000-01 Jomo Cosmos 30 13 **45 20**
2001-02 Grasshoppers 25 1 **25 1**
2002-03 Auxerre 27 7
2003-04 Auxerre 3 0
2004-05 Auxerre 31 11
2005-06 Auxerre 11 1 **72 19**
2005-06 Portsmouth 16 1
2006-07 Portsmouth 31 6
2007-08 Portsmouth 23 12
2007-08 Manchester C 13 3
2008-09 Manchester C 8 1
2009-10 Manchester C 2 0 **23 4**
2009-10 *Sunderland* 8 0 **8 0**
2010-11 Blackburn R 18 3 **18 3**
2011-12 Portsmouth 18 1 **88 20**

NORRIS, David (M) 378 49
H: 5 7 W: 11 06 b.Stamford 22-2-81
Source: Boston U.
1999-2000 Bolton W 0 0
2000-01 Bolton W 0 0
2001-02 Bolton W 0 0
2001-02 *Hull C* 6 1 **6 1**
2002-03 Bolton W 0 0
2002-03 Plymouth Arg 33 6
2003-04 Plymouth Arg 45 5
2004-05 Plymouth Arg 35 3
2005-06 Plymouth Arg 45 2
2006-07 Plymouth Arg 41 6
2007-08 Plymouth Arg 27 5 **226 27**
2007-08 Ipswich T 9 1
2008-09 Ipswich T 37 3
2009-10 Ipswich T 24 1
2010-11 Ipswich T 36 8 **106 13**
2011-12 Portsmouth 40 8 **40 8**

RICARDO ROCHA (D) 313 8
H: 6 0 W: 12 08 b.Santo Tirso 3-10-78
Honours: Portugal 6 full caps.
1998-99 Famalicao 28 2 **28 2**
1999-2000 Braga 25 1
2000-01 Braga 19 0
2000-01 Braga B 8 0 **8 0**
2001-02 Braga 25 2 **69 3**
2002-03 Benfica 27 0
2003-04 Benfica 25 0
2004-05 Benfica 25 0
2005-06 Benfica 26 0
2006-07 Benfica 12 3 **115 3**
2006-07 Tottenham H 9 0
2007-08 Tottenham H 5 0
2008-09 Tottenham H 0 0 **14 0**
2009-10 Standard Liege 7 0 **7 0**
2009-10 Portsmouth 10 0
2010-11 Portsmouth 29 0
2011-12 Portsmouth 33 0 **72 0**

STOCKFORD, Lewis (M) 0 0
b.Portsmouth 1-10-92
Source: Scholar.
2011-12 Portsmouth 0 0

TALLACK, Lewis (D) 0 0
b.Luton 4-10-92
Source: Scholar.
2011-12 Portsmouth 0 0

THOMPSON, Dan (F) 0 0
b. 4-7-94
Source: Hampton & Richmond Bor.
2011-12 Portsmouth 0 0

VARNEY, Luke (F) 267 60
H: 5 11 W: 11 00 b.Leicester 28-9-82
Source: Quorn.
2002-03 Crewe Alex 0 0
2003-04 Crewe Alex 8 1
2004-05 Crewe Alex 26 4
2005-06 Crewe Alex 27 5
2006-07 Crewe Alex 34 17 **95 27**
2007-08 Charlton Ath 39 8
2008-09 Charlton Ath 18 2 **57 10**
2008-09 *Sheffield W* 4 2
2008-09 Derby Co 10 1
2009-10 Derby Co 1 0
2009-10 *Sheffield W* 39 9 **43 11**
2010-11 Derby Co 1 0 **12 1**
2010-11 *Blackpool* 30 5 **30 5**
2011-12 Portsmouth 30 6 **30 6**

WALLACE, Jed (M) 0 0
b.Reading 15-12-93
Source: Lewes.
2011-12 Portsmouth 0 0

WALSHE, Carl (F) 0 0
b.Dublin 7-10-92
Source: Scholar.
2010-11 Portsmouth 0 0
2011-12 Portsmouth 0 0

WARD, Joel (D) 110 7
H: 6 2 W: 11 13 b.Emsworth 29-10-89
Source: Scholar.
2008-09 Portsmouth 0 0
2008-09 *Bournemouth* 21 1 **21 1**
2009-10 Portsmouth 3 0
2010-11 Portsmouth 42 3
2011-12 Portsmouth 44 3 **89 6**

WEBSTER, Adam (D) 3 0
H: 6 1 W: 11 11 b.West Wittering 4-1-95
Source: Scholar.
2011-12 Portsmouth 3 0 **3 0**

PRESTON NE (66)

ALEXANDER, Graham (D) 833 107
H: 5 10 W: 12 07 b.Coventry 10-10-71
Source: Trainee. *Honours:* Scotland B, 40 full caps.
1989-90 Scunthorpe U 0 0
1990-91 Scunthorpe U 1 0
1991-92 Scunthorpe U 36 5
1992-93 Scunthorpe U 41 5
1993-94 Scunthorpe U 41 4
1994-95 Scunthorpe U 40 4 **159 18**
1995-96 Luton T 37 1
1996-97 Luton T 45 2
1997-98 Luton T 39 8
1998-99 Luton T 29 4 **150 15**
1998-99 Preston NE 10 0
1999-2000 Preston NE 46 6
2000-01 Preston NE 34 5
2001-02 Preston NE 45 6
2002-03 Preston NE 45 10
2003-04 Preston NE 45 9
2004-05 Preston NE 42 7
2005-06 Preston NE 40 3
2006-07 Preston NE 42 6
2007-08 Preston NE 3 0
2007-08 Burnley 43 1
2008-09 Burnley 46 9
2009-10 Burnley 33 7
2010-11 Burnley 32 3 **154 20**
2011-12 Preston NE 18 2 **370 54**

ARESTIDOU, Andreas (G) 9 0
H: 6 2 W: 13 00 b.Lambeth 6-12-89
Source: Scholar.
2007-08 Blackburn R 0 0
2008-09 Blackburn R 0 0
2009-10 Shrewsbury T 2 0 **2 0**
2010-11 Preston NE 0 0
2011-12 Preston NE 7 0 **7 0**

ASHBEE, Ian (M) 473 21
H: 6 1 W: 13 07 b.Birmingham 6-9-76
Source: Trainee. *Honours:* England Youth.
1994-95 Derby Co 1 0
1995-96 Derby Co 0 0
1996-97 Derby Co 0 0 **1 0**
1996-97 Cambridge U 18 0
1997-98 Cambridge U 27 1
1998-99 Cambridge U 31 4
1999-2000 Cambridge U 45 1
2000-01 Cambridge U 44 3
2001-02 Cambridge U 38 2 **203 11**
2002-03 Hull C 31 1
2003-04 Hull C 39 2
2004-05 Hull C 40 1
2005-06 Hull C 6 0
2006-07 Hull C 35 1
2007-08 Hull C 42 3
2008-09 Hull C 31 1
2009-10 Hull C 0 0
2010-11 Hull C 19 1 **243 10**
2010-11 Preston NE 19 0
2011-12 Preston NE 7 0 **26 0**

BARTON, Adam (M) 50 1
H: 5 11 W: 12 01 b.Clitheroe 7-1-91
Source: Scholar. *Honours:* Eire Under-21. Northern Ireland 1 full cap.
2008-09 Preston NE 0 0
2009-10 Preston NE 1 0
2010-11 Preston NE 33 1
2011-12 Preston NE 16 0 **50 1**

BILLINGTON, Alex (D) 0 0
b.Kirkham 18-5-93
Source: Blackburn R Scholar.
2011-12 Preston NE 0 0

BROWN, Aaron (D) 77 5
H: 6 4 W: 14 07 b.Birmingham 23-6-83
Source: Stafford R, Tamworth.
2005-06 Reading 0 0
2005-06 *Bournemouth* 4 0 **4 0**
2006-07 Reading 0 0
2007-08 *Walsall* 0 0

2007-08 Reading 0 0
From Redditch U.
2008-09 Yeovil T 23 3 **23 3**
From AFC Telford U, Truro C.
2009-10 Burton Alb 1 0 **1 0**
2009-10 Aldershot T 12 1
2010-11 Leyton Orient 5 0 **5 0**
2010-11 *Stockport Co* 17 1 **17 1**
2011-12 Aldershot T 11 0 **23 1**
2011-12 Preston NE 4 0 **4 0**

CLARK, Luke (D) 2 0
b.Preston 24-5-94
Source: Scholar.
2011-12 Preston NE 2 0 **2 0**

CLUCAS, Seanan (M) 3 0
H: 5 10 W: 12 00 b.Dungannon 8-11-92
Source: Scholar. *Honours:* Northern Ireland Youth, Under-21.
2011-12 Preston NE 1 0 **1 0**
2011-12 *Burton Alb* 2 0 **2 0**

COMRIE, Dominic (G) 0 0
b.Bury 20-10-92
Source: Scholar.
2011-12 Preston NE 0 0

COUTTS, Paul (M) 130 4
H: 5 9 W: 11 11 b.Aberdeen 22-7-88
Source: Cove R. *Honours:* Scotland Under-21.
2008-09 Peterborough U 37 0
2009-10 Peterborough U 16 0 **53 0**
2009-10 Preston NE 13 1
2010-11 Preston NE 23 1
2011-12 Preston NE 41 2 **77 4**

CUMMINS, Graham (F) 182 78
H: 6 2 W: 11 11 b.Cork 29-12-87
2006 Cobh Ramblers 14 5
2007 Cobh Ramblers 35 11
2008 Cobh Ramblers 28 1 **77 17**
2009 Waterford U 28 17 **28 17**
2010 Cork C 32 18
2011 Cork C 30 24 **62 42**
2011-12 Preston NE 15 2 **15 2**

DALEY, Keammar (M) 8 1
H: 5 8 W: 10 00 b.Kingston 18-2-88
Source: Meadhaven, Tivoli Gardens.
Honours: Jamaica Youth, Under-23, 23 full caps, 2 goals.
2011-12 Preston NE 8 1 **8 1**

DEVINE, Daniel (D) 15 1
H: 6 0 W: 11 00 b.Belfast 7-9-92
Source: Scholar.
2010-11 Preston NE 2 0
2011-12 Preston NE 13 1 **15 1**

DOUGLAS, Jamie (F) 6 1
H: 5 11 W: 12 00 b.Cookstown 4-7-92
Source: Scholar.
2010-11 Preston NE 2 0
2011-12 Preston NE 4 1 **6 1**

GRAY, David (F) 72 0
H: 5 11 W: 11 02 b.Edinburgh 4-5-88
Source: Scholar. *Honours:* Scotland Under-21.
2005-06 Manchester U 0 0
2006-07 Manchester U 0 0
2007-08 Manchester U 0 0
2007-08 *Crewe Alex* 1 0 **1 0**
2008-09 Manchester U 0 0
2008-09 *Plymouth Arg* 14 0
2009-10 Manchester U 0 0
2009-10 *Plymouth Arg* 12 0 **26 0**
2010-11 Preston NE 22 0
2011-12 Preston NE 23 0 **45 0**

HAYHURST, Will (M) 2 0
H: 5 10 W: 11 02 b.Longridge 24-2-94
Source: Scholar.
2011-12 Preston NE 2 0 **2 0**

HOLROYD, Chris (F) 114 13
H: 5 11 W: 12 03 b.Macclesfield 24-10-86
Source: Crewe Alex Scholar.
2005-06 Chester C 0 0
2006-07 Chester C 22 0
2007-08 Chester C 25 4
2008-09 Chester C 0 0 **47 4**
From Cambridge U.
2009-10 Brighton & HA 13 0
From Cambridge U.
2010-11 Brighton & HA 3 0 **16 0**
2010-11 *Stevenage* 12 6 **12 6**
2010-11 *Bury* 4 1 **4 1**
From Cambridge U.
2011-12 Rotherham U 15 1 **15 1**
2011-12 Preston NE 20 1 **20 1**

HUME, Iain (F) 382 95
H: 5 7 W: 11 02 b.Ontario 31-10-83
Source: Juniors. *Honours:* Canada Youth, Under-20, 35 full caps, 5 goals.
1999-2000 Tranmere R 3 0
2000-01 Tranmere R 10 0
2001-02 Tranmere R 14 0
2002-03 Tranmere R 35 6
2003-04 Tranmere R 40 10
2004-05 Tranmere R 42 15
2005-06 Tranmere R 6 1 **150 32**
2005-06 Leicester C 37 9
2006-07 Leicester C 45 13
2007-08 Leicester C 40 11 **122 33**
2008-09 Barnsley 15 4
2009-10 Barnsley 35 5
2010-11 Barnsley 1 0 **51 9**
2010-11 Preston NE 31 12
2011-12 Preston NE 28 9 **59 21**

HUNT, Nicky (D) 184 2
H: 6 1 W: 13 07 b.Westhoughton 3-9-83
Source: Scholar. *Honours:* England Under-21.
2000-01 Bolton W 1 0
2001-02 Bolton W 0 0
2002-03 Bolton W 0 0
2003-04 Bolton W 31 1
2004-05 Bolton W 29 0
2005-06 Bolton W 20 0
2006-07 Bolton W 33 0
2007-08 Bolton W 14 0
2008-09 Bolton W 0 0
2008-09 *Birmingham C* 11 0 **11 0**
2009-10 Bolton W 0 0 **128 1**
2009-10 *Derby Co* 21 0 **21 0**
2010-11 Bristol C 7 0
2011-12 Bristol C 0 0 **7 0**
2011-12 Preston NE 17 1 **17 1**

LEATHER, Scott (D) 2 0
H: 6 1 W: 10 12 b.Sale 30-9-92
Source: Scholar.
2010-11 Preston NE 2 0
2011-12 Preston NE 0 0 **2 0**

MAYOR, Danny (M) 67 2
H: 6 0 W: 11 12 b.Leyland 18-10-90
Source: Scholar.
2008-09 Preston NE 0 0
2008-09 *Tranmere R* 3 0 **3 0**
2009-10 Preston NE 7 0
2010-11 Preston NE 21 0
2011-12 Preston NE 36 2 **64 2**

McLAUGHLIN, Conor (D) 28 0
H: 6 0 W: 11 02 b.Belfast 26-7-91
Source: Scholar. *Honours:* Northern Ireland Under-21, 1 full cap.
2009-10 Preston NE 0 0
2010-11 Preston NE 7 0
2011-12 Preston NE 17 0 **24 0**
2011-12 *Shrewsbury T* 4 0 **4 0**

McLEAN, Brian (D) 139 8
H: 6 2 W: 13 00 b.Rutherglen 28-2-85
2005-06 Rangers 0 0
2005-06 *Motherwell* 30 3
2006-07 Motherwell 5 0
2007-08 Motherwell 9 0
2008-09 Motherwell 12 2 **56 5**
2009-10 Falkirk 36 0
2010-11 Falkirk 31 2 **67 2**
2011-12 Preston NE 16 1 **16 1**

McLELLAN, Michael (F) 0 0
b.Belfast 22-1-93
Source: Scholar. *Honours:* Northern Ireland Youth.
2011-12 Preston NE 0 0

MELLOR, Neil (F) 194 56
H: 6 0 W: 13 05 b.Sheffield 4-11-82
Source: Scholar.
2001-02 Liverpool 0 0
2002-03 Liverpool 3 0
2003-04 Liverpool 0 0
2003-04 *West Ham U* 16 2 **16 2**
2004-05 Liverpool 9 2
2005-06 Liverpool 0 0
2005-06 *Wigan Ath* 3 1 **3 1**
2006-07 Liverpool 0 0 **12 2**
2006-07 Preston NE 5 1
2007-08 Preston NE 36 9
2008-09 Preston NE 33 10
2009-10 Preston NE 39 10
2010-11 Preston NE 0 0
2010-11 *Sheffield W* 33 13 **33 13**
2011-12 Preston NE 17 8 **130 38**

MIDDLETON, Doyle (M) 3 0
H: 5 6 W: 10 10 b.Southport 11-4-94
Source: Scholar. *Honours:* Scotland Youth.
2010-11 Preston NE 2 0
2011-12 Preston NE 1 0 **3 0**

MILLER, George (M) 7 0
H: 5 9 W: 12 02 b.Eccleston 25-11-91
Source: Scholar.
2009-10 Preston NE 0 0
2010-11 Preston NE 1 0
2011-12 Preston NE 6 0 **7 0**

MORGAN, Craig (D) 271 8
H: 6 0 W: 11 04 b.Flint 18-6-85
Source: Scholar. *Honours:* Wales Youth, Under-21, 23 full caps.
2001-02 Wrexham 2 0
2002-03 Wrexham 6 1
2003-04 Wrexham 18 0
2004-05 Wrexham 26 0
2005-06 Milton Keynes D 40 0
2006-07 Milton Keynes D 3 0 **43 0**
2006-07 *Wrexham* 1 0 **53 1**
2006-07 Peterborough U 23 1
2007-08 Peterborough U 41 2
2008-09 Peterborough U 27 0
2009-10 Peterborough U 34 1 **125 4**
2010-11 Preston NE 31 2
2011-12 Preston NE 19 1 **50 3**

NICHOLSON, Barry (M) 377 45
H: 5 7 W: 9 01 b.Dumfries 24-8-78
Honours: Scotland Under-21, 3 full caps.
1995-96 Rangers 0 0
1996-97 Rangers 0 0
1997-98 Rangers 0 0
1998-99 Rangers 6 0
1999-2000 Rangers 2 0 **8 0**
2000-01 Dunfermline Ath 36 3
2001-02 Dunfermline Ath 37 7
2002-03 Dunfermline Ath 38 5
2003-04 Dunfermline Ath 36 5
2004-05 Dunfermline Ath 27 3 **174 23**
2005-06 Aberdeen 33 2
2006-07 Aberdeen 31 6
2007-08 Aberdeen 38 5 **102 13**
2008-09 Preston NE 37 3
2009-10 Preston NE 4 0
2010-11 Preston NE 22 4
2011-12 Preston NE 30 2 **93 9**

PARRY, Paul (M) 271 30
H: 5 11 W: 12 12 b.Chepstow 19-8-80
Source: Hereford U. *Honours:* Wales 12 full caps, 1 goal.
2003-04 Cardiff C 17 1
2004-05 Cardiff C 24 4
2005-06 Cardiff C 27 1
2006-07 Cardiff C 42 6
2007-08 Cardiff C 41 10
2008-09 Cardiff C 40 2 **191 24**
2009-10 Preston NE 17 2
2010-11 Preston NE 23 0
2011-12 Preston NE 40 4 **80 6**

PROCTER, Andy (M) 254 29
H: 6 0 W: 12 04 b.Blackburn 13-3-83
Source: Great Harwood T.
2006-07 Accrington S 43 3
2007-08 Accrington S 43 10
2008-09 Accrington S 37 3
2009-10 Accrington S 44 5
2010-11 Accrington S 43 6
2011-12 Accrington S 25 2 **235 29**
2011-12 Preston NE 19 0 **19 0**

PROCTOR, Jamie (F) 44 4
H: 6 2 W: 12 03 b.Preston 25-3-92
Source: Scholar.
2009-10 Preston NE 1 0
2010-11 Preston NE 5 1
2010-11 *Stockport Co* 7 0 **7 0**
2011-12 Preston NE 31 3 **37 4**

ROBERTSON, Chris (D) **141 7**
H: 6 3 W: 11 08 b.Dundee 11-10-85
Source: Scholar.
2005-06 Sheffield U 0 0
2005-06 *Chester C* 1 0 **1 0**
2006-07 Sheffield U 0 0
2006-07 Torquay U 9 1
2009-10 Torquay U 45 2
2010-11 Torquay U 43 2
2011-12 Torquay U 25 1 **122 6**
2011-12 Preston NE 18 1 **18 1**

RUSSELL, Darel (M) **453 36**
H: 5 10 W: 11 09 b.Mile End 22-10-80
Source: Trainee. *Honours:* England Youth.
1997-98 Norwich C 1 0
1998-99 Norwich C 13 1
1999-2000 Norwich C 33 4
2000-01 Norwich C 41 2
2001-02 Norwich C 23 0
2002-03 Norwich C 21 0
2003-04 Stoke C 46 4
2004-05 Stoke C 45 2
2005-06 Stoke C 37 3
2006-07 Stoke C 43 7 **171 16**
2007-08 Norwich C 39 4
2008-09 Norwich C 38 4
2009-10 Norwich C 35 3 **244 18**
2010-11 Preston NE 25 0
2011-12 Preston NE 2 0 **27 0**
2011-12 *Charlton Ath* 11 2 **11 2**

SMITH, Steven (D) **92 1**
H: 5 8 W: 10 08 b.Bellshill 30-4-85
2004-05 Rangers 4 0
2005-06 Rangers 18 0
2006-07 Rangers 17 1
2007-08 Rangers 0 0
2008-09 Rangers 5 0
2009-10 Rangers 12 0 **56 1**
2010-11 Norwich C 7 0 **7 0**
2010-11 *Aberdeen* 16 0 **16 0**
2011-12 Preston NE 13 0 **13 0**
Transferred to Portland Timbers April 2012.

STUCKMANN, Thorsten (G) **309 0**
H: 6 6 W: 14 11 b.Gutersloh 17-3-81
2000-01 Pr Munster 25 0
2001-02 Pr Munster 19 0
2002-03 Pr Munster 30 0 **74 0**
2003-04 E Braunschweig 21 0
2004-05 E Braunschweig 36 0
2005-06 E Braunschweig 34 0
2006-07 E Braunschweig 34 0 **125 0**
2007-08 A Aachen 16 0
2008-09 A Aachen 34 0
2009-10 A Aachen 31 0
2010-11 A Aachen 1 0 **82 0**
2011-12 Preston NE 28 0 **28 0**

TSOUMOU, Juvhel (F) **72 11**
H: 6 1 W: 13 00 b.Brazzaville 27-12-90
Honours: Germany Youth.
2008-09 Eint Frankfurt 6 0
2008-09 Eint Frankfurt II 8 3
2009-10 Eint Frankfurt 4 1 **10 1**
2009-10 Eint Frankfurt II 21 2 **29 5**
2010-11 Al Aachen 6 0 **6 0**
2011-12 Preston NE 16 3 **16 3**
2011-12 *Plymouth Arg* 11 2 **11 2**

TURNER, Iain (G) **78 1**
H: 6 3 W: 12 10 b.Stirling 26-1-84
Source: Riverside BC. *Honours:* Scotland Youth, Under-21, B.
2002-03 Stirling A 14 0 **14 0**
2002-03 Everton 0 0
2003-04 Everton 0 0
2004-05 Everton 0 0
2004-05 *Doncaster R* 8 0 **8 0**
2005-06 Everton 3 0
2005-06 *Wycombe W* 3 0 **3 0**
2006-07 Everton 1 0
2006-07 *Crystal Palace* 5 0 **5 0**
2006-07 *Sheffield W* 11 0 **11 0**
2007-08 Everton 0 0
2008-09 Everton 0 0
2008-09 *Nottingham F* 3 0 **3 0**
2009-10 Everton 0 0
2010-11 Everton 0 0 **4 0**
2010-11 *Coventry C* 2 0 **2 0**
2010-11 *Preston NE* 17 0
2011-12 Preston NE 11 1 **28 1**

WRIGHT, Bailey (D) **15 1**
H: 5 9 W: 13 05 b.Melbourne 28-7-92
Source: Scholar.
2010-11 Preston NE 2 0
2011-12 Preston NE 13 1 **15 1**

ZIBAKA, Brandon (F) **0 0**
H: 6 0 W: 13 03 b.Camden 20-5-95
Source: Scholar.
2011-12 Preston NE 0 0

QPR (67)

AGYEMANG, Patrick (F) **385 65**
H: 6 1 W: 12 00 b.Walthamstow 29-9-80
Source: Trainee. *Honours:* Ghana 3 full caps, 1 goal.
1998-99 Wimbledon 0 0
1999-2000 Wimbledon 0 0
1999-2000 *Brentford* 12 0 **12 0**
2000-01 Wimbledon 29 4
2001-02 Wimbledon 33 4
2002-03 Wimbledon 33 5
2003-04 Wimbledon 26 7 **121 20**
2003-04 Gillingham 20 6
2004-05 Gillingham 13 2 **33 8**
2004-05 Preston NE 27 4
2005-06 Preston NE 42 6
2006-07 Preston NE 31 7
2007-08 Preston NE 22 4 **122 21**
2007-08 QPR 17 8
2008-09 QPR 20 2
2009-10 QPR 17 3
2009-10 *Bristol C* 7 0 **7 0**
2010-11 QPR 19 2
2011-12 QPR 2 0 **75 15**
2011-12 *Millwall* 2 0 **2 0**
2011-12 *Stevenage* 13 1 **13 1**

ANDRADE, Bruno (M) **3 0**
H: 5 9 W: 11 09 b.Aveiro 2-10-93
Source: Scholar.
2010-11 QPR 1 0
2011-12 QPR 1 0 **2 0**
2011-12 *Aldershot T* 1 0 **1 0**

BALANTA, Angelo (F) **74 15**
H: 5 10 W: 11 11 b.Colombia 1-7-90
Source: Scholar.
2007-08 QPR 11 1
2008-09 QPR 10 1
2008-09 *Wycombe W* 11 3 **11 3**
2009-10 QPR 4 0
2010-11 QPR 0 0
2010-11 *Milton Keynes D* 18 6
2011-12 QPR 0 0 **25 2**
2011-12 *Milton Keynes D* 20 4 **38 10**

BARTON, Joey (M) **242 25**
H: 5 11 W: 12 05 b.Huyton 2-9-82
Source: Scholar. *Honours:* England Under-21, 1 full cap.
2001-02 Manchester C 0 0
2002-03 Manchester C 7 1
2003-04 Manchester C 28 1
2004-05 Manchester C 31 1
2005-06 Manchester C 31 6
2006-07 Manchester C 33 6 **130 15**
2007-08 Newcastle U 23 1
2008-09 Newcastle U 9 1
2009-10 Newcastle U 15 1
2010-11 Newcastle U 32 4
2011-12 Newcastle U 2 0 **81 7**
2011-12 QPR 31 3 **31 3**

BORROWDALE, Gary (D) **179 0**
H: 6 0 W: 12 01 b.Sutton 16-7-85
Source: Scholar. *Honours:* England Youth, Under-20.
2002-03 Crystal Palace 13 0
2003-04 Crystal Palace 23 0
2004-05 Crystal Palace 7 0
2005-06 Crystal Palace 30 0
2006-07 Crystal Palace 25 0 **98 0**
2007-08 Coventry C 21 0
2008-09 Coventry C 0 0 **21 0**
2008-09 *Colchester U* 4 0 **4 0**
2008-09 QPR 0 0
2008-09 *Brighton & HA* 12 0 **12 0**
2009-10 QPR 21 0
2009-10 *Charlton Ath* 10 0 **10 0**
2010-11 QPR 1 0
2010-11 *Carlisle U* 1 0 **1 0**
2011-12 QPR 0 0 **22 0**
2011-12 *Barnet* 11 0 **11 0**

BOTHROYD, Jay (F) **323 76**
H: 6 3 W: 14 13 b.Islington 7-5-82
Source: Trainee. *Honours:* England Schools, Youth, Under-20, Under-21, 1 full cap.
1999-2000 Arsenal 0 0
2000-01 Coventry C 8 0
2001-02 Coventry C 31 6
2002-03 Coventry C 33 8 **72 14**
2003-04 *Perugia* 26 4 **26 4**
2004-05 Blackburn R 11 1 **11 1**
2005-06 Charlton Ath 18 2 **18 2**
2006-07 Wolverhampton W33 9
2007-08 Wolverhampton W22 3 **55 12**
2007-08 *Stoke C* 4 0 **4 0**
2008-09 Cardiff C 39 12
2009-10 Cardiff C 40 11
2010-11 Cardiff C 37 18 **116 41**
2011-12 QPR 21 2 **21 2**

BROWN, Ben (D) **0 0**
Source: Scholar.
2011-12 QPR 0 0

BUZSAKY, Akos (M) **210 31**
H: 5 11 W: 11 09 b.Hungary 7-5-82
Source: MTK, Porto. *Honours:* Hungary Under-21, 20 full caps, 2 goals.
2004-05 Plymouth Arg 15 1
2005-06 Plymouth Arg 34 4
2006-07 Plymouth Arg 36 3
2007-08 Plymouth Arg 11 0 **96 8**
2007-08 QPR 27 10
2008-09 QPR 11 1
2009-10 QPR 39 10
2010-11 QPR 19 0
2011-12 QPR 18 2 **114 23**

CAMPBELL, Dudley (F) **192 57**
H: 5 10 W: 11 00 b.Hammersmith 12-11-81
Source: Aston Villa Trainee, QPR, Chesham U, Stevenage B, Yeading.
2005-06 Brentford 23 9 **23 9**
2005-06 Birmingham C 11 0
2006-07 Birmingham C 32 9 **43 9**
2007-08 Leicester C 28 4
2008-09 Leicester C 7 0
2008-09 *Blackpool* 20 9
2009-10 Leicester C 3 0
2009-10 *Derby Co* 8 3 **8 3**
2009-10 *Blackpool* 15 8
2010-11 Leicester C 3 1 **41 5**
2010-11 Blackpool 31 13 **66 30**
2011-12 QPR 11 1 **11 1**

CERNY, Radek (G) **298 1**
H: 6 1 W: 14 02 b.Prague 18-2-74
Honours: Czech Republic 3 full caps.
1992-93 Slavia Prague 0 0
1993-94 *Ceske* 4 0
1994-95 *Ceske* 3 0 **7 0**
1995-96 *Union Cheb* 12 0 **12 0**
1995-96 *Tatran* 8 0 **8 0**
1996-97 Slavia Prague 7 0
1997-98 Slavia Prague 6 0
1998-99 Slavia Prague 25 0
1999-2000 Slavia Prague 30 1
2000-01 Slavia Prague 30 0
2001-02 Slavia Prague 16 0
2002-03 Slavia Prague 25 0
2003-04 Slavia Prague 22 0
2004-05 Tottenham H 3 0
2004-05 Slavia Prague 16 0 **177 1**
2005-06 Tottenham H 0 0
2006-07 Tottenham H 0 0
2007-08 Tottenham H 13 0 **16 0**
2008-09 QPR 42 0
2009-10 QPR 29 0
2010-11 QPR 2 0
2011-12 QPR 5 0 **78 0**

CHAMPION, Fred (M) **0 0**
b.Shepherds Bush 18-1-94
Source: Tottenham H Scholar.
2011-12 QPR 0 0

CISSE, Djibril (F) **357 167**
H: 6 0 W: 13 00 b.Arles 12-8-81
Honours: France Under 21, 41 full caps, 9 goals.
1998-99 Auxerre 1 0
1999-2000 Auxerre 2 0
2000-01 Auxerre 25 8
2001-02 Auxerre 29 22

2002-03	Auxerre	33	14		
2003-04	Auxerre	38	26	**128**	**70**
2004-05	Liverpool	16	4		
2005-06	Liverpool	33	9	**49**	**13**
2006-07	*Marseille*	21	8		
2007-08	Marseille	35	16		
2008-09	Marseille	2	0	**58**	**24**
2008-09	*Sunderland*	35	10	**35**	**10**
2009-10	Panathinaikos	28	23		
2010-11	Panathinaikos	33	20	**61**	**43**
2011-12	Lazio	18	1	**18**	**1**
2011-12	QPR	8	6	**8**	**6**

CONNOLLY, Matthew (D) **143 5**
H: 6 1 W: 11 03 b.Barnet 24-9-87
Source: Scholar. *Honours:* England Youth.

2005-06	Arsenal	0	0		
2006-07	Arsenal	0	0		
2006-07	*Bournemouth*	5	1	**5**	**1**
2007-08	Arsenal	0	0		
2007-08	*Colchester U*	16	2	**16**	**2**
2007-08	QPR	20	0		
2008-09	QPR	35	0		
2009-10	QPR	19	2		
2010-11	QPR	36	0		
2011-12	QPR	6	0	**116**	**2**
2011-12	*Reading*	6	0	**6**	**0**

COOK, Lee (M) **270 21**
H: 5 8 W: 11 10 b.Hammersmith 3-8-82
Source: Aylesbury U.

1999-2000	Watford	0	0		
2000-01	Watford	4	0		
2001-02	Watford	10	0		
2002-03	Watford	4	0		
2002-03	*York C*	7	1	**7**	**1**
2002-03	*QPR*	13	1		
2003-04	Watford	41	7	**59**	**7**
2004-05	QPR	42	2		
2005-06	QPR	40	4		
2006-07	QPR	37	3		
2007-08	Fulham	0	0		
2007-08	Charlton Ath	9	0		
2008-09	Fulham	0	0		
2008-09	QPR	34	1		
2009-10	QPR	16	1		
2010-11	QPR	0	0		
2011-12	QPR	0	0	**182**	**12**
2011-12	*Leyton Orient*	9	1	**9**	**1**
2011-12	*Charlton Ath*	4	0	**13**	**0**

DERRY, Shaun (M) **550 12**
H: 5 10 W: 10 13 b.Nottingham 6-12-77
Source: Trainee.

1995-96	Notts Co	12	0		
1996-97	Notts Co	39	2		
1997-98	Notts Co	28	2	**79**	**4**
1997-98	Sheffield U	12	0		
1998-99	Sheffield U	26	0		
1999-2000	Sheffield U	34	0	**72**	**0**
1999-2000	Portsmouth	9	1		
2000-01	Portsmouth	28	0		
2001-02	Portsmouth	12	0	**49**	**1**
2002-03	Crystal Palace	39	1		
2003-04	Crystal Palace	37	2		
2004-05	Crystal Palace	7	0		
2004-05	*Nottingham F*	7	0	**7**	**0**
2004-05	Leeds U	7	2		
2005-06	Leeds U	41	0		
2006-07	Leeds U	23	1		
2007-08	Leeds U	0	0	**71**	**3**
2007-08	Crystal Palace	30	0		
2008-09	Crystal Palace	39	0		
2009-10	Crystal Palace	46	0	**198**	**3**
2010-11	QPR	45	0		
2011-12	QPR	29	1	**74**	**1**

DIAKITE, Samba (M) **104 1**
H: 6 1 W: 11 13 b.Montfermeil 24-1-89
Honours: Mali 5 full caps.

2007-08	Valenciennes B	7	0	**7**	**0**
2008-09	Olympique Noisy-le-Sec	28	0	**28**	**0**
2009-10	Nancy B	19	0	**19**	**0**
2009-10	Nancy	3	0		
2010-11	Nancy	23	0		
2011-12	Nancy	15	0	**41**	**0**
2011-12	QPR	9	1	**9**	**1**

DOUGHTY, Michael (M) **21 0**
H: 6 1 W: 12 10 b.Westminster 20-11-92
Source: Scholar. *Honours:* Wales Youth.

2010-11	QPR	0	0		
2011-12	QPR	0	0		
2011-12	*Crawley T*	16	0	**16**	**0**
2011-12	*Aldershot T*	5	0	**5**	**0**

DYER, Kieron (M) **316 32**
H: 5 8 W: 10 01 b.Ipswich 29-12-78
Source: Trainee. *Honours:* England Youth, Under-21, B, 33 full caps.

1996-97	Ipswich T	13	0		
1997-98	Ipswich T	41	4		
1998-99	Ipswich T	37	5		
1999-2000	Newcastle U	30	3		
2000-01	Newcastle U	26	5		
2001-02	Newcastle U	18	3		
2002-03	Newcastle U	35	2		
2003-04	Newcastle U	25	1		
2004-05	Newcastle U	23	4		
2005-06	Newcastle U	11	0		
2006-07	Newcastle U	22	5		
2007-08	Newcastle U	0	0	**190**	**23**
2007-08	West Ham U	2	0		
2008-09	West Ham U	7	0		
2009-10	West Ham U	10	0		
2010-11	West Ham U	11	0	**30**	**0**
2010-11	*Ipswich T*	4	0	**95**	**9**
2011-12	QPR	1	0	**1**	**0**

EHMER, Max (M) **60 0**
H: 6 2 W: 11 00 b.Frankfurt 3-2-92
Source: Scholar.

2009-10	QPR	0	0		
2010-11	QPR	0	0		
2010-11	*Yeovil T*	27	0		
2011-12	QPR	0	0		
2011-12	*Yeovil T*	24	0	**51**	**0**
2011-12	*Preston NE*	9	0	**9**	**0**

EPHRAIM, Hogan (F) **142 10**
H: 5 9 W: 10 06 b.Islington 31-3-88
Source: Scholar. *Honours:* England Youth.

2004-05	West Ham U	0	0		
2005-06	West Ham U	0	0		
2006-07	West Ham U	0	0		
2006-07	*Colchester U*	21	1	**21**	**1**
2007-08	West Ham U	0	0		
2007-08	QPR	29	3		
2008-09	QPR	27	1		
2009-10	QPR	22	0		
2009-10	*Leeds U*	3	0	**3**	**0**
2010-11	QPR	28	3		
2011-12	QPR	2	0	**108**	**7**
2011-12	*Charlton Ath*	5	1	**5**	**1**
2011-12	*Bristol C*	5	1	**5**	**1**

FAURLIN, Alejandro (M) **169 13**
H: 6 1 W: 12 06 b.Argentina 9-8-86

2004	Rosario Central	1	0		
2005	Rosario Central	0	0		
2006	Rosario Central	0	0	**1**	**0**
2007	Atletico Rafaela	40	1	**40**	**1**
2008-09	Instituto	27	7	**27**	**7**
2009-10	QPR	41	1		
2010-11	QPR	40	3		
2011-12	QPR	20	1	**101**	**5**

FERDINAND, Anton (D) **254 5**
H: 6 2 W: 11 00 b.Peckham 18-2-85
Source: Trainee. *Honours:* England Youth, Under-20, Under-21.

2002-03	West Ham U	0	0		
2003-04	West Ham U	20	0		
2004-05	West Ham U	29	1		
2005-06	West Ham U	33	2		
2006-07	West Ham U	31	0		
2007-08	West Ham U	25	2		
2008-09	West Ham U	0	0	**138**	**5**
2008-09	Sunderland	31	0		
2009-10	Sunderland	24	0		
2010-11	Sunderland	27	0		
2011-12	Sunderland	3	0	**85**	**0**
2011-12	QPR	31	0	**31**	**0**

FITZPATRICK, David (M) **0 0**
b.Surbiton 10-2-95
Source: Scholar.

2011-12	QPR	0	0		

GABBIDON, Daniel (D) **330 10**
H: 6 0 W: 13 05 b.Cwmbran 8-8-79
Source: Trainee. *Honours:* Wales Youth, Under-21, 46 full caps.

1998-99	WBA	2	0		
1999-2000	WBA	18	0		
2000-01	WBA	0	0	**20**	**0**
2000-01	Cardiff C	43	3		
2001-02	Cardiff C	44	3		
2002-03	Cardiff C	24	0		
2003-04	Cardiff C	41	3		
2004-05	Cardiff C	45	1	**197**	**10**
2005-06	West Ham U	32	0		
2006-07	West Ham U	18	0		
2007-08	West Ham U	10	0		
2008-09	West Ham U	0	0		
2009-10	West Ham U	10	0		
2010-11	West Ham U	26	0	**96**	**0**
2011-12	QPR	17	0	**17**	**0**

GIBBONS, Jordan (M) **0 0**
b. 18-11-93
Source: Scholar.

2011-12	QPR	0	0		

HALL, Fitz (D) **247 11**
H: 6 3 W: 13 00 b.Leytonstone 20-12-80
Source: Barnet Trainee, Chesham U.

2001-02	Oldham Ath	4	1		
2002-03	Oldham Ath	40	4	**44**	**5**
2003-04	Southampton	11	0	**11**	**0**
2004-05	Crystal Palace	36	2		
2005-06	Crystal Palace	39	1	**75**	**3**
2006-07	Wigan Ath	24	0		
2007-08	Wigan Ath	1	0	**25**	**0**
2007-08	QPR	14	0		
2008-09	QPR	24	2		
2009-10	QPR	14	0		
2009-10	*Newcastle U*	7	0	**7**	**0**
2010-11	QPR	19	1		
2011-12	QPR	14	0	**85**	**3**

HARRIMAN, Michael (D) **1 0**
H: 5 6 W: 11 10 b.Chichester 23-10-92
Source: Scholar. *Honours:* Eire Youth.

2010-11	QPR	0	0		
2011-12	QPR	1	0	**1**	**0**

HELGUSON, Heidar (F) **386 125**
H: 5 10 W: 12 09 b.Akureyri 22-8-77
Source: Throttur. *Honours:* Iceland Youth, Under-21, 55 full caps, 12 goals.

1998	Lillestrom	19	2		
1999	Lillestrom	25	16	**44**	**18**
1999-2000	Watford	16	6		
2000-01	Watford	33	8		
2001-02	Watford	34	6		
2002-03	Watford	30	11		
2003-04	Watford	22	8		
2004-05	Watford	39	16		
2005-06	Fulham	27	8		
2006-07	Fulham	30	4	**57**	**12**
2007-08	Bolton W	6	2		
2008-09	Bolton W	1	0	**7**	**2**
2008-09	QPR	20	5		
2009-10	QPR	5	1		
2009-10	*Watford*	29	11	**203**	**66**
2010-11	QPR	34	13		
2011-12	QPR	16	8	**75**	**27**

HEWITT, Troy (F) **6 0**
H: 6 0 W: 12 05 b.Newham 10-2-90
Source: Clapton, Ilford, Harrow B.

2010-11	QPR	0	0		
2011-12	QPR	0	0		
2011-12	*Dagenham & R*	6	0	**6**	**0**

HILL, Clint (D) **422 27**
H: 6 0 W: 11 06 b.Liverpool 19-10-78
Source: Trainee.

1997-98	Tranmere R	14	0		
1998-99	Tranmere R	33	4		
1999-2000	Tranmere R	29	5		
2000-01	Tranmere R	34	5		
2001-02	Tranmere R	30	2	**140**	**16**
2002-03	Oldham Ath	17	1	**17**	**1**
2003-04	Stoke C	12	0		
2004-05	Stoke C	32	1		
2005-06	Stoke C	13	0		
2006-07	Stoke C	18	2		
2007-08	Stoke C	5	0	**80**	**3**
2007-08	Crystal Palace	28	3		
2008-09	Crystal Palace	43	1		
2009-10	Crystal Palace	43	1	**114**	**5**
2010-11	QPR	44	2		
2011-12	QPR	22	0	**66**	**2**
2011-12	*Nottingham F*	5	0	**5**	**0**

HITCHCOCK, Tom (F) **8 0**
H: 5 11 W: 12 08 b.Hemel Hempstead 1-10-92
Source: Scholar.

2009-10	Blackburn R	0	0		
2010-11	Blackburn R	0	0		
2011-12	Blackburn R	0	0		

2011-12	*Plymouth Arg*	8	0	**8**	**0**
2011-12	QPR	0	0		

HULSE, Rob (F) **361 112**
H: 6 1 W: 12 04 b.Crewe 25-10-79
Source: Trainee.

1998-99	Crewe Alex	0	0		
1999-2000	Crewe Alex	4	1		
2000-01	Crewe Alex	33	11		
2001-02	Crewe Alex	41	12		
2002-03	Crewe Alex	38	22	**116**	**46**
2003-04	WBA	33	10		
2004-05	WBA	5	0	**38**	**10**
2004-05	*Leeds U*	13	6		
2005-06	Leeds U	39	12	**52**	**18**
2006-07	Sheffield U	29	8		
2007-08	Sheffield U	21	0	**50**	**8**
2008-09	Derby Co	44	15		
2009-10	Derby Co	37	12		
2010-11	Derby Co	1	1	**82**	**28**
2010-11	QPR	21	2		
2011-12	QPR	2	0	**23**	**2**

KENNY, Paddy (G) **488 0**
H: 6 1 W: 14 01 b.Halifax 17-5-78
Source: Bradford PA. *Honours:* Eire 7 full caps.

1998-99	Bury	0	0		
1999-2000	Bury	46	0		
2000-01	Bury	46	0		
2001-02	Bury	41	0		
2002-03	Bury	0	0	**133**	**0**
2002-03	Sheffield U	45	0		
2003-04	Sheffield U	27	0		
2004-05	Sheffield U	40	0		
2005-06	Sheffield U	46	0		
2006-07	Sheffield U	34	0		
2007-08	Sheffield U	40	0		
2008-09	Sheffield U	44	0		
2009-10	Sheffield U	2	0	**278**	**0**
2010-11	QPR	44	0		
2011-12	QPR	33	0	**77**	**0**

LENNOX, Aaron (G) **0 0**
b.Sydney 19-2-93
Source: Australia IoS.

2011-12	QPR	0	0		

MACKIE, Jamie (F) **170 32**
H: 5 8 W: 11 00 b.Dorking 22-9-85
Source: Leatherhead. *Honours:* Scotland 5 full caps, 2 goals.

2003-04	Wimbledon	13	0	**13**	**0**
2004-05	Milton Keynes D	3	0	**3**	**0**
From Exeter C					
2007-08	Plymouth Arg	13	3		
2008-09	Plymouth Arg	43	5		
2009-10	Plymouth Arg	42	8	**98**	**16**
2010-11	QPR	25	9		
2011-12	QPR	31	7	**56**	**16**

MURPHY, Brian (G) **131 0**
H: 6 0 W: 13 00 b.Waterford 7-5-83
Honours: Eire Under-21.

2000-01	Manchester C	0	0		
2001-02	Manchester C	0	0		
2002-03	Manchester C	0	0		
2002-03	*Oldham Ath*	0	0		
2002-03	*Peterborough U*	1	0	**1**	**0**
From Waterford					
2003-04	Swansea C	11	0		
2004-05	Swansea C	2	0		
2005-06	Swansea C	0	0		
2006-07	Swansea C	0	0	**13**	**0**
2007	Bohemians	29	0		
2008	Bohemians	33	0		
2009	Bohemians	35	0	**97**	**0**
2009-10	Ipswich T	16	0		
2010-11	Ipswich T	4	0		
2011-12	Ipswich T	0	0	**20**	**0**
2011-12	QPR	0	0		

OLLEY, Luke (D) **0 0**
b.Sidcup 22-3-93
Source: Scholar.

2011-12	QPR	0	0		

ONUOHA, Nedum (D) **142 4**
H: 6 2 W: 12 04 b.Warri 12-11-86
Source: Scholar. *Honours:* England Youth, Under-20, Under-21.

2004-05	Manchester C	17	0		
2005-06	Manchester C	10	0		
2006-07	Manchester C	18	0		
2007-08	Manchester C	16	1		
2008-09	Manchester C	23	1		
2009-10	Manchester C	10	1		
2010-11	Manchester C	0	0		
2010-11	*Sunderland*	31	1	**31**	**1**
2011-12	Manchester C	1	0	**95**	**3**
2011-12	QPR	16	0	**16**	**0**

PARMENTER, Taylor (D) **0 0**
b.Bromley 9-9-92
Source: Scholar.

2009-10	QPR	0	0		
2010-11	QPR	0	0		
2011-12	QPR	0	0		

PERONE, Bruno (D) **1 0**
H: 6 3 W: 13 10 b.Sao Paulo 6-7-87
Source: Noroeste, Corinthians Paranaense, Figueirense, Tombense, Mirascol (loan), Xerex (loan).

2011-12	QPR	1	0	**1**	**0**

RAMAGE, Peter (D) **150 2**
H: 6 3 W: 11 02 b.Whitley Bay 22-11-83
Source: Trainee.

2003-04	Newcastle U	0	0		
2004-05	Newcastle U	4	0		
2005-06	Newcastle U	23	0		
2006-07	Newcastle U	21	0		
2007-08	Newcastle U	3	0	**51**	**0**
2008-09	QPR	31	0		
2009-10	QPR	33	2		
2010-11	QPR	4	0		
2011-12	QPR	0	0	**68**	**2**
2011-12	*Crystal Palace*	17	0	**17**	**0**
2011-12	*Birmingham C*	14	0	**14**	**0**

SENDLES-WHITE, Jamie (D) **0 0**
b.Kingston
Source: Scholar.

2011-12	QPR	0	0		

SHARIFF, Mo (F) **0 0**
b.Newham 5-3-93
Source: Slough T Youth.

2010-11	QPR	0	0		
2011-12	QPR	0	0		

SHITTU, Dan (D) **281 27**
H: 6 2 W: 16 03 b.Lagos 2-9-80
Honours: Nigeria 32 full caps.

1999-2000	Charlton Ath	0	0		
2000-01	Charlton Ath	0	0		
2000-01	*Blackpool*	17	2	**17**	**2**
2001-02	Charlton Ath	0	0		
2001-02	QPR	27	2		
2002-03	QPR	43	7		
2003-04	QPR	20	0		
2004-05	QPR	34	4		
2005-06	QPR	45	4		
2006-07	Watford	30	1		
2007-08	Watford	39	7	**69**	**8**
2008-09	Bolton W	10	0		
2009-10	Bolton W	0	0		
2010-11	Bolton W	0	0	**10**	**0**
2010-11	Millwall	9	0	**9**	**0**
2010-11	QPR	7	0		
2011-12	QPR	0	0	**176**	**17**

SKAPETIS, Petros (F) **0 0**
Source: South Melbourne.

2011-12	QPR	0	0		

SMITH, Tommy (F) **467 93**
H: 5 8 W: 11 04 b.Hemel Hempstead 22-5-80
Source: Trainee. *Honours:* England Youth, Under-21.

1997-98	Watford	1	0		
1998-99	Watford	8	2		
1999-2000	Watford	22	2		
2000-01	Watford	43	11		
2001-02	Watford	40	11		
2002-03	Watford	35	7		
2003-04	Watford	0	0		
2003-04	Sunderland	35	4	**35**	**4**
2004-05	Derby Co	42	11		
2005-06	Derby Co	43	8		
2006-07	Derby Co	5	1	**90**	**20**
2006-07	Watford	32	1		
2007-08	Watford	44	7		
2008-09	Watford	44	17		
2009-10	Watford	4	2	**273**	**60**
2009-10	Portsmouth	16	1		
2010-11	Portsmouth	3	0	**19**	**1**
2010-11	QPR	33	6		
2011-12	QPR	17	2	**50**	**8**

SUTHERLAND, Frankie (M) **0 0**
H: 5 9 W: 10 00 b.Hillingdon 6-12-93
Source: Scholar. *Honours:* Eire Youth.

2010-11	QPR	0	0		
2011-12	QPR	0	0		

TAARABT, Adel (M) **129 29**
H: 5 9 W: 10 12 b.Marseille 24-5-89
Honours: France Youth. Morocco 10 full caps, 3 goals.

2006-07	Lens	1	0	**1**	**0**
2006-07	Tottenham H	2	0		
2007-08	Tottenham H	6	0		
2008-09	Tottenham H	1	0		
2008-09	*QPR*	7	1		
2009-10	Tottenham H	0	0	**9**	**0**
2009-10	*QPR*	41	7		
2010-11	QPR	44	19		
2011-12	QPR	27	2	**119**	**29**

TAIWO, Taye (D) **211 18**
H: 6 0 W: 12 02 b.Lagos 16-4-85
Honours: Nigeria 53 full caps, 5 goals.

2004-05	Marseille	4	0		
2005-06	Marseille	30	1		
2006-07	Marseille	38	3		
2007-08	Marseille	28	3		
2008-09	Marseille	35	3		
2009-10	Marseille	27	3		
2010-11	Marseille	30	4	**192**	**17**
2011-12	AC Milan	4	0	**4**	**0**
2011-12	QPR	15	1	**15**	**1**

On loan from AC Milan.

TRANI, Tommaso (G) **0 0**
b.Florence 30-12-93
Source: AC Milan Youth.

2011-12	QPR	0	0		

TRAORE, Armand (D) **65 1**
H: 6 1 W: 12 12 b.Paris 8-10-89
Source: Monaco. *Honours:* France Youth. Senegal 3 full caps.

2006-07	Arsenal	0	0		
2007-08	Arsenal	3	0		
2008-09	Arsenal	0	0		
2008-09	*Portsmouth*	19	1	**19**	**1**
2009-10	Arsenal	9	0		
2010-11	Arsenal	0	0		
2010-11	*Juventus*	10	0	**10**	**0**
2011-12	Arsenal	1	0	**13**	**0**
2011-12	QPR	23	0	**23**	**0**

VINE, Rowan (F) **314 58**
H: 5 11 W: 12 10 b.Basingstoke 21-9-82
Source: Scholar.

2000-01	Portsmouth	2	0		
2001-02	Portsmouth	11	0		
2002-03	Portsmouth	0	0		
2002-03	*Brentford*	42	10		
2003-04	Portsmouth	0	0		
2003-04	*Colchester U*	35	6	**35**	**6**
2004-05	Portsmouth	0	0	**13**	**0**
2004-05	*Luton T*	45	9		
2005-06	Luton T	31	10		
2006-07	Luton T	26	12	**102**	**31**
2006-07	Birmingham C	17	1		
2007-08	Birmingham C	0	0	**17**	**1**
2007-08	QPR	33	6		
2008-09	QPR	5	1		
2009-10	QPR	31	1		
2010-11	QPR	0	0		
2010-11	*Hull C*	5	0	**5**	**0**
2010-11	*Milton Keynes D*	17	1	**17**	**1**
2010-11	*Brentford*	0	0	**42**	**10**
2011-12	QPR	0	0	**69**	**8**
2011-12	*Exeter C*	5	0	**5**	**0**
2011-12	*Gillingham*	9	1	**9**	**1**

WRIGHT-PHILLIPS, Shaun (M) **331 39**
H: 5 5 W: 10 01 b.Lewisham 25-10-81
Source: Scholar. *Honours:* England Under-21, 36 full caps, 6 goals.

1998-99	Manchester C	0	0		
1999-2000	Manchester C	4	0		
2000-01	Manchester C	15	0		
2001-02	Manchester C	35	8		
2002-03	Manchester C	31	1		
2003-04	Manchester C	34	7		
2004-05	Manchester C	34	10		
2005-06	Chelsea	27	0		
2006-07	Chelsea	27	2		
2007-08	Chelsea	27	2		
2008-09	Chelsea	1	0	**82**	**4**
2008-09	Manchester C	27	5		

2009-10 Manchester C 30 4
2010-11 Manchester C 7 0
2011-12 Manchester C 0 0 **217 35**
2011-12 QPR 32 0 **32 0**

YOUNG, Luke (D) 378 9
H: 6 0 W: 12 04 b.Harlow 19-7-79
Source: Trainee. *Honours:* England Youth, Under-21, 7 full caps.
1997-98 Tottenham H 0 0
1998-99 Tottenham H 15 0
1999-2000 Tottenham H 20 0
2000-01 Tottenham H 23 0 **58 0**
2001-02 Charlton Ath 34 0
2002-03 Charlton Ath 32 0
2003-04 Charlton Ath 24 0
2004-05 Charlton Ath 36 2
2005-06 Charlton Ath 32 1
2006-07 Charlton Ath 29 1 **187 4**
2007-08 Middlesbrough 35 1 **35 1**
2008-09 Aston Villa 34 1
2009-10 Aston Villa 16 0
2010-11 Aston Villa 23 1
2011-12 Aston Villa 2 0 **75 2**
2011-12 QPR 23 2 **23 2**

ZAMORA, Bobby (F) 380 128
H: 6 1 W: 11 11 b.Barking 16-1-81
Source: Trainee. *Honours:* England Under-21, 2 full caps.
1999-2000 Bristol R 4 0 **4 0**
1999-2000 *Brighton & HA* 6 6
2000-01 Brighton & HA 43 28
2001-02 Brighton & HA 41 28
2002-03 Brighton & HA 35 14 **125 76**
2003-04 Tottenham H 16 0 **16 0**
2003-04 West Ham U 17 5
2004-05 West Ham U 34 7
2005-06 West Ham U 34 6
2006-07 West Ham U 32 11
2007-08 West Ham U 13 1 **130 30**
2008-09 Fulham 35 2
2009-10 Fulham 27 8
2010-11 Fulham 14 5
2011-12 Fulham 15 5 **91 20**
2011-12 QPR 14 2 **14 2**

Scholars
Adekunle Oluwatobi Aliu; Buck Jordan Winston Bryan; Daly James Christopher; Downs Jake Louis; Hubble Conor Stephen James; Koeris Justin Vernon; Lumley Joseph Patrick; Nguemkam Monthe Emmanuel Gaetan; Simmonds Bradley Michael.

READING (68)

ANDERSEN, Mikkel (G) 64 0
H: 6 5 W: 12 08 b.Copenhagen 17-12-88
Source: AB Copenhagen. *Honours:* Denmark Youth, Under-21.
2006-07 Reading 0 0
2007-08 Reading 0 0
2008-09 Reading 0 0
2008-09 *Brentford* 1 0 **1 0**
2008-09 *Brighton & HA* 5 0 **5 0**
2009-10 Reading 0 0
2009-10 *Bristol R* 39 0
2010-11 Reading 0 0
2010-11 *Bristol R* 19 0 **58 0**
2011-12 Reading 0 0

ANTONIO, Michael (M) 94 13
H: 6 0 W: 11 11 b.Wandsworth 28-3-90
Source: Tooting & M.
2008-09 Reading 0 0
2008-09 *Cheltenham T* 9 0 **9 0**
2009-10 Reading 1 0
2009-10 *Southampton* 28 3 **28 3**
2010-11 Reading 21 1
2011-12 Reading 6 0 **28 1**
2011-12 *Colchester U* 15 4 **15 4**
2011-12 *Sheffield W* 14 5 **14 5**

ARNOLD, Nick (D) 0 0
b.Tadley 3-7-93
Source: Scholar.
2011-12 Reading 0 0

BASEYA, Cedric (M) 26 0
H: 6 4 W: 14 07 b.Bretigny 19-12-87
Source: Scholar.
2006-07 Southampton 0 0
2007-08 Southampton 1 0 **1 0**
2007-08 *Crewe Alex* 3 0 **3 0**
2008-09 Lille 1 0
2009-10 *Le Havre* 19 0 **19 0**
2010-11 Lille 0 0 **1 0**
2011-12 Cherbourg 0 0
2011-12 Reading 0 0
2011-12 *Barnet* 2 0 **2 0**

BIGNALL, Nicholas (F) 48 4
H: 5 10 W: 11 12 b.Reading 11-7-90
Source: Scholar.
2008-09 Reading 0 0
2008-09 *Northampton T* 5 1 **5 1**
2008-09 *Cheltenham T* 13 1 **13 1**
2009-10 Reading 1 0
2009-10 *Stockport Co* 11 2 **11 2**
2010-11 Reading 0 0
2010-11 *Southampton* 3 0 **3 0**
2010-11 *Bournemouth* 5 0 **5 0**
2010-11 *Brentford* 6 0 **6 0**
2011-12 Reading 0 0 **1 0**
2011-12 *Exeter C* 3 0 **3 0**
2011-12 *Wycombe W* 1 0 **1 0**

CHURCH, Simon (F) 144 28
H: 6 0 W: 13 04 b.Amersham 10-12-88
Source: Scholar. *Honours:* Wales Under-21, 15 full caps, 1 goal.
2007-08 Reading 0 0
2007-08 *Crewe Alex* 12 1 **12 1**
2007-08 *Yeovil T* 6 0 **6 0**
2008-09 Reading 0 0
2008-09 *Wycombe W* 9 0 **9 0**
2008-09 *Leyton Orient* 13 5 **13 5**
2009-10 Reading 36 10
2010-11 Reading 37 5
2011-12 Reading 31 7 **104 22**

CUMMINGS, Shaun (D) 87 0
H: 6 0 W: 11 10 b.Hammersmith 25-2-89
2007-08 Chelsea 0 0
2008-09 Chelsea 0 0
2008-09 *Milton Keynes D* 32 0 **32 0**
2009-10 Chelsea 0 0
2009-10 *WBA* 3 0 **3 0**
2009-10 Reading 8 0
2010-11 Reading 10 0
2011-12 Reading 34 0 **52 0**

CYWKA, Thomasz (M) 52 5
H: 5 10 W: 11 09 b.Gliwice 27-6-88
Source: Gwarek Zabrze. *Honours:* Poland Youth, Under-21.
2006-07 Wigan Ath 0 0
2006-07 *Oldham Ath* 4 0 **4 0**
2007-08 Wigan Ath 0 0
2008-09 Wigan Ath 0 0
2009-10 Wigan Ath 0 0
2009-10 *Derby Co* 5 0
2010-11 Derby Co 31 4
2011-12 Derby Co 8 1 **44 5**
2011-12 Reading 4 0 **4 0**

D'ATH, Lawson (M) 14 1
H: 5 9 W: 12 02 b.Witney 24-12-92
Source: Scholar.
2010-11 Reading 0 0
2011-12 Reading 0 0
2011-12 *Yeovil T* 14 1 **14 1**

EDWARDS, Cameron (M) 1 0
H: 5 11 W: 12 00 b.Sydney 27-3-92
2010-11 Perth Glory 1 0 **1 0**
2011-12 Reading 0 0

EDWARDS, Ryan (M) 0 0
b.Sydney 17-11-93
Source: Perth Glory. *Honours:* Australia Under-20.
2011-12 Reading 0 0

FEDERICI, Adam (G) 153 1
H: 6 2 W: 14 02 b.Nowra 31-1-85
Honours: Australia Youth, Under-20, Under-21, 6 full caps.
2005-06 Reading 0 0
2006-07 Reading 2 0
2007-08 Reading 0 0
2008-09 Reading 15 1
2008-09 *Southend U* 10 0 **10 0**
2009-10 Reading 46 0
2010-11 Reading 34 0
2011-12 Reading 46 0 **143 1**

GAGE, Ethan (D) 60 2
H: 5 11 b.Calgary 8-5-91
Honours: Canada Youth.
2007-08 Whitecaps Res 16 2
2008 Vancouver W'Caps6 0
2009 Vancouver W'Caps17 0
2009 *Whitecaps Res* 1 0
2010 Vancouver W'Caps7 0 **30 0**
2010 *Whitecaps Res* 13 0 **30 2**
2010-11 Reading 0 0
2011-12 Reading 0 0

GODDARD, John (M) 0 0
b.Sandhurst 2-6-93
Source: Scholar.
2011-12 Reading 0 0

GORKSS, Kaspars (D) 317 20
H: 6 3 W: 13 05 b.Riga 6-11-81
Honours: Latvia 44 full caps, 4 goals.
2002 Auda Riga 28 0 **28 0**
2003 Oster 8 0
2004 Oster 24 1 **32 1**
2005 Assyriska 23 0 **23 0**
2006 Ventspils 28 5 **28 5**
2006-07 Blackpool 10 0
2007-08 Blackpool 40 5 **50 5**
2008-09 QPR 31 0
2009-10 QPR 41 3
2010-11 QPR 42 3
2011-12 QPR 0 0 **114 6**
2011-12 Reading 42 3 **42 3**

GRIFFIN, Andy (D) 323 6
H: 5 9 W: 10 10 b.Billinge 7-3-79
Source: Trainee. *Honours:* England Youth, Under-21.
1996-97 Stoke C 34 1
1997-98 Stoke C 23 1
1997-98 Newcastle U 4 0
1998-99 Newcastle U 14 0
1999-2000 Newcastle U 3 1
2000-01 Newcastle U 19 0
2001-02 Newcastle U 4 0
2002-03 Newcastle U 27 1
2003-04 Newcastle U 5 0 **76 2**
2004-05 Portsmouth 22 0
2005-06 Portsmouth 22 0
2006-07 Portsmouth 0 0 **44 0**
2006-07 *Stoke C* 33 2
2007-08 Derby Co 15 0 **15 0**
2007-08 Stoke C 15 0
2008-09 Stoke C 20 0
2009-10 Stoke C 0 0 **125 4**
2009-10 *Reading* 21 0
2010-11 Reading 33 0
2011-12 Reading 9 0 **63 0**

GUNNARSSON, Brynjar (M) 380 31
H: 6 1 W: 12 01 b.Reykjavik 16-10-75
Honours: Iceland Youth, Under-21, 74 full caps, 4 goals.
1995 KR 16 1
1996 KR 18 0
1997 KR 16 0 **50 1**
1998 Moss 5 2 **5 2**
1999-2000 Stoke C 22 1
2000-01 Stoke C 46 5
2001-02 Stoke C 23 5
2002-03 Stoke C 40 5
2003-04 Nottingham F 13 0 **13 0**
2003-04 *Stoke C* 3 0 **134 16**
2004-05 Watford 36 3 **36 3**
2005-06 Reading 29 4
2006-07 Reading 23 3
2007-08 Reading 20 0
2008-09 Reading 27 2
2009-10 Reading 26 0
2010-11 Reading 12 0
2011-12 Reading 5 0 **142 9**

HARTE, Ian (D) 379 63
H: 5 11 W: 12 06 b.Drogheda 31-8-77
Source: Trainee. *Honours:* Eire 63 full caps, 11 goals.
1995-96 Leeds U 4 0
1996-97 Leeds U 14 2
1997-98 Leeds U 12 0
1998-99 Leeds U 35 4
1999-2000 Leeds U 33 6
2000-01 Leeds U 29 7
2001-02 Leeds U 36 5
2002-03 Leeds U 27 3
2003-04 Leeds U 23 1 **213 28**
2004-05 Levante 24 1

2005-06 Levante 0 0
2006-07 Levante 6 0 **30 1**
2007-08 Sunderland 8 0 **8 0**
2008-09 Blackpool 4 0 **4 0**
2008-09 Carlisle U 3 1
2009-10 Carlisle U 45 16
2010-11 Carlisle U 4 2 **52 19**
2010-11 Reading 40 11
2011-12 Reading 32 4 **72 15**

HECTOR, Michael (D) 38 4
H: 6 4 W: 12 13 b.Newham 19-7-92
Source: Scholar.
2009-10 Reading 0 0
2010-11 Reading 0 0
2011 *Dundalk* 11 2 **11 2**
2011-12 Reading 0 0
2011-12 *Barnet* 27 2 **27 2**

HOWARD, Brian (M) 292 40
H: 5 8 W: 11 00 b.Winchester 23-1-83
Source: Trainee. *Honours:* England Schools, Youth, Under-20.
1999-2000 Southampton 0 0
2000-01 Southampton 0 0
2001-02 Southampton 0 0
2002-03 Southampton 0 0
2003-04 Swindon T 35 4
2004-05 Swindon T 35 5 **70 9**
2005-06 Barnsley 31 5
2006-07 Barnsley 42 8
2007-08 Barnsley 41 13
2008-09 Barnsley 7 1 **121 27**
2008-09 Sheffield U 26 2
2009-10 Sheffield U 4 0 **30 2**
2009-10 Reading 34 2
2010-11 Reading 24 0
2011-12 Reading 1 0 **59 2**
2011-12 *Millwall* 12 0 **12 0**

HUNT, Noel (F) 265 62
H: 5 8 W: 11 05 b.Waterford 26-12-82
Honours: Eire Under-21, B, 3 full caps.
2002-03 Dunfermline Ath 12 1
2003-04 Dunfermline Ath 13 2
2004-05 Dunfermline Ath 23 1
2005-06 Dunfermline Ath 32 4 **80 8**
2006-07 Dundee U 28 10
2007-08 Dundee U 36 13 **64 23**
2008-09 Reading 37 11
2009-10 Reading 10 2
2010-11 Reading 33 10
2011-12 Reading 41 8 **121 31**

JOYCE, Danny (D) 4 0
b.Dublin 5-6-92
Source: Scholar.
2009-10 Reading 0 0
2010-11 Reading 0 0
2011 *Bohemians* 4 0 **4 0**
2011-12 Reading 0 0

KARACAN, Jem (M) 139 8
H: 5 10 W: 11 13 b.Lewisham 21-2-89
Source: Scholar. *Honours:* Turkey Youth, Under-21.
2007-08 Reading 0 0
2007-08 *Bournemouth* 13 1 **13 1**
2007-08 *Millwall* 7 0 **7 0**
2008-09 Reading 15 1
2009-10 Reading 27 0
2010-11 Reading 40 3
2011-12 Reading 37 3 **119 7**

KEBE, Jimmy (M) 191 31
H: 6 2 W: 11 07 b.Paris 19-1-84
Honours: Mali 8 full caps, 3 goals.
2005-06 Lens 0 0
2006-07 *Chateauroux* 18 2 **18 2**
2007-08 Lens 0 0
2007-08 *Boulogne* 16 5 **16 5**
2007-08 Reading 5 0
2008-09 Reading 41 2
2009-10 Reading 42 10
2010-11 Reading 36 9
2011-12 Reading 33 3 **157 24**

LE FONDRE, Adam (F) 286 119
H: 5 9 W: 11 04 b.Stockport 2-12-86
Source: Trainee.
2004-05 Stockport Co 20 4
2005-06 Stockport Co 22 6
2006-07 Stockport Co 21 7 **63 17**
2006-07 *Rochdale* 7 4
2007-08 Rochdale 46 16
2008-09 Rochdale 44 18
2009-10 Rochdale 1 0 **98 38**
2009-10 Rotherham U 44 25
2010-11 Rotherham U 45 23
2011-12 Rotherham U 4 4 **93 52**
2011-12 Reading 32 12 **32 12**

LEIGERTWOOD, Mikele (D) 338 21
H: 6 1 W: 11 04 b.Enfield 12-11-82
Source: Scholar.
2001-02 Wimbledon 1 0
2001-02 *Leyton Orient* 8 0 **8 0**
2002-03 Wimbledon 28 0
2003-04 Wimbledon 27 2 **56 2**
2003-04 Crystal Palace 12 0
2004-05 Crystal Palace 20 1
2005-06 Crystal Palace 27 0 **59 1**
2006-07 Sheffield U 19 0
2007-08 Sheffield U 2 0 **21 0**
2007-08 QPR 40 5
2008-09 QPR 42 2
2009-10 QPR 40 5
2010-11 QPR 9 0 **131 12**
2010-11 *Reading* 22 1
2011-12 Reading 41 5 **63 6**

LOCKE, Simon (G) 0 0
H: 6 1 W: 11 11 b.Newbury 15-10-91
Source: Scholar.
2010-11 Reading 0 0
2011-12 Reading 0 0

LOSASSO, Charlie (M) 0 0
b.Marlow 11-11-92
Source: Scholar.
2011-12 Reading 0 0

MACDONALD, Angus (D) 2 0
b.Winchester 15-10-92
Source: Scholar.
2011-12 Reading 0 0
2011-12 *Torquay U* 2 0 **2 0**

MANSET, Mathieu (F) 87 16
H: 6 1 W: 13 08 b.Metz 5-8-89
Source: Le Havre.
2009-10 Hereford U 29 3
2010-11 Hereford U 21 7 **50 10**
2010-11 Reading 13 2
2011-12 Reading 15 3 **28 5**
2011-12 *Shanghai S* 9 1 **9 1**

McANUFF, Jobi (M) 425 46
H: 5 11 W: 11 05 b.Edmonton 9-11-81
Source: Scholar. *Honours:* Jamaica 1 full cap.
2000-01 Wimbledon 0 0
2001-02 Wimbledon 38 4
2002-03 Wimbledon 31 4
2003-04 Wimbledon 27 5 **96 13**
2003-04 West Ham U 12 1
2004-05 West Ham U 1 0 **13 1**
2004-05 Cardiff C 43 2 **43 2**
2005-06 Crystal Palace 41 8
2006-07 Crystal Palace 34 5 **75 13**
2007-08 Watford 39 2
2008-09 Watford 40 3
2009-10 Watford 3 0 **82 5**
2009-10 Reading 36 3
2010-11 Reading 40 4
2011-12 Reading 40 5 **116 12**

McCARTHY, Alex (G) 80 0
H: 6 4 W: 11 12 b.Guildford 3-12-89
Source: Scholar. *Honours:* England Under-21.
2008-09 Reading 0 0
2008-09 *Aldershot T* 4 0 **4 0**
2009-10 Reading 0 0
2009-10 *Yeovil T* 44 0 **44 0**
2010-11 Reading 13 0
2010-11 *Brentford* 3 0 **3 0**
2011-12 Reading 0 0 **13 0**
2011-12 *Leeds U* 6 0 **6 0**
2011-12 *Ipswich T* 10 0 **10 0**

McCLEARY, Garath (M) 111 13
H: 5 10 W: 12 06 b.Oxford 15-5-87
Source: Bromley.
2007-08 Nottingham F 8 1
2008-09 Nottingham F 39 1
2009-10 Nottingham F 24 0
2010-11 Nottingham F 18 2
2011-12 Nottingham F 22 9 **111 13**
2011-12 Reading 0 0

McHUGH, Carl (D) 0 0
b.Co. Donegal 5-2-93
Source: Scholar. *Honours:* Eire Youth.
2011-12 Reading 0 0

MILLS, Jack (D) 7 0
H: 6 0 W: 11 02 b.Reading 26-3-92
Source: Scholar. *Honours:* England Youth.
2010-11 Reading 0 0
2010-11 *Telstar* 7 0 **7 0**
2011-12 Reading 0 0

MILLS, Joseph (D) 73 2
H: 5 9 W: 11 00 b.Swindon 30-10-89
Source: Scholar.
2006-07 Southampton 0 0
2007-08 Southampton 0 0
2008-09 Southampton 8 0
2008-09 *Scunthorpe U* 14 0 **14 0**
2009-10 Southampton 16 0
2010-11 Southampton 2 0
2010-11 *Doncaster R* 18 2 **18 2**
2011-12 Southampton 0 0 **26 0**
2011-12 Reading 15 0 **15 0**

MORRISON, Sean (D) 77 7
H: 6 4 W: 14 00 b.Plymouth 8-1-91
Source: Plymouth Arg.
2007-08 Swindon T 2 0
2008-09 Swindon T 20 1
2009-10 Swindon T 9 1
2009-10 *Southend U* 8 0 **8 0**
2010-11 Swindon T 19 4 **50 6**
2010-11 Reading 0 0
2010-11 *Huddersfield T* 0 0
2011-12 Reading 0 0
2011-12 *Huddersfield T* 19 1 **19 1**

MURPHY, David (F) 0 0
b.Wexford 18-4-93
Source: Scholar.
2011-12 Reading 0 0

OBITA, Jordan (M) 11 3
H: 5 11 W: 11 08 b.Oxford 8-12-93
Source: Scholar. *Honours:* England Youth.
2010-11 Reading 0 0
2011-12 Reading 0 0
2011-12 *Barnet* 5 0 **5 0**
2011-12 *Gillingham* 6 3 **6 3**

PEARCE, Alex (D) 154 14
H: 6 0 W: 11 10 b.Wallingford 9-11-88
Source: Scholar. *Honours:* Scotland Youth, Under-21.
2006-07 Reading 0 0
2006-07 *Northampton T* 15 1 **15 1**
2007-08 Reading 0 0
2007-08 *Bournemouth* 11 0 **11 0**
2007-08 *Norwich C* 11 0 **11 0**
2008-09 Reading 16 1
2008-09 *Southampton* 9 2 **9 2**
2009-10 Reading 25 4
2010-11 Reading 21 1
2011-12 Reading 46 5 **108 11**

RAYMOND, Frankie (M) 0 0
b.Chislehurst 18-11-92
Source: Scholar.
2010-11 Reading 0 0
2011-12 Reading 0 0

ROBERTS, Jason (F) 438 137
H: 6 0 W: 14 01 b.Acton 25-1-78
Source: Hayes. *Honours:* Grenada 22 full caps, 12 goals.
1997-98 Wolverhampton W 0 0
1997-98 *Torquay U* 14 6 **14 6**
1997-98 *Bristol C* 3 1 **3 1**
1998-99 Bristol R 37 16
1999-2000 Bristol R 41 22 **78 38**
2000-01 WBA 43 14
2001-02 WBA 14 7
2002-03 WBA 32 3
2003-04 WBA 0 0 **89 24**
2003-04 *Portsmouth* 10 1 **10 1**
2003-04 Wigan Ath 14 8
2004-05 Wigan Ath 45 21
2005-06 Wigan Ath 34 8 **93 37**
2006-07 Blackburn R 18 4
2007-08 Blackburn R 26 3
2008-09 Blackburn R 26 7
2009-10 Blackburn R 29 5
2010-11 Blackburn R 25 5
2011-12 Blackburn R 10 0 **134 24**
2011-12 Reading 17 6 **17 6**

ROBSON-KANU, Hal (F) **122 18**
H: 5 7 W: 11 08 b.Acton 21-5-89
Honours: England Youth, Under-20. Wales Under-21, 7 full caps.

2007-08	Reading	0	0		
2007-08	*Southend U*	8	3		
2008-09	Reading	0	0		
2008-09	*Southend U*	14	2	**22**	**5**
2008-09	*Swindon T*	20	4	**20**	**4**
2009-10	Reading	17	0		
2010-11	Reading	27	5		
2011-12	Reading	36	4	**80**	**9**

SAMUEL, Dominic (F) **0 0**
b.Southwark 1-4-94
Source: Scholar. *Honours:* England Youth.

2011-12	Reading	0	0		

SHEPPARD, Karl (F) **67 23**
b.Shelbourne 14-2-91
Source: Scholar. *Honours:* Eire Under-21.

2007-08	Everton	0	0		
2008-09	Everton	0	0		
2009-10	Everton	0	0		
2010	Galway U	33	8	**33**	**8**
2011	Shamrock R	34	15	**34**	**15**
2011-12	Reading	0	0		

TABB, Jay (M) **300 31**
H: 5 7 W: 10 00 b.Tooting 21-2-84
Source: Trainee. *Honours:* Eire Under-21.

2000-01	Brentford	2	0		
2001-02	Brentford	3	0		
2002-03	Brentford	5	0		
2003-04	Brentford	36	9		
2004-05	Brentford	40	5		
2005-06	Brentford	42	6	**128**	**20**
2006-07	Coventry C	31	3		
2007-08	Coventry C	42	5		
2008-09	Coventry C	22	3	**95**	**11**
2008-09	Reading	9	0		
2009-10	Reading	28	0		
2010-11	Reading	21	0		
2011-12	Reading	19	0	**77**	**0**

TANNER, Craig (F) **0 0**
b.Reading 27-10-94
Source: Scholar.

2011-12	Reading	0	0		

TAYLOR, Jake (M) **34 3**
H: 5 10 W: 12 01 b.Ascot 1-12-91
Source: Scholar. *Honours:* Wales Under-21.

2010-11	Reading	1	0		
2011-12	Reading	0	0	**1**	**0**
2011-12	*Aldershot T*	3	0	**3**	**0**
2011-12	*Exeter C*	30	3	**30**	**3**

TSHIBOLA, Aaron (M) **0 0**
b.Newham 2-1-95
Source: Scholar.

2011-12	Reading	0	0		

UGWU, Chigozie (F) **0 0**
b.Oxford 22-4-93
Source: Scholar.

2011-12	Reading	0	0		

WALCOTT, Jacob (M) **14 2**
H: 5 10 W: 11 00 b.Abingdon 29-6-92
Source: Scholar.

2010-11	Reading	0	0		
2010-11	*Telstar*	14	2	**14**	**2**
2011-12	Reading	0	0		

WILLIAMS, Brett (F) **29 5**
H: 6 2 W: 12 07 b.Southampton 1-12-87
Source: Eastleigh.

2010-11	Reading	0	0		
2011-12	Reading	0	0		
2011-12	*Rotherham U*	11	2	**11**	**2**
2011-12	*Northampton T*	18	3	**18**	**3**

ROCHDALE (69)

ABADAKI, Godwin (F) **2 0**
H: 5 11 W: 12 04 b.Kwara 21-10-93
Source: Scholar.

2011-12	Rochdale	2	0	**2**	**0**

ADAMS, Nicky (F) **205 19**
H: 5 10 W: 11 00 b.Bolton 16-10-86
Source: Scholar. *Honours:* Wales Under-21.

2005-06	Bury	15	1		
2006-07	Bury	19	1		
2007-08	Bury	43	12	**77**	**14**
2008-09	Leicester C	12	0		
2008-09	*Rochdale*	14	1		
2009-10	Leicester C	18	0	**30**	**0**
2009-10	*Leyton Orient*	6	0	**6**	**0**
2010-11	Brentford	7	0	**7**	**0**
2010-11	Rochdale	30	0		
2011-12	Rochdale	41	4	**85**	**5**

AKPA AKPRO, Jean-Louis (F) **174 24**
H: 6 0 W: 10 12 b.Toulouse 4-1-85

2004-05	Toulouse	13	0		
2005-06	Toulouse	14	3	**27**	**3**
2006-07	*Brest*	15	2	**15**	**2**
2007-08	FC Brussels	3	0	**3**	**0**
2008-09	Grimsby T	20	3		
2009-10	Grimsby T	36	5	**56**	**8**
2010-11	Rochdale	32	4		
2011-12	Rochdale	41	7	**73**	**11**

AMANKWAAH, Kevin (D) **264 7**
H: 6 1 W: 12 12 b.Harrow 19-5-82
Source: Scholar. *Honours:* England Youth.

1999-2000	Bristol C	5	0		
2000-01	Bristol C	14	0		
2001-02	Bristol C	24	1		
2002-03	Bristol C	1	0		
2002-03	*Torquay U*	6	0	**6**	**0**
2003-04	Bristol C	5	0		
2003-04	*Cheltenham T*	12	0	**12**	**0**
2004-05	Bristol C	5	0	**54**	**1**
2004-05	Yeovil T	15	0		
2005-06	Yeovil T	38	1	**53**	**1**
2006-07	Swansea C	29	0		
2007-08	Swansea C	0	0	**29**	**0**
2008-09	Swindon T	31	2		
2009-10	Swindon T	36	3		
2010-11	Swindon T	19	0		
2011-12	Swindon T	0	0	**86**	**5**
2011-12	Burton Alb	8	0	**8**	**0**
2011-12	Rochdale	16	0	**16**	**0**

BARNES-HOMER, Matt (M) **6 0**
H: 5 11 W: 12 05 b.Dudley 25-1-86
From Willenhall T.

2006-07	Wycombe W	1	0	**1**	**0**

From Kidderminster H, Luton T.

2011-12	Rochdale	5	0	**5**	**0**

BARRY-MURPHY, Brian (M) **446 17**
H: 5 10 W: 13 01 b.Cork 27-7-78
Honours: Eire Youth, Under-21.

1995-96	Cork City	13	0		
1996-97	Cork City	25	0		
1997-98	Cork City	15	1		
1998-99	Cork City	27	1	**80**	**2**
1999-2000	Preston NE	1	0		
2000-01	Preston NE	14	0		
2001-02	Preston NE	4	0		
2001-02	*Southend U*	8	1	**8**	**1**
2002-03	Preston NE	2	0	**21**	**0**
2002-03	*Hartlepool U*	7	0	**7**	**0**
2002-03	Sheffield W	17	0		
2003-04	Sheffield W	41	0	**58**	**0**
2004-05	Bury	45	6		
2005-06	Bury	40	3		
2006-07	Bury	14	0		
2007-08	Bury	31	1		
2008-09	Bury	42	2		
2009-10	Bury	46	1	**218**	**13**
2010-11	Rochdale	32	0		
2011-12	Rochdale	22	1	**54**	**1**

BYRNE, Callum (M) **0 0**
b. 5-2-92
Source: Scholar.

2010-11	Rochdale	0	0		
2011-12	Rochdale	0	0		

BYRNE, Neil (D) **3 0**
b.Dublin 2-2-93
Source: Scholar. *Honours:* Eire Youth.

2010-11	Nottingham F	0	0		
2011-12	Nottingham F	0	0		
2011-12	Rochdale	3	0	**3**	**0**

DONNELLY, George (F) **72 18**
H: 6 2 W: 13 03 b.Liverpool 28-5-88
Source: Skelmersdale U.

2008-09	Plymouth Arg	2	0		
2009-10	Plymouth Arg	0	0		
2009-10	*Stockport Co*	19	4		
2010-11	Plymouth Arg	0	0	**2**	**0**
2010-11	*Stockport Co*	23	8	**42**	**12**

From Fleetwood T

2011-12	Macclesfield T	28	6	**28**	**6**
2011-12	Rochdale	0	0		

EDWARDS, Matty (G) **8 0**
H: 6 2 W: 12 11 b.Birkenhead 22-8-90
Source: Leeds U. *Honours:* Scotland Under-21.

2008-09	Leeds U	0	0		
2009-10	Rochdale	0	0		
2010-11	Rochdale	1	0		
2011-12	Rochdale	7	0	**8**	**0**

GRAY, Reece (F) **8 2**
H: 5 7 W: 8 08 b.Oldham 1-9-92
Source: Scholar.

2009-10	Rochdale	2	0		
2010-11	Rochdale	2	1		
2011-12	Rochdale	4	1	**8**	**2**

GRIMES, Ashley (M) **88 25**
H: 6 0 W: 11 02 b.Swinton 9-12-86
Source: Scholar.

2006-07	Manchester C	0	0		
2006-07	*Swindon T*	4	0	**4**	**0**
2007-08	Manchester C	0	0		
2008-09	Millwall	17	2		
2009-10	Millwall	4	0		
2010-11	Millwall	0	0	**21**	**2**
2010-11	*Lincoln C*	27	15	**27**	**15**
2011-12	Rochdale	36	8	**36**	**8**

HACKNEY, Simon (M) **171 19**
H: 5 8 W: 9 13 b.Manchester 5-2-84
Source: Woodley Sports.

2005-06	Carlisle U	30	6		
2006-07	Carlisle U	18	2		
2007-08	Carlisle U	43	8		
2008-09	Carlisle U	22	1	**113**	**17**
2008-09	Colchester U	17	0		
2009-10	Colchester U	17	1		
2009-10	*Morecambe*	8	1	**8**	**1**
2010-11	Colchester U	1	0	**35**	**1**
2010-11	*Oxford U*	13	0	**13**	**0**
2011-12	Rochdale	2	0	**2**	**0**

HOLNESS, Marcus (D) **108 4**
H: 6 0 W: 12 02 b.Swinton 8-12-88
Source: Scholar.

2007-08	Oldham Ath	0	0		
2007-08	Rochdale	19	0		
2008-09	Rochdale	8	0		
2009-10	Rochdale	11	0		
2010-11	Rochdale	46	1		
2011-12	Rochdale	24	3	**108**	**4**

JONES, Gary (M) **534 76**
H: 5 11 W: 12 05 b.Birkenhead 3-6-77
Source: Caernarfon T.

1997-98	Swansea C	8	0	**8**	**0**
1997-98	Rochdale	17	2		
1998-99	Rochdale	20	0		
1999-2000	Rochdale	39	7		
2000-01	Rochdale	44	8		
2001-02	Rochdale	20	5		
2001-02	Barnsley	25	1		
2002-03	Barnsley	31	1		
2003-04	Barnsley	0	0	**56**	**2**
2003-04	Rochdale	26	4		
2004-05	Rochdale	39	8		
2005-06	Rochdale	42	4		
2006-07	Rochdale	27	3		
2007-08	Rochdale	43	7		
2008-09	Rochdale	28	0		
2009-10	Rochdale	34	4		
2010-11	Rochdale	46	17		
2011-12	Rochdale	45	5	**470**	**74**

JORDAN, Stephen (D) **177 0**
H: 6 1 W: 13 00 b.Warrington 6-3-82
Source: Scholarship.

1998-99	Manchester C	0	0		
1999-2000	Manchester C	0	0		
2000-01	Manchester C	0	0		
2001-02	Manchester C	0	0		
2002-03	Manchester C	1	0		
2002-03	*Cambridge U*	11	0	**11**	**0**
2003-04	Manchester C	2	0		
2004-05	Manchester C	19	0		
2005-06	Manchester C	18	0		
2006-07	Manchester C	13	0	**53**	**0**
2007-08	Burnley	21	0		
2008-09	Burnley	27	0		
2009-10	Burnley	25	0		
2010-11	Burnley	0	0	**73**	**0**
2010-11	Sheffield U	15	0	**15**	**0**

2010-11 *Huddersfield T* 6 0 6 0
2011-12 Rochdale 19 0 19 0

KENNEDY, Jason (M) 237 18
H: 6 1 W: 13 02 b.Stockton 11-9-86
Source: Scholar.
2004-05 Middlesbrough 1 0
2005-06 Middlesbrough 3 0
2006-07 Middlesbrough 0 0
2006-07 *Boston U* 13 1 13 1
2006-07 *Bury* 12 0 12 0
2007-08 Middlesbrough 0 0 4 0
2007-08 *Livingston* 18 2 18 2
2007-08 *Darlington* 13 2
2008-09 Darlington 46 5 59 7
2009-10 Rochdale 42 0
2010-11 Rochdale 45 4
2011-12 Rochdale 44 4 131 8

LUCAS, David (G) 306 0
H: 6 1 W: 13 07 b.Preston 23-11-77
Source: Trainee. *Honours:* England Youth.
1995-96 Preston NE 1 0
1995-96 *Darlington* 6 0
1996-97 Preston NE 2 0
1996-97 *Darlington* 7 0 13 0
1996-97 *Scunthorpe U* 6 0 6 0
1997-98 Preston NE 6 0
1998-99 Preston NE 30 0
1999-2000 Preston NE 6 0
2000-01 Preston NE 29 0
2001-02 Preston NE 24 0
2002-03 Preston NE 21 0
2003-04 Preston NE 2 0 121 0
2003-04 *Sheffield W* 17 0
2004-05 Sheffield W 34 0
2005-06 Sheffield W 18 0
2006-07 Sheffield W 0 0 69 0
2006-07 Barnsley 3 0
2007-08 Barnsley 0 0 3 0
2007-08 Leeds U 3 0
2008-09 Leeds U 13 0 16 0
2009-10 Swindon T 41 0
2010-11 Swindon T 21 0 62 0
2011-12 Rochdale 16 0 16 0

MINIHAN, Sam (D) 1 0
H: 6 1 W: 11 09 b.Rochdale 16-2-94
Source: Scholar.
2011-12 Rochdale 1 0 1 0

THOMPSON, Joe (M) 140 15
H: 6 0 W: 9 07 b.Rochdale 5-3-89
Source: Scholar.
2005-06 Rochdale 1 0
2006-07 Rochdale 13 0
2007-08 Rochdale 11 1
2008-09 Rochdale 30 5
2009-10 Rochdale 36 6
2010-11 Rochdale 32 2
2011-12 Rochdale 17 1 140 15

TUTTE, Andrew (M) 64 3
H: 5 9 W: 10 10 b.Huyton 21-9-90
Source: Scholar. *Honours:* England Youth, Under-20.
2007-08 Manchester C 0 0
2008-09 Manchester C 0 0
2009-10 Manchester C 0 0
2010-11 Manchester C 0 0
2010-11 *Rochdale* 7 0
2010-11 *Shrewsbury T* 2 0 2 0
2010-11 *Yeovil T* 15 2 15 2
2011-12 Rochdale 40 1 47 1

TWADDLE, Marc (D) 154 7
H: 6 1 W: 13 00 b.Glasgow 27-8-86
2003-04 Falkirk 3 0
2004-05 Falkirk 0 0
2005-06 Falkirk 6 0
2006-07 Falkirk 16 2
2007-08 Partick Th 33 2
2008-09 Partick Th 30 0 63 2
2009-10 Falkirk 33 1
2010-11 Falkirk 31 2 89 5
2011-12 Rochdale 2 0 2 0

WIDDOWSON, Joe (D) 127 1
H: 6 0 W: 12 00 b.Forest Gate 28-3-89
Source: Scholar.
2007-08 West Ham U 0 0
2007-08 *Rotherham U* 3 0 3 0
2008-09 West Ham U 0 0
2008-09 *Grimsby T* 20 1
2009-10 Grimsby T 38 0 58 1
2010-11 Rochdale 34 0
2011-12 Rochdale 32 0 66 0

ROTHERHAM U (70)

ANNERSON, Jamie (G) 9 0
H: 6 2 W: 13 02 b.Sheffield 1-11-88
Source: Scholar. *Honours:* England Youth.
2005-06 Sheffield U 0 0
2006-07 Sheffield U 0 0
2007-08 *Rotherham U* 0 0
2007-08 *Chesterfield* 0 0
2007-08 Sheffield U 0 0
2008-09 Sheffield U 0 0
2008-09 *Rotherham U* 0 0
2009-10 Rotherham U 0 0
2010-11 Rotherham U 9 0
2011-12 Rotherham U 0 0 9 0
2011-12 *Bradford C* 0 0

BANKS, Oliver (D) 1 1
H: 6 3 W: 11 11 b.Rotherham 21-9-92
Source: Scholar.
2010-11 Rotherham U 1 1
2011-12 Rotherham U 0 0 1 1

BRADLEY, Mark (D) 138 6
H: 6 0 W: 11 05 b.Dudley 14-1-88
Source: Scholar. *Honours:* Wales Youth, Under-21, 1 full cap.
2004-05 Walsall 1 0
2005-06 Walsall 3 0
2006-07 Walsall 1 0
2007-08 Walsall 35 3
2008-09 Walsall 28 2
2009-10 Walsall 28 0 96 5
2010-11 Rotherham U 21 0
2011-12 Rotherham U 21 1 42 1

BROWN, Troy (D) 36 3
H: 6 1 W: 12 01 b.Croydon 17-9-90
Source: Fulham Scholar. *Honours:* Wales Under-21.
2009-10 Ipswich T 1 0
2010-11 Ipswich T 12 0 13 0
2011-12 Rotherham U 6 1 6 1
2011-12 *Aldershot T* 17 2 17 2

CRESSWELL, Ryan (D) 115 10
H: 5 9 W: 10 05 b.Rotherham 22-12-87
Source: Scholar.
2006-07 Sheffield U 0 0
2007-08 Sheffield U 0 0
2007-08 *Rotherham U* 3 0
2007-08 *Morecambe* 2 0 2 0
2007-08 *Macclesfield T* 19 1 19 1
2008-09 Bury 25 1
2009-10 Bury 28 0 53 1
2010-11 Rotherham U 22 4
2011-12 Rotherham U 16 4 41 8

DENTON, Alec (F) 1 0
b.Sheffield 30-7-94
Source: Scholar.
2011-12 Rotherham U 1 0 1 0

EVANS, Gary (F) 193 40
H: 6 0 W: 12 08 b.Stockport 26-4-88
Source: Crewe Alex.
2007-08 Macclesfield T 42 7
2008-09 Macclesfield T 40 12 82 19
2009-10 Bradford C 43 11
2010-11 Bradford C 36 3 79 14
2011-12 Rotherham U 32 7 32 7

FOSTER, Luke (D) 44 2
H: 6 2 W: 12 08 b.Mexborough 8-9-85
Source: Scholar.
2004-05 Sheffield W 0 0
2005-06 Lincoln C 16 1
2006-07 Lincoln C 0 0 16 1
From Stalybridge C, Oxford U, Mansfield T.
2010-11 Stevenage 23 1 23 1
From Stalybridge C, Oxford U, Mansfield T.
2011-12 Rotherham U 5 0 5 0

GRABBAN, Lewis (F) 153 35
H: 6 0 W: 11 03 b.Croydon 12-1-88
Source: Scholar.
2005-06 Crystal Palace 0 0
2006-07 Crystal Palace 8 1
2006-07 *Oldham Ath* 9 0 9 0
2007-08 Crystal Palace 2 0 10 1
2007-08 *Motherwell* 6 0 6 0
2007-08 Millwall 13 3
2008-09 Millwall 31 6
2009-10 Millwall 11 0
2009-10 *Brentford* 7 2
2010-11 Millwall 1 0 56 9
2010-11 Brentford 22 5 29 7
2011-12 Rotherham U 43 18 43 18

HARRISON, Danny (M) 309 20
H: 5 11 W: 12 04 b.Liverpool 4-11-82
Source: Scholar.
2001-02 Tranmere R 1 0
2002-03 Tranmere R 12 0
2003-04 Tranmere R 32 2
2004-05 Tranmere R 32 0
2005-06 Tranmere R 35 2
2006-07 Tranmere R 12 1 124 5
2007-08 Rotherham U 44 4
2008-09 Rotherham U 33 1
2009-10 Rotherham U 37 4
2010-11 Rotherham U 30 4
2011-12 Rotherham U 41 2 185 15

MARSHALL, Marcus (F) 87 5
H: 5 10 W: 11 06 b.Hammersmith 7-10-89
Source: Scholar.
2007-08 Blackburn R 0 0
2008-09 Blackburn R 0 0
2009-10 Blackburn R 0 0
2009-10 *Rotherham U* 22 0
2010-11 Rotherham U 36 3
2011-12 Rotherham U 15 1 73 4
2011-12 *Macclesfield T* 14 1 14 1

MULLINS, John (D) 246 13
H: 5 11 W: 12 07 b.Hampstead 6-11-85
Source: Scholar.
2004-05 Reading 0 0
2004-05 *Kidderminster H* 21 2 21 2
2005-06 Reading 0 0
2006-07 Mansfield T 43 2
2007-08 Mansfield T 43 2 86 4
2008-09 Stockport Co 33 3
2009-10 Stockport Co 36 1 69 4
2010-11 Rotherham U 35 1
2011-12 Rotherham U 35 2 70 3

NAYLOR, Richard (D) 419 41
H: 6 1 W: 13 07 b.Leeds 28-2-77
Source: Trainee.
1995-96 Ipswich T 0 0
1996-97 Ipswich T 27 4
1997-98 Ipswich T 5 2
1998-99 Ipswich T 30 5
1999-2000 Ipswich T 36 8
2000-01 Ipswich T 13 1
2001-02 Ipswich T 14 1
2001-02 *Millwall* 3 0 3 0
2001-02 *Barnsley* 8 0 8 0
2002-03 Ipswich T 17 2
2003-04 Ipswich T 39 5
2004-05 Ipswich T 46 6
2005-06 Ipswich T 42 3
2006-07 Ipswich T 25 0
2007-08 Ipswich T 7 0
2008-09 Ipswich T 23 0 324 37
2008-09 Leeds U 22 1
2009-10 Leeds U 29 2
2010-11 Leeds U 15 1 66 4
2011-12 Doncaster R 13 0 13 0
2011-12 Rotherham U 5 0 5 0

NEWEY, Tom (D) 322 7
H: 5 10 W: 10 02 b.Sheffield 31-10-82
Source: Scholar.
2000-01 Leeds U 0 0
2001-02 Leeds U 0 0
2002-03 Leeds U 0 0
2002-03 *Cambridge U* 6 0
2002-03 *Darlington* 7 1 7 1
2003-04 Leyton Orient 34 2
2004-05 Leyton Orient 20 1 54 3
2004-05 *Cambridge U* 16 0 22 0
2005-06 Grimsby T 38 1
2006-07 Grimsby T 43 1
2007-08 Grimsby T 42 1
2008-09 Grimsby T 24 0
2008-09 *Rochdale* 2 0 2 0
2009-10 Grimsby T 0 0 147 3
2009-10 Bury 32 0 32 0
2010-11 Rotherham U 38 0
2011-12 Rotherham U 20 0 58 0

PRINGLE, Ben (M) **46 4**
H: 5 8 W: 11 10 b.Whitley Bay 25-7-88
Source: WBA Scholar, Newcastle Blue Star, Morpeth T, Ilkeston T.
2009-10 Derby Co 5 0
2010-11 Derby Co 15 0 **20 0**
2010-11 *Torquay U* 5 0 **5 0**
2011-12 Rotherham U 21 4 **21 4**

RAYNES, Michael (D) **207 5**
H: 6 4 W: 12 00 b.Wythenshawe 15-10-87
Source: Scholar.
2004-05 Stockport Co 19 0
2005-06 Stockport Co 25 1
2006-07 Stockport Co 9 0
2007-08 Stockport Co 27 0
2008-09 Stockport Co 35 3
2009-10 Stockport Co 25 1 **140 5**
2009-10 Scunthorpe U 12 0
2010-11 Scunthorpe U 22 0 **34 0**
2011-12 Rotherham U 33 0 **33 0**

REVELL, Alex (F) **259 53**
H: 6 3 W: 13 00 b.Cambridge 7-7-83
Source: Scholar.
2000-01 Cambridge U 4 0
2001-02 Cambridge U 24 2
2002-03 Cambridge U 9 0
2003-04 Cambridge U 20 3 **57 5**
From Braintree T.
2006-07 Brighton & HA 38 7
2007-08 Brighton & HA 21 6 **59 13**
2007-08 Southend U 8 0
2008-09 Southend U 23 4
2009-10 Southend U 3 0 **34 4**
2009-10 *Swindon T* 10 2 **10 2**
2009-10 Wycombe W 15 6 **15 6**
2010-11 Leyton Orient 39 13
2011-12 Leyton Orient 5 0 **44 13**
2011-12 Rotherham U 40 10 **40 10**

SCHOFIELD, Danny (M) **395 54**
H: 5 10 W: 11 02 b.Doncaster 10-4-80
Source: Brodsworth MW.
1998-99 Huddersfield T 1 0
1999-2000 Huddersfield T 2 0
2000-01 Huddersfield T 1 0
2001-02 Huddersfield T 40 8
2002-03 Huddersfield T 30 2
2003-04 Huddersfield T 40 8
2004-05 Huddersfield T 33 5
2005-06 Huddersfield T 41 9
2006-07 Huddersfield T 35 5
2007-08 Huddersfield T 25 2 **248 39**
2008-09 Yeovil T 39 4
2009-10 Yeovil T 4 1 **43 5**
2009-10 Millwall 36 7
2010-11 Millwall 31 2 **67 9**
2011-12 Rotherham U 37 1 **37 1**

TAYLOR, Jason (M) **225 15**
H: 6 1 W: 11 03 b.Ashton-under-Lyne 28-1-87
Source: Scholar.
2005-06 Oldham Ath 0 0
2005-06 *Stockport Co* 9 0
2006-07 Stockport Co 45 1
2007-08 Stockport Co 42 4
2008-09 Stockport Co 8 1 **104 6**
2008-09 Rotherham U 15 1
2009-10 Rotherham U 2 0
2009-10 *Rochdale* 23 1 **23 1**
2010-11 Rotherham U 42 5
2011-12 Rotherham U 39 2 **98 8**

TONGE, Dale (D) **200 1**
H: 5 10 W: 10 06 b.Doncaster 7-5-85
Source: Scholar.
2003-04 Barnsley 1 0
2004-05 Barnsley 14 0
2005-06 Barnsley 24 0
2006-07 Barnsley 6 0 **45 0**
2006-07 *Gillingham* 3 0 **3 0**
2007-08 Rotherham U 37 0
2008-09 Rotherham U 39 1
2009-10 Rotherham U 21 0
2010-11 Rotherham U 23 0
2011-12 Rotherham U 32 0 **152 1**

WARNE, Paul (M) **464 58**
H: 5 10 W: 11 07 b.Norwich 8-5-73
Source: Wroxham.
1997-98 Wigan Ath 25 2
1998-99 Wigan Ath 11 1 **36 3**
1998-99 Rotherham U 19 8
1999-2000 Rotherham U 43 10
2000-01 Rotherham U 44 7
2001-02 Rotherham U 25 0
2002-03 Rotherham U 40 1
2003-04 Rotherham U 35 1
2004-05 Rotherham U 24 1
2004-05 *Mansfield T* 7 1 **7 1**
2005-06 Oldham Ath 40 9
2006-07 Oldham Ath 46 9 **86 18**
2007-08 Yeovil T 33 1
2008-09 Yeovil T 44 4 **77 5**
2009-10 Rotherham U 14 2
2010-11 Rotherham U 11 1
2011-12 Rotherham U 3 0 **258 31**

WARRINGTON, Andy (G) **345 0**
H: 6 3 W: 12 13 b.Sheffield 10-6-76
Source: Trainee.
1994-95 York C 0 0
1995-96 York C 6 0
1996-97 York C 27 0
1997-98 York C 17 0
1998-99 York C 11 0 **61 0**
2003-04 Doncaster R 46 0
2004-05 Doncaster R 34 0
2005-06 Doncaster R 9 0
2006-07 Doncaster R 0 0 **89 0**
2006-07 Bury 20 0 **20 0**
2007-08 Rotherham U 46 0
2008-09 Rotherham U 38 0
2009-10 Rotherham U 46 0
2010-11 Rotherham U 38 0
2011-12 Rotherham U 7 0 **175 0**

SCUNTHORPE U (71)

BARCHAM, Andy (F) **165 29**
H: 5 8 W: 11 10 b.Basildon 16-12-86
Source: Scholar.
2005-06 Tottenham H 0 0
2006-07 Tottenham H 0 0
2007-08 Tottenham H 0 0
2007-08 *Leyton Orient* 25 1 **25 1**
2008-09 Tottenham H 0 0
2008-09 Gillingham 33 6
2009-10 Gillingham 42 7
2010-11 Gillingham 24 6 **99 19**
2011-12 Scunthorpe U 41 9 **41 9**

BYRNE, Cliff (D) **276 9**
H: 6 0 W: 12 11 b.Dublin 27-4-82
Honours: Eire Youth, Under-21.
1999-2000 Sunderland 0 0
2000-01 Sunderland 0 0
2001-02 Sunderland 0 0
2002-03 Sunderland 0 0
2002-03 *Scunthorpe U* 13 0
2003-04 Scunthorpe U 39 1
2004-05 Scunthorpe U 29 1
2005-06 Scunthorpe U 32 1
2006-07 Scunthorpe U 24 0
2007-08 Scunthorpe U 25 0
2008-09 Scunthorpe U 43 2
2009-10 Scunthorpe U 36 2
2010-11 Scunthorpe U 21 2
2011-12 Scunthorpe U 14 0 **276 9**

CANAVAN, Niall (D) **30 2**
H: 6 3 W: 12 00 b.Guiseley 11-4-91
Source: Scholar. *Honours:* Eire Under-21.
2009-10 Scunthorpe U 7 1
2010-11 Scunthorpe U 8 0
2010-11 *Shrewsbury T* 3 0 **3 0**
2011-12 Scunthorpe U 12 1 **27 2**

COLLINS, Michael (M) **206 20**
H: 6 0 W: 11 00 b.Halifax 30-4-86
Source: Scholar. *Honours:* Eire Youth, Under-21.
2004-05 Huddersfield T 8 0
2005-06 Huddersfield T 17 1
2006-07 Huddersfield T 43 4
2007-08 Huddersfield T 41 2
2008-09 Huddersfield T 36 9
2009-10 Huddersfield T 28 3 **173 19**
2010-11 Scunthorpe U 32 1
2011-12 Scunthorpe U 1 0 **33 1**

DUFFY, Mark (M) **125 8**
H: 5 9 W: 11 05 b.Liverpool 7-10-85
Source: Vauxhall M, Prescot C, Southport.
2008-09 Morecambe 9 1
2009-10 Morecambe 35 4
2010-11 Morecambe 22 0 **66 5**
2010-11 Scunthorpe U 22 1
2011-12 Scunthorpe U 37 2 **59 3**

GIBBONS, Robbie (M) **8 0**
H: 5 11 W: 12 00 b.Dublin 8-10-91
Source: Scholar.
2008-09 Nottingham F 0 0
2009-10 Nottingham F 0 0
2010-11 Nottingham F 0 0
2011-12 Alki 4 0 **4 0**
2011-12 Ermis 0 0
2011-12 Scunthorpe U 4 0 **4 0**

GODDEN, Matthew (F) **6 0**
H: 6 1 W: 12 03 b.Canterbury 29-7-91
Source: Scholar.
2009-10 Scunthorpe U 0 0
2010-11 Scunthorpe U 5 0
2011-12 Scunthorpe U 1 0 **6 0**

GRANT, Robert (M) **135 27**
H: 5 11 W: 12 00 b.Liverpool 1-7-90
Source: Scholar.
2006-07 Accrington S 1 0
2007-08 Accrington S 7 0
2008-09 Accrington S 15 1
2009-10 Accrington S 42 14
2010-11 Scunthorpe U 27 0
2010-11 *Rochdale* 6 2 **6 2**
2011-12 Scunthorpe U 29 7 **56 7**
2011-12 *Accrington S* 8 3 **73 18**

JENNINGS, Connor (F) **4 0**
H: 6 0 W: 12 00 b.Manchester 21-1-91
Source: Stalybridge C.
2011-12 Scunthorpe U 4 0 **4 0**

LILLIS, Josh (G) **71 0**
H: 6 0 W: 12 08 b.Derby 24-6-87
Source: Scholar.
2006-07 Scunthorpe U 1 0
2007-08 Scunthorpe U 3 0
2008-09 Scunthorpe U 5 0
2008-09 *Notts Co* 5 0 **5 0**
2009-10 Scunthorpe U 8 0
2009-10 *Grimsby T* 4 0 **4 0**
2009-10 *Rochdale* 1 0
2010-11 Scunthorpe U 15 0
2010-11 *Rochdale* 23 0 **24 0**
2011-12 Scunthorpe U 6 0 **38 0**

MOZIKA, Damien (M) **105 7**
H: 6 0 W: 11 13 b.Corbell-Essonnes 15-4-87
2006-07 Nancy 0 0
2007-08 *Louhans* 28 0 **28 0**
2008-09 Chester C 22 2 **22 2**
From Tarbiat Yazd.
2010-11 Bury 33 2
From Tarbiat Yazd.
2011-12 Bury 4 1 **37 3**
2011-12 Scunthorpe U 18 2 **18 2**

NELSON, Michael (D) **400 28**
H: 6 2 W: 13 03 b.Gateshead 15-3-82
Source: Bishop Auckland.
2000-01 Bury 2 1
2001-02 Bury 31 2
2002-03 Bury 39 5 **72 8**
2003-04 Hartlepool U 40 3
2004-05 Hartlepool U 43 1
2005-06 Hartlepool U 43 2
2006-07 Hartlepool U 42 1
2007-08 Hartlepool U 45 2
2008-09 Hartlepool U 46 5 **259 14**
2009-10 Norwich C 31 3
2010-11 Norwich C 8 2 **39 5**
2010-11 Scunthorpe U 20 0
2011-12 Scunthorpe U 10 1 **30 1**

NOLAN, Eddie (D) **134 2**
H: 6 0 W: 13 05 b.Waterford 5-8-88
Source: Scholar. *Honours:* Eire Under-21, 3 full caps.
2005-06 Blackburn R 0 0
2006-07 Blackburn R 0 0
2006-07 *Stockport Co* 4 0 **4 0**
2007-08 Blackburn R 0 0
2007-08 *Hartlepool U* 11 0 **11 0**
2008-09 Blackburn R 0 0
2008-09 Preston NE 21 0
2009-10 Preston NE 19 0
2009-10 *Sheffield W* 14 1 **14 1**
2010-11 Preston NE 0 0 **40 0**
2010-11 Scunthorpe U 35 0
2011-12 Scunthorpe U 30 1 **65 1**

O'CONNOR, Michael (M) **184 15**
H: 6 1 W: 11 08 b.Belfast 6-10-87
Source: Scholar. *Honours:* Northern Ireland Youth, Under-21, B, 10 full caps.

2005-06	Crewe Alex	2	0		
2006-07	Crewe Alex	29	0		
2007-08	Crewe Alex	23	0		
2008-09	Crewe Alex	23	3	**77**	**3**
2008-09	*Lincoln C*	10	1	**10**	**1**
2009-10	Scunthorpe U	32	2		
2010-11	Scunthorpe U	32	8		
2011-12	Scunthorpe U	33	1	**97**	**11**

PALMER, Ashley (D) **1 0**
H: 6 1 W: 11 13 b.Pontefract 9-11-92
Source: Scholar.

2010-11	Scunthorpe U	0	0		
2011-12	Scunthorpe U	1	0	**1**	**0**

REID, Paul (D) **291 8**
H: 6 2 W: 11 08 b.Carlisle 18-2-82
Source: Trainee. *Honours:* England Youth, Under-20.

1998-99	Carlisle U	0	0		
1999-2000	Carlisle U	19	0		
2000-01	Rangers	0	0		
2001-02	Rangers	0	0		
2001-02	*Preston NE*	1	1	**1**	**1**
2002-03	Rangers	0	0		
2002-03	*Northampton T*	19	0		
2003-04	Northampton T	33	2	**52**	**2**
2004-05	Barnsley	41	3		
2005-06	Barnsley	33	0		
2006-07	Barnsley	37	0		
2007-08	Barnsley	3	0	**114**	**3**
2007-08	*Carlisle U*	1	0	**20**	**0**
2008-09	Colchester U	26	1		
2009-10	Colchester U	12	0		
2010-11	Colchester U	18	0	**56**	**1**
2010-11	Scunthorpe U	12	0		
2011-12	Scunthorpe U	36	1	**48**	**1**

ROBERTSON, Jordan (F) **90 17**
H: 6 0 W: 12 06 b.Sheffield 12-2-88
Source: Scholar.

2006-07	Sheffield U	0	0		
2006-07	*Torquay U*	9	2	**9**	**2**
2006-07	*Northampton T*	17	3	**17**	**3**
2007-08	Sheffield U	0	0		
2007-08	*Dundee U*	14	3	**14**	**3**
2007-08	*Oldham Ath*	3	1	**3**	**1**
2008-09	Sheffield U	0	0		
2008-09	*Southampton*	10	1	**10**	**1**
2008-09	*Ferencvaros*	8	3	**8**	**3**
2009-10	Sheffield U	0	0		
2009-10	*Bury*	4	1	**4**	**1**
2010-11	St Johnstone	6	0	**6**	**0**
2011-12	Scunthorpe U	19	3	**19**	**3**

RYAN, James (M) **157 24**
H: 5 8 W: 11 08 b.Maghull 6-9-88
Source: Scholar. *Honours:* Eire Youth, Under-21.

2006-07	Liverpool	0	0		
2007-08	Liverpool	0	0		
2007-08	*Shrewsbury T*	4	0	**4**	**0**
2008-09	Accrington S	44	10		
2009-10	Accrington S	39	3		
2010-11	Accrington S	46	9	**129**	**22**
2011-12	Scunthorpe U	24	2	**24**	**2**

SLOCOMBE, Sam (G) **31 0**
H: 6 0 W: 11 11 b.Scunthorpe 5-6-88
Source: Bottesford T.

2008-09	Scunthorpe U	0	0		
2009-10	Scunthorpe U	1	0		
2010-11	Scunthorpe U	2	0		
2011-12	Scunthorpe U	28	0	**31**	**0**

THEWLIS, Jordan (F) **0 0**
b.Scunthorpe 24-10-92
Source: Scholar.

2011-12	Scunthorpe U	0	0		

THOMPSON, Gary (M) **151 27**
H: 6 0 W: 14 02 b.Kendal 24-11-80
Source: Scholar.

2007-08	Morecambe	40	7	**40**	**7**
2008-09	Scunthorpe U	24	3		
2009-10	Scunthorpe U	36	9		
2010-11	Scunthorpe U	12	1		
2011-12	Scunthorpe U	39	7	**111**	**20**

TOGWELL, Sam (M) **262 9**
H: 5 11 W: 12 04 b.Beaconsfield 14-10-84
Source: Scholar.

2002-03	Crystal Palace	1	0		
2003-04	Crystal Palace	0	0		
2004-05	Crystal Palace	0	0		
2004-05	*Oxford U*	4	0	**4**	**0**
2004-05	*Northampton T*	8	0	**8**	**0**
2005-06	Crystal Palace	0	0	**1**	**0**
2005-06	*Port Vale*	27	2	**27**	**2**
2006-07	Barnsley	44	1		
2007-08	Barnsley	22	1	**66**	**2**
2008-09	Scunthorpe U	40	2		
2009-10	Scunthorpe U	41	2		
2010-11	Scunthorpe U	36	0		
2011-12	Scunthorpe U	39	1	**156**	**5**

WINT, Aron (F) **0 0**
b.Coventry 20-10-92
Source: Scholar.

2011-12	Scunthorpe U	0	0		

WRIGHT, Andrew (M) **87 0**
H: 6 1 W: 13 07 b.Formby 15-1-85
Source: Liverpool Scholar.
From West Virginia Univ, Cape Cod Crusaders.

2007-08	Scunthorpe U	2	0		
2008-09	Scunthorpe U	28	0		
2009-10	Scunthorpe U	19	0		
2010-11	Scunthorpe U	20	0		
2011-12	Scunthorpe U	18	0	**87**	**0**

SHEFFIELD U (72)

ADAMS, Jack (F) **0 0**
b.Nottingham 19-7-92
Source: Scholar.

2011-12	Sheffield U	0	0		

BEATTIE, James (F) **418 125**
H: 6 1 W: 13 06 b.Lancaster 27-2-78
Source: Trainee. *Honours:* England Under-21, 5 full caps.

1994-95	Blackburn R	0	0		
1995-96	Blackburn R	0	0		
1996-97	Blackburn R	1	0		
1997-98	Blackburn R	3	0	**4**	**0**
1998-99	Southampton	35	5		
1999-2000	Southampton	18	0		
2000-01	Southampton	37	11		
2001-02	Southampton	28	12		
2002-03	Southampton	38	23		
2003-04	Southampton	37	14		
2004-05	Southampton	11	3	**204**	**68**
2004-05	Everton	11	1		
2005-06	Everton	32	10		
2006-07	Everton	33	2	**76**	**13**
2007-08	Sheffield U	39	22		
2008-09	Sheffield U	23	12		
2008-09	Stoke C	16	7		
2009-10	Stoke C	22	3	**38**	**10**
2010-11	Rangers	7	0	**7**	**0**

On loan from Rangers.

2010-11	Blackpool	9	0	**9**	**0**

On loan from Rangers.

2011-12	Sheffield U	18	0	**80**	**34**

BROWN, Connor (D) **0 0**
b.Sheffield 2-10-91
Source: Scholar.

2010-11	Sheffield U	0	0		
2011-12	Sheffield U	0	0		

CHAPELL, Jordan (M) **0 0**
H: 5 10 W: 10 09 b.Sheffield 8-9-91

2011-12	Sheffield U	0	0		

COLLINS, Neill (D) **328 17**
H: 6 3 W: 12 07 b.Irvine 2-9-83
Honours: Scotland Under-21, B.

2000-01	Queen's Park	4	0		
2001-02	Queen's Park	28	0	**32**	**0**
2002-03	Dumbarton	33	2		
2003-04	Dumbarton	30	2	**63**	**4**
2004-05	Sunderland	11	0		
2005-06	Sunderland	0	0		
2005-06	*Hartlepool U*	22	0	**22**	**0**
2005-06	*Sheffield U*	2	0		
2006-07	Sunderland	7	1	**18**	**1**
2006-07	Wolverhampton W	22	2		
2007-08	Wolverhampton W	39	3		
2008-09	Wolverhampton W	23	4		
2009-10	Wolverhampton W	0	0	**84**	**9**
2009-10	Preston NE	21	1	**21**	**1**
2009-10	*Leeds U*	9	0		
2010-11	Leeds U	21	0	**30**	**0**
2010-11	Sheffield U	14	0		
2011-12	Sheffield U	42	2	**58**	**2**

CONNEELY, Seamus (D) **86 2**
b.Galway 9-7-88
Honours: Eire Under-21.

2008	Galway U	20	0		
2009	Galway U	34	2		
2010	Galway U	32	0	**86**	**2**
2010-11	Sheffield U	0	0		
2011-12	Sheffield U	0	0		

CRESSWELL, Richard (F) **546 119**
H: 6 0 W: 11 08 b.Bridlington 20-9-77
Source: Trainee. *Honours:* England Under-21.

1995-96	York C	16	1		
1996-97	York C	17	0		
1996-97	*Mansfield T*	5	1	**5**	**1**
1997-98	York C	26	4		
1998-99	York C	36	16	**95**	**21**
1998-99	Sheffield W	7	1		
1999-2000	Sheffield W	20	1		
2000-01	Sheffield W	4	0	**31**	**2**
2000-01	Leicester C	8	0	**8**	**0**
2000-01	*Preston NE*	11	2		
2001-02	Preston NE	40	13		
2002-03	Preston NE	42	16		
2003-04	Preston NE	45	2		
2004-05	Preston NE	46	16		
2005-06	Preston NE	3	0	**187**	**49**
2005-06	Leeds U	16	5		
2006-07	Leeds U	22	4	**38**	**9**
2007-08	Stoke C	43	11		
2008-09	Stoke C	29	0		
2009-10	Stoke C	2	0	**74**	**11**
2009-10	Sheffield U	31	12		
2010-11	Sheffield U	35	5		
2011-12	Sheffield U	42	9	**108**	**26**

CUFF, Sean (G) **0 0**
b.Middlesbrough 21-5-93
Source: Scholar.

2011-12	Sheffield U	0	0		

DOYLE, Micky (M) **366 23**
H: 5 10 W: 11 00 b.Dublin 8-7-81
Source: Celtic. *Honours:* Eire Under-21, 1 full cap.

2003-04	Coventry C	40	5		
2004-05	Coventry C	44	2		
2005-06	Coventry C	44	0		
2006-07	Coventry C	40	3		
2007-08	Coventry C	42	7		
2008-09	Coventry C	37	2		
2009-10	Coventry C	0	0		
2009-10	*Leeds U*	42	0	**42**	**0**
2010-11	Coventry C	18	1	**265**	**20**
2010-11	Sheffield U	16	0		
2011-12	Sheffield U	43	3	**59**	**3**

ERTL, Johannes (D) **197 6**
H: 6 2 W: 12 08 b.Graz 13-11-82
Honours: Austria 7 full caps.

2003-04	*Kalzdorf*	11	3	**11**	**3**
2004-05	Sturm Graz	26	0		
2005-06	Sturm Graz	27	0		
2006-07	Sturm Graz	5	0	**58**	**0**
2006-07	FK Austria	24	1		
2007-08	FK Austria	24	2	**48**	**3**
2008-09	Crystal Palace	12	0		
2009-10	Crystal Palace	33	0	**45**	**0**
2010-11	Sheffield U	28	0		
2011-12	Sheffield U	7	0	**35**	**0**

EVANS, Ched (F) **147 53**
H: 6 0 W: 12 00 b.Rhyl 28-12-88
Source: Scholar. *Honours:* Wales Under-21, 13 full caps, 2 goals.

2006-07	Manchester C	0	0		
2007-08	Manchester C	0	0		
2007-08	*Norwich C*	28	10	**28**	**10**
2008-09	Manchester C	16	1	**16**	**1**
2009-10	Sheffield U	33	4		
2010-11	Sheffield U	34	9		
2011-12	Sheffield U	36	29	**103**	**42**

FLYNN, Ryan (M) **95 12**
H: 5 8 W: 10 00 b.Falkirk 4-9-88
Source: Scholar. *Honours:* Scotland Youth.

2006-07	Liverpool	0	0		
2007-08	*Hereford U*	0	0		

2007-08 Liverpool 0 0
2008-09 Liverpool 0 0
2009-10 Liverpool 0 0
2009-10 Falkirk 36 5
2010-11 Falkirk 33 5 **69** **10**
2011-12 Sheffield U 26 2 **26** **2**

HARRIOTT, Matty (M) **6** **0**
H: 6 0 W: 12 10 b.Luton 23-9-92
Source: Scholar.
2010-11 Sheffield U 2 0
2011-12 Sheffield U 0 0 **2** **0**
2011-12 *Burton Alb* 4 0 **4** **0**

HOWARD, Mark (G) **66** **0**
H: 6 0 W: 11 13 b.Southwark 21-9-86
2005-06 Falkirk 8 0 **8** **0**
2006-07 Cardiff C 0 0
2006-07 Swansea C 0 0
2007-08 St Mirren 10 0
2008-09 St Mirren 33 0
2009-10 St Mirren 2 0 **45** **0**
2010-11 Aberdeen 9 0 **9** **0**
2011-12 Blackpool 4 0 **4** **0**
2011-12 Sheffield U 0 0

KENNEDY, Terry (D) **1** **0**
H: 5 10 W: 12 04 b.Barnsley 14-11-93
Source: Scholar.
2010-11 Sheffield U 1 0
2011-12 Sheffield U 0 0 **1** **0**

LESCINEL, Jean-Francois (M) **101** **1**
H: 6 2 W: 12 04 b.Guyane 2-10-86
Source: Paris St Germain, Sedan. *Honours:* Haiti 1 full cap.
2006-07 Falkirk 8 0 **8** **0**
2006-07 Guingamp 12 0 **12** **0**
2008-09 Swindon T 5 0
2009-10 Swindon T 33 0
2010-11 Swindon T 18 1 **56** **1**
2011-12 Sheffield U 25 0 **25** **0**

LONG, George (G) **3** **0**
H: 6 0 W: 12 05 b.Sheffield 5-11-93
Source: Scholar. *Honours:* England Youth.
2010-11 Sheffield U 1 0
2011-12 Sheffield U 2 0 **3** **0**

LOWTON, Matt (M) **83** **10**
H: 5 11 W: 12 04 b.Chesterfield 9-6-89
Source: Scholar.
2008-09 Sheffield U 0 0
2009-10 Sheffield U 2 0
2009-10 *Ferencvaros* 5 0 **5** **0**
2010-11 Sheffield U 32 4
2011-12 Sheffield U 44 6 **78** **10**

MAGUIRE, Harry (D) **49** **1**
H: 6 2 W: 12 06 b.Mosborough 5-3-93
Source: Scholar.
2010-11 Sheffield U 5 0
2011-12 Sheffield U 44 1 **49** **1**

McALLISTER, David (M) **99** **27**
H: 5 10 W: 11 09 b.Dublin 29-12-88
2008 Drogheda U 0 0
2008 *Shelbourne* 16 7
2009 Shelbourne 30 16 **46** **23**
2010 St Patrick's Ath 32 3 **32** **3**
2010-11 Sheffield U 2 1
2011-12 Sheffield U 4 0 **6** **1**
2011-12 *Shrewsbury T* 15 0 **15** **0**

McDONALD, Kevin (M) **189** **20**
H: 6 2 W: 13 03 b.Carnoustie 4-11-88
Honours: Scotland Youth, Under-21.
2005-06 Dundee 26 3
2006-07 Dundee 31 2
2007-08 Dundee 34 9 **91** **14**
2008-09 Burnley 25 1
2009-10 Burnley 26 1
2010-11 Burnley 0 0 **51** **2**
2010-11 *Scunthorpe U* 5 1 **5** **1**
2010-11 *Notts Co* 11 0 **11** **0**
2011-12 Sheffield U 31 3 **31** **3**

McFADZEAN, Callum (D) **0** **0**
b.Sheffield 16-1-94
Source: Scholar.
2010-11 Sheffield U 0 0
2011-12 Sheffield U 0 0

MONTGOMERY, Nick (M) **351** **9**
H: 5 9 W: 11 08 b.Leeds 28-10-81
Source: Scholar. *Honours:* Scotland Under-21, B.
2000-01 Sheffield U 27 0
2001-02 Sheffield U 31 2
2002-03 Sheffield U 23 0
2003-04 Sheffield U 36 3
2004-05 Sheffield U 25 1
2005-06 Sheffield U 39 1
2006-07 Sheffield U 26 0
2007-08 Sheffield U 20 0
2008-09 Sheffield U 28 0
2009-10 Sheffield U 39 1
2010-11 Sheffield U 35 0
2011-12 Sheffield U 20 1 **349** **9**
2011-12 *Millwall* 2 0 **2** **0**

MORGAN, Chris (D) **432** **20**
H: 6 1 W: 12 03 b.Barnsley 9-11-77
Source: Trainee.
1996-97 Barnsley 0 0
1997-98 Barnsley 11 0
1998-99 Barnsley 19 0
1999-2000 Barnsley 37 0
2000-01 Barnsley 40 1
2001-02 Barnsley 42 4
2002-03 Barnsley 36 2 **185** **7**
2003-04 Sheffield U 32 1
2004-05 Sheffield U 41 2
2005-06 Sheffield U 39 3
2006-07 Sheffield U 24 1
2007-08 Sheffield U 25 2
2008-09 Sheffield U 41 2
2009-10 Sheffield U 37 2
2010-11 Sheffield U 8 0
2011-12 Sheffield U 0 0 **247** **13**

MURRAY, Shane (M) **0** **0**
b.Dublin 27-2-92
Source: Scholar.
2011-12 Sheffield U 0 0

PHILLISKIRK, Daniel (M) **8** **0**
H: 5 10 W: 11 05 b.Oldham 10-4-91
Source: Scholar.
2008-09 Chelsea 0 0
2009-10 Chelsea 0 0
2010-11 Chelsea 0 0
2010-11 *Oxford U* 1 0
2010-11 *Sheffield U* 3 0
2011-12 Sheffield U 0 0 **3** **0**
2011-12 *Oxford U* 4 0 **5** **0**

PORTER, Chris (F) **274** **83**
H: 6 1 W: 12 09 b.Wigan 12-12-83
Source: School.
2002-03 Bury 2 0
2003-04 Bury 37 9
2004-05 Bury 32 9 **71** **18**
2005-06 Oldham Ath 31 7
2006-07 Oldham Ath 35 21 **66** **28**
2007-08 Motherwell 37 14
2008-09 Motherwell 22 9 **59** **23**
2008-09 Derby Co 5 3
2009-10 Derby Co 21 4
2010-11 Derby Co 18 2 **44** **9**
2011-12 Sheffield U 34 5 **34** **5**

QUINN, Stephen (M) **234** **20**
H: 5 6 W: 9 08 b.Dublin 4-4-86
Source: Trainee. *Honours:* Eire Under-21.
2005-06 Sheffield U 0 0
2005-06 *Milton Keynes D* 15 0 **15** **0**
2005-06 *Rotherham U* 16 0 **16** **0**
2006-07 Sheffield U 15 2
2007-08 Sheffield U 19 2
2008-09 Sheffield U 43 7
2009-10 Sheffield U 44 4
2010-11 Sheffield U 37 1
2011-12 Sheffield U 45 4 **203** **20**

SIMONSEN, Steve (G) **327** **0**
H: 6 2 W: 12 08 b.South Shields 3-4-79
Source: Trainee. *Honours:* England Youth, Under-21.
1996-97 Tranmere R 0 0
1997-98 Tranmere R 30 0
1998-99 Tranmere R 5 0 **35** **0**
1998-99 Everton 0 0
1999-2000 Everton 1 0
2000-01 Everton 1 0
2001-02 Everton 25 0
2002-03 Everton 2 0
2003-04 Everton 1 0 **30** **0**
2004-05 Stoke C 31 0
2005-06 Stoke C 45 0
2006-07 Stoke C 46 0
2007-08 Stoke C 36 0
2008-09 Stoke C 5 0
2009-10 Stoke C 3 0 **166** **0**
2009-10 *Sheffield U* 7 0
2010-11 Sheffield U 45 0
2011-12 Sheffield U 44 0 **96** **0**

TAYLOR, Andy (D) **126** **3**
H: 5 11 W: 11 07 b.Blackburn 14-3-86
Source: Scholar. *Honours:* England Youth, Under-20, Under-21.
2004-05 Blackburn R 0 0
2005-06 Blackburn R 0 0
2005-06 *QPR* 3 0 **3** **0**
2005-06 *Blackpool* 3 0 **3** **0**
2006-07 Blackburn R 0 0
2006-07 *Crewe Alex* 4 0 **4** **0**
2006-07 *Huddersfield T* 8 0 **8** **0**
2007-08 Blackburn R 0 0
2007-08 Tranmere R 30 2
2008-09 Tranmere R 39 1 **69** **3**
2009-10 Sheffield U 26 0
2010-11 Sheffield U 9 0
2011-12 Sheffield U 4 0 **39** **0**

TONNE, Erik (M) **4** **1**
H: 5 11 W: 12 02 b.Trondheim 7-5-91
Source: Strindheim.
2010-11 Sheffield U 2 0
2011-12 Sheffield U 2 1 **4** **1**

WARREN, Mark (D) **0** **0**
b.Sydney 11-2-92
Source: Central Coast Mariners.
2010-11 Sheffield U 0 0
2011-12 Sheffield U 0 0

WILLIAMS, Marcus (D) **196** **0**
H: 5 8 W: 10 07 b.Doncaster 8-4-86
Source: Scholar.
2003-04 Scunthorpe U 1 0
2004-05 Scunthorpe U 4 0
2005-06 Scunthorpe U 29 0
2006-07 Scunthorpe U 35 0
2007-08 Scunthorpe U 34 0
2008-09 Scunthorpe U 26 0
2009-10 Scunthorpe U 37 0
2010-11 Reading 3 0
2010-11 *Peterborough U* 3 0 **3** **0**
2010-11 *Scunthorpe U* 5 0 **171** **0**
2011-12 Reading 0 0 **3** **0**
2011-12 Sheffield U 19 0 **19** **0**

WILLIAMSON, Lee (M) **389** **36**
H: 5 10 W: 10 04 b.Derby 7-6-82
Source: Trainee.
1999-2000 Mansfield T 4 0
2000-01 Mansfield T 15 0
2001-02 Mansfield T 46 3
2002-03 Mansfield T 40 0
2003-04 Mansfield T 35 0
2004-05 Mansfield T 4 0 **144** **3**
2004-05 Northampton T 37 0 **37** **0**
2005-06 Rotherham U 37 4
2006-07 Rotherham U 19 5 **56** **9**
2006-07 Watford 5 0
2007-08 Watford 32 2
2008-09 Watford 34 2 **71** **4**
2008-09 *Preston NE* 5 1 **5** **1**
2009-10 Sheffield U 20 3
2010-11 Sheffield U 16 3
2011-12 Sheffield U 40 13 **76** **19**

SHEFFIELD W (73)

BEEVERS, Mark (D) **148** **3**
H: 6 4 W: 13 00 b.Barnsley 21-11-89
Source: Scholar. *Honours:* England Youth.
2006-07 Sheffield W 2 0
2007-08 Sheffield W 28 0
2008-09 Sheffield W 34 0
2009-10 Sheffield W 35 0
2010-11 Sheffield W 28 2
2011-12 Sheffield W 7 0 **134** **2**
2011-12 *Milton Keynes D* 14 1 **14** **1**

BENNETT, Julian (D) **182** **14**
H: 6 1 W: 13 00 b.Nottingham 17-12-84
Source: Scholar.
2003-04 Walsall 1 0
2004-05 Walsall 31 2
2005-06 Walsall 19 1 **51** **3**
2005-06 Nottingham F 18 2
2006-07 Nottingham F 30 2
2007-08 Nottingham F 34 4
2008-09 Nottingham F 12 0
2009-10 Nottingham F 0 0

2010-11 Nottingham F 3 0 **97 8**
2010-11 *Crystal Palace* 13 1 **13 1**
2011-12 Sheffield W 21 2 **21 2**

BUXTON, Lewis (D) 257 4
H: 6 1 W: 13 11 b.Newport (IW) 10-12-83
Source: School.
2000-01 Portsmouth 0 0
2001-02 Portsmouth 29 0
2002-03 Portsmouth 1 0
2002-03 *Exeter C* 4 0 **4 0**
2002-03 *Bournemouth* 17 0
2003-04 Portsmouth 0 0
2003-04 *Bournemouth* 26 0 **43 0**
2004-05 Portsmouth 0 0 **30 0**
2004-05 Stoke C 16 0
2005-06 Stoke C 32 1
2006-07 Stoke C 1 0
2007-08 Stoke C 4 0
2008-09 Stoke C 0 0 **53 1**
2008-09 Sheffield W 32 1
2009-10 Sheffield W 28 0
2010-11 Sheffield W 30 1
2011-12 Sheffield W 37 1 **127 3**

BYWATER, Steve (G) 286 0
H: 6 2 W: 12 10 b.Manchester 7-6-81
Source: Trainee. *Honours:* England Youth, Under-20, Under-21.
1997-98 Rochdale 0 0
1998-99 West Ham U 0 0
1999-2000 West Ham U 4 0
1999-2000 *Wycombe W* 2 0 **2 0**
1999-2000 *Hull C* 4 0 **4 0**
2000-01 West Ham U 1 0
2001-02 West Ham U 0 0
2001-02 *Wolverhampton W* 0 0
2001-02 *Cardiff C* 0 0
2002-03 West Ham U 0 0
2003-04 West Ham U 17 0
2004-05 West Ham U 36 0
2005-06 West Ham U 1 0
2005-06 *Coventry C* 14 0 **14 0**
2006-07 West Ham U 0 0 **59 0**
2006-07 Derby Co 37 0
2007-08 Derby Co 18 0
2007-08 *Ipswich T* 17 0 **17 0**
2008-09 Derby Co 31 0
2009-10 Derby Co 42 0
2010-11 Derby Co 22 0
2010-11 *Cardiff C* 8 0 **8 0**
2011-12 Derby Co 0 0 **150 0**
2011-12 Sheffield W 32 0 **32 0**

COKE, Giles (M) 211 24
H: 6 0 W: 11 11 b.Westminster 3-6-86
Source: Kingstonian.
2004-05 Mansfield T 9 0
2005-06 Mansfield T 40 4
2006-07 Mansfield T 21 1 **70 5**
2007-08 Northampton T 20 5
2008-09 Northampton T 32 2 **52 7**
2009-10 Motherwell 32 2 **32 2**
2010-11 Sheffield W 27 4
2011-12 Sheffield W 0 0 **27 4**
2011-12 *Bury* 30 6 **30 6**

JAMESON, Arron (G) 2 0
H: 6 3 W: 13 01 b.Sheffield 7-11-89
Source: Scholar.
2008-09 Sheffield W 0 0
2009-10 Sheffield W 0 0
2010-11 Sheffield W 2 0
2011-12 Sheffield W 0 0 **2 0**

JOHNSON, Jermaine (M) 241 32
H: 5 11 W: 11 05 b.Kingston, Jamaica 25-6-80
Source: Tivoli Gardens. *Honours:* Jamaica 62 full caps, 9 goals.
2001-02 Bolton W 10 0
2002-03 Bolton W 2 0
2003-04 Bolton W 0 0 **12 0**
2003-04 Oldham Ath 20 5
2004-05 Oldham Ath 19 4
2005-06 Oldham Ath 0 0 **39 9**
2006-07 Bradford C 27 4 **27 4**
2006-07 Sheffield W 7 2
2007-08 Sheffield W 35 1
2008-09 Sheffield W 37 3
2009-10 Sheffield W 34 5
2010-11 Sheffield W 26 4
2011-12 Sheffield W 24 4 **163 19**

JOHNSON, Reda (D) 97 12
H: 6 2 W: 13 10 b.Marseille 21-3-88
Honours: Benin 9 full caps.
2005-06 Gueugnon 0 0
2006-07 Gueugnon 0 0
2007-08 Amiens 8 0
2008-09 Amiens 7 0 **15 0**
2009-10 Plymouth Arg 25 0
2010-11 Plymouth Arg 17 2 **42 2**
2010-11 Sheffield W 16 3
2011-12 Sheffield W 24 7 **40 10**

JONES, Daniel (D) 118 4
H: 6 2 W: 13 00 b.Rowley Regis 14-7-86
Source: Scholar.
2005-06 Wolverhampton W 1 0
2006-07 Wolverhampton W 8 0
2007-08 Wolverhampton W 1 0
2007-08 *Northampton T* 33 3 **33 3**
2008-09 Wolverhampton W 0 0
2008-09 *Oldham Ath* 23 1 **23 1**
2009-10 Wolverhampton W 0 0 **10 0**
2009-10 *Notts Co* 7 0 **7 0**
2009-10 *Bristol R* 17 0 **17 0**
2010-11 Sheffield W 25 0
2011-12 Sheffield W 3 0 **28 0**

JONES, Mike (M) 186 22
H: 5 11 W: 12 04 b.Birkenhead 15-8-87
Source: Scholar.
2005-06 Tranmere R 1 0
2006-07 Tranmere R 0 0
2006-07 *Shrewsbury T* 13 1 **13 1**
2007-08 Tranmere R 9 1 **10 1**
2008-09 Bury 46 4
2009-10 Bury 41 5
2010-11 Bury 42 8
2011-12 Bury 24 3 **153 20**
2011-12 Sheffield W 10 0 **10 0**

JONES, Rob (D) 256 22
H: 6 7 W: 12 02 b.Stockton 30-11-79
Source: Gateshead.
2002-03 Stockport Co 0 0
2003-04 Stockport Co 16 2 **16 2**
2003-04 *Macclesfield T* 1 0 **1 0**
2004-05 Grimsby T 20 1
2005-06 Grimsby T 40 4 **60 5**
2006-07 Hibernian 34 4
2007-08 Hibernian 30 0
2008-09 Hibernian 32 4 **96 8**
2009-10 Scunthorpe U 28 1
2010-11 Scunthorpe U 14 1 **42 2**
2010-11 *Sheffield W* 8 1
2011-12 Sheffield W 33 4 **41 5**

KASNIK, David (D) 0 0
H: 6 1 W: 12 00 b.Slovenia 16-1-87
2011-12 Sheffield W 0 0
On loan from Olimpija Ljubljana.

LINES, Chris (M) 209 23
H: 6 2 W: 12 00 b.Bristol 30-11-88
Source: Youth.
2005-06 Bristol R 4 0
2006-07 Bristol R 7 0
2007-08 Bristol R 27 3
2008-09 Bristol R 45 4
2009-10 Bristol R 42 10
2010-11 Bristol R 42 3
2011-12 Bristol R 1 0 **168 20**
2011-12 Sheffield W 41 3 **41 3**

LLERA, Miguel (D) 157 17
H: 6 3 W: 13 12 b.Seville 7-8-79
Source: Recretivo B, San Fernando (loan), Alicante.
2005-06 Gimnastic 27 3
2006-07 Gimnastic 12 2 **39 5**
2007-08 Heracles 13 1 **13 1**
2008-09 Milton Keynes D 34 2 **34 2**
2009-10 Charlton Ath 25 4
2010-11 Charlton Ath 15 1
2011-12 Charlton Ath 0 0 **40 5**
2011-12 *Brentford* 11 0 **11 0**
2011-12 Sheffield W 20 4 **20 4**

LOWE, Ryan (F) 406 122
H: 5 10 W: 12 08 b.Liverpool 18-9-78
Source: Burscough.
2000-01 Shrewsbury T 30 4
2001-02 Shrewsbury T 38 7
2002-03 Shrewsbury T 39 9
2003-04 Shrewsbury T 0 0
2004-05 Shrewsbury T 30 3 **137 23**
2004-05 Chester C 8 4
2005-06 Chester C 32 10
2005-06 Crewe Alex 0 0
2006-07 Crewe Alex 37 8
2007-08 Crewe Alex 27 4 **64 12**
2007-08 *Stockport Co* 4 0 **4 0**
2008-09 Chester C 45 16 **85 30**
2009-10 Bury 39 18
2010-11 Bury 46 27
2011-12 Bury 5 4 **90 49**
2011-12 Sheffield W 26 8 **26 8**

MADINE, Gary (F) 142 36
H: 6 1 W: 12 00 b.Gateshead 24-8-90
Source: Scholar.
2007-08 Carlisle U 11 0
2008-09 Carlisle U 14 1
2008-09 *Rochdale* 3 0 **3 0**
2009-10 Carlisle U 20 4
2009-10 *Coventry C* 9 0 **9 0**
2009-10 *Chesterfield* 4 0 **4 0**
2010-11 Carlisle U 21 8 **66 13**
2010-11 Sheffield W 22 5
2011-12 Sheffield W 38 18 **60 23**

MORRISON, Clinton (F) 527 148
H: 6 0 W: 12 00 b.Tooting 14-5-79
Source: Trainee. *Honours:* Eire Under-21, 36 full caps, 9 goals.
1996-97 Crystal Palace 0 0
1997-98 Crystal Palace 1 1
1998-99 Crystal Palace 37 12
1999-2000 Crystal Palace 29 13
2000-01 Crystal Palace 45 14
2001-02 Crystal Palace 45 22
2002-03 Birmingham C 28 6
2003-04 Birmingham C 32 4
2004-05 Birmingham C 26 4
2005-06 Birmingham C 1 0 **87 14**
2005-06 Crystal Palace 40 13
2006-07 Crystal Palace 41 12
2007-08 Crystal Palace 43 16 **281 103**
2008-09 Coventry C 45 10
2009-10 Coventry C 46 11 **91 21**
2010-11 Sheffield W 35 6
2011-12 Sheffield W 19 1 **54 7**
2011-12 *Milton Keynes D* 6 3 **6 3**
2011-12 *Brentford* 8 0 **8 0**

NYONI, Cecil (M) 0 0
b.Bulawayo 1-9-92
Source: Scholar.
2011-12 Sheffield W 0 0

O'CONNOR, James (M) 484 33
H: 5 8 W: 11 00 b.Dublin 1-9-79
Source: Trainee. *Honours:* Eire Youth, Under-21.
1996-97 Stoke C 0 0
1997-98 Stoke C 0 0
1998-99 Stoke C 4 0
1999-2000 Stoke C 42 6
2000-01 Stoke C 44 8
2001-02 Stoke C 43 2
2002-03 Stoke C 43 0 **176 16**
2003-04 WBA 30 0
2004-05 WBA 0 0 **30 0**
2004-05 Burnley 21 2
2005-06 Burnley 46 3
2006-07 Burnley 43 3
2007-08 Burnley 29 3 **139 11**
2008-09 Sheffield W 41 0
2009-10 Sheffield W 44 3
2010-11 Sheffield W 36 2
2011-12 Sheffield W 18 1 **139 6**
Transferred to Orlando City January 2012.

O'DONNELL, Richard (G) 30 0
H: 6 2 W: 13 05 b.Sheffield 12-9-88
Source: Scholar.
2007-08 Sheffield W 0 0
2007-08 *Rotherham U* 0 0
2007-08 *Oldham Ath* 4 0 **4 0**
2008-09 Sheffield W 0 0
2009-10 Sheffield W 0 0
2010-11 Sheffield W 9 0
2011-12 Sheffield W 6 0 **15 0**
2011-12 *Macclesfield T* 11 0 **11 0**

O'GRADY, Chris (F) 267 56
H: 6 3 W: 12 04 b.Nottingham 25-1-86
Source: Trainee. *Honours:* England Youth.
2002-03 Leicester C 1 0
2003-04 Leicester C 0 0
2004-05 Leicester C 0 0
2004-05 *Notts Co* 9 0 **9 0**
2005-06 Leicester C 13 1

2005-06 *Rushden & D* 22 4 **22 4**
2006-07 Leicester C 10 0 **24 1**
2006-07 Rotherham U 13 4
2007-08 Rotherham U 38 9 **51 13**
2008-09 Oldham Ath 13 0
2008-09 *Bury* 6 0 **6 0**
2008-09 *Bradford C* 2 0 **2 0**
2008-09 *Stockport Co* 18 2 **18 2**
2009-10 Oldham Ath 0 0 **13 0**
2009-10 Rochdale 43 22
2010-11 Rochdale 46 9
2011-12 Rochdale 1 0 **90 31**
2011-12 Sheffield W 32 5 **32 5**

OLIVER, Vadaine (F) 0 0
b.Sheffield 21-10-91
Source: Scholar.
2010-11 Sheffield W 0 0
2011-12 Sheffield W 0 0

OTSEMOBOR, John (D) 219 6
H: 5 10 W: 12 07 b.Liverpool 23-3-83
Source: Trainee. *Honours:* England Youth, Under-20.
1999-2000 Liverpool 0 0
2000-01 Liverpool 0 0
2001-02 Liverpool 0 0
2002-03 Liverpool 0 0
2002-03 *Hull C* 9 3 **9 3**
2003-04 Liverpool 4 0
2003-04 *Bolton W* 1 0 **1 0**
2004-05 Liverpool 0 0 **4 0**
2004-05 *Crewe Alex* 14 1
2005-06 Rotherham U 10 0 **10 0**
2005-06 Crewe Alex 16 0
2006-07 Crewe Alex 27 0 **57 1**
2007-08 Norwich C 43 1
2008-09 Norwich C 37 0
2009-10 Norwich C 13 1 **93 2**
2009-10 Southampton 19 0 **19 0**
2010-11 Sheffield W 15 0
2011-12 Sheffield W 11 0 **26 0**

PALMER, Liam (M) 23 1
H: 6 2 W: 12 10 b.Worksop 19-9-91
Source: Scholar. *Honours:* Scotland Under-21.
2010-11 Sheffield W 9 0
2011-12 Sheffield W 14 1 **23 1**

PRUTTON, David (M) 387 24
H: 5 10 W: 13 00 b.Hull 12-9-81
Source: Trainee. *Honours:* England Youth, Under-21.
1998-99 Nottingham F 0 0
1999-2000 Nottingham F 34 2
2000-01 Nottingham F 42 1
2001-02 Nottingham F 43 3
2002-03 Nottingham F 24 1
2002-03 Southampton 12 0
2003-04 Southampton 27 1
2004-05 Southampton 23 1
2005-06 Southampton 17 0
2006-07 Southampton 3 1 **82 3**
2006-07 *Nottingham F* 12 2 **155 9**
2007-08 Leeds U 43 4
2008-09 Leeds U 16 0
2009-10 Leeds U 6 0 **65 4**
2009-10 Colchester U 19 3 **19 3**
2010-11 Swindon T 41 3 **41 3**
2011-12 Sheffield W 25 2 **25 2**

REYNOLDS, Mark (D) 180 4
H: 5 11 W: 10 07 b.Motherwell 7-5-87
2005-06 Motherwell 1 0
2006-07 Motherwell 35 2
2007-08 Motherwell 38 0
2008-09 Motherwell 36 0
2009-10 Motherwell 26 2
2010-11 Motherwell 19 0 **155 4**
2010-11 Sheffield W 7 0
2011-12 Sheffield W 3 0 **10 0**
2011-12 *Aberdeen* 15 0 **15 0**

SEDGWICK, Chris (M) 515 34
H: 5 11 W: 11 10 b.Sheffield 28-4-80
Source: Trainee.
1997-98 Rotherham U 4 0
1998-99 Rotherham U 33 4
1999-2000 Rotherham U 38 5
2000-01 Rotherham U 21 2
2001-02 Rotherham U 44 1
2002-03 Rotherham U 43 1
2003-04 Rotherham U 40 2
2004-05 Rotherham U 20 2 **243 17**
2004-05 Preston NE 24 3
2005-06 Preston NE 46 4
2006-07 Preston NE 43 1
2007-08 Preston NE 42 2
2008-09 Preston NE 40 1
2009-10 Preston NE 34 1 **229 12**
2010-11 Sheffield W 33 4
2011-12 Sheffield W 10 1 **43 5**

SEMEDO, Jose (D) 236 5
H: 6 0 W: 12 08 b.Setubal 11-1-85
Honours: Portugal Under-21.
2004-05 Sporting Lisbon 0 0
2004-05 *Casa Pia* 34 2 **34 2**
2005-06 *Feirense* 18 0 **18 0**
2006-07 *Cagliari* 3 0 **3 0**
2007-08 Charlton Ath 37 0
2008-09 Charlton Ath 18 0
2009-10 Charlton Ath 38 1
2010-11 Charlton Ath 42 1 **135 2**
2011-12 Sheffield W 46 1 **46 1**

WEAVER, Nick (G) 316 0
H: 6 4 W: 14 07 b.Sheffield 2-3-79
Source: Trainee. *Honours:* England Under-21.
1995-96 Mansfield T 1 0
1996-97 Mansfield T 0 0 **1 0**
1996-97 Manchester C 0 0
1997-98 Manchester C 0 0
1998-99 Manchester C 45 0
1999-2000 Manchester C 45 0
2000-01 Manchester C 31 0
2001-02 Manchester C 25 0
2002-03 Manchester C 0 0
2003-04 Manchester C 0 0
2004-05 Manchester C 1 0
2005-06 Manchester C 0 0
2005-06 *Sheffield W* 14 0
2006-07 Manchester C 25 0 **172 0**
2007-08 Charlton Ath 45 0
2008-09 Charlton Ath 22 0 **67 0**
2009-10 Dundee U 18 0 **18 0**
2009-10 Burnley 0 0
2010-11 Sheffield W 36 0
2011-12 Sheffield W 8 0 **58 0**

SHREWSBURY T (74)

AINSWORTH, Lionel (F) 148 18
H: 5 9 W: 9 10 b.Nottingham 1-10-87
Source: Scholar. *Honours:* England Youth.
2005-06 Derby Co 2 0
2006-07 Derby Co 0 0 **2 0**
2006-07 *Bournemouth* 7 0 **7 0**
2006-07 *Wycombe W* 7 0 **7 0**
2007-08 Hereford U 15 4
2007-08 Watford 8 0
2008-09 Watford 7 0 **15 0**
2008-09 *Hereford U* 7 3 **22 7**
2008-09 Huddersfield T 14 0
2009-10 Huddersfield T 11 0
2009-10 *Brentford* 9 0 **9 0**
2010-11 Shrewsbury T 33 9
2010-11 *Huddersfield T* 0 0 **25 0**
2011-12 Shrewsbury T 21 2 **54 11**
2011-12 *Burton Alb* 7 0 **7 0**

BRADSHAW, Tom (F) 40 10
H: 5 5 W: 11 02 b.Shrewsbury 27-7-92
Source: Aberystwyth T. *Honours:* Wales Youth.
2009-10 Shrewsbury T 6 3
2010-11 Shrewsbury T 26 6
2011-12 Shrewsbury T 8 1 **40 10**

CANSDELL-SHERRIFF, Shane (D) 322 22
H: 5 11 W: 11 08 b.Sydney 10-11-82
Source: NSW Academy. *Honours:* Australia Youth, Under-23.
1999-2000 Leeds U 0 0
2000-01 Leeds U 0 0
2001-02 Leeds U 0 0
2002-03 Leeds U 0 0
2002-03 *Rochdale* 3 0 **3 0**
2003-04 Aarhus 29 4
2004-05 Aarhus 26 2
2005-06 Aarhus 27 1 **82 7**
2006-07 Tranmere R 43 3
2007-08 Tranmere R 44 3 **87 6**
2008-09 Shrewsbury T 31 2
2009-10 Shrewsbury T 41 1
2010-11 Shrewsbury T 41 2
2011-12 Shrewsbury T 37 4 **150 9**

COLLINS, James S (F) 83 28
H: 6 2 W: 13 08 b.Coventry 1-12-90
Source: Scholar. *Honours:* Eire Under-21.
2008-09 Aston Villa 0 0
2009-10 Aston Villa 0 0
2009-10 *Darlington* 7 2 **7 2**
2010-11 Aston Villa 0 0
2010-11 *Burton Alb* 10 4 **10 4**
2010-11 Shrewsbury T 24 8
2011-12 Shrewsbury T 42 14 **66 22**

GOLDSON, Connor (D) 7 0
H: 6 3 W: 13 05 b.York 18-12-92
Source: Youth.
2010-11 Shrewsbury T 3 0
2011-12 Shrewsbury T 4 0 **7 0**

GORNELL, Terry (F) 132 29
H: 5 11 W: 12 04 b.Liverpool 16-12-89
Source: Scholar.
2008-09 Tranmere R 10 1
2008-09 *Accrington S* 11 4
2009-10 Tranmere R 27 2
2010-11 Tranmere R 3 0 **40 3**
2010-11 Accrington S 40 13 **51 17**
2011-12 Shrewsbury T 41 9 **41 9**

GRANDISON, Jermaine (D) 64 2
H: 6 4 W: 13 03 b.Birmingham 15-12-90
Source: Scholar.
2008-09 Coventry C 2 0
2009-10 Coventry C 3 0
2010-11 Coventry C 0 0 **5 0**
2010-11 *Tranmere R* 8 0 **8 0**
2010-11 Shrewsbury T 13 0
2011-12 Shrewsbury T 38 2 **51 2**

HAZELL, Reuben (D) 356 12
H: 5 11 W: 12 05 b.Birmingham 24-4-79
Source: Trainee.
1996-97 Aston Villa 0 0
1997-98 Aston Villa 0 0
1998-99 Aston Villa 0 0
1999-2000 Tranmere R 23 1
2000-01 Tranmere R 13 0
2001-02 Tranmere R 6 0 **42 1**
2001-02 Torquay U 19 0
2002-03 Torquay U 46 1
2003-04 Torquay U 19 1
2004-05 Torquay U 0 0 **84 2**
2005-06 Chesterfield 33 0
2006-07 Chesterfield 39 2
2007-08 Chesterfield 0 0 **72 2**
2007-08 Oldham Ath 34 1
2008-09 Oldham Ath 43 3
2009-10 Oldham Ath 41 3
2010-11 Oldham Ath 33 0 **151 7**
2011-12 Shrewsbury T 7 0 **7 0**

JACOBSON, Joe (D) 161 5
H: 5 11 W: 12 06 b.Cardiff 17-11-86
Source: Scholar. *Honours:* Wales Under-21.
2005-06 Cardiff C 1 0
2006-07 Cardiff C 0 0 **1 0**
2006-07 *Accrington S* 6 1
2006-07 *Bristol R* 11 0
2007-08 Bristol R 40 1
2008-09 Bristol R 22 0 **73 1**
2009-10 Oldham Ath 15 0
2010-11 Oldham Ath 1 0 **16 0**
2010-11 Accrington S 26 2 **32 3**
2011-12 Shrewsbury T 39 1 **39 1**

LESLIE, Steven (M) 123 11
H: 5 10 W: 11 02 b.Glasgow 5-11-87
2005-06 Shrewsbury T 1 0
2006-07 Shrewsbury T 5 0
2007-08 Shrewsbury T 17 1
2008-09 Shrewsbury T 27 0
2009-10 Shrewsbury T 34 6
2010-11 Shrewsbury T 18 0
2010-11 *Hereford U* 11 2
2011-12 Shrewsbury T 0 0 **102 7**
2011-12 *Hereford U* 10 2 **21 4**

MALE, Luke (M) 0 0
b.Dudley 1-3-93
Source: Scholar.
2011-12 Shrewsbury T 0 0

McALLISTER, Sean (M) 110 5
H: 5 8 W: 10 07 b.Bolton 15-8-87
Source: Scholar.
2005-06 Sheffield W 2 0
2006-07 Sheffield W 6 1
2007-08 Sheffield W 8 0

2007-08 *Mansfield T* 7 0 **7 0**
2007-08 *Bury* 0 0
2008-09 Sheffield W 40 3
2009-10 Sheffield W 12 0 **68 4**
2010-11 Shrewsbury T 18 0
2011-12 Shrewsbury T 17 1 **35 1**

MORGAN, Marvin (F) 145 34
H: 6 4 W: 12 08 b.Manchester 13-4-83
Source: Wealdstone, Yeading, Woking.
2008-09 Aldershot T 32 6
2009-10 Aldershot T 40 15
2010-11 Aldershot T 19 5 **91 26**
2010-11 *Dagenham & R* 12 0 **12 0**
2011-12 Shrewsbury T 42 8 **42 8**

NEAL, Chris (G) 65 0
H: 6 2 W: 12 04 b.St Albans 23-10-85
Source: Scholar.
2004-05 Preston NE 1 0
2005-06 Preston NE 0 0
2006-07 Preston NE 0 0
2006-07 *Shrewsbury T* 0 0
2007-08 *Morecambe* 0 0
2007-08 Preston NE 0 0
2008-09 Preston NE 0 0 **1 0**
2009-10 Shrewsbury T 7 0
2010-11 Shrewsbury T 22 0
2011-12 Shrewsbury T 35 0 **64 0**

REGAN, Carl (D) 289 3
H: 5 11 W: 11 12 b.Liverpool 14-1-80
Source: Trainee. *Honours:* England Youth.
1997-98 Everton 0 0
1998-99 Everton 0 0
1999-2000 Everton 0 0
2000-01 Barnsley 27 0
2001-02 Barnsley 10 0
2002-03 Barnsley 0 0 **37 0**
2002-03 Hull C 38 0
2003-04 Hull C 0 0 **38 0**
From Droylsden.
2004-05 Chester C 6 0
2005-06 Chester C 41 0 **47 0**
2006-07 Macclesfield T 38 2
2007-08 Macclesfield T 20 0 **58 2**
2007-08 Milton Keynes D 9 1
2008-09 Milton Keynes D 27 0 **36 1**
2009-10 Bristol R 35 0
2010-11 Bristol R 21 0 **56 0**
2010-11 *Notts Co* 4 0 **4 0**
2011-12 Shrewsbury T 13 0 **13 0**

RICHARDS, Matt (D) 328 26
H: 5 8 W: 11 00 b.Harlow 26-12-84
Source: Scholar. *Honours:* England Under-21.
2001-02 Ipswich T 0 0
2002-03 Ipswich T 13 0
2003-04 Ipswich T 44 1
2004-05 Ipswich T 24 1
2005-06 Ipswich T 38 4
2006-07 Ipswich T 28 2
2007-08 Ipswich T 0 0
2007-08 *Brighton & HA* 28 0
2008-09 *Brighton & HA* 23 1 **51 1**
2008-09 Wycombe W 0 0
2008-09 *Notts Co* 1 0 **1 0**
2008-09 Ipswich T 1 0 **148 8**
2009-10 Walsall 40 4
2010-11 Walsall 46 8 **86 12**
2011-12 Shrewsbury T 42 5 **42 5**

SHARPS, Ian (D) 416 16
H: 6 3 W: 14 07 b.Warrington 23-10-80
Source: Trainee.
1998-99 Tranmere R 1 0
1999-2000 Tranmere R 0 0
2000-01 Tranmere R 0 0
2001-02 Tranmere R 29 0
2002-03 Tranmere R 30 3
2003-04 Tranmere R 27 1
2004-05 Tranmere R 44 1
2005-06 Tranmere R 39 1 **170 6**
2006-07 Rotherham U 38 2
2007-08 Rotherham U 33 2
2008-09 Rotherham U 45 4
2009-10 Rotherham U 44 0 **160 8**
2010-11 Shrewsbury T 43 1
2011-12 Shrewsbury T 43 1 **86 2**

SMITH, Benjamin (G) 63 0
H: 6 1 W: 12 11 b.Whitley Bay 5-9-86
Source: Newcastle U Scholar.
2006-07 Stockport Co 0 0
2006-07 Doncaster R 13 0
2007-08 Doncaster R 0 0
2007-08 *Lincoln C* 9 0 **9 0**
2008-09 Doncaster R 0 0
2009-10 Doncaster R 2 0 **15 0**
2009-10 *Morecambe* 3 0 **3 0**
2010-11 Shrewsbury T 25 0
2011-12 Shrewsbury T 11 0 **36 0**

TAYLOR, Jon (M) 55 6
H: 5 11 W: 12 04 b.Liverpool 23-12-89
Source: Youth.
2009-10 Shrewsbury T 2 0
2010-11 Shrewsbury T 20 6
2011-12 Shrewsbury T 33 0 **55 6**

WRIGHT, Mark (M) 309 51
H: 5 11 W: 11 00 b.Wolverhampton 24-2-82
Source: Scholar.
2000-01 Walsall 4 0
2001-02 Walsall 0 0
2002-03 Walsall 5 0
2003-04 Walsall 11 2
2004-05 Walsall 37 2
2005-06 Walsall 30 2
2006-07 Walsall 37 3 **124 9**
2007-08 Milton Keynes D 34 13
2008-09 Milton Keynes D 32 5 **66 18**
2009-10 Brighton & HA 4 0 **4 0**
2009-10 Bristol R 24 0
2010-11 Bristol R 0 0 **24 0**
2010-11 Shrewsbury T 45 14
2011-12 Shrewsbury T 46 10 **91 24**

WROE, Nicky (M) 175 20
H: 5 11 W: 10 02 b.Sheffield 28-9-85
Source: Scholar.
2002-03 Barnsley 1 0
2003-04 Barnsley 2 1
2004-05 Barnsley 31 0
2005-06 Barnsley 12 0
2006-07 Barnsley 3 0 **49 1**
2006-07 *Bury* 5 0 **5 0**
From York C.
2009-10 Torquay U 45 9
2010-11 Torquay U 20 3 **65 12**
2010-11 Shrewsbury T 18 3
2011-12 Shrewsbury T 38 4 **56 7**

SOUTHAMPTON (75)

BARNARD, Lee (F) 166 61
H: 5 10 W: 10 10 b.Romford 18-7-84
Source: Trainee.
2002-03 Tottenham H 0 0
2002-03 *Exeter C* 3 0 **3 0**
2003-04 Tottenham H 0 0
2004-05 Tottenham H 0 0
2004-05 *Leyton Orient* 8 0 **8 0**
2004-05 *Northampton T* 5 0 **5 0**
2005-06 Tottenham H 3 0
2006-07 Tottenham H 0 0
2007-08 Tottenham H 0 0 **3 0**
2007-08 *Crewe Alex* 10 3 **10 3**
2007-08 Southend U 15 9
2008-09 Southend U 35 11
2009-10 Southend U 25 15 **75 35**
2009-10 Southampton 20 9
2010-11 Southampton 36 14
2011-12 Southampton 6 0 **62 23**

BIALKOWSKI, Bartosz (G) 31 0
H: 6 3 W: 12 10 b.Braniewo 6-7-87
Honours: Poland Under-20, Under-21.
2004-05 Gornik Zabrze 7 0 **7 0**
2005-06 Southampton 5 0
2006-07 Southampton 8 0
2007-08 Southampton 1 0
2008-09 Southampton 0 0
2009-10 Southampton 7 0
2009-10 *Barnsley* 2 0 **2 0**
2010-11 Southampton 0 0
2011-12 Southampton 1 0 **22 0**

BUTTERFIELD, Danny (D) 412 9
H: 5 10 W: 11 06 b.Boston 21-11-79
Source: Trainee. *Honours:* England Youth.
1997-98 Grimsby T 7 0
1998-99 Grimsby T 12 0
1999-2000 Grimsby T 29 0
2000-01 Grimsby T 30 1
2001-02 Grimsby T 46 2 **124 3**
2002-03 Crystal Palace 46 1
2003-04 Crystal Palace 45 4
2004-05 Crystal Palace 7 0
2005-06 Crystal Palace 13 0
2006-07 Crystal Palace 28 0
2007-08 Crystal Palace 30 0
2008-09 Crystal Palace 26 1
2008-09 *Charlton Ath* 12 0 **12 0**
2009-10 Crystal Palace 37 0 **232 6**
2010-11 Southampton 34 0
2011-12 Southampton 10 0 **44 0**

CHAMBERS, Calum (M) 0 0
b.Petersfield 20-1-95
Source: Scholar.
2011-12 Southampton 0 0

CHAPLOW, Richard (M) 246 24
H: 5 9 W: 9 03 b.Accrington 2-2-85
Source: Scholar. *Honours:* England Youth, Under-20, Under-21.
2002-03 Burnley 5 0
2003-04 Burnley 39 5
2004-05 Burnley 21 2 **65 7**
2004-05 WBA 4 0
2005-06 WBA 7 0
2005-06 *Southampton* 11 1
2006-07 WBA 28 1
2007-08 WBA 5 0 **44 1**
2007-08 Preston NE 12 3
2008-09 Preston NE 25 3
2009-10 Preston NE 31 2
2010-11 Preston NE 0 0 **68 8**
2010-11 Southampton 33 4
2011-12 Southampton 25 3 **69 8**

CONNOLLY, David (F) 385 149
H: 5 9 W: 11 00 b.Willesden 6-6-77
Source: Trainee. *Honours:* Eire Under-21, 41 full caps, 9 goals.
1994-95 Watford 2 0
1995-96 Watford 11 8
1996-97 Watford 13 2 **26 10**
1997-98 Feyenoord 10 2
1998-99 Wolverhampton W32 6 **32 6**
1999-2000 *Excelsior* 32 29 **32 29**
2000-01 Feyenoord 15 5 **25 7**
2001-02 Wimbledon 35 18
2002-03 Wimbledon 28 24 **63 42**
2003-04 West Ham U 39 10 **39 10**
2004-05 Leicester C 44 13
2005-06 Leicester C 5 4 **49 17**
2005-06 Wigan Ath 17 1
2006-07 Wigan Ath 2 0 **19 1**
2006-07 Sunderland 36 13
2007-08 Sunderland 3 0
2008-09 Sunderland 0 0 **39 13**
2009-10 Southampton 20 5
2010-11 Southampton 15 3
2011-12 Southampton 26 6 **61 14**

CORK, Jack (D) 201 6
H: 6 0 W: 10 12 b.Carshalton 25-6-89
Source: Scholar. *Honours:* England Youth, Under-20, Under-21.
2006-07 Chelsea 0 0
2006-07 *Bournemouth* 7 0 **7 0**
2007-08 Chelsea 0 0
2007-08 *Scunthorpe U* 34 2 **34 2**
2008-09 Chelsea 0 0
2008-09 *Southampton* 23 0
2008-09 *Watford* 19 0 **19 0**
2009-10 Chelsea 0 0
2009-10 *Coventry C* 21 0 **21 0**
2009-10 *Burnley* 11 1
2010-11 Chelsea 0 0
2010-11 *Burnley* 40 3 **51 4**
2011-12 Southampton 46 0 **69 0**

DAVIS, Kelvin (G) 594 0
H: 6 1 W: 11 05 b.Bedford 29-9-76
Source: Trainee. *Honours:* England Youth, Under-21.
1993-94 Luton T 1 0
1994-95 Luton T 9 0
1994-95 *Torquay U* 2 0 **2 0**
1995-96 Luton T 6 0
1996-97 Luton T 0 0
1997-98 Luton T 32 0
1997-98 *Hartlepool U* 2 0 **2 0**
1998-99 Luton T 44 0 **92 0**
1999-2000 Wimbledon 0 0
2000-01 Wimbledon 45 0
2001-02 Wimbledon 40 0
2002-03 Wimbledon 46 0 **131 0**
2003-04 Ipswich T 45 0
2004-05 Ipswich T 39 0 **84 0**

2005-06	Sunderland	33	0	**33**	**0**
2006-07	Southampton	38	0		
2007-08	Southampton	35	0		
2008-09	Southampton	46	0		
2009-10	Southampton	40	0		
2010-11	Southampton	46	0		
2011-12	Southampton	45	0	**250**	**0**

DE RIDDER, Steve (F) **176 37**
H: 5 10 W: 11 07 b.Gent 25-2-87

2006-07	Gent	1	0	**1**	**0**
2006-07	Hamme	16	5		
2007-08	Hamme	34	17	**50**	**22**
2008-09	De Graafschap	29	0		
2009-10	De Graafschap	33	9		
2010-11	De Graafschap	31	3	**93**	**12**
2011-12	Southampton	32	3	**32**	**3**

DEAN, Harlee (M) **27 1**
H: 6 0 W: 11 10 b.Basingstoke 26-7-91
Source: Scholar.

2008-09	Dagenham & R	0	0		
2009-10	Dagenham & R	1	0	**1**	**0**
2010-11	Southampton	0	0		
2011-12	Southampton	0	0		
2011-12	*Brentford*	26	1	**26**	**1**

DICKSON, Ryan (M) **148 6**
H: 5 10 W: 11 05 b.Saltash 14-12-86
Source: Scholar.

2004-05	Plymouth Arg	3	0		
2005-06	Plymouth Arg	0	0		
2006-07	Plymouth Arg	2	0		
2006-07	*Torquay U*	9	1	**9**	**1**
2007-08	Plymouth Arg	0	0	**5**	**0**
2007-08	Brentford	31	0		
2008-09	Brentford	39	1		
2009-10	Brentford	27	2	**97**	**3**
2010-11	Southampton	23	1		
2011-12	Southampton	0	0	**23**	**1**
2011-12	*Yeovil T*	5	1	**5**	**1**
2011-12	*Leyton Orient*	9	0	**9**	**0**

DO PRADO, Guilherme (F) **212 49**
H: 6 2 W: 12 04 b.Sao Paulo 31-12-81

2002	Portuguese Santista	22	7	**22**	**7**
2002-03	Catania	6	0	**6**	**0**
2003-04	Perugia	17	0		
2004-05	Perugia	17	4	**34**	**4**
2005-06	Fiorentina	0	0		
2006-07	Fiorentina	0	0		
2006-07	Spezia	12	1	**12**	**1**
2007-08	*Mantoba*	14	2	**14**	**2**
2008-09	Pro Patria	14	7	**14**	**7**
2009-10	Cesena	34	9	**34**	**9**
2010-11	Southampton	34	9		
2011-12	Southampton	42	10	**76**	**19**

On loan from Cesena.

DOBLE, Ryan (M) **18 1**
H: 6 3 W: 13 00 b.Blaenavon 1-2-91
Source: Scholar. *Honours:* Wales Under-21.

2008-09	Southampton	0	0		
2009-10	Southampton	0	0		
2010-11	Southampton	0	0		
2010-11	*Stockport Co*	3	1	**3**	**1**
2010-11	*Oxford U*	3	0	**3**	**0**
2011-12	Southampton	0	0		
2011-12	*Bournemouth*	7	0	**7**	**0**
2011-12	*Bury*	5	0	**5**	**0**

FONTE, Jose (D) **268 17**
H: 6 2 W: 12 08 b.Penafiel 22-12-83
Source: Sporting Lisbon, Salgueiros.
Honours: Portugal Under-21.

2004-05	Felgueiros	28	1	**28**	**1**
2005-06	Setubal	15	0	**15**	**0**
2005-06	Benfica	1	0	**1**	**0**
2005-06	*Pacos*	11	1	**11**	**1**
2006-07	*Amadora*	25	1	**25**	**1**
2007-08	Crystal Palace	22	1		
2008-09	Crystal Palace	38	4		
2009-10	Crystal Palace	22	1	**82**	**6**
2009-10	Southampton	21	0		
2010-11	Southampton	43	7		
2011-12	Southampton	42	1	**106**	**8**

FORECAST, Tommy (G) **4 0**
H: 6 2 W: 11 10 b.Newham 15-10-86
Source: Scholar.

2005-06	Tottenham H	0	0		
2006-07	Tottenham H	0	0		
2007-08	Tottenham H	0	0		
2008-09	Southampton	0	0		
2009-10	Southampton	0	0		
2009-10	*Grimsby T*	4	0	**4**	**0**
2010-11	Southampton	0	0		
2011-12	Southampton	0	0		

FORTE, Jonathan (M) **235 38**
H: 6 0 W: 12 02 b.Sheffield 25-7-86
Source: Scholar. *Honours:* England Youth. Barbados 2 full caps.

2003-04	Sheffield U	7	0		
2004-05	Sheffield U	22	1		
2005-06	Sheffield U	1	0		
2005-06	*Doncaster R*	13	4		
2005-06	*Rotherham U*	11	4	**11**	**4**
2006-07	Sheffield U	0	0	**30**	**1**
2006-07	*Doncaster R*	41	5	**54**	**9**
2007-08	Scunthorpe U	38	4		
2008-09	Scunthorpe U	8	0		
2008-09	*Notts Co*	18	8		
2009-10	Scunthorpe U	28	2		
2010-11	Scunthorpe U	24	3	**98**	**9**
2010-11	Southampton	10	2		
2011-12	Southampton	1	0	**11**	**2**
2011-12	*Preston NE*	3	0	**3**	**0**
2011-12	*Notts Co*	10	5	**28**	**13**

FOX, Danny (D) **273 14**
H: 5 11 W: 12 06 b.Winsford 29-5-86
Source: Scholar. *Honours:* England Under-21, Scotland 1 full cap.

2004-05	Everton	0	0		
2004-05	*Stranraer*	11	1	**11**	**1**
2005-06	Walsall	33	0		
2006-07	Walsall	44	3		
2007-08	Walsall	22	3	**99**	**6**
2007-08	Coventry C	18	1		
2008-09	Coventry C	39	5		
2009-10	Coventry C	0	0	**57**	**6**
2009-10	Celtic	15	0	**15**	**0**
2009-10	Burnley	14	1		
2010-11	Burnley	35	0		
2011-12	Burnley	1	0	**50**	**1**
2011-12	Southampton	41	0	**41**	**0**

HAMMOND, Dean (M) **324 36**
H: 6 0 W: 11 09 b.Hastings 7-3-83
Source: Scholar.

2002-03	Brighton & HA	4	0		
2003-04	Brighton & HA	0	0		
2003-04	*Leyton Orient*	8	0	**8**	**0**
2004-05	Brighton & HA	30	4		
2005-06	Brighton & HA	41	4		
2006-07	Brighton & HA	37	8		
2007-08	Brighton & HA	24	5	**136**	**21**
2007-08	Colchester U	13	0		
2008-09	Colchester U	41	5		
2009-10	Colchester U	2	0	**56**	**5**
2009-10	Southampton	40	5		
2010-11	Southampton	41	4		
2011-12	Southampton	43	1	**124**	**10**

HARDING, Dan (D) **280 7**
H: 6 0 W: 11 11 b.Gloucester 23-12-83
Source: Scholar. *Honours:* England Under-21.

2002-03	Brighton & HA	1	0		
2003-04	Brighton & HA	23	0		
2004-05	Brighton & HA	43	1	**67**	**1**
2005-06	Leeds U	20	0	**20**	**0**
2006-07	Ipswich T	42	0		
2007-08	Ipswich T	30	1		
2008-09	Ipswich T	1	0	**73**	**1**
2008-09	*Southend U*	19	1	**19**	**1**
2008-09	*Reading*	3	0	**3**	**0**
2009-10	Southampton	42	3		
2010-11	Southampton	36	0		
2011-12	Southampton	20	1	**98**	**4**

HOLMES, Lee (M) **142 11**
H: 5 8 W: 10 06 b.Mansfield 2-4-87
Source: Scholar. *Honours:* FA Schools, England Youth.

2002-03	Derby Co	2	0		
2003-04	Derby Co	23	2		
2004-05	Derby Co	3	0		
2004-05	*Swindon T*	15	1		
2005-06	Derby Co	18	0		
2006-07	Derby Co	0	0		
2006-07	*Bradford C*	16	0	**16**	**0**
2007-08	Derby Co	0	0	**46**	**2**
2007-08	*Walsall*	19	4	**19**	**4**
2008-09	Southampton	11	0		
2009-10	Southampton	5	0		
2010-11	Southampton	7	0		
2011-12	Southampton	6	1	**29**	**1**
2011-12	*Oxford U*	7	2	**7**	**2**
2011-12	*Swindon T*	10	1	**25**	**2**

HOOIVELD, Jos (D) **197 14**
H: 6 3 W: 11 11 b.Zeijen 22-4-83

2002-03	Heerenveen	1	0		
2003-04	Heerenveen	12	0	**13**	**0**
2004-05	Zwolle	14	2		
2005-06	Zwolle	30	1	**44**	**3**
2006-07	Kapfenberger	14	0	**14**	**0**
2007	Inter Turku	26	0		
2008	Inter Turku	26	4	**52**	**4**
2009	AIK Stockholm	28	0	**28**	**0**
2009-10	Celtic	2	0		
2010-11	Celtic	5	0	**7**	**0**
2011-12	Southampton	39	7	**39**	**7**

On loan from Celtic.

HOSKINS, Sam (F) **8 2**
H: 5 8 W: 10 07 b.Dorchester 4-2-93
Source: Scholar.

2011-12	Southampton	0	0		
2011-12	*Preston NE*	0	0		
2011-12	*Rotherham U*	8	2	**8**	**2**

ISGROVE, Lloyd (M) **0 0**
b.Yeovil 12-1-93
Source: Scholar.

2011-12	Southampton	0	0		

JAIDI, Radhi (D) **187 18**
H: 6 2 W: 14 00 b.Tunis 30-8-75
Source: Esperance. *Honours:* Tunisia 101 full caps, 7 goals.

2004-05	Bolton W	27	5		
2005-06	Bolton W	16	3	**43**	**8**
2006-07	Birmingham C	38	6		
2007-08	Birmingham C	18	0		
2008-09	Birmingham C	30	0		
2009-10	Birmingham C	0	0	**86**	**6**
2009-10	Southampton	27	1		
2010-11	Southampton	31	3		
2011-12	Southampton	0	0	**58**	**4**

LALLANA, Adam (M) **170 36**
H: 5 8 W: 11 06 b.St Albans 10-5-88
Source: Scholar. *Honours:* England Youth, Under-21.

2005-06	Southampton	0	0		
2006-07	Southampton	1	0		
2007-08	Southampton	5	1		
2007-08	*Bournemouth*	3	0	**3**	**0**
2008-09	Southampton	40	1		
2009-10	Southampton	44	15		
2010-11	Southampton	36	8		
2011-12	Southampton	41	11	**167**	**36**

LAMBERT, Ricky (F) **469 184**
H: 6 2 W: 14 08 b.Liverpool 16-2-82
Source: Trainee.

1999-2000	Blackpool	3	0		
2000-01	Blackpool	0	0	**3**	**0**
2000-01	Macclesfield T	9	0		
2001-02	Macclesfield T	35	8	**44**	**8**
2001-02	Stockport Co	0	0		
2002-03	Stockport Co	29	2		
2003-04	Stockport Co	40	12		
2004-05	Stockport Co	29	4	**98**	**18**
2004-05	Rochdale	15	6		
2005-06	Rochdale	46	22		
2006-07	Rochdale	3	0	**64**	**28**
2006-07	Bristol R	36	8		
2007-08	Bristol R	46	14		
2008-09	Bristol R	45	29		
2009-10	Bristol R	1	1	**128**	**52**
2009-10	Southampton	45	30		
2010-11	Southampton	45	21		
2011-12	Southampton	42	27	**132**	**78**

LEE, Tadanari (F) **185 51**
H: 6 0 W: 11 09 b.Tokyo 19-12-85
Honours: Japan Under-23, 11 full caps, 2 goals.

2004	FC Tokyo	0	0		
2005	Kashiwa Reysol	8	0		
2006	Kashiwa Reysol	31	8		
2007	Kashiwa Reysol	30	10		
2008	Kashiwa Reysol	19	4		
2009	Kashiwa Reysol	20	2	**108**	**24**
2009	Sanfrecce	8	0		
2010	Sanfrecce	30	11		
2011	Sanfrecce	32	15	**70**	**26**
2011-12	Southampton	7	1	**7**	**1**

MARTIN, Aaron (D) **20 1**
H: 6 3 W: 11 13 b.Newport (IW) 29-9-89
Source: Eastleigh.

2009-10	Southampton	2	0		

2010-11	Southampton	8	0		
2011-12	Southampton	10	1	**20**	**1**

McQUEEN, Sam (M) **0 0**
b.Southampton 6-2-95
Source: Scholar.

2011-12	Southampton	0	0		

MOORE, Corby (M) **0 0**
b.Salisbury 21-11-93
Source: Scholar.

2011-12	Southampton	0	0		

PUNCHEON, Jason (M) **231 38**
H: 5 9 W: 12 05 b.Croydon 26-6-86
Source: Scholar.

2003-04	Wimbledon	8	0	**8**	**0**
2004-05	Milton Keynes D	25	1		
2005-06	Milton Keynes D	1	0		
2006-07	Barnet	37	5		
2007-08	Barnet	41	10	**78**	**15**
2008-09	Plymouth Arg	6	0		
2008-09	*Milton Keynes D*	27	4		
2009-10	Plymouth Arg	0	0	**6**	**0**
2009-10	*Milton Keynes D*	24	7	**77**	**12**
2009-10	Southampton	19	3		
2010-11	Southampton	15	0		
2010-11	*Millwall*	7	5	**7**	**5**
2010-11	*Blackpool*	11	3	**11**	**3**
2011-12	Southampton	8	0	**42**	**3**
2011-12	*QPR*	2	0	**2**	**0**

REED, Harrison (M) **0 0**
b. 27-1-95
Source: Scholar.

2011-12	Southampton	0	0		

REEVES, Ben (D) **7 0**
H: 5 10 W: 10 07 b.Verwood 19-11-91
Source: Scholar.

2008-09	Southampton	0	0		
2009-10	Southampton	0	0		
2010-11	Southampton	0	0		
2011-12	Southampton	2	0	**2**	**0**
2011-12	*Dagenham & R*	5	0	**5**	**0**

RICHARDSON, Frazer (D) **255 5**
H: 5 11 W: 11 12 b.Rotherham 29-10-82
Source: Trainee. *Honours:* England Youth, Under-20.

1999-2000	Leeds U	0	0		
2000-01	Leeds U	0	0		
2001-02	Leeds U	0	0		
2002-03	Leeds U	0	0		
2002-03	*Stoke C*	7	0		
2003-04	Leeds U	4	0		
2003-04	*Stoke C*	6	1	**13**	**1**
2004-05	Leeds U	38	1		
2005-06	Leeds U	23	1		
2006-07	Leeds U	22	0		
2007-08	Leeds U	39	1		
2008-09	Leeds U	23	0	**149**	**3**
2009-10	Charlton Ath	38	1	**38**	**1**
2010-11	Southampton	21	0		
2011-12	Southampton	34	0	**55**	**0**

ROBINSON, Andreas (M) **0 0**
b.Bournemouth 16-10-92
Source: Scholar.

2011-12	Southampton	0	0		

SCHNEIDERLIN, Morgan (M) **141 3**
H: 5 11 W: 11 11 b.Obernai 8-11-89
Honours: France Youth.

2007-08	Strasbourg	5	0	**5**	**0**
2008-09	Southampton	30	0		
2009-10	Southampton	37	1		
2010-11	Southampton	27	0		
2011-12	Southampton	42	2	**136**	**3**

SEABORNE, Danny (D) **96 1**
H: 6 0 W: 11 10 b.Barnstaple 5-3-87
Source: Scholar.

2008-09	Exeter C	33	1		
2009-10	Exeter C	19	0	**52**	**1**
2009-10	Southampton	16	0		
2010-11	Southampton	24	0		
2011-12	Southampton	4	0	**44**	**0**

SEIDI, Alberto (F) **0 0**
b.Guinea-Bissau 20-11-92
Source: Scholar.

2010-11	Southampton	0	0		
2011-12	Southampton	0	0		

SHARP, Billy (F) **248 119**
H: 5 9 W: 11 00 b.Sheffield 5-2-86
Source: Scholar.

2004-05	Sheffield U	2	0		
2004-05	*Rushden & D*	16	9	**16**	**9**
2005-06	Sheffield U	0	0		
2005-06	Scunthorpe U	37	23		
2006-07	Scunthorpe U	45	30	**82**	**53**
2007-08	Sheffield U	29	4		
2008-09	Sheffield U	22	4		
2009-10	Sheffield U	0	0	**53**	**8**
2009-10	*Doncaster R*	33	15		
2010-11	Doncaster R	29	15		
2011-12	Doncaster R	20	10	**82**	**40**
2011-12	Southampton	15	9	**15**	**9**

SHAW, Luke (D) **0 0**
H: 6 1 W: 11 11 b.Kingston 12-7-95
Source: Scholar.

2011-12	Southampton	0	0		

SINCLAIR, Jake (F) **0 0**
Source: Scholar.

2011-12	Southampton	0	0		

STEPHENS, Jack (D) **5 0**
b.Torpoint 27-1-94
Source: Scholar. *Honours:* England Youth.

2010-11	Plymouth Arg	5	0	**5**	**0**
2010-11	Southampton	0	0		
2011-12	Southampton	0	0		

TURNBULL, Jordan (D) **0 0**
b.Swindon 30-10-94
Source: Scholar.

2011-12	Southampton	0	0		

WARD-PROWSE, James (M) **0 0**
b.Portsmouth 1-11-94
Source: Scholar. *Honours:* England Youth.

2011-12	Southampton	0	0		

SOUTHEND U (76)

ASANTE, Kyle (F) **9 1**
H: 5 9 W: 10 10 b.Chelmsford 13-11-91
Source: Scholar.

2009-10	Southend U	0	0		
2010-11	Southend U	9	1		
2011-12	Southend U	0	0	**9**	**1**

BALDWIN, Pat (D) **243 2**
H: 6 3 W: 12 07 b.City of London 12-11-82
Source: Chelsea Academy.

2002-03	Colchester U	19	0		
2003-04	Colchester U	4	0		
2004-05	Colchester U	38	0		
2005-06	Colchester U	25	0		
2006-07	Colchester U	38	1		
2007-08	Colchester U	26	0		
2008-09	Colchester U	35	0		
2009-10	Colchester U	7	0		
2009-10	*Bristol R*	6	0	**6**	**0**
2009-10	*Southend U*	18	1		
2010-11	Colchester U	11	0		
2011-12	Colchester U	5	0	**208**	**1**
2011-12	Southend U	2	0	**20**	**1**
2011-12	*Exeter C*	9	0	**9**	**0**

BARKER, Chris (D) **479 3**
H: 6 2 W: 13 08 b.Sheffield 2-3-80
Source: Alfreton.

1998-99	Barnsley	0	0		
1999-2000	Barnsley	29	0		
2000-01	Barnsley	40	0		
2001-02	Barnsley	44	3	**113**	**3**
2002-03	Cardiff C	40	0		
2003-04	Cardiff C	39	0		
2004-05	*Stoke C*	4	0	**4**	**0**
2004-05	Cardiff C	39	0		
2005-06	Cardiff C	41	0		
2006-07	Cardiff C	0	0	**159**	**0**
2006-07	*Colchester U*	38	0	**38**	**0**
2007-08	QPR	25	0	**25**	**0**
2008-09	Plymouth Arg	40	0		
2009-10	Plymouth Arg	14	0		
2010-11	Plymouth Arg	0	0	**54**	**0**
2010-11	Southend U	43	0		
2011-12	Southend U	43	0	**86**	**0**

BENTLEY, Daniel (G) **1 0**
H: 6 2 W: 11 05 b.Wickford 13-7-93
Source: Scholar.

2011-12	Southend U	1	0	**1**	**0**

BENYON, Elliot (F) **105 27**
H: 5 9 W: 10 01 b.High Wycombe 29-8-87
Source: Scholar.

2005-06	Bristol C	0	0		
2006-07	Bristol C	0	0		
2009-10	Torquay U	45	11		
2010-11	Torquay U	23	13	**68**	**24**
2010-11	Swindon T	12	1		
2011-12	Swindon T	0	0	**12**	**1**
2011-12	*Wycombe W*	9	0	**9**	**0**
2011-12	Southend U	16	2	**16**	**2**

CLOHESSY, Sean (D) **134 2**
H: 5 11 W: 12 07 b.Croydon 12-12-86
Source: Arsenal Scholar.

2005-06	Gillingham	20	1		
2006-07	Gillingham	6	0		
2007-08	Gillingham	17	0	**43**	**1**

From Salisbury C.

2010-11	Southend U	46	1		

From Salisbury C.

2011-12	Southend U	45	0	**91**	**1**

CORR, Barry (F) **131 31**
H: 6 3 W: 12 07 b.Co Wicklow 2-4-85
Honours: Eire Youth.

2001-02	Leeds U	0	0		
2002-03	Leeds U	0	0		
2003-04	Leeds U	0	0		
2004-05	Leeds U	0	0		
2005-06	Sheffield W	16	0		
2006-07	Sheffield W	1	0	**17**	**0**
2006-07	*Bristol C*	3	0	**3**	**0**
2006-07	*Swindon T*	8	3		
2007-08	Swindon T	17	5		
2008-09	Swindon T	11	2	**36**	**10**
2009-10	Exeter C	34	3	**34**	**3**
2010-11	Southend U	41	18		
2011-12	Southend U	0	0	**41**	**18**

COUGHLAN, Graham (D) **449 39**
H: 6 2 W: 13 07 b.Dublin 18-11-74
Source: Bray Wanderers.

1995-96	Blackburn R	0	0		
1996-97	Blackburn R	0	0		
1996-97	*Swindon T*	3	0	**3**	**0**
1997-98	Blackburn R	0	0		
1998-99	Livingston	6	0		
1999-2000	Livingston	29	0		
2000-01	Livingston	21	2	**56**	**2**
2001-02	Plymouth Arg	46	11		
2002-03	Plymouth Arg	42	5		
2003-04	Plymouth Arg	46	7		
2004-05	Plymouth Arg	43	2	**177**	**25**
2005-06	Sheffield W	33	4		
2006-07	Sheffield W	18	1	**51**	**5**
2006-07	*Burnley*	2	0	**2**	**0**
2007-08	Rotherham U	45	1	**45**	**1**
2008-09	Shrewsbury T	42	4		
2009-10	Shrewsbury T	36	2	**78**	**6**
2010-11	Southend U	33	0		
2011-12	Southend U	4	0	**37**	**0**

CRAWFORD, Harry (F) **33 3**
H: 6 1 W: 12 04 b.Watford 10-12-91
Source: Scholar.

2009-10	Southend U	7	1		
2010-11	Southend U	23	2		
2011-12	Southend U	3	0	**33**	**3**

DAILLY, Christian (D) **549 31**
H: 6 1 W: 12 10 b.Dundee 23-10-73
Source: 'S' Form. *Honours:* Scotland Schools, Youth, Under-21, B, 67 full caps, 6 goals.

1990-91	Dundee U	18	5		
1991-92	Dundee U	8	0		
1992-93	Dundee U	14	4		
1993-94	Dundee U	38	4		
1994-95	Dundee U	33	4		
1995-96	Dundee U	30	1	**141**	**18**
1996-97	Derby Co	36	3		
1997-98	Derby Co	30	1		
1998-99	Derby Co	1	0	**67**	**4**
1998-99	Blackburn R	17	0		
1999-2000	Blackburn R	43	4		
2000-01	Blackburn R	10	0	**70**	**4**
2000-01	West Ham U	12	0		
2001-02	West Ham U	38	0		
2002-03	West Ham U	26	0		
2003-04	West Ham U	43	2		
2004-05	West Ham U	3	0		
2005-06	West Ham U	22	0		
2006-07	West Ham U	14	0		
2007-08	West Ham U	0	0	**158**	**2**
2007-08	*Southampton*	11	0	**11**	**0**

2007-08	Rangers	13	2		
2008-09	Rangers	9	0	**22**	**2**
2009-10	Charlton Ath	44	1		
2010-11	Charlton Ath	32	0	**76**	**1**
2011-12	Portsmouth	1	0	**1**	**0**
2011-12	Southend U	3	0	**3**	**0**

DICKINSON, Liam (F) 209 60
H: 6 4 W: 11 07 b.Salford 4-10-85
Source: Woodley Sports.

2005-06	Stockport Co	21	7		
2006-07	Stockport Co	33	7		
2007-08	Stockport Co	40	19	**94**	**33**
2008-09	*Huddersfield T*	13	6	**13**	**6**
2008-09	*Blackpool*	7	4	**7**	**4**
2008-09	*Leeds U*	8	0	**8**	**0**
2008-09	Derby Co	0	0		
2009-10	Brighton & HA	27	4	**27**	**4**
2009-10	*Peterborough U*	9	3	**9**	**3**
2010-11	Barnsley	3	0	**3**	**0**
2010-11	*Walsall*	4	0	**4**	**0**
2010-11	*Rochdale*	14	0	**14**	**0**
2011-12	Plymouth Arg	0	0		
2011-12	Southend U	30	10	**30**	**10**

FERDINAND, Kane (D) 58 9
H: 6 1 W: 13 07 b.Newham 7-10-92
Source: Scholar. *Honours:* Eire Youth.

2010-11	Southend U	22	2		
2011-12	Southend U	36	7	**58**	**9**

FLOOD, Anto (F) 53 15
H: 6 3 W: 11 11 b.Dublin 31-12-84
Source: St Patrick's Ath, Dundalk, Shelbourne.

2010	Galway U	16	7	**16**	**7**
2010	Orebro	3	0	**3**	**0**
2011	Bohemians	33	8	**33**	**8**
2011-12	Southend U	1	0	**1**	**0**

GILBERT, Peter (D) 220 4
H: 5 11 W: 12 00 b.Newcastle 31-7-83
Source: Scholar. *Honours:* Wales Under-21.

2001-02	Birmingham C	0	0		
2002-03	Birmingham C	0	0		
2003-04	Birmingham C	0	0		
2003-04	Plymouth Arg	40	1		
2004-05	Plymouth Arg	38	0	**78**	**1**
2005-06	Leicester C	5	0	**5**	**0**
2005-06	Sheffield W	17	0		
2006-07	Sheffield W	6	0		
2006-07	*Doncaster R*	4	0	**4**	**0**
2007-08	Sheffield W	10	0		
2008-09	Sheffield W	8	0	**41**	**0**
2009-10	Oldham Ath	5	0	**5**	**0**
2009-10	Northampton T	30	0	**30**	**0**
2010-11	Southend U	26	0		
2011-12	Southend U	31	3	**57**	**3**

GRANT, Anthony (M) 206 10
H: 5 10 W: 11 01 b.Lambeth 4-6-87
Source: Scholar. *Honours:* England Youth.

2004-05	Chelsea	1	0		
2005-06	Chelsea	0	0		
2005-06	*Oldham Ath*	2	0	**2**	**0**
2006-07	Chelsea	0	0		
2006-07	*Wycombe W*	40	0	**40**	**0**
2007-08	Chelsea	0	0	**1**	**0**
2007-08	*Luton T*	4	0	**4**	**0**
2007-08	*Southend U*	10	0		
2008-09	Southend U	35	1		
2009-10	Southend U	38	0		
2010-11	Southend U	43	8		
2011-12	Southend U	33	1	**159**	**10**

HALL, Ryan (M) 93 21
H: 5 10 W: 10 04 b.Dulwich 4-1-88
Source: Scholar.

2005-06	Crystal Palace	0	0		
2006-07	Crystal Palace	0	0		
2007-08	Crystal Palace	1	0	**1**	**0**
2007-08	*Dagenham & R*	8	2	**8**	**2**
From Bromley.					
2010-11	Southend U	41	9		
From Bromley.					
2011-12	Southend U	43	10	**84**	**19**

HARRIS, Neil (F) 479 140
H: 5 10 W: 12 08 b.Thurrock 12-7-77
Source: Cambridge C.

1997-98	Millwall	3	0		
1998-99	Millwall	39	15		
1999-2000	Millwall	38	25		
2000-01	Millwall	42	27		
2001-02	Millwall	21	4		
2002-03	Millwall	40	12		
2003-04	Millwall	38	9		
2004-05	Millwall	12	1		
2004-05	*Cardiff C*	3	1	**3**	**1**
2004-05	Nottingham F	13	0		
2005-06	Nottingham F	1	0		
2005-06	*Gillingham*	36	6	**36**	**6**
2006-07	Nottingham F	19	1	**33**	**1**
2006-07	Millwall	21	5		
2007-08	Millwall	27	3		
2008-09	Millwall	35	8		
2009-10	Millwall	32	13		
2010-11	Millwall	26	2	**374**	**124**
2011-12	Southend U	33	8	**33**	**8**

JAMES-LEWIS, Merrick (M) 1 0
H: 6 0 W: 11 11 b.Lambeth 21-5-92
Source: Scholar.

2010-11	Southend U	0	0		
2011-12	Southend U	1	0	**1**	**0**

JOHNSON, Jemal (F) 177 22
H: 5 8 W: 11 09 b.New Jersey 3-5-84
Source: Scholar.

2001-02	Blackburn R	0	0		
2002-03	Blackburn R	0	0		
2003-04	Blackburn R	0	0		
2004-05	Blackburn R	3	0		
2005-06	Blackburn R	3	0		
2005-06	*Preston NE*	3	1	**3**	**1**
2005-06	*Darlington*	9	3	**9**	**3**
2006-07	Blackburn R	0	0	**6**	**0**
2006-07	Wolverhampton W	20	3		
2006-07	*Leeds U*	5	0	**5**	**0**
2007-08	Wolverhampton W	0	0	**20**	**3**
2007-08	Milton Keynes D	39	5		
2008-09	Milton Keynes D	33	5		
2009-10	Milton Keynes D	17	1		
2009-10	*Stockport Co*	16	2	**16**	**2**
2010-11	Milton Keynes D	7	1	**96**	**12**
2010-11	*Port Vale*	6	0	**6**	**0**
2010-11	Lokomotiv Sofia	11	1	**11**	**1**
2011-12	Southend U	5	0	**5**	**0**

Transferred to Lokomotiv Sofia January 2011.

KALALA, Jean-Paul (M) 186 10
H: 5 10 W: 12 02 b.Lubumbashi 16-2-82
Honours: DR Congo 6 full caps.

2003-04	Nice	2	0		
2004-05	Nice	0	0	**2**	**0**
2005-06	Grimsby T	21	5		
2006-07	Yeovil T	38	1		
2007-08	Oldham Ath	20	0		
2008-09	Oldham Ath	0	0		
2008-09	*Grimsby T*	21	2	**42**	**7**
2009-10	Oldham Ath	0	0	**20**	**0**
2009-10	Yeovil T	34	1		
2010-11	Yeovil T	15	0	**87**	**2**
2010-11	Bristol R	11	0	**11**	**0**
2011-12	Southend U	24	1	**24**	**1**

LEONARD, Ryan (D) 18 1
H: 6 0 W: 11 01 b.Plympton 24-5-92
Source: Scholar.

2009-10	Plymouth Arg	1	0		
2010-11	Plymouth Arg	0	0	**1**	**0**
2011-12	Southend U	17	1	**17**	**1**

MARTIN, David J (M) 133 13
H: 5 9 W: 10 10 b.Erith 3-6-85
Source: Dartford.

2006-07	Crystal Palace	5	0		
2007-08	Crystal Palace	9	0	**14**	**0**
2007-08	Millwall	11	2		
2008-09	Millwall	44	4		
2009-10	Millwall	20	3	**75**	**9**
2009-10	*Derby Co*	11	1		
2010-11	Derby Co	2	0		
2010-11	*Notts Co*	10	0	**10**	**0**
2011-12	Derby Co	0	0	**13**	**1**
2011-12	*Walsall*	4	0	**4**	**0**
2011-12	Southend U	17	3	**17**	**3**

MOHSNI, Bilel (D) 54 18
H: 6 3 W: 11 11 b.Tunisia 21-7-87
Source: Les Ulis, Saint-Georges, Sainte Genevieve Sp.

2010-11	Southend U	23	5		
2011-12	Southend U	31	13	**54**	**18**

MORRIS, Glenn (G) 181 0
H: 6 0 W: 12 03 b.Woolwich 20-12-83
Source: Scholar.

2001-02	Leyton Orient	2	0		
2002-03	Leyton Orient	23	0		
2003-04	Leyton Orient	27	0		
2004-05	Leyton Orient	12	0		
2005-06	Leyton Orient	4	0		
2006-07	Leyton Orient	3	0		
2007-08	Leyton Orient	16	0		
2008-09	Leyton Orient	26	0		
2009-10	Leyton Orient	11	0	**124**	**0**
2010-11	Southend U	33	0		
2011-12	Southend U	24	0	**57**	**0**

NESBITT, Teddy (D) 2 0
H: 5 9 W: 11 02 b.East Ham 6-9-93
Source: Scholar.

2010-11	Southend U	2	0		
2011-12	Southend U	0	0	**2**	**0**

PATERSON, Matthew (F) 55 7
H: 5 10 W: 10 10 b.Dunfermline 18-10-89
Source: Scholar. *Honours:* Scotland Youth.

2008-09	Southampton	11	1		
2009-10	Southampton	7	1	**18**	**2**
2009-10	Southend U	16	2		
2010-11	Southend U	11	0		
2010-11	*Stockport Co*	10	3	**10**	**3**
2011-12	Southend U	0	0	**27**	**2**

PHILLIPS, Mark (D) 174 9
H: 6 2 W: 11 00 b.Lambeth 27-1-82
Source: Scholarship.

1999-2000	Millwall	0	0		
2000-01	Millwall	0	0		
2001-02	Millwall	1	0		
2002-03	Millwall	7	0		
2003-04	Millwall	0	0		
2004-05	Millwall	25	1		
2005-06	Millwall	22	0		
2006-07	Millwall	12	0	**67**	**1**
2006-07	*Darlington*	8	0	**8**	**0**
2007-08	Inactive	0	0		
2008-09	Brentford	33	1		
2009-10	Brentford	22	0	**55**	**1**
2010-11	Southend U	5	0		
2011-12	Southend U	39	7	**44**	**7**

PROSSER, Luke (D) 71 4
H: 6 2 W: 12 04 b.Waltham Cross 28-5-88
Source: Scholar.

2005-06	Port Vale	0	0		
2006-07	Port Vale	0	0		
2007-08	Port Vale	5	0		
2008-09	Port Vale	26	1		
2009-10	Port Vale	2	1	**33**	**2**
2010-11	Southend U	17	1		
2011-12	Southend U	21	1	**38**	**2**

SAWYER, Lee (M) 63 3
H: 5 10 W: 10 03 b.Leytonstone 10-9-89
Source: Scholar. *Honours:* England Youth.

2007-08	Chelsea	0	0		
2008-09	Chelsea	0	0		
2008-09	*Southend U*	12	1		
2008-09	*Coventry C*	2	0	**2**	**0**
2008-09	*Wycombe W*	9	1	**9**	**1**
2009-10	Chelsea	0	0		
2009-10	*Southend U*	6	0		
2009-10	Barnet	7	1	**7**	**1**
From Woking.					
2010-11	Southend U	17	0		
From Woking.					
2011-12	Southend U	10	0	**45**	**1**

STEVENS, Jamie (M) 1 0
b.Grays 10-10-92
Source: Scholar. *Honours:* Northern Ireland Youth.

2010-11	Southend U	1	0		
2011-12	Southend U	0	0	**1**	**0**

STURROCK, Blair (F) 249 31
H: 5 10 W: 12 09 b.Dundee 25-8-81
Source: Dundee U.

2000-01	Brechin C	27	6	**27**	**6**
2001-02	Plymouth Arg	19	1		
2002-03	Plymouth Arg	20	1		
2003-04	Plymouth Arg	24	0		
2004-05	Plymouth Arg	0	0	**63**	**2**
2004-05	Kidderminster H	22	5	**22**	**5**
2005-06	Rochdale	31	6		
2006-07	Rochdale	0	0	**31**	**6**
2006-07	Swindon T	19	3		
2007-08	Swindon T	21	3		
2008-09	Swindon T	10	0	**50**	**6**
2008-09	*Bournemouth*	4	0	**4**	**0**
From Mansfield T.					
2010-11	Southend U	43	6		
From Mansfield T.					
2011-12	Southend U	9	0	**52**	**6**

TIMLIN, Michael (M) 170 11
H: 5 8 W: 11 08 b.New Cross 19-3-85
Source: Trainee. *Honours:* Eire Youth, Under-21.

2002-03	Fulham	0	0		
2003-04	Fulham	0	0		
2004-05	Fulham	0	0		
2005-06	Fulham	0	0		
2005-06	*Scunthorpe U*	1	0	**1**	**0**
2005-06	*Doncaster R*	3	0	**3**	**0**
2006-07	Fulham	0	0		
2006-07	*Swindon T*	24	1		
2007-08	Fulham	0	0		
2007-08	*Swindon T*	10	1		
2008-09	Swindon T	41	2		
2009-10	Swindon T	21	0		
2010-11	Swindon T	22	2		
2010-11	*Southend U*	8	1		
2011-12	Swindon T	1	0	**119**	**6**
2011-12	Southend U	39	4	**47**	**5**

WOODYARD, Alex (M) 3 0
H: 5 9 W: 10 00 b.Gravesend 3-5-93
Source: Scholar.

2010-11	Southend U	3	0		
2011-12	Southend U	0	0	**3**	**0**

STEVENAGE (77)

ASHTON, Jon (D) 189 3
H: 6 2 W: 13 12 b.Nuneaton 4-10-82
Source: Scholar.

2000-01	Leicester C	0	0		
2001-02	Leicester C	7	0		
2002-03	*Notts Co*	4	0	**4**	**0**
2003-04	Leicester C	0	0	**7**	**0**
2003-04	Oxford U	34	0		
2004-05	Oxford U	30	0		
2005-06	Oxford U	33	1	**97**	**1**
From Rushden & D, Grays Ath.					
2010-11	Stevenage	38	1		
2011-12	Stevenage	43	1	**81**	**2**

BEARDSLEY, Chris (F) 116 14
H: 6 0 W: 12 12 b.Derby 28-2-84
Source: Scholar.

2002-03	Mansfield T	5	0		
2003-04	Mansfield T	15	1		
2004-05	Doncaster R	4	0	**4**	**0**
2004-05	Kidderminster H	25	5	**25**	**5**
2005-06	Mansfield T	3	0		
2006-07	Mansfield T	10	0	**33**	**1**
From Rushden & D, York C, Kettering T.					
2010-11	Stevenage	23	1		
2011-12	Stevenage	31	7	**54**	**8**

BOSTWICK, Michael (D) 84 9
H: 6 4 W: 14 00 b.Eltham 17-5-88

2006-07	Millwall	0	0		
From Rushden & D, Ebbsfleet U.					
2010-11	Stevenage	41	2		
2011-12	Stevenage	43	7	**84**	**9**

BYROM, Joel (M) 40 4
H: 6 0 W: 12 04 b.Accrington 14-9-86
Source: Scholar.

2004-05	Blackburn R	0	0		
2005-06	Blackburn R	0	0		
2006-07	Accrington S	1	0	**1**	**0**
From Clitheroe, Southport, Clitheroe, Northwich Vic.					
2010-11	Stevenage	7	0		
2011-12	Stevenage	32	4	**39**	**4**

CHARLES, Darius (M) 93 7
H: 6 1 W: 13 05 b.Ealing 10-12-87
Source: Scholar.

2004-05	Brentford	1	0		
2005-06	Brentford	2	0		
2006-07	Brentford	17	1		
2007-08	Brentford	17	0	**37**	**1**
From Ebbsfleet U.					
2010-11	Stevenage	28	2		
2011-12	Stevenage	28	4	**56**	**6**

COWAN, Don (F) 48 8
H: 5 10 W: 13 05 b.New York 16-11-89

2009	Shamrock R	5	0		
2010	Shamrock R	3	0	**8**	**0**
2010	*Longford T*	13	0		
2011	Longford T	19	8	**32**	**8**
2011-12	Stevenage	8	0	**8**	**0**

DAY, Chris (G) 272 0
H: 6 2 W: 13 07 b.Whipps Cross 28-7-75
Source: Trainee. *Honours:* England Youth, Under-21.

1992-93	Tottenham H	0	0		
1993-94	Tottenham H	0	0		
1994-95	Tottenham H	0	0		
1995-96	Tottenham H	0	0		
1996-97	Crystal Palace	24	0	**24**	**0**
1997-98	Watford	0	0		
1998-99	Watford	0	0		
1999-2000	Watford	11	0		
2000-01	Watford	0	0	**11**	**0**
2000-01	*Lincoln C*	14	0	**14**	**0**
2001-02	QPR	16	0		
2002-03	QPR	12	0		
2003-04	QPR	29	0		
2004-05	QPR	30	0	**87**	**0**
2004-05	*Preston NE*	6	0	**6**	**0**
2005-06	Oldham Ath	30	0	**30**	**0**
2006-07	Millwall	5	0		
2007-08	Millwall	5	0	**10**	**0**
2010-11	Stevenage	46	0		
2011-12	Stevenage	44	0	**90**	**0**

EDWARDS, Phil (D) 225 23
H: 5 8 W: 11 03 b.Bootle 8-11-85
Source: Scholar.

2005-06	Wigan Ath	0	0		
2006-07	Accrington S	33	1		
2007-08	Accrington S	31	1		
2008-09	Accrington S	46	0		
2009-10	Accrington S	46	8		
2010-11	Accrington S	44	13	**200**	**23**
2011-12	Stevenage	22	0	**22**	**0**
2011-12	*Rochdale*	3	0	**3**	**0**

FREEMAN, Luke (F) 40 9
H: 6 0 W: 10 00 b.Dartford 22-3-92
Source: Scholar.

2007-08	Gillingham	1	0	**1**	**0**
2008-09	Arsenal	0	0		
2009-10	Arsenal	0	0		
2010-11	Arsenal	0	0		
2010-11	*Yeovil T*	13	2	**13**	**2**
2011-12	Arsenal	0	0		
2011-12	Stevenage	26	7	**26**	**7**

HENRY, Ronnie (D) 89 0
H: 5 11 W: 11 10 b.Hemel Hempstead 2-1-84
Source: Trainee.

2002-03	Tottenham H	0	0		
2002-03	*Southend U*	3	0	**3**	**0**
2004	Dublin C	12	0	**12**	**0**
2010-11	Stevenage	42	0		
2011-12	Stevenage	32	0	**74**	**0**

JULIAN, Alan (G) 92 0
H: 6 2 W: 13 07 b.Ashford 11-3-83
Source: Trainee. *Honours:* Northern Ireland Youth, Under-21.

2001-02	Brentford	0	0		
2002-03	Brentford	3	0		
2003-04	Brentford	13	0		
2004-05	Brentford	0	0	**16**	**0**
From Stevenage B.					
2008-09	Gillingham	4	0		
2009-10	Gillingham	30	0		
2010-11	Gillingham	39	0	**73**	**0**
2011-12	Stevenage	3	0	**3**	**0**

LAIRD, Scott (D) 90 12
H: 5 11 W: 11 05 b.Taunton 15-5-88
Source: Scholar.

2006-07	Plymouth Arg	0	0		
2007-08	Plymouth Arg	0	0		
2010-11	Stevenage	44	4		
2011-12	Stevenage	46	8	**90**	**12**

LONG, Stacy (M) 71 4
H: 5 8 W: 10 00 b.Farnborough 11-1-85
Source: Scholar. *Honours:* England Under-20, Youth.

2001-02	Charlton Ath	0	0		
2002-03	Charlton Ath	0	0		
2003-04	Charlton Ath	0	0		
2004-05	Charlton Ath	0	0		
2005-06	Notts Co	19	1	**19**	**1**
From Ebbsfleet U.					
2010-11	Stevenage	22	2		
From Ebbsfleet U.					
2011-12	Stevenage	30	1	**52**	**3**

MAY, Ben (F) 232 31
H: 6 3 W: 12 12 b.Gravesend 10-3-84
Source: Juniors.

2000-01	Millwall	0	0		
2001-02	Millwall	0	0		
2002-03	Millwall	10	1		
2002-03	*Colchester U*	6	0		
2003-04	Millwall	0	0		
2003-04	*Brentford*	41	7		
2004-05	Millwall	8	1		
2004-05	*Colchester U*	14	1	**20**	**1**
2004-05	Brentford	10	1	**51**	**8**
2005-06	Millwall	39	10		
2006-07	Millwall	13	2		
2007-08	Millwall	8	0	**78**	**14**
2007-08	Scunthorpe U	21	1		
2008-09	Scunthorpe U	23	2		
2009-10	Scunthorpe U	1	0	**45**	**3**
2010-11	Stevenage	20	1		
2011-12	Stevenage	7	0	**27**	**1**
2011-12	*Barnet*	11	4	**11**	**4**

MOUSINHO, John (M) 194 15
H: 6 1 W: 12 07 b.Hounslow 30-4-86
Source: Univ of Notre Dame.

2005-06	Brentford	7	0		
2006-07	Brentford	34	0		
2007-08	Brentford	23	2	**64**	**2**
2008-09	Wycombe W	34	2		
2009-10	Wycombe W	39	1	**73**	**3**
2010-11	Stevenage	38	7		
2011-12	Stevenage	19	3	**57**	**10**

MURPHY, Darren (M) 115 11
H: 6 0 W: 11 11 b.Cork 28-7-85

2003	Cobh Ramblers	26	2		
2004	Cobh Ramblers	23	2		
2005	Cobh Ramblers	5	0		
2006	Cobh Ramblers	21	5	**75**	**9**
2007	Cork C	9	1		
2008	Cork C	23	1	**32**	**2**
2010-11	Stevenage	5	0		
2011-12	Stevenage	0	0	**5**	**0**
2011-12	*Aldershot T*	3	0	**3**	**0**

MYRIE-WILLIAMS, Jennison (F) 144 10
H: 5 11 W: 12 08 b.Lambeth 17-5-88
Source: Scholar. *Honours:* England Youth.

2005-06	Bristol C	1	0		
2006-07	Bristol C	25	2		
2007-08	Bristol C	0	0		
2007-08	*Cheltenham T*	12	0		
2007-08	*Tranmere R*	25	3	**25**	**3**
2008-09	Bristol C	0	0		
2008-09	*Cheltenham T*	5	1	**17**	**1**
2008-09	*Carlisle U*	8	0	**8**	**0**
2008-09	*Hereford U*	15	2	**15**	**2**
2009-10	Bristol C	0	0	**26**	**2**
2009-10	Dundee U	24	1	**24**	**1**
2010-11	St Johnstone	6	0	**6**	**0**
2011-12	Stevenage	17	0	**17**	**0**
2011-12	*Port Vale*	6	1	**6**	**1**

REID, Craig (F) 63 8
H: 5 10 W: 11 10 b.Coventry 17-12-85
Honours: Ipswich T Scholar.

2004-05	Coventry C	0	0		
2005-06	Coventry C	0	0		
2006-07	Cheltenham T	6	0		
2007-08	Cheltenham T	8	0	**14**	**0**
From Grays Ath, Newport Co.					
2010-11	Stevenage	20	2		
2011-12	Stevenage	29	6	**49**	**8**

ROBERTS, Mark (D) 129 12
H: 6 1 W: 12 00 b.Northwich 16-10-83
Source: Scholar.

2002-03	Crewe Alex	0	0		
2003-04	Crewe Alex	0	0		
2004-05	Crewe Alex	6	0		
2005-06	Crewe Alex	0	0		
2005-06	*Chester C*	1	0	**1**	**0**
2006-07	Crewe Alex	0	0	**6**	**0**
2007-08	Accrington S	34	0	**34**	**0**
From Northwich Vic.					
2010-11	Stevenage	42	6		
2011-12	Stevenage	46	6	**88**	**12**

SHROOT, Robin (M) 44 4
H: 5 9 W: 11 05 b.Hammersmith 26-3-88
Source: Staines T, AFC Wimbledon, Harrow Borough. *Honours:* Northern Ireland Under-21.

2008-09	Birmingham C	0	0		
2008-09	*Walsall*	5	0	**5**	**0**

2009-10 Birmingham C 0 0
2009-10 *Burton Alb* 7 0 **7 0**
2010-11 Birmingham C 0 0
2010-11 *Cheltenham T* 7 1 **7 1**
2011-12 Stevenage 25 3 **25 3**

SINCLAIR, Robert (M) 31 2
H: 5 10 W: 11 02 b.Bedford 29-8-89
Source: Scholar.
2007-08 Luton T 0 0
From Salisbury C.
2010-11 Stevenage 27 2
2011-12 Stevenage 0 0 **27 2**
2011-12 *Aldershot T* 4 0 **4 0**

THALASSITIS, Michael (F) 3 0
H: 6 1 W: 13 00 b.Enfield 19-1-93
Source: Youth.
2011-12 Stevenage 3 0 **3 0**

WILSON, Lawrie (D) 88 10
H: 5 11 W: 11 06 b.London 11-9-87
Source: Charlton Ath.
2006-07 Colchester U 0 0
2010-11 Stevenage 42 5
2011-12 Stevenage 46 5 **88 10**

WINN, Peter (M) 32 2
H: 6 0 W: 11 09 b.Cleethorpes 19-12-88
Source: Scholar.
2006-07 Scunthorpe U 0 0
2007-08 Scunthorpe U 4 0
2008-09 Scunthorpe U 0 0
2009-10 Scunthorpe U 0 0 **4 0**
2010-11 Stevenage 28 2
2011-12 Stevenage 0 0 **28 2**

STOKE C (78)

ARISMENDI, Diego (M) 101 3
H: 6 2 W: 12 13 b.Montevideo 25-1-88
Honours: Uruguay 2 full caps.
2006-07 Nacional 10 0
2007-08 Nacional 21 1
2008-09 Nacional 24 1 **55 2**
2009-10 Stoke C 0 0
2009-10 *Brighton & HA* 6 0 **6 0**
2010-11 Stoke C 0 0
2010-11 *Barnsley* 31 1 **31 1**
2011-12 Stoke C 0 0
2011-12 *Huddersfield T* 9 0 **9 0**

BACHMANN, Daniel (G) 0 0
b.Vienna 9-7-94
Source: Scholar.
2011-12 Stoke C 0 0

BEGOVIC, Asmir (G) 99 0
H: 6 5 W: 13 01 b.Trebinje 20-6-87
Source: La Louviere. *Honours:* Canada Under-20, Bosnia 12 full caps.
2006-07 Portsmouth 0 0
2006-07 *Macclesfield T* 3 0 **3 0**
2007-08 Portsmouth 0 0
2007-08 *Bournemouth* 8 0 **8 0**
2007-08 *Yeovil T* 2 0
2008-09 Portsmouth 2 0
2008-09 *Yeovil T* 14 0 **16 0**
2009-10 Portsmouth 9 0 **11 0**
2009-10 *Ipswich T* 6 0 **6 0**
2009-10 Stoke C 4 0
2010-11 Stoke C 28 0
2011-12 Stoke C 23 0 **55 0**

BRUNT, Ryan (F) 15 1
H: 6 1 W: 11 11 b.Birmingham 26-5-93
Source: Scholar.
2011-12 Stoke C 0 0
2011-12 *Tranmere R* 15 1 **15 1**

COLLINS, Danny (D) 238 8
H: 6 2 W: 11 13 b.Buckley 6-8-80
Source: Buckley T. *Honours:* Wales 12 full caps.
2004-05 Chester C 12 1 **12 1**
2004-05 Sunderland 14 0
2005-06 Sunderland 23 1
2006-07 Sunderland 38 0
2007-08 Sunderland 36 1
2008-09 Sunderland 35 1
2009-10 Sunderland 3 0 **149 3**
2009-10 Stoke C 25 0
2010-11 Stoke C 25 0
2011-12 Stoke C 0 0 **50 0**

2011-12 *Ipswich T* 16 3 **16 3**
2011-12 *West Ham U* 11 1 **11 1**

CROUCH, Peter (F) 386 105
H: 6 7 W: 13 03 b.Macclesfield 30-1-81
Source: Trainee. *Honours:* England Youth, Under-20, Under-21, B, 42 full caps, 22 goals.
1998-99 Tottenham H 0 0
1999-2000 Tottenham H 0 0
2000-01 QPR 42 10 **42 10**
2001-02 Portsmouth 37 18
2001-02 Aston Villa 7 2
2002-03 Aston Villa 14 0
2003-04 Aston Villa 16 4 **37 6**
2003-04 *Norwich C* 15 4 **15 4**
2004-05 Southampton 27 12 **27 12**
2005-06 Liverpool 32 8
2006-07 Liverpool 32 9
2007-08 Liverpool 21 5 **85 22**
2008-09 Portsmouth 38 11
2009-10 Portsmouth 0 0 **75 29**
2009-10 Tottenham H 38 8
2010-11 Tottenham H 34 4
2011-12 Tottenham H 1 0 **73 12**
2011-12 Stoke C 32 10 **32 10**

CUVELIER, Florent (M) 18 4
H: 6 0 W: 11 05 b.Brussels 12-9-92
Source: Scholar. *Honours:* Belgium Youth.
2009-10 Portsmouth 0 0
2010-11 Stoke C 0 0
2011-12 Stoke C 0 0
2011-12 *Walsall* 18 4 **18 4**

DAVIES, Andrew (D) 159 5
H: 6 3 W: 14 08 b.Stockton 17-12-84
Source: Scholar. *Honours:* England Youth, Under-20, Under-21.
2002-03 Middlesbrough 1 0
2003-04 Middlesbrough 10 0
2004-05 Middlesbrough 3 0
2004-05 *QPR* 9 0 **9 0**
2005-06 Middlesbrough 12 0
2005-06 *Derby Co* 23 3 **23 3**
2006-07 Middlesbrough 23 0
2007-08 Middlesbrough 4 0
2007-08 Southampton 23 0
2008-09 Southampton 0 0 **23 0**
2008-09 Stoke C 2 0
2008-09 *Preston NE* 5 0 **5 0**
2009-10 Stoke C 0 0
2009-10 *Sheffield U* 8 0 **8 0**
2010-11 Stoke C 0 0
2010-11 *Walsall* 3 0 **3 0**
2010-11 *Middlesbrough* 6 0 **59 0**
2011-12 Stoke C 0 0 **2 0**
2011-12 *Crystal Palace* 1 0 **1 0**
2011-12 *Bradford C* 26 2 **26 2**

DELAP, Rory (M) 491 32
H: 6 3 W: 13 00 b.Sutton Coldfield 6-7-76
Source: Trainee. *Honours:* Eire Under-21, B, 11 full caps.
1992-93 Carlisle U 1 0
1993-94 Carlisle U 1 0
1994-95 Carlisle U 3 0
1995-96 Carlisle U 19 3
1996-97 Carlisle U 32 4
1997-98 Carlisle U 9 0 **65 7**
1997-98 Derby Co 13 0
1998-99 Derby Co 23 0
1999-2000 Derby Co 34 8
2000-01 Derby Co 33 3 **103 11**
2001-02 Southampton 28 2
2002-03 Southampton 24 0
2003-04 Southampton 27 1
2004-05 Southampton 37 2
2005-06 Southampton 16 0 **132 5**
2005-06 Sunderland 6 1
2006-07 Sunderland 6 0 **12 1**
2006-07 Stoke C 2 0
2007-08 Stoke C 44 2
2008-09 Stoke C 34 2
2009-10 Stoke C 36 0
2010-11 Stoke C 37 2
2011-12 Stoke C 26 2 **179 8**

DIAO, Salif (M) 215 2
H: 6 1 W: 12 08 b.Kedougou 10-2-77
Honours: Senegal 39 full caps, 4 goals.
1996-97 Epinal 2 0 **2 0**
1996-97 Monaco 0 0
1997-98 Monaco 12 0
1998-99 Monaco 14 0
1999-2000 Monaco 1 0 **27 0**

2000-01 Sedan 26 0
2001-02 Sedan 22 0 **48 0**
2002-03 Liverpool 26 1
2003-04 Liverpool 3 0
2004-05 Liverpool 8 0
2004-05 *Birmingham C* 2 0 **2 0**
2005-06 Liverpool 0 0
2005-06 *Portsmouth* 11 0 **11 0**
2006-07 Liverpool 0 0 **37 1**
2006-07 Stoke C 27 0
2007-08 Stoke C 11 0
2008-09 Stoke C 20 0
2009-10 Stoke C 16 1
2010-11 Stoke C 8 0
2011-12 Stoke C 6 0 **88 1**

ETHERINGTON, Matthew (M) 384 37
H: 5 10 W: 10 12 b.Truro 14-8-81
Source: School. *Honours:* England Youth, Under-21.
1996-97 Peterborough U 1 0
1997-98 Peterborough U 2 0
1998-99 Peterborough U 29 3
1999-2000 Peterborough U 19 3 **51 6**
1999-2000 Tottenham H 5 0
2000-01 Tottenham H 6 0
2001-02 *Bradford C* 13 1 **13 1**
2001-02 Tottenham H 11 0
2002-03 Tottenham H 23 1 **45 1**
2003-04 West Ham U 35 5
2004-05 West Ham U 39 4
2005-06 West Ham U 33 2
2006-07 West Ham U 27 0
2007-08 West Ham U 18 3
2008-09 West Ham U 13 2 **165 16**
2008-09 Stoke C 14 0
2009-10 Stoke C 34 5
2010-11 Stoke C 32 5
2011-12 Stoke C 30 3 **110 13**

FULLER, Ricardo (F) 340 90
H: 6 3 W: 12 10 b.Kingston, Jamaica 31-10-79
Source: Tivoli Gardens. *Honours:* Jamaica 60 full caps, 11 goals.
2000-01 Crystal Palace 8 0 **8 0**
2001-02 Hearts 27 8 **27 8**
From Tivoli Gardens.
2002-03 Preston NE 18 9
2003-04 Preston NE 38 17
2004-05 Preston NE 2 1 **58 27**
2004-05 Portsmouth 31 1 **31 1**
2005-06 Southampton 30 9
2005-06 *Ipswich T* 3 2 **3 2**
2006-07 Southampton 1 0 **31 9**
2006-07 Stoke C 30 10
2007-08 Stoke C 42 15
2008-09 Stoke C 34 11
2009-10 Stoke C 35 3
2010-11 Stoke C 28 4
2011-12 Stoke C 13 0 **182 43**

HIGGINBOTHAM, Danny (D) 321 22
H: 6 2 W: 13 01 b.Manchester 29-12-78
Source: Trainee.
1997-98 Manchester U 1 0
1998-99 Manchester U 0 0
1999-2000 Manchester U 3 0 **4 0**
2000-01 Derby Co 26 0
2001-02 Derby Co 37 1
2002-03 Derby Co 23 2 **86 3**
2002-03 Southampton 9 0
2003-04 Southampton 27 0
2004-05 Southampton 21 1
2005-06 Southampton 37 3 **94 4**
2006-07 Stoke C 44 7
2007-08 Stoke C 1 0
2007-08 Sunderland 21 3
2008-09 Sunderland 1 0 **22 3**
2008-09 Stoke C 28 1
2009-10 Stoke C 24 1
2010-11 Stoke C 10 2
2011-12 Stoke C 2 0 **109 11**
2011-12 *Nottingham F* 6 1 **6 1**

HUTH, Robert (D) 196 14
H: 6 3 W: 14 07 b.Berlin 18-8-84
Source: Scholar. *Honours:* Germany Youth, Under-21, 19 full caps, 2 goals.
2001-02 Chelsea 1 0
2002-03 Chelsea 2 0
2003-04 Chelsea 16 0
2004-05 Chelsea 10 0
2005-06 Chelsea 13 0 **42 0**
2006-07 Middlesbrough 12 1

2007-08 Middlesbrough 13 1
2008-09 Middlesbrough 24 0
2009-10 Middlesbrough 4 0 **53 2**
2009-10 Stoke C 32 3
2010-11 Stoke C 35 6
2011-12 Stoke C 34 3 **101 12**

JEROME, Cameron (F) 277 65
H: 6 1 W: 13 06 b.Huddersfield 14-8-86
Honours: England Under-21.
2004-05 Cardiff C 29 6
2005-06 Cardiff C 44 18 **73 24**
2005-06 Birmingham C 0 0
2006-07 Birmingham C 38 7
2007-08 Birmingham C 33 7
2008-09 Birmingham C 43 9
2009-10 Birmingham C 32 11
2010-11 Birmingham C 34 3
2011-12 Birmingham C 1 0 **181 37**
2011-12 Stoke C 23 4 **23 4**

JONES, Kenwyne (F) 240 65
H: 6 2 W: 13 06 b.Trinidad & Tobago 5-10-84
Source: W Connection. *Honours:* Trindad & Tobago Youth, Under-23, 49 full caps, 7 goals.
2004-05 Southampton 2 0
2004-05 *Sheffield W* 7 7 **7 7**
2004-05 *Stoke C* 13 3
2005-06 Southampton 34 4
2006-07 Southampton 34 14
2007-08 Southampton 1 1 **71 19**
2007-08 Sunderland 33 7
2008-09 Sunderland 29 10
2009-10 Sunderland 32 9 **94 26**
2010-11 Stoke C 34 9
2011-12 Stoke C 21 1 **68 13**

LUND, Matthew (M) 18 2
H: 6 0 W: 11 13 b.Manchester 21-11-90
Source: Crewe Alex. *Honours:* Northern Ireland Under-21.
2009-10 Stoke C 0 0
2010-11 Stoke C 0 0
2010-11 *Hereford U* 2 0 **2 0**
2011-12 Stoke C 0 0
2011-12 *Oldham Ath* 3 0 **3 0**
2011-12 *Bristol R* 13 2 **13 2**

MOULT, Louis (F) 16 1
H: 6 0 W: 13 05 b.Stoke 14-5-92
Source: Scholar.
2009-10 Stoke C 1 0
2010-11 Stoke C 0 0
2010-11 *Bradford C* 11 1 **11 1**
2011-12 Stoke C 0 0 **1 0**
2011-12 *Accrington S* 4 0 **4 0**

NASH, Carlo (G) 243 0
H: 6 5 W: 14 01 b.Bolton 13-9-73
Source: Clitheroe.
1996-97 Crystal Palace 21 0
1997-98 Crystal Palace 0 0 **21 0**
1998-99 Stockport Co 43 0
1999-2000 Stockport Co 38 0
2000-01 Stockport Co 8 0 **89 0**
2000-01 Manchester C 6 0
2001-02 Manchester C 23 0
2002-03 Manchester C 9 0 **38 0**
2003-04 Middlesbrough 1 0
2004-05 Middlesbrough 2 0 **3 0**
2004-05 Preston NE 7 0
2005-06 Preston NE 46 0
2006-07 Preston NE 29 0 **82 0**
2007-08 Wigan Ath 0 0
2007-08 *Stoke C* 10 0
2008-09 Wigan Ath 0 0
2008-09 Everton 0 0
2009-10 Everton 0 0
2010-11 Stoke C 0 0
2011-12 Stoke C 0 0 **10 0**

PALACIOS, Wilson (D) 127 1
H: 5 10 W: 11 11 b.La Ceiba 29-7-84
Source: Olimpia. *Honours:* Honduras 79 full caps, 5 goals.
2007-08 Birmingham C 7 0 **7 0**
2007-08 Wigan Ath 16 0
2008-09 Wigan Ath 21 0 **37 0**
2008-09 Tottenham H 11 0
2009-10 Tottenham H 33 1
2010-11 Tottenham H 21 0
2011-12 Tottenham H 0 0 **65 1**
2011-12 Stoke C 18 0 **18 0**

PENNANT, Jermaine (M) 268 15
H: 5 9 W: 10 06 b.Nottingham 15-1-83
Honours: England Schools, Youth, Under-21.
1998-99 Notts Co 0 0
1998-99 Arsenal 0 0
1999-2000 Arsenal 0 0
2000-01 Arsenal 0 0
2001-02 Arsenal 0 0
2001-02 *Watford* 9 2
2002-03 Arsenal 5 3
2002-03 *Watford* 12 0 **21 2**
2003-04 Arsenal 0 0
2003-04 *Leeds U* 36 2 **36 2**
2004-05 Arsenal 7 0 **12 3**
2004-05 Birmingham C 12 0
2005-06 Birmingham C 38 2 **50 2**
2006-07 Liverpool 34 1
2007-08 Liverpool 18 2
2008-09 Liverpool 3 0 **55 3**
2008-09 *Portsmouth* 13 0 **13 0**
2009-10 Zaragoza 25 0 **25 0**
2010-11 Stoke C 29 3
2011-12 Stoke C 27 0 **56 3**

ROSSI, Karim (F) 0 0
b.Zurich 1-5-94
Source: Scholar.
2011-12 Stoke C 0 0

SHAWCROSS, Ryan (D) 171 15
H: 6 3 W: 13 13 b.Buckley 4-10-87
Source: Scholar. *Honours:* England Under-21.
2006-07 Manchester U 0 0
2007-08 Manchester U 0 0
2007-08 Stoke C 41 7
2008-09 Stoke C 30 3
2009-10 Stoke C 28 2
2010-11 Stoke C 36 1
2011-12 Stoke C 36 2 **171 15**

SHOTTON, Ryan (D) 88 6
H: 6 3 W: 13 05 b.Stoke 30-9-88
Source: Scholar.
2006-07 Stoke C 0 0
2007-08 Stoke C 0 0
2008-09 Stoke C 0 0
2008-09 *Tranmere R* 33 5 **33 5**
2009-10 Stoke C 0 0
2009-10 *Barnsley* 30 0 **30 0**
2010-11 Stoke C 2 0
2011-12 Stoke C 23 1 **25 1**

SIDIBE, Mamady (F) 305 41
H: 6 4 W: 12 02 b.Bamako 18-12-79
Source: CA Paris. *Honours:* Mali 14 full caps, 3 goals.
2001-02 Swansea C 31 7 **31 7**
2002-03 Gillingham 30 3
2003-04 Gillingham 41 5
2004-05 Gillingham 35 2 **106 10**
2005-06 Stoke C 42 6
2006-07 Stoke C 43 9
2007-08 Stoke C 35 4
2008-09 Stoke C 22 3
2009-10 Stoke C 24 2
2010-11 Stoke C 2 0
2011-12 Stoke C 0 0 **168 24**

SMAJL, Suljevic (M) 0 0
Source: Dalkurd.
2011-12 Stoke C 0 0

SOARES, Tom (M) 202 16
H: 6 0 W: 11 04 b.Reading 10-7-86
Source: Scholar. *Honours:* England Youth, Under-20, Under-21.
2003-04 Crystal Palace 3 0
2004-05 Crystal Palace 22 0
2005-06 Crystal Palace 44 1
2006-07 Crystal Palace 37 3
2007-08 Crystal Palace 39 6
2008-09 Crystal Palace 4 1 **149 11**
2008-09 Stoke C 7 0
2008-09 *Charlton Ath* 11 1 **11 1**
2009-10 Stoke C 0 0
2009-10 *Sheffield W* 25 2 **25 2**
2010-11 Stoke C 0 0
2011-12 Stoke C 0 0 **7 0**
2011-12 *Hibernian* 10 2 **10 2**

SORENSEN, Thomas (G) 405 0
H: 6 4 W: 13 10 b.Fredericia 12-6-76
Source: Odense. *Honours:* Denmark Youth, Under-21, B, 101 full caps.
1998-99 Sunderland 45 0
1999-2000 Sunderland 37 0
2000-01 Sunderland 34 0
2001-02 Sunderland 34 0
2002-03 Sunderland 21 0 **171 0**
2003-04 Aston Villa 38 0
2004-05 Aston Villa 36 0
2005-06 Aston Villa 36 0
2006-07 Aston Villa 29 0
2007-08 Aston Villa 0 0 **139 0**
2008-09 Stoke C 36 0
2009-10 Stoke C 33 0
2010-11 Stoke C 10 0
2011-12 Stoke C 16 0 **95 0**

SULJEVIC, Smajl (M) 0 0
b.Borlange 15-7-94
Source: Dalkurd.
2011-12 Stoke C 0 0

TONGE, Michael (M) 314 24
H: 6 0 W: 11 10 b.Manchester 7-4-83
Source: Scholar. *Honours:* England Youth, Under-20, Under-21.
2000-01 Sheffield U 2 0
2001-02 Sheffield U 30 3
2002-03 Sheffield U 44 6
2003-04 Sheffield U 46 4
2004-05 Sheffield U 34 2
2005-06 Sheffield U 30 3
2006-07 Sheffield U 27 2
2007-08 Sheffield U 45 1
2008-09 Sheffield U 4 0 **262 21**
2008-09 Stoke C 10 0
2009-10 Stoke C 0 0
2009-10 *Preston NE* 7 0
2009-10 *Derby Co* 18 2 **18 2**
2010-11 Stoke C 2 0
2010-11 *Preston NE* 5 1 **12 1**
2011-12 Stoke C 0 0 **12 0**
2011-12 *Barnsley* 10 0 **10 0**

TUNCAY, Sanli (F) 347 111
H: 5 10 W: 11 00 b.Sakarya 16-1-82
Honours: Turkey 79 full caps, 22 goals.
2000-01 Sakarya 31 16
2001-02 Sakarya 35 16 **66 32**
2002-03 Fenerbahce 29 9
2003-04 Fenerbahce 31 19
2004-05 Fenerbahce 31 7
2005-06 Fenerbahce 27 13
2006-07 Fenerbahce 33 9 **151 57**
2007-08 Middlesbrough 34 8
2008-09 Middlesbrough 33 7
2009-10 Middlesbrough 3 2 **70 17**
2009-10 Stoke C 30 4
2010-11 Stoke C 14 1
2011-12 Stoke C 0 0 **44 5**
2011-12 *Bolton W* 16 0 **16 0**
Transferred to Wolfsburg January 2011.

UPSON, Matthew (D) 315 10
H: 6 1 W: 11 04 b.Eye 18-4-79
Source: Trainee. *Honours:* England Youth, Under-21, 21 full caps, 2 goals.
1995-96 Luton T 0 0
1996-97 Luton T 1 0 **1 0**
1996-97 Arsenal 0 0
1997-98 Arsenal 5 0
1998-99 Arsenal 5 0
1999-2000 Arsenal 8 0
2000-01 Arsenal 2 0
2000-01 *Nottingham F* 1 0 **1 0**
2000-01 *Crystal Palace* 7 0 **7 0**
2001-02 Arsenal 14 0
2002-03 Arsenal 0 0 **34 0**
2002-03 *Reading* 14 0 **14 0**
2002-03 Birmingham C 14 0
2003-04 Birmingham C 30 0
2004-05 Birmingham C 36 2
2005-06 Birmingham C 24 1
2006-07 Birmingham C 9 2 **113 5**
2006-07 West Ham U 2 0
2007-08 West Ham U 29 1
2008-09 West Ham U 37 0
2009-10 West Ham U 33 3
2010-11 West Ham U 30 0 **131 4**
2011-12 Stoke C 14 1 **14 1**

WALTERS, Jon (F) 337 64
H: 6 0 W: 12 06 b.Birkenhead 20-9-83
Source: Blackburn R Scholar. *Honours:* Eire Youth, Under-21, B, 10 full caps, 1 goal.
2001-02 Bolton W 0 0
2002-03 Bolton W 4 0
2002-03 *Hull C* 11 5
2003-04 Bolton W 0 0 **4 0**

2003-04	Crewe Alex	0	0		
2003-04	*Barnsley*	8	0	**8**	**0**
2003-04	Hull C	16	1		
2004-05	Hull C	21	1	**48**	**7**
2004-05	*Scunthorpe U*	3	0	**3**	**0**
2005-06	Wrexham	38	5	**38**	**5**
2006-07	Chester C	26	9	**26**	**9**
2006-07	Ipswich T	16	4		
2007-08	Ipswich T	40	13		
2008-09	Ipswich T	36	5		
2009-10	Ipswich T	43	8		
2010-11	Ipswich T	1	0	**136**	**30**
2010-11	Stoke C	36	6		
2011-12	Stoke C	38	7	**74**	**13**

WHELAN, Glenn (M) **287 17**

H: 5 11 W: 12 07 b.Dublin 13-1-84

Source: Scholar. *Honours:* Eire Youth, Under-21, B, 42 full caps, 2 goals.

2000-01	Manchester C	0	0		
2001-02	Manchester C	0	0		
2002-03	Manchester C	0	0		
2003-04	Manchester C	0	0		
2003-04	*Bury*	13	0	**13**	**0**
2004-05	Sheffield W	36	2		
2005-06	Sheffield W	43	1		
2006-07	Sheffield W	38	7		
2007-08	Sheffield W	25	2	**142**	**12**
2007-08	Stoke C	14	1		
2008-09	Stoke C	26	1		
2009-10	Stoke C	33	2		
2010-11	Stoke C	29	0		
2011-12	Stoke C	30	1	**132**	**5**

WHITEHEAD, Dean (M) **413 24**

H: 5 11 W: 12 06 b.Abingdon 12-1-82

Source: Trainee.

1999-2000	Oxford U	0	0		
2000-01	Oxford U	20	0		
2001-02	Oxford U	40	1		
2002-03	Oxford U	18	1		
2003-04	Oxford U	44	7	**122**	**9**
2004-05	Sunderland	42	5		
2005-06	Sunderland	37	3		
2006-07	Sunderland	45	4		
2007-08	Sunderland	27	1		
2008-09	Sunderland	34	0		
2009-10	Sunderland	0	0	**185**	**13**
2009-10	Stoke C	36	0		
2010-11	Stoke C	37	2		
2011-12	Stoke C	33	0	**106**	**2**

WILKINSON, Andy (D) **147 0**

H: 5 11 W: 11 00 b.Stone 6-8-84

Source: Scholar.

2001-02	Stoke C	0	0		
2002-03	Stoke C	0	0		
2003-04	Stoke C	3	0		
2004-05	Stoke C	1	0		
2004-05	*Shrewsbury T*	9	0	**9**	**0**
2005-06	Stoke C	6	0		
2006-07	Stoke C	4	0		
2006-07	*Blackpool*	7	0	**7**	**0**
2007-08	Stoke C	23	0		
2008-09	Stoke C	22	0		
2009-10	Stoke C	25	0		
2010-11	Stoke C	22	0		
2011-12	Stoke C	25	0	**131**	**0**

WILSON, Marc (M) **130 4**

H: 6 2 W: 12 07 b.Lisburn 17-8-87

Source: Scholar. *Honours:* Eire Under-21, 1 full cap.

2005-06	Portsmouth	0	0		
2005-06	*Yeovil T*	2	0	**2**	**0**
2006-07	Portsmouth	0	0		
2006-07	*Bournemouth*	19	3		
2007-08	Portsmouth	0	0		
2007-08	*Bournemouth*	7	0	**26**	**3**
2007-08	*Luton T*	4	0	**4**	**0**
2008-09	Portsmouth	3	0		
2009-10	Portsmouth	28	0		
2010-11	Portsmouth	4	0	**35**	**0**
2010-11	Stoke C	28	1		
2011-12	Stoke C	35	0	**63**	**1**

WOODGATE, Jonathan (D) **253 6**

H: 6 2 W: 12 06 b.Middlesbrough 22-1-80

Source: Trainee. *Honours:* England Youth, Under-21, 8 full caps.

1996-97	Leeds U	0	0		
1997-98	Leeds U	0	0		
1998-99	Leeds U	25	2		
1999-2000	Leeds U	34	1		
2000-01	Leeds U	14	1		
2001-02	Leeds U	13	0		
2002-03	Leeds U	18	0	**104**	**4**
2002-03	Newcastle U	10	0		
2003-04	Newcastle U	18	0	**28**	**0**
2004-05	Real Madrid	0	0		
2005-06	Real Madrid	9	0	**9**	**0**
2006-07	Middlesbrough	30	0		
2007-08	Middlesbrough	16	0	**46**	**0**
2007-08	Tottenham H	12	1		
2008-09	Tottenham H	34	1		
2009-10	Tottenham H	3	0		
2010-11	Tottenham H	0	0	**49**	**2**
2011-12	Stoke C	17	0	**17**	**0**

Scholars

Barrington Marcel; Clarkson Michael Thomas; Dawson Lucas Jay; Debayo Joseph Akinlolu Onolapo; Eve Dale Donald; Hall Andrew Stephen; Hall Jadan; Musungu Andrew; Nardiello Jack Barrie; O'Reilly Ryan; Parry Immanuel Denchi; Richardson Jordan; Scott Kristian Adrian.

SUNDERLAND (79)

ADAMS, Blair (D) **29 0**

H: 5 11 W: 11 05 b.South Shields 8-9-91

Source: Scholar. *Honours:* England Under-20.

2010-11	Sunderland	0	0		
2011-12	Sunderland	0	0		
2011-12	*Brentford*	7	0	**7**	**0**
2011-12	*Northampton T*	22	0	**22**	**0**

ANGELERI, Marcos (D) **161 3**

H: 6 0 W: 10 10 b.La Plata 4-7-83

Honours: Argentina 4 full caps.

2005-06	Estudiantes	29	1		
2006-07	Estudiantes	29	1		
2007-08	Estudiantes	34	0		
2008-09	Estudiantes	49	1		
2009-10	Estudiantes	18	0	**159**	**3**
2010-11	Sunderland	2	0		
2011-12	Sunderland	0	0	**2**	**0**

ARMSTRONG, James (M) **0 0**

b.Sunderland 10-5-93

Source: Scholar.

2011-12	Sunderland	0	0		

BAGNALL, Liam (D) **0 0**

H: 5 11 W: 10 04 b.Newry 17-5-92

Source: Scholar. *Honours:* Northern Ireland Under-21.

2009-10	Sunderland	0	0		
2010-11	Sunderland	0	0		
2011-12	Sunderland	0	0		

BARDSLEY, Phillip (D) **178 5**

H: 5 11 W: 11 13 b.Salford 28-6-85

Source: Trainee. *Honours:* Scotland 12 full caps.

2003-04	Manchester U	0	0		
2004-05	Manchester U	0	0		
2005-06	Manchester U	8	0		
2005-06	*Burnley*	6	0	**6**	**0**
2006-07	Manchester U	0	0		
2006-07	*Rangers*	5	1	**5**	**1**
2006-07	*Aston Villa*	13	0	**13**	**0**
2007-08	Manchester U	0	0	**8**	**0**
2007-08	*Sheffield U*	16	0	**16**	**0**
2007-08	Sunderland	11	0		
2008-09	Sunderland	28	0		
2009-10	Sunderland	26	0		
2010-11	Sunderland	34	3		
2011-12	Sunderland	31	1	**130**	**4**

BRAMBLE, Titus (D) **282 10**

H: 6 2 W: 13 10 b.Ipswich 31-7-81

Source: Trainee. *Honours:* England Under-21.

1998-99	Ipswich T	4	0		
1999-2000	Ipswich T	0	0		
1999-2000	*Colchester U*	2	0	**2**	**0**
2000-01	Ipswich T	26	1		
2001-02	Ipswich T	18	0	**48**	**1**
2002-03	Newcastle U	16	0		
2003-04	Newcastle U	29	0		
2004-05	Newcastle U	19	1		
2005-06	Newcastle U	24	2		
2006-07	Newcastle U	17	0	**105**	**3**
2007-08	Wigan Ath	26	2		
2008-09	Wigan Ath	35	1		
2009-10	Wigan Ath	35	2	**96**	**5**
2010-11	Sunderland	23	0		
2011-12	Sunderland	8	1	**31**	**1**

BROWN, Wes (D) **252 4**

H: 6 1 W: 13 08 b.Manchester 13-10-79

Source: Trainee. *Honours:* England Schools, Youth, Under-21, 23 full caps, 1 goal.

1996-97	Manchester U	0	0		
1997-98	Manchester U	2	0		
1998-99	Manchester U	14	0		
1999-2000	Manchester U	0	0		
2000-01	Manchester U	28	0		
2001-02	Manchester U	17	0		
2002-03	Manchester U	22	0		
2003-04	Manchester U	17	0		
2004-05	Manchester U	21	1		
2005-06	Manchester U	19	0		
2006-07	Manchester U	22	0		
2007-08	Manchester U	36	1		
2008-09	Manchester U	8	1		
2009-10	Manchester U	19	0		
2010-11	Manchester U	7	0	**232**	**3**
2011-12	Sunderland	20	1	**20**	**1**

CAMPBELL, Frazier (F) **92 21**

H: 5 11 W: 12 04 b.Huddersfield 13-9-87

Source: Scholar. *Honours:* England Youth, Under-21, 1 full cap.

2005-06	Manchester U	0	0		
2006-07	Manchester U	0	0		
2007-08	Manchester U	1	0		
2007-08	*Hull C*	34	15	**34**	**15**
2008-09	Manchester U	1	0		
2008-09	*Tottenham H*	10	1	**10**	**1**
2009-10	Manchester U	0	0	**2**	**0**
2009-10	Sunderland	31	4		
2010-11	Sunderland	3	0		
2011-12	Sunderland	12	1	**46**	**5**

CATTERMOLE, Lee (M) **170 4**

H: 5 10 W: 11 13 b.Stockton 21-3-88

Source: Scholar. *Honours:* England Youth, Under-21.

2005-06	Middlesbrough	14	1		
2006-07	Middlesbrough	31	1		
2007-08	Middlesbrough	24	1	**69**	**3**
2008-09	Wigan Ath	33	1		
2009-10	Wigan Ath	0	0	**33**	**1**
2009-10	Sunderland	22	0		
2010-11	Sunderland	23	0		
2011-12	Sunderland	23	0	**68**	**0**

COLBACK, Jack (M) **97 5**

H: 5 9 W: 11 05 b.Killingworth 24-10-89

Source: Scholar. *Honours:* England Youth.

2007-08	Sunderland	0	0		
2008-09	Sunderland	0	0		
2009-10	Sunderland	1	0		
2009-10	*Ipswich T*	37	4		
2010-11	Sunderland	11	0		
2010-11	*Ipswich T*	13	0	**50**	**4**
2011-12	Sunderland	35	1	**47**	**1**

COOK, Jordan (F) **30 5**

H: 5 10 W: 10 10 b.Hetton-le-Hole 20-3-90

Source: Scholar.

2007-08	Sunderland	0	0		
2008-09	Sunderland	0	0		
2009-10	Sunderland	0	0		
2009-10	*Darlington*	5	0	**5**	**0**
2010-11	Sunderland	3	0		
2010-11	*Walsall*	8	1	**8**	**1**
2011-12	Sunderland	0	0	**3**	**0**
2011-12	*Carlisle U*	14	4	**14**	**4**

EGAN, John (D) **2 0**

H: 6 1 W: 11 11 b.Cork 20-10-92

Source: Scholar. *Honours:* Eire Youth, Under-21.

2009-10	Sunderland	0	0		
2010-11	Sunderland	0	0		
2011-12	Sunderland	0	0		
2011-12	*Crystal Palace*	1	0	**1**	**0**
2011-12	*Sheffield U*	1	0	**1**	**0**

ELLIOTT, Brett (M) **0 0**

b.Jarrow 30-5-93

Source: Scholar.

2011-12	Sunderland	0	0		

ELMOHAMADY, Ahmed (M) **129 15**

H: 5 11 W: 12 10 b.El Mahalla El-Kubra 9-9-87

Honours: Egypt 51 full caps, 2 goals.

2003-04	Ghazi Al-Mehalla	0	0		
2004-05	Ghazi Al-Mehalla	14	4		

2005-06 Ghazi Al-Mehalla 3 0 **17 4**
2006-07 ENPPI 12 2
2007-08 ENPPI 6 1
2008-09 ENPPI 28 6
2009-10 ENPPI 12 1 **58 10**
2010-11 Sunderland 36 0
2011-12 Sunderland 18 1 **54 1**
On loan from ENPPI.

GARDNER, Craig (M) 131 17
H: 5 10 W: 11 13 b.Solihull 25-11-86
Source: Scholar. *Honours:* England Under-21.
2004-05 Aston Villa 0 0
2005-06 Aston Villa 8 0
2006-07 Aston Villa 13 2
2007-08 Aston Villa 23 3
2008-09 Aston Villa 14 0
2009-10 Aston Villa 1 0 **59 5**
2009-10 Birmingham C 13 1
2010-11 Birmingham C 29 8 **42 9**
2011-12 Sunderland 30 3 **30 3**

GORDON, Craig (G) 226 0
H: 6 4 W: 12 02 b.Edinburgh 31-12-82
Honours: Scotland Under-21, 40 full caps.
2000-01 Hearts 0 0
2001-02 Hearts 0 0
2002-03 Hearts 1 0
2003-04 Hearts 29 0
2004-05 Hearts 38 0
2005-06 Hearts 36 0
2006-07 Hearts 34 0 **138 0**
2007-08 Sunderland 34 0
2008-09 Sunderland 12 0
2009-10 Sunderland 26 0
2010-11 Sunderland 15 0
2011-12 Sunderland 1 0 **88 0**

GORRIN, Alejandro (M) 0 0
b.Tenerife 1-8-93
Source: Scholar.
2011-12 Sunderland 0 0

GYAN, Asamoah (F) 191 72
H: 5 11 W: 12 08 b.Acrra 22-11-85
Honours: Ghana 59 full caps, 28 goals.
2003-04 Udinese 1 0
2004-05 Modena 27 7
2005-06 Modena 25 8 **52 15**
2006-07 Udinese 25 8
2007-08 Udinese 13 3 **39 11**
2008-09 Rennes 16 1
2009-10 Rennes 29 13
2010-11 Rennes 3 0 **48 14**
2010-11 Sunderland 31 10
2011-12 Sunderland 3 0 **34 10**
2011-12 *Al Ain* 18 22 **18 22**

JI, Dong-Won (F) 52 12
H: 6 2 W: 12 04 b.Jeju 28-5-91
Honours: South Korea Under-23, 17 full caps, 8 goals.
2010 Chunnam Dragons22 7
2011 Chunnam Dragons11 3 **33 10**
2011-12 Sunderland 19 2 **19 2**

KILGALLON, Matthew (D) 221 7
H: 6 1 W: 12 10 b.York 8-1-84
Source: Scholar. *Honours:* England Youth, Under-20, Under-21.
2000-01 Leeds U 0 0
2001-02 Leeds U 0 0
2002-03 Leeds U 2 0
2003-04 Leeds U 8 2
2003-04 *West Ham U* 3 0 **3 0**
2004-05 Leeds U 26 0
2005-06 Leeds U 25 1
2006-07 Leeds U 19 0 **80 3**
2006-07 Sheffield U 6 0
2007-08 Sheffield U 40 2
2008-09 Sheffield U 40 1
2009-10 Sheffield U 21 1 **107 4**
2009-10 Sunderland 7 0
2010-11 Sunderland 0 0
2010-11 *Middlesbrough* 2 0 **2 0**
2010-11 *Doncaster R* 12 0 **12 0**
2011-12 Sunderland 10 0 **17 0**

KING, Lewis (G) 0 0
b.Derby 8-5-93
Source: Scholar.
2011-12 Sunderland 0 0

KNOTT, Billy (M) 20 3
H: 5 8 W: 11 02 b.Canvey Island 28-11-92
Source: Scholar. *Honours:* England Under-20.
2010-11 Sunderland 0 0
2011-12 Sunderland 0 0
2011-12 *AFC Wimbledon* 20 3 **20 3**

KYRGIAKOS, Sotirios (D) 266 20
H: 6 3 W: 14 06 b.Trikala 23-7-79
Honours: Greece 61 full caps, 4 goals.
1998-99 Panathinaikos 0 0
1999-2000 Agios 28 1
2000-01 Agios 25 2 **53 3**
2001-02 Panathinaikos 18 1
2002-03 Panathinaikos 24 0
2003-04 Panathinaikos 6 1
2004-05 Panathinaikos 12 3 **60 5**
2004-05 Rangers 15 0
2005-06 Rangers 28 1 **43 1**
2006-07 Eintracht Frankfurt 27 5
2007-08 Eintracht Frankfurt 24 3 **51 8**
2008-09 AEK Athens 19 0 **19 0**
2009-10 Liverpool 14 1
2010-11 Liverpool 16 2 **30 3**
2011-12 Wolfsburg 7 0 **7 0**
2011-12 Sunderland 3 0 **3 0**
On loan from Wolfsburg.

LAING, Louis (D) 12 0
H: 5 11 W: 12 00 b.Newcastle 6-3-93
Source: Scholar. *Honours:* England Youth.
2009-10 Sunderland 0 0
2010-11 Sunderland 1 0
2011-12 Sunderland 0 0 **1 0**
2011-12 *Wycombe W* 11 0 **11 0**

LARSSON, Sebastian (M) 219 26
H: 5 11 W: 11 02 b.Eskilstuna 6-6-85
Source: Trainee. *Honours:* Sweden Under-21, 44 full caps, 6 goals.
2002-03 Arsenal 0 0
2003-04 Arsenal 0 0
2004-05 Arsenal 0 0
2005-06 Arsenal 3 0
2006-07 Arsenal 0 0 **3 0**
2006-07 Birmingham C 43 4
2007-08 Birmingham C 35 6
2008-09 Birmingham C 38 1
2009-10 Birmingham C 33 4
2010-11 Birmingham C 35 4 **184 19**
2011-12 Sunderland 32 7 **32 7**

LIDDLE, Michael (D) 35 0
H: 5 6 W: 11 00 b.Hounslow 25-12-89
Source: Scholar. *Honours:* Eire Under-21.
2007-08 Sunderland 0 0
2008-09 Sunderland 0 0
2008-09 *Carlisle U* 22 0 **22 0**
2009-10 Sunderland 0 0
2010-11 Sunderland 0 0
2010-11 *Leyton Orient* 1 0 **1 0**
2011-12 Sunderland 0 0
2011-12 *Accrington S* 12 0 **12 0**

LYNCH, Craig (F) 2 0
H: 5 9 W: 10 01 b.Chester-le-Street 25-3-92
Source: Scholar.
2010-11 Sunderland 2 0
2011-12 Sunderland 0 0 **2 0**

MADDEN, Daniel (D) 0 0
H: 5 10 W: 14 02 b.Sunderland 10-9-90
Source: Scholar.
2008-09 Sunderland 0 0
2009-10 Sunderland 0 0
2010-11 Sunderland 0 0
2011-12 Sunderland 0 0

MANDRON, Mikael (F) 0 0
b.Boulogne 11-10-94
Source: Scholar.
2011-12 Sunderland 0 0

MARRS, Liam (D) 0 0
b.North Shields 26-11-92
Source: Scholar.
2011-12 Sunderland 0 0

McCARTNEY, George (D) 306 2
H: 5 11 W: 11 02 b.Belfast 29-4-81
Source: Trainee. *Honours:* Northern Ireland Schools, Youth, Under-21, 34 full caps, 1 goal.
1998-99 Sunderland 0 0
1999-2000 Sunderland 0 0
2000-01 Sunderland 2 0
2001-02 Sunderland 18 0
2002-03 Sunderland 24 0
2003-04 Sunderland 41 0
2004-05 Sunderland 36 0
2005-06 Sunderland 13 0
2006-07 West Ham U 22 0
2007-08 West Ham U 38 1
2008-09 West Ham U 1 0
2008-09 Sunderland 16 0
2009-10 Sunderland 25 0
2010-11 Sunderland 0 0
2010-11 *Leeds U* 32 0 **32 0**
2011-12 Sunderland 0 0 **175 0**
2011-12 *West Ham U* 38 1 **99 2**

McCLEAN, James (M) 96 23
H: 5 11 W: 11 00 b.Derry 22-4-89
Honours: Northern Ireland Under-21. Eire 3 full caps.
2009 Derry C 27 1
2010 Derry C 30 10
2011 Derry C 16 7 **73 18**
2011-12 Sunderland 23 5 **23 5**

MEYLER, David (M) 24 0
H: 6 3 W: 11 09 b.Cork 29-5-89
Honours: Eire Under-21.
2008 Cork C 2 0 **2 0**
2008-09 Sunderland 0 0
2009-10 Sunderland 10 0
2010-11 Sunderland 5 0
2011-12 Sunderland 7 0 **22 0**

MIGNOLET, Simon (G) 174 1
H: 6 4 W: 13 10 b.St Truiden 6-3-88
Honours: Belgium Under-21, 10 full caps.
2006-07 St Truiden 2 0
2007-08 St Truiden 25 0
2008-09 St Truiden 35 1
2009-10 St Truiden 37 0
2010-11 St Truiden 23 0 **122 1**
2010-11 Sunderland 23 0
2011-12 Sunderland 29 0 **52 0**

MITCHELL, Adam (M) 0 0
b.Barnard Castle 3-4-93
Source: Scholar.
2011-12 Sunderland 0 0

NOBLE, Ryan (F) 17 2
H: 6 0 W: 11 00 b.Sunderland 6-11-91
Source: Scholar. *Honours:* England Youth.
2009-10 Sunderland 0 0
2009-10 *Watford* 0 0
2010-11 Sunderland 3 0
2010-11 *Derby Co* 1 0
2011-12 Sunderland 2 0 **5 0**
2011-12 *Derby Co* 2 0 **3 0**
2011-12 *Hartlepool U* 9 2 **9 2**

O'SHEA, John (D) 295 11
H: 6 3 W: 13 07 b.Waterford 30-4-81
Source: Waterford. *Honours:* Eire Youth, Under-21, 79 full caps, 1 goal.
1998-99 Manchester U 0 0
1999-2000 Manchester U 0 0
1999-2000 *Bournemouth* 10 1 **10 1**
2000-01 Manchester U 0 0
2001-02 Manchester U 9 0
2002-03 Manchester U 32 0
2003-04 Manchester U 33 2
2004-05 Manchester U 23 2
2005-06 Manchester U 34 1
2006-07 Manchester U 32 4
2007-08 Manchester U 28 0
2008-09 Manchester U 30 0
2009-10 Manchester U 15 1
2010-11 Manchester U 20 0 **256 10**
2011-12 Sunderland 29 0 **29 0**

PICKFORD, Jordan (G) 0 0
b.Washington 7-3-94
Source: Scholar. *Honours:* England Youth.
2010-11 Sunderland 0 0
2011-12 Sunderland 0 0

REED, Adam (M) 26 0
H: 5 5 W: 10 03 b.Hartlepool 8-5-91
Source: Scholar.
2009-10 Sunderland 0 0
2010-11 Sunderland 0 0
2010-11 *Brentford* 11 0 **11 0**
2011-12 Sunderland 0 0
2011-12 *Bradford C* 4 0 **4 0**
2011-12 *Leyton Orient* 11 0 **11 0**

RICHARDSON, Kieran (M) 186 19
H: 5 9 W: 11 13 b.Greenwich 21-10-84
Source: Scholar. *Honours:* England Under-21, 8 full caps, 2 goals.
2002-03 Manchester U 2 0
2003-04 Manchester U 0 0
2004-05 Manchester U 2 0
2004-05 *WBA* 12 3 **12 3**
2005-06 Manchester U 22 1
2006-07 Manchester U 15 1 **41 2**
2007-08 Sunderland 17 3
2008-09 Sunderland 32 4
2009-10 Sunderland 29 1
2010-11 Sunderland 26 4
2011-12 Sunderland 29 2 **133 14**

RIVEROS, Cristian (M) 280 34
H: 5 10 W: 11 13 b.Saldivar 16-10-81
Honours: Paraguay 60 full caps, 12 goals.
2002 Sportivo San Lorenzo 14 0 **14 0**
2003 Tacuary 29 1
2004 Tacuary 30 3
2005 Tacuary 18 3 **77 7**
2005 Libertad 17 4
2006 Libertad 24 4
2007 Libertad 7 1 **48 9**
2007-08 Cruz Azul 32 5
2008-09 Cruz Azul 31 5
2009-10 Cruz Azul 30 4 **93 14**
2010-11 Sunderland 12 1
2011-12 Sunderland 0 0 **12 1**
2011-12 *Kayseri* 36 3 **36 3**

SESSEGNON, Stephane (M) 258 34
H: 5 8 W: 11 05 b.Allahe 1-6-84
Honours: Benin 45 full caps, 8 goals.
2003-04 Requins 2 0 **2 0**
2004-05 Creteil 35 5
2005-06 Creteil 33 5 **68 10**
2006-07 Le Mans 31 1
2007-08 Le Mans 30 5 **61 6**
2008-09 Paris St Germain 34 5
2009-10 Paris St Germain 29 3
2010-11 Paris St Germain 14 0 **77 8**
2010-11 Sunderland 14 3
2011-12 Sunderland 36 7 **50 10**

TOUNKARA, Oumare (F) 52 8
H: 6 1 W: 12 08 b.Paris 25-5-90
Source: Sedan.
2009-10 Sunderland 0 0
2010-11 Sunderland 0 0
2010-11 *Oldham Ath* 44 7
2011-12 Sunderland 0 0
2011-12 *Oldham Ath* 8 1 **52 8**

TURNER, Michael (D) 295 18
H: 6 4 W: 13 05 b.Lewisham 9-11-83
Source: Scholar.
2001-02 Charlton Ath 0 0
2002-03 Charlton Ath 0 0
2002-03 *Leyton Orient* 7 1 **7 1**
2003-04 Charlton Ath 0 0
2004-05 Charlton Ath 0 0
2004-05 Brentford 45 1
2005-06 Brentford 46 2 **91 3**
2006-07 Hull C 43 3
2007-08 Hull C 44 5
2008-09 Hull C 38 4
2009-10 Hull C 4 0 **129 12**
2009-10 Sunderland 29 2
2010-11 Sunderland 15 0
2011-12 Sunderland 24 0 **68 2**

VAUGHAN, David (M) 323 25
H: 5 7 W: 11 00 b.Abergele 18-2-83
Source: Scholar. *Honours:* Wales Youth, Under-21, 29 full caps, 1 goal.
2000-01 Crewe Alex 1 0
2001-02 Crewe Alex 13 0
2002-03 Crewe Alex 32 3
2003-04 Crewe Alex 31 0
2004-05 Crewe Alex 44 6
2005-06 Crewe Alex 34 5
2006-07 Crewe Alex 29 4
2007-08 Crewe Alex 1 0 **185 18**
2007-08 Real Sociedad 7 1 **7 1**
2008-09 Blackpool 33 1
2009-10 Blackpool 41 1
2010-11 Blackpool 35 2 **109 4**
2011-12 Sunderland 22 2 **22 2**

WATSON, Jordan (M) 0 0
b.Cyprus 7-4-93
Honours: Northern Ireland Youth.
2009-10 Sunderland 0 0
2010-11 Sunderland 0 0
2011-12 Sunderland 0 0

WESTWOOD, Keiren (G) 267 0
H: 6 1 W: 13 10 b.Manchester 23-10-84
Source: Scholar. *Honours:* Eire 10 full caps.
2001-02 Manchester C 0 0
2002-03 Manchester C 0 0
2003-04 Manchester C 0 0
2003-04 *Oldham Ath* 0 0
2004-05 Manchester C 0 0
2005-06 Manchester C 0 0
2005-06 Carlisle U 35 0
2006-07 Carlisle U 46 0
2007-08 Carlisle U 46 0 **127 0**
2008-09 Coventry C 46 0
2009-10 Coventry C 44 0
2010-11 Coventry C 41 0 **131 0**
2011-12 Sunderland 9 0 **9 0**

WICKHAM, Connor (F) 81 14
H: 6 0 W: 14 01 b.Hereford 31-3-93
Source: School. *Honours:* England Youth, Under-21.
2008-09 Ipswich T 2 0
2009-10 Ipswich T 26 4
2010-11 Ipswich T 37 9 **65 13**
2011-12 Sunderland 16 1 **16 1**

WILSON, Ben (G) 0 0
b.Stanley 9-8-92
Source: Scholar.
2010-11 Sunderland 0 0
2011-12 Sunderland 0 0

Scholars
Agnew Liam John; Burn Jonathan David; Callaghan Anthony; Cartwright Andrew; Dixon Joel Stephen; Gibbons Lewis Michael Edward; Holland Ross Kieran; Honeyman George Christopher; Hope Callum Alfred; Laidler Jordan Lee; Lane Glen; Lawson Carl; Maddison Jonathan; Martin Kieran; McNamee Thomas Gerard; Noble Reece Paul; Oliver Connor; Thomas Nathan.

SWANSEA C (80)

AGUSTIEN, Kemy (M) 177 8
H: 5 10 W: 11 05 b.Tilburg 20-8-86
Honours: Holland Under-21.
2004-05 Willem II 21 1
2005-06 Willem II 34 2 **55 3**
2006-07 *Roda JC* 31 2 **31 2**
2007-08 AZ 25 2 **25 2**
2008-09 *Birmingham C* 18 0 **18 0**
2009-10 *RKC Waalwijk* 19 1 **19 1**
2010-11 Swansea C 8 0
2010-11 *Crystal Palace* 8 0 **8 0**
2011-12 Swansea C 13 0 **21 0**

ALFEI, Daniel (D) 1 0
H: 5 11 W: 12 02 b.Swansea 23-2-92
Source: Scholar. *Honours:* Wales Youth, Under-21.
2010-11 Swansea C 1 0
2011-12 Swansea C 0 0 **1 0**

ALLEN, Joe (M) 127 7
H: 5 6 W: 9 10 b.Carmarthen 14-3-90
Source: Scholar. *Honours:* Wales Under-21, 8 full caps.
2006-07 Swansea C 1 0
2007-08 Swansea C 6 0
2008-09 Swansea C 23 1
2009-10 Swansea C 21 0
2010-11 Swansea C 40 2
2011-12 Swansea C 36 4 **127 7**

BEATTIE, Craig (F) 161 31
H: 6 0 W: 11 07 b.Glasgow 16-1-84
Honours: Scotland Under-21, 7 full caps, 1 goal.
2003-04 Celtic 10 1
2004-05 Celtic 11 4
2005-06 Celtic 14 6
2006-07 Celtic 16 2 **51 13**
2007-08 WBA 21 3
2007-08 *Preston NE* 2 0 **2 0**
2008-09 WBA 7 1
2008-09 *Crystal Palace* 15 5 **15 5**
2008-09 *Sheffield U* 13 1 **13 1**
2009-10 WBA 3 0 **31 4**
2009-10 Swansea C 23 3
2010-11 Swansea C 22 4
2011-12 Swansea C 0 0 **45 7**
2011-12 *Watford* 4 1 **4 1**
Transferred to Hearts February 2012.

BESSONE, Fede (D) 66 1
H: 5 11 W: 11 13 b.Cordoba 23-1-84
Source: Barcelona B, Espanyol B.
2007-08 *Gimnastic* 10 0 **10 0**
2008-09 Swansea C 15 0
2009-10 Swansea C 21 1
2010-11 Leeds U 6 0
2010-11 *Charlton Ath* 13 0 **13 0**
2011-12 Leeds U 0 0 **6 0**
2011-12 Swansea C 1 0 **37 1**

BODDE, Ferrie (M) 215 24
H: 5 10 W: 12 06 b.Delft 4-5-82
2000-01 Den Haag 4 0
2001-02 Den Haag 27 3
2002-03 Den Haag 28 2
2003-04 Den Haag 27 1
2004-05 Den Haag 29 2
2005-06 Den Haag 19 2
2006-07 Den Haag 27 1 **161 11**
2007-08 Swansea C 33 6
2008-09 Swansea C 17 7
2009-10 Swansea C 4 0
2010-11 Swansea C 0 0
2011-12 Swansea C 0 0 **54 13**

BRITTON, Leon (M) 372 11
H: 5 6 W: 10 00 b.Merton 16-9-82
Source: Trainee. *Honours:* England Youth.
1999-2000 West Ham U 0 0
2000-01 West Ham U 0 0
2001-02 West Ham U 0 0
2002-03 West Ham U 0 0
2002-03 *Swansea C* 25 0
2003-04 Swansea C 42 3
2004-05 Swansea C 30 1
2005-06 Swansea C 38 4
2006-07 Swansea C 41 2
2007-08 Swansea C 40 0
2008-09 Swansea C 43 0
2009-10 Swansea C 36 0
2010-11 Sheffield U 24 0 **24 0**
2010-11 Swansea C 17 1
2011-12 Swansea C 36 0 **348 11**

CORNELL, David (G) 25 0
H: 5 11 W: 11 07 b.Gorseinon 28-3-91
Source: Scholar. *Honours:* Wales Youth, Under-21.
2009-10 Swansea C 0 0
2010-11 Swansea C 0 0
2011-12 Swansea C 0 0
2011-12 *Hereford U* 25 0 **25 0**

DAVIES, Ben (D) 0 0
b.Neath 24-4-93
Source: Scholar. *Honours:* Wales Youth.
2011-12 Swansea C 0 0

DOBBIE, Stephen (F) 244 85
H: 5 10 W: 11 00 b.Glasgow 5-12-82
2002-03 Rangers 0 0
2002-03 *Northern Spirit* 3 3 **3 3**
2003-04 Hibernian 28 2
2004-05 Hibernian 7 0 **35 2**
2004-05 *St Johnstone* 8 2
2005-06 St Johnstone 20 1 **28 3**
2006-07 *Dumbarton* 17 10 **17 10**
2006-07 Queen of the S 15 10
2007-08 Queen of the S 36 16
2008-09 Queen of the S 32 23 **83 49**
2009-10 Swansea C 6 0
2009-10 *Blackpool* 16 4
2010-11 Swansea C 41 9
2011-12 Swansea C 8 0 **55 9**
2011-12 *Blackpool* 7 5 **23 9**

DONNELLY, Rory (F) 49 20
H: 6 2 W: 12 10 b.Belfast 18-2-92
2010-11 Cliftonville 31 7
2011-12 Cliftonville 18 13 **49 20**
2011-12 Swansea C 0 0

DONNELLY, Scott (M) 113 21
H: 5 8 W: 11 10 b.Hammersmith 25-12-87
Source: Scholar.
2004-05 QPR 2 0

2005-06 QPR 8 0
2006-07 QPR 3 0 **13 0**
From Wealdstone.
2008-09 Aldershot T 20 1
2009-10 Aldershot T 43 13 **63 14**
2010-11 Swansea C 1 0
2010-11 *Wycombe W* 18 3
2011-12 Swansea C 0 0 **1 0**
2011-12 *Wycombe W* 18 4 **36 7**

DYER, Nathan (M) 205 15
H: 5 5 W: 9 00 b.Trowbridge 29-11-87
Source: Scholar. *Honours:* England Youth.
2005-06 Southampton 17 0
2005-06 *Burnley* 5 2 **5 2**
2006-07 Southampton 18 0
2007-08 Southampton 17 1
2008-09 Southampton 4 0 **56 1**
2008-09 *Sheffield U* 7 1 **7 1**
2008-09 *Swansea C* 17 2
2009-10 Swansea C 40 2
2010-11 Swansea C 46 2
2011-12 Swansea C 34 5 **137 11**

EDWARDS, Gwion (M) 0 0
b.Carmarthen 1-3-93
Source: Scholar. *Honours:* Wales Youth.
2011-12 Swansea C 0 0

GOWER, Mark (M) 353 40
H: 5 11 W: 11 12 b.Edmonton 5-10-78
Source: Trainee. *Honours:* England Schools, Youth.
1996-97 Tottenham H 0 0
1997-98 Tottenham H 0 0
1998-99 Tottenham H 0 0
1998-99 *Motherwell* 9 1 **9 1**
1999-2000 Tottenham H 0 0
2000-01 Tottenham H 0 0
2000-01 Barnet 14 1
2001-02 Barnet 0 0
2002-03 Barnet 0 0 **14 1**
2003-04 Southend U 40 6
2004-05 Southend U 38 6
2005-06 Southend U 40 6
2006-07 Southend U 43 8
2007-08 Southend U 42 9 **203 35**
2008-09 Swansea C 36 0
2009-10 Swansea C 31 1
2010-11 Swansea C 40 2
2011-12 Swansea C 20 0 **127 3**

GRAHAM, Danny (F) 272 89
H: 5 11 W: 12 05 b.Gateshead 12-8-85
Source: Trainee. *Honours:* England Youth, Under-20.
2003-04 Middlesbrough 0 0
2003-04 *Darlington* 9 2 **9 2**
2004-05 Middlesbrough 11 1
2005-06 Middlesbrough 3 0
2005-06 *Derby Co* 14 0 **14 0**
2005-06 *Leeds U* 3 0 **3 0**
2006-07 Middlesbrough 1 0 **15 1**
2006-07 *Blackpool* 4 1 **4 1**
2006-07 *Carlisle U* 11 7
2007-08 Carlisle U 45 14
2008-09 Carlisle U 44 15 **100 36**
2009-10 Watford 46 14
2010-11 Watford 45 23 **91 37**
2011-12 Swansea C 36 12 **36 12**

LITA, Leroy (F) 286 83
H: 5 7 W: 11 12 b.DR Congo 28-12-84
Source: Scholar. *Honours:* England Under-21.
2002-03 Bristol C 15 2
2003-04 Bristol C 26 5
2004-05 Bristol C 44 24 **85 31**
2005-06 Reading 26 11
2006-07 Reading 33 7
2007-08 Reading 14 1
2007-08 *Charlton Ath* 8 3 **8 3**
2008-09 Reading 10 1 **83 20**
2008-09 *Norwich C* 16 7 **16 7**
2009-10 Middlesbrough 40 8
2010-11 Middlesbrough 38 12 **78 20**
2011-12 Swansea C 16 2 **16 2**

LUCAS, Lee (M) 2 0
H: 5 11 W: 11 08 b.Aberdare 10-6-92
Source: Scholar. *Honours:* Wales Youth, Under-21.
2010-11 Swansea C 1 0
2011-12 Swansea C 0 0 **1 0**
2011-12 *Burton Alb* 1 0 **1 0**

MARCH, Kurtis (M) 0 0
b.Swansea 30-4-93
Source: Scholar. *Honours:* Wales Youth.
2011-12 Swansea C 0 0

MONK, Garry (D) 270 3
H: 6 0 W: 12 10 b.Bedford 6-3-79
Source: Trainee.
1995-96 Torquay U 5 0
1996-97 Southampton 0 0
1997-98 Southampton 0 0
1998-99 Southampton 4 0
1998-99 *Torquay U* 6 0 **11 0**
1999-2000 Southampton 2 0
1999-2000 *Stockport Co* 2 0 **2 0**
2000-01 Southampton 2 0
2000-01 *Oxford U* 5 0 **5 0**
2001-02 Southampton 2 0
2002-03 Southampton 1 0
2002-03 *Sheffield W* 15 0 **15 0**
2003-04 Southampton 0 0 **11 0**
2003-04 Barnsley 17 0 **17 0**
2004-05 Swansea C 34 0
2005-06 Swansea C 33 1
2006-07 Swansea C 2 0
2007-08 Swansea C 32 1
2008-09 Swansea C 40 1
2009-10 Swansea C 23 0
2010-11 Swansea C 29 0
2011-12 Swansea C 16 0 **209 3**

MOORE, Luke (F) 198 32
H: 5 11 W: 11 13 b.Birmingham 13-2-86
Source: Trainee. *Honours:* FA Schools, England Youth, Under-21.
2002-03 Aston Villa 0 0
2003-04 Aston Villa 7 0
2003-04 *Wycombe W* 6 4 **6 4**
2004-05 Aston Villa 25 1
2005-06 Aston Villa 27 8
2006-07 Aston Villa 13 4
2007-08 Aston Villa 15 1 **87 14**
2007-08 *WBA* 10 0
2008-09 WBA 21 1
2009-10 WBA 26 4
2010-11 WBA 0 0 **57 5**
2010-11 *Derby Co* 13 4 **13 4**
2010-11 *Swansea C* 15 3
2011-12 Swansea C 20 2 **35 5**

MORAS, Vangelis (D) 218 6
H: 6 5 W: 14 00 b.Larissa 26-8-81
Honours: Greece 16 full caps.
2000-01 Larissa 19 1 **19 1**
2001-02 Proodeftki 10 1
2002-03 Proodeftki 18 0 **28 1**
2003-04 AEK Athens 25 0
2004-05 AEK Athens 19 0
2005-06 AEK Athens 13 0
2006-07 AEK Athens 15 0 **72 0**
2007-08 Bologna 28 2
2008-09 Bologna 31 2
2009-10 Bologna 20 0
2010-11 Bologna 19 0 **98 4**
2011-12 Swansea C 1 0 **1 0**
Transferred to Cesena January 2012.

OBENG, Curtis (D) 0 0
H: 5 6 W: 10 05 b.Manchester 14-2-89
Honours: England Youth.
2007-08 Manchester C 0 0
2008-09 Manchester C 0 0
From Wrexham
2011-12 Swansea C 0 0

ORLANDI, Andrea (M) 140 8
H: 6 0 W: 12 01 b.Barcelona 3-8-84
2005-06 Alaves 0 0
2005-06 *Barcelona* 1 0 **1 0**
2005-06 *Barcelona B* 32 4
2006-07 *Barcelona B* 35 1 **67 5**
2007-08 Swansea C 8 0
2008-09 Swansea C 11 1
2009-10 Swansea C 30 1
2010-11 Swansea C 20 0
2011-12 Swansea C 3 1 **72 3**

RANGEL, Angel (D) 227 7
H: 5 11 W: 11 09 b.Barcelona 28-10-82
Source: Tortosa, Reus Deportiu, Girona, Sant Andreu.
2006-07 Terrassa 34 2 **34 2**
2007-08 Swansea C 43 2
2008-09 Swansea C 40 1
2009-10 Swansea C 38 0
2010-11 Swansea C 38 2
2011-12 Swansea C 34 0 **193 5**

RICHARDS, Jazz (M) 29 0
H: 6 1 W: 12 04 b.Swansea 12-4-91
Source: Scholar. *Honours:* Wales Under-21, 1 full cap.
2009-10 Swansea C 15 0
2010-11 Swansea C 6 0
2011-12 Swansea C 8 0 **29 0**

ROUTLEDGE, Wayne (M) 289 24
H: 5 6 W: 11 02 b.Sidcup 7-1-85
Source: Scholar. *Honours:* England Youth, Under-20, Under-21.
2001-02 Crystal Palace 2 0
2002-03 Crystal Palace 26 4
2003-04 Crystal Palace 44 6
2004-05 Crystal Palace 38 0 **110 10**
2005-06 Tottenham H 3 0
2005-06 *Portsmouth* 13 0 **13 0**
2006-07 Tottenham H 0 0
2006-07 *Fulham* 24 0 **24 0**
2007-08 Tottenham H 2 0 **5 0**
2007-08 Aston Villa 1 0
2008-09 Aston Villa 1 0 **2 0**
2008-09 *Cardiff C* 9 2 **9 2**
2008-09 QPR 19 1
2009-10 QPR 25 2
2009-10 Newcastle U 17 3
2010-11 Newcastle U 17 0 **34 3**
2010-11 *QPR* 20 5 **64 8**
2011-12 Swansea C 28 1 **28 1**

SIGURDSSON, Gylfi (M) 114 38
H: 6 1 W: 12 02 b.Reykjavik 9-9-89
Source: Scholar. *Honours:* Iceland Youth, Under-21, 8 full caps, 1 goal.
2007-08 Reading 0 0
2008-09 Reading 0 0
2008-09 *Shrewsbury T* 5 1 **5 1**
2008-09 *Crewe Alex* 15 3 **15 3**
2009-10 Reading 38 16
2010-11 Reading 4 2 **42 18**
2010-11 Hoffenheim 28 9
2011-12 Hoffenheim 6 0 **34 9**
2011-12 Swansea C 18 7 **18 7**
On loan from Hoffenheim.

SINCLAIR, Scott (F) 153 33
H: 5 10 W: 10 00 b.Bath 26-3-89
Source: Bristol R Schoolboy. *Honours:* England Youth, Under-21.
2004-05 Bristol R 2 0 **2 0**
2005-06 Chelsea 0 0
2006-07 Chelsea 2 0
2006-07 *Plymouth Arg* 15 2 **15 2**
2007-08 Chelsea 1 0
2007-08 *QPR* 9 1 **9 1**
2007-08 *Charlton Ath* 3 0 **3 0**
2007-08 *Crystal Palace* 6 2 **6 2**
2008-09 Chelsea 2 0
2008-09 *Birmingham C* 14 0 **14 0**
2009-10 Chelsea 0 0 **5 0**
2009-10 *Wigan Ath* 18 1 **18 1**
2010-11 Swansea C 43 19
2011-12 Swansea C 38 8 **81 27**

SITU, Darnel (D) 0 0
H: 6 2 W: 12 02 b.Rouen 18-3-92
Source: Lens. *Honours:* France Youth.
2011-12 Swansea C 0 0

SMITH, Jordan (M) 0 0
b.Swansea 20-4-93
Source: Scholar. *Honours:* Wales Youth.
2011-12 Swansea C 0 0

TATE, Alan (D) 287 5
H: 6 1 W: 13 05 b.Seaham 2-9-82
Source: Scholar.
2000-01 Manchester U 0 0
2001-02 Manchester U 0 0
2002-03 Manchester U 0 0
2002-03 *Swansea C* 27 0
2003-04 Manchester U 0 0
2003-04 Swansea C 26 1
2004-05 Swansea C 23 0
2005-06 Swansea C 43 0
2006-07 Swansea C 38 1
2007-08 Swansea C 21 1
2008-09 Swansea C 25 1
2009-10 Swansea C 39 1
2010-11 Swansea C 40 0
2011-12 Swansea C 5 0 **287 5**

TAYLOR, Neil (D) **91 0**
H: 5 9 W: 10 02 b.Ruthin 7-2-89
Source: Scholar. *Honours:* Wales Youth, Under-21, 9 full caps.

2007-08	Wrexham	26	0	**26**	**0**
2010-11	Swansea C	29	0		
2011-12	Swansea C	36	0	**65**	**0**

THOMAS, Casey (M) **3 0**
H: 5 9 W: 10 09 b.Port Talbot 14-11-90
Source: Scholar. *Honours:* Wales Youth, Under-21.

2009-10	Swansea C	1	0		
2010-11	Swansea C	0	0		
2011-12	Swansea C	0	0	**1**	**0**
2011-12	*Colchester U*	2	0	**2**	**0**

TREMMEL, Gerhard (G) **94 0**
H: 6 3 W: 14 00 b.Munich 16-11-78

2006-07	Energie Cottbus	1	0		
2007-08	Energie Cottbus	24	0		
2008-09	Energie Cottbus	34	0		
2009-10	Energie Cottbus	34	0	**93**	**0**
2011-12	Swansea C	1	0	**1**	**0**

VORM, Michel (G) **208 0**
H: 6 0 W: 13 03 b.Nieuwegein 20-10-83
Honours: Holland 9 full caps.

2005-06	Den Bosch	35	0	**35**	**0**
2006-07	Utrecht	33	0		
2007-08	Utrecht	11	0		
2008-09	Utrecht	26	0		
2009-10	Utrecht	33	0		
2010-11	Utrecht	33	0	**136**	**0**
2011-12	Swansea C	37	0	**37**	**0**

WALSH, Joe (D) **0 0**
H: 5 11 W: 11 00 b.Cardiff 15-5-92
Source: Scholar. *Honours:* Wales Youth.

2010-11	Swansea C	0	0		
2011-12	Swansea C	0	0		

WILLIAMS, Ashley (D) **340 14**
H: 6 0 W: 11 02 b.Wolverhampton 23-8-84
Source: Hednesford T. *Honours:* Wales 33 full caps, 2 goals.

2003-04	Stockport Co	10	0		
2004-05	Stockport Co	44	1		
2005-06	Stockport Co	36	1		
2006-07	Stockport Co	46	1		
2007-08	Stockport Co	26	0	**162**	**3**
2007-08	*Swansea C*	3	0		
2008-09	Swansea C	46	2		
2009-10	Swansea C	46	5		
2010-11	Swansea C	46	3		
2011-12	Swansea C	37	1	**178**	**11**

Scholars
Bray Alexander George; Davies Thomas Oliver; Evans Samuel; Jones Henry Lloyd; Loveridge James; Sheehan Joshua Luke; Shephard Liam; Tancock Scott Russell; Waters Nathan; Williams Luke David.

SWINDON T (81)

BENSON, Paul (F) **158 61**
H: 6 1 W: 11 01 b.Southend 12-10-79
Source: White Notley.

2007-08	Dagenham & R	22	6		
2008-09	Dagenham & R	33	17		
2009-10	Dagenham & R	45	17		
2010-11	Dagenham & R	3	0	**103**	**40**
2010-11	Charlton Ath	32	10		
2011-12	Charlton Ath	1	0	**33**	**10**
2011-12	Swindon T	22	11	**22**	**11**

BODIN, Billy (M) **41 8**
H: 5 11 W: 11 00 b.Swindon 24-3-92
Honours: Wales Youth, Under-21.

2009-10	Swindon T	0	0		
2010-11	Swindon T	5	0		
2011-12	Swindon T	11	3	**16**	**3**
2011-12	*Torquay U*	17	5	**17**	**5**
2011-12	*Crewe Alex*	8	0	**8**	**0**

CADDIS, Paul (D) **105 5**
H: 5 7 W: 10 07 b.Irvine 19-4-88

2007-08	Celtic	2	0		
2008-09	Celtic	5	0		
2008-09	*Dundee U*	11	0	**11**	**0**
2009-10	Celtic	10	0	**17**	**0**
2010-11	Swindon T	38	1		
2011-12	Swindon T	39	4	**77**	**5**

CIBOCCHI, Alessandro (D) **18 0**
H: 5 11 W: 11 07 b.Terni 18-9-82

2011-12	Swindon T	18	0	**18**	**0**

COMAZZI, Alberto (D) **324 5**
H: 5 10 W: 10 10 b.Novara 16-4-79

1996-97	AC Milan	1	0		
1997-98	AC Milan	1	0	**2**	**0**
1998-99	Como	30	0		
1999-2000	Como	29	1	**59**	**1**
2000-01	Monza	29	0	**29**	**0**
2001-02	Lazio	0	0		
2002-03	Verona	31	0		
2003-04	Verona	41	0		
2004-05	Verona	31	0		
2005-06	Verona	16	1		
2006-07	Verona	26	1		
2007-08	Verona	25	1		
2008-09	Verona	0	0		
2008-09	*Ancona*	30	0	**30**	**0**
2009-10	Verona	23	0	**193**	**3**
2010-11	Spezia	7	1	**7**	**1**
2011-12	Swindon T	4	0	**4**	**0**

CONNELL, Alan (F) **246 52**
H: 6 0 W: 12 00 b.Enfield 5-2-83
Source: Ipswich T Trainee.

2002-03	Bournemouth	13	6		
2003-04	Bournemouth	7	0		
2004-05	Bournemouth	34	2		
2005-06	Torquay U	22	7	**22**	**7**
2006-07	Hereford U	44	9	**44**	**9**
2007-08	Brentford	42	12		
2008-09	Brentford	2	0	**44**	**12**
2008-09	Bournemouth	12	0		
2009-10	Bournemouth	38	5	**104**	**13**
From Grimsby T.					
2011-12	Swindon T	32	11	**32**	**11**

COX, Lee (M) **76 3**
H: 6 1 W: 12 02 b.Leicester 26-6-90
Source: Scholar.

2007-08	Leicester C	0	0		
2008-09	Leicester C	0	0		
2008-09	*Yeovil T*	0	0		
2009-10	Inverness CT	35	2		
2010-11	Inverness CT	27	1		
2011-12	Inverness CT	7	0	**69**	**3**
2011-12	Swindon T	7	0	**7**	**0**

DE VITA, Raffaele (F) **105 26**
H: 6 0 W: 11 09 b.Rome 23-9-87
Source: Scholar.

2005-06	Blackburn R	0	0		
2006-07	Blackburn R	0	0		
2007-08	Blackburn R	0	0		
2008-09	Livingston	7	1		
2009-10	Livingston	29	9		
2010-11	Livingston	31	12	**67**	**22**
2011-12	Swindon T	38	4	**38**	**4**

DEVERA, Joe (D) **205 4**
H: 6 2 W: 12 00 b.Southgate 6-2-87

2005-06	Barnet	0	0		
2006-07	Barnet	26	0		
2007-08	Barnet	41	0		
2008-09	Barnet	34	1		
2009-10	Barnet	33	0		
2010-11	Barnet	43	1	**177**	**2**
2011-12	Swindon T	28	2	**28**	**2**

ESAJAS, Etienne (F) **107 8**
H: 5 7 W: 10 03 b.Amsterdam 4-11-84
Source: Ajax.

2005-06	Vitesse	11	1		
2006-07	Vitesse	21	2	**32**	**3**
2007-08	Sheffield W	18	0		
2008-09	Sheffield W	22	3		
2009-10	Sheffield W	20	2	**60**	**5**
2010-11	Helmond Sp	9	0	**9**	**0**
2011-12	Swindon T	6	0	**6**	**0**

FERRY, Simon (M) **105 3**
H: 5 8 W: 11 00 b.Dundee 11-1-88

2005-06	Celtic	0	0		
2006-07	Celtic	0	0		
2007-08	Celtic	0	0		
2008-09	Celtic	0	0		
2009-10	Celtic	0	0		
2009-10	Swindon T	40	2		
2010-11	Swindon T	21	0		
2011-12	Swindon T	44	1	**105**	**3**

FLINT, Aiden (D) **35 2**
H: 6 2 W: 12 00 b.Pinxton 11-7-89
Source: Alfreton T.

2010-11	Swindon T	3	0		
2011-12	Swindon T	32	2	**35**	**2**

FODERINGHAM, Wesley (G) **33 0**
H: 6 1 W: 12 00 b.Hammersmith 14-1-91
Source: Scholar.

2009-10	Fulham	0	0		
2010-11	Crystal Palace	0	0		
2011-12	Crystal Palace	0	0		
2011-12	Swindon T	33	0	**33**	**0**

GABILONDO, Lander (M) **169 17**
H: 5 8 W: 10 10 b.San Sebastian 30-4-87

2006-07	Real Sociedad II	28	4		
2007-08	Real Sociedad II	37	4		
2008-09	Real Sociedad II	34	5	**99**	**13**
2009-10	Osasuna II	35	0		
2010-11	Osasuna II	25	4	**60**	**4**
2011-12	Swindon T	10	0	**10**	**0**

KENNEDY, Callum (D) **41 1**
H: 6 1 W: 12 10 b.Chertsey 9-11-89
Source: Scholar.

2007-08	Swindon T	0	0		
2008-09	Swindon T	4	0		
2009-10	Swindon T	8	0		
2010-11	Swindon T	3	0		
2010-11	*Gillingham*	3	0	**3**	**0**
2010-11	*Rotherham U*	5	0	**5**	**0**
2011-12	Swindon T	18	1	**33**	**1**

KERROUCHE, Mehdi (F) **115 51**
H: 5 10 W: 10 10 b.Douai 11-10-85

2006-07	Cambrai	18	9	**18**	**9**
2006-07	KSK Ronse	23	11	**23**	**11**
2007-08	USM Alger	5	1	**5**	**1**
2008-09	Ajaccio	16	7	**16**	**7**
2009-10	Naval	18	5	**18**	**5**
2010-11	Al-Oruba	18	12	**18**	**12**
2011-12	Swindon T	13	6	**13**	**6**
2011-12	*Oxford U*	4	0	**4**	**0**

LANZANO, Mattia (G) **42 0**
H: 6 1 W: 13 05 b.Grosseto 4-7-90

2008-09	Piacenza	0	0		
2009-10	*Poggibonsi*	20	0	**20**	**0**
2010-11	Gavorrano	16	0	**16**	**0**
2011-12	Swindon T	6	0	**6**	**0**

MAGERA, Lukas (F) **232 49**
H: 6 4 W: 14 00 b.Opava 17-1-83
Honours: Czech Republic Under-21, 4 full caps.

2003-04	Banik Ostrava	14	1		
2004-05	Banik Ostrava	13	3		
2004-05	Kladno (loan)	12	3	**12**	**3**
2005-06	Banik Ostrava	29	5		
2006-07	Banik Ostrava	27	3		
2007-08	Banik Ostrava	27	9		
2008-09	Timisoara	30	4		
2009-10	Timisoara	26	10		
2010-11	Timisoara	29	7	**85**	**21**
2011-12	Swindon T	12	1	**12**	**1**
2011-12	*Banik Ostrava*	13	3	**123**	**24**

McCORMACK, Alan (M) **255 23**
H: 5 8 W: 11 00 b.Dublin 10-1-84
Source: Stella Maris BC.

2002-03	Preston NE	0	0		
2003-04	Preston NE	5	0		
2003-04	*Leyton Orient*	10	0	**10**	**0**
2004-05	Preston NE	3	0		
2004-05	*Southend U*	7	2		
2005-06	Preston NE	0	0		
2005-06	*Motherwell*	24	2	**24**	**2**
2006-07	Preston NE	3	0	**11**	**0**
2006-07	Southend U	22	3		
2007-08	Southend U	42	8		
2008-09	Southend U	34	2		
2009-10	Southend U	41	3	**146**	**18**
2010-11	Charlton Ath	24	1	**24**	**1**
2011-12	Swindon T	40	2	**40**	**2**

RISSER, Oliver (M) **171 8**
H: 6 3 W: 13 10 b.Windhoek 17-9-80
Honours: Namibia 27 full caps.

2003-04	Bor Dortmund II	20	1		
2004-05	Bor Dortmund II	13	0	**33**	**1**
2005-06	Sandhausen	28	0	**28**	**0**
2006	Breidablik	6	0	**6**	**0**
2006-07	Bonner	32	2	**32**	**2**
2007-08	Hannover II	7	0	**7**	**0**
2008	Manglerud Star	7	1	**7**	**1**

2009 Lyn 7 0
2010 Lyn 11 1 **18 1**
2010 Kuopio 8 0 **8 0**
2011-12 Swindon T 32 3 **32 3**

RITCHIE, Matt (M) 140 31
H: 5 8 W: 11 00 b.Gosport 10-9-89
Source: Scholar.
2008-09 Portsmouth 0 0
2008-09 *Dagenham & R* 37 11 **37 11**
2009-10 Portsmouth 2 0
2009-10 *Notts Co* 16 3 **16 3**
2009-10 *Swindon T* 4 0
2010-11 Portsmouth 5 0 **7 0**
2010-11 Swindon T 36 7
2011-12 Swindon T 40 10 **80 17**

ROONEY, Luke (M) 73 8
H: 5 8 W: 11 07 b.Southwark 28-12-90
Source: Scholar.
2009-10 Gillingham 13 2
2010-11 Gillingham 23 1
2011-12 Gillingham 17 3 **53 6**
2011-12 Swindon T 20 2 **20 2**

SAID, Abdul (M) 0 0
b.Somalia 22-2-93
Source: Scholar.
2011-12 Swindon T 0 0

SCOTT, Mark (G) 0 0
H: 5 9 W: 12 04 b.Fleet 3-1-91
Source: Scholar.
2007-08 Swindon T 0 0
2008-09 Swindon T 0 0
2009-10 Swindon T 0 0
2010-11 Swindon T 0 0
2011-12 Swindon T 0 0

SMITH, Chris (D) 1 0
b.Stoke 12-10-90
Source: Stone Dominoes.
2011-12 Swindon T 1 0 **1 0**

SMITH, Jonathan (M) 38 3
H: 6 3 W: 11 02 b.Preston 17-10-86
Source: Morecambe, Forest Green R, York C.
2011-12 Swindon T 38 3 **38 3**

SMITH, Phil (G) 117 0
H: 6 1 W: 13 11 b.Harrow 14-12-79
Source: Trainee.
1997-98 Millwall 0 0
1998-99 Millwall 5 0 **5 0**
From Folkestone, Dover, Margate, Crawley
2006-07 Swindon T 31 0
2007-08 Swindon T 15 0
2008-09 Swindon T 25 0
2009-10 Swindon T 6 0
2010-11 Swindon T 27 0
2011-12 Swindon T 8 0 **112 0**

STOREY, Miles (F) 6 0
H: 5 11 W: 11 00 b.West Bromwich 4-1-94
Source: Scholar.
2010-11 Swindon T 2 0
2011-12 Swindon T 4 0 **6 0**

THOMPSON, Nathan (D) 8 0
H: 5 7 W: 11 02 b.Chester 9-11-90
Source: Scholar.
2009-10 Swindon T 0 0
2010-11 Swindon T 3 0
2011-12 Swindon T 5 0 **8 0**

TORQUAY U (82)

ATIENO, Taiwo (F) 131 23
H: 6 2 W: 12 13 b.Brixton 6-8-85
Source: Scholar.
2003-04 Walsall 3 0
2004-05 Walsall 0 0
2004-05 *Rochdale* 13 2 **13 2**
2004-05 *Chester C* 4 1 **4 1**
2005-06 Walsall 2 0 **5 0**
2005-06 *Darlington* 3 0 **3 0**
2007 Puerto Rico Is 10 5
2008 Puerto Rico Is 22 4 **32 9**
From Charleston Battery.
2009 Rochester Rhinos 17 2 **17 2**
2010-11 Luton T 13 3 **13 3**
2010-11 Stevenage 1 0 **1 0**
2011-12 Torquay U 43 6 **43 6**

ELLIS, Mark (D) 89 8
H: 6 2 W: 12 04 b.Kingsbridge 30-9-88
Source: Exeter C.
2007-08 Bolton W 0 0
2009-10 Torquay U 27 3
2010-11 Torquay U 27 2
2011-12 Torquay U 35 3 **89 8**

HALPIN, Saul (M) 5 0
H: 6 1 W: 12 00 b.Bodmin 31-5-91
Source: Scholar.
2009-10 Torquay U 0 0
2010-11 Torquay U 4 0
2011-12 Torquay U 1 0 **5 0**

HOWE, Rene (F) 158 40
H: 6 0 W: 14 03 b.Bedford 22-10-86
Source: Kettering T.
2007-08 Peterborough U 15 1
2007-08 *Rochdale* 20 9 **20 9**
2008-09 Peterborough U 0 0
2008-09 *Morecambe* 37 10 **37 10**
2009-10 Peterborough U 0 0
2009-10 *Lincoln C* 17 5 **17 5**
2009-10 *Gillingham* 18 2 **18 2**
2010-11 Peterborough U 0 0 **15 1**
2010-11 *Bristol R* 12 1 **12 1**
2011-12 Torquay U 39 12 **39 12**

LATHROPE, Damon (M) 58 0
H: 5 8 W: 10 02 b.Stevenage 28-10-89
Source: Scholar.
2007-08 Norwich C 0 0
2008-09 Norwich C 0 0
2009-10 Norwich C 0 0
2010-11 Torquay U 18 0
2011-12 Torquay U 40 0 **58 0**

LEADBITTER, Daniel (D) 2 0
H: 6 0 W: 11 00 b.Newcastle 17-10-90
Source: Newcastle U Scholar.
2011-12 Torquay U 2 0 **2 0**

MACKLIN, Lloyd (M) 29 0
H: 5 9 W: 12 03 b.Camberley 2-8-91
Source: Scholar.
2007-08 Swindon T 0 0
2008-09 Swindon T 2 0
2009-10 Swindon T 9 0 **11 0**
2009-10 *Torquay U* 4 0
2010-11 Torquay U 10 0
2011-12 Torquay U 4 0 **18 0**

MANSELL, Lee (D) 265 27
H: 5 10 W: 11 10 b.Gloucester 28-10-82
Source: Scholar.
2000-01 Luton T 18 5
2001-02 Luton T 11 1
2002-03 Luton T 1 0
2003-04 Luton T 16 2
2004-05 Luton T 1 0 **47 8**
2005-06 Oxford U 44 1 **44 1**
2006-07 Torquay U 45 4
2009-10 Torquay U 39 2
2010-11 Torquay U 45 0
2011-12 Torquay U 45 12 **174 18**

McPHEE, Chris (F) 131 6
H: 5 11 W: 11 09 b.Eastbourne 20-3-83
Source: Scholar.
1999-2000 Brighton & HA 4 0
2000-01 Brighton & HA 0 0
2001-02 Brighton & HA 2 0
2002-03 Brighton & HA 2 0
2003-04 Brighton & HA 29 4
2004-05 Brighton & HA 16 0
2005-06 Brighton & HA 7 0 **60 4**
2005-06 *Swindon T* 8 0 **8 0**
2006-07 Torquay U 37 0
From Ebbsfleet U, Weymouth, Kidderminster H.
2011-12 Torquay U 26 2 **63 2**

MORRIS, Ian (D) 175 13
H: 6 0 W: 11 05 b.Dublin 27-2-87
Source: Scholar. *Honours:* Eire Under-21.
2003-04 Leeds U 0 0
2004-05 Leeds U 0 0
2005-06 Leeds U 0 0
2005-06 *Blackpool* 30 3 **30 3**
2006-07 Leeds U 0 0
2006-07 Scunthorpe U 28 3
2007-08 Scunthorpe U 25 3
2008-09 Scunthorpe U 20 1
2008-09 *Carlisle U* 6 0 **6 0**
2009-10 Scunthorpe U 3 0
2009-10 *Chesterfield* 7 0
2010-11 Scunthorpe U 0 0 **76 7**
2010-11 *Chesterfield* 19 1 **26 1**
2011-12 Torquay U 37 2 **37 2**

NICHOLSON, Kevin (D) 220 10
H: 5 8 W: 12 05 b.Derby 2-10-80
Source: Trainee. *Honours:* England Schools.
1997-98 Sheffield W 0 0
1998-99 Sheffield W 0 0
1999-2000 Sheffield W 0 0
2000-01 Sheffield W 1 0 **1 0**
From Forest Green R.
2000-01 Northampton T 7 0 **7 0**
2000-01 Notts Co 11 2
2001-02 Notts Co 24 1
2002-03 Notts Co 37 0
2003-04 Notts Co 23 0 **95 3**
From Scarborough, Forest Green R.
2009-10 Torquay U 27 0
From Scarborough, Forest Green R.
2010-11 Torquay U 44 3
From Scarborough, Forest Green R.
2011-12 Torquay U 46 4 **117 7**

O'KANE, Eunan (M) 119 16
H: 5 8 W: 13 04 b.Derry 10-7-90
Honours: Northern Ireland Schools, Youth, Under-21. Eire Under-21.
2007-08 Everton 0 0
2008-09 Everton 0 0
2009-10 Coleraine 13 4 **13 4**
2009-10 Torquay U 16 1
2010-11 Torquay U 45 6
2011-12 Torquay U 45 5 **106 12**

OASTLER, Joe (D) 71 0
H: 5 10 W: 11 03 b.Portsmouth 3-7-90
Source: Portsmouth Scholar.
2008-09 QPR 0 0
2009-10 QPR 1 0
2010-11 QPR 0 0 **1 0**
2010-11 *Torquay U* 25 0
2011-12 Torquay U 45 0 **70 0**

OLEJNIK, Robert (G) 148 0
H: 6 0 W: 15 06 b.Vienna 26-11-86
Source: Scholar. *Honours:* Austria Under-21.
2004-05 Aston Villa 0 0
2005-06 Aston Villa 0 0
2006-07 Aston Villa 0 0
2006-07 *Lincoln C* 0 0
2007-08 Falkirk 13 0
2008-09 Falkirk 15 0
2009-10 Falkirk 38 0
2010-11 Falkirk 36 0 **102 0**
2011-12 Torquay U 46 0 **46 0**

PALMER, Ed (D) 0 0
b.Torquay 13-11-91
Source: Scholar.
2010-11 Torquay U 0 0
2011-12 Torquay U 0 0

RICE, Martin (G) 0 0
b.Exeter 7-3-86
Source: Exeter C, Torquay U, Truro C.
2011-12 Torquay U 0 0

ROWE-TURNER, Lathanial (D) 36 1
H: 6 1 W: 13 00 b.Leicester 12-11-89
Source: Scholar.
2007-08 Leicester C 0 0
2008-09 Leicester C 0 0
2008-09 *Cheltenham T* 1 0 **1 0**
2009-10 Leicester C 0 0
2009-10 Torquay U 6 0
2010-11 Torquay U 8 1
2011-12 Torquay U 21 0 **35 1**

SAAH, Brian (M) 128 2
H: 6 3 W: 12 03 b.Rush Green 16-12-86
Source: Scholar.
2003-04 Leyton Orient 6 0
2004-05 Leyton Orient 12 0
2005-06 Leyton Orient 3 0
2006-07 Leyton Orient 32 0
2007-08 Leyton Orient 25 1
2008-09 Leyton Orient 15 0 **93 1**
From Cambridge U.
2011-12 Torquay U 35 1 **35 1**

SPEAR, Ray (F) 0 0
b.Plymouth 19-9-92
Source: Scholar.
2011-12 Torquay U 0 0

STEVENS, Danny (M) **106 12**
H: 5 5 W: 9 09 b.Enfield 26-11-86
Source: Tottenham H Scholar.
2004-05 Luton T 0 0
2005-06 Luton T 1 0
2006-07 Luton T 0 0 **1 0**
2009-10 Torquay U 27 1
2010-11 Torquay U 37 3
2011-12 Torquay U 41 8 **105 12**

YEOMAN, Ashley (F) **1 0**
H: 5 10 W: 12 01 b.Kingsbridge 25-2-92
Source: Scholar.
2010-11 Torquay U 0 0
2011-12 Torquay U 1 0 **1 0**

TOTTENHAM H (83)

ALNWICK, Ben (G) **47 0**
H: 6 2 W: 13 12 b.Prudhoe 1-1-87
Source: Scholar. *Honours:* England Youth, Under-21.
2003-04 Sunderland 0 0
2004-05 Sunderland 3 0
2005-06 Sunderland 5 0
2006-07 Sunderland 11 0 **19 0**
2006-07 Tottenham H 0 0
2007-08 Tottenham H 0 0
2007-08 *Luton T* 4 0 **4 0**
2007-08 *Leicester C* 8 0 **8 0**
2008-09 Tottenham H 0 0
2008-09 *Carlisle U* 6 0 **6 0**
2009-10 Tottenham H 1 0
2009-10 *Norwich C* 3 0 **3 0**
2010-11 Tottenham H 0 0
2010-11 *Leeds U* 0 0
2010-11 *Doncaster R* 0 0
2011-12 Tottenham H 0 0 **1 0**
2011-12 *Leyton Orient* 6 0 **6 0**

ARCHER, Jordan (G) **0 0**
b.Walthamstow 12-4-93
Source: Scholar. *Honours:* Scotland Youth. From Brackley T, Thurrock, Margate.
2011-12 Tottenham H 0 0

ASSOU-EKOTTO, Benoit (M) **206 3**
H: 5 10 W: 10 12 b.Arras 24-3-84
Honours: Cameroon B, 17 full caps.
2003-04 Lens 3 0
2004-05 Lens 29 0
2005-06 Lens 34 0 **66 0**
2006-07 Tottenham H 16 0
2007-08 Tottenham H 1 0
2008-09 Tottenham H 29 0
2009-10 Tottenham H 30 1
2010-11 Tottenham H 30 0
2011-12 Tottenham H 34 2 **140 3**

BALE, Gareth (D) **153 26**
H: 6 0 W: 11 10 b.Cardiff 16-7-89
Source: Scholar. *Honours:* Wales Youth, Under-21, 33 full caps, 6 goals.
2005-06 Southampton 2 0
2006-07 Southampton 38 5 **40 5**
2007-08 Tottenham H 8 2
2008-09 Tottenham H 16 0
2009-10 Tottenham H 23 3
2010-11 Tottenham H 30 7
2011-12 Tottenham H 36 9 **113 21**

BASSONG, Sebastien (D) **163 3**
H: 6 2 W: 11 07 b.Paris 9-7-86
Honours: France Under-21. Cameroon 16 full caps.
2005-06 Metz 23 0
2006-07 Metz 37 1
2007-08 Metz 19 0 **79 1**
2008-09 Newcastle U 30 0
2009-10 Newcastle U 0 0 **30 0**
2009-10 Tottenham H 28 1
2010-11 Tottenham H 12 1
2011-12 Tottenham H 5 0 **45 2**
2011-12 *Wolverhampton W* 9 0 **9 0**

BENTLEY, David (F) **189 18**
H: 5 10 W: 11 03 b.Peterborough 27-8-84
Source: Scholar. *Honours:* England Youth, Under-20, Under-21, B, 7 full caps.
2001-02 Arsenal 0 0
2002-03 Arsenal 0 0
2003-04 Arsenal 1 0
2004-05 Arsenal 0 0
2004-05 *Norwich C* 26 2 **26 2**
2005-06 Arsenal 0 0 **1 0**
2005-06 Blackburn R 29 3
2006-07 Blackburn R 36 4
2007-08 Blackburn R 37 6 **102 13**
2008-09 Tottenham H 25 1
2009-10 Tottenham H 15 2
2010-11 Tottenham H 2 0
2010-11 *Birmingham C* 13 0 **13 0**
2011-12 Tottenham H 0 0 **42 3**
2011-12 *West Ham U* 5 0 **5 0**

BOSTOCK, John (M) **31 4**
H: 5 10 W: 11 11 b.Camberwell 13-10-91
Honours: England Youth.
2007-08 Crystal Palace 4 0 **4 0**
2008-09 Tottenham H 0 0
2009-10 Tottenham H 0 0
2009-10 *Brentford* 9 2 **9 2**
2010-11 Tottenham H 0 0
2010-11 *Hull C* 11 2 **11 2**
2011-12 Tottenham H 0 0
2011-12 *Sheffield W* 4 0 **4 0**
2011-12 *Swindon T* 3 0 **3 0**

BUTTON, David (G) **90 0**
H: 6 3 W: 13 00 b.Stevenage 27-2-89
Source: Scholar. *Honours:* England Youth.
2005-06 Tottenham H 0 0
2006-07 Tottenham H 0 0
2007-08 *Rochdale* 0 0
2007-08 Tottenham H 0 0
2008-09 Tottenham H 0 0
2008-09 *Bournemouth* 4 0 **4 0**
2008-09 *Luton T* 0 0
2008-09 *Dagenham & R* 3 0 **3 0**
2009-10 Tottenham H 0 0
2009-10 *Crewe Alex* 10 0 **10 0**
2009-10 *Shrewsbury T* 26 0 **26 0**
2010-11 Tottenham H 0 0
2010-11 *Plymouth Arg* 30 0 **30 0**
2011-12 Tottenham H 0 0
2011-12 *Leyton Orient* 1 0 **1 0**
2011-12 *Doncaster R* 7 0 **7 0**
2011-12 *Barnsley* 9 0 **9 0**

BYRNE, Nathan (D) **20 0**
H: 5 10 W: 10 10 b.St Albans 5-6-92
Source: Scholar.
2010-11 Tottenham H 0 0
2010-11 *Brentford* 11 0 **11 0**
2011-12 Tottenham H 0 0
2011-12 *Bournemouth* 9 0 **9 0**

CARROLL, Tommy (M) **24 1**
b.Watford 28-5-92
Source: Scholar.
2010-11 Tottenham H 0 0
2010-11 *Leyton Orient* 12 0 **12 0**
2011-12 Tottenham H 0 0
2011-12 *Derby Co* 12 1 **12 1**

CAULKER, Steven (D) **99 2**
H: 6 3 W: 12 00 b.Feltham 29-12-91
Honours: England Youth. Under-21.
2009-10 Tottenham H 0 0
2009-10 *Yeovil T* 44 0 **44 0**
2010-11 Tottenham H 0 0
2010-11 *Bristol C* 29 2 **29 2**
2011-12 Tottenham H 0 0
2011-12 *Swansea C* 26 0 **26 0**

CEBALLOS, Cristian (M) **0 0**
b.Barcelona 3-12-92
Source: Barcelona Youth.
2011-12 Tottenham H 0 0

CORLUKA, Vedran (D) **214 13**
H: 6 3 W: 13 03 b.Zagreb 9-2-86
Honours: Croatia Youth, Under-21, 57 full caps, 3 goals.
2003-04 Dynamo Zagreb 0 0
2004-05 Inter Zapresic 27 4 **27 4**
2005-06 Dynamo Zagreb 32 3
2006-07 Dynamo Zagreb 29 4 **61 7**
2007-08 Manchester C 35 0
2008-09 Manchester C 3 1 **38 1**
2008-09 Tottenham H 34 0
2009-10 Tottenham H 29 1
2010-11 Tottenham H 15 0
2011-12 Tottenham H 3 0 **81 1**
2011-12 *Leverkusen* 7 0 **7 0**
Transferred to Lokomotiv Moscow June 2012.

CUDICINI, Carlo (G) **244 0**
H: 6 1 W: 12 08 b.Milan 6-9-73
Honours: Italy Youth, Under-21.
1991-92 AC Milan 0 0
1992-93 AC Milan 0 0
1993-94 Como 6 0 **6 0**
1994-95 AC Milan 0 0
1995-96 AC Milan 0 0
1995-96 Prato 30 0 **30 0**
1996-97 Lazio 1 0 **1 0**
1997-98 Castel di Sangro 14 0
1998-99 Castel di Sangro 32 0 **46 0**
1999-2000 Chelsea 1 0
2000-01 Chelsea 24 0
2001-02 Chelsea 28 0
2002-03 Chelsea 36 0
2003-04 Chelsea 26 0
2004-05 Chelsea 3 0
2005-06 Chelsea 4 0
2006-07 Chelsea 8 0
2007-08 Chelsea 10 0
2008-09 Chelsea 2 0 **142 0**
2008-09 Tottenham H 4 0
2009-10 Tottenham H 7 0
2010-11 Tottenham H 8 0
2011-12 Tottenham H 0 0 **19 0**

DAWKINS, Simon (F) **50 8**
H: 5 10 W: 11 01 b.Edgware 1-12-87
Source: Scholar.
2005-06 Tottenham H 0 0
2006-07 Tottenham H 0 0
2007-08 Tottenham H 0 0
2008-09 Tottenham H 0 0
2008-09 *Leyton Orient* 11 0 **11 0**
2009-10 Tottenham H 0 0
2010-11 Tottenham H 0 0
2010-11 *San Jose E* 26 6
2011-12 Tottenham H 0 0
2011-12 *San Jose E* 13 2 **39 8**

DAWSON, Michael (D) **260 13**
H: 6 2 W: 12 02 b.Leyburn 18-11-83
Source: School. *Honours:* England Youth, Under-21, B, 4 full caps.
2000-01 Nottingham F 0 0
2001-02 Nottingham F 1 0
2002-03 Nottingham F 38 5
2003-04 Nottingham F 30 1
2004-05 Nottingham F 14 1 **83 7**
2004-05 Tottenham H 5 0
2005-06 Tottenham H 32 0
2006-07 Tottenham H 37 1
2007-08 Tottenham H 27 1
2008-09 Tottenham H 16 1
2009-10 Tottenham H 29 2
2010-11 Tottenham H 24 1
2011-12 Tottenham H 7 0 **177 6**

DEFOE, Jermain (F) **381 141**
H: 5 7 W: 10 04 b.Beckton 7-10-82
Source: Charlton Ath. *Honours:* England Youth, Under-21, B, 48 full caps, 15 goals.
1999-2000 West Ham U 0 0
2000-01 West Ham U 1 0
2000-01 *Bournemouth* 29 18 **29 18**
2001-02 West Ham U 35 10
2002-03 West Ham U 38 8
2003-04 West Ham U 19 11 **93 29**
2003-04 Tottenham H 15 7
2004-05 Tottenham H 35 13
2005-06 Tottenham H 36 9
2006-07 Tottenham H 34 10
2007-08 Tottenham H 19 4
2007-08 Portsmouth 12 8
2008-09 Portsmouth 19 7 **31 15**
2008-09 Tottenham H 8 3
2009-10 Tottenham H 34 18
2010-11 Tottenham H 22 4
2011-12 Tottenham H 25 11 **228 79**

FALQUE, Iago (M) **38 12**
H: 5 8 W: 11 00 b.Vigo 4-4-90
Honours: Spain Youth, Under-21.
2008-09 Barcelona B 1 1 **1 1**
2008-09 Juventus 0 0
2009-10 Juventus 0 0
2009-10 *Bari* 0 0
2010-11 Juventus 0 0
2010-11 *Villarreal B* 36 11 **36 11**
2011-12 Tottenham H 0 0
2011-12 *Southampton* 1 0 **1 0**
On loan from Juventus.

FREDERICKS, Ryan (M) **0** **0**
H: 5 8 W: 11 10 b.Potters Bar 10-10-92
Source: Scholar.

2010-11	Tottenham H	0	0		
2011-12	Tottenham H	0	0		

FRIEDEL, Brad (G) **503** **1**
H: 6 3 W: 14 00 b.Lakewood 18-5-71
Honours: USA 82 full caps.

1996	Columbus Crew	9	0		
1997	Columbus Crew	29	0	**38**	**0**
1997-98	Liverpool	11	0		
1998-99	Liverpool	12	0		
1999-2000	Liverpool	2	0		
2000-01	Liverpool	0	0	**25**	**0**
2000-01	Blackburn R	27	0		
2001-02	Blackburn R	36	0		
2002-03	Blackburn R	37	0		
2003-04	Blackburn R	36	1		
2004-05	Blackburn R	38	0		
2005-06	Blackburn R	38	0		
2006-07	Blackburn R	38	0		
2007-08	Blackburn R	38	0	**288**	**1**
2008-09	Aston Villa	38	0		
2009-10	Aston Villa	38	0		
2010-11	Aston Villa	38	0	**114**	**0**
2011-12	Tottenham H	38	0	**38**	**0**

GALLAS, William (D) **405** **26**
H: 6 0 W: 12 12 b.Asnieres 17-8-77
Honours: France Under-21, 84 full caps, 5 goals.

1996-97	Caen	18	0	**18**	**0**
1997-98	Marseille	3	0		
1998-99	Marseille	30	0		
1999-2000	Marseille	22	0		
2000-01	Marseille	30	2	**85**	**2**
2001-02	Chelsea	30	1		
2002-03	Chelsea	38	4		
2003-04	Chelsea	29	0		
2004-05	Chelsea	28	2		
2005-06	Chelsea	34	5		
2006-07	Chelsea	0	0	**159**	**12**
2006-07	Arsenal	21	3		
2007-08	Arsenal	31	4		
2008-09	Arsenal	23	2		
2009-10	Arsenal	26	3		
2010-11	Arsenal	0	0	**101**	**12**
2010-11	Tottenham H	27	0		
2011-12	Tottenham H	15	0	**42**	**0**

GALLIFUOCO, Giancarlo (M) **0** **0**
b.Sydney 12-1-94
Source: Sutherland Sharks.

2011-12	Tottenham H	0	0		

GIOVANI (F) **83** **12**
H: 5 8 W: 12 03 b.Monterrey 11-5-89
Honours: Mexico Youth, 58 full caps, 14 goals.

2006-07	Barcelona B	0	0		
2007-08	Barcelona	28	3	**28**	**3**
2008-09	Tottenham H	6	0		
2008-09	*Ipswich T*	8	4	**8**	**4**
2009-10	Tottenham H	1	0		
2009-10	*Galatasaray*	14	0	**14**	**0**
2010-11	Tottenham H	3	0		
2010-11	*Santander*	16	5	**16**	**5**
2011-12	Tottenham H	7	0	**17**	**0**

GOMES, Heurelho (G) **282** **0**
H: 6 3 W: 12 13 b.Minas Gerais 15-2-81
Source: Democrata. *Honours:* Brazil Under-23, 11 full caps.

2001	Cruzeiro	0	0		
2002	Cruzeiro	14	0		
2003	Cruzeiro	40	0		
2004	Cruzeiro	5	0	**59**	**0**
2004-05	PSV Eindhoven	30	0		
2005-06	PSV Eindhoven	32	0		
2006-07	PSV Eindhoven	32	0		
2007-08	PSV Eindhoven	34	0	**128**	**0**
2008-09	Tottenham H	34	0		
2009-10	Tottenham H	31	0		
2010-11	Tottenham H	30	0		
2011-12	Tottenham H	0	0	**95**	**0**

HUDDLESTONE, Tom (M) **225** **9**
H: 6 2 W: 11 02 b.Nottingham 28-12-86
Source: Scholar. *Honours:* England Youth, Under-20, Under-21, 3 full caps.

2003-04	Derby Co	43	0		
2004-05	Derby Co	45	0	**88**	**0**
2005-06	Tottenham H	4	0		
2005-06	*Wolverhampton W*	13	1	**13**	**1**
2006-07	Tottenham H	21	1		
2007-08	Tottenham H	28	3		
2008-09	Tottenham H	22	0		
2009-10	Tottenham H	33	2		
2010-11	Tottenham H	14	2		
2011-12	Tottenham H	2	0	**124**	**8**

JANSSON, Oscar (G) **12** **0**
H: 6 0 W: 12 13 b.Orebro 23-12-90
Source: Scholar.

2007-08	Tottenham H	0	0		
2008-09	Tottenham H	0	0		
2009-10	Tottenham H	0	0		
2009-10	*Exeter C*	7	0	**7**	**0**
2010-11	Tottenham H	0	0		
2010-11	*Northampton T*	4	0	**4**	**0**
2011-12	Tottenham H	0	0		
2011-12	*Bradford C*	1	0	**1**	**0**

JENAS, Jermaine (M) **296** **34**
H: 5 11 W: 11 00 b.Nottingham 18-2-83
Source: Scholar. *Honours:* England Youth, Under-21, B, 21 full caps, 1 goal.

1999-2000	Nottingham F	0	0		
2000-01	Nottingham F	1	0		
2001-02	Nottingham F	28	4	**29**	**4**
2001-02	Newcastle U	12	0		
2002-03	Newcastle U	32	6		
2003-04	Newcastle U	31	2		
2004-05	Newcastle U	31	1		
2005-06	Newcastle U	4	0	**110**	**9**
2005-06	Tottenham H	30	6		
2006-07	Tottenham H	25	6		
2007-08	Tottenham H	29	4		
2008-09	Tottenham H	32	4		
2009-10	Tottenham H	19	1		
2010-11	Tottenham H	19	0		
2011-12	Tottenham H	0	0	**154**	**21**
2011-12	*Aston Villa*	3	0	**3**	**0**

KABOUL, Younes (D) **176** **12**
H: 6 2 W: 13 07 b.Annemasse 4-1-86
Honours: France Under-21, 5 full caps, 1 goal.

2004-05	Auxerre	12	1		
2005-06	Auxerre	9	0		
2006-07	Auxerre	31	2	**52**	**3**
2007-08	Tottenham H	21	3		
2008-09	Portsmouth	20	1		
2009-10	Portsmouth	19	3	**39**	**4**
2009-10	Tottenham H	10	0		
2010-11	Tottenham H	21	1		
2011-12	Tottenham H	33	1	**85**	**5**

KANE, Harry (F) **40** **12**
H: 6 0 W: 10 00 b.Chingford 28-7-93
Source: Scholar. *Honours:* England Youth.

2010-11	Tottenham H	0	0		
2010-11	*Leyton Orient*	18	5	**18**	**5**
2011-12	Tottenham H	0	0		
2011-12	*Millwall*	22	7	**22**	**7**

KHUMALO, Bongani (D) **141** **12**
H: 6 2 W: 12 13 b.Swaziland 6-1-87
Honours: South Africa 26 full caps, 1 goal.

2005-06	Pretoria Univ	22	0		
2006-07	Pretoria Univ	28	4	**50**	**4**
2007-08	Supersport U	25	4		
2008-09	Supersport U	23	3		
2009-10	Supersport U	26	1		
2010-11	Supersport U	7	0	**81**	**8**
2010-11	Tottenham H	0	0		
2010-11	*Preston NE*	6	0	**6**	**0**
2011-12	Tottenham H	0	0		
2011-12	*Reading*	4	0	**4**	**0**

KING, Ledley (D) **268** **10**
H: 6 2 W: 14 05 b.Bow 12-10-80
Source: Trainee. *Honours:* England Youth, B, Under-21, 21 full caps, 2 goals.

1998-99	Tottenham H	1	0		
1999-2000	Tottenham H	3	0		
2000-01	Tottenham H	18	1		
2001-02	Tottenham H	32	0		
2002-03	Tottenham H	25	0		
2003-04	Tottenham H	29	1		
2004-05	Tottenham H	38	2		
2005-06	Tottenham H	26	3		
2006-07	Tottenham H	21	0		
2007-08	Tottenham H	4	0		
2008-09	Tottenham H	24	1		
2009-10	Tottenham H	20	2		
2010-11	Tottenham H	6	0		
2011-12	Tottenham H	21	0	**268**	**10**

KRANJCAR, Niko (M) **267** **51**
H: 6 1 W: 12 13 b.Zagreb 13-8-84
Honours: Croatia Youth, Under-21, 73 full caps, 15 goals.

2001-02	Dynamo Zagreb	24	3		
2002-03	Dynamo Zagreb	21	4		
2003-04	Dynamo Zagreb	24	10		
2004-05	Dynamo Zagreb	16	2	**85**	**19**
2004-05	Hajduk Split	13	1		
2005-06	Hajduk Split	32	10		
2006-07	Hajduk Split	5	3	**50**	**14**
2006-07	Portsmouth	24	2		
2007-08	Portsmouth	34	4		
2008-09	Portsmouth	21	3		
2009-10	Portsmouth	4	0	**83**	**9**
2009-10	Tottenham H	24	6		
2010-11	Tottenham H	13	2		
2011-12	Tottenham H	12	1	**49**	**9**

LANCASTER, Cameron (F) **5** **0**
H: 6 0 W: 11 09 b.Camden 5-11-92
Source: Scholar.

2010-11	Tottenham H	0	0		
2010-11	*Dagenham & R*	4	0	**4**	**0**
2011-12	Tottenham H	1	0	**1**	**0**

LENNON, Aaron (M) **234** **22**
H: 5 6 W: 10 03 b.Leeds 16-4-87
Source: Trainee. *Honours:* England Youth, Under-21, B, 19 full caps.

2003-04	Leeds U	11	0		
2004-05	Leeds U	27	1	**38**	**1**
2005-06	Tottenham H	27	2		
2006-07	Tottenham H	26	3		
2007-08	Tottenham H	29	2		
2008-09	Tottenham H	35	5		
2009-10	Tottenham H	22	3		
2010-11	Tottenham H	34	3		
2011-12	Tottenham H	23	3	**196**	**21**

LIVERMORE, Jake (M) **72** **2**
H: 5 9 W: 12 08 b.Enfield 14-11-89
Source: Scholar.

2006-07	Tottenham H	0	0		
2007-08	Tottenham H	0	0		
2007-08	*Milton Keynes D*	5	0	**5**	**0**
2008-09	Tottenham H	0	0		
2008-09	*Crewe Alex*	0	0		
2009-10	Tottenham H	1	0		
2009-10	*Derby Co*	16	1	**16**	**1**
2009-10	*Peterborough U*	9	1	**9**	**1**
2010-11	Tottenham H	0	0		
2010-11	*Ipswich T*	12	0	**12**	**0**
2010-11	*Leeds U*	5	0	**5**	**0**
2011-12	Tottenham H	24	0	**25**	**0**

LUONGO, Massimo (F) **0** **0**
H: 5 8 W: 11 10 b.Sydney 25-9-92
Source: Rushden & D.

2010-11	Tottenham H	0	0		
2011-12	Tottenham H	0	0		

MASON, Ryan (F) **52** **6**
H: 5 9 W: 10 00 b.Enfield 13-6-91
Source: Scholar. *Honours:* England Youth.

2007-08	Tottenham H	0	0		
2008-09	Tottenham H	0	0		
2009-10	Tottenham H	0	0		
2009-10	*Yeovil T*	28	6	**28**	**6**
2010-11	Tottenham H	0	0		
2010-11	*Doncaster R*	15	0		
2011-12	Tottenham H	0	0		
2011-12	*Doncaster R*	4	0	**19**	**0**
2011-12	*Millwall*	5	0	**5**	**0**

MODRIC, Luka (M) **238** **44**
H: 5 8 W: 10 03 b.Zadar 9-9-85
Honours: Croatia Youth, Under-21, 57 full caps, 8 goals.

2004-05	Inter Zapresic	18	4	**18**	**4**
2004-05	Dinamo Zagreb	6	0		
2005-06	Dinamo Zagreb	32	8		
2006-07	Dinamo Zagreb	30	6		
2007-08	Dinamo Zagreb	25	13	**93**	**27**
2008-09	Tottenham H	34	3		
2009-10	Tottenham H	25	3		
2010-11	Tottenham H	32	3		
2011-12	Tottenham H	36	4	**127**	**13**

NAUGHTON, Kyle (M) **140** **6**
H: 5 11 W: 11 07 b.Sheffield 11-11-88
Honours: England Under-21.

2006-07	Sheffield U	0	0		
2007-08	*Gretna*	18	0	**18**	**0**
2007-08	Sheffield U	0	0		
2008-09	Sheffield U	40	1		

2009-10	Sheffield U	0	0	**40**	**1**
2009-10	Tottenham H	1	0		
2009-10	*Middlesbrough*	15	0	**15**	**0**
2010-11	Tottenham H	0	0		
2010-11	*Leicester C*	34	5	**34**	**5**
2011-12	Tottenham H	0	0	**1**	**0**
2011-12	*Norwich C*	32	0	**32**	**0**

NELSEN, Ryan (D) 258 15
H: 5 11 W: 14 02 b.Christchurch, NZ 18-10-77
Honours: New Zealand Under-23, 45 full caps, 7 goals.

2001	DC United	19	0		
2002	DC United	20	4		
2003	DC United	25	1		
2004	DC United	17	2	**81**	**7**
2004-05	Blackburn R	15	0		
2005-06	Blackburn R	31	0		
2006-07	Blackburn R	12	0		
2007-08	Blackburn R	22	0		
2008-09	Blackburn R	35	1		
2009-10	Blackburn R	28	4		
2010-11	Blackburn R	28	3		
2011-12	Blackburn R	1	0	**172**	**8**
2011-12	Tottenham H	5	0	**5**	**0**

NICHOLSON, Jake (M) 2 0
H: 6 0 W: 11 07 b.Harrow 19-7-92
Source: Scholar.

2010-11	Tottenham H	0	0		
2010-11	*MyPa*	2	0	**2**	**0**
2011-12	Tottenham H	0	0		

OBIKA, Jonathan (F) 95 20
H: 6 0 W: 12 00 b.Enfield 12-9-90
Source: Scholar. *Honours:* England Youth, Under-20.

2008-09	Tottenham H	0	0		
2008-09	*Yeovil T*	10	4		
2009-10	Tottenham H	0	0		
2009-10	*Yeovil T*	22	6		
2009-10	*Millwall*	12	2	**12**	**2**
2010-11	Tottenham H	0	0		
2010-11	*Crystal Palace*	7	0	**7**	**0**
2010-11	*Peterborough U*	1	1	**1**	**1**
2010-11	*Swindon T*	5	0	**5**	**0**
2010-11	*Yeovil T*	11	3		
2011-12	Tottenham H	0	0		
2011-12	*Yeovil T*	27	4	**70**	**17**

OYENUGA, Kudus (F) 2 0
H: 5 9 W: 11 00 b.Walthamstow 18-3-93
Source: Scholar.

2010-11	Tottenham H	0	0		
2011-12	Tottenham H	0	0		
2011-12	*Bury*	1	0	**1**	**0**
2011-12	*St Johnstone*	1	0	**1**	**0**

PARKER, Scott (M) 346 25
H: 5 9 W: 11 10 b.Lambeth 13-10-80
Source: Trainee. *Honours:* England Schools, Youth, Under-21, 17 full caps.

1997-98	Charlton Ath	3	0		
1998-99	Charlton Ath	4	0		
1999-2000	Charlton Ath	15	1		
2000-01	Charlton Ath	20	1		
2000-01	*Norwich C*	6	1	**6**	**1**
2001-02	Charlton Ath	38	1		
2002-03	Charlton Ath	28	4		
2003-04	Charlton Ath	20	2	**128**	**9**
2003-04	Chelsea	11	1		
2004-05	Chelsea	4	0	**15**	**1**
2005-06	Newcastle U	26	1		
2006-07	Newcastle U	29	3	**55**	**4**
2007-08	West Ham U	18	1		
2008-09	West Ham U	28	1		
2009-10	West Ham U	31	2		
2010-11	West Ham U	32	5		
2011-12	West Ham U	4	1	**113**	**10**
2011-12	Tottenham H	29	0	**29**	**0**

PARRETT, Dean (M) 31 3
H: 5 10 W: 11 04 b.Hampstead 16-11-91
Source: Scholar. *Honours:* England Youth, Under-20.

2008-09	Tottenham H	0	0		
2009-10	Tottenham H	0	0		
2009-10	*Aldershot T*	4	0	**4**	**0**
2010-11	Tottenham H	0	0		
2010-11	*Plymouth Arg*	8	1	**8**	**1**
2010-11	*Charlton Ath*	9	1	**9**	**1**
2011-12	Tottenham H	0	0		
2011-12	*Yeovil T*	10	1	**10**	**1**

PAVLYUCHENKO, Roman (F) 315 101
H: 6 2 W: 12 04 b.Mostovskoy 15-12-81
Honours: Russia 50 full caps, 21 goals.

1999	Dinamo Stavropol	31	1	**31**	**1**
2000	Rotor Volgograd II	13	3	**13**	**3**
2000	Rotor Volgograd	16	5		
2001	Rotor Volgograd	28	5		
2002	Rotor Volgograd	22	4	**66**	**14**
2003	Spartak Moscow	27	10		
2004	Spartak Moscow	26	10		
2005	Spartak Moscow	25	11		
2006	Spartak Moscow	27	18		
2007	Spartak Moscow	22	14	**127**	**63**
2008-09	Tottenham H	28	5		
2009-10	Tottenham H	16	5		
2010-11	Tottenham H	29	9		
2011-12	Tottenham H	5	1	**78**	**20**

Transferred to Lokomotiv Moscow January 2012.

PIENAAR, Steven (M) 247 28
H: 5 10 W: 10 06 b.Westbury 17-3-82
Honours: South Africa 60 full caps, 3 goals.

2001-02	Ajax	8	1		
2002-03	Ajax	31	5		
2003-04	Ajax	16	3		
2004-05	Ajax	24	4		
2005-06	Ajax	15	2	**94**	**15**
2006-07	Bor Dortmund	25	0	**25**	**0**
2007-08	Everton	28	2		
2008-09	Everton	28	2		
2009-10	Everton	30	4		
2010-11	Everton	18	1		
2010-11	Tottenham H	8	0		
2011-12	Tottenham H	2	0	**10**	**0**
2011-12	*Everton*	14	4	**118**	**13**

PRITCHARD, Alex (M) 0 0
b.Grays 3-5-93
Source: Scholar.

2011-12	Tottenham H	0	0		

RANIERI, Mirko (G) 18 0
b.Assisi 8-2-92
Source: Perugia. *Honours:* Italy Youth.

2008-09	Tottenham H	0	0		
2009-10	Tottenham H	0	0		
2009-10	Ipswich T	0	0		
2010-11	Tottenham H	0	0		
2011-12	Tottenham H	0	0		
2011-12	*Viareggio*	18	0	**18**	**0**

ROSE, Danny (M) 40 1
H: 5 8 W: 11 11 b.Doncaster 2-6-90
Source: Leeds U. *Honours:* England Youth, Under-21.

2007-08	Tottenham H	0	0		
2008-09	Tottenham H	0	0		
2008-09	*Watford*	7	0	**7**	**0**
2009-10	Tottenham H	1	1		
2010-11	Tottenham H	4	0		
2010-11	*Bristol C*	17	0	**17**	**0**
2011-12	Tottenham H	11	0	**16**	**1**

SAHA, Louis (F) 368 117
H: 6 1 W: 12 08 b.Paris 8-8-78
Honours: France Youth, Under-21, 20 full caps, 4 goals.

1997-98	Metz	21	1		
1998-99	Metz	3	0		
1998-99	Newcastle U	11	1	**11**	**1**
1999-2000	Metz	23	4	**47**	**5**
2000-01	Fulham	43	27		
2001-02	Fulham	36	8		
2002-03	Fulham	17	5		
2003-04	Fulham	21	13	**117**	**53**
2003-04	Manchester U	12	7		
2004-05	Manchester U	14	1		
2005-06	Manchester U	19	7		
2006-07	Manchester U	24	8		
2007-08	Manchester U	17	5		
2008-09	Manchester U	0	0	**86**	**28**
2008-09	Everton	24	6		
2009-10	Everton	33	13		
2010-11	Everton	22	7		
2011-12	Everton	18	1	**97**	**27**
2011-12	Tottenham H	10	3	**10**	**3**

SANDRO (M) 85 5
H: 6 2 W: 11 11 b.Riachinho 15-3-89
Honours: Brazil 9 full caps, 1 goal.

2008	Internacional	7	2		
2009	Internacional	27	1		
2010	Internacional	9	1	**43**	**4**
2010-11	Tottenham H	19	1		
2011-12	Tottenham H	23	0	**42**	**1**

SMITH, Adam (D) 78 3
H: 5 8 W: 10 07 b.Leytonstone 29-4-91
Source: Scholar. *Honours:* England Youth, Under-20, Under-21.

2007-08	Tottenham H	0	0		
2008-09	Tottenham H	0	0		
2009-10	Tottenham H	0	0		
2009-10	*Wycombe W*	3	0	**3**	**0**
2009-10	*Torquay U*	16	0	**16**	**0**
2010-11	Tottenham H	0	0		
2010-11	*Bournemouth*	38	1	**38**	**1**
2011-12	Tottenham H	1	0	**1**	**0**
2011-12	*Milton Keynes D*	17	2	**17**	**2**
2011-12	*Leeds U*	3	0	**3**	**0**

TAPPING, Callum (M) 0 0
H: 5 10 W: 11 00 b.Edinburgh 5-6-93
Source: Scholar.

2010-11	Tottenham H	0	0		
2011-12	Tottenham H	0	0		
2011-12	*Hearts*	0	0		

TOWNSEND, Andros (M) 89 9
H: 6 0 W: 12 00 b.Chingford 16-7-91
Source: Scholar. *Honours:* England Youth.

2008-09	Tottenham H	0	0		
2008-09	*Yeovil T*	10	1	**10**	**1**
2009-10	Tottenham H	0	0		
2009-10	*Leyton Orient*	22	2	**22**	**2**
2009-10	*Milton Keynes D*	9	2	**9**	**2**
2010-11	Tottenham H	0	0		
2010-11	*Ipswich T*	13	1	**13**	**1**
2010-11	*Watford*	3	0	**3**	**0**
2010-11	*Millwall*	11	2	**11**	**2**
2011-12	Tottenham H	0	0		
2011-12	*Leeds U*	6	1	**6**	**1**
2011-12	*Birmingham C*	15	0	**15**	**0**

VAN DER VAART, Rafael (M) 310 116
H: 5 9 W: 11 09 b.Heemskerk 11-2-83
Honours: Holland 99 full caps, 19 goals.

1999-2000	Ajax	1	0		
2000-01	Ajax	27	7		
2001-02	Ajax	20	14		
2002-03	Ajax	21	18		
2003-04	Ajax	26	7		
2004-05	Ajax	22	6	**117**	**52**
2005-06	Hamburg	19	9		
2006-07	Hamburg	26	8		
2007-08	Hamburg	29	12	**74**	**29**
2008-09	Real Madrid	32	5		
2009-10	Real Madrid	26	6	**58**	**11**
2010-11	Tottenham H	28	13		
2011-12	Tottenham H	33	11	**61**	**24**

WALKER, Kyle (D) 112 3
H: 5 10 W: 11 07 b.Sheffield 28-5-90
Source: Scholar. *Honours:* England Youth, Under-21, 2 full caps.

2008-09	Sheffield U	2	0		
2008-09	*Northampton T*	9	0	**9**	**0**
2009-10	Tottenham H	2	0		
2009-10	*Sheffield U*	26	0	**28**	**0**
2010-11	Tottenham H	1	0		
2010-11	*QPR*	20	0	**20**	**0**
2010-11	*Aston Villa*	15	1	**15**	**1**
2011-12	Tottenham H	37	2	**40**	**2**

WALLER-LARSEN, Jesse (M) 0 0
H: 5 8 W: 12 02 b.Hornsey 26-12-92
Source: Scholar.

2011-12	Tottenham H	0	0		

Scholars
Ball Dominic; Barthram Jack Patrick; Bentaleb Nabil; Bush Mason; Coulibaly Souleymane; Coulthirst Shaquile Tyshan; Dombaxe Laste; Ekong William Paul; Gardiner Thomas James; Granger Billy; Lameiras Ruben; McEvoy Kenneth; McQueen Alexander Luke; McQueen Darren; Michael-Percil Roman; Miles Jonathan David; Modeste Oliver Thomas Jack; Munns Jack Frederick; Smith Samuel Henry Tyson; Stewart Kevin Linford; Ward Grant Antony; Zapata-Caicedo Victor Manuel.

TRANMERE R (84)

AKINS, Lucas (F) 102 8
H: 5 10 W: 11 07 b.Huddersfield 25-2-89
Source: Scholar.

2006-07	Huddersfield T	2	0		
2007-08	Huddersfield T	3	0	**5**	**0**
2008-09	Hamilton A	11	0		
2008-09	*Partick Th*	9	1	**9**	**1**
2009-10	Hamilton A	0	0	**11**	**0**
2010-11	Tranmere R	33	2		
2011-12	Tranmere R	44	5	**77**	**7**

BAKAYOGO, Zaoumana (D) 97 1
H: 5 9 W: 10 08 b.Paris 11-8-86
Source: Paris St Germain. *Honours:* Ivory Coast Under-23.

2006-07	Millwall	5	0		
2007-08	Millwall	10	0	**15**	**0**
From Alfortville.					
2009-10	Tranmere R	29	0		
2010-11	Tranmere R	27	1		
2011-12	Tranmere R	26	0	**82**	**1**

BUCHANAN, David (M) 255 2
H: 5 7 W: 11 03 b.Rochdale 6-5-86
Source: Scholar. *Honours:* Northern Ireland Youth, Under-21.

2004-05	Bury	3	0		
2005-06	Bury	23	0		
2006-07	Bury	41	0		
2007-08	Bury	35	0		
2008-09	Bury	46	0		
2009-10	Bury	38	0	**186**	**0**
2010-11	Hamilton A	28	1	**28**	**1**
2011-12	Tranmere R	41	1	**41**	**1**

COLLISTER, Joe (G) 10 0
H: 6 0 W: 13 10 b.Hoylake 15-12-91
Source: Scholar.

2009-10	Tranmere R	3	0		
2010-11	Tranmere R	7	0		
2011-12	Tranmere R	0	0	**10**	**0**

COUGHLIN, Andy (G) 2 0
H: 6 3 W: 14 04 b.Bootle 31-1-93
Source: Scholar.

2010-11	Tranmere R	0	0		
2011-12	Tranmere R	2	0	**2**	**0**

DEVANEY, Martin (M) 388 56
H: 5 11 W: 12 00 b.Cheltenham 1-6-80
Source: Trainee.

1997-98	Coventry C	0	0		
1998-99	Coventry C	0	0		
1999-2000	Cheltenham T	26	6		
2000-01	Cheltenham T	34	10		
2001-02	Cheltenham T	25	1		
2002-03	Cheltenham T	40	6		
2003-04	Cheltenham T	40	5		
2004-05	Cheltenham T	38	10	**203**	**38**
2005-06	Watford	0	0		
2005-06	Barnsley	38	6		
2006-07	Barnsley	41	5		
2007-08	Barnsley	34	4		
2008-09	Barnsley	26	0		
2009-10	Barnsley	11	0		
2009-10	*Milton Keynes D*	5	0	**5**	**0**
2010-11	Barnsley	6	0	**156**	**15**
2010-11	*Walsall*	4	1	**4**	**1**
2011-12	Tranmere R	20	2	**20**	**2**

GOODISON, Ian (D) 406 12
H: 6 1 W: 13 04 b.St James, Jamaica 21-11-72
Source: Olympic Gardens. *Honours:* Jamaica 113 full caps, 9 goals.

1999-2000	Hull C	18	0		
2000-01	Hull C	36	1		
2001-02	Hull C	16	0		
2002-03	Hull C	0	0	**70**	**1**
From Seba U.					
2003-04	Tranmere R	12	0		
2004-05	Tranmere R	44	1		
2005-06	Tranmere R	38	1		
2006-07	Tranmere R	40	0		
2007-08	Tranmere R	42	0		
2008-09	Tranmere R	33	1		
2009-10	Tranmere R	44	3		
2010-11	Tranmere R	40	4		
2011-12	Tranmere R	43	1	**336**	**11**

HOLMES, Danny (D) 85 3
H: 6 0 W: 11 13 b.Birkenhead 6-1-89

2007-08	Tranmere R	0	0		
2008-09	Tranmere R	1	0		
2009-10	The New Saints	32	0		
2010-11	The New Saints	26	3	**58**	**3**
2011-12	Tranmere R	26	0	**27**	**0**

KAY, Michael (D) 28 1
H: 6 0 W: 11 05 b.Consett 12-9-89
Source: Scholar.

2007-08	Sunderland	0	0		
2008-09	Sunderland	0	0		
2009-10	Sunderland	0	0		
2010-11	Sunderland	0	0		
2010-11	*Tranmere R*	22	1		
2011-12	Tranmere R	6	0	**28**	**1**

KIRBY, Jake (M) 1 0
H: 5 11 W: 12 04 b.Liverpool 9-5-94
Source: Scholar.

2011-12	Tranmere R	1	0	**1**	**0**

LABADIE, Joss (M) 95 15
H: 5 7 W: 11 02 b.Croydon 31-8-90

2008-09	WBA	0	0		
2008-09	*Shrewsbury T*	1	0		
2009-10	WBA	0	0		
2009-10	*Shrewsbury T*	13	5	**14**	**5**
2009-10	*Cheltenham T*	11	0	**11**	**0**
2009-10	*Tranmere R*	9	3		
2010-11	Tranmere R	34	2		
2011-12	Tranmere R	27	5	**70**	**10**

McCHRYSTAL, Mark (D) 115 3
H: 6 1 W: 13 07 b.Derry 26-6-84
Source: Scholar. *Honours:* Northern Ireland Under-21.

2001-02	Wolverhampton W	0	0		
2003	Derry C	5	0		
2003	*Institute*	6	0	**6**	**0**
2004	Derry C	9	1		
2005	Derry C	9	0		
2006-07	Partick Th	15	1	**15**	**1**
2007	Derry C	3	0		
2008	Derry C	11	0		
2009	Derry C	13	0	**50**	**1**
2009-10	Lisburn Distillery	3	0	**3**	**0**
2010-11	Tranmere R	23	0		
2011-12	Tranmere R	18	1	**41**	**1**

McGURK, Adam (F) 52 7
H: 5 9 W: 12 13 b.Larne 24-1-89
Source: Scholar. *Honours:* Northern Ireland Under-21.

2005-06	Aston Villa	0	0		
2006-07	Aston Villa	0	0		
2007-08	Aston Villa	0	0		
2008-09	Aston Villa	0	0		
2009-10	Aston Villa	0	0		
From Hednesford T.					
2010-11	Tranmere R	21	3		
2011-12	Tranmere R	31	4	**52**	**7**

POWER, Max (M) 4 0
H: 5 11 W: 11 13 b.Bebington 27-7-93
Source: Scholar.

2010-11	Tranmere R	0	0		
2011-12	Tranmere R	4	0	**4**	**0**

RAVEN, David (D) 189 1
H: 6 0 W: 11 04 b.West Kirby 10-3-85
Source: Scholar. *Honours:* England Youth, Under-20.

2001-02	Liverpool	0	0		
2002-03	Liverpool	0	0		
2003-04	Liverpool	0	0		
2004-05	Liverpool	1	0		
2005-06	Liverpool	0	0	**1**	**0**
2005-06	*Tranmere R*	11	0		
2006-07	Carlisle U	36	0		
2007-08	Carlisle U	43	1		
2008-09	Carlisle U	41	0		
2009-10	Carlisle U	16	0	**136**	**1**
2010-11	Shrewsbury T	24	0	**24**	**0**
2011-12	Tranmere R	17	0	**28**	**0**

ROBINSON, Andy (M) 275 50
H: 5 8 W: 11 04 b.Birkenhead 3-11-79
Source: Cammell Laird.

2002-03	Tranmere R	0	0		
2003-04	Swansea C	37	8		
2004-05	Swansea C	37	8		
2005-06	Swansea C	39	12		
2006-07	Swansea C	39	7		
2007-08	Swansea C	40	8	**192**	**43**
2008-09	Leeds U	32	2		
2009-10	Leeds U	6	0		
2009-10	*Tranmere R*	5	1		
2010-11	Leeds U	0	0	**38**	**2**
2010-11	Tranmere R	15	0		
2011-12	Tranmere R	25	4	**45**	**5**

SHOWUNMI, Enoch (F) 247 43
H: 6 3 W: 14 11 b.Kilburn 21-4-82
Source: Willesden Constantine. *Honours:* Nigeria 2 full caps.

2003-04	Luton T	26	7		
2004-05	Luton T	35	6		
2005-06	Luton T	41	1	**102**	**14**
2006-07	Bristol C	33	10		
2007-08	Bristol C	17	3	**50**	**13**
2007-08	*Sheffield W*	10	0	**10**	**0**
2008-09	Leeds U	8	2		
2009-10	Leeds U	7	0	**15**	**2**
2010-11	Tranmere R	43	11		
2011-12	Tranmere R	27	3	**70**	**14**

STOCKTON, Cole (F) 1 0
H: 6 1 W: 11 11 b.Huyton 13-3-94
Source: Scholar.

2011-12	Tranmere R	1	0	**1**	**0**

TAYLOR, Ash (M) 97 3
H: 6 0 W: 12 00 b.Bromborough 2-9-90
Source: Scholar. *Honours:* Wales Youth.

2008-09	Tranmere R	1	0		
2009-10	Tranmere R	33	1		
2010-11	Tranmere R	26	0		
2011-12	Tranmere R	37	2	**97**	**3**

TIRYAKI, Mustafa (F) 30 3
H: 6 2 W: 13 03 b.Hackney 2-8-87
Source: Maidenhead U, Havant & W.

2011-12	Tranmere R	30	3	**30**	**3**

WEIR, Robbie (M) 57 3
H: 5 9 W: 11 07 b.Belfast 9-12-88
Source: Scholar. *Honours:* Northern Ireland Under-21, B.

2007-08	Sunderland	0	0		
2008-09	Sunderland	0	0		
2009-10	Sunderland	0	0		
2010-11	Sunderland	0	0		
2010-11	*Tranmere R*	18	0		
2011-12	Tranmere R	39	3	**57**	**3**

WELSH, John (M) 199 14
H: 5 7 W: 12 02 b.Liverpool 10-1-84
Source: Scholar. *Honours:* England Youth, Under-20, Under-21.

2000-01	Liverpool	0	0		
2001-02	Liverpool	0	0		
2002-03	Liverpool	0	0		
2003-04	Liverpool	1	0		
2004-05	Liverpool	3	0		
2005-06	Liverpool	0	0	**4**	**0**
2005-06	Hull C	32	2		
2006-07	Hull C	18	1		
2007-08	Hull C	0	0		
2007-08	*Chester C*	6	0	**6**	**0**
2008-09	Hull C	0	0	**50**	**3**
2008-09	*Carlisle U*	4	0	**4**	**0**
2008-09	*Bury*	5	0	**5**	**0**
2009-10	Tranmere R	45	4		
2010-11	Tranmere R	41	4		
2011-12	Tranmere R	44	3	**130**	**11**

WILLIAMS, Owain fon (G) 145 0
H: 6 1 W: 12 09 b.Penygroes 17-3-87
Source: Scholar. *Honours:* Wales Youth, Under-21.

2005-06	Crewe Alex	0	0		
2006-07	Crewe Alex	0	0		
2007-08	Crewe Alex	0	0		
2008-09	Stockport Co	33	0		
2009-10	Stockport Co	44	0		
2010-11	Stockport Co	5	0	**82**	**0**
2010-11	*Bury*	6	0	**6**	**0**
2010-11	Rochdale	22	0	**22**	**0**
2011-12	Tranmere R	35	0	**35**	**0**

WALSALL (85)

BEEVERS, Lee (D) 296 12
H: 6 2 W: 11 07 b.Doncaster 4-12-83
Source: Scholar. *Honours:* Wales Youth, Under-21.

2000-01	Ipswich T	0	0		
2001-02	Ipswich T	0	0		
2002-03	Ipswich T	0	0		
2002-03	*Boston U*	1	0		
2003-04	Boston U	40	2		

2004-05 Boston U 31 1 **72** **3**
2004-05 Lincoln C 8 0
2005-06 Lincoln C 33 1
2006-07 Lincoln C 44 5
2007-08 Lincoln C 37 1
2008-09 Lincoln C 44 2 **166** **9**
2009-10 Colchester U 4 0
2010-11 Colchester U 19 0 **23** **0**
2011-12 Walsall 35 0 **35** **0**

BOWERMAN, George (F) **22** **3**
H: 5 10 W: 10 07 b.Sedgley 6-11-91
Source: Scholar.
2010-11 Walsall 0 0
2011-12 Walsall 22 3 **22** **3**

BUTLER, Andy (D) **272** **29**
H: 6 0 W: 13 00 b.Doncaster 4-11-83
Source: Scholar.
2003-04 Scunthorpe U 35 2
2004-05 Scunthorpe U 37 10
2005-06 Scunthorpe U 16 1
2006-07 Scunthorpe U 11 1
2006-07 *Grimsby T* 4 0 **4** **0**
2007-08 Scunthorpe U 36 2 **135** **16**
2008-09 Huddersfield T 42 4
2009-10 Huddersfield T 11 0 **53** **4**
2009-10 *Blackpool* 7 0 **7** **0**
2010-11 Walsall 31 4
2011-12 Walsall 42 5 **73** **9**

BUTLIN, Joey (F) **0** **0**
b.Birmingham 17-3-93
Source: Scholar.
2011-12 Walsall 0 0

CHAMBERS, Adam (D) **272** **12**
H: 5 10 W: 11 12 b.Sandwell 20-11-80
Source: Trainee. *Honours:* England Youth.
1998-99 WBA 0 0
1999-2000 WBA 0 0
2000-01 WBA 11 1
2001-02 WBA 32 0
2002-03 WBA 13 0
2003-04 WBA 0 0
2003-04 *Sheffield W* 11 0 **11** **0**
2004-05 WBA 0 0 **56** **1**
2004-05 Kidderminster H 2 0 **2** **0**
2006-07 Leyton Orient 38 4
2007-08 Leyton Orient 45 3
2008-09 Leyton Orient 33 1
2009-10 Leyton Orient 29 1
2010-11 Leyton Orient 29 0 **174** **9**
2011-12 Walsall 29 2 **29** **2**

DEARDS, Connor (F) **0** **0**
b.Birmingham 19-1-93
Source: Scholar.
2011-12 Walsall 0 0

GNAKPA, Claude (D) **110** **10**
H: 6 0 W: 13 05 b.Marseille 9-6-83
Source: Montpellier, Marignane, Beaucaire, Santander, Alaves, Vaduz.
2006-07 Swindon T 0 0
2007-08 Peterborough U 28 0 **28** **0**
2008-09 Luton T 27 1
2009-10 Luton T 35 8 **62** **9**
2011-12 Walsall 20 1 **20** **1**
Transferred to Inverness CT January 2012.

GRIGG, Will (M) **58** **8**
H: 5 11 W: 11 00 b.Solihull 3-7-91
Source: Scholar. *Honours:* Northern Ireland Youth, Under-21, 1 full cap.
2008-09 Walsall 1 0
2009-10 Walsall 0 0
2010-11 Walsall 28 4
2011-12 Walsall 29 4 **58** **8**

GROF, David (G) **23** **0**
H: 6 3 W: 14 02 b.Budapest 17-4-89
2008-09 Hibernian 0 0
2009-10 Hibernian 0 0
2010-11 Notts Co 0 0
2011-12 Walsall 23 0 **23** **0**

HURST, Kevan (M) **240** **18**
H: 5 10 W: 11 07 b.Chesterfield 27-8-85
Source: Sheffield U Scholar.
2003-04 *Boston U* 7 1 **7** **1**
2004-05 Sheffield U 1 0
2004-05 *Stockport Co* 14 1 **14** **1**
2005-06 Sheffield U 0 0
2005-06 *Chesterfield* 37 4
2006-07 Sheffield U 0 0 **1** **0**
2006-07 *Chesterfield* 25 3 **62** **7**

2006-07 *Scunthorpe U* 13 0
2007-08 Scunthorpe U 33 1
2008-09 Scunthorpe U 20 2 **66** **3**
2009-10 Carlisle U 33 2
2010-11 Carlisle U 2 0 **35** **2**
2010-11 *Morecambe* 21 2 **21** **2**
2011-12 Walsall 34 2 **34** **2**

JARVIS, Ryan (F) **195** **26**
H: 6 1 W: 11 11 b.Fakenham 11-7-86
Source: Scholar. *Honours:* FA Schools, England Youth.
2002-03 Norwich C 3 0
2003-04 Norwich C 12 1
2004-05 Norwich C 4 1
2004-05 *Colchester U* 6 0 **6** **0**
2005-06 Norwich C 4 1
2006-07 Norwich C 5 0
2006-07 *Leyton Orient* 14 6
2007-08 Norwich C 1 0 **29** **3**
2007-08 *Kilmarnock* 9 1 **9** **1**
2007-08 *Notts Co* 17 2 **17** **2**
2008-09 Leyton Orient 31 0
2009-10 Leyton Orient 42 8
2010-11 Leyton Orient 11 2 **98** **16**
2010-11 *Northampton T* 3 0 **3** **0**
2011-12 Walsall 19 2 **19** **2**
2011-12 *Torquay U* 14 2 **14** **2**

JONES, Jake (M) **0** **0**
b.Solihull 6-4-93
Source: Scholar.
2011-12 Walsall 0 0

LANCASHIRE, Oliver (D) **87** **2**
H: 6 1 W: 11 10 b.Basingstoke 13-12-88
Source: Scholar.
2006-07 Southampton 0 0
2007-08 Southampton 0 0
2008-09 Southampton 11 0
2009-10 Southampton 2 0 **13** **0**
2009-10 *Grimsby T* 25 1 **25** **1**
2010-11 Walsall 29 0
2011-12 Walsall 20 1 **49** **1**

LEDESMA, Emmanuel (M) **64** **8**
H: 5 11 W: 12 02 b.Quilmes 24-5-88
2007-08 Genoa 1 0 **1** **0**
2008-09 *Salernitana* 8 1 **8** **1**
2008-09 *QPR* 17 1 **17** **1**
2009-10 *Novara* 8 1 **8** **1**
2010-11 Crotone 10 0 **10** **0**
2010-11 Walsall 10 1
2011-12 Walsall 10 4 **20** **5**

MACKEN, Jon (F) **466** **112**
H: 5 11 W: 12 04 b.Manchester 7-9-77
Source: Trainee. *Honours:* England Youth. Eire 1 full cap.
1996-97 Manchester U 0 0
1997-98 Preston NE 29 6
1998-99 Preston NE 42 8
1999-2000 Preston NE 44 22
2000-01 Preston NE 38 19
2001-02 Preston NE 31 8 **184** **63**
2001-02 Manchester C 8 5
2002-03 Manchester C 5 0
2003-04 Manchester C 15 1
2004-05 Manchester C 23 1 **51** **7**
2005-06 Crystal Palace 24 2
2006-07 Crystal Palace 1 0 **25** **2**
2006-07 *Ipswich T* 14 4 **14** **4**
2006-07 Derby Co 8 0
2007-08 Derby Co 3 0 **11** **0**
2007-08 Barnsley 29 7
2008-09 Barnsley 45 9
2009-10 Barnsley 31 4
2010-11 Barnsley 0 0 **105** **20**
2010-11 Walsall 39 9
2011-12 Walsall 37 7 **76** **16**

NICHOLLS, Alex (M) **191** **24**
H: 5 10 W: 11 00 b.Stourbridge 9-12-87
Source: Scholar.
2005-06 Walsall 8 0
2006-07 Walsall 0 0
2007-08 Walsall 19 2
2008-09 Walsall 45 6
2009-10 Walsall 37 4
2010-11 Walsall 37 5

2011-12 Walsall 45 7 **191** **24**

PATERSON, Jamie (F) **48** **3**
H: 5 9 W: 10 07 b.Coventry 20-12-91
Source: Scholar.
2010-11 Walsall 14 0
2011-12 Walsall 34 3 **48** **3**

PETERLIN, Anton (D) **90** **5**
H: 5 11 W: 11 05 b.San Francisco 4-4-87
2007 Cal Poly Mustangs 12 0 **12** **0**
2007 San Francisco Seals 16 3 **16** **3**
2008 Ventura CF 16 2
2009 Ventura CF 8 0 **24** **2**
2009-10 Everton 0 0
2010-11 Plymouth Arg 12 0 **12** **0**
2011-12 Walsall 26 0 **26** **0**

SADLER, Matthew (D) **200** **1**
H: 5 11 W: 11 08 b.Birmingham 26-2-85
Source: Scholar. *Honours:* England Youth.
2001-02 Birmingham C 0 0
2002-03 Birmingham C 2 0
2003-04 Birmingham C 0 0
2003-04 *Northampton T* 7 0 **7** **0**
2004-05 Birmingham C 0 0
2005-06 Birmingham C 8 0
2006-07 Birmingham C 36 0
2007-08 Birmingham C 5 0 **51** **0**
2007-08 Watford 15 0
2008-09 Watford 15 0
2009-10 Watford 0 0
2009-10 *Stockport Co* 20 0 **20** **0**
2010-11 Watford 0 0 **30** **0**
2010-11 *Shrewsbury T* 46 0 **46** **0**
2011-12 Walsall 46 1 **46** **1**

SMITH, Manny (D) **124** **7**
H: 6 2 W: 12 03 b.Birmingham 8-11-88
Source: Scholar.
2005-06 Walsall 0 0
2006-07 Walsall 3 0
2007-08 Walsall 4 0
2008-09 Walsall 26 0
2009-10 Walsall 33 4
2010-11 Walsall 25 2
2011-12 Walsall 33 1 **124** **7**

TAUNDRY, Richard (D) **152** **3**
H: 5 9 W: 12 10 b.Walsall 15-2-89
Source: Scholar.
2007-08 Walsall 21 0
2008-09 Walsall 38 0
2009-10 Walsall 30 3
2010-11 Walsall 28 0
2011-12 Walsall 35 0 **152** **3**

WALKER, Jim (G) **482** **0**
H: 5 11 W: 13 04 b.Sutton-in-Ashfield 9-7-73
Source: Trainee.
1991-92 Notts Co 0 0
1992-93 Notts Co 0 0
1993-94 Walsall 31 0
1994-95 Walsall 4 0
1995-96 Walsall 26 0
1996-97 Walsall 36 0
1997-98 Walsall 46 0
1998-99 Walsall 46 0
1999-2000 Walsall 43 0
2000-01 Walsall 44 0
2001-02 Walsall 43 0
2002-03 Walsall 41 0
2003-04 Walsall 43 0
2004-05 West Ham U 10 0
2005-06 West Ham U 3 0
2006-07 West Ham U 0 0
2007-08 West Ham U 0 0
2008-09 West Ham U 0 0
2008-09 *Colchester U* 16 0 **16** **0**
2009-10 West Ham U 0 0 **13** **0**
2010-11 Walsall 26 0
2011-12 Walsall 24 0 **453** **0**

WESTLAKE, Darryl (D) **67** **1**
H: 5 9 W: 11 00 b.Sutton Coldfield 1-3-91
Source: Scholar.
2009-10 Walsall 22 0
2010-11 Walsall 28 1
2011-12 Walsall 17 0 **67** **1**

WATFORD (86)

ASSOMBALONGA, Britt (F) **4 0**
H: 5 9 W: 11 13 b.Kinshasa 6-12-92
Source: Youth.
2010-11 Watford 0 0
2011-12 Watford 4 0 **4 0**

BENNETT, Dale (D) **27 1**
H: 5 11 W: 12 02 b.Enfield 6-1-90
Source: Scholar.
2008-09 Watford 0 0
2009-10 Watford 10 0
2010-11 Watford 10 0
2011-12 Watford 2 0 **22 0**
2011-12 *Brentford* 5 1 **5 1**

BOND, Jonathan (G) **12 0**
H: 6 3 W: 13 03 b.Hemel Hempstead 19-5-93
Source: Scholar. *Honours:* Wales Youth, Under-21.
2010-11 Watford 0 0
2011-12 Watford 1 0 **1 0**
2011-12 *Dagenham & R* 5 0 **5 0**
2011-12 *Bury* 6 0 **6 0**

BONHAM, Jack (G) **0 0**
b.Stevenage 14-9-93
Source: Scholar. *Honours:* Eire Youth.
2010-11 Watford 0 0
2011-12 Watford 0 0

BRYAN, Michael (M) **20 0**
H: 5 8 W: 10 00 b.Hayes 21-2-90
Honours: Northern Ireland Under-21, 2 full caps.
2008-09 Watford 0 0
2009-10 Watford 7 0
2010-11 Watford 5 0
2011-12 Watford 0 0 **12 0**
2011-12 *Bradford C* 8 0 **8 0**

BUABEN, Prince (M) **129 8**
H: 6 0 W: 11 09 b.Akosombo 23-4-88
Honours: Ghana 2 full caps.
2007-08 Dundee U 24 3
2008-09 Dundee U 22 1
2009-10 Dundee U 34 2
2010-11 Dundee U 19 1 **99 7**
2011-12 Watford 30 1 **30 1**

CONNOLLY, Kyle (D) **0 0**
b.Watford 18-7-94
Source: Youth.
2011-12 Watford 0 0

DEENEY, Troy (F) **202 41**
H: 5 11 W: 12 00 b.Solihull 29-6-88
Source: Chelmsley T.
2006-07 Walsall 1 0
2007-08 Walsall 35 1
2008-09 Walsall 45 12
2009-10 Walsall 42 14 **123 27**
2010-11 Watford 36 3
2011-12 Watford 43 11 **79 14**

DICKINSON, Carl (D) **168 3**
H: 6 1 W: 12 04 b.Swadlincote 31-3-87
Source: Scholar.
2004-05 Stoke C 1 0
2005-06 Stoke C 5 0
2006-07 Stoke C 13 0
2006-07 *Blackpool* 7 0 **7 0**
2007-08 Stoke C 27 0
2008-09 Stoke C 5 0
2008-09 *Leeds U* 7 0 **7 0**
2009-10 Stoke C 0 0
2009-10 *Barnsley* 28 1 **28 1**
2010-11 Stoke C 0 0 **51 0**
2010-11 *Portsmouth* 36 0 **36 0**
2011-12 Watford 39 2 **39 2**

DOYLEY, Lloyd (D) **331 1**
H: 5 10 W: 12 13 b.Whitechapel 1-12-82
Source: Scholar.
2000-01 Watford 0 0
2001-02 Watford 20 0
2002-03 Watford 22 0
2003-04 Watford 9 0
2004-05 Watford 29 0
2005-06 Watford 44 0
2006-07 Watford 21 0
2007-08 Watford 36 0
2008-09 Watford 37 0
2009-10 Watford 44 1
2010-11 Watford 36 0
2011-12 Watford 33 0 **331 1**

EUSTACE, John (M) **341 30**
H: 5 11 W: 11 12 b.Solihull 3-11-79
Source: Trainee.
1996-97 Coventry C 0 0
1997-98 Coventry C 0 0
1998-99 Coventry C 0 0
1998-99 Dundee U 11 1 **11 1**
1999-2000 Coventry C 16 1
2000-01 Coventry C 32 2
2001-02 Coventry C 6 0
2002-03 Coventry C 32 4 **86 7**
2002-03 *Middlesbrough* 1 0 **1 0**
2003-04 Stoke C 26 5
2004-05 Stoke C 7 0
2005-06 Stoke C 0 0
2006-07 Stoke C 15 0
2006-07 *Hereford U* 8 0 **8 0**
2007-08 Stoke C 26 0 **74 5**
2007-08 Watford 13 0
2008-09 Watford 17 2
2008-09 *Derby Co* 9 1 **9 1**
2009-10 Watford 42 4
2010-11 Watford 41 6
2011-12 Watford 39 4 **152 16**

FORSYTH, Craig (M) **114 15**
H: 6 0 W: 12 00 b.Carnoustie 24-2-89
2006-07 Dundee 1 0
2007-08 Dundee 0 0
2007-08 *Montrose* 9 0 **9 0**
2008-09 Dundee 1 0
2008-09 *Arbroath* 26 2 **26 2**
2009-10 Dundee 24 2
2010-11 Dundee 33 8 **59 10**
2011-12 Watford 20 3 **20 3**

GARNER, Joe (F) **153 35**
H: 5 10 W: 11 02 b.Blackburn 12-4-88
Source: Scholar. *Honours:* England Schools, Youth.
2004-05 Blackburn R 0 0
2005-06 Blackburn R 0 0
2006-07 Blackburn R 0 0
2006-07 *Carlisle U* 18 5
2007-08 Carlisle U 31 14 **49 19**
2008-09 Nottingham F 28 7
2009-10 Nottingham F 18 2
2010-11 Nottingham F 0 0
2010-11 *Huddersfield T* 16 0 **16 0**
2010-11 *Scunthorpe U* 18 6 **18 6**
2011-12 Nottingham F 2 0 **48 9**
2011-12 Watford 22 1 **22 1**

GILMARTIN, Rene (G) **51 0**
H: 6 5 W: 13 06 b.Dublin 31-5-87
Source: St Patrick's BC. *Honours:* Eire Youth, Under-21.
2005-06 Walsall 2 0
2006-07 Walsall 0 0
2007-08 Walsall 0 0
2008-09 Walsall 11 0
2009-10 Walsall 22 0 **35 0**
2010-11 Watford 0 0
2011-12 Watford 2 0 **2 0**
2011-12 *Yeovil T* 8 0 **8 0**
2011-12 *Crawley T* 6 0 **6 0**

HOBAN, Tommie (D) **1 0**
H: 6 2 W: 11 13 b.Walthamstow 24-1-94
Source: Scholar. *Honours:* Eire Youth.
2010-11 Watford 1 0
2011-12 Watford 0 0 **1 0**

HODSON, Lee (D) **81 1**
H: 5 11 W: 11 02 b.Boreham Wood 2-10-91
Source: Scholar. *Honours:* Northern Ireland Under-21, 8 full caps.
2008-09 Watford 1 0
2009-10 Watford 31 0
2010-11 Watford 29 1
2011-12 Watford 20 0 **81 1**

HOGG, Jonathan (M) **69 1**
H: 5 7 W: 10 05 b.Middlesbrough 6-12-88
Source: Scholar.
2007-08 Aston Villa 0 0
2008-09 Aston Villa 0 0
2009-10 Aston Villa 0 0
2009-10 *Darlington* 5 1 **5 1**
2010-11 Aston Villa 5 0
2010-11 *Portsmouth* 19 0 **19 0**
2011-12 Aston Villa 0 0 **5 0**
2011-12 Watford 40 0 **40 0**

ISAAC, Chez (M) **0 0**
b.Hatfield 16-11-92
Source: Scholar.
2011-12 Watford 0 0

IWELUMO, Chris (F) **447 103**
H: 6 3 W: 15 03 b.Coatbridge 1-8-78
Source: Juniors. *Honours:* Scotland B, 4 full caps.
1996-97 St Mirren 14 0
1997-98 St Mirren 12 0 **26 0**
1998-99 Aarhus Fremad 27 4 **27 4**
1999-2000 Stoke C 3 0
2000-01 Stoke C 2 1
2000-01 *York C* 12 2 **12 2**
2000-01 *Cheltenham T* 4 1 **4 1**
2001-02 Stoke C 38 10
2002-03 Stoke C 32 5
2003-04 Stoke C 9 0 **84 16**
2003-04 Brighton & HA 10 4 **10 4**
2004-05 Aachen 9 0 **9 0**
2005-06 Colchester U 46 17
2006-07 Colchester U 46 18 **92 35**
2007-08 Charlton Ath 46 10 **46 10**
2008-09 Wolverhampton W 31 14
2009-10 Wolverhampton W 15 0 **46 14**
2009-10 *Bristol C* 7 2 **7 2**
2010-11 Burnley 45 11 **45 11**
2011-12 Watford 39 4 **39 4**

JAMES, Tom (D) **0 0**
b.Leamington 19-11-88
Source: Stratford T.
2011-12 Watford 0 0

JENKINS, Ross (M) **81 2**
H: 5 11 W: 12 06 b.Watford 9-11-90
Source: Scholar. *Honours:* England Under-20.
2008-09 Watford 29 1
2009-10 Watford 24 0
2010-11 Watford 19 1
2011-12 Watford 9 0 **81 2**

LOACH, Scott (G) **176 0**
H: 6 1 W: 13 01 b.Nottingham 27-5-88
Source: Lincoln C Scholar. *Honours:* England Under-21.
2006-07 Watford 0 0
2007-08 Watford 0 0
2007-08 *Morecambe* 2 0 **2 0**
2007-08 *Bradford C* 20 0 **20 0**
2008-09 Watford 31 0
2009-10 Watford 46 0
2010-11 Watford 46 0
2011-12 Watford 31 0 **154 0**

MARIAPPA, Adrian (D) **216 4**
H: 5 10 W: 11 12 b.Harrow 3-10-86
Source: Scholar. *Honours:* Jamaica 3 full caps.
2005-06 Watford 3 0
2006-07 Watford 19 0
2007-08 Watford 25 0
2008-09 Watford 39 1
2009-10 Watford 46 1
2010-11 Watford 45 1
2011-12 Watford 39 1 **216 4**

MASSEY, Gavin (F) **31 3**
H: 5 11 W: 11 06 b.Watford 14-10-92
Source: Scholar.
2009-10 Watford 1 0
2010-11 Watford 3 0
2011-12 Watford 3 0 **7 0**
2011-12 *Yeovil T* 16 3 **16 3**
2011-12 *Colchester U* 8 0 **8 0**

McGINN, Stephen (M) **111 9**
H: 5 9 W: 10 01 b.Glasgow 2-12-88
Honours: Scotland Under-21.
2006-07 St Mirren 4 1
2007-08 St Mirren 25 2
2008-09 St Mirren 26 1
2009-10 St Mirren 18 3 **73 7**
2009-10 Watford 9 0
2010-11 Watford 29 2
2011-12 Watford 0 0 **38 2**

MENSAH, Bernard (F) **0 0**
b.Hounslow 29-12-94
Source: Scholar.
2011-12 Watford 0 0

MINGOIA, Piero (M) 5 0
H: 5 6 W: 10 12 b.Enfield 20-10-91
Source: Scholar.
2010-11 Watford 5 0
2011-12 Watford 0 0 **5 0**
2011-12 *Brentford* 0 0

MIRFIN, David (D) 277 14
H: 6 3 W: 13 00 b.Sheffield 18-4-85
Source: Scholar.
2002-03 Huddersfield T 1 0
2003-04 Huddersfield T 21 2
2004-05 Huddersfield T 41 4
2005-06 Huddersfield T 31 1
2006-07 Huddersfield T 38 1
2007-08 Huddersfield T 29 1 **161 9**
2008-09 Scunthorpe U 33 0
2009-10 Scunthorpe U 37 1
2010-11 Scunthorpe U 23 3
2011-12 Watford 4 0 **4 0**
2011-12 *Scunthorpe U* 19 1 **112 5**

MURRAY, Sean (M) 20 7
H: 5 9 W: 10 10 b.Abbots Langley 11-10-93
Source: Scholar. *Honours:* Eire Youth.
2010-11 Watford 2 0
2011-12 Watford 18 7 **20 7**

NOSWORTHY, Nyron (D) 371 7
H: 6 0 W: 12 08 b.Brixton 11-10-80
Source: Trainee. *Honours:* Jamaica 3 full caps.
1998-99 Gillingham 3 0
1999-2000 Gillingham 29 1
2000-01 Gillingham 10 0
2001-02 Gillingham 29 0
2002-03 Gillingham 39 2
2003-04 Gillingham 27 2
2004-05 Gillingham 37 0 **174 5**
2005-06 Sunderland 30 0
2006-07 Sunderland 29 0
2007-08 Sunderland 29 0
2008-09 Sunderland 16 0
2009-10 Sunderland 10 0
2009-10 *Sheffield U* 19 0
2010-11 Sunderland 0 0
2010-11 *Sheffield U* 32 0 **51 0**
2011-12 Sunderland 0 0 **114 0**
2011-12 Watford 32 2 **32 2**

TAYLOR, Martin (D) 293 17
H: 6 4 W: 15 00 b.Ashington 9-11-79
Source: Trainee. *Honours:* England Youth, Under-21.
1997-98 Blackburn R 0 0
1998-99 Blackburn R 3 0
1999-2000 Blackburn R 6 0
1999-2000 *Darlington* 4 0 **4 0**
1999-2000 *Stockport Co* 7 0 **7 0**
2000-01 Blackburn R 16 3
2001-02 Blackburn R 19 0
2002-03 Blackburn R 33 2
2003-04 Blackburn R 11 0 **88 5**
2003-04 Birmingham C 12 1
2004-05 Birmingham C 7 0
2005-06 Birmingham C 21 0
2006-07 Birmingham C 31 0
2007-08 Birmingham C 4 0
2007-08 *Norwich C* 8 1 **8 1**
2008-09 Birmingham C 24 1
2009-10 Birmingham C 0 0 **99 2**
2009-10 Watford 19 2
2010-11 Watford 46 6
2011-12 Watford 22 1 **87 9**

THOMPSON, Adam (D) 30 1
H: 6 2 W: 12 10 b.Harlow 28-9-92
Source: Scholar. *Honours:* Northern Ireland Under-21, 2 full caps.
2010-11 Watford 10 1
2011-12 Watford 0 0 **10 1**
2011-12 *Brentford* 20 0 **20 0**

WALKER, Josh (M) 89 7
H: 5 11 W: 11 13 b.Newcastle 21-2-89
Source: Scholar. *Honours:* England Schools, Youth, Under-20.
2005-06 Middlesbrough 1 0
2006-07 Middlesbrough 0 0
2006-07 *Bournemouth* 6 0 **6 0**
2007-08 *Aberdeen* 8 0 **8 0**
2007-08 Middlesbrough 0 0
2008-09 Middlesbrough 6 0
2009-10 Middlesbrough 1 0 **8 0**
2009-10 *Northampton T* 3 0
2009-10 *Rotherham U* 15 3 **15 3**
2010-11 Watford 5 0
2010-11 *Stevenage* 1 0
2010-11 *Northampton T* 19 0 **22 0**
2011-12 Watford 1 0 **6 0**
2011-12 *Stevenage* 5 1 **6 1**
2011-12 *Scunthorpe U* 18 3 **18 3**

WHICHELOW, Matt (M) 27 4
H: 5 7 W: 11 10 b.Islington 28-9-91
Source: Scholar.
2010-11 Watford 19 3
2011-12 Watford 2 0 **21 3**
2011-12 *Exeter C* 2 0 **2 0**
2011-12 *Wycombe W* 4 1 **4 1**

YEATES, Mark (F) 253 37
H: 5 8 W: 13 03 b.Dublin 11-1-85
Source: Trainee. *Honours:* Eire Youth, Under-21.
2002-03 Tottenham H 0 0
2003-04 Tottenham H 1 0
2003-04 *Brighton & HA* 9 0 **9 0**
2004-05 Tottenham H 2 0
2004-05 *Swindon T* 4 0 **4 0**
2005-06 Tottenham H 0 0
2005-06 *Colchester U* 44 5
2006-07 Tottenham H 0 0 **3 0**
2006-07 *Hull C* 5 0 **5 0**
2006-07 *Leicester C* 9 1 **9 1**
2007-08 Colchester U 29 8
2008-09 Colchester U 43 12 **116 25**
2009-10 Middlesbrough 19 1 **19 1**
2009-10 Sheffield U 20 2
2010-11 Sheffield U 35 5 **55 7**
2011-12 Watford 33 3 **33 3**

WBA (87)

ALLAN, Scott (M) 27 2
H: 5 9 W: 11 00 b.Glasgow 28-11-91
Honours: Scotland Youth, Under-21.
2010-11 Dundee U 0 0
2010-11 *Forfar Ath* 4 1 **4 1**
2011-12 Dundee U 8 0 **8 0**
2011-12 WBA 0 0
2011-12 *Portsmouth* 15 1 **15 1**

ANDREWS, Keith (M) 304 37
H: 6 0 W: 12 04 b.Dublin 13-9-80
Source: Trainee. *Honours:* Eire Youth, 32 full caps, 3 goals.
1997-98 Wolverhampton W 0 0
1998-99 Wolverhampton W 0 0
1999-2000 Wolverhampton W 2 0
2000-01 Wolverhampton W 22 0
2000-01 *Oxford U* 4 1 **4 1**
2001-02 Wolverhampton W 11 0
2002-03 Wolverhampton W 9 0
2003-04 Wolverhampton W 1 0
2003-04 *Stoke C* 16 0 **16 0**
2003-04 *Walsall* 10 2 **10 2**
2004-05 Wolverhampton W 20 0 **65 0**
2005-06 Hull C 26 0
2006-07 Hull C 3 0 **29 0**
2006-07 Milton Keynes D 34 6
2007-08 Milton Keynes D 41 12
2008-09 Milton Keynes D 1 0 **76 18**
2008-09 Blackburn R 33 4
2009-10 Blackburn R 32 1
2010-11 Blackburn R 5 0
2011-12 Blackburn R 0 0 **70 5**
2011-12 *Ipswich T* 20 9 **20 9**
2011-12 WBA 14 2 **14 2**

BERAHINO, Saido (F) 22 10
H: 5 10 W: 11 13 b.Burundi 4-8-93
Source: Scholar. *Honours:* England Youth, Under-20.
2010-11 WBA 0 0
2011-12 WBA 0 0
2011-12 *Northampton T* 14 6 **14 6**
2011-12 *Brentford* 8 4 **8 4**

BROWN, Kayleden (M) 11 0
H: 6 2 W: 12 08 b.Derry 15-4-92
Source: Scholar. *Honours:* Wales Youth.
2010-11 WBA 0 0
2010-11 *Tranmere R* 4 0 **4 0**
2010-11 *Dagenham & R* 3 0 **3 0**
2010-11 *Port Vale* 4 0 **4 0**
2011-12 WBA 0 0

BRUNT, Chris (M) 311 55
H: 6 1 W: 13 04 b.Belfast 14-12-84
Source: Trainee. *Honours:* Northern Ireland Under-21, Under-23, 36 full caps, 1 goal.
2002-03 Middlesbrough 0 0
2003-04 Middlesbrough 0 0
2003-04 Sheffield W 9 2
2004-05 Sheffield W 42 4
2005-06 Sheffield W 44 7
2006-07 Sheffield W 44 11
2007-08 Sheffield W 1 0 **140 24**
2007-08 WBA 34 4
2008-09 WBA 34 8
2009-10 WBA 40 13
2010-11 WBA 34 4
2011-12 WBA 29 2 **171 31**

COX, Simon (F) 169 57
H: 5 10 W: 10 12 b.Reading 28-4-87
Source: Scholar. *Honours:* Eire 15 full caps, 3 goals.
2005-06 Reading 2 0
2006-07 Reading 0 0
2006-07 *Brentford* 13 0 **13 0**
2006-07 *Northampton T* 8 3 **8 3**
2007-08 Reading 0 0 **2 0**
2007-08 Swindon T 36 15
2008-09 Swindon T 45 29 **81 44**
2009-10 WBA 28 9
2010-11 WBA 19 1
2011-12 WBA 18 0 **65 10**

DANIELS, Donervorn (D) 0 0
b.Montserrat 24-11-93
Source: Scholar.
2011-12 WBA 0 0

DANIELS, Luke (G) 96 0
H: 6 1 W: 12 10 b.Bolton 5-1-88
Source: Manchester U Scholar. *Honours:* England Youth.
2006-07 WBA 0 0
2007-08 *Motherwell* 2 0 **2 0**
2007-08 WBA 0 0
2008-09 WBA 0 0
2008-09 *Shrewsbury T* 38 0 **38 0**
2009-10 WBA 0 0
2009-10 *Tranmere R* 37 0 **37 0**
2010-11 WBA 0 0
2010-11 *Charlton Ath* 0 0
2010-11 *Rochdale* 1 0 **1 0**
2010-11 *Bristol R* 9 0 **9 0**
2011-12 WBA 0 0
2011-12 *Southend U* 9 0 **9 0**

DAWSON, Craig (D) 95 19
H: 6 0 W: 12 04 b.Rochdale 6-5-90
Source: Radcliffe B. *Honours:* England Under-21.
2008-09 Rochdale 0 0
2009-10 Rochdale 42 9
2010-11 WBA 0 0
2010-11 *Rochdale* 45 10 **87 19**
2011-12 WBA 8 0 **8 0**

DORRANS, Graham (F) 196 38
H: 5 9 W: 11 07 b.Glasgow 5-5-87
Honours: Scotland Youth, Under-21, 8 full caps.
2006-07 Livingston 8 0
2006-07 *Partick T* 15 5 **15 5**
2006-07 Livingston 34 5
2007-08 Livingston 34 11 **76 16**
2008-09 WBA 8 0
2009-10 WBA 45 13
2010-11 WBA 21 1
2011-12 WBA 31 3 **105 17**

DOWNING, Paul (D) 32 0
H: 6 1 W: 12 06 b.Taunton 26-10-91
Source: Scholar.
2009-10 WBA 0 0
2009-10 *Hereford U* 6 0
2010-11 WBA 0 0
2010-11 *Hereford U* 0 0 **6 0**
2010-11 *Swansea C* 0 0
2011-12 WBA 0 0
2011-12 *Barnet* 26 0 **26 0**

EDGE, Jamie (M) 0 0
b.Cheltenham 9-9-93
Source: Scholar.
2010-11 Arsenal 0 0
2011-12 Arsenal 0 0
2011-12 WBA 0 0

ELFORD-ALLIYU, Lateef (F) **34 7**
H: 5 8 W: 10 12 b.Ibadan 1-6-92
Source: Scholar.

2009-10	WBA	0	0		
2009-10	*Hereford U*	1	0	**1**	**0**
2010-11	WBA	0	0		
2010-11	*Tranmere R*	16	5		
2011-12	WBA	0	0		
2011-12	*Tranmere R*	4	0	**20**	**5**
2011-12	*Bury*	13	2	**13**	**2**

FORTUNE, Marc-Antoine (F) **358 74**
H: 6 0 W: 11 13 b.Cayenne 2-7-81

2000-01	Angouleme	18	3		
2001-02	Angouleme	36	12	**54**	**15**
2002-03	Nancy	19	1		
2002-03	Lille	15	0	**15**	**0**
2003-04	Rouen	34	10	**34**	**10**
2004-05	Brest	33	10	**33**	**10**
2005-06	Utrecht	31	6		
2006-07	Utrecht	22	5	**53**	**11**
2006-07	Nancy	15	5		
2007-08	Nancy	37	6		
2008-09	Nancy	19	1	**90**	**13**
2009-10	Celtic	30	10		
2010-11	Celtic	2	0	**32**	**10**
2010-11	WBA	25	2		
2011-12	WBA	17	2	**42**	**4**
2011-12	*Doncaster R*	5	1	**5**	**1**

FULOP, Marton (G) **146 0**
H: 6 6 W: 14 07 b.Budapest 3-5-83
Source: MTK, Elore, Bodajk. *Honours:* Hungary Under-21, 24 full caps.

2004-05	Tottenham H	0	0		
2004-05	*Chesterfield*	7	0	**7**	**0**
2005-06	Tottenham H	0	0		
2005-06	*Coventry C*	31	0	**31**	**0**
2006-07	Tottenham H	0	0		
2006-07	Sunderland	5	0		
2007-08	Sunderland	1	0		
2007-08	*Leicester C*	24	0	**24**	**0**
2007-08	*Stoke C*	0	0		
2008-09	Sunderland	26	0		
2009-10	Sunderland	13	0	**45**	**0**
2009-10	*Manchester C*	3	0	**3**	**0**
2010-11	Ipswich T	35	0	**35**	**0**
2011-12	WBA	1	0	**1**	**0**

GAYLE, Cameron (D) **0 0**
H: 5 11 W: 11 00 b.Birmingham 22-11-92
Source: Scholar.

2010-11	WBA	0	0
2011-12	WBA	0	0

GERA, Zoltan (M) **355 62**
H: 6 0 W: 11 11 b.Pecs 22-4-79
Source: Hakarny. *Honours:* Hungary 73 full caps, 21 goals.

1999-2000	Pecsi	15	4	**15**	**4**
2000-01	Ferencvaros	32	7		
2001-02	Ferencvaros	27	8		
2002-03	Ferencvaros	26	6		
2003-04	Ferencvaros	30	11	**115**	**32**
2004-05	WBA	38	6		
2005-06	WBA	15	2		
2006-07	WBA	40	5		
2007-08	WBA	43	8		
2008-09	Fulham	32	2		
2009-10	Fulham	27	2		
2010-11	Fulham	27	1	**86**	**5**
2011-12	WBA	3	0	**139**	**21**

HURST, James (D) **20 0**
H: 5 8 W: 11 11 b.Sutton Coldfield 31-1-92
Source: Scholar. *Honours:* England Youth, Under-20.

2008-09	Portsmouth	0	0		
2009-10	Portsmouth	0	0		
2010-11	Portsmouth	0	0		
2010-11	WBA	1	0		
2011-12	WBA	0	0	**1**	**0**
2011-12	*Blackpool*	2	0	**2**	**0**
2011-12	*Shrewsbury T*	7	0	**7**	**0**
2011-12	*Chesterfield*	10	0	**10**	**0**

JARA, Gonzalo (D) **202 5**
H: 5 10 W: 12 02 b.Chile 29-8-85
Honours: Chile 51 full caps, 3 goals.

2002	Huachipato	0	0		
2003	Huachipato	17	1		
2004	Huachipato	11	0		
2005	Huachipato	23	0		
2006	Huachipato	18	1	**69**	**2**
2007	Colo Colo	23	1		
2008	Colo Colo	25	0		
2009	Colo Colo	16	0	**64**	**1**
2009-10	WBA	22	1		
2010-11	WBA	29	1		
2011-12	WBA	4	0	**55**	**2**
2011-12	*Brighton & HA*	14	0	**14**	**0**

JONES, Billy (M) **310 21**
H: 5 11 W: 13 00 b.Shrewsbury 24-3-87
Source: Scholar. *Honours:* England Youth, Under-20.

2003-04	Crewe Alex	27	1		
2004-05	Crewe Alex	20	0		
2005-06	Crewe Alex	44	6		
2006-07	Crewe Alex	41	1	**132**	**8**
2007-08	Preston NE	29	0		
2008-09	Preston NE	44	3		
2009-10	Preston NE	44	4		
2010-11	Preston NE	43	6	**160**	**13**
2011-12	WBA	18	0	**18**	**0**

LONG, Shane (F) **207 52**
H: 5 10 W: 11 02 b.Co. Tipperary 22-1-87
Honours: Eire Youth, B, Under-21, 27 full caps, 7 goals.

2005	Cork C	1	0	**1**	**0**
2005-06	Reading	11	3		
2006-07	Reading	21	2		
2007-08	Reading	29	3		
2008-09	Reading	37	9		
2009-10	Reading	31	6		
2010-11	Reading	44	21		
2011-12	Reading	1	0	**174**	**44**
2011-12	WBA	32	8	**32**	**8**

MANTOM, Sam (M) **19 3**
H: 5 9 W: 11 00 b.Stourbridge 20-2-92
Source: Scholar.

2010-11	WBA	0	0		
2010-11	*Tranmere R*	2	0	**2**	**0**
2010-11	*Oldham Ath*	4	0	**4**	**0**
2011-12	WBA	0	0		
2011-12	*Walsall*	13	3	**13**	**3**

MATTOCK, Joe (D) **130 2**
H: 5 11 W: 12 05 b.Leicester 15-5-90
Source: Scholar. *Honours:* England Youth, Under-21.

2006-07	Leicester C	4	0		
2007-08	Leicester C	31	0		
2008-09	Leicester C	31	1		
2009-10	Leicester C	0	0	**66**	**1**
2009-10	WBA	29	0		
2010-11	WBA	0	0		
2010-11	*Sheffield U*	13	0	**13**	**0**
2011-12	WBA	0	0	**29**	**0**
2011-12	*Portsmouth*	7	0	**7**	**0**
2011-12	*Brighton & HA*	15	1	**15**	**1**

McAULEY, Gareth (D) **293 22**
H: 6 3 W: 13 00 b.Larne 5-12-79
Source: Coleraine. *Honours:* Northern Ireland Schools, B, 36 full caps, 2 goals.

2004-05	Lincoln C	37	3		
2005-06	Lincoln C	35	5	**72**	**8**
2006-07	Leicester C	30	3		
2007-08	Leicester C	44	2	**74**	**5**
2008-09	Ipswich T	35	0		
2009-10	Ipswich T	41	5		
2010-11	Ipswich T	39	2	**115**	**7**
2011-12	WBA	32	2	**32**	**2**

MORRISON, James (M) **204 20**
H: 5 10 W: 10 06 b.Darlington 25-5-86
Source: Trainee. *Honours:* England Youth, Under-20. Scotland 20 full caps, 1 goal.

2003-04	Middlesbrough	1	0		
2004-05	Middlesbrough	14	0		
2005-06	Middlesbrough	24	1		
2006-07	Middlesbrough	28	2	**67**	**3**
2007-08	WBA	35	4		
2008-09	WBA	30	3		
2009-10	WBA	11	1		
2010-11	WBA	31	4		
2011-12	WBA	30	5	**137**	**17**

MULUMBU, Youssef (M) **151 12**
H: 5 9 W: 10 03 b.Kinshasa 25-1-87
Honours: France Youth, Under-21. DR Congo 12 full caps.

2006-07	Paris St Germain	12	0		
2007-08	Paris St Germain	1	0		
2007-08	*Amiens*	23	1	**23**	**1**
2008-09	Paris St Germain	0	0	**13**	**0**
2008-09	WBA	6	0		
2009-10	WBA	40	3		
2010-11	WBA	34	7		
2011-12	WBA	35	1	**115**	**11**

MYHILL, Boaz (G) **324 0**
H: 6 3 W: 14 06 b.California 9-11-82
Source: Scholar. *Honours:* England Youth, Under-20. Wales 10 full caps.

2000-01	Aston Villa	0	0		
2001-02	Aston Villa	0	0		
2001-02	*Stoke C*	0	0		
2002-03	Aston Villa	0	0		
2002-03	*Bristol C*	0	0		
2002-03	*Bradford C*	2	0	**2**	**0**
2003-04	Aston Villa	0	0		
2003-04	*Macclesfield T*	15	0	**15**	**0**
2003-04	*Stockport Co*	2	0	**2**	**0**
2003-04	Hull C	23	0		
2004-05	Hull C	45	0		
2005-06	Hull C	45	0		
2006-07	Hull C	46	0		
2007-08	Hull C	43	0		
2008-09	Hull C	28	0		
2009-10	Hull C	27	0	**257**	**0**
2010-11	WBA	6	0		
2011-12	WBA	0	0	**6**	**0**
2011-12	*Birmingham C*	42	0	**42**	**0**

NABI, Adil (F) **0 0**
H: 5 9 W: 10 10 b.Birmingham 28-2-94
Source: Scholar.

2010-11	WBA	0	0
2011-12	WBA	0	0

O'NEIL, Liam (D) **14 0**
b.Cambridge 31-7-93
Source: Histon.

2011-12	WBA	0	0		
2011-12	*VPS*	14	0	**14**	**0**

ODEMWINGIE, Peter (F) **256 78**
H: 6 0 W: 11 09 b.Tashkent 15-7-81
Honours: Nigeria 55 full caps, 9 goals.

2002-03	La Louviere	14	2		
2003-04	La Louviere	27	5		
2004-05	La Louviere	3	2	**44**	**9**
2004-05	Lille	20	4		
2005-06	Lille	26	14		
2006-07	Lille	29	5	**75**	**23**
2007	Lok Moscow	14	4		
2008	Lok Moscow	26	10		
2009	Lok Moscow	25	7		
2010	Lok Moscow	10	0	**75**	**21**
2010-11	WBA	32	15		
2011-12	WBA	30	10	**62**	**25**

OLSSON, Jonas (D) **277 15**
H: 6 4 W: 12 08 b.Landskrona 10-3-83
Honours: Sweden Under-21, 10 full caps.

2002	Landskrona	0	0		
2003	Landskrona	22	0		
2004	Landskrona	22	1		
2005	Landskrona	12	0	**56**	**1**
2005-06	NEC Nijmegen	34	0		
2006-07	NEC Nijmegen	32	2		
2007-08	NEC Nijmegen	27	3	**93**	**5**
2008-09	WBA	28	2		
2009-10	WBA	43	4		
2010-11	WBA	24	1		
2011-12	WBA	33	2	**128**	**9**

REID, Steven (M) **309 27**
H: 6 0 W: 12 07 b.Kingston 10-3-81
Source: Trainee. *Honours:* England Youth. Eire Under-21, 23 full caps, 2 goals.

1997-98	Millwall	1	0		
1998-99	Millwall	25	0		
1999-2000	Millwall	21	0		
2000-01	Millwall	37	7		
2001-02	Millwall	35	5		
2002-03	Millwall	20	6	**139**	**18**
2003-04	Blackburn R	16	0		
2004-05	Blackburn R	28	2		
2005-06	Blackburn R	34	4		
2006-07	Blackburn R	3	0		
2007-08	Blackburn R	24	0		
2008-09	Blackburn R	4	0		
2009-10	Blackburn R	4	0	**113**	**6**
2009-10	*QPR*	2	0	**2**	**0**
2009-10	*WBA*	10	1		
2010-11	WBA	23	1		
2011-12	WBA	22	1	**55**	**3**

RIDGEWELL, Liam (D) **249 16**
H: 5 10 W: 10 03 b.Bexley 21-7-84
Source: Scholar. *Honours:* England Youth, Under-20, Under-21.

2001-02	Aston Villa	0	0		
2002-03	Aston Villa	0	0		
2002-03	*Bournemouth*	5	0	**5**	**0**
2003-04	Aston Villa	11	0		
2004-05	Aston Villa	15	0		
2005-06	Aston Villa	32	5		
2006-07	Aston Villa	21	1	**79**	**6**
2007-08	Birmingham C	35	1		
2008-09	Birmingham C	36	1		
2009-10	Birmingham C	31	3		
2010-11	Birmingham C	36	4		
2011-12	Birmingham C	14	0	**152**	**9**
2011-12	WBA	13	1	**13**	**1**

ROOFE, Kemar (M) **0 0**
b.Walsall 6-1-93
Source: Scholar.

2011-12	WBA	0	0

SAWYERS, Romaine (M) **8 0**
H: 5 9 W: 11 00 b.Birmingham 2-11-91
Source: Scholar.

2009-10	WBA	0	0		
2010-11	WBA	0	0		
2010-11	*Port Vale*	1	0	**1**	**0**
2011-12	WBA	0	0		
2011-12	*Shrewsbury T*	7	0	**7**	**0**

SCHARNER, Paul (D) **341 34**
H: 6 3 W: 12 09 b.Scheibbs 11-3-80
Source: St Polten. *Honours:* Austria Youth, Under-21, 39 full caps.

1998-99	FK Austria	4	0		
1999-2000	FK Austria	12	0		
2000-01	FK Austria	14	0		
2001-02	FK Austria	16	1		
2002-03	FK Austria	29	1		
2003-04	FK Austria	9	1	**84**	**3**
2003-04	Salzburg	13	2		
2004	Brann	7	1		
2004-05	Salzburg	5	1	**18**	**3**
2005	Brann	25	6	**32**	**7**
2005-06	Wigan Ath	16	3		
2006-07	Wigan Ath	25	3		
2007-08	Wigan Ath	37	4		
2008-09	Wigan Ath	29	0		
2009-10	Wigan Ath	38	4		
2010-11	Wigan Ath	0	0	**145**	**14**
2010-11	WBA	33	4		
2011-12	WBA	29	3	**62**	**7**

SHOREY, Nicky (D) **377 12**
H: 5 9 W: 10 08 b.Romford 19-2-81
Source: Trainee. *Honours:* England B, 2 full caps.

1999-2000	Leyton Orient	7	0		
2000-01	Leyton Orient	8	0	**15**	**0**
2000-01	Reading	0	0		
2001-02	Reading	32	0		
2002-03	Reading	43	2		
2003-04	Reading	35	2		
2004-05	Reading	44	3		
2005-06	Reading	40	2		
2006-07	Reading	37	1		
2007-08	Reading	36	2	**267**	**12**
2008-09	Aston Villa	21	0		
2009-10	Aston Villa	3	0	**24**	**0**
2009-10	*Nottingham F*	9	0	**9**	**0**
2009-10	*Fulham*	9	0	**9**	**0**
2010-11	WBA	28	0		
2011-12	WBA	25	0	**53**	**0**

TAMAS, Gabriel (D) **251 12**
H: 6 2 W: 12 02 b.Brasov 9-11-83
Honours: Romania 57 full caps, 3 goals.

1998-99	Brasov	1	0		
1999-2000	Brasov	0	0	**1**	**0**
2000-01	Tractorul	15	1		
2001-02	Tractorul	19	2	**34**	**3**
2002-03	Din Bucharest	19	4		
2003-04	Galatasaray	6	0	**6**	**0**
2004	Spartak Moscow	14	0		
2004-05	Din Bucharest	13	0		
2005-06	Din Bucharest	14	1		
2006	Spartak Moscow	3	0	**17**	**0**
2006-07	Celta Vigo	29	0	**29**	**0**
2007-08	Auxerre	27	0	**27**	**0**
2008-09	Din Bucharest	22	0		
2009-10	Din Bucharest	12	2	**80**	**7**
2009-10	WBA	23	2		
2010-11	WBA	26	0		
2011-12	WBA	8	0	**57**	**2**

TCHOYI, Somen (M) **188 30**
H: 6 3 W: 13 10 b.Douala 29-3-83
Honours: Cameroon 15 full caps, 2 goals.

2005	Odd	22	1		
2006	Odd	8	0	**30**	**1**
2006	Stabaek	15	3		
2007	Stabaek	26	4		
2008	Stabaek	8	1	**49**	**8**
2008-09	Salzburg	32	6		
2009-10	Salzburg	36	8	**68**	**14**
2010-11	WBA	23	6		
2011-12	WBA	18	1	**41**	**7**

THOMAS, Jerome (M) **205 21**
H: 5 9 W: 11 09 b.Wembley 23-3-83
Source: Scholar. *Honours:* England Youth, Under-20, Under-21.

2001-02	Arsenal	0	0		
2001-02	*QPR*	4	1		
2002-03	Arsenal	0	0		
2002-03	*QPR*	6	2	**10**	**3**
2003-04	Arsenal	0	0		
2003-04	Charlton Ath	1	0		
2004-05	Charlton Ath	24	3		
2005-06	Charlton Ath	25	1		
2006-07	Charlton Ath	20	3		
2007-08	Charlton Ath	32	0		
2008-09	Charlton Ath	1	0	**103**	**7**
2008-09	Portsmouth	3	0		
2009-10	Portsmouth	0	0	**3**	**0**
2009-10	WBA	27	7		
2010-11	WBA	33	3		
2011-12	WBA	29	1	**89**	**11**

THORNE, George (M) **19 0**
H: 6 2 W: 13 01 b.Chatham 4-1-93
Source: Scholar. *Honours:* England Youth.

2009-10	WBA	1	0		
2010-11	WBA	1	0		
2011-12	WBA	3	0	**5**	**0**
2011-12	*Portsmouth*	14	0	**14**	**0**

WOOD, Chris (F) **99 21**
H: 6 3 W: 12 10 b.Auckland 7-12-91
Honours: New Zealand Youth, 23 full caps, 4 goals.

2008-09	WBA	2	0		
2009-10	WBA	18	1		
2010-11	WBA	1	0		
2010-11	*Barnsley*	7	0	**7**	**0**
2010-11	*Brighton & HA*	29	8	**29**	**8**
2011-12	WBA	0	0	**21**	**1**
2011-12	*Birmingham C*	23	9	**23**	**9**
2011-12	*Bristol C*	19	3	**19**	**3**

Scholars
Ambalu Joel; Atkinson Wesley; Birch Aaron; Francis Jordan; Garmston Bradley; Jones Alexander; Lewis Shane; McCalla Kieran; O'Sullivan Mani; Rose Jack Joseph; Winwood Ryan Stephen.

WEST HAM U (88)

ABDULLAH, Ahmad (F) **11 0**
H: 5 8 W: 10 01 b.Saudi Arabia 12-11-91
Source: Scholar.

2008-09	West Ham U	0	0		
2009-10	West Ham U	0	0		
2010-11	West Ham U	0	0		
2011-12	West Ham U	0	0		
2011-12	*Swindon T*	6	0	**6**	**0**
2011-12	*Dagenham & R*	5	0	**5**	**0**

BALDOCK, Sam (F) **123 38**
H: 5 7 W: 10 07 b.Buckingham 15-3-89
Source: Scholar. *Honours:* England Under-20.

2005-06	Milton Keynes D	0	0		
2006-07	Milton Keynes D	1	0		
2007-08	Milton Keynes D	5	0		
2008-09	Milton Keynes D	40	12		
2009-10	Milton Keynes D	20	5		
2010-11	Milton Keynes D	30	12		
2011-12	Milton Keynes D	4	4	**100**	**33**
2011-12	West Ham U	23	5	**23**	**5**

BARRERA, Pablo (M) **107 18**
H: 5 9 W: 10 03 b.Mexico City 21-6-87
Honours: Mexico Youth, 49 full caps, 6 goals.

2005-06	UNAM	1	0		
2006-07	UNAM	5	0		
2007-08	UNAM	24	4		
2008-09	UNAM	14	2		
2009-10	UNAM	28	11	**72**	**17**
2010-11	West Ham U	14	0		

On loan to Zaragoza.

2011-12	West Ham U	1	0	**15**	**0**
2011-12	*Zaragoza*	20	1	**20**	**1**

BOA MORTE, Luis (F) **335 47**
H: 5 9 W: 12 06 b.Lisbon 4-8-77
Source: Sporting Lisbon, Lourihanense (loan). *Honours:* Portugal Youth, Under-21, 28 full caps, 1 goal.

1997-98	Arsenal	15	0		
1998-99	Arsenal	8	0		
1999-2000	Arsenal	2	0	**25**	**0**
1999-2000	Southampton	14	1		
2000-01	Southampton	0	0	**14**	**1**
2000-01	*Fulham*	39	18		
2001-02	Fulham	23	1		
2002-03	Fulham	29	2		
2003-04	Fulham	33	9		
2004-05	Fulham	31	8		
2005-06	Fulham	35	6		
2006-07	Fulham	15	0	**205**	**44**
2006-07	West Ham U	14	1		
2007-08	West Ham U	27	0		
2008-09	West Ham U	27	0		
2009-10	West Ham U	1	1		
2010-11	West Ham U	22	0		
2011-12	West Ham U	0	0	**91**	**2**

CAREW, John (F) **356 123**
H: 6 5 W: 14 11 b.Oslo 5-9-79
Source: Lorenskog. *Honours:* Norway Youth, Under-21, 91 full caps, 24 goals.

1998	Valerenga	18	7		
1999	Valerenga	15	7	**33**	**14**
1999	Rosenborg	8	10		
2000	Rosenborg	10	8	**18**	**18**
2000-01	Valencia	37	11		
2001-02	Valencia	15	1		
2002-03	Valencia	32	8	**84**	**20**
2003-04	Roma	20	8	**20**	**8**
2004-05	Besiktas	24	13	**24**	**13**
2005-06	Lyon	26	9		
2006-07	Lyon	9	1	**35**	**10**
2006-07	Aston Villa	11	3		
2007-08	Aston Villa	32	13		
2008-09	Aston Villa	27	11		
2009-10	Aston Villa	33	10		
2010-11	Aston Villa	10	0	**113**	**37**
2010-11	*Stoke C*	10	1	**10**	**1**
2011-12	West Ham U	19	2	**19**	**2**

COLE, Carlton (F) **260 57**
H: 6 3 W: 14 02 b.Croydon 12-11-83
Source: Scholar. *Honours:* England Youth, Under-20, Under-21, 7 full caps.

2000-01	Chelsea	0	0		
2001-02	Chelsea	3	1		
2002-03	Chelsea	13	3		
2002-03	*Wolverhampton W*	7	1	**7**	**1**
2003-04	Chelsea	0	0		
2003-04	*Charlton Ath*	21	4	**21**	**4**
2004-05	Chelsea	0	0		
2004-05	*Aston Villa*	27	3	**27**	**3**
2005-06	Chelsea	9	0	**25**	**4**
2006-07	West Ham U	17	2		
2007-08	West Ham U	31	4		
2008-09	West Ham U	27	10		
2009-10	West Ham U	30	10		
2010-11	West Ham U	35	5		
2011-12	West Ham U	40	14	**180**	**45**

COLLISON, Jack (M) **78 9**
H: 6 0 W: 13 10 b.Watford 2-10-88
Source: Scholar. *Honours:* Wales Under-21, 11 full caps.

2007-08	West Ham U	2	0		
2008-09	West Ham U	20	3		
2009-10	West Ham U	22	2		
2010-11	West Ham U	3	0		
2011-12	West Ham U	31	4	**78**	**9**

DEMEL, Guy (D) **212 11**
H: 6 2 W: 13 12 b.Paris 13-6-81
Honours: Ivory Coast 35 full caps.

1999-2000	Nimes	1	0	**1**	**0**
2000-01	Arsenal	0	0		
2001-02	Bor Dortmund II	16	3		
2002-03	Bor Dortmund II	24	6	**40**	**9**
2002-03	Bor Dortmund	4	0		
2003-04	Bor Dortmund	13	0		
2004-05	Bor Dortmund	16	0	**33**	**0**

2005-06 Hamburg 22 1
2006-07 Hamburg 8 0
2007-08 Hamburg 26 0
2008-09 Hamburg 28 0
2009-10 Hamburg 26 1
2010-11 Hamburg 21 0 **131 2**
2011-12 West Ham U 7 0 **7 0**

DIOP, Papa Bouba (M) 258 25
H: 6 4 W: 14 12 b.Dakar 28-1-78
Source: Espoir, Jaraaf, Vevey Sports.
Honours: Senegal 63 full caps, 11 goals.
1999-2000 Neuchatel Xamax 0 0
2000-01 Neuchatel Xamax 18 4 **18 4**
2000-01 Grasshoppers 11 1
2001-02 Grasshoppers 18 4 **29 5**
2001-02 Lens 5 0
2002-03 Lens 16 3
2003-04 Lens 26 3 **47 6**
2004-05 Fulham 29 6
2005-06 Fulham 22 2
2006-07 Fulham 23 0
2007-08 Fulham 2 0 **76 8**
2007-08 Portsmouth 25 0
2008-09 Portsmouth 16 0
2009-10 Portsmouth 12 0 **53 0**
2010-11 AEK Athens 19 1 **19 1**
2011-12 West Ham U 16 1 **16 1**

DRIVER, Callum (D) 8 1
H: 5 8 W: 11 11 b.Sidcup 23-10-92
Source: Scholar.
2011-12 West Ham U 0 0
2011-12 *Burton Alb* 8 1 **8 1**

FANIMO, Matthias (M) 0 0
b.Lambeth 28-1-94
Source: Scholar. *Honours:* England Youth.
2011-12 West Ham U 0 0

FAUBERT, Julien (M) 246 15
H: 5 10 W: 11 08 b.Le Havre 1-8-83
Honours: France 1 full cap, 1 goal.
2002-03 Cannes 26 1
2003-04 Cannes 19 3 **45 4**
2004-05 Bordeaux 36 1
2005-06 Bordeaux 34 5
2006-07 Bordeaux 26 3 **96 9**
2007-08 West Ham U 7 0
2008-09 West Ham U 20 0
2008-09 *Real Madrid* 2 0 **2 0**
2009-10 West Ham U 33 1
2010-11 West Ham U 9 0
2011-12 West Ham U 34 1 **103 2**

FAYE, Aboulaye (M) 286 14
H: 6 2 W: 13 10 b.Dakar 26-2-78
Source: Ndiambour Louga. *Honours:* Senegal 35 full caps, 3 goals.
2001-02 Jeanne D'Arc 32 4 **32 4**
2002-03 Lens 15 0
2003-04 Lens 19 0 **34 0**
2004-05 Istres 28 0 **28 0**
2005-06 Bolton W 27 1
2006-07 Bolton W 32 2
2007-08 Bolton W 1 0 **60 3**
2007-08 Newcastle U 22 1 **22 1**
2008-09 Stoke C 36 3
2009-10 Stoke C 31 2
2010-11 Stoke C 14 1 **81 6**
2011-12 West Ham U 29 0 **29 0**

GREEN, Rob (G) 442 0
H: 6 3 W: 14 09 b.Chertsey 18-1-80
Source: Trainee. *Honours:* England Youth, B, 12 full caps.
1997-98 Norwich C 0 0
1998-99 Norwich C 2 0
1999-2000 Norwich C 3 0
2000-01 Norwich C 5 0
2001-02 Norwich C 41 0
2002-03 Norwich C 46 0
2003-04 Norwich C 46 0
2004-05 Norwich C 38 0
2005-06 Norwich C 42 0 **223 0**
2006-07 West Ham U 26 0
2007-08 West Ham U 38 0
2008-09 West Ham U 38 0
2009-10 West Ham U 38 0
2010-11 West Ham U 37 0
2011-12 West Ham U 42 0 **219 0**

HALL, Robert (F) 18 5
H: 6 2 W: 10 05 b.Aylesbury 20-10-93
Source: Academy. *Honours:* England Youth.
2010-11 West Ham U 0 0
2011-12 West Ham U 3 0 **3 0**
2011-12 *Oxford U* 13 5 **13 5**
2011-12 *Milton Keynes D* 2 0 **2 0**

ILUNGA, Herita (D) 255 2
H: 5 11 W: 11 09 b.Kinshasa 25-2-82
Honours: DR Congo 32 full caps, 1 goal.
2002-03 Espanyol B 0 0
2003-04 St Etienne 32 0
2004-05 St Etienne 37 1
2005-06 St Etienne 30 1
2006-07 St Etienne 36 0 **135 2**
2007-08 Toulouse 35 0 **35 0**
2008-09 West Ham U 35 0
2009-10 West Ham U 16 0
2010-11 West Ham U 11 0
2011-12 West Ham U 4 0 **66 0**
2011-12 *Doncaster R* 19 0 **19 0**

JOHN, George (D) 0 0
H: 6 3 W: 13 00 b.Washington 20-3-87
Source: Washington H.
2011-12 West Ham U 0 0
On loan from Dallas.

KURUCZ, Peter (G) 21 0
H: 6 2 W: 13 09 b.Budapest 30-5-88
Honours: Hungary Under-21.
2008-09 *Ujpest* 0 0
2008-09 *Tatabanya* 9 0 **9 0**
2009-10 West Ham U 1 0
2010-11 West Ham U 0 0
2011-12 West Ham U 0 0 **1 0**
2011-12 *Rochdale* 11 0 **11 0**

LARKINS, Jake (G) 0 0
b.Barking 11-1-94
Source: Scholar.
2010-11 West Ham U 0 0
2011-12 West Ham U 0 0

LEE, Elliot (F) 0 0
b.Co. Durham 16-12-94
Source: Scholar.
2011-12 West Ham U 0 0

LEE, Oliver (M) 29 3
H: 5 11 W: 12 07 b.Hornchurch 11-7-91
Source: Scholar.
2009-10 West Ham U 0 0
2010-11 West Ham U 0 0
2010-11 *Dagenham & R* 5 0
2011-12 West Ham U 0 0
2011-12 *Dagenham & R* 16 3 **21 3**
2011-12 *Gillingham* 8 0 **8 0**

LLETGET, Sebastian (M) 0 0
H: 5 10 W: 10 11 b.San Francisco 3-9-92
Honours: USA Youth.
2010-11 West Ham U 0 0
2011-12 West Ham U 0 0

MAYNARD, Nicky (F) 198 78
H: 5 11 W: 11 00 b.Winsford 11-12-86
Source: Scholar.
2005-06 Crewe Alex 1 1
2006-07 Crewe Alex 31 16
2007-08 Crewe Alex 27 14 **59 31**
2008-09 Bristol C 43 11
2009-10 Bristol C 42 20
2010-11 Bristol C 13 6
2011-12 Bristol C 27 8 **125 45**
2011-12 West Ham U 14 2 **14 2**

McCALLUM, Paul (F) 0 0
H: 6 3 W: 12 00 b.Streatham 28-7-93
Source: Dulwich Hamlet.
2010-11 West Ham U 0 0
2011-12 West Ham U 0 0
2011-12 *Rochdale* 0 0

MONCUR, George (M) 20 2
H: 5 9 W: 10 00 b.Swindon 18-8-93
Source: Scholar. *Honours:* England Youth.
2010-11 West Ham U 0 0
2011-12 West Ham U 0 0
2011-12 *AFC Wimbledon* 20 2 **20 2**

MONTANO, Cristian (F) 38 10
H: 5 11 W: 12 00 b.Cali 11-12-91
Source: Scholar.
2010-11 West Ham U 0 0
2011-12 West Ham U 0 0
2011-12 *Notts Co* 15 4 **15 4**
2011-12 *Swindon T* 4 1 **4 1**
2011-12 *Dagenham & R* 10 3 **10 3**
2011-12 *Oxford U* 9 2 **9 2**

MONTENEGRO, Brian (F) 0 0
H: 5 10 W: 12 00 b.Asuncion 18-6-93
Source: Tacuary, Dep Maldonado. *Honours:* Paraguay Youth.
2011-12 West Ham U 0 0

MORRISON, Ravel (M) 1 0
H: 5 9 W: 11 02 b.Wythenshawe 2-2-93
Source: Scholar. *Honours:* England Youth.
2009-10 Manchester U 0 0
2010-11 Manchester U 0 0
2011-12 Manchester U 0 0
2011-12 West Ham U 1 0 **1 0**

NOBLE, Mark (M) 204 23
H: 5 11 W: 12 00 b.West Ham 8-5-87
Source: Scholar. *Honours:* England Youth, Under-21.
2004-05 West Ham U 13 0
2005-06 West Ham U 5 0
2005-06 *Hull C* 5 0 **5 0**
2006-07 West Ham U 10 2
2006-07 *Ipswich T* 13 1 **13 1**
2007-08 West Ham U 31 3
2008-09 West Ham U 29 3
2009-10 West Ham U 27 2
2010-11 West Ham U 26 4
2011-12 West Ham U 45 8 **186 22**

NOLAN, Kevin (M) 423 81
H: 6 0 W: 14 00 b.Liverpool 24-6-82
Source: Scholar. *Honours:* England Youth, Under-20, Under-21.
1999-2000 Bolton W 4 0
2000-01 Bolton W 31 1
2001-02 Bolton W 35 8
2002-03 Bolton W 33 1
2003-04 Bolton W 37 9
2004-05 Bolton W 36 4
2005-06 Bolton W 36 9
2006-07 Bolton W 31 3
2007-08 Bolton W 33 5
2008-09 Bolton W 20 0 **296 40**
2008-09 Newcastle U 11 0
2009-10 Newcastle U 44 17
2010-11 Newcastle U 30 12 **85 29**
2011-12 West Ham U 42 12 **42 12**

NOUBLE, Frank (F) 62 8
H: 6 3 W: 12 08 b.Lewisham 24-9-91
Source: Chelsea Scholar. *Honours:* England Youth.
2009-10 West Ham U 8 0
2009-10 *WBA* 3 0 **3 0**
2009-10 *Swindon T* 8 0 **8 0**
2010-11 West Ham U 2 0
2010-11 *Swansea C* 6 1 **6 1**
2010-11 *Barnsley* 4 0
2010-11 *Charlton Ath* 9 1 **9 1**
2011-12 West Ham U 3 1 **13 1**
2011-12 *Gillingham* 13 5 **13 5**
2011-12 *Barnsley* 6 0 **10 0**

O'BRIEN, Joey (M) 101 3
H: 5 11 W: 10 13 b.Dublin 17-2-86
Source: Scholar. *Honours:* Eire Youth, Under-21, 3 full caps.
2004-05 Bolton W 1 0
2004-05 *Sheffield W* 15 2
2005-06 Bolton W 23 0
2006-07 Bolton W 0 0
2007-08 Bolton W 19 0
2008-09 Bolton W 7 0
2009-10 Bolton W 0 0
2010-11 Bolton W 0 0 **50 0**
2010-11 *Sheffield W* 4 0 **19 2**
2011-12 West Ham U 32 1 **32 1**

O'NEIL, Gary (M) 324 27
H: 5 10 W: 11 00 b.Beckenham 18-5-83
Source: Scholar. *Honours:* England Youth, Under-20, Under-21.
1999-2000 Portsmouth 1 0
2000-01 Portsmouth 10 1
2001-02 Portsmouth 33 1
2002-03 Portsmouth 31 3
2003-04 Portsmouth 3 2
2003-04 *Walsall* 7 0 **7 0**
2004-05 Portsmouth 24 2
2004-05 *Cardiff C* 9 1 **9 1**
2005-06 Portsmouth 36 6
2006-07 Portsmouth 35 1
2007-08 Portsmouth 2 0 **175 16**
2007-08 Middlesbrough 26 0
2008-09 Middlesbrough 29 4

2009-10 Middlesbrough 36 4
2010-11 Middlesbrough 18 0 **109 8**
2010-11 West Ham U 8 0
2011-12 West Ham U 16 2 **24 2**

PIQUIONNE, Frederic (F) 341 73
H: 6 2 W: 12 00 b.New Caledonia 8-12-78
Source: Martinique. *Honours:* France B, 1 full cap.
2000-01 Nimes 8 3 **8 3**
2001-02 Rennes 20 3
2002-03 Rennes 31 10
2003-04 Rennes 32 5 **83 18**
2004-05 St Etienne 37 11
2005-06 St Etienne 34 6
2006-07 St Etienne 18 6 **89 23**
2006-07 Monaco 14 5
2007-08 Monaco 32 7 **46 12**
2008-09 Lyon 19 2 **19 2**
On loan from Lyon.
2009-10 Portsmouth 34 5 **34 5**
On loan from Lyon.
2010-11 West Ham U 34 6
On loan from Lyon.
2011-12 West Ham U 20 2 **54 8**
2011-12 *Doncaster R* 8 2 **8 2**

POTTS, Danny (D) 3 0
H: 5 8 W: 11 00 b.Barking 13-4-94
Source: Scholar. *Honours:* England Youth.
2011-12 West Ham U 3 0 **3 0**

REID, Winston (D) 118 5
H: 6 3 W: 13 10 b.North Shore 3-7-88
Honours: Denmark Youth, Under-21. New Zealand 10 full caps, 1 goal.
2005-06 Midtjylland 9 0
2006-07 Midtjylland 11 0
2007-08 Midtjylland 9 0
2008-09 Midtjylland 25 2
2009-10 Midtjylland 29 0 **83 2**
2010-11 West Ham U 7 0
2011-12 West Ham U 28 3 **35 3**

RUDDOCK, Pelly (M) 0 0
b.Hendon
Source: Boreham Wood.
2011-12 West Ham U 0 0

SEARS, Freddie (F) 94 4
H: 5 8 W: 10 01 b.Hornchurch 27-11-89
Source: Scholar. *Honours:* England Youth, Under-21.
2007-08 West Ham U 7 1
2008-09 West Ham U 17 0
2009-10 West Ham U 1 0
2009-10 *Crystal Palace* 18 0 **18 0**
2009-10 *Coventry C* 10 0 **10 0**
2010-11 West Ham U 11 1
2010-11 *Scunthorpe U* 9 0 **9 0**
2011-12 West Ham U 10 0 **46 2**
2011-12 *Colchester U* 11 2 **11 2**

SPENCE, Jordan (D) 53 0
H: 6 2 W: 12 07 b.Woodford 24-5-90
Source: Scholar. *Honours:* England Youth, Under-21.
2007-08 West Ham U 0 0
2008-09 West Ham U 0 0
2008-09 *Leyton Orient* 20 0 **20 0**
2009-10 West Ham U 1 0
2009-10 *Scunthorpe U* 9 0 **9 0**
2010-11 West Ham U 2 0
2010-11 *Bristol C* 11 0
2011-12 West Ham U 0 0 **3 0**
2011-12 *Bristol C* 10 0 **21 0**

STECH, Marek (G) 10 0
H: 6 3 W: 14 00 b.Prague 28-1-90
Source: Sparta Prague, West Ham U Scholar. *Honours:* Czech Republic Youth, Under-21.
2008-09 West Ham U 0 0
2008-09 *Wycombe W* 2 0 **2 0**
2009-10 West Ham U 0 0
2009-10 *Bournemouth* 1 0 **1 0**
2010-11 West Ham U 0 0
2011-12 West Ham U 0 0
2011-12 *Yeovil T* 5 0 **5 0**
2011-12 *Leyton Orient* 2 0 **2 0**

TAYLOR, Matthew (D) 459 63
H: 5 11 W: 12 03 b.Oxford 27-11-81
Source: Trainee. *Honours:* England Youth, Under-21.
1998-99 Luton T 0 0
1999-2000 Luton T 41 4
2000-01 Luton T 45 1
2001-02 Luton T 43 11 **129 16**
2002-03 Portsmouth 35 7
2003-04 Portsmouth 30 0
2004-05 Portsmouth 32 1
2005-06 Portsmouth 34 6
2006-07 Portsmouth 35 8
2007-08 Portsmouth 13 1 **179 23**
2007-08 Bolton W 16 3
2008-09 Bolton W 34 10
2009-10 Bolton W 37 8
2010-11 Bolton W 36 2 **123 23**
2011-12 West Ham U 28 1 **28 1**

TOMBIDES, Dylan (F) 0 0
b.Perth 8-3-94
Source: Scholar.
2011-12 West Ham U 0 0

TOMKINS, James (D) 111 6
H: 6 3 W: 11 10 b.Basildon 29-3-89
Source: Scholar. *Honours:* England Schools, Youth, Under-21.
2005-06 West Ham U 0 0
2006-07 West Ham U 0 0
2007-08 West Ham U 6 0
2008-09 West Ham U 12 1
2008-09 *Derby Co* 7 0 **7 0**
2009-10 West Ham U 23 0
2010-11 West Ham U 19 1
2011-12 West Ham U 44 4 **104 6**

TURGOTT, Blair (M) 0 0
b.Bromley 22-5-94
Source: Scholar. *Honours:* England Youth.
2011-12 West Ham U 0 0

VAZ TE, Ricardo (F) 101 23
H: 6 2 W: 12 07 b.Lisbon 1-10-86
Source: Trainee. *Honours:* Portugal Youth, Under-20, Under-21.
2003-04 Bolton W 1 0
2004-05 Bolton W 7 0
2005-06 Bolton W 22 3
2006-07 Bolton W 25 0
2006-07 *Hull C* 6 0 **6 0**
2007-08 Bolton W 1 0
2008-09 Bolton W 2 0
2009-10 Bolton W 0 0
2010-11 Bolton W 0 0 **58 3**
2011-12 Barnsley 22 10 **22 10**
2011-12 West Ham U 15 10 **15 10**

VOSE, Dominic (M) 0 0
b.Lambeth 23-11-93
Source: Academy.
2010-11 West Ham U 0 0
2011-12 West Ham U 0 0

WEAREN, Eoin Patrick (D) 2 0
b.Dublin 2-10-92
Source: Scholar.
2009-10 West Ham U 0 0
2010-11 West Ham U 0 0
2011-12 West Ham U 0 0
2011-12 *Dagenham & R* 2 0 **2 0**

WIGAN ATH (89)

AL-HABSI, Ali (G) 144 0
H: 6 4 W: 12 06 b.Oman 30-12-81
Source: Al-Nasser, Al-Mudhaibi. *Honours:* Oman 74 full caps.
2003 Lyn 13 0
2004 Lyn 24 0
2005 Lyn 25 0 **62 0**
2005-06 Bolton W 0 0
2006-07 Bolton W 0 0
2007-08 Bolton W 10 0
2008-09 Bolton W 0 0
2009-10 Bolton W 0 0
2010-11 Bolton W 0 0 **10 0**
2010-11 *Wigan Ath* 34 0
2011-12 Wigan Ath 38 0 **72 0**

ALCARAZ, Antolin (D) 239 13
H: 6 0 W: 12 08 b.Roque Gonzalez 30-7-82
Honours: Paraguay 19 full caps, 2 goals.
2002-03 Beira-Mar 7 0
2003-04 Beira-Mar 24 1
2004-05 Beira-Mar 24 1
2005-06 Beira-Mar 31 0
2006-07 Beira-Mar 26 3 **112 5**
2007-08 Club Brugge 10 1
2008-09 Club Brugge 29 3
2009-10 Club Brugge 29 1 **68 5**
2010-11 Wigan Ath 34 1
2011-12 Wigan Ath 25 2 **59 3**

BEAUSEJOUR, Jean (M) 270 33
H: 5 10 W: 12 08 b.Santiago 1-6-84
Honours: Chile 43 full caps, 3 goals.
2002 Univ Catolica 1 0
2003 Univ Concepcion 30 3 **30 3**
2004 Univ Catolica 15 3 **16 3**
2004-05 Servette 11 1 **11 1**
2005-06 Gremio 55 7 **55 7**
2006-07 Gent 0 0
2007-08 Cobreloa 22 0 **22 0**
2008 O'Higgins 34 13 **34 13**
2008-09 America 17 0
2009-10 America 28 3
2010-11 America 2 0 **47 3**
2010-11 Birmingham C 17 2
2011-12 Birmingham C 22 1 **39 3**
2011-12 Wigan Ath 16 0 **16 0**

BINGHAM, Rakish (F) 0 0
b.Newham 25-10-93
Source: Scholar.
2011-12 Wigan Ath 0 0

BOOTHMAN, Steven (M) 0 0
b.Wigan 18-9-92
Source: Scholar.
2011-12 Wigan Ath 0 0

BOSELLI, Mauro (F) 176 60
H: 6 0 W: 11 11 b.Buenos Aires 22-5-85
Honours: Argentina Youth, 4 full caps, 1 goal.
2002-03 Boca Juniors 1 0
2003-04 Boca Juniors 0 0
2004-05 Boca Juniors 10 2
2005-06 Malaga 32 5 **32 5**
2006-07 Boca Juniors 12 4
2007-08 Boca Juniors 21 4 **44 10**
2008-09 Estudiantes 25 10
2009-10 Estudiantes 31 22
2010-11 Wigan Ath 8 0
2010-11 *Genoa* 7 2 **7 2**
2011-12 Wigan Ath 0 0 **8 0**
2011-12 *Estudiantes* 29 11 **85 43**

BOYCE, Emmerson (D) 413 17
H: 6 0 W: 12 03 b.Aylesbury 24-9-79
Source: Trainee. *Honours:* Barbados 2 full caps.
1997-98 Luton T 0 0
1998-99 Luton T 1 0
1999-2000 Luton T 30 1
2000-01 Luton T 42 3
2001-02 Luton T 37 0
2002-03 Luton T 34 0
2003-04 Luton T 42 4 **186 8**
2004-05 Crystal Palace 27 0
2005-06 Crystal Palace 42 2 **69 2**
2006-07 Wigan Ath 34 0
2007-08 Wigan Ath 25 0
2008-09 Wigan Ath 27 1
2009-10 Wigan Ath 24 3
2010-11 Wigan Ath 22 0
2011-12 Wigan Ath 26 3 **158 7**

BREEZE, Jonathan (M) 0 0
b.Birkenhead 22-10-91
Source: Scholar. *Honours:* Northern Ireland Under-21.
2010-11 Wigan Ath 0 0
2011-12 Wigan Ath 0 0

BUXTON, Adam (D) 0 0
H: 6 1 W: 12 10 b.Liverpool 12-5-92
Source: Scholar.
2010-11 Wigan Ath 0 0
2011-12 Wigan Ath 0 0

CALDWELL, Gary (D) 329 15
H: 5 11 W: 11 10 b.Stirling 12-4-82
Source: Trainee. *Honours:* Scotland Under-21, 48 full caps, 2 goals.
1998-99 Newcastle U 0 0
1999-2000 Newcastle U 0 0
2000-01 Newcastle U 0 0
2001-02 Newcastle U 0 0
2001-02 *Darlington* 4 0 **4 0**
2001-02 *Hibernian* 11 0
2002-03 Newcastle U 0 0
2002-03 *Coventry C* 36 0 **36 0**
2003-04 Newcastle U 0 0
2003-04 *Derby Co* 9 0 **9 0**

2003-04 Hibernian 17 1
2004-05 Hibernian 37 3
2005-06 Hibernian 34 1 **99 5**
2006-07 Celtic 21 0
2007-08 Celtic 35 1
2008-09 Celtic 36 3
2009-10 Celtic 14 1 **106 5**
2009-10 Wigan Ath 16 2
2010-11 Wigan Ath 23 0
2011-12 Wigan Ath 36 3 **75 5**

CHOW, Tim (M) 0 0
b.Wigan 18-1-94
Source: Scholar.
2011-12 Wigan Ath 0 0

CRUSAT, Albert (M) 259 39
H: 5 5 W: 10 03 b.Barcelona 13-5-82
Honours: Spain Youth.
2002-03 Espanyol 5 0 **5 0**
2003-04 Rayo Vallecano 5 1 **5 1**
2004-05 Lleida 35 4 **35 4**
2005-06 Almeria 34 8
2006-07 Almeria 34 11
2007-08 Almeria 34 3
2008-09 Almeria 30 1
2009-10 Almeria 33 7
2010-11 Almeria 34 3 **199 33**
2011-12 Wigan Ath 15 1 **15 1**

CRUYFF, Jessua (D) 0 0
b.Amsterdam 11-3-93
Source: Barcelona Youth.
2011-12 Wigan Ath 0 0

DAWSON, Adam (M) 0 0
b.Bury 5-10-92
Source: Bury Scholar.
2011-12 Wigan Ath 0 0

DI SANTO, Franco (F) 142 22
H: 6 4 W: 13 01 b.Mendoza 7-4-89
Source: Audax Italiano. *Honours:* Argentina Under-20.
2006 Audax Italiano 18 6
2007 Audax Italiano 37 7 **55 13**
2007-08 Chelsea 0 0
2008-09 Chelsea 8 0
2009-10 Chelsea 0 0
2009-10 *Blackburn R* 22 1 **22 1**
2010-11 Chelsea 0 0 **8 0**
2010-11 Wigan Ath 25 1
2011-12 Wigan Ath 32 7 **57 8**

DIAME, Mohamed (M) 162 8
H: 6 1 W: 11 02 b.Creteil 14-6-87
Honours: Senegal 12 full caps.
2006-07 Lens 0 0
2007-08 Linares 31 1 **31 1**
2008-09 Rayo Vallecano 35 2 **35 2**
2009-10 Wigan Ath 34 1
2010-11 Wigan Ath 36 1
2011-12 Wigan Ath 26 3 **96 5**

DICKO, Nouha (M) 55 16
H: 5 8 W: 11 00 b.Paris 14-5-92
2009-10 Strasbourg B 18 4
2010-11 Strasbourg B 24 8 **42 12**
2010-11 Strasbourg 3 0 **3 0**
2011-12 Wigan Ath 0 0
2011-12 *Blackpool* 10 4 **10 4**

FIGUEROA, Maynor (D) 170 5
H: 5 11 W: 12 02 b.Jutiapa 2-5-83
Honours: Honduras 87 full caps, 2 goals.
2000-01 Victoria La Ceiba 2 0
2001-02 Victoria La Ceiba 22 2 **24 2**
2007-08 Wigan Ath 2 0
2008-09 Wigan Ath 38 1
2009-10 Wigan Ath 35 1
2010-11 Wigan Ath 33 1
2011-12 Wigan Ath 38 0 **146 3**

GIRVAN, Michael (M) 0 0
b.Liverpool 21-10-92
Source: Scholar.
2011-12 Wigan Ath 0 0

GOHOURI, Steve (D) 266 38
H: 6 2 W: 13 01 b.Treichville 8-2-81
Honours: Ivory Coast 13 full caps, 3 goals.
1999-2000 Paris St Germain B 1 0 **1 0**
1999-2000 Bnei Yehuda 13 4 **13 4**
2000-01 Yverdon 34 9
2001-02 Yverdon 18 2
2002-03 Yverdon 20 1 **72 12**
2002-03 Bologna 0 0
2003-04 Vaduz 18 5
2004-05 Vaduz 28 5
2005-06 Vaduz 7 0 **53 10**
2005-06 Young Boys 20 5
2006-07 Young Boys 16 3 **36 8**
2006-07 Mgladbach 14 0
2007-08 Mgladbach 17 0
2008-09 Mgladbach 15 2 **46 2**
2009-10 Mgladbach II 3 0 **3 0**
2009-10 Wigan Ath 5 1
2010-11 Wigan Ath 27 1
2011-12 Wigan Ath 10 0 **42 2**

GOLOBART, Roman (D) 22 2
H: 6 4 W: 13 10 b.Barcelona 21-3-92
Source: Espanyol.
2010-11 Wigan Ath 0 0
2011-12 Wigan Ath 0 0
2011-12 *Inverness CT* 22 2 **22 2**

GOMEZ, Jordi (M) 131 19
H: 5 10 W: 11 09 b.Barcelona 24-5-85
2006-07 Espanyol B 21 0 **21 0**
2007-08 Espanyol 2 0 **2 0**
On loan from Espanyol.
2008-09 Swansea C 44 12
2009-10 Swansea C 0 0 **44 12**
2009-10 Wigan Ath 23 1
2010-11 Wigan Ath 13 1
2011-12 Wigan Ath 28 5 **64 7**

JONES, David (M) 165 22
H: 5 11 W: 10 10 b.Southport 4-11-84
Source: Trainee. *Honours:* England Youth, Under-21.
2003-04 Manchester U 0 0
2004-05 Manchester U 0 0
2005-06 Manchester U 0 0
2005-06 *Preston NE* 24 3 **24 3**
2005-06 NEC Nijmegen 17 6 **17 6**
2006-07 Manchester U 0 0
2006-07 Derby Co 28 6
2007-08 Derby Co 14 1 **42 7**
2008-09 Wolverhampton W 34 4
2009-10 Wolverhampton W 20 1
2010-11 Wolverhampton W 12 1 **66 6**
2011-12 Wigan Ath 16 0 **16 0**

KIERNAN, Rob (D) 20 0
H: 6 1 W: 11 13 b.Rickmansworth 13-1-91
Source: Scholar. *Honours:* Eire Under-21.
2008-09 Watford 0 0
2009-10 Watford 0 0
2009-10 *Kilmarnock* 4 0 **4 0**
2010-11 Watford 0 0
2010-11 *Yeovil T* 3 0 **3 0**
2010-11 *Bradford C* 8 0 **8 0**
2010-11 *Wycombe W* 2 0 **2 0**
2011-12 Wigan Ath 0 0
2011-12 *Accrington S* 3 0 **3 0**

KIRKLAND, Chris (G) 194 0
H: 6 5 W: 14 08 b.Barwell 2-5-81
Source: Trainee. *Honours:* England Youth, Under-21, 1 full cap.
1997-98 Coventry C 0 0
1998-99 Coventry C 0 0
1999-2000 Coventry C 0 0
2000-01 Coventry C 23 0
2001-02 Coventry C 1 0 **24 0**
2001-02 Liverpool 1 0
2002-03 Liverpool 8 0
2003-04 Liverpool 6 0
2004-05 Liverpool 10 0
2005-06 Liverpool 0 0
2005-06 *WBA* 10 0 **10 0**
2006-07 Liverpool 0 0 **25 0**
2006-07 Wigan Ath 26 0
2007-08 Wigan Ath 37 0
2008-09 Wigan Ath 32 0
2009-10 Wigan Ath 32 0
2010-11 Wigan Ath 4 0
2010-11 *Leicester C* 3 0 **3 0**
2011-12 Wigan Ath 0 0 **131 0**
2011-12 *Doncaster R* 1 0 **1 0**

LANGLEY, Josh (M) 0 0
b.Warrington 13-8-92
Source: Scholar.
2010-11 Wigan Ath 0 0
2011-12 Wigan Ath 0 0

MALONEY, Shaun (M) 202 47
H: 5 7 W: 10 01 b.Miri 24-1-83
Honours: Scotland Under-20, Under-21, B, 20 full caps, 1 goal.
1999-2000 Celtic 0 0
2000-01 Celtic 4 0
2001-02 Celtic 16 5
2002-03 Celtic 20 3
2003-04 Celtic 17 5
2004-05 Celtic 2 0
2005-06 Celtic 36 13
2006-07 Celtic 9 0
2006-07 Aston Villa 8 1
2007-08 Aston Villa 22 4 **30 5**
2008-09 Celtic 21 4
2009-10 Celtic 10 4
2010-11 Celtic 21 5
2011-12 Celtic 3 0 **159 39**
2011-12 Wigan Ath 13 3 **13 3**

McARTHUR, James (M) 217 12
H: 5 6 W: 9 13 b.Glasgow 7-10-87
Honours: Scotland 7 full caps, 1 goal.
2004-05 Hamilton A 6 0
2005-06 Hamilton A 20 1
2006-07 Hamilton A 36 1
2007-08 Hamilton A 34 4
2008-09 Hamilton A 37 2
2009-10 Hamilton A 35 1 **168 9**
2010-11 Wigan Ath 18 0
2011-12 Wigan Ath 31 3 **49 3**

McCARTHY, James (M) 172 18
H: 5 11 W: 11 05 b.Glasgow 12-11-90
Honours: Eire Youth, Under-21, 3 full caps.
2006-07 Hamilton A 23 1
2007-08 Hamilton A 35 7
2008-09 Hamilton A 37 6 **95 14**
2009-10 Wigan Ath 20 1
2010-11 Wigan Ath 24 3
2011-12 Wigan Ath 33 0 **77 4**

McCORMACK, Jamie (D) 0 0
b.Edinburgh 1-2-92
Source: Hearts Youth.
2011-12 Wigan Ath 0 0

McMANAMAN, Callum (F) 20 2
H: 5 9 W: 11 03 b.Huyton 25-4-91
Source: Scholar. *Honours:* England Youth, Under-20.
2008-09 Wigan Ath 1 0
2009-10 Wigan Ath 0 0
2010-11 Wigan Ath 3 0
2011-12 Wigan Ath 2 0 **6 0**
2011-12 *Blackpool* 14 2 **14 2**

MORRIS, Callum (M) 0 0
b.Birkenhead 12-9-92
Source: Scholar.
2011-12 Wigan Ath 0 0

MOSES, Victor (M) 131 19
H: 5 10 W: 11 07 b.Lagos 12-12-90
Source: Scholar. *Honours:* England Youth, Under-21.
2007-08 Crystal Palace 13 3
2008-09 Crystal Palace 27 2
2009-10 Crystal Palace 18 6 **58 11**
2009-10 Wigan Ath 14 1
2010-11 Wigan Ath 21 1
2011-12 Wigan Ath 38 6 **73 8**

MUSTOE, Jordan (M) 18 0
H: 5 11 W: 11 11 b.Birkenhead 28-1-91
Source: Scholar.
2009-10 Wigan Ath 0 0
2010-11 Wigan Ath 0 0
2011-12 Wigan Ath 0 0
2011-12 *Barnet* 18 0 **18 0**

MYLER, Sean (M) 0 0
b.Widnes 7-6-93
Source: Scholar.
2011-12 Wigan Ath 0 0

NICHOLLS, Lee (G) 9 0
b.Huyton 5-10-92
Source: Scholar. *Honours:* England Youth.
2009-10 Wigan Ath 0 0
2010-11 Wigan Ath 0 0
2010-11 *Hartlepool U* 0 0
2010-11 *Shrewsbury T* 0 0
2010-11 *Sheffield W* 0 0
2011-12 Wigan Ath 0 0
2011-12 *Accrington S* 9 0 **9 0**

PISCU (ADRIAN LOPEZ) (D) **44 1**
H: 6 0 W: 12 00 b.As Pontes 25-2-87
2006-07 La Coruna 0 0
2007-08 La Coruna B 12 0 **12 0**
2007-08 La Coruna 15 0
2008-09 La Coruna 8 1
2009-10 La Coruna 3 0 **26 1**
2010-11 Wigan Ath 1 0
2011-12 Wigan Ath 5 0 **6 0**

POLLITT, Mike (G) **503 0**
H: 6 4 W: 15 03 b.Farnworth 29-2-72
Source: Trainee.
1990-91 Manchester U 0 0
1990-91 *Oldham Ath* 0 0
1991-92 Bury 0 0
1992-93 Lincoln C 27 0
1993-94 Lincoln C 30 0 **57 0**
1994-95 Darlington 40 0
1995-96 Darlington 15 0 **55 0**
1995-96 Notts Co 0 0
1996-97 Notts Co 8 0
1997-98 Notts Co 2 0 **10 0**
1997-98 *Oldham Ath* 16 0 **16 0**
1997-98 *Gillingham* 6 0 **6 0**
1997-98 *Brentford* 5 0 **5 0**
1997-98 Sunderland 0 0
1998-99 Rotherham U 46 0
1999-2000 Rotherham U 46 0
2000-01 Chesterfield 46 0 **46 0**
2001-02 Rotherham U 46 0
2002-03 Rotherham U 41 0
2003-04 Rotherham U 43 0
2004-05 Rotherham U 45 0 **267 0**
2005-06 Wigan Ath 24 0
2006-07 Wigan Ath 3 0
2006-07 *Ipswich T* 1 0 **1 0**
2006-07 *Burnley* 4 0 **4 0**
2007-08 Wigan Ath 1 0
2008-09 Wigan Ath 3 0
2009-10 Wigan Ath 4 0
2010-11 Wigan Ath 1 0
2011-12 Wigan Ath 0 0 **36 0**

REDMOND, Daniel (D) **18 5**
b.Liverpool 2-3-91
Source: Scholar.
2009-10 Wigan Ath 0 0
2010-11 Wigan Ath 0 0
2011-12 Wigan Ath 0 0
2011-12 *Hamilton A* 18 5 **18 5**

ROBINSON, Jordan (D) **0 0**
b.Yarm 28-4-91
Source: Middlesbrough Scholar.
2010-11 Wigan Ath 0 0
2011-12 Wigan Ath 0 0

RODALLEGA, Hugo (F) **269 101**
H: 5 11 W: 11 05 b.Valle del Cauca 25-7-85
Honours: Colombia 43 full caps, 8 goals.
2004 Quindio 32 31 **32 31**
2005 Dep Cali 26 12 **26 12**
2005-06 Monterrey 14 3
2006-07 Atlas 17 5 **17 5**
2006-07 Monterrey 15 1 **29 4**
2007-08 Necaxa 36 16
2008-09 Necaxa 17 9 **53 25**
2008-09 Wigan Ath 15 3
2009-10 Wigan Ath 38 10
2010-11 Wigan Ath 36 9
2011-12 Wigan Ath 23 2 **112 24**

RUGG, Jordan (M) **0 0**
b.Liverpool 15-9-91
Source: Scholar.
2010-11 Wigan Ath 0 0
2011-12 Wigan Ath 0 0

SAMMON, Conor (F) **182 34**
H: 5 10 W: 11 11 b.Dublin 13-4-87
Honours: Eire Under-21.
2005 UCD 7 0
2006 UCD 31 7
2007 UCD 31 6 **69 13**
2008 Derry C 16 3 **16 3**
2008-09 Kilmarnock 17 1
2009-10 Kilmarnock 25 1
2010-11 Kilmarnock 23 15 **65 17**
2010-11 Wigan Ath 7 1
2011-12 Wigan Ath 25 0 **32 1**

STAM, Ronnie (M) **223 7**
H: 5 9 W: 9 11 b.Breda 18-6-84
2002-03 NAC Breda 1 0
2003-04 NAC Breda 21 1
2004-05 NAC Breda 14 0
2005-06 NAC Breda 28 1
2006-07 NAC Breda 27 2
2007-08 NAC Breda 29 0
2008-09 NAC Breda 1 0 **121 4**
2008-09 Twente 24 1
2009-10 Twente 33 1 **57 2**
2010-11 Wigan Ath 25 1
2011-12 Wigan Ath 20 0 **45 1**

THOMAS, Hendry (M) **55 0**
H: 5 11 W: 12 08 b.La Ceiba 23-2-85
Source: Club Olimpija. *Honours:* Honduras 52 full caps, 2 goals.
2009-10 Wigan Ath 31 0
2010-11 Wigan Ath 24 0
2011-12 Wigan Ath 0 0 **55 0**

WATSON, Ben (M) **257 30**
H: 5 10 W: 10 11 b.Camberwell 9-7-85
Source: Scholar. *Honours:* England Under-21.
2002-03 Crystal Palace 5 0
2003-04 Crystal Palace 16 1
2004-05 Crystal Palace 21 0
2005-06 Crystal Palace 42 4
2006-07 Crystal Palace 25 3
2007-08 Crystal Palace 42 5
2008-09 Crystal Palace 18 5 **169 18**
2008-09 Wigan Ath 10 2
2009-10 Wigan Ath 5 1
2009-10 *QPR* 16 2 **16 2**
2009-10 *WBA* 7 1 **7 1**
2010-11 Wigan Ath 29 3
2011-12 Wigan Ath 21 3 **65 9**

WATSON, Ryan (M) **0 0**
b.Crewe 7-7-93
Source: Scholar.
2011-12 Wigan Ath 0 0

Scholars
Ainscough Luke Joseph; Anderson Bradley David; Christian Patrick; Cottrill Michael Alan; Gibson Jamie; Hare Calvin; Johnstone Bram; Kerwin Joel; Lynch Jonathon Paul; Mason Andrew; Meadows Ryan Walter; Phillips Jack; Sheego Abubakar Ahmed; Thompson Omar Marquis.

WOLVERHAMPTON W (90)

BATTH, Danny (D) **72 3**
H: 6 3 W: 13 05 b.Brierley Hill 21-9-90
Source: Scholar.
2009-10 Wolverhampton W 0 0
2009-10 *Colchester U* 17 1 **17 1**
2010-11 Wolverhampton W 0 0
2010-11 *Sheffield U* 1 0 **1 0**
2010-11 *Sheffield W* 10 0
2011-12 Wolverhampton W 0 0
2011-12 *Sheffield W* 44 2 **54 2**

BERRA, Christophe (D) **234 4**
H: 6 1 W: 12 10 b.Edinburgh 31-1-85
Honours: Scotland Under-21, B, 20 full caps, 2 goals.
2003-04 Hearts 6 0
2004-05 Hearts 12 0
2005-06 Hearts 12 1
2006-07 Hearts 35 1
2007-08 Hearts 35 2
2008-09 Hearts 23 0 **123 4**
2008-09 Wolverhampton W 15 0
2009-10 Wolverhampton W 32 0
2010-11 Wolverhampton W 32 0
2011-12 Wolverhampton W 32 0 **111 0**

CASSIDY, Jake (F) **10 5**
H: 5 10 W: 11 02 b.Glan Conwy 9-2-93
Source: Airbus UK. *Honours:* Wales Youth, Under-21.
2010-11 Wolverhampton W 0 0
2011-12 Wolverhampton W 0 0
2011-12 *Tranmere R* 10 5 **10 5**

CRADDOCK, Jody (D) **520 20**
H: 6 0 W: 12 04 b.Redditch 25-7-75
Source: Christchurch.
1993-94 Cambridge U 20 0
1994-95 Cambridge U 38 0
1995-96 Cambridge U 46 3
1996-97 Cambridge U 41 1 **145 4**
1997-98 Sunderland 32 0
1998-99 Sunderland 6 0
1999-2000 Sunderland 19 0
1999-2000 *Sheffield U* 10 0 **10 0**
2000-01 Sunderland 34 0
2001-02 Sunderland 30 1
2002-03 Sunderland 25 1 **146 2**
2003-04 Wolverhampton W 32 1
2004-05 Wolverhampton W 42 1
2005-06 Wolverhampton W 18 0
2006-07 Wolverhampton W 34 4
2007-08 Wolverhampton W 23 1
2007-08 *Stoke C* 4 0 **4 0**
2008-09 Wolverhampton W 17 1
2009-10 Wolverhampton W 33 5
2010-11 Wolverhampton W 15 1
2011-12 Wolverhampton W 1 0 **215 14**

DAVIS, David (M) **47 2**
H: 5 8 W: 12 03 b.Smethwick 20-2-91
Source: Scholar.
2009-10 Wolverhampton W 0 0
2009-10 *Darlington* 5 0 **5 0**
2010-11 Wolverhampton W 0 0
2010-11 *Walsall* 7 0 **7 0**
2010-11 *Shrewsbury T* 19 2 **19 2**
2011-12 Wolverhampton W 7 0 **7 0**
2011-12 *Chesterfield* 9 0 **9 0**

DE VRIES, Dorus (G) **340 0**
H: 6 1 W: 12 08 b.Bewerwijk 29-12-80
1999-2000 Telstar 1 0
2000-01 Telstar 27 0
2001-02 Telstar 27 0
2002-03 Telstar 26 0 **81 0**
2003-04 Den Haag 18 0
2004-05 Den Haag 32 0
2005-06 Den Haag 0 0 **50 0**
2006-07 Dunfermline Ath 27 0 **27 0**
2007-08 Swansea C 46 0
2008-09 Swansea C 40 0
2009-10 Swansea C 46 0
2010-11 Swansea C 46 0 **178 0**
2011-12 Wolverhampton W 4 0 **4 0**

DOHERTY, Matthew (M) **14 2**
b.Dublin 17-1-92
Source: Bohemians. *Honours:* Eire Youth.
2010-11 Wolverhampton W 0 0
2011-12 Wolverhampton W 1 0 **1 0**
2011-12 *Hibernian* 13 2 **13 2**

DOYLE, Kevin (F) **290 93**
H: 5 11 W: 12 06 b.Adamstown 18-9-83
Source: Adamstown, Wexford, St Patrick's Ath. *Honours:* Eire Under-21, 50 full caps, 10 goals.
2004 Cork C 32 13
2005 Cork C 11 7 **43 20**
2005-06 Reading 45 18
2006-07 Reading 32 13
2007-08 Reading 36 6
2008-09 Reading 41 18 **154 55**
2009-10 Wolverhampton W 34 9
2010-11 Wolverhampton W 26 5
2011-12 Wolverhampton W 33 4 **93 18**

EBANKS-BLAKE, Sylvan (F) **203 68**
H: 5 10 W: 13 04 b.Cambridge 29-3-86
Source: Scholar. *Honours:* England Under-21.
2004-05 Manchester U 0 0
2005-06 Manchester U 0 0
2006-07 Plymouth Arg 41 10
2007-08 Plymouth Arg 25 11 **66 21**
2007-08 Wolverhampton W 20 12
2008-09 Wolverhampton W 41 25
2009-10 Wolverhampton W 23 2
2010-11 Wolverhampton W 30 7
2011-12 Wolverhampton W 23 1 **137 47**

EBANKS-LANDELL, Ethan (M) **0 0**
H: 5 6 W: 11 02 b.Oldbury 16-12-92
Source: Scholar.
2009-10 Wolverhampton W 0 0
2010-11 Wolverhampton W 0 0
2011-12 Wolverhampton W 0 0

EDWARDS, Dave (M) **237 25**
H: 5 11 W: 11 04 b.Shrewsbury 3-2-86
Source: Scholar. *Honours:* Wales Youth, Under-21, 24 full caps, 3 goals.
2002-03 Shrewsbury T 1 0
2003-04 Shrewsbury T 0 0
2004-05 Shrewsbury T 27 5
2005-06 Shrewsbury T 30 2
2006-07 Shrewsbury T 45 5 **103 12**
2007-08 Luton T 19 4 **19 4**
2007-08 Wolverhampton W 10 1

2008-09	Wolverhampton W	44	3		
2009-10	Wolverhampton W	20	1		
2010-11	Wolverhampton W	15	1		
2011-12	Wolverhampton W	26	3	**115**	**9**

ELOKOBI, George (D) **133** **4**

H: 5 10 W: 13 02 b.Cameroon 31-1-86

Source: Dulwich Hamlet.

2004-05	Colchester U	0	0		
2004-05	*Chester C*	5	0	**5**	**0**
2005-06	Colchester U	12	1		
2006-07	Colchester U	10	0		
2007-08	Colchester U	17	1	**39**	**2**
2007-08	Wolverhampton W	15	0		
2008-09	Wolverhampton W	4	0		
2009-10	Wolverhampton W	22	0		
2010-11	Wolverhampton W	27	2		
2011-12	Wolverhampton W	9	0	**77**	**2**
2011-12	*Nottingham F*	12	0	**12**	**0**

FLETCHER, Steven (F) **252** **73**

H: 6 1 W: 12 00 b.Shrewsbury 26-3-87

Honours: Scotland Under-20, Under-21, B, 8 full caps, 1 goal.

2003-04	Hibernian	5	0		
2004-05	Hibernian	20	5		
2005-06	Hibernian	34	8		
2006-07	Hibernian	31	6		
2007-08	Hibernian	32	13		
2008-09	Hibernian	34	11	**156**	**43**
2009-10	Burnley	35	8	**35**	**8**
2010-11	Wolverhampton W	29	10		
2011-12	Wolverhampton W	32	12	**61**	**22**

FOLEY, Kevin (D) **314** **7**

H: 5 9 W: 11 11 b.Luton 1-11-84

Source: Scholar. *Honours:* Eire B, Under-21, 8 full caps.

2002-03	Luton T	2	0		
2003-04	Luton T	33	1		
2004-05	Luton T	39	2		
2005-06	Luton T	38	0		
2006-07	Luton T	39	0		
2007-08	Luton T	0	0	**151**	**3**
2007-08	Wolverhampton W	44	1		
2008-09	Wolverhampton W	45	1		
2009-10	Wolverhampton W	25	0		
2010-11	Wolverhampton W	33	2		
2011-12	Wolverhampton W	16	0	**163**	**4**

FORDE, Anthony (M) **6** **0**

b.Limerick 16-11-93

Source: Scholar. *Honours:* Eire Youth.

2011-12	Wolverhampton W	6	0	**6**	**0**

GORMAN, Johnny (M) **1** **0**

H: 5 9 W: 11 00 b.Sheffield 26-10-92

Honours: Northern Ireland Youth, Under-21, 9 full caps.

2009-10	Wolverhampton W	0	0		
2010-11	Wolverhampton W	0	0		
2011-12	Wolverhampton W	1	0	**1**	**0**

GRIFFITHS, Leigh (F) **126** **52**

H: 5 07 W: 10 01 b.Leith 20-8-90

Honours: Scotland Youth, Under-21, B.

2006-07	Livingston	4	1		
2007-08	Livingston	18	5		
2008-09	Livingston	27	17	**49**	**23**
2009-10	Dundee	29	13		
2010-11	Dundee	18	8	**47**	**21**
2010-11	Wolverhampton W	0	0		
2011-12	Wolverhampton W	0	0		
2011-12	*Hibernian*	30	8	**30**	**8**

GUEDIOURA, Adiene (M) **148** **14**

H: 6 1 W: 12 08 b.La Roche-sur-Yon 12-11-85

Honours: Algeria 13 full caps, 1 goal.

2004-05	Sedan	0	0		
2005-06	Noisy-Le-Sec	15	1	**15**	**1**
2006-07	L'Entente	21	3	**21**	**3**
2007-08	Creteil	24	6	**24**	**6**
2008-09	Kortrijk	10	0	**10**	**0**
2008-09	Charleroi	12	0		
2009-10	Charleroi	13	1	**25**	**1**
2009-10	Wolverhampton W	14	1		
2010-11	Wolverhampton W	10	1		
2011-12	Wolverhampton W	10	0	**34**	**2**
2011-12	*Nottingham F*	19	1	**19**	**1**

HAMMILL, Adam (M) **167** **15**

H: 5 11 W: 11 07 b.Liverpool 25-1-88

Source: Scholar. *Honours:* England Youth, Under-21.

2005-06	Liverpool	0	0		
2006-07	Liverpool	0	0		
2006-07	*Dunfermline Ath*	13	1	**13**	**1**
2007-08	Liverpool	0	0		
2007-08	*Southampton*	25	0	**25**	**0**
2008-09	Liverpool	0	0		
2008-09	*Blackpool*	22	1	**22**	**1**
2008-09	*Barnsley*	14	1		
2009-10	Liverpool	0	0		
2009-10	Barnsley	39	4		
2010-11	Barnsley	25	8	**78**	**13**
2010-11	Wolverhampton W	10	0		
2011-12	Wolverhampton W	9	0	**19**	**0**
2011-12	*Middlesbrough*	10	0	**10**	**0**

HARRIS, Louis (M) **2** **0**

H: 6 0 W: 12 05 b.Sutton Coldfield 7-12-92

Source: Scholar.

2011-12	Wolverhampton W	0	0		
2011-12	*Notts Co*	2	0	**2**	**0**

HEMMINGS, Ashley (M) **35** **2**

H: 5 8 W: 11 06 b.Lewisham 3-3-91

Source: Scholar.

2008-09	Wolverhampton W	2	0		
2008-09	*Cheltenham T*	1	0	**1**	**0**
2009-10	Wolverhampton W	0	0		
2010-11	Wolverhampton W	0	0		
2010-11	*Torquay U*	9	0	**9**	**0**
2011-12	Wolverhampton W	0	0	**2**	**0**
2011-12	*Plymouth Arg*	23	2	**23**	**2**

HENNESSEY, Wayne (G) **167** **0**

H: 6 0 W: 11 06 b.Anglesey 24-1-87

Source: Scholar. *Honours:* Wales Schools, Youth, Under-21, 38 full caps.

2004-05	Wolverhampton W	0	0		
2005-06	Wolverhampton W	0	0		
2006-07	Wolverhampton W	0	0		
2006-07	*Bristol C*	0	0		
2006-07	*Stockport Co*	15	0	**15**	**0**
2007-08	Wolverhampton W	46	0		
2008-09	Wolverhampton W	35	0		
2009-10	Wolverhampton W	13	0		
2010-11	Wolverhampton W	24	0		
2011-12	Wolverhampton W	34	0	**152**	**0**

HENRY, Karl (M) **340** **8**

H: 6 0 W: 12 00 b.Wolverhampton 26-11-82

Source: Trainee. *Honours:* England Youth, Under-20.

1999-2000	Stoke C	0	0		
2000-01	Stoke C	0	0		
2001-02	Stoke C	24	0		
2002-03	Stoke C	18	1		
2003-04	Stoke C	20	0		
2003-04	*Cheltenham T*	9	1	**9**	**1**
2004-05	Stoke C	34	0		
2005-06	Stoke C	24	0	**120**	**1**
2006-07	Wolverhampton W	34	3		
2007-08	Wolverhampton W	40	3		
2008-09	Wolverhampton W	43	0		
2009-10	Wolverhampton W	34	0		
2010-11	Wolverhampton W	29	0		
2011-12	Wolverhampton W	31	0	**211**	**6**

HUNT, Steve (M) **366** **54**

H: 5 9 W: 10 10 b.Port Laoise 1-8-80

Source: Trainee. *Honours:* Eire Under-21, B, 39 full caps, 1 goal.

1999-2000	Crystal Palace	3	0		
2000-01	Crystal Palace	0	0	**3**	**0**
2001-02	Brentford	35	4		
2002-03	Brentford	42	7		
2003-04	Brentford	40	11		
2004-05	Brentford	19	3	**136**	**25**
2005-06	Reading	38	2		
2006-07	Reading	35	4		
2007-08	Reading	37	5		
2008-09	Reading	46	6		
2009-10	Reading	0	0	**156**	**17**
2009-10	Hull C	27	6	**27**	**6**
2010-11	Wolverhampton W	20	3		
2011-12	Wolverhampton W	24	3	**44**	**6**

IHIEKWE, Michael (D) **0** **0**

b.Liverpool 20-11-92

Source: Scholar.

2011-12	Wolverhampton W	0	0		

IKEME, Carl (G) **76** **0**

H: 6 2 W: 13 09 b.Sutton Coldfield 8-6-86

Source: Scholar.

2005-06	Wolverhampton W	0	0		
2005-06	*Stockport Co*	9	0	**9**	**0**
2006-07	Wolverhampton W	1	0		
2007-08	Wolverhampton W	0	0		
2008-09	Wolverhampton W	12	0		
2009-10	Wolverhampton W	0	0		
2009-10	*Charlton Ath*	4	0	**4**	**0**
2009-10	*Sheffield U*	2	0	**2**	**0**
2009-10	*QPR*	17	0	**17**	**0**
2010-11	Wolverhampton W	0	0		
2010-11	*Leicester C*	5	0	**5**	**0**
2011-12	Wolverhampton W	1	0	**14**	**0**
2011-12	*Middlesbrough*	10	0	**10**	**0**
2011-12	*Doncaster R*	15	0	**15**	**0**

ISMAIL, Zeli (M) **0** **0**

b.Serbia 12-12-93

Source: Scholar.

2010-11	Wolverhampton W	0	0		
2011-12	Wolverhampton W	0	0		

JARVIS, Matthew (M) **272** **31**

H: 5 8 W: 11 10 b.Middlesbrough 22-5-86

Source: Scholar. *Honours:* England 1 full cap.

2003-04	Gillingham	10	0		
2004-05	Gillingham	30	3		
2005-06	Gillingham	35	3		
2006-07	Gillingham	35	6	**110**	**12**
2007-08	Wolverhampton W	26	1		
2008-09	Wolverhampton W	28	3		
2009-10	Wolverhampton W	34	3		
2010-11	Wolverhampton W	37	4		
2011-12	Wolverhampton W	37	8	**162**	**19**

JOHNSON, Roger (D) **379** **33**

H: 6 3 W: 11 00 b.Ashford (Middlesex) 28-4-83

Source: Trainee.

1999-2000	Wycombe W	1	0		
2000-01	Wycombe W	1	0		
2001-02	Wycombe W	7	1		
2002-03	Wycombe W	33	3		
2003-04	Wycombe W	28	2		
2004-05	Wycombe W	42	6		
2005-06	Wycombe W	45	7	**157**	**19**
2006-07	Cardiff C	32	2		
2007-08	Cardiff C	42	5		
2008-09	Cardiff C	45	5	**119**	**12**
2009-10	Birmingham C	38	0		
2010-11	Birmingham C	38	2	**76**	**2**
2011-12	Wolverhampton W	27	0	**27**	**0**

JONSSON, Eggert (D) **159** **13**

H: 6 2 W: 11 05 b.Reykjavik 18-8-88

Honours: Iceland Under-21, 13 full caps.

2005	Fjaroabyggo	22	5	**22**	**5**
2005-06	Hearts	0	0		
2006-07	Hearts	3	0		
2007-08	Hearts	28	1		
2008-09	Hearts	30	3		
2009-10	Hearts	28	3		
2010-11	Hearts	29	0		
2011-12	Hearts	16	1	**134**	**8**
2011-12	Wolverhampton W	3	0	**3**	**0**

KIGHTLY, Michael (F) **139** **26**

H: 5 10 W: 10 10 b.Basildon 24-1-86

Source: Scholar. *Honours:* England Under-21.

2002-03	Southend U	1	0		
2003-04	Southend U	11	0		
2004-05	Southend U	1	0	**13**	**0**

From Grays Ath.

2006-07	Wolverhampton W	24	8		
2007-08	Wolverhampton W	21	4		
2008-09	Wolverhampton W	38	8		
2009-10	Wolverhampton W	9	0		
2010-11	Wolverhampton W	4	0		
2011-12	Wolverhampton W	18	3	**114**	**23**
2011-12	*Watford*	12	3	**12**	**3**

KOSTRNA, Kristian (D) **0** **0**

b.Trnava 15-12-93

Source: Scholar. *Honours:* Slovakia Youth.

2011-12	Wolverhampton W	0	0		

MAIERHOFER, Stefan (F) **209** **92**

H: 6 8 W: 14 11 b.Vienna 16-8-82

Honours: Austria 10 full caps, 1 goal.

2002-03	First Vienna	0	0		
2003-04	Langenrohr	28	10		
2004-05	Langenrohr	25	16	**53**	**26**
2005-06	Bayern Munich II	28	10		
2006-07	Bayern Munich II	14	11	**42**	**21**
2006-07	Bayern Munich	2	0	**2**	**0**
2006-07	Koblenz	14	3	**14**	**3**
2007-08	Furth	10	2	**10**	**2**
2007-08	Rapid Vienna	11	7		
2008-09	Rapid Vienna	35	23		
2009-10	Rapid Vienna	3	1	**49**	**31**

2009-10 Wolverhampton W 8 1
2009-10 *Bristol C* 3 0 **3 0**
2010-11 Wolverhampton W 0 0
2010-11 *Duisburg* 27 8 **27 8**
2011-12 Wolverhampton W 1 0 **9 1**

McALINDEN, Liam (F) 0 0
b.Cannock 26-9-93
Source: Scholar. *Honours:* Northern Ireland Youth.
2010-11 Wolverhampton W 0 0
2011-12 Wolverhampton W 0 0

McCAREY, Aaron (G) 0 0
b.Monaghan 14-1-92
Source: Monaghan U. *Honours:* Eire Youth, Under-21.
2009-10 Wolverhampton W 0 0
2010-11 Wolverhampton W 0 0
2011-12 Wolverhampton W 0 0

MENDEZ-LAING, Nathaniel (M) 41 6
H: 5 10 W: 11 12 b.Birmingham 15-4-92
Source: Scholar.
2009-10 Wolverhampton W 0 0
2010-11 Wolverhampton W 0 0
2010-11 *Peterborough U* 33 5 **33 5**
2011-12 Wolverhampton W 0 0
2011-12 *Sheffield U* 8 1 **8 1**

MILIJAS, Nenad (M) 288 59
H: 6 2 W: 13 09 b.Belgrade 30-4-83
Honours: Serbia 25 full caps, 4 goals.
1999-2000 Zemun 2 0
2000-01 Zemun 10 0
2001-02 Zemun 28 1
2002-03 Zemun 27 2
2003-04 Zemun 26 3
2004-05 Zemun 22 3
2005-06 Zemun 15 9 **130 18**
2005-06 Red Star Belgrade 10 4
2006-07 Red Star Belgrade 25 5
2007-08 Red Star Belgrade 28 10
2008-09 Red Star Belgrade 33 18 **96 37**
2009-10 Wolverhampton W 19 2
2010-11 Wolverhampton W 23 2
2011-12 Wolverhampton W 20 0 **62 4**

MOLI, David (F) 0 0
b.Kinshasa 30-11-94
Source: Liverpool Scholar.
2011-12 Wolverhampton W 0 0

MOUYOKOLO, Steven (D) 64 1
H: 6 3 W: 13 08 b.Melun 24-1-87
2007-08 Gueugnon 22 0 **22 0**
From Chateauroux B.
2008-09 Boulogne 13 0 **13 0**
2009-10 Hull C 21 1 **21 1**
2010-11 Wolverhampton W 4 0
2011-12 Wolverhampton W 0 0 **4 0**
2011-12 *Sochaux* 4 0 **4 0**

O'HARA, Jamie (M) 126 16
H: 5 11 W: 12 04 b.Dartford 25-9-86
Source: Scholar. *Honours:* England Youth, Under-21.
2004-05 Tottenham H 0 0
2005-06 Tottenham H 0 0
2005-06 *Chesterfield* 19 5 **19 5**
2006-07 Tottenham H 0 0
2007-08 Tottenham H 17 1
2007-08 *Millwall* 14 2 **14 2**
2008-09 Tottenham H 15 1
2009-10 Tottenham H 2 0
2009-10 *Portsmouth* 26 2 **26 2**
2010-11 Tottenham H 0 0 **34 2**
2010-11 *Wolverhampton W* 14 3
2011-12 Wolverhampton W 19 2 **33 5**

PRICE, Jack (M) 0 0
b.Shrewsbury 19-12-92
Source: Scholar.
2011-12 Wolverhampton W 0 0

RECKORD, Jamie (D) 24 0
H: 5 10 W: 11 11 b.Wolverhampton 9-3-92
Source: Scholar.
2010-11 Wolverhampton W 0 0
2010-11 *Northampton T* 7 0 **7 0**
2011-12 Wolverhampton W 0 0
2011-12 *Scunthorpe U* 17 0 **17 0**

SPRAY, James (F) 3 0
H: 6 0 W: 12 01 b.Halesowen 2-12-92
Source: Scholar.
2009-10 Wolverhampton W 0 0
2010-11 Wolverhampton W 0 0
2011-12 Wolverhampton W 0 0
2011-12 *Accrington S* 3 0 **3 0**

STEARMAN, Richard (D) 230 9
H: 6 2 W: 10 08 b.Wolverhampton 19-8-87
Source: Scholar. *Honours:* England Youth, Under-21.
2004-05 Leicester C 8 1
2005-06 Leicester C 34 3
2006-07 Leicester C 35 1
2007-08 Leicester C 39 2 **116 7**
2008-09 Wolverhampton W 37 1
2009-10 Wolverhampton W 16 1
2010-11 Wolverhampton W 31 0
2011-12 Wolverhampton W 30 0 **114 2**

VOKES, Sam (F) 143 30
H: 6 1 W: 13 10 b.Lymington 21-10-89
Source: Scholar. *Honours:* Wales Under-21, 21 full caps, 4 goals.
2006-07 Bournemouth 13 4
2007-08 Bournemouth 41 12 **54 16**
2008-09 Wolverhampton W 36 6
2009-10 Wolverhampton W 5 0
2009-10 *Leeds U* 8 1 **8 1**
2010-11 Wolverhampton W 2 0
2010-11 *Bristol C* 1 0 **1 0**
2010-11 *Sheffield U* 6 1 **6 1**
2010-11 *Norwich C* 4 1 **4 1**
2011-12 Wolverhampton W 4 0 **47 6**
2011-12 *Burnley* 9 2 **9 2**
2011-12 *Brighton & HA* 14 3 **14 3**

WARD, Stephen (D) 255 18
H: 5 11 W: 12 02 b.Dublin 20-8-85
Honours: Eire Youth, Under-21, B, 15 full caps, 2 goals.
2003 Bohemians 6 0
2004 Bohemians 16 2
2005 Bohemians 29 7
2006 Bohemians 21 2 **72 11**
2006-07 Wolverhampton W 18 3
2007-08 Wolverhampton W 29 0
2008-09 Wolverhampton W 42 0
2009-10 Wolverhampton W 22 0
2010-11 Wolverhampton W 34 1
2011-12 Wolverhampton W 38 3 **183 7**

WINNALL, Sam (F) 29 9
H: 5 9 W: 11 04 b.Wolverhampton 19-1-91
Source: Scholar.
2009-10 Wolverhampton W 0 0
2010-11 Wolverhampton W 0 0
2010-11 *Burton Alb* 19 7 **19 7**
2011-12 Wolverhampton W 0 0
2011-12 *Hereford U* 8 2 **8 2**
2011-12 *Inverness CT* 2 0 **2 0**

ZUBAR, Ronald (D) 221 7
H: 6 1 W: 12 08 b.Guadeloupe 20-9-85
Honours: France Under-21, Guadeloupe 1 full cap.
2002-03 Caen 7 0
2003-04 Caen 24 1
2004-05 Caen 34 1
2005-06 Caen 31 0 **96 2**
2006-07 Marseille 34 0
2007-08 Marseille 21 1
2008-09 Marseille 17 1 **72 2**
2009-10 Wolverhampton W 23 1
2010-11 Wolverhampton W 15 1
2011-12 Wolverhampton W 15 1 **53 3**

Scholars
Cotman Aljaz; Cranston Jordan Christopher; Dell Dominic; Flatt Jonathan; Gibson Jacob; Ifil Luke Anton; Iorfa Dominic; Kellermann James Aaron; Kempton Jake Anthony; O'Neill Gary; Parry Robbie; Schofield Ryan; Whittall Sam.

WYCOMBE W (91)

AINSWORTH, Gareth (M) 514 103
H: 5 10 W: 12 05 b.Blackburn 10-5-73
Source: Blackburn R Trainee.
1991-92 Preston NE 5 0
1992-93 Cambridge U 4 1 **4 1**
1992-93 Preston NE 26 0
1993-94 Preston NE 38 11
1994-95 Preston NE 16 1
1995-96 Preston NE 2 0
1995-96 Lincoln C 31 12
1996-97 Lincoln C 46 22
1997-98 Lincoln C 6 3 **83 37**
1997-98 Port Vale 40 5
1998-99 Port Vale 15 5 **55 10**
1998-99 Wimbledon 8 0
1999-2000 Wimbledon 2 2
2000-01 Wimbledon 12 2
2001-02 Wimbledon 2 0
2001-02 *Preston NE* 5 1 **92 13**
2002-03 Wimbledon 12 2 **36 6**
2002-03 *Walsall* 5 1 **5 1**
2002-03 Cardiff C 9 0 **9 0**
2003-04 QPR 29 6
2004-05 QPR 22 2
2005-06 QPR 43 9
2006-07 QPR 22 1
2007-08 QPR 24 3
2008-09 QPR 0 0
2009-10 QPR 1 0 **141 21**
2009-10 Wycombe W 14 2
2010-11 Wycombe W 43 10
2011-12 Wycombe W 32 2 **89 14**

BASEY, Grant (D) 107 5
H: 6 2 W: 13 12 b.Bromley 30-11-88
Source: Scholar. *Honours:* Wales Under-21.
2007-08 Charlton Ath 8 1
2007-08 *Brentford* 8 0 **8 0**
2008-09 Charlton Ath 19 0
2009-10 Charlton Ath 19 0
2010-11 Charlton Ath 0 0 **46 1**
2010-11 Barnet 11 1 **11 1**
2010-11 Peterborough U 7 1
2011-12 Peterborough U 3 0 **10 1**
2011-12 Wycombe W 32 2 **32 2**

BEAVON, Stuart (F) 113 27
H: 5 7 W: 10 10 b.Reading 5-5-84
Source: Dicot T, Weymouth.
2008-09 Wycombe W 8 0
2009-10 Wycombe W 25 3
2010-11 Wycombe W 37 3
2011-12 Wycombe W 43 21 **113 27**

BETSY, Kevin (M) 398 53
H: 6 1 W: 12 00 b.Woking 20-3-78
Source: Woking.
1998-99 Fulham 7 1
1999-2000 Fulham 2 0
1999-2000 *Bournemouth* 5 0 **5 0**
1999-2000 *Hull C* 2 0 **2 0**
2000-01 Fulham 5 0
2001-02 Fulham 1 0 **15 1**
2001-02 Barnsley 10 0
2002-03 Barnsley 39 5
2003-04 Barnsley 45 10
2004-05 Barnsley 0 0 **94 15**
2004-05 *Hartlepool U* 6 1 **6 1**
2004-05 Oldham Ath 36 5 **36 5**
2005-06 Wycombe W 42 8
2006-07 Wycombe W 29 5
2006-07 Bristol C 17 1
2007-08 Bristol C 1 0 **18 1**
2007-08 *Yeovil T* 5 1 **5 1**
2007-08 *Walsall* 16 2 **16 2**
2008-09 Southend U 41 3
2009-10 Southend U 2 0 **43 3**
2009-10 Wycombe W 39 5
2010-11 Wycombe W 45 6
2011-12 Wycombe W 3 0 **158 24**

BLOOMFIELD, Matt (M) 252 23
H: 5 9 W: 11 00 b.Felixstowe 8-2-84
Source: Scholar. *Honours:* England Youth, Under-20.
2001-02 Ipswich T 0 0
2002-03 Ipswich T 0 0
2003-04 Ipswich T 0 0
2003-04 Wycombe W 12 1
2004-05 Wycombe W 26 2
2005-06 Wycombe W 39 5
2006-07 Wycombe W 41 4
2007-08 Wycombe W 35 4
2008-09 Wycombe W 20 0
2009-10 Wycombe W 14 2
2010-11 Wycombe W 34 3
2011-12 Wycombe W 31 2 **252 23**

BULL, Nikki (G) 128 0
H: 6 2 W: 12 08 b.Hastings 2-10-81
Source: Scholarship.
1999-2000 QPR 0 0
2000-01 QPR 0 0
2001-02 QPR 0 0
2008-09 Aldershot T 30 0 **30 0**

2009-10 Brentford 6 0 **6 0**
2010-11 Wycombe W 46 0
2011-12 Wycombe W 46 0 **92 0**

DUNNE, Charles (F) 3 0
H: 5 9 W: 11 09 b.Lambeth 13-2-93
Source: Scholar.
2011-12 Wycombe W 3 0 **3 0**

FOSTER, Danny (D) 173 4
H: 5 10 W: 12 10 b.Enfield 23-9-84
Source: Trainee.
2002-03 Tottenham H 0 0
2003-04 Tottenham H 0 0
2004-05 Tottenham H 0 0
2005-06 Tottenham H 0 0
2006-07 Tottenham H 0 0
2007-08 Dagenham & R 32 1
2008-09 Dagenham & R 38 2 **70 3**
2009-10 Brentford 36 0 **36 0**
2010-11 Wycombe W 38 1
2011-12 Wycombe W 29 0 **67 1**

GRANT, Joel (F) 133 20
H: 6 0 W: 12 01 b.Acton 26-8-87
Source: Scholar.
2005-06 Watford 7 0
2006-07 Watford 0 0 **7 0**
From Aldershot T.
2008-09 Crewe Alex 28 2
2009-10 Crewe Alex 43 9
2010-11 Crewe Alex 25 5 **96 16**
2011-12 Wycombe W 30 4 **30 4**

HALLS, John (M) 161 4
H: 6 0 W: 11 11 b.Islington 14-2-82
Source: Scholar. *Honours:* England Youth, Under-20.
2000-01 Arsenal 0 0
2001-02 Arsenal 0 0
2001-02 *Colchester U* 6 0 **6 0**
2002-03 Arsenal 0 0
2003-04 Arsenal 0 0
2003-04 Stoke C 34 0
2004-05 Stoke C 22 0
2005-06 Stoke C 13 2 **69 2**
2005-06 Reading 1 1
2006-07 Reading 0 0
2007-08 Reading 1 0
2007-08 *Preston NE* 4 0 **4 0**
2007-08 *Crystal Palace* 5 0 **5 0**
2007-08 *Sheffield U* 6 0 **6 0**
2008-09 Reading 0 0 **2 1**
2008-09 Brentford 23 0 **23 0**
2009-10 Aldershot T 16 0
2010-11 Aldershot T 23 1 **39 1**
2011-12 Wycombe W 7 0 **7 0**

INGRAM, Matt (G) 0 0
b. 18-12-93
Source: Scholar.
2011-12 Wycombe W 0 0

JOHNSON, Leon (D) 275 8
H: 6 1 W: 13 05 b.Shoreditch 10-5-81
Source: Scholarship.
1999-2000 Southend U 0 0
2000-01 Southend U 20 1
2001-02 Southend U 28 2 **48 3**
2002-03 Gillingham 18 0
2003-04 Gillingham 20 0
2004-05 Gillingham 8 0
2005-06 Gillingham 28 1
2006-07 Gillingham 24 1 **98 2**
2007-08 Wycombe W 45 0
2008-09 Wycombe W 29 2
2009-10 Wycombe W 5 0
2010-11 Wycombe W 23 1
2011-12 Wycombe W 27 0 **129 3**

KEWLEY-GRAHAM, Jesse (M) 1 0
H: 5 10 W: 11 11 b.Hounslow 15-6-93
Source: Scholar.
2011-12 Wycombe W 1 0 **1 0**

KRETZSCHMAR, Max (M) 0 0
Source: Scholar.
2011-12 Wycombe W 0 0

LEWIS, Stuart (M) 131 4
H: 5 10 W: 11 06 b.Welwyn 15-10-87
Source: Scholar. *Honours:* England Youth.
2005-06 Tottenham H 0 0
2006-07 Tottenham H 0 0
2006-07 Barnet 4 0 **4 0**
From Stevenage B.
2007-08 Gillingham 10 0
2008-09 Gillingham 21 0
2009-10 Gillingham 20 1 **51 1**
2010-11 Dagenham & R 10 0 **10 0**
2010-11 Wycombe W 25 2
2011-12 Wycombe W 41 1 **66 3**

McCLURE, Matt (F) 20 1
H: 5 10 W: 11 00 b.Slough 17-11-91
Source: Scholar.
2010-11 Wycombe W 8 0
2011-12 Wycombe W 12 1 **20 1**

McCOY, Marvin (D) 49 0
H: 5 11 W: 11 00 b.Walthamstow 2-10-88
Source: Watford Scholar.
2007-08 Hereford U 0 0
From Leyton, Wealdstone.
2010-11 Wycombe W 21 0
From Leyton, Wealdstone.
2011-12 Wycombe W 28 0 **49 0**

McNAMEE, Anthony (M) 231 8
H: 5 6 W: 10 03 b.Kensington 13-7-84
Source: Scholar. *Honours:* England Youth, Under-20.
2001-02 Watford 7 1
2002-03 Watford 23 0
2003-04 Watford 2 0
2004-05 Watford 14 0
2005-06 Watford 38 1
2006-07 Watford 7 0
2006-07 *Crewe Alex* 5 0 **5 0**
2007-08 Watford 0 0 **91 2**
2007-08 Swindon T 19 2
2008-09 Swindon T 43 0
2009-10 Swindon T 17 1 **79 3**
2009-10 Norwich C 17 1
2010-11 Norwich C 17 0 **34 1**
2011-12 Milton Keynes D 7 0 **7 0**
2011-12 Wycombe W 15 2 **15 2**

MOONEY, Jason (G) 0 0
H: 6 9 W: 14 00
Source: Ards, Bangor, Ards Rangers, Comber Rec.
2011-12 Wycombe W 0 0

RENDELL, Scott (F) 119 34
H: 6 1 W: 13 00 b.Ashford (Middlesex) 21-10-86
Source: Aldershot T, Reading, Crawley T, Cambridge U.
On loan from Cambridge U.
2007-08 Peterborough U 10 3
2008-09 Peterborough U 3 1
2008-09 *Yeovil T* 5 0 **5 0**
2009-10 Peterborough U 0 0 **13 4**
2009-10 *Torquay U* 35 12 **35 12**
2010-11 Wycombe W 37 14
2011-12 Wycombe W 6 1 **43 15**
2011-12 *Bristol R* 5 0 **5 0**
2011-12 *Oxford U* 18 3 **18 3**

SANDELL, Andy (D) 137 17
H: 5 11 W: 11 09 b.Calne 8-9-83
Source: Bath C.
2005-06 Bristol R 0 0
2006-07 Bristol R 36 3
2008-09 Bristol R 0 0 **36 3**
From Salisbury C.
2008-09 Aldershot T 29 2
2009-10 Aldershot T 29 5 **58 7**
2010-11 Wycombe W 32 7
2011-12 Wycombe W 11 0 **43 7**

SCOWEN, Josh (M) 2 0
b.Cheshunt 28-3-93
Source: Scholar.
2010-11 Wycombe W 2 0
2011-12 Wycombe W 0 0 **2 0**

STEWART, Anthony (D) 4 0
H: 5 10 W: 12 03 b.Brixton 18-9-92
Source: Scholar.
2011-12 Wycombe W 4 0 **4 0**

STREVENS, Ben (M) 262 55
H: 6 1 W: 12 00 b.Edgware 24-5-80
Source: Wingate & Finchley.
1998-99 Barnet 0 0
1999-2000 Barnet 6 0
2000-01 Barnet 28 4
2005-06 Barnet 35 5 **69 9**
From Crawley T.
2007-08 Dagenham & R 46 15
2008-09 Dagenham & R 46 14 **92 29**
2009-10 Brentford 25 6 **25 6**
2010-11 Wycombe W 40 7
2011-12 Wycombe W 36 4 **76 11**

TAYLOR, Olly (F) 0 0
Source: Scholar.
2011-12 Wycombe W 0 0

TUNNICLIFFE, James (D) 111 4
H: 6 4 W: 12 03 b.Denton 17-1-89
Source: Scholar.
2005-06 Stockport Co 1 0
2006-07 Stockport Co 5 0
2007-08 Stockport Co 5 0
2008-09 Stockport Co 30 0 **41 0**
2009-10 Brighton & HA 17 2
2009-10 *Milton Keynes D* 9 1 **9 1**
2010-11 Brighton & HA 0 0 **17 2**
2010-11 *Bristol R* 25 0 **25 0**
2011-12 Wycombe W 17 1 **17 1**
2011-12 *Crewe Alex* 2 0 **2 0**

WINFIELD, Dave (D) 97 6
H: 6 3 W: 13 08 b.Aldershot 24-3-88
Source: Youth.
2008-09 Aldershot T 10 0
2009-10 Aldershot T 25 2 **35 2**
2010-11 Wycombe W 37 2
2011-12 Wycombe W 25 2 **62 4**

YEOVIL T (92)

AGARD, Kieran (F) 38 7
H: 5 10 W: 10 10 b.Newham 10-10-89
Source: Scholar.
2006-07 Everton 0 0
2007-08 Everton 0 0
2008-09 Everton 0 0
2009-10 Everton 1 0
2010-11 Everton 0 0 **1 0**
2010-11 *Kilmarnock* 8 1 **8 1**
2010-11 *Peterborough U* 0 0
2011-12 Yeovil T 29 6 **29 6**

AYLING, Luke (D) 85 0
H: 5 11 W: 10 08 b.Lambeth 25-8-91
2009-10 Arsenal 0 0
2009-10 *Yeovil T* 4 0
2010-11 Yeovil T 37 0
2011-12 Yeovil T 44 0 **85 0**

BAGGRIDGE, Rhys (D) 0 0
b.Neath 14-10-92
Source: Scholar.
2011-12 Yeovil T 0 0

BELSON, Flavien (M) 51 3
H: 6 2 W: 12 02 b.Le Havre 22-2-87
Honours: France Youth, Guadeloupe 4 full caps.
2004-05 Metz B 12 1
2005-06 Metz 4 0
2006-07 Metz 0 0
2007-08 Metz 6 0 **10 0**
2008-09 Milton Keynes D 13 0 **13 0**
2009-10 Metz B 7 2 **19 3**
2009-10 Cannes 3 0 **3 0**
2010-11 Dives 5 0 **5 0**
2011-12 Yeovil T 1 0 **1 0**

BLIZZARD, Dominic (M) 172 10
H: 6 2 W: 12 04 b.High Wycombe 2-9-83
Source: Scholar.
2001-02 Watford 0 0
2002-03 Watford 0 0
2003-04 Watford 2 1
2004-05 Watford 17 1
2005-06 Watford 10 0
2006-07 Watford 0 0 **29 2**
2006-07 *Stockport Co* 7 0
2006-07 *Milton Keynes D* 8 0 **8 0**
2007-08 Stockport Co 27 1
2008-09 Stockport Co 31 3 **65 4**
2009-10 Bristol R 34 1
2010-11 Bristol R 5 0 **39 1**
2010-11 *Port Vale* 1 0 **1 0**
2011-12 Yeovil T 30 3 **30 3**

CLARKE, Lewis (D) 0 0
b.Weymouth 8-3-93
Source: Scholar.
2011-12 Yeovil T 0 0

CLOWES, Robert (F) 0 0
b.Taunton 24-2-93
Source: Scholar.

2011-12	Yeovil T	0	0		

EDGAR, Anthony (M) 13 1
H: 5 8 W: 11 00 b.Newham 30-9-90
Source: Scholar.

2009-10	West Ham U	0	0		
2009-10	*Bournemouth*	3	0	**3**	**0**
2010-11	West Ham U	0	0		
2011-12	Yeovil T	10	1	**10**	**1**

FALLON, Rory (F) 345 68
H: 6 2 W: 11 09 b.Gisbourne 20-3-82
Source: North Shore U. *Honours:* England Youth. New Zealand 11 full caps, 3 goals.

1998-99	Barnsley	0	0		
1999-2000	Barnsley	0	0		
2000-01	Barnsley	1	0		
2001-02	Barnsley	9	0		
2001-02	*Shrewsbury T*	11	0	**11**	**0**
2002-03	Barnsley	26	7		
2003-04	Barnsley	16	4	**52**	**11**
2003-04	Swindon T	19	6		
2004-05	Swindon T	31	3		
2004-05	*Yeovil T*	6	1		
2005-06	Swindon T	25	12	**75**	**21**
2005-06	Swansea C	17	4		
2006-07	Swansea C	24	8	**41**	**12**
2006-07	Plymouth Arg	15	1		
2007-08	Plymouth Arg	29	7		
2008-09	Plymouth Arg	44	5		
2009-10	Plymouth Arg	33	5		
2010-11	Plymouth Arg	28	4	**149**	**22**
2010-11	*Ipswich T*	6	1	**6**	**1**
2011-12	Yeovil T	5	0	**11**	**1**

Transferred to Aberdeen September 2011.

GIBSON, Billy (M) 9 0
H: 6 2 W: 11 07 b.Harrow 30-9-90
Source: Scholar.

2008-09	Watford	0	0		
2009-10	Watford	0	0		
2010-11	Yeovil T	4	0		
2011-12	Yeovil T	5	0	**9**	**0**

GILBERT, Kerrea (D) 83 1
H: 5 6 W: 11 03 b.Willesden 28-2-87
Source: Scholar. *Honours:* England Youth.

2005-06	Arsenal	2	0		
2006-07	Arsenal	0	0		
2006-07	*Cardiff C*	24	0	**24**	**0**
2007-08	Arsenal	0	0		
2007-08	*Southend U*	5	0	**5**	**0**
2008-09	Arsenal	0	0		
2008-09	*Leicester C*	34	1	**34**	**1**
2009-10	Arsenal	0	0	**2**	**0**
2009-10	*Peterborough U*	10	0	**10**	**0**
2011-12	Yeovil T	8	0	**8**	**0**

Transferred to Shamrock R February 2012.

HAYNES-BROWN, Curtis (D) 10 0
H: 6 2 W: 13 00 b.Ipswich 15-4-89
Source: Colchester U Scholar, AFC Sudbury, Lowestoft T.

2011-12	Yeovil T	10	0	**10**	**0**

HINDS, Richard (D) 276 12
H: 6 2 W: 12 02 b.Sheffield 22-8-80
Source: Schoolboy.

1998-99	Tranmere R	2	0		
1999-2000	Tranmere R	6	0		
2000-01	Tranmere R	29	0		
2001-02	Tranmere R	10	0		
2002-03	Tranmere R	8	0	**55**	**0**
2003-04	Hull C	39	1		
2004-05	Hull C	6	0	**45**	**1**
2004-05	*Scunthorpe U*	7	0		
2005-06	Scunthorpe U	42	6		
2006-07	Scunthorpe U	44	2	**93**	**8**
2007-08	Sheffield W	38	2		
2008-09	Sheffield W	14	0		
2009-10	Sheffield W	11	0		
2010-11	Sheffield W	4	0		
2011-12	Sheffield W	0	0	**67**	**2**

From Lincoln C.

2011-12	Yeovil T	16	1	**16**	**1**

HUNTINGTON, Paul (D) 135 10
H: 6 3 W: 12 08 b.Carlisle 17-9-87
Source: Scholar. *Honours:* England Youth.

2005-06	Newcastle U	0	0		
2006-07	Newcastle U	11	1		
2007-08	Newcastle U	0	0	**11**	**1**
2007-08	Leeds U	17	2		
2008-09	Leeds U	4	0		
2009-10	Leeds U	0	0	**21**	**2**
2009-10	Stockport Co	26	0	**26**	**0**
2010-11	Yeovil T	40	5		
2011-12	Yeovil T	37	2	**77**	**7**

JONES, Nathan (M) 452 11
H: 5 6 W: 10 06 b.Rhondda 28-5-73
Source: Cardiff C Trainee, Maesteg Park, Ton Pentre, Merthyr T.

1995-96	Luton T	0	0		

From Badajoz, Numaicia

1997-98	Southend U	39	0		
1998-99	Southend U	17	0		
1998-99	*Scarborough*	9	0	**9**	**0**
1999-2000	Southend U	43	2	**99**	**2**
2000-01	Brighton & HA	40	4		
2001-02	Brighton & HA	36	2		
2002-03	Brighton & HA	28	1		
2003-04	Brighton & HA	36	0		
2004-05	Brighton & HA	19	0	**159**	**7**
2005-06	Yeovil T	43	0		
2006-07	Yeovil T	42	1		
2007-08	Yeovil T	31	1		
2008-09	Yeovil T	21	0		
2009-10	Yeovil T	18	0		
2010-11	Yeovil T	8	0		
2011-12	Yeovil T	22	0	**185**	**2**

MACLEAN, Steve (F) 261 76
H: 5 11 W: 12 06 b.Edinburgh 23-8-82
Honours: Scotland Under-21.

2002-03	Rangers	3	0	**3**	**0**
2003-04	Scunthorpe U	42	23	**42**	**23**
2004-05	Sheffield W	36	18		
2005-06	Sheffield W	6	2		
2006-07	Sheffield W	41	12	**83**	**32**
2007-08	Cardiff C	15	1	**15**	**1**
2007-08	Plymouth Arg	17	3		
2008-09	Plymouth Arg	21	2		
2009-10	Plymouth Arg	3	0		
2009-10	*Aberdeen*	16	5	**16**	**5**
2010-11	Plymouth Arg	7	0	**48**	**5**
2010-11	*Oxford U*	31	6	**31**	**6**
2011-12	Yeovil T	20	3	**20**	**3**
2011-12	*Cheltenham T*	3	1	**3**	**1**

N'GALA, Bondz (D) 71 3
H: 6 0 W: 12 03 b.Forest Gate 13-9-89
Source: Scholar.

2007-08	West Ham U	0	0		
2008-09	West Ham U	0	0		
2008-09	*Milton Keynes D*	3	0	**3**	**0**
2009-10	West Ham U	0	0		
2009-10	*Scunthorpe U*	2	0	**2**	**0**
2009-10	*Plymouth Arg*	9	0		
2010-11	Plymouth Arg	26	1	**35**	**1**
2011-12	Yeovil T	31	2	**31**	**2**

O'BRIEN, Alan (M) 100 1
H: 5 10 W: 10 10 b.Dublin 20-2-85
Source: Scholar. *Honours:* Eire Youth, B, Under-21, 5 full caps.

2001-02	Newcastle U	0	0		
2002-03	Newcastle U	0	0		
2003-04	Newcastle U	0	0		
2004-05	Newcastle U	0	0		
2005-06	Newcastle U	3	0		
2005-06	*Carlisle U*	5	1	**5**	**1**
2006-07	Newcastle U	2	0	**5**	**0**
2007-08	Hibernan	23	0	**23**	**0**
2008-09	Hibernian	24	0	**24**	**0**
2009-10	Swindon T	9	0		
2010-11	Swindon T	21	0	**30**	**0**
2011-12	Yeovil T	13	0	**13**	**0**

SLOWE, Alistair (M) 0 0
H: 5 11 W: 11 13 b.Brighton 16-10-88
Source: Cantonments, Onisilos Sotira.

2010-11	Northampton T	0	0		
2011-12	Yeovil T	0	0		

STEWART, Gareth (G) 165 0
H: 6 0 W: 12 08 b.Preston 3-2-80
Source: Trainee. *Honours:* England Schools, Youth.

1996-97	Blackburn R	0	0		
1997-98	Blackburn R	0	0		
1998-99	Blackburn R	0	0		
1999-2000	Bournemouth	3	0		
2000-01	Bournemouth	35	0		
2001-02	Bournemouth	45	0		
2002-03	Bournemouth	1	0		
2003-04	Bournemouth	0	0		
2004-05	Bournemouth	0	0		
2005-06	Bournemouth	42	0		
2006-07	Bournemouth	20	0		
2007-08	Bournemouth	18	0		
2008-09	Bournemouth	0	0	**164**	**0**
2011-12	Yeovil T	1	0	**1**	**0**

UPSON, Edward (M) 73 4
H: 5 10 W: 11 07 b.Bury St Edmunds 21-11-89
Source: Scholar. *Honours:* England Youth.

2006-07	Ipswich T	0	0		
2007-08	Ipswich T	0	0		
2008-09	Ipswich T	0	0		
2009-10	Ipswich T	0	0		
2009-10	*Barnet*	9	1	**9**	**1**
2010-11	Yeovil T	23	0		
2011-12	Yeovil T	41	3	**64**	**3**

WILLIAMS, Andy (F) 227 40
H: 5 11 W: 11 09 b.Hereford 14-8-86
Source: Pershore College.

2006-07	Hereford U	41	8		
2007-08	Bristol R	41	4		
2008-09	Bristol R	4	1		
2008-09	*Hereford U*	26	2	**67**	**10**
2009-10	Bristol R	43	3	**88**	**8**
2010-11	Yeovil T	37	6		
2011-12	Yeovil T	35	16	**72**	**22**

WILLIAMS, Gavin (M) 238 30
H: 5 10 W: 11 05 b.Pontypridd 20-6-80
Source: Hereford U. *Honours:* Wales 2 full caps.

2003-04	Yeovil T	42	9		
2004-05	Yeovil T	13	2		
2004-05	West Ham U	10	1		
2005-06	West Ham U	0	0	**10**	**1**
2005-06	Ipswich T	12	1		
2006-07	Ipswich T	29	2		
2007-08	Ipswich T	13	0	**54**	**3**
2008-09	Bristol C	35	3		
2009-10	Bristol C	14	0		
2009-10	*Yeovil T*	8	5		
2010-11	Bristol C	3	0	**52**	**3**
2010-11	*Yeovil T*	12	1		
2010-11	Bristol R	19	2	**19**	**2**
2011-12	Yeovil T	28	4	**103**	**21**

WOODS, Michael (M) 5 1
H: 6 0 W: 12 07 b.Pocklington 6-4-90
Source: Scholar. *Honours:* England Youth.

2006-07	Chelsea	0	0		
2007-08	Chelsea	0	0		
2008-09	Chelsea	0	0		
2009-10	Chelsea	0	0		
2010-11	Chelsea	0	0		
2010-11	*Notts Co*	0	0		
2011-12	Chelsea	0	0		
2011-12	Yeovil T	5	1	**5**	**1**

YOUGA, Kelly (D) 97 2
H: 6 1 W: 12 00 b.Bangui 22-9-85
Source: Lyon.

2005-06	Charlton Ath	0	0		
2005-06	*Bristol C*	4	0	**4**	**0**
2006-07	Charlton Ath	0	0		
2006-07	*Bradford C*	11	0	**11**	**0**
2007-08	Charlton Ath	11	0		
2007-08	*Scunthorpe U*	19	1	**19**	**1**
2008-09	Charlton Ath	33	1		
2009-10	Charlton Ath	18	0		
2010-11	Charlton Ath	0	0		
2011-12	Charlton Ath	0	0	**62**	**1**
2011-12	Yeovil T	1	0	**1**	**0**

BLUE SQUARE PREMIER ROLL-CALL

FLEETWOOD TOWN

Player	*H*	*W*	*Birthplace*	*DOB*	*Source*
Scott Davies (G)	6 0	11 00	Blackpool	27 2 87	Morecambe
Shaun Beeley (D)	5 10	11 05	Stockport	21 11 88	Southport
Paul Edwards (M)	5 10	12 02	Manchester	1 1 80	Barrow
Anthony Barry (M)	5 7	10 01	Liverpool	29 5 86	Chester C
Steve McNulty (D)	6 1	13 12	Liverpool	26 9 83	Barrow
Nathan Pond (M)				5 1 85	Lancaster C
Sean Clancy (M)	5 8	9 13	Liverpool	16 9 87	Burscough
Jamie Milligan (M)	5 7	9 13	Blackpool	3 1 80	AFC Fylde
Magno Vieira (F)	5 10	11 13	Bahia	13 2 85	Ebbsfleet U
Peter Till (M)	5 11	11 05	Birmingham	7 9 85	York C
Junior Brown (M)	5 9	10 10	Crewe	7 5 89	Northwich Vic
Alan Goodall (D)	5 9	11 07	Birkenhead	2 12 81	Stockport Co
Andrew Mangan (F)	5 9	11 09	Liverpool	30 8 86	Wrexham
Keith Briggs (M)	6 0	11 05	Glossop	11 12 81	Kidderminster H
Danzelle St Louis-Hamilton (G)	6 3	12 11	Stevenage	7 5 90	Darlington
Stefan Cox (M)				17 9 91	Tooting & M
Jamie McGuire (M)	5 7	11 00	Birkenhead	13 11 83	Droylsden
Gareth Seddon (F)	5 9	12 04	Burnley	23 5 80	Kettering T
Paul Linwood (D)	6 2	12 08	Birkenhead	24 10 83	Grimsby T

YORK CITY

Player	*H*	*W*	*Birthplace*	*DOB*	*Source*
Paul Musselwhite (G)	6 2	14 05	Portsmouth	22 12 68	Lincoln C
Lanre Oyebanjo (D)	6 1	11 05	London	27 4 90	Histon
James Meredith (D)	6 1	11 07	Albury	4 4 88	Shrewsbury T
Chris Smith (D)	5 11	11 00	Derby	30 6 81	Mansfield T
David McGurk (D)	6 0	11 11	Middlesbrough	30 9 82	Darlington
Daniel Parslow (D)	5 11	12 06	Rhymney Valley	11 9 85	Cardiff C
Jamie Reed (F)	6 0	12 04	Chester	13 8 87	Bangor C
Scott Kerr (M)	5 9	12 10	Leeds	11 12 81	Lincoln C
Jason Walker (F)	5 9	11 00	Barrow	21 2 84	Luton T
Ashley Chambers (F)	5 10	11 07	Leicester	1 3 90	Leicester C
Danny Pilkington (F)	5 9	11 09	Blackburn	25 5 90	Stockport Co
Eugen Bopp (M)	6 0	12 10	Kiev	5 9 83	Carl Zeiss Jena
Michael Potts (M)				26 11 91	Blackburn R
Jamal Fyfield (D)				17 3 89	Maidenhead U
Matty Blair (M)			Warwick	5 7 90	Kidderminster H
Adriano Moke (M)	5 9	10 01		11 1 90	Jerez Industrial
Scott Brown (M)	5 9	10 03	Chester	8 5 85	Fleetwood T
Jon Challinor (M)	5 11	11 11	Northampton	2 12 80	Kettering T
Matthew Blinkhorn (F)	6 0	10 10	Blackpool	2 3 85	Sligo R
Chris Doig (D)	6 2	12 06	Dumfries	13 2 81	Aldershot T
Michael Ingham (G)	6 4	13 10	Preston	9 7 80	Hereford U

ENGLISH LEAGUE PLAYERS – INDEX

Abadaki, Godwin 69
Abdou, Nadjim 52
Abdullah, Ahmad 88
Abe, Yuki 45
Abeid, Mehdi 55
Abu, Mohammed 49
Ada, Patrick 19
Adam, Charlie 47
Adams, Blair 79
Adams, Jack 72
Adams, Nicky 69
Addai, Alex 10
Addison, Miles 33
Adebayor, Emmanuel 49
Adebola, Dele 42
Ademeno, Charlie 2
Adeyemi, Tom 57
Adjei, Samuel 55
Adomah, Albert 16
Adorjan, Krisztian 47
Affane, Amin 24
Afobe, Benik 4
Agard, Kieran 92
Agbonlahor, Gabriel 5
Agdestein, Torbjorn 15
Agger, Daniel 47
Aguero, Sergio 49
Agustien, Kemy 80
Agyemang, Patrick 67
Ainsley, Jack 43
Ainsworth, Gareth 91
Ainsworth, Lionel 74
Airey, Philip 55
Ajose, Nicholas 62
Akinde, John 29
Akinfenwa, Adebayo 56
Akins, Lucas 84
Akpa Akpro, Jean-Louis 69
Akpan, Hope 29
Al-Habsi, Ali 89
Albrighton, Marc 5
Alcaraz, Antolin 89
Alcock, Craig 62
Aldred, Tom 27
Alessandra, Lewis 54
Alex 24
Alexander, Gary 14
Alexander, Graham 66
Aley, Zach 9
Alfei, Daniel 80
Allan, Scott 87
Allen, Charlie 59
Allen, Joe 80
Allinson, Lloyd 41
Allott, Mark 26
Almond, Louis 10
Almunia, Manuel 4
Alnwick, Ben 83
Alnwick, Jak 55
Alonso, Marcus 11
Alonso, Mikel 23
Altman, Omri 37
Amankwaah, Kevin 69
Ambrose, Darren 31
Ameobi, Sam 55
Ameobi, Shola 55
Amond, Padraig 1
Amoo, David 47
Amos, Ben 50
Andersen, Mikkel 68
Anderson 50
Anderson, Myles 9
Anderson, Paul 58
Anderson, Russell 33
Anderson, Tom 18
Andrade, Bruno 67
Andre Santos, Clarindo 4
Andrew, Calvin 31
Andrew, Danny 25
Andrews, Keith 87
Andrews, Zac 16
Aneke, Chuks 4
Anelka, Nicolas 24
Angel 10
Angeleri, Marcos 79
Angha, Martin 4
Anichebe, Victor 35
Ankergren, Casper 15
Annerson, Jamie 70
Ansah, Zak 4
Antelmi, Patrick 65
Anthony, Byron 17
Antonio, Michael 68
Anyinsah, Joe 17
Appiah, Kwesi 31
Aquilani, Alberto 47
Arber, Mark 32
Arca, Julio 51
Archer, Jordan 83
Archibald-Henville, Troy 36
Arestidou, Andreas 66
Arfield, Scott 41
Arismendi, Diego 78
Armstrong, James 79
Arnold, Nick 68
Arquin, Yoann 40
Arshavin, Andrei 4
Artell, Dave 30
Arter, Harry 12
Arteta, Mikel 4
Arthur, Chris 56
Arthurworrey, Stephen 37
Asante, Akwasi 8
Asante, Kyle 76
Ashbee, Ian 66
Ashdown, Jamie 65
Ashton, James 24
Ashton, Jon 77
Assombalonga, Britt 86
Assou-Ekotto, Benoit 83
Assulin, Gai 49
Atieno, Taiwo 82
Atkins, Ross 33
Atkinson, Chris 41
Atkinson, David 51
Atkinson, Will 42
Austin, Charlie 18
Austin, Neil 39
Austin, Ryan 19
Ayala, Daniel 57
Ayling, Luke 92
Ba, Demba 55
Bachmann, Daniel 78
Bagayoko, Mamadou 34
Baggridge, Rhys 92
Bagnall, Liam 79
Bailey, James 33
Bailey, Nicky 51
Baines, Leighton 35
Baio, Yalany 47
Baird, Chris 37
Bakare, Michael 48
Bakayogo, Zaoumana 84
Baker, Adam 13
Baker, Carl 28
Baker, Nathan 5
Balanta, Angelo 67
Baldock, George 53
Baldock, Sam 88
Baldwin, Jack 39
Baldwin, Pat 76
Bale, Gareth 83
Balkestein, Pim 14
Ball, Callum 33
Ball, David 62
Ball, Matt 57
Balotelli, Mario 49
Bamba, Souleymane 45
Bamford, Patrick 24
Bamogo, Habib 34
Banks, Oliver 70
Bannan, Barry 5
Banton, Jason 47
Banya, Charlie 37
Barcham, Andy 71
Bardsley, Phillip 79
Barker, Chris 76
Barker, George 15
Barker, Shaun 33
Barkhuizen, Tom 10
Barkley, Ross 35
Barmby, Nick 42
Barnard, Lee 75
Barnes, Ashley 15
Barnes, Giles 34
Barnes-Homer, Matt 69
Barnett, Charlie 1
Barnett, Leon 57
Barnett, Tyrone 62
Barrera, Pablo 88
Barrett, Adam 12
Barroilhet, Richard 37
Barron, Scott 52
Barry, Gareth 49
Barry-Murphy, Brian 69
Bartlett, Adam 40
Bartley, Kyle 4
Bartley, Marvyn 18
Barton, Adam 66
Barton, Joey 67
Basey, Grant 91
Baseya, Cedric 68
Basham, Chris 10
Basso, Adriano 42
Bassong, Sebastien 83
Bates, Jon-Jo 32
Bates, Matthew 51
Bateson, Jonathan 48
Batt, Damian 61
Batt, Shaun 52
Bath, Danny 90
Baudry, Mathieu 12
Bauza, Guillem 36
Baxendale, James 34
Baxter, Jose 35
Bean, Marcus 14
Beardsley, Chris 77
Beattie, Craig 80
Beattie, James 72
Beausejour, Jean 89
Beavon, Stuart 91
Bebe 50
Becchio, Luciano 44
Beck, Mark 22
Beckford, Jermaine 45
Bednar, Roman 10
Beevers, Lee 85
Beevers, Mark 73
Begovic, Asmir 78
Belezika, Glenn 60
Belford, Cameron 20
Belford, Tyrell 47
Bell, David 28
Bell, Lee 30
Bellamy, Craig 47
Bellamy, Liam 14
Belson, Flavien 92
Bembo-Lita, Djenny 60
Ben Arfa, Hatem 55
Ben Haim, Tal 65
Ben Youssef, Syam 46
Benali, Ahmed 49
Benayoun, Yossi 24
Bencherif, Hamza 59
Bender, Tom 27
Bendtner, Nicklas 4
Bennett, Alan 25
Bennett, Dale 86
Bennett, Elliott 57
Bennett, Ian 41
Bennett, Joe 51
Bennett, Julian 73
Bennett, Kyle 34
Bennett, Mason 33
Bennett, Rhys 11
Bennett, Ryan 57
Bennett, Scott 36
Benson, Paul 81
Bent, Darren 5
Bentley, Daniel 76
Bentley, David 83
Bentley, Jim 54
Benyon, Elliot 76
Berahino, Saido 87
Berbatov, Dimitar 50
Bergkamp, Rowland 15
Bergqvist, Doug 3
Berra, Christophe 90
Berrett, James 22
Berry, Durrell 63
Bertrand, Ryan 24
Bessone, Fede 80
Best, Leon 55
Betsy, Kevin 91
Bettinelli, Marcus 37
Bevan, Scott 17
Beye, Habib 34
Bhasera, Onismor 63
Bialkowski, Bartosz 75
Bidwell, Jake 35
Bigirimana, Gael 28
Bignall, Nicholas 68
Bignot, Paul 10
Bijev, Villyan 47
Bikey, Andre 18
Billington, Alex 66
Bilyaletdinov, Diniyar 35
Bingham, Billy 32
Bingham, Rakish 89
Birchall, Adam 38
Bishop, Andy 20
Bishop, Neil 59
Black, Paul 60
Blackman, Jamal 24
Blackman, Nick 9
Blackstock, Dexter 58
Blake, Darcy 21
Blake, Jack 58
Blake, Robbie 11
Blake, Ryan 14
Blakeman, Adam 11
Blanchard, Maximo 63
Blanchett, Danny 19
Blizzard, Dominic 92
Bloomfield, Matt 91
Boa Morte, Luis 88
Boateng, Daniel 4
Boateng, George 58
Boateng, Michael 17
Bodde, Ferrie 80
Boden, Scott 26
Bodin, Billy 81
Bogdan, Adam 11
Bogdanovic, Daniel 10
Bolasie, Yannick 16
Bolder, Adam 19
Bolger, Cian 45
Bolton, James 48
Bond, Andy 27
Bond, Jonathan 86
Bonham, Jack 86
Boothman, Steven 89
Borrowdale, Gary 67
Boselli, Mauro 89
Bosingwa, Jose 24
Bostock, John 83
Bostwick, Michael 77
Bothelo, Pedro 4
Bothroyd, Jay 67
Bouazza, Hameur 52
Bouhbenna, Rachid 34
Bouzanis, Dean 60
Bover, Ruben 23
Bowditch, Dean 53
Bowerman, George 85
Bowery, Jordan 26
Bowles, Gary 12
Bowyer, Lee 43
Boyata, Dedryck 49
Boyce, Emmerson 89
Boyd, Adam 39
Boyd, George 62
Bradley, Mark 70
Bradley, Sonny 42
Bradshaw, Tom 74
Brady, Robert 50
Bramble, Titus 79
Branagan, Richie 20
Branston, Guy 13
Brayford, John 33
Breen, Sean 54
Breeze, Jonathan 89
Breeze, Matthew 62
Breimyr, Henrik 3
Brezovan, Peter 15
Bridcutt, Liam 15
Bridge, Wayne 49
Briggs, Matthew 37
Brill, Dean 6
Brislen-Hall, George 4
Brisley, Shaun 62
Brister, Alex 37
Britton, Leon 80
Brobbel, Ryan 51
Brodie, Richard 29
Bromby, Leigh 44
Brooke, Ryan 60
Brown, Aaron 66
Brown, Alex 38
Brown, Ben 67
Brown, Chris 34
Brown, Connor 72
Brown, James 39
Brown, Jordan 30
Brown, Kayleden 87
Brown, Lee 17
Brown, Michael 44
Brown, Nat 48
Brown, Reece 50
Brown, Scott P 25
Brown, Sebastian 2
Brown, Troy 70
Brown, Wayne 61
Brown, Wayne 17
Brown, Wes 79
Browning, Tyias 35
Bruce, Alex 44
Bruma, Jeffrey 24
Bruna, Gerardo 10
Brunt, Chris 87
Brunt, Ryan 78
Brunt, Thomas 38
Bryan, Joe 16
Bryan, Michael 86
Bryson, Craig 33
Buaben, Prince 86
Bubb, Bradley 3
Buchanan, David 84
Buckley, Will 15
Bull, Nikki 91
Bullard, Jimmy 43
Bullock, Lee 13
Bulman, Dannie 29
Bunn, Harry 49
Bunn, Mark 9
Burch, Rob 59
Burge, Lee 28
Burge, Ryan 34
Burgess, Ben 59
Burke, Chris 8
Burke, Cormac 43
Burke, Graham 5
Burn, Dan 37
Burns, Andrew 13
Burns, Ryan 60
Burrow, Jordan 54
Burton, Alan 1
Bush, Chris 2
Butcher, Lee 46
Butland, Jack 8
Butler, Andy 85
Butlin, Joey 85
Butterfield, Danny 75
Butterfield, Jacob 7
Button, David 83
Buxton, Adam 89
Buxton, Jake 33
Buxton, Lewis 73
Buzsaky, Akos 67
Byrne, Callum 69
Byrne, Cliff 71
Byrne, Mark 6
Byrne, Nathan 83
Byrne, Neil 69
Byrne, Shane 45
Byrom, Joel 77
Bywater, Steve 73
Cabaye, Yohan 55
Cadamarteri, Danny 41
Caddis, Paul 81
Cadogan, Kieron 31
Cahill, Gary 24
Cahill, Tim 35
Cain, Michael 45
Caira, Reece 5
Cairney, Tom 42

Cairns, Alex 44
Calderon, Inigo 15
Caldwell, Gary 89
Caldwell, Steven 8
Cameron, Courtney 5
Cameron, Nathan 28
Camp, Lee 58
Campbell, Adam 55
Campbell, Dudley 67
Campbell, Frazier 79
Campbell, Joel 4
Campbell, Stuart 17
Campbell-Ryce, Jamal 16
Canavan, Niall 71
Canham, Sean 40
Cansdell-Sherriff, Shane 74
Capaldi, Tony 61
Caprice, Jake 31
Carayol, Mustapha 17
Carew, John 88
Carey, Lewis 16
Carey, Louis 16
Carlisle, Clarke 18
Carlton, Danny 54
Carmichael, Josh 12
Carr, Matthew 60
Carr, Stephen 8
Carragher, Jamie 47
Carrick, Michael 50
Carrington, Mark 20
Carroll, Andy 47
Carroll, Tommy 83
Carruthers, Samir 5
Carson, Josh 43
Carson, Trevor 20
Carter, Joe 38
Carver, Marcus 1
Cassidy, Jake 90
Cathcart, Craig 10
Cattermole, Lee 79
Caulker, Steven 83
Ceballos, Cristian 83
Cech, Petr 24
Cerny, Radek 67
Cestor, Mike 46
Chadwick, Luke 53
Chadwick, Nick 63
Chalmers, Lewis 48
Chalobah, Nathaniel 24
Chamakh, Marouane 4
Chamberlain, Elliott 45
Chambers, Adam 85
Chambers, Calum 75
Chambers, James 34
Chambers, Luke 58
Chambers, Michael 31
Champion, Fred 67
Chantler, Chris 22
Chapell, Jordan 72
Chaplow, Richard 75
Chapman, Adam 61
Charles, Anthony 56
Charles, Darius 77
Charnock, Kieran 54
Chenoweth, Ollie 63
Chester, James 42
Chicksen, Adam 53
Chilvers, Liam 59
Chimbonda, Pascal 34
Chippendale, Aiden 41
Chopra, Michael 43
Chorley, Ben 46
Chow, Tim 89
Christie, Cyrus 28
Church, Simon 68
Cibocchi, Alessandro 81
Cisak, Aleksander 60
Cisse, Djibril 67
Cisse, Kalifa 16
Cisse, Papiss 55
Clark, Ciaran 5
Clark, Jordan 7
Clark, Luke 66
Clarke, Billy 29
Clarke, Jordan 28
Clarke, Leon 23
Clarke, Lewis 92
Clarke, Nathan 41
Clarke, Ollie 17
Clarke, Peter 41
Clarke, Ryan 61
Clarke, Tom 41
Clarkson, David 16
Clay, Craig 26
Clayton, Adam 44
Clayton, Harry 30
Clayton, Max 30
Clement, Jordan 3
Cleverley, Tom 50
Clichy, Gael 49
Clifford, Billy 24
Clifford, Conor 24
Clingan, Sammy 28
Clist, Simon 40
Clohessy, Sean 76
Clough, Charlie 17
Clowes, Robert 92
Clucas, Sam 40
Clucas, Seanan 66
Clyne, Nathaniel 31
Coady, Conor 47
Coates, Sebastian 47
Cofie, John 50
Cohen, Chris 58
Coid, Danny 1
Coke, Giles 73
Coker, Ben 27
Colback, Jack 79
Colbeck, Joe 40
Cole, Aaron 33
Cole, Ashley 24
Cole, Carlton 88
Cole, Jake 63
Cole, Joe 47
Cole, Larnell 50
Coleman, Seamus 35
Coleman , Alex 18
Coles, Danny 36
Colgan, Nick 41
Collin, Adam 22
Collins, Charlie 53
Collins, Danny 78
Collins, James M 5
Collins, James S 74
Collins, Jamie 3
Collins, Lee 7
Collins, Michael 71
Collins, Neill 72
Collins, Sam 39
Collis, Steve 62
Collison, Jack 88
Collister, Joe 84
Coloccini, Fabricio 55
Comazzi, Alberto 81
Compton, Jack 13
Comrie, Dominic 66
Conlan, Luke 18
Conneely, Seamus 72
Connell, Alan 81
Connolly, David 75
Connolly, Kyle 86
Connolly, Mark 11
Connolly, Matthew 67
Connolly, Paul 44
Connolly, Reece 3
Connolly, Ryan 33
Connor, Dan 40
Constable, James 61
Conway, Craig 21
Cook, Jordan 79
Cook, Lee 67
Cook, Steve 12
Cooper, Liam 42
Cooper, Shaun 12
Coppinger, James 34
Coquelin, Francis 4
Corbett, Andy 19
Cork, Jack 75
Corker, Ashley 56
Corluka, Vedran 83
Cornell, David 80
Corr, Barry 76
Cort, Leon 23
Cosgrove, Jonathan 37
Cotterill, David 7
Cotton, Robert 9
Coughlan, Graham 76
Coughlin, Andy 84
Coulson, Charlie 62
Courtois, Thibaut 24
Cousins, Jordan 23
Cousins, Mark 27
Coutts, Paul 66
Cowan, Don 77
Cowie, Don 21
Cowperthwaite, Niall 54
Cox, Dean 46
Cox, Lee 81
Cox, Sam 6
Cox, Simon 87
Coyne, Danny 51
Craddock, Jody 90
Craddock, Tom 61
Craig, Tony 52
Crainey, Stephen 10
Craney, Ian 1
Cranie, Martin 28
Crawford, Harry 76
Cregg, Patrick 20
Cresswell, Aaron 43
Cresswell, Richard 72
Cresswell, Ryan 70
Croft, Lee 33
Crofts, Andrew 57
Cronin, Lance 17
Crooks, Matt 41
Cropper, Cody 43
Crouch, Peter 78
Crowe, Jason 56
Crusat, Albert 89
Cruyff, Jessua 89
Cudicini, Carlo 83
Cudworth, Jack 48
Cuellar, Carlos 5
Cuff, Sean 72
Cullen, Mark 42
Culshaw, Joe 54
Cummings, Shaun 68
Cummings, Warren 12
Cummins, Graham 66
Cunningham, Greg 49
Cunnington, Adam 32
Cureton, Jamie 46
Curran, Craig 22
Cuthbert, Scott 46
Cuvelier, Florent 78
Cywka, Thomasz 68
D'Ath, Lawson 68
Daehli, Mats 50
Dagnall, Chris 7
Dailly, Christian 76
Daley, Keammar 66
Daley, Luke 63
Daley, Omar 13
Dalibard, Benoit 40
Dalla Valle, Lauri 37
Daniel, Colin 48
Daniels, Brendon 30
Daniels, Charlie 12
Daniels, Donervorn 87
Daniels, Greg 48
Daniels, Luke 87
Dann, Scott 9
Danns, Neil 45
Darby, Stephen 47
Darikwa, Tendayi 26
Darlow, Karl 58
Davies, Adam 35
Davies, Andrew 78
Davies, Arron 56
Davies, Ben 33
Davies, Ben 80
Davies, Callum 38
Davies, Craig 7
Davies, Curtis 8
Davies, Kevin 11
Davies, Mark 11
Davies, Scott 29
Davies, Simon 37
Davies, Steve 33
Davila, Ulises 24
Davis, Claude 29
Davis, David 90
Davis, Harry 30
Davis, Joe 64
Davis, Kelvin 75
Davis, Liam 61
Davis, Sean 11
Dawkin, Josh 57
Dawkins, Simon 83
Dawson, Aaron 36
Dawson, Adam 89
Dawson, Andy 42
Dawson, Craig 87
Dawson, Michael 83
Dawson, Stephen 7
Day, Chris 77
Day, Jamie 29
Day, Joe 62
De Bruyne, Kevin 24
De Gea, David 50
De Jong, Nigel 49
De Laet, Ritchie 50
De Ridder, Steve 75
De Silva, Kyle 31
De Vita, Raffaele 81
De Vries, Dorus 90
Deaman, Jack 8
Dean, Harlee 75
Dean, Luke 13
Deards, Connor 85
Deegan, Gary 28
Deen-Conteh, Aziz 24
Deeney, Saul 33
Deeney, Troy 86
Deering, Sam 6
Defoe, Jermain 83
Delac, Matej 24
Delaney, Damien 43
Delap, Rory 78
Delfouneso, Nathan 5
Della-Verde, Lyle 37
Delph, Fabian 5
Dembele, Moussa 37
Demel, Guy 88
Demontagnac, Ishmel 59
Dempsey, Clint 37
Dempster, John 29
Denilson 4
Dennehy, Darren 6
Dennis, Louis 32
Denton, Alec 70
Derbyshire, Matt 58
Derry, Shaun 67
Devaney, Martin 84
Devera, Joe 81
Devine, Daniel 66
Devine, Danny 5
Devitt, Jamie 42
Di Santo, Franco 89
Diaby, Abou 4
Diagne, Tony 48
Diagouraga, Toumani 14
Diakite, Samba 67
Diallo, Bradley 60
Diame, Mohamed 89
Diamond, Zander 60
Diao, Salif 78
Diarra, Mahamadou 37
Dickenson, Ben 15
Dicker, Gary 15
Dickinson, Carl 86
Dickinson, Liam 76
Dicko, Nouha 89
Dickson, Ryan 75
Dier, Eric 35
Digby, Paul 7
Dikgacoi, Kagisho 31
Dillon, Kealan 42
Dilo, Christopher 9
Diop, Papa Bouba 88
Diouf, El Hadji 34
Distin, Sylvain 35
Djilali, Kieran 2
Djourou, Johan 4
Do Prado, Guilherme 75
Dobbie, Stephen 80
Dobie, Luke 51
Doble, Ryan 75
Dodd, Adam 10
Dodds, Louis 64
Doe, Scott 32
Doherty, Gary 23
Doherty, Matthew 90
Doig, Chris 3
Dolan, Matthew 51
Donacien, Janoi 5
Donaldson, Clayton 14
Donaldson, Ryan 55
Done, Matt 7
Donegan, Tom 37
Doni 47
Donnelly, George 69
Donnelly, Rory 80
Donnelly, Scott 80
Donovan, Landon 35
Dorman, Andy 31
Dorrans, Graham 87
Doughty, Michael 67
Douglas, Jamie 66
Douglas, Jonathan 14
Doumbe, Stephen 53
Downes, Aaron 26
Downing, Paul 87
Downing, Stewart 47
Doyle, Colin 8
Doyle, Conor 33
Doyle, Kevin 90
Doyle, Micky 72
Doyle, Nathan 7
Doyley, Lloyd 86
Draper, Ross 48
Drennan, Michael 5
Drenthe, Roysten 35
Drinkwater, Daniel 45
Driver, Callum 88
Drogba, Didier 24
Drummond, Stuart 54
Drury, Adam 57
Drury, Adam 49
Drury, Andy 43
Duberry, Michael 61
Dudgeon, Joe 42
Duff, Damien 37
Duff, Michael 18
Duffy, Darryl 25
Duffy, Mark 71
Duffy, Richard 36
Duffy, Shane 35
Dugdale, Adam 30
Duguid, Karl 27
Duke, Matt 13
Dumbuya, Mustapha 34
Dummett, Paul 55
Dunbavin, Ian 1
Dunk, Lewis 15
Dunn, Chris 28
Dunn, David 9
Dunn, Jack 47
Dunne, Alan 52
Dunne, Charles 91
Dunne, James 36
Dunne, Richard 5
Dyer, Jack 19
Dyer, Kieron 67
Dyer, Lloyd 45
Dyer, Nathan 80
Dzeko, Edin 49
Eagles, Chris 11
Eardley, Neal 10
Earnshaw, Robert 21
East, Daniel 15
East, Danny 42
Easter, Jermaine 31
Eastham, Ashley 10
Eastman, Tom 27
Eastmond, Craig 4
Easton, Brian 18
Eastwood, Freddy 28
Eaves, Tom 11
Ebanks-Blake, Sylvan 90
Ebanks-Landell, Ethan 90
Ebecilio, Kyle 4
Eccleston, Nathan 47
Eckersley, Tom 11
Edgar, Anthony 92
Edgar, David 18
Edge, Jamie 87
Edmans, Rob 32
Edmundsson, Joan 55
Edwards, Cameron 68
Edwards, Carlos 43
Edwards, Curtis 51
Edwards, Dave 90
Edwards, Gwion 80
Edwards, Joe 16
Edwards, Matty 69
Edwards, Mike 59
Edwards, Phil 77
Edwards, Rob 36
Edwards, Rob 7
Edwards, Ryan 68
Edwards, Ryan 9
Egan, John 79
Eger, Marcel 14
Ehmer, Max 67
Eisfeld, Thomas 4
Ekangamene, Charni 50
Ekim, Josh 14
El-Abd, Adam 15
Elabdellaoui, Omar 49

Elder, Nathan 40
Elford-Alliyu, Lateef 87
Elito, Medy 32
Ellington, Nathan 43
Elliot, Rob 55
Elliott, Brett 79
Elliott, Marvin 16
Elliott, Steve 25
Elliott, Wade 8
Ellis, Mark 82
Ellison, Kevin 54
Elmohamady, Ahmed 79
Elokobi, George 90
Elphick, Tommy 15
Emerton, Brett 9
Emerton, Danny 42
Emilsson, Kristjan 47
Emmanuel-Thomas, Jay 43
Emnes, Marvin 51
Ephraim, Hogan 67
Errington, Jack 18
Ertl, Johannes 72
Esajas, Etienne 81
Essam, Connor 38
Essien, Michael 24
Etheridge, Neil 37
Etherington, Matthew 78
Etuhu, Dickson 37
Etuhu, Kelvin 65
Euell, Jason 23
Eustace, John 86
Evans, Adam 18
Evans, Alex 21
Evans, Ched 72
Evans, Corry 42
Evans, Daniel 29
Evans, Gary 70
Evans, Jack 38
Evans, Jonny 50
Evans, Micah 9
Evans, Will 40
Evatt, Ian 10
Evina, Cedric 23
Evra, Patrice 50
Fabianski, Lukasz 4
Fabio 50
Fabio Aurelio 47
Facey, Delroy 40
Fagan, Craig 13
Fahey, Keith 8
Fairhurst, Waide 48
Fallon, Rory 92
Falque, Iago 83
Fanimo, Matthias 88
Farah, Ibrahim 21
Faubert, Julien 88
Faurlin, Alejandro 67
Faye, Aboulaye 88
Fazlic, Dino 11
Featherstone, Nicky 40
Federici, Adam 68
Feeney, Liam 52
Feeney, Warren 63
Fellaini, Marouane 35
Fenton, Nick 54
Fenwick, Bayan 31
Ferdinand, Anton 67
Ferdinand, Kane 76
Ferdinand, Rio 50
Ferguson, Barry 10
Ferguson, Shane 55
Fernandez, Hugo 9
Fernandez, Jesus 47
Ferry, Simon 81
Feruz, Islam 24
Field, Adam 41
Fielding, Frank 33
Figueroa, Maynor 89
Findley, Robbie 58
Fish, Matt 38
Fisher, Tom 48
Fitzpatrick, David 67
Flahavan, Darryl 12
Flanagan, John 47
Flanagan, Tom 53
Fleck, John 10
Fleetwood, Stuart 40
Fleming, Andy 54
Fleming, Greg 26
Fletcher, Carl 63
Fletcher, Darren 50
Fletcher, Matthew 61
Fletcher, Steve 12
Fletcher, Steven 90
Fletcher, Wes 18
Flinders, Scott 39
Flint, Aiden 81
Flitney, Ross 38
Flood, Anto 76
Flynn, Michael 13
Flynn, Ryan 72
Foderingham, Wesley 81
Fogden, Wes 12
Folan, Caleb 8
Folan, Stephen 55
Foley, Kevin 90
Fontaine, Liam 16
Fonte, Jose 75
Forbes, Terrell 46
Ford, Simon 26
Forde, Anthony 90
Forde, David 52
Forecast, Tommy 75
Formica, Mauro 9
Fornasier, Michele 50
Forrester, Anton 35
Forrester, Harry 14
Forshaw, Adam 35
Forssell, Mikael 44
Forster, Fraser 55
Forster-Caskey, Jake 15
Forsyth, Craig 86
Forte, Jonathan 75
Fortune, Jon 36
Fortune, Marc-Antoine 87
Foster, Ben 8
Foster, Danny 91
Foster, Luke 70
Foster, Ricky 16
Foster, Stephen 7
Fowler, Jake 51
Fox, Danny 75
Fox, David 57
Frampton, Andrew 38
Francis, Simon 12
Francomb, George 57
Franks, Fraser 2
Franks, Jonathan 51
Fraser, Tom 6
Frear, Elliott 36
Frecklington, Lee 62
Fredericks, Ryan 83
Freeman, Kieron 58
Freeman, Luke 77
Frei, Kerim 37
Friedel, Brad 83
Friend, George 34
Frimpong, Emmanuel 4
Fry, Matt 13
Fryatt, Matty 42
Fryers, Zeki 50
Fuller, Barry 38
Fuller, Ricardo 78
Fulop, Marton 87
Furman, Dean 60
Futacs, Marko 65
Futcher, Ben 20
Gabbidon, Daniel 67
Gabilondo, Lander 81
Gage, Ethan 68
Gain, Peter 32
Galindo, Samuel 4
Gallagher, Jake 52
Gallagher, Paul 45
Gallas, William 83
Gallifuoco, Giancarlo 83
Galloway, Brendon 53
Gambin, Luke 6
Gameiro, Corey 37
Garbutt, Luke 35
Garcia, Richard 42
Gardner, Anthony 31
Gardner, Craig 79
Gardner, Gary 5
Gardner, Ricardo 11
Garner, Joe 86
Garratt, Ben 30
Garry, Ryan 12
Garvan, Owen 31
Gayle, Cameron 87
Gayle, Dwight 32
Gayle, Ian 32
Gazzaniga, Paulo 38
Gecov, Marcel 37
Gelson 45
Geohaghon, Exodus 6
Gera, Zoltan 87
Gerken, Dean 16
German, Antonio 14
Gerrard, Anthony 21
Gerrard, Paul 60
Gerrard, Steven 47
Gervinho 4
Gestede, Rudy 21
Ghilas, Kamel 42
Gibbons, Jordan 67
Gibbons, Robbie 71
Gibbs, Kieran 4
Gibson, Ben 51
Gibson, Billy 92
Gibson, Darron 35
Giggs, Ryan 50
Gilbert, Kerrea 92
Gilbert, Peter 76
Gilbey, Alex 27
Gilks, Matthew 10
Gill, Matthew 17
Gillespie, Mark 22
Gillespie, Steven 27
Gillett, Simon 34
Gilligan, Ryan 56
Gilmartin, Rene 86
Giovani 83
Girvan, Michael 89
Given, Shay 5
Giverin, Luke 50
Givet, Gael 9
Gleeson, Stephen 53
Gnahore, Eddy 8
Gnakpa, Claude 85
Gobern, Oscar 41
Goddard, John 68
Goddard, Jordan 17
Godden, Matthew 71
Gohouri, Steve 89
Golbourne, Scott 7
Goldson, Connor 74
Golobart, Roman 89
Gomes, Heurelho 83
Gomez, Jordi 89
Gomis, Morgaro 8
Gonzalez, David 15
Goodison, Ian 84
Goodwillie, David 9
Goodwin, Shamir 15
Gordon, Ben 24
Gordon, Craig 79
Gorkss, Kaspars 68
Gorman, Johnny 90
Gornell, Terry 74
Gorrin, Alejandro 79
Gosling, Dan 55
Gosling, Jake 36
Gough, Conor 23
Goulding, Jeff 25
Goulon, Herold 9
Gounet, Antoine 14
Gow, Alan 36
Gower, Mark 80
Grabban, Lewis 70
Gradel, Max 44
Graham, Bagasan 25
Graham, Danny 80
Graham, Jordan 5
Grandin, Elliot 10
Grandison, Jermaine 74
Grant, Alex 65
Grant, Anthony 76
Grant, Joel 91
Grant, John 48
Grant, Lee 18
Grant, Peter 62
Grant, Robert 71
Gray, Andy 7
Gray, Dan 26
Gray, David 66
Gray, Reece 69
Green, Danny 23
Green, Danny J 32
Green, Dominic 32
Green, Mike 64
Green, Paul 33
Green, Rob 88
Green, Ryan 40
Greening, Jonathan 58
Greer, Gordon 15
Gregory, Steven 12
Grella, Mike 20
Grella, Vince 9
Griffin, Andy 68
Griffith, Anthony 64
Griffiths, Jamie 43
Griffiths, Leigh 90
Griffiths, Sam 14
Griffiths, Scott 62
Grigg, Will 85
Grimes, Ashley 69
Grimmer, Jack 37
Grof, David 85
Grounds, Jonathan 51
Grygera, Zdenek 37
Gudjonsson, Joey 41
Guedioura, Adiene 90
Gueye, Magaye 35
Guidetti, John 49
Gulacsi, Peter 47
Gunnarsson, Aron 21
Gunnarsson, Brynjar 68
Gunter, Chris 58
Gurrieri, Andres 19
Guthrie, Danny 55
Guthrie, Jon 30
Guthrie, Kurtis 1
Gutierrez, Jonas 55
Guttridge, Luke 56
Guy, Lewis 53
Guzan, Brad 5
Gwillim, Gareth 2
Gyan, Asamoah 79
Hackett, Chris 52
Hackney, Simon 69
Hahnemann, Marcus 35
Haining, Will 54
Hajrovic, Sead 4
Haldane, Lewis 64
Halford, Greg 65
Hall, Asa 61
Hall, Fitz 67
Hall, Freddy 56
Hall, Grant 15
Hall, Robert 88
Hall, Ryan 76
Halliche, Rafik 37
Halliday, Andrew 51
Halls, John 91
Halpin, Saul 82
Halstead, Mark 10
Hamer, Ben 23
Hamilton, Bradley 27
Hammar, Johan 35
Hammill, Adam 90
Hammond, Dean 75
Hamshaw, Matt 48
Hancox, Mitch 8
Hands, Reece 9
Hanford, Daniel 40
Hangeland, Brede 37
Hanley, Grant 9
Hanley, Raheem 9
Hannah, Ross 13
Hansen, Martin 47
Hanson, James 13
Harding, Ben 56
Harding, Dan 75
Harding, Mitch 17
Harewood, Marlon 58
Hargreaves, Owen 49
Harley, Jon 59
Harley, Ryan 15
Haroun, Faris 51
Harper, James 42
Harper, Steve 55
Harper-Penman, Ged 63
Harrad, Shaun 20
Harriman, Michael 67
Harriott, Callum 23
Harriott, Matty 72
Harris, Ashley 65
Harris, Courtney 37
Harris, Kedeem 21
Harris, Louis 90
Harris, Neil 76
Harris, Robert 10
Harrison, Byron 2
Harrison, Danny 70
Harrison, Ellis 17
Harrold, Matt 17
Harrop, Max 20
Hart, Joe 49
Harte, Ian 68
Hartley, Peter 39
Harvey, Alex-Ray 18
Haslam, Steven 39
Hassan, Callum 39
Hassell, Bobby 7
Hatfield, Will 1
Hatton, Sam 2
Hawkes, Darren 38
Hawkins, Lewis 39
Hawley, Karl 59
Haworth, Andrew 20
Hayden, Isaac 4
Hayes, Paul 23
Hayhurst, Will 66
Haynes, Danny 23
Haynes-Brown, Curtis 92
Hayter, James 34
Hazell, Reuben 74
Healy, Colin 43
Heath, Joe 40
Heath, Matt 27
Heaton, Tom 21
Hector, Michael 68
Heitinga, Johnny 35
Helan, Jeremy 49
Helguson, Heidar 67
Hemmings, Ashley 90
Henderson, Conor 4
Henderson, Darius 52
Henderson, Ian 27
Henderson, Jeff 55
Henderson, Joe 28
Henderson, Jordan 47
Henderson, Stephen 65
Hendrick, Jeff 33
Henley, Adam 9
Hennessey, Wayne 90
Henry, Charlie 3
Henry, James 52
Henry, Karl 90
Henry, Ronnie 77
Henry, Thierry 4
Henshall, Alex 49
Herd, Ben 3
Herd, Chris 5
Hernandez, Javier 50
Heskey, Emile 5
Heslop, Simon 61
Hessey, Sean 1
Hester, Paddy 12
Hewitt, Elliott 48
Hewitt, Steven 18
Hewitt, Troy 67
Hibbert, Dave 62
Hibbert, Tony 35
Higginbotham, Danny 78
Higginbotham, Kallum 41
Higgins, Andrew 65
Higgs, Shane 56
Hilario 24
Hill, Clint 67
Hill, Matt 10
Hills, Lee 31
Hinds, Richard 92
Hines, Seb 51
Hines, Zavon 18
Hird, Samuel 34
Hitchcock, Tom 67
Hoban, Tommie 86
Hobbs, Jack 42
Hodson, Lee 86
Hoesen, Danny 37
Hogan, Dave 32
Hogg, Jonathan 86
Hoilett, Junior 9
Holden, Darren 39
Holden, Dean 26
Holden, Stuart 11
Holland, Jack 31
Hollands, Danny 23
Hollis, Haydn 59
Holloway, Aaron 16
Holmes, Danny 84
Holmes, Lee 75
Holmes, Ricky 6
Holness, Charlie 31
Holness, Marcus 69
Holohan, Gavan 42
Holroyd, Chris 66
Holt, Andy 56
Holt, Grant 57

Hooiveld, Jos 75
Hoolahan, Wes 57
Hooman, Harry 25
Hope, Hallam 35
Hopper, Ryan 1
Hopper, Tom 45
Horwood, Evan 39
Hoskins, Sam 75
Hoskins, Will 15
Hoult, Russell 40
Hourihane, Conor 63
Howard, Brian 68
Howard, Mark 72
Howard, Steve 45
Howard, Tim 35
Howe, Rene 82
Howell, Dean 29
Howell, Luke 32
Howieson, Cameron 18
Howson, Jonathan 57
Hoyte, Gavin 4
Hoyte, Justin 51
Hreidarsson, Hermann 28
Hubbins, Luke 8
Huddlestone, Tom 83
Hudson, Danny 20
Hudson, Mark 21
Hughes, Aaron 37
Hughes, Andy 23
Hughes, Bryan 1
Hughes, Caspar 30
Hughes, Connor 60
Hughes, Jeff 59
Hughes, Lee 59
Hughes, Mark 20
Hughes, Mark 6
Hughes, Will 33
Hulse, Rob 67
Hume, Iain 66
Humphreys, Richie 39
Hunt, David 29
Hunt, Jack 41
Hunt, Lewis 13
Hunt, Nicky 66
Hunt, Noel 68
Hunt, Stephen 59
Hunt, Steve 90
Hunter, Garry 54
Huntington, Paul 92
Hurst, James 87
Hurst, Kevan 85
Husband, James 34
Husband, Stephen 10
Huseklepp, Erik 65
Hussey, Chris 28
Hutchinson, Sam 24
Huth, Robert 78
Hutton, Alan 5
Huws, Emyr 49
Hyam, Luke 43
Hylton, Danny 3
Ibe, Jordan 47
Ibehre, Jabo 53
Ibrahim, Abdisalam 49
Ihiekwe, Michael 90
Ikeme, Carl 90
Ilesanmi, Femi 32
Ilunga, Herita 88
Ince, Rohan 24
Ince, Thomas 10
Ince, Tom 10
Ingham, Roger 36
Ingimarsson, Ivar 43
Ingram, Matt 91
Ings, Danny 18
Inman, Bradden 55
Ireland, Daniel 28
Ireland, Stephen 5
Isaac, Chez 86
Isgrove, Lloyd 75
Ismail, Zeli 90
Ivanovic, Branislav 24
Iversen, Steffen 31
Iwelumo, Chris 86
Izzet, Kem 27
Jaaskelainen, Jussi 11
Jackman, Danny 38
Jackson, Adam 51
Jackson, Joe 18
Jackson, Johnnie 23
Jackson, Josef 18
Jackson, Marlon 16
Jackson, Ryan 2
Jackson, Simeon 57
Jacobs, Michael 56
Jacobson, Joe 74
Jagielka, Phil 35
Jaidi, Radhi 75
Jalal, Shwan 12
James, David 16
James, Kingsley 64
James, Lloyd 27
James, Luke 39
James, Matthew 50
James, Tom 86
James, Tony 19
James-Lewis, Merrick 76
Jameson, Arron 73
Jansson, Oscar 83
Januzaj, Adrian 50
Jara, Gonzalo 87
Jarvis, Matthew 90
Jarvis, Nathaniel 21
Jarvis, Ryan 85
Jedinak, Mile 31
Jefferies, Darren 17
Jeffers, Shaun 28
Jelavic, Nikica 35
Jenas, Jermaine 83
Jenkins, Ross 86
Jenkinson, Carl 4
Jennings, Connor 71
Jensen, Brian 18
Jerome, Cameron 78
Jervis, Jake 8
Jevons, Phil 54
Ji, Dong-Won 79
Johansen, Eirik 49
John, George 88
John-Baptiste, Alex 10
John-Lewis, Lemell 20
Johnson, Adam 49
Johnson, Andy 37
Johnson, Brad 57
Johnson, Brett 2
Johnson, Damien 63
Johnson, Daniel 5
Johnson, Glen 47
Johnson, Huw 2
Johnson, Jemal 76
Johnson, Jermaine 73
Johnson, John 56
Johnson, Lee 16
Johnson, Leon 91
Johnson, Michael 49
Johnson, Oli 61
Johnson, Paul 39
Johnson, Reda 73
Johnson, Roger 90
Johnson, Sam 64
Johnstone, Samuel 50
Jolley, Christian 2
Jombati, Sido 25
Jones, Andrai 20
Jones, Billy 87
Jones, Billy 36
Jones, Brad 47
Jones, Chris 33
Jones, Daniel 73
Jones, Darren 3
Jones, David 89
Jones, Gary 69
Jones, Jake 85
Jones, Jamie 46
Jones, Joe 45
Jones, Kenwyne 78
Jones, Mike 73
Jones, Nathan 92
Jones, Paul 62
Jones, Phil 50
Jones, Reece 2
Jones, Richie 13
Jones, Rob 73
Jonsson, Eggert 90
Jordan, Stephen 69
Jorenen, Jesse 37
Jose Enrique 47
Joyce, Danny 68
Joyce, Luke 1
Juan, Jimmy 26
Judge, Alan 59
Julian, Alan 77
Jutkiewicz, Lucas 51
Kabba, Steven 6
Kaboul, Younes 83
Kacaniklic, Alex 37
Kadar, Tamas 55
Kakuta, Gael 24
Kalala, Jean-Paul 76
Kalas, Tomas 24
Kalou, Salomon 24
Kamau, Michael 14
Kamdjo, Clovis 6
Kane, Harry 83
Kane, Todd 24
Kanu, Nwankwo 65
Karacan, Jem 68
Kasami, Pajtim 37
Kasim, Yaser 15
Kasnik, David 73
Kavanagh, Graham 22
Kavanagh, Sean 37
Kay, Antony 41
Kay, Michael 84
Kay, Scott 48
Kaziboni, Greg 56
Kean, Jake 9
Keane, Kallum 36
Keane, Michael 50
Keane, Robbie 5
Keane, Will 50
Kearns, Daniel 62
Kebe, Jimmy 68
Kedwell, Danny 38
Kee, Billy 19
Keegan, Paul 34
Keinan, Dekel 21
Kelly, Julian 59
Kelly, Martin 47
Kelly, Sam 35
Kelly, Stephen 37
Kennedy, Callum 81
Kennedy, Jason 69
Kennedy, Kieran 49
Kennedy, Mark 43
Kennedy, Terry 72
Kennedy, Tom 45
Kenny, Paddy 67
Keogh, Andy 52
Keogh, Richard 28
Keohane, Jimmy 36
Kermorgant, Yann 23
Kerr, Fraser 8
Kerrouche, Mehdi 81
Kettings, Chris 10
Kewley-Graham, Jesse 91
Khumalo, Bongani 83
Kiernan, Brendan 2
Kiernan, Rob 89
Kightly, Michael 90
Kilbane, Kevin 42
Kilgallon, Matthew 79
Kilkenny, Neil 16
King, Andy 45
King, Josh 50
King, Ledley 83
King, Lewis 79
King, Marlon 8
King, Simon 38
King, Tom 31
Kink, Tarmo 51
Kinniburgh, Steve 61
Kirby, Jake 84
Kirkland, Chris 89
Kisnorbo, Patrick 44
Kiss, Filip 21
Kitson, Dave 65
Kitson, Neal 56
Klasnic, Ivan 11
Knight, Zat 11
Knott, Billy 79
Knowles, Dominic 18
Knowles, James 9
Kolarov, Aleksandar 49
Kompany, Vincent 49
Konchesky, Paul 45
Koral, Michael 30
Koren, Robert 42
Koscielny, Laurent 4
Kostrna, Kristian 90
Kovacs, Janos 40
Kozluk, Rob 13
Kranjcar, Niko 83
Kretzschmar, Max 91
Krul, Tim 55
Krysiak, Artur 36
Kuipers, Michels 29
Kuqi, Shefki 60
Kurucz, Peter 88
Kuszczak, Tomasz 50
Kuyt, Dirk 47
Kyrgiakos, Sotirios 79
Labadie, Joss 84
Lacey, Patrick 13
Ladapo, Freddie 27
Lafferty, Danny 18
Laing, Louis 79
Lainton, Robert 11
Laird, Marc 46
Laird, Scott 77
Lalkovic, Milan 24
Lallana, Adam 75
Lambert, Ricky 75
Lampard, Frank 24
Lancashire, Oliver 85
Lancaster, Cameron 83
Lane, Jack 48
Lane, Patrick 45
Langley, Josh 89
Langmead, Kelvin 56
Lansbury, Henri 4
Lanzano, Mattia 81
Lappin, Simon 57
Larkin, Colin 39
Larkins, Jake 88
Larrauri, Pier 45
Larrieu, Romain 63
Larsson, Sebastian 79
Lascelles, Jamaal 58
Lathrope, Damon 82
Lawlor, Ian 49
Lawrence, Byron 43
Lawrence, Liam 65
Lawrence, Matt 38
Lazaar, Mehdi 18
Le Fondre, Adam 68
Leach, Daniel 6
Leacock, Dean 46
Leadbitter, Daniel 82
Leadbitter, Grant 43
Leather, Scott 66
Lecointe, Matt 63
Ledesma, Emmanuel 85
Lee, Alan 41
Lee, Charlie 38
Lee, Chung Yong 11
Lee, Elliot 88
Lee, Kieran 60
Lee, Oliver 88
Lee, Richard 14
Lee, Tadanari 75
Lee, Tommy 26
Lee-Barrett, Arran 43
Lees, Tom 44
Legge, Leon 14
Legzdins, Adam 33
Leigertwood, Mikele 68
Leitch-Smith, AJ 30
Lenihan, Darragh 9
Lennon, Aaron 83
Lennox, Aaron 67
Lennox, Joe 63
Leonard, Ryan 76
Lescinel, Jean-Francois 72
Lescott, Jolean 49
Leslie, Steven 74
Lester, Jack 26
Leven, Peter 61
Lewington, Chris 32
Lewington, Dean 53
Lewis, Joe 62
Lewis, Stuart 91
Lewis, Theo 25
Lichaj, Eric 5
Lidakevicius, Lukas 7
Liddle, Gary 39
Liddle, Michael 79
Lillis, Josh 71
Lindegaard, Anders 50
Lindfield, Craig 1
Lines, Chris 73
Linganzi, Amine 9
Lingard, Jesse 50
Lisbie, Kevin 46
Lita, Leroy 80
Little, Andrew 64
Little, Mark 62
Livermore, Jake 83
Livesey, Danny 22
Llera, Miguel 73
Lletget, Sebastian 88
Lloyd, Ryan 64
Loach, Scott 86
Lobjoit, Billy 46
Locke, Simon 68
Lockwood, Adam 34
Loft, Doug 64
Logan, Conrad 45
Logan, Richard 36
Logan, Shaleum 14
Lonergan, Andrew 44
Long, George 72
Long, Kevin 18
Long, Shane 87
Long, Stacy 77
Losasso, Charlie 68
Love, Archie 18
Lovell, Stephen 12
Lovelock, Thomas 46
Lovenkrands, Peter 55
Low, Josh 25
Lowe, Jason 9
Lowe, Keith 25
Lowe, Ryan 73
Lowry, Jamie 26
Lowry, Shane 52
Lowton, Matt 72
Loy, Rory 22
Lua-Lua, Lomano 10
LuaLua, Kazenga 15
Lucas 47
Lucas, David 69
Lucas, Lee 80
Luiz, David 24
Lukaku, Romelu 24
Lund, Matthew 78
Lundstram, John 35
Lunt, Kenny 40
Luongo, Massimo 83
Luscombe, Nathan 39
Lussey, Jordan 47
Lynch, Chris 18
Lynch, Craig 79
Lynch, David 18
Lynch, Joel 58
M'Changama, Youssouf 60
M'Voto, Jean-Yves 60
MacDonald, Alex 18
MacDonald, Angus 68
MacDonald, Charlie 53
MacDonald, Shaun 12
Macheda, Federico 50
Mackail-Smith, Craig 15
Macken, Jon 85
MacKenzie, Gary 53
Mackie, Jamie 67
Macklin, Lloyd 82
MacLean, Steve 92
Madden, Daniel 79
Madden, Patrick 22
Madine, Gary 73
Madjo, Guy 3
Maduako, Jideofo 45
Magera, Lukas 81
Maghoma, Jacques 19
Magri, Sam 65
Maguire, Chris 33
Maguire, Harry 72
Maher, Kevin 32
Mahon, Gavin 59
Maierhofer, Stefan 90
Main, Curtis 51
Mainwaring, Matty 42
Majewski, Radoslaw 58
Makoun, Jean II 5
Male, Luke 74
Malone, Scott 12
Maloney, Shaun 89
Malouda, Florent 24
Mambo, Yado 23
Mancini, Andrea 49
Mandron, Mikael 79
Mannone, Vito 4
Mansell, Lee 82
Manset, Mathieu 68
Mantom, Sam 87
March, Kurtis 80
Mariappa, Adrian 86
Marney, Dean 18
Marquis, John 52
Marrow, Alex 31

Marrs, Liam 79
Marsh-Brown, Keanu 60
Marshall, Andy 5
Marshall, Ben 45
Marshall, David 21
Marshall, Marcus 70
Marshall, Mark 6
Marshall, Paul 64
Martin, Aaron 75
Martin, Alan 30
Martin, Carl 30
Martin, Chris 57
Martin, Chris 64
Martin, David E 53
Martin, David J 76
Martin, Joe 38
Martin, Lee 43
Martin, Malaury 51
Martin, Russell 57
Martinez, Damian 4
Martis, Shelton 34
Marveaux, Sylvain 55
Mason, Joe 21
Mason, Ryan 83
Massey, Gavin 86
Mata, Juan 24
Mattis, Dwayne 48
Mattock, Joe 87
May, Ben 77
Maynard, Nicky 88
Mayor, Danny 66
McAleny, Conor 35
McAlinden, Liam 90
McAllister, David 72
McAllister, Jamie 16
McAllister, Sean 74
McAnuff, Jobi 68
McArthur, James 89
McAuley, Gareth 87
McCallum, Gavin 6
McCallum, Paul 88
McCann, Chris 18
McCann, Grant 62
McCann, Joe 44
McCarey, Aaron 90
McCartan, Shay 18
McCarthy, Alex 68
McCarthy, James 89
McCarthy, Luke 20
McCarthy, Patrick 31
McCartney, George 79
McChrystal, Mark 84
McClean, James 79
McCleary, Garath 68
McClure, Matt 91
McCombe, Jamie 41
McCombe, John 64
McCormack, Alan 81
McCormack, Jamie 89
McCormack, Ross 44
McCoy, Marvin 91
McCready, Chris 54
McCrory, Damien 32
McDermott, Donal 12
McDermott, Greg 55
McDermott, Sean 4
McDonald, Clayton 64
McDonald, Cody 28
McDonald, Gary 54
McDonald, Kevin 72
McDonald, Scott 51
McEachran, Josh 24
McEveley, James 7
McFadden, James 35
McFadzean, Callum 72
McFadzean, Kyle 29
McGee, Joe 54
McGinn, Niall 14
McGinn, Stephen 86
McGinty, Sean 50
McGivern, Ryan 49
McGiveron, Matthew 47
McGlashan, Jermaine 25
McGleish, Scott 17
McGoldrick, David 58
McGovern, John-Paul 22
McGrath, John 19
McGrath, Philip 60
McGugan, Lewis 58
McGurk, Adam 84
McHugh, Carl 68
McIntyre, Kevin 1
McKee, Joe 18
McKenna, Ben 22
McKenna, Paul 42
McKoy, Nick 56
McLaggon, Kane 17
McLaren, Connor 52
McLaren, Paul 61
McLaughlin, Conor 66
McLaughlin, Jon 13
McLaughlin, Ryan 47
McLean, Aaron 42
McLean, Brian 66
McLellan, Michael 66
McLeod, Izale 6
McLoughlin, Ian 53
McMahon, Sam 34
McMahon, Tony 51
McManaman, Callum 89
McManus, Stephen 51
McNamee, Anthony 91
McNaughton, Callum 2
McNaughton, Kevin 21
McNish, Callum 36
McNulty, Jim 7
McPake, James 28
McPhail, Stephen 21
McPhee, Chris 82
McQueen, Sam 75
McQuilkin, James 40
McQuoid, Josh 52
McShane, Paul 42
McSheffrey, Gary 28
McSweeney, Leon 46
Meade, Jernade 4
Meades, Jonathan 21
Meadows, Danny 58
Mears, Tyrone 11
Mee, Ben 18
Mekki, Adam 3
Mellish, Jordan 39
Mellor, David 60
Mellor, Kelvin 30
Mellor, Neil 66
Mendez-Laing, Nathaniel 90
Mendy, Alex 26
Mendy, Arnaud 48
Mensah, Bernard 86
Meppen-Walters, Courtney 49
Merrifield, Frankie 2
Mersin, Yusuf 47
Mertesacker, Per 4
Meyler, David 79
Michalik, Lubomir 22
Middleton, Doyle 66
Midson, Jack 2
Miele, Brandon 55
Mignolet, Simon 79
Mikel, John Obi 24
Mildenhall, Steve 52
Milijas, Nenad 90
Millar, Kirk 60
Miller, Ashley 38
Miller, George 66
Miller, Ishmael 58
Miller, Kenny 21
Miller, Kern 7
Miller, Lee 22
Miller, Shaun 30
Miller, Tommy 41
Mills, Andy 48
Mills, Ben 48
Mills, Danny 62
Mills, Jack 68
Mills, Joseph 68
Mills, Matthew 45
Mills, Pablo 29
Milner, James 49
Milton, Harry 53
Mingoia, Piero 86
Minihan, Sam 69
Minkwitz, Ronny 37
Minshull, Lee 2
Miquel, Ignasi 4
Mirfin, David 86
Mitchel-King, Mat 2
Mitchell, Adam 79
Mitchell, Chris 13
Mitchell, Liam 59
Mitrovic, Marko 24
Miyaichi, Ryo 4
Mkandawire, Tamika 52
Modeste, Anthony 9
Modric, Luka 83
Mohammed, Kaid 25
Mohsni, Bilel 76
Mokoena, Aaron 65
Molesley, Mark 12
Moli, David 90
Molina, Hugo 9
Moloney, Brendan 58
Moncur, George 88
Monk, Garry 80
Monkhouse, Andy 39
Montano, Cristian 88
Monteiro, Elton 4
Montenegro, Brian 88
Montgomery, Nick 72
Montrose, Lewis 38
Mooney, David 46
Mooney, Jason 91
Moore, Byron 30
Moore, Corby 75
Moore, Darren 19
Moore, Ethan 25
Moore, Liam 45
Moore, Luke 80
Moore, Luke 2
Moore, Sammy 2
Moore, Simon 14
Morais, Filipe 60
Moras, Vangelis 80
Morch, Mats 33
Morgan, Adam 47
Morgan, Chris 72
Morgan, Craig 66
Morgan, David 58
Morgan, Dean 26
Morgan, Marvin 74
Morgan, Paul 48
Morgan, Wes 45
Morison, Steven 57
Morris, Aaron 3
Morris, Callum 89
Morris, Glenn 76
Morris, Ian 82
Morris, Josh 9
Morrison, Clinton 73
Morrison, James 87
Morrison, Michael 23
Morrison, Ravel 88
Morrison, Sean 68
Morsy, Sam 64
Moses, Victor 89
Moult, Louis 78
Mousinho, John 77
Moussa, Franck 45
Moussi, Guy 58
Mouyokolo, Steven 90
Moxey, Dean 31
Moyo, Yven 55
Mozika, Damien 71
Muamba, Fabrice 11
Mucha, Jan 35
Muggeridge, Henry 16
Mukendi, Vinny 48
Mulley, James 2
Mullins, Hayden 65
Mullins, John 70
Mulumbu, Youssef 87
Munn, Bradley 19
Murdoch, Sean 1
Murphy, Brian 67
Murphy, Danny 37
Murphy, Darren 77
Murphy, Daryl 43
Murphy, David 8
Murphy, David 68
Murphy, Joe 28
Murphy, Luke 30
Murphy, Peter 22
Murphy, Peter 1
Murphy, Rhys 4
Murray, Glenn 31
Murray, Paul 39
Murray, Ronan 43
Murray, Sean 86
Murray, Shane 72
Mustoe, Jordan 89
Mutch, Jordon 8
Mwaruwari, Benjamin 65
Mwasilie, Joe 54
Myhill, Boaz 87
Myler, Sean 89
Myrie-Williams, Jennison 77
N'Daw, Guirane 8
N'Diaye, Alassane 6
N'Gala, Bondz 92
N'Gog, David 11
N'Guessan, Dany 52
N'Zogbia, Charles 5
N'Zonzi, Steven 9
Na Bangna, Buomesca 37
Nabi, Adil 87
Nacho 47
Nani 50
Napper, Byron 29
Nardiello, Daniel 36
Nash, Carlo 78
Nasri, Samir 49
Naughton, Kyle 83
Navarro, Alan 15
Naylor, Lee 21
Naylor, Richard 70
Naylor, Tom 33
Naysmith, Gary 41
Neal, Chris 74
Needham, Matthew 26
Neilson, Scott 29
Neita, Nigel 4
Nelsen, Ryan 83
Nelson, Curtis 63
Nelson, Michael 71
Nelson, Stuart 59
Nelson-Addy, Ebby 5
Nesbitt, Teddy 76
Neville, Phil 35
Newell, Joe 62
Newey, Tom 70
Newton, Conor 55
Ngoo, Michael 47
Nicholas, George 59
Nicholls, Alex 85
Nicholls, Lee 89
Nichols, Tom 36
Nicholson, Barry 66
Nicholson, Jake 83
Nicholson, Kevin 82
Nimely-Tchuimeni, Alex 49
Nish, Colin 39
Niven, Derek 26
Nkumu, Archange 24
Noble, David 36
Noble, Liam 22
Noble, Mark 88
Noble, Ryan 79
Noble-Lazarus, Reuben 7
Nolan, Eddie 71
Nolan, Kevin 88
Noone, Craig 15
Norburn, Oliver 45
Norris, David 65
Norris, Luke 14
Norwood, Oliver 50
Nosworthy, Nyron 86
Nouble, Frank 88
Novak, Lee 41
Nsiala, Aristote 35
Ntambwe, Brice 8
Ntlhe, Kgosietsile 62
Nugent, Dave 45
Nuhu, Razak 49
Nunez, Ramon 44
Nurse, Jon 32
Nyatanga, Lewin 16
Nyoni, Cecil 73
Nzuzi, Patrick 55
O'Brien, Aiden 52
O'Brien, Alan 92
O'Brien, Andy 44
O'Brien, Jim 7
O'Brien, Joey 88
O'Brien, Liam 6
O'Brien, Luke 36
O'Brien, Mark 33
O'Connor, Anthony 9
O'Connor, James 34
O'Connor, James 73
O'Connor, Kevin 14
O'Connor, Michael 71
O'Dea, Darren 44
O'Donnell, Richard 73
O'Donovan, Roy 28
O'Flynn, John 36
O'Grady, Chris 73
O'Halloran, Michael 11
O'Halloran, Stephen 22
O'Hara, Jamie 90
O'Kane, Eunan 82
O'Keefe, Stuart 31
O'Neil, Gary 88
O'Neil, Liam 87
O'Reilly, Daniel 37
O'Shea, Jay 53
O'Shea, John 79
O'Sullivan, John 9
O'Toole, John 27
Oakley, Matthew 45
Oastler, Joe 82
Obadeyi, Temitope 11
Obafemi, Affy 46
Obeng, Curtis 80
Oberschmidt, Max 37
Obertan, Gabriel 55
Obika, Jonathan 83
Obita, Jordan 68
Odejayi, Kayode 27
Odemwingie, Peter 87
Odubajo, Moses 46
Ofori-Twumasi, Nana 56
Ogbeche, Bart 51
Ogogo, Abu 32
Okuonghae, Magnus 27
Olejnik, Robert 82
Oli, Dennis 38
Oliver, Kyle 51
Oliver, Luke 13
Oliver, Vadaine 73
Olley, Luke 67
Olofinjana, Seyi 42
Olsson, Jonas 87
Olsson, Marcus 9
Olsson, Martin 9
Omeruo, Kenneth 24
Omozusi, Elliot 46
Onuoha, Nedum 67
Orenuga, Femi 35
Orlandi, Andrea 80
Ormerod, Brett 10
Orr, Bradley 9
Osborn, Alex 32
Osborn, Ben 58
Osborne, Harry 23
Osborne, Karleigh 14
Osei-Kuffour, Jo 38
Osifuwa, Adetayo 2
Osman, Abdul 56
Osman, Leon 35
Oster, John 34
Oswell, Jason 30
Otsemobor, John 73
Overson, Dean 13
Owen, Gareth 64
Owen, Michael 50
Owusu, Lloyd 6
Oxlade-Chamberlain, Alex 4
Oxley, Mark 42
Oyeleke, Emmanuel 14
Oyenuga, Kudus 83
Ozyakup, Oguzhan 4
Pablo 8
Pacheco, Daniel 47
Pack, Marlon 25
Packwood, Will 8
Painter, Marcos 15
Palacios, Wilson 78
Palmer, Ashley 71
Palmer, Chris 19
Palmer, Ed 82
Palmer, Liam 73
Panayiotou, Harry 45
Panther, Manny 3
Pantilimon, Costel 49
Pantsil, John 45
Pappoe, Daniel 24
Parish, Elliot 21
Park, Cameron 51
Park, Chu-Young 4
Park, Ji-Sung 50
Parker, Ben 44
Parker, Josh 60
Parker, Scott 83
Parkes, Jordan 6
Parkes, Tom 45
Parkin, Jon 21
Parkinson, Dan 54

Parmenter, Taylor 67
Parr, Jonathan 31
Parrett, Dean 83
Parrish, Andy 54
Parry, Paul 66
Parsons, Alex 12
Parsons, Matthew 31
Partington, Joe 12
Paterson, Jamie 85
Paterson, Jim 17
Paterson, Martin 18
Paterson, Matthew 76
Paulo Ferreira 24
Pavlyuchenko, Roman 83
Payne, Jack 38
Payne, Josh 3
Payne, Sanchez 44
Payne, Stefan 38
Payne, Tim 9
Paynter, Billy 44
Pearce, Alex 68
Pearce, Jason 44
Pearce, Krystian 59
Pearson, Greg 19
Pearson, Greg 41
Pearson, Stephen 16
Pedersen, Morten 9
Pedroza, Antonio 31
Peet, Robert 42
Pell, Harry 40
Pelosi, Marc 47
Peltier, Lee 45
Peniket, Richard 37
Penn, Russ 25
Pennant, Jermaine 78
Pentney, Carl 27
Perch, James 55
Perkins, David 7
Perone, Bruno 67
Peterlin, Anton 85
Peters, Jaime 43
Petersson, Kristoffer 47
Petrov, Martin 11
Petrov, Stilian 5
Petrovic, Radosav 9
Petrucci, Davide 50
Phillip, Adam 24
Phillips, Jimmy 19
Phillips, Kevin 10
Phillips, Mark 76
Phillips, Matthew 10
Phillips, Steve 30
Philliskirk, Daniel 24
Piazon, Lucas 24
Picken, Phil 20
Pickford, Jordan 79
Pidgeley, Lenny 36
Pienaar, Steven 83
Pierre, Aaron 14
Pilatos, Bruno 51
Pilkington, Anthony 57
Pinney, Nathaniel 31
Piquionne, Frederic 88
Pirez, Jhon 24
Piscu (Adrian Lopez) 89
Pitman, Brett 16
Pittman, Jon-Paul 61
Pivkovski, Filip 9
Pizarro, David 49
Platt, Clive 28
Plummer, Ellis 49
Pogba, Paul 50
Pogrebnyak, Pavel 37
Poke, Michael 15
Pollitt, Mike 89
Poole, James 39
Poole, Kevin 19
Pope, Nick 23
Pope, Tom 64
Popo, Tosan 23
Porter, Chris 72
Porter, George 46
Porter, Max 2
Potter, Alfie 61
Potter, Darren 53
Potts, Danny 88
Powell, Daniel 53
Powell, Lamar 17
Powell, Nick 30
Power, Max 84
Poyet, Diego 23
Pratley, Darren 11
Preece, David 7
Price, Jack 90
Price, Jason 54
Price, Lewis 31
Pringle, Ben 70
Prior, Jason 2
Priskin, Tamas 43
Pritchard, Alex 83
Pritchard, Bradley 23
Pritchard, Josh 37
Procter, Andy 66
Proctor, Jamie 66
Prosser, Luke 76
Prutton, David 73
Pugh, Danny 44
Pugh, Marc 12
Pulis, Anthony 3
Puncheon, Jason 75
Purcell, Tadhg 56
Purches, Stephen 12
Purdie, Rob 40
Purkiss, Ben 40
Purse, Darren 63
Pusic, Martin 42
Quinn, Paul 21
Quinn, Stephen 72
Rachubka, Paul 44
Racon, Therry 52
Radford, Oscar 34
Rafael 50
Rafferty, Andy 39
Raglan, Charlie 64
Ralls, Joe 21
Ralph, Nathan 62
Ramage, Peter 67
Ramires 24
Ramsden, Simon 13
Ramsey, Aaron 4
Ramsey-Dickson, Kristian 19
Rance, Dean 38
Randall, Mark 26
Rangel, Angel 80
Ranger, Nile 55
Ranieri, Mirko 83
Rankine, Michael 3
Raul Meireles 24
Raven, David 84
Ravenhill, Ricky 13
Ray, George 30
Raymond, Frankie 68
Raynes, Michael 70
Razak, Abdul 49
Reach, Adam 51
Ream, Tim 11
Reckord, Jamie 90
Redmond, Daniel 89
Redmond, Nathan 8
Redshaw, Jack 54
Redwood, Leon 15
Reece, Charlie 17
Reed, Adam 79
Reed, Harrison 75
Reed, Jake 32
Rees, Josh 4
Reeves, Ben 75
Reeves, Jake 14
Regan, Carl 74
Regan, Matthew 58
Reid, Andy 58
Reid, Bobby 16
Reid, Craig 77
Reid, Izak 54
Reid, Kyel 13
Reid, Paul 71
Reid, Reuben 60
Reid, Steven 87
Reid, Winston 88
Reina, Jose 47
Rekik, Karim 49
Rendell, Scott 91
Reo-Coker, Nigel 11
Revell, Alex 70
Reynolds, Duran-Rhys 32
Reynolds, Mark 73
Rhodes, Jordan 41
Ribeiro, Christian 16
Ricardo Rocha 65
Rice, Martin 82
Richards, Eliot 17
Richards, Garry 38
Richards, Jamie 63
Richards, Jazz 80
Richards, Jordan 39
Richards, Justin 19
Richards, Marc 64
Richards, Matt 74
Richards, Micah 49
Richardson, Frazer 75
Richardson, Kieran 79
Richardson, Leam 1
Richardson, Michael 55
Ricketts, Rohan 36
Ricketts, Sam 11
Ridehalgh, Liam 41
Ridgewell, Liam 87
Rigg, Sean 64
Riise, Bjorn Helge 37
Riise, John Arne 37
Riley, Joe 11
Ripley, Connor 51
Risser, Oliver 81
Risser, Wilko 3
Ritchie, Matt 81
Riveros, Cristian 79
Robert, Fabien 34
Roberts, Adam 48
Roberts, Connor 35
Roberts, Gareth 33
Roberts, Gary 64
Roberts, Gary 41
Roberts, Jason 68
Roberts, Jordan 3
Roberts, Mark 77
Roberts, Michael 47
Roberts, Will 28
Robertson, Chris 66
Robertson, Gregor 26
Robertson, Jordan 71
Robinson, Andreas 75
Robinson, Andy 84
Robinson, Anton 41
Robinson, Bradley 49
Robinson, Jack 47
Robinson, Jake 56
Robinson, Jordan 89
Robinson, Paul 52
Robinson, Paul 9
Robinson, Paul 11
Robinson, Theo 33
Robson, Barry 51
Robson, Matty 22
Robson-Kanu, Hal 68
Roche, Barry 54
Rochina, Ruben 9
Rodallega, Hugo 89
Roddan, Craig 47
Rodgers, Anton 15
Rodman, Alex 3
Rodney, Nialle 13
Rodriguez, Jay 18
Rodriguez, Maxi 47
Rodwell, Jack 35
Roe, Phil 64
Rogers, Robbie 44
Roman Olle, Joan Angel 49
Romeu, Oriol 24
Roofe, Kemar 87
Rooney, Adam 8
Rooney, Luke 81
Rooney, Wayne 50
Rose, Danny 83
Rose, Danny 7
Rose, Michael 27
Rose, Richard 32
Rosenior, Liam 42
Rosicky, Tomas 4
Rossi, Karim 78
Rothwell, Zach 20
Routledge, Shaun 54
Routledge, Wayne 80
Rowbotham, Josh 39
Rowe, Dominic 13
Rowe, Tommy 62
Rowe-Turner, Lathanial 82
Rowlands, Martin 27
Rudd, Declan 57
Ruddock, Pelly 88
Ruddy, John 57
Ruffels, Joshua 28
Rugg, Jordan 89
Ruiz, Bryan 37
Rusnak, Albert 49
Russell, Darel 66
Rutherford, Greg 39
Ryan, James 71
Sa, Orlando 37
Saah, Brian 82
Sadler, Matthew 85
Sage, James 62
Sagna, Bakari 4
Saha, Louis 83
Said, Abdul 81
Salcido, Carlos 37
Salgado, Michel 9
Salihu, Lumbardh 56
Sam, Lloyd 44
Sama, Stephen 47
Samba, Christopher 9
Sammon, Conor 89
Sammons, Ashley 8
Sampayo, Ben 15
Sampson, Jack 11
Samuel, Dominic 68
Sandaza, Fran 15
Sandell, Andy 91
Sanderson, Jordan 27
Sandro 83
Santa Cruz, Roque 49
Santiago, Jordan 21
Santon, Davide 55
Santos, Francisco 35
Sarcevic, Antoni 30
Saunders, Matthew 32
Saunders, Sam 14
Savage, Bas 56
Savic, Stefan 49
Saville, George 24
Saville, Jack 6
Sawyer, Gary 17
Sawyer, Lee 76
Sawyers, Romaine 87
Scannell, Damian 32
Scannell, Sean 31
Scapuzzi, Luca 49
Scharner, Paul 87
Schlupp, Jeffrey 45
Schmeichel, Kasper 45
Schneiderlin, Morgan 75
Schofield, Danny 70
Scholes, Paul 50
Schumacher, Steven 20
Schwarzer, Mark 37
Scotland, Jason 43
Scott, Josh 32
Scott, Mark 81
Scowen, Josh 91
Seaborne, Danny 75
Seabright, Jordan 12
Sears, Freddie 88
Sedgwick, Chris 73
Seidi, Alberto 75
Seip, Marcel 13
Sekajja, Ibra 31
Semedo, Jose 73
Senda, Danny 6
Senderos, Philippe 37
Sendles-White, Jamie 67
Sercombe, Liam 36
Serrano, Juan Jose 5
Sessegnon, Stephane 79
Severn, James 33
Shackell, Jason 33
Shariff, Mo 67
Sharp, Billy 75
Sharps, Ian 74
Shaw, Luke 75
Shawcross, Ryan 78
Shea, James 4
Shearer, Scott 29
Sheehan, Alan 59
Shelley, Danny 30
Shelvey, Jonjo 47
Shephard, Chris 36
Sheppard, Karl 68
Sheringham, Charlie 12
Shittu, Dan 67
Shorey, Nicky 87
Shotton, Ryan 78
Showunmi, Enoch 84
Shroot, Robin 77
Shuker, Chris 64
Sidibe, Mamady 78
Sidwell, Steve 37
Siegrist, Benjamin 5
Sigurdsson, Gylfi 80
Silva, David 49
Silva, Joao 35
Silva, Toni 47
Silva, Wellington 4
Simek, Frankie 22
Simmonds, Ryan 15
Simonsen, Steve 72
Simpson, Danny 55
Simpson, Jay 42
Simpson, Josh 29
Simpson, Robbie 60
Sims, Jared 63
Sinclair, Emile 62
Sinclair, Jake 75
Sinclair, Robert 77
Sinclair, Scott 80
Situ, Darnel 80
Skapetis, Petros 67
Skarz, Joe 20
Skrtel, Martin 47
Skuse, Cole 16
Slane, Paul 53
Slew, Jordan 9
Slocombe, Sam 71
Slowe, Alistair 92
Smajl, Suljevic 78
Smalley, Deane 61
Smalling, Chris 50
Smallwood, Richard 51
Smikle, Brian 25
Smith, Adam 3
Smith, Adam 83
Smith, Adam 45
Smith, Alan 55
Smith, Alex 37
Smith, Ben 29
Smith, Benjamin 74
Smith, Bradley 47
Smith, Chris 81
Smith, Jack 52
Smith, Jamie 46
Smith, Jamie 55
Smith, Jimmy 46
Smith, Jonathan 81
Smith, Jordan 80
Smith, Korey 57
Smith, Manny 85
Smith, Matt 60
Smith, Michael 17
Smith, Michael 23
Smith, Nathan 26
Smith, Paul 58
Smith, Phil 81
Smith, Steven 66
Smith, Tommy 67
Smith, Tommy 43
Smithies, Alex 41
Snedker, Dean 56
Snodgrass, Robert 44
Soares, Tom 78
Soderberg, Ole 55
Sodje, Efe 20
Sodje, Sam 59
Sokolik, Jakub 47
Solano, Nolberto 39
Solly, Chris 23
Somma, Davide 44
Somogyi, Csaba 37
Song Billong, Alexandre 4
Sonko, Ibrahima 43
Sordell, Marvin 11
Sorensen, Thomas 78
Soukouna, Ladjie 63
Southern, Keith 10
Sowah, Lennard 52
Sparrow, Matt 15
Spear, Ray 82
Spearing, Jay 47
Spector, Jonathan 8
Speiss, Fabien 59
Spence, Jordan 88
Spencer, James 41
Speroni, Julian 31
Spicer, John 59
Spillane, Michael 32
Spiller, Danny 38
Spray, James 90
Spring, Matthew 46
Springthorpe, Mason 35
Spurr, Tommy 34
Squillaci, Sebastien 4
St Ledger-Hall, Sean 45

Stam, Ronnie 89
Stam, Stefan 40
Stanislas, Junior 18
Stanley, Craig 17
Stanton, Nathan 19
Stead, Jon 16
Stearman, Richard 90
Stech, Marek 88
Steele, Jason 51
Steele, Luke 7
Steer, Jed 57
Steinsson, Gretar Rafn 11
Stephens, Dale 23
Stephens, Jack 75
Stephens, James 47
Stephenson, Darren 13
Sterling, Raheem 47
Stevens, Danny 82
Stevens, Enda 5
Stevens, Jamie 76
Stevenson, Ryan 43
Stewart, Anthony 91
Stewart, Cameron 42
Stewart, Damion 16
Stewart, Gareth 92
Stewart, Jon 18
Stewart, Jordan 52
Stewart, Mark 13
Stieber, Andras 5
Stirling, Jude 59
Stock, Brian 34
Stockdale, David 37
Stockford, Lewis 65
Stockley, Jayden 12
Stockton, Cole 84
Stones, John 7
Storey, Miles 81
Stracqualursi, Denis 35
Straker, Anthony 3
Streete, Remie 55
Strevens, Ben 91
Strong, Jamie 15
Strugnell, Dan 12
Strutton, Charlie 2
Stuart, Jamie 2
Stuckmann, Thorsten 66
Sturridge, Daniel 24
Sturrock, Blair 76
Suarez, Denis 49
Suarez, Luis 47
Suljevic, Smajl 78
Sullivan, John 23
Sullivan, Neil 34
Summerfield, Luke 25
Surman, Andrew 57
Suso 47
Sutherland, Craig 10
Sutherland, Frankie 67
Swan, George 49
Sweeney, Anthony 39
Sweeney, Peter 20
Swinglehurst, Steven 22
Syers, Dave 13
Sylvestre, Ludovic 10
Symes, Michael 12
Szczesny, Wojciech 4
Taarabt, Adel 67
Tabb, Jay 68
Taft, George 45
Taiwo, Soloman 21
Taiwo, Taye 67
Taiwo, Tom 22
Talbot, Drew 26
Tallack, Lewis 65
Tamas, Gabriel 87
Tankovic, Muamer 37
Tanner, Craig 68
Tapping, Callum 83
Taricco, Mauricio 15
Tarkowski, James 60
Tate, Alan 80
Taudul, Mateusz 35
Taundry, Richard 85
Tavernier, James 55
Taylor, Alistair 7
Taylor, Andrew 21
Taylor, Andy 72
Taylor, Ash 84
Taylor, Charlie 6
Taylor, Charlie 44
Taylor, Chris 60
Taylor, Cleveland 19
Taylor, Connor 5
Taylor, Jake 68
Taylor, Jason 70
Taylor, Jon 74
Taylor, Lyle 12
Taylor, Maik 8
Taylor, Martin 86
Taylor, Matthew 88
Taylor, Matthew 23
Taylor, Nat 1
Taylor, Neil 80
Taylor, Olly 91
Taylor, Paul 62
Taylor, Quade 31
Taylor, Rhys 24
Taylor, Rob 64
Taylor, Ryan 16
Taylor, Ryan 55
Taylor, Steven 55
Taylor, Stuart 49
Taylor-Fletcher, Gary 10
Tchoyi, Somen 87
Tehoue, Jonathan 46
Teixeira, Joao Carlos 47
Terry, John 24
Tevez, Carlos 49
Thalassitis, Michael 77
Theophanous, Louie 2
Thewlis, Jordan 71
Thirlwell, Paul 22
Thomas, Casey 80
Thomas, Conor 28
Thomas, Hendry 89
Thomas, Jerome 87
Thomas, Michael 48
Thomas, Simon 41
Thomas, Wesley 12
Thompson, Adam 86
Thompson, Curtis 59
Thompson, Dan 65
Thompson, Gary 71
Thompson, Joe 69
Thompson, Josh 26
Thompson, Nathan 81
Thompson, O'Neil 7
Thompson, Zac 44
Thomson, Kevin 51
Thorne, George 87
Thornton, Kevin 56
Thorpe, Tom 50
Threlfall, Robbie 13
Tierney, Marc 57
Timlin, Michael 76
Ting, Daniel 30
Tiote, Cheik 55
Tiryaki, Mustafa 84
Tisdale, Paul 36
Todd, Andy 40
Togwell, Sam 71
Tombides, Dylan 88
Tomkins, James 88
Tomlin, Gavin 32
Tomlin, Lee 62
Tomlinson, Ben 48
Tomlinson, Stuart 64
Tomsett, Liam 10
Tonge, Dale 70
Tonge, Michael 78
Tonkin, Anthony 61
Tonne, Erik 72
Tootle, Matt 30
Toral Harper, Jon-Miquel 4
Torres, Fernando 24
Torres, Sergio 29
Tounkara, Oumare 79
Toure, Kolo 49
Toure, Yaya 49
Townsend, Andros 83
Townsend, Conor 42
Townsend, Michael 40
Tozer, Ben 56
Trani, Tommaso 67
Traore, Armand 67
Treacy, Keith 18
Tremarco, Carl 48
Tremmel, Gerhard 80
Trippier, Keiran 18
Trotman, Neal 26
Trotta, Marcello 37
Trotter, Liam 52
Tshibola, Aaron 68
Tsoumou, Juvhel 66
Tubbs, Matt 12
Tudgay, Marcus 58
Tully, Steve 36
Tuncay, Sanli 78
Tunchev, Aleksandar 45
Tunnicliffe, James 91
Tunnicliffe, Ryan 50
Turgott, Blair 88
Turnbull, Jordan 75
Turnbull, Paul 56
Turnbull, Ross 24
Turner, Ben 21
Turner, Iain 66
Turner, Jack 2
Turner, Lewis 44
Turner, Michael 79
Turner, Nathan 44
Turton, Oliver 30
Tutte, Andrew 69
Twaddle, Marc 69
Tyson, Nathan 33
Uchechi, Danny 45
Uddin, Anwar 6
Ugwu, Chigozie 68
Upson, Edward 92
Upson, Matthew 78
Usai, Sebastian 9
Valencia, Antonio 50
Valles, Enric 8
Van Aanholt, Patrick 24
Van der Vaart, Rafael 83
Van Persie, Robin 4
Van Velzen, Gyliano 50
Varney, Luke 65
Vassell, Darius 45
Vassell, Isaac 63
Vaughan, David 79
Vaughan, James 57
Vayrynen, Mika 44
Vaz Te, Ricardo 88
Veiga, Jose Manuel 48
Vela, Carlos 4
Vela, Joshua 11
Vellios, Apostolos 35
Vermaelen, Thomas 4
Vermijl, Marnick 50
Veseli, Frederic 50
Vicente, Rodriguez 15
Vidic, Nemanja 50
Vigen Christensen, Lasse 37
Vilhete, Mauro 6
Vincelot, Romain 15
Vincent, Ashley 27
Vincenti, Peter 3
Vine, Rowan 67
Virgo, Adam 17
Vokes, Sam 90
Vorm, Michel 80
Vose, Dominic 88
Vuckic, Haris 55
Vukcevic, Simon 9
Wabara, Reece 49
Waghorn, Martyn 45
Wagstaff, Scott 23
Waite, Tyrell 59
Wakefield, Josh 12
Walcott, Jacob 68
Walcott, Theo 4
Walker, Jim 85
Walker, Josh 86
Walker, Kyle 83
Walker, Mitch 15
Walker, Sam 24
Wallace, James 35
Wallace, Jed 65
Wallace, Murray 41
Wallace, Ross 18
Waller-Larsen, Jesse 83
Walsh, Joe 80
Walsh, Phil 32
Walshe, Carl 65
Walters, Jon 78
Walton, Simon 63
Ward, Charlie 5
Ward, Danny 41
Ward, Danny 47
Ward, Darren 52
Ward, Elliot 57
Ward, Jamie 33
Ward, Joel 65
Ward, Stephen 90
Ward-Prowse, James 75
Warne, Paul 70
Warnock, Stephen 5
Warren, Freddie 23
Warren, Mark 72
Warrington, Andy 70
Wassmer, Charlie 29
Watkiss, Ben 26
Watson, Ben 89
Watson, Jordan 79
Watson, Ryan 89
Watt, Sanchez 4
Weale, Chris 45
Wearen, Eoin Patrick 88
Weaver, Nick 73
Webber, Danny 44
Webster, Aaron 19
Webster, Adam 65
Webster, Byron 56
Wedderburn, Nathanial 56
Wedgbury, Sam 48
Weimann, Andreas 5
Weir, Robbie 84
Weir, Tyler 40
Weiss, Vladimir 49
Welbeck, Danny 50
Weldon, Paul 51
Wellard, Ricky 2
Wellens, Richard 45
Wells, Nahki 13
Welsh, Andy 22
Welsh, John 84
Wesolowski, James 60
Westcarr, Craig 26
Westlake, Darryl 85
Weston, Curtis 38
Weston, Myles 14
Westwood, Ashley 30
Westwood, Ashley M 56
Westwood, Keiren 79
Wharton, Theo 21
Wheater, David 11
Whelan, Glenn 78
Whelpdale, Chris 38
Whichelow, Matt 86
Whight, Joe 43
Whing, Andrew 61
Whitaker, Danny 26
Whitbread, Zak 57
White, Aidan 44
White, Andrew 30
White, John 27
Whitehead, Dean 78
Whiteley, Lewis 59
Whittingham, Peter 21
Wholey, Jake 59
Wickham, Aaron 29
Wickham, Connor 79
Widdowson, Joe 69
Wiggins, Rhoys 23
Wilbraham, Aaron 57
Wildig, Aaron 21
Wilkinson, Andy 78
Wilkinson, Luke 32
Williams, Andy 92
Williams, Aryn 18
Williams, Ashley 80
Williams, Ben 27
Williams, Brett 68
Williams, Danny 40
Williams, Derrick 5
Williams, Gavin 92
Williams, George 53
Williams, Jon 31
Williams, Luke 51
Williams, Marcus 72
Williams, Owain fon 84
Williams, Rhys 51
Williams, Robbie 63
Williams, Ryan 37
Williams, Sam 32
Williams, Shaun 53
Williams, Steve 13
Williams, Tony 20
Williamson, Ben 64
Williamson, Lee 72
Williamson, Mike 55
Willis, Jordan 28
Willis, Liam 1
Wilshere, Jack 4
Wilson, Ben 79
Wilson, Brian 27
Wilson, Callum 28
Wilson, Danny 47
Wilson, Glenn 29
Wilson, James 16
Wilson, Laurence 54
Wilson, Lawrie 77
Wilson, Lewis 56
Wilson, Marc 78
Wilson, Mark 61
Wilson, Ross 18
Winchester, Carl 60
Winfield, Dave 91
Winn, Peter 77
Winnall, Sam 90
Winnard, Dean 1
Wint, Aron 71
Wisdom, Andre 47
Wiseman, Scott 7
Witham, Alex 33
Wood, Chris 87
Wood, Richard 28
Wood, Sam 14
Woodall, Brian 32
Woodards, Danny 17
Woodgate, Jonathan 78
Woodley, Aaron 61
Woodman, Craig 14
Woodrow, Cauley 37
Woods, Calum 41
Woods, Gary 34
Woods, Martin 34
Woods, Michael 92
Woodyard, Alex 76
Woolford, Martyn 16
Wootton, Lee 32
Wootton, Scott 50
Wordsworth, Anthony 27
Worley, Harry 61
Worner, Ross 3
Worrall, David 20
Wotton, Paul 63
Wren, James 19
Wright, Andrew 71
Wright, Bailey 66
Wright, David 31
Wright, Jake 61
Wright, Josh 52
Wright, Mark 74
Wright, Richard 43
Wright, Stephen 39
Wright-Phillips, Bradley 23
Wright-Phillips, Shaun 67
Wroe, Nicky 74
Wyke, Charlie 51
Wynter, Alex 31
Xisco 55
Yadolahi, Neil 18
Yakubu, Ayegbeni 9
Yates, Adam 64
Yeates, Mark 86
Yennaris, Nico 4
Yeoman, Ashley 82
Yiadom, Andy 6
Yobo, Joseph 35
Youga, Kelly 92
Young, Ashley 50
Young, Jamie 3
Young, Lewis 56
Young, Luke 67
Young, Luke 63
Yussuf, Abdi 19
Yussuff, Rashid 2
Zabaleta, Pablo 49
Zaha, Wilfred 31
Zakuani, Gaby 62
Zamora, Bobby 67
Zebroski, Chris 17
Zemmama, Merouane 51
Zibaka, Brandon 66
Zigic, Nikola 8
Zoko, Francois 22
Zola, Calvin 19
Zubar, Ronald 90
Zubar, Stephane 12

REFEREEING AND THE LAWS OF THE GAME

Although there are minimal alterations to the Laws for the 2012–13 season there is one which is of fundamental importance and which brings technology to the playing of the game for the first time. This historical change was announced on 5 July 2012 when the President of FIFA Sepp Blatter announced that following a nine months test process started in August 2010 the International Board (IFAB) and FIFA unanimously approved the introduction of goal-line technology. Two variants of the technology were trialled, namely Hawkeye and GoalRef, and the companies installing the systems have to test them at each stadium before they can be utilised in competitive matches. IFAB was at pains to point out that the technology will only be used for goal-line decisions and for no other areas of the game. Only the referee will be notified of the decision made as to whether the ball has crossed the goal-line and he/she will still be the sole arbiter as to whether to award or disallow a goal. The decision to implement the technology will necessitate Law Changes particularly amendments to Law 1 (field of play); Law 2 (the ball); Law 5 (the Referee) and Law 10 (method of scoring). The Premier League has indicated they may try if possible to commence running the new systems by the start of 2013 even though it would be mid-season. Decisions will have to be made as to whether one or both systems will be utilised.

The verdict on the technology was made despite strong attempts by UEFA to have the decision delayed for further consideration and to continue with the additional assistants system (AAR) currently employed throughout European competitions. There was some consolation for UEFA in that after a two year experiment, AAR was held to be satisfactory enough for IFAB to universally approve their future use. As a result of this decision the Laws will again need amendments and a separate section inserted regarding their use. The system has been strongly criticised in the past on the grounds amongst other things that nobody other than the referee knows whether they have made a decision or not and is still susceptible to error. A short Law change is now needed, following the introduction of technology, which will mean the approval and permission of communication equipment between match officials details of which will also be inserted into the Laws. However the term "radio equipment" has been replaced with the more modern term "electronic equipment".

There is one vital change to the playing of the game relating to the "drop ball" insofar as in future if an uncontested drop ball is kicked into an opponent's goal, a goal kick is awarded whereas if it is kicked directly into the team's own goal a corner kick is awarded. This should prevent unintentional or unsporting goals occurring over which the referee has no control.

There are also some minor changes to the Laws on handball where the word "blatantly" has been removed; now where tie-up tape is applied externally to the socks it must be the same colour as the rest of the sock; vanishing spray to mark out where defenders stand at free kicks has been sanctioned provided it is agreed by the relevant association, and associations can also designate in their rules how many substitutes can be nominated up to 12 in number but only three can still be used.

IFAB further agreed to allow temporarily during a trial period, the wearing of headscarves. The colour, material and design which are to be allowed will be fully defined and confirmed during their Annual Business Meeting (ABM) to be held in October 2012 in Glasgow, Scotland. This decision removes the ban imposed in 2007 on the grounds of safety. Further consideration will also be given at the ABM of what is known as the "triple punishment" consisting of fouls, misconduct and sending-off offences; although no clues were given as to what alterations if any will be implemented. They also usefully agreed to discuss how they can improve consultation with the game at large.

The FA has in 2012 revised their "Laws of the Game for Small-Sided Football" which has been done to better reflect the way this type of football is being currently played by over 1.2 million adults in this country.

By common consent the officiating at Euro 2012 was especially good apart from one goal-line blip. The referee for the Final between Italy and Spain was Pedro Proenca of Portugal who also refereed the UEFA Champions League Final. Wolfgang Stark of Germany refereed the UEFA Europa Cup Final; whilst domestically the referee for the men's FA Cup Final was Phil Dowd; the womens FA Cup Final went to Natalie Walker; the referee for the Carling Cup Final was Mark Clattenberg and for the women's Premier League Cup Final – Paul Forrester.

KEN GOLDMAN

NATIONAL LIST OF REFEREES FOR SEASON 2012–13

REFEREES

The oldest National list referee Peter Walton has retired to take up a post in the USA but the current National list of referees and their assistants is as follows:

ADCOCK, JG (James) Nottinghamshire
ATKINSON, M (Martin) West Yorkshire
ATTWELL, SB (Stuart) Warwickshire
BATES, A (Tony) Staffordshire
BERRY, CJ (Carl) Surrey
BOND, DS (Darren) Lancashire
BOOTH, R (Russell) Nottinghamshire
BOYESON, C (Carl) East Yorkshire
BRATT, SJ (Steve) West Midlands
BROWN, M (Mark) East Yorkshire
CLATTENBURG, M (Mark) County Durham
CLARK, RM (Richard) Northumberland
COLLINS, LM (Lee) Surrey
COOTE, D (David) Nottinghamshire
DAVIES, A (Andy) Hampshire
DEADMAN, D (Darren) Cambridgeshire
DEAN, ML (Mike) Wirral
DOWD, P (Phil) Staffordshire
DRYSDALE, D (Darren) Lincolnshire
DUNCAN, SAJ (Scott) Newcastle-upon-Tyne
D'URSO, AP (Andy) Essex
EAST, R (Roger) Wiltshire
ELTRINGHAM, G (Geoff) Tyne & Wear
FOY, CJ (Chris) Merseyside
FRIEND, KA (Kevin) Leicestershire
GIBBS, PN (Phil) West Midlands
GRAHAM F (Fred) Essex
HAINES, A (Andy) Tyne & Wear
HALSEY, MR (Mark) Lancashire
HARRINGTON, T (Tony) Cleveland
HAYWOOD, M (Mark) West Yorkshire
HEYWOOD, M (Mark) Cheshire
HOOPER, SA (Simon) Wiltshire
ILDERTON, EL (Eddie) Tyne & Wear
JONES, MJ (Michael) Cheshire
KETTLE, TM (Trevor) Rutland
LANGFORD, O (Oliver) West Midlands
LEWIS, RL (Rob) Shropshire
LININGTON, JJ (James) Isle of Wight
MADLEY, AJ (Andy) West Yorkshire
MADLEY, RJ (Bobby) West Yorkshire
MALONE, BJ (Brendan) Wiltshire
MARRINER, AM (André) West Midlands
MARTIN, SJ (Stephen) Staffordshire
MASON, LS (Lee) Lancashire
MATHIESON, SW (Scott) Cheshire
MILLER, NS (Nigel) County Durham
MILLER, P (Pat) Bedfordshire
MOHAREB, D (Dean) Cheshire
MOSS, J (Jon) West Yorkshire
NAYLOR, MA (Michael) South Yorkshire
OLIVER, M (Michael) Northumberland
PAWSON, CL (Craig) South Yorkshire
PHILLIPS, DJ (David) West Sussex
PROBERT, LW (Lee) Wiltshire
ROBINSON, TJ (Tim) West Sussex
RUSHTON, SJ (Steve) Staffordshire
RUSSELL, MP (Mick) Hertfordshire
SALISBURY, G (Graham) Lancashire
SARGINSON, CD (Chris) Staffordshire
SCOTT, GD (Graham) Oxfordshire
SHELDRAKE, D (Darren) Surrey
SHOEBRIDGE, RL (Rob) Derbyshire
SIMPSON, J (Jeremy) Lancashire
STROUD, KP (Keith) Hampshire
SUTTON, GJ (Gary) Lincolnshire
SWARBRICK, ND (Neil) Lancashire
TANNER, SJ, (Steve) Somerset
TAYLOR, A (Anthony) Cheshire
TIERNEY, P Paul) Lancashire
WARD, GL (Gavin) Surrey
WAUGH, J (Jock) South Yorkshire
WEBB, D (David) County Durham
WEBB, HM (Howard) South Yorkshire
WHITESTONE, D (Dean) Northamptonshire
WILLIAMSON, IG, (Iain) Berkshire
WOOLMER, KA (Andy) Northamptonshire
WRIGHT, KK (Kevin) Cambridgeshire

ASSISTANT REFEREES

AKERS, C (Chris) South Yorkshire
AMEY, JR (Justin) Dorset
AMPHLETT, MJ (Marvyn) Worcestershire
ARTIS, SG (Stephen) Norfolk
ASTLEY, MA (Mark) Manchester
ATKIN, R (Robert) Lincolnshire
ATKIN, RT (Ryan) London
ATKIN, W (Warren) Sussex
AVENT, D (David) Northamptonshire
BACKHOUSE, A (Anthony) Cumbria
BANKES, P (Peter) Merseyside
BARRATT, W (Wayne) Worcestershire
BARROW, SJ (Simon) Staffordshire
BARTLETT, R (Richard) Cheshire
BECK, SP (Simon) Bedfordshire
BENNETT, A (Andrew) Devon
BENNETT, SP (Simon) Staffordshire
BENTON, DK (David) South Yorkshire
BESWICK, G (Gary) County Durham
BETTS, L (Lee) Norfolk
BINGHAM, M (Michael) Birmingham
BLACKLEDGE, M (Mike) Cambridgeshire
BLUNDEN, D (Darren) Kent
BREAKSPEAR, CT (Charles) Surrey
BRISTOW, M (Matthew) Manchester
BROADBENT, W (Warren) Durham
BROMLEY, A (Adam) Devon
BROOK, C (Carl) East Sussex
BROOKS, J (John) Leicestershire
BRYAN, DS (Dave) Lincolnshire
BULL, M (Michael) Essex
BULL, W (William) Hampshire
BUONASSISI, M (Mathew) Northamptonshire
BURT, S (Stuart) Northamptonshire
BUSBY, J (John) Oxfordshire
BUSHELL, DD (David) London
BUTLER, S (Stuart) Kent
CAIRNS, MJ (Mike) Somerset
CANN, DJ (Darren) Norfolk
CHILD, SA (Stephen) Kent
CLARK, J (Joseph) Staffordshire
CLAYTON, A (Alan) Cheshire
CLAYTON, S (Simon) County Durham
COGGINS, A (Anthony) Oxfordshire
COLLIN, J (Jake) Liverpool
COOK, D (Daniel) Hampshire
COOK, P (Paul) East Riding
COOK, SJ (Steve) Derbyshire
COOPER, IJ (Ian) Kent
COOPER, N (Nicholas) Suffolk
COPELAND, SJ (Steven) Merseyside
COY, M (Martin) Durham
CROPP, B (Barry) Lancashire
CROUCH, IJ (Ian) Kent
CRYSELL, A (Adam) Essex
CURRY, PE (Paul) Northumberland
DALY, SDJ (Stephen) Middlesex
DAVIES, N (Neil) Cheshire
DAVISON, PA (Paul) Cleveland
DENTON, MJ (Michael) Lancashire
DERMOTT, P (Philip) Cheshire
DERRIEN, M (Mark) Dorset
DICICCO, M (Matthew) North Riding
DUDLEY, IA (Ian) Nottinghamshire
DUNCAN, M (Mark) Cheshire
DUNN, C (Carl) Staffordshire
DWYER, M (Mark) West Riding
EATON, D (Derek) Gloucestershire

ELLIS, R (Rob) West Midlands
ENGLAND, DJH (Darren) South Yorkshire
EVANS, K (Karl) Lancashire
EVETTS, GS (Gary) Hertfordshire
FARRIES, J (John) Oxfordshire
FEARN, AE (Amy) Leicestershire
FISSENDEN, I (Ian) Kent
FITCH, C (Carl) Suffolk
FLETCHER, R (Russell) Derbyshire
FLYNN, J (John) Wiltshire
FOLEY, MJ (Matt) London
FORD, D (Declan) Lincolnshire
FOX, A (Andrew) Birmingham
GANFIELD, RS (Ron) Somerset
GARRATT, AM (Andy) West Midlands
GARRATT, S (Sarah) Birmingham
GEORGE, M (Mike) Norfolk
GIBBONS, N (Nicholas) Lancashire
GILLETT, A (Adrian) Berkshire & Buckinghamshire
GOOCH, P (Peter) Lancashire
GORDON, B (Barry) County Durham
GRAHAM, P (Paul) Manchester
GRATTON, D (Danny) Staffordshire
GREENHALGH, N (Nick) Lancashire
GREENWOOD, AH (Alf) North Yorkshire
GRIFFITHS, M (Mark) South Yorkshire
GRUNNILL, W (Wayne) Yorkshire
HAIR, NA (Neil) Cambridgeshire
HALLIDAY, A (Andy) North Yorkshire
HANDLEY, D (Darren) Lancashire
HARRIS, P (Paul) Kent
HART, G (Glen) Durham
HATZIDAKIS, C (Constantine) Kent
HAYCOCK, KW (Ken) West Yorkshire
HAYWARD, K (Kevin) Staffordshire
HENDLEY, AR (Andy) West Midlands
HICKS, C (Craig) Surrey
HILLIER, J(Jake) Hertfordshire
HILTON, G (Gary) Lancashire
HOBBIS, N (Nick) Birmingham
HOBDAY, P (Paul) Birmingham
HODGES, R (Robert) Berkshire & Buckinghamshire
HODSKINSON, P (Paul) Lancashire
HOLDERNESS, BC (Barry) Essex
HOLMES, AR (Adrian) West Yorkshire
HOPKINS, AJ (Adam) Devon
HOPKINS, JD (John) Essex
HORWOOD, GD (Graham) Bedfordshire
HOWES, M (Mark) Birmingham
HUDSON, S (Shaun) Durham
HULL, J (Joe) Cheshire
HULME, R (Richard) Somerset
HUNT, J (Jonathan) Liverpool
HUSSIN, (Ian) Liverpool
HUTCHINSON, AD (Andrew) Cheshire
HUXTABLE, B (Brett) Devon
HYDE, RA (Robert) London
IHRINGOVA, A (Sasa) Shropshire
JERDEN, GJN (Gary) Essex
JOHNSON, G (Gordon) Liverpool
JOHNSON, KA (Kevin) Somerset
JOHNSON, RL (Ryan) Manchester
JONES, MT (Mark) Nottinghamshire
JONES, RJ (Robert) Merseyside
JOYCE, R (Ross) Cleveland
KAVANAGH, C (Chris) Lancashire
KAYE, E (Elliott) Essex
KELLY, P (Paul) Kent
KENDALL, R (Richard) Bedfordshire
KETTLEWELL, PT (Paul) Lancashire
KHATIB, B (Billy) Sunderland
KINSELEY, N (Nick) Essex
KIRKUP, PJ (Peter) Northamptonshire
KNAPP, SC (Simon) Bristol
KNOWLES, CJ (Chris) Northamptonshire
LAVER, AA (Andrew) Hampshire
LAW, GC (Geoff) Leicestershire
LAW, J (John) Worcestershire
LAWSON, KD (Keith) South Humberside
LEACH, D (Daniel) Oxfordshire
LEDGER, S (Scott) Yorkshire
LENNARD, HW (Harry) East Sussex
LIDDLE, G (Geoffrey) Durham
LINDEN, W (Wes) Middlesex
LONG, SJ (Simon) Suffolk
LUCAS, S (Simeon) Lancashire
LUGG, N (Nigel) Surrey
LYMER, C (Colin) Hampshire
McCALLUM, DA (Dave) Tyne & Wear
McDONOUGH, M (Mick) Newcastle-upon-Tyne
MACKAY, R (Rob) Bedfordshire
MAGILL, JP (John) Essex
MARGETTS, DS (David) Essex
MARKHAM, DR (Danny) Tyne & Wear
MARSDEN, PR (Paul) Lancashire
MARTIN, RJ (Richard) Weston-super-Mare
MASSEY, SL (Sian) Coventry
MATTHEWS, A (Adam) Gloucestershire
MATTOCKS, KJ (Kevin) Lancashire
MCGRATH, M (Matthew) East Riding
MEESON, DP (Daniel) Staffordshire
MELLOR, M (Mark) Hertfordshire
MERCHANT, R (Rob) Staffordshire
MEREDITH, S (Steven) Nottinghamshire
METCALFE, RL (Lee) Lancashire
MUGE, G (Gavin) Bedfordshire
MULLARKEY, M (Mike) Devon
MURPHY, N (Nigel) Nottinghamshire
NEWBOLD, AM (Andy) Leicestershire
NORCOTT, WG (Wade) Essex
NUNN, AJ (Adam) Wiltshire
O'BRIEN, J (John) London
O'DONNELL, CJ (Chris) Bedfordshire
OLDHAM, SA (Scott) Lancashire
PARRY, MJ (Matthew) Liverpool
PEART, T (Tony) North Yorkshire
PERRY, MS (Marc) West Midlands
PLANE, S (Steven) Worcestershire
PLOWRIGHT, DP (David) Nottinghamshire
POLLOCK, RM (Bob) Merseyside
PORTER, W (Wayne) Lincolnshire
POTTAGE, M (Mark) Dorset
POWELL, CI (Chris) Dorset
RADFORD, N (Neil) Worcester
RAMSEY, T (Thomas) Essex
RATHBONE, I (Ian) Northamptonshire
REES, P (Paul) Bristol
RICHARDS, DC (Ceri) Carmarthenshire
RICHARDSON, D (David) West Yorkshire
ROBATHAN, DM (Daniel) Surrey
ROBERTS, B (Bob) Lancashire
ROCK, DK (David) Hertfordshire
RODGERS, T (Thomas) Durham
ROSS, SJ (Stephen) Lincolnshire
RUBERY, SP (Steve) Essex
RUSSELL, GR (Geoff) Northampton
RUSSELL, M (Mark) Bristol
SALISBURY, M (Michael) Lancashire
SALIY, O (Oleksandr) Middlesex
SANNERUDE, A (Adrian) Suffolk
SCHOLES, MS (Mark) Buckinghamshire
SCOTT, JW (John) Buckinghamshire
SCREGG, AJ (Andrew) Liverpool
SHARP, N (Neil) Durham
SIDDALL, I (Iain) Lancashire
SLAUGHTER, A (Ashley) Sussex
SMALLWOOD, W (William) Cheshire
SMART, E (Edward) Birmingham
SMITH, N (Nigel) Derbyshire
SMITH, S (Stephen) County Durham
STOCKBRIDGE, SM (Seb) Tyne & Wear
STORRIE, D (David) West Yorkshire
STOTT, GT (Gary) Manchester
STREET, DR (Duncan) West Yorkshire
STRETTON, GS (Guy) Leicestershire
SWABEY, L (Lee) Devon
TANKARD, A (Anthony) South Yorkshire
TAYLOR, G (Grant) Birmingham
THOMPSON, PI (Paul) Chesterfield
TONER, B (Ben) Lancashire
TRANTER, A (Adrian) Dorset
TRELEAVEN, D (Dean) West Sussex
TURNER, A (Andrew) Devon
TURNER, GB (Glenn) Derbyshire
TYAS, J (Jason) West Yorkshire
VENAMORE, L (Lee) Kent
WATTS, AS (Adam) Worcestershire
WEBB, MP (Michael) Surrey
WEST, RJ (Richard) East Yorkshire
WHITELEY, J (Jason) West Yorkshire
WHITTON, RP (Rob) Essex
WIGGLESWORTH, RJ (Richard) Doncaster
WILKES, MJ (Matthew) West Midlands
WILSON, J (James) Manchester
WILSON, M (Marc) Cambridgeshire
WOOD, T (Tim) Gloucestershire
WOOLFORD, DM (David) Hampshire
WOOTTON, R (Ricky) West Riding
WRIGHT, P (Peter) Merseyside
YATES, O (Oliver) Staffordshire
YOUNG, A (Alan) Cambridgeshire

TRANSFERS 2011–12

JUNE 2011	From	To	Fee in £
28 Barnett, Tyrone	Macclesfield T	Crawley T	150,000
20 Bencherif, Hamza	Macclesfield T	Notts Co	undisclosed
14 Bennett, Elliott	Brighton & HA	Norwich C	undisclosed
6 Buckley, William E.	Watford	Brighton & HA	1,000,000
1 Deering, Sam	Oxford U	Barnet	undisclosed
21 Done, Matthew	Rochdale	Barnsley	undisclosed
30 Gardner, Craig	Birmingham C	Sunderland	5,000,000
29 Green, Daniel R.	Dagenham & R	Charlton Ath	undisclosed
1 Greer, Gordon	Swindon T	Brighton & HA	undisclosed
20 Harrold, Matthew	Shrewsbury T	Bristol R	undisclosed
8 Henderson, Jordan	Sunderland	Liverpool	16,000,000
30 Hobbs, Jack	Leicester C	Hull C	800,000
1 Jones, Robert W.	Scunthorpe U	Sheffield W	undisclosed
1 Leigertwood, Mikele B.	QPR	Reading	undisclosed
23 McNulty, Jimmy	Brighton & HA	Barnsley	undisclosed
6 Morison, Steve	Millwall	Norwich C	2,800,000
16 Nolan, Kevin A.J.	Newcastle U	West Ham U	4,000,000
21 Peltier, Lee A.	Huddersfield T	Leicester C	750,000
30 Philliskirk, Daniel	Chelsea	Sheffield U	Free
1 Pringle, Benjamin P.	Derby Co	Rotherham U	Free
14 Smith, Jonathan P.	York C	Swindon T	30,000
28 Spurr, Thomas	Sheffield W	Doncaster R	200,000
29 Stephens, Dale	Oldham Ath	Charlton Ath	350,000
29 Wickham, Connor	Ipswich T	Sunderland	13,000,000
30 Wiggins, Rhoys	AFC Bournemouth	Charlton Ath	undisclosed
21 Wiseman, Scott N.K.	Rochdale	Barnsley	undisclosed
TEMPORARY TRANSFERS			
29 Addison, Miles V.E.	Derby Co	Barnsley	
JULY 2011			
7 Adam, Charles G.	Blackpool	Liverpool	9,000,000
5 Ajose, Nicholas O.	Manchester U	Peterborough U	undisclosed
1 Al Habsi, Ali	Bolton W	Wigan Ath	4,000,000
7 Alcock, Craig	Yeovil T	Peterborough U	undisclosed
5 Barrett, Adam	Crystal Palace	AFC Bournemouth	undisclosed
12 Birchall, Adam S.	Dover Ath	Gillingham	undisclosed
6 Brown, Wesley M.	Manchester U	Sunderland	1,000,000
14 Bruna, Gerardo A.B.	Liverpool	Blackpool	undisclosed
1 Carayol, Mustapha	Lincoln C	Bristol R	undisclosed
7 Cisak, Aleksander	Accrington S	Oldham Ath	undisclosed
4 Clichy, Gael	Arsenal	Manchester C	7,000,000
19 Connell, Alan J.	Grimsby T	Swindon T	115,000
7 Cork, Jack F.P.	Chelsea	Southampton	undisclosed
20 Daley, Luke A.	Norwich C	Plymouth Arg	undisclosed
15 Dance, James	Crawley T	Luton T	undisclosed
29 Dickinson, Carl	Stoke C	Watford	250,000
15 Downing, Stewart	Aston Villa	Liverpool	20,000,000
1 Dunn, Chris	Northampton T	Coventry C	undisclosed
26 Eagles, Christopher M.	Burnley	Bolton W	1,500,000
1 Edmans, Robert M.	Chelmsford C	Dagenham & R	undisclosed
25 Elding, Anthony L.	Rochdale	Grimsby T	undisclosed
25 Emmanuel-Thomas, Jay A.A.	Arsenal	Ipswich T	undisclosed
19 Fairhurst, Waide S.	Doncaster R	Macclesfield T	undisclosed
6 Evina, Cedric D.	Oldham Ath	Charlton Ath	undisclosed
21 Ferguson, Barry	Birmingham C	Blackpool	750,000
18 Given, Seamus J.J.	Manchester C	Aston Villa	3,500,000
1 Graham, Daniel A.W.	Watford	Swansea C	3,500,000
18 Greening, Jonathan	Fulham	Nottingham F	undisclosed
1 Gregory, Steven M.	AFC Wimbledon	AFC Bournemouth	undisclosed
8 Gunnarsson, Aron E.M.	Coventry C	Cardiff C	undisclosed
7 Halford, Gregory	Wolverhampton W	Portsmouth	undisclosed
23 Haynes-Brown, Curtis L.	Lowestoft T	Yeovil T	undisclosed
1 Henderson, Darius A.	Sheffield U	Millwall	undisclosed
4 Henderson, Stephen	Bristol C	Portsmouth	undisclosed
29 Hourihane, Conor	Ipswich T	Plymouth Arg	undisclosed
18 Iwelumo, Christopher	Burnley	Watford	undisclosed
12 Johnson, Roger	Birmingham C	Wolverhampton W	7,000,000
1 Jones, Philip A.	Blackburn R	Manchester U	16,500,000
1 Kedwell, Daniel T.	AFC Wimbledon	Gillingham	60,000
12 Konchesky, Paul M.	Liverpool	Leicester C	1,500,000
1 Lee, Charlie	Peterborough U	Gillingham	undisclosed
1 Legzdins, Adam R.	Burton Alb	Derby Co	undisclosed
25 Lonergan, Andrew	Preston NE	Leeds U	undisclosed
4 Mackail-Smith, Craig	Peterborough U	Brighton & HA	undisclosed

25 Mason, Joseph	Plymouth Arg	Cardiff C	250,000
1 McKenna, Paul S.	Nottingham F	Hull C	Free
26 Mears, Tyrone	Burnley	Bolton W	1,500,000
7 Mills, Matthew C.	Reading	Leicester C	5,000,000
8 Morrison, Michael B.	Sheffield W	Charlton Ath	undisclosed
4 N'Gala, Bondz	Plymouth Arg	Yeovil T	Free
29 N'Zogbia, Charles	Wigan Ath	Aston Villa	9,500,000
1 O'Hara, Jamie	Tottenham H	Wolverhampton W	5,000,000
7 O'Shea, John F.	Manchester U	Sunderland	undisclosed
1 Pearce, Jason D.	AFC Bournemouth	Portsmouth	350,000
19 Pilkington, Anthony	Huddersfield T	Norwich C	2,000,000
1 Reed, Jake	Great Yarmouth T	Dagenham & R	undisclosed
1 Reid, Izak G.	Macclesfield T	Morecambe	undisclosed
30 Rice, Martin	Truro C	Torquay U	undisclosed
1 Robinson, Theo	Millwall	Derby Co	undisclosed
1 Schmeichel, Kasper P.	Leeds U	Leicester C	undisclosed
1 Shackell, Jason	Barnsley	Derby Co	undisclosed
1 Smalley, Deane	Oldham Ath	Oxford U	undisclosed
4 St Ledger-Hall, Sean P.	Preston NE	Leicester C	1,200,000
22 Taylor, Matthew S.	Bolton W	West Ham U	undisclosed
14 Taylor, Ryan	Rotherham U	Bristol C	undisclosed
1 Tomlinson, Ben	Worksop T	Macclesfield T	undisclosed
1 Tyson, Nathan	Nottingham F	Derby Co	undisclosed
1 Varney, Luke I.	Derby Co	Portsmouth	750,000
15 Vincelot, Romain M.G.	Dagenham & R	Brighton & HA	undisclosed
11 Ward, Daniel C.	Bolton W	Huddersfield T	undisclosed
1 Whelpdale, Chris	Peterborough U	Gillingham	undisclosed
13 Yeates, Mark	Sheffield U	Watford	undisclosed
1 Young, Ashley	Aston Villa	Manchester U	16,000,000
6 Zebroski, Christopher	Torquay U	Bristol R	undisclosed

TEMPORARY TRANSFERS

12 Addison, Miles – Derby Co – Barnsley; 25 Atkinson, Christopher R. – Huddersfield T – Darlington; 28 Batth, Daniel T. – Wolverhampton W – Sheffield W; 12 Benyon, Elliot P. – Swindon T – Wycombe W; 21 Brady, Robert – Manchester U – Hull C; 7 Brodie, Richard J. – Crawley T – Fleetwood T; 14 Carlisle, Clarke J. – Burnley – Preston NE; 18 Cooper, Liam D.I. – Hull C – Huddersfield T; 26 Cullen, Mark – Hull C – Bury; 13 Darby, Stephen – Liverpool – Rochdale; 1 De Laet, Ritchie R.A. – Manchester U – Norwich C; 13 Donnelly, Scott P. – Swansea C – Wycombe W; 26 Ehmer, Maximillian A. – QPR – Yeovil T; 26 Green, Matthew J. – Torquay U – Mansfield T; 21 Gulacsi, Peter – Liverpool – Hull C; 27 Hansen, Martin – Liverpool – Bradford C; 29 Hitchcock, Thomas J. – Blackburn R – Plymouth Arg; 20 Johnson, Damien M. – Plymouth Arg – Huddersfield T; 26 Khumalo, Bongani – Tottenham H – Reading; 14 Logan, Conrad J. – Leicester C. – Rotherham U; 29 Mason, Ryan G. – Tottenham H – Doncaster R; 18 Mee, Benjamin – Manchester C – Burnley; 26 Naughton, Kyle – Tottenham H – Norwich C; 11 N'Diaye, Alassane – Crystal Palace – Southend U; 22 Noble, Liam T. – Sunderland – Carlisle U; 29 Parkes, Thomas P.W. – Leicester C – Burton Alb; 31 Taylor, Jake W.T. – Reading – Aldershot T; 11 Tunnicliffe, Ryan – Manchester U – Peterborough U; 13 Walker, Samuel C. – Chelsea – Northampton T

AUGUST 2011

31 Arteta, Mikel	Everton	Arsenal	10,000,000
12 Ayala, Daniel	Liverpool	Norwich C	undisclosed
30 Baldock, Samuel	Milton Keynes D	West Ham U	undisclosed
26 Barton, Joseph A.	Newcastle U	QPR	Free
31 Beckford, Jermaine P.A.	Everton	Leicester C	2,500,000
4 Campbell, Dudley J.	Blackpool	QPR	1,200,000
2 Cresswell, Aaron	Tranmere R	Ipswich T	undisclosed
31 Crouch, Peter J.	Tottenham H	Stoke C	10,000,000
6 Daley, Luke A.	Norwich C	Plymouth Arg	undisclosed
31 Dann, Scott	Birmingham C	Blackburn R	7,000,000
3 Dickinson, Carl M.	Stoke C	Watford	250,000
5 Dikgacoi, Kagisho	Fulham	Crystal Palace	600,000
30 Elliot, Robert	Charlton Ath	Newcastle U	undisclosed
31 Elliott, Wade P.	Burnley	Birmingham C	undisclosed
31 Feeney, Liam M.	AFC Bournemouth	Millwall	undisclosed
31 Ferdinand, Anton J.	Sunderland	QPR	undisclosed
11 Fox, Daniel	Burnley	Southampton	1,800,000
31 Garner, Joseph A.	Nottingham F	Watford	400,000
3 Goodwillie, David	Dundee U	Blackburn R	2,800,000
24 Gorkss, Kaspars	QPR	Reading	undisclosed
4 Gornell, Terence M.	Accrington S	Shrewsbury T	undisclosed
1 Hamer, Benjamin J.	Reading	Charlton Ath	undisclosed
31 Hargreaves, Owen L.	Manchester U	Manchester C	Free
22 Harley, Ryan	Swansea C	Brighton & HA	undisclosed
31 Harrad, Shaun	Northampton T	Bury	undisclosed
18 Hines, Zavon	West Ham U	Burnley	250,000
31 Hogg, Jonathan	Aston Villa	Watford	undisclosed
31 Hutton, Alan	Tottenham H	Aston Villa	undisclosed
5 Ince, Thomas	Liverpool	Blackpool	undisclosed
19 Ings, Daniel W.J.	AFC Bournemouth	Burnley	undisclosed
31 Jerome, Cameron Z.R.	Birmingham C	Stoke C	undisclosed
11 Jose Enrique	Newcastle U	Liverpool	7,000,000
25 Kee, Billy R.	Torquay U	Burton Alb	20,000

27 Le Fondre, Adam J.	Rotherham U	Reading	350,000
27 Lenihan, Darragh	Middlesbrough	Blackburn R	undisclosed
12 Lines, Christopher J.	Bristol R	Sheffield W	50,000
9 Long, Shane P.	Reading	WBA	4,500,000
30 Lowe, Ryan T.	Bury	Sheffield W	undisclosed
26 MacDonald, Charles L.	Brentford	Milton Keynes D	1,000,000
26 MacDonald, Shaun B.	Swansea C	AFC Bournemouth	125,000
4 McDermott, Donal	Manchester C	Huddersfield T	undisclosed
31 McDonald, Cody	Norwich C	Coventry C	undisclosed
15 Miller, Ishmael A.	WBA	Nottingham F	1,200,000
23 Miller, Lee A.	Middlesbrough	Carlisle U	undisclosed
22 Mills, Joseph N.	Southampton	Reading	undisclosed
2 Morrison, Michael B.	Sheffield W	Charlton Ath	undisclosed
31 Mozika, Damien	Bury	Scunthorpe U	undisclosed
24 Nasri, Samir	Arsenal	Manchester C	23,000,000
1 N'Gala, Bondz	Plymouth Arg	Yeovil T	Free
31 N'Gog, David	Liverpool	Bolton W	4,000,000
31 N'Guessen, Dany-Gale D.	Leicester C	Millwall	undisclosed
8 Obertan, Gabriel	Manchester C	Newcastle U	undisclosed
11 O'Grady, Christopher J.	Rochdale	Sheffield W	350,000
8 Oxlade-Chamberlain, Alexander M.D.		Southampton	Arsenal
12,000,000			
31 Pablo Ibanez	WBA	Birmingham C	undisclosed
31 Palacios, Wilson R.	Tottenham H	Stoke C	6,000,000
31 Parker, Scott M.	West Ham U	Tottenham H	6,000,000
3 Pell, Harry D.B.	Bristol R	Hereford U	undisclosed
31 Raul Meireles	Liverpool	Chelsea	11,500,000
5 Raynes, Michael	Scunthorpe U	Rotherham U	undisclosed
31 Revell, Alexander D.	Leyton Orient	Rotherham U	undisclosed
2 Robinson, Anton D.	AFC Bournemouth	Huddersfield T	250,000
31 Sinclair, Emile A.	Macclesfield T	Peterborough U	undisclosed
31 Slew, Jordan M.	Sheffield U	Blackburn R	1,000,000
12 Smith, Steven	Norwich C	Preston NE	Free
31 Stanislas, Junior	West Ham U	Burnley	undisclosed
2 Taylor, Ryan P.	Rotherham U	Bristol C	undisclosed
29 Traore, Armand	Arsenal	QPR	undisclosed
5 Treacy, Keith	Preston NE	Burnley	undisclosed
31 Turner, Ben H.	Coventry C	Cardiff C	750,000
26 Westcarr, Craig N.	Notts Co	Chesterfield	undisclosed
31 Wright-Philips, Shaun C.	Manchester C	QPR	undisclosed
31 Yakubu, Ayegbeni	Everton	Blackburn R	1,500,000
26 Young, Luke P.	Aston Villa	QPR	undisclosed

TEMPORARY TRANSFERS

31 Abdulla, Ahmed M. – West Ham U – Swindon T; 31 Adeyemi, Thomas O. – Norwich C – Oldham Ath; 4 Almond, Louis J. – Blackpool – Barrow; 12 Andrews, Keith J. – Blackburn R – Ipswich T; 15 Antonio, Michail G. – Reading – Colchester U; 5 Arnold, Steven J.W. – Wycombe W – Hayes & Yeading; 1 Atkins, Ross M. – Derby Co – Burton Alb; 12 Atkinson, William H. – Hull C – Plymouth Arg; 3 Balanta, Angelo J. – QPR – Milton Keynes D; 19 Balkestein, Pim – Brentford – Rochdale; 31 Ball, David M. – Peterborough U – Rochdale; 25 Barkhuizen, Thomas J. – Blackpool – Hereford U; 25 Barnes-Homer, Matt – Luton T – Rochdale; 20 Bates, Jon-jo D. – Dagenham & R – Harrow Bor; 31 Beevers, Mark G. – Sheffield W – Milton Keynes D; 31 Benali, Ahmed – Manchester C – Rochdale; 31 Bender, Thomas J. – Colchester U – Accrington S; 31 Bentley,David M. – Tottenham H – West Ham U; 1 Bergqvist, Jan D. – Aldershot T – Farnborough T; 5 Bignall, Nicholas C. – Reading – Exeter C; 25 Bodin, Billy P. – Swindon T – Torquay U; 4 Bolger, Cian T. – Leicester C – Bristol R; 12 Bond, Jonathan H. – Watford – Brackley T; 10 Breeze, Matthew C. – Peterborough U – Histon; 22 Breimyr, Henrik M. – Aldershot T – Eastleigh; 31 Brown, Jordan – West Ham U – Aldershot T; 16 Brown, Reece – Manchester U – Doncaster R; 11 Bryan, Michael A. – Watford – Bradford C; 25 Butlin, Joey – Walsall – Solihull Moors; 25 Button, David R.E. – Tottenham H – Leyton Orient; 1 Byrne, Nathan W. – Tottenham H – AFC Bournemouth; 31 Byrne, Shane W. – Leicester C – Bury; 19 Cestor, Mike B. – Leyton Orient – Woking; 15 Chamberlain, Elliott C. – Leicester C – Stockport Co; 19 Clarke, Nathan – Huddersfield T – Oldham Ath; 12 Clayton, Harry S. – Crewe Alex – Market Drayton T; 1 Clement, Jordan K. – Aldershot T – Maidenhead U; 18 Clist, Simon J. – Oxford U – Hereford U; 31 Coke, Giles C. – Sheffield W – Bury; 31 Cole, Aaron E. – Derby Co – Eastwood T; 1 Connolly, Reece W. – Aldershot T – Farnborough T; 19 Cornell, David J. – Swansea C – Hereford U; 29 Cort, Leon T.A. – Burnley – Charlton Ath; 26 Daniels, Gregg – Macclesfield T – Newcastle T; 5 Davies, Andrew J. – Stoke C – Crystal Palace; 25 Dean, Luke A. – Bradford C – Hinckley U; 20 Dennis, Louis H. – Dagenham & R – Grays Ath; 31 Devitt, Jamie M. – Hull C – Bradford C; 31 Dixon, Terry N. – Bradford C – FC Halifax T; 11 Doble, Ryan A. – Southampton – AFC Bournemouth; 19 Doughty, Michael E. – QPR – Crawley T; 23 Drinkwater, Daniel N. – Manchester U – Barnsley; 31 Duffy, Shane P.M. – Everton – Scunthorpe U; 25 Eastham, Ashley – Blackpool – Bury; 26 Ellison, James – Burton Alb – Alfreton T; 12 Essam, Connor – Gillingham – Bishop's Stortford; 27 Evans, William G. – Swindon T – Hereford U; 16 Fletcher, Wesleigh J. – Burnley – Accrington S; 5 Forecast, Tommy S. – Southampton – Thurrock; 31 Franks, Jonathan I. – Middlesbrough – Oxford U; 19 Futcher, Benjamin P. – Bury – Mansfield T; 13 Gayle, Dwight D.B. – Dagenham & R – Bishop's Stortford; 20 Gayle, Ian G. – Dagenham & R – Grays Ath; 5 Gibson, Benjamin J. – Middlesbrough – Plymouth Arg; 19 Gilligan, Ryan J. – Northampton T – Newport Co; 17 Gordon, Benjamin L. – Chelsea – Peterborough U; 13 Gough, Conor J.J. – Charlton Ath – Salisbury C; 26 Grella, Michele – Leeds U – Brentford; 31 Griffiths, Jamie – Ipswich T – Plymouth Arg; 26 Grounds, Jonathan M. – Middlesbrough – Chesterfield; 9 Guy, Lewis B. – Milton Keynes D – Oxford U; 20 Harvey, Alex-Ray – Burnley – Fleetwood T; 12 Hassan, Emmanuel – Hartlepool U – Harrogate T; 19 Hawkes, Daren G. – Gillingham – Ramsgate; 12 Haynes, Kyle J. – Cheltenham T – Hednesford T; 22 Hester, Patrick – AFC Bournemouth – Bashley; 27 Hogg, Jonathan – Aston Villa – Watford; 31 Hurst, James – WBA – Blackpool; 3 Ikeme, Carl – Wolverhampton W – Middlesbrough; 15 James-Lewis, Merrick A. – Southend U – Braintree T; 9 Jansson, Oscar – Tottenham H – Bradford C; 26 Johnson, Lee D. – Bristol C – Chesterfield; 4 Johnson, Michael – Manchester C – Leicester C; 30 Johnson, Samuel W. – Port Vale – Stafford R; 3

Kean, Jacob K. – Blackburn R – Rochdale; 16 Keogh, Andrew D. – Wolverhampton W – Leeds U; 26 Kettings, Christopher D. – Blackpool – Birmingham C; 5 Kilbane, Kevin D. – Hull C – Derby Co; 31 King, Simon D.R. – Gillingham – Plymouth Arg; 5 Kinnisburgh, Steven S. – Oxford U – Cambridge U; 19 Lalkovic, Milan – Chelsea – Doncaster R; 26 Lane, Jack F. – Macclesfield T – Newcastle T; 9 Langmead, Kelvin S. – Peterborough U – Northampton T; 31 Lansbury, Henri G. – Arsenal – West Ham U; 5 Lee, Oliver R. – West Ham U – Dagenham & R; 5 Long, Kevin F. – Burnley – Accrington S; 5 LuaLua, Kazenga – Newcastle U – Brighton & HA; 3 Lund, Matthew C. – Stoke C – Oldham Ath; 1 Malone, Scott L. – Wolverhampton W – AFC Bournemouth; 17 Marshall, Ben – Stoke C – Sheffield W; 12 McCartney, George – Sunderland – West Ham U; 12 McClure, Matthew G. – Wycombe W – Hayes & Yeading; 4 McGivern, Ryan – Manchester C – Crystal Palace; 31 McGivern, Ryan – Manchester C – Bristol C; 5 Mendez-Laing, Nathaniel – Wolverhampton W – Sheffield U; 3 Miller, Kern A. – Barnsley – Accrington S; 8 Mills, Daniel P. – Peterborough U – Tamworth; 5 Montano, Cristian A. – West Ham U – Notts Co; 12 Mooney, Jason B. – Wycombe W – Oxford C; 5 Moore, Liam S. – Leicester C – Bradford C; 19 Moult, Louis E. – Stoke C – Accrington S; 19 Murphy, David P. – Reading – Cirencester T; 3 Myhill, Glyn O. – WBA – Birmingham C; 31 Nelson, Mitchell A. – AFC Bournemouth – Lincoln C; 15 Napper, Byron J. – Crawley T – Weymouth; 8 N'Guessen, Dany-Gael D. – Leicester C – Millwall; 24 Norwood, Oliver J. – Manchester U – Scunthorpe U; 5 Obika, Jonathan – Tottenham H – Yeovil T; 25 Osborn, Alexander S. – Dagenham & R – Thurrock; 19 Osborne, Leon A. – Bradford C – Southport; 16 Oyenuga, Kudus – Tottenham H – Bury; 23 Park, Cameron – Middlesbrough – Barnsley; 13 Parsons, Alexander A. – AFC Bournemouth – Wimborne T; 19 Pope, Nicholas D. – Charlton Ath – Harrow Bor; 31 Puncheon, Jason D.I. – Plymouth Arg – QPR; 5 Purkiss, Ben – Oxford U – Darlington; 5 Ramage, Peter I. – QPR – Crystal Palace; 12 Rance, Dean J.R. – Gillingham – Bishop's Stortford; 12 Raymond, Frankie J. – Reading – Eastleigh; 13 Reynolds, Duran-Rhys – Southend U – St Neots T; 31 Richards, Jamie A. – Plymouth Arg – Barnstaple T; 5 Richardson, Michael – Newcastle U – Leyton Orient; 12 Saville, Jack W. – Southampton – Hayes & Yeading; 11 Severn, James A.R.M. – Derby Co – Eastwood T; 3 Shea, James – Arsenal – Dagenham & R; 31 Simpson, Jay-Alistaire F. – Hull C – Millwall; 16 Smith, Adam J. – Tottenham H – Milton Keynes D; 3 Spence, Jordan J. – West Ham U – Bristol C; 1 Spencer, James C. – Huddersfield T – Cheltenham T; 3 Steer, Jed J. – Norwich C – Yeovil T; 25 Stephenson, Darren C.A. – Bradford C – Hinckley U; 19 Stephenson, Timothy J. – AFC Bournemouth – Weymouth; 5 Stockdale, David A. – Fulham – Ipswich T; 13 Strugnell, Daniel – AFC Bournemouth – Wimborne T; 31 Swallow, Ben – Bristol R – Bath C; 12 Tavernier, James H. – Newcastle U – Carlisle U; 1 Taylor, Jake W.T. – Reading – Aldershot T; 19 Thomas, Daniel – AFC Bournemouth – Welling U; 12 Thomas, Michael D. – Macclesfield T – Leek T; 25 Thompson, Adam L. – Watford – Brentford; 31 Timlin, Michael A. – Swindon T – Southend U; 3 Trippier, Kieran J. – Manchester C – Burnley; 5 Tunchev, Aleksandar – Leicester C – Crystal Palace; 23 Turner, Jake S.P. – Scunthorpe U – Brigg T; 31 Waghorn, Martyn T. – Leicester C – Hull C; 30 Walker, Joshua – Watford – Stevenage; 26 Weimann, Andreas – Aston Villa – Watford; 11 Weir, Tyler C. – Hereford U – Gloucester C; 13 Wilkinson, Luke A. – Dagenham & R – Boreham Wood; 30 Williams, Brett A. – Reading – Rotherham U; 5 Wood, Chris – WBA – Birmingham C; 26 Vine, Rowan L. – QPR – Exeter C; 31 Winn, Peter H. – Stevenage – Cambridge U; 26 Winnall, Sam T. – Wolverhampton W – Hereford U; 15 Woodley, Aaron R. – Oxford U – Banbury U; 26 Woodyard, Alexander J. – Southend U – Farnborough; 20 Wootton, Lee S. – Dagenham & R – Harrow Bor; 3 Wootton, Scott J. – Manchester U – Peterborough U; 1 Worsfold, Max N. – Aldershot T – Maidenhead U

SEPTEMBER 2011 TEMPORARY TRANSFERS

8 Adams, Blair – Sunderland – Brentford; 16 Agdestein, Torbjorn – Brighton & HA – Bath C; 22 Ajose, Nicholas – Peterborough U – Scunthorpe U; 30 Almunia, Manuel – Arsenal – West Ham U; 9 Alnwick, Ben R. – Tottenham H – Leyton Orient; 23 Amoo, David O.S. – Liverpool – Bury; 29 Andrade, Bruno M.C. – QPR – Aldershot T; 1 Arnold, Steven J.W. – Wycombe W – Hayes & Yeading; 9 Asante, Kyle E.K. – Southend U – Concord R; 8 Baggridge, Rhys W. – Yeovil T – Gillingham T; 30 Baldock, George H.I. – Milton Keynes D – Northampton T; 30 Banton, Jason – Leicester C – Burton Alb; 23 Baxter, Jose – Everton – Tranmere R; 30 Borrowdale, Gary I. – QPR – Barnet; 10 Brooke, Ryan M. – Oldham Ath – Barrow; 23 Brown, Alexander S. – Gillingham – Whitstable T; 22 Burrow, Jordan – Chesterfield – Boston U; 8 Butland, Jack – Birmingham C – Cheltenham T; 20 Bywater, Stephen – Derby Co – Sheffield W; 30 Canham, Sean – Hereford U – Bath C; 19 Carey, Lewis T. – Bristol C – Gloucester C; 12 Carson, Trevor – Sunderland – Bury; 23 Chilvers, Liam C. – Notts Co – Port Vale; 22 Clark, Matthew W. – Swindon T – Oxford C; 9 Clarke, Leon M. – Swindon T – Chesterfield; 9 Clarke, Thomas – Huddersfield T – Leyton Orient; 16 Clarkson, David – Bristol C – Brentford; 9 Clough, Charlie – Bristol R – Bath C; 9 Collins, Daniel – Stoke C – Ipswich T; 24 Davies, Andrew J. – Stoke C – Bradford C; 30 Davisson, Benjamin J. – Charlton Ath – Welling U; 22 Dawson, Aaron P. – Exeter C – Tiverton T; 19 Deards, Connor A.J. – Walsall – Redditch U; 23 Dempster, John – Crawley T – Kettering T; 16 Donaldson, Ryan M. – Newcastle U – Tranmere R; 9 Donnelly, George – Fleetwood T – Macclesfield T; 15 Drury, Andrew M. – Ipswich T – Crawley T; 13 Eastman, Thomas M. – Colchester U – Crawley T; 30 Elder, Nathan – Hayes & Yeading – Hereford U; 23 Forecast, Tommy S. – Southampton – Bromley; 23 Franks, Fraser G. – AFC Wimbledon – Hayes & Yeading; 8 Furzer, Jack L. – Exeter C – Bideford; 23 Gallinagh, Andrew A.R. – Cheltenham T – Bath C; 29 Garbutt, Luke – Everton – Cheltenham T; 9 Griffiths, Scott R. – Peterborough U – Crawley T; 12 Hall, Robert – West Ham U – Oxford U; 19 Hassan, Emmanuel – Hartlepool U – Whitby T; 16 Haworth, Andrew A.D. – Bury – Oxford U; 29 Hewitt, Troy R. – QPR – Dagenham & R; 24 Hill, Clinton S. – QPR – Nottingham F; 20 Hollis, Haydn J. – Notts Co – Barrow; 26 Howard, Ryan R.W.B. – Reading – Millwall; 16 Isaac, Chez J.T. – Watford – Boreham Wood; 13 Jackson, Marlon M. – Bristol C – Northampton T; 9 Jarvis, Nathaniel S. – Cardiff C – Newport Co; 29 Jervis, Jake M. – Birmingham C – Swindon T; 26 Johnson, Oliver T. – Norwich C – Yeovil T; 9 Johnstone, Samuel L. – Manchester U – Scunthorpe U; 30 Kennedy, Thomas G. – Leicester C – Peterborough U; 30 Kewley-Graham, Jesse J. – Wycombe W – Staines T; 19 Kovacs, Janos – Hereford U – Luton T; 16 Lacey, Patrick S. – Bradford C – Vauxhall Motors; 8 Llera, Miguel A. – Charlton Ath – Brentford; 10 Lovelock, Thomas J. – Leyton Orient – Chertsey T; 16 Mambo, Yado M. – Charlton Ath – Ebbsfleet U; 13 Martin, David J. – Derby Co – Walsall; 12 Massey, Gavin A. – Watford – Yeovil T; 16 McGoldrick, David J. – Nottingham F – Sheffield W; 9 McNaughton, Callum J. – West Ham U – AFC Wimbledon; 23 Milton, Harry T. – Milton Keynes D – Aveley; 23 Mitchell, Liam – Notts Co – Lewes; 16 Montgomery, Graeme – Aldershot T – Eastleigh; 24 Morrison, Clinton H. – Sheffield W – Milton Keynes D; 23 Mukendi, Vinny K. – Macclesfield T – Southport; 23 Murphy, David P. – Reading – Hungerford T; 9 Nesbitt, Teddy – Southend U – Concord R; 23 Nicholas, George A. – Notts Co – Lewes; 23 Norburn, Oliver L. – Leicester C – Bristol R; 16 Nouble, Frank H. – West Ham U – Gillingham; 2 Okus, Conor E. – Dagenham & R – Havant & W'ville; 30 Osei-Kuffour, Jonathan – Bristol R – Gillingham; 23 Parish, Elliott C. – Aston Villa – Cardiff C; 21 Parkin, Jonathan – Cardiff C – Doncaster R; 13 Pentney, Carl – Colchester U – Chelmsford C; 23 Peters, Jaime B. – Ipswich T – AFC Bournemouth; 12 Pittman, Jon P. – Oxford U – Crawley T; 23 Pugh, Daniel A. – Stoke C – Leeds U; 15 Purcell, Tadhg – Northampton T – Darlington; 9 Purkiss, Ben – Oxford U – Darlington; 30 Raglan, Charles J.C. – Port Vale – Hinckley U; 29 Reed, Adam M. – Sunderland – Bradford C; 28 Ridehalgh, Liam – Huddersfield T – Swindon T; 27 Riise, Bjorn H.S. – Fulham – Portsmouth; 29 Rowe, Dominic R. – Bradford C – Barrow; 26 Rowlands, Martin C. – QPR – Wycombe W; 8 Sekajja,

Ibra – Crystal Palace – Kettering T; 30 Shelvey, Jonjo – Liverpool – Blackpool; 10 Simpson, Robbie – Huddersfield T – Oldham Ath; 16 Smith, Adam C. – Leicester C – Chesterfield; 23 Smith, Ben P. – Crawley T – Kettering T; 9 Stockford, Lewis J. – Portsmouth – Salisbury C; 27 Swinglehurst, Steven – Carlisle U – Kendal T; 16 Tallack, Lewis J. – Portsmouth – Dorchester T; 21 Taylor, Jake W.T. – Reading – Exeter C; 19 Tchuimeni-Nimely, Alex – Manchester C – Middlesbrough; 10 Thomas, Wesley A.N. – Crawley T – AFC Bournemouth; 12 Tunchev, Aleksandar – Leicester C – Crystal Palace; 30 Wabara, Reece – Manchester C – Ipswich T; 23 Walker, Paul H. – Northampton T – Brackley T; 26 Warren, Freddie R. – Charlton Ath – Kettering T; 2 Watson, Karlton A.J. – Nottingham F – Eastwood T; 15 Whichelow, Matthew R. – Watford – Exeter C; 8 White, Andrew I. – Crewe Alex – Stafford R; 23 Whiteley, Lewis – Notts Co – Bishop's Stortford; 13 Williams, Marcus V. – Reading – Sheffield U

OCTOBER 2011

5 Fogden, Wesley K.	Havant & W'ville	AFC Bournemouth	undisclosed
20 Sheringham, Charles E.W.	Dartford	AFC Bournemouth	undisclosed

TEMPORARY TRANSFERS

13 Agyemang, Patrick – QPR – Millwall; 28 Asante, Kyle E.K. – Southend U – Canvey Island; 6 Basey, Grant W. – Peterborough U – Wycombe W; 25 Beattie, Craig – Swansea C – Watford; 27 Bennett, Dale O. – Watford – Brentford; 21 Berahino, Saldo – WBA – Northampton T; 25 Bignall, Nicholas C. – Reading – Wycombe W; 21 Bird, David A. – Cheltenham T – Kidderminster H; 28 Blake, Ryan G. – Brentford – Farnborough T; 22 Boateng, Michael K.A. – Bristol R – Tonbridge Angels; 14 Boden, Scott D. – Chesterfield – Macclesfield T; 14 Branston, Guy P.B. – Bradford C – Rotherham U; 21 Brown, Connor A. – Sheffield U – Eastwood T; 7 Brunt, Thomas J. – Gillingham – Ashford U; 5 Clarke, Lewis P. – Yeovil T – Poole T; 14 Clarke, William C. – Blackpool – Sheffield U; 27 Cook, Steve A. – Brighton & HA – AFC Bournemouth; 22 Cox, Samuel P. – Barnet – Boreham Wood; 25 Cunningham, Gregory R. – Manchester C – Nottingham F; 25 Daniels, Luke M. – WBA – Southend U; 25 Davies, Callum J. – Gillingham – Thurrock; 27 Davies, Scott M.E. – Crawley T – Aldershot T; 6 Day, Joseph D. – Peterborough U – Alfreton T; 3 Dean, Luke A. – Bradford C – Harrogate T; 14 Dobie, Luke J. – Middlesbrough – Accrington S; 31 Donnelly, George – Fleetwood T – Macclesfield T; 28 Dovey, Jack M. – Southampton – Eastleigh; 14 Dunne, Charles – Wycombe W – Staines T; 21 Eccleston, Nathan – Liverpool – Rochdale; 14 Foderingham, Wesley A. – Crystal Palace – Swindon T; 14 Gayle, Ian G. – Dagenham & R – Kingstonian; 20 Green, Michael J. – Port Vale – Eastleigh; 14 Harley, Jon – Notts Co – Rotherham U; 24 Harper, Stephen A. – Newcastle U – Brighton & HA; 14 Hatfield, William H. – Leeds U – Accrington S; 14 Helan, Jeremy – Manchester C – Carlisle U; 21 Holland, Jack – Crystal Palace – Farnborough T; 4 Ilunga, Herita – West Ham U – Doncaster R; 18 Jackson, Ryan O. – AFC Wimbledon – Fleetwood T; 21 James, Kingsley T. – Port Vale – Chasetown; 21 Jara, Gonzalo A.R. – WBA – Brighton & HA; 13 Kightly, Michael J. – Wolverhampton W – Watford; 13 Kirkland, Christopher E. – Wigan Ath – Doncaster R; 6 Leslie, Steven – Shrewsbury T – Hereford U; 13 Losasso, Charlie C. – Reading – Salisbury C; 6 Lynch, David C.W. – Burnley – Droylsden; 22 McLaggon, Kayne S. – Bristol R – Tonbridge Angels; 17 McManaman, Callum H. – Wigan Ath – Blackpool; 17 McManaman, Callum H. – Wigan Ath – Blackpool; 16 Mambo, Yado M. – Charlton Ath – Ebbsfleet U; 7 Mekki, Adam R. – Aldershot T – Dorchester T; 13 Montano, Cristian A.C. – West Ham U – Swindon T; 10 Nelson, Mitchell A. – AFC Bournemouth – Lincoln C; 28 Niven, Derek – Chesterfield – Northampton T; 28 Nosworthy, Nyron – Sunderland – Watford; 7 Ntlhe, Kgosietsile – Peterborough U – St Albans C; 1 Oakley, Matthew – Leicester C – Exeter C; 21 Orenuga, Femi K. – Everton – Notts Co; 7 Overson, Dean J. – Burnley – Vauxhall Motors; 27 Paynter, William P. – Leeds U – Brighton & HA; 14 Phillips, Matthew – Blackpool – Sheffield U; 21 Philliskirk, Daniel – Sheffield U – Oxford U; 20 Potter, Luke A. – Barnsley – Alfreton T; 21 Purse, Darren J. – Millwall – Yeovil T; 7 Radford, Oscor S. – Doncaster R – Matlock T; 28 Razak, Abdul – Manchester C – Portsmouth; 7 Redwood, Leon N. – Brighton & HA – Dover Ath; 21 Reece, Charles T. – Bristol R – Gloucester C; 7 Rendell, Scott D. – Wycombe W – Bristol R; 3 Reynolds, Duran-Rhys – Dagenham & R – Met Police; 7 Robinson, Adam J. – Bradford C – Blyth Spartans; 21 Rodney, Nialle – Bradford C – Darlington; 10 Sandell, Andrew – Wycombe W – Forest Green R; 7 Scott, Mark J. – Swindon T – Oxford C; 21 Scowen, Josuha C. – Wycombe W – Hemel Hempstead T; 7 Smith, Nathan A. – Mansfield T – Aldershot T; 4 Spray, James M.K.T. – Wolverhampton W – Accrington S; 28 Spear, Ray B.K. – Torquay U – Bideford; 14 Stech, Marek – West Ham U – Yeovil T; 7 Stephenson, Darren C.A. – Bradford C – Woodley Sp; 14 Stockford, Lewis J. – Portsmouth – Salisbury C; 7 Taylor, Alistair W. – Barnsley – Worksop T; 7 Thalassitis, Michael – Stevenage – Boreham Wood; 21 Thompson, Curtis L. – Nots Co – Lincoln C; 12 Vose, Dominic J.S. – West Ham U – Braintree T; 13 Wassmer, Charlie – Crawley T – Fleetwood T; 13 Wilson, Glenn M. – Crawley T – Fleetwood T; 28 Wilson, Mark A. – Doncaster R – Walsall; 28 Woodley, Jordan A. – Brighton & HA – Hastings U

NOVEMBER 2011

16 LuaLua, Kazenga	Newcastle U	Brighton & HA	undisclosed

TEMPORARY TRANSFERS

24 Aldred, Thomas M. – Colchester U – Torquay U; 24 Amadi Holloway, Aaron J. – Bristol C – Bath C; 22 Aneke, Chukwuemeka, A.A. – Arsenal – Stevenage; 24 Assombalonga, Britt – Watford – Wealdstone; 22 Baker, Nathan L. – Aston Villa – Millwall; 24 Ball, David M. – Peterborough U – Rochdale; 24 Banks, Oliver – Rotherham U – Buxton; 24 Baseya, Cedric – Reading – Barnet; 24 Baxendale, James – Doncaster R – Buxton; 17 Bergkamp, Roland A.M. – Brighton & HA – Rochdale; 22 Beye, Habib – Aston Villa – Doncaster R; 24 Bidwell, Jake – Everton – Brentford; 4 Bignot, Paul J. – Blackpool – Plymouth Arg; 4 Bond, Jonathan H. – Watford – Forest Green R; 24 Bruce, Alex S. – Leeds U – Huddersfield T; 24 Bryan, Joseph E. – Bristol C – Bath C; 17 Bubb, Bradley – Aldershot T – Basingstoke T; 4 Bunn, Harry – Manchester C – Rochdale; 18 Butlin, Joey – Walsall – Sutton Coldfield T; 24 Chadwick, Nicholas G. – Stockport Co – Plymouth Arg; 24 Chantler, Christopher S. – Manchester C – Carlisle U; 24 Charnock, Kieran J. – Morecambe – Fleetwood T; 23 Clayton, Harry S. – Crewe Alex – Stafford R; 4 Clifford, Conor – Chelsea – Yeovil T; 12 Clowes, Robert N. – Yeovil T – Wimborne T; 24 Cole, Aaron E. – Derby Co – Stockport Co; 18 Collins, Daniel – Stoke C – Ipswich T; 18 Connerton, Jordan S. – Crewe Alex – Kendal T; 24 Cook, Lee – QPR – Leyton Orient; 24 Craig, Tony A. – Millwall – Leyton Orient; 24 Cunnington – Adam – Kettering T – Dagenham & R; 24 Daniels, Charlie – Leyton Orient – AFC Bournemouth; 19 Davies, Andrew J. – Stoke C – Bradford C; 18 Davisson, Benjamin J. – Charlton Ath – Welling U; 17 Day, Jamie R. – Crawley T – Aldershot T; 24 Dean, Harlee J. – Southampton – Brentford; 22 Dempster, John – Crawley T – Mansfield T; 11 Dorman, Andrew J. – Crystal Palace – Bristol R; 3 Downing, Paul – WBA – Barnet; 24 Doyle, Nathan L.R. – Barnsley – Preston NE; 4 Elder, Nathan – Hayes & Yeading – Hereford U; 10 Ellison, James – Burton Alb – Chester; 15 Ephraim, Hogan – QPR – Charlton Ath; 1 Evans, Micah – Blackburn R – Accrington S; 24 Farah, Ibrahim H. – Cardiff C – Tamworth; 4 Fisher, Thomas M. – Macclesfield T – Hyde U; 24 Fletcher, Wesleigh J. – Burnley – Crewe Alex; 8 Forte, Jonathan R.J. – Southampton – Preston NE; 24 Fortune, Marc-Antoine – WBA – Doncaster R; 8 Francis, Simon C. – Charlton Ath – AFC Bournemouth; 17 Freeman, Luke A. – Arsenal – Stevenage; 24 Gardner, Gary – Aston Villa – Coventry C; 21 Geohaghon, Exodus I. – Darlington – Dagenham & R; 24 Gilmartin,

Rene – Watford – Yeovil T; 17 Goodman, Jake P. – Millwall – Staines T; 24 Goulon, Herold – Blackburn R – Doncaster R; 11 Gray, Daniel E. – Chesterfield – Macclesfield T; 24 Griffiths, Scott R. – Peterborough U – Chesterfield; 24 Guthrie, Kurtis O. – Accrington S – Southport; 24 Guy, Lewis B. – Milton Keynes D – Oxford U; 24 Hackett, Christopher J. – Millwall – Exeter C; 16 Hall, Robert – West Ham U – Oxford U; 24 Halliday, Andrew – Middlesbrough – Walsall; 11 Halstead, Mark J. – Blackpool – Stockport Co; 3 Hector, Michael A.J. – Reading – Barnet; 24 Hemmings, Ashley J. – Wolverhampton W – Plymouth Arg; 24 Henry, Charles – Luton T – Aldershot T; 4 Holden, Dean T.J. – Chesterfield – Rochdale; 24 Holland, Jack – Crystal Palace – Farnborough T; 8 Hoskins, Samuel T. – Southampton – Preston NE; 22 Hudson, Daniel A. – Bury – Mossley; 18 Hurst, James – WBA – Shrewsbury T; 10 Ikeme, Carl – Wolverhampton W – Doncaster R; 24 Jackson, Marlon M. – Bristol C – Cheltenham T; 24 Jarvis, Nathaniel S. – Cardiff C – Newport Co; 4 Johnson, Paul A. – Hartlepool U – Workington; 11 Jones, Jake – Walsall – Redditch U; 24 Keinan, Dekel – Cardiff C – Crystal Palace; 1 Kettings, Christopher D. – Blackpool – Woodley Sp; 4 Kovacs, Janos – Hereford U – Luton T; 21 Llera, Miguel A. – Blackpool – Sheffield W; 11 Lovelock, Thomas J. – Leyton Orient – Chertsey T; 18 Lovelock, Thomas J. – Leyton Orient – Farnborough T; 24 Lowry, Jamie – Chesterfield – Crewe Alex; 24 Lowry, Shane T. – Aston Villa – Millwall; 24 MacDonald, Angus – Reading – Basingstoke T; 24 Madjo, Guy B. – Stevenage – Port Vale; 3 Mancini, Andreas – Manchester C – Oldham Ath; 18 Martin, Christopher H. – Norwich C – Crystal Palace; 24 Mattock, Joseph W. – WBA – Portsmouth; 23 McCallum, Gavin K. – Lincoln C – Barnet; 4 McCarthy, Alex S. – Reading – Leeds U; 24 McCarthy, Luke J. – Bury – Grimsby T; 24 McCombe, Jamie P. – Huddersfield T – Preston NE; 24 McNamee, Anthony – Milton Keynes D – Wycombe W; 17 Montano, Cristian A. – West Ham U – Dagenham & R; 24 Murray, Ronan M. – Ipswich T – Swindon T; 24 Myrie-Williams, Jennison – Stevenage – Port Vale; 15 Naylor, Tom – Mansfield T – Derby Co; 9 Obadeyi, Temitope – Bolton W – Chesterfield; 24 O'Connor, Shane E. – Ipswich T – Port Vale; 4 Owusu, Lloyd M. – Barnet – Hayes & Yeading; 17 Panther, Emmanuel – Aldershot T – Grimsby T; 17 Parish, Elliott C. – Aston Villa – Cardiff C; 23 Parkin, Jonathan – Cardiff C – Huddersfield T; 4 Pearson, Gregory C. – Huddersfield – Blyth Spartans; 24 Pearson, Gregory E. – Burton Alb – Aldershot T; 4 Pearson, Stephen P. – Derby Co – Bristol C; 4 Peniket, Richard J. – Fulham – Hereford U; 14 Pentney, Carl – Colchester U – Hayes & Yeading; 4 Pinney, Nathaniel B. – Crystal Palace – Ebbsfleet U; 23 Priskin, Tamas – Ipswich T – Derby Co; 18 Pugh, Daniel A. – Stoke C – Leeds U; 24 Purse, Darren J. – Millwall – Plymouth Arg; 24 Rachubka, Paul S. – Leeds U – Tranmere R; 22 Ranger, Nile – Newcastle U – Barnsley; 18 Ravenhill, Richard J. – Notts Co – Bradford C; 24 Reach, Adam M. – Middlesbrough – Darlington; 24 Reid, Bobby – Bristol C – Cheltenham T; 3 Ribeiro, Christian M. – Bristol C – Carlisle U; 24 Rodney, Nialle – Bradford C – Mansfield T; 24 Russell, Darel F.R. – Preston NE – Charlton Ath; 25 Said, Abdul K.H. – Swindon T – Fairford T; 7 Saville, Jack W. – Southampton – Barnet; 3 Scapuzzi, Luca – Manchester C – Oldham Ath; 25 Scott, Mark J. – Swindon T – Salisbury C; 25 Smith, Ben P. – Crawley T – Woking; 23 Smith, Nathan A. – Mansfield T – Aldershot T; 4 Soderberg, Ole P. – Newcastle U – Chesterfield; 18 Spillane, Michael E. – Brentford – Dagenham & R; 4 Stockley, Jayden C. – AFC Bournemouth – Accrington S; 15 Sutherland, Craig S. – Blackpool – Plymouth Arg; 22 Tavernier, James H. – Newcastle U – Sheffield W; 4 Thomas, Casey E. – Swansea C – Colchester U; 24 Thorne, George L.E. – WBA – Portsmouth; 24 Townsend, Conor S. – Hull C – Grimsby T; 3 Trotman, Neal A. – Rochdale – Chesterfield; 24 Trotta, Marcello – Fulham – Wycombe W; 18 Vokes, Samuel M. – Wolverhampton W – Burnley; 3 Wallace, James R. – Everton – Shrewsbury T; 24 Watt, Herschel O.S. – Arsenal – Sheffield W; 8 Wildig, Aaron K. – Cardiff C – Shrewsbury T'; 24 Wood, Samuel J. – Brentford – Rotherham U; 2 Woodyard, Alexander J. – Southend U – Farnborough T

DECEMBER 2011 TEMPORARY TRANSFERS

13 Baggridge, Rhys W. – Yeovil T – Poole T; 6 Carey, Lewis T. – Bristol C – Gloucester C; 7 Chamberlain, Elliott C. – Leicester C – AFC Telford U; 8 Cudworth, Jack R. – Macclesfield T – Colwyn Bay; 1 Dodd, Adam J. – Blackpool – Altrincham; 16 Ebigbeyi-Popo, Tosan E. – Charlton Ath – Chelmsford C; 16 Essam, Connor – Gillingham – Dartford; 12 Evans, Jack P. – Gillingham – Welling U; 14 Gough, Conor J.J. – Charlton Ath – Eastbourne Bor; 16 Gray, Reece A. – Rochdale – Hyde U; 5 Hawkes, Daren G. – Gillingham – Maidstone U; 9 James-Lewis, Merrick A. – Southend U – Bishop's Stortford; 15 Lacey, Patrick S. – Bradford C – Vauxhall Motors; 16 Lane, Jack F. – Macclesfield T – Woodley Sp; 1 Locke, Simon J. – Reading – Forest Green R; 1 Macklin, Lloyd J. – Torquay U – Salisbury C; 2 McLaren, Connor G.D. – Millwall – Lewes; 2 McLellan, Michael – Preston NE – Workington; 2 Milton, Harry T. – Milton Keynes D – Aveley; 23 Muggeridge, Henry J. – Bristol C – Cleveland T; 5 Nelson, Mitchell A. – AFC Bournemouth – Lincoln C; 16 Parkinson, Daniel J. – Morecambe – Colwyn Bay; 24 Pavett, Jordan L. – Swindon T – Heybridge Swifts; 23 Pentney, Carl – Colchester U – Hayes & Yeading; 22 Pope, Nicholas D. – Charlton Ath – Welling U; 9 Sekajja, Ibra – Crystal Palace – Bromley; 20 Stephenson, Darren C.A. – Bradford C – Woodley Sp; 21 Tomsett, Liam R. – Blackpool – Altrincham; 2 Warren, Freddie R. – Charlton Ath – Bromley; 12 Wint, Aron L. – Scunthorpe U – Belper T

JANUARY 2012

31 Bamford, Patrick J.	Nottingham F	Chelsea	1,500,000
1 Basey, Grant W.	Peterborough U	Wycombe W	Free
25 Beausejour, Jean A.E.	Birmingham C	Wigan Ath	3,500,000
31 Bennett, Ryan	Peterborough U	Norwich C	3,200,000
2 Benson, Paul A.	Charlton Ath	Swindon T	exch.
1 Benyon, Elliot P.	Swindon T	Southend U	undisclosed
16 Cahill, Gary J.	Bolton W	Chelsea	7,000,000
6 Chantler, Christopher S.	Manchester C	Carlisle U	undisclosed
1 Clarke, Leon M.	Swindon T	Charlton Ath	exch.
5 Cook, Steve A.	Brighton & HA	AFC Bournemouth	150,000
9 Dagnall, Christopher	Scunthorpe U	Barnsley	undisclosed
5 Daniels, Charlie	Leyton Orient	AFC Bournemouth	undisclosed
31 Dawson, Stephen J.	Leyton Orient	Barnsley	undisclosed
20 Drinkwater, Daniel N.	Manchester U	Leicester C	undisclosed
1 Evans, William G.	Swindon T	Hereford U	Free
10 Foderingham, Wesley A.	Crystal Palace	Swindon T	undisclosed
1 Francis, Simon C.	Charlton Ath	AFC Bournemouth	undisclosed
12 Freeman, Luke A.	Arsenal	Stevenage	undisclosed
13 Gibson, Darron	Manchester U	Everton	500,000
30 Golbourne, Julio S.	Exeter C	Barnsley	undisclosed
31 Harding, Benjamin S.	Wycombe W	Northampton T	Free
13 Harrison, Byron J.	Stevenage	AFC Wimbledon	undisclosed
13 Haynes, Danny L.	Barnsley	Charlton Ath	undisclosed
3 Holden, Dean T.J.	Chesterfield	Rochdale	undisclosed

20 Holroyd, Christopher	Rotherham U	Preston NE	undisclosed
23 Howson, Jonathan M.	Leeds U	Norwich C	2,000,000
17 Hreidarsson, Hermann	Portsmouth	Coventry C	undisclosed
12 Jones, Michael D.	Bury	Sheffield W	undisclosed
17 Jutkiewicz, Lukas I.P.	Coventry C	Middlesbrough	1,300,000
31 Keogh, Andrew D.	Wolverhampton W	Millwall	undisclosed
30 Lowry, Shane T.	Aston Villa	Millwall	500,000
20 Madjo, Guy B.	Stevenage	Aldershot T	30,000
6 Malone, Scott L.	Wolverhampton W	AFC Bournemouth	150,000
31 Marshall, Ben	Stoke C	Leicester C	undisclosed
5 Martin, David J.	Derby Co	Southend U	undisclosed
31 Mathurin-Harris, Kadeem R.	Wycombe W	Cardiff C	undisclosed
31 Maynard, Nicholas D.	Bristol C	West Ham U	undisclosed
31 McDermott, Donal	Huddersfield T	AFC Bournemouth	undisclosed
20 McGlashan, Jermain	Aldershot T	Cheltenham T	75,000
13 McNaughton, Callum J.	West Ham U	AFC Wimbledon	Free
20 Mee, Benjamin T.	Manchester C	Burnley	undisclosed
31 Morgan, Westley N.	Nottingham F	Leicester C	1,000,000
31 Morrison, Ravel R.	Manchester U	West Ham U	650,000
12 Noble, Liam T.	Sunderland	Carlisle U	Free
12 Nosworthy, Nyron	Sunderland	Watford	undisclosed
26 Onuoha, Chinedum	Manchester C	QPR	2,500,000
31 Orr, Bradley J.	QPR	Blackburn R	Free
13 Osei-Kuffour, Jonathan	Bristol R	Gillingham	undisclosed
5 Parish, Elliott C.	Aston Villa	Cardiff C	undisclosed
27 Procter, Andrew J.	Accrington S	Preston NE	undisclosed
3 Pugh, Daniel A.	Stoke C	Leeds U	undisclosed
31 Ridgewell, Liam M.	Birmingham C	WBA	undisclosed
31 Robertson, Christopher	Torquay U	Preston NE	undisclosed
20 Rooney, Luke W.	Gillingham	Swindon T	undisclosed
31 Saha, Louis	Everton	Tottenham H	undisclosed
31 Sharp, Billy L.	Doncaster R	Southampton	1,850,000
31 Sordell, Marvin A.	Watford	Bolton W	3,500,000
1 Thomas, Wesley A.N.	Crawley T	AFC Bournemouth	undisclosed
5 Timlin, Michael A.	Swindon T	Southend U	undisclosed
13 Trippier, Kieran J.	Manchester C	Burnley	undisclosed
5 Trotman, Neal A.	Rochdale	Chesterfield	undisclosed
30 Tubbs, Matthew S.	Crawley T	AFC Bournemouth	800,000
31 Vaz Te, Ricardo J.	Barnsley	West Ham U	undisclosed
31 Veseli, Frederic	Manchester C	Manchester U	undisclosed
31 Williams, Ryan D.	Portsmouth	Fulham	undisclosed
31 Zamora, Robert L.	Fulham	QPR	4,500,000

TEMPORARY TRANSFERS

5 Abdulla, Ahmed M. – West Ham U – Dagenham & R; 2 Adams, Blair – Sunderland – Northampton T; 1 Addison, Miles – Derby Co – Barnsley; 5 Adeyemi, Thomas O. – Norwich C – Oldham Ath; 31 Ajose, Nicholas – Peterborough U – Chesterfield; 20 Alabi, Rasheed T. – Millwall – Hampton & Richmond Bor; 31 Almond, Louis J. – Blackpool – Lincoln C; 30 Aneke, Chukwuemeka A.A. – Arsenal – Stevenage; 1 Asante, Akwasi – Birmingham C – Northampton T; 27 Asante, Kyle E.K. – Southend U – Thurrock; 26 Atkinson, William H. – Hull C – Bradford C; 12 Banks, Oliver I. – Rotherham U – Stalybridge C; 9 Barkhuizen, Thomas J. – Blackpool – Hereford U; 21 Boateng, Daniel – Arsenal – Swindon T; 31 Bassong, Sebastian A. – Tottenham H – Wolverhampton W; 3 Batth, Daniel T. – Wolverhampton W – Sheffield W; 19 Bembo Leta, Djenny – Oldham Ath – Stalybridge C; 1 Bennett, Dale O. – Watford – Brentford; 31 Bennett, Ryan – Norwich C – Peterborough U; 26 Bignot, Paul J. – Blackpool – Plymouth Arg; 19 Blake, Ryan G. – Brentford – Hampton & Richmond Bor; 1 Bogdanovic, Daniel – Blackpool – Rochdale; 2 Bolger, Cian T. – Leicester C – Bristol R; 30 Bostock, John – Tottenham H – Sheffield W; 6 Bradley, Sonny – Hull C – Aldershot T; 26 Breeze, Matthew C. – Peterborough U – Histon; 31 Bridge, Wayne M. – Manchester C – Sunderland; 31 Brooke, Ryan M. – Oldham Ath – AFC Telford U; 6 Brown, Troy A.F. – Rotherham U – Aldershot T; 26 Brunt, Ryan S. – Stoke C – Tranmere R; 27 Brunt, Thomas J. – Gillingham – Leatherhead; 9 Bubb, Bradley – Aldershot T – Eastleigh; 3 Bunn, Harry – Manchester C – Preston NE; 2 Button, David R.E. – Tottenham H – Doncaster R; 26 Cadogan, Kieron J.N. – Crystal Palace – Rotherham U; 31 Cairns, Alex T. – Leeds U – Barrow; 1 Canham, Sean – Hereford U – Bath C; 13 Carey, Lewis T. – Bristol C – Gloucester C; 31 Carlisle, Clarke J. – Burnley – Northampton T; 20 Carroll, Thomas J. – Tottenham H – Derby Co; 13 Carson, Trevor – Sunderland – Hull C; 13 Cestor, Mike B. – Leyton Orient – Woking; 27 Chapman, Adam – Oxford U – Newport Co; 27 Chenoweth, Oliver R. – Plymouth Arg – Truro C; 1 Chicksen, Adam T. – Milton Keynes D – Leyton Orient; 27 Clarke, Lewis P. – Yeovil T – Weymouth; 20 Clay, Craig W. – Chesterfield – Alfreton T; 23 Clayton, Harry S. – Crewe Alex – Newcastle T; 27 Clowes, Robert N. – Yeovil T – Bridgwater T; 13 Coke, Giles C. – Sheffield W – Bury; 13 Collins, Charlie J. – Milton Keynes D – Aldershot T; 27 Connerton, Jordan S. – Crewe Alex – Nantwich T; 31 Connolly, Matthew T.M. – QPR – Reading; 19 Cook, Jordan A. – Sunderland – Carlisle U; 27 Cox, Samuel P. – Barnet – Boreham Wood; 9 Cuff, Sean A. – Sheffield U – Cambridge U; 1 Cunningham, Gregory R. – Manchester C – Nottingham F; 27 Cuvelier, Florent – Stoke C – Walsall; 30 Darikwa, Tendayi D. – Chesterfield – Hinckley U; 3 Davies, Andrew J. – Stoke C – Bradford C; 14 Davis, David L. – Wolverhampton W – Chesterfield; 2 Day, Joseph D. – Peterborough U – Alfreton T; 6 Dean, Harlee J. – Southampton – Brentford; 3 Deards, Connor A.J. – Walsall – Hinckley U; 23 Delfouneso, Nathan – Aston Villa – Leicester C; 20 Delph, Fabian – Aston Villa – Leeds U; 27 Dicko, Nouha – Wigan Ath – Blackpool; 9 Dickson, Ryan A. – Southampton – Yeovil T; 17 Doble, Ryan A. – Southampton – Bury; 30 Dorman, Andrew J. – Crystal Palace – Bristol R; 1 Downes, Aaron T. – Chesterfield – Bristol R; 7 Drinkwater, Daniel N. – Manchester U – Barnsley; 5 Driver, Callum C.J. – West Ham U – Burton Alb; 6 Dumbuya, Mustapha S.M. – Doncaster R – Crystal Palace; 16 Ebigbeyi-Popo, Tosan E. – Charlton Ath – Chelmsford C; 12 Edwards, Joseph R. – Bristol C – Yeovil T; 7 Egan, John – Sunderland – Crystal Palace; 16 Elford-Alliyu, Lateef – WBA – Tranmere R; 12 Euell, Jason J. – Charlton Ath – AFC Wimbledon; 20 Falque, Yago – Tottenham H – Southampton; 20 Fisher, Thomas M. – Macclesfield T – Droylsden; 27 Forte, Jonathan R.J. – Southampton – Notts Co; 13 Freeman, Kieron S. – Nottingham F – Notts Co; 1 Frimpong, Emmanuel Y. – Arsenal –

Wolverhampton W; 20 Futcher, Benjamin P. – Bury – AFC Telford U; 20 Gayle, Ian G. – Dagenham & R – Kingstonian; 31 Gough, Conor J.J. – Charlton Ath – Eastbourne Bor; 10 Griffiths, Scott R. – Peterborough U – Rotherham U; 30 Guedioura, Adlene – Wolverhampton W – Nottingham F; 17 Hajrovic, Sead – Arsenal – Barnet; 1 Harding, Benjamin S. – Wycombe W – Northampton T; 25 Harper, James A.J. – Hull C – Wycombe W; 1 Harrop, Max – Bury – Blyth S; 10 Harvey, Alex-Ray – Burnley – Barrow; 31 Hawley, Karl L. – Notts Co – Crawley T; 12 Haworth, Andrew A.D. – Bury – Bradford C; 3 Hector, Michael A.J. – Reading – Barnet; 13 Hemmings, Ashley J. – Wolverhampton W – Plymouth Arg; 31 Higginbotham, Daniel J. – Stoke C – Nottingham F; 31 Hoskins, William R. – Brighton & HA – Sheffield U; 27 Hoyte, Gavin A. – Arsenal – AFC Wimbledon; 23 Hubbins, Luke A. – Birmingham C – Tamworth; 27 Hudson, Daniel A. – Bury – Mossley; 6 Hughes, Caspar D.S. – Crewe Alex – Chasetown; 11 Hurst, James – WBA – Chesterfield; 1 Isaac, Chez J.T. – Watford – Tamworth; 10 Jackson, Josef J. – Burnley – Barrow; 31 Jackson, Ryan O. – AFC Wimbledon – Cambridge U; 31 Jara, Gonzalo A. – WBA – Brighton & HA; 1 Jarvis, Nathaniel S. – Cardiff C – Newport Co; 1 Jervis, Jake M. – Birmingham C – Preston NE; 26 Johnson, Brett – AFC Wimbledon – Cambridge U; 13 Jones, Reece N. – AFC Wimbledon – Carshalton Ath; 14 Jutkiewicz, Lukas I.P. – Coventry C – Middlesbrough; 30 Kacaniklic, Alexander – Fulham – Watford; 1 Kane, Harry – Tottenham H – Millwall; 27 Kettings, Christopher D. – Blackpool – Morecambe; 27 Kiernan, Brendan J. – AFC Wimbledon – Braintree T; 14 King, Joshua C.K. – Manchester U – Hull C; 13 Knott, Billy S. – Sunderland – AFC Wimbledon; 2 Kurucz, Peter – West Ham U – Rochdale; 17 Laing, Louis M. – Sunderland – Wycombe W; 27 Long, Kevin F. – Burnley – Rochdale; 1 Losasso, Charlie C. – Reading – Salisbury C; 27 Lucas, Lee P. – Swansea C – Burton Alb; 30 Lund, Matthew C. – Stoke C – Bristol R; 10 Lynch, David C.W. – Burnley – Stalybridge C; 1 Macheda, Federico – Manchester U – QPR; 31 Mainwaring, Matthew T. – Hull C – Stockport Co; 5 Mannone, Vito – Arsenal – Hull C; 27 Marrow, Alexander J. – Crystal Palace – Preston NE; 27 Marshall, Marcus J.L. – Rotherham U – Macclesfield T; 6 Martin, Christopher H. – Norwich C – Crystal Palace; 1 Mason, Ryan G. – Tottenham H – Millwall; 19 Massey, Gavin A. – Watford – Colchester U; 31 Mattock, Joseph W. – WBA – Brighton & HA; 12 McAllister, David J. – Sheffield U – Shrewsbury T; 20 McAllister, James R. – Bristol C – Preston NE; 31 McCallum, Paul L.M. – West Ham U – Rochdale; 10 McCarthy, Alex S. – Reading – Ipswich T; 31 McDonald, Alex – Burnley – Plymouth Arg; 13 McQuilkin, James R.L. – Hereford U – Kidderminster H; 20 McQuoid, Joshua J.B. – Millwall – Burnley; 13 McShane, Paul D. – Hull C – Crystal Palace; 13 Mills, Daniel P. – Peterborough U – Kettering T; 5 Mingoia, Pietro – Watford – Brentford; 12 Minshull, Lee B. – AFC Wimbledon – Newport Co; 31 Mirfin, David M. – Watford – Scunthorpe U; 30 Miyaichi, Ryo – Arsenal – Bolton W; 10 Moncur, George – West Ham U – AFC Wimbledon; 24 Morrison, Sean J. – Reading – Huddersfield T; 19 Mukendi, Vinny K. – Macclesfield T – Southport; 30 Murphy, Rhys P.E. – Arsenal – Preston NE; 20 Murray, Ronan M. – Ipswich T – Swindon T; 31 Mustoe, Jordan D. – Wigan Ath – Barnet; 27 Nesbitt, Teddy – Southend U – Great Wakering R; 6 Nichols, Tom A. – Exeter C – Dorchester T; 19 Noble, Ryan – Sunderland – Derby Co; 31 Norwood, Oliver J. – Manchester U – Coventry C; 6 Nsiala, Aristote – Everton – Accrington S; 10 Obika, Jonathan – Tottenham H – Yeovil T; 27 Obita, Jordan J. – Reading – Barnet; 1 O'Brien, Aiden A. – Millwall – Staines T; 12 Odubajo, Moses A.A.J. – Leyton Orient – Sutton U; 3 Ormerod, Brett R. – Blackpool – Rochdale; 27 Palmer, Ashley J. – Scunthorpe U – Southport; 26 Parker, Ben B.C. – Leeds U – Carlisle U;20 Parkes, Jordan D. – Barnet – Farnborough T; 31 Parkin, Jonathan – Cardiff C – Scunthorpe U; 13 Parrett, Dean G. – Tottenham H – Yeovil T; 18 Parsons, Alexander A. – AFC Bournemouth – Bashley; 6 Paterson, Matthew – Southend U – Forest Green R; 12 Payne, Joshua J. – Oxford U – Aldershot T; 13 Pearson, Gregory E. – Burton Alb – Crewe Alex; 31 Pienaar, Steven – Tottenham H – Everton; 9 Pinney, Nathaniel B. – Crystal Palace – Ebbsfleet U; 1 Poke, Michael H. – Brighton & HA – Bristol R; 20 Procter, Andrew J. – Accrington S – Preston NE; 10 Ray, George E. – Crewe Alex – Leek T; 30 Reckord, Jamie – Wolverhampton W – Scunthorpe U; 27 Redshaw, Jack – Morecambe – Altrincham; 31 Rendell, Scott D. – Wycombe W – Oxford U; 2 Reynolds, Duran-Rhys – Dagenham & R – Met Police; 13 Ribeiro, Christian M. – Bristol C – Scunthorpe U; 6 Ridehalgh, Liam – Huddersfield T – Chesterfield; 5 Russell, Darel F.R. – Preston NE – Charlton Ath; 12 Sampson, Jack – Bolton W – Southend U; 27 Sawyers, Romaine T. – WBA – Shrewsbury T; 31 Shephard, Christopher J. – Exeter C – Bath C; 2 Simpson, Robbie – Huddersfield T – Oldham Ath; 19 Smalley, Deane A.M. – Oxford U – Bradford C; 6 Smith, Adam C. – Leicester C – Lincoln C; 31 Smith, Adam J. – Tottenham H – Leeds U; 30 Smith, Alan – Newcastle U – Milton Keynes D; 31 Smith, Ben P. – Crawley T – Aldershot T; 25 Smith, Korey A. – Norwich C – Barnsley; 17 Smith, Michael J. – Charlton Ath – Accrington S; 3 Spencer, James C. – Huddersfield T – Cheltenham T; 27 Stephenson, Darren C.A. – Bradford C – Stocksbridge PS; 6 Stewart, Damion D. – Bristol C – Notts Co; 31 Symes, Michael – AFC Bournemouth – Rochdale; 27 Taiwo, Soloman O. – Cardiff C – Leyton Orient; 31 Tavernier, James H. – Newcastle U – Milton Keynes D; 1 Taylor, Charles J. – Leeds U – Bradford C; 31 Taylor, Jake W.T. – Reading – Exeter C; 2 Taylor, Rhys F. – Chelsea – Rotherham U; 13 Tchuimeni-Nimely, Alex – Manchester C – Coventry C; 6 Thomas Daniel A. – AFC Bournemouth – AFC Totton; 6 Thompson, Daniel A. – Portsmouth – Havant & W'ville; 6 Ting, Daniel S. – Crewe Alex – Market Drayton; 13 Tomlin, Gavin G. – Dagenham & R – Gillingham; 25 Tonge, Michael W.E. – Stoke C – Barnsley; 31 Tonne, Erik – Sheffield U – York C; 1 Townsend, Andros – Tottenham H – Leeds U; 31 Tsoumou, Hama J.F. – Preston NE – Plymouth Arg; 23 Turnbull, Paul D. – Northampton T – Stockport Co; 31 Ugwu, Chigozie E. – Reading – Ebbsfleet U; 30 Vokes, Samuel M. – Wolverhampton W – Brighton & HA; 13 Walker, Joshua – Watford – Scunthorpe U; 19 Walker, Samuel C. – Chelsea – Yeovil T; 20 Wallace, James R. – EvertonT – Tranmere R; 1 Walsh, Phillip – Dagenham & R – Hayes & Yeading; 27 Watt, Herschel O.S. – Arsenal – Crawley T; 20 Weale, Christopher – Leicester C – Northampton T; 5 Wearen, Eoin P. – West Ham U – Dagenham & R; 9 Weir, Tyler C. – Hereford U – Worcester C; 31 Whichelow, Matthew R. – Watford – Wycombe W; 19 Wildig, Aaron K. – Cardiff C – Shrewsbury T; 1 Wilson, Callum E.G. – Coventry C – Tamworth; 1 Wilson, Daniel – Liverpool – Blackpool; 13 Wood, Chris – WBA – Bristol C; 12 Wood, Samuel J. – Brentford – Rotherham U; 27 Woodley, Aaron R. – Oxford U – Oxford C; Wootton, Scott J. – Manchester U – Nottingham F

FEBRUARY 2012 TEMPORARY TRANSFERS

24 Abadaki, Godwin O.E. – Rochdale – Hyde U; 24 Addison, Miles – Derby Co – AFC Bournemouth; 24 Allan, Scott – WBA – Portsmouth; 23 Annerson, Jamie P. – Rotherham U – Bradford C; 17 Anthony, Byron – Bristol R – Hereford U; 24 Antonio, Michail G. – Reading – Sheffield W; 17 Arnott, Craig W. – Colchester U – Leiston; 8 Assombalonga, Britt C. – Wealdstone – Watford; 10 Assombalonga, Britt C. – Watford – Braintree T; 17 Assulin, Gai – Manchester C – Brighton & HA; 21 Barnett, Tyrone – Crawley T – Peterborough U; 21 Batt, Shaun A.S.P. – Millwall – Crawley T; 10 Berahino, Saido – WBA – Brentford; 23 Bond, Jonathan H. – Watford – Dagenham & R; 15 Bonham, Jack E. – Watford – Harrow Borough; 8 Briggs, Matthew – Fulham – Peterborough U; 15 Brisley, Shaun R. – Macclesfield – Peterborough U; 21 Butland, Jack – Birmingham C – Cheltenham T; 24 Carson, Trevor – Sunderland – Bury; 24 Connolly, Mark G. – Bolton W – Macclesfield T; 22 Cronin, Lance – Bristol R – Ebbsfleet U; 9 D'Ath, Lawson M. – Reading – Yeovil T; 24 Davis, Sean – Bolton W – Bristol C; 17 Devitt, Jamie M. – Hull C – Accrington S; 10 Dickson, Ryan A. – Southampton – Leyton Orient; 24 Doherty, Gary M.T. – Charlton Ath – Wycombe W; 20 Duke, Matthew – Bradford C – Northampton T; 21 Eastmond, Craig L. – Arsenal – Wycombe W; 21 Elford-Alliyu, Lateef – WBA – Bury; 9 Elokobi, George N. – Wolverhampton W – Nottingham F; 17 Euell, Jason J. – Charlton Ath – AFC

Wimbledon; 23 Forshaw, Adam – Everton – Brentford; 22 Franks, Jonathan I. – Middlesbrough – Yeovil T; 12 Freeman, Kieron S. – Nottingham F – Notts Co; 20 Futcher, Benjamin P. – Bury – Macclesfield T; 7 Gallagher, Jake F. – Millwall – Staines T; 9 Gibson, Benjamin J. – Middlesbrough – York C; 16 Gilmartin, Rene – Watford – Crawley T; 24 Gray, Reece A. – Rochdale – Hyde U; 29 Gregory, Corey L. – Sheffield U – Leicester C; 22 Grounds, Jonathan M. – Middlesbrough – Yeovil T; 21 Hackett, Christopher J. – Millwall – Wycombe W; 8 Harrad, Shaun – Bury – Rotherham U; 10 Hawkes, Daren G. – Maidstone U – Gillingham; 24 Hayes, Paul E. – Charlton Ath – Wycombe W; 2 Hoban, Thomas M. – Watford – Wealdstone; 15 Hollis, Haydn J. – Notts Co – Hinckley U; 13 Holmes, Lee D. – Southampton – Oxford U; 24 Huseklepp, Erik – Portsmouth – Birmingham C; 24 Jones, Reece N. – AFC Wimbledon – Hampton & Richmond Bor; 9 Kerrouche, Mehdi – Swindon T – Oxford U; 3 Koral, Michael D. – Crewe Alex – Congleton T; 22 Kuszczak, Tomasz – Manchester U – Watford; 17 Lee, Oliver R. – West Ham U – Gillingham; 24 Liddle, Michael W. – Sunderland – Accrington S; 9 MacDonald, Angus L. – Reading – Torquay U; 24 Mainwaring, Matthew T. – Hull C – Stockport Co; 27 McGinty, Sean A. – Manchester U – Morecambe; 14 McManus, Stephen – Middlesbrough – Bristol C; 8 Montano, Cristian A. – West Ham U – Notts Co; 17 Mulley, James A. – AFC Wimbledon – Hayes & Yeading; 10 Murphy, Darren – Stevenage – Aldershot T; 24 Nicholls, Lee A. – Wigan Ath – Accrington S; 24 O'Donnell, Richard M. – Sheffield W – Macclesfield T; 7 Osborn, Alexander S. – Dagenham & R – Chelmsford C; 10 Parkes, Thomas P.W. – Leicester C – Bristol R; 24 Parkinson, Daniel J. – Morecambe – Vauxhall Motors; 28 Raglan, Charles J.C. – Port Vale – Chasetown; 24 Ramsey-Dickson, Kristian – Burton Alb – Mickleover Sp; 17 Razak, Abdul – Manchester C – Brighton & HA; 1 Reece, Charles T. – Bristol R – Tamworth; 23 Reeves, Benjamin N. – Southampton – Dagenham & R; 20 Scott, Mark J. – Swindon T – Salisbury C; 17 Sears, Fred – West Ham U – Colchester U; 14 Silva, Brito E.T. – Liverpool – Northampton T; 24 Stech, Marek – West Ham U – Leyton Orient; 15 Stockford, Lewis J. – Portsmouth – AFC Totton; 11 Taylor, Lyle J.A. – AFC Bournemouth – Hereford U; 17 Thalassitis, Michael – Stevenage – Hayes & Yeading; 9 Thompson, Adam L. – Watford – Brentford; 18 Thorne, George L.E. – WBA – Portsmouth; 24 Ting, Daniel S. – Crewe Alex – Market Drayton T; 24 Townsend, Andros – Tottenham H – Birmingham C; 23 Trotta, Marcello – Fulham – Watford; 9 Tunnicliffe, James M. – Wycombe W – Crewe Alex; 17 Vilhete, Mauro A.D.S. – Barnet – Boreham Wood; 10 Vuckic, Haris – Newcastle U – Cardiff C; 18 Walker, Joshua – Watford – Scunthorpe U; 21 Walshe, Carl D. – Portsmouth – Frome T; 20 Warren, Freddie R. – Charlton Ath – Hayes & Yeading; 3 White, Andrew I. – Crewe Alex – Nantwich T; 24 Wilkinson, Luke A. – Dagenham & R – Dartford; 10 Williams, Brett A. – Reading – Northampton T; 1 Worsfold, Max N. – Aldershot T – Dorchester T

MARCH 2012

13 Payne, Joshua J.	Oxford U	Aldershot T	undisclosed

TEMPORARY TRANSFERS

20 Adebola, Bamberdele – Hull C – Notts Co; 13 Adeyemi, Thomas O. – Norwich C – Oldham Ath; 2 Adjei, Samuel – Newcastle U – Hartlepool U; 22 Afobe, Benik – Arsenal – Reading; 9 Agyemang, Patrick – QPR – Stevenage; 6 Ainsworth, Lionel G.R. – Shrewsbury T – Burton Alb; 17 Akinde, John J.A. – Crawley T – Dagenham & R; 8 Alexander, Gary G. – Brentford – Crawley T; 22 Aley, Zachery G. – Blackburn R – Macclesfield T; 29 Allinson, Lloyd J. – Huddersfield T – Ilkeston T; 21 Amoo, David O.S. – Liverpool – Bury; 2 Andrew, Calvin H. – Crystal Palace – Leyton Orient; 16 Andrew, Daniel K. – Cheltenham T – Mansfield T; 22 Aneke, Chukwuemeka A.A. – Arsenal – Preston NE; 20 Anthony, Byron – Bristol R – Hereford U; 16 Arismendi, Hugo D. – Stoke C – Huddersfield T; 23 Baggridge, Rhys W. – Yeovil T – Weymouth; 22 Baldock, George H.I. – Milton Keynes D – Tamworth; 16 Baldwin, Patrick M. – Southend U – Exeter C; 9 Balkestein, Pim – Brentford – AFC Wimbledon; 15 Ball, Matthew – Norwich C – Macclesfield T; 12 Baudry, Mathieu M.G. – AFC Bournemouth – Dagenham & R; 22 Baxendale, James R. – Doncaster R – Hereford U; 3 Belford, Cameron D. – Bury – Southend U; 13 Bellamy, Liam J. – Brentford – Ebbsfleet U; 2 Bergqvist, Jan D. – Aldershot T – Farnborough T; 22 Bikey, Andre S. – Burnley – Bristol C; 22 Bodin, Billy P. – Swindon T – Crewe Alex; 22 Bogdanovic, Daniel – Blackpool – Notts Co; 22 Bond, Jonathan H. – Watford – Bury; 22 Bostock, John – Tottenham H – Swindon T; 2 Brown, Connor A. – Sheffield U – Hinckley U; 2 Brown, Reece – Manchester U – Oldham Ath; 27 Built, Michael C. – Northampton T – Bedford T; 16 Bunn, Harry – Manchester C – Oldham Ath; 22 Burgess, Benjamin K. – Notts Co – Cheltenham T; 9 Burns, Andrew – Bradford C – Harrogate T; 20 Button, David R.E. – Tottenham H – Barnsley; 8 Campbell-Ryce, Jamal J. – Bristol C – Leyton Orient; 6 Carr, Matthew D. – Oldham Ath – Woodley Sp; 16 Cassidy, Jake A. – Wolverhampton W – Tranmere R; 21 Cestor, Mike – Leyton Orient – Woking; 22 Chambers, James A. – Doncaster R – Hereford U; 17 Clarke, Leon M. – Charlton Ath – Crawley T; 9 Clarke, Nathan – Huddersfield T – Bury; 9 Clough, Charlie – Bristol R – AFC Telford U; 22 Clucas, Martin S. – Preston NE – Burton Alb; 22 Collins, Charlie J. – Milton Keynes D – Tamworth; 9 Collins, Daniel – Stoke C – West Ham U; 16 Collins, Lee – Port Vale – Barnsley; 9 Connelly, Seamus J. – Sheffield U – Alfreton T; 2 Connerton, Jordan S. – Crewe Alex – Workington; 22 Cook, Jordan A. – Sunderland – Carlisle U; 20 Cook, Lee – QPR – Charlton Ath; 9 Crooks, Matt D.R. – Huddersfield T – AFC Halifax T; 22 Cudworth, Jack R. – Macclesfield T – Barrow; 16 Cuff, Sean – Sheffield W – Worksop T; 2 Cummings, Warren T. – AFC Bournemouth – Crawley T; 8 Cunnington, Adam – Dagenham & R – Alfreton T; 2 Cureton, Jamie – Leyton Orient – Exeter C; 22 Curran, Craig – Carlisle U – Morecambe; 16 Dagnall, Christopher – Barnsley – Bradford C; 20 Dalla Valle, Lauri – Fulham – Exeter C; 8 Darlow, Karl – Nottingham F – Newport Co; 20 Dean, Luke – Bradford C – Harrogate T; 22 Dobbie, Stephen – Swansea C – Blackpool; 5 Doughty, Michael E. – QPR – Aldershot T; 21 Eastham, Ashley – Blackpool – Bury; 22 Eastwood, Freddy – Coventry C – Southend U; 22 Edmans, Robert M. – Dagenham & R – Dover Ath; 9 Edwards, Philip L. – Stevenage – Rochdale; 6 Egan, John – Sunderland – Sheffield U; 16 Ehmer, Maximilian A. – QPR – Preston NE; 22 Ephraim, Hogan – QPR – Bristol C; 22 Evans, Daniel J. – Crawley T – Hayes & Yeading; 9 Fisher, Thomas M. – Macclesfield T – Drolysden; 22 Fletcher, Steven M. – AFC Bournemouth – Plymouth Arg; 21 Franks, Fraser G. – AFC Wimbledon – Newport Co; 29 Gallagher, Jake F. – Millwall – Met Police; 22 Gibson, William – Yeovil T – Braintree T; 9 Godden, Matthew J. – Scunthorpe U – Gainsborough T; 16 Grant, Robert – Scunthorpe U – Accrington S; 9 Green, Daniel J. – Dagenham & R – Dover Ath; 29 Guthrie, Jonathan N. – Crewe Alex – Leek T; 16 Hall, Robert – West Ham U – Milton Keynes D; 22 Hamilton, Bradley – Colchester U – Chelmsford C; 1 Hammill, Adam – Wolverhampton W – Middlesbrough; 16 Hannah, Ross – Bradford C – AFC Halifax T; 6 Harriott, Matthew A. – Sheffield U – Burton Alb; 22 Harris, Louis D. – Wolverhampton W – Notts Co; 16 Henderson, Stephen – Portsmouth – West Ham U; 22 Higginbotham, Kallum M. – Huddersfield T – Barnsley; 6 Hill, Matthew C. – Blackpool – Sheffield U; 2 Hills, Lee M. – Crystal Palace – Southend U; 22 Hines, Zavon – Burnley – AFC Bournemouth; 5 Hoban, Thomas M. – Watford – Wealdstone; 22 Hollis, Haydn J. – Notts Co – Darlington; 16 Holmes,Lee D. – Southampton – Swindon T; 3 Holness, Charlie H.V. – Crystal Palace – Leatherhead; 15 Hoskins, Samuel T. – Southampton – Rotherham U; 2 Hudson, Daniel A. – Bury – Mossley; 2 Hughes, Casper D.S. – Crewe Alex – Nantwich T; 2 Ikeme, Carl – Wolverhampton W – Doncaster R; 2 James, Lloyd R.S. – Colchester U – Crawley T; 16 James-Lewis, Merrick – Southend U – Carshalton Ath; 1 Jarvis, Ryan R. – Walsall – Torquay U; 16 Johnson, Paul A. – Hartlepool U – Darlington; 22 Keinan, Dekel – Cardiff C – Bristol C; 16 Kiernan, Robert S. – Wigan Ath – Accrington S; 6 Lane, Jack F. – Macclesfield T – Leek T; 12

Lascelles, Jamaal – Nottingham F – Stevenage; 6 Lawrence, Liam – Portsmouth – Cardiff C; 20 Legzdins, Adam R. – Derby Co – Burton Alb; 9 Lewis, Theo A. – Cheltenham T – Gloucester C; 10 MacDonald, Alex – Burnley – Plymouth Arg; 22 MacLean, Steven – Yeovil T – Cheltenham T; 9 Maguire, Christopher – Derby Co – Portsmouth; 6 Mantom, Samuel S. – WBA – Walsall; 16 Massey, Gavin A. – Watford – Colchester U; 10 May, Ben S. – Stevenage – Barnet; 22 McAleny, Conor M. – Everton – Scunthorpe U; 22 McConville, Sean J. – Stockport Co – Rochdale; 9 McDermott, Sean – Arsenal – Leeds U; 22 McEveley, James – Barnsley – Swindon T; 1 McGleish, Scott – Bristol R – Barnet; 20 McLaren, Connor G.D. – Millwall – Welling U; 2 McLaughlin, Conor G. – Preston NE – Shrewsbury T; 22 Meadows, Daniel T. – Nottingham F – Alfreton T; 22 Mingoia, Pietro – Watford – Hayes & Yeading; 22 Molesley, Mark – AFC Bournemouth – Aldershot T; 16 Montano, Cristian A.C. – West Ham U – Oxford U; 19 Montgomery, Nicholas A. – Sheffield U – Millwall; 8 Morgan, Dean L. – Chesterfield – Oxford U; 22 Morris, Joshua F. – Blackburn R – Yeovil T; 22 Morrison, Clinton H. – Sheffield W – Brentford; 16 Moussa, Franck – Leicester C – Chesterfield; 29 Mulley, James A. – AFC Wimbledon – Wealdstone; 16 Mullins, Hayden – Portsmouth – Reading; 12 Nappa, Byron J. – Crawley T – Weymouth; 9 Nesbitt, Teddy – Southend U – Thurrock; 19 N'Guessen, Diombo D-G. – Millwall – Charlton Ath; 20 Noble, Ryan – Sunderland – Hartlepool U; 8 Nouble, Frank H. – West Ham U – Barnsley; 23 Nyoni, Cecil – Sheffield W – Frickley Ath; 15 Obadeyi, Temitope – Bolton W – Rochdale; 2 Obita, Jordan J. – Reading – Gillingham; 13 O'Brien, Aiden A. – Millwall – Hayes & Yeading; 22 O'Halloran, Michael F. – Bolton W – Sheffield U; 26 Overson, Dean J. – Bradford C – Bradford PA; 9 Palmer, Ashley – Scunthorpe U – Harrogate T; 8 Parker, Joshua K.S. – Oldham Ath – Dagenham & R; 17 Parkin, Jonathan – Cardiff C – Scunthorpe U; 10 Payne, Sanchez – Leeds U – Buxton; 21 Pell, Harry D.B. – Hereford U – Cambridge U; 6 Piquionne, Frederic – West Ham U – Doncaster R; 1 Porter, Max – AFC Wimbledon – Newport Co; 6 Rachubka, Paul S. – Leeds U – Leyton Orient; 1 Ramage, Peter I. – QPR – Birmingham C; 2 Rance, Dean J.R. – Gillingham – Dover Ath; 22 Ranger, Nile – Newcastle U – Sheffield W; 9 Reed, Adam M. – Sunderland – Leyton Orient; 22 Rekik, Kerim – Manchester C – Portsmouth; 6 Roberts, Adam J. – Macclesfield T – Leek T; 22 Roberts, Connor S. – Everton – Colwyn Bay; 6 Robinson, Paul P. – Bolton W – Leeds U; 14 Sam, Lloyd E. – Leeds U – Notts Co; 22 Scapuzzi, Luca – Manchester C – Portsmouth; 13 Sinclair, Robert J. – Stevenage – Aldershot T; 3 Slew, Jordan M. – Blackburn R – Stevenage; 14 Smith, Mathieu – Oldham Ath – Macclesfield T; 13 Stephenson, Darren C.A. – Bradford C – Southport; 2 Stewart, Jonathan – Burnley – Alfreton T; 30 Stockford, Lewis J. – Portsmouth – AFC Totton; 2 Strugnell, Daniel – AFC Bournemouth – Bashley; 2 Strutton, Charles – AFC Wimbledon – Maidenhead U; 13 Tallack, Lewis J. – Portsmouth – Poole T; 13 Taylor, Maik S. – Leeds U – Millwall; 8 Tehoue, Jonathan – Leyton Orient – Swindon T; 1 Tiryaki, Mustafa – Tranmere R – Cambridge U; 22 Tounkara, Oumare – Sunderland – Oldham Ath; 22 Treacy, Keith – Burnley – Sheffield W; 22 Vine, Rowan L. – QPR – Gillingham; 6 Walker, Mitchell C.A. – Brighton & HA – Eastbourne Bor; 21 Wallace, Jed F. – Portsmouth – Farnborough T; 17 Wassmer, Charlie – Crawley T – Dagenham & R; 22 Wickham, Arron L. – Crawley T – Hayes & Yeading; 25 Wilkinson, Luke A. – Dagenham & R – Dartford; 21 Wilson, Glenn M. – Crawley T – Woking; 9 Wilson, Ross S. – Burnley – Silsden; 8 Winn, Peter H. – Stevenage – Grimsby T; 5 Wint, Aron L. – Scunthorpe U – FC Halifax T; 22 Wright, Andrew D. – Scunthorpe U – Grimsby T; 9 Wyke, Charles T. – Middlesbrough – Kettering T; 22 Yennaris, Nicholas – Arsenal – Notts Co

APRIL 2012

30 Barnett, Tyrone	Crawley T	Peterborough U	1,000,000

TEMPORARY TRANSFERS

20 Allan, Scott – WBA – Portsmouth; 15 Ball, Matthew – Norwich C – Macclesfield T; 15 Baudry, Mathieu – AFC Bournemouth – Dagenham & R; 11 Bellamy, Liam J. – Brentford – Ebbsfleet U; 1 Brown, Reece – Manchester U – Oldham Ath; 9 Burns, Andrew J. – Bradford C – Harrogate T; 16 Button, David R. – Tottenham H – Barnsley; 4 Cassidy, Jake A. – Wolverhampton W – Tranmere R; 4 Clarke, Oliver A. – Bristol R – Cleveland T; 10 Conneely, Seamus – Sheffield U – Alfreton T; 11 Crooks, Matt – Huddersfield T – FC Halifax T; 1 Cummings, Warren T. – AFC Bournemouth – Crawley T; 10 Cunnington, Adam P. – Dagenham & R – Alfreton T; 10 D'Ath, Lawson M. – Reading – Yeovil T; 20 Dean, Luke A. – Bradford C – Harrogate T; 4 Dummett, Paul – Newcastle U – Gateshead; 10 Fisher, Thomas – Macclesfield T – Droylsden; 22 Gibson, William M.H. – Yeovil T – Braintree T; 29 Guthrie, John – Crewe Alex – Leek T; 1 Hajrovic, Sead – Arsenal – Barnet; 11 Hoban, Thomas – Watford – Wealdstone; 3 Hughes, Casper – Crewe Alex – Nantwich T; 8 Ikeme, Carl – Wolverhampton W – Doncaster R; 1 James, Lloyd S.R. – Colchester U – Crawley T; 10 Knott, Billy S. – Sunderland – AFC Wimbledon; 8 Lewis, Theo A. – Cheltenham T – Gloucester C; 5 Maguire, Christopher – Derby Co – Portsmouth; 3 Mantom, Sam – WBA – Walsall; 1 McAllister, David – Sheffield U – Shrewsbury T; 7 McGleish, Scott – Bristol R – Barnet; 29 McLaren, Connor G.D. – Millwall – Welling U; 10 Moncur, George – West Ham U – AFC Wimbledon; 16 Montano, Cristian A. – West Ham U – Oxford U; 27 Mooney, Jason – Wycombe W – Oxford C; 10 Morgan, Dean – Chesterfield – Oxford U; 10 Nouble, Frank H. – West Ham U – Barnsley; 22 Nyoni, Cecil – Sheffield W – Frickley Ath; 10 Palmer, Ashley J. – Scunthorpe U – Harrogate T; 8 Parker, Joshua K.S. – Oldham Ath – Dagenham & R; 7 Rachubka, Paul S. – Leeds U – Leyton Orient; 1 Ramsey-Dickson, Kristian – Burton Alb – Mickleover Sp; 1 Reckord, Jamie – Wolverhampton W – Scunthorpe U; 19 Rekik, Karim – Manchester C – Portsmouth; 28 Ripley, Connor J. – Middlesbrough – Oxford U; 10 Robinson, Paul P. – Bolton W – Leeds U; 1 Strugnell, Daniel S. – AFC Bournemouth – Bashley; 1 Strutton, Charles – AFC Wimbledon – Maidenhead U; 13 Tallack, Lewis – Portsmouth – Poole T; 1 Taylor, Jake W.T. – Reading – Exeter C; 11 Thompson, Adam L. – Watford – Brentford; 22 Treacy, Keith P. – Burnley – Sheffield W

MAY 2012

8 Brisley, Shaun R.	Macclesfield T	Peterborough U	undisclosed
10 Collins, Lee	Port Vale	Barnsley	undisclosed
15 Donnelly, George	Macclesfield T	Rochdale	undisclosed
8 Pearce, Jason D.	Portsmouth	Leeds U	undisclosed

TEMPORARY TRANSFERS

4 Gough, Conor J.J. – Charlton Ath – Bristol R; 5 Martinez, Damain E. – Arsenal – Oxford U

THE NEW FOREIGN LEGION 2011–12

JULY/AUGUST 2011	*From*	*To*	*Fee in £*
Aguero, Sergio	Atletico Madrid	Manchester C	38,000,000
Cabaye, Yohan	Lille	Newcastle U	4,300,000
Coates, Sebastian	Nacional	Liverpool	undisclosed
Crusat, Albert	Almeria	Wigan Ath	2,000,000
De Gea, David	Atletico Madrid	Manchester U	17,800,000
Drenthe, Royston	Real Madrid	Everton	Loan
Formica, Mauro	Newell's Old Boys	Blackburn R	3,500,000
Gecov, Marcel	Slovan Liberec	Fulham	Free
Gervinho	Lille	Arsenal	10,700,000
Grygera, Zdenek	Juventus	Fulham	Free
Ji, Dong-Won	Chunnam Dragons	Sunderland	2,000,000
Kasami, Pajtim	Palermo	Fulham	4,000,000
Lukaku, Romelu	Anderlecht	Chelsea	18,000,000
Mata, Juan	Valencia	Chelsea	27,000,000
Marveaux, Sylvain	Rennes	Newcastle U	Free
Mertesacker, Per	Werder Bremen	Arsenal	undisclosed
Moras, Vangelis	Bologna	Swansea C	undisclosed
Park, Chu-Young	Monaco	Arsenal	undisclosed
Perone, Bruno	Tombense	QPR	undisclosed
Petrovic, Radosav	Partizan Belgrade	Blackburn R	undisclosed
Romeu, Oriol	Barcelona	Chelsea	4,700,000
Ruiz, Bryan	Twente	Fulham	10,600,000
Sa, Orlando	Porto	Fulham	Free
Santon, Davide	Internazionale	Newcastle U	5,000,000
Santos, Andre	Fenerbahce	Arsenal	6,200,000
Savic, Stefan	Partizan Belgrade	Manchester C	6,000,000
Stracqualursi, Denis	Tigre	Everton	Loan
Vellios, Apostolos	Iraklis	Everton	250,000
Vorm, Michel	Utrecht	Swansea C	1,500,000
Vukcevic, Simon	Sporting Lisbon	Blackburn R	3,000,000
JANUARY/FEBRUARY 2012			
Cisse, Papisse Demba	Freiburg	Newcastle U	10,000,000
Diakite, Samba	Nancy	QPR	Loan
Diarra, Mahamadou	Monaco	Fulham	undisclosed
Frei, Kerim	Grasshoppers	Fulham	undisclosed
Jelavic, Nikica	Rangers	Everton	5,500,000
Jonsson, Eggert	Hearts	Wolverhampton W	250,000
Kasami, Pajtim	Palermo	Fulham	undisclosed
Miyaichi, Ryo	Arsenal	Bolton W	Loan
Modeste, Anthony	Bordeaux	Blackburn R	Loan
Olssson, Marcus	Halmstad	Blackburn R	Free
Pizzaro, David	Roma	Manchester C	Loan
Pogrebnyak, Pavel	Stuttgart	Fulham	1,500,000
Ream, Tim	New York Red Bulls	Bolton W	2,500,000
Tremmel, Gerhard	Salzburg	Swansea C	undisclosed
Vuckic, Haris	Domzale	Newcastle U	undisclosed

THE THINGS THEY SAID . . .

While he may well be a Scottish Knight, Sir Alex Ferguson knows how much his English players at Old Trafford are worth to the national team:
"The FA may realise one day who has produced more players for their country than any other club in the world. Maybe they will get some joy from it at some point in their lives and realise how important we are to England. You understand? They treat us like s***."

Richard Scudamore would seem to have sorted out just how much technology is needed to improve the game:
"A ball crossing a line is a matter of fact. Anything else is a matter of opinion."

Arsene Wenger has his definite views on the purchase of players:
"We are not in a supermarket where you go to a shelf and you ask where are the centre backs or the strikers?"

The Arsenal manager also has his say on the answer to divers:
"But a dive in the box sometimes . . . I think sometimes you see it properly after the game. If an obvious dive is punished by a three-match ban, the players would not do it any more."

If the words uttered by Fabio Capello are symptomatic of the malaise affecting football management, just where are the teams who have no interest in winning?
"For my whole life as a manager I've been under fire. The teams I coached wanted to win every game."

On departure from his role as England manager following the row over John Terry, Fabio Capello said:
"They insulted me and damaged my authority. What really hit me and forced me to take this decision was the much vaunted Anglo-Saxon sense of justice, that everyone is innocent until proven guilty."

In the wake of the summer riots in England, PFA chief executive Gordon Taylor gave his views on how football could respond in a correct manner:
"Clubs and players need to show the best example in these difficult times."

The PFA CEO on the question of salaries:
"The game is about players. People don't complain about Brad Pitt's wages."

Our own Wayne Rooney added to the various comments:
"These riots are nuts. Why would people do this to their own country? Stop, please."

Ricardo Teixeira, the head honcho of the Brazilian FA, has been a critic of England and surprisingly, too, his own national team's most famous footballer, Pele. He even failed to invite him to the World Cup draw until the government intervened. The famous one responded:
"This is not good for Brazil. Some people talk more than they know. With Ricardo we always have some confusion or misunderstanding, when he does interviews."

Brevity is often the best policy. Liverpool's US owner John W. Henry obviously thinks so:
"Mr Ferguson is a genius." (Presumably he meant Sir Alex.)

Sir Alex Ferguson admitted he was "really emotional" after Manchester United marked his 25th anniversary in charge by renaming Old Trafford's North Stand and commissioning a statue in his honour:
"I couldn't believe and I didn't expect that. I have to thank the club because it is fantastic of them to do that. I am really proud."

After Harry Redknapp was cleared in court of tax-evasion charges he was understandably emotional:
"My family have been put through it these last five years and I am looking forward to getting home and getting away from all this. It has been a nightmare. This is a case that should never have come to court, it is unbelievable. It was a unanimous decision, absolutely, unanimous, there was no case to answer."

Rio Ferdinand with a view on racism:
"Tell me I have just read Sepp Blatter's comments on racism in football wrong. I feel stupid for thinking that football was taking a leading role against racism."

After arguably the most exciting and dramatic end to any championship when Manchester City snatched victory from the famous jaws of defeat there were many opinions of the outcome. City manager Roberto Mancini said:
"It was a crazy finish. After this, I feel 90 years old! I am very proud of my players. To beat a strong team like United is fantastic and we deserve a title."

Sir Alex Ferguson described the climax as "cruel" and said it would take a century for City to catch up on comparable histories with Manchester United and affirmed the depth of talent at Old Trafford:
"It is a good experience for them even if it's a bad one. We have a lot of young players and they will be around in five, six or ten years at United."

Other views on the 20th Premier League wrap-up included:
"I think watching or hearing about football today is not good for my heart." **(Fabrice Muamba)**

"It was an unbelievable afternoon of football. Now City can go on and dominate for a while." **(Alan Shearer)**

"What an end to the season and what a league we play in – no other like it in the world." **(Phil Neville)**

"I played in that game against Arsenal at Anfield in 1989. This was far more dramatic." **(Alan Hansen)**

Sam Allardyce was generous in his praise of opponents Blackpool as West Ham United won back Premier League status:
"I told you it was going to be difficult. Blackpool were equally as good as us. But our finishing power counted in the end. We managed to swing it right at the death."

Chelsea won the shoot-out against Bayern Munich to take the Champions League trophy despite just one corner (from which they scored) against the Germans' 20 and being out-shot in the match 34 to nine. But hero marksman Didier Drogba said:
"I believe a lot in destiny. It was written a long time ago that we would win but we did not know it and we had to believe. This team is amazing. I want to dedicate this to the managers and players we had before."

Chelsea manager Roberto Di Matteo was mindful that it might have been his swansong at Stamford Bridge:
"I want a holiday. It's not important. I respect whatever is decided. We have players that have a big heart and passion and motivation and desire."

Before the Euro 2012 finals former England international Sol Campbell was mindful of the racist abuse that could be faced in Poland and the Ukraine:
"Stay at home, watch it on TV. Don't even risk it . . . because you could end up coming back in a coffin."

Mario Balotelli, Manchester City and Italy, put his own perspective on the issue of racism:
"I'm black and proud to have African roots. I think I'm lucky to be black. People say about me that I'm a black boy who has fun, earns money and has girls. It's not like that. It's too easy to judge people through what you see."

Caught up in the latest match-fixing scandal to hit Italian football, Domenico Criscito, dropped from Cesare Prandelli's squad, protested:
"I have nothing to do with this. I was only out for dinner with some Genoa fans."

In an unfortunate reminder of the comedy series "Allo, Allo", Germany's assistant coach had to apologise for suggesting:
"The Germans should wear steel helmets and stand tall." *(His name: Herr Flick!)*

The press did its best to predict trouble in the Spanish camp with Real Madrid and Barcelona players likely to be at odds with each other. Sergio Busquets summed it up:
"It is difficult to be friends with someone who does not play with you every day of the year. There is no problem. We can talk or have a drink. We are all here for the same reason."

On the eve of the Group D decider in Euro 2012 being played between England and Ukraine, Michel Platini again reiterated his objection to goal-line technology being introduced, claiming the effectiveness of five officials. Alas subsequent events overshadowed his remarks as there was a clear instance of the ball crossing the line without a goal being awarded:
"With five, officials see everything. They don't take decisions without being fully aware. There's also a uniformity of refereeing. For example, they don't call unintentional handballs. That uniformity has led to more flowing football. Goal-line technology isn't a problem."

Gary Neville, who went from being England's No.2 to becoming England's No.2 (!), remarked on the unusual lack of hype pre-Euro 2012:
"There seems to be the lowest expectation I've ever known going into a tournament but the fact is, in tournaments gone past, it's been fine lines."

Only a matter of days later with England about to meet Italy in the quarter-finals, his attitude changed dramatically:
"I think there are four or five players in our squad who I genuinely believe would be in any team in this tournament – even Spain. When I look at Wayne Rooney, Joe Hart, John Terry, Ashley Cole and Joleon Lescott, you'd go a long way to find players at this tournament who are better in those positions than they are."

England captain Steven Gerrard was caught up in the realisation that after years of frustration the Italian game could prove a watershed:
"Since I made my England debut I've dreamed of doing well in these major tournaments. Up to now it hasn't happened. I'm hoping it'll be different this time. To lose any quarter-final match hurts so much."

England's most capped goalkeeper Peter Shilton gave advice to Joe Hart in case there was a penalty shoot-out against Italy:
"Wait as long as you can on the line and be as big as you can and fill as much of the goal as you can. The moment you dive, there's a large space left for him to score. If you stay still, arms out, occupying space, he's got to hit the corners of the target to beat you." (*Needless to say Joe was unable to save one.*)

Roy Hodgson commenting on the aftermath of being knocked out by Italy in the post-match penalty shoot-out:
"When we took it to penalties I was hoping this was our tournament but the practising didn't help. I can't fault the players as a lot of them were running on empty."

Post-tournament criticism of Wayne Rooney was answered by the England manager:
"We haven't noticed anything with his fitness levels. But of course I think we put a lot of expectations on him. He certainly tried very hard, but he didn't have his best game. I think he would admit that, but I don't think fitness itself was a particular factor."

Former England manager Fabio Capello had a sarcastic swipe at the England striker in a reference to Sir Alex Ferguson, Rooney's boss at Manchester United:
"After watching the last game, I think that Rooney understands only the Scottish accent."

On the eve of the Euro 2012 final, Spain's midfield maestro Xavi responded to the criticism that his team's no-strike formation was boring:
"Fans identify with us, we enjoy it, people the world over love it. For us, not only is it not boring – but we are having fun on the pitch."

ENGLISH LEAGUE HONOURS 1888–2012

FA PREMIER LEAGUE

MAXIMUM POINTS: *a* 126; *b* 114.
**Won or placed on goal average (ratio), goal difference or most goals scored. ††Not promoted after play-offs.*

	First	*Pts*	*Second*	*Pts*	*Third*	*Pts*
1992–93*a*	Manchester U	84	Aston Villa	74	Norwich C	72
1993–94*a*	Manchester U	92	Blackburn R	84	Newcastle U	77
1994–95*a*	Blackburn R	89	Manchester U	88	Nottingham F	77
1995–96*b*	Manchester U	82	Newcastle U	78	Liverpool	71
1996–97*b*	Manchester U	75	Newcastle U*	68	Arsenal*	68
1997–98*b*	Arsenal	78	Manchester U	77	Liverpool	65
1998–99*b*	Manchester U	79	Arsenal	78	Chelsea	75
1999–2000*b*	Manchester U	91	Arsenal	73	Leeds U	69
2000–01*b*	Manchester U	80	Arsenal	70	Liverpool	69
2001–02*b*	Arsenal	87	Liverpool	80	Manchester U	77
2002–03*b*	Manchester U	83	Arsenal	78	Newcastle U	69
2003–04*b*	Arsenal	90	Chelsea	79	Manchester U	75
2004–05*b*	Chelsea	95	Arsenal	83	Manchester U	77
2005–06*b*	Chelsea	91	Manchester U	83	Liverpool	82
2006–07*b*	Manchester U	89	Chelsea	83	Liverpool*	68
2007–08*b*	Manchester U	87	Chelsea	85	Arsenal	83
2008–09*b*	Manchester U	90	Liverpool	86	Chelsea	83
2009–10*b*	Chelsea	86	Manchester U	85	Arsenal	75
2010–11*b*	Manchester U	80	Chelsea*	71	Manchester C	71
2011–12*b*	Manchester C*	89	Manchester U	89	Arsenal	70

FOOTBALL LEAGUE CHAMPIONSHIP

MAXIMUM POINTS: 138

2004–05	Sunderland	94	Wigan Ath	87	Ipswich T††	85
2005–06	Reading	106	Sheffield U	90	Watford	81
2006–07	Sunderland	88	Birmingham C	86	Derby Co	84
2007–08	WBA	81	Stoke C	79	Hull C	75
2008–09	Wolverhampton W	90	Birmingham C	83	Sheffield U††	80
2009–10	Newcastle U	102	WBA	91	Nottingham F††	79
2010–11	QPR	88	Norwich C	84	Swansea C*	80
2011–12	Reading	89	Southampton	88	West Ham U	86

FIRST DIVISION

MAXIMUM POINTS: 138

1992–93	Newcastle U	96	West Ham U*	88	Portsmouth††	88
1993–94	Crystal Palace	90	Nottingham F	83	Millwall††	74
1994–95	Middlesbrough	82	Reading††	79	Bolton W	77
1995–96	Sunderland	83	Derby Co	79	Crystal Palace††	75
1996–97	Bolton W	98	Barnsley	80	Wolverhampton W††	76
1997–98	Nottingham F	94	Middlesbrough	91	Sunderland††	90
1998–99	Sunderland	105	Bradford C	87	Ipswich T††	86
1999–2000	Charlton Ath	91	Manchester C	89	Ipswich T	87
2000–01	Fulham	101	Blackburn R	91	Bolton W	87
2001–02	Manchester C	99	WBA	89	Wolverhampton W††	86
2002–03	Portsmouth	98	Leicester C	92	Sheffield U††	80
2003–04	Norwich C	94	WBA	86	Sunderland††	79

FOOTBALL LEAGUE CHAMPIONSHIP 1

MAXIMUM POINTS: 138

2004–05	Luton T	98	Hull C	86	Tranmere R††	79
2005–06	Southend U	82	Colchester U	79	Brentford††	76
2006–07	Scunthorpe U	91	Bristol C	85	Blackpool	83
2007–08	Swansea C	92	Nottingham F	82	Doncaster R	80
2008–09	Leicester C	96	Peterborough U	89	Milton Keynes D††	87
2009–10	Norwich C	95	Leeds U	86	Millwall	85
2010–11	Brighton & HA	95	Southampton	92	Huddersfield T††	87
2011–12	Charlton Ath	101	Shefield W	93	Sheffield U††	90

SECOND DIVISION

MAXIMUM POINTS: 138

1992–93	Stoke C	93	Bolton W	90	Port Vale††	89
1993–94	Reading	89	Port Vale	88	Plymouth Arg*††	85
1994–95	Birmingham C	89	Brentford††	85	Crewe Alex††	83
1995–96	Swindon T	92	Oxford U	83	Blackpool††	82
1996–97	Bury	84	Stockport Co	82	Luton T††	78
1997–98	Watford	88	Bristol C	85	Grimsby T	72
1998–99	Fulham	101	Walsall	87	Manchester C	82
1999–2000	Preston NE	95	Burnley	88	Gillingham	85
2000–01	Millwall	93	Rotherham U	91	Reading††	86
2001–02	Brighton & HA	90	Reading	84	Brentford*††	83
2002–03	Wigan Ath	100	Crewe Alex	86	Bristol C††	83
2003–04	Plymouth Arg	90	QPR	83	Bristol C††	82

FOOTBALL LEAGUE CHAMPIONSHIP 2

MAXIMUM POINTS: 138

2004–05	Yeovil T	83	Scunthorpe U*	80	Swansea C	80
2005–06	Carlisle U	86	Northampton T	83	Leyton Orient	81
2006–07	Walsall	89	Hartlepool U	88	Swindon T	85
2007–08	Milton Keynes D	97	Peterborough U	92	Hereford U	88

	First	*Pts*	*Second*	*Pts*	*Third*	*Pts*
2008–09	Brentford	85	Exeter C	79	Wycombe W*	78
2009–10	Notts Co	93	Bournemouth	83	Rochdale	82
2010–11	Chesterfield	86	Bury	81	Wycombe W	80
2011–12	Swindon T	93	Shrewsbury T	88	Crawley T	84

THIRD DIVISION

MAXIMUM POINTS: ***a*** **126;** ***b*** **138.**

1992–93*a*	Cardiff C	83	Wrexham	80	Barnet	79
1993–94*a*	Shrewsbury T	79	Chester C	74	Crewe Alex	73
1994–95*a*	Carlisle U	91	Walsall	83	Chesterfield	81
1995–96*b*	Preston NE	86	Gillingham	83	Bury	79
1996–97*b*	Wigan Ath*	87	Fulham	87	Carlisle U	84
1997–98*b*	Notts Co	99	Macclesfield T	82	Lincoln C	72
1998–99*b*	Brentford	85	Cambridge U	81	Cardiff C	80
1999–2000*b*	Swansea C	85	Rotherham U	84	Northampton T	82
2000–01	Brighton & HA	92	Cardiff C	82	Chesterfield¶	80
2001–02	Plymouth Arg	102	Luton T	97	Mansfield T	79
2002–03	Rushden & D	87	Hartlepool U	85	Wrexham	84
2003–04	Doncaster R	92	Hull C	88	Torquay U*	81

¶9pts deducted for irregularities.

FOOTBALL LEAGUE

MAXIMUM POINTS: ***a*** **44;** ***b*** **60**

1888–89*a*	Preston NE	40	Aston Villa	29	Wolverhampton W	28
1889–90*a*	Preston NE	33	Everton	31	Blackburn R	27
1890–91*a*	Everton	29	Preston NE	27	Notts Co	26
1891–92*b*	Sunderland	42	Preston NE	37	Bolton W	36

FIRST DIVISION to 1991–92

MAXIMUM POINTS: ***a*** **44;** ***b*** **52;** ***c*** **60;** ***d*** **68;** ***e*** **76;** ***f*** **84;** ***g*** **126;** ***h*** **120;** ***k*** **114.**

1892–93*c*	Sunderland	48	Preston NE	37	Everton	36
1893–94*c*	Aston Villa	44	Sunderland	38	Derby Co	36
1894–95*c*	Sunderland	47	Everton	42	Aston Villa	39
1895–96*c*	Aston Villa	45	Derby Co	41	Everton	39
1896–97*c*	Aston Villa	47	Sheffield U*	36	Derby Co	36
1897–98*c*	Sheffield U	42	Sunderland	37	Wolverhampton W*	35
1898–99*d*	Aston Villa	45	Liverpool	43	Burnley	39
1899–1900*d*	Aston Villa	50	Sheffield U	48	Sunderland	41
1900–01*d*	Liverpool	45	Sunderland	43	Notts Co	40
1901–02*d*	Sunderland	44	Everton	41	Newcastle U	37
1902–03*d*	The Wednesday	42	Aston Villa*	41	Sunderland	41
1903–04*d*	The Wednesday	47	Manchester C	44	Everton	43
1904–05*d*	Newcastle U	48	Everton	47	Manchester C	46
1905–06*e*	Liverpool	51	Preston NE	47	The Wednesday	44
1906–07*e*	Newcastle U	51	Bristol C	48	Everton*	45
1907–08*e*	Manchester U	52	Aston Villa*	43	Manchester C	43
1908–09*e*	Newcastle U	53	Everton	46	Sunderland	44
1909–10*e*	Aston Villa	53	Liverpool	48	Blackburn R*	45
1910–11*e*	Manchester U	52	Aston Villa	51	Sunderland*	45
1911–12*e*	Blackburn R	49	Everton	46	Newcastle U	44
1912–13*e*	Sunderland	54	Aston Villa	50	Sheffield W	49
1913–14*e*	Blackburn R	51	Aston Villa	44	Middlesbrough*	43
1914–15*e*	Everton	46	Oldham Ath	45	Blackburn R*	43
1919–20*f*	WBA	60	Burnley	51	Chelsea	49
1920–21*f*	Burnley	59	Manchester C	54	Bolton W	52
1921–22*f*	Liverpool	57	Tottenham H	51	Burnley	49
1922–23*f*	Liverpool	60	Sunderland	54	Huddersfield T	53
1923–24*f*	Huddersfield T*	57	Cardiff C	57	Sunderland	53
1924–25*f*	Huddersfield T	58	WBA	56	Bolton W	55
1925–26*f*	Huddersfield T	57	Arsenal	52	Sunderland	48
1926–27*f*	Newcastle U	56	Huddersfield T	51	Sunderland	49
1927–28*f*	Everton	53	Huddersfield T	51	Leicester C	48
1928–29*f*	Sheffield W	52	Leicester C	51	Aston Villa	50
1929–30*f*	Sheffield W	60	Derby Co	50	Manchester C*	47
1930–31*f*	Arsenal	66	Aston Villa	59	Sheffield W	52
1931–32*f*	Everton	56	Arsenal	54	Sheffield W	50
1932–33*f*	Arsenal	58	Aston Villa	54	Sheffield W	51
1933–34*f*	Arsenal	59	Huddersfield T	56	Tottenham H	49
1934–35*f*	Arsenal	58	Sunderland	54	Sheffield W	49
1935–36*f*	Sunderland	56	Derby Co*	48	Huddersfield T	48
1936–37*f*	Manchester C	57	Charlton Ath	54	Arsenal	52
1937–38*f*	Arsenal	52	Wolverhampton W	51	Preston NE	49
1938–39*f*	Everton	59	Wolverhampton W	55	Charlton Ath	50
1946–47*f*	Liverpool	57	Manchester U*	56	Wolverhampton W	56
1947–48*f*	Arsenal	59	Manchester U*	52	Burnley	52
1948–49*f*	Portsmouth	58	Manchester U*	53	Derby Co	53
1949–50*f*	Portsmouth*	53	Wolverhampton W	53	Sunderland	52
1950–51*f*	Tottenham H	60	Manchester U	56	Blackpool	50
1951–52*f*	Manchester U	57	Tottenham H*	53	Arsenal	53
1952–53*f*	Arsenal*	54	Preston NE	54	Wolverhampton W	51
1953–54*f*	Wolverhampton W	57	WBA	53	Huddersfield T	51
1954–55*f*	Chelsea	52	Wolverhampton W*	48	Portsmouth*	48
1955–56*f*	Manchester U	60	Blackpool*	49	Wolverhampton W	49
1956–57*f*	Manchester U	64	Tottenham H*	56	Preston NE	56
1957–58*f*	Wolverhampton W	64	Preston NE	59	Tottenham H	51
1958–59*f*	Wolverhampton W	61	Manchester U	55	Arsenal*	50

	First	Pts	Second	Pts	Third	Pts
1959–60*f*	Burnley	55	Wolverhampton W	54	Tottenham H	53
1960–61*f*	Tottenham H	66	Sheffield W	58	Wolverhampton W	57
1961–62*f*	Ipswich T	56	Burnley	53	Tottenham H	52
1962–63*f*	Everton	61	Tottenham H	55	Burnley	54
1963–64*f*	Liverpool	57	Manchester U	53	Everton	52
1964–65*f*	Manchester U*	61	Leeds U	61	Chelsea	56
1965–66*f*	Liverpool	61	Leeds U*	55	Burnley	55
1966–67*f*	Manchester U	60	Nottingham F*	56	Tottenham H	56
1967–68*f*	Manchester C	58	Manchester U	56	Liverpool	55
1968–69*f*	Leeds U	67	Liverpool	61	Everton	57
1969–70*f*	Everton	66	Leeds U	57	Chelsea	55
1970–71*f*	Arsenal	65	Leeds U	64	Tottenham H*	52
1971–72*f*	Derby Co	58	Leeds U*	57	Liverpool*	57
1972–73*f*	Liverpool	60	Arsenal	57	Leeds U	53
1973–74*f*	Leeds U	62	Liverpool	57	Derby Co	48
1974–75*f*	Derby Co	53	Liverpool*	51	Ipswich T	51
1975–76*f*	Liverpool	60	QPR	59	Manchester U	56
1976–77*f*	Liverpool	57	Manchester C	56	Ipswich T	52
1977–78*f*	Nottingham F	64	Liverpool	57	Everton	55
1978–79*f*	Liverpool	68	Nottingham F	60	WBA	59
1979–80*f*	Liverpool	60	Manchester U	58	Ipswich T	52
1980–81*f*	Aston Villa	60	Ipswich T	56	Arsenal	53
1981–82*g*	Liverpool	87	Ipswich T	83	Manchester U	78
1982–83*g*	Liverpool	82	Watford	71	Manchester U	70
1983–84*g*	Liverpool	80	Southampton	77	Nottingham F*	74
1984–85*g*	Everton	90	Liverpool*	77	Tottenham H	77
1985–86*g*	Liverpool	88	Everton	86	West Ham U	84
1986–87*g*	Everton	86	Liverpool	77	Tottenham H	71
1987–88*h*	Liverpool	90	Manchester U	81	Nottingham F	73
1988–89*k*	Arsenal*	76	Liverpool	76	Nottingham F	64
1989–90*k*	Liverpool	79	Aston Villa	70	Tottenham H	63
1990–91*k*	Arsenal†	83	Liverpool	76	Crystal Palace	69
1991–92*g*	Leeds U	82	Manchester U	78	Sheffield W	75

No official competition during 1915–19 and 1939–46; Regional Leagues operated. †2 pts deducted.

SECOND DIVISION to 1991–92

MAXIMUM POINTS: ***a*** **44;** ***b*** **56;** ***c*** **60;** ***d*** **68;** ***e*** **76;** ***f*** **84;** ***g*** **126;** ***h*** **132;** ***k*** **138.**

	First	Pts	Second	Pts	Third	Pts
1892–93*a*	Small Heath	36	Sheffield U	35	Darwen	30
1893–94*b*	Liverpool	50	Small Heath	42	Notts Co	39
1894–95*c*	Bury	48	Notts Co	39	Newton Heath*	38
1895–96*c*	Liverpool*	46	Manchester C	46	Grimsby T*	42
1896–97*c*	Notts Co	42	Newton Heath	39	Grimsby T	38
1897–98*c*	Burnley	48	Newcastle U	45	Manchester C	39
1898–99*d*	Manchester C	52	Glossop NE	46	Leicester Fosse	45
1899–1900*d*	The Wednesday	54	Bolton W	52	Small Heath	46
1900–01*d*	Grimsby T	49	Small Heath	48	Burnley	44
1901–02*d*	WBA	55	Middlesbrough	51	Preston NE*	42
1902–03*d*	Manchester C	54	Small Heath	51	Woolwich A	48
1903–04*d*	Preston NE	50	Woolwich A	49	Manchester U	48
1904–05*d*	Liverpool	58	Bolton W	56	Manchester U	53
1905–06*e*	Bristol C	66	Manchester U	62	Chelsea	53
1906–07*e*	Nottingham F	60	Chelsea	57	Leicester Fosse	48
1907–08*e*	Bradford C	54	Leicester Fosse	52	Oldham Ath	50
1908–09*e*	Bolton W	52	Tottenham H*	51	WBA	51
1909–10*e*	Manchester C	54	Oldham Ath*	53	Hull C*	53
1910–11*e*	WBA	53	Bolton W	51	Chelsea	49
1911–12*e*	Derby Co*	54	Chelsea	54	Burnley	52
1912–13*e*	Preston NE	53	Burnley	50	Birmingham	46
1913–14*e*	Notts Co	53	Bradford PA*	49	Woolwich A	49
1914–15*e*	Derby Co	53	Preston NE	50	Barnsley	47
1919–20*f*	Tottenham H	70	Huddersfield T	64	Birmingham	56
1920–21*f*	Birmingham*	58	Cardiff C	58	Bristol C	51
1921–22*f*	Nottingham F	56	Stoke C*	52	Barnsley	52
1922–23*f*	Notts Co	53	West Ham U*	51	Leicester C	51
1923–24*f*	Leeds U	54	Bury*	51	Derby Co	51
1924–25*f*	Leicester C	59	Manchester U	57	Derby Co	55
1925–26*f*	Sheffield W	60	Derby Co	57	Chelsea	52
1926–27*f*	Middlesbrough	62	Portsmouth*	54	Manchester C	54
1927–28*f*	Manchester C	59	Leeds U	57	Chelsea	54
1928–29*f*	Middlesbrough	55	Grimsby T	53	Bradford PA*	48
1929–30*f*	Blackpool	58	Chelsea	55	Oldham Ath	53
1930–31*f*	Everton	61	WBA	54	Tottenham H	51
1931–32*f*	Wolverhampton W	56	Leeds U	54	Stoke C	52
1932–33*f*	Stoke C	56	Tottenham H	55	Fulham	50
1933–34*f*	Grimsby T	59	Preston NE	52	Bolton W*	51
1934–35*f*	Brentford	61	Bolton W*	56	West Ham U	56
1935–36*f*	Manchester U	56	Charlton Ath	55	Sheffield U*	52
1936–37*f*	Leicester C	56	Blackpool	55	Bury	52
1937–38*f*	Aston Villa	57	Manchester U*	53	Sheffield U	53
1938–39*f*	Blackburn R	55	Sheffield U	54	Sheffield W	53
1946–47*f*	Manchester C	62	Burnley	58	Birmingham C	55
1947–48*f*	Birmingham C	59	Newcastle U	56	Southampton	52
1948–49*f*	Fulham	57	WBA	56	Southampton	55
1949–50*f*	Tottenham H	61	Sheffield W*	52	Sheffield U*	52

	First	*Pts*	*Second*	*Pts*	*Third*	*Pts*
1950–51*f*	Preston NE	57	Manchester C	52	Cardiff C	50
1951–52*f*	Sheffield W	53	Cardiff C*	51	Birmingham C	51
1952–53*f*	Sheffield U	60	Huddersfield T	58	Luton T	52
1953–54*f*	Leicester C*	56	Everton	56	Blackburn R	55
1954–55*f*	Birmingham C*	54	Luton T*	54	Rotherham U	54
1955–56*f*	Sheffield W	55	Leeds U	52	Liverpool*	48
1956–57*f*	Leicester C	61	Nottingham F	54	Liverpool	53
1957–58*f*	West Ham U	57	Blackburn R	56	Charlton Ath	55
1958–59*f*	Sheffield W	62	Fulham	60	Sheffield U*	53
1959–60*f*	Aston Villa	59	Cardiff C	58	Liverpool*	50
1960–61*f*	Ipswich T	59	Sheffield U	58	Liverpool	52
1961–62*f*	Liverpool	62	Leyton Orient	54	Sunderland	53
1962–63*f*	Stoke C	53	Chelsea*	52	Sunderland	52
1963–64*f*	Leeds U	63	Sunderland	61	Preston NE	56
1964–65*f*	Newcastle U	57	Northampton T	56	Bolton W	50
1965–66*f*	Manchester C	59	Southampton	54	Coventry C	53
1966–67*f*	Coventry C	59	Wolverhampton W	58	Carlisle U	52
1967–68*f*	Ipswich T	59	QPR*	58	Blackpool	58
1968–69*f*	Derby Co	63	Crystal Palace	56	Charlton Ath	50
1969–70*f*	Huddersfield T	60	Blackpool	53	Leicester C	51
1970–71*f*	Leicester C	59	Sheffield U	56	Cardiff C*	53
1971–72*f*	Norwich C	57	Birmingham C	56	Millwall	55
1972–73*f*	Burnley	62	QPR	61	Aston Villa	50
1973–74*f*	Middlesbrough	65	Luton T	50	Carlisle U	49
1974–75*f*	Manchester U	61	Aston Villa	58	Norwich C	53
1975–76*f*	Sunderland	56	Bristol C*	53	WBA	53
1976–77*f*	Wolverhampton W	57	Chelsea	55	Nottingham F	52
1977–78*f*	Bolton W	58	Southampton	57	Tottenham H*	56
1978–79*f*	Crystal Palace	57	Brighton & HA*	56	Stoke C	56
1979–80*f*	Leicester C	55	Sunderland	54	Birmingham C*	53
1980–81*f*	West Ham U	66	Notts Co	53	Swansea C*	50
1981–82*g*	Luton T	88	Watford	80	Norwich C	71
1982–83*g*	QPR	85	Wolverhampton W	75	Leicester C	70
1983–84*g*	Chelsea*	88	Sheffield W	88	Newcastle U	80
1984–85*g*	Oxford U	84	Birmingham C	82	Manchester C	74
1985–86*g*	Norwich C	84	Charlton Ath	77	Wimbledon	76
1986–87*g*	Derby Co	84	Portsmouth	78	Oldham Ath††	75
1987–88*h*	Millwall	82	Aston Villa*	78	Middlesbrough	78
1988–89*k*	Chelsea	99	Manchester C	82	Crystal Palace	81
1989–90*k*	Leeds U*	85	Sheffield U	85	Newcastle U††	80
1990–91*k*	Oldham Ath	88	West Ham U	87	Sheffield W	82
1991–92*k*	Ipswich T	84	Middlesbrough	80	Derby Co	78

No official competition during 1915–19 and 1939–46; Regional Leagues operated.

THIRD DIVISION to 1991–92

MAXIMUM POINTS: 92; 138 FROM 1981–82.

	First	Pts	Second	Pts	Third	Pts
1958–59	Plymouth Arg	62	Hull C	61	Brentford*	57
1959–60	Southampton	61	Norwich C	59	Shrewsbury T*	52
1960–61	Bury	68	Walsall	62	QPR	60
1961–62	Portsmouth	65	Grimsby T	62	Bournemouth*	59
1962–63	Northampton T	62	Swindon T	58	Port Vale	54
1963–64	Coventry C*	60	Crystal Palace	60	Watford	58
1964–65	Carlisle U	60	Bristol C*	59	Mansfield T	59
1965–66	Hull C	69	Millwall	65	QPR	57
1966–67	QPR	67	Middlesbrough	55	Watford	54
1967–68	Oxford U	57	Bury	56	Shrewsbury T	55
1968–69	Watford*	64	Swindon T	64	Luton T	61
1969–70	Orient	62	Luton T	60	Bristol R	56
1970–71	Preston NE	61	Fulham	60	Halifax T	56
1971–72	Aston Villa	70	Brighton & HA	65	Bournemouth*	62
1972–73	Bolton W	61	Notts Co	57	Blackburn R	55
1973–74	Oldham Ath	62	Bristol R*	61	York C	61
1974–75	Blackburn R	60	Plymouth Arg	59	Charlton Ath	55
1975–76	Hereford U	63	Cardiff C	57	Millwall	56
1976–77	Mansfield T	64	Brighton & HA	61	Crystal Palace*	59
1977–78	Wrexham	61	Cambridge U	58	Preston NE*	56
1978–79	Shrewsbury T	61	Watford*	60	Swansea C	60
1979–80	Grimsby T	62	Blackburn R	59	Sheffield W	58
1980–81	Rotherham U	61	Barnsley*	59	Charlton Ath	59
1981–82	Burnley*	80	Carlisle U	80	Fulham	78
1982–83	Portsmouth	91	Cardiff C	86	Huddersfield T	82
1983–84	Oxford U	95	Wimbledon	87	Sheffield U*	83
1984–85	Bradford C	94	Millwall	90	Hull C	87
1985–86	Reading	94	Plymouth Arg	87	Derby Co	84
1986–87	Bournemouth	97	Middlesbrough	94	Swindon T	87
1987–88	Sunderland	93	Brighton & HA	84	Walsall	82
1988–89	Wolverhampton W	92	Sheffield U*	84	Port Vale	84
1989–90	Bristol R	93	Bristol C	91	Notts Co	87
1990–91	Cambridge U	86	Southend U	85	Grimsby T*	83
1991–92	Brentford	82	Birmingham C	81	Huddersfield T	78

FOURTH DIVISION (1958–1992)

MAXIMUM POINTS: 92; 138 FROM 1981–82.

	First	*Pts*	*Second*	*Pts*	*Third*	*Pts*	*Fourth*	*Pts*
1958–59	Port Vale	64	Coventry C*	60	York C	60	Shrewsbury T	58
1959–60	Walsall	65	Notts Co*	60	Torquay U	60	Watford	57
1960–61	Peterborough U	66	Crystal Palace	64	Northampton T*	60	Bradford PA	60
1961–62†	Millwall	56	Colchester U	55	Wrexham	53	Carlisle U	52
1962–63	Brentford	62	Oldham Ath*	59	Crewe Alex	59	Mansfield T*	57
1963–64	Gillingham*	60	Carlisle U	60	Workington	59	Exeter C	58
1964–65	Brighton & HA	63	Millwall*	62	York C	62	Oxford U	61
1965–66	Doncaster R*	59	Darlington	59	Torquay U	58	Colchester U*	56
1966–67	Stockport Co	64	Southport*	59	Barrow	59	Tranmere R	58
1967–68	Luton T	66	Barnsley	61	Hartlepools U	60	Crewe Alex	58
1968–69	Doncaster R	59	Halifax T	57	Rochdale*	56	Bradford C	56
1969–70	Chesterfield	64	Wrexham	61	Swansea C	60	Port Vale	59
1970–71	Notts Co	69	Bournemouth	60	Oldham Ath	59	York C	56
1971–72	Grimsby T	63	Southend U	60	Brentford	59	Scunthorpe U	57
1972–73	Southport	62	Hereford U	58	Cambridge U	57	Aldershot*	56
1973–74	Peterborough U	65	Gillingham	62	Colchester U	60	Bury	59
1974–75	Mansfield T	68	Shrewsbury T	62	Rotherham U	59	Chester*	57
1975–76	Lincoln C	74	Northampton T	68	Reading	60	Tranmere R	58
1976–77	Cambridge U	65	Exeter C	62	Colchester U*	59	Bradford C	59
1977–78	Watford	71	Southend U	60	Swansea C*	56	Brentford	56
1978–79	Reading	65	Grimsby T*	61	Wimbledon*	61	Barnsley	61
1979–80	Huddersfield T	66	Walsall	64	Newport Co	61	Portsmouth*	60
1980–81	Southend U	67	Lincoln C	65	Doncaster R	56	Wimbledon	55
1981–82	Sheffield U	96	Bradford C*	91	Wigan Ath	91	Bournemouth	88
1982–83	Wimbledon	98	Hull C	90	Port Vale	88	Scunthorpe U	83
1983–84	York C	101	Doncaster R	85	Reading*	82	Bristol C	82
1984–85	Chesterfield	91	Blackpool	86	Darlington	85	Bury	84
1985–86	Swindon T	102	Chester C	84	Mansfield T	81	Port Vale	79
1986–87	Northampton T	99	Preston NE	90	Southend U	80	Wolverhampton W††	79
1987–88	Wolverhampton W	90	Cardiff C	85	Bolton W	78	Scunthorpe U††	77
1988–89	Rotherham U	82	Tranmere R	80	Crewe Alex	78	Scunthorpe U††	77
1989–90	Exeter C	89	Grimsby T	79	Southend U	75	Stockport Co††	74
1990–91	Darlington	83	Stockport Co*	82	Hartlepool U	82	Peterborough U	80
1991–92†*	Burnley	83	Rotherham U*	77	Mansfield T	77	Blackpool	76

†*Maximum points:* 88 owing to Accrington Stanley's resignation.
†**Maximum points:* 126 owing to Aldershot being expelled (and only 23 teams started the competition).

THIRD DIVISION—SOUTH (1920–1958)

1920–21 SEASON AS THIRD DIVISION. MAXIMUM POINTS: *a* 84; *b* 92.

1920–21*a*	Crystal Palace	59	Southampton	54	QPR	53
1921–22*a*	Southampton*	61	Plymouth Arg	61	Portsmouth	53
1922–23*a*	Bristol C	59	Plymouth Arg*	53	Swansea T	53
1923–24*a*	Portsmouth	59	Plymouth Arg	55	Millwall	54
1924–25*a*	Swansea T	57	Plymouth Arg	56	Bristol C	53
1925–26*a*	Reading	57	Plymouth Arg	56	Millwall	53
1926–27*a*	Bristol C	62	Plymouth Arg	60	Millwall	56
1927–28*a*	Millwall	65	Northampton T	55	Plymouth Arg	53
1928–29*a*	Charlton Ath*	54	Crystal Palace	54	Northampton T*	52
1929–30*a*	Plymouth Arg	68	Brentford	61	QPR	51
1930–31*a*	Notts Co	59	Crystal Palace	51	Brentford	50
1931–32*a*	Fulham	57	Reading	55	Southend U	53
1932–33*a*	Brentford	62	Exeter C	58	Norwich C	57
1933–34*a*	Norwich C	61	Coventry C*	54	Reading*	54
1934–35*a*	Charlton Ath	61	Reading	53	Coventry C	51
1935–36*a*	Coventry C	57	Luton T	56	Reading	54
1936–37*a*	Luton T	58	Notts Co	56	Brighton & HA	53
1937–38*a*	Millwall	56	Bristol C	55	QPR*	53
1938–39*a*	Newport Co	55	Crystal Palace	52	Brighton & HA	49
1939–46	Competition cancelled owing to war. Regional Leagues operated.					
1946–47*a*	Cardiff C	66	QPR	57	Bristol C	51
1947–48*a*	QPR	61	Bournemouth	57	Walsall	51
1948–49*a*	Swansea T	62	Reading	55	Bournemouth	52
1949–50*a*	Notts Co	58	Northampton T*	51	Southend U	51
1950–51*b*	Nottingham F	70	Norwich C	64	Reading*	57
1951–52*b*	Plymouth Arg	66	Reading*	61	Norwich C	61
1952–53*b*	Bristol R	64	Millwall*	62	Northampton T	62
1953–54*b*	Ipswich T	64	Brighton & HA	61	Bristol C	56
1954–55*b*	Bristol C	70	Leyton Orient	61	Southampton	59
1955–56*b*	Leyton Orient	66	Brighton & HA	65	Ipswich T	64
1956–57*b*	Ipswich T*	59	Torquay U	59	Colchester U	58
1957–58*b*	Brighton & HA	60	Brentford*	58	Plymouth Arg	58

THIRD DIVISION—NORTH (1921–1958)

MAXIMUM POINTS: *a* 76; *b* 84; *c* 80; *d* 92.

1921–22*a*	Stockport Co	56	Darlington*	50	Grimsby T	50
1922–23*a*	Nelson	51	Bradford PA	47	Walsall	46
1923–24*b*	Wolverhampton W	63	Rochdale	62	Chesterfield	54
1924–25*b*	Darlington	58	Nelson*	53	New Brighton	53
1925–26*b*	Grimsby T	61	Bradford PA	60	Rochdale	59
1926–27*b*	Stoke C	63	Rochdale	58	Bradford PA	55
1927–28*b*	Bradford PA	63	Lincoln C	55	Stockport Co	54

	First	*Pts*	*Second*	*Pts*	*Third*	*Pts*
1928–29*b*	Bradford C	63	Stockport Co	62	Wrexham	52
1929–30*b*	Port Vale	67	Stockport Co	63	Darlington*	50
1930–31*b*	Chesterfield	58	Lincoln C	57	Wrexham*	54
1931–32*c*	Lincoln C*	57	Gateshead	57	Chester	50
1932–33*b*	Hull C	59	Wrexham	57	Stockport Co	54
1933–34*b*	Barnsley	62	Chesterfield	61	Stockport Co	59
1934–35*b*	Doncaster R	57	Halifax T	55	Chester	54
1935–36*b*	Chesterfield	60	Chester*	55	Tranmere R	55
1936–37*b*	Stockport Co	60	Lincoln C	57	Chester	53
1937–38*b*	Tranmere R	56	Doncaster R	54	Hull C	53
1938–39*b*	Barnsley	67	Doncaster R	56	Bradford C	52
1939–46	Competition cancelled owing to war. Regional Leagues operated.					
1946–47*b*	Doncaster R	72	Rotherham U	64	Chester	56
1947–48*b*	Lincoln C	60	Rotherham U	59	Wrexham	50
1948–49*b*	Hull C	65	Rotherham U	62	Doncaster R	50
1949–50*b*	Doncaster R	55	Gateshead	53	Rochdale*	51
1950–51*d*	Rotherham U	71	Mansfield T	64	Carlisle U	62
1951–52*d*	Lincoln C	69	Grimsby T	66	Stockport Co	59
1952–53*d*	Oldham Ath	59	Port Vale	58	Wrexham	56
1953–54*d*	Port Vale	69	Barnsley	58	Scunthorpe U	57
1954–55*d*	Barnsley	65	Accrington S	61	Scunthorpe U*	58
1955–56*d*	Grimsby T	68	Derby Co	63	Accrington S	59
1956–57*d*	Derby Co	63	Hartlepools U	59	Accrington S*	58
1957–58*d*	Scunthorpe U	66	Accrington S	59	Bradford C	57

PROMOTED AFTER PLAY-OFFS

(NOT ACCOUNTED FOR IN PREVIOUS SECTION)

1986–87	Aldershot to Division 3
1987–88	Swansea C to Division 3
1988–89	Leyton Orient to Division 3
1989–90	Sunderland to Division 1; Notts Co to Division 2; Cambridge U to Division 3
1990–91	Notts Co to Division 1; Tranmere R to Division 2; Torquay U to Division 3
1991–92	Blackburn R to Premier League; Peterborough U to Division 1
1992–93	Swindon T to Premier League; WBA to Division 1; York C to Division 2
1993–94	Leicester C to Premier League; Burnley to Division 1; Wycombe W to Division 2
1994–95	Huddersfield T to Division 1
1995–96	Leicester C to Premier League; Bradford C to Division 1; Plymouth Arg to Division 2
1996–97	Crystal Palace to Premier League; Crewe Alex to Division 1; Northampton T to Division 2
1997–98	Charlton Ath to Premier League; Colchester U to Division 2
1998–99	Watford to Premier League; Scunthorpe U to Division 2
1999–2000	Peterborough U to Division 2
2000–01	Walsall to Division 1; Blackpool to Division 2
2001–02	Birmingham C to Premier League; Stoke C to Division 1; Cheltenham T to Division 2
2002–03	Wolverhampton W to Premier League; Cardiff C to Division 1; Bournemouth to Division 2
2003–04	Crystal Palace to Premier League; Brighton & HA to Division 1; Huddersfield T to Division 2
2004–05	West Ham U to Premier League; Sheffield W to Championship; Southend U to Championship 1
2005–06	Watford to Premier League; Barnsley to Championship; Cheltenham T to Championship 1
2006–07	Derby Co to Premier League; Blackpool to Championship; Bristol R to Championship 1
2007–08	Hull C to Premier League; Doncaster R to Championship; Stockport Co to Championship 1
2008–09	Burnley to Premier League; Scunthorpe U to Championship; Gillingham to Championship 1
2009–10	Blackpool to Premier League; Millwall to Championship; Dagenham & R to Championship 1
2010–11	Swansea C to Premier League; Peterborough U to Championship; Stevenage to Championship 1
2011–12	West Ham U to Premier League; Huddersfield T to Championship; Crewe Alex to Championship 1

LEAGUE TITLE WINS

FA PREMIER LEAGUE – Manchester U 12, Arsenal 3, Chelsea 3, Blackburn R 1, Manchester C 1.

FOOTBALL LEAGUE CHAMPIONSHIP – Reading 2, Sunderland 2, Newcastle U 1, QPR 1, WBA 1, Wolverhampton W 1.

LEAGUE DIVISION 1 – Liverpool 18, Arsenal 10, Everton 9, Sunderland 8, Aston Villa 7, Manchester U 7, Newcastle U 5, Sheffield W 4, Huddersfield T 3, Leeds U 3, Manchester C 3, Portsmouth 3, Wolverhampton W 3, Blackburn R 2, Burnley 2, Derby Co 2, Nottingham F 2, Preston NE 2, Tottenham H 2; Bolton W, Charlton Ath, Chelsea, Crystal Palace, Fulham, Ipswich T, Middlesbrough, Norwich C, Sheffield U, WBA 1 each.

FOOTBALL LEAGUE CHAMPIONSHIP 1 – Brighton & HA 1, Charlton Ath 1, Leicester C 1, Luton T 1, Norwich C 1, Scunthorpe U 1, Southend U 1, Swansea C 1.

LEAGUE DIVISION 2 – Leicester C 6, Manchester C 6, Birmingham C (one as Small Heath) 5, Sheffield W 5, Derby Co 4, Liverpool 4, Preston NE 4, Ipswich T 3, Leeds U 3, Middlesbrough 3, Notts Co 3, Stoke C 3, Aston Villa 2, Bolton W 2, Burnley 2, Bury 2, Chelsea 2, Fulham 2, Grimsby T 2, Manchester U 2, Millwall 2, Norwich C 2, Nottingham F 2, Tottenham H 2, WBA 2, West Ham U 2, Wolverhampton W 2; Blackburn R, Blackpool, Bradford C, Brentford, Brighton & HA, Bristol C, Coventry C, Crystal Palace, Everton, Huddersfield T, Luton T, Newcastle U, QPR, Oldham Ath, Oxford U, Plymouth Arg, Reading, Sheffield U, Sunderland, Swindon T, Watford, Wigan Ath 1 each.

FOOTBALL LEAGUE CHAMPIONSHIP 2 – Brentford 1, Carlisle U 1, Chesterfield 1, Milton Keynes D 1, Notts Co 1, Swindon T 1, Walsall 1, Yeovil T 1.

LEAGUE DIVISION 3 – Brentford 2, Carlisle U 2, Oxford U 2, Plymouth Arg 2, Portsmouth 2, Preston NE 2, Shrewsbury T 2; Aston Villa, Blackburn R, Bolton W, Bournemouth, Bradford C, Brighton & HA, Bristol R, Burnley, Bury, Cambridge U, Cardiff C, Coventry C, Doncaster R. Grimsby T, Hereford U, Hull C, Leyton Orient, Mansfield T, Northampton T, Notts Co, Oldham Ath, QPR, Reading, Rotherham U, Rushden & D Southampton, Sunderland, Swansea C, Watford, Wigan Ath, Wolverhampton W, Wrexham 1 each.

LEAGUE DIVISION 4 – Chesterfield 2, Doncaster R 2, Peterborough U 2; Brentford, Brighton & HA, Burnley, Cambridge U, Darlington, Exeter C, Gillingham, Grimsby T, Huddersfield T, Lincoln C, Luton T, Mansfield T, Millwall, Northampton T, Notts Co, Port Vale, Reading, Rotherham U, Sheffield U, Southend U, Southport, Stockport Co, Swindon T, Walsall, Watford, Wimbledon, Wolverhampton W, York C 1 each.

LEAGUE TITLE WINS TO 1957–58

DIVISION 3 (South) – Bristol C 3, Charlton Ath 2, Ipswich T 2, Millwall 2, Notts Co 2, Plymouth Arg 2, Swansea T 2; Brentford, Brighton & HA, Bristol R, Cardiff C, Coventry C, Crystal Palace, Fulham, Leyton Orient, Luton T, Newport Co, Norwich C, Nottingham F, Portsmouth, QPR, Reading, Southampton 1 each.

DIVISION 3 (North) – Barnsley 3, Doncaster R 3, Lincoln C 3, Chesterfield 2, Grimsby T 2, Hull C 2, Port Vale 2, Stockport Co 2; Bradford C, Bradford PA, Darlington, Derby Co, Nelson, Oldham Ath, Rotherham U, Scunthorpe U, Stoke C, Tranmere R, Wolverhampton W 1 each.

RELEGATED CLUBS

1891–92 League extended. Newton Heath, Sheffield W and Nottingham F admitted. *Second Division formed* including Darwen.
1892–93 In Test matches, Sheffield U and Darwen won promotion in place of Notts Co and Accrington S.
1893–94 In Tests, Liverpool and Small Heath won promotion. Newton Heath and Darwen relegated.
1894–95 After Tests, Bury promoted, Liverpool relegated.
1895–96 After Tests, Liverpool promoted, Small Heath relegated.
1896–97 After Tests, Notts Co promoted, Burnley relegated.
1897–98 Test system abolished after success of Stoke C and Burnley. League extended. Blackburn R and Newcastle U elected to First Division. *Automatic promotion and relegation introduced.*

FA PREMIER LEAGUE TO DIVISION 1

1992–93 Crystal Palace, Middlesbrough, Nottingham F
1993–94 Sheffield U, Oldham Ath, Swindon T
1994–95 Crystal Palace, Norwich C, Leicester C, Ipswich T
1995–96 Manchester C, QPR, Bolton W
1996–97 Sunderland, Middlesbrough, Nottingham F
1997–98 Bolton W, Barnsley, Crystal Palace
1998–99 Charlton Ath, Blackburn R, Nottingham F
1999–2000 Wimbledon, Sheffield W, Watford
2000–01 Manchester C, Coventry C, Bradford C
2001–02 Ipswich T, Derby Co, Leicester C
2002–03 West Ham U, WBA, Sunderland
2003–04 Leicester C, Leeds U, Wolverhampton W.

FA PREMIER LEAGUE TO CHAMPIONSHIP

2004–05 Crystal Palace, Norwich C, Southampton
2005–06 Birmingham C, WBA, Sunderland
2006–07 Sheffield U, Charlton Ath, Watford
2007–08 Reading, Birmingham C, Derby Co
2008–09 Newcastle U, Middlesbrough, WBA
2009–10 Burnley, Hull C, Portsmouth
2010–11 Birmingham C, Blackpool, West Ham U
2011–12 Bolton W, Blackburn R, Wolverhampton W

DIVISION 1 TO DIVISION 2

1898–99 Bolton W and Sheffield W
1899–1900 Burnley and Glossop
1900–01 Preston NE and WBA
1901–02 Small Heath and Manchester C
1902–03 Grimsby T and Bolton W
1903–04 Liverpool and WBA
1904–05 League extended. Bury and Notts Co, two bottom clubs in First Division, re-elected.
1905–06 Nottingham F and Wolverhampton W
1906–07 Derby Co and Stoke C
1907–08 Bolton W and Birmingham C
1908–09 Manchester C and Leicester Fosse
1909–10 Bolton W and Chelsea
1910–11 Bristol C and Nottingham F
1911–12 Preston NE and Bury
1912–13 Notts Co and Woolwich Arsenal
1913–14 Preston NE and Derby Co
1914–15 Tottenham H and Chelsea*
1919–20 Notts Co and Sheffield W
1920–21 Derby Co and Bradford PA
1921–22 Bradford C and Manchester U
1922–23 Stoke C and Oldham Ath
1923–24 Chelsea and Middlesbrough
1924–25 Preston NE and Nottingham F
1925–26 Manchester C and Notts Co
1926–27 Leeds U and WBA
1927–28 Tottenham H and Middlesbrough
1928–29 Bury and Cardiff C
1929–30 Burnley and Everton
1930–31 Leeds U and Manchester U
1931–32 Grimsby T and West Ham U
1932–33 Bolton W and Blackpool
1933–34 Newcastle U and Sheffield U
1934–35 Leicester C and Tottenham H
1935–36 Aston Villa and Blackburn R
1936–37 Manchester U and Sheffield W
1937–38 Manchester C and WBA
1938–39 Birmingham C and Leicester C
1946–47 Brentford and Leeds U
1947–48 Blackburn R and Grimsby T
1948–49 Preston NE and Sheffield U
1949–50 Manchester C and Birmingham C
1950–51 Sheffield W and Everton
1951–52 Huddersfield T and Fulham
1952–53 Stoke C and Derby Co
1953–54 Middlesbrough and Liverpool
1954–55 Leicester C and Sheffield W
1955–56 Huddersfield T and Sheffield U
1956–57 Charlton Ath and Cardiff C
1957–58 Sheffield W and Sunderland
1958–59 Portsmouth and Aston Villa
1959–60 Luton T and Leeds U
1960–61 Preston NE and Newcastle U
1961–62 Chelsea and Cardiff C
1962–63 Manchester C and Leyton Orient
1963–64 Bolton W and Ipswich T
1964–65 Wolverhampton W and Birmingham C
1965–66 Northampton T and Blackburn R
1966–67 Aston Villa and Blackpool
1967–68 Fulham and Sheffield U
1968–69 Leicester C and QPR
1969–70 Sunderland and Sheffield W
1970–71 Burnley and Blackpool
1971–72 Huddersfield T and Nottingham F
1972–73 Crystal Palace and WBA
1973–74 Southampton, Manchester U, Norwich C
1974–75 Luton T, Chelsea, Carlisle U
1975–76 Wolverhampton W, Burnley, Sheffield U
1976–77 Sunderland, Stoke C, Tottenham H
1977–78 West Ham U, Newcastle U, Leicester C
1978–79 QPR, Birmingham C, Chelsea
1979–80 Bristol C, Derby Co, Bolton W
1980–81 Norwich C, Leicester C, Crystal Palace
1981–82 Leeds U, Wolverhampton W, Middlesbrough
1982–83 Manchester C, Swansea C, Brighton & HA
1983–84 Birmingham C, Notts Co, Wolverhampton W
1984–85 Norwich C, Sunderland, Stoke C
1985–86 Ipswich T, Birmingham C, WBA
1986–87 Leicester C, Manchester C, Aston Villa
1987–88 Chelsea**, Portsmouth, Watford, Oxford U
1988–89 Middlesbrough, West Ham U, Newcastle U
1989–90 Sheffield W, Charlton Ath, Millwall
1990–91 Sunderland and Derby Co
1991–92 Luton T, Notts Co, West Ham U
1992–93 Brentford, Cambridge U, Bristol R
1993–94 Birmingham C, Oxford U, Peterborough U
1994–95 Swindon T, Burnley, Bristol C, Notts Co
1995–96 Millwall, Watford, Luton T
1996–97 Grimsby T, Oldham Ath, Southend U
1997–98 Manchester C, Stoke C, Reading
1998–99 Bury, Oxford U, Bristol C
1999–2000 Walsall, Port Vale, Swindon T
2000–01 Huddersfield T, QPR, Tranmere R
2001–02 Crewe Alex, Barnsley, Stockport Co
2002–03 Sheffield W, Brighton & HA, Grimsby T
2003–04 Walsall, Bradford C, Wimbledon

***Relegated after play-offs.*

**Subsequently re-elected to Division 1 when League was extended after the War.*

FOOTBALL LEAGUE CHAMPIONSHIP TO FOOTBALL LEAGUE CHAMPIONSHIP 1

2004–05 Gillingham, Nottingham F, Rotherham U
2005–06 Crewe Alex, Millwall, Brighton & HA
2006–07 Southend U, Luton T, Leeds U
2007–08 Leicester C, Scunthorpe U, Colchester U
2008–09 Norwich C, Southampton, Charlton Ath
2009–10 Sheffield W, Plymouth Arg, Peterborough U
2010–11 Preston NE, Sheffield U, Scunthorpe U
2011–12 Portsmouth, Coventry C, Doncaster R

DIVISION 2 TO DIVISION 3

1920–21 Stockport Co
1921–22 Bradford PA and Bristol C
1922–23 Rotherham Co and Wolverhampton W
1923–24 Nelson and Bristol C
1924–25 Crystal Palace and Coventry C
1925–26 Stoke C and Stockport Co
1926–27 Darlington and Bradford C
1927–28 Fulham and South Shields
1928–29 Port Vale and Clapton Orient
1929–30 Hull C and Notts Co
1930–31 Reading and Cardiff C
1931–32 Barnsley and Bristol C
1932–33 Chesterfield and Charlton Ath
1933–34 Millwall and Lincoln C
1934–35 Oldham Ath and Notts Co
1935–36 Port Vale and Hull C
1936–37 Doncaster R and Bradford C
1937–38 Barnsley and Stockport Co
1938–39 Norwich C and Tranmere R
1946–47 Swansea T and Newport Co
1947–48 Doncaster R and Millwall
1948–49 Nottingham F and Lincoln C
1949–50 Plymouth Arg and Bradford PA
1950–51 Grimsby T and Chesterfield
1951–52 Coventry C and QPR
1952–53 Southampton and Barnsley
1953–54 Brentford and Oldham Ath
1954–55 Ipswich T and Derby Co
1955–56 Plymouth Arg and Hull C
1956–57 Port Vale and Bury
1957–58 Doncaster R and Notts Co
1958–59 Barnsley and Grimsby T
1959–60 Bristol C and Hull C
1960–61 Lincoln C and Portsmouth
1961–62 Brighton & HA and Bristol R
1962–63 Walsall and Luton T
1963–64 Grimsby T and Scunthorpe U
1964–65 Swindon T and Swansea T
1965–66 Middlesbrough and Leyton Orient
1966–67 Northampton T and Bury
1967–68 Plymouth Arg and Rotherham U
1968–69 Fulham and Bury
1969–70 Preston NE and Aston Villa
1970–71 Blackburn R and Bolton W
1971–72 Charlton Ath and Watford
1972–73 Huddersfield T and Brighton & HA
1973–74 Crystal Palace, Preston NE, Swindon T
1974–75 Millwall, Cardiff C, Sheffield W
1975–76 Oxford U, York C, Portsmouth
1976–77 Carlisle U, Plymouth Arg, Hereford U
1977–78 Blackpool, Mansfield T, Hull C
1978–79 Sheffield U, Millwall, Blackburn R
1979–80 Fulham, Burnley, Charlton Ath
1980–81 Preston NE, Bristol C, Bristol R
1981–82 Cardiff C, Wrexham, Orient
1982–83 Rotherham U, Burnley, Bolton W
1983–84 Derby Co, Swansea C, Cambridge U
1984–85 Notts Co, Cardiff C, Wolverhampton W
1985–86 Carlisle U, Middlesbrough, Fulham
1986–87 Sunderland**, Grimsby T, Brighton & HA
1987–88 Huddersfield T, Reading, Sheffield U**
1988–89 Shrewsbury T, Birmingham C, Walsall
1989–90 Bournemouth, Bradford C, Stoke C
1990–91 WBA and Hull C
1991–92 Plymouth Arg, Brighton & HA, Port Vale
1992–93 Preston NE, Mansfield T, Wigan Ath, Chester C
1993–94 Fulham, Exeter C, Hartlepool U, Barnet
1994–95 Cambridge U, Plymouth Arg, Cardiff C, Chester C, Leyton Orient
1995–96 Carlisle U, Swansea C, Brighton & HA, Hull C
1996–97 Peterborough U, Shrewsbury T, Rotherham U, Notts Co
1997–98 Brentford, Plymouth Arg, Carlisle U, Southend U
1998–99 York C, Northampton T, Lincoln C, Macclesfield T
1999–2000 Cardiff C, Blackpool, Scunthorpe U, Chesterfield
2000–01 Bristol R, Luton T, Swansea C, Oxford U
2001–02 Bournemouth, Bury, Wrexham, Cambridge U
2002–03 Cheltenham T, Huddersfield T, Mansfield T Northampton T
2003–04 Grimsby T, Rushden & D, Notts Co, Wycombe W

FOOTBALL LEAGUE CHAMPIONSHIP 1 TO FOOTBALL LEAGUE CHAMPIONSHIP 2

2004–05 Torquay U, Wrexham, Peterborough U, Stockport Co
2005–06 Hartlepool U, Milton Keynes D, Swindon T, Walsall
2006–07 Chesterfield, Bradford C, Rotherham U, Brentford
2007–08 Bournemouth, Gillingham, Port Vale, Luton T
2008–09 Northampton T, Crewe Alex, Cheltenham T, Hereford U
2009–10 Gillingham, Wycombe W, Southend U, Stockport Co
2010–11 Dagenham & R, Bristol R, Plymouth Arg, Swindon T
2011–12 Wycombe W, Chesterfield, Exeter C, Rochdale

DIVISION 3 TO DIVISION 4

1958–59 Stockport Co, Doncaster R, Notts Co, Rochdale
1959–60 York C, Mansfield T, Wrexham, Accrington S
1960–61 Tranmere R, Bradford C, Colchester U, Chesterfield
1961–62 Torquay U, Lincoln C, Brentford, Newport Co
1962–63 Bradford PA, Brighton & HA, Carlisle U, Halifax T
1963–64 Millwall, Crewe Alex, Wrexham, Notts Co
1964–65 Luton T, Port Vale, Colchester U, Barnsley
1965–66 Southend U, Exeter C, Brentford, York C
1966–67 Swansea T, Darlington, Doncaster R, Workington
1967–68 Grimsby T, Colchester U, Scunthorpe U, Peterborough U (demoted)
1968–69 Northampton T, Hartlepool, Crewe Alex, Oldham Ath
1969–70 Bournemouth, Southport, Barrow, Stockport Co
1970–71 Reading, Bury, Doncaster R, Gillingham
1971–72 Mansfield T, Barnsley, Torquay U, Bradford C
1972–73 Rotherham U, Brentford, Swansea C, Scunthorpe U
1973–74 Cambridge U, Shrewsbury T, Southport, Rochdale
1974–75 Bournemouth, Tranmere R, Watford, Huddersfield T
1975–76 Aldershot, Colchester U, Southend U, Halifax T
1976–77 Reading, Northampton T, Grimsby T, York C
1977–78 Port Vale, Bradford C, Hereford U, Portsmouth
1978–79 Peterborough U, Walsall, Tranmere R, Lincoln C
1979–80 Bury, Southend U, Mansfield T, Wimbledon
1980–81 Sheffield U, Colchester U, Blackpool, Hull C
1981–82 Wimbledon, Swindon T, Bristol C, Chester
1982–83 Reading, Wrexham, Doncaster R, Chesterfield
1983–84 Scunthorpe U, Southend U, Port Vale, Exeter C
1984–85 Burnley, Orient, Preston NE, Cambridge U
1985–86 Lincoln C, Cardiff C, Wolverhampton W, Swansea C
1986–87 Bolton W**, Carlisle U, Darlington, Newport Co
1987–88 Rotherham U**, Grimsby T, York C, Doncaster R
1988–89 Southend U, Chesterfield, Gillingham, Aldershot
1989–90 Cardiff C, Northampton T, Blackpool, Walsall
1990–91 Crewe Alex, Rotherham U, Mansfield T
1991–92 Bury, Shrewsbury T, Torquay U, Darlington

** *Relegated after play-offs.*

APPLICATIONS FOR RE-ELECTION

FOURTH DIVISION

Eleven: Hartlepool U.
Seven: Crewe Alex.
Six: Barrow (lost League place to Hereford U 1972), Halifax T, Rochdale, Southport (lost League place to Wigan Ath 1978), York C.
Five: Chester C, Darlington, Lincoln C, Stockport Co, Workington (lost League place to Wimbledon 1977).
Four: Bradford PA (lost League place to Cambridge U 1970), Newport Co, Northampton T.
Three: Doncaster R, Hereford U.
Two: Bradford C, Exeter C, Oldham Ath, Scunthorpe U, Torquay U.
One: Aldershot, Colchester U, Gateshead (lost League place to Peterborough U 1960), Grimsby T, Swansea C, Tranmere R, Wrexham, Blackpool, Cambridge U, Preston NE.
Accrington S resigned and Oxford U were elected 1962.
Port Vale were forced to re-apply following expulsion in 1968.
Aldershot expelled March 1992. Maidstone U resigned August 1992.

THIRD DIVISIONS NORTH & SOUTH

Seven: Walsall.
Six: Exeter C, Halifax T, Newport Co.
Five: Accrington S, Barrow, Gillingham, New Brighton, Southport.
Four: Rochdale, Norwich C.
Three: Crystal Palace, Crewe Alex, Darlington, Hartlepool U, Merthyr T, Swindon T.
Two: Aberdare Ath, Aldershot, Ashington, Bournemouth, Brentford, Chester, Colchester U, Durham C, Millwall, Nelson, QPR, Rotherham U, Southend U, Tranmere R, Watford, Workington.
One: Bradford C, Bradford PA, Brighton & HA, Bristol R, Cardiff C, Carlisle U, Charlton Ath, Gateshead, Grimsby T, Mansfield T, Shrewsbury T, Torquay U, York C.

LEAGUE STATUS FROM 1986–87

RELEGATED FROM LEAGUE

1986–87 Lincoln C
1987–88 Newport Co
1988–89 Darlington
1989–90 Colchester U
1990–91 —
1991–92 —
1992–93 Halifax T
1993–94 —
1994–95 —
1995–96 —
1996–97 Hereford U
1997–98 Doncaster R
1998–99 Scarborough
1999–2000 Chester C
2000–01 Barnet
2001–02 Halifax T
2002–03 Shrewsbury T, Exeter C
2003–04 Carlisle U, York C
2004–05 Kidderminster H, Cambridge U
2005–06 Oxford U, Rushden & D
2006–07 Boston U, Torquay U
2007–08 Mansfield T, Wrexham
2008–09 Chester C, Luton T
2009–10 Grimsby T, Darlington
2010–11 Lincoln C, Stockport Co
2011–12 Hereford U, Macclesfield T

PROMOTED TO LEAGUE

1986–87 Scarborough
1987–88 Lincoln C
1988–89 Maidstone U
1989–90 Darlington
1990–91 Barnet
1991–92 Colchester U
1992–93 Wycombe W
1993–94 —
1994–95 —
1995–96 —
1996–97 Macclesfield T
1997–98 Halifax T
1998–99 Cheltenham T
1999–2000 Kidderminster H
2000–01 Rushden & D
2001–02 Boston U
2002–03 Yeovil T, Doncaster R
2003–04 Chester C, Shrewsbury T
2004–05 Barnet, Carlisle U
2005–06 Accrington S, Hereford U
2006–07 Dagenham & R, Morecambe
2007–08 Aldershot T, Exeter C
2008–09 Burton Alb, Torquay U
2009–10 Stevenage B, Oxford U
2010–11 Crawley T, AFC Wimbledon
2011–12 Fleetwood T, York C

LEAGUE ATTENDANCES SINCE 1946–47

Season	*Matches*	*Total*	*Div. 1*	*Div. 2*	*Div. 3 (S)*	*Div. 3 (N)*
1946–47	1848	35,604,606	15,005,316	11,071,572	5,664,004	3,863,714
1947–48	1848	40,259,130	16,732,341	12,286,350	6,653,610	4,586,829
1948–49	1848	41,271,414	17,914,667	11,353,237	6,998,429	5,005,081
1949–50	1848	40,517,865	17,278,625	11,694,158	7,104,155	4,440,927
1950–51	2028	39,584,967	16,679,454	10,780,580	7,367,884	4,757,109
1951–52	2028	39,015,866	16,110,322	11,066,189	6,958,927	4,880,428
1952–53	2028	37,149,966	16,050,278	9,686,654	6,704,299	4,708,735
1953–54	2028	36,174,590	16,154,915	9,510,053	6,311,508	4,198,114
1954–55	2028	34,133,103	15,087,221	8,988,794	5,996,017	4,051,071
1955–56	2028	33,150,809	14,108,961	9,080,002	5,692,479	4,269,367
1956–57	2028	32,744,405	13,803,037	8,718,162	5,622,189	4,601,017
1957–58	2028	33,562,208	14,468,652	8,663,712	6,097,183	4,332,661
		Total	*Div. 1*	*Div. 2*	*Div. 3*	*Div. 4*
1958–59	2028	33,610,985	14,727,691	8,641,997	5,946,600	4,276,697
1959–60	2028	32,538,611	14,391,227	8,399,627	5,739,707	4,008,050
1960–61	2028	28,619,754	12,926,948	7,033,936	4,784,256	3,874,614
1961–62	2015	27,979,902	12,061,194	7,453,089	5,199,106	3,266,513
1962–63	2028	28,885,852	12,490,239	7,792,770	5,341,362	3,261,481
1963–64	2028	28,535,022	12,486,626	7,594,158	5,419,157	3,035,081
1964–65	2028	27,641,168	12,708,752	6,984,104	4,436,245	3,512,067
1965–66	2028	27,206,980	12,480,644	6,914,757	4,779,150	3,032,429
1966–67	2028	28,902,596	14,242,957	7,253,819	4,421,172	2,984,648
1967–68	2028	30,107,298	15,289,410	7,450,410	4,013,087	3,354,391
1968–69	2028	29,382,172	14,584,851	7,382,390	4,339,656	3,075,275
1969–70	2028	29,600,972	14,868,754	7,581,728	4,223,761	2,926,729
1970–71	2028	28,194,146	13,954,337	7,098,265	4,377,213	2,764,331
1971–72	2028	28,700,729	14,484,603	6,769,308	4,697,392	2,749,426
1972–73	2028	25,448,642	13,998,154	5,631,730	3,737,252	2,081,506
1973–74	2027	24,982,203	13,070,991	6,326,108	3,421,624	2,163,480
1974–75	2028	25,577,977	12,613,178	6,955,970	4,086,145	1,992,684
1975–76	2028	24,896,053	13,089,861	5,798,405	3,948,449	2,059,338
1976–77	2028	26,182,800	13,647,585	6,250,597	4,152,218	2,132,400
1977–78	2028	25,392,872	13,255,677	6,474,763	3,332,042	2,330,390
1978–79	2028	24,540,627	12,704,549	6,153,223	3,374,558	2,308,297
1979–80	2028	24,623,975	12,163,002	6,112,025	3,999,328	2,349,620
1980–81	2028	21,907,569	11,392,894	5,175,442	3,637,854	1,701,379
1981–82	2028	20,006,961	10,420,793	4,750,463	2,836,915	1,998,790
1982–83	2028	18,766,158	9,295,613	4,974,937	2,943,568	1,552,040
1983–84	2028	18,358,631	8,711,448	5,359,757	2,729,942	1,557,484
1984–85	2028	17,849,835	9,761,404	4,030,823	2,667,008	1,390,600
1985–86	2028	16,488,577	9,037,854	3,551,968	2,490,481	1,408,274
1986–87	2028	17,379,218	9,144,676	4,168,131	2,350,970	1,715,441
1987–88	2030	17,959,732	8,094,571	5,341,599	2,751,275	1,772,287
1988–89	2036	18,464,192	7,809,993	5,887,805	3,035,327	1,791,067
1989–90	2036	19,445,442	7,883,039	6,867,674	2,803,551	1,891,178
1990–91	2036	19,508,202	8,618,709	6,285,068	2,835,759	1,768,666
1991–92	2064*	20,487,273	9,989,160	5,809,787	2,993,352	1,694,974
		Total	*FA Premier*	*Div. 1*	*Div. 2*	*Div. 3*
1992–93	2028	20,657,327	9,759,809	5,874,017	3,483,073	1,540,428
1993–94	2028	21,683,381	10,644,551	6,487,104	2,972,702	1,579,024
1994–95	2028	21,856,020	11,213,168	6,044,293	3,037,752	1,560,807
1995–96	2036	21,844,416	10,469,107	6,566,349	2,843,652	1,965,308
1996–97	2036	22,783,163	10,804,762	6,931,539	3,195,223	1,851,639
1997–98	2036	24,692,608	11,092,106	8,330,018	3,503,264	1,767,220
1998–99	2036	25,435,542	11,620,326	7,543,369	4,169,697	2,102,150
1999-2000	2036	25,341,090	11,668,497	7,810,208	3,700,433	2,161,952
2000–01	2036	26,030,167	12,472,094	7,909,512	3,488,166	2,160,395
2001–02	2036	27,756,977	13,043,118	8,352,128	3,963,153	2,398,578
2002–03	2036	28,343,386	13,468,965	8,521,017	3,892,469	2,460,935
2003–04	2036	29,197,510	13,303,136	8,772,780	4,146,495	2,975,099
		Total	*FA Premier*	*Championship*	*Championship 1*	*Championship 2*
2004–05	2036	29,245,870	12,878,791	9,612,761	4,270,674	2,483,644
2005–06	2036	29,089,084	12,871,643	9,719,204	4,183,011	2,315,226
2006–07	2036	29,541,949	13,058,115	10,057,813	4,135,599	2,290,422
2007–08	2036	29,914,212	13,708,875	9,397,036	4,412,023	2,396,278
2008–09	2036	29,881,966	13,527,815	9, 877,552	4,171,834	2,304,765
2009–10	2036	30,057,892	12,977,251	9,909,882	5,043,099	2,127,660
2010–11	2036	29,459,105	13,406,990	9,595,236	4,150,547	2,306,332
2011–12	2036	29,454,401	13,148,465	9,784,100	4,091,897	2,429,939

**Figures include matches played by Aldershot.*
Football League official total for their three divisions in 2001–02 was 14,716,162.

ENGLISH LEAGUE ATTENDANCES 2011–12

FA BARCLAYCARD PREMIERSHIP ATTENDANCES

	Average Gate			*Season 2011–12*	
	2010–11	2011–12	+/–%	Highest	Lowest
Arsenal	60,025	60,000	–0.04	60,111	59,643
Aston Villa	37,193	33,873	–8.93	40,053	30,100
Blackburn Rovers	24,999	22,551	–9.79	26,532	18,003
Bolton Wanderers	22,869	23,669	+3.50	26,901	20,028
Chelsea	41,435	41,478	+0.10	41,830	40,651
Everton	36,038	33,228	–7.80	39,517	29,561
Fulham	25,042	25,293	+1.00	25,700	23,555
Liverpool	42,820	44,253	+3.35	45,071	40,106
Manchester City	45,880	47,044	+2.54	48,000	46,321
Manchester United	75,109	75,387	+0.37	75,627	74,719
Newcastle United	47,717	49,935	+4.65	52,389	42,684
Norwich City	25,386	26,605	+4.80	26,819	26,107
Queens Park Rangers	15,635	17,295	+10.62	18,076	15,195
Stoke City	26,858	27,225	+1.37	27,789	26,500
Sunderland	40,011	39,095	–2.29	47,751	32,296
Swansea City	15,507	19,946	+28.63	20,605	18,985
Tottenham Hotspur	35,703	36,026	+0.90	36,274	35,172
West Bromwich Albion	24,682	24,798	+0.47	26,358	22,474
Wigan Athletic	16,812	18,633	+10.83	22,187	15,796
Wolverhampton Wanderers	27,695	25,682	–7.27	27,494	22,657

TOTAL ATTENDANCES: 13,148,465 (380 games)
Average 34,601 (–1.93%)
HIGHEST: 75,627 Manchester U v Wolverhampton W
LOWEST: 15,195 QPR v Bolton W
HIGHEST AVERAGE: 75,387 Manchester U
LOWEST AVERAGE: 17,295 QPR

FOOTBALL LEAGUE: CHAMPIONSHIP ATTENDANCES

	Average Gate			*Season 2011–12*	
	2010–11	2011–12	+/–%	Highest	Lowest
Barnsley	11,855	10,331	–12.86	17,499	8,900
Birmingham City	25,461	19,126	–24.88	25,516	16,253
Blackpool	15,779	12,764	–19.11	14,141	11,414
Brighton & Hove Albion	7,351	20,027	+172.44	20,968	18,412
Bristol City	14,604	13,907	–4.77	19,003	12,017
Burnley	14,930	14,048	–5.91	17,226	12,355
Cardiff City	23,193	22,100	–4.71	25,109	20,366
Coventry City	16,309	15,118	–7.30	22,240	12,054
Crystal Palace	15,390	15,219	–1.11	21,002	11,853
Derby County	25,892	26,020	+0.49	33,010	22,040
Doncaster Rovers	10,258	9,341	–8.94	12,962	7,572
Hull City	21,168	18,790	–11.23	22,676	16,604
Ipswich Town	19,614	18,266	–6.87	24,763	15,650
Leeds United	27,299	23,283	–14.71	33,366	19,469
Leicester City	23,666	23,036	–2.66	27,720	19,806
Middlesbrough	16,268	17,557	+7.92	27,794	14,366
Millwall	12,438	11,484	–7.67	16,085	9,062
Nottingham Forest	23,274	21,578	–7.29	27,356	12,712
Peterborough United	6,449	9,110	+41.26	13,517	6,351
Portsmouth	15,707	15,015	–4.41	19,879	11,261
Reading	17,681	19,219	+8.70	24,026	15,124
Southampton	22,160	26,419	+19.22	32,363	21,014
Watford	13,151	12,703	–3.41	16,314	10,592
West Ham United	33,492	30,923	–7.67	35,000	25,680

TOTAL ATTENDANCES: 9,784,100 (552 games)
Average 17,725 (+1.97%)
HIGHEST: 35,000 West Ham U v Hull C
LOWEST: 6,351 Peterborough U v Cardiff C
HIGHEST AVERAGE: 30,923 West Ham U
LOWEST AVERAGE: 9,110 Peterborough U

Premiership and Football League attendance averages and highest crowd figures for 2011–12 are unofficial.

FOOTBALL LEAGUE: DIVISION 1 ATTENDANCES

	Average Gate			*Season 2011–12*	
	2010–11	2011–12	+/–%	Highest	Lowest
AFC Bournemouth	7,103	5,881	–17.20	8,034	4,563
Brentford	5,172	5,643	+9.11	8,095	4,124
Bury	3,313	3,552	+7.21	6,970	2,072
Carlisle United	5,207	5,247	+0.77	7,721	3,694
Charlton Athletic	15,582	17,401	+11.67	26,749	13,264
Chesterfield	6,972	6,530	–6.34	9,279	5,087
Colchester United	4,246	3,865	–8.97	6,643	2,923
Exeter City	5,393	4,474	–17.04	6,045	3,474
Hartlepool United	2,933	4,960	+69.11	6,800	4,004
Huddersfield Town	13,733	14,144	+2.99	18,646	11,043
Leyton Orient	4,581	4,298	–6.18	6,196	3,258
Milton Keynes Dons	8,512	8,659	+1.73	15,938	6,405
Notts County	6,586	6,807	+3.36	12,410	4,741
Oldham Athletic	4,392	4,432	+0.91	8,032	2,408
Preston North End	11,767	11,820	+0.45	17,518	9,148
Rochdale	3,537	3,108	–12.13	5,361	1,930
Scunthorpe United	5,547	4,339	–21.78	6,047	3,409
Sheffield United	20,632	18,701	–9.36	30,043	15,783
Sheffield Wednesday	17,817	21,336	+19.75	38,082	16,185
Stevenage	2,898	3,558	+22.77	5,351	2,419
Tranmere Rovers	5,467	5,130	–6.16	8,526	4,153
Walsall	3,845	4,274	+11.16	8,603	3,250
Wycombe Wanderers	4,495	4,843	+7.74	7,097	3,259
Yeovil Town	4,291	3,984	–7.15	5,635	3,121

TOTAL ATTENDANCES: 4,070,897 (552 games)
Average 7,375 (–1.92%)
HIGHEST: 38,082 Sheffield W v Wycombe W
LOWEST: 1,930 Rochdale v Exeter C
HIGHEST AVERAGE: 21,336 Sheffield W
LOWEST AVERAGE: 3,108 Rochdale

FOOTBALL LEAGUE: DIVISION 2 ATTENDANCES

	Average Gate			*Season 2011–12*	
	2010–11	2011–12	+/–%	Highest	Lowest
Accrington Stanley	1,867	1,784	–4.45	3,275	1,308
AFC Wimbledon	3,390	4,294	+26.67	4,634	3,678
Aldershot Town	2,487	2,864	+15.16	4,110	1,871
Barnet	2,249	2,265	+0.71	4,422	1,509
Bradford City	11,127	10,171	–8.59	17,014	2,149
Bristol Rovers	6,253	6,035	–3.49	8,427	5,024
Burton Albion	2,947	2,809	–4.68	3,608	1,714
Cheltenham Town	2,980	3,424	+14.9	5,288	2,035
Crawley Town	2,534	3,256	+28.49	4,723	2,184
Crewe Alexandra	4,119	4,124	+0.12	6,919	3,142
Dagenham & Redbridge	2,769	2,090	–24.52	3,259	1,446
Gillingham	5,230	5,146	–1.61	7,750	3,248
Hereford United	2,516	2,553	+1.47	5,143	1,599
Macclesfield Town	1,816	2,229	+22.74	4,214	1,527
Morecambe	2,647	2,141	–19.12	4,025	1,207
Northampton Town	4,604	4,808	+4.43	6,860	3,643
Oxford United	7,277	7,451	+2.39	11,825	5,653
Plymouth Argyle	8,613	6,828	–20.72	12,836	5,018
Port Vale	5,532	4,819	–12.89	6,356	3,714
Rotherham United	3,667	3,498	–4.61	5,368	2,447
Shrewsbury Town	5,875	5,769	–1.80	9,441	4,871
Southend United	5,344	5,999	+12.26	9,782	4,580
Swindon Town	8,457	8,410	–0.56	12,864	6,304
Torquay United	2,630	2,869	+9.09	4,157	2,018

TOTAL ATTENDANCES: 2,429,939 (552 games)
Average 4,402 (+5.36%)
HIGHEST: 17,014 Bradford C v Hereford U
LOWEST: 1,207 Morecambe v Cheltenham T
HIGHEST AVERAGE: 10,171 Bradford C
LOWEST AVERAGE: 1,784 Accrington S

LEAGUE CUP FINALISTS 1961–2012

Played as a two-leg final until 1966. All subsequent finals at Wembley until 2000, then at Millennium Stadium, Cardiff.

Year	*Winners*	*Runners-up*	*Score*
1961	Aston Villa	Rotherham U	0-2, 3-0 (aet)
1962	Norwich C	Rochdale	3-0, 1-0
1963	Birmingham C	Aston Villa	3-1, 0-0
1964	Leicester C	Stoke C	1-1, 3-2
1965	Chelsea	Leicester C	3-2, 0-0
1966	WBA	West Ham U	1-2, 4-1
1967	QPR	WBA	3-2
1968	Leeds U	Arsenal	1-0
1969	Swindon T	Arsenal	3-1 (aet)
1970	Manchester C	WBA	2-1 (aet)
1971	Tottenham H	Aston Villa	2-0
1972	Stoke C	Chelsea	2-1
1973	Tottenham H	Norwich C	1-0
1974	Wolverhampton W	Manchester C	2-1
1975	Aston Villa	Norwich C	1-0
1976	Manchester C	Newcastle U	2-1
1977	Aston Villa	Everton	0-0, 1-1 (aet), 3-2 (aet)
1978	Nottingham F	Liverpool	0-0 (aet), 1-0
1979	Nottingham F	Southampton	3-2
1980	Wolverhampton W	Nottingham F	1-0
1981	Liverpool	West Ham U	1-1 (aet), 2-1

MILK CUP

1982	Liverpool	Tottenham H	3-1 (aet)
1983	Liverpool	Manchester U	2-1 (aet)
1984	Liverpool	Everton	0-0 (aet), 1-0
1985	Norwich C	Sunderland	1-0
1986	Oxford U	QPR	3-0

LITTLEWOODS CUP

1987	Arsenal	Liverpool	2-1
1988	Luton T	Arsenal	3-2
1989	Nottingham F	Luton T	3-1
1990	Nottingham F	Oldham Ath	1-0

RUMBELOWS LEAGUE CUP

1991	Sheffield W	Manchester U	1-0
1992	Manchester U	Nottingham F	1-0

COCA-COLA CUP

1993	Arsenal	Sheffield W	2-1
1994	Aston Villa	Manchester U	3-1
1995	Liverpool	Bolton W	2-1
1996	Aston Villa	Leeds U	3-0
1997	Leicester C	Middlesbrough	1-1 (aet), 1-0 (aet)
1998	Chelsea	Middlesbrough	2-0 (aet)

WORTHINGTON CUP

1999	Tottenham H	Leicester C	1-0
2000	Leicester C	Tranmere R	2-1
2001	Liverpool	Birmingham C	1-1 (aet)
Liverpool won 5-4 on penalties			
2002	Blackburn R	Tottenham H	2-1
2003	Liverpool	Manchester U	2-0

CARLING CUP

2004	Middlesbrough	Bolton W	2-1
2005	Chelsea	Liverpool	3-2 (aet)
2006	Manchester U	Wigan Ath	4-0
2007	Chelsea	Arsenal	2-1
2008	Tottenham H	Chelsea	2-1 (aet)
2009	Manchester U	Tottenham H	0-0 (aet)
Manchester U won 4-1 on penalties			
2010	Manchester U	Aston Villa	2-1
2011	Birmingham C	Arsenal	2-1
2012	Liverpool	Cardiff C	2-2 (aet)
Liverpool won 3-2 on penalties.			

LEAGUE CUP WINS

Liverpool 8, Aston Villa 5, Chelsea 4, Manchester U 4, Nottingham F 4, Tottenham H 4, Leicester C 3, Arsenal 2, Birmingham C 2, Manchester C 2, Norwich C 2, Wolverhampton W 2, Blackburn R 1, Leeds U 1, Luton T 1, Middlesbrough 1, Oxford U 1, QPR 1, Sheffield W 1, Stoke C 1, Swindon T 1, WBA 1.

APPEARANCES IN FINALS

Liverpool 11, Aston Villa 8, Manchester U 8, Arsenal 7, Tottenham H 7, Chelsea 6, Nottingham F 6, Leicester C 5, Norwich C 4, Birmingham C 3, Manchester C 3, Middlesbrough 3, WBA 3, Bolton W 2, Everton 2, Leeds U 2, Luton T 2, QPR 2, Sheffield W 2, Stoke C 2, West Ham U 2, Wolverhampton W 2, Blackburn R 1, Cardiff C 1, Newcastle U 1, Oldham Ath 1, Oxford U 1, Rochdale 1, Rotherham U 1, Southampton 1, Sunderland 1, Swindon T 1, Tranmere R 1, Wigan Ath 1.

APPEARANCES IN SEMI-FINALS

Arsenal 14, Liverpool 14, Aston Villa 13, Tottenham H 13, Manchester U 12, Chelsea 10, West Ham U 8, Manchester C 7, Blackburn R 6, Nottingham F 6, Birmingham C 5, Leeds U 5, Leicester C 5, Middlesbrough 5, Norwich C 5, Bolton W 4, Burnley 4, Crystal Palace 4, Everton 4, Ipswich T 4, Sheffield W 4, WBA 4, QPR 3, Sunderland 3, Swindon T 3, Wolverhampton W 3, Bristol C 2, Cardiff C 2, Coventry C 2, Derby Co 2, Luton T 2, Oxford U 2, Plymouth Arg 2, Southampton 2, Stoke C 2, Tranmere R 2, Watford 2, Wimbledon 2, Blackpool 1, Bury 1, Carlisle U 1, Chester C 1, Huddersfield T 1, Newcastle U 1, Oldham Ath 1, Peterborough U 1, Rochdale 1, Rotherham U 1, Sheffield U 1, Shrewsbury T 1, Stockport Co 1, Walsall 1, Wigan Ath 1, Wycombe W 1.

CARLING CUP 2011–12

■ *Denotes player sent off.*

PRELIMINARY ROUND

Friday, 29 July 2011

Crawley T (1) 3 *(Akpan 38, Torres 53, Tubbs 64)*

AFC Wimbledon (1) 2 *(Moore L 26, Midson 46)* 3204

Crawley T: Kuipers; Hunt, Howell, Bulman, McFadzean, Dempster, Simpson (Smith), Torres, Tubbs (Akinde), Barnett (Wilson), Akpan■.
AFC Wimbledon: Brown; Hatton, Gwillim (Bush), Porter, Stuart, Johnson, Yussuff, Wellard (Moore S), Jolley (Ademeno), Midson, Moore L.

FIRST ROUND

Tuesday, 9 August 2011

Accrington S (0) 0

Scunthorpe U (0) 2 *(Dagnall 82 (pen), Barcham 90)* 1356

Accrington S: Murdoch; Winnard, McIntyre, Long, Miller, Procter, Lindfield (Hessey), Barnett (Murphy), Guthrie (Taylor), Craney, Joyce.
Scunthorpe U: Lillis; Wright, Nolan, Togwell, Nelson, Reid, Ryan (Barcham), Collins, Dagnall (Robertson), Duffy M, Thompson (Grant).

Barnsley (0) 0

Morecambe (0) 2 *(Carlton 49, Ellison 86)* 4331

Barnsley: Steele; Hassell (Wiseman), McEveley, Edwards, McNulty, Butterfield, Addison, O'Brien, Davies (Done), Haynes, Vaz Te (Perkins).
Morecambe: Roche; Haining, Wilson, McDonald, McCready, Fenton, Reid, Drummond, Alessandra (Ellison), Carlton (Parrish), Hunter.

Bournemouth (2) 5 *(Pugh 32, Cooper 35, Feeney 57, Taylor 88, 90)*

Dagenham & R (0) 0 3681

Bournemouth: Flahavan; Byrne, Malone (Cummings), Cooper, Barrett, Gregory, Pugh, Molesley (Ward), Taylor, Fletcher (Stockley), Feeney.
Dagenham & R: Shea; Ogogo, McCrory, Howell, Doe, Arber, Elito (Reed), Ilesanmi, Nurse, Williams (Woodall), Tomlin (Green Danny J).

Brighton & HA (0) 1 *(Barnes 67 (pen))*

Gillingham (0) 0 16,295

Brighton & HA: Ankergren; Calderon, Painter, Bridcutt, Dunk, Greer, Vincelot, Dicker, Barnes, Noone, Buckley.
Gillingham: Flitney; Fuller (Fish), Martin, Lee C (Weston), Lawrence, Frampton, Whelpdale, Payne J, Kedwell, Spiller (Payne S), Montrose.

Burnley (0) 6 *(Rodriguez 57 (pen), 66 (pen), 93, 106, Austin 83, Wallace 91)*

Burton Alb (0) 3 *(Taylor 72, Zola 85, Maghoma 90)* 4069

Burnley: Grant; Trippier, Fox, Bikey, Mee, McCann, Elliott, Marney (Bartley), Rodriguez (Fletcher), Austin (Edgar), Wallace.
Burton Alb: Atkins; Corbett, Webster, Stanton, James, Bolder, Taylor, Maghoma, Richards (Yussuf), Zola (McGrath), Palmer (Phillips).
aet.

Bury (1) 3 *(Bishop 33, Lowe 75, 88)*

Coventry C (1) 1 *(O'Donovan 26)* 2997

Bury: Belford; Jones M, Skarz, Hughes, Sodje, Mozika, Worrall, Schumacher (Sweeney), Lowe (Harrop), Bishop (John-Lewis), Jones A.
Coventry C: Murphy; Christie, Hussey, Cranie, Keogh, Wood (McPake), Bell, Bigirimana, Jutkiewicz, O'Donovan, McSheffrey (Thomas).

Cheltenham T (1) 1 *(Summerfield 29)*

Milton Keynes D (1) 4 *(Baldock S 41, Ibehre 46, Lewington 61, Balanta 64)* 1625

Cheltenham T: Brown; Lowe, Andrew, Pack, Bennett, Elliott, Mohamed, Low (Smikle), Spencer (Duffy), Goulding (Penn), Summerfield.
Milton Keynes D: Martin; Chicksen, Lewington, Potter (Chadwick), MacKenzie, Williams S, Ibehre (Powell), Gleeson, Baldock S, Bowditch, Balanta (O'Shea).

Derby Co (0) 2 *(Maguire 46, Robinson 78)*

Shrewsbury T (3) 3 *(Morgan 16, 37, Collins 34)* 7073

Derby Co: Fielding; Brayford, Kilbane, Maguire, O'Brien, Shackell (Roberts), Croft (Cywka), Pearson, Davies S, Robinson, Davies B.
Shrewsbury T: Smith; Regan, Cansdell-Sherriff, Richards, Sharps, Hazell, Ainsworth, Wroe, Collins (Gornell), Morgan (Grandison), Wright.

Doncaster R (2) 3 *(Brown C 5 (pen), Mason 29, Bennett 59)*

Tranmere R (0) 0 4339

Doncaster R: Woods G; Hird, Spurr, Friend, Naylor (Keegan), Oster, Coppinger, Mason (Baxendale), Brown C (Barnes), Bennett, Gillett.
Tranmere R: fon Williams; Kay, Bakayogo, Weir, Goodison, McChrystal (Raven), Devaney (Akins), Welsh, Tiryaki (Showunmi), McGurk, Robinson.

Exeter C (0) 2 *(Bauza 63, Shephard 90)*

Yeovil T (0) 0 3856

Exeter C: Krysiak; Tully, Golbourne, Dunne, Archibald-Henville, Duffy, Sercombe, Noble, Bignall (Nichols), Logan (Bauza) (McNish), Shephard.
Yeovil T: Steer; Ayling, Jones, Haynes-Brown, Huntington, Wotton, Williams A (Agard), Upson, Fallon (Obika), Williams G, Edgar (MacLean).

Hartlepool U (0) 1 *(Sweeney 80)*

Sheffield U (1) 1 *(Quinn 29)* 2774

Hartlepool U: Flinders; Austin, Horwood, Liddle (Murray), Collins, Hartley, Solano (Luscombe), Sweeney, Nish, Boyd (Poole), Monkhouse.
Sheffield U: Simonsen; Lowton, Lescinel, Montgomery, Collins, Maguire, Mendez-Laing (Slew), Doyle (Philliskirk), Cresswell, Williamson (McAllister), Quinn.
aet; Sheffield U won 4-3 on penalties.

Hereford U (0) 1 *(Arquin 90)*

Brentford (0) 0 1767

Hereford U: Bartlett; Green, Heath, Pell, Purdie, Stam, Lunt, McQuilkin, Fleetwood, Facey (Arquin), Colbeck.
Brentford: Moore; Logan (Alexander), O'Connor, Bean (Weston), Eger, Osborne, Saunders (Reeves), Douglas, Donaldson, MacDonald, Wood.

Hull C (0) 0

Macclesfield T (1) 2 *(Sinclair 17, 59)* 4826

Hull C: Basso; East, Dawson, McKenna, Chester, Hobbs, Devitt, Harper, Simpson, Fryatt, Pusic (Barmby).
Macclesfield T: Veiga; Bateson, Tremarco, Diagne, Brown, Brisley, Chalmers (Hamshaw), Draper, Sinclair (Kay), Tomlinson, Wedgbury.

Ipswich T (1) 1 *(Emmanuel-Thomas 11)*

Northampton T (1) 2 *(Tozer 39, Turnbull 54)* 9401

Ipswich T: Lee-Barrett; Peters, Cresswell, Healy, Ainsley, Smith, Drury (Martin), Hyam (Leadbitter), Emmanuel-Thomas, Scotland, Ellington.
Northampton T: Walker; Ofori-Twumasi, Corker, Turnbull, Westwood, Webster, Davies, Tozer, Jacobs (McKoy), Savage (Langmead), Robinson (Young).

Leeds U (0) 3 *(Nunez 46, 75, McCormack 70)*
Bradford C (1) 2 *(Compton 30, Flynn 57)* 17,667
Leeds U: Lonergan; Connolly (Lees), Parker, Howson, O'Brien (Bromby), Kisnorbo, Nunez, Clayton, McCormack (Taylor), Sam, Brown.
Bradford C: Jansson; Moore, Threlfall, Flynn, Branston, Williams, Mitchell (Hannah), Syers (Jones), Stewart (Rodney), Hanson, Compton.

Nottingham F (1) 3 *(McGugan 30, Findley 56, Morgan 120)*
Notts Co (1) 3 *(Edwards 16, Westcarr 76, Hughes L 98)* 21,605
Nottingham F: Smith; Moloney, Cohen, Chambers, Morgan, Majewski, Anderson (Garner), Greening, Findley, McGugan (Boateng), Reid (Tudgay).
Notts Co: Nelson; Kelly (Westcarr), Sheehan, Edwards, Pearce, Bencherif, Bishop, Ravenhill (Montano), Hughes L, Hawley, Hughes J (Stirling).
aet; Nottingham F won 4-3 on penalties.

Oldham Ath (1) 1 *(Reid 24 (pen))*
Carlisle U (0) 1 *(McGovern 57)* 1786
Oldham Ath: Cisak; Lee, Black, Furman, Diamond (Mellor), M'Voto, Morais (Parker), Wesolowski (Winchester), Reid, Smith, Taylor.
Carlisle U: Collin; Taiwo, Robson, McGovern, Livesey, Murphy, Thirlwell, Berrett, Curran (Loy), Zoko, Noble (Welsh).
aet; Carlisle U won 4-2 on penalties.

Plymouth Arg (0) 0
Millwall (1) 1 *(N'Guessan 14)* 4781
Plymouth Arg: Cole; Soukouna (Copp), Gibson, Walton, Zubar, Nelson, Daley, Hourihane, Sims (Lecointe), Hitchcock, Williams.
Millwall: Mildenhall; Smith, Barron, Racon (Mkandawire), Purse, Craig, Hackett, Abdou, Marquis, N'Guessan (Bouazza), Stewart.

Port Vale (1) 2 *(Roberts 24, Loft 83 (pen))*
Huddersfield T (2) 4 *(Novak 29, 38, Hunt 58, Roberts 67)* 3014
Port Vale: Martin; Yates, Green (McDonald), Griffith, McCombe, Collins, Rigg, Roberts (Williamson), Burge, Pope (Haldane), Loft.
Huddersfield T: Bennett; Hunt, Naysmith, Miller, Cooper, McCombe, Gobern, Arfield, Novak (Lee), McDermott (Ward), Roberts.

Portsmouth (0) 0
Barnet (1) 1 *(Hughes 30)* 4464
Portsmouth: Henderson; Ward, Rocha (Kanu), Mokoena, Halford, Dailly, Lawrence (Williams), Mullins, Kitson, Varney, Norris.
Barnet: Brill; Senda, Parkes, Hughes, Uddin, Kamdjo, Fraser, Byrne, Price, McLeod (Taylor), Marshall (Holmes).

Preston NE (1) 3 *(Tootle 3 (og), Mellor 84, Hume 90)*
Crewe Alex (2) 2 *(Miller 18, Artell 40)* 5401
Preston NE: Turner; McLean, Parry, Alexander, Carlisle, Devine, Clucas (Nicholson), Barton (Mayor), Proctor (Coutts), Mellor, Hume.
Crewe Alex: Phillips; Tootle, Davis, Leitch-Smith (Shelley), Artell, Dugdale, Bell, Powell, Miller, Murphy, Moore.

Rochdale (1) 3 *(Grimes 19, 111, Mattis 103 (og))*
Chesterfield (1) 2 *(Whitaker 11, 95 (pen))* 1718
Rochdale: Lucas; Darby, Widdowson, Holness, Trotman, Tutte, Kennedy (Thompson), Jones, Akpa Akpro, Grimes, Adams.
Chesterfield: Lee; Holden (Lester), Smith, Niven (Clay), Downes, Mattis, Talbot, Allott, Morgan, Boden (Bowery), Whitaker.
aet.

Rotherham U (1) 1 *(Mills 13 (og))*
Leicester C (1) 4 *(Gallagher 36, Schlupp 53, 63, 71)* 3717
Rotherham U: Warrington; Marshall (Tonge), Newey, Harrison, Cresswell, Raynes, Pringle (Evans), Taylor J, Grabban (Holroyd), Le Fondre, Schofield.
Leicester C: Schmeichel; Oakley, Konchesky (Nugent), Moussa (Gelson), Mills, Ball, Johnson (Danns), Schlupp, Gallagher, Waghorn, Dyer.

Southampton (2) 4 *(De Ridder 16, Lambert 27, Chaplow 81, Forte 90)*
Torquay U (1) 1 *(Mansell 17)* 6541
Southampton: Bialkowski; Butterfield, Dickson, Schneiderlin, Martin, Seaborne, De Ridder (Hammond), Chaplow, Lambert, Do Prado (Forte), Holmes (Lallana).
Torquay U: Olejnik; Oastler, Nicholson (Rowe-Turner), Mansell, Robertson, Saah, McPhee (Stevens), O'Kane, Howe, Atieno, Morris (Macklin).

Southend U (1) 1 *(Phillips 32)*
Leyton Orient (1) 1 *(Richardson 23)* 4847
Southend U: Morris; Clohessy, Prosser, Kalala, Coughlan, Phillips (Mohsni), Ferdinand (Grant), Johnson (Sawyer), Harris, Dickinson, Hall.
Leyton Orient: Butcher; Omozusi, Daniels, Chorley, Cuthbert, Smith Jimmy, Spring (Porter), Richardson, Revell (Cureton), Tehoue■, Cox (Forbes).
aet; Leyton Orient won 4-3 on penalties.

Stevenage (1) 3 *(Long 32, Bostwick 80, Beardsley 117)*
Peterborough U (1) 4 *(Ball 16, 65, Boyd 96, Tomlin 120 (pen))* 2414
Stevenage: Julian; Wilson, Charles, Henry, Ashton, Roberts, Bostwick, Edwards (Winn), Harrison (Beardsley), Long (Shroot), Laird.
Peterborough U: Jones; Little, Basey (Alcock), Bennett, Zakuani, Tunnicliffe (Wootton), Rowe, Frecklington, Ball (Taylor), Tomlin, Boyd.
aet.

Walsall (0) 0
Middlesbrough (2) 3 *(Emnes 17, 37, 52 (pen))* 3564
Walsall: Walker; Westlake, Sadler, Butler, Lancashire, Taundry, Gnakpa (Peterlin), Chambers■, Jarvis (Bowerman), Macken (Nicholls), Hurst.
Middlesbrough: Coyne; McMahon, Bennett, Bailey (Park), Hines, McManus, Hoyte, Martin, Emnes (Williams R), Zemmama (Miller), Smallwood.

Wycombe W (2) 3 *(Donnelly 2, Grant 12, Beavon 105)*
Colchester U (2) 3 *(Odejayi 27, Henderson 41, Gillespie 98 (pen))* 1430
Wycombe W: Bull; McCoy, Sandell, Halls, Tunnicliffe, Johnson (Winfield), Harris (Rendell), Harding, Beavon, Donnelly (Ibe), Grant.
Colchester U: Cousins; Wilson, Rose, Izzet, Okuonghae, Heath, O'Toole (James), Wordsworth, Odejayi (Coker), Henderson, Vincent (Gillespie).
aet; Wycombe W won 5-4 on penalties.

Wednesday, 10 August 2011

Oxford U (1) 1 *(Clist 30)*
Cardiff C (1) 3 *(Conway 12, Whittingham 98, Jarvis 120)* 5435
Oxford U: Clarke; Batt, Davis, Clist (Leven), Duberry, Wright, Whing, Hall A, Constable, Pittman (Guy), Potter (Smalley).
Cardiff C: Heaton; Naylor, Quinn, Farah, Evans, Gyepes, Taiwo (Whittingham), Taylor (Ralls), Gestede (Jarvis), Parkin, Conway.
aet.

Thursday, 11 August 2011

Sheffield W (0) 0
Blackpool (0) 0 5240
Sheffield W: O'Donnell; Otsemobor, Reynolds, O'Connor, Beevers, Johnson R, Coke, Nyoni, Uchechi (Tumilty), Madine (Morrison C), Jones D (Palmer).
Blackpool: Halstead; Basham (Llera), Harris, Angel, Hill, Eastham■, Eardley, Sylvestre, Ince (Barkhuizen), Sutherland (Bruna), Clarke.
aet; Sheffield W won 4-2 on penalties.

Tuesday, 23 August 2011

Bristol R (1) 1 *(Harrold 5)*

Watford (1) 1 *(Sordell 2)* 4432

Bristol R: Bevan; Anthony, Brown L, Virgo, Bolger (Smith), Stanley, Zebroski (Carayol), Gill, Harrold (Brown W), McGleish, Osei-Kuffour.
Watford: Gilmartin; Doyley, Dickinson, Eustace, Mirfin, Mariappa, Yeates (Massey), Walker (Buaben), Sordell, Deeney, Forsyth.
aet; Bristol R won 4-2 on penalties.

Charlton Ath (1) 2 *(Benson 25, Euell 64)*

Reading (0) 1 *(Morrison 73)* 6668

Charlton Ath: Hamer; Francis, Hughes, Pritchard, Doherty (Morrison), Mambo, Green, Izquiredo (Solly), Benson (Wagstaff), Euell, Evina.
Reading: McCarthy; Cummings, Harte (Mills), Howard, Morrison, Khumalo, Tabb, Obita (Robson-Kanu), Manset, Church, McAnuff.

Crystal Palace (0) 2 *(Zaha 54, 58)*

Crawley T (0) 0 8901

Crystal Palace: Price; Ramage (McCarthy), Parsons, Dorman, Davies, Moxey (Parr), Ambrose, O'Keefe, Andrew, Zaha, Williams (Murray).
Crawley T: Shearer; Hunt, Howell, Akpan (Neilson), McFadzean, Wassmer, Davies (Wilson), Torres, Tubbs (Thomas), Barnett, Simpson.

Wednesday, 24 August 2011

Bristol C (0) 0

Swindon T (0) 1 *(De Vita 71)* 7708

Bristol C: Gerken (James); Spence, McAllister, Wilson, Nyatanga, Skuse, Campbell-Ryce (Adomah), Kilkenny, Taylor, Pitman, Woolford (Stead).
Swindon T: Smith P; Caddis, Kennedy, Flint, Devera, Smith J (McCormack), Ritchie, Ferry, Connell (De Vita), Clarke (Magera), Gabilondo.

West Ham U (1) 1 *(Stanislas 16)*

Aldershot T (0) 2 *(Guttridge 78, Hylton 89)* 19,879

West Ham U: Boffin; Faubert, Reid, Nolan, McNaughton■, McCartney, Sears, Barrera (Taylor), Carew (Ilunga), Piquionne (Nouble), Stanislas.
Aldershot T: Young; Herd, Straker, Guttridge, Jones, Morris, Vincenti (McGlashan), Collins J, Hylton (Pulis), Taylor (Rankine), Rodman.

SECOND ROUND

Tuesday, 23 August 2011

Aston Villa (0) 2 *(Lichaj 80, Delfouneso 88)*

Hereford U (0) 0 21,058

Aston Villa: Guzan; Lichaj, Herd (Beye), Makoun, Dunne, Clark, Albrighton, Bannan, Bent (Weimann), N'Zogbia (Delfouneso), Ireland.
Hereford U: Cornell; Williams, Heath, Pell, Green, Townsend, Colbeck, Featherstone, Fleetwood (John), Facey (Arquin), McQuilkin (Lunt).

Bournemouth (0) 1 *(Lovell 48)*

WBA (2) 4 *(Thomas 7, Fortune 42, 78, Cox 53)* 6911

Bournemouth: Flahavan; Byrne, Malone, Cooper, Barrett, Arter, Pugh, Molesley (Baudry), Taylor (Stockley), Lovell (Purches), Feeney.
WBA: Fulop; Jones, Dawson, Thorne (Mantom), Cech, McAuley, Jara, Thomas (Mattock), Fortune (Bednar), Cox, Dorrans.

Brighton & HA (0) 1 *(Mackail-Smith 96)*

Sunderland (0) 0 17,090

Brighton & HA: Ankergren; Calderon, Painter, Bridcutt, Greer (Vincelot) (Taricco), Dunk, Harley (LuaLua), Navarro, Barnes, Mackail-Smith, Noone.
Sunderland: Westwood; Elmohamady, Richardson, Ferdinand, Brown, Cattermole (Wickham), Larsson, Colback, Vaughan (Ji), Sessegnon, Gardner (Gyan).
aet.

Burnley (1) 3 *(Rodriguez 38, Elliott 64, McCann 105)*

Barnet (0) 2 *(Kabba 73, Holmes 90)* 4273

Burnley: Grant; Trippier, Easton, Duff (Edgar), Mee, Marney, Elliott, Treacy (McCann), Rodriguez, Austin (Hines), Wallace.
Barnet: Brill; Senda, Parkes, Hughes, Uddin (Geohaghon), Kamdjo, Deering (Holmes), Byrne, Price (Kabba), McLeod, Marshall.
aet.

Bury (1) 2 *(Jones M 40, Lowe 53)*

Leicester C (1) 4 *(Schlupp 21, Gallagher 70, Dyer 77, Danns 90)* 3779

Bury: Belford; Picken (McCarthy), Skarz, Jones A, Sodje, Sweeney, Worrall, Mozika, Lowe, John-Lewis, Jones M (Oyenuga).
Leicester C: Weale; Peltier, Ball, Moussa (King), Mills, St Ledger-Hall, Abe, Oakley, Gallagher (Gelson), Schlupp (Danns), Dyer.

Cardiff C (2) 5 *(Gyepes 16, Parkin 17, Cowie 90, 117, Conway 96)*

Huddersfield T (0) 3 *(Rhodes 53, 88, Ward 70)* 6829

Cardiff C: Heaton; Keinan, Quinn, Blake, Naylor (Taylor), Gyepes, Cowie, Ralls (Whittingham), Gestede, Parkin (Miller), Conway.
Huddersfield T: Bennett; Hunt, Naysmith, Miller, Clarke P, McCombe, McDermott (Roberts), Robinson (Gobern), Rhodes, Novak (Lee), Ward.
aet.

Doncaster R (1) 1 *(Hayter 2)*

Leeds U (1) 2 *(Nunez 30, 83)* 8505

Doncaster R: Woods G; Dumbuya, Hird, Friend, Naylor (O'Connor), Oster, Gillett (Stock), Barnes (Wilson), Hayter, Bennett, Spurr.
Leeds U: Rachubka; Connolly, White (Taylor), Howson, O'Brien (Kisnorbo), O'Dea, Sam, Thompson, Keogh, McCormack (Gradel), Nunez.

Millwall (2) 2 *(Bouazza 34, Mkandawire 45)*

Morecambe (0) 0 3443

Millwall: Mildenhall; Dunne, Stewart, Mkandawire, Craig, Ward, Hackett (Henry), Abdou, Marquis, McQuoid, Bouazza (Barron).
Morecambe: Roche; Parrish, Wilson, McDonald, Haining, Charnock, Reid, Hunter (Jevons), Alessandra, Carlton (Drummond), Ellison (Parkinson).

Northampton T (0) 0

Wolverhampton W (2) 4 *(Ebanks-Blake 31, 77, Milijas 37, Vokes 88)* 5512

Northampton T: Walker; Johnson, Corker, Turnbull, Langmead, Webster, Young, Tozer (Jacobs), Davies (McKoy), Akinfenwa (Salihu), Robinson.
Wolverhampton W: De Vries; Doherty, Reckord, Milijas, Elokobi, Craddock, Kightly, Foley (Davis), Ebanks-Blake (Griffiths), Vokes, Hammill (Forde).

Norwich C (0) 0

Milton Keynes D (2) 4 *(Chadwick 21, 60, Baldock S 28, Powell 67)* 13,009

Norwich C: Rudd; Martin R, Drury, Smith, Ayala (De Laet), Whitbread (Lappin), Surman, Fox, Wilbraham, Jackson, Hoolahan (Morison).
Milton Keynes D: Martin; Smith Adam, Lewington, Potter, MacKenzie, Williams S, Ibehre (Balanta), Gleeson, Baldock S (O'Shea), Bowditch (Powell), Chadwick.

QPR (0) 0

Rochdale (1) 2 *(Akpa Akpro 5, Jones 81)* 4755

QPR: Murphy; Orr (Harriman), Connolly, Andrade, Shittu, Perone, Rowlands (Derry), Taarabt, Cook (Hewitt), Bothroyd, Ephraim.
Rochdale: Lucas; Darby, Widdowson, Holness, Balkestein, Tutte, Kennedy, Jones, Akpa Akpro, Grimes (Thompson), Adams.

Shrewsbury T (1) 3 *(Morgan 19, Wright 67, Wroe 90)*

Swansea C (1) 1 *(Cansdell-Sherriff 10 (og))* 4063

Shrewsbury T: Smith; Grandison (Goldson), Jacobson, McAllister S, Sharps, Cansdell-Sherriff, Ainsworth, Wroe, Gornell, Morgan (Collins), Wright.
Swansea C: Moreira; Alfei, Walsh (Taylor), Allen, Tate, Williams, Orlandi (Dobbie), Lita, Moore (Sinclair), Graham, Gower.

Wycombe W (0) 1 *(Benyon 66 (pen))*

Nottingham F (2) 4 *(Miller 3, McGugan 6 (pen), Findley 62, Majewski 75)* 2866

Wycombe W: Bull; McCoy, Foster, Lewis (Harris), Winfield, Johnson, Betsy, Bloomfield, Benyon, Rendell (Harding), Grant (Ibe).
Nottingham F: Camp; Gunter, Lynch, Chambers, Morgan, Majewski, McGugan (Freeman), Greening, Miller (Garner), Findley (Tudgay), Cohen.

Wednesday, 24 August 2011

Blackburn R (3) 3 *(Rochina 3, 4, Goodwillie 7)*

Sheffield W (0) 1 *(Morrison C 50)* 8607

Blackburn R: Bunn; Emerton, Martin Olsson, Nzonzi (Dunn), Givet, Hanley (Lowe), Rochina (Hoilett), Petrovic, Goodwillie, Formica, Pedersen.
Sheffield W: O'Donnell; Otsemobor (Lines), Reynolds, Batth, Johnson R, O'Connor, Sedgwick, Coke, Uchechi, Madine (Morrison C), Palmer.

Bolton W (0) 2 *(Tuncay 56, Petrov 73)*

Macclesfield T (1) 1 *(Sinclair 11)* 6777

Bolton W: Bogdan; Riley, Alonso (Blakeman), Pratley, Knight, Wheater, Eagles (Davies K), Davies M, Blake, Tuncay, Petrov (O'Halloran).
Macclesfield T: Veiga; Hewitt, Tremarco, Kay, Brown, Brisley, Chalmers (Mendy), Draper, Sinclair (Mukendi), Diagne, Wedgbury (Hamshaw).

Everton (3) 3 *(Cresswell 31 (og), Anichebe 37, Arteta 42)*

Sheffield U (1) 1 *(Cresswell 28)* 17,173

Everton: Mucha; Hibbert, Baines, Rodwell (Saha), Heitinga, Jagielka, Barkley (Neville), Fellaini, Anichebe, Osman (Baxter), Arteta.
Sheffield U: Simonsen; Lowton, Lescinel, Doyle, Collins, Maguire, Flynn (Porter), Williamson, Cresswell (Bogdanovic), Harriott (McAllister), Quinn.

Exeter C (0) 1 *(Nardiello 80 (pen))*

Liverpool (1) 3 *(Suarez 23, Rodriguez 55, Carroll 58)* 8290

Exeter C: Krysiak; Jones, Coles (Nichols), Dunne, Archibald-Henville, Duffy, Shephard (McNish), Noble, Bauza (Keohane), Nardiello, Golbourne.
Liverpool: Reina; Flanagan, Robinson, Wilson, Skrtel, Adam (Shelvey), Henderson, Spearing, Suarez (Downing), Raul Meireles (Carroll), Rodriguez.

Peterborough U (0) 0

Middlesbrough (2) 2 *(Robson 4, Hines 27)* 5012

Peterborough U: Jones; Little, Alcock (Tunnicliffe), Bennett, Wootton, McCann (Gordon), Rowe, Frecklington, Taylor (Ball), Tomlin, Boyd.
Middlesbrough: Coyne; McMahon, Hines, Bailey, Bates, McManus, Robson (Smallwood), Haroun, Emnes (Williams R), Martin (Arca), Bennett.

Thursday, 25 August 2011

Scunthorpe U (1) 1 *(Dagnall 15)*

Newcastle U (0) 2 *(Taylor R 80, Sammy Ameobi 112)* 4408

Scunthorpe U: Lillis; Wright, Nolan, Togwell, Nelson, Canavan, Ryan, Norwood, Dagnall (Duffy M), Grant (Thompson), Barcham.
Newcastle U: Krul; Simpson, Taylor R, Cabaye, Coloccini, Williamson (Taylor S), Marveaux, Gosling (Vuckic), Best, Ba (Sammy Ameobi), Lovenkrands.
aet.

Tuesday, 30 August 2011

Aldershot T (1) 2 *(Rankine 45, Livesey 75 (og))*

Carlisle U (0) 0 2809

Aldershot T: Worner; Herd, Straker, Guttridge, Jones, Morris, Vincenti (Pulis), Collins J, Rankine, Hylton (Mekki), Rodman (McGlashan).
Carlisle U: Collin; Berrett, Robson, McGovern (Loy), Livesey, O'Halloran, Taiwo, Noble, Curran, Zoko, Welsh (Thirlwell).

Leyton Orient (2) 3 *(Mooney 18, Chorley 23 (pen), Dawson 90)*

Bristol R (0) 2 *(Zebroski 69, Richards 90)* 1881

Leyton Orient: Button; Cuthbert (Laird), Daniels, Chorley, Forbes, Smith Jimmy, McSweeney (Omozusi), Dawson, Mooney (Tehoue), Cureton, Cox.
Bristol R: Bevan; Smith, Brown L, Virgo (Woodards), Anthony, Stanley, Brown W, Gill (Campbell), Zebroski, McGleish, Carayol (Richards).

Swindon T (0) 1 *(Kerrouche 84)*

Southampton (2) 3 *(Do Prado 17, Forte 30, Lambert 90)* 7452

Swindon T: Smith P; Caddis, Kennedy, Flint, Comazzi, Smith J, Ritchie, Ferry (McCormack), Connell (Kerrouche), Clarke, Gabilondo (Esajas).
Southampton: Bialkowski; Richardson, Harding, Cork, Seaborne, Martin, Holmes (Hammond), Schneiderlin, Do Prado (Hoskins), Forte (Lambert), Lallana.

Tuesday, 13 September 2011

Charlton Ath (0) 0

Preston NE (1) 2 *(Russell 11, Mayor 67)* 5130

Charlton Ath: Sullivan; Francis (Wagstaff), Evina, Pritchard, Doherty, Cort, Green (Popo), Hughes, Benson (Mambo), Euell, Izquiredo.
Preston NE: Arestidou; Clucas, Parry, Ashbee, Carlisle, Morgan, Mayor, Coutts, Tsoumou, Russell, Barton (Zibaka).

Crystal Palace (2) 2 *(Ambrose 24, Williams 30)*

Wigan Ath (0) 1 *(Watson 90)* 7649

Crystal Palace: Price; Ramage (Marrow), Moxey, Tunchev, McCarthy, Wright, Ambrose (Dorman), O'Keefe, Zaha, Murray, Williams (Jedinak).
Wigan Ath: Al Habsi; McArthur (Dicko), Figueroa, McCarthy, Van Aanholt, Piscu, Thomas (Watson), Maloney, Sammon, Crusat (McManaman), Jones.

THIRD ROUND

Tuesday, 20 September 2011

Aldershot T (0) 2 *(Rankine 47, Hylton 78)*

Rochdale (1) 1 *(Grimes 45)* 3334

Aldershot T: Worner; Herd, Brown J, Guttridge, Jones, Morris, McGlashan (Vincenti), Collins J, Rankine, Hylton, Rodman.
Rochdale: Edwards; Darby, Widdowson, Holness, Balkestein, Tutte (Barnes-Homer), Kennedy (Barry-Murphy), Jones, Akpa Akpro (Thompson), Grimes, Adams.

Arsenal (1) 3 *(Gibbs 33, Oxlade-Chamberlain 58, Benayoun 78)*

Shrewsbury T (1) 1 *(Collins 16)* 46,539

Arsenal: Fabianski; Jenkinson, Gibbs, Frimpong (Ozyakup), Djourou, Miquel, Benayoun, Coquelin, Chamakh, Park (Miyaichi), Oxlade-Chamberlain (Aneke).
Shrewsbury T: Smith; Grandison, Jacobson, McAllister S (Richards), Hazell, Goldson, Ainsworth (Taylor J), Wroe, Collins (Bradshaw), Morgan, Wright.

Aston Villa (0) 0

Bolton W (0) 2 *(Eagles 54, Kakuta 77)* 22,261

Aston Villa: Given; Hutton, Warnock, Collins, Dunne, Petrov, Albrighton (N'Zogbia), Bannan, Agbonlahor, Delfouneso, Ireland.
Bolton W: Bogdan; Steinsson (Robinson), Gardner, Muamba (Davies M), Cahill, Wheater, Eagles, Holden, N'Gog (Davies K), Kakuta, Pratley.

Blackburn R (1) 3 *(Roberts 44 (pen), Rochina 71, Vukcevic 75)*

Leyton Orient (0) 2 *(Mooney 64, Cox 86)* 7104

Blackburn R: Bunn; Lowe, Martin Olsson, Petrovic, Givet, Hanley, Vukcevic (Formica), Grella, Roberts, Blackman (Hoilett), Rochina (Yakubu).
Leyton Orient: Butcher; Omozusi, Daniels (Cestor), Chorley, Forbes, Smith Jimmy (Laird), Spring, Clarke, Mooney (McSweeney), Porter, Cox.

Burnley (0) 2 *(Trippier 59, Bikey 89)*

Milton Keynes D (1) 1 *(Powell 6)* 4134

Burnley: Grant; Trippier, Easton, Bikey, Edgar, Bartley, Wallace, Marney (McCann), Rodriguez, Hines (Austin), Treacy.
Milton Keynes D: Martin; Chicksen, Lewington, Baldock G, Flanagan, Williams S, Powell, Potter (McNamee), Bowditch (Collins), Ibehre, Chadwick.

Crystal Palace (1) 2 *(Zaha 18, Andrew 52)*

Middlesbrough (0) 1 *(Zemmama 55)* 5448

Crystal Palace: Price; Marrow, Moxey, O'Keefe, McCarthy, Gardner, Zaha (Scannell), Williams (Ramage), Andrew, Murray (Iversen), Parr.
Middlesbrough: Coyne; McMahon (Bates), Hoyte, Smallwood (Emnes), Williams R, McManus, Zemmama, Thomson, Nimely, McDonald, Arca (Haroun).

Leeds U (0) 0

Manchester U (3) 3 *(Owen 15, 32, Giggs 45)* 31,031

Leeds U: Lonergan; Lees, White, Howson, O'Dea, Bromby, Clayton, McCormack (Nunez), Keogh (Vayrynen), Becchio (Forssell), Snodgrass.
Manchester U: Amos; Valencia, Fabio, Biram Diouf (Welbeck), Fryers, Carrick, Park, Macheda (Cole), Berbatov, Owen, Giggs (Pogba).

Nottingham F (0) 3 *(Findley 46, Derbyshire 66, Tudgay 114)*

Newcastle U (1) 4 *(Lovenkrands 39, 60 (pen), Simpson 93, Coloccini 120)* 10,208

Nottingham F: Camp; Gunter, Moloney, Moussi (Majewski), Morgan, Lynch, McGugan (Reid), Greening, Findley, Derbyshire (Miller), Tudgay.
Newcastle U: Elliot; Simpson, Ferguson, Gosling (Sammy Ameobi), Coloccini, Perch, Abeid, Guthrie, Ben Arfa (Shola Ameobi), Lovenkrands (Obertan), Marveaux.
aet.

Stoke C (0) 0

Tottenham H (0) 0 15,023

Stoke C: Sorensen; Shotton, Wilson, Huth, Upson, Palacios (Diao), Pennant, Whelan, Jones (Crouch), Jerome (Walters), Etherington.
Tottenham H: Gomes; Corluka, Assou-Ekotto, Livermore, Kaboul, Bassong, Carroll, Sandro (Luongo), Pavlyuchenko, Van der Vaart (Defoe), Giovani (Townsend).
aet; Stoke C won 7-6 on penalties.

Wolverhampton W (3) 5 *(Edwards 3, Hammill 7, Elokobi 38, Spray 77, Guedioura 88)*

Millwall (0) 0 7749

Wolverhampton W: De Vries; Doherty, Elokobi, Milijas, Berra, Stearman, Guedioura, Edwards (Kightly), Vokes, Hunt (Spray), Hammill (Jarvis).
Millwall: Mildenhall; Smith, Stewart, Dunne, Craig, Ward, Henry, Abdou, Marquis, N'Guessan (O'Brien), Bouazza (Barron).

Wednesday, 21 September 2011

Brighton & HA (0) 1 *(Barnes 90 (pen))*

Liverpool (1) 2 *(Bellamy 7, Kuyt 81)* 21,897

Brighton & HA: Ankergren; Calderon, Vincelot, Bridcutt, Cook, Greer, Sparrow (Barnes), Navarro (LuaLua), Buckley (Vicente), Mackail-Smith, Noone.
Liverpool: Reina; Kelly (Flanagan), Robinson, Carragher, Coates, Spearing, Kuyt, Lucas, Suarez (Gerrard), Bellamy, Rodriguez.

Cardiff C (1) 2 *(Cowie 33, Gestede 82)*

Leicester C (1) 2 *(Howard 40, Dyer 66)* 8697

Cardiff C: Marshall; Blake, Taylor (Naylor), Mason (Conway), Quinn, Keinan, Cowie, McPhail (Gunnarsson), Gestede, Earnshaw, Kiss.
Leicester C: Weale; Pantsil, Ball, Danns, Mills (Peltier), St Ledger-Hall, Johnson (Abe), Moussa (Gelson), Howard, Schlupp, Dyer.
aet; Cardiff C won 7-6 on penalties.

Chelsea (0) 0

Fulham (0) 0 37,632

Chelsea: Cech (Turnbull); Paulo Ferreira, Bertrand, Romeu, David Luiz, Alex■, McEachran (Terry), Lukaku, Kalou, Sturridge (Lampard), Malouda.
Fulham: Schwarzer; Kelly, Grygera, Frei, Baird, Senderos, Gecov (Sidwell), Briggs, Sa (Dembele), Kasami (Zamora), Ruiz.
aet; Chelsea won 4-3 on penalties.

Everton (0) 2 *(Fellaini 89, Neville 103)*

WBA (0) 1 *(Brunt 57 (pen))* 17,647

Everton: Mucha; Neville, Baines, Rodwell, Heitinga, Jagielka, Coleman (Gueye), Barkley (Vellios), Drenthe, Fellaini, Stracqualursi (Cahill).
WBA: Fulop; Jones, Mattock, Thorne (Scharner), McAuley, Olsson (Dawson), Dorrans, Tchoyi, Odemwingie, Cox (Morrison), Brunt.
aet.

Manchester C (2) 2 *(Hargreaves 17, Balotelli 38)*

Birmingham C (0) 0 25,070

Manchester C: Pantilimon; Onuoha, Bridge (Rekik), Razak (Scapuzzi), Toure K, Savic, Zabaleta, Hargreaves (Milner), Balotelli, Tevez, Kolarov.
Birmingham C: Doyle; Spector, Murphy, N'Daw, Davies, Pablo, Burke, Fahey (Gomis), Redmond (King), Rooney (Zigic), Beausejour.

Southampton (1) 2 *(Hooiveld 27, Lallana 66)*

Preston NE (0) 1 *(Barton 51)* 7414

Southampton: Bialkowski; Butterfield, Dickson, Schneiderlin, Martin, Hooiveld (Fonte), Holmes, Chaplow, De Ridder (Lallana), Forte (Lambert), Reeves.
Preston NE: Arestidou; Clucas (Mellor), Smith (Carlisle), Ashbee, Morgan, Wright, Daley (Gray), Russell, Tsoumou, Barton, Mayor.

FOURTH ROUND

Tuesday, 25 October 2011

Aldershot T (0) 0

Manchester U (2) 3 *(Berbatov 15, Owen 41, Valencia 48)* 7044

Aldershot T: Worner; Herd, Straker, Guttridge, Jones, Morris, McGlashan, Vincenti (Collins J), Rankine (Smith A), Hylton, Rodman (Bubb).
Manchester U: Amos; Fabio, Fryers (Keane M), Cleverley (Pogba), Jones, Vidic, Valencia, Park, Berbatov, Owen, Biram Diouf (Morrison).

Arsenal (0) 2 *(Arshavin 53, Park 56)*

Bolton W (0) 1 *(Muamba 47)* 56,628

Arsenal: Fabianski; Yennaris, Miquel, Coquelin, Vermaelen (Boateng), Squillaci, Benayoun, Frimpong (Ozyakup), Park, Arshavin, Oxlade-Chamberlain (Miyaichi).
Bolton W: Bogdan; Steinsson, Gardner, Muamba, Cahill, Knight, Pratley (N'Gog), Davies M, Klasnic, Kakuta (Eagles), Tuncay (Blake).

Cardiff C (1) 1 *(Mason 40)*

Burnley (0) 0 11,601

Cardiff C: Heaton; McNaughton, Taylor, Gunnarsson, Hudson, Gerrard, Cowie, McPhail, Mason, Whittingham, Conway (Kiss).
Burnley: Grant; Trippier, Easton, Edgar, Mee, McCann (Wallace), Treacy (Austin), Marney, Rodriguez, Hines, MacDonald (Bartley).

Crystal Palace (0) 2 *(Ambrose 73, Easter 82 (pen))*
Southampton (0) 0 11,865

Crystal Palace: Price; Clyne, Moxey, O'Keefe, McCarthy, Ramage, Parr (Zaha), Dikgacoi, Ambrose (Jedinak), Easter, Williams (Gardner).
Southampton: Bialkowski; Butterfield, Harding, Schneiderlin, Martin, Reeves (Do Prado), De Ridder, Ward-Prowse, Forte (Barnard), Cork, Holmes (Lambert).

Wednesday, 26 October 2011

Blackburn R (1) 4 *(Rochina 5, Yakubu 64 (pen), Pedersen 99, Givet 120)*
Newcastle U (0) 3 *(Guthrie 89, Cabaye 90, Lovenkrands 105 (pen))* 10,682

Blackburn R: Bunn; Lowe, Martin Olsson, Petrovic, Givet, Samba, Rochina (Vukcevic), Hoilett (Hanley), Yakubu (Formica), Goodwillie, Pedersen.
Newcastle U: Krul; Simpson (Sammy Ameobi), Santon, Cabaye, Coloccini, Perch, Marveaux (Obertan), Guthrie, Ba, Ben Arfa (Lovenkrands), Gutierrez.
aet.

Everton (0) 1 *(Saha 83)*
Chelsea (1) 2 *(Kalou 38, Sturridge 116)* 23,170

Everton: Mucha; Neville (Hibbert), Baines, Rodwell (Stracqualursi), Distin, Heitinga, Bilyaletdinov (Coleman), Fellaini, Saha, Drenthe■, Cahill.
Chelsea: Turnbull■; Ivanovic, Bertrand, Romeu, Alex, David Luiz, Lukaku (Cech), McEachran (Mikel), Anelka, Kalou (Sturridge), Malouda.
aet.

Stoke C (1) 1 *(Jones 44)*
Liverpool (0) 2 *(Suarez 54, 85)* 24,934

Stoke C: Sorensen; Huth, Wilson, Whelan, Shawcross, Woodgate, Shotton (Pennant), Delap, Jones (Crouch), Walters, Etherington (Jerome).
Liverpool: Reina; Kelly, Agger, Spearing, Carragher (Skrtel), Coates, Henderson, Lucas, Carroll, Suarez (Kuyt), Rodriguez (Bellamy).

Wolverhampton W (1) 2 *(Milijas 18, O'Hara 65)*
Manchester C (3) 5 *(Johnson A 37, Nasri 39, Dzeko 40, 64, De Vries 50 (og))* 12,436

Wolverhampton W: De Vries; Doherty, Ward, Edwards (Henry), Craddock, Elokobi, Guedioura, Milijas (Hammill), Doyle (O'Hara), Vokes, Hunt.
Manchester C: Pantilimon; Zabaleta, Kolarov, De Jong, Toure K, Savic, Razak (Milner), Scapuzzi (Rekik), Dzeko, Johnson A, Nasri (Suarez).

QUARTER-FINALS

Tuesday, 29 November 2011

Arsenal (0) 0
Manchester C (0) 1 *(Aguero 83)* 60,028

Arsenal: Fabianski; Djourou, Miquel (Vermaelen), Coquelin, Squillaci, Koscielny, Benayoun, Frimpong, Chamakh, Park (Gervinho), Oxlade-Chamberlain (Arshavin).
Manchester C: Pantilimon; Zabaleta, Savic, De Jong, Toure K, Onuoha, Nasri, Hargreaves (Razak), Kolarov (Aguero), Dzeko, Johnson A.

Cardiff C (1) 2 *(Miller 19, Gerrard 50)*
Blackburn R (0) 0 19,436

Cardiff C: Heaton; McNaughton, Taylor, Gunnarsson, Gerrard, Turner, Cowie, Whittingham, Miller, Kiss (McPhail), Conway (Ralls).
Blackburn R: Bunn; Lowe, Givet, Dunn, Dann, Hanley, Petrovic (Rochina), Blackman (Yakubu), Goodwillie (Roberts), Formica, Pedersen.

Chelsea (0) 0
Liverpool (0) 2 *(Rodriguez 58, Kelly 63)* 40,511

Chelsea: Turnbull; Bosingwa, Bertrand, Romeu, Alex, David Luiz, McEachran (Ramires), Lampard, Torres, Lukaku (Mata), Malouda (Anelka).
Liverpool: Reina; Kelly, Jose Enrique, Spearing, Carragher, Coates, Henderson, Lucas (Adam), Carroll, Bellamy (Kuyt), Rodriguez (Skrtel).

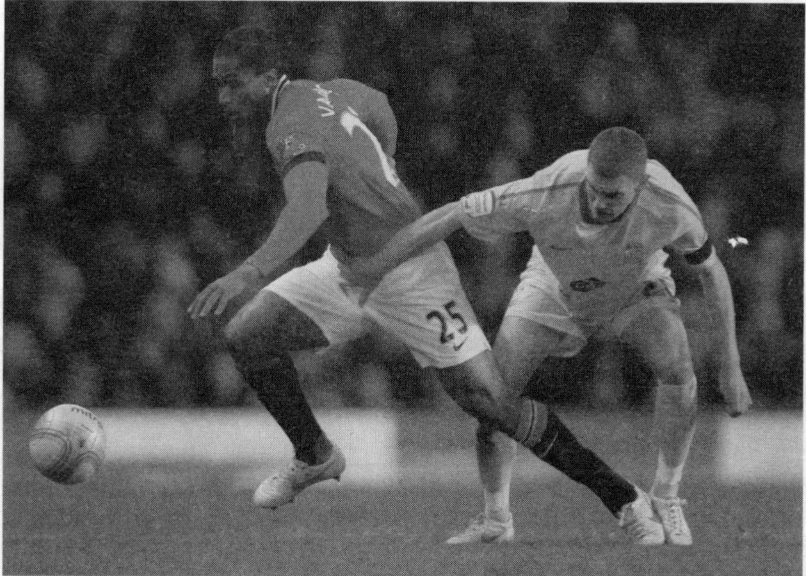

Manchester United's Antonio Valencia skips past Crystal Palace's Stuart O'Keefe in their Carling Cup quarter-final tie at Old Trafford at the end of November. Palace sprung a major surprise by winning 2-1 after extra time. (Action Images/Jason Cairnduff)

Wednesday, 30 November 2011

Manchester U (0) 1 *(Macheda 69 (pen))*

Crystal Palace (0) 2 *(Ambrose 65, Murray 98)* 52,624

Manchester U: Amos; Rafael (Pogba), Fabio (Fryers), Gibson, Smalling, Evans, Valencia, Park, Berbatov (Morrison), Macheda, Biram Diouf.
Crystal Palace: Price; Clyne, Moxey (Ambrose), Gardner, McCarthy, Wright, O'Keefe, Dikgacoi, Zaha, Easter (Murray), Scannell (Parr).
aet.

SEMI-FINAL FIRST LEG

Tuesday, 10 January 2012

Crystal Palace (1) 1 *(Gardner 43)*

Cardiff C (0) 0 22,147

Crystal Palace: Speroni; Ramage, Parr, Dikgacoi, McCarthy, Gardner, Ambrose, Jedinak, Martin (Scannell), Murray, Zaha (Easter).
Cardiff C: Heaton; McNaughton (Blake), Taylor, Gunnarsson, Hudson, Turner, Cowie, Whittingham, Miller, Mason (McPhail), Ralls.

Wednesday, 11 January 2012

Manchester C (0) 0

Liverpool (1) 1 *(Gerrard 13 (pen))* 36,017

Manchester C: Hart; Richards, Clichy, De Jong (Kolarov), Lescott, Savic, Milner, Barry, Aguero, Balotelli (Nasri), Johnson A (Dzeko).
Liverpool: Reina; Kelly, Johnson, Skrtel, Agger, Spearing (Adam), Henderson, Gerrard, Carroll, Bellamy (Carragher), Downing (Jose Enrique).

SEMI-FINAL SECOND LEG

Tuesday, 24 January 2012

Cardiff C (1) 1 *(Gardner 7 (og))*

Crystal Palace (0) 0 25,652

Cardiff C: Heaton; Blake (McNaughton), Taylor, Gunnarsson, Gerrard, Turner, Cowie (Gestede), Whittingham, Miller, McPhail (Kiss), Conway.
Crystal Palace: Speroni; Clyne, Parr, Gardner, McCarthy■, Dikgacoi, Ambrose (McShane), Jedinak, Martin (Scannell), Murray (Easter), Zaha.
aet; Cardiff C won 3-1 on penalties.

Wednesday, 25 January 2012

Liverpool (1) 2 *(Gerrard 41 (pen), Bellamy 74)*

Manchester C (1) 2 *(De Jong 31, Dzeko 67)* 44,590

Liverpool: Reina; Johnson, Jose Enrique, Skrtel, Agger, Adam, Henderson, Gerrard, Bellamy (Kelly), Kuyt (Carroll), Downing.
Manchester C: Hart; Richards, Kolarov, Barry, Lescott, Savic (Aguero), Zabaleta, De Jong (Johnson A), Dzeko, Silva, Nasri.

CARLING CUP FINAL

Sunday, 26 February 2012

Cardiff C (1) 2 Liverpool (0) 2

(at Wembley Stadium, attendance 89,044)

Cardiff C: Heaton; McNaughton (Blake), Taylor, Gunnarsson, Hudson (Gerrard), Turner, Cowie, Whittingham, Miller, Gestede, Mason (Kiss).
Scorers: Mason 19, Turner 118.

Liverpool: Reina; Johnson, Jose Enrique, Skrtel, Agger (Carragher), Adam, Henderson (Bellamy), Gerrard, Carroll (Kuyt), Suarez, Downing.
Scorers: Skrtel 60, Kuyt 108.

aet; Liverpool won 3-2 on penalties.

Referee: M. Clattenburg (Tyne & Wear).

Liverpool's Dirk Kuyt, Charlie Adam, Steven Gerrard, Jamie Carragher and Luis Suarez celebrate beating Cardiff City to win the Carling Cup final after a penalty shoot-out at Wembley in February. (Action Images/John Sibley)

JOHNSTONE'S PAINT TROPHY 2011–12

▪ *Denotes player sent off.*

NORTHERN SECTION FIRST ROUND

Tuesday, 30 August 2011

Bradford C (0) 0

Sheffield W (0) 0 3519

Bradford C: Jansson; Moore, Threlfall, Flynn, Branston, Oliver, Mitchell (Bryan), Jones, Hanson, Stewart (Hannah), Compton (O'Brien).
Sheffield W: Weaver (O'Donnell); Semedo (Coke), Reynolds, Obileye, Beevers, O'Connor, Sedgwick, Prutton (Nyoni), Morrison C, Uchechi, Palmer.
Bradford C won 3-1 on penalties.

Burton Alb (0) 1 *(Richards 73)*

Sheffield U (0) 2 *(McAllister 76, Tonne 80)* 2725

Burton Alb: Atkins; Corbett, Blanchett, Austin, Moore, McGrath, Maghoma, Dyer, Richards, Zola (Yussuf), Phillips.
Sheffield U: Long; Lowton, Mendez-Laing (Tonne), Doyle, Collins, Maguire, McAllister, Flynn, Porter (Harriott), Slew, Philliskirk (Parrino).

Bury (0) 0

Crewe Alex (0) 0 1295

Bury: Belford; Picken, Skarz, Eastham, Jones A, Sweeney, Worrall, Cregg, Oyenuga (Harrop), Bishop, Haworth (McCarthy).
Crewe Alex: Phillips; Westwood, Davis, Murphy, Artell, Dugdale, Bell, Hughes (Clayton), Miller, Shelley, Sarcevic (Mellor).
Crewe Alex won 4-2 on penalties.

Northampton T (1) 1 *(Jacobs 41)*

Huddersfield T (1) 2 *(McDermott 39, Novak 82)* 1776

Northampton T: Walker; Johnson, Tozer, Turnbull, Langmead, Webster, Davies, McKoy (Corker) (Westwood), Jacobs, Akinfenwa (Savage), Young.
Huddersfield T: Bennett; Hunt, Woods, Robinson, Cooper, Kay, Gobern, McDermott (Ward), Rhodes (Novak), Lee, Roberts (Arfield).

Scunthorpe U (0) 2 *(Grant 59, 66)*

Hartlepool U (0) 0 1763

Scunthorpe U: Lillis; Nolan, Palmer (Wright), Togwell, Reid, Nelson, Duffy M, Collins, Barcham (Ryan), Grant (Wint), Thompson.
Hartlepool U: Flinders; Austin, Horwood (Sweeney), Liddle, Haslam, Hartley, Monkhouse (Brown), Luscombe, Poole (Larkin), Boyd, Humphreys.

Tranmere R (0) 1 *(Taylor 88)*

Port Vale (0) 1 *(Taylor R 50)* 2546

Tranmere R: fon Williams; Kay, Bakayogo, Weir, McChrystal (Raven), Taylor, Welsh, Labadie, Tiryaki, Akins (Robinson) (Power), Devaney.
Port Vale: Martin; Yates, Owen, Griffith, McCombe, McDonald, Burge, Collins, Haldane (Williamson), Dodds (Roberts), Taylor R (Pope).
Tranmere R won 4-2 on penalties.

Walsall (2) 2 *(Jarvis 17, Taundry 35)*

Shrewsbury T (0) 1 *(Butler 48 (og))* 2605

Walsall: Grof; Westlake, Sadler, Butler, Smith, Taundry, Gnakpa (Peterlin), Chambers, Jarvis (Beevers), Nicholls, Hurst.
Shrewsbury T: Neal C; Grandison, Jacobson, McAllister S (Wroe), Hazell, Cansdell-Sherriff, Ainsworth (Wright), Leslie, Bradshaw, Gornell (Morgan), Richards.

Tuesday, 6 September 2011

Accrington S (1) 3 *(Lindfield 35, Dunbavin 86, Procter 90)*

Carlisle U (0) 2 *(McGovern 61, Zoko 68)* 1069

Accrington S: Dunbavin; Murphy, Winnard (Hessey), McIntyre, Bender, Procter, Lindfield, Craney (Amond), Guthrie (Fletcher), Moult, Joyce.
Carlisle U: Collin; Tavernier, O'Halloran, Noble, Livesey, Murphy▪, Welsh (McGovern), Berrett▪, Miller, Curran (Loy), Zoko (Taiwo).

SOUTHERN SECTION FIRST ROUND

Tuesday, 30 August 2011

Bournemouth (1) 4 *(Pugh 39, Stockley 66, 77, MacDonald 84)*

Hereford U (1) 1 *(Barkhuizen 12)* 2489

Bournemouth: Jalal; Purches, Cummings, Cooper, Barrett, MacDonald (Baudry), Gregory (Arter), Pugh, Lovell (Stockley), Doble, Byrne.
Hereford U: Bartlett (Cornell); Evans W, Heath, Pell (McQuilkin), Townsend, Stam, Barkhuizen, Lunt, Winnall, Arquin (Fleetwood), Clist.

Cheltenham T (2) 2 *(Spencer 14, Goulding 42)*

Torquay U (0) 1 *(Macklin 60)* 1247

Cheltenham T: Brown; Jombati, Andrew, Pack (Bird), Lowe, Hooman, Smikle, Summerfield, Spencer, Goulding (Duffy), Mohamed (Graham).
Torquay U: Rice; Oastler, Rowe-Turner, Mansell (O'Kane), Ellis, Saah, Bodin, Lathrope, Howe (Halpin), McPhee (Atieno), Macklin.

Colchester U (1) 1 *(Baldwin 16)*

Barnet (2) 3 *(Holmes 7, McLeod 19 (pen), Kabba 74)* 1747

Colchester U: Williams; Wilson, Rose, Izzet, Heath (Eastman), Baldwin, Bond (Wordsworth), James, Gillespie, Henderson, Antonio (Odejayi).
Barnet: Brill; Senda, Parkes, Hughes, Kamdjo, Geohaghon, Deering (Kabba), Byrne, Holmes (Dennehy), McLeod▪, Marshall (Taylor).

Exeter C (1) 1 *(Dunne 42)*

Plymouth Arg (0) 1 *(Daley 60)* 3940

Exeter C: Pidgeley; Tully, Duffy, Dunne, Archibald-Henville, Coles, Nichols (Logan), Noble, Vine (Shephard), Nardiello, Golbourne.
Plymouth Arg: Larrieu; Nelson, Gibson, Fletcher C, Walton, Soukouna, Daley, Hourihane, Hitchcock, Atkinson, Williams.
Exeter C won 3-0 on penalties.

Milton Keynes D (2) 3 *(MacDonald 19, Chadwick 30, Douglas 85 (og))*

Brentford (1) 3 *(Thompson 27, Alexander 56, 82)* 4175

Milton Keynes D: Martin; Smith Adam, Chicksen, Baldock G, Flanagan, Williams S▪, Powell (Lewington), O'Shea (Potter), Bowditch, MacDonald (Gleeson), Chadwick.
Brentford: Lee; Thompson, Woodman, Douglas, Eger, Osborne, O'Connor (Reeves), Bean, Alexander, Forrester (Wood), Weston (Grella).
Brentford won 4-3 on penalties.

Southend U (1) 1 *(Dickinson 25 (pen))*

Crawley T (0) 0 2053

Southend U: Morris; Clohessy, Prosser, Ferdinand, Barker, Phillips, Grant, Leonard, Harris (Johnson) (Mohsni), Dickinson▪, Sawyer (Hall).
Crawley T: Kuipers; Wilson, McFadzean, Bulman (Hunt), Dempster (Neilson), Wassmer, Smith, Torres, Tubbs, Akinde (Thomas), Akpan.

Tuesday, 6 September 2011

Wycombe W (1) 3 *(Beavon 9, 57, 76)*

Bristol R (0) 1 *(Harrold 58)* 771

Wycombe W: Bull; McCoy, Sandell, Benyon, Johnson, Tunnicliffe, Lewis (Harding), Bloomfield (Donnelly), Beavon (Harris), Rendell, Betsy.
Bristol R: Bevan; Smith, Woodards (Boateng), Anthony, Brown L, Campbell, Brown W, Gill (Stanley), Harrold, McGleish, Richards.

Wednesday, 7 September 2011

Leyton Orient (0) 1 *(Mooney 88)*

Dagenham & R (0) 1 *(Williams 64)* 1420

Leyton Orient: Butcher; Omozusi (Odubajo), Daniels, Chorley, Forbes, Smith Jimmy, Laird, Dawson (McSweeney), Mooney, Tehoue (Porter), Cox.
Dagenham & R: Shea; Ogogo (Rose), Ilesanmi, Bingham, Doe, Walsh, Scannell, Lee, Williams, Tomlin (Green Danny J), Gain.
Dagenham & R won 14-13 on penalties.

NORTHERN SECTION SECOND ROUND

Tuesday, 4 October 2011

Huddersfield T (0) 2 *(Miller 63 (pen), Clarke P 70)*

Bradford C (0) 2 *(Kay 55 (og), Oliver 64)* 10,489

Huddersfield T: Colgan; Hunt, Naysmith, Robinson, Clarke P, Cooper (Kay), Gobern (Miller), McDermott (Roberts), Lee, Novak, Ward.
Bradford C: Duke; Moore, Threlfall, Flynn, Branston, Oliver, Mitchell (Davies), O'Brien, Hannah (Rodney), Stewart, Compton (Reid).
Bradford C won 4-3 on penalties.

Morecambe (0) 2 *(Jevons 83, Ellison 90)*

Preston NE (2) 2 *(McLean 3, Tsoumou 21)* 4385

Morecambe: Roche; Haining, Reid, Hunter, Charnock (Parrish), Fenton, Wilson, Drummond (McDonald), Alessandra, Jevons, Price (Ellison).
Preston NE: Arestidou; Gray, Smith, Ashbee, Carlisle, McLean, Daley (Miller), Barton, Proctor (Mayor), Tsoumou, Parry.
Preston NE won 7-6 on penalties.

Notts Co (1) 1 *(Hawley 43)*

Chesterfield (0) 3 *(Randall 64, Morgan 68, Bowery 77)* 2293

Notts Co: Nelson; Edwards (Sodje), Harley, Ravenhill, Pearce (Thompson), Bencherif, Demontagnac, Spicer (Hughes L), Hawley, Allen, Judge.
Chesterfield: Fleming; Talbot, Grounds, Johnson■, Holden, Downes, Mendy, Clay (Darikwa), Randall, Bowery (Westcarr), Morgan (Boden).

Rochdale (0) 1 *(Ball 49)*

Walsall (0) 1 *(Hurst 66)* 2089

Rochdale: Kean; Darby, Twaddle, Benali (Grimes), Trotman, Holness, Kennedy, Barry-Murphy, Barnes-Homer (Adams), Ball, Thompson (Akpa Akpro).
Walsall: Walker; Westlake, Sadler, Chambers (Taundry), Butler, Smith, Gnakpa (Hurst), Peterlin, Grigg (Jarvis), Nicholls, Martin.
Rochdale won 3-1 on penalties.

Rotherham U (0) 1 *(Revell 69)*

Sheffield U (1) 2 *(Porter 9, Evans 90)* 6737

Rotherham U: Warrington; Tonge, Newey, Harrison, Bradley (Mullins), Raynes, Pringle, Taylor J, Grabban, Revell (Holroyd), Schofield.
Sheffield U: Long; Lowton, Lescinel, Montgomery, Collins, Maguire, Flynn (McAllister), McDonald, Evans, Porter (Mendez-Laing) (Philliskirk), Cresswell.

Scunthorpe U (0) 0

Oldham Ath (1) 1 *(Kuqi 26)* 2106

Scunthorpe U: Johnstone; Wright, Nolan, O'Connor, Duffy S, Nelson, Thompson, Ajose (Duffy M), Norwood (Mozika), Grant, Barcham.
Oldham Ath: Cisak; Lee, Diallo (Mellor), Wesolowski, Diamond, Clarke, Morais (Millar), Adeyemi, Reid, Kuqi (Smith), Taylor.

Wednesday, 5 October 2011

Crewe Alex (0) 1 *(Clayton 76)*

Macclesfield T (0) 0 2271

Crewe Alex: Phillips; Tootle, Davis, Hughes (Westwood), Turton (Martin C), Dugdale, Sarcevic (Leitch-Smith), Murphy, Moore, Clayton, Powell.
Macclesfield T: Collis; Bateson, Tremarco, Kay, Brown, Brisley (Hamshaw) (Roberts), Wedgbury, Chalmers, Tomlinson, Draper (Grant), Diagne.

Wednesday, 12 October 2011

Accrington S (0) 0

Tranmere R (1) 1 *(Taylor 39)* 1509

Accrington S: Dunbavin; McIntyre, Winnard, Long, Murphy, Procter, Coid (Lindfield), Craney, Amond (Fletcher), Guthrie, Joyce.
Tranmere R: fon Williams; Kay, Buchanan, Labadie, Goodison, Taylor, Akins (Weir), Welsh, Tiryaki, Baxter, Bakayogo (McGurk).

SOUTHERN SECTION SECOND ROUND

Tuesday, 4 October 2011

AFC Wimbledon (0) 2 *(Hatton 54 (pen), Yussuff 58)*

Stevenage (1) 2 *(Wilson 7, Roberts 90)* 1416

AFC Wimbledon: Turner; Hatton, Jackson, McNaughton (Porter), Minshull, Johnson, Bush, Mulley, Moore S (Wellard), Midson (Ademeno), Yussuff.
Stevenage: Julian; Henry, Laird (Harrison), Roberts, Ashton, Bostwick, Wilson, Mousinho, Beardsley (Walker), Reid, Shroot (Charles).
AFC Wimbledon won 4-3 on penalties.

Aldershot T (0) 1 *(Hylton 76)*

Oxford U (0) 2 *(Hall R 49, Smalley 52)* 1429

Aldershot T: Young; Herd, Straker, Pulis (Guttridge), Jones, Brown A, Andrade (McGlashan), Collins J, Hylton, Vincenti (Rankine), Rodman.
Oxford U: Brown; Batt, Davis, Payne (Constable), Whing, Wright, Hall A, Heslop (McLaren), Hall R, Smalley, Leven.

Bournemouth (3) 3 *(Pugh 16, 25, Ngala 30 (og))*

Yeovil T (0) 2 *(MacLean 63, Ehmer 88)* 3265

Bournemouth: Jalal; Purches (Partington), Cummings, Cooper, Barrett, Zubar, Gregory, Pugh, Taylor (Stockley) (Symes), Fletcher, Peters.
Yeovil T: Steer; Haynes-Brown, Gilbert (MacLean), Ehmer, Huntington, Ngala, Gibson, Wotton, Massey, Johnson (Edgar), O'Brien (Agard).

Dagenham & R (0) 1 *(McCrory 66)*

Southend U (1) 3 *(Hall 30, 74, Harris 90)* 2395

Dagenham & R: Lewington; Hewitt (Reed), McCrory, Bingham, Doe (Ilesanmi), Walsh, Arber, Maher, Rose, Tomlin (Green Danny J), Woodall.
Southend U: Morris; Clohessy, Gilbert, Kalala, Barker, Mohsni, Grant (Harris), Timlin, Sturrock, Leonard, Hall.

Exeter C (0) 1 *(Nardiello 72)*

Swindon T (2) 2 *(Jervis 18, 35)* 2627

Exeter C: Krysiak; Tully, Duffy (Shephard), Dunne, Archibald-Henville, Coles, Whichelow (Jones), Nichols (Logan), Bauza, Nardiello, Golbourne.
Swindon T: Lanzano; Caddis, Cibocchi (Thompson), Smith J (Risser), Devera, McCormack, Ritchie, Abdulla, Connell (Kerrouche), Jervis, Gabilondo.

Gillingham (1) 1 *(Richards 5)*

Barnet (1) 3 *(McLeod 11 (pen), 84, Marshall 72)* 1278

Gillingham: Gazzaniga; Fish (Whelpdale), Frampton (Davies), Montrose, Jackman, Richards, Weston, Rooney, Osei-Kuffour (Kedwell), Nouble, Payne S.
Barnet: O'Brien; Kamdjo, Borrowdale, Hughes, Uddin, Leach, Deering (Vilhete), Byrne, Taylor (Kabba), McLeod (Owusu), Marshall.

Wycombe W (0) 1 *(Betsy 62)*

Cheltenham T (1) 3 *(Duffy 37, 75, Smikle 50)* 931

Wycombe W: Bull; McCoy, Foster, Harding, Johnson, Tunnicliffe, Lewis (Bloomfield), Harris, Rendell (Strevens), Benyon (Ibe), Betsy.
Cheltenham T: Brown; Jombati, Garbutt, Pack (Lewis), Lowe, Hooman, Smikle, Summerfield, Spencer (Duffy), Goulding, Graham (Andrew).

Wednesday, 5 October 2011

Charlton Ath (0) 0

Brentford (2) 3 *(Adams 2, O'Connor 24 (pen), Diagouraga 61)* 3486

Charlton Ath: Sullivan; Hughes, Evina, Alonso, Doherty, Taylor (Morrison), Green, Stephens (Euell), Hayes, Wagstaff, Jackson (Kermorgant).
Brentford: Moore; Thompson (Saunders), Woodman, O'Connor, Eger, Llera, Diagouraga, Bean, Adams (Wood), Clarkson (Grella), Weston.

NORTHERN SECTION QUARTER-FINALS

Tuesday, 8 November 2011

Oldham Ath (1) 3 *(Kuqi 12, 59, Scapuzzi 72)*

Crewe Alex (0) 1 *(Powell 54)* 2163

Oldham Ath: Gerrard; Lee, Black, Furman, Mvoto, Diamond, Scapuzzi (Morais), Adeyemi, Simpson (Mancini), Kuqi (Smith), Taylor.
Crewe Alex: Phillips; Tootle, Martin C, Westwood, Artell, Dugdale, Sarcevic (Clayton), Murphy, Miller, Moore (Shelley), Powell.

Rochdale (0) 1 *(Bunn 52)*

Preston NE (1) 1 *(Barton 35)* 2395

Rochdale: Lucas; Darby, Jordan, Holness, Barry-Murphy, Tutte, Kennedy, Bunn (Adams), Akpa Akpro, Jones, Eccleston (Grimes).
Preston NE: Stuckmann; McLaughlin (Alexander), Parry, Ashbee (Clark), Carlisle, Morgan, Nicholson, Barton, Tsoumou, Forte, Mayor.
Preston NE won 4-2 on penalties.

Sheffield U (1) 1 *(Phillips 27)*

Bradford C (1) 1 *(Flynn 40)* 5692

Sheffield U: Simonsen; Parrino (Lowton), Williams, McDonald, Collins, Maguire, Phillips, Doyle, Evans (Tonne), Porter, Clarke.
Bradford C: McLaughlin; Ramsden, O'Brien, Flynn, Seip, Oliver, Mitchell, Jones, Fagan, Hannah (Devitt), Compton (Hanson).
Bradford C won 6-5 on penalties.

Wednesday, 9 November 2011

Chesterfield (1) 4 *(Mendy 44, Bowery 54, 80, Westcarr 90)*

Tranmere R (1) 3 *(McGurk 9, Showunmi 70, Tiryaki 72)* 3152

Chesterfield: Soderberg; Talbot (Ford), Smith, Johnson (Allott), Mattis (Whitaker), Downes, Mendy, Grounds, Obadeyi, Westcarr, Bowery.
Tranmere R: fon Williams; Holmes, Buchanan, Weir, McChrystal, Taylor, Akins, Welsh, Tiryaki (Power), McGurk (Labadie), Bakayogo (Showunmi).

SOUTHERN SECTION QUARTER-FINALS

Tuesday, 8 November 2011

Brentford (2) 6 *(Saunders 5, Grella 23, 48, 82, 84, Logan 77)*

Bournemouth (0) 0 3015

Brentford: Lee; Logan, Woodman, Douglas, Eger, Llera (Legge), Saunders (McGinn), Diagouraga, Donaldson (Alexander), Grella, Weston.
Bournemouth: Jalal; Purches (Molesley), Cummings, Cook, Barrett, Arter, Pugh, Malone, Symes (Fletcher), Fogden (Sheringham), Peters.

Cheltenham T (0) 0

Barnet (1) 2 *(Marshall 44, Taylor 68)* 1388

Cheltenham T: Brown; Jombati, Andrew, Summerfield (Lewis), Lowe, Hooman, Smikle, Penn (Pack), Spencer (Duffy), Goulding, Graham.
Barnet: Brill; Senda, Borrowdale, Hughes, Dennehy, Downing, Deering, Byrne, Marshall (Parkes), McLeod (Taylor), Kamdjo.

Oxford U (0) 0

Southend U (1) 1 *(Hall 15)* 2415

Oxford U: Brown■; Batt (Whing), Kinniburgh, McLaren (Payne), Worley, Wright, Hall A, Heslop, Franks, Smalley, Potter (Craddock■).
Southend U: Daniels; Clohessy, Gilbert, Ferdinand, Barker, Mohsni, Grant■, Leonard (Sawyer), Sturrock (Dickinson), Timlin, Hall.

Swindon T (0) 1 *(Risser 68)*

AFC Wimbledon (0) 1 *(Yussuff 82)* 4329

Swindon T: Smith P; Caddis, Ridehalgh, Flint, Devera, Risser, Ritchie (Esajas), Ferry, De Vita, Kerrouche (Magera) (Gabilondo), Connell.
AFC Wimbledon: Brown; Franks, Bush, Mulley, Stuart, McNaughton, Yussuff, Wellard, Jolley (Ademeno), Midson (Minshull), Djilali (Porter).
Swindon T won 3-1 on penalties.

NORTHERN SECTION SEMI-FINAL

Tuesday, 6 December 2011

Oldham Ath (0) 2 *(Adeyemi 61, Kuqi 80)*

Bradford C (0) 0 5697

Oldham Ath: Cisak; Lee, Black, Wesolowski, Mvoto, Clarke, Scapuzzi, Adeyemi, Simpson, Kuqi, Parker.
Bradford C: McLaughlin; Moore, Seip, Dean (Fagan), Davies, Oliver, Mitchell, Jones, Hanson, Wells (Hannah), Compton (Reid).

Preston NE (1) 1 *(McCombe 16)*

Chesterfield (1) 1 *(Westcarr 27)* 5835

Preston NE: Stuckmann; Gray, Parry, Alexander, McCombe, Morgan, Coutts, Doyle, Proctor, Mellor, Mayor.
Chesterfield: Lee; Talbot (Mattis), Griffiths, Downes, Ford, Whitaker, Mendy, Allott, Westcarr, Bowery (Clarke), Morgan.
Chesterfield won 4-2 on penalties.

SOUTHERN SECTION SEMI-FINAL

Tuesday, 6 December 2011

Barnet (0) 0

Brentford (0) 0 1970

Barnet: Brill; Senda, Borrowdale, Hughes, Hector, Downing, Deering, Kamdjo, Byrne (Holmes), McLeod, Marshall.
Brentford: Lee; Logan, Bidwell, Douglas, Eger, Dean, Saunders, Bean (Reeves), Donaldson (Grella), Diagouraga, McGinn (Alexander).
Barnet won 5-3 on penalties.

Southend U (0) 1 *(Sturrock 62)*

Swindon T (0) 2 *(Caddis 68, Murray 81)* 3981

Southend U: Daniels; Clohessy, Gilbert, Ferdinand (Sawyer), Barker, Mohsni, Grant, Prosser (Dickinson), Sturrock, Harris (Kalala), Hall.
Swindon T: Foderingham; Caddis, Cibocchi, Risser (Ferry), Flint, McCormack, Ritchie, Smith J, Connell (Magera), Jervis (Murray), Gabilondo.

NORTHERN SECTION FINAL FIRST LEG

Wednesday, 18 January 2012

Chesterfield (0) 2 *(Boden 49, Whitaker 67 (pen))*

Oldham Ath (0) 1 *(Simpson 58)* 5724

Chesterfield: Lee; Hurst, Robertson, Davis, Thompson, Ford, Talbot, Juan (Allott), Lester, Boden (Bowery), Whitaker (Mendy).
Oldham Ath: Cisak; Parker, Lee, Wesolowski, Tarkowski, Mvoto, Adeyemi, Simpson, Scapuzzi (Morais), Kuqi (Smith), Taylor.

NORTHERN SECTION FINAL SECOND LEG

Monday, 30 January 2012

Oldham Ath (0) 0

Chesterfield (0) 1 *(Lester 88)* 5622

Oldham Ath: Cisak; Lee, Black, Wesolowski (Smith), Diamond (Tarkowski), Mvoto, Morais (Marsh-Brown), Adeyemi, Simpson, Kuqi, Taylor.
Chesterfield: Lee; Hurst, Robertson, Davis, Thompson, Ford, Talbot, Allott, Lester (Bowery), Boden (Morgan), Lowry.

SOUTHERN SECTION FINAL FIRST LEG

Tuesday, 10 January 2012

Barnet (0) 1 *(Hughes 72)*

Swindon T (1) 1 *(Flint 44)* 3915

Barnet: Brill; Senda (Taylor) (Byrne), Saville, Hughes, Hector, Downing, Kamdjo, Holmes, Deering, McLeod, Marshall.

Swindon T: Foderingham; Caddis, Cibocchi (Devera), Smith J, Flint, McCormack, Ritchie, Ferry, Murray, Magera (Connell), Gabilondo (De Vita).

SOUTHERN SECTION FINAL SECOND LEG

Tuesday, 7 February 2012

Swindon T (1) 1 *(Connell 17)*

Barnet (0) 0 10,406

Swindon T: Foderingham; Caddis, Kennedy (Murray), Smith J, Devera, McCormack, Ritchie, Ferry (Risser), De Vita (Cibocchi), Connell, Benson.

Barnet: Brill; Hector, Saville, Hughes, Dennehy, Downing, Kamdjo (Obita), Byrne (Taylor■), Deering (Mustoe), McLeod, Holmes.

JOHNSTONE'S PAINT TROPHY FINAL

Sunday, 25 March 2012

(at Wembley Stadium, attendance 49,602)

Chesterfield (0) 2 Swindon T (0) 0

Chesterfield: Lee; Hurst, Smith, Moussa (Randall), Thompson, Ford, Talbot, Allott, Lester (Westcarr), Bowery (Boden), Mendy.
Scorers: Risser 47 (og), Westcarr 90.

Swindon T: Foderingham; Devera, McEveley (Cibocchi), Smith J (Bostock), Risser (Murray), McCormack, Ritchie, Ferry, Benson, Connell, Holmes.

Referee: T. Bates (Staffordshire).

FOOTBALL LEAGUE COMPETITION ATTENDANCES

LEAGUE CUP ATTENDANCES

Season	*Attendances*	*Games*	*Average*
1960–61	1,204,580	112	10,755
1961–62	1,030,534	104	9,909
1962–63	1,029,893	102	10,097
1963–64	945,265	104	9,089
1964–65	962,802	98	9,825
1965–66	1,205,876	106	11,376
1966–67	1,394,553	118	11,818
1967–68	1,671,326	110	15,194
1968–69	2,064,647	118	17,497
1969–70	2,299,819	122	18,851
1970–71	2,035,315	116	17,546
1971–72	2,397,154	123	19,489
1972–73	1,935,474	120	16,129
1973–74	1,722,629	132	13,050
1974–75	1,901,094	127	14,969
1975–76	1,841,735	140	13,155
1976–77	2,236,636	147	15,215
1977–78	2,038,295	148	13,772
1978–79	1,825,643	139	13,134
1979–80	2,322,866	169	13,745
1980–81	2,051,576	161	12,743
1981–82	1,880,682	161	11,681
1982–83	1,679,756	160	10,498
1983–84	1,900,491	168	11,312
1984–85	1,876,429	167	11,236
1985–86	1,579,916	163	9,693
1986–87	1,531,498	157	9,755
1987–88	1,539,253	158	9,742
1988–89	1,552,780	162	9,585
1989–90	1,836,916	168	10,934
1990–91	1,675,496	159	10,538
1991–92	1,622,337	164	9,892
1992–93	1,558,031	161	9,677
1993–94	1,744,120	163	10,700
1994–95	1,530,478	157	9,748
1995–96	1,776,060	162	10,963
1996–97	1,529,321	163	9,382
1997–98	1,484,297	153	9,701
1998–99	1,555,856	153	10,169
1999–2000	1,354,233	153	8,851
2000–01	1,501,304	154	9,749
2001–02	1,076,390	93	11,574
2002–03	1,242,478	92	13,505
2003–04	1,267,729	93	13,631
2004–05	1,313,693	93	14,216
2005–06	1,072,362	93	11,531
2006–07	1,098,403	93	11,811
2007–08	1,332,841	94	14,179
2008–09	1,329,753	93	14,298
2009–10	1,376,405	93	14,800
2010–11	1,197,917	93	12,881
2011–12	1,209,684	93	13,007

CARLING CUP 2011–12

Round	*Aggregate*	*Games*	*Average*
Preliminary + One	212,806	36	5,911
Two	177,281	24	7,387
Three	271,188	16	16,949
Four	158,360	8	19,795
Quarter-finals	172,599	4	43,150
Semi-finals	128,406	4	32,102
Final	89,044	1	89,044
Total	1,209,684	93	13,007

JOHNSTONE'S PAINT TROPHY 2011–12

Round	*Aggregate*	*Games*	*Average*
One	35,140	16	2,196
Two	48,706	16	3,044
Area Quarter-finals	24,549	8	3,069
Area Semi-finals	17,483	4	4,371
Area finals	25,667	4	6,417
Final	49,602	1	49,602
Total	201,147	49	4,105

FA CUP FINALS 1872–2012

1872 and 1874–92	Kennington Oval	1911	Replay at Old Trafford
1873	Lillie Bridge	1912	Replay at Bramall Lane
1886	Replay at Derby (Racecourse Ground)	1915	Old Trafford, Manchester
1893	Fallowfield, Manchester	1920–22	Stamford Bridge
1894	Everton	1923–2000	Wembley
1895–1914	Crystal Palace	1970	Replay at Old Trafford
1901	Replay at Bolton	2001–2006	Millennium Stadium, Cardiff
1910	Replay at Everton	2007 to date	Wembley

Year	*Winners*	*Runners-up*	*Score*
1872	Wanderers	Royal Engineers	1-0
1873	Wanderers	Oxford University	2-0
1874	Oxford University	Royal Engineers	2-0
1875	Royal Engineers	Old Etonians	2-0 (after 1-1 draw aet)
1876	Wanderers	Old Etonians	3-0 (after 1-1 draw aet)
1877	Wanderers	Oxford University	2-1 (aet)
1878	Wanderers*	Royal Engineers	3-1
1879	Old Etonians	Clapham R	1-0
1880	Clapham R	Oxford University	1-0
1881	Old Carthusians	Old Etonians	3-0
1882	Old Etonians	Blackburn R	1-0
1883	Blackburn Olympic	Old Etonians	2-1 (aet)
1884	Blackburn R	Queen's Park, Glasgow	2-1
1885	Blackburn R	Queen's Park, Glasgow	2-0
1886	Blackburn R†	WBA	2-0 (after 0-0 draw)
1887	Aston Villa	WBA	2-0
1888	WBA	Preston NE	2-1
1889	Preston NE	Wolverhampton W	3-0
1890	Blackburn R	The Wednesday	6-1
1891	Blackburn R	Notts Co	3-1
1892	WBA	Aston Villa	3-0
1893	Wolverhampton W	Everton	1-0
1894	Notts Co	Bolton W	4-1
1895	Aston Villa	WBA	1-0
1896	The Wednesday	Wolverhampton W	2-1
1897	Aston Villa	Everton	3-2
1898	Nottingham F	Derby Co	3-1
1899	Sheffield U	Derby Co	4-1
1900	Bury	Southampton	4-0
1901	Tottenham H	Sheffield U	3-1 (after 2-2 draw)
1902	Sheffield U	Southampton	2-1 (after 1-1 draw)
1903	Bury	Derby Co	6-0
1904	Manchester C	Bolton W	1-0
1905	Aston Villa	Newcastle U	2-0
1906	Everton	Newcastle U	1-0
1907	The Wednesday	Everton	2-1
1908	Wolverhampton W	Newcastle U	3-1
1909	Manchester U	Bristol C	1-0
1910	Newcastle U	Barnsley	2-0 (after 1-1 draw)
1911	Bradford C	Newcastle U	1-0 (after 0-0 draw)
1912	Barnsley	WBA	1-0 (aet, after 0-0 draw)
1913	Aston Villa	Sunderland	1-0
1914	Burnley	Liverpool	1-0
1915	Sheffield U	Chelsea	3-0
1920	Aston Villa	Huddersfield T	1-0 (aet)
1921	Tottenham H	Wolverhampton W	1-0
1922	Huddersfield T	Preston NE	1-0
1923	Bolton W	West Ham U	2-0
1924	Newcastle U	Aston Villa	2-0
1925	Sheffield U	Cardiff C	1-0
1926	Bolton W	Manchester C	1-0
1927	Cardiff C	Arsenal	1-0
1928	Blackburn R	Huddersfield T	3-1
1929	Bolton W	Portsmouth	2-0
1930	Arsenal	Huddersfield T	2-0
1931	WBA	Birmingham	2-1
1932	Newcastle U	Arsenal	2-1
1933	Everton	Manchester C	3-0
1934	Manchester C	Portsmouth	2-1
1935	Sheffield W	WBA	4-2
1936	Arsenal	Sheffield U	1-0
1937	Sunderland	Preston NE	3-1
1938	Preston NE	Huddersfield T	1-0 (aet)
1939	Portsmouth	Wolverhampton W	4-1
1946	Derby Co	Charlton Ath	4-1 (aet)

Year	*Winners*	*Runners-up*	*Score*
1947	Charlton Ath	Burnley	1-0 (aet)
1948	Manchester U	Blackpool	4-2
1949	Wolverhampton W	Leicester C	3-1
1950	Arsenal	Liverpool	2-0
1951	Newcastle U	Blackpool	2-0
1952	Newcastle U	Arsenal	1-0
1953	Blackpool	Bolton W	4-3
1954	WBA	Preston NE	3-2
1955	Newcastle U	Manchester C	3-1
1956	Manchester C	Birmingham C	3-1
1957	Aston Villa	Manchester U	2-1
1958	Bolton W	Manchester U	2-0
1959	Nottingham F	Luton T	2-1
1960	Wolverhampton W	Blackburn R	3-0
1961	Tottenham H	Leicester C	2-0
1962	Tottenham H	Burnley	3-1
1963	Manchester U	Leicester C	3-1
1964	West Ham U	Preston NE	3-2
1965	Liverpool	Leeds U	2-1 (aet)
1966	Everton	Sheffield W	3-2
1967	Tottenham H	Chelsea	2-1
1968	WBA	Everton	1-0 (aet)
1969	Manchester C	Leicester C	1-0
1970	Chelsea	Leeds U	2-1 (aet)
	(after 2-2 draw, after extra time)		
1971	Arsenal	Liverpool	2-1 (aet)
1972	Leeds U	Arsenal	1-0
1973	Sunderland	Leeds U	1-0
1974	Liverpool	Newcastle U	3-0
1975	West Ham U	Fulham	2-0
1976	Southampton	Manchester U	1-0
1977	Manchester U	Liverpool	2-1
1978	Ipswich T	Arsenal	1-0
1979	Arsenal	Manchester U	3-2
1980	West Ham U	Arsenal	1-0
1981	Tottenham H	Manchester C	3-2
	(after 1-1 draw, after extra time)		
1982	Tottenham H	QPR	1-0
	(after 1-1 draw, after extra time)		
1983	Manchester U	Brighton & HA	4-0
	(after 2-2 draw, after extra time)		
1984	Everton	Watford	2-0
1985	Manchester U	Everton	1-0 (aet)
1986	Liverpool	Everton	3-1
1987	Coventry C	Tottenham H	3-2 (aet)
1988	Wimbledon	Liverpool	1-0
1989	Liverpool	Everton	3-2 (aet)
1990	Manchester U	Crystal Palace	1-0
	(after 3-3 draw, after extra time)		
1991	Tottenham H	Nottingham F	2-1 (aet)
1992	Liverpool	Sunderland	2-0
1993	Arsenal	Sheffield W	2-1 (aet)
	(after 1-1 draw, after extra time)		
1994	Manchester U	Chelsea	4-0
1995	Everton	Manchester U	1-0
1996	Manchester U	Liverpool	1-0
1997	Chelsea	Middlesbrough	2-0
1998	Arsenal	Newcastle U	2-0
1999	Manchester U	Newcastle U	2-0
2000	Chelsea	Aston Villa	1-0
2001	Liverpool	Arsenal	2-1
2002	Arsenal	Chelsea	2-0
2003	Arsenal	Southampton	1-0
2004	Manchester U	Millwall	3-0
2005	Arsenal	Manchester U	0-0 (aet)
	(Arsenal won 5-4 on penalties)		
2006	Liverpool	West Ham U	3-3 (aet)
	(Liverpool won 3-1 on penalties)		
2007	Chelsea	Manchester U	1-0 (aet)
2008	Portsmouth	Cardiff C	1-0
2009	Chelsea	Everton	2-1
2010	Chelsea	Portsmouth	1-0
2011	Manchester C	Stoke C	1-0
2012	Chelsea	Liverpool	2-1

***** *Won outright, but restored to the Football Association.* † *A special trophy was awarded for third consecutive win.*

FA CUP WINS

Manchester U 11, Arsenal 10, Tottenham H 8, Aston Villa 7, Chelsea 7, Liverpool 7, Blackburn R 6, Newcastle U 6, Everton 5, Manchester C 5, The Wanderers 5, WBA 5, Bolton W 4, Sheffield U 4, Wolverhampton W 4, Sheffield W 3, West Ham U 3, Bury 2, Nottingham F 2, Old Etonians 2, Portsmouth 2, Preston NE 2, Sunderland 2, Barnsley 1, Blackburn Olympic 1, Blackpool 1, Bradford C 1, Burnley 1, Cardiff C 1, Charlton Ath 1, Clapham R 1, Coventry C 1, Derby Co 1, Huddersfield T 1, Ipswich T 1, Leeds U 1, Notts Co 1, Old Carthusians 1, Oxford University 1, Royal Engineers 1, Southampton 1, Wimbledon 1.

APPEARANCES IN FINALS

Manchester U 18, Arsenal 17, Liverpool 14, Everton 13, Newcastle U 13, Chelsea 11, Aston Villa 10, WBA 10, Manchester C 9, Tottenham H 9, Blackburn R 8, Wolverhampton W 8, Bolton W 7, Preston NE 7, Old Etonians 6, Sheffield U 6, Sheffield W 6, Huddersfield T 5, Portsmouth 5, *The Wanderers 5, West Ham U 5, Derby Co 4, Leeds U 4, Leicester C 4, Oxford University 4, Royal Engineers 4, Southampton 4, Sunderland 4, Blackpool 3, Burnley 3, Cardiff C 3, Nottingham F 3, Barnsley 2, Birmingham C 2, *Bury 2, Charlton Ath 2, Clapham R 2, Notts Co 2, Queen's Park (Glasgow) 2, *Blackburn Olympic 1, *Bradford C 1, Brighton & HA 1, Bristol C 1, *Coventry C 1, Crystal Palace 1, Fulham 1, *Ipswich T 1, Luton T 1, Middlesbrough 1, Millwall 1, *Old Carthusians 1, QPR 1, Stoke C 1, Watford 1, *Wimbledon 1.

** Denotes undefeated.*

APPEARANCES IN SEMI-FINALS

Manchester U 27, Arsenal 26, Everton 25, Liverpool 23, Aston Villa 20, Chelsea 20, WBA 20, Tottenham H 19, Blackburn R 18, Newcastle U 17, Sheffield W 16, Bolton W 14, Wolverhampton W 14, Derby Co 13, Sheffield U 13, Nottingham F 12, Sunderland 12, Manchester C 11, Southampton 11, Preston NE 10, Birmingham C 9, Burnley 8, Leeds U 8, Leicester C 8, Huddersfield T 7, Portsmouth 7, West Ham U 7, Old Etonians 6, Fulham 6, Oxford University 6, Notts Co 5, The Wanderers 5, Watford 5, Cardiff C 4, Luton T 4, Millwall 4, Queen's Park (Glasgow) 4, Royal Engineers 4, Stoke C 4, Barnsley 3, Blackpool 3, Clapham R 3, Crystal Palace (professional club) 3, Ipswich T 3, Middlesbrough 3, Norwich C 3, Old Carthusians 3, Oldham Ath 3, The Swifts 3, Blackburn Olympic 2, Bristol C 2, Bury 2, Charlton Ath 2, Grimsby T 2, Swansea T 2, Swindon T 2, Wimbledon 2, Bradford C 1, Brighton & HA 1, Cambridge University 1, Chesterfield 1, Coventry C 1, Crewe Alex 1, Crystal Palace (amateur club) 1, Darwen 1, Derby Junction 1, Glasgow R 1, Hull C 1, Marlow 1, Old Harrovians 1, Orient 1, Plymouth Arg 1, Port Vale 1, QPR 1, Reading 1, Shropshire W 1, Wycombe W 1, York C 1.

FA CUP ATTENDANCES 1969–2012

	1st Round	2nd Round	3rd Round	4th Round	5th Round	6th Round	Semi-finals & Final	Total	No. of matches	Average per match
2011–12	155,858	92,267	640,700	391,214	250,666	194,971	262,064	1,987,740	151	13,164
2010–11	169,259	101,291	637,202	390,524	284,311	164,092	250,256	1,996,935	150	13,313
2009–10	147,078	100,476	613,113	335,426	288,604	144,918	254,806	1,884,421	151	12,480
2008–09	161,526	96,923	631,070	529,585	297,364	149,566	264,635	2,131,669	163	13,078
2007–08	175,195	99,528	704,300	356,404	276,903	142,780	256,210	2,011,320	152	13,232
2006–07	168,884	113,924	708,628	478,924	340,612	230,064	177,810	2,218,846	158	14,043
2005–06	188,876	107,456	654,570	388,339	286,225	163,449	177,723	1,966,638	160	12,291
2004–05	161,197	98,702	602,152	477,472	339,082	127,914	193,233	1,999,752	146	13,697
2003–04	162,738	117,967	624,732	347,964	292,521	156,780	167,401	1,870,103	149	12,551
2002–03	189,905	104,103	577,494	404,599	242,483	156,244	175,498	1,850,326	150	12,336
2001–02	198,369	119,781	566,284	330,434	249,190	173,757	171,278	1,809,093	148	12,224
2000–01	171,689	122,061	577,204	398,241	256,899	100,663	177,778	1,804,535	151	11,951
1999–2000	181,485	127,728	514,030	374,795	182,511	105,443	214,921	1,700,913	158	10,765
1998–99	191,954	132,341	609,486	431,613	359,398	181,005	202,150	2,107,947	155	13,599
1997–98	204,803	130,261	629,127	455,557	341,290	192,651	172,007	2,125,696	165	12,883
1996–97	209,521	122,324	651,139	402,293	199,873	67,035	191,813	1,843,998	151	12,211
1995–96	185,538	115,669	748,997	391,218	274,055	174,142	156,500	2,046,199	167	12,252
1994–95	219,511	125,629	640,017	438,596	257,650	159,787	174,059	2,015,249	161	12,517
1993–94	190,683	118,031	691,064	430,234	172,196	134,705	228,233	1,965,146	159	12,359
1992–93	241,968	174,702	612,494	377,211	198,379	149,675	293,241	2,047,670	161	12,718
1991–92	231,940	117,078	586,014	372,576	270,537	155,603	201,592	1,935,340	160	12,095
1990–91	194,195	121,450	594,592	530,279	276,112	124,826	196,434	2,038,518	162	12,583
1989–90	209,542	133,483	683,047	412,483	351,423	123,065	277,420	2,190,463	170	12,885
1988–89	212,775	121,326	690,199	421,255	206,781	176,629	167,353	1,966,318	164	12,173
1987–88	204,411	104,561	720,121	443,133	281,461	119,313	177,585	2,050,585	155	13,229
1986–87	209,290	146,761	593,520	349,342	263,550	119,396	195,533	1,877,400	165	11,378
1985–86	171,142	130,034	486,838	495,526	311,833	184,262	192,316	1,971,951	168	11,738
1984–85	174,604	137,078	616,229	320,772	269,232	148,690	242,754	1,909,359	157	12,162
1983–84	192,276	151,647	625,965	417,298	181,832	185,382	187,000	1,941,400	166	11,695
1982–83	191,312	150,046	670,503	452,688	260,069	193,845	291,162	2,209,625	154	14,348
1981–82	236,220	127,300	513,185	356,987	203,334	124,308	279,621	1,840,955	160	11,506
1980–81	246,824	194,502	832,578	534,402	320,530	288,714	339,250	2,756,800	169	16,312
1979–80	267,121	204,759	804,701	507,725	364,039	157,530	355,541	2,661,416	163	16,328
1978–79	243,773	185,343	880,345	537,748	243,683	263,213	249,897	2,604,002	166	15,687
1977–78	258,248	178,930	881,406	540,164	400,751	137,059	198,020	2,594,578	160	16,216
1976–77	379,230	192,159	942,523	631,265	373,330	205,379	258,216	2,982,102	174	17,139
1975–76	255,533	178,099	867,880	573,843	471,925	206,851	205,810	2,759,941	161	17,142
1974–75	283,956	170,466	914,994	646,434	393,323	268,361	291,369	2,968,903	172	17,261
1973–74	214,236	125,295	840,142	747,909	346,012	233,307	273,051	2,779,952	167	16,646
1972–73	259,432	169,114	938,741	735,825	357,386	241,934	226,543	2,928,975	160	18,306
1971–72	277,726	236,127	986,094	711,399	486,378	230,292	248,546	3,158,562	160	19,741
1970–71	329,687	230,942	956,683	757,852	360,687	304,937	279,644	3,220,432	162	19,879
1969–70	345,229	195,102	925,930	651,374	319,893	198,537	390,700	3,026,765	170	17,805

THE E.ON FA CUP 2011–12

PRELIMINARY AND QUALIFYING ROUNDS

EXTRA PRELIMINARY ROUND

Bedlington Terriers v Whickham	1-0
Tow Law T v Marske U	1-2
Stokesley SC v Newcastle Benfield	1-6
Penrith v North Shields	1-1, 1-0
West Auckland C v Northallerton T	1-1, 1-2
Spennymoor T v Esh Winning	1-0
Ryton & Crawcrook Alb v Ashington	0-1
Gillford Park v Hebburn T	1-2
Newton Aycliffe v Billingham Syn	2-7
Crook T v Billingham T	2-6
Chester-le-Street T v South Shields	1-1, 1-2
West Auckland T v Dunston UTS	2-2, 1-5
Jarrow Roofing Boldon CA v Guisborough T	1-2
Sunderland RCA v Birtley T	7-0
Shildon v Consett	2-1
Whitehaven v Norton & Stockton A	3-0
Whitley Bay v Bishop Auckland	2-1
Scarborough Ath v Hallam	4-0
Thackley v Askern Villa	2-1
Maltby Main v Glasshoughton Wel	1-2
Silsden v Rossington Main	1-1, 2-2
Silsden won 4-2 on penalties.	
Pontefract Coll v Yorkshire Amat	2-0
Parkgate v Grimsby Bor	4-1
AFC Emley v Hall Road R	1-4
Hemsworth MW v Tadcaster Alb	1-2
Nostell MW v Armthorpe Wel	2-3
Selby T v Liversedge	1-4
Pickering T v Dinnington T	2-0
Staveley MW v Winterton R	4-0
Barton T OB v Bridlington T	2-2, 3-2
Squires Gate v Colne	1-0
Formby v Alsager T	3-0
Winsford U v Maine Road	1-1, 0-1
Runcorn T v Brighouse T	4-1
Padiham v Ashton Ath	1-2
Holker OB v Leek CSOB	3-0
Bacup Bor v AFC Blackpool	2-3
St Helens T v Atherton LR	0-2
Atherton Coll v Irlam	4-0
Chadderton v Cheadle T	2-8
Congleton T v Eccleshill U	3-1
Barnoldswick T v Ramsbottom U	0-2
Bootle v Wigan Robin Park	2-0
AFC Liverpool v Runcorn Linnets	2-2, 1-3
Retford U v Gresley	0-2
Holbeach U v Lincoln Moorlands R	3-1
Deeping R v Spalding U	2-1
Holbrook Sp v Greenwood Meadows	1-1, 2-0
Glossop NE v Boston T	2-4
Dunkirk v Arnold T	0-2
Radcliffe Olym v Heanor T	2-3
Borrowash Vic v Sleaford T	5-1
Gedling MW v Louth T	0-0, 1-2
Shirebrook T v Blackstones	2-1
Nuneaton Griff v Stratford T	0-7
Rocester v Wolverhampton Cas	3-1
Southam U v Tipton T	0-2
Coleshill T v Brockton	5-1
Highgate U v Willenhall T	2-0
Westfields v Norton U	2-4
Castle Vale v Heath Hayes	3-1
Bustleholme v Eccleshall	0-1
Lye T v Coventry Sphinx	0-5
Studley v Walsall Wood	2-1
Boldmere St M v Bartley Green	5-2
Malvern T v Causeway U	0-0, 0-5
Bridgnorth T v Ellesmere R	6-0
Atherstone T v Cadbury Ath	1-0
Tividale v Alvechurch	1-2
Gornal Ath v Shifnal T	2-2, 4-3
Stone Dominoes v Wellington	3-2
Cradley T v Continental Star	2-2, 2-3
Bloxwich U v AFC Wulfrunians	2-2, 0-3
Pegasus Jun v Bewdley T	1-1, 1-2
Friar Lane & Epworth withdrew v Loughborough Univ w.o.	
Thrapston T v Irchester U	3-2
Oadby T v Northampton Spencer	6-1
Rushden & Higham U v Cogenhoe U	2-3
Rothwell Cor v Wellingborough T	1-0
Bugbrooke St M v Anstey Nomads	2-1
Long Eaton U v Huntingdon T	0-4
Long Buckby v Stewarts & Lloyds C	1-0
Thurnby Nirvana v Desborough T	3-3, 5-0
Rothwell T v Raunds T	2-1
Barrow T v Kirby Muxloe	3-2
Daventry U v Bardon Hill Sp	2-1
Yaxley v Godmanchester R	0-2
Stanway R v Hadleigh U	2-3
King's Lynn T v Whitton U	6-1
Woodbridge T v Gorleston	2-2, 1-2
St Ives T v Debenham LC	3-2
Wroxham v Dereham T	3-1
Ipswich W v Newmarket T	3-1
Mildenhall T v Brantham Ath	0-4
Walsham-le-Willows v Thetford T	3-1
March T U v Kirkley & Pakefield	2-1
Ely C v Diss T	4-0
Stowmarket T v Haverhill R	1-4
Felixstowe & Walton U v Norwich U	1-0
Long Melford w.o. v Saffron Walden T removed	
Wisbech T v Halstead T	4-0
Great Yarmouth T v FC Clacton	0-3
Burnham Ram v Barking	1-1, 1-0
Hadley v Cockfosters	2-2, 0-0
Cockfosters won 5-4 on penalties.	
Haringey Bor v AFC Kempston R	2-0
Witham T v Bedford	4-1
St Margaretsbury v Dunstable T	0-3
Enfield 1893 v London Colney	3-1
Kings Langley v Stotfold	5-2
Tie awarded to Stotfold, Kings Langley removed.	
Colney Heath v Langford	3-1
Clapton v Stansted	0-1
Crawley Green v Berkhamsted	1-2
Hullbridge Sp v Royston T	1-3
Broxbourne Bor V&E v Hoddesdon T	4-0
Harringey & Waltham Dev v Bowers & Pitsea	4-1
Sawbridgeworth T v Hatfield T	2-2, 1-2
AFC Dunstable v Eton Manor	3-1
Biggleswade U v Leverstock Green	2-1
Takeley v Southend Manor	3-3, 2-3
London APSA v Basildon U	1-0
Oxhey Jets v Wodson Park	6-0
Barkingside v Hertford T	1-3
Bethnal Green U v Kentish T	2-1
Holmer Green v Harefield U	2-4
Sandhurst T v Thame U	2-3
Witney T v Newport Pagnell T	0-4
Tring Ath v Hanwell T	1-0
Wokingham & Emmbrook v Holyport	4-1
Staines Lammas v Clanfield 85	3-0
Bicester T removed v Bedfont Sp w.o.	
Old Woodstock T v Wantage T	1-2
Ascot U v Wembley	1-2
Abingdon T v Milton U	4-0
Kidlington v Hillingdon Bor	4-2
Hanworth Villa v Shrivenham	4-2
Ardley U v Flackwell Heath	3-0
Aylesbury U v Bracknell T	4-0
Reading T v Binfield	0-0, 0-3
Molesley v Egham T	0-3
Raynes Park Vale v Hassocks	3-1
Farnham T v Guildford C	1-0
Wick v Redhill	0-3
VCD Ath v Bookham	1-1, 2-0
Erith & Belvedere v St Francis R	2-0
Lancing v Horsham YMCA	2-2, 5-2
Chichester C v Fisher	2-2, 1-6
Pagham v Herne Bay	1-2
Colliers Wood U v Chessington & Hook U	1-1, 1-2
Ringmer v Deal T	0-2
Arundel v Sidley U	2-2, 5-1
Three Bridges v Camberley T	1-6
Sevenoaks T v Ash U	4-0
Shoreham v Holmesdale	3-1

Corinthian v Dorking	4-3
Mole Valley S.C.R. v Lordswood	2-3
Westfield v Peacehaven & Telscombe	3-6
Tunbridge Wells v Warlingham	1-0
South Park v AFC Uckfield	1-0
Greenwich Bor v Horley T	1-2
Banstead Ath v Woodstock Sp	3-0
Littlehampton T v Beckenham T	1-3
Erith T v Crowborough Ath	6-2
Selsey v Mile Oak	2-2, 2-1
Epsom & Ewell v Croydon	3-1
Cobham v Badshot Lea	2-2, 1-4
Hailsham T v Lingfield	0-4
Bridport v Hayling U	2-2, 2-0
Cowes Sp v Newport (IW)	1-4
Verwood T v Horndean	0-4
Romsey T v Brading T	0-1
Downton v Brockenhurst	3-3, 2-4
Alresford T v Devizes T	4-0
Totton & Eling v Fareham T	5-1
Cove v AFC Portchester	0-2
Petersfield T v Hartley Wintney	1-2
Hamworth U v Bournemouth	1-2
Shrewton U v Fleet Spurs	1-0
Winchester C v Ringwood T	5-0
Whitchurch U v Bemerton Heath Harl	3-2
Alton T v New Milton T	1-1, 6-0
Lymington T v Sherborne T	3-2
Blackfield & Langley v GE Hamble	3-1
Gillingham T v Newbury	1-2
Moneyfields v Christchurch	2-0
Welton R v Larkhall Ath	0-5
Melksham T v Almondsbury UWE	3-2
Hallen v Calne T	3-0
Fairford T v Wellington	3-0
Street v Shortwood U	0-2
Radstock T v Wootton Bassett T	2-1
Brislington v Lydney T	4-1
Pewsey Vale v Bishop Sutton	0-2
Slimbridge v Bradford T	3-1
Merthyr T v Bitton	2-2, 2-1
Bristol Manor Farm v Longwell Green Sp	1-1, 2-3
Hengrove Ath v Wells C	0-3
Highworth T v Odd Down	1-4
Corsham T v Cadbury Heath	1-6
Bodmin T v Falmouth T	6-3
Dawlish T removed v Tavistock w.o.	
St Blazey v Saltash U	1-0
Chard T v Torpoint Ath	1-2
Willand R v Barnstaple T	0-1
Buckland Ath v Ilfracombe T	4-0

PRELIMINARY ROUND

Erith & Belvedere v Selsey	4-1
Wakefield v Thackley	1-0
Causeway U v Leek T	3-4
AFC Dunstable v Grays Ath	2-3
Aylesbury U v North Leigh	0-0, 2-4
Slough T v Binfield	3-1
Romford v Royston T	3-2
Lingfield v Fisher	4-1
Newcastle Benfield v South Shields	1-1, 3-0
Dunston UTS v Durham C	4-0
Spennymoor T v Sunderland RCA	1-0
Guisborough T v Shildon	0-1
Bedlington Terriers v Billingham T	6-0
Whitley Bay v Marske U	2-0
Hebburn T v Whitehaven	2-2, 4-2
Penrith v Billingham Syn	3-2
Ashington v Northallerton T	2-1
Liversedge v Pickering T	2-2, 3-3
Pickering T won 5-4 on penalties.	
Armthorpe Wel v Brigg T	2-0
Silsden v Harrogate Railway Ath	1-1, 0-2
Pontefract Coll v Tadcaster Alb	2-3
Garforth T v Sheffield	3-2
Ossett T v Glasshoughton Wel	0-0, 3-1
Scarborough Ath v Barton T OB	2-2, 1-0
Goole v Staveley MW	1-1, 1-3
Parkgate v Hall Road R	2-2, 0-2
Tie awarded to Parkgate, Hall Road R fielded an ineligible player.	
AFC Blackpool v AFC Fylde	1-1, 2-3
Trafford v Cheadle T	3-0
Ossett Alb v Witton Alb	0-6
Cammell Laird v Atherton LR	3-1
Clitheroe v Skelmersdale U	4-0
Prescot Cables v Warrington T	0-2
Mossley v Runcorn Linnets	0-0, 0-4
Formby v Lancaster C	1-4
Squires Gate v Atherton Coll	1-0
Curzon Ashton v Bamber Bridge	1-1, 2-3
Woodley Sp v Bootle	3-1
Radcliffe Bor v Holker OB	3-0
Maine Road v Ashton Ath	0-0, 3-2
Congleton T v Runcorn T	0-6
Deeping R v Belper T	2-1
New Mills v Rainworth MW	3-2
Arnold T v Lincoln U	5-1
Grantham T v Stamford	1-0
Gresley v Shirebrook T	1-1, 3-2
Hucknall T v Holbeach U	0-0, 3-1
Borrowash Vic v Carlton T	1-3
Holbrook Sp v Lough T	1-3
Heanor T v Boston T	2-1
Castle Vale v AFC Wulfrunians	1-1, 3-3
AFC Wulfrunians won 5-4 on penalties.	
Newcastle T v Studley	6-2
Alvechurch v Eccleshall	1-1, 3-2
Bedworth U v Sutton Coldfield T	2-1
Rugby T v Gornal Ath	0-0, 3-4
Kidsgrove Ath v Atherstone T	5-1
Rocester v Halesowen T	2-1
Stratford T v Coventry Sphinx	2-1
Market Drayton T v Bewdley T	0-2
Continental Star v Bridgnorth T	1-2
Romulus v Norton U	3-1
Tipton T v Highgate U	4-1
Shepshed Dyn v Thrapston T	0-0, 1-2
Rothwell T v Barrow T	2-7
Thurnby Nirvana v St Neots T	2-0
Cogenhoe U v Loughborough Dyn	1-2
Rothwell Cor v Long Buckby	2-5
Woodford U v Daventry T	0-0, 0-5
Quorn v Oadby T	0-0, 3-1
Loughborough Univ v Godmanchester R	4-1
Coalville T v Daventry U	3-4
Bugbrooke St M v Huntingdon T	1-2
Leiston v FC Clacton	5-0
Needham Market v Felixstowe & Walton U	4-1
Haverhill R v Brantham Ath	3-2
Ely C v Walsham-le-Willows	1-1, 2-1
King's Lynn T v Soham T R	2-1
March T U v Wisbech T	1-1, 2-3
Hadleigh U v Heybridge Swifts	1-4
St Ives T v AFC Sudbury	0-0, 2-3
Maldon & Tiptree v Ipswich W	9-0
Wroxham v Long Melford	1-0
Gorleston v Harlow T	2-0
Burnham Ram v Hertford T	3-3, 2-2
Hertford T won 3-2 on penalties.	
Dunstable T v Bethnal Green U	1-1, 3-0
Potters Bar T v Broxbourne Bor V&E	1-3
Stotfold v Enfield T	2-1
Tilbury v Biggleswade U	3-1
Hatfield T v Enfield 1893	1-1, 2-1
Great Wakering R v Oxhey Jets	1-1, 0-1
Haringey Bor v Berkhamsted	0-1
Cheshunt v Southend Manor	0-0, 2-4
Waltham Forest v Ilford	1-1, 3-2
Waltham Abbey v Ware	6-1
Colney Heath v Brentwood T	0-1
Barton R v Witham T	3-0
Stansted v London APSA	4-0
Cockfosters v Redbridge	1-2
Biggleswade T v Haringey & Waltham Dev	5-5, 2-1
Newport Pagnell T v Thame U	1-1, 1-1
Thame U won 4-2 on penalties.	
Wokingham & Emmbrook v Kidlington	3-0
Bedfont Sp v Hanworth Villa	1-1, 0-2
Beaconsfield SYCOB v Northwood	2-1
Abingdon T v Didcot T	2-2, 2-3
Wantage T v Abingdon U	1-2
Leighton T v Uxbridge	2-0
Wembley v Ardley U	1-1, 2-1
AFC Hayes v Tring Ath	4-2
Chalfont St Peter v Aylesbury	4-2
Burnham v Ashford Town (Middlesex)	2-1
North Greenford U v Bedfont T	2-1
Staines Lammas v Harefield U	2-2, 2-0
Marlow v Thatcham T	1-0
Chatham T v Croydon Ath	1-0

Badshot Lea v Chertsey T 0-1
Folkestone Invicta v Whyteleafe 2-2, 2-1
Corinthian v Maidstone U 0-9
Walton & Hersham v Tunbridge Wells 3-1
Thamesmead T v Burgess Hill T 3-0
Crawley Down v Farnham T 2-1
Merstham v Egham T 1-1, 3-2
Dulwich Hamlet v Eastbourne T 2-0
Sittingbourne v Peacehaven & Telscombe 2-1
Whitstable T v Worthing 1-3
Epsom & Ewell v Chipstead 1-2
Banstead Ath v Arundel 3-1
Whitehawk v Ramsgate 0-0, 1-0
Beckenham T v Walton Cas 3-1
Chessington & Hook U v Hythe T 0-1
Lordswood v VCD Ath 0-1
Bognor Regis T v Camberley T 5-1
Shoreham v Lancing 1-0
Herne Bay v Deal T 3-0
Horley T v Corinthian Cas 3-1
Raynes Park Vale v Faversham T 0-1
Sevenoaks T v Redhill 1-3
Erith T v South Park 2-0
Totton & Eling v Bournemouth 1-2
Sholing v Newbury 9-1
Shrewton U v Hungerford T 0-1
Fleet T v Alton T 4-3
Wimborne T v Godalming T 1-2
Whitchurch U v Brading T 2-1
AFC Portchester v Newport (IW) 2-2, 1-2
Moneyfields v Gosport Bor 2-1
Winchester C v Blackfield & Langley 1-3
Andover removed v Poole T w.o.
Alresford T v Hartley Wintney 1-4
Lymington T v Brockenhurst 1-1, 1-2
Horndean v Bridport 3-1
Yate T v Melksham T 10-1
Merthyr T v Longwell Green Sp 1-0
Slimbridge v Cadbury Heath 1-2
Fairford T v Cinderford T 1-3
Shortwood U v Bishop Sutton 1-1, 1-4
Paulton R v Clevedon T 1-2
Mangotsfield U v Hallen 1-0
Tie awarded to Hallen; Mangotsfield U fielded an ineligible player.
Larkhall Ath v Odd Down 4-0
Bishop's Cleeve v Wells C 0-1
Radstock T v Brislington 1-2
St Blazey v Tavistock 1-2
Barnstaple T v Bodmin T 1-2
Taunton T v Buckland Ath 1-1, 2-0
Bideford v Tiverton T 4-0
Torpoint Ath v Bridgwater T 2-5
Stourport Swifts v Stone Dominoes 1-1, 1-2
Ramsbottom U v Salford C 2-1
Boldmere St M v Coleshill T 2-2, 1-0

FIRST QUALIFYING ROUND

Bamber Bridge v Warrington T 0-4
Ramsbottom U v Nantwich T 1-2
Grays Ath v Aveley 1-2
Wokingham & Emmbrook v North Greenford U 1-2
Romulus v Bridgnorth T 1-2
Spennymoor T v Dunston UTS 3-0
Bedlington Ter v Newcastle Benfield 4-0
Kendal T v Whitley Bay 1-0
Hebburn T v Penrith 2-0
Shildon v Ashington 0-0, 2-2
Ashington won 5-3 on penalties.
Armthorpe Wel v Stocksbridge PS 1-1, 1-3
Garforth T v Frickley Ath 0-2
Pickering T v Staveley MW 2-2, 0-4
Parkgate v Whitby T 1-3
Wakefield v Ossett T 4-0
North Ferriby U v Worksop T 1-0
Bradford PA v Harrogate Railway Ath 8-0
Tadcaster Alb v Scarborough Ath 3-0
Ashton U v Runcorn T 5-1
FC U of Manchester v Woodley Sp 1-1, 4-1
Squires Gate v Runcorn Linnets 0-0, 0-1
Lancaster C v Maine Road 5-1
AFC Fylde v Chorley 1-1, 1-0
Witton Alb v Marine 2-0
Burscough v Clitheroe 2-2. 2-5
Cammell Laird v Radcliffe Bor 1-2
Trafford v Northwich Vic 0-2

Deeping R v New Mills 5-1
Louth T v Buxton 0-2
Grantham T v Arnold T 2-0
Mickleover Sp v Gresley 4-2
Matlock T v Hucknall T 2-0
Carlton T v Heanor T 1-0
Evesham U v Rocester 4-0
Leamington v Boldmere St M 5-0
Leek T v Tipton T 2-0
Kidsgrove Ath v Gornal Ath 3-0
Chasetown v Alvechurch 6-2
Rushall Olym v Bedworth U 1-0
Bewdley T v Stourbridge 1-2
Redditch U v Hednesford T 0-2
AFC Wulfrunians v Stafford R 2-3
Newcastle T v Stratford T 5-5, 2-6
Barwell v Stone Dominoes 3-2
Thurnby Nirvana v Barrow T 1-1, 1-3
Long Buckby v Thrapston T 4-1
Huntingdon T v Daventry T 1-3
Quorn v Loughborough Univ 2-1
Loughborough Dyn v Daventry U 3-1
Cambridge C v Maldon & Tiptree 2-2, 1-2
Needham Market v Ely C 1-1, 4-3
Leiston v AFC Sudbury 0-1
Bury T v Gorleston 3-0
Heybridge Swifts v Lowestoft T 1-2
Wisbech T v Wroxham 1-4
King's Lynn T v Haverhill R 1-0
Tilbury v Arlesey T 1-2
Waltham Forest v Hitchin T 2-0
St Albans C v Berkhamsted 0-0, 3-0
Wingate & Finchley v Redbridge 0-3
Barton R v Hatfield T 1-1, 1-2
AFC Hornchurch v Concord R 1-3
Canvey Island v Stansted 4-1
Hemel Hempstead T v Brentwood T 0-0, 0-0
Hemel Hempstead T won 4-2 on penalties.
Hertford T v Oxhey Jets 0-1
East Thurrock U v Bedford T 1-0
Biggleswade T v Waltham Abbey 3-1
Billericay T v Stotfold 4-0
Dunstable T v Broxbourne Bor V&E 7-0
Southend Manor v Romford 4-2
Burnham v Chalfont St Peter 1-0
Leatherhead v North Leigh 5-1
Chesham U v Staines Lammas 3-2
Leighton T v Abingdon U 4-1
Oxford C v Didcot T 1-1, 3-0
Banbury U v Slough T 1-3
AFC Hayes v Hendon 0-3
Harrow Bor v Marlow 2-0
Thame U v Brackley T 2-0
Hanworth Villa v Wembley 1-0
Wealdstone v Beaconsfield SYCOB 0-2
Carshalton Ath v Faversham T 3-0
Herne Bay v Erith T 2-3
Margate v Tooting & Mitcham U 3-0
Chertsey T v Lewes 4-1
Hastings U v Cray W 0-3
Bognor Regis T v Sittingbourne 1-0
Beckenham T v Met Police 4-2
Chatham T v Worthing 0-1
Banstead Ath v Maidstone U 1-9
Merstham v Walton & Hersham 2-1
Crawley Down v VCD Ath 0-2
Horley T v Dulwich Hamlet 0-4
Chipstead v Redhill 3-1
Shoreham v Thamesmead T 0-2
Hythe T v Erith & Belvedere 5-2
Folkestone Invicta v Whitehawk 0-3
Horsham v Lingfield 2-2, 4-2
Hungerford T v Horndean 3-1
Whitchurch U v Brockenhurst 2-0
Sholing v Blackfield & Langley 2-1
Poole T v Kingstonian 3-0
Bournemouth v Newport (IW) 2-1
Hartley Wintney v Bashley 1-0
AFC Totton v Fleet T 2-0
Godalming T v Moneyfields 1-1, 3-1
Chippenham T v Wells C 3-0
Chippenham T removed; tie awarded to Wells C.
Merthyr T v Cinderford T 1-1, 0-2
Yate T v Larkhall Ath 1-0
Swindon Supermarine v Cirencester T 3-2

Hallen v Frome T 2-2, 1-1
Frome T won 4-2 on penalties.
Clevedon T v Brislington 3-2
Bishop Sutton v Cadbury Heath 0-4
Bideford v Bridgwater T 2-1
Weymouth v Taunton T 0-0, 3-1
Tavistock v Bodmin T 1-3

SECOND QUALIFYING ROUND
Northwich Vic v Nantwich T 1-2
Stalybridge C v Guiseley 1-2
Workington v Droylsden 1-2
FC Halifax T v Tadcaster Alb 2-1
Wakefield v Kendal T 1-4
Stocksbridge PS v Colwyn Bay 3-1
Clitheroe v Radcliffe Bor 1-3
Staveley MW v Hyde 0-3
Blyth Spartans v Bedlington Ter 2-1
Ashton U v Spennymoor T 0-3
AFC Fylde v Gainsborough T 2-2, 1-2
Hebburn T v Runcorn Linnets 1-0
FC U of Manchester v Lancaster C 0-1
Bradford PA v Warrington T 3-1
Whitby T v North Ferriby U 2-1
Frickley Ath v Harrogate T 1-1, 2-1
Altrincham v Witton Alb 0-2
Ashington v Vauxhall Motors 3-3, 1-0
Histon v Corby T 1-1, 1-3
Mickleover Sp v Barrow T 1-4
Stafford R v Stratford T 2-4
Deeping R v Leek T 0-2
Buxton v Rushall Olym 1-2
Matlock T v Hinckley U 1-3
Eastwood T v Evesham U 0-3
Barwell v Stourbridge 0-2
Chasetown v Grantham T 1-2
Bridgnorth T v Long Buckby 0-2
Carlton T v Hednesford T 0-1
Daventry T v Leamington 2-1
Needham Market v Nuneaton T 0-3
Solihull Moors v Loughborough Dyn 2-0
Boston U v Kidsgrove Ath 0-0, 0-2
Kings Lynn T v Quorn 4-2
Chipstead v Billericay T 0-3
Oxhey Jets v Hendon 1-2
Hanworth Villa v Aveley 1-0
Cray W v Erith T 5-0
Arlesey T v Hampton & Richmond Bor 6-2
Redbridge v Bury T 1-0
Slough T v Boreham Wood 3-2
East Thurrock U v St Albans C 3-3, 3-1
Southend Manor v Chertsey T 4-2
Dover Ath v Carshalton Ath 3-0
North Greenford U v Hythe T 2-1
Chelmsford C v Tonbridge Angels 3-0
Sutton U v Dulwich Hamlet 5-1
Wroxham v Concord R 2-2, 2-1
Dartford v Harrow Bor 5-0
Margate v Thamesmead T 0-0, 6-1
Bromley v Welling U 2-1
Leighton T v Hatfield T 3-0
Whitehawk v Maldon & Tiptree 0-0, 1-2
Staines T v Beaconsfield SYCOB 0-0, 2-0
Burnham v Horsham 2-2, 3-2
Dunstable T v Chesham U 2-1
Biggleswade T v Leatherhead 1-1, 1-2
Canvey Island v Bishop's Stortford 0-1
Maidstone U v Bognor Regis T 2-3
Merstham v AFC Sudbury 0-2
Lowestoft T v Hemel Hempstead T 3-0
VCD Ath v Thurrock 2-2, 0-1
Worthing v Beckenham T 0-0, 2-1
Havant & Waterlooville v Sholing 4-1
Frome T v Basingstoke T 0-0, 0-2
Thame U v Oxford C 1-3
Bournemouth v Truro C 0-0, 2-3
Dorchester T v Weston Super M 0-1
Whitchurch U v Gloucester C 0-2
Wells C v Woking 0-7
Salisbury C v Swindon Supermarine 3-0
Yate T v Bodmin T 1-1, 1-4
Godalming T v Worcester C 2-1
Poole T v Cadbury Heath 4-0

Eastleigh v Cinderford T 3-1
Weymouth v Hungerford T 3-3, 3-1
Hartley Wintney v Bideford 2-1
Maidenhead U v Farnborough 1-1, 3-2
Clevedon T v AFC Totton 1-2
Waltham Forest v Eastbourne Bor 0-3

THIRD QUALIFYING ROUND
Nantwich T v Kendal T 2-1
Radcliffe Bor v Hebburn T 2-4
Lancaster C v FC Halifax T 0-3
Whitby T v Blyth Spartans 1-2
Gainsborough T v Frickley Ath 2-0
Hyde v Bradford PA 0-1
Ashington v Guiseley 1-0
Witton Alb v Spennymoor T 3-1
Droylsden v Stocksbridge PS 4-1
King's Lynn T v Stratford T 3-2
Daventry T v Nuneaton T 1-2
Hednesford T v Corby T 2-4
Kidsgrove Ath v Long Buckby 2-1
Hinckley U v Leek T 3-3, 2-1
Solihull Moors v Grantham T 3-2
Barrow T v Rushall Olym 0-3
Stourbridge v Evesham U 5-0
Billericay T v Leatherhead 0-3
Worthing v Staines T 0-2
Redbridge v Dunstable T 3-0
Eastbourne Bor v AFC Sudbury 1-0
Lowestoft T v Chelmsford C 2-5
Cray W v Dartford 1-2
Maldon & Tiptree v Hendon 1-3
Thurrock v Arlesey T 0-0, 1-4
Burnham v Bishop's Stortford 2-5
Slough T v Hanworth Villa 2-2, 1-3
East Thurrock U v North Greenford U 3-3, 3-0
Dover Ath v Wroxham 3-1
Margate v Bromley 2-3
Southend Manor v Leighton T 5-0
Sutton U v Bognor Regis T 4-0
Basingstoke T v Hartley Wintney 4-0
Bodmin T v Godalming T 1-1, 1-5
Gloucester C v Truro C 7-2
AFC Totton v Weymouth 4-2
Eastleigh v Oxford C 1-3
Salisbury C v Poole T 6-1
Weston Super M v Havant & Waterlooville 3-2
Maidenhead U v Woking 4-1

FOURTH QUALIFYING ROUND
Tamworth v King's Lynn T 2-1
Droylsden v Blyth Spartans 0-0, 1-2
Stourbridge v Rushall Olym 5-0
Kidsgrove Ath v Bradford PA 0-2
Gateshead v Hebburn T 3-0
Grimsby T v Ashington 5-0
Wrexham v York C 2-1
Mansfield T v Fleetwood T 1-1, 0-5
Nantwich T v Nuneaton T 1-0
Alfreton T v Lincoln C 1-1, 2-1
AFC Telford U v Gainsborough T 5-0
Southport v Stockport Co 1-0
Solihull Moors v FC Halifax T 0-1
Kidderminster H v Corby T 0-0, 1-4
Darlington v Hinckley U 1-1, 0-3
Witton Alb v Barrow 1-4
Dover Ath v Bath C 0-1
Bishop's Stortford v Salisbury C 1-2
Eastbourne Bor v East Thurrock U 1-2
Chelmsford C v Gloucester C 1-1, 1-0
Hayes & Yeading U v Cambridge U 2-6
Godalming T v Maidenhead U 0-5
Sutton U v Leatherhead 3-3, 3-2
Weston Super M v Oxford C 2-3
AFC Totton v Hanworth Villa 3-2
Basingstoke T v Staines T 2-1
Arlesey T v Forest Green R 2-1
Dartford v Bromley 1-2
Luton T v Hendon 5-1
Kettering T v Southend Manor 3-1
Redbridge v Ebbsfleet U 2-0
Newport Co v Braintree T 4-3

THE E.ON FA CUP 2011–12

COMPETITION PROPER

■ *Denotes player sent off.*

FIRST ROUND

Friday, 11 November 2011

Cambridge U (0) 2 *(Coulson 53, 90)*

Wrexham (1) 2 *(Morrell 20, 60)* 2782

Cambridge U: Naisbitt; Roberts, Jennings, Coulson, McAuley, Shaw, Carew (Marriott), Jarvis (Patrick), Gash (Charles), Berry, Dunk.
Wrexham: Mayebi; Westwood, Ashton, Creighton (Hunt), Knight-Percival, Clarke, Tolley, Fowler, Wright D, Morrell (Cieslewicz), Pogba (Speight).

Saturday, 12 November 2011

AFC Totton (3) 8 *(Davies 13, 90, Gosney 29 (pen), 52, Charles 32, Brown 64, 74, 79)*

Bradford PA (1) 1 *(Clayton 30)* 2315

AFC Totton: Porter; Hill, Baddeley, Campbell, Whisken, Scott (Richardson), Pettefer, Davies, Sherborne (Osman), Charles (Brown), Gosney.
Bradford PA: Lamb; Clayton, Drury■, O'Brien, Iqbal, Riley, Daly (Deacey), Hotte, Marshall■, Greaves (Ahmed), Boshell (Beadle).

AFC Wimbledon (0) 0

Scunthorpe U (0) 0 2933

AFC Wimbledon: Brown; Hatton, Bush, Porter, Stuart, Johnson B, Moore S, Yussuff (Wellard), Jolley, Midson (Ademeno), Djilali (Jackson).
Scunthorpe U: Slocombe; Wright, Nolan, Togwell, Nelson, Canavan, Duffy M, O'Connor, Dagnall (Thompson), Grant, Ajose.

Alfreton T (0) 0

Carlisle U (4) 4 *(Miller 24, Loy 33, Berrett 41, Noble 45)* 1488

Alfreton T: Day; Law (Mullan), Brown A, Streete, Young, Franks, Hall, Church, Clayton, Wilson A (Jarman), Arnold (Senior).
Carlisle U: Collin; Ribeiro, Robson, Thirlwell (Zoko), Livesey, Michalik, McGovern (Curran), Berrett (Taiwo), Miller, Loy, Noble.

Barrow (1) 1 *(Rutherford 16)*

Rotherham U (0) 2 *(Grabban 82, 87 (pen))* 3030

Barrow: Hurst; Pearson M (Nicholas), Skelton, Owen, Bolland, Smith, Rutherford, Baker, Almond (Cook), Mackreth, Boyes.
Rotherham U: Logan; Tonge, Newey, Harrison, Branston, Foster (Schofield), Evans, Taylor J, Grabban, Revell, Holroyd (Williams).

Blyth Spartans (0) 0

Gateshead (1) 2 *(Shaw 14, Cummins 54)* 2763

Blyth Spartans: Knight; Slaughter, Cave (Forster), Phillips, Groves, Pearson, Mason (Offiong), Hooks, Armstrong (Taylor), Mole, Emms.
Gateshead: Alnwick; Baxter (Henderson), Carruthers, Gate, Curtis, Clark, Brittain (Moore), Turnbull, Shaw, Fisher, Cummins (Nix).

Bournemouth (1) 3 *(Purches 20, Zubar 59, Malone 60)*

Gillingham (1) 3 *(Payne J 37, Jackman 71, Kedwell 90)* 4282

Bournemouth: Flahavan; Francis, Cummings, Arter, Barrett, Zubar, Purches, Malone, Thomas G, Symes, Pugh.
Gillingham: Gazzaniga; Fish, Martin, Lee C, Lawrence, Frampton, Whelpdale (Oli), Payne J (Montrose), Kedwell, Rooney (Payne S), Jackman.

Bradford C (0) 1 *(Wells 84)*

Rochdale (0) 0 3579

Bradford C: McLaughlin; Moore (Ramsden), O'Brien, Flynn, Williams, Oliver, Mitchell, Jones, Hannah (Wells), Devitt (Hanson), Compton.
Rochdale: Lucas; Holden, Jordan, Holness, Barry-Murphy, Tutte (Eccleston), Kennedy, Jones, Bunn, Akpa Akpro, Adams (Grimes).

Brentford (1) 1 *(Saunders 9)*

Basingstoke T (0) 0 3553

Brentford: Lee; Logan, Adams, Diagouraga, Eger, Llera (Legge), Saunders, O'Connor (Bean), Alexander, Grella (Donaldson), McGinn.
Basingstoke T: Bayes; Smart, Little, Rice, Gasson, Lake, Ogunbote (Lockyer), McAuley, Sills, Sam-Yorke (Pratt), Warner.

Bristol R (1) 3 *(McGleish 26 (pen), Carayol 74, Zebroski 90)*

Corby T (0) 1 *(Reynolds 62)* 3787

Bristol R: Bevan; Woodards, Brown L, Sawyer, Bolger, Stanley (Goddard), Carayol, Dorman, Harrold, McGleish (Richards), Zebroski.
Corby T: MacKenzie; Gordon, Mayo, Reynolds, Gulliver, Hibbert (Malone), Hall (Ives), Ozmen (Spruce), Rhead, Rogan, Smith.

Bury (0) 0

Crawley T (0) 2 *(Barnett 49, Doughty 82)* 2436

Bury: Belford; Picken, Skarz, Schumacher, Hughes■, Eastham, Byrne, Sweeney (Worrall), Harrad (Amoo), Bishop, Jones M.
Crawley T: Shearer; Hunt (Dempster), Howell, Bulman, McFadzean (Doughty), Mills, Drury, Torres, Tubbs (Akpan), Barnett, Simpson.

Chelmsford C (2) 4 *(Palmer 11, Parker 45, Rainford 63 (pen), 87)*

AFC Telford U (0) 0 1430

Chelmsford C: Searle; Miller, Palmer, Tann, Clark, Rainford, Whitely (Benjamin), Corcoran, Ibe, Cornhill, Morgan (Parker).
AFC Telford U: Young; Salmon, Newton, Davies (Farrell), Preston (Rooney), Killock, Mills, Trainer, Sharp, Brown (Weir-Daley), Adams.

Chesterfield (0) 1 *(Bowery 59)*

Torquay U (1) 3 *(Stevens 20, Howe 72, Nicholson 88)* 4332

Chesterfield: Soderberg; Talbot, Grounds, Trotman, Mattis (Smith), Whitaker, Mendy, Allott, Westcarr, Clarke (Clay), Bowery.
Torquay U: Olejnik; Oastler, Nicholson, Mansell, Ellis, Saah, Lathrope, O'Kane, Howe (Atieno), Morris (McPhee), Stevens (Rowe-Turner).

Crewe Alex (1) 1 *(Moore 19)*

Colchester U (0) 4 *(James 60, 90, Bond 77, Coker 87)* 2325

Crewe Alex: Phillips; Tootle, Martin C, Westwood■, Artell, Dugdale, Bell (Mellor), Murphy, Moore, Leitch-Smith (Hughes), Powell (Sarcevic).
Colchester U: Williams B; Wilson, Coker, James, Okuonghae, Heath, Bond, Vincent (Duguid), Odejayi, Henderson, Thomas (Izzet).

Dagenham & R (1) 1 *(Woodall 41)*

Bath C (1) 1 *(Canham S 11)* 1225

Dagenham & R: Lewington; Ogogo, McCrory, Walsh, Rose, Ilesanmi, Green Danny J, Gain, Nurse, Woodall (Green Dominic), Scannell (Scott).
Bath C: Garner; Simpson, Gallinagh, Rollo (Clough), Jones, Burnell, Russell, Connolly, Watkins, Canham S (Phillips), Cook (Stonehouse).

East Thurrock U (0) 0
Macclesfield T (1) 3 *(Tremarco 43, Hamshaw 61, Donnelly 65)* 1207
East Thurrock U: Wray; Sammons, Stephen, Wood, Peddie, Gilbey, Newby (Elbi), Cohen, Higgins, Ruel, Collins.
Macclesfield T: Veiga; Bateson, Tremarco, Chalmers (Fairhurst), Brown, Brisley, Wedgbury, Draper, Donnelly (Roberts), Boden (Hamshaw), Daniel.

Exeter C (0) 1 *(Noble 90)*
Walsall (1) 1 *(Wilson 21)* 3026
Exeter C: Pidgeley; Tully, Coles, Dunne, Archibald-Henville, Sercombe, Shephard (Duffy), Noble, O'Flynn (Logan), Nardiello (Frear), Golbourne.
Walsall: Grof; Beevers, Sadler, Wilson, Butler, Smith, Paterson (Jarvis), Chambers, Nicholls, Macken (Grigg), Gnakpa (Taundry).

Fleetwood T (1) 2 *(Mangan 25, Vardy 80)*
Wycombe W (0) 0 2711
Fleetwood T: Davies; Beeley, Goodall, Milligan, McNulty, Pond, Clancy (Briggs), McGuire, Mangan (Vieira), Brodie■, Vardy (Till).
Wycombe W: Bull; Foster, Basey, Rowlands (Ibe), Winfield (Benyon), Johnson, Lewis, Donnelly, Harris (Rendell), Strevens, Grant.

Hartlepool U (0) 0
Stevenage (1) 1 *(Laird 10 (pen))* 2744
Hartlepool U: Flinders■; Austin, Humphreys (Boyd), Liddle, Wright, Hartley, Solano (Luscombe), Sweeney, Poole, Monkhouse, Horwood (Rafferty).
Stevenage: Day; Henry, Laird, Roberts, Ashton, Bostwick, Wilson, Mousinho (Long), Beardsley (Byrom), Reid (Harrison), Shroot.

Hereford U (0) 0
Yeovil T (1) 3 *(Upson 25, Williams A 57, Blizzard 72)* 2469
Hereford U: Cornell; Purdie, Heath, Pell, Green, Townsend, Featherstone (Evans W), McQuilkin (Arquin), Elder, Clucas (Facey), Clist.
Yeovil T: Stewart; Ayling, N'Gala, Ehmer, Huntington, Wotton, Blizzard, Upson, Williams A, Johnson (Gibson), Agard.

Hinckley U (0) 2 *(Gray 78, Kerry 88)*
Tamworth (0) 2 *(Christie 83 (pen), Patterson 90)* 1906
Hinckley U: Haystead■; Oddy, Dudley, Lavery, Raglan, Belcher, Kerry, Gooding, Joyce (Newton), Gray (Holt), Byrne (Hinds).
Tamworth: Hedge; Tait, Kanyuka, Smith (McDonald), Green, Francis, Patterson, Cain (Shariff), Christie, Barrow, Thomas (Mills).

Leyton Orient (1) 3 *(Spring 7, Porter 57, Smith Jimmy 79)*
Bromley (0) 0 4452
Leyton Orient: Alnwick; McSweeney, Daniels, Smith Jimmy, Cuthbert, Forbes, Spring (Laird), Dawson, Mooney, Porter (Odubajo), Cox (Cureton).
Bromley: Forecast; Udoji, Patterson, Harwood, Dolan, Gilman, Hill (Smith), Waldren (Goldberg), Araba (McBean), Williams, Rhule■.

Luton T (0) 1 *(Watkins 80)*
Northampton T (0) 0 4799
Luton T: Pilkington K; Osano, Howells, Keane (Crow), Kovacs, Pilkington G, Lawless, Hand, O'Connor, Morgan-Smith (Willmott), Kissock (Watkins).
Northampton T: Walker; Johnson (Holt), Young (Davies), Crowe, Westwood, Langmead, Jacobs, Tozer, Berahino, Akinfenwa, Arthur (Turnbull).

Maidenhead U (1) 1 *(Thomas 7)*
Aldershot T (0) 1 *(Rankine 78)* 2283
Maidenhead U: Beasant; Behzadi, Solomon, Brown, Henry, Scarborough, Powell, Hendry (Fagan), Holgate, Thomas (Wall), Tilson-Lascaris (Williams).
Aldershot T: Young; Herd, Straker, Guttridge, Jones, Brown A, McGlashan (Bubb), Collins J, Vincenti (Rankine), Hylton, Davies (Rodman).

Milton Keynes D (2) 6 *(Doumbe 28, Bowditch 30, 54, Powell 66, O'Shea 76, Williams G 90)*
Nantwich T (0) 0 4110
Milton Keynes D: Martin; Chicksen, Baldock G, Doumbe, Flanagan, Williams S, Powell (O'Shea), Chadwick (Galloway), Bowditch, MacDonald (Williams G), Balanta.
Nantwich T: Brain; Lowe, Solovjovs, Maguire (Jack), Bailey, Moss, Cook, Summerskill, Mills, Brunt (Lennon), McLachlan (Mitchell).

Newport Co (0) 0
Shrewsbury T (1) 1 *(Gornell 41)* 2362
Newport Co: Potter; Rodgers, Hughes, Doherty (Buchanan), Yakubu, Hatswell (Warren), Rose D, Pipe, McAllister, Foley, Knights (Jarvis).
Shrewsbury T: Neal C; Cansdell-Sherriff, Jacobson, McAllister S (Wroe), Sharps, Grandison (Goldson), Wright, Wildig, Gornell, Morgan, Richards.

Notts Co (1) 4 *(Hawley 34, 89, Judge 47, Sheehan 80)*
Accrington S (0) 1 *(Joyce 85)* 3613
Notts Co: Nelson; Kelly, Sheehan, Edwards, Pearce, Mahon (Allen), Bishop (Bencherif), Judge, Burgess, Hawley, Hughes J (Demontagnac).
Accrington S: Murdoch; McIntyre, Winnard, Hughes (Dobie), Hessey, Procter■, Evans, Barnett (Bender), Coid (Amond), Stockley, Joyce.

Oldham Ath (3) 3 *(Kuqi 4 (pen), Simpson 13, Furman 35)*
Burton Alb (0) 1 *(Zola 71)* 3102
Oldham Ath: Cisak; Lee, Mellor (Black), Wesolowski, Diamond, Mvoto, Scapuzzi (Morais), Furman, Simpson (Adeyemi), Kuqi, Taylor.
Burton Alb: Atkins; Corbett, Blanchett, Stanton, Austin■, McGrath, Taylor (James), Bolder (Palmer), Maghoma, Zola, Phillips (Gurrieri).

Plymouth Arg (1) 3 *(Feeney 4, Fletcher C 70, Bhasera 88)*
Stourbridge (1) 3 *(Drake 37, Rowe 53, Gebbis 82 (pen))* 6173
Plymouth Arg: Larrieu; Bignot, Williams■, Fletcher C, Nelson, Walton, Atkinson, Hourihane■, Lecointe, Feeney (Vassell), Bhasera.
Stourbridge: Solly; Rock (Evans), Lloyd, McCone, Gebbis, Bennett, Smith, Broadhurst, Rowe, Billingham, Drake (Craddock).

Port Vale (0) 0
Grimsby T (0) 0 4450
Port Vale: Tomlinson; Yates, Taylor R, Griffith, McCombe, Collins, Loft, Rigg (Morsy), Dodds, Pope, Roberts.
Grimsby T: McKeown; Wood, Townsend, Panther (Artus), Kempson, L'Anson, Thanoj, Disley, Duffy (Elding), Hearn (Makofo), Coulson.

Preston NE (0) 0
Southend U (0) 0 6609
Preston NE: Stuckmann; McLaughlin, Parry, Ashbee, Carlisle, Morgan, Nicholson (Middleton), Coutts, Tsoumou, Clark (Zibaka), Mayor.
Southend U: Daniels; Clohessy, Gilbert, Kalala (Mohsni), Barker, Phillips, Leonard, Ferdinand, Dickinson, Timlin, Hall.

Redbridge (0) 0
Oxford C (0) 0 465
Redbridge: Rafis; Turpin, Durrant, Haywood, Golby, Trenkel, Bradbury (Stamp), Hopkins, Murray (St Hilaire), Gardner, Gordon (Robinson).
Oxford C: McCloughin; Clarke, Learoyd, Ballard, Pond, Blossom, Lyon, Benjamin (Martin), Barcelos, Basham (Steele), Ashton.

Salisbury C (1) 3 *(Fitchett 12, Reid 55 (pen), Kelly 89)*

Arlesey T (1) 1 *(Sinclair 41)* 1298

Salisbury C: Smith; Ruddick, Brett, Adelsbury, Webb, Giles (Casey), Clarke (Kelly), Anderson, Fitchett, Reid (Wright), Knight.
Arlesey T: Osborn; Deeney, Perpetuini, Frater, Brown, Sinclair, Mason, Allinson (Goss), Dillon, Sinclair, Marsh (Patrick).

Sheffield U (2) 3 *(Evans 12, 19, Flynn 71)*

Oxford U (0) 0 7991

Sheffield U: Simonsen; Lowton, Williams, Montgomery, Collins, Maguire, Williamson (McAllister), Doyle, Evans, Cresswell, Quinn (Flynn).
Oxford U: Clarke; Batt, Kinniburgh, McLaren (Constable), Whing, Wright, Leven (Payne), Heslop, Franks (Worley), Smalley, Hall A.

Southport (0) 1 *(Akrigg 71)*

Barnet (0) 2 *(Kamdjo 59, Taylor 90)* 1939

Southport: McMillan; Lever (Carden), Owens (Brown), Akrigg, Grand, Poku, Whalley, Moogan, Aley (Davis), Gray, Ledsham.
Barnet: Brill; Senda, Borrowdale (Saville), Hughes, Dennehy, Downing, Deering, Byrne, Taylor, Kamdjo, Marshall (Parkes).

Sutton U (0) 1 *(Watkins 64)*

Kettering T (0) 0 1532

Sutton U: Scriven; Telfer (El-Salahi), Bray, Beautyman, Downer, Page, Riviere, Watkins, Griffiths, Dundas, Orilonishe (Taggart).
Kettering T: Walker; Sangare, Kelly (Ifil P), Meechan, Swaibu, Ifil J, Dawkin, Bridges, Cunnington, Marna, Verma (Ashikodi).

Swindon T (2) 4 *(Flint 36, De Vita 39, Kerrouche 76, Ferry 87)*

Huddersfield T (1) 1 *(Novak 22)* 5728

Swindon T: Foderingham; Caddis, Kennedy, Flint, McCormack, Risser, Ritchie, Ferry, De Vita (Smith J), Connell (Kerrouche), Gabilondo (Esajas).
Huddersfield T: Colgan; Woods, Naysmith (Cadamarteri), Miller, McCombe, Kay, McDermott (Arfield), Robinson, Lee, Novak, Roberts (Ward).

Tranmere R (0) 0

Cheltenham T (1) 1 *(Duffy 21 (pen))* 3211

Tranmere R: fon Williams; Raven, Buchanan, Weir, Goodison, Taylor, Akins (Labadie), Welsh, Tiryaki (Showunmi), Robinson, McGurk (Devaney).
Cheltenham T: Brown; Lowe, Jombati, Pack, Bennett, Elliott, Low (Smikle), Penn (Hooman), Duffy (Goulding), Mohamed, Summerfield.

Sunday, 13 November 2011

FC Halifax T (0) 0

Charlton Ath (1) 4 *(Taylor 40, Jackson 80, Hollands 82, Pritchard 90)* 4601

FC Halifax T: Eastwood; Toulson, McManus, Hardy, Hogan, Lowe■, Rainford (Anderson), Baker, Holland (St Juste), Gregory, Garner (Winter).
Charlton Ath: Sullivan; Solly, Evina, Hollands (Pritchard), Morrison, Taylor, Wagstaff, Hughes, Hayes (Wright-Phillips), Euell (Smith), Jackson.

Morecambe (0) 1 *(Wilson 62 (pen))*

Sheffield W (1) 2 *(Lines 18, O'Grady 52)* 4160

Morecambe: Roche; Parrish (Haining), Wilson, McDonald, McCready, Fenton, Reid (Alessandra), Drummond, Carlton, Ellison, Hunter (Jevons).
Sheffield W: O'Donnell; Buxton, Bennett, Batth, Johnson R, Semedo, Lines, O'Connor, O'Grady, Madine, Johnson J (Sedgwick).

FIRST ROUND REPLAYS

Tuesday, 22 November 2011

Aldershot T (2) 2 *(Rodman 15, Guttridge 34)*

Maidenhead U (0) 0 2181

Aldershot T: Young; Herd, Straker, Guttridge (Vincenti), Jones, Morris, McGlashan (Hylton), Collins J, Rankine (Mekki), Davies, Rodman.
Maidenhead U: Beasant; Behzadi, Solomon, Brown, Saroya (McKain), Scarborough, Powell, Hendry, Holgate, Thomas (Williams), Stanislaus (Wall).

Gillingham (1) 3 *(Weston 21, Richards 75, Payne S 82)*

Bournemouth (0) 2 *(Frampton 55 (og), Arter 90)* 4321

Gillingham: Flitney; Lee C, Martin, Montrose, Frampton, Richards, Whelpdale (Payne S), Weston (Rance), Kedwell, Oli (Fish), Payne J.
Bournemouth: Flahavan; Francis, Cummings (Gregory), Arter, Barrett, Zubar, Purches (Cooper), Malone, Thomas G, Symes (Fletcher), Pugh.

Grimsby T (0) 1 *(Makofo 59)*

Port Vale (0) 0 1906

Grimsby T: McKeown; Wood, Townsend, Panther, Pearson, L'Anson, Makofo (Eagle), Disley, Hearn, Elding, Coulson.
Port Vale: Martin; Yates (Roe), Collins, Griffith, McCombe, McDonald (Kozluk), Morsy (Rigg), Roberts, Dodds, Pope, Taylor R.

Oxford C (1) 1 *(Steele 20)*

Redbridge (0) 2 *(Gordon 70, Bradbury 102)* 1175

Oxford C: McCloughlin; Clarke, Learoyd, Ballard, Pond, Blossom, Lyon (Isaac), Basham, Barcelos (Martin), Steele, Ashton (Benjamin).
Redbridge: Rafis; Sendall (Haywood), Durrant, Turpin, Golby, Trenkel, Bradbury, Hopkins (Gardner), Dark, Robinson (Murray), Gordon.
aet.

Scunthorpe U (0) 0

AFC Wimbledon (0) 1 *(Moore L 66)* 2036

Scunthorpe U: Slocombe; Wright, Nolan, Togwell (Norwood), Nelson, Canavan, Duffy M (Thompson), O'Connor, Dagnall, Grant, Barcham.
AFC Wimbledon: Brown; Jackson (Midson), Bush, Wellard, Stuart, Johnson B, Hatton, Moore S (Porter), Ademeno (Mulley), Moore L, Yussuff.

Southend U (0) 1 *(Dickinson 55)*

Preston NE (0) 0 4537

Southend U: Daniels; Clohessy, Gilbert, Mohsni, Barker, Phillips (Kalala), Ferdinand, Timlin, Harris (Sturrock), Dickinson, Hall.
Preston NE: Stuckmann; Gray (McLaughlin), Parry, Barton (Middleton), Carlisle, Morgan, Nicholson, Coutts, Tsoumou (Zibaka), Mellor, Mayor.

Stourbridge (0) 2 *(McCone 52, Evans 73)*

Plymouth Arg (0) 0 2519

Stourbridge: Solly; Rock (Canavan), Lloyd, McCone, Gebbis (Dyson), Bennett, Smith, Broadhurst, Rowe, Billingham, Evans (Craddock).
Plymouth Arg: Cole; Bignot■, Bhasera, Nelson, Gibson, Walton, Daley (Berry), Hourihane, Feeney (Vassell), Fletcher C (Lecointe), Atkinson.

Tamworth (0) 1 *(St Aimie 90)*

Hinckley U (0) 0 1583

Tamworth: Hedge; Tait, Habergham, Bradley, Francis, Kanyuka, McDonald, Patterson (Barrow), Shariff, St Aimie, Thomas (Christie).
Hinckley U: Hinds; Oddy, Dudley, Lavery, Raglan, Belcher (Joyce), Kerry, Gooding, Newton, Gray, Byrne.

Wrexham (0) 2 *(Pogba 59, Wright D 76)*

Cambridge U (0) 1 *(Wylde 87)* 2606

Wrexham: Mayebi; Obeng, Ashton, Creighton, Knight-Percival, Harris, Tolley (Fowler), Clarke, Wright D, Morrell (Speight), Pogba.

Cambridge U: Naisbitt; Roberts, Jennings, Coulson, Wylde, Shaw, Carew, Jarvis (Berry), Gash (Charles), Hughes, Dunk (Patrick).

Wednesday, 23 November 2011

Bath C (0) 1 *(Connolly 71)*

Dagenham & R (1) 3 *(Woodall 20, Nurse 100, 115)* 1704

Bath C: Garner; Simpson, Stonehouse, Burnell (Rollo), Gallinagh, Clough, Watkins, Connolly, Canham S (Murray), Russell (Phillips), Hogg.
Dagenham & R: Lewington; Ogogo, McCrory, Rose, Doe, Ilesanmi, Green Dominic (Elito), Gain, Nurse, Woodall (Scott), Tomlin.
aet.

Walsall (0) 3 *(Macken 64, Nicholls 69, Bowerman 98)*

Exeter C (1) 2 *(Logan 41, Frear 77)* 2089

Walsall: Walker; Beevers, Sadler, Taundry, Lancashire, Butler, Wilson (Peterlin), Chambers, Grigg (Bowerman), Macken (Jarvis), Nicholls.
Exeter C: Krysiak; Tully, Golbourne, Dunne, Archibald-Henville, Coles, Sercombe, Duffy (Keohane), O'Flynn (Nichols), Logan, Shephard (Frear).
aet.

SECOND ROUND

Friday, 2 December 2011

Fleetwood T (0) 2 *(Charnock 82, Milligan 89 (pen))*

Yeovil T (1) 2 *(Upson 32, Clifford 49)* 3319

Fleetwood T: Davies; Beeley (McNulty), Goodall, McGuire, Charnock, Pond, Clancy (Till), Milligan, Mangan (Brodie), Seddon, Vardy.
Yeovil T: Stewart; Ayling, Ehmer, N'Gala, Huntington, Wotton, Blizzard, Upson, Williams A (Johnson), Agard, Clifford (MacLean).

Saturday, 3 December 2011

Barnet (0) 1 *(McLeod 87)*

Milton Keynes D (1) 3 *(Potter 39, MacDonald 78, Powell 88)* 2608

Barnet: Brill; Senda, Kamdjo, Hughes (Holmes), Hector, Saville, Downing, Byrne (Baseya), Deering, McLeod, Marshall.
Milton Keynes D: Martin (McLoughlin); Smith Adam, Lewington, Flanagan, MacKenzie, Williams S, Ibehre, Potter (Chicksen), Bowditch, MacDonald (Powell), Balanta.

Bradford C (2) 3 *(Hannah 9, Bush 14 (og), Fagan 70 (pen))*

AFC Wimbledon (0) 1 *(Midson 50)* 3432

Bradford C: McLaughlin; Ramsden, Seip, Flynn, Davies, Oliver, Fagan (Dean), Ravenhill, Hanson, Hannah (Wells), Reid (Compton).
AFC Wimbledon: Brown; Hatton (Minshull), Bush, Wellard, Stuart, Johnson B, Mulley, Moore S, Jolley (Ademeno), Midson, Moore L (Kiernan).

Brentford (0) 0

Wrexham (1) 1 *(Tolley 33)* 3452

Brentford: Lee; Logan, Woodman (Donaldson), Douglas, Legge, Dean, Saunders, Diagouraga, Alexander, Grella (McGinn), Weston (Oyeleke).
Wrexham: Mayebi; Obeng, Ashton, Creighton, Knight-Percival, Harris, Cieslewicz (Morrell), Fowler, Wright D, Speight (Pogba), Tolley.

Charlton Ath (0) 2 *(Morrison 64, Euell 90)*

Carlisle U (0) 0 7461

Charlton Ath: Sullivan; Solly, Wiggins, Hollands, Morrison, Cort, Green (Kermorgant), Pritchard, Hayes (Wright-Phillips), Wagstaff, Evina (Euell).
Carlisle U: Collin; Ribeiro, Robson, Thirlwell (Madden), Michalik (Chantler), Murphy, McGovern, Berrett, Miller, Loy (Zoko), Noble.

Chelmsford C (1) 1 *(Cornhill 35)*

Macclesfield T (0) 1 *(Diagne 64)* 2919

Chelmsford C: Searle; Miller, Palmer, Tann, Clark, Parker, Whitely, Corcoran, Ibe, Cornhill, Akurang.
Macclesfield T: Veiga; Bateson, Diagne, Mendy, Brown, Brisley, Hamshaw, Wedgbury, Donnelly, Mukendi, Daniel.

Colchester U (0) 0

Swindon T (0) 1 *(Ritchie 59)* 3035

Colchester U: Williams B; Wilson, Coker, Izzet (James), Okuonghae (Eastman), Heath, Bond, Wordsworth, Odejayi, Henderson, Vincent (Gillespie).
Swindon T: Foderingham; Caddis, Ridehalgh, Risser, Flint, McCormack, Ritchie, Smith J, De Vita (Cibocchi), Kerrouche (Murray), Magera (Connell).

Crawley T (2) 5 *(Tubbs 31 (pen), 36, 79 (pen), Drury 83, McFadzean 90)*

Redbridge (0) 0 2494

Crawley T: Shearer; Hunt, Howell, Bulman (Akpan), Davis, McFadzean, Drury, Torres (Akinde), Tubbs, Barnett (Doughty), Simpson.
Redbridge: Rafis; Haywood, Durrant■, Turpin, Golby, Trenkel, Bradbury, Dark (Hopkins), Gardner, Robinson (Murray), Gordon.

Dagenham & R (0) 1 *(Nurse 81)*

Walsall (0) 1 *(Gnakpa 76)* 1237

Dagenham & R: Shea; Rose, Ogogo, Spillane, Doe, Ilesanmi, Scannell (Tomlin), Scott, Nurse, Woodall (Walsh), Gain.
Walsall: Walker; Beevers, Sadler, Taundry, Lancashire, Smith, Halliday (Gnakpa), Chambers, Grigg (Bowerman), Macken (Jarvis■), Nicholls.

Gateshead (0) 1 *(Fisher 62)*

Tamworth (1) 2 *(Francis 29, Patterson 90)* 1163

Gateshead: Alnwick; Baxter (Odhiambo), Carruthers■, Gate (Marwood), Curtis, Clark, Brittain (Rents), Turnbull, Shaw, Fisher, Moore.
Tamworth: Hedge; Tait, Habergham, Courtney (Bradley) (McDonald), Francis, Kanyuka, Mills, Green, Patterson, St Aimie, Thomas (Barrow).

Leyton Orient (0) 0

Gillingham (1) 1 *(Weston 45)* 3763

Leyton Orient: Alnwick; Clarke, McSweeney, Chorley (Forbes), Cuthbert, Dawson, Spring, Porter (Mooney), Cook, Lisbie, Laird (Cureton).
Gillingham: Flitney; Lee C, Martin, Montrose, Frampton, Richards, Weston (Fish), Payne J, Kedwell, Payne S (Oli), Jackman.

Luton T (1) 2 *(O'Connor 40, 51)*

Cheltenham T (2) 4 *(Duffy 2, Pack 45, Summerfield 64, Penn 90)* 4516

Luton T: Pilkington K; Gleeson, Howells, Keane (Kissock), Kovacs, Pilkington G, Lawless, Watkins, O'Connor, Crow, Willmott.
Cheltenham T: Brown; Jombati, Bennett, Pack, Lowe, Low, Penn, Summerfield, Duffy■, Spencer (Goulding), Mohamed (Smikle).

Salisbury C (0) 0

Grimsby T (0) 0 2161

Salisbury C: Scott; Adelsbury, Brett, Webb, Dutton, Giles, Alexis, Anderson, Fitchett (Macklin), Reid, Williams (Knight).
Grimsby T: McKeown; Green, Townsend, Wood, Pearson, L'Anson, Panther (Thanoj), Disley, Hearn, Elding (Duffy), Coulson.

Sheffield U (0) 3 *(Ellis 68 (og), Evans 69, 78)*

Torquay U (1) 2 *(Howe 3, Stevens 90)* 10,105

Sheffield U: Simonsen; Lowton, Williams (Lescinel), McAllister (McDonald), Collins, Maguire, Williamson, Doyle, Evans, Cresswell (Porter), Quinn.
Torquay U: Olejnik; Oastler, Nicholson, Mansell, Robertson, Ellis, Bodin, O'Kane, Howe, Morris (Atieno), Stevens.

Sheffield W (0) 1 *(Lowe 49)*

Aldershot T (0) 0 10,162

Sheffield W: O'Donnell; Tavernier, Bennett, Semedo, Jones R, Johnson R, Sedgwick (Prutton), Lines, O'Grady, Lowe (Morrison), Palmer (Johnson J).
Aldershot T: Young; Herd, Straker, Guttridge, Jones, Morris, Smith A, Collins J (Davies), Rankine (McGlashan), Hylton, Rodman (Pearson).

Shrewsbury T (0) 2 *(Sharps 48, Wroe 83 (pen))*

Rotherham U (1) 1 *(Grabban 42 (pen))* 4048

Shrewsbury T: Neal C; Hurst, Jacobson, Richards, Sharps, Cansdell-Sherriff, Ainsworth (Taylor), Wroe, Gornell (Collins), Morgan, Wright.
Rotherham U: Logan; Marshall■, Newey, Harrison, Branston (Raynes), Mullins (Holroyd), Wood, Williams (Tonge), Grabban, Revell, Schofield.

Southend U (0) 1 *(Hall 67)*

Oldham Ath (1) 1 *(Wesolowski 39)* 4613

Southend U: Daniels; Clohessy, Gilbert, Kalala (Harris), Barker, Phillips, Ferdinand, Timlin, Dickinson (Sturrock), Mohsni, Hall.
Oldham Ath: Cisak; Lee, Black, Wesolowski, Diamond (Clarke), Mvoto, Scapuzzi (Morais), Furman (Smith), Simpson, Kuqi, Adeyemi.

Stourbridge (0) 0

Stevenage (0) 3 *(Beardsley 65, 77, Shroot 90)* 3067

Stourbridge: Solly; Rock (Craddock), Lloyd, McCone, Canavan (Dovey), Bennett, Smith, Broadhurst, Rowe, Billingham, Evans (Drake).
Stevenage: Day; Henry (Byrom), Laird, Roberts, Ashton, Edwards, Wilson (Shroot), Bostwick, Beardsley, May (Harrison), Freeman.

Sunday, 4 December 2011

AFC Totton (0) 1 *(Sherborne 71)*

Bristol R (3) 6 *(Anyinsah 8, Carayol 10, Woodards 13, Anthony 64, Richards 72, 90)* 2236

AFC Totton: Porter; Hill (Richardson), Baddeley, Campbell, Whisken, Scott, Pettefer, Davies, Sherborne (Charles), Brown (Osman), Gosney.
Bristol R: Bevan; Woodards, Brown L, Sawyer, Anthony, Norburn (Jefferies), Anyinsah (Swallow■), Dorman, Harrold, Zebroski, Carayol (Richards).

Sutton U (0) 0

Notts Co (1) 2 *(Hughes J 35, 90)* 3704

Sutton U: Scriven; Telfer (Orilonishe), El-Salahi (Murray■), Piper, Downer, Page, Riviere, Watkins, Griffiths, Beautyman, Dundas (Taggart).
Notts Co: Nelson; Kelly, Sheehan, Sodje (Edwards), Pearce, Mahon, Bishop, Judge, Burgess (Demontagnac), Hawley (Bencherif), Hughes J.

SECOND ROUND REPLAYS

Tuesday, 13 December 2011

Grimsby T (0) 2 *(Duffy 90, 92)*

Salisbury C (0) 3 *(Fitchett 46, Dutton 100, Anderson 113 (pen))* 1880

Grimsby T: McKeown; Wood (Duffy), Townsend, Panther (Artus), Pearson, L'Anson, McCarthy (Makofo), Disley, Hearn, Elding, Coulson.
Salisbury C: Scott; Adelsbury, Brett, Dutton, Webb, Giles, Alexis (Knight), Anderson, Fitchett, Reid (Kelly), Williams (Macklin).
aet.

Oldham Ath (0) 1 *(Taylor 58)*

Southend U (0) 0 4207

Oldham Ath: Cisak; Lee, Black, Wesolowski, Diamond, Clarke, Scapuzzi (Morais), Furman, Adeyemi (Parker), Kuqi, Taylor.
Southend U: Daniels; Clohessy, Gilbert, Mohsni■, Barker (Prosser), Phillips, Grant, Timlin, Harris (Ferdinand), Sturrock, Leonard (Hall).

Walsall (0) 0

Dagenham & R (0) 0 1802

Walsall: Walker; Westlake, Beevers, Taundry (Gnakpa), Lancashire (Butler), Smith, Peterlin, Chambers, Nicholls, Macken, Paterson (Bowerman).
Dagenham & R: Lewington; Ogogo, Ilesanmi, Doe, Rose, Maher (Bingham), Spillane, Scott (Elito), Nurse, Woodall, Gain (Green Danny J).
aet; Dagenham & R won 3-2 on penalties.

Yeovil T (0) 0

Fleetwood T (1) 2 *(McGuire 28, Vardy 90)* 3276

Yeovil T: Stewart; Ayling, Ehmer, N'Gala■, Huntington, Wotton (Gibson), Williams A, Upson, MacLean (O'Brien), Agard, Clifford (Williams G).
Fleetwood T: Davies; Beeley, Goodall, Cavanagh, McNulty■, Pond, Briggs, McGuire, Mangan, Vardy, Till (Charnock).

Wednesday, 14 December 2011

Macclesfield T (1) 1 *(Tremarco 26)*

Chelmsford C (0) 0 1607

Macclesfield T: Veiga; Bateson, Tremarco, Diagne, Brown, Brisley, Hamshaw, Wedgbury, Donnelly (Mukendi), Daniel, Mendy.
Chelmsford C: Searle; Miller, Palmer, Tann, Clark, Parker, Modeste (Rainford), Corcoran, Ibe, Cornhill, Akurang (Morgan).

THIRD ROUND

Friday, 6 January 2012

Liverpool (2) 5 *(Bellamy 30, Gerrard 45 (pen), Shelvey 68, Carroll 89, Downing 90)*

Oldham Ath (1) 1 *(Simpson 28)* 44,556

Liverpool: Reina; Kelly, Fabio Aurelio (Flanagan), Spearing, Carragher, Coates, Rodriguez, Gerrard, Bellamy (Downing), Kuyt (Carroll), Shelvey.
Oldham Ath: Cisak; Lee, Taylor, Wesolowski (Morais), Diamond, Mvoto, Adeyemi, Furman, Simpson (Smith), Kuqi, Scapuzzi (Parker).

Saturday, 7 January 2012

Barnsley (1) 2 *(Vaz Te 29, 65)*

Swansea C (1) 4 *(Rangel 30, Graham 46, 89, Dyer 54)* 7380

Barnsley: Steele; Hassell (Wiseman), McEveley, Addison, Foster, McNulty, Vaz Te, Drinkwater, Davies, Done (Noble-Lazarus), Perkins (Gray).
Swansea C: Tremmel; Rangel, Taylor, Orlandi (Sigurdsson), Monk, Williams, Britton, Agustien (Allen), Dyer (Sinclair), Graham, Routledge.

Birmingham C (0) 0

Wolverhampton W (0) 0 14,594

Birmingham C: Doyle; Spector, Murphy, N'Daw (Fahey), Davies, Ridgewell (Caldwell), Elliott, Mutch (Beausejour), Rooney, Redmond, Gomis.
Wolverhampton W: De Vries; Stearman, Ward, Jonsson, Berra, Johnson (Foley), Kightly, Henry, Ebanks-Blake, Doyle (Fletcher), Hunt (Jarvis).

Brighton & HA (0) 1 *(Forster-Caskey 48)*

Wrexham (0) 1 *(Cieslewicz 62)* 18,573

Brighton & HA: Brezovan; Sampayo, Vincelot, Forster-Caskey, Hall, Calderon, Sparrow, Navarro (Rodgers), LuaLua (Agdestein), Barnes, Buckley (Kasim).
Wrexham: Mayebi; Obeng, Ashton, Creighton, Knight-Percival, Harris, Clarke (Keates), Tolley, Morrell (Little), Speight, Cieslewicz (Hunt).

Bristol R (0) 1 *(McGleish 90)*

Aston Villa (1) 3 *(Albrighton 35, Agbonlahor 64, Clark 78)* 10,883

Bristol R: Poke; Woodards, Sawyer, Downes, Bolger, Stanley, Anyinsah (McLaggon), Dorman, Richards (Brown L), Zebroski, Carayol (McGleish).
Aston Villa: Guzan; Hutton, Warnock, Collins (Gardner), Dunne, Petrov (Bannan), Albrighton, Clark, Bent, Heskey (Agbonlahor), Ireland.

Coventry C (1) 1 *(McSheffrey 5)*
Southampton (0) 2 *(Ward-Prowse 64, Martin 82)* 9000
Coventry C: Dunn; Christie, Cranie, Thomas, Keogh, Wood (Hussey), Deegan, Baker, O'Donovan (Jeffers), McSheffrey, Bigirimana (Ruffels).
Southampton: Bialkowski; Harding (Stephens), Cork, Schneiderlin, Hooiveld, Martin, Ward-Prowse (Reeves), Hammond, Lallana, Doble (Hoskins), Fox.

Crawley T (0) 1 *(Tubbs 73)*
Bristol C (0) 0 3779
Crawley T: Shearer; Hunt, Howell, Bulman, Davis, Mills, Simpson (Akinde), Torres, Tubbs (Akpan), Barnett (Neilson), McFadzean.
Bristol C: James; Wilson, McGivern (Pitman), Skuse, Nyatanga, Carey, Pearson■, Kilkenny (Clarkson), Adomah (Bolasie), Maynard, Woolford.

Dagenham & R (0) 0
Millwall (0) 0 3396
Dagenham & R: Lewington; Abdulla, Ilesanmi, Doe, Spillane, Bingham, Ogogo, Green Dominic, Nurse, Woodall, Wearen (Reed).
Millwall: Mildenhall; Dunne, Barron, Smith, Robinson, Ward, Trotter, Henry, Marquis (McQuoid), Kane (Batt), Feeney (Bouazza).

Derby Co (1) 1 *(Robinson 9)*
Crystal Palace (0) 0 10,113
Derby Co: Fielding; Brayford, Roberts, Bailey, Barker, Shackell, Green, Bryson, Robinson, Ball (Buxton), Ward.
Crystal Palace: Price; Dumbuya, Parsons, Egan, Ramage, Garvan, Pedroza (Iversen), O'Keefe, Andrew, De Silva (Cadogan), Wright (Sekajia).

Doncaster R (0) 0
Notts Co (1) 2 *(Hughes J 37, 70 (pen))* 9535
Doncaster R: Button; O'Connor, Beye, Hird, Lockwood, Stock, Coppinger (Diouf), Barnes (Woods M), Hayter, Bagayoko (Oster), Bennett.
Notts Co: Nelson; Kelly (Harley), Sheehan, Chilvers, Stewart, Bencherif, Bishop, Judge, Hughes L (Burgess), Hawley, Hughes J.

Everton (1) 2 *(Heitinga 5, Baines 79 (pen))*
Tamworth (0) 0 27,564
Everton: Howard; Coleman (Baines), Neville, Heitinga, Distin, Bilyaletdinov, Donovan, Fellaini, Anichebe (Stracqualursi), McFadden (Drenthe), Gueye.
Tamworth: Collister; Tait, Habergham, Courtney (McDonald), Francis, Kanyuka, McKoy, Barrow, Christie (St Aimie), Patterson, Thomas (Shariff).

Fleetwood T (0) 1 *(Vardy 70)*
Blackpool (1) 5 *(LuaLua 24, Phillips M 47, 77, 81, Ince 55)* 5092
Fleetwood T: Davies; Beeley, Brown, Cavanagh, McNulty, Pond, Till, McGuire, Mangan, Vardy, Milligan (Clancy).
Blackpool: Howard; Eardley, Harris, Basham, John Baptiste, Wilson, Angel (Phillips K), Sylvestre, LuaLua (Taylor-Fletcher), Ince, Phillips M.

Fulham (1) 4 *(Dempsey 8, 61, 81 (pen), Duff 87)*
Charlton Ath (0) 0 20,317
Fulham: Stockdale; Kelly, Riise J, Murphy (Sidwell), Senderos, Hangeland, Frei (Duff), Dempsey, Dembele (Kasami), Zamora, Ruiz.
Charlton Ath: Sullivan; Solly, Wiggins (Evina), Hollands (Hughes), Morrison, Taylor, Green (Wagstaff), Pritchard, Kermorgant, Wright-Phillips, Jackson.

Gillingham (1) 1 *(Kedwell 16)*
Stoke C (2) 3 *(Walters 34, Jerome 43, Huth 49)* 9872
Gillingham: Flitney; Lee C, Frampton, Payne J, Lawrence (Rooney), Richards, Whelpdale, Montrose (Payne S), Kedwell (Oli), Jackman, Weston.
Stoke C: Begovic; Woodgate, Upson, Huth, Shawcross, Palacios (Whitehead), Shotton (Whelan), Delap, Jones (Fuller), Walters, Jerome.

Hull C (2) 3 *(McLean 27, Cairney 32, Stewart 90)*
Ipswich T (0) 1 *(Scotland 57)* 10,246
Hull C: Mannone; McShane, Dudgeon, McKenna (Olofinjana), Cooper, Hobbs, Stewart, Cairney, McLean (Simpson), Brady, Garcia (Evans).
Ipswich T: Lee-Barrett; Edwards, Cresswell, Delaney (Smith), Sonko, Leadbitter, Emmanuel-Thomas, Hyam (Chopra), Murphy D, Ellington (Scotland), Carson.

Macclesfield T (1) 2 *(Daniel 16, Mendy 68)*
Bolton W (1) 2 *(Klasnic 7, Wheater 77)* 5757
Macclesfield T: Veiga; Bateson, Tremarco, Diagne, Brown, Brisley, Hamshaw (Hewitt), Wedgbury, Donnelly, Daniel, Mendy.
Bolton W: Bogdan; Riley, Robinson, Pratley (N'Gog), Wheater, Knight, Eagles, Reo-Coker, Klasnic, Davies K (Davies M), Petrov.

Middlesbrough (1) 1 *(Emnes 40)*
Shrewsbury T (0) 0 12,631
Middlesbrough: Steele (Coyne); Hoyte, Bennett, Smallwood, Bates, Williams R, Martin (Kink), Thomson, Emnes, McDonald, Ogbeche.
Shrewsbury T: Neal C; Hurst, Jacobson, McAllister S, Sharps, Cansdell-Sherriff, Ainsworth (Collins), Richards, Gornell (Taylor), Morgan, Wright.

Milton Keynes D (0) 1 *(Bowditch 65)*
QPR (0) 1 *(Helguson 89)* 19,506
Milton Keynes D: Martin; Smith Adam, Lewington, Potter, MacKenzie (Doumbe), Williams S, Ibehre, Gleeson, Bowditch, Powell, Chadwick.
QPR: Cerny; Young, Hill, Derry (Buzsaky), Hall, Gabbidon, Mackie, Smith, Campbell (Helguson), Macheda (Bothroyd), Faurlin.

Newcastle U (0) 2 *(Ben Arfa 70, Gutierrez 90)*
Blackburn R (1) 1 *(Goodwillie 35)* 30,876
Newcastle U: Krul; Simpson (Taylor R), Santon, Cabaye, Coloccini, Williamson, Obertan (Shola Ameobi), Abeid (Gosling), Ben Arfa, Best, Gutierrez.
Blackburn R: Bunn; Olsson (Lowe), Henley, Nzonzi, Givet, Hanley, Vukcevic, Petrovic, Rochina (Formica), Goodwillie (Slew), Pedersen.

Norwich C (2) 4 *(Holt 6, Jackson 12, Surman 60, Morison 73)*
Burnley (1) 1 *(Rodriguez 15)* 22,898
Norwich C: Rudd; Martin R, Drury, Crofts, Ayala, Whitbread, Surman, Fox, Jackson (Morison), Holt (Wilbraham), Hoolahan (Bennett E).
Burnley: Grant; Bikey (MacDonald), Easton, Edgar, Mee, McCann, Wallace (Bartley), Marney, Rodriguez, Paterson, Austin (Stanislas).

Nottingham F (0) 0
Leicester C (0) 0 18,477
Nottingham F: Camp; Gunter, Freeman, Chambers, Lynch, Moussi, McCleary (Anderson), Greening, Tudgay (Blackstock), McGugan, Reid (Harewood).
Leicester C: Schmeichel; Peltier, Konchesky, Danns, Mills, Tunchev, Abe (Wellens), King, Schlupp (Beckford), Nugent, Gallagher (Dyer).

Reading (0) 0
Stevenage (1) 1 *(Charles 21)* 11,295
Reading: Federici; Cummings (D'Ath), Harte, Leigertwood, Pearce, Gorkss, Tabb (Antonio), Robson-Kanu, Church, Le Fondre (Manset), McAnuff.
Stevenage: Day; Henry, Laird, Roberts, Ashton, Bostwick, Wilson, Byrom, Charles (Shroot), Beardsley (Edwards), Freeman (Harrison).

Sheffield U (1) 3 *(Porter 18, Evans 60, Webb 72 (og))*
Salisbury C (0) 1 *(Macklin 86)* 10,488
Sheffield U: Simonsen; Ertl, Lescinel, McDonald, Collins, Maguire, Williamson (Chapell), Doyle, Evans, Porter (Beattie), Flynn (Cresswell).
Salisbury C: Scott; Webb, Brett, Adelsbury, Dutton, Giles, Clarke (Losasso), Anderson, Fitchett (Knight), Reid (Macklin), Williams.

Swindon T (1) 2 *(Connell 40, Benson 76)*

Wigan Ath (1) 1 *(McManaman 35)* 13,238

Swindon T: Foderingham; Caddis, Kennedy, Smith J, Flint, McCormack, Ritchie, Ferry, De Vita (Cibocchi), Connell (Magera), Murray (Benson).
Wigan Ath: Al Habsi; Boyce, Mustoe, Thomas (Gomez), Caldwell, Piscu, Maloney (Moses), Watson, Di Santo, McManaman (Sammon), McArthur.

Tottenham H (2) 3 *(Defoe 24, Pavlyuchenko 43, Giovani 87)*

Cheltenham T (0) 0 35,672

Tottenham H: Cudicini; Bassong, Rose, Kranjcar, Dawson (Carroll), Livermore, Lennon (Bostock), Pienaar, Pavlyuchenko, Defoe (Falque), Giovani.
Cheltenham T: Brown; Jombati, Garbutt, Pack, Bennett, Elliott, Low (Smikle), Penn (Goulding), Spencer (Duffy), Mohamed, Summerfield.

Watford (2) 4 *(Deeney 3, Sordell 40, Forsyth 56, 59)*

Bradford C (1) 2 *(Hanson 8, Wells 88)* 8935

Watford: Bond; Doyley, Dickinson, Eustace, Nosworthy, Mariappa, Yeates (James), Forsyth, Sordell (Iwelumo), Deeney (Garner), Hogg.
Bradford C: McLaughlin; Seip, Threlfall, Ravenhill (Dean), Davies, Oliver, Fagan, Jones (Bullock), Hanson (Hannah), Wells, Taylor.

WBA (2) 4 *(Odemwingie 7, Cox 33, 61, 90)*

Cardiff C (1) 2 *(Earnshaw 36, Mason 50)* 12,454

WBA: Foster; Jones, Shorey, Jara (Tchoyi), McAuley (Tamas), Dawson, Thorne (Fortune), Morrison, Odemwingie, Cox, Dorrans.
Cardiff C: Heaton; Quinn, Naylor, Blake, Gerrard, Keinan (Wharton), Kiss, McPhail, Gestede (Mason), Earnshaw, Conway.

Sunday, 8 January 2012

Chelsea (0) 4 *(Mata 48, Ramires 85, 87, Lampard 90)*

Portsmouth (0) 0 41,529

Chelsea: Cech; Bosingwa, Cole (Bertrand), Ramires, Terry, David Luiz, Raul Meireles, Lampard, Torres (Lukaku), Mata, Malouda (Romeu).
Portsmouth: Henderson; Mokoena, Halford, Mullins (Huseklepp), Pearce, Rocha (Williams), Lawrence, Norris, Kitson, Futacs, Ward.

Manchester C (0) 2 *(Kolarov 48, Aguero 65)*

Manchester U (3) 3 *(Rooney 10, 40, Welbeck 30)* 46,808

Manchester C: Pantilimon; Richards, Kolarov, Company■, Lescott, De Jong, Johnson A (Savic), Milner, Aguero, Silva (Zabaleta), Nasri (Hargreaves).
Manchester U: Lindegaard; Smalling, Evra, Carrick, Ferdinand, Jones, Valencia, Giggs, Welbeck (Anderson), Rooney, Nani (Scholes).

Peterborough U (0) 0

Sunderland (0) 2 *(Larsson 48, McClean 58)* 8954

Peterborough U: Lewis; Alcock, Rowe (Little), Bennett, Zakuani, Wootton (Kearns), Tunnicliffe, Tomlin, Taylor, Sinclair (Newell), Boyd.
Sunderland: Mignolet; Gardner (Elmohamady), Bardsley, O'Shea, Kilgallon, Larsson, Cattermole, McClean, Sessegnon (Ji), Vaughan (Meyler), Richardson.

Sheffield W (0) 1 *(O'Grady 88)*

West Ham U (0) 0 17,916

Sheffield W: Weaver; Otsemobor, Bennett (Lowe), Batth, Jones R, Semedo, Tavernier (Jones D), Lines, O'Grady, Johnson J, Johnson R (Morrison).
West Ham U: Boffin; O'Brien, Potts, O'Neil (Montenegro), Reid, McCartney, Lansbury, Sears (Hall), Baldock, Carew (Nouble), Collison.

Monday, 9 January 2012

Arsenal (0) 1 *(Henry 78)*

Leeds U (0) 0 59,615

Arsenal: Szczesny; Koscielny, Coquelin (Yennaris), Squillaci, Miquel, Song Billong, Ramsey, Chamakh (Walcott), Arshavin, Arteta, Oxlade-Chamberlain (Henry).
Leeds U: Lonergan; Thompson, White, Lees, O'Dea, Townsend, Pugh, Clayton, Vayrynen (Brown), Becchio (McCormack), Nunez (Forssell).

THIRD ROUND REPLAYS

Tuesday, 17 January 2012

Bolton W (2) 2 *(Davies K 1, Petrov 26)*

Macclesfield T (0) 0 9466

Bolton W: Bogdan; Riley, Ricketts (Robinson), Davies M, Boyata, Wheater, Tuncay (O'Halloran), Reo-Coker, Klasnic (N'Gog), Davies K, Petrov.
Macclesfield T: Veiga; Bateson (Whiteoak), Tremarco, Diagne, Brown, Brisley, Hamshaw (Mukendi), Wedgbury (Fairhurst), Hewitt, Daniel, Mendy.

Leicester C (2) 4 *(Boateng 7 (og), Beckford 30, 50, 57)*

Nottingham F (0) 0 16,210

Leicester C: Schmeichel; Peltier, Konchesky, Danns, Mills, St Ledger-Hall, Wellens, Beckford (Howard), Gallagher, Nugent, Dyer (Kennedy).
Nottingham F: Camp; Gunter, Cunningham, Moussi, Lynch, Boateng (McGugan), Anderson, Greening (McGoldrick), Harewood (Blackstock), Findley, Reid.

Millwall (2) 5 *(Henderson 7, 59, 63 (pen), Kane 41, 65)*

Dagenham & R (0) 0 3751

Millwall: Forde; Smith, Barron, Abdou, Robinson, Ward, Trotter (Wright), Bouazza, Kane (McQuoid), Henderson (Batt), Feeney.
Dagenham & R: Lewington; Ogogo, Ilesanmi, Doe, Spillane, Rose (Wearen), Green Danny J, Bingham, Nurse, Green Dominic (Reed), Abdulla (Edmans).

QPR (0) 1 *(Gabbidon 73)*

Milton Keynes D (0) 0 10,855

QPR: Kenny; Young, Hill, Derry, Ferdinand, Gabbidon, Wright-Phillips, Buzsaky (Helguson), Macheda (Smith), Bothroyd (Orr), Mackie.
Milton Keynes D: Martin; Smith Adam, Lewington, Doumbe, Williams S, Potter, Ibehre, Gleeson, Bowditch (O'Shea), MacDonald, Chadwick (Powell).

Wednesday, 18 January 2012

Wolverhampton W (0) 0

Birmingham C (0) 1 *(Elliott 74)* 10,153

Wolverhampton W: De Vries; Doherty (Ward), Elokobi, Jonsson (Guedioura), Berra, Stearman, Hammill, Milijas, Ebanks-Blake, Doyle (Fletcher), Hunt.
Birmingham C: Doyle; Spector, Murphy, Caldwell, Davies, Gomis (Fahey), Redmond (Burke), Mutch, Rooney, Beausejour, Elliott.

Wrexham (1) 1 *(Morrell 23)*

Brighton & HA (0) 1 *(Barnes 77)* 8316

Wrexham: Mayebi; Obeng, Ashton, Creighton, Knight-Percival, Harris, Clarke, Tolley (Keates), Wright D (Little), Morrell (Hunt), Cieslewicz.
Brighton & HA: Brezovan; Calderon, Vincelot, Bridcutt, Dunk, Hall, Sparrow, Navarro (Barnes), Hoskins (Agdestein), Mackail-Smith, Buckley.
aet; Brighton & HA won 5-4 on penalties.

FOURTH ROUND

Friday, 27 January 2012

Everton (1) 2 *(Stracqualursi 27, Fellaini 73)*

Fulham (1) 1 *(Murphy 14 (pen))* 25,300

Everton: Howard; Neville, Baines, Gibson, Duffy, Heitinga, Donovan, Fellaini, Stracqualursi (Anichebe), Cahill, Gueye (Drenthe).
Fulham: Stockdale; Kelly, Riise J, Murphy (Trotta), Hughes, Hangeland, Duff (Zamora), Baird (Sidwell), Johnson A, Dempsey, Ruiz.

Swindon Town's Paul Benson celebrates scoring his side's second goal as Wigan Athletic goalkeeper Ali Al Habsi watches. Swindon won 2-1 at the County Ground in the FA Cup third round. (Action Images/Steven Paston)

Watford (0) 0

Tottenham H (1) 1 *(Van der Vaart 42)* 15,384

Watford: Loach; Hodson, Doyley, Eustace, Nosworthy, Mariappa, Deeney, Buaben, Sordell, Garner (Whichelow), Murray (Yeates).
Tottenham H: Cudicini; Walker, Rose, Modric (Lennon), Kaboul, Dawson, Van der Vaart, Parker, Defoe (Pienaar), Adebayor (Pavlyuchenko), Livermore.

Saturday, 28 January 2012

Blackpool (0) 1 *(Phillips K 90 (pen))*

Sheffield W (0) 1 *(Morrison 52)* 14,042

Blackpool: Gilks; Eardley, Harris, Southern (Taylor-Fletcher), Cathcart, Wilson, Basham, Angel (Ince), Phillips K, Clarke (Dicko), Phillips M.
Sheffield W: Bywater; Buxton, Beevers, Batth, Jones R, Palmer (Johnson J), Prutton, Lines, Morrison (O'Grady), Lowe (Otsemobor), Sedgwick.

Bolton W (1) 2 *(Pratley 45, Eagles 56)*

Swansea C (1) 1 *(Moore 43)* 11,597

Bolton W: Bogdan; Riley, Ricketts, Pratley (Muamba), Boyata, Wheater, Eagles (Tuncay), Reo-Coker, N'Gog (Davies K), Davies M, Petrov.
Swansea C: Tremmel; Richards, Bessone, Agustien, Monk, Williams, Routledge (Graham), McEachran, Lita (Dyer), Moore, Gower (Allen).

Brighton & HA (0) 1 *(Williamson 76 (og))*

Newcastle U (0) 0 21,558

Brighton & HA: Brezovan; Calderon, El-Abd, Bridcutt, Dunk, Greer, Sparrow (Navarro), Forster-Caskey (Harley), Barnes, Mackail-Smith (Hoskins), Buckley.
Newcastle U: Krul; Simpson, Santon (Gosling), Cabaye, Perch, Williamson, Ben Arfa (Ferguson), Guthrie (Taylor R), Shola Ameobi, Best, Gutierrez.

Derby Co (0) 0

Stoke C (1) 2 *(Jerome 5, Huth 81)* 22,247

Derby Co: Fielding; Brayford, Roberts, Bailey (Tyson), Barker, Shackell (Naylor), Green, Hendrick, Ball, Bryson (Buxton), Ward.
Stoke C: Begovic; Wilkinson, Wilson, Huth, Shawcross, Whelan, Walters, Whitehead, Jerome (Fuller), Crouch (Jones), Etherington (Pennant).

Hull C (0) 0

Crawley T (0) 1 *(Tubbs 57)* 14,473

Hull C: Mannone; East, Dudgeon, Evans, Cooper, Hobbs, Garcia (Olofinjana), Cairney, Brady (McLean), Fryatt, King (Cullen).
Crawley T: Shearer; Hunt, Howell, Bulman, Davis, Mills, Watt (Akpan), Torres (Neilson), Tubbs (Simpson), Barnett, McFadzean.

Leicester C (1) 2 *(Beckford 5, 53)*

Swindon T (0) 0 19,942

Leicester C: Schmeichel; Peltier, Konchesky (Kennedy), Danns, Mills, St Ledger-Hall, Gallagher, Wellens, Beckford (Howard), Nugent (Hopper), Dyer.
Swindon T: Foderingham; Caddis, Cibocchi, Risser, Devera, McCormack, Ritchie, Ferry (Thompson), De Vita (Gabilondo), Connell (Murray), Benson.

Liverpool (1) 2 *(Agger 21, Kuyt 88)*

Manchester U (1) 1 *(Park 39)* 43,952

Liverpool: Reina; Kelly, Jose Enrique, Skrtel, Carragher (Adam), Agger, Henderson, Gerrard (Bellamy), Carroll, Rodriguez (Kuyt), Downing.
Manchester U: De Gea; Rafael, Evra, Carrick, Smalling, Evans, Valencia, Giggs (Berbatov), Welbeck, Scholes (Hernandez), Park.

Millwall (0) 1 *(Henderson 86)*

Southampton (1) 1 *(Lambert 31)* 8278

Millwall: Forde; Smith, Barron, Abdou, Craig, Ward, Henry (Hackett), Trotter, Kane (N'Guessan), Henderson, Feeney.
Southampton: Bialkowski; Richardson, Fox, Hammond, Martin, Harding, Puncheon (Shaw), Reeves, Lambert, Barnard (Lee), De Ridder (Holmes).

QPR (0) 0

Chelsea (0) 1 *(Mata 62 (pen))* 15,728

QPR: Kenny; Young, Hill, Barton, Ferdinand, Hall, Wright-Phillips, Buzsaky (Hulse), Helguson (Macheda), Smith, Mackie.
Chelsea: Cech; Ivanovic, Cole, Ramires (Romeu), Terry, David Luiz, Raul Meireles, Sturridge, Torres, Mata (Essien), Malouda.

Sheffield U (0) 0

Birmingham C (2) 4 *(Redmond 18, Rooney 38, 78, Elliott 58)* 18,072

Sheffield U: Simonsen; Lowton, Lescinel (Williams), McDonald, Collins, Maguire, Williamson, Doyle, Evans, Cresswell (Flynn), Quinn (Porter).
Birmingham C: Doyle; Spector, Murphy, Caldwell, Davies, Gomis, Burke (Gnahore), Mutch (Reilly), Redmond, Rooney, Elliott.

Stevenage (1) 1 *(Stewart 12 (og))*

Notts Co (0) 0 4439

Stevenage: Day; Henry, Laird, Roberts, Ashton, Bostwick, Wilson, Byrom, Beardsley (May), Charles (Long), Freeman (Shroot).
Notts Co: Nelson; Kelly (Stirling), Sheehan, Chilvers, Stewart, Mahon (Sodje), Bishop, Judge, Hughes L, Forte (Demontagnac), Hughes J.

WBA (0) 1 *(Fortune 54)*

Norwich C (1) 2 *(Holt 35, Jackson 85)* 17,434

WBA: Foster; Jara (McAuley), Mattock, Mulumbu, Dawson, Tamas, Thomas (Tchoyi), Morrison, Fortune (Long), Cox, Dorrans.
Norwich C: Steer; Martin R, Drury, Crofts, Ayala, Whitbread, Bennett E, Fox, Pilkington (Lappin), Holt (Jackson), Hoolahan (Wilbraham).

Sunday, 29 January 2012

Arsenal (0) 3 *(Van Persie 54 (pen), 61 (pen), Walcott 57)*

Aston Villa (2) 2 *(Dunne 33, Bent 45)* 60,019

Arsenal: Fabianski; Coquelin, Koscielny, Song Billong, Mertesacker, Vermaelen, Walcott (Henry), Ramsey, Oxlade-Chamberlain (Sagna), Van Persie, Rosicky (Arteta).
Aston Villa: Given; Hutton, Warnock, Cuellar, Dunne, Petrov (Bannan), Ireland, Clark, Bent, Keane, Agbonlahor (Gardner).

Sunderland (0) 1 *(Campbell 59)*

Middlesbrough (1) 1 *(Robson 16)* 33,275

Sunderland: Mignolet; Bardsley, Richardson, Gardner, O'Shea, Brown (Turner), Larsson, Vaughan (Colback), Wickham (Campbell), Sessegnon, McClean.
Middlesbrough: Coyne (Ripley); Hoyte, McMahon, Hines, Bates, Williams R, Robson, Jutkiewicz, Emnes, McDonald, Haroun.

FOURTH ROUND REPLAYS

Tuesday, 7 February 2012

Sheffield W (0) 0

Blackpool (2) 3 *(Phillips M 7, LuaLua 14, Sylvestre 54)* 10,274

Sheffield W: Bywater; Otsemobor, Johnson R (Semedo), Batth, Jones R, Palmer, Sedgwick, Lines, Morrison, Lowe, Bennett.
Blackpool: Gilks; Eardley, Harris (Dicko), Angel, John Baptiste, Wilson, LuaLua, Sylvestre, Phillips K (Fleck), Ince, Phillips M (Bruna).

Southampton (1) 2 *(Lallana 35, Lambert 77)*

Millwall (1) 3 *(Trotter 17, N'Guessan 79, Feeney 90)* 8493

Southampton: Bialkowski; Richardson, Harding, Chaplow (Reeves), Martin, Fonte, Lallana, Hammond, Lee, Do Prado (Lambert), De Ridder (Barnard).
Millwall: Forde; Dunne, Barron, Mason, Craig, Ward, Wright, Trotter, Kane, Henry, N'Guessan (Feeney).

Wednesday, 8 February 2012

Middlesbrough (0) 1 *(Jutkiewicz 57)*

Sunderland (1) 2 *(Colback 32, Sessegnon 113)* 26,707

Middlesbrough: Steele; Hines, Bennett, Hoyte, Bates, Williams R, McMahon, Thomson (Smallwood), Jutkiewicz (Reach), Main, Arca (Emnes).
Sunderland: Mignolet; Bardsley, Richardson, Gardner, O'Shea, Turner, Larsson (Elmohamady), Colback, Campbell (Wickham), Sessegnon (Meyler), McClean.
aet.

FIFTH ROUND

Saturday, 18 February 2012

Chelsea (0) 1 *(Sturridge 62)*

Birmingham C (1) 1 *(Murphy 20)* 36,870

Chelsea: Cech; Ivanovic, Bertrand, Mikel (Kalou), Cahill, David Luiz, Ramires, Sturridge, Torres (Drogba), Mata (Lampard), Raul Meireles.
Birmingham C: Doyle; Carr (Spector), Murphy, Gomis, Davies, Pablo, Elliott (Burke), Mutch, Rooney (Jervis), Fahey, Redmond.

Everton (2) 2 *(Drenthe 1, Stracqualursi 6)*

Blackpool (0) 0 38,347

Everton: Howard; Hibbert, Baines, Gibson (Barkley), Distin, Heitinga, Neville, Fellaini, Stracqualursi (Vellios), Drenthe, Gueye (Coleman).
Blackpool: Gilks; John Baptiste, Harris, Angel (Dicko), Cathcart, Wilson, Basham, Sylvestre, Phillips K, Ince (LuaLua), Taylor-Fletcher (Bednar).

Millwall (0) 0

Bolton W (1) 2 *(Miyaichi 4, N'Gog 59)* 11,134

Millwall: Mildenhall; Dunne, Barron, Smith (Wright), Robinson, Lowry, Feeney (Bouazza), Trotter, Kane (Henry), Henderson, Keogh.
Bolton W: Bogdan; Steinsson, Ricketts, Muamba, Ream, Wheater, Tuncay, Reo-Coker, N'Gog, Miyaichi (Eagles), Davies M (Pratley).

Norwich C (1) 1 *(Hoolahan 23)*

Leicester C (1) 2 *(St Ledger-Hall 5, Nugent 71)* 26,658

Norwich C: Steer; Martin R, Drury, Fox (Johnson B), Barnett, Ward, Bennett E, Pilkington, Morison (Vaughan), Jackson (Wilbraham), Hoolahan.
Leicester C: Schmeichel; Peltier, Kennedy (Konchesky), Danns, St Ledger-Hall, Morgan, Marshall (Delfouneso), Wellens, Beckford, Nugent, Dyer.

Sunderland (1) 2 *(Richardson 40, Oxlade-Chamberlain 78 (og))*

Arsenal (0) 0 26,042

Sunderland: Mignolet; Bardsley, Richardson, Turner, O'Shea, Cattermole, Larsson, Gardner, McClean, Sessegnon (Campbell), Colback.
Arsenal: Fabianski; Sagna, Coquelin (Squillaci) (Rosicky), Song Billong, Djourou, Vermaelen, Gervinho, Ramsey (Walcott), Oxlade-Chamberlain, Van Persie, Arteta.

Sunday, 19 February 2012

Crawley T (0) 0

Stoke C (1) 2 *(Walters 42 (pen), Crouch 52)* 4214

Crawley T: Gilmartin; Hunt (Neilson), Howell, Bulman, Davis, Mills, Simpson, Torres, Watt, Barnett, McFadzean.
Stoke C: Begovic; Shotton, Upson, Collins, Shawcross, Whelan, Whitehead, Delap■, Crouch, Jerome (Wilkinson), Walters.

Liverpool (2) 6 *(Skrtel 5, Bridcutt 44 (og), 71 (og), Carroll 57, Dunk 74 (og), Suarez 85)*

Brighton & HA (1) 1 *(LuaLua 17)* 43,490

Liverpool: Reina; Johnson, Jose Enrique, Skrtel, Carragher, Adam, Henderson (Rodriguez), Gerrard (Shelvey), Carroll, Suarez, Downing (Kuyt).
Brighton & HA: Brezovan; Calderon, El-Abd (Mackail-Smith), Bridcutt, Dunk, Greer, LuaLua, Navarro, Barnes, Vokes (Vicente), Buckley (Noone).

Stevenage (0) 0

Tottenham H (0) 0 6332

Stevenage: Day; Henry, Laird, Roberts, Ashton, Bostwick, Wilson, Byrom, Beardsley (May), Charles (Cowan), Freeman (Edwards).
Tottenham H: Cudicini; Walker (Kranjcar), Rose (Lennon), Nelsen, Dawson, Kaboul, Livermore, Parker, Saha, Defoe, Bale.

FIFTH ROUND REPLAYS

Tuesday, 6 March 2012

Birmingham C (0) 0

Chelsea (0) 2 *(Mata 54, Raul Meireles 60)* 21,822

Birmingham C: Doyle; Spector, N'Daw (King), Pablo, Davies, Gomis, Redmond, Mutch, Rooney (Burke), Zigic, Elliott.
Chelsea: Cech; Ivanovic, Bertrand, Mikel, Cahill, David Luiz, Ramires (Lampard), Kalou (Sturridge), Torres, Mata (Essien), Raul Meireles.

Wednesday, 7 March 2012

Tottenham H (1) 3 *(Defoe 26, 75, Adebayor 55 (pen))*

Stevenage (1) 1 *(Byrom 4 (pen))* 35,757

Tottenham H: Cudicini; Nelsen, Rose, Kranjcar (Livermore), Dawson (Walker), Kaboul, Lennon (Adebayor), Parker, Van der Vaart, Defoe, Bale.
Stevenage: Day; Henry, Laird, Roberts, Ashton, Bostwick, Wilson, Byrom, Beardsley (Reid), Charles (Myrie-Williams), Shroot.

SIXTH ROUND

Saturday, 17 March 2012

Everton (1) 1 *(Cahill 23)*

Sunderland (1) 1 *(Bardsley 12)* 38,875

Everton: Howard; Neville, Baines, Fellaini, Distin, Heitinga, Coleman (Gueye), Osman, Jelavic, Cahill, Drenthe (Stracqualursi).
Sunderland: Mignolet; Bardsley, Bridge, Turner, O'Shea, Gardner, Larsson, Colback, Campbell (Vaughan), Bendtner, McClean.

Sunday, 18 March 2012

Chelsea (2) 5 *(Cahill 12, Kalou 17, Torres 67, 85, Raul Meireles 90)*

Leicester C (0) 2 *(Beckford 77, Marshall 88)* 38,276

Chelsea: Cech; Bosingwa, Bertrand, Mikel, Cahill, Ivanovic (David Luiz), Raul Meireles, Kalou (Essien), Torres, Sturridge, Mata (Malouda).
Leicester C: Schmeichel; St Ledger-Hall (Schlupp), Konchesky, Danns, Morgan, Bamba, Gallagher (Peltier), Wellens (Marshall), Beckford, Nugent, Dyer.

Liverpool (1) 2 *(Suarez 23, Downing 57)*

Stoke C (1) 1 *(Crouch 26)* 43,962

Liverpool: Reina; Kelly (Coates), Jose Enrique, Spearing, Carragher, Skrtel, Rodriguez (Kuyt), Gerrard, Carroll, Suarez (Henderson), Downing.
Stoke C: Sorensen; Wilkinson, Wilson, Huth, Shawcross, Whelan, Shotton (Pennant), Whitehead (Delap), Crouch, Walters, Etherington (Jerome).

Tottenham H (1) 1 *(Walker 11)*

Bolton W (1) 1 *(Bale 6 (og))*

Abandoned 41 minutes; Muamba suffered serious cardiac event.

Tuesday, 27 March 2012

Tottenham H (0) 3 *(Nelsen 74, Bale 77, Saha 90)*

Bolton W (0) 1 *(Davies K 89)* 30,718

Tottenham H: Cudicini; Walker, Assou-Ekotto, Modric, Nelsen, King, Livermore, Parker (Defoe), Van der Vaart (Rose), Adebayor (Saha), Bale.
Bolton W: Bogdan; Alonso, Ricketts, Pratley (Ream), Knight, Boyata (Davies K), Davies M, Reo-Coker, Klasnic, Miyaichi (Tuncay), Eagles.

Spaniard Juan Mata scores Chelsea's second goal as the west London club came from behind to beat their north London rivals, Spurs, in this FA Cup semi-final tie at Wembley in the middle of April. (Action Images/Carl Recine)

SIXTH ROUND REPLAY

Tuesday, 27 March 2012

Sunderland (0) 0

Everton (1) 2 *(Jelavic 24, Vaughan 57 (og))* 43,140

Sunderland: Mignolet; Bardsley, Bridge (Campbell), Turner, Kyrgiakos (Vaughan), Cattermole, Larsson, Gardner, Bendtner, Sessegnon, McClean.
Everton: Howard; Neville, Baines, Gibson, Distin, Heitinga, Gueye (Jagielka), Fellaini, Jelavic (Stracqualursi), Cahill (Hibbert), Osman.

SEMI-FINALS (at Wembley)

Saturday, 14 April 2012

Liverpool (0) 2 *(Suarez 62, Carroll 87)*

Everton (1) 1 *(Jelavic 24)* 87,231

Liverpool: Jones; Johnson, Agger, Spearing, Carragher, Skrtel, Henderson (Rodriguez), Gerrard, Carroll, Suarez, Downing (Bellamy).
Everton: Howard; Neville, Baines (Anichebe), Gibson, Distin, Heitinga, Gueye (Coleman), Fellaini, Jelavic, Cahill, Osman.

Sunday, 15 April 2012

Tottenham H (0) 1 *(Bale 56)*

Chelsea (1) 5 *(Drogba 43, Mata 49, Ramires 77, Lampard 81, Malouda 90)* 85,731

Tottenham H: Cudicini; Walker, Assou-Ekotto, Modric, Gallas, King, Lennon, Parker (Sandro), Van der Vaart (Defoe), Adebayor, Bale.
Chelsea: Cech; Bosingwa, Cole, Mikel, Terry, David Luiz (Cahill), Ramires (Malouda), Lampard, Kalou, Drogba (Torres), Mata.

THE FA CUP FINAL

Saturday, 5 May 2012

(at Wembley Stadium, attendance 89,102)

Chelsea (1) 2 Liverpool (0) 1

Chelsea: Cech; Bosingwa, Cole, Mikel, Terry, Ivanovic, Ramires (Raul Meireles), Lampard, Kalou, Drogba, Mata (Malouda).
Scorers: Ramires 11, Drogba 52.

Liverpool: Reina; Johnson, Jose Enrique, Spearing (Carroll), Agger, Skrtel, Henderson, Gerrard, Suarez, Bellamy (Kuyt), Downing.
Scorer: Carroll 64.

Referee: P. Dowd (Staffordshire).

Didier Drogba, something of a Wembley scoring specialist, finds the net for Chelsea's second goal in their 2-1 FA Cup final victory over Liverpool at Wembley. (Reuters/Eddie Keogh)

BLUE SQUARE PREMIER 2011–12

Fleetwood Town came within a win of overtaking Crawley Town's record-breaking 105 points. As in 2010–11 the champions were well-placed in the financial field as well as the playing area. They also added to the coffers with a handsome transfer fee for one of their players.

With the Blue Square Premier League now awash with former Football League clubs each year, the competition to return to their former status is producing increased intensity. And with one automatic slot for the title winners and just one through the play-offs, the competition is formidable.

Neither Lincoln City nor Stockport County, the two clubs relegated, were able to finish in either play-off contention or maintain any kind of challenge. Indeed both had concerns over staying out of the bottom four.

Mid-way through September with almost a quarter of the fixtures completed, it was Luton Town leading the field unbeaten after ten matches, though they had drawn five of them. At this stage their advantage was merely on goal difference and in fact there was a four-way tie on the same number of points! The prospects for a close campaign seemed reasonable with Wrexham, Gateshead and Fleetwood bracketed with them.

Mansfield Town were fifth, just a point adrift again ahead of the surprise packets thus far in newcomers Braintree Town level on points. AFC Telford United were in the bottom half along with Alfreton Town. Back in the Conference arena were Ebbsfleet United, but at this juncture third from the bottom.

By mid-November and with twenty matches already taken into account, the picture was beginning to take on a different slant. Wrexham and Fleetwood in that order were five points ahead of the next club Southport, followed by Cambridge United and York City in the play-off zone and Gateshead just outside it. Luton had slipped to seventh.

The bottom four were Hayes & Yeading, Newport County, Alfreton and Bath City, with Grimsby Town, Kettering Town, Stockport, AFC Telford and Lincoln City hovering just above them. As far as Kettering were concerned, they had moved into Rushden's old ground but were experiencing financial problems of their own as were Darlington, then in mid-table.

Come mid-February and with most clubs having completed 32 Blue Square matches, it was interesting to note that ten of the fourteen ex-League clubs were in the top half, the remaining four just above the relegation foursome of Alfreton, Kettering and Hayes with Bath still at the foot.

However, one of those just out of the danger areas was Darlington now in administration and with ten points deducted. There were also strong indications that neither they nor Kettering might finish the season.

Fleetwood were now top but Wrexham had a game in hand. Luton, York and Southport came next. Grimsby had improved to be in sixth position while Braintree had slipped to the middle of the table.

After 41 games Fleetwood had opened a nine-point lead over Wrexham, who still had that game in hand. Mansfield had climbed to third with York fourth and Southport still fifth. In the cellar area, Kettering had joined Darlington with a points deduction of three points over a fixture problem, that pair coupled with Hayes and Bath still last.

Fleetwood hoisted the century with a win at York after Wrexham had lost at home to Alfreton. Kidderminster Harriers had taken the last play-off spot having been thereabouts most of the season. On 10 April Fleetwood entertained Wrexham with a crowd of 4,994 at their Highbury ground. Wrexham managed a 1-1 draw despite finishing with ten men, but it was certainly their last chance of overhauling the leaders, 11 points behind. And it was Fleetwood's 100th League goal.

Yet Fleetwood did it the hard way. They then drew with Lincoln and had to rely the following day on Wrexham failing to beat Grimsby Town before being crowned. Mansfield, York and Luton reached the play-offs, York emerging to join Fleetwood in the Football League. Hayes, Darlington, Bath and Kettering were relegated.

Tenth for Forest Green Rovers was an improvement but 13th was disappointing for Barrow, one above Ebbsfleet while 18th was less than Tamworth might have imagined.

BLUE SQUARE PREMIER ATTENDANCES BY CLUB 2011–12

	Aggregate 2011–12	*Average 2011–12*	*Highest Attendance 2011–12*	
Luton Town	140,560	6,111	8,415	v. Kidderminster H
Wrexham	87,549	3,806	5,812	v. AFC Telford U
Stockport County	84,567	3,676	6,393	v. Tamworth
Grimsby Town	76,085	3,308	6,672	v. Lincoln C
York City	71,700	3,117	4,295	v. Wrexham
Mansfield Town	61,685	2,681	4,830	v. Lincoln C
Cambridge United	55,956	2,432	4,796	v. Luton T
Lincoln City	53,990	2,347	5,506	v. Grimsby T
Fleetwood Town	52,079	2,264	4,994	v. Wrexham
AFC Telford United	52,066	2,263	4,591	v. Wrexham
Darlington	50,658	2,202	6,413	v. York C
Kidderminster Harriers	48,191	2,095	3,565	v. Mansfield T
Kettering Town	32,187	1,399	3,247	v. Luton T
Newport County	31,042	1,349	1,675	v. Grimsby T
Southport	29,669	1,289	2,589	v. Fleetwood T
Barrow	29,015	1,261	2,190	v. York C
Tamworth	25,237	1,097	1,923	v. Wrexham
Alfreton Town	24,454	1,063	3,354	v. Mansfield T
Forest Green Rovers	23,796	1,034	1,848	v. Stockport Co
Ebbsfleet United	23,396	1,017	1,651	v. Luton T
Braintree Town	20,603	895	2,029	v. Cambridge U
Gateshead	19,381	842	1,604	v. York C
Bath City	18,942	823	1,158	v. Luton T
Hayes & Yeading	8,671	377	1,015	v. Luton T

BLUE SQUARE PREMIER 2011–12

(P) *Promoted into division at end of 2010–11 season.* (R) *Relegated into division at end of 2010–11 season.*

		Total						*Home*					*Away*						
		P	*W*	*D*	*L*	*F*	*A*	*W*	*D*	*L*	*F*	*A*	*W*	*D*	*L*	*F*	*A*	*GD*	*Pts*
1	Fleetwood T	46	31	10	5	102	48	13	8	2	50	25	18	2	3	52	23	54	103
2	Wrexham	46	30	8	8	85	33	16	3	4	48	17	14	5	4	37	16	52	98
3	Mansfield T	46	25	14	7	87	48	14	6	3	50	25	11	8	4	37	23	39	89
4	York C¶	46	23	14	9	81	45	11	6	6	43	24	12	8	3	38	21	36	83
5	Luton T	46	22	15	9	78	42	15	4	4	48	15	7	11	5	30	27	36	81
6	Kidderminster H	46	22	10	14	82	63	10	7	6	44	32	12	3	8	38	31	19	76
7	Southport	46	21	13	12	72	69	8	8	7	36	39	13	5	5	36	30	3	76
8	Gateshead	46	21	11	14	69	62	11	8	4	39	26	10	3	10	30	36	7	74
9	Cambridge U	46	19	14	13	57	41	11	6	6	31	16	8	8	7	26	25	16	71
10	Forest Green R	46	19	13	14	66	45	11	5	7	37	25	8	8	7	29	20	21	70
11	Grimsby T	46	19	13	14	79	60	12	4	7	51	28	7	9	7	28	32	19	70
12	Braintree T (P)	46	17	11	18	76	80	11	5	7	39	34	6	6	11	37	46	–4	62
13	Barrow	46	17	9	20	62	76	12	6	5	39	25	5	3	15	23	51	–14	60
14	Ebbsfleet U (P)	46	14	12	20	69	84	7	6	10	34	39	7	6	10	35	45	–15	54
15	Alfreton T (P)	46	15	9	22	62	86	8	6	9	39	48	7	3	13	23	38	–24	54
16	Stockport Co (R)	46	12	15	19	58	74	8	7	8	35	28	4	8	11	23	46	–16	51
17	Lincoln C (R)	46	13	10	23	56	66	8	6	9	32	24	5	4	14	24	42	–10	49
18	Tamworth	46	11	15	20	47	70	7	9	7	30	30	4	6	13	17	40	–23	48
19	Newport County AFC	46	11	14	21	53	65	8	6	9	22	22	3	8	12	31	43	–12	47
20	AFC Telford U (P)	46	10	16	20	45	65	9	6	8	24	26	1	10	12	21	39	–20	46
21	Hayes & Yeading U	46	11	8	27	58	90	5	5	13	26	41	6	3	14	32	49	–32	41
22	Darlington	46	11	13	22	47	73	8	7	8	24	24	3	6	14	23	49	–26	36
23	Bath C	46	7	10	29	43	89	5	4	14	27	41	2	6	15	16	48	–46	31
24	Kettering T	46	8	9	29	40	100	5	5	13	25	47	3	4	16	15	53	–60	30

Darlington deducted 10 points. Kettering T deducted 3 points. ¶York C promoted via play-offs.

BLUE SQUARE PREMIER LEADING GOALSCORERS 2011–12

	Club	*League*	*Play-Offs*	*FA Cup*	*Total*
Jamie Vardy	(Fleetwood T)	31	0	3	34
Matt Green	(Mansfield T)	29	0	0	29
Jon Shaw	(Gateshead)	27	0	3	30
Liam Hearn	(Grimsby T)	26	0	2	28
Tony Gray	(Southport)	24	0	0	24
Jake Speight	(Wrexham)	21	0	0	21
Andrew Mangan	(Fleetwood T)	19	0	2	21
Calum Willock	(Ebbsfleet U)	19	0	0	19
Yan Klukowski	(Forest Green R)	18	0	0	18
Jason Walker	(York C)	18	0	0	18
Ben Wright	(Braintree T)	17	0	1	18
Andy Cook	(Barrow)	17	0	0	17

BLUE SQUARE PREMIER LEAGUE PLAY-OFFS

▪ *Denotes player sent off.*

SEMI-FINAL FIRST LEG

Wednesday, 2 May 2012

York C (1) 1 *(Geohaghon 42 (og))*

Mansfield T (1) 1 *(Dyer 26)* 6057

York C: Ingham; Parslow, Meredith, Smith, Doig, Fyfield, Challinor, McLaughlin (Moke), Walker, Chambers, Blair.
Mansfield T: Marriott; Riley (Andrew), Sutton, Howell, O'Neill, Geohaghon, Murray, Meikle (Briscoe), Dyer (Rhead), Green▪, Roberts.

Thursday, 3 May 2012

Luton T (2) 2 *(Gray 22, Fleetwood 30)*

Wrexham (0) 0 9012

Luton T: Tyler; Osano, Howells, Keane, Kovacs, Pilkington G, Lawless, Watkins (Kissock), Fleetwood (McAllister), Gray (Morgan-Smith), Willmott.
Wrexham: Mayebi; Wright S, Ashton, Creighton, Knight-Percival, Harris, Cieslewicz (Hunt), Keates, Morrell (Wright D), Pogba, Tolley.

SEMI-FINAL SECOND LEG

Monday, 7 May 2012

Mansfield T (0) 0

York C (0) 1 *(Blair 111)* 7295

Mansfield T: Marriott; O'Neill, Sutton▪, Roberts, Geohaghon, Riley, Howell (Rhead), Meikle, Dyer, Briscoe (Stevenson), Murray.
York C: Ingham; Parslow, Meredith, Smith, Doig (Fyfield), McLaughlin (Potts), Challinor (Moke), Oyebanjo, Walker, Chambers, Blair.
aet.

Wrexham (0) 2 *(Cieslewicz 63, Morrell 77)*

Luton T (1) 1 *(Pilkington G 25 (pen))* 9087

Wrexham: Mayebi; Alfei, Ashton, Creighton, Knight-Percival, Harris (Tolley), Little, Keates, Wright D (Cieslewicz), Speight, Pogba (Morrell).
Luton T: Tyler; Osano, Howells, Keane (McAllister), Kovacs, Pilkington G, Lawless, Watkins, Fleetwood (Taylor), Gray (Morgan-Smith), Willmott.

FINAL (at Wembley)

Sunday, 20 May 2012

Luton T (1) 1 *(Gray 2)*

York C (1) 2 *(Chambers 26, Blair 47)* 39,265

Luton T: Tyler; Osano, Howells, Keane, Kovacs, Pilkington G, Lawless, Watkins (McAllister) (O'Connor), Fleetwood (Kissock), Gray, Willmott.
York C: Ingham; Challinor (Brown), Gibson, Smith, Doig, Parslow, Oyebanjo, Blair, Walker (McLaughlin), Chambers (Reed), Meredith.
Referee: J. Simpson (Lancs).

BLUE SQUARE NORTH & SOUTH 2011–12

(P) *Promoted into division at end of 2010–11 season.* (R) *Relegated into division at end of 2010–11 season.*

BLUE SQUARE NORTH 2011–12

		Total						*Home*					*Away*						
		P	*W*	*D*	*L*	*F*	*A*	*W*	*D*	*L*	*F*	*A*	*W*	*D*	*L*	*F*	*A*	*GD*	*Pts*
1	Hyde U	42	27	9	6	90	36	15	5	1	55	17	12	4	5	35	19	54	90
2	Guiseley	42	25	10	7	87	50	15	3	3	52	24	10	7	4	35	26	37	85
3	FC Halifax T (P)	42	21	11	10	80	59	10	5	6	41	33	11	6	4	39	26	21	74
4	Gainsborough Trinity	42	23	5	14	74	60	14	2	5	38	22	9	3	9	36	38	14	74
5	Nuneaton T¶	42	22	12	8	73	41	13	4	4	36	19	9	8	4	37	22	32	72
6	Stalybridge Celtic	42	20	11	11	83	64	13	2	6	48	33	7	9	5	35	31	19	71
7	Worcester C	42	18	11	13	63	58	10	7	4	31	20	8	4	9	32	38	5	65
8	Altrincham (R)	42	17	10	15	90	71	10	6	5	49	31	7	4	10	41	40	19	61
9	Droylsden	42	16	11	15	83	86	10	6	5	46	35	6	5	10	37	51	–3	59
10	Bishop's Stortford	42	17	7	18	70	75	8	4	9	35	30	9	3	9	35	45	–5	58
11	Boston U	42	15	9	18	60	67	6	8	7	28	29	9	1	11	32	38	–7	54
12	Harrogate T	42	14	11	17	59	68	7	8	6	25	25	7	3	11	34	43	–9	53
13	Colwyn Bay (P)	42	15	8	19	55	70	9	3	9	31	39	6	5	10	24	31	–15	53
14	Gloucester C	42	15	7	20	53	60	8	3	10	25	27	7	4	10	28	33	–7	52
15	Histon (R)	42	12	15	15	67	72	5	9	7	41	41	7	6	8	26	31	–5	51
16	Corby T	42	14	8	20	65	71	6	1	14	33	43	8	7	6	32	28	–6	50
17	Workington	42	13	11	18	55	61	8	6	7	31	28	5	5	11	24	33	–6	50
18	Vauxhall Motors	42	14	8	20	63	78	8	4	9	27	33	6	4	11	36	45	–15	50
19	Solihull Moors	42	13	10	19	44	54	9	4	8	29	25	4	6	11	15	29	–10	49
20	Hinckley U	42	13	9	20	75	90	5	5	11	36	43	8	4	9	39	47	–15	48
21	Blyth Spartans	42	7	13	22	51	81	5	5	11	30	38	2	8	11	21	43	–30	34
22	Eastwood T	42	4	8	30	37	105	1	7	13	22	53	3	1	17	15	52	–68	20

Nuneaton Town deducted 6 points. ¶Nuneaton T promoted via play-offs.

BLUE SQUARE SOUTH 2011–12

		Total						*Home*					*Away*						
		P	*W*	*D*	*L*	*F*	*A*	*W*	*D*	*L*	*F*	*A*	*W*	*D*	*L*	*F*	*A*	*GD*	*Pts*
1	Woking	42	30	7	5	92	41	15	4	2	43	18	15	3	3	49	23	51	97
2	Dartford¶	42	26	10	6	89	40	15	4	2	52	19	11	6	4	37	21	49	88
3	Welling U	42	24	9	9	79	47	14	6	1	42	18	10	3	8	37	29	32	81
4	Sutton U (P)	42	20	14	8	68	53	12	6	3	39	24	8	8	5	29	29	15	74
5	Basingstoke T	42	20	11	11	65	50	10	6	5	35	29	10	5	6	30	21	15	71
6	Chelmsford C	42	18	13	11	67	44	8	5	8	33	25	10	8	3	34	19	23	67
7	Dover Ath	42	17	15	10	62	49	7	8	6	26	24	10	7	4	36	25	13	66
8	Boreham Wood	42	17	10	15	66	58	11	5	5	43	26	6	5	10	23	32	8	61
9	Tonbridge Angels (P)	42	15	12	15	70	67	10	4	7	41	34	5	8	8	29	33	3	57
10	Salisbury C (P)	42	15	12	15	55	54	9	4	8	27	21	6	8	7	28	33	1	57
11	Dorchester T	42	16	8	18	58	65	7	4	10	30	37	9	4	8	28	28	–7	56
12	Eastleigh	42	15	9	18	57	63	10	5	6	36	25	5	4	12	21	38	–6	54
13	Weston Super Mare	42	14	9	19	58	71	8	6	7	34	35	6	3	12	24	36	–13	51
14	Truro C (P)	42	13	9	20	65	80	7	3	11	33	37	6	6	9	32	43	–15	48
15	Staines T	42	12	10	20	53	63	4	6	11	25	39	8	4	9	28	24	–10	46
16	Farnborough	42	15	6	21	52	79	9	0	12	21	32	6	6	9	31	47	–27	46
17	Bromley	42	10	15	17	52	66	4	10	7	23	24	6	5	10	29	42	–14	45
18	Eastbourne Borough (R)	42	12	9	21	54	69	7	4	10	29	33	5	5	11	25	36	–15	45
19	Havant & Waterlooville	42	11	11	20	64	75	7	6	8	39	34	4	5	12	25	41	–11	44
20	Maidenhead U	42	11	10	21	49	74	4	6	11	25	41	7	4	10	24	33	–25	43
21	Hampton & Richmond B	42	10	12	20	53	69	3	7	11	22	39	7	5	9	31	30	–16	42
22	Thurrock	42	5	11	26	33	84	2	7	12	13	36	3	4	14	20	48	–51	26

Farnborough deducted 5 points. ¶Dartford promoted via play-offs.

BLUE SQUARE NORTH & SOUTH PLAY-OFFS

BLUE SQUARE NORTH

SEMI-FINALS FIRST LEG

Gainsborough Trinity 2 *(Connor 6, 13)*
FC Halifax T 2 *(Gregory 44, 85)* 2380

Nuneaton T 1 *(Glover 2)*
Guiseley 1 *(Wilson 90)* 1476

SEMI-FINALS SECOND LEG

FC Halifax T 0
Gainsborough Trinity 1 *(Clarke 65)* 3468

Guiseley 0
Nuneaton T 1 *(Brown 2)* 1676

FINAL

Gainsborough Trinity 0
Nuneaton T 1 *(Brown 17)* 3280

BLUE SQUARE SOUTH

SEMI-FINALS FIRST LEG

Sutton U 1 *(Holloway 67 og)*
Welling U 2 *(Clarke 25, Healy 71)* 1255

Basingstoke T 0
Dartford 1 *(Noble 46)* 1691

SEMI-FINALS SECOND LEG

Welling U 0
Sutton U 0 1408

Dartford 2 *(Bradbrook 57, Wilkinson 73)*
Basingstoke T 1 *(McAuley 68)* 2210

FINAL

Dartford 1 *(Noble 4)*
Welling 0 4088

AFC TELFORD UNITED Blue Square Premier

Ground: The New Bucks Head Stadium, Watling Street, Wellington, Telford, Shropshire TF1 2TU.
Tel: (01952) 640 064. *Fax:* (01952) 640 021. *Year Formed:* 2004. *Record Gate:* 5,710 (2007 v Burscough).
Nickname: The Bucks or Lillywhites. *Manager:* Andy Sinton. *Secretary:* Sharon Bowyer.
Colours: White shirts with black trim, black shorts, white and black stockings.

AFC TELFORD UNITED 2011–12 LEAGUE RECORD

Match No.	Date	Venue	Opponents	Result		H/T Score	Lg Pos.	Goalscorers	Attendance
1	Aug 16	A	Cambridge U	L	0-1	0-0	—		2482
2	20	A	York C	W	1-0	0-0	16	Farrell [86]	2723
3	23	H	Lincoln C	L	1-2	0-0	—	Mills [90]	2323
4	27	H	Newport Co	W	2-1	1-1	15	Davies [17], Newton (pen) [57]	2147
5	29	A	Tamworth	D	2-2	0-1	—	Rooney [70], Meechan [79]	1316
6	Sept 3	A	Southport	L	2-3	2-3	17	Mills [33], Brown [35]	1123
7	10	H	Stockport Co	D	1-1	0-0	17	Newton (pen) [49]	2375
8	13	H	Luton T	L	0-2	0-1	—		2640
9	17	H	Bath C	W	2-1	1-1	15	Sharp [3], Brown [46]	2093
10	20	A	Mansfield T	D	1-1	0-0	—	Sharp [86]	2481
11	24	A	Fleetwood T	D	2-2	1-0	15	Killock [43], Newton [58]	1686
12	27	H	Alfreton T	W	1-0	0-0	—	Sharp [68]	1871
13	Oct 1	H	Hayes & Y	D	1-1	1-0	13	Davies [38]	1941
14	8	A	Barrow	L	1-2	0-1	14	Farrell [58]	1109
15	11	A	Kidderminster H	D	2-2	1-2	—	Adams [8], Sharp [75]	2440
16	15	H	Ebbsfleet U	L	0-2	0-1	15		2004
17	18	A	Forest Green R	L	1-2	0-1	—	Proudlock [77]	632
18	22	H	Gateshead	L	1-2	0-1	19	Preston [65]	2484
19	Nov 5	A	Darlington	L	0-1	0-1	20		1680
20	19	H	Mansfield T	D	0-0	0-0	19		2203
21	26	H	Barrow	W	1-0	0-0	17	Jones [77]	1814
22	29	A	Luton T	D	1-1	0-1	—	Newton [55]	5399
23	Dec 3	A	Bath C	L	1-3	1-1	17	Jones [45]	761
24	6	H	York C	D	0-0	0-0	—		1601
25	17	A	Braintree T	L	1-2	1-1	18	Smith [7]	605
26	26	H	Wrexham	L	0-2	0-1	18		4591
27	Jan 1	A	Wrexham	L	0-4	0-2	18		5812
28	7	H	Kettering T	W	3-1	1-1	17	Sharp [43], Trainer [46], Jackson [86]	2035
29	21	H	Cambridge U	L	1-2	0-1	17	Sharp [53]	1903
30	24	A	Stockport Co	D	2-2	2-0	—	Sharp [16], Jones [34]	2831
31	28	A	Grimsby T	L	0-2	0-0	18		3704
32	Feb 18	H	Braintree T	W	1-0	0-0	18	Brooke [75]	1776
33	25	A	Lincoln C	D	1-1	1-1	18	Perry [24]	2438
34	Mar 3	A	Alfreton T	D	0-0	0-0	19		940
35	10	H	Southport	L	0-1	0-0	20		2025
36	13	H	Kidderminster H	W	2-1	1-0	—	Trainer [3], Blackburn [66]	2192
37	17	H	Fleetwood T	L	1-4	0-2	17	Brown [74]	2313
38	20	A	Kettering T	L	1-2	0-0	—	Sharp [85]	939
39	24	A	Hayes & Y	D	0-0	0-0	18		307
40	27	H	Forest Green R	W	2-0	2-0	—	Sharp 2 [8, 38]	1674
41	31	H	Darlington	D	3-3	1-2	18	Sharp [9], Davies [52], Trainer [60]	1908
42	Apr 6	A	Newport Co	D	0-0	0-0	—		1540
43	14	A	Ebbsfleet U	L	2-3	0-2	20	Proudlock [66], Brooke [74]	875
44	17	H	Tamworth	W	1-0	0-0	—	Trainer [77]	3477
45	21	H	Grimsby T	D	0-0	0-0	20		2676
46	28	A	Gateshead	L	0-3	0-0	20		606

Final League Position: 20

GOALSCORERS

League (45): Sharp 11, Newton 4 (2 pens), Trainer 4, Brown 3, Davies 3, Jones 3, Brooke 2, Farrell 2, Mills 2, Proudlock 2, Adams 1, Blackburn 1, Jackson 1, Killock 1, Meechan 1, Perry 1, Preston 1, Rooney 1, Smith 1.
FA Cup (5): Pitt 2, Sharp 2, Killock 1.

Young 46	Valentine 35 + 2	Newton 33	Davies 29 + 5	Preston 25 + 3	Killock 32 + 3	Reid 4 + 1	Trainer 34 + 2	Meechan 2 + 3	Brown 29 + 5	Adams 14 + 6	Farrell 7 + 9	Samuels 7 + 10	Rooney 7 + 9	Salmon 38	King 2 + 2	Mills 7 + 9	Whitehead 13 + 1	Sharp 32 + 5	Rodgers 8 + 3	Proudlock 6 + 12	Platt 2 + 1	Weir-Daley — + 2	Pitt 4	Smith 15 + 2	Cain 15 + 8	Jones 9 + 6	Chamberlain 1 + 1	Blackburn 19	Perry 13 + 6	Jackson 8	Futcher 3	Brooke 6 + 5	Kinniburgh 1	*Match No.*
1	2	3	4^{3}	5	6	7	8	9^{1}	10	11^{2}	12	13	14																					1
1	11	3	4	5	6	7^{1}	8	13	10^{3}		14	12		2	9^{2}																			2
1	11	3	4	5	6	7^{1}	8	9^{3}	10		13			2^{2}	14	12																		3
1	11	3	4	5	6^{1}		8		10^{2}		13	7		2		9	12																	4
1	11	3	4	5			8	12	10		14	7^{3}	13	2^{2}		9^{1}	6																	5
1	7^{1}	3	4^{2}	5			8	14	10			12	13	2^{3}		11	6	9																6
1		3			6	7^{2}	8		10^{3}		14	11	9^{1}	2		12	5	13	4															7
1		3	4^{1}		6		8		12	13	14	7		2^{3}		9	5	10	11^{2}															8
1	14	3			6		8		9	11		7^{3}	4^{1}	2		12	5	10^{2}		13														9
1	7	3	4	5	6		8		10^{1}	11^{2}		13		2				9		12														10
1	7	3	4	5	6		8		10^{1}	11^{3}		14		2				9^{2}	12	13														11
1	7	3	4	5	6		8		10	11				2^{1}		12		9^{2}		13														12
1	2	3	4	5	6		8			11						12		10		9^{2}	7^{1}	13												13
1	2^{2}	3	4	5	6		8			11	9					12		10		13	7^{1}													14
1		3		5	6		8^{2}			11	9			2		12		10	4^{1}	13			7											15
1		3	12	5	6		8^{1}			11	9^{2}			2		4		10		13	14		7^{3}											16
1	12	3	4		6		8		13	11	9^{3}			2		14	5^{1}			10			7^{2}											17
1		3	4	5	6		14		10	11				2	7^{1}	8^{3}		12		9^{2}		13												18
1		3	4	5	6	12	14		10^{2}	11^{3}	13			2		8		9					7^{1}											19
1	7	3	4^{2}		6					13	9^{1}			2	14		5	10^{3}						8	11	12								20
1	3	11^{1}	8^{3}		6					14	12			2			5	10■						4	7	13	9^{2}							21
1	3	11	8	14	6				12	13	10^{3}			2			5							4	7^{2}	9^{1}								22
1	11	3	4^{1}		6■				13	12	10^{2}		14	2			5							7^{3}	8	9								23
1	3	11		6			8		10				12	2			5							4	7	9^{1}								24
1	11	3		5	6		8		10	14			9^{1}	2				12						4^{3}	7^{2}		13							25
1	3	9^{3}	4	12^{2}	6		8■		13	11		14		2			5^{1}	10							7									26
1	3	9			6					11			8	2^{1}		12	5	10^{2}	4						7	13								27
1	3^{2}			13	6		8					14		2				10^{3}						4	7^{1}	12		5	9	11				28
1	3		12				8^{1}					14	13	2^{3}				10						4^{2}	7	11		6	9		5			29
1	3				14		8■					13		2				10	12					4^{3}	7	11^{2}		6	9^{1}		5			30
1	3											13	8	2^{2}				10	4						7	9		6	12	11^{1}	5			31
1	2	3	14		6				7^{1}				8^{3}					10						4	12	11		5	9^{2}			13		32
1	2	3	13		6				8				7					11^{1}						4^{2}	14	10		5	9^{3}			12		33
1	2■	3	8		6				7									12						4	13	11^{2}		5	9^{1}			10		34
1		3	11	5								7^{1}	13	2				10						4^{2}	8			6	12			9		35
1		3	11	5			8		4^{2}					2				10^{1}							13			6	9	7		12		36
1			4^{2}	5	14		8		7					2				10							13			6	9^{1}	11		12	3^{3}	37
1	2	3^{3}	14	5			8		7									10						4^{2}	13			6	12	11		9^{1}		38
1	3		7^{3}	5^{1}	12		8		10					2				13	4	14								6	9^{2}	11				39
1	3		4^{2}		6		8		7					2				10^{3}		12				13	14			5	9^{1}	11				40
1	3		4		5		8		7					2				10		12					13			6	9^{1}	11^{2}				41
1	3		4		6		8		7					2				10^{2}	12	13					11			5	9^{1}					42
1	3		4^{1}		6		8		7			2						10		13				12	11^{3}			5	9^{2}			14		43
1	3			6			8		7					2				10		9^{2}				4^{1}		12		5	13			11		44
1	3			5			8		7				13	2				10^{1}	4	9^{2}								6	12			11		45
1	3			5			8		7				14	2				10	4^{3}	9^{2}						13		6	12			11^{1}		46

FA Cup

Fourth Qualifying Round			
	Gainsborough T	(a)	5-0
First Round	Chelmsford C	(a)	0-4

ALFRETON TOWN

Blue Square Premier

Ground: The Impact Arena, North Street, Alfreton, Derbyshire DE55 7FZ. *Tel:* (01773) 830 277 or (01773) 836 164. *Year Formed:* 1959. *Record Gate:* 5,023 (1960 v Matlock T). *Nickname:* The Reds. *Manager:* Nicky Law. *Secretary:* Bryan Rudkin. *Colours:* All red.

ALFRETON TOWN 2011–12 LEAGUE RECORD

Match No.	Date	Venue	Opponents	Result		H/T Score	Lg Pos.	Goalscorers	Attendance
1	Aug 13	A	Hayes & Y	L	1-3	0-2	—	Mullan [70]	262
2	16	H	Southport	D	0-0	0-0	—		777
3	20	H	Forest Green R	L	1-6	1-3	23	Streete [13]	686
4	23	A	Darlington	D	1-1	0-0	—	Jarman (pen) [83]	1965
5	27	H	Wrexham	L	1-4	1-2	24	Jarman (pen) [21]	1165
6	29	A	York C	W	1-0	1-0	—	Mackin (pen) [43]	3166
7	Sept 3	A	Gateshead	L	0-2	0-0	23		991
8	10	H	Braintree T	L	0-1	0-1	22		656
9	17	A	Kidderminster H	L	1-3	1-1	23	Broughton (pen) [31]	1939
10	20	H	Barrow	W	2-1	0-1	—	Brown [73], Ellison [90]	678
11	24	H	Ebbsfleet U	D	2-2	0-2	21	Brown [49], Jarman [64]	661
12	27	A	AFC Telford U	L	0-1	0-0	—		1871
13	Oct 1	A	Grimsby T	L	2-5	1-0	22	Clayton [18], Jarman (pen) [90]	2941
14	8	H	Kettering T	D	1-1	1-0	22	Brown [24]	851
15	11	H	Lincoln C	L	1-3	1-3	—	Clayton [18]	1232
16	15	A	Cambridge U	L	0-3	0-2	23		2741
17	18	H	Fleetwood T	L	1-4	0-1	—	Clayton [70]	625
18	22	A	Mansfield T	L	2-3	2-0	23	Brown [13], Clayton [21]	2982
19	Nov 5	A	Forest Green R	L	1-4	0-0	23	Wilson, A [62]	764
20	19	H	Gateshead	D	1-1	1-0	23	Clayton [37]	651
21	26	H	Hayes & Y	W	3-2	0-0	23	Arnold [64], Moult, J [89], Jarman [90]	600
22	29	A	Barrow	L	0-1	0-1	—		963
23	Dec 3	A	Southport	L	1-2	0-0	23	Quinn [63]	1061
24	6	H	Newport Co	W	3-2	2-1	—	Church [28], Moult, J [38], Jarman [89]	579
25	17	A	Stockport Co	D	0-0	0-0	23		2802
26	26	H	Tamworth	W	5-2	3-0	22	Brown [1], Arnold [3], Moult, J [36], Wilson, A [55], Jarman [67]	1012
27	Jan 1	A	Tamworth	D	2-2	1-1	21	Streete [43], Brown [62]	1241
28	7	H	Grimsby T	L	2-5	1-3	21	Arnold [33], Wilson, M [73]	1924
29	21	H	Kidderminster H	L	0-2	0-0	21		990
30	24	A	Bath C	W	3-0	1-0	—	Connolly (og) [17], Jarman (pen) [88], Clay [90]	739
31	28	A	Luton T	L	0-1	0-1	22		5658
32	Feb 18	H	Darlington	W	3-1	1-1	21	Arnold 2 [33, 69], Clayton [58]	950
33	25	A	Fleetwood T	L	0-4	0-2	21		1929
34	Mar 3	H	AFC Telford U	D	0-0	0-0	20		940
35	6	H	Stockport Co	W	6-1	3-0	—	Jarman 3 (2 pens) [1, 37 (p), 86 (p)], Wilson, A [25], Clayton [68], Arnold [77]	1115
36	10	A	Lincoln C	W	1-0	1-0	17	Moult, J [45]	2253
37	17	A	Kettering T	W	2-0	2-0	16	Kempson [4], Moult, J [10]	1093
38	20	H	Mansfield T	L	3-6	3-4	—	Moult, J [6], Jarman [21], Brown [45]	3354
39	24	H	Cambridge U	W	2-1	1-1	16	Thorpe (og) [1], Wilson, A [54]	965
40	27	A	Ebbsfleet U	W	2-1	1-1	—	Cunnington [35], Law [48]	687
41	31	A	Braintree T	W	2-1	1-1	15	Cunnington [23], Brown [63]	620
42	Apr 6	A	Wrexham	W	1-0	1-0	—	Wilson, A [43]	4673
43	9	H	York C	L	0-2	0-0	15		1603
44	14	H	Luton T	D	0-0	0-0	15		1654
45	21	A	Newport Co	L	0-1	0-1	15		1239
46	28	H	Bath C	W	2-1	2-1	15	Meadows [17], Wilson, A [20]	786

Final League Position: 15

GOALSCORERS

League (62): Jarman 12 (6 pens), Brown 8, Clayton 7, Arnold 6, Moult, J 6, Wilson, A 6, Cunnington 2, Streete 2, Broughton 1 (1 pen), Church 1, Clay 1, Ellison 1, Kempson 1, Law 1, Mackin 1 (1 pen), Meadows 1, Mullan 1, Quinn 1, Wilson, M 1, own goals 2.
FA Cup (3): Jarman 2 (2 pens), Brown 1.

Lowson 20	Law 30 + 8	Franklin 37 + 2	Streete 40 + 3	Young 28 + 2	Wilson M 12 + 2	Brown 38 + 2	Jarman 25 + 14	Clayton 30 + 10	Senior 7 + 12	Arnold 27 + 1	Mullan 16 + 18	Moult J 33 + 4	Hall 5 + 7	Wilson A 26 + 7	Franks 21 + 2	Mackin 11	Hawes 2 + 2	Ellison 1 + 7	Brogan — + 2	Holdsworth 2 + 2	Broughton 2	Day 15	Stevenson 3	Potter 2	Church 6	Quinn 17	Eagle 2 + 1	Moult L 1	Clay 2 + 2	Kempson 13	Stewart 11	Deverdics 3 + 3	Conneely 8 + 1	Cunnington 7 + 4	Meadows 3 + 1	*Match No.*
1	2	3	4	5	6	7	8^{1}	9^{3}	10^{2}	11	12	13	14																							1
1	2	3	4	5	6	7		9		11	10^{1}	8^{2}	13	12																						2
1	2	3	4	5	6	7	13	9	14	11^{3}	10^{1}	8^{2}		12																						3
1	2	3	4		6	7	13	9	10^{2}	11^{1}			12		5	8																				4
1		3	4		6	7	10^{1}	9^{3}	14		12		2		5	8	11^{2}	13																		5
1		3	4	5	6	7	12	9^{1}	10^{2}		11				2	8		13																		6
1		3	4	5	2	7^{1}	8^{2}		10		11^{3}				6	9		13	12	14																7
1	2		4	5		7	14	9^{3}	10^{2}		8^{1}				6	11		13	12	3																8
1	2	3	4^{2}	5	6	7	12	9	13			8^{3}	14		11▪						10^{1}															9
1	2	3	4	5	6	7	10^{3}	9^{2}	14		12	8^{1}				11		13																		10
1	2	3	4		6^{2}	7	10	9^{3}			13	8			5	11^{1}		14		12																11
1	2^{2}	3	4^{1}	5		7			10		14	8	13		6		12	9^{3}		11																12
1		3		5		7	11	9^{1}	14		13	8	4^{2}		2		6^{3}	12▪			10▪															13
	2	3	4		5^{1}	7	10	9^{3}	14		11	8^{2}		13	12	6						1														14
		3	4	5		7	12	9	14		8^{3}	13		10^{2}	2	11						1	6^{1}													15
	2	3^{3}	4	5		7		9	12		13		14	10^{1}	6	11						1	8^{2}													16
	2	3^{3}	4▪	14		7		9	13		10	12	8^{1}		5	11						1	6^{2}													17
	2^{1}			5▪		7	12	9^{3}	14		11^{2}	8	4	10▪	3		13					1		6												18
	2		4	5		3	8^{2}	9^{1}	10	12	13		7	11								1		6												19
		3	4	5		14	12	9	13	11^{2}	2	8		10^{1}	6^{3}							1			7											20
		3	4	5			13	9^{2}		11	7▪	8		10^{1}								1			2	6	12									21
	13	3	4	5			14	9^{1}	12	11		8		10^{3}								1			2	6	7^{2}									22
	12	3	4	5		14	13	9^{2}		11		8		10^{1}								1			2	6	7^{3}									23
	2^{2}	3	4	5		7	12	9^{1}		11		8		13								1			10	6										24
	2		4	5		3	9	12		11		8		10^{1}								1			7	6										25
	2^{3}	3^{1}	4	5	12	7	9	13		11	14	8		10^{2}								1				6										26
	2	3	4	5		7	9	12		11^{1}		8		10								1				6										27
	2^{1}	3	4	5	15	7	9	13		11	12	8		10^{2}								1^{G}				6										28
1	2	3	4	5			10	12		11^{2}	7	8^{1}		13												6		9▪								29
1	14		4	5		3	10	12		11	7^{3}	8^{2}		9^{1}	2											6			13							30
1	14	12	4	3		2	9	13		10^{2}	7^{3}	8			6^{1}														11	5						31
1	13		4	3		2▪	7	9^{3}		11		8^{2}	14	10^{1}												6			12	5						32
1	12		4^{1}	3	7		10	9^{3}			13	8		14	2											6			11^{2}	5						33
	12	3	4			7	9	8		11^{1}	13			10^{2}	2▪											6				5	1					34
	2	3	4			7^{1}	10	8		11	13	6		9^{2}																5	1	12				35
	2	3	4^{1}				7	9^{2}		11		6		10																5	1	8	12	13		36
	2^{3}	3	12				7	9^{1}		11	14	4		10^{2}																5	1	8	6	13		37
	2	3	4^{1}	12		7	8^{2}	9^{3}		11	13	6		10																5	1			14		38
		3	4			2	7	13		11		8		9																5^{1}	1	12	6	10^{2}		39
	2	3	4			7				11^{1}	12	6		9^{2}	13											8					1		5	10		40
	2	3	4			7		12			11	8		9^{1}												6					1		5	10		41
	2	3	12			7				11^{2}	13	4		9												6^{1}				5	1		8	10		42
	2^{2}	3	4			7	12				11^{3}	8		9																5	1	13	6^{1}	10	14	43
	2	3	14			7	9	12		11^{1}				13	6															5	1	8^{3}		10^{2}	4	44
1	14	12	4			3	13	11				8		9	6															5^{1}			7	10^{2}	2^{3}	45
1	2^{3}	3				7	10			11^{2}	12	14		9^{1}	5											6							8	13	4	46

FA Cup

Fourth Qualifying Round	Lincoln C	(h)	1-1
		(a)	2-1
First Round	Carlisle U	(h)	0-4

BARROW

Blue Square Premier

Ground: Furness Building Society Stadium, Wilkie Road, Barrow-in-Furness, Cumbria LA14 5UW.
Tel: (01229) 828 227. *Year Formed:* 1901. *Record Gate:* 16,854 (1954 v Swansea T, FA Cup 3rd rd).
Nickname: Bluebirds. *Managers:* Dave Bayliss and Darren Sheridan.
Colours: White shirts, blue shorts, white stockings.

BARROW 2011–12 LEAGUE RECORD

Match No.	Date	Venue	Opponents	Result		H/T Score	Lg Pos.	Goalscorers	Attendance
1	Aug 13	H	Tamworth	D	1-1	0-1	—	Boyes [69]	1371
2	16	A	York C	L	1-3	0-2	—	Boyes [81]	3075
3	20	A	Bath C	W	1-0	0-0	15	Boyes [66]	781
4	23	H	Fleetwood T	W	4-0	3-0	—	Cook 3 [11, 38, 81], Edwards (og) [37]	1482
5	27	H	Gateshead	L	1-2	1-2	10	Boyes [33]	1291
6	29	A	Southport	L	1-2	1-0	—	Rutherford [45]	1204
7	Sept 3	A	Ebbsfleet U	W	2-1	1-1	12	Boyes [17], Smith [79]	983
8	10	H	Wrexham	W	3-1	0-1	9	Bolland [53], Boyes 2 [63, 85]	1463
9	17	H	Mansfield T	L	2-3	1-2	11	Almond [26], Boyes [56]	1244
10	20	A	Alfreton T	L	1-2	1-0	—	Hollis [41]	678
11	24	A	Newport Co	D	2-2	1-1	13	Boyes [5], Baker (pen) [90]	1315
12	27	H	Lincoln C	W	1-0	1-0	—	Baker (pen) [45]	1181
13	Oct 1	A	Luton T	L	1-5	1-1	12	Mackreth [2]	5613
14	8	H	AFC Telford U	W	2-1	1-0	12	Boyes (pen) [21], Baker [83]	1109
15	11	A	Grimsby T	L	2-5	1-2	—	Smith [19], Mackreth [54]	2675
16	15	H	Hayes & Y	W	3-1	2-0	12	Cook 3 [1, 32, 48]	1074
17	18	A	Darlington	W	1-0	1-0	—	Boyes [23]	1786
18	22	H	Kidderminster H	W	3-1	3-1	11	Boyes [18], Cook [21], Rowe [23]	1246
19	Nov 5	A	Lincoln C	L	1-2	0-2	12	Pearson, M [90]	2090
20	19	H	York C	D	0-0	0-0	12		2190
21	26	A	AFC Telford U	L	0-1	0-0	14		1814
22	29	H	Alfreton T	W	1-0	1-0	—	Cook [10]	963
23	Dec 3	H	Ebbsfleet U	D	1-1	1-0	11	Cook [6]	1047
24	17	A	Hayes & Y	D	1-1	1-1	12	Mackreth [23]	313
25	26	H	Stockport Co	W	1-0	1-0	10	Bolland [42]	2103
26	Jan 1	A	Stockport Co	L	2-3	0-2	12	Baker 2 (1 pen) [57, 67 (p)]	3301
27	7	H	Darlington	W	3-0	2-0	11	Boyes [15], Cook 2 [32, 63]	2144
28	10	A	Fleetwood T	L	1-4	0-1	—	Jackson [70]	2091
29	21	A	Tamworth	W	3-2	1-1	11	Smith [11], Cook 2 [79, 84]	1222
30	24	H	Grimsby T	D	2-2	1-1	—	Boyes [21], Jackson [90]	1081
31	28	A	Braintree T	L	0-1	0-0	11		685
32	Feb 18	H	Kettering T	W	3-0	1-0	11	Baker (pen) [20], Cook 2 [78, 83]	1090
33	21	H	Luton T	W	1-0	0-0	—	Harvey [73]	925
34	25	H	Forest Green R	D	1-1	0-1	10	Cook [64]	1194
35	Mar 3	A	Kidderminster H	W	2-1	2-1	9	Mackreth [20], Baker (pen) [25]	2135
36	6	H	Bath C	L	0-1	0-1	—		1190
37	10	A	Wrexham	L	0-2	0-1	18		3432
38	13	A	Cambridge U	L	0-1	0-0	—		1651
39	17	A	Mansfield T	L	0-7	0-4	11		2510
40	24	H	Braintree T	L	0-4	0-3	13		939
41	31	A	Forest Green R	L	0-3	0-0	13		1070
42	Apr 7	A	Gateshead	L	0-2	0-1	13		701
43	9	H	Southport	D	2-2	1-1	13	Jackson [7], Baker [71]	918
44	14	H	Cambridge U	L	1-3	1-2	13	Mackreth [20]	870
45	21	A	Kettering T	D	1-1	0-1	13	Boyes [81]	896
46	28	H	Newport Co	W	3-1	1-1	13	Cook [7], Baker [51], Boyes [69]	900

Final League Position: 13

GOALSCORERS

League (62): Cook 17, Boyes 16 (1 pen), Baker 9 (5 pens), Mackreth 5, Jackson 3, Smith 3, Bolland 2, Almond 1, Harvey 1, Hollis 1, Pearson, M 1, Rowe 1, Rutherford 1, own goal 1.
FA Cup (5): Boyes 4, Rutherford 1.

Hurst 31	Lomax 22 + 4	Skelton 43	Quinn 18	Bolland 28 + 1	Hulbert 7 + 1	Rutherford 32 + 8	Baker 31 + 8	Almond 10 + 13	Ferrell 13 + 2	Boyes 39 + 3	Sheridan 1 + 1	Cook 34 + 3	Mackreth 36 + 7	Smith 36 + 4	Pearson M 9 + 1	Owen 31 + 2	Brooke 1 + 5	Moyo 4 + 5	Hollis 2 + 1	Nicholas 11 + 9	Rowe 6 + 4	Hone 25 + 1	Pearson S 14	Harvey 10 + 3	Jackson 2 + 4	Turner 5	Edwards 4	Dixon — + 1	Cudworth 1	*Match No.*
1	2	3	4	5	6^{2}	7^{3}	8^{1}	9	10	11	12	13	14																	1
1	2■	3	4	5^{3}		7		9^{2}	10	11	6^{1}	12	13	8	14															2
1		3	4		12	7		9^{1}	10	11		8	6	2	5															3
1	13	3	4		6^{1}	7	12	14	10	11		9^{3}	8^{2}	2	5															4
1		3	4		6	7	12	13	10^{1}	11		9	8	2^{2}	5															5
1	13	3	4		6^{1}	7	12	14	10	11		9^{3}	8	2^{2}	5															6
1	2	3	4	13		7		12		11		9^{1}	8	6	5^{2}	10														7
1	2	3	4	5^{1}		7	12	9^{2}		11			8	10		6	13													8
1	2	3	4			7		9^{1}		11			10	8		6	12	5												9
1	2	3■	4		6	7		9^{1}		11			10	12		8			5											10
1	2		5		6	7	8	9	10	11				3^{1}			12			4										11
1	3		5		6^{1}		8	9^{2}		11		10■	7^{3}	2		12	13	14		4										12
1	2		5				8	9^{1}	13	11			7			6	10^{2}	3		4	12									13
1	2	3	5			13	12	9^{3}		11			8	7^{1}		6	14			4	10^{2}									14
1	2	3	5			12	8			11			10	7		6			13	4^{2}	9^{1}									15
1		3	5				8	12		11		9^{1}	10	2	6	4					7									16
1		3					8			11		9	10	2	6	4			5	12	7^{1}									17
1		3	5			12	8	13		11		9^{2}	10	2	6	4					7^{1}									18
1		3	5			7^{1}	8	12		11		9^{2}	10	2	6	4					13									19
1		3		5		7	8	12		11		9^{1}	10^{2}	2		4					13	6								20
1		3		5		7	8	14	4	11		9^{3}	10^{1}	2^{2}						13	12	6								21
		3		5^{1}		7	8		4	11		9	13	2						12	10^{2}	6	1							22
	2	3		5		7	8	12	4^{2}	11^{1}		9	10			13						6	1							23
	2	3		5		7	12	13	8^{1}	11^{2}		9	10			4						6	1							24
1	2	3		5		7	8	12		11		9^{1}	10^{2}	13		4						6								25
1	2^{1}	3		5		7	8	13		11		9^{2}	10	12		4						6								26
1	12	3		5		7^{2}	8		10	11		9^{3}		2		4^{1}		13		14		6								27
1		3		5		7	8			11		9^{1}	10	2								6		4	12					28
	2	3		5		7	8			11		12		10				13		14		6^{2}	1	4^{3}	9^{1}					29
	2■	3		5			8			11		9	10^{2}	7				12		4^{1}		6	1		13					30
		3		5			8			11		9■	10^{1}	7				2		4		6	1		12■					31
		3		5		12	8		14			9	10^{2}	2		4^{3}				13		6	1	7		11^{1}				32
		3		5		12	8					9	10	2		4						6	1	7		11^{1}				33
		3		5		12	8					9	10	2		4						6	1	7		11^{1}				34
		3		5		12	8			13		9	10^{3}	2		4				14		6	1	7^{2}		11^{1}				35
		3		5		7	8^{2}			11		9	10^{1}	2		4				13		6	1	12						36
	14	3		5		12	8■			13		9	10	2		4^{3}						6	1	7^{1}		11^{2}				37
	2	11		5		7				10		9^{1}	12	8		4				13		6	1				3^{2}			38
	3	11		5		7				10^{2}		9	12	8		4						6	1^{G}	13			2^{1}	15		39
		3		5		7	8			12		9	10^{2}	2		4^{1}						6		11	13				1	40
1	2	3^{1}		5		7	8^{2}			10		9	12	14		4^{3}						6		13			11			41
1	2	11^{2}		5		7	12					9■	13	10		4^{1}						6		8			3			42
1		3				7	12			9^{1}			10	2		4				5		6		11	8					43
1		3				7	8		9	11			10	2		4^{1}		12		5		6								44
1		3		5		7	8			11		9	10			6		2		4										45
1	2	3		5^{1}		7	8			11		9	10			6				4		12								46

FA Cup

Fourth Qualifying Round	Witton Alb	(a)	4-1
First Round	Rotherham U	(h)	1-2

BATH CITY

Blue Square South

Ground: Twerton Park, Twerton, Bath BA2 1DB. *Tel:* (01225) 423 087. *Fax:* (01225) 481 391. *Year Formed:* 1889.
Record Gate: 18,020 (1960 v Brighton & HA). *Nickname:* The Romans. *Manager:* Adie Britton.
Secretary: Quentin Edwards. *Colours:* Black and white stripes.

BATH CITY 2011–12 LEAGUE RECORD

Match No.	Date	Venue	Opponents	Result		H/T Score	Lg Pos.	Goalscorers	Attendance
1	Aug 13	A	Mansfield T	D	1-1	1-1	—	Connolly 35	3997
2	16	H	Wrexham	L	0-2	0-0	—		1075
3	20	H	Barrow	L	0-1	0-0	22		781
4	23	A	Hayes & Y	D	1-1	0-1	—	Murray 90	172
5	27	H	Tamworth	L	0-2	0-1	22		656
6	29	A	Forest Green R	L	0-3	0-2	—		1344
7	Sept 10	H	Southport	L	1-2	0-1	24	Watkins 79	663
8	13	A	York C	L	0-1	0-0	—		2030
9	17	A	AFC Telford U	L	1-2	1-1	24	Watkins 22	2093
10	20	H	Luton T	D	1-1	0-1	—	Phillips 72	1158
11	24	H	Kettering T	L	0-1	0-1	24		734
12	27	A	Ebbsfleet U	L	0-3	0-1	—		816
13	Oct 1	A	Lincoln C	L	0-2	0-2	24		2244
14	8	H	Darlington	W	2-0	0-0	24	Canham, S 69, Phillips 71	1156
15	11	H	Cambridge U	L	3-4	2-2	—	Clough 12, Canham, M 2 (2 pens) 25, 79	788
16	15	A	Braintree T	D	3-3	1-2	24	Jones 3, Watkins 71, Phillips 90	703
17	18	H	Stockport Co	L	0-2	0-0	—		919
18	22	A	Fleetwood T	L	1-4	0-2	24	Stonehouse 74	1451
19	Nov 5	H	Grimsby T	D	2-2	0-1	24	Canham, M (pen) 57; Canham, S 72	993
20	19	A	Southport	L	1-2	0-0	24	Canham, S 76	1021
21	26	H	Mansfield T	D	1-1	1-1	24	Watkins 19	816
22	29	A	Cambridge U	D	1-1	0-1	—	Hogg 53	2267
23	Dec 3	H	AFC Telford U	W	3-1	1-1	24	Murray 26, Canham, M (pen) 55, Bryan 83	761
24	6	A	Kidderminster H	L	1-4	1-2	—	Murray 6	1472
25	17	A	Kettering T	D	1-1	0-0	24	Murray 51	1096
26	Jan 3	H	Newport Co	W	3-2	2-1	—	Connolly 23, Canham, S 30, Murray 47	1147
27	7	H	Braintree T	D	1-1	1-0	24	Canham, S 5	956
28	21	A	Grimsby T	L	0-6	0-2	24		3836
29	24	H	Alfreton T	L	0-3	0-1	—		739
30	28	A	Wrexham	L	0-2	0-1	24		3583
31	Feb 14	A	Newport Co	L	0-1	0-1	—		1130
32	18	H	Ebbsfleet U	L	2-3	0-1	24	Jones 61, Canham, S 90	693
33	21	H	Hayes & Y	L	0-1	0-1	—		512
34	25	H	Kidderminster H	L	1-2	0-1	24	Canham, S 88	676
35	Mar 3	A	Luton T	L	0-2	0-1	24		5745
36	6	A	Barrow	W	1-0	1-0	—	Canham, S 27	1190
37	17	H	Lincoln C	W	2-1	2-0	24	Canham, M (pen) 2, Watkins 4	760
38	20	A	Gateshead	L	0-1	0-0	—		512
39	24	A	Stockport Co	L	0-4	0-1	24		3744
40	27	H	York C	L	0-1	0-0	—		565
41	31	H	Fleetwood T	L	1-4	0-2	24	Connolly 81	762
42	Apr 6	A	Tamworth	W	1-0	0-0	—	Cook 78	957
43	9	H	Forest Green R	L	0-2	0-1	24		983
44	14	A	Darlington	D	2-2	0-1	24	Russell 83, Murray 89	1420
45	21	H	Gateshead	W	4-2	3-0	23	Connolly 4, Canham, M (pen) 8, Gallinagh 13, Canham, S 55	649
46	28	A	Alfreton T	L	1-2	1-2	23	Murray (pen) 25	786

Final League Position: 23

GOALSCORERS

League (43): Canham, S 9, Murray 7 (1 pen), Canham, M 6 (6 pens), Watkins 5, Connolly 4, Phillips 3, Jones 2, Bryan 1, Clough 1, Cook 1, Gallinagh 1, Hogg 1, Russell 1, Stonehouse 1.
FA Cup (3): Canham, S. 1, Connolly 1, Gallinagh 1.

Garner 36	Simpson 34 + 2	Stonehouse 32 + 6	Preece 25 + 4	Jones 39 + 1	Burnell 32 + 1	Russell 17 + 14	Connolly 41 + 2	Watkins 28 + 9	Phillips 24 + 7	Hogg 34 + 8	Murray 15 + 19	Cook 13 + 11	Mills 2 + 2	Rollo 7 + 9	Canham M 36 + 2	Egan — + 8	Carvalho-Landell 1	Swallow 7 + 2	Clough 10 + 2	Agdestein 3	Gallinagh 32	Canham S 22 + 2	Matthews 10	Bryan 1 + 3	Amadi-Holloway 3 + 2	Shephard 1 + 4	Doherty 1	Smith — + 3	Match No.
1	2	3	4	5	6	7^{1}	8	9	10^{2}	11	12	13																	1
1	2	3	4	5	6^{2}	8^{1}	12	9	10	11	7^{3}	14	13																2
1	2	3	4	5		7	8		10	11	12	9^{1}	6^{2}	13															3
1	2	3	4^{3}	5	6^{1}	14	8	9	10	11	12	13	7^{2}																4
1	2	3	4^{2}	5	6	7^{3}	8		10	11	12	9^{1}			13	14													5
1	2	3	4	5^{1}	6	14	8^{3}	7	10	11	13		12				9^{2}												6
1	2	3	4^{3}	5	13	14	8	9	10	11^{1}		12			6^{2}			7											7
1	2	3	12	5	6		8	9	10^{1}						11	13		7^{2}	4										8
1	2	3		5	6^{2}	12		9^{1}	10	13					11			7	4	8									9
1	2	3■	14	5	6		8		10^{2}	12	13^{3}				9			7	4■	11^{1}									10
1	2^{3}		5		4^{1}		8	13	10	11	14			12	6			7		9^{2}	3								11
1	2	3						9^{1}	10	11		12		4	8			7	6		5								12
1		14		2	3^{3}	8		9^{2}	10^{1}	11	13				4			7	5		6	12							13
1		3		5	7^{2}	12	8		10^{3}	11		14		13	4				6		2	9^{1}							14
1		3		5	7^{1}	13	8^{3}	12	10	11^{2}	14				6				4		2	9							15
1	2^{2}	3		5		14	8	13	10	11^{3}				12	6				4^{1}		7	9							16
1	2^{3}	3^{2}	12	5^{1}		14	8	11	10					4	6			13			7	9							17
1	2	3				10^{2}	8	7		11	13			5	4^{1}			12			6	9							18
1	2	14		5		12	8^{2}	7^{3}	10^{1}	11	13			6	4■						3	9							19
1	2	13		5	4^{3}	7^{1}	8	11	14	12		9^{2}							6		3	10							20
	2			5			8	7	14	3	12				4^{3}				6		11	9^{2}	1	10^{1}	13				21
	2			5	6	13	8	7	12	11					4						3	9^{2}	1		10^{1}				22
	2	14		5	6^{2}		8		10	11	7^{3}				4				13		3		1	12	9^{1}				23
	2			5	6		8	13	10^{2}	9	7^{3}				4				12		3^{1}		1	14	11				24
	2	3		5	6		8	10		11	7^{2}	9^{1}			4								1	13	12				25
	2	3		5	6	12	8	10^{2}	14	11	7^{1}	13			4							9^{3}	1						26
	2	3	12	5	6^{1}	7^{3}	8	10	13	11				14	4							9^{2}	1						27
	2	11		5	6	14	8		13	10^{3}	7^{1}	12			4						3	9^{2}	1						28
1	2			5■	6	10	8		12	11^{1}	7				4						3	9■							29
1	2	3	5		4^{3}	10	8	12	9^{2}		7^{1}	13		14	11						6								30
1	2	3	5		9^{2}	13	8	11	10	12					4^{1}						6					7			31
1	2		6^{2}	5	4^{1}		8	7	10	11					12						3	9				13			32
	2^{1}		6	5			8	14	10^{2}	11	7			12	4^{3}						3	9	1			13			33
		3	6	5	10		8	12		11^{3}	7^{2}	14									2	9	1			13	4^{1}		34
1		3	6	5	2		8	10^{2}		11^{1}	13				4						7	9				12			35
1		3	6	5	11		8	7			12	9^{1}		14	4^{3}	13					2	10^{2}							36
1		3	6	5	7^{3}	13	8	11^{1}		14	12	9^{2}			4						2	10							37
1		3	6	5	7^{2}		8			11	12	10^{1}			4^{3}	14					2	9						13	38
1		3	6	5	4^{1}		8			11	7^{3}	13			10	14					2	9^{2}						12	39
1	2	3	6		11	10^{3}	8	12		13	7^{2}	9			4	14					5^{1}								40
1	2^{1}	11	6	12	5	10	8	7^{3}		13	14	9			4^{2}						3								41
1	12	3	6	5		8^{3}	14	13		10	7^{2}	9		4	11						2^{1}								42
1	2	3	6^{2}	5		10	8	7^{1}		11	12	9		4		13													43
1		14	6	5		10	8	7		11	12	9^{2}		2^{3}	4^{1}						3	13							44
1	2		6	5^{1}		11	8	10		14	7^{3}			12	4						3	9^{2}						13	45
1	12	14	6^{2}	5		2	8^{1}	10		11	7	9^{3}			4	13					3								46

FA Cup

Fourth Qualifying Round	Dover Ath	(a)	1-0
First Round	Dagenham & R	(a)	1-1
		(h)	1-3

BRAINTREE TOWN

Blue Square Premier

Ground: The Amlin Stadium, Clockhouse Way, Braintree, Essex CM7 3RD. *Tel:* (01376) 345 617. *Fax:* (01376) 330 976. *Year Formed:* 1898. *Record Gate:* 2,029 (2002 v Cambridge U). *Nickname:* The Iron. *Manager:* Alan Devonshire. *Colours:* Orange shirts, blue shorts, orange stockings.

BRAINTREE TOWN 2011–12 LEAGUE RECORD

Match No.	*Date*	*Venue*	*Opponents*	*Result*		*H/T Score*	*Lg Pos.*	*Goalscorers*	*Attendance*
1	Aug 13	A	Darlington	L	0-1	0-0	—		2268
2	16	H	Grimsby T	W	5-0	2-0	—	Davis ^{44}, Marks 2 $^{45, 57}$, Yiadom ^{54}, Quinton ^{90}	1006
3	20	H	Mansfield T	D	1-1	0-0	9	Bailey-Dennis ^{54}	875
4	23	A	Forest Green R	W	2-0	1-0	—	Wright ^{35}, Yiadom ^{90}	1033
5	27	A	Luton T	L	1-3	1-3	9	Wright ^{20}	5703
6	29	H	Ebbsfleet U	L	2-3	1-0	—	Reason 2 (1 pen) $^{15 (p), 69}$	697
7	Sept 3	H	Lincoln C	W	1-0	1-0	11	Yiadom ^{31}	1182
8	10	A	Alfreton T	W	1-0	1-0	8	Chilaka ^{18}	656
9	17	H	Newport Co	W	1-0	1-0	9	Wright ^{20}	786
10	20	A	Hayes & Y	W	2-1	1-1	—	Yiadom ^{22}, Reason ^{55}	209
11	24	A	Southport	W	4-0	2-0	3	Chilaka ^{27}, Marks ^{45}, Reason ^{56}, Yiadom ^{66}	938
12	27	H	Tamworth	W	3-1	1-1	—	Reason 2 $^{29, 89}$, Yiadom ^{62}	840
13	Oct 1	H	Fleetwood T	L	1-2	1-1	4	Davis ^{21}	1005
14	8	A	York C	L	2-6	1-4	7	Marks ^{45}, Thomas ^{62}	2640
15	11	A	Kettering T	L	1-2	0-0	—	Marks ^{59}	1115
16	15	H	Bath C	D	3-3	2-1	8	Wright ^{19}, McCammon ^{22}, Paine ^{48}	703
17	18	A	Kidderminster H	L	4-5	2-1	—	Marks ^{26}, Wright 2 (1 pen) $^{33, 67 (p)}$, Thomas ^{63}	1301
18	22	H	Darlington	W	3-1	1-0	9	Stevens ^{44}, Davis ^{51}, Marks ^{58}	864
19	Nov 5	A	Gateshead	D	2-2	0-1	9	Reason (pen) ^{47}, Yiadom ^{55}	745
20	19	H	Forest Green R	L	1-5	1-3	10	Marks ^{28}	1005
21	26	H	Wrexham	D	0-0	0-0	10		957
22	29	A	Tamworth	L	0-1	0-0	—		742
23	Dec 3	A	Mansfield T	L	1-4	1-1	14	Wright ^{8}	1790
24	6	H	Hayes & Y	L	0-3	0-0	—		454
25	17	H	AFC Telford U	W	2-1	1-1	13	Wright 2 (1 pen) $^{45 (p), 77}$	605
26	26	A	Cambridge U	L	0-2	0-1	14		3717
27	Jan 1	H	Cambridge U	W	3-2	0-0	14	Reason ^{51}, Marks ^{55}, Wright ^{77}	2029
28	7	A	Bath C	D	1-1	0-1	14	Marks ^{90}	956
29	21	H	Stockport Co	D	2-2	0-0	13	Thomas ^{58}, Symons ^{61}	833
30	24	A	Fleetwood T	L	1-3	1-2	—	Paine ^{5}	1791
31	28	H	Barrow	W	1-0	0-0	13	Thomas ^{79}	685
32	Feb 14	A	Lincoln C	D	3-3	1-1	—	Reason 2 $^{4, 54}$, Assombalonga ^{88}	1616
33	18	A	AFC Telford U	L	0-1	0-0	13		1776
34	25	H	Kettering T	W	2-1	2-0	13	Wright (pen) ^{15}, Marks ^{45}	730
35	Mar 3	A	Grimsby T	D	1-1	0-0	13	Marks ^{59}	3688
36	6	A	Newport Co	W	4-3	3-2	—	Assombalonga 2 $^{22, 49}$, Marks ^{32}, Wright ^{35}	1101
37	10	H	Gateshead	W	3-1	2-0	11	Assombalonga 2 $^{5, 55}$, Wright ^{6}	650
38	17	H	Kidderminster H	L	1-4	1-1	12	Wright ^{6}	610
39	24	A	Barrow	W	4-0	3-0	12	Thomas ^{25}, Reason (pen) ^{29}, Wright ^{45}, Guy ^{90}	939
40	27	H	Southport	D	0-0	0-0	—		637
41	31	H	Alfreton T	L	1-2	1-1	12	Gibson ^{33}	620
42	Apr 7	H	Luton T	W	3-1	1-1	12	Bailey-Dennis ^{5}, Marks ^{70}, Gibson (pen) ^{90}	1703
43	9	A	Ebbsfleet U	D	1-1	1-1	12	Wright (pen) ^{34}	938
44	14	A	Stockport Co	D	1-1	0-1	12	Quinton ^{90}	3199
45	21	H	York C	L	0-1	0-0	12		1127
46	28	A	Wrexham	L	1-5	0-2	12	Wright ^{52}	3303

Final League Position: 12

GOALSCORERS

League (76): Wright 17 (4 pens), Marks 14, Reason 11 (3 pens), Yiadom 7, Assombalonga 5, Thomas 5, Davis 3, Bailey-Dennis 2, Chilaka 2, Gibson 2 (1 pen), Paine 2, Quinton 2, Guy 1, McCammon 1, Stevens 1, Symons 1.
FA Cup (3): Davis 1, Wright 1, Yiadom 1.

McDonald 46	O'Connor 23 + 5	Thomas 43	Bailey-Dennis 34 + 3	Paine 40 + 1	Reason 44	Symons 35 + 6	Davis 39	Marks 41 + 1	Wright 40 + 1	James-Lewis 2 + 2	Yiadom 24 + 4	Chilaka 6 + 19	Quinton 12 + 30	Constantine — + 1	Peters 23 + 3	McLeod — + 1	Johnson 5 + 10	Stevens 5 + 4	McCammon 1 + 4	Vose 1 + 4	Wells 25 + 1	Pooley — + 2	Kiernan 3 + 1	Assombalonga 5	Guy 1 + 7	Appoil-Kupi — + 2	Gibson 8	Bentley — + 1	*Match No.*
1	2	3	4	5	6^{1}	7^{3}	8	9	10^{2}	11	12	13	14																1
1	2	3	4	5	6^{3}	7	8	9^{2}	10^{1}		11	13	14	12															2
1	2	3	4	5	6^{1}	7	8	9	10^{2}		11	13	12																3
1		3	4	5	6	7	8	9	10^{2}	11^{1}	12	13			2														4
1	13	3	4	5	6	7^{2}	8	9^{1}	10^{3}		11	12	14		2														5
1	12	3	4	5	6	7^{1}	8	9	10^{2}	14	11^{3}	13			2														6
1		3	4	5	6^{2}	7	8	9	10^{1}		11	12	13		2														7
1		3	4	5	6^{1}	7	8		10^{3}	14	11^{2}	9	13		2	12													8
1	14	3	4	5	6	7	8	12	10^{3}		11^{2}	9^{1}	13		2														9
1		3	4	5	6^{1}	7	8	9	10^{2}		11	13	12		2														10
1		3	4	5	6	7	8^{2}	9^{3}			11^{1}	10	13		2		12	14											11
1		3	4	5	6^{3}	7	8	9	12		11^{2}	10^{1}	13		2		14												12
1		3	4^{3}	5	6	7^{1}	8	9	10^{2}		11		12		2		13	14											13
1	2	3	4		6	7	8^{3}	9^{2}	10^{1}		14■		12				11	5■	13										14
1	5	3	4		6	7^{2}	8	9	10						2		11^{1}		13	12									15
1		3	4	5	6^{1}	7	8		10^{2}				12		2		11		9	13									16
1		3	4	5	6^{3}	7^{2}	8	9	10				12		2		13		14	11^{1}									17
1		3		5	6	14	8	9	10^{2}		7^{1}		11^{3}		2			4	13	12									18
1		3		5	6	7		9	10^{1}		8^{3}	14	11^{2}		2		13	4		12									19
1		3		5■	6^{2}	13	8	9	10^{3}		4	14	7^{1}		2			11			12								20
1	2	3■	4		6^{3}	7	8	9^{1}	10^{2}		11	13					12	14			5								21
1	3		4		6^{2}	7^{3}	8■		10		11	9	14		2^{1}		13	12			5								22
1		3			6	7		9	10^{1}		11	12	8				2	4			5								23
1		3	4	5	6■	7^{2}		9	10^{1}		11	13	12				8				2								24
1		3	4	5		7^{1}	8	9	10^{3}		2	14	11^{2}		12		13				6								25
1	2■	3	4	5		7^{2}	8	9			11	12	10^{1}				13				6								26
1		3		5	6	7	8^{1}	9	10^{2}		11^{3}	13	14		2		12				4								27
1	12	3		5	6^{1}	7	8^{3}	9	10^{2}		11	13	14		2						4								28
1	2	3	4^{1}	12	6^{3}	7	8	9	10^{2}		11	13	14								5								29
1	2	3	4	8	6^{3}	7^{1}		9^{2}	10■		11	13	12								5	14							30
1		3	4	2	6	7^{1}	8	9			13	10^{2}	12								5		11						31
1	13	3	4	5	6	7^{1}	8	9					12								2		11^{2}	10■					32
1	11^{2}	3	4	5	6		8	9					12		2						7	13	10^{1}						33
1		3	4	5	6		8	9	10^{1}				11								2		12	7					34
1	4	3	12	5	6^{1}	7		9	10^{2}				11								2			8	13				35
1	4	3	12	5	6	7		9^{1}	10				11								2			8^{2}	13				36
1	2	3	12	5	6	7		9^{1}	10^{2}				11								4			8	13				37
1	2	3		5	6	7^{1}	8	9	10^{3}				11^{2}		12						4				13	14			38
1	2	3	4	5	6		8^{2}	9	10^{1}				13								11				12	14	7^{3}		39
1	2	3	4	5	6^{1}		8	9	10				12								11						7		40
1	2^{1}	3	4	5	6	12	8^{2}	9	10^{3}				13								11				14		7		41
1	7	3	4	5	6		8	9^{2}	10^{1}				12		13						11						2		42
1	11	3		5	6^{1}	7	8	9	10				12		2												4		43
1	7			5	6	12	8	9	10^{1}				11		2						4						3		44
1	11		4	5	6^{2}	12	8	9■	10				13		2^{1}						3				14		7^{3}		45
1	2^{1}	3	4	5	6^{2}	13	8		10				12								11				9^{3}		7	14	46

FA Cup
Fourth Qualifying Round
Newport Co (a) 3-4

CAMBRIDGE UNITED — Blue Square Premier

Ground: R Costings Abbey Stadium, Newmarket Road, Cambridge CB5 8LN. *Tel:* (01223) 566 500. *Fax:* (01223) 729 220. *Year Formed:* 1912. *Record Gate:* 14,000 (1970 v Chelsea, Friendly). *Nickname:* The U's. *Manager:* Jez George. *Secretary:* Claire Osbourn. *Colours:* Navy and sky blue shirts, sky blue shorts, sky blue stockings.

CAMBRIDGE UNITED 2011–12 LEAGUE RECORD

Match No.	Date	Venue	Opponents	Result		H/T Score	Lg Pos.	Goalscorers	Attendance
1	Aug 13	A	Wrexham	D	1-1	0-1	—	Platt ^{90}	4206
2	16	H	AFC Telford U	W	1-0	0-0	—	Dunk ^{50}	2482
3	20	H	Kidderminster H	L	1-2	0-2	13	Gash ^{58}	2171
4	23	A	Grimsby T	L	1-2	1-1	—	Wylde ^{30}	2616
5	27	H	Hayes & Y	W	2-1	0-0	12	Platt ^{54}, Berry ^{85}	1778
6	29	A	Kettering T	D	0-0	0-0	—		2000
7	Sept 3	A	Newport Co	W	1-0	1-0	5	Charles ^{15}	1515
8	10	H	Forest Green R	D	1-1	0-1	10	Carew (pen) ^{78}	2408
9	17	A	Gateshead	D	1-1	1-1	12	Carew ^{16}	904
10	20	H	Ebbsfleet U	W	2-0	2-0	—	Winn ^{10}, Shaw ^{32}	1911
11	24	H	Darlington	W	2-0	1-0	9	Gash ^{23}, Shaw ^{62}	2300
12	27	A	Luton T	W	1-0	0-0	—	McAuley ^{60}	6274
13	Oct 1	A	Southport	L	0-1	0-1	9		1104
14	6	H	Stockport Co	D	2-2	1-1	—	Berry ^{12}, Patrick ^{74}	2047
15	11	A	Bath C	W	4-3	2-2	—	Gash ^{16}, Carew ^{40}, Berry ^{76}, Shaw ^{84}	788
16	15	H	Alfreton T	W	3-0	2-0	6	Berry ^{29}, Dunk 2 $^{41, 52}$	2741
17	18	A	York C	D	2-2	2-1	—	Dunk ^{8}, Gash ^{31}	2711
18	21	H	Lincoln C	W	2-0	1-0	—	Carew 2 $^{23, 90}$	2875
19	Nov 5	A	Mansfield T	W	2-1	0-0	3	Dunk 2 $^{57, 62}$	2046
20	19	H	Luton T	D	1-1	0-1	4	Hughes ^{77}	4796
21	26	A	Kidderminster H	D	0-0	0-0	4		1899
22	29	H	Bath C	D	1-1	1-0	—	Hughes ^{21}	2267
23	Dec 6	A	Ebbsfleet U	D	0-0	0-0	—		964
24	17	A	Darlington	L	0-2	0-1	6		1784
25	26	H	Braintree T	W	2-0	1-0	7	Gash ^{36}, Berry ^{58}	3717
26	Jan 1	A	Braintree T	L	2-3	0-0	8	Jennings ^{88}, Shaw ^{90}	2029
27	5	H	Southport	W	3-0	2-0	—	Marriott ^{7}, Roberts ^{29}, Gash ^{72}	1840
28	10	H	Grimsby T	L	0-1	0-1	—		2436
29	21	A	AFC Telford U	W	2-1	1-0	7	Roberts ^{45}, Shaw ^{56}	1903
30	28	H	Tamworth	L	0-1	0-0	10		2281
31	Feb 18	A	Fleetwood T	L	0-1	0-1	10		2068
32	Mar 3	A	Forest Green R	L	1-2	0-0	12	Berry ^{75}	1005
33	6	H	Mansfield T	L	1-2	1-1	—	Jennings ^{6}	1738
34	10	A	Stockport Co	W	1-0	1-0	13	Tiryaki ^{14}	5957
35	13	H	Barrow	W	1-0	0-0	—	Pugh ^{88}	1651
36	17	H	Gateshead	L	0-1	0-0	10		2344
37	20	H	Newport Co	D	1-1	1-0	—	Dawkin ^{24}	1815
38	24	A	Alfreton T	L	1-2	1-1	11	Pugh (pen) ^{30}	965
39	31	H	Wrexham	D	1-1	0-0	11	Shaw ^{48}	3014
40	Apr 3	A	Lincoln C	W	1-0	0-0	—	Shaw ^{47}	1978
41	7	A	Hayes & Y	D	0-0	0-0	11		336
42	9	H	Kettering T	W	2-0	1-0	11	Pugh ^{10}, Pell ^{80}	2578
43	14	A	Barrow	W	3-1	2-1	11	Gash ^{16}, Pell ^{38}, Roberts ^{58}	870
44	17	H	York C	L	0-1	0-0	—		2211
45	21	H	Fleetwood T	W	2-0	2-0	10	Eades ^{17}, McAuley ^{31}	2555
46	28	A	Tamworth	D	2-2	1-1	9	Marriott 2 $^{31, 49}$	1137

Final League Position: 9

GOALSCORERS

League (57): Gash 7, Shaw 7, Berry 6, Dunk 6, Carew 5 (1 pen), Marriott 3, Pugh 3 (1 pen), Roberts 3, Hughes 2, Jennings 2, McAuley 2, Pell 2, Platt 2, Charles 1, Dawkin 1, Eades 1, Patrick 1, Tiryaki 1, Winn 1, Wylde 1.
FA Cup (9): Berry 2, Carew 2, Coulson 2, Charles 1, Patrick 1, Wylde 1.

Naisbitt 45	Roberts 40	Kinniburgh 2 + 1	Coulson 32	Wylde 20 + 2	Shaw 41 + 1	Carew 29	Berry 40 + 3	Marriott 10 + 1	Charles 6 + 13	Dunk 18 + 5	Gash 32 + 8	Platt 2 + 3	Jarvis 36 + 5	McAuley 28 + 3	Jennings 41	Patrick 1 + 18	Eades 8 + 2	Thorpe 13 + 13	Winn 10 + 3	Murtagh — + 7	Hughes 9 + 12	Hudson 13 + 5	Johnson 2	Pugh 10 + 3	Jackson 3 + 2	Tiryaki 5 + 1	Dawkin 2 + 3	Pell 7	Ambrusics 1	Hurst — + 1	Corker — + 1	Brighton — + 2	*Match No.*
1	2	3	4	5	6	7	8	9[2]	10[3]	11[1]	12	13	14																				1
1	2	3	4	5	6	7	8	9[2]	10[1]	11	12		13																				2
1	2	14	4	5	6	7	8	9[1]	10	11[2]	12	13		3[3]																			3
1	2		4	5	6	7[1]	8		13	11■	9	12	10[2]		3																		4
1	2		4	5	6	7	8	9[2]			10[1]	11[3]	13	14	3	12																	5
1	2		4	5	6	7	10					9[1]	8		3	12	11[2]	13															6
1	2		4	5	6	7	8		10[2]				11		3	13		12	9[1]														7
1			4	5	6	7	12		10		9[3]		8[1]	2	3	13			11[2]	14													8
1	2		4		6	7[3]	8			12	9[2]		10	5	3	14			11[1]	13													9
1	2		4		6	7	8[1]		12	14	9[2]		10	5	3				11[3]	13													10
1	2		4		6	7[2]	8		12		9[1]		10	5	3	13			11														11
1	2		4		6	7	8		12	13	9[1]		10	5	3				11[2]														12
1	2		4		6	7[3]	8		12		9		10[1]	5	3	14			11[2]	13													13
1	2		4			7[1]	6	10[2]	13	14	9[3]		8	5	3	12			11														14
1	2		4		6	7[2]	10		13	11[1]	9		8	5	3	12																	15
1	2[3]		4		6	7[1]	10		12	11[2]	9		8	5	3			14	13														16
1			4	13	6	7	10[3]		14	11[1]	9		8	5	3■			2[2]	12														17
1	3		4	14	6	7	10		12	11	9[1]		8[2]	5				2[3]		13													18
1	2		4	3	6	7[1]	10		12	11[2]	9		8	5		13																	19
1	2		4	5	6	7	10[2]				9		8		3	12			11[1]		13												20
1			4	5	6	7					9		8	14	3	12		2[3]	11[1]	13	10[2]												21
1	2		4	5	6	7[3]			11[1]		9[2]		8		3	13			14	12	10												22
1	2		4	5	6	7[3]	10			11[1]	9		8[2]		3	12		14			13												23
1	2		4	5	6	7	10		12	11[2]	9[3]		8[1]		3	14					13												24
1	2		4	5	6	7[1]	8	10		11	9				3			12															25
1	2		4	5	6		8	10[1]	14	11[3]	9				3	13		7[2]			12												26
1	2		4	5[1]	6	7	8	10[2]		11[3]	9		13		3			14				12											27
1	2		4		6	7[1]	8	10[2]		11			13		3			12			9	5											28
1	2		4[1]		6	7	10			11[2]	9		8	12	3			13				5											29
1	2				6	7[2]	10			11	9		8[1]		3			13			14	5	4[3]	12									30
1	2				6[3]		10[1]			11	9		8		3			13			14	5	4	12	7[2]								31
1	2				6[2]		8						11	4	3	14	10[1]				12	5		13	7	9[3]							32
1	2				6		8	13						4	3		11[1]				12	5		10	7	9[2]							33
1	2		4		6		7[3]						8	5	3		11[2]	12			14			10		9[1]	13						34
1	2		4		6						13		8	5	3		11[3]	7[1]			14			10		9[2]	12						35
1	2		4[1]		6[2]		13				9		8	5	3		11[3]	7				12		10			14						36
1	2			5[3]			6				9[1]		8	4	3			7[2]				14		10	13	12	11						37
1	2						14				12		8	5	3			7[2]				6[3]		10	13	9[1]	11	4					38
1	2			4[3]	6		7				13		11	5	3			12			9[1]	14		10[2]				8					39
1	2			5[1]	6		7				13		11	4	3		14				9[3]	12		10[2]				8					40
	2						7				12		8	5	3		10[1]	13			11[2]	6		9				4	1				41
1	2				11		7				9			5	3			8[2]			13	6		10[1]				4		12			42
1	2[1]				6[2]		8				9		11	4	3			7			12	5						10			13		43
1					6[2]		7				9		8	4	3		12	2[1]			11	5						10				13	44
1					6		7				9		10	4	3	12	11[1]	2			8	5											45
1					14		7	11[3]		12	9[1]		8	4	3[2]	6		2			10	5										13	46

FA Cup

Fourth Qualifying Round	Hayes & Yeading	(a)	6-2
First Round	Wrexham	(h)	2-2
		(a)	1-2

DARLINGTON

Evo-Stik Northern

Ground: The Northern Echo Arena, Neasham Road, Darlington DL2 1DL (expected to play at Shildon 2012–13). *Tel:* (01325) 387 000. *Year Formed:* 1883. *Record Gate:* 21,023 (1960 v Bolton W, League Cup 3rd rd, 14 November, at Feethams). *Nickname:* The Quakers. *Manager:* Martin Gray. *Secretary:* Colin Galloway. *Colours:* White with black trim.

DARLINGTON 2011–12 LEAGUE RECORD

Match No.	*Date*	*Venue*	*Opponents*	*Result*		*H/T Score*	*Lg Pos.*	*Goalscorers*	*Attendance*
1	Aug 13	H	Braintree T	W	1-0	0-0	—	Hatch [83]	2268
2	16	A	Fleetwood T	D	0-0	0-0	—		1811
3	20	A	Tamworth	L	0-1	0-0	14		977
4	23	H	Alfreton T	D	1-1	0-0	—	Walshaw [47]	1965
5	27	A	Grimsby T	W	2-1	2-0	7	Taylor, G [11], Arnison [41]	2887
6	29	H	Lincoln C	W	3-1	1-0	—	Bowman 2 [1, 50], Campbell [55]	2252
7	Sept 3	H	Mansfield T	L	0-2	0-2	6		2647
8	10	A	Luton T	L	0-2	0-1	11		5952
9	17	H	Hayes & Y	D	1-1	0-0	14	Bowman [88]	1809
10	20	A	York C	D	2-2	2-1	—	Walshaw [12], Bridge-Wilkinson (pen) [32]	2844
11	24	A	Cambridge U	L	0-2	0-1	16		2300
12	27	H	Southport	L	0-3	0-1	—		637
13	Oct 1	H	Newport Co	W	2-0	2-0	16	Bridge-Wilkinson (pen) [31], Purcell [45]	1785
14	8	A	Bath C	L	0-2	0-0	16		1156
15	11	A	Stockport Co	W	4-3	2-2	—	Chandler 2 [2, 61], Walshaw [32], Taylor, G [85]	2671
16	15	H	Kidderminster H	W	1-0	0-0	13	Sanchez-Munoz [80]	1763
17	18	H	Barrow	L	0-1	0-1	—		1786
18	22	A	Braintree T	L	1-3	0-1	14	Lee [80]	864
19	Nov 5	H	AFC Telford U	W	1-0	1-0	14	Bridge-Wilkinson (pen) [20]	1680
20	19	A	Ebbsfleet U	W	3-1	1-0	14	Hatch 2 [20, 71], Hopson [90]	1087
21	26	H	Tamworth	W	2-0	0-0	11	Rundle [55], Hopson [90]	1752
22	30	A	Wrexham	L	1-2	1-0	—	Bridge-Wilkinson (pen) [35]	3171
23	Dec 3	H	Forest Green R	D	0-0	0-0	9		1693
24	6	A	Kettering T	D	0-0	0-0	—		924
25	17	H	Cambridge U	W	2-0	1-0	11	Rundle [37], Reach [69]	1784
26	26	A	Gateshead	D	1-1	0-0	12	Bridge-Wilkinson (pen) [82]	1522
27	Jan 1	H	Gateshead	L	0-1	0-0	13		2581
28	7	A	Barrow	L	0-3	0-2	16		2144
29	21	H	Fleetwood T	L	0-1	0-1	16		5638
30	24	A	Hayes & Y	L	2-3	0-2	—	Barton [81], Pele (og) [90]	550
31	28	H	York C	D	2-2	1-0	17	Rundle [43], McReady [49]	6413
32	Feb 14	A	Southport	L	0-2	0-1	—		847
33	18	A	Alfreton T	L	1-3	1-1	20	Bowman [27]	950
34	21	A	Mansfield T	L	2-5	1-2	—	Bridge-Wilkinson [3], McReady [72]	1697
35	Mar 3	H	Stockport Co	L	0-1	0-0	21		2202
36	13	H	Luton T	D	1-1	0-0	—	Bowman (pen) [86]	1382
37	17	H	Ebbsfleet U	L	0-2	0-0	22		1796
38	24	A	Kidderminster H	L	1-3	1-1	22	Bowman [17]	1635
39	27	H	Wrexham	L	2-4	0-1	—	Rundle [69], Bowman [71]	1401
40	31	A	AFC Telford U	D	3-3	2-1	22	Broughton [19], Bowman [30], Lambert [82]	1908
41	Apr 7	H	Grimsby T	D	0-0	0-0	22		2212
42	9	A	Lincoln C	L	0-5	0-4	22		2274
43	14	H	Bath C	D	2-2	1-0	22	Hollis [34], Rundle [81]	1420
44	17	A	Newport Co	D	0-0	0-0	—		1249
45	21	A	Forest Green R	L	0-2	0-1	22		1131
46	28	H	Kettering T	W	3-1	1-0	22	Bowman 2 [31, 48], Ford (og) [74]	1792

Final League Position: 22

GOALSCORERS

League (47): Bowman 10 (1 pen), Bridge-Wilkinson 6 (5 pens), Rundle 5, Hatch 3, Walshaw 3, Chandler 2, Hopson 2, McReady 2, Taylor, G 2, Arnison 1, Barton 1, Broughton 1, Campbell 1, Hollis 1, Lambert 1, Lee 1, Purcell 1, Reach 1, Sanchez-Munoz 1, own goals 2.
FA Cup (1): Bowman 1.

Russell 22 / Nixon 1	Purkiss 12	Taylor G 19	Chandler 23 + 1	Lee 24 / Johnson 9	Miller 16	Atkinson 10 + 5 / Hollis 9	Bridge-Wilkinson 23 + 5	Hatch 17 + 5	Walshaw 15 + 3	Taylor K 35 + 1	McReady 30 + 7	Bowman 28 + 12	Campbell 4 + 8	Smith — + 1	Arnison 31 + 3	Rundle 36 + 2	Sanchez-Munoz 5 + 3	Brown 30	Purcell 5	Brough 2 + 4	Soderberg 6	Geohaghon 5	Rodney 1	Gray J 3 + 8	Hopson 14 + 1	Reach 2 + 3	Harrison 7 + 3	Ramshaw 4 + 7	Pickford 17	Barton — + 4	Gray P 1 + 1	Lambert — + 13	Bagnall 2	Keltie 14 + 1	Ferguson 2 + 4	Broughton 11	Wainwright 11 + 1	Match No.
1	2	3	4[1]	5	6	7	8[2]	9	10[3]	11	12	13	14																									1
1	2	3	4	5	6	7	13	9	10[1]	11		8[2]	12																									2
1	2	3	4[2]	5	6	7	12	9[3]	10	11	13	8[1]		14																								3
1	2	3	4[3]	5	6	7[1]	8	9[2]	10	11	12	13	14																									4
1	2	4		5	6		14	13	10	3	8	12	11[3]		7[1]	9[2]																						5
1	2	3	13	5	6			14	12	11	4	9[3]	10[1]		7	8[2]																						6
1	2	3		5	6	12		13	14	11[1]	4[2]	9	10[3]		7	8																						7
1	2	3		5▮	6	4	13	9[3]	10[1]			12	14		7	11[2]	8																					8
1	5	7	4[3]		6	13	8		10			12			2	11[1]		3	9[2]	14																		9
1	2	7	4	5	6		8	12	10[2]			13				11		3[3]	9[1]	14																		10
1	2	7	4	5			8[3]		10			12	13		14	11[2]	6	3	9[1]																			11
1	2[1]	7	4	5			14	6	10[3]			9	13		12	11		3		8[2]																		12
		6	4	5			8	7	10[3]	3	11[1]	13	14		2				9[2]	12	1																	13
		6		5		12	8	11	10[2]	3	7	14	13		2[1]				9[3]	4	1																	14
		2	4			8		9	10	11		12				7	6	3[1]			1	5																15
		2	4			8		9	10[1]	11	13	12				7[2]	6	3			1	5																16
		2	4			8		9	10[3]	11[2]	13	14				7	6[1]	3		12	1	5																17
		2	4	5		8		12		3[2]	14	10				7[3]		11			1	6	9[1]	13														18
1		3	4[1]	6		12	10		13	14	2	9	11[2]		7							5		8[3]														19
1			4	5	6		8	9			7[1]				2	11		3						12	10													20
1			4	5	6		8	9			7[2]				2	11	12	3[1]							10	13												21
1			4	5	6		8			3	7[2]	9[1]			2	11	14							12	10[3]	13												22
1			4[1]	5	6	12	8			10					2	11	14							13	9[3]	7[2]	3											23
1			4	5	6	8[1]		10		3	7				2	11									9	12												24
1			4	5	6		8	9[2]			13				2	11[1]		3						12	10	7												25
1			4	6			8	5[1]		11	7[2]				2	10		3						13	9		12											26
1			4	5			8			6	7	10			2	11		3							9													27
1			4				8	5[1]		6	7[2]	10			2	11[3]		3						13	9		12	14										28
				5			8			6	7[1]	10			2	11[3]		3						4[2]	9		13	14	1	12								29
							8			6	7[1]	9			2	11[2]								10[3]	5		4	14	1	12	3	13						30
							8			6	7	9			2[1]	11		3						13	4[2]		5	10	1		12							31
							8			6	7	10[3]				11[2]		3							9[1]		5	12	1			13	2	4	14			32
							8			6	7	9			2	11		3[3]							13		5	4[2]	1			12		10[1]	14			33
							8			6	11	9[1]			7	12											5	4	1			13	2	10[2]	3			34
							8			6	7	9			2			3									5	4▮	1					12		10	11[1]	35
										6	7	5			2	11		3							9[1]				1			12		4		10	8	36
				5						6	7[2]	9			2	11[1]		3										13	1			12		4		10	8	37
				5		3				6[1]	7[2]	9			2	12		4										13	1					8		10	11	38
				5		4				6		9			2[1]	11		3										13	1	14		12		8[3]		10[2]	7	39
				5		4				6	7[1]	9				11		3											1			12		8		10	2	40
				5		4				6	7	9				11[1]		3											1			12		8		10	2	41
				5▮		4[2]				6	7	9			12	11		3											1					8	13	10	2[1]	42
						6					7	9			5	11		3											1			12		8	4	10	2[1]	43
				5		6					7	9			2	11		3											1	13		12		8		10[2]	4[1]	44
				5		4				6	7[3]	9[1]			2[2]	11		3											1			12		8	13	10▮	14	45
1				5		4				6	7	9			2	11		3														12		8			10[1]	46

FA Cup
Fourth Qualifying Round

Hinckley U	(h)	1-1
	(a)	0-3

EBBSFLEET UNITED Blue Square Premier

Ground: Stonebridge Road, Northfleet, Kent DA11 9BA. *Tel:* (01474) 533 796. *Fax:* (01474) 324 754.
Year Formed: 1946. *Record Gate:* 12,036 (1963 v Sunderland FA Cup 4th rd). *Nickname:* The Fleet.
Manager: Liam Daish. *Secretary:* Peter Danzey. *Colours:* Red shirts with white trim, white shorts, red stockings.

EBBSFLEET UNITED 2011–12 LEAGUE RECORD

Match No.	*Date*	*Venue*	*Opponents*	*Result*		*H/T Score*	*Lg Pos.*	*Goalscorers*	*Attendance*
1	Aug 13	H	York C	L	1-2	0-0	—	Willock [80]	1522
2	16	A	Tamworth	L	0-1	0-0	—		921
3	20	A	Stockport Co	D	1-1	0-0	21	West [76]	3674
4	23	H	Newport Co	D	1-1	0-1	—	West [90]	992
5	27	H	Forest Green R	D	1-1	1-0	21	Shakes [35]	889
6	29	A	Braintree T	W	3-2	0-1	—	Phipp (pen) [61], Ginty (pen) [87], Willock [90]	697
7	Sept 3	H	Barrow	L	1-2	1-1	19	Enver-Marum [12]	983
8	10	A	Kidderminster H	D	2-2	1-1	20	Enver-Marum [38], Herd [90]	1788
9	17	H	Fleetwood T	L	1-3	1-0	20	Willock [40]	974
10	20	A	Cambridge U	L	0-2	0-2	—		1911
11	24	A	Alfreton T	D	2-2	2-0	22	Enver-Marum [5], Willock [45]	661
12	27	H	Bath C	W	3-0	1-0	—	Willock 2 [24, 75], West [53]	816
13	Oct 1	A	Wrexham	L	0-1	0-0	20		2849
14	8	H	Gateshead	L	0-1	0-1	21		947
15	11	H	Luton T	D	2-2	0-1	—	West 2 [77, 90]	1651
16	15	A	AFC Telford U	W	2-0	1-0	19	Darvill [24], Willock [56]	2004
17	18	H	Grimsby T	W	3-1	2-1	—	West [14], Shakes [38], Willock [74]	1143
18	22	A	Kettering T	D	2-2	2-1	16	Willock (pen) [22], Darvill [33]	1402
19	Nov 5	A	Newport Co	W	1-0	1-0	15	Shakes [20]	1412
20	12	H	Stockport Co	W	2-1	0-1	—	Willock [81], Pinney [88]	1119
21	19	H	Darlington	L	1-3	0-1	15	Willock [66]	1087
22	26	A	Lincoln C	L	0-3	0-1	15		2111
23	29	H	Kidderminster H	D	3-3	0-1	—	Willock 2 (1 pen) [55 (p), 70], Pinney [72]	731
24	Dec 3	A	Barrow	D	1-1	0-1	16	Enver-Marum [87]	1047
25	6	H	Cambridge U	D	0-0	0-0	—		964
26	17	A	Grimsby T	L	3-4	2-3	16	Pinney [25], Mambo [28], Shakes [90]	2818
27	26	H	Hayes & Y	W	3-1	1-0	16	West [42], Phipp 2 [51, 61]	1176
28	Jan 17	A	Hayes & Y	W	2-1	1-0	—	Willock 2 [41, 77]	266
29	21	A	York C	L	2-3	0-1	14	Pinney [50], Willock [87]	2973
30	24	H	Tamworth	W	3-0	0-0	—	Enver-Marum [54], Pinney 2 [61, 88]	746
31	28	H	Mansfield T	L	0-3	0-2	14		1085
32	Feb 18	A	Bath C	W	3-2	1-0	14	Pinney [8], Shakes [79], Ugwu [90]	693
33	21	A	Fleetwood T	L	2-6	1-4	—	Enver-Marum 2 [15, 86]	1411
34	25	H	Southport	L	1-2	1-1	15	Ugwu [29]	907
35	Mar 3	A	Gateshead	W	3-2	0-1	13	Barrett [55], Enver-Marum [78], Ugwu (pen) [88]	754
36	13	H	Wrexham	L	0-5	0-2	—		990
37	17	A	Darlington	W	2-0	0-0	14	Enver-Marum [49], Ugwu [50]	1796
38	24	H	Kettering T	W	1-0	1-0	14	Shakes [20]	957
39	27	H	Alfreton T	L	1-2	1-1	—	Enver-Marum [7]	687
40	31	A	Mansfield T	L	0-1	0-0	14		2630
41	Apr 6	A	Forest Green R	L	1-3	1-0	—	Lorraine [20]	1058
42	9	H	Braintree T	D	1-1	1-1	14	Willock (pen) [30]	938
43	14	H	AFC Telford U	W	3-2	2-0	14	West [27], Enver-Marum 2 [45, 62]	875
44	17	A	Luton T	L	0-3	0-1	—		5526
45	21	A	Southport	D	3-3	1-2	14	Shakes [15], Enver-Marum [89], Willock [90]	1231
46	28	H	Lincoln C	L	2-3	1-3	14	Willock (pen) [24], Bellamy [66]	1217

Final League Position: 14

GOALSCORERS

League (69): Willock 19 (4 pens), Enver-Marum 13, West 8, Pinney 7, Shakes 7, Ugwu 4 (1 pen), Phipp 3 (1 pen), Darvill 2, Barrett 1, Bellamy 1, Ginty 1 (1 pen), Herd 1, Lorraine 1, Mambo 1.
FA Cup (0).

Welch 2	Stone 44 + 1	Herd 18 + 4	Fakinos 7 + 5	Easton 6	Simpemba 17 + 3	West 35 + 1	Marwa 39 + 2	Enver-Marum 34 + 4	Shakes 25 + 16	Phipp 32 + 8	Stavrinou 5 + 7	Willock 38 + 5	Azeez 2 + 13	Howe 37 + 4	Edwards 31	Ginty — + 13	Mambo 24	Lorraine 30 + 1	Darvill 4 + 5	Pinney 17 + 8	Barrett 19 + 7	Adams — + 1	Ugwu 8 + 1	McNeil 3 + 1	Cronin 10	Smith 12 + 1	Bellamy 7 + 4	*Match No.*
1	2	3	4[1]	5	6	7	8	9	10[2]	11■	12	13																1
1	2[3]	3	13	5	6	7	8	9	4[1]		11[2]	10	12	14														2
	2	3	4[1]	5	6	7	8	9	13		11	10[2]		12	1													3
	2[2]	3	4	5	6	7	8	9	14		11[1]	10[3]		12	1	13												4
	13	3	4[1]	5	6	7[2]	8	9	12	11[3]	14	10		2	1													5
	2	3		5	6		8	9	7[2]	11		10	12	4[1]	1	13												6
	5	3	13		6		8	9	4[3]	11[2]	14	10[1]	7	2	1	12												7
	2	3	12		6		8	9	7[3]	11	4[1]	10[2]	14	5	1	13												8
	2[3]	3			6	7[2]	8	9	13	11[1]	4	10		12	1	14	5											9
	2	3[1]	14		6		8	9	7	11[3]		10[2]	12	4	1	13	5											10
	2	3	13		6		8	9[1]	7[3]	11		10	4[2]		1	12	5	14										11
	2	14	4[1]		6	7[2]	8		12	11		10		9[3]	1	13	5	3										12
	3[3]		4[1]		6	7	8		12	11		10[2]	13	9	1	14	5	2										13
	3	9[1]			6	7	8[2]			11		10	12	4	1	13	5	2										14
	3		4[1]			7	8[3]			11	12	10	14	9	1	13	5	2	6[2]									15
	3					7	8		6[3]	11[1]	12	10	14	9	1	13	5	2	4[2]									16
	3				12	7	8		4	11		9		6	1		5	2	10[1]									17
	2				12	7	8		4[3]	11[2]	13	9		3	1	14	5■	6	10[1]									18
	2					7[1]	8		4	12		10		6	1		5	3	13	9[2]	11							19
	2					7	8	12		11[1]		10		3	1		5	6		9	4							20
	2					7	8	12	4[1]	13		9		3	1		5	6	14	10[3]	11[2]							21
	2				14	7	8	12	4[1]	13		9[3]		3	1		5■	6		10	11[2]							22
	2				5	7[2]	8	11[1]	12	4		9		3	1			6	13	10								23
		2			5	7	8	11	13	4[1]		9[2]		3	1			6	14	10[3]	12							24
	2					7[1]	8	11	12	4		9[2]		3	1		5	6		10	13							25
	2				6	7	8	11[3]	12	4[2]		9		3	1		5		14	10[1]	13							26
	2					7	8	10[2]	12	4		13		3	1		5	6		9[1]	11							27
	2					7[2]	8	13	11	4[1]		9		3	1		5	6		10	12							28
	2	3[1]					8	11		4		9	12	6	1		5			10	7							29
	2					7[3]	8[1]	11		4		9[2]	13	3	1		5	6		10	12	14						30
	2					7[2]		11	12	4		10	13	3	1		5	6		9	8[1]							31
	2						8	10[6]	13	4[2]		9		3	1■		5	6		11[1]	12		7	15				32
	2						8	11	13	14		9		3[1]			5	6[2]		10[3]	7		4		1	12		33
	2						8	11	7	4		9[2]					5[1]	6		13	12		10		1	3		34
	2	12					8	11[3]	4	3[1]	14	9[2]						6		13	7		10		1	5		35
	5	3				12		11	7	4					1			6		9[1]	8		10				2	36
	2					7[2]		11	10	4[1]			14	3				6		13	8		9[3]		1	5	12	37
	2					7[2]	12	10	11	14				3				6		13	8		9[3]		1	5	4[1]	38
	2					7	8	10[1]	4[3]			12		3				6		14	11[2]		9		1	5	13	39
	2					7	8[3]	10[2]	4			14		3				6		9[1]	11		13		1	5	12	40
	2					7	8[3]	10	4[1]	14		9		3				6		12	11[2]				1	5	13	41
	2	12				7	8	10	13	4[2]		9[3]		3[1]				6		14					1	5	11	42
	2	12				7	13	10	14	4[1]		9[2]		3				6■			8[3]				1	5	11	43
	4	2				7	8[1]	10	6			12[2]	13	3							11			1		5	9	44
	2	3				7[1]		10	11	12		9		6							8			1		5	4	45
	4	3				7[2]		10	8	12		9		2						13	11[1]			1		5	6	46

FA Cup
Fourth Qualifying Round
Redbridge (a) 0-2

FLEETWOOD TOWN — FL Championship 2

Ground: Highbury Stadium, Fleetwood, Lancashire FY7 6TX. *Tel:* (01253) 770 702. *Fax:* (0871) 770 702.
Year Formed: 1908. *Record Gate:* 6,150 (1965 v Rochdale). *Nickname:* The Trawlermen or The Cod Army.
Manager: Micky Mellon. *Secretary:* Steve Edwards. *Colours:* All white with red trim.

FLEETWOOD TOWN 2011–12 LEAGUE RECORD

Match No.	Date	Venue	Opponents	Result		H/T Score	Lg Pos.	Goalscorers	Attendance
1	Aug 13	A	Grimsby T	W	2-0	0-0	—	Mangan [57], Donnelly [90]	4061
2	16	H	Darlington	D	0-0	0-0	—		1811
3	20	H	Hayes & Y	W	1-0	0-0	3	Milligan [85]	1376
4	23	A	Barrow	L	0-4	0-3	—		1482
5	26	H	York C	D	0-0	0-0	—		2111
6	29	A	Wrexham	L	0-2	0-1	—		4283
7	Sept 3	A	Kettering T	W	3-2	3-0	8	Vardy 2 [1, 40], Seddon [38]	1209
8	10	H	Gateshead	W	3-1	0-0	6	Mangan [51], Vardy 2 [79, 90]	1388
9	17	A	Ebbsfleet U	W	3-1	0-1	7	Vieira 2 [49, 70], Vardy [82]	974
10	20	H	Kidderminster H	W	5-2	1-0	—	Seddon [45], Vieira 2 [46, 67], Mangan [57], Brodie [77]	1316
11	24	H	AFC Telford U	D	2-2	0-1	4	Brodie 2 [76, 90]	1686
12	27	A	Stockport Co	W	4-2	1-1	—	Vieira [2], Clancy [49], Cox [57], Mangan [90]	3023
13	Oct 1	A	Braintree T	W	2-1	1-1	2	Milligan (pen) [20], Clancy [65]	1005
14	8	H	Forest Green R	D	0-0	0-0	3		1687
15	11	H	Newport Co	L	1-4	1-3	—	Seddon [1]	1277
16	14	A	Lincoln C	W	3-1	0-1	—	Jackson 2 [53, 72], Mangan [65]	2332
17	18	A	Alfreton T	W	4-1	1-0	—	Brodie (pen) [37], Vardy 3 [47, 58, 61]	625
18	22	H	Bath C	W	4-1	2-0	2	McGuire [43], Vardy 2 [45, 90], Seddon [83]	1451
19	Nov 5	A	Luton T	W	2-1	1-0	2	Vardy [11], Milligan (pen) [67]	6361
20	19	H	Stockport Co	W	2-1	0-0	2	Mangan [53], Vardy [66]	3021
21	26	A	Gateshead	D	1-1	0-1	2	Vardy [72]	768
22	29	H	Kettering T	W	3-0	2-0	—	Charnock [24], Mangan [32], Clancy [69]	1221
23	Dec 17	A	Newport Co	W	1-0	0-0	2	Cavanagh [75]	1011
24	20	A	Hayes & Y	W	3-1	1-1	—	Briggs [14], Vieira [74], Mangan (pen) [82]	264
25	26	H	Southport	D	2-2	1-1	2	Mangan (pen) [18], Brodie [88]	3029
26	Jan 1	A	Southport	W	6-0	3-0	2	Brodie 2 [4, 29], Milligan (pen) [28], Vardy 2 [52, 90], Mangan [79]	2589
27	10	H	Barrow	W	4-1	1-0	—	Till [5], Vardy 2 [48, 84], Rose [54]	2091
28	21	A	Darlington	W	1-0	1-0	2	Rose [44]	5638
29	24	H	Braintree T	W	3-1	2-1	—	Vieira 2 (1 pen) [34 (p), 51], Vardy [44]	1791
30	28	A	Forest Green R	W	2-1	1-1	1	Vieira [44], Atkinson [90]	922
31	Feb 4	H	Tamworth	D	2-2	1-2	—	Mangan [1], Vardy [55]	1911
32	18	H	Cambridge U	W	1-0	1-0	1	Mangan [3]	2068
33	21	H	Ebbsfleet U	W	6-2	4-1	—	Seddon [16], Cavanagh [23], Vardy 3 [29, 48, 58], Mangan (pen) [43]	1411
34	25	H	Alfreton T	W	4-0	2-0	1	Pond [18], Seddon 2 [37, 56], Lowson (og) [84]	1929
35	Mar 3	A	Tamworth	W	3-0	1-0	1	Mangan 2 (1 pen) [25 (p), 90], Vardy [88]	958
36	6	H	Grimsby T	W	2-1	0-1	—	Mangan (pen) [77], Vardy [90]	2447
37	9	A	Kidderminster H	W	2-0	0-0	—	Mangan [53], Vaughan (og) [61]	2341
38	13	A	Mansfield T	D	1-1	0-0	—	Vardy [81]	3132
39	17	A	AFC Telford U	W	4-1	2-0	1	Mangan 2 [4, 15], Vardy 2 [83, 90]	2313
40	24	H	Mansfield T	W	2-0	0-0	1	Beeley [50], Vardy [64]	3106
41	31	A	Bath C	W	4-1	2-0	1	Vardy [11], Cavanagh [36], Gallinagh (og) [72], Brodie [76]	762
42	Apr 7	A	York C	W	1-0	0-0	1	Brodie [73]	4048
43	10	H	Wrexham	D	1-1	0-0	—	Seddon [59]	4994
44	13	H	Lincoln C	D	2-2	1-2	—	Vardy 2 [45, 49]	4511
45	21	A	Cambridge U	L	0-2	0-2	1		2555
46	28	H	Luton T	L	0-2	0-1	1		4446

Final League Position: 1

GOALSCORERS

League (102): Vardy 31, Mangan 19 (5 pens), Brodie 9 (1 pen), Vieira 9 (1 pen), Seddon 8, Milligan 4 (3 pens), Cavanagh 3, Clancy 3, Jackson 2, Rose 2, Atkinson 1, Beeley 1, Briggs 1, Charnock 1, Cox 1, Donnelly 1, McGuire 1, Pond 1, Till 1, own goals 3.
FA Cup (13): Milligan 3 (1 pen), Vardy 3, Mangan 2, Brodie 1, Charnock 1, Clancy 1, McGuire 1, Seddon 1.

Davies 46	Barry 2	Edwards 7	Flynn 3	McNulty 39	Goodall 29 + 2	Atkinson 15 + 2	Brown J 18 + 3	Mangan 39 + 2	Vieira 16 + 8	McGuire 34 + 4	Brodie 16 + 18	Seddon 22 + 16	Donnelly 2 + 3	Cox 3 + 3	Briggs 8 + 8	Milligan 19 + 6	Harvey 3 + 2	Hughes 1	Holmes 3	Vardy 34 + 2	Linwood 3	Beeley 32 + 1	Clancy 7 + 4	Brown S 3 + 1	Pond 29 + 5	Wilson 5	Jackson 4	Wassmer 3	Till 9 + 9	Crowther — + 3	Charnock 4	Cavanagh 23	Rose 8 + 2	Fowler 17 + 2	Allen — + 2	Rowe — + 2	Match No.
1	2	3[2]	4	5	6	7	8	9[3]	10[1]	11	12	13	14																								1
1	4[2]		2	5	3	6	7	9[1]		11	12	14	10	8[3]	13																						2
1		3	4	5	6[1]	7	8[3]		13	11	9	14	10[2]			2	12																				3
1		3		5	12	6			14	11	9	10[3]	13		7[2]	4	8	2[1]																			4
1		3		5		6	11[1]		10	8	9					12	4		2	7																	5
1		3		5		6	8[1]		10	11	9[3]		14		13	12	4[2]		2	7																	6
1		3				6			10[2]	11	13	9		8[1]	14	4[3]	12		2	7	5																7
1		3				5		12	10	11	13	9[2]		4[1]	14	8[3]				7	6	2															8
1						5	3	9[1]	10	11		8				4				7	6	2	12														9
1				5	14	6	3[3]	9	10	11	12	8[1]			13	4[2]				7■		2															10
1				5		6	3	9	10		12	8[3]		14	7	11						2[2]	4[1]	13													11
1				5		6	3	9	10[1]					12[2]	11	8						2	4	7	13												12
1				5		6	3	9			10			13	11	4						2	8[2]	7[1]	12												13
1				5		6[1]	3	9		14	10	13			8[3]	4						2	7[2]	11	12												14
1				5	3	6[1]	11	9[2]		8	13	10■				4				7		2			12												15
1				5			11	9		4	10[1]					8[2]				7			12		13	2	3	6									16
1				5			3	9		8[2]	10[1]	12				13				7[3]			14		6	2	11	4									17
1							3	9[2]		4	10[1]	12				8				7			13		6	2	11	5									18
1				5			3[1]	14		8	10[3]	12			13	4				9		2	7[2]		6		11										19
1				5[1]	3			9		8		13				4				10		12	7[2]		6	2			11[3]	14							20
1					3			9	12			7				4				10		2			6				11[1]		5	8					21
1					3			9[2]	10	2		13				4							7		6	8			11[1]	12	5						22
1					3		13	9[2]		8		12			7					10		2			6				11[1]		5■	4					23
1				5	3		14	9	13	8		10			7[2]					12		2			6[3]				11[1]			4					24
1				5	3[2]		13	9	10[3]	7■	14	8[1]			12					11		2			6							4					25
1				5			3	9			10■	13			7[2]	8[1]				11		2			6							4	12				26
1				5	3			9	14	8[3]		13								10		2			6				11[2]			4	7[1]	12			27
1				5	3			9		13	11	10[1]										2			6							4	8	7[2]	12		28
1				5	3	14		9[3]	10[2]		12	13								11		2[1]			6							4	7	8			29
1				5[1]	3	12		9	10	14	13									11[3]		2			6							4	7[2]	8			30
1				5	3			9	10		12									11		2			6							4	7[1]	8			31
1				5	3			9	10[2]	12	8[1]	13								11		2			6							4		7			32
1				5	3			9	10[1]	8	13	11				14				7[2]					6							2	12	4[3]			33
1				5	3			9	12[2]	8	14	10[3]								11					6				13			2	7[1]	4			34
1				4	5			9		8		10[1]								11		2			6				12			3		7			35
1				5			3	9		8	12	10[1]								11		2			6				13			4		7[2]			36
1				5	3			9		8	11[2]	10[1]								7		2			6				13			4		12			37
1				5	3			9[2]		8	10[1]	13								11		2			6				12			4		7			38
1				5	3			9		8	10[1]									11		2			6				12			4		7			39
1				5	3			9		7	12	10[2]								13		2			6				11[1]			4		8			40
1				5	3			9	14	11[2]	12	10[1]								7[3]		2			6				13			4		8			41
1				5	3			9	12[3]	7	13	14								10		2			6				11[2]			4[1]		8			42
1				5	3			9		4	14	8[3]			12	7[1]				10		2			6				13				11[2]				43
1				5	3			9		8		10								11		2			6				12			4[1]		7			44
1				5	3			9		7[2]		8[1]				13				10		2							11[3]	14	6			4		12	45
1				5	3			9				10[2]				14				11[3]		2			6							4	7[1]	8	13	12	46

FA Cup

Fourth Qualifying Round	Mansfield T	(a)	1-1
		(h)	5-0
First Round	Wycombe W	(h)	2-0
Second Round	Yeovil T	(h)	2-2
		(a)	2-0
Third Round	Blackpool	(h)	1-5

FOREST GREEN ROVERS Blue Square Premier

Ground: The New Lawn, Smiths Way, Nailsworth, Gloucestershire GL6 0FG. *Tel:* (01453) 834 860. *Fax:* (01453) 835 291. *Year Formed:* 1890. *Record Gate:* 4,836 (2009 v Derby Co, FA Cup 3rd rd) *Nickname:* Rovers. *Manager:* David Hockaday. *Secretary:* Philip Catherall. *Colours:* Black and white striped shirts, black shorts, red stockings.

FOREST GREEN ROVERS 2011–12 LEAGUE RECORD

Match No.	*Date*	*Venue*	*Opponents*	*Result*		*H/T Score*	*Lg Pos.*	*Goalscorers*	*Atten-dance*
1	Aug 12	H	Stockport Co	D	1-1	1-0	—	Styche [21]	1848
2	16	A	Luton T	D	1-1	0-0	—	Griffin [52]	6061
3	20	A	Alfreton T	W	6-1	3-1	7	Turley [4], Streete (og) [89], Griffin [16], Styche 2 [22, 76], Klukowski [90]	686
4	23	H	Braintree T	L	0-2	0-1	—		1033
5	27	A	Ebbsfleet U	D	1-1	0-1	13	Styche [71]	889
6	29	H	Bath C	W	3-0	2-0	—	Styche 2 [14, 61], Stokes [31]	1344
7	Sept 3	H	Grimsby T	L	0-1	0-1	13		1181
8	10	A	Cambridge U	D	1-1	1-0	13	Griffin [9]	2408
9	17	H	Southport	L	2-3	0-1	16	Norwood [86], Klukowski [90]	873
10	20	A	Tamworth	W	1-0	1-0	—	Green (og) [3]	783
11	24	A	Lincoln C	D	1-1	1-0	12	McDonald [2]	2076
12	27	H	Newport Co	D	1-1	0-1	—	Griffin [66]	1203
13	Oct 1	H	Mansfield T	D	1-1	1-1	15	Forbes [41]	893
14	8	A	Fleetwood T	D	0-0	0-0	13		1687
15	11	A	Hayes & Y	L	0-2	0-0	—		251
16	15	H	Kettering T	L	0-1	0-0	17		823
17	18	H	AFC Telford U	W	2-1	1-0	—	Griffin [31], Killock (og) [90]	632
18	22	A	Stockport Co	W	1-0	1-0	13	Klukowski [36]	3391
19	Nov 5	H	Alfreton T	W	4-1	0-0	13	Taylor 3 [49, 77, 80], Griffin [90]	764
20	19	A	Braintree T	W	5-1	3-1	13	Klukowski 2 [6, 78], Griffin [27], Taylor [45], Henderson [80]	1005
21	26	H	York C	D	1-1	0-0	12	Norwood [90]	1157
22	29	A	Southport	W	3-1	3-0	—	Turley [7], Klukowski 2 (1 pen) [20 (p), 31]	978
23	Dec 3	A	Darlington	D	0-0	0-0	10		1693
24	6	H	Tamworth	W	3-1	2-1	—	Thomson [15], Stokes [39], Klukowski (pen) [73]	732
25	17	H	Lincoln C	L	0-2	0-1	9		969
26	26	A	Kidderminster H	L	0-1	0-0	11		2491
27	Jan 1	H	Kidderminster H	D	1-1	1-0	10	Klukowski [35]	1542
28	7	A	Mansfield T	L	0-1	0-0	12		2008
29	21	A	Newport Co	D	0-0	0-0	12		1325
30	24	H	Wrexham	W	1-0	0-0	—	Taylor [48]	1109
31	28	H	Fleetwood T	L	1-2	1-1	12	Taylor [31]	922
32	Feb 18	H	Gateshead	W	2-1	1-1	12	Wright [25], Henderson [79]	751
33	21	A	Kettering T	W	3-1	2-0	—	Collins 2 [2, 40], Klukowski [77]	830
34	25	A	Barrow	D	1-1	1-0	11	Klukowski [3]	1194
35	Mar 3	H	Cambridge U	W	2-1	0-0	11	Uwezu [83], Wright [85]	1005
36	10	A	Grimsby T	L	1-2	1-1	12	Klukowski (pen) [18]	3294
37	17	H	Hayes & Y	L	1-3	0-1	13	Uwezu [63]	781
38	20	H	Luton T	W	3-0	1-0	—	Klukowski [35], Taylor 2 [74, 89]	975
39	24	A	Wrexham	W	2-1	0-1	10	Taylor [64], Norwood [90]	4451
40	27	A	AFC Telford U	L	0-2	0-2	—		1674
41	31	H	Barrow	W	3-0	0-0	10	Klukowski 3 (1 pen) [49 (p), 52, 90]	1070
42	Apr 6	H	Ebbsfleet U	W	3-1	0-1	—	Forbes [47], Taylor [62], Styche [90]	1058
43	9	A	Bath C	W	2-0	1-0	9	Klukowski [44], Styche [74]	983
44	14	A	Gateshead	L	0-1	0-0	10		579
45	21	H	Darlington	W	2-0	1-0	8	Forbes [4], Klukowski [67]	1131
46	28	A	York C	L	0-1	0-0	10		3391

Final League Position: 10

GOALSCORERS

League (66): Klukowski 18 (4 pens), Taylor 10, Styche 8, Griffin 7, Forbes 3, Norwood 3, Collins 2, Henderson 2, Stokes 2, Turley 2, Uwezu 2, Wright 2, McDonald 1, Thomson 1, own goals 3.
FA Cup (1): Hodgkiss 1.

Bulman 5	Hodgkiss 46	Imudia 1 + 1	Allen 10 + 6	Graham 21 + 7	Todd 2	Rowe 22 + 6	Norwood 34 + 4	Styche 9 + 7	Griffin 19 + 9	Forbes 40 + 1	Klukowski 38 + 8	Turk 2 + 10	Henry — + 1	Stokes 45	Turley 38 + 1	Matthews — + 3	McDonald 6 + 5	Bittner 19 + 1	Taylor 27 + 2	Bangura 11 + 1	Thomson 19 + 9	Oshodi 30	Sandell 3	Bond 4	Uwezu 8 + 17	Henderson 14 + 8	Paterson — + 1	Russell 18	Wright 3 + 4	Collins 12	Pook — + 7	*Match No.*
1	2	3^{3}	4	5	6^{1}	7	8^{2}	9	10	11	12	13	14																			1
1	2		4^{2}	5		7^{1}	8	9	10	11	12	13		3	6																	2
1	2		4	5		7		9^{2}	10^{1}	11	8			3	6	12	13															3
1	2	13	4^{2}	5		7^{3}		9	10	11	8	12		3	6^{1}	14																4
1	2		4	5		7		9^{3}	10^{2}	11	8^{1}	14		3	6	13	12															5
	2		12	5		7	8	9^{3}	13	11	14	4^{1}		3	6		10^{2}	1														6
	2		4^{1}	5		7	8	9	10^{2}	11^{3}	12	14		3	6		13	1														7
	2		4^{1}	5		7	14	9^{2}	10	11	12			3	6		8^{3}	1	13													8
	2		4^{1}	5		7^{2}	14		10	11	12			3	6		9^{3}	1	8	13												9
	2			5		7^{3}	10^{2}	9^{1}	13	11	8	14		3	6		12	1		4												10
	2		14	5		4	10		13	11^{2}	8	12		3	6		9^{3}	1		7^{1}												11
	2			5		13	10		9	11	8	4^{2}		3	6		7^{1}	1			12											12
	2		14	3		4	9^{3}		10^{2}	11	8			5	6		13	1	12		7^{1}											13
	2			5			9		10^{2}	11	8	13		3			7^{1}	1		6	12	4										14
	2			5		10^{2}	8		13	7	12			3^{3}	14			1		6	9^{1}	4	11									15
	2		13	12		9^{2}	7		10		8			3	6^{1}			1		4		5	11									16
	2		8^{2}	5		7	10		9		13	12		3				1		4^{1}	14	6	11^{3}									17
	2					7	10		9	11	8^{1}			3	5			1		6	12	4										18
	2					7			10	11	8			3	5				9^{1}	4		6		1	12							19
	2					4			10^{1}	11	8			3	5				9^{3}	7^{2}	13	6		1	14	12						20
	2					7^{2}	12		10^{1}	11	8			3	5				9	4		6		1	13							21
	2^{1}			14		12	11		13		8			3	5				9	4	7^{3}	6		1		10^{2}						22
	2					4^{2}	7^{1}			11	8			3	5			1	9		10	6			12	13						23
	2					12			13	11	8			3	5			1	9		4	6			7^{1}	10^{2}						24
	2					12	13			11	8^{2}			3	5▮			1	9		4	6			7^{1}	10						25
	2			6		10^{1}	7		13	11	8	12		3				1	9		5				4^{2}							26
	2			13			7^{1}		10	11	8			3	5			1	9^{2}		4	6			12							27
	2						7		10^{1}	11	8			3	5			1			4	6			13	9^{2}	12▮					28
	2		14				7^{3}		13	11	8			3	5				9^{2}		4	6			12	10^{1}		1				29
	2		12				7^{3}		14	11^{1}	8			3	5				9^{2}		4	6			13	10		1				30
	2		11				7				8			3	5			15	9		4	6			12	10^{1}		1^{6}				31
	2			14			7				8			3	5				9		4^{1}	6^{3}				13		1	10^{2}	11	12	32
	2						7^{1}			12	8			3	5				9^{2}		4	6				10^{3}		1	13	11	14	33
	2			6			7^{2}			11	8			3	5						4				13	12		1	9^{1}	10▮		34
	2						7^{3}			11^{2}	8			3	5				9		4	6			14	10^{1}		1	12		13	35
	2			5			7^{3}			11	8			3					9^{2}		4	6			13	10^{1}		1	12		14	36
	2						7			11	8^{3}			3	5				9^{1}		4^{2}	6			12	10		1	14		13	37
	2						7			11^{3}	8^{2}			3	5				9		13	6			12	10^{1}		1		4	14	38
	2						7			11^{2}	8			3	5				9^{3}			6			12	14		1	10^{1}	4	13	39
	2			12	6▮		7^{3}	14		11^{2}	8			3	5				9^{1}						10	13		1		4		40
	2			13				14		11	8			3	5^{2}				9^{3}		7^{1}	6			10	12		1		4		41
	2			13				14		11	8			3	5				9^{3}		12	6^{1}			10^{2}	7		1		4		42
	2			5		14	7	13		11	8^{3}			3					9^{1}			6			10^{2}	12		1		4		43
	2			5			7^{1}	13		11	8			3					9^{3}		14	6			12	10^{2}		1		4		44
	2					10^{1}	7^{3}	13		11	8			3	5				9^{2}		12	6			14			1		4		45
	2					13	7	12		11	8			3	5				9^{1}			6			10^{2}			1		4		46

FA Cup
Fourth Qualifying Round
Arlesey T (a) 1-2

GATESHEAD

Blue Square Premier

Ground: Gateshead International Stadium, Neilson Road, Gateshead NE10 0EF. *Tel:* (0191) 478 3883. *Fax:* (0191) 440 0404. *Year Formed:* 1889 (Reformed 1977). *Record Gate:* 24,348 (1927 v Swansea T, FA Cup Quarter-Final). *Nickname:* The Tynesiders, The Heed. *Manager:* Ian Bogie. *Secretary:* Mike Coulson. *Colours:* White shirts, black shorts and stockings.

GATESHEAD 2011–12 LEAGUE RECORD

Match No.	*Date*	*Venue*	*Opponents*	*Result*		*H/T Score*	*Lg Pos.*	*Goalscorers*	*Attendance*
1	Aug 13	A	Kidderminster H	W	3-2	2-2	—	Shaw (pen) [4], Cummins [19], Gate [80]	1636
2	16	H	Mansfield T	W	3-0	2-0	—	Shaw [33], Odubade [41], Curtis [59]	825
3	20	H	Kettering T	D	1-1	1-0	1	Shaw (pen) [6]	661
4	23	A	Southport	W	3-1	1-1	—	Moore [17], Turnbull [75], Shaw (pen) [84]	957
5	27	A	Barrow	W	2-1	2-1	2	Shaw 2 [22, 26]	1291
6	29	H	Grimsby T	W	1-0	0-0	—	Shaw [58]	1132
7	Sept 3	H	Alfreton T	W	2-0	0-0	2	Gate 2 [60, 81]	991
8	10	A	Fleetwood T	L	1-3	0-0	2	Odubade [90]	1388
9	17	H	Cambridge U	D	1-1	1-1	1	Gilles [33]	904
10	20	A	Lincoln C	L	0-1	0-0	—		1587
11	24	A	Hayes & Y	W	3-2	3-0	2	Shaw 3 [22, 34, 45]	218
12	27	H	York C	W	3-2	2-1	—	Shaw 3 (1 pen) [3, 26, 69 (p)]	1604
13	Oct 1	H	Tamworth	D	1-1	1-0	1	Curtis [23]	770
14	4	H	Wrexham	L	1-4	0-1	—	Gate [62]	1258
15	8	A	Ebbsfleet U	W	1-0	1-0	2	Henderson [40]	947
16	15	A	Luton T	L	1-5	0-2	5	Shaw [77]	6285
17	18	H	Southport	L	2-3	2-0	—	Shaw [23], Odubade [27]	737
18	22	A	AFC Telford U	W	2-1	1-0	6	Odubade [29], Preston (og) [84]	2484
19	Nov 5	H	Braintree T	D	2-2	1-0	6	Cummins [35], Brittain [62]	745
20	19	A	Alfreton T	D	1-1	0-1	6	Moore [68]	651
21	26	H	Fleetwood T	D	1-1	1-0	7	Brittain [11]	768
22	29	A	Mansfield T	D	1-1	0-1	—	Shaw [68]	1513
23	Dec 6	A	Stockport Co	W	1-0	0-0	—	Shaw [59]	2366
24	17	A	Wrexham	L	1-2	1-2	7	Cummins [20]	3161
25	26	H	Darlington	D	1-1	0-0	8	Brittain [53]	1522
26	Jan 1	A	Darlington	W	1-0	0-0	7	Shaw [90]	2581
27	7	H	Stockport Co	W	2-0	0-0	7	Shaw (pen) [61], Moore [64]	846
28	10	H	Kidderminster H	W	2-1	1-0	—	Gilles [25], Odubade [47]	724
29	21	H	Lincoln C	D	3-3	2-1	6	Shaw [28], Odubade 2 [45, 53]	870
30	24	A	Kettering T	L	1-2	0-0	—	Shaw [89]	804
31	28	H	Newport Co	L	2-3	1-0	8	Hatch [45], Shaw [53]	704
32	Feb 18	A	Forest Green R	L	1-2	1-1	8	Cummins [13]	751
33	22	A	York C	W	2-1	1-0	—	Cummins 2 [2, 57]	2683
34	Mar 3	H	Ebbsfleet U	L	2-3	1-0	10	Cummins [15], Shaw [90]	754
35	6	H	Hayes & Y	W	2-0	1-0	—	Gate [34], Shaw [63]	465
36	10	A	Braintree T	L	1-3	0-2	9	Chandler [90]	650
37	17	A	Cambridge U	W	1-0	0-0	8	Hatch [47]	2344
38	20	H	Bath C	W	1-0	0-0	—	Shaw [67]	512
39	24	A	Tamworth	D	1-1	1-1	8	Shaw [27]	968
40	31	A	Newport Co	L	0-1	0-1	9		1261
41	Apr 7	H	Barrow	W	2-0	1-0	8	Gate [37], Cummins [77]	701
42	9	A	Grimsby T	L	0-2	0-1	10		2938
43	14	H	Forest Green R	W	1-0	0-0	8	Shaw [59]	579
44	21	A	Bath C	L	2-4	0-3	11	Cummins [72], Hatch [79]	649
45	24	H	Luton T	D	0-0	0-0	—		703
46	28	H	AFC Telford U	W	3-0	0-0	8	Hatch [48], Gilles [53], Gate [71]	606

Final League Position: 8

GOALSCORERS

League (69): Shaw 27 (5 pens), Cummins 9, Gate 7, Odubade 7, Hatch 4, Brittain 3, Gilles 3, Moore 3, Curtis 2, Chandler 1, Henderson 1, Turnbull 1, own goal 1.
FA Cup (6): Shaw 3, Fisher 2, Cummins 1.

Farman 25	Odhiambo 20 + 5	Carruthers 19 + 2	Gate 36 + 3	Curtis 38	Clark 40	Cummins 41 + 2	Turnbull 38 + 3	Shaw 43	Fisher 7 + 13	Odubade 27 + 2	Moore 13 + 11	Nix 2 + 6	Mulligan 2 + 12	Rents 24 + 5	Baxter 24 + 3	Gilles 19 + 8	Moyes 1	Brittain 10 + 10	Henderson 5 + 1	Alnwick 6	Marwood 5 + 16	Deasy 15	Chandler 13	Airey 1 + 1	Hatch 8 + 3	O'Brien 11 + 1	Dummett 10	Magnay 3 + 1	*Match No.*
1	2	3	4	5	6	7[2]	8	9	10[1]	11[3]	12	13	14																1
1	2[2]	3	4	5	6	7[3]	8	9	10[1]	11	12	14	13																2
1	2	3	4	5	6	7[2]	8	9	10[1]	11	12		13																3
1	2	3	4	5	6	7[1]	8	9	12	11[2]	10			13															4
1	2[3]	3[1]	4	5	6	7	8	9[2]		11	10		13	12	14														5
1	2		4	5	6	7[1]	8	9	12	11[3]	10[2]	13	14	3															6
1	2		4	5	6	7	8	9		11	10			3															7
1	2		4	5	6	7[2]	8		13	11	9[1]		10	3		12													8
1	2	12	4	5	6	7	8	9	13	10				3[1]		11[2]													9
1	2	3[1]	4[2]	5	6	7[3]	8	9		10		13	14	12		11													10
1	2	3	4	5	6	7	8	9[2]	12	10			13			11[1]													11
1	2		4[1]	5	6	7	8	9		10		12	13	3		11[2]													12
1	2		4	5[2]	6[1]	7	8	9	14	10			13	3	12	11[3]													13
1	2[2]	5	4			7[1]	8	9	14	10				3	13	11[3]	6	12											14
1		3	4	5		7	8	9	12	10[2]					2	11[1]		13	6										15
1		3	4	5		7[2]	8	9	12	10[3]		14			2	11[1]		13	6										16
		3	4	5		7[1]	8	9	12	10					2	11■		13	6[2]	1									17
	2	3	4	5			8	9		10		7[2]	11[1]	13				12	6	1									18
		3	4[1]	5	6	11	8	9	10		12		13		2			7[2]		1									19
		3	4	5	6	11[3]	8	9	10[1]		12		14		2			7[2]		1	13								20
		3	4[2]	5	6	11[3]	8	9	14		10				2			7[1]	13	1	12								21
		13	4	5	6		8	9	12		11[1]	7		3					10[2]	1	2								22
	2		4	5	6		8	9	10		7			3		11[1]		12				1							23
	2		4[3]	5	6	11	8	9[1]			10		12	3		7[2]		13			14	1							24
		3■	4	5	6	11[1]	8	9	12		10[2]			14	2			7[3]			13	1							25
				5	6	11	8	9	10[2]	13	4			3	2	12		7[1]				1							26
				5	6	11	8	9		10[1]	4			3	2	7					12	1							27
	14			5	6	11[3]	4	9		8[2]	10			3	2	7[1]		13			12	1							28
	12	6		5		11[1]	8	9[2]		10				3	2						7■	1	4	13					29
				5	6	11[1]	8	9		10	14			3	2[3]			12				1	4	7[2]	13				30
	13			5	6	12	8	9		10				3[2]	2			7[1]				1	4■		11				31
	2		4	5	6	11	8			10	13			3		7[1]					12	1				9[2]			32
			4	5	6	11	8	9		10[2]	13			3	2						12	1				7[1]			33
1			14	5	6	11[1]	8	9						3	2	12					10[2]		4		13	7[3]			34
1			4[3]	5	6	11[2]	13	9							2	12					10		7			8[1]	3	14	35
1			4[2]	5	6	14	13	9							2			12			7[1]		8		10[3]	11	3		36
1	13			5	6	11	8	9							2			7[2]			12		4		10[1]		3		37
1		3	13	5	6	11[3]	8[2]	9							2	14		7[1]			12		4		10				38
1		3	4	5	6	11[1]		9			13				8	14		7[2]			12		2		10[3]				39
1			13		6	11		9							2	12		7[1]					4		10	8[2]	3	5■	40
1	2		4		6	11[1]		9			13			3		10					12		7			8[2]	5		41
1			4		6	11[1]		9		12	14			3	2	10[3]					13		7			8[2]	5		42
			4		6	11		9		10[2]				3	2	12					13	1	7[1]			8	5		43
	12		4		6	11	14	9		10				3[3]	2[1]	7[2]						1			13	8	5		44
	2		4		6	11	8									7					12	1			9	10[1]	3	5	45
			4		6	11[2]	8	9[1]						3		7					12	1			10	13	5	2	46

FA Cup

Fourth Qualifying Round	Hebburn	(h)	3-0
First Round	Blyth Spartans	(a)	2-0
Second Round	Tamworth	(h)	1-2

GRIMSBY TOWN

Blue Square Premier

Ground: Blundell Park, Cleethorpes, NE Lincolnshire DN35 7PY. *Tel:* (01472) 605 050. *Fax:* (01472) 693 665.
Year Formed: 1878. *Record Gate:* 31,657 (1937 v Wolverhampton W). *Nickname:* Mariners.
Team Managers: Rob Scott & Paul Hurst. *Secretary:* Ian Fleming. *Colours:* Black and white stripes.

GRIMSBY TOWN 2011–12 LEAGUE RECORD

Match No.	Date	Venue	Opponents	Result		H/T Score	Lg Pos.	Goalscorers	Attendance
1	Aug 13	H	Fleetwood T	L	0-2	0-0	—		4061
2	16	A	Braintree T	L	0-5	0-2	—		1006
3	20	A	Newport Co	D	0-0	0-0	24		1675
4	23	H	Cambridge U	W	2-1	1-1	—	Thompson [28], Duffy [64]	2616
5	27	H	Darlington	L	1-2	0-2	20	Makofo [51]	2887
6	29	A	Gateshead	L	0-1	0-0	—		1132
7	Sept 3	A	Forest Green R	W	1-0	1-0	18	Coulson [44]	1181
8	10	H	Hayes & Y	W	3-0	1-0	15	Duffy 2 [32, 47], Wood [86]	2835
9	17	A	Stockport Co	L	0-2	0-1	17		3943
10	20	H	Kettering T	W	2-1	0-1	—	Elding [48], Coulson [84]	2470
11	24	H	Wrexham	L	1-3	1-1	17	Hearn [29]	3515
12	27	A	Kidderminster H	D	1-1	0-1	—	Elding [90]	1807
13	Oct 1	H	Alfreton T	W	5-2	0-1	14	Hearn 4 [57, 60, 70, 86], Elding [90]	2941
14	8	A	Mansfield T	L	1-2	1-0	15	Coulson [31]	2982
15	11	H	Barrow	W	5-2	2-1	—	Hearn 3 [5, 45, 76], Elding 2 [83, 85]	2675
16	15	A	York C	L	1-2	1-1	14	Disley [4]	3872
17	18	A	Ebbsfleet U	L	1-3	1-2	—	Elding [1]	1143
18	21	H	Luton T	L	0-1	0-0	—		3239
19	Nov 5	A	Bath C	D	2-2	1-0	16	Makofo 2 [11, 51]	993
20	19	H	Newport Co	D	2-2	0-2	16	Makofo [79], Elding (pen) [87]	2701
21	26	A	Kettering T	W	2-1	1-0	16	Hearn 2 [13, 63]	1354
22	29	H	Stockport Co	W	7-0	5-0	—	Coulson [18], Hearn 3 [22, 45, 58], Elding [32], Green [35], L'Anson [64]	2254
23	Dec 6	H	Mansfield T	D	0-0	0-0	—		2553
24	17	H	Ebbsfleet U	W	4-3	3-2	15	Hearn 2 [2, 13], Antwi [11], Coulson [49]	2818
25	26	A	Lincoln C	W	2-1	0-1	13	Garner [52], Hearn [61]	5506
26	Jan 1	H	Lincoln C	W	3-1	2-0	11	Hearn [25], Coulson [45], Elding (pen) [52]	6672
27	7	A	Alfreton T	W	5-2	3-1	10	Hearn 2 [11, 40], Coulson [29], Garner [61], Duffy [90]	1924
28	10	A	Cambridge U	W	1-0	1-0	—	Elding [24]	2436
29	21	H	Bath C	W	6-0	2-0	9	Hearn 3 [21, 46, 57], Gallinagh (og) [41], Hughes-Mason [77], Church [85]	3836
30	24	A	Barrow	D	2-2	1-1	—	Hearn [10], Garner [73]	1081
31	28	H	AFC Telford U	W	2-0	0-0	7	Duffy [81], Artus [89]	3704
32	Feb 17	A	Southport	W	2-1	1-1	—	Miller [45], Hearn [82]	1934
33	Mar 3	H	Braintree T	D	1-1	0-0	8	Hearn [65]	3688
34	6	A	Fleetwood T	L	1-2	1-0	—	Cavanagh (og) [19]	2447
35	10	H	Forest Green R	W	2-1	1-1	7	Hearn [13], Townsend [90]	3294
36	13	H	York C	L	2-3	0-1	—	Elding [74], Coulson [81]	4250
37	17	H	Tamworth	D	0-0	0-0	9		3206
38	20	A	Hayes & Y	W	2-1	1-0	—	Duffy [30], Pearson [56]	392
39	24	A	Luton T	D	1-1	0-0	9	Hughes-Mason [87]	6419
40	27	A	Tamworth	D	1-1	0-0	—	Miller [61]	892
41	31	H	Kidderminster H	L	1-2	1-0	8	Wright [39]	3194
42	Apr 7	A	Darlington	D	0-0	0-0	9		2212
43	9	H	Gateshead	W	2-0	1-0	8	Pearson 2 [16, 56]	2938
44	14	A	Wrexham	D	2-2	0-1	9	Elding [64], Thanoj [82]	2917
45	21	A	AFC Telford U	D	0-0	0-0	9		2676
46	28	H	Southport	L	0-1	0-0	11		3738

Final League Position: 11

GOALSCORERS

League (79): Hearn 26, Elding 12 (2 pens), Coulson 8, Duffy 6, Makofo 4, Garner 3, Pearson 3, Hughes-Mason 2, Miller 2, Antwi 1, Artus 1, Church 1, Disley 1, Green 1, L'Anson 1, Thanoj 1, Thompson 1, Townsend 1, Wood 1, Wright 1, own goals 2.
FA Cup (8): Duffy 3, Hearn 2, Eagle 1, Makofo 1, Southwell 1.

McKeown 46	Silk 21 + 3	Ridley 12	Thanoj 14 + 9	L'Anson 12 + 1	Garner 13 + 1	Makofo 15 + 3	Disley 44	Hearn 42	Elding 27 + 16	Coulson 38 + 5	Wood 28 + 4	Spencer 1 + 6	Artus 23 + 6	Pearson 27 + 3	Kempson 18 + 1	Duffy 17 + 18	Thompson 3	Church 15 + 6	Green 5 + 1	Eagle 3 + 8	Townsend 27	Panther 7	Antwi 4	McCarthy 4 + 1	Miller 20	Hughes-Mason 2 + 9	Soares 8 + 3	Winn 6 + 4	Wright 4	Southwell — + 1	*Match No.*
1	2^1	3	4^2	5	6	7	8	9	10^3	11	12	13	14																		1
1		3		5^2		7^1	8	9	10^3	11	2	13	6	4	12	14															2
1		3				13	8	9^1	12	11	2	14	6	4	5■	10^3	7^2														3
1		3				7	8	9	13	12	2		6	4	5	10^2	11^1														4
1		3^2		13		10^3	8	11		12	2	14	6	4	5	9	7^1														5
1				2		13	8	10	14	11^1	3	12	6	4	5	9^2		7^3													6
1						7^2	8	10^3	13	11	2	9^1	6	3	5	12			4	14											7
1						7^2	8	9	14	11	2		6^1	4	5	10^3		12	3	13											8
1						7^2	8	9	12	11	3		6^3	4	5	10^1		14	2	13											9
1						7^1	8	9	10	12	2			6	5			4	3	11											10
1		3				7^2	8	9	10^3	12	2		13	6	5	14		4		11^1											11
1	13	3		2^2		7	8		12	11			10^1	6	5	9		4													12
1	14	3				7^1	8	10	13	11	2^3			6	5	9^2		4		12											13
1	14	3			6	13	8	10	12	11	2^3				5	9^1		4		7^2											14
1	2	3			6	7^1	8	10	13	11					5	9^2		4		12											15
1	2	3			6		8	10	12	7			11		5	9^1		4													16
1	2	3^2			6		8	9	10^3	7	14		11^1		5	13		4		12											17
1	2			6		11^1	8	9	10^2	7	3	14			5	13		4^3		12											18
1			4	6		7	8	10	12	11	2				5	9^1					3										19
1			11^1	6^2		7	8	10	14		2			13	5	9^3				12	3	4									20
1				6			8	9	10^2	11	2					13			12		3	4	5	7^1							21
1			12	6			8^1	9	10	11^2	2			14					7		3	4	5^3	13							22
1			12	6			8	9	10^2	11	2					13					3	4^1	5	7							23
1			13	6			8^1	9	10	11	2		12								3	4	5	7^2							24
1				6^1	12		8	9	10	11	2		13	5							3	4		7^2							25
1			12		6		8^1	9	10	11	2		7								3	4■			5						26
1	2		4		6		8	9^2	10^1	11			7			12					3				5	13					27
1	2		4		6		8	9	10^1	11			7			12					3				5						28
1	2		4^1		6		8	9^2	10^3	11			7			14		12			3				5	13					29
1	2		4		5		8	9	10^1	11			7			12					3				6						30
1	2		4		6		8	9^2	10^1	11			7			12					3				5	13					31
1	2		4		6^1		8^3	9	10^2	11			7	12		13		14			3				5						32
1	2		4				8	9		11				6		10					3				5	12	7^1				33
1	2		12				8	9	10	11				6				4			3				5		7^1				34
1	2		12				8	9^3	10	11				6		14		4^1			3				5		7^2	13			35
1	2		4^1				8		10	11	13			6		12					3				5		9^2	7			36
1	2						8	9	10^1	11^2	4			6		12					3				5	14	13	7^3			37
1			12				8		10^2	11	2			6		9		4■			3				5	13		7^1			38
1	2						8		12	11	7^3			3		9^1					6				5	14	13	10^2	4		39
1							8	9	10^1	11^3	2		13	6		12					3				5	14	7^2		4		40
1								9	10^2	11	2		8^3	6		13		12			3				5	14		7^1	4		41
1	2		4		6			10	13	12			14	5		9^2					3						7^1	11^3	8		42
1	2		13				8	10		11			7	6				4^2			3				5	9^1		12			43
1	2		12				8	9	13	11^3	5		7	6				4^1							3	10^2	14				44
1			4^1				8^2	9	10		2		11	6				13			3				5		7	12			45
1	2^1		4				8	9	10^3		12		11	6							3				5		7^2	13		14	46

FA Cup

Fourth Qualifying Round

	Ashington	(h)	5-0
First Round	Port Vale	(a)	0-0
		(h)	1-0
Second Round	Salisbury C	(a)	0-0
		(h)	2-3

HAYES & YEADING UNITED

Blue Square South

Ground: For the 2011–12 season, all matches were played at Woking FC's ground, Kingfield Stadium, Kingfield Road, Woking GU22 9AA. *Tel:* (0208) 573 2075. *Fax:* (0208) 573 0933. *Year Formed:* 2007. *Record Gate:* 1,234 (2009 v Histon, Blue Square Premier). *Nickname:* United. *Manager:* Nas Bashir. *Secretary:* John Bond Jr. *Colours:* Red shirts, black shorts, black stockings.

HAYES & YEADING 2011–12 LEAGUE RECORD

Match No.	*Date*	*Venue*	*Opponents*	*Result*		*H/T Score*	*Lg Pos.*	*Goalscorers*	*Attendance*
1	Aug 13	H	Alfreton T	W	3-1	2-0	—	McClure[9], Pacquette[30], Crockford[73]	262
2	16	A	Newport Co	L	0-4	0-1	—		1519
3	20	A	Fleetwood T	L	0-1	0-0	17		1376
4	23	H	Bath C	D	1-1	1-0	—	Pacquette[45]	172
5	27	A	Cambridge U	L	1-2	0-0	18	Bentley[49]	1778
6	30	H	Luton T	D	2-2	2-2	—	Soares 2[4, 45]	1015
7	Sept 4	H	Tamworth	W	1-0	0-0	15	Pacquette[49]	359
8	10	A	Grimsby T	L	0-3	0-1	19		2835
9	17	A	Darlington	D	1-1	0-0	18	Soares[68]	1809
10	20	H	Braintree T	L	1-2	1-1	—	Joseph-Dubois[13]	209
11	24	H	Gateshead	L	2-3	0-3	20	Soares (pen)[72], Collins[83]	218
12	27	A	Kettering T	W	5-3	3-1	—	Collins[7], Soares 2 (1 pen)[17 (p), 83], Joseph-Dubois[22], Mackie[55]	1119
13	Oct 1	A	AFC Telford U	D	1-1	0-1	18	Pacquette[85]	1941
14	9	H	Wrexham	L	0-2	0-0	18		625
15	11	H	Forest Green R	W	2-0	0-0	—	Collins 2[61, 83]	251
16	15	A	Barrow	L	1-3	0-2	18	Soares (pen)[58]	1074
17	18	A	Tamworth	L	1-2	1-0	—	Soares (pen)[15]	742
18	22	H	York C	L	2-4	1-2	20	Soares[45], Williams[90]	525
19	Nov 5	A	Stockport Co	D	3-3	1-2	21	Sinclair[13], Soares 2[75, 88]	2804
20	19	H	Kidderminster H	L	1-3	0-1	21	Cadmore[65]	289
21	26	A	Alfreton T	L	2-3	0-0	21	Arnold (og)[88], Soares[90]	600
22	29	H	Newport Co	L	0-4	0-3	—		303
23	Dec 6	A	Braintree T	W	3-0	0-0	—	Williams 2[56, 88], Collins[63]	454
24	17	H	Barrow	D	1-1	1-1	21	Wishart[40]	313
25	20	H	Fleetwood T	L	1-3	1-1	—	Collins[36]	264
26	26	A	Ebbsfleet U	L	1-3	0-1	21	Collins[80]	1176
27	Jan 7	A	Kidderminster H	L	1-3	1-0	23	Williams[28]	1732
28	17	H	Ebbsfleet U	L	1-2	0-1	—	Soares[46]	266
29	21	A	Mansfield T	L	2-3	1-1	23	Owusu[31], Soares[55]	1872
30	24	H	Darlington	W	3-2	2-0	—	Soares (pen)[4], Wishart[6], Collins[60]	550
31	28	H	Southport	L	0-2	0-1	23		294
32	Feb 18	A	Wrexham	L	1-4	0-2	23	Thalassitis[88]	3845
33	21	A	Bath C	W	1-0	1-0	—	Thalassitis[38]	512
34	Mar 3	A	York C	L	0-2	0-0	22		2603
35	6	A	Gateshead	L	0-2	0-1	—		465
36	10	H	Kettering T	W	1-0	0-0	21	Wishart[84]	253
37	17	A	Forest Green R	W	3-1	1-0	21	Cadmore[40], Thalassitis[68], Wishart[81]	781
38	20	H	Grimsby T	L	1-2	0-1	—	Hand (pen)[87]	392
39	24	H	AFC Telford U	D	0-0	0-0	21		307
40	27	H	Lincoln C	L	1-2	0-0	—	Pele[70]	327
41	31	A	Southport	W	2-1	1-0	21	Hand (pen)[14], Owusu[90]	1147
42	Apr 7	H	Cambridge U	D	0-0	0-0	21		336
43	9	A	Luton T	L	2-4	1-2	21	Wishart[21], Kovacs (og)[56]	6003
44	14	H	Mansfield T	L	1-3	1-1	21	Mingoia[37]	487
45	21	A	Lincoln C	W	1-0	0-0	21	Mingoia[60]	2585
46	28	H	Stockport Co.	L	1-2	1-1	21	Owusu[15]	654

Final League Position: 21

GOALSCORERS

League (58): Soares 15 (5 pens), Collins 8, Wishart 5, Pacquette 4, Williams 4, Owusu 3, Thalassitis 3, Cadmore 2, Hand 2 (2 pens), Joseph-Dubois 2, Mingoia 2, Bentley 1, Crockford 1, Mackie 1, McClure 1, Pele 1, Sinclair 1, own goals 2.
FA Cup (2): Crockford 1, Soares 1 (pen).

Arnold 31	Argent 16 + 1	John 12 / Gladwin 1 + 1	Hand 26	Cadmore 46	Bentley 32 + 2	Soares 31 / Evans — + 4	Crockford 10 + 9	Joseph-Dubois 20 + 2 / Walsh 16 + 1	Pacquette 13 + 5	McClure 1 / Rose 3 + 1	Elder 2 + 4	Federico — + 1 / Bell-Baggie — + 1	Williams 38 + 1	Wishart 22 + 14	Bayley 5 + 4	Saville 2 + 2 / Pele 16 + 2	Ujah 16	Mackie 7 + 4 / Bassele 1 + 3	Collins 18 + 17	Noble — + 2 / Koo-Boothe 1	Franks 7	Preddie 3 + 4 / Berry — + 1	Spence 19 + 1	Marsaud — + 3 / Mulley 1	Lee 13 + 6	Sinclair 2 / Thalassitis 5	Owusu 13 + 8	Legg — + 1 / Warren — + 7	Pentney 9	Folkes 7 + 1 / Monteiro 1	Morris 2 + 1	Wynters 2 / O'Brien 6 + 1	Gameiao 1 + 4	Bettamer — + 7 / Mingoia 7 + 1	Beasant 3	Ajala 3 + 7	Moutaouakil 15 + 1 / Wickham 1 + 1	*Match No.*
1	2	3	4	5	6	7	8	9	10^{1}	11^{2}	12	13																										1
1	2	3	4	5^{3}	6	7		9^{1}	10		11^{2}		8	12	13	14																						2
1	2	3	4	5	6	7^{1}		9	10^{2}		13		11	12	14		8^{3}																					3
1	2	3	4	5	6	7	8^{3}	9^{2}	10^{1}		12		11	13	14																							4
1		3	4	5	6	7^{3}		9	13		10^{2}		14	11^{1}	2		8	12																				5
1		3^{1}	4	5	6	7	8^{2}	9^{3}	10				11	14	2	12		13																				6
1			4	5	6	7	12	9^{2}	10^{3}		14		11	13	2	3	8^{1}																					7
1	2			5	6	7	8	14	10^{3}				11	13		3	4^{1}	12	9^{2}																			8
1	2^{3}	3		5	6	7	8	9^{1}	10^{2}				11	12	4			14	13																			9
1		3		5	6	7	8	9^{2}	10				11	4^{1}	2				13	12																		10
1^{G}	2	3		5	6	7	8	9	10^{2}					11^{1}				12	13	4	15																11
	2			5	6	7^{3}	14	9^{2}	12				11	13				8	10^{1}		4	1	3															12
	2^{1}			5	6	7	13	9	14				10		12			8	11^{3}		4^{2}	1	3															13
1		3		5	6^{3}	7	14	9	12				10					8^{2}	11^{1}		4		2	13														14
1				5	6	7	13	9^{3}	10^{1}				11				3	8^{2}	12		4		2	14														15
1		3		5	6^{3}	7	12	9					11	13			4	8^{1}	10^{2}				2	14														16
1				5	6	7^{3}	13	9	12				11				4	8^{2}	10^{1}		3		2		14													17
1	14	3		5	6	7	8^{2}		10				11				2	4^{1}	12		9^{3}				13													18
1^{G}	2^{1}			5	6	7		9^{2}					11				3		13			15			4	8	10	12										19
	2^{1}			5	6	7	13	14					10^{3}				3		12						4■	11^{2}	9		1	8								20
				5	6	7			10^{2}				11				4				15					9		1^{G}	8^{1}	2	3	12	13				21
				5	6	7							11	12			4		13			1					9^{3}			8^{1}	2	3	10^{2}	14				22
	2			5	6^{1}	7							11	3			4		9^{2}						8						14		12	13	1	10^{3}		23
		14		5		7^{1}	8^{3}	9					11	3			6		10^{2}						4								12	13	1		2	24
			4	5		7	12	9^{G}						3			6		10			15			8^{1}					11				13	1■	2^{2}		25
		4^{1}		5		7^{2}	8	9^{3}					11	3			6		10										1	2			14	13		12		26
				5		7		2		6^{3}		13	8^{1}	11											4		9		1	10				14		12	3^{2}	27
			4	5		7		9		6^{2}			11	3		12		14	13								10^{3}		1	8^{1}							2	28
			4	5		7		9		6^{1}				3		11		13	12						8^{2}		10^{3}		1							14	2	29
			4	5		7^{2}		9		14				3		6			11						8^{3}		10^{1}		1	13						12	2	30
			4	5		7		9					8	3^{3}		11			14	6^{2}		12			13		10^{1}		1								2	31
			4	5	14			6					8	11^{2}		2			9				12	7^{3}		10	13		1								3^{1}	32
1	2^{1}		4	5	8^{2}			6					11			7			14				3			10^{3}	9										13	12	33
1			4	5	8^{1}			3					9	13		7^{3}			14				6■			10	11^{2}	12									2	34
1			4^{2}	5				3					8	14						9					7	10^{1}	11^{3}	12■		6						13	2	35
1			4	5	7^{3}			6					8	12		11^{2}			9^{1}				3		13		14						10					2	36
1			4	5	8			9					7^{3}	12		6^{1}			14				3		13	10^{2}						11					2	37
1			4	5	14			6						10		13			9^{2}				3		8^{1}		12						11				7^{3}	2	38
1			4	5	8^{1}			6■					10	11^{3}		7							3		12		13					9^{2}		14			2	39
1			4	5		13								10^{3}	11^{2}		6							3		8		12	14				9^{1}		7			2	40
1			4	5		13								10	11^{2}		6			9^{1}				3		8		12	14						7^{3}			2	41
1	2		4	5									10	11^{2}		6			9^{1}				3		8■		12	14				13		7^{3}				42
1	2		4	5	8^{3}			12					10	11		6			13				3					14				9^{1}		7^{2}				43
1	2		4	5	8^{3}			9					10	11^{2}		6			14				3				12	13						7^{1}				44
1			4■	5	8	13		9					11^{1}	3		6		12	10^{3}				2											7^{2}			14	45
1				5	4^{2}	14		10						3		6		11^{3}	13				2				9							7		12	8^{1}	46

FA Cup
Fourth Qualifying Round
Cambridge U (h) 2-6

KETTERING TOWN Evo-Stik Southern Premier

Ground: Nene Park, Irthlingborough, Northants NN9 5QF. *Tel:* (01933) 652 000. *Year Formed:* 1872. *Record Gate:* 11,536 v Peterborough U. *Nickname:* Poppies. *Manager:* John Beck. *Colours:* Red shirts, black and white trim, red shorts, black stockings.

KETTERING TOWN 2011–12 LEAGUE RECORD

Match No.	Date	Venue	Opponents	Result		H/T Score	Lg Pos.	Goalscorers	Attendance
1	Aug 13	H	Newport Co	W	3-2	0-1	—	Marna 2 (1 pen) $^{51, 90 (p)}$, Cunnington ^{60}	2047
2	16	A	Stockport Co	L	0-1	0-0	—		3429
3	20	A	Gateshead	D	1-1	0-1	12	McKenzie ^{63}	661
4	23	H	York C	L	1-5	1-4	—	McKenzie ^{43}	1595
5	27	A	Mansfield T	L	0-3	0-1	19		2051
6	29	H	Cambridge U	D	0-0	0-0	—		2000
7	Sept 3	H	Fleetwood T	L	2-3	0-3	22	Marna 2 $^{74, 82}$	1209
8	10	A	Lincoln C	W	2-0	0-0	18	Marna ^{63}, Ashikodi (pen) ^{82}	2269
9	17	H	Tamworth	L	0-2	0-1	19		1955
10	20	A	Grimsby T	L	1-2	1-0	—	Ashikodi ^{28}	2470
11	24	A	Bath C	W	1-0	1-0	18	Sangare ^{2}	734
12	27	H	Hayes & Y	L	3-5	1-3	—	Ashikodi ^{44}, Cunnington ^{57}, Marna ^{90}	1119
13	Oct 1	H	Kidderminster H	L	0-1	0-1	21		1301
14	8	A	Alfreton T	D	1-1	0-1	20	Cunnington (pen) ^{72}	851
15	11	H	Braintree T	W	2-1	0-0	—	Cunnington ^{55}, Verma ^{71}	1115
16	15	A	Forest Green R	W	1-0	0-0	16	Cunnington ^{52}	823
17	18	A	Newport Co	L	1-3	1-1	—	Ashikodi ^{45}	1249
18	22	H	Ebbsfleet U	D	2-2	1-2	17	Bridges ^{13}, Dawkin ^{50}	1402
19	Nov 5	H	Southport	L	2-3	0-2	19	Hughes-Mason ^{58}, Ashikodi ^{77}	1368
20	18	A	Tamworth	D	2-2	2-1	—	Ashikodi ^{2}, Marna ^{16}	1197
21	26	H	Grimsby T	L	1-2	0-1	19	Bridges ^{90}	1354
22	29	A	Fleetwood T	L	0-3	0-2	—		1221
23	Dec 3	A	York C	L	0-7	0-4	20		2899
24	6	H	Darlington	D	0-0	0-0	—		924
25	17	H	Bath C	D	1-1	0-0	20	Jones ^{84}	1096
26	26	A	Luton T	L	0-5	0-2	20		7164
27	Jan 1	H	Luton T	L	0-5	0-2	22		3247
28	7	A	AFC Telford U	L	1-3	1-1	22	Marna ^{5}	2035
29	21	A	Wrexham	L	1-4	0-1	22	Sangare ^{67}	4066
30	24	H	Gateshead	W	2-1	0-0	—	Mills ^{57}, Verma ^{85}	804
31	28	H	Lincoln C	W	1-0	1-0	20	Verma (pen) ^{36}	1417
32	Feb 18	A	Barrow	L	0-3	0-1	22		1090
33	21	H	Forest Green R	L	1-3	0-2	—	Mills ^{90}	830
34	25	A	Braintree T	L	1-2	0-2	22	Sangare ^{60}	730
35	Mar 3	H	Wrexham	L	0-1	0-1	23		1377
36	10	A	Hayes & Y	L	0-1	0-0	23		253
37	13	A	Southport	D	0-0	0-0	—		753
38	17	H	Alfreton T	L	0-2	0-2	23		1093
39	20	H	AFC Telford U	W	2-1	0-0	—	Wyke ^{50}, Joyce ^{60}	939
40	24	A	Ebbsfleet U	L	0-1	0-1	23		957
41	31	H	Stockport Co	L	1-3	0-2	23	Westwood ^{76}	1281
42	Apr 7	H	Mansfield T	L	0-3	0-1	23		1818
43	9	A	Cambridge U	L	0-2	0-1	23		2578
44	14	A	Kidderminster H	L	1-6	1-1	23	Ford ^{19}	1967
45	21	H	Barrow	D	1-1	1-0	24	Bridges ^{45}	896
46	28	A	Darlington	L	1-3	0-1	24	Wyke (pen) ^{59}	1792

Final League Position: 24

GOALSCORERS

League (40): Marna 8 (1 pen), Ashikodi 6 (1 pen), Cunnington 5 (1 pen), Bridges 3, Sangare 3, Verma 3 (1 pen), McKenzie 2, Mills 2, Wyke 2 (1 pen), Dawkin 1, Ford 1, Hughes-Mason 1, Jones 1, Joyce 1, Westwood 1.
FA Cup (3): Marna 2, McKenzie 1.

			Jones 2 + 8			Mills 17 + 1			Ralph 13 + 1			Hornby 3 + 1		Wyke 12			Ford 7 + 3			Westwood 9		Joyce 8 + 1				York 5 + 3		Gray 8 + 1		Van Engel 1 + 4		Jack 3		Petranyuk — + 3		Palmer 1		
Walker 40	Ifil P 22 + 1	Davis 36	Cunnington 9 + 3	Ifil J 28	Parry 1	Challinor 2 + 2	Verma 22	Marna 15 + 2	Ashikodi 16 + 1	Kelly 26 + 1	Dobson — + 1	Taft 10 + 4	McKenzie 6 + 3	Meechan 17 + 4	Thomson — + 4	Noubissie 26 + 6	Clapham 2 + 1	Navarro 13 + 3	Williams 1	Dossou — + 1	Sekajia 1 + 1	Koo-Boothe 10 + 3	Bridges 33 + 2	Sangare 27 + 2	Dempster 5	Smith 3	Warren 1	O'Leary 11	Hughes-Mason 9 + 3	Cross — + 2	Dawkin 9 + 3	Swaibu 5 + 1	Haxhia 3 + 1	Deeney 3	Dance 1 + 2	Roper 1	Pryor 3 + 6	*Match No.*
1	2	3	4[1]	5	6	7	8	9	10	11	12																											1
1	2	3■		5		7[1]	8	9	11	6		4	10[2]	12	13																							2
1	2			5		12	8	9	7[2]	11		4	10[1]	3■	13	6																						3
1	2			5		13	8	9	7	11[2]		14	10[3]		12	6[1]	3	4																				4
1	2	3		5			8	9	10	12		4		11	13			7[2]	6[1]																			5
1	2	3		5				9	10	11[1]		4		7		6		8		12																		6
1	2	3	13	5				9	10			4		11[3]		7	12	6[1]			8[2]	14																7
1	2	3	13	5				9	10[3]			4		12		11	6[2]				14	8	7[1]															8
1	2	3	4	5				9	10			8	13	12		11[2]						6	7[1]															9
1	2	3	12	5				9[1]	10			7	14			11[2]		13■				4	8[3]	6														10
1		3	4	5			8[1]		10[3]			12	14			2						13	11	9	6[2]	7												11
1		3	10	5[1]				12■	9■							2						13	8	7	6	11	4[2]											12
1			10							3		12		8		13		7[2]				6[1]		2	5	11		4	9[3]	14								13
1		3	9	5■			10[1]			11		12	8	7										2	6			4										14
1		3	9				8			11		5	10[1]	7[2]								6	13	2				4	12									15
1		3	9				7[2]	13	10[1]	11		2		4								6		5				8	12									16
1	12	3	9■				8[3]		10[2]	11				2[1]								7	14	5	6■			4			13							17
1	2	3					7[1]		10[3]	11				8				12				6■	9	5				4[2]	14		13							18
1	2						7[1]	10	12	3				4									8	6					9		11	5						19
1■				6			11[6]	10	9	3				4				7[2]				5	8	2[1]							12	13	15					20
		3												4[2]		12		2[1]				6	9					8	10		7	5	1	11	13			21
		3		6												4							9					8	10		7	5	1	11[2]	12	2[1]	13	22
		3		6												2		8					9					4[1]	10		7	5	1	11			12	23
1		3	12	6												2		4					8						10[2]	13	9	5			11[1]		7	24
1		3	13	6									10	12		2		4[2]					8	5					11		9						7[1]	25
1	2	3	11	6[1]												13		5					8	12				4	10		9						7[2]	26
1	2■	3[2]	12					10								7		6					8	5				4	11[1]		9						13	27
1		3	12				7	10		11				6[1]		4		2[2]					8	5							9						13	28
1		3		6		9[1]	7	10■	12	11				4		2[2]							8	5													13	29
1		3	12	6		9	7		10[1]	11				4		2							8	5														30
1		3		6		9	7		10	11				4		2							8	5														31
1	4[1]	3	12	6		9	8		10	11						2							7	5														32
1		3	12	6		9	7		10	11		4[1]				2							8	5														33
1	2	3		6		9	8		10	11[1]		7				12■							4	5														34
1	2	3	7			9	8		10			4[1]		11			12						6	5[2]													13	35
1	2	3	12			8	7[2]		4	11		13		9						5		10[1]	6															36
1	2	3■				11			8					9			7			5		10	4	6														37
1	2	3		6[2]		11								9		13	12					7	4	5		8[1]		10										38
1	2	3				11								9		12	8[3]			4		7[2]	6	5[1]		13		10		14								39
1	2[1]	3				8								9		6	7[2]			5		11	4	12				10		13								40
		3[1]		6[2]		12			8	11				9		4	14			5				2		13		10		7[3]		1						41
						10			3	11				9[2]		7				4■		8	6	5[1]		2		12		13		1						42
						10			3	11				9		4[3]	6	13				8[1]	5			2		7		12[2]		1■		14				43
1				6		8[1]			3	11				9[2]			7			5		12	4			2		10						13				44
1						8			3	11[1]				9		2	7			5			6			4		10						12				45
1						11								9		2	4			6		7	5	8		12		10								3[1]		46

FA Cup

Fourth Qualifying Round			
	Southend Manor	(h)	3-1
First Round	Sutton U	(a)	0-1

KIDDERMINSTER HARRIERS Blue Square Premier

Ground: Aggborough Stadium, Hoo Road, Kidderminster DY10 1NB. *Tel:* (01562) 823 931. *Fax:* (01562) 827 329.
Year Formed: 1886. *Record Gate:* 9,155 (1948 v Hereford U). *Nickname:* Harriers. *Manager:* Steve Burr.
Secretary: David Colwell. *Colours:* Red shirts, white shorts, red stockings.

KIDDERMINSTER HARRIERS 2011–12 LEAGUE RECORD

Match No.	Date	Venue	Opponents	Result		H/T Score	Lg Pos.	Goalscorers	Attendance
1	Aug 13	H	Gateshead	L	2-3	2-2	—	Wright, N [20], Storer [25]	1636
2	16	A	Lincoln C	W	1-0	1-0	—	Gittings [42]	2448
3	20	A	Cambridge U	W	2-1	2-0	6	Guinan 2 [40, 44]	2171
4	23	H	Stockport Co	D	1-1	0-1	—	Phelan [88]	1886
5	27	H	Southport	W	2-0	0-0	4	Byrne [79], Williams, Marc [81]	1763
6	29	A	Newport Co	W	3-1	0-0	—	Byrne [49], Miller (og) [65], Jones [80]	1672
7	Sept 3	A	Wrexham	L	0-2	0-1	3		4102
8	10	H	Ebbsfleet U	D	2-2	1-1	4	Jones [11], Wright, N [74]	1788
9	17	H	Alfreton T	W	3-1	1-1	5	Williams, Marc [39], Guinan [51], Vincent [89]	1939
10	20	A	Fleetwood T	L	2-5	0-1	—	Vaughan (pen) [69], Matt [90]	1316
11	24	A	Mansfield T	W	3-0	3-0	7	Storer [6], Wright, N [7], Vaughan (pen) [23]	2522
12	27	H	Grimsby T	D	1-1	1-0	—	Wright, N [16]	1807
13	Oct 1	A	Kettering T	W	1-0	1-0	5	Jamile [42]	1301
14	8	H	Luton T	L	1-2	0-1	8	Sharpe [87]	3332
15	11	H	AFC Telford U	D	2-2	2-1	—	Matt [13], Preston (og) [39]	2440
16	15	A	Darlington	L	0-1	0-0	11		1763
17	18	H	Braintree T	W	5-4	1-2	—	Wright, N 2 (1 pen) [27, 77 (p)], Vincent 2 [51, 55], Gittings [58]	1301
18	22	A	Barrow	L	1-3	1-3	12	Matt [35]	1246
19	Nov 5	H	Tamworth	W	2-0	2-0	8	Vaughan (pen) [6], Guinan [18]	1797
20	19	A	Hayes & Y	W	3-1	1-0	8	Vaughan (pen) [28], Gittings 2 [70, 87]	289
21	26	H	Cambridge U	D	0-0	0-0	8		1899
22	29	A	Ebbsfleet U	D	3-3	1-0	—	Hankin [5], Wright, N [80], Matt [84]	731
23	Dec 6	H	Bath C	W	4-1	2-1	—	Guinan [33], Matt 2 [45, 66], Byrne [88]	1472
24	19	A	York C	W	3-2	3-1	—	Byrne [5], Gittings [21], Matt [33]	2830
25	26	H	Forest Green R	W	1-0	0-0	6	Byrne [67]	2491
26	Jan 1	A	Forest Green R	D	1-1	0-1	6	Matt [90]	1542
27	7	H	Hayes & Y	W	3-1	0-1	5	Guinan [82], Matt [89], Wright, N [90]	1732
28	10	A	Gateshead	L	1-2	0-1	—	Wright, N (pen) [80]	724
29	21	A	Alfreton T	W	2-0	0-0	5	Malbon [89], Bradley [90]	990
30	24	H	York C	D	1-1	0-0	—	McQuilkin [85]	2417
31	28	A	Stockport Co	L	1-2	0-1	5	Wright, N [56]	3728
32	Feb 18	H	Lincoln C	D	1-1	0-1	7	Guinan [90]	2081
33	21	H	Wrexham	L	0-1	0-1	—		2492
34	25	A	Bath C	W	2-1	1-0	6	Byrne 2 [18, 54]	676
35	Mar 3	H	Barrow	L	1-2	1-2	7	Malbon [31]	2135
36	9	H	Fleetwood T	L	0-2	0-0	—		2341
37	13	A	AFC Telford U	L	1-2	0-1	—	Malbon [53]	2192
38	17	A	Braintree T	W	4-1	1-1	7	Marshall [42], Byrne 2 [51, 69], Malbon [60]	610
39	20	A	Tamworth	D	0-0	0-0	—		924
40	24	H	Darlington	W	3-1	1-1	7	Hankin [26], Malbon [54], Rowe [89]	1635
41	31	A	Grimsby T	W	2-1	0-1	7	Malbon [55], Rowe [90]	3194
42	Apr 7	A	Southport	W	2-1	1-1	5	Malbon [41], Jones [90]	1544
43	9	H	Newport Co	W	3-2	0-2	5	Wright, N 3 (1 pen) [86 (p), 89, 90]	2275
44	14	H	Kettering T	W	6-1	1-1	4	Wright, N 2 (1 pen) [25 (p), 54], Malbon [72], Rowe [74], Jones [82], Williams, Mike [89]	1967
45	21	A	Luton T	L	0-1	0-0	6		8415
46	28	H	Mansfield T	L	0-3	0-0	6		3565

Final League Position: 6

GOALSCORERS

League (82): Wright, N 15 (4 pens), Byrne 9, Matt 9, Malbon 8, Guinan 7, Gittings 5, Jones 4, Vaughan 4 (4 pens), Rowe 3, Vincent 3, Hankin 2, Storer 2, Williams, Marc 2, Bradley 1, Jamile 1, Marshall 1, McQuilkin 1, Phelan 1, Sharpe 1, Williams, Mike 1, own goals 2.
FA Cup (1): Guinan 1.

Lewis 12	Vaughan 40	Williams Mike 28	Vincent 21 + 7	Jones 38 + 1	Marshall 23	Storer 38 + 1	Gittings 25 + 5	Guinan 25 + 13	Williams Marc 10 + 12	Wright N 23 + 20	Medley 7 + 6	Phelan 8 + 7	Matt 23 + 8	Byrne 20 + 6	Hankin 23 + 4	Sharpe 21 + 1	Demetriou 23 + 3	Wright T — + 2	Lyness 6	Jamile 1	Briscoe 11 + 2	Thompson-Brown — + 3	Cresswell — + 3	Bird 4	Breeden 28	Hendrie 13 + 2	Bradley 7 + 8	Malbon 14 + 3	McQuilkin — + 2	Johnson 11 + 1	Rowe 3 + 12	*Match No.*
1	2	3	4	5	6	7	8^{2}	9^{3}	10^{1}	11	12	13	14																			1
1	2	3	4	5	6	7	8^{2}	9^{1}	10	11^{3}	14	13	12																			2
1	2	3	4	5	6	7	8^{3}	9	10^{2}	11^{1}	14	13	12																			3
1	2	3	4	5	6	7	8	9^{2}	10^{3}	11^{1}	12	13	14																			4
1	2	3	4^{1}	5	6	7			10	13	11^{2}	8	9^{3}	12	14																	5
1	2^{3}	3		5	6	7	12	9	10^{2}		13	8^{1}		11	4	14																6
1	2	3	4	5	6	7^{1}	14	9^{2}	12		10^{3}		13	11	8																	7
1	2	3	14	5	6	7	8^{2}	9^{1}		10		4	12	11^{3}	13																	8
1	2	3	12	5	6	7		9^{2}	10	11		4^{1}	13	8																		9
1	2	3	4^{1}	5	6	7		9■	10^{3}	13		8	14	12	11^{2}																	10
1	2	3		5		4	8^{2}		12	9	7^{1}	13	10^{3}	11		6	14															11
1	2	3		5		4■	8		12	9^{3}	7^{1}	14	10^{2}	11		6		13														12
	2	3	12	5			8		13	9^{2}	7	4^{1}		11		6		14	1	10^{3}												13
	2	3^{2}	11	4^{1}		6	8		14	10	7^{3}	13	9			5			1		12											14
	2■		7			4	8	13	10^{1}	11			9^{2}			3	5		1		6	12										15
			7		6	4^{3}	8^{2}	9^{1}	13	11			10			2	3		1		5	12	14									16
			7		6	4	10^{2}	14	13	11	12	8^{1}	9^{3}			2	3		1		5											17
			4		6		8	14	13	10	11^{2}		9^{3}			2	3		1		5^{1}		12	7								18
	2		13				8	9	10	12		11^{2}			7^{1}	6	3				5			4	1							19
	2		7^{3}				8	9^{2}	13	12			10		11^{1}	6	3				5		14	4	1							20
	2		7			12	8	9^{3}		14			10		11^{2}	6	3				5			4^{1}	1	13						21
	2			12		7^{2}	8^{3}	9		14			10	13	11	6	3				5^{1}				1	4						22
	2			4		6		9^{1}	13	11^{3}			10	12	7	5	3					14			1	8^{2}						23
	2			5		8	10^{1}	14	13	12			9^{2}	11	7	6	3								1	4^{3}						24
	2		12	5		8	10	13					9^{2}	11	7	6	3								1	4^{1}						25
	2		11^{1}	5		4	10^{3}	13	14	12			9		7^{2}	6	3								1	8						26
	2		11^{1}	5		4	10^{2}	14		12			9		7^{3}	6	3								1	8	13					27
	2			5■		8	10^{1}	12		13			9	14	7^{2}	6	3								1	4	11^{3}					28
		6		5		7	13	9		8			11^{1}			2^{2}	3				14				1	4^{3}	10	12				29
		6		5		8				9			10		7^{1}	2	3								1	4^{2}	11	12	13			30
		3		5		8	10			11^{3}			9		12	6^{1}	2								1	4	7^{2}	13	14			31
	2	3	13	5		4^{2}		14		9			10^{3}				6								1	8	7			11^{1}	12	32
	2	3		5		6		12		8^{2}			10^{3}	11	13						4				1		7	9^{1}			14	33
	2	3		5		4	7	12		14			10^{1}	11							6				1			9^{2}		13	8^{3}	34
	2	3		5		6	12	14		13				11							4^{1}				1	8^{3}		9		7	10^{2}	35
	2	6		5			14	9^{2}		12				11			3								1	7^{3}	4	8		10^{1}	13	36
	2			5	6	4	8^{3}	9^{2}		10				11^{1}			3								1	13	12	7			14	37
	2			5	6	4^{3}		9^{2}		12				11	7		3								1		14	8^{1}		10	13	38
	2			5	6	4^{3}		9^{1}		12				11	7		3								1		14	8		10^{2}	13	39
	2		12	5	6	4		9^{2}		14				11	7^{3}		3								1			8^{1}		10	13	40
	2	3		5	6	4		9^{1}		13				11	7										1			8		10^{2}	12	41
	2	3	8	5	6			9^{1}		13				11	7^{3}		14								1			4		10^{2}	12	42
	2	3	8	5	6			9^{2}		12				11^{3}	7^{1}										1		14	4		10	13	43
	2	3	8	5	6	4		9^{1}		10^{2}					7		13								1		14	11^{3}			12	44
	2	3	8	5	6	4^{2}		14		9^{1}					7^{3}										1		13	10		11	12	45
	2■	3	8	5	6	4^{2}				14				12	7^{1}										1		13	11^{3}		9	10	46

FA Cup
Fourth Qualifying Round

Corby T	(h)	0-0
	(a)	1-4

LINCOLN CITY — Blue Square Premier

Ground: Sincil Bank Stadium, Sincil Bank, Lincoln LN5 8LD. *Tel:* (01522) 880 011. *Fax:* (01522) 880 020.
Year Formed: 1884. *Record Gate:* 23,196 v Derby Co, League Cup 4th rd, 15 November 1967.
Nickname: 'The Red Imps' *Manager:* David Holdsworth. *Colours:* Grey shirts with dark blue sleeves, dark blue shorts, dark blue stockings.

LINCOLN CITY 2011–12 LEAGUE RECORD

Match No.	Date	Venue	Opponents	Result		H/T Score	Lg Pos.	Goalscorers	Attendance
1	Aug 13	A	Southport	D	2-2	1-1	—	Smith[29], Perry[50]	1687
2	16	H	Kidderminster H	L	0-1	0-1	—		2448
3	19	H	Wrexham	L	1-2	1-1	—	Smith[45]	2211
4	23	A	AFC Telford U	W	2-1	0-0	—	Perry 2[75, 80]	2323
5	26	H	Stockport Co	D	1-1	1-1	—	Power[8]	2152
6	29	A	Darlington	L	1-3	0-1	—	Power[71]	2252
7	Sept 3	A	Braintree T	L	0-1	0-1	21		1182
8	10	H	Kettering T	L	0-2	0-0	22		2269
9	17	A	Luton T	L	0-1	0-0	22		6316
10	20	H	Gateshead	W	1-0	0-0	—	Fuseini[77]	1587
11	24	H	Forest Green R	D	1-1	0-1	19	Hone[60]	2076
12	27	A	Barrow	L	0-1	0-1	—		1181
13	Oct 1	H	Bath C	W	2-0	2-0	19	Smith[19], McCallum[30]	2244
14	8	A	Tamworth	L	0-4	0-1	19		1232
15	11	A	Alfreton T	W	3-1	3-1	—	Smith 2[11, 13], McCallum[24]	1232
16	14	H	Fleetwood T	L	1-3	1-0	—	O'Keefe[42]	2332
17	18	H	Mansfield T	D	1-1	0-0	—	McCallum[76]	2944
18	21	A	Cambridge U	L	0-2	0-1	—		2875
19	Nov 5	H	Barrow	W	2-1	2-0	18	Smith[20], Christophe[22]	2090
20	19	A	Wrexham	L	0-2	0-1	20		3424
21	26	H	Ebbsfleet U	W	3-0	1-0	18	Platt[38], Russell[74], Nutter[80]	2111
22	29	A	York C	L	0-2	0-1	—		3155
23	Dec 3	A	Newport Co	L	0-1	0-1	19		1270
24	6	H	Luton T	D	1-1	0-1	—	Hinds[77]	2049
25	17	A	Forest Green R	W	2-0	1-0	17	Power (pen)[42], Laurent[72]	969
26	26	H	Grimsby T	L	1-2	1-0	17	Platt[33]	5506
27	Jan 1	A	Grimsby T	L	1-3	0-2	17	Taylor[59]	6672
28	7	H	York C	L	0-2	0-0	18		3048
29	21	A	Gateshead	D	3-3	1-2	18	Pacquette 2[7, 82], Smith[87]	870
30	24	H	Southport	W	2-0	1-0	—	Christophe[7], Pacquette[53]	1615
31	28	A	Kettering T	L	0-1	0-1	16		1417
32	Feb 14	H	Braintree T	D	3-3	1-1	—	Louis[1], Thompson[56], Almond[90]	1616
33	18	A	Kidderminster H	D	1-1	1-0	17	Louis[21]	2081
34	25	H	AFC Telford U	D	1-1	1-1	17	Blackburn (og)[32]	2438
35	Mar 3	A	Mansfield T	L	1-2	0-0	18	McCammon[90]	4830
36	10	H	Alfreton T	L	0-1	0-1	19		2253
37	17	A	Bath C	L	1-2	0-2	20	Lloyd[76]	760
38	24	H	Newport Co	W	2-0	2-0	19	McCammon[25], Nutter[33]	1951
39	27	A	Hayes & Y	W	2-1	0-0	—	Louis[68], Miller[73]	327
40	31	H	Tamworth	W	4-0	2-0	17	Bore[7], Thomas (2 ogs)[30, 82], Power (pen)[48]	2213
41	Apr 3	H	Cambridge U	L	0-1	0-0	—		1978
42	7	A	Stockport Co	L	0-4	0-2	19		3975
43	9	H	Darlington	W	5-0	4-0	17	Lloyd 2[21, 39], Taylor[33], Louis 2[37, 74]	2274
44	13	A	Fleetwood T	D	2-2	2-1	—	Taylor[8], Louis[20]	4511
45	21	H	Hayes & Y	L	0-1	0-0	19		2585
46	28	A	Ebbsfleet U	W	3-2	3-1	17	Howe (og)[15], Bore[27], Taylor[33]	1217

Final League Position: 17

GOALSCORERS

League (56): Smith 7, Louis 6, Power 4 (2 pens), Taylor 4, Lloyd 3, McCallum 3, Pacquette 3, Perry 3, Bore 2, Christophe 2, McCammon 2, Nutter 2, Platt 2, Almond 1, Fuseini 1, Hinds 1, Hone 1, Laurent 1, Miller 1, O'Keefe 1, Russell 1, Thompson 1, own goals 4.
FA Cup (2): Smith 2.

Anyon 38	Watts 11	Nutter 46	Fuseini 15 + 2	Gowling 36 + 1	Hone 9	McCallum 17 + 1 / Almond 3 + 2	Power 42	Perry 14 + 9 / Rodney 2 + 4	Smith 18 + 7	Russell 17 + 9	Barraclough 4 + 8	Taylor 10 + 14	O'Keefe 4 + 6	Sinclair 23 + 1 / McCammon 2 + 4	Nicolau 14 + 5	Christophe 22 + 5	Nelson 9 + 1	Arnaud — + 1 / Miller 8	Cunningham 2	Thomas — + 1 / Cobb — + 1	Thompson 26 + 1	Farman 8	Anderson 1	Platt 14	Laurent 5 + 9	Hinds 8 / Robinson — + 1	Medley — + 6	Sheridan 12 + 7	Beardsley — + 1	Williams 10 + 1	Watson 3 + 2	Lloyd 3 + 9	Pacquette 9 + 4	Broughton 1	Robson 15	Bore 11	Louis 14	*Match No.*
1	2	3	4	5	6	7^{1}	8	9^{2}	10^{3}	11	12	13	14																									1
1	2	3	4	5		7^{1}	8	9	10^{3}	11^{2}	13	12	14	6																								2
1	2	3	4^{1}	5		7	8	12	10	11	13	9^{2}		6																								3
1	2	3	4	5		7^{3}	8	12	10^{2}	11	13	9^{1}		6	14																							4
1	2	3	4	5		7	8	9^{2}	13	11	10^{1}	12		6																								5
1		3	4	5	6	7	8	9^{3}	10^{2}	11	14	13		2^{1}		12																						6
1		3	4	5		7^{1}	8	9^{2}	13	11	10	12				2	6																					7
1		3	4	5		13	8	12	10^{2}	11	7	9^{1}				2■	6																					8
1	2	3	4^{3}			7^{2}	8	9	13	11	10^{1}		14	6	12		5■																					9
1		3	4	5	6	7^{2}	8	9^{1}	12	11	13			2		10																						10
1		3	10	5	6	11	8	9^{1}	12	4			13	2		7^{2}																						11
1		3	11^{1}	5	6	7	8		10	9	12		13	2^{3}		4^{2}	14																					12
1		3	11^{1}	5	6	9^{2}	8	14	10^{3}	7	12		13	2		4																						13
1	4	3	10		5	7	8		9					2	11^{1}	6		12																				14
1	2	3	12		6	10^{2}	8	14	9^{3}			13			11	4	5		7^{1}																			15
1	2	3	13		5	10	8	14	9^{3}				7^{1}	12	11	4^{2}	6																					16
1	2	3	6^{1}			10	8	13	9^{2}					4	11	12	5		7^{3}	14																		17
1	2	3				10	8	12	9^{2}				7^{1}	6	11	4	5				13																	18
		3^{1}		13				9	10				8^{2}	2	11	4	6					1	5	7	12													19
		3					8	9	10^{1}	14			4^{3}	2	11^{2}		6					1		7	12	5	13											20
		3		6			4	9		11^{2}				2							8	1		7	13	5	12	10^{1}										21
		3		6			4	9^{1}		11^{2}				2	14						8	1		7	13	5	12	10^{3}										22
		3		6			4^{2}	9		14				2		8					10	1		11^{1}	7^{3}	5	12	13										23
		3		6			4	9^{1}		7^{2}		13		2		8^{3}					11	1		10	12	5		14										24
		3		5			8			13		9^{2}		2		4					7	1		10^{1}	11^{3}	6	12	14										25
		3		5^{1}			7	13		14				2		4					8^{3}	1		11	9^{2}	6		10	12									26
1		3					7		13	14		9		2		4^{2}					8			11^{3}		5	12	10^{1}		6								27
1		3					10		9^{3}			12		2	11^{2}	4					8			7^{1}						6	5	13	14					28
1		3		5			4■		9						11^{2}						8			7^{1}				13		6		12	10	2				29
1		3		5					9^{1}	13					11^{3}	4					8			7^{2}				14		6		12	10		2			30
1		3		5						12					11^{3}	4					8			7^{1}				9^{2}		6	14	13	10		2			31
1		3		5		12		13		14					11^{1}	4					8			7^{2}							6		10^{3}			2	9	32
1		3		5		9	7	11^{1}		13						4					8									6			12			2	10^{2}	33
1		3		5		11^{2}	4	13				12				14					8									6			10^{1}		2	7^{3}	9	34
1		3		5		12	6			11^{1}		13		14							8									4			10^{2}		2	7^{3}	9	35
1		3		5		9^{2}	4					13		14							8							12		6			10^{1}		2	7^{3}	11	36
1		3		5			7					9^{3}		13		4^{1}					8				14			11		6		12	10^{2}		2			37
1		3		5			4							10^{2}		14		6			8				13			11^{3}				12			2	7^{1}	9	38
1		3		5			7					13		10^{1}	12			6			8				11^{2}			4							2		9	39
1		3		5			4	14				12						6			8							11^{3}				13	10^{1}		2	7^{2}	9	40
1		3		5			4	14				10^{1}			11^{2}			6			8				12			7^{3}				13			2		9	41
1		3		5			4					14		13	11^{1}			6			8^{3}				10^{2}			7				12			2		9	42
1		3		5			4					9^{2}						6			8				13			12				11	14		2	7^{1}	10^{3}	43
1		3		5			4					9				13					8									12	6^{1}	11^{2}			2	7	10	44
1		3		5			4	10^{2}	14									6		12	8					13						11^{1}			2	7^{3}	9	45
1		3		5			4					9			13			6			8							11^{2}			14		12		2^{3}	7	10^{1}	46

FA Cup
Fourth Qualifying Round

Alfreton T	(a)	1-1
	(h)	1-2

LUTON TOWN

Blue Square Premier

Ground: Kenilworth Stadium, 1 Maple Road, Luton LU4 8AW. *Tel:* (01582) 411 622. *Year Formed:* 1885.
Record Gate: 30, 869 (1959 v Blackpool, FA Cup 6th rd replay). *Nickname:* The Hatters. *Manager:* Paul Buckle.
Secretary: Paul Buckle. *Colours:* Orange shirts, white shorts, orange stockings.

LUTON TOWN 2011–12 LEAGUE RECORD

Match No.	*Date*	*Venue*	*Opponents*	*Result*	*H/T Score*	*Lg Pos.*	*Goalscorers*	*Attendance*
1	Aug 16	H	Forest Green R	D 1-1	0-0	—	Beckwith [70]	6061
2	20	H	Southport	W 5-1	1-1	10	Watkins [41], Antwi [71], Morgan-Smith [73], Willmott [77], Crow [78]	5681
3	23	A	Mansfield T	D 1-1	0-1	—	Antwi [78]	2592
4	27	H	Braintree T	W 3-1	3-1	6	Morgan-Smith 2 [12, 44], Howells [45]	5703
5	30	A	Hayes & Y	D 2-2	2-2	—	Morgan-Smith [26], Crow [28]	1015
6	Sept 2	A	Stockport Co	D 1-1	1-0	—	Lawless [5]	3389
7	10	H	Darlington	W 2-0	1-0	7	Crow [31], Fleetwood [71]	5952
8	13	A	AFC Telford U	W 2-0	1-0	—	Morgan-Smith 2 [8, 46]	2640
9	17	H	Lincoln C	W 1-0	0-0	2	Fleetwood [84]	6316
10	20	A	Bath C	D 1-1	1-0	—	Morgan-Smith [45]	1158
11	24	A	York C	L 0-3	0-3	6		3570
12	27	H	Cambridge U	L 0-1	0-0	—		6274
13	Oct 1	H	Barrow	W 5-1	1-1	6	Willmott 2 [12, 46], Watkins [55], Dance [61], Morgan-Smith [75]	5613
14	8	A	Kidderminster H	W 2-1	1-0	5	Willmott 2 [39, 82]	3332
15	11	A	Ebbsfleet U	D 2-2	1-0	—	Morgan-Smith [44], Dance [71]	1651
16	15	H	Gateshead	W 5-1	2-0	3	Howells 2 [34, 44], O'Connor [70], Hand 2 [79, 90]	6285
17	18	H	Wrexham	L 0-1	0-0	—		7270
18	21	A	Grimsby T	W 1-0	0-0	—	Wright [73]	3239
19	Nov 5	H	Fleetwood T	L 1-2	0-1	7	Kovacs [90]	6361
20	19	A	Cambridge U	D 1-1	1-0	7	Fleetwood [18]	4796
21	26	A	Newport Co	W 1-0	0-0	6	Crow [90]	1511
22	29	H	AFC Telford U	D 1-1	1-0	—	Willmott [41]	5399
23	Dec 6	A	Lincoln C	D 1-1	1-0	—	Crow [36]	2049
24	17	A	Tamworth	W 3-1	1-0	5	Crow 2 [38, 53], Dance [56]	1467
25	26	H	Kettering T	W 5-0	2-0	5	Howells [20], O'Connor [27], Lawless [49], Fleetwood [80], Willmott [85]	7164
26	Jan 1	A	Kettering T	W 5-0	2-0	3	Howells [4], Watkins [9], Kovacs [62], Taylor [74], Fleetwood [90]	3247
27	7	H	Newport Co	W 2-0	1-0	3	O'Connor [35], Crow [66]	6108
28	10	H	Stockport Co	W 1-0	0-0	—	O'Connor (pen) [73]	5588
29	21	A	Southport	D 3-3	2-2	3	Crow [39], Watkins [45], O'Connor [47]	1665
30	25	H	Mansfield T	D 0-0	0-0	—		5261
31	28	H	Alfreton T	W 1-0	1-0	3	Pilkington, G (pen) [39]	5658
32	Feb 18	H	Tamworth	W 3-0	1-0	3	Fleetwood [14], Kovacs [63], Francis (og) [81]	5833
33	21	A	Barrow	L 0-1	0-0	—		925
34	Mar 3	H	Bath C	W 2-0	1-0	3	Kovacs [17], Watkins [81]	5745
35	7	A	Wrexham	L 0-2	0-2	—		4206
36	13	A	Darlington	D 1-1	0-0	—	Fleetwood [90]	1382
37	20	A	Forest Green R	L 0-3	0-1	—		975
38	24	H	Grimsby T	D 1-1	0-0	5	Gray [60]	6419
39	30	H	York C	L 1-2	1-0	—	Gray [5]	5925
40	Apr 7	A	Braintree T	L 1-3	1-1	7	Gray [7]	1703
41	9	H	Hayes & Y	W 4-2	2-1	7	Fleetwood 2 [13, 44], Keane [53], Gray [71]	6003
42	14	A	Alfreton T	D 0-0	0-0	7		1654
43	17	H	Ebbsfleet U	W 3-0	1-0	—	Fleetwood 2 [45, 46], McAllister [90]	5526
44	21	H	Kidderminster H	W 1-0	0-0	5	Willmott [67]	8415
45	24	A	Gateshead	D 0-0	0-0	—		703
46	28	A	Fleetwood T	W 2-0	1-0	5	Pond (og) [10], Gray [70]	4446

Final League Position: 5

GOALSCORERS

League (78): Fleetwood 11, Crow 9, Morgan-Smith 9, Willmott 8, Gray 5, Howells 5, O'Connor 5 (1 pen), Watkins 5, Kovacs 4, Dance 3, Antwi 2, Hand 2, Lawless 2, Beckwith 1, Keane 1, McAllister 1, Pilkington, G. 1 (1 pen), Taylor 1, Wright 1, own goals 2.
FA Cup (8): O'Connor 4 (1 pen), Dance 1, Fleetwood 1, Watkins 1, Wright 1.
Play-Offs (4): Gray 2, Fleetwood 1, Pilkington, G. 1 (pen).

Pilkington K 12	Osano 28	Asafu-Adjaye 7 + 2	Keane 33	Beckwith 8	Antwi 12	Lawless 38	Howells 42	Barnes-Homer 1	O'Connor 21 + 13	Dance 21 + 5	Willmott 29 + 10	Tyler 34	Watkins 20 + 14	Crow 23 + 6	Morgan-Smith 15 + 2	Gleeson 8 + 2	Walker — + 1	Kissock 7 + 14	Fleetwood 22 + 15	Hand 11 + 2	Kovacs 37	Samuel — + 1	Blackett 5 + 4	Pilkington G 33	Carden 1	Wright 1 + 3	Taylor 15 + 2	Brunt — + 5	McAllister 4 + 10	Poku 5 + 5	Boucaud 4 + 3	Henry — + 2	Woolley — + 1	Gray 9	*Match No.*
1	2	3	4	5	6	7	8	9[1]	10	11	12																								1
	2	14	4	5	6	7	8		10[2]	11[1]	3	1	9[3]	12	13																				2
	2	3[1]		5	6		8		9[2]	11		1	4	10	7	12	13																		3
	2		4	5	6	7[1]	3		13	8[3]	11	1	12	10[2]	9			14																	4
	2	12	4	5	6	7	3[1]		14	8[2]	11	1	13	10[3]	9																				5
	2	3	4		6	7				12	11	1	8	10[2]	9			5[1]	13																6
			4	5	6	7	2			12	11	1		10[2]	8[1]			13	9	3															7
		3■	4	5	6	7	2		13	12	11[3]	1	14	10[1]	8				9[2]																8
				5■	6	2	3		13	7	11[2]	1	12	10[1]	8[3]			14	9	4															9
					6	7	3		12	2[1]	14	1		10[3]	8			11[2]	9	4	5	13													10
			4		6	7[2]	3		12	2	11	1	13	14				10[1]	9[3]	8	5														11
			4		6		3		12	2	11[2]	1	14	10[1]	8			13	9	7[3]	5														12
	2		4				3		9[1]	7	11	1	8[2]	12	10			13		6	5														13
	2		4						10[1]	9[2]	11	1		13	8				12	7	5		3	6											14
	2								10[1]	9	11	1	13		8[2]				12	4	5		3	6	7										15
	2		4				7		12[2]	10	11[3]	1			8[1]			14	9	13	5		3	6											16
	2		4				7		10[2]	8	11	1						13	9[1]		5		3	6		12									17
	2						3		12	7[1]	11[2]	1	8	14				13	9[3]	4	5			6		10									18
	2		4			7[3]	3		8[2]		11[1]	1	14		10			13	9		5			6		12									19
1	2					7	8		10	11[1]			13						9	4[2]	5			6			3	12							20
1	2					7	4		10[1]	8	13			14					9[3]	11	5			6			3[2]	12							21
1	2		4			7	3		12	8[1]	11		14	10[3]					9[2]		5			6				13							22
1			4			7■	3		9[3]	13	11[2]		8	10		2				12■	5			6[1]				14							23
1			4			7	8			9[3]			11[1]	10[2]		2		12	13		5			6		14	3								24
1			4			7	11[1]		9[2]		12		8	10[3]		2		13	14		5			6			3								25
1	2		4			7[3]	11		10[1]	8[2]	13		9						14		5			6			3	12							26
1			4			7	11		9	12	14		8	10[2]		2[1]			13		5			6[3]			3								27
1						7	11		13	8[1]	12		4	10		2			9[2]		5			6			3								28
1						7	11		9				8	10	12	2		4[1]			5			6			3								29
1						7	11		9				4	10[2]	8[1]	2			12		5			6			3		13						30
						7	8		14		11[3]	1	4[1]	10[2]		2			13		5			6			3		9	12					31
	2[1]					7	8		10[3]		14	1	12					11[2]	9		5			6			3		13		4				32
			2			7	11		8			1	12					13	9		5			6			3		10[2]		4[1]				33
		2	4[2]			7	9[3]				11	1	12	10				8[1]	14		5			6			3				13				34
		2	4			7	11		9[1]		13	1		10				14■			5			6			3[3]		12		8[2]				35
		2				7					11	1	8[2]	10[1]					12		5■			6			3		9[3]	4		13	14		36
	2		4			7[3]	3		10[2]		11	1	8[1]						9		5			6					13		12	14			37
	2		4			7	3[2]				11[1]	1		10					13		5		12	6						8				9	38
	2		4			7	3				11	1	13	10[1]					14		5			6					12	8[3]				9[2]	39
	2		4			7[3]	11		9[2]			1							14		5		3	6					13	12	8[1]			10	40
	2		4			7	3				11[3]	1						12	9[2]		5		14	6					13	8				10[1]	41
	2[1]		4			7	3		13		11[3]	1				12			9		5			6						8[2]	14			10	42
	2		4			7	3				11[3]	1	8[1]						9		5		12	6					13	14				10[2]	43
	2		4			7	3				11[3]	1	8[1]						9[2]		5		14	6					13	12				10	44
	2		4			7	3				11[2]	1	8[1]						9		5			6			13		14	12[3]				10	45
	2		4			7[1]	3				13	1	8					11	14		5			6			12		9[2]					10[3]	46

FA Cup

Fourth Qualifying Round			
	Hendon	(h)	5-1
First Round	Northampton T	(h)	1-0
Second Round	Cheltenham T	(h)	2-4

Play-Offs

Semi-Final	Wrexham	(h)	2-0
		(a)	1-2
Final	York C		1-2
(at Wembley).			

MANSFIELD TOWN

Blue Square Premier

Ground: Field Mill Ground, Quarry Lane, Mansfield, Notts NG18 5DA. *Tel:* (01623) 482 482. *Fax:* (01623) 482 495.
Year Formed: 1897. *Record Gate:* 24,467 (1953 v Nottingham F, FA Cup 3rd rd). *Nickname:* The Stags.
Manager: Paul Cox. *Secretary:* Catherine Hannant. *Colours:* Yellow shirts, blue shorts, blue stockings.

MANSFIELD TOWN 2011–12 LEAGUE RECORD

Match No.	*Date*	*Venue*	*Opponents*	*Result*		*H/T Score*	*Lg Pos.*	*Goalscorers*	*Attendance*
1	Aug 13	H	Bath C	D	1-1	1-1	—	Connor ^{3}	3997
2	16	A	Gateshead	L	0-3	0-2	—		825
3	20	A	Braintree T	D	1-1	0-0	18	Briscoe ^{47}	875
4	23	H	Luton T	D	1-1	1-0	—	Green ^{26}	2592
5	27	H	Kettering T	W	3-0	1-0	14	Briscoe ^{11}, Green ^{51}, Dyer ^{64}	2051
6	29	A	Stockport Co	W	1-0	0-0	—	O'Neill ^{67}	3571
7	Sept 3	A	Darlington	W	2-0	2-0	4	Green 2 $^{5, 15}$	2647
8	10	H	Newport Co	W	5-0	2-0	3	Green ^{11}, Briscoe 2 $^{33, 72}$, Dyer ^{56}, O'Neill ^{75}	2324
9	17	A	Barrow	W	3-2	2-1	4	Green ^{4}, Futcher ^{29}, Meikle ^{81}	1244
10	20	H	AFC Telford U	D	1-1	0-0	—	Green ^{72}	2481
11	24	H	Kidderminster H	L	0-3	0-3	8		2522
12	27	A	Wrexham	W	3-1	1-0	—	Wright (og) ^{41}, Green (pen) ^{67}, Connor ^{90}	3478
13	Oct 1	A	Forest Green R	D	1-1	1-1	8	Dyer ^{1}	893
14	8	H	Grimsby T	W	2-1	0-1	6	O'Neill ^{72}, Connor ^{78}	2982
15	15	H	Southport	L	1-3	0-2	9	Connor ^{76}	2406
16	18	A	Lincoln C	D	1-1	0-0	—	Green ^{86}	2944
17	22	H	Alfreton T	W	3-2	0-2	8	Green (pen) ^{75}, Meikle ^{86}, Todd ^{90}	2982
18	Nov 5	H	Cambridge U	L	1-2	0-0	10	Green ^{55}	2046
19	19	A	AFC Telford U	D	0-0	0-0	9		2203
20	26	A	Bath C	D	1-1	1-1	9	Meikle ^{24}	816
21	29	H	Gateshead	D	1-1	1-0	—	Dyer ^{10}	1513
22	Dec 3	H	Braintree T	W	4-1	1-1	8	Dempster ^{24}, Green 2 $^{49, 67}$, Meikle ^{60}	1790
23	6	A	Grimsby T	D	0-0	0-0	—		2553
24	17	A	Southport	L	1-3	0-0	10	Dempster ^{48}	1006
25	26	H	York C	D	1-1	1-0	9	Green ^{11}	3551
26	Jan 1	A	York C	D	2-2	1-0	9	Green ^{14}, Verma ^{72}	4284
27	7	H	Forest Green R	W	1-0	0-0	9	Meikle ^{64}	2008
28	21	H	Hayes & Y	W	3-2	1-1	10	Dyer ^{38}, Green ^{67}, Hutchinson (pen) ^{90}	1872
29	25	A	Luton T	D	0-0	0-0	—		5261
30	28	A	Ebbsfleet U	W	3-0	2-0	9	Green ^{22}, Roberts 2 $^{38, 90}$	1085
31	Feb 18	A	Newport Co	L	0-1	0-1	9		1285
32	21	H	Darlington	W	5-2	2-1	—	Dempster ^{15}, Green 3 (1 pen) $^{44, 70, 75 (p)}$, Briscoe ^{86}	1697
33	25	H	Tamworth	W	2-1	0-0	7	Smith ^{76}, Green ^{87}	2221
34	Mar 3	H	Lincoln C	W	2-1	0-0	6	Dyer ^{47}, Roberts ^{58}	4830
35	6	A	Cambridge U	W	2-1	1-1	—	Dyer ^{10}, Briscoe ^{57}	1738
36	10	A	Tamworth	W	1-0	1-0	4	Green ^{13}	1600
37	13	H	Fleetwood T	D	1-1	0-0	—	Geohaghon ^{90}	3132
38	17	H	Barrow	W	7-0	4-0	3	Briscoe 3 $^{9, 17, 67}$, Howell ^{28}, Meikle ^{41}, Green ^{54}, Rhead ^{77}	2510
39	20	A	Alfreton T	W	6-3	4-3	—	Howell 2 $^{17, 43}$, Briscoe ^{31}, Green 2 $^{33, 90}$, Geohaghon ^{89}	3354
40	24	A	Fleetwood T	L	0-2	0-0	3		3106
41	31	H	Ebbsfleet U	W	1-0	0-0	3	Green ^{82}	2630
42	Apr 7	A	Kettering T	W	3-0	1-0	3	Meikle ^{14}, Green ^{63}, Rhead ^{86}	1818
43	9	H	Stockport Co	W	2-1	0-0	3	Smith ^{47}, Briscoe ^{53}	3883
44	14	A	Hayes & Y	W	3-1	1-1	3	Howell ^{5}, Dyer ^{67}, Green ^{71}	487
45	20	H	Wrexham	W	2-0	1-0	—	Howell ^{13}, Marriott ^{61}	3665
46	28	A	Kidderminster H	W	3-0	0-0	3	Stevenson ^{56}, Briscoe ^{78}, Green ^{87}	3565

Final League Position: 3

GOALSCORERS

League (87): Green 29 (3 pens), Briscoe 12, Dyer 8, Meikle 7, Howell 5, Connor 4, Dempster 3, O'Neill 3, Roberts 3, Geohaghon 2, Rhead 2, Smith 2, Futcher 1, Hutchinson 1 (1 pen), Marriott 1, Stevenson 1, Todd 1, Verma 1, own goal 1.
FA Cup (1): Dyer 1.
Play-Offs (1): Dyer 1.

Marriott 45	Bell 1	O'Neill 43	Worthington 8 + 9	Naylor 5	Riley 26 + 2	Briscoe 25 + 13	Todd 6 + 2	Connor 4 + 11	Green 44 + 1	Murray 39	Dyer 42 + 3	Meikle 33 + 9	Kendrick 15	Stevenson 6 + 1	Smith 8 + 4	Wood — + 1	Howell 28 + 5	Futcher 13	Sutton 39 + 2	Bolland 4 + 6	Freeman 9	Hegarty 2	Moult — + 1	Thompson 6 + 1	Verma 4 + 1	Rodney — + 2	Dempster 11 + 1	Kelly — + 1	Roberts 16 + 1	Hutchinson 5 + 7	Edwards 2 + 1	Rhead 2 + 13	Geohaghon 13	Andrew 1 + 4	Redmond 1	*Match No.*
1	2	3	4	5	6	7	8	9^{1}	10^{2}	11	12	13																								1
1		2	4^{1}	5■	6	7		9^{2}	10^{3}	11	12		3	8	13	14																				2
1		2			6	7		12	10	11	9^{1}	8	3				4	5																		3
1		2			6	7			10	11	9	8	3				4	5																		4
1		2	13		6^{2}	7		14	10	11^{3}	9^{1}	8	3				4	5	12																	5
1		2	13			7		12	10	11	9^{1}	8^{2}	3				4	5	6																	6
1		2	13			7^{2}		12	10	11	9	8^{1}	3				4	5	6																	7
1		2	13			7		14	10	11	9^{3}	8^{1}	3		12		4^{2}	5	6																	8
1		2	13			7^{2}		12	10	11	9^{1}	8^{3}	3				4	5	6	14																9
1		2				7			10	11	9	8^{1}	3		12		4	5	6																	10
1		2	12			7■			10	11	9	8^{2}	3				4^{1}	5	6	13																11
1		3	7^{1}	2■			8	13	10^{2}	11	9						4	5	6	12																12
1		2	7		5		9^{1}	13	10^{3}	8	11^{2}	14	3				4■		6	12																13
1		2	7	3			8	12	10	11	9	4^{1}						5	6																	14
1		2	4	3^{1}	12	7^{3}	8^{2}	13	10	11	9	14						5	6																	15
1		2			6	12	13	9	10	11	7^{1}	8^{2}	3						5	4																16
1		2			6		12	9	10	11	7	8	3^{1}						5	4																17
1		3							10	11	9	8					4	6	5		2	7^{1}	12													18
1		2						12	9	8	7	10					4		5		3	11^{1}		6												19
1		2				12			9^{2}		7	11					8		6	4^{1}	3^{3}			5	10	13	14									20
1						13			9	11	10	8		4^{2}					5	12	3			2	7^{1}		6									21
1						13			9	11	10^{2}	8^{1}		4^{3}					5	14	3			2	7	12	6									22
1						12			10	11	9	8		4^{1}					5	7	3			2			6									23
1		2				7			10	11	9	8^{1}					4		6■		3^{2}			12			5	13								24
1		2			6	12			10^{1}	11	9	8					4				3				7		5									25
1		2	14		6				10^{2}	11	9	8		13			4^{1}		5		3				12				7^{3}							26
1		2			13	7^{1}			10	11	9	8	3				12		6								5^{2}		4^{3}	14						27
1		2				13			10	7	9^{1}	4^{2}	3		11		14		5								6		8^{3}	12						28
1		2			6	13			10	7	9	12			11^{1}				5								4		8	3^{2}						29
1		3			6	12			10^{1}	8	9	13			11^{2}		14		2								5		4	7^{3}						30
1		3			6				10	8	7^{1}				11^{2}		13		2								5		4	9^{3}	12	14				31
1		2				12			10	8	11^{3}	13			7^{2}				6								5		4	9^{1}	3	14				32
1		3				7			10	11^{3}	9^{2}	8^{1}			13		14		6										4		2	12	5			33
1		3	13		6	7			10		9	12			11^{1}		8		2										4^{2}				5			34
1		2			6	7			10^{2}		9	8^{1}					11		3										4	13		12	5			35
1		2			6	7^{1}			10^{2}		9	8					11		3										4	13		12	5			36
1		2	7^{2}		6	12			10	11	9	8^{1}					4		3													13	5			37
1		3			6	7			10^{1}	11	9^{3}	8					4		2^{2}											14		12	5	13		38
1		2			6	7			10	11	9	8^{1}					4		3													12	5			39
1		2			6	12			10	11^{2}	9	8^{1}					4		3^{3}										7			14	5	13		40
1		2			6	7^{3}			10	8	9	14			11^{2}				3^{1}										4			13	5	12		41
1		2	14		6	7^{1}			10^{2}		9	8					11		3										4^{3}	13		12	5			42
1		2			6	7			10	8^{2}	14	12			11^{1}		4		3										13			9^{3}	5			43
1		2			6	13			10		9	11^{2}					8		3										4	7^{1}		12	5			44
1		2			6	7^{1}				8	9	10		11			4^{2}		3													12	5	13		45
		2^{1}	11		6	7^{2}	8		14					10					12					5					4	13		9		3^{3}	1	46

FA Cup
Fourth Qualifying Round

Fleetwood T	(h)	1-1
	(a)	0-5

Play-Offs
Semi-Final

York C	(a)	1-1
	(h)	0-1

NEWPORT COUNTY

Blue Square Premier

Ground: Newport Stadium, Stadium Way, Newport International Sports Village, Newport NP19 4PT (moving to Rodney Parade). *Tel:* (01633) 662 262. *Fax:* (01633) 666 107. *Year Formed:* 1912. *Record Gate:* 4,616 (at Newport Stadium 2006 v Swansea C). *Nickname:* The Ironsides. *Manager:* Justin Edinburgh. *Secretary:* Mike Everett. *Colours:* Red shirts, black shorts.

NEWPORT COUNTY 2011–12 LEAGUE RECORD

Match No.	Date	Venue	Opponents	Result		H/T Score	Lg Pos.	Goalscorers	Attendance
1	Aug 13	A	Kettering T	L	2-3	1-0	—	Buchanan [6], Rose, D [61]	2047
2	16	H	Hayes & Y	W	4-0	1-0	—	Rogers [14], Buchanan [53], Rose, D 2 [62, 66]	1519
3	20	H	Grimsby T	D	0-0	0-0	11		1675
4	23	A	Ebbsfleet U	D	1-1	1-0	—	Buchanan [4]	992
5	27	A	AFC Telford U	L	1-2	1-1	16	Rose, D [41]	2147
6	29	H	Kidderminster H	L	1-3	0-0	—	Foley [50]	1672
7	Sept 3	H	Cambridge U	L	0-1	0-1	20		1515
8	10	A	Mansfield T	L	0-5	0-2	21		2324
9	17	A	Braintree T	L	0-1	0-1	21		786
10	20	H	Stockport Co	D	1-1	1-0	—	Rose, D [31]	1205
11	24	H	Barrow	D	2-2	1-1	23	Jarvis [9], Rose, D [73]	1315
12	27	A	Forest Green R	D	1-1	1-0	—	Jarvis [38]	1203
13	Oct 1	A	Darlington	L	0-2	0-2	23		1785
14	8	H	Southport	L	0-3	0-3	23		1576
15	11	A	Fleetwood T	W	4-1	3-1	—	Foley 3 [15, 29, 59], Rose, D (pen) [23]	1277
16	15	H	Tamworth	L	1-2	0-0	22	Knights [74]	1310
17	18	H	Kettering T	W	3-1	1-1	—	Rose, D 3 (1 pen) [34 (p), 53, 61]	1249
18	22	A	Wrexham	D	0-0	0-0	22		4232
19	Nov 5	H	Ebbsfleet U	L	0-1	0-1	22		1412
20	19	A	Grimsby T	D	2-2	2-0	22	Hatswell [2], Jarvis [17]	2701
21	26	H	Luton T	L	0-1	0-0	22		1511
22	29	A	Hayes & Y	W	4-0	3-0	—	Rose, D [22], Foley [38], Yakubu 2 [45, 75]	303
23	Dec 3	H	Lincoln C	W	1-0	1-0	18	Yakubu [24]	1270
24	6	A	Alfreton T	L	2-3	1-2	—	Buchanan [4], Warren [60]	579
25	17	H	Fleetwood T	L	0-1	0-0	19		1011
26	Jan 3	A	Bath C	L	2-3	1-2	—	Jarvis [13], Warren [54]	1147
27	7	A	Luton T	L	0-2	0-1	20		6108
28	21	H	Forest Green R	D	0-0	0-0	20		1325
29	28	A	Gateshead	W	3-2	0-1	21	Buchanan [57], Foley [89], Harris [90]	704
30	Feb 11	A	Stockport Co	D	2-2	0-1	—	Sandell [50], Harris [87]	3565
31	14	H	Bath C	W	1-0	1-0	—	Minshull [12]	1130
32	18	H	Mansfield T	W	1-0	1-0	16	Foley [33]	1285
33	21	A	Tamworth	L	1-2	1-0	—	Foley (pen) [6]	815
34	Mar 3	A	Southport	D	1-1	1-1	17	Yakubu [40]	1105
35	6	H	Braintree T	L	3-4	2-3	—	Foley [29], Warren [44], Rose, R [90]	1101
36	20	A	Cambridge U	D	1-1	0-1	—	Sandell (pen) [86]	1815
37	24	A	Lincoln C	L	0-2	0-2	20		1951
38	31	H	Gateshead	W	1-0	1-0	20	Charles [12]	1261
39	Apr 3	H	York C	W	2-1	1-1	—	Jarvis [33], Rose, R [70]	1241
40	6	H	AFC Telford U	D	0-0	0-0	—		1540
41	9	A	Kidderminster H	L	2-3	2-0	19	Reid [1], Foley [37]	2275
42	14	A	York C	D	1-1	1-0	19	Jarvis [4]	2824
43	17	H	Darlington	D	0-0	0-0	—		1249
44	21	H	Alfreton T	W	1-0	1-0	17	Rose, R [38]	1239
45	24	H	Wrexham	L	0-1	0-1	—		1431
46	28	A	Barrow	L	1-3	1-1	19	Yakubu [15]	900

Final League Position: 19

GOALSCORERS

League (53): Rose, D 11 (2 pens), Foley 10 (1 pen), Jarvis 6, Buchanan 5, Yakubu 5, Rose, R 3, Warren 3, Harris 2, Sandell 2 (1 pen), Charles 1, Hatswell 1, Knights 1, Minshull 1, Reid 1, Rogers 1.
FA Cup (4): Foley 1, Jarvis 1, McAllister 1, Rodgers 1.

Potter 16	Robson 7	Baker 17 + 3	Miller 20 + 4	Yakubu 26	Doherty 18 + 1	Rose D 24	Rogers 7 + 7	Buchanan 26 + 10	Selino 1	Velez 3 + 1	McAllister 19 + 6	Foley 32 + 9	Rodgers 31 + 5	Jardim 3 + 4	Hughes 36 + 2	Gilligan 3 + 1	Warren 35	Thompson 22 + 1	Greening — + 1	Jarvis 20 + 11	Pipe 33 + 1	Knights 12 + 10	Hatswell 9 + 3	Matthews 6 + 3	Harris 1 + 8	Charles 13	Sandell 10	Minshull 17	Chapman 4 + 1	Reid 5 + 7	Rose R 5 + 7	Porter 13	Evans 3	Franks 1	Darlow 8	*Match No.*
1	2	3	4	5	6	7	8	9	10^{2}	11^{1}	12	13																								1
1		3	4	5	6	7	8^{3}	9		14	10^{2}	13	2	11^{1}	12																					2
1		3	4	5	6	7	8	9			10		2	11																						3
1		3	4	5	6^{1}	7	12	9^{3}			10	13	2	14	11	8^{2}																				4
1^{G}			4	6	8■	7	13■	9			10	12	2^{2}	11^{1}	3		5	15																		5
			4	6■		7		9^{1}		11^{2}	10	8	2	12	3		5■	1	13																	6
		12	4		6^{1}	7		9^{2}		11	10	8	2	13	3		5	1																		7
	2	3	4	6	8	7		9^{1}			10		11^{2}	13			5	1		12																8
	2^{3}		4		11	7	8	12			9^{1}	13	14		6		5	1		10	3^{2}															9
	2		4			7	8	14			9	10^{2}			3	12	5	1		11^{3}	6^{1}	13														10
	2	3	4			7	8				9	10					5	1		11	6															11
	2	3	4			7^{1}	8	14			12	10^{2}				6	5	1		9^{3}	11	13														12
	2		4			7	12	9^{2}			13	14	3			6^{3}	5	1		10	8	11^{1}														13
		3^{1}	4^{2}		8	7		11^{3}			9	13	2		12		5	1		10		14	6													14
			14		4	7	13	8			9^{1}	10^{3}	2		3		5	1		12		11^{2}	6													15
1					4	7					9	10^{1}	2		3		5			12	8	11	6													16
1			13		4^{1}	7	12				9	10	2^{2}		3		5			14	8^{3}	11	6													17
1			12		4	7					9	10	2		3		5			13	8^{1}	11^{2}	6													18
1			14	5	4^{3}	7					9^{2}	10	2		3					13	8^{1}	11	6	12												19
1			4	5	8^{2}		13	11^{1}			14	12	2		3					10^{3}	7		6	9												20
1				2	4	7		11^{1}			12	10	3		5						8		6	9												21
1			4	6	8^{3}	7		12			9^{1}	11^{2}	2		3		5				14	13		10												22
1			4	6		7		11^{1}			12	10^{2}	2		3		5				8	13		9												23
1			4	6		7		11				10	2				5				8		3	9												24
1			4^{2}	6	13	7		12			9		2		3		5				8	11		10^{1}												25
1			4^{1}	6^{3}	8			12			9^{2}		2		3		5			10	7	11		14	13											26
		14		6^{3}				7^{1}				8	2		3		5	1		10^{2}	4			12	13	9■	11									27
				6■				9^{2}				8	2		3		5	1		10	7^{1}	12			13		11	4								28
		3^{2}						9				8	2		6		5	1		10^{1}	7^{3}	14			13		11	4	12							29
		3^{1}						12				10	2		6^{2}		5	1		13	7				14	9^{3}	11■	4	8							30
		3						11^{1}				10	2		6		5	1			7				14	9^{2}		4	8^{3}	12	13					31
		3						9				10	12		4		5^{1}	1		8	2					11^{2}		6	7	13						32
		3		6^{2}			13	9^{3}				8			5			1		10^{1}	2				14	11		4	7	12						33
				6								10	2		3■		5	1		12	7					9^{1}	11	4			13	8^{2}				34
		3		6								10	2				5	1		9	7						11	4			12	8^{1}				35
								9^{1}					2		6		5^{2}	1		10		11^{3}	13		12		3			14	8	4	7			36
												10	2		6			1		12	7				9^{2}	11^{1}	3	8			13	4		5		37
								9				7			6		5			11	2					10^{1}	3	4			12	8			1	38
								9^{1}				7			6		5			11^{2}	2					10	3	4		13	12	8			1	39
				6				12				7			3		5			11^{1}	8	14				10^{3}		4		13	9^{2}	2			1	40
		3^{3}		6				14				10	13		5					12	2					7		4		9^{1}	11^{2}	8			1	41
		3^{3}		6				13				7	12		5					10^{2}	2	11^{1}	14					4		9		8			1	42
		3										7			6		5			10^{1}	2	11						4		9	12	8			1	43
				6								7			3		5			12	2	13				10^{2}		4		9	11^{1}	8			1	44
				6				10^{3}				7	13		3		5				2^{2}	12	14			11^{1}				9		8	4		1	45
		12		6				9				14	2		3		5^{1}	1				11^{3}						4		13	10^{2}	8	7			46

FA Cup

Fourth Qualifying Round	Braintree T	(h)	4-3
First Round	Shrewsbury T	(h)	0-1

SOUTHPORT

Blue Square Premier

Ground: Haig Avenue, Southport PR8 6JZ. *Tel:* (01704) 533 422. *Year Formed:* 1881.
Record Gate: 20,010 (1932 v Newcastle U). *Nickname:* The Sandgrounders. *Manager:* Liam Watson.
Secretary: Ken Hilton. *Colours:* Yellow and black shirts, black shorts.

SOUTHPORT 2011–12 LEAGUE RECORD

Match No.	*Date*	*Venue*	*Opponents*	*Result*		*H/T Score*	*Lg Pos.*	*Goalscorers*	*Attendance*
1	Aug 13	H	Lincoln C	D	2-2	1-1	—	Kissock [41], Whalley [51]	1687
2	16	A	Alfreton T	D	0-0	0-0	—		777
3	20	A	Luton T	L	1-5	1-1	19	Brown [8]	5681
4	23	H	Gateshead	L	1-3	1-1	—	Gray [15]	957
5	27	A	Kidderminster H	L	0-2	0-0	23		1763
6	29	H	Barrow	W	2-1	0-1	—	Gray [57], Lee [80]	1204
7	Sept 3	H	AFC Telford U	W	3-2	3-2	16	Whalley [14], Walker [17], Lee [20]	1123
8	10	A	Bath C	W	2-1	1-0	12	Walker [3], Gray [77]	663
9	17	A	Forest Green R	W	3-2	1-0	10	Davis [33], Grand [48], Whalley [73]	873
10	20	H	Wrexham	D	0-0	0-0	—		1710
11	24	H	Braintree T	L	0-4	0-2	11		938
12	27	A	Darlington	W	3-0	1-0	—	Grand [7], Lee [52], Gray [64]	637
13	Oct 1	H	Cambridge U	W	1-0	1-0	10	Owens [3]	1104
14	8	A	Newport Co	W	3-0	3-0	9	Grand [30], Ledsham [40], Gray [44]	1576
15	11	H	York C	D	1-1	0-0	—	Mukendi [81]	1107
16	15	A	Mansfield T	W	3-1	2-0	7	Todd (og) [25], Whalley [38], Gray [48]	2406
17	18	A	Gateshead	W	3-2	0-2	—	Whalley 2 [67, 75], Mukendi [89]	737
18	22	H	Tamworth	D	1-1	1-0	7	Gray [14]	1310
19	Nov 5	A	Kettering T	W	3-2	2-0	5	Grand [18], Gray 2 (1 pen) [24 (p), 88]	1368
20	19	H	Bath C	W	2-1	0-0	3	Gray 2 [87, 89]	1021
21	26	A	Stockport Co	W	1-0	0-0	3	Ledsham [74]	4540
22	29	H	Forest Green R	L	1-3	0-3	—	Owens [64]	978
23	Dec 3	H	Alfreton T	W	2-1	0-0	3	Guthrie [71], Gray [72]	1061
24	6	A	Wrexham	L	0-2	0-1	—		3256
25	17	H	Mansfield T	W	3-1	0-0	3	Lever 2 (1 pen) [50, 89 (p)], Brown [90]	1006
26	26	A	Fleetwood T	D	2-2	1-1	3	Gray 2 [13, 50]	3029
27	Jan 1	H	Fleetwood T	L	0-6	0-3	4		2589
28	5	A	Cambridge U	L	0-3	0-2	—		1840
29	21	H	Luton T	D	3-3	2-2	8	Gray [10], Mukendi [33], Pilkington, K (og) [59]	1665
30	24	A	Lincoln C	L	0-2	0-1	—		1615
31	28	A	Hayes & Y	W	2-0	1-0	6	Akrigg [22], Sheridan [67]	294
32	Feb 14	H	Darlington	W	2-0	1-0	—	Ledsham [8], Whalley [49]	847
33	17	H	Grimsby T	L	1-2	1-1	—	Elding (og) [28]	1934
34	25	A	Ebbsfleet U	W	2-1	1-1	4	Gray 2 (2 pens) [38, 89]	907
35	Mar 3	H	Newport Co	D	1-1	1-1	5	Ellison [18]	1105
36	10	A	AFC Telford U	W	1-0	0-0	5	Ledsham [50]	2025
37	13	H	Kettering T	D	0-0	0-0	—		753
38	17	H	Stockport Co	W	5-0	1-0	5	Gray 2 (1 pen) [41, 73 (p)], Piergianni (og) [64], Whalley 2 [70, 76]	1648
39	24	A	York C	W	2-1	0-0	4	Owens [64], Gray [69]	3465
40	27	A	Braintree T	D	0-0	0-0	—		637
41	31	H	Hayes & Y	L	1-2	0-1	5	Gray (pen) [59]	1147
42	Apr 7	H	Kidderminster H	L	1-2	1-1	6	Moogan [16]	1544
43	9	A	Barrow	D	2-2	1-1	6	Stephenson [33], Gray (pen) [90]	918
44	14	A	Tamworth	D	2-2	2-0	6	Whalley [11], Gray (pen) [23]	830
45	21	H	Ebbsfleet U	D	3-3	2-1	7	Owens [16], Ellison [22], Gray (pen) [59]	1231
46	28	A	Grimsby T	W	1-0	0-0	7	Stephenson [87]	3738

Final League Position: 7

GOALSCORERS

League (72): Gray 24 (8 pens), Whalley 10, Grand 4, Ledsham 4, Owens 4, Lee 3, Mukendi 3, Brown 2, Ellison 2, Lever 2 (1 pen), Stephenson 2, Walker 2, Akrigg 1, Davis 1, Guthrie 1, Kissock 1, Moogan 1, Sheridan 1, own goals 4.
FA Cup (2): Akrigg 1, Owens 1.

McMillan 43	Lee 17	Owens 37 + 2	Akrigg 40 + 3	Grand 42	Smith 37	Whalley 41	Ledsham 37 + 2	Kissock 4	Gray 44	Brown 11 + 9	Daly — + 6	Lever 23 + 8	Benjamin 7 + 18	Osborne 1 + 3	Davis 14 + 4	Moogan 26 + 1	Nemes 3	Walker 7 + 5	Poku 21 + 1	Ordish — + 2	Carden 2 + 19	Mukendi 11 + 2	Aley 2 + 1	Parry 20 + 4	Guthrie 2 + 3	Ellison 6 + 9	Sheridan 2 + 1	O'Keefe 5 + 2	Putterill — + 2	Stephenson 1 + 5	*Match No.*
1	2	3^{2}	4	5	6	7	8	9	10^{3}	11^{1}	12	13	14																		1
1	2		4	5	6	7	8	9	10^{1}		12	3	11																		2
1	2	13	4■	5	6	7	8	9^{1}	10^{3}	11^{2}		3	12	14																	3
1■	2			5	11^{1}	7	8^{2}	9	10^{3}	13		3	12	14	4	6															4
	2		12	5^{1}		7	8		10^{3}			3	11	9^{2}	4	6	1	13	14												5
	2	3	4			7^{2}			10^{1}	11^{3}		14	12		5	6	1	9	8	13											6
	2	3^{2}	4			7			10^{1}	11^{3}		13	14	12	5	6	1	9	8												7
1	2	3	4			7^{3}	13		10	11^{2}	12				5	8		9^{1}	6	14											8
1	2			5		7^{2}	8		10^{3}	13	12	3			6	4		9^{1}	11		14										9
1	2		12	5		7	13		10^{3}	11	14	3^{1}			6	8■		9^{2}	4												10
1	2	12	4	5	11	7	8		10^{2}	3^{1}	13				6			9^{3}				14									11
1	2	11	4	5	3	7	8		10	6^{2}								12			13	9^{1}									12
1	7	3	4	5	2	11^{3}	8		10							13		12	6^{2}		14	9^{1}									13
1	2	6	4	5	3	7^{1}	8		10^{2}	12								13	11		14	9^{3}									14
1		3	4	5	2■	7	11		10^{2}			12				8		9^{1}	6			13									15
1	2	3	4	5		7	11		10^{1}							8		12	6			9									16
1	2	3	4	5		7	11		10^{2}			12				8^{1}			6		13	9									17
1	2^{1}		4^{2}	5		7	11		10	12		3			13				6			9	8								18
1		3	4	5	2^{1}	7	11		10			12				8			6				9								19
1		3	4	5	2	7^{3}	11		10	9^{1}		12	8^{2}						6		14		13								20
1		9^{3}	4	5	2	7■	11		10^{1}	14		3				8			6^{2}		13			12							21
1		10	4	5	2^{1}		11■			7^{2}		3	13			8			6		14			12	9^{3}						22
1		11	4	5	2				10^{2}			3	13		14	8			6		7^{1}			12	9^{3}						23
1		7	4	5	2		11^{1}		10	9^{2}		3				8^{3}			6		13			14	12						24
1		11	4^{1}	5	2	7	10^{3}			14		3			12	8			6		9^{2}				13						25
1		6		5	2	7			10^{1}			3			4	9			8					11	12						26
1		9	4	3	2	7			10^{3}	12			14		5^{1}	8			6^{2}		13			11							27
1		9	12	5	2	7			10	13		3^{3}	14		6^{1}	8■			4					11^{2}							28
1		6	4	5	2	7	11		10			3^{1}	12									9^{2}		8		13					29
1		3	4	5	2	7^{1}	8		10^{3}	13			6								14	9^{2}		11		12					30
1		3	4	5	2	7^{1}	8		10^{3}				13								12	9		11		14	6^{2}				31
1		3	4	5	2	7	8		10^{3}				13								14	9^{1}		11		12	6^{2}				32
1		3	4	5	2	7	6		10							8^{1}						9^{2}		11		12	13				33
1		3	4	5	2	7	8		10				12			6^{1}					13			11		9^{2}					34
1		3	4	5	2	7	6		10															11		9^{1}		8	12		35
1		3	4	5	2	7^{1}	6		10^{2}				14								12			11		9^{3}		8	13■		36
1		3	4	5	2	7^{2}	8		10												13			11		9^{1}		6■		12	37
1		6	4	5	2	7^{2}	8		10^{3}			3	12								14			11		9^{1}				13	38
1		9	4	6	3		7		10^{1}			8	2		5						12			11							39
1		9	4	6	2		7		10			3	8		5									11							40
1		9	4	5	2	7^{1}	8		10			3	13											11				6^{2}		12	41
1		9^{2}	4	5	2	7	6		10			3	12			8^{1}								11		13					42
1			4^{1}	5	2	7	6		10			3	13		12	8										14		11^{3}		9^{2}	43
1		9	4	6	2	7	3^{2}		10			12			5^{1}	8								11		13					44
1		6	4	5	2	7			10			3^{3}				8					14			11^{2}		9^{1}		13		12	45
1		5	4		2	7^{2}	9		10^{1}			3	6^{3}			8								11		12		14		13	46

FA Cup

Fourth Qualifying Round	Stockport Co	(h)	1-0
First Round	Barnet	(h)	1-2

STOCKPORT COUNTY — Blue Square Premier

Ground: Edgeley Park, Hardcastle Road, Edgeley, Stockport, Cheshire SK3 9DD. *Tel:* (0161) 286 8888 (ext 257). *Fax:* (0161) 429 7392. *Year Formed:* 1883. *Record Gate:* 27,833 v Liverpool, FA Cup 5th rd, 11 February 1950. *Nickname:* 'County' or 'Hatters'. *Director of Football:* Jim Gannon. *Colours:* Reflex blue shirts with one broad white band, reflex blue shorts, white stockings.

STOCKPORT COUNTY 2011–12 LEAGUE RECORD

Match No.	Date	Venue	Opponents	Result		H/T Score	Lg Pos.	Goalscorers	Attendance
1	Aug 12	A	Forest Green R	D	1-1	0-1	—	Chadwick ^{78}	1848
2	16	H	Kettering T	W	1-0	0-0	—	Holden ^{60}	3429
3	20	H	Ebbsfleet U	D	1-1	0-0	8	Chadwick ^{68}	3674
4	23	A	Kidderminster H	D	1-1	1-0	—	Elliott ^{27}	1886
5	26	A	Lincoln C	D	1-1	1-1	—	Elliott ^{44}	2152
6	29	H	Mansfield T	L	0-1	0-0	—		3571
7	Sept 2	H	Luton T	D	1-1	0-1	—	McConville ^{90}	3389
8	10	A	AFC Telford U	D	1-1	0-0	16	German ^{51}	2375
9	17	H	Grimsby T	W	2-0	1-0	13	McConville ^{23}, Elliott ^{61}	3943
10	20	A	Newport Co	D	1-1	0-1	—	Elliott ^{82}	1205
11	24	A	Tamworth	D	1-1	0-0	14	Chadwick ^{48}	1381
12	27	H	Fleetwood T	L	2-4	1-1	—	German 2 $^{30, 71}$	3023
13	Oct 1	H	York C	L	1-2	0-0	17	Paton ^{90}	3753
14	6	A	Cambridge U	D	2-2	1-1	—	Chadwick ^{3}, Whitehead ^{63}	2047
15	11	H	Darlington	L	3-4	2-2	—	Chadwick ^{3}, Paton 2 $^{12, 52}$	2671
16	15	A	Wrexham	L	0-4	0-2	20		3874
17	18	A	Bath C	W	2-0	0-0	—	Chadwick ^{63}, Paton ^{90}	919
18	22	H	Forest Green R	L	0-1	0-1	18		3391
19	Nov 5	H	Hayes & Y	D	3-3	2-1	17	Elliott ^{27}, Piergianni 2 $^{30, 57}$	2804
20	12	A	Ebbsfleet U	L	1-2	1-0	—	Chadwick (pen) ^{21}	1119
21	19	A	Fleetwood T	L	1-2	0-0	18	McConville (pen) ^{59}	3021
22	26	H	Southport	L	0-1	0-0	20		4540
23	29	A	Grimsby T	L	0-7	0-5	—		2254
24	Dec 6	H	Gateshead	L	0-1	0-0	—		2366
25	17	H	Alfreton T	D	0-0	0-0	22		2802
26	26	A	Barrow	L	0-1	0-1	23		2103
27	Jan 1	H	Barrow	W	3-2	2-0	19	Sheridan 2 (1 pen) $^{10, 84 (p)}$, Connor ^{32}	3301
28	7	A	Gateshead	L	0-2	0-0	19		846
29	10	A	Luton T	L	0-1	0-0	—		5588
30	21	A	Braintree T	D	2-2	0-0	19	Connor ^{67}, Rowe, Danny L ^{90}	833
31	24	H	AFC Telford U	D	2-2	0-2	—	O'Donnell ^{67}, Piergianni ^{82}	2831
32	28	H	Kidderminster H	W	2-1	1-0	19	McConville ^{21}, Rowe, Danny L ^{55}	3728
33	Feb 11	H	Newport Co	D	2-2	1-0	—	Rowe, Danny M 2 $^{8, 60}$	3565
34	18	A	York C	L	1-2	0-0	19	Rowe, Danny L ^{52}	3370
35	25	H	Wrexham	W	1-0	1-0	19	Mayebi (og) ^{27}	4518
36	Mar 3	A	Darlington	W	1-0	0-0	16	Rowe, Danny L (pen) ^{60}	2202
37	6	A	Alfreton T	L	1-6	0-3	—	Rose ^{90}	1115
38	10	H	Cambridge U	L	0-1	0-1	16		5957
39	17	A	Southport	L	0-5	0-1	18		1648
40	24	H	Bath C	W	4-0	1-0	17	Hattersley ^{14}, Elliott 2 $^{55, 82}$, Piergianni ^{61}	3744
41	31	A	Kettering T	W	3-1	2-0	19	Hattersley ^{29}, Newton ^{45}, Darkwah ^{90}	1281
42	Apr 7	H	Lincoln C	W	4-0	2-0	17	Hattersley ^{6}, Rowe, Danny L 2 $^{11, 55}$, Darkwah ^{90}	3975
43	9	A	Mansfield T	L	1-2	0-0	18	Rose ^{89}	3883
44	14	H	Braintree T	D	1-1	1-0	18	Hattersley ^{15}	3199
45	21	H	Tamworth	W	2-0	0-0	16	O'Donnell ^{48}, Hattersley ^{77}	6393
46	28	A	Hayes & Y	W	2-1	1-1	16	Hattersley ^{7}, Connor ^{70}	654

Final League Position: 16

GOALSCORERS

League (58): Chadwick 7 (1 pen), Elliott 7, Hattersley 6, Rowe, Danny L 6 (1 pen), McConville 4 (1 pen), Paton 4, Piergianni 4, Connor 3, German 3, Darkwah 2, O'Donnell 2, Rose 2, Rowe, Danny M 2, Sheridan 2 (1 pen), Holden 1, Newton 1, Whitehead 1, own goal 1.
FA Cup (0).

Glennon 24	McCann 11 + 8	Holden 29 + 4	Sheridan 24 + 3	Bounab 10 + 1	Hall 1	Routledge 12 + 2 / King 5	Miles 11 + 3	Gritton 6 + 5 / Newton 7	Chadwick 17 + 2	Fraughan 6 + 3 / Brownhill — + 2	Elliott 33 + 9	Piergianni 39 + 2	O'Donnell 32 + 2	Chamberlain — + 5	Parker — + 1	Halls 29 + 1	Rowe Danny M 17 + 9	McConville 21 + 2	Nolan 18 + 13	Blackburn 12 + 3	German 10 + 6	Paton 15	Whitehead 4 + 13	Edwards 11	Lynch 5 + 1	Darkwah — + 7	Halstead 4	Cole 7 + 9	Say — + 1	Connor 19 + 2	Rowe Danny L 11 + 4	Ormson 13	Mainwaring 15	Turnbull 14	Rose 6 + 4	Hattersley 8	Hirmer — + 1	*Match No.*
1	2	3	4	5	6	7	8^{2}	9^{1}	10	11	12	13																										1
1	2	3	4	5^{1}		7	8^{2}		10	11^{3}	9	6	12	13	14																							2
1		3	4			7		9^{2}	10	11	13	6	5	12		2	8^{1}																					3
1	2	3	4	14		7	8^{2}		10^{1}		9	6	5	12			13	11^{3}																				4
1	12	3	4	2^{1}		7	8^{2}		10^{3}		9	6	5	13				11	14																			5
1	2	3	4^{3}				14	9^{1}	12		10	6	5	13			7^{2}	11	8																			6
1	4^{3}	3^{2}				7			10^{1}	13	12	6	5				8	11	14	2	9																	7
1		3	4^{2}						10^{1}		12	6	5			2		11	13	7	9	8																8
1	12						14		13		10	6	5			2	3	11^{3}	8	7	9^{2}	4^{1}																9
1	12	13									10	3	5			2^{1}	6	11	8	7	9^{2}	4																10
1	2	3	4						10		9^{1}	6	5				13	11^{2}	14	7	12	8^{3}																11
1	2	3	13				12		10			6	5				4^{1}		8	7^{2}	9	11^{3}	14															12
1		3	13	5			11^{1}		10^{3}		14	6							8	7^{2}	9	4	12	2														13
1	14		4	2			7^{3}		10^{2}		9	6■	5						8	13		11^{1}	12	3														14
1	14	3	4^{3}	6^{1}			11		10		9^{2}		5						8	12	13	7		2														15
1			4^{2}			12	7^{1}		10^{3}		14	3	5						8	6	9	11	13	2														16
1	4					7	11^{1}		10			6	5						8^{2}	13	14	9^{3}	12	3	2													17
1	7					4	11^{1}		10	14		6	5						8		12	9^{3}	13	2	3^{2}													18
1	13					4	11^{2}		10		9^{1}	6	5						8			7		3	2	12												19
	8	3		5		4			10^{3}		9	6				12	11^{1}		13		14	7^{2}		2			1											20
		3	8^{1}	6		4					10		5				12	11			9	7			2		1											21
		3		6		13		14			10		5			2^{3}		11	8^{2}	4	9	7^{1}					1	12										22
	8	3^{1}		6				10^{2}			13		5			2	11			4	9^{3}		14		12		1	7										23
1		3				4				14	10		5			6	8	11^{2}		7^{3}	12				2^{1}			9	13									24
1		3^{1}	13								10	6	5			2	9	11		7^{2}				8		12				4								25
1		3	7^{3}					14		10	9	6	5^{1}			2	12	11^{2}						8				13		4								26
1	12	2	8					13		7^{2}	10	6	5			3^{1}								9				11		4								27
1	12	3^{2}	8					9		11	14	6^{1}	5			2	13											7		4	10^{3}							28
		3	8					9^{3}			14	6	5			2	10		12				11^{1}					7^{2}		4	13	1						29
		3	8^{2}								10	6	5			2^{3}	9	13	14									7^{1}		4	12	1	11					30
		3^{1}									10^{3}	6	5			2^{2}	9	7					14					13		4	12	1	11	8				31
		2						12			10^{1}	6	5			3		9^{3}	13									14		4	7	1	11^{2}	8				32
		3									10	6^{1}	5			2^{2}	7	9	12									13		4	14	1	11^{3}	8				33
		3									10	12	5^{1}			2		7	6				14					13		4^{3}	9	1	11^{2}	8				34
		12									10	5				2	4^{1}	7^{2}	8				14					13			9^{3}	1	11	6	3			35
		12									10	5				2	9^{1}	7^{2}	4				13							14	6^{3}	1	11	8	3			36
		3						14			10^{3}	6				2^{1}		7	4									12		13	9	1	11^{2}	8	5			37
		14									10^{2}	6				2	3^{1}	12					13					7		4	9	1	11	8^{3}	5			38
			6^{1}									5				3^{2}		7	12							13				4	9	1■	11	8	2	10^{6}	15	39
						1		3			10^{3}	5				2	13		12				14							4	9		11	8	6^{1}	7^{2}		40
			6			1		3			10	5				2	13									12				4	9^{2}		11	8		7^{1}		41
			6^{1}			1		3			10^{3}	5				2			12							13				4	11		7	8	14	9^{2}		42
			6^{2}			1		3			10	5				2	12		11							13				4			7^{1}	8	14	9^{3}		43
			6			1		3		14	9	5	12			2							11^{2}					13		4			7	8^{1}		10^{3}		44
		8^{2}	7					3^{1}		13	9	6	5			2			12				11							4		1			14	10^{3}		45
			7					3			10^{3}	6	5			2	12		8				11^{1}			13				4		1			14	9^{2}		46

FA Cup
Fourth Qualifying Round
Southport (a) 0-1

TAMWORTH

Blue Square Premier

Ground: The Lamb Ground, Kettlebrook, Tamworth B77 1AA. *Tel:* (01827) 65798. *Fax:* (01827) 62236.
Year Formed: 1933. *Record Gate:* 4,920 (1948 v Atherstone T). *Nickname:* The Lambs. *Manager:* Marcus Law.
Secretary: Rod Hadley. *Colours:* Red shirts with white trim, white shorts, red stockings.

TAMWORTH 2011–12 LEAGUE RECORD

Match No.	*Date*	*Venue*	*Opponents*	*Result*		*H/T Score*	*Lg Pos.*	*Goalscorers*	*Attendance*
1	Aug 13	A	Barrow	D	1-1	1-0	—	Christie (pen)[31]	1371
2	16	H	Ebbsfleet U	W	1-0	0-0	—	Bradley[71]	921
3	20	H	Darlington	W	1-0	0-0	4	Christie (pen)[83]	977
4	23	A	Wrexham	L	0-3	0-1	—		3353
5	27	A	Bath C	W	2-0	1-0	5	Thomas[31], Shariff[90]	656
6	29	H	AFC Telford U	D	2-2	1-0	—	St Aimie 2[41, 67]	1316
7	Sept 4	A	Hayes & Y	L	0-1	0-0	7		359
8	10	H	York C	W	2-1	0-0	5	St Aimie (pen)[53], Christie (pen)[73]	1012
9	17	A	Kettering T	W	2-0	1-0	6	Thomas[30], Christie[80]	1955
10	20	H	Forest Green R	L	0-1	0-1	—		783
11	24	H	Stockport Co	D	1-1	0-0	10	Christie[90]	1381
12	27	A	Braintree T	L	1-3	1-1	—	McDonald[30]	840
13	Oct 1	A	Gateshead	D	1-1	0-1	11	Christie (pen)[77]	770
14	8	H	Lincoln C	W	4-0	1-0	11	St Aimie 2[12, 87], Christie (pen)[61], Francis[64]	1232
15	15	A	Newport Co	W	2-1	0-0	10	St Aimie[47], Christie[59]	1310
16	18	H	Hayes & Y	W	2-1	0-1	—	St Aimie[83], Patterson[90]	742
17	22	A	Southport	D	1-1	0-1	10	Christie (pen)[50]	1310
18	Nov 5	A	Kidderminster H	L	0-2	0-2	11		1797
19	18	H	Kettering T	D	2-2	1-2	—	Patterson (pen)[41], Mills[55]	1197
20	26	A	Darlington	L	0-2	0-0	13		1752
21	29	H	Braintree T	W	1-0	0-0	—	Mills[56]	742
22	Dec 6	A	Forest Green R	L	1-3	1-2	—	Shariff[19]	732
23	17	H	Luton T	L	1-3	0-1	14	Mills[76]	1467
24	26	A	Alfreton T	L	2-5	0-3	15	McDonald[78], Tait[86]	1012
25	Jan 1	H	Alfreton T	D	2-2	1-1	15	Courtney[17], Christie[49]	1241
26	14	H	Wrexham	L	1-2	0-2	—	Wilson[54]	1923
27	21	H	Barrow	L	2-3	1-1	15	Patterson 2[7, 49]	1222
28	24	A	Ebbsfleet U	L	0-3	0-0	—		746
29	28	A	Cambridge U	W	1-0	0-0	15	McDonald[50]	2281
30	Feb 4	A	Fleetwood T	D	2-2	2-1	—	Patterson[9], Barrow[40]	1911
31	18	A	Luton T	L	0-3	0-1	15		5833
32	21	H	Newport Co	W	2-1	0-1	—	Barrow[83], Thomas[85]	815
33	25	A	Mansfield T	L	1-2	0-0	14	Marna[54]	2221
34	Mar 3	H	Fleetwood T	L	0-3	0-1	15		958
35	6	A	York C	D	0-0	0-0	—		2249
36	10	H	Mansfield T	L	0-1	0-1	15		1600
37	17	A	Grimsby T	D	0-0	0-0	15		3206
38	20	H	Kidderminster H	D	0-0	0-0	—		924
39	24	H	Gateshead	D	1-1	1-1	15	Marna (pen)[44]	968
40	27	H	Grimsby T	D	1-1	0-0	—	Taylor[67]	892
41	31	A	Lincoln C	L	0-4	0-2	16		2213
42	Apr 6	H	Bath C	L	0-1	0-0	—		957
43	14	H	Southport	D	2-2	0-2	16	Christie[53], Gudger[63]	830
44	17	A	AFC Telford U	L	0-1	0-0	—		3477
45	21	A	Stockport Co	L	0-2	0-0	18		6393
46	28	H	Cambridge U	D	2-2	1-1	18	Marna 2[16, 54]	1137

Final League Position: 18

GOALSCORERS

League (47): Christie 11 (6 pens), St Aimie 7 (1 pen), Patterson 5 (1 pen), Marna 4 (1 pen), McDonald 3, Mills 3, Thomas 3, Barrow 2, Shariff 2, Bradley 1, Courtney 1, Francis 1, Gudger 1, Tait 1, Taylor 1, Wilson 1.
FA Cup (7): Patterson 3, St Aimie 2, Christie 1 (pen), Francis 1.

Hedge 43	Tait 40 + 1	Barrow 26 + 4	McDonald 21 + 9	Green 40	Kanyuka 11	Smith 15 + 1	Cain 12 + 4	Christie 22 + 11	Patterson 26 + 14	Thomas 24 + 13	St Aimie 18 + 12	Shariff 13 + 11	Bradley 15 + 2	Mills 9 + 11	Francis 35 + 1	Reynolds 2 + 1	Habergham 28 + 2	Valentim — + 1	Lake-Gaskin 1	Courtney 18 + 1	Farah 1 + 2	Gudger 6 + 5	Collister 3	Wilson 3	McKoy 14	Oji 12	Isaac 8 + 1	Hubbins 1	Headley — + 1	Marna 10 + 1	Reece 4 + 3	Taylor 6 + 2	Nix 9 + 2	Baldock 3	Collins 6	Grayson 1 + 3	Healy — + 1	*Match No.*
1	2	3	4^3	5	6	7	8	9^1	10^2	11	12	13	14																									1
1	2	3		5	6	7	8	9^1	10^3	11^2	14	12	4	13																								2
1	2	3	4	5		14	8^3	12	10	13		11^1	7	9^2	6																							3
1	2	3	13			7		9^2	10	11^1	12	14	6	8^3	5	4																						4
1	2	3		5		7	12	9^3	8^2	11	14	13	4	10^1	6																							5
1	2	3	4	5		7^2	8		12	11^1	10	9^3	13	14	6																							6
1	2			5		7	8^2	9^1	12	11^3	10	13	4	14	6		3																					7
1	2			5		7	14	13	11^1	12	10	9^3	4	8^2	6		3																					8
1	2		14	5		7	13	12		11^3	10	9^1	6	8^2	4		3																					9
1	2			5		7	8^1	13		11	10	12	4	9^2	6^3		3	14																				10
1	2			5		7	8^3	12	13	11	10^1	9^2	4	14	6		3																					11
1	2		8	5		7		9	10^3	11^1	14	12	4^2	13	6		3																					12
1	2			6		7	8	10			12	11	4	9^1	5		3																					13
1	2	12	7	6			8^2	9^1			10	11	4	13	5		3																					14
1	2			6			8	9			10	7	4		5		3		11																			15
1	2	11^1		4	6	7	8^3	9	14	12	10				5^2		3			13																		16
1	2^1			8	6	7^2	12	9	13	11^3	10			14	5		3			4																		17
1	12		14	5	2	4^3	8	9	7^2	11	10^1	13			6		3																					18
1	2	3^3	7	5				13	8^1	11	12	10^2	4	9	6		14																					19
1	2		8^3	5	6			9^2	13	11	10	7^1	4	12			3				14																	20
1	7		13	4^2	6			14	10^3	11	12			8	5		3			2	9^1																	21
1	2	11^2	4^3	8	6				9	13	10	7^1		12	5		3				14																	22
1	2	8		7■	6			14	9^2	11^1	10^3			13	5■	12	3			4																		23
1	2	7	4		6				9^2	11^3	10	13		12		8^1	3			5		14																24
	2	11			6			9				10			5		3			4		7	1	8														25
	2			8				9	10^2	11^1		13			5^3					4		12	1	7	3	6	14											26
	2■		6^1	3				9^3	10	13		14								4		12	1	7^2	8	5	11											27
1			11	7					10^2	12		9			5					6		8			4		2	3^1	13									28
1		3	9	6					10						5					2		11			4	8	7											29
1		3	6					13	10						5					2		12			4	8■	7			9^1	11^2							30
1	2	3	6^2	4				14	9	13	12				5										8		7			10^3	11^1							31
1	2	3	6	5				11	14	13	9^2									4					8		7^1			10^3	12							32
1	2	3	7^1	6				9	10^3	12	14									5					4		11			8^2	13							33
1	2		4	6					7^2		13				14		3			5^3					8		11^1			10		9	12					34
1	2	12		6					13	11	10^2				5		3^1								4						7	9	8					35
1	2	13	14	6					12	11	10^1				5		3								4						7^2	9	8^3					36
1	2	11^1		6					10	12					5		3			4					7	8						9						37
1	2	11		8					9	13	14				5^1		3^2			4					7	6				10^3	12							38
1	2	7^3	13	6					12	11					5		3													10			8	4^2	9^1	14		39
1	2	7^2	13						14	11^1					5		3									6				10^3		12	8	4	9			40
1	2	4	12						13	11					5		3									6						9^2	8	7^1	10^3	14		41
1	2	9	13	5				12	14	11							3^1								4^2	6				10			8		7^3			42
1	2^2	3^3	4	5				9	10								14					11				6				12			8		7^1	13		43
1		14	7	5				9	10^3	13							3			2		11^2				6						12	8			4^1		44
1		3	4	8				9	7^2	12					5					2		11^1				6^3						10	14				13	45
1	2	11	6	3				9	12						5					4		13								10			8^1		7^2			46

FA Cup

Fourth Qualifying Round			
	King's Lynn	(h)	2-1
First Round	Hinckley U	(a)	2-2
		(h)	1-0
Second Round	Gateshead	(a)	2-1
Third Round	Everton	(a)	0-2

WREXHAM

Blue Square Premier

Ground: Racecourse Ground, Mold Road, Wrexham LL11 2AH. *Tel:* (01978) 262 129. *Fax:* (01978) 357 821.
Year Formed: 1872. *Record Gate:* 34,445 (1957 v Manchester U, FA Cup 4th rd). *Nickname:* Red Dragons.
Manager: Andy Morrell. *Secretary:* Geraint Parry. *Colours:* Red shirts, white shorts, red stockings.

WREXHAM 2011–12 LEAGUE RECORD

Match No.	*Date*	*Venue*	*Opponents*	*Result*		*H/T Score*	*Lg Pos.*	*Goalscorers*	*Attendance*
1	Aug 13	H	Cambridge U	D	1-1	1-0	—	Morrell [17]	4206
2	16	A	Bath C	W	2-0	0-0	—	Morrell 2 [78, 79]	1075
3	19	A	Lincoln C	W	2-1	1-1	—	Tolley [29], Harris [56]	2211
4	23	H	Tamworth	W	3-0	1-0	—	Reynolds (og) [18], Tolley [78], Cieslewicz [82]	3353
5	27	A	Alfreton T	W	4-1	2-1	1	Speight 3 (1 pen) [13, 32, 57 (p)], Pogba [90]	1165
6	29	H	Fleetwood T	W	2-0	1-0	—	Speight [2], Morrell [59]	4283
7	Sept 3	H	Kidderminster H	W	2-0	1-0	1	Tolley [24], Wright, D [48]	4102
8	10	A	Barrow	L	1-3	1-0	1	Speight [40]	1463
9	17	H	York C	L	0-3	0-3	3		3872
10	20	A	Southport	D	0-0	0-0	—		1710
11	24	A	Grimsby T	W	3-1	1-1	1	Pogba [16], Harris [62], Fowler [68]	3515
12	27	H	Mansfield T	L	1-3	0-1	—	Fowler [64]	3478
13	Oct 1	H	Ebbsfleet U	W	1-0	0-0	3	Speight (pen) [78]	2849
14	4	A	Gateshead	W	4-1	1-0	—	Wright, D [4], Clarke [49], Moyes (og) [59], Keates (pen) [78]	1258
15	9	A	Hayes & Y	W	2-0	0-0	1	Knight-Percival [59], Pogba [61]	625
16	15	H	Stockport Co	W	4-0	2-0	1	Knight-Percival 2 [3, 46], Morrell [23], Speight [75]	3874
17	18	A	Luton T	W	1-0	0-0	—	Pogba [73]	7270
18	22	H	Newport Co	D	0-0	0-0	1		4232
19	Nov 5	A	York C	D	0-0	0-0	1		4295
20	19	H	Lincoln C	W	2-0	1-0	1	Pogba 2 (1 pen) [11, 61 (p)]	3424
21	26	A	Braintree T	D	0-0	0-0	1		957
22	30	H	Darlington	W	2-1	0-1	—	Cieslewicz [78], Speight [81]	3171
23	Dec 6	H	Southport	W	2-0	1-0	—	Speight (pen) [44], Cieslewicz [78]	3256
24	17	H	Gateshead	W	2-1	2-1	1	Pogba [3], Wright, D [35]	3161
25	26	A	AFC Telford U	W	2-0	1-0	1	Clarke [13], Speight [67]	4591
26	Jan 1	H	AFC Telford U	W	4-0	2-0	1	Killock (og) [34], Creighton [35], Speight [74], Cieslewicz [86]	5812
27	14	A	Tamworth	W	2-1	2-0	—	Tolley [5], Speight [29]	1923
28	21	H	Kettering T	W	4-1	1-0	1	Morrell [5], Creighton [53], Colbeck 2 [77, 90]	4066
29	24	A	Forest Green R	L	0-1	0-0	—		1109
30	28	H	Bath C	W	2-0	1-0	2	Obeng [13], Speight (pen) [48]	3583
31	Feb 18	H	Hayes & Y	W	4-1	2-0	2	Speight [16], Creighton [44], Harris [58], Pogba [74]	3845
32	21	A	Kidderminster H	W	1-0	1-0	—	Morrell [45]	2492
33	25	A	Stockport Co	L	0-1	0-1	2		4518
34	Mar 3	A	Kettering T	W	1-0	1-0	2	Tolley [24]	1377
35	7	H	Luton T	W	2-0	2-0	—	Wright, D [6], Keates [39]	4206
36	10	H	Barrow	W	2-0	1-0	2	Wright, D [34], Speight [52]	3432
37	13	A	Ebbsfleet U	W	5-0	2-0	—	Pogba [27], Morrell 2 [44, 68], Leslie [57], Speight (pen) [78]	990
38	24	H	Forest Green R	L	1-2	1-0	2	Speight (pen) [20]	4451
39	27	A	Darlington	W	4-2	1-0	—	Speight 2 (1 pen) [44, 90 (p)], Knight-Percival [65], Pogba [86]	1401
40	31	A	Cambridge U	D	1-1	0-0	2	Ogleby [90]	3014
41	Apr 6	H	Alfreton T	L	0-1	0-1	—		4673
42	10	A	Fleetwood T	D	1-1	0-0	—	Speight [53]	4994
43	14	H	Grimsby T	D	2-2	1-0	2	Speight [23], Westwood [72]	2917
44	20	A	Mansfield T	L	0-2	0-1	—		3665
45	24	A	Newport Co	W	1-0	1-0	—	Cieslewicz [10]	1431
46	28	H	Braintree T	W	5-1	2-0	2	Morrell [19], Cieslewicz [42], Pogba [59], Wright, D [88], Ashton (pen) [90]	3303

Final League Position: 2

GOALSCORERS

League (85): Speight 21 (7 pens), Pogba 11 (1 pen), Morrell 10, Cieslewicz 6, Wright, D. 6, Tolley 5, Knight-Percival 4, Creighton 3, Harris 3, Clarke 2, Colbeck 2, Fowler 2, Keates 2 (1 pen), Ashton 1 (1 pen), Leslie 1, Obeng 1, Ogleby 1, Westwood 1, own goals 3.
FA Cup (9): Morrell 3, Cieslewicz 1, Knight-Percival 1, Pogba 1, Tolley 1, Wright, D. 1, own goal 1.
Play-Offs (2): Cieslewicz 1, Morrell 1.

Maxwell 10	Obeng 29	Ashton 43	Creighton 38 + 1	Knight-Percival 43	Harris 38	Tolley 29 + 5	Fowler 14 + 3	Wright D 26 + 6	Speight 33 + 5	Morrell 31 + 10	Cieslewicz 18 + 26	Pogba 27 + 10	Tomassen — + 2	Clarke 19 + 8	Taylor — + 1	Mayebi 36	Keates 23 + 5	Westwood 12 + 2	Little 3 + 14	Anoruo — + 3	Hunt 4 + 9	Moss — + 1	Colbeck 1 + 3	Alfei 5	Leslie 10 + 3	Wright S 10 + 1	Ogleby 2 + 4	Clowes 1	Walker 1	Evans — + 1	Match No.
1	2^{3}	3	4	5	6	7	8	9^{2}	10	11^{1}	12	13	14																		1
1	2	3	4	5	6	7	8	9^{2}	10^{1}	11	13	12																			2
1	2	3	4	5	6	7	8	9	10^{1}	11	12																				3
1	2	3	4	5	6	7	8^{2}	9	10^{1}	11^{3}	12		13	14																	4
1	2	3	4	5	6	7	8	9^{2}	10^{3}	11^{1}	12	13			14																5
1	2	3	4	5	6	7	8	9^{2}	10	11^{1}	12	13																			6
	2	3	4	5	6	7	8	9^{3}	10^{2}	11^{1}	12	14				1	13														7
	2	3^{2}		5	6	7^{3}	8	9■	10	11^{1}	12					1	13	4	14												8
	2^{1}	3	12	5	6	7^{3}	8		10	11^{2}	14	9				1	13	4													9
1	2■	3	4	5	6^{2}		8		10	11^{3}	12	9^{1}					7		13	14											10
1		3	4	5	6		8		10^{1}	12	11	9					7	2													11
1	2	3^{3}	4	5■	6	13	8	9	10^{2}	14	12	11^{1}					7														12
	2	3	4		6	8		10^{1}	11	9^{2}	13	12		14		1	7	5^{3}													13
	2	3	4	5	6^{1}			10^{2}		9^{3}	11	13		8		1	7		14		12										14
	2	3	4	5		6		10^{1}	13	9^{2}	7	12		11^{3}		1	8				14										15
	2	3	4	5	6^{2}	7		13	12	9^{1}	11	10^{3}		14		1	8														16
	2	3	4	5	6	8			10^{1}	12	11	9				1	7														17
	2	3	4	5	6	8^{1}		13	10^{3}	14	11	9^{2}		12		1	7														18
	2	3	4	5	6	8^{2}	13	12		9^{1}	7^{3}	10		11		1					14										19
	2	3	4	5	6^{2}	7	13	9	12	10^{1}		11		8		1															20
	2	3	4	5	6	7^{2}	13	9	12	10^{3}	14	11^{1}		8		1															21
	2	3	4		6			9	13	10^{2}	7^{3}			8^{1}		1		5	12		11	14									22
	2	3	4	5	6	7^{2}	8	9	10^{1}	13	12	11				1															23
	2	3	4	5	6	12	8^{1}	9	10^{2}		13	11		7		1															24
	2	3	4	5	6^{1}	7		9^{3}	10^{2}		13	11		8		1	12		14												25
	2	3	4	5	6	8			10^{1}		7	11		9		1			12												26
	2	3	4	5	6^{2}	8		12	10^{1}	9^{3}	7			11		1	13		14												27
	2	3	4	5	6^{2}					9^{3}	7			11^{1}		1	8		10	14	12		13								28
	2	3	4	5	6					9	7	10^{1}		11^{2}		1	8		12^{3}		13		14								29
	2	3	4	5	6	7			10^{3}	9	11^{1}					1	8^{2}			14	12		13								30
		3	4	5	6				10	9^{1}	11	12		8		1					13			2	7^{2}						31
		3	4^{3}	5	6				10	9^{2}	11^{1}	12		8		1		14			13			2	7						32
		3		5	6■			13	10^{2}	9^{1}	14	11		7		1		4	12					2	8^{3}						33
		3		5		7		9^{3}	10^{1}	13	12	11		4		1		6	14						8^{2}	2					34
		3		5	6	7		9	10^{1}	13	12	11^{2}				1	8	4								2					35
		3		6		7^{1}		9■	10^{2}	14	13	11^{3}		12		1	4	5							8	2					36
		3		6		7			10^{3}	9^{1}	12	11		13		1	4	5							8^{2}	2	14				37
		3	4	5	6^{1}				10^{2}	9	13	11		12		1	8		14						7^{3}	2					38
			4	5	6	14			10^{3}	9^{2}	13	11				1	8		12		3				7^{1}	2					39
			4	5	6^{1}	7				9	11^{2}	10				1	8		12		3^{3}				14	2	13				40
		3	4	5		8^{3}		10^{2}		9	14	11				1	6		12						7^{1}	2	13				41
		3	4	5		14		9^{1}	10^{2}			11		7■		1	6	13	8^{3}					2			12				42
		3	4^{1}	5				9	10^{3}		14	11				1	6	7	8^{2}					2	13	12					43
		3	4	5	6^{1}			9^{2}	10^{3}	14	12			7		1	8								13	2	11				44
1						12		9^{2}		13	7			3				5			8		4^{3}		11		10^{1}	2	6	14	45
		3	4	5	6^{2}	8^{1}		14		9^{3}	7	11		12		1	10				13					2					46

FA Cup

Fourth Qualifying Round			
	York C	(h)	2-1
First Round	Cambridge U	(a)	2-2
		(h)	2-1
Second Round	Brentford	(a)	1-0
Third Round	Brighton & HA	(a)	1-1
		(h)	1-1

Play-Offs

Semi-Final	Luton T	(a)	0-2
		(h)	2-1

YORK CITY

FL Championship 2

Ground: Bootham Cresent, York YO30 7AQ. *Tel:* (01904) 624 447. *Fax:* (01904) 631 457. *Year Formed:* 1922.
Record Gate: 28,123 (1938 v Huddersfield T, FA Cup 6th rd). *Nickname:* Minster Men.
Manager: Gary Mills. *Secretary:* Lisa Charlton. *Colours:* Red shirts, navy shorts, navy stockings.

YORK CITY 2011–12 LEAGUE RECORD

Match No.	Date	Venue	Opponents	Result		H/T Score	Lg Pos.	Goalscorers	Attendance
1	Aug 13	A	Ebbsfleet U	W	2-1	0-0	—	Walker 2 (1 pen) 83 (p), 90	1522
2	16	H	Barrow	W	3-1	2-0	—	Walker 7, McLaughlin 45, Blair 90	3075
3	20	H	AFC Telford U	L	0-1	0-0	5		2723
4	23	A	Kettering T	W	5-1	4-1	—	Boucaud 20, Walker 2 21, 31, Moke 39, Pilkington 90	1595
5	26	A	Fleetwood T	D	0-0	0-0	—		2111
6	29	H	Alfreton T	L	0-1	0-1	—		3166
7	Sept 10	A	Tamworth	L	1-2	0-0	14	Walker 84	1012
8	13	H	Bath C	W	1-0	0-0	—	Reed 88	2030
9	17	A	Wrexham	W	3-0	3-0	8	McLaughlin 4, Chambers 21, Reed 24	3872
10	20	H	Darlington	D	2-2	1-2	—	Reed 2, Walker 79	2844
11	24	H	Luton T	W	3-0	3-0	5	Chambers 2 9, 45, Walker 31	3570
12	27	A	Gateshead	L	2-3	1-2	—	Walker 23, Curtis (og) 87	1604
13	Oct 1	A	Stockport Co	W	2-1	0-0	7	Blair 52, Walker 86	3753
14	8	H	Braintree T	W	6-2	4-1	4	Chambers 15, McLaughlin 2 28, 41, Fyfield 37, Walker (pen) 72, Moke 85	2640
15	11	A	Southport	D	1-1	0-0	—	Chambers 62	1107
16	15	H	Grimsby T	W	2-1	1-1	4	Walker 34, Chambers 86	3872
17	18	H	Cambridge U	D	2-2	1-2	—	Walker 2 21, 89	2711
18	22	A	Hayes & Y	W	4-2	2-1	3	Walker 14, Challinor 19, McLaughlin 61, Chambers 76	525
19	Nov 5	H	Wrexham	D	0-0	0-0	4		4295
20	19	A	Barrow	D	0-0	0-0	5		2190
21	26	A	Forest Green R	D	1-1	0-0	5	Reed (pen) 83	1157
22	29	H	Lincoln C	W	2-0	1-0	—	Pilkington 4, McLaughlin 56	3155
23	Dec 3	H	Kettering T	W	7-0	4-0	4	Reed 2 6, 12, Challinor 30, Blair 45, McLaughlin 50, Chambers 65, Ashikodi 77	2899
24	6	A	AFC Telford U	D	0-0	0-0	—		1601
25	19	H	Kidderminster H	L	2-3	1-3	—	Blair 20, McGurk 68	2830
26	26	A	Mansfield T	D	1-1	0-1	4	Henderson 62	3551
27	Jan 1	H	Mansfield T	D	2-2	0-1	5	Blair 77, Fyfield 90	4284
28	7	A	Lincoln C	W	2-0	0-0	4	Blair 2 64, 72	3048
29	21	H	Ebbsfleet U	W	3-2	1-0	4	Blair 2 10, 53, Meredith 67	2973
30	24	A	Kidderminster H	D	1-1	0-0	—	Smith 57	2417
31	28	A	Darlington	D	2-2	0-1	4	Smith 60, Chambers 61	6413
32	Feb 18	H	Stockport Co	W	2-1	0-0	4	Reed 84, Blinkhorn 90	3370
33	22	H	Gateshead	L	1-2	0-1	—	Reed 65	2683
34	Mar 3	H	Hayes & Y	W	2-0	0-0	4	Oyebanjo 57, Walker (pen) 90	2603
35	6	H	Tamworth	D	0-0	0-0	—		2249
36	13	A	Grimsby T	W	3-2	1-0	—	Reed 19, Smith 47, Fyfield 90	4250
37	24	H	Southport	L	1-2	0-0	6	Reed 84	3465
38	27	A	Bath C	W	1-0	0-0	—	McLaughlin 50	565
39	30	A	Luton T	W	2-1	0-1	—	McLaughlin 81, Meredith 86	5925
40	Apr 3	A	Newport Co	L	1-2	1-1	—	McLaughlin 39	1241
41	7	H	Fleetwood T	L	0-1	0-0	4		4048
42	9	A	Alfreton T	W	2-0	0-0	4	Blair 69, Oyebanjo 76	1603
43	14	H	Newport Co	D	1-1	0-1	5	Walker 59	2824
44	17	A	Cambridge U	W	1-0	0-0	—	Walker 64	2211
45	21	A	Braintree T	W	1-0	0-0	4	Tonne 75	1127
46	28	H	Forest Green R	W	1-0	0-0	4	Moke 82	3391

Final League Position: 4

GOALSCORERS

League (81): Walker 18 (3 pens), Blair 10, McLaughlin 10, Reed 10 (1 pen), Chambers 9, Fyfield 3, Moke 3, Smith 3, Challinor 2, Meredith 2, Oyebanjo 2, Pilkington 2, Ashikodi 1, Blinkhorn 1, Boucaud 1, Henderson 1, McGurk 1, Tonne 1, own goal 1.
FA Cup (1): McLaughlin 1.
Play-Offs (4): Blair 2, Chambers 1, own goal 1.

Ingham 43	Oyebanjo 19 + 2	Meredith 43	Smith 31	McGurk 18 + 1	Boucaud 23	Moke 11 + 15	McLaughlin 42 + 2	Walker 29 + 1	Chambers 34 + 8	Blair 37 + 4	Potts 2 + 8	Reed 17 + 18	Fyfield 25 + 8	Kerr 33 + 1	Pilkington 10 + 8	Challinor 35 + 4	Parslow 17 + 10	Henderson 2 + 4	Ashikodi 2 + 6	Brown 6 + 1	Blinkhorn 3 + 12	Gibson 8	Doig 10	Swallow — + 2	Bopp 1 + 1	Tonne 2 + 1	Musselwhite 3	Kelly — + 1	Match No.
1	2	3	4	5	6	7	8	9	10	11																			1
1	2	3	4	5	6	7[1]	8	9[2]	10	11	12	13																	2
1	2	3	4	5	6[3]	7[2]	8	9	10	11[1]		12	13	14															3
1	2	3	4	5	6	7[2]	8[1]	9[3]	10			12	13	11	14														4
1	2	3	4	5	6[3]	7[2]	8[1]	9	10				14	11	13	12													5
1		3[3]	4	5	6[2]	7	8[1]	9	10			12	14	11		13	2												6
1	2	3	4	5		7[1]	13	9	10	11[2]		12		6		8[3]		14											7
1		3		5	6			9	10[3]	13		14	4	11	8[2]	7[1]	2	12											8
1		3		5	6[2]		8	9	10	12	13	7[1]	4	11		2													9
1		3		5	6[1]	12	8	9	10			7	4	11		2													10
1		3		5	6	12	8	9[3]	10[2]	13		7[1]	4	11		2		14											11
1		3		5	6	13	8[2]	9	10[3]	12		7[1]	4	11		2		14											12
1		3	4		6[1]		8[2]	9	10	7	12		5	11		2	13												13
1		3	4		6[1]	13	7	9[3]	10[2]	8		14	5	11		2	12												14
1		3	4		6[1]		8	9	10	7	12		5	11		2													15
1		3	4		6[1]	12	8	9[2]	10	7			5	11		2	13												16
1		3	4		6[2]	12	8[3]	9	10	7[1]	14	13	5	11		2													17
1		3	4		6	12	8[3]	9[1]	10[2]	7	14	13	5	11		2													18
1		3	4		6[2]	12	8	9	10	7[1]	13		5	11		2													19
1		3	4[2]	13	6■		8[1]	9■	10[3]	7			5	11	12	2	14												20
1	2	3	4				6[2]		10	8		12	5	11	13	7[3]	14		9[1]										21
1	13	3		5			4		10[2]	9		7	6	11	8[1]	2			12										22
1	13	3		5		14	4		10[3]	9		7[1]	6	11[2]	8	2			12										23
1		3		5	4[2]		8	9[3]	10[1]	7		13	6	11	12	2			14										24
1		3		5	4[1]	12	8		10[3]	7			6	11	9[2]	2	14		13										25
1	2	3	4	5			8		12	9		13	7[1]	11			6	10[2]											26
1	2	3		5[2]	4		8		10[3]	7		12	13	11	14		6	9[1]											27
1		3	4				6		12	10		9[1]		11	8	2	5			7									28
1		3	6				4			9		7[1]	13	11	10[2]	2	5			8■	12								29
1		3	6			8	4		13	9		7[1]		11	10[2]	2	5				12								30
1		3	6		4[2]		8		13	9		12	14	11	7[1]	2	5				10[3]								31
1			6				4	9[1]	8	10[2]		12		11		2				7[3]	13	3	5	14					32
1			6				4	8[2]	10[3]	9		14		11		2				7[1]	12	3	5	13					33
1	2	3				13	4	9	10[3]	8				11		7	12				14	5[1]	6[2]						34
1	2	3					4[3]	8[1]	10	9[2]		14	6	11	13	7	5				12								35
1		3	4				7	9[1]		8		10	6	11		2	5				12								36
1	7	11	4			12	14		10[3]	9		8	6[1]			2	5				13	3[2]							37
1	7	3	6			13	4		10[2]	9		8[3]				2	12			11[1]	14		5						38
1	2	3	6				4[3]	9	12	7		10[1]				11[2]	14					8	5		13				39
1	7	3				13	4[2]		14	9[1]		8[3]	6			11	2		12		10	5							40
1	2	11				12	4		13	9		8[2]					6				14	3	5		7[1]	10[3]			41
1	2	3	4[1]			8	11			9		7[3]	12		10[2]	13	6				14		5						42
1	2	11	4			7[1]	6	13	12	9		10[3]			8[2]	14	3						5						43
	2[2]	3	4				11	9[3]	8	10	13					7	12				14	6■	5[1]				1		44
		3	4				8[1]	9[3]	10[2]	11	7		6			2	5		14	13						12	1		45
						4					3	12	6		13	7	2		9[1]	11	10[2]		5			8[3]	1	14	46

FA Cup
Fourth Qualifying Round
Wrexham (a) 1-2

Play-Offs
Semi-Final Mansfield T (h) 1-1
(a) 1-0
Final Luton T 2-1
(at Wembley).

REVIEW OF THE SCOTTISH SEASON 2011–12

Glasgow Rangers no longer in existence, the newco Rangers not allowed to take their place in the Scottish Premier League and forced to go cap in hand to the Scottish Football League for clemency and acceptance. Such was the situation after the second half of 2011–12 as it resulted in the complete demise of one of the two most famous Scottish clubs. Just how such a calamity caused by financial misdemeanour and mismanagement could have occurred is not for discussion at this time.

Docked ten points for entering administration there was no question of relegation. Indeed Rangers still finished second, 11 points ahead of third placed Motherwell. Naturally Celtic had little more to do than tread carefully 20 points in front at the finale, to end Rangers' three successive titles in almost bizarre circumstances. Celtic had, however, lost in the final of the Scottish Communities League Cup to Kilmarnock, who already in mid-March were struggling to make the cut for the top six in the table. Moreover the William Hill Scottish Cup was disputed between the two Edinburgh clubs Hearts and Hibs; a rare meeting at this stage of the competition, the last dating back to before the turn of the 20th century.

Once again Scottish domestic football is at a crisis point. It has an unsettling effect on everything. The national team has to concentrate on qualifying for World Cup 2014 in Brazil having missed out on Euro 2012. Placed third at the halfway stage behind leaders Spain and the Czech Republic, the Scots though with a match in hand of all of their rivals, were five points adrift in what was considered a tough group.

A draw with the Czechs and a decent display and narrow defeat against Spain was an encouraging sign, but not sufficient to break into the top two qualifiers for Poland and the Ukraine in the summer. Yet again in a matter of priorities, the situation at home has to be put in order.

Leaving out the drama of Rangers, the SPL still itches for expansion into two divisions. Such an event would throw the Scottish Football League into a spin. The summer months before the start of a new season are not the time for snap decisions, yet it seems inevitable that they will occur.

As to 2011–12, with the title moving to Parkhead, the other concerns homed in on places for Europe. Yet it was Celtic's devastating spell of 17 consecutive wins to the end of February which set them apart from everyone else.

They called upon the services of no fewer than 32 players, none of them ever present and only one of whom managed to miss just one league game. Hooper was also the top scorer with 24 League goals including all five in the tail end match against Hearts. Only four times did opponents prevent Celtic from scoring a goal.

Motherwell were a pretty consistent choice for third place, though significantly losing all four games to Celtic and only managing one draw with Rangers! Dundee United showed greater staying power for finishing fourth, noticeably improving in the second half of the campaign.

Hearts, not out of the top six from the end of August, had their best two runs in spells of five without defeat and earned their reward in the Scottish Cup that highlighted the dire season endured by their Edinburgh rivals Hibernian. Hibs, within a couple of weeks of the final matches were not entirely certain of avoiding relegation. Hibs' only second home win was against relegated Dunfermline Athletic. Only Inverness Caley Thistle, bottom at the end of November, seemed at one time to be seriously involved in the demotion battle, though Aberdeen would not have been delighted with ninth position, were at the bottom early December and scored only 36 goals.

St Johnstone finished sixth and but for just one point from the last seven games might have been higher placed, leaving Killie as mentioned in the bottom six group along with St Mirren.

Kilmarnock paid dearly for beating Celtic in a cup final; The Hoops won 6-0 at Rugby Park. They did win 1-0 away to Rangers on 18 February, the last occasion in sixth spot. Draw specialists St Mirren divided the spoils 16 times including five times in succession. Goals, too, were scarce, 39 in total. Indeed apart from Celtic and Rangers, scoring was low everywhere. The average number of goals per game was 2.06, an uninspiring average and a third of teams overall were unable to score at least one goal in fixtures played.

There was no joy in European competitions, Rangers disappointing and Celtic, given a reprieve by the banishment of their opponents, were unable to take advantage of the situation (see European Review).

Promoted to the SPL, Ross County romped away with the Scottish League Championship. Only that games in hand might have produced an upset prevented them gaining the prize much earlier. Thirty-five matches undefeated was an outstanding performance. Queen of the South suffered relegation, Cowdenbeath won the automatic slot and Dumbarton impressively won their play-off matches to move up while Ayr United also lost First Division status.

Long-time Third Division leaders Stranraer had again slipped away but recovered in the play-offs only to lose on penalties in the final that enabled Albion Rovers to retain Second Division status. Stirling Albion suffered the drop, to be replaced by Third Division winners Alloa Athletic.

SCOTTISH LEAGUE TABLES 2011–12

(P) *Promoted into division at end of 2010–11 season.* (R) *Relegated into division at end of 2010–11 season.*

CLYDESDALE BANK SCOTTISH PREMIER LEAGUE 2011–12

		Total						*Home*					*Away*						
		P	*W*	*D*	*L*	*F*	*A*	*W*	*D*	*L*	*F*	*A*	*W*	*D*	*L*	*F*	*A*	*GD*	*Pts*
1	Celtic	38	30	3	5	84	21	17	1	1	41	6	13	2	4	43	15	63	93
2	Rangers*	38	26	5	7	77	28	12	5	2	38	14	14	0	5	39	14	49	73
3	Motherwell	38	18	8	12	49	44	9	3	7	27	24	9	5	5	22	20	5	62
4	Dundee U	38	16	11	11	62	50	8	6	5	27	16	8	5	6	35	34	12	59
5	Hearts	38	15	7	16	45	43	11	0	8	30	19	4	7	8	15	24	2	52
6	St Johnstone	38	14	8	16	43	50	6	2	10	20	30	8	6	6	23	20	−7	50
7	Kilmarnock	38	11	14	13	44	61	7	7	6	29	35	4	7	7	15	26	−17	47
8	St Mirren	38	9	16	13	39	51	6	6	7	23	25	3	10	6	16	26	−12	43
9	Aberdeen	38	9	14	15	36	44	6	8	5	22	16	3	6	10	14	28	−8	41
10	Inverness CT	38	10	9	19	42	60	5	5	9	19	27	5	4	10	23	33	−18	39
11	Hibernian	38	8	9	21	40	67	2	7	10	17	30	6	2	11	23	37	−27	33
12	Dunfermline Ath (P)	38	5	10	23	40	82	1	7	11	22	44	4	3	12	18	38	−42	25

**Rangers deducted 10 points; Top 6 teams split after 33 games.*

IRN-BRU SCOTTISH FOOTBALL LEAGUE FIRST DIVISION 2011–12

		Total						*Home*					*Away*						
		P	*W*	*D*	*L*	*F*	*A*	*W*	*D*	*L*	*F*	*A*	*W*	*D*	*L*	*F*	*A*	*GD*	*Pts*
1	Ross Co	36	22	13	1	72	32	11	7	0	40	14	11	6	1	32	18	40	79
2	Dundee	36	15	10	11	53	43	7	5	6	25	20	8	5	5	28	23	10	55
3	Falkirk	36	13	13	10	53	48	9	6	3	29	21	4	7	7	24	27	5	52
4	Hamilton A (R)	36	14	7	15	55	56	8	3	7	33	30	6	4	8	22	26	−1	49
5	Livingston (P)	36	13	9	14	56	54	5	6	7	26	29	8	3	7	30	25	2	48
6	Partick Th	36	12	11	13	50	39	7	6	5	27	16	5	5	8	23	23	11	47
7	Raith R	36	11	11	14	46	49	7	4	7	24	21	4	7	7	22	28	−3	44
8	Morton	36	10	12	14	40	55	5	5	8	24	29	5	7	6	16	26	−15	42
9	Ayr U (P)	36	9	11	16	44	67	5	7	6	22	25	4	4	10	22	42	−23	38
10	Queen of the S	36	7	11	18	38	64	6	5	7	21	31	1	6	11	17	33	−26	32

IRN-BRU SCOTTISH FOOTBALL LEAGUE SECOND DIVISION 2011–12

		Total						*Home*					*Away*						
		P	*W*	*D*	*L*	*F*	*A*	*W*	*D*	*L*	*F*	*A*	*W*	*D*	*L*	*F*	*A*	*GD*	*Pts*
1	Cowdenbeath (R)	36	20	11	5	68	29	13	4	1	37	10	7	7	4	31	19	39	71
2	Arbroath (P)	36	17	12	7	76	51	10	5	3	44	23	7	7	4	32	28	25	63
3	Dumbarton¶	36	17	7	12	61	61	10	2	6	30	30	7	5	6	31	31	0	58
4	Airdrie U	36	14	10	12	68	60	9	4	5	43	30	5	6	7	25	30	8	52
5	Stenhousemuir	36	15	6	15	54	49	9	2	7	32	23	6	4	8	22	26	5	51
6	East Fife	36	14	6	16	55	57	7	4	7	27	29	7	2	9	28	28	−2	48
7	Forfar Ath	36	11	9	16	59	72	6	5	7	33	34	5	4	9	26	38	−13	42
8	Brechin C	36	10	11	15	47	62	5	6	7	24	30	5	5	8	23	32	−15	41
9	Albion R (P)	36	10	7	19	43	66	6	6	6	25	22	4	1	13	18	44	−23	37
10	Stirling Alb (R)	36	9	7	20	46	70	4	5	9	22	29	5	2	11	24	41	−24	34

¶Dumbarton promoted via play-offs.

IRN-BRU SCOTTISH FOOTBALL LEAGUE THIRD DIVISION 2011–12

		Total						*Home*					*Away*						
		P	*W*	*D*	*L*	*F*	*A*	*W*	*D*	*L*	*F*	*A*	*W*	*D*	*L*	*F*	*A*	*GD*	*Pts*
1	Alloa Ath (R)	36	23	8	5	70	39	13	4	1	43	13	10	4	4	27	26	31	77
2	Queen's Park	36	19	6	11	70	48	10	4	4	41	17	9	2	7	29	31	22	63
3	Stranraer	36	17	7	12	77	57	10	2	6	43	33	7	5	6	34	24	20	58
4	Elgin C	36	16	9	11	68	60	11	3	4	43	17	5	6	7	25	43	8	57
5	Peterhead (R)	36	15	6	15	51	53	7	5	6	25	23	8	1	9	26	30	−2	51
6	Annan Ath	36	13	10	13	53	53	7	5	6	28	26	6	5	7	25	27	0	49
7	Berwick R	36	12	12	12	61	58	6	5	7	30	28	6	7	5	31	30	3	48
8	Montrose	36	11	5	20	58	75	7	3	8	34	33	4	2	12	24	42	−17	38
9	Clyde	36	8	11	17	35	50	5	5	8	24	23	3	6	9	11	27	−15	35
10	East Stirling	36	6	6	24	38	88	5	4	9	24	33	1	2	15	14	55	−50	24

ABERDEEN

Year Formed: 1903. *Ground & Address:* Pittodrie Stadium, Pittodrie St, Aberdeen AB24 5QH. *Telephone:* 01224 650400. *Fax:* 01224 644173. *E-mail:* feedback@afc.co.uk *Website:* www.afc.co.uk
Ground Capacity: all seated: 21,421. *Size of Pitch:* 115yd × 72yd.
Chairman: Stewart Milne. *Secretary:* David Johnston.
Manager: Craig Brown. *Assistant Manager:* Archie Knox. *U-19 Coach:* Neil Cooper.
Club Nicknames: The Dons, The Reds, The Dandies.
Previous Grounds: None.
Record Attendance: 45,061 v Hearts, Scottish Cup 4th rd, 13 Mar 1954.
Record Transfer Fee received: £1.75 million for Eoin Jess to Coventry City (February 1996).
Record Transfer Fee paid: £1m+ for Paul Bernard from Oldham Athletic (September 1995).
Record Victory: 13-0 v Peterhead, Scottish Cup, 9 Feb 1923.
Record Defeat: 0-9 v Celtic, Premier League, 6 Nov 2010.
Most Capped Player: Alex McLeish, 77 (Scotland).
Most League Appearances: 556: Willie Miller, 1973-90.
Most League Goals in Season (Individual): 38: Benny Yorston, Division I, 1929-30.
Most Goals Overall (Individual): 199: Joe Harper, 1969-72; 1976-81.

ABERDEEN 2011–12 LEAGUE RECORD

Match No.	*Date*	*Venue*	*Opponents*	*Result*		*H/T Score*	*Lg Pos.*	*Goalscorers*	*Attendance*
1	July 23	H	St Johnstone	D	0-0	0-0	—		10,001
2	30	A	St Mirren	L	0-1	0-0	—		5011
3	Aug 7	H	Celtic	L	0-1	0-0	—		12,497
4	13	A	Hearts	L	0-3	0-2	11		13,374
5	20	H	Inverness CT	W	2-1	2-0	10	Milsom [12], Vernon [27]	7989
6	28	A	Rangers	L	0-2	0-1	11		44,070
7	Sept 11	A	Hibernian	D	0-0	0-0	11		8972
8	17	H	Kilmarnock	D	2-2	1-2	10	Considine [37], Mawene [53]	7672
9	24	A	Motherwell	L	0-1	0-0	11		4348
10	30	H	Dunfermline Ath	W	4-0	3-0	—	Vernon 3 [6, 35, 80], Fyvie [45]	8333
11	Oct 15	H	Dundee U	W	3-1	1-0	7	Arnason [14], Mawene [51], Considine [60]	10,256
12	23	A	Celtic	L	1-2	0-1	7	Jack [59]	49,037
13	29	H	Rangers	L	1-2	0-0	10	Foster [82]	15,468
14	Nov 19	H	Motherwell	L	1-2	1-1	11	Vernon [10]	8779
15	26	A	Dunfermline Ath	D	3-3	1-0	11	Considine [45], Keddie (og) [81], Magennis [88]	4149
16	Dec 3	A	Kilmarnock	L	0-2	0-1	12		4367
17	10	H	St Mirren	D	2-2	2-1	10	Vernon [1], Fallon [17]	9452
18	13	A	St Johnstone	W	2-1	1-0	—	Vernon [13], Jack [79]	1607
19	17	H	Hibernian	W	1-0	0-0	9	Vernon (pen) [59]	7137
20	24	A	Inverness CT	L	1-2	0-0	9	Fallon [76]	5888
21	28	H	Hearts	D	0-0	0-0	9		9210
22	Jan 2	A	Dundee U	W	2-1	0-1	9	Chalali [67], Arnason [86]	11,471
23	14	H	Kilmarnock	D	0-0	0-0	9		8324
24	21	A	Rangers	D	1-1	0-0	8	Arnason [63]	46,648
25	28	H	Dunfermline Ath	W	1-0	1-0	6	Vernon [24]	8081
26	Feb 11	A	Hibernian	D	0-0	0-0	7		10,100
27	19	H	St Johnstone	D	0-0	0-0	8		6936
28	25	A	St Mirren	D	1-1	0-0	7	Vernon [59]	3627
29	Mar 3	H	Celtic	D	1-1	1-1	7	Blackman (og) [44]	13,127
30	17	A	Motherwell	L	0-1	0-1	—		4637
31	24	H	Inverness CT	L	0-1	0-1	8		8939
32	31	A	Hearts	L	0-3	0-1	9		13,292
33	Apr 7	H	Dundee U	W	3-1	1-1	8	Mackie [12], Clark [68], Jack [78]	8439
34	21	A	Inverness CT	W	2-0	0-0	8	Golobart (og) [46], Gillet (og) [89]	3487
35	28	A	Dunfermline Ath	L	0-3	0-0	8		3501
36	May 2	H	Hibernian	L	1-2	0-2	—	Vernon [53]	5281
37	5	A	Kilmarnock	D	1-1	1-0	9	Masson [30]	3893
38	12	H	St Mirren	D	0-0	0-0	9		10,716

Final League Position: 9

Honours
League Champions: Division I 1954-55. Premier Division 1979-80, 1983-84, 1984-85; *Runners-up:* Division I 1910-11, 1936-37, 1955-56, 1970-71, 1971-72. Premier Division 1977-78, 1980-81, 1981-82, 1988-89, 1989-90, 1990-91, 1992-93, 1993-94.
Scottish Cup Winners: 1947, 1970, 1982, 1983, 1984, 1986, 1990; *Runners-up:* 1937, 1953, 1954, 1959, 1967, 1978, 1993, 2000.
League Cup Winners: 1955-56, 1976-77, 1985-86, 1989-90, 1995-96; *Runners-up:* 1946-47, 1978-79, 1979-80, 1987-88, 1988-89, 1992-93, 1999-2000.
Drybrough Cup Winners: 1971, 1980.

European: *European Cup:* 12 matches (1980-81, 1984-85, 1985-86); *Cup Winners' Cup:* 39 matches (1967-68, 1970-71, 1978-79, 1982-83 winners, 1983-84 semi-finals, 1986-87, 1990-91, 1993-94); *UEFA Cup:* 56 matches (*Fairs Cup:* 1968-69. *UEFA Cup:* 1971-72, 1972-73, 1973-74, 1977-78, 1979-80, 1981-82, 1987-88, 1988-89, 1989-90, 1991-92, 1994-95, 1996-97, 2000-01, 2002-03, 2007-08). *Europa League:* 2 matches (2009–10).

Club colours: All red.

Goalscorers: *League (36):* Vernon 11 (1 pen), Arnason 3, Considine 3, Jack 3, Fallon 2, Mawene 2, Chalali 1, Clark 1, Foster 1, Fyvie 1, Mackie 1, Magennis 1, Masson 1, Milsom 1, own goals 4.
Scottish Cup (10): Fallon 4, Vernon 2, Chalili 1, Considine 1, Fyvie 1, Megginson 1.
Scottish Communities Cup (4): Mackie 2, Fallon 1, McArdle 1.

Gonzalez D 14	Jack R 30 + 1	Foster R 22	Osbourne I 22 + 1	Mawene Y 19 + 3	Considine A 36	Pawlett P 5 + 16	Milsom R 22	Vernon S 34 + 1	Mackie D 8 + 11	Fyvie F 26 + 1	Arnason K 31 + 2	Magennis J 13 + 10	Robertson C 9	Paton M — + 2	Megginson M 7 + 9	Low N — + 2	McArdle R 20 + 5	Clark C 16 + 8	Chalali M 4 + 12	Brown J 20	Fallon R 18 + 4	Reynolds M 16	Hughes S 3 + 2	Rae G 12	Uchechi D — + 1	Anderson R 4 + 2	Langfield J 4	Smith C — + 2	Masson J 3 + 1	McManus D — + 2	Fraser R — + 3	*Match No.*
1	2■	3	4	5	6	7^1	8	9^2	10	11	12	13																				1
1		3	4		6	7^2	8	9^3	10		5	11^1	2	12	13	14																2
1		3	4		6	7^1	8	9	10^3		5	11^2		12	13	14	2															3
1	13	3	4	5	6	12	8	9^3	10^1	11	7	14					2^2															4
1	2	3	4	5^3	6		8	9		11^2	7	10^1			12		14	13														5
1	7^1	3	4	5	6	12	8	9^2		11	10	13					2^3		14													6
1		3	4	5	6	13	8	9^3	14	11^2	10	12					2	7^1														7
	2^2	3	4	5	6	12	8^3	14		11	7							13	10^1	1	9											8
1	2	3	4	5	6	12	8	9^3			11	14			13			7^1			10^2											9
1	2^3	3	4	5	6	13	8	9		11^2	7							14	12		10^1											10
1	2	3	4	5	6		8	9^3	14	11^2	7	12						13			10^1											11
1	2■	3	4	5	6		8	9^1	12	11	7								13		10^2											12
1		3	4	5	6		9^1		12	11^2	8	14					2	7^3	13		10■											13
1		3	4	5	6	12	8	9	14	11^2		13					2^1	7	10^3													14
1	7^2	3	4	5	6	13	8		12	11		10						2			9^1											15
		3	4	5	6	13	8	9^1		11		12			14		2^2	7		1	10^3											16
	2	3	4	5	6	13	8^2	9		11■	7								12	1	10^1											17
	2	3	4	5^1	6■	14	8	9			11						12	7^3	13	1	10^2											18
	2	3	4	13		12■	8	9		11^3	6						5	14	7^1	1	10^2											19
	2^3	3	4	5	6		8	9^2	12		11	10^1			14			7		1	13											20
	2	3	4	5	6		8	9	7^1		11	13						12		1	10^2											21
	2	3	4		6	7^1	8^3	9		11	5						12	14	13	1	10^2											22
	7				6			9^1		11	4		5		13		2	8	10^2	1	12	3										23
	2							9	12	11	4	8	3				5	7		1	10^1	6										24
	7				6			9		11^1	4	10^2	3				2	8	12	1		5	13									25
	7			14	6			9	13	11		10^1	3^3		8^2		2		12	1		5	4									26
	2				6			9	13	11	4				10^3		5		14	1		3	8^1	7^2	12							27
	7			5^1	6	13		9		11	4				10^2		2			1	12	3		8								28
	2			13	6	12		9		11^1	4				7		5			1	10^2	3		8								29
	11^3				6	13		9			8		3^2		12		2	7	14	1	10^1	5		4								30
	7				6	12		9			8^1		3		10^3		2	11^2	13	1	14	5		4								31
					6	11^1		9	10		5^3		8^2		12		2	7		1		3	14	4		13						32
	7				6^1			9	10^3	14	13		3				2	8		1		5	11^2	4		12						33
	2^3				6					11	4	10			7^2		13	14			9^1	5		8		3	1	12				34
	2				6			9^3	12	11		10			8^1			7^2				5		4		3	1		13	14		35
	2				6			9		11^1	4	10										3		7		5	1	12	8^2		13	36
	7				6			9			5	8					2			1	10^1	3		4					11^2	12	13	37
	2		13		6			9	10		4^2	8^1					12					3		7		5	1		11^3		14	38

AIRDRIE UNITED

Year Formed: 1965. *Ground & Address:* Shyberry Excelsior Stadium, Broomfield Park, Craigneuk Avenue, Airdrie ML6 8QZ. *Telephone:* (Stadium) 01236 622000. *Fax:* 01236 626002. *Postal Address:* 60 St Enoch Square, Glasgow G1 4AG.
E-mail: annmarie@airdrieunitedfc.com *Website:* www.airdrieunited.com
Ground Capacity: all seated: 10,171. *Size of Pitch:* 105m × 67m.
Chairman: Jim Ballantyne. *Secretary:* Ann Marie Ballantyne.
Manager: Jimmy Boyle. *First Team Coaches:* Paul Jack and Alan Lawrence.
Club Nickname: The Diamonds.
Record Attendance: 5924 v Motherwell, Scottish Cup 3rd rd, 6 Jan 2007.
Record Victory: 11-0 v Gala Fairydean, Scottish Cup 3rd rd, 19 Nov 2011.
Record Defeat: 1-6 v Morton, Second Division, 1 Nov 2003.
Most League Appearances: 222, Paul Lovering 2004-12.
Most League Goals in Season (Individual): 19: Alan Russell, 2007-08.
Most Goals Overall (Individual): 33: Stephen McKeown, 2002-08.

AIRDRIE UNITED 2011–12 LEAGUE RECORD

Match No.	Date	Venue	Opponents	Result		H/T Score	Lg Pos.	Goalscorers	Attendance
1	Aug 6	H	Dumbarton	W	3-0	2-0	—	Johnston 2 [6, 63], Donnelly [9]	887
2	13	A	East Fife	L	0-2	0-1	4		759
3	20	H	Cowdenbeath	L	1-5	1-2	8	Donnelly [6]	834
4	27	A	Forfar Ath	L	2-3	2-2	9	Stephenson [23], Lynch [29]	432
5	Sept 10	H	Albion R	W	4-0	4-0	7	Lynch [9], Donnelly 2 [11, 45], Stephenson (pen) [41]	1368
6	17	A	Arbroath	L	1-3	0-1	7	Owens [65]	761
7	24	H	Stirling A	D	1-1	1-1	7	Boyle [4]	709
8	Oct 1	H	Stenhousemuir	W	5-2	3-0	5	Donnelly 2 [10, 66], Lovering [27], Boyle [45], Blockley [83]	698
9	15	A	Brechin C	D	1-1	1-0	5	Donnelly [14]	455
10	22	A	Dumbarton	D	1-1	1-1	5	Stephenson [37]	285
11	29	H	East Fife	L	1-3	0-1	7	Donnelly [74]	849
12	Nov 5	A	Albion R	L	2-7	1-3	9	Stephenson [23], Owens (pen) [74]	1109
13	12	H	Forfar Ath	D	4-4	1-1	9	Donnelly 3 [32, 58, 73], Boyle [82]	635
14	26	H	Arbroath	D	3-3	1-2	7	Lovering (pen) [6], Donnelly 2 [68, 71]	687
15	Dec 3	A	Stirling A	W	4-1	2-1	7	Donnelly 2 [13, 58], Lovering (pen) [29], McLaren [49]	711
16	10	A	Stenhousemuir	D	1-1	0-1	7	McLaren [69]	698
17	17	H	Brechin C	L	2-3	0-1	—	Donnelly 2 [69, 83]	643
18	26	A	Forfar Ath	W	3-2	2-2	4	Lynch [42], McLaren [45], Morton [90]	579
19	Jan 2	H	Albion R	W	1-0	0-0	4	Stephenson [71]	1490
20	14	A	Cowdenbeath	L	0-2	0-1	5		408
21	21	H	Dumbarton	L	2-3	2-1	6	Donnelly [15], Boyle [36]	743
22	28	H	Stirling A	W	4-1	2-0	—	Boyle [3], Lovering [17], McLaren [73], Sally [84]	730
23	Feb 11	A	Brechin C	D	1-1	0-1	5	Holmes [72]	483
24	18	H	Stenhousemuir	L	0-3	0-1	7		685
25	25	A	East Fife	L	0-2	0-1	7		535
26	29	A	Arbroath	D	2-2	0-2	—	Holmes [49], Boyle [78]	728
27	Mar 3	H	Cowdenbeath	D	1-1	1-0	7	Lynch [39]	702
28	10	A	Albion R	W	1-0	1-0	7	MacDonald [27]	1134
29	17	H	Forfar Ath	W	3-0	0-0	7	Bain [54], Lovering (pen) [75], McLaren [86]	621
30	24	H	Arbroath	W	2-0	0-0	6	Lovering [73], McLaren [90]	689
31	31	A	Stirling A	W	2-0	2-0	5	Donnelly 2 [20, 31]	677
32	Apr 7	A	Stenhousemuir	W	3-0	2-0	4	Lynch [7], McLaren [45], Blockley [81]	903
33	14	H	Brechin C	W	4-1	3-1	4	Holmes 2 [7, 86], Donnelly [14], Lovering (pen) [23]	802
34	21	A	Dumbarton	L	1-2	0-0	4	McLaren [56]	1088
35	28	H	East Fife	W	2-0	0-0	4	Lynch [51], Bain [88]	1223
36	May 5	A	Cowdenbeath	D	0-0	0-0	4		1345

Final League Position: 4

Honours
League Champions: Second Division 2003-04; *Runners-up:* Second Division 2007-08.
League Challenge Cup Winners: 2008-09; *Runners-up:* 2003-04.

Club colours: Shirt: White with red trim. Shorts: White. Stockings: White.

Goalscorers: *League (68):* Donnelly 21, McLaren 8, Lovering 7 (4 pens), Boyle 6, Lynch 6, Stephenson 5 (1 pen), Holmes 4, Bain 2, Blockley 2, Johnston 2, Owens 2 (1 pen), MacDonald 1, Morton 1, Sally 1.
Scottish Cup (13): Boyle 3, Donnelly 3, Stevenson 3, Lovering 2 (1 pen), Holmes 1, McLaren 1.
Scottish Communities Cup (7): Donnelly 3, Owens 2 (2 pens), Bain 1, Holmes 1.
Ramsdens Cup (0).
Play-Offs (5): Holmes 3, Bain 1, McLaren 1.

McKane P 9	Bain J 31 + 3	Lilley D 31	Stallard K 29 + 2	Malone C 5 + 1	Johnston P 9 + 4	Owens G 11 + 9	Stephenson J 28 + 3	Keast F 7 + 7	Donnelly R 33	Holmes D 21 + 11	Devlin R 6 + 9	Boyle J 12 + 14	Sally S 1 + 10	Lynch S 29	Lovering P 25 + 1	Blockley N 19 + 4	Burns D 1	Morton S 4 + 5	Woodburn A 1	Hill C 4 + 3	Fairley C 12	Green K 4 + 1	McLaren W 20 + 3	Goodall G 2 + 1	MacDonald C 14	Adam G 14	Duncan A 1 + 1	Lamie R 7 + 3	McNeil E 6	Watt L — + 1	*Match No.*
1	2	3	4	5	6	7^{1}	8	9^{2}	10	11^{3}	12	13	14																		1
1	2	4	3	5	6^{2}	8	7	9^{1}	10^{3}	11	12	13	14																		2
1	2	3	4	5	6^{1}	7	9	14	10	11^{2}	12		13	8^{3}																	3
1	2	4^{1}	3	12	6^{2}		10^{3}		9	14				7	5	8	11	13													4
1	2	3	4			12	6		10^{2}	11		13		8	5	7^{1}			9^{3}	14											5
	2	4	3			6	9^{1}	12	11	10	14	13		8^{3}	5^{2}	7					1										6
1	2	3^{2}	4	5	12	8^{1}	9	6	11	14		10^{3}		7						13											7
1	2	3■	4		12		9	6^{1}	11	13	7	10^{2}		8^{3}	5	14															8
	2		4■				9	7^{2}	11	13	8	10^{1}		6	3	12				5^{3}	1	14									9
	2					13	9	6^{2}	10^{1}	11	7			8	5			12		3	1	4■									10
	2	4				13	9	6^{2}	11	10^{1}	8			7	5■			12		3	1										11
	2	4■	3	5^{1}		7	8		11	12	6	14	10^{2}					9^{3}		13	1										12
	2		3		6^{2}	7^{3}	8		11	14	5	12				13		10^{1}		4	1		9								13
	2		3		6^{2}	12	7^{1}		11	13	14	10^{3}		8	5						1	4	9								14
	2	3	5		6	7			10^{2}	11	12	13		8^{1}	4						1		9								15
	2	3	4		6^{1}	8^{3}	12		11	10^{2}	14	13		7	5						1		9								16
	2	3^{1}	4		6^{2}	13	8	14	10		12■	11^{3}		7	5						1		9								17
1	6	4	3				10		11^{1}					7		8		12				2	9	5							18
1	6	3	4				11		10					7	5	8						2	9								19
	2	3	4				6^{3}		11	10	13	12		8^{2}	5	7		14			1		9^{1}								20
	5		3			13	8^{2}		11^{3}			10^{1}	14	7	4	6					1		9	12	2■						21
	5	2				12	8^{1}		11^{2}	14		10^{3}	13	7	4	6							9		3	1					22
		3	4			13	7		11^{3}	12		10^{1}	14	8	2	6^{2}							9		5	1					23
	2^{1}	5	4			12	8		11	13		6^{2}	14	9	3^{3}	10							7			1					24
	5	4				9			10	11				7■	12	8							6^{G}	2^{1}		1■	15	3			25
	6	4	2^{1}		14	8^{2}			10	11		13			5	7^{3}							9		3		1	12			26
	6	3			13				11	10^{2}		9^{1}		7	5	8							12		2	1		4			27
	2	4	13				8^{3}	12		11		7^{1}		9	3	10							14		6^{2}	1		5			28
	6	3	14				9		10	11^{1}		12		7	5	8^{2}							13		2	1		4^{3}			29
	6	3^{3}	4					13	11^{2}	12		10^{1}		8	5								9		7	1		14	2		30
	6^{2}	3	4				12	13	11	10				8									9^{1}		7	1		5	2		31
	6^{2}	3	7				12		10	11^{3}		14		8■		13							9^{1}		4	1		5	2		32
	12	3	6				7^{1}		11^{2}	10			13		5	8							9^{3}		4	1			2	14	33
	12	4^{3}	6				7		10■	11^{2}			13		5	8^{1}							9		3	1		14	2		34
	13	3	2				6			10^{1}		12		8	5	7		11^{2}					9■		4	1					35
		4	6				9^{2}	13		10^{3}		12	14	8		7		11^{1}							3	1		5	2		36

ALBION ROVERS

Year Formed: 1882. *Ground & Address:* Cliftonhill Stadium, Main St, Coatbridge ML5 3RB. *Telephone/Fax:* 01236 606334.
E-mail: info@albionroversfc.com *Website:* albionroversfc.com
Ground capacity: 1,249 (seated 489). *Size of Pitch:* 110yd × 72yd.
Chairman and Secretary: Frank Meade ACMA.
Manager: Paul Martin. *Assistant Manager:* Todd Lumsden. *Physio:* John McMenamy.
Club Nickname: The Wee Rovers.
Previous Grounds: Cowheath Park, Meadow Park, Whifflet.
Record Attendance: 27,381 v Rangers, Scottish Cup 2nd rd, 8 Feb 1936.
Record Transfer Fee received: £40,000 from Motherwell for Bruce Cleland.
Record Transfer Fee paid: £7000 for Gerry McTeague to Stirling Albion, September 1989.
Record Victory: 12-0 v Airdriehill, Scottish Cup, 3 Sept 1887.
Record Defeat: 1-11 v Partick Th, League Cup, 11 Aug 1993.
Most Capped Player: Jock White, 1 (2), Scotland.
Most League Appearances: 399: Murdy Walls, 1921-36.
Most League Goals in Season (Individual): 41: Jim Renwick, Division II, 1932-33.
Most Goals Overall (Individual): 105: Bunty Weir, 1928-31.

ALBION ROVERS 2011–12 LEAGUE RECORD

Match No.	*Date*	*Venue*	*Opponents*	*Result*		*H/T Score*	*Lg Pos.*	*Goalscorers*	*Attendance*
1	Aug 6	A	Arbroath	L	2-6	2-2	—	Boyle 2 [31, 37]	661
2	13	H	Forfar Ath	W	1-0	0-0	8	Love [89]	352
3	20	A	Stirling A	D	2-2	0-1	6	Chaplain [82], Russell [88]	617
4	27	H	Brechin C	L	1-2	1-1	8	Gilmartin [8]	386
5	Sept 10	A	Airdrie U	L	0-4	0-4	9		1368
6	17	H	Stenhousemuir	D	1-1	0-0	8	Acqua [83]	369
7	24	A	Cowdenbeath	L	1-2	0-2	9	Chaplain [83]	304
8	Oct 15	H	East Fife	L	0-3	0-1	10		403
9	18	A	Dumbarton	L	1-2	0-1	—	Lawless [68]	406
10	22	H	Arbroath	W	1-0	1-0	10	Gemmell [13]	338
11	29	A	Forfar Ath	W	2-0	1-0	10	Love 2 [45, 58]	436
12	Nov 5	H	Airdrie U	W	7-2	3-1	7	Chaplain 3 [13, 29, 88], O'Byrne 2 [36, 90], Gemmell 2 [56, 61]	1109
13	12	A	Brechin C	W	4-1	2-0	5	O'Byrne [17], McStay [21], Love [66], Chaplain (pen) [90]	455
14	26	A	Stenhousemuir	L	0-3	0-0	6		561
15	Dec 3	H	Cowdenbeath	D	3-3	1-1	6	Love [2], Lawless 2 [64, 72]	207
16	10	H	Dumbarton	W	3-1	2-1	4	Gemmell 2 [5, 25], Love [60]	489
17	26	H	Brechin C	L	0-1	0-1	5		414
18	Jan 2	A	Airdrie U	L	0-1	0-0	7		1490
19	14	H	Stirling A	L	0-1	0-1	7		455
20	21	A	Arbroath	L	1-6	1-3	8	Gemmell [24]	616
21	24	A	East Fife	L	0-2	0-0	—		390
22	Feb 11	H	East Fife	D	1-1	0-0	8	Halsman [83]	348
23	14	A	Cowdenbeath	L	0-3	0-3	—		302
24	18	A	Dumbarton	L	0-1	0-0	9		657
25	25	H	Forfar Ath	D	2-2	1-2	9	Gemmell [5], Love [78]	312
26	Mar 3	A	Stirling A	L	0-3	0-2	10		511
27	6	H	Stenhousemuir	W	1-0	0-0	—	Werndly [83]	268
28	10	H	Airdrie U	L	0-1	0-1	10		1134
29	17	A	Brechin C	L	1-2	0-0	10	Love [68]	421
30	24	A	Stenhousemuir	W	2-1	1-1	9	Werndly [33], McStay [50]	486
31	31	H	Cowdenbeath	W	1-0	1-0	9	Werndly [7]	402
32	Apr 7	H	Dumbarton	D	1-1	1-1	9	Ferry [20]	471
33	14	A	East Fife	W	2-1	2-0	9	Chaplain [14], Gemmell [40]	566
34	21	H	Arbroath	D	1-1	0-0	8	Love [49]	407
35	28	A	Forfar Ath	L	0-4	0-3	9		554
36	May 5	H	Stirling A	L	1-2	1-0	9	Gemmell [5]	462

Final League Position: 9

Honours
League Champions: Division II 1933-34, Second Division 1988-89; *Runners-up:* Division II 1913-14, 1937-38, 1947-48.
Promoted to Second Division: 2010-11 (play-offs).
Scottish Cup Runners-up: 1920.

Club colours: All red.

Goalscorers: *League (43):* Gemmell 9, Love 9, Chaplain 7 (1 pen), Lawless 3, O'Byrne 3, Werndly 3, Boyle 2, McStay 2, Acqua 1, Ferry 1, Gilmartin 1, Halsman 1, Russell 1.
Scottish Cup (0).
Scottish Communities Cup (2): Boyle 1, Chaplain 1 (pen).
Ramsdens Cup (0).
Play-Offs (5): Chaplain 3 (1 pen), Gemmell 1, Love 1.

Gaston D 29 + 1	Dempsie A 1	Stevenson A 33 + 1	Donnelly R 4	Reid A 35	Donnelly C 18	McStay R 24 + 8	Boyle C 18 + 4	Gilmartin J 5 + 10	Canning S 8	Scott A 7 + 7	Acqua L — + 13	Russell B 20 + 1	Fahey C 6 + 2	Crawford D 1	Lumsden T 22	Chaplain S 26 + 4	Love R 25 + 9	Hamilton C 1 + 6	O'Byrne M 30 + 1	Gemmell J 28 + 1	Marriott S 16 + 6	Ferry D 5 + 2	Lawless S 10	Reilly T — + 5	Halsman J 7	Pierce S 1	Quinn P — + 2	Hunter R 1	Werndly J 9 + 3	McKay D 5 + 3	McGowan J 1	*Match No.*
1▪	2	3	4^{1}	5	6	7	8^{2}	9	10^{6}	11	12	13	15▪																			1
		8		2	3	6	11^{1}	10^{2}		9^{3}	13	5		1	4	7	12	14														2
		2		5	6	7	8^{1}	9^{2}		10^{3}	12	3	1		4	11	13	14														3
15		4		5	6	7▪	9^{6}	8^{2}		11		3	1▪		2^{1}	10	13		12													4
1		3	5▪	4			6	13	7	11^{1}						8	9^{2}	12	2	10												5
1		3		5			7^{2}		6	8^{1}	13					11	9^{3}	12	4	10	2	14										6
1		5		6		8	9^{2}		7^{1}		13	4			3	11▪		12	2	10												7
1		6		2		8^{3}	7	13		12	14	5			4		9	11^{1}	3	10^{2}												8
1		6		2		8	7^{2}			9^{1}	13	5			4		10	12	3				11									9
1		4		6			7	13		12	14				2	8^{3}	10^{1}		3	11	5		9^{2}									10
1		5		6		12	8^{1}	13		14					3	7	9^{3}		2	11	4^{2}		10									11
1		5		6	7	13		14		12					3	8	9^{1}		2	10^{3}	4^{2}		11									12
1		4		5	6	7				12						8	9^{1}		2	11	3		10									13
1		3		2	5	7									8	10	6^{1}		4	11			9	12								14
1		5		6	7	13									4	8^{2}	9^{1}		3	11	2		10	12								15
1		4		6	7	12		14							3	8	9		2	11^{3}	5^{1}		10^{2}	13								16
1		4		6	7	14		9^{1}		13					3	8	10^{2}		2		5^{3}		11	12								17
1		3		5	7	6^{2}				14					4	8	9^{1}		2	11	13		10^{3}	12								18
1		5		6	7	12	8	14			13				2	9	10^{2}		3^{1}	11	4^{3}											19
1		4		5	6	8	9^{2}		7^{3}						2		12			11	14				3	10^{1}	13					20
1		3		4	5	7	6		8								9^{2}		2	11		12					13	10^{1}				21
1			4	2		6			8			5^{2}	13			7	12		3						11				9^{1}	10		22
		4		5	6	7^{2}	9^{3}		8				1			13	14		2	11					3				12	10^{1}		23
		3		7	8							2	1			10	11^{1}		6	13	4^{2}				5				12	9		24
		6		2	3	13						5	1		4^{2}	8	12			10	7				9					11^{1}		25
		2		8	9^{1}	7	13					5	1			6	11		3	10	12				4^{2}							26
1		13		5		6	10					3					12		2	11	4	9^{2}							7	8^{1}		27
1		3		8		13	12					4				7^{2}	9^{3}		5	10	6				2^{1}				11	14		28
1		5		6		8						4			3	10	13		2	11		7^{2}							9^{1}	12		29
1		2		9		8						3				6	11		5	10	12								7		4^{1}	30
1		5		6		7^{1}	12	14				4				13	10^{2}		3	11	2	9^{3}							8			31
1		6		2		7					13	5			4^{3}	12	8^{1}		3	11	14	9^{2}							10			32
1		5		6		7	12	13				4				9^{2}	10^{1}		2	11	3								8▪			33
1		2		8		7	9^{1}				13	5			4	6	11^{2}		3	10										12		34
1		2▪	9			8	6▪				13	3			4	7^{1}	11^{2}		5	10^{3}	12								14			35
1				6		7		14			13	4			3	12	9^{3}		2	10	5^{1}	8							11^{2}			36

ALLOA ATHLETIC

Year Formed: 1878. *Ground & Address:* Recreation Park, Clackmannan Rd, Alloa FK10 1RY. *Telephone:* 01259 722695. *Fax:* 01259 210886. *E-mail:* fcadmin@alloaathletic.co.uk *Website:* www.alloaathletic.co.uk
Ground Capacity: total: 3,100, seated: 400. *Size of Pitch:* 101m × 69m.
Honorary President: George Ormiston. *Chairman:* Mike Mulraney. *Secretary:* Ewen G. Cameron.
Player-Manager: Paul Hartley. *Assistant Manager:* Paddy Connolly. *Coach:* Ronnie Scott. *Physio:* Jim Law.
Club Nicknames: The Wasps, The Hornets.
Previous Grounds: West End Public Park, Gabberston Park, Belleview Park.
Record Attendance: 13,000 v Dunfermline Athletic, Scottish Cup 3rd rd replay, 26 Feb 1939.
Record Transfer Fee received: £100,000 for Martin Cameron to Bristol Rovers.
Record Transfer Fee paid: £26,000 for Ross Hamilton from Stenhousemuir.
Record Victory: 9-0 v Selkirk, Scottish Cup First Round, 28 November 2005.
Record Defeat: 0-10 v Dundee, Division II, 8 Mar 1947 v Third Lanark, League Cup, 8 Aug 1953.
Most Capped Player: Jock Hepburn, 1, Scotland.
Most League Goals in Season (Individual): 49: 'Wee' Willie Crilley, Division II, 1921-22.

ALLOA ATHLETIC 2011–12 LEAGUE RECORD

Match No.	*Date*	*Venue*	*Opponents*	*Result*		*H/T Score*	*Lg Pos.*	*Goalscorers*	*Attendance*
1	Aug 6	A	Stranraer	W	3-2	1-2	—	McCord, Ryan (pen) ^{2}, Gordon ^{59}, Cawley ^{84}	306
2	13	H	Clyde	D	2-2	1-1	3	McCord, Ryan ^{31}, Docherty ^{61}	705
3	20	A	Annan Ath	L	0-2	0-1	4		516
4	27	H	Peterhead	W	2-1	0-1	4	Cawley 2 $^{46, 67}$	507
5	Sept 10	A	East Stirling	W	1-0	1-0	3	Gordon ^{45}	419
6	17	A	Queen's Park	W	3-1	2-0	2	Cawley 2 $^{9, 28}$, Doyle ^{84}	589
7	24	H	Montrose	W	4-2	2-2	2	McCord, Ryan (pen) ^{4}, Cawley 2 $^{28, 79}$, Gordon ^{51}	461
8	Oct 1	A	Elgin C	L	0-5	0-3	3		522
9	15	H	Berwick R	D	1-1	1-1	3	Holmes ^{7}	442
10	Nov 5	H	Stranraer	W	1-0	0-0	2	McCord, Ryan ^{58}	502
11	8	A	Clyde	W	1-0	1-0	—	Holmes ^{2}	654
12	12	A	Peterhead	D	1-1	0-0	2	One ^{77}	528
13	26	H	East Stirling	D	1-1	0-0	—	Campbell ^{83}	421
14	Dec 3	A	Montrose	D	1-1	0-1	2	Gordon ^{79}	313
15	10	H	Queen's Park	W	1-0	1-0	2	Doyle ^{6}	449
16	17	A	Berwick R	D	2-2	1-0	3	McCord, Ryan ^{44}, May ^{61}	362
17	26	H	Elgin C	W	3-0	1-0	1	Docherty ^{16}, Cawley ^{59}, McCord, Ryan ^{90}	491
18	Jan 2	A	East Stirling	W	3-1	1-1	1	May 3 $^{2, 46, 74}$	531
19	14	H	Annan Ath	W	1-0	1-0	1	May ^{30}	635
20	21	A	Stranraer	W	4-0	2-0	1	Docherty ^{25}, May 2 $^{40, 69}$, Masterton ^{60}	475
21	28	H	Montrose	W	2-0	0-0	1	McKinnon ^{87}, May ^{90}	508
22	31	H	Peterhead	W	3-1	2-1	—	Gordon ^{13}, Docherty ^{37}, May ^{65}	429
23	Feb 4	A	Queen's Park	W	2-1	2-0	1	Cawley ^{29}, Little (og) ^{41}	711
24	11	H	Berwick R	L	0-1	0-0	1		544
25	18	A	Elgin C	L	0-3	0-2	1		600
26	25	H	Clyde	W	1-0	0-0	1	Young ^{76}	719
27	Mar 3	A	Annan Ath	W	2-1	1-1	1	Young ^{7}, May ^{77}	642
28	10	H	East Stirling	W	5-1	2-1	1	Winters ^{26}, May ^{43}, Harding ^{60}, McCord, Ross ^{72}, Campbell ^{81}	579
29	17	A	Peterhead	W	1-0	1-0	1	May ^{20}	488
30	24	H	Queen's Park	W	4-0	1-0	1	Winters 2 $^{14, 58}$, May ^{86}, Holmes ^{90}	807
31	31	A	Montrose	W	2-0	0-0	1	McCord, Ryan 2 (1 pen) $^{80 (p), 83}$	390
32	Apr 7	H	Elgin C	W	8-1	2-0	1	Nicolson (og) ^{30}, May 4 $^{44, 46, 65, 75}$, Winters ^{49}, McCord, Ryan ^{82}, Campbell ^{83}	730
33	14	A	Berwick R	L	0-5	0-3	1		486
34	21	H	Stranraer	W	3-1	2-1	1	McCord, Ryan 2 $^{13, 68}$, Winters ^{34}	617
35	28	A	Clyde	D	1-1	1-0	1	May ^{6}	748
36	May 5	H	Annan Ath	D	1-1	0-1	1	May ^{87}	2551

Final League Position: 1

Honours
League Champions: Division II 1921-22; Third Division 1997-98, 2011-12. *Runners-up:* Division II 1938-39. Second Division 1976-77, 1981-82, 1984-85, 1988-89, 1999-2000, 2001-02.
League Challenge Cup Winners: 1999-2000; *Runners-up:* 2001-02.

Club colours: Shirt: Gold with black trim. Shorts: Black. Stockings: Black.

Goalscorers: *League (70):* May 19, McCord, Ryan 11 (3 pens), Cawley 9, Gordon 5, Winters 5, Docherty 4, Campbell 3, Holmes 3, Doyle 2, Young 2, Harding 1, Masterton 1, McCord, Ross 1, McKinnon 1, One 1, own goals 2.
Scottish Cup (2): Cawley 1, Masterton 1.
Scottish Communities Cup (0).
Ramsdens Cup (2): McCord, Ross 1, Wright 1.

Bain S 30	Harding R 35	Gordon B 32 + 1	Smith S 3	Doyle M 36	Docherty M 22 + 7	McCord Ross 10 + 18	McCord Ryan 32	Holmes G 33 + 1	One A 3 + 11	Cawley K 32 + 3	Caddis R — + 2	Innes P 3 + 4	Wright M 1 + 6	McDowall C 6 + 2	Locke N 1	Campbell C 1 + 14	Young D 32	Winters R 20 + 7	Howarth S — + 2	McCullagh M 9 + 4	Masterton S 8 + 6	Forrest F 3 + 2	O'Brien K 1 + 1	McHattie K 5	May S 22	McKinnon R 16	*Match No.*
1	2	3	4	5	6^{1}	7^{3}	8	9	10^{2}	11	12■	13	14														1
1■	2	3	4^{2}	5	9	8^{6}	7	6	12	10		13	11^{1}	15													2
	3	2	4	5	8^{2}	12	7	6	10^{3}	11			14	1	9^{1}	13											3
1	3	2		4	5	9^{2}	7	10		11	12	6				13	8^{1}										4
1	3	2		4	5	6^{1}	8	9	14	11^{3}		12				13	7	10^{2}									5
1	4	3		2	5	12	8	9^{1}		11^{2}		6^{3}				13	7	10	14								6
1	2	3		4	5	8	7	6^{1}	14	11^{3}						13	9	10^{2}	12								7
1■	3	2		4	5■	6^{1}	7	9		11		14		13			8^{3}	10^{2}		12							8
	4	3		2		13	8	9^{2}	14	11		7^{1}		1			6^{3}	10		5	12						9
	6	3■		2		13	9^{3}	7^{2}		11			14	1			8	10^{1}		5	12	4					10
	4			5	12	13	8	9		10^{3}			14	1			7	11^{1}		2	6^{2}	3■					11
	4	3		5	13	9^{2}	8	6	12	11^{3}			14	1			7	10^{1}		2							12
1	4	3^{1}		5	7^{3}	13		9	10^{2}	11						14	6	8		2		12					13
1	4	3		5	6		8	9^{3}	13	11						14	7	10^{2}		2^{1}			12				14
1	2	3		7	13	8		6^{2}		10						12	5	9^{1}						4	11		15
1	4	3		2	5		6	8^{3}	12	11						13	7	14					9^{1}		10^{2}		16
1	4	3■		2	6		8	9^{2}		10^{1}							7				13	12		5	11		17
1	4			2	6		8	9^{1}		10							7				12	3		5	11		18
1	3			4	6		7	11		9							8			2				5	10		19
1	3	4		2	9		6		13	11							7	12			8^{1}			5	10^{2}		20
1	4	3		2	6^{1}	12		8^{3}	13	11							7	14			9^{2}				10	5	21
1	4	3^{1}		2	6	13		8		10							7			12	9^{2}				11	5	22
1	4	3		2	9		8	6		11^{1}							7	12							10	5	23
1	4	3		2	6^{2}	12	8	9^{1}	13	11							7^{3}	14							10	5	24
1	4	3		5	6^{1}	14	8^{3}	9	13	10^{2}							7	12							11	2	25
1	4	3		2			7	12		9							8	11^{1}			6				10	5	26
1	4	3		2		9^{1}	8	10									6	12		13	7				11	5^{2}	27
1	4	3		2		13	6	9		12						14	7	10^{1}			8^{2}				11^{3}	5	28
1	4	3		2	9^{1}	12	8	6		13							7	11^{2}							10	5	29
1	4	3		2		13	6	8		9^{2}						12	7	10^{1}							11	5	30
1	4■	3		2	13	14	7	8		9^{2}							6^{3}	11^{1}		12					10	5	31
1		4		3	13	12	6	8^{2}		11						14	7^{1}	9^{3}		5					10	2	32
	3	14		5^{1}	8	9^{2}	6			12			13	1		11^{3}				2	7				10	4	33
1	4	3		2		12	8^{1}	6		9^{3}						14	7	11^{2}			13				10	5	34
1	3	4		5	12	13	7	6		11^{2}						14	8^{3}	9							10	2^{1}	35
1	4	3		2	13	14	8	6^{3}		9							7^{1}	11			12				10	5^{2}	36

ANNAN ATHLETIC

Year Formed: 1942. *Ground & Address:* Galabank, North Street, Annan DG12 5DQ. *Telephone:* 01461 204108.
E-mail: annanathleticfc@aol.com *Website:* www.annanathleticfc.com
Ground capacity: 3,000 (426 seated). *Size of Pitch:* 100m × 69m.
Chairman: Henry McLelland.
Secretary: Alan Irving.
Manager: Harry Cairney.
Assistant Manager: Andy Aitken.
Coaches: Pietro Baldotto.
Club Nicknames: Galabankies, Black and Golds.
Most League Appearances: 99: Steven Sloan, 2008-12.
Most League Goals in Season (Individual): 15: Mike Jack, 2008-09.
Most Goals Overall (Individual): 21: Graeme Bell, 2008-12.

ANNAN ATHLETIC 2011–12 LEAGUE RECORD

Match No.	Date	Venue	Opponents	Result		H/T Score	Lg Pos.	Goalscorers	Attendance
1	Aug 6	H	Queen's Park	W	5-2	2-2	—	Cox [32], Bell [45], Gibson 2 [59, 65], Sloan [62]	511
2	13	A	Peterhead	W	3-2	1-2	1	McKechnie 2 [19, 50], Harty (pen) [73]	448
3	20	H	Alloa Ath	W	2-0	1-0	1	Harty [33], Cox [64]	516
4	27	H	Clyde	W	1-0	1-0	1	Sloan [29]	644
5	Sept 10	A	Stranraer	L	2-4	1-1	2	Gibson [44], Muirhead (pen) [64]	396
6	17	A	Montrose	W	3-2	1-2	1	Gibson 2 [16, 84], McKechnie [90]	308
7	24	H	East Stirling	W	3-0	3-0	1	Sloan [10], Cox 2 [25, 33]	511
8	Oct 1	A	Berwick R	W	1-0	0-0	1	Gibson [71]	412
9	15	H	Elgin C	D	1-1	0-1	1	Gibson [74]	417
10	Nov 5	A	Queen's Park	D	0-0	0-0	1		502
11	8	H	Peterhead	W	2-0	2-0	—	Muirhead (pen) [10], Steele [11]	388
12	12	A	Clyde	D	0-0	0-0	1		668
13	Dec 3	A	East Stirling	L	0-1	0-1	1		215
14	6	H	Stranraer	L	0-3	0-2	—		304
15	10	H	Montrose	W	2-1	2-0	1	O'Connor 2 [33, 35]	402
16	24	H	Berwick R	D	2-2	2-0	—	Watson, P. [18], Harty [41]	598
17	31	A	Stranraer	L	2-4	1-1	3	Harty (pen) [36], O'Connor [59]	592
18	Jan 7	H	Clyde	W	1-0	0-0	3	O'Connor [64]	505
19	14	A	Alloa Ath	L	0-1	0-1	3		635
20	21	H	Queen's Park	L	2-3	1-1	4	Winters [2], O'Connor [90]	507
21	28	H	East Stirling	D	2-2	1-2	3	Winters [5], Steele [57]	401
22	Feb 4	A	Montrose	D	1-1	0-1	3	Muirhead (pen) [78]	246
23	11	H	Elgin C	D	1-1	1-1	4	Steele [17]	413
24	18	A	Berwick R	W	3-1	2-0	4	Cox [19], Winters [20], O'Connor [59]	389
25	25	A	Peterhead	L	2-3	2-0	5	Muirhead 2 (1 pen) [15 (p), 45]	453
26	Mar 3	H	Alloa Ath	L	1-2	1-1	5	O'Connor [33]	642
27	6	A	Elgin C	L	0-3	0-2	—		588
28	10	H	Stranraer	L	1-3	1-2	5	Swinglehurst [4]	491
29	17	A	Clyde	D	1-1	0-1	5	Winters [70]	503
30	24	H	Montrose	L	1-2	1-2	5	Muirhead (pen) [27]	418
31	31	A	East Stirling	W	4-0	1-0	5	Bell [5], McGowan [62], Steele [70], Underwood [83]	235
32	Apr 7	H	Berwick R	D	1-1	1-0	5	Muirhead (pen) [24]	430
33	14	A	Elgin C	W	2-1	2-1	5	McKechnie 2 [26, 38]	715
34	21	A	Queen's Park	L	0-2	0-1	5		623
35	28	H	Peterhead	L	0-3	0-1	5		408
36	May 5	A	Alloa Ath	D	1-1	1-0	6	Bell [31]	2551

Final League Position: 6

Honours
East of Scotland Premier League: Winners (4).
East of Scotland League Cup: Winners (1).
East of Scotland Div 1: Winners (1).
South of Scotland League: Winners (2).
South of Scotland League Cup: Winners (4).
Scottish Challenge Cup South: Winners (1).
Scottish Qualifying Cup South: Winners (1).

Club colours: Shirt: Gold with black trim. Shorts: Black. Stockings: Gold.

Goalscorers: *League (53):* Gibson 7, Muirhead 7 (6 pens), O'Connor 7, Cox 5, McKechnie 5, Harty 4 (2 pens), Steele 4, Winters 4, Bell 3, Sloan 3, McGowan 1, Swinglehurst 1, Underwood 1, Watson, P. 1.
Scottish Cup (4): Cox 1, Gilfillan 1, Muirhead 1, Watson, P. 1.
Scottish Communities Cup (1): Cox 1.
Ramsdens Cup (7): Harty 4, Cox 2, Muirhead 1.

Summersgill C 11	Gibson S 23	Aitken A 3	McGowan M 35	Watson P 34	Sloan S 30 + 6	Jardine C 26 + 3	McKechnie J 18 + 9	Cox D 31	Harty I 11 + 2	Bell G 16 + 5	Holms R — + 1	Atkinson J — + 3	O'Connor S 23 + 4	Muirhead A 26 + 1	Steele J 19 + 9	Neilson K 2 + 3	Gilfillan B 8 + 12	MacBeth J 9 + 10	Mitchell A 25	Wild G 2 + 1	Mitchell D 8 + 6	Winters D 11 + 6	McKenna B 12 + 2	Swinglehurst S 13 + 1	Underwood L — + 1	*Match No.*
1	2	3	4	5	6	7	8^1	9	10	11^2	12	13														1
1	2	3	4	5	6	8	7	9	10	12			11^1													2
1	2■	3	4	5	6^1	7^2	8	9	10	11				12	13											3
1			4	6	7	8^1	9	10		11				2	12	3	5^2	13								4
1	4		2^3	3	9^2	8	7		10^1			14	11	5	12		6	13								5
1	4		3	5	7^2	8	6	9		11^1			10^3	2	13		12	14								6
1	3^1		4	5	6^2	7	8^3	9		10			11		14	2	12	13								7
	3		4	7^2	12			9	11	8^1			10		5		6	2	1	13						8
1	3		4	5	12	6	7	9	10^1	8							11	2								9
1	3^2		4	5	6^1	8	7^3	9		10			12	2	14	13	11									10
	3		4	7	13	8	12	11^1		9			10	2	5^2	14		6^3	1							11
	4		3	5■	6^1	7	8^2	9		11			10	2		13	12		1							12
1	3		5		13		14	10	12	11^1				2	7		8	6^3		4	9^2					13
			3	7	10		9^1		11			13	8^2	4	6		5^3	12	1	2	14					14
	3		4	6	7		12	9^2	10				11^1	2■	5		13		1		8					15
	3		4■	6	7		12	9	10				11^1		5^2		13	2	1		8					16
	3			5	6^1	8		9	10				11	2			12	4	1		7					17
	4		3	5	6	7		9^2	10	12			11^1	2	13				1		8					18
	3		5	4	6^2	7^1		9		14			11	2	13				1		8	10^3	12			19
	3		4	5	13	8^2		9	14				11	2^1	12				1		7	10	6^3			20
1			5	4	12	7^3	14	9					11	2	8^1						13	10	6^2	3		21
			3	7	8		9^1	10						2	6		4		1		12		11	5		22
			4	7	6			11					10		2			12	1		8^1	9	3	5		23
			5	3	8^1	13	12	9					10^2	2	6				1			11	7	4		24
			5	4	7	8		9^2					11^1	2				13	1		12	10	6	3		25
	3		5		8	7	12	9					11^1	2					1			10	6	4		26
	4^2		5	8	9	7^1	12■	11		13				2				14	1			10^3	6	3		27
	3		5	2	8	14		9		12			11^2	6	7^3				1			10^1	13	4		28
			4	8	6^1	12		11■					10	5	2^2			13	1			9	7	3		29
			4	6	9	8	14						11^3	2	5		13	12	1			10^2	7	3^1		30
			4	6	9	8^3	10			11^1				2	5			3	1		12	14	7^2		13	31
			3	6	10	7	8^2			11^3			12	2	5		13	4	1			14	9^1			32
			5	4	6	8^3	9	11		10^1				2	7		12	3^2	1			14		13		33
			5	7	6^1	8^2	9	11					10^3	2	3		13		1		14	12		4		34
	2		4	6	7^1	8^2	9	11		10^3			12		5		13		1			14		3		35
	2		5	6	9^3	7^2	8	10		11^1			12		4		13		1			14		3		36

ARBROATH

Year Formed: 1878. *Ground & Address:* Gayfield Park, Arbroath DD11 1QB. *Telephone:* 01241 872157. *Fax:* 01241 431125. *E-mail:* afc@gayfield.fsnet.co.uk *Website:* www.arbroathfc.co.uk
Ground Capacity: 4,165 (seated 860; standing 3,305). *Size of Pitch:* 115yd × 71yd.
Chairman: John D. Christison. *Secretary:* Dr Gary Callon. *Administrator:* Mike Cargill.
Manager: Paul Sheerin. *Assistant Manager:* Stewart Petrie. *Physio:* Frank Kenny.
Club Nicknames: The Red Lichties, The Smokies.
Previous Grounds: None.
Record Attendance: 13,510 v Rangers, Scottish Cup 3rd rd, 23 Feb 1952.
Record Transfer Fee received: £120,000 for Paul Tosh to Dundee (Aug 1993).
Record Transfer Fee paid: £20,000 for Douglas Robb from Montrose (1981).
Record Victory: 36-0 v Bon Accord, Scottish Cup 1st rd, 12 Sept 1885.
Record Defeat: 1-9 v Celtic, League Cup 3rd rd, 25 Aug 1993.
Most Capped Player: Ned Doig, 2 (5), Scotland.
Most League Appearances: 445: Tom Cargill, 1966-81.
Most League Goals in Season (Individual): 45: Dave Easson, Division II, 1958-59.
Most Goals Overall (Individual): 120: Jimmy Jack, 1966-71.

ARBROATH 2011–12 LEAGUE RECORD

Match No.	Date	Venue	Opponents	Result	H/T Score	Lg Pos.	Goalscorers	Attendance
1	Aug 6	H	Albion R	W 6-2	2-2	—	Sheerin 2 (2 pens) [7, 58], Sibanda [29], Malcolm [46], McAnespie [51], Bryce [80]	661
2	13	A	Stenhousemuir	L 0-2	0-1	3		492
3	20	H	East Fife	W 3-0	1-0	3	Swankie [28], Doris 2 (1 pen) [69, 81 (p)]	723
4	27	H	Stirling A	W 4-2	1-1	1	McPherson (og) [10], Doris (pen) [51], Sheerin [56], Swankie [65]	670
5	Sept 10	A	Dumbarton	W 4-3	2-3	1	Sibanda [14], Swankie 2 [27, 46], Doris (pen) [68]	640
6	17	H	Airdrie U	W 3-1	1-0	1	McAnespie [6], Doris [63], Swankie [90]	761
7	24	A	Brechin C	W 3-2	1-1	1	Sibanda [36], Doris (pen) [78], Swankie [88]	911
8	Oct 1	H	Cowdenbeath	D 1-1	0-1	1	Falkingham [58]	857
9	15	A	Forfar Ath	D 1-1	1-0	2	Sibanda [12]	908
10	22	A	Albion R	L 0-1	0-1	2		338
11	29	H	Stenhousemuir	W 1-0	0-0	2	Doris (pen) [84]	572
12	Nov 5	H	Dumbarton	W 4-3	3-0	2	McAnespie [21], Malcolm [23], Swankie [26], Doris [79]	723
13	12	A	Stirling A	W 1-0	0-0	2	Malcolm [90]	573
14	26	A	Airdrie U	D 3-3	2-1	2	Swankie [2], Doris (pen) [42], Falkingham [56]	687
15	Dec 3	H	Brechin C	D 1-1	0-0	2	Falkingham [63]	1104
16	10	A	Cowdenbeath	D 0-0	0-0	2		437
17	Jan 2	A	Dumbarton	L 2-3	2-1	2	Doris [26], Falkingham [32]	585
18	14	A	East Fife	D 2-2	1-1	2	Malcolm [31], Swankie [78]	617
19	21	H	Albion R	W 6-1	3-1	2	Sibanda [5], Swankie 2 [28, 56], Falkingham [34], Sheerin [85], Samuel [90]	616
20	Feb 1	H	Stirling A	W 2-0	2-0	—	Doris [9], Sheerin [45]	901
21	11	A	Forfar Ath	W 4-2	2-0	2	Malcolm [17], Samuel [41], Sibanda [75], Sheerin [82]	794
22	14	A	Brechin C	D 1-1	0-0	—	Doris [71]	703
23	18	H	Cowdenbeath	D 1-1	1-0	2	Innes [42]	1125
24	22	H	Forfar Ath	W 4-1	3-1	—	Samuel [20], Doris 3 [44, 45, 72]	789
25	25	A	Stenhousemuir	W 3-1	2-0	2	Doris [9], Falkingham 2 [37, 88]	563
26	29	H	Airdrie U	D 2-2	2-0	—	Gibson 2 [9, 42]	728
27	Mar 3	H	East Fife	D 2-2	2-2	2	Caddis 2 [6, 15]	842
28	10	H	Dumbarton	W 2-0	2-0	2	Innes [24], Doris [27]	824
29	17	A	Stirling A	D 1-1	0-1	2	Falkingham [89]	537
30	24	A	Airdrie U	L 0-2	0-0	2		689
31	31	H	Brechin C	L 2-3	1-2	2	Doris 2 (2 pens) [21, 58]	917
32	Apr 7	A	Cowdenbeath	W 3-2	2-1	2	Doris 2 [25, 75], McAnespie [29]	671
33	14	H	Forfar Ath	L 0-1	0-0	2		998
34	21	A	Albion R	D 1-1	0-0	2	Sibanda [72]	407
35	28	H	Stenhousemuir	L 0-2	0-2	2		643
36	May 5	A	East Fife	W 3-1	2-0	2	Samuel [8], Caddis [29], Sibanda [72]	597

Final League Position: 2

Honours
League Champions: Third Division 2010-11. *League Runners-up:* Division II 1934-35, 1958-59, 1967-68, 1971-72; Second Division 2000-01; Third Division 1997-98, 2007-08. *Promoted to Second Division:* 2007-08 (play-offs).
Scottish Cup: Quarter-finals 1993.

Club colours: Shirt: Maroon with white trim. Shorts: White. Stockings: White.

Goalscorers: *League (76):* Doris 21 (8 pens), Swankie 11, Falkingham 8, Sibanda 8, Sheerin 6 (2 pens), Malcolm 5, McAnespie 4, Samuel 4, Caddis 3, Gibson 2, Innes 2, Bryce 1, own goal 1.
Scottish Cup (1): Sheerin 1 (pen).
Scottish Communities Cup (0).
Ramsdens Cup (1): Elfverson 1.
Play-Offs (1): Malcolm 1.

Hill D 35	Baxter M 29	Malcolm S 31	Wedderburn C 22 + 5	McAnespie K 24 + 1	Gibson K 13 + 14	Kerr B 33 + 2	Falkingham J 34 + 1	Sheerin P 27 + 3	Sibanda L 19 + 15	Swankie G 28 + 5	Girvan G 4 + 1	Bryce L — + 10	Mair J 1 + 2	Busch B 19 + 1	Doris S 33	Elfverson J — + 5	Ardallany P 4 + 6	Birse C 1 + 2	Strachan M — + 1	Brown K 5 + 4	Monti C 2	Caddis L 10 + 10	Samuel C 8 + 5	Connelly C 1	Innes C 12	White M 1	McWalter K — + 1	Robertson D — + 1	*Match No.*
1	2	3	4	5^{1}	6	7	8^{2}	9	10	11^{3}	12	13	14																1
1	5	3	12		6^{3}	7	8	9	10^{2}	11	2	13	14	4^{1}															2
1	5	3	2		7^{1}	12	6	8	10^{3}	9^{2}		14		4	11	13													3
1			2			8	9	7^{3}	5	10	4	12		3	11^{2}		6^{1}	13	14										4
1			3		13	6	7^{2}	9	8^{1}	10^{3}	2	14		4	11		12			5									5
1	2	3		5	12	7	8^{2}	9	13	10		14		4	11^{3}		6^{1}												6
1	2	4		3^{3}	8^{2}	7	6	9^{1}	12	11				5	10		14			13									7
1	2	4		3	8^{1}	6	7		9^{2}	11				5	10	13	12												8
1	2	3		5	13	8	9	10	7^{2}			12		4	11^{3}	14				6^{1}									9
1	2	4	3	5	13	7	6^{2}		9	10					11	12	8^{1}												10
1	2		3^{1}	5		8	6		13	10		14		4	11		7^{2}			12	9^{3}								11
1	2	3	4	5	13	7	8		6^{2}	10		14			11^{3}		12				9^{1}								12
1	2	4	3	9	14	7	6		8^{1}	10^{3}		12			11		13			5^{2}									13
1	2		3	6	12	8	7	13	9^{1}	10				4	11							5^{2}							14
1	2	3	4	6	8	10	7^{2}	13	12	9					11							5^{1}							15
1	2	5	3	7		6	8		9^{1}	10					11		12					4							16
1	2	3	4	6	13	8	7^{2}	9^{3}	12	10					11					14		5^{1}							17
1	6	3^{3}	4		14	7	8	9	10^{2}	13				2	11					5^{1}		12							18
1	5	3	4		13	7	6^{2}	9	8^{1}	10^{3}				2	11							14	12						19
1		4^{3}	5	10	13	8	7	9	12	6				2^{1}	11					14				3^{2}					20
1	2^{2}	3	4	14	13	7	8^{3}	6	12	9					10								11^{1}		5				21
1	5	3	2			7	6	9	8^{1}	10					11^{2}							13	12		4				22
1	5		4			7	6	9	12^{2}	8				2	11							13	10^{1}		3				23
1		3	4	5	8	7	6	9^{3}	12	13				2^{1}	10							14	11^{2}						24
1		3	2	5	8^{2}	7	6	9	12	10^{1}					11^{3}	14						13			4				25
1		3		5	8	7		9	6^{1}	10				2	11							12			4				26
1	3	4			8^{1}	12	7	9^{2}	14	13				2	10							6	11^{3}		5				27
1	2	3		6	14	8	7	9		12				13	10							5^{3}	11^{1}		4^{2}				28
1	2	3	13	6^{2}		8	7	9		12					10							5	11^{1}		4				29
1	2^{2}	3	12	6^{1}		8	7	9	13				10^{3}		11							5	14		4				30
1	5	3	4		12■	7^{1}	6	8^{3}	14	11				2	10							13	9^{2}						31
1	2	3	13	5		7	6	9	8^{1}	10^{2}					11								12		4				32
1	2	3		5		7	8	9	6^{1}	10^{2}					11			13				12			4				33
1	2	3	14	9	8^{1}	7	6	13	12	10^{2}					11							5			4^{3}				34
1		3	4		8	7^{3}	14	9	6^{1}	10^{2}	2				11					5		12	13						35
	2	3		6	8		9^{2}	7	12					4				10^{1}				5	11^{3}			1	13	14	36

AYR UNITED

Year Formed: 1910. *Ground & Address:* Somerset Park, Tryfield Place, Ayr KA8 9NB. *Telephone:* 01292 263435. *Fax:* 01292 281314. *E-mail:* info@ayrunitedfc.co.uk *Website:* ayrunitedfc.co.uk
Ground Capacity: 10,185, seated: 1,597. *Size of Pitch:* 101m × 66m.
Chairman and Managing Director: Lachlan Cameron.
Manager: Mark Roberts. *Assistant Manager:* tba. *Physio:* Ryan MacLeod.
Club Nickname: The Honest Men.
Previous Grounds: None.
Record Attendance: 25,225 v Rangers, Division I, 13 Sept 1969.
Record Transfer Fee received: £300,000 for Steven Nicol to Liverpool (Oct 1981).
Record Transfer Fee paid: £90,000 for Mark Campbell from Stranraer (March 1999).
Record Victory: 11-1 v Dumbarton, League Cup, 13 Aug 1952.
Record Defeat: 0-9 in Division I v Rangers (1929); v Hearts (1931); B Division v Third Lanark (1954).
Most Capped Player: Jim Nisbet, 3, Scotland.
Most League Appearances: 459: John Murphy, 1963-78.
Most League League and Cup Goals in Season (Individual): 66: Jimmy Smith, 1927-28.
Most League and Cup Goals Overall (Individual): 213: Peter Price, 1955-61.

AYR UNITED 2011–12 LEAGUE RECORD

Match No.	Date	Venue	Opponents	Result		H/T Score	Lg Pos.	Goalscorers	Attendance
1	Aug 6	H	Hamilton A	L	1-2	1-1	—	McGowan [8]	1750
2	13	A	Dundee	D	1-1	1-1	7	Moffat [14]	4686
3	20	H	Falkirk	D	2-2	1-2	8	Wardlaw [29], Malone [60]	1938
4	27	H	Raith R	W	2-1	1-1	5	Moffat [23], Robertson, R [90]	1570
5	Sept 10	A	Morton	L	1-4	0-3	9	Roberts (pen) [88]	2018
6	17	A	Partick Th	L	0-4	0-0	10		2639
7	24	H	Queen of the S	W	1-0	0-0	8	Roberts [84]	1582
8	Oct 1	A	Ross Co	L	0-4	0-1	10		2121
9	15	H	Livingston	D	0-0	0-0	8		1390
10	22	H	Dundee	L	1-3	0-1	10	Roberts (pen) [83]	1390
11	29	A	Hamilton A	W	3-2	0-2	8	Moffat [52], Robertson, J [57], Smith [90]	1699
12	Nov 5	H	Morton	L	0-1	0-1	9		1570
13	12	A	Raith R	W	1-0	1-0	8	Graham (og) [10]	2038
14	30	H	Partick Th	D	0-0	0-0	—		1122
15	Dec 3	A	Queen of the S	L	1-4	1-1	9	Wardlaw [45]	1478
16	26	H	Raith R	D	1-1	0-1	9	Tiffoney [63]	1407
17	Jan 2	A	Morton	L	1-3	1-1	9	Moffat [19]	2108
18	14	A	Falkirk	D	0-0	0-0	9		3091
19	21	H	Hamilton A	D	2-2	2-0	9	Dodd [32], Malone [45]	1310
20	Feb 11	H	Queen of the S	D	1-1	0-0	10	Moffat [85]	1475
21	18	A	Ross Co	D	1-1	0-1	10	Tomsett [79]	2390
22	21	A	Partick Th	L	2-4	1-0	—	Parker [4], McGowan [88]	1439
23	25	H	Livingston	W	3-1	1-1	9	Geggan 2 [33, 56], Malone [53]	1312
24	29	H	Ross Co	L	2-3	0-2	—	Parker 2 [52, 75]	1096
25	Mar 3	H	Falkirk	W	1-0	0-0	9	Geggan [73]	1621
26	6	A	Livingston	W	2-1	1-1	—	Roberts (pen) [20], McGowan [66]	859
27	17	A	Raith R	D	2-2	0-1	8	Roberts (pen) [64], Malone [79]	1861
28	24	H	Morton	D	0-0	0-0	8		1669
29	27	A	Dundee	L	1-4	0-1	—	Roberts [77]	3136
30	31	A	Queen of the S	L	1-2	0-2	8	Moffat [78]	2079
31	Apr 7	H	Partick Th	L	1-3	0-2	9	Dodd [79]	1761
32	11	H	Ross Co	L	1-3	0-0	—	Trouten [63]	1389
33	14	A	Livingston	W	1-0	1-0	9	Roberts [24]	1375
34	21	A	Hamilton A	L	2-3	1-1	9	Roberts [17], McGowan [59]	1645
35	28	H	Dundee	W	3-2	0-1	9	Parker 2 [61, 84], Robertson, R [89]	1656
36	May 5	A	Falkirk	L	2-3	0-1	9	Moffat 2 [51, 81]	3445

Final League Position: 9

Honours
League Champions: Division II 1911-12, 1912-13, 1927-28, 1936-37, 1958-59, 1965-66. Second Division 1987-88, 1996-97; *Runners-up:* Division II 1910-11, 1955-56, 1968-69. Second Divison 2008-09. *Promoted to First Division:* 2008-09 (play-offs). *Promoted to First Division:* 2010-11 (play-offs).
Scottish Cup: Semi-finals 2002.
League Cup: Runners-up: 2001-02.
B&Q Cup Runners-up: 1990-91, 1991-92.

Club colours: Shirt: Black and white halves. Shorts: White. Stockings: White with black trim.

Goalscorers: *League (44):* Moffat 8, Roberts 8 (4 pens), Parker 5, Malone 4, McGowan 4, Geggan 3, Dodd 2, Robertson R. 2, Wardlaw 2, Robertson, J. 1, Smith 1, Tiffoney 1, Tomsett 1, Trouten 1, own goal 1.
Scottish Cup (8): Trouten 3 (1 pen), Geggan 2, McGowan 1, Roberts 1 (pen), Robertson, R. 1.
Scottish Communities Cup (6): Roberts 2, Malone 1, Smith 1, Trouten 1, Wardlaw 1.
Ramsdens Cup (5): Campbell 1, Geggan 1, McKernan 1, Paterson 1, Robertson, R. 1.
Play-Off (1): Geggan 1.

Cuthbert K 35	Robertson J 27	Malone E 31	Smith C 34	Campbell M 7 + 2	Geggan A 34	Trouten A 16 + 7	Burke A 1 + 2	McGowan M 33	Moffat M 31 + 5	Roberts M 27 + 8	McKernan J 16 + 4	Wardlaw G 10 + 15	Armstrong G 2 + 2	Robertson R 9 + 11	Duff S 3	Tiffoney J 28 + 2	Connolly R 1 + 8	Paterson R 1 + 1	McManus T 2 + 3	Dodd A 13 + 3	Tomsett L 15 + 1	Parker K 14 + 2	Higgins S 1	Hutchinson S 1 + 1	Longridge J 1 + 1	McWilliams R 1	Crawford R 1	McGill D 1	Wyllie A — + 1	*Match No.*
1	2	3^{3}	4	5	6	7	8^{1}	9	10	11^{2}	12	13	14																	1
1	3		2	4	6	5^{1}		8	12	11	7	10^{2}	9	13																2
1	2	5	3	4■	6			8	9	11^{1}	7	10^{2}	13	12																3
1	3	4	2		7			6	9	11^{1}	8	10		13	5^{2}	12														4
1	2	5	4	3	8	14		9	11	13	7^{3}	10^{2}			6^{1}		12													5
1	2	4		3	7	12		6	10	11^{3}	8	13			5^{2}	14	9^{1}													6
1		3	4		6	11		7^{1}	9^{2}	10	8			5		2	13	12												7
1		4	2		6	9		8^{2}	10	11	7^{1}	12		3		5	13													8
1	2	4	3^{3}		7	6	14	9^{2}	10	11	8^{1}	12		13		5														9
1	3	2			7	8^{1}	14	10^{2}	11	4	9^{3}	13		5		6	12													10
1	3	5	4		7	6^{1}		9	11	13	12	10^{2}		8		2														11
1	2	4	3		8			9	10	12	7^{2}	11^{1}		5		6	13													12
1	3	5	4		7	8		9	11^{2}	13		10^{1}		6		2	12													13
1	2	4	3		8	6		9	10^{2}	11^{1}	7	12				5			13											14
1	2	4■	3		8	6		9^{1}	10^{2}	14	7	11^{3}				5	12		13											15
1	3		4		5	7		9	11^{3}	14	8	10^{2}		2^{1}		6	13		12											16
1	2	4	3		7	6		8	9	10		12		13		5^{2}			11^{1}											17
1	2	4	3		8			6	9	10	7					5			11^{1}	12										18
1	4	3	2		6			8	10^{1}	11^{2}	9	13				5				7	12									19
1	4^{2}	3	5	13	6			11^{3}	14	12						2				7	8	9	10^{1}							20
1		3	2		6^{1}			8	10	11^{2}	12	13		14		4				5	7	9^{3}								21
1	2^{1}	3	4		7			6	9^{3}	11^{2}	14	13		12						5	8	10								22
1		4	5		6			11	7	10		12				2				3	8	9^{1}								23
1		3	2		6			8	9	11^{1}		12				4				5	7	10								24
1		2	3		8			7	9	10						4				6	5	11								25
1		3	4		7			9	6	11						2				5	8	10								26
1	2	4	3					9	12	11		13		5		6				7^{1}	8	10^{2}								27
1	4	2	3		7	13		8^{2}	12	11^{3}				14		9				5	6	10^{1}								28
1	3	2^{1}	4		8	7		6	11	10						5				9		12								29
1	4		3	2	8	6			9	11						5				12	7	10^{1}								30
1	3	2	4		6	9^{1}		7	10^{2}	11^{3}		14				5				12■	8	13								31
1	2	3	5	4^{1}	6	12		9	14	13		11^{2}				7^{3}					8	10								32
1	2^{2}	4	3		6	12		8	9^{3}	11^{1}		14		13		5					7	10								33
1		3■	2		7	12		8	9	11^{2}				13		4				5	6	10^{1}								34
1	2^{1}		3		6	7			11	10				14		4				5^{2}	8	9		12^{3}	13					35
			3	12		13			11		4		2^{3}	8				10^{2}						6	5	1	7	9^{1}	14	36

BERWICK RANGERS

Year Formed: 1881. *Ground & Address:* Shielfield Park, Tweedmouth, Berwick-upon-Tweed TD15 2EF. *Telephone:* 01289 307424. *Fax:* 01289 309424. *Email:* club@berwickrangersfc.co.uk *Website:* berwickrangers.net
Ground Capacity: 4,131, seated: 1,366. *Size of Pitch:* 110yd × 70yd.
Chairman: Brian Porteous. *Vice-Chairman:* Moray McLaren. *Football Secretary:* Dennis McCleary.
Manager: Ian Little. *Assistant Manager:* Robbie Horn. *Physio:* Jamie Dougal. *Ground/Kit:* Ian Oliver.
Club Nicknames: The Borderers, Black and Gold, The Dream Team.
Previous Grounds: Bull Stob Close, Pier Field, Meadow Field, Union Park, Old Shielfield.
Record Attendance: 13,283 v Rangers, Scottish Cup 1st rd, 28 Jan 1967.
Record Victory: 8-1 v Forfar Ath, Division II, 25 Dec 1965; v Vale of Leithen, Scottish Cup, Dec 1966.
Record Defeat: 1-9 v Hamilton A, First Division, 9 Aug 1980.
Most League Appearances: 435: Eric Tait, 1970-87.
Most League Goals in Season (Individual): 33: Ken Bowron, Division II, 1963-64.
Most Goals Overall (Individual): 115: Eric Tait, 1970-87.

BERWICK RANGERS 2011–12 LEAGUE RECORD

Match No.	*Date*	*Venue*	*Opponents*	*Result*		*H/T Score*	*Lg Pos.*	*Goalscorers*	*Attendance*
1	Aug 6	A	Elgin C	L	1-4	0-2	—	Currie, P [84]	534
2	13	H	East Stirling	W	4-2	1-0	6	Currie, P 2 (1 pen) [9 (p), 90], Gray, D [50], McLaren [71]	441
3	20	A	Stranraer	L	1-2	0-0	7	McLaren [77]	260
4	27	A	Queen's Park	D	1-1	1-0	6	McDonald [20]	504
5	Sept 10	H	Montrose	L	1-2	1-1	8	McLaren [11]	368
6	17	H	Peterhead	W	2-1	2-1	6	McLaren 2 [12, 43]	334
7	24	A	Clyde	W	4-1	1-0	5	Gray, D [41], Gribben 2 [54, 56], Smith, E [90]	618
8	Oct 1	H	Annan Ath	L	0-1	0-0	7		412
9	15	A	Alloa Ath	D	1-1	1-1	7	McLeod [16]	442
10	Nov 5	H	Elgin C	D	1-1	1-1	7	Gribben [45]	327
11	9	A	East Stirling	W	3-1	2-1	—	Gribben 2 (1 pen) [7, 66 (p)], McLean [31]	310
12	12	H	Queen's Park	W	2-0	0-0	5	Noble [80], Gray, D [82]	449
13	26	A	Montrose	W	5-3	2-1	—	Gribben 2 [20, 25], Noble 2 [60, 79], Gray, R [90]	328
14	Dec 3	H	Clyde	L	0-2	0-1	5		410
15	17	H	Alloa Ath	D	2-2	0-1	5	Deland [78], Gray, D [84]	362
16	20	A	Peterhead	L	0-1	0-1	—		438
17	24	A	Annan Ath	D	2-2	0-2	—	Gibson (og) [77], Gribben [82]	598
18	Jan 2	H	Montrose	D	2-2	1-0	5	Deland [15], Greenhill [62]	455
19	14	H	Stranraer	D	2-2	2-1	5	Notman [10], Currie, L [32]	438
20	21	A	Elgin C	L	0-4	0-2	6		438
21	Feb 11	A	Alloa Ath	W	1-0	0-0	6	Gray, D (pen) [59]	544
22	14	A	Clyde	D	2-2	1-2	—	Walker [29], Gray, D [90]	351
23	18	H	Annan Ath	L	1-3	0-2	6	Gribben (pen) [80]	389
24	21	A	Queen's Park	D	2-2	1-1	—	Gribben [21], Greenhill [90]	413
25	25	H	East Stirling	L	0-2	0-1	6		349
26	28	H	Peterhead	L	0-1	0-0	—		278
27	Mar 3	A	Stranraer	W	3-1	1-1	6	Noble [27], McLaren [68], Ferguson [80]	330
28	10	A	Montrose	D	1-1	0-0	7	Gray, D [80]	318
29	17	H	Queen's Park	L	1-4	0-0	7	Greenhill [57]	428
30	24	A	Peterhead	W	2-1	1-0	6	Handling 2 [23, 56]	396
31	31	H	Clyde	W	3-0	2-0	6	Handling 2 [31, 35], Currie, L [88]	389
32	Apr 7	A	Annan Ath	D	1-1	0-1	6	Forster [72]	430
33	14	H	Alloa Ath	W	5-0	3-0	6	Handling 2 [13, 51], Currie, L [14], Harding (og) [34], Noble [58]	486
34	21	H	Elgin C	D	3-3	2-1	6	McDonald [1], Forster [45], Noble [53]	411
35	28	A	East Stirling	L	1-2	0-2	7	Currie, L (pen) [70]	277
36	May 5	H	Stranraer	W	1-0	0-0	7	Handling [70]	402

Final League Position: 7

Honours
League Champions: Second Division 1978-79. Third Division 2006-07; *Runners-up:* Second Division 1993-94. Third Division 1999-2000, 2005-06 (not promoted).
Scottish Cup: Quarter-finals 1953-54, 1979-80.
League Cup: Semi-finals 1963-64.
League Challenge Cup: Quarter-finals 2004-05.

Club colours: Shirt: Black with gold vertical stripes. Shorts: Black. Stockings: Black.

Goalscorers: *League (61):* Gribben 10 (2 pens), Gray, D. 7 (1 pen), Handling 7, McLaren 6, Noble 6, Currie, L. 4 (1 pen), Currie, P. 3 (1 pen), Greenhill 3, Deland 2, Forster 2, McDonald 2, Ferguson 1, Gray, R. 1, McLean 1, McLeod 1, Notman 1, Smith, E. 1, Walker 1, own goals 2.
Scottish Cup (0).
Scottish Communities Cup (3): Currie, P. 1, Gray, D. 1, Noble 1.
Ramsdens Cup (4): Currie, L. 2, Gray, D. 1, Greenhill 1, McDonald 1.

Barclay J 29	Walker R 9 + 7	McLeod C 14	Thompson S 18	McLean A 24 + 3	Smith D 1 + 3	Currie P 4	McDonald K 29 + 1	McLaren F 15 + 10	Gray D 16 + 14	Noble S 24 + 8	Gribben D 18 + 9	Smith E 7 + 6	Greenhill D 18 + 8	Townsley C 28	Currie L 33	Notman S 29	Deland M 13 + 5	Little I 4	Lavery D 2 + 6	Gray R 17 + 1	Ponton A 1 + 1	Ferguson J 5 + 7	Tulloch S 4	Forster J 10	McGlinchey C 10 + 1	Bejaoui Y 7	Handling D 7	Miller B — + 4	Match No.
1	2^{2}	3	4	5	6	7	8	9^{1}	10	11^{3}	12	13	14																1
1	2	4	5^{3}			8	9	12	10^{1}	11^{2}	13	14	7	3	6														2
1		5	3	12		8	9	13	14	10^{3}	11^{2}	2	7^{1}	4	6														3
1	12	3	4			8^{1}	9	10	14	13	11^{2}		7^{3}	2	5	6													4
1		3	4				8	7	12	10^{1}	11			2■	5	6	9												5
1		2	3	6			8	7	10^{2}	13	11	12			4	5		9^{1}											6
1		2	3	6	13		9	7^{2}	11^{3}	14	10	12			4	5		8^{1}											7
1		2	3	6	14		8	7^{3}	10^{1}	12	11■	13			4	5		9^{2}											8
1	14	2	3	7	12		9	6^{1}	10^{3}	11		13	8^{2}		5	4													9
1		3		13			6		9^{2}		11^{3}	4	7■	2	8	5	12	10^{1}	14										10
1	2^{3}			5			7		13	10^{1}	11^{2}	4		3	8	9			12	6	14								11
1		3^{1}		12			6		14	11^{3}	10^{2}	2		4	8	7	5		13	9									12
1			3	5			9		13	10^{2}	11	2			7	8^{1}	4		12	6									13
1				5			8		13	10	11^{1}	2		3	7	6	4^{2}		12	9									14
1			5	3			8		13	11	10^{2}		6	4	7	2	12		9^{1}										15
1			5	3			8	13	14	10	11^{3}	4^{1}	9^{2}	2	6	7	12												16
1	12		4	3			9		10	13	14		7^{1}	2	8	6■	5^{2}		11^{3}										17
1			3	6			9	12	11^{2}	10^{1}	13		7	2	8		4				5								18
1	2			5			6	9^{2}	10^{3}	14	11^{1}		13	3	7	8	4		12										19
1	2			5			9■	6	11^{2}	13	10^{1}		12	3	8	7	4												20
1		2	4	5				6^{3}	11	10^{2}	13		9	3		7■	12			8^{1}		14							21
1	6	4	5^{1}	2				9^{2}	11	10	13		8	3	7		12												22
1	4■	3^{1}		6				12	10^{2}	11^{3}	13		7	2	8	9	5					14							23
1			3	6^{2}			8	12			10		13	2	9	5				7^{1}		11	4						24
1			4	5			6	13	12	11^{3}	10^{1}		8^{2}	3	7					9		14	2						25
1	6^{2}							9	11^{3}	12	14			3	8	7				13		10^{1}	4	2	5				26
1	13							6^{2}		11	10^{3}		12	4	8	7				9^{1}		14	3	2	5				27
1								6^{1}	12	11			13	4	7	8	2			9^{2}		10		3	5				28
1							13		11	10^{1}	12		9^{2}	3	7	8	2			6^{3}		14		4	5				29
	12						7		13	10^{1}				4	8	6	2			9				3■	5	1	11^{2}		30
	14			4			6		12				13	3	8	7	5^{3}			9^{1}		11^{2}			2	1	10		31
				5			8		12				13	3■	9	7				6		10^{1}		2	4	1	11^{2}		32
	14			5^{3}			6	13		10^{1}			7^{2}		8	4				9				2	3	1	11	12	33
				5■			6	13		11			7^{1}		8	4				9^{2}				2	3	1	10	12	34
							6	13		11^{2}			8	3	7^{3}	5■				9		12		2	4^{1}	1	10	14	35
	4			5			8	6^{2}		11			7	3						9^{1}		14		2	12	1	10^{3}	13■	36

BRECHIN CITY

Year Formed: 1906. *Ground & Address:* Glebe Park, Trinity Rd, Brechin, Angus DD9 6BJ. *Telephone:* 01356 622856.
Fax: 01382 206331. *E-mail:* secretary@brechincityfc.com *Website:* www.brechincity.com
Ground Capacity: total: 3,960, seated: 1,519. *Size of Pitch:* 110yd × 67yd.
Chairman: Kenneth Ferguson. *Vice-Chairman:* Martin Smith. *Secretary:* Gus Fairlie.
Manager: Jim Weir. *Assistant Manager:* Kevin McGowne. *Physio:* Tom Gilmartin.
Club Nicknames: The City, The Hedgemen.
Previous Grounds: Nursery Park.
Record Attendance: 8122 v Aberdeen, Scottish Cup 3rd rd, 3 Feb 1973.
Record Transfer Fee received: £100,000 for Scott Thomson to Aberdeen (1991) and Chris Templeman to Morton (2004).
Record Transfer Fee paid: £16,000 for Sandy Ross from Berwick Rangers (1991).
Record Victory: 12-1 v Thornhill, Scottish Cup 1st rd, 28 Jan 1926.
Record Defeat: 0-10 v Airdrieonians, Albion R and Cowdenbeath, all in Division II, 1937-38.
Most League Appearances: 459: David Watt, 1975-89.
Most League Goals in Season (Individual): 26: Ronald McIntosh, Division II, 1959-60.
Most Goals Overall (Individual): 131: Ian Campbell, 1977-85.

BRECHIN CITY 2011–12 LEAGUE RECORD

Match No.	Date	Venue	Opponents	Result		H/T Score	Lg Pos.	Goalscorers	Attendance
1	Aug 6	H	Stenhousemuir	W	2-0	0-0	—	McKenna [71], McManus [80]	442
2	13	A	Cowdenbeath	L	1-3	1-1	6	Brady [37]	308
3	20	H	Dumbarton	D	3-3	0-2	5	Fusco [46], McManus (pen) [52], McKenna [56]	427
4	27	A	Albion R	W	2-1	1-1	5	McManus (pen) [30], Dunlop [90]	386
5	Sept 10	H	Forfar Ath	L	0-1	0-0	5		651
6	17	A	East Fife	D	1-1	0-1	6	Lister [57]	501
7	24	H	Arbroath	L	2-3	1-1	6	Buist [29], McManus (pen) [82]	911
8	Oct 1	A	Stirling A	L	0-1	0-1	7		555
9	15	H	Airdrie U	D	1-1	0-1	8	King (pen) [51]	455
10	22	A	Stenhousemuir	D	1-1	1-1	9	King (pen) [29]	681
11	29	H	Cowdenbeath	W	1-0	0-0	6	King [53]	418
12	Nov 5	A	Forfar Ath	D	0-0	0-0	5		661
13	12	H	Albion R	L	1-4	0-2	7	Lister [81]	455
14	26	H	East Fife	L	0-2	0-2	8		503
15	Dec 3	A	Arbroath	D	1-1	0-0	8	McManus [90]	1104
16	17	A	Airdrie U	W	3-2	1-0	—	Lister [34], McManus [79], McKenna [82]	643
17	26	A	Albion R	W	1-0	1-0	6	McManus [38]	414
18	Jan 2	H	Forfar Ath	W	2-1	0-1	5	McManus 2 [51, 59]	776
19	14	A	Dumbarton	L	0-1	0-0	6		572
20	Feb 11	H	Airdrie U	D	1-1	1-0	7	McManus [26]	483
21	14	H	Arbroath	D	1-1	0-0	—	McLean [81]	703
22	18	A	Stirling A	W	3-2	0-1	6	Ferry (og) [53], Hodge [83], McKenzie [87]	479
23	21	H	Stenhousemuir	W	1-0	0-0	—	McKenzie [70]	347
24	25	A	Cowdenbeath	L	0-1	0-0	6		332
25	28	H	Stirling A	L	1-3	0-2	—	McManus [63]	362
26	Mar 3	H	Dumbarton	D	2-2	2-0	6	McManus [30], McKenzie [34]	459
27	6	A	East Fife	D	2-2	2-2	—	McManus [21], McKenna [34]	416
28	10	A	Forfar Ath	L	1-4	0-3	6	Buist [46]	584
29	17	H	Albion R	W	2-1	0-0	6	McKenzie (pen) [54], King [90]	421
30	24	H	East Fife	L	1-3	1-1	7	Moyes [16]	525
31	31	A	Arbroath	W	3-2	2-1	7	McKenzie [6], McManus 2 [14, 65]	917
32	Apr 7	H	Stirling A	L	1-2	0-1	7	Buist [86]	468
33	14	A	Airdrie U	L	1-4	1-3	7	Hodge [31]	802
34	21	A	Stenhousemuir	L	1-2	0-1	7	Lister [82]	541
35	28	H	Cowdenbeath	D	2-2	2-1	7	McKenzie 2 (1 pen) [22 (p), 25]	487
36	May 5	A	Dumbarton	L	2-4	0-0	8	King [53], Molloy [88]	636

Final League Position: 8

Honours

League Champions: C Division 1953-54. Second Division 1982-83, 1989-90, 2004-05. Third Division 2001-02. *Runners-up:* Second Division 1992-93, 2002-03. Third Division 1995-96.
League Challenge Cup Runners-up 2002-03. Semi-finals 2001-02.

Club colours: Shirt: Red with white trim. Shorts: White. Stockings: Red.

Goalscorers: *League (47):* McManus 15 (3 pens), McKenzie 7 (2 pens), King 5 (2 pens), Lister 4, McKenna 4, Buist 3, Hodge 2, Brady 1, Dunlop 1, Fusco 1, McLean 1, Molloy 1, Moyes 1, own goal 1.
Scottish Cup (4): McManus 2, King 1, Molloy 1.
Scottish Communities Cup (2): King 1, McKenna 1.
Ramsdens Cup (1): McKenna 1.

Nelson C 34	Buist S 30 + 1	Dunlop M 32	McLauchlan G 8 + 1	McLean P 30	Janczyk N 12	Molloy C 31	Brady G 25 + 3	McManus P 24 + 6	McKenna D 23 + 11	Weir G 5 + 7	Carcary D 2 + 9	King C 13 + 11	Lister J 15 + 11	Fusco G 20 + 9	McClune D 6 + 6	Crawford S 9 + 11	Smith S 11 + 1	Hodge B 23 + 2	Moyes E 14 + 1	McKenzie R 16 + 1	Lindsay J 9	Scott D 2	Adam M 1	Webster S 1	*Match No.*
1	2	3	4	5	6	7	8	9^{3}	10^{2}	11^{1}	12	13	14												1
1	4	5	3	2	8	7	6	11^{1}	9	10^{2}	12	13													2
1	5^{2}	3	4	2	6	7		10^{3}	11	14	9	8^{1}		12	13										3
1	13	5	3	4	7^{3}	8	14	9	10		11^{1}			6	2	12^{2}									4
1		5	3	4		8	7^{3}	10^{1}	9		12■	11^{2}	13	6	2	14									5
1	4	5	3^{1}	2	8				11	12			10	9		7	6								6
1	4	5		2	8			13	9^{1}	11^{2}			10	7		6	3	12							7
1	3	5		2	6		12	13	9^{1}	10		14	11■	8^{3}		7^{2}	4								8
1	4	5		2	6			12	13	10^{1}		11^{2}		8		9	3	7							9
1	3	4		2	8	6^{2}		11^{3}		12		10^{1}		7	13	14	5	9■							10
1	3	4		2	7	6		10^{2}	14	13		9^{3}	11^{1}	8	12		5								11
1	4	5		2	6	7^{3}	14	10^{2}		13		9^{1}	11	8	12		3								12
1	3	4		2	7^{1}	6		10^{2}	14			11^{3}	13	8		12	5	9							13
1	3	4		2		7	6		10^{3}		14	9	11	8^{2}	5^{1}	13	12								14
1	4	5		2		7	6	12	14		13	11^{3}	10^{1}			9^{2}	3	8							15
1	4	3		2		7	8	13	12		14	10^{1}	11^{2}			6^{3}	5	9							16
1	3	4		2		6	7	10^{1}	9	12			11				5	8							17
1	3^{1}	4	12	2		7	6	11^{2}	9^{3}	13			10	14	5			8							18
1		4	3^{1}	2		6	7	10	11^{3}			13		14	5	9^{2}		8	12						19
1	3	4		2		7■	6	11	9				10^{2}	12	5^{1}			8		13					20
1	5	4		2			8	11^{3}	13				12	7		14		9	3	10^{2}	6^{1}				21
	4	3		2		9	8	11^{2}	13				12	7^{1}				6	5	10		1			22
1	3			5		7	8	10^{3}	11					13	12^{2}	14		6	4^{1}	9	2				23
1	4	3		2^{1}		6	7	11^{2}	9					12		13		8		10	5				24
1	3	2				8	7	11^{2}	12			13		5		6				10	4^{1}		9		25
1		2				7	6	11^{1}	12				10	5				8	3	9	4				26
1		3		2		6	7	11	10^{1}							12		8	4	9	5				27
1	2					6	7	10	11^{1}			13	12	5				8	3	9^{2}	4				28
1	5	4		2		8	7	12	13			14	11^{1}					9	3	10^{3}	6^{2}				29
1	4	3		2		7	6	11	9^{2}			12^{3}	13	14				8^{1}	5	10					30
1	3	5		2		8	7	10^{3}	6^{2}			12	14	13				9	4	11^{1}					31
1	3	5		2		7	6^{2}		11^{3}			10	14	12		13		8^{1}	4	9					32
1			3	2		8	7	11^{3}	13			10^{1}	14	6^{2}				12	4	9	5				33
1	2	4				7	8		10^{2}		13	14	12	5		6^{1}		9	3	11^{3}					34
1	3	2				7	6		11^{1}		13	12	10^{2}	5				8	4	9					35
	3					7			9^{3}		13	11^{2}	10	6	12	14		5	4	8		1		2^{1}	36

CELTIC

Year Formed: 1888. *Ground & Address:* Celtic Park, Glasgow G40 3RE. *Telephone:* 0871 226 1888. *Fax:* 0141 551 4223. *E-mail:* customerservices@celticfc.co.uk *Website:* www.celticfc.net
Ground Capacity: all seated: 60,355. *Size of Pitch:* 105m × 68m.
Chairman: Ian P. Bankier. *Chief Executive:* Peter Lawwell. *Secretary:* Robert Howat.
Manager: Neil Lennon. *Assistant Manager:* Johan Mjallby. *First Team Coaches:* Alan Thompson and Garry Parker. *Physio:* Graham Parsons.
Club Nicknames: The Bhoys, The Hoops, The Celts. *Previous Grounds:* None.
Record Attendance: 92,000 v Rangers, Division I, 1 Jan 1938.
Record Transfer Fee received: £6,500,000 for Stilian Petrov to Aston Villa (August 2007).
Record Transfer Fee paid: £6,000,000 for Chris Sutton from Chelsea (July 2000).
Record Victory: 11-0 Dundee, Division I, 26 Oct 1895.
Record Defeat: 0-8 v Motherwell, Division I, 30 Apr 1937.
Most Capped Player: Pat Bonner 80, Republic of Ireland.
Most League Appearances: 486: Billy McNeill, 1957-75.
Most League Goals in Season (Individual): 50: James McGrory, Division I, 1935-36.
Most Goals Overall (Individual): 397: James McGrory, 1922-39.

Honours
League Champions: (43 times) Division I 1892-93, 1893-94, 1895-96, 1897-98, 1904-05, 1905-06, 1906-07, 1907-08, 1908-09, 1909-10, 1913-14, 1914-15, 1915-16, 1916-17, 1918-19, 1921-22, 1925-26, 1935-36, 1937-38, 1953-54, 1965-66, 1966-67, 1967-68, 1968-69, 1969-70, 1970-71, 1971-72, 1972-73, 1973-74. Premier Division 1976-77, 1978-79, 1980-81, 1981-82, 1985-86, 1987-88, 1997-98, 2000-01, 2001-02, 2003-04, 2005-06, 2006-07, 2007-08, 2011-12. *Runners-up:* 31 times.
Scottish Cup Winners: (35 times) 1892, 1899, 1900, 1904, 1907, 1908, 1911, 1912, 1914, 1923, 1925, 1927, 1931, 1933, 1937, 1951, 1954, 1965, 1967, 1969, 1971, 1972, 1974, 1975, 1977, 1980, 1985, 1988, 1989, 1995, 2001, 2004, 2005, 2007, 2011. *Runners-up:* 18 times.

CELTIC 2011–12 LEAGUE RECORD

Match No.	Date	Venue	Opponents	Result		H/T Score	Lg Pos.	Goalscorers	Attendance
1	July 24	A	Hibernian	W	2-0	1-0	—	Stokes [14], Ki [63]	12,523
2	Aug 7	A	Aberdeen	W	1-0	0-0	—	Stokes [74]	12,497
3	13	H	Dundee U	W	5-1	2-1	2	Stokes [4], Hooper [33], Ki [58], Ledley [71], Forrest [90]	50,589
4	21	H	St Johnstone	L	0-1	0-0	3		40,268
5	28	A	St Mirren	W	2-0	2-0	3	Hooper 2 [6, 12]	6223
6	Sept 10	H	Motherwell	W	4-0	2-0	2	Forrest 2 [9, 74], Ledley [33], Ki [67]	48,793
7	18	A	Rangers	L	2-4	2-1	2	Hooper [34], El Kaddouri [41]	50,221
8	24	H	Inverness CT	W	2-0	2-0	2	Ledley [28], Forrest [33]	47,382
9	Oct 2	A	Hearts	L	0-2	0-0	3		14,749
10	15	A	Kilmarnock	D	3-3	0-3	3	Stokes 2 [73, 76], Mulgrew [80]	8011
11	23	H	Aberdeen	W	2-1	1-0	3	Ki [17], Mulgrew [72]	49,037
12	29	H	Hibernian	D	0-0	0-0	3		48,670
13	Nov 6	A	Motherwell	W	2-1	1-1	2	Stokes [14], Hooper [80]	10,440
14	19	A	Inverness CT	W	2-0	0-0	2	Stokes 2 [61, 72]	6435
15	23	H	Dunfermline Ath	W	2-1	2-0	—	Hooper [6], Forrest [13]	41,000
16	26	H	St Mirren	W	5-0	2-0	2	Samaras [4], Hooper 3 [8, 53, 57], McGeouch [72]	48,406
17	Dec 4	A	Dundee U	W	1-0	1-0	2	Hooper [12]	10,980
18	10	H	Hearts	W	1-0	0-0	2	Wanyama [72]	49,023
19	18	A	St Johnstone	W	2-0	0-0	2	Hooper [60], Ki [64]	6759
20	24	H	Kilmarnock	W	2-1	1-0	2	Samaras 2 [45, 53]	49,352
21	28	H	Rangers	W	1-0	0-0	1	Ledley [52]	58,658
22	Jan 2	A	Dunfermline Ath	W	3-0	2-0	1	Stokes [18], Wanyama [40], Mulgrew [69]	10,140
23	14	H	Dundee U	W	2-1	2-0	1	Hooper [12], Wanyama [17]	50,139
24	21	A	St Mirren	W	2-0	0-0	1	Forrest [71], Brown [88]	6129
25	Feb 8	A	Hearts	W	4-0	3-0	—	Brown [3], Wanyama [20], Ledley [31], Hooper [60]	14,787
26	11	H	Inverness CT	W	1-0	1-0	1	Ledley [16]	50,014
27	19	A	Hibernian	W	5-0	2-0	1	Stokes [14], Hooper 2 [20, 52], Mulgrew [47], Ki [77]	12,161
28	22	H	Dunfermline Ath	W	2-0	1-0	—	Mulgrew [32], Forrest [75]	45,000
29	25	H	Motherwell	W	1-0	0-0	1	Hooper [59]	53,486
30	Mar 3	A	Aberdeen	D	1-1	1-1	1	Stokes [28]	13,127
31	25	A	Rangers	L	2-3	0-1	1	Brown (pen) [89], Rogne [90]	50,191
32	Apr 1	H	St Johnstone	W	2-0	0-0	1	Samaras [66], Millar (og) [70]	57,848
33	7	A	Kilmarnock	W	6-0	4-0	1	Mulgrew 2 [8, 35], Loovens [17], Hooper 2 [45, 90], Ledley [88]	15,926
34	22	A	Motherwell	W	3-0	0-0	1	Watt 2 [63, 66], Cha [83]	8760
35	29	H	Rangers	W	3-0	2-0	1	Mulgrew [17], Commons [31], Hooper [54]	58,546
36	May 3	H	St Johnstone	W	1-0	1-0	—	Stokes [28]	50,297
37	6	A	Dundee U	L	0-1	0-1	1		9144
38	13	H	Hearts	W	5-0	3-0	1	Hooper 5 (1 pen) [5, 8, 39 (p), 66, 87]	58,875

Final League Position: 1

League Cup Winners: (14 times) 1956-57, 1957-58, 1965-66, 1966-67, 1967-68, 1968-69, 1969-70, 1974-75, 1982-83, 1997-98, 1999-2000, 2000-01, 2005-06, 2008-09; *Runners-up:* 15 times.

European: *European Cup:* 140 matches (1966-67 winners, 1967-68, 1968-69, 1969-70 runners-up, 1970-71, 1971-72, 1972-73, 1973-74 semi-finals, 1974-75, 1977-78, 1979-80, 1981-82, 1982-83, 1986-87, 1988-89, 1998-99, 2001-02, 2002-03, 2003-04, 2004-05, 2005-06, 2006-07, 2007-08, 2008-09, 2009-10, 2010-11). *Cup Winners' Cup:* 28 matches (1963-64 semi-finals, 1965-66 semi-finals, 1975-76, 1980-81, 1984-85, 1985-86, 1989-90, 1995-96). *UEFA Cup:* 75 matches (*Fairs Cup:* 1962-63, 1964-65. *UEFA Cup:* 1976-77, 1983-84, 1987-88, 1991-92, 1992-93, 1993-94, 1996-97, 1997-98, 1998-99, 1999-2000, 2000-01, 2001-02, 2002-03 runners-up, 2003-04 quarter-finals). *Europa League:* 16 matches (2009-10, 2010-11, 2011-12).

Club colours: Shirt: Emerald green and white hoops. Shorts: White with emerald green trim. Stockings: White with emerald green trim.

Goalscorers: *League (84):* Hooper 24 (1 pen), Stokes 12, Mulgrew 8, Forrest 7, Ledley 7, Ki 6, Samaras 4, Wanyama 4, Brown 3 (1 pen), Watt 2, Cha 1, Commons 1, El Kaddouri 1, Loovens 1, McGeouch 1, Rogne 1, own goal 1.
Scottish Cup (10): Stokes 4, Brown 2 (2 pens), Samaras 2, Hooper 1, Ledley 1.
Scottish Communities Cup (9): Stokes 3, Forrest 2, Hooper 2, Brown 1 (pen), own goal 1.
Europa League (7): Hooper 2, Stokes 2, Ki 1 (pen), Ledley 1, Mulgrew 1.

Zaluska L 5	Wilson M 5 + 2	Izaguirre E 9 + 3	Ki S 21 + 9	Loovens G 11	Wilson K 14 + 1	Kayal B 18 + 1	Ledley J 31 + 1	Stokes A 25 + 9	Hooper G 34 + 3	Commons K 16 + 8	Forrest J 23 + 6	Samaras G 20 + 6	Maloney S 1 + 2	Matthews A 25 + 2	Majstorovic D 15 + 2	Mulgrew C 29 + 1	Brown S 20 + 2	McCourt P — + 13	Forster F 33	Wanyama V 24 + 5	Cha D 11 + 4	El Kaddouri B 5 + 1	Bangura M 2 + 8	Rogne T 15 + 2	McGeouch D 1 + 5	Brozek P 1 + 2	Lustig M 3 + 1	Blackman A 1 + 2	Twardzik F — + 1	Watt T — + 3	Ibrahim R — + 1	*Match No.*
1	2	3	4	5	6	7	8	9^{2}	10^{3}	11^{1}	12	13	14																			1
1		3^{1}	4		6	7	8^{2}	9^{3}	10	11	13	14		2	5	12																2
1	2		4		6		8	9^{3}	10^{2}	11^{1}	12		13		5	3	7	14														3
	12		4				8^{3}	9		11^{2}	14		10	2	5	3^{1}	7	13	1	6												4
			4^{1}		6	7	12	9	10		11				5	3	8		1		2											5
			4		6	7^{3}	8^{2}	9^{1}	10	13	11			2		5			1	14		3	12									6
	2		4	5	6	7		12	10		13	9^{3}				11■	8^{2}		1			3^{1}	14									7
			4^{2}	6		7	8	9^{3}	10^{1}		11	13		2	5			14	1			3	12									8
	13		4					12	10	11■	7			2^{2}	5	6		14	1	8		3^{3}	9^{1}									9
			4			7^{1}	8	9	10^{2}		11			2	5	6			1	12	3^{3}	14	13									10
			4	5^{1}		7	3	9	10		11			2	12	6		13	1	8^{2}												11
	3		8^{2}			7^{1}	4	9	10^{3}		11	14		2		6		12	1	13				5								12
						7		10	12	8^{1}	11^{3}	9^{2}		2	5			13	1	6	3			4	14							13
			12			7	6	8	10	14	11^{3}	9^{2}		2	5			13	1	3		4^{1}										14
			4			8	3	9^{2}	10	11^{1}	7	13		2	5			12	1	6												15
				4		7	3	8	10^{2}		11^{1}	9^{3}		2	5			13	1	6			14		12							16
			13	4^{1}		7		8^{2}	10		11	9		2	5		12		1	6	3											17
			13	4^{1}		7^{2}		8^{3}	10		11	9			5	3	12		1	6	2		14									18
			4			7^{2}			10^{3}		11	9			5^{1}	6	8		1	3	2		14	12	13							19
			4^{3}		12	7	3		10		11^{1}	9^{2}				5	8		1	6	2		13	14								20
			12			7^{1}	3	13	10^{2}		11	9		2		5	8		1	6				4								21
		14	12				3	8	10^{1}		11	9		2^{2}		5	7		1	6^{3}	13			4								22
		3^{2}	12				11	8^{1}	10	13		9		2		5	7		1	6				4								23
			7^{1}				3	12	10	13	11^{3}	9^{2}		14		5	8		1	6	2			4								24
					5		11	13	10^{2}		7	9		2	12	3	8^{3}		1	6				4^{1}		14						25
			12		4		11		10^{1}	13	7^{2}	9		2	5■	3	8		1	6												26
		14	12		4		11	9	10^{2}	13	7			2		3	8		1	6^{1}				5^{3}								27
		3^{1}	4		6		11	9^{2}	10	7	13	12				5	8^{3}		1		2					14						28
			8		4		11	12	10^{2}	14	7^{3}	9		2		3			1	6^{1}	13			5								29
					6		11	9	10	8^{2}	7					4			1	12	14			5	13		2^{3}	3^{1}				30
		12	7^{2}				11^{3}	10^{1}	14	13		9		3		4	8		1	6■	2■			5								31
			13	5			6	7^{2}	10^{3}	11		9		12		3	8		1					4			2^{1}	14				32
			7	5	3		4	13	10	11		9^{2}		2		6^{3}	8^{1}		1									14	12			33
1		3	8^{1}				11		10	7^{3}						5		12		6	2			4		9^{2}	14			13		34
		3		5			11	14	10^{1}	7^{2}		9^{3}		2		6	8	12	1	4										13		35
1	2^{2}	3			4		8	10	12	11^{3}										6	13		9	5	7^{1}						14	36
		11					6	9^{1}	10	7				3		5	8^{3}		1	13				4^{2}	14		2			12		37
		3		5		12	11^{2}	14	10	7^{3}		9		2		4	8^{1}	13	1	6												38

CLYDE

Year Formed: 1877. *Ground & Address:* Broadwood Stadium, Cumbernauld, G68 9NE. *Telephone:* 01236 451511. *Fax:* 01236 733490. *E-mail:* info@clydefc.co.uk *Website:* www.clydefc.co.uk
Ground Capacity: all seated: 8,006. *Size of Pitch:* 112yd × 76yd.
Chairman: John Alexander. *Secretary:* John D. Taylor.
Manager: Jim Duffy. *Assistant Manager:* Chic Charnley. *Physio:* Iain McKinlay.
Club Nickname: The Bully Wee.
Previous Grounds: Barrowfield Park 1877-97, Shawfield Stadium 1897-1986, Firhill Stadium 1986-91, Douglas Park 1991-94.
Record Attendance: 52,000 v Rangers, Division I, 21 Nov 1908.
Record Transfer Fee received: £200,000 from Blackburn R for Gordon Greer (May 2001).
Record Transfer Fee paid: £14,000 for Harry Hood from Sunderland (1966).
Record Victory: 11-1 v Cowdenbeath, Division II, 6 Oct 1951.
Record Defeat: 0-11 v Dumbarton, Scottish Cup 4th rd, 22 Nov, 1879; v Rangers, Scottish Cup 4th rd, 13 Nov 1880.
Most Capped Player: Tommy Ring, 12, Scotland.
Most League Appearances: 420: Brian Ahern, 1971-81; 1987-88.
Most League Goals in Season (Individual): 32: Bill Boyd, 1932-33.

CLYDE 2011–12 LEAGUE RECORD

Match No.	*Date*	*Venue*	*Opponents*	*Result*		*H/T Score*	*Lg Pos.*	*Goalscorers*	*Attendance*
1	Aug 6	H	Peterhead	W	2-0	1-0	—	Sweeney [45], McDonald [75]	711
2	13	A	Alloa Ath	D	2-2	1-1	2	Sweeney 2 (1 pen) [21, 80 (p)]	705
3	20	H	Montrose	W	1-0	0-0	2	McDonald [50]	700
4	27	A	Annan Ath	L	0-1	0-1	3		644
5	Sept 10	H	Queen's Park	L	0-2	0-0	5		650
6	17	A	Elgin C	W	3-0	2-0	7	Cusack 2 [12, 26], Neill [68]	728
7	24	H	Berwick R	L	1-4	0-1	6	Neill [48]	618
8	Oct 1	A	Stranraer	D	0-0	0-0	5		363
9	15	H	East Stirling	W	7-1	3-0	5	McDonald [14], Brown [19], Neill [31], Gallagher [77], Oliver [81], Cusack [82], Archdeacon [90]	617
10	Nov 5	A	Peterhead	D	0-0	0-0	6		517
11	8	H	Alloa Ath	L	0-1	0-1	—		654
12	12	H	Annan Ath	D	0-0	0-0	7		668
13	Dec 3	A	Berwick R	W	2-0	1-0	6	Sweeney (pen) [25], Cusack [86]	410
14	13	A	Queen's Park	L	0-3	0-1	—		402
15	17	A	East Stirling	D	1-1	0-1	7	Cusack [90]	490
16	26	H	Stranraer	D	1-1	1-1	7	Neill [28]	556
17	Jan 2	H	Queen's Park	L	1-2	1-1	7	White [45]	668
18	7	A	Annan Ath	L	0-1	0-0	7		505
19	14	A	Montrose	L	0-4	0-0	7		365
20	21	H	Peterhead	L	0-1	0-1	7		456
21	Feb 11	H	East Stirling	W	3-0	1-0	7	Sweeney (pen) [19], Sloss [46], Neill [66]	507
22	14	H	Berwick R	D	2-2	2-1	—	Brown [6], Neill [13]	351
23	18	A	Stranraer	L	0-1	0-0	8		385
24	21	H	Elgin C	L	1-2	1-0	—	Niven (og) [23]	352
25	25	A	Alloa Ath	L	0-1	0-0	8		719
26	28	A	Elgin C	D	1-1	1-0	—	Pollock [37]	611
27	Mar 3	H	Montrose	L	1-2	0-0	8	Crighton (og) [54]	476
28	17	H	Annan Ath	D	1-1	1-0	8	Pollock [26]	503
29	20	A	Queen's Park	L	0-3	0-2	—		658
30	24	H	Elgin C	L	0-2	0-0	9		450
31	31	A	Berwick R	L	0-3	0-2	9		389
32	Apr 7	H	Stranraer	W	2-1	0-1	8	Brannan [55], Belkouche (og) [63]	506
33	14	A	East Stirling	W	1-0	0-0	8	Neill [76]	434
34	21	A	Peterhead	D	1-1	0-0	9	Gallagher [90]	497
35	28	H	Alloa Ath	D	1-1	0-1	8	Scullion [65]	748
36	May 5	A	Montrose	L	0-5	0-2	9		450

Final League Position: 9

Honours
League Champions: Division II 1904-05, 1951-52, 1956-57, 1961-62, 1972-73. Second Division 1977-78, 1981-82, 1992-93, 1999-2000.
Runners-up: Division II 1903-04, 1905-06, 1925-26, 1963-64. First Division 2002-03, 2003-04.
Scottish Cup Winners: 1939, 1955, 1958; *Runners-up:* 1910, 1912, 1949.
League Challenge Cup Runners-up: 2006-07.

Club colours: Shirt: Red and white halves. Shorts: Black. Stockings: Red.

Goalscorers: *League (35):* Neill 7, Cusack 5, Sweeney 5 (3 pens), McDonald 3, Brown 2, Gallagher 2, Pollock 2, Archdeacon 1, Brannan 1, Oliver 1, Scullion 1, Sloss 1, White 1, own goals 3.
Scottish Cup (1): Neill 1.
Scottish Communities Cup (4): Archdeacon 1, Gray 1, Sweeney 1 (pen), own goal 1.
Ramsdens Cup (3): McDonald 2, Fitzpatrick 1.

Mental F 11	Gray I 30 + 2	Sharp L 35	Brown G 19 + 4	Scullion P 14 + 7	McQueen B 29	Sweeney J 32 + 1	Hay P 29	Oliver M 17 + 12	Cusack L 18	McDonald S 18 + 10	McMullan P 1 + 3	Irvine C 1 + 8	Archdeacon M 1 + 11	Gallagher D 25	Neill J 33	Kane R 10 + 15	Sloss J 4 + 5	Ramsay D 2 + 3	Fitzpatrick D — + 4	Combe A 1	Crawford D 12	Marr J 16 + 1	White J 6	Fulton D 1 + 1	Finlayson K 1	Brannan K 9	Pollock J 8 + 1	Feely N 12	Daw K — + 2	Dickie G 1 + 1	*Match No.*
1	2^{2}	3	4	5	6	7	8	9^{1}	10	11^{3}	12	13	14																		1
1	13	3	2^{2}		5	8	9		10	11	4^{1}		14	6	7^{3}	12															2
1		3	2		5	6	8	13	9^{1}	11^{2}			12	4	7	10^{3}	14														3
1		4^{3}	2^{1}		5	7	8	9^{2}	10			14	11	3	6	12		13													4
1	2	4			5	6	7	14	10^{2}	11	12		13	3	8^{3}	9^{1}															5
1	5	4	2		6	8	9		10^{2}	11^{1}			12	3	7^{3}	13			14												6
1	5	4	2^{1}		6	7	8	14	10	11^{2}			13	3	9^{3}	12															7
1	9	5	2		4	6	8	12	11^{1}	10				3	7^{2}	13															8
1	6	5	2^{1}		3	8	9	13	11	10^{2}	12		14	4	7^{3}																9
1	2	5		13	4	6	7■	9^{2}	11	10^{1}			12	3	8																10
1	6^{1}	5	2^{3}		3	8		13	10	11				4	7	9^{2}	12		14												11
	12	3	2^{1}	13	5	7	8	14	10	11■				4	6^{3}		9^{2}			1											12
	2	5		6	4	9	7	12	11^{2}			13			8						1	3	10^{1}								13
	5	2		4	3	6^{1}	7	11	9						8^{2}		13		12		1		10								14
	2	5		6^{1}	4		8	9	11	13		14			7^{3}	12					1	3	10^{2}								15
	2	3		9	4	7	5		11						6						1	8	10								16
	2	3			5	8■		9	11^{3}	13		7^{1}	14		6	12					1	4	10^{2}								17
	2	4		6^{1}	3		7	9^{2}	11	12					8	13					1	5	10								18
	2	5		3	4		6	11		10			14		7^{3}	9^{2}	12		13		1			8^{1}							19
	2^{1}	5		6^{2}	4	9	8^{3}	12		13					7						1	3		14	10	11					20
	2	3		13	4	6	8^{2}	11		10			14		7	12	5^{1}				1					9^{3}					21
	7■	5	2^{1}	12	4	8		3		11					6		9				1	13				10^{2}					22
		5	2^{2}		4	12	7	9^{1}		10^{3}		13		3	8	14					1	6				11					23
	2^{3}	3	14		5	8	9			13				4	10	7^{2}					1	6^{1}				11	12				24
	2		5		4	8	9			12				3	11	10						6					7^{1}	1			25
	2	5	12		4	8	6			10^{1}				3	7^{2}	13										11	9	1			26
	6	3^{1}	2	12	5	8	7^{2}			13				4		9										11	10	1			27
	5	2		12		9	10^{1}	13		11^{2}				3	6	8		14				4					7^{3}	1			28
	2	5		10	4	9		11^{2}		12				3	6							8^{1}					7	1	13		29
	2	5	14	12	3	8		13		11^{2}				4	10^{3}	9						6^{1}					7	1			30
	4	5	2			7		11		14				3	8^{1}	12	9^{2}										6	1	13	10^{3}	31
	2	3	5^{1}	11		7	8	9						4	6	12		13								10^{2}		1			32
	2	4	14	6		9	7^{3}	13						5	8	12						3				11^{1}	10^{2}	1			33
	2	5^{3}	6	8^{2}		10		11		13		14		3	9	12		7^{1}				4						1			34
		3	6	2		10	9^{1}	11				12		5	8	7						4						1			35
	11	5	2^{1}	8		10	4^{3}	6				14		7			13	9^{2}				3						1		12	36

COWDENBEATH

Year Formed: 1881. *Ground & Address:* Central Park, Cowdenbeath KY4 9QQ. *Telephone:* 01383 610166. *Fax:* 01383 512132.
E-mail: bluebrazil@cowdenbeathfc.com *Website:* www.cowdenbeathfc.com
Ground Capacity: total: 4,370, seated: 1,431. *Size of Pitch:* 98m × 59m.
Chairman: Donald Findlay QC. *Vice Chairman:* John Lints. *Secretary:* Alex Anderson.
Club Nicknames: The Blue Brazil, Cowden, The Miners.
Manager: Colin Cameron. *Assistant Manager:* Lee Makel. *Physio:* Ian McIvor.
Previous Grounds: North End Park, Cowdenbeath.
Record Attendance: 25,586 v Rangers, League Cup quarter-final, 21 Sept 1949.
Record Transfer Fee received: £30,000 for Nicky Henderson to Falkirk (March 1994).
Record Victory: 12-0 v Johnstone, Scottish Cup 1st rd, 21 Jan 1928.
Record Defeat: 1-11 v Clyde, Division II, 6 Oct 1951.
Most Capped Player: Jim Paterson, 3, Scotland.
Most League and Cup Appearances: 491 Ray Allan 1972-75, 1979-89.
Most League Goals in Season (Individual): 54, Rab Walls, Division II, 1938-39.
Most Goals Overall (Individual): 127, Willie Devlin, 1922-26, 1929-30.

COWDENBEATH 2011–12 LEAGUE RECORD

Match No.	*Date*	*Venue*	*Opponents*	*Result*		*H/T Score*	*Lg Pos.*	*Goalscorers*	*Attendance*
1	Aug 6	A	Forfar Ath	D	2-2	1-0	—	Ramsay [11], Coult [78]	469
2	13	H	Brechin C	W	3-1	1-1	2	Ramsay [13], McKenzie [67], Morton [80]	308
3	20	A	Airdrie U	W	5-1	2-1	1	Robertson [37], Linton 2 [45, 67], Coult [50], Morton [78]	834
4	27	A	Stenhousemuir	L	1-3	0-0	3	Adamson [69]	621
5	Sept 10	H	East Fife	W	3-2	1-1	2	Stewart [17], Park (og) [52], Robertson [76]	540
6	17	A	Dumbarton	W	4-0	2-0	2	McKenzie [8], Robertson [19], Morton [68], Linton [86]	615
7	24	H	Albion R	W	2-1	2-0	2	Naismith 2 (1 pen) [21, 37 (p)]	304
8	Oct 1	A	Arbroath	D	1-1	1-0	2	O'Brien [19]	857
9	15	H	Stirling A	W	2-0	1-0	1	Morton (pen) [33], McKenzie [46]	312
10	22	H	Forfar Ath	W	3-1	0-0	1	Coult [60], Stewart 2 [68, 72]	339
11	29	A	Brechin C	L	0-1	0-0	1		418
12	Nov 5	A	East Fife	W	3-1	0-1	1	Linton [48], Robertson [62], Morton [90]	1022
13	12	H	Stenhousemuir	W	2-0	1-0	1	Stewart [15], Coult [87]	374
14	26	H	Dumbarton	D	0-0	0-0	1		271
15	Dec 3	A	Albion R	D	3-3	1-1	1	Ramsay [16], Robertson [67], Stewart [81]	207
16	10	H	Arbroath	D	0-0	0-0	1		437
17	26	A	Stenhousemuir	W	2-0	1-0	1	Stewart [37], Coult [88]	576
18	Jan 2	H	East Fife	W	4-0	1-0	1	Morton [10], Cameron [60], Ramsay [75], McKenzie [90]	485
19	14	H	Airdrie U	W	2-0	1-0	1	McKenzie [37], Ramsay (pen) [58]	408
20	21	A	Forfar Ath	L	0-1	0-1	1		475
21	Feb 11	H	Stirling A	W	4-1	1-1	1	Coult 3 [12, 48, 59], McKenzie [84]	341
22	14	H	Albion R	W	3-0	3-0	—	Coult 2 [10, 26], McKenzie [21]	302
23	18	A	Arbroath	D	1-1	0-1	1	McKenzie [60]	1125
24	21	A	Stirling A	D	1-1	0-1	—	Coult [56]	329
25	25	H	Brechin C	W	1-0	0-0	1	Lyle [90]	332
26	Mar 3	A	Airdrie U	D	1-1	0-1	7	Ramsay (pen) [50]	702
27	6	A	Dumbarton	W	2-0	1-0	—	Mbu [3], McKenzie [73]	812
28	10	A	East Fife	W	1-0	1-0	1	McKenzie [43]	926
29	17	H	Stenhousemuir	D	0-0	0-0	1		367
30	24	H	Dumbarton	W	4-1	3-1	1	McKenzie 2 [19, 81], Coult [29], Mbu [38]	380
31	31	A	Albion R	L	0-1	0-1	1		402
32	Apr 7	H	Arbroath	L	2-3	1-2	1	McKenzie 2 (1 pen) [5, 46 (p)]	671
33	14	A	Stirling A	W	2-0	1-0	1	Coult [6], McKenzie [89]	568
34	21	H	Forfar Ath	W	2-0	0-0	1	McKenzie 2 [72, 83]	930
35	28	A	Brechin C	D	2-2	1-2	1	McKenzie [30], Armstrong [54]	487
36	May 5	H	Airdrie U	D	0-0	0-0	1		1345

Final League Position: 1

Honours
League Champions: Division II 1913-14, 1914-15, 1938-39. Second Division 2011-12. Third Division 2005-06. *Runners-up:* Division II 1921-22, 1923-24, 1969-70. Second Division 1991-92. Third Division 2000-01, 2008-09. *Promoted to First Division:* 2009-10 (play-offs).
Scottish Cup: Quarter-finals 1931.
League Cup: Semi-finals 1959-60, 1970-71.

Club colours: Shirt: Royal blue. Shorts: White. Stockings: Red.

Goalscorers: *League (68):* McKenzie 18 (1 pen), Coult 13, Morton 6 (1 pen), Ramsay 6 (2 pens), Stewart 6, Robertson 5, Linton 4, Mbu 2, Naismith 2 (1 pen), Adamson 1, Armstrong 1, Cameron 1, Lyle 1, O'Brien 1, own goal 1.
Scottish Cup (5): Robertson 2, Coult 1, Linton 1, Stewart 1.
Scottish Communities Cup (2): Ramsey 2.
Ramsdens Cup (1): Coult 1.

Bejaoui Y 5	Armstrong J 33 + 1	Mbu J 31	Adamson K 30 + 1	Linton S 30 + 3	Brett D 16 + 1	Cameron C 20 + 2	Morton J 12 + 6	Robertson J 35	Ramsay M 19 + 5	Stewart G 16 + 13	Coult L 20 + 12	McKenzie M 31 + 5	Winter C 3 + 6	Makel L 1 + 2	Miller K 2 + 3	Byrne P — + 2	Milne L 2 + 5	O'Brien T 11 + 4	Naismith K 7 + 2	Flynn T 30	Cowan D 15	Cusack L 5 + 8	Lyle D 12 + 6	Fisher G 9 + 1	Wilson L 1	Match No.
1	2	3	4	5	6	7	8^{2}	9	10	11^{1}	12	13														1
1	3	4^{2}	5	9^{3}	2	8	13	7	11^{1}		10	6	12	14												2
1		2^{3}	3	4	6	9^{2}	11	8		12	5^{1}	10	7		13	14										3
1	3	2	4	5			9	8		12	11^{1}	10		7^{2}	6		13									4
1	2		3	4	5	9	7^{1}	8		11		12						6	10							5
	2		3	4	5	8^{3}	13	7		10^{1}	12	9	14					6	11^{2}	1						6
	2		3	4	5		12	8		11^{1}		7^{3}	13		9^{2}		14	6	10	1						7
	3		2	4	5	6^{2}	12	9		10	14	8^{1}	13					7	11^{3}	1						8
	3	4	5	9		8^{1}	10^{2}	7		11	13	6^{3}	12		14					1	2					9
	3	4	5	6			10^{1}	8		11^{2}	12	7	9					13		1	2					10
	3	4	5^{2}	6			10	9	13	11	12	7	8^{1}							1	2					11
	3	4	5	6		14	10	7		11^{2}	13	9^{1}						8^{3}	12	1	2					12
	3	4	5	6^{2}		14	9	7		11^{3}	13	12						8	10^{1}	1	2					13
	12	3	4	10^{3}		7	9	8		11	14	13						5^{1}	6^{2}	1	2					14
	3	4	5	6^{2}		7	13	8	9	14	11	12							10^{1}	1	2^{3}					15
		3	4	5^{2}		9	12	8	10^{3}	14	11	7^{1}						6	13	1	2					16
	3	4		5		7	9	8	10	11^{1}	12	6								1	2					17
	3	4^{1}	12	5		6	11^{3}	8	7	10^{2}	14	9					13			1	2					18
	3	4	5^{1}	12		7		8	9^{3}		10	6					14			1	2	11^{2}	13			19
	5	4		3		6^{2}		8	9^{1}	14	10	7	13							1	2	11^{3}	12			20
	5	4	3	12				8	7	14	10^{3}	9								1	6^{2}	13	11^{1}	2		21
	2	3	4		6			8^{3}	9	12	11^{1}	7^{2}					14			1		13	10	5		22
	4	3^{1}	2	12■	6			8	9	13	10^{2}	7								1			11	5		23
	2	3	4		6			9	8^{1}	12	10	7								1		13	11^{2}	5		24
	2	3	4		6			8	9^{1}	11		7								1		12	10	5		25
	3	4	2	5				8	9	12	11^{1}	7								1		13	10^{2}	6		26
	3	4	5	2				8	9^{1}	13	11^{2}	7^{3}						12		1		14	10	6		27
	3	4	5	7				9	14	10^{1}	12	8						13		1	2^{3}		11	6^{2}		28
	3		4	2		8		7	9		11	6						5		1		12	10^{1}			29
	2	3	4	5	6	8^{1}		9			10	7								1		11^{2}	13	12		30
	2	3	4	5	6^{1}	7		9	12		11	8								1		10^{2}	13			31
	3	4	5■	6	9	8^{2}		7	13		11^{3}	10						12		1			14	2^{1}		32
	3	4		5	12	7		8	9	14	11^{3}	6								1	2^{1}	10^{2}	13			33
	3	4		5	2	8		7	9	11		6								1			10			34
	4	3		2^{2}	5				9^{1}		10	6^{3}			12	13	7	8				14	11		1	35
	3	4	5	2				7^{3}	13	12	11^{1}	6		14			9^{2}	8		1			10			36

DUMBARTON

Year Formed: 1872. *Ground:* Dumbarton Football Stadium, Castle Road, Dumbarton G82 1JJ. *Telephone:* 01389 762569. *Fax:* 01389 762629. *E-mail:* david_prophet58@hotmail.com *Website:* www.dumbartonfootballclub.com
Ground Capacity: total: 2,025. *Size of Pitch:* 110yd × 75yd.
Joint Chairmen: Colin Hosie and Alan Jardine. *Club Secretary:* David Prophet. *Chief Executive Officer:* Gilbert Lawrie.
Manager: Alan Adamson. *Assistant Manager:* Jack Ross. *Physio:* Ahmed Habib.
Club Nickname: The Sons.
Previous Grounds: Broadmeadow, Ropework Lane, Townend Ground, Boghead Park, Cliftonhill Stadium.
Record Attendance: 18,000 v Raith Rovers, Scottish Cup, 2 Mar 1957.
Record Transfer Fee received: £125,000 for Graeme Sharp to Everton (March 1982).
Record Transfer Fee paid: £50,000 for Charlie Gibson from Stirling Albion (1989).
Record Victory: 13-1 v Kirkintilloch Central. 1st rd, 1 Sept 1888.
Record Defeat: 1-11 v Albion Rovers, Division II; 30 Jan, 1926: v Ayr United, League Cup, 13 Aug 1952.
Most Capped Player: James McAulay, 9, Scotland.
Most League Appearances: 297: Andy Jardine, 1957-67.
Most Goals in Season (Individual): 38: Kenny Wilson, Division II, 1971-72. *(League and Cup):* 46 Hughie Gallacher, 1955-56.
Most Goals Overall (Individual): 169: Hughie Gallacher, 1954-62 (including C Division 1954-55). *(League and Cup):* 202 Hughie Gallacher, 1954-62

DUMBARTON 2011–12 LEAGUE RECORD

Match No.	*Date*	*Venue*	*Opponents*	*Result*		*H/T Score*	*Lg Pos.*	*Goalscorers*	*Attendance*
1	Aug 6	A	Airdrie U	L	0-3	0-2	—		887
2	13	H	Stirling A	L	1-5	1-1	10	Agnew [8]	706
3	20	A	Brechin C	D	3-3	2-0	10	Agnew 2 [11, 89], Lyden [28]	427
4	27	A	East Fife	W	6-0	4-0	6	McBride [17], Prunty 4 [20, 33, 79, 85], Lyden [45]	635
5	Sept 10	H	Arbroath	L	3-4	3-2	8	Prunty [5], Gilhaney [17], Nicoll [38]	640
6	17	H	Cowdenbeath	L	0-4	0-2	9		615
7	24	A	Forfar Ath	W	2-0	1-0	8	Winters [32], Prunty [61]	493
8	Oct 15	A	Stenhousemuir	L	1-3	0-2	9	Agnew [85]	529
9	18	H	Albion R	W	2-1	1-0	—	McKinnon [13], Agnew [51]	406
10	22	H	Airdrie U	D	1-1	1-1	8	Gilhaney (pen) [29]	285
11	29	A	Stirling A	W	1-0	0-0	5	Agnew [84]	602
12	Nov 5	A	Arbroath	L	3-4	0-3	6	McNiff 2 [51, 83], Agnew [65]	723
13	12	H	East Fife	W	3-0	1-0	4	Agnew [34], Gilhaney [60], Lithgow [68]	678
14	26	A	Cowdenbeath	D	0-0	0-0	5		271
15	Dec 3	H	Forfar Ath	D	1-1	1-0	4	Walker [16]	443
16	10	A	Albion R	L	1-3	1-2	5	Prunty [37]	489
17	Jan 2	H	Arbroath	W	3-2	1-2	6	Prunty [20], Lithgow [84], Walker [90]	585
18	14	H	Brechin C	W	1-0	0-0	7	Prunty [89]	572
19	21	A	Airdrie U	W	3-2	1-2	4	Lithgow [34], Agnew [67], Walker [88]	743
20	Feb 11	A	Stenhousemuir	W	2-1	2-0	4	Lithgow [36], Devlin (og) [45]	0
21	14	A	Forfar Ath	D	1-1	1-1	—	Prunty [44]	284
22	18	H	Albion R	W	1-0	0-0	3	Prunty [61]	657
23	21	A	East Fife	W	2-1	0-1	—	Gilhaney [52], Graham [79]	397
24	25	H	Stirling A	W	4-1	0-1	3	Graham [46], Agnew [73], Gilhaney 2 [80, 87]	722
25	28	H	Stenhousemuir	W	3-0	2-0	—	Prunty [1], Gilhaney [32], Agnew [74]	557
26	Mar 3	A	Brechin C	D	2-2	0-2	3	Prunty (pen) [57], Agnew [73]	459
27	6	H	Cowdenbeath	L	0-2	0-1	—		812
28	10	A	Arbroath	L	0-2	0-2	3		824
29	17	H	East Fife	L	0-4	0-3	3		713
30	24	A	Cowdenbeath	L	1-4	1-3	3	Dargo [33]	380
31	31	H	Forfar Ath	W	1-0	0-0	3	Paterson (og) [56]	513
32	Apr 7	A	Albion R	D	1-1	1-1	3	Agnew [38]	471
33	14	H	Stenhousemuir	L	0-2	0-2	3		728
34	21	H	Airdrie U	W	2-1	0-0	3	Prunty [61], Lovering (og) [67]	1088
35	28	A	Stirling A	W	2-1	0-0	3	Jacobs (og) [78], Dargo [90]	709
36	May 5	H	Brechin C	W	4-2	0-0	3	Dargo 3 [59, 62, 72], Thomson [90]	636

Final League Position: 3

Honours
League Champions: Division I 1890-91 (shared with Rangers), 1891-92. Division II 1910-11, 1971-72. Second Division 1991-92. Third Division 2008-09; *Runners-up:* First Division 1983-84. Division II 1907-08. Second Division 1994-95. Third Division 2001-02.
Scottish Cup Winners: 1883; *Runners-up:* 1881, 1882, 1887, 1891, 1897.

Club colours: Shirt: White with yellow and black horizontal stripe. Shorts: White. Stockings: White.

Goalscorers: *League (61):* Prunty 14 (1 pen), Agnew 13, Gilhaney 7 (1 pen), Dargo 5, Lithgow 4, Walker 3, Graham 2, Lyden 2, McNiff 2, McBride 1, McKinnon 1, Nicoll 1, Thomson 1, Winters 1, own goals 4.
Scottish Cup (0).
Scottish Communities Cup (0).
Ramsdens Cup (3): Gilhaney 1 (pen), Prunty 1, Walker 1..
Play-Offs (8): Wallace 3, Dargo 2, Prunty 2, Gilhaney 1.

Grindlay S 26	Lyden J 5 + 1	Nugent P 30 + 3	Lithgow A 32	Nicoll K 26 + 3	Borris R 6 + 10	Agnew S 35	Gilhaney M 33 + 1	Brannan K 1 + 10	Walker P 22 + 14	Hempstead J 1 + 1	Ramage G — + 5	Metcalf R — + 1	Ewings J 9	Monaghan A 1	Creaney J 32	McNiff M 28 + 1	Winters D 2 + 10	Prunty B 32 + 1	McBride M 5	Kennedy D 7 + 1	McKinnon R 6 + 1	Wallace A 16 + 6	McKell G 1 + 1	Lemont M 7 + 5	Graham A 10 + 7	Finnie R 11 + 3	Dargo C 7 + 2	Gray D 2 + 1	Mptata A 2 + 2	Gastal A 1	Thomson G — + 1	*Match No.*
1	2	3	4	5	6¹	7	8	9	10	11²	12	13																				1
		3	5	7		6	9²		12	14	13		1	2	4	8	10³	11¹														2
	2	12	3▪	7		8	9	13	11³				1		4	5	14	10¹	6²													3
	2	3		7		8³	9	12	11²		14		1		4	5	13	10	6¹													4
	2	3		6		7	9	13	11²		14		1		4³	5	12	10	8¹													5
			3	7		8	9³	14	11				1			4²	12	10¹	6	2	5	13										6
1		2	4	7	14	8	9³	13	11¹						3	5	12	10²			6											7
1		2	3	8³	12	9	7	14	11						5	4²		10			6¹	13										8
1		2	3			7	6	12	11						5	4		10¹			9	8										9
1		2	3	7¹		8	9		10						4	6	13	11²			5	12										10
1		2	3	7	12	8	9		11²						4	6	13	10			5¹											11
1		2	3	7	8²	6	9		11¹						4	5	12	10					13									12
		2	4		7³	8	10	14	12				1		3	6	11¹	9²			13	5										13
		2	3	8¹	7	9	12		11				1		5	6	13	10²				4										14
		2	4		6²	8	9	13	11¹				1		5		12	10		3		7										15
	14	2	4		8¹	7	9	12	11²		13		1		5³			10		3		6										16
1		2	3	6	13	7²	9		12						5			10				4		8	11¹							17
1			3	6	12	7	8		13						4	5		10						9¹	11²	2						18
1		14	3	6	13	7	8		12						4	5		10						9²	11¹	2³						19
1		3	4			8	9		10²						5¹	7		11				6		12	13	2						20
1		4	5	13		8	9		10						3¹	7		11				6²		12		2						21
1		4	5	7³		8	9		11²						3	6		10				14		12	13	2¹						22
1		2	3		14	8	9		10²						4			11³	7			6		13	12	5¹						23
1		5	4	13	14	6	11		9						3²	7						2¹		10³	8	12						24
1		2	4		13	6	8²		12						3	7		9				5		10³	11¹	14						25
1		2	3	12		6	8		13						5	7		10				4¹		9	11²							26
1		2	3	6	12²	7	8		13						4³	5		10						9¹	11	14						27
1		3	4	8		7	9		14						5²	6		11¹							12	2³	10	13				28
1		2	3	7		8	9		10³							5		14		12		4¹			13		11	6²				29
1		2	3	7³		8	9		12						5	6		10²				14			13	4¹	11					30
1			4	8		7	9		13						3			10²		5					12	2	11		6¹			31
1		12	3	6		10	8		14						5			11³		4		7²		13		2¹	9					32
1		2		6		7			12						4²	8¹		11		3		5			9		10		13			33
1		2	3	6		7	9		11						4	5		10¹							8		12					34
1		2	4	6¹		7	8		10²						3	5		11				12			9³		13		14			35
	4	5		8					13							12				3		6	9³			2¹	10	7	11²	1	14	36

DUNDEE

Year Formed: 1893. *Ground & Address:* Dens Park Stadium, Sandeman St, Dundee DD3 7JY. *Telephone:* 01382 889966.
Fax: 01382 832284. *E-mail:* laura@dundeefc.co.uk *Website:* www.thedees.co.uk
Ground Capacity: all seated: 11,760. *Size of Pitch:* 101m × 66m.
Operations/Company Secretary: Jim Thomson. *Club Secretary:* Laura Hayes (tel: 01382 826104; mob: 07855 410 929).
Email: laura@dundeefc.co.uk
Manager: Barry Smith. *Assistant Manager:* Ray Farningham. *Youth Development Coach:* Gordon Wallace. *Physio:* Karen Gibson.
Club Nicknames: The Dark Blues or The Dee.
Previous Grounds: Carolina Port 1893-98.
Record Attendance: 43,024 v Rangers, Scottish Cup, 1953.
Record Transfer Fee received: £1,200,000 for Robert Douglas to Celtic (2000).
Record Transfer Fee paid: £600,000 for Fabian Caballero (2000).
Record Victory: 10-0 Division II v Alloa, 9 Mar 1947 and v Dunfermline Ath, 22 Mar 1947.
Record Defeat: 0-11 v Celtic, Division I, 26 Oct 1895.
Most Capped Player: Alex Hamilton, 24, Scotland.
Most League Appearances: 400: Barry Smith, 1995-2006.
Most League Goals in Season (Individual): 52: Alan Gilzean, 1960-64.
Most Goals Overall (Individual): 113: Alan Gilzean 1960-64.

DUNDEE 2011–12 LEAGUE RECORD

Match No.	Date	Venue	Opponents	Result		H/T Score	Lg Pos.	Goalscorers	Attendance
1	Aug 6	A	Partick Th	W	1-0	0-0	—	Lockwood (pen) [90]	3065
2	13	H	Ayr U	D	1-1	1-1	3	Hyde [30]	4686
3	20	A	Livingston	L	2-4	0-2	6	Irvine [61], McNeil (og) [65]	1966
4	27	H	Morton	L	0-1	0-1	9		4096
5	Sept 10	A	Raith R	W	1-0	0-0	4	Riley [86]	2459
6	17	A	Falkirk	L	1-2	1-0	9	Milne [45]	3576
7	24	H	Hamilton A	L	0-1	0-0	10		4186
8	Oct 1	A	Queen of the S	D	0-0	0-0	9		1649
9	15	H	Ross Co	L	1-2	1-1	10	Lockwood (pen) [25]	4030
10	22	A	Ayr U	W	3-1	1-0	9	Weston [16], McIntosh [71], Milne [87]	1390
11	29	H	Partick Th	L	0-1	0-1	10		4263
12	Nov 5	H	Raith R	W	1-0	0-0	7	Conroy [83]	4258
13	12	A	Morton	W	2-1	1-1	6	Rae [42], Conroy [56]	2201
14	26	H	Falkirk	W	4-2	2-1	3	Rae [8], Hyde 2 [11, 67], Milne [85]	4507
15	Dec 3	A	Hamilton A	W	6-1	3-0	3	Milne 3 [21, 37, 49], O'Donnell [39], Riley [71], Rae [83]	1964
16	10	H	Queen of the S	W	2-1	2-0	2	Hyde [8], Riley [25]	5019
17	17	A	Ross Co	D	1-1	1-0	3	Milne [35]	3046
18	26	H	Morton	L	0-1	0-1	3		5862
19	Jan 2	A	Raith R	W	1-0	1-0	3	Hyde [37]	3629
20	14	H	Livingston	W	3-0	1-0	3	Conroy [19], McGregor [74], Riley [82]	4176
21	21	A	Partick Th	D	0-0	0-0	3		2425
22	Feb 11	H	Hamilton A	D	2-2	0-1	3	Conroy [53], Milne (pen) [79]	4065
23	18	A	Queen of the S	D	1-1	0-1	3	Lockwood [89]	1682
24	21	A	Falkirk	D	1-1	0-1	—	Finnigan [87]	3089
25	25	H	Ross Co	D	1-1	1-1	3	Conroy (pen) [33]	5003
26	Mar 3	A	Livingston	W	3-2	1-1	3	McCluskey 2 [26, 88], Finnigan [56]	2052
27	17	A	Morton	W	2-0	1-0	2	Conroy 2 (1 pen) [15 (p), 55]	1610
28	20	A	Hamilton A	L	1-3	1-1	—	Conroy (pen) [30]	1366
29	24	H	Raith R	D	1-1	1-1	2	Finnigan [6]	4118
30	27	H	Ayr U	W	4-1	1-0	—	McCluskey [20], Milne [62], Conroy [89], Hyde [90]	3136
31	Apr 7	H	Falkirk	W	3-1	2-1	2	O'Donnell [11], Conroy (pen) [36], Milne [57]	3896
32	10	H	Queen of the S	D	1-1	0-0	—	O'Donnell [53]	3371
33	14	A	Ross Co	L	0-3	0-1	2		4350
34	21	H	Partick Th	L	0-3	0-1	2		3682
35	28	A	Ayr U	L	2-3	1-0	2	Conroy [14], Milne [70]	1656
36	May 5	H	Livingston	W	1-0	0-0	2	Reid [48]	3675

Final League Position: 2

Honours
League Champions: Division I 1961-62. First Division 1978-79, 1991-92, 1997-98. Division II 1946-47; *Runners-up:* Division I 1902-03, 1906-07, 1908-09, 1948-49. First Division 1980-81, 2007-08, 2009-10.
Scottish Cup Winners: 1910; *Runners-up:* 1925, 1952, 1964, 2003.
League Cup Winners: 1951-52, 1952-53, 1973-74; *Runners-up:* 1967-68, 1980-81, 1995-96.
League Challenge Cup Winners: 2009-10.
B&Q (Centenary) Cup Winners: 1990-91; *Runners-up:* 1994-95.

European: *European Cup:* 8 matches (1962-63 semi-finals). *Cup Winners' Cup:* 2 matches: (1964-65).
UEFA Cup: 22 matches: (*Fairs Cup:* 1967-68 semi-finals. *UEFA Cup:* 1971-72, 1973-74, 1974-75, 2003-04).

Club colours: Shirt: Navy blue with one white and red band. Shorts: White. Stockings: Navy blue.

Goalscorers: *League (53):* Conroy 11 (4 pens), Milne 11 (1 pen), Hyde 6, Riley 4, Finnigan 3, Lockwood 3 (2 pens), McCluskey 3, O'Donnell 3, Rae 3, Irvine 1, McGregor 1, McIntosh 1, Reid 1, Weston 1, own goal 1.
Scottish Cup (4): Milne 2, Conroy 1, Rae 1.
Scottish Communities Cup (4): Milne 2, Lockwood 1 (pen), McCluskey 1.
Ramsdens Cup (2): Milne 1, O'Donnell 1.

Douglas R 36	Irvine G 35	Weston R 20 + 5	McKeown C 23 + 4	Lockwood M 34	Chisholm R 13 + 5	McCluskey J 20 + 8	O'Donnell S 33	Conroy R 32 + 3	McIntosh L 11 + 7	Hyde J 14 + 12	Riley N 19 + 6	McGregor N 26 + 1	Harkins G 1	Milne S 30 + 1	Bayne G 7 + 11	Benedictis K 11 + 3	Masterton S — + 1	Rae G 12 + 1	Gibson J — + 1	Elliot C 1 + 5	Finnigan C 4 + 1	McBride K 11	Fotheringham M 2 + 6	Reid J 1	*Match No.*
1	2	3	4	5	6	7²	8	9	10¹	11	12	13													1
1		4	3	2	6	9	8		12	10¹	5		7	11											2
1	2	4²	3	5	7¹	9	8	12		13	6			11	10										3
1	2	4	3	5	8³	13	7	9	14	12	6²			11	10¹										4
1	8		3	5²	13	12	7■	9¹			6	4		11	10	2									5
1	7	12	3	5	8²	13		9			6	4¹		11	10	2									6
1	2	13	5	3	10³	11	4	14			7	6²		9		8¹	12								7
1	2		3	5	6¹	10²	9	12	14		7	4		11³	13	8									8
1	6		4	5			7	9	12		8	3		11	10²	2¹		13							9
1	2	5		3			6	9	11		8	4		10				7							10
1■	2	5	12	3²		13	6	9¹	10⁶		8	4		11				7	15						11
1	2	4²	13	3		14	7	9	11	12³	8	5						6		10¹					12
1	2	4		5	13		6	9	10¹	12²	8	3		11				7							13
1	2	5		3			8	9		11¹	6	4		10				7		12					14
1	2	4		5		13	6	9		10¹	8	3		11²				7		12					15
1	2	4		5		14	7¹	9		11²	8■	3		10³		12		6		13					16
1	2	3		5	12	6¹	8■	9		10³		4		11²	14			7		13					17
1	2	5²	13	3	7³			9		10	6	4		11¹	14			8		12					18
1	2		3	5	6	12		9	13	10¹	8²	4		11				7							19
1	2		4	5	6	8¹	9	10		12	13³	3		11²	14			7							20
1	2	13	3	5²	6	11	7	9		12		4		10				8¹							21
1	2	13	4	5	7	6²	8	9		10¹		3		11	12										22
1	2	6³	4	5	12	7²	8	9		10	13	3¹		11		14									23
1	2	4		5	8¹	6	7	9		11²		3		10	13						12				24
1	2	5		3		6	7	9		10²		4		12	13						11	8¹			25
1	2	4²	13	5		6	8	9				3		11¹	12						10	7			26
1	2		4	5		6	7	9²		12		3			11¹						10	8	13		27
1	2		4	5		6	8	9	13	10²		3			11							7¹	12		28
1	2		4	5		6²	8	9		12		3		10³	14						11¹	7	13		29
1	2		4	3		6	8	9	11²	13				10¹	12	5						7			30
1	2		4	3	14	6¹	8	9	10²	13				11³		5						7	12		31
1	2	5	3			6¹	7	9	10	13	14			11³		4²						8	12		32
1	2	12	4	5			7	9	11		13			10¹		3						8■	6²		33
1	5	2		4		8¹	7	11	9	10²	12	3■				13							6		34
1	2¹	5	4	3			7	11	12		9			10		6						8			35
1	2		4				7	3	9¹	12	11²			10³	14	5						8	13	6	36

DUNDEE UNITED

Year Formed: 1909 (1923). *Ground & Address:* Tannadice Park, Tannadice St, Dundee DD3 7JW. *Telephone:* 01382 833166. *Fax:* 01382 889398. *E-mail:* enquiries@dundeeunited.co.uk *Website:* www.dundeeunitedfc.co.uk
Ground Capacity: total: 14,223 all seated: stands: east 2,868, west 2,096, south 2,201, Fair Play 1601, George Fox 5151, executive boxes 292. *Size of Pitch:* 110yd × 72yd.
Chairman: Stephen Thompson, OBE. *Vice-Chairman:* Cath Thompson. *Secretary:* Spence Anderson.
Manager: Peter Houston. *Assistant Manager:* Paul Hegarty. *First Team Coach:* Gary Kirk. *Physio:* Jeff Clarke.
Club Nickname: The Terrors.
Previous Grounds: None.
Record Attendance: 28,000 v Barcelona, Fairs Cup, 16 Nov 1966.
Record Transfer Fee received: £4,000,000 for Duncan Ferguson from Rangers (July 1993).
Record Transfer Fee paid: £750,000 for Steven Pressley from Coventry C (July 1995).
Record Victory: 14-0 v Nithsdale Wanderers, Scottish Cup 1st rd, 17 Jan 1931.
Record Defeat: 1-12 v Motherwell, Division II, 23 Jan 1954.
Most Capped Player: Maurice Malpas, 55, Scotland.
Most League Appearances: 618, Maurice Malpas, 1980-2000.
Most Appearances in European Matches: 76, Dave Narey (record for Scottish player).
Most League Goals in Season (Individual): 41: John Coyle, Division II, 1955-56.
Most Goals Overall (Individual): 158: Peter McKay, 1947-54.

DUNDEE UNITED 2011–12 LEAGUE RECORD

Match No.	Date	Venue	Opponents	Result		H/T Score	Lg Pos.	Goalscorers	Attendance
1	July 24	H	Kilmarnock	D	1-1	0-0	—	Swanson [70]	6232
2	31	A	Hearts	W	1-0	1-0	—	Daly [38]	13,821
3	Aug 6	H	St Mirren	D	1-1	0-1	—	Daly [67]	6594
4	13	A	Celtic	L	1-5	1-2	7	Russell [31]	50,589
5	20	H	Dunfermline Ath	L	0-1	0-0	8		6527
6	27	A	St Johnstone	D	3-3	1-3	8	Douglas [2], Gunning [63], Mackay-Steven [80]	4480
7	Sept 10	H	Rangers	L	0-1	0-0	9		10,156
8	17	H	Inverness CT	W	3-1	2-1	8	Dalla Valle [13], Swanson [43], Daly [71]	6497
9	24	A	Hibernian	D	3-3	2-1	8	Daly 2 [28, 68], Swanson [33]	9360
10	Oct 1	H	Motherwell	L	1-3	0-2	8	Daly [77]	6073
11	15	A	Aberdeen	L	1-3	0-1	9	Dalla Valle [79]	10,256
12	22	H	St Johnstone	D	0-0	0-0	10		6707
13	29	A	Dunfermline Ath	W	4-1	2-0	8	Dixon [13], Dalla Valle [18], Russell [75], Mackay-Steven [82]	3979
14	Nov 5	A	Rangers	L	1-3	0-1	8	Daly [73]	45,600
15	19	H	Hearts	W	1-0	1-0	7	Robertson [24]	6925
16	26	A	Motherwell	D	0-0	0-0	8		4487
17	Dec 4	H	Celtic	L	0-1	0-1	8		10,980
18	10	A	Inverness CT	W	3-2	0-1	7	Russell 2 [51, 78], Golobart (og) [64]	3142
19	17	A	Kilmarnock	D	1-1	0-0	7	Dixon [90]	4007
20	24	H	Hibernian	W	3-1	0-1	6	Russell [59], Daly 2 [76, 88]	8168
21	28	A	St Mirren	D	2-2	2-2	6	Daly [31], Armstrong [35]	3811
22	Jan 2	H	Aberdeen	L	1-2	1-0	6	Daly [6]	11,471
23	14	A	Celtic	L	1-2	0-2	7	Rankin [50]	50,139
24	21	H	Motherwell	D	1-1	1-0	6	Craigan (og) [28]	5969
25	Feb 11	A	St Johnstone	W	5-1	1-0	6	Anderson (og) [35], Davidson (og) [61], Russell [84], Daly [89], Lacny [90]	4319
26	18	H	St Mirren	D	0-0	0-0	7		6363
27	21	H	Kilmarnock	W	4-0	0-0	—	Daly (pen) [56], Dixon [58], Rankin [70], Robertson [84]	5232
28	25	A	Hearts	W	2-0	1-0	5	Daly [41], Gunning [85]	13,176
29	Mar 5	H	Inverness CT	W	3-0	1-0	—	Rankin [15], Robertson [52], Russell [78]	5994
30	17	H	Rangers	W	2-1	1-0	—	Watson [37], Daly [47]	9464
31	24	A	Hibernian	W	2-0	0-0	4	Russell [66], Mackay-Steven [73]	9161
32	31	H	Dunfermline Ath	W	3-0	0-0	4	Daly 2 [49, 83], Robertson [80]	6654
33	Apr 7	A	Aberdeen	L	1-3	1-1	5	Daly [29]	8439
34	21	A	St Johnstone	W	2-0	1-0	4	Robertson [32], Rankin [90]	5826
35	28	H	Hearts	D	2-2	1-1	4	Flood [32], Mackay-Steven [65]	7001
36	May 2	A	Rangers	L	0-5	0-3	—		43,383
37	6	H	Celtic	W	1-0	1-0	4	Robertson [21]	9144
38	13	A	Motherwell	W	2-0	1-0	4	Russell [8], Daly [82]	7456

Final League Position: 4

Honours
League Champions: Premier Division 1982-83. Division II 1924-25, 1928-29; *Runners-up:* Division II 1930-31, 1959-60. First Division Runners-up 1995-96.
Scottish Cup Winners: 1994, 2010; *Runners-up:* 1974, 1981, 1985, 1987, 1988, 1991, 2005.
League Cup Winners: 1979-80, 1980-81; *Runners-up:* 1981-82, 1984-85, 1997-98, 2007-08.
League Challenge Cup Runners-up: 1995-96.
Summer Cup Runners-up: 1964-65. *Scottish War Cup Runners-up:* 1939-40.

European: *European Cup:* 8 matches (1983-84, semi-finals). *Cup Winners' Cup:* 10 matches (1974-75, 1988-89, 1994-95). *UEFA Cup:* 86 matches (*Fairs Cup:* 1966-67, 1969-70, 1970-71. *UEFA Cup:* 1975-76, 1977-78, 1978-79, 1979-80, 1980-81, 1981-82, 1982-83, 1984-85, 1985-86, 1986-87 runners-up, 1987-88, 1989-90, 1990-91, 1993-94, 1997-98, 2005-06). *Europa League:* 4 matches (2010-2011, 2011-12).

Club colours: Shirt: Tangerine with black trim. Shorts: Black. Stockings: Tangerine with black hoop.

Goalscorers: *League (62):* Daly 19 (1 pen), Russell 9, Robertson 6, Mackay-Steven 4, Rankin 4, Dalla Valle 3, Dixon 3, Swanson 3, Gunning 2, Armstrong 1, Douglas 1, Flood 1, Lacny 1, Watson 1, own goals 4.
Scottish Cup (8): Russell 4, Gunning 1, Mackay-Steven 1, Rankin 1, Robertson 1.
Scottish Communities Cup (4): Daly 2, Dow 1, Russell 1.
Europa League (3): Daly 1 (pen), Goodwillie 1, Watson 1.

Pernis D 38	Dillon S 26 + 2	Dixon P 37	Douglas B 5 + 5	Watson K 14 + 3	Armstrong S 11 + 12	Flood W 30 + 2	Daly J 35 + 1	Goodwillie D 1	Russell J 33 + 4	Rankin J 38	Kenneth G 20 + 5	Swanson D 6 + 8	Mackay-Steven G 24 + 7	Severin S 2	Allan S 4 + 4	Robertson S 34 + 3	Gunning G 29 + 2	Dow R 3 + 7	Dalla Valle L 5 + 7	Marsh-Brown K — + 1	Neilson R 21	Ryan R 2 + 12	Lacny M — + 4	Gauld R — + 1	*Match No.*
1	2	3	4^{2}	5	6^{1}	7	8	9	10^{3}	11	12	13	14												1
1	2	3	13	5		7	9		10	11	6			4^{1}	8^{2}	12									2
1	2	3		5		7	9		10	11	6		13	4^{1}	8	12^{2}									3
1	2	3		5	12	7^{2}	9		10	11	4				6^{1}	8	13								4
1	2	3	4^{1}			7	9		10^{2}	11	5	12				8	6	13							5
1	2	3	4^{1}		8^{2}	7^{3}			10	11	5	12	14			13	6		9						6
1		3		2		7			10[illegible]	11	5	4				8	6	12	9^{1}						7
1		3		2		7	12			11	5	8				4	6	10^{1}	9^{2}	13					8
1		3	12	2		7	9		10^{1}	11	5	8				4	6								9
1		3		2		7	9		13	11	5	10^{3}	14			4^{2}	6	8^{1}	12						10
1		3			14	7	9		8^{2}	11	5	10^{1}	13		2^{3}	4	6		12						11
1		3	8^{1}	2		7^{3}	9		14	11	5				13	4	6	12	10^{2}						12
1		3		2	14	7	5		10	11			12		13	4^{3}	6	8^{2}	9^{1}						13
1		3		2		7	9		10^{2}	11	5		8^{1}			4	6	12	13						14
1		3	12		13	7	9		8^{2}	11	5		10^{1}			4	6				2				15
1	12	3				7	9		10^{1}	11	5		8^{2}			4	6		13		2				16
1		3			12	7^{3}	9		10	11	5		8^{2}			4^{1}	6	14	13		2				17
1	2	3			10	7^{1}	9		12	11			8			4	6				5				18
1	2	3			7		9		10	11^{1}	13		8			4	6^{2}		12		5				19
1	2	3			7		9		10^{2}	11	12		8		13	4	6				5^{1}				20
1	2	3			7^{1}	13	9		10	11			8^{2}		12	4	6				5				21
1	2	3			7^{2}	12	9		10	11^{3}			8^{1}			4	6		14		5	13			22
1	2	3^{2}	13		12	7^{1}	9		10	11	5	14	8^{3}			4					6				23
1	2	3			7^{2}		9		10	11	5	14	8^{3}			4	12				6^{1}	13			24
1	12	3			7^{2}		9		10	11	5^{1}		8^{3}			4	6				2	13	14		25
1	2	3			7^{1}		9		10	11			8			4	6				5		12		26
1	2	3			13	7	9^{1}		10^{2}	11			8^{3}			4	6				5	14	12		27
1	2		3		12	7	9		10	11			8^{1}			4^{2}	6				5	13			28
1	2	3			12	7	9^{2}		10^{3}	11			8^{1}			4	6				5	13	14		29
1	2	3		5	13	7	9		10^{2}	11			8^{1}			4	6					12			30
1	2	3		5^{2}		7^{3}	9^{1}		10	11	13	14	8			4	6					12			31
1	2	3			12	7^{2}	9		10	11		14	8^{1}			4^{3}	6				5	13			32
1	2	3			13	7^{1}	9		10	11		12	8^{2}			4^{3}	6				5	14			33
1	2	3		12		7	9		10	11			8^{2}			4	6^{1}				5	13			34
1	2	3				7	9		10^{1}	11	5		8			4					6	12			35
1	2	3	13	12		7	9		10^{3}	11	5^{1}		8^{2}			4		14			6				36
1	2	3		12		7	9		13	11	14		8^{2}			4	6^{3}				5^{1}	10			37
1	2	3		5	6^{2}		9		10^{3}	11		8^{1}	13			4		12				7		14	38

DUNFERMLINE ATHLETIC

Year Formed: 1885. *Ground & Address:* East End Park, Halbeath Rd, Dunfermline KY12 7RB.
Telephone: 01383 724295. *Fax:* 01383 745 959. *E-mail:* enquiries@dafc.co.uk
Website: www.dafc.co.uk
Ground Capacity: all seated: 12,509. *Size of Pitch:* 115yd × 71yd.
Chairman: John Yorkston. *Chief Executive:* Bill Hodgins.
Manager: Jim Jefferies. *Assistant Manager:* Gerry McCabe. *Physio:* Kenny Murray. *Head of Youth Development:* Steven Wright.
Club Nickname: The Pars.
Previous Grounds: None.
Record Attendance: 27,816 v Celtic, Division I, 30 Apr 1968.
Record Transfer Fee received: £650,000 for Jackie McNamara to Celtic (Oct 1995).
Record Transfer Fee paid: £540,000 for Istvan Kozma from Bordeaux (Sept 1989).
Record Victory: 11-2 v Stenhousemuir, Division II, 27 Sept 1930.
Record Defeat: 1-11 v Hibernian, Scottish Cup, 3rd rd replay, 26 Oct 1889.
Most Capped Player: Colin Miller 16 (61), Canada.
Most League Appearances: 497: Norrie McCathie, 1981-96.
Most League Goals in Season (Individual): 53: Bobby Skinner, Division II, 1925-26.
Most Goals Overall (Individual): 154: Charles Dickson, 1954-64.

DUNFERMLINE ATHLETIC 2011–12 LEAGUE RECORD

Match No.	*Date*	*Venue*	*Opponents*	*Result*		*H/T Score*	*Lg Pos.*	*Goalscorers*	*Attendance*
1	July 25	H	St Mirren	D	0-0	0-0	—		5035
2	Aug 6	H	Inverness CT	D	3-3	1-0	—	Kirk 2 [26, 52], Hardie [90]	3378
3	13	A	St Johnstone	W	1-0	1-0	5	Kirk [30]	3466
4	20	A	Dundee U	W	1-0	0-0	4	Burns [85]	6527
5	27	H	Motherwell	L	2-4	0-2	5	Cardle 2 [69, 88]	4462
6	Sept 10	A	Kilmarnock	L	2-3	1-2	7	Thomson, J [14], Thomson, R [49]	4222
7	17	H	Hibernian	D	2-2	0-1	7	Thomson, R [53], Hanlon (og) [63]	4116
8	24	H	Rangers	L	0-4	0-2	9		7577
9	30	A	Aberdeen	L	0-4	0-3	—		8333
10	Oct 15	H	Hearts	L	0-2	0-1	11		5694
11	22	A	Inverness CT	D	1-1	0-1	11	Buchanan (pen) [86]	3241
12	29	H	Dundee U	L	1-4	0-2	11	Kirk [55]	3979
13	Nov 5	A	Hibernian	W	1-0	1-0	10	McCann [3]	9531
14	19	A	St Mirren	L	1-2	0-2	10	Cardle [63]	4363
15	23	A	Celtic	L	1-2	0-2	—	Barrowman [86]	41,000
16	26	H	Aberdeen	D	3-3	0-1	10	Barrowman [54], Graham [62], Buchanan [69]	4149
17	Dec 3	A	Rangers	L	1-2	1-2	11	Cardle [31]	47,305
18	17	A	Hearts	L	0-4	0-2	12		11,988
19	24	H	St Johnstone	L	0-3	0-1	12		4474
20	Jan 2	H	Celtic	L	0-3	0-2	12		10,140
21	14	H	Hibernian	L	2-3	1-1	12	Kirk [14], Buchanan [82]	6780
22	21	A	Kilmarnock	W	3-0	1-0	12	Barrowman [42], Cardle [60], Buchanan [87]	4016
23	24	A	Motherwell	L	1-3	0-1	—	Kirk [62]	3772
24	28	A	Aberdeen	L	0-1	0-1	12		8081
25	Feb 7	H	Kilmarnock	D	1-1	1-1	—	Kirk [44]	2303
26	11	H	Rangers	L	1-4	1-2	12	Kirk [16]	7464
27	18	H	Inverness CT	D	1-1	1-0	12	Cardle [45]	2881
28	22	A	Celtic	L	0-2	0-1	—		45,000
29	25	A	St Johnstone	L	1-3	0-2	12	Burns [73]	3732
30	Mar 3	H	Motherwell	L	0-2	0-0	12		3523
31	24	H	St Mirren	D	1-1	0-1	12	Cardle [46]	3753
32	31	A	Dundee U	L	0-3	0-0	12		6654
33	Apr 7	H	Hearts	L	1-2	0-0	12	Zaliukas (og) [85]	4700
34	21	A	St Mirren	D	4-4	1-2	12	McMillan [24], Graham [56], Buchanan [71], Kirk [88]	3616
35	28	H	Aberdeen	W	3-0	0-0	12	Cardle [56], Kirk 2 [68, 77]	3501
36	May 2	A	Inverness CT	D	0-0	0-0	—		6036
37	7	A	Hibernian	L	0-4	0-3	—		15,281
38	12	H	Kilmarnock	L	1-2	1-0	12	Willis [20]	3276

Final League Position: 12

Honours
League Champions: First Division 1988-89, 1995-96, 2010-11. Division II 1925-26. Second Division 1985-86; *Runners-up:* First Division 1986-87, 1993-94, 1994-95, 1999-2000. Division II 1912-13, 1933-34, 1954-55, 1957-58, 1972-73. Second Division 1978-79.
Scottish Cup Winners: 1961, 1968; *Runners-up:* 1965, 2004, 2007.
League Cup Runners-up: 1949-50, 1991-92, 2005-06.
League Challenge Cup Runners-up: 2007-08.

European: *Cup Winners' Cup:* 14 matches (1961-62, 1968-69 semi-finals). *UEFA Cup:* 32 matches (*Fairs Cup:* 1962-63, 1964-65, 1965-66, 1966-67, 1969-70. *UEFA Cup:* 2004-05, 2007-08).

Club colours: Shirt: White and black stripes. Shorts: White. Stockings: White.

Goalscorers: *League (40):* Kirk 11, Cardle 8, Buchanan 5 (1 pen), Barrowman 3, Burns 2, Graham 2, Thomson, R. 2, Hardie 1, McCann 1, McMillan 1, Thomson, J. 1, Willis 1, own goals 2.
Scottish Cup (2): Barrowman 2.
Scottish Communities Cup (3): Barrowman 1, Buchanan 1, Kirk 1.

Gallacher P 18	Thomson J 12	McCann A 22 + 1	Mason G 32	Potter J 15 + 1	Keddie A 36	Cardle J 24 + 12	Hardie M 18 + 10	McDougall S 2 + 10	Kirk A 23 + 13	Graham D 33 + 5	Barrowman A 13 + 9	Burns P 21 + 4	Thomson R 11 + 14	Dowie A 30	Willis P 11 + 10	Easton C 3	Buchanan L 14 + 13	Boyle P 20 + 1	Clarke P — + 3	Phinn N — + 1	Smith C 14	Turner I 5	Rutkiewicz K 8	Kerr M 13	McMillan J 11	Hutton K 8 + 1	Fernandez B 1	Match No.
1	2	3	4	5	6	7	8	9¹	10³	11²	12	13	14															1
1	2	3	4²	5	6	7	8	12	10¹	13	9	11																2
1	2	3	4	5■	6	7²	8	13	10¹	12		9		11														3
1	2	3	4		6	7	8		10¹	9	12	11		5														4
1	2	3	4²		6	7	8		10	12	9¹	11³	14	5	13													5
1	2	3	4²	14	6³	7			10	11		8	12	5	13	9¹												6
1	2	3	4		6	7			10¹	11	12	9	8	5														7
1	2	3	4		6	7²			12	11	9³	8	10¹	5	13		14											8
1	7	11	4²	2	6	13			12	3	9	8	14	5¹		10³												9
1		3	4	6		7¹			10³	11		8	9²	5	14		12	2	13									10
1	2¹	3	4	5	6	7		14	10²	11³		9	12				13	8										11
1	2	3	4■	5	6			14	10²	9		7	12			8¹		11³	13									12
1		11		5	6	13	14	12	10³	8		3	7	2	4²		9¹											13
1		3		4	5	13		14	10³	11	12	7	2		6		9¹	8²										14
1			4	5	6	13			10³	3	9	11	7¹	2	8²		14	12										15
1			4	5	6		12		10²	11	9	8¹		2	3³		13	7		14								16
1			4	5	6	7¹	10²		14	11	9³		12	2	3			8	13									17
1			4³	5	6	12	8		13	11	9¹	7	14	2	3		10²											18
	2				6	11	8²		12	10	9³	4	13	5	7¹		14	3			1							19
			4¹	5	6	12	8		13	10	9³	11		2	7²		14	3			1							20
			4¹	2	5	7	8		10³	11²	9		12	6	14		13	3				1						21
			4		6	7	13		12	11	9¹		14	2			10²	3				1	5	8³				22
			4		6	7²	14		12	11	9¹			2	13		10³	3				1	5	8				23
			4³		6	12	14		13	11			8	2	10¹		9²	3				1	5	7				24
					6	12	13	14	10²	11		8¹					9³	3				1	5	7	2	4		25
			4³		6	14	12		10	11		8	13				9²	3			1		5	7¹	2			26
			4³		6	7¹	8²		10	11		12	14				13	3			1		5		2	9		27
		12			6	7²	14			11		8	4	2	13		9³	3			1		5¹			10		28
		5	4		6	7	8		14	11¹		12	10	2	13		9³	3²			1							29
		3	4³		6	7¹	10²	14		11	13		8	5	12		9				1				2			30
		3	4		6	7	8	14	12	11²				5			9¹				1			10³	2	13		31
		3	8³		6	7	9		10²	12				4	14		13				1		5	11	2¹			32
		3	4		6	12		13	10²	9				5	7³		14				1			11¹	2	8		33
		3	4³		6	12	10		14	11	13			5			9²				1			7	2¹	8		34
			4		6	7	9²		10³	11¹	13	12	14	5				3			1			2		8		35
		3	4¹		6	7	12		10³	11²	13			5			14				1			2	9	8		36
		6¹	4			12	9		10²	11	13			5			14	3			1			7	2	8³		37
					6	7¹	14	10²	12	13			4	5	8		9³	3						11	2		1	38

EAST FIFE

Year Formed: 1903. *Ground & Address:* Bayview Stadium, Harbour View, Methil, Fife KY8 3RW. *Telephone:* 01333 426323. *Fax:* 01333 426376. *E-mail:* office@eastfife.org. *Website:* www.eastfife.org
Ground Capacity: 1,992. *Size of Pitch:* 105m × 65m.
Chairman: Sid Columbine. *Secretary:* Jim Stevenson.
Manager: Gordon Durie. *Assistant Manager:* Gordon Chisholm. *Physio:* Brian McNeill.
Club Nickname: The Fifers.
Previous Ground: Bayview Park.
Record Attendance: 22,515 v Raith Rovers, Division I, 2 Jan 1950.
Record Transfer Fee received: £150,000 for Paul Hunter from Hull C (March 1990).
Record Transfer Fee paid: £70,000 for John Sludden from Kilmarnock (July 1991).
Record Victory: 13-2 v Edinburgh City, Division II, 11 Dec 1937.
Record Defeat: 0-9 v Hearts, Division I, 5 Oct 1957.
Most Capped Player: George Aitken, 5 (8), Scotland.
Most League Appearances: 517: David Clarke, 1968-86.
Most League Goals in Season (Individual): 41: Jock Wood, Division II; 1926-27 and Henry Morris, Division II, 1947-48.
Most Goals Overall (Individual): 225: Phil Weir, 1922-35.

EAST FIFE 2011–12 LEAGUE RECORD

Match No.	*Date*	*Venue*	*Opponents*	*Result*		*H/T Score*	*Lg Pos.*	*Goalscorers*	*Attendance*
1	Aug 6	A	Stirling A	L	0-1	0-0	—		688
2	13	H	Airdrie U	W	2-0	1-0	—	Johnstone [36], Linn [64]	759
3	20	A	Arbroath	L	0-3	0-1	7		723
4	27	H	Dumbarton	L	0-6	0-4	10		635
5	Sept 10	A	Cowdenbeath	L	2-3	1-1	10	Wallace [3], Muir [62]	540
6	17	H	Brechin C	D	1-1	1-0	10	Wallace [8]	501
7	24	A	Stenhousemuir	L	1-2	0-1	10	Wallace [56]	642
8	Oct 1	H	Forfar Ath	W	4-3	3-2	9	Ovenstone [15], Muir [32], Ogleby [44], Wallace [83]	533
9	15	A	Albion R	W	3-0	1-0	7	Johnstone 2 [38, 51], Linn [83]	403
10	22	H	Stirling A	W	1-0	0-0	4	Wallace [88]	617
11	29	A	Airdrie U	W	3-1	1-0	4	Wallace [34], Johnstone [81], Linn [85]	849
12	Nov 5	H	Cowdenbeath	L	1-3	1-0	4	Wallace [6]	1022
13	12	A	Dumbarton	L	0-3	0-1	6		678
14	26	A	Brechin C	W	2-0	2-0	4	Linn [1], Ogleby [22]	503
15	Dec 3	H	Stenhousemuir	L	1-3	0-1	5	Linn [80]	508
16	Jan 2	A	Cowdenbeath	L	0-4	0-1	8		485
17	14	H	Arbroath	D	2-2	1-1	8	Cook [6], Hislop [52]	617
18	21	A	Stirling A	W	1-0	0-0	7	Wallace [51]	608
19	24	H	Albion R	W	2-0	0-0	—	Sloan [77], Linn [88]	390
20	28	A	Stenhousemuir	L	0-1	0-0	—		687
21	Feb 11	A	Albion R	D	1-1	0-0	6	Wallace [57]	348
22	18	H	Forfar Ath	W	4-0	3-0	5	Sloan 2 (1 pen) [11 (p), 15], Hislop [36], Wallace [70]	526
23	21	H	Dumbarton	L	1-2	1-0	—	Linn [23]	397
24	25	H	Airdrie U	W	2-0	1-0	5	Sloan (pen) [42], Johnstone [87]	535
25	28	A	Forfar Ath	L	2-3	1-2	—	Sloan (pen) [19], Wallace (pen) [90]	432
26	Mar 3	A	Arbroath	D	2-2	2-2	2	Sloan [28], Hislop [43]	842
27	6	H	Brechin C	D	2-2	2-2	—	Sloan 2 (1 pen) [25 (p), 45]	416
28	10	H	Cowdenbeath	L	0-1	0-1	5		926
29	17	A	Dumbarton	W	4-0	3-0	5	Wallace 2 [4, 24], Grindlay (og) [23], Dalziel [51]	713
30	24	A	Brechin C	W	3-1	1-1	5	Wallace 3 [31, 59, 90]	525
31	31	H	Stenhousemuir	D	1-1	1-0	6	Wallace [8]	742
32	Apr 7	A	Forfar Ath	W	4-1	2-1	5	Dalziel 2 [15, 90], Wallace 2 [18, 53]	559
33	14	H	Albion R	L	1-2	0-2	6	Muir [82]	566
34	21	H	Stirling A	W	1-0	0-0	6	Wallace (pen) [90]	495
35	28	A	Airdrie U	L	0-2	0-0	6		1223
36	May 5	H	Arbroath	L	1-3	0-2	6	Muir [90]	597

Final League Position: 6

Honours
League Champions: Division II 1947-48. Third Division 2007-08. *Runners-up:* Division II 1929-30, 1970-71. Second Division 1983-84, 1995-96. Third Division 2002-03.
Scottish Cup Winners: 1938; *Runners-up:* 1927, 1950.
League Cup Winners: 1947-48, 1949-50, 1953-54.

Club colours: Shirt: Black with gold sleeves. Shorts: Black with gold trim. Stockings: Black.

Goalscorers: *League (55):* Wallace 20 (2 pens), Sloan 8 (4 pens), Linn 7, Johnstone 5, Muir 4, Dalziel 3, Hislop 3, Ogleby 2, Cook 1, Ovenstone 1, own goal 1.
Scottish Cup (5): Ogleby 2, Linn 1, Sloan 1, Wallace 1.
Scottish Communities Cup (7): Wallace 2, Dalziel 1, Linn 1, Ogleby 1, Park 1, Sloan 1.
Ramsdens Cup (9): Wallace 4, Ogleby 3 (1 pen), Linn 1, Young 1.

Ridgers M 13	Cowan D 2 + 1	Campbell S 22	Ovenstone J 19 + 4	Muir D 25 + 6	Johnstone C 16 + 12	Park M 14	Young L 2 + 1	Linn R 35	Ogleby R 13 + 1	Wallace R 32	Sloan R 16 + 16	Dalziel S 10 + 16	Durie S 29 + 1	Smith D 26 + 4	Hislop S 14 + 13	Brown M 15 + 1	White D 27	McQuade P 3 + 9	Innes C 1	Cook A 22 + 4	Brown R 8 + 1	McCormack D 16	Janczyk N 16 + 2	Martin J — + 3	Devlin J — + 1	Collier A — + 1	*Match No.*
1	2	3	4	5	6^{1}	7	8	9	10^{2}	11	12	13															1
1^{6}	13	4	3	5▮	6^{2}	7		9	10^{1}	11			2	8	12	15											2
	8	4	3		5	6^{2}	9^{1}	7			13	12	2	11	10	1											3
		3	4	5	6	7	12^{2}	9	14	11	13		2	8^{1}	10^{3}	1											4
1			3	5	6^{3}	7		9^{2}	10	11	12	13	2	8^{1}			4	14									5
1				5	6^{1}	7		9	10	11^{2}		13	2	8			4		3	12							6
1			4	6	14	8		10^{3}	7^{1}	11	13	12	2	9^{2}			3			5							7
1			3	5	6^{1}	7		9^{2}	10^{3}	11	13	14	2	8			4			12							8
1			4	7	9^{1}	5		6	8	11^{2}			2	10^{3}	14		3	13		12							9
1			3	6^{1}	7^{2}	5		10	11^{3}	9	12		2	8			4	14		13							10
1			4	6	7	5		10	11^{1}	9^{3}	8^{2}		2	13	12		3	14									11
1			4	7	6^{1}	5		10^{2}	11^{3}	9	12		2	8	14		3	13									12
			4	6	7^{1}			11		9	14		2	8^{3}	10^{2}	1	3	13		5	12						13
1		4	12	6		7		10	11^{2}	9			2	8	13		3			5^{1}							14
1		3	5	6		7^{1}		10	11^{2}	9	12		2	8^{3}	14		4	13									15
1		2	5	8^{1}				10	11	9	12		6	7						4		3					16
		3			7^{1}			10		9	12	13	2		11^{2}	1	4			5		6	8				17
		6			7^{1}			10		9^{3}	14	13	2	12	11^{2}		3			5	1	4▮	8				18
		3	5	6	12			10^{3}			13	11		8		1	4	9^{2}		2			7^{1}	14			19
		3	5	6	12			10			13	14		8^{1}	11^{3}	1	4	9^{2}		2			7				20
		3		6	12			10^{3}		9	8^{1}	13	2	14	11^{2}		4			5	1		7				21
		3		6				10		9^{2}	8	12	2		11^{1}		4	13		5	1		7				22
		3^{1}	12	6	14			10		9	8^{3}	11^{2}	2		13	1	4			5		7					23
		5		2	12			11^{3}		7	8^{1}	13			10^{2}		4			3	1	6	9		14		24
		3		6	14			10		9	8^{3}	12		13	11^{1}		4			5	1	2	7^{2}				25
		4^{2}			14			10		9	8^{3}	12	13	7	11^{1}	1	5▮			3		2	6				26
				12	13			10^{2}		7	6	11^{3}	8	4	9	1				3		2	5^{1}	14			27
								10		9	8	12	2	7	11^{1}		4			5	1	3	6^{2}	13			28
			14	13				10		9	8	11^{1}	2	6^{2}			3	12		5	1	4	7^{3}				29
				13				10		9	8	11^{1}	2	7	12	1	5			3		4	6^{2}				30
			12	14				10		9	8	11^{2}	2	6	13	1	4▮			5^{1}		3	7^{3}				31
		3	2	12	13			9^{2}		10	6^{3}	11	5	8^{1}	14	1						4	7				32
		4	5	12	13			10^{3}		9	8^{2}	11	2	6	14	1						3	7^{1}				33
		3		6	12			11		8	9^{1}	13	2		10^{2}	1	4			5		7^{3}	14				34
		7		8	6^{1}						9^{2}	10	2	4	12		3▮	11		5	1		13				35
		3	4	6	7^{1}			10		9^{2}	12	11		8	13	1^{6}				5		2				15	36

EAST STIRLINGSHIRE

Year Formed: 1880. *Ground & Address:* Club moving to new premises. *Present contact:* 202 Stirling Road, Larbert, Falkirk FK5 3NJ. *Telephone:* 01324 557 862. *Fax:* 01324 557 862.
E-mail: fceaststirlingshire@gmail.com *Website:* www.eaststirlingfc.com
Ground Capacity: 3,776 (626 seated). *Size of Pitch:* 110yd × 72yd.
Chairman: Les Thomson. *Vice-Chairman:* Andy Miller.
Head Coach: John Coughlin. *Assistant Manager:* Matthew Kerr. *Physio:* Steve O'Neill.
Club Nickname: The Shire.
Previous Grounds: Burnhouse, Randyford Park, Merchiston Park, New Kilbowie Park, Firs Park.
Record Attendance: 12,000 v Partick Th, *Scottish Cup* 3rd rd, 21 Feb 1921.
Record Transfer Fee received: £35,000 for Jim Docherty to Chelsea (1978).
Record Transfer Fee paid: £6,000 for Colin McKinnon from Falkirk (March 1991).
Record Victory: 11-2 v Vale of Bannock, *Scottish Cup* 2nd rd, 22 Sept 1888.
Record Defeat: 1-12 v Dundee United, Division II, 13 Apr 1936.
Most Capped Player: Humphrey Jones, 5 (14), Wales.
Most League Appearances: 415: Gordon Russell, 1983-2001.
Most League Goals in Season (Individual): 36: Malcolm Morrison, Division II, 1938-39.

EAST STIRLINGSHIRE 2011–12 LEAGUE RECORD

Match No.	Date	Venue	Opponents	Result		H/T Score	Lg Pos.	Goalscorers	Attendance
1	Aug 6	H	Montrose	W	1-0	0-0	—	Jackson (pen) [79]	282
2	13	A	Berwick R	L	2-4	0-1	8	Love, A (pen) [75], Gibson [88]	441
3	20	H	Peterhead	L	0-2	0-1	10		287
4	27	A	Elgin C	L	0-2	0-1	9		578
5	Sept 10	H	Alloa Ath	L	0-1	0-1	10		419
6	17	H	Stranraer	L	1-3	1-1	10	Stirling [19]	271
7	24	A	Annan Ath	L	0-3	0-3	10		511
8	Oct 1	H	Queen's Park	L	1-3	0-0	10	Love, A [89]	384
9	15	A	Clyde	L	1-7	0-3	10	Coyne [82]	617
10	Nov 5	A	Montrose	L	1-2	1-1	10	Stirling [13]	315
11	9	H	Berwick R	L	1-3	1-2	—	Coyne [17]	310
12	12	H	Elgin C	D	1-1	1-1	10	Coyne [40]	234
13	26	A	Alloa Ath	D	1-1	0-0	—	Hunter [65]	421
14	Dec 3	H	Annan Ath	W	1-0	1-0	9	Coyne [39]	215
15	10	A	Stranraer	L	0-6	0-3	9		276
16	17	H	Clyde	D	1-1	1-0	9	Turner [45]	490
17	24	A	Queen's Park	L	0-2	0-1	—		504
18	Jan 2	H	Alloa Ath	L	1-3	1-1	10	Beveridge [6]	531
19	7	A	Elgin C	L	1-3	1-1	10	Coyne (pen) [45]	531
20	14	A	Peterhead	L	0-1	0-1	10		451
21	21	H	Montrose	W	3-1	1-0	10	Lurinsky 2 (1 pen) [38, 49 (p)], Turner [55]	248
22	28	A	Annan Ath	D	2-2	2-1	10	Maxwell [12], Lurinsky [24]	401
23	Feb 4	H	Stranraer	D	2-2	1-1	10	Maxwell [3], Horner [46]	275
24	11	A	Clyde	L	0-3	0-1	10		507
25	18	H	Queen's Park	L	1-2	0-0	10	Maxwell [74]	346
26	25	A	Berwick R	W	2-0	1-0	10	Dingwall [40], Turner [84]	349
27	Mar 3	H	Peterhead	W	6-3	5-1	10	Hunter [10], Devlin [23], Lurinsky (pen) [33], Maxwell [38], Stirling 2 [41, 90]	277
28	10	A	Alloa Ath	L	1-5	1-2	10	Lurinsky [1]	579
29	17	H	Elgin C	D	2-2	1-1	10	Turner [7], Stirling [58]	264
30	24	A	Stranraer	L	1-4	0-3	10	Turner [90]	304
31	31	H	Annan Ath	L	0-4	0-1	10		235
32	Apr 7	A	Queen's Park	L	1-5	0-1	10	Ramage [79]	477
33	14	H	Clyde	L	0-1	0-0	10		434
34	21	A	Montrose	L	1-3	1-1	10	Turner [15]	329
35	28	H	Berwick R	W	2-1	2-0	10	Horner [6], Sheerin [18]	277
36	May 5	A	Peterhead	L	0-2	0-1	10		494

Final League Position: 10

Honours
League Champions: Division II 1931-32; C Division 1947-48. *Runners-up:* Division II 1962-63. Second Division 1979-80. Division Three 1923-24.

Club colours: Shirt: Black and white hoops. Shorts: Black. Stockings: Black and white hoops.

Goalscorers: *League (38):* Turner 6, Coyne 5 (1 pen), Lurinsky 5 (2 pens), Stirling 5, Maxwell 4, Horner 2, Hunter 2, Love, A. 2 (1 pen), Beveridge 1, Devlin 1, Dingwall 1, Gibson 1, Jackson 1 (1 pen), Ramage 1, Sheerin 1.
Scottish Cup (4): Coyne 1, Gibson 1, Stirling 1, Team 1.
Scottish Communities Cup (0).
Ramsdens Cup (2): Love, A. 1, Turner 1.

Antell C 35	Chisholm I 18 + 2	Cane D 25 + 1	Beveridge S 11	Dingwall J 27 + 2	Stirling A 35	Hunter M 30 + 2	Love A 13 + 2	Jackson S 31 + 2	Turner K 28 + 5	Lurinsky A 20 + 7	Sheerin J 9 + 10	Team F 5 + 13	Frances R 15	Gibson N — + 8	Maxwell S 26 + 2	Savage J 1 + 2	Scott C 5 + 3	Coyne B 11	Love S — + 3	Horner L 25	Winter C 4	Benton J 5 + 2	Ramage G 3 + 7	Devlin R 10 + 2	Fulton S 2 + 6	Gillespie K 1 + 6	Glasgow J — + 2	Tart S — + 4	Campbell J — + 1	Hay G 1	Gordon C — + 1	*Match No.*
1	2	3	4	5	6	7	8^{2}	9	10^{1}	11	12	13																			1
1	2			4	5	7	6	9■	11^{3}	10^{1}	8^{2}		3	12	13	14															2
1	2	3	4		6	8	9^{1}		12	13	10^{2}		5	14	7	11^{3}															3
1	2	3		5	6	14	9		12	11^{2}	10^{1}	13	4		7		8^{3}														4
1	2^{1}	4	3		6	8	9	11	10^{2}	12	13	14	5				7^{3}														5
1	2	4	3	5	6■	8	9	12	11^{2}	13	10^{3}	14	7^{1}																		6
1	2	4	3	6^{1}		7	8	9^{2}	11	10^{3}		14	5	13			12														7
1	2		3	4	5	7	8	9	11^{3}	10^{2}		14		12		13	6^{1}														8
1	2		3		5	6	8	9	10^{2}	13			4		7^{1}			11	12												9
1	2		3	5	4	6	7	9	10^{2}			12		13	8^{1}			11													10
1	2		3		4	7	8^{1}	9		11^{2}				12	5			10	13	6											11
1	2	3		13	4	6	7■	10		14		9^{3}			5^{2}		12	11		8^{1}											12
1	2	4			7	6^{1}		13	12	10		8			5			11^{2}		9	3										13
1		2			3	6		8	14	10^{3}		9^{2}			5		12	11	13	7	4^{1}										14
1		3		2	4	6^{3}	12	8	13	9^{1}		10^{2}		14	5			11		7											15
1		3		2	4	7	12	10	11^{2}	13					8^{1}			9		6	5										16
1		4		5	6	8^{1}	9^{2}	2	11	13				14	12			10^{3}		7	3										17
1	13	3	2	12	4			8	11^{3}	9		14			5^{1}		6^{2}	10		7											18
1	12	3	2^{1}		4	13		8	9^{3}	11	14				5		6^{2}	10		7											19
1	2	3		4^{3}	5	7		9	10^{1}	11^{2}	12	14			8					6		13									20
1	2	3		4	5	6		9	11^{3}	10^{1}		14			7^{2}					8			12	13							21
1	5	3^{1}		2	8	7		4	11	9^{2}					10					6			13	12							22
1	2			3	4	6		9	11^{2}	10^{1}	12				7					8			13	5							23
1	5	4		3^{3}	2			11		9^{2}	12	13			7					6			10	8^{1}	14						24
1		2		3^{3}	4	7		9	11^{1}	10^{2}	14	12			8					6			13	5							25
1				3	4	6		9	11^{1}	10		12	2		8					7				5							26
1		4		2	8	7			11^{2}	9^{1}	13		3		6■					10				5	12						27
1		13		5	8	7		3	11	6^{1}			4							9^{2}		12	10^{3}	2	14						28
1				3	4	6		10	11^{1}		12		2■		8					9		7		5							29
1		3		4	2	7		11	10		13				8					9^{2}		5^{1}	12	6^{3}		14					30
1		4^{1}		3^{2}	5	6^{3}		10	11				2		8					9				7	13	12	14				31
1				3	4			10	11^{3}		9^{1}		2		8							7^{2}	12	5■	6	14		13			32
1		2		3	4			9	11		6^{3}				7					8		5^{2}	10^{1}		14	13	12				33
1		2		4	5	6		9	10^{1}		8^{2}	11^{3}	3							7						12		13	14			34
1				4	5	6		10	11^{3}		9^{1}		3■		7^{2}					8			14		12	2		13			35
		2		3	4	7^{1}		10	11		9^{3}									6		5			8^{2}	13		14		1	12	36

ELGIN CITY

Year Formed: 1893. *Ground and Address:* Borough Briggs, Borough Briggs Road, Elgin IV30 1AP.
Telephone: 01343 551114. *Fax:* 01343 547921. *E-mail:* elgincityfc@ukonline.co.uk *Website:* www.elgincity.com
Ground Capacity: 3,927, seated 478, standing 3,449. *Size of pitch:* 111yd × 72yd.
Chairman: Graham Tatters. *Secretary:* Ian A. Allan.
Manager: Ross Jack. *Assistant Manager:* Barry Wilson. *Physios:* Lynda Anderson and Eilidh Paterson.
Previous names: 1893-1900 Elgin City, 1900–03 Elgin City United, 1903– Elgin City.
Club Nicknames: City or Black & Whites.
Previous Grounds: Association Park 1893-95; Milnfield Park 1895-1909; Station Park 1909-19; Cooper Park 1919-21.
Record Attendance: 12,608 v Arbroath, Scottish Cup, 17 Feb 1968.
Record Transfer Fee received: £32,000 for Michael Teasdale to Dundee (Jan 1994).
Record Transfer Fee paid: £10,000 to Fraserburgh for Russell McBride (July 2001).
Record Victory: 18-1 v Brora Rangers, North of Scotland Cup, 6 Feb 1960.
Record Defeat: 1-14 v Hearts, Scottish Cup, 4 Feb 1939.
Most League Appearances: 224: David Hind, 2001-09.
Most League Goals in Season (Individual): 20: Martin Johnston, 2005-06.
Most Goals Overall (Individual): 39: Martin Johnston, 2005-07.

ELGIN CITY 2011–12 LEAGUE RECORD

Match No.	*Date*	*Venue*	*Opponents*	*Result*	*H/T Score*	*Lg Pos.*	*Goalscorers*	*Attendance*
1	Aug 6	H	Berwick R	W 4-1	2-0	—	Gunn 4 (1 pen) [17, 20 (p), 51, 70]	534
2	13	A	Montrose	L 0-3	0-2	5		349
3	20	H	Queen's Park	W 2-0	2-0	3	Beveridge [7], Gunn [29]	591
4	27	H	East Stirling	W 2-0	1-0	2	Gunn 2 [30, 81]	578
5	Sept 10	A	Peterhead	W 3-1	3-0	1	Gunn [4], Nicolson [8], Duff [45]	596
6	17	H	Clyde	L 0-3	0-2	4		728
7	24	A	Stranraer	L 0-1	0-1	4		365
8	Oct 1	H	Alloa Ath	W 5-0	3-0	4	Beveridge 2 [21, 78], Cameron [43], Leslie 2 (2 pens) [45, 56]	522
9	15	A	Annan Ath	D 1-1	1-0	4	Beveridge [4]	417
10	Nov 5	A	Berwick R	D 1-1	1-1	7	Gunn [34]	327
11	8	H	Montrose	W 3-1	2-1	—	O'Donoghue 2 [10, 17], Crooks [66]	461
12	12	A	East Stirling	D 1-1	1-1	3	Gunn [1]	234
13	Dec 3	H	Stranraer	D 1-1	1-0	3	Millar [9]	520
14	26	A	Alloa Ath	L 0-3	0-1	6		491
15	Jan 2	A	Peterhead	L 0-3	0-2	6		626
16	7	H	East Stirling	W 3-1	1-1	5	Leslie [43], MacPhee [73], Crooks [90]	531
17	14	A	Queen's Park	L 0-6	0-1	6		344
18	21	H	Berwick R	W 4-0	2-0	5	Millar 2 [35, 53], MacPhee [37], Leslie [49]	438
19	28	A	Stranraer	L 2-5	2-2	5	Nicolson 2 [13, 41]	285
20	Feb 11	A	Annan Ath	D 1-1	1-1	5	Niven [29]	413
21	14	H	Peterhead	W 6-1	1-0	—	Ross (og) [25], Millar [53], McAllister (og) [55], MacDonald (og) [70], Cameron [89], Gunn [90]	431
22	18	H	Alloa Ath	W 3-0	2-0	5	Millar [1], Gunn [37], Leslie [67]	600
23	21	A	Clyde	W 2-1	0-1	—	Moore [53], Durnan [55]	352
24	25	A	Montrose	W 3-2	2-1	4	Gunn 3 [6, 42, 70]	401
25	28	H	Clyde	D 1-1	0-1	—	Wilson [89]	611
26	Mar 3	H	Queen's Park	D 1-1	1-1	4	Niven [9]	792
27	6	H	Annan Ath	W 3-0	2-0	—	Gunn [28], Muirhead (og) [35], Niven [78]	588
28	10	H	Peterhead	L 1-2	1-1	4	Nicolson [2]	1072
29	17	A	East Stirling	D 2-2	1-1	4	Niven [41], MacPhee (pen) [84]	264
30	24	A	Clyde	W 2-0	0-0	4	Crooks [57], Cameron [78]	450
31	31	H	Stranraer	L 1-2	0-0	4	MacPhee [58]	685
32	Apr 7	A	Alloa Ath	L 1-8	0-2	4	Millar [51]	730
33	14	H	Annan Ath	L 1-2	1-2	4	Millar [6]	715
34	21	A	Berwick R	D 3-3	1-2	4	Durnan [23], Crooks [75], Gunn [77]	411
35	28	H	Montrose	W 2-1	1-0	4	Gunn [35], MacPhee [56]	901
36	May 5	A	Queen's Park	W 3-1	1-0	4	MacPhee [4], Crooks [72], Duff [81]	527

Final League Position: 4

Honours
Scottish Cup: Quarter-finals 1968.
Highland League Champions: winners 15 times.
Scottish Qualifying Cup (North): winners 7 times.
North of Scotland Cup: winners 17 times.
Highland League Cup: winners 5 times.
Inverness Cup: winners twice.

Club colours: Shirt: Black and white stripes. Shorts: Black. Stockings: Red.

Goalscorers: *League (68):* Gunn 18 (1 pen), Millar 7, MacPhee 6 (1 pen), Crooks 5, Leslie 5 (2 pens), Beveridge 4, Nicolson 4, Niven 4, Cameron 3, Duff 2, Durnan 2, O'Donoghue 2, Moore 1, Wilson 1, own goals 4.
Scottish Cup (7): Gunn 3, Cameron 1, Crooks 1, Nicolson 1, own goal 1.
Scottish Communities Cup (1): Cameron 1.
Ramsdens Cup (2): Cameron 1, Leslie 1.
Play-Offs (1): Millar 1.

Clark A 33	Niven D 34 + 1	Duff J 32 + 1	Kaczan P 11	Nicolson M 35	O'Donoghue R 16 + 8	Cameron B 26 + 1	Beveridge G 20 + 9	Moore D 31	Gunn C 30 + 4	Leslie S 28 + 1	Lawrie B — + 8	Crooks J 12 + 19	Frizzel C 2 + 6	MacPhee A 30 + 3	Edwards S 1 + 4	Wilson B 3 + 8	Innes G — + 2	Millar P 17 + 7	McMullan P 9 + 9	Calder J 3 + 2	Durnan M 15 + 2	Cooper A 8	Forbes F — + 1	McLean C — + 2	Halford L — + 1	*Match No.*
1	2	3	4	5	6	7^{1}	8	9	10^{2}	11^{3}	12	13	14													1
1	2	4^{3}	3	6	5^{1}		11	7	9	10		13	8^{2}	12	14											2
1	7	3	2	4	12		8^{3}	9	10^{2}	11	14	6^{1}	13	5												3
1	5	3	2	6	13		7^{3}	9	10	11		8^{2}	12	4^{1}		14										4
1	4	3	2	5		8	7	9■	10^{1}	11	13		12	6^{2}												5
1	5	3	2^{1}	6	12	7^{3}	8		10	11	14	13	9^{2}	4												6
1	6	3	2	4	8^{3}	10^{1}	7^{2}	9		11		12	13	5			14									7
1	5	3	2	6		7^{1}	8	9^{2}	10	11^{3}	12	13	14	4												8
1	2^{2}	3	4	6	13	10^{3}	8	9	7^{1}	11		12		5	14											9
1	12	3	2^{2}	6	5	7	14	9	10^{3}	11		8^{1}		4	13											10
1	2	3		5	6	7^{1}	12	9	10^{3}	8		11^{2}		4	13			14								11
1	4		2^{1}	6	5	11^{3}	12	9	10	8	14	7^{2}			3			13								12
1	5	3		4	7	6	2	9	10	8^{1}	13	12						11^{2}								13
1	2	3		6	5	11^{1}	8	9	10		13	7^{2}		4				12								14
1■	2	3		5	6		9	10	11^{2}	8^{1}		13		4				7^{6}	12	15						15
	2	3		6	14	12	9	10^{3}	11	8^{1}		13		4				7^{2}	5	1						16
1	2	4		7^{3}	13		8^{1}	9	11	10		12		5			14		6^{2}		3					17
1	2^{3}	3^{1}		7	12	9	14	10	13	11^{2}				6				8	5		4					18
1	3	2		8	6	7^{2}	14	5	12			13		11				10^{1}	9^{3}		4					19
1	5	3		6^{1}		9^{3}	11	10	12	8		13		2				7^{2}	14		4■					20
1	4	2		5		8	7	10	11	9				3				6^{1}	12							21
1	4	3		7	6	11^{3}		10	8	9^{2}		12		2				5^{1}	14		13					22
1	2	4		5	6^{1}	11		10	9^{2}	8		13		3				7^{3}	14		12					23
1	2	4		7		8^{2}		9	11	10		12		5				6^{1}	13		3					24
1	2	4		6		8^{2}		10	11	9^{3}		12		5		14		7^{1}	13		3					25
1	2	3		7	14	8^{2}		9	10	11^{3}		12		4		13		6^{1}			5					26
1	2	3^{2}		6	7^{1}			9^{3}	10	8		11		5		14		13	12		4					27
1	2	3		6		7^{1}	13	9	10	8^{3}		11^{2}		5		14		12			4					28
1	2	3^{2}		7			8	10	9^{3}			11^{1}		4		14		12	13		5■	6				29
1				5		9	7	10	8^{1}			11		3		4			2			6	12			30
1	5	4		7		11^{1}		10	8	12		9^{3}		2		14		13	3^{2}			6				31
1■	3			8			11^{1}	10	12					2		9		6	4^{6}	15	5^{2}	7		13		32
	2	3		4	7^{3}	6^{2}	14		10	9■				12		13		11		1	5^{1}	8				33
	2	3		6	8^{1}	10	12		11			14		13				9^{3}	5^{2}	1	4	7				34
1	2	3		6		9	13		11	10^{2}		12		5				8^{1}			4	7				35
1	2^{2}	13			7		10					11		4		9^{1}		6	5		3	8^{3}		14	12	36

FALKIRK

Year Formed: 1876. *Ground & Address:* The Falkirk Stadium, Westfield, Falkirk FK2 9DX. *Telephone:* 01324 624121.
Fax: 01324 612418. *Email:* post@falkirkfc.co.uk *Website:* www.falkirkfc.co.uk
Ground Capacity: seated: 8,000. *Size of Pitch:* 105m × 68m.
Chairman: Martin Ritchie. *Managing Director:* George Craig. *Secretary:* Alex Blackwood.
Manager: Steven Pressley.
Club Nickname: The Bairns.
Previous Grounds: Randyford 1876-81; Blinkbonny Grounds 1881-83; Brockville Park 1883-2003.
Record Attendance: 23,100 v Celtic, Scottish Cup 3rd rd, 21 Feb 1953.
Record Transfer Fee received: £380,000 for John Hughes to Celtic (Aug 1995).
Record Transfer Fee paid: £225,000 to Chelsea for Kevin McAllister (Aug 1991).
Record Victory: 12-1 v Laurieston, Scottish Cup 2nd rd, 23 Sept 1893.
Record Defeat: 1-11 v Airdrieonians, Division I, 28 Apr 1951.
Most Capped Player: Alex Parker, 14 (15), Scotland and Russell Latapy, Trinidad & Tobago.
Most League Appearances: 450: Tom Ferguson, 1919-32.
Most League Goals in Season (Individual): 43: Evelyn Morrison, Division I, 1928-29.
Most Goals Overall (Individual): 86: Dougie Moran, 1957-61 and 1964-67.

FALKIRK 2011–12 LEAGUE RECORD

Match No.	Date	Venue	Opponents	Result		H/T Score	Lg Pos.	Goalscorers	Attendance
1	Aug 6	A	Raith R	L	0-1	0-1	—		2695
2	13	H	Partick Th	W	2-1	1-1	5	El Alaguie 8, Higginbotham 50	3036
3	20	A	Ayr U	D	2-2	2-1	5	Higginbotham 8, El Alaguie 44	1938
4	27	H	Ross Co	D	1-1	0-0	6	El Alaguie 87	3009
5	Sept 10	A	Livingston	D	1-1	0-0	6	Millar, M (pen) 90	2229
6	17	H	Dundee	W	2-1	0-1	3	Weatherston 79, El Alaguie 86	3576
7	24	A	Morton	L	2-3	2-1	—	Weatherston 17, Alston 24	2621
8	Oct 1	A	Hamilton A	W	1-0	1-0	4	El Alaguie 39	2367
9	15	H	Queen of the S	W	1-0	0-0	3	Dods 90	3094
10	22	A	Partick Th	D	2-2	1-0	2	El Alaguie 35, Higginbotham 85	2851
11	29	H	Raith R	W	2-0	0-0	2	Alston 77, Dods 82	3628
12	Nov 5	H	Livingston	W	4-3	3-0	2	El Alaguie 12, Wallace 17, Brown (og) 39, Weatherston 85	3691
13	12	A	Ross Co	L	1-3	1-1	2	Wallace 10	4108
14	26	A	Dundee	L	2-4	1-2	2	Weston (og) 35, Fulton, J 74	4507
15	Dec 3	H	Morton	W	1-0	0-0	2	El Alaguie 58	3114
16	10	H	Hamilton A	D	0-0	0-0	3		3024
17	17	A	Queen of the S	W	5-1	1-1	2	Sibbald 2 43, 77, El Alaguie 2 73, 86, Higginbotham 81	1466
18	26	H	Ross Co	D	1-1	0-0	2	Duffie 77	4383
19	Jan 2	A	Livingston	W	2-1	1-0	2	El Alaguie 12, Higginbotham 72	2967
20	14	H	Ayr U	D	0-0	0-0	2		3091
21	21	A	Raith R	D	2-2	1-2	2	El Alaguie 36, Dods 63	2026
22	Feb 11	A	Morton	D	0-0	0-0	2		1757
23	18	A	Hamilton A	W	1-0	1-0	2	Dods 45	1843
24	21	H	Dundee	D	1-1	1-0	—	El Alaguie 27	3089
25	25	H	Queen of the S	W	3-0	2-0	2	El Alaguie 35, Gibson 36, Dods 79	2982
26	Mar 3	A	Ayr U	L	0-1	0-0	2		1621
27	10	H	Partick Th	D	1-1	0-1	2	Millar, M (pen) 52	3257
28	17	A	Ross Co	L	1-2	0-2	3	Millar, M 62	4302
29	20	H	Morton	L	0-2	0-0	—		2538
30	24	H	Livingston	L	2-5	1-2	3	El Alaguie 29, Weatherston 79	2939
31	Apr 7	A	Dundee	L	1-3	1-2	3	Millar, M 24	3896
32	10	H	Hamilton A	W	3-0	0-0	—	Millar, M 2 (1 pen) 58 (p), 60, El Alaguie 81	2461
33	14	A	Queen of the S	D	0-0	0-0	3		1446
34	21	H	Raith R	L	2-3	1-2	3	El Alaguie 9, Alston 68	3024
35	28	A	Partick Th	D	1-1	0-1	3	Alston 71	2586
36	May 5	H	Ayr U	W	3-2	1-0	3	Scobbie (pen) 7, El Alaguie 56, Alston 63	3445

Final League Position: 3

Honours
League Champions: Division II 1935-36, 1969-70, 1974-75. First Division 1990-91, 1993-94, 2002-03, 2004-05. Second Division 1979-80; *Runners-up:* Division I 1907-08, 1909-10. First Division 1985-86, 1988-89, 1997-98, 1998-99. Division II 1904-05, 1951-52, 1960-61.
Scottish Cup Winners: 1913, 1957; *Runners-up:* 1997, 2009. *League Cup Runners-up:* 1947-48. *B&Q Cup Winners:* 1993-94. *League Challenge Cup Winners:* 1997-98, 2004-05, 2011-12.

European: *Europa League:* 2 matches (2009-10).

Club colours: Shirt: Navy blue with white seams. Shorts: White. Stockings: Red.

Goalscorers: *League (53):* El Alaguie 18, Millar, M. 6 (3 pens), Alston 5, Dods 5, Higginbotham 5, Weatherston 4, Sibbald 2, Wallace 2, Duffie 1, Fulton, J. 1, Gibson 1, Scobbie 1 (1 pen), own goals 2.
Scottish Cup (3): Alston 1, Dods 1, El Alagui 1.
Scottish Communities Cup (12): El Alagui 5, Fulton, J. 2, Graham 1, Higginbotham 1, Millar, M. 1, Sibbald 1, own goal 1.
Ramsdens Cup (11): El Alagui 3, Dods 2, Higginbotham 2, Millar, M. 2, Bennett 1, Sibbald 1.

McGovern M 35	Duffie K 30	Dods D 34	Bennett R 8 + 10	Scobbie T 30	Fulton J 23 + 9	Fulton D 4 + 2	Murdoch S 25 + 1	Sibbald C 22 + 4	El Alaguie F 33	Higginbotham K 20	Graham A — + 3	Wallace M 32 + 2	Alston B 14 + 10	Weatherston D 25 + 1	Brisbane S — + 2	Millar M 33	Millar R 1 + 4	Kingsley S 8 + 7	White J 4 + 6	Gibson W 10 + 2	Faulds K 4 + 5	Bowman G 1 + 1	Dick L — + 1	*Match No.*
1	2	3■	4	5	6^{1}	7	8	9^{2}	10	11	12	13												1
1	2		3	5	12	6	7		10	11		4	8^{1}	9^{2}	13									2
1	2	3	4	5	12		6	8	10	11				9^{1}		7								3
1	2	3		5	6^{3}	12	8	9^{1}	10	11	14	13	4^{2}			7								4
1	2	3		5	6		7■	9^{1}	10	11■		4	12			8								5
1	2	3	13	5	7^{1}			10	11			4	6	9^{2}		8	12							6
1	2	3	12	5	14		8	13	11	10		4^{1}	6^{3}	9^{2}		7								7
1	2	3	4	5	7^{1}		12	9	11	10			13	6^{2}		8								8
1	2	4		3	13		6	11^{2}	9	10		5	12	8^{1}		7								9
1	2	3	12	5^{1}	8^{2}		6		10	11		4	14	9		7^{3}	13							10
1		2	5		13	6^{1}	7			11	12	3	9	10^{2}		8		4						11
1		3	2				6		10	11		4	8^{1}	9		7	12	5						12
1	2	4		3^{3}	12		6		10	11		5	8^{1}	9^{2}		7	14	13						13
1	2	3	13		6		8		11	9		4	12			7	10^{1}	5^{2}						14
1	2	3	14	5	6^{1}		7	9^{2}	10	11^{3}		4		12		8		13						15
1	2	3		5	12		6	9^{1}	10	11		4		8		7								16
1	2	3	13	5	12		7^{1}	9^{2}	11	10^{3}		4		8		6		14						17
1	2	3	13	5	6			9^{1}	11	10^{2}		4	12	8		7								18
1	2	3		5	8^{1}	12		6	10	11		4		9		7								19
1	2	3		5			7	9^{1}	11	10		4	12	8^{2}		6			13					20
1	2	3		5			7		10	11		4	9	6		8								21
1	2	3		5	6^{2}		7	13				4	9^{1}	11		8			10	12				22
1	2	3		5	13		7	10	11			4	6^{1}			8^{2}		12	14	9^{3}				23
1	2	3		5	6		7	10^{2}	11			4	12			8		13		9^{1}				24
1	2	3	12	5	7		8	13	11			4							10^{1}	9^{2}	6			25
1	2	4	12	3	7		6^{2}	13	10			5				8			11^{1}	9				26
1	5■	4		2	9		8	11	10			3				7			12	6^{1}				27
1■			2	3	7		6		10■			5	12	11^{1}		8		4^{2}	13	9^{6}		15		28
1		3	12	5	8		2^{1}					4	10^{3}	6		7		13	11^{2}	9	14			29
	2	3		5	6				11			4	9^{1}	10		8				12	7	1		30
1	2	4			6			9	10			5		11		8		3			7			31
1	2	3		5	6			9	10			4		11^{2}		7		12		8^{1}	13			32
1	2	3		5		8		6^{1}	10			4		11		7				9	12			33
1	5	4			8^{2}			7	10			3	13	9		11		2^{3}	14	6^{1}	12			34
1		3	2		7			9	11			4	8	10^{1}		6		5			12			35
1		2		4^{2}	8			10	11^{3}			3	6		12	7^{1}		5	14		9		13	36

FORFAR ATHLETIC

Year Formed: 1885. *Ground & Address:* Station Park, Carseview Road, Forfar DD8 3BT. *Telephone:* 01307 463576.
Fax: 01307 466956. *E-mail:* pat@ramsayladders.co.uk *Website:* www.forfarathletic.co.uk
Ground Capacity: 5,177 (739 seated). *Size of Pitch:* 103m × 64m.
Chairman: Alastair Donald. *Vice Chairman:* Jim Farquhar. *Secretary:* David McGregor.
Manager: Dick Campbell. *Assistant Manager:* Ian Campbell. *Physios:* Duncan Sangster and Donald Ritchie.
Club Nicknames: Loons, The Sky Blues.
Previous Grounds: None.
Record Attendance: 10,780 v Rangers, Scottish Cup 2nd rd, 2 Feb 1970.
Record Transfer Fee received: £65,000 for David Bingham to Dunfermline Ath (September 1995).
Record Transfer Fee paid: £50,000 for Ian McPhee from Airdrieonians (1991).
Record Victory: 14-1 v Lindertis, Scottish Cup 1st rd, 1 Sept 1988.
Record Defeat: 2-12 v King's Park, Division II, 2 Jan 1930.
Most League Appearances: 484: Ian McPhee, 1978-88 and 1991-98.
Most League Goals in Season (Individual): 45: Dave Kilgour, Division II, 1929-30.
Most Goals Overall: 124: John Clark, 1978-91.

FORFAR ATHLETIC 2011–12 LEAGUE RECORD

Match No.	*Date*	*Venue*	*Opponents*	*Result*		*H/T Score*	*Lg Pos.*	*Goalscorers*	*Attendance*
1	Aug 6	H	Cowdenbeath	D	2-2	0-1	—	McCulloch [58], Templeman (pen) [62]	469
2	13	A	Albion R	L	0-1	0-0	9		352
3	20	H	Stenhousemuir	L	2-3	0-2	9	Templeman [55], Mowat [57]	372
4	27	H	Airdrie U	W	3-2	2-2	7	Crawford 2 [11, 43], Fotheringham [64]	432
5	Sept 10	A	Brechin C	W	1-0	0-0	6	Templeman [61]	651
6	17	A	Stirling A	W	4-2	1-1	4	Shaughnessy [34], Templeman 2 [61, 78], Low [75]	551
7	24	H	Dumbarton	L	0-2	0-1	4		493
8	Oct 1	A	East Fife	L	3-4	2-3	6	Ovenstone (og) [40], Byers [19], Shaughnessy [53]	533
9	15	H	Arbroath	D	1-1	0-1	6	Shaughnessy [82]	908
10	22	A	Cowdenbeath	L	1-3	0-0	7	Low [75]	339
11	29	H	Albion R	L	0-2	0-1	9		436
12	Nov 5	H	Brechin C	D	0-0	0-0	8		661
13	12	A	Airdrie U	D	4-4	1-1	8	Templeman 2 [17, 64], Motion [62], Byers [79]	635
14	Dec 3	A	Dumbarton	D	1-1	0-1	9	Motion [90]	443
15	26	H	Airdrie U	L	2-3	2-2	9	Templeman [15], Motion [18]	579
16	Jan 2	A	Brechin C	L	1-2	1-0	10	Templeman [39]	776
17	14	A	Stenhousemuir	W	3-2	1-1	10	Templeman 2 [43, 80], Fotheringham [90]	454
18	21	H	Cowdenbeath	W	1-0	1-0	9	Low [45]	475
19	24	H	Stirling A	D	2-2	1-0	—	Coyne 2 [21, 60]	361
20	Feb 11	H	Arbroath	L	2-4	0-2	9	Fotheringham 2 [80, 89]	794
21	14	H	Dumbarton	D	1-1	1-1	—	Hilson [30]	284
22	18	A	East Fife	L	0-4	0-3	8		526
23	22	A	Arbroath	L	1-4	1-3	—	Coyne [13]	789
24	25	A	Albion R	D	2-2	2-1	8	Hilson [2], Templeman [22]	312
25	28	H	East Fife	W	3-2	2-1	—	Low [4], Templeman 2 (1 pen) [15 (p), 64]	432
26	Mar 3	H	Stenhousemuir	L	1-2	0-1	8	Low [56]	374
27	6	A	Stirling A	D	2-2	0-1	—	Tulloch [62], Templeman [65]	371
28	10	H	Brechin C	W	4-1	3-0	8	Fotheringham 2 (1 pen) [20, 67 (p)], Low [32], Byers [43]	584
29	17	A	Airdrie U	L	0-3	0-0	8		621
30	24	H	Stirling A	W	4-3	3-1	8	Fotheringham [12], Coyne [15], Templeman [23], Byers [90]	462
31	31	A	Dumbarton	L	0-1	0-0	8		513
32	Apr 7	H	East Fife	L	1-4	1-2	8	Byers [32]	559
33	14	A	Arbroath	W	1-0	0-0	8	Ross [60]	998
34	21	A	Cowdenbeath	L	0-2	0-0	9		930
35	28	H	Albion R	W	4-0	3-0	8	Byers 2 [3, 30], Ross [28], Coyne [84]	554
36	May 5	A	Stenhousemuir	W	2-1	2-1	7	McMillan (og) [4], Fotheringham [22]	759

Final League Position: 7

Honours

League Champions: Second Division 1983-84. Third Division 1994-95; *Runners-up:* 1996-97. C Division 1948-49. *Third Division* 2009-10. *Promoted to Second Division:* 2009-10 (play-offs).
Scottish Cup: Semi-finals 1982.
League Cup: Semi-finals 1977-78.
League Challenge Cup: Semi-finals 2004-05.

Club colours: Shirt: Sky blue and white stripes. Shorts: White. Stockings: White.

Goalscorers: *League (59):* Templeman 16 (2 pens), Fotheringham 8 (1 pen), Byers 7, Low 6, Coyne 5, Motion 3, Shaughnessy 3, Crawford 2, Hilson 2, Ross 2, McCulloch 1, Mowat 1, Tulloch 1, own goals 2.
Scottish Cup (4): Templeman 2, Gibson 1, Ross 1.
Scottish Communities Cup (2): Crawford 1, Templeman 1.
Ramsdens Cup (1): Gibson 1.

Paterson G 20 + 1	Wilson C 11 + 6	Tulloch S 13 + 2	Ross G 27 + 3	Mowat D 20 + 3	McCulloch M 28	Hegarty C 20 + 4	Byers K 13 + 16	Gibson G 4 + 12	Templeman C 32 + 1	Crawford S 11	Campbell R 12 + 11	Motion K 13 + 12	Campbell I 21 + 1	Bolochewecкyj M 16 + 8	Girvan G — + 1	McHugh A 6	Bishop J 8	Fotheringham M 22 + 4	Shaughnessy J 26	Low N 28 + 1	Brown J 3 + 1	Langfield J 2	McCallum M 10	Hilson D 19	Coyne B 9 + 7	Sellars B 2 + 2	Bryce L — + 3	Ried D — + 1	Match No.
1	2	3	4	5	6	7	8	9^1	10^2	11	12	13																	1
1	6	4	2	7	3	8^1			11	10^3	13	9^2	5	12	14														2
			2	12	8	7^1	9^2	14	10^3	11	13		5	4		1	3	6											3
	6	3	2	5	7		13	12	14	10	11^1	9^2		4		1		8^3											4
	14	4	2	5	7	12	8	13	10^3	11^2						1		9^1	3	6									5
	6^2	4^1	2	5	8	13		14	10	11				12		1		9	3	7^3									6
	5^1	3	2^2	6	8				10	11	13					1		9	4	7	12								7
15					3	2	7^1	13	10^6	11	12			5		1■		8	4	6	9^2								8
1				7^1		2	13		11	10	14	12	5	3■				6^3	4	9	8^2								9
1		12				5	13^3		10	11	14	6^1	4				2	7	3	9	8^2								10
1	13		12^2		4^1	6	7	14	9	11	10^3		5				2		3	8									11
1	14		8			2	6^3	12	10		11^1	13	3				4	7	5	9^2									12
1			6	4		7	13		11		10^2	12	3				2	8	5	9^1									13
	2		7	8			12	6^1	10		11^2	13	5	14			3		4	9^3		1							14
			5	12	2	7■	8^2	10^3	11		13	9	4	6^1					3	14		1							15
1	11	12	5^2	6	2		14		10		9	8^3	4^1	7				13	3										16
		5^1	7^2	8^3	2		14		10		6	13		3				12	4	9			1	11					17
	14	3	2			6^2	12		10		8^3	13		5					4	7			1	9	11^1				18
			2		4	6^1	12		10		8^2	13		5					3	7			1	9	11				19
			5	7^3	2		14		11		8		12	4^1				13	3	6			1	10	9^2				20
	2				4		6		11			13	3					8	5	9^2			1	10^1	12	7^3	14		21
	2			12	5		6^1		10		14		4					8^3	3	9			1	11	13	7^2			22
			12	5	2	7			11			13	4	6^1					3	8			1	9^2	10^3		14		23
			2	7	4	8^2	14		10			9^3	5	3				13					1	6	11^1		12		24
1	13		2^2	4	3	7		12	9				5					6		8				11	10^1				25
1			2	5	3	6^2	14	12	10^3			13	4					7		8				9	11^1				26
1		5	6	4	2	8■			11^2				3^1	12				9^3		7				10	13	14			27
1	2	3	5	6	4		7	13				8						10^2		9^1				11				12	28
1	2^2	4	5	7	3		6^1					8		13				11		9				10	12				29
1		4		5	2		13	14	9^2			6		12				7^3	3^1	8				11	10				30
1		4	5			6^3	12	9^1	11		13	8		14					3	7^2			2	10					31
1			2^3		5	12	8^2		11		13	6^1	3	9				7	4					10	14				32
1			12		2	6^1	14		10		11^3		5	13			3^2	8	4	7				9					33
1			8				12		7		10^2	14		2			3	11^1	4	9^3			5	6	13				34
1			2		5	13	8		11^3			7^1	3	9^2					4	6				10■	14	12			35
1	13		6		2	8^2		12				9	5	4				7	3	10					11^1				36

HAMILTON ACADEMICAL

Year Formed: 1874. *Ground:* New Douglas Park, Cadzow Avenue, Hamilton ML3 0FT. *Telephone:* 01698 368650. *Fax:* 01698 285422. *E-mail:* scott@acciesfc.co.uk *Website:* www.acciesfc.co.uk
Ground Capacity: 6,078. *Size of Pitch:* 115yd × 75yd.
Chairman: Les Gray. *Secretary:* Scott A. Struthers BA.
Manager: Billy Reid. *Physio:* Sarah Boyd.
Club Nickname: The Accies.
Previous Grounds: Bent Farm, South Avenue, South Haugh, Douglas Park, Cliftonhill Stadium, Firhill Stadium.
Record Attendance: 28,690 v Hearts, Scottish Cup 3rd rd, 3 Mar 1937 (at Douglas Park); 5,895 v Rangers, 28 February 2009 (at New Douglas Park).
Record Transfer Fee received: £1,200,000 from Wigan Ath for James McCarthy (July 2009).
Record Transfer Fee paid: £180,000 for Tomas Cerny from Sigma Olomouc (July 2009).
Record Victory: 11-1 v Chryston, Lanarkshire Cup, 28 Nov 1885.
Record Defeat: 1-11 v Hibernian, Division I, 6 Nov 1965.
Most Capped Player: Colin Miller, 29 (61), Canada, 1988-94.
Most League Appearances: 452: Rikki Ferguson, 1974-88.
Most League Goals in Season (Individual): 35: David Wilson, Division I; 1936-37.
Most Goals Overall (Individual): 246: David Wilson, 1928-39.

HAMILTON ACADEMICAL 2011–12 LEAGUE RECORD

Match No.	*Date*	*Venue*	*Opponents*	*Result*		*H/T Score*	*Lg Pos.*	*Goalscorers*	*Attendance*
1	Aug 6	A	Ayr U	W	2-1	1-1	—	McLaughlin 2 [29, 57]	1750
2	13	H	Ross Co	W	5-1	3-0	1	McLaughlin [23], Crawford [39], Chambers (pen) [42], Paterson [57], Anderson [90]	1744
3	20	A	Partick Th	D	1-1	0-0	1	Mensing [76]	2501
4	27	H	Livingston	D	1-1	0-0	1	Crawford [78]	2051
5	Sept 10	A	Queen of the S	L	0-1	0-0	2		1514
6	17	H	Raith R	D	2-2	0-1	2	Spence [66], Lyle [73]	1982
7	24	A	Dundee	W	1-0	0-0	2	McLaughlin [64]	4186
8	Oct 1	H	Falkirk	L	0-1	0-1	3		2367
9	15	A	Morton	W	2-0	0-0	2	Currie, P [72], Anderson [77]	2264
10	22	A	Ross Co	L	0-1	0-1	3		2431
11	29	H	Ayr U	L	2-3	2-0	5	Currie, P (pen) [17], Spence [45]	1699
12	Nov 5	H	Queen of the S	W	3-1	1-1	3	Paterson [17], Imrie [82], Anderson [90]	1836
13	12	A	Livingston	L	0-1	0-0	4		1738
14	26	A	Raith R	L	2-3	1-1	6	Imrie [16], McLaughlin [90]	1416
15	Dec 3	H	Dundee	L	1-6	0-3	7	Imrie [86]	1964
16	10	A	Falkirk	D	0-0	0-0	7		3024
17	26	H	Livingston	L	0-1	0-0	7		1456
18	Jan 2	A	Queen of the S	W	2-1	2-0	10	Imrie 2 [5, 15]	1282
19	13	H	Partick Th	W	1-0	0-0	—	Spence [87]	2401
20	21	A	Ayr U	D	2-2	0-2	5	Spence [46], Redmond [53]	1310
21	Feb 11	A	Dundee	D	2-2	1-0	6	McShane [12], Ryan [85]	4065
22	14	H	Morton	L	1-2	0-2	—	Ryan [85]	1356
23	18	H	Falkirk	L	0-1	0-1	7		1843
24	21	H	Raith R	W	2-1	1-0	—	Canning [45], Mensing [63]	1276
25	25	A	Morton	W	2-1	2-0	4	McShane [11], Ryan [30]	1594
26	Mar 3	A	Partick Th	L	0-2	0-1	5		2111
27	10	H	Ross Co	L	0-2	0-2	6		1743
28	17	A	Livingston	W	4-0	3-0	5	McShane [3], Redmond [12], Routledge 2 [28, 81]	1066
29	20	H	Dundee	W	3-1	1-1	—	McLaughlin [35], McShane [50], Stewart [56]	1366
30	24	H	Queen of the S	W	3-0	0-0	4	Spence [72], Redmond [84], Ryan [90]	1631
31	Apr 7	A	Raith R	L	1-2	1-0	4	McLaughlin [23]	1526
32	10	A	Falkirk	L	0-3	0-0	—		2461
33	14	H	Morton	W	4-3	2-0	4	Weatherson (og) [16], McShane 2 [17, 51], Mensing [63]	1423
34	21	H	Ayr U	W	3-2	1-1	4	McShane 2 [24, 89], Redmond [58]	1645
35	28	A	Ross Co	L	1-5	0-2	5	McAlister [46]	4737
36	May 5	H	Partick Th	D	2-2	2-2	4	Redmond [26], McShane [30]	1978

Final League Position: 4

Honours

League Champions: Division II 1903-04. First Division 1985-86, 1987-88, 2007-08; Third Division 2000-01. *Runners-up:* Division II 1952-53, 1964-65; Second Division 1996-97, 2003-04.
Scottish Cup Runners-up: 1911, 1935. *League Cup:* Semi-finalists three times. *League Challenge Cup Runners-up:* 2005-06, 2011-12. *B&Q Cup Winners:* 1991-92, 1992-93.

Club colours: Shirt: Red and white hoops. Shorts: White. Stockings: White.

Goalscorers: *League (55):* McShane 9, McLaughlin 7, Imrie 5, Redmond 5, Spence 5, Ryan 4, Anderson 3, Mensing 3, Crawford 2, Currie, P. 2 (1 pen), Paterson 2, Routledge 2, Canning 1, Chambers 1 (1 pen), Lyle 1, McAlister 1, Stewart 1, own goal 1.
Scottish Cup (0).
Scottish Communities Cup (1): Chambers 1 (pen).
Ramsdens Cup (6): Chambers 1 (pen), Crawford 1, Hopkirk 1, McLaughlin 1, Mensing 1, Spence 1.

Cerny T 11	Hendrie s 22 + 3	McLaughlin M 23	McAlister J 36	Gillespie G 12 + 4	Mensing S 34	Anderson G 7 + 13	Crawford A 16 + 3	Imrie D 18 + 1 / Currie B 3 + 1	Hopkirk D 1 + 2	Kirkpatrick J 2 + 5	Lyle D 3 + 6	Canning M 31 + 1	McLaren W — + 3	Chambers J 5 + 5	Paterson M 10 + 4	Kilday L 13	Wilkie K — + 1	Fraser G 3 + 1 / Jivanda J 1	Spence G 11 + 18	Gordon Z 7 + 1	Devlin M 1 + 2	Currie P 3 + 6	Hutton D 18 + 1	McBride K 5 + 1	Ryan A 13 + 8	Millar K 2 / Watson C — + 1	Christie S 3	Smith G 3 / MacGregor G — + 1	Coombe A 1	McGlinchey C 1	Neil A 17	Redmond D 18	McShane J 17	Routledge J 15 + 1	Stewart M 8 + 5	Martin J 1	Longridge L 1 + 1	*Match No.*
1	2^3	3	4	5	6	7	8^2	9	10	11^1	12	13	14																									1
1	4	3	5	8^2	7	13	6	10^3	12		14	2		9^1	11																							2
1	4		5	6	8		9^1	10			14	3	13	7^2	11^3	2	12																					3
1	4^1	3▮	5	7^2	6▮		8	10	13		11^3	2		9				12	14																			4
1	4^1		5	7			8	9				3	14	6^2	10^3				11	2	12	13																5
1		3	4	5	6	12	8	9			13	2		7^1	10^2				11																			6
1		6	2	13	5	8^1	11^2	7			9	4		12	14				10^3	3																		7
1^G	5		2	7	4	12	8	9			10^1	3			11^2				13			6	15															8
1	4	3	5		6	14	8^2	10							12				11	2		13		7^3	9^1													9
		5	11		4	13	9^3	6			14	3							10	2^1		8	1	7^2	12													10
		4^1	2	5	7	12	8^2	9			14	3		13	10				11			6^3	1															11
		4	5		2	7	9^1	13				3		14	10^2			8	11			12	1	6^3														12
	12	4	7		2	9		5		14		3		13	10			8^1	11^2				1	6^3														13
	5	4	9	6^1	3	11	14	7						12	10				13	2^3			1			8^2												14
		3	8		5	9^1	14	7				2^2			11				12	4	6		1	13		10^3												15
	6^2	4	10		5	12	9	8				3			14	2^1						13		7			1	11^3										16
			8		2		6^2	5				3			13			9^1	11			12						10	1	4	7							17
	5^1	4▮	9		6			8				3				2			14	12		13			10^2		1	11^3			7							18
1	5		9		3	12	14	8				4				2			13						10^1						6	7^3	11^2					19
1	3		10		5		8^2					4				2			9		13				12						7	6	11^1					20
	5^3		9		4		8^1					3				2			11^2				1		14						7	6	10	12	13			21
	5^2		9	12	4	13						3								2^1					14		1				6	8	10	7	11^3			22
	4		8		3	13						2							12				1		11						6	5	10^2	7	9^1			23
	4		9		2	8^1						3							13				1		12						6	7	11	5	10^2			24
	14		8		3	12						2				4			13				1		9^2						5	6	10^1	7	11^3			25
	12	3	8									2				4			13				1		10^1						7	5	11	6	9^2			26
	5		2		3	13				12		4											1		10						7	6		8	11^2	9^1		27
		3^1	9	12	5							2				4			14				1		10^3						7	6	11^2	8	13			28
		4^3	9		2	14						3				5			12				1		13						6	8	10^1	7	11^2			29
		4	5		7					12		3				2^1			13				1		14						6	9	10^3	8	11^2			30
	5	2^1	9	12	3							4											1		10						8	7^3	11^2	6	14		13	31
	4^G	3	9		5			15				2							13				1▮		10^1						7	6	11^2	8	12			32
	4	3	9		5			1				2							12						11^2						7▮	8	10^1	6	13			33
	5	3	2	9^1	6			1		12		4							13						11^2							7	10	8				34
	4^2		9	8	3					12						5		2	14				1		10^3	13						7^1	11	6				35
		4▮	2	8	3			1		11^2						5			14						12			13				7^3	10	6			9^1	36

HEART OF MIDLOTHIAN

Year Formed: 1874. *Ground & Address:* Tynecastle Stadium, McLeod Street, Edinburgh EH11 2NL. *Telephone:* 0871 663 1874. *Fax:* 0131 200 7222. *E-mail:* hearts@homplc.co.uk *Website:* www.heartsfc.co.uk
Ground Capacity: 17,402. *Size of Pitch:* 100m × 64m.
Chairman: Roman Romanov. *Non-Executive Directors:* Sergejus Fedotovas, Julija Goncaruk, Vitalijus Vasiliauskas.
Manager: tba. *First Team Coach:* Gary Locke. *Physio:* Rob Marshall.
Club Nicknames: Hearts, Jambos.
Previous Grounds: The Meadows 1874, Powderhall 1878, Old Tynecastle 1881, (Tynecastle Park, 1886).
Record Attendance: 53,396 v Rangers, Scottish Cup 3rd rd, 13 Feb 1932 (57,857 v Barcelona, 28 July 2007 at Murrayfield).
Record Transfer Fee received: £9,000,000 for Craig Gordon to Sunderland (August 2008).
Record of Transfer paid: £850,000 for Mirsad Beslija to Genk (January 2006).
Record Victory: 21-0 v Anchor, EFA Cup, 30 Oct 1880.
Record Defeat: 1-8 v Vale of Leven, Scottish Cup, 1888.
Most Capped Player: Steven Pressley, 32, Scotland.
Most League Appearances: 515: Gary Mackay, 1980-97.
Most League Goals in Season (Individual): 44: Barney Battles, 1930-31.
Most Goals Overall (Individual): 214: John Robertson, 1983-98.

HEART OF MIDLOTHIAN 2011–12 LEAGUE RECORD

Match No.	*Date*	*Venue*	*Opponents*	*Result*		*H/T Score*	*Lg Pos.*	*Goalscorers*	*Attendance*
1	July 23	A	Rangers	D	1-1	1-0	—	Obua [16]	49,083
2	31	H	Dundee U	L	0-1	0-1	—		13,821
3	Aug 7	A	Motherwell	L	0-1	0-0	—		5685
4	13	H	Aberdeen	W	3-0	2-0	8	Novikovas [24], Sutton 2 [35, 52]	13,374
5	21	A	Kilmarnock	D	0-0	0-0	7		5328
6	28	H	Hibernian	W	2-0	1-0	4	Stevenson [39], Webster [69]	15,868
7	Sept 10	A	Inverness CT	D	1-1	0-0	5	Elliott [81]	4106
8	17	H	St Mirren	W	2-0	1-0	4	Hamill (pen) [43], Mair (og) [70]	12,572
9	25	A	St Johnstone	L	0-2	0-1	4		2770
10	Oct 2	H	Celtic	W	2-0	0-0	4	Skacel [58], Stevenson [81]	14,749
11	15	A	Dunfermline Ath	W	2-0	1-0	4	Webster [42], Templeton [76]	5694
12	23	H	Rangers	L	0-2	0-1	5		15,495
13	29	H	Kilmarnock	L	0-1	0-0	5		12,829
14	Nov 5	A	St Mirren	D	0-0	0-0	5		4771
15	19	A	Dundee U	L	0-1	0-1	6		6925
16	26	H	Inverness CT	W	2-1	0-0	5	Skacel [46], Jonsson [76]	12,021
17	Dec 3	H	St Johnstone	L	1-2	0-1	5	Taouil [86]	12,815
18	10	A	Celtic	L	0-1	0-0	5		49,023
19	17	H	Dunfermline Ath	W	4-0	2-0	5	Elliott [2], Taouil [27], Templeton [71], Skacel [90]	11,988
20	24	H	Motherwell	W	2-0	2-0	5	Black [17], Elliott [28]	13,300
21	28	A	Aberdeen	D	0-0	0-0	5		9210
22	Jan 2	A	Hibernian	W	3-1	0-0	4	McGowan [58], Webster [83], Skacel [90]	15,013
23	14	H	St Mirren	W	5-2	2-2	3	Zaliukas [1], Skacel 3 [23, 64, 68], Sutton [90]	12,462
24	21	A	Inverness CT	L	0-1	0-0	3		3812
25	Feb 8	H	Celtic	L	0-4	0-3	—		14,787
26	11	A	Kilmarnock	D	1-1	0-0	4	Santana [90]	4327
27	18	A	Motherwell	L	0-3	0-2	4		5489
28	25	H	Dundee U	L	0-2	0-1	6		13,176
29	Mar 3	A	Rangers	W	2-1	0-1	5	Black [58], Hamill [79]	47,276
30	18	H	Hibernian	W	2-0	1-0	—	Beattie [28], Santana [90]	15,128
31	24	A	St Johnstone	L	1-2	1-1	6	Holt [29]	4365
32	31	H	Aberdeen	W	3-0	1-0	6	McGowan [27], Skacel 2 [53, 89]	13,292
33	Apr 7	A	Dunfermline Ath	W	2-1	0-0	6	Glen [49], Barr [53]	4700
34	21	H	Rangers	L	0-3	0-2	6		14,842
35	28	A	Dundee U	D	2-2	1-1	6	Skacel [35], Novikovas [83]	7001
36	May 1	H	Motherwell	L	0-1	0-1	—		9185
37	6	H	St Johnstone	W	2-0	1-0	5	Skacel [21], Webster [58]	12,543
38	13	A	Celtic	L	0-5	0-3	5		58,875

Final League Position: 5

Honours
League Champions: Division I 1894-95, 1896-97, 1957-58, 1959-60. First Division 1979-80; *Runners-up:* Division I 1893-94, 1898-99, 1903-04, 1905-06, 1914-15, 1937-38, 1953-54, 1956-57, 1958-59, 1964-65. Premier Division 1985-86, 1987-88, 1991-92; *Runners-up:* 2005-06. First Division 1977-78, 1982-83.
Scottish Cup Winners: 1891, 1896, 1901, 1906, 1956, 1998, 2006, 2012; *Runners-up:* 1903, 1907, 1968, 1976, 1986, 1996.
League Cup Winners: 1954-55, 1958-59, 1959-60, 1962-63; *Runners-up:* 1961-62, 1996-97.

European: *European Cup:* 8 matches (1958-59, 1960-61, 2006-07). *Cup Winners' Cup:* 10 matches (1976-77, 1996-97, 1998-99). *UEFA Cup:* 47 matches (*Fairs Cup:* 1961-62, 1963-64, 1965-66. *UEFA Cup:* 1984-85, 1986-87, 1988-89, 1990-91, 1992-93, 1993-94, 2000-01, 2003-04, 2004-05, 2006-07). *Europa League:* 6 matches (2010-11, 2011-12).

Club colours: Shirt: Maroon with white panels. Shorts: White with maroon side panels. Stockings: Maroon with white tops.

Goalscorers: *League (45):* Skacel 11, Webster 4, Elliott 3, Sutton 3, Black 2, Hamill 2 (1 pen), McGowan 2, Novikovas 2, Santana 2, Stevenson 2, Taouil 2, Templeton 2, Barr 1, Beattie 1, Glen 1, Holt 1, Jonsson 1, Obua 1, Zaliukas 1, own goal 1.
Scottish Cup (14): Skacel 5, Beattie 2 (1 pen), Hamill 2 (1 pen), Barr 1, Grainger 1 (pen), Smith 1, Templeton 1, Zaliukas 1.
Scottish Communities Cup (1): Robinson 1.
Europa League (5): Stevenson 2, Driver 1, Hamill 1 (pen), Skacel 1.

Kello M 20	McGowan R 23 + 5	Grainger D 27	Jonsson E 14 + 2	Zaliukas M 36	Webster A 31	Templeton D 20 + 7	Black I 28 + 1	Sutton J 9 + 5	Obua D 11 + 8	Taouil M 15 + 9	Mrowiec A 27 + 2	Elliott S 19 + 7	Stevenson R 15 + 4	Novikovas A 4 + 11	Skacel R 19 + 10	Hamill J 28 + 1	Driver A 15 + 6	Robinson S 14 + 6	McHattie K — + 1	MacDonald J 17 + 1	Smith G — + 6	Barr D 13 + 2	Santana S 3 + 10	Glen G 4 + 4	Beattie C 4 + 1	Holt J 1 + 1	Ridgers M 1 + 1	Prychynenko D — + 3	Match No.
1	2	3	4	5	6^1	7^2	8^3	9	10	11	12	13	14																1
1	2	3	4	5		7	8	9^3	11		6^1	10^2	14	12	13														2
1	2	3	4	5		7^2	8	12			10		9	14	13	6^3	11^1												3
1	14	3	4^3	5		7		9			8		10^2	11^1	12	2		6	13										4
1		3		5	6	12		14	10		7	9^3	8		13	2	11^1	4^2											5
1^G		3	12	5	6		8		10^1		4	9	7^2	13		2	11			15									6
		3	14	5^2	6	12	8		11^3	13	7	10	4	9^1		2				1									7
		3	4	5		12	8^3	13	11	6^1	7	10^2	9			2		14		1									8
		3		5	6^3	14	8		9^1	11	4	10^2	7			2		13		1	12								9
		3	4	5	6	9^2	8^3		12		7		10	13	11^1	2				1	14								10
1		3	4	5	6	9	8^1	14	13	12	7		10^3		11^2	2													11
1		3	4^1	5	6	9	8^2		14	12	7		10		11^3	2					13								12
1		3^3	4	5^2	6	9	8■				7	12	10^1	14	11	2					13								13
1	3		4	5	6	9^3			12	8^1	7^2	13	10		11	2	14												14
1	3		4	5	6	9		10^3		12	7^1	14	8	13	11	2^2													15
1	2		4	5	6	7^3		9^2	8	13	12		10^1		11	3		14											16
1	3		4	5	6^1	9^3		10	13	8	7	12	14		11	2^2													17
1	3		4	5		9^2	8^1		13	6	7	12	10			2	14	11^3											18
1	3			5	6	9^2	8			4^1	7	10^3	14	13	12	2		11											19
1	3			5	6	9^1	8^3			4	7	10			14	2^2	12	11				13							20
1	3			5	6	9	12^2	10	4^3	14	7			13	11^1		8					2							21
1	3			5	6	9^3	8	13		4^1	7	10			14	2	12	11^2											22
1				5■	6		8^2	9	12		7	10^1		14	11^3	2		4				3	13						23
1	3				6	12	8^2	9	14		7	10^1			11	2		4				5^3	13						24
	8	3^2		5	6					9	7	10			13	2	11^1	4^3		1			14	12					25
	12	3^1		5	6		8			4	7^3	9			10	2■	11^2			1	14		13						26
	2	3		5	6	9^1	8^3		7	14	4	10			12		11^2	13		1									27
	12	3		5^2			8^1		7^3	4		10			11	2	14	9		1		6	13						28
	14	3		5	6		8^2			13	9					2	11	7		1		4^1		10^3	12				29
	13	3			6		8^2			7		9^1			10^3	2	11	12		1		5	14		4				30
	2	3		5	6									9^2		12	11	8		1^G		4	13	10		7^1	15		31
	2	3		5	6		8^1								10	7^3	11			1		4	12	13	9^2			14	32
	2	3		5			8^3							13	10	7	11^2	4		1		6	12	9^1				14	33
	2	3		5	6	13	8					9^1			10		11^3			1		4^2	12	14	7				34
	2^2	3		5	6	13	8					12		14	10		11^3			1		4	7		9^1				35
	2	3		5	6	9	8^3			11^1		10^2			12		14			1		4	7	13					36
	2	3		5	6		8			13		10^2			9		11	12			14	4^1	7^3				1		37
	2	3		5	6^3	9				4^1	7			11^2				8		1		14		10		13		12	38

HIBERNIAN

Year Formed: 1875. *Ground & Address:* Easter Road Stadium, 12 Albion Place, Edinburgh EH7 5QG. *Telephone:* 0131 661 2159. *Fax:* 0131 659 6488. *E-mail:* club@hibernianfc.co.uk *Website:* www.hibernianfc.co.uk
Ground Capacity: total: 17,400. *Size of Pitch:* 112yd × 74yd.
Chairman: Rod Petrie. *Chief Executive:* Scott Lindsay. *Club Secretary:* Garry O'Hagan.
Manager: Pat Fenlon. *Assistant Manager:* Billy Brown. *Physio:* Calum Rea.
Club Nickname: Hibees.
Previous Grounds: Meadows 1875-78, Powderhall 1878-79, Mayfield 1879-80, First Easter Road 1880-92, Second Easter Road 1892-.
Record Attendance: 65,860 v Hearts, Division I, 2 Jan 1950.
Record Transfer Fee received: £4,400,000 for Scott Brown from Celtic (2007).
Record of Transfer paid: £700,000 to LDU Quito for Ulises de la Cruz (2001).
Record Victory: 22-1 v 42nd Highlanders, 3 Sept 1881.
Record Defeat: 0-10 v Rangers, 24 Dec 1898.
Most Capped Player: Lawrie Reilly, 38, Scotland.
Most League Appearances: 446: Arthur Duncan.
Most League Goals in Season (Individual): 42: Joe Baker, 1959-60.
Most Goals Overall (Individual): 364: Gordon Smith, 1941-1959.

HIBERNIAN 2011–12 LEAGUE RECORD

Match No.	Date	Venue	Opponents	Result	H/T Score	Lg Pos.	Goalscorers	Attendance
1	July 24	H	Celtic	L 0-2	0-1	—		12,523
2	30	A	Inverness CT	W 1-0	0-0	—	O'Connor [90]	3600
3	Aug 14	A	Kilmarnock	L 1-4	1-2	9	O'Connor [13]	4182
4	20	H	St Mirren	L 1-2	1-2	11	O'Connor [25]	8886
5	28	A	Hearts	L 0-2	0-1	12		15,868
6	Sept 11	H	Aberdeen	D 0-0	0-0	12		8972
7	17	A	Dunfermline Ath	D 2-2	1-0	11	Sproule [37], O'Connor [51]	4116
8	24	H	Dundee U	D 3-3	1-2	10	O'Connor [22], Robertson (og) [72], Agogo [74]	9360
9	28	H	St Johnstone	W 3-2	2-1	—	Sproule [17], O'Connor 2 (1 pen) [37, 63 (p)]	8323
10	Oct 1	A	Rangers	L 0-1	0-0	10		44,430
11	15	H	Motherwell	L 0-1	0-1	10		8518
12	22	A	St Mirren	W 3-2	3-2	9	Griffiths 2 [6, 41], O'Hanlon [37]	4273
13	29	A	Celtic	D 0-0	0-0	9		48,670
14	Nov 5	H	Dunfermline Ath	L 0-1	0-1	9		9531
15	19	H	Kilmarnock	D 1-1	0-1	9	Griffiths [49]	8169
16	26	A	St Johnstone	L 1-3	1-2	9	Towell [26]	3782
17	Dec 10	H	Rangers	L 0-2	0-0	11		11,380
18	17	A	Aberdeen	L 0-1	0-0	11		7137
19	24	A	Dundee U	L 1-3	1-0	11	Griffiths [23]	8168
20	28	H	Inverness CT	D 1-1	1-1	11	O'Connor [8]	6923
21	Jan 2	H	Hearts	L 1-3	0-0	11	Zaliukas (og) [59]	15,013
22	14	A	Dunfermline Ath	W 3-2	1-1	11	Griffiths 2 [33, 83], O'Connor [75]	6780
23	21	H	St Johnstone	L 2-3	0-1	11	Griffiths (pen) [70], Booth [84]	8772
24	28	A	Rangers	L 0-4	0-1	11		44,057
25	Feb 11	H	Aberdeen	D 0-0	0-0	11		10,100
26	19	H	Celtic	L 0-5	0-2	11		12,161
27	22	A	Motherwell	L 3-4	1-0	—	Osbourne [18], Doherty [66], Sproule [85]	8065
28	25	A	Kilmarnock	W 3-1	1-0	11	Soares 2 [17, 66], O'Donovan [46]	4283
29	Mar 3	H	St Mirren	D 0-0	0-0	11		9211
30	18	A	Hearts	L 0-2	0-1	—		15,128
31	24	H	Dundee U	L 0-2	0-0	11		9161
32	Apr 1	A	Inverness CT	W 3-2	0-0	11	Hanlon [64], O'Connor [75], Griffiths [85]	3274
33	8	H	Motherwell	D 1-1	1-0	11	O'Connor [30]	7110
34	22	H	Kilmarnock	L 0-1	0-1	11		8877
35	29	A	St Mirren	L 0-1	0-0	11		3305
36	May 2	A	Aberdeen	W 2-1	2-0	—	Reynolds (og) [7], O'Hanlon [17]	5281
37	7	H	Dunfermline Ath	W 4-0	3-0	—	Doherty [5], Doyle [11], O'Connor (pen) [15], Hanlon [81]	15,281
38	12	A	Inverness CT	L 0-2	0-0	11		4457

Final League Position: 11

Honours
League Champions: Division I 1902-03, 1947-48, 1950-51, 1951-52. First Division 1980-81, 1998-99. Division II 1893-94, 1894-95, 1932-33; *Runners-up:* Division I 1896-97, 1946-47, 1949-50, 1952-53, 1973-74, 1974-75.
Scottish Cup Winners: 1887, 1902; *Runners-up:* 1896, 1914, 1923, 1924, 1947, 1958, 1972, 1979, 2001, 2012.
League Cup Winners: 1972-73, 1991-92, 2006-07; *Runners-up:* 1950-51, 1968-69, 1974-75, 1993-94, 2003-04.

European: *European Cup:* 6 matches (1955-56 semi-finals). *Cup Winners' Cup:* 6 matches (1972-73). *UEFA Cup:* 63 matches (*Fairs Cup:* 1960-61 semi-finals, 1961-62, 1962-63, 1965-66, 1967-68, 1968-69, 1970-71. *UEFA Cup:* 64 matches (1973-74, 1974-75, 1975-76, 1976-77, 1978-79, 1989-90, 1992-93, 2001-02, 2005-06). *Europa League:* 2 matches (2010-11).

Club colours: Shirt: Green with white sleeves. Shorts: White. Stockings: Green.

Goalscorers: *League (40):* O'Connor 12 (2 pens), Griffiths 8 (1 pen), Sproule 3, Doherty 2, Hanlon 2, O'Hanlon 2, Soares 2, Agogo 1, Booth 1, Doyle 1, O'Donovan 1, Osbourne 1, Towell 1, own goals 3.
Scottish Cup (9): Griffiths 3 (1 pen), Doyle 2, McPake 1, O'Connor 1, O'Donovan 1, Wotherspoon 1.
Scottish Communities Cup (8): O'Connor 3, Scott 2, Sodje 1, Sproule 1, own goal 1.

Stack G 30	Wotherspoon D 20 + 10	Booth C 10 + 2	Hanlon P 35	O'Hanlon S 22	Murray I 13 + 2	Sproule I 26 + 8	Palsson V 12 + 3	O'Connor G 27 + 6	Stevenson L 27 + 2	Thornhill M 5 + 1	Stephens D 14 + 3	Galbraith D 7 + 9	Crawford D — + 2	De Graaf E — + 1	Agogo J 9 + 3	Osbourne I 29 + 1	Airey P — + 1	Sodje A — + 12	Scott M 8 + 7	Towell R 11 + 3	Griffiths L 24 + 6	Hart M 6	Caldwell R — + 1	Doyle E 6 + 7	Brown M 7	Francomb G 11 + 3	Soares T 9 + 1	McPake J 11	Stanton S — + 2	Kujabi P 12 + 1	Doherty M 11 + 2	Claros J 10	O'Donovan R 5 + 9	Grant P 1	*Match No.*
1	2	3	4	5[1]	6[3]	7	8	9	10[2]	11	12	13	14																						1
1	2[2]	3	4		6	7[3]	8	9	10[1]	11	5	12	14	13																					2
1	7[3]	3	4		6	8	2	9	10[2]	11[1]	5				12	13	14																		3
1	7	3	4		6	11	2[1]	9		10[2]	5	12				8[3]		13	14																4
1		3	4	5	6	7[1]		9		11[3]					10[2]	8		12	14	2	13														5
1		12	4	5	6[1]	7[3]	8	9							10[2]	11		14	3	2	13														6
1	14	3	4	5		7[3]	8	9[1]							12	6		13	11	2	10[2]														7
1	7[1]	13	4	5	6	12	8	9			14				10[3]	3				2	11[2]														8
1			4	5	6	7[2]	8	9[3]	13						10	3		14	12	2	11[1]														9
1	12		4	5	3	11[2]	7[3]	9							10	6		14	8[1]	2	13														10
1	12		4	5	3	11	2[1]	9				13			10	6[3]			8[2]	7	14														11
1	7		4	5	3		14	9[3]	13			11[2]			10	6		12		2	8[1]														12
1	2		4	5		13	14	9[2]	8	12	3	11			10[1]	6					7[3]														13
1	2		4	5		12		9[3]	8[2]		3	11			10[1]	6		14		13	7														14
1	10		4	5		7[3]		9	8		3	11[2]				6			14	13	12	2[1]													15
1	7		4	5		9			11		3	13			14	6		12	8[2]	2[1]	10[3]														16
1	7		4	5		11		9[2]	3		8	12				6		13			10[3]	2[1]	14												17
1	7		4	5		10[2]		9	3		8	11						12	6	13		2[1]													18
1	7		4	5	14	11[3]	8		9		3	13						12	6[1]		10	2[2]													19
1	7	3		5	14	8[3]	13	9	4		6	11							12	2[2]	10[1]														20
1		3	4	5	2	7	8	12	11			9[1]							6[2]		10			13											21
	11[1]	3	5			7		12	8		6	14				4[3]					10	2		9[2]	1	13									22
	12	3	5			11[2]		9[3]	8		4	14				6					10	2		13	1	7[1]									23
	7		4	5[1]		11			9		13					8			12					10[2]	1	2	3[3]	6■	14						24
1	7			5				9	11							4								10[1]		2				3	6	8	12		25
1	7		6					13	11							4					9[3]			10[2]		12		5		3	2[1]	8	14		26
1			4			7		9	11							6			14		10[1]					2		5		12	3[2]	8[3]	13		27
1			4			13			11							6					10[1]			12		2	7	5		3		8	9[2]		28
1	12		4			7[1]		14	11							6					10					2[2]		5		3	13	8	9[3]		29
1	7[2]		4					13	11												10			14		2[1]	6	5		3	12	8	9[3]		30
1	14		4			12		13	7							6					10					2	11[1]			3	5	8[3]	9[2]		31
1			4			7		9	8							6[2]				11[1]	10[3]			13			12	5		3	2		14		32
1	12		4			11[1]		9	8							6					10[2]						7	5		3	2		13		33
	13		4			11[2]		9[1]	7							6					10			14	1			5		3[3]	2	8	12		34
	14		4			13			8■							6					10			9[1]	1	7[2]	11	5		3[3]	2		12		35
	13		4	5		14		9[1]								6					10[3]				1	7[2]	11			3	2	8	12		36
			4			14		9[2]	11							6								10[3]	1	12	7	5		3[1]	2	8	13		37
	7			5	6	11		9[1]			3										12			14		8	4[2]		13		2		10[3]	1	38

INVERNESS CALEDONIAN THISTLE

Year Formed: 1994. *Ground & Address:* Tulloch Caledonian Stadium, Stadium Road, Inverness IV1 1FF. *Telephone:* 01463 222880. *Fax:* 01463 227479. *E-mail:* jim.falconer@ictfc.co.uk *Website:* www.ictfc.co.uk
Ground Capacity (seated): 7,780. *Size of Pitch:* 115yd × 75yd.
Chairman: Graham Cameron. *Club Secretary:* Jim Falconer.
Club Nicknames: Caley Thistle, ICT.
Manager: Terry Butcher. *Assistant Manager:* Maurice Malpas. *Physios:* John McCreadie and Fiona Hogg.
Record Attendance: 7753 v Rangers, SPL, 20 January 2008.
Record Victory: 8-1, v Annan Ath, Scottish Cup 3rd rd, 24 January 1998.
Record Defeats: 0-5, v Celtic, Premier League, 15 September 2007 and 0-5, v Rangers, Premier League, 1 November 2008.
Most League Appearances: 490: Ross Tokely, 1995-2012.
Most League Goals in Season: 27: Iain Stewart, 1996-97; Denis Wyness, 2002-03.
Most Goals Overall (Individual): 118: Denis Wyness, 2000-03, 2005-08.

Honours
Scottish Cup: Semi-finals 2003, 2004; Quarter-finals 1996.

INVERNESS CALEDONIAN THISTLE 2011–12 LEAGUE RECORD

Match No.	*Date*	*Venue*	*Opponents*	*Result*		*H/T Score*	*Lg Pos.*	*Goalscorers*	*Attendance*
1	July 23	A	Motherwell	L	0-3	0-2	—		4190
2	30	H	Hibernian	L	0-1	0-0	—		3600
3	Aug 6	A	Dunfermline Ath	D	3-3	0-1	—	Tansey 2 [46, 83], Hayes [76]	3378
4	13	H	Rangers	L	0-2	0-0	12		6623
5	20	A	Aberdeen	L	1-2	0-2	12	Foran [79]	7989
6	27	H	Kilmarnock	W	2-1	1-1	10	Tade [26], Shinnie, G [89]	3348
7	Sept 10	H	Hearts	D	1-1	0-0	10	Tade [50]	4106
8	17	A	Dundee U	L	1-3	1-2	12	Ross [16]	6497
9	24	A	Celtic	L	0-2	0-2	12		47,382
10	Oct 1	H	St Mirren	W	2-1	1-1	12	Shinnie, A [31], Tade [78]	3249
11	15	A	St Johnstone	L	0-2	0-1	12		2909
12	22	H	Dunfermline Ath	D	1-1	1-0	12	Tade [33]	3241
13	29	H	Motherwell	L	2-3	1-1	12	Davis [4], Shinnie, A [76]	3188
14	Nov 5	A	Kilmarnock	W	6-3	1-1	12	Shinnie, A 3 [39, 60, 66], Hayes [53], Tade 2 [62, 83]	5626
15	19	H	Celtic	L	0-2	0-0	12		6435
16	26	A	Hearts	L	1-2	0-0	12	Tokely [58]	12,021
17	Dec 3	A	St Mirren	W	2-1	1-1	9	Shinnie, A [11], Hayes [69]	3675
18	10	H	Dundee U	L	2-3	1-0	9	Hayes [2], McKay [47]	3142
19	17	A	Rangers	L	1-2	0-0	10	Shinnie, A [67]	43,701
20	24	H	Aberdeen	W	2-1	0-0	10	Golobart [64], Tade [69]	5888
21	28	A	Hibernian	D	1-1	1-1	10	Hayes [41]	6923
22	Jan 14	A	Motherwell	W	1-0	0-0	10	Tade [67]	4152
23	21	H	Hearts	W	1-0	0-0	10	Sutherland [49]	3812
24	28	H	St Mirren	D	0-0	0-0	10		3044
25	Feb 11	A	Celtic	L	0-1	0-1	10		50,014
26	18	A	Dunfermline Ath	D	1-1	0-1	10	Ross [73]	2881
27	26	H	Rangers	L	1-4	1-3	10	Williams [40]	6416
28	Mar 5	A	Dundee U	L	0-3	0-1	—		5994
29	10	H	Kilmarnock	D	1-1	0-1	—	Golobart [83]	3060
30	24	A	Aberdeen	W	1-0	1-0	10	Tade [10]	8939
31	28	H	St Johnstone	L	0-1	0-1	—		3035
32	Apr 1	H	Hibernian	L	2-3	0-0	10	Tansey (pen) [60], Hayes [83]	3274
33	7	A	St Johnstone	D	0-0	0-0	10		3326
34	21	H	Aberdeen	L	0-2	0-0	10		3487
35	28	A	Kilmarnock	L	3-4	2-1	10	McKay 2 [29, 35], Williams [90]	3848
36	May 2	H	Dunfermline Ath	D	0-0	0-0	—		6036
37	5	A	St Mirren	W	1-0	0-0	10	Foran [85]	3540
38	12	H	Hibernian	W	2-0	0-0	10	Tansey [62], Hayes (pen) [71]	4457

Final League Position: 10

League Champions: First Division 2003-04, 2009-10. Third Division 1996-97; *Runners-up:* Second Division 1998-99.
League Challenge Cup Winners: 2003-04. *Runners-up:* 1999-2000, 2009-10.

Club colours: Shirt: Blue with red stripes. Shorts: Blue. Stockings: Blue with red tops.

Goalscorers: *League (42):* Tade 9, Hayes 7 (1 pen), Shinnie, A. 7, Tansey 4 (1 pen), McKay 3, Foran 2, Golobart 2, Ross 2, Williams 2, Davis 1, Shinnie, G. 1, Sutherland 1, Tokely 1.
Scottish Cup (4): Hayes 2, Shinnie, A. 1, Tansey 1.
Scottish Communities Cup (0).

Esson R 33	Proctor D 9 + 8	Gillet K 25	Shinnie A 15 + 4	Tokely R 28 + 1	Aldred T 2 + 2	Hayes J 25 + 1	Tansey G 33 + 3	Foran R 37	Tade G 30 + 6	Ross N 18 + 11	Sutherland S 9 + 19	Shinnie G 25 + 1	Piermayr T 16 + 4	Tudur-Jones O 8 + 7	Doran A 7 + 3	Hogg C 9	Golobart R 18 + 4	Morrison G 3 + 1	McKay W 17 + 5	Davis D 14	Chippendale A 1 + 4	Meekings J 18 + 1	Cox L 4 + 3	Williams S 6 + 3	Gnakpa C 2 + 5	Winnall S 1 + 1	Tuffey J 5	*Match No.*
1	2	3	4^{1}	5	6	7	8	9	10^{2}	11	12	13																1
1		3		5	6	7	8	9	10^{2}	11^{1}	13		2	4	12													2
1	12^{2}	3^{1}		5	13	7	8	9	10	14			2	4	11^{3}	6												3
1				5■	12	7	8	9	10^{1}	13	14	3	2	4^{2}	11^{3}	6												4
1			4^{1}			7^{3}	8	9	14	11^{2}	13	3	2		12	5	6	10										5
1			13	2				9^{2}	10^{1}	11	12	3	7		8^{3}	5	6	4	14									6
1			4^{2}	5			12	9^{3}	10	11	14	7	2				3	6		8^{1}	13							7
1	12		4	5			8	9^{2}	10	11	13	3	2				6^{1}			7								8
1	6^{1}		14	5			8	9	10	11	13	3	2^{3}				12			4	7^{2}							9
1	6		4	5			3	9^{2}	10^{1}	11	13	2	7							8	12							10
1	6		4^{3}	5			8	9	10^{1}	11^{2}	12	3	2						14	7	13							11
1	6		4^{2}	5			8	9	10^{3}	11	14	3	2^{1}							7		12	13					12
1		3	7^{3}	5		13	8	9	10^{2}		11		14			6■	12			4		2^{1}						13
1	6	3	11	5		7^{2}	8	9	10								14	12		4^{1}	13	2^{3}						14
1	12	2	4	3		7	8■	9^{2}	10^{1}		13					5				11		6						15
1	12	3	4^{2}	6		7	8	9	10^{3}	13	14					5				11		2^{1}						16
1		3	4	5		7	8	9^{1}	13							6	2		10^{2}	11			12					17
1		3	4^{2}	5		7	8	9	14	13						6^{1}	2		10^{3}	11■			12					18
1		2	12	5		7	8^{1}	9	10		13	3					4		11^{2}				6					19
1		3				7	12	9	10		13	6	2				5		11^{2}	4			8^{1}					20
1		3				7	12	9	10			6	2		13		5		11^{2}	8			4^{1}					21
1	13	4				7	8		10	11^{1}		3	2				5		9^{2}				6	12				22
1	2	5		12		7	8	9	10^{2}	4^{1}	11								13			3		6				23
1	6	3		5		7	8	9	10^{2}	11	4^{1}											2			12	13		24
1		6				7	8	9		11	10^{2}	3	12	13								2^{1}		5■	4			25
1	5	6				7	8	9		11	4^{2}	10		13					12			2			3^{1}			26
1	12	5				7	8	9	10^{3}	11^{2}		2		14					4			3^{1}		6	13			27
1		3		5			8	9	7	11^{1}	4			13			6		10^{2}			2			12			28
1				5			8	9^{3}	7^{1}	13	4	3		14			6		10			2			12	11^{2}		29
	13			5			8^{2}	9	10		7	3	12	4^{3}			6		11^{1}			2■		14			1	30
				5			8	9	10^{1}	12	7^{2}	3	2	4			6		11						13		1	31
		11^{1}		5		7	4^{2}	9	10^{3}	12	14	3		13			6		8			2					1	32
		11		5^{1}		7^{2}	8	9	14	13		3		4			6		10^{3}			2		12			1	33
	14	3				7^{3}		9	10^{2}	13	12			4	11		6		8^{1}			2		5			1	34
1				5		7■	8	9	13			3		4	11^{1}		12		10^{2}			2		6				35
1		4	12	5			8	9	14	11^{2}	13	3^{1}			7				10^{3}			2		6				36
1		6	4^{3}			7	8	9	10	12		3	13		11^{1}		5		14			2^{2}						37
1		5	4^{1}	2		7^{3}	8	9	10^{2}	14	13	3	6	12					11									38

KILMARNOCK

Year Formed: 1869. *Ground & Address:* Rugby Park, Kilmarnock KA1 2DP. *Telephone:* 01563 545300. *Fax:* 01563 522181. *Email:* kirstencallaghan@kilmarnockfc.co.uk *Website:* www.kilmarnockfc.co.uk
Ground Capacity: all seated: 18,128. *Size of Pitch:* 115yd × 74yd.
Chairman: Michael Johnston. *Secretary:* Kirsten Callaghan.
Manager: Kenny Shiels. *Assistant Manager:* Jimmy Nicholl.
Club Nickname: Killie.
Previous Grounds: Rugby Park (Dundonald Road); The Grange; Holm Quarry; Present ground since 1899.
Record Attendance: 35,995 v Rangers, Scottish Cup, 10 Mar 1962.
Record Transfer Fee received: £2,000,000 for Stephen Naismith to Rangers (2007).
Record Transfer Fee paid: £300,000 for Paul Wright from St Johnstone (1995).
Record Victory: 11-1 v Paisley Academical, Scottish Cup, 18 Jan 1930 (15-0 v Lanemark, Ayrshire Cup, 15 Nov 1890).
Record Defeat: 1-9 v Celtic, Division I, 13 Aug 1938.
Most Capped Player: Joe Nibloe, 11, Scotland.
Most League Appearances: 481: Alan Robertson, 1972-88.
Most League Goals in Season (Individual): 34: Harry 'Peerie' Cunningham 1927-28; Andy Kerr 1960-61.
Most Goals Overall (Individual): 148: Willy Culley, 1912-23.

KILMARNOCK 2011–12 LEAGUE RECORD

Match No.	*Date*	*Venue*	*Opponents*	*Result*		*H/T Score*	*Lg Pos.*	*Goalscorers*	*Attendance*
1	July 24	A	Dundee U	D	1-1	0-0	—	McKeown ^{46}	6232
2	30	H	Motherwell	D	0-0	0-0	—		4867
3	Aug 14	H	Hibernian	W	4-1	2-1	4	Heffernan 2 $^{3, 71}$, Hanlon (og) ^{41}, Dayton ^{65}	4182
4	21	H	Hearts	D	0-0	0-0	6		5328
5	27	A	Inverness CT	L	1-2	1-1	7	Shiels ^{35}	3348
6	Sept 10	H	Dunfermline Ath	W	3-2	2-1	4	Heffernan 2 (1 pen) $^{32 (p), 45}$, Kroca ^{62}	4222
7	17	A	Aberdeen	D	2-2	2-1	5	Heffernan ^{15}, Shiels ^{28}	7672
8	24	A	St Mirren	L	0-3	0-2	7		5013
9	27	A	Rangers	L	0-2	0-0	—		43,761
10	Oct 1	H	St Johnstone	L	1-2	1-1	7	Pascali ^{36}	4059
11	15	H	Celtic	D	3-3	3-0	8	Shiels ^{26}, Heffernan ^{40}, Fowler ^{45}	8011
12	22	A	Motherwell	D	0-0	0-0	8		4184
13	29	A	Hearts	W	1-0	0-0	7	Shiels (pen) ^{55}	12,829
14	Nov 5	H	Inverness CT	L	3-6	1-1	7	Shiels 2 (1 pen) $^{12, 73 (p)}$, Heffernan ^{90}	5626
15	19	A	Hibernian	D	1-1	1-0	8	Pascali ^{37}	8169
16	27	H	Rangers	W	1-0	0-0	7	Pascali ^{80}	9506
17	Dec 3	H	Aberdeen	W	2-0	1-0	6	Harkins ^{5}, Dayton ^{65}	4367
18	17	H	Dundee U	D	1-1	0-0	6	Dayton ^{51}	4007
19	24	A	Celtic	L	1-2	0-1	8	Racchi ^{87}	49,352
20	28	A	St Johnstone	L	0-2	0-2	8		2394
21	Jan 2	H	St Mirren	W	2-1	1-1	7	Heffernan ^{34}, Racchi ^{89}	5986
22	14	A	Aberdeen	D	0-0	0-0	6		8324
23	21	H	Dunfermline Ath	L	0-3	0-1	7		4016
24	Feb 7	A	Dunfermline Ath	D	1-1	1-1	—	Fowler ^{21}	2303
25	11	H	Hearts	D	1-1	0-0	8	Heffernan ^{79}	4327
26	18	A	Rangers	W	1-0	1-0	6	Shiels ^{12}	50,268
27	21	A	Dundee U	L	0-4	0-0	—		5232
28	25	H	Hibernian	L	1-3	0-1	8	Shiels ^{83}	4283
29	Mar 3	H	St Johnstone	D	0-0	0-0	8		3768
30	10	A	Inverness CT	D	1-1	1-0	—	Golobart (og) ^{31}	3060
31	24	H	Motherwell	W	2-0	0-0	7	Heffernan 2 (1 pen) $^{50, 62 (p)}$	6878
32	31	A	St Mirren	L	2-4	1-1	7	Van Tornhout ^{13}, Shiels ^{89}	4365
33	Apr 7	H	Celtic	L	0-6	0-4	7		15,926
34	22	A	Hibernian	W	1-0	1-0	7	Shiels (pen) ^{44}	8877
35	28	H	Inverness CT	W	4-3	1-2	7	Fowler ^{14}, Nelson ^{66}, Shiels 2 $^{80, 85}$	3848
36	May 2	H	St Mirren	L	0-2	0-2	—		3645
37	5	H	Aberdeen	D	1-1	0-1	7	Shiels ^{53}	3893
38	12	A	Dunfermline Ath	W	2-1	0-1	7	Kelly ^{86}, Winchester ^{89}	3276

Final League Position: 7

Honours
League Champions: Division I 1964-65. Division II 1897-98, 1898-99; *Runners-up:* Division I 1959-60, 1960-61, 1962-63, 1963-64. First Division 1975-76, 1978-79, 1981-82, 1992-93. Division II 1953-54, 1973-74. Second Division 1989-90.
Scottish Cup Winners: 1920, 1929, 1997; *Runners-up:* 1898, 1932, 1938, 1957, 1960.
League Cup Winners: 2011-12; *Runners-up:* 1952-53, 1960-61, 1962-63, 2000-01, 2006-07.

European: *European Cup:* 4 matches (1965-66). *Cup Winners' Cup:* 4 matches (1997-98). *UEFA Cup:* 32 matches (*Fairs Cup:* 1964-65, 1966-67, 1969-70, 1970-71. *UEFA Cup:* 1998-99, 1999-2000, 2001-02).

Club colours: Shirts: Light and dark blue stripes. Shorts: Dark blue with light blue stripes. Stockings: White with dark blue tops.

Goalscorers: *League (44):* Shiels 13 (3 pens), Heffernan 11 (2 pens), Dayton 3, Fowler 3, Pascali 3, Racchi 2, Harkins 1, Kelly 1, Kroca 1, McKeown 1, Nelson 1, Van Tornhout 1, Winchester 1, own goals 2.
Scottish Cup (3): Heffernan 1, Pascali 1, Shiels 1.
Scottish Communities Cup (9): Heffernan 3, Harkins 2, Hutchinson 1, Shiels 1, Sissoko 1, Van Tournhout 1.

Bell C 32	Clancy T 1	McKeown R 18	Dayton J 13 + 16	Kroca Z 13 + 1	Ada P 3	Pascali M 24	Fowler J 34 + 3	Hutchinson B 3 + 1	Kelly L 33 + 1	Harkins G 29 + 1	Silva D 3 + 13	Hay G 20 + 4	Buijs D 12 + 2	O'Leary R 7 + 1	Heffernan P 26 + 3	Shiels D 33 + 2	Galan J — + 4	Fisher G 3 + 3	Pursehouse A 8	Racchi D 9 + 10	Panikvar L 2	Sissoko M 24 + 3	Gros W 2 + 6	Jaakkola A 5	Kennedy M 2 + 9	Davidson R — + 1	Gordon B 17	Toshney L 12	Nelson M 15	Van Tornhout D 6 + 5	Johnson L 7 + 2	Johnston C — + 2	Letheren K 1 + 1	Barbour R 1 + 1	Winchester J — + 2	*Match No.*
1	2	3^{2}	4	5	6	7	8	9	10	11^{1}	12	13																								1
1		3	4	5		7	8	9^{2}	10^{3}	11^{1}	12		2	6	13	14																				2
1		3	4^{3}	5		7	14		8	11^{1}	9^{2}		2	6	10	12	13																			3
1		3	4		6	7	12		8	11^{2}			2	5^{1}	10	9	13																			4
1		3	4	5	6	7	2^{2}	9^{1}	8				11			10	12	13																		5
1		3	4^{3}	5		7	6		8^{1}	11^{2}					10	9	14	13	2	12																6
1			4^{1}	5		7	2		8	11^{2}		3			10	9				12	6	13														7
1			13	5		7	2	14	8^{2}	11^{3}	12	4			10	9					3^{1}	6														8
1		3^{2}	12	5		7	2		8	11^{1}	14	13			10	9^{3}		4				6														9
1		3^{1}	8^{2}	5		7	4					12			10	9		11^{3}	2	13		6	14													10
		3				7	4		8	11			5		10	9			2			6		1												11
		3	12			6	4		8	11^{1}			7		10	9			2			5		1												12
		3				5	4		8	11	12		7^{2}		10	9			2^{1}	13		6		1												13
		3^{3}	13			5	4^{1}		8^{2}	11	12	14	7		10	9			2			6		1												14
		3	13			6	4		8	12		11^{3}	2		10^{1}	9				7^{2}		5		1	14											15
1		3				6	4		8	11	13	7	2^{1}		10^{3}	9				12^{2}		5	14													16
1		3	12			5	2			11^{2}	7	8^{3}			10^{1}	9		4				6			13	14										17
1		3	7^{2}	5		6			8	11^{3}	13	4			10^{1}	9			2			14			12											18
1		2	12			5	4		8	11		3^{3}	7^{1}		10	9^{2}				13		6			14											19
1		2^{1}	7^{2}			6	4		8	11^{3}	13	3			10	9				12		5			14											20
1				12		6	4		8		13	3			10	9^{3}		14	2^{1}	7		5			11^{2}											21
1				7		5	4		8			11^{1}			10	9				2		6	12^{2}		13		3									22
1			13	5		2	4		8^{1}	11	12	7^{2}			10	9						6					3									23
1			13			5	4		8			3			10^{2}	9				7^{1}							11	2	6	12						24
1							4		8			3			10	9						5					11	2	6	7■						25
1			12				4		8			11			10	9^{2}				13		5					3	2	6		7^{1}					26
1			14				4		8■			3			10^{2}	9^{3}						5			13		11	2	6	12	7^{1}					27
1			8^{3}				2			11^{2}		7	12		10	9						5			14		3		6	13	4^{1}					28
1			12				2		8	11	13	7^{2}	14			9■				4^{3}		5					3		6	10^{1}						29
1							12		10	11	7^{2}		4		13					8^{3}		5			9^{1}		3	2	6		14					30
1^{G}				6			4			11		3			10^{1}								13				7	2	5	9^{2}	8	12	15			31
1			12				4^{3}		14	11		7^{1}				9				13		5					3	2	6	10	8^{2}					32
1			12				4		8	11		2^{1}			14	9						5					3		6	10^{3}	7^{2}			13		33
1			7^{2}				4		8	11^{3}	13			5		9				10^{1}		14					3	2	6		12					34
1			7^{2}				4		8	11^{1}				5^{3}		9				10			12				3	2	6	13					14	35
1			12				4		8	11				5		9				7^{2}			13		14		3	2^{1}	6	10^{3}						36
1							4^{1}		8	11^{2}				14		9				12		5^{3}	10				3	2	6	13	7					37
			14				4		8	11^{3}				5		9							10^{2}				3	2	6			13	1	7^{1}	12	38

LIVINGSTON

Year Formed: 1974. *Ground:* The Braidwood Motor Company Stadium, Almondvale Stadium Road, Livingston EH54 7DN. *Telephone:* 01506 417000. *Fax:* 01506 418888. *Email:* info@livingstonfc.co.uk *Website:* www.livingstonfc.co.uk
Ground Capacity: 10,005 (all seated). *Size of Pitch:* 107yd × 75yd.
Chairman: Gordon McDougall. *Vice Chairman:* Robert Wilson.
Manager: John Hughes. *Director of Football:* John Collins. *Physio:* Andy Mackenzie.
Club Nickname: Livi Lions.
Previous Grounds: Meadowbank Stadium (as Meadowbank Thistle).
Record Attendance: 10,024 v Celtic, Premier League, 18 Aug 2001.
Record Transfer Fee received: £1,000,000 for David Fernandez to Celtic (June 2002).
Record Transfer Fee paid: £120,000 for Wes Hoolahan from Shelbourne (December 2005).
Record Victory: 7-0 v Queen of the South, Scottish Cup, 29 Jan 2000.
Record Defeat: 0-8 v Hamilton A. Division II, 14 Dec 1974.
Most Capped Player (under 18): Ian Little.
Most League Appearances: 446: Walter Boyd, 1979-89.
Most League Goals in Season (Individual): 22: Leigh Griffiths, 2008-09; Iain Russell, 2010-11.
Most Goals Overall (Individual): 64: David Roseburgh, 1986-93.

LIVINGSTON 2011–12 LEAGUE RECORD

Match No.	*Date*	*Venue*	*Opponents*	*Result*		*H/T Score*	*Lg Pos.*	*Goalscorers*	*Attendance*
1	Aug 6	H	Queen of the S	D	2-2	0-2	—	Sinclair 56, Russell, I (pen) 85	1444
2	13	A	Morton	L	1-2	0-1	6	Russell, I (pen) 55	2025
3	20	H	Dundee	W	4-2	2-0	4	Russell, I 4, Deuchar 2 13, 59, Jacobs, Keaghan 90	1966
4	27	A	Hamilton A	D	1-1	0-0	4	Boulding 90	2051
5	Sept 10	H	Falkirk	D	1-1	0-0	5	Russell, I 70	2229
6	17	A	Ross Co	D	1-1	1-1	6	Sinclair 40	2047
7	24	H	Partick Th	W	2-1	1-0	3	Deuchar 29, Jacobs, Kyle 90	2251
8	Oct 1	H	Raith R	D	1-1	0-0	6	McNulty 67	2011
9	15	A	Ayr U	D	0-0	0-0	5		1390
10	22	H	Morton	D	1-1	1-1	5	Russell, I (pen) 34	1740
11	29	A	Queen of the S	W	2-0	1-0	3	McNulty 6, Fotheringham 64	1556
12	Nov 5	A	Falkirk	L	3-4	0-3	5	Barr, B 56, Jacobs, Keaghan 62, Fotheringham 78	3691
13	12	H	Hamilton A	W	1-0	0-0	3	McNulty 52	1738
14	26	H	Ross Co	L	0-3	0-0	4		1628
15	Dec 3	A	Partick Th	L	1-2	1-2	5	Deuchar 45	2026
16	10	A	Raith R	W	1-0	0-0	5	Barr, C 56	1604
17	26	A	Hamilton A	W	1-0	0-0	5	Barr, B 70	1456
18	Jan 2	H	Falkirk	L	1-2	0-1	5	McNulty 66	2967
19	14	A	Dundee	L	0-3	0-1	7		4176
20	21	H	Queen of the S	D	2-2	1-1	6	Fox 40, Scougall 73	1286
21	28	A	Ross Co	L	0-3	0-1	—		2514
22	Feb 11	H	Partick Th	W	3-1	1-0	4	McNulty 37, Watson 46, Jacobs, Kyle 52	1824
23	18	H	Raith R	W	4-0	1-0	4	Jacobs, Kyle 17, McNulty 3 (1 pen) 48, 60, 70 (p)	1929
24	25	A	Ayr U	L	1-3	1-1	5	Cummings 11	1312
25	Mar 3	H	Dundee	L	2-3	1-1	6	McNulty 39, McGregor (og) 46	2052
26	6	H	Ayr U	L	1-2	1-1	—	Jacobs, Keaghan 12	859
27	10	A	Morton	W	3-1	2-1	5	McNulty 5, Russell, I 41, Barr, C 51	1396
28	17	H	Hamilton A	L	0-4	0-3	6		1066
29	24	A	Falkirk	W	5-2	2-1	6	Boulding 2 36, 41, Barr, B 2 71, 84, Russell, I (pen) 74	2939
30	31	A	Partick Th	W	3-2	1-1	5	Boulding 2 20, 46, Russell, I 50	1871
31	Apr 7	H	Ross Co	L	1-3	0-1	6	Boulding 46	2004
32	10	A	Raith R	W	3-0	2-0	—	Boulding 3 (1 pen) 17 (p), 45, 55	1541
33	14	H	Ayr U	L	0-1	0-1	5		1375
34	21	A	Queen of the S	W	4-0	2-0	5	Boulding 2 27, 88, McNulty 38, Jacobs, Keaghan 72	1403
35	28	H	Morton	D	0-0	0-0	4		1571
36	May 5	A	Dundee	L	0-1	0-0	5		3675

Final League Position: 5

Honours
League Champions: First Division 2000-01. Second Division 1986-87, 1998-99, 2010-11. Third Division 1995-96, 2009-10;
Runners-up: Second Division 1982-83. First Division 1987-88.
Scottish Cup: Semi-finals 2001, 2004.
League Cup Winners: 2003-04. Semi-finals 1984-85. *B&Q Cup:* Semi-finals 1992-93, 1993-94, 2001.
League Challenge Cup Runners-up: 2000-01.

European: *UEFA Cup:* 4 matches (2002-03).

Club colours: Shirt: Yellow. Shorts: Black. Stockings: Yellow.

Goalscorers: *League (56):* Boulding 11 (1 pen), McNulty 11 (1 pen), Russell, I. 8 (4 pens), Barr, B. 4, Deuchar 4, Jacobs, Keaghan 4, Jacobs, Kyle 3, Barr, C. 2, Fotheringham 2, Sinclair 2, Cummings 1, Fox 1, Scougall 1, Watson 1, own goal 1.
Scottish Cup (7): McNulty 4, Barr, R. 1, Boulding 1, Deuchar 1.
Scottish Communities Cup (6): Russell, I. 2, Boulding 1, Jacobs, Keaghan 1, McNulty 1, Talbot 1.
Ramsdens Cup (12): Deuchar 3, Russell, I. 3, Barr, R. 2, Scougall 1, Sinclair 1, own goals 2.

McNeil A 36	Brown J 8 + 2	Sinclair D 6 + 8	Talbot J 25	Barr C 35	Watson P 32	Fox L 21 + 1	Jacobs Keaghan 30 + 1	Barr B 34 + 2	Russell I 17 + 9	Boulding R 12 + 13	Deuchar K 14 + 5	Scougall S 20 + 4	Jacobs Kyle 29 + 5	McNulty M 25 + 5	Doherty R 8 + 3	Travis M — + 1	Fotheringham M 11	Cummings D 5 + 6	Ross M 8	Russie A — + 8	MacDonald C 1 + 3	Fordyce C 8 + 2	Easton D — + 2	McCann K 10	Scott M 1	Beaumont J — + 2	Gray L — + 2	Downie J — + 1	Match No.
1	2	3	4	5	6	7	8	9[2]	10	11[1]	12	13																	1
1	2	4[1]	3	5[2]	6	7	8	9	11	12	10		13																2
1	2	14	5	3	4	7	6	9[1]	10[2]	13	11[3]	8	12																3
1	2[2]		5	3[1]	4	7	6	9	11	13		8	12	10															4
1	2[2]	12	5	4	3	6[1]	8	9	11		10	7	13																5
1	13	6	2	4	5▪	8	9[1]	12	11	14	10[2]	3[3]	7																6
1	2[1]		4	3		7		9	10		11[2]	8	5	13	6	12													7
1	2[2]		5	3	4	7		6	11	13	10[1]	9	8	12															8
1		14	4	2	3	6		9	11[1]	12		7	5	10[2]			8[3]	13											9
1		6[1]	5	3	4		12	9	11[2]		13	7	14	10			8		2[3]										10
1			5	3	4		6	9	12		10		7	11[1]			8		2										11
1	2[1]		5	3	4		6	9		12	11[2]		8	10			7			13									12
1			4	2	3		6[1]	8		10[2]	11	12	5	9[3]			7	13		14									13
1	12		5[1]	3	4	13	6	8	14	11▪	9[2]		2	10[3]			7												14
1				3	4	8	7	9	12		11[1]		5	10			6				2								15
1		8	4	3	5	6		9[2]			12		10	11[1]			7	13	2										16
1			5[1]	3	4	9	6	10		13	11[2]		7	12			8		2										17
1				3	4	7[3]	8	5	12	14	10[1]		6	11			9		2[2]			13							18
1		13		2	3	7[2]	6	9	11[3]		10[1]	14	5	12			8▪		4										19
1		6	5	3	4	8[1]	7	9[2]	11	14	13	12		10[3]					2										20
1			5[1]	3	4	7	8	12	11[3]	10[2]	13	9	6	14					2										21
1			2	4	3	8[2]	9	6	12			7[3]	11	10[1]	5			13					14						22
1			5	4	3	7[3]	11	9	13			8[1]	6	10[2]	2			12					14						23
1			3	5	4	8[1]	11	7	12	13			6	9[2]	2			10											24
1				4	3	7[1]	11	9	12			8	6	10	2			5[2]				13							25
1			5	4	3	7	10	9	12			8[1]	6	11	2														26
1			5	4	3		9	7	11	14			8[3]	10[2]	13					12				2	6[1]				27
1			5▪	4	3		9	6[1]	11	14		8	7	10[2]	13					12[3]				2					28
1		12					8	6	11	10[2]		5	7	9[1]	2					13		4		3					29
1		12		4			8	6[1]	10[2]	11		5	7	9	13							3		2					30
1		13	5[1]	4			8	9		11		7[2]	6	10[3]						14	12	3		2					31
1				4	3		9[3]	6		11		8[1]	7	10				12			13	5[2]		2		14			32
1				4	3		9	6		11			7	10				8[1]				5		2			12		33
1				3	4		6	10[1]		11			7	9[3]				8[2]		14	12	5		2			13		34
1		12		4	3		9[1]	6		11		8	7	10								5		2					35
1				5	4			6		11		9	8		7			10[3]		13		3		2[1]		12[2]		14	36

MONTROSE

Year Formed: 1879. *Ground & Address:* Links Park, Wellington St, Montrose DD10 8QD. *Telephone:* 01674 673200. *Fax:* 01674 677311. *E-mail:* montrosefootballclub@tesco.net *Website:* www.montrosefc.co.uk
Ground Capacity: total: 3,292, seated: 1,338. *Size of Pitch:* 113yd × 70yd.
Chairman: Derek Sim. *Vice-Chairman:* John Crawford. *Secretary:* Malcolm J. Watters.
Manager: Stuart Garden. *Assistant Manager:* Lee Wilkie. *Physio:* Craig Smith.
Club Nickname: The Gable Endies.
Previous Grounds: None.
Record Attendance: 8983 v Dundee, Scottish Cup 3rd rd, 17 Mar 1973.
Record Transfer Fee received: £50,000 for Gary Murray to Hibernian (Dec 1980).
Record Transfer Fee paid: £17,500 for Jim Smith from Airdrieonians (Feb 1992).
Record Victory: 12-0 v Vale of Leithen, Scottish Cup 2nd rd, 4 Jan 1975.
Record Defeat: 0-13 v Aberdeen, 17 Mar 1951.
Most Capped Player: Alexander Keillor, 2 (6), Scotland.
Most League Appearances: 432: David Larter, 1987-98.
Most League Goals in Season (Individual): 28: Brian Third, Division II, 1972-73.

MONTROSE 2011–12 LEAGUE RECORD

Match No.	Date		Venue	Opponents	Result		H/T Score	Lg Pos.	Goalscorers	Attendance
1	Aug	6	A	East Stirling	L	0-1	0-0	—		282
2		13	H	Elgin C	W	3-0	2-0	4	Boyle 2 [11, 36], Crawford (pen) [50]	349
3		20	A	Clyde	L	0-1	0-0	5		700
4		27	H	Stranraer	L	0-6	0-2	10		302
5	Sept	10	A	Berwick R	W	2-1	1-1	7	Winter [23], Pierce (pen) [81]	368
6		17	H	Annan Ath	L	2-3	2-1	8	Boyle 2 [13, 44]	308
7		24	A	Alloa Ath	L	2-4	2-2	8	Campbell [27], Boyle [37]	461
8	Oct	1	H	Peterhead	W	2-1	1-1	8	Masson [41], Boyle [66]	359
9		15	A	Queen's Park	L	1-3	1-0	8	Boyle [30]	529
10	Nov	5	H	East Stirling	W	2-1	1-1	8	Johnston [2], Smart [60]	315
11		8	A	Elgin C	L	1-3	1-2	—	Johnston [29]	461
12		12	A	Stranraer	D	4-4	0-3	8	Pierce 2 (1 pen) [64 (p), 69], Winter 2 [70, 74]	326
13		26	H	Berwick R	L	3-5	1-2	—	Boyle [9], Lunan [50], Cameron [86]	328
14	Dec	3	H	Alloa Ath	D	1-1	1-0	8	Johnston [15]	313
15		10	A	Annan Ath	L	1-2	0-2	8	Winter (pen) [54]	402
16		26	A	Peterhead	W	3-2	1-0	8	Strachan (og) [15], McGowan [62], Crawford [90]	566
17	Jan	2	A	Berwick R	D	2-2	0-1	8	Johnston [46], Boyle [58]	455
18		7	H	Stranraer	L	1-3	1-1	8	Boyle [3]	257
19		14	H	Clyde	W	4-0	0-0	8	McGowan [51], Johnston [53], Winter [75], McNalley [90]	365
20		21	A	East Stirling	L	1-3	0-1	8	Winter [59]	248
21		28	A	Alloa Ath	L	0-2	0-0	9		508
22	Feb	4	H	Annan Ath	D	1-1	1-0	8	Winter [45]	246
23		11	A	Queen's Park	L	0-5	0-1	9		426
24		18	H	Peterhead	L	1-3	0-1	9	Boyle [62]	358
25		25	H	Elgin C	L	2-3	1-2	9	Masson [29], Boyle [51]	401
26		28	H	Queen's Park	L	0-1	0-0	—		303
27	Mar	3	A	Clyde	W	2-1	0-0	9	Cameron [50], Boyle [64]	476
28		10	H	Berwick R	D	1-1	0-0	9	Boyle [49]	318
29		17	A	Stranraer	L	1-3	1-0	9	Boyle [45]	287
30		24	A	Annan Ath	W	2-1	2-1	8	Wood, G [5], Winter (pen) [43]	418
31		31	H	Alloa Ath	L	0-2	0-0	8		390
32	Apr	7	A	Peterhead	L	1-2	0-1	9	Crawford [55]	458
33		14	H	Queen's Park	W	3-1	1-1	9	Crighton [41], Boyle [51], Winter [63]	336
34		21	H	East Stirling	W	3-1	1-1	8	Boyle 2 [24, 83], Wood, G [72]	329
35		28	A	Elgin C	L	1-2	0-1	9	Boyle [75]	901
36	May	5	H	Clyde	W	5-0	2-0	8	Boyle 3 [20, 41, 75], Masson [54], Campbell [72]	450

Final League Position: 8

Honours
League Champions: Second Division 1984-85; *Runners-up:* Second Division 1990-91. Third Division 1994-95.
Scottish Cup: Quarter-finals 1973, 1976.
League Cup: Semi-finals 1975-76.
B&Q Cup: Semi-finals 1992-93.
League Challenge Cup: Semi-finals 1996-97.

Club colours: Shirt: Royal blue with white trim. Shorts: White with blue trim. Stockings: Blue with white trim.

Goalscorers: *League (58):* Boyle 22, Winter 9 (2 pens), Johnston 5, Crawford 3 (1 pen), Masson 3, Pierce 3 (2 pens), Cameron 2, Campbell 2, McGowan 2, Wood, G. 2, Crighton 1, Lunan 1, McNalley 1, Smart 1, own goal 1.
Scottish Cup (5): Winter 2 (1 pen), Lunan 1, Masson 1, Pierce 1.
Scottish Communities Cup (1): Winter 1.
Ramsdens Cup (1): McPhee 1.

Andrews M 25	Crighton S 25 + 1	Campbell A 28	Smart J 21 + 1	Cameron D 34	Johnston S 28 + 4	Crawford J 23 + 5	Masson T 30 + 3	McGowan D 11 + 4	Winter J 31 + 2	Boyle M 36	McPhee S 4 + 16	Pierce S 8 + 6	Lunan P 20 + 2	Dimilta D — + 6	McNalley S 25 + 5	Masterton S 1	Wood S 11	Young L 22	Wood G 12 + 4	Brown K 1	Match No.
1	2	3	4■	5	6^2	7	8^3	9^1	10	11	12	13	14								1
1	4	3		2	10^2	7	6	9^1	8	11	13		5	12							2
1	4	3		2	10^3	7^1	6	9	8^2	11	14		5■	13	12						3
1	2	3	4■	5		8	7	10^1		11	9	12			6						4
1	4	3		5		7	9■		8	10		11	6		2						5
1	4	5		3		7			9	10	12	11	6		2	8^1					6
1	3^1	4		5		7^2	9	12	6	10	13	11	8		2						7
1		4	3	5	12		7		8	10	9^1	11	2		6						8
1	3	4		5	12		7		8	10	9^1	11	2		6						9
1	2	4	3	5	11	6^1	8^2		13	10		9	7		12						10
1	2	4	3^2	6	11	5	8^1		7	10	12	9^3		14	13						11
1	4	3	2	7	10	6^1	13		9^2	11		12	8		5						12
1	4^1	3		5	10^3	12	8		7	9	13	11^2	6	14	2						13
	2		3	5	11		7		8	10		12	6		4		1	9^1			14
	4^2		3	7	11		6		5	10	12	13	8		2		1	9^1			15
	2	3	4	5	9	12	7	11^1	8	10							1	6			16
	2	3	4	5	10	12	7	11^2	6	9		13					1	8^1			17
	4		3	2	10	5	8	11	7	9							1	6			18
	3		4	5	10^3	2^2	6	11^1	7	9	14				13		1	8	12		19
	3		4	5	9	2^3	7^2	8^1	6	11	12		13		14		1		10		20
1		3	4	5	10		6		7	9					2			8	11		21
1	12	3	4	6■	11		5		8	10					2			7	9^1		22
1		4^1	3		9	12		6	8	10					2			7	11	5	23
1	2^2	3	4	5	11	13	7	9^1	8	10								6	12		24
1		3	4	5	9		6^1	12	8	10					2			7	11		25
1		3		5	11		7	12	6	10			4■		2			8^1	9		26
1	3		4	6	11	5	8			10					2			7	9		27
1	3		4	6	9	5	7^1		12	10					2			8	11		28
1		4	3■	6	9^2	5	12		8^1	10	13				2			7	11		29
1		3		6	9	4			8	10	12		5		2			7	11^1		30
1		3■		6	10	4	13		8	11	9^2		5	12	2			7^1			31
1	4			5^1	11	3	6^2	14	8	10	13		7	12	2			9^3			32
	5	3			11^1	4	6		8	10	13		7		2		1	9^2	12		33
		3		4	11^1	5	7		8	10			6		2		1	9	12		34
		3	14	5^3	12	4	6^2		8	10	13		7		2		1	9^1	11		35
	2	4		5	13	8	9^1			10	12		3		6		1	7	11^2		36

MORTON

Year Formed: 1874. *Ground & Address:* Cappielow Park, Sinclair St, Greenock PA15 2TY. *Telephone:* 01475 723571. *Fax:* 01475 781084. *E-mail:* info@gmfc.net *Website:* www.gmfc.net
Ground Capacity: total: 11,612, seated: 6,062. *Size of Pitch:* 110yd × 71yd.
Chairman: Douglas Rae. *Chief Executive:* Gillian Donaldson. *Company Secretary:* Mary Davidson.
Manager: Allan Moore. *Assistant Manager:* Mark McNally. *Physio:* Alyson Hendry.
Club Nickname: The Ton.
Previous Grounds: Grant Street 1874, Garvel Park 1875, Cappielow Park 1879, Ladyburn Park 1882, (Cappielow Park 1883).
Record Attendance: 23,500 v Celtic, 29 April 1922.
Record Transfer Fee received: £350,000 for Neil Orr to West Ham U.
Record Transfer Fee paid: £150,000 for Alan Mahood from Nottingham Forest (August 1998).
Record Victory: 11-0 v Carfin Shamrock, Scottish Cup 1st rd, 13 Nov 1886.
Record Defeat: 1-10 v Port Glasgow Ath, Division II, 5 May, 1894 and v St Bernards, Division II, 14 Oct 1933.
Most Capped Player: Jimmy Cowan, 25, Scotland.
Most League Appearances: 534: Derek Collins, 1987-98, 2001-05.
Most League Goals in Season (Individual): 58: Allan McGraw, Division II, 1963-64.
Most Goals Overall (Individual): 117: Allan McGraw, 1961-66.

MORTON 2011–12 LEAGUE RECORD

Match No.	*Date*	*Venue*	*Opponents*	*Result*		*H/T Score*	*Lg Pos.*	*Goalscorers*	*Attendance*
1	Aug 6	A	Ross Co	D	0-0	0-0	—		2249
2	13	H	Livingston	W	2-1	1-0	4	Tidser [9], MacDonald (pen) [64]	2025
3	20	A	Raith R	D	1-1	1-1	3	Di Giacomo [38]	2109
4	27	A	Dundee	W	1-0	1-0	2	MacDonald [7]	4096
5	Sept 10	H	Ayr U	W	4-1	3-0	1	MacDonald 2 [10, 13], Jackson [11], Weatherson (pen) [89]	2018
6	17	A	Queen of the S	L	1-4	0-4	1	MacDonald [87]	1699
7	24	H	Falkirk	W	3-2	1-2	1	MacDonald 2 (1 pen) [6, 54 (p)], Jackson [58]	2621
8	30	A	Partick Th	L	0-5	0-2	—		3380
9	Oct 15	H	Hamilton A	L	0-2	0-0	4		2264
10	22	A	Livingston	D	1-1	1-1	4	O'Brien [16]	1740
11	29	H	Ross Co	L	0-2	0-1	6		1748
12	Nov 5	A	Ayr U	W	1-0	1-0	4	O'Brien [23]	1570
13	12	H	Dundee	L	1-2	1-1	5	Jackson [5]	2201
14	26	H	Queen of the S	D	2-2	1-1	5	Jackson [17], Weatherson [82]	1352
15	Dec 3	A	Falkirk	L	0-1	0-0	6		3114
16	10	H	Partick Th	L	1-2	0-1	7	McGeouch [53]	1849
17	26	A	Dundee	W	1-0	1-0	6	Jackson [22]	5862
18	Jan 2	H	Ayr U	W	3-1	1-1	6	O'Brien [44], Campbell [64], Di Giacomo [89]	2108
19	14	H	Raith R	D	1-1	0-0	5	O'Brien [65]	1739
20	28	A	Queen of the S	L	1-2	0-0	—	Campbell [75]	1444
21	Feb 11	H	Falkirk	D	0-0	0-0	7		1757
22	14	A	Hamilton A	W	2-1	2-0	—	Campbell [24], O'Brien [29]	1356
23	18	A	Partick Th	D	0-0	0-0	5		2305
24	25	H	Hamilton A	L	1-2	0-2	7	O'Brien [85]	1594
25	Mar 3	A	Raith R	L	0-5	0-1	7		1480
26	10	H	Livingston	L	1-3	1-2	7	MacDonald [22]	1396
27	13	A	Ross Co	D	2-2	0-1	—	Campbell [87], Weatherson (pen) [90]	2325
28	17	H	Dundee	L	0-2	0-1	7		1610
29	20	A	Falkirk	W	2-0	0-0	—	Tidser [56], Campbell [82]	2538
30	24	A	Ayr U	D	0-0	0-0	7		1669
31	Apr 7	H	Queen of the S	D	2-2	1-0	7	Bachirou [32], MacDonald [62]	1622
32	10	H	Partick Th	W	1-0	1-0	—	MacDonald [8]	1637
33	14	A	Hamilton A	L	3-4	0-2	7	Mensing (og) [78], McGeouch [84], Young [89]	1423
34	21	H	Ross Co	D	1-1	1-1	7	Smyth [41]	1306
35	28	A	Livingston	D	0-0	0-0	7		1571
36	May 5	H	Raith R	L	1-3	0-1	8	Hawke [77]	1813

Final League Position: 8

Honours
League Champions: First Division 1977-78, 1983-84, 1986-87. Division II 1949-50, 1963-64, 1966-67. Second Division 1994-95, 2006-07. Third Division 2002-03. *Runners-up:* Division 1 1916-17, Division II 1899-1900, 1928-29, 1936-37.
Scottish Cup Winners: 1922; *Runners-up:* 1948. *League Cup Runners-up:* 1963-64.
B&Q Cup Runners-up: 1992-93.

European: *UEFA Cup:* 2 matches (*Fairs Cup:* 1968-69).

Club colours: Shirt: Blue and white hoops. Shorts: White with blue trim. Stockings: White.

Goalscorers: *League (40):* MacDonald 10 (2 pens), O'Brien 6, Campbell 5, Jackson 5, Weatherson 3 (2 pens), Di Giacomo 2, McGeouch 2, Tidser 2, Bachirou 1, Hawke 1, Smyth 1, Young 1, own goal 1.
Scottish Cup (6): MacDonald 2 (1 pen), Campbell 1, Jackson 1, O'Brien 1, Weatherson 1.
Scottish Communities Cup (6): Jackson 2, Di Giacomo 1, MacDonald 1, Tidser 1, Weatherson 1.
Ramsdens Cup (14): Di Giacomo 5, Jackson 4, MacDonald 2, Campbell 1, O'Brien 1, Weatherson 1.

Stewart C 17	Evans G 31 + 2	Smyth M 28	McCaffrey S 6	Forsyth R 26	Tidser M 22 + 3	Bachirou F 28 + 2	O'Brien D 32	Di Giacomo P 16 + 8	MacDonald P 30 + 5	Jackson A 20 + 9	Weatherson P 19 + 12	Campbell A 16 + 16	McCann K 10 + 1	McGeouch D 13 + 13	Graham A 25 + 2	Fitzharris S 3 + 7	McGinley M 2	Cervi D 7	Young D 18 + 1	O'Ware T 13 + 1	Hawke L — + 2	Little C 1	Combe A 10	Flannigan I 3 + 1	Kasubandi J — + 2	Ramsay C — + 1	Frizzell A — + 1	*Match No.*
1	2	3	4	5	6	7	8	9	10^{1}	11^{2}	12	13																1
1	4		5▪	3	6	7	8^{3}	9	10	11^{1}	13	12	2^{2}	14														2
1	3	4		5	6		8	9	10^{2}	11^{1}	13	12	2	7														3
1	3	8	4	5	7		9	6	10^{3}	11^{2}	14		2^{1}	13	12													4
1	3	6	4	5	7^{3}		8^{2}	9	10^{1}	11	12			14	2	13												5
1	3	6	4	5	7^{2}	13	8^{3}	9	10	11^{1}	12				2	14												6
1	2	6	4^{1}	5		7	8		10	11		13	12	14	3^{2}	9^{3}												7
1	4^{1}	7		5		8	9^{3}	13	10	11		14	2	12	3▪	6^{2}												8
1	2	3		4		6	7^{1}	8	9	10	11	12	5															9
	4	3^{1}		5		11	9	6	13		10^{2}	12	7	8	2		1											10
1	4	3		5		9	10^{3}	6	11^{2}		12	13	7	8	2^{1}	14												11
	4			5		7^{2}	8	9	10^{1}	11	12		2	13	3			1	6									12
	4			5^{1}		7	8	9^{2}	10	11	12	14	2^{3}		3	13		1	6									13
	5	4					8	9	10^{2}	11^{3}	13	14	2^{1}	7		12		1	6	3								14
	2	3					9	6^{1}	12	10^{2}	11^{3}	13		8	4	14		1	7	5								15
	2	4			13	12	8			11^{3}	10	14		6	3	9^{1}		1	7^{2}	5								16
	2	5			7^{3}	8	9		13	10^{2}	12	11^{1}		6	4			1	14	3								17
	2	4			8	7	9	14	12	10^{3}	13	11^{1}		6^{2}	3			1		5								18
1		3			6	5	7	9^{1}	11^{3}		8	10^{2}		12	2	13				4	14							19
1	2	4			8	7	9	13	12		10	11		6^{2}	3							5^{1}						20
1	3	2^{2}		4	6	7	8^{3}	14	10	12	9	11^{1}			13				5									21
1	3			5	8	7	9		10	12	4	11^{1}							6	2								22
1	3			4	7	5	6	8^{1}	10	13	9	11^{2}		12						2								23
1	3			4	7	5	8	13	10	12	9	11^{1}		6^{2}						2								24
	3			4	5	7	8	13	10	12	9	11^{1}					1		6	2^{2}								25
1		3		5	12	7	8	9^{1}	10	11^{2}	4	13		14	2				6^{3}									26
	12	3		5	7	8^{3}	9		10	11^{1}	4	13		14	2^{2}								1	6				27
	13	3		4	7^{3}	6	8		10	11^{1}	9▪	12		14	2				5^{2}				1					28
	3	4		5	8	7	9		10			11			2				6				1					29
	5	4		2	7	8^{2}	6^{1}		11	14		10^{3}		13	3				9				1	12				30
					7	6			10	12	9	11		8^{1}	2				4	3			1	5				31
	2	4		5	9	7			10	14		11^{3}		13	3				8	12^{2}			1	6^{1}				32
	2	4^{1}		5		8^{2}			10	12	9	11^{3}		6	3				7				1		13	14		33
	2	5		4			8		10	11^{2}	9	13		6^{1}	3				7				1		12			34
	2	6			12	7	9^{1}	13	10		3	11^{2}			4				8	5			1					35
	2	5			8^{3}	7		12	10		9	11^{2}			3				6	4^{1}	13		1				14	36

MOTHERWELL

Year Formed: 1886. *Ground & Address:* Fir Park Stadium, Motherwell ML1 2QN. *Telephone:* 01698 333333. *Fax:* 01698 338001.
E-mail: mfcenquiries@motherwellfc.co.uk *Website:* www.motherwellfc.co.uk
Ground Capacity: all seated: 13,742. *Size of Pitch:* 110yd × 75yd.
Manager: Stuart McCall. *Assistant Manager:* Kenny Black. *Physio:* John Porteous.
Club Nicknames: The Well, The Steelmen.
Previous Grounds: Roman Road, Dalziel Park.
Record Attendance: 35,632 v Rangers, Scottish Cup 4th rd replay, 12 Mar 1952.
Record Transfer Fee received: £1,750,000 for Phil O'Donnell to Celtic (September 1994).
Record Transfer Fee paid: £500,000 for John Spencer from Everton (Jan 1999).
Record Victory: 12-1 v Dundee U, Division II, 23 Jan 1954.
Record Defeat: 0-8 v Aberdeen, Premier Division, 26 Mar 1979.
Most Capped Player: Stephen Craigan, 54, Northern Ireland.
Most League Appearances: 626: Bobby Ferrier, 1918-37.
Most League Goals in Season (Individual): 52: Willie McFadyen, Division I, 1931-32.
Most Goals Overall (Individual): 283: Hugh Ferguson, 1916-25.

MOTHERWELL 2011–12 LEAGUE RECORD

Match No.	Date	Venue	Opponents	Result		H/T Score	Lg Pos.	Goalscorers	Attendance
1	July 23	H	Inverness CT	W	3-0	2-0	—	Hammell 25, Murphy 28, Lasley 77	4190
2	30	A	Kilmarnock	D	0-0	0-0	—		4867
3	Aug 7	H	Hearts	W	1-0	0-0	—	Murphy 60	5685
4	13	A	St Mirren	W	1-0	0-0	1	Hateley 90	5105
5	21	H	Rangers	L	0-3	0-2	2		10,092
6	27	A	Dunfermline Ath	W	4-2	2-0	2	Higdon 2 11, 90, Murphy 26, Humphrey 55	4462
7	Sept 10	A	Celtic	L	0-4	0-2	3		48,793
8	17	H	St Johnstone	L	0-3	0-1	3		4336
9	24	H	Aberdeen	W	1-0	0-0	3	McHugh 84	4348
10	Oct 1	A	Dundee U	W	3-1	2-0	2	Lasley 14, Higdon 2 (1 pen) 45, 64 (p)	6073
11	15	A	Hibernian	W	1-0	1-0	2	Murphy 8	8518
12	22	H	Kilmarnock	D	0-0	0-0	2		4184
13	29	A	Inverness CT	W	3-2	1-1	2	Hutchinson 39, Lasley 77, Hateley 87	3188
14	Nov 6	H	Celtic	L	1-2	1-1	3	Higdon 11	10,440
15	19	A	Aberdeen	W	2-1	1-1	3	Higdon 6, Daley 53	8779
16	26	H	Dundee U	D	0-0	0-0	3		4487
17	Dec 10	A	St Johnstone	W	3-0	2-0	3	Daley 16, Murphy 2 28, 68	2885
18	17	H	St Mirren	D	1-1	0-0	3	Higdon 48	4557
19	24	A	Hearts	L	0-2	0-2	3		13,300
20	Jan 2	A	Rangers	L	0-3	0-1	3		44,893
21	14	H	Inverness CT	L	0-1	0-0	4		4152
22	21	A	Dundee U	D	1-1	0-1	5	Higdon 85	5969
23	24	H	Dunfermline Ath	W	3-1	1-0	—	Ojamaa 29, Law 52, Humphrey 80	3772
24	28	H	St Johnstone	W	3-2	1-1	3	Ojamaa 2 22, 65, Lasley 75	4520
25	Feb 11	A	St Mirren	D	0-0	0-0	3		4204
26	18	H	Hearts	W	3-0	2-0	3	Webster (og) 37, Murphy 41, Law 65	5489
27	22	H	Hibernian	W	4-3	0-1	—	Higdon 3 (2 pens) 47 (p), 70, 75 (p), Murphy 63	8065
28	25	A	Celtic	L	0-1	0-0	3		53,486
29	Mar 3	A	Dunfermline Ath	W	2-0	0-0	3	Higdon 64, Ojamaa 70	3523
30	17	H	Aberdeen	W	1-0	1-0	—	Hammell 22	4637
31	24	A	Kilmarnock	L	0-2	0-0	3		6878
32	31	H	Rangers	L	1-2	1-1	3	Ojamaa 6	9063
33	Apr 8	A	Hibernian	D	1-1	0-1	3	Law 81	7110
34	22	H	Celtic	L	0-3	0-0	3		8760
35	28	H	St Johnstone	W	5-1	2-0	3	Higdon (pen) 17, Law 20, Murphy 52, Ojamaa 2 83, 87	4743
36	May 1	A	Hearts	W	1-0	1-0	—	Higdon 29	9185
37	5	A	Rangers	D	0-0	0-0	3		45,962
38	13	H	Dundee U	L	0-2	0-1	3		7456

Final League Position: 3

Honours
League Champions: Division I 1931-32. First Division 1981-82, 1984-85. Division II 1953-54, 1968-69; *Runners-up:* Premier Division 1994-95. Division I 1926-27, 1929-30, 1932-33, 1933-34. Division II 1894-95, 1902-03. *Scottish Cup:* 1952, 1991; *Runners-up:* 1931, 1933, 1939, 1951, 2011.
League Cup Winners: 1950-51; *Runners-up:* 1954-55, 2004-05. *Scottish Summer Cup:* 1944, 1965.

European: *Cup Winners' Cup:* 2 matches (1991-92). *UEFA Cup:* 8 matches (1994-95, 1995-96, 2008-09). *Europa League:* 12 matches (2009-10, 2010-11).

Club colours: Shirt: Amber with maroon band. Shorts: Amber with maroon stripe. Stockings: Amber with maroon top.

Goalscorers: *League (49):* Higdon 14 (4 pens), Murphy 9, Ojamaa 7, Lasley 4, Law 4, Daley 2, Hammell 2, Hateley 2, Humphrey 2, Hutchinson 1, McHugh 1, own goal 1.
Scottish Cup (11): Murphy 4, Law 2, Ojamaa 2, Daley 1, Hateley 1, Hutchinson 1.
Scottish Communities Cup (6): Higdon 2, Hateley 1, Lasley 1, Law 1, Lawless 1.

Randolph D 38	Hateley T 38	Hammell S 37	Hutchinson S 29 + 1	Craigan S 24 + 2	Lasley K 32	Humphrey C 23 + 12	Jennings S 33 + 1	Higdon M 35	Murphy J 32 + 4	Law N 38	Smith G — + 1	McHugh R 1 + 8	Saunders S 1 + 1	Carswell S 4 + 10	Forbes R 1 + 3	Clancy T 24 + 2	Daley O 11 + 14	Page J 2 + 2	Hughes S 2 + 2	Ojamaa H 12 + 6	Cummins A 1	*Match No.*
1	2	3	4	5	6	7	8	9^{1}	10	11	12											1
1	2	3	4	5	6	7	8		10	11		9										2
1	2	3		5	6■	7	8	9	10^{1}	11			4	12								3
1	2	3	4	5		7	8^{1}	9	10	11				12	6							4
1	2	3	4	5	6	7	8	9	10	11												5
1	2	3		5	6	7	8	9	10	11						4						6
1	6	3	4^{1}	5	7	12	8^{2}	9	10	11				13		2						7
1	2	3		5	6	7	8^{1}	9	10^{2}	11		13				4	12					8
1	2	3		5	6	7^{1}	8	9	10^{2}	11^{3}		13				4	12	14				9
1	2	3		5	6	7^{2}	8	9	10^{1}	11				12		4	13					10
1	2	3		5	4	7^{1}	8	9	10	11						6	12					11
1	2	3		5	4	7^{1}	8	9	10^{2}	11		12				6	13					12
1	8	3^{1}	2	5	4	7^{2}		9	10	11				14	12^{3}	6	13					13
1	2	3	14	5	6	7^{2}	8^{1}	9	10^{3}	11				12		4■	13					14
1	6	3	4	5	2	12	8	9	10	11							7^{1}					15
1	2	3	4^{2}	5	6^{3}	7^{1}	8	9	12	11				14			10	13				16
1	6	3	4	5	11^{1}	13	8	9	10	2							7^{2}		12			17
1	2	3	4	5	6^{2}	12	8	9	10	11							7^{1}		13			18
1	2	3	4	5	6			9	10^{2}	11		13		12			7		8^{1}			19
1	2	3	4	5	8	12		9	10^{2}	11						7	13		6^{1}			20
1	6	3	4	5^{3}	8	12	14	9	10	11^{2}						2	7^{1}			13		21
1	2	3	4	5	6		8	9	10	11							7^{1}			12		22
1	2	3	4	5■	6	14	8	9	10^{1}	11^{3}		13				12				7^{2}		23
1	2	3	4		6	12	8		10^{1}	11						5	7			9		24
1	2	3	4		6	12	8	9	10^{1}	11						5				7		25
1	2	3	4		6■		8	9	10	11						5	12			7^{1}		26
1	2	3	4	14		12	6	9	10^{2}	11^{3}				13		5	8^{1}			7		27
1	2	3	4		6	12	8	9	10^{1}	11						5	13			7^{2}		28
1	2	3	4^{2}	13		12	6	9	10	11						5	8^{1}			7		29
1	2	3				7	8	9		11		12		4				5		10^{1}	6	30
1	2	3	4			7	8	9^{2}	13	11^{1}		12		6		5	14			10^{3}		31
1	2	3	4		6	7	8	9		11^{1}						5	12			10		32
1	3		4		6	7^{3}		9	12	11			14	8^{2}		2	13	5■		10^{1}		33
1	2	3	4			7	8	9	13	11				6^{2}		5	10^{1}			12		34
1	2	3	4		6^{3}	7	8^{1}	9	10^{2}	11				13	14	5				12		35
1	2	3	4		6	7^{2}	8	9	10^{1}	11						5	13			12		36
1	2	3	4		6	7	8		9	11		12				5				10^{1}		37
1	2	3^{1}	4	5^{3}	6	7	8	9	10	11^{2}					14	12				13		38

PARTICK THISTLE

Year Formed: 1876. *Ground & Address:* Firhill Stadium, 80 Firhill Rd, Glasgow G20 7AL. *Telephone:* 0141 579 1971. *Fax:* 0141 945 1525. *E-mail:* mail@ptfc.co.uk *Website:* www.ptfc.co.uk
Ground Capacity: total: 13,141, seated: 10,921. *Size of Pitch:* 105yd × 68yd.
Acting Chairman: David Beattie. *Secretary:* Antonia Kerr.
Manager: Jackie McNamara. *Assistant Manager:* Simon Donnelly. *Coach:* Ian Cameron. *Head of Youth Development:* Gerry Britton. *Physio:* Kenny Crichton.
Club Nickname: The Jags.
Previous Grounds: Jordanvale Park; Muirpark; Inchview; Meadowside Park.
Record Attendance: 49,838 v Rangers, Division I, 18 Feb 1922. *Ground Record:* 54,728, Scotland v Ireland, 25 Feb 1928.
Record Transfer Fee received: £200,000 for Mo Johnston to Watford.
Record Transfer Fee paid: £85,000 for Andy Murdoch from Celtic (Feb 1991).
Record Victory: 16-0 v Royal Albert, Scottish Cup 1st rd, 17 Jan 1931.
Record Defeat: 0-10 v Queen's Park, Scottish Cup, 3 Dec 1881.
Most Capped Player: Alan Rough, 51 (53), Scotland.
Most League Appearances: 410: Alan Rough, 1969-82.
Most League Goals in Season (Individual): 41: Alex Hair, Division I, 1926-27.

PARTICK THISTLE 2011–12 LEAGUE RECORD

Match No.	*Date*	*Venue*	*Opponents*	*Result*		*H/T Score*	*Lg Pos.*	*Goalscorers*	*Attendance*
1	Aug 6	H	Dundee	L	0-1	0-0	—		3065
2	13	A	Falkirk	L	1-2	1-1	10	Doolan [36]	3036
3	20	H	Hamilton A	D	1-1	0-0	9	Elliot [66]	2501
4	27	H	Queen of the S	W	2-1	1-0	8	Doolan [20], Elliot [85]	2045
5	Sept 10	A	Ross Co	D	2-2	0-1	8	Cairney (pen) [73], Erskine [89]	2189
6	17	H	Ayr U	W	4-0	0-0	4	Rowson [49], Cairney [65], Erskine [73], Doolan (pen) [90]	2639
7	24	A	Livingston	L	1-2	0-1	6	Elliot [51]	2251
8	30	H	Morton	W	5-0	2-0	—	O'Donnell [3], Doolan [29], Elliot [76], Erskine [82], Stewart [89]	3380
9	Oct 15	A	Raith R	L	0-2	0-1	7		1769
10	22	H	Falkirk	D	2-2	0-1	6	Rowson [48], Erskine [90]	2851
11	29	A	Dundee	W	1-0	1-0	4	Cairney (pen) [26]	4263
12	Nov 5	H	Ross Co	L	0-1	0-1	6		2472
13	12	A	Queen of the S	D	0-0	0-0	7		1728
14	30	A	Ayr U	D	0-0	0-0	—		1122
15	Dec 3	H	Livingston	W	2-1	2-1	4	Balatoni [26], Deuchar (og) [33]	2026
16	10	A	Morton	W	2-1	1-0	4	Rowson [39], Doolan [88]	1849
17	17	H	Raith R	L	0-1	0-0	4		1918
18	26	H	Queen of the S	W	1-0	0-0	4	Doolan [48]	2261
19	Jan 13	A	Hamilton A	L	0-1	0-0	—		2401
20	21	H	Dundee	D	0-0	0-0	4		2425
21	Feb 11	A	Livingston	L	1-3	0-1	5	Cairney [88]	1824
22	18	H	Morton	D	0-0	0-0	6		2305
23	21	H	Ayr U	W	4-2	0-1	—	Doolan 2 [55, 64], Cairney 2 (1 pen) [81 (p), 90]	1439
24	25	A	Raith R	L	1-2	1-0	6	Doolan [28]	1535
25	Mar 3	H	Hamilton A	W	2-0	1-0	4	Doolan [18], Erskine [65]	2111
26	6	A	Ross Co	L	0-3	0-2	—		2200
27	10	A	Falkirk	D	1-1	1-0	4	Cairney [45]	3257
28	17	A	Queen of the S	W	5-0	2-0	4	Doolan 2 [17, 64], O'Donnell [42], Erskine [69], Elliot [85]	1689
29	24	H	Ross Co	L	0-1	0-1	5		2480
30	31	H	Livingston	L	2-3	1-1	6	Cairney [7], Sinclair [54]	1871
31	Apr 7	A	Ayr U	W	3-1	2-0	5	Erskine [27], Doolan [33], McGuigan [90]	1761
32	10	A	Morton	L	0-1	0-1	—		1637
33	14	H	Raith R	D	1-1	0-0	6	Welsh [64]	1832
34	21	A	Dundee	W	3-0	1-0	6	Cairney 3 (1 pen) [35, 81, 90 (p)]	3682
35	28	H	Falkirk	D	1-1	1-0	6	McGuigan [24]	2586
36	May 5	A	Hamilton A	D	2-2	2-2	6	Bannigan [36], Welsh [42]	1978

Final League Position: 6

Honours
League Champions: First Division 1975-76, 2001-02; *Runners-up:* 2008-09. Division II 1896-97, 1899-1900, 1970-71; Second Division 2000-01; *Runners-up:* First Division 1991-92. Division II 1901-02. *Promoted to First Division:* 2005-06 (play-offs).
Scottish Cup Winners: 1921; *Runners-up:* 1930; *Semi-finals:* 2002.
League Cup Winners: 1971-72; *Runners-up:* 1953-54, 1956-57, 1958-59.
League Challenge Cup: Quarter-finals 2004-05.

European: *Fairs Cup:* 4 matches (1963-64). *UEFA Cup:* 2 matches (1972-73). *Intertoto Cup:* 4 matches 1995-96.

Club colours: Shirt: Yellow with thin red stripes. Shorts: Black. Stockings: Black.

Goalscorers: *League (50):* Doolan 13 (1 pen), Cairney 11 (4 pens), Erskine 7, Elliot 5, Rowson 3, McGuigan 2, O'Donnell 2, Welsh 2, Balatoni 1, Bannigan 1, Sinclair 1, Stewart 1, own goal 1.
Scottish Cup (5): Cairney 3, Elliot 1, Erskline 1.
Scottish Communities Cup (1): Cairney 1.
Ramsdens Cup (2): Rowson 1, Stewart 1.

Fox S 31	Kinniburgh W 4 + 1	Archibald A 33	Sinclair A 29	Paton P 33	Cairney P 35	Rowson D 28 + 1	Robertson S 18 + 3	Erskine C 23 + 12	Stewart T 8 + 13	Doolan K 28 + 6	Balatoni C 21 + 3	Campbell J — + 2	Flannigan I 2 + 3	Elliot C 18 + 11	Lindsay J — + 1	Hutton K 12	O'Donnell S 28 + 3	Bannigan S 9 + 5	Scully R 5	Dargo C 3 + 1	Burns K 1 + 4	Cole D 6	Naismith K 4 + 4	Welsh S 10 + 2	Griffin G — + 2	Sekhon A 1	Wilson D 1	McGuigan M 4 + 3	McAleer C — + 1	Halsman B 1	*Match No.*
1	2^{1}	3	4	5	6^{2}	7	8^{3}	9	10	11	12	13	14																		1
1	2	3	4	5	6	7	8	10^{1}	9	11			12																		2
1		3	4^{3}	5	6	7	8^{2}		10^{1}	11	2	13	9	12	14																3
1		3	4	5	6	7	8	12	13	10	2^{2}		9^{1}	11																	4
1		4	5	2	6	8	3	12	9^{1}	10				11		7															5
1		2^{2}	3	4	6^{3}	7	5^{1}	8		10	12		14	11		9	13														6
1		3	4	5	6	7		8^{1}	13	11^{2}	2			10		9	12														7
1		4	5	2	6	7^{3}		13	12	11^{1}	3			10		8	9^{2}	14													8
1		3	4	5^{2}	6	7		13	12	10	2			11^{1}		9	8														9
1		2	3	6	8	9		12	13	10^{2}	7			11		4	5^{1}														10
		3	2	6	11	9		10^{3}	12	13	7			8^{2}		4	5^{1}	14	1												11
		2	3	5	7	8		9^{1}	13	10	6			11^{2}		4	12		1												12
1		4	9	2	8	7^{2}	14	13	11	10^{1}	3			12		6	5^{3}														13
1		2	3	6	8^{1}			9	10^{2}	12	7			11		4	5			13											14
1		2	3	7	9	10		12		13	8			6^{2}		4	5			11^{1}											15
1		3	4	7	8	9		12		13	6			10^{2}		5	2			11^{1}											16
1		2^{3}	3	5	7	8	14	12	13	9	6			11^{2}			4			10^{1}											17
1		3	4	6	7	8		12	11^{2}	10	5						2	9^{1}			13										18
1		4■	5	6	7^{3}	8		12	14	10				13			2				11^{1}	3	9^{2}								19
1			5	7	6	8	4	12	10^{1}	13				11^{2}			2					3	9								20
1				9	7	5^{1}	8	10		11				12			3	4^{2}				2	14	6^{3}	13						21
1		4	5	7	6^{1}	8		9	12	10				11			2					3									22
1		4	5	8	6	7		9^{2}		10				11^{1}			2	13				3	12								23
1		4	5	7■	6^{2}	8	12	9		10				13			2					3	11^{1}								24
1		3			6^{3}	8	7	9^{2}	12	10^{1}	5			11			2	14					13			4					25
1	9^{1}		3		5		7	8	14		4			10^{3}			2				12		11	13			6^{2}				26
1		4	2	8	7	6	10	5		11	9^{1}			13			3^{2}							12							27
	12	4	3	6	7^{2}	8	5^{1}	10	13	11^{3}				14			2		1					9							28
	10	2		4	8	6		9		11				12			3^{1}	7^{2}	1				13	5							29
		3	4	6	7	8^{1}	5^{2}	9		11							2	12	1					10				13			30
1		4	3	5	7		6	10^{1}		11							2	8						9				12			31
1		3	4^{2}	6	7		5^{1}	10		11	12						2^{3}	9						8				13	14		32
1		3		5	7			10		11^{1}	6			12			2	4						8				9			33
1		3		8	7		11	4^{1}			10			12			2	9			13			6				5^{2}			34
1		3			6		8	11^{1}		12	4			14			2	5						9	13			10^{3}		7^{2}	35
1		3		8		12	7	9		11	4^{2}						2^{1}	5			13			6				10			36

PETERHEAD

Year Formed: 1891. *Ground and Address:* Balmoor Stadium, Balmoor Terrace, Peterhead AB42 1EQ.
Telephone: 01779 478256. *Fax:* 01779 490682. *E-mail:* office@peterheadfc.co.uk *Website:* www.peterheadfc.co.uk
Ground Capacity: 3,250, seated 1,000.
Chairman: Rodger Morrison. *Vice-Chairman:* Ian Grant. *Secretary:* Brian McCombie.
Manager: Jim McInally. *Assistant coaches:* David Nicholls and Craig Tully. *Physio:* Greig Smith.
Club Nickname: Blue Toon.
Previous Ground: Recreation Park.
Record Attendance: 8,643 v Raith R, Scottish Cup 4th rd replay, 25 Feb 1987 (Recreation Park); 4,465 v Celtic, Scottish Cup 4th rd, 8 Jan 2012 (at Balmoor)
Record Victory: 17-0 v Fort William, 1998-99 (in Highland League).
Record Defeat: 0-13 v Aberdeen, Scottish Cup, 1923-24.
Most League Appearances: 262: Martin Bavidge, 2003-12.
Most League Goals in Season (Individual): 21: Iain Stewart, 2002-03; 21, Scott Michie, 2004-05.
Most Goals Overall (Individual): 93: Martin Bavidge, 2003-12.

PETERHEAD 2011–12 LEAGUE RECORD

Match No.	Date	Venue	Opponents	Result		H/T Score	Lg Pos.	Goalscorers	Attendance
1	Aug 6	A	Clyde	L	0-2	0-1	—		711
2	13	H	Annan Ath	L	2-3	2-1	9	Deasley [8], McAllister [41]	448
3	20	A	East Stirling	W	2-0	1-0	6	Deasley [38], McAllister (pen) [68]	287
4	27	A	Alloa Ath	L	1-2	1-0	8	McAllister [30]	507
5	Sept 10	H	Elgin C	L	1-3	0-3	9	Sellars [46]	596
6	17	A	Berwick R	L	1-2	1-2	9	McAllister (pen) [15]	334
7	24	H	Queen's Park	D	1-1	0-0	9	Bavidge [73]	478
8	Oct 1	A	Montrose	L	1-2	1-1	9	McAllister [12]	359
9	15	H	Stranraer	L	1-3	0-2	9	McAllister [68]	405
10	Nov 5	H	Clyde	D	0-0	0-0	9		517
11	8	A	Annan Ath	L	0-2	0-2	—		388
12	12	H	Alloa Ath	D	1-1	0-0	9	McDowall (og) [87]	528
13	Dec 3	A	Queen's Park	D	1-1	0-0	10	McAllister [48]	431
14	17	A	Stranraer	L	1-2	0-0	10	Deasley [58]	290
15	20	H	Berwick R	W	1-0	1-0	—	McAllister (pen) [45]	438
16	26	H	Montrose	L	2-3	0-1	9	Strachan [74], Bavidge [89]	566
17	Jan 2	H	Elgin C	W	3-0	2-0	9	McAllister (pen) [21], Sharp [45], Ross, S [72]	626
18	14	H	East Stirling	W	1-0	1-0	9	Wyness [35]	451
19	21	A	Clyde	W	1-0	1-0	9	Bavidge [3]	456
20	28	H	Queen's Park	W	2-1	0-1	7	McAllister 2 (1 pen) [62, 67 (p)]	505
21	31	A	Alloa Ath	L	1-3	1-2	—	McAllister [35]	429
22	Feb 11	H	Stranraer	D	1-1	1-1	8	McAllister (pen) [42]	435
23	14	A	Elgin C	L	1-6	0-1	—	Redman [80]	431
24	18	A	Montrose	W	3-1	1-0	7	Webster [32], Ross, D [51], Bavidge [54]	358
25	25	H	Annan Ath	W	3-2	0-2	7	Tully [55], Bavidge 2 [60, 79]	453
26	28	A	Berwick R	W	1-0	0-0	—	Bavidge [83]	278
27	Mar 3	A	East Stirling	L	3-6	1-5	7	Sharp [1], MacDonald [50], McBain [57]	277
28	10	A	Elgin C	W	2-1	1-1	6	Bavidge [38], Redman [53]	1072
29	17	H	Alloa Ath	L	0-1	0-1	6		488
30	24	H	Berwick R	L	1-2	0-1	7	McAllister (pen) [49]	396
31	31	A	Queen's Park	W	1-0	0-0	7	McAllister [54]	441
32	Apr 7	H	Montrose	W	2-1	1-0	7	McAllister 2 [9, 65]	458
33	14	A	Stranraer	W	3-0	1-0	7	McAllister 2 [34, 75], McBain [82]	291
34	21	H	Clyde	D	1-1	0-0	7	Gray (og) [48]	497
35	28	A	Annan Ath	W	3-0	1-0	6	Deasley [21], MacDonald [49], McAllister [84]	408
36	May 5	H	East Stirling	W	2-0	1-0	5	Redman [12], Ross, S [50]	494

Final League Position: 5

Honours
Third Division Runners up: 2004-05.
Scottish Cup: Quarter-finals 2001.
Highland League Champions: winners 5 times.
Scottish Qualifying Cup (North): winners 6 times.
North of Scotland Cup: winners 5 times.
Aberdeenshire Cup: winners: 20 times.

Club colours: Shirt: Royal blue shirts with two white stripes. Shorts: White. Stockings: Royal blue and white hoops.

Goalscorers: *League (51):* McAllister 20 (7 pens), Bavidge 8, Deasley 4, Redman 3, MacDonald 2, McBain 2, Ross, S. 2, Sharp 2, Ross, D. 1, Sellars 1, Strachan 1, Tully 1, Webster 1, Wyness 1, own goals 2.
Scottish Cup (6): Bavidge 2, McAllister 1, MacDonald 1, Redman 1, Ross, S. 1.
Scottish Communities Cup (0).
Ramsdens Cup (4): McAllister 2 (1 pen), Deasley 1, Redman 1.

Jellema R 18 + 3	Davidson L 8 + 11	Donald D 34 + 2	McBain R 29	Rattray A 4 + 2	Redman J 33	Sharp G 20 + 8	Watson P 5 + 1	Deasley B 23 + 6	Bavidge M 26 + 6	McAllister R 33 + 1	Conway A 4 + 5	Ross D 14 + 9	Duffy N 1	MacDonald C 31 + 1	Sellars B 8	Wyness D 8 + 21	Wood G 3 + 1	Bishop J 3	Ross S 22 + 2	Jarvie P 17	Strachan R 26 + 2	Robertson S — + 4	Kelly D — + 1	Tully C 10 + 1	Webster G 5 + 2	Smith R 6 + 2	Duncan R 5	Match No.
1	2	3	4	5	6	7^{2}	8	9	10^{1}	11	12	13																1
		2	4		6	12	7^{3}	9	11^{2}	10	8^{1}	14	1	3	5	13												2
1	4	2	5	3	7	12		9^{1}	11	10		8			6													3
1	5^{1}	2	4	3	7	13		9	11^{3}	10	14	8^{2}		12	6													4
1		2	5	3	6	12	8^{1}	13	14	9				4	7	10^{2}	11^{3}											5
1		2	4^{3}	14	8^{2}	7	13	9	12	11					6		10^{1}	3	5									6
	7	2				9			5^{3}	11	10^{1}	12		3	8	14		4	6^{2}	1	13							7
	5	2				7^{2}			11	10	9^{3}	14		3	8^{1}		13	4	6	1	12							8
		2		12			5^{2}	9	10	11	6^{1}			4	8^{3}	14	3		13	1	7							9
1	5	2			7			9		11^{1}		8		4		10			3		6	12						10
1		2			7		6^{1}	11		10		9		3		8			5		4		12					11
1	5	2			7			9	12	10		8		4		11^{1}			3		6							12
1		2^{1}	5		7	12		9	11^{2}	10		8		3		13			4		6							13
1		2	5		7	8^{3}		10^{1}	12	11^{2}		9		3		13			4		6	14						14
1	14	3	2		8	7^{1}		10	12	9^{2}		11^{3}		4		13			5		6							15
1		2	5^{3}		7	8^{2}		11	12	10	14	9^{1}		4		13			3		6							16
		2	5		7	8		13	11^{1}	10^{3}	14	9^{2}		4		12			3	1	6							17
	12	2	5		8	7^{2}		9	11		13			4		10			3^{1}	1	6							18
	14	2	5^{3}		7	12		9^{2}	11	10		13		4		8^{1}			3	1	6							19
		5	6		8	12		9^{2}	10^{3}	11		13		4		14				1	3			2	7^{1}			20
		2	5		8	7^{2}		12	11	10		9^{1}		3		13			4^{3}	1	6			14				21
15		2	5		7	6^{2}		9^{1}	11	10		13		4		12			3	1^{6}	8							22
		2	5		7	8^{3}		13	11	10		9^{1}		4		14			3^{2}	1	6					12		23
		5	7		9				11	10^{1}		12		4		13				1	6			3	8^{2}	2		24
15	2^{1}	13	5		8	9			11	10▮		6		4		12				1^{6}				3	7^{2}			25
1		13	4		6	5		12	10			9^{1}		3		11^{2}					7			2	8			26
1	13	5^{2}	2		8	9		12		11				3▮		10^{3}					7	14		4	6^{1}			27
	13	2	4		8	7		9	11^{2}	10^{1}						12				1	5			3			6	28
		5	6		7	9^{2}		11		10		12		4		13				1	2			3^{1}			8	29
		2	5^{3}		7	9^{1}			11	10				4		14			12	1	6			3^{2}		13	8	30
1	14	5	2		8	9^{1}			10^{2}	11^{3}				4		13			3		7				12		6	31
1	14	5	7		8				11	10^{3}				3					2		6^{1}	13			12^{2}	4	9	32
	12	5	7		8			9	11	10^{2}				3		13			2	1				6^{1}		4		33
15	12	5			8			9	11^{2}	10^{1}				4		13			3	1^{6}	6			7		2		34
1	12	5	7		8	9^{2}		10	11	13				3					2		6^{1}					4		35
1	13	5	7^{1}		8	12		9	11^{3}	10^{2}				4		14			3		6					2		36

QUEEN OF THE SOUTH

Year Formed: 1919. *Ground & Address:* Palmerston Park, Dumfries DG2 9BA. *Telephone:* 01387 254853.
Fax: 01387 240470. *E-mail:* admin@qosfc.com *Website:* www.qosfc.com
Ground Capacity: 6,412 *Size of Pitch:* 112yd × 73yd.
Chairman: David Rae. *Vice-Chairman:* Craig Paterson. *Club Secretary:* Eric Moffat.
Manager: Allan Johnston. *Assistant Manager:* Sandy Clark. *Physio:* John Kerr.
Club Nickname: The Doonhamers.
Previous Grounds: None.
Record Attendance: 26,552 v Hearts, Scottish Cup 3rd rd, 23 Feb 1952.
Record Transfer Fee received: £250,000 for Andy Thomson to Southend U (1994).
Record Transfer Fee paid: £30,000 for Jim Butter from Alloa Athletic (1995).
Record Victory: 11-1 v Stranraer, Scottish Cup 1st rd, 16 Jan 1932.
Record Defeat: 2-10 v Dundee, Division I, 1 Dec 1962.
Most Capped Player: Billy Houliston, 3, Scotland.
Most League Appearances: 731: Allan Ball, 1963-82.
Most League Goals in Season (Individual): 37: Jimmy Gray, Division II, 1927-28.
Most Goals in Season: 41: Jimmy Rutherford, 1931-32.
Most Goals Overall (Individual): 250: Jim Patterson, 1949-63.

QUEEN OF THE SOUTH 2011–12 LEAGUE RECORD

Match No.	Date	Venue	Opponents	Result		H/T Score	Lg Pos.	Goalscorers	Attendance
1	Aug 6	A	Livingston	D	2-2	2-0	—	McLaughlin [19], Brighton [32]	1444
2	13	H	Raith R	L	1-3	1-0	8	Smith (pen) [45]	1602
3	20	A	Ross Co	L	0-2	0-0	10		2065
4	27	A	Partick Th	L	1-2	0-1	10	Campbell [61]	2045
5	Sept 10	H	Hamilton A	W	1-0	0-0	10	Johnston [51]	1514
6	17	H	Morton	W	4-1	4-0	7	Smith 3 [20, 35, 38], Brighton [30]	1699
7	24	A	Ayr U	L	0-1	0-0	9		1582
8	Oct 1	H	Dundee	D	0-0	0-0	8		1649
9	15	A	Falkirk	L	0-1	0-0	9		3094
10	22	A	Raith R	W	2-0	1-0	8	McLaughlin [18], Brighton [75]	1523
11	29	H	Livingston	L	0-2	0-1	9		1556
12	Nov 5	A	Hamilton A	L	1-3	1-1	10	Smith [31]	1836
13	12	H	Partick Th	D	0-0	0-0	10		1728
14	26	A	Morton	D	2-2	1-1	10	McLaughlin [2], McKenna [57]	1352
15	Dec 3	H	Ayr U	W	4-1	1-1	8	McKenna [31], McLaughlin (pen) [71], Carmichael [72], Simmons [89]	1478
16	10	A	Dundee	L	1-2	0-2	8	Higgins [56]	5019
17	17	H	Falkirk	L	1-5	1-1	9	McLaughlin [34]	1466
18	26	A	Partick Th	L	0-1	0-0	10		2261
19	Jan 2	H	Hamilton A	L	1-2	0-2	10	McGuffie [82]	1282
20	14	H	Ross Co	D	0-0	0-0	10		1314
21	21	A	Livingston	D	2-2	1-1	10	Brighton [16], McGuffie (pen) [81]	1286
22	28	H	Morton	W	2-1	0-0	—	Parkin 2 [58, 65]	1444
23	Feb 11	A	Ayr U	D	1-1	0-0	9	Simmons [76]	1475
24	18	H	Dundee	D	1-1	1-0	8	Parkin [44]	1682
25	25	A	Falkirk	L	0-3	0-2	10		2982
26	Mar 3	A	Ross Co	L	1-2	0-1	10	McGuffie [57]	2578
27	10	H	Raith R	W	1-0	0-0	10	Reilly [82]	1561
28	17	H	Partick Th	L	0-5	0-2	10		1689
29	24	A	Hamilton A	L	0-3	0-0	10		1631
30	31	H	Ayr U	W	2-1	2-0	10	Johnston [14], Parkin [24]	2079
31	Apr 7	A	Morton	D	2-2	0-1	10	Parkin [60], Carmichael [79]	1622
32	10	A	Dundee	D	1-1	0-0	—	Potter [82]	3371
33	14	H	Falkirk	D	0-0	0-0	10		1446
34	21	H	Livingston	L	0-4	0-2	10		1403
35	28	A	Raith R	L	1-3	0-1	10	Carmichael [58]	2400
36	May 5	H	Ross Co	L	3-5	2-2	10	Carmichael [10], Parkin [15], Reilly [53]	1323

Final League Position: 10

Honours
League Champions: Division II 1950-51. Second Division 2001-02. *Runners-up:* Division II 1932-33, 1961-62, 1974-75. Second Division 1980-81, 1985-86.
Scottish Cup Runners-up: 2007-08.
League Cup: semi-finals 1950-51, 1960-61.
B&Q Cup: semi-finals 1991-92. *League Challenge Cup Winners:* 2002-03; *Runners-up:* 1997-98, 2010-11.

European: *UEFA Cup:* 2 matches (2008-09).

Club colours: Shirt: Royal blue with white trim. Shorts: Royal blue. Stockings: Royal blue.

Goalscorers: *League (38):* Parkin 6, McLaughlin 5 (1 pen), Smith 5 (1 pen), Brighton 4, Carmichael 4, McGuffie 3 (1 pen), Johnston 2, McKenna 2, Reilly 2, Simmons 2, Campbell 1, Higgins 1, Potter 1.
Scottish Cup (3): Carmichael 1, McGuffie 1 (pen), McLaughlin 1.
Scottish Communities Cup (5): Brighton 2, Carmichael 1, Clark 1, Johnston 1.
Ramsdens Cup (0).

McKenzie R 2	Reid C 26	Higgins C 31 + 1	Campbell M 15	McGuffie R 26 + 4	Simmons S 23 + 6	Clark N 19 + 11	McLaughlin S 35	Brighton T 15 + 6	Smith K 17 + 6	Carmichael D 27 + 7	Reid A 23 + 5	Smylie R — + 8	McShane I 1 + 3	Robinson L 34	Johnston A 31	McKenna S 24 + 6	Holt K 13 + 4	Black S 3 + 3	McCusker M — + 7	Reilly G 3 + 11	Parkin S 15	Potter J 12 + 1	Orsi D 1 + 1	*Match No.*
1	2■	3	4	5	6	7	8	9^2	10^1	11	12	13												1
1		5	4	3	7	6^1	8	9	11■	10	2		12											2
	2	3	5		4	12	8	9		10	6	13	11^2	1	7^1									3
	2	4	3		8	12	9	13	10^2	11^1	5			1	6	7								4
	3	5	4^2	13	7	14	9	10^3	11^1	12	2			1	6	8								5
	2	5	3	4	8	12	9	10^1	11^3	13				1	6^2	7	14							6
	2	3	5	6	4	12	11	9^2		10^3		14		1	7^1	8	13							7
		5	3	4	8	10^3		9^1		11	2	14	13	1	6^2	7	12							8
	2^1	3	4	5	7	13	8^3	9	10	11^2	12			1	6			14						9
	2	5	3	4	8	9^1	7	12	11		10			1	6^2				13					10
	2^3	5^2	3	4	7		8	11^1	10		9			1	6	13	14		12					11
	2	5	3	4	8	10^1	9		11	13				1	6^2	7			12					12
	2	4		3		11^1	8	13	10^2	6				1	9	7	5		12					13
	2	3			13		8	10	11^1	9				1	5^2	6	7	4	12					14
	2	3			8	12	9	11^2	13	10	4			1	5^1	7	6							15
	3	2^2			5^1	13	8	14	11	10	12			1	6	7	9■	4^3						16
	2	4	3		7	10	8^2		11	12	5			1	9^1	6			13					17
	2		3	4	7^3	10	9	12	11^2	14	5			1	6	8^1			13					18
	2	12	3^1	4	7	9	8		11	10	5			1		6^2				13				19
	2	4		3		9	7	11^1		10				1	8	6	5			12				20
	2■	4		3		9	6	11^2		10	12	14		1	8	7^3	5^1			13				21
		4		3	12	6	8			9	2	13		1	7^1		5			11^2	10			22
		6		5	12	13	8			11	3			1	7	4^1				10^2	9	2		23
	3			2	7^1	9	8			10	5			1	6^2	12				13	11	4		24
	2^1	3		6	7	9^3	8			10^2	5	14		1		12				13	11	4		25
	2	5		3		10	9	13		12	6			1	7^3	8				14	11^2	4^1		26
		5		3	13		8^2	11^1	12	9^3	2			1	7	6				14	10	4		27
		5		3	13		8^2	9^1	14	11	2			1	7^3	6				12	10	4		28
	5	4		2	14	11^1	9^3			12	6^2			1	8	7				13	10	3		29
	3	4		13	6	12	9^1			10				1	8	5^2	7				11	2		30
	2	4		12	6	14	7		13	10				1	9^3	5^1	8^2				11	3		31
	2^1	3^3		12	7	9	8^2		13	10	5			1	6	14					11	4		32
		3		4	8^1	11^2	9^3		13	6	2			1	7	12	5	14			10			33
		4■		3		8^3	7^2		11^1	9	2			1	6	14	5			13	10	12		34
				3			7		11^1	9	2^3			1	6^2	8	5	14		12	10	4	13	35
				2			7^3			9	12	13	14	1		6	5^1	4		11	10	3	8^2	36

QUEEN'S PARK

Year Formed: 1867. *Ground & Address:* Hampden Park, Mount Florida, Glasgow G42 9BA. *Telephone:* 0141 632 1275. *Fax:* 0141 636 1612. *E-mail:* secretary@queensparkfc.co.uk *Website:* queensparkfc.co.uk
Ground Capacity: all seated: 52,000. *Size of Pitch:* 115yd × 75yd.
President: Alan Hutchison. *Secretary:* Alistair MacKay. *Treasurer:* David Gordon.
Head Coach: Gardner Spiers. *Physios:* R. C. Findlay and A. Myles.
Club Nickname: The Spiders.
Previous Grounds: 1st Hampden (Recreation Ground); (Titwood Park was used as an interim measure between 1st & 2nd Hampdens); 2nd Hampden (Cathkin); 3rd Hampden.
Record Attendance: 95,772 v Rangers, Scottish Cup, 18 Jan 1930.
Record for Ground: 149,547 Scotland v England, 1937.
Record Transfer Fee received: Not applicable due to amateur status.
Record Transfer Fee paid: Not applicable due to amateur status.
Record Victory: 16-0 v St. Peters, Scottish Cup 1st rd, 29 Aug 1885.
Record Defeat: 0-9 v Motherwell, Division I, 26 Apr 1930.
Most Capped Player: Walter Arnott, 14, Scotland.
Most League Appearances: 532: Ross Caven, 1982-2002.
Most League Goals in Season (Individual): 30: William Martin, Division I, 1937-38.
Most Goals Overall (Individual): 163: James B. McAlpine, 1919-33.

QUEEN'S PARK 2011–12 LEAGUE RECORD

Match No.	Date	Venue	Opponents	Result		H/T Score	Lg Pos.	Goalscorers	Attendance
1	Aug 6	A	Annan Ath	L	2-5	2-2	—	Smith 2 [18, 27]	511
2	13	H	Stranraer	W	2-0	1-0	7	Longworth [34], Daly [46]	626
3	20	A	Elgin C	L	0-2	0-2	9		591
4	27	H	Berwick R	D	1-1	0-1	7	Daly [60]	504
5	Sept 10	A	Clyde	W	2-0	0-0	6	Longworth [82], Daly [86]	650
6	17	H	Alloa Ath	L	1-3	0-2	7	Quinn [86]	589
7	24	A	Peterhead	D	1-1	0-0	7	Watt [52]	478
8	Oct 1	A	East Stirling	W	3-1	0-0	6	Watt [54], Murray [80], McBride [83]	384
9	15	H	Montrose	W	3-1	0-1	6	Daly [55], Longworth 2 [81, 87]	529
10	29	A	Stranraer	W	3-2	1-2	3	Longworth [12], Smith [72], Watt [89]	390
11	Nov 5	H	Annan Ath	D	0-0	0-0	4		502
12	12	A	Berwick R	L	0-2	0-0	6		449
13	Dec 3	H	Peterhead	D	1-1	0-0	7	Murray [82]	431
14	10	A	Alloa Ath	L	0-1	0-1	7		449
15	13	H	Clyde	W	3-0	1-0	—	Burns [4], Smith [63], Daly [84]	402
16	24	H	East Stirling	W	2-0	1-0	—	Watt [38], Smith [67]	504
17	Jan 2	A	Clyde	W	2-1	1-1	4	Longworth [6], Daly [78]	668
18	14	H	Elgin C	W	6-0	1-0	4	McBride [35], Longworth 4 [53, 67, 71, 78], Smith [80]	344
19	21	A	Annan Ath	W	3-2	1-1	3	McBride 2 (2 pens) [19, 51], Smith [88]	507
20	28	A	Peterhead	L	1-2	1-0	4	Burns [34]	505
21	Feb 4	H	Alloa Ath	L	1-2	0-2	4	Daly [85]	711
22	11	H	Montrose	W	5-0	1-0	3	Longworth 2 [5, 77], McBride [50], Daly [63], Quinn [90]	426
23	18	A	East Stirling	W	2-1	0-0	3	Longworth 2 [79, 90]	346
24	21	H	Berwick R	D	2-2	1-1	—	Watt [26], Quinn [90]	413
25	25	H	Stranraer	W	3-2	1-2	3	Murray 2 [33, 62], Ronald [81]	637
26	28	A	Montrose	W	1-0	0-0	—	Longworth [89]	303
27	Mar 3	A	Elgin C	D	1-1	1-1	2	Daly [37]	792
28	17	A	Berwick R	W	4-1	0-0	3	Brough [54], McBride [61], Forster (og) [64], Daly [79]	428
29	20	H	Clyde	W	3-0	2-0	—	Longworth [7], Watt [10], McBride [89]	658
30	24	A	Alloa Ath	L	0-4	0-1	3		807
31	31	H	Peterhead	L	0-1	0-0	3		441
32	Apr 7	H	East Stirling	W	5-1	1-0	3	Longworth [32], Quinn 2 [49, 57], Burns [67], McBride (pen) [88]	477
33	14	A	Montrose	L	1-3	1-1	3	Quinn [25]	336
34	21	H	Annan Ath	W	2-0	1-0	2	Longworth [30], Watt [71]	623
35	28	A	Stranraer	W	3-2	1-0	2	Longworth 2 [10, 65], Quinn [67]	458
36	May 5	H	Elgin C	L	1-3	0-1	2	Smith [88]	527

Final League Position: 2

Honours
League Champions: Division II 1922-23. B Division 1955-56. Second Division 1980-81. Third Division 1999-2000.
Promoted to Second Division: 2006-07 (play-offs).
Scottish Cup Winners: 1874, 1875, 1876, 1880, 1881, 1882, 1884, 1886, 1890, 1893; *Runners-up:* 1892, 1900.
FA Cup Runners-up: 1884, 1885.

Club colours: Shirt: White with thin black hoops. Shorts: White. Stockings: White.

Goalscorers: *League (70):* Longworth 20, Daly 10, McBride 8 (3 pens), Smith 8, Quinn 7, Watt 7, Murray 4, Burns 3, Brough 1, Ronald 1, own goal 1.
Scottish Cup (7): Smith 3, Burns 1, Longworth 1, McBride 1 (pen), Murray 1.
Scottish Communities Cup (1): Daly 1.
Ramsdens Cup (0).
Play-Offs (1): Quinn 1.

Parry N 34	Little R 33	Brough J 22	Meggatt D 31	Gallagher P 10 + 7	McGinn P 34	Anderson D 29	Daly M 18 + 12	Smith C 14 + 13	Watt I 29 + 3	Murray D 19 + 7	Longworth J 33 + 2	Kennedy K — + 1	Urquhart A 2	Burns S 20 + 6	Stewart P 4 + 6	Quinn T 6 + 15	Capuano G 5 + 1	Bradley P 12 + 1	Lauchlan G 1	McBride M 29	Ronald O 7 + 12	Lockhead B — + 1	Strain A 2	Baillie S 2	McVey C — + 1	*Match No.*
1	2	3	4	5	6	7	8	9	10^{2}	11^{1}	12	13														1
1	3	4	5	2	6		8^{2}	9^{3}	14		11		7^{1}	10	12	13										2
1	3	4	5	7	2		10	6^{1}	12		11			9	13		8^{2}									3
1	2	3	4	5^{2}	6	8	9^{3}			13	10		7^{1}	11	12	14										4
1	3		5^{1}	12	2		8^{3}	13		10	11			9^{2}	7	14	6	4								5
1	3			4	2		10^{3}	14	12	9	7			11^{1}	8	13		5	6^{2}							6
1	2	5			4	7	10^{3}	13	9^{2}	8^{1}	11			12		14		3		6						7
1	6■	3	4		7	2			9	10	11					8				5						8
1		2	3	14	5	7	8^{2}	12	10^{1}	11	6			9	13					4^{3}						9
1	2	3^{1}	4		6	7^{2}	8^{3}	14	11	12	9			10	13					5						10
1	3		4	7	2		10	12	9^{1}	11	8			5						6						11
1	3		4		2	6	13	12	9^{2}	11	10			5	7^{1}					8						12
1	2	3	4		6	7	13	10^{2}	9^{1}	11	8				12					5						13
1	2	5	4		3	7	13	10^{1}	9^{2}	8	11			12						6						14
1	2	3	4		6	8	14	10	9^{2}		12			11^{3}	7^{1}					5	13					15
1	3	4	5^{2}	12	2	8	13	10^{3}	9	11	7			14						6^{1}						16
1	2	3		13	5	6	12	10^{1}	8^{3}	9	11			7						4^{2}	14					17
1	2	3	4		6	7	14	10	9^{2}	11^{1}	8^{3}			12						5	13					18
1	2		4	3	6	7		10	8		11			9						5						19
1	2		4	3	6	7	12	10	8^{2}		11			9^{1}		13				5						20
1	3		5	4	2	8	12	10^{2}	9^{1}		7			11						6	13					21
1	3	4	5		2	8	10^{3}		9^{2}	11^{1}	7			12		13				6	14					22
1		2	3		5	6	7^{1}		10	11^{2}	9			8		12				4	13					23
1	2		3		6	7	8^{2}	13	10^{3}		9			11^{1}		14		4		5	12					24
1	2		3		6	7		10^{1}	9	11^{2}	8					12		4		5	13					25
1	2	3	4		6	7		10^{1}	8^{2}	9	11					12				5	13					26
1■	3		4		7	8	6^{1}		10^{6}	9^{2}	11					12		5		2	13	15				27
	5	4	3	14		9^{2}	12		11		10					7^{1}	13	2		6^{3}	8		1			28
1	3	4	5^{2}		2	8	10^{3}		11^{1}	12	7					14		13		6	9					29
1	2	3■		14	6	7	9^{1}		10^{2}	13	11					12		4		5	8^{3}					30
1	4		3		5		11^{3}	14	10^{1}	12	8					13	9	2		7	6^{2}					31
1	2		3		6	7		13	10	11^{1}	9^{3}			12		8^{2}		4		5	14					32
1	3				6	8	14	13		12	11			10		9^{3}		4^{1}		5	7^{2}			2		33
1	2	3	4		6	7		13	10^{1}	14	9			11^{3}		8^{2}				5	12					34
1	2	3	4	12	6	8^{1}	13				10			11		9	5				7^{2}					35
			4	3			9^{2}	13	10					11			6^{1}	5		7	8		1	2	12	36

RAITH ROVERS

Year Formed: 1883. *Ground & Address:* Stark's Park, Pratt St, Kirkcaldy KY1 1SA. *Telephone:* 01592 263514. *Fax:* 01592 642833. *E-mail:* info@raithrovers.net *Website:* www.raithroversfc.com
Ground Capacity: all seated: 10,104. *Size of Pitch:* 113yd × 70yd.
General Manager & Secretary: Bob Mullen.
Manager: John McGlynn. *Assistant Manager:* Paul Smith.
Club Nickname: Rovers.
Previous Grounds: Robbie's Park.
Record Attendance: 31,306 v Hearts, Scottish Cup 2nd rd, 7 Feb 1953.
Record Transfer Fee received: £900,000 for Steve McAnespie to Bolton Wanderers (Sept 1995).
Record Transfer Fee paid: £225,000 for Paul Harvey from Airdrieonians (1996).
Record Victory: 10-1 v Coldstream, Scottish Cup 2nd rd, 13 Feb 1954.
Record Defeat: 2-11 v Morton, Division II, 18 Mar 1936.
Most Capped Player: David Morris, 6, Scotland.
Most League Appearances: 430: Willie McNaught, 1946-51.
Most League Goals in Season (Individual): 38: Norman Haywood, Division II, 1937-38.
Most Goals Overall (Individual): 154: Gordon Dalziel (League), 1987-94.

RAITH ROVERS 2011–12 LEAGUE RECORD

Match No.	Date	Venue	Opponents	Result		H/T Score	Lg Pos.	Goalscorers	Attendance
1	Aug 6	H	Falkirk	W	1-0	1-0	—	Hamill ^{45}	2695
2	13	A	Queen of the S	W	3-1	0-1	2	Baird 2 $^{67, 77}$, Graham ^{88}	1602
3	20	H	Morton	D	1-1	1-1	2	Reynolds ^{31}	2109
4	27	A	Ayr U	L	1-2	1-1	3	Hamill ^{34}	1570
5	Sept 10	H	Dundee	L	0-1	0-0	3		2459
6	17	A	Hamilton A	D	2-2	1-0	5	Baird ^{45}, Hamill ^{62}	1982
7	24	H	Ross Co	L	0-1	0-0	7		1479
8	Oct 1	A	Livingston	D	1-1	0-0	7	Graham ^{60}	2011
9	15	H	Partick Th	W	2-0	1-0	6	Ellis ^{31}, Baird ^{56}	1769
10	22	H	Queen of the S	L	0-2	0-1	7		1523
11	29	A	Falkirk	L	0-2	0-0	7		3628
12	Nov 5	A	Dundee	L	0-1	0-0	8		4258
13	12	H	Ayr U	L	0-1	0-1	9		2038
14	26	H	Hamilton A	W	3-2	1-1	8	Holt ^{9}, Prychynenko ^{61}, Smith ^{79}	1416
15	Dec 3	A	Ross Co	L	2-4	2-2	10	Walker, A 2 $^{12, 36}$	2698
16	10	H	Livingston	L	0-1	0-0	10		1604
17	17	A	Partick Th	W	1-0	0-0	8	Baird ^{66}	1918
18	26	A	Ayr U	D	1-1	1-0	8	Baird ^{42}	1407
19	Jan 2	H	Dundee	L	0-1	0-1	8		3629
20	14	A	Morton	D	1-1	0-0	8	Murray ^{55}	1739
21	21	H	Falkirk	D	2-2	2-1	8	Murray ^{27}, Baird ^{33}	2026
22	Feb 11	H	Ross Co	D	1-1	0-0	8	Walker, J ^{89}	1702
23	18	A	Livingston	L	0-4	0-1	9		1929
24	21	A	Hamilton A	L	1-2	0-1	—	Graham ^{59}	1276
25	25	H	Partick Th	W	2-1	0-1	8	Graham ^{63}, Baird ^{72}	1535
26	Mar 3	H	Morton	W	5-0	1-0	8	Graham 2 $^{35, 46}$, Baird ^{59}, Walker, J ^{86}, Williamson ^{90}	1480
27	10	A	Queen of the S	L	0-1	0-0	9		1561
28	17	H	Ayr U	D	2-2	1-0	9	Graham ^{13}, Casalinuovo ^{90}	1861
29	24	A	Dundee	D	1-1	1-1	9	Casalinuovo ^{45}	4118
30	31	A	Ross Co	D	1-1	0-0	9	Clarke (pen) ^{90}	3379
31	Apr 7	H	Hamilton A	W	2-1	0-1	8	Casalinuovo ^{55}, Walker, A ^{61}	1526
32	10	H	Livingston	L	0-3	0-2	—		1541
33	14	A	Partick Th	D	1-1	0-0	8	Paton (og) ^{74}	1832
34	21	A	Falkirk	W	3-2	2-1	8	Graham 3 (1 pen) $^{24 (p), 45, 69}$	3024
35	28	H	Queen of the S	W	3-1	1-0	8	Graham ^{15}, Baird ^{54}, Clarke ^{90}	2400
36	May 5	A	Morton	W	3-1	1-0	7	Walker, J ^{16}, Clarke 2 $^{52, 54}$	1813

Final League Position: 7

Honours
League Champions: First Division 1992-93, 1994-95. Second Division 2008-09. Division II 1907-08, 1909-10 (shared), 1937-38, 1948-49; *Runners-up:* Division II 1908-09, 1926-27, 1966-67. Second Division 1975-76, 1977-78, 1986-87.
Scottish Cup Runners-up: 1913. *League Cup Winners:* 1994-95. *Runners-up:* 1948-49.

European: *UEFA Cup:* 6 matches (1995-96).

Club colours: Shirt: Navy blue with white trim. Shorts: White. Stockings: White.

Goalscorers: *League (46):* Graham 11 (1 pen), Baird 10, Clarke 4 (1 pen), Casalinuovo 3, Hamill 3, Walker, A. 3, Walker, J. 3, Murray 2, Ellis 1, Holt 1, Prychynenko 1, Reynolds 1, Smith 1, Williamson 1, own goal 1.
Scottish Cup (1): Clarke 1.
Scottish Communities Cup (4): Baird 1, Thomson 1, Walker, A. 1, Williamson 1.
Ramsdens Cup (2): Baird 2.

McGurn D 34	Donaldson R 21	Murray G 36	Ellis L 30 + 2	Dyer W 30 + 4	Davidson I 21 + 2	Williamson I 17 + 10	Walker A 36	Hamill J 30 + 3	Baird J 34 + 1	Graham B 19 + 5	Thomson D 6 + 8	Reynolds S 1 + 10	Hill D 28 + 1	McBride S 1 + 3	Callachan R 1 + 5	Prychynenko D 4 + 1	Wilson C — + 1	Holt J 3 + 2	Walker J 10 + 13	Smith D 6 + 2	Clarke P 7 + 8	Casalinuovo D 9 + 6	Laidlaw R 2	Thomson J 9	Stewart J 1 + 3	Vaughan L — + 1	Match No.
1	2	3	4	5	6¹	7	8	9	10	11²	12	13															1
1	2	3	5	12		6	7	9	10	11²	8	13	4¹														2
1	2	3	4	12		6	7	9	10		8³	11²	5¹	13	14												3
1	2	3	5	12		6	7	9	10	11			4¹		8▪												4
1	2	3	5			6²	7	9	10	11	8¹	13	4	12													5
1	2¹	6	4	3		7²	8	9	10³	11	12	13	5	14													6
1	2	3	6¹	5	12	7²	8	9³	10	11	13	14	4														7
1	2	4	7	5	6¹	12	8	9	11²	10³	13	14	3▪														8
1	2	3	4	5	6¹	7	8	9	10	11					12												9
1	2	3	4	5	6²	7¹	8	9	10	11	13	12															10
1	2	3	4	5		7¹	8	9	10	11²	12	13	6														11
1	2	5	4¹	3		7²	8	9	10	11		13	6			12											12
1		2	3	5		6³	8		10	11	7²	13	4¹		14	9	12										13
1		2	3	5			6	12	11	13			4			10		7²	8¹	9							14
1		2	3¹	5	12		6		11	13	14		4			10		7³	8²	9							15
1		3	4	2	5		8	14	10	12			13			7²		6¹	11³	9							16
1	2	6	4	5²	7	12	8	10	11				3						13	9¹							17
1	2	4	5		6¹	12²	7³	9	10		13		3					14	8	11							18
1	2	3	5	12	6		7³	8	10				4¹					14	9²	11	13						19
1	2	3		5	4	6	7	8	9²										13	12	10	11¹					20
1	2³	4	14	5	3	6¹	7	8	9										13	12	10	11²					21
1	2	4		5	3	6	7	8	10	12									13		9¹	11²					22
1	2	4	14	5	3▪	6²	7	8	11						13				12		9¹	10³					23
1	2	6	4	5			8	9	10	11¹			3						7²		13	12					24
1	2	4	3	5	8		7¹	9	10	11²			6						12		13						25
		6	4	5	7	12	8	9	11²	10³			3¹						13			14	1	2			26
		7	4	5	6	14	8	9³	10²				3						13		12	11¹	1	2			27
1		3	6	5	7		8	9²	10¹	11▪			4³						12		13	14		2			28
1		3	6	5	7		8	9	10³				4²						14		12	11¹		2	13		29
1		6	4	3	7	12	8	9					5¹						13		10	11²		2			30
1		7	5	6	3	14	8³	9¹	10				4						12		13	11²		2			31
1		6	3	5		12	7	13	11	14			4						9²			10³		2	8¹		32
1		6	4	3		7³	8		13	9	2		5	11²					12		10¹				14		33
1		8	4¹	2		14	7	6	11²	10	5		3						9³			13			12		34
1		3		5	6	14	8	9	10²	11¹			4						7³		12	13		2			35
1		4		5	6		8	9	10				3³		12				7¹		11²	13		2		14	36

RANGERS

Year Formed: 1873. *Ground & Address:* Ibrox Stadium, 150 Edmiston Drive, Glasgow G51 2XD. New club The Rangers Football Club Ltd from June 2012.
Telephone: 0871 702 1972. *Fax:* 0870 600 1978. *Website:* www.rangers.co.uk
Ground Capacity: all seated: 51,082. *Size of Pitch:* 105m × 68m.
Manager: Ally McCoist. *Assistant Manager:* Kenny McDowall. *Physio:* Pip Yeates. *Head of Football Administration:* Andrew Dickson.
Club Nickname: The Gers.
Previous Grounds: Flesher's Haugh, Burnbank, Kinning Park, Old Ibrox.
Record Attendance: 118,567 v Celtic, Division I, 2 Jan 1939.
Record Transfer Fee received: £9,000,000 for Alan Hutton to Tottenham H (January 2008).
Record Transfer Fee paid: £12,000,000 for Tore Andre Flo from Chelsea (November 2000).
Record Victory: 14-2 v Blairgowrie, Scottish Cup 1st rd, 20 Jan, 1934. *Record Defeat:* 2-10 v Airdrieonians; 1886.
Most Capped Player: Ally McCoist, 60, Scotland.
Most League Appearances: 496: John Greig, 1962-78.
Most League Goals in Season (Individual): 44: Sam English, Division I, 1931-32.
Most Goals Overall (Individual): 355: Ally McCoist; 1985-98.

Honours
League Champions: (54 times) Division I 1890-91 (shared), 1898-99, 1899-1900, 1900-01, 1901-02, 1910-11, 1911-12, 1912-13, 1917-18, 1919-20, 1920-21, 1922-23, 1923-24, 1924-25, 1926-27, 1927-28, 1928-29, 1929-30, 1930-31, 1932-33, 1933-34, 1934-35, 1936-37, 1938-39, 1946-47, 1948-49, 1949-50, 1952-53, 1955-56, 1956-57, 1958-59, 1960-61, 1962-63, 1963-64, 1974-75. Premier Division: 1975-76, 1977-78, 1986-87, 1988-89, 1989-90, 1990-91, 1991-92, 1992-93, 1993-94, 1994-95, 1995-96, 1996-97, 1998-99, 1999-2000, 2002-03, 2004-05, 2008-09, 2009-10, 2010-11; *Runners-up:* 30 times.

RANGERS 2011–12 LEAGUE RECORD

Match No.	Date	Venue	Opponents	Result		H/T Score	Lg Pos.	Goalscorers	Attendance
1	July 23	H	Hearts	D	1-1	0-1	—	Naismith [58]	49,083
2	30	A	St Johnstone	W	2-0	1-0	—	Naismith [31], Jelavic [50]	6459
3	Aug 13	A	Inverness CT	W	2-0	0-0	3	Jelavic (pen) [60], Edu [68]	6623
4	21	A	Motherwell	W	3-0	2-0	1	Naismith [20], Lafferty [45], Wylde [85]	10,092
5	28	H	Aberdeen	W	2-0	1-0	1	Davis [15], Naismith [90]	44,070
6	Sept 10	A	Dundee U	W	1-0	0-0	1	Lafferty [61]	10,156
7	18	H	Celtic	W	4-2	1-2	1	Naismith 2 [23, 90], Jelavic [55], Lafferty [67]	50,221
8	24	A	Dunfermline Ath	W	4-0	2-0	1	Bocanegra [9], Edu [17], Naismith 2 [51, 81]	7577
9	27	H	Kilmarnock	W	2-0	0-0	—	Jelavic [64], Wylde [66]	43,761
10	Oct 1	H	Hibernian	W	1-0	0-0	1	Lafferty [68]	44,430
11	15	H	St Mirren	D	1-1	0-0	1	Jelavic [48]	47,034
12	23	A	Hearts	W	2-0	1-0	1	Naismith [21], Jelavic [74]	15,495
13	29	A	Aberdeen	W	2-1	0-0	1	Lafferty [58], Jelavic (pen) [70]	15,468
14	Nov 5	H	Dundee U	W	3-1	1-0	1	Jelavic 3 (1 pen) [19, 63 (p), 82]	45,600
15	19	H	St Johnstone	D	0-0	0-0	1		45,279
16	27	A	Kilmarnock	L	0-1	0-0	1		9506
17	Dec 3	H	Dunfermline Ath	W	2-1	2-1	1	Keddie (og) [22], Jelavic (pen) [29]	47,305
18	10	A	Hibernian	W	2-0	0-0	1	Jelavic 2 (1 pen) [61 (p), 69]	11,380
19	17	H	Inverness CT	W	2-1	0-0	1	Bocanegra [55], Lafferty [83]	43,701
20	24	A	St Mirren	L	1-2	1-2	1	Wallace [11]	6711
21	28	A	Celtic	L	0-1	0-0	2		58,658
22	Jan 2	H	Motherwell	W	3-0	1-0	2	Healy [35], Aluko [55], Craigan (og) [73]	44,893
23	14	A	St Johnstone	W	2-1	1-0	2	Jelavic 2 [24, 81]	6577
24	21	H	Aberdeen	D	1-1	0-0	2	Edu [67]	46,648
25	28	H	Hibernian	W	4-0	1-0	2	Davis 2 [27, 90], Healy [55], Aluko [72]	44,057
26	Feb 11	A	Dunfermline Ath	W	4-1	2-1	2	Healy [24], McCulloch [39], Aluko [71], Kerkar [85]	7464
27	18	H	Kilmarnock	L	0-1	0-1	2		50,268
28	26	A	Inverness CT	W	4-1	3-1	2	Davis [6], Aluko [16], Little [36], McCulloch [72]	6416
29	Mar 3	H	Hearts	L	1-2	1-0	2	Davis [45]	47,276
30	17	A	Dundee U	L	1-2	0-1	—	Aluko [60]	9464
31	25	H	Celtic	W	3-2	1-0	2	Aluko [11], Little [72], Wallace [77]	50,191
32	31	A	Motherwell	W	2-1	1-1	2	Whittaker [9], McCulloch [89]	9063
33	Apr 7	H	St Mirren	W	3-1	2-0	2	McCulloch [1], Little [40], Lafferty (pen) [60]	46,998
34	21	A	Hearts	W	3-0	2-0	2	Aluko [29], Little 2 [35, 88]	14,842
35	29	A	Celtic	L	0-3	0-2	2		58,546
36	May 2	H	Dundee U	W	5-0	3-0	—	Whittaker [6], Aluko 2 [17, 20], Ness [57], Bedoya [84]	43,383
37	5	H	Motherwell	D	0-0	0-0	2		45,962
38	13	A	St Johnstone	W	4-0	1-0	2	McCulloch [23], Aluko 3 [56, 62, 73]	6459

Final League Position: 2

Scottish Cup Winners: (33 times) 1894, 1897, 1898, 1903, 1928, 1930, 1932, 1934, 1935, 1936, 1948, 1949, 1950, 1953, 1960, 1962, 1963, 1964, 1966, 1973, 1976, 1978, 1979, 1981, 1992, 1993, 1996, 1999, 2000, 2002, 2003, 2008, 2009; *Runners-up:* 17 times.
League Cup Winners: (27 times) 1946-47, 1948-49, 1960-61, 1961-62, 1963-64, 1964-65, 1970-71, 1975-76, 1977-78, 1978-79, 1981-82, 1983-84, 1984-85, 1986-87, 1987-88, 1988-89, 1990-91, 1992-93, 1993-94, 1996-97, 1998-99, 2001-02, 2002-03, 2004-05, 2007-08, 2009-10, 2010-11; *Runners-up:* 7 times.

European: *European Cup:* 161 matches (1956-57, 1957-58, 1959-60 semi-finals, 1961-62, 1963-64, 1964-65, 1975-76, 1976-77, 1978-79, 1987-88, 1989-90, 1990-91, 1991-92, 1992-93 final pool, 1993-94, 1994-95, 1995-96; 1996-97, 1997-98, 1999-2000, 2000-01, 2001-02, 2003-04, 2004-05, 2005-06, 2007-08, 2008-09, 2009-10, 2010-11, 2011-12).
Cup Winners' Cup: 54 matches (1960-61, 1962-63, 1966-67 runners-up, 1969-70, 1971-72 winners, 1973-74, 1977-78, 1979-80, 1981-82, 1983-84).
UEFA Cup: 88 matches (*Fairs Cup:* 1967-68, 1968-69 semi-finals, 1970-71. *UEFA Cup:* 1982-83, 1984-85, 1985-86, 1986-87, 1988-89, 1997-98, 1998-99, 1999-2000, 2000-01, 2001-02, 2002-03, 2004-05, 2006-07, 2007-08 runners-up). *Europa League:* 6 matches (2010-11, 2011-12).

Club colours: Shirt: Royal blue with red and white trim. Shorts: White. Stockings: Black with red tops.

Goalscorers: *League (77):* Jelavic 15 (5 pens), Aluko 12, Naismith 9, Lafferty 7 (1 pen), Davis 5, Little 5, McCulloch 5, Edu 3, Healy 3, Bocanegra 2, Wallace 2, Whittaker 2, Wylde 2, Bedoya 1, Kerkar 1, Ness 1, own goals 2.
Scottish Cup (4): Healy 1, Jelavic 1, Kerkar 1, own goal 1.
Scottish Communities Cup (2): Goian 1, Jelavic 1.
Champions League (1): Jelavic 1. *Europa League (2):* Bocanegra 1, Juanma Ortiz 1.

McGregor A 37	Whittaker S 24+1	Papac S 21	Broadfoot K 11+5	Bougherra M 2	McCulloch L 20+6	Juanma Ortiz P 5+5	Davis S 33	Jelavic N 21+1	Naismith S 11	Edu M 34+2	Wylde G 13+8	Wallace L 26+2	Goian D 33	Bartley K 18+1	Ness J 3+2	Perry R 8+4	McMillan J 1+1	Lafferty K 14+6	Fleck J —+4	Kerkar S 5+10	Healy D 6+5	Bocanegra C 29	Bedoya A 5+7	McKay M 2+1	Hemmings K —+4	Aluko S 19+2	Bendiksen T 1+2	Alexander N 1	Celik M —+5	Little A 6+4	McCabe R 8+1	Mitchell A 1+1	McKay B —+1	*Match No.*
1	2	3	4	5	6	7^1	8	9	10	11	12																							1
1	2	11		5	6^1	12	8	9	10	7^2	13	3	4																					2
1			4			7^2	8	9	10	11■	13	3	2	5^1	6	12																		3
1						7	8	9^3	10		6^2	3	4			5	2	11^1	12	13	14													4
1	12		2				8	9	7	6	11		4^1			5		10^2				3	13											5
1	2		4		12	7	8		10	6^1	11^2		5					9				3		13										6
1	2	3			12		8	9^2	7	6	11		5					10^1			13	4												7
1	2	3				12	8	9^3	7	6	11^2		5					10^1			14	4	13											8
1	2	3^3	14			7^1	8	9		6	11	12	5					10^2				4	13											9
1	2	3					8	9		6	11	13	5		12			10^2				4	7^1											10
1	2		14		12	13	7	9	8	6^1	11^2	3^3	5					10				4												11
1	2^3	11^1	14		8		7	12	9	6	13	3	5					10^2				4												12
1	2	11			8		7	9	10^1	6		3	5					12				4												13
1	2	11					7	9		6	12■	3^1	5	8								4	13	10^2										14
1	2		3				8	9		6			5					10	12			4	7^2	11^1	13									15
1	3		2		8		7	9		6^2			5			4		10^1	14				13		12	11^3								16
1	2		3				7	9		8	11		5	6				12								10	4^1							17
1	2				6	13	8	9		7^2	11	3	5	10^1								4					12							18
1	2	11^3			12		8	9		7^1	10	3		5				13				4	6^2				14							19
1	2	3			6■		8	9		12	7^1	11	5■	14				10^2				4^3				13								20
1		3	2		6^1		8	9		12	14	11^2		5				10			13	4				7^3								21
1		3					8			6^2		11^3	5	2			13	9^1	12	14	10	4				7								22
		3				13	8	9		6		11^1	5	4						12	10^2	2				7		1						23
1		3					8	9		6	12	11^1	5	2						13	10^2	4				7								24
1		3			13		8			6^2	7^1	11	5	2						14	10^3	4				9			12					25
1		3^3	12		9		8			6		11	5	2^1						14	10^2	4				7			13					26
1		11■	2^3		10		8			6		3	5^1			12				14	9^2	4				7			13					27
1			3		6		8			11	13		5			2				9^1		4			14	7^2			12	10^3				28
1					11		8					3	5			2				10		4				7^1			12	9	6			29
1					6		8			4		3				5				10			11^2		13	12				9	2	7^1		30
1	2	3			10		8			7		11^3	5					12		14		4■				9^2				13	6^1			31
1	7	3^1			10		8			6^2		11	5	2		4		12								9				13				32
1		3			10		8^1			6			5	2				13		7^2		4				11				9^3	12	14		33
1	2				10					6		3	5^1	8		13				12		4				7^2				9	11			34
1	3				10					6		8	5	2	12					13		4				11				9^2	7^1			35
1	3		12		13					6		11	5	2	8^1					9^2		4	14			10^3					7			36
1	3				10					6		11	5^1	2	8^3	12						4	13			9				14	7^2			37
1	7		2		10					6		3		4		5					13		11^3			9^1				14	8^2		12	38

ROSS COUNTY

Year Formed: 1929. *Ground & Address:* Victoria Park Stadium, Jubilee Road, Dingwall IV15 9QZ. *Telephone:* 01349 860860. *Fax:* 01349 866277. *E-mail:* donnie.macbean@rosscountyfootballclub.co.uk
Website: www.rosscountyfootballclub.co.uk
Ground Capacity: 6,700. *Size of Ground:* 105 × 68m.
Chairman: Rory MacGregor. *Secretary:* Donnie MacBean.
Manager: Derek Adams. *Assistant Manager:* Stuart Balmer. *Director of Football:* George Adams. *Physio:* Douglas Sim.
Club Nickname: The Staggies.
Record Attendance: 6600, benefit match v Celtic, 31 August 1970.
Record Transfer Fee Received: £200,000 for Neil Tarrant to Aston Villa (April 1999).
Record Transfer Fee Paid: £50,000 for Derek Holmes from Hearts (1999).
Record Victory: 11-0 v St Cuthbert Wanderers, Scottish Cup, 11 Dec 1993.
Record Defeat: 1-10 v Inverness Thistle, Highland League.
Most League Appearances: 230: Mark McCulloch, 2002-2009.
Most League Goals in Season: 24: Andrew Barrowman, 2007-08.
Most League Goals (Overall): 47: Sean Higgins, 2002-09.

ROSS COUNTY 2011–12 LEAGUE RECORD

Match No.	Date	Venue	Opponents	Result		H/T Score	Lg Pos.	Goalscorers	Attendance
1	Aug 6	H	Morton	D	0-0	0-0	—		2249
2	13	A	Hamilton A	L	1-5	0-3	9	Byrne [77]	1744
3	20	H	Queen of the S	W	2-0	0-0	7	Craig 2 [87, 90]	2065
4	27	A	Falkirk	D	1-1	0-0	7	Craig [75]	3009
5	Sept 10	H	Partick Th	D	2-2	1-0	7	Brittain (pen) [13], Gardyne [46]	2189
6	17	H	Livingston	D	1-1	1-1	8	Brittain (pen) [45]	2047
7	24	A	Raith R	W	1-0	0-0	4	Boyd [82]	1479
8	Oct 1	H	Ayr U	W	4-0	1-0	2	Brittain [5], Lawson [64], Morrow [69], Vigurs [87]	2121
9	15	A	Dundee	W	2-1	1-1	1	McMenamin [39], Quinn [63]	4030
10	22	H	Hamilton A	W	1-0	1-0	1	Munro [31]	2431
11	29	A	Morton	W	2-0	1-0	1	Kettlewell [34], Stewart (og) [90]	1748
12	Nov 5	A	Partick Th	W	1-0	1-0	1	Vigurs [26]	2472
13	12	H	Falkirk	W	3-1	1-1	1	Kettlewell [4], Gardyne [52], Miller [83]	4108
14	26	A	Livingston	W	3-0	0-0	1	Gardyne [65], McMenamin 2 [72, 74]	1628
15	Dec 3	H	Raith R	W	4-2	2-2	1	Quinn [28], McMenamin 2 [45, 62], Gardyne [81]	2698
16	17	H	Dundee	D	1-1	0-1	1	McMenamin [82]	3046
17	26	A	Falkirk	D	1-1	0-0	1	McMenamin [90]	4383
18	Jan 14	A	Queen of the S	D	0-0	0-0	1		1314
19	28	H	Livingston	W	3-0	1-0	—	McMenamin 2 [28, 82], Morrow [87]	2514
20	Feb 11	A	Raith R	D	1-1	0-0	1	Craig [53]	1702
21	18	H	Ayr U	D	1-1	1-0	1	Munro [7]	2390
22	25	A	Dundee	D	1-1	1-1	1	Kettlewell [11]	5003
23	29	A	Ayr U	W	3-2	2-0	—	Brittain 3 (1 pen) [16, 38 (p), 80]	1096
24	Mar 3	H	Queen of the S	W	2-1	1-0	1	Vigurs [23], Gardyne [72]	2578
25	6	H	Partick Th	W	3-0	2-0	—	McMenamin [30], Vigurs [36], Gardyne [50]	2200
26	10	A	Hamilton A	W	2-0	2-0	1	McMenamin [7], Boyd [16]	1743
27	13	H	Morton	D	2-2	1-0	—	Gardyne [32], Brittain [58]	2325
28	17	H	Falkirk	W	2-1	2-0	1	Brittain (pen) [19], Quinn [25]	4302
29	24	A	Partick Th	W	1-0	1-0	1	McMenamin [44]	2480
30	31	H	Raith R	D	1-1	0-0	1	Lawson [85]	3379
31	Apr 7	A	Livingston	W	3-1	1-0	1	McMenamin 2 [38, 69], Vigurs [86]	2004
32	11	A	Ayr U	W	3-1	0-0	—	Gardyne [46], McMenamin [67], Morrow [84]	1389
33	14	H	Dundee	W	3-0	1-0	1	Gardyne 2 [9, 64], McMenamin [61]	4350
34	21	A	Morton	D	1-1	1-1	1	McMenamin [6]	1306
35	28	H	Hamilton A	W	5-1	2-0	1	McMenamin [5], Brittain 2 [40, 54], Kettlewell [46], Gardyne [77]	4737
36	May 5	A	Queen of the S	W	5-3	2-2	1	Kettlewell [11], Gardyne 2 [39, 77], McMenamin [57], Byrne [90]	1323

Final League Position: 1

Honours
League Champions: First Division 2011-12. Second Division 2007-08. Third Division 1998-99.
Scottish Cup Runners-up: 2009-10.
League Challenge Cup Winners: 2006-07, 2010-11; *Runners-up:* 2004-05, 2008-09.

Club colours: Shirt: Navy blue with white V. Shorts: Navy blue with white flashes. Stockings: Navy blue with white ring.

Goalscorers: *League (72):* McMenamin 19, Gardyne 13, Brittain 10 (4 pens), Kettlewell 5, Vigurs 5, Craig 4, Morrow 3, Quinn 3, Boyd 2, Byrne 2, Lawson 2, Munro 2, Miller 1, own goal 1.
Scottish Cup (13): Gardyne 4, Brittain 2 (2 pens), Byrne 2, Vigurs 2, Craig 1, Lawson 1, Morrow 1.
Scottish Communities Cup (4): Craig 1, Flynn 1, Gardyne 1, McMenamin 1.
Ramsdens Cup (1): Morrison 1.

Fraser M 36	Miller G 36	Munro G 35	Flynn J 3 + 4	Morrison S 23 + 1	Kettlewell S 27 + 1	Corcoran M 6 + 26	Brittain R 34 + 1	Gardyne M 30 + 4	McMenamin C 34	Craig S 7 + 18	Byrne K 1 + 12	Quinn R 15 + 13	Boyd S 34 + 1	Fitzpatrick M 13	Lawson P 31 + 2	Duncan R — + 4	Vigurs I 27 + 3	Morrow S 4 + 7	Match No.
1	2	3	4	5	6	7^{1}	8	9	10	11	12								1
1	2	4	3■	5	6	14	7	9^{1}	10^{2}	11	13	8^{3}	12						2
1	2	5			6■	9	12	7^{2}	10^{3}	14	11^{1}	8	4	3	13				3
1	2	4^{2}	13	14		12	6	9^{3}	11^{1}	10		8	3	5	7				4
1	2■	4	13			9^{1}	6	10		11^{2}	12	7	3	5	8^{3}	14			5
1	2^{2}	4			13	9^{1}	8	12	10	11■		7^{3}	3	5	14		6		6
1	2	3					5	10^{2}	11^{1}		13	6	4	8	7		9	12	7
1	2	4				12	7		11		13	9^{2}	3	5	8^{3}	14	6	10^{1}	8
1	2	3				12	9	13	11			6	4	5	7^{1}		8	10^{2}	9
1	2	4			7	13	6	12	11^{3}		14		3	5	8		9^{2}	10^{1}	10
1	2	4			8	12	6	10^{2}	11^{1}		13		3	5	7		9		11
1	2	3			9	14	8	10^{3}	11^{2}		13	12	4	5	6^{1}		7		12
1	2	4			7^{3}	13	8	10	11^{2}			12	3	5	6	14	9^{1}		13
1	2	4			7^{1}		8^{2}	10	11^{3}	14		12	3	5	6	13	9		14
1	2	4			8	13	6^{2}	10	11			12	3	5^{1}	7		9		15
1	2	4		5^{1}	8^{2}	14		10^{3}	11	12	13	6	3		7		9		16
1	2	4		5	7	13	6^{2}	11^{1}	10		14	12	3		8		9^{3}		17
1	2	3		5	7		6	11	10^{2}	12	13		4		8^{1}		9		18
1	2	4		5	7	12	6	10^{2}	11^{3}	13		8^{1}	3				9	14	19
1	2	3		4		9	8		11	10^{1}			5		6		7	12	20
1	2	4		5		8^{3}	9	12	11	10^{1}		13	3		6^{2}		7	14	21
1	2	4		5	6	12	8	10^{1}	11^{2}	13			3		7		9		22
1	2	3		5^{1}	6	12	8	10	11^{2}	13		14	4		7^{3}		9		23
1	2	4		5	7^{3}	12	6^{1}	10	11	13		14	3		8		9^{2}		24
1	2	4	14	5^{2}	8^{3}	13	6	10	11^{1}	12			3		7		9		25
1	2	3		5	7	12	6	10^{2}	11	13		14	4		8^{3}		9^{1}		26
1	2	4		5	8^{1}	13	6^{2}	10	11^{3}	14		12	3		7		9		27
1	2	5	14	3	8^{1}	12	9	11^{2}	10	13		7^{3}	4		6				28
1	2	4		5	6	13	7	10	11^{2}			9^{1}	3		8		12		29
1	2	5		3	8	14	7	10^{1}		12		9^{3}	4		6		13	11^{2}	30
1	2	3		5	7^{1}	14	8	11	10^{3}	13		9^{2}	4		6		12		31
1	2	5		3	7^{1}		8	10^{2}	11^{3}	14		12	4		6		9	13	32
1	2	4		5		12	9^{1}	10^{2}	11^{3}	14		7■	3		6		8	13	33
1	2	4		5^{1}	8	12	6^{2}	10^{3}	11	13			3		7		9	14	34
1	2		4	5	7	13	9^{3}	10^{2}	11	12		14	3		6		8^{1}		35
1	2	4		5	8	14	7	10^{2}	11^{3}		13	12	3		6		9^{1}		36

ST JOHNSTONE

Year Formed: 1884. *Ground & Address:* McDiarmid Park, Crieff Road, Perth PH1 2SJ. *Telephone:* 01738 459090. *Fax:* 01738 625 771. *Email:* karin@perthsaints.co.uk *Website:* www.perthstjohnstonefc.co.uk
Ground Capacity: all seated: 10,673. *Size of Pitch:* 115yd × 75yd.
Chairman: Steve Brown.
Manager: Steve Lomas. *Assistant Manager:* Tommy Wright. *Youth Coach:* Tommy Campbell. *Physio:* John Kerr.
Club Nickname: Saints.
Previous Grounds: Recreation Grounds, Muirton Park.
Record Attendance: (McDiarmid Park): 10,545 v Dundee, Premier Division, 23 May 1999.
Record Transfer Fee received: £1,750,000 for Calum Davidson to Blackburn R (March 1998).
Record Transfer Fee paid: £400,000 for Billy Dodds from Dundee (1994).
Record Victory: 9-0 v Albion R, League Cup, 9 Mar 1946.
Record Defeat: 1-10 v Third Lanark, Scottish Cup, 24 Jan 1903.
Most Capped Player: Nick Dasovic, 26, Canada.
Most League Appearances: 298: Drew Rutherford, 1976-85.
Most League Goals in Season (Individual): 36: Jimmy Benson, Division II, 1931-32.
Most Goals Overall (Individual): 140: John Brogan, 1977-83.

ST JOHNSTONE 2011–12 LEAGUE RECORD

Match No.	Date	Venue	Opponents	Result		H/T Score	Lg Pos.	Goalscorers	Attendance
1	July 23	A	Aberdeen	D	0-0	0-0	—		10,001
2	30	H	Rangers	L	0-2	0-1	—		6459
3	Aug 13	H	Dunfermline Ath	L	0-1	0-1	10		3466
4	21	A	Celtic	W	1-0	0-0	9	MacKay [60]	40,268
5	27	H	Dundee U	D	3-3	3-1	9	Sandaza 2 (1 pen) [34 (p), 45], Craig [37]	4480
6	Sept 10	A	St Mirren	D	0-0	0-0	8		3855
7	17	A	Motherwell	W	3-0	1-0	6	Clancy (og) [20], Sandaza [75], Craig [85]	4336
8	25	H	Hearts	W	2-0	1-0	5	Sheridan 2 [30, 55]	2770
9	28	A	Hibernian	L	2-3	1-2	—	Craig [19], Sheridan [88]	8323
10	Oct 1	A	Kilmarnock	W	2-1	1-1	5	Sandaza [22], Sheridan [73]	4059
11	15	H	Inverness CT	W	2-0	1-0	5	Sandaza [12], MacKay [65]	2909
12	22	A	Dundee U	D	0-0	0-0	4		6707
13	29	H	St Mirren	L	0-1	0-0	4		2939
14	Nov 19	A	Rangers	D	0-0	0-0	4		45,279
15	26	H	Hibernian	W	3-1	2-1	4	Sandaza [38], Haber [45], MacKay [47]	3782
16	Dec 3	A	Hearts	W	2-1	1-0	4	Craig [3], Maybury (pen) [79]	12,815
17	10	H	Motherwell	L	0-3	0-2	4		2885
18	13	H	Aberdeen	L	1-2	0-1	—	Haber [90]	1607
19	18	H	Celtic	L	0-2	0-0	4		6759
20	24	A	Dunfermline Ath	W	3-0	1-0	4	Smith (og) [38], Sandaza [52], Craig [59]	4474
21	28	H	Kilmarnock	W	2-0	2-0	4	Sandaza 2 [26, 45]	2394
22	Jan 14	H	Rangers	L	1-2	0-1	5	Bocanegra (og) [68]	6577
23	21	A	Hibernian	W	3-2	1-0	4	Croft [30], Craig [71], Sandaza [87]	8772
24	28	A	Motherwell	L	2-3	1-1	5	Morris [45], Sandaza (pen) [81]	4520
25	Feb 11	H	Dundee U	L	1-5	0-1	5	Anderson [66]	4319
26	19	A	Aberdeen	D	0-0	0-0	5		6936
27	25	H	Dunfermline Ath	W	3-1	2-0	4	Davidson, M [33], Davidson, C [35], Croft [78]	3732
28	Mar 3	A	Kilmarnock	D	0-0	0-0	4		3768
29	17	A	St Mirren	W	3-0	1-0	—	Croft [2], McCracken [76], Sandaza [85]	3768
30	24	H	Hearts	W	2-1	1-1	5	Davidson, M [35], Sandaza (pen) [77]	4365
31	28	A	Inverness CT	W	1-0	1-0	—	Sandaza (pen) [41]	3035
32	Apr 1	A	Celtic	L	0-2	0-0	—		57,848
33	7	H	Inverness CT	D	0-0	0-0	4		3326
34	21	H	Dundee U	L	0-2	0-1	5		5826
35	28	A	Motherwell	L	1-5	0-2	5	Craig (pen) [59]	4743
36	May 3	A	Celtic	L	0-1	0-1	—		50,297
37	6	A	Hearts	L	0-2	0-1	6		12,543
38	13	H	Rangers	L	0-4	0-1	6		6459

Final League Position: 6

Honours
League Champions: First Division 1982-83, 1989-90, 1996-97, 2008-09. Division II 1923-24, 1959-60, 1962-63; *Runners-up:* Division II 1931-32. First Division 2005-06, 2006-07. Second Division 1987-88.
Scottish Cup: Semi-finals 1934, 1968, 1989, 1991, 2007, 2008.
League Cup Runners-up: 1969-70, 1998-99.
League Challenge Cup Winners: 2007-08; *Runners-up:* 1996-97.

European: *UEFA Cup:* 10 matches (1971-72, 1999-2000).

Club colours: Shirt: Royal blue. Short: White. Stockings: Royal blue.

Goalscorers: *League (43):* Sandaza 14 (4 pens), Craig 7 (1 pen), Sheridan 4, Croft 3, MacKay 3, Davidson, M. 2, Haber 2, Anderson 1, Davidson, C. 1, Maybury 1 (1 pen), McCracken 1, Morris 1, own goals 3.
Scottish Cup (4): Davidson, M. 2, Sheridan 1, Sandaza 1.
Scottish Communities Cup (3): Sandaza 2, Wright 1.

Enckelman P 25	MacKay D 36	Davidson C 26	Morris J 28	Wright F 23	Anderson S 26 + 3	Millar C 26 + 4	Robertson D 10 + 6	Sheridan C 25 + 3	Davidson M 24 + 2	Craig L 36	Haber M 14 + 17	Moon K 13 + 6	May S — + 1	Finnigan C 3 + 8	McCracken D 27 + 1	Sandaza F 28 + 1	Maybury A 15 + 7	Higgins S — + 3	Adams J 6 + 1	Gibson W 1 + 10	Parkin S 1 + 1	Croft L 10 + 1	Compton J — + 3	Mannus A 13	Keatings J — + 4	Oyenuga K — + 1	Riordan D 2 + 2	Match No.
1	2	3	4	5	6	7	8^{3}	9^{2}	10	11^{1}	12	13	14															1
1	2	3	4	5	6	12	8^{1}	9^{2}	10		11	7		13														2
1	2		4	5			13	9^{1}	8	3	11^{2}	6		10	7	12												3
1	2	3	4	5				9^{1}	8	11	13				6	10^{2}	7	12										4
1	2	3^{1}	4	5			8	9^{3}		11					6	10	13	14	7	12^{2}								5
1	2			5	14	7	8	9^{2}		11				13	6^{3}	10	3		4^{1}	12								6
1	2			5	6	7^{3}		9^{1}		11	13	8				10^{2}	3	12	4	14								7
1	2				6	7	12	9		11	13	8			5	10^{2}	3			4^{1}								8
1	2		4		6	7	13	9		11	14	8^{2}			5^{3}	10	3^{1}			12								9
1	2	5	4		6	12	7^{2}	9		11	14	8^{1}				10^{3}	3			13								10
1	2	3	4	5	6	7		9^{1}	14	11	12	8^{3}				10^{2}				13								11
1	2	3	4	5	6	7				11^{2}	9^{1}	8		12		10				13								12
1	2	3	4	5^{1}	6	7		9	13	11^{3}	14	8^{2}				10	12											13
1	2	3	4^{1}	5	6	7			8	11	13	10		12		9^{2}												14
1	2	3		5	6	7		9^{1}	8	11	12	4				10												15
1	2	3		5^{1}	6	7			8	11	10	4		9^{2}	12		13											16
1	2	3			6	7	4^{1}		8	11	10			9^{2}	5					12	13							17
1	2	3			6	7			8	11	10			13	5^{2}		4^{1}			12	9							18
1	2				6	7	9^{1}		8	11^{2}	10	4		12	5		3			13								19
1	2	3	4^{1}		6	7			8^{3}	11	10	12		13	5	9^{2}	14											20
1	2	3^{2}	4		6	7^{1}			8	11	10	14		12	5	9^{3}	13											21
1	2	3	4		6		7^{1}	12	8	11	9				5	10												22
1	2	3	4		6			13	8	11	9^{2}				5	10						7^{1}	12					23
1	2	3	4		6			13	8	11^{2}	9^{1}				5	10						7	12					24
1	2	3	4		6	7^{2}	13	9		11	12				5	10						8^{1}						25
	2	3	4	5		7^{1}		9^{2}	8	11	13				6	10						12		1				26
	2	3	4^{1}	5		12		9	8	11	13				6	10^{2}						7^{3}		1	14			27
	2	3		5		7		9■	8	11	12				6	10^{1}						4		1				28
	2	3^{1}	4	5		7	13		8	11^{3}					6	10	12					9^{2}		1	14			29
	2		4	5		12		9	8^{1}	11					6	10	3					7		1				30
	2		4^{2}	5	13	7	12	9^{1}		11					6	10	3					8		1				31
	2		4^{1}	5		7		9		11		12			6	10	3					8^{2}		1		13		32
	2		4		6	7		9^{2}		11	13	12			5	10	3					8^{1}		1				33
	2			5	12		7	9	8		13	14			6^{1}	10■	3		4^{3}					1			11^{2}	34
			4	5	3		7^{1}		8	11^{2}	9				6		2						12	1	13		10	35
		3	4		6	7^{1}		9	8	11	13				5		2		10^{2}					1			12	36
	2	3^{3}	4		6	7^{1}		9	8^{2}	11	10				5		14		13					1			12	37
	2	3	4	5	6	7		9^{1}		11						10			8					1	12			38

ST MIRREN

Year Formed: 1877. *Ground & Address:* St Mirren Park, Greenhill Road, Paisley PA3 1RU. *Telephone:* 0141 889 2558.
Fax: 0141 848 6444. *E-mail:* info@saintmirren.net *Website:* www.saintmirren.net
Ground Capacity: 10,476 (all seated). *Size of Pitch:* 105yd × 68yd.
Chairman: Stewart Gilmour. *Vice-Chairman:* George Campbell. *Secretary:* Chris Stewart.
Manager: Danny Lennon. *First Team Coach:* Tommy Craig. *Youth Development Officer:* David Longwell. *Physio:* Gerry Docherty.
Club Nickname: The Buddies.
Previous Grounds: Short Roods 1877-79, Thistle Park Greenhill 1879-83, Westmarch 1883-94, Love Street 1894-2009.
Record Attendance: 47,438 v Celtic, League Cup, 20 Aug 1949.
Record Transfer Fee received: £850,000 for Ian Ferguson to Rangers (1988).
Record Transfer Fee paid: £400,000 for Thomas Stickroth from Bayer Uerdingen (1990).
Record Victory: 15-0 v Glasgow University, Scottish Cup 1st rd, 30 Jan 1960.
Record Defeat: 0-9 v Rangers, Division I, 4 Dec 1897.
Most Capped Player: Godmundor Torfason, 29, Iceland.
Most League Appearances: 399: Hugh Murray, 1997-2012.
Most League Goals in Season (Individual): 45: Dunky Walker, Division I, 1921-22.
Most Goals Overall (Individual): 221: David McCrae, 1923-34.

ST MIRREN 2011–12 LEAGUE RECORD

Match No.	Date	Venue	Opponents	Result		H/T Score	Lg Pos.	Goalscorers	Attendance
1	July 25	A	Dunfermline Ath	D	0-0	0-0	—		5035
2	30	H	Aberdeen	W	1-0	0-0	—	Hasselbaink [50]	5011
3	Aug 6	A	Dundee U	D	1-1	1-0	—	Thompson [11]	6594
4	13	H	Motherwell	L	0-1	0-0	6		5105
5	20	A	Hibernian	W	2-1	2-1	5	Thompson [42], Thomson [45]	8886
6	28	H	Celtic	L	0-2	0-2	6		6223
7	Sept 10	H	St Johnstone	D	0-0	0-0	6		3855
8	17	A	Hearts	L	0-2	0-1	9		12,572
9	24	H	Kilmarnock	W	3-0	2-0	6	McGowan 2 (1 pen) [32, 45 (p)], Hasselbaink [85]	5013
10	Oct 1	A	Inverness CT	L	1-2	1-1	6	McAusland [23]	3249
11	15	A	Rangers	D	1-1	0-0	6	Thompson [90]	47,034
12	22	H	Hibernian	L	2-3	2-3	6	McGowan 2 [32, 34]	4273
13	29	A	St Johnstone	W	1-0	0-0	6	McLean [81]	2939
14	Nov 5	H	Hearts	D	0-0	0-0	6		4771
15	19	H	Dunfermline Ath	W	2-1	2-0	5	McLean [25], Hasselbaink [45]	4363
16	26	A	Celtic	L	0-5	0-2	6		48,406
17	Dec 3	H	Inverness CT	L	1-2	1-1	7	Thompson [45]	3675
18	10	A	Aberdeen	D	2-2	1-2	8	McLean [34], Carey [52]	9452
19	17	A	Motherwell	D	1-1	0-0	8	Goodwin [59]	4557
20	24	H	Rangers	W	2-1	2-1	7	Mooy [44], McGowan [45]	6711
21	28	H	Dundee U	D	2-2	2-2	7	Thompson [27], Carey [32]	3811
22	Jan 2	A	Kilmarnock	L	1-2	1-1	8	Mair [10]	5986
23	14	A	Hearts	L	2-5	2-2	8	McGowan (pen) [13], Thompson [19]	12,462
24	21	H	Celtic	L	0-2	0-0	9		6129
25	28	A	Inverness CT	D	0-0	0-0	9		3044
26	Feb 11	H	Motherwell	D	0-0	0-0	9		4204
27	18	A	Dundee U	D	0-0	0-0	9		6363
28	25	H	Aberdeen	D	1-1	0-0	9	Hasselbaink [57]	3627
29	Mar 3	A	Hibernian	D	0-0	0-0	9		9211
30	17	H	St Johnstone	L	0-3	0-1	—		3768
31	24	A	Dunfermline Ath	D	1-1	1-0	9	Thompson [38]	3753
32	31	H	Kilmarnock	W	4-2	1-1	8	Thompson 2 [24, 83], Thomson [61], Hasselbaink [66]	4365
33	Apr 7	A	Rangers	L	1-3	0-2	9	McGowan [49]	46,998
34	21	H	Dunfermline Ath	D	4-4	2-1	9	Hasselbaink [4], Thompson 3 [43, 48, 67]	3616
35	29	H	Hibernian	W	1-0	0-0	9	McLean [65]	3305
36	May 2	A	Kilmarnock	W	2-0	2-0	—	McGowan [9], Thompson [45]	3645
37	5	H	Inverness CT	L	0-1	0-0	8		3540
38	12	A	Aberdeen	D	0-0	0-0	8		10,716

Final League Position: 8

Honours
League Champions: First Division 1976-77, 1999-2000, 2005-06; *Runners-up:* 2004-05. Division II 1967-68; *Runners-up:* 1935-36.
Scottish Cup Winners: 1926, 1959, 1987; *Runners-up:* 1908, 1934, 1962.
League Cup Runners-up: 1955-56, 2009-10.
League Challenge Cup Winners: 2005-06.
B&Q Cup Runners-up: 1993-94. *Anglo-Scottish Cup:* 1979-80.

European: *Cup Winners' Cup:* 4 matches (1987-88). *UEFA Cup:* 10 matches (1980-81, 1983-84, 1985-86).

Club colours: Shirt: Black and white vertical stripes. Shorts: White. Stockings: White.

Goalscorers: *League (39):* Thompson 13, McGowan 8 (2 pens), Hasselbaink 6, McLean 4, Carey 2, Thomson 2, Goodwin 1, Mair 1, McAusland 1, Mooy 1.
Scottish Cup (6): Carey 2, Hasselbaink 1, Teale 1, Thompson 1, own goal 1.
Scottish Communities Cup (6): Thompson 2, Goodwin 1, Hasselbaink 1 (pen), Teale 1, own goal 1.

Samson C 38	Van Zanten D 35	Tesselaar J 33	McGregor D 6 + 3	Mair L 34	Goodwin J 31	McGowan P 37	Thomson S 19 + 5	Thompson S 34 + 1	Hasselbaink N 22 + 12	Teale G 21 + 13	Carey G 20 + 9	McShane J 1 + 9	McAusland M 31 + 1	McLean K 24 + 4	Haddad I 4 + 6	McQuade P — + 1	McKee J — + 2	Barron D 12 + 5	Mooy A 3 + 5	Murray H 1 + 6	Reilly T — + 4	Imrie D 12 + 2	Naismith J — + 2	*Match No.*
1	2	3	4	5	6	7	8	9	10	11														1
1	2	3	4	5	6	7	8	9^{1}	10^{2}	11	12	13												2
1	2	3	4^{2}	5	6	7	8	9^{3}	10■	11^{1}		12	13	14										3
1	2	3		5	6	7		9		11	8^{1}	12	4	10										4
1	2	3		5	6	10^{2}	8	9^{3}		11^{1}		12	4	7	13	14								5
1	2	3		5	6^{3}	7	8	9	10^{2}	11^{1}		12	4	14			13							6
1	2	3		5	6	7	8^{1}	9	10	11		12			4									7
1	2^{3}	3		5	6	7^{1}	8	9	10^{2}	11		14		13	4		12							8
1	2	3		5	6^{3}	7	8	9^{2}	12	11	14		4	10^{1}				13						9
1	2	3		5	6	7	8^{2}	9^{3}	10	11^{1}	14		4	12				13						10
1	2	3		5	6^{2}	7	8^{3}	9	10^{1}	12		14	4	11	13									11
1	2	3		5	6	10	8^{1}	9	12	11^{2}	13		4	7										12
1	2	3		5	6	8		9^{2}	12		10	7^{1}	4	11	13									13
1	2^{1}	3		5	6	10^{3}		9	13	11^{2}	8		4	7	14			12						14
1	2	3		5	6	11^{3}	8^{1}	9	10	14	12^{2}		4	7	13									15
1	2^{2}	3		5	6	10		12	9	11^{1}	14		4	7	8^{3}			13						16
1		3		5^{1}	6	8		9	10^{3}	11^{2}	13	14	4	2	7			12						17
1	2	7			5^{2}	10		9	12	11^{1}	6		4	8	13			3						18
1	2	3			6	7		9	10^{1}	13	11^{2}		4	8				5	12					19
1	2	3		5		6		9^{3}	14	12	7^{1}		4	8				11	10^{2}	13				20
1	2	3		5		6		9	13	12	7^{1}		4	8				11	10^{2}					21
1	2	3		5		8	12	9^{3}	13	14	7^{1}		4	6				11	10^{2}					22
1	2^{1}	3		5		10	12	9	13	7^{2}	8^{3}		4	6				11			14			23
1	2	3		5		7		9		13	8^{2}		4	6				11^{1}	12			10		24
1	2	3		5		10	6^{2}	9		13	7^{1}		4					11		12		8		25
1		3		5	6	10		9	12	11	8^{1}		4					2				7		26
1		3		5	6	7	9		12	11^{1}	8^{2}		4					2	13			10		27
1	2			5	6	7	9^{2}		10^{3}	13	8		4^{1}					3			14	11	12	28
1	2			5	6		8	9	10	11				4^{2}				3	12	7^{1}			13	29
1	2^{1}			5	6	7	8^{2}		10	11	3		4						13	12		9		30
1	2			5	6	8	12	9	10	11^{1}	3		4									7		31
1	2	3	14	5	6^{2}	7	8	9	10^{3}		11^{1}		4							13		12		32
1	2^{2}	3■	12	5		10	8	9	11^{1}		13		4	6^{3}						14		7		33
1	2			5	6	7		9	10^{2}	12	3		4	8							13	11^{1}		34
1	2	3	14	5	6^{3}	7	12	9	10^{2}		11^{1}		4■	8								13		35
1	2	3	4	5	6	11^{3}	12	9	10^{1}	14	13			7								8^{2}		36
1	2	3	5		6	11		9	10^{2}	13			4	7^{3}						12	14	8^{1}		37
1	2	3	5		6	8		9	13	12	11^{1}		4	7								10^{2}		38

STENHOUSEMUIR

Year Formed: 1884. *Ground & Address:* Ochilview Park, Gladstone Rd, Stenhousemuir FK5 4QL. *Telephone:* 01324 562992. *Fax:* 01324 562980. *E-mail:* info@stenhousemuirfc.com *Website:* www.stenhousemuirfc.com
Ground Capacity: 3,776 (626 seated). *Size of Pitch:* 110yd × 72yd.
Chairman: Martin McNairney. *Vice Chairman:* Bill Darroch. *Secretary/General Manager:* Margaret Kilpatrick.
Manager: Dave Irons. *Assistant Manager:* Kevin McGoldrick. *Physio:* Laura Chimimba.
Club Nickname: The Warriors.
Previous Grounds: Tryst Ground 1884-86, Goschen Park 1886-90.
Record Attendance: 12,500 v East Fife, Scottish Cup 4th rd, 11 Mar 1950.
Record Transfer Fee received: £70,000 for Euan Donaldson to St Johnstone (May 1995).
Record Transfer Fee paid: £20,000 to Livingston for Ian Little (June 1995); £20,000 to East Fife for Paul Hunter (September 1995).
Record Victory: 9-2 v Dundee U, Division II, 16 Apr 1937.
Record Defeat: 2-11 v Dunfermline Ath, Division II, 27 Sept 1930.
Most League Appearances: 434: Jimmy Richardson, 1957-73.
Most League Goals in Season (Individual): 32: Robert Taylor, Division II, 1925-26.

STENHOUSEMUIR 2011–12 LEAGUE RECORD

Match No.	*Date*	*Venue*	*Opponents*	*Result*	*H/T Score*	*Lg Pos.*	*Goalscorers*	*Attendance*
1	Aug 6	A	Brechin C	L 0-2	0-0	—		442
2	13	H	Arbroath	W 2-0	1-0	7	Ferguson [13], Rodgers [56]	492
3	20	A	Forfar Ath	W 3-2	2-0	4	Ferguson [22], Kean [25], Thomson [62]	372
4	27	H	Cowdenbeath	W 3-1	0-0	2	Rodgers [56], McHale [72], Ferguson [77]	621
5	Sept 10	A	Stirling A	D 2-2	1-0	3	Paton (pen) [39], Thomson [69]	649
6	17	A	Albion R	D 1-1	0-0	3	Murray [67]	369
7	24	H	East Fife	W 2-1	1-0	3	Kean [19], Rodgers [88]	642
8	Oct 1	A	Airdrie U	L 2-5	0-3	3	Hamilton, C [51], Kean [56]	698
9	15	H	Dumbarton	W 3-1	2-0	3	Rodgers [29], McMillan 2 [45, 77]	529
10	22	H	Brechin C	D 1-1	1-1	3	Dickson [40]	681
11	29	A	Arbroath	L 0-1	0-0	3		572
12	Nov 5	H	Stirling A	W 4-0	0-0	3	Kean 2 [54, 80], McMillan [63], Ferguson [69]	829
13	12	A	Cowdenbeath	L 0-2	0-1	3		374
14	26	H	Albion R	W 3-0	0-0	3	Kean [57], Rodgers 2 [80, 85]	561
15	Dec 3	A	East Fife	W 3-1	1-0	3	Kean [15], Rodgers [48], Quinn [90]	508
16	10	H	Airdrie U	D 1-1	1-0	3	Rodgers [4]	698
17	26	H	Cowdenbeath	L 0-2	0-1	3		576
18	Jan 2	A	Stirling A	L 1-3	0-0	3	Thomson [83]	578
19	14	H	Forfar Ath	L 2-3	1-1	3	McMillan [42], McCulloch (og) [71]	454
20	28	H	East Fife	W 1-0	0-0	—	Rodgers [59]	687
21	Feb 11	H	Dumbarton	L 1-2	0-2	3	Smith [76]	0
22	18	A	Airdrie U	W 3-0	1-0	4	Dickson [4], Smith 2 [46, 66]	685
23	21	A	Brechin C	L 0-1	0-0	—		347
24	25	H	Arbroath	L 1-3	0-2	4	Kean [70]	563
25	28	A	Dumbarton	L 0-3	0-2	—		557
26	Mar 3	A	Forfar Ath	W 2-1	1-0	4	Ferguson [13], Kean [53]	374
27	6	A	Albion R	L 0-1	0-0	—		268
28	10	H	Stirling A	W 4-0	1-0	4	Kean [2], Rodgers 2 [55, 81], Campbell [57]	674
29	17	A	Cowdenbeath	D 0-0	0-0	4		367
30	24	H	Albion R	L 1-2	1-1	4	Rodgers [25]	486
31	31	A	East Fife	D 1-1	0-1	4	Ferguson (pen) [81]	742
32	Apr 7	H	Airdrie U	L 0-3	0-2	6		903
33	14	A	Dumbarton	W 2-0	2-0	5	Ferguson (pen) [5], Rodgers [11]	728
34	21	H	Brechin C	W 2-1	1-0	5	Thomson [17], Anderson [60]	541
35	28	A	Arbroath	W 2-0	2-0	5	Anderson [11], Rodgers [20]	643
36	May 5	H	Forfar Ath	L 1-2	1-2	5	Anderson [15]	759

Final League Position: 5

Honours
League Champions: Third Division runners-up: 1998-99. *Promoted to Second Division:* 2008-09 (play-offs).
Scottish Cup: Semi-finals 1902-03. Quarter-finals 1948-49, 1949-50, 1994-95.
League Cup: Quarter-finals 1947-48, 1960-61, 1975-76.
League Challenge Cup Winners: 1995-96.

Club colours: Shirt: Maroon with light blue trim. Shorts: White. Stockings: Maroon.

Goalscorers: *League (54):* Rodgers 14, Kean 10, Ferguson 7 (2 pens), McMillan 4, Thomson 4, Anderson 3, Smith 3, Dickson 2, Campbell 1, Hamilton, C. 1, McHale 1, Murray 1, Paton 1 (1 pen), Quinn 1, own goal 1.
Scottish Cup (4): Rodgers 3, Kean 1.
Scottish Communities Cup (3): Paton 2, Lyle 1.
Ramsdens Cup (1): Kean 1.

McCluskey C 8	Lyle W 27 + 2	Paton E 24 + 2	Corrigan M 19	McMillan R 29 + 1	McKinlay K 26 + 3	Thomson I 29 + 5	Ferguson B 31	Dickson S 15 + 10	Murray S 22 + 8	Kean S 36	McHale P 12 + 5	Plenderleith G — + 4	Rodgers A 28 + 5	Quinn P 2 + 11	Fraser S — + 3	McCafferty J 1 + 4	Brown A 27 + 1	Hamilton C 6 + 2	Hamilton J — + 2	Campbell J 6 + 1	Lawson A 5 + 4	Smith G 5 + 5	Devlin M 12 + 1	Anderson K 6 + 1	Fitzharris S 2 + 1	Deuchar K 6 + 3	Devlin N 6	Miller K 5	Shaw D 1	*Match No.*
1	2	3	4	5[3]	6	7	8[1]	9[2]	10	11	12	13	14																	1
1	2	8	3		4	12	6[1]	5	9	11	7		10[2]	13																2
1	2	4	3	14	5	12	7[1]	6	9[3]	11[2]	8		10		13															3
1	2	11	3	4		5	6		9	10[2]	8[1]		7[3]	14	13	12														4
	5	8[1]	3	2		7	6	4[3]	9	11		12	10[2]	13		14	1													5
	2	5	4	3[1]		8	7	6	9	10			11	12			1													6
	2	6	3	4		8	7[1]	12	9	11			10				1	5												7
	2	7[1]	3	4		8[3]	6	12	9[2]	10			11		13	14	1	5												8
1	2		4	3		8	7[2]	9	6	10			11[1]	12				5	13											9
1	2	5	3	4[1]	12	8[2]	7	6	9	11			10	13																10
1■	2	5	3[G]	4	12	8[2]	7	13	9	11			10				15	6[1]												11
	2	5	3	4	8	13	7[3]		9	11		14		12		10[1]	1	6[2]												12
	2	4	3		5	8	7	13	9	10			12	11[1]			1	6[2]												13
	2	7	3		4	8	6[1]	5	9[2]	10[3]	12		11	14			1	13												14
	2	5	3	4	6	7	8	13	9[2]	10			11[1]	12			1													15
	2	7	3	4	5[2]	8	6[1]	14	9[3]	10	12		11				1	13												16
	2[1]	5	3	4	6	8		12	9	10	7[2]		11	13			1													17
	12		2	3	4	8	6	5	9[1]	11			10	13			1			7[2]										18
1	2		3	4	5	13	6	9[3]		11	8	12		10[1]						7[2]	14									19
	2	4[1]			6	5	7	12	9[2]	10	8		11				1				3	13								20
	2	5[2]		4■	6■	8	7[1]	9		11	12		10[3]				1			14		13	3							21
	4					9	8	5[2]		11	6					13	1			7[1]	2	10	3	12						22
	5			4	13	8	7	6		11	9[2]		12				1				2	10[1]	3							23
	12			3	4	5	7	8	13	10[2]	6		9				1					11	2[1]							24
	2			4	7[2]	5	6	8[1]	12	11	14		9[3]				1				13	10	3							25
	2	12		3	6	5	7[1]		13	11	8[3]		14				1				4				9[2]	10				26
		4		3	5	6			12	10	7[2]		9				1				2	13			8[1]	11				27
	2	7[1]		4	5	8			9[3]	10			12				1			6	13	14	3[2]			11				28
	2[2]			3	5	6			12	9			8				1		13	7		11[1]	4			10				29
	3[2]			2	7	8			4[1]	9	5		11				1			6	14	12			13[3]	10				30
					5	4	6		12	11			9				1						3	8		10[1]	2	7		31
		12		3	5[3]	4	7		6[1]	11			10[2]				1						14	9		13	2	8		32
		5		4	6		7		13	10			11[2]										3	9[1]		12	2	8■	1	33
		5		4	6	8	7	12		10			11				1						3	9[1]			2			34
		5		3	6		8	12		10			11				1						7	9[1]			2	4		35
		5		3[1]	6	12	7		13	11			10[3]				1						8	9		14	2	4[2]		36

STIRLING ALBION

Year Formed: 1945. *Ground & Address:* Forthbank Stadium, Springkerse, Stirling FK7 7UJ. *Telephone:* 01786 450399. *Fax:* 01786 448592. *Email:* stirlingalbion@btconnect.com *Website:* www.stirlingalbionfc.co.uk
Ground Capacity: 3,808, seated: 2,508. *Size of Pitch:* 110yd × 74yd.
Manager: Greig McDonald. *Assistant Manager:* John Blackley.
Club Nickname: The Binos.
Previous Grounds: Annfield 1945-92.
Record Attendance: 26,400 (at Annfield) v Celtic, Scottish Cup 4th rd, 14 Mar 1959; 3808 v Aberdeen, Scottish Cup 4th rd, 15 February 1996 (Forthbank).
Record Transfer Fee received: £90,000 for Stephen Nicholas to Motherwell (Mar 1999).
Record Transfer Fee paid: £25,000 for Craig Taggart from Falkirk (Aug 1994).
Record Victory: 20-0 v Selkirk, Scottish Cup 1st rd, 8 Dec 1984.
Record Defeat: 0-9 v Dundee U, Division I, 30 Dec 1967; 0-9 v Ross Co Scottish Cup 5th rd, 6 Feb 2010.
Most League Appearances: 504: Matt McPhee, 1967-81.
Most League Goals in Season (Individual): 27: Joe Hughes, Division II, 1969-70.
Most Goals Overall (Individual): 129: Billy Steele, 1971-83.

STIRLING ALBION 2011–12 LEAGUE RECORD

Match No.	Date	Venue	Opponents	Result	H/T Score	Lg Pos.	Goalscorers	Attendance
1	Aug 6	H	East Fife	W 1-0	0-0	—	Davieson [76]	688
2	13	A	Dumbarton	W 5-1	1-1	—	Smith [5], Cook [46], Flood [48], Dillon [56], Crawley [69]	706
3	20	H	Albion R	D 2-2	1-0	2	Jacobs [34], Davieson (pen) [76]	617
4	27	A	Arbroath	L 2-4	1-1	4	Cook [38], Dillon [49]	670
5	Sept 10	H	Stenhousemuir	D 2-2	0-1	4	Davieson [59], Cook (pen) [89]	649
6	17	H	Forfar Ath	L 2-4	1-1	5	Davieson (pen) [45], Smith [83]	551
7	24	A	Airdrie U	D 1-1	1-1	5	Davieson [37]	709
8	Oct 1	H	Brechin C	W 1-0	1-0	4	Smith [19]	555
9	15	A	Cowdenbeath	L 0-2	0-1	4		312
10	22	A	East Fife	L 0-1	0-0	6		617
11	29	H	Dumbarton	L 0-1	0-0	8		602
12	Nov 5	A	Stenhousemuir	L 0-4	0-0	10		829
13	12	H	Arbroath	L 0-1	0-0	10		573
14	Dec 3	H	Airdrie U	L 1-4	1-2	10	Bonar [45]	711
15	Jan 2	H	Stenhousemuir	W 3-1	0-0	9	Cook [54], Thom [69], Flood [90]	578
16	14	A	Albion R	W 1-0	1-0	9	McLeish [11]	455
17	21	H	East Fife	L 0-1	0-0	10		608
18	24	A	Forfar Ath	D 2-2	0-1	—	McSorley [79], Davieson [88]	361
19	28	A	Airdrie U	L 1-4	0-2	—	Ferry [90]	730
20	Feb 1	A	Arbroath	L 0-2	0-2	—		901
21	11	A	Cowdenbeath	L 1-4	1-1	10	Thom [36]	341
22	18	H	Brechin C	L 2-3	1-0	10	Ferry [33], McLean (og) [75]	479
23	21	H	Cowdenbeath	D 1-1	1-0	—	Thom [28]	329
24	25	A	Dumbarton	L 1-4	1-0	10	Davidson [3]	722
25	28	A	Brechin C	W 3-1	2-0	—	Cook [42], Ferry [44], Thom [62]	362
26	Mar 3	H	Albion R	W 3-0	2-0	9	Cook 2 [20, 78], Kelbie [23]	511
27	6	H	Forfar Ath	D 2-2	1-0	—	Ferry [18], McSorley [88]	371
28	10	A	Stenhousemuir	L 0-4	0-1	9		674
29	17	H	Arbroath	D 1-1	1-0	9	Davidson [20]	537
30	24	A	Forfar Ath	L 3-4	1-3	10	Kelbie [22], Smith [63], Ferry [89]	462
31	31	H	Airdrie U	L 0-2	0-2	10		677
32	Apr 7	A	Brechin C	W 2-1	1-0	10	Ferry [33], Cook [82]	468
33	14	H	Cowdenbeath	L 0-2	0-1	10		568
34	21	A	East Fife	L 0-1	0-0	10		495
35	28	H	Dumbarton	L 1-2	0-0	10	Davidson [57]	709
36	May 5	A	Albion R	W 2-1	0-1	10	Day [61], Brass [75]	462

Final League Position: 10

Honours
League Champions: Division II 1952-53, 1957-58, 1960-61, 1964-65. Second Division 1976-77, 1990-91, 1995-96, 2009-10; *Runners-up:* Division II 1948-49, 1950-51. Second Division 2006-07. Third Division 2003-04. *Promoted to First Division:* 2006-07 (play-offs).
League Cup: Semi-finals 1961-62.

Club colours: All red with white trim.

Goalscorers: *League (46):* Cook 8 (1 pen), Davieson 6 (2 pens), Ferry 6, Smith 4, Thom 4, Davidson 3, Dillon 2, Flood 2, Kelbie 2, McSorley 2, Bonar 1, Brass 1, Crawley 1, Day 1, Jacobs 1, McLeish 1, own goal 1.
Scottish Cup (1): Smith 1.
Scottish Communities Cup (0).
Ramsdens Cup (3): Bonar 2 (1 pen), McPherson 1.

Filler S 13 + 1	Jacobs D 26 + 6	Allison B 28	Thom G 34	Dillon S 15 + 2	Cook A 24 + 9	Smith D 29 + 4	Flood J 10 + 12	McSorley D 22 + 3	McCulloch M 18 + 2	Davieson S 19 + 1	Bonar L 9 + 7	Crawley J 26 + 3	Brass G 1 + 1	Fagan S 21 + 1	McPherson D 3 + 6	Ashe D — + 2	Nicholas S 1 + 9	McLeish C 13 + 5	Reidford C 22	McDonald G — + 1	Ferry M 19 + 2	Weir G 16 + 1	Kelbie K 10 + 4	Davidson S 8 + 5	Day S — + 3	McCunnie J 7 + 1	Cleland J 1	McGeachie R 1	*Match No.*
1	2	3	4	5	6^{2}	7	8^{1}	9	10	11	12	13																	1
1	2	5	6	3	7	11	8^{1}		10	9^{2}	12	4	13																2
1	2	3	4	6	12	9	7^{1}		8	11^{2}	13	10		5															3
1	2		5■	3	6	9			7	10	11^{1}	4			8^{2}	12	13												4
1	2	3		5^{1}	9	11			4	10	13	8^{3}		7	12		6^{2}	14											5
1	2	3	4		12	10	6^{2}	13	5	11		8^{3}		7			14	9^{1}											6
1	2	3	4		12	11	9^{1}		8	10	6^{2}	5		7	13														7
1	2	3^{3}	4	13	14	10	9^{2}		8	11	6	5		7^{1}			12												8
1	2	3	4		11^{2}		10^{3}		7	9	8^{1}	5		6	13		12	14											9
1	2	4	5	3	6	10^{2}	12		9	11		7			8^{1}		13												10
1	5	2	3	4	6^{2}	11	12	8^{1}	9	10		7		13															11
1	2	3	4	6^{1}		10		7^{2}	9	11	12	5		8	13														12
	2	3	4		5	10	9^{1}	6	8	11		13		7^{2}			12		1										13
	4	2	3		5^{1}	10	12	7^{2}		11	8^{3}			6			14	9	1	13									14
	5	3	4		2^{1}	11	12	8^{3}		10	9^{2}	14		6			13	7	1										15
		2	3		5	9		8	13	10^{1}	11^{2}	4■		6				7	1		12								16
	4	3^{3}	2		5	9	14	7	12	10^{2}	11			6^{1}				8	1		13								17
	4		2	3	5^{2}	10^{3}	13	12	8	11	14			6^{1}				9	1		7								18
	4	3■	2		14	12	9	6	5	11^{3}	10^{2}							7^{1}	1		8	13							19
	3		4	5	2	10^{2}	13	6^{1}	7	12	14			9^{3}					1		8	11							20
	2	4	5	3	9^{2}	11	12■	6^{1}	7										1		8	10^{3}	13	14					21
	12	3	2	4	13	8^{2}		6				5^{1}						14	1		7	9	10^{3}	11					22
		2	3		13	12		6				4		5				8^{2}	1		7	10	11^{1}	9					23
	14		3	4	13	12		7				2		8^{2}				5^{3}	1		6	10	9^{1}	11■					24
	12		2	3^{1}	5^{2}	10		7				4		6				8	1		9	11	13						25
	12	4	3		2^{1}			7				5		9	14			6	1		8	10^{2}	11^{3}		13				26
	13	5^{3}	4		2	12	14	7				3		9^{2}				6^{1}	1		8	11	10						27
	2		4		6^{2}	7^{1}	13	3	8									9	1		5	11^{3}	10	14	12				28
			2			8		5				3		4	12				1		6	10	11^{1}	9		7			29
	12	2			13	9		6				3		4^{1}					1		7	10	8	11^{2}		5			30
	2	4	3		6	9		8^{1}				5^{3}						12	1		7	10	11^{2}	14		13			31
	2	4	3		6^{2}	9		12				5					14	13	1		8	10^{3}		11^{1}		7			32
15	2	4	3		6	10						5							1^{G}		8	9	12	11^{1}		7			33
1	2	3	4		6^{2}	9	13					5									8	10	11^{1}	12		7			34
	2	4	3	14	6	9	12					5							1		8	10^{2}	13	11^{1}		7^{3}			35
			4	3			9	7				5	11		10^{3}	12					8^{2}			14	13	6^{1}	1	2	36

STRANRAER

Year Formed: 1870. *Ground & Address:* Stair Park, London Rd, Stranraer DG9 8BS. *Telephone and Fax:* 01776 703271.
E-mail: secretary@stranraerfc.org *Website:* www.stranraerfc.org
Ground Capacity: 5,600, seated: 1,830. *Size of Pitch:* 110yd × 70yd.
Chairman: Alex Connor. *Vice Chairman:* Robert Rice. *Secretary:* Hilde Law.
Manager: Keith Knox. *Assistant Manager:* Stephen Aitken. *Physio:* Walter Cannon.
Club Nicknames: The Blues, The Clayholers.
Previous Grounds: None.
Record Attendance: 6500 v Rangers, Scottish Cup 1st rd, 24 Jan 1948.
Record Transfer Fee received: £90,000 for Mark Campbell to Ayr U (1999).
Record Transfer Fee paid: £15,000 for Colin Harkness from Kilmarnock (Aug 1989).
Record Victory: 9-0 v St Cuthbert Wanderers, Scottish Cup 2nd rd, 23 Oct 2010; 9-0 v Wigtown & Bladnoch, Scottish Cup 2nd rd, 22 Oct 2011.
Record Defeat: 1-11 v Queen of the South, Scottish Cup 1st rd, 16 Jan 1932.
Most League Appearances: 301: Keith Knox, 1986-90; 1999-2001.
Most League Goals in Season (Individual): 59: Tommy Sloan.

STRANRAER 2011–12 LEAGUE RECORD

Match No.	*Date*	*Venue*	*Opponents*	*Result*	*H/T Score*	*Lg Pos.*	*Goalscorers*	*Attendance*
1	Aug 6	H	Alloa Ath	L 2-3	2-1	—	Aitken [17], Winter [35]	306
2	13	A	Queen's Park	L 0-2	0-1	10		626
3	20	H	Berwick R	W 2-1	0-0	8	Aitken [62], Malcolm [64]	260
4	27	A	Montrose	W 6-0	2-0	5	McColm 2 [38, 42], Aitken [46], Moore 2 [68, 79], Malcolm [72]	302
5	Sept 10	H	Annan Ath	W 4-2	1-1	4	Aitken 2 (1 pen) [29, 83 (p)], McColm 2 [55, 71]	396
6	17	A	East Stirling	W 3-1	1-1	3	Noble [12], McColm [70], Moore [90]	271
7	24	H	Elgin C	W 1-0	1-0	3	Shepherd [15]	365
8	Oct 1	H	Clyde	D 0-0	0-0	2		363
9	15	A	Peterhead	W 3-1	2-0	2	McKeown [12], Stirling [39], Moore [90]	405
10	29	H	Queen's Park	L 2-3	2-1	2	Grehan [23], Malcolm [29]	390
11	Nov 5	A	Alloa Ath	L 0-1	0-0	3		502
12	12	H	Montrose	D 4-4	3-0	4	Winter [7], Malcolm 2 [18, 19], Grehan [53]	326
13	Dec 3	A	Elgin C	D 1-1	0-1	4	Stirling [63]	520
14	6	A	Annan Ath	W 3-0	2-0	—	McColm [18], Grehan [31], Stirling [79]	304
15	10	H	East Stirling	W 6-0	3-0	3	Stirling 2 (1 pen) [30 (p), 32], Winter [33], McColm [58], Taggart [63], Moore [83]	276
16	17	H	Peterhead	W 2-1	0-0	1	Moore [80], Stirling [90]	290
17	26	A	Clyde	D 1-1	1-1	2	Grehan [18]	556
18	31	H	Annan Ath	W 4-2	1-1	1	Winter 2 [41, 69], Stirling (pen) [61], Malcolm [88]	592
19	Jan 7	A	Montrose	W 3-1	1-1	1	Winter 2 [38, 83], Malcolm [73]	257
20	14	A	Berwick R	D 2-2	1-2	2	McColm [6], Malcolm [75]	438
21	21	H	Alloa Ath	L 0-4	0-2	2		475
22	28	H	Elgin C	W 5-2	2-2	2	Moore 2 [22, 71], Malcolm [33], Stirling (pen) [53], Taggart [68]	285
23	Feb 4	A	East Stirling	D 2-2	1-1	2	Stirling [33], Aitken (pen) [89]	275
24	11	A	Peterhead	D 1-1	1-1	2	Malcolm [1]	435
25	18	H	Clyde	W 1-0	0-0	2	Stirling [54]	385
26	25	A	Queen's Park	L 2-3	2-1	2	Malcolm [24], Aitken [42]	637
27	Mar 3	H	Berwick R	L 1-3	1-1	3	McColm [45]	330
28	10	A	Annan Ath	W 3-1	2-1	2	Aitken (pen) [13], McKeown [45], Malcolm [87]	491
29	17	H	Montrose	W 3-1	0-1	2	Moore [58], Malcolm 2 [65, 90]	287
30	24	H	East Stirling	W 4-1	3-0	2	Malcolm [9], Moore [17], Devlin (og) [45], Stirling [52]	304
31	31	A	Elgin C	W 2-1	0-0	2	Moore [67], Stirling [74]	685
32	Apr 7	A	Clyde	L 1-2	1-0	2	Moore [6]	506
33	14	H	Peterhead	L 0-3	0-1	2		291
34	21	A	Alloa Ath	L 1-3	1-2	3	Gallagher [25]	617
35	28	H	Queen's Park	L 2-3	0-1	3	Grehan [64], Aitken (pen) [73]	458
36	May 5	A	Berwick R	L 0-1	0-0	3		402

Final League Position: 3

Honours
League Champions: Second Division 1993-94, 1997-98; *Runners up:* 2004-05, 2007-08. Third Division 2003-04.
Qualifying Cup Winners: 1937.
Scottish Cup: Quarter-finals 2003
League Challenge Cup Winners: 1996-97.

Club colours: Shirt: Royal blue with white trim. Shorts: White with royal blue trim. Stockings: Royal blue.

Goalscorers: *League (77):* Malcolm 15, Moore 12, Stirling 12 (3 pens), Aitken 9 (4 pens), McColm 9, Winter 7, Grehan 5, McKeown 2, Taggart 2, Gallagher 1, Noble 1, Shepherd 1, own goal 1.
Scottish Cup (10): Winter 3, Grehan 2, Malcolm 2, Aitken 1, McColm 1, McKeown 1.
Scottish Communities Cup (1): Gallagher 1.
Ramsdens Cup (0).
Play-Offs (8): Grehan 2, Malcolm 2, Winter 2, McKeown 1, Moore 1.

Mitchell David 24	Kane J 29 + 3	McKeown F 33	Kennedy R 2	Shepherd N 12 + 12	Noble S 30 + 1	Aitken C 24 + 2	Murphy P 2 + 2	Gallagher G 24 + 3	Winter S 27 + 8	Malcolm C 34 + 1	McColm S 16 + 16	Mitchell Danny 6 + 3	Cochrane A — + 4	Moore M 9 + 22	McGregor D 25	Durnan M 4	Taggart S 24	Stirling S 24 + 2	Grehan M 22 + 5	Marshall R 12 + 1	Agnew D — + 4	Carnaghan A — + 1	Borris R 8	Belkouche Z 5 + 1	Dougan B — + 1	*Match No.*
1	2	3	4	5^{1}	6	7	8^{2}	9	10^{3}	11	12	13	14													1
1	2	4	3	5^{3}	6^{1}	8	9	10	7^{2}	11	14	12		13												2
1	2	5		9		6	12	7	13	10^{3}	11^{2}	8	14		3^{1}	4										3
1	2	4		7		8		6^{2}	13	10	11^{1}	9		12	3	5										4
1	2	4		6	5	7	14	9^{1}	12	10^{3}	11^{2}	8		13		3										5
1	2	4		5^{1}	6	8		7	13	10	11^{2}	9		12		3										6
1	2	3		4^{2}	6	8		7		10	11^{3}	9^{1}		13			5	12	14							7
1	2	4		6^{1}	5			9^{2}	13	11	12	8		10^{3}			3	7	14							8
1	2	4		14	5	8^{1}		6	9^{3}	10		12		13			3	7	11^{2}							9
1	5	3			6	9		4	7^{2}	10	13			12			2	8	11^{1}							10
1		3			6	7		5	9	10	13			12	4^{1}		2^{2}	8	11							11
1■	12	3			6^{1}	8		5^{2}	7	10	13				2		4	9	11^{G}	15						12
	4	3		13	5				7	10^{1}	9^{2}			12	6		2	8	11	1						13
	8	3			5			14	6	9^{3}	11^{2}			12	4		2	7	10^{1}	1	13					14
	6	3			5			12	8^{2}	10	9			13	2^{1}		4	7^{3}	11	1	14					15
	8	4			5				6^{1}	10	9			12	3		2	7	11	1						16
	5	4			3			2	6	10	9^{1}			12	8			7	11	1						17
	8	3		13	5			2	6	11^{3}	10^{1}		14	12	4			7	9^{2}	1						18
	6^{3}	4		13	5			2	7	10	9^{1}			12	3			8	11^{2}	1		14				19
	8	4^{1}		13	5			2	6	10	9^{2}			12	3			7	11	1						20
	7	3		13	5			2	6^{2}	10	9^{1}			12	4			8	11^{3}	1	14					21
	7	5		3	6	13			8	11^{3}	14			10^{1}	2		4	9^{2}	12	1						22
	9^{2}	4		5^{1}	6	13			7	11^{3}	14			10	3		2	8	12	1						23
1	2	4			5	8^{1}		9	12	10^{2}	14			13	3		6	7	11^{3}							24
1	6	3			9	7^{2}		5	13	10^{1}				12	2		4	8	11							25
	6^{2}	3■		12	9	8		4	7	10	13				2		5^{1}		11	1						26
1	4			13	5	8^{3}			7	9	11		14	12	3^{2}		2	6	10^{1}							27
1		4			5	8			6	10^{2}	13			12	3		2	7	11^{1}				9			28
1	14	4		13	5	8^{3}			6	11	12			10^{1}	3		2	7					9^{2}			29
1	6	3		12	4	8			5	11^{2}	13			10^{3}	2			7	14				9^{1}			30
1	14	3		13		7			9	11				12	4		5^{3}	8	10^{1}				6^{2}	2		31
1		5				8		13	6	11	12			10	4		2	7^{2}					9	3^{1}		32
1	5	3		6		9		8^{1}	12	11^{2}				10			2						7	4	13	33
1	6	3^{1}		4	14	8		5	7	13	10^{2}						2		11				9^{3}	12		34
1	4^{2}			14	6	8		3	7^{3}		13			10			2	12	11				9^{1}	5		35
1					6	8		5	7	9	12			10^{1}	4		2		11		13			3^{2}		36

SCOTTISH LEAGUE PLAY-OFFS 2011–12

■ *Denotes player sent off.*

DIVISION 1 SEMI-FINALS FIRST LEG

Wednesday, 9 May 2012

Airdrie U (0) 0

Ayr U (0) 0 1871

Airdrie U: Adam; Stallard, McDonald, Lovering, Lilley, Bain, Lynch, Blockley, Stevenson, Donnelly, Holmes.
Ayr U: Cuthbert; Malone, Longridge, Smith, Tiffoney, Trouten (Campbell), Geggan, Tomsett (McKernon), Moffat, Roberts, Parker (Robertson R).

Dumbarton (1) 2 *(Wallace 16, Prunty 61)*

Arbroath (1) 1 *(Malcolm 6)* 911

Dumbarton: Grindlay; Nugent, Lithgow, Creaney, Wallace, McNiff, Nicoll, Agnew, Gilhaney (Gray), Prunty (Walker), Dargo.
Arbroath: Hill; Baxter, Malcolm, Innes, McAnespie, Sheerin (Gibson), Falkingham, Kerr, Doris, Birse (Caddis), Samuel (Sibanda).

DIVISION 1 SEMI-FINALS SECOND LEG

Saturday, 12 May 2012

Arbroath (0) 0

Dumbarton (0) 0 1454

Arbroath: Hill; Baxter, Malcolm, Innes, Caddis (Kerr), McAnespie, Falkingham, Gibson, Sheerin (Samuel), Swankie, Doris.
Dumbarton: Grindlay; Kennedy, Lithgow, Creaney, Wallace, McNiff, Agnew, Nicoll, Gilhaney, Prunty (Graham), Dargo (Walker).

Ayr U (0) 1 *(Geggan 64)*

Airdrie U (0) 3 *(Holmes 55, 65, McLaren 85)* 2782

Ayr U: Cuthbert; Malone, Smith, Campbell, Tiffoney■, Longridge, McKernon (McGowan), Geggan, Trouten, Roberts, Moffat (Parker).
Airdrie U: Adam; Bain, Lamie (Green) (McLaren), Lilley, Stallard, McNeil, Stevenson, Blockley, Lynch, Holmes, Donnelly (Boyle).

DIVISION 1 FINAL FIRST LEG

Wednesday, 16 May 2012

Dumbarton (2) 2 *(Prunty 29, Wallace 32)*

Airdrie U (1) 1 *(Bain 42)* 1746

Dumbarton: Grindlay; Nugent■, Creaney, Lithgow, Wallace (Gray), Agnew, Nicoll, McNiff, Gilhaney (Lamont), Prunty, Walker (Graham).
Airdrie U: Adam; Stallard, Lovering, MacDonald (McNeil), Lilley, Lynch, Bain (McLaren), Blockley, Stevenson, Holmes, Donnelly (Boyle).

DIVISION 1 FINAL SECOND LEG

Sunday, 20 May 2012

Airdrie U (1) 1 *(Holmes 35)*

Dumbarton (3) 4 *(Dargo 9, 21, Gilhaney 45, Wallace 65)* 2914

Airdrie U: Adam; McNeil, Stallard (Lamie), Lilley, Lovering, Stevenson, Lynch (Bain■), Blockley, McLaren, Holmes, Donnelly (Boyle).
Dumbarton: Grindlay; Finnie, Lithgow, Creaney, McNiff, Wallace, Nicoll, Gilhaney (Lamont), Agnew, Prunty (Graham), Dargo (Walker).

DIVISION 2 SEMI-FINALS FIRST LEG

Wednesday, 9 May 2012

Elgin C (0) 1 *(Millar 53)*

Albion R (0) 0 1248

Elgin C: Clark; Niven, Duff, Nicolson, Durnan, Cameron, Leslie (MacPhee), Cooper, Moore (O'Donoghue), Gunn, Millar (Crooks).
Albion R: Gaston; Reid, Donnelly, O'Byrne■, Russell, McStay, Ferry, Lumsden, Werndly (Marriott), Gemmell, Love (Pierce).

Stranraer (2) 3 *(Winter 17, 68, Malcolm 22)*

Queen's Park (0) 1 *(Quinn 48)* 481

Stranraer: David Mitchell; Taggart, McGregor, McKeown, Noble, Winter, Stirling, Aitken, Borris (Gallagher), Malcolm, Grehan (Moore).
Queen's Park: Parry; Brough, Little, Meggatt, Capuano, Gallagher, McGinn, Quinn, Watt (Smith), Longworth, Burns (Ronald) (Daly).

DIVISION 2 SEMI-FINALS SECOND LEG

Saturday, 12 May 2012

Albion R (0) 2 *(Gemmell 62, Chaplain 90)*

Elgin C (0) 0 827

Albion R: Gaston; Marriott, Russell, Stevenson, Reid, Donnelly, Canning, Boyle (Love), Chaplain, Pierce (Werndly), Gemmell.
Elgin C: Clark; Durnan, Duff, Niven, Nicolson, Cooper, Millar (O'Donoghue), Moore, Lesley, Cameron, Gunn.

Queen's Park (0) 0

Stranraer (2) 2 *(Malcolm 12, Grehan 20)* 1188

Queen's Park: Parry; Little, Brough, Bradley, McBride, McGinn, Anderson (Gallagher), Watt, Smith (Quinn), Longworth, Murray (Meggatt).
Stranraer: David Mitchell; Taggart, McGregor, McKeown, Gallagher, Noble, Winter (Kane), Aitken, Stirling, Malcolm (McColm), Grehan (Moore).

DIVISION 2 FINAL FIRST LEG

Wednesday, 16 May 2012

Stranraer (1) 2 *(McKeown 39, Moore 90)*

Albion R (0) 0 506

Stranraer: David Mitchell; Taggart, McKeown, McGregor, Gallagher, Noble, Winter, Aitken, Stirling, Malcolm, Grehan (Moore).
Albion R: Gaston; Donnelly, Lumsden, O'Byrne, Russell, Stevenson, Canning, McStay, Boyle (Marriott), Pierce (Love), Gemmell.

DIVISION 2 FINAL SECOND LEG

Sunday, 20 May 2012

Albion R (3) 3 *(Chaplain 6, 33 (pen), Love 25)*

Stranraer (1) 1 *(Grehan 27)* 1008

Albion R: Gaston; Reid, Donnelly, Stevenson, O'Byrne, Ferry (Werndly), Boyle (Russell), Love, Canning, Chaplain (McStay), Acqua.
Stranraer: David Mitchell; Taggart, McGregor, McKeown, Noble, Winter (Borris), Aitken, Stirling, Gallagher (McColm), Malcolm (Moore), Grehan.
aet; Albion R won 5-3 on penalties.

SCOTTISH LEAGUE HONOURS 1890–2012

*On goal average (ratio)/difference. †Held jointly after indecisive play-off. ‡Won on deciding match. ¶Two points deducted for fielding ineligible player. Competition suspended 1940–45 during war; Regional Leagues operating. ‡‡Two points deducted for registration irregularities. §Not promoted after play-offs. §§Ten points deducted for entering administration.

PREMIER LEAGUE

Maximum points: 108

	First	*Pts*	*Second*	*Pts*	*Third*	*Pts*
1998–99	Rangers	77	Celtic	71	St Johnstone	57
1999–2000	Rangers	90	Celtic	69	Hearts	54
			Maximum points: 114			
2000–01	Celtic	97	Rangers	82	Hibernian	66
2001–02	Celtic	103	Rangers	85	Livingston	58
2002–03	Rangers*	97	Celtic	97	Hearts	63
2003–04	Celtic	98	Rangers	81	Hearts	68
2004–05	Rangers	93	Celtic	92	Hibernian*	61
2005–06	Celtic	91	Hearts	74	Rangers	73
2006–07	Celtic	84	Rangers	72	Aberdeen	65
2007–08	Celtic	89	Rangers	86	Motherwell	60
2008–09	Rangers	86	Celtic	82	Hearts	59
2009–10	Rangers	87	Celtic	81	Dundee U	63
2010–11	Rangers	93	Celtic	92	Hearts	63
2011–12	Celtic	93	Rangers§§	73	Motherwell	62

PREMIER DIVISION

Maximum points: 72

	First	*Pts*	*Second*	*Pts*	*Third*	*Pts*
1975–76	Rangers	54	Celtic	48	Hibernian	43
1976–77	Celtic	55	Rangers	46	Aberdeen	43
1977–78	Rangers	55	Aberdeen	53	Dundee U	40
1978–79	Celtic	48	Rangers	45	Dundee U	44
1979–80	Aberdeen	48	Celtic	47	St Mirren	42
1980–81	Celtic	56	Aberdeen	49	Rangers*	44
1981–82	Celtic	55	Aberdeen	53	Rangers	43
1982–83	Dundee U	56	Celtic*	55	Aberdeen	55
1983–84	Aberdeen	57	Celtic	50	Dundee U	47
1984–85	Aberdeen	59	Celtic	52	Dundee U	47
1985–86	Celtic*	50	Hearts	50	Dundee U	47
			Maximum points: 88			
1986–87	Rangers	69	Celtic	63	Dundee U	60
1987–88	Celtic	72	Hearts	62	Rangers	60
			Maximum points: 72			
1988–89	Rangers	56	Aberdeen	50	Celtic	46
1989–90	Rangers	51	Aberdeen*	44	Hearts	44
1990–91	Rangers	55	Aberdeen	53	Celtic*	41
			Maximum points: 88			
1991–92	Rangers	72	Hearts	63	Celtic	62
1992–93	Rangers	73	Aberdeen	64	Celtic	60
1993–94	Rangers	58	Aberdeen	55	Motherwell	54
			Maximum points: 108			
1994–95	Rangers	69	Motherwell	54	Hibernian	53
1995–96	Rangers	87	Celtic	83	Aberdeen*	55
1996–97	Rangers	80	Celtic	75	Dundee U	60
1997–98	Celtic	74	Rangers	72	Hearts	67

FIRST DIVISION

Maximum points: 52

	First	*Pts*	*Second*	*Pts*	*Third*	*Pts*
1975–76	Partick Th	41	Kilmarnock	35	Montrose	30
			Maximum points: 78			
1976–77	St Mirren	62	Clydebank	58	Dundee	51
1977–78	Morton*	58	Hearts	58	Dundee	57
1978–79	Dundee	55	Kilmarnock*	54	Clydebank	54
1979–80	Hearts	53	Airdrieonians	51	Ayr U*	44
1980–81	Hibernian	57	Dundee	52	St Johnstone	51
1981–82	Motherwell	61	Kilmarnock	51	Hearts	50
1982–83	St Johnstone	55	Hearts	54	Clydebank	50
1983–84	Morton	54	Dumbarton	51	Partick Th	46
1984–85	Motherwell	50	Clydebank	48	Falkirk	45
1985–86	Hamilton A	56	Falkirk	45	Kilmarnock	44
			Maximum points: 88			
1986–87	Morton	57	Dunfermline Ath	56	Dumbarton	53
1987–88	Hamilton A	56	Meadowbank Th	52	Clydebank	49

	First	*Pts*	*Second*	*Pts*	*Third*	*Pts*
			Maximum points: 78			
1988–89	Dunfermline Ath	54	Falkirk	52	Clydebank	48
1989–90	St Johnstone	58	Airdrieonians	54	Clydebank	44
1990–91	Falkirk	54	Airdrieonians	53	Dundee	52
			Maximum points: 88			
1991–92	Dundee	58	Partick Th*	57	Hamilton A	57
1992–93	Raith R	65	Kilmarnock	54	Dunfermline Ath	52
1993–94	Falkirk	66	Dunfermline Ath	65	Airdrieonians	54
			Maximum points: 108			
1994–95	Raith R	69	Dunfermline Ath*	68	Dundee	68
1995–96	Dunfermline Ath	71	Dundee U*	67	Morton	67
1996–97	St Johnstone	80	Airdieonians	60	Dundee*	58
1997–98	Dundee	70	Falkirk	65	Raith R*	60
1998–99	Hibernian	89	Falkirk	66	Ayr U	62
1999–2000	St Mirren	76	Dunfermline Ath	71	Falkirk	68
2000–01	Livingston	76	Ayr U	69	Falkirk	56
2001–02	Partick Th	66	Airdrieonians	56	Ayr U	52
2002–03	Falkirk	81	Clyde	72	St Johnstone	67
2003–04	Inverness CT	70	Clyde	69	St Johnstone	57
2004–05	Falkirk	75	St Mirren*	60	Clyde	60
2005–06	St Mirren	76	St Johnstone	66	Hamilton A	59
2006–07	Gretna	66	St Johnstone	65	Dundee*	53
2007–08	Hamilton A	76	Dundee	69	St Johnstone	58
2008–09	St Johnstone	65	Partick Th	55	Dunfermline Ath	51
2009–10	Inverness CT	73	Dundee	61	Dunfermline Ath	58
2010–11	Dunfermline Ath	70	Raith R	60	Falkirk	58
2011–12	Ross Co	79	Dundee	55	Falkirk	52

SECOND DIVISION

	First	*Pts*	*Second*	*Pts*	*Third*	*Pts*
			Maximum points: 52			
1975–76	Clydebank*	40	Raith R	40	Alloa Ath	35
			Maximum points: 78			
1976–77	Stirling Alb	55	Alloa Ath	51	Dunfermline Ath	50
1977–78	Clyde*	53	Raith R	53	Dunfermline Ath	48
1978–79	Berwick R	54	Dunfermline Ath	52	Falkirk	50
1979–80	Falkirk	50	East Stirling	49	Forfar Ath	46
1980–81	Queen's Park	50	Queen of the S	46	Cowdenbeath	45
1981–82	Clyde	59	Alloa Ath*	50	Arbroath	50
1982–83	Brechin C	55	Meadowbank Th	54	Arbroath	49
1983–84	Forfar Ath	63	East Fife	47	Berwick R	43
1984–85	Montrose	53	Alloa Ath	50	Dunfermline Ath	49
1985–86	Dunfermline Ath	57	Queen of the S	55	Meadowbank Th	49
1986–87	Meadowbank Th	55	Raith R*	52	Stirling Alb*	52
1987–88	Ayr U	61	St Johnstone	59	Queen's Park	51
1988–89	Albion R	50	Alloa Ath	45	Brechin C	43
1989–90	Brechin C	49	Kilmarnock	48	Stirling Alb	47
1990–91	Stirling Alb	54	Montrose	46	Cowdenbeath	45
1991–92	Dumbarton	52	Cowdenbeath	51	Alloa Ath	50
1992–93	Clyde	54	Brechin C*	53	Stranraer	53
1993–94	Stranraer	56	Berwick R	48	Stenhousemuir*	47
			Maximum points: 108			
1994–95	Morton	64	Dumbarton	60	Stirling Alb	58
1995–96	Stirling Alb	81	East Fife	67	Berwick R	60
1996–97	Ayr U	77	Hamilton A	74	Livingston	64
1997–98	Stranraer	61	Clydebank	60	Livingston	59
1998–99	Livingston	77	Inverness CT	72	Clyde	53
1999–2000	Clyde	65	Alloa Ath	64	Ross Co	62
2000–01	Partick Th	75	Arbroath	58	Berwick R*	54
2001–02	Queen of the S	67	Alloa Ath	59	Forfar Ath	53
2002–03	Raith R	59	Brechin C	55	Airdrie U	54
2003–04	Airdrie U	70	Hamilton A	62	Dumbarton	60
2004–05	Brechin C	72	Stranraer	63	Morton	62
2005–06	Gretna	88	Morton§	70	Peterhead*§	57
2006–07	Morton	77	Stirling Alb	69	Raith R§	62
2007–08	Ross Co	73	Airdrie U	66	Raith R§	60
2008–09	Raith R	76	Ayr U	74	Brechin C§	62
2009–10	Stirling Alb*	65	Alloa Ath§	65	Cowdenbeath	54
2010–11	Livingston	82	Ayr U*	59	Forfar Ath§	59
2011–12	Cowdenbeath	71	Arbroath§	63	Dumbarton	58

THIRD DIVISION

	First	*Pts*	*Second*	*Pts*	*Third*	*Pts*
			Maximum points: 108			
1994–95	Forfar Ath	80	Montrose	67	Ross Co	60
1995–96	Livingston	72	Brechin C	63	Inverness CT	57

	First	*Pts*	*Second*	*Pts*	*Third*	*Pts*
1996–97	Inverness CT	76	Forfar Ath*	67	Ross Co	67
1997–98	Alloa Ath	76	Arbroath	68	Ross Co*	67
1998–99	Ross Co	77	Stenhousemuir	64	Brechin C	59
1999–2000	Queen's Park	69	Berwick R	66	Forfar Ath	61
2000–01	Hamilton A*	76	Cowdenbeath	76	Brechin C	72
2001–02	Brechin C	73	Dumbarton	61	Albion R	59
2002–03	Morton	72	East Fife	71	Albion R	70
2003–04	Stranraer	79	Stirling Alb	77	Gretna	68
2004–05	Gretna	98	Peterhead	78	Cowdenbeath	51
2005–06	Cowdenbeath*	76	Berwick R§	76	Stenhousemuir§	73
2006–07	Berwick R	75	Arbroath§	70	Queen's Park	68
2007–08	East Fife	88	Stranraer	65	Montrose§	59
2008–09	Dumbarton	67	Cowdenbeath§	63	East Stirling§	61
2009–10	Livingston	78	Forfar Ath	63	East Stirling§	61
2010–11	Arbroath	66	Albion R	61	Queen's Park*§	59
2011–12	Alloa Ath	77	Queen's Park§	63	Stranraer§	58

DIVISION 1 to 1974–75

Maximum points: *a* 36; *b* 44; *c* 40; *d* 52; *e* 60; *f* 68; g 76; *h* 84.

1890–91*a*	Dumbarton†	29	Rangers†	29	Celtic	21
1891–92*b*	Dumbarton	37	Celtic	35	Hearts	34
1892–93*a*	Celtic	29	Rangers	28	St Mirren	20
1893–94*a*	Celtic	29	Hearts	26	St Bernard's	23
1894–95*a*	Hearts	31	Celtic	26	Rangers	22
1895–96*a*	Celtic	30	Rangers	26	Hibernian	24
1896–97*a*	Hearts	28	Hibernian	26	Rangers	25
1897–98*a*	Celtic	33	Rangers	29	Hibernian	22
1898–99*a*	Rangers	36	Hearts	26	Celtic	24
1899–1900*a*	Rangers	32	Celtic	25	Hibernian	24
1900–01*c*	Rangers	35	Celtic	29	Hibernian	25
1901–02*a*	Rangers	28	Celtic	26	Hearts	22
1902–03*b*	Hibernian	37	Dundee	31	Rangers	29
1903–04*d*	Third Lanark	43	Hearts	39	Celtic*	38
1904–05*d*	Celtic‡	41	Rangers	41	Third Lanark	35
1905–06*e*	Celtic	49	Hearts	43	Airdrieonians	38
1906–07*f*	Celtic	55	Dundee	48	Rangers	45
1907–08*f*	Celtic	55	Falkirk	51	Rangers	50
1908–09*f*	Celtic	51	Dundee	50	Clyde	48
1909–10*f*	Celtic	54	Falkirk	52	Rangers	46
1910–11*f*	Rangers	52	Aberdeen	48	Falkirk	44
1911–12*f*	Rangers	51	Celtic	45	Clyde	42
1912–13*f*	Rangers	53	Celtic	49	Hearts*	41
1913–14*g*	Celtic	65	Rangers	59	Hearts*	54
1914–15*g*	Celtic	65	Hearts	61	Rangers	50
1915–16*g*	Celtic	67	Rangers	56	Morton	51
1916–17*g*	Celtic	64	Morton	54	Rangers	53
1917–18*f*	Rangers	56	Celtic	55	Kilmarnock*	43
1918–19*f*	Celtic	58	Rangers	57	Morton	47
1919–20*h*	Rangers	71	Celtic	68	Motherwell	57
1920–21*h*	Rangers	76	Celtic	66	Hearts	50
1921–22*h*	Celtic	67	Rangers	66	Raith R	51
1922–23*g*	Rangers	55	Airdrieonians	50	Celtic	46
1923–24*g*	Rangers	59	Airdrieonians	50	Celtic	46
1924–25*g*	Rangers	60	Airdrieonians	57	Hibernian	52
1925–26*g*	Celtic	58	Airdrieonians*	50	Hearts	50
1926–27*g*	Rangers	56	Motherwell	51	Celtic	49
1927–28*g*	Rangers	60	Celtic*	55	Motherwell	55
1928–29*g*	Rangers	67	Celtic	51	Motherwell	50
1929–30*g*	Rangers	60	Motherwell	55	Aberdeen	53
1930–31*g*	Rangers	60	Celtic	58	Motherwell	56
1931–32*g*	Motherwell	66	Rangers	61	Celtic	48
1932–33*g*	Rangers	62	Motherwell	59	Hearts	50
1933–34*g*	Rangers	66	Motherwell	62	Celtic	47
1934–35*g*	Rangers	55	Celtic	52	Hearts	50
1935–36*g*	Celtic	66	Rangers*	61	Aberdeen	61
1936–37*g*	Rangers	61	Aberdeen	54	Celtic	52
1937–38*g*	Celtic	61	Hearts	58	Rangers	49
1938–39*g*	Rangers	59	Celtic	48	Aberdeen	46
1946–47*e*	Rangers	46	Hibernian	44	Aberdeen	39
1947–48*e*	Hibernian	48	Rangers	46	Partick Th	36
1948–49*e*	Rangers	46	Dundee	45	Hibernian	39
1949–50*e*	Rangers	50	Hibernian	49	Hearts	43
1950–51*e*	Hibernian	48	Rangers*	38	Dundee	38
1951–52*e*	Hibernian	45	Rangers	41	East Fife	37

	First	*Pts*	*Second*	*Pts*	*Third*	*Pts*
1952–53*e*	Rangers*	43	Hibernian	43	East Fife	39
1953–54*e*	Celtic	43	Hearts	38	Partick Th	35
1954–55*e*	Aberdeen	49	Celtic	46	Rangers	41
1955–56*f*	Rangers	52	Aberdeen	46	Hearts*	45
1956–57*f*	Rangers	55	Hearts	53	Kilmarnock	42
1957–58*f*	Hearts	62	Rangers	49	Celtic	46
1958–59*f*	Rangers	50	Hearts	48	Motherwell	44
1959–60*f*	Hearts	54	Kilmarnock	50	Rangers*	42
1960–61*f*	Rangers	51	Kilmarnock	50	Third Lanark	42
1961–62*f*	Dundee	54	Rangers	51	Celtic	46
1962–63*f*	Rangers	57	Kilmarnock	48	Partick Th	46
1963–64*f*	Rangers	55	Kilmarnock	49	Celtic*	47
1964–65*f*	Kilmarnock*	50	Hearts	50	Dunfermline Ath	49
1965–66*f*	Celtic	57	Rangers	55	Kilmarnock	45
1966–67*f*	Celtic	58	Rangers	55	Clyde	46
1967–68*f*	Celtic	63	Rangers	61	Hibernian	45
1968–69*f*	Celtic	54	Rangers	49	Dunfermline Ath	45
1969–70*f*	Celtic	57	Rangers	45	Hibernian	44
1970–71*f*	Celtic	56	Aberdeen	54	St Johnstone	44
1971–72*f*	Celtic	60	Aberdeen	50	Rangers	44
1972–73*f*	Celtic	57	Rangers	56	Hibernian	45
1973–74*f*	Celtic	53	Hibernian	49	Rangers	48
1974–75*f*	Rangers	56	Hibernian	49	Celtic	45

DIVISION 2 to 1974–75

Maximum points: a 76; *b* 72; *c* 68; *d* 52; *e* 60; *f* 36; *g* 44.

	First	Pts	Second	Pts	Third	Pts
1893–94*f*	Hibernian	29	Cowlairs	27	Clyde	24
1894–95*f*	Hibernian	30	Motherwell	22	Port Glasgow	20
1895–96*f*	Abercorn	27	Leith Ath	23	Renton	21
1896–97*f*	Partick Th	31	Leith Ath	27	Kilmarnock*	21
1897–98*f*	Kilmarnock	29	Port Glasgow	25	Morton	22
1898–99*f*	Kilmarnock	32	Leith Ath	27	Port Glasgow	25
1899–1900*f*	Partick Th	29	Morton	28	Port Glasgow	20
1900–01*f*	St Bernard's	25	Airdrieonians	23	Abercorn	21
1901–02*g*	Port Glasgow	32	Partick Th	31	Motherwell	26
1902–03*g*	Airdrieonians	35	Motherwell	28	Ayr U*	27
1903–04*g*	Hamilton A	37	Clyde	29	Ayr U	28
1904–05*g*	Clyde	32	Falkirk	28	Hamilton A	27
1905–06*g*	Leith Ath	34	Clyde	31	Albion R	27
1906–07*g*	St Bernard's	32	Vale of Leven*	27	Arthurlie	27
1907–08*g*	Raith R	30	Dumbarton*‡‡	27	Ayr U	27
1908–09*g*	Abercorn	31	Raith R*	28	Vale of Leven	28
1909–10*g*	Leith Ath‡	33	Raith R	33	St Bernard's	27
1910–11*g*	Dumbarton	31	Ayr U	27	Albion R	25
1911–12*g*	Ayr U	35	Abercorn	30	Dumbarton	27
1912–13*d*	Ayr U	34	Dunfermline Ath	33	East Stirling	32
1913–14*g*	Cowdenbeath	31	Albion R	27	Dunfermline Ath*	26
1914–15*d*	Cowdenbeath*	37	St Bernard's*	37	Leith Ath	37
1921–22*a*	Alloa Ath	60	Cowdenbeath	47	Armadale	45
1922–23*a*	Queen's Park	57	Clydebank¶	50	St Johnstone¶	45
1923–24*a*	St Johnstone	56	Cowdenbeath	55	Bathgate	44
1924–25*a*	Dundee U	50	Clydebank	48	Clyde	47
1925–26*a*	Dunfermline Ath	59	Clyde	53	Ayr U	52
1926–27*a*	Bo'ness	56	Raith R	49	Clydebank	45
1927–28*a*	Ayr U	54	Third Lanark	45	King's Park	44
1928–29*b*	Dundee U	51	Morton	50	Arbroath	47
1929–30*a*	Leith Ath*	57	East Fife	57	Albion R	54
1930–31*a*	Third Lanark	61	Dundee U	50	Dunfermline Ath	47
1931–32*a*	East Stirling*	55	St Johnstone	55	Raith R*	46
1932–33*c*	Hibernian	54	Queen of the S	49	Dunfermline Ath	47
1933–34*c*	Albion R	45	Dunfermline Ath*	44	Arbroath	44
1934–35*c*	Third Lanark	52	Arbroath	50	St Bernard's	47
1935–36*c*	Falkirk	59	St Mirren	52	Morton	48
1936–37*c*	Ayr U	54	Morton	51	St Bernard's	48
1937–38*c*	Raith R	59	Albion R	48	Airdrieonians	47
1938–39*c*	Cowdenbeath	60	Alloa Ath*	48	East Fife	48
1946–47*d*	Dundee	45	Airdrieonians	42	East Fife	31
1947–48*e*	East Fife	53	Albion R	42	Hamilton A	40
1948–49*e*	Raith R*	42	Stirling Alb	42	Airdrieonians*	41
1949–50*e*	Morton	47	Airdrieonians	44	Dunfermline Ath*	36
1950–51*e*	Queen of the S*	45	Stirling Alb	45	Ayr U*	36
1951–52*e*	Clyde	44	Falkirk	43	Ayr U	39
1952–53*e*	Stirling Alb	44	Hamilton A	43	Queen's Park	37
1953–54*e*	Motherwell	45	Kilmarnock	42	Third Lanark*	36
1954–55*e*	Airdrieonians	46	Dunfermline Ath	42	Hamilton A	39

	First	*Pts*	*Second*	*Pts*	*Third*	*Pts*
1955–56*b*	Queen's Park	54	Ayr U	51	St Johnstone	49
1956–57*b*	Clyde	64	Third Lanark	51	Cowdenbeath	45
1957–58*b*	Stirling Alb	55	Dunfermline Ath	53	Arbroath	47
1958–59*b*	Ayr U	60	Arbroath	51	Stenhousemuir	46
1959–60*b*	St Johnstone	53	Dundee U	50	Queen of the S	49
1960–61*b*	Stirling Alb	55	Falkirk	54	Stenhousemuir	50
1961–62*b*	Clyde	54	Queen of the S	53	Morton	44
1962–63*b*	St Johnstone	55	East Stirling	49	Morton	48
1963–64*b*	Morton	67	Clyde	53	Arbroath	46
1964–65*b*	Stirling Alb	59	Hamilton A	50	Queen of the S	45
1965–66*b*	Ayr U	53	Airdrieonians	50	Queen of the S	47
1966–67*a*	Morton	69	Raith R	58	Arbroath	57
1967–68*b*	St Mirren	62	Arbroath	53	East Fife	49
1968–69*b*	Motherwell	64	Ayr U	53	East Fife*	48
1969–70*b*	Falkirk	56	Cowdenbeath	55	Queen of the S	50
1970–71*b*	Partick Th	56	East Fife	51	Arbroath	46
1971–72*b*	Dumbarton*	52	Arbroath	52	Stirling Alb	50
1972–73*b*	Clyde	56	Dumfermline Ath	52	Raith R*	47
1973–74*b*	Airdrieonians	60	Kilmarnock	58	Hamilton A	55
1974–75*a*	Falkirk	54	Queen of the S*	53	Montrose	53

Elected to First Division: 1894 Clyde; 1895 Hibernian; 1896 Abercorn; 1897 Partick Th; 1899 Kilmarnock; 1900 Morton and Partick Th; 1902 Port Glasgow and Partick Th; 1903 Airdrieonians and Motherwell; 1905 Falkirk and Aberdeen; 1906 Clyde and Hamilton A; 1910 Raith R; 1913 Ayr U and Dumbarton.

RELEGATED FROM PREMIER LEAGUE

1998–99 Dunfermline Ath
1999–2000 *No relegation due to League reorganization*
2000–01 St Mirren
2001–02 St Johnstone
2002–03 *No relegated team*
2003–04 Partick Th
2004–05 Dundee
2005–06 Livingston
2006–07 Dunfermline Ath
2007–08 Gretna
2008–09 Inverness CT
2009–10 Falkirk
2010–11 Hamilton A
2011–12 Dunfermline Ath

RELEGATED FROM PREMIER DIVISION

1974–75 *No relegation due to League reorganization*
1975–76 Dundee, St Johnstone
1976–77 Hearts, Kilmarnock
1977–78 Ayr U, Clydebank
1978–79 Hearts, Motherwell
1979–80 Dundee, Hibernian
1980–81 Kilmarnock, Hearts
1981–82 Partick Th, Airdrieonians
1982–83 Morton, Kilmarnock
1983–84 St Johnstone, Motherwell
1984–85 Dumbarton, Morton
1985–86 *No relegation due to League reorganization*
1986–87 Clydebank, Hamilton A
1987–88 Falkirk, Dunfermline Ath, Morton
1988–89 Hamilton A
1989–90 Dundee
1990–91 *None*
1991–92 St Mirren, Dunfermline Ath
1992–93 Falkirk, Airdrieonians
1993–94 *See footnote*
1994–95 Dundee U
1995–96 Partick Th, Falkirk
1996–97 Raith R
1997–98 Hibernian

RELEGATED FROM DIVISION 1

1975–76 Dunfermline Ath, Clyde
1976–77 Raith R, Falkirk
1977–78 Alloa Ath, East Fife
1981–82 East Stirling, Queen of the S
1982–83 Dunfermline Ath, Queen's Park
1983–84 Raith R, Alloa Ath
1984–85 Meadowbank Th, St Johnstone
1985–86 Ayr U, Alloa Ath
1986–87 Brechin C, Montrose
1987–88 East Fife, Dumbarton
1988–89 Kilmarnock, Queen of the S
1989–90 Albion R, Alloa Ath
1990–91 Clyde, Brechin C
1992–93 Meadowbank Th, Cowdenbeath
1993–94 *See footnote*
1994–95 Ayr U, Stranraer
1995–96 Hamilton A, Dumbarton
1978–79 Montrose, Queen of the S
1979–80 Arbroath, Clyde
1980–81 Stirling Alb, Berwick R
1996–97 Clydebank, East Fife
1997–98 Partick Th, Stirling Alb
1998–99 Hamilton A, Stranraer
1999–2000 Clydebank
2000–01 Morton, Alloa Ath
2001–02 Raith R
2002–03 Alloa Ath, Arbroath
2003–04 Ayr U, Brechin C
2004–05 Partick Th, Raith R
2005–06 Stranraer, Brechin C
2006–07 Airdrie U, Ross Co
2007–08 Stirling Alb
2008–09 Clyde
2009–10 Airdrie U, Ayr U
2010–11 Cowdenbeath, Stirling Alb
2011–12 Ayr U, Queen of the S

RELEGATED FROM DIVISION 2

1994–95 Meadowbank Th, Brechin C
1995–96 Forfar Ath, Montrose
1996–97 Dumbarton, Berwick R
1997–98 Stenhousemuir, Brechin C
1998–99 East Fife, Forfar Ath
1999–2000 Hamilton A**
2000–01 Queen's Park, Stirling Alb
2001–02 Morton
2002–03 Stranraer, Cowdenbeath
2003–04 East Fife, Stenhousemuir
2004–05 Arbroath, Berwick R
2005–06 Dumbarton
2006–07 Stranraer, Forfar Ath
2007–08 Cowdenbeath, Berwick R
2008–09 Stranraer, Queen's Park
2009–10 Arbroath, Clyde
2010–11 Alloa Ath, Peterhead
2011–12 Stirling Alb

RELEGATED FROM DIVISION 1 (TO 1973–74)

1921–22 *Queen's Park, Dumbarton, Clydebank
1922–23 Albion R, Alloa Ath
1923–24 Clyde, Clydebank
1924–25 Third Lanark, Ayr U
1925–26 Raith R, Clydebank
1926–27 Morton, Dundee U
1927–28 Dunfermline Ath, Bo'ness
1928–29 Third Lanark, Raith R
1929–30 St Johnstone, Dundee U
1930–31 Hibernian, East Fife
1931–32 Dundee U, Leith Ath
1932–33 Morton, East Stirling
1933–34 Third Lanark, Cowdenbeath
1934–35 St Mirren, Falkirk
1935–36 Airdrieonians, Ayr U
1936–37 Dunfermline Ath, Albion R
1937–38 Dundee, Morton
1938–39 Queen's Park, Raith R
1946–47 Kilmarnock, Hamilton A
1947–48 Airdrieonians, Queen's Park
1948–49 Morton, Albion R
1949–50 Queen of the S, Stirling Alb
1950–51 Clyde, Falkirk
1951–52 Morton, Stirling Alb
1952–53 Motherwell, Third Lanark
1953–54 Airdrieonians, Hamilton A
1954–55 *No clubs relegated*
1955–56 Stirling Alb, Clyde
1956–57 Dunfermline Ath, Ayr U
1957–58 East Fife, Queen's Park
1958–59 Queen of the S, Falkirk
1959–60 Arbroath, Stirling Alb
1960–61 Ayr U, Clyde
1961–62 St Johnstone, Stirling Alb
1962–63 Clyde, Raith R
1963–64 Queen of the S, East Stirling
1964–65 Airdrieonians, Third Lanark
1965–66 Morton, Hamilton A
1966–67 St Mirren, Ayr U
1967–68 Motherwell, Stirling Alb
1968–69 Falkirk, Arbroath
1969–70 Raith R, Partick Th
1970–71 St Mirren, Cowdenbeath
1971–72 Clyde, Dunfermline Ath
1972–73 Kilmarnock, Airdrieonians
1973–74 East Fife, Falkirk

*Season 1921–22 – only 1 club promoted, 3 clubs relegated. ***15pts deducted for failing to field a team.*

Scottish League Championship wins: Rangers 54, Celtic 43, Aberdeen 4, Hearts 4, Hibernian 4, Dumbarton 2, Dundee 1, Dundee U 1, Kilmarnock 1, Motherwell 1, Third Lanark 1.

At the end of the 1993–94 season four divisions were created assisted by the admission of two new clubs Ross County and Caledonian Thistle. Only one club was promoted from Division 1 and Division 2. The three relegated from the Premier joined with teams finishing second to seventh in Division 1 to form the new Division 1. Five relegated from Division 1 combined with those who finished second to sixth to form a new Division 2 and the bottom eight in Division 2 linked with the two newcomers to form a new Division 3. At the end of the 1997–98 season the nine clubs remaining in the Premier Division plus the promoted team from Division 1 formed a breakaway Premier League. At the end of the 1999–2000 season two teams were added to the Scottish League. There was no relegation from the Premier League but two promoted from the First Division and three from each of the Second and Third Divisions. One team was relegated from the First Division and one from the Second Division, leaving 12 teams in each division. In season 2002–03, Falkirk were not promoted to the Premier League due to the failure of their ground to meet League rules. Inverness CT were promoted after a previous refusal in 2003–04 because of ground sharing. At the end of 2005–06 the Scottish League introduced play-offs for the team finishing second from the bottom of Division 1 against the winners of the second, third and fourth finishing teams in Division 2 and with a similar procedure for Division 2 and Division 3.

From 1946–47 to 1955–56 the two divisions were known as A and B. A division 3 had existed for three years from 1923–24 and was revived for three more seasons from 1946–47 as Division C when it included reserve teams.

SCOTTISH LEAGUE ATTENDANCES 2011–12

PREMIER LEAGUE

	Average	*Highest*	*Lowest*
Aberdeen	9,296	15,468	5,281
Celtic	50,283	58,875	40,268
Dundee U	7,481	11,471	5,232
Dunfermline Ath	4,799	10,140	2,303
Hearts	13,381	15,868	9,185
Hibernian	9,909	15,281	6,923
Inverness CT	4,181	6,623	3,035
Kilmarnock	5,537	15,926	3,645
Motherwell	5,946	10,440	3,772
Rangers	46,324	50,268	43,383
St Johnstone	4,169	6,759	1,607
St Mirren	4,492	6,711	3,305

FIRST DIVISION

	Average	*Highest*	*Lowest*
Ayr U	1,500	1,938	1,096
Dundee	4,223	5,862	3,136
Falkirk	3,187	4,383	2,461
Hamilton A	1,764	2,401	1,276
Livingston	1,774	2,967	859
Morton	1,814	2,621	1,306
Partick Th	2,344	3,380	1,439
Queen of the S	1,550	2,079	1,282
Raith R	1,932	3,629	1,416
Ross Co	2,873	4,737	2,047

SECOND DIVISION

	Average	*Highest*	*Lowest*
Airdrie U	833	1,490	621
Albion R	462	1,134	207
Arbroath	803	1,125	572
Brechin C	516	911	347
Cowdenbeath	469	1,345	271
Dumbarton	630	1,088	285
East Fife	599	1,022	390
Forfar Ath	512	908	284
Stenhousemuir	594	903	0
Stirling Alb	572	711	329

THIRD DIVISION

	Average	*Highest*	*Lowest*
Alloa Ath	672	2,551	421
Annan Ath	472	644	304
Berwick R	396	486	278
Clyde	566	748	351
East Stirling	321	531	215
Elgin C	627	1,072	431
Montrose	334	450	246
Peterhead	487	626	396
Queen's Park	519	711	344
Stranraer	354	592	260

SCOTTISH LEAGUE CUP FINALS 1946–2012

Season	*Winners*	*Runners-up*	*Score*
1946–47	Rangers	Aberdeen	4-0
1947–48	East Fife	Falkirk	4-1 after 0-0 draw (*aet.*)
1948–49	Rangers	Raith R	2-0
1949–50	East Fife	Dunfermline Ath	3-0
1950–51	Motherwell	Hibernian	3-0
1951–52	Dundee	Rangers	3-2
1952–53	Dundee	Kilmarnock	2-0
1953–54	East Fife	Partick Th	3-2
1954–55	Hearts	Motherwell	4-2
1955–56	Aberdeen	St Mirren	2-1
1956–57	Celtic	Partick Th	3-0 after 0-0 draw
1957–58	Celtic	Rangers	7-1
1958–59	Hearts	Partick Th	5-1
1959–60	Hearts	Third Lanark	2-1
1960–61	Rangers	Kilmarnock	2-0
1961–62	Rangers	Hearts	3-1 after 1-1 draw
1962–63	Hearts	Kilmarnock	1-0
1963–64	Rangers	Morton	5-0
1964–65	Rangers	Celtic	2-1
1965–66	Celtic	Rangers	2-1
1966–67	Celtic	Rangers	1-0
1967–68	Celtic	Dundee	5-3
1968–69	Celtic	Hibernian	6-2
1969–70	Celtic	St Johnstone	1-0
1970–71	Rangers	Celtic	1-0
1971–72	Partick Th	Celtic	4-1
1972–73	Hibernian	Celtic	2-1
1973–74	Dundee	Celtic	1-0
1974–75	Celtic	Hibernian	6-3
1975–76	Rangers	Celtic	1-0
1976–77	Aberdeen	Celtic	2-1
1977–78	Rangers	Celtic	2-1 (*aet.*)
1978–79	Rangers	Aberdeen	2-1
1979–80	Dundee U	Aberdeen	3-0 after 0-0 draw (*aet.*)
1980–81	Dundee U	Dundee	3-0
1981–82	Rangers	Dundee U	2-1
1982–83	Celtic	Rangers	2-1
1983–84	Rangers	Celtic	3-2
1984–85	Rangers	Dundee U	1-0
1985–86	Aberdeen	Hibernian	3-0
1986–87	Rangers	Celtic	2-1
1987–88	Rangers	Aberdeen	3-3
		(aet; Rangers won 5-3 on penalties)	
1988–89	Rangers	Aberdeen	3-2 (*aet.*)
1989–90	Aberdeen	Rangers	2-1
1990–91	Rangers	Celtic	2-1
1991–92	Hibernian	Dunfermline Ath	2-0
1992–93	Rangers	Aberdeen	2-1 (*aet.*)
1993–94	Rangers	Hibernian	2-1
1994–95	Raith R	Celtic	2-2
		(aet; Raith R won 6-5 on penalties)	
1995–96	Aberdeen	Dundee	2-0
1996–97	Rangers	Hearts	4-3
1997–98	Celtic	Dundee U	3-0
1998–99	Rangers	St Johnstone	2-1
1999–2000	Celtic	Aberdeen	2-0
2000–01	Celtic	Kilmarnock	3-0
2001–02	Rangers	Ayr U	4-0
2002–03	Rangers	Celtic	2-1
2003–04	Livingston	Hibernian	2-0
2004–05	Rangers	Motherwell	5-1
2005–06	Celtic	Dunfermline Ath	3-0
2006–07	Hibernian	Kilmarnock	5-1
2007–08	Rangers	Dundee U	2-2
		(aet; Rangers won 3-2 on penalties)	
2008–09	Celtic	Rangers	2-0 (*aet.*)
2009–10	Rangers	St Mirren	1-0
2010–11	Rangers	Celtic	2-1 (*aet.*)
2011–12	Kilmarnock	Celtic	1-0

SCOTTISH LEAGUE CUP WINS

Rangers 27, Celtic 14, Aberdeen 5, Hearts 4, Dundee 3, East Fife 3, Hibernian 3, Dundee U 2, Kilmarnock 1, Livingston 1, Motherwell 1, Partick Th 1, Raith R 1.

APPEARANCES IN FINALS

Rangers 34, Celtic 29, Aberdeen 12, Hibernian 9, Dundee 6, Dundee U 6, Hearts 6, Kilmarnock 6, Partick Th 4, Dunfermline Ath 3, East Fife 3, Motherwell 3, Raith R 2, St Johnstone 2, St Mirren 2, Ayr U 1, Falkirk 1, Livingston 1, Morton 1, Third Lanark 1.

SCOTTISH COMMUNITIES LEAGUE CUP 2011–12

■ *Denotes player sent off.*

FIRST ROUND

Saturday, 30 July 2011

Airdrie U (2) 5 *(Donnelly 35, 81, Owens 32 (pen), 78 (pen), Bain 88)*

Stirling Alb (0) 0 705

Airdrie U: McKane; Bain, Lilley, Stallard, Malone, Johnston (Sally), Devlin, Owens (Lovering), Keast (Boyle), Donnelly, Holmes.
Stirling Alb: Filler■; Jacobs, Allison, Thom, Crawley, Flood (McSorley), Fagan■, McCulloch, MacPherson (Cook), Bonar (Smith), Davidson.

Albion R (1) 2 *(Chaplain 33 (pen), Boyle 90)*

Falkirk (1) 4 *(El Alagui 15, 67, Fulton J 50, Higginbotham 69)* 602

Albion R: Fahey; Dempsie, Marriott (Gilmartin), Stevenson, Reid, Donnelly, McStay, Chaplain, Love (Boyle), Gemmell, Scott (Acqua).
Falkirk: McGovern; Dods, Scobbie, Duffie, Bennett, Higginbotham, Murdoch, Millar, Fulton J (Graham), El Alagui, Sibbald (Fulton D).

Alloa Ath (0) 0

Morton (1) 3 *(Di Giacomo 29, Jackson 67, Weatherson 90)* 683

Alloa Ath: Bain; Harding, Gordon, Docherty, Ryan McCord, Holmes, Doyle, Ross McCord (Campbell), Innes (Caddis), One (Wright), Cawley.
Morton: Stewart; McCaffrey, Smyth, Forsyth, Evans, O'Brien, Tidser (McGeough), Bachirou, Di Giacomo, Jackson (Weatherson), MacDonald (Campbell).

Annan Ath (1) 1 *(Cox 21)*

Dunfermline Ath (1) 2 *(Barrowman 18, Kirk 51)* 767

Annan Ath: Summersgill; Aitken, McGowan, Watson P, Muirhead (Steele), Gibson, Sloan (McKechnie), Gilfillan, O'Connor (Bell), Cox, Harty.
Dunfermline Ath: Gallacher; Potter, Thomson J, Keddie, Dowie, McCann, Mason (Thomson R), Burns (McDougall), Cardle, Barrowman, Kirk (Buchanan).

Brechin C (1) 2 *(McKenna 26, King 114)*

Clyde (1) 4 *(McLauchlan 20 (og), Sweeney 97 (pen), Archdeacon 105, Gray 119)* 402

Brechin C: Nelson; McLauchlan, Buist■, Dunlop, Molloy, Brady, McClune, Janczyk, McKenna (McManus), Weir (Lister), Carcary (King).
Clyde: Hutchison; Hay, Sharp, Gray, Irvine (Archdeacon), Neill, Scullion, Cusack, McQueen, Sweeney (Tully), McDonald (Brown).
aet.

Cowdenbeath (2) 2 *(Ramsay 28, 40)*

Stenhousemuir (1) 2 *(Lyle 4, Paton 53)* 293

Cowdenbeath: Bejaoui; Adamson, Mbu, Brett, Cameron, Ramsay, Winter, Robertson, Stewart, Coult (McKenzie), Morton (Linton).
Stenhousemuir: Brown (McCluskey); Corrigan, Paton, Lyle, McMillan, McHale (Thomson), Ferguson (Plenderleith), Murray, Dickson, Kean, Rodgers.
aet; Stenhousemuir won 4-3 on penalties.

Dumbarton (0) 0

Dundee (0) 4 *(Milne 48, 73, McCluskey 67, Lockwood 84 (pen))* 870

Dumbarton: Grindlay; Lithgow, Nugent, Nicoll (Monaghan), Lyden, Agnew, McBride (Wallace), Ramage (Metcalfe), Prunty, Gilhaney, Brannan.
Dundee: Douglas; Irvine, McKeown, Weston, Lockwood, McCluskey (Riley), Chisholm, O'Donnell, Conroy, Milne, McIntosh (Hyde).

East Fife (0) 2 *(Ogleby 60, Wallace 72)*

Elgin C (0) 1 *(Cameron 73)* 514

East Fife: Ridgers; Campbell, Ovenstone, Durie, Park, Smith, Muir, Johnstone, Wallace (Dalziel), Linn (Young), Ogleby.
Elgin C: Clark; Duff, Kaczan, Niven, Moore, O'Donoghue, Cameron (Crooks), Nicolson, Beveridge (Frizzel), Gunn, Leslie.

East Stirling (0) 0

Ayr U (2) 3 *(Trouten 39, Roberts 45, 52)* 535

East Stirling: Sorley; Dingwall, Chisholm, Love A, Cane, Frances, Stirling, Hunter, Jackson (Scott), Lurinsky (Team), Turner (Sheerin).
Ayr U: Cuthbert; Smith, Malone, Robertson J, Campbell, Burke, Trouten, McGowan, Geggan (Robertson R), Roberts (Paterson), Moffat (Wardlaw).

Forfar Ath (1) 2 *(Crawford 43, Templeman 61)*

Peterhead (0) 0 452

Forfar Ath: Adam; Ross, Wilson, McCulloch, Tulloch, Mowat, Byers, Fotheringham (Gibson), Hegarty (Motion), Crawford, Templeman (Campbell R).
Peterhead: Jellema; McBain, Rattray, MacDonald, Sellars (Ross S), Watson, Redman, McAllister, Deasley (Wyness), Bavidge, Conway (Sharp).

Livingston (4) 6 *(Boulding 2, Russell I 7, 22, Keaghan Jacobs 33, Talbot 66, McNulty 72)*

Arbroath (0) 0 804

Livingston: McNeil; Barr C, Brown, Talbot, Watson P, Fox (Kyle Jacobs), Keaghan Jacobs, Sinclair, Barr B, Boulding (Deuchar), Russell I (McNulty).
Arbroath: Hill; Malcolm, Wedderburn, Baxter, Kerr (Elfverson), Sheerin, McAnespie, Gibson (Bryce), Falkingham, Sibanda (Girvan), Doris■.

Montrose (1) 1 *(Winter 20)*

Raith R (1) 4 *(Williamson 31, Walker A 52, Baird 54, Thomson 77)* 614

Montrose: Andrews; Campbell, Smart■, Crighton, McGowan (Johnstone), Masson, Cameron, McNally■, Winter, Boyle (Lunan), Dimilta (Pierce).
Raith R: McGurn; Murray, Dyer, Ellis, Walker A, Hamill, Donaldson, Thomson (Callachan), Baird (Reynolds), Williamson, Graham (Walls).

Partick Th (1) 1 *(Cairney 28)*

Berwick R (1) 3 *(Gray D 33, Noble 73, Currie P 79 (pen))* 1255

Partick Th: Fox; Kinniburgh, Paton■, Balatoni■, Flannigan (Bannigan), Rowson, Cairney (Robertson), Erskine (Campbell), Sinclair, Stewart, Doolan.
Berwick R: Barclay; McLean (Gall), McLeod, Thomson, Currie L, McDonald■, Walker, Currie P, Gray D (Gribben), Noble, McLaren (Smith D).

Queen of the S (1) 2 *(Carmichael 19, Brighton 78)*

Stranraer (1) 1 *(Gallagher 15)* 1511

Queen of the S: McKenzie; Higgins, Reid C, Campbell, Simmons, McGuffie (Reid A), McLaughlin, Clark (McKenna), Carmichael, Smith (Smylie), Brighton.
Stranraer: David Mitchell; Devine (Shepherd), Gallagher, Kennedy (Danny Mitchell), McKeown, Noble, Aitken, Murphy, Kane, Winter (McColm), Malcolm.

Ross Co (0) 2 *(McMenamin 58, Flynn 75)*

Queen's Park (1) 1 *(Daly 5)* 949

Ross Co: Fraser; Munro, Boyd (Miller), Flynn, Fitzpatrick, Duncan, Brittain, Corcoran (Gardyne), Kettlewell, McMenamin (Byrne), Craig.
Queen's Park: Parry; Little, McGinn, Meggatt■, Brough, Burns (Bradley), Gallagher, Anderson, Watt (Murray), Daly, Smith.

SECOND ROUND

Tuesday, 23 August 2011

Aberdeen (1) 1 *(Mackie 16)*

Dundee (0) 0 5722

Aberdeen: Brown; Considine, Foster, Jack, Arnason (Mawene), Clark (Chalali), Osbourne, Fyvie (McArdle), Pawlett, Magennis, Mackie.
Dundee: Douglas; Irvine, McKeown, Weston, Lockwood, Riley, Chisholm, O'Donnell, Conroy, Bayne (Hyde), Milne.

Airdrie U (2) 2 *(Holmes 27, Donnelly 41)*

Raith R (0) 0 683

Airdrie U: McKane; Bain, Stallard, Lilley, Lovering, Keast (Owens), Lynch (Hill), Blockley, Stevenson, Holmes, Donnelly (Morton).
Raith R: McGurn; Donaldson, Murray, Ellis, Dyer, Thomson (Hill), Walker A, Hamill, McBride (Callachan), Baird, Reynolds (Graham).

East Fife (1) 2 *(Linn 4, Dalziel 54)*

Dunfermline Ath (1) 1 *(Buchanan 12)* 1262

East Fife: Brown; Durie, Ovenstone, Hislop, Park, Linn, Young, Smith, Johnstone, Dalziel (Sloan), Wallace.
Dunfermline Ath: Gallacher; Thomson J, Dowie (Thomson R), Rutkiewicz, McCann, Burns, Keddie, Graham, McDougall (Willis), Barrowman, Buchanan (Kirk).

Hamilton A (1) 1 *(Chambers 2 (pen))*

Ross Co (0) 2 *(Gardyne 65, Craig 82)* 828

Hamilton A: Cerny; McAlister, Canning, Kilday, Gordon (Crawford), Gillespie, Mensing, Chambers (Wilkie), McLaren, Paterson (Anderson), Imrie.
Ross Co: Fraser; Miller, Boyd, Munro, Fitzpatrick, Lawson, Brittain, Quinn, Corcoran (McMenamin), Gardyne, Byrne (Craig).

Hibernian (2) 5 *(Scott 11, 58, Sodje 38, O'Connor 51, Sproule 87)*

Berwick R (0) 0 4936

Hibernian: Brown; O'Hanlon, Hanlon, Booth (Smith), Wotherspoon, Sproule, Palsson, Scott, Galbraith, O'Connor (Crawford), Sodje (Thornhill).
Berwick R: Barclay; Walker, Townsley, McLeod, Thomson, Currie L, Currie P (Smith E), Greenhill (Notman), McLaren, Noble (Gribben), Gray D.

Morton (2) 3 *(Tidser 17, MacDonald 27, Jackson 79)*

St Mirren (1) 4 *(Teale 8, Thompson 55, 66, Hasselbaink 60 (pen))* 4959

Morton: Stewart; McCann, Evans, McCaffrey, Forsyth, Di Giacomo, McGeouch (Jackson), Smyth, Tidser, O'Brien (Weatherson), MacDonald.
St Mirren: Samson; Van Zanten, Tesselaar, McAusland, Mair, Goodwin, Thomson, McGowan, Thompson, Hasselbaink (McShane), Teale (Haddad).

Queen of the S (1) 3 *(Brighton 29, Johnston 58, Clark 61)*

Forfar Ath (0) 0 1008

Queen of the S: Robinson; Reid C, Campbell, Higgins, Reid A, Johnston (McShane), McKenna, Simmons (McGuffie), McLaughlin, Brighton (Clark), Carmichael.
Forfar Ath: McHugh; Wilson, Bolochoweckyj (Tulloch), Ross, Mowat, Campbell I (Byers), McCulloch, Fotheringham, Motion, Crawford, Templeman (Campbell R).

Wednesday, 24 August 2011

Ayr U (0) 1 *(Malone 60)*

Inverness CT (0) 0 987

Ayr U: Cuthbert; Robertson J, Malone, Smith, Campbell (Armstrong), McKernan, McGowan, Geggan, Wardlaw, Roberts (Tiffoney), Moffat (Robertson R).
Inverness CT: Tuffey; Tokely, Hogg, Shinnie G, Golobart, Piermayr, Hayes (Ross), Morrison (Tade), Sutherland (Shinnie A), Doran, Foran.

Clyde (0) 0

Motherwell (2) 4 *(Higdon 17, Law 41, Hateley 51, Lawless 85)* 1778

Clyde: Hutchison; Brown, Gallagher, Sharp, McQueen, Neill (Archdeacon), Hay, Sweeney, Kane (Oliver), Cusack, McDonald (Gray).
Motherwell: Hollis; Hutchinson, Page, Halsman, Hateley, Lasley (Humphrey), Law (Carswell), Lawless, Forbes, Higdon (Smith), McHugh.

Falkirk (0) 3 *(Sibbald 49, Ferguson 46 (og), El Alagui 90)*

Stenhousemuir (1) 1 *(Paton 25)* 2134

Falkirk: McGovern; Duffie, Dods, Bennett, Scobbie, Fulton J, Millar, Murdoch, Sibbald (Fulton D), El Alagui, Higginbotham.
Stenhousemuir: McCluskey; Lyle, Corrigan, Paton, McKinlay, Dickson (Quinn), Ferguson (McMillan), McHale, Murray, Kean, Rodgers.

St Johnstone (3) 3 *(Sandaza 18, 25, Wright 13)*

Livingston (0) 0 2439

St Johnstone: Enckelman; MacKay, Gibson, Morris, Anderson, Wright (Maybury), Adams, Davidson M (Robertson), Sheridan (Haber), Sandaza, Craig.
Livingston: McNeil; Brown, Barr C, Watson P, Talbot, Keaghan Jacobs, Fox, Scougall, Kyle Jacobs (Barr R), Russell I (McNulty), Deuchar (Boulding).

THIRD ROUND

Tuesday, 20 September 2011

Aberdeen (1) 3 *(McArdle 40, Mackie 46, Fallon 90)*

East Fife (1) 3 *(Wallace 31, Park 54, Sloan 57)* 3964

Aberdeen: Gonzalez; McArdle, Considine, Foster, Jack (Chalali), Clark, Arnason, Pawlett, Magennis, Vernon (Osbourne), Mackie (Fallon).
East Fife: Ridgers; Durie, Campbell, White (Hislop), Muir, Park, Sloan (Cook), Smith, Wallace (Dalziel), Linn, Ogleby.
aet; East Fife won 4-3 on penalties.

Airdrie U (0) 0

Dundee U (1) 2 *(Dow 11, Daly 76)* 1252

Airdrie U: McKane; Bain, Stallard, Lilley (Hill), Malone, Stevenson, Lynch, Owens, Keast (Johnston), Boyle (Holmes), Donnelly.
Dundee U: Pernis; Dixon, Kenneth, Douglas, Gunning, Flood, Dow, Swanson (Mackay-Steven), Rankin, Armstrong (Daly), Dalla Valle.

Kilmarnock (2) 5 *(Harkins 2, Heffernan 41, 59, 70, Hutchinson 74)*

Queen of the S (0) 0 3091

Kilmarnock: Bell; Fowler, Kroca, Sissoko, Fisher (Galan), Harkins, Panikvar (Hay), Pascali, Kelly (Hutchinson), Shiels, Heffernan.
Queen of the S: Robinson; Reid A, Higgins, Reid C, Campbell, Simmons, Johnston (Carmichael), McKenna, McLaughlin (Brighton), Clark, Smith■.

Motherwell (2) 2 *(Lasley 30, Higdon 40)*

Hibernian (1) 2 *(O'Connor 19, 87)* 3909

Motherwell: Randolph; Clancy, Hammell, Hateley, Craigan, Lasley (Forbes), Humphrey (Daley), Jennings (McHugh), Higdon, Murphy, Law.
Hibernian: Brown; Towell, Murray (Agogo), Scott, Hanlon, O'Hanlon, Wotherspoon, Sproule (Galbraith) (Booth), O'Connor, Griffiths, Palsson.
aet; Hibernian won 7-6 on penalties.

St Johnstone (0) 0

St Mirren (2) 2 *(Adams 39 (og), Goodwin 45)* 2296

St Johnstone: Enckelman; MacKay, Maybury, Millar, Wright (McCracken), Anderson, Adams (Robertson), Higgins (Gibson), Sheridan, Sandaza, Craig.
St Mirren: Samson; Van Zanten, Tesselaar, McAusland, Mair, Goodwin, Thomson (McShane), McLean, Thompson, Hasselbaink (McGowan), Teale.

Wednesday, 21 September 2011

Ayr U (0) 1 *(Wardlaw 63)*

Hearts (0) 1 *(Robinson 49)* 2517

Ayr U: Cuthbert; Smith, Malone, Robertson J (Robertson R), Tiffoney, Trouten, McGowan, Geggan, McKernan, Wardlaw (Roberts), Moffat.
Hearts: Balogh; Barr, Grainger, Jonsson, Zaliukas, McGowan, Templeton (Taouil), Robinson, Novikovas (Driver), Sutton (Smith), Skacel.
aet; Ayr U won 4-1 on penalties.

Falkirk (0) 3 *(El Alagui 58, 73, Millar M 90)*

Rangers (0) 2 *(Goian 82, Jelavic 86)* 6493

Falkirk: McGovern; Dods, Scobbie, Duffie, Wallace, Bennett, Millar M, Fulton J, Sibbald, Weatherston (Alston), El Alagui.
Rangers: Alexander; Whittaker, Papac, Bocanegra, Goian, McCulloch, Bedoya (Naismith), Davis, Healy (Jelavic), Lafferty, Wylde.

Ross Co (0) 0

Celtic (1) 2 *(Hooper 13, Boyd 52 (og))* 5367

Ross Co: Fraser; Munro, Miller, Boyd, Lawson (Corcoran), Fitzpatrick, Brittain, Quinn, Vigurs (Byrne), McMenamin (Kettlewell), Gardyne.
Celtic: Forster; Wilson K (Wanyama), El Kaddouri, Matthews, Majstorovic, Mulgrew, Kayal, Ledley, Stokes (Bangura), Hooper (George), Forrest.

QUARTER-FINALS

Tuesday, 25 October 2011

Dundee U (0) 2 *(Russell 73, Daly 96)*

Falkirk (0) 2 *(El Alagui 70, Graham 118)* 4188

Dundee U: Pernis; Watson, Dixon, Robertson (Armstrong), Kenneth, Gunning, Flood, Douglas, Daly, Dalla Valle (Russell), Rankin.
Falkirk: McGovern; Duffie (Dick), Kingsley, Dods, Wallace, Murdoch, Weatherston, Fulton J (Graham), El Alagui, Higginbotham, Alston (Fulton D).
aet; Falkirk won 5-4 on penalties.

Kilmarnock (0) 2 *(Sissoko 73, Harkins 81)*

East Fife (0) 0 4029

Kilmarnock: Jaakkola; Buijs, Pursehouse, Fowler (Dayton), McKeown (Hay), Sissoko, Kelly (Silva), Pascali, Shiels, Heffernan, Harkins.
East Fife: Ridgers; Durie, Park, Ovenstone, White, Muir, Linn, Smith (McQuade), Ogleby■, Wallace, Sloan (Johnstone).

St Mirren (0) 0

Ayr U (0) 1 *(Smith 81)* 4570

St Mirren: Samson; Van Zanten, Tesselaar, McAusland, Mair, Goodwin (McShane), McLean, Thomson (Hasselbaink), Thompson, McGowan, Teale (Carey).
Ayr U: Cuthbert; Tiffoney, Malone, Robertson J, Trouten, Geggan, Robertson R, Moffat, Wardlaw, McGowan, Smith.

Wednesday, 26 October 2011

Hibernian (1) 1 *(Majstorovic 4 (og))*

Celtic (0) 4 *(Forrest 46, 58, Stokes 64, Hooper 69)* 10,569

Hibernian: Brown; Wotherspoon, Murray, Stephens, Hanlon, Osbourne, Sproule■, Griffiths, O'Connor (Stevenson), Agogo (Sodje), Palsson (Galbraith).
Celtic: Forster; Matthews, Wilson M, Ledley, Majstorovic, Rogne, Kayal (Wanyama), Ki, Stokes, Hooper (McCourt), Forrest (Cha).

SEMI-FINALS

Saturday, 28 January 2012

Ayr U (0) 0

Kilmarnock (0) 1 *(Shiels 109)* 25,057

Ayr U: Cuthbert; Tiffoney, Malone, Robertson J, Smith, Geggan, Trouten (Tomsett), McKernon (Dodd), Moffat, Wardlaw (Roberts), McGowan.
Kilmarnock: Bell; Fowler, Gordon, Dayton (Silva), Pascali, Nelson, Hay (Buijs), Kelly, Shiels, Heffernan, Harkins (Racchi).
aet.

Sunday, 29 January 2012

Falkirk (1) 1 *(Fulton J 40)*

Celtic (1) 3 *(Brown 27 (pen), Stokes 56, 86)* 30,000

Falkirk: McGovern; Duffie, Scobbie, Dods, Wallace, Murdoch, Weatherston (White), Millar M, El Alagui, Higginbotham (Sibbald), Fulton J (Alston).
Celtic: Forster; Cha (Matthews), Izaguirre (Ki), Rogne, Mulgrew, Wanyama, Forrest, Brown, Stokes (Commons), Hooper, Ledley.

FINAL (at Hampden Park.)

Sunday, 18 March 2012

Celtic (0) 0

Kilmarnock (0) 1 *(Van Tornhout 84)* 49,572

Celtic: Forster; Matthews, Mulgrew, Rogne (Ki), Wilson K, Wanyama, Forrest, Brown, Stokes, Hooper (Samaras), Ledley (Commons).
Kilmarnock: Bell; Fowler, Gordon, Buijs (Johnson), Sissoko (Kroca), Nelson, Hay, Kelly, Shiels, Heffernan, Harkins (Van Tornhout).

LEAGUE CHALLENGE FINALS 1991–2012

Year	*Winners*	*Runners-up*	*Score*
1990–91	Dundee	Ayr U	3-2
1991–92	Hamilton A	Ayr U	1-0
1992–93	Hamilton A	Morton	3-2
1993–94	Falkirk	St Mirren	3-0
1994–95	Airdrieonians	Dundee	3-2
1995–96	Stenhousemuir	Dundee U	0-0
	(aet; Stenhousemuir won 5-4 on penalties)		
1996–97	Stranraer	St Johnstone	1-0
1997–98	Falkirk	Queen of the S	1-0
1998–99	no competition		
1999–2000	Alloa Ath	Inverness CT	4-4
	(aet; Alloa Ath won 5-4 on penalties)		
2000–01	Airdrieonians	Livingston	2-2
	(aet; Airdrieonians won 3-2 on penalties)		
2001–02	Airdrieonians	Alloa Ath	2-1
2002–03	Queen of the S	Brechin C	2-0
2003–04	Inverness CT	Airdrie U	2-0
2004–05	Falkirk	Ross Co	2-1
2005–06	St Mirren	Hamilton A	2-1
2006–07	Ross Co	Clyde	1-1
	(aet; Ross Co won 5-4 on penalties)		
2007–08	St Johnstone	Dunfermline Ath	3-2
2008–09	Airdrie U	Ross Co	2-2
	(aet; Airdrie U won 3-2 on penalties)		
2009–10	Dundee	Inverness CT	3-2
2010–11	Ross Co	Queen of the S	2-0
2011–12	Falkirk	Hamilton A	1-0

THE RAMSDENS CUP 2011–12

■ *Denotes player sent off.*

FIRST ROUND NORTH-EAST

Saturday, 23 July 2011

Arbroath (0) 1 *(Elfverson 77)*

Dundee (0) 2 *(Milne 79, O'Donnell 90)* 1761

Arbroath: Hill; Malcolm, Baxter, Busch, Kerr (Sibanda), Sheerin, Swankie, McAnespie, Falkingham (Elfverson), Bryce (Gibson), Doris.
Dundee: Douglas; Irvine, Weston, Lockwood, Benedictus (McKeown), McCluskey, Chisholm, O'Donnell, Conroy, Milne, Hyde (McIntosh).

Brechin C (1) 1 *(McKenna 40)*

Falkirk (2) 2 *(Bennett 26, Dods 33)* 596

Brechin C: Scott; McLauchlan, Buist, McLean, Dunlop, Brady (McClune), Fusco, McKenna, McManus (Lister), Weir (King), Carcary.
Falkirk: McGovern; Dods, Scobbie, Duffie, Kingsley, Bennett, Higginbotham, Murdoch, Millar, Alston (Sibbald), El Alagui.

Deveronvale (0) 1 *(McKenzie 58)*

Stirling Alb (1) 3 *(Bonar 19 (pen), 48, MacPherson 63)* 400

Deveronvale: Gray; Fraser, Hendry, Dlugonski, Rae, Meldrum (Blackhall), Rodger, Barclay, Cowie, McKenzie (Mountford), Lombardi.
Stirling Alb: Filler; Allison, Thom (McSorley), McCulloch, Jacobs, Crawley, Fagan, Flood, Davidson, Bonar, MacPherson (Cook).

Forfar Ath (1) 1 *(Gibson 29)*

Buckie Th (1) 1 *(MacMillan 33)* 416

Forfar Ath: Paterson; Ross, Wilson, McCulloch, Tulloch, Fotheringham (Byers), Hegarty, Motion (Mowat), Crawford, Templeman, Gibson.
Buckie Th: Main; Morrison, MacKinnon, Shewan, Stewart, Davidson, Napier (Sutherland), MacRae, Charlesworth (Scott), Low (Clark), MacMillan.
aet; Forfar Ath won 5-4 on penalties.

Montrose (0) 1 *(McPhee 73)*

East Fife (3) 6 *(Linn 16, Ogleby 27, 51, 63 (pen), Wallace 31, Young 64)* 404

Montrose: Andrews; Campbell, Smart, Crighton (McPhee), Crawford, Masson, Cameron, McNally, Johnstone, Boyle, Dimilta (Pierce).
East Fife: Ridgers; Campbell, Ovenstone, Durie, Park, Smith (Young), Muir, Johnstone, Wallace (Sloan), Linn, Ogleby (Dalziel).

Peterhead (1) 2 *(Deasley 30, McAllister 60)*

Alloa Ath (1) 2 *(Ross McCord 16, Wright 73)* 443

Peterhead: Jellema; McBain, Donald, MacDonald, Sellars, Watson, Redman, McAllister, Deasley, Bavidge (Ross D), Conway (Sharp).
Alloa Ath: Bain; Harding, Gordon, Young, Docherty, Ryan McCord, Holmes, Doyle, Ross McCord, One (Campbell), Cawley (Wright).
aet; Peterhead won 5-4 on penalties.

Raith R (0) 2 *(Baird 51, 77)*

Cowdenbeath (0) 1 *(Coult 80)* 1098

Raith R: McGurn; Murray, Dyer, Ellis, Walker A, Hamill, Davidson (Thomson), Donaldson, Baird, Williamson, Graham (Reynolds).
Cowdenbeath: Bejaoui; Adamson, Mbu, Linton (Milne), Brett, Cameron (Miller), Ramsay (Coult), Winter, Robertson, Stewart, Morton.

Ross Co (1) 1 *(Morrison 2)*

Elgin C (1) 2 *(Cameron 37, Leslie 61)* 1368

Ross Co: Fraser; Munro, Morrison, Miller (Byrne), Flynn, Lawson (Duncan), Brittain, Vigurs (Corcoran), McMenamin, Craig, Gardyne.
Elgin C: Clark; Duff, Kaczan, Niven, Moore (Lawrie), O'Donoghue (Crooks), Cameron (Frizzel), Nicolson, Beveridge, Gunn, Leslie.

FIRST ROUND SOUTH-WEST

Saturday, 23 July 2011

Airdrie U (0) 0

Livingston (0) 5 *(Sinclair 50, Russell I 55, 67, Barr B 82, 90)* 719

Airdrie U: McKane; Lovering, Stallard, Malone, Woodburn (Keast), Bain, Devlin, Donnelly, Blockley, Holmes (Morton), Boyle (Sally).
Livingston: Jamieson; Barr C (Travis), Brown, Talbot, Watson P, Fox, Keaghan Jacobs, Sinclair (Docherty), Barr B, Deuchar (McNulty), Russell I.

Albion R (0) 0

Annan Ath (1) 2 *(Cox 29, Harty 81)* 247

Albion R: Gaston; Dempsie, Reid, Marriott, McStay, Chaplain, Stevenson, Donnelly (Russell), Boyle (Love), Gemmell (Gilmartin), Hamilton.
Annan Ath: Summersgill; Aitken, McGowan, Watson P, Steele (McKechnie), Muirhead, Gibson, Sloan, O'Connor, Cox, Bell (Harty).

Ayr U (0) 2 *(Campbell 94, Geggan 115)*

Queen of the S (0) 0 1272

Ayr U: Cuthbert; Smith, Malone, Robertson J, Campbell, Trouten, McGowan, Geggan, Burke (Tiffoney), Wardlaw (Roberts), Moffat (Robertson R).
Queen of the S: McKenzie; Higgins, Reid C, Campbell, Simmons, Johnston (Carmichael), McGuffie, McKenna, McLaughlin, Smith (Clark), Brighton.
aet.

Clyde (1) 2 *(Fitzpatrick 36, McDonald 51)*

Berwick R (2) 2 *(Currie L 4, Gray D 10)* 472

Clyde: Mentel; Tully, Hay, Sharp, Brown, Neill, Scullion, Cusack (Gray), Sweeney, Fitzpatrick (Irvine), McDonald (Oliver).
Berwick R: Barclay; McLean, McLeod, Thomson, Currie L, McDonald, Walker (Smith E), Currie P, Gray D, Noble (Smith D), McLaren.
aet; Berwick R won 4-3 on penalties.

Partick Th (1) 2 *(Rowson 20, Stewart 82)*

Stenhousemuir (0) 1 *(Kean 86)* 1292

Partick Th: Fox; Kinniburgh, Paton, Balatoni, Flannigan, Rowson, Erskine (Campbell), Sinclair, Bannigan, Stewart, Doolan (Grehan).
Stenhousemuir: McCluskey; Corrigan, Paton, Lyle, McMillan, McHale (Dickson), McKinlay, Ferguson (Thomson), Murray, Kean, Rodgers (Plenderleith).

Queen's Park (0) 0

Hamilton A (0) 2 *(Crawford 72, Hopkirk 81)* 748

Queen's Park: Parry; Little, McGinn, Meggatt, Brough, Gallagher, Anderson, Urquhart, Watt (Burns), Daly, Smith.
Hamilton A: Cerny; McLaughlin, Mensing, McAlister, Gillespie (Chambers), Kirkpatrick (McLaren), Crawford, Anderson, Hopkirk, Imrie, Lyle (Hendrie).

Stranraer (0) 0

Morton (2) 8 *(Jackson 19, 42, 77, 86, Di Giacomo 53, 54, 64, 69)* 374

Stranraer: David Mitchell; Devine, Gallagher (Kane), Noble, Aitken, Murphy, Danny Mitchell, Winter, Kennedy, Moore (Cochrane), Malcolm (McColm).
Morton: Stewart; Smyth, Forsyth, Evans, McCaffrey (Weatherson), O'Brien, Tidser, Bachirou (Campbell), Di Giacomo, Jackson, MacDonald (McGeough).

Sunday, 24 July 2011

Dumbarton (0) 3 *(Prunty 54, Gilhaney 61 (pen), Walker 90)*

East Stirling (0) 2 *(Love A 66, Turner 70)* 454

Dumbarton: Grindlay; Lyden■, Lithgow, Nugent (Wallace), Nicoll, Agnew, McBride (Ramage), Prunty, Gilhaney, Walker, Brannan (Metcalfe).
East Stirling: Antell; Dingwall, Chisholm, Love A, Cane, Frances, Stirling, Hunter (Sheerin), Jackson, Lurinsky (Savage), Turner (Team).

SECOND ROUND

Tuesday, 9 August 2011

Annan Ath (2) 4 *(Harty 20, 48, 87, Muirhead 31)*

Peterhead (0) 2 *(Redman 49, McAllister 75 (pen))* 359

Annan Ath: Mitchell A; Muirhead, Gibson, Neilson, McGowan, Steele, Gilfillan, Bell (Sloan), Cox (McKechnie), Harty, O'Connor (Watson P).
Peterhead: Duffy; Davidson, MacDonald, McBain, Donald, Sharp (Bavidge), Watson, Redman, Conway, McAllister, Deasley.

Ayr U (1) 3 *(Paterson 43, McKernan 76, Robertson R 79)*

Raith R (0) 0 227

Ayr U: Cuthbert; Smith, Robertson J, Robertson R, Campbell, Tiffoney (McGowan), McKernan, Armstrong, Paterson (Trouten), Wardlaw, Moffat.
Raith R: McGurn; Donaldson, Murray, Dyer, Ellis, Williamson, Walker A, Thomson (McBride), Hamill, Graham (Reynolds), Baird.

Dumbarton (0) 0

Berwick R (0) 2 *(Greenhill 55, Currie L 89)* 334

Dumbarton: Ewings; Monaghan, Nugent, Lithgow, McBride (Wallace), Ramage (Brannan), McNiff, Agnew (Metcalf), Gilhaney, Prunty, Walker.
Berwick R: Barclay; Walker, Townsley, McLeod, Thomson, Currie L, Greenhill (Smith E), Currie P (Gribben), McDonald, Gray D, Noble.

East Fife (0) 2 *(Wallace 52, 77)*

Elgin C (0) 0 408

East Fife: Brown; Durie, Ovenstone, Campbell, Muir, Johnstone (Young), Park, Smith (Sloan), Linn, Dalziel (Hislop), Wallace.
Elgin C: Clark; Niven, Kaczan, Duff, O'Donoghue, Nicolson, Moore (McPhee), Gunn, Cameron (Frizzel), Beveridge, Leslie (Crooks).

Falkirk (1) 1 *(El Alagui 43)*

Dundee (0) 0 1791

Falkirk: McGovern; Duffie, Dods, Bennett, Scobbie, Fulton J, Murdoch, Millar M, Sibbald (Fulton D), Higginbotham, El Alagui.
Dundee: Douglas; Irvine, McKeown, Weston, Lockwood, Riley, McGregor (Webster), O'Donnell, McCluskey, Conroy (Rennie), Hyde.

Forfar Ath (0) 0

Morton (0) 5 *(O'Brien 56, Weatherson 59, MacDonald 61, 75, Campbell 78)* 448

Forfar Ath: Paterson; Ross, Bishop, McCulloch, Campbell I, Fotheringham, Byers (Hegarty), Mowat, Campbell R (Motion), Templeman (Gibson), Crawford.
Morton: Stewart; Evans, McCaffrey (Little), Forsyth, Tidser (McGeouch), Bachirou, O'Brien, Di Giacomo, MacDonald, Jackson (Campbell), Weatherson.

Hamilton A (0) 1 *(Chambers 86 (pen))*

Partick Th (0) 0 1362

Hamilton A: Cerny; Canning, Kilday, McAlister, Mensing, Chambers, Gillespie, McLaren, Hopkirk (Crawford), Lyle (Anderson), Paterson (Imrie).
Partick Th: Fox; Balatoni, Lindsay, Sinclair (Flannigan), Paton, Robertson, Erskine, Cairney, Rowson, Grehan (Doolan), Stewart.

Livingston (3) 5 *(Deuchar 23, 34, 90, Jacobs 36 (og), Thom 87 (og))*

Stirling Alb (0) 0 549

Livingston: McNeil; Brown, Sinclair, Barr C (Travis), MacDonald, Watson, Kyle Jacobs, Keaghan Jacobs (Gray), Scougal, Deuchar, Boulding (McNulty).
Stirling Alb: Filler; Jacobs (Cook), Ashe, Dillon, Crawley, Thom, MacPherson, Hunter (Davidson), Brass, Smith (Flood), Bonar.

QUARTER-FINALS

Sunday, 4 September 2011

Ayr U (0) 0

Annan Ath (0) 1 *(Cox 58)* 1232

Ayr U: Cuthbert; Malone, Robertson R, Robertson J, Smith, Tiffoney (McGowan), Trouten, Connolly, Burke (Moffat), Armstrong, Paterson (Roberts).
Annan Ath: Summersgill; Gibson, McGowan, Muirhead, Watson P, McKechnie, Jardine (Steele), Sloan, Harty, O'Connor (Bell), Cox (Gilfillan).

Berwick R (0) 1 *(McDonald 52)*

Livingston (1) 2 *(Scougall 12, Russell I 85)* 567

Berwick R: Barclay; Townsley, McLeod, Thompson, Currie L, Notman, McLaren, McDonald, Greenhill (Ponton), Noble, Gray D (Gribben).
Livingston: McNeil; Brown, MacDonald, Watson P, Talbot, Sinclair, Keaghan Jacobs, Scougall (Fox), Barr R, Boulding (Deuchar), Russell I.

East Fife (1) 1 *(Wallace 27)*

Falkirk (1) 4 *(Millar M 42, Higginbotham 52, 87, Sibbald 54)* 1064

East Fife: Brown; Durie, Ovenstone, Campbell, Muir, Johnstone (Young), Park, Sloan (Cook), Linn, McQuade (Hislop), Wallace.
Falkirk: McGovern; Duffie, Dods, Wallace, Scobbie, Fulton J (Fulton D), Murdoch, Millar M, Sibbald (Alston), Weatherston (Bennett), Higginbotham.

Hamilton A (2) 2 *(Spence 18, Mensing 33)*

Morton (1) 1 *(Di Giacomo 10)* 1496

Hamilton A: Cerny; Canning, McLaughlin, Hendrie, McAlister, Crawford, Chambers, Mensing, Imrie, Spence (Lyle), Paterson (McLaren).
Morton: Stewart; McCann (Bachirou), Evans, Graham, Forsyth, Smyth, McGeouch (Campbell), Tidser, O'Brien, Di Giacomo, MacDonald (Jackson).

SEMI-FINALS

Sunday, 9 October 2011

Annan Ath (0) 0

Falkirk (3) 3 *(Millar M 10, El Alagui 25, 42)* 1575

Annan Ath: Summersgill; MacBeth (Steele), Gibson, Watson P, McGowan, Sloan, Gilfillan, Jardine (McKechnie), Cox, Harty, O'Connor (Bell).
Falkirk: McGovern; Wallace, Dods, Bennett, Scobbie, Weatherston (Fulton J), Murdoch, Millar M, Sibbald (Alston), El Alagui, Higginbotham (Fulton D).

Hamilton A (1) 1 *(McLaughlin 43)*

Livingston (0) 0 1418

Hamilton A: Cerny; McLaughlin (Chambers), Canning, Hendrie, Gordon, McAlister, Mensing, Crawford, Imrie, Lyle (Spence), Ryan (Paterson).
Livingston: McNeil; Barr C, Watson P, Talbot, Sinclair, Kyle Jacobs (Docherty), Scougall, Fox (Boulding), Barr R, Deuchar (McNulty), Russell I.

FINAL (at Livingston)

Sunday, 1 April 2012

Falkirk (1) 1 *(Dods 2)*

Hamilton A (0) 0 5210

Falkirk: McGovern; Duffie, Dods, Wallace, Scobbie, Gibson, Fulton J, Millar M, Sibbald (Alston), Weatherston, El Alagui.
Hamilton A: Hutton; Mensing, McLaughlin (Ryan), Kilday, Routledge, Redmond, Neil, McAlister, Kirkpatrick (Hendrie), Stewart (Spence), McShane.
Referee: B. Winter.

SCOTTISH CUP FINALS 1874–2012

Year	*Winners*	*Runners-up*	*Score*
1874	Queen's Park	Clydesdale	2-0
1875	Queen's Park	Renton	3-0
1876	Queen's Park	Third Lanark	2-0 after 1-1 draw
1877	Vale of Leven	Rangers	3-2 after 0-0 and 1-1 draws
1878	Vale of Leven	Third Lanark	1-0
1879	Vale of Leven*	Rangers	
1880	Queen's Park	Thornlibank	3-0
1881	Queen's Park†	Dumbarton	3-1
1882	Queen's Park	Dumbarton	4-1 after 2-2 draw
1883	Dumbarton	Vale of Leven	2-1 after 2-2 draw
1884	Queen's Park‡	Vale of Leven	
1885	Renton	Vale of Leven	3-1 after 0-0 draw
1886	Queen's Park	Renton	3-1
1887	Hibernian	Dumbarton	2-1
1888	Renton	Cambuslang	6-1
1889	Third Lanark§	Celtic	2-1
1890	Queen's Park	Vale of Leven	2-1 after 1-1 draw
1891	Hearts	Dumbarton	1-0
1892	Celtic¶	Queen's Park	5-1
1893	Queen's Park	Celtic	2-1
1894	Rangers	Celtic	3-1
1895	St Bernard's	Renton	2-1
1896	Hearts	Hibernian	3-1
1897	Rangers	Dumbarton	5-1
1898	Rangers	Kilmarnock	2-0
1899	Celtic	Rangers	2-0
1900	Celtic	Queen's Park	4-3
1901	Hearts	Celtic	4-3
1902	Hibernian	Celtic	1-0
1903	Rangers	Hearts	2-0 after 1-1 and 0-0 draws
1904	Celtic	Rangers	3-2
1905	Third Lanark	Rangers	3-1 after 0-0 draw
1906	Hearts	Third Lanark	1-0
1907	Celtic	Hearts	3-0
1908	Celtic	St Mirren	5-1
1909	••		
1910	Dundee	Clyde	2-1 after 2-2 and 0-0 draws
1911	Celtic	Hamilton A	2-0 after 0-0 draw
1912	Celtic	Clyde	2-0
1913	Falkirk	Raith R	2-0
1914	Celtic	Hibernian	4-1 after 0-0 draw
1920	Kilmarnock	Albion R	3-2
1921	Partick Th	Rangers	1-0
1922	Morton	Rangers	1-0
1923	Celtic	Hibernian	1-0
1924	Airdrieonians	Hibernian	2-0
1925	Celtic	Dundee	2-1
1926	St Mirren	Celtic	2-0
1927	Celtic	East Fife	3-1
1928	Rangers	Celtic	4-0
1929	Kilmarnock	Rangers	2-0
1930	Rangers	Partick Th	2-1 after 0-0 draw
1931	Celtic	Motherwell	4-2 after 2-2 draw
1932	Rangers	Kilmarnock	3-0 after 1-1 draw
1933	Celtic	Motherwell	1-0
1934	Rangers	St Mirren	5-0
1935	Rangers	Hamilton A	2-1
1936	Rangers	Third Lanark	1-0
1937	Celtic	Aberdeen	2-1
1938	East Fife	Kilmarnock	4-2 after 1-1 draw
1939	Clyde	Motherwell	4-0
1947	Aberdeen	Hibernian	2-1
1948	Rangers	Morton	1-0 after 1-1 draw
1949	Rangers	Clyde	4-1
1950	Rangers	East Fife	3-0
1951	Celtic	Motherwell	1-0
1952	Motherwell	Dundee	4-0
1953	Rangers	Aberdeen	1-0 after 1-1 draw
1954	Celtic	Aberdeen	2-1
1955	Clyde	Celtic	1-0 after 1-1 draw
1956	Hearts	Celtic	3-1
1957	Falkirk	Kilmarnock	2-1 after 1-1 draw
1958	Clyde	Hibernian	1-0
1959	St Mirren	Aberdeen	3-1
1960	Rangers	Kilmarnock	2-0
1961	Dunfermline Ath	Celtic	2-0 after 0-0 draw
1962	Rangers	St Mirren	2-0
1963	Rangers	Celtic	3-0 after 1-1 draw

Year	*Winners*	*Runners-up*	*Score*
1964	Rangers	Dundee	3-1
1965	Celtic	Dunfermline Ath	3-2
1966	Rangers	Celtic	1-0 after 0-0 draw
1967	Celtic	Aberdeen	2-0
1968	Dunfermline Ath	Hearts	3-1
1969	Celtic	Rangers	4-0
1970	Aberdeen	Celtic	3-1
1971	Celtic	Rangers	2-1 after 1-1 draw
1972	Celtic	Hibernian	6-1
1973	Rangers	Celtic	3-2
1974	Celtic	Dundee U	3-0
1975	Celtic	Airdrieonians	3-1
1976	Rangers	Hearts	3-1
1977	Celtic	Rangers	1-0
1978	Rangers	Aberdeen	2-1
1979	Rangers	Hibernian	3-2 after 0-0 and 0-0 draws
1980	Celtic	Rangers	1-0
1981	Rangers	Dundee U	4-1 after 0-0 draw
1982	Aberdeen	Rangers	4-1 (aet)
1983	Aberdeen	Rangers	1-0 (aet)
1984	Aberdeen	Celtic	2-1 (aet)
1985	Celtic	Dundee U	2-1
1986	Aberdeen	Hearts	3-0
1987	St Mirren	Dundee U	1-0 (aet)
1988	Celtic	Dundee U	2-1
1989	Celtic	Rangers	1-0
1990	Aberdeen	Celtic	0-0 (aet)
		(Aberdeen won 9-8 on penalties)	
1991	Motherwell	Dundee U	4-3 (aet)
1992	Rangers	Airdrieonians	2-1
1993	Rangers	Aberdeen	2-1
1994	Dundee U	Rangers	1-0
1995	Celtic	Airdrieonians	1-0
1996	Rangers	Hearts	5-1
1997	Kilmarnock	Falkirk	1-0
1998	Hearts	Rangers	2-1
1999	Rangers	Celtic	1-0
2000	Rangers	Aberdeen	4-0
2001	Celtic	Hibernian	3-0
2002	Rangers	Celtic	3-2
2003	Rangers	Dundee	1-0
2004	Celtic	Dunfermline Ath	3-1
2005	Celtic	Dundee U	1-0
2006	Hearts	Gretna	1-1 (aet)
		(Hearts won 4-2 on penalties)	
2007	Celtic	Dunfermline Ath	1-0
2008	Rangers	Queen of the S	3-2
2009	Rangers	Falkirk	1-0
2010	Dundee U	Ross Co	3-0
2011	Celtic	Motherwell	3-0
2012	Hearts	Hibernian	5-1

*Vale of Leven awarded cup, Rangers failing to appear for replay after 1-1 draw.
†After Dumbarton protested the first game, which Queen's Park won 2-1.
‡Queen's Park awarded cup, Vale of Leven failing to appear.
§Replay by order of Scottish FA because of playing conditions in first match, won 3-0 by Third Lanark.
¶After mutually protested game which Celtic won 1-0.
••Owing to riot, the cup was withheld after two drawn games between Celtic and Rangers 2-2 and 1-1.

SCOTTISH CUP WINS

Celtic 35, Rangers 33, Queen's Park 10, Hearts 8, Aberdeen 7, Clyde 3, Kilmarnock 3, St Mirren 3, Vale of Leven 3, Dundee U 2, Dunfermline Ath 2, Falkirk 2, Hibernian 2, Motherwell 2, Renton 2, Third Lanark 2, Airdrieonians 1, Dumbarton 1, Dundee 1, East Fife 1, Morton 1, Partick Th 1, St Bernard's 1.

APPEARANCES IN FINAL

Celtic 54, Rangers 50, Aberdeen 15, Hearts 14, Hibernian 12, Queen's Park 12, Dundee U 9, Kilmarnock 8, Motherwell 7, Vale of Leven 7, Clyde 6, Dumbarton 6, St Mirren 6, Third Lanark 6, Dundee 5, Dunfermline Ath 5, Renton 5, Airdrieonians 4, Falkirk 4, East Fife 3, Hamilton A 2, Morton 2, Partick Th 2, Albion R 1, Cambuslang 1, Clydesdale 1, Gretna 1, Queen of the S 1, Raith R 1, Ross Co 1, St Bernard's 1, Thornlibank 1.

WILLIAM HILL SCOTTISH CUP 2011–12

■ *Denotes player sent off.*

FIRST ROUND

Rothes v Clachnacuddin	0-3
Fort William v Bo'ness U	0-4
Edinburgh C v Brora R	3-0
Nairn Co v Selkirk	2-1
Fraserburgh v Civil Service S	4-3
Wigtown & B v Preston Ath	2-0
Lossiemouth v Auchinleck T	1-2
Huntly v Newton Stewart	6-1
Forres Mechs v Irvine Meadow	2-2, 3-6
Dalbeattie Star v Inverurie Loco W	1-6
Wick Acad v Coldstream	9-1
Glasgow Univ v Cove R	0-4
Vale of Leithen v Girvan	1-0
Gala Fairydean v Hawick R A	8-1
Culter v Burntisland S	4-0
Edinburgh Univ v Whitehill Wel	0-3
St Cuthbert W v Keith	0-2

Golspie S received a bye.

SECOND ROUND

Clachnacuddin v Inverurie Loco W	1-1, 2-3
Vale of Leithen v Cove R	3-2
Gala Fairydean v Golspie S	5-2
Bo'ness U v Whitehill Wel	2-1
Fraserburgh v Elgin C	0-0, 2-5
Wigtown & B v Stranraer	0-9
Peterhead v Nairn Co	2-0
Wick Acad v Keith	0-1
Culter v Spartans	0-2

Spartans expelled for fielding ineligible player.

Alloa Ath v Annan Ath	2-2, 0-2
Deveronvale v Berwick R	4-0
Auchinleck T v Threave R	8-1
East Stirling v Buckie T	1-1, 4-2
Huntly v Queen's Park	0-3
Montrose v Clyde	2-1
Edinburgh C v Irvine Meadow	0-1

THIRD ROUND

Saturday, 19 November 2011

Airdrie U (5) 11 *(Lovering 28 (pen), 69, Boyle 31, 42, 65, Stevenson 34, 37, 57, McLaren 59, Donnelly 77, Holmes 81)*
Gala Fairydean (0) 0 732
Airdrie U: Fairley; Lilley, Lovering, Stallard, McLaren, Stevenson (Burns 71), Bain, Boyle (Holmes 71), Donnelly, Johnston, Lynch (Owens 58).
Gala Fairydean: Turnbull; Hay G, Young, Brown, Lothian, Wilson, Hunter (McBride 64), Hay J (Jackson 78), Livingstone, Brunton (Grass 73), Rossi.

Auchinleck T (1) 3 *(Milliken 39, McCann 50, Young 65)*
Vale of Leithen (1) 1 *(McKenna 26)* 750
Auchinleck T: Leishman; Pope, Collins, McGoldrick (Park 61), Slavin, White, Young, Latta, Spence (Connolly 76), Milliken, McCann (Gillies 71).
Vale of Leithen: Wilson; Lee (Hill 85), Miller, Sproule, Hall, Greenhill (Devlin 66), Martin, Lauder (Paterson 85), McKenna, Radzynski, Moffat.

Ayr U (1) 2 *(Robertson R 10, Trouten 55 (pen))*
Montrose (1) 2 *(Masson 24, Winter 57 (pen))* 988
Ayr U: Cuthbert; Smith, Malone, Robertson J, Robertson R (Connolly 59), Tiffoney, Trouten (McKernan 82), McGowan, Geggan, Wardlaw (Roberts 59), Moffat.
Montrose: Andrews; Smart, Crighton, Lunan, Masson, Cameron, McNally, Winter, Johnstone, Boyle, Pierce (McPhee 82).

Bo'ness U (0) 0
Cowdenbeath (1) 3 *(Robertson 38, Linton 66, Coult 87)* 1176
Bo'ness U: Christie; Gibb, Snowdon, Hunter■, Shields, Walker, Nimmo (Taggart 76), Donnelly, Duffy, Scanlon■, Tarditi (Stewart 46).
Cowdenbeath: Flynn; Cowan, Adamson, Mbu, Linton, Cameron, Ramsay (Coult 61), Robertson, O'Brien, Naismith (McKenzie 79), Stewart.

Brechin C (1) 3 *(Molloy 26, King 77, McManus 90)*
Dumbarton (0) 0 447
Brechin C: Nelson; Buist, McLean, Dunlop, Molloy (Carcary 70), Brady, McClune, Hodge, McKenna, King (McManus 80), Lister (Weir 90).
Dumbarton: Ewings; Lithgow, Nugent, Creaney (Brannan 78), Wallace, McKinnon, Borris (Ramage 69), McNiff, Prunty, Gilhaney, Winters (Walker 70).

Culter (1) 1 *(Stott 19)*
Partick Th (1) 1 *(Cairney 6)* 1113
Culter: Farquhar; Kelly, Sim (Donald 77), Seivwright, Robertson, Wilson, Youngson (Shand 86), Stott, McKimmie (McWilliam 67), McAllister, McBain.
Partick Th: Fox; Archibald, Paton, Sinclair, Balatoni (Robertson 35), Rowson, Cairney, Erskine, Bannigan, Stewart (Dargo 46), Doolan (Elliot 76).

East Fife (2) 5 *(Ogleby 13, 44, Wallace 49, Linn 71, Sloan 79)*
East Stirling (0) 0 585
East Fife: Brown M; Campbell, White, Cook, Durie, Smith (Ovenstone 61), Muir (Johnstone 36), Sloan, Wallace, Linn, Ogleby (Hislop 73).
East Stirling: Antell; Chisholm, Cane, Stirling, Hunter, Jackson, Horner, Maxwell, Team (Turner 78), Lurinsky (Gibson 63), Coyne.

Elgin C (1) 1 *(Gunn 37)*
Queen's Park (0) 1 *(McBride 58 (pen))* 799
Elgin C: Clark; Duff, Niven, Moore, O'Donoghue, Cameron (Millar 88), Nicolson, Beveridge, Gunn, McPhee, Leslie (Crooks 65).
Queen's Park: Parry; Little, McGinn, Meggatt, Brough, McBride, Anderson, Murray, Watt, Daly (Smith 68), Longworth.

Inverurie Loco W (1) 2 *(Park 25, McLean 57)*
Peterhead (3) 4 *(Redman 18, Ross S 22, MacDonald 44, McAllister 74)* 998
Inverurie Loco W: Coull (Strachan 74); Reid, Park, Thomson, Scott, Maitland, Begg, Ross (Young 81), McLean, Gauld (Michie 81), Brodhurst.
Peterhead: Jellema; Donald, MacDonald, Ross S, Strachan (McBain 68), Redman, Davidson (Wyness 78), McAllister (Sharp 81), Deasley, Bavidge, Ross D.

Irvine Meadow (0) 0
Livingston (4) 6 *(McNulty 5, 26, 40, Boulding 41, Deuchar 51, Barr R 90)* 1500
Irvine Meadow: Wadrope (Hewitt 42); Robertson, Ryan, Turner (McGuinness 66), Hamilton, McLennan, McGeown, MacDonald, Fleming, Barr (Strain 61), Hughes.
Livingston: McNeil; Barr C, Talbot, Watson, Fotheringham, Keaghan Jacobs (Scougall 61), Barr R, Kyle Jacobs, Deuchar (Fox 71), Boulding, McNulty (Russell I 44).

Keith (0) 0

Arbroath (0) 1 *(Sheerin 90 (pen))* 350

Keith: Shearer; Niddrie■, Lonie (Keith S 76), Keith C, Donaldson (McGovern 46), McNamee, Farrell, MacAskill, Lennox (Smith 70), Walker, Phillips.
Arbroath: Hill; Wedderburn, Baxter, Busch, Kerr, Swankie, McAnespie, Gibson (Elfverson 70), Falkingham, Bryce (Sheerin 79), Doris (Sibanda 90).

Morton (3) 5 *(O'Brien 15, MacDonald 21, Jackson 38, Weatherson 72, Campbell 74)*

Deveronvale (1) 1 *(Noble 45)* 1406

Morton: Deans; McCann, Graham, Evans, O'Ware, Young, O'Brien, McGeough, Di Giacomo (Fitzharris 75), Jackson (Campbell 67), MacDonald (Weatherson 58).
Deveronvale: Blanchard; Fraser, Rodger, Blackhall, Barclay, Cowie (Rae 85), Henderson (Hendry 80), McKenzie R (Carstairs 84), Watt, Duncan, Noble.

Ross Co (2) 4 *(Gardyne 9, 70, 90, Lawson 27)*

Albion R (0) 0 1353

Ross Co: Fraser; Munro, Miller, Boyd, Lawson, Fitzpatrick, Brittain, Vigurs (Quinn 46), Kettlewell (Corcoran 63), McMenamin (Byrne 72), Gardyne.
Albion R: Gaston; Reid, O'Byrne, Marriott, McStay, Chaplain (Acquah 80), Stevenson, Donnelly, Scott (Reilly 61), Gemmell (Canning 80), Hamilton.

Stenhousemuir (4) 4 *(Kean 9, Rodgers 17, 22, 37)*

Annan Ath (0) 0 602

Stenhousemuir: Brown; Corrigan, Paton, Lyle, McMillan, McKinlay, Ferguson (Dickson 46), Murray (Plenderleith 65), Thomson, Kean, Rodgers (Quinn 84).
Annan Ath: Mitchell A; McGowan, Watson P (Neilson 46), Muirhead, Gibson (Wild 46), Sloan, Jardine, McKechnie, O'Connor (Gilfillan 54), Cox, Bell.

Stirling Alb (1) 1 *(Smith 26)*

Dundee (1) 2 *(Conroy 31, Milne 61)* 1473

Stirling Alb: Reidford; Allison, Thom, Jacobs, Fagan, Smith, McLeish (McDonald 86), Cook (MacPherson 80), Davidson, McSorley, Nicholas (Flood 67).
Dundee: Douglas; Irvine, McGregor, Weston, Lockwood, Rae, O'Donnell, Riley, Conroy (McCluskey 83), Milne (Chisholm 89), McIntosh (Elliot 54).

Stranraer (0) 1 *(McKeown 89)*

Forfar Ath (1) 1 *(Templeman 32)* 340

Stranraer: David Mitchell; McGregor (Moore 84), Gallagher■, Taggart, McKeown, Noble (McColm 78), Aitken (Shepherd 8), Winter, Stirling, Grehan, Malcolm.
Forfar Ath: Paterson; Ross, Campbell I, Bishop, Mowat, Shaughnessy, Fotheringham (Byers 80), Hegarty (Wilson 60), Low (Motion 90), Templeman, Campbell R.

THIRD ROUND REPLAYS

Saturday, 26 November 2011

Forfar Ath (0) 3 *(Ross 67, Templeman 76, Gibson 87)*

Stranraer (0) 0 423

Forfar Ath: Paterson; Hegarty, Campbell I (Motion), Bishop (Bolocheweckyj), Shaughnessy, Mowat, Fotheringham, Ross, Campbell R (Gibson), Templeman, Low.
Stranraer: David Mitchell; Taggart, Noble, McGregor, McKeown, Kane, Winter (McColm), Stirling, Malcolm, Grehan, Shepherd (Moore).

Partick Th (3) 4 *(Elliot 1, Cairney 26, 29, Erskine 47)*

Culter (0) 0 1864

Partick Th: Fox; Paton, Sinclair, Robertson, O'Donnell, Archibald, Cairney, Rowson (Dargo), Stewart, Elliot (Bannigan), Erskine (Doolan).
Culter: Farquhar; Sim, Robertson, Kelly, Seivwright, McAllister, McBain (Shand), Wilson (Crosbie), Youngson (McWilliam), McKimmie, Stott.

Queen's Park (2) 3 *(Murray 11, Smith 43, 87)*

Elgin C (0) 1 *(Gunn 74)* 513

Queen's Park: Parry; McGinn, Meggatt, Little, Brough, Anderson, Watt (Daly), McBride, Smith (Stewart), Longworth, Murray (Burns).
Elgin C: Clark■; Niven, McPhee (Millar), O'Donoghue, Duff, Beveridge, Gunn, Crooks (Calder), Cameron (Leslie), Nicolson, Moore.

Tuesday, 22 November 2011

Montrose (0) 1 *(Winter 81)*

Ayr U (1) 2 *(Trouten 28, 73)* 575

Montrose: Andrews; Smart, Crighton, Lunan (McGowan), Masson, Cameron, McNally, Winter, Johnstone, Boyle (Dimilta 77), Pierce (McPhee 61).
Ayr U: Cuthbert; Smith, Malone, Robertson J, Tiffoney, Trouten, McGowan (Connolly 78), Geggan, McKernan, Roberts (Wardlaw 82), Moffat.

FOURTH ROUND

Saturday, 7 January 2012

Airdrie U (0) 2 *(Donnelly 85, 90)*

Dundee U (2) 6 *(Rankin 17, Robertson 43, Russell 62, 68, 84, Mackay-Steven 71)* 2434

Airdrie U: Fairley; Lilley, Lovering, Stallard, Green (Holmes), McLaren, Stevenson (Devlin), Bain, Donnelly, Blockley, Lynch (Johnston).
Dundee U: Pernis; Dillon, Dixon, Robertson, Kenneth, Armstrong (Ryan), Flood, Mackay-Steven, Daly (Dalla Valle), Russell, Rankin (Douglas).

Cowdenbeath (1) 2 *(Stewart 1, Robertson 69)*

Hibernian (2) 3 *(Griffiths 18, Doyle 27, Wotherspoon 54)* 2670

Cowdenbeath: Flynn; Cowan, Armstrong, Adamson, Mbu, Linton (Coult), Cameron, Ramsay, Robertson, McKenzie, Stewart.
Hibernian: Brown; Hart, Hanlon, O'Hanlon, Booth, Sproule, Stevenson, Galbraith (Towell), Wotherspoon, Griffiths, Doyle (Sodje).

Dundee (0) 1 *(Milne 46)*

Kilmarnock (1) 1 *(Pascali 32)* 3446

Dundee: Douglas; Irvine, McGregor, McKeown, Lockwood, Rae, McCluskey (Hyde), Chisholm, O'Donnell, Conroy, Milne.
Kilmarnock: Bell; Hay, McKeown, Pascali, Sissoko, Fowler, Racchi, Dayton (Gros), Shiels, Heffernan, Kelly.

Falkirk (2) 2 *(Dods 7, El Alagui 21)*

East Fife (0) 0 2475

Falkirk: McGovern; Dods, Scobbie, Duffie, Wallace, Murdoch, Millar M, Sibbald, Weatherston (Alston), Higginbotham (Fulton D), El Alagui.
East Fife: Brown M; McCormack, White, Cook, Durie, Janczyk, Smith (Johnstone), Muir (Campbell), McQuade (Hislop), Wallace, Linn.

Forfar Ath (0) 0

Aberdeen (2) 4 *(Vernon 31, Chalali 41, Fallon 71, Megginson 84)* 3747

Forfar Ath: Paterson; Ross (Byers), Wilson, Campbell I, McCulloch, Tulloch, Mowat (Motion), Fotheringham, Templeman (Gibson), Campbell R, Hilson.
Aberdeen: Brown; Jack, Arnason, Osbourne (Fallon), McArdle, Robertson, Pawlett (Clark), Reynolds, Vernon, Chalali (Megginson), Fyvie.

Hearts (0) 1 *(Smith 84)*

Auchinleck T (0) 0 8895

Hearts: MacDonald; Barr (Glen), Mullen, Robinson, Grainger (Morton), Webster, Driver, Black, Novikovas (Templeton), Smith, Skacel.
Auchinleck T: Leishman; Pope, Pettigrew, Robb, McGoldrick, White (Park), Young, Latta, Faulds (Slavin), Spence, Milliken (McCann).

Inverness CT (0) 1 *(Hayes 90)*

Dunfermline Ath (1) 1 *(Barrowman 30)* 1601

Inverness CT: Tuffey; Gillet■, Golobart, Davis (Tansey), Piermayr, Shinnie G, Cox (Meekings), Hayes, Foran, Tade, McKay (Doran).
Dunfermline Ath: Smith; Potter, Dowie, Burns, Boyle, Keddie, Cardle (Mason), Hardie (Thomson), Barrowman, Kirk (Buchanan), Graham.

Livingston (1) 1 *(McNulty 43)*

Ayr U (1) 2 *(Geggan 39, McGowan 52)* 932

Livingston: McNeil; Barr C, Watson, Fordyce, Fotheringham, Keaghan Jacobs (Boulding), Barr R, Kyle Jacobs (Fox), Scougall, Russell I, McNulty.
Ayr U: Cuthbert; Smith, Malone, Robertson J, Tiffoney, Trouten (McKernan), McGowan, Geggan, McManus (Wardlaw), Roberts (Robertson R), Moffat.

Motherwell (2) 4 *(Daley 5, Murphy 21, 71, Ojamaa 90)*

Queen's Park (0) 0 4286

Motherwell: Randolph; Clancy, Hammell, Craigan, Hateley, Page, Daley (Lawless), Forbes (Humphrey), McHugh (Ojamaa), Murphy, Law.
Queen's Park: Parry; Little, McGinn, Meggatt, Brough, McBride (Gallagher), Anderson, Murray (Burns), Watt, Smith (Daly), Longworth.

Partick Th (0) 0

Queen of the S (0) 1 *(Carmichael 89)* 2454

Partick Th: Fox; Archibald, Paton, Sinclair, O'Donnell, Flannigan (Dargo), Robertson, Cairney, Erskine, Stewart (Elliot), Doolan.
Queen of the S: Robinson; Reid A (Reilly), McGuffie, Higgins, Reid C, Simmons (McKenna), Johnston, McLaughlin, Clark, Holt, Carmichael.

Raith R (1) 1 *(Clarke 39)*

Morton (0) 2 *(Campbell 67, MacDonald 76 (pen))* 1581

Raith R: McGurn; Murray, Ellis, Donaldson, Walker A, Hamill, Davidson, Baird, Clarke, Williamson (Walker J), Casalinuovo (Smith).
Morton: Stewart; Smyth, Graham, O'Ware, Young (Weatherson), O'Brien, McGeough (Di Giacomo), Tidser, Bachirou, Jackson (MacDonald), Campbell.

Ross Co (1) 7 *(Vigurs 5, 75, Brittain 52 (pen), Gardyne 62, Craig 71, Byrne 87, 88)*

Stenhousemuir (0) 0 1421

Ross Co: Fraser; Munro, Morrison, Miller, Boyd, Lawson (Cooper), Brittain, Vigurs, Kettlewell (Byrne), Craig, Gardyne (Quinn).
Stenhousemuir: Brown; Corrigan, Lyle, McMillan■, McHale, McKinlay, Ferguson, Thomson, Campbell (Rodgers), Dickson (Lawson), Kean (Plenderleith).

St Johnstone (1) 2 *(Davidson M 6, Sandaza 46)*

Brechin C (1) 1 *(McManus 26)* 2467

St Johnstone: Enckelman; McCracken, Maybury, Anderson, MacKay, Craig, Morris, Davidson M, Finnigan, Sandaza (Robertson), Haber.
Brechin C: Nelson; McLauchlan■, McLean, Dunlop, Molloy, Brady, Fusco (Crawford), Hodge, McKenna (King), McManus, Lister (Carcary).

St Mirren (0) 0

Hamilton A (0) 0 3091

St Mirren: Samson; Van Zanten, Tesselaar, McAusland, Mair, Barron, Carey (Teale), Mooy (McShane), McGowan, Hasselbaink, McLean.
Hamilton A: Hutton; Canning, McLaughlin, Crawford (Anderson), Kilday, Hendrie, Mensing, Imrie, McAlister, Gillespie (Currie P), Spence (Ryan).

Sunday, 8 January 2012

Arbroath (0) 0

Rangers (2) 4 *(Healy 18, Wedderburn 22 (og), Jelavic 59, Kerkar 77)* 5895

Arbroath: Hill; Malcolm, Wedderburn, Baxter, Kerr (Gibson), Sheerin (Bryce), Swankie, McAnespie, Falkingham, Caddis (Sibanda), Doris.
Rangers: McGregor; Bartley (McMillan), Papac, Bocanegra, Goian, Wallace (Kerkar), Edu, Healy, Jelavic, Fleck, Aluko (Wylde).

Peterhead (0) 0

Celtic (1) 3 *(Stokes 36, 57, 82)* 4600

Peterhead: Jarvie; McBain, Donald, MacDonald, Ross S, Strachan, Sharp (Deasley), Redman, McAllister, Bavidge (Wyness), Ross D (Davidson).
Celtic: Zaluska; Cha, Wilson K, Ki, Izaguirre, Mulgrew (McGeough), Brown, Stokes, Samaras (Twardzik), McCourt, Ledley (Wanyama).

FOURTH ROUND REPLAYS

Tuesday, 17 January 2012

Kilmarnock (2) 2 *(Heffernan 34, Shiels 43)*

Dundee (0) 1 *(Rae 63)* 4618

Kilmarnock: Bell; Pascali, Hay (Racchi), Fowler, Kroca, Sissoko, McKeown, Kelly, Shiels, Heffernan, Harkins.
Dundee: Douglas; Irvine, Lockwood, O'Donnell, McGregor, McKeown, Chisholm (Bayne), Rae, McCluskey, Milne, Conroy.

Wednesday, 18 January 2012

Dunfermline Ath (1) 1 *(Barrowman 40)*

Inverness CT (0) 3 *(Hayes 54, Shinnie A 93, Tansey 110)* 1594

Dunfermline Ath: Smith; Dowie, Boyle, Thomson, Rutkiewicz (Potter), Keddie, Cardle, Hardie, Barrowman (Buchanan), Kirk, Graham (Willis).
Inverness CT: Tuffey; Piermayr, Shinnie G, Golobart (Proctor), Tokely, Cox (Shinnie A), Hayes, Tansey, Foran, Tade, McKay (Ross).
aet.

Tuesday, 17 January 2012

Hamilton A (0) 0

St Mirren (1) 1 *(Carey 21)* 1520

Hamilton A: Cerny; Kilday, Hendrie, Canning, Mensing, McLaughlin, Imrie, McAlister, Anderson (Spence), Crawford, Ryan (Martin).
St Mirren: Samson; Van Zanten, Tesselaar, McAusland, Mair, McLean, Teale, McGowan, Thompson, Carey (Thomson), Barron.

FIFTH ROUND

Saturday, 4 February 2012

Aberdeen (0) 1 *(Vernon 67)*

Queen of the S (0) 1 *(McLaughlin 54)* 6785

Aberdeen: Brown; McArdle, Jack (Megginson), Arnason, Reynolds, Considine, Clark (Magennis), Hughes, Vernon, Fallon (Chalali), Fyvie.
Queen of the S: Robinson; Reid C, Reid A, McKenna, McGuffie, Higgins, Johnston (Simmons), McLaughlin, Parkin, Brighton (Reilly), Carmichael.

Hibernian (1) 1 *(Doyle 15)*
Kilmarnock (0) 0 8198

Hibernian: Stack; Doherty, Kujabi, Hanlon, McPake, Osbourne, Wotherspoon (Scott), Soares, O'Connor (Sproule), Doyle (O'Donovan), Stevenson.
Kilmarnock: Bell; Fowler, Gordon, Racchi, Pascali, Nelson, Dayton (Van Tornhout), Kelly, Shiels, Heffernan, Hay (Silva).

Inverness CT (0) 0
Celtic (1) 2 *(Samaras 33, Brown 68 (pen))* 5743

Inverness CT: Tuffey; Meekings, Shinnie G, Proctor, Tokely, Gillet, Hayes (Winnall), Tansey, Foran, Tade (Gnakpa), Ross (Sutherland).
Celtic: Forster; Wilson K, Matthews, Rogne, Mulgrew, Ledley (Twardzik), Brown, Wanyama, Samaras, Hooper (Stokes), Commons (Forrest).

Motherwell (5) 6 *(Hateley 9, Murphy 29, 67, Hutchinson 33, Ojamaa 35, Law 41)*
Morton (0) 0 5139

Motherwell: Randolph; Hateley, Hammell, Hutchinson, Clancy (Page), Ojamaa, Jennings, Higdon, Murphy, Lasley (Carswell), Law (Humphrey).
Morton: Stewart; Evans, Little, Smyth (Weatherson), Graham, Tidser, McGeouch, Bachirou, MacDonald, Campbell (Young), O'Brien (Di Giacomo).

St Mirren (1) 1 *(Thompson 43)*
Ross Co (1) 1 *(Brittain 40 (pen))* 3334

St Mirren: Samson; Van Zanten, Barron (Carey), McAusland, Mair, Goodwin, Tesselaar, Mooy (Hasselbaink), Thompson, McGowan, Teale (Thomson).
Ross Co: Fraser; Miller, Morrison, Boyd, Munro, Kettlewell, Craig (Morrow), Vigurs, McMenamin (Byrne), Brittain, Corcoran.

Sunday, 5 February 2012

Hearts (1) 1 *(Templeton 10)*
St Johnstone (0) 1 *(Sheridan 77)* 9185

Hearts: MacDonald; Hamill, McGowan, Robinson, Zaliukas, Webster, Mrowiec, Black, Templeton (Driver), Elliott, Skacel (Taouil).
St Johnstone: Enckelman; MacKay■, Davidson C, Morris, McCracken, Anderson, Croft (Keatings), Robertson (Sheridan), Sandaza, Davidson M (Millar), Craig.

Rangers (0) 0
Dundee U (2) 2 *(Gunning 16, Russell 35)* 17,822

Rangers: McGregor; Bartley, Papac (Wylde), Bocanegra, Goian, Edu, Celik (Kerkar), Davis, Aluko, Healy (Little), Wallace.
Dundee U: Pernis; Neilson, Dixon, Robertson, Kenneth, Gunning (Dillon), Armstrong (Flood), Mackay-Steven (Lacny), Daly, Russell, Rankin.

Wednesday, 15 February 2012

Ayr U (1) 2 *(Geggan 19, Roberts 57 (pen))*
Falkirk (1) 1 *(Alston 6)* 1873

Ayr U: Cuthbert; Tiffoney, Malone, Campbell (Wardlaw), Smith, Geggan, Dodd, Tomsett, Moffat, Roberts, Trouten (McGowan).
Falkirk: McGovern; Duffie, Scobbie, Dods, Wallace, Murdoch, Alston (Fulton J), Millar M, El Alagui, Gibson (White), Sibbald (Bennett).

FIFTH ROUND REPLAYS

Tuesday, 14 February 2012

Queen of the S (0) 1 *(McGuffie 58 (pen))*
Aberdeen (1) 2 *(Fyvie 21, Considine 90)* 3102

Queen of the S: Robinson; Reid C, Reid A, McKenna, McGuffie, Higgins (Holt), Johnston (Simmons), McLaughlin, Parkin, Clark, Carmichael.
Aberdeen: Brown; McArdle, Reynolds, Hughes, Mawene, Considine, Arnason, Megginson (Uchechi), Vernon, Fallon (Mackie), Fyvie.

Ross Co (0) 1 *(Morrow 55)*
St Mirren (1) 2 *(Teale 14, Hasselbaink 53)* 2334

Ross Co: Malin; Miller, Morrison, Boyd, Flynn, Duncan, Craig, Gardyne (Byrne), Morrow, Quinn (Cooper), Corcoran.
St Mirren: Samson; Barron, Tesselaar, McAusland, Mair, Goodwin, McGowan, Carey, Thompson■, Hasselbaink (Mooy), Teale.

St Johnstone (0) 1 *(Davidson M 84)*
Hearts (0) 2 *(Hamill 90 (pen), Zaliukas 117)* 3404

St Johnstone: Mannus; Anderson (Oyenuga), Maybury (Haber), Morris, Wright, McCracken, Millar (Croft), Davidson M, Sheridan, Sandaza, Craig.
Hearts: MacDonald; Hamill, Grainger (McGowan), Robinson, Zaliukas, Webster, Mrowiec, Taouil (Santana), Obua (Templeton), Elliott, Skacel.
aet.

QUARTER-FINALS

Saturday, 10 March 2012

Ayr U (0) 0
Hibernian (2) 2 *(O'Donovan 6, Griffiths 19 (pen))* 5991

Ayr U: Cuthbert; Tiffoney, Dodd, Malone, Smith, Geggan (McKernan), Moffat, Tomsett, Parker, Roberts (Wardlaw), McGowan (Robertson R).
Hibernian: Stack; Francomb, Kujabi (Doherty), Hanlon, McPake, Osbourne, Sproule (Wotherspoon), Claros, O'Donovan, Griffiths (O'Connor), Stevenson.

Hearts (1) 2 *(Beattie 37, Skacel 48)*
St Mirren (1) 2 *(Carey 27, Zaliukas 84 (og))* 8859

Hearts: MacDonald; McGowan, Grainger, Taouil, Zaliukas, Webster, Mrowiec (Skacel), Black, Beattie, Elliott, Driver.
St Mirren: Samson; Van Zanten, Carey, McLean (Murray), Mair, Goodwin, McGowan, Thomson, Thompson, Hasselbaink, Teale.

Sunday, 11 March 2012

Dundee U (0) 0
Celtic (0) 4 *(Ledley 53, Samaras 71, Stokes 86, Brown 90 (pen))* 12,270

Dundee U: Pernis; Dillon, Dixon, Robertson, Neilson■, Gunning (Lacny), Flood (Armstrong), Mackay-Steven (Kenneth), Daly, Russell, Rankin.
Celtic: Forster (Zaluska), Matthews, Ledley, Rogne, Mulgrew, Wanyama, Forrest, Brown, Samaras, Hooper (McCourt), Stokes (Commons).

Motherwell (0) 1 *(Law 79)*
Aberdeen (2) 2 *(Fallon 5, 41)* 7640

Motherwell: Randolph; Hateley, Hammell, Hutchinson (Page), Clancy, Lasley■, Ojamaa, Jennings, Higdon, Murphy (Humphrey), Law.
Aberdeen: Brown; McArdle, Jack (Clark), Robertson, Reynolds, Considine, Arnason, Megginson (Pawlett), Vernon, Fallon, Fyvie (Mawene).

QUARTER-FINAL REPLAY

Wednesday, 21 March 2012

St Mirren (0) 0
Hearts (1) 2 *(Hamill 31, Skacel 86)* 5291

St Mirren: Samson; Van Zanten, Carey, McAusland, Mair, Goodwin, Murray (Tesselaar 70), Thomson, Thompson, Hasselbaink, Teale (Mooy).
Hearts: MacDonald; McGowan, Grainger, Barr, Zaliukas, Webster, Hamill, Black (Robinson), Beattie (Glen), Skacel (Santana), Driver.

SEMI-FINALS (at Hampden Park)

Saturday, 14 April 2012

Aberdeen (0) 1 *(Fallon 59)*

Hibernian (1) 2 *(O'Connor 3, Griffiths 85)* 28,278

Aberdeen: Brown; McArdle (Magennis), Robertson, Arnason, Reynolds, Considine, Clark (Mackie), Hughes, Vernon, Fallon, Jack (Fyvie).
Hibernian: Stack (Brown); Doherty, Kujabi, Hanlon, McPake, Osbourne, Soares, Claros (Wotherspoon), O'Connor (Francomb), Griffiths, Sproule.

Sunday, 15 April 2012

Celtic (0) 1 *(Hooper 87)*

Hearts (0) 2 *(Skacel 47, Beattie 90 (pen))* 36,609

Celtic: Forster; Lustig (Wanyama), Wilson K, Loovens, Mulgrew, Ledley, Ki, Brown (McGeough), Samaras (Stokes), Hooper, Commons.
Hearts: MacDonald; McGowan, Grainger, Barr, Zaluikas, Webster, Robinson (Beattie), Black (Santana), Elliott (Prychynenko), Skacel, Driver.

WILLIAM HILL SCOTTISH CUP FINAL

Saturday, 19 May 2012

Hibernian (1) 1 Hearts (2) 5

Hibernian: Brown; Doherty, Kujabi■, Hanlon, McPake, Osbourne, Soares (Francomb), Claros (Sproule), O'Connor (Doyle), Griffiths, Stevenson.
Scorer: McPake 41.

Hearts: MacDonald; McGowan, Grainger, Barr, Zaliukas, Webster, Santana (Beattie), Black (Robinson), Elliott, Skacel, Driver (Taouil).
Scorers: Barr 15, Skacel 27, 75, Grainger 48 (pen), McGowan 50.

Referee: C. Thomson.

Stephen Elliott of Hearts attempts to fend off a challenge by Pa Kujabi of Hibernian in the first all-Edinburgh Scottish Cup Final since 1896. Hibs finished with ten men and Hearts won 5-1. (Action Images/Ed Sykes)

WELSH FOOTBALL 2011–12

Another eventful season was inevitably overshadowed by the inexplicable death of Gary Speed in November at the age of 42.

When the national manager was found hanged at his home, it was assumed he had committed suicide. The internet, but not the press, was suddenly awash with unfounded and outlandish rumours and the subsequent inquest, in reaching a narrative verdict, failed to shed much more light on his death.

The timing of Speed's demise was bizarre: the team had won half of his 10 games in charge since he'd replaced John Toshack – including four of the last five which had returned Wales to the top 50 in FIFA's world rankings. He had just finalised the 2014 World Cup qualifying fixture list and, despite experiencing domestic difficulties, he seemed in good spirits during an appearance on BBC TV's *Football Focus* the day before he died.

As speculation about Speed's death continued, the Welsh FA moved sure-footedly but sensitively to appoint his successor and it was no surprise when Chris Coleman, another much respected former international in his early forties, was chosen. Wales lost 1-0 to Costa Rica in an emotional memorial match for Speed in Cardiff in February and went down 2-0 to Mexico in New Jersey in Coleman's first game in charge in May.

Swansea City once again became the victims of their own success after finishing an impressive 11th on their return to the top flight. In 2009, they lost manager Roberto Martinez to Wigan and, three years later, Brendan Rodgers was lured away to Liverpool. The Northern Irishman's determination to stick to his passing principles resulted in a number of notable victories – especially over Manchester City and Arsenal at the Liberty Stadium – but a total of 44 goals in 38 games suggested that although possession may be nine-tenths of the law, it doesn't add up to much in a game of football without an end product. Like Rodgers' favourite team, Barcelona, Swansea might consider developing a Plan B or even a Plan C – although that seems unlikely following the appointment of the ex-Barcelona and Real Madrid player, Michael Laudrup, as their new manager.

For the second successive season, Cardiff City reached the play-offs but missed out on the final at Wembley. New manager Malky Mackay deserves huge credit for taking his rebuilt squad to the semi-finals but the Bluebirds were ultimately outclassed by a more experienced West Ham side in both games. Their supporters had already visited the home of English football though when Cardiff turned in a spirited performance against Liverpool in the Carling Cup final – only to lose on penalties. A controversial rebranding – including the club's main colours being changed from blue to red – was introduced in June as part of a further £100 million investment by its Malaysian owners as they seek to increase Cardiff's appeal in the Far East. Following the death of former Cardiff manager Eddie May in April, they agreed for his ashes to be scattered at the club's new memorial park.

It was déjà vu for Wrexham too when, with manager Dean Saunders having left for Doncaster in September, their automatic promotion campaign stalled as Fleetwood won the Blue Square Premier title. Like last year, the Red Dragons couldn't muster enough firepower to beat Luton in the play-off semi-finals – with player-manager Andy Morrell admitting that a lacklustre first-half performance in the first leg had sealed their fate – just as it had a year earlier. Despite the disappointment, everyone involved with the club must be congratulated on helping to secure its financial future under the auspices of the Wrexham Supporters' Trust. At the other end of the table, Newport County struggled for most of the season – first under Anthony Hudson and then Justin Edinburgh. The former Spurs defender guided the Exiles to safety before taking them to the FA Trophy Final at Wembley where they lost 2-0 to York. Colwyn Bay finished comfortably in mid-table in their first season in the Blue Square North while Merthyr Town secured back-to-back promotions by winning the Toolstation Western League Premier Division title and moving up to the Southern League Division One.

European football provided little joy for Welsh clubs with Bangor suffering a record 10-0 defeat in the second leg of their Champions League tie against HJK Helsinki as they lost 13-0 on aggregate. In the Europa League, The New Saints were knocked out 8-3 by Midtjylland of Denmark, Llanelli went down 6-2 to Georgia's Dinamo Tbilisi while Aalesund of Norway beat Neath 6-1. Domestically, The New Saints completed a league and cup double and will play in the Champions League while runners-up Bangor, European play-off winners Llanelli and Welsh Cup losing finalists Cefn Druids will compete in the Europa League – Llanelli having qualified for Europe for the seventh successive season. Neath finished third in the Welsh Premier League but, having been refused both domestic and UEFA licences, were then wound up in the High Court.

A week after Coleman took up his new role, the FAW launched its strategic plan and vision for the future of Welsh football. "The message has been clear on the badge for years: *Gorau Chwarae Cyd Chwarae* – best play is team play. Our messages are clear: greater team work, better communication, a longer term perspective through evolution and winning more." Progress is certainly being made and although qualifying for Brazil 2014 from a group consisting of Scotland, Belgium, Serbia, Croatia and Toshack's Macedonia won't be easy, there could surely be no more lasting legacy to his predecessor if, with the help of such established stars as Craig Bellamy, Aaron Ramsey and Gareth Bale, Coleman managed to pull it off.

GRAHAME LLOYD

CORBETT SPORTS WELSH PREMIER LEAGUE 2011–12

		Total						*Home*					*Away*						
		P	*W*	*D*	*L*	*F*	*A*	*W*	*D*	*L*	*F*	*A*	*W*	*D*	*L*	*F*	*A*	*GD*	*Pts*
1	The New Saints	32	23	5	4	75	31	12	2	2	46	19	11	3	2	29	12	44	74
2	Bangor C	32	22	3	7	72	45	11	2	3	40	25	11	1	4	32	20	27	69
3	Neath Ath	32	18	8	6	60	36	11	2	3	34	16	7	6	3	26	20	24	62
4	Llanelli	32	18	5	9	63	37	9	1	6	33	19	9	4	3	30	18	26	59
5	Bala T	32	14	7	11	48	41	6	5	5	24	17	8	2	6	24	24	7	49
6	Prestatyn T	32	8	4	20	41	63	5	2	9	21	32	3	2	11	20	31	–22	28
7	Airbus UK Broughton	32	10	9	13	48	50	6	6	4	29	25	4	3	9	19	25	–2	39
8	Aberystwyth T	32	8	10	14	45	50	4	6	6	23	26	4	4	8	22	24	–5	33
9	Port Talbot T	32	8	9	15	39	51	6	4	6	21	22	2	5	9	18	29	–12	33
10	Afan Lido	32	7	11	14	40	55	5	5	6	18	20	2	6	8	22	35	–15	32
11	Carmarthen T	32	10	2	20	33	67	8	1	7	22	25	2	1	13	11	42	–34	32
12	Newtown	32	7	5	20	44	82	5	3	8	20	31	2	2	12	24	51	–38	23

Top 6 teams split after 22 games. Aberystwyth T deducted 1 point. Newtown deducted 3 points.

PREVIOUS WELSH LEAGUE WINNERS

1993	Cwmbran Town	1998	Barry Town	2003	Barry Town	2008	Llanelli
1994	Bangor City	1999	Barry Town	2004	Rhyl	2009	Rhyl
1995	Bangor City	2000	TNS	2005	TNS	2010	The New Saints
1996	Barry Town	2001	Barry Town	2006	TNS	2011	Bangor C
1997	Barry Town	2002	Barry Town	2007	TNS	2012	The New Saints

MACWHIRTER WELSH LEAGUE 2011–12

		P	*W*	*D*	*L*	*F*	*A*	*GD*	*Pts*
1	Cambrian & Clydach	30	16	10	4	78	25	53	58
2	Taffs Well	30	16	4	10	60	42	18	52
3	Haverfordwest Co	30	15	7	8	58	43	15	52
4	Bryntirion Ath	30	16	3	11	52	43	9	51
5	AFC Porth	30	13	9	8	54	36	18	48
6	Barry T	30	12	10	8	48	37	11	46
7	Goytre U	30	12	8	10	71	55	16	44
8	Bridgend T	30	13	5	12	50	41	9	44
9	Ton Pentre	30	9	16	5	48	40	8	43
10	Pontardawe T	30	11	9	10	48	53	–5	42
11	West End	30	11	5	14	53	62	–9	38
12	Cwmbran Celtic	30	12	2	16	32	54	–22	38
13	Aberaman Ath	30	8	9	13	46	55	–9	33
14	Cwmaman Institute	30	7	8	15	36	59	–23	29
15	Cardiff Corinthians	30	6	10	14	50	67	–17	28
16	Caerau (Ely)	30	4	3	23	37	109	–72	15

HUWS GRAY-FITLOCK CYMRU ALLIANCE LEAGUE 2011–12

		P	*W*	*D*	*L*	*F*	*A*	*GD*	*Pts*
1	Gap Connah's Quay	30	21	5	4	89	23	66	68
2	Rhyl	30	19	5	6	80	22	58	62
3	Buckley T	30	19	4	7	67	43	24	61
4	Porthmadog	30	19	5	6	68	41	27	59
5	Penrhyncoch	30	17	4	9	56	44	12	55
6	Cefn Druids	30	17	3	10	58	42	16	54
7	Caersws	30	17	4	9	68	49	19	52
8	Llandudno T	30	14	7	9	55	40	15	49
9	Flint Town U	30	13	7	10	59	47	12	46
10	Conwy U	30	10	7	13	59	65	–6	37
11	Guilsfield	30	10	4	16	41	58	–17	34
12	Ruthin T	30	6	7	17	28	60	–32	25
13	Penycae	30	7	4	19	30	76	–46	25
14	Llanrhaeadr YM	30	3	9	18	40	77	–37	18
15	Llangefni T	30	4	2	24	32	96	–64	14
16	Rhos Aelwyd	30	2	7	21	29	76	–47	13

Caersws deducted 3 points; Porthmadog deducted 3 points.

WELSH CUP 2011–12

QUALIFYING ROUND ONE NORTH

Acrefair Y v Coedpoeth U 0-4
Amlwch T v Rhydymwyn 0-5
Barmouth & Dyffryn v Aberdyfi 3-1
Bethel v Caernarfon W 1-2
Blaenau Ffestiniog v Caernarfon T 3-7
Bow Street v Mold Alex 1-9
Brymbo v Penmaenmawr Phoenix 0-1
Builth Wells v Llanberis 3-2
Carno v Trearddur Bay 4-2
Connah's Quay T v Kerry 3-1
Dyffryn N V v Llanllyfni 1-2
FC Nomads of Connah's Q v Llay M W 3-2
Gaerwen v Llandudno J 2-1
Glan Conwy v Overton Rec 4-1
Greenfield v FC Cefn 0-4
Gwalchmai v Dolgellau Ath 6-4
Johnstown Y v Llandrindod Wells 1-3
Kinmel Bay S P v Chirk AAA 1-1
Chirk AAA won 5-4 on penalties.
Llandyrnog U v Holywell T 1-0
Llanfyllin v Brickfield R 1-5
Llanrwst U v Llangollen U 0-1
Llanystumdwy v Bro Goronwy 2-6
Montgomery T v Machynlleth 8-0
Nefyn U v Presteigne St A 5-0
Penyffordd v Glantraeth 2-5
Pontrhydfendigaid v Castell Alun C 4-2
Pwllheli v Llanrug U 1-3
Rhayader T v Hawarden R 3-3
Hawarden R won 3-2 on penalties.
Rhosgoch R v Halkyn U 2-1
Tregaron Turfs v Llanfair U 0-4
Tywn Bryncrug v Llanfair PG 3-2
Venture Comm v Bodedern 3-0
Waterloo R v Berriew 1-3

QUALIFYING ROUND ONE SOUTH

Aber Valley YMCA v Garw 8-3
Abercarn U v Llanharry 8-3
AFC Abercynon withdrew v Perthcelyn U w.o.
AFC Llwydcoed v Croesyceliog 3-1

Bettws v Trefelin	0-4
Brecon Cor v Undy Ath	1-6
Bridgend St v Treforest	2-0
Briton Ferry L v Treharris Ath W	3-1
Cadoxton Barry v UWIC	0-1
Cardiff Hibs v Caerau	0-2
Cornelly U v Ely R	0-6
Cwmbran T v Hirwaun Wel	2-1
Dinas Powys v Blanrhondda	6-1
Ferndale withdrew v Goytre w.o.	
Graig v STM Sp	4-5
Kenfig Hill v Caerleon	1-1
Caerleon won 4-2 on penalties.	
Llangeinor v Merthyr Saints	2-4
Llantwit Fadre v Baglan Dragons	2-1
Llanwern v Fleur de Lys Wel	1-2
Newport CS v Cwmamman U	3-2
Penrhiwceiber Con v Aberbargoed Buds	1-3
Penrhiwceiber R v Aberaeron	2-5
Pentwynmawr Ath v Abertillery Blue birds	0-5
Pontyclun v Penygraig	2-0
Talgarth T v Nelson Cavaliers	2-3
Tata Steel v Carnetown	3-2
Tonyrefail v RTB Ebbw Vale	3-2
Tredegar Ath v Risca U	0-3
Tredegar T v Cardiff Grange Harle	3-2
Treowen Stars v Pontypridd T	4-3
Trethomas Blue birds v Splott Alb	0-1

SECOND QUALIFYING ROUND NORTH

Barmouth & Dyffryn v Hawarden R	4-1
Brickfield R v Builth Wells	1-4
Carnaerfon T v Penmaenmawr Phoenix	8-0
Caernarfon W v Bethesda Ath	1-5
Chirk AAA v Berriew	1-0
Coedpoeth U v Gaerwen	5-1
FC Cefn v FC Nomads of Connah's Quay	3-1
Glantraeth v Pontrhydfendigaid	9-0
Gresford Ath v Mold Alex	3-2
Gwalchmai v Llansantffraid Vill	3-2
Holyhead Hotspur v Llanfair U	4-3
Lex XI v Connah's Quay T	1-3
Llandyrnog U v Llanrug U	1-2
Llangollen U v Carno	1-2
Llanidloes T v Glan Conwy	4-3
Llanllyfni v Venture Com	0-3
Montgomery T v Bro Goronwy	5-0
Nefyn U v Llandrindod Wells	2-3
Rhydymwyn v Denbigh T	0-5
Rhosgoch R v Corwen Amat	2-1
Tywyn Bryncrug v Newbridge-on-Wye	1-3

SECOND QUALIFYING ROUND SOUTH

Aber Valley YMCA v Abertillery Blue birds	3-6
Aberbargoed Buds v Abercarn U	4-0
Ammanford v Dinas Powys	1-3
Bridgend St v UWIC	2-3
Briton Ferry L v Tata Steel	0-1
Caerleon v Newport YMCA	2-0
Cwmbran T v Pontyclun	3-1
Fleur de Lys Wel v Undy Ath	3-5
Garden Vill v Caldicot T	1-1
Caldicot T won 4-2 on penalties.	
Goytre v Llantwit Fardre	1-0
Merthyr T v Caerau	5-1
Monmouth T v Tredegar T	6-2
Nelson Cavaliers v Aberaeron	0-6
Newcastle Emlyn v Ely R	0-0
Newcastle Emlyn won 4-2 on penalties.	
Perthcelyn U v Merthyr Saints	5-6
Risca U v Tonyrefail	4-0
Splott Alb v AFC Llwydcoed	1-0
STM Sp v Newport CS	2-3
Trefelin v Treowen Stars	1-2

FIRST ROUND NORTH

Barmouth & Dyffryn v Ruthin T	4-1
Buckley T v Penrhyncoch	4-0
Caersws v Conwy U	1-1
Caersws won 4-2 on penalties.	
Carno v Coedpoeth U	0-2
Cefn Druids v Caernarfon T	6-1
Flint T U v Chirk AAA	5-1
Connah's Quay N v Gwalchmai	7-2
Llandrindod Wells v Llanrug U	3-3
Llandrindod Wells won 4-1 on penalties.	
Llangefni T v Denbigh T	2-3
Llanidloes T v Glantraeth	4-3
Llanrhaeadr ym M v Holyhead Hotspur	1-6
Montgomery T v Connah's Quay T	4-0
Penycae v FC Cefn	1-2
Porthmadog v Bethesda Ath	3-1
Rhos Aelwyd v Guilsfield	0-1
Rhyl v Gresford Ath	5-0
Venture Com v Llandudno T	1-3

FIRST ROUND SOUTH

Abertillery Blue birds v Caerau	0-2
AFC Porth v Aberbargoed Buds	2-0
Bridgend T v Splott Alb	2-0
Bryntirion Ath v Cwmbran T	3-1
Caerleon v Aberaman Ath	1-0
Caldicot T v Newport CS	2-4
Cambrian & Clydach v Monmouth T	5-1
Cardiff Cor v Cwmaman Inst	2-0
Dinas Powys v Builth Wells	0-2
Goytre v Aberaeron	3-1
Goytre U v Ton Pentre	1-0
Merthyr T v Barry T	0-3
Pontardawe T v Treowen Stars	3-0
Rhosgoch R v Merthyr Saints	2-6
Risca U v Newbridge-on-Wye	0-4
Taff's Well v Undy Ath	5-4
Tata Steel v Newcastle Emlyn	3-1
UWIC v Haverfordwest Co	0-2
West End v Cwmbran C	2-0

SECOND ROUND NORTH

Barmouth & Dyffryn v Caersws	0-3
Buckley T v Holyhead Hotspur	5-2
Cefn Druids v Coedpoeth U	8-0
Denbigh T v Flint T U	1-2
Guilsfield v Llandudno T	1-3
Llanidloes T v Connah's Quay N	0-2
Montgomery T v FC Cefn	3-7
Porthmadog v Rhyl	2-3

SECOND ROUND SOUTH

AFC Porth v Pontardawe T	3-0
Bridgend T v Tata Steel	5-3
Bryntirion Ath v Goytre	5-2
Builth Wells v Taff's Well	0-5
Caerau v Goytre U	1-8
Caerleon v Merthyr Saints	3-4
Cambrian & Clydach v Llandrindod Wells	2-0
Haverfordwest Co v Barry T	1-2
Newport CS v Newbridge-on-Wye	2-0
West End v Cardiff Cor	2-1

THIRD ROUND

Flint T U v Newport CS	3-0
Port Talbot T v Afan Lido	0-1
The New Saints v Bryntirion Ath	6-0
AFC Porth v Cambrian & Clydach	0-0
AFC Porth won 4-3 on penalties.	
Wrexham v Airbus UK	1-2
Carmarthen T v Bridgend T	2-1
Caersws v Llandudno T	0-1
Buckley T v Taff's Well	4-3
Neath v West End	4-0
FC Cefn v Aberystwyth T	1-6
Newtown v Rhyl	1-2
Bangor C v Llanelli	2-4
Prestatyn T v Goytre U	6-2
Newport Co v Barry T	3-2
Connah's Quay N v Cefn Druids	1-2
Merthyr Saints v Bala T	0-6

FOURTH ROUND

Rhyl v Llanelli	3-3
aet; Llanelli won 5-4 on penalties.	
Afan Lido v Airbus UK	2-2
aet; Airbus UK won 5-4 on penalties.	
Buckley T v Bala T	2-4

Flint T U v Neath	1-3
Aberystwyth T v Llandudno T	1-1
aet; Aberystwyth T won 5-4 on penalties.	
The New Saints v Newport Co	4-0
Prestatyn T v Cefn Druids	0-2
Carmarthen T v AFC Porth	3-1

QUARTER-FINALS

Aberystwyth T v Cefn Druids	0-1
Airbus UK v Carmarthen T	3-1
Bala T v Llanelli	1-1
aet; Bala T won 5-4 on penalties.	
The New Saints v Neath	1-0

SEMI-FINALS

Bala T v The New Saints	0-4
Airbus UK v Cefn Druids	1-4

FINAL (at Bangor)

5 May 2012

Cefn Druids (0) 0

The New Saints (2) 2 *(Draper 13, Darlington 15)* 731

Cefn Druids: Mullock; Harris, Price, Hesp, McElmeel, Hughes, Griffiths, Quinn (Edwards 88), Cann, Swarbrick (Speed 90), Duckett.
The New Saints: Harrison; Spender, Marriott, Baker, Evans, Seargeant, Edwards (Ruscoe 84), Draper (Ward 77), Darlington, Jones, Fraughan (Roberts 68).
Referee: K. Parry.

PREVIOUS WELSH CUP WINNERS

1878	Wrexham Town	1910	Wrexham	1952	Rhyl	1984	Shrewsbury Town
1879	White Star Newtown	1911	Wrexham	1953	Rhyl	1985	Shrewsbury Town
1880	Druids	1912	Cardiff City	1954	Flint Town United	1986	Wrexham
1881	Druids	1913	Swansea Town	1955	Barry Town	1987	Merthyr Tydfil
1882	Druids	1914	Wrexham	1956	Cardiff City	1988	Cardiff City
1883	Wrexham	1915	Wrexham	1957	Wrexham	1989	Swansea City
1884	Oswestry United	1920	Cardiff City	1958	Wrexham	1990	Hereford United
1885	Druids	1921	Wrexham	1959	Cardiff City	1991	Swansea City
1886	Druids	1922	Cardiff City	1960	Wrexham	1992	Cardiff City
1887	Chirk	1923	Cardiff City	1961	Swansea Town	1993	Cardiff City
1888	Chirk	1924	Wrexham	1962	Bangor City	1994	Barry Town
1889	Bangor	1925	Wrexham	1963	Borough United	1995	Wrexham
1890	Druids	1926	Ebbw Vale	1964	Cardiff City	1996	TNS
1891	Shrewsbury Town	1927	Cardiff City	1965	Cardiff City	1997	Barry Town
1892	Chirk	1928	Cardiff City	1966	Swansea Town	1998	Bangor City
1893	Wrexham	1929	Connah's Quay	1967	Cardiff City	1999	Inter Cable-Tel
1894	Chirk	1930	Cardiff City	1968	Cardiff City	2000	Bangor City
1895	Newtown	1931	Wrexham	1969	Cardiff City	2001	Barry Town
1896	Bangor	1932	Swansea Town	1970	Cardiff City	2002	Barry Town
1897	Wrexham	1933	Chester	1971	Cardiff City	2003	Barry Town
1898	Druids	1934	Bristol City	1972	Wrexham	2004	Rhyl
1899	Druids	1935	Tranmere Rovers	1973	Cardiff City	2005	TNS
1900	Aberystwyth	1936	Crewe Alexandra	1974	Cardiff City	2006	Rhyl
1901	Oswestry United	1937	Crewe Alexandra	1975	Wrexham	2007	Carmarthen Town
1902	Wellington Town	1938	Shrewsbury Town	1976	Cardiff City	2008	Bangor C
1903	Wrexham	1939	South Liverpool	1977	Shrewsbury Town	2009	Bangor C
1904	Druids	1940	Wellington Town	1978	Wrexham	2010	Bangor C
1905	Wrexham	1947	Chester	1979	Shrewsbury Town	2011	Llanelli
1906	Wellington Town	1948	Lovell's Athletic	1980	Newport County	2012	The New Saints
1907	Oswestry United	1949	Merthyr Tydfil	1981	Swansea City		
1908	Chester	1950	Swansea Town	1982	Swansea City		
1909	Wrexham	1951	Merthyr Tydfil	1983	Swansea City		

THE LOOSEMORES OF CARDIFF CHALLENGE CUP 2011–12

FIRST ROUND FIRST LEG

Afan Lido v Aberystwyth T	2-0
Airbus UK v Bala T	4-1
Carmarthen T v Port Talbot T	1-0
Prestatyn T v Newtown	1-1

FIRST ROUND SECOND LEG

Aberystwyth T v Afan Lido	1-0
Bala T v Airbus UK	2-1
Port Talbot T v Carmarthen T	3-1
Newtown v Prestatyn T	2-1

SECOND ROUND FIRST LEG

The New Saints v Airbus UK	2-1
Llanelli v Neath	0-0
Port Talbot T v Afan Lido	0-2
Bangor v Newtown	1-1

SECOND ROUND SECOND LEG

Airbus UK v The New Saints	0-1
Neath v Llanelli	4-2
Newtown v Bangor	5-1
Afan Lido v Port Talbot T	0-0

SEMI-FINAL FIRST LEG

Neath v Afan Lido	0-1
The New Saints v Newtown	3-2

SEMI-FINAL SECOND LEG

Afan Lido v Neath	2-1
Newtown v The New Saints	1-0

FINAL (at Aberystwyth)

28 April 2012

Afan Lido (1) 1 *(Jones M 42)*

Newtown (0) 1 *(Rushton 90)* 301

aet; Afan Lido won 3-2 on penalties.
Afan Lido: Morris; Sheehan, James, Hanford, Evans, Payne, Thomas D (Thomas L 65), Finselbach (D'Auria 110), Jones M (Rickett 79), Hill, Jeanne.
Newtown: Thomas; Partridge (Wright 82), Penk, Cook, Jones A, Sutton, Millington, Mills-Evans, Rushton, Boundford (Blenkinsop 25), Price.
Referee: K. Morgan.

NORTHERN IRISH FOOTBALL 2011–12

Internationally a far from memorable season but domestically yet another glory, glory one for Linfield, their sixth Irish League and Cup double in seven years – a remarkable ratio.

Crusaders, known as "the Working Man's club", made an immense impact winning the Setanta All Ireland Sports Cup, defeating Derry City in a dramatic penalty shoot-out, but form temporarily slumped when outclassed 4-1 by Linfield in the JJB Sports Irish Cup Final.

For manager Stephen Baxter – nicknamed Stanley after the Scottish comedian – it had been a phenomenal year operating on a limited budget. Players gave him the utmost support and commitment while management revealed a progressive outlook in refurbishing Seaview with further improvements ongoing. It is a policy which paid off.

Linfield's David Jeffrey, "The Special One", picked up the Manager of the Year award and other accolades by numerous supporters clubs. He is now about to overtake the 30 trophy record of his mentor Roy Coyle, currently Football Director at arch rivals Glentoran.

Irish football needs a charismatic character such as "Big Davy" who has the ability to motivate players, make them walk tall and provide the media with forthright and controversial comment.

It has been a nightmare scenario, however, for the Glens and their former manager Scott Young. They failed to win a major trophy which, by their normal standards, can only be described as catastrophic.

Eddie Patterson, ex-Cliftonville, who has succeeded Young, faces a formidable challenge to restore pride and prestige at a club experiencing serious cash difficulties. The Glens, pride of East Belfast, whose presence is vital to a competitive Irish Premiership, are determined to get back on track and according to officials, have ambitious plans to sell the Oval and relocate at a new stadium within the next few years.

Agreement was reached with Linfield, owners of Windsor Park, the international football stadium, to stage Northern Ireland matches and other events there. It replaced the old one which had been operational since the fifties and had a couple of decades still to run. Linfield, negotiated a 51-year lease with the Irish FA for the administration of the stadium which will be run by a separate company and whose responsibility also includes upkeep and maintenance of the facilities.

The entire project will cost £29.5m funded primarily by the government and should be completed by 2016. Linfield have been guaranteed £200,000 per annum; they will play all their matches at Windsor Park, a name that is sacrosanct and must be included in any commercial naming agreement. The Blues will have their own administrative and social accommodation and the Irish FA staff will also be located there. Midgley Park, the reserve pitch area and city council's leisure centre are not included in the new arrangements but, perhaps sooner rather than later, they will be incorporated, making Windsor Park one of the top drawer sporting facilities in Ireland. Irish FA President Jim Shaw predicts: "When completed, Windsor will be a model for others to follow."

Huge progress has been made in developing youth, junior and women's football. The grass roots and community relations departments are surging ahead, but alas, controversy still exists over the Republic "poaching" young players who have been developed through the Northern Ireland coaching system up to Under-21 level and then opt for the Republic.

There does not appear to be an easy solution to the problem. Players are free to make their own choice and it is not illegal under FIFA rules. Once a player appears for a country in a competitive fixture, there can be no going back. The die is cast.

Another World Cup qualifying series is just around the corner. Northern Ireland are in the same group as Russia, Portugal, Israel, Azerbaijan and Luxembourg. Qualifying for the finals in Brazil 2014 seems remote; a mission impossible. But manager Michael O'Neill assures everyone the approach will be positive.

Ballinamallard United, a junior side from County Fermanagh who won promotion to the Irish Premiership, promise entertaining football measuring up to all opposition. They have been the real success story of Irish football 2012.

DR MALCOLM BRODIE MBE

CARLING PREMIERSHIP 2011–12

SECTION A	P	W	D	L	F	A	GD	Pts
Linfield	38	27	4	7	79	29	50	85
Portadown	38	22	5	11	72	47	25	71
Cliftonville	38	21	6	11	83	62	21	69
Coleraine	38	18	12	8	61	38	23	66
Crusaders	38	18	10	10	63	47	16	64
Glentoran	38	16	9	13	67	52	15	57

SECTION B	P	W	D	L	F	A	GD	Pts
Ballymena U	38	14	8	16	66	71	–5	50
Donegal Celtic	38	12	5	21	44	80	–36	41
Dungannon Swifts	38	8	11	19	42	71	–29	35
Glenavon	38	8	10	20	60	71	–11	34
Lisburn Distillery	38	8	8	22	56	84	–28	32
Carrick Rangers	38	7	10	21	50	91	–41	31

IFA RESERVE LEAGUE 2011–12

	P	W	D	L	F	A	GD	Pts
Cliftonville Olympic	33	23	6	4	99	35	64	75
Glentoran II	33	23	3	7	86	38	48	72
Crusaders Res	33	19	7	7	84	45	39	64
Glenavon Res	33	19	4	10	85	53	32	61
Linfield Swifts	33	20	0	13	91	47	44	60
Donegal Celtic Res	33	13	5	15	59	71	–12	44
Lisburn Distillery II	33	13	2	18	62	73	–11	41
Carrick Rangers Res	33	11	4	18	72	82	–10	37
Coleraine Res	33	10	5	18	68	92	–24	35
Portadown Res	33	9	6	18	31	86	–55	33
Ballymena U Res	33	9	3	21	46	85	–39	30
Dungannon Swifts Res	33	5	3	25	35	111	–76	18

PLAY-OFFS

FIRST LEG

Lisburn Distillery 0, Newry City 0

SECOND LEG

Newry City 2, Lisburn Distillery 3

Carrick Rangers relegated.

BELFAST TELEGRAPH CHAMPIONSHIP

DIVISION ONE	P	W	D	L	F	A	GD	Pts
Ballinamallard U	26	20	3	3	62	24	38	63
Newry C	26	15	6	5	51	22	29	51
Institute	26	13	4	9	37	34	3	43
Bangor	26	12	6	8	45	34	11	42
Ards	26	11	6	9	39	31	8	39
Limavady U	26	12	2	12	48	43	5	38
Loughgall	26	11	5	10	45	41	4	38
Dergview	26	8	10	8	38	37	1	34
H&W Welders	26	10	4	12	30	35	–5	34
Larne	26	9	5	12	37	47	–10	32
Tobermore U	26	8	7	11	34	44	–10	31
Warrenpoint T	26	7	7	12	34	37	–3	28
Banbridge T	26	5	4	17	30	70	–40	19
Glebe Rangers	26	3	7	16	25	56	–31	16

**Newry City deducted three points (re-awarded to Institute) for fielding an ineligible player on 12 August 2011.*

DIVISION TWO	P	W	D	L	F	A	GD	Pts
Coagh U	30	19	6	5	81	41	40	63
Dundela	30	20	2	8	79	46	33	62
Knockbreda	30	19	4	7	70	31	39	61
Lurgan Celtic	30	17	6	7	73	40	33	57
Queen's University	30	18	1	11	63	38	25	55
Ballyclare Comrades	30	16	4	10	60	46	14	52
Annagh U	30	15	6	9	59	51	8	51
Wakehurst	30	14	5	11	59	48	11	47
Ballymoney U	30	12	3	15	51	45	6	39
Portstewart	30	11	4	15	43	56	–13	37
Armagh C	30	9	6	15	39	52	–13	33
Sport & Leisure Swifts	30	9	5	16	46	59	–13	32
PSNI	30	8	5	17	36	67	–31	29
Moyola Park	30	9	2	19	34	71	–37	29
Killymoon Rangers	30	7	3	20	34	72	–38	24
Chimney Corner	30	5	2	23	26	90	–64	17

**Armagh City deducted nine points (re-awarded between Coagh United, Lurgan Celtic and Portstewart) for fielding an ineligible player in three fixtures.*

IRISH LEAGUE CHAMPIONSHIP WINNERS

1891	Linfield	1913	Glentoran	1940	Belfast Celtic	1970	Glentoran	1993	Linfield
1892	Linfield	1914	Linfield	1948	Belfast Celtic	1971	Linfield	1994	Linfield
1893	Linfield	1915	Belfast Celtic	1949	Linfield	1972	Glentoran	1995	Crusaders
1894	Glentoran	1920	Belfast Celtic	1950	Linfield	1973	Crusaders	1996	Portadown
1895	Linfield	1921	Glentoran	1951	Glentoran	1974	Coleraine	1997	Crusaders
1896	Distillery	1922	Linfield	1952	Glenavon	1975	Linfield	1998	Cliftonville
1897	Glentoran	1923	Linfield	1953	Glentoran	1976	Crusaders	1999	Glentoran
1898	Linfield	1924	Queen's Island	1954	Linfield	1977	Glentoran	2000	Linfield
1899	Distillery	1925	Glentoran	1955	Linfield	1978	Linfield	2001	Linfield
1900	Belfast Celtic	1926	Belfast Celtic	1956	Linfield	1979	Linfield	2002	Portadown
1901	Distillery	1927	Belfast Celtic	1957	Glentoran	1980	Linfield	2003	Glentoran
1902	Linfield	1928	Belfast Celtic	1958	Ards	1981	Glentoran	2004	Linfield
1903	Distillery	1929	Belfast Celtic	1959	Linfield	1982	Linfield	2005	Glentoran
1904	Linfield	1930	Linfield	1960	Glenavon	1983	Linfield	2006	Linfield
1905	Glentoran	1931	Glentoran	1961	Linfield	1984	Linfield	2007	Linfield
1906	Cliftonville	1932	Linfield	1962	Linfield	1985	Linfield	2008	Linfield
	Distillery	1933	Belfast Celtic	1963	Distillery	1986	Linfield	2009	Glentoran
1907	Linfield	1934	Linfield	1964	Glentoran	1987	Linfield	2010	Linfield
1908	Linfield	1935	Linfield	1965	Derry City	1988	Glentoran	2011	Linfield
1909	Linfield	1936	Belfast Celtic	1966	Linfield	1989	Linfield	2012	Linfield
1910	Cliftonville	1937	Belfast Celtic	1967	Glentoran	1990	Portadown		
1911	Linfield	1938	Belfast Celtic	1968	Glentoran	1991	Portadown		
1912	Glentoran	1939	Belfast Celtic	1969	Linfield	1992	Glentoran		

BELFAST TELEGRAPH CHAMPIONSHIP (Previously First Division)

1996	Coleraine	2002	Lisburn Distillery	2008	Loughgall
1997	Ballymena United	2003	Dungannon Swifts	2009	Portadown
1998	Newry Town	2004	Loughgall	2010	Loughgall
1999	Distillery	2005	Armagh City	2011	Carrick Rangers
2000	Omagh Town	2006	Crusaders	2012	Ballinamallard U
2001	Ards	2007	Institute		

IFA YOUTH LEAGUE 2011–12

SECTION A	*P*	*W*	*D*	*L*	*F*	*A*	*GD*	*Pts*
Crusaders Colts	22	15	1	6	52	20	32	46
Ballinamallard U III	22	13	4	5	53	30	23	43
Cliftonville Strollers	22	12	4	6	55	25	30	40
Linfield Rangers	22	12	2	8	42	36	6	38
Newington YC	22	10	6	6	56	58	–2	36
Glenavon III	22	10	5	7	51	43	8	35
Glentoran Colts	22	10	1	11	58	37	21	31
Carrick Rangers Colts	22	9	3	10	45	62	–17	30
Donegal Celtic Youth	22	5	6	11	44	56	–12	21
Lisburn Distillery III	22	6	3	13	40	54	–14	21
Dungannon Swifts Youth	22	5	4	13	42	71	–29	19
Institute Colts	22	2	7	13	30	76	–46	13

SECTION B	*P*	*W*	*D*	*L*	*F*	*A*	*GD*	*Pts*
Coleraine Colts	20	17	2	1	74	16	58	53
Ballymena U III	20	15	2	3	79	27	52	47
Newry City Wanderers	20	13	5	2	58	16	42	44
Limavady U Youth	20	9	6	5	49	39	10	33
Crewe U Youth	20	8	3	9	70	59	11	27
Portadown III	20	8	3	9	47	49	–2	27
Ballymoney U Colts	20	6	3	11	43	51	–8	21
Annagh U Youth	20	5	3	12	35	77	–42	18
Ballyclare Comrades Colts	20	5	2	13	30	49	–19	17
Tandragee R Youth	20	3	5	12	34	69	–35	14
Larne FC	20	3	2	15	21	88	–67	11

IFA RESERVE LEAGUE 2011–12

	P	*W*	*D*	*L*	*F*	*A*	*Pts*
Cliftonville Olympic	33	23	6	4	99	35	75
Glentoran II	33	23	3	7	86	38	72
Crusaders Reserves	33	19	7	7	84	45	64
Glenavon Reserves	33	19	4	10	85	53	61
Linfield Swifts	33	20	0	13	91	47	60
Donegal Celtic Reserves	33	13	5	15	59	71	44
Lisburn Distillery II	33	13	2	18	62	73	41
Carrick Rangers Reserves	33	11	4	18	72	82	37
Coleraine Reserves	33	10	5	18	68	92	35
Portadown Reserves	33	9	6	18	31	86	33
Ballymena U Reserves	33	9	3	21	46	85	30
Dungannon Swifts Reserves	33	5	3	25	35	111	18

SETANTA SPORTS CUP 2011–12

FIRST ROUND FIRST LEG
Bray Wanderers v Glentoran 2-4
Lisburn Distillery v Derry City 0-4
Bohemians v Portadown 2-1
Cliftonville v St Patrick's Ath 1-0

FIRST ROUND SECOND LEG
Glentoran v Bray Wanderers 3-0
Derry City v Lisburn Distillery 3-0
Portadown v Bohemians 0-1
St Patrick's Ath v Cliftonville 0-1

QUARTER-FINALS FIRST LEG
Linfield v Derry City 1-1
Sligo Rovers v Glentoran 2-0
Crusaders v Bohemians 0-0
Shamrock Rovers v Cliftonville 2-0

QUARTER-FINALS SECOND LEG
Derry City v Linfield 3-1
Glentoran v Sligo Rovers 1-1
Bohemians v Crusaders 0-2
Cliftonville v Shamrock Rovers 2-0
Shamrock Rovers won 3-1 on penalties.

SEMI-FINALS FIRST LEG
Crusaders v Sligo Rovers 2-0
Shamrock Rovers v Derry City 0-3

SEMI-FINALS SECOND LEG
Sligo Rovers v Crusaders 2-1
Derry City v Shamrock Rovers 0-2

FINAL

12 May 2012, 3275
(at The Oval, Belfast).

Crusaders (0) 2 *(Coates 85, 90)*

Derry C (0) 2 *(Patterson 80, 102 (pen))*

Crusaders: O'Neill; Leeman, Coates, Magowan, McBride■, Watson, Caddell (Gargan 112), Morrow, Dallas, Adamson (McKeown 91), Rainey (Snoddy 98).
Derry C: Doherty; McCaffrey, Madden, McEleney S, McBride (McCallion 106), Higgins, Molloy, McDaid, Patterson, McEleney P, McLaughlin (Morrison 63).
aet: Crusaders won 5-4 on penalties.
Referee: R. Crangle.
■ *Denotes player sent off.*

SETANTA SPORTS CUP WINNERS

2004–05 Linfield
2005–06 Drogheda United
2006–07 Drogheda United
2007–08 Cork City
2009–10 Bohemians
2010–11 Shamrock Rovers
2011–12 Crusaders

JJB SPORTS IRISH CUP 2011–12

SIXTH ROUND

Ballymena United v Derriaghy CC	3-1
Ballymoney United v Newry City	1-6
Coleraine v Ballinamallard United	3-0
Coagh United v Newbuildings	1-1, 4-1
Dungannon Swifts v Newington YC	3-0
Glenavon v Crusaders	0-4
Linfield v Carrick Rangers	5-1
Donegal Celtic v Cliftonville	1-0

QUARTER-FINALS

Coleraine v Crusaders	0-2
Donegal Celtic v Dungannon Swifts	1-1, 0-1
Linfield v Coagh United	4-0
Newry City v Ballymena United	1-2

Ballymena United ejected for fielding ineligible player.

SEMI-FINALS

Dungannon Swifts v Crusaders *(at Mourneview Park, Lurgan)*	0-1
Newry City v Linfield *(at The Oval)*	0-7

FINAL

(at Windsor Park, 5 May 2012)

Linfield 4 *(McAllister 28, 41, Carvill 63, Mulgrew 83)*

Crusaders 1 *(Coates 66)*

Linfield: Blayney; Murphy, Curran, Lowry, Thompson, Carvill, Garrett (Casement 70), Ervin, Mulgrew (Burns BJ 80), Albert Watson, McAllister (Fordyce 90).

Crusaders: O'Neill; McKeown (Leeman 40), McBride, Aidan Watson, Magowan, Morrow, Adamson, Rainey, Caddell, Dallas, McMaster (Owens 46).

Referee: R. Crangle.

N.B. Linfield played in white instead of traditional blue.

IRISH CUP FINALS (from 1946–47)

1946–47 Belfast Celtic 1, Glentoran 0
1947–48 Linfield 3, Coleraine 0
1948–49 Derry City 3, Glentoran 1
1949–50 Linfield 2, Distillery 1
1950–51 Glentoran 3, Ballymena U 1
1951–52 Ards 1, Glentoran 0
1952–53 Linfield 5, Coleraine 0
1953–54 Derry City 1, Glentoran 0
1954–55 Dundela 3, Glenavon 0
1955–56 Distillery 1, Glentoran 0
1956–57 Glenavon 2, Derry City 0
1957–58 Ballymena U 2, Linfield 0
1958–59 Glenavon 2, Ballymena U 0
1959–60 Linfield 5, Ards 1
1960–61 Glenavon 5, Linfield 1
1961–62 Linfield 4, Portadown 0
1962–63 Linfield 2, Distillery 1
1963–64 Derry City 2, Glentoran 0
1964–65 Coleraine 2, Glenavon 1
1965–66 Glentoran 2, Linfield 0
1966–67 Crusaders 3, Glentoran 1
1967–68 Crusaders 2, Linfield 0
1968–69 Ards 4, Distillery 2
1969–70 Linfield 2, Ballymena U 1
1970–71 Distillery 3, Derry City
1971–72 Coleraine 2, Portadown 1
1972–73 Glentoran 3, Linfield 2
1973–74 Ards 2, Ballymena U 1
1974–75 Coleraine 1:0:1, Linfield 1:0:0
1975–76 Carrick Rangers 2, Linfield 1
1976–77 Coleraine 4, Linfield 1
1977–78 Linfield 3, Ballymena U 1
1978–79 Cliftonville 3, Portadown 2
1979–80 Linfield 2, Crusaders 0
1980–81 Ballymena U 1, Glenavon 0
1981–82 Linfield 2, Coleraine 1
1982–83 Glentoran 1:2, Linfield 1:1
1983–84 Ballymena U 4, Carrick Rangers 1
1984–85 Glentoran 1:1, Linfield 1:0
1985–86 Glentoran 2, Coleraine 1
1986–87 Glentoran 1, Larne 0
1987–88 Glentoran 1, Glenavon 0
1988–89 Ballymena U 1, Larne 0
1989–90 Glentoran 3, Portadown 0
1990–91 Portadown 2, Glenavon 1
1991–92 Glenavon 2, Linfield 1
1992–93 Bangor 1:1:1, Ards 1:1:0
1993–94 Linfield 2, Bangor 0
1994–95 Linfield 3, Carrick Rangers 1
1995–96 Glentoran 1, Glenavon 0
1996–97 Glenavon 1, Cliftonville 0
1997–98 Glentoran 1, Glenavon 0
1998–99 *Portadown awarded trophy after Cliftonville were eliminated for using an ineligible player in semi-final.*
1999–2000 Glentoran 1, Portadown 0
2000–01 Glentoran 1, Linfield 0
2001–02 Linfield 2, Portadown 1
2002–03 Coleraine 1, Glentoran 0
2003–04 Glentoran 1, Coleraine 0
2004–05 Portadown 5, Larne 1
2005–06 Linfield 2, Glentoran 1
2006–07 Linfield 2, Dungannon Swifts 2 *(aet; Linfield won 3-2 on penalties).*
2007–08 Linfield 2, Coleraine 1
2008–09 Crusaders 1, Cliftonville 0
2009–10 Linfield 2, Portadown 1
2010–11 Linfield 2, Crusaders 1
2011–12 Linfield 4, Crusaders 1

ULSTER CUP WINNERS

1949 Linfield
1950 Larne
1951 Glentoran
1952 *No competition*
1953 Glentoran
1954 Crusaders
1955 Glenavon
1956 Linfield
1957 Linfield
1958 Distillery
1959 Glenavon
1960 Linfield
1961 Ballymena U
1962 Linfield
1963 Crusaders
1964 Linfield
1965 Coleraine
1966 Glentoran
1967 Linfield
1968 Coleraine
1969 Coleraine
1970 Linfield
1971 Linfield
1972 Coleraine
1973 Ards
1974 Linfield
1975 Coleraine
1976 Glentoran
1977 Linfield
1978 Linfield
1979 Linfield
1980 Ballymena U
1981 Glentoran
1982 Glentoran
1983 Glentoran
1984 Linfield
1985 Coleraine
1986 Coleraine
1987 Larne
1988 Glentoran
1989 Glentoran
1990 Portadown
1991 Bangor
1992 Linfield
1993 Crusaders
1994 Bangor
1995 Portadown
1996 Portadown
1997 Coleraine
1998 Ballyclare Comrades
1999 Distillery
2000 *No competition*
2001 *No competition*
2002 *No competition*
2003 Dungannon Swifts *(Confined to First Division clubs)*
2004–2012 *No competition*

ROLL OF HONOUR SEASON 2011–12

Competition	*Winner*	*Runner-up*
Carling Irish Premiership	Linfield	Portadown
JJB Sports Irish Cup	Linfield	Crusaders
Irish Championship Division One	Ballinamallard United	Newry City
Irish Championship Division Two	Coagh United	Dundela
Irn Bru League Cup	Crusaders	Coleraine
County Antrim Shield	Cliftonville	Glentoran
Steel & Sons Cup	Bangor	Larne
Co Antrim Junior Shield	Basement YM	Valley Rangers
Setanta Sports Cup	Crusaders	Derry City
Coca-Cola Irish Junior Cup	Strathroy Harps	St Marys
Mid Ulster Cup (Senior)	Newry City	Glenavon
Harry Cavan Youth Cup	Ballinamallard United	Glenavon III
George Wilson Mem Cup	Glentoran II	Cliftonville Olympic
North West Senior Cup	Institute	Coleraine
The Fermanagh Mulhern Cup	Enniskillen Town United	Tummery Athletic
Britton Rose Bowl	Northern Amateur FL	Scottish Amateur FA
Coca-Cola Intermediate Cup	Newry City	Dergview
Best Programme Award	Glentoran*	Cliftonville
Groundsman of the Year	Mervyn Nixon (Ballinamallard United)	

**13th successive season.*

AWARDS

ULSTER FOOTBALLER OF THE YEAR
(Castlereagh Glentoran Supporters Club).
Chris Morrow *(Crusaders).*

NORTHERN IRELAND PLAYER OF THE YEAR
(Northern Ireland Football Writers' Association)
Gary McCutcheon *(Ballymena United).*

FIRST DIVISION PLAYER OF THE YEAR
Chris Curran *(Ballinamallard United).*

MANAGER OF THE YEAR
David Jeffrey *(Linfield).*

OUTSTANDING NON SENIOR TEAM
Ballinamallard United

INTERNATIONAL PERSONALITY
Johnny Evans *(Manchester United).*

CARLING LEADING SCORER (PREMIER DIVISION)
Gary McCutcheon*(Ballymena United)* 34

CARLING TEAM OF THE YEAR (NIFWA)
O'Neill *(Crusaders)*
Ervin *(Linfield)*
Beverland *(Coleraine)*
Watson *(Linfield)*
Pennan *(Portadown)*
Lowry *(Linfield)*
Gault *(Linfield)*
Johnston *(Cliftonville)*
Morrow *(Crusaders)*
Tipton *(Portadown)*
McCutcheon *(Ballymena United)*

TOP GOALSCORERS 2011–12

All competitions

Gary McCutcheon (Ballymena U)	34
Matthew Tipton (Portadown)	27
Curtis Allen (Coleraine)	24
Gary Liggett (Lisburn Distillery)	23
David Rainey (Crusaders)	20
Kevin Braniff (Portadown)	19
Peter Thompson (Linfield)	19
Chris Scannell (Cliftonville)	18
Rory Donnelly (Cliftonville)	17
Philip Lowry (Linfield)	16
Mark McAllister (Linfield)	16
Gary Hamilton (Glenavon) *(11 for Glentoran).*	15
Joe Gormley (Cliftonville)	14
Diarmuid O'Carroll (Cliftonville) *(10 for Glenavon).*	14
Jordan Owens (Crusaders)	14
Darren Boyce (Glentoran)	13
Colin Coates (Crusaders)	13
Bryan McCaul (Glenavon)	13
Darren Murray (Donegal Celtic)	13
Leon Knight (Glentoran) *(9 for Coleraine).*	12
Richard Gibson (Glentoran)	11
Paul Heatley (Carrick Rangers)	11
Ryan Henderson (Donegal Celtic)	11
Colin Nixon (Glentoran)	11
Timmy Adamson (Crusaders)	10
Stuart Dallas (Crusaders)	10
Chris Morrow (Crusaders)	10

CARLING PLAYER OF THE MONTH

Month	*Player*	*Team*
August	Jamie Mulgrew	Linfield
September	Matthew Tipton	Portadown
October	Gary Hamilton	Glentoran/Glenavon
November	Barry Johnston	Cliftonville
December	William Murphy	Linfield
January	Chris Morrow	Crusaders
February	Niall Morgan	Dungannon Swifts
March	Peter Thompson	Linfield
April	James Costello	Ballymena United

CARLING MANAGER OF THE MONTH

Month	*Manager*	*Team*
August	Ronnie McFall	Portadown
September	Ronnie McFall	Portadown
October	Scott Young	Glentoran
November	Tommy Breslin	Cliftonville
December	Oran Kearney	Coleraine
January	Stephen Baxter	Crusaders
February	David Jeffrey	Linfield
March	Stephen Baxter	Crusaders
April	Glenn Ferguson	Ballymena United

CHAMPIONSHIP PLAYER OF THE MONTH

Month	*Player*	*Team*
August	Nathan McConnell	Ards
September	Ricky Copeland	Newry City
October	Andy Crawford	Ballinamallard United
November	Ben Browne	Bangor
December	Keith Johnston	Warrenpoint Town
January	Gary Workman	Larne
February	Marty Havern	Newry City
March	David Kee	Ballinamallard United
April	Darragh Hanaphy	Newry City

EUROPEAN FOOTBALL REVIEW 2011–12

Given that as soon as Villas-Boas had had his chips at Stamford Bridge, the media decided to write off the ageing Chelsea squad as a threat either at home or abroad, the fact that the Blues went on to win the Champions League against pretty formidable odds, it was the minimal digital salute to the wiseacres. In fairness there were no disparaging remarks aimed at Roberto Di Matteo, handed the hot potato.

Yet the knock-out round seemed to have put an end to it. Trailing by two goals away to Napoli, Chelsea turned it round and had an impressive 4-1 win at home. It got better, generally here and there against Benfica, then the epic semi-final clashes with Barcelona, said to be the finest team on this and any planet, indeed of all time. A precious leveller at The Bridge, an amazing rearguard action and subsequent draw with ten men at the heart of Catalonia stunned the critics.

Even the final was gained the hard way. On Bayern Munich's own pitch and needing a shoot-out to take the trophy, there were heroes all round with Petr Cech at one end, Didier Drogba at the other at the forefront. It was just as well for Chelsea abroad; the rest of the English entry fared less spectacularly.

Arsenal put up a tremendous fightback against AC Milan. Having conceded four goals in Italy they pulled three back at the Emirates and came close to forcing extra time at the elimination point. But neither of the Mancunian clubs excelled in top company. Both failed to finish higher than third at the group stage and were banished to the Europa League only for Manchester City and Manchester United respectively to lose out to Sporting Lisbon and Athletic Bilbao in the third round.

There was increased representation for the Europa with the addition of Birmingham City, winners of the Carling Cup but relegated to the Football League Championship, Fulham, Stoke City and Tottenham Hotspur all involved.

Fulham, no strangers to the competition, as beaten finalists in 2010, were in from the first qualifying round and were not disgraced in losing at the group stage in what was their fourteenth match. Neither did Birmingham, remembered from flying the flag for the city in the old Fairs Cup, neglect to put in a good shift in Group H.

Stoke City, beginning at the third qualifying round, surprised everyone except themselves by negotiating Group E successfully before losing out to Valencia in the second round. However, Tottenham Hotspur disappointed in their group section.

Scotland's effort fell away even earlier in the Champions League. Rangers, before the club disintegrated as an entity, were even defeated at Ibrox by Malmo, then Maribor in the Europa before exit. In the Europa League Celtic were granted a reprieve after losing to Sion, when the Swiss team was thrown out for fielding ineligible players. But again only third place was reached in the group stage.

Hearts, starting in the third qualifying round, showed better staying power before conceding five goals to Spurs in the play-off round. Dundee United in the second qualifying round were unfortunate to lose on the away goals rule to Slask Wroclaw.

For Wales, Bangor City conceded ten goals away to HJK Helsinki in the Champions League, Northern Ireland's champions Linfield held BATE Borisov in one leg of their tie but Shamrock Rovers famously battled on for the Republic into the Europa and Group A.

Overall in the Europa, Cliftonville held The New Saints in one leg, the Welsh team in turn going out to Midtjylland. Glentoran beat Renova in a penalty shoot-out before bowing to Vorskla. Neath went out quietly but Llanelli surprised Dinamo Tbilisi at home. St Patrick's Athletic and Sligo Rovers each negotiated two rounds.

What about Europe's teams? Champions League favourites Barcelona (as we know) and Real Madrid slipped up in the semi-finals, but at least Spain was represented in the Europa final where Atletico beat Athletic in the double AA affair.

Stoke City's Kenwyne Jones and Dynamo Kiev's Ognjen Vukojevic dispute possession during their UEFA Europa League Group E match at the Britannia Stadium in December. The game ended 1-1. (PA)

EUROPEAN CUP FINALS

EUROPEAN CUP FINALS 1956–1992

Year	Winners		Runners-up		Venue	Attendance	Referee
1956	Real Madrid	4	Reims	3	Paris	38,000	Ellis (E)
1957	Real Madrid	2	Fiorentina	0	Madrid	124,000	Horn (Ho)
1958	Real Madrid	3	AC Milan	2 *(aet)*	Brussels	67,000	Alsteen (Bel)
1959	Real Madrid	2	Reims	0	Stuttgart	80,000	Dutsch (WG)
1960	Real Madrid	7	Eintracht Frankfurt	3	Glasgow	135,000	Mowat (S)
1961	Benfica	3	Barcelona	2	Berne	28,000	Dienst (Sw)
1962	Benfica	5	Real Madrid	3	Amsterdam	65,000	Horn (Ho)
1963	AC Milan	2	Benfica	1	Wembley	45,000	Holland (E)
1964	Internazionale	3	Real Madrid	1	Vienna	74,000	Stoll (A)
1965	Internazionale	1	Benfica	0	Milan	80,000	Dienst (Sw)
1966	Real Madrid	2	Partizan Belgrade	1	Brussels	55,000	Kreitlein (WG)
1967	Celtic	2	Internazionale	1	Lisbon	56,000	Tschenscher (WG)
1968	Manchester U	4	Benfica	1 *(aet)*	Wembley	100,000	Lo Bello (I)
1969	AC Milan	4	Ajax	1	Madrid	50,000	Ortiz (Sp)
1970	Feyenoord	2	Celtic	1 *(aet)*	Milan	50,000	Lo Bello (I)
1971	Ajax	2	Panathinaikos	0	Wembley	90,000	Taylor (E)
1972	Ajax	2	Internazionale	0	Rotterdam	67,000	Helies (F)
1973	Ajax	1	Juventus	0	Belgrade	93,500	Guglovic (Y)
1974	Bayern Munich	1	Atletico Madrid	1	Brussels	49,000	Loraux (Bel)
Replay	Bayern Munich	4	Atletico Madrid	0	Brussels	23,000	Delcourt (Bel)
1975	Bayern Munich	2	Leeds U	0	Paris	50,000	Kitabdjian (F)
1976	Bayern Munich	1	St Etienne	0	Glasgow	54,864	Palotai (H)
1977	Liverpool	3	Moenchengladbach	1	Rome	57,000	Wurtz (F)
1978	Liverpool	1	FC Brugge	0	Wembley	92,000	Corver (Ho)
1979	Nottingham F	1	Malmo	0	Munich	57,500	Linemayr (A)
1980	Nottingham F	1	Hamburg	0	Madrid	50,000	Garrido (P)
1981	Liverpool	1	Real Madrid	0	Paris	48,360	Palotai (H)
1982	Aston Villa	1	Bayern Munich	0	Rotterdam	46,000	Konrath (F)
1983	Hamburg	1	Juventus	0	Athens	80,000	Rainea (R)
1984	Liverpool	1	Roma	1	Rome	69,693	Fredriksson (Se)
	(aet; Liverpool won 4-2 on penalties)						
1985	Juventus	1	Liverpool	0	Brussels	58,000	Daina (Sw)
1986	Steaua Bucharest	0	Barcelona	0	Seville	70,000	Vautrot (F)
	(aet; Steaua won 2-0 on penalties)						
1987	Porto	2	Bayern Munich	1	Vienna	59,000	Ponnet (Bel)
1988	PSV Eindhoven	0	Benfica	0	Stuttgart	70,000	Agnolin (I)
	(aet; PSV won 6-5 on penalties)						
1989	AC Milan	4	Steaua Bucharest	0	Barcelona	97,000	Tritschler (WG)
1990	AC Milan	1	Benfica	0	Vienna	57,500	Kohl (A)
1991	Red Star Belgrade	0	Marseille	0	Bari	56,000	Lanese (I)
	(aet; Red Star won 5-3 on penalties)						
1992	Barcelona	1	Sampdoria	0 *(aet)*	Wembley	70,827	Schmidhuber (G)

UEFA CHAMPIONS LEAGUE FINALS 1993–2012

Year	Winners		Runners-up		Venue	Attendance	Referee
1993	Marseille*	1	AC Milan	0	Munich	64,400	Rothlisberger (Sw)
1994	AC Milan	4	Barcelona	0	Athens	70,000	Don (E)
1995	Ajax	1	AC Milan	0	Vienna	49,730	Craciunescu (R)
1996	Juventus	1	Ajax	1	Rome	67,000	Vega (Sp)
	(aet; Juventus won 4-2 on penalties)						
1997	Borussia Dortmund	3	Juventus	1	Munich	59,000	Puhl (H)
1998	Real Madrid	1	Juventus	0	Amsterdam	47,500	Krug (G)
1999	Manchester U	2	Bayern Munich	1	Barcelona	90,000	Collina (I)
2000	Real Madrid	3	Valencia	0	Paris	78,759	Braschi (I)
2001	Bayern Munich	1	Valencia	1	Milan	71,500	Jol (Ho)
	(aet; Bayern Munich won 5-4 on penalties)						
2002	Real Madrid	2	Leverkusen	1	Glasgow	52,000	Meier (Sw)
2003	AC Milan	0	Juventus	0	Manchester	63,215	Merk (G)
	(aet; AC Milan won 3-2 on penalties)						
2004	Porto	3	Monaco	0	Gelsenkirchen	52,000	Nielsen (D)
2005	Liverpool	3	AC Milan	3	Istanbul	65,000	González (Sp)
	(aet; Liverpool won 3-2 on penalties)						
2006	Barcelona	2	Arsenal	1	Paris	79,500	Hauge (N)
2007	AC Milan	2	Liverpool	1	Athens	74,000	Fandel (G)
2008	Manchester U	1	Chelsea	1	Moscow	69,552	Michel (Slo)
	(aet; Manchester U won 6-5 on penalties)						
2009	Barcelona	2	Manchester U	0	Rome	62,467	Busacca (Sw)
2010	Internazionale	2	Bayern Munich	0	Madrid	74,954	Webb (E)
2011	Barcelona	3	Manchester U	1	Wembley	87,695	Kassai (H)
2012	Chelsea	1	Bayern Munich	1	Munich	69,901	Proença (P)
	(aet; Chelsea won 4-3 on penalties)						

**Subsequently stripped of title.*

UEFA CHAMPIONS LEAGUE 2011–12

■ *Denotes player sent off.*

FIRST QUALIFYING ROUND FIRST LEG

Tuesday, 28 June 2011

FC Santa Coloma (0) 0

F91 Dudelange (0) 2 *(Legros 57, Caillet 79)* 300

FC Santa Coloma: Ricart Fernandez; Javi Sanchez, Ribolleda, Genis Garcia, Sonejee, Xinos, Jimenez, Bousenine, Urbani N (Mercade 80), Romero (Urbani M 60), Renato Mota (Pousa 67).
F91 Dudelange: Joubert; Caillet, Wiggers, Rentmeister, Benzouien, Sanchez D'Avolio, Payal (Bensi 82), Legros, Da Mota (Olle Nicolle 70), Joachim (Gruszczynski 52), Melisse.

Tre Fiori (0) 0

Valletta (1) 3 *(Denni 43, Effiong 50, Agius G 70 (pen))* 544

Tre Fiori: Bertozzi; Andreini, Benedettini, Ballanti, Tarini (Grini 46), Vannoni, Canarezza, Lisi, Macina (Zenunay 56), Simoncini, Giunta (Amici 65).
Valletta: Hogg; Caruana (Scicluna 71), Borg, Denni, Falzon, Pace, Agius E, Briffa, Fenech (Agius G 54), Effiong (Zammit 60), William Barbosa.

FIRST QUALIFYING ROUND SECOND LEG

Tuesday, 5 July 2011

F91 Dudelange (0) 2 *(Abdullei 60, 89)*

FC Santa Coloma (0) 0 1015

F91 Dudelange: Joubert; Caillet, Wiggers, Tournut (Payal 73), Rentmeister, Sanchez D'Avolio, Olle Nicolle, Bensi (Da Mota 68), Legros, Melisse, Gruszczynski (Abdullei 55).
FC Santa Coloma: Ricart Fernandez; Nastri (Txema 67), Javi Sanchez, Fite, Ribolleda, Urbani M (Bousenine 18), Xinos, Jimenez, Pousa, Urbani N (Juli Sanchez 57), Romero.

Wednesday, 6 July 2011

Valletta (0) 2 *(Zammit 58 (pen), William Barbosa 88)*

Tre Fiori (1) 1 *(Lisi 21 (pen))* 1616

Valletta: Hogg; Scicluna, Borg, Falzon, Pace, Agius E, Denni (Fenech 39), Agius G, Zammit, Effiong (Sammut 77), Zongo (William Barbosa 59).
Tre Fiori: Cola; Andreini, Vendemini■, Grini, Vannoni, Canarezza (Grana 79), Lisi, Simoncini, Amici (Zenunay 65), Giunta (Stolfi 90), Baizan.

SECOND QUALIFYING ROUND FIRST LEG

Tuesday, 12 July 2011

Maribor (2) 2 *(Arghus 36, Ibraimi 45)*

F91 Dudelange (0) 0 5500

Maribor: Pridigar; Rajcevic, Arghus (Vidovic 90), Ibraimi, Viler, Mezga, Mertelj, Beric, Mejac, Marcos Tavares (Velikonja 81), Filipovic (Cvijanovic 66).
F91 Dudelange: Joubert; Caillet, Wiggers, Tournut, Benzouien, Sanchez D'Avolio, Olle Nicolle (Da Mota 73), Payal, Legros (Gruszczynski 78), Melisse, Abdullei.

Mogren (1) 1 *(Zec M 14)*

Litex (0) 2 *(Todorov 77, 79)* 1500

Mogren: Scekic; Batak (Bogic 46), Lakic, Simovic, Kapisoda, Zec M (Vujovic 62), Ivanovic, Culafic (Zec R 87), Bozovic D, Matic, Gluscevic.
Litex: Vinicius; Berberovic, Nikolov, Bodurov, Zanev, Jelenkovic, Yanev, Tom, Thiago Miracema (Tsvetanov 71), Milanov G (Flores 78), Celio Codo (Todorov 64).

Pyunik (0) 0

Viktoria Plzen (3) 4 *(Bakos 7, 40 (pen), Horvath 28 (pen), Kolar 72)* 3000

Pyunik: Israyelyan; Hovsepyan S, Artak Yedigaryan, Haroyan, Malakyan, Aleksanyan (Manoyan 46), Hovhannisyan K (Gagik Poghosyan 46), Voskanyan, Ghukas Poghosyan (Minasyan 64), Yuspashyan, Hovhannisyan H.
Viktoria Plzen: Pavlik; Cisovsky, Bystron (Sevinsky 70), Rajtoral, Trapp, Petrzela (Fillo 83), Kolar, Horvath, Pilar (Duris 73), Jiracek, Bakos.

Shamrock R (1) 1 *(Turner 34)*

Flora (0) 0 5026

Shamrock R: Mannus; O'Donnell (O'Neill 83), Oman, Sullivan, Sives, Stevens, Turner (McCormack 71), Finn, Dennehy, Kelly (McCabe 76), Twigg.
Flora: Pedok; Palatu, Kams, Jurgenson, Baranov, Minkenen, Mosnikov, Luts, Beglarishvili (Herrem 46), Henri Anier (Hannes Anier 88), Alliku (Mashichev 71).

Slovan Bratislava (1) 2 *(Sebo 41, Guede 81)*

Tobol (0) 0 5128

Slovan Bratislava: Putnocky; Had, Dobrotka, Bagayoko, Guede, Zofcak, Grendel (Milinkovic 63), Stepanovsky (Kolcak 76), Sebo, Kladrubsky, Halenar■.
Tobol: Petukhov; Ovshinov, Bogdan (Yurin 71), Kislitsyn, Kucera, Volkov, Sljivic, Bekric (Bogdanov 57), Kuantayev, Zebelyan, Dzholchiev (Gridin 64).

Valletta (1) 2 *(Mifsud 43, William Barbosa 90 (pen))*

Ekranas (3) 3 *(Umeh 15, Gleveckas 22, Radavicius 41 (pen))* 1608

Valletta: Hogg; Caruana, Azzopardi, Borg, Pace (Effiong 46), Agius E, Briffa, Fenech (Sammut 79), Mifsud, Agius G, William Barbosa.
Ekranas: Zubas; Dedura, Gleveckas, Matovic, Joksas, Radavicius (Skinderis 83), Andelkovic, Kucys, Vertelis, Mauro Alonso (Velicka 80), Umeh (Markevicius 65).

Wednesday, 13 July 2011

Bangor C (0) 0

HJK Helsinki (1) 3 *(Sadik 14, 55, Sorsa 89)* 1189

Bangor C: Idzi; Morley, Roberts, Brewerton, Johnston, Garside, Hoy, Davies, Jones (Wilson 68), Ward (Smyth 67), Bull (Edwards 67).
HJK Helsinki: Wallen; Kansikas, Lindstrom, Sumusalo, Moren, Riihilahti, Bah, Mannstrom (Sorsa 63), Ring, Sadik (Fowler 71), Pukki (Parikka 82).
Played at Rhyl.

Dinamo Zagreb (1) 3 *(Badelj 38, Krstanovic 46, 65 (pen))*

Neftci (0) 0 33,266

Dinamo Zagreb: Kelava; Tonel, Vida, Ibanez, Leko, Sammir, Alispahic (Kovacic 88), Badelj, Vrsaljko, Beciraj (Rukavina 67), Krstanovic (Tomecak 80).
Neftci: Stamenkovic; Mitreski (Huseynov 44), Melikov, Abishov, Denis, Georgievski, Abdullayev (Imamverdiyev 77), Rodriguinho (Nasimov 71), Alessandro, Mpenza, Flavinho.

Linfield (1) 1 *(Fordyce 5)*

BATE Borisov (1) 1 *(Renan 38 (pen))* 1212

Linfield: Blayney; Casement (Burns BJ 82), Ervin, Watson, Armstrong, Garrett, Lowry, Hanley, Fordyce, Carvill (McCaul 90), Thompson (McAllister 77).
BATE Borisov: Gutor; Filipenko, Yurevich, Bordachev, Simic, Likhtarovich (Olekhnovich 76), Nekhajchik, Renan, Volodko. A, Pavlov (Rudik 86), Skavysh (Kontsevoy 70).

Maccabi Haifa (1) 5 *(Amasha 45, 71, 73, Yampolsky 72, Golasa 81)*

Borac (1) 1 *(Raspudic 24)* 9750

Maccabi Haifa: Davidovich; Buljat, Meshumar, Vered (Azulay 66), Gustavo Boccoli (Dvalishvili 39), Golasa, Yahaya, Tawatha, Pilyavskiy, Amasha, Katan (Yampolsky 61).
Borac: Avdukic; Markovic (Petric 69), Stakic, Zaric, Raspudic, Krunic, Kovacevic, Stupar, Grahovac (Sakan 64), Stajic (Vidakovic 81), Mikic.

Malmo (0) 2 *(Rexhepi 58, Holm 77 (og))*

HB (0) 0 12,501

Malmo: Melicharek; Andersson, Halsti, Ricardinho, Jansson, Pekalski (Mutavdzic 89), Durmaz, Wilton Figueiredo, Larsson, Mehmeti (Nazari O 88), Rexhepi (Nilsson 82).
HB: Gestson; Jorgensen, Lag, Rubeksen, Holm, Samuelsen (Jon Poulsen 90), Thorleifsson (Mouritsen K 90), Nielsen, Benjaminsen, Poulsen R, Flotum (Nolsoe 87).

Partizan Belgrade (0) 4 *(Vukic 48, Eduardo 58, Scepovic 74, Emini 76 (og))*

Skendija 79 (0) 0 15,324

Partizan Belgrade: Stojkovic; Rankovic, Volkov, Ivanov, Aksentijevic, Ilic S (Tomic 67), Vukic, Kamara, Babovic, Eduardo (Jovancic 76), Scepovic (Markovic L 87).
Skendija 79: Zendeli; Elmazovski (Neziri 84), Cuculi, Berisha, Nikitovic, Mustafi, Redjepi (Nafiu 67), Useini (Selmani 88), Emini, Hasani, Sali.

Rosenborg (1) 5 *(Skjelbred 43, Dorsin 48, Henriksen 72, Prica 76, Olsen 86)*

Breidablik (0) 0 4943

Rosenborg: Orlund; Dorsin, Lustig, Larsen, Wangberg, Skjelbred, Winsnes, Henriksen, Svensson (Bakenga 70), Moldskred (Midtsjo 86), Prica (Olsen 79).
Breidablik: Kale; Adalsteinsson, Jonsson, Arsaelsson, Kristjansson, Elisabetarson, Steindorsson (Bjorgvinsson 90), Margeirsson (Sigurgeirsson 90), Haraldsson, Gardarsson (Yeoman 77), Macallister.

Skenderbeu (0) 0

Apoel (0) 2 *(Nuno Morais 52, Gustavo Manduca 56)* 5000

Skenderbeu: Shehi; Arapi R, Vrapi, Eloy (Radas 46), Orelesi, Bicaj, Allmuca (Bernardo 67), Muzaka, Shkembi, Bratic (Biskup 85), Dos Santos.
Apoel: Chiotis; Paulo Jorge, William, Poursaitidis, Kontis, Nuno Morais, Marcinho (Adorno 72), Charalambidis (Alexandrou 86), Solari, Gustavo Manduca (Satsias 81), Helio Pinto.

Skonto Riga (0) 0

Wisla (1) 1 *(Rode 40 (og))* 5200

Skonto Riga: Malins; Kacanovs, Smirnovs, Rode, Laizans■, Tarasovs, Fertovs, Mingazov, Petersons (Smart 66), Sabala (Blanks 76), Karasausks (Fabinho 63).
Wisla: Pareiko; Jaliens, Lamey, Chavez, Sobolewski, Wilk, Malecki, Paljic, Meliksson (Gargula 86), Iliev, Genkov (Biton 75).

Sturm Graz (0) 2 *(Szabics 69, Kienast 90)*

Videoton (0) 0 11,500

Sturm Graz: Gratzei; Standfest, Burgstaller, Feldhofer, Purcher, Bukva (Wolf 36), Holzl, Muratovic (Kienast 62), Weber, Koch (Foda 82), Szabics.
Videoton: Tujvel; Horvath, Liptak, Hector Sanchez, Alvaro Brachi, Vasiljevic (Sandor 63), Polonkai (Nagy 81), Mitrovic, Elek, Gosztonyi (Walter Fernandez 73), Andre Alves.

Zestafoni (3) 3 *(Gelashvili 14, Dvali 23, 40)*

Dacia (0) 0 4458

Zestafoni: Kvaskhvadze; Oniani, Eliava, Khidesheli, Gongadze, Daushvili, Dzaria (Gorgiashvili 71), Grigalashvili, Aptsiauri (Babunashvili 88), Gelashvili (Tsinamdzgvrishvili 69), Dvali.
Dacia: Gaiduchevici; Dimovski, Gamezardashvili, Dobre, Atanackovic (Mamah 42), Mihaliov, Cojocari, Onica (Orbu 78), Tumbasevic, Stjepanovic, Nechaev (Dedov 46).

SECOND QUALIFYING ROUND SECOND LEG

Tuesday, 19 July 2011

BATE Borisov (0) 2 *(Nekhajchik 58, Pavlov 61)*

Linfield (0) 0 5200

BATE Borisov: Gutor; Filipenko, Yurevich, Shitov, Simic, Likhtarovich (Olekhnovich 78), Nekhajchik, Renan (Volodko A 64), Pavlov, Patotsky, Kontsevoy (Rodionov 80).
Linfield: Blayney; Casement (Burns BJ 70), Ervin, Watson, Armstrong, Garrett, Lowry, Hanley, Fordyce (McCaul 76), Carvill, McAllister (Burns A 62).

Ekranas (1) 1 *(Dedura 5)*

Valletta (0) 0 3000

Ekranas: Zubas; Dedura, Matovic, Joksas, Tomkevicius, Radavicius, Andelkovic, Kucys, Vertelis (Ribokas 83), Mauro Alonso (Velicka 70), Umeh (Moroz 89).
Valletta: Hogg; Azzopardi, Borg, Falzon, Agius E, Sammut (Denni 55), Fenech, Mifsud, Agius G, Effiong (Zammit 67), William Barbosa.

F91 Dudelange (0) 1 *(Da Mota 54)*

Maribor (1) 3 *(Mezga 26, 76 (pen), Beric 72)* 1152

F91 Dudelange: Joubert; Caillet■, Wiggers, Tournut, Rentmeister, Benzouien, Sanchez D'Avolio, Payal (Malget 62), Bensi (Gruszczynski 66), Da Mota■, Abdullei (Olle Nicolle 80).
Maribor: Pridigar; Rajcevic, Arghus, Cvijanovic, Mezga, Mertelj, Beric (Volas 79), Milec, Velikonja (Marcos Tavares 64), Mejac, Filipovic (Gabriel 60).

Flora (0) 0

Shamrock R (0) 0 2970

Flora: Pedok; Palatu, Kams, Jurgenson, Baranov, Minkenen, Mosnikov (Beglarishvili 72), Luts, Mashichev (Peitre 84), Henri Anier, Alliku (Dupikov 10).
Shamrock R: Mannus; Oman, Sullivan, Sives, Stevens, Turner (O'Donnell 82), Finn, McCormack, Kelly, Dennehy, Twigg.

HB (0) 1 *(Benjaminsen 70)*

Malmo (0) 1 *(Wilton Figueiredo 90)* 688

HB: Gestson; Mortensen, Jorgensen, Rubeksen, Holm, Samuelsen, Thorleifsson (Davidsen 89), Nielsen, Benjaminsen, Poulsen R (Mouritsen K 88), Flotum (Nolsoe 74).
Malmo: Melicharek; Andersson, Halsti, Ricardinho, Jansson, Pekalski, Durmaz, Wilton Figueiredo, Larsson, Mehmeti (Mutavdzic 85), Rexhepi (Hamad 63).

HJK Helsinki (2) 10 *(Ring 37, Sadik 44, Zeneli 47, 54, Rafinha 52, Pukki 64, 67, Kastrati 66, 88, Parikka 71)*

Bangor C (0) 0 5944

HJK Helsinki: Wallen; Lindstrom, Sumusalo, Moren, Rafinha, Zeneli, Riihilahti (Fowler 59), Bah, Ring, Sadik (Kastrati 59), Pukki (Parikka 69).
Bangor C: Idzi; Morley, Roberts, Brewerton, Johnston, Hoy (Williams 56), Davies (Garside 73), Jones (Walsh 56), Ward, Wilson, Bull.

Litex (1) 3 *(Zanev 3, Todorov 49 (pen), Yanev 80)*

Mogren (0) 0 4000

Litex: Vinicius; Berberovic (Josse 77), Nikolov, Bodurov, Zanev, Jelenkovic, Yanev, Tom (Thiago Miracema 67), Milanov G, Todorov (Flores 72), Tsvetanov.
Mogren: Todorovic; Batak (Tatar 59), Lakic, Simovic, Kapisoda, Ivanovic, Culafic (Bakic 74), Mirkovic, Matic, Gluscevic, Dordevic (Vujovic 62).

Neftci (0) 0

Dinamo Zagreb (0) 0 7000

Neftci: Stamenkovic; Melikov, Abishov, Denis, Georgievski (Seyidov 85), Abdullayev (Huseynov 46), Rodriguinho (Imamverdiyev 6), Amirjanov, Mpenza, Flavinho, Nasimov.
Dinamo Zagreb: Kelava; Tonel, Vida, Ibanez, Leko, Sammir (Calello 89), Alispahic (Kovacic 80), Badelj, Vrsaljko, Beciraj (Rukavina 72), Krstanovic.

Skendija 79 (0) 0

Partizan Belgrade (0) 1 *(Jovancic 68)* 5000

Skendija 79: Zendeli; Cuculi, Berisha, Nikitovic, Mustafi, Useini■, Emini (Bilbilovski 86), Hasani, Neziri, Selmani (Taipi 75), Sali (Iseni 46).
Partizan Belgrade: Ilic R; Rankovic, Volkov, Ivanov, Aksentijevic, Ilic S, Vukic (Ninkovic 77), Kamara, Tomic (Babovic 46), Eduardo (Jovancic 64), Scepovic.

Tobol (0) 1 *(Stepanovsky 62 (og))*

Slovan Bratislava (1) 1 *(Kladrubsky 16)* 6800

Tobol: Petukhov; Ovshinov, Bogdan, Kislitsyn (Kuantayev 60), Kucera, Volkov, Sljivic, Kostyuk (Bogdanov 61), Zebelyan, Dzholchiev, Gridin.
Slovan Bratislava: Putnocky; Had, Dobrotka, Bagayoko (Cikos 85), Guede, Ivana (Kiss 65), Zofcak, Milinkovic (Kuzma 76), Stepanovsky, Sebo, Kladrubsky.

Viktoria Plzen (3) 5 *(Bakos 38, 42, Kolar 45, 57, Pilar 90)*

Pyunik (0) 1 *(Malakyan 49)* 5400

Viktoria Plzen: Pavlik; Cisovsky, Limbersky, Bystron, Rajtoral, Petrzela (Duris 65), Kolar (Darida 81), Horvath, Pilar, Jiracek, Bakos (Hora 74).
Pyunik: Israyelyan; Hovsepyan, Artak Yedigaryan, Haroyan, Malakyan, Aleksanyan, Manoyan (Bakalyan 79), Hovhannisyan K (Gagik Poghosyan 54), Manucharyan, Yuspashyan, Hovhannisyan H (Ghukas Poghosyan 59).

Wisla (0) 2 *(Malecki 51, Iliev 64)*

Skonto Riga (0) 0 19,300

Wisla: Pareiko; Jaliens, Lamey (Jovanovic 88), Chavez, Sobolewski (Nunez 75), Wilk, Malecki, Paljic, Meliksson, Iliev (Jirsak 86), Genkov.
Skonto Riga: Malins; Kacanovs, Smirnovs, Rode, Smart (Fabinho 55), Tarasovs, Fertovs, Mingazov■, Maksimenko, Sabala (Blanks 67), Nathan Junior (Petersons 73).

Wednesday, 20 July 2011

Apoel (0) 4 *(Solari 59, Ailton Almeida 66, Adorno 80, Charalambidis 86)*

Skenderbeu (0) 0 11,271

Apoel: Chiotis; Marcelo Oliveira, William, Poursaitidis (Solomou 81), Kontis, Nuno Morais, Charalambidis, Solari (Ailton Almeida 62), Gustavo Manduca, Helio Pinto (Jahic 72), Adorno.
Skenderbeu: Shehi; Radas (Sulejmanovic 72), Arapi R, Vrapi, Orelesi (Biskup 46), Bicaj, Allmuca, Muzaka, Shkembi, Bratic, Dos Santos (Bernardo 72).

Borac (2) 3 *(Krunic 9, 34, Vidakovic 84)*

Maccabi Haifa (1) 2 *(Dvalishvili 24, 54)* 4000

Borac: Avdukic; Markovic, Stakic, Zaric, Raspudic, Krunic, Kovacevic (Stupar 66), Grahovac, Vidakovic, Stajic (Stefan Dujakovic 87), Mikic (Sinisa Dujakovic 90).
Maccabi Haifa: Davidovich; Buljat, Meshumar, Vered (Ghadir 75), Gustavo Boccoli (Yampolsky 57), Golasa, Yahaya, Tawatha, Pilyavskiy, Dvalishvili, Amasha (Azulay 68).

Breidablik (1) 2 *(Macallister 28, Steindorsson 82)*

Rosenborg (0) 0 747

Breidablik: Kale; Adalsteinsson, Jonsson, Arsaelsson, Kristjansson, Elisabetarson, Steindorsson (Illugason 90), Margeirsson, Haraldsson (Yeoman 74), Gardarsson (Bjorgvinsson 68), Macallister.
Rosenborg: Orlund; Dorsin, Lustig, Larsen (Lago 63), Wangberg, Skjelbred (Svensson 72), Winsnes, Henriksen, Prica, Olsen, Bakenga (Moldskred 46).

Dacia (1) 2 *(Popovici 20, Orbu 90 (pen))*

Zestafoni (0) 0 4000

Dacia: Gaiduchevici; Dimovski, Popovici (Pavlov 84), Mamah, Ilescu, Mihaliov, Cojocari, Dedov (Krkotic 71), Tumbasevic (Nechaev 77), Orbu, Stjepanovic.
Zestafoni: Kvaskhvadze; Oniani, Eliava, Khidesheli (Kobakhidze 86), Gongadze■, Daushvili, Dzaria, Grigalashvili, Aptsiauri (Gorgiashvili 82), Gelashvili, Dvali (Aladashvili 59).

Videoton (3) 3 *(Elek 27, Sandor 32, Liptak 45)*

Sturm Graz (2) 2 *(Holzl 28, Feldhofer 39)* 8780

Videoton: Tujvel; Horvath, Liptak, Hector Sanchez, Alvaro Brachi, Sandor (Nikolic 76), Nagy, Mitrovic, Elek (Polonkai 65), Gosztonyi (Walter Fernandez 79), Andre Alves.
Sturm Graz: Gratzei; Standfest, Burgstaller, Feldhofer, Purcher (Popkhadze 46), Holzl, Wolf (Ehrenreich 83), Muratovic, Weber, Koch, Szabics (Kienast 46).

THIRD QUALIFYING ROUND FIRST LEG

Tuesday, 26 July 2011

Apoel (0) 0

Slovan Bratislava (0) 0 14,553

Apoel: Chiotis; Paulo Jorge, William, Poursaitidis, Kontis, Nuno Morais, Charalambidis, Solari (Ailton Almeida 59), Gustavo Manduca (Marcinho 59), Helio Pinto, Adorno (Trickovski 72).
Slovan Bratislava: Putnocky; Had, Dobrotka, Bagayoko, Cikos (Ivana 86), Guede, Zofcak, Grendel (Milinkovic 61), Stepanovsky (Pauschek 71), Sebo, Kladrubsky.

Dynamo Kiev (0) 0

Rubin (1) 2 *(Kasaev 6, Natcho 68 (pen))* 16,430

Dynamo Kiev: Shovkovskiy; Diakathe, El Kaddouri, Danilo Silva, Khacheridi, Gusev (Ninkovic 78), Eremenko (Aliyev 86), Vukojevic (Milevskiy 55), Lukman, Brown, Yarmolenko.
Rubin: Ryzhikov; Bocchetti, Ansaldi, Sharonov, Kverkvelia, Gokdeniz, Noboa, Natcho (Dzhalilov 90), Kasaev (Nemov 69), Kislyak, Dyadyun (Medvedev 60).

Ekranas (0) 0

BATE Borisov (0) 0 2989

Ekranas: Zubas; Dedura, Samusiovas, Tomkevicius, Radavicius (Skinderis 72), Andelkovic■, Kucys, Vertelis, Ribokas (Velicka 46), Mauro Alonso (Moroz 59), Umeh.
BATE Borisov: Gutor; Filipenko, Yurevich, Shitov, Simic, Likhtarovich (Rudik 61), Nekhajchik, Renan (Rodionov 67), Olekhnovich, Patotsky (Gordeychuk 76), Kontsevoy.

Genk (0) 2 *(Vossen 70 (pen), Ogunjimi 90)*

Partizan Belgrade (0) 1 *(Tomic 65)* 12,735

Genk: Koteles; Joneleit, Ngongca■, Tozser, Hubert (Barda 71), Pudil, Jose Nadson, Nwanganga, De Bruyne, Buffel (Vanden Borre 46), Vossen (Ogunjimi 85).
Partizan Belgrade: Stojkovic; Rankovic, Rnic, Volkov, Ivanov, Ilic S, Vukic (Markovic S 90), Kamara, Babovic■, Eduardo (Jovancic 68), Scepovic (Tomic 53).

Litex (1) 1 *(Tom 45)*

Wisla (1) 2 *(Lamey 19, Meliksson 76)* 6800

Litex: Vinicius; Berberovic, Nikolov, Bodurov, Zanev, Jelerkovic, Yanev, Tom, Milanov (Josse 86), Todorov (Celio Codo 65), Tsvetanov (Flores 73).
Wisla: Jovanic; Jaliens, Lamey, Diaz, Chavez, Sobolewski, Wilk, Meliksson, Iliev (Kirm 66), Nunez (Gargula 77), Genkov (Jovanovic 87).

Rangers (0) 0

Malmo (1) 1 *(Larsson 18)* 28,828

Rangers: McGregor; Whittaker, Papac, Bougherra, Weir (Juanma Ortiz 29), Wallace, Davis, McCulloch, Jelavic, Naismith, Edu.
Malmo: Melicharek; Andersson, Halsti, Jansson, Hamad, Pekalski, Durmaz, Wilton Figueiredo (Rexhepi 69), Mutavdzic, Larsson (Yago 81), Mehmeti (Nazari A 54).

Twente (1) 2 *(Janko 34 (pen), 57)*

Vaslui (0) 0 12,800

Twente: Mihaylov; Wisgerhof, Cornelisse, Buysse, Douglas, Leugers, Brama, Bajrami (John 71), Berghuis (Vogelsang 76), Janko (Rendla 85), De Jong.
Vaslui: Cerniauskas; Milanov, Canu (Farkas 60), Papp, Sanmartean, Jovanovic, Pavlovic, Wesley, Costin (Milisavljevic 63), Temwanjira (Bello 70), Adailton.

Zestafoni (0) 1 *(Gelashvili 74)*

Sturm Graz (0) 1 *(Wolf 78)* 14,700

Zestafoni: Kvaskhvadze; Oniani, Eliava (Chankotadze 88), Aladashvili (Benashvili 82), Kobakhidze, Daushvili (Gorgiashvili 57), Dzaria, Grigalashvili, Aptsiauri, Gelashvili, Dvali.
Sturm Graz: Gratzei; Burgstaller, Popkhadze, Ehrenreich, Neuhold, Wolf, Muratovic, Weber, Foda (Koch 83), Kainz (Stangl 90), Kienast (Haas 82).

Wednesday, 27 July 2011

Benfica (0) 2 *(Nolito 71, Gaitan 88)*

Trabzonspor (0) 0 37,341

Benfica: Artur Moraes; Luisao, Garay, Emerson, Aimar (Witsel 74), Javi Garcia, Perez (Nolito 54), Ruben Amorim (Pereira 64), Gaitan, Saviola, Cardozo.
Trabzonspor: Tolga; Glowacki; Remzi, Celustka, Zokora, Serkan, Alanzinho (Aykut 67), Colman, Burak, Paulo Henrique, Mierzejewski (Pawel Brozek 85).

FC Copenhagen (1) 1 *(Ottesen 4)*

Shamrock R (0) 0 11,571

FC Copenhagen: Wiland; Ottesen, Jorgensen, Thomsen (Sigurdsson 46), Bengtsson, Grindheim, Claudemir, Diouf, Bolanos, Delaney (Absalonsen 61), Cesar Santin (Nordstrand 70).
Shamrock R: Thompson; Rice (Kilduff 90), Oman (Murray 83), Sullivan, Sives, Stevens, Finn, McCormack, Kelly (McCabe 54), Dennehy, Twigg.

HJK Helsinki (1) 1 *(Ring 14)*

Dinamo Zagreb (1) 2 *(Rafinha 19 (og), Sammir 77)* 10,153

HJK Helsinki: Wallen; Lindstrom, Sumusalo, Ojala, Rafinha, Zeneli (Sorsa 62), Riihilahti, Bah, Ring, Sadik (Litmanen 78), Pukki (Pelvas 82).
Dinamo Zagreb: Kelava; Tonel, Vida, Ibanez, Leko, Sammir (Calello 90), Alispahic (Kovacic 69), Badelj, Vrsaljko, Beciraj (Rukavina 59), Krstanovic.

Maccabi Haifa (1) 2 *(Dvalishvili 8 (pen), Yampolsky 70)*

Maribor (1) 1 *(Marcos Tavares 27)* 9600

Maccabi Haifa: Saranov (Davidovich 46); Buljat, Osman, Meshumar, Vered, Golasa, Tawatha, Pilyavskiy (Falach 82), Dvalishvili, Amasha, Ghadir (Yampolsky 46).
Maribor: Handanovic; Rajcevic, Arghus, Cvijanovic, Ibraimi, Mezga (Filipovic 90), Mertelj, Beric, Milec, Mejac, Marcos Tavares (Volas 75).

Odense (0) 1 *(Reginiussen 90)*

Panathinaikos (0) 1 *(Leto 47)* 10,055

Odense: Wessels; Mendy (Gislason 46) (Djemba-Djemba 68), Ruud, Reginiussen, Christensen, Chris Sorensen, Johansson, Andreasen, Kadrii, Utaka, Jensen (Hoegh 85).
Panathinaikos: Tzorvas; Boumsong, Sarriegi, Vyntra, Spiropoulos, Katsouranis, Simao, Ninis (Karagounis 77), Marinos, Leto, Petropoulos (Owusu-Abeyie 72).

Rosenborg (0) 0

Viktoria Plzen (1) 1 *(Pilar 33)* 8028

Rosenborg: Orlund; Dorsin, Lustig, Larsen, Wangberg, Skjelbred, Winsnes, Henriksen, Svensson (Olsen 73), Moldskred (Bakenga 82), Prica.
Viktoria Plzen: Pavlik (Danek 16); Cisovsky, Limbersky, Bystron, Rajtoral, Petrzela (Duris 78), Kolar, Horvath, Pilar (Sevinsky 88), Jiracek, Bakos.

Standard Liege (0) 1 *(Gonzalez 90)*

Zurich (0) 1 *(Mehmedi 78)* 13,727

Standard Liege: Sinan; Van Damme, Pocognoli (Benteke 87), Felipe, Kanu, Opare, Buyens, Camara (Gonzalez 84), Tchite, Nong (Batshuayi 84), Leye.
Zurich: Leoni; Beda, Koch P, Jorge Teixeira, Ricardo Rodriguez, Djuric (Koch R 90), Margairaz (Kukuruzovic 23), Aegerter, Alphonse, Nikci, Mehmedi (Drmic 87).

THIRD QUALIFYING ROUND SECOND LEG

Tuesday, 2 August 2011

BATE Borisov (2) 3 *(Rodionov 18, Renan 35, Gordeychuk 89)*

Ekranas (1) 1 *(Velicka 22)* 5360

BATE Borisov: Gutor; Filipenko, Yurevich, Shitov, Simic, Likhtarovich (Olekhnovich 74), Nekhajchik, Baga (Rudik 85), Renan■, Patotsky (Gordeychuk 46), Rodionov.
Ekranas: Zubas; Dedura, Joksas, Samusiovas, Tomkevicius (Ribokas 81), Radavicius (Moroz 61), Kucys, Vertelis, Mauro Alonso, Velicka (Markevicius 69), Umeh.

Panathinaikos (1) 3 *(Boumsong 37, Toche 50, Petropoulos 90)*

Odense (1) 4 *(Johansson 12, Ruud 58, Kadrii 80, Andreasen 88)*

Panathinaikos: Tzorvas; Boumsong, Josu Sarriegi, Vyntra, Spiropoulos, Katsouranis (Karagounis 74), Simao, Ninis, Marinos (Toche 20), Leto, Cleyton (Petropoulos 67).
Odense: Wessels; Mendy■, Ruud, Reginiussen, Christensen, Chris Sorensen, Johansson, Djemba-Djemba, Andreasen, Kadrii (Hoegh 89), Utaka (Traore 87).
Behind closed doors.

Shamrock R (0) 0

FC Copenhagen (1) 2 *(N'Doye 42, Bolanos 73)* 5901

Shamrock R: Thompson; Murray, Sullivan, Sives, Stevens, Turner, Finn (Rice 75), McCormack, Dennehy, McCabe (Kelly 65), Twigg (Kilduff 75).
FC Copenhagen: Wiland; Ottesen, Sigurdsson, Jorgensen, Bengtsson, Grindheim, Kristensen (Absalonsen 90), Claudemir, Diouf (Cesar Santin 83), Bolanos (Delaney 79), N'Doye.

Wednesday, 3 August 2011

Dinamo Zagreb (0) 1 *(Ibanez 90)*

HJK Helsinki (0) 0 25,370

Dinamo Zagreb: Kelava; Tonel, Vida, Ibanez, Leko, Sammir, Alispahic (Kovacic 19), Badelj, Vrsaljko, Beciraj (Cufre 83), Krstanovic (Rukavina 55).
HJK Helsinki: Wallen; Lindstrom, Sumusalo, Ojala, Rafinha, Zeneli (Sorsa 58), Riihilahti (Mannstrom 62), Bah, Ring, Sadik, Pukki (Pelvas 75).

Malmo (0) 1 *(Hamad 80)*

Rangers (1) 1 *(Jelavic 24)* 19,084

Malmo: Melicharek; Andersson, Ricardinho■, Jansson, Hamad, Pekalski, Durmaz, Wilton Figueiredo, Mutavdzic (Rexhepi 46), Larsson, Mehmeti (Stenstrom 33).
Rangers: McGregor; Whittaker■, Wallace, Edu, Bougherra■, McCulloch, Juanma Ortiz (Hemmings 84), Davis, Jelavic, Naismith, Papac.

Maribor (1) 1 *(Marcos Tavares 32)*

Maccabi Haifa (1) 1 *(Vered 10)* 12,000

Maribor: Handanovic; Rajcevic, Vidovic, Cvijanovic (Volas 66), Ibraimi, Mezga (Velikonja 81), Mertelj, Beric, Milec, Mejac (Trajkovski 80), Marcos Tavares.
Maccabi Haifa: Davidovich; Buljat, Meshumar, Falach, Vered (Osman 90), Gustavo Boccoli, Golasa, Yahaya, Tawatha, Dvalishvili (Ghadir 88), Amasha (Yampolsky 54).

Partizan Belgrade (1) 1 *(Tomic 40)*

Genk (0) 1 *(Vossen 58 (pen))* 24,511

Partizan Belgrade: Stojkovic; Rnic, Miljkovic, Volkov, Ivanov, Ilic S (Ninkovic 86), Vukic, Kamara, Tomic (Babic 51), Eduardo, Scepovic (Markovic 77).
Genk: Koteles; Vanden Borre, Joneleit, Tozser, Hubert, Pudil, Jose Nadson, De Bruyne, Durwael, Vossen (Barda 68), Ogunjimi (Nwanganga 86).

Rubin (1) 2 *(Dyadyun 19, Medvedev 88)*

Dynamo Kiev (0) 1 *(Gusev 90)* 19,820

Rubin: Ryzhikov; Bocchetti, Kaleshin, Sharonov, Kverkvelia, Gokdeniz, Noboa (Lebedenko 89), Natcho, Kasaev (Nemov 73), Kislyak, Dyadyun (Medvedev 81).
Dynamo Kiev: Shovkovskiy; Diakathe, Popov, Danilo Silva (Shevchenko 63), Gusev, Yussuf, Eremenko, Vukojevic, Lukman (Garmash 46), Brown, Yarmolenko.

Slovan Bratislava (0) 0

Apoel (0) 2 *(Ailton Almeida 57, Gustavo Manduca 90)* 9318

Slovan Bratislava: Putnocky; Had, Dobrotka, Bagayoko, Cikos (Szarka 85), Guede, Zofcak, Grendel■, Stepanovsky (Milinkovic 61), Sebo, Kladrubsky.
Apoel: Chiotis; Paulo Jorge, William, Poursaitidis, Kontis, Nuno Morais, Marcinho (Jahic 89), Gustavo Manduca, Ailton Almeida (Charalambidis 79), Helio Pinto, Trickovski (Solari 84).

Sturm Graz (0) 1 *(Kienast 68)*

Zestafoni (0) 0 10,058

Sturm Graz: Gratzei; Burgstaller, Popkhadze, Ehrenreich, Holzl, Wolf (Kainz 85), Muratovic, Weber, Dudic, Szabics (Bodul 74), Kienast (Haas 90).
Zestafoni: Kvaskhvadze; Oniani, Eliava, Aladashvili, Kobakhidze, Daushvili (Gorgiashvili 52), Dzaria (Tsinamdzgvrishvili 80), Grigalashvili, Aptsiauri (Babunashvili 76), Gelashvili, Dvali.

Trabzonspor (1) 1 *(Paulo Henrique 32)*

Benfica (1) 1 *(Nolito 19)* 32,060

Trabzonspor: Tolga; Glowacki, Remzi, Celustka, Zokora, Serkan (Halil Altintop 79), Piotr Brozek (Mustafa 63), Colman, Burak, Paulo Henrique (Alanzinho 44), Mierzejewski■.
Benfica: Artur Moraes; Luisao, Garay, Emerson, Pereira, Aimar (Matic 64), Javi Garcia, Witsel, Gaitan (Bruno Cesar 87), Saviola (Jara 75), Nolito.

Vaslui (0) 0

Twente (0) 0 5280

Vaslui: Cerniauskas; Balace, Farkas, Papp, Sanmartean (Milisavljevic 60), Jovanovic (Milanov 73), Wesley, Costin, Neagu (Annang 78), Temwanjira, Adailton.
Twente: Mihaylov; Wisgerhof, Cornelisse, Tiendalli, Douglas, Brama, Janssen, Berghuis, Ruiz (John 74), Janko (Landzaat 86), De Jong.

Viktoria Plzen (0) 3 *(Bakos 56, Kolar 60, Petrzela 78)*

Rosenborg (1) 2 *(Lustig 45, Prica 77)* 5124

Viktoria Plzen: Danek; Cisovsky (Sevinsky 32), Limbersky, Bystron, Rajtoral, Petrzela (Fillo 89), Kolar, Horvath, Pilar, Jiracek, Bakos (Duris 82).
Rosenborg: Orlund; Dorsin, Lustig, Larsen, Wangberg, Winsnes, Henriksen, Svensson (Midtsjo 80), Moldskred (Bakenga 68), Fredheim Holm (Olsen 85), Prica.

Wisla (1) 3 *(Meliksson 42, 56 (pen), Wilk 84)*

Litex (0) 1 *(Bodurov 68)* 23,050

Wisla: Pareiko; Jaliens, Lamey (Jovanovic 86), Diaz, Chavez, Sobolewski, Nunez, Kirm, Meliksson (Paljic 84), Malecki (Wilk 75), Genkov.
Litex: Vinicius; Nikolov, Bodurov, Zanev, Milanov I, Jelenkovic■, Yanev (Tsvetkov 62), Tom, Thiago Miracema, Milanov G (Celio Codo 72), Tsvetanov (Todorov 52).

Zurich (0) 1 *(Mehmedi 58)*

Standard Liege (0) 0 10,500

Zurich: Leoni; Beda, Koch P, Jorge Teixeira, Ricardo Rodriguez, Djuric (Barmettler 83), Aegerter, Kukuruzovic, Alphonse (Koch R 90), Nikci, Mehmedi (Chermiti 80).
Standard Liege: Sinan; Van Damme, Pocognoli (Camara 61), Felipe, Kanu, Opare (Goreux 34), Gonzalez, Buyens■, Tchite, Nong (Benteke 61), Leye.

PLAY-OFF ROUND FIRST LEG

Tuesday, 16 August 2011

Arsenal (1) 1 *(Walcott 4)*

Udinese (0) 0 58,159

Arsenal: Szczesny; Sagna, Gibbs (Djourou 46) (Jenkinson 56), Song Billong, Vermaelen, Koscielny, Walcott, Ramsey, Gervinho, Chamakh, Rosicky (Frimpong 73).
Udinese: Handanovic; Danilo, Benatia, Isla, Armero, Ekstrand, Neuton (Pasquale 59), Pinzi (Abdi 87), Asamoah, Agyemang-Badu, Di Natale.

BATE Borisov (0) 1 *(Simic 59)*

Sturm Graz (1) 1 *(Weber 12)* 15,550

BATE Borisov: Gutor; Filipenko, Yurevich, Bordachev (Volodko A 82), Simic, Nekhajchik, Baga, Olekhnovich, Patotsky (Gordeychuk 46), Rodionov (Rudik 69), Kontsevoy.
Sturm Graz: Gratzei; Standfest, Burgstaller, Popkhadze, Saumel, Bukva, Holzl (Ehrenreich 88), Weber, Dudic, Szabics (Muratovic 71), Kienast.

FC Copenhagen (0) 1 *(Ottesen 69)*

Viktoria Plzen (0) 3 *(Ottesen 52 (og), Pilar 59, Fillo 79)* 19,148

FC Copenhagen: Wiland; Ottesen, Jorgensen, Thomsen, Bengtsson, Grindheim, Kristensen, Claudemir (Absalonsen 65), Diouf (Nordstrand 56), Bolanos, N'Doye.
Viktoria Plzen: Cech; Cisovsky, Limbersky, Bystron, Rajtoral, Trapp, Petrzela (Fillo 76), Kolar, Horvath, Pilar (Hora 90), Duris (Sevinsky 89).

Lyon (2) 3 *(Gomis 10, Kverkvelia 40 (og), Briand 71)*

Rubin (1) 1 *(Dyadyun 3)* 35,468

Lyon: Lloris; Reveillere, Cissokho (Pjanic 52), Kone, Lovren, Kallstrom, Michel Bastos, Gonalons, Gomis, Briand (Pied 82), Lopez.
Rubin: Ryzhikov; Bocchetti, Kuzmin, Kaleshin, Sharonov, Kverkvelia, Gokdeniz, Noboa, Natcho, Kasaev (Lebedenko 69), Dyadyun (Medvedev 36).

Twente (1) 2 *(De Jong 6, Ruiz 80)*

Benfica (2) 2 *(Cardozo 21, Nolito 35)* 20,000

Twente: Mihaylov; Wisgerhof, Cornelisse, Tiendalli (Buysse 75), Douglas, Landzaat (Janko 46), Brama, Bajrami (John 58), Janssen, Ruiz, De Jong.
Benfica: Artur Moraes; Luisao, Garay, Emerson, Pereira, Aimar (Saviola 64), Javi Garcia, Witsel, Gaitan (Ruben Amorim 56), Cardozo (Matic 87), Nolito.

Wednesday, 17 August 2011

Bayern Munich (1) 2 *(Schweinsteiger 8, Robben 72)*

Zurich (0) 0 66,000

Bayern Munich: Neuer; Lahm, Rafinha, Boateng, Badstuber, Robben, Schweinsteiger, Ribery, Luiz Gustavo, Kroos (Muller 57), Gomez.
Zurich: Leoni; Beda■, Jorge Teixeira, Koch R, Ricardo Rodriguez, Djuric, Barmettler (Buff 67), Aegerter, Schonbachler (Nikci 55), Chermiti (Drmic 84), Mehmedi.

Dinamo Zagreb (1) 4 *(Sammir 4, 61 (pen), Rukavina 56, Beciraj 84)*

Malmo (1) 1 *(Mehmeti 17)* 30,065

Dinamo Zagreb: Kelava; Tonel, Vida, Ibanez, Leko, Calello (Kovacic 86), Sammir (Situm 90), Badelj, Vrsaljko, Rukavina, Krstanovic (Beciraj 61).
Malmo: Melicharek; Andersson, Halsti, Jansson, Hamad, Pekalski, Durmaz, Wilton Figueiredo (Rexhepi 67), Mutavdzic (Aubynn 66), Larsson, Mehmeti (Vinzents 74).

Maccabi Haifa (2) 2 *(Amasha 8, Dvalishvili 28)*

Genk (0) 1 *(Barda 61)* 19,170

Maccabi Haifa: Davidovich; Meshumar, Cohen I, Falach, Vered, Gustavo Boccoli (Yampolsky 65), Golasa (Cohen T 82), Yahaya, Tawatha, Dvalishvili, Amasha (Azriel 73).
Genk: Koteles; Joneleit, Tozser, Hubert, Pudil, Jose Nadson, Hyland (Camus 89), Nwanganga, Durwael, Vossen (Buffel 79), Barda.

Odense (0) 1 *(Andreasen 84)*
Villarreal (0) 0 13,002
Odense: Wessels; Ruud, Christensen, Chris Sorensen, Hoegh, Johansson, Djemba-Djemba, Andreasen, Traore, Kadrii, Gislason (Jensen 81).
Villarreal: Diego Lopez; Marchena (Ruben 85), Zapata, Musacchio, Joan Oriol, Mario, Cani, Borja Valero (Senna 84), Soriano, Rossi, Nilmar (Camunas 83).

Wisla (0) 1 *(Malecki 71)*
Apoel (0) 0 22,545
Wisla: Pareiko; Jaliens, Diaz, Chavez, Jovanovic, Sobolewski, Nunez, Meliksson, Iliev (Wilk 68), Malecki (Kirm 90), Genkov.
Apoel: Chiotis; Paulo Jorge, William, Kontis, Nuno Morais, Marcinho (Jahic 80), Solomou, Gustavo Manduca (Charalambidis 46), Ailton Almeida, Helio Pinto, Trickovski (Solari 85).

PLAY-OFF ROUND SECOND LEG

Tuesday, 23 August 2011

Apoel (1) 3 *(Pareiko 29 (og), Ailton Almeida 54, 87)*
Wisla (0) 1 *(Wilk 71)* 21,665
Apoel: Chiotis; Paulo Jorge, William (Alexandrou 85), Poursaitidis, Kontis, Nuno Morais, Marcinho (Jahic 90), Gustavo Manduca (Charalambidis 85), Ailton Almeida, Helio Pinto, Trickovski.
Wisla: Pareiko; Jaliens (Jovanovic 80), Lamey, Diaz, Chavez, Sobolewski (Iliev 58), Wilk, Nunez, Meliksson, Malecki (Kirm 80), Genkov.

Genk (2) 2 *(Vossen 35, Buffel 41)*
Maccabi Haifa (1) 1 *(Golasa 37)* 13,753
Genk: Koteles; Joneleit, Ngongca, Tozser, Hubert, Pudil, Jose Nadson, Nwanganga (Ogunjimi 68), Buffel (Limbombe 110), Vossen, Barda (Vanden Borre 96).
Maccabi Haifa: Davidovich; Meshumar, Cohen I■, Falach, Vered (Katan 79), Gustavo Boccoli (Yampolsky 46), Golasa, Yahaya, Tawatha, Dvalishvili, Amasha (Cohen T 112).
aet; Genk won 4-1 on penalties.

Malmo (0) 2 *(Wilton Figueiredo 69, Jansson 86)*
Dinamo Zagreb (0) 0 15,331
Malmo: Melicharek; Vinzents, Halsti, Ricardinho, Jansson, Hamad, Pekalski (Aubynn 81), Durmaz (Miiko Albornoz 79), Wilton Figueiredo, Larsson, Mehmeti (Rexhepi 78).
Dinamo Zagreb: Kelava; Cufre, Tonel, Vida, Leko, Calello, Sammir (Situm 81), Badelj, Vrsaljko■, Rukavina (Krstanovic 87), Beciraj (Kovacic 58).

Villarreal (0) 3 *(Rossi 50, 66, Marchena 82)*
Odense (0) 0 18,404
Villarreal: Diego Lopez; Zapata, Musacchio, Joan Oriol, Senna, Cani (Rodriguez 84), Camunas (Marchena 75), Borja Valero■, Soriano, Rossi, Nilmar (Ruben 84).
Odense: Wessels; Mendy (Chris Sorensen 80), Ruud, Reginiussen, Christensen, Johansson, Djemba-Djemba, Andreasen, Traore (Utaka 80), Kadrii■, Gislason (Jensen 57).

Zurich (0) 0
Bayern Munich (1) 1 *(Gomez 7)* 23,400
Zurich: Leoni; Koch P, Jorge Teixeira, Ricardo Rodriguez, Djuric (Brunner 66), Barmettler, Aegerter (Gajic 65), Buff, Schonbachler, Chermiti, Mehmedi (Drmic 78).
Bayern Munich: Neuer; Lahm, Van Buyten, Boateng, Badstuber, Schweinsteiger, Ribery, Luiz Gustavo, Kroos (Tymoschuk 65), Gomez (Petersen 46), Muller (Alaba 72).

Wednesday, 24 August 2011

Benfica (0) 3 *(Witsel 46, 66, Luisao 59)*
Twente (0) 1 *(Ruiz 85)* 48,353
Benfica: Artur Moraes; Luisao, Garay, Emerson, Pereira, Aimar, Javi Garcia, Witsel, Gaitan (Bruno Cesar 73), Cardozo (Saviola 84), Nolito (Matic 74).
Twente: Mihaylov; Wisgerhof, Cornelisse, Tiendalli, Douglas, Brama (Landzaat 76), Janssen (John 60), Berghuis (Bajrami 60), Ruiz, Janko, De Jong.

Rubin (0) 1 *(Natcho 77)*
Lyon (0) 1 *(Kone 87)* 20,620
Rubin: Ryzhikov; Kaleshin, Sharonov, Kverkvelia, Gokdeniz, Lebedenko (Martins 69), Nemov, Noboa, Natcho, Kislyak, Dyadyun (Medvedev 69).
Lyon: Lloris; Reveillere, Cissokho, Kone, Lovren, Kallstrom, Michel Bastos, Gonalons, Gomis (Pjanic 83), Briand, Lopez (Pied 90).

Sturm Graz (0) 0
BATE Borisov (1) 2 *(Volodko A 36, Simic 69)* 14,528
Sturm Graz: Gratzei; Standfest, Burgstaller, Popkhadze, Saumel, Bukva (Haas 46), Holzl (Muratovic 74), Wolf (Kainz 60), Weber, Dudic, Szabics.
BATE Borisov: Gutor; Filipenko, Yurevich, Simic, Nekhajchik, Baga, Renan (Rudik 59), Volodko A, Olekhnovich, Rodionov (Bordachev 77), Kontsevoy (Gordeychuk 67).

Udinese (1) 1 *(Di Natale 39)*
Arsenal (0) 2 *(Van Persie 55, Walcott 70)* 26,031
Udinese: Handanovic; Danilo, Benatia (Pasquale 87), Isla (Denis 83), Armero, Ekstrand, Neuton, Pinzi (Fabbrini 63), Asamoah, Agyemang-Badu, Di Natale.
Arsenal: Szczesny; Sagna, Jenkinson, Song Billong, Vermaelen, Djourou, Walcott (Arshavin 90), Ramsey, Gervinho (Traore 86), Van Persie, Frimpong (Rosicky 46).

Viktoria Plzen (0) 2 *(Bakos 68, Duris 90)*
FC Copenhagen (1) 1 *(Bolanos 32)* 19,350
Viktoria Plzen: Cech; Cisovsky, Limbersky, Bystron, Rajtoral, Petrzela (Fillo 82), Kolar, Horvath (Trapp 86), Pilar, Jiracek, Bakos (Duris 77).
FC Copenhagen: Wiland; Ottesen, Jorgensen, Thomsen (Sigurdsson 83), Bengtsson, Grindheim, Bolanos (Diouf 74), Delaney, Cesar Santin (Absalonsen 64), Nordstrand, N'Doye.

GROUP STAGE

GROUP A

Wednesday, 14 September 2011

Manchester C (0) 1 *(Kolarov 74)*

Napoli (0) 1 *(Cavani 69)* 44,026

Manchester C: Hart; Zabaleta, Kolarov (Clichy 75), Kompany, Lescott, Barry, Nasri (Johnson A 76), Toure Y, Aguero, Dzeko (Tevez 81), Silva.
Napoli: De Sanctis; Aronica, Zuniga, Cannavaro, Campagnaro, Maggio, Gargano, Inler, Hamsik (Santana 89), Cavani (Pandev 84), Lavezzi (Dzemaili 57).

Villarreal (0) 0

Bayern Munich (1) 2 *(Kroos 7, Rafinha 76)* 19,168

Villarreal: Diego Lopez; Marchena, Zapata, Musacchio, Catala, Mario, Senna (Cani 46), De Guzman (Camunas 72), Soriano, Rossi, Nilmar (Ruben 58).
Bayern Munich: Neuer; Lahm, Van Buyten (Rafinha 22), Boateng, Badstuber, Schweinsteiger, Ribery, Tymoschuk, Kroos (Luiz Gustavo 80), Gomez (Petersen 46), Muller.

Tuesday, 27 September 2011

Bayern Munich (2) 2 *(Gomez 38, 45)*

Manchester C (0) 0 66,000

Bayern Munich: Neuer; Lahm, Rafinha, Van Buyten, Boateng, Schweinsteiger, Ribery (Robben 90), Luiz Gustavo, Kroos (Tymoschuk 82), Gomez (Petersen 90), Muller.
Manchester C: Hart; Richards, Clichy, Kompany, Toure K, Barry (Kolarov 73), Nasri (Milner 70), Toure Y, Aguero, Dzeko (De Jong 55), Silva.

Napoli (2) 2 *(Hamsik 14, Cavani 17 (pen))*

Villarreal (0) 0 46,747

Napoli: De Sanctis; Dossena, Aronica, Zuniga, Cannavaro, Campagnaro, Gargano, Inler, Hamsik (Mascara 79), Cavani (Pandev 71), Lavezzi (Santana 88).
Villarreal: Diego Lopez; Rodriguez (Camunas 33), Zapata, Musacchio, Catala, Senna (Mubarak 83), De Guzman (Perez 83), Cani, Soriano, Rossi, Nilmar.

Tuesday, 18 October 2011

Manchester C (1) 2 *(Marchena 43 (og), Aguero 90)*

Villarreal (1) 1 *(Cani 4)* 43,326

Manchester C: Hart; Zabaleta, Kolarov, De Jong (Aguero 62), Lescott, Kompany, Nasri (Milner 80), Toure Y, Dzeko, Silva, Johnson A (Barry 40).
Villarreal: Diego Lopez; Marchena, Rodriguez, Zapata, Catala, De Guzman (Marcos Gullon 88), Cani (Mario 82), Borja Valero, Soriano, Hernan Perez (Mubarak 80), Rossi.

Napoli (1) 1 *(Badstuber 39 (og))*

Bayern Munich (1) 1 *(Kroos 2)* 46,000

Napoli: De Sanctis; Aronica, Zuniga, Cannavaro, Campagnaro, Maggio, Gargano, Inler (Santana 90), Hamsik (Mascara 90), Cavani (Dzemaili 81), Lavezzi.
Bayern Munich: Neuer; Lahm, Van Buyten, Boateng, Badstuber, Schweinsteiger, Ribery (Alaba 90), Tymoschuk, Kroos, Gomez (Luiz Gustavo 90), Muller.

Wednesday, 2 November 2011

Bayern Munich (3) 3 *(Gomez 17, 23, 42)*

Napoli (1) 2 *(Fernandez 45, 79)* 61,523

Bayern Munich: Neuer; Lahm, Van Buyten, Boateng, Badstuber■, Schweinsteiger (Tymoschuk 53), Ribery (Alaba 80), Luiz Gustavo, Kroos, Gomez, Muller.
Napoli: De Sanctis; Aronica (Dossena 42), Zuniga■, Campagnaro, Fernandez, Dzemaili (Pandev 84), Maggio, Inler, Hamsik, Cavani, Lavezzi.

Villarreal (0) 0

Manchester C (2) 3 *(Toure Y 30, 71, Balotelli 45 (pen))* 19,358

Villarreal: Diego Lopez; Marchena, Rodriguez, Musacchio, Catala, Mario, De Guzman (Angel Lopez 78), Borja Valero, Hernan Perez (Joan Oriol 84), Mubarak (Gerard Bordas 77), Joselu.
Manchester C: Hart; Zabaleta, Clichy, Kompany, Savic, De Jong, Milner, Toure Y (Aguero 74), Balotelli (Kolarov 83), Silva (Johnson A 65), Nasri.

Tuesday, 22 November 2011

Bayern Munich (2) 3 *(Ribery 3, 69, Gomez 23)*

Villarreal (0) 1 *(De Guzman 50)* 66,000

Bayern Munich: Neuer; Lahm, Rafinha, Van Buyten, Boateng, Robben (Olic 76), Ribery (Pranjic 81), Tymoschuk, Kroos, Alaba, Gomez (Muller 72).
Villarreal: Diego Lopez; Marchena, Angel Lopez (Senna 69), Musacchio, Joan Oriol, Mario, De Guzman (Mubarak 62), Borja Valero (Joselu 78), Soriano, Hernan Perez, Ruben.

Napoli (1) 2 *(Cavani 18, 49)*

Manchester C (1) 1 *(Balotelli 33)* 57,575

Napoli: De Sanctis; Dossena (Fernandez 88), Aronica, Cannavaro, Campagnaro, Maggio, Gargano, Inler (Dzemaili 59), Hamsik, Cavani (Pandev 83), Lavezzi.
Manchester C: Hart; Zabaleta (Johnson A 86), Kolarov, Kompany, Lescott, De Jong (Nasri 71), Silva, Toure Y, Balotelli, Dzeko (Aguero 81), Milner.

Wednesday, 7 December 2011

Manchester C (1) 2 *(Silva 37, Toure Y 52)*

Bayern Munich (0) 0 46,002

Manchester C: Hart; Savic, Clichy, Kompany, Lescott, Barry, Silva (Johnson A 84), Toure Y (Balotelli 81), Aguero, Dzeko (De Jong 77), Nasri.
Bayern Munich: Butt; Rafinha, Boateng, Badstuber, Contento, Tymoschuk, Pranjic, Luiz Gustavo, Alaba, Olic, Petersen (Usami 81).

Villarreal (0) 0

Napoli (0) 2 *(Inler 65, Hamsik 76)* 15,350

Villarreal: Diego Lopez; Angel Lopez, Zapata (Rodriguez 76), Musacchio, Joan Oriol, Senna (Joselu 73), De Guzman, Soriano, Hernan Perez, Nilmar (Camunas 64), Ruben.
Napoli: De Sanctis; Oronica, Zuniga (Grava 90), Cannavaro, Campagnaro, Maggio, Gargano, Inler, Hamsik (Dzemaili 79), Cavani (Pandev 82), Lavezzi.

Group A Table	*P*	*W*	*D*	*L*	*F*	*A*	*Pts*
Bayern Munich	6	4	1	1	11	6	13
Napoli	6	3	2	1	10	6	11
Manchester C	6	3	1	2	9	6	10
Villarreal	6	0	0	6	2	14	0

GROUP B

Wednesday, 14 September 2011

Internazionale (0) 0

Trabzonspor (0) 1 *(Celustka 76)* 24,444

Internazionale: Julio Cesar; Lucio, Zanetti, Jonathan, Nagatomo, Ranocchia, Sneijder, Cambiasso, Obi (Alvarez 55), Pazzini (Milito 55), Zarate (Philippe Coutinho 77).
Trabzonspor: Tolga; Cech, Glowacki, Remzi, Celustka, Zokora, Serkan, Alanzinho (Sapara 64), Colman, Paulo Henrique (Vittek 74), Halil Altintop (Aykut 87).

Lille (1) 2 *(Sow 45, Pedretti 57)*

CSKA Moscow (0) 2 *(Doumbia 72, 90)* 15,274

Lille: Landreau; Rozehnal, Basa, Debuchy, Beria, Balmont, Rio Mavuba, Pedretti (Gueye 76), Obraniak (Cole 76), Hazard, Sow (Rodelin 86).
CSKA Moscow: Gabulov; Berezutski A, Berezutski V, Ignashevich, Nababkin, Aldonin (Mamaev 80), Cauna (Oliseh 67), Dzagoev, Tosic, Vagner Love, Doumbia (Semberas 90).

Tuesday, 27 September 2011

CSKA Moscow (1) 2 *(Dzagoev 45, Vagner Love 77)*

Internazionale (2) 3 *(Lucio 6, Pazzini 23, Zarate 79)* 35,000

CSKA Moscow: Gabulov; Berezutski V, Ignashevich, Berezutski A, Nababkin, Aldonin, Mamaev (Tosic 68), Dzagoev, Oliseh, Vagner Love, Doumbia.
Internazionale: Julio Cesar; Lucio, Zanetti, Samuel, Chivu (Crisetig 90), Nagatomo, Cambiasso, Alvarez (Jonathan 84), Obi, Milito, Pazzini (Zarate 49).

Trabzonspor (0) 1 *(Colman 75 (pen))*

Lille (1) 1 *(Sow 30)* 17,349

Trabzonspor: Tolga; Cech (Sapara 82), Glowacki, Remzi, Celustka, Zokora, Serkan, Alanzinho (Mierzejewski 66), Colman, Paulo Henrique, Halil Altintop (Pawel Brozek 90).
Lille: Landreau; Rozehnal, Basa, Debuchy, Beria, Cole (Obraniak 76), Balmont, Rio Mavuba, Pedretti, Hazard, Sow.

Tuesday, 18 October 2011

CSKA Moscow (1) 3 *(Doumbia 29, 86, Cauna 76)*

Trabzonspor (0) 0 18,000

CSKA Moscow: Gabulov; Berezutski V, Ignashevich, Berezutski A, Fedotov, Aldonin, Mamaev (Semberas 70), Dzagoev, Tosic (Cauna 62), Vagner Love, Doumbia (Rahimic 87).
Trabzonspor: Tolga; Cech (Sapara 75), Glowacki, Remzi, Celustka, Zokora, Serkan, Alanzinho (Pawel Brozek 46), Colman, Halil Altintop (Aykut 90), Mierzejewski.

Lille (0) 0

Internazionale (1) 1 *(Pazzini 21)* 16,996

Lille: Enyeama; Basa, Debuchy, Beria, Chedjou, Cole (Obraniak 74), Balmont (Gueye 80), Rio Mavuba, Pedretti (Payet 63), Hazard, Sow.
Internazionale: Julio Cesar; Lucio, Zanetti, Maicon, Chivu, Nagatomo, Sneijder (Stankovic 67), Cambiasso, Thiago Motta, Pazzini (Milito 81), Zarate (Obi 63).

Wednesday, 2 November 2011

Internazionale (1) 2 *(Samuel 18, Milito 65)*

Lille (0) 1 *(Tulio de Melo 83)* 24,299

Internazionale: Castellazzi; Lucio, Zanetti, Samuel, Chivu, Sneijder (Alvarez 67), Cambiasso, Stankovic, Thiago Motta, Milito (Obi 90), Zarate (Pazzini 79).
Lille: Landreau; Rozehnal, Debuchy, Beria, Chedjou, Cole (Payet 71), Rio Mavuba, Pedretti, Hazard, Jelen (Tulio de Melo 46), Sow (Obraniak 60).

Trabzonspor (0) 0

CSKA Moscow (0) 0 19,516

Trabzonspor: Tolga; Cech, Glowacki, Remzi, Celustka, Zokora, Serkan (Alanzinho 61), Colman, Burak, Halil Altintop (Paulo Henrique 61), Mierzejewski (Aykut 81).
CSKA Moscow: Gabulov; Berezutski V, Ignashevich, Berezutski A, Schennikov (Nababkin 46), Aldonin, Mamaev (Semberas 79), Dzagoev, Tosic (Cauna 70), Vagner Love, Doumbia■.

Tuesday, 22 November 2011

CSKA Moscow (0) 0

Lille (0) 2 *(Berezutski V 49 (og), Sow 64)* 19,100

CSKA Moscow: Gabulov; Berezutski V, Ignashevich (Schennikov 75), Berezutski A, Nababkin, Aldonin, Mamaev, Cauna (Serderov 87), Dzagoev, Oliseh, Vagner Love.
Lille: Landreau; Rozehnal, Debuchy, Beria, Chedjou, Cole (Payet 87), Balmont, Rio Mavuba, Hazard (Tulio de Melo 90), Gueye, Sow (Jelen 74).

Trabzonspor (1) 1 *(Halil Altintop 23)*

Internazionale (1) 1 *(Alvarez 18)* 21,611

Trabzonspor: Tolga; Cech; Glowacki, Remzi, Celustka, Zokora, Serkan (Mierzejewski 64), Alanzinho (Paulo Henrique 85), Colman, Burak, Halil Altintop.
Internazionale: Julio Cesar; Lucio, Zanetti, Samuel, Chivu, Nagatomo, Cambiasso, Stankovic, Alvarez (Faraoni 89), Milito (Pazzini 86), Zarate (Philippe Coutinho 69).

Wednesday, 7 December 2011

Internazionale (0) 1 *(Cambiasso 51)*

CSKA Moscow (0) 2 *(Doumbia 50, Berezutski V 87)* 23,295

Internazionale: Castellazzi; Zanetti, Samuel, Chivu (Zarate 46), Nagatomo, Ranocchia, Faraoni, Cambiasso, Philippe Coutinho (Caldirola 46), Obi (Alvarez 70), Milito.
CSKA Moscow: Gabulov; Berezutski V, Ignashevich, Berezutski A, Nababkin, Semberas (Aldonin 77), Mamaev, Dzagoev, Oliseh (Cauna 77), Vagner Love, Doumbia (Schennikov 90).

Lille (0) 0

Trabzonspor (0) 0 16,375

Lille: Landreau; Basa, Debuchy, Beria (Bonnart 84), Chedjou, Cole (Obraniak 69), Balmont, Rio Mavuba, Hazard, Payet (Rodelin 89), Sow.
Trabzonspor: Tolga; Cech, Glowacki, Remzi, Celustka (Mierzejewski 33), Zokora, Serkan, Alanzinho (Paulo Henrique 65), Colman, Burak (Mustafa 90), Halil Altintop.

Group B Table	*P*	*W*	*D*	*L*	*F*	*A*	*Pts*
Internazionale	6	3	1	2	8	7	10
CSKA Moscow	6	2	2	2	9	8	8
Trabzonspor	6	1	4	1	3	5	7
Lille	6	1	3	2	6	6	6

GROUP C

Wednesday, 14 September 2011

Basle (1) 2 *(Frei F 39, Frei A 84 (pen))*

Otelul (0) 1 *(Pena 58)* 30,126

Basle: Sommer; Steinhofer, Abraham, Park, Dragovic, Huggel■, Cabral, Frei F (Pak 90), Xhaka G (Zoua 78), Frei A (Kovac 90), Streller.
Otelul: Grahovac; Costin, Salageanu■, Rapa, Perendija, Giurgiu, Ilie (Frunza 89), Ibeh, Antal, Filip (Viglianti 86), Pena (Paraschiv 71).

Benfica (1) 1 *(Cardozo 24)*

Manchester U (1) 1 *(Giggs 42)* 63,822

Benfica: Artur Moraes; Luisao, Garay, Emerson, Pereira, Aimar (Matic 75), Javi Garcia, Witsel, Ruben Amorim (Nolito 56), Gaitan (Bruno Cesar 90), Cardozo.
Manchester U: Lindegaard; Smalling, Evra, Carrick, Fabio (Jones 78), Evans, Valencia (Nani 69), Fletcher (Hernandez 68), Giggs, Rooney, Park.

Tuesday, 27 September 2011

Manchester U (2) 3 *(Welbeck 16, 17, Young 90)*

Basle (0) 3 *(Frei F 58, Frei A 60, 76 (pen))* 73,115

Manchester U: De Gea; Fabio (Nani 69), Evra, Carrick, Ferdinand, Jones, Valencia, Anderson (Berbatov 82), Welbeck, Giggs (Park 61), Young.
Basle: Sommer; Steinhofer, Abraham, Park, Dragovic, Cabral, Frei F (Chipperfield 77), Xhaka G, Frei A (Xhaka T 89), Streller (Pak 81), Zoua.

Otelul (0) 0

Benfica (1) 1 *(Bruno Cesar 40)* 6824

Otelul: Grahovac; Costin, Skubic, Perendija, Ljubinkovic, Giurgiu, Bus (Frunza 65), Ibeh (Viglianti 46), Antal, Filip, Pena (Punosevac 69).
Benfica: Artur Moraes; Luisao, Garay, Emerson, Pereira, Javi Garcia, Witsel, Gaitan (Rodrigo 77), Bruno Cesar (Ruben Amorim 81), Saviola (Nolito 63), Cardozo.

Tuesday, 18 October 2011

Basle (0) 0

Benfica (1) 2 *(Bruno Cesar 20, Cardozo 75)* 33,000

Basle: Sommer; Steinhofer, Abraham, Park, Dragovic, Huggel (Chipperfield 85), Frei F (Zoua 66), Shaqiri, Xhaka G (Cabral 80), Frei A, Streller.
Benfica: Artur Moraes; Luisao, Garay, Emerson■, Pereira (Miguel Vitor 78), Aimar (Nolito 67), Javi Garcia, Witsel, Gaitan, Bruno Cesar, Rodrigo (Cardozo 70).

Otelul (0) 0

Manchester U (0) 2 *(Rooney 64 (pen), 90 (pen))* 28,047

Otelul: Grahovac; Costin, Salageanu, Rapa, Perendija■, Giurgiu, Frunza (Ilie 83), Antal, Neagu (Pena 72), Filip, Punosevac (Viglianti 87).
Manchester U: Lindegaard; Fabio (Jones 76), Evra, Carrick, Smalling, Vidic■, Valencia (Evans 71), Anderson, Hernandez, Rooney, Nani.

Wednesday, 2 November 2011

Benfica (1) 1 *(Rodrigo 4)*

Basle (0) 1 *(Huggel 64)* 39,270

Benfica: Artur Moraes; Luisao, Garay, Pereira, Luis Martins (Miguel Vitor 64), Aimar (Cardozo 73), Witsel, Gaitan (Nolito 82), Matic, Bruno Cesar, Rodrigo.
Basle: Sommer; Steinhofer, Abraham, Park, Dragovic, Chipperfield (Kusunga 89), Huggel, Frei F, Shaqiri, Xhaka G (Cabral 81), Zoua (Pak 90).

Manchester U (1) 2 *(Valencia 8, Sarghi 87 (og))*

Otelul (0) 0 74,847

Manchester U: De Gea; Jones, Fabio, Anderson (Park 80), Ferdinand, Evans (Fryers 89), Valencia, Owen (Hernandez 11), Berbatov, Rooney, Nani.
Otelul: Grahovac; Sarghi, Costin, Salageanu, Rapa, Giurgiu (Paraschiv 81), Ilie (Frunza 53), Antal (Iorga 61), Neagu, Filip, Pena.

Tuesday, 22 November 2011

Manchester U (1) 2 *(Berbatov 30, Fletcher 59)*

Benfica (1) 2 *(Jones 3 (og), Aimar 61)* 74,873

Manchester U: De Gea; Fabio (Smalling 82), Evra, Carrick, Ferdinand, Jones, Valencia (Hernandez 80), Fletcher, Berbatov, Young, Nani.
Benfica: Artur Moraes; Luisao (Miguel Vitor 58), Garay, Emerson, Pereira, Aimar (Ruben Amorim 83), Javi Garcia, Witsel, Gaitan (Matic 67), Bruno Cesar, Rodrigo.

Otelul (0) 2 *(Giurgiu 75, Antal 81)*

Basle (3) 3 *(Frei F 10, Frei A 14, Streller 37)* 5787

Otelul: Grahovac; Sarghi, Salageanu, Rapa, Perendija, Giurgiu, Iorga (Ilie 67), Antal, Neagu (Viglianti 67), Filip, Pena.
Basle: Sommer; Steinhofer, Abraham, Park, Dragovic, Huggel (Cabral 44), Frei F, Shaqiri (Zoua 82), Xhaka G, Frei A (Chipperfield 74), Streller.

Wednesday, 7 December 2011

Basle (1) 2 *(Streller 9, Frei A 85)*

Manchester U (0) 1 *(Jones 89)* 36,000

Basle: Sommer; Steinhofer, Abraham, Park, Dragovic, Cabral, Frei F, Shiqiri (Stocker 90), Xhaka G (Chipperfield 83), Frei A (Kusunga 87), Streller.
Manchester U: De Gea; Smalling, Evra, Jones, Ferdinand, Vidic (Evans 44), Park (Macheda 82), Giggs, Nani, Rooney, Young (Welbeck 64).

Benfica (1) 1 *(Cardozo 7)*

Otelul (0) 0 35,155

Benfica: Artur Moraes; Garay, Emerson, Jardel, Aimar (Rodrigo 70), Javi Garcia, Witsel, Ruben Amorim, Gaitan, Bruno Cesar (Nolito 57), Cardozo (Saviola 79).
Otelul: Grahovac; Rapa, Perendija, Paraschiv, Giurgiu, Ilie (Ljubinkovic 21), Iorga, Antal (Frunza 81), Benga, Neagu (Pena 70), Filip.

Group C Table	*P*	*W*	*D*	*L*	*F*	*A*	*Pts*
Benfica	6	3	3	0	8	4	12
Basle	6	3	2	1	11	10	11
Manchester U	6	2	3	1	11	8	9
Otelul	6	0	0	6	3	11	0

GROUP D

Wednesday, 14 September 2011

Ajax (0) 0

Lyon (0) 0 49,504

Ajax: Vermeer; Vertonghen, Van der Wiel, Alderweireld, Boilesen, Janssen (Anita 70), De Jong, Eriksen, Sulejmani (Ebecilio 85), Sigthorsson (Bulykin 81), Boerrigter.
Lyon: Lloris; Reveillere, Cissokho, Kone, Lovren, Kallstrom, Michel Bastos, Grenier, Gonalons (Fofana 90), Gomis (Belfodil 85), Briand.

Dinamo Zagreb (0) 0

Real Madrid (0) 1 *(Di Maria 53)* 27,055

Dinamo Zagreb: Kelava; Tonel, Vida, Ibanez, Leko, Calello (Situm 87), Sammir, Tomecak, Badelj, Kovacic (Pokrivac 62), Rukavina (Beciraj 75).
Real Madrid: Casillas; Sergio Ramos, Ricardo Carvalho, Pepe, Fabio Coentrao, Marcelo■, Xabi Alonso, Ozil (Higuain 78), Di Maria (Diarra 78), Cristiano Ronaldo, Benzema (Arbeloa 82).

Tuesday, 27 September 2011

Lyon (2) 2 *(Gomis 23, Kone 42)*

Dinamo Zagreb (0) 0 34,432

Lyon: Lloris; Reveillere, Cissokho, Kone, Lovren, Kallstrom, Michel Bastos, Grenier (Pied 79), Gonalons, Gomis (Lacazette 63), Briand.
Dinamo Zagreb: Kelava; Tonel, Vida, Ibanez, Leko, Calello, Pokrivac (Rukavina 74), Sammir, Badelj (Tomecak 46), Kovacic (Simunic 46), Beciraj.

Real Madrid (2) 3 *(Cristiano Ronaldo 25, Kaka 41, Benzema 49)*

Ajax (0) 0 70,320

Real Madrid: Casillas; Sergio Ramos, Ricardo Carvalho, Arbeloa, Varane, Kaka (Di Maria 75), Xabi Alonso, Ozil (Hamit Altintop 84), Khedira, Cristiano Ronaldo, Benzema (Higuain 75).
Ajax: Vermeer; Vertonghen, Van der Wiel, Anita, Alderweireld, Janssen (Enoh 51), De Jong, Eriksen, Sulejmani (Ebecilio 71), Sigthorsson, Boerrigter (Serero 83).

Tuesday, 18 October 2011

Dinamo Zagreb (0) 0

Ajax (0) 2 *(Boerrigter 49, Eriksen 90)* 28,000

Dinamo Zagreb: Kelava; Simunic, Tonel, Vida, Ibanez, Leko, Calello (Tomecak 80), Sammir, Badelj (Kovacic 46), Rukavina, Beciraj (Pokrivac 70).
Ajax: Vermeer; Vertonghen, Van der Wiel, Anita, Alderweireld, Janssen, De Jong, Enoh, Eriksen (Lodeiro 90), Sulejmani, Boerrigter (Bulykin 70).

Real Madrid (1) 4 *(Benzema 19, Khedira 47, Lloris 55 (og), Sergio Ramos 81)*

Lyon (0) 0 76,102

Real Madrid: Casillas; Sergio Ramos, Pepe, Arbeloa, Marcelo, Xabi Alonso, Ozil (Kaka 66), Khedira (Fabio Coentrao 61), Di Maria, Cristiano Ronaldo, Benzema (Higuain 72).
Lyon: Lloris; Reveillere, Cissokho, Kone, Lovren, Kallstrom, Michel Bastos, Gourcuff (Ederson 66), Fofana, Gomis (Dabo 80), Briand.

Wednesday, 2 November 2011

Ajax (2) 4 *(Van der Wiel 20, Sulejmani 25, De Jong 65, Lodeiro 90)*

Dinamo Zagreb (0) 0 49,707

Ajax: Vermeer; Vertonghen, Van der Wiel, Anita, Alderweireld, Janssen, De Jong, Enoh, Eriksen (Lodeiro 80), Sulejmani (Lukoki 72), Boerrigter (Ebecilio 77).
Dinamo Zagreb: Kelava; Simunic, Vida, Ibanez, Leko, Calello (Tomecak 46), Sammir (Situm 72), Badelj, Vrsaljko, Kovacic, Rukavina (Beciraj 56).

Lyon (0) 0

Real Madrid (1) 2 *(Cristiano Ronaldo 24, 69 (pen))* 40,099

Lyon: Lloris; Cris, Dabo, Reveillere, Lovren (Kone 38), Kallstrom, Ederson (Belfodil 84), Gourcuff, Gonalons, Gomis (Lacazette 75), Briand.
Real Madrid: Casillas; Sergio Ramos, Pepe, Fabio Coentrao (Albiol 64), Xabi Alonso, Ozil, Diarra, Khedira, Di Maria (Jose Callejon 83), Cristiano Ronaldo, Benzema (Higuain 71).

Tuesday, 22 November 2011

Lyon (0) 0

Ajax (0) 0 35,070

Lyon: Lloris; Cris, Reveillere, Cissokho, Lovren, Kallstrom, Michel Bastos, Gourcuff, Gomis, Briand (Lacazette 85), Lopez (Ederson 73).
Ajax: Vermeer; Vertonghen, Van der Wiel (Blind 67), Anita, Alderweireld, Janssen, Lodeiro (Lukoki 89), Enoh, Eriksen, Sulejmani, Ebecilio (Klaassen 85).

Real Madrid (4) 6 *(Benzema 2, 66, Jose Callejon 6, 49, Higuain 9, Ozil 20)*

Dinamo Zagreb (0) 2 *(Beciraj 81, Tomecak 90)* 65,415

Real Madrid: Adan; Sergio Ramos (Albiol 46), Fabio Coentrao, Varane, Xabi Alonso (Granero 46), Nuri, Ozil (Hamit Altintop 46), Diarra, Jose Callejon, Benzema, Higuain.
Dinamo Zagreb: Kelava; Cufre, Tonel, Vida (Ademi 63), Ibanez, Calello, Sammir (Tomecak 82), Alispahic (Leko 46), Badelj, Kovacic, Beciraj.

Wednesday, 7 December 2011

Ajax (0) 0

Real Madrid (2) 3 *(Jose Callejon 14, 90, Higuain 41)* 51,557

Ajax: Vermeer; Vertonghen, Van der Wiel, Anita, Blind, Janssen (Klaassen 76), Lodeiro (Bulykin 74), Enoh, Eriksen, Sulejmani, Ebecilio.
Real Madrid: Adan; Albiol, Arbeloa (Pedro Mendes 67), Fabio Coentrao, Varane, Kaka, Nuri, Granero (Xabi Alonso 59), Jose Callejon, Benzema (Hamit Altintop 54), Higuain.

Dinamo Zagreb (1) 1 *(Kovacic 40)*

Lyon (1) 7 *(Gomis 45, 48, 52, 70, Gonalons 48, Lopez 65, Briand 76)* 16,457

Dinamo Zagreb: Kelava; Vida, Ibanez, Leko■, Calello, Sammir (Alispahic 66), Ademi, Badelj, Vrsaljko, Kovacic (Pokrivac 80), Beciraj (Situm 55).
Lyon: Lloris; Dabo, Cissokho, Kone, Lovren (Lopez 55), Gourcuff, Fofana, Gonalons, Gomis, Briand, Lacazette (Ederson 65).

Group D Table	*P*	*W*	*D*	*L*	*F*	*A*	*Pts*
Real Madrid	6	6	0	0	19	2	18
Lyon	6	2	2	2	9	7	8
Ajax	6	2	2	2	6	6	8
Dinamo Zagreb	6	0	0	6	3	22	0

GROUP E

Tuesday, 13 September 2011

Chelsea (0) 2 *(David Luiz 67, Mata 90)*

Leverkusen (0) 0 33,820

Chelsea: Cech; Bosingwa, Cole, Mikel, Ivanovic, David Luiz (Alex 76), Raul Meireles (Lampard 63), Mata, Torres, Sturridge (Anelka 64), Malouda.
Leverkusen: Leno; Kadlec, Reinartz, Toprak, Castro, Ballack (Renato Augusto 66), Rolfes, Sam (Derdiyok 73), Bender (Balitsch 80), Kiessling, Schurrle.

Genk (0) 0

Valencia (0) 0 20,248

Genk: Koteles; Simaeys, Ngongca, Tozser, Hubert, Pudil, Ndabashinze, Jose Nadson, Nwanganga (Ogunjimi 63), Buffel (Camus 85), Vossen (Barda 79).
Valencia: Diego Alves; Miguel, Mathieu, Rami, Victor Ruiz, Mehmet, Banega, Feghouli (Pablo Hernandez 69), Dani Parejo (Aduriz 74), Soldado, Piatti (Canales 79).

Wednesday, 28 September 2011

Leverkusen (1) 2 *(Bender 30, Ballack 90)*

Genk (0) 0 25,138

Leverkusen: Leno; Kadlec (Ballack 80), Reinartz, Toprak, Castro, Rolfes, Renato Augusto (Balitsch 65), Sam, Bender, Kiessling (Derdiyok 90), Schurrle.
Genk: Koteles; Simaeys, Ngongca, Tozser, Hubert (Nwanganga 78), Pudil, Jose Nadson (Hyland 69), De Bruyne, Buffel, Vossen (Barda 46), Ogunjimi.

Valencia (0) 1 *(Soldado 87 (pen))*

Chelsea (0) 1 *(Lampard 56)* 33,791

Valencia: Diego Alves; Miguel, Mathieu (Piatti 59), Rami, Jordi Alba, Victor Ruiz, Albelda, Banega (Jonas 73), Pablo Hernandez (Feghouli 73), Canales, Soldado.
Chelsea: Cech; Bosingwa, Cole, Mikel, Terry, David Luiz, Ramires (Raul Meireles 66), Lampard (Kalou 83), Torres (Anelka 72), Mata, Malouda.

Wednesday, 19 October 2011

Chelsea (4) 5 *(Raul Meireles 8, Torres 11, 27, Ivanovic 42, Kalou 72)*

Genk (0) 0 38,518

Chelsea: Cech; Bosingwa (Alex 78), Cole (Paulo Ferreira 46), Raul Meireles, Ivanovic, David Luiz, Romeu, Lampard (Kalou 68), Torres, Anelka, Malouda.
Genk: Koteles; Vanden Borre, Masuero (Camus 46), Ngongca, Tozser, Pudil, Hyland, De Bruyne, Buffel, Vossen (Nwanganga 81), Barda (Ndabashinze 71).

Leverkusen (0) 2 *(Schurrle 52, Sam 56)*

Valencia (1) 1 *(Jonas 24)* 26,384

Leverkusen: Leno; Kadlec, Reinartz (Friedrich 46), Omer, Castro, Ballack, Rolfes, Sam (Schwaab 90), Bender, Kiessling (Derdiyok 81), Schurrle.
Valencia: Diego Alves; Miguel, Mathieu, Rami, Jordi Alba (Canales 65), Victor Ruiz, Albelda (Aduriz 82), Banega, Pablo Hernandez (Feghouli 65), Soldado, Jonas.

Tuesday, 1 November 2011

Genk (0) 1 *(Vossen 61)*

Chelsea (1) 1 *(Ramires 26)* 22,584

Genk: Koteles; Vanden Borre, Ngongca, Tozser, Camus, Jose Nadson, Hyland, Nwanganga (Limbombe 82), De Bruyne, Buffel (Ndabashinze 69), Vossen (Barda 87).
Chelsea: Cech; Bosingwa, Cole, Ramires (Lampard 66), Ivanovic, David Luiz, Raul Meireles, Romeu (Mata 77), Torres, Anelka (Sturridge 66), Malouda.

Valencia (1) 3 *(Jonas 1, Soldado 65, Rami 75)*

Leverkusen (1) 1 *(Kiessling 31)* 37,047

Valencia: Diego Alves; Miguel, Mathieu, Rami, Victor Ruiz, Mehmet, Banega (Costa 24), Feghouli (Piatti 59), Pablo Hernandez, Soldado, Jonas (Jordi Alba 74).
Leverkusen: Leno; Friedrich, Kadlec, Omer, Castro, Ballack, Rolfes, Sam (Jorgensen 84), Bender (Reinartz 79), Kiessling (Derdiyok 77), Schurrle.

Wednesday, 23 November 2011

Leverkusen (0) 2 *(Derdiyok 73, Friedrich 90)*

Chelsea (0) 1 *(Drogba 48)* 29,285

Leverkusen: Leno; Friedrich, Kadlec (Derdiyok 71), Schwaab (Schurrle 57), Omer, Castro, Ballack, Rolfes, Sam, Bender, Kiessling (Oczipka 83).
Chelsea: Cech; Ivanovic, Bosingwa, Ramires, Terry, David Luiz (Alex 69), Raul Meireles (Mikel 80), Lampard, Sturridge, Drogba, Mata (Malouda 66).

Valencia (4) 7 *(Jonas 10, Soldado 13, 36, 39, Pablo Hernandez 68, Aduriz 70, Costa 81)*

Genk (0) 0 35,086

Valencia: Diego Alves; Miguel, Mathieu, Rami, Victor Ruiz (Dani Parejo 46), Mehmet, Costa, Feghouli (Piatti 57), Pablo Hernandez, Soldado (Aduriz 65), Jonas.
Genk: Koteles; Vanden Borre, Tozser, Camus, Pudil, Jose Nadson, Hyland (Limbombe 61), De Bruyne, Buffel, Vossen (Sarr 46), Barda (Nwanganga 71).

Tuesday, 6 December 2011

Chelsea (2) 3 *(Drogba 3, 76, Ramires 22)*

Valencia (0) 0 41,109

Chelsea: Cech; Ivanovic, Cole, Ramires (Mikel 65), Terry, David Luiz, Raul Meireles, Romeu, Sturridge, Drogba (Torres 78), Mata (Malouda 83).
Valencia: Diego Alves; Mathieu, Barragan, Rami, Jordi Alba (Aduriz 55), Victor Ruiz, Albelda, Costa (Dani Parejo 77), Feghouli (Pablo Hernandez 65), Soldado, Jonas.

Genk (1) 1 *(Vossen 30)*

Leverkusen (0) 1 *(Derdiyok 79)* 21,187

Genk: Koteles; Vanden Borre, Simaeys, Ngongca, Tozser, Camus, Pudil, Ndabashinze, Jose Nadson, Vossen (Barda 81), Limbombe (Buffel 75).
Leverkusen: Leno; Kadlec (Oczipka 73), Schwaab, Reinartz (Jorgensen 87), Castro, Ballack, Rolfes, Sam, Bender, Derdiyok, Schurrle (Kiessling 68).

Group E Table	P	W	D	L	F	A	Pts
Chelsea	6	3	2	1	13	4	11
Leverkusen	6	3	1	2	8	8	10
Valencia	6	2	2	2	12	7	8
Genk	6	0	3	3	2	16	3

GROUP F

Tuesday, 13 September 2011

Borussia Dortmund (0) 1 *(Perisic 88)*

Arsenal (1) 1 *(Van Persie 42)* 65,590

Borussia Dortmund: Weidenfeller; Hummels, Piszczek, Subotic, Schmelzer, Kehl (Blaszczykowski 68), Bender, Grosskreutz (Perisic 69), Gotze, Kagawa (Mohamed Zidan 85), Lewandowski.
Arsenal: Szczesny; Sagna, Gibbs, Song Billong, Mertesacker, Koscielny, Benayoun, Arteta, Walcott (Frimpong 77), Van Persie (Chamakh 86), Gervinho (Andre Santos 86).

Olympiakos (0) 0

Marseille (0) 1 *(Gonzalez 51)* 30,040

Olympiakos: Costanzo; Mellberg, Modesto, Holebas, Papadopoulos A, Torosidis, David Fuster (Ibagaza 67), Francisco Yeste (Djebbour 55), Abdoun, Fejsa (Makoun 67), Mirallas.
Marseille: Mandanda; Morel, Diawara, Traore, Azpilicueta, N'Koulou, Gonzalez (Kabore 76), Diarra, Amalfitano, Cheyrou (Fanni■ 81), Remy (Ayew J 68).

Wednesday, 28 September 2011

Arsenal (2) 2 *(Oxlade-Chamberlain 8, Andre Santos 20)*

Olympiakos (1) 1 *(David Fuster 27)* 59,676

Arsenal: Szczesny; Sagna, Andre Santos, Song Billong, Mertesacker, Frimpong, Arteta, Rosicky, Chamakh (Van Persie 71), Arshavin (Gibbs 83), Oxlade-Chamberlain (Ramsey 67).
Olympiakos: Costanzo; Mellberg, Holebas, Marcano, Torosidis, Ibagaza, David Fuster (Pantelic 79), Orbaiz (Modesto 75), Fejsa, Mirallas (Abdoun 75), Djebbour.

Marseille (1) 3 *(Ayew A 20, 69 (pen), Remy 62)*

Borussia Dortmund (0) 0 26,142

Marseille: Mandanda; Morel, Diawara, Azpilicueta, N'Koulou, Gonzalez (Amalfitano 73), Diarra, Valbuena, Kabore, Remy (Ayew J■ 72), Ayew A (Sabo 89).
Borussia Dortmund: Weidenfeller; Hummels, Piszczek, Subotic, Schmelzer, Kehl, Bender, Grosskreutz (Perisic 63), Gotze, Kagawa (Blaszczykowski 63), Lewandowski (Barrios 73).

Wednesday, 19 October 2011

Marseille (0) 0

Arsenal (0) 1 *(Ramsey 90)* 33,258

Marseille: Mandanda; Morel, Diawara, Azpilicueta, N'Koulou, Gonzalez (Amalfitano 73), Diarra, Cheyrou (Kabore 87), Valbuena, Remy (Gignac 69), Ayew A.
Arsenal: Szczesny; Jenkinson (Djourou 62), Andre Santos, Song Billong, Mertesacker, Koscielny, Arteta, Walcott (Gervinho 67), Arshavin (Ramsey 78), Van Persie, Rosicky.

Olympiakos (2) 3 *(Holebas 8, Djebbour 40, Modesto 78)*

Borussia Dortmund (1) 1 *(Lewandowski 26)* 29,638

Olympiakos: Costanzo; Mellberg, Modesto, Holebas, Papadopoulos A, Marcano, Makoun (Maniatis 73), Ibagaza, Orbaiz, Mirallas (Fetfatzidis 90), Djebbour (Pantelic 87).
Borussia Dortmund: Weidenfeller; Hummels, Piszczek, Subotic, Schmelzer, Perisic, Bender, Gundogan (Leitner 56), Gotze (Grosskreutz 81), Kagawa (Blaszczykowski 66), Lewandowski.

Tuesday, 1 November 2011

Arsenal (0) 0

Marseille (0) 0 59,961

Arsenal: Szczesny; Jenkinson, Andre Santos, Song Billong, Mertesacker, Vermaelen, Walcott, Ramsey (Rosicky 66), Gervinho (Arshavin 77), Park (Van Persie 62), Arteta.
Marseille: Mandanda; Morel, Fanni, Diawara, N'Koulou, Diarra, Cheyrou, Valbuena (Gonzalez 74), Remy (Amalfitano 68), Ayew A, Ayew J (Gignac 84).

Borussia Dortmund (1) 1 *(Grosskreutz 7)*

Olympiakos (0) 0 65,590

Borussia Dortmund: Weidenfeller; Hummels, Piszczek, Subotic, Schmelzer, Kehl, Perisic (Blaszczykowski 75), Grosskreutz, Gotze (Kagawa 66), Leitner (Felipe Santana 86), Lewandowski.
Olympiakos: Megyeri; Mellberg, Modesto, Holebas, Papadopoulos A, Marcano (Abdoun 67), Ibagaza (Pantelic 80), Orbaiz, Fejsa (Makoun 59), Mirallas, Djebbour.

Wednesday, 23 November 2011

Arsenal (0) 2 *(Van Persie 49, 86)*

Borussia Dortmund (0) 1 *(Kagawa 90)* 59,531

Arsenal: Szczesny; Koscielny (Djourou 83), Andre Santos, Song Billong, Mertesacker, Vermaelen, Walcott (Diaby 85), Ramsey, Gervinho (Benayoun 74), Van Persie, Arteta.
Borussia Dortmund: Weidenfeller; Hummels, Piszczek, Schmelzer, Felipe Santana, Kehl (Barrios 64), Bender (Leitner 25), Grosskreutz, Gotze (Perisic 28), Kagawa, Lewandowski.

Marseille (0) 0

Olympiakos (0) 1 *(Fetfatzidis 82)* 25,392

Marseille: Mandanda; Diawara, Traore, N'Koulou, Diarra, Cheyrou (M'Bia 61), Valbuena (Gonzalez 73), Kabore, Remy, Ayew A, Ayew J (Gignac 61).
Olympiakos: Megyeri; Mellberg, Modesto, Holebas (Fetfatzidis 75), Papadopoulos A, Marcano, Torosidis, Maniatis, David Fuster (Francisco Yeste 54), Mirallas, Djebbour (Potouridis 88).

Tuesday, 6 December 2011

Borussia Dortmund (2) 2 *(Blaszczykowski 23, Hummels 32 (pen))*

Marseille (1) 3 *(Remy 45, Ayew A 85, Valbuena 87)* 65,590

Borussia Dortmund: Weidenfeller; Hummels, Piszczek, Felipe Santana, Kehl (Antonio da Silva 32), Blaszczykowski, Lowe, Gundogan, Gotze (Perisic 46), Barrios (Kagawa 63), Lewandowski.
Marseille: Mandanda; Diawara, Traore, Azpilicueta, N'Koulou, Gonzalez (Ayew J 67), Diarra, Amalfitano, M'Bia (Cheyrou 46), Remy (Valbuena 73), Ayew A.

Olympiakos (2) 3 *(Djebbour 16, David Fuster 36, Modesto 89)*

Arsenal (0) 1 *(Benayoun 57)* 30,816

Olympiakos: Megyeri; Mellberg, Modesto, Holebas (Orbaiz 37), Papadopoulos A, Marcano, Torosidis, Maniatis, David Fuster (Abdoun 64), Mirallas, Djebbour (Papazoglou 90).
Arsenal: Fabianski (Mannone 25); Djourou, Andre Santos (Miquel 51), Coquelin (Rosicky 67), Squillaci, Vermaelen, Benayoun, Frimpong, Chamakh, Arshavin, Oxlade-Chamberlain.

Group F Table	P	W	D	L	F	A	Pts
Arsenal	6	3	1	2	7	6	11
Marseille	6	3	1	2	7	4	10
Olympiakos	6	3	0	3	8	6	9
Borussia Dortmund	6	1	1	4	6	12	4

GROUP G

Tuesday, 13 September 2011

Apoel (0) 2 *(Gustavo Manduca 72, Ailton Almeida 75)*

Zenit (0) 1 *(Zyryanov 63)* 21,269

Apoel: Chiotis; Paulo Jorge, Marcelo Oliveira, William, Poursaitidis (Solomou 74), Nuno Morais, Marcinho (Jahic 65), Gustavo Manduca (Alexandrou 89), Ailton Almeida, Helio Pinto, Trickovski.

Zenit: Malafeev; Bruno Alves■, Anyukov, Lombaerts, Criscito, Hubocan (Bukharov 89), Danny, Shirokov (Faizulin 75), Zyryanov (Lazovic 80), Denisov, Kerzhakov.

Porto (1) 2 *(Hulk 28, Kleber 51)*

Shakhtar Donetsk (1) 1 *(Luiz Adriano 13)* 36,612

Porto: Helton; Fucile, Pereira, Otamendi, Maicon, Defour, Joao Moutinho, Fernando (Belluschi 61), Hulk (Silvestre Varela 78), Rodriguez J, Kleber (Djalma 69).
Shakhtar Donetsk: Rybka; Srna, Chygrynskiy■, Rat, Rakitskiy■, Willian (Hubschman 82), Fernandinho, Jadson (Alex Teixeira 65), Mkhitaryan, Luiz Adriano, Eduardo Da Silva (Kucher 42).

Wednesday, 28 September 2011

Shakhtar Donetsk (0) 1 *(Jadson 64)*

Apoel (0) 1 *(Trickovski 61)* 47,014

Shakhtar Donetsk: Rybka; Srna, Kucher, Rat, Hubschman, Chizhov, Willian, Jadson (Eduardo Da Silva 81), Alex Teixeira (Douglas Costa 65), Mkhitaryan, Luiz Adriano (Seleznev 76).
Apoel: Chiotis; Paulo Jorge, Marcelo Oliveira, Jahic (Marcinho 58), William, Poursaitidis, Nuno Morais, Gustavo Manduca (Charalambidis 7), Ailton Almeida (Solari 77), Helio Pinto, Trickovski.

Zenit (1) 3 *(Shirokov 19, 63, Danny 72)*

Porto (1) 1 *(Rodriguez J 10)* 21,405

Zenit: Malafeev; Anyukov, Lombaerts, Criscito, Hubocan, Danny, Shirokov, Faizulin, Zyryanov (Huszti 86), Denisov, Kerzhakov (Bukharov 90).
Porto: Helton; Fucile■, Rolando, Pereira, Otamendi, Belluschi (Defour 72), Joao Moutinho, Fernando, Rodriguez J (Souza 46), Hulk, Kleber (Silvestre Varela 33).

Wednesday, 19 October 2011

Porto (1) 1 *(Hulk 13)*

Apoel (1) 1 *(Ailton Almeida 19)* 32,512

Porto: Helton; Sapunaru, Rolando, Pereira, Otamendi, Joao Moutinho (Defour 78), Guarin, Fernando (Belluschi 69), Rodriguez J (Silvestre Varela 69), Hulk, Kleber.
Apoel: Chiotis (Urko 52); Kaka, Marcelo Oliveira, William, Poursaitidis, Nuno Morais, Charalambidis, Gustavo Manduca (Jahic 72), Ailton Almeida, Helio Pinto, Trickovski (Adorno 90).

Shakhtar Donetsk (2) 2 *(Willian 15, Luiz Adriano 45)*

Zenit (1) 2 *(Shirokov 33, Faizulin 60)* 50,578

Shakhtar Donetsk: Rybka; Srna, Chygrynskiy, Rat, Hubschman, Chizhov (Kucher 73), Willian, Fernandinho, Jadson (Mkhitaryan 67), Douglas Costa (Alex Teixeira 75), Luiz Adriano.
Zenit: Malafeev; Bruno Alves, Lombaerts, Criscito, Hubocan, Danny, Shirokov, Faizulin, Zyryanov (Semak 90), Denisov, Bukharov (Lazovic 74).

Tuesday, 1 November 2011

Apoel (1) 2 *(Ailton Almeida 42 (pen), Gustavo Manduca 90)*

Porto (0) 1 *(Hulk 89 (pen))* 22,301

Apoel: Urko; Paulo Jorge, Marcelo Oliveira, Poursaitidis, Nuno Morais, Charalambidis, Solomou, Gustavo Manduca (Alexandrou 90), Ailton Almeida (Jahic 77), Helio Pinto, Trickovski (Solari 85).
Porto: Helton; Fucile, Rolando, Pereira, Mangala, Belluschi (Defour 76), Joao Moutinho, Fernando (Guarin 60), Silvestre Varela (Rodriguez J 60), Hulk, Kleber.

Zenit (1) 1 *(Lombaerts 45)*

Shakhtar Donetsk (0) 0 21,405

Zenit: Malafeev; Anyukov, Lombaerts, Criscito, Hubocan, Danny (Lazovic 85), Shirokov, Faizulin, Zyryanov, Denisov, Bukharov (Semak 81).
Shakhtar Donetsk: Rybka; Srna, Kucher, Hubschman, Shevchuk, Rakitskiy, Willian, Alex Teixeira (Douglas Costa 68), Mkhitaryan, Luiz Adriano (Seleznev 77), Eduardo Da Silva.

Wednesday, 23 November 2011

Shakhtar Donetsk (0) 0

Porto (0) 2 *(Hulk 79, Rat 90 (og))* 42,565

Shakhtar Donetsk: Rybka; Kucher, Rat, Hubschman, Rakitskiy, Willian (Alex Teixeira 69), Fernandinho, Kobin (Douglas Costa 87), Mkhitaryan, Luiz Adriano, Eduardo Da Silva (Jadson 59).
Porto: Helton; Rolando, Pereira, Otamendi, Maicon, Defour (Souza 88), Joao Moutinho, Fernando, Rodriguez J (Silvestre Varela 81), Djalma (Rodriguez C 73), Hulk.

Zenit (0) 0

Apoel (0) 0 21,500

Zenit: Malafeev; Anyukov, Lombaerts, Criscito, Hubocan, Danny, Shirokov (Lazovic 88), Faizulin, Zyryanov (Bystrov 55), Denisov, Bukharov.
Apoel: Urko; Paulo Jorge, Marcelo Oliveira, Nuno Morais, Charalambidis, Solomou, Alexandrou (Ilia 46), Gustavo Manduca, Ailton Almeida (Jahic 67), Helio Pinto, Trickovski (Adorno 90).

Tuesday, 6 December 2011

Apoel (0) 0

Shakhtar Donetsk (0) 2 *(Luiz Adriano 62, Seleznev 78)* 22,537

Apoel: Urko; Paulo Jorge, Marcelo Oliveira, Jahic, Poursaitidis, Nuno Morais, Marcinho (Belaid 60), Charalambidis (Adorno 77), Alexandrou, Gustavo Manduca (Solari 68), Trickovski.
Shakhtar Donetsk: Rybka; Srna, Kucher, Hubschman, Shevchuk, Rakitskiy, Willian (Moreno 84), Fernandinho, Mkhitaryan, Douglas Costa (Eduardo Da Silva 78), Luiz Adriano (Seleznev 73).

Porto (0) 0

Zenit (0) 0 46,512

Porto: Helton; Rolando, Pereira, Otamendi (Belluschi 82), Maicon, Defour (Kleber 46), Joao Moutinho, Fernando, Rodriguez J, Djalma (Silvestre Varela 68), Hulk.
Zenit: Malafeev; Anyukov, Lombaerts, Criscito, Hubocan, Semak, Danny, Shirokov (Zyryanov 46), Faizulin (Bystrov 57), Denisov, Lazovic (Bruno Alves 82).

Group G Table	*P*	*W*	*D*	*L*	*F*	*A*	*Pts*
Apoel	6	2	3	1	6	6	9
Zenit	6	2	3	1	7	5	9
Porto	6	2	2	2	7	7	8
Shakhtar Donetsk	6	1	2	3	6	8	5

GROUP H

Tuesday, 13 September 2011

Barcelona (1) 2 *(Pedro 36, David Villa 50)*

AC Milan (1) 2 *(Alexandre Pato 1, Thiago Silva 90)* 89,861

Barcelona: Valdes; Abidal, Dani Alves, Mascherano, Iniesta (Fabregas 39), Xavi, Keita (Puyol 67), Busquets, Messi, David Villa (Afellay 84), Pedro.
AC Milan: Abbiati; Nesta, Zambrotta, Thiago Silva, Abate, Van Bommel (Aquilani 77), Boateng (Ambrosini 34), Seedorf, Nocerino, Cassano (Emanuelson 62), Alexandre Pato.

Viktoria Plzen (1) 1 *(Bakos 45)*

BATE Borisov (0) 1 *(Renan 69)* 19,541

Viktoria Plzen: Cech; Cisovsky, Limbersky (Trapp 78), Bystron, Rajtoral, Petrzela (Duris 69), Kolar, Horvath, Pilar (Hora 88), Jiracek, Bakos.
BATE Borisov: Gutor; Filipenko, Bordachev, Simic, Baga, Renan (Kontsevoy 71), Volodko A, Rudik, Olekhnovich, Gordeychuk (Volodko M 83), Kezman (Alex 75).

Wednesday, 28 September 2011

AC Milan (0) 2 *(Ibrahimovic 53 (pen), Cassano 66)*

Viktoria Plzen (0) 0 66,859

AC Milan: Abbiati; Nesta, Antonini (Taiwo 78), Thiago Silva, Abate (Sciglio 87), Van Bommel, Emanuelson, Seedorf (Aquilani 71), Nocerino, Ibrahimovic, Cassano.
Viktoria Plzen: Cech; Cisovsky, Limbersky, Bystron, Rajtoral, Petrzela, Kolar (Darida 90), Horvath, Pilar (Fillo 76), Jiracek, Bakos (Duris 67).

BATE Borisov (0) 0

Barcelona (3) 5 *(Volodko A 19 (og), Pedro 22, Messi 38, 56, David Villa 90)* 29,555

BATE Borisov: Gutor; Filipenko, Bordachev, Simic, Baga, Renan (Kurlovich 82), Volodko A, Rudik (Aleksiyan 60), Olekhnovich, Kezman (Skavysh 56), Kontsevoy.
Barcelona: Valdes; Puyol, Abidal (Adriano Correia 61), Dani Alves, Mascherano, Xavi (Fabregas 59), Keita, Thiago Alcantara, Messi, David Villa, Pedro (Maxwell 69).

Wednesday, 19 October 2011

AC Milan (1) 2 *(Ibrahimovic 33, Boateng 70)*

BATE Borisov (0) 0 66,040

AC Milan: Abbiati; Nesta (Mexes 84), Taiwo, Bonera, Abate, Van Bommel, Boateng (Emanuelson 78), Aquilani, Nocerino, Ibrahimovic, Cassano (Robinho 62).
BATE Borisov: Gutor; Radkov, Yurevich, Bordachev, Simic, Likhtarovich (Olekhnovich 66), Baga, Renan (Pavlov 77), Volodko A, Kezman (Skavysh 71), Kontsevoy.

Barcelona (1) 2 *(Iniesta 10, David Villa 82)*

Viktora Plzen (0) 0 74,376

Barcelona: Valdes; Abidal, Dani Alves, Adriano Correia, Mascherano, Iniesta (Keita 85), Xavi, Busquets, Messi, David Villa (Cuenca 88), Pedro.
Viktora Plzen: Cech; Cisovsky, Limbersky, Bystron, Rajtoral, Petrzela (Darida 86), Kolar, Horvath, Pilar (Fillo 75), Jiracek, Bakos (Duris 57).

Tuesday, 1 November 2011

BATE Borisov (0) 1 *(Renan 55 (pen))*

AC Milan (1) 1 *(Ibrahimovic 22)* 29,100

BATE Borisov: Gutor; Radkov, Yurevich, Bordachev, Simic, Likhtarovich (Olekhnovich 63), Baga (Pavlov 76), Renan, Volodko A, Skavysh, Kontsevoy (Gordeychuk 84).
AC Milan: Abbiati; Nesta (Bonera 67), Taiwo, Thiago Silva, Abate, Boateng, Ambrosini, Aquilani (Seedorf 69), Nocerino, Robinho (Ganz 83), Ibrahimovic.

Viktoria Plzen (0) 0

Barcelona (2) 4 *(Messi 24 (pen), 45, 90, Fabregas 72)* 20,145

Viktoria Plzen: Pavlik; Cisovsky■, Limbersky, Bystron, Rajtoral, Petrzela, Kolar (Duris 68), Horvath (Reznik 78), Pilar, Jiracek, Bakos (Sevinsky 24).
Barcelona: Valdes; Puyol, Abidal (Sanchez 73), Dani Alves (Maxwell 71), Adriano Correia, Pique, Fabregas, Busquets (Keita 65), Thiago Alcantara, Messi, Cuenca.

Wednesday, 23 November 2011

AC Milan (1) 2 *(Ibrahimovic 20, Boateng 54)*

Barcelona (2) 3 *(Van Bommel 14 (og), Messi 31 (pen), Xavi 63)* 78,927

AC Milan: Abbiati; Nesta (Bonera 66), Zambrotta, Thiago Silva, Abate, Van Bommel (Nocerino 72), Boateng, Seedorf, Aquilani, Robinho (Alexandre Pato 46), Ibrahimovic.
Barcelona: Valdes; Puyol, Abidal, Mascherano, Fabregas (Pedro 80), Xavi, Keita, Busquets, Thiago Alcantara (Dos Santos 90), Messi, David Villa (Sanchez 68).

BATE Borisov (0) 0

Viktoria Plzen (1) 1 *(Bakos 42)* 26,520

BATE Borisov: Gutor; Filipenko, Yurevich, Bordachev, Simic, Baga, Renan, Volodko A, Pavlov (Gordeychuk 69), Skavysh (Kezman 77), Kontsevoy (Rudik 75).
Viktoria Plzen: Cech; Sevinsky, Limbersky, Bystron, Rajtoral, Petrzela (Fillo 83), Kolar, Horvath, Pilar (Reznik 90), Jiracek, Bakos (Duris 80).

Tuesday, 6 December 2011

Barcelona (1) 4 *(Sergi Roberto 35, Montoya 60, Pedro 63, 89 (pen))*

BATE Borisov (0) 0 37,374

Barcelona: Pinto; Maxwell, Fontas, Bartra, Montoya, Thiago Alcantara, Dos Santos (Muniesa 58), Sergi Roberto (Riverola 79), Rafinha (Gerard 70), Pedro, Cuenca.
BATE Borisov: Gutor; Filipenko, Yurevich, Bordachev, Simic, Likhtarovich (Olekhnovich 67), Baga, Renan (Kezman 77), Volodko A, Pavlov (Gordeychuk 64), Kontsevoy.

Viktoria Plzen (0) 2 *(Bystron 89, Duris 90)*

AC Milan (0) 2 *(Alexandre Pato 47, Robinho 48)* 19,854

Viktoria Plzen: Cech; Cisovsky, Limbersky, Bystron, Rajtoral, Petrzela, Kolar (Duris 67), Horvath, Pilar (Hora 84), Jiracek (Darida 28), Bakos.
AC Milan: Amelia; Taiwo (Zambrotta 90), Bonera, Mexes, Sciglio, Emanuelson, Seedorf, Ambrosini, Nocerino (Thiago Silva 40), Robinho (Cristante 81), Alexandre Pato.

Group H Table	*P*	*W*	*D*	*L*	*F*	*A*	*Pts*
Barcelona	6	5	1	0	20	4	16
AC Milan	6	2	3	1	11	8	9
Viktoria Plzen	6	1	2	3	4	11	5
BATE Borisov	6	0	2	4	2	14	2

KNOCK-OUT STAGE

KNOCK-OUT ROUND FIRST LEG

Tuesday, 14 February 2012

Leverkusen (0) 1 *(Kadlec 52)*

Barcelona (1) 3 *(Sanchez 41, 55, Messi 88)* 29,412

Leverkusen: Leno; Friedrich, Kadlec, Corluka (Da Costa 90), Schwaab, Reinartz, Castro, Rolfes (Kiessling 77), Renato Augusto, Bender, Schurrle (Bellarabi 90).
Barcelona: Valdes; Puyol, Abidal, Dani Alves, Adriano Correia (Pedro 70), Mascherano, Fabregas, Iniesta (Thiago Alcantara 61), Busquets, Messi, Sanchez (Cuenca 86).

Lyon (0) 1 *(Lacazette 58)*

Apoel (0) 0 32,010

Lyon: Lloris; Cris, Reveillere, Cissokho, Kone, Kallstrom, Ederson (Gourcuff 71), Michel Bastos, Gonalons, Lopez, Lacazette (Briand 58).
Apoel: Chiotis; Paulo Jorge, Kaka, William, Poursaitidis, Nuno Morais, Charalambidis (Gustavo Manduca 82), Helder Sousa (Marcinho 72), Ailton Almeida (Solari 67), Helio Pinto, Trickovski.

Wednesday, 15 February 2012

AC Milan (2) 4 *(Boateng 15, Robinho 38, 49, Ibrahimovic 79 (pen))*

Arsenal (0) 0 64,462

AC Milan: Abbiati; Mexes, Antonini, Thiago Silva, Abate, Van Bommel, Boateng (Ambrosini 70), Seedorf (Emanuelson 12), Nocerino, Robinho (Alexandre Pato 84), Ibrahimovic.
Arsenal: Szczesny; Sagna, Gibbs (Oxlade-Chamberlain 66), Song Billong, Vermaelen, Koscielny (Djourou 44), Arteta, Ramsey, Walcott (Henry 46), Van Persie, Rosicky.

Zenit (1) 3 *(Shirokov 27, 88, Semak 71)*

Benfica (1) 2 *(Pereira 20, Cardozo 87)* 18,200

Zenit: Zhevnov; Bruno Alves, Anyukov, Lombaerts, Hubocan, Shirokov, Faizulin (Rosina 89), Zyryanov (Semak 46), Denisov, Kerzhakov, Kanunnikov (Bystrov 66).
Benfica: Artur Moraes; Luisao, Garay, Emerson, Pereira, Witsel, Gaitan (Miguel Vitor 90), Matic, Bruno Cesar (Nolito 76), Cardozo, Rodrigo (Aimar 30).

Tuesday, 21 February 2012

CSKA Moscow (0) 1 *(Wernbloom 90)*

Real Madrid (1) 1 *(Cristiano Ronaldo 28)* 50,000

CSKA Moscow: Chepchugov; Berezutski V, Ignashevich, Berezutski A, Schennikov, Wernbloom, Aldonin (Honda 68), Dzagoev, Tosic (Necid 82), Doumbia, Musa (Oliseh 64).
Real Madrid: Casillas; Sergio Ramos, Pepe, Arbeloa, Fabio Coentrao, Xabi Alonso, Ozil (Albiol 85), Khedira, Jose Callejon (Kaka 75), Cristiano Ronaldo, Benzema (Higuain 16).

Napoli (2) 3 *(Lavezzi 39, 65, Cavani 45)*

Chelsea (1) 1 *(Mata 27)* 52,495

Napoli: De Sanctis; Aronica, Zuniga, Cannavaro, Campagnaro, Maggio, Gargano, Inler, Hamsik (Pandev 82), Cavani, Lavezzi (Dzemaili 74).
Chelsea: Cech; Bosingwa (Cole 12), Ivanovic, Ramires, Cahill, David Luiz, Raul Meireles (Essien 70), Sturridge, Drogba, Mata, Malouda (Lampard 70).

Wednesday, 22 February 2012

Basle (0) 1 *(Stocker 86)*

Bayern Munich (0) 0 36,000

Basle: Sommer; Steinhofer, Abraham, Park, Dragovic, Huggel, Frei F (Stocker 66), Shaqiri (Zoua 83), Xhaka G, Frei A (Cabral 90), Streller.
Bayern Munich: Neuer; Lahm, Rafinha, Boateng, Badstuber, Robben, Ribery (Muller 71), Tymoschuk, Kroos (Olic 89), Alaba, Gomez.

Marseille (0) 1 *(Ayew A 90)*

Internazionale (0) 0 37,646

Marseille: Mandanda; Morel, Diawara, Azpilicueta (Fanni 80), N'Koulou, Diarra, Amalfitano, Cheyrou (Kabore 84), Valbuena, Brandao (Ayew J 73), Ayew A.
Internazionale: Julio Cesar; Lucio, Zanetti, Maicon (Nagatomo 46), Samuel, Chivu, Sneijder, Cambiasso, Stankovic, Forlan, Zarate (Obi 64).

KNOCK-OUT ROUND SECOND LEG

Tuesday, 6 March 2012

Arsenal (3) 3 *(Koscielny 7, Rosicky 26, Van Persie 43 (pen))*

AC Milan (0) 0 59,973

Arsenal: Szczesny; Sagna, Gibbs, Song Billong, Vermaelen, Koscielny, Walcott (Park 84), Rosicky, Gervinho, Van Persie, Oxlade-Chamberlain (Chamakh 75).
AC Milan: Abbiati; Mexes, Thiago Silva, Abate, Van Bommel, Emanuelson, Mesbah (Bonera 90), Nocerino, Robinho, Ibrahimovic, El Shaarawy (Aquilani 70).

Benfica (1) 2 *(Pereira 45, Nelson Oliveira 90)*

Zenit (0) 0 48,909

Benfica: Artur Moraes; Luisao, Emerson, Pereira, Jardel, Javi Garcia, Witsel, Gaitan (Matic 72), Bruno Cesar, Cardozo (Nelson Oliveira 80), Rodrigo (Nolito 62).
Zenit: Malafeev; Anyukov (Bruno Alves 53), Lombaerts, Criscito, Hubocan, Bystrov (Lazovic 46), Semak, Shirokov, Zyryanov (Faizulin 70), Denisov, Kerzhakov.

Wednesday, 7 March 2012

Apoel (1) 1 *(Gustavo Manduca 9)*

Lyon (0) 0 18,500

Apoel: Chiotis; Paulo Jorge, Marcelo Oliveira, William, Poursaitidis, Nuno Morais, Charalambides (Marcinho 77), Helder Sousa (Alexandrou 94), Solari (Trickovski 74), Gustavo Manduca■, Ailton Almeida.
Lyon: Lloris; Cris, Reveillere, Cissokho, Kone, Kallstrom, Ederson (Gomis 73), Michel Bastos, Gonalons, Briand (Lacazette 100), Lopez.
aet; Apoel won 4-3 on penalties.

Arsenal's Laurent Koscielny scores against AC Milan during their Champions League last 16 second leg match at the Emirates Stadium in early March. Having lost the first leg 4-0 in Italy, Arsenal's 3-0 victory was a brave response to the deficit. (Reuters/Eddie Keogh)

Barcelona (2) 7 *(Messi 25, 42, 49, 58, 84, Tello 55, 62)*

Leverkusen (0) 1 *(Bellarabi 90)* 75,632

Barcelona: Valdes; Dani Alves, Adriano Correia (Muniesa 63), Pique, Mascherano, Fabregas, Iniesta (Tello 53), Xavi (Keita 53), Busquets, Messi, Pedro.
Leverkusen: Leno; Kadlec, Schwaab, Reinartz, Toprak, Castro, Rolfes, Renato Augusto (Oczipka 67), Bender (Schurrle 55), Kiessling, Derdiyok (Bellarabi 55).

Tuesday, 13 March 2012

Bayern Munich (3) 7 *(Robben 11, 81, Muller 42, Gomez 44, 50, 61, 67)*

Basle (0) 0 66,000

Bayern Munich: Neuer; Lahm, Boateng, Badstuber, Robben (Tymoschuk 82), Ribery (Pranjic 79), Luiz Gustavo, Kroos, Alaba, Gomez, Muller (Schweinsteiger 70).
Basle: Sommer; Steinhofer (Degen 70), Abraham, Park, Dragovic, Cabral, Frei F (Stocker 61), Shaqiri (Zoua 80), Xhaka G, Frei A, Streller.

Internazionale (0) 2 *(Milito 75, Pazzini 90 (pen))*

Marseille (0) 1 *(Brandao 89)* 62,632

Internazionale: Julio Cesar; Lucio, Zanetti, Maicon, Samuel, Nagatomo, Sneijder (Obi 58), Stankovic, Poli (Cambiasso 74), Forlan (Pazzini 58), Milito.
Marseille: Mandanda■; Morel, Diawara, Azpilicueta, N'Koulou, Diarra, Amalfitano, M'Bia, Valbuena (Cheyrou 76), Remy (Brandao 88), Ayew A (Bracigliano 90).

Wednesday, 14 March 2012

Chelsea (1) 4 *(Drogba 28, Terry 47, Lampard 75 (pen), Ivanovic 105)*

Napoli (0) 1 *(Inler 55)* 37,784

Chelsea: Cech; Ivanovic, Cole, Essien, Terry (Bosingwa 98), David Luiz, Ramires, Lampard, Sturridge (Torres 63), Drogba, Mata (Malouda 95).
Napoli: De Sanctis; Aronica (Vargas 110), Zuniga, Cannavaro, Campagnaro, Maggio (Dossena 37), Gargano, Inler, Hamsik (Pandev 106), Cavani, Lavezzi.
aet.

Real Madrid (1) 4 *(Higuain 26, Cristiano Ronaldo 55, 90, Benzema 70)*

CSKA Moscow (0) 1 *(Tosic 77)* 67,743

Real Madrid: Casillas; Sergio Ramos, Pepe, Arbeloa, Marcelo, Kaka (Granero 75), Xabi Alonso, Ozil (Diarra 88), Khedira, Cristiano Ronaldo, Higuain (Benzema 69).
CSKA Moscow: Chepchugov; Berezutski V, Ignashevich, Berezutski A, Schennikov, Wernbloom, Aldonin (Mamaev 46), Dzagoev, Tosic (Necid 81), Doumbia, Musa (Oliseh 60).

QUARTER-FINALS FIRST LEG

Tuesday, 27 March 2012

Apoel (0) 0

Real Madrid (0) 3 *(Benzema 74, 90, Kaka 82)* 22,385

Apoel: Chiotis; Paulo Jorge, Marcelo Oliveira (Kaka 13), William, Poursaitidis, Nuno Morais, Charalambides, Alexandrou (Helder Sousa 46), Ailton Almeida, Helio Pinto (Solari 72), Trickovski.
Real Madrid: Casillas; Sergio Ramos, Pepe, Arbeloa, Fabio Coentrao (Marcelo 64), Nuri (Grenero 84), Ozil, Khedira, Cristiano Ronaldo, Benzema, Higuain (Kaka 64).

Benfica (0) 0

Chelsea (0) 1 *(Kalou 75)* 60,830

Benfica: Artur Moraes; Luisao, Emerson, Pereira, Jardel, Aimar (Matic 69), Javi Garcia (Nolito 81), Witsel, Gaitan, Bruno Cesar (Rodrigo 69), Cardozo.
Chelsea: Cech; Paulo Ferreira (Bosingwa 80), Cole, Mikel, Terry, David Luiz, Raul Meireles (Lampard 68), Ramires, Torres, Kalou (Sturridge 82), Mata.

Wednesday, 28 March 2012

AC Milan (0) 0

Barcelona (0) 0 76,169

AC Milan: Abbiati; Nesta (Mesbah 74), Bonera, Mexes, Antonini, Boateng (Emanuelson 67), Seedorf, Ambrosini, Nocerino, Robinho (El Shaarawy 52), Ibrahimovic.
Barcelona: Valdes; Puyol, Dani Alves, Pique, Mascherano, Iniesta (Tello 65), Xavi, Keita, Busquets, Messi, Sanchez (Pedro 76).

Marseille (0) 0

Bayern Munich (1) 2 *(Gomez 44, Robben 69)* 31,683

Marseille: Elinton Andrade; Morel, Fanni, Azpilicueta, N'Koulou, Diarra (Cheyrou 71), Amalfitano (Brandao 68), M'Bia, Valbuena, Remy, Ayew A.
Bayern Munich: Neuer; Lahm, Boateng, Badstuber, Robben, Ribery (Pranjic 78), Luiz Gustavo, Kroos (Tymoschuk 63), Alaba, Gomez, Muller (Schweinsteiger 70).

QUARTER-FINALS SECOND LEG

Tuesday, 3 April 2012

Barcelona (2) 3 *(Messi 11 (pen), 41 (pen), Iniesta 53)*

AC Milan (1) 1 *(Nocerino 32)* 94,629

Barcelona: Valdes; Puyol, Dani Alves, Pique (Adriano Correia 75), Mascherano, Fabregas (Keita 78), Iniesta, Xavi (Thiago Alcantara 63), Busquets, Messi, Cuenca.
AC Milan: Abbiati; Nesta, Mexes, Antonini, Abate, Boateng (Alexandre Pato 69), Seedorf (Aquilani 61), Ambrosini, Nocerino, Robinho, Ibrahimovic.

Bayern Munich (2) 2 *(Olic 13, 37)*

Marseille (0) 0 66,000

Bayern Munich: Neuer; Lahm, Boateng, Badstuber, Ribery, Tymoschuk, Luiz Gustavo, Kroos (Pranjic 67), Alaba, Olic (Gomez 75), Muller (Rafinha 39).
Marseille: Mandanda; Morel (Amalfitano 46), Fanni, Azpilicueta, N'Koulou, Cheyrou, M'Bia, Valbuena, Remy (Kabore 63), Brandao (Gignac 74), Ayew A.

Wednesday, 4 April 2012

Chelsea (1) 2 *(Lampard 21 (pen), Raul Meireles 90)*

Benfica (0) 1 *(Javi Garcia 85)* 37,264

Chelsea: Cech; Ivanovic, Cole, Mikel, Terry (Cahill 60), David Luiz, Ramires, Lampard, Torres (Drogba 88), Kalou, Mata (Raul Meireles 79).
Benfica: Artur Moraes; Emerson, Pereira■, Capdevila, Aimar, Javi Garcia, Witsel, Gaitan (Yannick Djalo 61), Matic, Bruno Cesar (Rodrigo 72), Cardozo (Nelson Oliveira 57).

Real Madrid (2) 5 *(Cristiano Ronaldo 26, 75, Kaka 37, Jose Callejon 80, Di Maria 84)*

Apoel (0) 2 *(Gustavo Manduca 67, Solari 82 (pen))* 50,865

Real Madrid: Casillas; Sergio Ramos, Pepe, Marcelo (Jose Callejon 46), Varane, Kaka, Nuri, Hamit Altintop, Granero (Albiol 65), Cristiano Ronaldo, Higuain (Di Maria 55).
Apoel: Urko; Paulo Jorge, Kaka, William, Poursaitidis, Nuno Morais, Marcinho, Charalambidis, Gustavo Manduca (Adorno 68), Ailton Almeida (Solari 70), Helio Pinto (Satsias 78).

SEMI-FINALS FIRST LEG

Tuesday, 17 April 2012

Bayern Munich (1) 2 *(Ribery 17, Gomez 90)*

Real Madrid (0) 1 *(Ozil 53)* 66,000

Bayern Munich: Neuer; Lahm, Boateng, Badstuber, Robben, Schweinsteiger (Muller 61), Ribery, Luiz Gustavo, Kroos, Alaba, Gomez.
Real Madrid: Casillas; Sergio Ramos, Pepe, Arbeloa, Fabio Coentrao, Xabi Alonso, Ozil (Marcelo 69), Khedira, Di Maria (Granero 79), Cristiano Ronaldo, Benzema (Higuain 84).

Wednesday, 18 April 2012

Chelsea (1) 1 *(Drogba 45)*

Barcelona (0) 0 38,039

Chelsea: Cech; Ivanovic, Cole, Mikel, Terry, Cahill, Ramires (Bosingwa 88), Lampard, Drogba, Mata (Kalou 74), Raul Meireles.
Barcelona: Valdes; Puyol, Dani Alves, Adriano Correia, Mascherano, Fabregas (Thiago Alcantara 78), Iniesta, Xavi (Cuenca 87), Busquets, Messi, Sanchez (Pedro 66).

SEMI-FINALS SECOND LEG

Tuesday, 24 April 2012

Barcelona (2) 2 *(Busquets 35, Iniesta 43)*

Chelsea (1) 2 *(Ramires 45, Torres 90)* 95,845

Barcelona: Valdes; Puyol, Pique (Dani Alves 26), Mascherano, Fabregas (Keita 74), Iniesta, Xavi, Busquets, Messi, Sanchez, Cuenca (Tello 67).
Chelsea: Cech; Ivanovic, Cole, Mikel, Terry■, Cahill (Bosingwa 12), Ramires, Lampard, Drogba (Torres 80), Mata (Kalou 58), Raul Meireles.

Wednesday, 25 April 2012

Real Madrid (2) 2 *(Cristiano Ronaldo 6 (pen), 14)*

Bayern Munich (1) 1 *(Robben 27 (pen))* 71,654

Real Madrid: Casillas; Sergio Ramos, Pepe, Arbeloa, Marcelo, Xabi Alonso, Ozil (Granero 111), Khedira, Di Maria (Kaka 75), Cristiano Ronaldo, Benzema (Higuain 106).
Bayern Munich: Neuer; Lahm, Boateng, Badstuber, Robben, Schweinsteiger, Ribery (Muller 95), Luiz Gustavo, Kroos, Alaba, Gomez.
aet; Bayern Munich won 3-1 on penalties: Alaba scored; Ronaldo saved; Gomez scored; Kaka saved; Kroos saved; Xabi Alonso scored; Lahm saved; Sergio Ramos missed; Schweinsteiger scored.

UEFA CHAMPIONS LEAGUE FINAL

Saturday, 19 May 2012

(at Munich, 69,901)

Bayern Munich (0) 1 *(Muller 83)* **Chelsea (0) 1** *(Drogba 88)*

Bayern Munich: Neuer; Lahm, Boateng, Contento, Robben, Schweinsteiger, Ribery (Olic 97), Tymoshchuk, Kroos, Gomez, Muller (Van Buyten 87).

Chelsea: Cech; Bosingwa, Cole, Mikel, Cahill, David Luiz, Mata, Lampard, Drogba, Kalou (Torres 84), Bertrand (Malouda 73).

aet; Chelsea won 4-3 on penalties: Lahm scored; Mata saved; Gomez scored; David Luiz scored; Neuer scored; Lampard scored; Olic saved; Cole scored; Schweinsteiger saved; Drogba scored.

Referee: Proenca (Portugal).

Chelsea's Didier Drogba scores the winning spot kick in the shoot-out to defeat Bayern Munich in the Champions League Final, played coincidentally at Bayern's Allianz Arena. Drogba had earlier scored an 88th minute equaliser to take the game into extra time. Chelsea then won 4-3 on penalties. (PA)

EUROPEAN CUP-WINNERS' CUP FINALS 1961–99

Year	Winners		Runners-up		Venue	Attendance	Referee
1961	Fiorentina	2	Rangers	0 *(1st Leg)*	Glasgow	80,000	Steiner (A)
	Fiorentina	2	Rangers	1 *(2nd Leg)*	Florence	50,000	Hernadi (H)
1962	Atletico Madrid	1	Fiorentina	1	Glasgow	27,389	Wharton (S)
Replay	Atletico Madrid	3	Fiorentina	0	Stuttgart	38,000	Tschenscher (WG)
1963	Tottenham Hotspur	5	Atletico Madrid	1	Rotterdam	49,000	Van Leuwen (Ho)
1964	Sporting Lisbon	3	MTK Budapest	3 *(aet)*	Brussels	3000	Van Nuffel (Bel)
Replay	Sporting Lisbon	1	MTK Budapest	0	Antwerp	19,000	Versyp (Bel)
1965	West Ham U	2	Munich 1860	0	Wembley	100,000	Szolt (H)
1966	Borussia Dortmund	2	Liverpool	1 *(aet)*	Glasgow	41,657	Schwinte (F)
1967	Bayern Munich	1	Rangers	0 *(aet)*	Nuremberg	69,480	Lo Bello (I)
1968	AC Milan	2	Hamburg	0	Rotterdam	53,000	Ortiz (Sp)
1969	Slovan Bratislava	3	Barcelona	2	Basle	19,000	Van Ravens (Ho)
1970	Manchester C	2	Gornik Zabrze	1	Vienna	8,000	Schiller (A)
1971	Chelsea	1	Real Madrid	1 *(aet)*	Athens	42,000	Scheurer (Sw)
Replay	Chelsea	2	Real Madrid	1 *(aet)*	Athens	35,000	Bucheli (Sw)
1972	Rangers	3	Moscow Dynamo	2	Barcelona	24,000	Ortiz (Sp)
1973	AC Milan	1	Leeds U	0	Salonika	45,000	Mihas (Gr)
1974	Magdeburg	2	AC Milan	0	Rotterdam	4000	Van Gemert (Ho)
1975	Dynamo Kiev	3	Ferencvaros	0	Basle	13,000	Davidson (S)
1976	Anderlecht	4	West Ham U	2	Brussels	58,000	Wurtz (F)
1977	Hamburg	2	Anderlecht	0	Amsterdam	65,000	Partridge (E)
1978	Anderlecht	4	Austria/WAC	0	Paris	48,679	Adlinger (WG)
1979	Barcelona	4	Fortuna Dusseldorf	3 *(aet)*	Basle	58,000	Palotai (H)
1980	Valencia	0	Arsenal	0	Brussels	36,000	Christov (Cz)
	(aet; Valencia won 5-4 on penalties)						
1981	Dynamo Tbilisi	2	Carl Zeiss Jena	1	Dusseldorf	9000	Lattanzi (I)
1982	Barcelona	2	Standard Liege	1	Barcelona	100,000	Eschweiler (WG)
1983	Aberdeen	2	Real Madrid	1 *(aet)*	Gothenburg	17,804	Menegali (I)
1984	Juventus	2	Porto	1	Basle	60,000	Prokop (EG)
1985	Everton	3	Rapid Vienna	1	Rotterdam	50,000	Casarin (I)
1986	Dynamo Kiev	3	Atletico Madrid	0	Lyon	39,300	Wohrer (A)
1987	Ajax	1	Lokomotiv Leipzig	0	Athens	35,000	Agnolin (I)
1988	Mechelen	1	Ajax	0	Strasbourg	39,446	Pauly (WG)
1989	Barcelona	2	Sampdoria	0	Berne	45,000	Courtney (E)
1990	Sampdoria	2	Anderlecht	0	Gothenburg	20,103	Galler (Sw)
1991	Manchester U	2	Barcelona	1	Rotterdam	42,000	Karlsson (Se)
1992	Werder Bremen	2	Monaco	0	Lisbon	16,000	D'Elia (I)
1993	Parma	3	Antwerp	1	Wembley	37,393	Assenmacher (G)
1994	Arsenal	1	Parma	0	Copenhagen	33,765	Krondl (CzR)
1995	Zaragoza	2	Arsenal	1	Paris	42,424	Ceccarini (I)
1996	Paris St Germain	1	Rapid Vienna	0	Brussels	37,500	Pairetto (I)
1997	Barcelona	1	Paris St Germain	0	Rotterdam	45,000	Merk (G)
1998	Chelsea	1	Stuttgart	0	Stockholm	30,216	Braschi (I)
1999	Lazio	2	Mallorca	1	Villa Park	33,021	Benko (A)

INTER-CITIES FAIRS CUP FINALS 1958–71

(Winners in italics)

Year	First Leg	Attendance	Second Leg	Attendance
1958	London 2 Barcelona 2	45,466	*Barcelona* 6 London 0	62,000
1960	Birmingham C 0 Barcelona 0	40,500	*Barcelona* 4 Birmingham C 1	70,000
1961	Birmingham C 2 Roma 2	21,005	*Roma* 2 Birmingham C 0	60,000
1962	Valencia 6 Barcelona 2	65,000	Barcelona 1 *Valencia* 1	60,000
1963	Dynamo Zagreb 1 Valencia 2	40,000	*Valencia* 2 Dynamo Zagreb 0	55,000
1964	*Zaragoza* 2 Valencia 1	50,000	(in Barcelona)	
1965	*Ferencvaros* 1 Juventus 0	25,000	(in Turin)	
1966	Barcelona 0 Zaragoza 1	70,000	Zaragoza 2 *Barcelona* 4	70,000
1967	Dynamo Zagreb 2 Leeds U 0	40,000	Leeds U 0 *Dynamo Zagreb* 0	35,604
1968	Leeds U 1 Ferencvaros 0	25,368	Ferencvaros 0 *Leeds U* 0	70,000
1969	Newcastle U 3 Ujpest Dozsa 0	60,000	Ujpest Dozsa 2 *Newcastle U* 3	37,000
1970	Anderlecht 3 Arsenal 1	37,000	*Arsenal* 3 Anderlecht 0	51,612
1971	Juventus 0 Leeds U 0 *(abandoned 51 minutes)*	42,000		
	Juventus 2 Leeds U 2	42,000	*Leeds U* 1* Juventus 1	42,483

UEFA CUP FINALS 1972–97

(Winners in italics)

Year	First Leg	Attendance	Second Leg	Attendance
1972	Wolverhampton W 1 Tottenham H 2	45,000	*Tottenham H* 1 Wolverhampton W 1	48,000
1973	Liverpool 0 Moenchengladbach 0 *(abandoned 27 minutes)*	44,967		
	Liverpool 3 Moenchengladbach 0	41,169	Moenchengladbach 2 *Liverpool* 0	35,000
1974	Tottenham H 2 Feyenoord 2	46,281	*Feyenoord* 2 Tottenham H 0	68,000
1975	Moenchengladbach 0 Twente 0	45,000	Twente 1 *Moenchengladbach* 5	24,500
1976	Liverpool 3 FC Brugge 2	56,000	FC Brugge 1 *Liverpool* 1	32,000
1977	Juventus 1 Athletic Bilbao 0	75,000	Athletic Bilbao 2 *Juventus* 1*	43,000
1978	Bastia 0 PSV Eindhoven 0	15,000	*PSV Eindhoven* 3 Bastia 0	27,000
1979	Red Star Belgrade 1 Moenchengladbach 1	87,500	*Moenchengladbach* 1 Red Star Belgrade 0	45,000
1980	Moenchengladbach 3 Eintracht Frankfurt 2	25,000	*Eintracht Frankfurt* 1* Moenchengladbach 0	60,000
1981	Ipswich T 3 AZ 67 Alkmaar 0	27,532	AZ 67 Alkmaar 4 *Ipswich T* 2	28,500
1982	Gothenburg 1 Hamburg 0	42,548	Hamburg 0 *Gothenburg* 3	60,000
1983	Anderlecht 1 Benfica 0	45,000	Benfica 1 *Anderlecht* 1	80,000
1984	Anderlecht 1 Tottenham H 1	40,000	*Tottenham H* 1[1] Anderlecht 1	46,258
1985	Videoton 0 Real Madrid 3	30,000	*Real Madrid* 0 Videoton 1	98,300
1986	Real Madrid 5 Cologne 1	80,000	Cologne 2 *Real Madrid* 0	15,000
1987	Gothenburg 1 Dundee U 0	50,023	Dundee U 1 *Gothenburg* 1	20,911
1988	Espanol 3 Bayer Leverkusen 0	42,000	*Bayer Leverkusen* 3[2] Espanol 0	22,000
1989	Napoli 2 Stuttgart 1	83,000	Stuttgart 3 *Napoli* 3	67,000
1990	Juventus 3 Fiorentina 1	45,000	Fiorentina 0 *Juventus* 0	32,000
1991	Internazionale 2 Roma 0	68,887	Roma 1 *Internazionale* 0	70,901
1992	Torino 2 Ajax 2	65,377	*Ajax* 0* Torino 0	40,000
1993	Borussia Dortmund 1 Juventus 3	37,000	*Juventus* 3 Borussia Dortmund 0	62,781
1994	Salzburg 0 Internazionale 1	47,500	*Internazionale* 1 Salzburg 0	80,326
1995	Parma 1 Juventus 0	23,000	Juventus 1 *Parma* 1	80,750
1996	Bayern Munich 2 Bordeaux 0	62,000	Bordeaux 1 *Bayern Munich* 3	36,000
1997	Schalke 1 Internazionale 0	56,824	Internazionale 1 *Schalke* 0[3]	81,670

**won on away goals* [1]*aet; Tottenham H won 4-3 on penalties* [2]*aet; Bayer Leverkusen won 3-2 on penalties*
[3]*aet; Schalke won 4-1 on penalties*

UEFA CUP FINALS 1998–2009

Year	Winners		Runners-up		Venue	Attendance	Referee
1998	Internazionale	3	Lazio	0	Paris	42,938	Nieto (Sp)
1999	Parma	3	Marseille	0	Moscow	61,000	Dallas (S)
2000	Galatasaray *(aet; Galatasaray won 4-1 on penalties)*	0	Arsenal	0	Copenhagen	38,919	Nieto (Sp)
2001	Liverpool *(aet; Liverpool won on sudden death)*	5	Alaves	4	Dortmund	65,000	Veissiere (F)
2002	Feyenoord	3	Borussia Dortmund	2	Rotterdam	45,000	Pereira (P)
2003	Porto *(aet)*	3	Celtic	2	Seville	52,972	Michel (Slo)
2004	Valencia	2	Marseille	0	Gothenburg	40,000	Collina (I)
2005	CSKA Moscow	3	Sporting Lisbon	1	Lisbon	48,000	Poll (E)
2006	Sevilla	4	Middlesbrough	0	Eindhoven	36,500	Fandel (G)
2007	Sevilla *(aet; Sevilla won 3-1 on penalties)*	2	Espanyol	2	Glasgow	50,670	Busacca (Sw)
2008	Zenit St Petersburg	2	Rangers	0	Manchester	43,878	Fröjdfeldt (Se)
2009	Shakhtar Donetsk *(aet)*	2	Werder Bremen	1	Istanbul	40,000	Chantalejo (Sp)

UEFA EUROPA LEAGUE FINALS 2010–12

Year	Winners		Runners-up		Venue	Attendance	Referee
2010	Atletico Madrid *(aet)*	2	Fulham	1	Hamburg	49,000	Rizzoli (I)
2011	Porto	1	Braga	0	Dublin	45,391	Carballo (Sp)
2012	Atletico Madrid	3	Athletic Bilbao	0	Bucharest	52,347	Stark (G)

UEFA EUROPA LEAGUE 2011–12

■ *Denotes player sent off.*

FIRST QUALIFYING ROUND FIRST LEG

Thursday, 30 June 2011

Aalesund (2) 4 *(Fuhre 35, Olsen M 37, Ulvestad 48 (pen), Sellin 77)*

Neath Ath (1) 1 *(Trundle 23)* 3847

Aalesund: Sandqvist; Arnefjord, Jaager, Tollas, Fuhre (Phillips 58), Barrantes, Olsen M (Flotre 78), Morrison, Ulvestad, Okoronkwo (Sellin 58), Parr.
Neath Ath: Kendall; Harris, Lewis, Hillier (Cummings 44), O'Leary, Collins, Fowler, Trundle, Jones C (Rees 86), Morgan (Hughes 53), Bowen.

Banants (0) 0

Metalurgi Rustavi (0) 1 *(Kobalia 48)* 4215

Banants: Nepogodov; Artur Yedigaryan, Daghbashyan (Petrosyan 46), Artashes Arakelyan, Hambardzumyan, Khachatryan, Dashyan, Voskanyan, Balabekan, Nor Gyozalyan (Du Bala 46), Bruno Correa (Sujyan 62).
Metalurgi Rustavi: Batiashvili; Orbeladze, Japaridze, Kvakhadze, Makhviladze, Maisuradze (Pavliashvili 84), Razmadze, Getsadze (Kavtaradze 74), Modebadze, Tkemaladze (Mikaberidze 90), Kobalia■.

Banga (0) 0

Karabakh (2) 4 *(Rashad A Sadygov 16, Nadirov 33, 70, Soltanov 88)* 1400

Banga: Pocius; Zelmikas, Usachev, Gudauskas, Urbaitis (Ostap 46) (Kulbis 60), Padaigis, Choruzijus (Kazlauskas 52), Tatiefang, Kura, Lipskis, Ekwegwo.
Karabakh: Pavlovic; Rashad F Sadygov, Teli, Medvedev, Agolli, Gurbanov (Soltanov 71), Rashad A Sadygov, Yusifov, Nedzipi (Garayev 80), Adamia (Imamaliyev 83), Nadirov.

Birkirkara (0) 0

Vllaznia (1) 1 *(Sukaj 2)* 776

Birkirkara: Jorge Mora; Zerafa (Grech 46), Buhagiar, Agius, Savinovs, Sciberras, Fenech P, De Cesare, Cilia, Muscat (Tabone 63), Camilli (David Silva 81).
Vllaznia: Vujadinovic; Alechenwu, Rajovic, Smajlaj, Sykaj, Popovic, Belisha, Nallbani, Vajushi (Shtubina 81), Gocaj (Hasani 88), Sukaj (Nimani 90).

Buducnost (0) 1 *(Boskovic 53)*

Flamurtari (1) 3 *(Shehaj 23, Xhafaj 63, Sakaj 65 (pen))* 2980

Buducnost: Dragojevic; Radovic, Golubovic (Padovic 64), Radunovic, Vukcevic P, Cicmil, Vukcevic NP, Onguene (Orahovac 73), Adrovic (Flavio 46), Boskovic, Mugosa.
Flamurtari: Mocka; Ahmataj, Sakaj, Veliu, Arberi (Grami 70), Licaj, Begaj, Kuqi, Lena, Xhafaj (Cutra 89), Shehaj (Idrizaj 57).

Daugava (0) 0

Tromso (2) 5 *(Johansen 26, Andersen 31, 60, Jenssen 47, Jama 72)* 1500

Daugava: Eltermanis; Simonovs, Shelenkov, Timofejevs, Tsintsadze, Afanasjevs, Logins (Kotyukov 72), Zizilevs (Vorobjovs 64), Kovalovs, Sokolovs, Ghonghadze (Kokins 53).
Tromso: Sahlmann; Bjorck, Yndestad (Nystrom 52), Norbye, Mbodji, Ciss, Jenssen, Andersen, Johansen, Abdellaoue (Moller 73), Drage (Jama 62).

Dinamo Tbilisi (1) 2 *(Kvekveskiri 4, Lekvtadze 71)*

Milsami Orhei (0) 0 12,000

Dinamo Tbilisi: Loria; Tomashvili, Rekhviashvili, Kakubava, Kvekveskiri, Odikadze, Koshkadze (Beraia 85), Lekvtadze, Jighauri, Robertinho (Tekturmanidze 64), Pantskhava (Akhalaia 72).
Milsami Orhei: Moraru; Stadiiciuc, Ionescu, Garla (Roman 84), Sosnovschi, Ademar, Grigoruta (Ochinca 68), Furdui, Mendizov, Boghiu, Bezimov (Traore 70).

Elfsborg (3) 4 *(Hiljemark 5, Elm 24, 90, Larsson 36)*

Fola Esch (0) 0 2109

Elfsborg: Christiansen; Karlsson, Andersson M, Augustsson, Svensson, Mobaeck, Ishizaki, Hult (Keene 55), Larsson (Yarsuvat 80), Hiljemark (Nordmark 55), Elm.
Fola Esch: Besic; Schnell, Geisbusch (Veiga 46), Ronny Souto, Carlos Helena, Christophe Pazos, Dallevedove (Mazurier 62), Klein, Kitenge, Boulahfari (Caldieri 77), Hornuss.

Ferencvaros (2) 3 *(Jozsi 31, Otten 33, Felipe Almeida 69)*

Ulisses (0) 0 6600

Ferencvaros: Ranilovic; Otten, Gruz, Fulop (Balog 73), Jozsi (Csizmadia 77), Maroti, Junior Ailton, Abdi, Andrezinho, Aleksandar Jovanovic, Olah (Felipe Almeida 63).
Ulisses: Malkov; Andrikyan, Ugrekhelidze, Hakhnazaryan, Grigoryan D (Jikia 55), Bareghamyan, Krasovski, Pato (Sahakyan 50), Adamyan, Grigoryan AG, Zokou (Nranyan 75).

Fulham (1) 3 *(Duff 33, Murphy 61 (pen), Johnson A 70)*

NSI (0) 0 14,910

Fulham: Schwarzer; Baird, Briggs, Murphy, Hughes, Hangeland, Duff, Etuhu (Sidwell 74), Johnson A, Zamora (Dalla Valle 79), Davies (Riise B 69).
NSI: Gango; Joensen, Mikkelsen, Danielsen (Frederiksberg A 78), Lakjuni, Hansen J, Mortensen (Olsen M 86), Jacobsen C, Petersen H, Frederiksberg J, Olsen K (Liknargotu 90).

Honka (0) 0

Kalju (0) 0 2100

Honka: Maanoja; Heilala, Heikkila, Aalto, Vasara, Aijala, Schuller, Tammilehto, Vayrynen (Koskinen 68), Dudu, Savage.
Kalju: Kutt; Koogas, Barengrub, Gutierrez, Puri, Kallaste, Viikmae, Konsa, Jevdokimov (Rantanen 82), Neemelo, Wakui (Mitsuyama 89).

IBV (0) 1 *(Andri Olafsson 50 (pen))*

St Patrick's Ath (0) 0 555

IBV: Saevarsson; Olafsson F, Christiansen, Garner, Valdimarsson, Sigurbjornsson, Andri Olafsson (Hughes 78), Mellor, Gudmundsson (Borgthorsson 86), Mawejje, Sytnik (Thorarinsson 74).
St Patrick's Ath: Rogers; Pender, Bermingham, Shortall, McMillan, Bradley, Mulcahy (Murphy 84), Doyle, Crowley (McFaul 61), North (Daly 76), Kavanagh.

IF (1) 1 *(Lakjuni 8)*

KR (2) 3 *(Finnbogason 22, Gudmundur Gunnarsson 30, Sigurdsson B 79)* 589

IF: Mikkelsen; Aki Petersen, Eliasen, Ellingsgaard J, Petersen U, Zachariasen (Ellingsgaard A 88), Jovevic (Frank Poulsen 72), Lakjuni, Lokin B, Lokin K, Saric (Lambanum 84).
KR: Halldorsson; Fridgeirsson (Josepsson 90), Gudmundur Gunnarsson, Sigurdarson, Amarsson, Gudjonsson (Olafsson 82), Sigurdsson B, Hauksson, Finnbogason (Jonsson G 69), Ludviksson, Baldvinsson.

Jagiellonia (0) 1 *(Frankowski 80)*

Irtysh (0) 0 4200

Jagiellonia: Sandomierski; Bartczak, Skerla, Norambuena, Thiago Rangel, Hermes (Seratlic 46), Burkhardt (Rogerio Maycon 88), Grzyb, Plizga (Makuszewski 73), Kupisz, Frankowski.
Irtysh: Tsirin; Coulibaly, Kuchma, Danaev, Mikhaylyuk■, Asanbaev (Zarechniy 46), Sergienko, Govedarica, Ivanov, Shabalin (Maltsev 86), Daskalov (Nikolic 77).

Kaerjeng (0) 1 *(Da Cruz 85)*

Hacken (0) 1 *(Ostberg 90)* 727

Kaerjeng: Winckel; Da Costa, Ramdedovic, Heller, Binsfeld, Sabotic, Martins (Fiorani 78), Rolandi (Andres 84), Corral, Piron (Da Cruz 65), Marinelli.
Hacken: Kallqvist; Ostberg, Forsell, Soderberg, Khan, Anklev (Williams 66), Chatto, Makondele, Elvby (Nystrom 87), Chibuike (Waris 86), Ranegie.

Koper (0) 1 *(Bubanja 84)*

Shakhtar (0) 1 *(Kukeyev 90 (pen))* 2500

Koper: Hasic; Dukic, Handanagic, Hadzic, Aljaz Struna (Marijanovic 88), Blazic, Vassiljev, Stojanovic (Karic 72), Guberac, Osterc, Bunderla (Bubanja 80).
Shakhtar: Mokin; Vasiljevic, Utabaev, Dzidic, Baizhanov, Kukeyev, Vicius, Konysbaev, Borantaev, Khizhnichenko (Dosmanbetov 90), Finonchenko (Raskovic 85).

Olimpik (1) 1 *(Ibekoyi 14)*

Minsk (1) 1 *(Voronkov 11)* 2900

Olimpik: Hasanzade; Krjauklis, Nabiyev, Nduka, Petrov, Benouahi, Khalilov (Kvirtia 71), Limani, Ikedia (Garayev 77), Krastovchev (Mammadov 46), Ibekoyi.
Minsk: Skinderis; Pjatrauskas, Razin, Sashcheko (Gigevich 90), Shegrikovich, Soro, Voronkov (Osipovich 73), Rakhmanov, Sachivko, Loshankov, Vasilyuk (Zenko 83).

Rad (4) 6 *(Stanojevic 6 (pen), 13, Valentini F 9 (og), Mrkela 24, Kojic 48, Prso 66)*

Tre Penne (0) 0 1500

Rad: Danilovic; Pajovic, Lekovic, Mitrovic, Pantic, Andric (Malbasic 75), Prso, Milivojevic (Raspopovic 80), Stanojevic, Mrkela, Kojic (Varga 70).
Tre Penne: Valentini F; Valentini S (Gasperoni 51), Zavoli, Raggini, Bonini, Cibelli, Francesconi■, Palazzi, Rossi (Chiaruzzi 59), Cardini, Pignieri (Valli 72).

Renova (1) 2 *(Janchevski 14 (pen), Bajrami 87)*

Glentoran (1) 1 *(Nixon 45)* 1500

Renova: Elezi; Stepanovski M, Stepanovski K (Simovski 47), Bajrami, Emini, Nuhiu F, Ristov, Statovci, Gashi, Trajkovski (Fetai 81), Janchevski (Ismaili 47).
Glentoran: Morris■; Nixon, Hill, Ward, McGovern■, Taylor, Clarke, Cherry (McGuigan 81), O'Hanlon (Murray 57), Boyce, Waterworth (Gibson 85).

Siroki (0) 0

Olimpija (0) 0 3500

Siroki: Bacak; Bertosa, Dzidic, Renato, Coric, Wagner, Silic, Serdarusic (Misic 46), Ivankovic, Zakaric (Varea 77), Roskam (Pinjuh A 77).
Olimpija: Dzafic; Sretenovic, Salkic, Andelkovic, Vrsic, Lovrecic, Skerjanc, Ivelja, Radujko, Fink (Omladic 78), Valencic (Besic■ 71).

Spartak Trnava (1) 3 *(Kone 29, Kascak 48, Tomacek 81)*

Zeta (0) 0 1737

Spartak Trnava: Raska; Gross, Diallo, Carnota, Kascak, Prochazka, Petras, Ciprys (Sabo 62), Bernath (Tomacek 46), Machovec, Kone (Gogolak 80).
Zeta: Ivanovic; Petrovic, Kaluderovic, Novovic, Zlaticanin, Pelicic, Burzanovic (Knezevic 53), Bozovic (Ladic 78), Dosljak, Korac, Skuletic.

The New Saints (1) 1 *(Darlington 26)*

Cliftonville (1) 1 *(Johnston 39)* 927

The New Saints: Harrison; Spender, Evans, Baker, Marriott, Jones, Ruscoe (Hogan 61), Edwards, Williams C (Partridge 71), Darlington, Sharp (Draper 74).
Cliftonville: Brown; Smyth, Seydak (Scannell 57), McVeigh, Catney, Johnston, McMullan (Lynch 75), Donnelly M, Caldwell, Garrett, Donnelly R (Gormley 52).

Trans (1) 1 *(Epikhin 34)*

Rabotnicki (1) 4 *(Velkoski K 15, Manevski 51, Petkovski 73, Grozdanovski 88)* 200

Trans: Vyalchinov; Kitto, Rimas, Grigorjev, Kazakov (Plotnikov 61), Bezykornovas, Bazjukin (Strockis 59), Cekulajevs, Leontovits (Fjodorov 55), Abramenko, Epikhin.
Rabotnicki: Dimitrievski; Kumbev, Stojanov (Petkovski 69), Lazarevski, Manevski (Angelov 90), Grozdanovski, Todorovski, Bogdanovic, Vujcic, Petrovic (Micevski 82), Velkoski K.

UE Santa Coloma (0) 0

Paksi (1) 1 *(Vayer 14)* 650

UE Santa Coloma: Rivas; Soria, Rubio, Codina, Roca, Martinez, Sirvan, Aloy (Lopez 90), Rodriguez (Blazquez 85), Luis Miguel, Bernat.
Paksi: Csernyanszki; Csehi, Eger, Heffler T, Fiola, Sifter, Bode (Kiss 68), Magasfoldi (Hrepka 68), Sipeki, Bartha (Haraszti 77), Vayer.

Varazdin (2) 5 *(Safaric N 4, 59, Glavica 40, Glavina 57, Vugrinec 78)*

Lusitanos (0) 1 *(Bertran 49)* 1200

Varazdin: Krklec; Susac, Brlecic (Grgec 77), Tkalcic (Antolic 59), Glavina, Safaric N, Simek, Conjar, Aganovic, Glavica (Pajac■ 65), Vugrinec.
Lusitanos: Benitez; Meza, Leonel Antunes, Fontan, Hugo Veloso (Reis 38), Bruno Silva, Bertran (Marinho 60), Pinto, Soares, Charles (Ferreira 67), Raya.

FIRST QUALIFYING ROUND SECOND LEG

Thursday, 7 July 2011

Cliftonville (0) 0

The New Saints (1) 1 *(Baker 4)* 1221

Cliftonville: Brown; Symth, Seydak, McVeigh, Catney (Scannell 73), Johnston, McMullan, Donnelly M, Caldwell, Garrett (Steele 85), Donnelly R (Gormley 53).
The New Saints: Harrison; Spender, Evans, Baker (Johnson 38), Marriott, Jones, Hogan, Ruscoe, Partridge (Williams C 64), Draper (Sharp 80), Williams M.

Flamurtari (1) 1 *(Shehaj 20)*

Buducnost (0) 2 *(Boskovic 72, 77 (pen))* 4000

Flamurtari: Mocka; Ahmataj, Sakaj, Veliu, Arberi (Licaj 59), Brahja, Begaj (Grami 71), Kuqi, Lena, Xhafaj, Shehaj (Idrizaj 61).
Buducnost: Dragojevic; Dikanovic, Radunovic, Tatar, Vukcevic P (Golubovic 59), Cicmil, Vukcevic NP, Onguene (Adrovic 71), Orahovac, Boskovic, Nikac (Flavio 64).

Fola Esch (0) 1 *(Alomerovic 74)*

Elfsborg (1) 1 *(Schnell 37 (og))* 703

Fola Esch: Besic; Schnell, Ronny Souto (Mazurier 58), Carlos Helena, Christophe Pazos (Caldieri 75), Dallevedove, Alomerovic, Veiga, Klein, Kitenge (Boulahfari 65), Hornuss.
Elfsborg: Christiansen; Karlsson, Jonsson, Augustsson (Klarstrom 67), Mobaeck, Ishizaki (Yarsuvat 46), Nordmark, Hiljemark (Larsson 57), Elm, Johansson, Jawo.

Glentoran (1) 2 *(Clarke 31, Murray 74)*

Renova (0) 1 *(Ismaili 59)* 1424

Glentoran: Hogg; Nixon, Hill, Ward, Johnny Taylor, O'Kane (Carson 62), Clarke, Cherry (Howland 106), O'Hanlon (Murray 71), Boyce, Waterworth.
Renova: Elezi; Stepanovski M, Simovski, Bajrami (Gafuri 90), Emini, Nuhiu F, Ristov, Statovci, Gashi (Janchevski■ 52), Trajkovski, Ismaili.
Glentoran won 3-2 on penalties.

Hacken (2) 5 *(Makonele 7 (pen), 82 (pen), Waris 42, Williams 65, Ranegie 84)*

Kaerjeng (0) 1 *(Da Cruz 48)* 934

Hacken: Kallqvist; Ostberg, Arkivuo, Soderberg, Joza, Anklev (Elvby 12), Chatto (Bjurstrom 78), Makondele, Nystrom, Williams (Ranegie 66), Waris.
Kaerjeng: Winckel; Leite, Ramdedovic, Heller, Binsfeld (Fiorani 81), Sabotic, Martins, Rolandi (Piron 60), Da Cruz, Corral (Andres 60), Marinelli.

Irtysh (2) 2 *(Coulibaly 37, Maltsev 43)*

Jagiellonia (0) 0 9560

Irtysh: Tsirin; Coulibaly, Kuchma, Chernyshov, Zarechniy (Siminidi 90), Danaev, Sergienko, Govedarica, Maltsev (Tleshev 62), Ivanov, Daskalov (Nikolic 79).
Jagiellonia: Sandomierski; Bartczak (Sidqy 57), Skerla, Norambuena, Thiago Rangel, Hermes (Burkhardt 46), Grzyb, Plizga, Kupisz, Rogerio Maycon (Frankowski 46), Seratlic.

Kalju (0) 0

Honka (0) 2 *(Savage 48, Dudu 77)* 2250

Kalju: Kutt; Koogas, Barengrub, Gutierrez, Puri, Kallaste, Rantanen (Viikmae 73), Konsa, Jevdokimov, Neemelo, Wakui.
Honka: Maanoja; Koskinen, Heilala, Heikkila, Aalto, Vasara (Otaru 75), Aijala, Schuller (Simpanen 83), Tammilehto, Dudu, Savage.

Karabakh (2) 3 *(Teli 29, Rashad A Sadygov 35, Agolli 77)*

Banga (0) 0 10,000

Karabakh: Veliyev; Rashad F Sadygov, Teli, Medvedev, Agolli, Rashad A Sadygov, Yusifov (Garayev 46), Ismayilov, Adamia, Nadirov (Isgandarov 70), Aliyev (Soltanov 59).
Banga: Pocius; Zelmikas, Usachev (Ratkus 86), Kazlauskas, Urbaitis, Padaigis, Bitinas, Kura (Gudauskas 68), Lipskis, Gailius (Kulbis 55), Bagdonas.

KR (2) 5 *(Baldvinsson 18, 56, Jonsson B 23, Finnbogason 47, Hauksson 90)*

IF (0) 1 *(Saric 88)* 877

KR: Halldorsson; Gunnar Gunnarsson, Fridgeirsson, Gudjonsson (Olafsson 38), Sigurdsson B, Hauksson, Jordao Diogo, Jonsson B (Gudmundur Gunnarsson 68), Finnbogason, Ludviksson (Josepsson 56), Baldvinsson.
IF: Mikkelsen; Aki Petersen, Eliasen, Ellingsgaard J, Petersen U (Lokin K 60), Zachariasen, Jovevic (Lambanum 60), Lakjuni, Lokin B, Muomaife (Frank Poulsen 71), Saric.

Lusitanos (0) 0

Varazdin (0) 1 *(Brlecic 62)* 450

Lusitanos: Benitez; Meza (Hugo Veloso 34), Leonel Antunes, Fontan, Peire, Martins, Bertran, Pinto, Soares (Maicon 61), Reis, Raya (Pereira 75).
Varazdin: Krklec (Mrmic 76); Susac, Brlecic, Tkalcic, Glavina, Safaric■, Simek, Conjar, Aganovic, Glavica (Antolic 68), Grgec (Gluhak 57).

Metalurgi Rustavi (1) 1 *(Mikaberidze 18)*

Banants (0) 1 *(Du Bala 72 (pen))* 3500

Metalurgi Rustavi: Batiashvili; Orbeladze, Japaridze, Kvakhadze, Makhviladze, Maisuradze, Razmadze, Getsadze (Pavliashvili 79), Modebadze, Tkemaladze (Aburjania 90), Mikaberidze (Kavtaradze 39).
Banants: Nepogodov; Artur Yedigaryan, Artashes Arakelyan (Daghbashyan 34), Hambardzumyan, Khachatryan, Petrosyan, Dashyan, Voskanyan (Bruno Correa 66), Sujyan (Hovhannisyan 58), Balabekyan, Du Bala.

Milsami Orhei (0) 1 *(Golban 90)*

Dinamo Tbilisi (0) 3 *(Koshkadze 73, Robertinho 89 (pen), 90)* 3000

Milsami Orhei: Moraru; Andronic, Stadiiciuc, Ionescu, Garla (Caio Suguino 82), Sosnovschi, Ademar (Golban 70), Grigoruta (Stoica 83), Furdui■, Mendizov, Boghiu.
Dinamo Tbilisi: Loria; Tomashvili, Rekhviashvili, Kakubava, Kvekveskiri, Odikadze, Koshkadze (Homola 79), Beraia (Jighauri 46), Lekvtadze (Kakhelishvili 65), Robertinho, Akhalaia.

Minsk (2) 2 *(Loshankov 5, Sashcheko 10)*

Olimpik (0) 1 *(Sachivko 66 (og))* 3000

Minsk: Skinderis; Osipovich, Razin, Sashcheko (Gigevich 78), Shegrikovic, Soro, Voronkov, Rakhmanov, Sachivko, Loshankov (Navikas 83), Zenko (Vasilyuk 68).
Olimpik: Hasanzade; Nabiyev, Nduka■, Petrov, Benouahi, Khalilov (Ikedia 46), Akhundov, Kvirtia, Limani (Mammadov 79), Krastovchev, Ibekoyi.

Neath Ath (0) 0

Aalesund (0) 2 *(Barrantes 53, Olsen M 79)* 600

Neath Ath: Kendall; Harris, Rees, Lewis, Hillier, O'Leary, Collins, Fowler (Jones C 63), Trundle, Hughes (Morgan 57), Bowen (Preen 83).
Aalesund: Sandqvist; Arnefjord, Skiri, Jalasto, Skagestad, Barrantes (Ulvestad 85), Larsen, Olsen M (Sandnes 81), Okoronkwo, Parr, Phillips (Flotre 58).

NSI (0) 0

Fulham (0) 0 1245

NSI: Gango; Hansen E, Joensen, Lakjuni, Hansen J, Mortensen (Danielsen 84), Petersen H, Toronjadze (Frederiksberg A 90), Frederiksberg J, Olsen K (Mikkelsen 90), Jacobsen C.
Fulham: Schwarzer; Kelly, Briggs, Sidwell, Senderos, Hangeland, Duff (Dalla Valle 86), Etuhu, Johnson A (Frei 72), Zamora, Greening (Riise B 76).

Olimpija (2) 3 *(Radujko 15, 18, Vrsic 49)*

Siroki (0) 0 4500

Olimpija: Dzafic; Sretenovic, Salkic, Andelkovic, Vrsic, Lovrecic (Ranic 72), Skerjanc, Radujko, Fink (Omladic 46), Jovic, Valencic (Smiljanic 85).
Siroki: Bacak; Bertosa, Dzidic, Renato, Coric, Wagner, Silic■, Ivankovic, Zakaric, Roskam, Misic (Pinjuh A 46).

Paksi (1) 4 *(Magasfoldi 11, 49, Bode 77, Heffler N 81)*

UE Santa Coloma (0) 0 2000

Paksi: Csernyanszki; Eger, Heffler T, Fiola, Sifter, Balo, Bode, Magasfoldi, Sipeki (Nagy 78), Bartha (Hrepka 69), Vayer (Heffler N 69).
UE Santa Coloma: Rivas; Soria, Rubio, Codina (Goncalves 63), Roca, Martinez, Sirvan, Aloy (Pedescoll 70), Rodriguez (Guida 75), Luis Miguel, Bernat.

Rabotnicki (1) 3 *(Petrovic 45, Manevski 81, Petkovski 90)*

Trans (0) 0 700

Rabotnicki: Dimitrievski; Kumbev, Stojanov, Lazarevski, Manevski, Grozdanovski (Angelov 83), Todorovski, Bogdanovic (Velkoski D 67), Vujcic, Petrovic (Petkovski 61), Velkoski K.
Trans: Vyalchinov; Kitto, Strockis, Rimas, Grigorjev, Bezykornovas, Bazjukin (Gruznov 64), Cekulajevs, Leontovits (Plotnikov 68), Abramenko, Epikhin (Fjodorov 59).

Shakhtar (1) 2 *(Konysbaev 45, 84)*

Koper (1) 1 *(Osterc 32)* 10,000

Shakhtar: Mokin; Kirov, Vasiljevic, Utabaev, Dzidic, Baizhanov, Kukeyev, Vicius, Konysbaev (Borovskiy 90), Khizhnichenko (Dosmanbetov 90), Finonchenko (Raskovic 89).
Koper: Hasic; Dukic, Handanagic, Hadzic (Karic 58), Aljaz Struna, Blazic, Vassiljev, Stojanovic (Stancic 67), Guberac, Osterc, Bubanja (Bunderla 79).

St Patrick's Ath (2) 2 *(Daly 24, Doyle 36)*

IBV (0) 0 2100

St Patrick's Ath: Rogers; Pender, Bermingham, Shortall (Murphy 84), McMillan E, Bradley, Doyle, McFaul, North (McMillan D 87), Kavanagh, Daly (Crowley 76).
IBV: Dhaira; Olafsson F (Hughes 74), Christiansen, Garner, Valdimarsson (Thorarinsson 81), Sigurbjornsson, Jeffs (Sytnik 62), Andri Olafsson, Mellor, Gudmundsson, Mawejje.

Tre Penne (1) 1 *(Cardini 32)*

Rad (2) 3 *(Kojic 27, 38, Stanojevic 75)* 521

Tre Penne: Valentini F; Macerata, Mikhaylovskiy, Raggini, Gasperoni (Olivieri 81), Bonini, Cibelli, Chiaruzzi, Cardini, Valli (Nanni 61), Pignieri (Di Giuli 72).
Rad: Danilovic; Pajovic (Randelovic 73), Lekovic, Mitrovic, Pantic (Raspopovic 79), Andric, Jovanovic (Prso 45), Milivojevic, Stanojevic, Mrkela, Kojic.

Tromso (1) 2 *(Moller 12, Tsintsadze 53 (og))*

Daugava (1) 1 *(Ghonghadze 33)* 2077

Tromso: Malmkvist; Bjorck, Norbye, Mbodji (Drage 57), Ciss, Rinde, Jenssen (Frantzen 77), Andersen, Nystrom, Jama, Moller (Johansen 57).
Daugava: Nerugals; Ulyanov, Kotyukov (Radevics 71), Chikhradze, Timotejevs, Tsintsadze, Afanasjevs, Logins, Kovalovs (Kokins 58), Sokolovs, Ghonghadze.

Ulisses (0) 0

Ferencvaros (1) 2 *(Abdi 34 (pen), Olah 90)* 1500

Ulisses: Malkov; Andrikyan, Ugrekhelidze (Manasyan 88), Hakhnazaryan, Sahakyan (Nranyan 88), Bareghamyan, Krasovski, Adamyan (Grigoryan D 59), Jikia, Grigoryan AG, Zokou.
Ferencvaros: Ranilovic; Otten, Balog, Gruz, Maroti (Rosa 46), Junior Ailton, Abdi (Olah 63), Andrezinho, Jovanovic, Felipe Almeida, Morales (Csizmadia 60).

Vllaznia (1) 1 *(Vajushi 4)*

Birkirkara (1) 1 *(David Silva 17)* 5000

Vllaznia: Vujadinovic; Alechenwu, Rajovic, Smajlaj, Sykaj, Popovic (Sinani 63), Belisha, Nallbani (Hasani 85), Vajushi, Gocaj (Shtubina 46), Sukaj.
Birkirkara: Jorge Mora; Zerafa, Buhagiar, Savinovs, Sciberras, Fenech P, Cilia (Tabone 66), Grech, Muscat, Camilli (Camenzuli 75), David Silva.

Zeta (0) 2 *(Dabic 79, Novovic 81)*

Spartak Trnava (0) 1 *(Ciprys 90)* 650

Zeta: Ivanovic; Petrovic, Kaluderovic, Radulovic MB (Dabic 75), Novovic, Zlaticanin, Pelicic (Dosljak 56), Burzanovic, Bozovic, Ladic (Kalacevic 64), Knezevic.
Spartak Trnava: Raska; Gross, Diallo, Carnota, Kascak, Prochazka, Petras, Machovec, Kone (Gogolak 46) (Banovic 86), Sabo■, Tomacek (Ciprys 70).

SECOND QUALIFYING ROUND FIRST LEG

Thursday, 14 July 2011

Anorthosis (2) 3 *(Vucicevic 9, Rezek 35, 71)*

Gagra (0) 0 6450

Anorthosis: Kozacik; Leiwakabessy, Sprockel, Tomasic, Colin, Janicio, Okkas (Andic 88), Rezek, Vucicevic, Evandro Roncatto (Laban 37), Laborde (Sielis 66).
Gagra: Sepiashvili; Tkeshelashvili, Sichinava (Koberidze 60), Kalandadze, Chkhetiani, Jishkariani, Khutsidze, Sharikadze (Chkuaseli 86), Nakonechniy (Gabedava 67), Kvantaliani, Ordynskyi.

Crusaders (0) 1 *(Adamson 54)*

Fulham (1) 3 *(Briggs 39, Zamora 74, Murphy 77 (pen))* 2477

Crusaders: O'Neill; McCann, Leeman, Magowan, McBride, McKeown, Watson (Faulkner 86), Dallas (Gargan 71), Adamson, Owens (Rainey 83), McMaster.
Fulham: Schwarzer; Baird, Briggs, Murphy, Hughes, Hangeland, Duff (Donegan 86), Etuhu (Sidwell 80), Johnson A (Riise B 79), Zamora, Frei.

Differdange (0) 0

Levadia (0) 0 674

Differdange: Weber; Rodrigues, Bukvic, Janisch, Kettenmeyer, Lebresne, Bettmer (Er Rafik 88), Leoni, Siebenaler, Caron, Franzoni (Piskor 77).
Levadia: Smisko; Kalimullin, Morozov, Teniste, Sarunas, Leitan, Nahk, Novikov (Volodin 57), Subbotin, Mizigurskis (Toomet 59), Pebre.

Domzale (0) 1 *(Pekic 47 (pen))*

Split (1) 2 *(Cop 41, Vitaic 76)* 1000

Domzale: Vidmar; Zec, Knezovic, Elsner, Apatic, Juninho, Drevensek (Geric 64), Teinovic, Aziri (Vuk 46), Pekic (Zadnikar 65), Horvat.
Split: Vukovic; Krizanac, Marcic, Vidic, Budisa, Vitaic, Simic, Erceg, Baraban (Rasic 72), Cop (Rebic 63), Golubovic (Barisic 88).

EB/Streymur (0) 1 *(Hansen A 90)*

Karabakh (1) 1 *(Aliyev 11)* 735

EB/Streymur: Torgard; Bo, Hansen G, Niclasen (Arnar Dam 80), Alex Santos, Samuelsen, Hansen P, Jacobsen, Udsen (Hanssen 70), Anghel, Hansen A.
Karabakh: Pavlovic; Rashad F Sadygov, Teli, Medvedev, Agolli, Rashad A Sadygov, Yusifov, Ismayilov, Adamia, Nadirov, Aliyev (Soltanov 70).

Ferencvaros (1) 2 *(Olah 38, Abdi 56)*

Aalesund (1) 1 *(Okoronkwo 27)* 8000

Ferencvaros: Ranilovic; Otten, Gruz, Fulop, Jozsi (Morales 65), Maroti, Junior Ailton, Abdi (Rosa 78), Andrezinho, Jovanovic, Olah (Felipe Almeida 64).
Aalesund: Grytebust; Arnefjord, Jaager, Tollas, Skagestad (Olsen M 74), Barrantes, Morrison, Ulvestad, Okoronkwo (Myklebust 62), Parr (Jalasto 67), Sellin.

FH (0) 1 *(Bjarnason 67)*

Nacional (1) 1 *(Edgar Costa 45)* 1140

FH: Gunnleifsson; Bjarnason, Vidarsson, Asgeirsson, Runarsson (Gunnlaugsson 84), Sverrisson, Bjornsson, Snorrason (Gudmundsson V 89), Gudnason (Sigurdsson H 73), Vilhjalmsson, Hallfredsson.
Nacional: Elisson; Felipe Lopes, Danielson, Nuno Pinto, Claudemir, Luis Alberto, Mihelic, Skolnik, Mateus, Candeias (Anselmo 68), Edgar Costa (Marcio Madeira 85).

Flamutari (0) 0

Jablonec (0) 2 *(Lafata 70, 76)* 2700

Flamutari: Mocka (Spaho 82); Ahmataj, Sakaj, Veliu, Arberi, Brahja, Begaj (Progni 56), Kuqi, Lena, Xhafaj, Shehaj (Idrizaj 76).
Jablonec: Spit; Benes, Jablonsky, Pitak, Pavlik, Jarolim, Loucka, Elias, Kovarik (Novak 63), Kopic (Vosahlik 72), Lafata (Tresnak 85).

Floriana (0) 0

AEK Larnaca (5) 8 *(Mrdakovic 4, Pavlou 12, Gonzalo Garcia 22, 42, 53, Linssen 36, Ruben Gomez 74, Mitidis 84)* 851

Floriana: Towns; Paris, Farrugia T, Bugeja, Doffo, Cassar, Joseph Borg (Borg C 56), Caruana (Darmanin 61), Micallef, Alcorse, Edilson.
AEK Larnaca: Alexandre Negri; Hofland, Dimech, Albert Serran, Van Dijk, Linssen, Pavlou (Mitidis 70), Priso, Demetriou, Gonzalo Garcia (Ruben Gomez 59), Mrdakovic (Kingsley 59).

Glentoran (0) 0

Vorskla (2) 2 *(Bezus 29, Januzi 38)* 1527

Glentoran: Hogg; Hill, McGovern, Martyn (O'Kane 75), Howland, Carson (O'Hanlon 75), Cherry, Boyce (Burrows 79), Gibson, Waterworth, Murray.
Vorskla: Velichko; Selin, Kurilov, Dallku, Chesnakov, Zakarlyuka (Oberemko 65), Kryvosheenko, Krasnoperov, Januzi, Osipenko (Rebenok 77), Bezus (Chichikov 82).

Hacken (1) 1 *(Ranegie 36 (pen))*

Honka (0) 0 448

Hacken: Kallqvist; Ostberg, Arkivuo, Soderberg, Chatto, Makondele (Waris 79), Nystrom, Elvby, Chibuike (Henriksson 70), Frolund, Ranegie.
Honka: Maanoja; Koskinen, Heilala, Heikkila, Aalto, Vasara (Otaru 79), Aijala, Schuller, Tammilehto, Dudu (Puustinen 87), Savage.

Iskra-Stal (1) 1 *(Ponomar 17)*

Varazdin (1) 1 *(Tkalcic 12)* 1200

Iskra-Stal: Melenciuc; Leshchuk, Uzbek, Novicov, Rudac, Porfireanu, Gorodetchi, Kourouma, Vishnyakov (Truhanov 70), Ponomar (Zacon 46), Suchu (Chebotarev 66).
Varazdin: Krklec; Susac, Brlecic, Tkalcic, Glavina, Simek, Conjar, Puncec, Glavica (Golubar 68), Vugrinec, Sacer (Aganovic 55).

Juvenes/Dogana (0) 0

Rabotnicki (0) 1 *(Petkovski 86)* 311

Juvenes/Dogana: Manzaroli; Selva, Bacciocchi, Cervellini, Frino, Ceci (Colombini E 67), Santini (Zafferani 90), Gasperoni■, Caminati (Casadei 78), Cavalli, Friguglietti.
Rabotnicki: Dimitrievski; Kumbev, Stojanov, Lazarevski, Manevski (Skenderovic 84), Todorovski, Bogdanovic (Petkovski 59), Vujcic, Petrovic (Trajkovski 75), Velkoski K, Velkoski D.

Kecskemeti (1) 1 *(Radanovic 23)*

Aktobe (0) 1 *(Mane 59)* 3400

Kecskemeti: Nemeth; Balogh, Radanovic, Mohl, Bori, Ebala, Kethevoama, Cukic (Savic 72), Litsingi (Gyurcso 63), Alempijevic, Dosso (Attila Simon 46).
Aktobe: Sidelnikov; Kenzhisariev (Badlo 87), Smakov, Chichulin, Primus, Kostic, Khayrullin, Logvinenko (Khokhlov 85), Averchenko (Maletic 71), Mane, Dilas.

KR (1) 3 *(Gudjonsson 25, Arnarsson 51, Finnbogason 55 (pen))*

Zilina (0) 0 1234

KR: Halldorsson; Fridgeirsson, Gudmundur Gunnarsson, Sigurdarson, Arnarsson (Olafsson A 75), Gudjonsson, Sigurdsson B, Hauksson, Finnbogason, Ludviksson, Baldvinsson.
Zilina: Dubravka; Piacek, Ofori, Mraz, Barcik, Pecovsky, Sulek■, Zlatkovic (Pich 57), Gergel, Lietava (Strihavka 65), Majtan (Ceesay 53).

KuPS (1) 1 *(Venalainen 16)*

Gaz Metan (0) 0 3190

KuPS: Hilander; Karkkainen, Holopainen, Nissinen, Joenmaki, Balogh, Nykanen, Ilo, Venalainen, Nwakaeme (Udah 65), Williams (Oravainen 57).
Gaz Metan: Plesca; Lazar, Khubutia (Breeveld 42), Buzean, Parvulescu (Petre 61), Zaharia, Hoban, Todea (Litu 67), Eric de Oliveira, Munteanu, Thaer Al Bawab.

Llanelli (1) 2 *(Follows 8, 51)*

Dinamo Tbilisi (0) 1 *(Odikadze 81 (pen))* 643

Llanelli: Morris; Jones S, Surman, Grist (Batley 89), Bowen, Corbisiero, Williams, Thomas K (Legg 67), Evans A, Follows (Jones R 72), Bond.
Dinamo Tbilisi: Loria; Homola, Rekhviashvili, Kakubava, Kvekveskiri, Xisco Munoz, Odikadze, Kakhelishvili (Albert Yague 70), Koshkadze, Jighauri (Tekturmanidze 65), Carlos Coto (Lekvtadze 57).

Maccabi Tel Aviv (3) 3 *(Konate 22, Atar 39, Israelevich 44)*

Xazar (1) 1 *(Muresan 45)* 8352

Maccabi Tel Aviv: Haimov; Vered, Nivaldo, Pavicevic, Ziv, Medunjanin (Lugasi 80), Israelevich, Dahan, Konate (Kaat 73), Atar, Dabbur (Micha 60).
Xazar: Agayev; Eder Bonfim, Allahverdiyev, Ricardo, Onofras, Muresan, Pit, Amirguliyev, Wobay (Diego Souza 46), Borbely (Doman 71), Joao Paulo (Opara 46).

Metalurg Skopje (0) 0

Lokomotiv Sofia (0) 0 4000

Metalurg Skopje: Pavlovic; Kralevski, Petkovski, Dragovic, Memedi, Zaharievski, Mitrev, Krstev, Nachevski (Ljamchevski 70), Ilijoski (Simonovski 89), Ejupi (Tenekedzhiev 53).
Lokomotiv Sofia: Galev; Dyakov, Dobrev, Savic, Lahchev, Karadzhinov, Yanev (Velev 74), Bozhinov, Pisarov (Manolov 78), Romanov, Andonov (Yordanov 58).

Metalurgi Rustavi (0) 1 *(Kvakhadze 73)*

Irtysh (0) 1 *(Daskalov 79)* 3000

Metalurgi Rustavi: Bediashvili; Orbeladze, Japaridze, Kvakhadze, Makhviladze, Maisuradze, Razmadze, Getsadze (Kavtaradze 78), Modebadze, Mikaberidze (Tkemaladze 84), Kobalia (Tatanashvili 64).
Irtysh: Tsirin; Coulibaly, Chernyshov, Balazic, Danaev, Sergienko (Asanbaev 88), Govedarica, Siminidi (Zarechniy 69), Tleshev (Maltsev 46), Ivanov, Daskalov.

Metalurgs Liepaya (0) 1 *(Kalns 61)*

Salzburg (3) 4 *(Alan 22, 44, 45, Cziommer 89)* 1750

Metalurgs Liepaya: Steinbors; Surnins, Jemelins (Mihadjuks 78), Kavaliauskas (Savalnieks 77), Cinikas, Valskis, Solonicins, Tamosauskas, Prohorenkovs, Kamess, Kalns.
Salzburg: Gustafsson; Pasanen, Schwegler, Hinteregger, Cziommer, Lindgren, Svento, Jantscher (Leonardo 76), Leitgeb, Zarate, Alan (Wallner 82).

Minsk (1) 1 *(Razin 22)*

Gaziantep (0) 1 *(Sachivko 51 (og))* 4200

Minsk: Skinderis■; Klimovich, Razin, Shegrikovich, Soro, Voronkov, Rakhmanov, Sachivko, Loshankov (Lesko 74), Vasilyuk (Gigevich 83), Zenko (Sashcheko 63).
Gaziantep: Mahmut; Serdar, Emre G, Senol, Nounkeu, Olcan (Ivan 90), Bekir, Wagner, Murat (Alper 79), Sosa (Popov 67), Cenk.

Olimpija (1) 2 *(Vrsic 45 (pen), 76)*

Bohemians (0) 0 6000

Olimpija: Dzafic; Sretenovic, Andelkovic, Vrsic, Lovrecic (Ranic 55), Skerjanc (Omladic 46), Radujko, Bozic, Fink (Cadikovski 78), Jovic, Valencic.
Bohemians: Murphy; Heary, Burns, Price, O'Brien, Brennan, Cahill, Bayly (Traynor 65), Cronin (Rossiter 87), Buckley, Fagan (Flood 63).

Orebro (0) 0

Sarajevo (0) 0 5529

Orebro: Alvbage; Haginge, Wikstrom, Wirtanen, Wowoah, Rama, Nordback, Gerzic, Astvald (Lushtaku 67), Staaf (Johansson 83), Paulinho.
Sarajevo: Hamzic; Belosevic, Torlak, Dupovac, Kojasevic (Bajraktarevic 90), Scepanovic, Comor, Handzic K, Obuca, Suljic (Smigalovic 83), Haskic (Handzic H 71).

Paksi (0) 1 *(Vayer 58)*

Tromso (1) 1 *(Andersen 26)* 1800

Paksi: Csernyanszki; Eger, Heffler T, Fiola, Sifter, Balo, Bode, Magasfoldi (Kiss 65), Sipeki (Szabo 83), Bartha (Haraszti 89), Vayer.
Tromso: Malmkvist; Bjorck, Norbye, Yndestad, Mbodji, Ciss, Jenssen, Andersen, Johansen (Jama 90), Abdellaoue (Moller 80), Drage (Nystrom 51).

Rad (0) 0

Olympiakos Volos (0) 1 *(Martin 87)* 2300

Rad: Danilovic; Pajovic, Lekovic, Mitrovic, Pantic, Andric (Malbasic 68), Jovanovic (Prso 80), Milivojevic, Stanojevic, Mrkela (Kosoric 90), Kojic.
Olympiakos Volos: Jakupovic; Szelesi, Sankare, Tomas, Alvarez, Umbides, Breska (Schembri 89), Rokas, Mitropoulos, Monje (Noe Acosta 80), Martin (Darbion 90).

Rudar (0) 0

FK Austria (1) 3 *(Barazite 35, 63, Jun 75)* 1150

Rudar: Mijatovic; Radusinovic, Igumanovic (Ivanovic 71), Adzic, Nestorovic, Franciskovic, Vlahovic, Brnovic (Rustemovic 59), Popovic (Mrdak 63), Jovanovic M, Jovanovic I.
FK Austria: Grunwald P; Ortlechner, Suttner (Gorgon 77), Leovac, Rogulj, Klein, Junuzovic, Liendl (Hlinka 67), Barazite, Stankovic, Linz (Jun 73).

Sant Julia (0) 0

Bnei Yehuda (1) 2 *(Balili 6, Marinkovic 56)* 448

Sant Julia: Perianes; Wagner, Varela, Miguel Ruiz, Peppe, Iguacel (Alves 70), Vicente Munoz (Albert Acosta 77), Riera (Gomez 54), Rodriguez F, Jacques, Salvat.
Bnei Yehuda: Aiyenugba; Azoz, Hadad, Mori, Ivaskevicius, Edri, Rali (Abu Zaid 72), Galvan, Menashe (Zairi 85), Balili (Agaiev 63), Marinkovic.

Shakhtar (0) 2 *(Vasiljevic 52, 86)*

St Patrick's Ath (0) 1 *(McMillan D 79)* 12,000

Shakhtar: Mokin; Kirov, Vasiljevic, Utabaev, Dzidic, Baizhanov (Dosmanbetov 90), Kukeyev, Vicius, Konysbaev (Borovskiy 90), Khizhnichenko, Finonchenko (Petronijevic 80).
St Patrick's Ath: Rogers; Pender, Bermingham, Shortall, McMillan E, Bradley (Guthrie 90), Murphy (McMillan D 63), Doyle, McFaul, Crowley (Daly 77), Kavanagh.

Shakhtyor (0) 0

Ventspils (0) 1 *(Kosmacovs 89)* 3020

Shakhtyor: Tsygalko; Polyakov, Kirenkin, Yanushkevich, Kolomyts, Rios (Balanovich 78), Rozhkov, Sitko, Grenkov, Komarovski, Alumona.
Ventspils: Vlasovs; Shibamura, Gabovs, Savcenkovs, Postnikov, Kosmacovs, Laizans, Sato (Tukura 66), Martinez (Maki 85), Kozacuks (Sukhanov 76), Rugins.

SK Tirana (0) 0

Spartak Trnava (0) 0 4000

SK Tirana: Lika I; Pisha, Dushku, Taku, Karabeci, Lika G (Bala 46), Kalari, Situma, Al Ajmi (Osmani 78), Kerciku, Essama (Hepple 67).
Spartak Trnava: Raska; Koubsky, Hanzel L, Diallo, Karhan, Malcharek, Vyskocil, Kascak, Prochazka, Petras (Gogolak 58), Tomacek (Bicak 86).

Slask (0) 1 *(Voskamp 75)*

Dundee U (0) 0 8300

Slask: Kelemen; Celeban, Pietrasiak, Socha, Mila, Spahic, Elsner, Dudek (Sztylka 87), Gancarczyk (Sobota 61), Cwielong (Voskamp 73), Diaz.
Dundee U: Pernis; Dillon, Dixon, Severin (Allan 88), Watson, Douglas, Flood, Rankin, Goodwillie, Daly, Russell.

Suduva (0) 1 *(Beniusis 88)*

Elfsborg (0) 1 *(Keene 78)* 2114

Suduva: Valincius; Radzius, Leimonas, Borovskis, Chvedukas, Slavickas, Urbsys (Grigaitis 60), Gu Bin, Eliosius (Beniusis 67), Loginov, Zhygalov (Luksys 77).
Elfsborg: Christiansen; Jonsson (Andersson M 80), Augustsson, Klarstrom, Svensson, Mobaeck, Ishizaki (Nordmark 82), Larsson (Nilsson 66), Hiljemark, Keene, Jawo.

Tauras (0) 2 *(Jerkovic 56 (pen), Seedorf 73)*

Den Haag (0) 3 *(Immers 71, 82 (pen), Gnedojus 90 (og))* 1400

Tauras: Borysenko; Gnedojus, Sirevicius, Zubavicius, Gedgaudas, Miguel Soares (Maciulis 63), Savastas, Martisauskis (Arlauskis 46), Seedorf, Borisovs, Jerkovic (Grigalevicius 70).
Den Haag: Coutinho; Kum, Derijck, Leeuwin, Ammi, Luksik■, Radosavljevic, Toornstra, Verhoek, Immers, Vicento (Chery 68) (Hocher 89).

The New Saints (0) 1 *(Evans 59)*

Midtjylland (0) 3 *(Hassan 65, Olsen 86 (pen), Albaek 90)* 914

The New Saints: Harrison; Spender, Evans, Baker, Marriott, Jones, Hogan, Ruscoe, Partridge (Williams C 72), Draper (Sharp 67), Williams M (Edwards 59).
Midtjylland: Jensen; Juelsgard Kristensen, Albrechtsen (Nielsen K 30), Ipsa, Pedersen, Poulsen, Olsen, Uzochukwu (Albaek 79), Hassan, Janssen, Igboun (Nworuh 65).

TPS Turku (0) 0

Westerlo (0) 1 *(Cabeke 90)* 3197

TPS Turku: Lehtovaara; Rahmonen, Heinikangas, Nyberg, Hurme, Pennanen, N'Galula, Lahde, Makinen (Saarinen 63), Kuqi, Aaritalo.
Westerlo: Deelkens; Van Hout (Marcao 80), Vanaudenaerde, De Petter, Corstjens, Farssi (Cabeke 90), De Greef, Delen, Bruls, Annab (Molenberghs 67), Ngolok.

Vaduz (0) 0

Vojvodina (0) 2 *(Oumarou 60, Ilic 70)* 1892

Vaduz: Jehle; Sara, Cerrone, Denicola, Rechsteiner (Zanni 66), Cvetinovic, Kienzl, Burgmeier, Rafinha (Tripodi 76), Merenda, Baron (Cecchini 76).
Vojvodina: Supic; Pavlovic, Trajkovic, Vulicevic, Mojsov, Stevanovic (Antwi 88), Merebashvili (Covic 59), Medojevic, Mitosevic, Oumarou, Ilic (Brankovic 82).

Valerenga (0) 1 *(Berre 68)*

Mika (0) 0 2312

Valerenga: Hirschfeld; Nordvik (Dos Santos 46), Muri, Nouri, Strandberg, Fellah, Zajic, Singh, Ogude, Boakye (Berre 30), Nielsen (Kone 68).
Mika: Kasparov; Poghosyan, Alex Henrique, Tadevosyan, Mkoyan, Mkrtchyan (Muradyan 73), Petrosyan, Pedro Lopez, Edney (Azatyan 74), Beglaryan, Mandricenco.

Vllaznia (0) 0

Thun (0) 0 6000

Vllaznia: Vujadinovic; Alechenwu (Sinani 83), Rajovic, Smajlaj, Sykaj, Popovic, Belisha, Nallbani (Hasani 67), Vajushi, Gocaj (Nimani 90), Sukaj.
Thun: Da Costa; Luthi, Reinmann, Matic, Schindelholz, Battig, Andrist (Wittwer 69), Demiri, Sanogo, Rama (Lustrinelli 62), Lezcano (Schneuwly 89).

Zeljeznicar (0) 1 *(Beslija 60)*

Serif (0) 0 10,000

Zeljeznicar: Karic; Bogicevic, Gerhardt, Savic, Beslija (Jamak 85), Zeba, Markovic, Svraka, Visca (Smajic 63), Adilovic (Ramic 90), Stanic.
Serif: Stoyanov; Samardzic, Kassenu, Metoua, Henrique (Cheptine 76), Zamaliyev, Bulat, Rouamba, Jhonatan, Balima, Jymmy Franca (Sosa 87).

SECOND QUALIFYING ROUND SECOND LEG

Thursday, 21 July 2011

Aalesund (0) 3 *(Barrantes 72 (pen), Fuhre 87, Post 119)*

Ferencvaros (1) 1 *(Olah 42)* 5122

Aalesund: Grytebust; Arnefjord, Jaager, Tollas, Barrantes, Olsen M, Morrison, Ulvestad (Post 63), Okoronkwo (Fuhre 80), Parr, Sellin (Myklebust 20).
Ferencvaros: Ranilovic; Otten, Gruz, Fulop, Jozsi (Balog 90), Maroti, Junior Ailton, Abdi (Rodenbucher 70), Andrezinho, Olah (Felipe Almeida 84), Morales.
aet.

AEK Larnaca (1) 1 *(Pavlou 26)*

Floriana (0) 0 1413

AEK Larnaca: Fortin; De Cler, Hofland, Dimech (Kastanas K 82), Albert Serran, Linssen, Skopelitis (Van Dijk 62), Ruben Gomez, Pavlou (Georgiou 72), Kingsley, Mitidis.
Floriana: Towns; Paris, Pisani, Farrugia T, Bugeja, Doffo, Cassar (Farrugia B 83), Joseph Borg, Micallef, Borg C (Caruana 70), Woods.

Aktobe (0) 0

Kecskemeti (0) 0 12,500

Aktobe: Sidelnikov; Kenzhisariev, Smakov, Chiculin, Primus, Kostic, Khayrullin, Logvinenko (Semenov 79), Maletic (Averchenko 90), Mane, Dilas (Lisenkov 75).
Kecskemeti: Rybansky; Balogh, Radanovic, Mohl, Ebala (Bertus 84), Savic, Kethevoama, Cukic (Dosso 84), Alempijevic, Tokoli, Gyurcso (Litsingi 72).

Bnei Yehuda (1) 2 *(Marinkovic 16, Galvan 89)*

Sant Julia (0) 0 1998

Bnei Yehuda: Aiyenugba; Azoz, Hadad, Mori, Ivaskevicius, Edri, Rali (Abu Zaid 60), Galvan, Menashe (Agaiev 60), Balili (Zairi 83), Marinkovic.
Sant Julia: Perianes; Wagner, Varela, Miguel Ruiz, Peppe, Iguacel (Moreno 66), Munoz, Rodriguez F (Josep 61), Jacques, Salvat, Gomez.

Bohemians (1) 1 *(Fagan 34)*

Olimpija (0) 1 *(O'Brien 81 (og))* 1802

Bohemians: Murphy; Heary, Burns (Cahill 61), Price, O'Brien, Rossiter (Downes 81), Brennan, Bayly (Forrester 71), Cronin, Buckley, Fagan.
Olimpija: Dzafic; Sretenovic (Kasnik 86), Salkic, Andelkovic, Vrsic, Lovrecic, Skerjanc, Radujko, Fink (Omladic 46), Jovic, Valencic (Cadikovski 73).

Den Haag (1) 2 *(Toornstra 45, Chery 80)*

Tauras (0) 0 13,111

Den Haag: Coutinho; Kum, Derijck, Leeuwin, Ammi, Chery (Van Duijn 86), Radosavljevic, Toornstra, Verhoek, Hocher (Vicento 71), Immers.
Tauras: Borysenko; Gnedojus, Sirevicius, Arlauskis, Zubavicius, Gedgaudas (Misiuk 77), Miguel Soares, Savastas (Borisovs 61), Martisauskis, Seedorf, Jerkovic.

Dinamo Tbilisi (3) 5 *(Xisco Munoz 7, 51, Albert Yague 11, Robertinho 27, Carlos Coto 55)*

Llanelli (0) 0 18,027

Dinamo Tbilisi: Loria; Tomashvili, Rekhviashvili, Kakubava (Homola 25), Kvekveskiri, Xisco Munoz (Jighauri 54), Odikadze, Koshkadze (Tekturmanidze 62), Albert Yague, Carlos Coto, Robertinho.
Llanelli: Morris; Jones S, Surman, Grist, Bowen (Holloway 69), Corbisiero (Venables 46), Williams, Thomas K, Evans A, Follows (Bond 35), Griffiths.

Dundee U (3) 3 *(Watson 2, Goodwillie 5, Daly 44 (pen))*

Slask (1) 2 *(Elsner 15, Dudek 74)* 11,306

Dundee U: Pernis; Dillon, Dixon, Severin (Swanson 77), Kenneth, Watson, Flood, Rankin, Goodwillie, Daly, Russell (Mackay-Steven 81).
Slask: Kelemen; Celeban, Pietrasiak, Socha, Mila, Spahic, Elsner, Dudek (Cetnarski 87), Gancarczyk (Sobota 63), Sztylka, Cwielong (Voskamp 35).

Elfsborg (1) 3 *(Elm 26, Augustsson 58, Hult 67)*

Suduva (0) 0 3417

Elfsborg: Covic; Karlsson, Augustsson, Klarstrom, Svensson, Mobaeck, Ishizaki (Keene 71), Hult, Larsson, Hiljemark (Nordmark 79), Elm (Jawo 76).
Suduva: Valincius; Radzius, Leimonas, Borovskis, Chvedukas, Slavickas, Urbsys (Beniusis 58), Gu Bin, Loginov, Wang Yang (Eliosius 35), Zhygalov (Luksys 70).

FK Austria (1) 2 *(Barazite 44, Jun 75)*

Rudar (0) 0 5100

FK Austria: Grunwald P; Ortlechner, Suttner, Rogulj (Wallner 61), Klein, Hlinka, Junuzovic (Salomon 72), Grunwald A, Koch, Barazite (Tadic 59), Jun.
Rudar: Vuklis; Radusinovic, Igumanovic (Sljivancanin 81), Adzic, Nestorovic, Franciskovic (Bambur 88), Vlahovic, Brnovic■, Rustemovic, Jovanovic M (Popovic 70), Jovanovic I.

Fulham (1) 4 *(Johnson A 19, Duff 56, Zamora 66, Sidwell 70)*

Crusaders (0) 0 15,676

Fulham: Schwarzer; Senderos, Briggs, Murphy, Hughes, Hangeland, Duff, Sidwell (Etuhu 71), Johnson A (Frei 71), Zamora, Riise J (Riise B 76).
Crusaders: O'Neill; McCann (Faulkner 86), Leeman, Magowan, McBride, McKeown, Watson, Dallas, Adamson (Halliday 84), Owens (Rainey 68), Gargan.

Gagra (2) 2 *(Gabedava 6, Tkeshelashvili 40)*

Anorthosis (0) 0 735

Gagra: Sepiashvili; Tkeshelashvili, Kalandadze, Chkhetiani, Jishkariani, Khutsidze (Tsitskhvaia 78), Sharikadze, Nakonechniy, Gabedava, Kvantaliani, Ordynsky.
Anorthosis: Kozacik; Leiwakabessy, Sprockel, Tomasic, Colin, Janicio, Laban, Okkas, Rezek, Vucicevic (Andic 90), Laborde (Sielis 90).

Gaz Metan (1) 2 *(Petre 36, Hoban 53)*

KuPS (0) 0 6000

Gaz Metan: Plesca; Lazar, Khubutia, Buzean, Parvulescu, Hoban, Petre (Zaharia 79), Todea, Eric de Oliveira, Munteanu (Breeveld 64), Thaer Al Bawab (Markovic 84).
KuPS: Hilander; Karkkainen, Holopainen (Hoivala 76), Nissinen, Joenmaki, Balogh, Nykanen, Paananen (Oravainen 40), Ilo (Kaivonurmi 61), Venalainen, Williams.

Gaziantep (1) 4 *(Emre G 28, Wagner 73, Popov 83, Olcan 90)*

Minsk (0) 1 *(Zenko 61)* 6499

Gaziantep: Karcemarskas; Serdar, Emre G, Ivan (Senol 86), Nounkeu, Olcan, Bekir (Murat 71), Wagner, Elyasa, Sosa, Cenk (Popov 81).
Minsk: Lesko; Klimovich, Razin, Sashcheko, Shegrikovich, Soro (Vasilyuk 62), Voronkov, Rakhmanov (Gigevich 87), Sachivko, Loshankov, Zenko (Khachaturyan 70).

Honka (0) 0

Hacken (1) 2 *(Chibuike 42, Forsell 85)* 2216

Honka: Maanoja; Koskinen, Heilala, Heikkila, Aalto, Vasara (Otaru 66), Aijala (Makijarvi 72), Schuller, Tammilehto, Dudu (Vayrynen 56), Savage.
Hacken: Kallqvist; Ostberg, Arkivuo, Soderberg, Chatto (Forsell 75), Bjurstrom (Nystrom 67), Makondele (Henriksson 46), Elvby, Chibuike, Frolund, Ranegie.

Irtysh (0) 0

Metalurgi Rustavi (1) 2 *(Kobalia 23, Modebadze 57)* 10,000

Irtysh: Tsirin; Coulibaly, Kuchma (Nikolic 62), Chernyshov (Mikhaylyuk 46), Zarechniy, Balazic, Sergienko, Govedarica, Maltsev (Tleshev 60), Ivanov, Daskalov.
Metalurgi Rustavi: Bediashvili; Orbeladze, Japaridze, Kvakhadze, Makhviladze, Maisuradze, Razmadze, Getsadze (Tatanashvili 64), Modebadze, Mikaberidze (Tkemaladze 79), Kobalia (Kavtaradze 75).

Jablonec (2) 5 *(Kovarik 25, 70, Pitak 30, 61, Lafata 55)*

Flamurtari (1) 1 *(Sakaj 36 (pen))* 3095

Jablonec: Spit; Benes, Jablonsky, Pitak, Pavlik, Jarolim (Vanek 34), Loucka, Elias, Kovarik (Novak 82), Kopic (Vosahlik 64), Lafata.
Flamurtari: Mocka; Sakaj, Veliu, Arberi, Brahja, Progni (Cutra 86), Begaj, Kuqi, Lena (Grami 67), Shehaj, Idrizaj (Licaj 46).

Karabakh (0) 0

EB/Streymur (0) 0 17,387

Karabakh: Pavlovic; Rashad F Sadygov, Teli, Medvedev, Agolli, Rashad A Sadygov, Yusifov, Ismayilov (Gurbanov 90), Adamia, Nadirov (Nedzipi 73), Aliyev.
EB/Streymur: Torgard; Hansen G, Djurhuus, Niclasen (Arnar Dam 83), Alex Santos, Bardur Olsen, Samuelsen, Hanssen, Jacobsen, Anghel, Hansen A.

Levadia (0) 0

Differdange (1) 1 *(Lebresne 32)* 1550

Levadia: Smisko; Kalimullin, Morozov, Teniste, Sarunas (Holst 65), Podholjuzin, Leitan, Nahk, Novikov (Taar 46), Toomet, Pebre (Subbotin 46).
Differdange: Weber; Rodrigues, Bukvic, Janisch, Kettenmeyer, Lebresne, Bettmer, Leoni, Siebenaler, Piskor (Franzoni 77), Caron (May 89).

Lokomotiv Sofia (0) 3 *(Yordanov 57 (pen), 85, Bozhinov 89)*

Metalurg Skopje (1) 2 *(Krstev 4, Ilijoski 62)* 3000

Lokomotiv Sofia: Galev; Dyakov, Dobrev, Savic, Atanasov (Velev 58), Karadzhinov (Yordanov 46), Yanev (Andonov 69), Bozhinov, Pisarov, Romanov, Mesic.
Metalurg Skopje: Pavlovic; Kralevski, Petkovski, Dragovic, Memedi■, Ljamchevski, Zaharievski (Gjorgievski 66), Mitrev, Krstev, Nachevski (Tenekedzhiev 60), Ilijoski (Ejupi 84).

Midtjylland (3) 5 *(Igboun 23, Nworuh 24, 52, Olsen 32 (pen), Hvilsom 90)*

The New Saints (0) 2 *(Darlington 55, 90)* 2650

Midtjylland: Jensen; Juelsgard Kristensen, Ipsa, Sivebaek (Uzochukwu 69), Lauridsen, Poulsen (Hvilsom 46), Olsen, Borring, Albaek, Nworuh, Igboun (Hansen 46).
The New Saints: Harrison; Evans, Baker, Marriott (Giglio 82), Jones, Hogan, Ruscoe (Sharp 46), Seargeant, Partridge (Williams C 62), Edwards, Darlington.

Mika (0) 0

Valerenga (0) 1 *(Dos Santos 49)* 2350

Mika: Kasparov; Poghosyan, Alex Henrique, Tadevosyan, Mkoyan, Grigoryan, Mkrtchyan (Mandricenco 41), Ishkhanyan (Azatyan 78), Pedro Lopez, Edney (Muradyan 62), Beglaryan.
Valerenga: Hirschfeld; Stoor, Nordvik, Muri, Strandberg, Dos Santos (Leigh 62), Fellah, Zajic (Kone 59), Singh, Ogude, Nielsen (Haidar 81).

Nacional (0) 2 *(Luis Alberto 55, Candeias 90)*

FH (0) 0 4783

Nacional: Elisson; Felipe Lopes, Danielson, Nuno Pinto, Luis Alberto, Mihelic (Elizeu 71), Skolnik (Todorovic 88), Mateus, Joao Aurelio, Edgar Costa, Oliver (Candeias 75).
FH: Gunnleifsson; Bjarnason, Vidarsson, Asgeirsson (Saevarsson 81), Runarsson (Gudmundsson V 81), Sverrisson, Sigurdsson H, Bjornsson (Gudnason 46), Snorrason, Vilhjalmsson, Hallfredsson.

Olympiakos Volos (0) 1 *(Martin 79 (pen))*

Rad (0) 1 *(Kojic 48)* 5994

Olympiakos Volos: Jakupovic; Szelesi, Sankare■, Tomas, Alvarez, Breska (Schembri 72), Rokas, Noe Acosta (Dolezaj 85), Mitropoulos, Monje (Darbion 90), Martin.
Rad: Danilovic; Pajovic, Raspopovic, Kosoric (Randelovic 62), Lekovic, Mitrovic, Andric (Stojiljkovic 77), Prso, Milivojevic, Stanojevic (Varga 81), Kojic.

Rabotnicki (1) 3 *(Manevski 35, Petkovski 50, Petrovic 56)*

Juvenes/Dogana (0) 0 1000

Rabotnicki: Dimitrievski; Kumbev, Stojanov, Lazarevski, Manevski, Todorovski, Vujcic, Petkovski (Trajkovski 61), Petrovic (Avramovski 60), Velkoski K (Micevski 75), Velkoski D.
Juvenes/Dogana: Gobbi; Selva, Bacciocchi, Cervellini, Frino, Ceci (Stefanelli 85), Santini (Zafferani 77), Colombini A (Casadei 59), Caminati, Cavalli, Friguglietti.

Salzburg (0) 0

Metalurgs Liepaya (0) 0 5100

Salzburg: Walke; Pasanen, Ulmer, Sekagya, Schwegler, Cziommer (Anton 78), Jantscher (Leonardo 54), Hierlander, Teigl, Offenbacher (Svento 75), Wallner.
Metalurgs Liepaya: Steinbors; Surnins, Zirnis, Jemelins (Mezs 45), Kavaliauskas (Golovins 77), Valskis, Solonicins, Tamosauskas, Prohorenkovs, Kamess, Kalns.

Sarajevo (0) 2 *(Haskic 47, 62)*

Orebro (0) 0 10,527

Sarajevo: Hamzic; Belosevic, Torlak, Dupovac, Kojasevic (Bajraktarevic 85), Scepanovic (Handzic H 90), Comor, Handzic K, Obuca, Suljic (Hadzic 81), Haskic.
Orebro: Alvbage; Haginge, Wirtanen, Wowoah, Rama (Berger 90), Johansson (Astvald 60), Nordback, Kihlberg, Gerzic, Staaf (Yasin 82), Paulinho.

Serif (0) 0

Zeljeznicar (0) 0 5120

Serif: Stoyanov; Samardzic, Kassenu, Metoua, Henrique, Zamaliyev, Bulat, Rata, Jhonatan (Dima 86), Balima, Sosa (Tarkhnishvili 73).
Zeljeznicar: Karic; Bogicevic, Gerhardt, Savic, Vasilic, Beslija (Stanic 57), Zeba (Jamak 90), Smajic, Markovic, Svraka, Adilovic (Ramic 82).

Spartak Trnava (1) 3 *(Tomacek 41, 85 (pen), Prochazka 66)*

SK Tirana (1) 1 *(Lika G 22)* 6182

Spartak Trnava: Raska; Koubsky, Hanzel L, Diallo, Karhan, Malcharek, Vyskocil (Petras 67), Kascak, Prochazka, Bernath (Gogolak 65), Tomacek (Ciprys 89).
SK Tirana: Lika I; Pisha, Pashaj, Dushku, Taku, Karabeci■, Lika G, Kalari, Al Ajmi (Essama 54), Kerciku (Hepple 70), Bala.

Split (0) 3 *(Cop 47, Vidic 72, Milovic 85)*

Domzale (0) 1 *(Horvat 46)* 2600

Split: Vukovic; Marcic, Vidic, Budisa, Milovic, Vitaic, Simic, Erceg, Baraban (Rasic 81), Cop (Obilinovic 73), Golubovic (Rebic 66).
Domzale: Vidmar; Zec, Knezovic, Elsner, Apatic (Diallo 83), Juninho, Drevensek (Zadnikar 69), Teinovic, Krcic (Smukavec 78), Horvat, Vuk.

St Patrick's Ath (1) 2 *(McMillan E 14, Doyle 70)*

Shakhtar (0) 0 2250

St Patrick's Ath: Rogers; Pender, Bermingham, Shortall, McMillan E, Bradley, Doyle (Murphy 86), McFaul, North (McMillan D 77), Kavanagh, Daly (Mulcahy 83).
Shakhtar: Mokin; Kirov, Vasiljevic, Utabaev (Borantaev 80), Dzidic, Petronijevic (Dosmanbetov 73), Baizhanov, Kukeyev, Vicius, Konysbaev, Khizhnichenko.

Thun (0) 2 *(Rama 89, Luthi 90)*

Vllaznia (1) 1 *(Sukaj 14)* 7193

Thun: Da Costa; Schneider, Reinmann (Luthi 61), Matic, Schindelholz, Battig, Demiri, Schneuwly (Andrist 27), Wittwer (Rama 70), Lustrinelli, Lezcano.
Vllaznia: Vujadinovic; Alechenwu, Rajovic■, Smajlaj, Sykaj, Popovic, Belisha, Nallbani, Vajushi (Hasani 75), Gocaj, Sukaj (Sinani 88).

Tromso (0) 0

Paksi (0) 3 *(Kiss 59, 77, Bode 62)* 2710

Tromso: Malmkvist; Bjorck, Norbye, Yndestad, Mbodji, Ciss, Jenssen, Andersen (Jama 67), Abdellaoue (Moller 65), Drage, Nystrom (Johansen 54).
Paksi: Csernyanszki; Eger, Heffler T, Fiola, Sifter, Balo, Bode, Sipeki, Bartha, Kiss, Vayer (Magasfoldi 79).

Varazdin (2) 3 *(Vugrinec 14, 70, Glavica 18)*

Iskra-Stal (1) 1 *(Novicov 41)* 2250

Varazdin: Krklec; Brlecic (Grgec 77), Tkalcic, Glavina, Simek, Conjar, Aganovic, Puncec, Glavica (Gluhak 89), Vugrinec, Sacer (Golubar 69).
Iskra-Stal: Melenciuc; Leshchuk, Uzbek, Novicov, Rudac (Naginaylov 82), Porfireanu, Gorodetchi (Truhanov 88), Kourouma (Ponomar 53), Vishnyakov, Shugladze, Suchu.

Ventspils (0) 3 *(Maki 51, 79 (pen), Martinez 90)*

Shakhtyor (1) 2 *(Kolomyts 6, Komarovski 73)* 2500

Ventspils: Vlasovs; Shibamura, Gabovs, Savcenkovs, Postnikov, Kosmacovs (Kato 80), Laizans (Sukhanov■ 64), Tukura, Martinez, Kozacuks (Maki 44), Rugins.
Shakhtyor: Tsygalko; Polyakov, Kirenkin, Yanushkevich, Kolomyts, Leonchik (Petrov 88), Balanovich, Sitko, Grenkov, Komarovski, Alumona (Sokol 63) (Rios 76).

Vojvodina (0) 1 *(Covic 87)*

Vaduz (1) 3 *(Cvetinovic 10, Merenda 78, 90)* 6800

Vojvodina: Supic; Pavlovic, Trajkovic, Vulicevic, Mojsov, Stevanovic, Merebashvili (Covic 46), Medojevic, Mitosevic (Ajuru 73), Oumarou, Ilic (Brankovic 89).
Vaduz: Jehle; Cerrone, Denicola (Bader 46), Rechsteiner, Cvetinovic, Kienzl, Sara, Burgmeier (Zanni 69), Rafinha (Ciccone 54), Merenda, Baron.

Vorskla (2) 3 *(Januzi 33, 73, Kurilov 36)*

Glentoran (0) 0 8000

Vorskla: Dolganski; Kurilov, Dallku, Chesnakov, Vovkodav, Oberemko (Matveev 46), Kryvosheenko (Osipenko 67), Rebenok, Markoski (Zakarlyuka 46), Januzi, Bezus.
Glentoran: Morris; Hill, McGovern, Johnny Taylor, Howland, Carson, Callacher (McGuigan 29), Cherry, O'Hanlon (Murray 63), Johnston (Beggs 71), Boyce.

Westerlo (0) 0

TPS Turku (0) 0 2814

Westerlo: De Winter; Van Hout, Vanaudenaerde, De Petter, Farssi, De Greef, Delen, Bruls, Annab (Dekelver 63), Ngolok, Marcao (Molenberghs 82).
TPS Turku: Lehtovaara; Heinikangas, Nyberg, Hurme, Uronen, Pennanen, Kolehmainen, N'Galula (Makinen 70), Lahde (Lehtonen 83), Kuqi, Aaritalo.

Xazar (0) 0

Maccabi Tel Aviv (0) 0 15,000

Xazar: Agayev; Eder Bonfim, Beqiri, Ricardo, Onofras (Allahverdiyev 67), Muresan, Pit, Amirguliyev, Doman (Wobay 52), Opara, Borbely (Joao Paulo 56).
Maccabi Tel Aviv: Haimov; Nivaldo, Pavicevic, Ziv, Saban, Medunjanin, Israelevich (Micha 73), Dahan, Konate (Colautti 85), Atar, Dabbur (Yeini 67).

Zilina (1) 2 *(Majtan 29, Ceesay 70)*

KR (0) 0 3412

Zilina: Dubravka; Ondras, Angelovic, Piacek, Ofori, Barcik, Pecovsky, Gergel (Strihavka 64), Lietava (Ceesay 46), Majtan, Pich (Zlatkovic 81).
KR: Halldorsson; Fridgeirsson, Gudmundur Gunnarsson, Sigurdarson, Arnarsson (Olafsson A 75), Gudjonsson, Sigurdsson B, Hauksson, Finnbogason, Ludviksson, Baldvinsson (Jonsson 82).

THIRD QUALIFYING ROUND FIRST LEG

Tuesday, 26 July 2011

Bnei Yehuda (1) 1 *(Galvan 41)*

Helsingborg (0) 0 3475

Bnei Yehuda: Aiyenugba; Azoz, Hadad, Mori, Ivaskevicius, Edri, Rali (Abu Zaid 68), Galvan, Menashe (Imses 90), Balili (Agaiev 81), Marinkovic.
Helsingborg: Hansson; Edman, Andersson C (Thern 90), Larsson, Holgersson, Bouaouzan (Wahlstedt 10), Gashi, Sundin, Mahlangu, Gerndt, Jonsson.

Thursday, 28 July 2011

Aalesund (1) 4 *(Okoronkwo 5, Barrantes 56, Larsen 72, Augustsson 74 (og))*

Elfsborg (0) 0 5769

Aalesund: Grytebust; Arnefjord, Jaager, Tollas, Skagestad (Jalasto 17), Fuhre (Carlsen 69), Barrantes, Larsen, Olsen (Myklebust 27), Morrison, Okoronkwo.
Elfsborg: Covic; Karlsson, Jonsson, Augustsson, Svensson, Mobaeck, Hult, Larsson (Nilsson 64), Hiljemark (Ishizaki 63), Keene, Jawo (Yarsuvat 85).

AEK Larnaca (0) 3 *(Van Dijk 62 (pen), Gonzalo Garcia 73, De Cler 90)*

Mlada Boleslav (0) 0 1977

AEK Larnaca: Alexandre Negri; De Cler, Hofland, Albert Serran, Van Dijk, Linssen, Pavlou (Kingsley 61), Priso (Ruben Gomez 90), Demetriou, Gonzalo Garcia (Skopelitis 87), Mrdakovic.
Mlada Boleslav: Miller; Neuwirth (Janicek 10), Prochazka, Rolko, Sirl, Opiela, Kudela, Kysela, Kulic (Stohanzl 60), Reznicek (Taborsky 77), Chramosta.

Alaniya (0) 1 *(Buraev 60)*

Aktobe (1) 1 *(Mane 11)* 23,000

Alaniya: Khomich; Grigoryev, Grachev, Bulgaru, Da Costa Goore, Dudiev (Buraev 51), Bikmaev (Tsarikaev 46), Gabulov, Khubulov (Stoyanov 80), Gigolaev, Danilo Neco.
Aktobe: Sidelnikov■; Kenzhisariev, Smakov, Chichulin (Badlo 75), Primus, Kostic, Khayrullin (Semenov 90), Logvinenko, Maletic, Mane, Dilas (Boychenko 69).

Anorthosis (0) 0

Rabotnicki (0) 2 *(Petrovic 71, Velkoski K 82)* 6500

Anorthosis: Ivankov; Leiwakabessy, Sprockel, Tomasic, Janicio, Laban, Okkas (Colin 71), Rezek, Vucicevic, Cristovao (Sielis 83), Laborde (Angelov 58).
Rabotnicki: Dimitrievski; Kumbev, Stojanov (Petrovic 38), Lazarevski, Manevski, Nastevski (Micevski 56), Todorovski, Bogdanovic, Vujcic, Velkoski K (Petkovski 89), Velkoski D.

Atletico Madrid (0) 2 *(Reyes 54, 74)*

Stromsgodset (0) 1 *(Storflor 80)* 30,056

Atletico Madrid: Joel; Miranda■, Felipe Luis, Dominguez, Silvio, Reyes, Tiago (Raul Garcia 80), Juanfran (Perea 78), Gabi, Forlan (Salvio 72), Adrian.
Stromsgodset: Kwarasey; Madsen, Andersen (Nuhu 72), Aas, Storflor, Konradsen, Sankoh (Nordkvelle 61), Vilsvik, Abu, Keita, Berget (Kamara 78).

AZ (0) 2 *(Wernbloom 64, Gudmundsson 88)*

Jablonec (0) 0 8871

AZ: Alvarado; Marcellis, Moisander, Viergever, Martens, Holman, Wernbloom, Elm, Poulsen, Benschop (Gudmundsson 65), Boymans (Falkenburg 90).
Jablonec: Spit; Pavlik, Loucka, Benes, Elias, Pitak, Jarolim (Tresnak 86), Jablonsky, Kovarik (Vosahlik 69), Kopic (Vanek 74), Lafata.

Bursa (0) 2 *(Serdar 52, Ibrahim 72)*

Gomel (1) 1 *(Kuzmianok 42)* 16,122

Bursa: Carson; Stepanov, Serdar, Ibrahim (Omer 82), Vederson, Kirita (Batalla 69), N'Diaye, Volkan, Ozan, Turgay, Sercan (Okan 88).
Gomel: Bushma; Kuzmianok, Matveichyk, Kontsevoy, Stasevich, Kashevski, Evseenko, Levitski (Gordya 90), Lisovyi (Platonov 59), Kozeka, Aleksievich (Stepanov 81).

Club Brugge (1) 4 *(Vleminckx 9, Victor Vazquez 55, Donk 71, Dirar 83)*

Karabakh (0) 1 *(Aliyev 62)* 22,213

Club Brugge: Coosemans; Stenman, Donk, Hoefkens, Almeback, Zimling, Dirar, Odjidja-Ofoe, Refaelov (Meunier 85), Vleminckx, Victor Vazquez.
Karabakh: Pavlovic; Rashad F Sadygov, Teli, Medvedev (Nedzipi 87), Garayev (Hashimov 81), Agolli, Yusifov, Ismayilov, Adamia, Nadirov (Gurbanov 13), Aliyev.

Differdange (0) 0

Olympiakos Volos (0) 3 *(Schembri 67, Noe Acosta 71, Solakis 90)* 743

Differdange: Weber (Hym 63); Rodrigues De Almeida, Bukvic, Janisch, Kettenmeyer (Ribeiro Alves 75), Lebresne, Bettmer, Leoni, Siebenaler (May 71), Caron, Franzoni.
Olympiakos Volos: Jakupovic; Szelesi, Tomas, Dolezaj, Alvarez, Darbion (Cascio 73), Schembri, Breska (Noe Acosta 67), Rokas, Monje, Martin (Solakis 84).

Dinamo Bucharest (2) 2 *(Susac 6 (og), Moti 16)*

Varazdin (2) 2 *(Sacer 43, Vugrinec 45)* 4380

Dinamo Bucharest: Balgradean; Moti, Scarlatache, Diabate, Munteanu, Alexe, Torje (Paun 78), Rus, Kone, Danciulescu (Tucudean 75), Niculae.
Varazdin: Krklec; Susac, Gluhak, Brlecic, Tkalcic, Glavina, Simek (Loncar 9), Aganovic (Grgec 82), Vugrinec, Golubar, Sacer (Trojak 74).

Gaziantep (0) 0

Legia (0) 1 *(Radovic 51)* 7852

Gaziantep: Karcemarskas; Serdar, Emre G, Ivan, Nounkeu, Olcan, Wagner, Elyasa (Pehlivan 58), Murat (Muhammet 85), Popov (Cenk 67), Sosa.
Legia: Skaba; Rzezniczak, Wawrzyniak, Komorowski, Zewlakow, Radovic, Vrdoljak, Borysiuk, Manu (Gol 81), Ljuboja (Zyro 90), Kucharczyk (Hubnik 62).

Hapoel Tel Aviv (2) 4 *(Kende 24, Tamuz 45, Damari 49, Cohen 82)*

Vaduz (0) 0 8822

Hapoel Tel Aviv: Edel; Pecalka, Kende, Ben Dayan, Tuama, Badir, Abutbul (Abass 83), Shivhon (Cohen 67), Yadin, Tamuz, Damari (Al Lala 77).
Vaduz: Jehle; Zanni, Cerrone, Ritzberger■, Bader, Oehri (Schwegler 46), Kienzl, Rafinha (Merenda 46), Hasler N, Hasler D (Ciccone 72), Baron.

Karpaty (1) 2 *(Fedetskiy 34, Voronkov 90)*

St Patrick's Ath (0) 0 13,000

Karpaty: Bogatinov; Oshchipko, Milosevic, Fedetskiy, Borja Gomez, Khudobyak, Tkachuk, Danilo Avelar (Martynyuk 19), Zenjov, Pacheco (Voronkov 61), Lucas (Cristobal 76).
St Patrick's Ath: Rogers; Pender, Bermingham, Shortall, McMillan E, Murphy (Carroll 72), Mulcahy, Doyle, McFaul, North (McMillan D 46), Daly (Crowley 65).

KR (1) 1 *(Baldvinsson 2)*

Dinamo Tbilisi (1) 4 *(Kakhelishvili 38, Albert Yague 50, Xisco Munoz 61 (pen), Lekvtadze 67)* 1200

KR: Halldorsson; Fridgejrsson, Gudmundur Gunnarsson, Sigurdarson, Arnarsson, Sigurdsson B (Jonsson E 65), Hauksson (Jonsson G 75), Olafsson A, Snorrason (Josepsson 80), Finnbogason, Baldvinsson.
Dinamo Tbilisi: Loria; Homola, Tomashvili, Rekhviashvili, Kvekveskiri (Pirtskhalava 80), Xisco Munoz (Jighauri 70), Odikadze, Kakhelishvili, Koshkadze, Albert Yague, Carlos Coto (Lekvtadze 65).

Levski (0) 2 *(Gadzhev 89, Ars 90)*

Spartak Trnava (0) 1 *(Tomacek 80 (pen))* 11,900

Levski: Iliev; Mulder, Starokin, Miliev, Risp, Greene, Gadzhev, Tasevski (Ars 56), Yovov (Raykov 77), Tsvetkov, Mladenov (Hristov 87).
Spartak Trnava: Raska; Koubsky, Gross (Cvirik 83), Hanzel, Diallo, Karhan, Kascak, Prochazka, Bicak (Petras 66), Bernath (Ciprys 69), Tomacek.

Mainz (1) 1 *(Bungert 31)*

Gaz Metan (0) 1 *(Thaer Al Bawab 60)* 15,759

Mainz: Muller H; Noveski, Svensson, Pospech, Bungert, Polanski, Soto, Ivanschitz (Choupo-Moting 62), Risse (Muller N 80), Stieber, Ujah (Allagui 62).
Gaz Metan: Plesca; Khubutia, Trtovac, Markovic, Parvulescu (Munteanu 8) (Zaharia 70), Petre (Buzean 84), Todea, Hoban, Breeveld, Litu, Thaer Al Bawab.

Metalurgi Rustavi (1) 2 *(Japaridze 41, Razmadze 56 (pen))*

Rennes (3) 5 *(Boukari 17, 31, Pitroipa 42, 70, Feret 49)* 10,312

Metalurgi Rustavi: Bediashvili (Batiashvili 46); Orbeladze, Japaridze, Kvakhadze, Murvelashvili■, Maisuradze, Razmadze, Getsadze (Tkemaladze 67), Modebadze, Mikaberidze (Makhviladze 32), Kobalia.
Rennes: Costil; Danze, Mangane, Kana Biyik, Theophile Catherine, Pitroipa (Tettey 72), Feret, Brahimi (Camara 61), M'Vila, Doumbia, Boukari (Montano 65).

Mitdjylland (0) 0

Guimaraes (0) 0 4579

Mitdjylland: Jensen; Afriyie, Juelsgard Kristensen, Ipsa, Nielsen, Poulsen, Albaek (Borring 87), Uzochukwu, Hassan, Nworuh (Janssen 72), Igboun.
Guimaraes: Nilson; Joao Paulo, Alex, Anderson Santana, El Adoua, N'Diaye, Pedro Mendes (Leonel Olimpio 71), Joao Alves, Targino (Maranhao 82), Marcelo Toscano, Faouzi (Edgar Silva 57).

Nacional (3) 3 *(Luis Alberto 13, Mateus 18, 45)*

Hacken (0) 0 4612

Nacional: Elisson; Felipe Lopes, Danielson, Nuno Pinto, Luis Alberto, Mihelic, Skolnik (Edgar Costa 81), Elizeu (Todorovic 69), Mateus (Candeias 85), Joao Aurelio, Rondon.
Hacken: Kallqvist; Ostberg, Arkivuo, Forsell, Soderberg, Bjurstrom, Makondele (Williams 80), Nystrom (Waris 68), Elvby, Chibuike, Ranegie.

Olimpija (0) 1 *(Vrsic 60)*

FK Austria (1) 1 *(Linz 33)* 7350

Olimpija: Dzafic; Sretenovic (Mlinar 12), Salkic, Andelkovic, Vrsic, Lovrecic (Bozic 77), Skerjanc, Omladic, Radujko, Jovic, Besic (Cadikovski 58).
FK Austria: Grunwald P; Ortlechner, Suttner, Rogulj, Klein, Hlinka, Junuzovic, Grunwald A (Leovac 56), Barazite, Stankovic (Koch 89), Linz (Jun 69).

Omonia (1) 3 *(Alexandre 37 (pen), Rengifo 58, Christofi 77)*

Den Haag (0) 0 12,326

Omonia: Georgallides; Alabi, Karipidis, Leandro De Almeida, Shpungin, Salatic, Efrem, Avraam, Alexandre (Tadic 85), Rengifo (Bruno Aguiar 72), Christofi (Davidson Morais 90).
Den Haag: Coutinho; Kum, Derijck, Leeuwin, Ammi, Luksik (Chery 70), Radosavljevic, Toornstra, Verhoek, Hocher (Vicento 46), Immers.

Paksi (1) 1 *(Sipeki 32)*

Hearts (1) 1 *(Hamill 45 (pen))* 3500

Paksi: Csernyanszki; Heffler, Fiola, Sifter, Balo, Bode, Magasfoldi (Montvai 66), Sipeki, Bartha, Kiss, Vayer.
Hearts: Kello; McGowan, Grainger, Jonsson, Zaliukas, Hamill, Mrowiec, Black, Sutton (Stevenson 79) (Elliott 90), Obua, Templeton (Novikovas 82).

Palermo (1) 2 *(Ilicic 13, Miccoli 90)*

Thun (1) 2 *(Luthi 6, Schneider 56)* 28,760

Palermo: Benussi; Cassani, Bovo, Mantovani, Balzaretti, Munoz (Bacinovic 61), Migliaccio (Acquah 80), Nocerino, Zahavi, Ilicic, Pinilla (Miccoli 38).
Thun: Da Costa; Luthi, Schneider, Matic, Schindelholz, Battig, Demiri (Hediger 88), Schneuwly, Wittwer, Lustrinelli (Sanogo 76), Lezcano (Andrist 77).

Ried (1) 2 *(Mader 33, Royer 46)*

Brondby (0) 0 4500

Ried: Gebauer; Glasner, Riegler, Reifeltshammer, Basala-Mazana (Hadzic 43), Mader, Lexa, Hinum (Karner 81), Ivan Carril, Royer, Hammerer (Guillem 70).
Brondby: Andersen; Goodson, Randrup (Larsen 64), Rasmussen, Stenderup, Kristiansen (Akharraz 82), Krohn-Dehli, Jensen, Thygesen, Nilsson, Agger (McGrath 59).

Salzburg (0) 1 *(Leonardo 75)*

Senica (0) 0 5900

Salzburg: Gustafsson; Pasanen, Sekagya, Schwegler, Cziommer, Lindgren (Wallner 46), Svento, Leitgeb, Leonardo, Zarate (Alex Rafael 67), Alan.
Senica: Bolek; Urbanek, Gorosito, Gajdosik, Pillar■, Kona, Wijlaars (Faleiro Kaka 74), Motha, Piroska, Kroupa (Valenta 84), Divis (Hosek 60).

Slask (0) 0

Lokomotiv Sofia (0) 0 7000

Slask: Kelemen; Wasiluk, Celeban, Pietrasiak, Mila, Cetnarski, Spahic, Elsner, Cwielong (Dudek 69), Sobota (Gancarczyk 83), Diaz (Voskamp 53).
Lokomotiv Sofia: Galev; Varbanov, Dobrev, Savic (Romanov 69), Atanasov, Lahchev, Ivanov, Velev (Dafchev 65), Pisarov, Goranov, Yordanov (Mesic 82).

Sparta Prague (2) 5 *(Kweuke 5, 69, 90, Sionko 36, Podany 89)*

Sarajevo (0) 0 11,626

Sparta Prague: Blazek; Zapotocny, Vidlicka, Repka, Pamic, Sionko (Kadlec 64), Vacek (Mares 90), Matejovsky, Husek, Juhar (Podany 90), Kweuke.
Sarajevo: Hamzic; Belosevic, Torlak, Maksumic, Kojasevic, Scepanovic (Bajraktarevic 86), Hadzic (Suljic 46), Comor, Handzic K, Obuca, Haskic (Handzic H 73).

Split (0) 0

Fulham (0) 0 4000

Split: Vukovic; Krizanac, Marcic, Vidic, Budisa, Milovic, Vitaic, Simic (Rebic 57), Erceg, Baraban (Rasic 85), Golubovic (Cop 70).
Fulham: Schwarzer; Baird, Briggs, Murphy, Hughes, Hangeland, Duff, Etuhu (Sidwell 76), Johnson A, Zamora (Kasami 81), Riise J.

Stoke C (1) 1 *(Walters 2)*

Hajduk Split (0) 0 26,322

Stoke C: Begovic; Wilkinson, Wilson, Whelan, Huth, Shawcross, Pennant (Whitehead 75), Delap, Jones, Walters, Etherington (Shotton 88).
Hajduk Split: Subasic; Inoha, Vejic, Maloca, Ruben Lima, Anas Sharbini (Ljubicic 90), Andric, Tomasov (Ahmad Sharbini 85), Brkljaca, Oremus, Vukusic (Vukovic 63).

Valerenga (0) 0

PAOK Salonika (0) 2 *(Vieirinha 72, Garcia 90)* 3019

Valerenga: Hirschfeld; Nordvik, Muri, Strandberg, Dos Santos, Berre, Fellah (Nielsen 68), Zajic (Stoor 84), Singh, Ogude, Leigh (Kone 57).
PAOK Salonika: Kresic; Cirillo, Lino, Malezas, Etto, Fotakis (Robert 90), Garcia, Lazar (Tsoukalas 80), Arias, Vieirinha, Athanasiadis (Papazoglou 90).

Ventspils (1) 1 *(Visnakovs 44)*

Red Star Belgrade (1) 2 *(Kaluderovic 10, Bruno Mezenga 90)* 3000

Ventspils: Vlasovs; Shibamura, Gabovs, Savcenkovs, Postnikov, Kosmacovs, Laizans, Tukura, Martinez (Abdultaofik 75), Rugins, Visnakovs.
Red Star Belgrade: Bajkovic; Tosic, Mikic, Reljic, Dimitrijevic (Vesovic 75), Kovacevic, Evandro (Cadu 46), Lazovic, Mijailovic, Kaluderovic (Bruno Mezenga 83), Borja.

Vorskla (0) 0

Sligo R (0) 0 8500

Vorskla: Velichko; Selin, Kurilov, Dallku, Chesnakov, Kryvosheenko (Sachko 81), Rebenok, Krasnoperov, Markoski (Zakarlyuka 46), Januzi, Bezus (Oberemko 73).
Sligo R: Clarke; McGuinness, Powell, Keane, Peers, Kirby, Ndo, Ryan, Cretaro (Davoren 77), Blinkhorn (Russell 90), Greene (Doyle 63).

Young Boys (2) 3 *(Farnerud 22, Degen 33, 79)*

Westerlo (1) 1 *(Bruls 34)* 11,163

Young Boys: Wolfli; Spycher, Nef, Veskovac, Degen, Silberbauer, Sutter, Costanzo (Schneuwly 71), Farnerud, N'Tsama, Ben Khalifa (Nuzzolo 57).
Westerlo: De Winter; Van Hout, Vanaudenaerde, De Petter, Corstjens, Farssi, Delen, Bruls, Annab (Molenberghs 64), Ngolok, Marcao (Dekelver 64).

Zeljeznicar (0) 0

Maccabi Tel Aviv (0) 2 *(Colautti 47, 56)* 10,000

Zeljeznicar: Karic; Bogicevic, Gerhardt, Kvesic, Savic (Jamak 70), Beslija (Selimovic 58), Zeba, Smajic, Markovic, Svraka, Adilovic (Visca 70).
Maccabi Tel Aviv: Haimov; Nivaldo, Pavicevic, Ziv, Saban, Lugasi (Alberman 69), Medunjanin, Dahan (Israelevich 46), Kaat (Colautti 46), Konate, Dabbur.

THIRD QUALIFYING ROUND SECOND LEG

Thursday, 4 August 2011

Aktobe (0) 1 *(Dilas 75)*

Alaniya (0) 1 *(Bikmaev 55)* 12,700

Aktobe: Boychenko; Kenzhisariev, Smakov, Chichulin, Primus■, Khayrullin, Logvinenko, Semenov (Badlo 62), Maletic, Mane, Dilas.
Alaniya: Khomich; Grigoryev, Grachev, Gnanou (Gigolaev 105), Da Costa Goore, Bikmaev, Gabulov, Stoyanov, Khubulov (Dudiev 47) (Buraev 81), Danilo Neco, Tsarikaev.
aet; Alaniya won 4-2 on penalties.

Brondby (2) 4 *(Kristiansen 40, Krohn-Dehli 45 (pen), Akharraz 53, 55)*

Ried (0) 2 *(Royer 71, Hadzic 88)* 7769

Brondby: Andersen; Goodson, Randrup, Rasmussen (Fredriksen 57), Stenderup, Akharraz (Agger 75), Kristiansen, Krohn-Dehli, Thygesen, Nilsson, McGrath (Jatta 86).
Ried: Gebauer; Riegler, Hadzic, Karner, Reifeltshammer, Basala-Mazana (Nacho Rodriguez 61), Mader, Lexa, Ivan Carril (Hinum 46), Royer, Hammerer (Nacho Casanova 61).

Den Haag (0) 1 *(Derijck 53)*

Omonia (0) 0 13,268

Den Haag: Coutinho; Kum, Derijck, Leeuwin, Ammi (Mulders 32), Chery, Immers, Radosavljevic (Hocher 77), Toornstra, Verhoek, Vicento (Brouwer 72).
Omonia: Georgallides; Iago Bouzon, Alabi, Leandro De Almedia, Shpungin, Salatic, Efrem (Margaca 46), Avraam, Tadic, Alexandre (Kaseke 79), Christofi (Davidson Morais 88).

Dinamo Tbilisi (0) 2 *(Albert Yague 48, Kakhelishvili 55)*

KR (0) 0 12,000

Dinamo Tbilisi: Loria; Homola, Tomashvili, Kakubava (Beraia 66), Odikadze, Pirtskhalava, Kakhelishvili, Koshkadze (Tekturmanidze 62), Jighauri■, Albert Yague (Lekvtadze 56), Robertinho.
KR: Halldorsson; Gunnar Gunnarsson, Sigurdarson (Fridgeirsson 77), Josepsson, Hauksson (Baldvinsson 49), Olafsson A, Snorrason, Jonsson E, Jonsson B, Jonsson G, Finnbogason (Ludviksson 64).

Elfsborg (0) 1 *(Ericsson 65)*

Aalesund (0) 1 *(Ulvestad 49 (pen))* 2686

Elfsborg: Covic; Jonsson, Augustsson, Klarstrom (Lans 61), Svensson, Mobaeck (Elm 46), Nordmark, Larsson, Wede, Nilsson (Ericsson 46), Yarsuvat.
Aalesund: Grytebust; Arnefjord, Jaager, Jalasto, Fuhre (Flotre 57), Post (Sandnes 84), Carlsen, Olsen, Morrison (Larsen 46), Ulvestad, Phillips.

FK Austria (1) 3 *(Barazite 18, 46, 69 (pen))*

Olimpija (0) 2 *(Vrsic 54, Jovic 59)* 7688

FK Austria: Grundwald P; Ortlechner, Margreitter, Suttner (Rogulj 82), Leovac, Klein, Junuzovic, Grundwald A■, Barazite (Koch 88), Jun, Linz (Gorgon 52).
Olimpija: Dzafic; Salkic, Andelkovic■, Vrsic, Lovrecic (Bozic 75), Omladic, Radujko, Mlinar, Fink (Valencic 56), Jovic, Cadikovski (Smiljanic 87).

Fulham (1) 2 *(Johnson A 19, Murphy 56 (pen))*

Split (0) 0 17,087

Fulham: Schwarzer; Senderos, Riise J, Murphy, Hughes, Hangeland, Duff (Kasami 89), Etuhu, Johnson A, Zamora (Dembele 76), Dempsey (Briggs 81).
Split: Vukovic; Krizanac, Marcic, Vidic, Budisa, Milovic, Vitaic (Rasic 75), Simic, Erceg, Baraban (Obilinovic 61), Cop (Jordan 83).

Gaz Metan (0) 1 *(Thaer Al Bawab 62)*

Mainz (1) 1 *(Risse 31)* 5600

Gaz Metan: Plesca; Lazar, Khubutia, Trtovac (Munteanu 82), Markovic (Petre 46), Buzean, Todea, Hoban, Breeveld, Roman (Litu 46), Thaer Al Bawab.
Mainz: Wetklo; Noveski, Svensson, Pospech (Sliskovic 91), Bungert, Polanski, Soto, Ivanschitz (Caligiuri 64), Baumgartlinger, Risse, Ujah (Allagui 54).
aet; Gaz Metan won 4-3 on penalties.

Gomel (1) 1 *(Aleksievich 41)*

Bursa (0) 3 *(N'Diaye 78, Insua 86, Turgay 90)* 13,100

Gomel: Bushma; Kuzmianok, Matveichyk, Kontsevoy (Stepanov 84), Stasevich, Kashevski, Evseenko, Levitski, Lisovyi (Zuev 72), Kozeka■, Aleksievich (Platonov 89).
Bursa: Carson; Stepanov, Serdar, Ibrahim, Vederson, Kirita (Insua 46), Batalla, N'Diaye (Svensson 88), Volkan (Sercan 75), Ozan, Turgay.

Guimaraes (1) 2 *(Faouzi 45, Targino 76)*

Midtjylland (1) 1 *(Nielsen 28)* 9062

Guimaraes: Nilson; Joao Paulo, Alex, Anderson Santana, El Adoua, N'Diaye, Pedro Mendes (Marcelo Toscano 46), Renan Teixeira (Leonel Olimpio 79), Barrientos (Targino 67), Edgar Silva, Faouzi.
Midtjylland: Jensen; Afriyie, Juelsgard Kristensen, Ipsa, Nielsen (Albrechtsen 46), Poulsen, Albaek (Janssen 80), Uzochukwu, Hassan, Nworuh, Igboun (Salami 61).

Hacken (1) 2 *(Makondele 28, 87)*

Nacional (1) 1 *(Rondon 40)* 808

Hacken: Kallqvist; Ostberg, Arkivuo, Forsell (Williams 57), Soderberg, Chatto (Elvby 79), Bjurstrom, Makondele, Henriksson, Chibuike, Waris.
Nacional: Elisson; Felipe Lopes, Danielson, Nuno Pinto, Todorovic, Mihelic (Candeias 78), Skolnik, Joao Aurelio, Elizeu (Edgar Costa 64), Mateus, Rondon (Oliver 78).

Hajduk Split (0) 0

Stoke C (0) 1 *(Milicevic 90 (og))* 33,000

Hajduk Split: Subasic; Milicevic, Maloca, Ruben Lima, Anas Sharbini, Andric, Tomasov (Kukoc 87), Brkljaca, Trebotic (Saric 69), Vukovic (Ahmad Sharbini 56), Vukusic.
Stoke C: Begovic; Huth, Wilson, Whelan, Shawcross, Woodgate, Pennant (Pugh 84), Whitehead, Jones (Diao 77), Walters (Shotton 86), Etherington.

Hearts (2) 4 *(Stevenson 34, 45, Driver 50, Skacel 75)*

Paksi (0) 1 *(Bode 89)* 12,811

Hearts: Kello; McGowan, Grainger, Jonsson, Zaliukas (Hamill 46), Mrowiec, Stevenson, Black, Templeton, Elliott (Sutton 13), Driver (Skacel 63).
Paksi: Csernyanszki; Eger, Heffler, Fiola, Sifter, Balo, Bode, Magasfoldi (Csehi 55), Sipeki, Bartha, Kiss (Montvai 79).

Helsingborg (1) 3 *(Lindstrom 3, 73, Gashi 61)*

Bnei Yehuda (0) 0 5002

Helsingborg: Hansson; Edman, Andersson C (Thern 86), Larsson, Holgersson, Baffo, Gashi (Patronen 89), Sundin, Lindstrom, Mahlangu, Jonsson (Aberg 90).
Bnei Yehuda: Aiyenugba; Azoz, Hadad, Mori, Ivaskevicius, Edri, Rali■, Galvan, Menashe (Zairi 79), Balili (Levi 82), Marinkovic (Agaiev 76).

Jablonec (0) 1 *(Loucka 80)*

AZ (1) 1 *(Benschop 45)* 4844

Jablonec: Spit; Pavlik, Loucka, Benes, Vanek (Tresnak 87), Pitak, Jablonsky, Kovarik, Novak (Stochl 59), Lafata, Vosahlik (Kopic 13).
AZ: Alvarado; Marcellis, Moisander, Viergever, Martens, Holman (Ortiz 66), Wernbloom, Elm (Falkenburg 77), Poulsen, Benschop, Boymans (Gudmundsson 71).

Karabakh (0) 1 *(Soltanov 87)*

Club Brugge (0) 0 8800

Karabakh: Pavlovic; Rashad F Sadygov, Teli, Medvedev, Garayev, Agolli, Rashad A Sadygov (Nedzipi 76), Yusifov, Ismayilov, Adamia (Soltanov 82), Aliyev.
Club Brugge: Coosemans; Donk, Hogli, Almeback, Vansteenkiste, Odjidja-Ofoe, Refaelov, Meunier (Lestienne 44), Van Acker, Vleminckx (Akpala 62), Victor Vazquez (Deschilder 65).

Legia (0) 0

Gaziantep (0) 0 20,118

Legia: Skaba; Rzezniczak, Wawrzyniak, Komorowski, Zewlakow, Radovic (Jedrzejczyk 90), Vrdoljak (Gol 46), Rybus (Hubnik 77), Borysiuk, Manu, Ljuboja.
Gaziantep: Karcemarskas; Serdar, Emre G, Ivan, Nounkeu, Olcan, Murat (Bekir 61), Popov (Wagner 73), Pehlivan (Alper 90), Sosa, Cenk.

Lokomotiv Sofia (0) 0

Slask (0) 0 2610

Lokomotiv Sofia: Galev; Varbanov, Dyakov (Garov 90), Dobrev, Atanasov, Lahchev, Yanev (Dafchev 46), Ivanov, Pisarov, Goranov, Mesic (Yordanov 75).
Slask: Kelemen; Wasiluk, Celeban, Pietrasiak, Spahic, Mila, Cetnarski, Elsner, Dudek (Sztylka 117), Sobota (Madej 82), Diaz (Voskamp 59).
aet; Slask won 4-3 on penalties.

Maccabi Tel Aviv (3) 6 *(Colautti 18, 45, Dahan 38, Atar 54, 86, Vasilic 82 (og))*

Zeljeznicar (0) 0 6013

Maccabi Tel Aviv: Haimov; Vered, Pavicevic, Ziv, Lugasi, Israelevich (Atar 46), Yeini, Dahan (Kaat 56), Micha, Konate, Colautti (Itzhaki 46).
Zeljeznicar: Karic; Stancheski, Gerhardt, Kvesic, Vasilic, Beslija (Selimovic 70), Zeba, Markovic, Svraka (Zolotic 70), Jamak (Visca 59), Adilovic.

Mlada Boleslav (0) 2 *(Reznicek 52 (pen), Stohanzl 74)*

AEK Larnaca (1) 2 *(Priso 43, Mrdakovic 76 (pen))* 2312

Mlada Boleslav: Miller; Janicek, Rolko, Sirl, Opiela, Kudela, Stohanzl, Zahustel (Taborsky 64), Kysela, Kulic (Chramosta 46), Reznicek.
AEK Larnaca: Fortin; De Cler, Hofland, Albert Serran, Van Dijk, Linssen (Dimech 83), Priso■, Demetriou, Gonzalo Garcia (Skopelitis 66), Mrdakovic, Kingsley (Ruben Gomez 60).

Olympiakos Volos (1) 3 *(Martin 30, Szelesi 57, Solakis 83)*

Differdange (0) 0 4267

Olympiakos Volos: Jose Roca; Szelesi, Sankare, Dolezaj, Alvarez, Zaradoukas (Rokas 75), Darbion, Schembri (Solakis 46), Noe Acosta (Breska 46), Monje, Martin.
Differdange: Weber; Afoun, Rodrigues de Almeida, Kintziger, Janisch, Lebresne, Bettmer, Leoni, Piskor (Franzoni 64), Caron (May 85), Er Rafik (Ribeiro Alves 78).
Olympiakos Volos demoted from Greek top division and excluded from play-off round.

PAOK Salonika (1) 3 *(Vieirinha 45, Athanasiadis 49, Fotakis 58)*

Valerenga (0) 0 22,168

PAOK Salonika: Kresic; Cirillo, Lino, Malezas, Etto, Fotakis, Garcia (Contreras 79), Ivic (Georgiadis 61), Arias, Vieirinha (Robert 69), Athanasiadis.
Valerenga: Hirschfeld; Nordvik (Leigh 46), Muri, Strandberg, Dos Santos, Berre, Fellah, Zajic (Nielsen 73), Singh, Ogude (Haestad 60), Kone.

Rabotnicki (0) 1 *(Kumbev 87)*

Anorthosis (0) 2 *(Rezek 50, Cristovao 64)* 10,000

Rabotnicki: Dimitrievski; Kumbev, Lazarevski, Manevski, Nastevski (Gligorov 76), Todorovski, Bogdanovic (Petkovski 73), Vujcic, Petrovic, Velkoski K, Velkoski D (Micevski 70).
Anorthosis: Ivankov; Sprockel, Colin, Janicio, Andic, Laban, Okkas, Rezek (Michail 89), Vucicevic (Marquinhos 57), Cristovao, Laborde (Angelov 72).

Red Star Belgrade (4) 7 *(Martinez 13 (og), Kaluderovic 23, 53, Lazovic 26, Borja 41, 75, Bruno Mezenga 60)*

Ventspils (0) 0 39,628

Red Star Belgrade: Bajkovic; Tosic, Vilotic, Mikic, Dimitrijevic, Kovacevic (Cosic 62), Cadu (Jankovic 67), Lazovic, Mijailovic, Kaluderovic (Bruno Mezenga 57), Borja.
Ventspils: Vlasovs; Shibamura, Gabovs, Savcenkovs, Postnikov (Mukins 80), Kosmacovs, Laizans, Tukura, Martinez (Sukhanov 46), Rugins■, Visnakovs (Abdultaofik 72).

Rennes (0) 2 *(Montano 75, Feret 85)*

Metalurgi Rustavi (0) 0 13,848

Rennes: Costil; Danze, Mangane, Kana Biyik, Theophile Catherine, Tettey, Pitroipa (Dalmat 73), Feret, Brahimi (Camara 11), M'Vila, Boukari (Montano 64).
Metalurgi Rustavi: Batiashvili; Orbeladze, Japaridze, Lomaia, Makhviladze, Kavtaradze (Aburjania 77), Maisuradze, Getsadze, Tatanashvili (Kobalia 61), Modebadze, Mikaberidze (Dobrovolski 56).

Sarajevo (0) 0

Sparta Prague (2) 2 *(Kweuke 20, Matejovsky 36)* 5600

Sarajevo: Hamzic; Belosevic■, Torlak, Dupovac, Kojasevic (Handzic H 69), Scepanovic (Maksumic 79), Comor, Handzic K, Obuca, Suljic (Trebinjac 58), Haskic.
Sparta Prague: Blazek; Brabec, Vidlicka, Repka, Pamic, Vacek, Matejovsky (Abena 83), Husek, Juhar, Kweuke (Keric 64), Kadlec (Mares 57).

Senica (0) 0

Salzburg (1) 3 *(Leonardo 10, Alan 57, 64)* 3273

Senica: Bolek; Gorosito, Pavlik, Gajdosik, Sima, Kona, Wijlaars, Motha, Piroska (Valenta 76), Kalabiska (Divis 58), Hosek (Kroupa 66).
Salzburg: Gustafsson; Ulmer, Sekagya, Schwegler, Hinteregger, Cziommer (Hierlander 74), Lindgren, Svento, Leitgeb, Leonardo (Jantscher 67), Alan (Wallner 68).

Sligo R (0) 0

Vorskla (2) 2 *(Zakarlyuka 16, Rebenok 17)* 3800

Sligo R: Clarke; McGuinness, Powell, Peers, Ventre, Kirby, Ndo, Ryan, Cretaro (Russell 69), Blinkhorn (Dillon 69), Greene (Doyle 55).
Vorskla: Dolganski; Selin, Kurilov, Dallku, Chesnakov, Zakarlyuka (Oberemko 46), Kryvosheenko, Rebenok, Krasnoperov (Osipenko 80), Markoski, Sachko (Bezus 68).

Spartak Trnava (0) 2 *(Tomacek 52, 59 (pen))*

Levski (1) 1 *(Ars 11)* 12,169

Spartak Trnava: Raska; Koubsky, Gross, Hanzel, Carnota■, Karhan, Vyskocil (Cvirik 118), Kascak, Prochazka, Bicak (Gogolak 72) (Ciprys 120), Tomacek.
Levski: Iliev; Mulder, Starokin, Miliev (Dimov 52), Risp, Greene■, Gadzhev, Yovov, Tsvetkov (Toni Calvo 69), Ars, Mladenov (Raykov 100).
aet; Spartak Trnava won 5-4 on penalties.

St Patrick's Ath (0) 1 *(McMillan E 57)*

Karpaty (1) 3 *(Zenjov 22, Khudobyak 64, Oshchipko 83)* 2109

St Patrick's Ath: Rogers; Pender, Bermingham, Shortall, McMillan E (Kenna 69), Bradley (Daly 23), Mulcahy, Doyle (North 61), McFaul, McMillan D, Kavanagh.
Karpaty: Tlumak; Oshchipko, Milosevic, Fedetskiy, Borja Gomez, Khudobyak, Tkachuk, Kopolovets (Voronkov 55), Martynyuk, Zenjov (Pacheco 68), Lucas (Cristobal 76).

Stromsgodset (0) 0

Atletico Madrid (1) 2 *(Adrian 13, Reyes 90)* 6807

Stromsgodset: Kwarasey; Madsen, Andersen, Aas, Kamara (Berget 69), Storflor, Konradsen (Nordkvelle 69), Sankoh, Vilsvik, Abu, Keita.
Atletico Madrid: Joel; Antonio Lopez, Perea, Dominguez, Silvio, Reyes, Gabi (Raul Garcia 74), Paulo Assuncao, Salvio (Juanfran 65), Forlan, Adrian (Filipe Luis 82).

Thun (0) 1 *(Lezcano 65)*

Palermo (0) 1 *(Gonzalez 49)* 7227

Thun: Da Costa; Luthi, Schneider, Matic, Schindelholz, Battig, Andrist, Demiri, Schneuwly (Hediger 77), Wittwer (Reinmann 90), Lezcano (Sanogo 90).
Palermo: Benussi; Cassani, Bovo, Mantovani, Balzaretti (Nocerino 46), Munoz, Migliaccio (Bertolo 78), Ilicic, Acquah, Miccoli, Gonzalez (Zahavi 63).

Vaduz (0) 2 *(Zanni 78, Rafinha 81)*

Hapoel Tel Aviv (1) 1 *(Damari 1)* 870

Vaduz: Jehle; Cerrone, Schwegler, Oehri (Zanni 73), Cvetinovic, Kienzl, Sara, Rafinha, Hasler N (Hasler D 62), Cecchini, Tripodi (Baron 62).
Hapoel Tel Aviv: Edel; Pecalka, Kende, Ben Dayan, Tuama, Badir, Abutbul (Abass 68), Shivhon (Cohen 71), Yadin, Tamuz, Damari (Al Lala 80).

Varazdin (1) 1 *(Golubar 14)*

Dinamo Bucharest (2) 2 *(Danciulescu 7, Munteanu 26)* 2600

Varazdin: Krklec; Gluhak, Tkalcic, Glavina, Safaric, Simek, Conjar, Aganovic, Vugrinec (Trojak 46), Golubar (Cerovecki 65), Sacer (Grgec 90).
Dinamo Bucharest: Balgradean; Moti, Scarlatache, Diabate, Munteanu, Alexe (Patrascu 64), Torje, Rus, Kone, Danciulescu, Niculae (Tucudean 89).

Westerlo (0) 0

Young Boys (1) 2 *(Schneuwly 5, N'Tsama 77)* 2388

Westerlo: Deelkens; Vanaudenaerde, De Petter (Adams 73), Corstjens, De Greef, Delen, Bruls, Annab (Molenberghs 59), Ngolok, Dekelver (Marcao 73), Liliu.
Young Boys: Wolfli; Spycher, Nef, Veskovac, Zverotic, Degen, Silberbauer (Doubai 59), Nuzzolo, Farnerud, Schneuwly (N'Tsama 65), Ben Khalifa (Costanzo 79).

PLAY-OFF ROUND FIRST LEG

Thursday, 18 August 2011

Aalesund (1) 2 *(Barrantes 14 (pen), 74)*

AZ (1) 1 *(Martens 30)* 5646

Aalesund: Grytebust; Arnefjord, Jaager, Matland, Tollas, Barrantes, Carlsen, Olsen (Sellin 82), Morrison, Myklebust (Okoronkwo 46), Phillips.
AZ: Alvarado; Marcellis, Poulsen, Moisander, Viergever, Martens (Falkenburg 69), Holman (Altidore 76), Wernbloom, Elm, Gudmundsson, Benschop.

AEK Athens (0) 1 *(Jose Carlos 87)*

Dinamo Tbilisi (0) 0 12,640

AEK Athens: Konstantopoulos; Dellas (Juan Cala 32), Karabelas, Georgeas, Manolas, Makos, Kafes, Jose Carlos, Gudjohnsen (Lagos 81), Liberopoulos (Leonardo 56), Beleck.
Dinamo Tbilisi: Loria; Tomashvili, Rekhviashvili, Kakubava, Xisco Munoz (Lekvtadze 90), Kakhelishvili (Carlos Coto 60), Odikadze, Mikel Alvaro, Koshkadze (Pirtskhalava 83), Kvekveskiri, Albert Yague.

Athletic Bilbao (0) 0

Trabzonspor (0) 0 26,000

Athletic Bilbao: Iraizoz; Amorebieta, San Jose, Gabilondo (Susaeta 46), Gurpegi, Javi Martinez, Iturraspe (Toquero 46), Ander Herrera, Llorente, Muniain, De Marcos (Aurtenetxe 63).
Trabzonspor: Tolga; Glowacki, Remzi, Celustka, Mustafa (Aykut 68), Serkan, Alanzinho (Baris 90), Colman, Burak■, Paulo Henrique (Badur 87), Halil Altintop.

Atletico Madrid (0) 2 *(Elias 68, 73)*

Guimaraes (0) 0 27,153

Atletico Madrid: Joel; Perea, Filipe Luis, Dominguez, Silvio (Elias 65), Reyes (Antonio Lopez 78), Tiago, Gabi, Mario Suarez (Juanfran 69), Salvio, Adrian.
Guimaraes: Nilson; Joao Paulo■, Alex, Anderson Santana, El Adoua, N'Diaye, Pedro Mendes, Barrientos (Targino 46), Leonel Olimpio, Marcelo Toscano (Joao Alves 74), Paulo Sergio (Faouzi 58).

Besiktas (1) 3 *(Sivok 20, Guti 75 (pen), Hugo Almeida 90)*

Alaniya (0) 0 18,430

Besiktas: Rustu; Ibrahim, Egemen, Sivok, Ismail, Simao (Holosko 31), Ernst, Guti, Manuel Fernandes, Hugo Almeida (Mehmet 90), Mustafa (Kavlak 60).
Alaniya: Khomich; Grigoryev, Grachev, Dudiev (Barbarouses 53), Pliev, Bikmaev, Bakaev, Gabulov, Danilo Neco (Khubulov 70), Zelaya (Bulgaru 37), Tsarikaev.

Braga (0) 0

Young Boys (0) 0 12,457

Braga: Quim; Paulo Vinicius, Imorou (Echiejile 23), Baiano, Ewerton, Hugo Viana, Marcio Mossoro (Helder Barbosa 70), Mahamat, Leandro Salino, Nuno Gomes (Meyong 70), Alan.
Young Boys: Benito; Spycher, Nef■, Veskovac, Zverotic, Silberbauer, Raimondi (Mayuka 62), Nuzzolo, Farnerud (Doubai 58), Ben Khalifa, Bienvenu (Affolter 78).

Bursa (1) 1 *(Vederson 36 (pen))*

Anderlecht (0) 2 *(Legear 53 (pen), Jovanovic 77)* 21,920

Bursa: Carson; Omer, Serdar, Ibrahim■, Vederson, Insua (Kirita 46), Batalla (Mehmet 84), N'Diaye, Volkan, Ozan (Sercan 59), Bangura.
Anderlecht: Proto; Safari, Odoi, Samuel, Biglia, Kljestan, Legear (Gillet 75), Kouyate, Fernando Canesin (De Sutter 88), Suarez, Kanu (Jovanovic 65).

Celtic (0) 0

Sion (0) 0 51,795

Celtic: Forster; Wilson M, Mulgrew, Ki, Majstorovic, Cha, Brown, Ledley, Samaras (McCourt 84), Stokes (Maloney 69), Commons (Forrest 56).
Sion: Vanins; Dingsdag, Buhler, Vanczak, Jose Goncalves, Adailton, Feindouno (Rodrigo 90), Obradovic (Gabri 85), Serey Die, Sio, Afonso (Mutsch 51).
Sion subsequently removed from competition with a 3-0 default.

Differdange (0) 0

Paris St Germain (1) 4 *(Gameiro 17, Bahebeck 71, Ceara 89, Menez 90)* 6153

Differdange: Weber; Bukvic, Rodrigues de Almeida, Janisch, Kettenmayer, Lebresne (Er Rafik 81), Bettmer, Leoni, Siebenaler, Caron (Piskor 88), Franzoni (Albanese 69).

Paris St Germain: Sirigu; Camara, Tiene, Ceara, Bisevac (N'Goyi 52), Matuidi (Kebano 79), Menez, Bodmer, Pastore, Gameiro (Maurice 66), Bahebeck.

Ekranas (0) 1 *(Samusiovas 82)*

Hapoel Tel Aviv (0) 0 2748

Ekranas: Zubas; Gleveckas, Joksas, Samusiovas, Tomkevicius, Radavicius, Kucys, Mauro Alonso (Skinderis 84), Velicka, Fofana (Moroz 56), Umeh (Markevicius 72).

Hapoel Tel Aviv: Edel; Fransman, Ben Dayan, Hotba, Tuama (Cohen 87), Badir, Abutbul, Yadin, Igiebor, Tamuz, Damari (Al Lala 69).

FK Austria (2) 3 *(Linz 7, Barazite 45, 61)*

Gaz Metan (1) 1 *(Breeveld 24)* 9100

FK Austria: Grunwald P; Ortlechner, Margreitter, Suttner, Klein, Hlinka, Junuzovic, Liendl (Gorgon 62), Barazite (Stankovic 68), Jun (Tadic 87), Linz.

Gaz Metan: Plesca; Lazar, Trtovac, Markovic, Buzean, Zaharia (Litu 57), Petre, Todea, Hoban (Bozesan 69), Breeveld, Thaer Al Bawab.

Fulham (2) 3 *(Hughes 38, Dempsey 43, 49)*

Dnepr (0) 0 14,823

Fulham: Schwarzer; Kelly, Briggs, Murphy (Etuhu 67), Hughes, Hangeland, Duff (Dembele 67), Sidwell, Kasami (Johnson 88), Zamora, Dempsey.

Dnepr: Lastuvka; Denisov, Mandzyuk, Cheberyachko, Boateng (Zozulya 56), Rotan, Giuliano (Oliynyk 70), Kulakov, Kravchenko, Kalinic, Konoplyanka.

Hannover (2) 2 *(Schlaudraff 6, 45)*

Sevilla (1) 1 *(Kanoute 37)* 43,500

Hannover: Zieler; Haggui, Schulz, Pogatetz, Rausch (Pander 81), Cherundolo, Sergio Pinto, Stindl, Schmiedebach (Hauger 90), Schlaudraff (Ya Konan 75), Abdellaoue.

Sevilla: Palop; Escude, Navarro, Spahic, Fazio (Medel 73), Trochowski, Jesus Navas, Armenteros (Perotti 46), Kanoute, Negredo (Manu 78), Coke.

Hearts (0) 0

Tottenham H (3) 5 *(Van der Vaart 5, Defoe 13, Livermore 28, Bale 63, Lennon 78)* 16,279

Hearts: Kello; Mrowiec (Obua 82), Grainger, Hamill, Webster, Zaliukas, Stevenson, Black, Sutton (Skacel 74), Templeton, Driver (Elliott 65).

Tottenham H: Gomes; Walker, Assou-Ekotto, Van der Vaart (Huddlestone 59), Kaboul, Dawson, Lennon, Kranjcar, Defoe (Pavlyuchenko 79), Livermore, Bale (Townsend 70).

HJK Helsinki (1) 2 *(Pukki 18, 54)*

Schalke (0) 0 10,504

HJK Helsinki: Wallen; Kansikas, Lindstrom, Lahti, Rafinha, Sorsa (Zeneli 86), Riihilahti, Bah, Ring, Sadik (Litmanen 67), Pukki (Perovuo 82).

Schalke: Fahrmann; Uchida, Howedes, Papadopoulos, Holtby (Baumjohann 77), Moravek (Gavranovic 59), Matip, Hoger, Draxler, Huntelaar, Marica (Jurado 59).

Lazio (2) 6 *(Hernanes 20, Mauri 39, Cisse 51, 65, Rocchi 87, Klose 90)*

Rabotnicki (0) 0 24,532

Lazio: Marchetti; Scaloni, Biava, Andre Dias, Radu, Brocchi (Matuzalem 63), Mauri (Lulic 72), Ledesma, Hernanes, Klose, Cisse (Rocchi 85).

Rabotnicki: Dimitrievski; Lazarevski, Najdoski, Manevski (Petkovski 85), Muarem (Gligorov 77), Todorovski, Micevski (Nastevski 43), Vujcic, Petrovic, Velkoski K, Velkoski D.

Legia (1) 2 *(Radovic 3, 69)*

Spartak Moscow (0) 2 *(Ari 52, 71)* 23,450

Legia: Skaba; Jedrzejczyk, Wawrzyniak, Komorowski, Zewlakow, Radovic, Rybus (Kucharczyk 63), Borysiuk, Gol, Manu (Zyro 90), Ljuboja.

Spartak Moscow: Dikan; Pareja, Rodri, Makeev, De Zeeuw (Ananidze 80), Kombarov K, Rafael Carioca, Ari, Welliton, Dzyuba (Zotov 57), Emenike (Kozlov 63).

Litex (1) 1 *(Yanev 13)*

Dynamo Kiev (1) 2 *(Ninkovic 7 (pen), Brown 77)* 5862

Litex: Vinicius; Josse (Milanov G 68), Bodurov, Zanev, Itoua Onanga (Nikolov 60), Milanov I, Yanev, Tom, Thiago Miracema, Tsvetkov, Celio Codo (Todorov 70).

Dynamo Kiev: Shovkovsky; Betao, Popov, Danilo Silva, Yussuf, Eremenko, Ninkovic (Lukman 60), Vukojevic, Milevskiy (Garmash 90), Brown, Yarmolenko (Aliyev 78).

Lokomotiv Moscow (2) 2 *(Yanbayev 34, Maicon 37)*

Spartak Trnava (0) 0 13,402

Lokomotiv Moscow: Guilherme; Manuel da Costa, Shishkin, Yanbayev, Durica, Tarasov, Glushakov, Ignatyev (Obinna 69), Ibricic (Alberto Zapater 65), Sychev (Caicedo 81), Maicon.

Spartak Trnava: Raska; Koubsky, Gross, Hanzel L, Diallo, Karhan, Vyskocil (Malcharek 54), Kascak, Prochazka, Bicak (Ciprys 90), Oravec (Bernath 72).

Maccabi Tel Aviv (0) 3 *(Konate 60, Atar 67 (pen), 90)*

Panathinaikos (0) 0 12,500

Maccabi Tel Aviv: Haimov; Nivaldo, Pavicevic, Vered, Lugasi, Yeini, Dahan (Medunjanin 53), Micha, Konate (Kaat 71), Atar, Dabbur (Colautti 46).

Panathinaikos: Tzorvas; Boumsong, Kante, Vyntra, Spiropoulos, Katsouranis, Owusu-Abeyie, Simao (Zeca 69), Ninis (Vitolo 55), Leto, Toche.

Maribor (0) 2 *(Ibraimi 52, Velikonja 90)*

Rangers (1) 1 *(Juanma Ortiz 31)* 10,900

Maribor: Handanovic; Rajcevic, Arghus, Ibraimi (Milec 86), Viler, Mezga, Mertelj, Beric, Mejac, Volas (Velikonja 79), Filipovic (Cvijanovic 68).

Rangers: McGregor; Goian, Bocanegra, Broadfoot, Wallace, McCulloch, Juanma Ortiz, Davis, Jelavic, Naismith (Lafferty 46), Edu.

Metalist Kharkiv (0) 0

Sochaux (0) 0 35,886

Metalist Kharkiv: Horyainov; Fininho, Torsiglieri, Villagra, Gueye, Cleiton Xavier, Torres (Valyaev 76), Sosa, Edmar, Cristaldo (Devic 60), Taison (Tkachev 90).

Sochaux: Richert; Sauget, Perquis, Mikari (Roudet 80), Corchia, Carliao, Martin, Boudebouz, Nogueira, Anin, Butin (Privat 83).

Nacional (0) 0

Birmingham C (0) 0 4323

Nacional: Elisson; Felipe Lopes, Danielson, Nuno Pinto, Luis Alberto, Mihelic (Diego Barcellos 46), Skolnik (Elizeu 46), Joao Aurelio, Mateus, Rondon, Edgar Costa (Candeias 69).

Birmingham C: Myhill; Carr, Murphy, Spector, Caldwell, Ridgewell, Burke, Davies, Wood, Redmond, Beausejour.

Nordsjaelland (0) 0

Sporting Lisbon (0) 0 3891

Nordsjaelland: Hansen; Parkhurst, Kildentoft, Bjelland, Stokholm, Christensen, Beckmann (Mikkelsen 60), Adu, Okore, Lawan (Laudrup 74), Granskov-Hansen (Rohde 82).

Sporting Lisbon: Rui Patricio; Anderson Polga, Rodriguez, Joao Pereira, Evaldo, Schaars, Jeffren (Izmailov 46), Rinaudo, Andre Santos (Fernandez 60), Helder Postiga (Rubio 68), Yannick Djalo.

Omonia (2) 2 *(Freddy 35, Leandro 45)*
Salzburg (1) 1 *(Alan 3)* 11,858
Omonia: Georgallides; Cherfa (Iago Bouzon 70), Karipidis, Leandro De Almeida, Shpungin, Salatic, Efrem, Avraam, Alexandre (Bruno Aguiar 81), Christofi (Margaca 65), Freddy.
Salzburg: Gustafsson; Ulmer, Sekagya, Schwegler (Jantscher 72), Hinteregger, Cziommer (Hierlander 22), Lindgren (Schiemer 86), Svento, Leitgeb, Leonardo, Alan.

PAOK Salonika (1) 2 *(Athanasiadis 15, Lino 56)*
Karpaty (0) 0 21,424
PAOK Salonika: Kresic; Cirillo, Contreras (Malezas 46), Lino, Etto, Fotakis, Garcia, Lazar (Georgiadis 72), Arias (Balafas 86), Vierinha, Athanasiadis.
Karpaty: Tlumak; Balazic, Oshchipko, Fedetskiy, Borja Gomez, Khudobyak, Tkachuk, Golodyuk, Cristobal (Voronkov 65), Zenjov (Pacheco 57), Lucas (Kravchenko 75).

Red Star Belgrade (1) 1 *(Cadu 17 (pen))*
Rennes (1) 2 *(Pitroipa 41, Montano 75)* 51,862
Red Star Belgrade: Bajkovic; Tosic, Vilotic, Mikic, Cosic, Dimitrijevic, Kovacevic, Cadu (Evandro 56), Lazovic (Vesovic 77), Kaluderovic (Bruno Mezenga 66), Borja.
Rennes: Costil; Danze, Mangane, Boye, Mavinga, Dalmat (M'Vila 61), Tettey, Feret, Pajot, Boukari (Montano 67), Pitroipa (Kembo-Ekoko 76).

Ried (0) 0
PSV Eindhoven (0) 0 5740
Ried: Gebauer; Riegler, Hadzic, Karner, Reifeltshammer, Ziegl (Ivan Carril 74), Lexa (Guillem 89), Hinum, Royer, Hammerer (Nacho Casanova 49), Nacho Rodriguez.
PSV Eindhoven: Isaksson; Pieters, Bouma, Marcelo (Verkoelen 90), Manolev (Tamata 46), Ojo, Wijnaldum, Strootman, Lens, Toivonen, Mertens (Labyad 52).

Rosenborg (0) 0
AEK Larnaca (0) 0 5081
Rosenborg: Orlund; Dorsin, Lago, Lustig, Wangberg (Ronning 46), Dockal, Issah, Henriksen, Svensson (Moldskred 72), Fredheim Holm (Bakenga 80), Prica.
AEK Larnaca: Alexandre Negri; De Cler, Ander Murillo, Dimech, Van Dijk, Linssen, Ruben Gomez (Alfa 78), Demetriou, Gonzalo Garcia (Mitidis 90), Mrdakovic, Kingsley (Pavlou 63).

Shamrock Rovers (0) 1 *(McCabe 81)*
Partizan Belgrade (1) 1 *(Tomic 14)* 4650
Shamrock Rovers: Thompson; Rice (Kilduff 76), Murray, Sullivan, Sives, Stevens, Finn (Turner 46), McCormack, Dennehy (O'Neill 58), McCabe, Twigg.
Partizan Belgrade: Stojkovic; Rankovic, Rnic, Ivanov, Stankovic, Ilic S (Markovic L 85), Kamara, Smiljanic, Tomic, Eduardo (Babovic 66), Jovancic (Markovic S 90).

Slask (1) 1 *(Mila 16)*
Rapid Bucharest (2) 3 *(Grigore 24, Roman 34, Apostol 80)* 7200
Slask: Kelemen; Wasiluk, Celeban, Pietrasiak, Socha, Mila, Cetnarski (Voskamp 46), Elsner, Dudek (Sztylka 72), Sobota (Madej 46), Diaz.
Rapid Bucharest: Coman; Marcos Antonio, Burca, Rui Duarte, Bozovic, Grigore (Apostol 57), Alexa, Roman, Herea, Surdu (Grigorie 85), Cassio (Pancu 76).

Slovan Bratislava (0) 1 *(Dobrotka 80)*
Roma (0) 0 10,548
Slovan Bratislava: Putnocky; Had, Dobrotka, Bagayoko, Cikos, Pauschek, Zofcak, Milinkovic (Kolcak 67), Sebo (Augustin 90), Kladrubsky, Lacny (Kuzma 74).
Roma: Stekelenburg; Burdisso, Cicinho, Cassetti, Jose Angel, Fabio Simplicio, Brighi (Perrotta 64), Viviani, Okaka (Borriello 76), Bojan, Caprari (Totti 72).

Standard Liege (0) 1 *(Tchite 60)*
Helsingborg (0) 0 10,457
Standard Liege: Sinan; Pocognoli, Goreux, Felipe, Belhocine, Kanu, Berrier (Mujangi Bia 74), Camara, Tchite, Leye (Nong 81), Benteke (Eninful 89).
Helsingborg: Hansson; Edman (Wahlstedt 9), Andersson C, Larsson, Holgersson (Alvaro Santos 74), Baffo, Gashi, Sundin (Thern 61), Lindstrom, Mahlangu, Jonsson.

Steaua (1) 2 *(Galamaz 16, Leandro Tatu 77)*
CSKA Sofia (0) 0 20,700
Steaua: Tatarusanu; Latovlevici, Galamaz (Geraldo Alves 59), Iliev, Martinovic (Rusescu 67), Nicolita, Brandan, Tanase, Bourceanu, Costea M (Nikolic 77), Leandro Tatu.
CSKA Sofia: M'Bolhi; Halilovic, Trifonov (Nelson 46), Bandalovski, Ademar, Stoyanov, Yanchev, Galchev, Zicu, Michel, Delev.

Thun (0) 0
Stoke C (1) 1 *(Pugh 18)* 7150
Thun: Da Costa■; Luthi, Reinmann, Matic, Schindelholz, Battig, Andrist, Demiri (Sanogo 70), Schneuwly (Wittwer 70), Lustrinelli (Rama 80), Lezcano.
Stoke C: Sorensen; Huth (Wilkinson 50), Tonge, Upson, Shawcross, Whitehead, Pugh, Wilson, Jones (Whelan 66), Walters, Etherington (Arismendi 73).

Vaslui (2) 2 *(Temwanjira 13, Milanov 36)*
Sparta Prague (0) 0 5170
Vaslui: Cerniauskas; Milanov, Balace, Farkas, Sanmartean (Annang 83), Zmeu, Costin, Willian, Neagu (Buhaescu 26), Temwanjira, Balaur (Jovanovic 82).
Sparta Prague: Blazek (Svenger 46); Zapotocny, Vidlicka, Repka, Pamic, Sionko (Kadlec 84), Vacek, Matejovsky, Husek, Juhar (Podany 68), Kweuke.

Vorskla (1) 2 *(Kryvosheenko 32, Rebenok 89)*
Dinamo Bucharest (0) 1 *(Niculae 58)* 9500
Vorskla: Dolganski; Selin, Kurilov, Dallku, Chesnakov, Kryvosheenko (Barannik 87), Rebenok, Krasnoperov, Markoski (Oberemko 46), Januzi (Gromov 77), Bezus.
Dinamo Bucharest: Balgradean; Moti, Scarlatache, Diabate, Grigore■, Munteanu (Alexe 75), Torje, Stoica, Kone, Danciulescu, Niculae (Ganea 86).

Zestafoni (0) 3 *(Gelashvili 59, 83, Dvali 63)*
Club Brugge (2) 3 *(Akpala 27, Refaelov 30, Hoefkens 72)* 7680
Zestafoni: Kvaskhvadze; Eliava, Sajaia, Ghonghadze (Benashvili 58), Kobakhidze, Gorgiashvili, Dzaria (Babunashvili 80), Grigalashvili, Aptsiauri, Gelashvili, Dvali (Tsinamdzgvrishvili 75).
Club Brugge: Coosemans; Donk, Hoefkens, Hogli, Almeback, Zimling, Dirar, Odjidja-Ofoe (Van Acker 60), Refaelov (Lestienne 70), Akpala (Meunier 81), Victor Vazquez.

PLAY-OFF ROUND SECOND LEG

Thursday, 25 August 2011

AEK Larnaca (1) 2 *(Van Dijk 21 (pen), 54 (pen))*
Rosenborg (0) 1 *(Henriksen 68)* 5342
AEK Larnaca: Fortin; De Cler, Hofland, Ander Murillo, Van Dijk, Skopelitis (Alfa 76), Priso, Demetriou, Gonzalo Garcia, Mrdakovic (Pavlou 35), Kingsley (Mitidis 79).
Rosenborg: Orlund; Ronning, Dorsin, Lago, Lustig, Dockal, Winsnes (Bakenga 46), Issah, Henriksen, Svensson, Prica.

Alaniya (0) 2 *(Gabulov 81, Danilo Neco 88)*
Besiktas (0) 0 10,000
Alaniya: Khomich; Grigoryev, Bulgaru, Da Costa Goore, Dudiev (Takazov 20), Pliev, Bikmaev (Gigolaev 73), Bakaev, Gabulov, Khubulov (Danilo Neco 49), Zelaya.
Besiktas: Rustu; Ibrahin■, Egemen, Sivok, Ismail, Ernst, Guti (Mehmet Aurelio 62), Manuel Fernandes, Kavlak (Ekrem 89), Hugo Almeida, Holosko (Mustafa 71).

Anderlecht (1) 2 *(Juhasz 38, Jovanovic 57)*

Bursa (1) 2 *(Turgay 5, Stepanov 68)* 15,551

Anderlecht: Proto; Juhasz, Safari, Odoi, Biglia, Kljestan, Gillet, Kouyate, De Sutter (Fernando Canesin 59), Jovanovic (Kanu 82), Suarez.
Bursa: Carson; Stepanov, Ibrahim, Vederson, Insua (Ismail 78), Svensson, Batalla, N'Diaye, Ahmet (Mehmet 74), Turgay, Bangura (Omer 86).

AZ (2) 6 *(Wernbloom 7, Altidore 24, 59, Martens 54, Holman 68, Moisander 90 (pen))*

Aalesund (0) 0 11,814

AZ: Alvarado; Marcellis, Poulsen, Moisander, Viergever, Martens (Maher 58), Holman, Wernbloom, Elm (Klavan 66), Beerens, Altidore (Benschop 63).
Aalesund: Grytebust; Arnefjord, Jaager, Matland (Sellin 46), Jalasto, Tollas (Skagestad 74), Barrantes (Larsen 67), Carlsen, Ulvestad, Okoronkwo, Phillips■.

Birmingham C (2) 3 *(Redmond 15, Murphy 24, Wood 86)*

Nacional (0) 0 27,698

Birmingham C: Myhill; Carr, Murphy, Caldwell, Davies, Spector, Burke (Asante 88), Beausejour, Wood (Jervis 89), Rooney, Redmond.
Nacional: Elisson; Felipe Lopes, Danielson, Claudemir (Edgar Costa 55), Tomasevic, Luis Alberto, Elizeu, Mateus (Oliver 64), Diego Barcellos (Mihelic 55), Candeias, Rondon.

Club Brugge (2) 2 *(Akpala 7, 26)*

Zestafoni (0) 0 23,725

Club Brugge: Coosemans; Donk, Hoefkens, Hogli, Almeback, Zimling, Dirar, Odjidja-Ofoe (Van Acker 78), Refaelov, Akpala (Meunier 71), Victor Vazquez (Blondel 65).
Zestafoni: Kvaskhvadze; Oniani, Eliava, Aladashvili (Sajaia 44), Kobakhidze, Gorgiashvili, Dzaria (Benashvili 33), Grigalashvili, Aptsiauri (Tsinamdzgvrishvili 57), Gelashvili, Dvali.

CSKA Sofia (0) 1 *(Michel 83)*

Steaua (0) 1 *(Tanase 74)* 17,200

CSKA Sofia: M'Bolhi; Halilovic (Vidanov 46), Bandalovski (Dechev 82), Ademar, Stoyanov, Yanchev, Galchev, Zicu (Kostov 78), Nelson, Michel, Delev.
Steaua: Tatarusanu; Latovlevici, Galamaz, Iliev, Nicolita, Prepelita (Bicfalvi 69), Brandan, Tanase (Nikolic 77), Bourceanu, Costea M (Rusescu 61), Leandro Tatu.

Dinamo Bucharest (1) 2 *(Torje 45, Tucudean 90)*

Vorskla (1) 3 *(Januzi 37, Barannik 72, 78)* 9641

Dinamo Bucharest: Balgradean; Moti, Scarlatache (Stoica 46), Diabate, Munteanu, Torje (Cazacu 84), Rus, Kone, Danciulescu, Ganea, Bakaj (Tucudean 52).
Vorskla: Dolganski; Selin, Dallku, Chesnakov, Matveev, Kryvosheenko, Rebenok (Gromov 82), Krasnoperov, Markoski, Januzi (Barannik 64), Bezus (Oberemko 46).

Dinamo Tbilisi (1) 1 *(Koshkadze 1)*

AEK Athens (0) 1 *(Leonardo 111 (pen))* 40,000

Dinamo Tbilisi: Loria; Tomashvili, Rekhviashvili, Kakubava■, Xisco Munoz (Kakhelishvili 105), Odikadze, Mikel Alvaro, Koshkadze (Jighauri 79), Kvekveskiri, Albert Yague, Robertinho (Carlos Coto 74).
AEK Athens: Konstantopoulos (Arabatzis 36); Karabelas, Georgeas, Juan Cala, Manolas, Makos, Lagos, Gentzoglou, Jose Carlos (Kafes 106), Gudjohnsen, Liberopoulos (Leonardo 63).
aet.

Dnepr (1) 1 *(Shakhov 22)*

Fulham (0) 0 12,750

Dnepr: Lastuvka; Denisov (Strinic 56), Mandzyuk, Cheberyachko (Rotan 57), Inkoom, Boateng, Giuliano (Antonov 72), Kravchenko, Shakhov, Kalinic, Konoplyanka.
Fulham: Schwarzer; Baird, Riise J (Briggs 22), Murphy, Hughes, Hangeland, Duff, Sidwell, Johnson, Dembele (Kasami 71), Dempsey (Etuhu 80).

Dynamo Kiev (0) 1 *(Milevskiy 74)*

Litex (0) 0 8100

Dynamo Kiev: Shovkovsky; Betao, Danilo Silva, Khacheridi, Yussuf (Popov 53), Eremenko, Aliyev (Garmash 75), Vukojevic, Milevskiy, Brown, Yarmolenko (Lukman 79).
Litex: Vinicius; Josse■, Bodurov, Zanev, Itoua Onanga, Milanov I, Yanev, Thiago Miracema (Djermanovic 80), Milanov G, Tsvetkov (Flores 61), Celio Codo (Todorov 66).

Gaz Metan (1) 1 *(Hoban 40)*

FK Austria (0) 0 3700

Gaz Metan: Plesca; Lazar, Trtovac, Markovic (Miclea 75), Vukadinovic, Petre, Todea (Roman 81), Hoban, Breeveld, Bratu (Litu 60), Thaer Al Bawab.
FK Austria: Grunwald P; Ortlechner, Margreitter, Suttner, Klein, Hlinka, Junuzovic, Grunwald A, Barazite (Stankovic 46), Jun (Rogulj 86), Linz.

Guimaraes (0) 0

Atletico Madrid (2) 4 *(Gabi 2 (pen), Adrian 18, 60, Salvio 81)* 10,330

Guimaraes: Nilson; Alex, Anderson Santana, El Adoua, N'Diaye, Pedro Mendes, Joao Alves (Targino 46), Barrientos (Soudani 66), Leonel Olimpio, Edgar Silva, Faouzi (Marcelo Toscano 46).
Atletico Madrid: Courtois; Miranda, Perea, Filipe Luis, Silvio, Reyes, Tiago (Elias 46), Gabi, Mario Suarez (Koke 67), Salvio, Adrian (Juanfran 71).

Hapoel Tel Aviv (1) 4 *(Cohen 37, Damari 53, Tamuz 81, Al Lala 90)*

Ekranas (0) 0 7500

Hapoel Tel Aviv: Edel; Fransman, Hotba, Shish, Badir, Abutbul, Igiebor, Gordana (Abass 86), Cohen (Tuama 74), Tamuz, Damari (Al Lala 86).
Ekranas: Zubas; Dedura, Gleveckas (Vertelis 69), Joksas, Samusiovas, Tomkevicius, Radavicius, Andelkovic (Mauro Alonso 79), Kucys, Velicka (Fofana 57), Umeh.

Helsingborg (0) 1 *(Jonsson 61 (pen))*

Standard Liege (2) 3 *(Leye 14, Berrier 35, Kanu 68)* 6656

Helsingborg: Hansson; Edman, Andersson C, Larsson, Holgersson, Gashi, Sundin (Alvaro Santos 72), Lindstrom, Mahlangu, Thern (Skjelvik 46), Jonsson (Ramadan 74).
Standard Liege: Sinan; Van Damme, Pocognoli, Felipe, Belhocine, Kanu, Opare, Buyens, Berrier (Camara 73), Leye (Mujangi Bia 83), Benteke (Nong 66).

Karpaty (1) 1 *(Lucas 45 (pen))*

PAOK Salonika (0) 1 *(Balafas 55)* 20,000

Karpaty: Bogatinov; Balazic, Oshchipko, Fedetskiy■, Borja Gomez, Khudobyak, Tkachuk, Golodyuk (Kravchenko 34), Cristobal (Pacheco 74), Batista (Kopolovets 67), Lucas.
PAOK Salonika: Kresic; Lino, Malezas, Balafas, Etto, Fotakis, Lazar (Tsoukalas 88), Georgiadis, Arias, Vierinha (Salpingidis 83), Athanasiadis (Robert 89).

Panathinaikos (0) 2 *(Boumsong 70, Toche 79)*

Maccabi Tel Aviv (0) 1 *(Medunjanin 61)* 15,503

Panathinaikos: Kotsolis; Boumsong, Kante, Vyntra (Karagounis 67), Spiropoulos, Katsouranis, Owusu-Abeyie, Ninis (Cleyton 66), Leto, Zeca, Toche.
Maccabi Tel Aviv: Haimov; Nivaldo, Pavicevic, Vered, Lugasi, Medunjanin (Alberman 76), Yeini, Dahan, Micha (Ziv 59), Konate■, Atar (Colautti 83).

Paris St Germain (0) 2 *(Nene 65, Afoun 79 (og))*

Differdange (0) 0 15,194

Paris St Germain: Douchez; Camara, Tiene, Ceara, Bisevac, Menez, Bodmer, Nene (Gameiro 78), Chantome (N'Goyi 82), Pastore, Hoarau (Maurice 58).
Differdange: Hym; Afoun, Bukvic, Rodrigues de Almeida, Janisch, Kettenmeyer (Lebresne 76), May (Diop 90), Bettmer, Leoni, Caron (Piskor 80), Er Rafik.

Partizan Belgrade (1) 1 *(Volkov 35)*
Shamrock R (0) 2 *(Sullivan 58, O'Donnell 113 (pen))* 13,706
Partizan Belgrade: Ilic R; Rankovic, Rnic, Volkov, Ivanov, Ilic S, Vukic (Babovic 58), Kamara■, Tomic, Eduardo (Markovic 85), Jovancic.
Shamrock R: Thompson; Rice, Murray, Sullivan, Sives, Stevens, Turner, Finn, Dennehy (Sheppard 46), McCabe (O'Donnell 68), Twigg (Kilduff 102).
aet.

PSV Eindhoven (0) 5 *(Toivonen 53, Lens 67, Wijnaldum 74, Labyad 79, Strootman 90)*
Ried (0) 0 23,000
PSV Eindhoven: Isaksson; Pieters, Bouma (Marcelo 81), Manolev, Wijnaldum (Ojo 88), Hutchinson, Strootman, Labyad (Zeefuik 83), Lens, Toivonen, Mertens.
Ried: Gebauer; Riegler, Hadzic, Reifeltshammer, Ziegl (Zulj 59), Basala-Mazana, Lexa, Hinum, Ivan Carril (Grasegger 82), Royer, Guillem (Nacho Rodriguez 68).

Rabotnicki (1) 1 *(Lazarevski 39)*
Lazio (1) 3 *(Rocchi 23, 77, Hernanes 74)* 7100
Rabotnicki: Dimitrievski (Shishkovski 90); Kumbev, Lazarevski, Manevski (Trajkovski 63), Muarem (Nastevski 61), Todorovski, Bogdanovic, Micevski, Vujcic, Petkovski, Velkoski K.
Lazio: Bizarri; Scaloni, Zauri, Diakite, Andre Dias (Biava 37), Cana, Mauri (Hernanes 57), Matuzalem, Lulic, Rocchi, Kozak (Ledesma 71).

Rangers (0) 1 *(Bocanegra 75)*
Maribor (0) 1 *(Volas 55)* 32,223
Rangers: McGregor; Bocanegra, Wallace (Perry 40), Broadfoot, Goian, Edu, Juanma Ortiz (Healy 67), Davis, Jelavic, Lafferty, Wylde.
Maribor: Handanovic; Rajcevic, Arghus, Ibraimi, Viler, Mezga (Cvijanovic 76), Mertelj, Beric (Marcos Tavares 86), Potokar (Milec 83), Volas, Filipovic.

Rapid Bucharest (1) 1 *(Pancu 12)*
Slask (0) 1 *(Sobota 90)* 3383
Rapid Bucharest: Coman; Marcos Antonio, Burca, Rui Duarte, Bozovic, Alexa, Apostol, Roman (Deac 59), Herea (Grigorie 81), Pancu, Surdu (Sburlea 88).
Slask: Kelemen; Pawelec, Wasiluk, Pietrasiak, Socha, Madej, Cetnarski, Elsner (Sztylka 78), Gancarczyk (Dudek 78), Sobota, Diaz (Voskamp 78).

Rennes (2) 4 *(Montano 10, M'Vila 19 (pen), Pajot 85, Kembo-Ekoko 90)*
Red Star Belgrade (0) 0 19,364
Rennes: Costil; Danze, Kana Biyik, Theophile Catherine, Boye, Tettey, Feret (Pajot 83), M'Vila, Boukari, Pitroipa (Kembo-Ekoko 62), Montano (Dalmat 71).
Red Star Belgrade: Bajkovic; Tosic, Vilotic, Mikic, Addy, Dimitrijevic, Kovacevic, Cadu, Lazovic, Mijailovic (Kaluderovic 46), Borja (Bruno Mezenga 75).

Roma (1) 1 *(Perrotta 11)*
Slovan Bratislava (0) 1 *(Stepanovsky 82)* 47,302
Roma: Stekelenburg; Burdisso, Cicinho (Rosi 9), Cassetti, Jose Angel, Perrotta, Fabio Simplicio, Viviani, Caprari (Verre 69), Totti (Okaka 74), Bojan.
Slovan Bratislava: Putnocky; Had, Dobrotka, Bagayoko, Cikos, Pauschek, Guede, Zofcak (Dosoudil 90), Grendel (Stepanovsky 66), Sebo (Lacny 89), Kladrubsky.

Salzburg (0) 1 *(Hinteregger 50)*
Omonia (0) 0 9100
Salzburg: Gustafsson; Pasanen■, Schiemer, Hinteregger, Jefferson Cardoso, Cziommer, Lindgren, Svento (Sekagya 87), Leitgeb, Leonardo (Hierlander 90), Alan (Teigl 69).
Omonia: Georgallides; Iago Bouzon, Karipidis, Leandro De Almeida (Makridis 79), Shpungin, Salatic (Rengifo 86), Kaseke, Avraam■, Alexandre (Margaca 68), Christofi, Freddy.

Schalke (2) 6 *(Huntelaar 15 (pen), 25, 49 (pen), 63, Papadopoulos 56, Draxler 82)*
HJK Helsinki (1) 1 *(Pukki 20)* 52,034
Schalke: Fahrmann; Fuchs, Howedes, Papadopoulos, Holtby, Matip, Hoger (Uchida 78), Draxler (Moravek 83), Raul, Huntelaar, Farfan (Marica 73).
HJK Helsinki: Wallen; Kansikas (Sumusalo 59), Lindstrom, Lahti, Rafinha, Sorsa, Riihilahti (Perovuo 79), Bah, Ring, Sadik (Zeneli 64), Pukki.

Sevilla (1) 1 *(Pogatetz 37 (og))*
Hannover (1) 1 *(Abdellaoue 23)* 33,026
Sevilla: Palop; Escude, Navarro, Alexis (Fazio 84), Coke, Trochowski (Campana 81), Jesus Navas, Medel■, Perotti, Kanoute, Negredo (Manu 63).
Hannover: Zieler; Haggui, Schulz, Pogatetz, Rausch (Pander 89), Cherundolo, Sergio Pinto, Stindl, Schmiedebach, Schiaudraff, Abdellaoue (Ya Konan 90).

Sion (1) 3 *(Feindouno 3 (pen), 63, Sio 82)*
Celtic (0) 1 *(Mulgrew 78)* 7100
Sion: Vanins; Dingsdag, Buhler, Vanczak, Adailton, Feindouno, Obradovic (Crettenand 69), Mutsch, Serey Die, Sio, Afonso (Prijovic 6).
Celtic: Forster; Cha, Mulgrew, Ki, Majstorovic■, Wilson K, Kayal (Forrest 72), Brown, Samaras, Hooper, Ledley (Commons 88).

Sochaux (0) 0
Metalist Kharkiv (3) 4 *(Sosa 6, Cristaldo 11, 41, Taison 51)* 8739
Sochaux: Richert; Sauget, Perquis (Peybernes 61), Mikari (Privat 41), Corchia, Carlao, Martin (Roudet 54), Boudebouz, Nogueira■, Anin, Maiga.
Metalist Kharkiv: Horyainov; Fininho (Taison 46), Torsiglieri, Villagra, Gueye, Pshenichnikh, Cleiton Xavier, Torres, Sosa (Valyaev 65), Edmar, Cristaldo (Devic 72).

Sparta Prague (0) 1 *(Pamic 59)*
Vaslui (0) 0 13,699
Sparta Prague: Svenger; Zapotocny, Brabec■, Kusnir, Pamic, Vacek, Matejovsky, Husek (Jarosik 52), Juhar (Podany■ 52), Kweuke, Kadlec (Mares 79).
Vaslui: Cerniauskas; Milanov, Balace (Buhaescu 14), Farkas, Sanmartean, Jovanovic, Zmeu, Pavlovic, Wesley (Annang 72), Temwanjira (Bello 89), Balaur.

Spartak Moscow (2) 2 *(Kombarov K 10, Kombarov D 27 (pen))*
Legia (2) 3 *(Kucharczyk 29, Rybus 43, Gol 90)* 19,345
Spartak Moscow: Dikan; Pareja, Parshivlyuk, Rodri, Rojo, Sheshukov, Kombarov K, Kombarov D, Rafael Carioca (De Zeeuw 46), Dzyuba, Emenike (Ari 62).
Legia: Kuciak; Jedrzejczyk, Wawrzyniak, Inaki Astiz (Ohayon 69), Zewlakow, Vrdoljak, Rybus (Rzezniczak 90), Borysiuk, Gol, Ljuboja, Kucharczyk (Zyro 84).

Spartak Trnava (1) 1 *(Yanbayev 38 (og))*
Lokomotiv Moscow (0) 1 *(Obinna 80 (pen))* 11,258
Spartak Trnava: Raska■; Koubsky, Cvirik, Hanzel L, Carnota■, Karhan, Vyskocil (Malcharek■ 61), Kascak, Bicak (Kone 72), Oravec (Slovenciak 78), Tomacek.
Lokomotiv Moscow: Guilherme; Manuel da Costa, Shishkin, Yanbayev, Durica, Tarasov (Ibricic 86), Loskov (Ozdoev 62), Glushakov, Obinna (Ignatyev 89), Sychev, Maicon.

Sporting Lisbon (0) 2 *(Andre Santos 77, Evaldo 82)*
Nordsjaelland (0) 1 *(Laudrup 90)* 24,028
Sporting Lisbon: Rui Patricio; Anderson Polga, Joao Pereira, Evaldo, Daniel Carrico, Schaars (Rinaudo 70), Izmailov (Carrillo 85), Capel, Andre Santos, Helder Postiga, Yannick Djalo (Bozhinov 62).
Nordsjaelland: Hansen; Parkhurst, Kildentoft, Bjelland, Gundelach, Stokholm, Christensen (Rohde 84), Beckmann (Mikkelsen 62), Okore, Lawan (Laudrup 66), Granskov-Hansen.

Stoke C (3) 4 *(Upson 24, Jones 31, 72, Whelan 38)*
Thun (0) 1 *(Wittwer 78)* 24,118
Stoke C: Sorensen; Wilkinson, Wilson (Collins 56), Whelan, Shawcross, Upson, Pennant (Soares 55), Whitehead, Jones, Walters (Shotton 63), Pugh.
Thun: Djukic; Luthi, Ghezal, Schneider (Hediger 66), Reinmann, Schindelholz, Battig, Andrist, Demiri (Wittwer 66), Sanogo, Lezcano (Rama 77).

Tottenham H (0) 0
Hearts (0) 0 24,053
Tottenham H: Cudicini; Corluka, Kane, Huddlestone, Dawson (Kaboul 46), Bassong, Carroll, Livermore (Nicholson 76), Pavlyuchenko, Fredericks (Kranjcar 61), Townsend.
Hearts: MacDonald; McGowan, Grainger, Jonsson, Zaliukas, Webster, Templeton, Robinson (Taouil 78), Smith (Suso Santana 82), Novikovas, Skacel (Mrowiec 72).

Trabzonspor
Athletic Bilbao
Trabzonspor replaced Fenerbahce in the Champions League, allowing Athletic Bilbao a walkover.

Young Boys (0) 2 *(Mayuka 61, Farnerud 81)*
Braga (1) 2 *(Helder Barbosa 24, Lima 78)* 15,012
Young Boys: Wolfli; Spycher, Veskovac (Doubai 84), Zverotic, Affolter, Silberbauer, Raimondi (Nuzzolo 46), Farnerud, Mayuka, Ben Khalifa■, Bienvenu (Degen 59).
Braga: Quim; Paulo Vinicius, Echiejile, Baiano, Ewerton, Hugo Viana (Marcio Mossoro 76), Mahamat, Leandro Salino (Vinicius 86), Alan, Lima, Helder Barbosa (Guilherme 60).

GROUP STAGE

GROUP A

Thursday, 15 September 2011

PAOK Salonika (0) 0
Tottenham H (0) 0 24,285
PAOK Salonika: Kresic; Contreras, Lino, Malezas, Etto, Fotakis (Ivic 62), Garcia, Arias, Vieirinha, Salpingidis, Athanasiadis.
Tottenham H: Cudicini; Walker, Townsend, Livermore, Corluka, Bassong, Iago Falque (Fredericks 81), Carroll, Pavlyuchenko, Kane, Giovani (Parrett 90).

Shamrock R (0) 0
Rubin (1) 3 *(Martins 2, Noboa 50, Gokdeniz 60)* 6290
Shamrock R: Thompson; O'Donnell, Rice, Murray, Sullivan, Sives, Stevens, Finn (Kilduff 56), McCormack (Dennehy 56), Ricketts (Turner 63), Twigg.
Rubin: Ryzhikov; Bocchetti, Cesar Navas, Kaleshin (Ansaldi 75), Sharonov, Gokdeniz, Ryazantsev, Noboa, Natcho, Haedo Valdez (Dyadyun 64), Martins (Bystrov 46).

Thursday, 29 September 2011

Rubin (0) 2 *(Haedo Valdez 52, Dyadyun 66)*
PAOK Salonika (1) 2 *(Athanasiadis 23, Fotakis 81)* 14,350
Rubin: Ryzhikov; Bocchetti, Cesar Navas, Kuzmin, Gokdeniz, Nemov, Noboa, Natcho, Kasaev (Bystrov 90), Haedo Valdez (Ryazantsev 77), Dyadyun.
PAOK Salonika: Kresic; Contreras (Cirillo 54), Lino, Malezas, Etto, Fotakis, Lazar (Ivic 72), Georgiadis, Arias (Balafas 51), Vieirinha, Athanasiadis.

Tottenham H (0) 3 *(Pavlyuchenko 60, Defoe 61, Giovani 65)*
Shamrock R (0) 1 *(Rice 51)* 24,782
Tottenham H: Cudicini; Walker, Carroll, Bassong, Corluka, Livermore, Lennon (Townsend 46), Rose (Kane 80), Pavlyuchenko, Defoe (Iago Falque 73), Giovani.
Shamrock R: Brush; O'Donnell (McCormack 46), Rice, Murray, Sullivan, Sives, Paterson (Stevens 46), Finn (Ricketts 73), Dennehy, McCabe, Twigg.

Thursday, 20 October 2011

PAOK Salonika (1) 2 *(Lazar 12, Vieirinha 63)*
Shamrock R (0) 1 *(Sheppard 48)* 12,776
PAOK Salonika: Chalkias; Cirillo, Lino (Sznaucer 29), Malezas, Etto, Lazar, Ivic, Arias, Vieirinha, Salpingidis (Papazoglou 88), Athanasiadis (Georgiadis 62).
Shamrock R: Thompson; O'Donnell, Rice, Murray, Oman, Sullivan, Stevens, Paterson (Finn 74), Turner (Kilduff 74), Dennehy, Sheppard (McCabe 84).

Tottenham H (1) 1 *(Pavlyuchenko 33)*
Rubin (0) 0 24,058
Tottenham H: Gomes; Walker, Rose, Carroll, Bassong, Livermore, Lennon (Modric 73), Sandro (Kaboul 73), Pavlyuchenko, Defoe, Giovani (Assou-Ekotto 65).
Rubin: Ryzhikov; Bocchetti, Cesar Navas, Kuzmin, Sharonov, Gokdeniz, Ryazantsev (Eremenko 78), Noboa, Natcho, Kasaev (Martins 61), Haedo Valdez.

Thursday, 3 November 2011

Rubin (0) 1 *(Natcho 56)*
Tottenham H (0) 0 21,250
Rubin: Ryzhikov; Bocchetti, Cesar Navas, Kaleshin, Sharonov, Gokdeniz, Ryazantsev (Eremenko 89), Noboa, Natcho, Kasaev (Ansaldi 83), Martins (Haedo Valdez 65).
Tottenham H: Cudicini; Carroll, Fredericks, Bassong, Gallas (Parrett 72), Livermore, Iago Falque, Pienaar, Pavlyuchenko (Kane 75), Defoe, Townsend.

Shamrock R (0) 1 *(Dennehy 51)*
PAOK Salonika (3) 3 *(Salpingidis 7, 38, Fotakis 36)* 6100
Shamrock R: Thompson; O'Donnell, Murray, Sullivan, Sives, Stevens, Turner (Kilduff 46), Dennehy, McCormack (Rice 70), McCabe (Twigg 46), Sheppard.
PAOK Salonika: Chalkias; Cirillo, Lino, Malezas, Sznaucer, Fotakis (Balafas 64), Lazar, Georgiadis (Apostolopoulos 88), Arias, Vieirinha, Salpingidis (Papazoglou 90).

Wednesday, 30 November 2011

Rubin (2) 4 *(Haedo Valdez 10, 51, Natcho 36, Martins 62)*
Shamrock R (1) 1 *(Oman 12)* 15,740
Rubin: Ryzhikov; Bocchetti, Cesar Navas, Kaleshin, Sharonov, Gokdeniz (Ansaldi 69), Ryazantsev (Dyadyun 71), Noboa, Natcho, Haedo Valdez (Kasaev 61), Martins.
Shamrock R: Thompson; Rice, Murray, Oman, Sullivan, Stevens, Paterson (Kilduff 70), Turner (Twigg 81), Finn (O'Donnell 70), Dennehy, Sheppard.

Tottenham H (1) 1 *(Modric 39 (pen))*
PAOK Salonika (2) 2 *(Salpingidis 6, Athanasiadis 14)* 26,229
Tottenham H: Gomes; Corluka, Rose (Bale 63), Modric, Bassong, Gallas, Lennon, Livermore, Kane (Iago Falque 71), Defoe, Pienaar (Walker 67).
PAOK Salonika: Chalkias; Contreras (Cirillo 80), Malezas, Etto, Fotakis, Garcia, Lazar (Arias 83), Georgiadis (Sznaucer 62), Stafylidis■, Salpingidis, Athanasiadis.

Thursday, 15 December 2011

PAOK Salonika (1) 1 *(Vieirinha 16 (pen))*

Rubin (0) 1 *(Haedo Valdez 48)* 26,173

PAOK Salonika: Glykos; Cirillo, Lino, Malezas, Etto, Garcia, Ivic (Fotakis 80), Georgiadis (Salpingidis 73), Arias (Lazar 84), Vieirinha, Athanasiadis.
Rubin: Ryzhikov■; Bocchetti, Kaleshin (Arlauskis 15), Ansaldi, Sharonov, Gokdeniz, Nemov, Noboa, Natcho, Haedo Valdez (Dyadyun 90), Martins (Bystrov 62).

Shamrock R (0) 0

Tottenham H (3) 4 *(Pienaar 29, Townsend 38, Defoe 45, Kane 90)* 7545

Shamrock R: Brush; Rice (O'Donnell 46), Murray, Oman, Sullivan, Stevens, Paterson, Turner, Finn (Twigg 57), Dennehy, Sheppard (Kilduff 74).
Tottenham H: Cudicini; Rose, Assou-Ekotto (Iago Falque 84), Livermore, Kaboul, Townsend, Pienaar, Kranjcar, Defoe (Kane 76), Giovani, Sandro.

Group A Table	*P*	*W*	*D*	*L*	*F*	*A*	*Pts*
PAOK Salonika	6	3	3	0	10	6	12
Rubin	6	3	2	1	11	5	11
Tottenham H	6	3	1	2	9	4	10
Shamrock R	6	0	0	6	4	19	0

GROUP B

Thursday, 15 September 2011

FC Copenhagen (0) 1 *(Nordstrand 54 (pen))*

Vorskla (0) 0 10,420

FC Copenhagen: Wiland; Ottesen, Sigurdsson, Thomsen, Bengtsson, Grindheim, Kristensen (Absalonsen 67), Bolanos, Delaney, Nordstrand (Cesar Santin 79), N'Doye.
Vorskla: Dolganski; Selin, Kurilov, Dallku, Chesnakov, Matveev, Kryvosheenko, Rebenok (Gromov 75), Krasnoperov, Januzi (Sachko 88), Bezus (Barannik 68).

Hannover (0) 0

Standard Liege (0) 0 43,540

Hannover: Zieler; Haggui, Pogatetz, Rausch, Cherundolo, Sergio Pinto (Hauger 75), Chahed, Stindl, Schmiedebach (Stoppelkamp 82), Schlaudraff, Abdellaoue (Ya Konan 46).
Standard Liege: Sinan; Van Damme, Pocognoli, Felipe, Kanu, Opare, Vainqueur, Buyens, Mujangi Bia (Buzaglo 74), Berrier (Gonzalez 82), Cyriac (Tchite 67).

Thursday, 29 September 2011

Standard Liege (0) 3 *(Seijas 57, Felipe 72, Kanu 79)*

FC Copenhagen (0) 0 13,368

Standard Liege: Sinan; Van Damme, Pocognoli, Felipe, Kanu, Opare, Vainqueur, Berrier, Seijas (Gonzalez 87), Buzaglo (Tchite 46), Leye (Cyriac 81).
FC Copenhagen: Wiland; Ottesen, Sigurdsson, Thomsen, Bengtsson, Grindheim, Claudemir, Bolanos, Delaney (Kristensen 66), Cesar Santin (Diouf 67), N'Doye.

Vorskla (0) 1 *(Kurilov 50)*

Hannover (2) 2 *(Abdellaoue 32, Pander 44)* 11,000

Vorskla: Dolganski; Selin, Kurilov, Dallku, Chesnakov (Markoski 75), Tkachuk, Kryvosheenko (Gromov 85), Rebenok, Krasnoperov, Sachko (Januzi 46), Bezus.
Hannover: Zieler; Haggui, Pander, Schulz (Rausch 85), Pogatetz, Cherundolo, Sergio Pinto, Lala (Schmiedebach 65), Stindl, Schlaudraff, Abdellaoue (Sobiech 76).

Thursday, 20 October 2011

Hannover (1) 2 *(Pander 29, Sergio Pinto 81)*

FC Copenhagen (0) 2 *(N'Doye 67, Cesar Santin 89)* 43,100

Hannover: Zieler; Haggui, Pander, Schulz (Rausch 72), Pogatetz, Cherundolo, Sergio Pinto, Stindl, Schlaudraff (Stoppelkamp 78), Ya Konan, Abdellaoue (Lala 84).
FC Copenhagen: Wiland; Ottesen, Sigurdsson, Thomsen, Bengtsson, Grindheim (Cesar Santin 84), Claudemir (Kristensen 54), Diouf (Oviedo 70), Bolanos, Delaney, N'Doye.

Standard Liege (0) 0

Vorskla (0) 0 13,496

Standard Liege: Sinan; Van Damme (Gonzalez 51), Pocognoli, Felipe, Kanu, Opare, Vainqueur, Buyens (Buzaglo 83), Mujangi Bia (Batshuayi 89), Seijas, Cyriac.
Vorskla: Dolganski; Selin, Kurilov, Dallku, Chesnakov, Tkachuk (Gromov 88), Kryvosheenko, Rebenok, Krasnoperov, Markoski (Oberemko 68), Bezus (Januzi 46).

Thursday, 3 November 2011

FC Copenhagen (0) 1 *(N'Doye 67)*

Hannover (0) 2 *(Schlaudraff 71, Stindl 75)* 27,853

FC Copenhagen: Wiland; Ottesen, Sigurdsson, Thomsen, Oviedo, Grindheim, Kristensen (Bergvold 76), Diouf (Absalonsen 84), Bolanos, Cesar Santin (Nordstrand 76), N'Doye.
Hannover: Zieler; Haggui, Pander (Rausch 46), Schulz, Pogatetz, Sergio Pinto, Chahed, Stindl, Schmiedebach, Schlaudraff (Eggimann 90), Abdellaoue (Ya Konan 90).

Vorskla (1) 1 *(Kurilov 5)*

Standard Liege (2) 3 *(Seijas 17, Kanu 45, Tchite 74)* 8000

Vorskla: Dolganski; Selin, Kurilov, Dallku, Chesnakov, Oberemko (Esin 82), Kryvosheenko, Rebenok (Barannik 71), Krasnoperov, Markoski, Januzi (Gromov 85).
Standard Liege: Sinan; Van Damme, Pocognoli, Ciman, Goreux, Kanu, Vainqueur, Mujangi Bia (Batshuayi 82), Seijas (Gonzalez 87), Tchite, Cyriac (Buyens 71).

Wednesday, 30 November 2011

Standard Liege (1) 2 *(Tchite 26, Cyriac 59)*

Hannover (0) 0 18,104

Standard Liege: Sinan; Pocognoli, Goreux, Felipe, Kanu, Vainqueur, Buyens (Belhocine 89), Mujangi Bia (Buzaglo 90), Seijas, Tchite, Cyriac (Gonzalez 87).
Hannover: Zieler; Haggui, Pander, Schulz (Rausch 63), Pogatetz, Cherundolo, Sergio Pinto, Stindl (Ya Konan 51), Schmiedebach, Schlaudraff, Abdellaoue (Sobiech 80).

Vorskla (1) 1 *(N'Doye 31 (og))*

FC Copenhagen (1) 1 *(N'Doye 37)* 3000

Vorskla: Velichko; Selin, Kurilov, Dallku, Peskov, Kryvosheenko (Esin 90), Rebenok, Krasnoperov, Markoski (Oberemko 69), Januzi, Bezus (Chesnakov 81).
FC Copenhagen: Wiland; Ottesen, Sigurdsson, Thomsen, Oviedo (Bengtsson 46), Grindheim, Claudemir, Diouf (Vingaard 46), Bolanos, Cesar Santin (Nordstrand 74), N'Doye.

Thursday, 15 December 2011

FC Copenhagen (0) 0

Standard Liege (1) 1 *(Batshuayi 31)* 9722

FC Copenhagen: Wiland; Ottesen, Sigurdsson, Oviedo, Gamboa, Claudemir, Diouf (Vingaard 46), Bolanos, Delaney (Grindheim 77), Cesar Santin (Nordstrand 46), N'Doye.
Standard Liege: Moris; Pocognoli (Felipe 55), Ciman, Goreux, Belhocine, Kanu, Gonzalez (Seijas 75), Buyens, Berrier, Camara, Batshuayi (Cyriac 81).

Hannover (2) 3 *(Rausch 25, Ya Konan 33, Sobiech 78)*

Vorskla (1) 1 *(Bezus 45 (pen))* 42,000

Hannover: Miller; Pander, Pogatetz, Eggimann, Rausch, Sergio Pinto (Schmiedebach 71), Lala, Chahed (Avevor 81), Stindl (Stoppelkamp 46), Ya Konan, Sobiech.
Vorskla: Dolganski; Selin, Chesnakov, Peskov, Oberemko (Tkachuk 72), Kryvosheenko (Gromov 65), Rebenok, Krasnoperov, Markoski, Januzi (Barannik 87), Bezus.

Group B Table	*P*	*W*	*D*	*L*	*F*	*A*	*Pts*
Standard Liege	6	4	2	0	9	1	14
Hannover	6	3	2	1	9	7	11
FC Copenhagen	6	1	2	3	5	9	5
Vorskla	6	0	2	4	4	10	2

GROUP C

Thursday, 15 September 2011

Hapoel Tel Aviv (0) 0

Rapid Bucharest (0) 1 *(Herea 55)* 9575

Hapoel Tel Aviv: Edel; Fransman (Cohen 90), Pecalka, Kende, Badir, Abutbul, Oremus (Tuama 73), Igiebor, Al Lala (Yadin■ 62), Tamuz, Damari.
Rapid Bucharest: Coman; Marcos Antonio, Burca, Roosevelt Ezequias, Rui Duarte, Grigore, Alexa, Deac, Roman (Surdu■ 80), Herea (Filipe Teixeira 85), Cassio (Pancu 53).

PSV Eindhoven (1) 1 *(Mertens 21)*

Legia (0) 0 13,524

PSV Eindhoven: Tyton; Pieters, Bouma, Marcelo, Manolev, Wijnaldum, Strootman, Lens (Ojo 73), Toivonen (Engelaar 89), Mertens, Matavz.
Legia: Kuciak; Jedrzejczyk, Wawrzyniak, Komorowski, Zewlakow, Vrdoljak, Rybus (Kosecki 81), Borysiuk, Gol (Zyro 65), Manu (Radovic 46), Ljuboja.

Thursday, 29 September 2011

Legia (0) 3 *(Ljuboja 67, Komorowski 72 (pen), Radovic 89)*

Hapoel Tel Aviv (1) 2 *(Tamuz 34, Al Lala 78)* 20,150

Legia: Kuciak; Jedrzejczyk, Wawrzyniak, Komorowski, Zewlakow, Radovic, Vrdoljak (Gol 46), Rybus (Wolski 82), Borysiuk, Ohayon (Zyro 46), Ljuboja.
Hapoel Tel Aviv: Edel; Fransman, Pecalka, Kende, Shish, Abutbul, Oremus (Badir 84), Igiebor, Abass (Tuama 12), Tamuz, Damari (Al Lala 76).

Rapid Bucharest (1) 1 *(Alexa 28)*

PSV Eindhoven (1) 3 *(Bouma 43, Toivonen 89, Matavz 90)* 21,320

Rapid Bucharest: Coman; Marcos Antonio, Burca, Rui Duarte, Bozovic, Grigore, Alexa, Deac, Roman (Filipe Teixeira 51), Herea (Apostol 74), Pancu (Cassio 83).
PSV Eindhoven: Isaksson; Pieters, Bouma, Marcelo, Manolev, Wijnaldum, Strootman, Lens (Labyad 72), Toivonen, Mertens, Matavz.

Thursday, 20 October 2011

Hapoel Tel Aviv (0) 0

PSV Eindhoven (0) 1 *(Wijnaldum 70 (pen))* 9468

Hapoel Tel Aviv: Edel; Fransman, Pecalka, Hotba, Shish, Abutbul, Oremus (Tuama 83), Igiebor (Gordana 60), Cohen, Tamuz, Damari (Al Lala 54).
PSV Eindhoven: Isaksson; Bouma, Marcelo, Manolev, Tamata, Engelaar (Strootman 46), Wijnaldum, Labyad (Lens 79), Toivonen, Mertens, Matavz.

Rapid Bucharest (0) 0

Legia (0) 1 *(Radovic 73)* 13,726

Rapid Bucharest: Coman; Marcos Antonio, Burca, Rui Duarte, Bozovic, Grigore (Sburlea 81), Alexa, Deac, Roman (Filipe Teixeira 27), Herea (Cassio 88), Pancu.
Legia: Kuciak; Jedrzejczyk, Wawrzyniak (Rzezniczak 81), Komorowski, Zewlakow, Radovic, Vrdoljak, Rybus (Zyro 90), Borysiuk, Gol (Manu 63), Ljuboja.

Thursday, 3 November 2011

Legia (0) 3 *(Radovic 54, 68, Kucharczyk 90)*

Rapid Bucharest (0) 1 *(Filipe Teixeira 65)* 30,786

Legia: Kuciak; Jedrzejczyk, Wawrzyniak, Komorowski, Zewlakow, Radovic (Wolski 90), Vrdoljak, Rybus (Kucharczyk 86), Borysiuk, Zyro (Gol■ 63), Ljuboja.
Rapid Bucharest: Draghia; Marcos Antonio, Burca, Rui Duarte, Bozovic, Alexa■, Filipe Teixeira, Deac, Herea (Pancu 73), Sburlea (Grigorie 54), Cassio (Grigore 29).

PSV Eindhoven (1) 3 *(Wijnaldum 12, Toivonen 59, Strootman 87)*

Hapoel Tel Aviv (2) 3 *(Damari 10, Tamuz 33, 47)* 23,500

PSV Eindhoven: Isaksson; Derijck (Lens 73), Marcelo, Manolev, Willems (Bouma 66), Wijnaldum, Strootman, Labyad, Toivonen, Mertens, Matavz.
Hapoel Tel Aviv: Edel; Pecalka, Hotba, Shish, Badir, Abutbul, Igiebor (Kende 90), Gordana■, Cohen (Al Lala 63), Tamuz, Damari (Fransman 74).

Wednesday, 30 November 2011

Legia (0) 0

PSV Eindhoven (1) 3 *(Zewlakow 32 (og), Mertens 59 (pen), Labyad 68)* 28,786

Legia: Kuciak■; Jedrzejczyk, Wawrzyniak, Komorowski, Zewlakow, Radovic, Vrdoljak, Rybus (Wolski 70), Borysiuk, Zyro (Kucharczyk 83), Ljuboja (Skaba 57).
PSV Eindhoven: Isaksson; Derijck, Marcelo (Ritzmaier 77), Manolev, Willems (Bouma 65), Engelaar, Wijnaldum, Strootman, Labyad, Lens, Mertens (Toivonen 71).

Rapid Bucharest (1) 1 *(Deac 43 (pen))*

Hapoel Tel Aviv (3) 3 *(Igiebor 12, Tamuz 39 (pen), Tuama 45)* 4529

Rapid Bucharest: Coman; Marcos Antonio, Burca (Oros 46), Bozovic, Grigorie (Sburlea 61), Grigore, Apostol, Deac, Roman, Cretu, Cassio (Pancu 54).
Hapoel Tel Aviv: Edel; Fransman, Pecalka (Badir 27), Kende, Shish, Tuama, Abutbul, Yadin (Abass 34), Igiebor, Tamuz (Al Lala 81), Damari.

Thursday, 15 December 2011

Hapoel Tel Aviv (1) 2 *(Tuama 33, Yadin 76)*

Legia (0) 0 5496

Hapoel Tel Aviv: Edel; Hotba, Shushan, Shish■, Tuama (Al Lala 78), Badir, Oremus, Yadin, Gordana (Abass 70), Tamuz, Damari (Abutbul 24).
Legia: Skaba; Rzezniczak, Choto, Kielbowicz (Ohayon 86), Inaki Astiz, Radovic, Rybus, Gol, Zyro (Kucharczyk 71), Lukasik (Wolski 60), Ljuboja.

PSV Eindhoven (0) 2 *(Manolev 75, Matavz 79)*

Rapid Bucharest (0) 1 *(Pancu 90)* 27,415

PSV Eindhoven: Tyton; Derijck, Marcelo, Marzo (Manolev 70), Willems, Engelaar (Toivonen 46), Wijnaldum, Ritzmaier, Labyad, Lens, Matavz.
Rapid Bucharest: Coman (Straton 34); Marcos Antonio, Oros, Rui Duarte, Bozovic, Grigorie, Grigore, Alexa, Deac, Surdu (Filipe Teixeira 36), Cassio (Pancu 72).

Group C Table	*P*	*W*	*D*	*L*	*F*	*A*	*Pts*
PSV Eindhoven	6	5	1	0	13	5	16
Legia	6	3	0	3	7	9	9
Hapoel Tel Aviv	6	2	1	3	10	9	7
Rapid Bucharest	6	1	0	5	5	12	3

GROUP D

Thursday, 15 September 2011

Lazio (1) 2 *(Cisse 35 (pen), Sculli 71)*

Vaslui (0) 2 *(Wesley 59, 63 (pen))* 15,390

Lazio: Marchetti; Zauri■, Diakite, Andre Dias, Ledesma, Matuzalem, Gonzalez (Konko 81), Lulic, Rocchi (Kozak 67), Cisse, Sculli (Hernanes 80).
Vaslui: Cerniauskas; Milanov, Farkas, Balaur, Sanmartean, Zmeu (Costin 87), Pavlovic, Milisavljevic, Wesley, Temwanjira (Bello 77), Adailton (Buhaescu 90).

Zurich (0) 0

Sporting Lisbon (2) 2 *(Insua 4, Van Wolfswinkel 21)* 13,060

Zurich: Leoni; Beda, Jorge Teixeira, Koch R, Rodriguez, Chikhaoui (Chermiti 59), Gajic, Buff (Margairaz 67), Alphonse, Schonbachler (Nikci 46), Mehmedi.
Sporting Lisbon: Rui Patricio; Onyewu, Rodriguez, Insua, Joao Pereira, Schaars, Bruno Pereirinha, Capel (Evaldo 74), Rinaudo, Van Wolfswinkel (Rubio 65), Carrillo (Andre Santos 59).

Thursday, 29 September 2011

Sporting Lisbon (2) 2 *(Van Wolfswinkel 21, Insua 45)*

Lazio (1) 1 *(Klose 40)* 33,725

Sporting Lisbon: Rui Patricio; Onyewu, Anderson Polga, Insua■, Joao Pereira, Schaars, Fernandez (Andre Santos 69), Capel (Daniel Carrico 74), Rinaudo, Van Wolfswinkel, Carrillo (Evaldo 52).
Lazio: Marchetti; Diakite, Konko, Andre Dias (Radu 69), Cana, Brocchi (Sculli 64), Hernanes, Gonzalez, Lulic, Klose (Cisse 46), Rocchi.

Vaslui (0) 2 *(Wesley 62 (pen), Temwanjira 77)*

Zurich (1) 2 *(Alphonse 32, Mehmedi 79)* 3000

Vaslui: Cerniauskas; Milanov, Farkas, Papp, Sanmartean, Pavlovic, Milisavljevic (Jovanovic 72), Wesley, Temwanjira, Adailton, Bello (Costin 46).
Zurich: Leoni; Koch P, Jorge Teixeira, Koch R■, Rodriguez, Aegerter, Zouaghi, Alphonse, Schonbachler (Chikhaoui 86), Chermiti (Barmettler 64), Nikci (Mehmedi 63).

Thursday, 20 October 2011

Sporting Lisbon (1) 2 *(Evaldo 43, Fernandez 70)*

Vaslui (0) 0 28,106

Sporting Lisbon: Rui Patricio; Anderson Polga, Joao Pereira, Evaldo, Daniel Carrico, Schaars, Fernandez, Bruno Pereirinha (Carrillo 62), Capel (Andre Martins 78), Rinaudo, Van Wolfswinkel (Bozhinov 74).
Vaslui: Cerniauskas; Milanov, Gladstone (Costin 71), Farkas, Papp, Sanmartean, Pavlovic, Milisavljevic, Wesley■, Adailton (Buhaescu 46), Bello (Jovanovic 79).

Zurich (1) 1 *(Nikci 23)*

Lazio (1) 1 *(Sculli 22)* 10,800

Zurich: Guatelli; Magnin, Beda, Koch P, Jorge Teixeira, Chikhaoui (Mehmedi 62), Djuric (Rodriguez 76), Margairaz, Aegerter, Alphonse (Drmic 81), Nikci.
Lazio: Marchetti; Diakite, Andre Dias, Radu, Cana (Rocchi 46), Matuzalem, Hernanes, Gonzalez (Ledesma 72), Lulic, Cisse (Kozak 79), Sculli.

Thursday, 3 November 2011

Lazio (0) 1 *(Brocchi 62)*

Zurich (0) 0 13,414

Lazio: Marchetti; Zauri (Konko 78), Diakite, Andre Dias, Radu, Cana, Ledesma, Lulic (Brocchi 46), Klose (Cisse 46), Rocchi, Sculli.
Zurich: Leoni; Beda, Koch P, Jorge Teixeira, Rodriguez, Chikhaoui (Magnin 62), Djuric (Schonbachler 77), Aegerter, Zouaghi, Alphonse, Mehmedi (Chermiti 66).

Vaslui (1) 1 *(Zmeu 30)*

Sporting Lisbon (0) 0 4000

Vaslui: Cerniauskas; Milanov, Farkas, Papp, Sanmartean (Gheorghiu 89), Zmeu, Pavlovic (Costin 79), Milisavljevic, Neagu (Jovanovic 42), Adailton, Bello.
Sporting Lisbon: Marcelo Boeck; Rodriguez, Evaldo, Daniel Carrico, Schaars, Fernandez (Rubio 65), Bruno Pereirinha, Capel, Rinaudo (Andre Santos 12), Bozhinov (Van Wolfswinkel 46), Carrillo.

Thursday, 1 December 2011

Sporting Lisbon (1) 2 *(Van Wolfswinkel 15, Bozhinov 58)*

Zurich (0) 0 25,309

Sporting Lisbon: Marcelo Boeck; Onyewu, Anderson Polga, Insua, Joao Pereira, Daniel Carrico, Schaars (Andre Santos 68), Capel, Andre Martins, Bozhinov, Van Wolfswinkel (Rubio 74).
Zurich: Leoni; Magnin, Koch P, Jorge Teixeira, Koch R, Chikhaoui (Chermiti 63), Djuric (Schonbachler 75), Aegerter (Mehmedi 62), Zouaghi, Buff, Nikci.

Vaslui (0) 0

Lazio (0) 0 7000

Vaslui: Cerniauskas; Milanov, Gladstone (Zmeu 71), Farkas, Papp, Sanmartean, Pavlovic, Milisavljevic, Buhaescu (Jovanovic 58), Temwanjira (Bello 90), Adailton.
Lazio: Marchetti; Diakite, Biava, Konko (Kozak 88), Radu, Cana, Hernanes, Gonzalez, Lulic (Sculli 59), Klose, Cisse (Rocchi 71).

Wednesday, 14 December 2011

Lazio (1) 2 *(Kozak 42, Sculli 55)*

Sporting Lisbon (0) 0 8295

Lazio: Bizarri; Diakite, Biava, Cavanda, Cana (Gonzalez 53), Ledesma, Hernanes (Zampa 73), Lulic, Cisse, Sculli, Kozak (Klose 85).
Sporting Lisbon: Marcelo Boeck; Onyewu (Joao Mario 76), Evaldo, Tiago Llori, Schaars (Daniel Carrico 69), Bruno Pereirinha, Andre Santos, Andre Martins, Bozhinov, Carrillo, Rubio (Insua 65).

Zurich (0) 2 *(Margairaz 69, Buff 90)*

Vaslui (0) 0 6200

Zurich: Guatelli; Beda, Koch P, Jorge Teixeira, Rodriguez, Djuric (Nikci 62), Margairaz, Aegerter (Buff 70), Zouaghi, Chermiti (Drmic 84), Mehmedi.
Vaslui: Cerniauskas (Puia 32); Milanov, Gladstone, Farkas, Balaur, Sanmartean (Willian 54), Jovanovic (Buhaescu 80), Pavlovic, Milisavljevic, Adailton, Bello.

Group D Table	*P*	*W*	*D*	*L*	*F*	*A*	*Pts*
Sporting Lisbon	6	4	0	2	8	4	12
Lazio	6	2	3	1	7	5	9
Vaslui	6	1	3	2	5	8	6
Zurich	6	1	2	3	5	8	5

GROUP E

Thursday, 15 September 2011

Besiktas (2) 5 *(Hugo Almeida 3, 28, Mehmet Aurelio 50, Egemen 53, Edu 88)*

Maccabi Tel Aviv (0) 1 *(Kaat 49)* 28,425

Besiktas: Rustu; Egemen, Sivok, Ismail, Simao (Kavlak 80), Ricardo Quaresma (Mustafa 86), Mehmet Aurelio, Dag, Manuel Fernandes, Necip, Hugo Almeida (Edu 58).
Maccabi Tel Aviv: Haimov; Nivaldo, Pavicevic, Ziv, Vered, Medunjanin, Yeini (Itzhaki 46), Dahan, Kaat, Colautti (Puncec 59), Dabbur (Atar 46).

Dynamo Kiev (0) 1 *(Vukojevic 90)*

Stoke C (0) 1 *(Jerome 55)* 14,550

Dynamo Kiev: Shovkovsky; Betao, Popov, Danilo Silva, Yussuf, Ninkovic (Aliyev 58), Vukojevic, Garmash (Lukman 46) (Brown 75), Milevskiy, Shevchenko, Yarmolenko.
Stoke C: Sorensen; Wilkinson, Shotton (Whitehead 81), Huth, Shawcross, Upson, Diao, Whelan, Jones, Jerome (Pennant 75), Palacios (Walters 87).

Thursday, 29 September 2011

Maccabi Tel Aviv (1) 1 *(Micha 44)*

Dynamo Kiev (1) 1 *(Brown 9)* 13,835

Maccabi Tel Aviv: Haimov; Nivaldo, Ziv, Vered, Medunjanin, Alberman (Lugasi 46), Yeini, Puncec (Israelevich 71), Micha, Colautti, Dabbur (Itzhaki 62).
Dynamo Kiev: Shovkovsky; Betao, Popov, Danilo Silva, Yussuf, Aliyev (Husyev 60), Vukojevic, Garmash (Lukman 27), Shevchenko, Brown (Milevskiy 83), Yarmolenko.

Stoke C (1) 2 *(Crouch 15, Walters 78 (pen))*

Besiktas (1) 1 *(Hilbert 14)* 23,551

Stoke C: Sorensen; Huth, Shotton, Upson, Shawcross, Palacios (Whelan 61), Whitehead, Delap, Crouch, Jerome (Walters 59), Etherington (Pennant 51).
Besiktas: Rustu; Egemen, Sivok, Ismail, Simao, Hilbert, Ricardo Quaresma, Mehmet Aurelio (Holosko 82), Manuel Fernandes, Necip (Ernst 75), Edu.

Thursday, 20 October 2011

Dynamo Kiev (0) 1 *(Garmash 90)*

Besiktas (0) 0 13,500

Dynamo Kiev: Shovkovsky; Betao, Popov, Mykhalyk, Husyev, Vukojevic, Garmash, Milevskiy (Aliyev 60), Shevchenko (Dudu 82), Brown, Yarmolenko.
Besiktas: Cenk; Egemen, Sivok, Ismail, Simao, Hilbert, Ernst, Ricardo Quaresma (Kavlak 90), Mehmet Aurelio, Necip, Edu (Holosko 73).

Stoke C (3) 3 *(Jones 12, Jerome 24, Shotton 32)*

Maccabi Tel Aviv (0) 0 22,756

Stoke C: Sorensen; Huth (Walters 76), Shotton, Upson, Shawcross, Whitehead, Wilson (Wilkinson 61), Diao, Jones, Jerome■, Etherington (Palacios 79).
Maccabi Tel Aviv: Haimov; Pavicevic (Vered 64), Ziv■, Saban, Medunjanin, Israelevich (Micha 75), Yeini, Puncec, Dahan, Konate, Atar (Colautti 42).

Thursday, 3 November 2011

Besiktas (0) 1 *(Egemen 68)*

Dynamo Kiev (0) 0 24,183

Besiktas: Cenk; Egemen, Sivok, Ismail, Simao (Holosko 90), Hilbert, Ernst, Ricardo Quaresma, Mehmet Aurelio (Necip 63), Kavlak, Hugo Almeida (Edu 87).
Dynamo Kiev: Shovkovsky; Betao, Danilo Silva, Khacheridi, Yussuf, Correa (Brown 75), Aliyev, Vukojevic, Garmash (Ninkovic 46), Milevskiy, Yarmolenko.

Maccabi Tel Aviv (0) 1 *(Colautti 90)*

Stoke C (0) 2 *(Whitehead 51, Crouch 64)* 10,368

Maccabi Tel Aviv: Levi; Pavicevic, Saban, Cohen (Vered 46), Lugasi, Medunjanin (Kaat 66), Zizov (Colautti 60), Yeini, Puncec, Konate, Atar.
Stoke C: Sorensen; Wilkinson, Higginbotham, Upson, Huth, Palacios (Arismendi 74), Shotton, Diao (Whelan 65), Jones, Walters (Crouch 61), Whitehead.

Thursday, 1 December 2011

Maccabi Tel Aviv (0) 2 *(Yeini 59, Lugasi 70)*

Besiktas (1) 3 *(Ricardo Quaresma 45, 90, Ibrahim 47)* 9420

Maccabi Tel Aviv: Levi; Pavicevic, Saban (Nivaldo 54), Vered, Alberman (Lugasi 64), Israelevich (Zizov 83), Yeini, Puncec, Colautti, Itzhaki, Atar.
Besiktas: Cenk; Ibrahim, Egemen, Sivok, Ismail, Hilbert, Ernst, Ricardo Quaresma (Julio Alves 90), Dag (Kavlak 61), Manuel Fernandes (Holosko 90), Hugo Almeida.

Stoke C (0) 1 *(Jones 81)*

Dynamo Kiev (1) 1 *(Upson 27 (og))* 23,774

Stoke C: Begovic; Huth, Shotton, Upson, Higginbotham, Palacios, Pennant (Whitehead 88), Diao (Fuller 70), Jones (Walters 84), Jerome, Delap.
Dynamo Kiev: Shovkovsky; Betao, Danilo Silva, Khacheridi, Husyev, Yussuf (Ninkovic 85), Aliyev, Vukojevic, Shevchenko (Leandro Almeida 73), Brown, Yarmolenko.

Wednesday, 14 December 2011

Besiktas (0) 3 *(Manuel Fernandes 59 (pen), Mustafa 74, Edu 82)*

Stoke C (1) 1 *(Fuller 29)* 26,118

Besiktas: Rustu; Egemen, Sivok, Ismail, Hilbert, Ernst, Manuel Fernandes, Kavlak, Necip (Julio Alves 77), Hugo Almeida (Edu 75), Holosko (Mustafa 46).
Stoke C: Begovic; Wilkinson (Pennant 27), Higginbotham, Arismendi, Upson■, Palacios, Diao, Delap, Jones, Fuller, Jerome.

Dynamo Kiev (2) 3 *(Yeini 12 (og), Husyev 17, 80)*

Maccabi Tel Aviv (0) 3 *(Vered 50, Atar 62, Dabbur 75)* 3850

Dynamo Kiev: Koval; Leandro Almeida■, Betao, Danilo Silva, Khacheridi■, Husyev, Ninkovic (Correa 68), Aliyev, Garmash, Brown (Milevskiy 66), Yarmolenko (Lukman 85).
Maccabi Tel Aviv: Haimov; Nivaldo, Saban (Cohen 87), Vered, Lugasi (Dabbur 60), Alberman, Yeini, Kaat, Micha (Zizov 70), Konate, Atar.

Group E Table	P	W	D	L	F	A	Pts
Besiktas	6	4	0	2	13	7	12
Stoke C	6	3	2	1	10	7	11
Dynamo Kiev	6	1	4	1	7	7	7
Maccabi Tel Aviv	6	0	2	4	8	17	2

GROUP F

Thursday, 15 September 2011

Paris St Germain (2) 3 *(Nene 35 (pen), Bodmer 44, Menez 67)*

Salzburg (0) 1 *(Sekagya 87)* 23,039

Paris St Germain: Douchez; Jallet, Camara, Armand, Lugano, Matuidi, Menez (Ceara 85), Bodmer (Kebano 64), Nene, Pastore, Mevlut.
Salzburg: Gustafsson; Schiemer, Sekagya, Cziommer (Ulmer 46), Lindgren, Svento, Jantscher, Leitgeb (Alex Rafael 66), Hierlander, Leonardo, Maierhofer (Wallner 78).

Slovan Bratislava (1) 1 *(Guede 34)*

Athletic Bilbao (2) 2 *(Susaeta 13, Muniain 40)* 6328

Slovan Bratislava: Putnocky; Had (Hartig 87), Dobrotka, Bagayoko, Pauschek, Guede, Zofcak, Milinkovic (Lacny 72), Grendel (Taborsky 60), Sebo, Kladrubsky.
Athletic Bilbao: Iraizoz; Iraola, Amorebieta, Gabilondo (David Lopez 75), Gurpegi, Javi Martinez, Susaeta, Iturraspe, Llorente (Toquero 88), Muniain, De Marcos.

Thursday, 29 September 2011

Athletic Bilbao (2) 2 *(Gabilondo 20, Susaeta 45)*

Paris St Germain (0) 0 23,487

Athletic Bilbao: Iraizoz; Iraola, Amorebieta, Aurtenetxe, Ekiza, Gabilondo (Ibai 78), Javi Martinez, Susaeta (Iturraspe 72), Llorente, Muniain (Toquero 81), De Marcos.
Paris St Germain: Douchez; Jallet, Tiene, Armand, Lugano, Bodmer (Matuidi 66), Sissoko■, Nene (Ceara 76), Chantome, Pastore (Bahebeck 58), Mevlut.

Salzburg (0) 3 *(Leonardo 60, Zarate 76, Svento 90)*

Slovan Bratislava (0) 0 7500

Salzburg: Gustafsson; Pasanen, Schiemer (Lindgren 88), Ulmer, Sekagya, Schwegler, Cziommer, Svento, Jantscher, Leonardo (Teigl 85), Zarate (Maierhofer 83).
Slovan Bratislava: Hrosso; Had, Dosoudil, Dobrotka, Bagayoko, Guede, Milinkovic, Grendel (Zofcak 54), Sebo, Kladrubsky (Stepanovsky 76), Lacny.

Thursday, 20 October 2011

Athletic Bilbao (0) 2 *(Llorente 69 (pen), 75 (pen))*

Salzburg (2) 2 *(Wallner 30, Leonardo 36)* 22,566

Athletic Bilbao: Iraizoz; Iraola (Ander Herrera 65), Amorebieta, Aurtenetxe, Ekiza (Gabilondo 46), Javi Martinez, Susaeta (Toquero 87), Iturraspe, Llorente, Muniain, De Marcos.
Salzburg: Gustafsson; Pasanen, Schiemer (Lindgren■ 59), Sekagya, Schwegler, Hinteregger, Cziommer, Svento, Leonardo, Wallner (Maierhofer 90), Zarate (Hierlander 90).

Slovan Bratislava (0) 0

Paris St Germain (0) 0 7238

Slovan Bratislava: Hrosso; Had, Dobrotka, Bagayoko, Guede (Taborsky 85), Zofcak, Milinkovic (Grendel 61), Stepanovsky, Sebo, Kladrubsky, Halenar (Lacny 46).
Paris St Germain: Douchez; Jallet, Camara, Tiene■, Armand, Lugano, Menez (Bahebeck 90), Nene, Chantome■, Pastore (Gameiro 71), Mevlut (Ceara 66).

Thursday, 3 November 2011

Paris St Germain (0) 1 *(Pastore 63)*

Slovan Bratislava (0) 0 32,046

Paris St Germain: Douchez; Armand, Lugano, Ceara, Sakho, Menez (Jallet 75), Bodmer, Sissoko, Nene (Bahebeck 75), Pastore (Gameiro 87), Mevlut.
Slovan Bratislava: Hrosso; Had, Dobrotka, Bagayoko, Guede (Stepanovsky 90), Zofcak (Lacny 70), Milinkovic, Sebo, Taborsky (Kuzma 86), Kladrubsky, Halenar.

Salzburg (0) 0

Athletic Bilbao (1) 1 *(Ander Herrera 37)* 10,350

Salzburg: Gustafsson; Pasanen, Schiemer, Sekagya (Teigl 85), Schwegler, Hinteregger, Cziommer (Wallner 69), Svento, Jantscher (Leonardo 61), Leitgeb, Maierhofer.
Athletic Bilbao: Iraizoz; Iraola, San Jose, Aurtenetxe, Javi Martinez, Susaeta (Inigo Perez 88), Iturraspe (Amorebieta 68), Ander Herrera, Llorente, Muniain (Toquero 46), De Marcos.

Thursday, 1 December 2011

Athletic Bilbao (1) 2 *(De Marcos 15, Susaeta 75)*

Slovan Bratislava (1) 1 *(Sebo 39)* 28,314

Athletic Bilbao: Iraizoz; Amorebieta, Aurtenetxe, Javi Martinez, Susaeta, Inigo Perez (Iraola 46), Iturraspe, Ander Herrera, Llorente (Toquero 46), Muniain, De Marcos.
Slovan Bratislava: Putnocky; Had, Dobrotka, Bagayoko, Kolcak (Pauschek 83), Guede, Zofcak (Lacny 83), Milinkovic (Grendel 87), Sebo, Kladrubsky, Halenar.

Salzburg (1) 2 *(Jantscher 20, Svento 90)*

Paris St Germain (0) 0 8304

Salzburg: Walke; Pasanen, Hinteregger, Jefferson Cardoso, Svento, Jantscher (Cziommer 59), Leitgeb, Hierlander, Leonardo, Maierhofer (Wallner 89), Zarate (Teigl 83).
Paris St Germain: Douchez; Jallet (Bahebeck 46), Camara, Tiene, Ceara, Bisevac, Bodmer, Sissoko (Matuidi 73), Nene, Chantome (Gameiro 62), Mevlut.

Wednesday, 14 December 2011

Paris St Germain (2) 4 *(Pastore 21, Bodmer 41, Inigo Perez 85 (og), Hoarau 90 (pen))*

Athletic Bilbao (1) 2 *(Aurtenetxe 4, David Lopez 55)* 37,114

Paris St Germain: Douchez; Camara, Tiene, Armand, Lugano, Ceara, Bodmer (Mevlut 77), Nene, Pastore, Gameiro (Jallet 75), Baheveck (Hoarau 65).
Athletic Bilbao: Raul; Iraola, San Jose, Aurtenetxe, Ekiza (Inigo Ruiz 88), Gabilondo (Muniain 69), David Lopez, Inigo Perez, Iturraspe, Toquero (Susaeta 60), Ibai.

Slovan Bratislava (2) 2 *(Lacny 3, 6)*

Salzburg (2) 3 *(Jantscher 19 (pen), Leonardo 24, Had 52 (og))* 4586

Slovan Bratislava: Hrosso; Had, Dobrotka, Kolcak (Taborsky 71), Pauschek, Guede (Hartig 85), Zofcak (Grendel 80), Sebo, Kladrubsky, Halenar, Lacny.
Salzburg: Walke; Pasanen, Ulmer (Schiemer 84), Hinteregger, Lindgren (Sekagya 82), Svento, Jantscher, Hierlander, Leonardo, Maierhofer (Wallner 90), Zarate.

Group F Table	P	W	D	L	F	A	Pts
Athletic Bilbao	6	4	1	1	11	8	13
Salzburg	6	3	1	2	11	8	10
Paris St Germain	6	3	1	2	8	7	10
Slovan Bratislava	6	0	1	5	4	11	1

GROUP G

Thursday, 15 September 2011

AZ (3) 4 *(Altidore 21, Elm 33 (pen), Maher 39, Holman 49)*

Malmo (0) 1 *(Larsson 72 (pen))* 11,905

AZ: Alvarado; Marcellis, Poulsen (Klavan 65), Moisander (Reijnen 70), Viergever, Holman, Wernbloom, Elm, Maher, Beerens (Gudmundsson 62), Altidore.
Malmo: Dahlin; Vinzents, Andersson, Ricardinho, Jansson, Hamad, Pekalski, Durmaz, Wilton Figueiredo (Mehmeti 67), Ranegie (Mutavdzic 56), Larsson (Rexhepi 84).

FK Austria (1) 1 *(Jun 7)*

Metalist Kharkiv (0) 2 *(Gueye 56, Cleiton Xavier 79 (pen))* 9120

FK Austria: Grunwald P; Margreitter, Suttner, Rogulj, Klein, Hlinka, Junuzovic, Grunwald A (Gorgon 80), Barazite, Jun (Stankovic 84), Linz.
Metalist Kharkiv: Horyainov; Torsiglieri, Villagra (Obradovic 38) (Berezovchuk 90), Gueye, Romanchuk, Cleiton Xavier, Torres, Sosa, Edmar, Cristaldo (Shelayev 85), Taison.

Thursday, 29 September 2011

Malmo (0) 1 *(Ranegie 82)*

FK Austria (2) 2 *(Barazite 17, Grunwald A 36)* 10,802

Malmo: Dahlin; Vinzents (Aubynn 88), Andersson, Ricardinho, Jansson, Hamad, Pekalski, Durmaz (Halsti 69), Wilton Figueiredo, Ranegie, Larsson (Mehmeti 37).
FK Austria: Grunwald P; Ortlechner, Margreitter, Suttner, Klein, Mader, Junuzovic (Dilaver 90), Grunwald A■, Gorgon, Barazite, Linz (Hlinka 70).

Metalist Kharkiv (0) 1 *(Taison 76)*

AZ (1) 1 *(Altidore 26)* 37,122

Metalist Kharkiv: Horyainov; Torsiglieri, Villagra, Gueye, Romanchuk, Cleiton Xavier, Torres (Devic 70), Sosa, Edmar, Cristaldo, Taison (Shelayev 90).
AZ: Alvarado; Klavan, Marcellis, Poulsen, Moisander, Wernbloom, Elm (Viergever 77), Maher, Beerens, Altidore (Benschop 82), Gudmundsson (Ortiz 78).

Thursday, 20 October 2011

AZ (0) 2 *(Hlinka 80 (og), Wernbloom 83)*

FK Austria (2) 2 *(Marcellis 18 (og), Gorgon 29)* 15,321

AZ: Alvarado; Klavan, Marcellis, Poulsen, Moisander■, Wernbloom, Elm, Maher (Altidore 73), Beerens (Lewis 69), Gudmundsson (Ortiz 80), Benschop.
FK Austria: Grunwald P; Ortlechner, Margreitter, Suttner, Klein, Hlinka, Mader, Junuzovic, Gorgon, Barazite (Linz 87), Jun.

Malmo (1) 1 *(Hamad 22)*

Metalist Kharkiv (2) 4 *(Cristaldo 32, Fininho 45, Edmar 58, Devic 73)* 8466

Malmo: Dahlin; Vinzents (Mehmeti 72), Andersson (Aubynn 84), Ricardinho, Jansson, Hamad, Pekalski, Durmaz (Larsson 61), Wilton Figueiredo, Mutavdzic, Ranegie.
Metalist Kharkiv: Horyainov; Fininho, Torsiglieri, Villagra, Gueye, Cleiton Xavier (Blanco 77), Torres, Sosa (Valyaev 76), Edmar, Cristaldo■, Taison (Devic 67).

Thursday, 3 November 2011

FK Austria (0) 2 *(Ortlechner 58, Barazite 61)*

AZ (2) 2 *(Elm 19 (pen), Wernbloom 44)* 10,450

FK Austria: Lindner; Ortlechner, Margreitter, Suttner, Klein, Mader, Junuzovic, Grunwald A (Liendl 58), Gorgon (Linz 46), Barazite, Jun (Stankovic 88).
AZ: Alvarado; Klavan, Poulsen, Reijnen, Viergever, Holman (Ortiz 68), Wernbloom, Elm, Maher, Beerens, Altidore (Benschop 87).

Metalist Kharkiv (0) 3 *(Taison 46, 56, Fininho 90)*

Malmo (0) 1 *(Ranegie 66)* 25,883

Metalist Kharkiv: Disljenkovic; Torsiglieri, Villagra, Gueye, Pshenichnikh, Shelayev (Fininho 46), Blanco, Torres, Edmar, Devic (Valyaev 90), Taison.
Malmo: Dahlin; Vinzents, Andersson, Halsti, Ricardinho, Hamad, Pekalski (Aubynn 71), Durmaz (Malm 81), Wilton Figueiredo, Ranegie, Larsson (Mehmeti 71).

Wednesday, 30 November 2011

Malmo (0) 0

AZ (0) 0 7632

Malmo: Dahlin; Vinzents, Andersson, Ricardinho, Jansson, Aubynn, Hamad, Durmaz (Malm 88), Mutavdzic (Wilton Figueiredo 74), Ranegie, Larsson (Mehmeti 65).
AZ: Alvarado; Klavan, Poulsen, Reijnen, Viergever, Holman (Gudmundsson 67), Elm, Falkenburg (Ortiz 74), Maher, Beerens (Benschop 24), Altidore.

Metalist Kharkiv (2) 4 *(Devic 16, Edmar 40, Gueye 60, Sosa 90)*

FK Austria (1) 1 *(Mader 19)* 25,810

Metalist Kharkiv: Disljenkovic; Fininho, Torsiglieri, Villagra, Gueye, Cleiton Xavier, Torres, Sosa (Radchenko 90), Edmar (Shelayev 88), Devic (Blanco 79), Taison.
FK Austria: Lindner; Margreitter, Suttner, Klein, Hlinka, Mader, Junuzovic, Grunwald A (Liendl 66), Gorgon (Stankovic 56), Barazite, Jun (Tadic 80).

Thursday, 15 December 2011

AZ (1) 1 *(Maher 37)*

Metalist Kharkiv (1) 1 *(Devic 36)* 13,268

AZ: Alvarado; Poulsen, Moisander, Reijnen, Viergever, Wernbloom, Elm, Maher, Beerens, Altidore, Gudmundsson (Holman 59).
Metalist Kharkiv: Horyainov; Torsiglieri, Villagra, Gueye, Romanchuk (Budnik 74), Pshenichnikh, Shelayev (Obradovic 61), Blanco (Berezovchuk 89), Valyaev, Edmar, Devic.

FK Austria (0) 2 *(Liendl 62, Barazite 80)*

Malmo (0) 0 9350

FK Austria: Lindner; Suttner, Wallner, Mally, Klein, Mader, Junuzovic (Stankovic 88), Liendl, Gorgon, Barazite (Jun 82), Linz (Grunwald A 78).
Malmo: Dahlin; Vinzents, Andersson (Mutavdzic 79) (Miiko Albornoz 84), Halsti, Ricardinho, Jansson, Aubynn, Hamad, Durmaz, Ranegie, Larsson (Nilsson 78).

Group G Table	P	W	D	L	F	A	Pts
Metalist Kharkiv	6	4	2	0	15	6	14
AZ	6	1	5	0	10	7	8
FK Austria	6	2	2	2	10	11	8
Malmo	6	0	1	5	4	15	1

GROUP H

Thursday, 15 September 2011

Birmingham C (0) 1 *(King 71)*

Braga (1) 3 *(Helder Barbosa 7, 88, Lima 59)* 21,747

Birmingham C: Myhill; Pablo, Murphy, Spector, N'Daw (Burke 60), Ridgewell, Carr, Elliott, King, Rooney (Wood 60), Redmond.
Braga: Quim; Paulo Vinicius, Echiejile, Baiano, Ewerton, Hugo Viana, Djalma, Nuno Gomes (Leandro Salino 73), Alan, Lima (Carlao 82), Helder Barbosa (Paulo Cesar 89).

Club Brugge (2) 2 *(Odjidja-Ofoe 7, Dirar 24)*

Maribor (0) 0 16,688

Club Brugge: Coosemans; Donk, Hoefkens, Hogli (Lestienne 90), Almeback, Zimling, Dirar, Odjidja-Ofoe, Refaelov (Meunier 74), Akpala, Victor Vazquez (Blondel 71).
Maribor: Handanovic; Rajcevic■, Arghus, Ibraimi (Beric 66), Viler, Mezga, Mertelj (Cvijanovic 75), Mejac (Milec 81), Marcos Tavares, Volas, Filipovic.

Thursday, 29 September 2011

Braga (0) 1 *(Helder Barbosa 53)*

Club Brugge (0) 2 *(Akpala 71, Donk 90)* 9145

Braga: Quim; Paulo Vinicius, Echiejile, Baiano, Ewerton, Hugo Viana, Marcio Mossoro (Leandro Salino 64), Djalma (Carlao 83), Alan, Lima, Helder Barbosa (Nuno Gomes 75).
Club Brugge: Coosemans; Donk, Hoefkens, Hogli, Almeback, Zimling, Odjidja-Ofoe, Refaelov (De Jonghe 74), Meunier (Blondel 90), Vleminckx (Akpala 32), Victor Vazquez.

Maribor (1) 1 *(Volas 29)*

Birmingham C (0) 2 *(Burke 64, Elliott 79)* 10,000

Maribor: Handanovic; Arghus, Cvijanovic (Ibraimi 71), Lesjak, Viler, Mezga (Crnic 86), Mertelj (Beric 81), Potokar, Milec, Marcos Tavares, Volas.
Birmingham C: Doyle; Pablo, Ridgewell, Spector, Caldwell, Gomis, Burke, Elliott, King (Zigic 65), Beausejour, Fahey.

Thursday, 20 October 2011

Club Brugge (1) 1 *(Akpala 3)*

Birmingham C (1) 2 *(Murphy 26, Wood 90)* 23,936

Club Brugge: Coosemans; Donk, Hogli, Almeback, Vansteenkiste (De Jonghe 60), Zimling, Blondel (Deschilder 82), Dirar, Odjidja-Ofoe, Refaelov (Meunier 63), Akpala.
Birmingham C: Myhill; Spector, Murphy, Caldwell, Pablo (Ridgewell 90), N'Daw, Burke, Elliott, Rooney (King 72), Zigic (Wood 73), Fahey.

Maribor (1) 1 *(Ibraimi 14)*

Braga (1) 1 *(Echiejile 44)* 8500

Maribor: Handanovic; Arghus, Trajkovski, Ibraimi, Lesjak, Mezga, Mertelj, Potokar, Milec, Marcos Tavares (Beric 74), Volas (Velikonja 85).
Braga: Quim; Paulo Vinicius, Echiejile, Baiano, Ewerton, Hugo Viana, Marcio Mossoro (Paulo Cesar 72), Djalma, Alan, Lima, Helder Barbosa (Leandro Salino 67).

Thursday, 3 November 2011

Birmingham C (0) 2 *(Beausejour 55, King 74 (pen))*

Club Brugge (2) 2 *(Meunier 39, Akpala 44)* 26,849

Birmingham C: Doyle; N'Daw, Murphy, Caldwell, Pablo, Spector, Elliott (Burke 66), Fahey, Rooney (Wood 66), Zigic (King 66), Beausejour.
Club Brugge: Kujovic; Donk, Van Gijseghem, Vansteenkiste, Zimling, Dirar, Odjidja-Ofoe, Meunier, Van Acker (Almeback 85), Akpala (Vleminckx 76), Victor Vazquez (Refaelov 81).

Braga (3) 5 *(Lima 4, Alan 7, Echiejile 38, Paulo Vinicius 85, Fran Merida 90)*

Maribor (0) 1 *(Volas 62)* 7185

Braga: Quim; Paulo Vinicius, Echiejile, Baiano, Ewerton, Hugo Viana (Fran Merida 86), Marcio Mossoro (Leandro Salino 65), Djalma, Alan, Lima, Helder Barbosa (Paulo Cesar 78).
Maribor: Handanovic; Rajcevic, Arghus, Trajkovski, Ibraimi, Lesjak (Filipovic 80), Mezga (Cvijanovic 63), Mertelj, Beric (Marcos Tavares 65), Milec, Volas.

Wednesday, 30 November 2011

Braga (0) 1 *(Hugo Viana 51)*

Birmingham C (0) 0 9957

Braga: Quim; Paulo Vinicius, Echiejile (Douglao 68), Ewerton, Hugo Viana, Marcio Mossoro (Fran Merida 84), Djalma, Leandro Salino, Alan, Lima, Helder Barbosa (Paulo Cesar 69).
Birmingham C: Myhill; N'Daw, Murphy, Caldwell, Davies, Spector, Burke, Fahey, Elliott (King 64), Zigic (Wood 76), Beausejour (Redmond 64).

Maribor (1) 3 *(Volas 11, 68, Donk 51 (og))*

Club Brugge (0) 4 *(Dirar 74, 77, Akpala 81, Donk 90)* 8000

Maribor: Handanovic; Rajcevic, Arghus, Trajkovski, Cvijanovic (Velikonja 85), Ibraimi (Lesjak 75), Mezga, Mertelj, Potokar, Marcos Tavares (Beric 86), Volas.
Club Brugge: Kujovic; Donk, Hoefkens, Almeback, De Jonghe, Zimling, Dirar, Odjidja-Ofoe (Victor Vazquez 73), Refaelov (Akpala 59), Meunier, Vleminckx.

Thursday, 15 December 2011

Birmingham C (1) 1 *(Rooney 24)*

Maribor (0) 0 21,634

Birmingham C: Doyle; Pablo, Murphy, Gomis (N'Daw 73), Davies, Spector, Beausejour, Fahey, Rooney (Mutch 79), Zigic, Redmond (Burke 88).
Maribor: Handanovic; Rajcevic, Arghus (Trajkovski 75), Vidovic, Cvijanovic (Ibraimi 67), Mezga, Mertelj, Potokar, Marcos Tavares (Velikonja 71), Volas, Filipovic.

Club Brugge (0) 1 *(Vleminckx 50)*

Braga (0) 1 *(Ewerton 65)* 21,050

Club Brugge: Kujovic; Donk, Hoefkens, Hogli, Almeback, Zimling, Dirar, Odjidja-Ofoe, Meunier (Refaelov 46), Vleminckx (Akpala 88), Victor Vazquez.
Braga: Quim; Echiejile■, Douglao, Ewerton, Hugo Viana (Marcio Mossoro 86), Djalma, Leandro Salino, Nuno Gomes (Paulo Cesar 60), Alan, Lima, Helder Barbosa (Carlao 78).

Group H Table	P	W	D	L	F	A	Pts
Club Brugge	6	3	2	1	12	9	11
Braga	6	3	2	1	12	6	11
Birmingham C	6	3	1	2	8	8	10
Maribor	6	0	1	5	6	15	1

GROUP I

Thursday, 15 September 2011

Atletico Madrid (1) 2 *(Falcao 3, Diego 69)*

Celtic (0) 0 28,960

Atletico Madrid: Courtois; Antonio Lopez, Miranda, Perea, Godin, Diego (Tiago 84), Gabi (Adrian 70), Mario Suarez, Arda, Koke (Reyes 57), Falcao.
Celtic: Forster; Wilson M (Matthews 80), Ki, Mulgrew, Wilson K, Loovens, Ledley (Bangura 78), Kayal, Samaras, Hooper, Forrest (Commons 83).

Udinese (1) 2 *(Di Natale 39, Armero 83)*

Rennes (1) 1 *(Hadji 18)* 15,100

Udinese: Handanovic; Danilo, Benatia, Isla, Armero, Neuton (Domizzi 46), Abdi, Doubai, Agyemang-Badu, Di Natale (Barreto 66), Fabbrini (Asamoah 70).
Rennes: Costil; Danze, Mangane (Kana Biyik 15), Boye, Mavinga, Dalmat, Tettey, M'Vila, Hadji, Kembo-Ekoko (Montano 71), Pitroipa (Boukari 59).

Thursday, 29 September 2011

Celtic (1) 1 *(Ki 3 (pen))*

Udinese (0) 1 *(Abdi 88 (pen))* 28,476

Celtic: Zaluska; Matthews, Wanyama, Ki, Majstorovic, Mulgrew, Kayal, Ledley (Wilson M 46), Bangura, Hooper, Forrest (Samaras 72).
Udinese: Handanovic; Basta (Benatia 46), Danilo, Ekstrand, Neuton, Abdi, Doubai, Pereyra (Isla 46), Agyemang-Badu, Battocchio, Fabbrini (Armero 67).

Rennes (0) 1 *(Montano 56)*

Atletico Madrid (0) 1 *(Juanfran 87)* 24,299

Rennes: Costil; Danze, Kana Biyik, Theophile Catherine, Dalmat (M'Vila 74), Tettey, Mandjeck, Feret, Doumbia, Kembo-Ekoko (Pitroipa 60), Montano (Hadji 69).
Atletico Madrid: Courtois; Miranda, Perea, Filipe Luis, Dominguez, Diego, Gabi (Reyes 73), Mario Suarez, Arda (Juanfran 80), Adrian (Salvio 63), Falcao.

Thursday, 20 October 2011

Rennes (1) 1 *(Cha 31 (og))*

Celtic (0) 1 *(Ledley 70)* 21,825

Rennes: Costil; Mangane, Kana Biyik, Mavinga (Theophile Catherine 77), Jebbour, Tettey, Feret, Brahimi (Pitroipa 59), Pajot, Boukari (Kembo-Ekoko 58), Hadji.
Celtic: Forster; Matthews, Mulgrew, Ki (Bangura 90), Loovens, Wanyama, Kayal, Ledley, Stokes, Cha, Forrest.

Udinese (0) 2 *(Benatia 88, Floro Flores 90)*

Atletico Madrid (0) 0 10,026

Udinese: Handanovic; Danilo, Benatia, Domizzi, Armero, Pinzi, Abdi (Fabbrini 46), Doubai (Asamoah 84), Pereyra (Basta 46), Agyemang-Badu, Floro Flores.
Atletico Madrid: Courtois; Miranda, Perea, Filipe Luis, Godin, Diego, Juanfran (Reyes 58), Gabi (Adrian 79), Paulo Assuncao, Falcao, Pizzi (Koke 85).

Thursday, 3 November 2011

Atletico Madrid (3) 4 *(Adrian 7, 12, Diego 37, Falcao 67)*

Udinese (0) 0 18,300

Atletico Madrid: Courtois; Antonio Lopez, Perea, Godin, Dominguez, Diego (Koke 70), Gabi, Mario Suarez, Arda, Adrian (Salvio 77), Falcao (Pizzi 83).
Udinese: Handanovic; Danilo, Domizzi (Basta 71), Ekstrand, Neuton, Doubai, Pereyra, Agyemang-Badu, Battocchio, Floro Flores (Isla 86), Fabbrini (Abdi 24).

Celtic (2) 3 *(Stokes 30, 43, Hooper 82)*

Rennes (1) 1 *(Mangane 2)* 28,578

Celtic: Forster; Matthews, Wanyama, Cha, Majstorovic, Loovens (Fraser 46), Kayal, McCourt (Commons 66), Stokes, Samaras, Forrest (Hooper 79).
Rennes: Costil; Danze, Mangane, Theophile Catherine, Tettey (Doumbia 46), Mandjeck, Feret (Hadji 70), M'Vila■, Pajot, Boukari (Montano 46), Pitroipa.

Wednesday, 30 November 2011

Celtic (0) 0

Atletico Madrid (1) 1 *(Arda 30)* 33,257

Celtic: Forster; Matthews, Ledley (Mulgrew 38), Loovens, Majstorovic, Wanyama (Hooper 46), Kayal, Ki, Samaras, Stokes (Brown 76), Forrest.
Atletico Madrid: Courtois; Miranda, Perea, Filipe Luis, Godin, Diego, Gabi (Paulo Assuncao 90), Mario Suarez, Arda (Juanfran 80), Salvio, Adrian (Falcao 68).

Rennes (0) 0

Udinese (0) 0 17,428

Rennes: Costil; Kana Biyik, Boye (Mandjeck 46), Mavinga, Jebbour, Dalmat (Doumbia 60), Tettey, Brahimi (Pitroipa 55), Pajot, Boukari, Hadji.
Udinese: Handanovic; Danilo, Benatia, Isla (Basta 61), Armero, Ekstrand, Doubai (Pinzi 82), Asamoah, Agyemang-Badu, Floro Flores, Fabbrini.

Thursday, 15 December 2011

Atletico Madrid (2) 3 *(Falcao 38 (pen), Dominguez 43, Arda 79)*

Rennes (0) 1 *(Mandjeck 86)* 24,371

Atletico Madrid: Sergio Asenjo; Perea (Miranda 65), Filipe Luis, Godin, Dominguez, Diego (Tiago 76), Paulo Assuncao, Arda (Juanfran 81), Koke, Adrian, Falcao.
Rennes: Diallo; Apam, Mavinga, Jebbour (Feret 87), Foulquier, Tettey, Mandjeck, Brahimi (Diarra 87), Doumbia, Pajot, Montano (Hadji 65).

Udinese (1) 1 *(Di Natale 45)*

Celtic (1) 1 *(Hooper 29)* 15,227

Udinese: Handanovic; Basta, Danilo, Benatia, Armero, Ekstrand, Abdi, Doubai (Isla 46), Asamoah, Agyemang-Badu (Pinzi 29), Di Natale.
Celtic: Forster; Cha, Mulgrew, Ki, Majstorovic, Wanyama, Kayal (Stokes 71), Brown, Samaras (Bangura 83), Hooper, Forrest.

Group I Table	*P*	*W*	*D*	*L*	*F*	*A*	*Pts*
Atletico Madrid	6	4	1	1	11	4	13
Udinese	6	2	3	1	6	7	9
Celtic	6	1	3	2	6	7	6
Rennes	6	0	3	3	5	10	3

GROUP J

Thursday, 15 September 2011

Maccabi Haifa (0) 1 *(Ghadir 54)*

AEK Larnaca (0) 0 11,110

Maccabi Haifa: Saranov; Meshumar, Dgani, Falach, Vered, Golasa, Yahaya, Tawatha, Amasha (De Jesus 73), Katan (Cohen 89), Ghadir (Gustavo Boccoli 65).
AEK Larnaca: Fortin; De Cler, Ander Murillo■, Dimech, Van Dijk, Linssen, Skopelitis (Kingsley 79), Ruben Gomez (Priso 65), Pavlou (Gonzalo Garcia 64), Demetriou, Mrdakovic.

Steaua (0) 0

Schalke (0) 0 18,000

Steaua: Tatarusanu; Latovlevici, Galamaz, Geraldo Alves, Gardos, Prepelita (Rusescu 67), Brandan, Tanase (Costea F 90), Bourceanu, Costea M (Nikolic 80), Leandro Tatu.
Schalke: Fahrmann; Uchida, Fuchs, Howedes, Papadopoulos, Holtby, Matip, Raul, Huntelaar, Farfan (Baumjohann 80), Marica (Draxler 73).

Thursday, 29 September 2011

AEK Larnaca (0) 1 *(Mrdakovic 59)*

Steaua (0) 1 *(Costea M 65)* 4058

AEK Larnaca: Fortin; De Cler, Dimech, Van Dijk, Linssen, Skopelitis, Priso, Demetriou, Gonzalo Garcia (Ruben Gomez 52), Mrdakovic (Pavlou 73), Kingsley (Gorka Pintado 60).
Steaua: Stanca; Emeghara (Martinovic 67), Latovlevici, Iliev, Gardos, Prepelita (Bicfalvi 90), Brandan■, Tanase (Costea F 76), Bourceanu, Costea M, Leandro Tatu.

Schalke (1) 3 *(Fuchs 8, 66, Jurado 82)*

Maccabi Haifa (1) 1 *(Vered 35)* 49,070

Schalke: Fahrmann; Metzelder, Fuchs, Howedes, Holtby (Papadopoulos 62), Matip (Jurado 62), Hoger, Draxler (Jones 77), Raul, Huntelaar, Farfan.
Maccabi Haifa: Saranov; Buljat, Osman, Falach, Vered, Gustavo Boccoli (Ghadir 68), Golasa, Yahaya, Tawatha, De Jesus (Dvalishvili 67), Amasha (Cohen 54).

Thursday, 20 October 2011

AEK Larnaca (0) 0

Schalke (3) 5 *(Holtby 23, Huntelaar 35, 88, Matip 40, Draxler 87)* 5344

AEK Larnaca: Fortin; De Cler, Dimech, Prodromou, Van Dijk, Linssen, Skopelitis (Kingsley 79), Ruben Gomez, Priso (Pavlou 58), Demetriou, Mrdakovic (Gorka Pintado 59).
Schalke: Unnerstall; Fuchs (Sarpei 62), Howedes, Papadopoulos, Jones (Hoger 68), Holtby, Matip, Draxler, Raul (Moravek 46), Huntelaar, Farfan.

Maccabi Haifa (3) 5 *(Amasha 10, 20, Katan 38 (pen), Tawatha 72, Vered 79)*
Steaua (0) 0 12,000
Maccabi Haifa: Saranov; Buljat, Meshumar, Dgani, Cohen (Azriel 60), Vered, Golasa, Yahaya, Tawatha, Amasha (Gustavo Boccoli 70), Katan (Turgeman 65).
Steaua: Stanca; Latovlevici, Geraldo Alves, Iliev■, Martinovic, Bicfalvi■, Bourceanu, Costea F (Rusescu 51), Costea M (Mustata 67), Nikolic, Leandro Tatu (Rosu 77).

Thursday, 3 November 2011

Schalke (0) 0
AEK Larnaca (0) 0 52,077
Schalke: Unnerstall; Uchida (Baumjohann 77), Fuchs, Papadopoulos, Jurado (Holtby 58), Moravek, Matip, Hoger, Draxler, Huntelaar, Marica (Farfan 58).
AEK Larnaca: Fortin; De Cler, Dimech, Van Dijk, Linssen, Ruben Gomez, Priso, Demetriou, Gonzalo Garcia, Mrdakovic (Mitidis 90), Kingsley (Prodromou 89).

Steaua (2) 4 *(Leandro Tatu 13, Costea F 28, Tanase 64, 84)*
Maccabi Haifa (2) 2 *(Meshumar 36, Katan 40)* 31,233
Steaua: Stanca; Latovlevici, Geraldo Alves, Martinovic, Gardos (Rusescu 3), Brandan, Tanase, Bourceanu, Costea F■, Costea M (Nastasie 85), Leandro Tatu (Nikolic 26).
Maccabi Haifa: Davidovich; Buljat, Meshumar, Falach, Vered (Yampolsky 33), Gustavo Boccoli (Dvalishvili 36), Golasa, Yahaya (Turgeman 68), Tawatha, Amasha, Katan.

Thursday, 1 December 2011

AEK Larnaca (1) 2 *(Gonzalo Garcia 14, Gorka Pintado 51)*
Maccabi Haifa (0) 1 *(Buljat 75)* 3132
AEK Larnaca: Alexandre Negri; De Cler, Hofland, Ander Murillo, Van Dijk, Linssen, Ruben Gomez, Priso (Dimech 86), Demetriou, Gonzalo Garcia (Mrdakovic 86), Gorka Pintado (Skopelitis 75).
Maccabi Haifa: Saranov; Buljat, Dgani (Yampolsky 46), Cohen I, Cohen T, Gustavo Boccoli (Azriel 46), Golasa, Tawatha, Dvalishvili, Amasha, Katan (Vered 55).

Schalke (1) 2 *(Papadopoulos 25, Raul 57)*
Steaua (1) 1 *(Rusescu 33)* 53,123
Schalke: Unnerstall; Fuchs, Papadopoulos, Jones, Baumjohann (Draxler 65), Jurado, Holtby (Moritz 78), Matip, Hoger, Raul, Huntelaar (Marica 83).
Steaua: Tatarusanu; Latovlevici (Prepelita 68), Geraldo Alves, Iliev, Martinovic, Bicfalvi, Brandan, Tanase, Bourceanu, Costea M (Rosu 88), Rusescu (Nikolic 69).

Wednesday, 14 December 2011

Maccabi Haifa (0) 0
Schalke (1) 3 *(Buljat 7 (og), Marica 84, Wiegel 90)* 11,234
Maccabi Haifa: Saranov; Buljat, Meshumar, Falach, Vered (Azriel 65), Golasa, Yahaya (Turgeman 80), Tawatha, Dvalishvili (Yampolsky 56), Amasha, Katan.
Schalke: Hildebrand; Metzelder, Uchida, Howedes (Sabah 58), Sergio Escudero, Baumjohann, Jurado (Langlitz 84), Moritz, Hoger, Draxler (Wiegel 65), Marica.

Steaua (0) 3 *(Rusescu 55 (pen), Nikolic 70, 85)*
AEK Larnaca (0) 1 *(Gorka Pintado 61)* 50,051
Steaua: Tatarusanu; Emeghara (Martinovic 64), Latovlevici, Geraldo Alves, Iliev, Prepelita (Leandro Tatu 67), Brandan, Tanase, Bourceanu, Rusescu (Bicfalvi 79), Nikolic.
AEK Larnaca: Alexandre Negri; De Cler, Hofland, Ander Murillo, Van Dijk (Kingsley 72), Linssen, Ruben Gomez, Priso, Demetriou, Gonzalo Garcia, Gorka Pintado (Mitidis 76).

Group J Table	*P*	*W*	*D*	*L*	*F*	*A*	*Pts*
Schalke	6	4	2	0	13	2	14
Steaua	6	2	2	2	9	11	8
Maccabi Haifa	6	2	0	4	10	12	6
AEK Larnaca	6	1	2	3	4	11	5

GROUP K

Thursday, 15 September 2011

Fulham (1) 1 *(Johnson 19)*
Twente (1) 1 *(Schwarzer 40 (og))* 14,120
Fulham: Schwarzer; Baird, Briggs (Senderos 81), Murphy, Grygera, Hangeland, Sidwell, Kasami (Duff 74), Dembele, Johnson (Zamora 66), Dempsey.
Twente: Mihaylov; Wisgerhof, Cornelisse, Tiendalli, Rosales, Douglas, Brama, Janssen (Landzaat 83), Fer, De Jong, John (Bajrami 68).

Wisla (0) 1 *(Kirm 54)*
Odense (1) 3 *(Johansson 36, Utaka 80, Jensen 90)* 12,950
Wisla: Pareiko; Jaliens, Lamey, Chavez, Sobolewski (Diaz 87), Nunez (Gargula 85), Paljic, Kirm, Meliksson, Iliev (Malecki 84), Biton.
Odense: Wessels; Mendy (Jensen 46), Ruud, Reginiussen, Christensen, Chris Sorensen, Johansson, Djemba-Djemba, Andreasen, Gislason (Christian Sorensen 90), Utaka (Fall 82).

Thursday, 29 September 2011

Odense (0) 0
Fulham (1) 2 *(Johnson 36, 88)* 7969
Odense: Wessels; Mendy, Ruud, Reginiussen, Christensen, Johansson, Djemba-Djemba (Skoubo 84), Andreasen, Traore■, Kadrii (Gislason 79), Fall (Utaka 68).
Fulham: Schwarzer; Kelly, Briggs, Murphy (Sidwell 77), Senderos, Hangeland, Duff, Etuhu, Johnson, Kasami (Orlando Sa 84), Dempsey.

Twente (2) 4 *(De Jong 32, Janko 45, 57, Janssen 80)*
Wisla (1) 1 *(Biton 9)* 20,000
Twente: Mihaylov; Wisgerhof, Tiendalli, Rosales, Douglas, Landzaat (Fer 84), Brama, Bajrami, Janko (Janssen 68), De Jong, John (Berghuis 83).
Wisla: Pareiko; Jaliens, Lamey, Diaz, Chavez, Sobolewski, Jirsak (Wilk 68), Nunez (Brud 85), Kirm, Iliev (Paljic 67), Biton.

Thursday, 20 October 2011

Odense (0) 1 *(Fall 71)*
Twente (2) 4 *(Brama 13, Bajrami 31, Chadli 65, De Jong 82)* 8036
Odense: Toppel; Mendy, Ruud, Reginiussen, Christensen, Chris Sorensen, Johansson (Jensen 76), Djemba-Djemba, Andreasen (Fall 69), Kadrii (Gislason 84), Utaka.
Twente: Mihaylov; Wisgerhof, Tiendalli, Rosales, Douglas, Landzaat (Fer 68), Brama, Bajrami, Janko (Chadli 62), De Jong, John (Janssen 77).

Wisla (0) 1 *(Biton 60)*
Fulham (0) 0 16,377
Wisla: Pareiko; Jaliens, Lamey, Diaz, Chavez■, Wilk, Gargula (Brud 79), Nunez, Kirm (Czekaj 90), Iliev (Boguski 86), Biton.
Fulham: Schwarzer; Kelly, Briggs (Frei 88), Gecov (Sidwell 75), Hughes, Hangeland, Duff, Etuhu, Johnson, Orlando Sa (Kasami 59), Dembele■.

Thursday, 3 November 2011

Fulham (2) 4 *(Duff 5, Johnson 30, 57, Sidwell 79)*
Wisla (1) 1 *(Kirm 9)* 20,319
Fulham: Schwarzer; Kelly, Riise J, Murphy (Sidwell 63), Baird, Hangeland, Duff, Etuhu, Johnson (Kasami 77), Zamora (Frei 72), Dempsey.
Wisla: Pareiko; Jaliens, Lamey, Diaz, Wilk, Gargula (Genkov 61), Nunez, Paljic, Kirm, Brud (Iliev 61), Biton (Jovanovic 88).

Twente (2) 3 *(Hoegh 35 (og), Landzaat 37, Fer 82)*
Odense (1) 2 *(Fall 11, 62)* 20,000
Twente: Mihaylov; Wisgerhof, Tiendalli, Rosales, Douglas, Landzaat (Janssen 74), Brama, Bajrami, Chadli (Fer 79), De Jong, John (Gouriye 90).
Odense: Wessels; Mendy, Ruud, Christensen, Chris Sorensen, Hoegh, Johansson, Traore (Reginiussen 79), Gislason, Skoubo (Andreasen 75), Fall (Utaka 83).

Thursday, 1 December 2011

Odense (0) 1 *(Jensen 51)*

Wisla (2) 2 *(Biton 20, Malecki 28)* 5824

Odense: Toppel; Mendy, Ruud, Christensen, Chris Sorensen, Hoegh (Reginiussen 15), Johansson, Andreasen, Skoubo (Fall 75), Utaka, Jensen (Kadrii 55).
Wisla: Pareiko; Lamey (Jovanovic 79), Diaz, Chavez, Wilk, Gargula, Nunez, Paljic, Kirm (Iliev 90), Malecki (Meliksson 82), Biton.

Twente (0) 1 *(Janko 89)*

Fulham (0) 0 25,250

Twente: Mihaylov; Wisgerhof, Tiendalli, Rosales, Douglas, Landzaat, Brama, Bajrami, Fer (John 46), Chadli (Janko 79), De Jong.
Fulham: Schwarzer; Kelly, Riise J, Murphy, Hughes, Hangeland, Duff (Frei 34), Etuhu, Johnson■, Zamora (Orlando Sa 87), Dembele (Kasami 83).

Wednesday, 14 December 2011

Fulham (2) 2 *(Dempsey 27, Frei 31)*

Odense (0) 2 *(Andreasen 64, Fall 90)* 15,757

Fulham: Etheridge; Kelly, Briggs, Baird, Hughes, Hangeland, Dempsey (Duff 72), Gecov, Dembele, Zamora (Orlando Sa 89), Frei.
Odense: Wessels; Mendy (Djemba-Djemba 86), Ruud, Reginiussen, Chris Sorensen, Hoegh, Andreasen, Kadrii (Johansson 69), Gislason, Utaka, Jensen (Fall 78).

Wisla (1) 2 *(Gargula 12, Genkov 46)*

Twente (1) 1 *(De Jong 40)* 15,500

Wisla: Pareiko; Diaz, Jovanovic, Bunoza, Wilk, Jirsak (Brud 90), Gargula, Nunez, Meliksson (Kirm 89), Boguski (Malecki 61), Genkov.
Twente: Marsman; Cornelisse, Bengtsson, Buysse, Roseler, Landzaat, Bajrami, Janssen, Chadli (John 46), Janko (Berghuis 65), De Jong (Gouriye 77).

Group K Table	*P*	*W*	*D*	*L*	*F*	*A*	*Pts*
Twente	6	4	1	1	14	7	13
Wisla	6	3	0	3	8	13	9
Fulham	6	2	2	2	9	6	8
Odense	6	1	1	4	9	14	4

GROUP L

Thursday, 15 September 2011

Anderlecht (3) 4 *(Suarez 16, 40, 84, Jovanovic 33)*

AEK Athens (1) 1 *(Leonardo 36)* 13,216

Anderlecht: Proto; Juhasz, Deschacht, Wasilewski, Biglia, Kljestan, Gillet, Kouyate (Safari 85), Fernando Canesin, Jovanovic (Iakovenko 80), Suarez (De Sutter 85).
AEK Athens: Konstantopoulos; Dellas, Karabelas, Georgeas, Manolas■, Vargas, Leonardo (Sialmas 71), Lagos (Jose Carlos 46), Gentzoglou, Gudjohnsen, Liberopoulos (Beleck 57).

Sturm Graz (1) 1 *(Szabics 14)*

Lokomotiv Moscow (2) 2 *(Obinna 28, Sychev 29)* 13,356

Sturm Graz: Cavlina; Standfest, Burgstaller, Feldhofer (Purcher 46), Popkhadze, Holzl (Kainz 21), Wolf, Muratovic (Haas 66), Weber, Szabics, Bodul.
Lokomotiv Moscow: Guilherme; Shishkin, Yanbayev, Durica, Burlak, Glushakov, Ibricic (Alberto Zapater 46), Ozdoev, Obinna (Ignatyev 69), Sychev (Caicedo 76), Maicon.

Thursday, 29 September 2011

AEK Athens (0) 1 *(Standfest 50 (og))*

Sturm Graz (0) 2 *(Burgstaller 87, Haas 90)* 10,074

AEK Athens: Arabatzis; Dellas■, Kontoes, Juan Cala, Guerreiro (Bougaidis 56), Vargas, Leonardo (Klonaridis 66), Lagos, Jose Carlos, Gudjohnsen, Beleck (Liberopoulos 77).
Sturm Graz: Cavlina; Standfest, Burgstaller, Popkhadze, Stangl (Saumel 56), Wolf (Bukva 40), Weber, Kainz (Haas 73), Dudic, Szabics, Bodul.

Lokomotiv Moscow (0) 0

Anderlecht (1) 2 *(Suarez 11, Mbokani 71)* 11,485

Lokomotiv Moscow: Guilherme; Manuel da Costa, Shishkin, Yanbayev (Ignatyev 78), Burlak, Alberto Zapater, Glushakov, Ozdoev (Loskov 41), Obinna, Sychev (Caicedo 78), Maicon.
Anderlecht: Proto; Juhasz, Safari, Wasilewski, Biglia, Kljestan, Gillet, Kouyate, Fernando Canesin (Mbokani 60), Suarez (Marecek 74), Kanu (Odoi 90).

Thursday, 20 October 2011

Lokomotiv Moscow (0) 3 *(Sychev 47, 71 (pen), Caicedo 90)*

AEK Athens (0) 1 *(Sialmas 89)* 8279

Lokomotiv Moscow: Guilherme; Manuel da Costa, Shishkin, Yanbayev, Burlak, Alberto Zapater, Glushakov, Ignatyev (Loskov 78), Ibricic (Caicedo 66), Sychev, Maicon (Obinna 46).
AEK Athens: Arabatzis; Kontoes, Karabelas, Juan Cala, Manolas, Vargas (Kafes 58), Lagos (Sialmas 73), Gentzoglou, Jose Carlos, Burns (Leonardo 65), Beleck.

Sturm Graz (0) 0

Anderlecht (0) 2 *(Gillet 66, Suarez 75)* 14,297

Sturm Graz: Cavlina; Burgstaller■, Ehrenreich, Saumel, Wolf (Holzl 79), Weber, Klem, Kainz (Feldhofer 69), Dudic, Szabics, Bodul (Haas 65).
Anderlecht: Proto; Juhasz, Safari, Wasilewski, Biglia (Marecek 80), Kljestan, Gillet, Kouyate, Mbokani (De Sutter 89), Jovanovic, Suarez (Fernando Canesin 86).

Thursday, 3 November 2011

AEK Athens (0) 1 *(Leonardo 60 (pen))*

Lokomotiv Moscow (0) 3 *(Glushakov 50, Maicon 72, Ignatyev 80)* 4042

AEK Athens: Arabatzis; Georgeas, Manolas, Helgason (Kontoes 46), Makos, Lagos, Gentzoglou, Jose Carlos, Burns (Leonardo 46), Sialmas (Guerreiro 69), Beleck.
Lokomotiv Moscow: Guilherme; Shishkin, Ilic, Durica, Burlak, Alberto Zapater, Torbinski (Maicon 61), Glushakov, Ignatyev (Nurov 81), Ibricic (Sychev 81), Obinna.

Anderlecht (1) 3 *(Gillet 23, Suarez 74, De Sutter 81)*

Sturm Graz (0) 0 15,460

Anderlecht: Proto; Juhasz, Safari, Wasilewski, Kljestan, Gillet (Kabasele 77), Marecek, Kouyate, Fernando Canesin (Badibanga 67), Jovanovic (De Sutter 70), Suarez.
Sturm Graz: Cavlina; Feldhofer■, Ehrenreich, Bukva, Holzl (Wolf 8), Weber, Koch, Klem, Dudic, Szabics (Haas 78), Kienast (Purcher 60).

Thursday, 1 December 2011

AEK Athens (1) 1 *(Sialmas 19)*

Anderlecht (2) 2 *(Gillet 4, 36)* 3703

AEK Athens: Konstantopoulos; Kontoes, Juan Cala, Manolas, Helgason (Vargas 46) (Leonardo 63), Guerreiro, Makos, Englezou, Klonaridis, Burns (Beleck 46), Sialmas.
Anderlecht: Proto; Juhasz, Safari (Odoi 54), Wasilewski, Kouyate, Kljestan, Gillet, Marecek (Fernando Canesin 70), Jovanovic, Suarez (De Sutter 83), Kanu.

Lokomotiv Moscow (0) 3 *(Maicon 62, Sychev 72 (pen), Glushakov 89)*

Sturm Graz (0) 1 *(Kainz 64)* 12,423

Lokomotiv Moscow: Amelchenko; Manuel da Costa, Shishkin, Yanbayev, Durica, Alberto Zapater, Torbinski (Ozdoev 77), Glushakov, Ignatyev, Ibricic (Maicon 57), Sychev (Minchenkov 86).
Sturm Graz: Cavlina; Standfest (Kainz 38), Popkhadze, Ehrenreich, Neuhold, Weber, Koch, Klem (Weinberger 77), Dudic, Kienast, Bodul (Haas 66).

Wednesday, 14 December 2011

Anderlecht (2) 5 *(Kljestan 33, Fernando Canesin 39, Wasilewski 57, Suarez 61, Gillet 78)*

Lokomotiv Moscow (1) 3 *(Ignatyev 21, Sychev 69 (pen), 89)* 14,609

Anderlecht: Proto; Juhasz, Safari, Wasilewski, Kouyate, Kljestan, Gillet (Badibanga 81), Marecek, Fernando Canesin (De Sutter 88), Jovanovic, Suarez (Mbokani 73).
Lokomotiv Moscow: Amelchenko; Manuel da Costa, Ilic, Ivanov■, Durica, Alberto Zapater, Torbinski (Ozdoev 46), Glushakov, Ignatyev, Maicon (Caicedo 55), Minchenkov (Sychev 46).

Sturm Graz (0) 1 *(Kainz 59)*

AEK Athens (2) 3 *(Manolas 10, Burns 43, Klonaridis 77)* 13,681

Sturm Graz: Cavlina; Standfest, Burgstaller, Popkhadze, Wolf (Haas 62), Koch, Muratovic (Bukva 73), Kainz (Ehrenreich 84), Dudic, Kienast, Bodul.
AEK Athens: Konstantopoulos; Kontoes, Juan Cala, Manolas, Bougaidis, Guerreiro, Makos, Englezou (Karabelas 54), Klonaridis (Tsoukalas 85), Burns (Beleck 63), Sialmas.

Group L Table	*P*	*W*	*D*	*L*	*F*	*A*	*Pts*
Anderlecht	6	6	0	0	18	5	18
Lokomotiv Moscow	6	4	0	2	14	11	12
AEK Athens	6	1	0	5	8	15	3
Sturm Graz	6	1	0	5	5	14	3

KNOCK-OUT STAGE

SECOND ROUND FIRST LEG

Tuesday, 14 February 2012

Braga (0) 0

Besiktas (1) 2 *(Sivok 37, Simao 58)* 9088

Braga: Quim; Douglao, Miguel Lopes (Paulo Cesar 74), Ewerton, Hugo Viana, Marcio Mossoro (Carlao 46), Custodio (Ruben Amorim 68), Leandro Salino, Alan, Lima, Helder Barbosa■.
Besiktas: Cenk; Ibrahim, Egemen, Sivok, Kayhan (Dag 88), Simao (Mustafa 90), Ernst, Ricardo Quaresma (Hugo Almeida 68), Manuel Fernandes, Kavlak, Necip.

Rubin (0) 0

Olympiakos (0) 1 *(David Fuster 71)* 1741

Rubin: Arlauskis; Bocchetti, Cesar Navas, Kuzmin, Sharonov, Gokdeniz, Nemov, Ryazantsev (Kasaev 83), Natcho, Haedo Valdez (Martins 81), Dyadyun (Ansaldi 46).
Olympiakos: Megyeri■; Mellberg (Papazoglou 33), Holebas, Marcano, Torosidis, Maniatis, Makoun, David Fuster (Carroll 74), Orbaiz, Mirallas, Djebbour (Modesto 81).

Thursday, 16 February 2012

Ajax (0) 0

Manchester U (0) 2 *(Young 59, Hernandez 85)* 48,966

Ajax: Vermeer; Vertonghen, Anita, Alderweireld, Koppers (Boilesen 63), Aissati, De Jong, Eriksen, Bulykin (Van Rhijn 60), Sulejmani, Ozbiliz (Lukoki 80).
Manchester U: De Gea; Jones, Fabio, Carrick, Ferdinand, Evans, Young (Valencia 76), Cleverley (Scholes 61), Hernandez, Rooney, Nani (Welbeck 86).

AZ (1) 1 *(Maher 35)*

Anderlecht (0) 0 13,744

AZ: Alvarado; Marcellis, Poulsen, Moisander, Viergever, Martens, Holman (Gudmundsson 78), Elm, Maher, Beerens, Benschop (Altidore 76).
Anderlecht: Proto; Juhasz, Safari (Deschacht 46), Wasilewski (Odoi 90), Kouyate, Biglia, Kljestan, Gillet, Fernando Canesin (Suarez 59), Mbokani, Jovanovic.

Hannover (0) 2 *(Sobiech 73, Schlaudraff 80 (pen))*

Club Brugge (0) 1 *(Lestienne 51)* 42,000

Hannover: Zieler; Pander, Pogatetz, Eggimann, Cherundolo (Chahed 76), Sergio Pinto (Sobiech 68), Stindl, Schmiedebach, Schlaudraff, Abdellaoue (Rausch 37), Diouf.
Club Brugge: Kujovic; Stenman, Donk, Hoefkens, Jordi Figueras, Zimling, Refaelov, Van Acker, Akpala (Vleminckx 87), Victor Vazquez, Lestienne (Meunier 74).

Lazio (1) 1 *(Klose 19)*

Atletico Madrid (2) 3 *(Adrian 25, Falcao 27, 63)* 30,604

Lazio: Marchetti; Zauri, Diakite, Biava (Stankevicius 46), Konko, Ledesma (Zampa 84), Matuzalem, Henanes, Gonzalez (Kozak 54), Candreva, Klose.
Atletico Madrid: Courtois; Miranda, Filipe Luis, Godin, Diego (Arda 72), Juanfran (Salvio 82), Gabi, Mario Suarez, Koke, Adrian (Perea 66), Falcao.

Legia (1) 2 *(Wawrzyniak 37, Gol 79)*

Sporting Lisbon (0) 2 *(Daniel Corrico 61, Andre Santos 88)* 27,234

Legia: Kuciak; Rzezniczak (Wolski 71), Jedrzejczyk, Wawrzyniak, Komorowski, Zewlakow, Vrdoljak, Rybus (Kosecki 61), Gol, Zyro, Ljuboja (Hubnik 82).
Sporting Lisbon: Rui Patricio; Onyewu, Anderson Polga, Insua, Joao Pereira, Schaars (Daniel Carrico 46), Izmailov (Bruno Pereirinha 46), Fernandez, Rinaudo, Van Wolfswinkel, Carrillo (Andre Santos 74).

Lokomotiv Moscow (0) 2 *(Glushakov 61 (pen), Caicedo 71)*

Athletic Bilbao (1) 1 *(Muniain 35)* 13,160

Lokomotiv Moscow: Guilherme; Shishkin, Yanbayev, Burlak, Belyaev, Alberto Zapater, Tarasov, Torbinski (Obinna 67), Glushakov (Ozdoev 88), Caicedo, Maicon (Sychev 90).
Athletic Bilbao: Iraizoz; Iraola, Amorebieta, Aurtenetxe (David Lopez 78), Javi Martinez, Susaeta, Iturraspe, Ander Herrera, Llorente, Muniain, De Marcos.

Porto (1) 1 *(Silvestre Varela 27)*

Manchester C (0) 2 *(Pereira 55 (og), Aguero 85)* 47,417

Porto: Helton; Rolando, Pereira, Danilo (Mangala 22) (Defour 89), Maicon, Gonzalez, Joao Moutinho, Fernando, Rodriguez J, Silvestre Varela (Kleber 77), Hulk.
Manchester C: Hart; Richards, Clichy, Kompany, Lescott, De Jong, Barry, Silva (Kolarov 83), Balotelli (Aguero 78), Toure Y, Nasri (Zabaleta 88).

Salzburg (0) 0

Metalist Kharkiv (3) 4 *(Taison 1, Cristaldo 37, 41, Devic 90)* 8100

Salzburg: Walke; Douglas (Maierhofer 26), Hinteregger, Cziommer, Mendes da Silva (Pasanen 46), Svento, Jantscher, Hierlander, Leonardo, Soriano, Zarate (Lindgren 63).
Metalist Kharkiv: Goryainov; Fininho, Torsiglieri, Villagra, Gueye, Cleiton Xavier (Torres 87), Blanco, Sosa, Edmar, Cristaldo (Marlos 66), Taison (Devic 75).

Steaua (0) 0

Twente (0) 1 *(John 53)* 49,588

Steaua: Tatarusanu; Dananae (Martinovic 46), Geraldo Alves, Chiriches, Bicfalvi, Prepelita (Costea F 66), Brandan, Tanase, Rusescu, Nikolic (Costea M 75), Leandro Tatu.
Twente: Mihaylov; Wisgerhof, Cornelisse, Rosales, Douglas, Brama, Janssen (Bengtsson 85), Fer, Chadli (Plet 90), De Jong, John (Bajrami 75).

Stoke C (0) 0

Valencia (1) 1 *(Mehmet Topal 36)* 24,185

Stoke C: Begovic; Wilkinson, Wilson (Shotton 69), Huth, Shawcross, Palacios (Whitehead 53), Pennant, Delap, Walters, Crouch (Jerome 69), Etherington.
Valencia: Guaita; Mathieu, Rami, Bruno (Miguel 81), Dealbert, Mehmet Topal, Costa, Feghouli, Aduriz (Soldado 79), Jonas, Piatti (Juan Bernat 89).

Trabzonspor (1) 1 *(Olcan 33)*

PSV Eindhoven (2) 2 *(Matavz 6, Toivonen 11)* 18,866

Trabzonspor: Tolga; Cech, Remzi, Celustka, Mustafa, Olcan, Serkan (Mierzejewski 78), Aykut, Colman (Alanzinho 46), Burak, Halil Altintop (Paulo Henrique 72).
PSV Eindhoven: Isaksson; Derijck, Marcelo, Manolev, Willems (Bouma 90), Hutchinson, Strootman, Lens, Toivonen, Mertens (Wijnaldum 78), Matavz.

Udinese (0) 0

PAOK Salonika (0) 0 11,641

Udinese: Handanovic; Basta, Pasquale, Danilo, Benatia, Domizzi, Armero, Pazienza, Pinzi (Fabbrini 57), Abdi, Floro Flores.
PAOK Salonika: Kresic; Cirillo, Sznaucer, Malezas, Fotakis, Garcia, Lazar, Georgiadis (Lino 84), Stafylidis, Salpingidis, Athanasiadis (Giannou 76).

Viktoria Plzen (1) 1 *(Darida 22)*

Schalke (0) 1 *(Huntelaar 75)* 11,435

Viktoria Plzen: Cech; Prochazka, Cisovsky, Limbersky, Rajtoral, Petrzela (Duris 66), Kolar (Wagner 89), Horvath, Pilar, Darida, Bakos (Berger 80).
Schalke: Unnerstall; Fuchs, Howedes, Papadopoulos, Jones, Matip, Hoger, Draxler, Raul (Marica 69), Huntelaar, Obasi (Farfan 62).

Wisla (0) 1 *(Genkov 88)*

Standard Liege (1) 1 *(Cyriac 28 (pen))* 19,000

Wisla: Pareiko; Diaz, Chavez, Jovanovic, Czekaj■, Wilk, Gargula (Kirm 78), Nunez, Meliksson, Malecki (Iliev 57), Genkov.
Standard Liege: Sinan; Pocognoli, Goreux (Ciman 46), Felipe, Kanu, Vainqueur, Buyens, Seijas (Bjarnason 81), Gakpe (Batshuayi 70), Tchite, Cyriac.

SECOND ROUND SECOND LEG

Wednesday, 22 February 2012

Manchester C (1) 4 *(Aguero 1, Dzeko 76, Silva 84, Pizarro 86)*

Porto (0) 0 39,538

Manchester C: Hart; Richards, Clichy, Kompany, Lescott, De Jong, Barry (Milner 58), Silva, Aguero (Pizarro 80), Toure Y, Nasri (Dzeko 69).
Porto: Helton; Rolando■, Otamendi (Sapunaru 63), Alex Sandro, Maicon, Gonzalez, Joao Moutinho, Fernando, Rodriguez J (Defour 80), Silvestre Varela (Rodriguez C 63), Hulk.

Thursday, 23 February 2012

Anderlecht (0) 0

AZ (0) 1 *(Martens 54)* 25,000

Anderlecht: Proto; Juhasz, Deschacht (Kabangu 61), Wasilewski, Kouyate, Biglia, Kljestan, Gillet, Mbokani, Jovanovic, Suarez.
AZ: Alvarado; Marcellis (Reijnen 55), Poulsen, Moisander, Viergever, Martens (Falkenburg 75), Holman, Elm, Maher, Beerens, Benschop (Altidore 44).

Athletic Bilbao (0) 1 *(Muniain 62)*

Lokomotiv Moscow (0) 0 35,000

Athletic Bilbao: Iraizoz; Iraola, Amorebieta■, Javi Martinez, Susaeta (San Jose 46), Iturraspe (Inigo Perez 46), Ander Herrera (Ekiza 68), Llorente, Muniain, Toquero, De Marcos.
Lokomotiv Moscow: Guilherme; Shishkin, Yanbayev, Burlak, Belyaev (Manuel da Costa 80), Alberto Zapater, Tarasov, Torbinski (Obinna 66), Glushakov, Ozdoev (Sychev 66), Caicedo.

Atletico Madrid (0) 1 *(Godin 48)*

Lazio (0) 0 30,000

Atletico Madrid: Courtois; Miranda (Silvio 70), Perea, Godin, Dominguez, Juanfran (Arda 58), Gabi, Paulo Assuncao, Salvio, Koke, Adrian (Falcao 61).
Lazio: Bizarri; Zauri, Diakite, Andre Dias, Mauri, Ledesma (Zampa 60), Matuzalem, Hernanes, Candreva (Gonzalez 57), Lulic (Rozzi 78), Kozak.

Besiktas (0) 0

Braga (1) 1 *(Lima 25)* 25,000

Besiktas: Cenk; Ibrahim, Egemen, Sivok, Kayhan (Dag 68), Simao, Ernst, Ricardo Quaresma (Sidnei 90), Manuel Fernandes, Kavlak, Necip (Hugo Almeida 33).
Braga: Quim; Echiejile, Douglao, Nuno Coelho, Hugo Viana, Ruben Amorim (Nuno Gomes 77), Djalma (Custodio 85), Leandro Salino, Alan, Lima, Paulo Cesar (Carlao 72).

Club Brugge (0) 0

Hannover (1) 1 *(Diouf 21)* 22,000

Club Brugge: Kujovic; Hoefkens, Hogli (Lestienne 62), Almeback, Jordi Figueras, Zimling, Refaelov, Meunier, Van Acker (Vleminckx 62), Akpala, Victor Vazquez.
Hannover: Zieler; Pander, Pogatetz, Eggimann, Sergio Pinto, Chahed, Stindl (Stoppelkamp 90), Schmiedebach, Schlaudraff (Rausch 74), Abdellaoue (Ya Konan 90), Diouf.

Manchester U (1) 1 *(Hernandez 6)*

Ajax (1) 2 *(Ozbiliz 37, Alderweireld 87)* 67,328

Manchester U: De Gea; Rafael, Fabio, Jones, Smalling, Park, Young (Evans 61), Cleverley (Scholes 61), Berbatov (Welbeck 72), Hernandez, Nani.
Ajax: Vermeer; Vertonghen, Anita, Alderweireld, Koppers (Klaassen 46), Van Rhijn, De Jong, Lodeiro (Blind 80), Eriksen (Serero 60), Sulejmani, Ozbiliz.

Metalist Kharkiv (1) 4 *(Hinteregger 28 (og), Cristaldo 62, Blanco 63, Marlos 87)*

Salzburg (0) 1 *(Jantscher 56)* 30,826

Metalist Kharkiv: Goryainov; Villagra (Obradovic 21), Gueye, Berezovchuk, Pshenichnikh, Cleiton Xavier, Blanco, Torres, Sosa, Cristaldo (Devic 63), Taison (Marlos 57).
Salzburg: Walke; Pasanen, Schiemer, Ulmer, Hinteregger, Lindgren (Sekagya 78), Svento, Jantscher, Leonardo (Savic 83), Soriano, Zarate (Teigl 65).

Olympiakos (1) 1 *(Djebbour 14)*

Rubin (0) 0 30,000

Olympiakos: Carroll; Mellberg, Papadopoulos, Marcano, Torosidis, Maniatis, Ibagaza (Makoun 72), David Fuster (Modesto 81), Orbaiz, Mirallas, Djebbour (Abdoun 88).
Rubin: Ryzhikov; Bocchetti, Cesar Navas, Kuzmin, Sharonov (Nemov 68), Gokdeniz, Ryazantsev, Natcho, Kislyak (Dyadyun 46), Haedo Valdez, Martins (Kasaev 63).

PAOK Salonika (0) 0

Udinese (2) 3 *(Danilo 6, Floro Flores 15, Domizzi 51 (pen))* 20,000

PAOK Salonika: Kresic; Cirillo, Lino, Sznaucer (Apostolopoulos 54), Malezas, Garcia, Lazar, Stafylidis (Georgiadis 31), Salpingidis, Giannou (Nimani 64), Athanasiadis.
Udinese: Handanovic; Basta, Pasquale, Danilo, Benatia (Ferronetti 86), Domizzi, Pazienza, Abdi (Battocchio 46), Asamoah, Floro Flores, Fabbrini (Armero 69).

PSV Eindhoven (3) 4 *(Mertens 15 (pen), Matavz 31, 53, Strootman 38)*

Trabzonspor (1) 1 *(Burak 43)* 18,300

PSV Eindhoven: Isaksson; Bouma, Marcelo, Manolev, Willems (Pieters 64), Wijnaldum, Strootman (Hutchinson 63), Labyad, Toivonen (Lens 68), Mertens, Matavz.
Trabzonspor: Tolga■; Cech, Remzi, Celustka, Mustafa, Zokora, Olcan (Halil Altintop 73), Aykut (Alanzinho 76), Colman, Burak, Paulo Henrique (Onur 46).

Schalke (1) 3 *(Huntelaar 8, 106, 120)*

Viktoria Plzen (0) 1 *(Rajtoral 88)* 50,000

Schalke: Hildebrand; Metzelder, Fuchs, Howedes, Papadopoulos, Matip, Hoger, Draxler (Baumjohann 79), Raul (Marica 120), Huntelaar, Farfan (Obasi 73).
Viktoria Plzen: Cech; Prochazka, Sevinsky, Cisovsky, Limbersky, Rajtoral, Petrzela (Duris 65), Kolar (Hora 80), Pilar (Berger 98), Darida, Bakos■.
aet.

Sporting Lisbon (0) 1 *(Fernandez 84)*

Legia (0) 0 20,144

Sporting Lisbon: Rui Patricio; Anderson Polga, Rodriguez (Xandao 71), Insua, Joao Pereira, Daniel Carrico, Schaars, Izmailov (Bruno Pereirinha 77), Fernandez, Van Wolfswinkel, Carrillo (Capel 70).
Legia: Kuciak; Rzezniczak (Wolski 69), Jedrzejczyk, Wawrzyniak, Komorowski, Zewlakow, Vrdoljak, Rybus, Gol (Hubnik 87), Zyro (Kucharczyk 59), Ljuboja.

Standard Liege (0) 0

Wisla (0) 0 23,000

Standard Liege: Sinan; Pocognoli, Ciman, Goreux (Gakpe 89), Felipe, Belhocine, Gershon, Bjarnason, Buyens, Tchite (Batshuayi 85), Cyriac (Opare 90).
Wisla: Pareiko; Jaliens, Diaz, Chavez, Jovanovic (Biton 76), Wilk (Jirsak 87), Gargula, Nunez■, Meliksson, Iliev (Kirm 67), Genkov.

Twente (1) 1 *(Chadli 29)*

Steaua (0) 0 28,000

Twente: Mihaylov; Wisgerhof, Cornelisse, Rosales, Douglas, Brama, Janssen (Bengtsson 80), Fer, Chadli, De Jong (Plet 90), John (Bajrami 54).
Steaua: Tatarusanu; Latovlevici, Geraldo Alves, Chiriches, Martinovic, Prepelita (Costea F 46), Brandan (Costea M 75), Tanase, Bourceanu, Rusescu, Leandro Tatu (Nikolic 62).

Valencia (1) 1 *(Jonas 24)*

Stoke C (0) 0 35,000

Valencia: Guaita; Rami, Bruno, Dealbert, Jordi Alba, Mehmet Topal, Dani Parejo, Pablo Hernandez, Aduriz, Jonas (Soldado 63), Piatti (Feghouli 63).
Stoke C: Sorensen; Woodgate, Palacios (Pennant 65), Diao, Huth, Collins, Arismendi (Shotton 65), Delap, Jones, Fuller, Jerome.

THIRD ROUND FIRST LEG

Thursday, 8 March 2012

Atletico Madrid (3) 3 *(Salvio 24, 27, Adrian 36)*

Besiktas (0) 1 *(Simao 53)* 40,000

Atletico Madrid: Courtois; Perea, Filipe Luis, Godin, Juanfran, Gabi, Mario Suarez, Salvio (Domingez 82), Koke (Saul 84), Adrian (Pizzi 62), Falcao.
Besiktas: Cenk; Ibrahim, Egemen, Sivok, Simao, Ernst, Ricardo Quaresma (Ismail 46), Manuel Fernandes, Kavlak, Necip (Edu 80), Mustafa (Holosko 74).

AZ (0) 2 *(Martens 63, Falkenburg 84)*

Udinese (0) 0 12,579

AZ: Alvarado; Marcellis, Poulsen, Moisander, Viergever, Martens (Falkenburg 78), Holman (Ortiz 86), Elm, Maher, Beerens (Gudmundsson 74), Altidore.
Udinese: Handanovic; Pasquale (Di Natale 80), Ferronetti, Danilo, Benatia, Domizzi, Armero, Pazienza, Pinzi, Asamoah, Floro Flores.

Manchester U (1) 2 *(Rooney 22, 90 (pen))*

Atheltic Bilbao (1) 3 *(Llorente 44, De Marcos 72, Muniain 89)* 67,000

Manchester U: De Gea; Rafael, Evra, Jones, Smalling (Carrick 55), Evans, Park (Anderson 61), Giggs (Nani 75), Hernandez, Rooney, Young.
Atheltic Bilbao: Iraizoz; Iraola, San Jose, Aurtenetxe, Javi Martinez, Susaeta, Iturraspe, Ander Herrera (Inigo Perez 84), Llorente (Toquero 81), Muniain, De Marcos.

Metalist Kharkiv (0) 0

Olympiakos (0) 1 *(David Fuster 50)* 11,000

Metalist Kharkiv: Goryainov; Fininho (Pshenichnikh 63), Torsiglieri, Villagra, Gueye, Cleiton Xavier, Blanco (Devic 63), Sosa, Edmar■, Cristaldo (Marlos 84), Taison.
Olympiakos: Megyeri; Mellberg, Papadopoulos, Marcano, Torosidis, Maniatis, Makoun (Modesto 77), David Fuster (Holebas 80), Orbaiz, Mirallas (Abdoun 89), Djebbour.

Sporting Lisbon (0) 1 *(Xandao 51)*

Manchester C (0) 0 34,371

Sporting Lisbon: Rui Patricio; Anderson Polga, Insua, Joao Pereira, Daniel Carrico, Xandao, Schaars, Izmailov (Bruno Pereirinha 59), Fernandez (Renato Neto 69), Capel (Carrillo 75), Van Wolfswinkel.
Manchester C: Hart; Kolarov, Clichy, Kompany (Lescott 12), Toure K, Barry (Nasri 59), Milner, De Jong, Aguero, Dzeko (Balotelli 71), Silva.

Standard Liege (2) 2 *(Buyens 27, Tchite 30)*

Hannover (1) 2 *(Stindl 22 (pen), Diouf 56)* 25,000

Standard Liege: Sinan; Van Damme (Seijas 80), Pocognoli, Ciman, Felipe, Kanu, Vainqueur, Buyens, Gakpe (Bjarnason 89), Tchite, Cyriac (Batshuayi 89).
Hannover: Zieler; Haggui, Pander, Eggimann, Rausch (Schulz 90), Cherundolo, Sergio Pinto, Chahed, Stindl, Ya Konan (Stoppelkamp 90), Diouf (Sobiech 60).

Twente (0) 1 *(De Jong 61 (pen))*

Schalke (0) 0 30,000

Twente: Mihaylov; Wisgerhof, Cornelisse, Rosales, Douglas, Brama, Janssen (Bajrami 85), Fer, Chadli, De Jong, John.
Schalke: Hildebrand; Uchida, Fuchs, Papadopoulos, Jones, Holtby (Moritz 90), Matip■, Hoger, Raul (Sergio Escudero 90), Marica, Obasi (Draxler 82).

Valencia (3) 4 *(Victor Ruiz 11, Soldado 13, 43 (pen), Piatti 56)*

PSV Eindhoven (0) 2 *(Toivonen 83 (pen), Wijnaldum 90)* 28,000

Valencia: Diego Alves; Ricardo Costa (Rami 24), Mathieu, Barragan, Victor Ruiz, Albelda, Dani Parejo, Pablo Hernandez, Soldado (Aduriz 76), Jonas (Juan Bernat 71), Piatti.
PSV Eindhoven: Isaksson; Derijck, Marcelo, Manolev, Willems (Pieters 34), Hutchinson, Strootman, Labyad, Toivonen, Mertens (Wijnaldum 75), Matavz (Lens 67).

THIRD ROUND SECOND LEG

Thursday, 15 March 2012

Athletic Bilbao (1) 2 *(Llorente 23, De Marcos 65)*

Manchester U (0) 1 *(Rooney 80)* 40,000

Athletic Bilbao: Iraizoz; Iraola, Amorebieta, Aurtenetxe, Javi Martinez, Susaeta, Iturraspe, Ander Herrera (Inigo Perez 82), Llorente (Toquero 40), Muniain (San Jose 88), De Marcos.
Manchester U: De Gea; Rafael, Evra, Carrick (Pogba 63), Ferdinand (Smalling 63), Evans, Park, Giggs (Welbeck 68), Young, Rooney, Cleverley.

Besiktas (0) 0

Atletico Madrid (1) 3 *(Adrian 26, Falcao 83, Salvio 90)* 23,000

Besiktas: Cenk; Ibrahim (Mehmet Aurelio 61), Egemen, Sivok, Ismail, Simao, Dag (Holosko 46), Manuel Fernandes, Kavlak, Edu (Mustafa 59), Hugo Almeida.
Atletico Madrid: Courtois; Miranda, Filipe Luis, Godin, Juanfran, Gabi (Dominguez 85), Mario Suarez, Arda (Paulo Assuncao 69), Koke (Salvio 73), Adrian, Falcao.

Hannover (2) 4 *(Abdellaoue 4, Kanu 21 (og), 73 (og), Sergio Pinto 90)*

Standard Liege (0) 0 43,000

Hannover: Zieler; Haggui, Pander (Schulz 46), Eggimann, Rausch, Cherundolo, Sergio Pinto, Stindl, Schmiedebach (Lala 85), Schlaudraff, Abdellaoue (Ya Konan 70).
Standard Liege: Sinan; Van Damme (Seijas 70), Pocognoli, Ciman (Opare 24), Felipe, Kanu, Vainqueur, Buyens, Gakpe■, Tchite, Cyriac (Batshuayi 82).

Manchester C (0) 3 *(Aguero 60, 82, Balotelli 75 (pen))*

Sporting Lisbon (2) 2 *(Fernandez 33, Van Wolfswinkel 40)* 38,021

Manchester C: Hart; Richards, Kolarov, Savic, Toure K, Pizarro (Dzeko 55), Silva (Nasri 66), Toure Y, Aguero, Balotelli, Johnson A (De Jong 46).
Sporting Lisbon: Rui Patricio; Anderson Polga, Insua, Daniel Carrico, Xandao, Schaars, Izmailov, Fernandez (Renato Neto 64), Bruno Pereirinha, Capel (Jeffren 63), Van Wolfswinkel (Carrillo 68).

Olympiakos (1) 1 *(Marcano 14)*

Metalist Kharkiv (0) 2 *(Villagra 81, Devic 86)* 30,000

Olympiakos: Megyeri; Holebas, Papadopoulos, Marcano, Torosidis, Maniatis (Modesto 59), Ibagaza (Makoun 46), David Fuster, Orbaiz (Diogo 88), Mirallas, Djebbour.
Metalist Kharkiv: Disljenkovic; Torsiglieri, Villagra, Gueye, Pshenichnikh, Cleiton Xavier, Blanco (Valyaev 90), Torres, Sosa, Marlos (Devic 46), Taison.

PSV Eindhoven (0) 1 *(Toivonen 64)*

Valencia (0) 1 *(Rami 47)* 22,000

PSV Eindhoven: Tyton; Pieters, Bouma (Derijck 76), Marcelo, Manolev, Wijnaldum, Strootman, Labyad, Toivonen, Mertens (Lens 80), Matavz.
Valencia: Diego Alves; Mathieu, Rami■, Bruno, Dealbert, Jordi Alba, Albelda (Mehmet Topal 75), Costa, Feghouli, Aduriz (Piatti 80), Jonas (Dani Parejo 85).

Schalke (1) 4 *(Huntelaar 29, 57 (pen), 81, Jones 71)*

Twente (1) 1 *(Janssen 14)* 52,000

Schalke: Hildebrand; Uchida, Fuchs, Papadopoulos, Jones (Moritz 88), Holtby, Matip, Draxler (Obasi 90), Raul, Huntelaar, Farfan (Marica 86).
Twente: Mihaylov; Tiendalli, Bengtsson, Rosales, Douglas, Leugers (Fer 51), Brama (Plet 76), Bajrami (John 57), Janssen, Chadli, De Jong.

Udinese (2) 2 *(Di Natale 3 (pen), 15)*

AZ (1) 1 *(Falkenburg 31)* 9500

Udinese: Handanovic; Ferronetti (Fabbrini 66), Benatia (Pasquale 11), Domizzi, Armero, Ekstrand, Pazienza (Abdi 78), Pinzi, Asamoah, Di Natale, Floro Flores.
AZ: Alvarado; Marcellis, Poulsen, Moisander, Viergever■, Holman (Gudmundsson 78), Elm, Falkenburg (Ortiz 83), Maher, Beerens (Klavan 11), Altidore.

QUARTER-FINALS FIRST LEG

Thursday, 29 March 2012

Atletico Madrid (1) 2 *(Falcao 9, Salvio 89)*

Hannover (1) 1 *(Diouf 38)* 23,000

Atletico Madrid: Courtois; Miranda, Filipe Luis, Godin, Juanfran, Gabi, Mario Suarez, Arda, Koke (Diego 61), Adrian (Salvio 70), Falcao.
Hannover: Zieler; Pander (Schulz 70), Pogatetz, Eggimann, Rausch, Cherundolo, Sergio Pinto, Stindl, Schmiedebach (Ya Konan 55), Schlaudraff, Diouf (Abdellaoue 82).

AZ (1) 2 *(Holman 45, Martens 79)*

Valencia (0) 1 *(Mehmet Topal 52)* 16,100

AZ: Alvarado; Klavan, Marcellis, Poulsen, Moisander, Martens, Holman, Elm, Maher, Altidore (Benschop 77), Gudmundsson.
Valencia: Diego Alves; Ricardo Costa, Mathieu (Piatti 77), Barragan, Dealbert, Jordi Alba, Mehmet Topal, Costa, Feghouli (Jonas 65), Pablo Hernandez, Soldado.

Schalke (1) 2 *(Raul 22, 60)*

Athletic Bilbao (1) 4 *(Llorente 20, 73, De Marcos 81, Muniain 90)* 52,000

Schalke: Hildebrand (Schober 46); Uchida, Fuchs, Papadopoulos, Jones, Matip, Hoger (Holtby 56), Draxler (Jurado 56), Raul, Huntelaar, Farfan.
Athletic Bilbao: Iraizoz; Iraola, Amorebieta, Aurtenetxe (Inigo Perez 70), Javi Martinez, Susaeta, Iturraspe, Anda Herrera (Ibai 46), Llorente, Muniain, De Marcos (Ekiza 85).

Sporting Lisbon (0) 2 *(Izmailov 51, Insua 64)*

Metalist Kharkiv (0) 1 *(Cleiton Xavier 90 (pen))* 27,000

Sporting Lisbon: Rui Patricio; Anderson Polga, Inusa, Joao Pereira, Daniel Carrico (Renato Neto 70), Xandao, Schaars, Izmailov (Carrillo 79), Fernandez, Capel (Jeffren 72), Van Wolfswinkel.
Metalist Kharkiv: Goryainov; Torsiglieri, Villagra, Obradovic, Gueye, Cleiton Xavier, Blanco (Marlos 77), Torres, Sosa (Valyaev 90), Cristaldo (Devic 65), Taison.

QUARTER-FINALS SECOND LEG

Thursday, 5 April 2012

Athletic Bilbao (1) 2 *(Ibai 41, Susaeta 55)*

Schalke (1) 2 *(Huntelaar 29, Raul 52)* 40,000

Athletic Bilbao: Iraizoz; Iraola, Amorebieta, Aurtenetxe, Ekiza, Javi Martinez, Susaeta, Ander Herrera (Ibai 30), Llorente (Toquero 59), Muniain, De Marcos.
Schalke: Unnerstall; Hoogland, Papadopoulos, Sergio Escudero, Jones, Jurado (Farfan 60), Holtby (Hoger 72), Matip, Raul, Huntelaar, Obasi (Marica 62).

Hannover (0) 1 *(Diouf 81)*

Atletico Madrid (0) 2 *(Adrian 63, Falcao 87)* 44,000

Hannover: Zieler; Pander (Sobiech 86), Schulz (Schmiedebach 73), Pogatetz, Eggimann, Rausch (Abdellaoue 71), Cherundolo, Sergio Pinto, Schlaudraff, Ya Konan, Diouf.
Atletico Madrid: Courtois; Miranda, Perea, Filipe Luis, Godin, Tiago, Diego (Domingez 88), Mario Suarez, Koke (Salvio 65), Adrian, Falcao.

Metalist Kharkiv (0) 1 *(Cristaldo 57)*

Sporting Lisbon (1) 1 *(Van Wolfswinkel 44)* 38,500

Metalist Kharkiv: Goryainov; Villagra, Obradovic, Berezovchuk, Pshenichnikh (Blanco 85), Cleiton Xavier, Torres (Marlos 71), Sosa, Edmar (Devic 46), Cristaldo, Taison.
Sporting Lisbon: Rui Patricio; Anderson Polga, Insua, Joao Pereira, Xandao, Schaars, Izmailov, Fernandez (Renato Neto 60), Capel (Evaldo 83), Andre Martins (Andre Santos 72), Van Wolfswinkel.

Valencia (2) 4 *(Rami 15, 17, Jordi Alba 56, Pablo Hernandez 80)*

AZ (0) 0 25,000

Valencia: Diego Alves; Ricardo Costa, Mathieu, Barragan, Rami, Jordi Alba, Mehmet Topal, Costa (Maduro 84), Feghouli (Pablo Hernandez 76), Soldado, Jonas (Dani Parejo 68).
AZ: Alvarado; Marcellis, Poulsen, Moisander, Viergever, Martens, Holman (Gudmundsson 46), Elm, Maher, Beerens (Falkenburg 79), Altidore (Benschop 69).

SEMI-FINALS FIRST LEG

Thursday, 19 April 2012

Atletico Madrid (1) 4 *(Falcao 18, 78, Miranda 49, Adrian 54)*

Valencia (1) 2 *(Jonas 45, Ricardo Costa 90)* 51,000

Atletico Madrid: Courtois; Miranda, Filipe Luis, Dominguez, Diego (Perea 88), Juanfran, Gabi, Mario Suarez, Arda (Tiago 81), Adrian (Salvio 90), Falcao.
Valencia: Diego Alves; Ricardo Costa, Mathieu, Rami, Jordi Alba (Piatti 72), Victor Ruiz, Mehmet Topal, Costa, Feghouli (Canales 72), Soldado, Jonas (Aduriz 79).

Sporting Lisbon (0) 2 *(Insua 76, Capel 80)*

Athletic Bilbao (0) 1 *(Aurtenetxe 54)* 37,213

Sporting Lisbon: Rui Patricio; Anderson Polga, Insua, Joao Pereira, Daniel Carrico (Carrillo 68), Xandao, Schaars, Izmailov, Capel (Bruno Pereirinha 84), Andre Martins (Rubio 76), Van Wolfswinkel.
Athletic Bilbao: Iraizoz; Iraola, Amorebieta, Aurtenetxe, Ekiza, Susaeta (Ibai 83), Iturraspe, Ander Herrera (San Jose 73), Llorente (Toquero 87), Muniain, De Marcos.

SEMI-FINALS SECOND LEG

Thursday, 26 April 2012

Athletic Bilbao (2) 3 *(Susaeta 17, Ibai 45, Llorente 88)*

Sporting Lisbon (1) 1 *(Van Wolfswinkel 44)* 37,000

Athletic Bilbao: Iraizoz; Iraola, Amorebieta, Aurtenetxe, Javi Martinez, Susaeta, Iturraspe, Ander Herrera (Inigo Perez 90), Llorente, Muniain (Ekiza 90), Ibai (Toquero 90).

Sporting Lisbon: Rui Patricio; Anderson Polga, Insua, Joao Pereira, Xandao, Schaars, Fernandez (Daniel Carrico 46), Bruno Pereirinha (Jeffren 63), Capel, Andre Martins (Carrillo 83), Van Wolfswinkel.

Valencia (0) 0

Atletico Madrid (0) 1 *(Adrian 60)* 35,000

Valencia: Diego Alves; Ricardo Costa, Barragan, Rami, Jordi Alba, Albelda, Feghouli, Dani Parejo (Costa 68), Canales (Mathieu 59), Soldado, Jonas (Aduriz 57).

Atletico Madrid: Courtois; Miranda, Filipe Luis, Godin, Tiago■, Diego (Koke 84), Juanfran, Mario Suarez (Gabi 46), Arda (Salvio 74), Adrian, Falcao.

UEFA EUROPA LEAGUE FINAL

Wednesday, 9 May 2012

(in Bucharest, 52,347)

Atletico Madrid (2) 3 *(Falcao 7, 34, Diego 85)* **Athletic Bilbao (0) 0**

Atletico Madrid: Courtois; Miranda, Filipe Luis, Godin, Diego (Koke 90), Juanfran, Gabi, Mario Suarez, Arda (Domingez 90), Adrian (Salvio 88), Falcao.

Athletic Bilbao: Iraizoz; Iraola, Amorebieta, Aurtenetxe (Ibai 46), Javi Martinez, Susaeta, Iturraspe (Inigo Perez 46), Ander Herrera (Toquero 63), Llorente, Muniain, De Marcos.

Referee: Stark (Germany).

Atletico Madrid's Falcao celebrates after scoring the opening goal against Athletic Bilbao during the Europa League Final at the National Arena in Bucharest. Atletico won 3-0. (PA)

UEFA CHAMPIONS LEAGUE 2012–13

PARTICIPATING CLUBS
This list is provisional and subject to final confirmation from UEFA.

UEFA CHAMPIONS LEAGUE GROUP STAGE
Chelsea FC (ENG) – holders
FC Barcelona (ESP)
Manchester United FC (ENG)
FC Bayern München (GER)
Real Madrid CF (ESP)
Arsenal FC (ENG)
FC Porto (POR)
AC Milan (ITA)
Valencia CF (ESP)
SL Benfica (POR)
FC Shakhtar Donetsk (UKR)
FC Zenit St Petersburg (RUS)
FC Schalke 04 (GER)
Manchester City FC (ENG)
Olympiacos FC (GRE)
AFC Ajax (NED)
Juventus (ITA)
Paris Saint-Germain FC (FRA)
Galatasaray AŞ (TUR)
Borussia Dortmund (GER)
Montpellier Hérault SC (FRA)
FC Nordsjælland (DEN)

UEFA CHAMPIONS LEAGUE PLAY-OFF – LEAGUE ROUTE
SC Braga (POR)
FC Spartak Moskva (RUS)
Udinese Calcio (ITA)
LOSC Lille Métropole (FRA)
Málaga CF (ESP
VfL Borussia Mönchengladbach (GER)

UEFA CHAMPIONS LEAGUE THIRD QUALIFYING ROUND – LEAGUE ROUTE
FC Dynamo Kyiv (UKR)
Panathinaikos FC (GRE)
FC København (DEN)
Fenerbahçe SK (TUR)
Club Brugge KV (BEL)
FC Vaslui (ROU)
Feyenoord (NED)
Motherwell (SCO)

UEFA CHAMPIONS LEAGUE THIRD QUALIFYING ROUND – CHAMPIONS ROUTE
RSC Anderlecht (BEL)
Celtic FC (SCO)
CFR 1907 Cluj (ROU)

UEFA CHAMPIONS LEAGUE SECOND QUALIFYING ROUND
FC Basel 1893 (SUI)
FC BATE Borisov (BLR)
FC Salzburg (AUT)
GNK Dinamo Zagreb (CRO)
MŠK Žilina (SVK)
FK Partizan (SRB)
Helsingborgs IF (SWE)
FC Sheriff (MDA)
Debreceni VSC (HUN)
NK Maribor (SVN)
FK Ventspils (LVA)
FC Slovan Liberec (CZE)
WKS Śląsk Wroclaw (POL)
HJK Helsinki (FIN)
AEL Limassol FC (CYP)
FK Ekranas (LTU)
FC Zestafoni (GEO)
Shamrock Rovers FC (IRL)
Hapoel Kiryat Shmona FC (ISR)
Molde FK (NOR)
FK Željezničar (BIH)
KR Reykjavík (ISL)
PFC Ludogorets Razgrad (BUL)
The New Saints FC (WAL)
FK Budućnost Podgorica (MNE)
FC Flora Tallinn (EST)
Neftçi PFK (AZE)
FC Shakhter Karagandy (KAZ)
KS Skënderbeu (ALB)
FK Vardar (MKD)
Ulisses FC (ARM)

UEFA CHAMPIONS LEAGUE FIRST QUALIFYING ROUND
Linfield FC (NIR)
F91 Dudelange (LUX)
Valletta FC (MLT)
SP Tre Penne (SMR)
FC Lusitans (AND)
B36 Tórshavn (FRO)

UEFA EUROPA LEAGUE 2012–13

The list below is provisional and subject to pending CAS decisions and final confirmation from UEFA.

UEFA EUROPA LEAGUE GROUP STAGE
Club Atlético de Madrid (ESP)
Olympique Lyonnais (FRA)*
Tottenham Hotspur FC (ENG)
Bayer 04 Leverkusen (GER)
FC Rubin Kazan (RUS)*
SSC Napoli (ITA)*
A. Académica de Coimbra (POR)*

UEFA EUROPA LEAGUE PLAY-OFFS
Sporting Clube de Portugal (POR)
PFC CSKA Moskva (RUS)
PSV Eindhoven (NED)*
FC Girondins de Bordeaux (FRA)
VfB Stuttgart (GER)
FC Metalist Kharkiv (UKR)
AZ Alkmaar (NED)
Hapoel Tel-Aviv FC (ISR)*
S.S. Lazio (ITA)
Trabzonspor AŞ (TUR)
Newcastle United FC (ENG)
Levante UD (ESP)
FC Dnipro Dnipropetrovsk (UKR)
FC Dinamo Bucureşti (ROU)*
Atromitos FC (GRE)
Heart of Midlothian FC (SCO)*
FC Midtjylland (DEN)
KSC Lokeren OV (BEL)*
FC Luzern (SUI)

UEFA EUROPA LEAGUE THIRD QUALIFYING ROUND

FC Internazionale Milano (ITA)
Liverpool FC (ENG)
Olympique de Marseille (FRA) [LCW]
Athletic Club (ESP)†
Hannover 96 (GER)
PAOK FC (GRE)
FC Steaua Bucureşti (ROU)
AC Sparta Praha (CZE)
sc Heerenveen (NED)
KRC Genk (BEL)
Bursaspor (TUR)
CS Marítimo (POR)
SK Rapid Wien (AUT)
FC Dinamo Moskva (RUS)
AC Omonia (CYP)*
FC Arsenal Kyiv (UKR)
Dundee United FC (SCO)
AC Horsens (DEN)

UEFA EUROPA LEAGUE SECOND QUALIFYING ROUND

APOEL FC (CYP)
Anorthosis Famagusta FC (CYP)
BSC Young Boys (SUI)
FC Viktoria Plzeň (CZE)
KAA Gent (BEL)
Legia Warszawa (POL)*
PFC Levski Sofia (BUL)
FK Crvena Zvezda (SRB)*
FC Metalurh Donetsk (UKR)*
PFC CSKA Sofia (BUL)
FC Anzhi Makhachkala (RUS)
Vitesse (NED)
FK Mladá Boleslav (CZE)
FC Rapid Bucureşti (ROU)
ŠK Slovan Bratislava (SVK)
HNK Hajduk Split (CRO)
Asteras Tripolis FC (GRE)
Bnei Yehuda Tel-Aviv FC (ISR)
Eskişehirspor (TUR)
SV Ried (AUT)†
AIK Solna (SWE)
AGF Århus (DEN)
Aalesunds FK (NOR)*
Maccabi Netanya FC (ISR)
Servette FC (SUI)
VfB Admira Wacker Mödling (AUT)
Ruch Chorzów (POL)
FC Spartak Trnava (SVK)
Tromsø IL (NOR)
NK Slaven Koprivnica (CRO)
FK Vojvodina (SRB)
Saint Johnstone FC (SCO)
FC Naftan Novopolotsk (BLR)*
FC Shakhtyor Soligorsk (BLR)
FC Inter Turku (FIN)
Videoton FC (HUN)
NK Široki Brijeg (BIH)
Skonto FC (LVA)*
PFC Lokomotiv Plovdiv 1936 (BUL)†
Sligo Rovers FC (IRL)*
FC Dila Gori (GEO)*
FC Milsami Orhei (MDA)*
VMFD Žalgiris (LTU)*

UEFA EUROPA LEAGUE FIRST QUALIFYING ROUND

FC Twente (NED)¶
KKS Lech Poznań (POL)
Rosenborg BK (NOR)
IF Elfsborg (SWE)
Kalmar FF (SWE)†
FC Aktobe (KAZ)
Saint Patrick's Athletic FC (IRL)
Stabæk Fotball (NOR)¶
FC Gomel (BLR)
FC Metalurgi Rustavi (GEO)
FK Sarajevo (BIH)
Bohemian FC (IRL)
FK Senica (SVK)
NK Osijek (CRO)†
FH Hafnarfjördur (ISL)
FC Levadia Tallinn (EST)*
FC Pyunik (ARM)
FC Dacia Chişinău (MDA)
FK Bakı (AZE)*
FK Borac Banja Luka (BIH)
SK Liepājas Metalurgs (LVA)
Bangor City FC (WAL)
FC Differdange 03 (LUX)
Budapest Honvéd FC (HUN)
FK Sūduva (LTU)
FK Jagodina (SRB)
Myllykosken Pallo-47 (FIN)¶
KF Tirana (ALB)*
NK Olimpija Ljubljana (SVN)
FK Renova (MKD)*
FC İnter Bakı (AZE)
FK Rudar Pljevlja (MNE)
KuPS Kuopio (FIN)†
FK Skendija 79 (MKD)
Birkirkara FC (MLT)
EB/Streymur (FRO)*
Xäzär Länkäran FK (AZE)
MTK Budapest (HUN)†
FK Metalurg Skopje (MKD)
FC Šiauliai (LTU)
FC Zimbru Chişinău (MDA)
JJK Jyväskylä (FIN)
KS Flamurtari (ALB)
Cliftonville FC (NIR)
FC Torpedo Kutaisi (GEO)
FC Santa Coloma (AND)*
Llanelli AFC (WAL)
Crusaders FC (NIR)†
AS Jeunesse Esch (LUX)
NK Celje (SVN)†
FC Daugava (LVA)
NK Mura (SVN)
FK Zeta (MNE)
ÍBV Vestmannaeyjar (ISL)
JK Trans Narva (EST)
Floriana FC (MLT)
Hibernians FC (MLT)†
FC Ordabasy Shymkent (KAZ)*
Thór Akureyri (ISL)†
FC Zhetysu Taldykorgan (KAZ)
JK Nõmme Kalju (EST)
NSÍ Runavík (FRO)
Portadown FC (NIR)
CS Grevenmacher (LUX)
FC Gandzasar Kapan (ARM)
FK Čelik Nikšić (MNE)*
FC USV Eschen-Mauren (LIE)*
KS Teuta (ALB)
Vikingur (FRO)
UE Santa Coloma (AND)
Cefn Druids AFC (WAL)†
FC Shirak (ARM)*
SP La Fiorita (SMR)*
AC Libertas (SMR)

* – cup winners; † – losing cup finalists; ¶ – Fair Play winners.

SUMMARY OF APPEARANCES

EUROPEAN CUP AND CHAMPIONS LEAGUE (1955–2012)

ENGLISH CLUBS
24 Manchester U
20 Liverpool
16 Arsenal
10 Chelsea
4 Leeds U
3 Everton, Newcastle U, Nottingham F
2 Aston Villa, Derby Co, Manchester C, Tottenham H, Wolverhampton W
1 Blackburn R, Burnley, Ipswich T

SCOTTISH CLUBS
30 Rangers
26 Celtic
3 Aberdeen, Hearts
1 Dundee, Dundee U, Hibernian, Kilmarnock

WELSH CLUBS
6 Barry T
5 The New Saints
2 Rhyl
1 Bangor C, Cwmbran T, Llanelli

NORTHERN IRELAND CLUBS
26 Linfield
12 Glentoran
3 Crusaders, Portadown
2 Glenavon
1 Ards, Cliftonville, Coleraine, Derry C, Distillery

REPUBLIC OF IRELAND CLUBS
8 Shamrock R
7 Dundalk
6 Bohemians, Shelbourne, Waterford
3 Derry C*, Drumcondra, St Patrick's Ath
2 Athlone T, Cork City, Limerick
1 Celtic, Cork Hibs, Cork Drogheda U, Sligo R

Winners: Celtic 1966–67; Manchester U 1967–68, 1998–99, 2007–08; Liverpool 1976–77, 1977–78, 1980–81, 1983–84, 2004–05; Nottingham F 1978–79, 1979–80; Aston Villa 1981–82; Chelsea 2011–12

Finalists: Celtic 1969–70; Leeds U 1974–75; Liverpool 1984–85, 2006–07; Arsenal 2005–06; Chelsea 2007–08; Manchester U 2008–09, 2010–11

UEFA EUROPA LEAGUE 2010–12

ENGLISH CLUBS
2 Aston Villa, Fulham, Liverpool, Manchester C
1 Birmingham C, Everton, Manchester U, Stoke C, Tottenham H

SCOTTISH CLUBS
3 Celtic
2 Dundee U, Hearts, Motherwell, Rangers
1 Aberdeen, Falkirk, Hibernian

WELSH CLUBS
3 Llanelli
2 Bangor C, Llanelli, The New Saints
1 Neath Ath, Port Talbot

NORTHERN IRELAND CLUBS
2 Cliftonville, Crusaders, Glentoran
1 Linfield, Lisburn Distillery, Portadown

REPUBLIC OF IRELAND CLUBS
2 Shamrock R, Sligo R
1 Bohemians, Derry C*, Dundalk, Sporting Fingal, St Patrick's Ath

Finalists: Fulham 2009–10

EUROPEAN CUP-WINNERS' CUP (1960–99)

ENGLISH CLUBS
6 Tottenham H **5** Chelsea, Liverpool, Manchester U **4** West Ham U **3** Arsenal, Everton **2** Manchester C **1** Ipswich T, Leeds U, Leicester C, Newcastle U, Southampton, Sunderland, WBA, Wolverhampton W

SCOTTISH CLUBS
10 Rangers **8** Aberdeen, Celtic **3** Dundee U, Hearts **2** Dunfermline Ath **1** Airdrieonians, Dundee, Hibernian, Kilmarnock, Motherwell, St Mirren

WELSH CLUBS
14 Cardiff C **8** Wrexham **7** Swansea C **3** Bangor C **1** Barry T, Borough U, Cwmbran T, Llansantfraid, Merthyr Tydfil, Newport Co

NORTHERN IRELAND CLUBS
9 Glentoran **5** Glenavon **4** Ballymena U, Coleraine **3** Crusaders, Linfield **2** Ards, Bangor **1** Derry C, Distillery, Carrick Rangers, Cliftonville, Portadown

REPUBLIC OF IRELAND CLUBS
6 Shamrock R **4** Shelbourne **3** Bohemians, Dundalk, Limerick, Waterford **2** Cork City, Cork Hibs, Derry C*, Galway U, Sligo R **1** Bray W, Cork Celtic, Finn Harps, Home Farm, St Patrick's Ath, University College Dublin

Winners: Tottenham H 1962–63; West Ham U 1964–65; Manchester C 1969–70; Chelsea 1970–71, 1997–98; Rangers 1971–72; Aberdeen 1982–83; Everton 1984–85; Manchester U 1990–91; Arsenal 1993–94

Finalists: Rangers 1960–61, 1966–67; Liverpool 1965–66; Leeds U 1972–73; West Ham U 1975–76; Arsenal 1979–80, 1994–95

EUROPEAN FAIRS CUP & UEFA CUP (1955–2009)

ENGLISH CLUBS
13 Leeds U, Liverpool **11** Aston Villa **10** Ipswich T, Newcastle U **9** Arsenal, Everton, Tottenham H **7** Manchester U **6** Blackburn R, Chelsea, Manchester C, Southampton **5** Nottingham F **4** Birmingham C, WBA, Wolverhampton W **3** Sheffield W **2** Bolton W, Derby Co, Leicester C, Middlesbrough, QPR, Stoke C, West Ham U **1** Burnley, Coventry C, Fulham, London Rep XI, Millwall, Norwich C, Portsmouth, Watford

SCOTTISH CLUBS
19 Dundee U **17** Rangers **16** Aberdeen, Celtic, Hibernian **13** Hearts **7** Dunfermline Ath, Kilmarnock **5** Dundee **3** Motherwell, St Mirren **2** Partick T, St Johnstone **1** Gretna, Livingston, Morton, Queen of the S, Raith R

WELSH CLUBS
5 Bangor C, TNS **3** Cwmbran T, Inter Cardiff (formerly Inter Cable-Tel), Rhyl **2** Barry T, Carmarthen T, Newtown **1** Afan Lido, Llanelli, Haverfordwest

** Now play in League of Ireland*

NORTHERN IRELAND CLUBS
18 Glentoran **9** Coleraine **8** Linfield, Portadown **5** Glenavon **3** Crusaders **1** Ards, Ballymena U, Bangor, Cliftonville, Dungannon Swifts

REPUBLIC OF IRELAND CLUBS
11 Bohemians **7** Shelbourne **6** Dundalk, St Patrick's Ath **5** Cork City, Shamrock R **4** Derry C* **3** Drogheda U, Finn Harps, Longford T **2** Drumcondra **1** Athlone T, Bray Wanderers, Cork Hibs, Galway U, Limerick

Winners: Leeds U 1967–68, 1970–71; Newcastle U 1968–69; Arsenal 1969–70, 1999–2000; Tottenham H 1971–72, 1983–84; Liverpool 1972–73, 1975–76, 2000–01; Ipswich T 1980–81

Finalists: London 1955–58, Birmingham C 1958–60, 1960–61; Leeds U 1966–67; Wolverhampton W 1971–72; Tottenham H 1973–74; Dundee U 1986–87; Celtic 2002–03; Middlesbrough 2005–06; Rangers 2007–08

FIFA CLUB WORLD CUP 2011

Formerly known as the FIFA Club World Championship, this tournament is played annually between the champion clubs from all 6 continental confederations, although since 2007 the champions of Oceania must play a qualifying play-off against the champion club of the host country.

FIFA CLUB WORLD CUP 2011

(Finals in Japan)

▪ *Denotes player sent off.*

QUARTER-FINAL PLAY-OFF

8 December 2011

Kashiwa Reysol (2) 2 *(Tanaka 37, Kudo 40)*

Auckland City (0) 0 18,754

Kashiwa Reysol: Sugeno; Kondo, Sakai (Mizuno 67), Masushima, Otani, Leandro Domingues, Jorge Wagner, Tanaka (Kitajima 85), Kudo, Barada (Kurisawa 82), Hashimoto.

Auckland City: Spoonley; Hogg, Berlanga, Pritchett, Mulligan, Exposito, Feneridis (Corrales 49), Dickinson (Tade 68), Vicelich, Riera (Koprivcic 69), Guerao.

QUARTER-FINALS

11 December 2011

Kashiwa Reysol (0) 1 *(Leandro Domingues 53)*

CF Monterrey (0) 1 *(Suazo 58)* 27,525

Kashiwa Reysol: Sugeno; Kondo, Sakai, Masushima, Otani, Leandro Domingues, Jorge Wagner, Tanaka, Kudo (Hayashi 106), Hashimoto, Kurisawa.

CF Monterrey: Orozco; Osorio, Chavez (Avoyi W 91), Perez L, Santana (De Nigris 97), Basanta, Zavala, Cardozo (Perez S 100), Delgado, Mier, Suazo.

aet; Kashiwa Reysol won 4-3 on penalties.

Esperance Tunis (0) 1 *(Darragi 60)*

Al-Sadd SC (1) 2 *(Al Khalfan 33, Koni 49)* 21,251

Esperance Tunis: Ben Cherifia; Yaya, Coulibaly (Afful 46), Darragi (Ayari 75), Chamman, Ndjeng, Bouazzi, Mouelhi, Traoui, Msakni, Hichri.

Al-Sadd SC: Saqr; Belhadj, Lee, Abdulmajid (Muhammad 72), Mohammed, Niang (Al Haydos 92), Keita, Abdulmajed, Al Khalfan (Ali 75), Albloushi, Koni.

MATCH FOR FIFTH PLACE

14 December 2011

CF Monterrey (2) 3 *(Mier 39, De Nigris 44, Zavala 47)*

Esperance Tunis (1) 2 *(Ndjeng 31, Mouelhi 76 (pen))* 13,639

CF Monterrey: Orozco; Chavez, Perez L (Morales 29), De Nigris, Santana (Meza 87), Basanta, Zavala, Cardozo, Avoyi W, Mier, Perez S.

Esperance Tunis: Ben Cherifia; Yaya, Coulibaly, Chamman (Ayari 54), Ndjeng, Bouazzi (Darragi 77), Mouelhi, Traoui, Afful, Msakni, Hichri.

SEMI-FINALS

14 December 2011

Kashiwa Reysol (0) 1 *(Sakai 54)*

Santos (2) 3 *(Neymar 19, Borges 24, Danilo 63)* 29,173

Kashiwa Reysol: Sugeno; Kondo, Sakai, Masushima, Otani, Leandro Dominges, Jorge Wagner, Tanaka (Sawa 65), Kudo (Kitajima 46), Hashimoto (Hyodo 80), Kurisawa.

Santos: Rafael Cabral; Edu Dracena, Danilo (Bruno Aguiar 90), Arouca, Durval, Henrique, Elano (Alan Kardec 59), Borges (Ibson 80), Ganso, Neymar, Bruno Rodrigo.

15 December 2011

Al-Sadd SC (0) 0

Barcelona (2) 4 *(Adriano 25, 43, Keita 64, Maxwell 81)* 66,298

Al-Sadd SC: Saqr; Belhadj, Lee, Abdulmajid, Mohammed, Niang (Ali 77), Keita (Al Haydos 85), Abdulmajed, Al Khalfan, Albloushi (Al Yazidi 65), Koni.

Barcelona: Valdes; Puyol, David Villa (Sanchez 39) (Cuenca 71), Iniesta, Thiago, Mascherano, Keita, Pedro, Adriano, Messi, Abidal (Maxwell 66).

MATCH FOR THIRD PLACE

18 December 2011

Kashiwa Reysol (0) 0

Al-Sadd SC (0) 0 60,527

Kashiwa Reysol: Sugeno; Kondo, Sakai, Masushima, Otani, Kitajima (Hayashi 81), Jorge Wagner, Tanaka (Sawa 75), Barada, Hashimoto, Mizuno.

Al-Sadd SC: Saqr; Belhadj, Lee, Abdulmajid, Al Hamad (Muhammad 93), Niang, Al Yazidi (Al Haydos 83), Keita, Abdulmajed, Al Klhalfan (Afif 73), Koni.

aet; Al-Sadd SC won 5-3 on penalties.

FINAL 2011

18 December 2011 (attendance 68,166)

Santos (0) 0

Barcelona (3) 4 *(Messi 17, 81, Xavi 24, Fabregas 45)*

Santos: Rafael Cabral; Edu Dracena, Leo, Danilo (Elano 31), Arouca, Durval, Henrique, Borges (Alan Kardec 79), Ganzo (Ibson 83), Neymar, Bruno Rodrigo.

Barcelona: Valdes; Dani Alves, Pique (Mascherano 56), Fabregas, Puyol (Fontas 85), Xavi, Iniesta, Abidal, Thiago (Pedro 79), Messi, Busquets.

PREVIOUS FINALS

2000 Corinthians beat Vaso de Gama 4-3 on penalties after 0-0 draw
2005 Sao Paulo beat Liverpool 1-0
2006 Internacional beat Barcelona 1-0
2007 AC Milan beat Boca Juniors 4-2
2008 Manchester U beat Liga De Quito 1-0
2009 Barcelona beat Estudiantes 2-1
2010 Internazionale beat TP Mazembe Englebert 3-0
2011 Barcelona beat Santos 4-0

WORLD CLUB CHAMPIONSHIP

Played annually up to 1974 and intermittently since then between the winners of the European Cup and the winners of the South American Champions Cup — known as the Copa Libertadores. In 1980 the winners were decided by one match arranged in Tokyo in February 1981 which remained the venue until 2004, when the match was superseded by the FIFA Club World Championship. AC Milan replaced Marseille who had been stripped of their European Cup title in 1993.

1960 Real Madrid beat Penarol 0-0, 5-1
1961 Penarol beat Benfica 0-1, 5-0, 2-1
1962 Santos beat Benfica 3-2, 5-2
1963 Santos beat AC Milan 2-4, 4-2, 1-0
1964 Inter-Milan beat Independiente 0-1, 2-0, 1-0
1965 Inter-Milan beat Independiente 3-0, 0-0
1966 Penarol beat Real Madrid 2-0, 2-0
1967 Racing Club beat Celtic 0-1, 2-1, 1-0
1968 Estudiantes beat Manchester United 1-0, 1-1
1969 AC Milan beat Estudiantes 3-0, 1-2
1970 Feyenoord beat Estudiantes 2-2, 1-0
1971 Nacional beat Panathinaikos* 1-1, 2-1
1972 Ajax beat Independiente 1-1, 3-0
1973 Independiente beat Juventus* 1-0
1974 Atlético Madrid* beat Independiente 0-1, 2-0
1975 Independiente and Bayern Munich could not agree dates; no matches.
1976 Bayern Munich beat Cruzeiro 2-0, 0-0
1977 Boca Juniors beat Borussia Moenchengladbach* 2-2, 3-0
1978 Not contested
1979 Olimpia beat Malmö* 1-0, 2-1
1980 Nacional beat Nottingham Forest 1-0
1981 Flamengo beat Liverpool 3-0
1982 Penarol beat Aston Villa 2-0
1983 Gremio Porto Alegre beat SV Hamburg 2-1
1984 Independiente beat Liverpool 1-0
1985 Juventus beat Argentinos Juniors 4-2 on penalties after a 2-2 draw
1986 River Plate beat Steaua Bucharest 1-0
1987 FC Porto beat Penarol 2-1 after extra time
1988 Nacional (Uru) beat PSV Eindhoven 7-6 on penalties after 1-1 draw
1989 AC Milan beat Atletico Nacional (Col) 1-0 after extra time
1990 AC Milan beat Olimpia 3-0
1991 Red Star Belgrade beat Colo Colo 3-0
1992 Sao Paulo beat Barcelona 2-1
1993 Sao Paulo beat AC Milan 3-2
1994 Velez Sarsfield beat AC Milan 2-0
1995 Ajax beat Gremio Porto Alegre 4-3 on penalties after 0-0 draw
1996 Juventus beat River Plate 1-0
1997 Borussia Dortmund beat Cruzeiro 2-0
1998 Real Madrid beat Vasco da Gama 2-1
1999 Manchester U beat Palmeiras 1-0
2000 Boca Juniors beat Real Madrid 2-1
2001 Bayern Munich beat Boca Juniors 1-0 after extra time
2002 Real Madrid beat Olimpia 2-0
2003 Boca Juniors beat AC Milan 3-1 on penalties after 1-1 draw
2004 Porto beat Once Caldas 8-7 on penalties after 0-0 draw

*European Cup runners-up; winners declined to take part.

EUROPEAN SUPER CUP 2011

Played annually between the winners of the European Champions' Cup and the European Cup-Winners' Cup (UEFA Cup from 2000; UEFA Europa League from 2010). AC Milan replaced Marseille in 1993–94.

■ *Denotes player sent off.*

EUROPEAN SUPER CUP 2011

26 August 2011, Monaco (attendance 18,048)

Barcelona (1) 2 *(Messi 39, Fabregas 88)* **Porto (0) 0**

Barcelona: Valdes; Abidal, Dani Alves, Adriano Correia (Busquets 63), Mascherano, Iniesta, Xavi, Keita, Messi, David Villa (Sanchez 60), Pedro (Fabregas 80).

Porto: Helton; Fucile, Sapunaru, Rolando■, Otamendi, Rodriguez (Silvestre Varela 68), Joao Moutinho, Souza (Fernando 77), Guarin■, Hulk, Kleber (Belluschi 77).

Referee: B. Kuipers (Holland).

PREVIOUS MATCHES

1972 Ajax beat Rangers 3-1, 3-2
1973 Ajax beat AC Milan 0-1, 6-0
1974 Not contested
1975 Dynamo Kiev beat Bayern Munich 1-0, 2-0
1976 Anderlecht beat Bayern Munich 4-1, 1-2
1977 Liverpool beat Hamburg 1-1, 6-0
1978 Anderlecht beat Liverpool 3-1, 1-2
1979 Nottingham F beat Barcelona 1-0, 1-1
1980 Valencia beat Nottingham F 1-0, 1-2
1981 Not contested
1982 Aston Villa beat Barcelona 0-1, 3-0
1983 Aberdeen beat Hamburg 0-0, 2-0
1984 Juventus beat Liverpool 2-0
1985 Juventus v Everton not contested due to UEFA ban on English clubs
1986 Steaua Bucharest beat Dynamo Kiev 1-0
1987 FC Porto beat Ajax 1-0, 1-0
1988 KV Mechelen beat PSV Eindhoven 3-0, 0-1
1989 AC Milan beat Barcelona 1-1, 1-0
1990 AC Milan beat Sampdoria 1-1, 2-0
1991 Manchester U beat Red Star Belgrade 1-0
1992 Barcelona beat Werder Bremen 1-1, 2-1
1993 Parma beat AC Milan 0-1, 2-0
1994 AC Milan beat Arsenal 0-0, 2-0
1995 Ajax beat Zaragoza 1-1, 4-0
1996 Juventus beat Paris St Germain 6-1, 3-1
1997 Barcelona beat Borussia Dortmund 2-0, 1-1
1998 Chelsea beat Real Madrid 1-0
1999 Lazio beat Manchester U 1-0
2000 Galatasaray beat Real Madrid 2-1
2001 Liverpool beat Bayern Munich 3-2
2002 Real Madrid beat Feyenoord 3-1
2003 AC Milan beat Porto 1-0
2004 Valencia beat Porto 2-1
2005 Liverpool beat CSKA Moscow 3-1
2006 Sevilla beat Barcelona 3-0
2007 AC Milan beat Sevilla 3-1
2008 Zenit beat Manchester U 2-1
2009 Barcelona beat Shakhtar Donetsk 1-0
2010 Atletico Madrid beat Internazionale 2-0
2011 Barcelona beat Porto 2-0

INTERNATIONAL DIRECTORY

The latest available information has been given regarding numbers of clubs and players registered with FIFA, the world governing body. Where known, official colours are listed. With European countries, League tables show a number of signs. * indicates relegated teams, + play-offs, *+ relegated after play-offs, ++ promoted.

There are 209 member associations. The four home countries, England, Scotland, Northern Ireland and Wales, are dealt with elsewhere in the Yearbook; but basic details appear in this directory. The following countries are not members of FIFA: Gibraltar, Kosovo, and Northern Cyprus.

There are a number of associate members and others who have affiliation to their confederations, but there is only one recent official addition and that is South Sudan. Of the many affiliated countries, they include Northern Mariana Islands, Reunion, Zanzibar, French Guiana, Saint-Martin, Sint Maarten, Kiribati, Niue and Tuvalu.

EUROPE

ALBANIA

The Football Association of Albania, Rruga Labinoti, Pallati Perballe Shkolles 'Gjuhet e Huaja'.
Founded: 1930; *National Colours:* Red shirts, black shorts, red stockings.

International matches 2011
Slovenia (h) 1-2, Belarus (h) 1-0, Bosnia (a) 0-2, Argentina (a) 0-4, Montenegro (h) 3-2, France (h) 1-2, Luxembourg (a) 1-2, France (a) 0-3, Romania (h) 1-1, Azerbaijan (h) 0-1, Macedonia (a) 0-0.

League Championship wins (1930–37; 1945–2012)
SK Tirana 24 (including 17 Nentori 8); Dinamo Tirana 18; Partizani Tirana 15; Vllaznia 9; Skenderbeu 3; Elbasan 2 (including Labinoti 1); Flamurtari 1; Teuta 1.

Cup wins (1948–2012)
Partizani Tirana 15; SK Tirana 15 (including 17 Nentori 8); Dinamo Tirana 13; Vllaznia 6; Teuta 3; Flamurtari 3; Elbasan 2 (including Labinoti 1); Besa 2; Apolonia 1.

Final League Table 2011–12

	P	*W*	*D*	*L*	*F*	*A*	*Pts*
Skenderbeu	26	17	6	3	45	16	57
Teuta	26	17	5	4	33	18	56
SK Tirana	26	16	5	5	33	21	53
Flamurtari	26	13	7	6	42	20	46
Kastrioti	26	11	5	10	37	30	38
Vllaznia	26	10	5	11	39	33	35
Bylis	26	9	8	9	40	37	35
Laci (–6)	26	11	7	8	26	28	34
Shkumbini	26	8	7	11	37	45	31
Tomori+	26	8	4	14	36	47	28
Kamza*+	26	7	6	13	22	32	27
Apolonia+	26	5	6	15	27	46	21
Pogradeci* (–3)	26	6	4	16	25	47	19
Dinamo Tirana* (–3)	26	3	7	16	19	41	13

Top scorer: Dervishi (Shkumbini) 20.
Cup Final: SK Tirana 1, Skenderbeu 0.

ANDORRA

Federacio Andorrana de Futbol, Avinguda Carlemany 67, 3er Pis, Apartado postal 65, Escaldes-Engordany, Principat D'Andorra.
Founded: 1994; *National Colours:* Yellow shirts, red shorts, blue stockings.

International matches 2011
Moldova (a) 1-2, Slovakia (h) 0-1, Slovakia (a) 0-1, Armenia (h) 0-3, Macedonia (a) 0-1, Republic of Ireland (h) 0-2, Russia (a) 0-6.

League Championship wins (1996–2012)
FC Santa Coloma 6; Principat 3; Encamp 2; Ranger's 2; St Julia 2; Constelacio 1; Lusitanos 1.

Cup wins (1991–2012)
FC Santa Coloma 9; Principat 6; St Julia 3; Constelacio 1; Lusitanos 1.

Qualifying League Table 2011–12

	P	*W*	*D*	*L*	*F*	*A*	*Pts*
FC Santa Coloma	14	10	2	2	51	9	32
Lusitanos	14	9	4	1	40	12	31
UE Santa Coloma	14	9	3	2	54	12	30
St Julia	14	8	4	2	47	14	28
Principat	14	3	3	8	17	27	12
Engordany	14	3	3	8	17	45	12
Inter Club	14	3	1	10	13	51	10
Ranger's	14	1	0	13	8	77	3

Championship Play-Offs

	P	*W*	*D*	*L*	*F*	*A*	*Pts*
Lusitanos	20	11	7	2	48	18	40
FC Santa Coloma	20	11	5	4	56	17	38
UE Santa Coloma	20	10	7	3	61	20	37
St Julia	20	10	6	4	57	22	36

Relegation Play-Offs

	P	*W*	*D*	*L*	*F*	*A*	*Pts*
Principat	20	8	3	9	32	32	27
Engordany	20	6	4	10	32	51	22
Inter Club+	20	5	3	12	34	65	18
Ranger's*	20	1	1	18	16	111	4

Top scorer: Bernat (UE Santa Coloma) 14.
Cup Final: Lusitanos 0, FC Santa Coloma 1.

ARMENIA

Football Federation of Armenia, Saryan 38, Yerevan, 375 010, Armenia.
Founded: 1992; *National Colours:* Red shirts, blue shorts, orange stockings.

International matches 2011
Georgia (a) 1-2, Russia (h) 0-0, Russia (a) 1-3, Lithuania (a) 0-3, Andorra (a) 3-0, Slovakia (a) 4-0, Macedonia (h) 4-1, Republic of Ireland (a) 1-2.

League Championship wins (1992–2011)
Pyunik 13 (including Homenetmen); Shirak Gyumri 4*; Ararat Yerevan 2*; Araks 2 (including Tsement); FC Yerevan 1; Ulysses 1.
*Includes one unofficial title.

Cup wins (1992–2012)
Mika 6; Ararat Yerevan 5; Pyunik 4; Tsement 2; Banants 2; Pyunik (including Homenetmen) 1; Shirak Gyumri 1.

Final League Table 2011

	P	*W*	*D*	*L*	*F*	*A*	*Pts*
Ulysses	28	15	8	5	38	22	53
Gandzasar	28	12	10	6	31	18	46
Pyunik	28	12	10	6	33	28	46
Banants	28	12	8	8	42	30	44
Mika	28	12	8	8	36	25	44
Impuls	28	10	7	11	37	36	37
Shirak	28	6	7	15	27	42	25
Ararat*	28	2	4	22	14	57	10

Top scorer: Bruno Correa (Banants) 16.
Cup Final: Shirak 1, Impuls 0.

AUSTRIA

Oesterreichischer Fussball-Bund, Ernst-Happel Stadion – Sektor A/F, Postfach 340, Meierestrasse 7, Wien 1021.
Founded: 1904; *National Colours:* White shirts, black shorts, white stockings.

International matches 2011
Holland (a) 1-3, Belgium (h) 0-2, Turkey (a) 0-2, Germany (h) 1-2, Latvia (h) 3-1, Slovakia (h) 1-2, Germany (a) 2-6, Turkey (h) 0-0, Azerbaijan (a) 4-1, Kazakhstan (a) 0-0, Ukraine (a) 1-2.

League Championship wins (1912–2012)
Rapid Vienna 32; FK Austria (formerly Amateure) 23; Tirol-Svarowski-Innsbruck 10; Admira-Energie-Wacker 8; Austria Salzburg 7; First Vienna 6; Wiener Sportklub 3; Sturm Graz 3; WAC 1; FAC 1; Hakoah 1; Linz ASK 1; WAF 1; Voest Linz 1; Graz 1; WAC 1; Wacker 1.

Cup wins (1919–2012)
FK Austria (formerly Amateure) 27; Rapid Vienna 14; TS Innsbruck (formerly Wacker Innsbruck) 7; Admira-Energie-Wacker (formerly Sportklub Admira & Admira-Energie) 5; Graz 4; Sturm Graz 4; First Vienna 3; WAC 3;

Ried 2; Linz ASK 1; Wacker Vienna 1; WAF 1; Wiener Sportklub 1; Kremser 1; Stockerau 1; Karnten 1; WAC 1; Kremser 1, Horn 1; Austria Salzburg 1.

Final League Table 2011–12

	P	*W*	*D*	*L*	*F*	*A*	*Pts*
Salzburg	36	19	11	6	60	30	68
Rapid Vienna	36	16	14	6	52	30	62
Admira	36	15	10	11	59	52	55
FK Austria	36	14	12	10	52	44	54
Sturm Graz	36	12	15	9	47	41	51
Ried	36	11	15	10	44	38	48
Wacker Innsbruck	36	10	15	11	36	45	45
Mattersburg	36	9	11	16	41	43	38
Neustadt	36	6	15	15	26	51	33
Kapfenberger*	36	5	8	23	21	64	23

Top scorers: Jantscher (Salzburg), Maierhofer (Salzburg) 14.
Cup Final: Salzburg 3, Ried 0.

AZERBAIJAN

Association of Football Federations of Azerbaijan, 42 Gussi Gadjiev Street, Baku 370 009.
Founded: 1992; *National Colours:* White shirts, blue shorts, white stockings.

International matches 2011
Hungary (a) 0-2, Belgium (a) 1-4, Kazakhstan (a) 1-2, Germany (h) 1-3, Macedonia (h) 0-1, Belgium (h) 1-1, Kazakhstan (h) 3-2, Austria (h) 1-4, Turkey (a) 0-1, Albania (a) 1-0.

League Championship wins (1992–2012)
Neftchi 7; Kapaz 3; Shamkir 3; Baku 2; Inter 2; Karabakh 1; Turan 1; Xazar 1.
Includes one unofficial title for Shamkir in 2002.

Cup wins (1992–2012)
Neftchi 5; Kapaz 4; Karabakh 3; Xazar 3; Baku 3; Inshatchi 1; Shafa 1.

Qualifying League Table 2011–12

	P	*W*	*D*	*L*	*F*	*A*	*Pts*
Neftchi	22	16	1	5	45	17	49
Inter	22	13	6	3	21	10	45
Xazar	22	13	5	4	33	19	44
Karabakh	22	12	5	5	27	14	41
Baku	22	10	5	7	27	22	35
Kabala	22	10	5	7	27	23	35
AZAL	22	8	5	9	35	35	29
Revan	22	6	7	9	23	29	25
Kapaz	22	6	4	12	26	38	22
Simurq	22	5	4	13	18	34	19
Sumqayit	22	4	3	15	16	37	15
Turan	22	3	2	17	13	33	11

Final League Table 2011–12

	P	*W*	*D*	*L*	*F*	*A*	*Pts*
Neftchi	32	20	3	9	55	30	63
Xazar	32	17	8	7	44	28	59
Inter	32	16	8	8	29	21	56
Karabakh	32	15	8	9	37	28	53
Kabala	32	15	7	10	43	32	52
Baku	32	15	5	12	42	36	50

Relegation Table 2011–12

	P	*W*	*D*	*L*	*F*	*A*	*Pts*
AZAL	32	12	8	12	44	44	44
Revan	32	10	11	11	39	39	41
Simurq	32	8	10	14	27	41	34
Kapaz	32	9	5	18	35	55	32
Turan	32	6	7	19	26	42	25
Sumqayit	32	6	6	20	27	52	24

No relegation in 2011–12.
Top scorer: Nasimov (Neftchi) 13.
Cup Final: Neftchi 0, Baku 2.

BELARUS

Belarus Football Federation, Kirova Street 8/2, Minsk 220 600, Belarus.
Founded: 1992; *National Colours:* Red shirts, green shorts, red stockings.

International matches 2011
Kazakhstan (h) 1-1, Albania (a) 0-1, Canada (h) 0-1, France (h) 1-1, Luxembourg (h) 2-0, Bulgaria (h) 1-0, Bosnia (h) 0-2, Bosnia (a) 0-1, Romania (a) 2-2, Poland (a) 0-2, Libya (h) 1-1.

League Championship wins (1992–2011)
BATE Borisov 8; Dynamo Minsk 7; Slavia Mozyr (formerly MPKC Mozyr) 2; Dnepr Mogilev 1; Belshina 1; Gomel 1; Shakhtyor 1.

Cup wins (1992–2012)
Belshina 3; Dynamo Minsk 3; Slavia Mozyr (formerly MPKC Mozyr) 2; MTZ-RIPA 2; BATE Borisov 2; Gomel 2; Naftan 2; Neman 1; Dynamo 93 Minsk 1; Lokomotiv 96 1; Shakhtyor 1; Dynamo Brest 1.

Final League Table 2011

	P	*W*	*D*	*L*	*F*	*A*	*Pts*
BATE Borisov	33	18	12	3	53	20	66
Shakhtyor	33	17	10	6	46	24	61
Gomel	33	13	15	5	36	24	54
Dynamo Minsk	33	14	7	12	50	43	49
Belshina	33	12	12	9	41	35	48
Torpedo Zhodino	33	9	14	10	37	41	41
Naftan	33	10	7	16	35	45	37
Neman	33	8	13	12	33	45	37
Minsk	33	8	11	14	33	40	35
Dynamo Brest	33	8	11	14	38	46	35
FK Vitebsk*+	33	8	8	17	29	46	32
Dnepr*	33	6	14	13	29	51	32

Top scorer: Renan (BATE Borisov) 13.
Cup Final: Naftan 2, Minsk 2
Naftan won 4-3 on penalties.

BELGIUM

Union Royale Belge Des Societes De Football Association, 145 Avenue Houba de Strooper, B-1020 Bruxelles.
Founded: 1895; *National Colours:* All red.

International matches 2011
Finland (h) 1-1, Austria (a) 2-0, Azerbaijan (h) 4-1, Turkey (h) 1-1, Slovenia (a) 0-0, Azerbaijan (a) 1-1, USA (h) 1-0, Kazakhstan (h) 4-1, Germany (a) 1-3, Romania (h) 2-1, France (a) 0-0.

League Championship wins (1896–2012)
Anderlecht 31; Club Brugge 13; Union St Gilloise 11; Standard Liege 10; Beerschot 7; RC Brussels 6; FC Liege 5; Daring Brussels 5; Antwerp 4; Mechelen 4; Lierse SK 4; Cercle Brugge 3; Genk 3; Beveren 2; RWD Molenbeek 1.

Cup wins (1912–14; 1927; 1935; 1954–2012)
Club Brugge 10; Anderlecht 9; Standard Liege 6; Racing Genk 3; Gent 3; Beerschot (became Germinal) 2; Waterschei (became Racing Genk) 2; Beveren 2; Antwerp 2; Lierse SK 2; Union St Gilloise 2; Cercle Brugge 2; Mechelen 1; FC Liege 1; Ekeren (became Germinal) 1; Westerlo 1; La Louviere 1; Zulte-Waregem 1; Daring 1; Germinal 1; Tournai 1; Racing 1; Waregem 1; Lokeren 1.

Qualifying League Table 2011–12

	P	*W*	*D*	*L*	*F*	*A*	*Pts*
Anderlecht	30	20	7	3	61	26	67
Club Brugge	30	19	4	7	51	32	61
Gent	30	17	5	8	63	35	56
Standard Liege	30	14	9	7	43	33	51
Genk	30	13	7	10	60	44	46
Kortrijk	30	13	7	10	39	36	46
Cercle Brugge	30	13	7	10	36	37	46
Lokeren	30	11	11	8	48	40	44
Mechelen	30	10	7	13	40	50	37
Mons	30	9	9	12	50	55	36
Beerschot	30	9	9	12	45	51	36
Lierse	30	6	13	11	24	36	31
Waregem	30	6	12	12	32	38	30
Leuven	30	7	8	15	38	58	29
Westerlo+	30	5	5	20	29	59	20
St Truiden+	30	3	10	17	32	61	19

Top scorer: Perbet (Mons) 22.

Championship Play-Off

	P	*W*	*D*	*L*	*F*	*A*	*Pts*
Anderlecht	10	5	3	2	16	8	52
Club Brugge	10	5	2	3	14	11	48
Genk	10	6	0	4	19	19	41
Gent	10	4	0	6	16	16	40
Standard Liege	10	2	3	5	10	17	35
Kortrijk	10	3	2	5	16	20	34

Europa League Qualifying Table A

	P	W	D	L	F	A	Pts
Cercle Brugge	6	3	2	1	16	10	11
Leuven	6	3	1	2	15	14	10
Lierse	6	1	4	1	7	7	7
Mechelen	6	1	1	4	7	14	4

Europa League Qualifying Table B

	P	W	D	L	F	A	Pts
Mons	6	3	2	1	8	4	11
Waregem	6	2	2	2	7	8	8
Beerschot	6	2	1	3	9	10	7
Lokeren	6	1	3	2	9	11	6

Europa League Tables A and B Finals

Mons 0, 2 Cercle Brugge 1, 3

Final

Cercle Brugge 1, 1 Gent 5, 2

Relegation Table

	P	W	D	L	F	A	Pts
Westerlo*+	4	3	0	1	12	6	12
St Truiden*	4	1	0	3	6	12	3

Top scorer: Perbet (Mons) 25.
Cup Final: Kortrijk 0, Lokeren 1.

BOSNIA-HERZEGOVINA

Football Federation of Bosnia & Herzegovina, Ferhadija 30, Sarajevo 71000.
Founded: 1992; *National Colours:* White shirts, blue shorts, white stockings.

International matches 2011

Mexico (h) 0-2, Romania (h) 2-1, Romania (a) 0-3, Albania (h) 2-0, Greece (h) 0-0, Belarus (a) 2-0, Belarus (h) 1-0, Luxembourg (h) 5-0, France (a) 1-1, Portugal (h) 0-0, Portugal (a) 2-6.

League Championship wins (1998–2012)

Zeljeznicar 5 Siroki 2; Sarajevo 2; Zrinjski 2; Brotnjo 1; Leotar 1; Modrica 1; Borac 1.

Cup wins (1998–2012)

Zeljeznicar 5; Sarajevo 3; Modrica 1; Orasje 1; Siroki 1; Zrinjski 1; Slavija 1; Borac 1.

Final League Table 2011–12

	P	W	D	L	F	A	Pts
Zeljeznicar	30	22	5	3	68	17	71
Siroki	30	18	9	3	48	17	63
Borac	30	17	4	9	46	26	55
Sarajevo	30	16	6	8	48	31	54
Olimpik	30	15	7	8	44	23	52
Zrinjski	30	12	9	9	47	41	45
Zvijezda	30	13	6	11	37	35	45
Travnik	30	10	5	15	42	53	35
Celik	30	8	10	12	31	39	34
Rudar	30	10	4	16	30	46	34
Velez	30	8	9	13	28	35	33
Leotar	30	9	6	15	27	40	33
GOSK Gabela	30	8	9	13	26	43	33
Slavija	30	10	2	18	36	61	32
Sloboda*	30	10	2	18	23	48	32
Kozara*	30	4	7	19	19	45	19

Top scorer: Adilovic (Zeljeznicar) 20.
Cup Final: Zeljeznicar 1, 0, Siroki 0, 0.

BULGARIA

Bulgarian Football Union, Karnigradska Street 19, BG-1000 Sofia.
Founded: 1923; *National Colours:* White shirts, green shorts, white stockings.

International matches 2011

Estonia (h) 2-2, Switzerland (h) 0-0, Cyprus (a) 1-0, Montenegro (a) 1-1, Belarus (a) 0-1, England (h) 0-3, Switzerland (a) 1-3, Ukraine (a) 0-3, Wales (h) 0-1.

League Championship wins (1925–2012)

CSKA Sofia 31; Levski Sofia 26; Slavia Sofia 7; Litex 4; Vladislav Varna 3; Lokomotiv Sofia 3; Botev Plovdiv (includes Trakija) 2; AC 23 Sofia 1; SC Sofia 1; Sokol Varna 1; Spartak Plovdiv 1; Tichka Varna 1; JSZ Sofia 1; Beroe Stara Zagora 1; Etur 1; Lokomotiv Plovdiv 1; Ludogorets 1.

Cup wins (1946–2012)

Levski Sofia 24; CSKA Sofia 19; Slavia Sofia 7; Lokomotiv Sofia 4; Litex 4; Botev Plovdiv (includes Trakija) 2; Spartak Plovdiv 1; Septemvri Sofia 1; Marek Dupnica 1; Spartak Varna 1; Sliven 1; Beroe 1; Ludogorets 1.

Final League Table 2011–12

	P	W	D	L	F	A	Pts
Ludogorets	30	22	4	4	73	16	70
CSKA Sofia	30	22	3	5	60	19	69
Levski Sofia	30	20	2	8	61	28	62
Chernomorets	30	17	9	4	57	23	60
Litex	30	17	8	5	57	28	59
Lokomotiv Plovdiv	30	17	6	7	44	39	57
Cherno More	30	16	4	10	46	25	52
Slavia Sofia	30	15	6	9	42	36	51
Minjor	30	8	12	10	35	40	36
Beroe	30	9	8	13	30	37	35
Montana	30	8	7	15	29	51	31
Botev	30	7	8	15	30	44	29
Lokomotiv Sofia	30	5	9	16	26	50	24
Vidima*	30	3	6	21	19	59	15
Kaliakara*	30	2	5	23	26	77	11
Svetkavitsa*	30	1	5	24	8	71	8

Top scorers: Junior Moraes (CKSA Sofia) 16, Stoyanov (Ludogorets) 16.
Cup Final: Lokomotiv Plovdiv 1, Ludogorets 2.

CHANNEL ISLANDS

Guernsey

League Championship wins (1894–2012)

Northerners 30; Rangers 17; Vale Recreation 15; St Martin's AC 13; Sylvans 10; Belgrave Wanderers 6; 2nd Batt Manchesters 3; 2nd Batt Royal Irish Regt 2; 2nd Batt Wiltshires 2; 10th Comp W Div Royal Artillery 1; 2nd Batt Leicesters 1; 2nd Batt PA Somerset Light Infantry 1; 2nd Middlesex Regt 1; Athletics 1; Band Comp 2nd Batt Royal Fusiliers 1; G&H Comp Royal Fusiliers 1; Grange 1; Yorkshire Regt (Green Howards) 1.

Final League Table 2011–12

	P	W	D	L	Pts
Northerners	18	15	2	1	47
St Martin's AC	18	10	3	5	33
Sylvans S&FC	18	10	2	6	32
Belgrave Wanderers	18	10	1	7	31
Vale Recreation	18	6	2	10	20
Rovers AC	18	4	2	12	14
Rangers	18	2	0	16	6

Jersey

League Championship wins (1905–2012)

Jersey Wanderers 20; First Tower United 19; St Paul's 14; Jersey Scottish 10; Beeches Old Boys 5; Magpies 4; 2nd Batt King's Own Regt 3; Oaklands 3; St Peter 3; 1st Batt Devon Regt 2; 1st Batt East Surrey Regt 2; Georgetown 2; Mechanics 2; YMCA 2; 2nd Batt East Surrey Regt 1; 20th Comp Royal Garrison Artillery 1; National Rovers 1; Sporting Academics 1; Trinity 1.

Final League Table 2011–12

	P	W	D	L	Pts
Jersey Scottish	16	13	2	1	41
St Paul's	16	8	3	5	27
Jersey Wanderers	16	8	3	5	27
Grouville	16	6	6	4	24
St Peter	16	7	3	6	24
St Ouen	16	5	3	8	18
Rozel Rovers	16	4	6	6	18
Trinity	16	4	3	9	15
First Tower United	16	1	3	12	6

Upton Park Trophy (For Guernsey & Jersey Winners)

Northerners AC 18; First Tower United 12; Jersey Wanderers 11; St Martin's AC 11; St Paul's 6; Rangers 5; Jersey Scottish 5; Vale Recreation 4; Belgrave Wanderers 4; Sylvans 3; Beeches Old Boys 3; Old St Paul's 3; Magpies 3; St Peter 2; Jersey Mechanics 1; Jersey YMCA 1; National Rovers 1; Sporting Academics 1; Trinity 1.
2012 Northerners AC 4, Jersey Scottish 0.

CROATIA

Croatian Football Federation, Rusanova 13, Zagreb, 10 3000, Croatia.
Founded: 1912; *National Colours:* Red & white shirts, white shorts, blue stockings.

International matches 2011

Czech Republic (h) 4-2, Georgia (a) 0-1, France (a) 0-0, Georgia (h) 2-1, Republic of Ireland (a) 0-0, Malta (a) 3-1, Israel (h) 3-1, Greece (a) 0-2, Latvia (h) 2-0, Turkey (a) 3-0, Turkey (h) 0-0.

League Championship wins (1941–46; 1992–2012)
Dinamo Zagreb (formerly Croatia Zagreb) 14; Hajduk Split 8; Gradjanski 1; Concordia 1; Zagreb 1.

Cup wins (1992–2012)
Dinamo Zagreb (formerly Croatia Zagreb) 12; Hajduk Split 5; Rijeka 2, Inker Zapresic 1; Osijek 1.

Final League Table 2011–12

	P	W	D	L	F	A	Pts
Dinamo Zagreb	30	23	6	1	73	11	75
Hajduk Split	30	16	6	8	50	24	54
Slaven	30	14	10	6	41	27	52
Split	30	14	8	8	43	32	50
Cibalia	30	13	6	11	35	35	45
Zagreb	30	13	6	11	36	42	45
Lokomotiva	30	12	8	10	33	33	44
Osijek	30	11	10	9	45	38	43
Istra	30	11	9	10	35	33	42
Zadar	30	11	7	12	29	44	40
Inter	30	11	5	14	33	33	38
Rijeka	30	9	11	10	29	29	38
Lucko*	30	6	13	11	2	36	31
Sibenik*	30	6	9	15	27	39	27
Karlovac* (–1)	30	6	7	17	25	53	24
Varazdin* (–1)	30	2	3	25	16	52	8

Top scorer: Beciraj (Dinamo Zagreb) 15.
Cup Final: Osijek 0, 1, Dinamo Zagreb 0, 3.

CYPRUS

Cyprus Football Association, 1 Stasinos Str., Engomi, P.O. Box 25071, Nicosia 2404.
Founded: 1934; *National Colours:* Blue shirts, white shorts, blue stockings.

International matches 2011
Sweden (h) 0-2, Romania (h) 1-1, Iceland (h) 0-0, Bulgaria (h) 0-1, Moldova (h) 3-2, Portugal (h) 0-4, Iceland (a) 0-1, Denmark (h) 1-4, Norway (a) 1-3, Scotland (h) 1-2.

League Championship wins (1935–2012)
Apoel 21; Omonia 20; Anorthosis 13; AEL 6; EPA 3; Olympiakos 3; Apollon 3; Pezoporikos 2; Cetinkaya 1; Trast 1.

Cup wins (1935–2012)
Apoel 19; Omonia 14; Anorthosis 10; AEL 6; Apollon 6; EPA 5; Trast 3; Cetinkaya 2; Olympiakos 1; Pezoporikos 1; Salamina 1; AEK 1; Apop 1.

Qualifying League Table 2011–12

	P	W	D	L	F	A	Pts
AEL	26	18	6	2	33	7	60
Omonia	26	17	6	3	47	16	57
Apoel	26	17	5	4	39	13	56
Anorthosis	26	15	7	4	30	12	52
AEK	26	11	9	6	33	21	42
Nea Salamis	26	10	6	10	33	41	36
Apollon	26	10	4	12	31	39	34
Alki	26	10	4	12	32	40	34
Olympiakos+	26	7	9	10	29	34	30
Enosis+	26	8	5	13	17	24	29
Ethnikos Achnas+	26	7	8	11	21	23	29
Aris+	26	7	6	13	27	35	27
Anagennisi*	26	2	5	19	16	45	11
Ermis*	26	1	4	21	12	50	7

Play-Offs League Table 2011-12

Group A	P	W	D	L	F	A	Pts
AEL	32	20	8	4	37	10	68
Apoel	32	20	6	6	46	19	66
Omonia	32	20	6	6	56	23	66
Anorthosis	32	17	8	7	36	22	59

Group B	P	W	D	L	F	A	Pts
AEK	32	13	10	9	40	27	49
Apollon	32	12	7	13	36	43	43
Nea Salamis	32	11	10	11	39	47	43
Alki	32	12	6	14	35	45	42

Relegation Table 2011-12

Group C	P	W	D	L	F	A	Pts
Ethnikos Achnas	32	10	10	12	31	30	40
Olympiakos	32	10	9	13	36	44	39
Enosis	32	11	5	16	26	29	38
Aris*	32	8	8	16	32	44	32

Top scorer: Freddy (Omonia) 17.
Cup Final: Omonia 1, AEL 0.

CZECH REPUBLIC

Football Association of Czech Republic, Diskarska 100, Prague 6 16017 – Strahov, Czech Republic.
Founded: 1901; *National Colours:* Red shirts, white shorts, blue stockings.

International matches 2011
Croatia (a) 2-4, Spain (a) 1-2, Liechtenstein (h) 2-0, Peru (a) 0-0, Japan (a) 0-0, Norway (a) 0-3, Scotland (a) 2-2, Ukraine (h) 4-0, Spain (h) 0-2, Lithuania (a) 4-1, Montenegro (h) 2-0, Montenegro (a) 1-0.

League Championship wins (1925–93)
Sparta Prague 19; Dukla Prague (prev. UDA, now Marila Pribram) 11; Slavia Prague 9; Slovan Bratislava (formerly NV Bratislava) 8; Spartak Trnava 5; Banik Ostrava 3; Inter-Bratislava 1; Spartak Hradec Kralove 1; Viktoria Zizkov 1; Zbrojovka Brno 1; Bohemians 1; Vitkovice 1.

Cup wins (1961–93)
Dukla Prague 8; Sparta Prague 8; Slovan Bratislava 5; Spartak Trnava 4; Banik Ostrava 3; Lokomotiva Kosice 2; TJ Gottwaldov 1; Dunajska Streda 1; Kosice 1.
From 1993–94, there were two separate countries; the Czech Republic and Slovakia.

League Championship wins (1994–2012)
Sparta Prague 11; Slavia Prague 3; Slovan Liberec 3; Banik Ostrava 1; Viktoria Plzen 1.

Cup wins (1994–2012)
Sparta Prague 4; Slavia Prague 4; Viktoria Zizkov 2; Teplice 2; Spartak Hradec Kralove 1; Jablonec 1; Slovan Liberec 1; Banik Osrava 1; Viktoria Plzen 1; Mlada 1; Sigma Olomouc 1.

Final League Table 2011–12

	P	W	D	L	F	A	Pts
Slovan Liberec	30	20	6	4	68	29	66
Sparta Prague	30	20	4	6	51	25	64
Viktoria Plzen	30	19	6	5	66	33	63
Mlada	30	15	5	10	49	34	50
Teplice	30	12	10	8	36	30	46
Dukla Prague	30	11	9	10	42	35	42
Slovacko	30	12	5	13	29	32	41
Jablonec	30	11	7	12	54	43	40
Pribram	30	11	6	13	44	56	39
Ceske	30	9	8	13	30	51	35
Sigma Olomouc	30	11	10	9	42	38	34
Slavia Prague	30	8	10	12	28	34	34
Hradec Kralove	30	8	7	15	22	38	31
Banik Ostrava	30	7	7	16	31	48	28
Bohemians*	30	6	6	18	20	54	24
Viktoria Zizkov*	30	5	4	21	23	55	19

Top scorer: Lafata (Jablonec) 25.
Cup Final: Sparta Prague 0, Sigma Olomouc 1.

DENMARK

Danish Football Association, Idraettens Hus, Brondby Stadion 20, DK-2605, Brondby.
Founded: 1889; *National Colours:* Red shirts, white shorts, red stockings.

International matches 2011
England (h) 1-2, Norway (a) 1-1, Slovakia (a) 2-1, Iceland (a) 2-0, Scotland (a) 1-2, Norway (h) 2-0, Cyprus (a) 4-1, Portugal (h) 2-1, Sweden (h) 2-0, Finland (h) 2-1.

League Championship wins (1913–2012)
KB Copenhagen 15; Brondby 10; B 93 Copenhagen 9; AB (Akademisk) 9; FC Copenhagen 9; B 1903 Copenhagen 7; Frem 6; Esbjerg BK 5; Vejle BK 5; AGF Aarhus 5; Hvidovre 3; OB Odense 3; AaB Aalborg 3; B 1909 Odense 2; Koge BK 2; Lyngby 2; Silkeborg 1; Herfolge 1; Nordsjaelland 1.

Cup wins (1955–2012)
AGF Aarhus 9; Vejle BK 6; Brondby 6; OB Odense 5; FC Copenhagen 5; Randers Freja 4; Lyngby 3; B 1909 Odense 2; Aab Aalborg 2; Esbjerg BK 2; Frem 2; B 1903 Copenhagen 2; Nordsjaelland 2; B 93 Copenhagen 1; KB Copenhagen 1; Vanlose 1; Hvidovre 1; B1913 Odense 1, AB (Akademisk) 1, Viborg 1; Silkeborg 1.

Final League Table 2011–12

	P	W	D	L	F	A	Pts
Nordsjaelland	33	21	5	7	49	22	68
FC Copenhagen	33	19	9	5	55	26	66
Midtjylland	33	17	7	9	50	40	58
Horsens	33	17	6	10	53	39	57

Aarhus	33	12	12	9	47	40	48
Sonderiyske	33	11	11	11	48	51	44
Aalborg	33	12	8	13	42	48	44
Silkeborg	33	11	10	12	51	47	43
Brondby	33	9	9	15	35	46	36
Odense	33	8	10	15	46	50	34
Lyngby*	33	8	4	21	32	60	28
Koge*	33	4	7	22	32	71	19

Top scorer: N'Doye (FC Copenhagen) 18.
Cup Final: Horsens 0, FC Copenhagen 1.

ENGLAND

The Football Association, Wembley Stadium, PO Box 1966, London SW1P 9EQ.
Founded: 1863; *National Colours:* White shirts with navy blue collar, navy shorts, white stockings.

ESTONIA

Estonian Football Association, Rapia 8/10, Tallinn 11312.
Founded: 1921; *National Colours:* Blue shirts, black shorts, white stockings.

International matches 2011
Bulgaria (a) 2-2, Uruguay (h) 2-0, Serbia (h) 1-1, Italy (a) 0-3, Faeroes (a) 0-2, Chile (a) 0-4, Uruguay (a) 0-3, Turkey (a) 0-3, Slovenia (a) 2-1, Northern Ireland (h) 4-1, Northern Ireland (a) 2-1, Ukraine (h) 0-2, Republic of Ireland (h) 0-4, Republic of Ireland (a) 1-1.

League Championship wins (1921–40; 1992–2011)
Sport 9; Flora Tallinn 9; Levadia Tallinn (includes Levadia Maardu) 8; Estonia 5; Tallinn JK 2; Norma 2; Lantana (formerly Nikol) 2; Kalev 2; Olimpia 1; VMK Tallinn 1.

Cup wins (1993–2012)
Levadia Tallinn (includes Levadia Maardu) 8; Flora Tallinn 5; Sadam 2; VMK Tallinn 2; Lantana (formerly Nikol) 1; Trans 1; Levadia Tallinn (pre-2004) 1; Norma 1.

Final League Table 2011

	P	*W*	*D*	*L*	*F*	*A*	*Pts*
Flora	36	26	8	2	100	24	86
Kalju	36	24	7	5	82	23	79
Trans	36	22	7	7	107	29	73
Levadia Tallinn	36	21	10	5	76	25	73
Kalev Sillamae	36	17	3	16	77	59	54
Paide	36	13	6	17	40	51	45
Tammeka	36	11	6	19	57	75	39
Viljandi	36	8	6	22	37	69	30
Kuressaare+	36	7	5	24	28	68	26
Ajax Lasnamae*	36	0	4	32	11	192	4

Top scorer: Cekulajevs (Trans) 46.
Cup Final: Trans 0, Levadia Tallinn 3.

FAEROE ISLANDS

Fotboltssamband Foroya, The Faeroes' Football Assn., Gundalur, P.O. Box 3028, FR-110, Torshavn.
Founded: 1979; *National Colours:* White shirts, blue shorts, white stockings.

International matches 2011
Slovenia (h) 0-2, Estonia (h) 2-0, Northern Ireland (a) 0-4, Italy (h) 0-1, Serbia (a) 1-3.

League Championship wins (1942–2011)
HB Torshavn 21; KI Klaksvik 17; B36 Torshavn 9; TB Tvoroyri 7; GI Gotu 6; B68 Toftir 3; SI Sorvag 1; IF Fuglafjordur 1; B71 Sandur 1; VB Vagur 1; NSI Runavik 1; EB/Streymur 1.

Cup wins (1955–2011)
HB Torshavn 26; GI Gotu 6; KI Klaksvik 5; TB Tvoroyri 5; B36 Torshavn 5; EB/Streymur 4; NSI Runavik 2; VB Vagur 1; B71 Sandur 1; Vikingur 1.

Final League Table 2011

	P	*W*	*D*	*L*	*F*	*A*	*Pts*
B36	27	21	4	2	63	28	67
EB/Streymur	27	19	3	5	66	33	60
Vikingur	27	18	5	4	62	31	59
NSI	27	11	8	8	58	47	41
KI	27	10	4	13	48	50	34
B68	27	9	5	13	44	44	32
IF	27	8	4	15	36	44	28
HB	27	7	5	15	46	56	26
07 Vestur*	27	6	6	15	30	65	24
B71*	27	3	2	22	25	80	11

Top scorer: Justinussen (Vikingur) 21.
Cup Final: EB/Streymur 3, IF 0.

FINLAND

Suomen Palloliitto Finlands Bollfoerbund, Urheilukatu 5, P.O. Box 191, Helsinki 00251.
Founded: 1907; *National Colours:* White shirts, blue shorts, white stockings.

International matches 2011
Belgium (a) 1-1, San Marino (a) 1-0, Portugal (a) 0-2, Sweden (a) 0-5, Latvia (a) 2-0, Moldova (h) 4-1, Holland (h) 0-2, Sweden (h) 1-2, Hungary (a) 0-0, Denmark (a) 1-2.

League Championship wins (1908–2011)
HJK Helsinki 24; Haka Valkeakoski 9; HPS Helsinki 9; TPS Turku 8; HIFK Helsinki 7; Tampere United (includes IKIssat and Ilves) 5; KuPS Kuopio 5; Kuusysi Lahti 5; KIF Helsinki 4; AIFK Turku 3; Reipas Lahti 3; VIFK Vaasa 3; Jazz Pori 2; KTP Kotka 2; OPS Oulu 2; VPS Vaasa 2; Unitas Helsinki 1; PUS Helsinki 1; Sudet Viipuri 1; HT Helsinki 1; Pyrkiva Turku 1; KPV Kokkola 1; TPV Tampere 1; MyPa Anjalankoski 1; Inter 1.

Cup wins (1955–2011)
Haka Valkeakoski 12; HJK Helsinki 11; Reipas Lahti 7; KTP Kotka 4; MyPa Anjalankoski 3; Tampere United (includes Ilves) 3; TPS Turku 3; KuPS Kuopio 2; Kuusysi Lahti 2; Mikkeli 2; PPojat 1; Drott (renamed Jaro) 1; HPS Helsinki 1; AIFK Turku 1; RoPS Rovaniemi 1; Jokerit (formerly PK-35) 1; Allianssi (formerly Atlantis) 1; Inter 1.

Final League Table 2011

	P	*W*	*D*	*L*	*F*	*A*	*Pts*
HJK Helsinki	33	26	3	4	86	23	81
Inter Turku	33	16	9	8	70	44	57
JJK	33	14	12	7	60	48	54
Honka	33	13	14	6	57	40	53
TPS Turku	33	13	11	9	48	44	50
KuPS	33	10	10	13	44	55	40
Mariehamn	33	10	8	15	39	47	38
MyPa	33	11	5	17	39	52	38
VPS	33	8	13	12	32	44	37
Haka	33	10	7	16	36	60	37
Jaro	33	7	10	16	49	64	31
RoPS*	33	5	8	20	39	78	23

Top scorer: Furuholm (Inter Turku) 22.
Cup Final: HJK Helsinki 2, KuPS 1.

FRANCE

Federation Francaise De Football, 60 Bis Avenue d'Iena, Paris 75116.
Founded: 1919; *National Colours:* Blue shirts, white shorts, red stockings.

International matches 2011
Brazil (h) 1-0, Luxembourg (a) 2-0, Croatia (h) 0-0, Belarus (a) 1-1, Ukraine (a) 4-1, Poland (a) 1-0, Chile (h) 1-1, Albania (a) 2-1, Romania (a) 0-0, Albania (h) 3-0, Bosnia (h) 1-1, USA (h) 1-0, Belgium (h) 0-0.

League Championship wins (1933–2012)
Saint Etienne 10; Olympique Marseille 9; Nantes 8; AS Monaco 7; Lyon 7; Stade de Reims 6; Girondins de Bordeaux 6; OGC Nice 4; Lille OSC (includes Olympique Lillois) 4; Paris St Germain 2; FC Sete 2; Sochaux 2; Racing Club Paris 1; Roubaix-Tourcoing 1; Strasbourg 1; Auxerre 1; Lens 1; Montpellier 1.

Cup wins (1918–2012)
Olympique Marseille 10; Paris St Germain 8; Saint Etienne 6; Lille OSC 6; AS Monaco 5; Racing Club Paris 5; Red Star 5; Lyon 5; Auxerre 4; Girondins de Bordeaux 3; OGC Nice 3; Nantes 3; Strasbourg 3; CAS Genereaux 2; Nancy 2; Sedan 2; FC Sete 2; Stade de Reims 2; SO Montpellier 2; Stade Rennes 2; Metz 2; Sochaux 2; AS Cannes 1; Club Français 1; Excelsior Roubaix 1; Le Havre 1; Olympique de Pantin 1; CA Paris 1; Toulouse 1; Bastia 1; Lorient 1; Guingamp 1.

Final League Table 2011–12

	P	*W*	*D*	*L*	*F*	*A*	*Pts*
Montpellier	38	25	7	6	68	34	82
Paris St Germain	38	23	10	5	75	41	79
Lille	38	21	11	6	72	39	74
Lyon	38	19	7	12	64	51	64
Bordeaux	38	16	13	9	53	41	61
Rennes	38	17	9	12	53	44	60
St Etienne	38	16	9	13	49	45	57
Toulouse	38	15	11	12	37	34	56

Evian TG	38	13	11	14	54	55	50
Marseille	38	12	12	14	45	41	48
Nancy	38	11	12	15	38	48	45
Valenciennes	38	12	7	19	40	50	43
Nice	38	10	12	16	39	46	42
Sochaux	38	11	9	18	40	60	42
Brest	38	8	17	13	31	38	41
Ajaccio	38	9	14	15	40	61	41
Lorient	38	9	12	17	35	49	39
Caen*	38	9	11	18	39	59	38
Dijon*	38	9	9	20	38	63	36
Auxerre*	38	7	13	18	46	57	34

Top scorers: Nene (Paris St Germain) 21, Giroud (Montpellier) 21.
Cup Final: Lyon 1, Quevilly 0.

GEORGIA

Georgian Football Federation, 76a Tchavtchavadze Avenue, Tbilisi 380062.
Founded: 1990; *National Colours:* All white.

International matches 2011
Armenia (h) 2-1, Croatia (h) 1-0, Israel (a) 0-1, Croatia (a) 1-2, Poland (a) 0-1, Latvia (h) 0-1, Malta (a) 1-1, Greece (h) 1-2, Moldova (h) 2-0.

League Championship wins (1990–2012)
Dinamo Tbilisi 13; Torpedo Kutaisi 3; WIT Georgia 2; Olimpi 2; Sioni 1; Zestafoni 1; Metalurg Rustavi 1.

Cup wins (1990–2012)
Dinamo Tbilisi 9; Lokomotivi 3; Torpedo Kutaisi 2; Ameri 2; Dynamo Batumi 1; Guria 1; Zestafoni 1; WIT 1; Gagra 1; Dila Gori 1.

Qualifying League Table 2011–12

	P	*W*	*D*	*L*	*F*	*A*	*Pts*
Zestafoni	22	17	3	2	45	17	54
Dinamo Tbilisi	22	14	3	5	44	24	45
Torpedo Kutaisi	22	13	4	5	33	19	43
Metalurg Rustavi	22	9	6	7	25	26	33
Merani	22	9	3	10	23	26	30
Baia	22	8	4	10	21	26	28
Dila Gori	22	7	5	10	29	28	26
Kolkheti	22	6	8	8	19	24	26
WIT	22	6	7	9	23	27	25
Spartaki	22	6	6	10	22	32	24
Gagra	22	6	3	13	21	32	21
Sioni	22	2	6	14	13	37	12

Championship Table 2011–12

	P	*W*	*D*	*L*	*F*	*A*	*Pts*
Metalurg Rustavi	28	17	4	7	39	28	55
Zestafoni	28	16	7	5	52	28	55
Torpedo Kutaisi	28	14	6	8	34	25	48
Dinamo Tbilisi	28	10	10	8	47	35	40
Dila Gori	28	10	7	11	38	32	37
Kolkheti	28	8	8	12	25	39	32
Baia	28	5	7	16	25	49	22
Merani	28	6	3	19	31	55	21

Top scorer: Dvali (Zestafoni) 20.
Cup Final: Dila Gori 4, Zestafoni 1.

GERMANY

Deutscher Fussball-Bund, Otto-Fleck-Schneise 6, Postfach 710265, Frankfurt Am Main 60492.
Founded: 1900; *National Colours:* White shirts, black shorts, white stockings.

International matches 2011
Italy (h) 1-1, Kazakhstan (h) 4-0, Australia (h) 1-2, Uruguay (h) 2-1, Austria (a) 2-1, Azerbaijan (a) 3-1, Brazil (h) 3-2, Austria (h) 6-2, Poland (a) 2-2, Turkey (a) 3-1, Belgium (h) 3-1, Ukraine (a) 3-3, Holland (h) 3-0.

League Championship wins (1903–2012)
Bayern Munich 22; 1.FC Nuremberg 9; Borussia Dortmund 8; Schalke 04 7; SV Hamburg 6; Borussia Moenchengladbach 5; VfB Stuttgart 5; 1.FC Kaiserslautern 4; Werder Bremen 4; VfB Leipzig 3; SpVgg Furth 3; 1.FC Cologne 3; Viktoria Berlin 2; Hertha Berlin 2; Hannover 96 2; Dresden SC 2; Munich 1860 1; Union Berlin 1; FC Freiburg 1; Phoenix Karlsruhe 1; Karlsruher FV 1; Holstein Kiel 1; Fortuna Dusseldorf 1; Rapid Vienna 1; VfR Mannheim 1; Rot-Weiss Essen 1; Eintracht Frankfurt 1; Eintracht Brunswick 1;Wolfsburg 1.

Cup wins (1935–2012)
Bayern Munich 15; Werder Bremen 6; 1.FC Cologne 4; Eintracht Frankfurt 4; Schalke 04 5; 1.FC Nuremberg 4; SV Hamburg 3; Moenchengladbach 3; VfB Stuttgart 3; Borussia Dortmund 3; Dresden SC 2; Fortuna Dusseldorf 2; Karlsruhe SC 2; Munich 1860 2; 1.FC Kaiserslautern 2; First Vienna 1; VfB Leipzig 1; Kickers Offenbach 1; Rapid Vienna 1; Rot-Weiss Essen 1; SW Essen 1; Bayer Uerdingen 1; Hannover 96 1; Leverkusen 1.

Final League Table 2011–12

	P	*W*	*D*	*L*	*F*	*A*	*Pts*
Borussia Dortmund	34	25	6	3	80	25	81
Bayern Munich	34	23	4	7	77	22	73
Schalke	34	20	4	10	74	44	64
Moenchengladbach	34	17	9	8	49	24	60
Leverkusen	34	15	9	10	52	44	54
Stuttgart	34	15	8	11	63	46	53
Hannover	34	12	12	10	41	45	48
Wolfsburg	34	13	5	16	47	60	44
Werder Bremen	34	11	9	14	49	58	42
Nuremberg	34	12	6	16	38	49	42
Hoffenheim	34	10	11	13	41	47	41
Freiburg	34	10	10	14	45	61	40
Mainz	34	9	12	13	47	51	39
Augsburg	34	8	14	12	36	49	38
Hamburg	34	8	12	14	35	57	36
Hertha Berlin+	34	7	10	17	38	64	31
Cologne*	34	8	6	20	39	75	30
Kaiserslautern*	34	4	11	19	24	54	23

Top scorer: Huntelaar (Schalke) 29.
Cup Final: Borussia Dortmund 5, Bayern Munich 2.

GIBRALTAR

Gibraltar Football Association, 32a Rosia Road, Gibraltar.
Founded: 1905. *National Colours:* Red shirts, white shorts, white stockings.

League Championship wins (1896–2012)
Prince of Wales 19; Glacis United 17; Britannia 14; Lincoln 12; Gibraltar United 11; Manchester United 7; Europa 6; Newcastle (formerly Lincoln) 5; St Theresas 3; Chief Construction 2; Exiles 2; Gibraltar FC 2; Jubilee 2; South United 2; Albion 1; Athletic 1; Commander of the Yard 1; Royal Soverign 1; St Joseph's 1.

Cup wins (1896–2012)
Lincoln 8; St Joseph's 8; Europa 5; Glacis United 5; Newcastle (formerly Lincoln) 4; Britannia 3; Gibraltar United 3; Manchester United 3; AARA 1; Gibraltar FC 1; HMS Hood 1; Lincoln ABG 1; Lincoln Reliance 1; Manchester United Reserves 1; Prince of Wales 1; St Theresas 1; 2nd Battalion RGS 1; 2nd Battalion The King's Regiment 1; 4th Battalion Royal Scots 1; RAF Gibraltar 1; RAF New Camp 1.

Final League Table 2011–12

	P	*W*	*D*	*L*	*F*	*A*	*Pts*
Lincoln	20	17	3	0	39	11	54
St Joseph's	20	10	8	2	29	15	38
Manchester U	20	9	4	7	19	18	31
Glacis U	20	7	4	9	23	24	25
Lions Gibraltar	20	4	6	10	21	21	18
Athletic Corinthians	20	0	1	19	11	53	1

Cup Final: St Joseph's 2, Lions Gibraltar 0.

GOZO

Gozo Football Association.
Founded: 1936.

League Championship wins (1938-2012)
Victoria Hotspurs 11; Nadur Youngsters 10; Sannat Lions 10; Ghajnsielem 6; Salesian Youths 6; Xewkija Tigers 5; Victoria Athletics 4; Xaghra United 4; Calypcians 1; Kercem Ajax 1; Victoria City 1; Victoria Stars 1; Victoria United 1; Xaghra Blue Stars 1; Xaghra Young Stars 1; Zebbug Rovers 1.

Cup wins (1972–2012)
Sannat Lions 9; Xewkija Tigers 8; Nadur Youngsters 7; Ghajnsielem 5; Xaghra United 4; S.K. Calyptians 1; Calypsians Bosco Youths 1; Victoria Hotspurs 1; Kercem Ajax 1; Quala St. Joseph 1.

Final League Table 2011-12

	P	W	D	L	F	A	Pts
Xewkija Tigers	17	13	3	1	46	15	42
Nadur Youngsters	17	13	2	2	58	27	41
Victoria Wanderers	17	5	6	6	31	31	21
Xaghra United	17	5	3	9	23	39	18
Sannat Lions	18	5	2	11	17	30	17
Victoria Hotspurs	18	4	4	10	24	40	16
Ghajnsielem	18	4	4	10	30	47	16

Cup Final: Xewkija Tigers 1, Xaghra United 0.

GREECE

Hellenic Football Federation, Singrou Avenue 137, Nea Smirni, 17121 Athens.
Founded: 1926; *National Colours:* Blue shirts, white shorts, blue stockings.

International matches 2011

Canada (h) 1-0, Malta (a) 1-0, Poland (h) 0-0, Malta (h) 3-1, Ecuador (h) 1-1, Bosnia (a) 0-0, Israel (a) 1-0, Latvia (a) 1-1, Croatia (h) 2-0, Georgia (a) 2-1, Russia (h) 1-1, Romania (a) 1-3.

League Championship wins (1928–2012)

Olympiakos 39; Panathinaikos 20; AEK Athens 11; Aris Salonika 3; PAOK Salonika 2; Larisa 1.

Cup wins (1932–2012)

Olympiakos 25; Panathinaikos 17; AEK Athens 14; PAOK Salonika 4; Panionios 2; Larisa 2; Aris Salonika 1; Ethnikos 1; Iraklis 1; Kastoria 1; OFI Crete 1.

Final League Table 2011–12

	P	W	D	L	F	A	Pts
Olympiakos	30	23	4	3	70	17	73
Panathinaikos	30	22	3	5	54	23	66
PAOK Salonika	30	14	8	8	45	27	50
Atromitos	30	13	11	6	32	26	50
AEK Athens	30	13	9	8	36	30	48
Asteras	30	13	6	11	30	34	45
Levadiakos	30	11	6	13	33	42	39
Giannina	30	10	8	12	30	35	38
Aris Salonika	30	10	10	10	29	33	37
OFI Crete	30	10	7	13	27	32	37
Xanthi	30	10	6	14	31	35	36
Panionios	30	9	6	15	26	34	33
Kerkyra	30	8	8	14	31	44	32
Ergotelis*	30	7	8	15	27	44	29
Panaitolikos*	30	7	7	16	23	37	28
Doxa*	30	4	5	21	11	42	17

Top scorer: Mirallas (Olympiakos) 20.
Cup Final: Atromitos 1, Olympiakos 2.

HOLLAND

Koninklijke Nederlandsche Voetbalbond, Woudenbergseweg 56–58, Postbus 515, NL-3700 AM, Zeist.
Founded: 1889; *National Colours:* Orange shirts, black shorts, orange stockings.

International matches 2011

Austria (h) 3-1, Hungary (a) 4-0, Hungary (h) 5-3, Brazil (a) 0-0, Uruguay (a) 1-1, San Marino (h) 11-0, Finland (a) 2-0, Moldova (h) 1-0, Sweden (a) 2-3, Switzerland (h) 0-0, Germany (a) 0-3.

League Championship wins (1898–2012)

Ajax Amsterdam 31; PSV Eindhoven 21; Feyenoord 14; HVV The Hague 8; Sparta Rotterdam 6; Go Ahead Deventer 4; HBS The Hague 3; Willem II Tilburg 3; RAP Amsterdam 2; RCH Heemstede 2; Heracles 2; ADO The Hague 2; AZ 67 Alkmaar 2; Quick The Hague 1; BVV Den Bosch 1; NAC Breda 1; Eindhoven 1; Enschede 1; Volewijckers Amsterdam 1; Limburgia 1; Rapid JC Den Heerlen 1; DOS Utrecht 1; DWS Amsterdam 1; Haarlem 1; SVV Schiedam 1; Be Quick Groningen 1; Twente 1.

Cup wins (1899–2012)

Ajax Amsterdam 18; Feyenoord 11; PSV Eindhoven 9; Quick The Hague 4; AZ 67 Alkmaar 3; Sparta Rotterdam 3; Utrecht 3; HFC Haarlem 3; Twente Enschede 3; DFC 2; Fortuna Geleen 2; Haarlem 2; HBS The Hague 2; RCH Haarlem 2; Roda JC 2; VOC 2; Wageningen 2; Willem II Tilburg 2; FC Den Haag (includes ADO) 2; Concordia Delft 1; CVV 1; Eindhoven 1; HVV The Hague 1; Longa 1; Quick Nijmegen 1; RAP Amsterdam 1; Roermond 1; Schoten 1; Velocitas Breda 1; Velocitas Groningen 1; VSV 1; VUC 1; VVV Groningen 1; ZFC Zaandam 1; NAC Breda 1; Heerenveen 1.

Final League Table 2011–12

	P	W	D	L	F	A	Pts
Ajax	34	23	7	4	93	36	76
Feyenoord	34	21	7	6	70	37	70
PSV Eindhoven	34	21	6	7	87	47	69
AZ	34	19	8	7	64	35	65
Heerenveen	34	18	10	6	79	59	64
Twente	34	17	9	8	82	46	60
Vitesse	34	15	8	11	48	43	53
NEC Nijmegen	34	13	6	15	42	45	45
Waalwijk	34	13	6	15	40	49	45
Roda JC	34	14	2	18	55	70	44
Utrecht	34	11	10	13	55	58	43
Heracles	34	11	7	16	52	62	40
NAC Breda	34	10	8	16	45	54	38
Groningen	34	10	7	17	41	61	37
Den Haag	34	8	8	18	38	67	32
VVV+	34	9	4	21	42	78	31
De Graafschap*+	34	6	6	22	36	74	24
Excelsior*	34	4	7	23	28	76	19

Top scorer: Dost (Heerenveen) 32.
Cup Final: PSV Eindhoven 3, Heracles 0.

HUNGARY

Hungarian Football Federation, Robert Karoly krt 61-65, Robert Haz Budapest 1134.
Founded: 1901; *National Colours:* Red shirts, white shorts, green stockings.

International matches 2011

Azerbaijan (h) 2-0, Holland (h) 0-4, Holland (a) 3-5, Luxembourg (a) 1-0, San Marino (a) 3-0, Iceland (a) 0-4, Sweden (h) 2-1, Moldova (a) 2-0, Finland (h) 0-0, Liechtenstein (h) 5-0, Poland (a) 1-2.

League Championship wins (1901–2012)

Ferencvaros 28; MTK-Hungaria Budapest 23; Ujpest 20; Kispest Honved 13; Vasas Budapest 6; Debrecen 6; Csepel 4; Raba Gyor 3; BTC 2; Nagyvarad 1; Vac 1; Dunaferr 1; Zalaegerszeg 1; Fehervar 1.

Cup wins (1910–2012)

Ferencvaros 20; MTK-Hungaria Budapest 12; Ujpest 8; Kispest Honved 7; Debrecen 5; Raba Gyor 4; Vasas Budapest 4; Diösgyör 2; Bocskai 1; III Ker 1; Soroksar 1; Szolnoki MAV 1; Siofok Banyasz 1; Bekescsaba 1; Pecsi 1; Matav 1; Fehervar 1; Kecskemeti 1.
Cup not regularly held until 1964.

Final League Table 2011–12

	P	W	D	L	F	A	Pts
Debrecen	30	22	8	0	64	18	74
Videoton	30	21	3	6	58	19	66
Gyor	30	20	3	7	56	31	63
Honved	30	13	7	10	48	40	46
Kecskemeti	30	13	6	11	48	38	45
Paksi	30	12	9	9	47	51	45
Diosgyor	30	13	4	13	42	43	43
Szombathelyi Haladas	30	9	11	10	39	37	38
Siofok	30	9	9	12	30	41	36
Kaposvari	30	7	14	9	35	42	35
Ferencvaros	30	9	7	14	31	36	34
Pecsi	30	8	10	12	36	50	34
Ujpest	30	8	8	14	34	46	32
Papa	30	8	6	16	26	40	30
Vasas*	30	5	9	16	29	51	22
Zalaegerszeg*	30	1	10	19	25	65	13

Top scorer: Coulibaly (Debrecen) 20.
Cup Final: MTK Budapest 3, Debrecen 3.
Debrecen won 8-7 on penalties.

ICELAND

Knattspyrnusamband Island, Laugardal, 104 Reykjavik.
Founded: 1929; *National Colours;* All blue.

International matches 2011

Cyprus (a) 0-0, Denmark (h) 0-2, Hungary (h) 4-0, Norway (a) 0-1, Cyprus (h) 1-0, Portugal (a) 3-5.

League Championship wins (1912–2011)

KR 25; Valur 20; Fram 18; IA Akranes 18; Vikingur 5; FH Hafnarfjordur 5; IBK Keflavik 4; IBV Vestmannaeyjar 3; KA Akureyri 1; Breidblik 1.

Cup wins (1960–2011)

KR 12; Valur 9; IA Akranes 9; Fram 7; IBV Vestmannaeyjar 4; IBK Keflavik 4; Fylkir 2; FH Hafnarfjordur 2; IBA Akureyri 1; Vikingur 1; Breidblik 1.

Final League Table 2011

	P	W	D	L	F	A	Pts
KR	22	13	8	1	44	22	47
FH	22	13	5	4	48	31	44
IBV	22	12	4	6	37	27	40
Stjarnan	22	10	7	5	51	35	37
Valur	22	10	6	6	28	23	36
Breidblik	22	7	6	9	34	42	27
Fylkir	22	7	4	11	34	44	25
Keflavik	22	7	3	12	27	32	24
Fram	22	6	6	10	20	28	24
Grindavik	22	5	8	9	26	37	23
Thor*	22	6	3	13	28	41	21
Vikingur*	22	3	6	13	24	39	15

Top scorer: Johannsson (Stjarnan) 15.
Cup Final: KR 2, Thor 0

REPUBLIC OF IRELAND

The Football Association of Ireland (Cumann Peile Na H-Eireann), National Sports Campus, Abbotstown, Dublin 15.
Founded: 1921; *National Colours:* Green shirts, white shorts, green and white stockings.

League Championship wins (1922–2011)
Shamrock Rovers 17; Shelbourne 13; Bohemians 10; Dundalk 9; Cork Athletic (formerly Cork United) 7; St Patrick's Athletic 7; Waterford 6; Drumcondra 5; St James's Gate 2; Sligo Rovers 2; Limerick 2; Athlone Town 2; Derry City 2; Cork City 2; Dolphin 1; Cork Hibernians 1; Cork Celtic 1; Drogheda United 1.

Cup wins (1922–2011)
Shamrock Rovers 24; Dundalk 9; Bohemians 8; Shelbourne 7; Drumcondra 5; Cork Athletic (formerly Cork United) 4; Derry City 4; Sligo 4; Cork City 2; St James's Gate 2; St Patrick's Athletic 2; Cork Hibernians 2; Limerick 2; Waterford 2; Bray Wanderers 2; Longford Town 2; Alton United 1; Athlone Town 1; Fordsons 1; Cork 1; Transport 1; Finn Harps 1; Home Farm 1; UCD 1; Galway United 1; Drogheda United 1; Sporting Fingal 1.

Final League Table 2011

	P	W	D	L	F	A	Pts
Shamrock Rovers	36	23	8	5	69	24	77
Sligo Rovers	36	22	7	7	73	19	73
Derry City	36	18	14	4	63	23	68
St Patrick's Ath	36	17	12	7	62	35	63
Bohemians	36	17	9	10	39	27	60
Bray Wanderers	36	15	6	15	53	50	51
Dundalk	36	11	11	14	50	53	44
UCD	36	10	4	22	42	80	34
Drogheda United	36	7	4	25	32	77	25
Galway United*+	36	1	3	32	20	115	6

Top scorer: Zayed (Derry City) 22.
Cup Final: Sligo Rovers 1, Shelbourne 1.
Sligo Rovers won 4-1 on penalties.

ISRAEL

Israel Football Association, Ramat-Gan Stadium, 299 Aba Hilell Street, Ramat-Gan 52134.
Founded: 1948; *National Colours:* Blue shirts, white shorts, blue stockings.

International matches 2011
Serbia (h) 0-2, Latvia (h) 2-1, Georgia (h) 1-0, Latvia (a) 2-1, Ivory Coast (a) 3-4, Greece (h) 0-1, Croatia (a) 1-3, Malta (a) 2-0.

League Championship wins (1932–2012)
Maccabi Tel Aviv 18; Maccabi Haifa 12; Hapoel Tel Aviv 10; Hapoel Petah Tikva 6; Beitar Jerusalem 6; Maccabi Netanya 5; Hakoah Ramat Gan 2; Hapoel Beersheba 2; Bnei Yehouda 1; British Police 1; Hapoel Kfar Saba 1; Hapoel Ramat Gan 1; Hapoel Haifa 1; Ironi Kiryat 1.

Cup wins (1928–2012)
Maccabi Tel Aviv 23; Hapoel Tel Aviv 16; Beitar Jerusalem 7; Maccabi Haifa 5; Hapoel Haifa 3; Hapoel Kfar Saba 3; Beitar Tel Aviv 2; Bnei Yehouda 2; Hakoah Ramat Gan 2; Hapoel Petah Tikva 2; Maccabi Petah Tikva 2; Maccabi Hashmonai Jerusalem 1; British Police 1; Gunners 1; Hapoel Jerusalem 1; Hapoel Yehud 1; Hapoel Lod 1; Maccabi Netanya 1; Hapoel Beersheba 1; Hapoel Ramat Gan 1; Hapoel Bnei Sakhnin 1.

Qualifying League Table 2011–12

	P	W	D	L	F	A	Pts
Ironi Kiryat	30	19	9	2	42	15	66
Hapoel Tel Aviv	30	14	10	6	53	27	49
Bnei Sakhnin	30	14	7	9	49	35	47
Ashdod	30	12	11	7	39	33	47
Maccabi Netanya	30	13	8	9	44	40	47
Maccabi Haifa	30	12	9	9	46	39	45
Maccabi Tel Aviv	30	13	5	12	41	32	44
Bnei Yehouda	30	11	10	9	38	27	43
Hapoel Acre	30	10	8	12	41	37	38
Ironi Ramat	30	9	10	11	29	38	37
Beitar Jerusalem	30	10	6	14	22	39	34
Hapoel Beersheba	30	9	5	16	33	54	32
Maccabi Petah Tikva	30	7	9	14	31	50	30
Hapoel Rishon	30	6	9	15	34	54	27
Hapoel Petah Tikva	30	6	10	14	28	45	19

Championship Play-Off Table 2011–12

	P	W	D	L	F	A	Pts
Ironi Kiryat	37	21	10	6	48	26	73
Hapoel Tel Aviv	37	16	14	7	63	35	59
Bnei Yehouda	37	16	11	10	53	36	59
Maccabi Netanya	37	17	8	12	54	48	59
Maccabi Haifa	37	16	10	11	56	44	58
Maccabi Tel Aviv	37	16	7	14	55	43	55
Ashdod	37	14	12	11	44	44	54
Bnei Sakhnin	37	15	7	15	60	53	50

Relegation Table 2011–12

	P	W	D	L	F	A	Pts
Beitar Jerusalem	37	15	7	15	32	44	50
Hapoel Acre	37	13	9	15	51	45	48
Ironi Ramat	37	11	13	13	37	45	46
Hapoel Haifa	37	11	11	15	41	43	44
Hapoel Beersheba	37	12	7	18	41	61	43
Maccabi Petah Tikva*	37	11	10	16	39	57	40
Hapoel Rishon*	37	6	9	22	39	70	27
Hapoel Petah Tikva*	37	8	11	18	36	55	26

Top scorer: Saba'a (Maccabi Netanya) 20.
Cup Final: Hapoel Tel Aviv 2, Maccabi Haifa 1.

ITALY

Federazione Italiana Giuoco Calcio, Via Gregorio Allegri 14, Roma 00198.
Founded: 1898; *National Colours:* Blue shirts, white shorts, blue stockings.

International matches 2011
Germany (a) 1-1, Slovenia (a) 1-0, Ukraine (a) 2-0, Estonia (h) 3-0, Republic of Ireland (a) 0-2, Spain (h) 2-1, Faeroes (a) 1-0, Slovenia (h) 1-0, Serbia (a) 1-1, Northern Ireland (h) 3-0, Poland (a) 2-0, Uruguay (h) 0-1.

League Championship wins (1898–2012)
Juventus 28 (excludes two titles revoked); Internazionale 18 (includes one title awarded); AC Milan 18; Genoa 9; Torino 7 (excludes one title revoked); Pro Vercelli 7; Bologna 7; AS Roma 3; Fiorentina 2; Lazio 2; Napoli 2; Casale 1; Novese 1; Cagliari 1; Verona 1; Sampdoria 1.

Cup wins (1928–2012)
AS Roma 9; Juventus 9; Internazionale 7; Fiorentina 6; AC Milan 5; Torino 5; Lazio 5; Sampdoria 4; Napoli 4; Parma 3; Bologna 2; Atalanta 1; Genoa 1; Vado 1; Venezia 1; Vicenza 1.

Final League Table 2011–12

	P	W	D	L	F	A	Pts
Juventus	38	23	15	0	68	20	84
AC Milan	38	24	8	6	74	33	80
Udinese	38	18	10	10	52	35	64
Lazio	38	18	8	12	56	47	62
Napoli	38	16	13	9	66	46	61
Internazionale	38	17	7	14	58	55	58
Roma	38	16	8	14	60	54	56
Parma	38	15	11	12	54	53	56
Bologna	38	13	12	13	41	43	51
Chievo	38	12	13	13	35	45	49
Catania	38	11	15	12	47	52	48
Atalanta	38	13	13	12	41	43	46
Fiorentina	38	11	13	14	37	43	46
Siena	38	11	11	16	45	45	44
Cagliari	38	10	13	15	37	46	43
Palermo	38	11	10	17	52	62	43
Genoa+	38	11	9	18	50	69	42
Lecce*	38	8	12	18	40	56	36
Novara*	38	7	11	20	35	65	32
Cesena*	38	4	10	24	24	60	22

Top scorer: Ibrahimovic (AC Milan) 28.
Cup Final: Juventus 0, Napoli 2.

KAZAKHSTAN

The Football Union of Kazakhstan, Satpayev Street, 29/3 Almaty 480 072, Kazakhstan.
Founded: 1914; *National Colours:* Blue shirts, blue shorts, yellow stockings.

International matches 2011
Belarus (a) 1-1, Germany (a) 0-4, Azerbaijan (h) 2-1, Syria (h) 1-1, Turkey (a) 1-2, Azerbaijan (a) 2-3, Belgium (a) 1-4, Austria (h) 0-0.

League Championship wins (1992–2011)
Irtysh (includes Ansat) 5; Aqtobe 5; Yelimai 3; Astana (includes Zhenis) 3; Kairat 2; Taraz 1; Tobol 1; Shakhtyor 1.

Cup wins (1992–2011)
Kairat 5; Astana (includes Zhenis) 3; Dostyk 1; Vostok 1; Yelimai 1; Irtysh 1; Kaisar 1; Taraz 1; Almaty 1; Tobol 1; Aqtobe 1; Atirau 1; Lokomotiv Astana 1; Ordabasy 1.

Qualifying League Table 2011

	P	*W*	*D*	*L*	*F*	*A*	*Pts*
Zhetysu	22	15	4	3	39	16	49
Astana	22	13	6	3	35	19	45
Shakhtyor	22	13	3	6	35	20	42
Aqtobe	22	12	5	5	39	19	41
Yertis	22	11	3	8	38	34	36
Ordabasy	22	8	7	7	28	19	31
Tobol	22	8	3	11	30	28	27
Taraz	22	6	3	13	15	24	21
Kairat	22	5	5	12	20	37	20
Atirau	22	4	8	10	15	30	20
Vostok	22	3	9	10	15	32	18
Kaisar	22	4	4	14	13	44	16

Championship Play-Off 2011

	P	*W*	*D*	*L*	*F*	*A*	*Pts*
Shakhtyor	32	19	6	7	52	29	42
Zhetysu	32	19	5	8	51	27	38
Aqtobe	32	15	9	8	53	31	34
Astana	32	16	7	9	50	37	33
Yertis	32	15	5	12	50	50	32
Ordabasy	32	11	10	11	41	36	28

Relegation Play-Off 2011

	P	*W*	*D*	*L*	*F*	*A*	*Pts*
Tobol	32	14	3	15	48	44	32
Kaisar	32	10	5	17	29	53	27
Taraz	32	10	5	17	30	39	25
Atirau	32	8	10	14	28	43	24
Kairat*	32	8	8	16	30	49	22
Vostok*	32	5	11	16	23	47	17

Top scorer: Bakayev (Zhetysu) 18.
Cup Final: Ordabasy 1, Tobol 0.

KOSOVO

Football Federation Kosova, Agim Ramadani 45, Prishtina, Kosovo 10000.
Founded: 1946; *National Colours:* Blue shirts, white shorts, blue stockings.

League Championship wins (1945–2012)
Prishtina 13; Vellaznimi 9; Trepca 7; Liria 5; Buduqnosti 4; Red Star 3; Rudari 3; Besa 3; Fushe-Kosova 2; Jedinstvo 2; Kosova Prishtina 2; Obiliqi 2; Slloga 2; Besiana 1; Drita 1; Dukagjini 1; KNI Ramiz Sadiku 1; KXEK Kosova 1; Proletari 1; Rudniku 1; Hysi 1.

Cup wins (1992–2012)
Liria 3; Besa 2; Flamurtari 2; Prishtina 2; Besiana 1; Drita 1; Gjilani 1; KEK-u 1; Kosova Prishtina 1; Trepca 1; Vellaznimi 1; Hysi 1; Trepca 89 1.

Superliga Final League Table 2011–12

	P	*W*	*D*	*L*	*F*	*A*	*Pts*
Prishtina	33	19	8	6	63	31	65
Trepca 89	33	17	10	6	54	29	61
Vellaznimi	33	15	10	8	43	38	55
Besa	33	13	9	11	46	40	48
Hysi	33	14	5	14	50	41	47
Drita	33	13	8	12	44	42	47
Drenica	33	13	7	13	42	32	46
Liria	33	13	5	15	44	50	44
Trepca	33	12	7	14	39	44	43
Lepenci+	33	11	9	13	35	42	42
KEK-u*	33	7	7	19	38	66	28
Gjilani*	33	6	5	22	25	68	23

Cup Final: Trepca 89 3, Ferizaj 0.

LATVIA

Latvian Football Federation, Augsiela 1, LV-1009, Riga.
Founded: 1921; *National Colours:* Carmine red shirts, white shorts, carmine red stockings.

International matches 2011
Bolivia (h) 2-1, Israel (a) 1-2, Israel (h) 1-2, Austria (a) 1-3, Finland (h) 0-2, Georgia (a) 1-0, Greece (h) 1-1, Malta (h) 2-0, Croatia (a) 0-2.

League Championship wins (1922–2011)
Skonto Riga 15; ASK Riga 9; RFK Riga 8; Sarkanais Metalurgs Liepaya 8; Olympija Liepaya 7; VEF Riga 6; Energija Riga 4; FK Ventspils 4; Elektrons Riga 3; Torpedo Riga 3; Daugava Liepaya 2; ODO Riga 2; Khimikis Daugavpils 2; RAF Yelgava 2; Keisermezhs Riga 2; Dinamo Riga 1; Zhmilyeva Team 1; Darba Rezervi 1; RER Riga 1; Starts Brotseni 1; Venta Ventspils 1; Yurnieks Riga 1; Alta Riga 1; Gauja Valmiera 1; Metalurgs Liepaya 1.

Cup wins (1937–2012)
Skonto Riga 8; Elektrons Riga 7; Sarkanais Metalurgs Liepaya 5; FK Ventspils 5; ODO Riga 3; VEF Riga 3; ASK Riga 3; Tseltnieks Riga 3; RAF Yelgava 3; RFK Riga 2; Daugava Liepaya 2; Starts Brotseni 2; Selmash Liepaya 2; Yurnieks Riga 2; Khimikis Daugavpils 2; Rigas Vilki 1; Dinamo Liepaya 1; Dinamo Riga 1; RER Riga 1; Voulkan Kouldiga 1; Baltika Liepaya 1; Venta Ventspils 1; Pilots Riga 1; Lielupe Yurmala 1; Energija Riga 1; Torpedo Riga 1; Daugava SKIF Riga 1; Tseltnieks Daugavpils 1; Olympija Riga 1; FK Riga 1; Metalurgs Liepaya 1; Daugava Daugavpils 1; Jelgava 1.

Final League Table 2011

	P	*W*	*D*	*L*	*F*	*A*	*Pts*
FK Ventspils	32	22	5	5	75	19	71
Metalurgs Liepaya	32	22	4	6	72	26	70
Daugava Daugavpils	32	19	6	7	58	30	63
Skonto Riga	32	17	9	6	62	21	60
FC Jurmala	32	12	8	12	46	43	44
Jelgava	32	13	4	15	47	54	43
Gulbene 2005	32	7	7	18	39	67	28
FK Jurmala	32	5	6	21	35	76	21
RFS/Olimps+	32	1	3	28	19	117	6

Top scorer: Nathan Junior (Skonto Riga) 22.
Cup Final: Skonto Riga 1, Metalurgs Liepaya 1.
Skonto Riga won 4-3 on penalties.

LIECHTENSTEIN

Liechtensteiner Fussball-Verband, Malbuner Huus Altenbach 11, Postfach 165, 9490 Vaduz.
Founded: 1934; *National Colours:* Blue shirts, red shorts, blue stockings.

International matches 2011
San Marino (a) 1-0, Czech Republic (a) 0-2, Lithuania (h) 2-0, Switzerland (h) 1-2, Lithuania (a) 0-0, Spain (a) 0-6, Scotland (h) 0-1, Hungary (a) 0-5.
Liechtenstein has no national league. Teams compete in Swiss regional leagues.

Cup wins (1937–2012)
Vaduz 40; Balzers 11; Triesen 8; Eschen/Mauren 5; Schaan 3.
Cup Final: Vaduz 2, Eschen/Mauren 2
Eschen/Mauren won 4-2 on penalties.

LITHUANIA

Lithuanian Football Federation, Seimyniskiu str. 15, 2005 Vilnius.
Founded: 1922; *National Colours:* Yellow shirts, green shorts, yellow stockings.

International matches 2011
Poland (h) 2-0, Spain (h) 1-3, Liechtenstein (a) 0-2, Norway (a) 0-1, Armenia (h) 3-0, Lithuania (a) 0-0, Scotland (a) 0-1, Czech Republic (h) 1-4.

League Championship wins (1990–2011)
FBK Kaunas 8 (including Zalgiris Kaunas 1); Ekranas Panevezys 6; Zalgiris Vilnius 3; Kareda 2; Inkaras Kaunas 2; Sirijus Klaipeda 1; ROMAR Mazeikiai 1.

Cup wins (1990–2012)
Zalgiris Vilnius 6; FBK Kaunas 4; Ekranas Panevezys 4; Kareda 2; Atlantas 2; Suduva 2; Sirijus Klaipeda 1; Lietuvos Makabi Vilnius 1; Inkaras Kaunas 1.

Final League Table 2011

	P	W	D	L	F	A	Pts
Ekranas	33	24	8	1	68	14	80
Zalgiris	33	22	6	5	56	17	72
Suduva	33	19	8	6	70	19	65
Siauliai	33	16	11	6	45	30	59
Kruoja	33	13	10	10	43	34	49
Banga	33	13	7	13	51	37	46
Tauras	33	11	12	10	50	38	45
Dainava	33	13	6	14	53	54	45
Mazeikiai*	33	9	9	15	36	54	36
Kaunas* (–6)	33	8	8	17	41	53	26
Atlantas*	33	3	2	28	28	121	11
Klaipeda*	33	2	3	28	19	89	9

Top scorer: Matulevicius (Zalgiris) 19.
Cup Final: Zalgiris 0, Ekranas 0
Zalgiris won 3-1 on penalties.

LUXEMBOURG

Federation Luxembourgeoise De Football (F.L.F.), 68 Rue De Gasperich, Luxembourg 1617.
Founded: 1908; *National Colours:* All red.

International matches 2011
Slovakia (h) 2-1, France (h) 0-2, Romania (a) 1-3, Hungary (h) 0-1, Belarus (a) 0-2, Portugal (a) 0-5, Romania (h) 0-2, Albania (h) 2-1, Bosnia (a) 0-5, Switzerland (h) 0-1.

League Championship wins (1910–2012)
Jeunesse Esch 28; Spora Luxembourg 11; Stade Dudelange 10; F91 Dudelange 10; Red Boys Differdange 6; Union Luxembourg 6; Avenir Beggen 6; US Hollerich-Bonnevoie 5; Fola Esch 5; Aris Bonnevoie 3; Progres Niedercorn 3; Sporting Club 2; Racing Club 1; National Schifflange 1; Grevenmacher 1.

Cup wins (1922–2012)
Red Boys Differdange 16 (now Differdange 03); Jeunesse Esch 12; Union Luxembourg 10; Spora Luxembourg 8; Avenir Beggen 7; F91 Dudelange 5; Stade Dudelange 4; Progres Niedercorn 4; Grevenmacher 4; Fola Esch 3; Alliance Dudelange 2; US Rumelange 2; Aris Bonnevoie 1; US Dudelange 1; Jeunesse Hautcharage 1; National Schifflange 1; Racing Club 1; SC Tetange 1; Swift Hesperange 1; Etzella Ettelbruck 1; CS Petange 1; FC Differdange 1.

Final League Table 2011–12

	P	W	D	L	F	A	Pts
F91 Dudelange	26	16	6	4	67	20	54
Jeunesse Esch	26	15	6	5	56	37	51
Grevenmacher	26	14	7	5	50	27	49
Differdange	26	13	9	4	64	26	48
Kaerjeng	26	12	7	7	37	35	43
Fola Esch	26	10	8	8	41	30	38
Hamm Benfica	26	12	2	12	54	47	38
Petange	26	10	6	10	29	37	36
Proges	26	9	6	11	32	35	33
Racing	26	7	11	8	40	41	32
Union Kayl-Tetange	26	8	5	13	39	51	29
Hesperange*+	26	7	5	14	34	53	26
Rumelange*	26	5	4	17	27	71	19
Ostert*	26	2	2	22	22	82	8

Top scorer: Rafik (Differdange) 23.
Cup Final: F91 Dudelange 4, Jeunesse Esch 2.

MACEDONIA

Football Association of Macedonia, VIII-ma Udarna Brigada 31-A, Skopje 1000.
Founded: 1948; *National Colours:* All red.

International matches 2011
Cameroon (h) 0-1, Republic of Ireland (a) 1-2, Republic of Ireland (h) 0-2, Azerbaijan (a) 1-0, Russia (a) 0-1, Andorra (h) 1-0, Armenia (a) 1-4, Slovakia (h) 1-1, Albania (h) 0-0.

League Championship wins (1993–2012)
Vardar 6; Sileks 3; Sloga Jugomagnat 3; Rabotnicki 3; Pobeda 2; Makedonija 1; Renova 1; Skendija 79 1.

Cup wins (1993–2012)
Vardar 5; Sloga Jugomagnat 3; Sileks 2; Rabotnicki 2; Pelister 1; Pobeda 1; Cement 1; Baskimi 1; Makedonija 1; Teteks 1; Metalurg 1; Renova 1.

Final League Table 2011–12

	P	W	D	L	F	A	Pts
Vardar	33	22	10	1	50	15	76
Metalurg	33	19	10	4	53	16	67
Skendija 79	33	20	6	7	53	28	66
Renova	33	13	13	7	56	38	52
Bregalnica	33	13	6	14	51	47	45
Sileks	33	13	3	17	42	51	42
Napredok	33	12	6	15	37	51	42
Rabotnicki	33	11	8	14	50	45	41
Turnovo+	33	10	8	15	34	42	38
Teteks+	33	8	11	14	23	48	35
Ohrid*	33	6	8	19	26	62	26
Oktomvri*	33	3	7	23	26	58	16

Top scorer: Ivanovski (Vardar) 24.
Cup Final: Renova 3, Rabotnicki 1.

MALTA

Malta Football Association, 280 St Paul Street, Valletta VLT07.
Founded: 1900; *National Colours:* Red shirts, white shorts, red stockings.

International matches 2011
Switzerland (h) 0-0, Greece (h) 0-1, Greece (a) 1-3, Central Africa (h) 2-1, Croatia (h) 1-3, Georgia (h) 1-1, Latvia (a) 0-2, Israel (h) 0-2.

League Championship wins (1910–2012)
Sliema Wanderers 26; Floriana 25; Valletta 21; Hibernians 10; Hamrun Spartans 7; Birkirkara 3; Rabat Ajax 2; St George's 1; KOMR 1; Marsaxlokk 1.

Cup wins (1935–2012)
Sliema Wanderers 20; Floriana 19; Valletta 12; Hibernians 9; Hamrun Spartans 6; Birkirkara 4; Gzira United 1; Melita 1; Zurrieq 1; Rabat Ajax 1.

Qualifying League Table 2011–12

	P	W	D	L	F	A	Pts
Valletta	22	17	4	1	52	17	55
Hibernians	22	15	6	1	55	16	51
Floriana	22	12	6	4	34	19	42
Sliema Wanderers	22	8	11	3	34	24	35
Birkirkara	22	11	2	9	34	29	35
Balzan Youths	22	9	4	9	28	34	31
Qormi	22	9	2	11	36	37	29
Mosta	22	6	5	11	23	35	23
Mqabba	22	5	5	12	25	43	20
Hamrun Spartans	22	5	4	13	31	52	19
Tarxien Rainbows	22	5	3	14	26	44	18
Marsaxlokk	22	3	2	17	25	53	11

Championship Table 2011–12

	P	W	D	L	F	A	Pts
Valletta	32	25	5	2	75	24	53
Hibernians	32	22	6	4	74	26	47
Birkirkara	32	17	4	11	55	37	38
Floriana	32	16	6	10	47	35	33
Sliema Wanderers	32	9	14	9	47	47	24
Balzan Youths	32	9	6	17	36	67	18

Relegation Table 2011–12

	P	W	D	L	F	A	Pts
Qormi	32	15	2	15	54	48	33
Mosta	32	10	8	14	45	47	27
Tarxien Rainbows	32	11	3	18	45	54	27
Hamrun Spartans	32	9	7	16	47	71	25
Mqabba*	32	9	7	16	40	55	24
Marsaxlokk*	32	5	2	25	34	88	8

Top scorer: Obiefule (Mosta) 34 (including 10 for Marsaxlokk).
Cup Final: Qormi 1, Hibernians 3.

MOLDOVA

Football Association of Moldova, 39 Tricolorului Str, 2012, Chisinau.
Founded: 1990; *National Colours:* Red shirts, blue shorts, red stockings.

International matches 2011
Poland (a) 0-1, Andorra (h) 2-1, Sweden (a) 1-2, Sweden (h) 1-4, Cyprus (a) 2-3, Finland (a) 1-4, Hungary (h) 0-2, Holland (a) 0-1, San Marino (h) 4-0, Georgia (a) 0-2.

League Championship wins (1992–2012)
Sheriff 11; Zimbru Chisinau 8; Constructorul 1; Dacia 1.

Cup wins (1992–2012)
Sheriff 7; Zimbru Chisinau 5; Tiligul 3; Constructorul 2; Comrat 1; Nistru Otaci 1; Iscra-Stali 1; Milsami-Ursidos 1.

Final League Table 2011–12

	P	*W*	*D*	*L*	*F*	*A*	*Pts*
Sheriff	33	25	6	2	75	18	81
Dacia	33	24	5	4	63	17	77
Zimbru Chisinau	33	17	10	6	47	24	61
Milsami-Ursidos	33	14	5	14	41	37	47
Olimpia	33	10	15	8	26	27	45
Tiraspol	33	10	12	11	36	32	42
Iscra-Stali	33	11	7	15	41	48	40
Nistru	33	10	9	14	30	41	39
Academia	33	6	13	14	32	48	31
Sfintul*	33	7	9	17	23	55	30
CSCA-Rapid	33	6	8	19	20	52	26
Costuleni	33	3	11	19	19	54	20

Sfintul did not obtain a licence for 2012–13 and were relegated.
Top scorer: Balima (Sheriff) 18.
Cup Final: CSCA-Rapid 0, Milsami-Ursidos 0.
Milsami-Ursidos won 5-3 on penalties.

MONTENEGRO

Football Association of Montenegro.
Founded: 1931.

International matches 2011

Uzbekistan (h) 1-0, Bulgaria (h) 1-1, Albania (a) 2-3, Wales (a) 1-2, England (h) 2-2, Switzerland (a) 0-2, Czech Republic (a) 0-2, Czech Republic (h) 0-1.

League Championship wins (2006–12)

Mogren 2; Buducnost 2; Zeta 1; Rudar 1.

Cup wins (2006–12)

Rudar 3; Mogren 1; Petrovac 1; Celik 1.

Final League Table 2011–12

	P	*W*	*D*	*L*	*F*	*A*	*Pts*
Buducnost	33	25	5	3	82	25	80
Rudar	33	23	8	2	60	20	77
Zeta	33	17	9	7	55	40	60
Mogren	33	15	9	9	54	37	54
Petrovac	33	13	9	11	36	39	48
Lovcen	33	10	10	13	32	42	40
Mladost	33.	10	7	16	32	45	37
Sutjeska	33	9	9	15	29	36	36
Decic*+	33	10	4	19	34	51	34
Grbalj	33	9	7	17	28	49	34
Berane*+ (–1)	33	8	5	20	32	54	28
Bokelj*	33	5	6	22	21	57	21

Top scorer: Adrovic (Buducnost) 22.
Cup Final: Celik 2, Rudar 1.

NORTHERN CYPRUS

Turkish Republic of Northern Cyprus.
Founded: 1955; *National Colours:* All red with white trim.

League Championship wins (1956–63; 1969–74; 1976–2012)

Cetinkaya 14; Gonyeli 9; Magusa 7; Dogan 6; Yenicami 5; BAF Ulku 4; Kucuk 4; Akincilar 1; Binatli 1.

Cup wins (1956-2011)

Cetinkaya 17; Gonyeli 8; Kucuk 6; Magusa 5; Yenicami 5; Turk Ocagi 4; Dogan 2; Binatli 1; Genclik 1; Lefke 1; Yalova 1.

Final League Table 2011–12

	P	*W*	*D*	*L*	*F*	*A*	*Pts*
Cetinkaya	26	19	4	3	61	21	61
Magusa	26	15	7	4	54	29	52
Kucuk	26	16	3	7	47	29	51
Yenicami	26	15	2	9	62	35	47
Cihangir	26	14	3	9	46	46	45
Lefke	26	11	6	9	45	36	39
Dogan Turk	26	11	6	9	54	47	39
Bagcil	26	9	10	7	40	32	37
Lapta	26	9	6	11	33	37	33
Ocagi	26	6	8	12	41	63	26
Duzkaya	26	6	6	14	35	52	24
Gocmenkov	26	6	5	15	25	55	23
Tatlisu	26	6	3	17	34	57	21
Gonyeli	26	3	3	20	29	67	12

Top scorer: Massa (Yenicami) 29.
Cup Final: Dogan Turk 2, Kucuk 2.
Dogan Turk won 6-4 on penalties.

NORTHERN IRELAND

Irish Football Association Ltd, 20 Windsor Avenue, Belfast BT9 6EE.
Founded: 1880; *National Colours:* Green shirts, white shorts, green stockings.

NORWAY

Norges Fotballforbund, Ullevaal Stadion, Sognsveien 75J, Serviceboks 1, Oslo 0855.
Founded: 1902; *National Colours:* Red shirts, white shorts, blue stockings.

International matches 2011

Poland (a) 0-1, Denmark (h) 1-1, Portugal (a) 0-1, Lithuania (h) 1-0, Czech Republic (h) 3-0, Iceland (h) 1-0, Denmark (a) 0-2, Cyprus (h) 3-1, Wales (a) 1-4.

League Championship wins (1938–2011)

Rosenborg Trondheim 22; Fredrikstad 9; Viking Stavanger 8; Lillestrom 5; Valerenga 5; Larvik Turn 3; Brann Bergen 3; Lyn Oslo 2; IK Start 2; Freidig 1; Fram 1; Skeid Oslo 1; Strömsgodset Drammen 1; Moss 1; Stabaek 1; Molde 1.

Cup wins (1902–2011)

Odd Grenland 12; Fredrikstad 11; Rosenborg Trondheim 9; Lyn Oslo 8; Skeid Oslo 8; Rosenborg Trondheim 8; Sarpsborg 6; Brann Bergen 6; Viking Stavanger 5; Lillestrom 5; Orn Horten 4; Strömsgodset Drammen 5; Valerenga 4; Frigg 3; Mjondalen 3; Bodo/Glimt 2; Mercantile 2; Tromso 2; Molde 2; Aalesund 2; Grane Nordstrand 1; Kvik Halden 1; Sparta 1; Gjovik/Lyn 1; Moss 1; Bryne 1; Stabaek 1.
(Known as the Norwegian Championship for HM The King's Trophy).

Final League Table 2011

	P	*W*	*D*	*L*	*F*	*A*	*Pts*
Molde	30	17	7	6	55	38	58
Tromso	30	15	8	7	56	34	53
Rosenborg	30	14	7	9	69	44	49
Brann	30	14	6	10	51	49	48
Odd	30	14	6	10	44	44	48
Haugesund	30	14	5	11	55	43	47
Valerenga	30	14	5	11	42	33	47
Stromsgodset	30	12	9	9	44	43	45
Aalesund	30	12	7	11	36	38	43
Stabaek	30	11	6	13	44	50	39
Viking	30	9	10	11	33	40	37
Fredrikstad	30	10	6	14	38	41	36
Lillestrom	30	9	7	14	46	52	34
Sogndal	30	8	10	12	24	31	34
Start*	30	7	5	18	39	61	26
Sarpsborg 08*	30	5	6	19	31	65	21

Top scorer: Abdellaoue (Tromso) 17.
Cup Final: Brann 1, Aalesund 2.

POLAND

Polish Football Association, Polski Zwiazek Pilki Noznej, Miodowa 1, Warsaw 00-080.
Founded: 1919; *National Colours:* White shirts, red shorts, white stockings.

International matches 2011

Moldova (h) 1-0, Norway (h) 1-0, Lithuania (a) 0-2, Greece (a) 0-0, Argentina (h) 2-1, France (h) 0-1, Georgia (h) 1-0, Mexico (h) 1-1, Germany (h) 2-2, South Korea (a) 2-2, Belarus (h) 2-0, Italy (h) 0-2, Hungary (h) 2-1.

League Championship wins (1921–2012)

Gornik Zabrze 14; Ruch Chorzow 14; Wisla Krakow 14; Legia Warsaw 8; Lech Poznan 6; Cracovia 5; Pogon Lwow 4; Widzew Lodz 4; Warta Poznan 2; Polonia Bytom 2; Stal Mielec 2; LKS Lodz 2; Polonia Warsaw 2; Zaglebie Lubin 2; Slask Wroclaw 2; Garbarnia Krakow 1; Szombierki Bytom 1.

Cup wins (1951–2012)

Legia Warsaw 15; Gornik Zabrze 6; Lech Poznan 5; Zaglebie Sosnowiec 4; GKS Katowice 3; Ruch Chorzow 3; Amica Wronki 3; Wisla Krakow 3; Slask Wroclaw 2; Polonia Warsaw 2; Groclin 2; Gwardia Warsaw 1; LKS Lodz 1; Stal Rzeszow 1; Arka Gdynia 1; Lechia Gdansk 1; Widzew Lodz 1; Miedz Legnica 1; Wisla Plock 1; Jagiellonia 1.

Final League Table 2011–12

	P	*W*	*D*	*L*	*F*	*A*	*Pts*
Slask	30	17	5	8	47	31	56
Ruch	30	16	7	7	44	28	55
Legia	30	15	8	7	42	17	53
Lech	30	15	7	8	42	22	52
Korona	30	13	9	8	34	29	48
Polonia W	30	13	6	11	33	32	45

	P	W	D	L	F	A	Pts
Wisla	30	12	7	11	29	26	43
Gornik Zabrze	30	11	9	10	36	30	42
Zaglebie	30	11	7	12	36	42	40
Jagiellonia	30	11	6	13	35	45	39
Widzew	30	9	12	9	25	26	39
Podbeskidzie	30	9	8	13	26	39	35
Lechia	30	7	10	13	21	30	31
GKS Belchatow	30	7	10	13	34	36	31
Lodzki*	30	5	9	16	23	53	24
Cracovia*	30	4	10	16	20	41	22

Top scorer: Rudnevs (Lech) 22.
Cup Final: Legia 3, Ruch 0.

PORTUGAL

Federacao Portuguesa De Futebol, Praca De Alegria N.25, Apartado 21.100, P-1127, Lisboa 1250-004.
Founded: 1914; *National Colours:* Red shirts, green shorts, red stockings.

International matches 2011
Argentina (a) 1-2, Chile (h) 1-1, Finland (h) 2-0, Norway (h) 1-0, Luxembourg (h) 5-0, Cyprus (a) 4-0, Iceland (h) 5-3, Denmark (a) 1-2, Bosnia (a) 0-0, Bosnia (h) 6-2.

League Championship wins (1935–2012)
Benfica 32; FC Porto 26; Sporting Lisbon 18; Belenenses 1; Boavista 1.

Cup wins (1939–2012)
Benfica 24; FC Porto 16; Sporting Lisbon 15; Boavista 5; Belenenses 3; Vitoria Setubal 3; Academica Coimbra 2; Leixoes 1; Sporting Braga 1; Estrela Amadora 1; Beira Mar 1.

Final League Table 2011–12

	P	W	D	L	F	A	Pts
Porto	30	23	6	1	69	19	75
Benfica	30	21	6	3	66	27	69
Braga	30	19	5	6	59	29	62
Sporting Lisbon	30	18	5	7	47	26	59
Maritimo	30	14	8	8	41	38	50
Guimaraes	30	14	3	13	40	40	45
Nacional	30	13	5	12	48	50	44
Olhanense	30	9	12	9	36	38	39
Gil Vicente	30	8	10	12	31	42	34
Pacos de Ferreira	30	8	7	15	35	53	31
Setubal	30	8	6	16	24	49	30
Academica	30	7	8	15	27	38	29
Beira-Mar	30	8	5	17	26	38	29
Rio Ave	30	7	7	16	33	42	28
Feirense*	30	5	9	16	27	49	24
Uniao de Leiria*	30	5	4	21	25	56	19

Top scorers: Cardozo (Benfica), Lima (Braga) 20.
Cup Final: Sporting Lisbon 0, Academica 1.

ROMANIA

Federatia Romana De Fotbal, House of Football, Str. Serg. Serbanica Vasile 12, Bucharest 73412.
Founded: 1909; *National Colours:* All yellow.

International matches 2011
Ukraine (h) 2-2, Cyprus (a) 1-1, Bosnia (a) 1-2, Luxembourg (h) 3-1, Bosnia (h) 3-0, Brazil (a) 0-1, Paraguay (a) 0-2, San Marino (a) 1-0, Luxembourg (a) 2-0, France (h) 0-0, Belarus (h) 2-2, Albania (a) 1-1, Belgium (a) 1-2, Greece (h) 3-1.

League Championship wins (1910–2012)
Steaua Bucharest 23; Dinamo Bucharest 18; Venus Bucharest 8; Chinezul Timisoara 6; UT Arad 6; Ripensia Timisoara 4; Uni Craiova 4; Petrolul Ploiesti 3; Rapid Bucharest 3; Cluj 3; Olimpia Bucharest 2; Colentina Bucharest 2; Arges Pitesti 2; ICO Oradea 1; Romano-Americana Bucharest 1; Prahova Ploiesti 1; Coltea Brasov 1; Juventus Bucharest 1; Metalochimia Resita 1; United Ploiesti 1; Unirea Tricolor 1; Unirea 1; Otelul 1.

Cup wins (1934–2012)
Steaua Bucharest 22; Rapid Bucharest 13; Dinamo Bucharest 13; Uni Craiova 6; Cluj 3; UT Arad 2; Ripensia Timisoara 2; Politehnica Timisoara 2; Petrolul Ploiesti 2; Metalochimia Resita 1; Universitata Cluj (includes Stiinta) 1; CFR Turnu Severin 1; Chimia Ramnicu Vilcea 1; Jiul Petrosani 1; Progresul Bucharest 1; Progresul Oradea (formerly ICO) 1; Ariesul Turda 1; Gloria Bistrita 1.

Final League Table 2011–12

	P	W	D	L	F	A	Pts
Cluj	34	21	8	5	63	31	71
Vaslui	34	22	4	8	58	29	70
Steaua	34	19	9	6	47	26	66
Rapid Bucharest	34	18	10	6	54	29	64
Dinamo Bucharest	34	18	8	8	57	32	62
Otelul	34	15	7	12	34	29	52
Univ Cluj	34	11	14	9	46	37	47
Pandurii	34	12	11	11	47	40	47
Brasov	34	13	6	15	39	34	45
Concordia	34	13	6	15	42	52	45
Ceahlaul	34	11	9	14	36	46	42
Astra	34	11	8	15	36	43	41
Gaz Metan	34	11	8	15	39	54	41
Petrolul	34	10	9	15	42	45	39
Targu*	34	8	11	15	34	47	35
Vointa*	34	8	8	18	24	45	32
Sportul*	34	6	12	16	33	55	30
Mioveni*	34	2	6	26	20	77	12

Top scorer: Wesley (Vaslui) 27.
Cup Final: Rapid Bucharest 0, Dinamo Bucharest 1.

RUSSIA

Football Union of Russia; Luzhnetskaya Naberezyhnaja 8, Moscow 119 992.
Founded: 1912; *National Colours:* All white.

International matches 2011
Iran (a) 0-1, Armenia (a) 0-0, Qatar (a) 1-1, Armenia (h) 3-1, Cameroon (h) 0-0, Serbia (h) 1-0, Macedonia (h) 1-0, Republic of Ireland (h) 0-0, Slovakia (a) 1-0, Andorra (h) 6-0, Greece (a) 1-1.

League Championship wins (1936–2012)
Spartak Moscow 21; Dynamo Kiev 13; Dynamo Moscow 11; CSKA Moscow 10; Zenit St Petersburg (formerly Zenit Leningrad) 4; Torpedo Moscow 3; Dinamo Tbilisi 2; Dnepr Dnepropetrovsk 2; Lokomotiv Moscow 2; Rubin 2; Saria Voroshilovgrad 1; Ararat Erevan 1; Dynamo Minsk 1; Spartak Vladikavkaz 1.

Cup wins (1936–2012)
Spartak Moscow 13; CSKA Moscow 11; Dynamo Kiev 9; Torpedo Moscow 7; Dynamo Moscow 7; Lokomotiv Moscow 7; Shakhtar Donetsk 4; Zenit St Petersburg (formerly Zenit Leningrad) 3; Dinamo Tbilisi 2; Ararat Erevan 2; Karpaty Lvov 1; SKA Rostov 1; Metalist Kharkov 1; Dnepr 1; Terek Groznyi 1; Rubin 1.

First Stage Final League Table 2011–12

	P	W	D	L	F	A	Pts
Zenit	30	17	10	3	59	25	61
CSKA Moscow	30	16	11	3	58	29	59
Dynamo Moscow	30	16	7	7	51	30	55
Spartak Moscow	30	15	8	7	48	33	53
Lokomotiv Moscow	30	15	8	7	49	30	53
Kuban	30	14	7	9	38	27	49
Rubin	30	13	10	7	40	27	49
Anzhi	30	13	9	8	38	32	48
Krasnodar	30	10	8	12	38	43	38
FK Rostov	30	8	8	14	31	45	32
Terek	30	8	7	15	29	45	31
Volga	30	8	4	18	24	40	28
Amkar	30	6	9	15	20	39	27
Krylia Sovekov	30	6	9	15	21	43	27
Spartak Nalchik	30	5	9	16	23	40	24
Tomsk	30	4	8	18	19	58	20

Top eight teams enter championship group; bottom eight teams enter relegation group.

Championship Group

	P	W	D	L	F	A	Pts
Zenit	44	24	16	4	85	40	88
Spartak Moscow	44	21	12	11	68	48	75
CSKA Moscow	44	19	16	9	72	47	73
Dynamo Moscow	44	20	12	12	66	50	72
Anzhi	44	19	13	12	54	42	70
Rubin	44	17	17	10	55	41	68
Lokomotiv Moscow	44	18	12	14	59	48	66
Kuban	44	15	16	13	50	45	61

Top scorer: Doumbia (CSKA Moscow) 28.
NB: Fourteen matches played in Championship and Relegation groups added to previous tables.

Relegation Group

	P	W	D	L	F	A	Pts
Krasnodar	44	16	13	15	58	61	61
Amkar	44	14	13	17	40	51	55
Terek	44	14	10	20	45	62	52
Krylia Sovekov	44	12	15	17	33	50	51
Rostov+	44	12	12	20	45	61	48
Volga+	44	12	5	27	37	60	41
Tomsk*	44	8	13	23	30	70	37
Spartak Nalchik*	44	7	13	24	39	60	34

Top Scorer: Doumbia (CSKA Moscow) 28.
Cup Final: Dynamo Moscow 0, Rubin 1.

SAN MARINO

Federazione Sammarinese Giuoco Calcio, Viale Campo dei Giudei, 14; Rep. San Marino 47890.
Founded: 1931; *National Colours:* All light blue.

International matches 2011
Liechtenstein (h) 0-1, Finland (h) 0-1, Hungary (h) 0-3, Romania (h) 0-1, Holland (a) 0-11, Sweden (h) 0-5, Moldova (a) 0-4.

League Championship wins (1986–2012)
Tre Fiori 7; Domagnono 4; Faetano 3; Folgore/Falciano 3; Murata 3; La Fiorita 2; Montevito 1; Libertas 1; Cosmos 1; Pennarossa 1; Tre Penne 1.

Cup wins (1937–2012)
Libertas 10; Domagnono 8; Tre Fiori 6; Juvenes 5; Tre Penne 5; Cosmos 4; Faetano 3; Murata 3; Dogana 2; Pennarossa 2; Juvenes/Dogana 2; La Fiorita 2.

Qualifying League Table 2012

Group A

	P	W	D	L	F	A	Pts
Libertas	21	10	9	2	37	24	39
Cosmos	21	10	5	6	29	23	35
Faetano	21	10	3	8	32	34	33
Pennarossa	21	9	3	9	25	28	30
Murata	21	9	3	9	30	32	30
San Giovanni	21	5	7	9	32	29	22
Cailungo	21	4	7	10	21	29	19
Domagnano	21	2	3	16	11	45	9

Group B

	P	W	D	L	F	A	Pts
Tre Fiori	20	15	4	1	44	14	49
La Fiorita	20	12	5	3	42	20	41
Tre Penne	20	11	3	6	37	24	36
Virtus	20	9	3	8	25	25	30
Fiorentino	20	8	3	9	30	33	27
Juvenes/Dogana	20	3	9	8	23	31	18
Folgore/Falciano	20	2	3	15	14	41	9

Play-Offs: Cosmos 1, Tre Penne 4; La Fiorita 1, Faetano 1 (Faetano won 4-2 on penalties); Cosmos 1, La Fiorita 0; Tre Penne 2, Faetano 1; Libertas 1, Tre Fiori 1 (Libertas won 4-3 on penalties); Cosmos 2, Faetano 1; Libertas 1, Tre Penne 1 (Libertas won 3-2 on penalties); Cosmos 0, Tre Fiori 0 (Tre Fiori won 6-5 on penalties); Tre Penne 2, Tre Fiori 1; Tre Penne 1, Libertas 0.
Top scorer: Menin (Cosmos) 11.
Cup Final: Pennarossa 2, La Fiorita 3.

SCOTLAND

The Scottish Football Association Ltd, Hampden Park, Glasgow G42 9AY.
Founded: 1873; *National Colours:* Dark blue shirts, white shorts, dark blue stockings.

SERBIA

Football Association of Serbia, Terazije 35, P.O. Box 263, 11000 Beograd.
Founded: 1919; *National Colours:* Blue shirts, white shorts, red stockings.

International matches 2011
Israel (a) 2-0, Northern Ireland (h) 2-1, Estonia (a) 1-1, South Korea (a) 1-2, Australia (a) 0-0, Russia (a) 0-1, Northern Ireland (a) 1-0, Faeroes (h) 3-1, Italy (h) 1-1, Slovenia (a) 0-1, Mexico (a) 0-2, Honduras (a) 0-2.

League Championship wins (1923–2012)
Red Star Belgrade 25; Partizan Belgrade 24; Hajduk Split 9; Gradjanski Zagreb 5; BSK Belgrade 5; Dinamo Zagreb 4; Jugoslavija Belgrade 2; Concordia Zagreb 2; FC Sarajevo 2; Vojvodina Novi Sad 2; HASK Zagreb 1; Zeljeznicar 1; Obilic 1.

Cup wins (1947–2012)
Red Star Belgrade 24; Partizan Belgrade 12; Hajduk Split 9; Dinamo Zagreb 8; BSK Belgrade (includes OFK) 2; Rijeka 2; Velez Mostar 2; Vardar Skopje 1; Borac Banjaluka 1; Sartid 1; Zeleznik 1.

Final League Table 2011–12

	P	W	D	L	F	A	Pts
Partizan Belgrade	30	26	2	2	67	12	80
Red Star Belgrade	30	21	5	4	57	18	68
Vojvodina	30	14	10	6	44	26	52
Jagodina	30	14	9	7	34	20	51
Sloboda	30	15	6	9	42	35	51
Radnicki	30	11	14	5	38	27	47
Spartak	30	11	10	9	31	31	43
OFK Belgrade	30	12	4	14	34	36	40
Javor	30	11	6	13	28	32	39
Rad	30	10	7	13	33	31	37
Hajduk Kula	30	9	6	15	28	44	33
Borca	30	7	9	14	18	39	30
Smederevo	30	9	2	19	22	42	29
Novi Pazar	30	6	10	14	21	41	28
Borac*	30	4	7	19	16	45	19
Metalac*	30	2	9	19	14	48	15

Top scorer: Spalevic (Radnicki) 19.
Cup Final: Red Star Belgrade 2, Borac 0.

SLOVAKIA

Slovak Football Association, Junacka 6, 83280 Bratislava, Slovakia.
Founded: 1993; *National Colours:* All blue and white.

International matches 2011
Luxembourg (a) 1-2, Andorra (a) 1-0, Denmark (h) 1-2, Andorra (h) 1-0, Austria (a) 2-1, Republic of Ireland (a) 0-0, Armenia (h) 0-4, Russia (h) 0-1, Macedonia (a) 1-1.

League Championship wins (1939–44; 1994–2012)
Slovan Bratislava 10; Zilina 6; Kosice 2; Inter Bratislava 2; Artmedia Petrzalka 2; Bystrica 1; OAP Bratislava 1; Ruzomberok 1.

Cup wins (1994–2012)
Slovan Bratislava 5; Inter Bratislava 3; Artmedia Petrzalka 2; Humenne 1; Spartak Trnava 1; Koba Senec 1; Matador Puchov 1; Bystrica 1; Ruzomberok 1; ViOn Zlate 1; Kosice 1; Zilina 1.

Final League Table 2011–12

	P	W	D	L	F	A	Pts
Zilina	33	19	10	4	52	27	67
Spartak Trnava	33	19	8	6	44	22	65
Slovan Bratislava	33	16	11	6	48	35	59
Senica	33	15	12	6	47	23	57
Trencin	33	12	12	9	51	49	48
Ruzomberok	33	11	11	11	39	34	44
Zlate	33	11	8	14	34	43	41
Nitra	33	9	12	12	33	39	39
Dukla	33	9	10	14	37	44	37
Tatran	33	7	12	14	23	35	33
Kosice	33	6	11	16	25	40	29
DAC*	33	5	1	27	21	63	16

Top scorer: Masaryk (Ruzomberok) 18.
Cup Final: Zilina 3, Senica 2.

SLOVENIA

Football Association of Slovenia, Nogometna zveza Slovenije, Cerinova 4, P.P. 3986, 1001 Ljubljana, Slovenia.
Founded: 1920; *National Colours:* White shirts with green sleeves, white shorts, white stockings.

International matches 2011
Albania (a) 2-1, Italy (h) 0-1, Northern Ireland (a) 0-0, Faeroes (a) 2-0, Belgium (h) 0-0, Estonia (h) 1-2, Italy (a) 0-1, Serbia (h) 1-0, USA (h) 2-3.

League Championship wins (1992–2012)
Maribor 10; SCT Olimpija 4; Gorica 4; Domzale 2; Koper 1.

Cup wins (1992–2012)
Maribor 7; SCT Olimpija 4; Gorica 2; Koper 2; Interblock 2; Mura 1; Rudar 1; Celje 1; Domzale 1.

Final League Table 2011–12

	P	W	D	L	F	A	Pts
Maribor	36	26	7	3	88	35	85
Olimpija	36	19	8	9	60	38	65
Mura	36	18	5	13	52	46	59
Koper	36	16	10	10	48	35	58
Gorica	36	14	11	11	49	37	53
Rudar	36	11	10	15	55	54	43
Domzale	36	11	7	18	39	52	40
Celje	36	9	10	17	44	56	37
Triglav*+	36	9	6	21	22	67	33
Nafta*	36	5	10	21	34	71	25

Top scorer: Vrsic (Olimpija) 22.
Cup Final: Celje 2, Maribor 2
Maribor won 3-2 on penalties.

SPAIN

Real Federacion Espanola De Futbol, Ramon y Cajal, s/n, Apartado Postale 385, Madrid 28230.
Founded: 1913; *National Colours:* Red shirts, blue shorts, blue stockings with red, blue and yellow border.

International matches 2011
Colombia (h) 1-0, Czech Republic (h) 2-1, Lithuania (a) 3-1, USA (a) 4-0, Venezuela (a) 3-0, Italy (a) 1-2, Chile (h) 3-2, Liechtenstein (h) 6-0, Czech Republic (a) 2-0, Scotland (h) 3-1, England (a) 0-1, Costa Rica (a) 2-2.

League Championship wins (1929–36; 1940–2012)
Real Madrid 32; Barcelona 21; Atletico Madrid 9; Athletic Bilbao 8; Valencia 6; Real Sociedad 2; Real Betis 1; Sevilla 1; La Coruna 1.

Cup wins (1903–2012)
Barcelona 26; Athletic Bilbao (including Vizcaya Bilbao 1) 23; Real Madrid 18; Atletico Madrid 9; Valencia 7; Real Zaragoza 6; Sevilla 5; Espanyol 4; Real Union de Irun 3; La Coruna 2; Real Sociadad (includes Ciclista) 2; Real Betis 2; Arenas 1; Racing de Irun 1; Real Sociedad 1; Mallorca 1.

Final League Table 2011–12

	P	*W*	*D*	*L*	*F*	*A*	*Pts*
Real Madrid	38	32	4	2	121	32	100
Barcelona	38	28	7	3	114	29	91
Valencia	38	17	10	11	59	44	61
Malaga	38	17	7	14	54	53	58
Atletico Madrid	38	15	11	12	53	46	56
Levante	38	16	7	15	54	50	55
Osasuna	38	13	15	10	44	61	54
Mallorca	38	14	10	14	42	46	52
Sevilla	38	13	11	14	48	47	50
Athletic Bilbao	38	12	13	13	49	52	49
Getafe	38	12	11	15	40	51	47
Real Sociedad	38	12	11	15	46	52	47
Betis	38	13	8	17	47	56	47
Espanyol	38	12	10	16	46	56	46
Rayo Vallecano	38	13	4	21	53	73	43
Zaragoza	38	12	7	19	36	61	43
Granada	38	12	6	20	35	56	42
Villarreal*	38	9	14	15	39	53	41
Gijon*	38	10	7	21	42	69	37
Santander*	38	4	15	19	28	63	27

Top scorer: Messi (Barcelona) 50.
Cup Final: Athletic Bilbao 0, Barcelona 3.

SWEDEN

Svenska Fotbollfoerbundet, Box 1216, S-17123 Solna.
Founded: 1904; *National Colours:* Yellow shirts, blue shorts, yellow stockings.

International matches 2011
Botswana (h) 2-1, Cyprus (a) 2-0, Ukraine (a) 1-1, Moldova (h) 2-1, Moldova (a) 4-1, Finland (h) 5-0, Ukraine (a) 1-0, Hungary (a) 1-2, San Marino (a) 5-0, Finland (a) 2-1, Holland (h) 3-2, Denmark (a) 0-2, England (a) 0-1.

League Championship wins (1896–2011)
IFK Gothenburg 19; Malmo FF 16; Orgryte 14; IFK Norrköping 12; Djurgaarden 11; AIK Stockholm 11; IF Helsingborg 7; GAIS Gothenburg 6; IF Elfsborg 5; Oster Vaxjo 4; Halmstad 4; Atvidaberg 2; IFK Eskilstuna 1; IF Gavic Brynas 1; IF Gothenburg 1; Fassbergs 1; IK Sleipner 1; Hammarby 1; Kalmar 1.

Cup wins (1941–2011)
Malmo FF 14; AIK Stockholm 8; IFK Norrköping 6; IFK Gothenburg 5; Helsingborg 5; Djurgaarden 4; Kalmar 3; Atvidaberg 2; IF Elfsborg 2; GAIS Gothenburg 1; IF Raa 1; Landskrona 1; Oster Vaxjo 1; Degerfors 1; Halmstad 1; Orgryte 1.

Final League Table 2011

	P	*W*	*D*	*L*	*F*	*A*	*Pts*
Helsingborg	30	18	9	3	55	27	63
AIK	30	18	4	8	46	27	58
Elfsborg	30	18	3	9	52	32	57
Malmo	30	15	9	6	37	30	54
GAIS Gothenburg	30	16	3	11	47	34	51
Hacken	30	14	7	9	52	32	49
IFK Gothenburg	30	13	6	11	42	34	45
Kalmar	30	13	5	12	39	34	44
Gefle	30	10	11	9	31	39	41
Mjallby	30	12	4	14	33	39	40
Djurgaarden	30	10	6	14	36	40	36
Orebro	30	11	3	16	36	45	36
Norrkoping	30	9	7	14	32	49	34
Syrianska+	30	8	4	18	27	44	28
Trelleborg*	30	7	4	19	39	64	25
Halmstad*	30	3	5	22	24	58	14

Top scorer: Ranegie (Malmo) 21 (including 18 for Hacken).
Cup Final: Helsingborg 3, Kalmar 1.

SWITZERLAND

Schweizerisher Fussballverband, Postfach 3000, Berne 15.
Founded: 1895; *National Colours:* Red shirts, white shorts, red stockings.

International matches 2011
Malta (a) 0-0, Bulgaria (a) 0-0, England (a) 2-2, Liechtenstein (a) 2-1, Bulgaria (h) 3-1, Wales (a) 0-2, Montenegro (h) 2-0, Holland (a) 0-0, Luxembourg (a) 1-0.

League Championship wins (1897–2012)
Grasshoppers 27; Servette 17; FC Basle 15; FC Zurich 12; Young Boys Berne 11; Lausanne 7; La Chaux-de-Fonds 3; FC Lugano 3; Winterthur 3; FC Aarau 3; Neuchatel Xamax 2; Sion 2; St Gallen 2; FC Anglo-American Club 1; FC Brühl 1; Cantonal-Neuchatel 1; Biel-Bienne 1; Bellinzona 1; FC Etoile La Chaux-de-Fonds 1; Lucerne 1.

Cup wins (1926–2012)
Grasshoppers 18; FC Sion 12; FC Basle 11; Lausanne 9; Servette 7; FC Zurich 7; La Chaux-de-Fonds 6; Young Boys Berne 6; FC Lugano 3; Lucerne 2; FC Grenchen 1; St Gallen 1; Urania Geneva 1; Young Fellows Zurich 1; FC Aarau 1; Wil 1.

Final League Table 2011–12

	P	*W*	*D*	*L*	*F*	*A*	*Pts*
Basle	34	22	8	4	78	33	74
Lucerne	34	14	12	8	46	32	54
Young Boys	34	13	12	9	52	38	51
Servette	34	14	6	14	45	53	48
Thun	34	11	10	13	38	41	43
Zurich	34	11	8	15	43	44	41
Lausanne	34	8	6	20	29	61	30
Neuchatel Xamax*	18	7	5	6	22	22	26
Grasshoppers+	34	7	5	22	32	66	26
Sion+ (–36)	34	15	8	11	40	35	17

Neuchatel Xamax licence revoked for financial irregularities and demoted. Sion deducted 36 points for fielding ineligible players but survived relegation play-off.
Top scorer: Frei A (Basle) 24.
Cup Final: Basle 1, Lucerne 1
Basle won 4-2 on penalties.

TURKEY

Turkiye Futbol Federasyonu, Konaklar Mah. Ihlamurlu Sok. 9, 4 Levent, Istanbul 80620.
Founded: 1923; *National Colours:* All white.

International matches 2011
South Korea (h) 0-0, Austria (h) 2-0, Belgium (a) 1-1, Estonia (h) 3-0, Kazakhstan (h) 2-1, Austria (a) 0-0, Germany (h) 1-3, Azerbaijan (h) 1-0, Croatia (h) 0-3, Croatia (a) 0-0.

League Championship wins (1959–2012)
Fenerbahce 18; Galatasaray 18; Besiktas 11; Trabzonspor 6; Bursa 1.

Cup wins (1963–2012)
Galatasaray 14; Besiktas 9; Trabzonspor 8; Fenerbahce 5; Goztepe Izmir 2; Altay Izmir 2; Ankaragucu 2; Genclerbirligi 2; Kocaelispor 2; Eskisehirspor 1; Bursapor 1; Sakaryaspor 1; Kayseri 1.

Qualifying League Table 2011–12

	P	W	D	L	F	A	Pts
Galatasaray	34	23	8	3	69	24	77
Fenerbahce	34	20	8	6	61	34	68
Trabzonspor	34	15	11	8	60	39	56
Besiktas	34	15	10	9	50	39	55
Eskisehir	34	14	8	12	42	41	50
Istanbul	34	14	8	12	48	49	50
Sivas	34	13	11	10	57	54	50
Bursa	34	13	10	11	44	35	49
Genclerbirligi	34	13	10	11	49	48	49
Gaziantep	34	13	9	12	39	33	48
Kayseri	34	13	5	16	42	39	44
Karabuk	34	13	5	16	44	56	44
Mersin	34	12	6	16	34	45	42
Ordu	34	10	12	12	28	34	42
Antalya	34	10	9	15	32	42	39
Samsung*	34	9	9	16	36	47	36
Manisa*	34	8	8	18	31	52	32
Ankaragucu*	34	2	5	27	22	77	11

Championship League Table 2011–12

	P	W	D	L	F	A	Pts
Galatasaray	6	2	3	1	9	6	48
Fenerbahce	6	4	1	1	9	4	47
Trabzonspor	6	1	2	3	5	10	33
Besiktas	6	1	2	3	5	8	33

Europa League Group

	P	W	D	L	F	A	Pts
Bursa	6	4	0	2	12	10	37
Eskisehir	6	3	2	1	12	7	36
Istanbul	6	2	1	3	10	14	32
Sivas	6	1	1	4	9	12	29

Top scorer: Burak (Trabzonspor) 33.
Cup Final: Bursa 0, Fenerbahce 4.

UKRAINE

Football Federation of Ukraine, Laboratorna Str. 1, P.O. Box 293, Kiev 03150.
Founded: 1991; *National Colours:* All yellow and blue.

International matches 2011
Romania (a) 2-2, Sweden (h) 1-1, Italy (h) 0-2, Uzbekistan (h) 2-0, France (h) 1-4, Sweden (h) 0-1, Uruguay (h) 2-3, Czech Republic (a) 0-4, Bulgaria (h) 3-0, Estonia (a) 2-0, Germany (h) 3-3, Austria (h) 2-1.

League Championship wins (1992–2012)
Dynamo Kiev 13; Shakhtar Donetsk 7; Tavriya Simferopol 1.

Cup wins (1992–2012)
Dynamo Kiev 9; Shakhtar Donetsk 8; Chernomorets Odessa 2; Vorskla 1; Tavriya Simferopol 1.

Final League Table 2011–12

	P	W	D	L	F	A	Pts
Shakhtar Donetsk	30	25	4	1	80	18	79
Dynamo Kiev	30	23	6	1	56	12	75
Metalist	30	16	11	3	54	32	59
Dnepr	30	15	7	8	52	35	52
Arsenal Kiev	30	14	9	7	44	27	51
Tavriya	30	12	9	9	43	36	45
Metalurg Donetsk	30	12	6	12	35	34	42
Vorskla	30	9	10	11	38	43	37
Chernomorets	30	10	7	13	32	42	37
Krivbas	30	9	6	15	22	38	33
Illichivets	30	8	8	14	28	42	32
Volyn	30	7	6	17	25	43	27
Zorya	30	6	8	16	34	58	26
Karpaty	30	5	8	17	27	51	23
Obolon*	30	4	9	17	17	42	21
Oleksandria*	30	4	8	18	24	58	20

Top scorer: Seleznyov (Shakhtar Donetsk) 14.
Cup Final: Metalurg Donetsk 1, Shakhtar Donetsk 2.

WALES

The Football Association of Wales Limited, 11/12 Neptune Court, Vanguard Way, Cardiff, CF24 5PJ.
Founded: 1876; *National Colours:* All red.

SOUTH AMERICA

ARGENTINA

Asociacion Del Futbol Argentina, Viamonte 1366/76, 1053 Buenos Aires.
Founded: 1893; *National Colours:* Light blue and white vertical striped shirts, dark blue shorts, white stockings.
International matches 2011
Portugal (h) 2-1, Venezuela (h) 4-1, USA (a) 1-1, Costa Rica (a) 0-0, Ecuador (h) 2-2, Paraguay (h) 4-2, Nigeria (a) 1-4, Poland (a) 1-2, Albania (h) 4-0, Bolivia (n) 1-1, Colombia (n) 0-0, Costa Rica (n) 3-0, Uruguay (n) 1-1, Venezuela (h) 1-0, Nigeria (h) 3-1, Brazil (h) 0-0, Brazil (a) 0-2, Chile (h) 4-1, Venezuela (a) 0-1, Bolivia (h) 1-1, Colombia (a) 2-1.

BOLIVIA

Federacion Boliviana De Futbol, Av. Libertador Bolivar No. 1168, Casilla de Correo 484, Cochabamba, Bolivia.
Founded: 1925; *National Colours:* Green shirts, white shorts, green stockings.
International matches 2011
Panama (a) 0-2, Guatemala (a) 1-1, Paraguay (h) 0-2, Paraguay (a) 0-0, Argentina (n) 1-1, Costa Rica (n) 0-2, Colombia (n) 0-2, Panama (h) 1-3, Peru (a) 2-2, Peru (h) 0-0, Uruguay (a) 2-4, Colombia (h) 1-2, Argentina (a) 1-1, Venezuela (a) 0-1.

BRAZIL

Confederacao Brasileira De Futebol, Rua Victor Civita 66, Bloco 1-Edificio 5-5 Andar, Barra da Tijuca, Rio De Janeiro 22775-040.
Founded: 1914; *National Colours:* Yellow shirts with green collar and cuffs, blue shorts, white stockings with green and yellow border.
International matches 2011
France (a) 0-1, Scotland (a) 2-0, Holland (h) 0-0, Romania (h) 1-0, Venezuela (n) 0-0, Paraguay (n) 2-2, Ecuador (n) 4-2, Paraguay (n) 0-0, Germany (a) 2-3, Ghana (h) 1-0, Argentina (a) 0-0, Argentina (h) 2-0, Costa Rica (a) 1-0, Mexico (a) 2-1, Gabon (a) 2-0, Egypt (h) 2-0.

CHILE

Federacion De Futbol De Chile, Avda. Quillin No. 5635, Casilla postal 3733, Correo Central, Santiago de Chile.
Founded: 1895; *National Colours:* Red shirts with blue collar and cuffs, blue shorts, white stockings.
International matches 2011
USA (a) 1-1, Portugal (a) 1-1, Colombia (h) 2-0, Estonia (h) 4-0, Paraguay (a) 0-0, Mexico (n) 2-1, Uruguay (n) 1-1, Peru (n) 1-0, Venezuela (n) 1-2, France (a) 1-1, Spain (a) 2-3, Mexico (a) 0-1, Argentina (a) 1-4, Peru (h) 4-2, Uruguay (a) 0-4, Paraguay (h) 2-0.

COLOMBIA

Federacion Colombiana De Futbol, Avenida 32, No. 16–22 piso 4o. Apartado Aereo 17602, Santafe de Bogota.
Founded: 1924; *National Colours:* Yellow shirts, blue shorts, red stockings.
International matches 2011
Spain (a) 0-1, Ecuador (h) 2-0, Chile (a) 0-2, Costa Rica (n) 1-0, Argentina (n) 0-0, Bolivia (n) 2-0, Peru (n) 0-2, Honduras (a) 2-0, Jamaica (a) 2-0, Bolivia (a) 2-1, Venezuela (h) 1-1, Argentina (h) 1-2.

ECUADOR

Federacion Ecuatoriana del Futbol, km 4 1/2 via a la Costa (Avda. del Bombero), PO Box 09-01-7447 Guayaquil.
Founded: 1925; *National Colours:* Yellow shirts, blue shorts, red stockings.
International matches 2011
Honduras (a) 1-1, Colombia (a) 0-2, Peru (a) 0-0, Argentina (a) 2-2, Mexico (a) 1-1, Canada (a) 2-2, Greece (h) 1-1, Paraguay (n) 0-0, Venezuela (n) 0-1, Brazil (n) 2-4, Costa Rica (a) 2-0, Jamaica (h) 5-2, Costa Rica (h) 4-0, Venezuela (h) 2-0, USA (a) 1-0, Paraguay (a) 1-2, Peru (h) 2-0.

PARAGUAY

Asociacion Paraguaya de Futbol, Estadio De Los Defensores del Chaco, Calles Mayor Martinez 1393, Asuncion.
Founded: 1906; *National Colours:* Red and white shirts, blue shorts, blue stockings.
International matches 2011
Mexico (a) 1-3, USA (a) 1-0, Argentina (a) 2-4, Bolivia (a) 2-0, Bolivia (h) 0-0, Romania (h) 2-0, Chile (h) 0-0, Ecuador (n) 0-0, Brazil (n) 2-2, Venezuela (n) 3-3, Brazil (n) 0-0, Venezuela (n) 0-0, Uruguay (n) 0-3, Panama (a) 2-0, Honduras (a) 3-0, Peru (a) 0-2, Uruguay (h) 1-1, Ecuador (h) 2-1, Chile (a) 0-2.

PERU

Federacion Peruana De Futbol, Av. Aviacion 2085, San Luis, Lima 30.
Founded: 1922; *National Colours:* White shirts with red stripe, white shorts with red lines, white stockings with red line.
International matches 2011
Panama (h) 1-0, Ecuador (h) 0-0, Japan (a) 0-0, Czech Republic (h) 0-0, Uruguay (n) 1-1, Mexico (n) 1-0, Chile (n) 0-1, Colombia (n) 2-0, Uruguay (n) 0-2, Venezuela (n) 4-1, Bolivia (h) 2-2, Bolivia (a) 0-0, Paraguay (h) 2-0, Chile (a) 2-4, Ecuador (a) 0-2.

URUGUAY

Asociacion Uruguaya De Futbol, Guayabo 1531, 11200 Montevideo.
Founded: 1900; *National Colours:* Sky blue shirts with white collar/cuffs, black shorts and stockings with sky blue borders.
International matches 2011
Estonia (a) 0-2, Republic of Ireland (a) 3-2, Germany (a) 1-2, Holland (h) 1-1, Estonia (h) 3-0, Peru (n) 1-1, Chile (n) 1-1, Mexico (n) 1-0, Argentina (n) 1-1, Peru (n) 2-0, Paraguay (n) 3-0, Ukraine (a) 3-2, Bolivia (h) 4-2, Paraguay (a) 1-1, Chile (h) 4-0, Italy (a) 1-0.

VENEZUELA

Federacion Venezolana De Futbol, Avda. Santos Erminy Ira, Calle las Delicias Torre Mega II, P.H. Sabana Grande, Caracas 1050.
Founded: 1926; *National Colours:* Burgundy shirts, white shorts and stockings.
International matches 2011
Costa Rica (h) 2-2, Argentina (a) 1-4, Jamaica (a) 2-0, Mexico (a) 1-1, Guatemala (a) 2-0, Spain (h) 0-3, Brazil (n) 0-0, Ecuador (n) 1-0, Paraguay (n) 3-3, Chile (n) 2-1, Paraguay (n) 0-0, Peru (n) 1-4, El Salvador (a) 1-2, Honduras (a) 0-2, Argentina (a) 0-1, Guinea (h) 2-1, Ecuador (a) 0-2, Argentina (h) 1-0, Colombia (a) 1-1, Bolivia (h) 1-0, Costa Rica (h) 0-2.

ASIA

AFGHANISTAN

Afghanistan Football Federation, PO Box 5099, Kabul.
Founded: 1933; *National Colours*: All white with red lines.
International matches 2011
Bhutan (a) 3-0, Bhutan (h) 2-0, Nepal (a) 0-1, Sri Lanka (a) 1-0, North Korea (a) 0-2, Palestine (h) 0-2, Palestine (a) 1-1, India (a) 1-1, Sri Lanka (a) 3-1, Bhutan (a) 8-1, Nepal (h) 1-0, India (a) 0-4.

AUSTRALIA

Soccer Australia Ltd, Level 3, East Stand, Stadium Australia, Edwin Flack Avenue, Homebush, NSW 2127.
Founded: 1961; *National Colours:* All green with gold trim.
International matches 2011
UAE (a) 0-0, India (a) 4-0, South Korea (a) 1-1, Bahrain (h) 1-0, Iraq (h) 1-0, Uzbekistan (a) 6-0, Japan (a) 0-1, Germany (a) 2-1, New Zealand (h) 3-0, Serbia (h) 0-0, Wales (a) 2-1, Thailand (h) 2-1, Saudi Arabia (a) 3-1, Malaysia (h) 5-0, Oman (h) 3-0, Oman (a) 0-1, Thailand (a) 1-0.

BAHRAIN

Bahrain Football Association, P.O. Box 5464, Manama.
Founded: 1957; *National Colours:* All red.
International matches 2011
North Korea (h) 0-1, South Korea (a) 1-2, India (h) 5-2, Australia (a) 0-1, Kuwait (h) 0-0, Oman (a) 1-1, Sudan (h) 1-0, Qatar (h) 0-0, Indonesia (a) 2-0, Iran (a) 0-6, Kuwait (a) 1-0, Iran (h) 1-1, Qatar (a) 0-0, Qatar (a) 2-2, Iraq (h) 3-0, Palestine (h) 3-1, Jordan (h) 1-0.

BANGLADESH

Bangladesh Football Federation, Bangabandhu National Stadium-1, Dhaka 1000.
Founded: 1972; *National Colours:* Orange shirts, white shorts, green stockings.
International matches 2011
Palestine (a) 0-2, Burma (a) 2-0, Philippines (h) 0-3, Pakistan (h) 3-0, Pakistan (a) 0-0, Lebanon (a) 0-4, Lebanon (h) 2-0, Pakistan (h) 0-0, Nepal (h) 0-1, Maldives (a) 1-3.

BHUTAN

Bhutan Football Federation, P.O. Box 365, Thimphu.
National Colours: All yellow and red.
International matches 2011
Nepal (a) 0-1, Nepal (a) 1-2, Afghanistan (h) 0-3, Afghanistan (a) 0-2, Sri Lanka (a) 0-3, India (a) 0-5, Afghanistan (h) 1-8.

BRUNEI DARUSSALAM

The Football Association of Brunei Darussalam, P.O. Box 2010, 1920 Bandar Seri Begawan BS 8674.
Founded: 1959; *Number of Clubs:* 22; *Number of Players:* 830; *National Colours:* Yellow shirts, black shorts, black and white stockings.
Telephone: 00673-2/382 761; *Fax:* 00673-2/382 760.

BURMA

Myanmar Football Federation, Youth Training Centre, Thingankyun Township, Yangon.
Founded: 1947; *National Colours:* Red shirts, white shorts, red stockings.
International matches 2011
Philippines (h) 1-1, Bangladesh (h) 0-2, Palestine (h) 1-3, Malaysia (a) 0-2, Mongolia (a) 0-1, Mongolia (h) 2-0, Thailand (a) 0-1, Thailand (a) 1-1, Oman (a) 0-2.

CAMBODIA

Cambodian Football Federation, Chaeng Maeng Village, Rd. Kab Srov, Sangkat Samrong Krom, Khan Dangkor, Phnom-Penh.
Founded: 1933; *National Colours:* All blue.
International matches 2011
Macau (h) 3-1, Macau (a) 2-3, Maldives (a) 0-4, Tajikistan (h) 0-3, Kyrgyzstan (h) 3-4, Laos (h) 4-2, Laos (a) 2-6.

CHINA PR

Football Association of The People's Republic of China, 9 Tiyuguan Road, Beijing 100763.
Founded: 1924; *National Colours:* All white.
International matches 2011
Kuwait (a) 2-0, Qatar (a) 0-2, Uzbekistan (h) 2-2, New Zealand (h) 1-1, Costa Rica (a) 2-2, Honduras (h) 3-0, Uzbekistan (h) 1-0, North Korea (h) 2-0, Laos (h) 7-2, Laos (a) 6-1, Jamaica (h) 1-0, Singapore (h) 2-1, Jordan (a) 1-2, UAE (h) 2-1, Iraq (h) 0-1, Iraq (a) 0-1, Singapore (a) 4-0.

CHINESE TAIPEI

Chinese Taipei Football Association, 2F No. Yu Men St., Taipei, Taiwan 104.
Founded: 1936; *National Colours:* Blue shirts and shorts, white stockings.
International matches 2011
Laos (h) 5-2, Laos (a) 1-1, India (a) 0-3, Turkmenistan (h) 0-2, Pakistan (a) 0-2, Malaysia (a) 1-2, Malaysia (h) 3-2, Singapore (a) 2-3, Macau (h) 3-0, Philippines (h) 0-0, Hong Kong (h) 0-6.

GUAM

Guam Football Association, P.O.Box 5093, Agana, Guam 96932.
Founded: 1975; *National Colours:* Blue shirts, white shorts, blue stockings.
International matches 2011
Soloman Islands (a) 0-7, New Caledonia (a) 0-9, American Samoa (a) 2-0, Vanuatu (h) 1-4.

HONG KONG

The Hong Kong Football Association Ltd, 55 Fat Kwong Street, Homantin, Kowloon, Hong Kong.
Founded: 1914; *National Colours:* All red.
International matches 2011
Malaysia (a) 0-2, Malaysia (h) 1-1, Saudi Arabia (a) 0-3, Saudi Arabia (h) 0-5, Philippines (h) 3-3, Macau (h) 5-1, Chinese Taipei (a) 6-0.

INDIA

All India Football Federation, Nehru Stadium (West Stand), Fatorda Margao-Goa 403 602.
Founded: 1937; *National Colours:* Sky blue shirts, navy blue shorts, sky and navy blue stockings.
International matches 2011
Australia (h) 0-4, Bahrain (a) 2-5, South Korea (a) 1-4, Chinese Taipei (h) 3-0, Pakistan (a) 3-1, Turkmenistan (a) 1-1, Maldives (a) 1-1, UAE (a) 0-3, UAE (h) 2-2, Trinidad & Tobago (a) 0-3, Guyana (a) 1-2, Malaysia (h) 1-1, Malaysia (h) 3-2, Zambia (h) 0-5, Afghanistan (h) 1-1, Bhutan (h) 5-0, Sri Lanka (h) 3-0, Maldives (h) 3-1, Afghanistan (h) 4-0.

INDONESIA

Football Association of Indonesia, Gelora Bung Karno, Pintu X-XI, Jakarta 10270.
Founded: 1930; *National Colours:* Red shirts, white shorts, red stockings.
International matches 2011
Turkmenistan (a) 1-1, Turkmenistan (h) 4-3, Palestine (h) 4-1, Jordan (a) 0-1, Iran (a) 0-3, Bahrain (h) 0-2, Saudi Arabia (h) 0-0, Qatar (h) 2-3, Qatar (a) 0-4, Iran (h) 1-4.

IRAN

IR Iran Football Federation, No. 16-4th deadend, Pakistan Street, PO Box 15316-6967 Shahid Beheshti Avenue, Tehran 15316.
Founded: 1920; *National Colours:* All white.
International matches 2011
Angola (h) 1-0, Iraq (a) 2-1, North Korea (h) 1-0, UAE (a) 3-0, South Korea (h) 0-1, Russia (h) 1-0, Madagascar (h) 1-0, Maldives (h) 4-0, Maldives (a) 1-0, Indonesia (h) 3-0, Qatar (a) 1-1, Palestine (h) 7-0, Bahrain (h) 6-0, Bahrain (a) 1-1, Indonesia (a) 4-1.

IRAQ

Iraqi Football Association, Olympic Committee Building, Palestine Street, PO Box 484, Baghdad.
Founded: 1948; *National Colours:* All black.
International matches 2011
Iran (h) 1-2, UAE (a) 1-0, North Korea (h) 1-0, Australia (a) 0-1, North Korea (a) 2-0, Kuwait (a) 0-1, Syria (h) 1-2, Kuwait (h) 0-1, Jordan (a) 1-1, Yemen (h) 2-0, Yemen (a) 0-0, Qatar (a) 1-0, Jordan (h) 0-2, Singapore (a) 2-0, China (a) 1-0, China (h) 1-0, Jordan (a) 3-1, Bahrain (a) 0-3, Qatar (a) 0-0.

JAPAN

Japan Football Association, JFA House, 3-10-15, Hongo, Bunkyo-ku, Tokyo 113-0033.
Founded: 1921; *National Colours:* Blue shirts, white shorts, blue stockings.
International matches 2011
Jordan (h) 1-1, Syria (a) 2-1, Saudi Arabia (a) 5-0, Qatar (a) 3-2, South Korea (h) 2-2, Australia (h) 1-0, Peru (h) 0-0, Czech Republic (h) 0-0, South Korea (h) 3-0, North Korea (h) 1-0, Uzbekistan (a) 1-1, Vietnam (h) 1-0, Tajikistan (h) 8-0, Tajikistan (a) 4-0, North Korea (a) 0-1.

JORDAN

Jordan Football Association, P.O. Box 962024 Al Hussein Sports City, 11196 Amman.
Founded: 1949; *National Colours:* All white and red.
International matches 2011
Uzbekistan (h) 2-2, Japan (a) 1-1, Saudi Arabia (h) 1-0, Syria (h) 2-1, Uzbekistan (a) 1-2, Kuwait (h) 1-1, North Korea (h) 1-1, Syria (h) 1-3, Yemen (h) 4-0, Saudi Arabia (h) 1-1, Iraq (h) 1-1, Nepal (h) 9-0, Nepal (a) 1-1, Tunisia (h) 3-3, Indonesia (h) 1-0, Iraq (a) 2-0, China (h) 2-1, Thailand (a) 0-0, Singapore (a) 3-0, Singapore (h) 2-0, Iraq (h) 1-3, Palestine (h) 4-1, Sudan (a) 0-0, Libya (a) 0-0, Kuwait (a) 2-0, Bahrain (a) 0-1.

KOREA, NORTH

Football Association of The Democratic People's Rep. of Korea, Kumsong-dong, Kwangbok Street, Mangyongdae Distr, PO Box 56, Pyongyang FNJ-PRK.
Founded: 1945; *National Colours:* All white.
International matches 2011
Bahrain (a) 1-0, UAE (h) 0-0, Iran (a) 0-1, Iraq (a) 0-1, Iraq (h) 0-2, Jordan (a) 1-1, Sri Lanka (h) 4-0, Nepal (a) 1-0, Afghanistan (h) 2-0, China (a) 0-2, Kuwait (a) 0-0, Japan (a) 0-1, Tajikistan (h) 1-0, Uzbekistan (h) 0-1, Uzbekistan (a) 0-1, Japan (h) 1-0.

KOREA, SOUTH

Korea Football Association, 1-131 Sinmunno, 2-ga, Jongno-Gu, Seoul 110-062.
Founded: 1928; *National Colours:* Red shirts, blue shorts, red stockings.
International matches 2011
Bahrain (h) 2-1, Australia (a) 1-1, India (h) 4-1, Iran (a) 1-0, Japan (a) 2-2, Uzbekistan (h) 3-2, Turkey (a) 0-0, Honduras (h) 4-0, Serbia (h) 2-1, Ghana (h) 2-1, Japan (a) 0-3, Lebanon (h) 6-0, Kuwait (a) 1-1, UAE (h) 2-1, UAE (a) 2-0, Lebanon (a) 1-2.

KUWAIT

Kuwait Football Association, P.O. Box 2029, Udiliya, Block 4 Al-Ittihad Street, Safat 13021.
Founded: 1952; *National Colours:* All blue.
International matches 2011
China (h) 0-2, Uzbekistan (a) 1-2, Qatar (a) 0-3, Bahrain (a) 0-0, Jordan (a) 1-1, Iraq (h) 1-0, Lebanon (a) 6-0, Oman (h) 1-1, Iraq (a) 2-0, Saudi Arabia (h) 1-0, Philippines (h) 3-0, Philippines (a) 2-1, North Korea (h) 0-0, Oman (a) 0-1, UAE (a) 3-2, South Korea (a) 1-1, Lebanon (a) 2-2, Bahrain (h) 0-1, Lebanon (h) 0-1, UAE (h) 2-1, Oman (a) 2-0, Saudi Arabia (a) 2-0, Jordan (h) 0-2, Palestine (h) 3-0.

KYRGYZSTAN

Football Federation of Kyrgyz Republic, PO Box 1484, Kurenkeeva Street 195, Bishkek 720040, Kyrgyzstan.
Founded: 1992; *National Colours:* Red shirts, white shorts, red stockings.
International matches 2011
Tajikistan (a) 0-1, Maldives (a) 1-2, Cambodia (a) 4-3, Uzbekistan (a) 0-4, Uzbekistan (h) 0-3.

LAOS

Federation Lao de Football, National Stadium, Kounboulo Street, PO Box 3777, Vientiane 856-21, Laos.
Founded: 1951; *National Colours:* All red.
International matches 2011
Chinese Taipei (a) 2-5, Chinese Taipei (h) 1-1, Cambodia (a) 2-4, Cambodia (h) 6-2, China (a) 2-7, China (h) 1-6.

LEBANON

Federation Libanaise De Football-Association, P.O. Box 4732, Verdun Street, Bristol, Radwan Centre Building, Beirut.
Founded: 1933; *National Colours:* Red shirts, white shorts, red stockings.
International matches 2011
Kuwait (h) 0-6, Oman (h) 0-1, UAE (a) 2-6, Bangladesh (h) 4-0, Bangladesh (a) 0-2, South Korea (a) 0-6, Syria (h) 2-3, UAE (h) 3-1, Kuwait (h) 2-2, Kuwait (a) 1-0, South Korea (h) 2-1.

MACAO

Associacao De Futebol De Macau (AFM), Ave. da Amizade 405, Seng Vo Kok, 13 Andar "A", Macau.
Founded: 1939; *National Colours:* All green.
International matches 2011
Cambodia (a) 1-3, Cambodia (h) 3-2, Vietnam (a) 0-6, Vietnam (h) 1-7, Chinese Taipei (a) 0-3, Hong Kong (a) 1-5, Philippines (a) 0-2.

MALAYSIA

Football Association of Malaysia, 3rd Floor, Wisma Fam, Jalan, SSA/9, Kelana Jaya Selangor Darul Ehsan 47301.
Founded: 1933; *National Colours:* All yellow and black.
International matches 2011
Hong Kong (h) 2-0, Hong Kong (a) 1-1, Burma (h) 2-0, Chinese Taipei (h) 2-1, Chinese Taipei (a) 2-3, Singapore (a) 3-5, Singapore (h) 1-1, Australia (a) 0-5, India (a) 1-1, India (a) 2-3.

MALDIVES REPUBLIC

Football Association of Maldives, National Stadium G. Banafsaa Magu 20-04, Male.
Founded: 1982; *National Colours:* Red shirts, Green shorts, white stockings.
International matches 2011
Cambodia (h) 4-0, Kyrgyzstan (h) 2-1, Tajikistan (h) 0-0, Singapore (a) 0-4, India (h) 1-1, Iran (a) 0-4, Iran (h) 0-1, Mauritius (h) 1-1, Comores (a) 2-2, Seychelles (a) 1-5, Seychelles (h) 3-0, Seychelles (h) 2-1, Nepal (h) 1-1, Pakistan (h) 0-0, Bangladesh (h) 3-1, India (a) 1-3.

MONGOLIA

Mongolia Football Federation, PO Box 259 Ulaan-Baatar 210646.
National Colours: White shirts, red shorts, white stockings.
International matches 2011
Philippines (a) 0-2, Philippines (h) 2-1, Burma (h) 1-0, Burma (a) 0-2.

NEPAL

All-Nepal Football Association, AMFA House, Ward No. 4, Bishalnagar, PO Box 12582, Kathmandu.
Founded: 1951; *National Colours:* All red.
International matches 2011
Bhutan (h) 1-0, Bhutan (h) 2-1, Afghanistan (h) 1-0, North Korea (h) 0-1, Sri Lanka (h) 0-0, Timor-Leste (h) 2-1, Timor-Leste (a) 5-0, Jordan (a) 0-9, Jordan (h) 1-1, Philippines (a) 0-4, Maldives (a) 1-1, Bangladesh (a) 1-0, Pakistan (a) 1-1, Afghanistan (a) 0-1.

OMAN

Oman Football Association, P.O. Box 3462, Ruwi Postal Code 112.
Founded: 1978; *National Colours:* All white.
International matches 2011
Tunisia (h) 2-1, Kuwait (a) 1-1, Lebanon (a) 1-0, Syria (h) 1-1, Burma (h) 2-0, Bahrain (h) 1-1, Kuwait (h) 1-0, Saudi Arabia (h) 0-0, Thailand (a) 0-3, Australia (a) 0-3, Qatar (a) 0-0, Australia (h) 1-0, Saudi Arabia (a) 0-0, Saudi Arabia (a) 0-0, Kuwait (h) 0-2.

PAKISTAN

Pakistan Football Federation, 6 National Hockey Stadium, Feroze Pure Road, Lahore, Pakistan.
Founded: 1948; *National Colours:* All green and white.
International matches 2011
Turkmenistan (h) 0-3, India (h) 1-3, Chinese Taipei (h) 2-0, Bangladesh (a) 0-3, Bangladesh (h) 0-0, Bangladesh (a) 0-0, Maldives (a) 0-0, Nepal (h) 1-1.

PALESTINE

Palestinian Football Federation, Al-Yarmouk, Gaza.
Founded: 1928; *National Colours:* White shirts, black shorts, white stockings.
International matches 2011
Tanzania (a) 0-1, Bangladesh (h) 2-0, Philippines (h) 0-0, Burma (a) 3-1, Afghanistan (a) 2-0, Afghanistan (h) 1-1, Thailand (a) 0-1, Thailand (h) 2-2, Indonesia (a) 1-4, Iran (a) 0-7, Jordan (a) 1-4, Libya (h) 1-1, Sudan (a) 2-0, Bahrain (a) 1-3, Kuwait (a) 0-3.

PHILIPPINES

Philippine Football Federation, Room 405, Building V, Philsports Complex, Meralco Avenue, Pasig City, Metro Manila.
Founded: 1907; *National Colours:* All blue.
International matches 2011
Mongolia (h) 2-0, Mongolia (a) 1-2, Burma (a) 1-1, Palestine (a) 0-0, Bangladesh (a) 3-0, Sri Lanka (a) 1-1, Sri Lanka (h) 4-0, Kuwait (a) 0-3, Kuwait (h) 1-2, Hong Kong (a) 3-3, Chinese Taipei (a) 0-0, Macau (h) 2-0, Singapore (a) 0-2, Nepal (h) 4-0.

QATAR

Qatar Football Association, 7th Floor, QNOC Building, Cornich, P.O. Box 5333, Doha.
Founded: 1960; *National Colours:* All white.
International matches 2011
Uzbekistan (h) 0-2, China (h) 2-0, Kuwait (h) 3-0, Japan (h) 2-3, Russia (h) 1-1, Vietnam (h) 3-0, Vietnam (a) 1-2, Iraq (h) 0-1, UAE (a) 1-3, Bahrain (a) 0-0, Iran (h) 1-1, Indonesia (a) 3-2, Oman (h) 0-0, Indonesia (h) 4-0, Bahrain (h) 0-0, Bahrain (h) 2-2, Iraq (h) 0-0.

SAUDI ARABIA

Saudi Arabian Football Federation, Al Mather Quarter (Olympic Complex), Prince Faisal Bin Fahad Street, P.O. Box 5844, Riyadh 11432.
Founded: 1959; *National Colours:* White shirts, green shorts, white stockings.
International matches 2011
Angola (h) 0-0, Syria (h) 1-2, Jordan (a) 0-1, Japan (h) 0-5, Jordan (a) 1-1, Kuwait (a) 0-1, Hong Kong (h) 3-0, Hong Kong (a) 5-0, Oman (a) 0-0, Australia (h) 1-3, Indonesia (a) 0-0, Thailand (a) 0-0, Thailand (h) 3-0, Oman (h) 0-0, Oman (h) 0-0, Kuwait (h) 0-2.

SINGAPORE

Football Association of Singapore, Jalan Besar Stadium, 100 Tyrwhitt Road, Singapore 207542.
Founded: 1892; *National Colours:* All red.
International matches 2011
Chinese Taipei (h) 3-2, Malaysia (h) 5-3, Malaysia (a) 1-1, Thailand (a) 0-0, China (a) 1-2, Iraq (h) 0-2, Philippines (h) 2-0, Jordan (h) 0-3, Jordan (a) 0-2, China (h) 0-4, Maldives (h) 4-0.

SRI LANKA

Football Federation of Sri Lanka, 100/9, Independence Avenue, Colombo 07.
Founded: 1939; *National Colours:* All white.
International matches 2011
Tajikistan (h) 2-2, Tajikistan (h) 0-2, North Korea (a) 0-4, Afghanistan (h) 0-1, Nepal (a) 0-0, Philippines (h) 1-1, Philippines (a) 0-4, Bhutan (h) 3-0, Afghanistan (h) 1-3, India (a) 0-3.

SYRIA

Syrian Football Federation, PO Box 421, Maysaloon Street, Damascus.
Founded: 1936; *National Colours:* All red.
International matches 2011
UAE (a) 0-2, Saudi Arabia (a) 2-1, Japan (h) 1-2, Jordan (a) 1-2, Iraq (a) 2-1, Jordan (a) 3-1, Oman (a) 1-1, Tajikistan (h) 0-3, Tajikistan (a) 0-3, Kazakhstan (a) 1-1, Lebanon (a) 3-2.

TAJIKISTAN

Tajikistan Football Federation, 22 Shotemur Ave., Dushanbe 734 025.
Founded: 1991; *National Colours:* All white.
International matches 2011
Kyrgyzstan (h) 1-0, Cambodia (a) 3-0, Maldives (a) 0-0, Sri Lanka (a) 2-2, Sri Lanka (a) 2-0, Syria (a) 3-0, Syria (h) 3-0, Uzbekistan (h) 0-1, North Korea (a) 0-1, Japan (a) 0-8, Japan (h) 0-4, Uzbekistan (a) 0-3.

THAILAND

The Football Association of Thailand, Gate 3, Rama I Road, Patumwan, Bangkok 10330.
Founded: 1916; *National Colours:* All red.
International matches 2011
Burma (h) 1-0, Burma (h) 1-1, Palestine (h) 1-0, Palestine (a) 2-2, Singapore (h) 0-0, Australia (a) 1-2, Oman (h) 3-0, Jordan (h) 0-0, Saudi Arabia (h) 0-0, Saudi Arabia (a) 0-3, Australia (h) 0-1.

TIMOR-LESTE

Federacao Futebol Timor-Leste, Rua 12 de Novembro Str., Cruz, Dili.
Founded: 2002; *National Colours:* Red shirts, black shorts, red stockings.
International matches 2011
Nepal (a) 1-2, Nepal (h) 0-5.

TURKMENISTAN

Football Association of Turkmenistan, 32 Belinskiy Street, Stadium Kopetdag, Ashgabat 744 001.
Founded: 1992; *National Colours:* Green shirts, white shorts, green stockings.
International matches 2011
Pakistan (a) 3-0, Chinese Taipei (a) 2-0, India (h) 1-1, Indonesia (h) 1-1, Indonesia (a) 3-4.

UNITED ARAB EMIRATES

United Arab Emirates Football Association, P.O. Box 916, Abu Dhabi.
Founded: 1971; *National Colours:* All white.
International matches 2011
Syria (h) 2-0, Australia (h) 0-0, North Korea (a) 0-0, Iraq (h) 0-1, Iran (h) 0-3, Lebanon (h) 6-2, India (h) 3-0, India (a) 2-2, Qatar (h) 3-1, Kuwait (h) 2-3, Lebanon (a) 1-3, China (a) 1-2, South Korea (a) 1-2, South Korea (h) 0-2, Kuwait (a) 1-2.

UZBEKISTAN

Uzbekistan Football Federation, Massiv Almazar Furkat Street 15/1, 700003 Tashkent, Uzbekistan.
Founded: 1946; *National Colours:* All white.
International matches 2011
Jordan (a) 2-2, Qatar (a) 2-0, Kuwait (h) 2-1, China (a) 2-2, Jordan (h) 2-1, Australia (h) 0-6, South Korea (a) 2-3, Montenegro (a) 0-1, Ukraine (a) 0-2, China (a) 0-1, Kyrgyzstan (h) 4-0, Kyrgyzstan (a) 3-0, Tajikistan (a) 1-0, Japan (h) 1-1, North Korea (a) 1-0, North Korea (h) 1-0, Tajikistan (h) 3-0.

VIETNAM

Vietnam Football Federation, 18 Ly van Phuc, Dong Da District, Hanoi 844.
Founded: 1962; *National Colours:* All red.
International matches 2011
Macau (h) 6-0, Macau (a) 7-1, Qatar (a) 0-3, Qatar (h) 2-1, Japan (a) 0-1.

YEMEN

Yemen Football Association, Quarter of Sport – Al Jeraf, Behind the Stadium of Ali Mushsen, Al Moreissy in the Sport, Al-Thawra City.
Founded: 1962; *National Colours:* All green.
International matches 2011
Jordan (a) 0-4, Iraq (a) 0-2, Iraq (h) 0-0.

CONCACAF

ANGUILLA

Anguilla Football Association, P.O. Box 1318, The Valley, Anguilla, BWI.
National Colours: Turquoise, white, orange and blue shirts and shorts, turquoise and orange stockings.
International matches 2011
US Virgin Islands (h) 0-0, Dominican Republic (h) 0-2, Dominican Republic (a) 0-4.

ANTIGUA & BARBUDA

The Antigua/Barbuda Football Association, Newgate Street, P.O. Box 773, St John's.
Founded: 1928; *National Colours:* Red, black, yellow and blue shirts, black shorts and stockings.
International matches 2011
Grenada (a) 2-2, St Vincent & The Grenadines (h) 1-0, St Vincent & The Grenadines (h) 2-2, Martinique (h) 1-0, Martinique (h) 1-2, Curacao (h) 5-2, US Virgin Islands (a) 8-1, Curacao (a) 1-0, US Virgin Islands (h) 10-0, Haiti (h) 1-0, Haiti (a) 1-2.

ARUBA

Arubaanse Voetbal Bond, Ferguson Street, Z/N P.O. Box 376, Oranjestad, Aruba.
Founded: 1932; *National Colours:* Yellow shirts, blue shorts, yellow and blue stockings.
International matches 2011
St Lucia (h) 4-2, St Lucia (a) 2-4, Surinam (a) 0-0.

BAHAMAS

Bahamas Football Association, Plaza on the Way, West Bay Street, P.O. Box N 8434, Nassau, NP.
Founded: 1967; *National Colours:* Yellow shirts, black shorts, yellow stockings.
International matches 2011
Turks & Caicos Islands (a) 4-0, Turks & Caicos Islands (h) 6-0.

BARBADOS

Barbados Football Association, Hildor No. 4, 10th Avenue, P.O. Box 1362, Belleville-St. Michael, Barbados.
Founded: 1910; *National Colours:* Royal blue and gold shirts, gold shorts, white, gold and blue stockings.
International matches 2011
Guyana (a) 0-1, Guyana (a) 2-3, St Vincent & The Grenadines (h) 0-0, Guyana (h) 1-1, St Lucia (h) 4-0, Guyana (a) 0-2, Trinidad & Tobago (h) 0-2, Guyana (h) 0-2, Trinidad & Tobago (a) 0-4, Bermuda (a) 1-2, Bermuda (h) 1-2.

BELIZE

Belize National Football Association, 26 Hummingbird Highway, Belmopan, P.O. Box 1742, Belize City.
Founded: 1980; *National Colours:* Red, white and black shirts, black shorts, red and black stockings.
International matches 2011
Panama (a) 0-2, El Salvador (h) 2-5, Nicaragua (a) 1-1, Monserrat (a) 5-2, Monserrat (h) 3-1, Grenada (a) 3-0, Guatemala (h) 1-2, Grenada (h) 1-4, Guatemala (a) 1-3, St Vincent & The Grenadines (h) 1-1, St Vincent & The Grenadines (a) 2-0.

BERMUDA

The Bermuda Football Association, 48 Cedar Avenue, Hamilton HM12.
Founded: 1928; *National Colours:* All blue.
International matches 2011
Trinidad & Tobago (a) 0-1, Guyana (a) 1-2, Trinidad & Tobago (h) 2-1, Guyana (h) 1-1, Barbados (h) 2-1, Barbados (a) 2-1.

BRITISH VIRGIN ISLANDS

British Virgin Islands Football Association, P.O. Box 29, Road Town, Tortola, BVI.
National Colours: Gold and green shirts, green shorts, and stockings.
International matches 2011
US Virgin Islands (a) 0-2, US Virgin (h) 1-2.

US VIRGIN ISLANDS

USVI Soccer Federation Inc., 54, Castle Coakley, PO Box 2346, Kingshill, St Croix 00851.
National Colours: Royal blue and gold shirts, royal blue shorts and stockings.
International matches 2011
Anguilla (a) 0-0, British Virgin Islands (h) 2-0, British Virgin Islands (a) 2-1, Haiti (a) 0-6, Antiqua (h) 1-8, Haiti (h) 0-7, Antigua (a) 0-10, Curacao (h) 0-3, Curacao (a) 1-6.

CANADA

The Canadian Soccer Association, Place Soccer Canada, 237 Metcalfe Street, Ottawa, ONT K2P 1R2.
Founded: 1912; *National Colours:* All red.
International matches 2011
Greece (a) 0-1, Belarus (a) 1-0, Ecuador (h) 2-2, USA (a) 0-2, Guadeloupe (h) 1-0, Panama (h) 1-1, St Lucia (h) 4-1, Puerto Rico (a) 3-0, St Lucia (a) 7-0, Puerto Rico (h) 0-0, St Kitts & Nevis (a) 0-0, St Kitts & Nevis (h) 4-0.

CAYMAN ISLANDS

Cayman Islands Football Association, PO Box 178 GT, Truman Bodden Sports Complex, Olympic Way Off Walkers Rd, George Town, Grand Cayman, Cayman Islands WI.
Founded: 1966; *National Colours:* Red and white shirts, blue and white shorts, white and red stockings.
International matches 2011
Surinam (a) 0-1, El Salvador (h) 1-4, Surinam (h) 0-1, El Salvador (a) 0-4, Dominican Republic (a) 0-4, Dominican Republic (h) 1-1.

COSTA RICA

Federacion Costarricense De Futbol, Costado Norte Estatua Leon Cortes, San Jose 670-1000.
Founded: 1921; *National Colours:* Red shirts, blue shorts, white stockings.
International matches 2011
Honduras (h) 1-1, Guatemala (a) 2-0, Panama (a) 1-1, Honduras (a) 1-2, Venezuela (a) 2-2, China (h) 2-2, Argentina (h) 0-0, Cuba (h) 5-0, El Salvador (h) 1-1, Mexico (a) 1-4, Honduras (h) 1-1, Colombia (a) 0-1, Bolivia (a) 2-0, Argentina (a) 0-3, Ecuador (h) 0-2, USA (a) 1-0, Ecuador (a) 0-4, Brazil (h) 0-1, Panama (a) 0-2, Spain (h) 2-2, Cuba (a) 1-1, Venezuela (a) 2-0.

CUBA

Asociacion de Futbol de Cuba, Calle 13 No. 661, Esq. C. Vedado, ZP 4, La Habana.
Founded: 1924; *National Colours:* All red, white and blue.
International matches 2011
El Salvador (h) 0-1, Panama (h) 0-2, Nicaragua (h) 1-1, Nicaragua (h) 2-1, Cost Rica (a) 0-5, Mexico (h) 0-5, El Salvador (a) 1-6, Costa Rica (h) 1-1.

CURACAO

(Formerly Netherlands Antilles)

Curacao Football Federation, Bonamweg 49, PO Box 341, Willemstad, Curacao.
Founded: 1921; *National Colours:* Blue shirts, red shorts and stockings.
International matches 2011
Dominican Republic (a) 0-1, Dominican Republic (a) 0-1, Antigua (a) 2-5, Haiti (h) 2-4, Surinam (a) 0-2, Surinam (a) 2-2, Antigua (h) 0-1, Haiti (a) 2-2, US Virgin Islands (a) 3-0, US Virgin Islands (h) 6-1, Surinam (a) 0-2.

DOMINICA

Dominica Football Association, 33 Great Marlborough Street, Roseau.
Founded: 1970; *National Colours:* Emerald green shirts, black shorts, green stockings.
International matches 2011
Nicaragua (h) 0-2, St Vincent & The Grenadines (a) 0-1, Panama (h) 0-5, Nicaragua (a) 0-1, Panama (a) 0-3.

DOMINICAN REPUBLIC

Federacion Dominicana De Futbol, Centro Olimpico Juan Pablo Duarte, Ensanche Miraflores, Apartado De Correos No. 1953, Santo Domingo.
Founded: 1953; *National Colours:* Navy blue shirts, white shorts, red stockings.
International matches 2011
Anguilla (a) 2-0, Anguilla (h) 4-0, Curacao (h) 1-0, Curacao (h) 1-0, El Salvador (a) 2-3, Surinam (h) 1-1, El Salvador (h) 1-2, Surinam (a) 3-1, Cayman Islands (h) 4-0, Cayman Islands (a) 1-1.

EL SALVADOR

Federacion Salvadorena De Futbol, Primera Calle Poniente No. 2025, San Salvador CA1029.
Founded: 1935; *National Colours:* All blue.
International matches 2011
Nicaragua (h) 2-0, Belize (a) 5-2, Panama (a) 0-2, Honduras (a) 0-2, Panama (a) 0-0, Haiti (h) 1-0, Cuba (a) 1-0, Jamaica (h) 2-3, Honduras (h) 2-2, Mexico (a) 0-5, Costa Rica (a) 1-1, Cuba (h) 6-1, Panama (a) 1-1, Venezuela (h) 2-1, Dominican Republic (h) 3-2, Cayman Islands (a) 4-1, Dominican Republic (a) 2-1, Cayman Islands (h) 4-0, Surinam (a) 3-1, Surinam (h) 4-0.

GRENADA

Grenada Football Association, P.O. Box 326, National Stadium, Queens Park, St George's, Grenada, W.I.
Founded: 1924; *National Colours:* Green and yellow striped shirts, red shorts, yellow stockings.
International matches 2011
St Kitts & Nevis (a) 0-0, St Kitts & Nevis (h) 0-1, Antigua (h) 2-2, Panama (a) 0-2, Jamaica (a) 0-4, Honduras (h) 1-7, Guatemala (a) 0-4, Belize (h) 0-3, StVincent & The Grenadines (a) 1-2, Belize (a) 4-1, St Vincent & The Grenadines (h) 1-1, Guatemala (a) 0-3, Guatemala (h) 1-4.

GUADELOUPE

Ligue Guadeloupeenne de Football, Rue de la Ville D'Orly, Bergevin, 97110, Pointe-a-Pitre.
Not affiliated to FIFA.
International matches 2011
Panama (a) 2-3, Canada (a) 0-1, USA (a) 0-1.

GUATEMALA

Federacion Nacional de Futbol de Guatemala, 2a Calle 15-57, Zona 15, Boulevard Vista Hermosa, Guatemala City 01009.
Founded: 1946; *National Colours:* Blue shirts, white shorts, blue stockings.
International matches 2011
Costa Rica (h) 0-2, Honduras (a) 1-3, Nicaragua (a) 2-1, Bolivia (h) 1-1, Venezuela (h) 0-2, Honduras (a) 0-0, Jamaica (a) 0-2, Grenada (h) 4-0, Mexico (a) 1-2, St Vincent & The Grenadines (h) 4-0, Belize (a) 2-1, St Vincent & The Grenadines (a) 3-0, Belize (h) 3-1, Grenada (h) 3-0, Grenada (a) 4-1.

GUYANA

Guyana Football Federation, 159 Rupununi Street, Bel Air Park, P.O. Box 10727, Georgetown.
Founded: 1902; *National Colours:* Green shirts and shorts, yellow stockings.
International matches 2011
Barbados (h) 1-0, Barbados (h) 3-2, Barbados (a) 1-1, India (h) 2-1, Barbados (h) 2-0, Bermuda (h) 2-1, Barbados (a) 2-0, Bermuda (a) 1-1, Trinidad & Tobago (h) 2-1, Trinidad & Tobago (a) 0-2.

HAITI

Federation Haitienne De Football, 128 Avenue Christiophe, P.O. Box 2258, Port-Au-Prince.
Founded: 1904; *National Colours:* Blue shirts, red shorts, blue stockings.
International matches 2011
El Salvador (a) 0-1, US Virgin Islands (h) 6-0, Curacao (a) 4-2, US Virgin Islands (a) 7-0, Curacao (h) 2-2, Antigua (a) 0-1, Antigua (h) 2-1.

HONDURAS

Federacion Nacional Autonoma De Futbol De Honduras, Colonia Florencia Norte, Ave Roble, Edificio Plaza America, Ave. Roble 1 y 2 Nivel, Tegucigalpa, D.C.
Founded: 1951; *National Colours:* All white.
International matches 2011
Costa Rica (a) 1-1, Guatemala (h) 3-1, El Salvador (h) 2-0, Costa Rica (h) 2-1, Ecuador (h) 1-1, South Korea (a) 0-4, China (a) 0-3, El Salvador (a) 2-2, Guatemala (h) 0-0, Grenada (a) 7-1, Jamaica (h) 0-1, Costa Rica (a) 1-1,

Mexico (h) 0-2, Venezuela (h) 2-0, Colombia (h) 0-2, Paraguay (h) 0-3, USA (a) 0-1, Jamaica (h) 2-1, Serbia (h) 2-0.

JAMAICA

Jamaica Football Federation Ltd, 20 St Lucia Crescent, Kingston 5.
Founded: 1910; *National Colours:* Gold shirts, black shorts, gold stockings.
International matches 2011
Venezuela (h) 0-2, El Salvador (a) 3-2, Grenada (h) 4-0, Guatemala (h) 2-0, Honduras (a) 1-0, USA (h) 0-2, China (a) 0-1, Ecuador (a) 2-5, Colombia (h) 0-2, Honduras (a) 1-2.

MARTINIQUE

2, Rue Saint John Perse, Nome Tartenson, BP 307, 97203 Fort de France.
Not affiliated to FIFA.
International matches 2011
Antigua (a) 0-1, Antigua (a) 2-1.

MEXICO

Federacion Mexicana De Futbol Asociacion, A.C., Colima No. 373, Colonia Roma Mexico DF 06700.
Founded: 1927; *National Colours:* Green shirts with white collar, white shorts, red stockings.
International matches 2011
Bosnia (h) 2-0, Paraguay (h) 3-1, Venezuela (h) 1-1, Ecuador (h) 1-1, New Zealand (h) 3-0, El Salvador (h) 5-0, Cuba (a) 5-0, Costa Rica (h) 4-1, Guatemala (h) 2-1, Honduras (a) 2-0, USA (a) 4-2, Chile (a) 1-2, Peru (a) 0-1, Uruguay (a) 0-1, USA (a) 1-1, Poland (a) 1-1, Chile (h) 1-0, Brazil (h) 1-2, Serbia (h) 2-0.

MONSERRAT

Monserrat Football Association Inc., P.O. Box 505, Woodlands, Monserrat.
National Colours: Green shirts with black and white stripes, green shorts with white stripes, green stockings with black and white stripes.
International matches 2011
Belize (h) 2-5, Belize (a) 1-3.

NICARAGUA

Federacion Nicaraguense De Futbol, Hospital Pautista 1, Cuadra avajo, 1 cuada al Sur y 1/2, Cuadra Abajo, Managua 976.
Founded: 1931; *National Colours:* Blue shirts, white shorts, blue stockings.
International matches 2011
El Salvador (a) 0-2, Panama (a) 0-2, Belize (h) 1-1, Guatemala (h) 1-2, Cuba (a) 1-1, Cuba (a) 0-2, Dominica (a) 2-0, Panama (h) 1-2, Panama (a) 1-5, Dominica (h) 1-0.

PANAMA

Federacion Panamena De Futbol, Estadio Rommel Fernandez, Puerta 24, Ave. Jose Aeustin Araneo, Apartado Postal 8-391, Zona 8, Panama.
Founded: 1937; *National Colours:* All red.
International matches 2011
Belize (h) 2-0, Nicaragua (h) 2-0, El Salvador (h) 2-0, Costa Rica (h) 1-1, El Salvador (h) 0-0, Peru (a) 0-1, Bolivia (h) 2-0, Cuba (a) 2-0, Grenada (h) 2-0, Guadeloupe (h) 3-2, USA (a) 2-1, Canada (a) 1-1, El Salvador (h) 1-1, USA (a) 0-1, Bolivia (a) 3-1, Paraguay (h) 0-2, Nicaragua (a) 2-1, Dominica (a) 5-0, Nicaragua (h) 5-1, Costa Rica (h) 2-0, Dominica (h) 3-0.

PUERTO RICO

Federacion Puertorriquena De Futbol, P.O. Box 193590 San Juan 00919.
Founded: 1940; *National Colours:* Red, blue and white shirts and shorts, red and blue stockings.
International matches 2011
St Kitts & Nevis (a) 0-0, Canada (h) 0-3, St Kitts & Nevis (h) 1-1, Canada (a) 0-0, St Lucia (a) 4-0, St Lucia (h) 3-0.

ST KITTS & NEVIS

St Kitts & Nevis Football Association, P.O. Box 465, Warner Park, Basseterre, St Kitts, W.I.
Founded: 1932; *National Colours:* Green and yellow shirts, red shorts, yellow stockings.
International matches 2011
Grenada (h) 0-0, Grenada (a) 1-0, Puerto Rico (h) 0-0, St Lucia (a) 4-2, Puerto Rico (a) 1-1, St Lucia (h) 1-1, Canada (h) 0-0, Canada (a) 0-4.

ST LUCIA

St Lucia National Football Association, PO Box 255, Sans Souci, Castries, St Lucia.
Founded: 1979; *National Colours:* White shirts and shorts with yellow, blue and black stripes, white, blue and yellow stockings.
International matches 2011
Aruba (a) 2-4, Aruba (h) 4-2, Barbados (a) 0-4, Canada (a) 1-4, St Kitts & Nevis (h) 2-4, Canada (h) 0-7, St Kitts & Nevis (a) 1-1, Puerto Rico (h) 0-4, Puerto Rico (a) 0-3.

ST VINCENT & THE GRENADINES

St Vincent & The Grenadines Football Federation, Sharpe Street, PO Box 1278, Saint George.
Founded: 1979; *National Colours:* Green shirts with yellow border, blue shorts, yellow stockings.
International matches 2011
Barbados (a) 0-0, Antigua (a) 0-1, Antigua (a) 2-2, Guatemala (a) 0-4, Dominica (h) 1-0, Grenada (h) 2-1, Guatemala (h) 0-3, Grenada (a) 1-1, Belize (a) 1-1, Belize (h) 0-2.

SURINAM

Surinaamse Voetbal Bond, Letitia Vriesde Laan 7, P.O. Box 1223, Paramaribo.
Founded: 1920; *National Colours:* White, green and red shirts, green and white shirts and stockings.
International matches 2011
Cayman Islands (h) 1-0, Dominican Republic (a) 1-1, Curacao (h) 2-0, Curacao (h) 2-2, Cayman Islands (a) 1-0, Dominican Republic (h) 1-3, El Salvador (h) 1-3, El Salvador (a) 0-4, Aruba (h) 0-0, Curacao (h) 2-0.

TRINIDAD & TOBAGO

Trinidad & Tobago Football Federation, 24–26 Dundonald Street, PO Box 400, Port of Spain.
Founded: 1908; *National Colours:* Red shirts, black shorts, white stockings.
International matches 2011
India (h) 3-0, Bermuda (h) 1-0, Barbados (a) 2-0, Bermuda (a) 1-2, Barbados (h) 4-0, Guyana (a) 1-2, Guyana (h) 2-0.

TURKS & CAICOS

Turks & Caicos Islands Football Association, P.O. Box 626, Tropicana Plaza, Leeward Highway, Providenciales.
National Colours: All white.
International matches 2011
Bahamas (h) 0-4, Bahamas (a) 0-6.

USA

US Soccer Federation, US Soccer House, 1801–1811 S. Prairie Avenue, Chicago, Illinois 60616.
Founded: 1913; *National Colours:* White shirts, blue shorts, white stockings.
International matches 2011
Chile (h) 1-1, Argentina (h) 1-1, Paraguay (h) 0-1, Spain (h) 0-4, Canada (h) 2-0, Panama (h) 1-2, Guadeloupe (h) 1-0, Jamaica (a) 2-0, Panama (h) 1-0, Mexico (h) 2-4, Mexico (h) 1-1, Costa Rica (h) 0-1, Belgium (a) 0-1, Honduras (h) 1-0, Ecuador (h) 0-1, France (a) 0-1, Slovenia (a) 3-2.

OCEANIA

AMERICAN SAMOA

American Samoa Football Association, P.O. Box 282, Pago Pago AS 96799.
National Colours: Navy blue shirts, white shorts, red stockings.
International matches 2011
Solomon Islands (h) 0-4, Guam (h) 0-2, New Caledonia (a) 0-8, Vanuatu (h) 0-8, Tonga (h) 2-1, Cook Islands (h) 1-1, Samoa (a) 0-1.

COOK ISLANDS

Cook Islands Football Association, Victoria Road, Tupapa, P.O. Box 29, Avarua, Rarotonga, Cook Islands.
Founded: 1971; *National Colours:* Green shirts with white sleeves, green shorts, white stockings.
International matches 2011
Papua New Guinea (a) 0-4, Tahiti (a) 0-7, Fiji (h) 1-4, Samoa (h) 2-3, American Samoa (a) 1-1, Tonga (a) 1-2.

FIJI

Fiji Football Association, PO Box 2514, Government Buildings, Suva.
Founded: 1938; *National Colours:* White shirts, blue shorts and stockings.
International matches 2011
Vanuatu (h) 2-0, Vanuatu (h) 1-2, Samoa (h) 3-0, Samoa (h) 5-1, Tahiti (h) 3-0, Cook Islands (a) 4-1, Papua New Guinea (a) 2-0, Solomon Islands (h) 1-2, Tahiti (a) 1-2.

NEW CALEDONIA

Federation Caledonienne de Football, 7 bis, Rue Suffren Quartien latin, BP 560, 99845 Noumea, New Caledonia.
Founded: 1928; *National Colours:* Grey shirts, red shorts, grey stockings.
International matches 2011
Vanuatu (a) 0-0, Tahiti (a) 3-1, Tahiti (a) 0-1, Vanuatu (h) 5-0, Guam (h) 9-0, American Samoa (h) 8-0, Solomon Islands (h) 1-2, Tahiti (h) 3-1, Solomon Islands (h) 2-0.

NEW ZEALAND

New Zealand Soccer Inc., PO Box 301 043, Albany, Auckland, New Zealand.
Founded: 1891; *National Colours:* All white.
International matches 2011
China (a) 1-1, Mexico (a) 0-3, Australia (a) 0-3.

PAPUA NEW GUINEA

Papua New Guinea Football Association, PO Box 957, Room II Level I, Haus Tisa, Lae.
Founded: 1962; *National Colours:* Red and yellow shirts, black shorts, yellow stockings.
International matches 2011
Cook Islands (h) 4-0, Tahiti (a) 1-1, Fiji (h) 0-2.

SAMOA

The Samoa Football Soccer Federation, P.O. Box 960, Apia.
Founded: 1968; *National Colours:* Blue, white and red shirts, blue and white shorts, red and blue stockings.
International matches 2011
Fiji (a) 0-3, Fiji (a) 1-5, Cook Islands (a) 3-2, Tonga (h) 1-1, American Samoa (h) 1-0.

SOLOMON ISLANDS

Solomon Islands Football Federation, PO Box 854, Honiara, Solomon Islands.
Founded: 1978; *National Colours:* Gold and blue shirts, blue and white shorts, white and blue stockings.
International matches 2011
Vanuatu (h) 2-1, Vanuatu (h) 0-0, Vanuatu (a) 0-0, Vanuatu (a) 0-2, Guam (h) 7-0, American Samoa (a) 4-0, Vanuatu (a) 0-1, New Caledonia (a) 2-1, Fiji (a) 2-1, New Caledonia (a) 0-2.

TAHITI

Federation Tahitienne de Football, Rue Coppenrath Stade de Fautana, PO Box 50858 Pirae 98716.
Founded: 1989; *National Colours:* Red shirts, white shorts, red stockings.
International matches 2011
New Caledonia (h) 1-3, New Caledonia (h) 1-0, Fiji (a) 0-3, Cook Islands (h) 7-0, Papua New Guinea (h) 1-1, New Caledonia (a) 1-3, Fiji (h) 2-1.

TONGA

Tonga Football Association, Tungi Arcade, Taufa'Ahau Road, P.O. Box 852, Nuku'Alofa, Tonga.
Founded: 1965; *National Colours:* Red shirts, white shorts, red stockings.
International matches 2011
American Samoa (a) 1-2, Samoa (a) 1-1, Cook Islands (h) 2-1.

VANUATU

Vanuatu Football Federation, P.O. Box 266, Port Vila, Vanuatu.
Founded: 1934; *National Colours:* Gold and black shirts, black shorts, gold and black stockings.
International matches 2011
New Caledonia (h) 0-0, Solomon Islands (a) 1-2, Solomon Islands (a) 0-0, Fiji (a) 0-2, Fiji (a) 2-1, Solomon Islands (h) 0-0, Solomon Islands (h) 2-0, New Caledonia (a) 0-5, Solomon Islands (h) 1-0, Guam (a) 4-1, American Samoa (a) 8-0.

AFRICA

ALGERIA

Federation Algerienne De Foot-ball, Chemin Ahmed Ouaked, Boite Postale No. 39, Dely-Ibrahim-Alger.
Founded: 1962; *National Colours:* Green shirts, white shorts, green stockings.
International matches 2011
Morocco (h) 1-0, Morocco (a) 0-4, Tanzania (a) 1-1, Central Africa (h) 2-0, Tunisia (h) 1-0.

ANGOLA

Federation Angolaise De Football, Compl. da Cidadela Desportiva, B.P. 3449, Luanda.
Founded: 1979; *National Colours:* Red shirts, black shorts, red stockings.
International matches 2011
Iran (a) 0-1, Saudi Arabia (a) 0-0, Kenya (a) 1-2, Kenya (h) 1-0, Liberia (a) 0-0, DR Congo (h) 1-2, Uganda (h) 2-0, Guinea-Bissau (a) 2-0, Zambia (h) 1-0, Namibia (h) 0-0.

BENIN

Federation Beninoise De Football, Stade Rene Pleven d'Akpakpa, B.P. 965, Cotonou 01.
Founded: 1962; *National Colours:* Green shirts, Yellow shorts, red stockings.
International matches 2011
Libya (a) 2-3, Ivory Coast (a) 1-2, Ivory Coast (h) 2-6, Burundi (a) 1-1, Rwanda (h) 0-1.

BOTSWANA

Botswana Football Association, P.O. Box 1396, Gabarone.
Founded: 1970; *National Colours:* Blue, white and black striped shirts, blue, white and black shorts and stockings.
International matches 2011
Sweden (h) 1-2, Mozambique (a) 1-1, Namibia (h) 1-1, Chad (a) 1-0, Swaziland (a) 0-0, Malawi (h) 0-0, Swaziland (a) 2-0, Kenya (h) 1-0, Lesotho (h) 1-2, Togo (a) 0-1, Nigeria (a) 0-0, Niger (a) 1-1.

BURKINA FASO

Federation Burkinabe De Foot-Ball, 01 B.P. 57, Ouagadougou 01.
Founded: 1960; *National Colours:* All green, red and white.
International matches 2011
Cape Verde Islands (h) 0-1, Namibia (h) 4-0, Namibia (a) 4-1, South Africa (a) 0-3, Equatorial Guinea (h) 1-0, Gambia (a) 1-1, Mali (h) 1-1, Guinea (a) 1-1.

BURUNDI

Federation De Football Du Burundi, Bulding Nyogozi, Boulevard de l'Uprona, B.P. 3426, Bujumbura.
Founded: 1948; *National Colours:* Red and white shirts, white and red shorts, green stockings.
International matches 2011
Uganda (a)-1-3, Tanzania (a) 1-1, Egypt (a) 0-3, Rwanda (a) 1-3, Rwanda (h) 3-1, Benin (h) 1-1, Ivory Coast (a) 1-2, Lesotho (a) 0-1, Lesotho (h) 2-2, Somalia (h) 4-1, Uganda (h) 0-1, Sudan (h) 0-2.

CAMEROON

Federation Camerounaise De Football, B.P. 1116, Yaounde.
Founded: 1959; *National Colours:* Green shirts, red shorts, yellow stockings.
International matches 2011
Macedonia (a) 1-0, Senegal (a) 0-1, Senegal (h) 0-0, Russia (a) 0-0, Mauritius (h) 5-0, DR Congo (a) 3-2, Equatorial Guinea (a) 1-1, Sudan (h) 3-1, Morocco (a) 1-1.

CAPE VERDE ISLANDS

Federacao Cabo-Verdiana De Futebol, Praia Cabo Verde, FCF CX, P.O. Box 234, Praia.
Founded: 1982; *National Colours:* Blue and white shirts and shorts, blue and red stockings.
International matches 2011
Burkina Faso (h) 1-0, Liberia (h) 4-2, Liberia (a) 0-1, Mali (a) 0-3, Zimbabwe (h) 2-1.

CENTRAL AFRICAN REPUBLIC

Federation Centrafricaine De Football, Immeuble Soca Constructa, B.P. 344, Bangui.
Founded: 1937; *National Colours:* Blue and white shirts, white shorts, blue stockings.
International matches 2011
Tanzania (a) 1-2, Tunisia (a) 0-3, Tanzania (h) 2-1, Malta (a) 1-2, Morocco (h) 0-0, Equatorial Guinea (a) 0-2, Algeria (a) 0-2.

CHAD

Federation Tchadienne de Football, B.P. 886, N'Djamena.
Founded: 1962; *National Colours:* Blue shirts, yellow shorts, red stockings.
International matches 2011
Equatorial Guinea (a) 0-2, Botswana (h) 0-1, Tunisia (a) 0-5, Malawi (h) 2-2, Tanzania (h) 1-2, Tanzania (a) 1-0.

COMOROS

Comoros FA, BP 798, Moroni.
Founded: 1979.
International matches 2011
Libya (a) 0-3, Libya (h) 1-1, Seychelles (a) 0-0, Maldives (h) 2-2, Mauritius (a) 0-2, Zambia (h) 1-2, Mozambique (a) 0-3, Mozambique (h) 0-1, Mozambique (a) 1-4.

CONGO

Federation Congolaise De Football, 80 Rue Eugene-Etienne, Centre Ville, PO Box 11, Brazzaville.
Founded: 1962; *National Colours:* Green shirts, yellow shorts, red stockings.
International matches 2011
Ghana (h) 0-3, Ghana (a) 1-3, Sudan (h) 0-1, Swaziland (a) 1-0, St Thomas & Principe (a) 5-0, St Thomas & Principe (h) 1-1.

CONGO DR

Federation Congolaise De Football-Association, Av. de l'Enseignemt 210, C/Kasa-Vubu, Kinshasa 1.
Founded: 1919; *National Colours:* Blue and yellow shirts, yellow and blue shorts, white and blue stockings.
International matches 2011
Kenya (h) 1-0, Sudan (h) 2-1, Uganda (h) 0-1, Kenya (h) 1-0, Gabon (h) 0-2, Mauritius (h) 3-0, Mauritius (a) 2-1, Gambia (a) 0-3, Angola (a) 2-1, Senegal (a) 0-2, Cameroon (h) 2-3, Lesotho (a) 3-0, Swaziland (a) 3-1, Swaziland (h) 5-1.

DJIBOUTI

Federation Djiboutienne de Football, Stade el Haoj Hassan Gouled, B.P. 2694, Djibouti.
Founded: 1977; *National Colours:* Green shirts, white shorts, blue stockings.
International matches 2011
Namibia (h) 0-4, Namibia (a) 0-4, Zimbabwe (a) 0-2, Tanzania (a) 0-3, Rwanda (a) 2-5.

EGYPT

Egyptian Football Association, 5 Gabalaya Street, Guezira, El Borg Post Office, Cairo.
Founded: 1921; *National Colours:* Red shirts, white shorts, black stockings.
International matches 2011
Tanzania (h) 5-1, Uganda (h) 1-0, Burundi (h) 3-0, Kenya (h) 5-1, Uganda (h) 3-1, South Africa (a) 0-1, South Africa (h) 0-0, Sierra Leone (a) 1-2, Niger (h) 3-0, Brazil (a) 0-2.

ERITREA

The Eritrean National Football Federation, Sematat Avenue 29–31, P.O. Box 3665, Asmara.
National Colours: Blue shirts, red shorts, green stockings.
International matches 2011
Sudan (h) 0-3, Rwanda (h) 1-1, Rwanda (a) 1-3.

ETHIOPIA

Ethiopia Football Federation, Addis Ababa Stadium, P.O. Box 1080, Addis Ababa.
Founded: 1943; *National Colours:* Green shirts, yellow shorts, red stockings.
International matches 2011
Nigeria (a) 0-4, Sudan (h) 1-2, Nigeria (h) 2-2, Guinea (a) 0-1, Malawi (h) 0-0, Madagascar (h) 4-2, Somalia (a) 0-0, Somalia (h) 5-0, Sudan (a) 1-1, Kenya (h) 0-2, Malawi (h) 1-1.

GABON

Federation Gabonaise De Football, B.P. 181, Libreville.
Founded: 1962; *National Colours:* Green, yellow and blue shirts, blue and yellow shorts, white stockings with tri-colour trims.
International matches 2011
Congo DR (a) 2-0, Gambia (h) 0-1, Guinea (h) 1-1, Niger (h) 1-0, Equatorial Guinea (h) 2-0, Brazil (h) 0-2, Ghana (a) 1-2.

GAMBIA

Gambia Football Association, Independence Stadium, Bakau, P.O. Box 523, Banjul.
Founded: 1952; *National Colours:* All red, blue and white.
International matches 2011
Guinea-Bissau (a) 1-3, Equatorial Guinea (a) 0-1, Gabon (a) 1-0, Liberia (a) 2-3, Congo DR (h) 3-0, Namibia (a) 0-1, Burkina Faso (h) 1-1.

GHANA

Ghana Football Association, National Sports Council, P.O. Box 1272, Accra.
Founded: 1957; *National Colours:* All yellow.
International matches 2011
Togo (h) 4-1, Congo (a) 3-0, England (a) 1-1, Congo (h) 3-1, South Korea (a) 1-2, Swaziland (h) 2-0, Brazil (a) 0-1, Sudan (a) 2-0, Nigeria (h) 0-0, Gabon (h) 2-1.

GUINEA

Federation Guineenne De Football, P.O. Box 3645, Conakry.
Founded: 1959; *National Colours:* Red shirts, yellow shorts, green stockings.
International matches 2011
Senegal (a) 0-3, Madagascar (a) 1-1, Madagascar (h) 4-1, Gabon (a) 1-1, Ethiopia (h) 1-0, Nigeria (a) 2-2, Senegal (h) 1-4, Burkina Faso (h) 1-1.

GUINEA-BISSAU

Federacao De Football Da Guinea-Bissau, Alto Bandim (Nova Sede), PO Box 375 Bissau 1035.
Founded: 1974; *National Colours:* Red, green and yellow shirts, green and yellow shorts, red, green and yellow stockings.
International matches 2011
Gambia (h) 3-1, Uganda (h) 0-1, Uganda (a) 0-2, Equatorial Guinea (a) 4-1, Kenya (a) 1-2, Angola (h) 0-2, Togo (h) 1-1, Togo (a) 0-1.

GUINEA, EQUATORIAL

Federacion Ecuatoguineana De Futbol, c/P Patricio Lumumba (Estadio La Paz), Malabo 1071.
Founded: 1986; *National Colours:* All red.
International matches 2011
Chad (h) 2-0, Gambia (h) 1-0, Guinea-Bissau (h) 1-4, Burkina Faso (a) 0-1, Central Africa (h) 3-0, Gabon (a) 0-2, Cameroon (h) 1-1, Madagascar (h) 2-0, Madagascar (a) 1-2.

IVORY COAST

Federation Ivoirienne De Football, 01 PO Box 1202, Abidjan 01.
Founded: 1960; *National Colours:* Orange shirts, black shorts, green stockings.
International matches 2011
Mali (h) 1-0, Benin (h) 2-1, Benin (a) 6-2, Israel (h) 4-3, Rwanda (a) 5-0, Burundi (h) 2-1, South Africa (a) 1-1.

KENYA

Kenya Football Federation, Nyayo National Stadium, P.O. Box 40234, Nairobi.
Founded: 1960; *National Colours:* All red.
International matches 2011
Sudan (h) 1-0, Congo DR (a) 0-1, Egypt (a) 1-5, Congo DR (a) 0-1, South Africa (a) 0-2, Angola (h) 2-1, Nigeria (a) 0-3, Angola (a) 0-1, Sudan (h) 1-2, Botswana (a) 0-1, Guinea-Bissau (h) 2-1, Uganda (a) 0-0, Seychelles (a) 3-0, Seychelles (h) 4-0, Malawi (h) 0-2, Ethiopia (a) 2-0, Sudan (h) 0-1.

LESOTHO

Lesotho Football Association, P.O. Box 1879, Maseru-100, Lesotho.
Founded: 1932; *National Colours:* Blue shirts, green shorts, white stockings.
International matches 2011
Swaziland (h) 0-0, Swaziland (h) 0-1, Botswana (a) 2-1, Namibia (a) 0-0, Congo DR (h) 0-3, Burundi (h) 1-0, Burundi (a) 2-2.

LIBERIA

Liberia Football Association, Broad and Center Streets, PO Box 10-1066, Monrovia 1000.
Founded: 1936; *National Colours:* Blue shirts, white shorts, red stockings.
International matches 2011
Cape Verde Islands (a) 2-4, Cape Verde Islands (h) 1-0, Gambia (h) 3-2, Angola (h) 0-0, Niger (h) 0-0, Zimbabwe (a) 0-3, Mali (h) 2-2.

LIBYA

Libyan Football Federation, Asayadi Street, Near Janat Al-Areet, P.O. Box 5137, Tripoli.
Founded: 1963; *National Colours:* Green and black shirts, black shorts and stockings.
International matches 2011
Benin (h) 3-2, Comoros (h) 3-0, Comoros (a) 1-1, Mozambique (h) 1-0, Zambia (a) 0-0, Belarus (a) 1-1, Sudan (h) 0-1, Palestine (a) 1-1, Jordan (h) 0-0.

MADAGASCAR

Federation Malagasy de Football, Immeuble Preservatrice Vie-Lot IBF-9B, Rue Rabearivelo-Antsahavola, PO Box 4409, Antananarivo 101.
Founded: 1961; *National Colours:* Red and green shirts, white and green shorts, green and white stockings.
International matches 2011
Guinea (h) 1-1, Guinea (a) 1-4, Iran (a) 0-1, Nigeria (h) 0-2, Ethiopia (a) 2-4, Equatorial Guinea (a) 0-2, Equatorial Guinea (h) 2-1.

MALAWI

Football Association of Malawi, Mpira House, Old Chileka Road, P.O. Box 865, Blantyre.
Founded: 1966; *National Colours:* Red shirts, white shorts, red and black stockings.
International matches 2011
Namibia (a) 2-1, Togo (h) 1-0, Swaziland (a) 1-1, Botswana (a) 0-0, Namibia (h) 0-1, Tunisia (h) 0-0, Ethiopia (a) 0-0, Chad (a) 2-2, Kenya (a) 2-0, Sudan (h) 0-0, Ethiopia (a) 1-1, Tanzania (a) 0-1.

MALI

Federation Malienne De Football, Avenue du Mali, Hamdallaye ACI 2000, PO Box 1020, Bamako 12582.
Founded: 1960; *National Colours:* Green shirts, yellow shorts, red stockings.
International matches 2011
Ivory Coast (a) 0-1, Zimbabwe (h) 1-0, Zimbabwe (a) 1-2, Tunisia (a) 2-4, Cape Verde Islands (h) 3-0, Liberia (a) 2-2, Burkina Faso (a) 1-1.

MAURITANIA

Federation De Foot-Ball De La Rep. Islamique. De Mauritanie, B.P. 566, Nouakchott.
Founded: 1961; *National Colours:* Green and yellow shirts, yellow shorts, green stockings.

MAURITIUS

Mauritius Football Association, Chancery House, 2nd Floor Nos. 303–305, 14 Lislet Geoffroy Street, Port Louis.
Founded: 1952; *National Colours:* All red.
International matches 2011
Congo DR (a) 0-3, Congo DR (h) 1-2, Maldives (a) 1-1, Seychelles (a) 1-2, Comoros (h) 2-0, Seychelles (a) 1-1, Cameroon (a) 0-5, Senegal (h) 0-2.

MOROCCO

Federation Royale Marocaine De Football, 51 Bis Av. Ibn Sina, PO Box 51, Agdal, Rabat 10 000.
Founded: 1955; *National Colours:* All green white and red.
International matches 2011
Niger (h) 3-0, Algeria (a) 0-1, Algeria (h) 4-0, Senegal (a) 2-0, Central Africa (a) 0-0, Tanzania (h) 3-1, Uganda (h) 0-1, Cameroon (h) 1-1.

MOZAMBIQUE

Federacao Mocambicana De Futebol, Av. Samora Machel 11-2, Caixa Postal 1467, Maputo.
Founded: 1978; *National Colours:* Red shirts, black shorts, red and black stockings.
International matches 2011
Botswana (h) 1-1, Zambia (h) 0-2, Tanzania (h) 2-0, Zambia (a) 0-3, Libya (a) 0-1, Comoros (h) 3-0, Comoros (a) 1-0, Comoros (h) 4-1.

NAMIBIA

Namibia Football Association, Abraham Mashego Street 8521, Katurua Council of Churches in Namibia, P.O. Box 1345, Windhoek 9000, Namibia.
Founded: 1990; *National Colours:* All red.
International matches 2011
Malawi (h) 1-2, Botswana (a) 1-1, Burkina Faso (a) 0-4, Burkina Faso (h) 1-4, Malawi (a) 1-0, Gambia (h) 1-0, Lesotho (h) 0-0, Djibouti (a) 4-0, Djibouti (h) 4-0, Angola (a) 0-0.

NIGER

Federation Nigerienne De Football, Rue de la Tapoa, PO Box 10299, Niamey.
Founded: 1967; *National Colours:* Orange shirts, white shorts, green stockings.
International matches 2011
Morocco (a) 0-3, Sierra Leone (h) 3-1, Sierra Leone (a) 0-1, Togo (h) 3-3, Liberia (a) 0-0, South Africa (h) 2-1, Gabon (a) 0-1, Egypt (a) 0-3, Botswana (h) 1-1.

NIGERIA

Nigeria Football Association, Plot 2033, Olusegun, Obasanjo Way, Zone 7, Wuse Abuja, PO Box 5101 Garki, Abuja, Nigeria.
Founded: 1945; *National Colours:* All green and white.
International matches 2011
Sierra Leone (h) 2-1, Ethiopia (h) 4-0, Kenya (h) 3-0, Argentina (h) 4-1, Ethiopia (a) 2-2, Madagascar (a) 2-0, Argentina (a) 1-3, Guinea (h) 2-2, Ghana (a) 0-0, Botswana (h) 0-0, Zambia (h) 2-0.

RWANDA

Federation Rwandaise De Football Amateur, B.P. 2000, Kigali.
Founded: 1972; *National Colours:* Red, green and yellow shirts, green shorts, red stockings.
International matches 2011
Burundi (h) 3-1, Burundi (a) 1-3, Ivory Coast (h) 0-5, Benin (a) 1-0, Eritrea (a) 1-1, Eritrea (h) 3-1, Tanzania (a) 1-0, Zimbabwe (h) 2-0, Djibouti (h) 5-2, Sudan (h) 2-1, Uganda (a) 2-2.

SENEGAL

Federation Senegalaise De Football, Stade Leopold Sedar Senghor, Route De L'Aeroport De Yoff, B.P. 130 21, Dakar.
Founded: 1960; *National Colours:* All white and green.
International matches 2011
Guinea (h) 3-0, Cameroon (h) 1-0, Cameroon (a) 0-0, Morocco (h) 0-2, Congo DR (h) 2-0, Mauritius (a) 2-0, Guinea (a) 4-1.

SEYCHELLES

Seychelles Football Federation, P.O. Box 843, People's Stadium, Victoria-Mahe, Seychelles.
Founded: 1979; *National Colours:* Red and green shirts and shorts, red stockings.
International matches 2011
Comoros (h) 0-0, Mauritius (h) 2-1, Maldives (h) 5-1, Mauritius (h) 1-1, Kenya (h) 0-3, Kenya (a) 0-4, Maldives (a) 0-3, Maldives (a) 1-2.

ST THOMAS AND PRINCIPE

Federation Santomense De Futebol, Rua Ex-Joao de Deus No. QXXIII-426/26, PO Box 440, Sao Tome.
Founded: 1975; *National Colours:* Green and red shirts, yellow shorts, green stockings.
International matches 2011
Congo (h) 0-5, Congo (a) 1-1.

SIERRA LEONE

Sierra Leone Football Association, 21 Battery Street, Kingtorn, P.O. Box 672, National Stadium, Brookfields, Freetown.
Founded: 1967; *National Colours:* Green and blue shirts, green, blue and white shorts and stockings.
International matches 2011
Nigeria (a) 1-2, Niger (a) 1-3, Niger (h) 1-0, Egypt (h) 2-1, South Africa (a) 0-0.

SOMALIA

Somali Football Federation, PO Box 222, Mogadishu BN 03040.
Founded: 1951; *National Colours:* Sky blue and white shirts and shorts, white and sky blue stockings.
International matches 2011
Ethiopia (h) 0-0, Ethiopia (a) 0-5, Burundi (a) 1-4, Uganda (h) 0-4.

SOUTH AFRICA

South African Football Association, First National Bank Stadium, PO Box 910, Johannesburg 2000, South Africa.
Founded: 1991; *National Colours:* White shirts with yellow striped sleeves, white shorts with yellow stripes, white stockings.
International matches 2011
Kenya (h) 2-0, Egypt (h) 1-0, Tanzania (a) 1-0, Egypt (a) 0-0, Burkina Faso (h) 3-0, Niger (a) 1-2, Sierra Leone (h) 0-0, Ivory Coast (h) 1-1, Zimbabwe (a) 1-2.

SUDAN

Sudan Football Association, Bladia Street, Khartoum.
Founded: 1936; *National Colours:* Red shirts, white shorts, black stockings.
International matches 2011
Kenya (a) 0-1, Congo DR (a) 1-2, Tanzania (a) 2-0, Swaziland (h) 3-0, Ethiopia (a) 2-1, Swaziland (a) 2-1, Kenya (a) 2-1, Eritrea (a) 3-0, Bahrain (a) 0-1, Congo (a) 1-0, Ghana (h) 0-2, Cameroon (a) 1-3, Uganda (h) 0-0, Ethiopia (h) 1-1, Malawi (a) 0-0, Kenya (a) 1-0, Burundi (a) 2-0, Rwanda (a) 1-2, Tanzania (h) 1-0, Libya (a) 1-0, Jordan (h) 0-0, Palestine (h) 0-2.

SWAZILAND

National Football Association of Swaziland, Sigwaca House, Plot 582, Sheffield Road, PO Box 641, Mbabane H100.
Founded: 1968; *National Colours:* Blue shirts, gold shorts, red stockings.
International matches 2011
Zambia (h) 0-4, Sudan (a) 0-3, Botswana (h) 0-0, Malawi (h) 1-1, Sudan (h) 1-2, Botswana (h) 0-2, Lesotho (a) 0-0, Lesotho (a) 1-0, Ghana (a) 0-2, Congo (h) 0-1, Congo DR (h) 1-3, Congo DR (a) 1-5.

TANZANIA

Football Association of Tanzania, Uhuru/Shaurimoyo Road, Karume Memorial Stadium, P.O. Box 1574, Ilala/Dar Es Salaam.
Founded: 1930; *National Colours:* Green, yellow and blue shirts, black shorts, green stockings with horizontal stripe.
International matches 2011
Egypt (a) 1-5, Burundi (h) 1-1, Uganda (a) 1-1, Sudan (h) 0-2, Palestine (h) 1-0, Central Africa (h) 2-1, Mozambique (a) 0-2, South Africa (h) 0-1, Central Africa (a) 1-2, Algeria (h) 1-1, Morocco (a) 1-3, Chad (a) 2-1, Chad (h) 0-1, Rwanda (h) 0-1, Djibouti (h) 3-0, Zimbabwe (h) 1-2, Malawi (h) 1-0, Uganda (h) 1-3, Sudan (h) 0-1.

TOGO

Federation Togolaise De Football, C.P. 5, Lome.
Founded: 1960; *National Colours:* White shirts, green shorts, red stockings with yellow and green stripes.
International matches 2011
Ghana (a) 1-4, Malawi (a) 0-1, Niger (a) 3-3, Botswana (h) 1-0, Tunisia (a) 0-2, Guinea-Bissau (a) 1-1,Guinea-Bissau (h) 1-0.

TUNISIA

Federation Tunisienne De Football, Maison des Federations Sportives, Cite Olympique, Tunis 1003.
Founded: 1956; *National Colours:* Red shirts, white shorts, red stockings.
International matches 2011
Oman (a) 1-2, Central Africa (h) 3-0, Chad (h) 5-0, Mali (h) 4-2, Jordan (a) 3-3, Malawi (a) 0-0, Togo (h) 2-0, Algeria (a) 0-1.

UGANDA

Federation of Uganda Football Associations, Plot No. 879, Kyadondo Block 8, Mengo Wakaliga Road, P.O. Box 22518, Kampala.
Founded: 1924; *National Colours:* All yellow, red and white.
International matches 2011
Burundi (h) 3-1, Egypt (a) 0-1, Tanzania (a) 1-1, Congo DR (a) 1-0, Egypt (a) 1-3, Guinea-Bissau (a) 1-0, Guinea-Bissau (h) 2-0, Angola (a) 0-2, Kenya (h) 0-0, Morocco (a) 1-0, Sudan (a) 0-0, Somalia (a) 4-0, Burundi (a) 0-1, Zimbabwe (a) 1-0, Tanzania (a) 3-1, Rwanda (h) 2-2.

ZAMBIA

Football Association of Zambia, Football House, Alick Nkhata Road, P.O. Box 34751, Lusaka.
Founded: 1929; *National Colours:* White and green shirts, green and white shorts, white and green stockings.
International matches 2011
Swaziland (a) 4-0, Mozambique (a) 2-0, Mozambique (h) 3-0, Zimbabwe (a) 0-2, Comoros (a) 2-1, Libya (h) 0-0, Nigeria (a) 0-2, India (a) 5-0, Angola (a) 0-1.

ZIMBABWE

Zimbabwe Football Association, P.O. Box CY 114, Causeway, Harare.
Founded: 1965; *National Colours:* All green and gold.
International matches 2011
Mali (a) 0-1, Mali (h) 2-1, Zambia (h) 2-0, Liberia (h) 3-0, Cape Verde Islands (a) 1-2, South Africa (h) 2-1, Djibouti (h) 2-0, Rwanda (a) 0-2, Tanzania (a) 2-1, Uganda (a) 0-1.

EURO 2012 QUALIFYING COMPETITION

■ *Denotes player sent off.*

GROUP A

Brussels, 3 September 2010, 41,126

Belgium (0) 0

Germany (0) 1 *(Klose 51)*

Belgium: Bailly; Kompany, Van Buyten, Vermaelen, Vertonghen, Alderweireld, Simons (Vossen 83), Fellaini, Hazard (Benteke 73), Dembele, Lukaku (Defour 73).
Germany: Neuer; Jansen (Westermann 46), Lahm, Mertesacker, Badstuber, Schweinsteiger, Ozil (Cacau 88), Khedira, Klose, Podolski (Kroos 70), Muller.
Referee: Hauge (Norway).

Astana, 3 September 2010, 15,800

Kazakhstan (0) 0

Turkey (2) 3 *(Arda 24, Hamit Altintop 26, Nihat 75)*

Kazakhstan: Sidelnikov; Popov, Kirov, Abdulin, Karpovich (Rodionov 64), Schmidtgal, Nurgaliev, Zhumaskaliev, Kislitsyn (Rozhkov 85), Ostapenko (Maltsev 72), Azovskiy.
Turkey: Onur; Sabri, Omer, Hakan Balta, Servet, Hamit Altintop, Emre B, Arda, Mehmet Aurelio (Kazim-Richards 89), Nihat (Selcuk I 82), Tuncay (Halil Altintop 80).
Referee: Vad II (Hungary).

Wals-Siezenheim, 7 September 2010, 22,500

Austria (0) 2 *(Linz R 89, Hoffer 90)*

Kazakhstan (0) 0

Austria: Macho; Pogatetz, Schiemer, Prodl, Fuchs, Dag, Kavlak, Jantscher (Alaba 66), Harnik (Hoffer 66), Janko (Maierhofer 78), Linz.
Kazakhstan: Sidelnikov; Popov, Kirov, Abdulin, Karpovich, Geteriev, Nurgaliev (Azovskiy 59), Zhumaskaliev, Kislitsyn (Rozhkov 75), Maltsev (Khizhnichenko 46), Averchenko.
Referee: Strahonja (Croatia).

Cologne, 7 September 2010, 43,751

Germany (3) 6 *(Westermann 28, Podolski 44, Klose 45, 90, Rashad F Sadygov 53 (og), Badstuber 86)*

Azerbaijan (0) 1 *(Javadov 57)*

Germany: Neuer; Lahm, Mertesacker (Westermann 11), Badstuber, Schweinsteiger (Cacau 78), Ozil, Khedira, Riether, Klose, Podolski, Muller (Marin 62).
Azerbaijan: Agayev K; Melikov, Allahverdiyev, Rashad F Sadygov, Abbasov, Shukurov, Yunisoglu (Huseynov V 56), Medvedev, Chertoganov (Rashad A Sadygov 64), Nadirov (Abdullayev 85), Javadov.
Referee: Strombergsson (Sweden).

Istanbul, 7 September 2010, 43,538

Turkey (0) 3 *(Hamit Altintop 48, Semih 66, Arda 78)*

Belgium (1) 2 *(Van Buyten 28, 69)*

Turkey: Onur; Sabri (Gokhan G 73), Omer, Servet, Ismail, Hamit Altintop, Emre B, Arda, Mehmet Aurelio, Selcuk I (Semih 47), Tuncay (Selcuk S 82).
Belgium: Bailly; Kompany■, Van Buyten, Vermaelen, Vertonghen, Alderweireld, Simons, Gillet (Hazard 82), Fellaini, Dembele (Mirallas 63), Lukaku (Witsel 76).
Referee: Skomina (Slovenia).

Vienna, 8 October 2010, 26,500

Austria (1) 3 *(Prodl 3, Arnautovic 53, 90)*

Azerbaijan (0) 0

Austria: Macho; Scharner, Schiemer, Prodl, Fuchs, Klein, Junuzovic (Baumgartlinger 78), Harnik (Kavlak 55), Maierhofer, Linz (Hoffer 59), Arnautovic.
Azerbaijan: Agayev K; Melikov, Allahverdiyev, Rashad F Sadygov, Abbasov, Shukurov, Yunisoglu, Mammadov E (Nadirov 59), Amirguliyev, Javadov (Rashad A Sadygov 74), Aliyev.
Referee: Vollquartz (Denmark).

Berlin, 8 October 2010, 74,244

Germany (1) 3 *(Klose 42, 87, Ozil 79)*

Turkey (0) 0

Germany: Neuer; Lahm, Mertesacker, Westermann, Badstuber, Ozil (Marin 90), Khedira, Kroos, Klose (Cacau 90), Podolski (Trasch 86), Muller.
Turkey: Volkan; Sabri, Omer, Gokhan G, Servet, Nuri (Sercan 78), Hamit Altintop, Emre B, Mehmet Aurelio (Tuncay 24), Ozer, Halil Altintop (Semih 68).
Referee: Webb (England).

Astana, 8 October 2010, 8500

Kazakhstan (0) 0

Belgium (0) 2 *(Ogunjimi 53, 70)*

Kazakhstan: Sidelnikov; Popov, Kirov, Abdulin, Karpovich, Geteriev, Schmidtgal, Nurgaliev (Rozhkov 74), Zhumaskaliev (Averchenko 87), Kislitsyn■, Khizhnichenko.
Belgium: Bailly; Van Buyten, Van Damme (Legear 79), Deschacht, Lombaerts, Alderweireld, Simons, Fellaini, Witsel, Vossen, Lukaku (Ogunjimi 46).
Referee: Borski (Poland).

Baku, 12 October 2010, 29,500

Azerbaijan (1) 1 *(Rashad F Sadygov 39)*

Turkey (0) 0

Azerbaijan: Agayev K; Melikov (Chertoganov 45), Allahverdiyev, Rashad F Sadygov, Abishov, Shukurov, Yunisoglu, Amirguliyev, Nadirov, Javadov (Huseynov V 85), Guliyev (Aliyev 72).
Turkey: Volkan; Ibrahim T, Hakan Balta, Gokhan G, Servet, Hamit Altintop, Emre B, Ozer (Nihat 46), Selcuk I (Halil Altintop 82), Tuncay (Sercan 62), Semih.
Referee: Deaconu (Romania).

Brussels, 12 October 2010, 25,000

Belgium (1) 4 *(Vossen 11, Fellaini 47, Ogunjimi 87, Lombaerts 90)*

Austria (2) 4 *(Schiemer 14, 62, Arnautovic 29, Harnik 90)*

Belgium: Bailly; Kompany, Vertonghen, Lombaerts, Alderweireld (Boyata 46), Simons (Lukaku 73), Fellaini (Hazard 81), Witsel, Legear, Vossen, Ogunjimi.
Austria: Macho; Scharner■, Schiemer, Prodl, Fuchs, Klein, Kavlak (Hoffer 57), Junuzovic (Pehlivan 73), Baumgartlinger, Maierhofer, Arnautovic (Harnik 88).
Referee: Dean (England).

Astana, 12 October 2010, 20,000

Kazakhstan (0) 0

Germany (0) 3 *(Klose 48, Gomez 76, Podolski 86)*

Kazakhstan: Sidelnikov; Popov, Irismetov (Rozhkov 68), Kirov, Abdulin, Geteriev, Schmidtgal, Nurgaliev (Averchenko 63), Zhumaskaliev, Azovskiy, Khizhnichenko (Finonchenko 79).
Germany: Neuer; Lahm, Mertesacker, Westermann, Badstuber, Ozil (Cacau 79), Khedira, Kroos, Klose (Gomez 56), Podolski, Muller (Marin 71).
Referee: Tudor (Romania).

Vienna, 25 March 2011, 45,000

Austria (0) 0

Belgium (1) 2 *(Witsel 6, 50)*

Austria: Macho; Pogatetz, Fuchs, Dragovic, Dag, Junuzovic (Korkmaz 68), Baumgartlinger, Alaba (Maierhofer 54), Harnik, Janko (Pehlivan 54), Arnautovic.
Belgium: Mignolet; Kompany, Van Buyten, Vertonghen, Ciman, Simons, Defour, Witsel, Chadli, Dembele, Ogunjimi (Mirallas 80).
Referee: Bezborodov (Russia).

Kaiserslautern, 26 March 2011, 47,849

Germany (3) 4 *(Klose 4, 88, Muller 25, 44)*

Kazakhstan (0) 0

Germany: Neuer; Lahm, Mertesacker, Aogo, Badstuber, Schweinsteiger (Kroos 77), Ozil, Khedira, Klose, Podolski (Gomez 65), Muller (Gotze 78).

Kazakhstan: Loria; Irismetov, Nurdauletov, Chichulin, Abdulin, Chernyshov, Geteriev (Ostapenko 81), Nurgaliev (Kukeev 60), Zhumaskaliev (Baizhanov 46), Konysbaev, Khizhnichenko.
Referee: Stavrev (Macedonia).

Brussels, 29 March 2011, 34,985

Belgium (3) 4 *(Vertonghen 12, Simons 32 (pen), Chadli 45, Vossen 74)*

Azerbaijan (1) 1 *(Abishov 16)*

Belgium: Mignolet; Van Buyten (Van Damme 80), Vertonghen, Lombaerts, Ciman, Simons, Defour (Odjidja-Ofoe 90), Witsel, Chadli, Dembele (Hazard 64), Vossen.
Azerbaijan: Agayev K; Rashad F Sadykov, Melikov, Abishov, Levin, Shukurov, Chertoganov, Mammadov E (Huseynov J 78), Amirguliyev, Javadov (Nadirov 76), Aliyev.
Referee: Stalhammar (Sweden).

Istanbul, 29 March 2011, 40,420

Turkey (1) 2 *(Arda 28, Gokhan G 78)*

Austria (0) 0

Turkey: Volkan; Hakan Balta, Gokhan G, Servet, Serdar, Nuri, Hamit Altintop, Arda (Mehmet Topal 87), Burak (Semih 72), Selcuk I, Mehmet E (Mehmet Topuz 63).
Austria: Macho; Scharner, Pogatetz, Fuchs, Dragovic, Dag, Baumgartlinger (Hoffer 46), Alaba, Pehlivan (Korkmaz 57), Harnik (Arnautovic 69), Maierhofer.
Referee: Kralovec (Czech Republic).

Vienna, 3 June 2011, 47,500

Austria (0) 1 *(Friedrich 50 (og))*

Germany (1) 2 *(Gomez 44, 90)*

Austria: Gratzei; Scharner, Pogatetz, Fuchs, Dag (Junuzovic 66), Klein, Kulovits, Baumgartlinger, Alaba, Harnik (Royer 81), Hoffer (Janko 88).
Germany: Neuer; Friedrich, Lahm, Hummels, Schmelzer, Ozil, Khedira (Badstuber 69), Kroos (Aogo 90), Gomez, Podolski (Schurrle 68), Muller.
Referee: Busacca (Switzerland).

Brussels, 3 June 2011, 44,185

Belgium (1) 1 *(Ogunjimi 4)*

Turkey (1) 1 *(Burak 22)*

Belgium: Mignolet; Kompany, Vertonghen (Vermaelen 46), Lombaerts, Alderweireld, Simons, Defour (Vossen 88), Witsel, Hazard (Mertens 60), Chadli, Ogunjimi.
Turkey: Volkan; Sabri, Caglar, Serdar, Kazim-Richards, Servet, Emre B, Arda (Semih 85), Selcuk S, Burak (Mehmet E 76), Selcuk I (Mehmet Topal 78).
Referee: Rizzoli (Italy).

Astana, 3 June 2011, 3000

Kazakhstan (0) 2 *(Gridin 57, 68)*

Azerbaijan (0) 1 *(Nadirov 63)*

Kazakhstan: Nesterenko; Smakov, Nurdauletov, Mukhtarov, Geteriev, Schmidtgal, Khayrullin (Kirov 82), Logvinenko (Rozhkov 65), Konysbaev, Ostapenko (Khizhnichenko 79), Gridin.
Azerbaijan: Agayev K; Rashad F Sadygov, Melikov, Abishov, Levin, Medvedev, Rashad A Sadygov, Huseynov J (Nadirov 61), Ismayilov, Javadov, Aliyev (Huseynov M 79).
Referee: Norris (Scotland).

Baku, 7 June 2011, 25,000

Azerbaijan (0) 1 *(Huseynov M 89)*

Germany (2) 3 *(Ozil 30, Gomez 41, Schurrle 90)*

Azerbaijan: Agayev K; Rashad F Sadygov, Melikov, Allahverdiyev, Abishov, Huseynov V, Chertoganov (Rashad A Sadygov 86), Amirguliyev, Ismayilov (Isayev 58), Nadirov, Javadov (Huseynov M 72).
Germany: Neuer; Lahm, Howedes, Aogo, Hummels, Badstuber, Ozil, Kroos (Gotze 81), Gomez, Podolski (Schurrle 78), Muller (Holtby 88).
Referee: Koukoulakis (Greece).

Baku, 2 September 2011, 9300

Azerbaijan (0) 1 *(Aliyev 86)*

Belgium (0) 1 *(Simons 55 (pen))*

Azerbaijan: Agayev K; Rashad F Sadygov, Allahverdiyev, Abishov (Amirguliyev 65), Shukurov, Nabiyev, Huseynov V, Chertoganov (Subasic 83), Ismayilov (Mammadov E 58), Javadov, Aliyev.
Belgium: Mignolet; Kompany, Vertonghen, Lombaerts, Alderweireld, Simons, Fellaini, Witsel, Hazard, Mertens, Lukaku (De Camargo 61).
Referee: Probert (England).

Gelsenkirchen, 2 September 2011, 53,313

Germany (3) 6 *(Klose 8, Ozil 23, 47, Podolski 28, Schurrle 84, Gotze 89)*

Austria (1) 2 *(Arnautovic 42, Harnik 51)*

Germany: Neuer; Lahm, Howedes (Boateng 46), Hummels, Badstuber, Schweinsteiger, Ozil, Kroos (Gotze 85), Klose, Podolski (Schurrle 74), Muller.
Austria: Gratzei; Pogatetz, Schiemer, Fuchs, Dag, Klein, Baumgartlinger, Alaba, Royer (Hoffer 73), Harnik, Arnautovic.
Referee: Tagliavento (Italy).

Istanbul, 2 September 2011, 47,756

Turkey (1) 2 *(Burak 31, Arda 90)*

Kazakhstan (0) 1 *(Konysbaev 55)*

Turkey: Volkan; Sabri, Egemen, Hakan Balta, Serdar, Emre B (Gokhan T 60), Kazim-Richards (Umut 82), Arda, Selcuk I■, Mehmet E (Selcuk S 51), Burak.
Kazakhstan: Mokin; Schmidtgal, Nurdauletov, Kirov, Gurman, Mukhtarov, Khayrullin (Ostapenko 67), Logvinenko, Konysbaev (Nuserbayev 86), Shakhmetov (Baizhanov 81), Gridin.
Referee: Turpin (France).

Vienna, 6 September 2011, 47,500

Austria (0) 0

Turkey (0) 0

Austria: Grunwald P; Pogatetz, Schiemer, Fuchs, Scharner, Dag, Baumgartlinger, Alaba, Royer (Hoffer 67), Harnik, Arnautovic (Maierhofer 90).
Turkey: Volkan; Sabri, Egemen, Hakan Balta, Servet, Arda, Selcuk S, Mehmet Topal, Yekta, Burak (Gokhan T 90), Umut.
Referee: Undiano (Spain).

Lenkeran, 6 September 2011, 9112

Azerbaijan (0) 3 *(Aliyev 53, Shukurov 62 (pen), Javadov 67)*

Kazakhstan (1) 2 *(Ostapenko 20, Yestigneev 78)*

Azerbaijan: Agayev K; Rashad F Sadygov, Shukurov, Nabiyev (Yunisoglu 13), Huseynov, Chertoganov (Subasic 46), Amirguliyev, Ismayilov (Abishov 87), Budak, Javadov, Aliyev.
Kazakhstan: Mokin; Rozhkov (Yevstigneev 77), Nurdauletov, Kirov, Gurman, Logvinenko, Kukeev (Khayrullin 59), Konysbaev, Ostapenko, Shakhmetov (Muzhikov 70), Gridin.
Referee: Hermansen (Denmark).

Baku, 7 October 2011, 6000

Azerbaijan (0) 1 *(Nadirov 74)*

Austria (1) 4 *(Ivanschitz 34, Janko 52, 62, Junuzovic 90)*

Azerbaijan: Agayev K; Rashad F Sadygov, Allahverdiyev, Abishov,Yunisoglu■, Huseynov V, Rashad A Sadygov (Amirguliyev 46), Ismayilov, Budak, Javadov (Nadirov 57), Aliyev.
Austria: Grunwald P; Prodl, Fuchs, Dragovic, Scharner, Dag, Ivanschitz (Royer 73), Baumgartlinger, Alaba, Janko (Hosiner 88), Arnautovic (Junuzovic 67).
Referee: Studer (Switzerland).

Brussels, 7 October 2011, 29,758

Belgium (2) 4 *(Simons 40 (pen), Hazard 43, Kompany 49, Yevstigneev 84 (og))*

Kazakhstan (0) 1 *(Nurdauletov 86 (pen))*

Belgium: Mignolet; Kompany, Van Buyten, Vertonghen, Ciman, Simons (Defour 75), Witsel, Hazard (Odjidja-Ofoe 63), Dembele, De Camargo (Ogunjimi 73), Mertens.
Kazakhstan: Loginovskiy; Rozhkov, Kirov, Mukhtarov, Kurgulin■, Karpovich (Shakhmetov 75), Kukeev (Nurdauletov 61), Yevstigneev, Muzhikov, Khizhnichenko, Tazhimbetov (Ostapenko 56).
Referee: Mazic (Serbia).

Istanbul, 7 October 2011, 49,532

Turkey (0) 1 *(Hakan Balta 79)*

Germany (1) 3 *(Gomez 35, Muller 66, Schweinsteiger 86 (pen))*

Turkey: Volkan; Sabri, Egemen, Hakan Balta, Gokhan G, Servet, Hamit Altintop, Arda (Kazim-Richards 70), Mehmet Aurelio (Umut 86), Selcuk I (Gokhan T 46), Burak.
Germany: Neuer; Lahm, Mertesacker, Boateng (Howedes 73), Badstuber, Schweinsteiger, Khedira, Gotze (Reus 89), Gomez, Podolski (Schurrle 62), Muller.
Referee: Atkinson (England).

Dusseldorf, 11 October 2011, 48,483

Germany (2) 3 *(Ozil 30, Schurrle 33, Gomez 48)*

Belgium (0) 1 *(Fellaini 46)*

Germany: Neuer; Lahm (Gundogan 84), Mertesacker, Howedes, Hummels, Ozil, Khedira, Kroos, Gomez (Cacau 77), Muller (Reus 71), Schurrle.
Belgium: Mignolet; Kompany, Vertonghen, Lombaerts, Ciman, Simons, Fellaini, Witsel, Hazard, Dembele (Mertens 65), Ogunjimi (Lukaku 46).
Referee: Moen (Norway).

Astana, 11 October 2011, 11,000

Kazakhstan (0) 0

Austria (0) 0

Kazakhstan: Sidelnikov; Schmidtgal, Rozhkov, Nurdauletov, Kirov, Gurman (Yevstigneev 77), Mukhtarov, Khayrullin, Nurgaliev (Muzhikov 46), Ostapenko, Gridin.
Austria: Grunwald P; Prodl, Fuchs, Dragovic, Scharner, Dag, Kulovits (Kavlak 74), Ivanschitz (Junuzovic 66), Alaba, Janko, Arnautovic (Maierhofer 83).
Referee: Kaasik (Estonia).

Istanbul, 11 October 2011, 32,174

Turkey (0) 1 *(Burak 60)*

Azerbaijan (0) 0

Turkey: Sinan; Sabri, Gokhan Z, Egemen, Hakan Balta, Hamit Altintop, Emre B (Gokhan T 78), Kazim-Richards (Selcuk I 58), Arda, Mehmet Topal, Burak (Umut 87).
Azerbaijan: Agayev K; Rashad F Sadygov, Abishov, Levin, Shukurov, Huseynov V, Chertoganov, Ismayilov (Mammadov E 46) (Isayev 85), Budak (Amirguliyev 90), Subasic, Nadirov.
Referee: Rasmussen (Denmark),

Group A Group A Table	P	W	D	L	F	A	Pts
Germany	10	10	0	0	34	7	30
Turkey	10	5	2	3	13	11	17
Belgium	10	4	3	3	21	15	15
Austria	10	3	3	4	16	17	12
Azerbaijan	10	2	1	7	10	26	7
Kazakhstan	10	1	1	8	6	24	4

GROUP B

Andorra la Vella, 3 September 2010, 1100

Andorra (0) 0

Russia (1) 2 *(Pogrebnyak 14, 64 (pen))*

Andorra: Gomes; Lima I, Jordi Rubio (Lorenzo 58), Marc Bernaus, Martinez C, Josep Ayala, Vieira, Moreno (Manolo Jimenez 76), Pujol (Mejias 89), Silva, Gomez.
Russia: Akinfeev; Berezutski V, Ignashevich, Anyukov, Bystrov (Dzagoev 61), Semshov, Bilyaletdinov, Shirokov, Zyryanov, Arshavin, Pogrebnyak (Pavlyuchenko 86).
Referee: Borg (Malta).

Erevan, 3 September 2010, 8600

Armenia (0) 0

Republic of Ireland (0) 1 *(Fahey 76)*

Armenia: Berezovskiy; Arzumanian, Arakelian, Hovespian, Artur Yedigarian (Manoian 68), Artak Yedigarian (Hambardzumian 71), Pachajian, Mkhitarian, Malakian (Manucharian 78), Mkrtchian K, Movsisian.
Republic of Ireland: Given; Dunne, Kilbane, Whelan, St Ledger-Hall, O'Shea, Lawrence, Green, Keane (Keogh 85), Doyle, McGeady (Fahey 68).
Referee: Szabo (Hungary).

Bratislava, 3 September 2010, 5980

Slovakia (0) 1 *(Holosko 90)*

Macedonia (0) 0

Slovakia: Mucha; Skrtel, Hubocan, Pekarik (Sylvestr 90), Salata (Kucka 76), Sapara, Hamsik, Strba, Stoch, Weiss (Jendrisek 61), Holosko.
Macedonia: Nuredinoski; Mitreski, Noveski, Shikov■, Popov, Shumulikoski, Georgievski, Despotovski (Lazevski 73), Pandev, Naumoski (Ristic 61), Trichkovski (Grncharov 80).
Referee: Circhetta (Switzerland).

Skopje, 7 September 2010, 9000

Macedonia (1) 2 *(Durovski 42, Naumoski 89 (pen))*

Armenia (1) 2 *(Movsisian 40, Manucharian 90)*

Macedonia: Nuredinoski; Mitreski, Noveski, Popov, Todorovski, Shumulikoski, Georgievski (Despotovski 67), Durovski (Ilijoski 75), Pandev, Ristic (Naumoski 62), Trichkovski.
Armenia: Berezovskiy; Arzumanian, Arakelian, Hovsepian, Artak Yedigarian, Pachajian (Artur Yedigarian 70), Mkhitarian, Malakian (Manucharian 58), Mkrtchian K (Mkoian 90), Manoian, Movsisian.
Referee: Berntsen (Norway).

Dublin, 7 September 2010, 40,283

Republic of Ireland (2) 3 *(Kilbane 15, Doyle 41, Keane 54)*

Andorra (1) 1 *(Martinez C 45)*

Republic of Ireland: Given; Dunne, Kilbane, Whelan (Gibson 61), St Ledger-Hall, O'Shea (Kelly 75), Lawrence, Green, Keane, Doyle (Keogh 82), McGeady.
Andorra: Gomes; Lima I, Escura, Marc Bernaus, Martinez C, Josep Ayala (Andorra 71), Vieira, Moreno (Manolo Jimenez 59), Pujol (Oscar Sonejee 86), Silva, Gomez.
Referee: Trattou (Cyprus).

Moscow, 7 September 2010, 27,052

Russia (0) 0

Slovakia (1) 1 *(Stoch 27)*

Russia: Akinfeev; Berezutski V, Ignashevich (Bilyaletdinov 81), Anyukov, Zhirkov, Semshov (Bystrov 61), Shirokov, Zyryanov, Arshavin, Dzagoev, Pogrebnyak (Pavlyuchenko 71).
Slovakia: Mucha; Skrtel, Zabavnik, Hubocan, Salata, Karhan (Sapara 73), Hamsik, Strba, Kucka (Jendrisek 58), Stoch (Pecalka 90), Holosko.
Referee: De Bleeckere (Belgium).

Andorra la Vella, 8 October 2010, 550

Andorra (0) 0

Macedonia (1) 2 *(Naumoski 42, Shikov 60)*

Andorra: Gomes; Escura, Marc Bernaus, Martinez C (Manolo Jimenez 74), Josep Ayala (Bousenine 86), Vieira, Vales, Meijas (Lorenzo 62), Moreno, Silva, Gomez.
Macedonia: Nuredinoski; Mitreski, Noveski, Lazarevski, Shikov, Shumulikoski (Grncharov 83), Georgievski (Durovski 34), Despotovski, Naumoski (Ibraimi 73), Ristic, Trichkovski.
Referee: Mazelka (Lithuania).

Erevan, 8 October 2010, 8500

Armenia (1) 3 *(Movsisian 23, Ghazarian 50, Mkhitarian 89)*

Slovakia (1) 1 *(Weiss 37)*

Armenia: Berezovskiy; Arzumanian (Arakelian 79), Hovsepian, Mkoian, Artak Yedigarian, Pachajian (Manucharian 46), Mkhitarian, Mkrtchian K, Pizzelli (Artur Yedigarian 72), Movsisian, Ghazarian.
Slovakia: Mucha; Skrtel, Zabavnik (Sebo 81), Pekarik, Salata, Karhan, Hamsik, Kopunek (Holosko 57), Stoch (Kucka 57), Weiss, Sestak.
Referee: Orsato (Italy).

Dublin, 8 October 2010, 50,411

Republic of Ireland (0) 2 *(Keane 72 (pen), Long 78)*

Russia (2) 3 *(Kerzhakov 10, Dzagoev 28, Shirokov 51)*

Republic of Ireland: Given; O'Shea, Kilbane, Whelan (Gibson 66), Dunne, St Ledger-Hall, Lawrence (Long 62), Green, Doyle (Fahey 71), Keane, McGeady.

Russia: Akinfeev; Berezutski V, Ignashevich, Anyukov, Zhirkov, Shirokov, Zyryanov (Semshov 68), Denisov, Dzagoev (Berezutski A 85), Kerzhakov (Pogrebnyak 80), Arshavin.
Referee: Blom (Holland).

Erevan, 12 October 2010, 12,000

Armenia (3) 4 *(Ghazarian 4, Mkhitarian 16, Movsisian 33, Pizzelli 52)*

Andorra (0) 0

Armenia: Berezovskiy; Arzumanian, Hovsepian, Artur Yedigarian, Mkoian, Artak Yedigarian, Mkhitarian, Pizzelli (Yuspashian 82), Manucharian, Movsisian (Goharian 54), Ghazarian (Malakian 67).
Andorra: Gomes; Lima I, Escura, Marc Bernaus, Martinez C (Jordi Rubio 87), Josep Ayala, Vieira, Vales (Andorra 64), Moreno (Manolo Jimenez 53), Silva, Gomez.
Referee: Mikulski (Poland).

Skopje, 12 October 2010, 10,500

Macedonia (0) 0

Russia (1) 1 *(Kerzhakov 8)*

Macedonia: Nuredinoski; Mitreski, Noveski, Shikov, Lazevski, Shumulikoski, Despotovski (Georgievski 77), Durovski (Alimi 80), Naumoski, Ibraimi (Ristic 49), Trichkovski.
Russia: Akinfeev; Berezutski V, Ignashevich, Anyukov, Zhirkov, Shirokov, Zyryanov, Denisov, Dzagoev (Berezutski A 62), Kerzhakov (Pogrebnyak 79), Arshavin (Bystrov 81).
Referee: Johannesson (Sweden).

Zilina, 12 October 2010, 10,892

Slovakia (1) 1 *(Durica 36)*

Republic of Ireland (1) 1 *(St Ledger-Hall 16)*

Slovakia: Mucha; Zabavnik, Hubocan, Salata, Durica, Karhan, Hamsik, Kucka, Weiss (Holosko 70), Jendrisek (Oravec 84), Sestak (Stoch 70).
Republic of Ireland: Given; O'Shea, Kilbane, Whelan, Dunne, St Ledger-Hall, Green (Gibson 41), Fahey (Keogh 71), Long, Keane, McGeady.
Referee: Mallenco (Spain).

Andorra la Vella, 26 March 2011, 850

Andorra (0) 0

Slovakia (1) 1 *(Sebo 21)*

Andorra: Gomis; Lima I, Jordi Rubio, Marc Bernaus, Garcia E, Martinez C, Josep Ayala (Juli Sanchez 81), Manolo Jimenez (Oscar Sonejee 87), Vales, Moreno, Gomez (Vieira 72).
Slovakia: Mucha; Skrtel, Pekarik, Durica, Kona, Hamsik, Luksik, Stoch (Salata 90), Vittek (Piroska 78), Jendrisek (Holosko 87), Sebo.
Referee: Masiah (Israel).

Erevan, 26 March 2011, 14,800

Armenia (0) 0

Russia (0) 0

Armenia: Berezovskiy; Arzumanian, Hovsepian, Mkoian, Mkhitarian, Malakian (Manucharian 49), Mkrtchian K, Hayrapetian (Artak Yedigarian 67), Pizzelli (Artur Yedigarian 57), Movsisian, Ghazarian.
Russia: Akinfeev; Berezutski V, Shishkin, Ignashevich, Zhirkov, Shirokov, Zyryanov, Denisov, Dzagoev, Kerzhakov (Pogrebnyak 78), Arshavin (Bilyaletdinov 90).
Referee: Thomson (Scotland).

Dublin, 26 March 2011, 33,200

Republic of Ireland (2) 2 *(McGeady 2, Keane 21)*

Macedonia (1) 1 *(Trichkovski 45)*

Republic of Ireland: Westwood; Dunne, O'Dea, Foley, Whelan, McGeady, Kilbane, Gibson (Fahey 77), Doyle (Long 20), Keane (McCarthy 87), Duff.
Macedonia: Nuredinoski; Novevski, Grncharov, Shikov, Popov, Shumulikoski, Demiri (Georgievski 84), Tasevski (Durovski 61), Pandev, Naumoski (Ristic 68), Trichkovski.
Referee: Vad II (Hungary).

Skopje, 4 June 2011, 29,500

Macedonia (0) 0

Republic of Ireland (2) 2 *(Keane 8, 36)*

Macedonia: Bogatinov; Noveski, Grncharov, Shikov, Popov, Shumulikoski, Despotovski (Durovski 57), Demiri (Savic 72), Pandev, Naumoski (Hasani 10), Trichkovski.
Republic of Ireland: Given; O'Dea, O'Shea, Kelly, McGeady, Hunt, Kilbane, Whelan, Andrews, Keane, Cox (Long 64).
Referee: Meyer (Germany).

St Petersburg, 4 June 2011, 18,000

Russia (1) 3 *(Pavlyuchenko 26, 59, 73 (pen))*

Armenia (1) 1 *(Pizzelli 25)*

Russia: Akinfeev; Berezutski V, Ignashevich, Anyukov (Yanbayev 74), Zhirkov, Semshov (Glushakov 69), Zyryanov (Dzagoev 82), Denisov, Torbinski, Pavlyuchenko, Arshavin.
Armenia: Berezovskiy; Arzumanian, Hovsepian, Mkoian, Pachajian (Manucharian 57), Mkhitarian K, Mkrtchian (Artak Yedigarian 89), Hayrapetian, Pizzelli (Artur Yedigarian 67), Movsisian, Ghazarian.
Referee: Lannoy (France).

Bratislava, 4 June 2011, 4300

Slovakia (0) 1 *(Karhan 63)*

Andorra (0) 0

Slovakia: Kello; Cech (Salata 83), Hubocan, Durica, Karhan, Hamsik, Jez, Kucka (Sestak 46), Vittek, Sebo, Holosko (Zofcak 74).
Andorra: Gomes; Lima I, Jordi Rubio, Marc Bernaus, Garcia E, Martinez C, Josep Ayala (Andorra 16), Manolo Jimenez (Salvat 86), Vieira, Vales, Silva (Gomez 64).
Referee: Jemini (Albania).

Andorra La Vella, 2 September 2011, 750

Andorra (0) 0

Armenia (1) 3 *(Pizzelli 35, Ghazarian 75, Mkhitarian 90 (pen))*

Andorra: Gomes; Lima I■, Jordi Rubio, Marc Bernaus, Garcia E, Martinez C, Josep Ayala (Juli Sanchez 87), Vales, Moreno (Vieira 80), Pujol, Silva (Gomez 72).
Armenia: Berezovskiy; Hovsepian, Aleksanian, Mkoian, Ghazarian (Badoian 89), Mkhitarian, Mkrtchian K, Hayrapetian, Pizzelli (Artur Yedigarian 83), Manucharian (Malakian 78), Sarkisov.
Referee: Kostadinov (Bulgaria).

Dublin, 2 September 2011, 35,480

Republic of Ireland (0) 0

Slovakia (0) 0

Republic of Ireland: Given; Dunne, O'Shea, Ward, St Ledger-Hall, McGeady (Hunt 84), Duff, Whelan, Andrews, Doyle (Cox 64), Keane.
Slovakia: Mucha; Cech, Skrtel, Pekarik, Durica, Karhan, Hamsik, Kucka (Guede 76), Stoch, Weiss (Jendrisek 85), Holosko (Vittek 88).
Referee: Proenca (Portugal).

Moscow, 2 September 2011, 31,028

Russia (1) 1 *(Semshov 41)*

Macedonia (0) 0

Russia: Malafeev; Berezutski V, Berezutski A, Anyukov, Zhirkov, Semshov (Pavlyuchenko 46), Shirokov, Zyryanov (Torbinski 60), Denisov, Arshavin, Kerzhakov (Glushakov 88).
Macedonia: Bogatinov; Noveski, Shikov, Popov, Georgievski (Hasani 66), Shumulikoski (Muarem 85), Ibraimi, Demiri, Pandev■, Ivanovski M (Trajkovski 75), Trichkovski.
Referee: Bulent (Turkey).

Skopje, 6 September 2011, 5000

Macedonia (0) 1 *(Ivanovski M 59)*

Andorra (0) 0

Macedonia: Bogatinov; Shikov, Popov, Mojsov, Georgievski, Shumulikoski, Ibraimi (Trajkovski 46), Muarem (Huseini 77), Hasani (Fazli 68), Ivanovski M, Trichkovski.
Andorra: Gomes; Jordi Rubio (Martinez A 26), Marc Bernaus, Garcia E, Martinez C, Josep Ayala, Oscar Sonejee, Vieira (Garcia M 83), Vales, Moreno, Silva (Gomez 74).
Referee: Whitby (Wales).

Moscow, 6 September 2011, 49,515

Russia (0) 0

Republic of Ireland (0) 0

Russia: Malafeev; Berezutski V, Berezutski A, Ignashevich, Anyukov, Zhirkov (Bilyaletdinov 76), Semshov, Shirokov, Zyryanov, Arshavin, Kerzhakov (Pavlyuchenko 54).
Republic of Ireland: Given; Dunne, O'Dea, Ward, Kelly, McGeady, Duff (Hunt 67), Whelan, Andrews, Doyle (Cox 59), Keane.
Referee: Brych (Germany).

Zilina, 6 September 2011, 7238

Slovakia (0) 0

Armenia (0) 4 *(Movsisian 57, Mkhitarian 70, Ghazarian 80, Sarkisov 90)*

Slovakia: Mucha; Cech (Jendrisek 76), Skrtel, Pekarik, Durica, Guede (Jez 55), Karhan, Hamsik, Stoch, Weiss (Sestak 71), Holosko.
Armenia: Berezovskiy; Hovsepian, Aleksanian, Artur Yedigarian (Yuspashian 90), Mkoian, Ghazarian, Mkhitarian, Mkrtchian K, Hayrapetian, Pizzelli (Manucharian 73), Movsisian (Sarkisov 85).
Referee: Borski (Poland).

Andorra La Vella, 7 October 2011, 860

Andorra (0) 0

Republic of Ireland (2) 2 *(Doyle 8, McGeady 20)*

Andorra: Gomes; Lima I (Oscar Sonejee 80), Marc Bernaus, Garcia E, Martinez C, Martinez A (Lorenzo 78), Josep Ayala, Vieira, Moreno, Pujol (Peppe 59), Silva.
Republic of Ireland: Given; O'Dea, O'Shea, Whelan (Fahey 64), St Ledger-Hall, Andrews, Duff (Hunt 75), McGeady, Doyle (Long 71), Keane, Ward.
Referee: Kovarik (Czech Republic).

Erevan, 7 October 2011, 14,403

Armenia (2) 4 *(Pizzelli 28, Mkhitarian 34, Ghazarian 69, Sarkisov 90)*

Macedonia (0) 1 *(Shikov 86)*

Armenia: Berezovskiy; Hovsepian, Aleksanian, Artur Yedigarian, Ghazarian (Malakian 83), Mkhitarian, Mkrtchian K (Sarkisov 75), Hayrapetian, Pizzelli (Manucharian 63), Movsisian, Yuspashian.
Macedonia: Bogatinov; Noveski, Shikov, Popov, Georgievski (Lazarevski 51), Shumulikoski■, Demiri, Muarem (Durovski 46), Ivanovski F (Mitreski 60), Ivanovski M, Trichkovski.
Referee: Schorgenhofer (Austria).

Zilina, 7 October 2011, 10,087

Slovakia (0) 0

Russia (0) 1 *(Dzagoev 71)*

Slovakia: Mucha; Skrtel, Hubocan, Pekarik, Durica, Karhan (Sebo 86), Hamsik, Kucka (Guede 73), Stoch, Jendrisek, Holosko (Weiss 73).
Russia: Malafeev; Berezutski V, Ignashevich, Anyukov, Zhirkov (Berezutski A 90), Shirokov, Zyryanov, Denisov, Arshavin, Dzagoev (Samedov 90), Pavlyuchenko (Pogrebnyak 87).
Referee: Eriksson (Sweden).

Skopje, 11 October 2011, 4100

Macedonia (0) 1 *(Noveski 80)*

Slovakia (0) 1 *(Piroska 54)*

Macedonia: Bogatinov; Noveski, Lazarevski, Shikov, Lazevski (Ivanovski F 64), Mojsov, Demiri, Grozdanoski (Petrov 46), Durovski, Trichkovski, Fazli (Trajkovski 84).
Slovakia: Mucha; Michalik, Hubocan (Cech 46), Pekarik, Salata, Hamsik, Jez (Grajciar 88), Kucka, Weiss, Jendrisek, Piroska (Holosko 87).
Referee: Chapron (France).

Dublin, 11 October 2011, 45,200

Republic of Ireland (1) 2 *(Aleksanyan 43 (og), Dunne 60)*

Armenia (0) 1 *(Mkhitarian 62)*

Republic of Ireland: Given; Kelly, O'Shea, Whelan (Fahey 76), Dunne, St Ledger-Hall, Duff, McGeady (Hunt 67), Doyle■, Cox (Walters 80), Andrews.
Armenia: Berezovskiy■; Hovsepian, Aleksanian, Mkoian, Ghazarian (Sarkisov 63), Mkhitarian, Malakian (Petrosian 28), Mkrtchian K, Hayrapetyin, Pizzelli (Manucharian 53), Movsisian.
Referee: Gonzalez (Spain).

Moscow, 11 October 2011, 38,790

Russia (4) 6 *(Dzagoev 5, 44, Ignashevich 26, Pavlyuchenko 30, Glushakov 59, Bilyaletdinov 78)*

Andorra (0) 0

Russia: Malafeev; Berezutski V, Shishkin, Ignashevich, Berezutski A, Semshov (Bilyaletdinov 72), Denisov, Arshavin, Glushakov (Samedov 80), Dzagoev, Pavlyuchenko (Pogrebnyak 73).
Andorra: Gomes; Lima I, Marc Bernaus, Garcia E, Martinez A, Peppe (Lorenzo 80), Vieira, Vales, Moreno, Pujol (Juli Sanchez 84), Gomez (Silva 70).
Referee: Hacmon (Israel).

Group B Table	P	W	D	L	F	A	Pts
Russia	10	7	2	1	17	4	23
Republic of Ireland	10	6	3	1	15	7	21
Armenia	10	5	2	3	22	10	17
Slovakia	10	4	3	3	7	10	15
Macedonia	10	2	2	6	8	14	8
Andorra	10	0	0	10	1	25	0

GROUP C

Tallinn, 11 August 2010, 5470

Estonia (0) 2 *(Saag 89, Piiroja 90)*

Faeroes (1) 1 *(Edmundsson 28)*

Estonia: Pareiko; Klavan, Piiroja, Jaager, Barengrub, Kruglov (Post 70), Dmitrijev, Puri (Purje 77), Vassiljev, Oper (Saag 62), Kink.
Faeroes: Nielsen; Borg (Poulsen 67), Benjaminsen, Gregersen, Davidsen, Naes, Samuelsen (Hansen J 74), Petersen J (Lokin 85), Holst, Edmundsson, Rubeksen.
Referee: Vucemilovic (Croatia).

Tallinn, 3 September 2010, 8600

Estonia (1) 1 *(Zenjov 31)*

Italy (0) 2 *(Cassano 60, Bonucci 63)*

Estonia: Pareiko; Klavan, Piiroja, Jaager, Rahn, Kruglov (Kink 82), Dmitrijev, Puri (Purje 77), Vunk, Vassiljev, Zenjov (Saag 64).
Italy: Sirigu; Bonucci, Cassani, Molinaro, Chiellini, De Rossi, Pirlo, Montolivo (Palombo 75), Pepe (Quagliarella 61), Cassano (Antonelli 80), Pazzini.
Referee: Velasco (Spain).

Torshavn, 3 September 2010, 1847

Faeroes (0) 0

Serbia (2) 3 *(Lazovic 14, Stankovic 18, Zigic 90)*

Faeroes: Nielsen; Rubeksen, Gregersen, Davidsen, Naes, Samuelsen, Petersen J (Hansen J 73), Benjaminsen, Udsen (Mouritsen 46), Holst (Hansen A 79), Edmundsson.
Serbia: Duricic; Vidic, Subotic, Rukavina, Obradovic (Lukovic 46), Stankovic (Petrovic 58), Krasic, Kuzmanovic, Zigic, Lazovic (Ninkovic 83), Jovanovic.
Referee: Toussaint (Luxembourg).

Maribor, 3 September 2010, 12,000

Slovenia (0) 0

Northern Ireland (0) 1 *(Evans C 70)*

Slovenia: Handanovic; Cesar, Jokic, Brecko, Mavric, Koren, Kirm (Dedic 74), Radosavljevic, Birsa, Novakovic (Ilicic 74), Ljubijankic (Matavz 88).
Northern Ireland: Taylor; Baird, McAuley, McCann (Lafferty 67), Hughes, Craigan, Cathcart, Davis, Healy (Evans C 67), Feeney, Brunt (Gorman 89).
Referee: Balaj (Romania).

Florence, 7 September 2010, 19,266

Italy (3) 5 *(Gilardino 11, De Rossi 22, Cassano 27, Quagliarella 81, Pirlo 90)*

Faeroes (0) 0

Italy: Viviano; Bonucci, De Silvestri, Chiellini, De Rossi (Palombo 76), Pirlo, Montolivio, Antonelli, Gilardino (Pazzini 59), Rossi (Quagliarella 58), Cassano.
Faeroes: Nielsen; Bo, Rubeksen, Gregersen, Davidsen, Samuelsen, Petersen J, Benjaminsen, Lokin (Naes 74), Edmundsson (Udsen 89), Mouritsen (Holst 75).
Referee: Kulbakov (Belarus).

Belgrade, 7 September 2010, 24,028

Serbia (0) 1 *(Zigic 86)*

Slovenia (0) 1 *(Novakovic 63)*

Serbia: Duricic; Vidic, Lukovic, Subotic, Rukavina, Stankovic (Kacar 71), Kuzmanovic, Tosic (Krasic 46), Zigic, Lazovic, Jovanovic (Ninkovic 64).
Slovenia: Handanovic; Cesar, Jokic, Brecko, Mavric, Koren, Kirm (Stevanovic 89), Radosavljevic, Birsa (Ljubijankic 77), Dedic (Ilic 77), Novakovic.
Referee: Olegario Benquerenca (Portugal).

Belfast, 8 October 2010, 15,200

Northern Ireland (0) 0

Italy (0) 0

Northern Ireland: Taylor; Baird, McAuley, Craigan, Hughes, Evans J, Davis, McCann (Evans C 80), Healy (Lafferty 66), Brunt (McGinn 71), Feeney.
Italy: Viviano; Bonucci, Cassani, Chiellini, Criscito, De Rossi, Pirlo, Mauri (Marchisio 79), Pepe (Rossi 84), Cassano, Borriello (Pazzini 74).
Referee: Chapron (France).

Belgrade, 8 October 2010, 12,000

Serbia (0) 1 *(Kuzmanovic 60)*

Estonia (0) 3 *(Kink 63, Vassiljev 73, Lukovic 90 (og))*

Serbia: Stojkovic; Vidic, Lukovic, Ivanovic, Lomic, Stankovic, Krasic, Kuzmanovic (Lazovic 79), Kacar (Tosic 46), Zigic, Jovanovic (Ninkovic 46).
Estonia: Pareiko; Klavan, Piiroja, Jaager, Rahn, Kruglove, Dmitrijev, Puri (Purje 70), Vassiljev, Kink (Saag 64), Zenjov (Vunk 88).
Referee: Layushkin (Russia).

Ljubljana, 8 October 2010, 15,750

Slovenia (2) 5 *(Matavz 25, 36, 66, Novakovic 72 (pen), Dedic 84)*

Faeroes (0) 1 *(Mouritsen 90)*

Slovenia: Handanovic; Cesar, Jokic, Brecko, Suler, Koren, Radosavljevic (Bacinovic 59), Ilicic, Birsa (Kirm 51), Novakovic (Dedic 73), Matavz.
Faeroes: Mikkelsen; Bo, Rubeksen, Gregersen, Naes, Benjaminsen, Hansen J, Lokin (Elttor 41), Udsen (Mouritsen 81), Holst (Petersen J 81), Edmundsson.
Referee: Todorov (Bulgaria).

Tallinn, 12 October 2010, 5722

Estonia (0) 0

Slovenia (0) 1 *(Sidorenkov 66 (og))*

Estonia: Pareiko; Klavan, Jaager, Sidorenkov, Rahn (Palatu 55), Kruglov, Dmitrijev, Puri (Purje 69), Vassalijev, Kink (Zenjov 59), Saag.
Slovenia: Handanovic; Cesar, Jokic, Brecko, Suler, Koren, Radosavljevic, Ilicic (Kirm 67), Birsa (Ljubijankic 90), Novakovic, Matavz (Dedic 53).
Referee: Skjerven (Norway).

Toftir, 12 October 2010, 1921

Faeroes (0) 1 *(Holst 60)*

Northern Ireland (0) 1 *(Lafferty 76)*

Faeroes: Mikkelsen; Gregersen, Davidsen, Naes, Samuelsen (Hansen A 78), Benjaminsen, Jacobsen, Udsen (Petersen J 68), Holst (Hansen J 85), Edmundsson, Elttor.
Northern Ireland: Taylor; Baird, McAuley, Craigan, Hughes, Evans J, Davis, McGinn (Evans C 83), Lafferty, Feeney (Healy 50), Brunt.
Referee: Zimmermann (Switzerland).

Genoa, 12 October 2010,

Italy (0) 0

Serbia (0) 0

Referee: Thomson (Scotland).
Abandoned 7 minutes; crowd trouble. Italy awarded the match 3-0.

Belgrade, 25 March 2011, 350

Serbia (0) 2 *(Pantelic 65, Tosic 74)*

Northern Ireland (1) 1 *(McAuley 40)*

Serbia: Brkic; Ivanovic, Bisevac, Subotic, Kolarov, Stankovic, Krasic (Petrovic 86), Milijas (Jovanovic 47), Tosic, Ljajic (Ninkovic 47), Pantelic.
Northern Ireland: Camp; Baird, Cathcart, McAuley, Hughes, Evans J (McCourt 86), Evans C, Clingan, Lafferty (Healy 46), Gorman (Feeney 78), Brunt.
Referee: Gumienny (Belgium).

Ljubljana, 25 March 2011, 15,790

Slovenia (0) 0

Italy (0) 1 *(Thiago Motta 73)*

Slovenia: Handanovic; Cesar, Jokic, Brecko (Andelkovic 70), Suler, Koren, Kirm, Radosavljevic, Birsa (Ilicic 74), Dedic (Ljubijankic 56), Novakovic.
Italy: Buffon; Bonucci, Chiellini, Balzaretti, Thiago Motta, Aquilani, Montolivo (Marchisio 87), Mauri (Nocerino 63), Maggio, Cassano (Rossi 74), Pazzini.
Referee: Brych (Germany).

Tallinn, 29 March 2011, 5185

Estonia (0) 1 *(Vassiljev 84)*

Serbia (1) 1 *(Pantelic 38)*

Estonia: Pareiko; Klavan, Piiroja, Jaager, Rahn, Kruglov, Dmitrijev, Puri (Purje 29), Vassiljev, Ahjupera (Oper 55), Saag (Kink 66).
Serbia: Brkic; Vidic, Ivanovic, Bisevac, Kolarov, Ninkovic (Trivunovic 14), Milijas, Tosic, Petrovic, Pantelic, Jovanovic (Zigic 74).
Referee: Nijhuis (Holland).

Belfast, 29 March 2011, 14,200

Northern Ireland (0) 0

Slovenia (0) 0

Northern Ireland: Camp; Baird, Cathcart, Craigan, McAuley, Evans J, Evans C (Boyce 90), McCann (McQuoid 72), Brunt, Feeney (McCourt 82), Clingan.
Slovenia: Handanovic; Jokic, Brecko, Mavric, Suler, Koren, Kirm, Bacinovic (Sukalo 90), Ilicic (Ljubijankic 29), Birsa, Novakovic (Dedic 84).
Referee: Kuipers (Holland).

Toftir, 3 June 2011, 974

Faeroes (0) 0

Slovenia (1) 2 *(Matavz 29, Baldvinsson 47 (og))*

Faeroes: Mikkelsen; Hansen E, Justinussen, Davidsen, Naes (Olsen S 81), Benjaminsen, Udsen (Danielsen 46), Baldvinsson, Holst (Mouritsen 75), Edmundsson, Elttor.
Slovenia: Handanovic; Cesar, Jokic, Brecko, Suler■, Koren, Bacinovic, Ilicic, Birsa (Mavric 47), Novakovic (Ljubijankic 55), Matavz (Kirm 76).
Referee: Drachta (Austria).

Modena, 3 June 2011, 19,434

Italy (2) 3 *(Rossi 21, Cassano 39, Pazzini 68)*

Estonia (0) 0

Italy: Buffon; Chiellini, Balzaretti, Ranocchia, Pirlo, Aquilani (Nocerino 24), Montolivo, Maggio, Marchisio, Rossi (Giovinco 79), Cassano (Pazzini 65).
Estonia: Pareiko; Klavan, Piiroja, Jaager, Teniste (Saag 59), Rahn, Kruglov, Puri, Vunk, Kink (Kams 78), Zenjov (Ahjupera 58).
Referee: Tudor (Romania).

Toftir, 7 June 2011, 1715

Faeroes (1) 2 *(Benjaminsen 43 (pen), Hansen A 47)*

Estonia (0) 0

Faeroes: Mikkelsen; Hansen E, Justinussen■, Gregersen, Danielsen, Naes, Benjaminsen, Baldvinsson, Holst (Mouritsen 85), Hansen A (Samuelsen 69), Elttor (Olsen S 90).
Estonia: Pareiko; Piiroja, Jaager, Rahn, Kruglov, Puri■, Vassiljev, Ahjupera (Kams 67), Kink, Saag (Mosnikov 83), Zenjov.
Referee: Munukka (Finland).

Belfast, 10 August 2011, 15,000

Northern Ireland (1) 4 *(Hughes 5, Davis 66, McCourt 71, 88)*

Faeroes (0) 0

Northern Ireland: Camp; Baird, McAuley (Cathcart 46), Hughes, Evans J, Clingan, Davis, McCann, Evans C (McGinn 59), Healy (Ward 83), McCourt.
Faeroes: Mikkelsen; Naes, Davidsen, Baldvinsson, Gregersen, Benjaminsen, Udsen, Olsen S (Danielsen 75), Holst (Hansen A 68), Edmundsson, Elttor (Mouritsen 75).
Referee: Aleckovic (Bosnia).

Torshavn, 2 September 2011, 5654

Faeroes (0) 0

Italy (1) 1 *(Cassano 11)*

Faeroes: Torgard; Justinussen (Samuelsen 87), Gregersen, Davidsen, Naes, Olsen S (Danielsen 76), Benjaminsen, Baldvinsson, Holst (Mouritsen 87), Edmundsson, Elttor.
Italy: Buffon; Chiellini, Criscito, Ranocchia, De Rossi, Pirlo, Thiago Motta (Aquilani 73), Montolivo, Maggio, Rossi (Pazzini 59), Cassano (Balotelli 85).
Referee: Bognar (Hungary).

Belfast, 2 September 2011, 15,148

Northern Ireland (0) 0

Serbia (0) 1 *(Pantelic 67)*

Northern Ireland: Camp; Baird, Hughes, McAuley, Cathcart, Evans J, Evans C (McGinn 59), Davis, Healy (McQuoid 84), McCann (Feeney 71), Brunt.
Serbia: Jorgacevic; Ivanovic, Subotic, Rajkovic, Kolarov, Stankovic, Kuzmanovic (Fejsa 89), Ninkovic (Petrovic 74), Tosic (Ljajic 79), Pantelic, Jovanovic.
Referee: Einwaller (Austria).

Ljubljana, 2 September 2011, 15,480

Slovenia (0) 1 *(Matavz 78)*

Estonia (1) 2 *(Vassiljev 29 (pen), Purje 81)*

Slovenia: Handanovic; Cesar, Ilic, Jokic, Brecko, Koren, Radosavljevic (Vrsic 56), Ilicic (Pecnik 82), Birsa, Novakovic (Ljubijankic 56), Matavz.
Estonia: Pareiko; Klavan, Piiroja (Stepanov 74), Jaager, Teniste, Rahn, Kruglov (Purje 69), Dmitrijev, Vunk, Vassiljev, Zenjov (Ahjupera 61).
Referee: Studer (Switzerland).

Tallinn, 6 September 2011, 8660

Estonia (2) 4 *(Vunk 28, Kink 32, Zenjov 59, Saag 90)*

Northern Ireland (1) 1 *(Piiroja 40 (og))*

Estonia: Pareiko; Klavan, Piiroja, Jaager, Rahn, Kruglov, Puri (Purje 63), Vunk, Vassiljev, Ahjupera (Zenjov 52), Kink (Saag 88).
Northern Ireland: Camp; Baird, Hughes, McAuley, Cathcart, Clingan, Davis, Brunt, Healy (McQuoid 65), McCann, McGinn (Feeney 65).
Referee: Stalhammar (Sweden).

Florence, 6 September 2011, 18,000

Italy (0) 1 *(Pazzini 85)*

Slovenia (0) 0

Italy: Buffon; Cassani, Chiellini, Balzaretti, Ranocchia, De Rossi, Pirlo, Thiago Motta (Marchisio 46), Montolivo (Balotelli 76), Rossi, Cassano (Pazzini 61).
Slovenia: Handanovic; Cesar, Jokic, Brecko, Suler, Vrsic (Pecnik 76), Koren, Kirm (Dedic 86), Radosavljevic, Birsa (Ilicic 57), Novakovic.
Referee: Moen (Norway).

Belgrade, 6 September 2011, 7500

Serbia (2) 3 *(Jovanovic 6, Tosic 23, Kuzmanovic 69)*

Faeroes (1) 1 *(Benjaminsen 37)*

Serbia: Jorgacevic; Ivanovic, Bisevac (Tomovic 46), Subotic, Kolarov, Stankovic (Petrovic 46), Kuzmanovic, Ninkovic (Fejsa 82), Tosic, Pantelic, Jovanovic.
Faeroes: Torgard; Gregersen, Davidsen, Danielsen, Naes, Samuelsen (Justinussen 73), Benjaminsen, Baldvinsson, Holst (Mouritsen 78), Edmundsson, Elttor.
Referee: Amirkhanyan (Armenia).

Belfast, 7 October 2011, 12,604

Northern Ireland (1) 1 *(Davis 22)*

Estonia (0) 2 *(Vassiljev 77 (pen), 84)*

Northern Ireland: Camp; Baird, Hodson, McCann (Healy 83), McAuley, Cathcart, Davis, Clingan (Evans C 32), McCourt, Lafferty (Feeney 69), Brunt.
Estonia: Pareiko; Klavan, Stepanov, Piiroja, Jaager, Kruglov, Dmitrijev, Puri (Purje 57), Vunk, Ahjupera (Zenjov 46), Kink (Vassiljev 65).
Referee: Grafe (Germany).

Belgrade, 7 October 2011, 35,000

Serbia (1) 1 *(Ivanovic 26)*

Italy (1) 1 *(Marchisio 2)*

Serbia: Jorgacevic; Ivanovic, Subotic, Rajkovic, Kolarov, Stankovic (Jovanovic 87), Krasic (Zigic 76), Fejsa (Petrovic 46), Ninkovic, Tosic, Pantelic.
Italy: Buffon; Barzagli, Bonucci, Chiellini, De Rossi, Pirlo, Montolivo (Aquilani 81), Maggio, Marchisio (Nocerino 70), Rossi, Cassano (Giovinco 66).
Referee: Proenca (Portugal).

Pescara, 11 October 2011, 19,480

Italy (1) 3 *(Cassano 22, 53, McAuley 74 (og))*

Northern Ireland (0) 0

Italy: Buffon (De Sanctis 81); Barzagli, Cassani, Chiellini, Balzaretti, De Rossi, Pirlo, Aquilani (Nocerino 69), Montolivo, Giovinco, Cassano (Osvaldo 56).
Northern Ireland: Taylor; Baird, Hodson, Evans C, McAuley, McGivern, Davis, Norwood (McLaughlin C 74), Little, Healy (Feeney 70), Gorman (McGinn 78).
Referee: Lahoz (Spain).

Maribor, 11 October 2011, 9848

Slovenia (1) 1 *(Vrsic 45)*

Serbia (0) 0

Slovenia: Handanovic; Cesar, Jokic, Brecko (Ilic 65), Suler, Vrsic (Birsa 75), Kirm, Bacinovic (Krhin 69), Radosavljevic, Ljubijankic, Matavz.
Serbia: Jorgacevic; Vidic, Ivanovic, Subotic, Kolarov, Stankovic, Ninkovic (Milijas 72), Tosic, Petrovic (Pantelic 51), Mrda, Jovanovic (Krasic 57).
Referee: De Bleeckere (Belgium).

Group C Table	*P*	*W*	*D*	*L*	*F*	*A*	*Pts*
Italy	10	8	2	0	20	2	26
Estonia	10	5	1	4	15	14	16
Serbia	10	4	3	3	13	12	15
Slovenia	10	4	2	4	11	7	14
Northern Ireland	10	2	3	5	9	13	9
Faeroes	10	1	1	8	6	26	4

GROUP D

Paris, 3 September 2010, 76,395

France (0) 0

Belarus (0) 1 *(Kislyak 86)*

France: Lloris; Sagna, Clichy, Mexes, Rami, Malouda, Diaby, M'Vila, Menez (Saha 69) (Gameiro 80), Remy (Valbuena 34), Hoarau.

Belarus: Zhevnov; Omelyanchuk, Tigorev, Yurevich, Shitov, Martynovich, Hleb A, Kulchiy, Kutuzov (Kislyak 74), Rodionov (Kornilenko 85), Hleb V (Putsila 89).
Referee: Collum (Scotland).

Luxembourg, 3 September 2010, 7327

Luxembourg (0) 0

Bosnia (3) 3 *(Ibricic 6, Pjanic 12, Dzeko 16)*

Luxembourg: Joubert; Hoffmann, Schnell, Kintziger, Mutsch, Gerson, Janisch, Peters, Bettmer (Laterza 86), Collette (Da Mota 76), Bensi (Kitenge 46).
Bosnia: Hasagic; Spahic, Nadarevic, Mujdza, Misimovic, Rahimic (Jahic 67), Pjanic (Zec 78), Lulic, Ibricic (Medunjanin 72), Ibisevic, Dzeko.
Referee: Banari (Moldova).

Piatra Neamt, 3 September 2010, 13,400

Romania (0) 1 *(Stancu 80)*

Albania (0) 1 *(Muzaka 88)*

Romania: Lobont; Tamas, Rat, Contra (Muresan 57), Radoi, Cocis (Herea 78), Torje, Deac, Florescu, Niculae (Stancu 64), Marica.
Albania: Beqaj; Vangjeli, Lila, Dallku, Curri, Cana, Skela (Lika 79), Agolli, Bulku, Duro (Muzaka 82), Bogdani (Salihi 57).
Referee: Schorgenhofer (Austria).

Tirana, 7 September 2010, 10,000

Albania (1) 1 *(Salihi 37)*

Luxembourg (0) 0

Albania: Beqaj; Dallku, Curri, Cana, Skela, Agolli, Bulku, Duro (Lila 90), Bogdani, Salihi, Muzaka (Hyka 80).
Luxembourg: Joubert; Hoffmann, Schnell, Kintziger, Blaise, Mutsch■, Payal, Peters, Bettmer (Collette 90), Laterza (Martino 82), Da Mota.
Referee: Trutz (Slovakia).

Minsk, 7 September 2010, 26,354

Belarus (0) 0

Romania (0) 0

Belarus: Zhevnov; Omelyanchuk, Yurevich, Shitov, Martynovich, Hleb A (Putsila 73), Kulchiy, Kislyak, Kutuzov (Krivets 87), Kornilenko (Rodionov 76), Hleb V.
Romania: Pantilimon; Chivu, Tamas, Rat, Maftei, Radoi, Torje (Cocis 46), Deac (Marica 83), Florescu, Stancu (Niculae 73), Bilasco.
Referee: Kralovec (Czech Republic).

Sarajevo, 7 September 2010, 28,000

Bosnia (0) 0

France (0) 2 *(Benzema 72, Malouda 78)*

Bosnia: Hasagic; Spahic, Nadarevic, Mujdza, Misimovic, Rahimic (Zec 74), Pjanic, Lulic, Ibricic, Ibisevic (Jahic 75), Dzeko.
France: Lloris; Sagna, Clichy, Mexes, Rami, Diarra A, Malouda (Matuidi 80), Valbuena, Diaby, M'Vila, Benzema.
Referee: Brych (Germany).

Tirana, 8 October 2010, 14,220

Albania (1) 1 *(Duro 45)*

Bosnia (1) 1 *(Ibisevic 21)*

Albania: Beqaj; Vangjeli, Lila, Dallku, Cana, Agolli, Bulku, Duro, Muzaka (Lika 65), Bogdani (Skela 46), Salihi (Hyka 85).
Bosnia: Hasagic (Begovic 46); Spahic, Mravac (Pandza 46), Mujdza, Misimovic, Medunjanin, Rahimic, Pjanic, Lulic, Ibisevic, Dzeko (Ibricic 89).
Referee: Jakobsson (Iceland).

Luxembourg, 8 October 2010, 1857

Luxembourg (0) 0

Belarus (0) 0

Luxembourg: Joubert; Hoffmann, Schnell, Kintziger, Blaise, Leweck, Payal (Kettenmeyer 77), Peters, Bettmer (Gerson 62), Laterza, Joachim (Da Mota 66).
Belarus: Zhevnov; Omelyanchuk, Tigorev (Rodionov 67), Yurevich (Molosh 87), Shitov, Martynovich, Kulchiy, Kalachev, Kislyak, Kornilenko■, Hleb V (Putsila 67).
Referee: Stavrev (Macedonia).

Paris, 9 October 2010, 79,299

France (0) 2 *(Remy 83, Gourcuff 90)*

Romania (0) 0

France: Lloris; Reveillere, Clichy, Mexes, Rami, Diarra A, Malouda, Valbuena (Remy 68), Nasri (Gourcuff 74), M'Vila, Benzema (Payet 86).
Romania: Pantilimon; Chivu, Tamas, Rat, Sapunaru, Radoi, Cocis (Roman 87), Florescu, Niculae (Marica 63), Zicu (Deac 46), Stancu.
Referee: Proenca (Portugal).

Mogilev, 12 October 2010, 7000

Belarus (1) 2 *(Rodionov 10, Krivets 77)*

Albania (0) 0

Belarus: Zhevnov; Omelyanchuk, Molosh (Yurevich 86), Tigorev, Shitov, Martynovich, Kulchiy (Krivets 75), Putsila (Hleb V 82), Kalachev, Kislyak, Rodionov.
Albania: Beqaj; Vangjeli, Lila, Dallku■, Teli, Skela (Kapllani 81), Agolli, Bulku (Muzaka 59), Duro, Lika (Bakaj 76), Salihi.
Referee: Rasmussen (Denmark).

Longeville-les-Metz, 12 October 2010, 24,710

France (1) 2 *(Benzema 22, Gourcuff 76)*

Luxembourg (0) 0

France: Lloris; Reveillere, Clichy, Mexes, Rami, Diarra A, Malouda (Payet 63), Diaby, Gourcuff, Benzema (Nasri 63), Hoarau (Remy 73).
Luxembourg: Joubert; Hoffmann, Schnell, Blaise, Mutsch, Leweck, Payal, Peters■, Bettmer (Da Mota 84), Laterza (Strasser 70), Joachim (Kitenge 53).
Referee: Jug (Slovenia).

Luxembourg, 25 March 2011, 8052

Luxembourg (0) 0

France (1) 2 *(Mexes 28, Gourcuff 72)*

Luxembourg: Joubert; Hoffmann, Schnell, Blaise, Mutsch, Gerson (Da Mota 71), Leweck (Plein 90), Payal, Bettmer, Laterza (Martino 54), Joachim.
France: Lloris; Sagna, Evra, Mexes, Rami, Malouda, Ribery, Nasri, Gourcuff, M'Vila, Benzema.
Referee: Hagen (Norway).

Tirana, 26 March 2011, 13,826

Albania (0) 1 *(Salihi 62)*

Belarus (0) 0

Albania: Ujkani; Vangjeli, Lila, Teli, Cana, Lala, Skela (Duro 80), Agolli, Bulku, Bogdani (Bakaj 75), Salihi (Muzaka 90).
Belarus: Veremko; Omelyanchuk, Molosh, Tigorev, Shitov, Martynovich, Kulchiy (Bychenok 62), Putsila (Sitko 82), Krivets (Kovel 46), Kislyak, Hleb V.
Referee: Strombergsson (Sweden).

Zenica, 26 March 2011, 13,000

Bosnia (0) 2 *(Ibisevic 63, Dzeko 83)*

Romania (1) 1 *(Marica 29)*

Bosnia: Hasagic; Spahic, Mravac, Mujdza, Misimovic (Ibricic 81), Medunjanin (Maletic 71), Rahimic, Pjanic, Lulic, Ibisevic (Muslimovic 76), Dzeko.
Romania: Pantilimon; Goian, Tamas, Rat, Rapa, Alexa, Torje (Cocis 71), Deac (Zicu 87), Florescu (Ropotan 76), Mutu, Marica.
Referee: Teixeira (Spain).

Ceahlaul, 29 March 2011, 13,500

Romania (1) 3 *(Mutu 24, 68, Zicu 78)*

Luxembourg (1) 1 *(Gerson 22)*

Romania: Tatarusanu; Tamas (Goian 65), Rat, Sapunaru, Gardos, Ropotan, Muresan, Mutu (Alexe 84), Marica, Zicu, Stancu (Torje 46).
Luxembourg: Joubert; Hoffmann, Schnell (Martino 90), Blaise, Mutsch, Gerson (Da Mota 58), Leweck, Payal, Peters, Bettmer (Laterza 81), Joachim.
Referee: Huseyin (Turkey).

Minsk, 3 June 2011, 26,500

Belarus (1) 1 *(Abidal 20 (og))*

France (1) 1 *(Malouda 22)*

Belarus: Veremko; Omelyanchuk, Tigorev, Bordachev, Shitov, Verkhovtsov, Martynovich, Trubila, Putsila (Kislyak 86), Kalachev (Hleb V 90), Varankov.
France: Lloris; Abidal, Sagna, Sakho, Rami, Diarra A, Malouda, Ribery, Nasri, Diaby (Remy 73), Benzema.
Referee: Fernandez (Spain).

Bucharest, 3 June 2011, 8200

Romania (2) 3 *(Mutu 37, Marica 41, 55)*

Bosnia (0) 0

Romania: Tatarusanu; Tamas, Rat, Sapunaru, Papp, Sanmartean (Tanase 63), Muresan, Torje, Bourceanu, Mutu (Surdu 83), Marica (Alexe 87).
Bosnia: Hasagic; Spahic, Mravac, Mujdza, Misimovic, Medunjanin (Ibisevic 46), Rahimic, Pjanic, Lulic, Ibricic (Muslimovic 64), Dzeko (Stilic 64).
Referee: Eriksson (Sweden).

Minsk, 7 June 2011, 8000

Belarus (0) 2 *(Kornilenko 48 (pen), Putsila 73)*

Luxembourg (0) 0

Belarus: Zhevnov; Omelyanchuk, Tigorev, Bordachev, Shitov, Verkhovtsov, Kulchiy (Kislyak 87), Trubila (Hleb V 62), Putsila, Kalachev, Varankov (Kornilenko 46).
Luxembourg: Joubert; Hoffmann, Martino, Schnell, Blaise, Malget (Kitenge 61), Gerson, Leweck (Collette 84), Payal, Peters, Da Mota (Laterza 77).
Referee: Salmanov (Azerbaijan).

Zenica, 7 June 2011, 10,000

Bosnia (0) 2 *(Medunjanin 67, Maletic 90)*

Albania (0) 0

Bosnia: Hasagic; Spahic, Pandza, Mujdza (Maletic 73), Misimovic, Medunjanin, Rahimic, Pjanic (Besic 77), Lulic, Ibisevic (Muslimovic 61), Dzeko.
Albania: Ujkani; Vangjeli, Dallku, Curri, Cana, Lala (Muzaka 72), Skela, Agolli (Lila■ 60), Bulku, Bogdani (Duro 46), Salihi.
Referee: Blom (Holland).

Tirana, 2 September 2011, 15,600

Albania (0) 1 *(Bogdani 46)*

France (2) 2 *(Benzema 11, M'Vila 18)*

Albania: Ujkani; Vangjeli, Dallku, Curri (Lala 24), Teli, Cana, Skela (Hyka 46), Agolli, Bulku (Bakaj 69), Bogdani, Salihi.
France: Lloris; Abidal, Kaboul, Reveillere, Evra, Diarra A, Malouda (Martin 81), Ribery, Nasri, M'Vila, Benzema.
Referee: Nikolaev (Russia).

Minsk, 2 September 2011, 28,500

Belarus (0) 0

Bosnia (2) 2 *(Salihovic 22 (pen), Medunjanin 24)*

Belarus: Zhevnov; Trubila, Shitov, Verkhovtsov, Martynovich, Kulchiy, Putsila, Zhavnerchik (Sitko 63), Kalachev, Kislyak, Kornilenko (Varankov 63).
Bosnia: Hasagic; Spahic, Papac, Pandza, Medunjanin (Muslimovic 88), Rahimic, Salihovic (Maletic 72), Pjanic, Lulic, Zahirovic, Dzeko (Misimovic 80).
Referee: Kassai (Hungary).

Luxembourg, 2 September 2011, 2812

Luxembourg (0) 0

Romania (2) 2 *(Torje 34, 45)*

Luxembourg: Joubert; Hoffmann (Bukvic 76), Schnell, Blaise, Mutsch, Gerson, Leweck, Payal, Bettmer, Da Mota (Janisch 61), Joachim (Kitenge 46).
Romania: Tatarusanu; Goian, Rat, Galamaz (Chiriches 62), Matel, Cocis, Lazar, Torje (Nicolita 76), Tanase, Marica (Stancu 86), Bucur.
Referee: Karasev (Russia).

Zenica, 6 September 2011, 12,000

Bosnia (0) 1 *(Misimovic 87)*

Belarus (0) 0

Bosnia: Begovic; Papac, Pandza (Misimovic 46), Mujdza, Medunjanin, Rahimic, Salihovic (Stilic 19), Lulic, Ibricic (Zec 64), Zahirovic, Dzeko.
Belarus: Zhevnov; Trubila, Shitov, Verkhovtsov, Martynovich■, Kulchiy, Putsila, Sitko (Varankov 77), Kalachev■, Kislyak, Kornilenko (Drahun 72).
Referee: Atkinson (England).

Luxembourg, 6 September 2011, 2132

Luxembourg (1) 2 *(Bettmer 27, Joachim 78)*

Albania (0) 1 *(Bogdani 64)*

Luxembourg: Joubert; Schnell, Bukvic, Blaise, Mutsch, Gerson, Leweck (Joachim 68), Payal (Pedro 88), Janisch, Bettmer, Da Mota (Bensi 70).
Albania: Ujkani; Vangjeli, Teli, Veliu (Bulku 62), Lala, Skela, Agolli■, Duro (Bakaj 46), Bogdani■, Salihi, Kapllani (Muzaka 46).
Referee: Kari (Finland).

Bucharest, 6 September 2011, 49,137

Romania (0) 0

France (0) 0

Romania: Tatarusanu; Goian, Rat, Luchin, Chiriches, Nicolita, Cocis, Lazar (Stancu 43), Tanase, Bourceanu, Marica (Bucur 90).
France: Lloris; Abidal, Sagna, Evra, Rami, Ribery, Valbuena (Remy 71), Cabaye (Nasri 75), M'Vila, Martin, Benzema.
Referee: Webb (England).

Zenica, 7 October 2011, 12,000

Bosnia (4) 5 *(Dzeko 12, Misimovic 15, 22 (pen), Pjanic 36, Medunjanin 51)*

Luxembourg (0) 0

Bosnia: Begovic; Spahic, Papac, Mujdza, Misimovic, Medunjanin (Ibricic 64), Rahimic (Zahirovic 59), Pjanic, Lulic (Maletic 66), Ibisevic, Dzeko.
Luxembourg: Joubert; Schnell, Bukvic, Blaise, Mutsch, Gerson, Leweck, Payal, Bettmer, Laterza (Janisch 83), Da Mota (Joachim 44).
Referee: Evans (Wales).

Paris, 7 October 2011, 65,239

France (2) 3 *(Malouda 11, Remy 38, Reveillere 67)*

Albania (0) 0

France: Lloris; Kaboul, Debuchy, Evra (Reveillere 46), Rami, Malouda, Nasri, Cabaye (Martin 47), M'Vila, Gomis (Cisse 80), Remy.
Albania: Ujkani; Vangjeli, Lila, Dallku, Cana, Duro, Muzaka (Januzi 74), Lika (Lilaj 81), Hyka (Bakaj 63), Roshi, Salihi.
Referee: Koukoulakis (Greece).

Bucharest, 7 October 2011, 29,486

Romania (1) 2 *(Mutu 19, 51 (pen))*

Belarus (1) 2 *(Kornilenko 45, Drahun 82)*

Romania: Pantilimon; Tamas, Rat, Moti, Matel, Sanmartean (Adrian Cristea 28), Lazar (Cocis 70), Torje, Bourceanu, Mutu, Marica (Stancu 80).
Belarus: Zhevnov; Omelyanchuk, Filipenko (Plaskonny 19), Bordachev (Veretilo 90), Verkhovtsov, Kulchiy, Krivets (Rudik 60), Nekhajchik, Drahun, Kislyak, Kornilenko.
Referee: Kelly (Republic of Ireland).

Tirana, 11 October 2011, 3000

Albania (1) 1 *(Salihi 24)*

Romania (0) 1 *(Luchin 77)*

Albania: Ujkani; Lila, Dallku, Teli, Cana, Lala, Bakaj (Hyka 67), Roshi (Muzaka 77), Lilaj, Bogdani (Januzi 46), Salihi.
Romania: Lung; Goian, Tamas, Latovlevici, Luchin, Nicolita (Torje 63), Cocis, Lazar (Bucur 87), Bourceanu, Mutu, Marica (Stancu 49).
Referee: Mazeika (Lithuania).

Paris, 11 October 2011, 78,467

France (0) 1 *(Nasri 78 (pen))*

Bosnia (1) 1 *(Dzeko 40)*

France: Lloris; Abidal, Reveillere, Evra, Rami, Malouda (Martin 61), Menez, Nasri, Cabaye (Gameiro 61), M'Vila, Remy (Diarra A 82).
Bosnia: Hasagic (Begovic 46); Spahic, Papac, Pandza, Mujdza (Maletic 61), Misimovic, Medunjanin (Zahirovic 71), Rahimic, Pjanic, Lulic, Dzeko.
Referee: Thomson (Scotland).

Group D Table	P	W	D	L	F	A	Pts
France	10	6	3	1	15	4	21
Bosnia	10	6	2	2	17	8	20
Romania	10	3	5	2	13	9	14
Belarus	10	3	4	3	8	7	13
Albania	10	2	3	5	7	14	9
Luxembourg	10	1	1	8	3	21	4

GROUP E

Chisinau, 3 September 2010, 10,300

Moldova (0) 2 *(Suvorov 69, Doros 73)*

Finland (0) 0

Moldova: Namasco; Epureanu, Bulgaru, Savinov, Cebotaru, Boret, Bordian, Josan (Suvorov 58), Frunza, Tigirlas (Bugaev 69), Doros (Andronic 75).
Finland: Fredrikson; Pasanen, Hyypia■, Heikkinen, Moisander, Eremenko R, Sparv, Eremenko A Jr (Forssell 81), Porokara (Vayrynen 75), Litmanen (Hamalainen 46), Johansson.
Referee: Malek (Poland).

Serravalle, 3 September 2010, 4127

San Marino (0) 0

Holland (2) 5 *(Kuyt 16 (pen), Huntelaar 38, 48, 67, Van Nistelrooy 90)*

San Marino: Simoncini A; Vitaioli F, Alessandro Della Valle (Bacciocchi 61), Simoncini D, Valentini C, Berretti, Vannucci, Mazza, Manuel Marani (Gasperoni A 76), Selva A, Vitaioli M (Ciacci 83).
Holland: Stekelenburg; Mathijsen, Maduro, Pieters, Van der Wiel, Sneijder, Van Bommel, De Jong (Van der Vaart 46), Kuyt (Van Nistelrooy 68), Elia (Afellay 59), Huntelaar.
Referee: Lee (Wales).

Stockholm, 3 September 2010, 32,304

Sweden (0) 2 *(Wernbloom 51, 73)*

Hungary (0) 0

Sweden: Isaksson (Wiland 46); Mellberg, Safari, Majstorovic, Lustig, Svensson (Kallstrom 33), Bajrami, Wernbloom, Ibrahimovic, Elmander (Larsson S 49), Toivonen.
Hungary: Kiraly; Juhasz, Laczko, Lazar, Liptak, Vadocz, Gera, Koman, Dzsudzsak (Huszti 46), Elek (Priskin 59), Rudolf (Hajnal 82).
Referee: Atkinson (England).

Rotterdam, 7 September 2010, 25,000

Holland (2) 2 *(Huntelaar 7, 16 (pen))*

Finland (1) 1 *(Forssell 18)*

Holland: Stekelenburg; Heitinga, Mathijsen, Van der Wiel, Anita, Sneijder, Van Bommel, Van der Vaart (Elia 64), De Jong, Afellay (Lens 74), Huntelaar (Van Nistelrooy 82).
Finland: Fredrikson; Pasanen, Heikkinen, Lampi, Moisander, Vayrynen, Eremenko R, Sparv, Hamalainen (Porokara 46), Forssell (Eremenko A Jr 81), Sjolund (Johansson 68).
Referee: Nikolaev (Russia).

Budapest, 7 September 2010, 9209

Hungary (0) 2 *(Rudolf 50, Koman 66)*

Moldova (0) 1 *(Suvorov 79)*

Hungary: Kiraly; Juhasz, Laczko, Lazar, Liptak, Gera, Koman (Vadocz 88), Dzsudzsak, Czvitkovics (Szalai 46), Elek, Rudolf (Vanczak 64).
Moldova: Namasco; Epureanu, Racu, Bulgaru, Bolohan, Cebotaru (Cojocari 71), Suvorov, Bordian, Josan (Doros 59), Frunza (Bugaev 84), Tigirlas.
Referee: Kovarik (Czech Republic).

Malmo, 7 September 2010, 21,083

Sweden (3) 6 *(Ibrahimovic 7, 77, Simoncini D 12 (og), Simoncini A 26 (og), Granqvist 51, Berg 90)*

San Marino (0) 0

Sweden: Wiland; Mellberg■, Safari, Majstorovic, Lustig, Kallstrom, Bajrami, Wernbloom (Elmander 69), Larsson S, Ibrahimovic (Berg 82), Toivonen (Granqvist 47).
San Marino: Simoncini A; Vitaioli F, Alesssandro Della Valle, Simoncini D, Bacciocchi (Valentini C 79), Vannucci, Chiaruzzi (Gasperoni A 72), Mazza, Manuel Marani (Berretti 56), Selva A, Vitaioli M.
Referee: McKeon (Republic of Ireland).

Budapest, 8 October 2010, 10,596

Hungary (4) 8 *(Rudolf 11, 25, Szalai 18, 27, 49, Koman 61, Dzsudszak 89, Gera 90 (pen))*

San Marino (0) 0

Hungary: Kiraly; Juhasz, Vanczak, Laczko, Vermes, Gera, Koman (Czvitkovics 79), Dzsudszak, Elek (Vadocz 64), Rudolf, Szalai (Priskin 64).
San Marino: Simoncini A; Vitaioli F, Alessandro Della Valle, Bacciocchi (Nicola Albani 53), Bollini (Cervellini 84), Valentini C, Berretti, Vannucci, Manuel Marani, Vitaioli M (Bugli 77), Montagna.
Referee: Kaasik (Estonia).

Chisinau, 8 October 2010, 10,500

Moldova (0) 0

Holland (1) 1 *(Huntelaar 37)*

Moldova: Namasco; Epureanu, Golovatenco, Racu, Bulgaru, Bolohan, Cebotaru (Andronic 69), Suvorov, Bordian, Frunza (Bugaev 46), Doros (Josan 78).
Holland: Stekelenburg; Heitinga, Mathijsen, Pieters, Van der Wiel, Sneijder, Van Bommel, Van der Vaart, Afellay (Emanuelson 90), Kuyt, Huntelaar.
Referee: Meyer (Germany).

Helsinki, 12 October 2010, 18,532

Finland (0) 1 *(Forssell 86)*

Hungary (0) 2 *(Szalai 50, Dzsudzsak 90)*

Finland: Jaaskelainen; Pasanen, Hyypia, Moisander, Vayrynen, Eremenko R, Sparv (Litmanen 72), Porokara (Eremenko A Jr 71), Heikkinen, Forssell, Sjolund (Kuqi 81).
Hungary: Kiraly; Juhasz, Laczko (Vanczak 86), Vermes, Liptak, Vadocz (Pinter 75), Gera, Dzsudzsak, Elek, Rudolf (Koman 46), Szalai.
Referee: Kelly (Republic of Ireland).

Amsterdam, 12 October 2010, 46,000

Holland (2) 4 *(Huntelaar 4, 55, Afellay 37, 59)*

Sweden (0) 1 *(Granqvist 69)*

Holland: Stekelenburg; Heitinga, Mathijsen, Pieters, Van der Wiel, Sneijder, Van Bommel (Brama 72), Van der Vaart, Afellay, Kuyt (Lens 29), Huntelaar (Van Nistelrooy 84).
Sweden: Isaksson; Granqvist, Safari (Wendt 46), Majstorovic, Lustig, Svensson, Wernbloom (Kallstrom 54), Larsson S, Ibrahimovic, Elmander, Toivonen (Berg 79).
Referee: Lannoy (France).

Serravalle, 12 October 2010, 714

San Marino (0) 0

Moldova (1) 2 *(Josan 20, Doros 86 (pen))*

San Marino: Simoncini A; Vitaioli F, Simoncini D, Bacciocchi, Cervellini (Berretti 60), Bollini (Ciacci 67), Vannucci, Mazza, Manuel Marani, Vitaioli M, Montagna (Coppini 82).
Moldova: Namasco; Epureanu, Golovatenco, Suvorov, Boret, Bordian, Cojocari (Savinov 82), Josan (Zmeu 69), Andronic, Frunza, Bugaev (Doros 62).
Referee: Courtney (Northern Ireland).

Helsinki, 17 November 2010, 8192

Finland (1) 8 *(Vayrynen 39, Hamalainen 49, 67, Forssell 51, 59, 78, Litmanen 71 (pen), Porokara 73)*

San Marino (0) 0

Finland: Fredrikson; Pasanen, Lampi, Moisander, Vayrynen, Eremenko R, Eremenko A Jr (Kuqi 80), Hamalainen (Porokara 70), Heikkinen, Forssell, Sjolund (Litmanen 46).
San Marino: Simoncini A; Vitaioli F (Vannucci 72), Alessandro Della Valle, Cervellini, Berretti (Alex Della Valle 67), Bugli, Coppini, Nicola Albani, Selva A, Vitaioli M, Montagna (Manuel Marani 79).
Referee: Matejek (Czech Republic).

Budapest, 25 March 2011, 23,817

Hungary (0) 0

Holland (2) 4 *(Van der Vaart 8, Afellay 45, Kuyt 54, Van Persie 62)*

Hungary: Kiraly; Juhasz, Vanczak, Laczko, Liptak, Gera, Koman (Vadocz 46), Dzsudzsak, Varga (Czvitkovics 46), Elek (Priskin 80), Rudolf.
Holland: Vorm; Heitinga, Mathijsen, Pieters, Van der Wiel, Sneijder, Van der Vaart (Van Nistelrooy 82), De Jong, Afellay (Elia 63), Kuyt (Strootman 82), Van Persie.
Referee: Velasco (Spain).

Amsterdam, 29 March 2011, 51,700

Holland (1) 5 *(Van Persie 13, Sneijder 61, Van Nistelrooy 73, Kuyt 78, 81)*

Hungary (0) 3 *(Rudolf 47, Gera 50, 75)*

Holland: Vorm; Heitinga, Mathijsen, Pieters (Emanuelson 64), Van der Wiel, Sneijder, Van der Vaart, De Jong, Afellay, Kuyt (Elia 90), Van Persie (Van Nistelrooy 46).
Hungary: Fulop; Juhasz, Vanczak, Laczko, Pinter (Koman 46), Lazar, Vadocz (Czvitkovics 90), Gera, Dzsudzsak, Rudolf, Priskin (Tokoli 73).
Referee: Moen (Norway).

Stockholm, 29 March 2011, 25,544

Sweden (1) 2 *(Lustig 30, Larsson S 32)*

Moldova (0) 1 *(Suvorov 90)*

Sweden: Isaksson; Wendt, Granqvist, Antonsson, Lustig, Kallstrom, Bajrami (Olsson 73), Wernbloom (Elm R 65), Larsson S, Ibrahimovic, Elmander (Gerndt 89).
Moldova: Namasco; Golovatenco, Racu, Armas, Bolohan, Cebotaru, Suvorov, Boret, Gatcan (Andronic 83), Frunza (Bugaev 46), Doros (Cheptine 72).
Referee: Kircher (Germany).

Chisinau, 3 June 2011, 10,500

Moldova (0) 1 *(Bugaev 61)*

Sweden (2) 4 *(Toivonen 11, Elmander 30, 58, Gerndt 88)*

Moldova: Namasco; Golovatenco, Racu, Armas, Bolohan, Ivanov, Cebotaru (Patras 78), Suvorov, Gatcan (Tigirlas 46), Bugaev, Doros (Boghiu 63).
Sweden: Isaksson; Mellberg, Wendt, Majstorovic, Lustig, Kallstrom, Svensson, Larsson S, Elmander (Gerndt 75), Toivonen (Wilhelmsson 68), Hysen (Wernbloom 40).
Referee: Marriner (England).

Serravalle, 3 June 2011, 1218

San Marino (0) 0

Finland (1) 1 *(Forssell 41)*

San Marino: Simoncini A; Vitaioli F (Bacciocchi 88), Alessandro Della Valle, Simoncici D, Cervellini, Bollini, Vannucci, Mazza (Berretti 77), Manuel Marani, Selva A, Vitaioli M (Montagna 80).
Finland: Hradecky; Pasanen, Raitala, Lampi, Moisander, Vayrynen, Eremenko A Jr (Riski 68), Hamalainen, Heikkinen, Hetemaj (Sjolund 84), Forssell (Sadik 90).
Referee: Sipailo (Latvia).

Serravalle, 7 June 2011, 1900

San Marino (0) 0

Hungary (1) 3 *(Liptak 41, Szabics 49, Koman 83)*

San Marino: Simoncini A; Vitaioli F (Alex Della Valle 46), Alessandro Della Valle, Benedettini, Cervellini, Bollini (Bacciocchi 80), Vannucci, Mazza, Manuel Marani (Berretti 64), Selva A, Vitaioli M.
Hungary: Kiraly; Juhasz, Vanczak, Laczko, Liptak (Pinter 87), Hajnal (Czvitkovics 71), Koman, Dzsudzsak, Elek, Szabics (Koltai 84), Nemeth.
Referee: Radovanovic (Montenegro).

Stockholm, 7 June 2011, 32,128

Sweden (3) 5 *(Kallstrom 11, Ibrahimovic 31, 35, 53, Bajrami 74)*

Finland (0) 0

Sweden: Isaksson; Mellberg, Wendt, Majstorovic, Lustig, Kallstrom, Svensson, Bajrami, Larsson S (Wilhelmsson 89), Elmander (Wernbloom 81), Toivonen (Ibrahimovic 25).
Finland: Jaakkola; Pasanen, Moisander, Toivio, Vayrynen, Eremenko R, Eremenko A Jr (Ring 79), Hamalainen (Halsti 46), Heikkinen (Aaritalo 46), Hetemaj, Forssell.
Referee: Gautier (France).

Helsinki, 2 September 2011, 9056

Finland (2) 4 *(Hamalainen 11, 43, Forssell 52 (pen), Armas 70 (og))*

Moldova (0) 1 *(Alexeev 85)*

Finland: Hradecky; Arkivuo, Raitala, Moisander, Toivio, Eremenko R, Hamalainen (Furuholm 76), Hetemaj, Sjolund (Pukki 61), Ring (Vayrynen 72), Forssell.
Moldova: Calancea; Epureanu, Golovatenco, Armas, Savinov, Cebotaru, Zmeu, Suvorov (Bordian 55), Boret, Ovseannicov (Alexeev 69), Doros (Cheptine 55).
Referee: Kakos (Greece).

Eindhoven, 2 September 2011, 35,000

Holland (3) 11 *(Van Persie 7, 65, 67, 79, Sneijder 12, 87, Heitinga 17, Kuyt 49, Huntelaar 56, 77, Wijnaldum 90)*

San Marino (0) 0

Holland: Stekelenburg; Heitinga, Mathijsen, Pieters, Van der Wiel, Sneijder, Van Bommel (Maduro 74), Strootman (Wijnaldum 86), Kuyt (Elia 74), Van Persie, Huntelaar.
San Marino: Simoncini A; Vitaioli F, Simoncini D (Bacciocchi 82), Andreini, Benedettini, Cervellini, Bollini (Gasperoni A 68), Vannucci, Mazza (Coppini 54), Selva A, Vitaioli M.
Referee: Liany (Israel).

Budapest, 2 September 2011, 23,500

Hungary (1) 2 *(Szabics 44, Rudolf 90)*

Sweden (0) 1 *(Wilhelmsson 61)*

Hungary: Kiraly; Laczko, Pinter, Korcsmar, Liptak (Sandor 74), Hajnal (Stieber 65), Koman, Varga, Elek, Rudolf, Szabics (Priskin 80).
Sweden: Isaksson; Wendt, Granqvist, Majstorovic, Lustig, Kallstrom (Wernbloom 88), Svensson (Elm R 53), Wilhelmsson, Larsson S (Toivonen 68), Ibrahimovic, Elmander.
Referee: Skomina (Slovenia).

Helsinki, 6 September 2011, 21,580

Finland (0) 0

Holland (1) 2 *(Strootman 29, De Jong 90)*

Finland: Hradecky; Pasanen (Raitala 78), Arkivuo, Moisander, Toivio, Eremenko A Jr, Hamalainen, Hetemaj■, Ring, Pukki (Vayrynen 61), Forssell (Sjolund 86).
Holland: Stekelenburg; Heitinga, Mathijsen, Pieters, Van der Wiel, Sneijder, Van Bommel, Strootman, Kuyt, Van Persie (Elia 68), Huntelaar (De Jong 68).
Referee: Grafe (Germany).

Chisinau, 6 September 2011, 10,500

Moldova (0) 0

Hungary (1) 2 *(Vanczak 7, Rudolf 83)*

Moldova: Gaiduchevici; Epureanu, Golovatenco, Armas, Savinov, Cebotaru, Zmeu (Bugaev 46), Suvorov, Cheptine (Doros 62), Boret, Alexeev (Tigirlas 73).
Hungary: Kiraly; Juhasz, Vanczak, Pinter (Sandor 64), Korcsmar (Laczko 69), Hajnal, Koman, Varga, Elek, Rudolf, Szabics (Vadocz 81).
Referee: Bebek (Croatia).

Serravalle, 6 September 2011, 2946

San Marino (0) 0

Sweden (0) 5 *(Kallstrom 64, Wilhelmsson 70, 90, Olsson 81, Hysen 89)*

San Marino: Valentini F; Vitaioli F, Simoncini D■, Bacciocchi, Cervellini, Bollini (Gasperoni A 83), Vannucci, Coppini (Andreini 71), Manuel Marani (Benedettini 56), Selva A, Vitaioli M.
Sweden: Isaksson; Olsson, Granqvist, Majstorovic, Lustig, Kallstrom, Wilhelmsson, Elm R (Svensson 65), Ibrahimovic, Elmander (Hysen 67), Toivonen (Larsson S 57).
Referee: McLean (Scotland).

Helsinki, 7 October 2011, 23,257

Finland (0) 1 *(Toivio 73)*

Sweden (1) 2 *(Larsson S 8, Olsson 52)*

Finland: Hradecky; Arkivuo, Raitala, Moisander, Toivio, Vayrynen (Furuholm 71), Eremenko R, Sparv, Hamalainen, Ring, Pukki (Forssell 60).
Sweden: Isaksson; Mellberg, Olsson, Majstorovic, Lustig, Kallstrom (Bajrami 87), Wilhelmsson (Svensson 54), Elm R, Larsson S (Toivonen 68), Ibrahimovic, Elmander.
Referee: Clattenburg (England).

Rotterdam, 7 October 2011, 47,226

Holland (1) 1 *(Huntelaar 40)*

Moldova (0) 0

Holland: Vorm; Mathijsen, Pieters, Van der Wiel, Bruma, Van Bommel, Van der Vaart (Elia 77), Strootman, Kuyt, Van Persie, Huntelaar.
Moldova: Namasco; Epureanu, Golovatenco, Racu, Bulgaru, Armas, Ivanov, Cebotaru, Suvorov (Zmeu 58), Cheptine (Ovseannicov 84), Alexeev (Bugaev 69).
Referee: Jug (Slovenia).

Budapest, 11 October 2011, 25,169

Hungary (0) 0

Finland (0) 0

Hungary: Kiraly; Juhasz, Vanczak, Korcsmar, Hajnal (Stieber 88), Koman, Varga, Sandor (Vadocz 60), Elek, Szabics, Priskin (Dzsudzsak 59).
Finland: Fredrikson; Arkivuo (Lampi 55), Raitala, Moisander, Toivio, Vayrynen, Sparv, Eremenko A Jr, Hamalainen (Pukki 84), Ring, Forssell (Furuholm 67).
Referee: Undiano (Spain).

Chisinau, 11 October 2011, 6534

Moldova (1) 4 *(Zmeu 30, Bacciocchi 62 (og), Suvorov 66, Andronic 87)*

San Marino (0) 0

Moldova: Gaiduchevici; Epureanu, Golovatenco, Racu (Andronic 70), Armas, Cebotaru (Tigirlas■ 78), Zmeu, Suvorov, Cheptine, Alexeev (Bugaev 61), Doros.
San Marino: Simoncini A; Alessandro Della Valle, Bacciocchi (Nicola Albani 89), Benedettini, Cervellini, Gasperoni A (Montagna 76), Berretti (Bugli 67), Vannucci, Coppini, Selva A, Vitaioli M.
Referee: Reinert (Faeroes).

Stockholm, 11 October 2011, 33,066

Sweden (1) 3 *(Kallstrom 15, Larsson S 52 (pen), Toivonen 54)*

Holland (1) 2 *(Huntelaar 23, Kuyt 50)*

Sweden: Isaksson; Mellberg, Olsson, Majstorovic, Lustig, Kallstrom, Svensson, Elm R, Larsson S, Elmander, Toivonen (Wernbloom 75).
Holland: Vorm; Mathijsen, Pieters, Van der Wiel, Bruma, Van Bommel, Van der Vaart, Strootman (De Jong 81), Kuyt (Elia 73), Van Persie, Huntelaar.
Referee: Cuneyt (Turkey).

Group E Table	*P*	*W*	*D*	*L*	*F*	*A*	*Pts*
Holland	10	9	0	1	37	8	27
Sweden	10	8	0	2	31	11	24
Hungary	10	6	1	3	22	14	19
Finland	10	3	1	6	16	16	10
Moldova	10	3	0	7	12	16	9
San Marino	10	0	0	10	0	53	0

GROUP F

Tel Aviv, 2 September 2010, 17,365

Israel (1) 3 *(Benayoun 7, 64 (pen), 75)*

Malta (1) 1 *(Pace 38)*

Israel: Awat; Ben Haim T, Bondarv, Ben Dayan, Benayoun, Cohen T, Zahavi (Vermouth 51), Refaelov, Almog Cohen, Kayal (Golasa 86), Sahar (Arbeitman 73).
Malta: Hogg; Caruana J, Mamo, Agius, Sciberras, Bajada, Briffa (Failla 82), Mifsud, Pace, Bogdanovic (Cohen 57), Herrera (Muscat 80).
Referee: Ennjimi (France).

Piraeus, 3 September 2010, 14,794

Greece (0) 1 *(Spiropoulos 72)*

Georgia (1) 1 *(Iashvili 3)*

Greece: Sifakis; Seitaridis (Mitroglou 71), Papadopoulos A, Torosidis, Papastathopoulos, Spiropoulos, Karagounis, Katsouranis, Samaras (Ninis 59), Gekas, Salpingidis.
Georgia: Revishvili; Kobiashvili, Khizanishvili, Kaladze, Amisulashvili, Asatiani, Kvirkvelia, Lobzhanidze, Gogua (Merebashvili 87), Iashvili (Ananidze 54), Dvalishvili (Gelashvili 60).
Referee: Gomez (Spain).

Riga, 3 September 2010, 7600

Latvia (0) 0

Croatia (1) 3 *(Petric 43, Olic 51, Srna 82)*

Latvia: Vanins; Gorkss, Mihadjuks, Ivanovs, Klava, Laizans (Astafjevs 87), Rafalskis, Rubins (Zigajevs 85), Cauna, Verpakovskis, Karlsons (Rudnevs 63).
Croatia: Runje; Simunic, Srna, Corluka, Strinic, Kranjcar, Rakitic, Vukojevic (Pranjic 70), Olic, Eduardo Da Silva (Jelavic 62), Petric (Mandzukic 84).
Referee: Kuipers (Holland).

Zagreb, 7 September 2010, 24,399

Croatia (0) 0

Greece (0) 0

Croatia: Runje; Simunic, Srna, Corluka, Strinic, Kranjcar, Modric, Pranjic, Vukojevic (Rakitic 57), Olic (Eduardo Da Silva 73), Petric (Jelavic 46).
Greece: Sifakis; Papadopoulos A, Torosidis (Seitaridis 90), Vyntra, Papastathopoulos, Tzavelas, Karagounis (Ninis 70), Katsouranis, Tziolis, Samaras, Salpingidis (Gekas 59).
Referee: Larsen (Denmark).

Tbilisi, 7 September 2010, 45,000

Georgia (0) 0

Israel (0) 0

Georgia: Revishvili; Kobiashvili, Khizanishvili, Kaladze, Amisulashvili, Asatiani, Lobzhanidze, Gogua (Aptsiauri 75), Ananidze, Iashvili (Siradze 46), Dvalishvili (Merebashvili 63).
Israel: Awat; Ben Haim T, Bondarv, Keinan, Ben Dayan, Benayoun, Cohen T (Zahavi 61), Refaelov (Vermouth 75), Almog Cohen, Kayal, Sahar (Arbeitman 53).
Referee: Kever (Switzerland).

Ta'Qali, 7 September 2010, 6255

Malta (0) 0

Latvia (1) 2 *(Gorkss 42, Verpakovskis 85)*

Malta: Hogg; Caruana J, Mamo (Fenech R 77), Muscat (Bogdanovic 59), Agius, Sciberras (Failla 77), Bajada, Briffa, Mifsud, Cohen, Pace.
Latvia: Vanins; Gorkss, Mihadjuks, Ivanovs, Klava, Laizans, Rafalskis (Astafjevs 82), Rubins, Cauna, Verpakovskis (Pereplotkins 90), Rudnevs (Karlsons 70).
Referee: Asumaa (Finland).

Tbilisi, 8 October 2010, 38,000

Georgia (0) 1 *(Siradze 90)*

Malta (0) 0

Georgia: Revishvili; Khizanishvili, Kaladze, Amisulashvili, Asatiani, Salukvadze, Kobiashvili, Gogua, Merebashvili (Siradze 46), Ananidze (Daushvili 73), Dvalishvili (Iashvili 46).
Malta: Haber; Caruana J, Mamo, Agius, Schembri (Fenech P 80), Sciberras (Fenech R 69), Bajada, Briffa, Mifsud, Cohen (Grima 90), Pace.
Referee: Black (Northern Ireland).

Piraeus, 8 October 2010, 13,520

Greece (0) 1 *(Torosidis 58)*

Latvia (0) 0

Greece: Sifakis; Papadopoulos A, Torosidis, Papastathopoulos, Tzvelas, Karagounis (Kafes 89), Katsouranis, Tziolis, Ninis (Fetfatzidis 83), Samaras, Mitroglou (Salpingidis 78).
Latvia: Vanins; Gorkss, Ivanovs, Zirnis, Klava, Laizans (Pereplotkins 82), Rubins (Zigajevs 66), Astafjevs, Cauna, Verpakovskis, Rudnevs (Karlsons 74).
Referee: Damato (Italy).

Tel Aviv, 9 October 2010, 33,421

Israel (0) 1 *(Shechter 81)*

Croatia (2) 2 *(Kranjcar 36 (pen), 41)*

Israel: Awat; Ben Haim T, Ziv, Keinan, Vermouth, Natcho, Cohen T (Colautti 51), Almog Cohen, Barda (Refaelov 56), Shechter, Alroey Cohen (Golasa 69).
Croatia: Runje; Simunic, Corluka, Schildenfeld, Strinic, Kranjcar, Modric, Pranjic, Rakitic (Vukojevic 77), Olic (Bilic 72), Eduardo Da Silva (Mandzukic 57).
Referee: Stark (Germany).

Piraeus, 12 October 2010, 16,935

Greece (1) 2 *(Salpingidis 22, Karagounis 63 (pen))*

Israel (0) 1 *(Spiropoulos 59 (og))*

Greece: Sifakis; Papadopoulos A, Vyntra, Papastathopoulos, Spiropoulos, Karagounis, Katsouranis, Ninis (Fetfatzidis 15), Kafes, Samaras (Mitroglou 81), Salpingidis (Maniatis 87).
Israel: Awat; Bondarv, Keinan, Gershon, Natcho (Vermouth 65), Cohen T (Alroey Cohen 69), Refaelov, Golasa, Almog Cohen, Colautti (Barda 75), Shechter.
Referee: Hansson (Sweden).

Riga, 12 October 2010, 4330

Latvia (0) 1 *(Cauna 90)*

Georgia (0) 1 *(Siradze 74)*

Latvia: Vanins; Gorkss, Ivanovs, Zirnis, Klava, Laizans (Grebis 82), Zigajevs (Pereplotkins 86), Rubins, Astafjevs, Cauna, Rudnevs.
Georgia: Revishvili; Kaladze, Amisulashvili, Asatiani, Kvirkvelia (Gogua 69), Lobzhanidze, Kobiashvili, Daushvili, Ananidze (Salukvadze 79), Iashvili (Koshkadze 87), Siradze.
Referee: De Sousa (Portugal).

Zagreb, 17 November 2010, 10,000

Croatia (2) 3 *(Kranjcar 19, 42, Kalinic 81)*

Malta (0) 0

Croatia: Runje; Srna, Corluka, Schildenfeld, Kranjcar, Modric, Pranjic, Rakitic (Ilicevic 69), Dujmovic, Eduardo Da Silva (Mandzukic 78), Petric (Kalinic 60).
Malta: Hogg; Caruana J, Grima, Hutchinson, Schembri (Fenech R 70), Sciberras (Fenech P 88), Bajada, Briffa, Mifsud, Pace, Bogdanovic (Sammut 83).
Referee: Duarte (Portugal).

Tbilisi, 26 March 2011, 55,000

Georgia (0) 1 *(Kobiashvili 90)*

Croatia (0) 0

Georgia: Revishvili; Khizanishvili, Kaladze, Amisulashvili, Salukvadze, Khubutia, Kobiashvili, Kankava, Daushvili (Siradze 46), Iashvili (Martsvaladze 62), Dvalishvili (Gogua 73).
Croatia: Runje; Srna, Corluka, Strinic, Lovren, Kranjcar (Jelavic 70), Modric, Rakitic (Perisic 61), Dujmovic, Petric (Pranjic 84), Kalinic.
Referee: Tagliavento (Italy).

Tel Aviv, 26 March 2011, 10,801

Israel (1) 2 *(Barda 16, Kayal 81)*

Latvia (0) 1 *(Gorkss 62)*

Israel: Awat; Ben Haim T, Ziv (Sahar 66), Cohen T, Tawatha, Gershon, Natcho, Refaelov (Vermouth 85), Kayal, Barda (Buzaglo 69), Damari.
Latvia: Vanins; Gorkss, Krjauklis, Kacanovs, Ivanovs, Rafalskis (Zigajevs 58), Lazdins, Rubins (Pereplotkins 58), Verpakovskis (Turkovs 73), Rudnevs, Lukjanovs.
Referee: Mazic (Serbia).

Ta'Qali, 26 March 2011, 10,605

Malta (0) 0

Greece (0) 1 *(Torosidis 90)*

Malta: Haber; Caruana J (Pace 46), Mamo, Agius, Hutchinson, Schembri (Cohen 90), Sciberras, Bajada (Fenech R 78), Briffa, Mifsud, Bogdanovic.
Greece: Tzorvas; Papadopoulos A, Torosidis, Papastathopoulos■, Tzavelas, Karagounis, Katsouranis, Ninis (Kone 81), Samaras, Liberopoulos (Mitroglou 70), Salpingidis (Fetfatzidis 61).
Referee: Weiner (Germany).

Tel Aviv, 29 March 2011, 13,716

Israel (0) 1 *(Ben Haim T II 59)*

Georgia (0) 0

Israel: Awat; Ben Haim T, Bondarv, Keinan, Gershon, Natcho (Ben Haim T II 52), Refaelov (Vermouth 63), Almog Cohen, Buzaglo, Kayal, Barda (Benayoun 71).
Georgia: Revishvili; Khizanishvili, Kaladze, Amisulashvili, Salukvadze, Khubutia, Kobiashvili, Kankava, Daushvili (Kvirkvelia 46), Iashvili (Dvalishvili 63), Martsvaladze (Siradze 73).
Referee: Fautrel (France).

Split, 3 June 2011, 28,000

Croatia (0) 2 *(Mandzukic 76, Kalinic 78)*

Georgia (1) 1 *(Kankava 16)*

Croatia: Runje; Simunic, Srna, Corluka, Modric, Pranjic, Perisic (Dujmovic 70), Vukojevic (Klasnic 70), Eduardo Da Silva, Jelavic (Kalinic 46), Mandzukic.
Georgia: Loria; Khizanishvili, Kaladze, Salukvadze, Kvirkvelia, Grigalava, Khubutia, Kashia (Ananidze 80), Kankava, Iashvili (Daushvili 62), Siradze (Dvalishvili 56).
Referee: Johannesson (Sweden).

Piraeus, 4 June 2011, 14,746

Greece (2) 3 *(Fetfatzidis 8, 64, Papadopoulos K 26)*

Malta (0) 1 *(Mifsud 54)*

Greece: Konstantopoulos; Torosidis, Papadopoulos K, Moras, Spiropoulos, Karagounis (Kafes 70), Katsouranis, Tziolis, Ninis (Christodoulopoulos 79), Fetfatzidis, Salpingidis (Mitroglou 90).
Malta: Hogg; Caruana J, Agius, Hutchinson (Fenech P 87), Schembri, Sciberras, Bajada (Failla 80), Briffa, Fenech R, Mifsud, Bogdanovic (Cohen 59).
Referee: Gil (Poland).

Riga, 4 June 2011, 6147

Latvia (0) 1 *(Cauna 62 (pen))*

Israel (2) 2 *(Benayoun 20, Ben Haim T 43 (pen))*

Latvia: Vanins; Gorkss, Krjauklis, Ivanovs, Klava, Rafalskis (Zigajevs 28), Lazdins, Cauna, Visnakovs (Rugins 71), Rudnevs, Pereplotkins (Gauracs 60).
Israel: Awat; Ben Haim T, Keinan, Shpungin, Gershon, Benayoun, Zahavi (Golasa 89), Refaelov (Ben Haim T II 79), Almog Cohen, Buzaglo (Natcho 69), Hemed.
Referee: Kelly (Republic of Ireland).

Tbilisi, 2 September 2011, 15,422

Georgia (0) 0

Latvia (0) 1 *(Cauna 64)*

Georgia: Loria; Khizanishvili, Kaladze, Amisulashvili (Dvalishvili 71), Kashia, Kobiashvili, Kankava, Targamadze, Ananidze (Grigalashvili 54), Iashvili (Siradze 55), Martsvaladze.
Latvia: Vanins; Gorkss, Krjauklis, Ivanovs, Klava, Lazdins (Laizans 88), Cauna, Visnakovs, Fertovs, Verpakovskis (Gauracs 77), Lukjanovs.
Referee: Trattou (Cyprus).

Tel Aviv, 2 September 2011, 13,100

Israel (0) 0

Greece (0) 1 *(Ninis 60)*

Israel: Awat; Ben Haim T, Ben Harush, Gershon, Spungin, Benayoun, Zahavi (Hemed 53), Refaelov, Almog Cohen (Natcho 61), Kayal, Shechter (Damari 55).
Greece: Sifakis; Papadopoulos A, Torosidis, Papadopoulos K, Zaradoukas, Karagounis, Katsouranis, Ninis (Fetfatzidis 77), Kafes (Makos 42), Samaras, Salpingidis (Maniatis 84).
Referee: Thomson (Scotland).

Ta'Qali, 2 September 2011, 6150

Malta (1) 1 *(Mifsud 38)*

Croatia (2) 3 *(Vukojevic 11, Badelj 32, Lovren 68)*

Malta: Hogg; Muscat, Agius, Hutchinson, Failla, Schembri, Sciberras, Briffa (Pace 74), Fenech R (Mamo 88), Mifsud (Woods 82), Cohen.
Croatia: Pletikosa; Srna, Corluka, Strinic, Lovren, Perisic (Dujmovic 67), Vukojevic, Badelj (Eduardo Da Silva 82), Vrsaljko, Klasnic (Kalinic 46), Mandzukic.
Referee: Chapron (France).

Zagreb, 6 September 2011, 13,688

Croatia (0) 3 *(Modric 47, Eduardo Da Silva 55, 57)*

Israel (1) 1 *(Hemed 44)*

Croatia: Pletikosa; Simunic, Srna, Corluka (Eduardo Da Silva 46), Strinic, Lovren, Kranjcar, Modric, Vukojevic (Dujmovic 46), Jelavic (Kalinic 87), Mandzukic.
Israel: Awat (Haimov 46); Ben Haim T■, Ben Harush, Gershon, Hutba, Benayoun, Cohen T (Golasa 57), Zahavi (Shechter 68), Kayal, Tawatha, Hemed.
Referee: Carballo (Spain).

Riga, 6 September 2011, 5415

Latvia (1) 1 *(Cauna 19)*

Greece (0) 1 *(Papadopoulos K 84)*

Latvia: Vanins; Krjauklis, Mihadjuks, Ivanovs, Klava, Cauna, Visnakovs (Zigajevs 83), Laizans, Fertovs, Verpakovskis (Rudnevs 68), Lukjanovs.
Greece: Sifakis; Papadopoulos K, Vyntra (Maniatis 71), Papastathopoulos, Zaradoukas, Karagounis, Makos (Georgiadis 81), Fetfatzidis (Tziolis 46), Samaras, Liberopoulos, Salpingidis.
Referee: Todorov (Bulgaria).

Ta'Qali, 6 September 2011, 5000

Malta (1) 1 *(Mifsud 25)*

Georgia (1) 1 *(Kankava 15)*

Malta: Hogg; Caruana J, Agius, Hutchinson, Failla, Schembri (Pace 76), Sciberras, Briffa, Fenech R (Bogdanovic 59), Mifsud, Cohen (Woods 90).
Georgia: Revishvili; Khizanishvili, Kaladze, Grigalava, Kashia, Kobiashvili, Kankava, Targamadze, Ananidze (Kobakhidze 77), Iashvili (Dvalishvili 61), Martsvaladze (Grigalashvili 66).
Referee: Van Boekel (Holland).

Piraeus, 7 October 2011, 27,200

Greece (0) 2 *(Samaras 71, Gekas 79)*

Croatia (0) 0

Greece: Tzorvas; Papadopoulos A, Torosidis (Vyntra 43), Papastathopoulos, Zaradoukas, Karagounis (Makos 87), Katsouranis, Tziolis (Fotakis 62), Samaras, Gekas, Salpingidis.
Croatia: Pletikosa; Simunic, Corluka (Vida 75), Strinic, Lovren, Kranjcar, Modric, Vukojevic, Eduardo Da Silva (Perisic 52), Jelavic (Kalinic 61), Mandzukic.
Referee: Webb (England).

Riga, 7 October 2011, 4315

Latvia (1) 2 *(Visnakovs 33, Rudnevs 83)*

Malta (0) 0

Latvia: Vanins; Gorkss, Mihadjuks, Ivanovs, Klava, Cauna, Visnakovs, Laizans (Rugins 76), Verpakovskis (Rubins 90), Rudnevs (Gauracs 88), Lukjanovs.
Malta: Hogg; Agius, Borg, Hutchinson, Failla, Schembri, Pace (Woods 70), Sciberras (Fenech P 83), Briffa, Fenech R (Mamo 82), Cohen.
Referee: Trutz (Slovakia).

Rijeka, 11 October 2011, 8370

Croatia (0) 2 *(Eduardo Da Silva 66, Mandzukic 72)*

Latvia (0) 0

Croatia: Pletikosa; Simunic, Srna, Corluka (Vida 33), Strinic, Lovren, Kranjcar (Perisic 60), Modric, Rakitic, Eduardo Da Silva, Mandzukic (Jelavic 84).
Latvia: Vanins; Gorkss, Mihadjuks, Ivanovs, Klava, Cauna, Visnakovs (Rubins 88), Laizans, Rudnevs, Pereplotkins (Gauracs 72), Rugins (Tarasovs 14).
Referee: Gautier (France).

Tbilisi, 11 October 2011, 7824

Georgia (1) 1 *(Targamadze 18)*

Greece (0) 2 *(Fotakis 79, Charisteas 85)*

Georgia: Revishvili; Khizanishvili, Kaladze, Amisulashvili, Kashia, Kobiashvili, Kankava (Lobzhanidze 42), Targamadze, Grigalashvili (Iashvili 51), Mchedlidze (Guruli 65), Martsvaladze.
Greece: Tzorvas; Papadopoulos K, Vyntra, Papastathopoulos, Spiropoulos, Karagounis, Katsouranis, Tziolis (Fotakis 56), Charisteas, Gekas (Kone 90), Salpingidis (Athanasiadis 68).
Referee: Orsato (Italy).

Ta'Qali, 11 October 2011, 2614

Malta (0) 0

Israel (1) 2 *(Refaelov 10, Gershon 90)*

Malta: Hogg; Caruana J (Borg 82), Mamo, Agius, Hutchinson, Sciberras, Fenech P (Herrera 64), Briffa, Fenech R, Mifsud, Woods (Caruana C 81).
Israel: Awat; Bondarv (Vermouth 57), Gershon, Natcho, Refaelov (Almog Cohen 50), Golasa, Buzaglo, Tawatha, Sahar (Ben Haim T II 78), Hemed, Biton.
Referee: Paixao (Portugal).

Group F Table	*P*	*W*	*D*	*L*	*F*	*A*	*Pts*
Greece	10	7	3	0	14	5	24
Croatia	10	7	1	2	18	7	22
Israel	10	5	1	4	13	11	16
Latvia	10	3	2	5	9	12	11
Georgia	10	2	4	4	7	9	10
Malta	10	0	1	9	4	21	1

GROUP G

Wembley, 3 September 2010, 73,426

England (1) 4 *(Defoe 3, 61, 86, Johnson A 83)*

Bulgaria (0) 0

England: Hart; Johnson G, Cole, Barry, Dawson (Cahill 56), Jagielka, Walcott (Johnson A 74), Gerrard, Defoe (Young A 87), Rooney, Milner.
Bulgaria: Mihaylov; Milanov, Stoyanov, Ivanov, Manolev (Minev 66), Petrov S, Yankov, Petrov M, Angelov, Popov (Peev 79), Bozhinov (Rangelov 63).
Referee: Kassai (Hungary).

Podgorica, 3 September 2010, 7442

Montenegro (1) 1 *(Vucinic 30)*

Wales (0) 0

Montenegro: Bozovic M; Basa, Dzudovic, Jovanovic, Zverotic, Pavicevic, Boskovic B (Bozovic V 74), Pekovic, Vukcevic (Beciraj 87), Vucinic, Dalovic (Novakovic 83).
Wales: Hennessey; Gunter, Bale, Collins J (Morgan C 75), Williams A, Ricketts, Edwards D (Earnshaw 68), Ledley, Morison (Church 78), Bellamy, Vaughan.
Referee: Kakos (Greece).

Sofia, 7 September 2010, 9470

Bulgaria (0) 0

Montenegro (1) 1 *(Zverotic 35)*

Bulgaria: Mihaylov; Milanov (Genchev 47), Stoyanov, Minev, Ivanov, Petrov S, Petrov M, Angelov, Peev (Domovchiyski 67), Popov, Rangelov (Bozhinov 47).
Montenegro: Bozovic M; Basa, Dzudovic, Jovanovic, Zverotic (Novakovic 68), Pavicevic, Boskovic B (Bozovic V 64), Pekovic, Vukcevic, Vucinic, Dalovic (Kascelan 77).
Referee: Bezborodov (Russia).

Basle, 7 September 2010, 37,500

Switzerland (0) 1 *(Shaqiri 71)*

England (1) 3 *(Rooney 10, Johnson A 69, Bent 88)*

Switzerland: Benaglio; Grichting, Lichtsteiner■, Ziegler, Von Bergen, Degen (Streller 64), Schwegler (Costanzo 83), Inler, Margairaz (Shaqiri 46), Frei, Derdiyok.
England: Hart; Johnson G, Cole, Barry, Lescott, Jagielka, Walcott (Johnson A 13), Gerrard, Defoe (Bent 70), Rooney (Wright-Phillips 79), Milner.
Referee: Rizzoli (Italy).

Podgorica, 8 October 2010, 10,750

Montenegro (0) 1 *(Vucinic 67)*

Switzerland (0) 0

Montenegro: Bozovic M; Basa, Dzudovic, Jovanovic, Savic, Boskovic B (Kascelan 46), Vukcevic (Beciraj 86), Zverotic, Novakovic, Vucinic, Balovic (Batak 90).
Switzerland: Wolfli; Grichting, Ziegler, Von Bergen, Schwegler, Inler, Sutter, Stocker (Yakin 76), Shaqiri (Barnetta 67), Frei, Streller (Derdiyok 67).
Referee: Gonzalez (Spain).

Cardiff, 8 October 2010, 14,061

Wales (0) 0

Bulgaria (0) 1 *(Popov 48)*

Wales: Hennessey; Gunter■, Bale, Collins D, Williams A, Collins J, Ricketts, Edwards D (Church 69), Morison (Robson-Kanu 82), Ledley (King 59), Vaughan.
Bulgaria: Mihaylov; Iliev (Vidanov 37), Ivanov, Bodurov, Zanev, Petrov S, Petrov M, Peev (Rangelov 72), Georgiev, Popov, Makriev (Yankov 87).
Referee: Eriksson (Sweden).

Wembley, 12 October 2010, 73,451

England (0) 0

Montenegro (0) 0

England: Hart; Johnson G, Cole, Barry, Ferdinand, Lescott, Young A (Wright-Phillips 74), Gerrard, Crouch (Davies 70), Rooney, Johnson A.
Montenegro: Bozovic M; Basa, Dzudovic, Jovanovic, Savic, Boskovic B (Beciraj 82), Pekovic, Vukcevic, Zverotic, Novakovic (Kascelan 62), Dalovic (Delibasic 77).
Referee: Grafe (Germany).

Basle, 12 October 2010, 26,000

Switzerland (2) 4 *(Stocker 9, 89, Streller 22, Inler 82 (pen))*

Wales (1) 1 *(Bale 13)*

Switzerland: Benaglio (Wolfli 8); Grichting, Lichtsteiner, Ziegler, Von Bergen, Barnetta, Schwegler (Gelson 90), Inler, Stocker, Frei (Derdiyok 79), Streller.
Wales: Hennessey; Blake (Ribeiro 54), Bale, Collins J, Williams A, Collins D, Edwards D (Morison 77), King, Church, Crofts, Vaughan (MacDonald 89).
Referee: Hamer (Luxembourg).

Sofia, 26 March 2011, 9600

Bulgaria (0) 0

Switzerland (0) 0

Bulgaria: Mihaylov; Ivanov, Manolev, Bandalovski, Zanev, Stoyanov, Petrov S, Georgiev, Popov (Angelov 85), Makriev (Genkov 52), Delev (Lazarov 81).
Switzerland: Wolfli; Grichting, Lichtsteiner, Ziegler, Von Bergen, Behrami (Gelson 17), Dzemaili, Inler, Stocker (Derdiyok 67), Frei, Streller (Gavranovic 77).
Referee: Collum (Scotland).

Cardiff, 26 March 2011, 68,959

Wales (0) 0

England (2) 2 *(Lampard 7 (pen), Bent 15)*

Wales: Hennessey; Gunter, Collins D, King (Vaughan 65), Collins J, Williams A, Crofts, Ramsey, Morison (Evans C 65), Bellamy, Ledley.
England: Hart; Johnson G, Cole, Parker (Jagielka 88), Terry, Dawson, Young A, Lampard, Bent, Rooney (Milner 70), Wilshere (Downing 82).
Referee: Benquerenca (Portugal).

Wembley, 4 June 2011, 84,459

England (1) 2 *(Lampard 37 (pen), Young A 51)*

Switzerland (2) 2 *(Barnetta 32, 35)*

England: Hart; Johnson G, Cole (Baines 30), Parker, Terry, Ferdinand, Walcott (Downing 77), Wilshere, Bent, Lampard (Young A 46), Milner.
Switzerland: Benaglio; Djourou, Senderos, Lichtsteiner, Ziegler, Barnetta (Emeghara 90), Behrami (Dzemaili 58), Inler, Shaqiri, Xhaka, Derdiyok (Mehmedi 74).
Referee: Skomina (Slovenia).

Podgorica, 4 June 2011, 11,500

Montenegro (0) 1 *(Dalovic 53)*

Bulgaria (0) 1 *(Popov 66)*

Montenegro: Bozovic M (Fatic 76); Basa, Zverotic (Jovetic 72), Pavicevic (Kascelan 82), Pejovic, Savic, Pekovic, Drincic, Bozovic V, Vucinic, Dalovic.
Bulgaria: Mihaylov; Ivanov, Manolev, Bodurov, Bandalovski, Zanev, Petrov S (Yankov 46), Petrov M (Delev 88), Yanev (Genkov 84), Marquinhos, Popov.
Referee: Yefet (Israel).

Sofia, 2 September 2011, 27,230

Bulgaria (0) 0

England (3) 3 *(Cahill 13, Rooney 21, 45)*

Bulgaria: Mihaylov; Milanov, Ivanov, Bodurov, Bandalovski (Sarmov 46), Zanev, Petrov S, Petrov M, Georgiev, Popov (Marquinhos 81), Genkov (Bozinhov 61).
England: Hart; Smalling, Cole, Barry (Lampard 80), Terry, Cahill, Young A (Milner 61), Parker, Walcott (Johnson A 83), Rooney, Downing.
Referee: De Bleeckere (Belgium).

Cardiff, 2 September 2011, 8194

Wales (1) 2 *(Morison 29, Ramsey 50)*

Montenegro (0) 1 *(Jovetic 71)*

Wales: Hennessey; Gunter, Bale (Earnshaw 90), Blake, Taylor N, Williams A, Ledley, Ramsey (Crofts 64), Morison (Robson-Kanu 83), Bellamy, Vaughan.
Montenegro: Bozovic M; Batak, Zverotic, Balic (Jovanovic 83), Savic, Pekovic, Drincic, Vukcevic, Vucinic (Delibasic 79), Jovetic, Dalovic (Damjanovic 57).
Referee: Banti (Italy).

Wembley, 6 September 2011, 77,128

England (1) 1 *(Young A 35)*

Wales (0) 0

England: Hart; Smalling, Cole, Lampard (Parker 73), Terry, Cahill, Young A, Barry, Milner, Rooney (Carroll 89), Downing (Johnson A 79).
Wales: Hennessey; Gunter, Bale, Blake, Taylor N, Williams A, Ledley, Crofts, Morison (Earnshaw 68), Collison (King 85), Ramsey.
Referee: Schorgenhofer (Austria).

Basle, 6 September 2011, 16,880

Switzerland (1) 3 *(Shaqiri 45, 62, 90)*

Bulgaria (1) 1 *(Ivanov 9)*

Switzerland: Benaglio; Djourou, Senderos, Lichtsteiner, Ziegler, Dzemaili, Inler, Shaqiri (Ben Khalifa 90), Xhaka (Gelson 88), Derdiyok, Mehmedi (Emeghara 83).
Bulgaria: Mihaylov; Milanov■, Iliev, Ivanov, Zanev, Petrov S, Petrov M (Gadzhev 60), Georgiev, Sarmov, Popov, Genkov (Bodurov 70).
Referee: Kralovec (Czech Republic).

Podgorica, 7 October 2011, 11,340

Montenegro (1) 2 *(Zverotic 45, Delibasic 90)*

England (2) 2 *(Young A 11, Bent 31)*

Montenegro: Bozovic M; Dzudovic, Zverotic, Savic, Pekovic, Vukcevic, Bozovic V (Delibasic 79), Kascelan (Jovanovic 46), Vucinic, Beciraj (Damjanovic 64), Jovetic.
England: Hart; Jones, Cole, Barry, Terry, Cahill, Walcott (Welbeck 76), Parker, Bent (Lampard 64), Rooney■, Young A (Downing 60).
Referee: Stark (Germany).

Swansea, 7 October 2011, 12,317

Wales (0) 2 *(Ramsey 60 (pen), Bale 71)*

Switzerland (0) 0

Wales: Hennessey; Gunter, Bale, Allen, Blake, Williams A, Crofts (Vaughan 81), Ramsey, Morison (Church 81), Bellamy, Taylor N.
Switzerland: Benaglio; Lichtsteiner, Ziegler■, Von Bergen, Klose, Behrami, Inler, Frei F (Emeghara 71), Shaqiri (Ricardo Rodriguez 62), Xhaka (Mehmedi 81), Derdiyok.
Referee: Kuipers (Holland).

Sofia, 11 October 2011, 1672

Bulgaria (0) 0

Wales (1) 1 *(Bale 45)*

Bulgaria: Mihaylov; Ivanov, Miliev, Manolev (Delev 52), Zanev, Terziev, Petrov S, Gadzhev, Popov (Rangelov 70), Tonev, Domovchiyski (Bozhinov 62).
Wales: Hennessey; Gunter, Bale, Blake (Matthews 41), Taylor N, Williams A, Crofts, Allen, Morison (Church 70), Bellamy, Ramsey.
Referee: Gil (Poland).

Basle, 11 October 2011, 19,997

Switzerland (0) 2 *(Derdiyok 51, Lichtsteiner 65)*

Montenegro (0) 0

Switzerland: Benaglio; Djourou, Lichtsteiner, Von Bergen, Ricardo Rodriguez, Behrami, Inler, Shaqiri (Degen 77), Xhaka (Gelson 83), Derdiyok (Emeghara 69), Mehmedi.
Montenegro: Bozovic M; Batak, Zverotic, Pejovic (Bozovic V 46), Bozovic D, Savic, Drincic (Grbic 72), Cetkovic, Damjanovic, Beciraj, Dalovic (Delibasic 67).
Referee: Benquerenca (Portugal).

Group G Table	P	W	D	L	F	A	Pts
England	8	5	3	0	17	5	18
Montenegro	8	3	3	2	7	7	12
Switzerland	8	3	2	3	12	10	11
Wales	8	3	0	5	6	10	9
Bulgaria	8	1	2	5	3	13	5

GROUP H

Reykjavik, 3 September 2010, 6137

Iceland (1) 1 *(Helguson 38)*

Norway (0) 2 *(Hangeland 59, Abdellaoue 75)*

Iceland: Gunnleifsson; Steinsson (Adalsteinsson 76), Ottesen, Sigurdsson K, Sigurdsson I, Jonsson, Gunnarsson A, Sigurdsson G, Gudmundsson J (Gislason 87), Helguson, Gunnarsson V (Bjarnason 76).
Norway: Knudsen; Riise J, Hangeland, Waehler, Hogli, Pedersen M, Hauger, Riise B (Iversen 57), Grindheim, Huseklepp (Ruud 76), Abdellaoue (Solli 88).
Referee: Banti (Italy).

Guimaraes, 3 September 2010, 9100

Portugal (2) 4 *(Hugo Almeida 8, Raul Meireles 29, Danny 50, Manuel Fernandes 60)*

Cyprus (2) 4 *(Aloneftis 3, Konstantinou 11, Okkas 57, Avraam 89)*

Portugal: Eduardo; Ricardo Carvalho, Miguel, Bruno Alves, Fabio Coentrao, Raul Meireles, Quaresma, Nani, Manuel Fernandes (Joao Moutinho 79), Danny (Liedson 61), Hugo Almeida (Yannick Djalo 84).
Cyprus: Georgallides; Charalambous, Ilia (Poursaitidis 66), Merkis, Aloneftis (Okkas 56), Charalambidis (Nikolaou 76), Makridis, Dobrasinovic, Satsias, Avraam, Konstantinou.
Referee: Clattenburg (England).

Copenhagen, 7 September 2010, 18,908

Denmark (0) 1 *(Kahlenberg 90)*

Iceland (0) 0

Denmark: Lindegaard; Agger, Kjaer, Jessen, Jacobsen, Kahlenberg, Poulsen C, Eriksen (Junker 56), Krohn-Dehli (Vingaard 77), Rommedahl, Pedersen (Skoubo 71).
Iceland: Gunnleifsson; Ottesen, Sigurdsson K, Sigurdsson I, Saevarsson, Gislason, Jonsson, Gunnarsson A, Sigurdsson G, Gudmundsson J (Bjarnason 90), Helguson (Sigurdsson R 77).
Referee: McDonald (Scotland).

Oslo, 7 September 2010, 24,535

Norway (1) 1 *(Huseklepp 21)*

Portugal (0) 0

Norway: Knudsen; Hangeland, Ruud, Waehler (Demidov 28), Hogli, Pedersen M, Hauger, Riise B, Grindheim (Jenssen 86), Carew (Abdellaoue 38), Huseklepp.
Portugal: Eduardo; Ricardo Carvalho, Bruno Alves, Silvio, Tiago (Danny 72), Raul Meireles, Quaresma (Liedson 84), Nani, Manuel Fernandes, Miguel Veloso, Hugo Almeida.
Referee: Duhamel (France).

Larnaca, 8 October 2010, 7648

Cyprus (0) 1 *(Okkas 58)*

Norway (2) 2 *(Riise J 2, Carew 42)*

Cyprus: Georgallides; Charalambous (Efrem 86), Poursaitidis, Merkis (Christofi 81), Aloneftis, Charalambidis (Satsias 46), Makridis, Dobrasinovic, Avraam, Okkas, Konstantinou.
Norway: Knudsen; Riise J, Hangeland, Waehler, Hogli, Pedersen, Hauger, Riise B (Moen 74), Grindheim, Carew (Abdellaoue 83), Huseklepp (Ruud 80).
Referee: Gumienny (Belgium).

Oporto, 8 October 2010, 27,117

Portugal (2) 3 *(Nani 29, 31, Cristiano Ronaldo 85)*

Denmark (0) 1 *(Ricardo Carvalho 79 (og))*

Portugal: Eduardo; Ricardo Carvalho, Pepe, Fabio Coentrao, Joao Pereira, Raul Meireles, Nani (Silvestre Varela 86), Joao Moutinho, Carlos Martins (Tiago 75), Cristiano Ronaldo, Hugo Almeida (Helder Postiga 69).
Denmark: Sorensen (Lindegaard 32), Kroldrup, Kvist (Lovenkrands 72), Kjaer, Jacobsen, Jensen (Eriksen 58), Poulsen C, Silberbauer, Vingaard, Rommedahl, Pedersen.
Referee: Braamhaar (Holland).

Copenhagen, 12 October 2010, 15,544

Denmark (0) 2 *(Rasmussen 48, Lorentzen 81)*

Cyprus (0) 0

Denmark: Lindegaard; Agger (Kroldrup 39), Kjaer, Jessen, Jacobsen, Poulsen C, Junker (Rasmussen 46), Krohn-Dehli (Eriksen 65), Rommedahl, Lorentzen, Pedersen.
Cyprus: Georgallides; Charalambous (Christou 28), Merkis, Satsias, Poursaitidis, Makrides, Dobrasinovic, Okkas, Konstantinou, Avraam (Garpozis 64), Aloneftis (Charalambides 54).
Referee: Fernandez (Spain).

Reykjavik, 12 October 2010, 9767

Iceland (1) 1 *(Helguson 17)*

Portugal (2) 3 *(Cristiano Ronaldo 3, Raul Meireles 27, Helder Postiga 72)*

Iceland: Gunnleifsson; Steinsson, Sigurdsson R, Sigurdsson K, Sigurdsson I (Adalsteinsson 86), Saevarsson (Gunnarsson V 85), Skulason, Danielsson, Bjarnason (Thorvaldsson 68), Helguson, Gudjohnsen.
Portugal: Eduardo; Ricardo Carvalho, Pepe, Fabio Coentrao, Joao Pereira, Raul Meireles, Nani (Danny 88), Joao Moutinho, Carlos Martins (Tiago 77), Cristiano Ronaldo, Hugo Almeida (Helder Postiga 66).
Referee: Einwaller (Austria).

Strovolos, 26 March 2011, 2088

Cyprus (0) 0

Iceland (0) 0

Cyprus: Georgallides; Poursaitidis (Ilia 61), Merkis, Sielis (Demetriou 46), Aloneftis, Charalambidis, Makridis, Dobrasinovic, Michael, Avraam, Christofi (Alexandrou 73).
Iceland: Magnusson; Hreidarsson, Sigurdsson K, Sigurdsson I, Saevarsson, Gislason (Finnbogason 63), Jonsson, Gunnarsson A, Gudmundsson J (Smarason 59), Sigurdsson G (Bjarnason 90), Helguson.
Referee: Ceferin (Slovenia).

Oslo, 26 March 2011, 24,828

Norway (0) 1 *(Huseklepp 81)*

Denmark (1) 1 *(Rommedahl 28)*

Norway: Jarstein; Riise J, Hangeland, Ruud (Braaten 78), Waehler, Pedersen, Hauger, Riise B, Grindheim, Huseklepp (Iversen 89), Abdellaoue.
Denmark: Sorensen; Agger, Kvist, Jacobsen, Jorgensen, Poulsen C (Poulsen J 70), Silberbauer, Eriksen, Krohn-Dehli (Enevoldsen 82), Rommedahl (Wass 90), Bendtner.
Referee: Rocchi (Italy).

Reykjavik, 4 June 2011, 7629

Iceland (0) 0

Denmark (0) 2 *(Schone 60, Eriksen 75)*

Iceland: Magnusson; Hreidarsson, Sigurdsson K, Saevarsson, Eiriksson, Skulason (Finnbogason 67), Gunnarsson A, Sigurdsson G, Helguson (Gudmundsson J 77), Gudjohnsen, Sigthorsson.
Denmark: Sorensen; Svensson, Kvist (Poulsen C 62), Kjaer, Jacobsen, Zimling, Poulsen S, Eriksen, Krohn-Dehli (Schone 46), Rommedahl, Bendtner.
Referee: Firat (Turkey).

Lisbon, 4 June 2011, 47,829

Portugal (0) 1 *(Helder Postiga 53)*

Norway (0) 0

Portugal: Eduardo; Pepe, Bruno Alves, Fabio Coentrao, Joao Pereira (Silvio 73), Raul Meireles, Nani (Silvestre Varela 86), Joao Moutinho, Carlos Martins (Ruben 69), Cristiano Ronaldo, Helder Postiga.
Norway: Jarstein; Riise J, Hangeland, Hogli, Demidov, Pedersen, Hauger, Riise B, Grindheim (Henriksen 83), Carew (Abdellaoue 60), Huseklepp (Braaten 75).
Referee: Cuneyt (Turkey).

Strovolos, 2 September 2011, 15,444

Cyprus (0) 0

Portugal (1) 4 *(Cristiano Ronaldo 35 (pen), 82, Hugo Almeida 84, Danny 90)*

Cyprus: Georgallides; Poursaitidis, Christou, Merkis, Charalambides (Alexandrou 63), Makridis (Nikolaou 38), Dobrasinovic■, Demetriou, Avraam, Okkas, Christofi (Efrem 80).
Portugal: Rui Patricio; Pepe, Bruno Alves, Fabio Coentrao, Joao Pereira, Raul Meireles, Nani (Danny 85), Joao Moutinho, Ruben (Miguel Veloso 63), Cristiano Ronaldo, Helder Postiga (Hugo Almeida 76).
Referee: Rocchi (Italy).

Oslo, 2 September 2011, 22,381

Norway (0) 1 *(Abdellaoue 88 (pen))*

Iceland (0) 0

Norway: Jarstein; Hangeland, Ruud, Waehler, Hogli, Hauger, Tettey, Grindheim (Carew 80), Huseklepp (Brenne 87), Parr (Braaten 68), Abdellaoue.
Iceland: Magnusson; Ottesen, Sigurdsson I, Valgardsson, Saevarsson, Jonsson, Danielsson (Bjarnason 90), Gislason, Gudjohnsen, Sigthorsson (Gunnarsson V 77), Gudmundsson J (Thorsteinsson 80).
Referee: Hategan (Romania).

Copenhagen, 6 September 2011, 37,167

Denmark (2) 2 *(Bendtner 24, 44)*

Norway (0) 0

Denmark: Sorensen; Agger, Kvist, Kjaer, Jacobsen, Boilesen, Krohn-Dehli (Schone 70), Zimling, Eriksen, Rommedahl (Silberbauer 65), Bendtner (Pedersen 90).
Norway: Jarstein; Riise J (Braaten 61), Hangeland, Ruud, Waehler (Demidov 46), Nordtveit, Hogli, Tettey, Grindheim, Huseklepp (Carew 69), Abdellaoue.
Referee: Lannoy (France).

Reykjavik, 6 September 2011, 5267

Iceland (1) 1 *(Sigthorsson 5)*

Cyprus (0) 0

Iceland: Halldorsson; Sigurdsson K, Valgardsson, Jonasson, Saevarsson, Bjarnason (Sigurdarson 84), Jonsson E, Danielsson, Gudjohnsen, Sigthorsson (Finnbogason 84), Gudmundsson J (Vihjalmsson 88).
Cyprus: Georgallides; Poursaitidis, Christou, Merkis, Charalambides (Pavlou 83), Satsias, Demetriou, Avraam, Okkas (Makridis 46), Alexandrou (Efrem 61), Christofi.
Referee: Jovanetic (Serbia).

Strovolos, 7 October 2011, 2408

Cyprus (1) 1 *(Avraam 45)*

Denmark (4) 4 *(Jacobsen 7, Rommedahl 11, 22, Krohn-Dehli 20)*

Cyprus: Georgallides; Poursaitidis (Solomou 46), Pelagias, Merkis, Charalambides, Dobrasinovic, Efrem, Demetriou (Satsias 71), Avraam, Konstantinou (Christofi 62), Alexandrou.
Denmark: Sorensen; Kvist, Kjaer, Poulsen S, Bjelland, Jacobsen (Silberbauer 82), Krohn-Dehli, Zimling (Jorgensen 68), Eriksen, Rommedahl (Poulsen C 71), Bendtner.
Referee: Strahonja (Croatia).

Oporto, 7 October 2011, 35,715

Portugal (3) 5 *(Nani 13, 21, Helder Postiga 45, Joao Moutinho 81, Eliseu 87)*

Iceland (0) 3 *(Jonasson 48, 68, Sigurdsson G 90 (pen))*

Portugal: Rui Patricio; Bruno Alves, Joao Pereira, Rolando, Raul Meireles (Miguel Veloso 59), Nani, Joao Moutinho, Carlos Martins (Ruben 72), Eliseu, Cristiano Ronaldo, Helder Postiga (Nuno Gomes 88).
Iceland: Magnusson; Ottesen, Sigurdsson K, Valgardsson, Jonasson (Vihjalmsson 89), Saevarsson, Bjarnason, Gunnarsson A, Sigurdsson G, Gislason (Smarason 89), Gudmundsson J (Finnbogason 81).
Referee: Nijhuis (Holland).

Copenhagen, 11 October 2011, 37,012

Denmark (1) 2 *(Krohn-Dehli 13, Bendtner 63)*

Portugal (0) 1 *(Cristiano Ronaldo 90)*

Denmark: Sorensen; Kvist, Kjaer, Bjelland, Jacobsen, Krohn-Dehli, Silberbauer (Poulsen S 76), Zimling (Poulsen C 70), Eriksen, Rommedahl (Poulsen J 87), Bendtner.
Portugal: Rui Patricio; Bruno Alves, Joao Pereira, Rolando, Raul Meireles, Nani, Joao Moutinho, Carlos Martins (Miguel Veloso 65), Eliseu (Ricardo Quaresma 65), Cristiano Ronaldo, Helder Postiga (Nuno Gomes 78).
Referee: Rizzoli (Italy).

Oslo, 11 October 2011, 13,490

Norway (2) 3 *(Pedersen 26, Carew 34, Hogli 65)*

Cyprus (1) 1 *(Okkas 42)*

Norway: Jarstein; Riise J, Ruud (Brenne 62), Waehler, Hogli, Demidov, Pedersen (Parr 46), Tettey (Jenssen 82), Grindheim, Carew, Huseklepp.
Cyprus: Kissas; Charalambous, Pelagias (Parpas 6), Merkis, Charalambides (Christofi 62), Dobrasinovic, Satsias, Demetriou, Solomou, Avraam, Okkas (Stavrou 81).
Referee: Collum (Scotland).

Group H Table	*P*	*W*	*D*	*L*	*F*	*A*	*Pts*
Denmark	8	6	1	1	15	6	19
Portugal	8	5	1	2	21	12	16
Norway	8	5	1	2	10	7	16
Iceland	8	1	1	6	6	14	4
Cyprus	8	0	2	6	7	20	2

GROUP I

Vaduz, 3 September 2010, 6100

Liechtenstein (0) 0

Spain (2) 4 *(Torres 18, 54, David Villa 26, David Silva 62)*

Liechtenstein: Jehle; Martin Stocklasa, Oehri (Vogt 46), Michael Stocklasa, Eberle (Rechsteiner 46), Burgmeier, Polverino, Wieser (Buchel R 82), Frick M, Erne, Hasler D.
Spain: Casillas; Marchena, Sergio Ramos, Pique, Capdevila, Iniesta (Pedro 65), Xabi Alonso, Xavi (Fabregas 46), Sergio Busquets, Torres (David Silva 58), David Villa.
Referee: Bulent (Turkey).

Kaunas, 3 September 2010, 5248

Lithuania (0) 0

Scotland (0) 0

Lithuania: Karcemarskas; Stankevicius, Skerla, Kijanskas, Mikoliunas (Poskus 71), Semberas, Cesnauskis E, Panka, Sernas (Luksa 80), Radavicius, Danilevicius (Ivaskevicius 90).
Scotland: McGregor; Hutton, Whittaker (Berra 90), McCulloch, Weir, McManus, Robson (McFadden 69), Brown (Morrison 76), Fletcher D, Miller, Naismith.
Referee: Cuneyt (Turkey).

Olomouc, 7 September 2010, 12,038

Czech Republic (0) 0

Lithuania (1) 1 *(Sernas 26)*

Czech Republic: Cech; Hubschman, Hubnik, Pospech, Kadlec M, Plasil, Polak (Stajner 75), Rosicky, Pudil (Bednar 83), Baros, Fenin (Necid 63).
Lithuania: Karcemarskas; Stankevicius, Skerla, Kijanskas, Mikoliunas (Luksa 76), Semberas, Cesnauskis E, Panka, Sernas (Poskus 65), Radavicius, Danilevicius (Ivaskevicius 90).
Referee: Yefet (Israel).

Hampden Park, 7 September 2010, 37,050

Scotland (0) 2 *(Miller 62, McManus 90)*

Liechtenstein (0) 1 *(Frick M 46)*

Scotland: McGregor; Hutton, Wallace L (Robson 54), McCulloch, Weir, McManus, Fletcher D, Brown, Boyd (Naismith 66), Miller, McFadden (Morrison 46).
Liechtenstein: Jehle; Martin Stocklasa, Oehri, Michael Stocklasa, Rechsteiner, Burgmeier, Polverino, Wieser (Buchel R 71), Frick M (D'Elia 79), Erne, Hasler D (Hasler N 90).
Referee: Shvetsov (Ukraine).

Prague, 8 October 2010, 14,922

Czech Republic (0) 1 *(Hubnik 69)*

Scotland (0) 0

Czech Republic: Cech; Hubschman, Hubnik, Suchy, Pospech, Kadlec M, Plasil (Rajnoch 90), Polak, Rosicky, Necid (Holek 84), Magera (Bednar 59).
Scotland: McGregor; Hutton, Whittaker, Morrison (Robson 84), Caldwell G (Iwelumo 76), Weir, McManus, Fletcher D, Mackie (Miller 78), Naismith, Dorrans.
Referee: Bebek (Croatia).

Salamanca, 8 October 2010, 16,800

Spain (0) 3 *(Llorente 47, 56, David Silva 79)*

Lithuania (0) 1 *(Sernas 54)*

Spain: Casillas; Puyol, Sergio Ramos (Arbeloa 83), Pique, Capdevila, Iniesta, David Silva, Cazorla, Sergio Busquets, David Villa (Pablo Hernandez 76), Llorente (Aduriz 77).
Lithuania: Karcemarskas; Stankevicius, Skerla, Kijanskas, Mikoliunas (Cesnauskis D 59), Semberas, Cesnauskis E (Poskus 84), Panka, Sernas, Radavicius, Danilevicius (Ivaskevicius 82).
Referee: Rocchi (Italy).

Vaduz, 12 October 2010, 2555

Liechtenstein (0) 0

Czech Republic (2) 2 *(Necid 12, Kadlec V 28)*

Liechtenstein: Jehle; Martin Stocklasa, Oehri, Michael Stocklasa, Rechsteiner, Burgmeier, Polverino, Wieser (Buchel R 84), Frick M, Beck T (Hasler N 67), Erne (Hanselmann 78).
Czech Republic: Cech; Hubschman, Hubnik, Suchy, Pospech, Kadlec M, Plasil, Polak (Stajner 59), Rosicky, Necid (Petrzela 89), Kadlec V (Bednar 64).
Referee: Sukhina (Russia).

Glasgow, 12 October 2010, 51,322

Scotland (0) 2 *(Naismith 58, Pique 66 (og))*

Spain (1) 3 *(David Villa 44 (pen), Iniesta 56, Llorente 79)*

Scotland: McGregor; Whittaker■, Bardsley, McCulloch (Adam 46), Weir, McManus, Morrison (Maloney 88), Fletcher D, Naismith, Miller, Dorrans (Mackie 80).
Spain: Casillas; Puyol, Sergio Ramos, Pique, Capdevila, Iniesta, Xabi Alonso, David Silva (Llorente 76), Cazorla (Pablo Hernandez 70), Sergio Busquets (Marchena 90), David Villa.
Referee: Busacca (Switzerland).

Grenada, 25 March 2011, 16,301

Spain (0) 2 *(David Villa 69, 72 (pen))*

Czech Republic (1) 1 *(Plasil 29)*

Spain: Casillas; Sergio Ramos, Arbeloa, Pique, Capdevila (Cazorla 58), Iniesta, Xabi Alonso (Torres 46), Xavi, Jesus Navas (Marchena 87), Sergio Busquets, David Villa.
Czech Republic: Cech; Hubschman, Hubnik, Sivok, Pospech, Kadlec M, Plasil, Rosicky, Pudil (Hlousek 78), Baros, Rezek (Necid 84).
Referee: Kassai (Hungary).

Budejovice, 29 March 2011, 6600

Czech Republic (1) 2 *(Baros 3, Kadlec M 70)*

Liechtenstein (0) 0

Czech Republic: Cech; Hubschman, Hubnik, Sivok, Pospech, Kadlec M, Plasil, Rosicky (Polak 84), Moravek (Hlousek 56), Baros, Lafata (Necid 59).
Liechtenstein: Jehle; Martin Stocklasa, Michael Stocklasa, Rechsteiner, Burgmeier, Buchel M (Kieber 10) (Christen A 81), Hasler N, Frick M, Beck T, Erne, Hasler D.
Referee: Hategan (Romania).

Kaunas, 29 March 2011, 9180

Lithuania (0) 1 *(Stankevicius 57)*

Spain (1) 3 *(Xavi 19, Kijanskas 70 (og), Mata 83)*

Lithuania: Karcemarskas; Zaliukas, Stankevicius, Skerla, Kijanskas, Mikoliunas (Radavicius 71), Semberas, Cesnauskis E, Panka, Sernas (Labukas 74), Danilevicius (Galkevicius 85).
Spain: Casillas; Albiol, Arbeloa, Pique (Sergio Ramos 89), Andoni Iraola, Xabi Alonso, Xavi, Javi Martinez, Cazorla (Mata 67), David Villa (David Silva 54), Llorente.
Referee: Duhamel (France).

Vaduz, 3 June 2011, 1886

Liechtenstein (2) 2 *(Erne 6, Polverino 36)*

Lithuania (0) 0

Liechtenstein: Buchel B; Ritzberger, Martin Stocklasa, Kaufmann, Burgmeier, Buchel M, Polverino, Hasler N, Fischer (Christen M 72), Beck T (Christen A 84), Erne (Hanselmann 87).
Lithuania: Setkus; Stankevicius (Labukas 46), Skerla, Kijanskas, Mikoliunas, Semberas, Cesnauskis E (Savenas 68), Panka, Sernas, Radavicius, Danilevicius (Cesnauskis D 46).
Referee: Kuchin (Kazakhstan).

Kaunas, 2 September 2011, 3500

Lithuania (0) 0

Liechtenstein (0) 0

Lithuania: Karcemarskas; Zaliukas, Klimavicius, Kijanskas, Cesnauskis D, Mikoliunas (Papsys 64), Semberas, Cesnauskis E■, Panka (Savenas 88), Danilevicius, Novikovas (Labukas 46).
Liechtenstein: Jehle; Ritzberger, Martin Stocklasa, Oehri (Kaufmann 52), Michael Stocklasa, Rechsteiner, Burgmeier, Buchel M (Kieber 90), Wieser (Hasler N 46), Frick M, Hasler D.
Referee: Johnsen (Norway).

Glasgow, 3 September 2011, 51,564

Scotland (1) 2 *(Miller 45, Fletcher D 82)*

Czech Republic (0) 2 *(Plasil 78, Kadlec M 90 (pen))*

Scotland: McGregor; Hutton, Bardsley (Wilson D 76), Adam (Cowie 79), Caldwell G, Berra, Brown, Fletcher D, Miller, Naismith (Robson 86), Morrison.
Czech Republic: Lastuvka; Hubschman, Hubnik, Sivok, Rajnoch, Kadlec M, Plasil, Rosicky, Petrzela (Rezek 56), Jiracek (Pekhart 77), Baros (Vacek 90).
Referee: Blom (Holland).

Glasgow, 6 September 2011, 34,071

Scotland (0) 1 *(Naismith 50)*

Lithuania (0) 0

Scotland: McGregor; Whittaker, Bardsley (Crainey 70), Bannan (Snodgrass 84), Caldwell G, Berra, Cowie, Fletcher D, Goodwillie, Naismith, Morrison (Dorrans 79).
Lithuania: Karcemarskas; Zaliukas, Klimavicius, Kijanskas (Danilevicius 61), Cesnauskis D, Mikoliunas (Beniusis 77), Semberas, Pilibaitis, Radavicius, Labukas (Novikovas 46), Sernas.
Referee: Jakobsson (Iceland).

Logrono, 6 September 2011, 15,660

Spain (3) 6 *(Negredo 33, 37, Xavi 44, Sergio Ramos 52, David Villa 60, 79)*

Liechtenstein (0) 0

Spain: Casillas; Sergio Ramos (Thiago Alcantara 55), Albiol, Arbeloa, Iniesta, Xabi Alonso, Xavi (Fabregas 46), Sergio Busquets, David Villa, Negredo (Llorente 62), Mata.
Liechtenstein: Jehle; Ritzberger, Martin Stocklasa, Michael Stocklasa, Rechsteiner, Burgmeier, Buchel M (Kieber 80), Wieser (Hasler N 70), Frick M, Beck T (Hanselmann 88), Hasler D.
Referee: Lechner (Austria).

Prague, 7 October 2011, 17,873

Czech Republic (0) 0

Spain (2) 2 *(Mata 7, Xabi Alonso 23)*

Czech Republic: Cech; Hubschman■, Hubnik, Sivok, Kadlec, Gebreselassie, Rosicky, Pudil, Kolar (Vacek 77), Jiracek, Baros (Pekhart 62).
Spain: Casillas; Sergio Ramos (Puyol 46), Albiol, Arbeloa, Pique, Xabi Alonso (Javi Martinez 70), Xavi, David Silva, Sergio Busquets, Torres (David Villa 61), Mata.
Referee: Taglivento (Italy).

Vaduz, 8 October 2011, 5636

Liechtenstein (0) 0

Scotland (1) 1 *(Mackail-Smith 32)*

Liechtenstein: Jehli; Ritzberger, Martin Stocklasa, Rechsteiner, Kaufmann, Buchel M (Kieber 71), Polverino, Hanselmann (Eberle 75), Hasler N, Frick M, Beck T.
Scotland: McGregor; Hutton, Bardsley, Caldwell G, Berra, Adam (Cowie 76), Morrison, Fletcher D, Naismith, Mackail-Smith, Bannan (Forrest 73).
Referee: Hagen (Norway).

Kaunas, 11 October 2011, 4000

Lithuania (0) 1 *(Sernas 68 (pen))*

Czech Republic (3) 4 *(Kadlec M 2 (pen), 85 (pen), Rezek 16, 45)*

Lithuania: Karcemarskas; Zaliukas, Stankevicius, Skerla, Mikoliunas, Ivaskevicius (Novikovas 46), Pilibaitis (Beniusis 74), Radavicius, Vicius, Sernas, Poskus (Panka 57).
Czech Republic: Cech; Hubnik■, Sivok, Kadlec M, Gebreselassie, Plasil, Rosicky, Pilar (Pudil 70), Jiracek, Baros (Pekhart 59), Rezek (Pospech 82).
Referee: Borbalan (Spain).

Alicante, 11 October 2011, 27,559

Spain (2) 3 *(David Silva 6, 44, David Villa 54)*

Scotland (0) 1 *(Goodwillie 66 (pen))*

Spain: Valdes; Puyol (Arbeloa 46), Sergio Ramos, Pique, Jordi Alba, Xavi (Llorente 64), David Silva (Thiago Alcantara 55), Cazorla, Sergio Busquets, David Villa, Pedro.
Scotland: McGregor; Hutton, Bardsley, Caldwell G, Berra, Adam (Forrest 63), Morrison, Fletcher D (Cowie 85), Naismith, Mackail-Smith, Bannan (Goodwillie 63).
Referee: Johannesson (Sweden).

Group I Table	*P*	*W*	*D*	*L*	*F*	*A*	*Pts*
Spain	8	8	0	0	26	6	24
Czech Republic	8	4	1	3	12	8	13
Scotland	8	3	2	3	9	10	11
Lithuania	8	1	2	5	4	13	5
Liechtenstein	8	1	1	6	3	17	4

PLAY-OFFS FIRST LEG

Zenica, 11 November 2011, 15,292

Bosnia (0) 0

Portugal (0) 0

Bosnia: Begovic; Spahic, Jahic, Misimovic (Ibricic 86), Medunjanin (Maletic 67), Rahimic, Salihovic (Ibisevic 68), Pjanic, Lulic, Zahirovic, Dzeko.
Portugal: Rui Patricio; Pepe, Bruno Alves, Fabio Coentrao, Joao Pereira, Raul Meireles (Ruben 82), Nani, Miguel Veloso, Joao Moutinho, Cristiano Ronaldo, Helder Postiga (Hugo Almeida 65).
Referee: Webb (England).

Prague, 11 November 2011, 14,560

Czech Republic (0) 2 *(Pilar 63, Sivok 90)*

Montenegro (0) 0

Czech Republic: Cech; Sivok, Kadlec M, Gebreselassie, Plasil, Rosicky, Pudil, Pilar (Kolar 90), Jiracek, Pekhart (Lafata 90), Rezek (Pospech 81).
Montenegro: Bozovic M; Dzudovic, Jovanovic, Pavicevic, Savic, Pekovic (Zverotic 80), Drincic, Vukcevic (Delibasic 89), Vucinic, Damjanovic (Bozovic V 61), Jovetic.
Referee: Atkinson (England).

Tallinn, 11 November 2011, 10,500

Estonia (0) 0

Republic of Ireland (1) 4 *(Andrews 13, Walters 67, Keane 71, 88 (pen))*

Estonia: Pareiko; Klavan, Stepanov■, Piiroja■, Jaager, Kruglov, Dmitrijev, Vunk (Lindpere 61), Vassiljev, Ahjupera (Voskoboinikov 55), Kink (Purje 67).
Republic of Ireland: Given; Kelly, Ward, St Ledger-Hall, Dunne, Whelan (Fahey 78), Duff (Hunt 73), McGeady, Walters (Cox 83), Keane, Andrews.
Referee: Kassai (Hungary).

Istanbul, 11 November 2011, 47,000

Turkey (0) 0

Croatia (2) 3 *(Olic 2, Mandzukic 32, Corluka 51)*

Turkey: Volkan; Sabri, Egemen, Hakan Balta, Remzi, Gokhan G (Gokhan T 46), Hamit Altintop, Emre B, Arda, Selcuk I (Mehmet Topal 69), Burak (Umut 81).
Croatia: Pletikosa; Simunic, Srna, Corluka, Schildenfeld, Vida, Modric, Rakitic (Pranjic 83), Dujmovic, Olic (Jelavic 85), Mandzukic (Eduardo Da Silva 90).
Referee: Brych (Germany).

PLAY-OFFS SECOND LEG

Zagreb, 15 November 2011, 26,371

Croatia (0) 0

Turkey (0) 0

Croatia: Pletikosa; Simunic, Srna, Schildenfeld, Vida, Modric, Pranjic, Rakitic, Vukojevic (Eduardo Da Silva 88), Olic (Perisic 61), Mandzukic (Jelavic 78).
Turkey: Sinan; Egemen, Caner (Gokhan T 36), Omer, Ismail, Hamit Altintop, Kazim-Richards, Selcuk S, Serkan, Selcuk I, Umut (Halil Altintop 71).
Referee: Pedro Proenca (Portugal).

Podgorica, 15 November 2011, 10,100

Montenegro (0) 0

Czech Republic (0) 1 *(Jiracek 81)*

Montenegro: Bozovic M; Dzudovic, Zverotic, Pavicevic, Savic, Drincic, Bozovic V (Dalovic 79), Vucinic, Damjanovic (Vukcevic 76), Beciraj (Delibasic 58), Jovetic.
Czech Republic: Cech; Hubnik, Sivok, Kadlec M, Gebreselassie, Plasil, Rosicky, Pilar (Kolar 69), Jiracek, Pekhart (Baros 84), Rezek (Pospech 60).
Referee: Rizzoli (Italy).

Lisbon, 15 November 2011, 45,000

Portugal (2) 6 *(Cristiano Ronaldo 8, 53, Nani 24, Helder Postiga 72, 82, Miguel Veloso 80)*

Bosnia (1) 2 *(Misimovic 41 (pen), Spahic 65)*

Portugal: Rui Patricio; Pepe, Bruno Alves, Fabio Coentrao, Joao Pereira, Raul Meireles (Ruben 63), Nani (Ricardo Quaresma 83), Miguel Veloso, Joao Moutinho, Cristiano Ronaldo, Helder Postiga (Carlos Martins 84).
Bosnia: Begovic; Spahic, Papac, Jahic, Misimovic, Medunjanin, Rahimic (Maletic 56), Pjanic (Besic 65), Lulic■, Zahirovic, Dzeko.
Referee: Stark (Germany).

Dublin, 15 November 2011, 51,151

Republic of Ireland (1) 1 *(Ward 32)*

Estonia (0) 1 *(Vassiljev 57)*

Republic of Ireland: Given; O'Shea, Ward, St Ledger-Hall, Dunne, Whelan, Duff (Fahey 79), Hunt (McGeady 59), Doyle, Keane (Cox 67), Andrews.
Estonia: Londak; Klavan, Jaager, Teniste, Rahn, Kruglov (Puri 18), Lindpere (Kink 54), Vunk, Vassiljev, Saag, Voskoboinikov (Purje 73).
Referee: Kuipers (Holland).

EURO 2012 FINALS REVIEW

Spanish masters boring? Yes, but only drilling devastatingly through the Italian defence to become a four-goal five-star class above everyone. Two banks of three in midfield and movement all over, first a cut-back by Cesc Fabregas for David Silva to head in, then Xavi's penetrating pass for Jordi Alba to gallop for number two. Second half goals were made in Stamford Bridge: Torres with the first and an assist from him to substitute Juan Mata for the second. To their credit Italy, down to ten through injury, behaved. A World Cup squeezed between two Euro titles, where next for Spain?

The group stages had provided the eyebrow-raising demise of Holland in two years since being runners-up in the World Cup. Though they lost by just one goal in each match, their overall performance was depressing. Robin Van Persie managed a goal, but was otherwise a shadow of the predatory Premier League sharp-shooter.

Conversely, Germany also in Group B won all three games, the only team so to do. Physical presence personified, they appeared comfortably in control. However, another surprise was the disintegration of the Russians, though their 4-1 win over the Czech Republic in the opener was flattering. They drew with Poland, the co-hosts, but then unexpectedly conceded to Greece, the real shakers in Group A. The Greeks began in the only ten-a-side affair drawing with the Poles before losing to the better-displays-than-results Czechs.

The bright-starting Danes in Group B faded, Portugal's ratings swung depending on the Cristiano Ronaldo mood. Off colour in one, then taking on the opposition single-handedly – and winning – in another. Spain, holders, World Cup winners and the favourites in Group C, had a quiet opening, playing possession and apparently unwilling to lose the ball by taking a shot at goal. Fielding a team without a striker in two of the matches yet scoring four in the one game with Fernando Torres in the starting line-up, albeit against the out-of-touch Republic of Ireland.

The Italians did hold the Spaniards in the first game but were unable to beat Croatia in another 1-1 and needed the win over the ten-finishing Irish to continue. Yet England were encouraged by taking the lead against the fancied French and gaining a deserved draw. Co-hosts Ukraine were boosted by two goals from Andrij Shevchenko to edge Sweden, only to concede a couple to France. In an exciting tussle with the Swedes, England took the lead, went behind and then sneaked it with a fluky back-heel from Danny Welbeck. But they all count. Though the returning Rooney headed in from a couple of inches, Ukraine missed the target from decent scoring positions. Thus neither co-host reached the last eight. France, already qualified, lost to Sweden.

Herald the quarter-finals: Portugal with Ronaldo almost back to his unplayable best, just edged it over an under-the-cosh Czech team, stretched for long periods. Germany, brimming with confidence, even rested a few players with the veteran Miroslav Klose as spearhead for his 120th cap. Greece even levelled early in the second half but eventually conceded four goals though converted a penalty harshly awarded for handling.

Spain decided to revert to their "ghost-striker" formation with six in midfield against France. They were at their most irritating and, camped in the first third of the French half, they dictated play without any real penetration. A downward header from Xabi Alonso opened the score and he finished it from the penalty spot. Then it was England against the Italians, who hit a post early on and enjoyed more possession, but lacked decisiveness. And so into extra time before penalties emerged and ended with England's poor shoot-out record confirmed.

The first semi-final also went to penalties. Spain – edging it over 120 minutes – and Portugal knew too much about each other and it was tediously scrappy. Only two real chances, one at either end: Rui Patricio spilled one but recovered; then in a swift four-against-two counter-attacking move, Ronaldo missed the target. He was also the fifth (unused) penalty taker! Yet the shock came in the other match.

Once Mario Balotelli had headed Italy into a surprise lead over the Germans, they were always the more dangerous team and deservedly added to the score after a defence-splitting aerial launch that the Manchester City striker duly despatched. Germany, denied an early penalty, had one awarded late on which was not an offence.

The Spanish national team celebrate winning the European Championship trophy after beating Italy 4-0 in the final in Kiev on 1st July.

EURO 2012 FINAL COMPETITION

▪ *Denotes player sent off.*

GROUP A

Warsaw, 8 June 2012, 56,070

Poland (1) 1 *(Lewandowski 17)*

Greece (0) 1 *(Salpingidis 51)*

Poland: Szczesny▪; Perquis, Boenisch, Wasilewski, Piszczek, Polanski, Obraniak, Murawski, Blaszczykowski, Rybus (Tyton 70), Lewandowski.
Greece: Chalkias; Holebas, Papadopoulos A (Papadopoulos K 37), Torosidis, Papastathopoulos▪, Maniatis, Karagounis, Katsouranis, Ninis (Salpingidis 46), Samaras, Gekas (Fortounis 68).
Referee: Velasco (Spain).

Wroclaw, 8 June 2012, 40,803

Russia (2) 4 *(Dzagoev 15, 79, Shirokov 24, Pavlyuchenko 82)*

Czech Republic (0) 1 *(Pilar 52)*

Russia: Malafeev; Ignashevich, Berezutski A, Anyukov, Zhirkov, Shirokov, Zyryanov, Denisov, Arshavin, Dzagoev (Kokorin 84), Kerzhakov (Pavlyuchenko 73).
Czech Republic: Cech; Hubnik, Sivok, Kadlec, Gebre Selassie, Plasil, Rosicky, Pilar, Jiracek (Petrzela 76), Baros (Lafata 85), Rezek (Hubschman 46).
Referee: Webb (England).

Wroclaw, 12 June 2012, 41,105

Greece (0) 1 *(Gekas 53)*

Czech Republic (2) 2 *(Jiracek 3, Pilar 6)*

Greece: Chalkias (Sifakis 23); Holebas, Torosidis, Papadopoulos K, Maniatis, Fotakis (Gekas 46), Karagounis, Katsouranis, Samaras, Salpingidis, Fortounis (Mitroglou 71).
Czech Republic: Cech; Sivok, Kadlec, Limbersky, Gebre Selassie, Plasil, Rosicky (Kolar 46), Hubschman, Pilar, Jiracek, Baros (Rajtoral 90).
Referee: Lannoy (France).

Warsaw, 12 June 2012, 55,920

Poland (0) 1 *(Blaszczykowski 57)*

Russia (1) 1 *(Dzagoev 37)*

Poland: Tyton; Perquis, Boenisch, Wasilewski, Piszczek, Dudka (Mierzejewski 73), Polanski (Matuszczyk 85), Obraniak (Pawel Brozek 90), Murawski, Blaszczykowski, Lewandowski.
Russia: Malafeev; Ignashevich, Berezutski A, Anyukov, Zhirkov, Shirokov, Zyryanov, Denisov, Arshavin, Dzagoev (Izmailov 79), Kerzhakov (Pavlyuchenko 70).
Referee: Stark (Germany).

Wroclaw, 16 June 2012, 41,480

Czech Republic (0) 1 *(Jiracek 72)*

Poland (0) 0

Czech Republic: Cech; Sivok, Kadlec, Limbersky, Gabre Selassie, Plasil, Hubschman, Kolar, Pilar (Rezek 88), Jiracek (Rajtoral 84), Baros (Pekhart 90).
Poland: Tyton; Perquis, Boenisch, Wasilewski, Piszczek, Dudka, Polanski (Grosicki 56), Obraniak (Pawel Brozek 73), Murawski (Mierzejewski 73), Blaszczykowski, Lewandowski.
Referee: Thomson (Scotland).

Warsaw, 16 June 2012, 55,614

Greece (1) 1 *(Karagounis 45)*

Russia (0) 0

Greece: Sifakis; Torosidis, Papadopoulos K, Papastathopoulos, Maniatis, Tzavelas, Karagounis (Makos 67), Katsouranis, Samaras, Gekas (Holebas 64), Salpingidis (Ninis 83).
Russia: Malafeev; Ignashevich, Berezutski A, Anyukov (Izmailov 81), Zhirkov, Shirokov, Denisov, Arshavin, Glushakov (Pogrebnyak 72), Dzagoev, Kerzhakov (Pavlyuchenko 46).
Referee: Eriksson (Sweden).

Group A Table	*P*	*W*	*D*	*L*	*F*	*A*	*Pts*
Czech Republic	3	2	0	1	4	5	6
Greece	3	1	1	1	3	3	4
Russia	3	1	1	1	5	3	4
Poland	3	0	2	1	2	3	2

GROUP B

Lvov, 9 June 2012, 32,990

Germany (0) 1 *(Gomez 72)*

Portugal (0) 0

Germany: Neuer; Lahm, Boateng, Hummels, Badstuber, Schweinsteiger, Ozil (Kroos 87), Khedira, Gomez (Klose 80), Podolski, Muller (Bender 90).
Portugal: Rui Patricio; Pepe, Bruno Alves, Fabio Coentrao, Joao Pereira, Raul Meireles (Silvestre Varela 80), Nani, Miguel Veloso, Joao Moutinho, Cristiano Ronaldo, Helder Postiga (Nelson Oliveira 70).
Referee: Lannoy (France).

Kharkiv, 9 June 2012, 35,923

Holland (0) 0

Denmark (1) 1 *(Krohn-Dehli 24)*

Holland: Stekelenburg; Heitinga, Vlaar, Van der Wiel (Kuyt 85), Willems, Robben, Sneijder, Van Bommel, De Jong (Van der Vaart 71), Afellay (Huntelaar 71), Van Persie.
Denmark: Andersen; Agger, Kjaer, Poulsen S, Jacobsen, Zemling, Kvist, Eriksen (Schone 74), Krohn-Dehli, Rommedahl (Mikkelsen 84), Bendtner.
Referee: Skomina (Slovenia).

Lvov, 13 June 2012, 31,840

Denmark (1) 2 *(Bendtner 41, 80)*

Portugal (2) 3 *(Pepe 24, Helder Postiga 36, Silvestre Varela 87)*

Denmark: Andersen; Agger, Kjaer, Poulsen S, Jacobsen, Zimling (Poulsen J 16), Kvist, Eriksen, Krohn-Dehli (Schone 90), Rommedahl (Mikkelsen 60), Bendtner.
Portugal: Rui Patricio; Pepe, Bruno Alves, Fabio Coentrao, Joao Pereira, Raul Meireles (Silvestre Varela 84), Nani (Rolando 89), Miguel Veloso, Joao Moutinho, Cristiano Ronaldo, Helder Postiga (Nelson Oliveira 64).
Referee: Thomson (Scotland).

Kharkiv, 13 June 2012, 37,750

Holland (0) 1 *(Van Persie 73)*

Germany (2) 2 *(Gomez 24, 38)*

Holland: Stekelenburg; Heitinga, Mathijsen, Van der Wiel, Willems, Robben (Kuyt 83), Sneijder, Van Bommel (Van der Vaart 46), De Jong, Afellay (Huntelaar 46), Van Persie.
Germany: Neuer; Lahm, Boateng, Hummels, Badstuber, Schweinsteiger, Ozil (Kroos 81), Khedira, Gomez (Klose 72), Podolski, Muller (Bender 90).
Referee: Eriksson (Sweden).

Lvov, 17 June 2012, 32,990

Denmark (1) 1 *(Krohn-Dehli 24)*

Germany (1) 2 *(Podolski 19, Bender 80)*

Denmark: Andersen; Agger, Kjaer, Poulsen S, Jacobsen, Poulsen J (Mikkelsen 82), Zimling (Poulsen C 79), Kvist, Eriksen, Krohn-Dehli, Bendtner.
Germany: Neuer; Lahm, Hummels, Badstuber, Schweinsteiger, Ozil, Khedira, Bender, Gomez (Klose 74), Podolski (Schurrle 64), Muller (Kroos 84).
Referee: Velasco (Spain).

Kharkiv, 17 June 2012, 37,445

Portugal (1) 2 *(Cristiano Ronaldo 28, 74)*

Holland (1) 1 *(Van der Vaart 11)*

Portugal: Rui Patricio; Pepe, Bruno Alves, Fabio Coentrao, Joao Pereira, Raul Meireles (Custodio 72), Nani (Rolando 87), Miguel Veloso, Joao Moutinho, Cristiano Ronaldo, Helder Postiga (Nelson Oliveira 64).
Holland: Stekelenburg; Mathijsen, Vlaar, Van der Wiel, Willems (Afellay 67), Robben, Sneijder, Van der Vaart, De Jong, Van Persie, Huntelaar.
Referee: Rizzoli (Italy).

Group B Table	P	W	D	L	F	A	Pts
Germany	3	3	0	0	5	2	9
Portugal	3	2	0	1	5	4	6
Denmark	3	1	0	2	4	5	3
Holland	3	0	0	3	2	5	0

GROUP C

Poznan, 10 June 2012, 39,550

Republic of Ireland (1) 1 *(St Ledger-Hall 19)*

Croatia (2) 3 *(Mandzukic 3, 48, Jelavic 43)*

Republic of Ireland: Given; Dunne, O'Shea, Ward, St Ledger-Hall, McGeady (Cox 54), Duff, Whelan, Andrews, Doyle (Walters 53), Keane (Long 75).
Croatia: Pletikosa; Srna, Corluka, Schildenfeld, Strinic, Modric, Rakitic (Dujmovic 90), Perisic (Eduardo da Silva 89), Vukojevic, Jelavic (Kranjcar 72), Mandzukic.
Referee: Kuipers (Holland).

Gdansk, 10 June 2012, 38,869

Spain (0) 1 *(Fabregas 64)*

Italy (0) 1 *(Di Natale 60)*

Spain: Casillas; Sergio Ramos, Arbeloa, Pique, Jordi Alba, Fabregas (Torres 74), Iniesta, Xabi Alonso, Xavi, David Silva (Jesus Navas 65), Busquets.
Italy: Buffon; Bonucci, Chiellini, De Rossi, Pirlo, Thiago Motta (Nocerino 90), Maggio, Marchisio, Giaccherini, Cassano (Giovinco 65), Balotelli (Di Natale 56).
Referee: Kassai (Hungary).

Poznan, 14 June 2012, 37,096

Italy (1) 1 *(Pirlo 39)*

Croatia (0) 1 *(Mandzukic 72)*

Italy: Buffon; Bonucci, Chiellini, De Rossi, Pirlo, Thiago Motta (Montolivo 63), Maggio, Marchisio, Giaccherini, Cassano (Giovinco 83), Balotelli (Di Natale 70).
Croatia: Pletikosa; Srna, Corluka, Schildenfeld, Strinic, Modric, Rakitic, Perisic (Pranjic 68), Vukojevic, Jelavic (Eduardo Da Silva 83), Mandzukic (Kranjcar 90).
Referee: Webb (England).

Gdansk, 14 June 2012, 39,150

Spain (1) 4 *(Torres 4, 70, David Silva 49, Fabregas 83)*

Republic of Ireland (0) 0

Spain: Casillas; Sergio Ramos, Arbeloa, Pique, Jordi Alba, Iniesta (Cazorla 80), Xabi Alonso (Javi Martinez 65), Xavi, David Silva, Busquets, Torres (Fabregas 74).
Republic of Ireland: Given; Dunne, O'Shea, Ward, St Ledger-Hall, McGeady, Duff (McClean 76), Whelan (Green 80), Andrews, Cox (Walters 46), Keane.
Referee: Proenca (Portugal).

Gdansk, 18 June 2012, 39,076

Croatia (0) 0

Spain (0) 1 *(Jesus Navas 88)*

Croatia: Pletikosa; Srna, Corluka, Schildenfeld, Vida (Jelavic 66), Strinic, Modric, Pranjic (Perisic 65), Rakitic, Vukojevic (Eduardo Da Silva 81), Mandzukic.
Spain: Casillas; Sergio Ramos, Arbeloa, Pique, Jordi Alba, Iniesta, Xabi Alonso, Xavi (Negredo 89), David Silva (Fabregas 73), Busquets, Torres (Jesus Navas 61).
Referee: Stark (Germany).

Poznan, 18 June 2012, 38,794

Italy (1) 2 *(Cassano 35, Balotelli 90)*

Republic of Ireland (0) 0

Italy: Buffon; Barzagli, Chiellini (Bonucci 57), Balzaretti, Abate, De Rossi, Pirlo, Thiago Motta, Marchisio, Cassano (Diamanti 63), Di Natale (Balotelli 75).
Republic of Ireland: Given; Dunne, O'Shea, Ward, St Ledger-Hall, McGeady (Long 65), Duff, Whelan, Andrews■, Doyle (Walters 76), Keane (Cox 86).
Referee: Cuneyt (Turkey).

Group C Table	P	W	D	L	F	A	Pts
Spain	3	2	1	0	6	1	7
Italy	3	1	2	0	4	2	5
Croatia	3	1	1	1	4	3	4
Republic of Ireland	3	0	0	3	1	9	0

GROUP D

Donetsk, 11 June 2012, 47,400

France (1) 1 *(Nasri 39)*

England (1) 1 *(Lescott 30)*

France: Lloris; Debuchy, Evra, Mexes, Rami, Diarra, Malouda (Martin 85), Ribery, Nasri, Cabaye (Ben Arfa 84), Benzema.
England: Hart; Johnson G, Cole, Gerrard, Terry, Lescott, Milner, Parker (Henderson 78), Welbeck (Walcott 90), Young, Oxlade-Chamberlain (Defoe 77).
Referee: Rizzoli (Italy).

Kiev, 11 June 2012, 64,290

Ukraine (0) 2 *(Schevchenko 55, 61)*

Sweden (0) 1 *(Ibrahimovic 52)*

Ukraine: Pyatov; Mykhalyk, Selin, Khacheridi, Husyev, Nazarenko, Tymoshchuk, Konoplyanka (Devic 90), Shevchenko (Milevskiy 81), Voronin (Rotan 85), Yarmolenko.
Sweden: Isaksson; Mellberg, Martin Olsson, Granqvist, Lustig, Kallstrom, Elm, Toivonen (Svensson 62), Larsson (Wilhelmsson 68), Ibrahimovic, Rosenberg (Elmander 71).
Referee: Cuneyt (Turkey).

Kiev, 15 June 2012, 64,640

Sweden (0) 2 *(Johnson G 49 (og), Mellberg 59)*

England (1) 3 *(Carroll 23, Walcott 64, Welbeck 78)*

Sweden: Isaksson; Mellberg, Olsson J, Martin Olsson, Granqvist (Lustig 66), Kallstrom, Svensson, Elm (Wilhelmsson 81), Larsson, Ibrahimovic, Elmander (Rosenberg 79).
England: Hart; Johnson G, Cole, Gerrard, Terry, Lescott, Milner (Walcott 61), Parker, Carroll, Welbeck (Oxlade-Chamberlain 90), Young.
Referee: Skomina (Slovenia).

Donetsk, 15 June 2012, 48,000

Ukraine (0) 0

France (0) 2 *(Menez 53, Cayabye 56)*

Ukraine: Pyatov; Mykhalyk, Selin, Khacheridi, Husyev, Nazarenko (Milevskiy 60), Tymoshchuk, Konoplyanka, Shevchenko, Voronin (Devic 46), Yarmolenko (Aliyev 68).
France: Lloris; Debuchy, Clichy, Mexes, Rami, Diarra, Ribery, Menez (Martin 73), Nasri, Cabaye (M'Vila 68), Benzema (Giroud 76).
Referee: Kuipers (Holland).

Donetsk, 19 June 2012, 48,700

England (0) 1 *(Rooney 48)*

Ukraine (0) 0

England: Hart; Johnson G, Cole, Gerrard, Terry, Lescott, Milner (Walcott 70), Parker, Welbeck (Carroll 82), Rooney (Oxlade-Chamberlain 87), Milner (Walcott 70).
Ukraine: Pyatov; Selin, Rakitskiy, Khacheridi, Husyev, Tymoshchuk, Konoplyanka, Garmash (Nazarenko 78), Milevskiy (Butko 77), Devic (Shevchenko 70), Yarmolenko.
Referee: Cassai (Hungary).

Kiev, 19 June 2012, 63,010

Sweden (0) 2 *(Ibrahimovic 54, Larsson 90)*

France (0) 0

Sweden: Isaksson; Mellberg, Olsson J, Martin Olsson, Granqvist, Kallstrom, Svensson (Holmen 78), Bajrami (Wilhelmsson 46), Toivonen (Wernbloom 78), Larsson, Ibrahimovic.
France: Lloris; Debuchy, Clichy, Mexes, Rami, Diarra, Ribery, Nasri (Menez 77), Ben Arfa (Malouda 59), M'Vila (Giroud 83), Benzema.
Referee: Proenca (Portugal).

Group D Table	P	W	D	L	F	A	Pts
England	3	2	1	0	5	3	7
France	3	1	1	1	3	3	4
Ukraine	3	1	0	2	2	4	3
Sweden	3	1	0	2	5	5	3

QUARTER-FINALS

Warsaw, 21 June 2012, 55,590

Czech Republic (0) 0

Portugal (0) 1 *(Cristiano Ronaldo 79)*

Czech Republic: Cech; Sivok, Kadlec, Limbersky, Gebre Selassie, Plasil, Hubschman (Pekhart 86), Pilar, Jiracek, Darida (Rezek 61), Baros.
Portugal: Rui Patricio; Pepe, Bruno Alves, Fabio Coentrao, Joao Pereira, Raul Meireles (Rolando 88), Nani (Custodio 84), Miguel Veloso, Joao Moutinho, Cristiano Ronaldo, Helder Postiga (Hugo Almeida 40).
Referee: Webb (England).

Gdansk, 22 June 2012, 38,751

Germany (1) 4 *(Lahm 39, Khedira 61, Klose 68, Reus 74)*

Greece (0) 2 *(Samaras 55, Salpingidis 89 (pen))*

Germany: Neuer; Lahm, Boateng, Hummels, Badstuber, Schweinsteiger, Ozil, Khedira, Reus (Gotze 80), Klose (Gomez 80), Schurrle (Muller 67).
Greece: Sifakis; Torosidis, Papadopoulos K, Papastathopoulos, Maniatis, Tzavelas (Fotakis 46), Katsouranis, Makos (Liberopoulos 72), Ninis (Gekas 46), Samaras, Salpingidis.
Referee: Skomina (Slovenia).

Donetsk, 23 June 2012, 47,000

Spain (1) 2 *(Xabi Alonso 19, 90 (pen))*

France (0) 0

Spain: Casillas; Sergio Ramos, Arbeloa, Pique, Jordi Alba, Fabregas (Torres 67), Iniesta (Cazorla 84), Xabi Alonso, Xavi, David Silva (Pedro 65), Busquets.
France: Lloris; Reveillere, Debuchy (Menez 64), Clichy, Rami, Koscielny, Malouda (Nasri 65); Ribery, Cabaye, M'Vila (Giroud 79), Benzema.
Referee: Rizzoli (Italy).

Kiev, 24 June 2012, 64,340

England (0) 0

Italy (0) 0

England: Hart; Johnson G, Cole, Gerrard, Terry, Lescott, Milner (Walcott 61), Parker (Henderson 94), Welbeck (Carroll 60), Rooney, Young A.
Italy: Buffon; Barzagli, Bonucci, Balzaretti, Abate (Maggio 90), De Rossi (Nocerino 80), Pirlo, Montolivo, Marchisio, Cassano (Diamanti 78), Balotelli.
Referee: Proenca (Portugal).
aet; Italy won 4-2 on penalties: Balotelli scored; Gerrard scored; Montolivo missed; Rooney scored; Pirlo scored; Young A hit bar; Nocerino scored; Cole saved; Diamanti scored.

SEMI-FINALS

Donetsk, 27 June 2012, 48,000

Portugal (0) 0

Spain (0) 0

Portugal: Rui Patricio; Pepe, Bruno Alves, Fabio Coentrao, Joao Pereira, Raul Meireles (Silvestre Varela 113), Nani, Miguel Veloso (Custodio 106), Joao Moutinho, Cristiano Ronaldo, Hugo Almeida (Nelson Oliveira 81).
Spain: Casillas; Sergio Ramos, Arbeloa, Pique, Jordi Alba, Iniesta, Xabi Alonso, Xavi (Pedro 87), David Silva (Jesus Navas 60), Busquets, Negredo (Fabregas 54).
Referee: Cuneyt (Turkey).
aet; Spain won 4-2 on penalties: Xabi Alonso saved; Joao Moutinho saved; Iniesta scored; Pepe scored; Pique scored; Nani scored; Sergio Ramos scored; Bruno Alves hit bar; Fabregas scored.

Warsaw, 28 June 2012, 55,540

Germany (0) 1 *(Ozil 90 (pen))*

Italy (2) 2 *(Balotelli 20, 36)*

Germany: Neuer; Lahm, Boateng (Muller 71), Hummels, Badstuber, Schweinsteiger, Ozil, Khedira, Kroos, Gomez (Klose 46), Podolski (Reus 46).
Italy: Buffon; Barzagli, Bonucci, Chiellini, Balzaretti, De Rossi, Pirlo, Montolivo (Thiago Motta 64), Marchisio, Cassano (Diamanti 58), Balotelli (Di Natale 70).
Referee: Lannoy (France).

EURO 2012 FINAL

Sunday, 1 July 2012

(in Kiev, attendance 63,170

Spain (2) 4 *(David Silva 14, Jordi Alba 41, Torres 84, Mata 88)* **Italy (0) 0**

Spain: Casillas; Sergio Ramos, Arbeloa, Pique, Jordi Alba, Fabregas (Torres 75), Iniesta (Mata 87), Xabi Alonso, Xavi, David Silva (Pedro 59), Busquets.

Italy: Buffon; Barzagli, Bonucci, Chiellini (Balzaretti 21), Abate, De Rossi, Pirlo, Montolivo (Thiago Motta 57), Marchisio, Cassano (Di Natale 46), Balotelli.

Referee: Proenca (Portugal).

EURO 2012 STATISTICS

Attendances:	1,440,896	**Number of goals:**	76
Average:	46,479	**Average:**	2.45

Number of red cards: 3 (two yellow-red)
Number of yellow cards: 123

Golden Boot winner: Fernando Torres (Spain).
(based on three goals, one assist and fewest minutes played).

UEFA squad of tournament:

Goalkeepers: Gianluigi Buffon (Italy), Iker Casillas (Spain), Manuel Neuer (Germany).

Defenders: Gerard Pique (Spain), Pepe (Portugal), Fabio Coentrao (Portugal), Philipp Lahm (Germany), Sergio Ramos (Spain), Jordi Alba (Spain).

Midfield: Daniele De Rossi (Italy), Steven Gerrard (England), Xavi (Spain), Andres Iniesta (Spain), Sami Khedira (Germany), Sergio Busquets (Spain), Mesut Ozil (Germany), Andrea Pirlo (Italy), Xabi Alonso (Spain).

Forwards: Mario Balotelli (Italy), Cesc Fabregas (Spain), Cristiano Ronaldo (Portugal), Zlatan Ibrahimovic (Sweden), David Silva (Spain).

WORLD CUP 2014 QUALIFYING COMPETITION

■ *Denotes player sent off.*

SOUTH AMERICA

Buenos Aires, 7 October 2011, 26,161

Argentina (2) 4 *(Higuain 7, 52, 63, Messi 25)*

Chile (0) 1 *(Fernandez 59)*

Argentina: Andujar; Zabaleta, Burdisso, Rojo, Otamendi, Di Maria (Gutierrez 85), Sosa (Salvio 79), Higuain, Messi, Banega (Rinaudo 72), Brana.
Chile: Bravo; Ponce, Isla, Carmona, Vidal, Suazo, Valdivia, Pinilla (Gonzalez M 54), Fernandez (Jorquera 81), Beausejour (Vargas 54), Jara.
Referee: Roldan (Colombia).

Quito, 7 October 2011, 32,278

Ecuador (2) 2 *(Ayovi J 15, Benitez 28)*

Venezuela (0) 0

Ecuador: Banguera; Erazo, Paredes, Noboa (Arroyo 76), Ayovi W, Benitez (Mendez 83), Suarez (Bolanos 68), Campos, Valencia, Ayovi J, Saritama.
Venezuela: Vega; Granados, Rey■, Velazquez, Flores F (Flores A 57), Di Giorgi, Meza, Maldonado (Feltscher F 72), Seijas, Lucena, Aristeguieta (Moreno 46).
Referee: Osses (Chile).

Lima, 7 October 2011, 39,600

Peru (0) 2 *(Guerrero 46, 71)*

Paraguay (0) 0

Peru: Fernandez; Rodriguez, Acasiete, Guizasola, Balbin, Vargas, Guerrero (Advincula 90), Farfan, Pizarro, Cruzado (Lobaton 89), Yotun.
Paraguay: Barreto D; Piris, Marecos (Samudio 25), Veron, Barreto E, Santa Cruz R, Estigarribia, Da Silva, Riveros, Pirez (Cardozo O 66), Ramirez (Pittoni 55).
Referee: Pezzotta (Argentina).

Montevideo, 7 October 2011, 25,500

Uruguay (3) 4 *(Suarez 3, Lugano 25, 71, Cavani 34)*

Bolivia (1) 2 *(Cardozo 17, Martins 87 (pen))*

Uruguay: Muslera; Lugano, Godin, Suarez, Forlan, Pereira A (Fucile 56), Pirez, Pereira M, Arevalo, Cavani (Rodriguez C 70), Caceres.
Bolivia: Arias; Gutierrez, Rivero, Flores (Chavez 81), Rojas (Vaca 60), Martins, Vargas, Robles, Raldes, Saucedo (Pena 46), Cardozo.
Referee: Carrillo (Peru).

La Paz, 11 October 2011, 33,155

Bolivia (0) 1 *(Flores 85)*

Colombia (0) 2 *(Pabon 48, Falcao 90)*

Bolivia: Vaca; Gutierrez (Campos 70), Alvarez (Chavez 77), Rivero, Flores, Martins (Andaveris 71), Robles, Raldes, Arce, Escobar, Cardozo.
Colombia: Ospina; Rodriguez, Sanchez, Armero, Aguilar, Pabon (Moreno 62), Guarin (Chara 70), Perea, Zuniga, Gutierrez (Falcao 79), Mosquera.
Referee: Amarilla (Paraguay).

Santiago, 11 October 2011, 39,000

Chile (2) 4 *(Ponce 2, Vargas 18, Medel 47, Suazo 63 (pen))*

Peru (0) 2 *(Pizarro 49, Farfan 59)*

Chile: Bravo; Ponce, Isla, Gonzalez M, Vidal, Suazo (Paredes 72), Valdivia (Carmona 90), Beausejour, Medel, Jara, Vargas (Fernandez 84).
Peru: Fernandez; Rodriguez, Acasiete (Chiroque 87), Balbin (Guizasola 46), Vargas, Guerrero, Farfan, Revoredo, Pizarro, Cruzado, Yotun (Lobaton 46).
Referee: Orosco (Bolivia).

Asuncion, 11 October 2011, 12,922

Paraguay (0) 1 *(Ortiz 90)*

Uruguay (0) 1 *(Forlan 67)*

Paraguay: Barreto D; Veron, Bonet (Perez 79), Cardozo O (Caballero 67), Barreto E, Estigarribia, Da Silva, Caceres (Santa Cruz R 77), Riveros, Valdez, Ortiz.
Uruguay: Muslera; Lugano, Godin, Suarez, Forlan (Rodriguez C 83), Pereira A (Gonzalez 64), Perez (Eguren 58), Pereira M, Arevalo, Cavani, Caceres.
Referee: Seneme (Brazil).

Anzoategui, 11 October 2011, 37,000

Venezuela (0) 1 *(Amorebieta 61)*

Argentina (0) 0

Venezuela: Vega; Vizcarrondo, Amorebieta, Cichero, Fedor (Moreno 89), Rincon, Gonzalez (Alvarez 83), Lucena, Rosales, Arango, Rondon J (Feltscher 76).
Argentina: Andujar; Demichelis, Zabaleta (Banega 66), Burdisso, Rojo, Otamendi, Di Maria (Pastore 84), Sosa (Palacio 74), Higuain, Messi, Mascherano.
Referee: Silvera (Uruguay).

Buenos Aires, 11 November 2011, 27,592

Argentina (0) 1 *(Lavezzi 60)*

Bolivia (0) 1 *(Martins 56)*

Argentina: Romero; Burdisso, Demichelis, Zabaleta, Rodriguez C, Mascherano (Sosa 82), Gago, Pastore, Alvarez (Lavezzi 59), Messi, Higuain.
Bolivia: Arias; Gutierrez, Mendez, Vargas, Rivero, Flores, Robles, Cardozo, Martins (Andaveris 77), Escobar (Chavez 84), Rojas (Segovia 54).
Referee: Vera (Ecuador).

Montevideo, 11 November 2011, 40,500

Uruguay (2) 4 *(Suarez 42, 45, 68, 74)*

Chile (0) 0

Uruguay: Muslera; Lugano, Caceres, Godin, Pereira, Perez, Gonzalez (Eguren 70), Arevalo, Ramirez (Abreu 58), Suarez (Rodriguez C 77), Cavani.
Chile: Bravo; Gonzalez M, Contreras, Isla, Ponce, Diaz (Mirosevic 61), Fernandez, Medel, Suazo (Paredes 61), Vargas (Canales 72), Campos.
Referee: Baldassi (Argentina).

Barranquilla, 12 November 2011, 49,612

Colombia (1) 1 *(Guarin 11)*

Venezuela (0) 1 *(Feltscher F 79)*

Colombia: Ospina; Yepes, Perea, Vallejo, Armero, Bolivar, Guarin, Rodriguez (Moreno 90), Gutierrez (Quintero 85), Martinez J, Pabon (Marrugo 77).
Venezuela: Vega; Amorebieta, Vizcarrondo, Rosales, Cichero, Arango, Gonzalez, Agnel Flores, Rincon (Guerra 84), Moreno (Feltscher F 71), Fedor (Rondon J 58).
Referee: Ponce (Ecuador).

Asuncion, 12 November 2011, 11,173

Paraguay (0) 2 *(Riveros 47, Veron 57)*

Ecuador (0) 1 *(Rojas 90)*

Paraguay: Barreto D; Da Silva, Veron, Bonet, Riveros, Estigarribia (Samudio 80), Caceres, Ayala, Ortiz, Haedo Valdez (Caballero 74), Barrios (Dos Santos 64).
Ecuador: Banguera; Achilier, Erazo, Saritama (Rojas 78), Valencia, Noboa, Ayovi W, Morante, Borja (Mendez 71), Suarez (Montero 59), Ayovi J.
Referee: Buitrago (Colombia).

Santiago, 15 November 2011, 44,726

Chile (1) 2 *(Contreras 28, Campos 86)*

Paraguay (0) 0

Chile: Bravo; Gonzalez M, Contreras, Isla, Ponce, Fernandez (Mirosevic 87), Medel, Aranguiz, Sanchez, Suazo (Campos 71), Vargas (Paredes 78).
Paraguay: Barreto D; Manzur, Veron, Bonet (Hernan Perez 46), Samudio, Barreto E, Dos Santos (Benitez 62), Riveros, Estigarribia (Cardozo 75), Aquino, Haedo Valdez.
Referee: Lopes (Brazil).

Barranquilla, 15 November 2011, 49,600

Colombia (1) 1 *(Pabon 45)*

Argentina (0) 2 *(Messi 61, Aguero 85)*

Colombia: Ospina; Yepes, Zuniga, Mosquera, Armero, Aguilar (Arias 77), Bolivar, Rodriguez, Ramos, Martinez J (Quintero 77), Pabon (Moreno 62).
Argentina: Romero; Burdisso (Desabato 38), Zabaleta, Rodriguez C, Fernandez, Mascherano, Brana, Guinazu (Aguero 46), Sosa, Messi, Higuain (Gago 86).
Referee: Filho (Brazil).

Quito, 15 November 2011, 34,481

Ecuador (0) 2 *(Mendez 70, Benitez 89)*

Peru (0) 0

Ecuador: Banguera; Campos, Erazo (Morante 37), Castillo, Saritama (Minda 81), Valencia, Ayovi W, Paredes, Benitez, Rojas (Mendez 46), Ayovi J.
Peru: Fernandez; Acasiete, Vilchez, Revoredo, Ramos, Vargas, Lobaton (Guevera 46), Retamoso, Guerrero, Pizarro (Chiroque 63), Farfan (Advincula 66).
Referee: Larrionda (Uruguay).

San Cristobal, 15 November 2011, 33,351

Venezuela (1) 1 *(Vizcarrondo 26)*

Bolivia (0) 0

Venezuela: Vega; Amorebieta, Vizcarrondo, Rosales, Cichero, Arango, Gonzalez (Feltscher F 63), Rincon, Julio Alvarez (Lucena 72), Maldonado (Feltscher R 78), Rondon J.
Bolivia: Arias; Raldes, Gutierrez, Christian Vargas, Rivero, Robles, Chavez, Cardozo (Andaveris 78), Marcelo Martins, Escobar (Campos 59), Segovia (Arce 59).
Referee: Buckley (Peru).

Buenos Aires, 2 June 2012, 50,000

Argentina (3) 4 *(Aguero 19, Higuain 29, Messi 31, Di Maria 76)*

Ecuador (0) 0

Argentina: Romero; Garay, Zabaleta, Gago, Di Maria (Maxi Rodriguez 82), Higuain (Lavezzi 73), Messi, Mascherano, Rodriguez C, Aguero (Sosa 62), Fernandez.
Ecuador: Dominguez; Guagua, Noboa, Ayovi W, Benitez (Ibarra 84), Suarez (Montero 46), Quinonez, Valencia, Saritama (Ayovi J 39), Achilier, Campos.
Referee: Rivera (Peru).

La Paz, 2 June 2012, 34,389

Bolivia (0) 0

Chile (1) 2 *(Aranguiz 45, Vidal 83)*

Bolivia: Vaca; Mendez, Gutierrez, Vargas, Rivero, Flores, Arce, Campos (Cardozo 56), Chumacero, Pedriel (Andaveris 70), Escobar (Pena 73).
Chile: Bravo; Contreras, Gonzalez O, Sanchez, Vidal, Suazo (Vargas 78), Rojas, Fernandez (Figueroa 73), Mena, Aranguiz (Leal 87), Diaz.
Referee: Intriago (Ecuador).

Montevideo, 2 June 2012, 57,000

Uruguay (1) 1 *(Forlan 38)*

Venezuela (0) 1 *(Rondon J 84)*

Uruguay: Muslera; Lugano (Coates 78), Godin, Suarez, Forlan (Abreu 88), Pereira A, Perez (Gonzalez 75), Pereira M, Arevalo, Cavani, Caceres.
Venezuela: Vega; Vizcarrondo, Amorebieta, Cichero, Rincon, Seijas (Perozo 88), Di Giorgi (Orozco 75), Rosales, Arango, Feltscher (Fedor 55), Rondon J.
Referee: Arias (Paraguay).

Lima, 3 June 2012, 35,724

Peru (0) 0

Colombia (0) 1 *(Rodriguez 51)*

Peru: Penny; Galliquio, Carrillo (Farfan 85), Guerrero, Revoredo (Rui Diaz 68), Ramos, Lobaton (Chiroque 57), Cruzado, Votun, Ramirez, Alvarez.
Colombia: Ospina; Yepes, Cuadrado (Ramirez 72), Sanchez, Armero, Falcao, Rodriguez (Martinez J 90), Pabon, Guarin (Mejia 86), Perea, Mosquera.
Referee: Pitana (Argentina).

La Paz, 9 June 2012, 17,320

Bolivia (1) 3 *(Pena 10, Escobar 70, 80)*

Paraguay (0) 1 *(Riveros 83)*

Bolivia: Galarza; Valverde, Vargas, Jimenez, Flores, Martins (Andaveris 84), Escobar (Cardozo 85), Pena, Chumacero, Mojica (Chavez 73), Barba.
Paraguay: Villar; Roman, Aranda (Perez 74), Zeballos, Mazacotte, Da Silva, Ramos (Benitez 58), Riveros, Torres, Valdez, Martinez.
Referee: Silvera (Uruguay).

Puerto La Cruz, 9 June 2012, 35,000

Venezuela (0) 0

Chile (0) 2 *(Fernandez 85, Aranguiz 90)*

Venezuela: Vega; Vizcarrondo, Chicero, Fedor (Del Valle 63), Seijas (Orozco 82), Di Giorgi, Rosales, Arango, Perozo, Rondon J, Alvarez (Guerra 63).
Chile: Bravo; Contreras (Figueroa 65), Gonzalez O, Sanchez, Vidal, Suazo (Pinto 79), Rojas (Gonzalez M 30), Fernandez, Mena, Aranguiz, Diaz.
Referee: Buitrago (Colombia).

Quito, 10 June 2012, 37,353

Ecuador (0) 1 *(Benitez 54)*

Colombia (0) 0

Ecuador: Dominguez; Erazo, Paredes, Noboa■, Rojas (Mendez 72), Montero (Saritama 78), Ayovi W, Benitez (Minda 90), Castillo, Valencia, Campos.
Colombia: Ospina; Yepes, Sanchez, Armero, Falcao, Rodriguez, Pabon, Guarin (Cuadrado 66), Perea (Zuniga 35), Soto (Muriel 73), Mosquera.
Referee: Seneme (Brazil).

Montevideo, 10 June 2012, 55,000

Uruguay (2) 4 *(Coates 15, Pereira M 30, Rodriguez C 63, Eguren 90)*

Peru (1) 2 *(Godin 40 (og), Guerrero 48)*

Uruguay: Muslera; Godin, Coates, Suarez (Eguren 90), Forlan (Rodriguez C 60), Pereira A (Ramirez 60), Perez, Pereira M, Arevalo, Cavani, Caceres.
Peru: Penny; Galliquio, Gonzales (Lobaton 46), Guerrero, Fernandez (Carrillo 76), Ramos, Advincula (Cueva 68), Cruzado, Yotun, Ramirez, Alvarez.
Referee: Pedro (Brazil).

OCEANIA

Samoa 1, American Samoa 0; Tonga 2, Cook Islands 1; Samoa 1, Tonga 1; American Samoa 1, Cook Islands 1; Cook Islands 2, Samoa 3; American Samoa 2, Tonga 1; American Samoa 2, Tonga 1; Cook Islands 2, Samoa 3; American Samoa 1, Cook Islands 1; Samoa 1, Tonga 1; Tonga 2, Cook Islands 1; Samoa 1, American Samoa 0; Samoa 1, Tahiti 10; Vanuatu 2, New Caldedonia 5; Fiji 0, New Zealand 1; Solomon Islands 1, Papua New Guinea 0; Vanuatu 5, Samoa 0; Tahiti 4, New Caledonia 3; Papua New Guinea 1, New Zealand 2; Fiji 0, Solomon Islands 0; New Caledonia 9, Samoa 0; Tahiti 4, Vanuatu 1; Papua New Guinea 1, Fiji 1; New Zealand 1, Solomon Islands 1; Samoa 1, Tahiti 10; Vanuatu 2, New Caledonia 5; Fiji 0, New Zealand 1; Vanuatu 5, Samoa 0; Tahiti 1, Solomon Islands 0; New Zealand 0, New Caledonia 2; Solomon Islands 3, New Zealand 4; Tahiti 1, New Caledonia 0.
The four semi-finalists from Round 2 are: New Caledonia, New Zealand, Solomon Islands and Tahiti.

ASIA

Singapore 0, China 4; Jordan 1, Iraq 3; Kuwait 2, UAE 1; North Korea 1, Japan 0; Lebanon 2, South Korea 1; Tajikistan 0, Japan 4; UAE 0, South Korea 2; Iraq 1, China 0; Kuwait 0, Lebanon 1; Jordan 2, Singapore 0; Uzbekistan 1, North Korea 0; Oman 1, Australia 0; Bahrain 1, Iran 1; Qatar 4, Indonesia 0; Saudi Arabia 3, Thailand 0; Uzbekistan 3, Tajikistan 0; Thailand 0, Australia 1; Qatar 0, Bahrain 0; Indonesia 1, Iran 4; Singapore 0, China 4; Saudi Arabia 0, Oman 0; Tajikistan 1, North Korea 1; Oman 2, Thailand 0; China 3, Jordan 1; UAE 4, Lebanon 2; Bahrain 10, Indonesia 0; Iraq 7, Singapore 1; Iran 2, Qatar 2; Japan 0, Uzbekistan 1; Australia 4, Saudi Arabia 2; South Korea 2, Kuwait 0; Uzbekistan 0, Iran 1; Jordan 1, Iraq 1; Japan 3, Oman 0; Lebanon 0, Qatar 1; Oman 0, Australia 0; Lebanon 1, Uzbekistan 1; Qatar 1, South Korea 4; Japan 6, Jordan 0; Iraq 1, Oman 1; South Korea 3, Lebanon 0; Iran 0, Qatar 0; Australia 1, Japan 1.

CONCACAF

Panama 3, Dominica 0; Curacao 6, US Virgin Islands 1; El Salvador 4, Surinam 0; Canada 4, St Kitts & Nevis 0; Trinidad & Tobago 3, Guyana 0 (match awarded); Grenada 1, Guatemala 4; St Vincent & the Grenadines 0, Belize 2; Haiti 2, Antigua & Barbuda 1; Barbados 1, Bermuda 2; Puerto Rico 3, St Lucia 0; Cayman Islands 1, Dominican Republic 1; Surinam 1, El Salvador 3; Guyana 2, Trinidad & Tobago 1; Dominican Republic 4, Cayman Islands 0; Bermuda 2, Barbados 1; Dominican Republic 4, Cayman Islands 0; Bermuda 2, Barbados 1; Belize 1, St Vincent & the Grenadines 1; US Virgin Islands 0, Curacao 3; Nicaragua 1, Dominica 0; Antigua & Barbuda 1, Haiti 0; Guyana 2, Trinidad & Tobago 1; St Kitts & Nevis 0, Canada 0; St Lucia 0, Puerto Rico 4 (match awarded); Guatemala 3, Grenada 0; Jamaica 2, Guatemala 1; USA 3, Antigua & Barbuda 1; Mexico 3, Guyana 1; Costa Rica 2, El Salvador 2; Cuba 0, Canada 1; Honduras 0, Panama 2; Guatemala 1, USA 1; Antigua & Barbuda 0, Jamaica 0; El Salvador 1, Mexico 2; Guyana 0, Costa Rica 4; Panama 1, Cuba 0; Canada 0, Honduras 0.

AFRICA

ROUND ONE FIRST LEG

St Thomas & Principe 0, Congo 5; Djibouti 0, Namibia 4; Comoros 0, Mozambique 1; Eritrea 1, Rwanda 1; Swaziland 1, DR Congo 3; Equatorial Guinea 2, Madagascar 0; Chad 1, Tanzania 2; Guinea-Bissau 1, Togo 1; Seychelles 0, Kenya 3; Lesotho 1, Burundi 0; Somalia 0, Ethiopia 0.

ROUND ONE SECOND LEG

Congo 1, St Thomas & Principe 1; Namibia 4, Djibouti 0; Mozambique 4, Comoros 1; Rwanda 3, Eritrea 1; DR Congo 5, Swaziland 1; Madagascar 2, Equatorial Guinea 1; Tanzania 0, Chad 1; Togo 1, Guinea-Bissau 0; Kenya 4, Seychelles 0; Burundi 2, Lesotho 2; Ethiopia 5, Somalia 0.

ROUND TWO

GROUP A	*P*	*W*	*D*	*L*	*F*	*A*	*Pts*
Ethiopia	2	1	1	0	3	1	4
Central African Rep	2	2	0	1	2	2	3
South Africa	2	0	2	0	2	2	2
Botswana	2	0	1	1	1	3	1

GROUP B	*P*	*W*	*D*	*L*	*F*	*A*	*Pts*
Tunisia	2	2	0	0	5	2	6
Sierra Leone	2	1	1	0	4	3	4
Equatorial Guinea	2	0	1	1	3	5	1
Cape Verde Islands	2	0	0	2	2	4	0

GROUP C	*P*	*W*	*D*	*L*	*F*	*A*	*Pts*
Ivory Coast	2	1	1	0	4	2	4
Tanzania	2	1	0	1	2	3	3
Morocco	2	0	2	0	3	3	2
Gambia	2	0	1	1	2	3	1

GROUP D	*P*	*W*	*D*	*L*	*F*	*A*	*Pts*
Sudan	2	1	1	0	2	0	4
Ghana	2	1	0	1	7	1	3
Zambia	2	1	0	1	1	2	3
Lesotho	2	0	1	1	0	7	1

GROUP E	*P*	*W*	*D*	*L*	*F*	*A*	*Pts*
Congo	2	1	1	0	1	0	4
Gabon	2	1	1	0	1	0	4
Burkina Faso	2	0	1	1	0	1	1
Niger	2	0	1	1	0	1	1

GROUP F	*P*	*W*	*D*	*L*	*F*	*A*	*Pts*
Nigeria	2	1	1	0	2	1	4
Namibia	2	1	0	1	1	1	3
Malawi	2	0	2	0	1	1	2
Kenya	2	0	1	1	0	1	1

GROUP G	*P*	*W*	*D*	*L*	*F*	*A*	*Pts*
Egypt	2	2	0	0	5	2	6
Guinea	2	1	0	1	3	3	3
Zambabwe	2	0	1	1	0	1	1
Mozambique	2	0	1	1	0	2	1

GROUP H	*P*	*W*	*D*	*L*	*F*	*A*	*Pts*
Benin	2	1	1	0	2	1	4
Algeria	2	1	0	1	5	2	3
Mali	2	1	0	1	2	2	3
Rwanda	2	0	1	1	1	5	1

GROUP I	*P*	*W*	*D*	*L*	*F*	*A*	*Pts*
Libya	2	1	1	0	3	2	4
DR Congo	2	1	0	1	2	1	3
Cameroon	2	1	0	1	2	2	3
Togo	2	0	1	1	1	3	1

GROUP J	*P*	*W*	*D*	*L*	*F*	*A*	*Pts*
Senegal	2	1	1	0	4	2	4
Uganda	2	0	2	0	2	2	2
Angola	2	0	2	0	1	1	2
Liberia	2	0	1	1	1	3	1

WORLD CUP 2014 FIXTURES

EUROPE

GROUP A

7 September 2012 – Wales v Belgium; Croatia v Macedonia
8 September 2012 – Scotland v Serbia
11 September 2012 – Scotland v Macedonia; Belgium v Croatia; Serbia v Wales
12 October 2012 – Wales v Scotland; Serbia v Belgium; Macedonia v Croatia
16 October 2012 – Belgium v Scotland; Macedonia v Serbia; Croatia v Wales
22 March 2013 – Croatia v Serbia; Scotland v Wales; Macedonia v Belgium
26 March 2013 – Wales v Croatia; Serbia v Scotland; Belgium v Macedonia
7 June 2013 – Belgium v Serbia; Croatia v Scotland
6 September 2013 – Macedonia v Wales; Serbia v Croatia; Scotland v Belgium
10 September 2013 – Macedonia v Scotland; Wales v Serbia
11 October 2013 – Wales v Macedonia; Croatia v Belgium
15 October 2013 – Scotland v Croatia; Belgium v Wales; Serbia v Macedonia

GROUP B

7 September 2012 – Malta v Armenia; Bulgaria v Italy
8 September 2012 – Denmark v Czech Republic
11 September 2012 – Italy v Malta; Bulgaria v Armenia
12 October 2012 – Bulgaria v Denmark; Czech Republic v Malta; Armenia v Italy
16 October 2012 – Czech Republic v Bulgaria; Italy v Denmark
22 March 2013 – Czech Republic v Denmark; Bulgaria v Malta
26 March 2013 – Armenia v Czech Republic; Denmark v Bulgaria; Malta v Italy
7 June 2013 – Armenia v Malta
8 June 2013 – Czech Republic v Italy
11 June 1013 – Denmark v Armenia
6 September 2013 – Malta v Denmark; Italy v Bulgaria; Czech Republic v Armenia
10 September 2013 – Malta v Bulgaria; Italy v Czech Republic; Armenia v Denmark
11 October 2013 – Armenia v Bulgaria; Malta v Czech Republic; Denmark v Italy
15 October 2013 – Italy v Armenia; Bulgaria v Czech Republic; Denmark v Malta

GROUP C

7 September 2012 – Germany v Faeroes; Kazakhstan v Republic of Ireland
11 September 2012 – Austria v Germany; Sweden v Kazakhstan
12 October 2012 – Faeroes v Sweden; Kazakhstan v Austria; Republic of Ireland v Germany
16 October 2012 – Faeroes v Republic of Ireland; Germany v Sweden; Austria v Kazakhstan

22 March 2013 – Sweden v Republic of Ireland; Austria v Faeroes; Kazakhstan v Germany
26 March 2013 – Republic of Ireland v Austria; Germany v Kazakhstan
7 June 2013 – Republic of Ireland v Faeroes; Austria v Sweden
11 June 2013 – Sweden v Faeroes
6 September 2013 – Republic of Ireland v Sweden; Germany v Austria; Kazakhstan v Faeroes
10 September 2013 – Kazakhstan v Sweden; Austria v Republic of Ireland; Faeroes v Germany
11 October 2013 – Sweden v Austria; Faeroes v Kazakhstan; Germany v Republic of Ireland
15 October 2013 – Faeroes v Austria; Republic of Ireland v Kazakhstan; Sweden v Germany

GROUP D
7 September 2012 – Andorra v Hungary; Holland v Turkey; Estonia v Romania
11 September 2012 – Turkey v Estonia; Hungary v Holland; Romania v Andorra
12 October 2012 – Holland v Andorra; Turkey v Romania; Estonia v Hungary
16 October 2012 – Andorra v Estonia; Hungary v Turkey; Romania v Holland
22 March 2013 – Andorra v Turkey; Holland v Estonia; Hungary v Romania
26 March 2013 – Holland v Romania; Estonia v Andorra; Turkey v Hungary
6 September 2013 – Estonia v Holland; Turkey v Andorra; Romania v Hungary
10 September 2013 – Romania v Turkey; Hungary v Estonia; Andorra v Holland
11 October 2013 – Holland v Hungary; Andorra v Romania; Estonia v Turkey
15 October 2013 – Hungary v Andorra; Romania v Estonia; Turkey v Holland

GROUP E
7 September 2012 – Slovenia v Switzerland; Albania v Cyprus; Iceland v Norway
11 September 2012 – Cyprus v Iceland; Norway v Slovenia; Switzerland v Albania
12 October 2012 – Albania v Iceland; Switzerland v Norway; Slovenia v Cyprus
16 October 2012 – Albania v Slovenia; Cyprus v Norway; Iceland v Switzerland
22 March 2013 – Switzerland v Cyprus; Slovenia v Iceland; Norway v Albania
7 June 2013 – Iceland v Slovenia; Cyprus v Switzerland; Albania v Norway
6 September 2013 – Norway v Cyprus; Switzerland v Iceland; Slovenia v Albania
10 September 2013 – Iceland v Albania; Norway v Switzerland; Cyprus v Slovenia
11 October 2013 – Slovenia v Norway; Albania v Switzerland; Iceland v Cyprus
15 October 2013 – Norway v Iceland; Switzerland v Slovenia; Cyprus v Albania

GROUP F
7 September 2012 – Luxembourg v Portugal; Russia v Northern Ireland; Azerbaijan v Israel
11 September 2012 – Northern Ireland v Luxembourg; Israel v Russia; Portugal v Azerbaijan
12 October 2012 – Luxembourg v Israel; Russia v Portugal
16 October 2012 – Israel v Luxembourg; Russia v Azerbaijan; Portugal v Northern Ireland
14 November 2012 – Northern Ireland v Azerbaijan
22 March 2013 – Luxembourg v Azerbaijan; Northern Ireland v Russia; Israel v Portugal
26 March 2013 – Northern Ireland v Israel; Azerbaijan v Portugal
7 June 2013 – Azerbaijan v Luxembourg; Portugal v Russia
6 September 2013 – Russia v Luxembourg; Northern Ireland v Portugal; Israel v Azerbaijan
10 September 2013 – Russia v Israel; Luxembourg v Northern Ireland
11 October 2013 – Portugal v Israel; Azerbaijan v Northern Ireland; Luxembourg v Russia
15 October 2013 – Portugal v Luxembourg; Azerbaijan v Russia; Israel v Northern Ireland

GROUP G
7 September 2012 – Latvia v Greece; Lithuania v Slovakia; Liechtenstein v Bosnia
11 September 2012 – Greece v Lithuania; Slovakia v Liechtenstein; Bosnia v Latvia
12 October 2012 – Greece v Bosnia; Liechtenstein v Lithuania; Slovakia v Latvia
16 October 2012 – Bosnia v Lithuania; Latvia v Liechtenstein; Slovakia v Greece
22 March 2013 – Bosnia v Greece; Slovakia v Lithuania; Liechteinstein v Latvia
7 June 2013 – Latvia v Bosnia; Lithuania v Greece; Liechtenstein v Slovakia
6 September 2013 – Latvia v Lithuania; Liechtenstein v Greece; Bosnia v Slovakia
10 September 2013 – Greece v Latvia; Slovakia v Bosnia; Lithuania v Liechtenstein
11 October 2013 – Bosnia v Liechtenstein; Lithuania v Latvia; Greece v Slovakia
15 October 2013 – Latvia v Slovakia; Greece v Liechtenstein; Lithuania v Bosnia

GROUP H
7 September 2012 – Montenegro v Poland; Moldova v England
11 September 2012 – Poland v Moldova; San Marino v Montenegro; England v Ukraine
12 October 2012 – England v San Marino; Moldova v Ukraine
16 October 2012 – Poland v England; Ukraine v Montenegro; San Marino v Moldova
14 November 2012 – Montenegro v San Marino
22 March 2013 – San Marino v England; Moldova v Montenegro; Poland v Ukraine
26 March 2013 – Montenegro v England; Ukraine v Moldova; Poland v San Marino
7 June 2013 – Moldova v Poland; Montenegro v Ukraine
6 September 2013 – Poland v Montenegro; Ukraine v San Marino; England v Moldova
10 September 2013 – San Marino v Poland; Ukraine v England
11 October 2013 – Ukraine v Poland; England v Montenegro; Moldova v San Marino
15 October 2013 – England v Poland; San Marino v Ukraine; Montenegro v Moldova

GROUP I
7 September 2012 – Georgia v Belarus; Finland v France
11 September 2012 – Georgia v Spain; France v Belarus
12 October 2012 – Belarus v Spain; Finland v Georgia
16 October 2012 – Spain v France; Belarus v Georgia
22 March 2013 – France v Georgia; Spain v Finland
26 March 2013 – France v Spain
7 June 2013 – Finland v Belarus
11 June 2013 – Belarus v Finland
6 September 2013 – Georgia v France; Finland v Spain
10 September 2013 – Belarus v France; Georgia v Finland
11 October 2013 – Spain v Belarus
15 October 2013 – France v Finland; Spain v Georgia

Competition still being played.

OLYMPICS 2012

Competition from 26 July to 11 August.

GROUP A
Great Britain, Senegal, UAE, Uruguay

GROUP B
Gabon, Mexico, South Korea, Switzerland

GROUP C
Belarus, Brazil, Egypt, New Zealand

GROUP D
Honduras, Japan, Morocco, Spain

THE WORLD CUP 1930–2010

Year	Winners		Runners-up		Venue	Attendance	Referee
1930	Uruguay	4	Argentina	2	Montevideo	90,000	Langenus (B)
1934	Italy*	2	Czechoslovakia	1	Rome	50,000	Eklind (Se)
1938	Italy	4	Hungary	2	Paris	45,000	Capdeville (F)
1950	Uruguay	2	Brazil	1	Rio de Janeiro	199,854	Reader (E)
1954	West Germany	3	Hungary	2	Berne	60,000	Ling (E)
1958	Brazi	5	Sweden	2	Stockholm	49,737	Guigue (F)
1962	Brazil	3	Czechoslovakia	1	Santiago	68,679	Latychev (USSR)
1966	England*	4	West Germany	2	Wembley	93,802	Dienst (Sw)
1970	Brazil	4	Italy	1	Mexico City	107,412	Glockner (EG)
1974	West Germany	2	Holland	1	Munich	77,833	Taylor (E)
1978	Argentina*	3	Holland	1	Buenos Aires	77,000	Gonella (I)
1982	Italy	3	West Germany	1	Madrid	90,080	Coelho (Br)
1986	Argentina	3	West Germany	2	Mexico City	114,580	Filho (Br)
1990	West Germany	1	Argentina	0	Rome	73,603	Mendez (Mex)
1994	Brazil*	0	Italy	0	Los Angeles	94,194	Puhl (H)
	(Brazil won 3-2 on penalties)						
1998	France	3	Brazil	0	St-Denis	75,000	Belqola (Mor)
2002	Brazil	2	Germany	0	Yokohama	69,029	Collina (I)
2006	Italy*	1	France	1	Berlin	69,000	Elizondo (Arg)
	(Italy won 5-3 on penalties)						
2010	Spain	1	Holland	0	Johannesburg	84,490	Webb (E)

*(*After extra time)*

GOALSCORING AND ATTENDANCES IN WORLD CUP FINAL ROUNDS

Venue	*Matches*	*Goals (av)*	*Attendance (av)*
1930 Uruguay	18	70 (3.9)	434,500 (24,138)
1934 Italy	17	70 (4.1)	395,000 (23,235)
1938 France	18	84 (4.6)	483,000 (26,833)
1950 Brazil	22	88 (4.0)	1,337,000 (60,772)
1954 Switzerland	26	140 (5.4)	943,000 (36,270)
1958 Sweden	35	126 (3.6)	868,000 (24,800)
1962 Chile	32	89 (2.8)	776,000 (24,250)
1966 England	32	89 (2.8)	1,614,677 (50,458)
1970 Mexico	32	95 (2.9)	1,673,975 (52,311)
1974 West Germany	38	97 (2.5)	1,774,022 (46,684)
1978 Argentina	38	102 (2.7)	1,610,215 (42,374)
1982 Spain	52	146 (2.8)	2,064,364 (38,816)
1986 Mexico	52	132 (2.5)	2,441,731 (46,956)
1990 Italy	52	115 (2.2)	2,515,168 (48,368)
1994 USA	52	141 (2.7)	3,567,415 (68,604)
1998 France	64	171 (2.6)	2,775,400 (43,366)
2002 Japan/S. Korea	64	161 (2.5)	2,705,566 (42,274)
2006 Germany	64	147 (2.3)	3,354,646 (52,416)
2010 South Africa	64	145 (2.3)	3,178,856 (49,670)

LEADING GOALSCORERS

Year	*Player*	*Goals*
1930	Guillermo Stabile (Argentina)	8
1934	Angelo Schiavio (Italy), Oldrich Nejedly (Czechoslovakia), Edmund Conen (Germany)	4
1938	Leonidas da Silva (Brazil)	8
1950	Ademir (Brazil)	9
1954	Sandor Kocsis (Hungary)	11
1958	Just Fontaine (France)	13
1962	Valentin Ivanov (USSR), Leonel Sanchez (Chile), Garrincha, Vava (both Brazil), Florian Albert (Hungary), Drazen Jerkovic (Yugoslavia)	4
1966	Eusebio (Portugal)	9
1970	Gerd Muller (West Germany)	10
1974	Grzegorz Lato (Poland)	7
1978	Mario Kempes (Argentina)	6
1982	Paolo Rossi (Italy)	6
1986	Gary Lineker (England)	6
1990	Salvatore Schillaci (Italy)	6
1994	Oleg Salenko (Russia) Hristo Stoichkov (Bulgaria)	6
1998	Davor Suker (Croatia)	6
2002	Ronaldo (Brazil)	8
2006	Miroslav Klose (Germany)	5
2010	Thomas Muller (Germany), David Villa (Spain), Wesley Sneijder (Holland), Diego Forlan (Uruguay)	5

EUROPEAN FOOTBALL CHAMPIONSHIP

(formerly EUROPEAN NATIONS' CUP)

Year	*Winners*		*Runners-up*		*Venue*	*Attendance*
1960	USSR	2	Yugoslavia	1	Paris	17,966
1964	Spain	2	USSR	1	Madrid	120,000
1968	Italy After 1-1 draw	2	Yugoslavia	0	Rome	60,000 75,000
1972	West Germany	3	USSR	0	Brussels	43,437
1976	Czechoslovakia	2	West Germany	2	Belgrade	45,000
	(Czechoslovakia won on penalties)					
1980	West Germany	2	Belgium	1	Rome	47,864
1984	France	2	Spain	0	Paris	48,000
1988	Holland	2	USSR	0	Munich	72,308
1992	Denmark	2	Germany	0	Gothenburg	37,800
1996	Germany	2	Czech Republic	1	Wembley	73,611
	(Germany won on sudden death)					
2000	France	2	Italy	1	Rotterdam	50,000
	(France won on sudden death)					
2004	Greece	1	Portugal	0	Lisbon	62,865
2008	Spain	1	Germany	0	Vienna	51,428
2012	Spain	4	Italy	0	Kiev	63,170

BRITISH AND IRISH INTERNATIONAL RESULTS 1872–2012

Note: In the results that follow, WC=World Cup, EC=European Championship, UI=Umbro International Trophy. TF = Tournoi de France. NC = Nations Cup. For Ireland, read Northern Ireland from 1921. *After extra time.

ENGLAND v SCOTLAND

Played: 110; England won 45, Scotland won 41, Drawn 24. Goals: England 192, Scotland 169.

			E	*S*
1872	30 Nov	Glasgow	0	0
1873	8 Mar	Kennington Oval	4	2
1874	7 Mar	Glasgow	1	2
1875	6 Mar	Kennington Oval	2	2
1876	4 Mar	Glasgow	0	3
1877	3 Mar	Kennington Oval	1	3
1878	2 Mar	Glasgow	2	7
1879	5 Apr	Kennington Oval	5	4
1880	13 Mar	Glasgow	4	5
1881	12 Mar	Kennington Oval	1	6
1882	11 Mar	Glasgow	1	5
1883	10 Mar	Sheffield	2	3
1884	15 Mar	Glasgow	0	1
1885	21 Mar	Kennington Oval	1	1
1886	31 Mar	Glasgow	1	1
1887	19 Mar	Blackburn	2	3
1888	17 Mar	Glasgow	5	0
1889	13 Apr	Kennington Oval	2	3
1890	5 Apr	Glasgow	1	1
1891	6 Apr	Blackburn	2	1
1892	2 Apr	Glasgow	4	1
1893	1 Apr	Richmond	5	2
1894	7 Apr	Glasgow	2	2
1895	6 Apr	Everton	3	0
1896	4 Apr	Glasgow	1	2
1897	3 Apr	Crystal Palace	1	2
1898	2 Apr	Glasgow	3	1
1899	8 Apr	Birmingham	2	1
1900	7 Apr	Glasgow	1	4
1901	30 Mar	Crystal Palace	2	2
1902	3 Mar	Birmingham	2	2
1903	4 Apr	Sheffield	1	2
1904	9 Apr	Glasgow	1	0
1905	1 Apr	Crystal Palace	1	0
1906	7 Apr	Glasgow	1	2
1907	6 Apr	Newcastle	1	1
1908	4 Apr	Glasgow	1	1
1909	3 Apr	Crystal Palace	2	0
1910	2 Apr	Glasgow	0	2
1911	1 Apr	Everton	1	1
1912	23 Mar	Glasgow	1	1
1913	5 Apr	Chelsea	1	0
1914	14 Apr	Glasgow	1	3
1920	10 Apr	Sheffield	5	4
1921	9 Apr	Glasgow	0	3
1922	8 Apr	Aston Villa	0	1
1923	14 Apr	Glasgow	2	2
1924	12 Apr	Wembley	1	1
1925	4 Apr	Glasgow	0	2
1926	17 Apr	Manchester	0	1
1927	2 Apr	Glasgow	2	1
1928	31 Mar	Wembley	1	5
1929	13 Apr	Glasgow	0	1
1930	5 Apr	Wembley	5	2
1931	28 Mar	Glasgow	0	2

			E	*S*
1932	9 Apr	Wembley	3	0
1933	1 Apr	Glasgow	1	2
1934	14 Apr	Wembley	3	0
1935	6 Apr	Glasgow	0	2
1936	4 Apr	Wembley	1	1
1937	17 Apr	Glasgow	1	3
1938	9 Apr	Wembley	0	1
1939	15 Apr	Glasgow	2	1
1947	12 Apr	Wembley	1	1
1948	10 Apr	Glasgow	2	0
1949	9 Apr	Wembley	1	3
WC1950	15 Apr	Glasgow	1	0
1951	14 Apr	Wembley	2	3
1952	5 Apr	Glasgow	2	1
1953	18 Apr	Wembley	2	2
WC1954	3 Apr	Glasgow	4	2
1955	2 Apr	Wembley	7	2
1956	14 Apr	Glasgow	1	1
1957	6 Apr	Wembley	2	1
1958	19 Apr	Glasgow	4	0
1959	11 Apr	Wembley	1	0
1960	9 Apr	Glasgow	1	1
1961	15 Apr	Wembley	9	3
1962	14 Apr	Glasgow	0	2
1963	6 Apr	Wembley	1	2
1964	11 Apr	Glasgow	0	1
1965	10 Apr	Wembley	2	2
1966	2 Apr	Glasgow	4	3
EC1967	15 Apr	Wembley	2	3
EC1968	24 Jan	Glasgow	1	1
1969	10 May	Wembley	4	1
1970	25 Apr	Glasgow	0	0
1971	22 May	Wembley	3	1
1972	27 May	Glasgow	1	0
1973	14 Feb	Glasgow	5	0
1973	19 May	Wembley	1	0
1974	18 May	Glasgow	0	2
1975	24 May	Wembley	5	1
1976	15 May	Glasgow	1	2
1977	4 June	Wembley	1	2
1978	20 May	Glasgow	1	0
1979	26 May	Wembley	3	1
1980	24 May	Glasgow	2	0
1981	23 May	Wembley	0	1
1982	29 May	Glasgow	1	0
1983	1 June	Wembley	2	0
1984	26 May	Glasgow	1	1
1985	25 May	Glasgow	0	1
1986	23 Apr	Wembley	2	1
1987	23 May	Glasgow	0	0
1988	21 May	Wembley	1	0
1989	27 May	Glasgow	2	0
EC1996	15 June	Wembley	2	0
EC1999	13 Nov	Glasgow	2	0
EC1999	17 Nov	Wembley	0	1

ENGLAND v WALES

Played: 101; England won 66, Wales won 14, Drawn 21. Goals: England 245, Wales 90.

			E	*W*
1879	18 Jan	Kennington Oval	2	1
1880	15 Mar	Wrexham	3	2
1881	26 Feb	Blackburn	0	1

			E	*W*
1882	13 Mar	Wrexham	3	5
1883	3 Feb	Kennington Oval	5	0
1884	17 Mar	Wrexham	4	0

			E	*W*
1885	14 Mar	Blackburn	1	1
1886	29 Mar	Wrexham	3	1
1887	26 Feb	Kennington Oval	4	0
1888	4 Feb	Crewe	5	1
1889	23 Feb	Stoke	4	1
1890	15 Mar	Wrexham	3	1
1891	7 May	Sunderland	4	1
1892	5 Mar	Wrexham	2	0
1893	13 Mar	Stoke	6	0
1894	12 Mar	Wrexham	5	1
1895	18 Mar	Queen's Club, Kensington	1	1
1896	16 Mar	Cardiff	9	1
1897	29 Mar	Sheffield	4	0
1898	28 Mar	Wrexham	3	0
1899	20 Mar	Bristol	4	0
1900	26 Mar	Cardiff	1	1
1901	18 Mar	Newcastle	6	0
1902	3 Mar	Wrexham	0	0
1903	2 Mar	Portsmouth	2	1
1904	29 Feb	Wrexham	2	2
1905	27 Mar	Liverpool	3	1
1906	19 Mar	Cardiff	1	0
1907	18 Mar	Fulham	1	1
1908	16 Mar	Wrexham	7	1
1909	15 Mar	Nottingham	2	0
1910	14 Mar	Cardiff	1	0
1911	13 Mar	Millwall	3	0
1912	11 Mar	Wrexham	2	0
1913	17 Mar	Bristol	4	3
1914	16 Mar	Cardiff	2	0
1920	15 Mar	Highbury	1	2
1921	14 Mar	Cardiff	0	0
1922	13 Mar	Liverpool	1	0
1923	5 Mar	Cardiff	2	2
1924	3 Mar	Blackburn	1	2
1925	28 Feb	Swansea	2	1
1926	1 Mar	Crystal Palace	1	3
1927	12 Feb	Wrexham	3	3
1927	28 Nov	Burnley	1	2
1928	17 Nov	Swansea	3	2
1929	20 Nov	Chelsea	6	0
1930	22 Nov	Wrexham	4	0
1931	18 Nov	Liverpool	3	1
1932	16 Nov	Wrexham	0	0
1933	15 Nov	Newcastle	1	2
EC2011	6 Sept	Wembley	1	0

			E	*W*
1934	29 Sept	Cardiff	4	0
1936	5 Feb	Wolverhampton	1	2
1936	17 Oct	Cardiff	1	2
1937	17 Nov	Middlesbrough	2	1
1938	22 Oct	Cardiff	2	4
1946	13 Nov	Manchester	3	0
1947	18 Oct	Cardiff	3	0
1948	10 Nov	Aston Villa	1	0
wc1949	15 Oct	Cardiff	4	1
1950	15 Nov	Sunderland	4	2
1951	20 Oct	Cardiff	1	1
1952	12 Nov	Wembley	5	2
wc1953	10 Oct	Cardiff	4	1
1954	10 Nov	Wembley	3	2
1955	27 Oct	Cardiff	1	2
1956	14 Nov	Wembley	3	1
1957	19 Oct	Cardiff	4	0
1958	26 Nov	Aston Villa	2	2
1959	17 Oct	Cardiff	1	1
1960	23 Nov	Wembley	5	1
1961	14 Oct	Cardiff	1	1
1962	21 Oct	Wembley	4	0
1963	12 Oct	Cardiff	4	0
1964	18 Nov	Wembley	2	1
1965	2 Oct	Cardiff	0	0
EC1966	16 Nov	Wembley	5	1
EC1967	21 Oct	Cardiff	3	0
1969	7 May	Wembley	2	1
1970	18 Apr	Cardiff	1	1
1971	19 May	Wembley	0	0
1972	20 May	Cardiff	3	0
wc1972	15 Nov	Cardiff	1	0
wc1973	24 Jan	Wembley	1	1
1973	15 May	Wembley	3	0
1974	11 May	Cardiff	2	0
1975	21 May	Wembley	2	2
1976	24 Mar	Wrexham	2	1
1976	8 May	Cardiff	1	0
1977	31 May	Wembley	0	1
1978	3 May	Cardiff	3	1
1979	23 May	Wembley	0	0
1980	17 May	Wrexham	1	4
1981	20 May	Wembley	0	0
1982	27 Apr	Cardiff	1	0
1983	23 Feb	Wembley	2	1
1984	2 May	Wrexham	0	1
wc2004	9 Oct	Old Trafford	2	0
wc2005	3 Sept	Cardiff	1	0
EC2011	26 Mar	Cardiff	2	0
EC2011	6 Sept	Wembley	1	0

ENGLAND v IRELAND

Played: 98; England won 75, Ireland won 7, Drawn 16. Goals: England 323, Ireland 81.

			E	*I*
1882	18 Feb	Belfast	13	0
1883	24 Feb	Liverpool	7	0
1884	23 Feb	Belfast	8	1
1885	28 Feb	Manchester	4	0
1886	13 Mar	Belfast	6	1
1887	5 Feb	Sheffield	7	0
1888	31 Mar	Belfast	5	1
1889	2 Mar	Everton	6	1
1890	15 Mar	Belfast	9	1
1891	7 Mar	Wolverhampton	6	1
1892	5 Mar	Belfast	2	0
1893	25 Feb	Birmingham	6	1
1894	3 Mar	Belfast	2	2
1895	9 Mar	Derby	9	0
1896	7 Mar	Belfast	2	0
1897	20 Feb	Nottingham	6	0
1898	5 Mar	Belfast	3	2
1899	18 Feb	Sunderland	13	2
1900	17 Mar	Dublin	2	0
1901	9 Mar	Southampton	3	0
1902	22 Mar	Belfast	1	0

			E	*I*
1903	14 Feb	Wolverhampton	4	0
1904	12 Mar	Belfast	3	1
1905	25 Feb	Middlesbrough	1	1
1906	17 Feb	Belfast	5	0
1907	16 Feb	Everton	1	0
1908	15 Feb	Belfast	3	1
1909	13 Feb	Bradford	4	0
1910	12 Feb	Belfast	1	1
1911	11 Feb	Derby	2	1
1912	10 Feb	Dublin	6	1
1913	15 Feb	Belfast	1	2
1914	14 Feb	Middlesbrough	0	3
1919	25 Oct	Belfast	1	1
1920	23 Oct	Sunderland	2	0
1921	22 Oct	Belfast	1	1
1922	21 Oct	West Bromwich	2	0
1923	20 Oct	Belfast	1	2
1924	22 Oct	Everton	3	1
1925	24 Oct	Belfast	0	0
1926	20 Oct	Liverpool	3	3
1927	22 Oct	Belfast	0	2

			E	*I*
1928	22 Oct	Everton	2	1
1929	19 Oct	Belfast	3	0
1930	20 Oct	Sheffield	5	1
1931	17 Oct	Belfast	6	2
1932	17 Oct	Blackpool	1	0
1933	14 Oct	Belfast	3	0
1935	6 Feb	Everton	2	1
1935	19 Oct	Belfast	3	1
1936	18 Nov	Stoke	3	1
1937	23 Oct	Belfast	5	1
1938	16 Nov	Manchester	7	0
1946	28 Sept	Belfast	7	2
1947	5 Nov	Everton	2	2
1948	9 Oct	Belfast	6	2
WC1949	16 Nov	Manchester	9	2
1950	7 Oct	Belfast	4	1
1951	14 Nov	Aston Villa	2	0
1952	4 Oct	Belfast	2	2
WC1953	11 Nov	Everton	3	1
1954	2 Oct	Belfast	2	0
1955	2 Nov	Wembley	3	0
1956	10 Oct	Belfast	1	1
1957	6 Nov	Wembley	2	3
1958	4 Oct	Belfast	3	3
1959	18 Nov	Wembley	2	1
1960	8 Oct	Belfast	5	2
1961	22 Nov	Wembley	1	1
1962	20 Oct	Belfast	3	1
1963	20 Nov	Wembley	8	3
1964	3 Oct	Belfast	4	3
1965	10 Nov	Wembley	2	1
EC1966	20 Oct	Belfast	2	0
EC1967	22 Nov	Wembley	2	0
1969	3 May	Belfast	3	1
1970	21 Apr	Wembley	3	1
1971	15 May	Belfast	1	0
1972	23 May	Wembley	0	1
1973	12 May	Everton	2	1
1974	15 May	Wembley	1	0
1975	17 May	Belfast	0	0
1976	11 May	Wembley	4	0
1977	28 May	Belfast	2	1
1978	16 May	Wembley	1	0
EC1979	7 Feb	Wembley	4	0
1979	19 May	Belfast	2	0
EC1979	17 Oct	Belfast	5	1
1980	20 May	Wembley	1	1
1982	23 Feb	Wembley	4	0
1983	28 May	Belfast	0	0
1984	24 Apr	Wembley	1	0
WC1985	27 Feb	Belfast	1	0
WC1985	13 Nov	Wembley	0	0
EC1986	15 Oct	Wembley	3	0
EC1987	1 Apr	Belfast	2	0
WC2005	26 Mar	Old Trafford	4	0
WC2005	7 Sept	Belfast	0	1

SCOTLAND v WALES

Played: 105; Scotland won 61, Wales won 21, Drawn 23. Goals: Scotland 241, Wales 120.

			S	*W*
1876	25 Mar	Glasgow	4	0
1877	5 Mar	Wrexham	2	0
1878	23 Mar	Glasgow	9	0
1879	7 Apr	Wrexham	3	0
1880	3 Apr	Glasgow	5	1
1881	14 Mar	Wrexham	5	1
1882	25 Mar	Glasgow	5	0
1883	12 Mar	Wrexham	3	0
1884	29 Mar	Glasgow	4	1
1885	23 Mar	Wrexham	8	1
1886	10 Apr	Glasgow	4	1
1887	21 Mar	Wrexham	2	0
1888	10 Mar	Edinburgh	5	1
1889	15 Apr	Wrexham	0	0
1890	22 Mar	Paisley	5	0
1891	21 Mar	Wrexham	4	3
1892	26 Mar	Edinburgh	6	1
1893	18 Mar	Wrexham	8	0
1894	24 Mar	Kilmarnock	5	2
1895	23 Mar	Wrexham	2	2
1896	21 Mar	Dundee	4	0
1897	20 Mar	Wrexham	2	2
1898	19 Mar	Motherwell	5	2
1899	18 Mar	Wrexham	6	0
1900	3 Feb	Aberdeen	5	2
1901	2 Mar	Wrexham	1	1
1902	15 Mar	Greenock	5	1
1903	9 Mar	Cardiff	1	0
1904	12 Mar	Dundee	1	1
1905	6 Mar	Wrexham	1	3
1906	3 Mar	Edinburgh	0	2
1907	4 Mar	Wrexham	0	1
1908	7 Mar	Dundee	2	1
1909	1 Mar	Wrexham	2	3
1910	5 Mar	Kilmarnock	1	0
1911	6 Mar	Cardiff	2	2
1912	2 Mar	Tynecastle	1	0
1913	3 Mar	Wrexham	0	0
1914	28 Feb	Glasgow	0	0
1920	26 Feb	Cardiff	1	1
1921	12 Feb	Aberdeen	2	1
1922	4 Feb	Wrexham	1	2
1923	17 Mar	Paisley	2	0
1924	16 Feb	Cardiff	0	2
1925	14 Feb	Tynecastle	3	1
1925	31 Oct	Cardiff	3	0
1926	30 Oct	Glasgow	3	0
1927	29 Oct	Wrexham	2	2
1928	27 Oct	Glasgow	4	2
1929	26 Oct	Cardiff	4	2
1930	25 Oct	Glasgow	1	1
1931	31 Oct	Wrexham	3	2
1932	26 Oct	Edinburgh	2	5
1933	4 Oct	Cardiff	2	3
1934	21 Nov	Aberdeen	3	2
1935	5 Oct	Cardiff	1	1
1936	2 Dec	Dundee	1	2
1937	30 Oct	Cardiff	1	2
1938	9 Nov	Edinburgh	3	2
1946	19 Oct	Wrexham	1	3
1947	12 Nov	Glasgow	1	2
1948	23 Oct	Cardiff	3	1
WC1949	9 Nov	Glasgow	2	0
1950	21 Oct	Cardiff	3	1
1951	14 Nov	Glasgow	0	1
1952	18 Oct	Cardiff	2	1
WC1953	4 Nov	Glasgow	3	3
1954	16 Oct	Cardiff	1	0
1955	9 Nov	Glasgow	2	0
1956	20 Oct	Cardiff	2	2
1957	13 Nov	Glasgow	1	1
1958	18 Oct	Cardiff	3	0
1959	4 Nov	Glasgow	1	1
1960	20 Oct	Cardiff	0	2
1961	8 Nov	Glasgow	2	0
1962	20 Oct	Cardiff	3	2
1963	20 Nov	Glasgow	2	1
1964	3 Oct	Cardiff	2	3
EC1965	24 Nov	Glasgow	4	1
EC1966	22 Oct	Cardiff	1	1
1967	22 Nov	Glasgow	3	2
1969	3 May	Wrexham	5	3

			S	W
1970	22 Apr	Glasgow	0	0
1971	15 May	Cardiff	0	0
1972	24 May	Glasgow	1	0
1973	12 May	Wrexham	2	0
1974	14 May	Glasgow	2	0
1975	17 May	Cardiff	2	2
1976	6 May	Glasgow	3	1
WC1976	17 Nov	Glasgow	1	0
1977	28 May	Wrexham	0	0
WC1977	12 Oct	Liverpool	2	0
1978	17 May	Glasgow	1	1
1979	19 May	Cardiff	0	3
1980	21 May	Glasgow	1	0
1981	16 May	Swansea	0	2
1982	24 May	Glasgow	1	0
1983	28 May	Cardiff	2	0
1984	28 Feb	Glasgow	2	1
WC1985	27 Mar	Glasgow	0	1
WC1985	10 Sept	Cardiff	1	1
1997	27 May	Kilmarnock	0	1
2004	18 Feb	Cardiff	0	4
2009	14 Nov	Cardiff	0	3
NC2011	25 May	Dublin	3	1

SCOTLAND v IRELAND

Played: 95; Scotland won 63, Ireland won 15, Drawn 17. Goals: Scotland 260, Ireland 81.

			S	I
1884	26 Jan	Belfast	5	0
1885	14 Mar	Glasgow	8	2
1886	20 Mar	Belfast	7	2
1887	19 Feb	Glasgow	4	1
1888	24 Mar	Belfast	10	2
1889	9 Mar	Glasgow	7	0
1890	29 Mar	Belfast	4	1
1891	28 Mar	Glasgow	2	1
1892	19 Mar	Belfast	3	2
1893	25 Mar	Glasgow	6	1
1894	31 Mar	Belfast	2	1
1895	30 Mar	Glasgow	3	1
1896	28 Mar	Belfast	3	3
1897	27 Mar	Glasgow	5	1
1898	26 Mar	Belfast	3	0
1899	25 Mar	Glasgow	9	1
1900	3 Mar	Belfast	3	0
1901	23 Feb	Glasgow	11	0
1902	1 Mar	Belfast	5	1
1902	9 Aug	Belfast	3	0
1903	21 Mar	Glasgow	0	2
1904	26 Mar	Dublin	1	1
1905	18 Mar	Glasgow	4	0
1906	17 Mar	Dublin	1	0
1907	16 Mar	Glasgow	3	0
1908	14 Mar	Dublin	5	0
1909	15 Mar	Glasgow	5	0
1910	19 Mar	Belfast	0	1
1911	18 Mar	Glasgow	2	0
1912	16 Mar	Belfast	4	1
1913	15 Mar	Dublin	2	1
1914	14 Mar	Belfast	1	1
1920	13 Mar	Glasgow	3	0
1921	26 Feb	Belfast	2	0
1922	4 Mar	Glasgow	2	1
1923	3 Mar	Belfast	1	0
1924	1 Mar	Glasgow	2	0
1925	28 Feb	Belfast	3	0
1926	27 Feb	Glasgow	4	0
1927	26 Feb	Belfast	2	0
1928	25 Feb	Glasgow	0	1
1929	23 Feb	Belfast	7	3
1930	22 Feb	Glasgow	3	1
1931	21 Feb	Belfast	0	0
1931	19 Sept	Glasgow	3	1
1932	12 Sept	Belfast	4	0
1933	16 Sept	Glasgow	1	2
1934	20 Oct	Belfast	1	2
1935	13 Nov	Edinburgh	2	1
1936	31 Oct	Belfast	3	1
1937	10 Nov	Aberdeen	1	1
1938	8 Oct	Belfast	2	0
1946	27 Nov	Glasgow	0	0
1947	4 Oct	Belfast	0	2
1948	17 Nov	Glasgow	3	2
1949	1 Oct	Belfast	8	2
1950	1 Nov	Glasgow	6	1
1951	6 Oct	Belfast	3	0
1952	5 Nov	Glasgow	1	1
1953	3 Oct	Belfast	3	1
1954	3 Nov	Glasgow	2	2
1955	8 Oct	Belfast	1	2
1956	7 Nov	Glasgow	1	0
1957	5 Oct	Belfast	1	1
1958	5 Nov	Glasgow	2	2
1959	3 Oct	Belfast	4	0
1960	9 Nov	Glasgow	5	2
1961	7 Oct	Belfast	6	1
1962	7 Nov	Glasgow	5	1
1963	12 Oct	Belfast	1	2
1964	25 Nov	Glasgow	3	2
1965	2 Oct	Belfast	2	3
1966	16 Nov	Glasgow	2	1
1967	21 Oct	Belfast	0	1
1969	6 May	Glasgow	1	1
1970	18 Apr	Belfast	1	0
1971	18 May	Glasgow	0	1
1972	20 May	Glasgow	2	0
1973	16 May	Glasgow	1	2
1974	11 May	Glasgow	0	1
1975	20 May	Glasgow	3	0
1976	8 May	Glasgow	3	0
1977	1 June	Glasgow	3	0
1978	13 May	Glasgow	1	1
1979	22 May	Glasgow	1	0
1980	17 May	Belfast	0	1
WC1981	25 Mar	Glasgow	1	1
1981	19 May	Glasgow	2	0
WC1981	14 Oct	Belfast	0	0
1982	28 Apr	Belfast	1	1
1983	24 May	Glasgow	0	0
1983	13 Dec	Belfast	0	2
1992	19 Feb	Glasgow	1	0
2008	20 Aug	Glasgow	0	0
NC2011	9 Feb	Dublin	3	0

WALES v IRELAND

Played: 94; Wales won 44, Ireland won 27, Drawn 23. Goals: Wales 189, Ireland 131.

			W	I
1882	25 Feb	Wrexham	7	1
1883	17 Mar	Belfast	1	1
1884	9 Feb	Wrexham	6	0
1885	11 Apr	Belfast	8	2
1886	27 Feb	Wrexham	5	0
1887	12 Mar	Belfast	1	4
1888	3 Mar	Wrexham	11	0
1889	27 Apr	Belfast	3	1

			W	I
1890	8 Feb	Shrewsbury	5	2
1891	7 Feb	Belfast	2	7
1892	27 Feb	Bangor	1	1
1893	8 Apr	Belfast	3	4
1894	24 Feb	Swansea	4	1
1895	16 Mar	Belfast	2	2
1896	29 Feb	Wrexham	6	1
1897	6 Mar	Belfast	3	4
1898	19 Feb	Llandudno	0	1
1899	4 Mar	Belfast	0	1
1900	24 Feb	Llandudno	2	0
1901	23 Mar	Belfast	1	0
1902	22 Mar	Cardiff	0	3
1903	28 Mar	Belfast	0	2
1904	21 Mar	Bangor	0	1
1905	18 Apr	Belfast	2	2
1906	2 Apr	Wrexham	4	4
1907	23 Feb	Belfast	3	2
1908	11 Apr	Aberdare	0	1
1909	20 Mar	Belfast	3	2
1910	11 Apr	Wrexham	4	1
1911	28 Jan	Belfast	2	1
1912	13 Apr	Cardiff	2	3
1913	18 Jan	Belfast	1	0
1914	19 Jan	Wrexham	1	2
1920	14 Feb	Belfast	2	2
1921	9 Apr	Swansea	2	1
1922	4 Apr	Belfast	1	1
1923	14 Apr	Wrexham	0	3
1924	15 Mar	Belfast	1	0
1925	18 Apr	Wrexham	0	0
1926	13 Feb	Belfast	0	3
1927	9 Apr	Cardiff	2	2
1928	4 Feb	Belfast	2	1
1929	2 Feb	Wrexham	2	2
1930	1 Feb	Belfast	0	7
1931	22 Apr	Wrexham	3	2
1931	5 Dec	Belfast	0	4
1932	7 Dec	Wrexham	4	1
1933	4 Nov	Belfast	1	1
1935	27 Mar	Wrexham	3	1
1936	11 Mar	Belfast	2	3
1937	17 Mar	Wrexham	4	1
1938	16 Mar	Belfast	0	1
1939	15 Mar	Wrexham	3	1
1947	16 Apr	Belfast	1	2
1948	10 Mar	Wrexham	2	0
1949	9 Mar	Belfast	2	0
WC1950	8 Mar	Wrexham	0	0
1951	7 Mar	Belfast	2	1
1952	19 Mar	Swansea	3	0
1953	15 Apr	Belfast	3	2
WC1954	31 Mar	Wrexham	1	2
1955	20 Apr	Belfast	3	2
1956	11 Apr	Cardiff	1	1
1957	10 Apr	Belfast	0	0
1958	16 Apr	Cardiff	1	1
1959	22 Apr	Belfast	1	4
1960	6 Apr	Wrexham	3	2
1961	12 Apr	Belfast	5	1
1962	11 Apr	Cardiff	4	0
1963	3 Apr	Belfast	4	1
1964	15 Apr	Swansea	2	3
1965	31 Mar	Belfast	5	0
1966	30 Mar	Cardiff	1	4
EC1967	12 Apr	Belfast	0	0
EC1968	28 Feb	Wrexham	2	0
1969	10 May	Belfast	0	0
1970	25 Apr	Swansea	1	0
1971	22 May	Belfast	0	1
1972	27 May	Wrexham	0	0
1973	19 May	Everton	0	1
1974	18 May	Wrexham	1	0
1975	23 May	Belfast	0	1
1976	14 May	Swansea	1	0
1977	3 June	Belfast	1	1
1978	19 May	Wrexham	1	0
1979	25 May	Belfast	1	1
1980	23 May	Cardiff	0	1
1982	27 May	Wrexham	3	0
1983	31 May	Belfast	1	0
1984	22 May	Swansea	1	1
WC2004	8 Sept	Cardiff	2	2
WC2005	8 Oct	Belfast	3	2
2007	6 Feb	Belfast	0	0
NC2011	27 May	Dublin	2	0

OTHER BRITISH INTERNATIONAL RESULTS 1908–2010

ENGLAND

		v ALBANIA	E	A
WC1989	8 Mar	Tirana	2	0
WC1989	26 Apr	Wembley	5	0
WC2001	28 Mar	Tirana	3	1
WC2001	5 Sept	Newcastle	2	0

		v ALGERIA	E	A
WC2010	18 June	Cape Town	0	0

		v ANDORRA	E	A
EC2006	2 Sept	Old Trafford	5	0
EC2007	28 Mar	Barcelona	3	0
WC2008	6 Sept	Barcelona	2	0
WC2009	10 June	Wembley	6	0

		v ARGENTINA	E	A
1951	9 May	Wembley	2	1
1953	17 May	Buenos Aires	0	0
(*abandoned after 21 mins*)				
WC1962	2 June	Rancagua	3	1
1964	6 June	Rio de Janeiro	0	1
WC1966	23 July	Wembley	1	0
1974	22 May	Wembley	2	2
1977	12 June	Buenos Aires	1	1
1980	13 May	Wembley	3	1
WC1986	22 June	Mexico City	1	2
1991	25 May	Wembley	2	2
WC1998	30 June	St Etienne	2	2
2000	23 Feb	Wembley	0	0
WC2002	7 June	Sapporo	1	0
2005	12 Nov	Geneva	3	2

		v AUSTRALIA	E	A
1980	31 May	Sydney	2	1
1983	11 June	Sydney	0	0
1983	15 June	Brisbane	1	0
1983	18 June	Melbourne	1	1
1991	1 June	Sydney	1	0
2003	12 Feb	West Ham	1	3

		v AUSTRIA	E	A
1908	6 June	Vienna	6	1
1908	8 June	Vienna	11	1
1909	1 June	Vienna	8	1
1930	14 May	Vienna	0	0
1932	7 Dec	Chelsea	4	3
1936	6 May	Vienna	1	2
1951	28 Nov	Wembley	2	2
1952	25 May	Vienna	3	2
WC1958	15 June	Boras	2	2
1961	27 May	Vienna	1	3
1962	4 Apr	Wembley	3	1
1965	20 Oct	Wembley	2	3
1967	27 May	Vienna	1	0
1973	26 Sept	Wembley	7	0
1979	13 June	Vienna	3	4
WC2004	4 Sept	Vienna	2	2
WC2005	8 Oct	Old Trafford	1	0
2007	16 Nov	Vienna	1	0

		v AZERBAIJAN	E	A
WC2004	13 Oct	Baku	1	0
WC2005	30 Mar	Newcastle	2	0

		v BELARUS	*E*	*B*
WC2008	15 Oct	Minsk	3	1
WC2009	14 Oct	Wembley	3	0

		v BELGIUM	*E*	*B*
1921	21 May	Brussels	2	0
1923	19 Mar	Highbury	6	1
1923	1 Nov	Antwerp	2	2
1924	8 Dec	West Bromwich	4	0
1926	24 May	Antwerp	5	3
1927	11 May	Brussels	9	1
1928	19 May	Antwerp	3	1
1929	11 May	Brussels	5	1
1931	16 May	Brussels	4	1
1936	9 May	Brussels	2	3
1947	21 Sept	Brussels	5	2
1950	18 May	Brussels	4	1
1952	26 Nov	Wembley	5	0
WC1954	17 June	Basle	4	4*
1964	21 Oct	Wembley	2	2
1970	25 Feb	Brussels	3	1
EC1980	12 June	Turin	1	1
WC1990	27 June	Bologna	1	0*
1998	29 May	Casablanca	0	0
1999	10 Oct	Sunderland	2	1
2012	2 June	Wembley	1	0

		v BOHEMIA	*E*	*B*
1908	13 June	Prague	4	0

		v BRAZIL	*E*	*B*
1956	9 May	Wembley	4	2
WC1958	11 June	Gothenburg	0	0
1959	13 May	Rio de Janeiro	0	2
WC1962	10 June	Vina del Mar	1	3
1963	8 May	Wembley	1	1
1964	30 May	Rio de Janeiro	1	5
1969	12 June	Rio de Janeiro	1	2
WC1970	7 June	Guadalajara	0	1
1976	23 May	Los Angeles	0	1
1977	8 June	Rio de Janeiro	0	0
1978	19 Apr	Wembley	1	1
1981	12 May	Wembley	0	1
1984	10 June	Rio de Janeiro	2	0
1987	19 May	Wembley	1	1
1990	28 Mar	Wembley	1	0
1992	17 May	Wembley	1	1
1993	13 June	Washington	1	1
UI1995	11 June	Wembley	1	3
TF1997	10 June	Paris	0	1
2000	27 May	Wembley	1	1
WC2002	21 June	Shizuoka	1	2
2007	1 June	Wembley	1	1
2009	14 Nov	Doha	0	1

		v BULGARIA	*E*	*B*
WC1962	7 June	Rancagua	0	0
1968	11 Dec	Wembley	1	1
1974	1 June	Sofia	1	0
EC1979	6 June	Sofia	3	0
EC1979	22 Nov	Wembley	2	0
1996	27 Mar	Wembley	1	0
EC1998	10 Oct	Wembley	0	0
EC1999	9 June	Sofia	1	1
EC2010	3 Sept	Wembley	4	0
EC2011	2 Sept	Sofia	3	0

		v CAMEROON	*E*	*C*
WC1990	1 July	Naples	3	2*
1991	6 Feb	Wembley	2	0
1997	15 Nov	Wembley	2	0
2002	26 May	Kobe	2	2

		v CANADA	*E*	*C*
1986	24 May	Burnaby	1	0

		v CHILE	*E*	*C*
WC1950	25 June	Rio de Janeiro	2	0
1953	24 May	Santiago	2	1
1984	17 June	Santiago	0	0
1989	23 May	Wembley	0	0
1998	11 Feb	Wembley	0	2

		v CHINA	*E*	*C*
1996	23 May	Beijing	3	0

		v CIS	*E*	*C*
1992	29 Apr	Moscow	2	2

		v COLOMBIA	*E*	*C*
1970	20 May	Bogota	4	0
1988	24 May	Wembley	1	1
1995	6 Sept	Wembley	0	0
WC1998	26 June	Lens	2	0
2005	31 May	New Jersey	3	2

		v CROATIA	*E*	*C*
1996	24 Apr	Wembley	0	0
2003	20 Aug	Ipswich	3	1
EC2004	21 June	Lisbon	4	2
EC2006	11 Oct	Zagreb	0	2
EC2007	21 Nov	Wembley	2	3
WC2008	10 Sept	Zagreb	4	1
WC2009	9 Sept	Wembley	5	1

		v CYPRUS	*E*	*C*
EC1975	16 Apr	Wembley	5	0
EC1975	11 May	Limassol	1	0

		v CZECHOSLOVAKIA	*E*	*C*
1934	16 May	Prague	1	2
1937	1 Dec	Tottenham	5	4
1963	29 May	Bratislava	4	2
1966	2 Nov	Wembley	0	0
WC1970	11 June	Guadalajara	1	0
1973	27 May	Prague	1	1
EC1974	30 Oct	Wembley	3	0
EC1975	30 Oct	Bratislava	1	2
1978	29 Nov	Wembley	1	0
WC1982	20 June	Bilbao	2	0
1990	25 Apr	Wembley	4	2
1992	25 Mar	Prague	2	2

		v CZECH REPUBLIC	*E*	*C*
1998	18 Nov	Wembley	2	0
2008	20 Aug	Wembley	2	2

		v DENMARK	*E*	*D*
1948	26 Sept	Copenhagen	0	0
1955	2 Oct	Copenhagen	5	1
WC1956	5 Dec	Wolverhampton	5	2
WC1957	15 May	Copenhagen	4	1
1966	3 July	Copenhagen	2	0
EC1978	20 Sept	Copenhagen	4	3
EC1979	12 Sept	Wembley	1	0
EC1982	22 Sept	Copenhagen	2	2
EC1983	21 Sept	Wembley	0	1
1988	14 Sept	Wembley	1	0
1989	7 June	Copenhagen	1	1
1990	15 May	Wembley	1	0
EC1992	11 June	Malmo	0	0
1994	9 Mar	Wembley	1	0
WC2002	15 June	Niigata	3	0
2003	16 Nov	Old Trafford	2	3
2005	17 Aug	Copenhagen	1	4
2011	9 Feb	Copenhagen	2	1

		v ECUADOR	*E*	*Ec*
1970	24 May	Quito	2	0
WC2006	25 June	Stuttgart	1	0

		v EGYPT	*E*	*Eg*
1986	29 Jan	Cairo	4	0
WC1990	21 June	Cagliari	1	0
2010	3 Mar	Wembley	3	1

		v ESTONIA	*E*	*Es*
EC2007	6 June	Tallinn	3	0
EC2007	13 Oct	Wembley	3	0

		v FIFA	*E*	*FIFA*
1938	26 Oct	Highbury	3	0
1953	21 Oct	Wembley	4	4
1963	23 Oct	Wembley	2	1

		v FINLAND	*E*	*F*
1937	20 May	Helsinki	8	0

			E	*F*
1956	20 May	Helsinki	5	1
1966	26 June	Helsinki	3	0
wc1976	13 June	Helsinki	4	1
wc1976	13 Oct	Wembley	2	1
1982	3 June	Helsinki	4	1
wc1984	17 Oct	Wembley	5	0
wc1985	22 May	Helsinki	1	1
1992	3 June	Helsinki	2	1
wc2000	11 Oct	Helsinki	0	0
wc2001	24 Mar	Liverpool	2	1

		v FRANCE	*E*	*F*
1923	10 May	Paris	4	1
1924	17 May	Paris	3	1
1925	21 May	Paris	3	2
1927	26 May	Paris	6	0
1928	17 May	Paris	5	1
1929	9 May	Paris	4	1
1931	14 May	Paris	2	5
1933	6 Dec	Tottenham	4	1
1938	26 May	Paris	4	2
1947	3 May	Highbury	3	0
1949	22 May	Paris	3	1
1951	3 Oct	Highbury	2	2
1955	15 May	Paris	0	1
1957	27 Nov	Wembley	4	0
EC1962	3 Oct	Sheffield	1	1
EC1963	27 Feb	Paris	2	5
wc1966	20 July	Wembley	2	0
1969	12 Mar	Wembley	5	0
wc1982	16 June	Bilbao	3	1
1984	29 Feb	Paris	0	2
1992	19 Feb	Wembley	2	0
EC1992	14 June	Malmo	0	0
TF1997	7 June	Montpellier	1	0
1999	10 Feb	Wembley	0	2
2000	2 Sept	Paris	1	1
EC2004	13 June	Lisbon	1	2
2008	26 Mar	Paris	0	1
2010	17 Nov	Wembley	1	2
EC2012	11 June	Donetsk	1	1

		v GEORGIA	*E*	*G*
wc1996	9 Nov	Tbilisi	2	0
wc1997	30 Apr	Wembley	2	0

		v GERMANY	*E*	*G*
1930	10 May	Berlin	3	3
1935	4 Dec	Tottenham	3	0
1938	14 May	Berlin	6	3
1991	11 Sept	Wembley	0	1
1993	19 June	Detroit	1	2
EC1996	26 June	Wembley	1	1*
EC2000	17 June	Charleroi	1	0
wc2000	7 Oct	Wembley	0	1
wc2001	1 Sept	Munich	5	1
2007	22 Aug	Wembley	1	2
2008	19 Nov	Berlin	2	1
wc2010	27 June	Bloemfontein	1	4

		v EAST GERMANY	*E*	*EG*
1963	2 June	Leipzig	2	1
1970	25 Nov	Wembley	3	1
1974	29 May	Leipzig	1	1
1984	12 Sept	Wembley	1	0

		v WEST GERMANY	*E*	*WG*
1954	1 Dec	Wembley	3	1
1956	26 May	Berlin	3	1
1965	12 May	Nuremberg	1	0
1966	23 Feb	Wembley	1	0
wc1966	30 July	Wembley	4	2*
1968	1 June	Hanover	0	1
wc1970	14 June	Leon	2	3*
EC1972	29 Apr	Wembley	1	3
EC1972	13 May	Berlin	0	0
1975	12 Mar	Wembley	2	0
1978	22 Feb	Munich	1	2
wc1982	29 June	Madrid	0	0
1982	13 Oct	Wembley	1	2
1985	12 June	Mexico City	3	0
1987	9 Sept	Dusseldorf	1	3
wc1990	4 July	Turin	1	1*

		v GHANA	*E*	*G*
2011	29 Mar	Wembley	1	1

		v GREECE	*E*	*G*
EC1971	21 Apr	Wembley	3	0
EC1971	1 Dec	Piraeus	2	0
EC1982	17 Nov	Salonika	3	0
EC1983	30 Mar	Wembley	0	0
1989	8 Feb	Athens	2	1
1994	17 May	Wembley	5	0
wc2001	6 June	Athens	2	0
wc2001	6 Oct	Old Trafford	2	2
2006	16 Aug	Old Trafford	4	0

		v HOLLAND	*E*	*H*
1935	18 May	Amsterdam	1	0
1946	27 Nov	Huddersfield	8	2
1964	9 Dec	Amsterdam	1	1
1969	5 Nov	Amsterdam	1	0
1970	14 Jun	Wembley	0	0
1977	9 Feb	Wembley	0	2
1982	25 May	Wembley	2	0
1988	23 Mar	Wembley	2	2
EC1988	15 June	Dusseldorf	1	3
wc1990	16 June	Cagliari	0	0
2005	9 Feb	Villa Park	0	0
wc1993	28 Apr	Wembley	2	2
wc1993	13 Oct	Rotterdam	0	2
EC1996	18 June	Wembley	4	1
2001	15 Aug	Tottenham	0	2
2002	13 Feb	Amsterdam	1	1
2006	15 Nov	Amsterdam	1	1
2009	12 Aug	Amsterdam	2	2
2012	29 Feb	Wembley	2	3

		v HUNGARY	*E*	*H*
1908	10 June	Budapest	7	0
1909	29 May	Budapest	4	2
1909	31 May	Budapest	8	2
1934	10 May	Budapest	1	2
1936	2 Dec	Highbury	6	2
1953	25 Nov	Wembley	3	6
1954	23 May	Budapest	1	7
1960	22 May	Budapest	0	2
wc1962	31 May	Rancagua	1	2
1965	5 May	Wembley	1	0
1978	24 May	Wembley	4	1
wc1981	6 June	Budapest	3	1
wc1982	18 Nov	Wembley	1	0
EC1983	27 Apr	Wembley	2	0
EC1983	12 Oct	Budapest	3	0
1988	27 Apr	Budapest	0	0
1990	12 Sept	Wembley	1	0
1992	12 May	Budapest	1	0
1996	18 May	Wembley	3	0
1999	28 Apr	Budapest	1	1
2006	30 May	Old Trafford	3	1
2010	11 Aug	Wembley	2	1

		v ICELAND	*E*	*I*
1982	2 June	Reykjavik	1	1
2004	5 June	City of Manchester	6	1
EC2007	24 Mar	Tel Aviv	0	0

		v REPUBLIC OF IRELAND	*E*	*RI*
1946	30 Sept	Dublin	1	0
1949	21 Sept	Everton	0	2
wc1957	8 May	Wembley	5	1
wc1957	19 May	Dublin	1	1
1964	24 May	Dublin	3	1
1976	8 Sept	Wembley	1	1
EC1978	25 Oct	Dublin	1	1
EC1980	6 Feb	Wembley	2	0
1985	26 Mar	Wembley	2	1
EC1988	12 June	Stuttgart	0	1
wc1990	11 June	Cagliari	1	1
EC1990	14 Nov	Dublin	1	1
EC1991	27 Mar	Wembley	1	1
1995	15 Feb	Dublin	0	1

(abandoned after 27 mins)

		v ISRAEL	*E*	*I*
1986	26 Feb	Ramat Gan	2	1
1988	17 Feb	Tel Aviv	0	0
EC2007	24 Mar	Tel Aviv	0	0
EC2007	8 Sept	Wembley	3	0

		v ITALY	*E*	*I*
1933	13 May	Rome	1	1
1934	14 Nov	Highbury	3	2
1939	13 May	Milan	2	2
1948	16 May	Turin	4	0
1949	30 Nov	Tottenham	2	0
1952	18 May	Florence	1	1
1959	6 May	Wembley	2	2
1961	24 May	Rome	3	2
1973	14 June	Turin	0	2
1973	14 Nov	Wembley	0	1
1976	28 May	New York	3	2
WC1976	17 Nov	Rome	0	2
WC1977	16 Nov	Wembley	2	0
EC1980	15 June	Turin	0	1
1985	6 June	Mexico City	1	2
1989	15 Nov	Wembley	0	0
WC1990	7 July	Bari	1	2
WC1997	12 Feb	Wembley	0	1
TF1997	4 June	Nantes	2	0
WC1997	11 Oct	Rome	0	0
2000	15 Nov	Turin	0	1
2002	27 Mar	Leeds	1	2
EC2012	24 June	Kiev	0	0

		v JAMAICA	*E*	*J*
2006	3 June	Old Trafford	6	0

		v JAPAN	*E*	*J*
UI1995	3 June	Wembley	2	1
2004	1 June	City of Manchester	1	1
2010	30 May	Graz	2	1

		v KAZAKHSTAN	*E*	*K*
WC2008	11 Oct	Wembley	5	1
WC2009	6 June	Almaty	4	0

		v KUWAIT	*E*	*K*
WC1982	25 June	Bilbao	1	0

		v LIECHTENSTEIN	*E*	*L*
EC2003	29 Mar	Vaduz	2	0
EC2003	10 Sept	Old Trafford	2	0

		v LUXEMBOURG	*E*	*L*
1927	21 May	Esch-sur-Alzette	5	2
WC1960	19 Oct	Luxembourg	9	0
WC1961	28 Sept	Highbury	4	1
WC1977	30 Mar	Wembley	5	0
WC1977	12 Oct	Luxembourg	2	0
EC1982	15 Dec	Wembley	9	0
EC1983	16 Nov	Luxembourg	4	0
EC1998	14 Oct	Luxembourg	3	0
EC1999	4 Sept	Wembley	6	0

		v MACEDONIA	*E*	*M*
EC2002	16 Oct	Southampton	2	2
EC2003	6 Sept	Skopje	2	1
EC2006	6 Sept	Skopje	1	0
EC2006	7 Oct	Old Trafford	0	0

		v MALAYSIA	*E*	*M*
1991	12 June	Kuala Lumpur	4	2

		v MALTA	*E*	*M*
EC1971	3 Feb	Valletta	1	0
EC1971	12 May	Wembley	5	0
2000	3 June	Valletta	2	1

		v MEXICO	*E*	*M*
1959	24 May	Mexico City	1	2
1961	10 May	Wembley	8	0
WC1966	16 July	Wembley	2	0
1969	1 June	Mexico City	0	0
1985	9 June	Mexico City	0	1
1986	17 May	Los Angeles	3	0
1997	29 Mar	Wembley	2	0
2001	25 May	Derby	4	0
2010	24 May	Wembley	3	1

		v MOLDOVA	*E*	*M*
WC1996	1 Sept	Chisinau	3	0
WC1997	10 Sept	Wembley	4	0

		v MONTENEGRO	*E*	*M*
EC1989	8 Mar	Tirana	2	0
2010	12 Oct	Wembley	0	0
EC2011	7 Oct	Podgorica	2	2

		v MOROCCO	*E*	*M*
WC1986	6 June	Monterrey	0	0
1998	27 May	Casablanca	1	0

		v NEW ZEALAND	*E*	*NZ*
1991	3 June	Auckland	1	0
1991	8 June	Wellington	2	0

		v NIGERIA	*E*	*N*
1994	16 Nov	Wembley	1	0
WC2002	12 June	Osaka	0	0

		v NORWAY	*E*	*N*
1937	14 May	Oslo	6	0
1938	9 Nov	Newcastle	4	0
1949	18 May	Oslo	4	1
1966	29 June	Oslo	6	1
WC1980	10 Sept	Wembley	4	0
WC1981	9 Sept	Oslo	1	2
WC1992	14 Oct	Wembley	1	1
WC1993	2 June	Oslo	0	2
1994	22 May	Wembley	0	0
1995	11 Oct	Oslo	0	0
2012	26 May	Oslo	1	0

		v PARAGUAY	*E*	*P*
WC1986	18 June	Mexico City	3	0
2002	17 Apr	Liverpool	4	0
WC2006	10 June	Frankfurt	1	0

		v PERU	*E*	*P*
1959	17 May	Lima	1	4
1962	20 May	Lima	4	0

		v POLAND	*E*	*P*
1966	5 Jan	Everton	1	1
1966	5 July	Chorzow	1	0
WC1973	6 June	Chorzow	0	2
WC1973	17 Oct	Wembley	1	1
WC1986	11 June	Monterrey	3	0
WC1989	3 June	Wembley	3	0
WC1989	11 Oct	Katowice	0	0
EC1990	17 Oct	Wembley	2	0
EC1991	13 Nov	Poznan	1	1
WC1993	29 May	Katowice	1	1
WC1993	8 Sept	Wembley	3	0
WC1996	9 Oct	Wembley	2	1
WC1997	31 May	Katowice	2	0
EC1999	27 Mar	Wembley	3	1
EC1999	8 Sept	Warsaw	0	0
WC2004	8 Sept	Katowice	2	1
WC2005	12 Oct	Old Trafford	2	1

		v PORTUGAL	*E*	*P*
1947	25 May	Lisbon	10	0
1950	14 May	Lisbon	5	3
1951	19 May	Everton	5	2
1955	22 May	Oporto	1	3
1958	7 May	Wembley	2	1
WC1961	21 May	Lisbon	1	1
WC1961	25 Oct	Wembley	2	0
1964	17 May	Lisbon	4	3
1964	4 June	São Paulo	1	1
WC1966	26 July	Wembley	2	1
1969	10 Dec	Wembley	1	0
1974	3 Apr	Lisbon	0	0
EC1974	20 Nov	Wembley	0	0
EC1975	19 Nov	Lisbon	1	1
WC1986	3 June	Monterrey	0	1
1995	12 Dec	Wembley	1	1
1998	22 Apr	Wembley	3	0
EC2000	12 June	Eindhoven	2	3
2002	7 Sept	Villa Park	1	1
2004	18 Feb	Faro	1	1
EC2004	24 June	Lisbon	2	2*
WC2006	1 July	Gelsenkirchen	0	0

		v ROMANIA	*E*	*R*
1939	24 May	Bucharest	2	0
1968	6 Nov	Bucharest	0	0
1969	15 Jan	Wembley	1	1
WC1970	2 June	Guadalajara	1	0
WC1980	15 Oct	Bucharest	1	2
WC1981	29 April	Wembley	0	0
WC1985	1 May	Bucharest	0	0
WC1985	11 Sept	Wembley	1	1
1994	12 Oct	Wembley	1	1
WC1998	22 June	Toulouse	1	2
EC2000	20 June	Charleroi	2	3

		v RUSSIA	*E*	*R*
EC2007	12 Sept	Wembley	3	0
EC2007	17 Oct	Moscow	1	2

		v SAN MARINO	*E*	*SM*
WC1992	17 Feb	Wembley	6	0
WC1993	17 Nov	Bologna	7	1

		v SAUDI ARABIA	*E*	*SA*
1988	16 Nov	Riyadh	1	1
1998	23 May	Wembley	0	0

		v SERBIA-MONTENEGRO	*E*	*S-M*
2003	3 June	Leicester	2	1

		v SLOVAKIA	*E*	*S*
EC2002	12 Oct	Bratislava	2	1
EC2003	11 June	Middlesbrough	2	1
2009	28 Mar	Wembley	4	0

		v SLOVENIA	*E*	*S*
2009	5 Sept	Wembley	2	1
WC2010	23 June	Port Elizabeth	1	0

		v SOUTH AFRICA	*E*	*SA*
1997	24 May	Old Trafford	2	1
2003	22 May	Durban	2	1

		v SOUTH KOREA	*E*	*SK*
2002	21 May	Seoguipo	1	1

		v SPAIN	*E*	*S*
1929	15 May	Madrid	3	4
1931	9 Dec	Highbury	7	1
WC1950	2 July	Rio de Janeiro	0	1
1955	18 May	Madrid	1	1
1955	30 Nov	Wembley	4	1
1960	15 May	Madrid	0	3
1960	26 Oct	Wembley	4	2
1965	8 Dec	Madrid	2	0
1967	24 May	Wembley	2	0
EC1968	3 Apr	Wembley	1	0
EC1968	8 May	Madrid	2	1
1980	26 Mar	Barcelona	2	0
EC1980	18 June	Naples	2	1
1981	25 Mar	Wembley	1	2
WC1982	5 July	Madrid	0	0
1987	18 Feb	Madrid	4	2
1992	9 Sept	Santander	0	1
EC 1996	22 June	Wembley	0	0
2001	28 Feb	Villa Park	3	0
2004	17 Nov	Madrid	0	1
2007	7 Feb	Old Trafford	0	1
2009	11 Feb	Seville	0	2
2011	12 Nov	Wembley	1	0

		v SWEDEN	*E*	*S*
1923	21 May	Stockholm	4	2
1923	24 May	Stockholm	3	1
1937	17 May	Stockholm	4	0
1947	19 Nov	Highbury	4	2
1949	13 May	Stockholm	1	3
1956	16 May	Stockholm	0	0
1959	28 Oct	Wembley	2	3
1965	16 May	Gothenburg	2	1
1968	22 May	Wembley	3	1
1979	10 June	Stockholm	0	0
1986	10 Sept	Stockholm	0	1
WC1988	19 Oct	Wembley	0	0
WC1989	6 Sept	Stockholm	0	0
EC1992	17 June	Stockholm	1	2
UI1995	8 June	Leeds	3	3

		v SWEDEN	*E*	*S*
EC1998	5 Sept	Stockholm	1	2
EC1999	5 June	Wembley	0	0
2001	10 Nov	Old Trafford	1	1
WC2002	2 June	Saitama	1	1
2004	31 Mar	Gothenburg	0	1
WC2006	20 June	Cologne	2	2
2011	15 Nov	Wembley	1	0
EC2012	15 June	Kiev	3	2

		v SWITZERLAND	*E*	*S*
1933	20 May	Berne	4	0
1938	21 May	Zurich	1	2
1947	18 May	Zurich	0	1
1948	2 Dec	Highbury	6	0
1952	28 May	Zurich	3	0
WC1954	20 June	Berne	2	0
1962	9 May	Wembley	3	1
1963	5 June	Basle	8	1
EC1971	13 Oct	Basle	3	2
EC1971	10 Nov	Wembley	1	1
1975	3 Sept	Basle	2	1
1977	7 Sept	Wembley	0	0
WC1980	19 Nov	Wembley	2	1
WC1981	30 May	Basle	1	2
1988	28 May	Lausanne	1	0
1995	15 Nov	Wembley	3	1
EC1996	8 June	Wembley	1	1
1998	25 Mar	Berne	1	1
EC2004	17 June	Coimbra	3	0
2008	6 Feb	Wembley	2	1
EC1989	8 Mar	Tirana	2	0
EC2010	7 Sept	Basle	3	1
EC2011	4 June	Wembley	2	2

		v TRINIDAD & TOBAGO	*E*	*TT*
WC2006	15 June	Nuremberg	2	0
2008	2 June	Port of Spain	3	0

		v TUNISIA	*E*	*T*
1990	2 June	Tunis	1	1
WC1998	15 June	Marseilles	2	0

		v TURKEY	*E*	*T*
WC1984	14 Nov	Istanbul	8	0
WC1985	16 Oct	Wembley	5	0
EC1987	29 Apr	Izmir	0	0
EC1987	14 Oct	Wembley	8	0
EC1991	1 May	Izmir	1	0
EC1991	16 Oct	Wembley	1	0
WC1992	18 Nov	Wembley	4	0
WC1993	31 Mar	Izmir	2	0
EC2003	2 Apr	Sunderland	2	0
EC2003	11 Oct	Istanbul	0	0

		v UKRAINE	*E*	*U*
2000	31 May	Wembley	2	0
2004	18 Aug	Newcastle	3	0
WC2009	1 Apr	Wembley	2	1
WC2009	10 Oct	Dnepr	0	1
EC2012	19 June	Donetsk	1	0

		v URUGUAY	*E*	*U*
1953	31 May	Montevideo	1	2
WC1954	26 June	Basle	2	4
1964	6 May	Wembley	2	1
WC1966	11 July	Wembley	0	0
1969	8 June	Montevideo	2	1
1977	15 June	Montevideo	0	0
1984	13 June	Montevideo	0	2
1990	22 May	Wembley	1	2
1995	29 Mar	Wembley	0	0
2006	1 Mar	Liverpool	2	1

		v USA	*E*	*USA*
WC1950	29 June	Belo Horizonte	0	1
1953	8 June	New York	6	3
1959	28 May	Los Angeles	8	1
1964	27 May	New York	10	0
1985	16 June	Los Angeles	5	0
1993	9 June	Foxboro	0	2
1994	7 Sept	Wembley	2	0
2005	28 May	Chicago	2	1
2008	28 May	Wembley	2	0
WC2010	12 June	Rustenburg	1	1

		v USSR	E	USSR
1958	18 May	Moscow	1	1
wc1958	8 June	Gothenburg	2	2
wc1958	17 June	Gothenburg	0	1
1958	22 Oct	Wembley	5	0
1967	6 Dec	Wembley	2	2
EC1968	8 June	Rome	2	0
1973	10 June	Moscow	2	1
1984	2 June	Wembley	0	2
1986	26 Mar	Tbilisi	1	0
EC1988	18 June	Frankfurt	1	3
1991	21 May	Wembley	3	1

		v YUGOSLAVIA	E	Y
1939	18 May	Belgrade	1	2
1950	22 Nov	Highbury	2	2
1954	16 May	Belgrade	0	1
1956	28 Nov	Wembley	3	0
1958	11 May	Belgrade	0	5
1960	11 May	Wembley	3	3
1965	9 May	Belgrade	1	1
1966	4 May	Wembley	2	0
EC1968	5 June	Florence	0	1
1972	11 Oct	Wembley	1	1
1974	5 June	Belgrade	2	2
EC1986	12 Nov	Wembley	2	0
EC1987	11 Nov	Belgrade	4	1
1989	13 Dec	Wembley	2	1

SCOTLAND

		v ARGENTINA	S	A
1977	18 June	Buenos Aires	1	1
1979	2 June	Glasgow	1	3
1990	28 Mar	Glasgow	1	0
2008	19 Nov	Glasgow	0	1

		v AUSTRALIA	S	A
wc1985	20 Nov	Glasgow	2	0
wc1985	4 Dec	Melbourne	0	0
1996	27 Mar	Glasgow	1	0
2000	15 Nov	Glasgow	0	2

		v AUSTRIA	S	A
1931	16 May	Vienna	0	5
1933	29 Nov	Glasgow	2	2
1937	9 May	Vienna	1	1
1950	13 Dec	Glasgow	0	1
1951	27 May	Vienna	0	4
wc1954	16 June	Zurich	0	1
1955	19 May	Vienna	4	1
1956	2 May	Glasgow	1	1
1960	29 May	Vienna	1	4
1963	8 May	Glasgow	4	1
(*abandoned after 79 mins*)				
wc1968	6 Nov	Glasgow	2	1
wc1969	5 Nov	Vienna	0	2
EC1978	20 Sept	Vienna	2	3
EC1979	17 Oct	Glasgow	1	1
1994	20 Apr	Vienna	2	1
wc1996	31 Aug	Vienna	0	0
wc1997	2 Apr	Celtic Park	2	0
2003	30 Apr	Glasgow	0	2
2005	17 Aug	Graz	2	2
2007	30 May	Vienna	1	0

		v BELARUS	S	B
wc1997	8 June	Minsk	1	0
wc1997	7 Sept	Aberdeen	4	1
wc2005	8 June	Minsk	0	0
wc2005	8 Oct	Glasgow	0	1

		v BELGIUM	S	B
1947	18 May	Brussels	1	2
1948	28 Apr	Glasgow	2	0
1951	20 May	Brussels	5	0
EC1971	3 Feb	Liège	0	3
EC1971	10 Nov	Aberdeen	1	0
1974	2 June	Brussels	1	2
EC1979	21 Nov	Brussels	0	2
EC1979	19 Dec	Glasgow	1	3
EC1982	15 Dec	Brussels	2	3
EC1983	12 Oct	Glasgow	1	1
EC1987	1 Apr	Brussels	1	4
EC1987	14 Oct	Glasgow	2	0
wc2001	24 Mar	Glasgow	2	2
wc2001	5 Sept	Brussels	0	2

		v BOSNIA	S	B
EC1999	4 Sept	Sarajevo	2	1
EC1999	5 Oct	Glasgow	1	0

		v BRAZIL	S	B
1966	25 June	Glasgow	1	1
1972	5 July	Rio de Janeiro	0	1
1973	30 June	Glasgow	0	1
wc1974	18 June	Frankfurt	0	0
1977	23 June	Rio de Janeiro	0	2
wc1982	18 June	Seville	1	4
1987	26 May	Glasgow	0	2
wc1990	20 June	Turin	0	1
wc1998	10 June	Saint-Denis	1	2
2011	27 Mar	Emirates	0	2

		v BULGARIA	S	B
1978	22 Feb	Glasgow	2	1
EC1986	10 Sept	Glasgow	0	0
EC1987	11 Nov	Sofia	1	0
EC1990	14 Nov	Sofia	1	1
EC1991	27 Mar	Glasgow	1	1
2006	11 May	Kobe	5	1

		v CANADA	S	C
1983	12 June	Vancouver	2	0
1983	16 June	Edmonton	3	0
1983	20 June	Toronto	2	0
1992	21 May	Toronto	3	1
2002	15 Oct	Easter Road	3	1

		v CHILE	S	C
1977	15 June	Santiago	4	2
1989	30 May	Glasgow	2	0

		v CIS	S	C
EC1992	18 June	Norrkoping	3	0

		v COLOMBIA	S	C
1988	17 May	Glasgow	0	0
1996	30 May	Miami	0	1
1998	23 May	New York	2	2

		v COSTA RICA	S	CR
wc1990	11 June	Genoa	0	1

		v CROATIA	S	C
wc2000	11 Oct	Zagreb	1	1
wc2001	1 Sept	Glasgow	0	0
2008	26 Mar	Glasgow	1	1

		v CYPRUS	S	C
wc1968	17 Dec	Nicosia	5	0
wc1969	11 May	Glasgow	8	0
wc1989	8 Feb	Limassol	3	2
wc1989	26 Apr	Glasgow	2	1
2011	11 Nov	Larnaca	2	1

		v CZECHOSLOVAKIA	S	C
1937	22 May	Prague	3	1
1937	8 Dec	Glasgow	5	0
wc1961	14 May	Bratislava	0	4
wc1961	26 Sept	Glasgow	3	2
wc1961	29 Nov	Brussels	2	4*
1972	2 July	Porto Alegre	0	0
wc1973	26 Sept	Glasgow	2	1
wc1973	17 Oct	Prague	0	1
wc1976	13 Oct	Prague	0	2
wc1977	21 Sept	Glasgow	3	1

v CZECH REPUBLIC			S	C
EC1999	31 Mar	Glasgow	1	2
EC1999	9 June	Prague	2	3
2008	30 May	Prague	1	3
2010	3 Mar	Glasgow	1	0
EC2010	8 Oct	Prague	0	1
EC2011	3 Sept	Glasgow	2	2

v DENMARK			S	D
1951	12 May	Glasgow	3	1
1952	25 May	Copenhagen	2	1
1968	16 Oct	Copenhagen	1	0
EC1970	11 Nov	Glasgow	1	0
EC1971	9 June	Copenhagen	0	1
WC1972	18 Oct	Copenhagen	4	1
WC1972	15 Nov	Glasgow	2	0
EC1975	3 Sept	Copenhagen	1	0
EC1975	29 Oct	Glasgow	3	1
WC1986	4 June	Nezahualcayotl	0	1
1996	24 Apr	Copenhagen	0	2
1998	25 Mar	Glasgow	0	1
2002	21 Aug	Glasgow	0	1
2004	28 Apr	Copenhagen	0	1
2011	10 Aug	Glasgow	2	1

v ECUADOR			S	E
1995	24 May	Toyama	2	1

v EGYPT			S	E
1990	16 May	Aberdeen	1	3

v ESTONIA			S	E
WC1993	19 May	Tallinn	3	0
WC1993	2 June	Aberdeen	3	1
WC1997	11 Feb	Monaco	0	0
WC1997	29 Mar	Kilmarnock	2	0
EC1998	10 Oct	Edinburgh	3	2
EC1999	8 Sept	Tallinn	0	0
2004	27 May	Tallinn	1	0

v FAEROES			S	F
EC1994	12 Oct	Glasgow	5	1
EC1995	7 June	Toftir	2	0
EC1998	14 Oct	Aberdeen	2	1
EC1999	5 June	Toftir	1	1
EC2002	7 Sept	Toftir	2	2
EC2003	6 Sept	Glasgow	3	1
EC2006	2 Sept	Celtic Park	6	0
EC2007	6 June	Toftir	2	0
2010	16 Nov	Aberdeen	3	0

v FINLAND			S	F
1954	25 May	Helsinki	2	1
WC1964	21 Oct	Glasgow	3	1
WC1965	27 May	Helsinki	2	1
1976	8 Sept	Glasgow	6	0
1992	25 Mar	Glasgow	1	1
EC1994	7 Sept	Helsinki	2	0
EC1995	6 Sept	Glasgow	1	0
1998	22 Apr	Edinburgh	1	1

v FRANCE			S	F
1930	18 May	Paris	2	0
1932	8 May	Paris	3	1
1948	23 May	Paris	0	3
1949	27 Apr	Glasgow	2	0
1950	27 May	Paris	1	0
1951	16 May	Glasgow	1	0
WC1958	15 June	Orebro	1	2
1984	1 June	Marseilles	0	2
WC1989	8 Mar	Glasgow	2	0
WC1989	11 Oct	Paris	0	3
1997	12 Nov	St Etienne	1	2
2000	29 Mar	Glasgow	0	2
2002	27 Mar	Paris	0	5
EC2006	7 Oct	Glasgow	1	0
EC2007	12 Sept	Paris	1	0

v GEORGIA			S	G
EC2007	24 Mar	Glasgow	2	1
EC2007	17 Oct	Tblisi	0	2

v GERMANY			S	G
1929	1 June	Berlin	1	1
1936	14 Oct	Glasgow	2	0
EC1992	15 June	Norrkoping	0	2
1993	24 Mar	Glasgow	0	1
1998	28 Apr	Bremen	1	0
EC2003	7 June	Glasgow	1	1
EC2003	10 Sept	Dortmund	1	2

v EAST GERMANY			S	EG
1974	30 Oct	Glasgow	3	0
1977	7 Sept	East Berlin	0	1
EC1982	13 Oct	Glasgow	2	0
EC1983	16 Nov	Halle	1	2
1985	16 Oct	Glasgow	0	0
1990	25 Apr	Glasgow	0	1

v WEST GERMANY			S	WG
1957	22 May	Stuttgart	3	1
1959	6 May	Glasgow	3	2
1964	12 May	Hanover	2	2
WC1969	16 Apr	Glasgow	1	1
WC1969	22 Oct	Hamburg	2	3
1973	14 Nov	Glasgow	1	1
1974	27 Mar	Frankfurt	1	2
WC1986	8 June	Queretaro	1	2

v GREECE			S	G
EC1994	18 Dec	Athens	0	1
EC1995	16 Aug	Glasgow	1	0

v HOLLAND			S	H
1929	4 June	Amsterdam	2	0
1938	21 May	Amsterdam	3	1
1959	27 May	Amsterdam	2	1
1966	11 May	Glasgow	0	3
1968	30 May	Amsterdam	0	0
1971	1 Dec	Rotterdam	1	2
WC1978	11 June	Mendoza	3	2
1982	23 Mar	Glasgow	2	1
1986	29 Apr	Eindhoven	0	0
EC1992	12 June	Gothenburg	0	1
1994	23 Mar	Glasgow	0	1
1994	27 May	Utrecht	1	3
EC1996	10 June	Birmingham	0	0
2000	26 Apr	Arnhem	0	0
EC2003	15 Nov	Glasgow	1	0
EC2003	19 Nov	Amsterdam	0	6
WC2009	28 Mar	Amsterdam	0	3
WC2009	9 Sept	Glasgow	0	1

v HONG KONG XI			S	HK
†2002	23 May	Hong Kong	4	0

†match not recognised by FIFA

v HUNGARY			S	H
1938	7 Dec	Glasgow	3	1
1954	8 Dec	Glasgow	2	4
1955	29 May	Budapest	1	3
1958	7 May	Glasgow	1	1
1960	5 June	Budapest	3	3
1980	31 May	Budapest	1	3
1987	9 Sept	Glasgow	2	0
2004	18 Aug	Glasgow	0	3

v ICELAND			S	I
WC1984	17 Oct	Glasgow	3	0
WC1985	28 May	Reykjavik	1	0
EC2002	12 Oct	Reykjavik	2	0
EC2003	29 Mar	Glasgow	2	1
WC2008	10 Sept	Reykjavik	2	1
WC2009	1 Apr	Glasgow	2	1

v IRAN			S	I
WC1978	7 June	Cordoba	1	1

v REPUBLIC OF IRELAND			S	RI
WC1961	3 May	Glasgow	4	1
WC1961	7 May	Dublin	3	0
1963	9 June	Dublin	0	1
1969	21 Sept	Dublin	1	1
EC1986	15 Oct	Dublin	0	0
EC1987	18 Feb	Glasgow	0	1
2000	30 May	Dublin	2	1

			S	RI
2003	12 Feb	Glasgow	0	2
NC2011	29 May	Dublin	0	1
		v ISRAEL	S	I
WC1981	25 Feb	Tel Aviv	1	0
WC1981	28 Apr	Glasgow	3	1
1986	28 Jan	Tel Aviv	1	0
		v ITALY	S	I
1931	20 May	Rome	0	3
WC1965	9 Nov	Glasgow	1	0
WC1965	7 Dec	Naples	0	3
1988	22 Dec	Perugia	0	2
WC1992	18 Nov	Glasgow	0	0
WC1993	13 Oct	Rome	1	3
WC2005	26 Mar	Milan	0	2
WC2005	3 Sept	Glasgow	1	1
EC2007	28 Mar	Bari	0	2
EC2007	17 Nov	Glasgow	3	1
		v JAPAN	S	J
1995	21 May	Hiroshima	0	0
2006	13 May	Saitama	0	0
2009	10 Oct	Yokohama	0	2
		v LATVIA	S	L
WC1996	5 Oct	Riga	2	0
WC1997	11 Oct	Glasgow	2	0
WC2000	2 Sept	Riga	1	0
WC2001	6 Oct	Glasgow	2	1
		v LIECHTENSTEIN	S	L
EC2010	7 Sept	Glasgow	2	1
EC2011	8 Oct	Vaduz	1	0
		v LITHUANIA	S	L
EC1998	5 Sept	Vilnius	0	0
EC1999	9 Oct	Glasgow	3	0
EC2003	2 Apr	Kaunas	0	1
EC2003	11 Oct	Glasgow	1	0
EC2006	6 Sept	Kaunas	2	1
EC2007	8 Sept	Glasgow	3	1
EC2010	3 Sept	Kaunas	0	0
EC2011	6 Sept	Glasgow	1	0
		v LUXEMBOURG	S	L
1947	24 May	Luxembourg	6	0
EC1986	12 Nov	Glasgow	3	0
EC1987	2 Dec	Esch	0	0
		v MACEDONIA	S	M
WC2008	6 Sept	Skopje	0	1
WC2009	5 Sept	Glasgow	2	0
		v MALTA	S	M
1988	22 Mar	Valletta	1	1
1990	28 May	Valletta	2	1
WC1993	17 Feb	Glasgow	3	0
WC1993	17 Nov	Valletta	2	0
1997	1 June	Valletta	3	2
		v MOLDOVA	S	M
EC2004	13 Oct	Chisinau	1	1
EC2005	4 June	Glasgow	2	0
		v MOROCCO	S	M
WC1998	23 June	St Etienne	0	3
		v NEW ZEALAND	S	NZ
WC1982	15 June	Malaga	5	2
2003	27 May	Tynecastle	1	1
		v NIGERIA	S	N
2002	17 Apr	Aberdeen	1	2
		v NORWAY	S	N
1929	28 May	Oslo	7	3
1954	5 May	Glasgow	1	0
1954	19 May	Oslo	1	1
1963	4 June	Bergen	3	4
1963	7 Nov	Glasgow	6	1
1974	6 June	Oslo	2	1
EC1978	25 Oct	Glasgow	3	2
EC1979	7 June	Oslo	4	0
WC1988	14 Sept	Oslo	2	1
WC1989	15 Nov	Glasgow	1	1

			S	N
1992	3 June	Oslo	0	0
WC1998	16 June	Bordeaux	1	1
2003	20 Aug	Oslo	0	0
WC2004	9 Oct	Glasgow	0	1
WC2005	7 Sept	Oslo	2	1
WC2008	11 Oct	Glasgow	0	0
WC2009	12 Aug	Oslo	0	4
		v PARAGUAY	S	P
WC1958	11 June	Norrkoping	2	3
		v PERU	S	P
1972	26 Apr	Glasgow	2	0
WC1978	3 June	Cordoba	1	3
1979	12 Sept	Glasgow	1	1
		v POLAND	S	P
1958	1 June	Warsaw	2	1
1960	4 June	Glasgow	2	3
WC1965	23 May	Chorzow	1	1
WC1965	13 Oct	Glasgow	1	2
1980	28 May	Poznan	0	1
1990	19 May	Glasgow	1	1
2001	25 Apr	Bydgoszcz	1	1
		v PORTUGAL	S	P
1950	21 May	Lisbon	2	2
1955	4 May	Glasgow	3	0
1959	3 June	Lisbon	0	1
1966	18 June	Glasgow	0	1
EC1971	21 Apr	Lisbon	0	2
EC1971	13 Oct	Glasgow	2	1
1975	13 May	Glasgow	1	0
EC1978	29 Nov	Lisbon	0	1
EC1980	26 Mar	Glasgow	4	1
WC1980	15 Oct	Glasgow	0	0
WC1981	18 Nov	Lisbon	1	2
WC1992	14 Oct	Glasgow	0	0
WC1993	28 Apr	Lisbon	0	5
2002	20 Nov	Braga	0	2
		v ROMANIA	S	R
EC1975	1 June	Bucharest	1	1
EC1975	17 Dec	Glasgow	1	1
1986	26 Mar	Glasgow	3	0
EC1990	12 Sept	Glasgow	2	1
EC1991	16 Oct	Bucharest	0	1
2004	31 Mar	Glasgow	1	2
		v RUSSIA	S	R
EC1994	16 Nov	Glasgow	1	1
EC1995	29 Mar	Moscow	0	0
		v SAN MARINO	S	SM
EC1991	1 May	Serravalle	2	0
EC1991	13 Nov	Glasgow	4	0
EC1995	26 Apr	Serravalle	2	0
EC1995	15 Nov	Glasgow	5	0
WC2000	7 Oct	Serravalle	2	0
WC2001	28 Mar	Glasgow	4	0
		v SAUDI ARABIA	S	SA
1988	17 Feb	Riyadh	2	2
		v SLOVENIA	S	Sl
WC2004	8 Sept	Glasgow	0	0
WC2005	12 Oct	Celje	3	0
2012	29 Feb	Koper	1	1
		v SOUTH AFRICA	S	SA
2002	20 May	Hong Kong	0	2
2007	22 Aug	Aberdeen	1	0
		v SOUTH KOREA	S	SK
2002	16 May	Busan	1	4
		v SPAIN	S	Sp
WC1957	8 May	Glasgow	4	2
WC1957	26 May	Madrid	1	4
1963	13 June	Madrid	6	2
1965	8 May	Glasgow	0	0
EC1974	20 Nov	Glasgow	1	2
EC1975	5 Feb	Valencia	1	1

			S	*Sp*
1982	24 Feb	Valencia	0	3
wc1984	14 Nov	Glasgow	3	1
wc1985	27 Feb	Seville	0	1
1988	27 Apr	Madrid	0	0
2004	3 Sept	Valencia	1	1

Match abandoned afer 60 minutes; floodlight failure.

EC2010	12 Oct	Glasgow	2	3
EC2011	11 Oct	Alicante	1	3

		v SWEDEN	*S*	*Sw*
1952	30 May	Stockholm	1	3
1953	6 May	Glasgow	1	2
1975	16 Apr	Gothenburg	1	1
1977	27 Apr	Glasgow	3	1
wc1980	10 Sept	Stockholm	1	0
wc1981	9 Sept	Glasgow	2	0
wc1990	16 June	Genoa	2	1
1995	11 Oct	Stockholm	0	2
wc1996	10 Nov	Glasgow	1	0
wc1997	30 Apr	Gothenburg	1	2
2004	17 Nov	Edinburgh	1	4
2010	11 Aug	Stockholm	0	3

		v SWITZERLAND	*S*	*Sw*
1931	24 May	Geneva	3	2
1948	17 May	Berne	1	2
1950	26 Apr	Glasgow	3	1
wc1957	19 May	Basle	2	1
wc1957	6 Nov	Glasgow	3	2
1973	22 June	Berne	0	1

		v SWITZERLAND	*S*	*Sw*
1976	7 Apr	Glasgow	1	0
EC1982	17 Nov	Berne	0	2
EC1983	30 May	Glasgow	2	2
EC1990	17 Oct	Glasgow	2	1
EC1991	11 Sept	Berne	2	2
wc1992	9 Sept	Berne	1	3
wc1993	8 Sept	Aberdeen	1	1
wc1996	18 June	Birmingham	1	0
2006	1 Mar	Glasgow	1	3

		v TRINIDAD & TOBAGO	*S*	*TT*
2004	30 May	Edinburgh	4	1

		v TURKEY	*S*	*T*
1960	8 June	Ankara	2	4

		v UKRAINE	*S*	*U*
EC2006	11 Oct	Kiev	0	2
EC2007	13 Oct	Glasgow	3	1

		v URUGUAY	*S*	*U*
wc1954	19 June	Basle	0	7
1962	2 May	Glasgow	2	3
1983	21 Sept	Glasgow	2	0
wc1986	13 June	Nezahualcoyotl	0	0

		v USA	*S*	*USA*
1952	30 Apr	Glasgow	6	0
1992	17 May	Denver	1	0
1996	26 May	New Britain	1	2
1998	30 May	Washington	0	0
2005	11 Nov	Glasgow	1	1
2012	26 May	Jacksonville	1	5

		v USSR	*S*	*USSR*
1967	10 May	Glasgow	0	2
1971	14 June	Moscow	0	1
wc1982	22 June	Malaga	2	2
1991	6 Feb	Glasgow	0	1

		v YUGOSLAVIA	*S*	*Y*
1955	15 May	Belgrade	2	2
1956	21 Nov	Glasgow	2	0
wc1958	8 June	Vasteras	1	1
1972	29 June	Belo Horizonte	2	2
wc1974	22 June	Frankfurt	1	1
1984	12 Sept	Glasgow	6	1
wc1988	19 Oct	Glasgow	1	1
wc1989	6 Sept	Zagreb	1	3

		v ZAIRE	*S*	*Z*
wc1974	14 June	Dortmund	2	0

WALES

		v ALBANIA	*W*	*A*
EC1994	7 Sept	Cardiff	2	0
EC1995	15 Nov	Tirana	1	1

		v ARGENTINA	*W*	*A*
1992	3 June	Tokyo	0	1
2002	13 Feb	Cardiff	1	1

		v ARMENIA	*W*	*A*
wc2001	24 Mar	Erevan	2	2
wc2001	1 Sept	Cardiff	0	0

		v AUSTRALIA	*W*	*A*
2011	10 Aug	Cardiff	1	2

		v AUSTRIA	*W*	*A*
1954	9 May	Vienna	0	2
EC1955	23 Nov	Wrexham	1	2
EC1974	4 Sept	Vienna	1	2
1975	19 Nov	Wrexham	1	0
1992	29 Apr	Vienna	1	1
EC2005	26 Mar	Cardiff	0	2
EC2005	30 Mar	Vienna	0	1

		v AZERBAIJAN	*W*	*A*
EC2002	20 Nov	Baku	2	0
EC2003	29 Mar	Cardiff	4	0
wc2004	4 Sept	Baku	1	1
wc2005	12 Oct	Cardiff	2	0
wc2008	6 Sept	Cardiff	1	0
wc2009	6 June	Baku	1	0

		v BELARUS	*W*	*B*
EC1998	14 Oct	Cardiff	3	2
EC1999	4 Sept	Minsk	2	1
wc2000	2 Sept	Minsk	1	2
wc2001	6 Oct	Cardiff	1	0

		v BELGIUM	*W*	*B*
1949	22 May	Liège	1	3
1949	23 Nov	Cardiff	5	1
EC1990	17 Oct	Cardiff	3	1
EC1991	27 Mar	Brussels	1	1
wc1992	18 Nov	Brussels	0	2
wc1993	31 Mar	Cardiff	2	0
wc1997	29 Mar	Cardiff	1	2
wc1997	11 Oct	Brussels	2	3

		v BOSNIA	*W*	*B*
2003	12 Feb	Cardiff	2	2

		v BRAZIL	*W*	*B*
wc1958	19 June	Gothenburg	0	1
1962	12 May	Rio de Janeiro	1	3
1962	16 May	São Paulo	1	3
1966	14 May	Rio de Janeiro	1	3
1966	18 May	Belo Horizonte	0	1
1983	12 June	Cardiff	1	1
1991	11 Sept	Cardiff	1	0
1997	12 Nov	Brasilia	0	3
2000	23 May	Cardiff	0	3
2006	5 Sept	Cardiff	0	2

		v BULGARIA	*W*	*B*
EC1983	27 Apr	Wrexham	1	0
EC1983	16 Nov	Sofia	0	1
EC1994	14 Dec	Cardiff	0	3
EC1995	29 Mar	Sofia	1	3
2006	15 Aug	Swansea	0	0
2007	22 Aug	Burgas	1	0
EC2010	8 Oct	Cardiff	0	1
EC2011	12 Oct	Sofia	1	0

		v CANADA	*W*	*C*
1986	10 May	Toronto	0	2
1986	20 May	Vancouver	3	0
2004	30 May	Wrexham	1	0

		v CHILE	*W*	*C*
1966	22 May	Santiago	0	2

		v COSTA RICA	*W*	*CR*
1990	20 May	Cardiff	1	0
2012	29 Feb	Cardiff	0	1

		v CROATIA	*W*	*C*
2002	21 Aug	Varazdin	1	1
2010	23 May	Osijek	0	2

		v CYPRUS	*W*	*C*
wc1992	14 Oct	Limassol	1	0
wc1993	13 Oct	Cardiff	2	0
2005	16 Nov	Limassol	0	1
EC2006	11 Oct	Cardiff	3	1
EC2007	13 Oct	Nicosia	1	3

		v CZECHOSLOVAKIA	*W*	*C*
wc1957	1 May	Cardiff	1	0
wc1957	26 May	Prague	0	2
EC1971	21 Apr	Swansea	1	3
EC1971	27 Oct	Prague	0	1
wc1977	30 Mar	Wrexham	3	0
wc1977	16 Nov	Prague	0	1
wc1980	19 Nov	Cardiff	1	0
wc1981	9 Sept	Prague	0	2
EC1987	29 Apr	Wrexham	1	1
EC1987	11 Nov	Prague	0	2
wc1993	28 Apr	Ostrava†	1	1
wc1993	8 Sept	Cardiff†	2	2

†*Czechoslovakia played as RCS (Republic of Czechs and Slovaks).*

		v CZECH REPUBLIC	*W*	*CR*
2002	27 Mar	Cardiff	0	0
EC2006	2 Sept	Teplice	1	2
EC2007	2 June	Cardiff	0	0

		v DENMARK	*W*	*D*
wc1964	21 Oct	Copenhagen	0	1
wc1965	1 Dec	Wrexham	4	2
EC1987	9 Sept	Cardiff	1	0
EC1987	14 Oct	Copenhagen	0	1
1990	11 Sept	Copenhagen	0	1
EC1998	10 Oct	Copenhagen	2	1
EC1999	9 June	Liverpool	0	2
2008	19 Nov	Brondby	1	0

		v ESTONIA	*W*	*E*
1994	23 May	Tallinn	2	1
2009	29 May	Llanelli	1	0

		v FINLAND	*W*	*F*
EC1971	26 May	Helsinki	1	0
EC1971	13 Oct	Swansea	3	0
EC1987	10 Sept	Helsinki	1	1
EC1987	1 Apr	Wrexham	4	0
wc1988	19 Oct	Swansea	2	2
wc1989	6 Sept	Helsinki	0	1
2000	29 Mar	Cardiff	1	2
EC2002	7 Sept	Helsinki	2	0
EC2003	10 Sept	Cardiff	1	1
wc2009	28 Mar	Cardiff	0	2
wc2009	10 Oct	Helsinki	1	2

		v FAEROES	*W*	*F*
wc1992	9 Sept	Cardiff	6	0
wc1993	6 June	Toftir	3	0

		v FRANCE	*W*	*F*
1933	25 May	Paris	1	1
1939	20 May	Paris	1	2
1953	14 May	Paris	1	6
1982	2 June	Toulouse	1	0

		v GEORGIA	*W*	*G*
EC1994	16 Nov	Tbilisi	0	5
EC1995	7 June	Cardiff	0	1
2008	20 Aug	Swansea	1	2

		v GERMANY	*W*	*G*
EC1995	26 Apr	Dusseldorf	1	1
EC1995	11 Oct	Cardiff	1	2
2002	14 May	Cardiff	1	0
EC2007	8 Sept	Cardiff	0	2
EC2007	21 Nov	Frankfurt	0	0
wc2008	15 Oct	Moenchengladbach	0	1
wc2009	1 Apr	Cardiff	0	2

		v EAST GERMANY	*W*	*EG*
wc1957	19 May	Leipzig	1	2
wc1957	25 Sept	Cardiff	4	1
wc1969	16 Apr	Dresden	1	2
wc1969	22 Oct	Cardiff	1	3

		v WEST GERMANY	*W*	*WG*
1968	8 May	Cardiff	1	1
1969	26 Mar	Frankfurt	1	1
1976	6 Oct	Cardiff	0	2
1977	14 Dec	Dortmund	1	1
EC1979	2 May	Wrexham	0	2
EC1979	17 Oct	Cologne	1	5
wc1989	31 May	Cardiff	0	0
wc1989	15 Nov	Cologne	1	2
EC1991	5 June	Cardiff	1	0
EC1991	16 Oct	Nuremberg	1	4

		v GREECE	*W*	*G*
wc1964	9 Dec	Athens	0	2
wc1965	17 Mar	Cardiff	4	1

		v HOLLAND	*W*	*H*
wc1988	14 Sept	Amsterdam	0	1
wc1989	11 Oct	Wrexham	1	2
1992	30 May	Utrecht	0	4
wc1996	5 Oct	Cardiff	1	3
wc1996	9 Nov	Eindhoven	1	7
2008	1 June	Rotterdam	0	2

		v HUNGARY	*W*	*H*
wc1958	8 June	Sanviken	1	1
wc1958	17 June	Stockholm	2	1
1961	28 May	Budapest	2	3
EC1962	7 Nov	Budapest	1	3
EC1963	20 Mar	Cardiff	1	1
EC1974	30 Oct	Cardiff	2	0
EC1975	16 Apr	Budapest	2	1
1985	16 Oct	Cardiff	0	3
2004	31 Mar	Budapest	2	1
2005	9 Feb	Cardiff	2	0

		v ICELAND	*W*	*I*
wc1980	2 June	Reykjavik	4	0
wc1981	14 Oct	Swansea	2	2
wc1984	12 Sept	Reykjavik	0	1
wc1984	14 Nov	Cardiff	2	1
1991	1 May	Cardiff	1	0
2008	28 May	Reykjavik	1	0

		v IRAN	*W*	*I*
1978	18 Apr	Teheran	1	0

		v REPUBLIC OF IRELAND	*W*	*RI*
1960	28 Sept	Dublin	3	2
1979	11 Sept	Swansea	2	1
1981	24 Feb	Dublin	3	1
1986	26 Mar	Dublin	1	0
1990	28 Mar	Dublin	0	1
1991	6 Feb	Wrexham	0	3
1992	19 Feb	Dublin	1	0
1993	17 Feb	Dublin	1	2
1997	11 Feb	Cardiff	0	0
EC2007	24 Mar	Dublin	0	1
EC2007	17 Nov	Cardiff	2	2
NC2011	8 Feb	Dublin	0	3

		v ISRAEL	*W*	*I*
wc1958	15 Jan	Tel Aviv	2	0
wc1958	5 Feb	Cardiff	2	0
1984	10 June	Tel Aviv	0	0
1989	8 Feb	Tel Aviv	3	3

		v ITALY	*W*	*I*
1965	1 May	Florence	1	4
wc1968	23 Oct	Cardiff	0	1
wc1969	4 Nov	Rome	1	4
1988	4 June	Brescia	1	0
1996	24 Jan	Terni	0	3
EC1998	5 Sept	Liverpool	0	2
EC1999	5 June	Bologna	0	4
EC2002	16 Oct	Cardiff	2	1
EC2003	6 Sept	Milan	0	4

		v JAMAICA	*W*	*J*
1998	25 Mar	Cardiff	0	0

		v JAPAN	*W*	*J*
1992	7 June	Matsuyama	1	0

		v KUWAIT	*W*	*K*
1977	6 Sept	Wrexham	0	0
1977	20 Sept	Kuwait	0	0

		v LATVIA	*W*	*L*
2004	18 Aug	Riga	2	0

		v LIECHTENSTEIN	*W*	*L*
2006	14 Nov	Swansea	4	0
wc2008	11 Oct	Cardiff	2	0
wc2009	14 Oct	Vaduz	2	0

		v LUXEMBOURG	*W*	*L*
EC1974	20 Nov	Swansea	5	0
EC1975	1 May	Luxembourg	3	1
EC1990	14 Nov	Luxembourg	1	0
EC1991	13 Nov	Cardiff	1	0
2008	26 Mar	Luxembourg	2	0
2010	11 Aug	Llanelli	5	1

		v MALTA	*W*	*M*
EC1978	25 Oct	Wrexham	7	0
EC1979	2 June	Valletta	2	0
1988	1 June	Valletta	3	2
1998	3 June	Valletta	3	0

		v MEXICO	*W*	*M*
wc1958	11 June	Stockholm	1	1
1962	22 May	Mexico City	1	2
2012	27 May	New Jersey	0	2

		v MOLDOVA	*W*	*M*
EC1994	12 Oct	Kishinev	2	3
EC1995	6 Sept	Cardiff	1	0

		v MONTENEGRO	*W*	*M*
2009	12 Aug	Podgorica	1	2
EC2010	3 Sept	Podgorica	0	1
EC2011	2 Sept	Cardiff	2	1

		v NEW ZEALAND	*W*	*NZ*
2007	26 May	Wrexham	2	2

		v NORWAY	*W*	*N*
EC1982	22 Sept	Swansea	1	0
EC1983	21 Sept	Oslo	0	0
1984	6 June	Trondheim	0	1
1985	26 Feb	Wrexham	1	1
1985	5 June	Bergen	2	4
1994	9 Mar	Cardiff	1	3
wc2000	7 Oct	Cardiff	1	1
wc2001	5 Sept	Oslo	2	3
2004	27 May	Oslo	0	0
2008	6 Feb	Wrexham	3	0
2011	12 Nov	Cardiff	4	1

		v PARAGUAY	*W*	*P*
2006	1 Mar	Cardiff	0	0

		v POLAND	*W*	*P*
wc1973	28 Mar	Cardiff	2	0
wc1973	26 Sept	Katowice	0	3
1991	29 May	Radom	0	0
wc2000	11 Oct	Warsaw	0	0
wc2001	2 June	Cardiff	1	2
wc2004	13 Oct	Cardiff	2	3

			W	*P*
wc2005	7 Sept	Warsaw	0	1
2009	11 Feb	Vila Real	0	1

		v PORTUGAL	*W*	*P*
1949	15 May	Lisbon	2	3
1951	12 May	Cardiff	2	1
2000	2 June	Chaves	0	3

		v QATAR	*W*	*Q*
2000	23 Feb	Doha	1	0

		v ROMANIA	*W*	*R*
EC1970	11 Nov	Cardiff	0	0
EC1971	24 Nov	Bucharest	0	2
1983	12 Oct	Wrexham	5	0
wc1992	20 May	Bucharest	1	5
wc1993	17 Nov	Cardiff	1	2

		v RUSSIA	*W*	*R*
EC2003	15 Nov	Moscow	0	0
EC2003	19 Nov	Cardiff	0	1
wc2008	10 Sept	Moscow	1	2
wc2009	9 Sept	Cardiff	1	3

		v SAN MARINO	*W*	*SM*
wc1996	2 June	Serravalle	5	0
wc1996	31 Aug	Cardiff	6	0
EC2007	28 Mar	Cardiff	3	0
EC2007	17 Oct	Serravalle	2	1

		v SAUDI ARABIA	*W*	*SA*
1986	25 Feb	Dahran	2	1

		v SERBIA-MONTENEGRO	*W*	*SM*
EC2003	20 Aug	Belgrade	0	1
EC2003	11 Oct	Cardiff	2	3

		v SLOVAKIA	*W*	*S*
EC2006	7 Oct	Cardiff	1	5
EC2007	12 Sept	Trnava	5	2

		v SLOVENIA	*W*	*Sl*
2005	17 Aug	Swansea	0	0

		v SPAIN	*W*	*S*
wc1961	19 Apr	Cardiff	1	2
wc1961	18 May	Madrid	1	1
1982	24 Mar	Valencia	1	1
wc1984	17 Oct	Seville	0	3
wc1985	30 Apr	Wrexham	3	0

		v SWEDEN	*W*	*S*
wc1958	15 June	Stockholm	0	0
1988	27 Apr	Stockholm	1	4
1989	26 Apr	Wrexham	0	2
1990	25 Apr	Stockholm	2	4
1994	20 Apr	Wrexham	0	2
2010	3 Mar	Swansea	0	1

		v SWITZERLAND	*W*	*S*
1949	26 May	Berne	0	4
1951	16 May	Wrexham	3	2
1996	24 Apr	Lugano	0	2
EC1999	31 Mar	Zurich	0	2
EC1999	9 Oct	Wrexham	0	2
EC2010	12 Oct	Basle	1	4
EC2011	8 Oct	Swansea	2	0

		v TRINIDAD & TOBAGO	*W*	*TT*
2006	27 May	Graz	2	1

		v TUNISIA	*W*	*T*
1998	6 June	Tunis	0	4

		v TURKEY	*W*	*T*
EC1978	29 Nov	Wrexham	1	0
EC1979	21 Nov	Izmir	0	1
wc1980	15 Oct	Cardiff	4	0
wc1981	25 Mar	Ankara	1	0
wc1996	14 Dec	Cardiff	0	0
wc1997	20 Aug	Istanbul	4	6

v REST OF UNITED KINGDOM			W	UK
1951	5 Dec	Cardiff	3	2
1969	28 July	Cardiff	0	1

v UKRAINE			W	U
wc2001	28 Mar	Cardiff	1	1
wc2001	6 June	Kiev	1	1

v USA			W	USA
2003	27 May	San Jose	0	2

v URUGUAY			W	U
1986	21 Apr	Wrexham	0	0

v USSR			W	USSR
wc1965	30 May	Moscow	1	2
wc1965	27 Oct	Cardiff	2	1
wc1981	30 May	Wrexham	0	0
wc1981	18 Nov	Tbilisi	0	3
1987	18 Feb	Swansea	0	0

v YUGOSLAVIA			W	Y
1953	21 May	Belgrade	2	5
1954	22 Nov	Cardiff	1	3
EC1976	24 Apr	Zagreb	0	2
EC1976	22 May	Cardiff	1	1
EC1982	15 Dec	Titograd	4	4
EC1983	14 Dec	Cardiff	1	1
1988	23 Mar	Swansea	1	2

NORTHERN IRELAND

v ALBANIA			NI	A
wc1965	7 May	Belfast	4	1
wc1965	24 Nov	Tirana	1	1
EC1982	15 Dec	Tirana	0	0
EC1983	27 Apr	Belfast	1	0
wc1992	9 Sept	Belfast	3	0
wc1993	17 Feb	Tirana	2	1
wc1996	14 Dec	Belfast	2	0
wc1997	10 Sept	Zurich	0	1
2010	3 Mar	Tirana	0	1

v ALGERIA			NI	A
wc1986	3 June	Guadalajara	1	1

v ARGENTINA			NI	A
wc1958	11 June	Halmstad	1	3

v ARMENIA			NI	A
wc1996	5 Oct	Belfast	1	1
wc1997	30 Apr	Erevan	0	0
EC2003	29 Mar	Erevan	0	1
EC2003	10 Sept	Belfast	0	1

v AUSTRALIA			NI	A
1980	11 June	Sydney	2	1
1980	15 June	Melbourne	1	1
1980	18 June	Adelaide	2	1

v AUSTRIA			NI	A
wc1982	1 July	Madrid	2	2
EC1982	13 Oct	Vienna	0	2
EC1983	21 Sept	Belfast	3	1
EC1990	14 Nov	Vienna	0	0
EC1991	16 Oct	Belfast	2	1
EC1994	12 Oct	Vienna	2	1
EC1995	15 Nov	Belfast	5	3
wc2004	13 Oct	Belfast	3	3
wc2005	12 Oct	Vienna	0	2

v AZERBAIJAN			NI	A
wc2004	9 Oct	Baku	0	0
wc2005	3 Sept	Belfast	2	0

v BARBADOS			NI	B
2004	30 May	Waterford	1	1

v BELGIUM			NI	B
wc1976	10 Nov	Liège	0	2
wc1977	16 Nov	Belfast	3	0
1997	11 Feb	Belfast	3	0

v BRAZIL			NI	B
wc1986	12 June	Guadalajara	0	3

v BULGARIA			NI	B
wc1972	18 Oct	Sofia	0	3
wc1973	26 Sept	Sheffield	0	0
EC1978	29 Nov	Sofia	2	0
EC1979	2 May	Belfast	2	0
wc2001	28 Mar	Sofia	3	4
wc2001	2 June	Belfast	0	1
2008	6 Feb	Belfast	0	1

v CANADA			NI	C
1995	22 May	Edmonton	0	2
1999	27 Apr	Belfast	1	1
2005	9 Feb	Belfast	0	1

v CHILE			NI	C
1989	26 May	Belfast	0	1
1995	25 May	Edmonton	1	2
2010	30 May	Chillan	0	1

v COLOMBIA			NI	C
1994	4 June	Boston	0	2

v CYPRUS			NI	C
EC1971	3 Feb	Nicosia	3	0
EC1971	21 Apr	Belfast	5	0
wc1973	14 Feb	Nicosia	0	1
wc1973	8 May	London	3	0
2002	21 Aug	Belfast	0	0

v CZECHOSLOVAKIA			NI	C
wc1958	8 June	Halmstad	1	0
wc1958	17 June	Malmo	2	1*

**After extra time*

v CZECH REPUBLIC			NI	C
wc2001	24 Mar	Belfast	0	1
wc2001	6 June	Teplice	1	3
wc2008	10 Sept	Belfast	0	0
wc2009	14 Oct	Prague	0	0

v DENMARK			NI	D
EC1978	25 Oct	Belfast	2	1
EC1979	6 June	Copenhagen	0	4
1986	26 Mar	Belfast	1	1
EC1990	17 Oct	Belfast	1	1
EC1991	13 Nov	Odense	1	2
wc1992	18 Nov	Belfast	0	1
wc1993	13 Oct	Copenhagen	0	1
wc2000	7 Oct	Belfast	1	1
wc2001	1 Sept	Copenhagen	1	1
EC2006	7 Oct	Copenhagen	0	0
EC2007	17 Nov	Belfast	2	1

v ESTONIA			NI	E
2004	31 Mar	Tallinn	1	0
2006	1 Mar	Belfast	1	0
EC2011	6 Sept	Tallinn	1	4
EC2011	7 Oct	Belfast	1	2

v FAEROES			NI	F
EC1991	1 May	Belfast	1	1
EC1991	11 Sept	Landskrona	5	0
EC2010	12 Oct	Toftir	1	1
EC2011	10 Aug	Belfast	4	0

v FINLAND			NI	F
wc1984	27 May	Pori	0	1
wc1984	14 Nov	Belfast	2	1
EC1998	10 Oct	Belfast	1	0
EC1998	9 Oct	Helsinki	1	4
2003	12 Feb	Belfast	0	1
2006	16 Aug	Helsinki	2	1

		v FRANCE	*NI*	*F*
1928	21 Feb	Paris	0	4
1951	12 May	Belfast	2	2
1952	11 Nov	Paris	1	3
wc1958	19 June	Norrkoping	0	4
1982	24 Mar	Paris	0	4
wc1982	4 July	Madrid	1	4
1986	26 Feb	Paris	0	0
1988	27 Apr	Belfast	0	0
1999	18 Aug	Belfast	0	1

		v GEORGIA	*NI*	*G*
2008	26 Mar	Belfast	4	1

		v GERMANY	*NI*	*G*
1992	2 June	Bremen	1	1
1996	29 May	Belfast	1	1
wc1996	9 Nov	Nuremberg	1	1
wc1997	20 Aug	Belfast	1	3
EC1999	27 Mar	Belfast	0	3
EC1999	8 Sept	Dortmund	0	4
2005	4 June	Belfast	1	4

		v WEST GERMANY	*NI*	*WG*
wc1958	15 June	Malmo	2	2
wc1960	26 Oct	Belfast	3	4
wc1961	10 May	Hamburg	1	2
1966	7 May	Belfast	0	2
1977	27 Apr	Cologne	0	5
EC1982	17 Nov	Belfast	1	0
EC1983	16 Nov	Hamburg	1	0

		v GREECE	*NI*	*G*
wc1961	3 May	Athens	1	2
wc1961	17 Oct	Belfast	2	0
1988	17 Feb	Athens	2	3
EC2003	2 Apr	Belfast	0	2
EC2003	11 Oct	Athens	0	1

		v HOLLAND	*NI*	*H*
1962	9 May	Rotterdam	0	4
wc1965	17 Mar	Belfast	2	1
wc1965	7 Apr	Rotterdam	0	0
wc1976	13 Oct	Rotterdam	2	2
wc1977	12 Oct	Belfast	0	1
2012	2 June	Amsterdam	0	6

		v HONDURAS	*NI*	*H*
wc1982	21 June	Zaragoza	1	1

		v HUNGARY	*NI*	*H*
wc1988	19 Oct	Budapest	0	1
wc1989	6 Sept	Belfast	1	2
2000	26 Apr	Belfast	0	1
2008	19 Nov	Belfast	0	2

		v ICELAND	*NI*	*I*
wc1977	11 June	Reykjavik	0	1
wc1977	21 Sept	Belfast	2	0
wc2000	11 Oct	Reykjavik	0	1
wc2001	5 Sept	Belfast	3	0
EC2006	2 Sept	Belfast	0	3
EC2007	12 Sept	Reykjavik	1	2

		v REPUBLIC OF IRELAND	*NI*	*RI*
EC1978	20 Sept	Dublin	0	0
EC1979	21 Nov	Belfast	1	0
wc1988	14 Sept	Belfast	0	0
wc1989	11 Oct	Dublin	0	3
wc1993	31 Mar	Dublin	0	3
wc1993	17 Nov	Belfast	1	1
EC1994	16 Nov	Belfast	0	4
EC1995	29 Mar	Dublin	1	1
1999	29 May	Dublin	1	0
NC2011	24 May	Dublin	0	5

		v ISRAEL	*NI*	*I*
1968	10 Sept	Jaffa	3	2
1976	3 Mar	Tel Aviv	1	1
wc1980	26 Mar	Tel Aviv	0	0
wc1981	18 Nov	Belfast	1	0
1984	16 Oct	Belfast	3	0
1987	18 Feb	Tel Aviv	1	1
2009	12 Aug	Belfast	1	1

		v ITALY	*NI*	*I*
wc1957	25 Apr	Rome	0	1
1957	4 Dec	Belfast	2	2
wc1958	15 Jan	Belfast	2	1
1961	25 Apr	Bologna	2	3
1997	22 Jan	Palermo	0	2
2003	3 June	Campobasso	0	2
2009	6 June	Pisa	0	3
EC2010	8 Oct	Belfast	0	0
EC2011	11 Oct	Pescara	0	3

		v LATVIA	*NI*	*L*
wc1993	2 June	Riga	2	1
wc1993	8 Sept	Belfast	2	0
EC1995	26 Apr	Riga	1	0
EC1995	7 June	Belfast	1	2
EC2006	11 Oct	Belfast	1	0
EC2007	8 Sept	Riga	0	1

		v LIECHTENSTEIN	*NI*	*L*
EC1994	20 Apr	Belfast	4	1
EC1995	11 Oct	Eschen	4	0
2002	27 Mar	Vaduz	0	0
EC2007	24 Mar	Vaduz	4	1
EC2007	22 Aug	Belfast	3	1

		v LITHUANIA	*NI*	*L*
wc1992	28 Apr	Belfast	2	2
wc1993	25 May	Vilnius	1	0

		v LUXEMBOURG	*NI*	*L*
2000	23 Feb	Luxembourg	3	1

		v MALTA	*NI*	*M*
wc1988	21 May	Belfast	3	0
wc1989	26 Apr	Valletta	2	0
2000	28 Mar	Valletta	3	0
wc2000	2 Sept	Belfast	1	0
wc2001	6 Oct	Valletta	1	0
2005	17 Aug	Ta'Qali	1	1

		v MEXICO	*NI*	*M*
1966	22 June	Belfast	4	1
1994	11 June	Miami	0	3

		v MOLDOVA	*NI*	*M*
EC1998	18 Nov	Belfast	2	2
EC1999	31 Mar	Chisinau	0	0

		v MONTENEGRO	*NI*	*M*
2010	11 Aug	Podgorica	0	2

		v MOROCCO	*NI*	*M*
1986	23 Apr	Belfast	2	1
2010	17 Nov	Belfast	1	1

		v NORWAY	*NI*	*N*
1922	25 May	Bergen	1	2
EC1974	4 Sept	Oslo	1	2
EC1975	29 Oct	Belfast	3	0
1990	27 Mar	Belfast	2	3
1996	27 Mar	Belfast	0	2
2001	28 Feb	Belfast	0	4
2004	18 Feb	Belfast	1	4
2012	29 Feb	Belfast	0	3

		v POLAND	*NI*	*P*
EC1962	10 Oct	Katowice	2	0
EC1962	28 Nov	Belfast	2	0
1988	23 Mar	Belfast	1	1
1991	5 Feb	Belfast	3	1
2002	13 Feb	Limassol	1	4
EC2004	4 Sept	Belfast	0	3
EC2005	30 Mar	Warsaw	0	1
wc2009	28 Mar	Belfast	3	2
wc2009	5 Sept	Chorzow	1	1

		v PORTUGAL	*NI*	*P*
wc1957	16 Jan	Lisbon	1	1
wc1957	1 May	Belfast	3	0
wc1973	28 Mar	Coventry	1	1
wc1973	14 Nov	Lisbon	1	1
wc1980	19 Nov	Lisbon	0	1
wc1981	29 Apr	Belfast	1	0
EC1994	7 Sept	Belfast	1	2

		v PORTUGAL	*NI*	*P*
EC1995	3 Sept	Lisbon	1	1
WC1997	29 Mar	Belfast	0	0
WC1997	11 Oct	Lisbon	0	1
2005	15 Nov	Belfast	1	1

		v ROMANIA	*NI*	*R*
WC1984	12 Sept	Belfast	3	2
WC1985	16 Oct	Bucharest	1	0
1994	23 Mar	Belfast	2	0
2006	27 May	Chicago	0	2

		v SAN MARINO	*NI*	*SM*
WC2008	15 Oct	Belfast	4	0
WC2009	11 Feb	Serravalle	3	0

		v ST KITTS & NEVIS	*NI*	*SK*
2004	2 June	Basseterre	2	0

		v SERBIA	*NI*	*S*
2009	14 Nov	Belfast	0	1
EC2011	25 Mar	Belgrade	1	2
EC2011	2 Sept	Belfast	0	1

		v SERBIA-MONTENEGRO	*NI*	*SM*
2004	28 Apr	Belfast	1	1

		v SLOVAKIA	*NI*	*S*
1998	25 Mar	Belfast	1	0
WC2008	6 Sept	Bratislava	1	2
WC2009	9 Sept	Belfast	0	2

		v SLOVENIA	*NI*	*S*
WC2008	11 Oct	Maribor	0	2
WC2009	1 Apr	Belfast	1	0
EC2010	3 Sept	Maribor	1	0
EC2011	29 Mar	Belfast	0	0

		v SOUTH AFRICA	*NI*	*SA*
1924	24 Sept	Belfast	1	2

		v SPAIN	*NI*	*S*
1958	15 Oct	Madrid	2	6
1963	30 May	Bilbao	1	1
1963	30 Oct	Belfast	0	1
EC1970	11 Nov	Seville	0	3
EC1972	16 Feb	Hull	1	1
WC1982	25 June	Valencia	1	0
1985	27 Mar	Palma	0	0
WC1986	7 June	Guadalajara	1	2
WC1988	21 Dec	Seville	0	4
WC1989	8 Feb	Belfast	0	2
WC1992	14 Oct	Belfast	0	0
WC1993	28 Apr	Seville	1	3
1998	2 June	Santander	1	4
2002	17 Apr	Belfast	0	5
EC2002	12 Oct	Albacete	0	3
EC2003	11 June	Belfast	0	0
EC2006	6 Sept	Belfast	3	2
EC2007	21 Nov	Las Palmas	0	1

		v SWEDEN	*NI*	*S*
EC1974	30 Oct	Solna	2	0
EC1975	3 Sept	Belfast	1	2
WC1980	15 Oct	Belfast	3	0
WC1981	3 June	Solna	0	1
1996	24 Apr	Belfast	1	2
EC2007	28 Mar	Belfast	2	1
EC2007	17 Oct	Stockholm	1	1

		v SWITZERLAND	*NI*	*S*
WC1964	14 Oct	Belfast	1	0
WC1964	14 Nov	Lausanne	1	2
1998	22 Apr	Belfast	1	0
2004	18 Aug	Zurich	0	0

		v THAILAND	*NI*	*T*
1997	21 May	Bangkok	0	0

		v TRINIDAD & TOBAGO	*NI*	*TT*
2004	6 June	Bacolet	3	0

		v TURKEY	*NI*	*T*
WC1968	23 Oct	Belfast	4	1
WC1968	11 Dec	Istanbul	3	0
EC1983	30 Mar	Belfast	2	1
EC1983	12 Oct	Ankara	0	1
WC1985	1 May	Belfast	2	0
WC1985	11 Sept	Izmir	0	0
EC1986	12 Nov	Izmir	0	0
EC1987	11 Nov	Belfast	1	0
EC1998	5 Sept	Istanbul	0	3
EC1999	4 Sept	Belfast	0	3
2010	26 May	New Britain	0	2

		v UKRAINE	*NI*	*U*
WC1996	31 Aug	Belfast	0	1
WC1997	2 Apr	Kiev	1	2
EC2002	16 Oct	Belfast	0	0
EC2003	6 Sept	Donetsk	0	0

		v URUGUAY	*NI*	*U*
1964	29 Apr	Belfast	3	0
1990	18 May	Belfast	1	0
2006	21 May	New Jersey	0	1

		v USSR	*NI*	*USSR*
WC1969	19 Sept	Belfast	0	0
WC1969	22 Oct	Moscow	0	2
EC1971	22 Sept	Moscow	0	1
EC1971	13 Oct	Belfast	1	1

		v YUGOSLAVIA	*NI*	*Y*
EC1975	16 Mar	Belfast	1	0
EC1975	19 Nov	Belgrade	0	1
WC1982	17 June	Zaragoza	0	0
EC1987	29 Apr	Belfast	1	2
EC1987	14 Oct	Sarajevo	0	3
EC1990	12 Sept	Belfast	0	2
EC1991	27 Mar	Belgrade	1	4
2000	16 Aug	Belfast	1	2

REPUBLIC OF IRELAND

		v ALBANIA	*RI*	*A*
WC1992	26 May	Dublin	2	0
WC1993	26 May	Tirana	2	1
EC2003	2 Apr	Tirana	0	0
EC2003	7 June	Dublin	2	1

		v ALGERIA	*RI*	*A*
1982	28 Apr	Algiers	0	2
2010	28 May	Dublin	3	0

		v ANDORRA	*RI*	*A*
WC2001	28 Mar	Barcelona	3	0
WC2001	25 Apr	Dublin	3	1
EC2010	7 Sept	Dublin	3	1
EC2011	7 Oct	Andorra La Vella	2	0

		v ARGENTINA	*RI*	*A*
1951	13 May	Dublin	0	1
†1979	29 May	Dublin	0	0
1980	16 May	Dublin	0	1
1998	22 Apr	Dublin	0	2
2010	11 Aug	Dublin	0	1

†*Not considered a full international.*

		v ARMENIA	*RI*	*A*
EC2010	3 Sept	Erevan	1	0
EC2011	11 Oct	Dublin	2	1

		v AUSTRALIA	*RI*	*A*
2003	19 Aug	Dublin	2	1
2009	12 Aug	Limerick	0	3

		v AUSTRIA	*RI*	*A*
1952	7 May	Vienna	0	6
1953	25 Mar	Dublin	4	0
1958	14 Mar	Vienna	1	3
1962	8 Apr	Dublin	2	3

			RI	*A*
EC1963	25 Sept	Vienna	0	0
EC1963	13 Oct	Dublin	3	2
1966	22 May	Vienna	0	1
1968	10 Nov	Dublin	2	2
EC1971	30 May	Dublin	1	4
EC1971	10 Oct	Linz	0	6
EC1995	11 June	Dublin	1	3
EC1995	6 Sept	Vienna	1	3

		v BELGIUM	*RI*	*B*
1928	12 Feb	Liège	4	2
1929	30 Apr	Dublin	4	0
1930	11 May	Brussels	3	1
WC1934	25 Feb	Dublin	4	4
1949	24 Apr	Dublin	0	2
1950	10 May	Brussels	1	5
1965	24 Mar	Dublin	0	2
1966	25 May	Liège	3	2
WC1980	15 Oct	Dublin	1	1
WC1981	25 Mar	Brussels	0	1
EC1986	10 Sept	Brussels	2	2
EC1987	29 Apr	Dublin	0	0
WC1997	29 Oct	Dublin	1	1
WC1997	16 Nov	Brussels	1	2

		v BOLIVIA	*RI*	*B*
1994	24 May	Dublin	1	0
1996	15 June	New Jersey	3	0
2007	26 May	Boston	1	1

		v BOSNIA	*RI*	*B*
2012	26 May	Dublin	1	0

		v BRAZIL	*RI*	*B*
1974	5 May	Rio de Janeiro	1	2
1982	27 May	Uberlandia	0	7
1987	23 May	Dublin	1	0
2004	18 Feb	Dublin	0	0
2008	6 Feb	Dublin	0	1
2010	2 Mar	Emirates	0	2

		v BULGARIA	*RI*	*B*
WC1977	1 June	Sofia	1	2
WC1977	12 Oct	Dublin	0	0
EC1979	19 May	Sofia	0	1
EC1979	17 Oct	Dublin	3	0
WC1987	1 Apr	Sofia	1	2
WC1987	14 Oct	Dublin	2	0
2004	18 Aug	Dublin	1	1
WC2009	28 Mar	Dublin	1	1
WC2009	6 June	Sofia	1	1

		v CAMEROON	*RI*	*C*
WC2002	1 June	Niigata	1	1

		v CANADA	*RI*	*C*
2003	18 Nov	Dublin	3	0

		v CHILE	*RI*	*C*
1960	30 Mar	Dublin	2	0
1972	21 June	Recife	1	2
1974	12 May	Santiago	2	1
1982	22 May	Santiago	0	1
1991	22 May	Dublin	1	1
2006	24 May	Dublin	0	1

		v CHINA	*RI*	*C*
1984	3 June	Sapporo	1	0
2005	29 Mar	Dublin	1	0

		v COLOMBIA	*RI*	*C*
2008	29 May	Fulham	1	0

		v CROATIA	*RI*	*C*
1996	2 June	Dublin	2	2
EC1998	5 Sept	Dublin	2	0
EC1999	4 Sept	Zagreb	0	1
2001	15 Aug	Dublin	2	2
2004	16 Nov	Dublin	1	0
2011	10 Aug	Dublin	0	0
EC2012	10 June	Poznan	1	3

		v CYPRUS	*RI*	*C*
WC1980	26 Mar	Nicosia	3	2
WC1980	19 Nov	Dublin	6	0
WC2001	24 Mar	Nicosia	4	0
WC2001	6 Oct	Dublin	4	0
WC2004	4 Sept	Dublin	3	0
WC2005	8 Oct	Nicosia	1	0
EC2006	7 Oct	Nicosia	2	5
EC2007	17 Oct	Dublin	1	1
2008	15 Oct	Dublin	1	0
WC2009	5 Sept	Nicosia	2	1

		v CZECHOSLOVAKIA	*RI*	*C*
1938	18 May	Prague	2	2
EC1959	5 Apr	Dublin	2	0
EC1959	10 May	Bratislava	0	4
WC1961	8 Oct	Dublin	1	3
WC1961	29 Oct	Prague	1	7
EC1967	21 May	Dublin	0	2
EC1967	22 Nov	Prague	2	1
WC1969	4 May	Dublin	1	2
WC1969	7 Oct	Prague	0	3
1979	26 Sept	Prague	1	4
1981	29 Apr	Dublin	3	1
1986	27 May	Reykjavik	1	0

		v CZECH REPUBLIC	*RI*	*C*
1994	5 June	Dublin	1	3
1996	24 Apr	Prague	0	2
1998	25 Mar	Olomouc	1	2
2000	23 Feb	Dublin	3	2
2004	31 Mar	Dublin	2	1
EC2006	11 Oct	Dublin	1	1
EC2007	12 Sept	Prague	0	1
2012	29 Feb	Dublin	1	1

		v DENMARK	*RI*	*D*
WC1956	3 Oct	Dublin	2	1
WC1957	2 Oct	Copenhagen	2	0
WC1968	4 Dec	Dublin	1	1
(abandoned after 51 mins)				
WC1969	27 May	Copenhagen	0	2
WC1969	15 Oct	Dublin	1	1
EC1978	24 May	Copenhagen	3	3
EC1979	2 May	Dublin	2	0
WC1984	14 Nov	Copenhagen	0	3
WC1985	13 Nov	Dublin	1	4
WC1992	14 Oct	Copenhagen	0	0
WC1993	28 Apr	Dublin	1	1
2002	27 Mar	Dublin	3	0
2007	22 Aug	Copenhagen	4	0

		v ECUADOR	*RI*	*E*
1972	19 June	Natal	3	2
2007	23 May	New Jersey	1	1

		v EGYPT	*RI*	*E*
WC1990	17 June	Palermo	0	0

		v ENGLAND	*RI*	*E*
1946	30 Sept	Dublin	0	1
1949	21 Sept	Everton	2	0
WC1957	8 May	Wembley	1	5
WC1957	19 May	Dublin	1	1
1964	24 May	Dublin	1	3
1976	8 Sept	Wembley	1	1
EC1978	25 Oct	Dublin	1	1
EC1980	6 Feb	Wembley	0	2
1985	26 Mar	Wembley	1	2
EC1988	12 June	Stuttgart	1	0
WC1990	11 June	Cagliari	1	1
EC1990	14 Nov	Dublin	1	1
EC1991	27 Mar	Wembley	1	1
1995	15 Feb	Dublin	1	0
(abandoned after 27 mins)				

		v ESTONIA	*RI*	*E*
WC2000	11 Oct	Dublin	2	0
WC2001	6 June	Tallinn	2	0
EC2011	11 Nov	Tallinn	4	0
EC2011	15 Nov	Dublin	1	1

		v FAEROES	*RI*	*F*
EC2004	13 Oct	Dublin	2	0
EC2005	8 June	Toftir	2	0

		v FINLAND	*RI*	*F*
wc1949	8 Sept	Dublin	3	0
wc1949	9 Oct	Helsinki	1	1
1990	16 May	Dublin	1	1
2000	15 Nov	Dublin	3	0
2002	21 Aug	Helsinki	3	0

		v FRANCE	*RI*	*F*
1937	23 May	Paris	2	0
1952	16 Nov	Dublin	1	1
wc1953	4 Oct	Dublin	3	5
wc1953	25 Nov	Paris	0	1
wc1972	15 Nov	Dublin	2	1
wc1973	19 May	Paris	1	1
wc1976	17 Nov	Paris	0	2
wc1977	30 Mar	Dublin	1	0
wc1980	28 Oct	Paris	0	2
wc1981	14 Oct	Dublin	3	2
1989	7 Feb	Dublin	0	0
wc2004	9 Oct	Paris	0	0
wc2005	7 Sept	Dublin	0	1
wc2009	14 Nov	Dublin	0	1
wc2009	18 Nov	Paris	1	1

		v GEORGIA	*RI*	*G*
EC2003	29 Mar	Tbilisi	2	1
EC2003	11 June	Dublin	2	0
wc2008	6 Sept	Mainz	2	1
wc2009	11 Feb	Dublin	2	1

		v GERMANY	*RI*	*G*
1935	8 May	Dortmund	1	3
1936	17 Oct	Dublin	5	2
1939	23 May	Bremen	1	1
1994	29 May	Hanover	2	0
wc2002	5 June	Ibaraki	1	1
EC2006	2 Sept	Stuttgart	0	1
EC2007	13 Oct	Dublin	0	0

		v WEST GERMANY	*RI*	*WG*
1951	17 Oct	Dublin	3	2
1952	4 May	Cologne	0	3
1955	28 May	Hamburg	1	2
1956	25 Nov	Dublin	3	0
1960	11 May	Dusseldorf	1	0
1966	4 May	Dublin	0	4
1970	9 May	Berlin	1	2
1975	1 Mar	Dublin	1	0†
1979	22 May	Dublin	1	3
1981	21 May	Bremen	0	3†
1989	6 Sept	Dublin	1	1

†*v West Germany 'B'*

		v GREECE	*RI*	*G*
2000	26 Apr	Dublin	0	1
2002	20 Nov	Athens	0	0

		v HOLLAND	*RI*	*N*
1932	8 May	Amsterdam	2	0
1934	8 Apr	Amsterdam	2	5
1935	8 Dec	Dublin	3	5
1955	1 May	Dublin	1	0
1956	10 May	Rotterdam	4	1
wc1980	10 Sept	Dublin	2	1
wc1981	9 Sept	Rotterdam	2	2
EC1982	22 Sept	Rotterdam	1	2
EC1983	12 Oct	Dublin	2	3
EC1988	18 June	Gelsenkirchen	0	1
wc1990	21 June	Palermo	1	1
1994	20 Apr	Tilburg	1	0
wc1994	4 July	Orlando	0	2
EC1995	13 Dec	Liverpool	0	2
1996	4 June	Rotterdam	1	3
wc2000	2 Sept	Amsterdam	2	2
wc2001	1 Sept	Dublin	1	0
2004	5 June	Amsterdam	1	0
2006	16 Aug	Dublin	0	4

		v HUNGARY	*RI*	*H*
1934	15 Dec	Dublin	2	4
1936	3 May	Budapest	3	3
1936	6 Dec	Dublin	2	3
1939	19 Mar	Cork	2	2
1939	18 May	Budapest	2	2
wc1969	8 June	Dublin	1	2
wc1969	5 Nov	Budapest	0	4
wc1989	8 Mar	Budapest	0	0
wc1989	4 June	Dublin	2	0
1991	11 Sept	Gyor	2	1
2012	4 June	Budapest	0	0

		v ICELAND	*RI*	*I*
EC1962	12 Aug	Dublin	4	2
EC1962	2 Sept	Reykjavik	1	1
EC1982	13 Oct	Dublin	2	0
EC1983	21 Sept	Reykjavik	3	0
1986	25 May	Reykjavik	2	1
wc1996	10 Nov	Dublin	0	0
wc1997	6 Sept	Reykjavik	4	2

		v IRAN	*RI*	*I*
1972	18 June	Recife	2	1
wc2001	10 Nov	Dublin	2	0
wc2001	15 Nov	Tehran	0	1

		v N. IRELAND	*RI*	*NI*
EC1978	20 Sept	Dublin	0	0
EC1979	21 Nov	Belfast	0	1
wc1988	14 Sept	Belfast	0	0
wc1989	11 Oct	Dublin	3	0
wc1993	31 Mar	Dublin	3	0
wc1993	17 Nov	Belfast	1	1
EC1994	16 Nov	Belfast	4	0
EC1995	29 Mar	Dublin	1	1
1999	29 May	Dublin	0	1
NC2011	24 May	Dublin	5	0

		v ISRAEL	*RI*	*I*
1984	4 Apr	Tel Aviv	0	3
1985	27 May	Tel Aviv	0	0
1987	10 Nov	Dublin	5	0
EC2005	26 Mar	Tel Aviv	1	1
EC2005	4 June	Dublin	2	2

		v ITALY	*RI*	*I*
1926	21 Mar	Turin	0	3
1927	23 Apr	Dublin	1	2
EC1970	8 Dec	Rome	0	3
EC1971	10 May	Dublin	1	2
1985	5 Feb	Dublin	1	2
wc1990	30 June	Rome	0	1
1992	4 June	Foxboro	0	2
wc1994	18 June	New York	1	0
2005	17 Aug	Dublin	1	2
wc2009	1 Apr	Bari	1	1
wc2009	10 Oct	Dublin	2	2
2011	7 June	Liege	2	0
EC2012	18 June	Poznan	0	2

		v JAMAICA	*RI*	*J*
2004	2 June	Charlton	1	0

		v LATVIA	*RI*	*L*
wc1992	9 Sept	Dublin	4	0
wc1993	2 June	Riga	2	1
EC1994	7 Sept	Riga	3	0
EC1995	11 Oct	Dublin	2	1

		v LIECHTENSTEIN	*RI*	*L*
EC1994	12 Oct	Dublin	4	0
EC1995	3 June	Eschen	0	0
wc1996	31 Aug	Eschen	5	0
wc1997	21 May	Dublin	5	0

		v LITHUANIA	*RI*	*L*
wc1993	16 June	Vilnius	1	0
wc1993	8 Sept	Dublin	2	0
wc1997	20 Aug	Dublin	0	0
wc1997	10 Sept	Vilnius	2	1

v LUXEMBOURG

			RI	L
1936	9 May	Luxembourg	5	1
wc1953	28 Oct	Dublin	4	0
wc1954	7 Mar	Luxembourg	1	0
EC1987	28 May	Luxembourg	2	0
EC1987	9 Sept	Dublin	2	1

v MACEDONIA

			RI	M
wc1996	9 Oct	Dublin	3	0
wc1997	2 Apr	Skopje	2	3
EC1999	9 June	Dublin	1	0
EC1999	9 Oct	Skopje	1	1
EC2011	26 Mar	Dublin	2	1
EC2011	4 June	Podgorica	2	0

v MALTA

			RI	M
EC1983	30 Mar	Valletta	1	0
EC1983	16 Nov	Dublin	8	0
wc1989	28 May	Dublin	2	0
wc1989	15 Nov	Valletta	2	0
1990	2 June	Valletta	3	0
EC1998	14 Oct	Dublin	5	0
EC1999	8 Sept	Valletta	3	2

v MEXICO

			RI	M
1984	8 Aug	Dublin	0	0
wc1994	24 June	Orlando	1	2
1996	13 June	New Jersey	2	2
1998	23 May	Dublin	0	0
2000	4 June	Chicago	2	2

v MONTENEGRO

			RI	M
wc2008	10 Sept	Podgorica	0	0
wc2009	14 Oct	Dublin	0	0

v MOROCCO

			RI	M
1990	12 Sept	Dublin	1	0

v NIGERIA

			RI	N
2002	16 May	Dublin	1	2
2004	29 May	Charlton	0	3
2009	29 May	Fulham	1	1

v NORWAY

			RI	N
wc1937	10 Oct	Oslo	2	3
wc1937	7 Nov	Dublin	3	3
1950	26 Nov	Dublin	2	2
1951	30 May	Oslo	3	2
1954	8 Nov	Dublin	2	1
1955	25 May	Oslo	3	1
1960	6 Nov	Dublin	3	1
1964	13 May	Oslo	4	1
1973	6 June	Oslo	1	1
1976	24 Mar	Dublin	3	0
1978	21 May	Oslo	0	0
wc1984	17 Oct	Oslo	0	1
wc1985	1 May	Dublin	0	0
1988	1 June	Oslo	0	0
wc1994	28 June	New York	0	0
2003	30 Apr	Dublin	1	0
2008	20 Aug	Oslo	1	1
2010	17 Nov	Dublin	1	2

v PARAGUAY

			RI	P
1999	10 Feb	Dublin	2	0
2010	25 May	Dublin	2	1

v POLAND

			RI	P
1938	22 May	Warsaw	0	6
1938	13 Nov	Dublin	3	2
1958	11 May	Katowice	2	2
1958	5 Oct	Dublin	2	2
1964	10 May	Kracow	1	3
1964	25 Oct	Dublin	3	2
1968	15 May	Dublin	2	2
1968	30 Oct	Katowice	0	1
1970	6 May	Dublin	1	2
1970	23 Sept	Dublin	0	2
1973	16 May	Wroclaw	0	2
1973	21 Oct	Dublin	1	0
1976	26 May	Poznan	2	0
1977	24 Apr	Dublin	0	0
1978	12 Apr	Lodz	0	3
1981	23 May	Bydgoszcz	0	3
1984	23 May	Dublin	0	0
1986	12 Nov	Warsaw	0	1
1988	22 May	Dublin	3	1
EC1991	1 May	Dublin	0	0
EC1991	16 Oct	Poznan	3	3
2004	28 Apr	Bydgoszcz	0	0
2008	19 Nov	Dublin	2	3

v PORTUGAL

			RI	P
1946	16 June	Lisbon	1	3
1947	4 May	Dublin	0	2
1948	23 May	Lisbon	0	2
1949	22 May	Dublin	1	0
1972	25 June	Recife	1	2
1992	7 June	Boston	2	0
EC1995	26 Apr	Dublin	1	0
EC1995	15 Nov	Lisbon	0	3
1996	29 May	Dublin	0	1
wc2000	7 Oct	Lisbon	1	1
wc2001	2 June	Dublin	1	1
2005	9 Feb	Dublin	1	0

v ROMANIA

			RI	R
1988	23 Mar	Dublin	2	0
wc1990	25 June	Genoa	0	0*
wc1997	30 Apr	Bucharest	0	1
wc1997	11 Oct	Dublin	1	1
2004	27 May	Dublin	1	0

v RUSSIA

			RI	R
1994	23 Mar	Dublin	0	0
1996	27 Mar	Dublin	0	2
2002	13 Feb	Dublin	2	0
EC2002	7 Sept	Moscow	2	4
EC2003	6 Sept	Dublin	1	1
EC2010	8 Oct	Dublin	2	3
EC2011	6 Sept	Moscow	0	0

v SAN MARINO

			RI	SM
EC2006	15 Nov	Dublin	5	0
EC2007	7 Feb	Serravalle	2	1

v SAUDI ARABIA

			RI	SA
wc2002	11 June	Yokohama	3	0

v SERBIA

			RI	S
2008	24 May	Dublin	1	1

v SCOTLAND

			RI	S
wc1961	3 May	Glasgow	1	4
wc1961	7 May	Dublin	0	3
1963	9 June	Dublin	1	0
1969	21 Sept	Dublin	1	1
EC1986	15 Oct	Dublin	0	0
EC1987	18 Feb	Glasgow	1	0
2000	30 May	Dublin	1	2
2003	12 Feb	Glasgow	2	0
NC2011	29 May	Dublin	1	0

v SLOVAKIA

			RI	S
EC2007	28 Mar	Dublin	1	0
EC2007	8 Sept	Bratislava	2	2
EC2010	12 Oct	Zilina	1	1
EC2011	2 Sept	Dublin	0	0

v SOUTH AFRICA

			RI	SA
2000	11 June	New Jersey	2	1
2009	8 Sept	Limerick	1	0

v SPAIN

			RI	S
1931	26 Apr	Barcelona	1	1
1931	13 Dec	Dublin	0	5
1946	23 June	Madrid	1	0
1947	2 Mar	Dublin	3	2
1948	30 May	Barcelona	1	2
1949	12 June	Dublin	1	4
1952	1 June	Madrid	0	6
1955	27 Nov	Dublin	2	2

			RI	S
EC1964	11 Mar	Seville	1	5
EC1964	8 Apr	Dublin	0	2
WC1965	5 May	Dublin	1	0
WC1965	27 Oct	Seville	1	4
WC1965	10 Nov	Paris	0	1
EC1966	23 Oct	Dublin	0	0
EC1966	7 Dec	Valencia	0	2
1977	9 Feb	Dublin	0	1
EC1982	17 Nov	Dublin	3	3
EC1983	27 Apr	Zaragoza	0	2
1985	26 May	Cork	0	0
WC1988	16 Nov	Seville	0	2
WC1989	26 Apr	Dublin	1	0
WC1992	18 Nov	Seville	0	0
WC1993	13 Oct	Dublin	1	3
WC2002	16 June	Suwon	1	1
EC2012	14 June	Gdansk	0	4

v SWEDEN

			RI	S
WC1949	2 June	Stockholm	1	3
WC1949	13 Nov	Dublin	1	3
1959	1 Nov	Dublin	3	2
1960	18 May	Malmo	1	4
EC1970	14 Oct	Dublin	1	1
EC1970	28 Oct	Malmo	0	1
1999	28 Apr	Dublin	2	0
2006	1 Mar	Dublin	3	0

v SWITZERLAND

			RI	S
1935	5 May	Basle	0	1
1936	17 Mar	Dublin	1	0
1937	17 May	Berne	1	0
1938	18 Sept	Dublin	4	0
1948	5 Dec	Dublin	0	1
EC1975	11 May	Dublin	2	1
EC1975	21 May	Berne	0	1
1980	30 Apr	Dublin	2	0
WC1985	2 June	Dublin	3	0
WC1985	11 Sept	Berne	0	0
1992	25 Mar	Dublin	2	1
EC2002	16 Oct	Dublin	1	2
EC2003	11 Oct	Basle	0	2
WC2004	8 Sept	Basle	1	1
WC2005	12 Oct	Dublin	0	0

v TRINIDAD & TOBAGO

			RI	TT
1982	30 May	Port of Spain	1	2

v TUNISIA

			RI	T
1988	19 Oct	Dublin	4	0

v TURKEY

			RI	T
EC1966	16 Nov	Dublin	2	1
EC1967	22 Feb	Ankara	1	2
EC1974	20 Nov	Izmir	1	1
EC1975	29 Oct	Dublin	4	0
1976	13 Oct	Ankara	3	3
1978	5 Apr	Dublin	4	2
1990	26 May	Izmir	0	0
EC1990	17 Oct	Dublin	5	0
EC1991	13 Nov	Istanbul	3	1
EC2000	13 Nov	Dublin	1	1
EC2000	17 Nov	Bursa	0	0
2003	9 Sept	Dublin	2	2

v URUGUAY

			RI	U
1974	8 May	Montevideo	0	2
1986	23 Apr	Dublin	1	1
2011	29 Mar	Dublin	2	3

v USA

			RI	USA
1979	29 Oct	Dublin	3	2
1991	1 June	Boston	1	1
1992	29 Apr	Dublin	4	1
1992	30 May	Washington	1	3
1996	9 June	Boston	1	2
2000	6 June	Boston	1	1
2002	17 Apr	Dublin	2	1

v USSR

			RI	USSR
WC1972	18 Oct	Dublin	1	2
WC1973	13 May	Moscow	0	1
EC1974	30 Oct	Dublin	3	0
EC1975	18 May	Kiev	1	2
WC1984	12 Sept	Dublin	1	0
WC1985	16 Oct	Moscow	0	2
EC1988	15 June	Hanover	1	1
1990	25 Apr	Dublin	1	0

v WALES

			RI	W
1960	28 Sept	Dublin	2	3
1979	11 Sept	Swansea	1	2
1981	24 Feb	Dublin	1	3
1986	26 Mar	Dublin	0	1
1990	28 Mar	Dublin	1	0
1991	6 Feb	Wrexham	3	0
1992	19 Feb	Dublin	0	1
1993	17 Feb	Dublin	2	1
1997	11 Feb	Cardiff	0	0
EC2007	24 Mar	Dublin	1	0
EC2007	17 Nov	Cardiff	2	2
NC2011	8 Feb	Dublin	3	0

v YUGOSLAVIA

			RI	Y
1955	19 Sept	Dublin	1	4
1988	27 Apr	Dublin	2	0
EC1998	18 Nov	Belgrade	0	1
EC1999	1 Sept	Dublin	2	1

OTHER BRITISH AND IRISH INTERNATIONAL MATCHES 2011–12

FRIENDLIES

Wembley, 12 November 2011, 87,189

England (0) 1 *(Lampard 49)*

Spain (0) 0

England: Hart; Johnson G, Cole, Jones (Rodwell 56), Jagielka, Lescott, Walcott (Downing 46), Parker (Walker 85), Bent (Welbeck 64), Lampard (Barry 57), Milner (Johnson A 76).
Spain: Casillas (Reina 46); Sergio Ramos (Puyol 74), Arbeloa, Jordi Alba, Iniesta (Cazorla 74), Xavi (Mata 46), Busquets (Torres 64), Xabi Alonso, Silva (Fabregas 46), David Villa.
Referee: F. De Bleeckere (Belgium).

Wembley, 15 November 2011, 48,876

England (1) 1 *(Barry 23)*

Sweden (0) 0

England: Hart (Carson 46); Walker, Baines, Jones, Cahill, Terry, Walcott (Milner 58), Rodwell (Sturridge 58), Zamora, Barry, Downing.
Sweden: Isaksson (Wiland 46); Lustig (Wilhelmsson 55), Mellberg (Olsson J 46), Majstorovic, Olsson M, Larsson, Kallstrom (Svensson 70), Ibrahimovic (Toivonen 46), Elmander, Wernbloom, Elm (Bajrami 87).
Referee: P. Kralovec (Czech Republic).

Wembley, 29 February 2012, 76,283

England (0) 2 *(Cahill 85, Young A 89)*

Holland (0) 3 *(Robben 57, 90, Huntelaar 58)*

England: Hart; Richards, Baines, Barry (Milner 46), Smalling (Jones 64), Cahill, Young A, Parker, Welbeck (Campbell 80), Gerrard (Sturridge 33) (Walcott 88), Johnson A (Downing 61).
Holland: Stekelenburg; Boulahrouz (Vlaar 82), Heitinga, Mathijsen, Pieters (Schaars 46), Van Bommel, Kuyt, De Jong N, Van Persie (Huntelaar 46) (De Jong L 62), Sneijder (Emanuelson 76), Robben.
Referee: F. Brych (Germany).

Oslo, 26 May 2012, 21,496

Norway (0) 0

England (1) 1 *(Young 9)*

Norway: Jarstein; Hogli (Ruud 40), Demidov, Hangeland, Riise J, Henriksen, Abdellaoue, Elyounoussi, Pedersen (Grindheim 63), Tettey (Jenssen 89), Braaten.
England: Green; Jones (Kelly 88), Baines, Gerrard (Barry 46) (Oxlade-Chamberlain 73), Jagielka, Lescott, Milner, Parker (Walcott 56), Carroll, Young A (Henderson 73), Downing (Johnson A 85).
Referee: M. Weiner (Germany).

Wembley, 2 June 2012, 85,091

England (1) 1 *(Welbeck 36)*

Belgium (0) 0

England: Hart; Johnson G, Cole, Gerrard (Henderson 83), Cahill (Lescott 19), Terry (Jagielka 70), Milner, Parker, Welbeck (Rooney 53), Young A (Defoe 66), Oxlade-Chamberlain (Walcott 66).
Belgium: Mignolet; Gillet, Vertonghen, Vermaelen, Simons, Mertens (Lukaku 72), Witsel, Mirallas (Chadli 59), Hazard, Fellaini, Dembele.
Referee: P. Rasmussen.

Glasgow, 10 August 2011, 17,582

Scotland (2) 2 *(Kvist Jorgensen 23 (og), Snodgrass 44)*

Denmark (1) 1 *(Eriksen 31)*

Scotland: McGregor; Bardsley, Caldwell G, Wilson D, Crainey, Morrison (Bannan 67), Brown (Cowie 21), Adam (Dorrans 57), Snodgrass (Hanley 88), Naismith (Forrest 74), Miller (Mackail-Smith 57).
Denmark: Sorensen; Poulsen C (Zimling 46), Agger (Jorgensen 58), Boilesen, Kjaer, Kvist, Eriksen, Jacobsen (Silberbauer 73), Rommedahl (Schone 46), Krohn-Delhi (Kadrii 76), Bendtner (Pedersen 46).
Referee: M. Borg (Malta).

Larnaca, 11 November, 2011, 1500

Cyprus (0) 1 *(Christofi 59)*

Scotland (1) 2 *(Miller 23, Mackie 56)*

Cyprus: Georgallides (Kissas 46); Merkis, Alexandrou (Katsis 69), Demetriou (Sielis 46), Parpas (Nicolaou 58), Satsias, Dobrasinovic (Vasilou 74), Solomou, Avraam (Mitidis 46), Christofi, Efrem.
Scotland: McGregor; Whittaker, Bardsley (Crainey 74), Berra, Caldwell G, Cowie, Fletcher D (McArthur 63), Morrison, Miller (Mackail-Smith 63), Mackie (Rhodes 87), Robson (Conway 80).
Referee: M. Levy (Israel).

Koper, 29 February 2012, 4200

Slovenia (1) 1 *(Kirm 33)*

Scotland (1) 1 *(Berra 39)*

Slovenia: Handanovic S; Brecko, Suler, Cesar, Jokic, Birsa (Vuckic 61), Kirm (Pecnik 88), Radosavljevic, Khrin (Matic 84), Dedic (Ljubjankic 82), Ilic.
Scotland: McGregor; Martin, Mulgrew, Caldwell G, Berra, Adam (Bannan 46), Forrest (Robson 86), McArthur, Mackie (Miller 79), Mackail-Smith (Snodgrass 60), Morrison (Dorrans 71).
Referee: A. Stavrev (Macedonia).

Jacksonville, 26 May 2012, 54,894

USA (2) 5 *(Donovan 4, 60, 65, Bradley 11, Jones 70)*

Scotland (1) 1 *(Cameron 15 (og))*

USA: Howard (Guzan 71); Cherundolo, Cameron, Bocanegra (Onyewu 63), Johnson (Castillo 72), Edu (Beckerman 64), Bradley, Jones, Donovan, Boyd (Gomez 64), Torres (Corona 68).
Scotland: McGregor; Bardsley (Martin 59), Mulgrew (Wallace 68), Webster (Berra 82), Caldwell G, McArthur (Whittaker 59), Phillips, Brown, Miller, Bannan (Cowie 51), Maloney (Mackail-Smith 83).
Referee: E. Bonilla (El Salvador).

Cardiff, 10 August 2011, 6378

Wales (0) 1 *(Blake 82)*

Australia (1) 2 *(Cahill 44, Kruse 60)*

Wales: Hennessey; Gunter (Matthews 62), Taylor N, Vaughan (Allen 70), Gabbidon (Blake 46), Williams A, Ramsey (Collison 47), Ledley, Bale, Earnshaw (Morison 62), Bellamy.
Australia: Schwarzer; Wilkshire (Kruse 46), Neill, Spiranovic, Zullo (Sarota 83), Emerton (Williams 48), Kilkenny, Valeri, McKay, Cahill (Troisi 70), McDonald (Jedinak 90).
Referee: K. Tohver (Estonia).

Cardiff, 12 November 2011, 12,637

Wales (2) 4 *(Bale 11, Bellamy 16, Vokes 88, 89)*

Norway (0) 1 *(Huseklepp 61)*

Wales: Hennessey; Gunter, Matthews, Williams A, Blake, Allen (Robson-Kanu 76), Crofts, Ramsey (King 90), Bellamy (Edwards D 90), Morison (Vokes 70), Bale.
Norway: Jarstein (Pettersen 46); Ruud, Waehler (Demidov 46), Hangeland, Riise J, Pedersen, Tettey, Grindheim (Brenne 54), Jenssen (Parr 85), Abdellaoui (Braaten 77), Huseklepp.
Referee: G. Grobelnik (Austria).

Cardiff, 29 February 2012, 23,193

Wales (0) 0

Costa Rica (1) 1 *(Campbell 7)*

Wales: Price; Gunter, Matthews (Ricketts 75), Allen (Collison 63), Blake, Williams A (Gabbidon 70), Robson-Kanu, Crofts, Morison (Vokes 68), Bellamy (Earnshaw 75), Vaughan (Ledley 70).
Costa Rica: Navas; Umana, Salvatierra, Miller, Cunningham (Diaz 88), Barrantes, Azofeifa, Wallace (Gabas 68), Oviedo, Ruiz, Campbell (McDonald 79).
Referee: H. Webb (England).

New Jersey, 27 May 2012, 35,518

Mexico (1) 2 *(De Nigris 43, 89)*

Wales (0) 0

Mexico: Corona; Meza, Salcido, Perez (Torres 71), Rodriguez, Andrade, Barrera (Marquez 76), Moreno, De Nigris, Giovani (Reyna 71), Zavala (Granados 64).
Wales: Brown; Matthews (Ricketts 60), Taylor N (Richards 80), Edwards D (King 71), Gunter, Williams A, Allen, Bellamy, Morison (Vokes 60), Ramsey, Robson-Kanu (Church 60).
Referee: R. Salazar (USA).

Belfast, 29 February 2012, 10,500

Northern Ireland (0) 0

Norway (1) 3 *(Nordtveit 44, Elyounoussi 88, Ruud 90)*

Northern Ireland: Camp; McAuley (Hodson 57), McGivern, Clingan, Hughes (Duff 46), Evans J, Evans C (McCann 46), Davis, Shiels, Paterson (Healy 73), Ferguson (McCourt 69).
Norway: Jarstein; Hogli (Ruud 87), Rogne, Demidov (Reginiussen 60), Riise J, Henriksen (Jenssen 78), Nordtveit, Grindheim (Elyounoussi 60), Pedersen, Abdellaoui (Braaten 46), Huseklepp (Berisha 66).
Referee: H. Jones (Wales).

Amsterdam, 2 June 2012, 50,000

Holland (4) 6 *(Van Persie 11, 29 (pen), Sneijder 15, Afellay 37, 51, Vlaar 78)*

Northern Ireland (0) 0

Holland: Stekelenburg; Van der Wiel, Heitinga, Vlaar, Willems (Schaars 78), Robben (Narsingh 82), Afellay, Van Bommel (Van der Vaart 57), De Jong, Sneijder (Kuyt 70), Van Persie (Huntelaar 57).
Northern Ireland: Camp (Carroll 46); McPake, Hodson, Duff (McArdle 62), Ferguson (Healy 81), Lafferty D (McGivern 46), McCann (Carson 46), Clingan, Norwood, Grigg, Little (McGinn 56).
Referee: R. Schorgenhofer (Austria).

Dublin, 10 August 2011, 20,179

Republic of Ireland (0) 0

Croatia (0) 0

Republic of Ireland: Given (Westwood 64); Kelly, Dunne, St Ledger-Hall, Ward, Duff (Treacy 83), Whelan (O'Dea 74), Gibson, Hunt (Keogh 64), Keane, Long (Cox 83).
Croatia: Pletikosa; Corluka (Vrsaljko 74), Lovren, Simunic, Strinic, Srna, Vekojevic (Dujmovic 87), Modric, Kranjcar (Ilicevic 65), Mandzukic (Kalinic 74), Eduardo (Olic 46).
Referee: T. Hagen (Norway).

Dublin, 29 February 2012, 37,741

Republic of Ireland (0) 1 *(Cox 87)*

Czech Republic (0) 1 *(Baros 50)*

Republic of Ireland: Given; O'Shea, Ward, Whelan (Hunt 63), O'Dea, St Ledger-Hall, Duff (Green 63), Andrews, Long (Cox 71), Keane (Walters 71), McGeady (McClean 79).
Czech Republic: Cech; Gebreselassie (Pilar 66), Limbersky, Sivok, Kadlec M, Petrzela (Rajtoral 66), Resek (Pekhart 88), Stajner (Kolar 59), Plasil, Baros (Lafata 59), Jiracek (Hubschman 46).
Referee: De Sousa (Portugal).

Dublin, 26 May 2012, 37,100

Republic of Ireland (0) 1 *(Long 78)*

Bosnia (0) 0

Republic of Ireland: Westwood; McShane (Kelly 78), Dunne (St Ledger-Hall 70), O'Dea, Ward, Duff (McGeady 46), Whelan (Andrews 46), Gibson, McClean, Keane (Long 62), Doyle (Walters 63).
Bosnia: Begovic; Medunjanin (Stevanovic 46), Pandza, Jahic, Mujdza (Zahirovic 56), Pjanic, Misimovic (Alispahic 81), Rahimic (Vrancic 46), Lulic, Dzeko, Ibisevic (Vranjes 70).
Referee: N. Haenni (Switzerland).

Budapest, 4 June 2012, 17,000

Hungary (0) 0

Republic of Ireland (0) 0

Hungary: Bogdan; Varga, Meszaros, Gyurcso (Koltai 86), Korcsmar, Halmosi (Kadar 69), Pinter (Vanczak 46), Koman, Dzsudzsak, Szakaly (Szabics 66), Szalai (Nemeth 79).
Republic of Ireland: Given (Westwood 46); O'Shea, St Ledger-Hall, Dunne, Ward, Duff (Hunt 63), Andrews (Gibson 66), Whelan (Green 85), McGeady, Keane (Cox 60), Doyle (Walters 46).
Referee: K. Hansen (Denmark).

INTERNATIONAL APPEARANCES 1872–2012

This is a list of full international appearances by Englishmen, Irishmen, Scotsmen and Welshmen in matches against the Home Countries and against foreign nations. It does not include unofficial matches against Commonwealth and Empire countries. The year indicated refers to the player's international debut season; i.e. 2005 is the 2004–05 season. **Bold** type indicates players who have made an international appearance in season 2011–12.

As at July 2012.

ENGLAND

Abbott, W. 1902 (Everton) 1
A'Court, A. 1958 (Liverpool) 5
Adams, T. A. 1987 (Arsenal) 66
Adcock, H. 1929 (Leicester C) 5
Agbonlahor, G. 2009 (Aston Villa) 3
Alcock, C. W. 1875 (Wanderers) 1
Alderson, J. T. 1923 (Crystal Palace) 1
Aldridge, A. 1888 (WBA, Walsall Town Swifts) 2
Allen, A. 1888 (Aston Villa) 1
Allen, A. 1960 (Stoke C) 3
Allen, C. 1984 (QPR, Tottenham H) 5
Allen, H. 1888 (Wolverhampton W) 5
Allen, J. P. 1934 (Portsmouth) 2
Allen, R. 1952 (WBA) 5
Alsford, W. J. 1935 (Tottenham H) 1
Amos, A. 1885 (Old Carthusians) 2
Anderson, R. D. 1879 (Old Etonians) 1
Anderson, S. 1962 (Sunderland) 2
Anderson, V. A. 1979 (Nottingham F, Arsenal, Manchester U) 30
Anderton, D. R. 1994 (Tottenham H) 30
Angus, J. 1961 (Burnley) 1
Armfield, J. C. 1959 (Blackpool) 43
Armitage, G. H. 1926 (Charlton Ath) 1
Armstrong, D. 1980 (Middlesbrough, Southampton) 3
Armstrong, K. 1955 (Chelsea) 1
Arnold, J. 1933 (Fulham) 1
Arthur, J. W. H. 1885 (Blackburn R) 7
Ashcroft, J. 1906 (Woolwich Arsenal) 3
Ashmore, G. S. 1926 (WBA) 1
Ashton, C. T. 1926 (Corinthians) 1
Ashton, D. 2008 (West Ham U) 1
Ashurst, W. 1923 (Notts Co) 5
Astall, G. 1956 (Birmingham C) 2
Astle, J. 1969 (WBA) 5
Aston, J. 1949 (Manchester U) 17
Athersmith, W. C. 1892 (Aston Villa) 12
Atyeo, P. J. W. 1956 (Bristol C) 6
Austin, S. W. 1926 (Manchester C) 1

Bach, P. 1899 (Sunderland) 1
Bache, J. W. 1903 (Aston Villa) 7
Baddeley, T. 1903 (Wolverhampton W) 5
Bagshaw, J. J. 1920 (Derby Co) 1
Bailey, G. R. 1985 (Manchester U) 2
Bailey, H. P. 1908 (Leicester Fosse) 5
Bailey, M. A. 1964 (Charlton Ath) 2
Bailey, N. C. 1878 (Clapham R) 19
Baily, E. F. 1950 (Tottenham H) 9
Bain, J. 1877 (Oxford University) 1
Baines, L. J. 2010 (Everton) 8
Baker, A. 1928 (Arsenal) 1
Baker, B. H. 1921 (Everton, Chelsea) 2
Baker, J. H. 1960 (Hibernian, Arsenal) 8
Ball, A. J. 1965 (Blackpool, Everton, Arsenal) 72
Ball, J. 1928 (Bury) 1
Ball, M. J. 2001 (Everton) 1
Balmer, W. 1905 (Everton) 1
Bamber, J. 1921 (Liverpool) 1
Bambridge, A. L. 1881 (Swifts) 3
Bambridge, E. C. 1879 (Swifts) 18
Bambridge, E. H. 1876 (Swifts) 1
Banks, G. 1963 (Leicester C, Stoke C) 73
Banks, H. E. 1901 (Millwall) 1
Banks, T. 1958 (Bolton W) 6
Bannister, W. 1901 (Burnley, Bolton W) 2
Barclay, R. 1932 (Sheffield U) 3
Bardsley, D. J. 1993 (QPR) 2
Barham, M. 1983 (Norwich C) 2
Barkas, S. 1936 (Manchester C) 5
Barker, J. 1935 (Derby Co) 11
Barker, R. 1872 (Herts Rangers) 1
Barker, R. R. 1895 (Casuals) 1
Barlow, R. J. 1955 (WBA) 1
Barmby, N. J. 1995 (Tottenham H, Middlesbrough, Everton, Liverpool) 23
Barnes, J. 1983 (Watford, Liverpool) 79
Barnes, P. S. 1978 (Manchester C, WBA, Leeds U) 22
Barnet, H. H. 1882 (Royal Engineers) 1
Barrass, M. W. 1952 (Bolton W) 3
Barrett, A. F. 1930 (Fulham) 1
Barrett, E. D. 1991 (Oldham Ath, Aston Villa) 3
Barrett, J. W. 1929 (West Ham U) 1
Barry, G. 2000 (Aston Villa, Manchester C) 53
Barry, L. 1928 (Leicester C) 5
Barson, F. 1920 (Aston Villa) 1
Barton, J. 1890 (Blackburn R) 1
Barton, J. 2007 (Manchester C) 1
Barton, P. H. 1921 (Birmingham) 7
Barton, W. D. 1995 (Wimbledon, Newcastle U) 3
Bassett, W. I. 1888 (WBA) 16
Bastard, S. R. 1880 (Upton Park) 1
Bastin, C. S. 1932 (Arsenal) 21
Batty, D. 1991 (Leeds U, Blackburn R, Newcastle U, Leeds U) 42
Baugh, R. 1886 (Stafford Road, Wolverhampton W) 2
Bayliss, A. E. J. M. 1891 (WBA) 1
Baynham, R. L. 1956 (Luton T) 3
Beardsley, P. A. 1986 (Newcastle U, Liverpool, Newcastle U) 59
Beasant, D. J. 1990 (Chelsea) 2
Beasley, A. 1939 (Huddersfield T) 1
Beats, W. E. 1901 (Wolverhampton W) 2
Beattie, J. S. 2003 (Southampton) 5
Beattie, T. K. 1975 (Ipswich T) 9
Beckham, D. R. J. 1997 (Manchester U, Real Madrid, LA Galaxy) 115
Becton, F. 1895 (Preston NE, Liverpool) 2
Bedford, H. 1923 (Blackpool) 2
Bell, C. 1968 (Manchester C) 48
Bennett, W. 1901 (Sheffield U) 2
Benson, R. W. 1913 (Sheffield U) 1
Bent, D. A. 2006 (Charlton Ath, Tottenham H, Sunderland, Aston Villa) 13
Bentley, D. M. 2008 (Blackburn R, Tottenham H) 7
Bentley, R. T. F. 1949 (Chelsea) 12
Beresford, J. 1934 (Aston Villa) 1
Berry, A. 1909 (Oxford University) 1
Berry, J. J. 1953 (Manchester U) 4
Bestall, J. G. 1935 (Grimsby T) 1
Betmead, H. A. 1937 (Grimsby T) 1
Betts, M. P. 1877 (Old Harrovians) 1
Betts, W. 1889 (Sheffield W) 1
Beverley, J. 1884 (Blackburn R) 3
Birkett, R. H. 1879 (Clapham R) 1
Birkett, R. J. E. 1936 (Middlesbrough) 1
Birley, F. H. 1874 (Oxford University, Wanderers) 2
Birtles, G. 1980 (Nottingham F) 3
Bishop, S. M. 1927 (Leicester C) 4
Blackburn, F. 1901 (Blackburn R) 3
Blackburn, G. F. 1924 (Aston Villa) 1
Blenkinsop, E. 1928 (Sheffield W) 26
Bliss, H. 1921 (Tottenham H) 1
Blissett, L. L. 1983 (Watford, AC Milan) 14
Blockley, J. P. 1973 (Arsenal) 1
Bloomer, S. 1895 (Derby Co, Middlesbrough) 23
Blunstone, F. 1955 (Chelsea) 5
Bond, R. 1905 (Preston NE, Bradford C) 8
Bonetti, P. P. 1966 (Chelsea) 7
Bonsor, A. G. 1873 (Wanderers) 2
Booth, F. 1905 (Manchester C) 1
Booth, T. 1898 (Blackburn R, Everton) 2

Bothroyd, J. 2011 (Cardiff C) 1
Bould, S. A. 1994 (Arsenal) 2
Bowden, E. R. 1935 (Arsenal) 6
Bower, A. G. 1924 (Corinthians) 5
Bowers, J. W. 1934 (Derby Co) 3
Bowles, S. 1974 (QPR) 5
Bowser, S. 1920 (WBA) 1
Bowyer, L. D. 2003 (Leeds U) 1
Boyer, P. J. 1976 (Norwich C) 1
Boyes, W. 1935 (WBA, Everton) 3
Boyle, T. W. 1913 (Burnley) 1
Brabrook, P. 1958 (Chelsea) 3
Bracewell, P. W. 1985 (Everton) 3
Bradford, G. R. W. 1956 (Bristol R) 1
Bradford, J. 1924 (Birmingham) 12
Bradley, W. 1959 (Manchester U) 3
Bradshaw, F. 1908 (Sheffield W) 1
Bradshaw, T. H. 1897 (Liverpool) 1
Bradshaw, W. 1910 (Blackburn R) 4
Brann, G. 1886 (Swifts) 3
Brawn, W. F. 1904 (Aston Villa) 2
Bray, J. 1935 (Manchester C) 6
Brayshaw, E. 1887 (Sheffield W) 1
Bridge W. M. 2002 (Southampton, Chelsea, Manchester C) 36
Bridges, B. J. 1965 (Chelsea) 4
Bridgett, A. 1905 (Sunderland) 11
Brindle, T. 1880 (Darwen) 2
Brittleton, J. T. 1912 (Sheffield W) 5
Britton, C. S. 1935 (Everton) 9
Broadbent, P. F. 1958 (Wolverhampton W) 7
Broadis, I. A. 1952 (Manchester C, Newcastle U) 14
Brockbank, J. 1872 (Cambridge University) 1
Brodie, J. B. 1889 (Wolverhampton W) 3
Bromilow, T. G. 1921 (Liverpool) 5
Bromley-Davenport, W. E. 1884 (Oxford University) 2
Brook, E. F. 1930 (Manchester C) 18
Brooking, T. D. 1974 (West Ham U) 47
Brooks, J. 1957 (Tottenham H) 3
Broome, F. H. 1938 (Aston Villa) 7
Brown, A. 1882 (Aston Villa) 3
Brown, A. 1971 (WBA) 1
Brown, A. S. 1904 (Sheffield U) 2
Brown, G. 1927 (Huddersfield T, Aston Villa) 9
Brown, J. 1881 (Blackburn R) 5
Brown, J. H. 1927 (Sheffield W) 6
Brown, K. 1960 (West Ham U) 1
Brown, W. 1924 (West Ham U) 1
Brown, W. M. 1999 (Manchester U) 23
Bruton, J. 1928 (Burnley) 3
Bryant, W. I. 1925 (Clapton) 1
Buchan, C. M. 1913 (Sunderland) 6
Buchanan, W. S. 1876 (Clapham R) 1
Buckley, F. C. 1914 (Derby Co) 1
Bull, S. G. 1989 (Wolverhampton W) 13
Bullock, F. E. 1921 (Huddersfield T) 1
Bullock, N. 1923 (Bury) 3
Burgess, H. 1904 (Manchester C) 4
Burgess, H. 1931 (Sheffield W) 4
Burnup, C. J. 1896 (Cambridge University) 1
Burrows, H. 1934 (Sheffield W) 3
Burton, F. E. 1889 (Nottingham F) 1
Bury, L. 1877 (Cambridge University, Old Etonians) 2
Butcher, T. 1980 (Ipswich T, Rangers) 77
Butler, J. D. 1925 (Arsenal) 1
Butler, W. 1924 (Bolton W) 1
Butt, N. 1997 (Manchester U, Newcastle U) 39
Byrne, G. 1963 (Liverpool) 2
Byrne, J. J. 1962 (Crystal Palace, West Ham U) 11
Byrne, R. W. 1954 (Manchester U) 33

Cahill, G. J. 2011 (Bolton W, Chelsea) 9
Callaghan, I. R. 1966 (Liverpool) 4
Calvey, J. 1902 (Nottingham F) 1
Campbell, A. F. 1929 (Blackburn R, Huddersfield T) 8
Campbell, F. L. 2012 (Sunderland) 1
Campbell, S. 1996 (Tottenham H, Arsenal, Portsmouth) 73
Camsell, G. H. 1929 (Middlesbrough) 9
Capes, A. J. 1903 (Stoke) 1
Carr, J. 1905 (Newcastle U) 2
Carr, J. 1920 (Middlesbrough) 2
Carr, W. H. 1875 (Owlerton, Sheffield) 1
Carragher, J. L. 1999 (Liverpool) 38
Carrick, M. 2001 (West Ham U, Tottenham H, Manchester U) 22
Carroll, A. T. 2011 (Newcastle U, Liverpool) 7
Carson, S. P. 2008 (Liverpool, WBA) 4
Carter, H. S. 1934 (Sunderland, Derby Co) 13
Carter, J. H. 1926 (WBA) 3
Catlin, A. E. 1937 (Sheffield W) 5
Chadwick, A. 1900 (Southampton) 2
Chadwick, E. 1891 (Everton) 7
Chamberlain, M. 1983 (Stoke C) 8
Chambers, H. 1921 (Liverpool) 8
Channon, M. R. 1973 (Southampton, Manchester C) 46
Charles, G. A. 1991 (Nottingham F) 2
Charlton, J. 1965 (Leeds U) 35
Charlton, R. 1958 (Manchester U) 106
Charnley, R. O. 1963 (Blackpool) 1
Charsley, C. C. 1893 (Small Heath) 1
Chedgzoy, S. 1920 (Everton) 8
Chenery, C. J. 1872 (Crystal Palace) 3
Cherry, T. J. 1976 (Leeds U) 27
Chilton, A. 1951 (Manchester U) 2
Chippendale, H. 1894 (Blackburn R) 1
Chivers, M. 1971 (Tottenham H) 24
Christian, E. 1879 (Old Etonians) 1
Clamp, E. 1958 (Wolverhampton W) 4
Clapton, D. R. 1959 (Arsenal) 1
Clare, T. 1889 (Stoke) 4
Clarke, A. J. 1970 (Leeds U) 19
Clarke, H. A. 1954 (Tottenham H) 1
Clay, T. 1920 (Tottenham H) 4
Clayton, R. 1956 (Blackburn R) 35
Clegg, J. C. 1872 (Sheffield W) 1
Clegg, W. E. 1873 (Sheffield W, Sheffield Alb) 2
Clemence, R. N. 1973 (Liverpool, Tottenham H) 61
Clement, D. T. 1976 (QPR) 5
Clough, B. H. 1960 (Middlesbrough) 2
Clough, N. H. 1989 (Nottingham F) 14
Coates, R. 1970 (Burnley, Tottenham H) 4
Cobbold, W. N. 1883 (Cambridge University, Old Carthusians) 9
Cock, J. G. 1920 (Huddersfield T, Chelsea) 2
Cockburn, H. 1947 (Manchester U) 13
Cohen, G. R. 1964 (Fulham) 37
Cole, A. 2001 (Arsenal, Chelsea) 98
Cole, A. A. 1995 (Manchester U) 15
Cole, C. 2009 (West Ham U) 7
Cole, J. J. 2001 (West Ham U, Chelsea) 56
Colclough, H. 1914 (Crystal Palace) 1
Coleman, E. H. 1921 (Dulwich Hamlet) 1
Coleman, J. 1907 (Woolwich Arsenal) 1
Collymore, S. V. 1995 (Nottingham F, Aston Villa) 3
Common, A. 1904 (Sheffield U, Middlesbrough) 3
Compton, L. H. 1951 (Arsenal) 2
Conlin, J. 1906 (Bradford C) 1
Connelly, J. M. 1960 (Burnley, Manchester U) 20
Cook, T. E. R. 1925 (Brighton) 1
Cooper, C. T. 1995 (Nottingham F) 2
Cooper, N. C. 1893 (Cambridge University) 1
Cooper, T. 1928 (Derby Co) 15
Cooper, T. 1969 (Leeds U) 20
Coppell, S. J. 1978 (Manchester U) 42
Copping, W. 1933 (Leeds U, Arsenal, Leeds U) 20
Corbett, B. O. 1901 (Corinthians) 1
Corbett, R. 1903 (Old Malvernians) 1
Corbett, W. S. 1908 (Birmingham) 3
Corrigan, J. T. 1976 (Manchester C) 9
Cottee, A. R. 1987 (West Ham U, Everton) 7
Cotterill, G. H. 1891 (Cambridge University, Old Brightonians) 4
Cottle, J. R. 1909 (Bristol C) 1
Cowan, S. 1926 (Manchester C) 3
Cowans, G. S. 1983 (Aston Villa, Bari, Aston Villa) 10
Cowell, A. 1910 (Blackburn R) 1
Cox, J. 1901 (Liverpool) 3
Cox, J. D. 1892 (Derby Co) 1
Crabtree, J. W. 1894 (Burnley, Aston Villa) 14
Crawford, J. F. 1931 (Chelsea) 1
Crawford, R. 1962 (Ipswich T) 2
Crawshaw, T. H. 1895 (Sheffield W) 10
Crayston, W. J. 1936 (Arsenal) 8

Creek, F. N. S. 1923 (Corinthians) 1
Cresswell, W. 1921 (South Shields, Sunderland, Everton) 7
Crompton, R. 1902 (Blackburn R) 41
Crooks, S. D. 1930 (Derby Co) 26
Crouch, P. J. 2005 (Southampton, Liverpool, Portsmouth, Tottenham H) 42
Crowe, C. 1963 (Wolverhampton W) 1
Cuggy, F. 1913 (Sunderland) 2
Cullis, S. 1938 (Wolverhampton W) 12
Cunliffe, A. 1933 (Blackburn R) 2
Cunliffe, D. 1900 (Portsmouth) 1
Cunliffe, J. N. 1936 (Everton) 1
Cunningham, L. 1979 (WBA, Real Madrid) 6
Curle, K. 1992 (Manchester C) 3
Currey, E. S. 1890 (Oxford University) 2
Currie, A. W. 1972 (Sheffield U, Leeds U) 17
Cursham, A. W. 1876 (Notts Co) 6
Cursham, H. A. 1880 (Notts Co) 8

Daft, H. B. 1889 (Notts Co) 5
Daley, A. M. 1992 (Aston Villa) 7
Danks, T. 1885 (Nottingham F) 1
Davenport, P. 1985 (Nottingham F) 1
Davenport, J. K. 1885 (Bolton W) 2
Davies, K. C. 2011 (Bolton W) 1
Davis, G. 1904 (Derby Co) 2
Davis, H. 1903 (Sheffield W) 3
Davison, J. E. 1922 (Sheffield W) 1
Dawson, J. 1922 (Burnley) 2
Dawson, M. R. 2011 (Tottenham H) 4
Day, S. H. 1906 (Old Malvernians) 3
Dean, W. R. 1927 (Everton) 16
Deane, B. C. 1991 (Sheffield U) 3
Deeley, N. V. 1959 (Wolverhampton W) 2
Defoe, J. C. 2004 (Tottenham H, Portsmouth, Tottenham H) 48
Devey, J. H. G. 1892 (Aston Villa) 2
Devonshire, A. 1980 (West Ham U) 8
Dewhurst, F. 1886 (Preston NE) 9
Dewhurst, G. P. 1895 (Liverpool Ramblers) 1
Dickinson, J. W. 1949 (Portsmouth) 48
Dimmock, J. H. 1921 (Tottenham H) 3
Ditchburn, E. G. 1949 (Tottenham H) 6
Dix, R. W. 1939 (Derby Co) 1
Dixon, J. A. 1885 (Notts Co) 1
Dixon, K. M. 1985 (Chelsea) 8
Dixon, L. M. 1990 (Arsenal) 22
Dobson, A. T. C. 1882 (Notts Co) 4
Dobson, C. F. 1886 (Notts Co) 1
Dobson, J. M. 1974 (Burnley, Everton) 5
Doggart, A. G. 1924 (Corinthians) 1
Dorigo, A. R. 1990 (Chelsea, Leeds U) 15
Dorrell, A. R. 1925 (Aston Villa) 4
Douglas, B. 1958 (Blackburn R) 36
Downing, S. 2005 (Middlesbrough, Aston Villa, Liverpool) 34
Downs, R. W. 1921 (Everton) 1
Doyle, M. 1976 (Manchester C) 5
Drake, E. J. 1935 (Arsenal) 5
Dublin, D. 1998 (Coventry C, Aston Villa) 4
Ducat, A. 1910 (Woolwich Arsenal, Aston Villa) 6
Dunn, A. T. B. 1883 (Cambridge University, Old Etonians) 4
Dunn, D. J. I. 2003 (Blackburn R) 1
Duxbury, M. 1984 (Manchester U) 10
Dyer, K. C. 2000 (Newcastle U, West Ham U) 33

Earle, S. G. J. 1924 (Clapton, West Ham U) 2
Eastham, G. 1963 (Arsenal) 19
Eastham, G. R. 1935 (Bolton W) 1
Eckersley, W. 1950 (Blackburn R) 17
Edwards, D. 1955 (Manchester U) 18
Edwards, J. H. 1874 (Shropshire Wanderers) 1
Edwards, W. 1926 (Leeds U) 16
Ehiogu, U. 1996 (Aston Villa, Middlesbrough) 4
Ellerington, W. 1949 (Southampton) 2
Elliott, G. W. 1913 (Middlesbrough) 3
Elliott, W. H. 1952 (Burnley) 5
Evans, R. E. 1911 (Sheffield U) 4
Ewer, F. H. 1924 (Casuals) 2

Fairclough, P. 1878 (Old Foresters) 1
Fairhurst, D. 1934 (Newcastle U) 1
Fantham, J. 1962 (Sheffield W) 1
Fashanu, J. 1989 (Wimbledon) 2
Felton, W. 1925 (Sheffield W) 1
Fenton, M. 1938 (Middlesbrough) 1
Fenwick, T. W. 1984 (QPR, Tottenham H) 20
Ferdinand, L. 1993 (QPR, Newcastle U, Tottenham H) 17
Ferdinand, R. G. 1998 (West Ham U, Leeds U, Manchester U) 81
Field, E. 1876 (Clapham R) 2
Finney, T. 1947 (Preston NE) 76
Fleming, H. J. 1909 (Swindon T) 11
Fletcher, A. 1889 (Wolverhampton W) 2
Flowers, R. 1955 (Wolverhampton W) 49
Flowers, T. D. 1993 (Southampton, Blackburn R) 11
Forman, Frank 1898 (Nottingham F 9
Forman, F. R. 1899 (Nottingham F) 3
Forrest, J. H. 1884 (Blackburn R) 11
Fort, J. 1921 (Millwall) 1
Foster, B. 2007 (Manchester U, Birmingham C) 5
Foster, R. E. 1900 (Oxford University, Corinthians) 5
Foster, S. 1982 (Brighton & HA) 3
Foulke, W. J. 1897 (Sheffield U) 1
Foulkes, W. A. 1955 (Manchester U) 1
Fowler, R. B. 1996 (Liverpool, Leeds U) 26
Fox, F. S. 1925 (Millwall) 1
Francis, G. C. J. 1975 (QPR) 12
Francis, T. 1977 (Birmingham C, Nottingham F, Manchester C, Sampdoria) 52
Franklin, C. F. 1947 (Stoke C) 27
Freeman, B. C. 1909 (Everton, Burnley) 5
Froggatt, J. 1950 (Portsmouth) 13
Froggatt, R. 1953 (Sheffield W) 4
Fry, C. B. 1901 (Corinthians) 1
Furness, W. I. 1933 (Leeds U) 1

Galley, T. 1937 (Wolverhampton W) 2
Gardner, A. 2004 (Tottenham H) 1
Gardner, T. 1934 (Aston Villa) 2
Garfield, B. 1898 (WBA) 1
Garraty, W. 1903 (Aston Villa) 1
Garrett, T. 1952 (Blackpool) 3
Gascoigne, P. J. 1989 (Tottenham H, Lazio, Rangers, Middlesbrough) 57
Gates, E. 1981 (Ipswich T) 2
Gay, L. H. 1893 (Cambridge University, Old Brightonians) 3
Geary, F. 1890 (Everton) 2
Geaves, R. L. 1875 (Clapham R) 1
Gee, C. W. 1932 (Everton) 3
Geldard, A. 1933 (Everton) 4
George, C. 1977 (Derby Co) 1
George, W. 1902 (Aston Villa) 3
Gerrard, S. G. 2000 (Liverpool) 96
Gibbins, W. V. T. 1924 (Clapton) 2
Gibbs, K. J. R. 2011 (Arsenal) 2
Gidman, J. 1977 (Aston Villa) 1
Gillard, I. T. 1975 (QPR) 3
Gilliat, W. E. 1893 (Old Carthusians) 1
Goddard, P. 1982 (West Ham U) 1
Goodall, F. R. 1926 (Huddersfield T) 25
Goodall, J. 1888 (Preston NE, Derby Co) 14
Goodhart, H. C. 1883 (Old Etonians) 3
Goodwyn, A. G. 1873 (Royal Engineers) 1
Goodyer, A. C. 1879 (Nottingham F) 1
Gosling, R. C. 1892 (Old Etonians) 5
Gosnell, A. A. 1906 (Newcastle U) 1
Gough, H. C. 1921 (Sheffield U) 1
Goulden, L. A. 1937 (West Ham U) 14
Graham, L. 1925 (Millwall) 2
Graham, T. 1931 (Nottingham F) 2
Grainger, C. 1956 (Sheffield U, Sunderland) 7
Gray, A. A. 1992 (Crystal Palace) 1
Gray, M. 1999 (Sunderland) 3
Greaves, J. 1959 (Chelsea, Tottenham H) 57
Green, F. T. 1876 (Wanderers) 1
Green, G. H. 1925 (Sheffield U) 8
Green, R. P. 2005 (Norwich C, West Ham U) 12
Greenhalgh, E. H. 1872 (Notts Co) 2
Greenhoff, B. 1976 (Manchester U, Leeds U) 18
Greenwood, D. H. 1882 (Blackburn R) 2

Gregory, J. 1983 (QPR) 6
Grimsdell, A. 1920 (Tottenham H) 6
Grosvenor, A. T. 1934 (Birmingham) 3
Gunn, W. 1884 (Notts Co) 2
Guppy, S. 2000 (Leicester C) 1
Gurney, R. 1935 (Sunderland) 1

Hacking, J. 1929 (Oldham Ath) 3
Hadley, H. 1903 (WBA) 1
Hagan, J. 1949 (Sheffield U) 1
Haines, J. T. W. 1949 (WBA) 1
Hall, A. E. 1910 (Aston Villa) 1
Hall, G. W. 1934 (Tottenham H) 10
Hall, J. 1956 (Birmingham C) 17
Halse, H. J. 1909 (Manchester U) 1
Hammond, H. E. D. 1889 (Oxford University) 1
Hampson, J. 1931 (Blackpool) 3
Hampton, H. 1913 (Aston Villa) 4
Hancocks, J. 1949 (Wolverhampton W) 3
Hapgood, E. 1933 (Arsenal) 30
Hardinge, H. T. W. 1910 (Sheffield U) 1
Hardman, H. P. 1905 (Everton) 4
Hardwick, G. F. M. 1947 (Middlesbrough) 13
Hardy, H. 1925 (Stockport Co) 1
Hardy, S. 1907 (Liverpool, Aston Villa) 21
Harford, M. G. 1988 (Luton T) 2
Hargreaves, F. W. 1880 (Blackburn R) 3
Hargreaves, J. 1881 (Blackburn R) 2
Hargreaves, O. 2002 (Bayern Munich, Manchester U) 42
Harper, E. C. 1926 (Blackburn R) 1
Harris, G. 1966 (Burnley) 1
Harris, P. P. 1950 (Portsmouth) 2
Harris, S. S. 1904 (Cambridge University, Old Westminsters) 6
Harrison, A. H. 1893 (Old Westminsters) 2
Harrison, G. 1921 (Everton) 2
Harrow, J. H. 1923 (Chelsea) 2
Hart, C. 2008 (Manchester C) 22
Hart, E. 1929 (Leeds U) 8
Hartley, F. 1923 (Oxford C) 1
Harvey, A. 1881 (Wednesbury Strollers) 1
Harvey, J. C. 1971 (Everton) 1
Hassall, H. W. 1951 (Huddersfield T, Bolton W) 5
Hateley, M. 1984 (Portsmouth, AC Milan, Monaco, Rangers) 32
Hawkes, R. M. 1907 (Luton T) 5
Haworth, G. 1887 (Accrington) 5
Hawtrey, J. P. 1881 (Old Etonians) 2
Haygarth, E. B. 1875 (Swifts) 1
Haynes, J. N. 1955 (Fulham) 56
Healless, H. 1925 (Blackburn R) 2
Hector, K. J. 1974 (Derby Co) 2
Hedley, G. A. 1901 (Sheffield U) 1
Hegan, K. E. 1923 (Corinthians) 4
Hellawell, M. S. 1963 (Birmingham C) 2
Henderson, J. B. 2011 (Sunderland, Liverpool) 5
Hendrie, L. A. 1999 (Aston Villa) 1
Henfrey, A. G. 1891 (Cambridge University, Corinthians) 5
Henry, R. P. 1963 (Tottenham H) 1
Heron, F. 1876 (Wanderers) 1
Heron, G. H. H. 1873 (Uxbridge, Wanderers) 5
Heskey, E. W. I. 1999 (Leicester C, Liverpool, Birmingham C, Wigan Ath, Aston Villa) 62
Hibbert, W. 1910 (Bury) 1
Hibbs, H. E. 1930 (Birmingham) 25
Hill, F. 1963 (Bolton W) 2
Hill, G. A. 1976 (Manchester U) 6
Hill, J. H. 1925 (Burnley, Newcastle U) 11
Hill, R. 1983 (Luton T) 3
Hill, R. H. 1926 (Millwall) 1
Hillman, J. 1899 (Burnley) 1
Hills, A. F. 1879 (Old Harrovians) 1
Hilsdon, G. R. 1907 (Chelsea) 8
Hinchcliffe, A. G. 1997 (Everton, Sheffield W) 7
Hine, E. W. 1929 (Leicester C) 6
Hinton, A. T. 1963 (Wolverhampton W, Nottingham F) 3
Hirst, D. E. 1991 (Sheffield W) 3
Hitchens, G. A. 1961 (Aston Villa, Internazionale) 7
Hobbis, H. H. F. 1936 (Charlton Ath) 2
Hoddle, G. 1980 (Tottenham H, Monaco) 53
Hodge, S. B. 1986 (Aston Villa, Tottenham H, Nottingham F) 24
Hodgetts, D. 1888 (Aston Villa) 6
Hodgkinson, A. 1957 (Sheffield U) 5
Hodgson, G. 1931 (Liverpool) 3
Hodkinson, J. 1913 (Blackburn R) 3
Hogg, W. 1902 (Sunderland) 3
Holdcroft, G. H. 1937 (Preston NE) 2
Holden, A. D. 1959 (Bolton W) 5
Holden, G. H. 1881 (Wednesbury OA) 4
Holden-White, C. 1888 (Corinthians) 2
Holford, T. 1903 (Stoke) 1
Holley, G. H. 1909 (Sunderland) 10
Holliday, E. 1960 (Middlesbrough) 3
Hollins, J. W. 1967 (Chelsea) 1
Holmes, R. 1888 (Preston NE) 7
Holt, J. 1890 (Everton, Reading) 10
Hopkinson, E. 1958 (Bolton W) 14
Hossack, A. H. 1892 (Corinthians) 2
Houghton, W. E. 1931 (Aston Villa) 7
Houlker, A. E. 1902 (Blackburn R, Portsmouth, Southampton) 5
Howarth, R. H. 1887 (Preston NE, Everton) 5
Howe, D. 1958 (WBA) 23
Howe, J. R. 1948 (Derby Co) 3
Howell, L. S. 1873 (Wanderers) 1
Howell, R. 1895 (Sheffield U, Liverpool) 2
Howey, S. N. 1995 (Newcastle U) 4
Huddlestone, T. A. 2010 (Tottenham H) 3
Hudson, A. A. 1975 (Stoke C) 2
Hudson, J. 1883 (Sheffield) 1
Hudspeth, F. C. 1926 (Newcastle U) 1
Hufton, A. E. 1924 (West Ham U) 6
Hughes, E. W. 1970 (Liverpool, Wolverhampton W) 62
Hughes, L. 1950 (Liverpool) 3
Hulme, J. H. A. 1927 (Arsenal) 9
Humphreys, P. 1903 (Notts Co) 1
Hunt, G. S. 1933 (Tottenham H) 3
Hunt, Rev. K. R. G. 1911 (Leyton) 2
Hunt, R. 1962 (Liverpool) 34
Hunt, S. 1984 (WBA) 2
Hunter, J. 1878 (Sheffield Heeley) 7
Hunter, N. 1966 (Leeds U) 28
Hurst, G. C. 1966 (West Ham U) 49

Ince, P. E. C. 1993 (Manchester U, Internazionale, Liverpool, Middlesbrough) 53
Iremonger, J. 1901 (Nottingham F) 2

Jack, D. N. B. 1924 (Bolton W, Arsenal) 9
Jackson, E. 1891 (Oxford University) 1
Jagielka, P. N. 2008 (Everton) 12
James. D. B. 1997 (Liverpool, Aston Villa, West Ham U, Manchester C, Portsmouth) 53
Jarrett, B. G. 1876 (Cambridge University) 3
Jarvis, M. T. 2011 (Wolverhampton W) 1
Jefferis, F. 1912 (Everton) 2
Jeffers, F. 2003 (Arsenal) 1
Jenas, J. A. 2003 (Newcastle U, Tottenham H) 21
Jezzard, B. A. G. 1954 (Fulham) 2
Johnson, A. 2005 (Crystal Palace, Everton) 8
Johnson, A. 2010 (Manchester C) 11
Johnson, D. E. 1975 (Ipswich T, Liverpool) 8
Johnson, E. 1880 (Saltley College, Stoke) 2
Johnson, G. M. C. 2004 (Chelsea, Portsmouth, Liverpool) 40
Johnson, J. A. 1937 (Stoke C) 5
Johnson, S. A. M. 2001 (Derby Co) 1
Johnson, T. C. F. 1926 (Manchester C, Everton) 5
Johnson, W. H. 1900 (Sheffield U) 6
Johnston, H. 1947 (Blackpool) 10
Jones, A. 1882 (Walsall Swifts, Great Lever) 3
Jones, H. 1923 (Nottingham F) 1
Jones, H. 1927 (Blackburn R) 6
Jones, M. D. 1965 (Sheffield U, Leeds U) 3
Jones, P. A. 2012 (Manchester U) 5
Jones, R. 1992 (Liverpool) 8
Jones, W. 1901 (Bristol C) 1
Jones, W. H. 1950 (Liverpool) 2
Joy, B. 1936 (Casuals) 1

Kail, E. I. L. 1929 (Dulwich Hamlet) 3

Kay, A. H. 1963 (Everton) 1
Kean, F. W. 1923 (Sheffield W, Bolton W) 9
Keegan, J. K. 1973 (Liverpool, SV Hamburg, Southampton) 63
Keen, E. R. L. 1933 (Derby Co) 4
Kelly, M. R. 2012 (Liverpool) 1
Kelly, R. 1920 (Burnley, Sunderland, Huddersfield T) 14
Kennedy, A. 1984 (Liverpool) 2
Kennedy, R. 1976 (Liverpool) 17
Kenyon-Slaney, W. S. 1873 (Wanderers) 1
Keown, M. R. 1992 (Everton, Arsenal) 43
Kevan, D. T. 1957 (WBA) 14
Kidd, B. 1970 (Manchester U) 2
King, L. B. 2002 (Tottenham H) 21
King, R. S. 1882 (Oxford University) 1
Kingsford, R. K. 1874 (Wanderers) 1
Kingsley, M. 1901 (Newcastle U) 1
Kinsey, G. 1892 (Wolverhampton W, Derby Co) 4
Kirchen, A. J. 1937 (Arsenal) 3
Kirkland, C. E. 2007 (Liverpool) 1
Kirton, W. J. 1922 (Aston Villa) 1
Knight, A. E. 1920 (Portsmouth) 1
Knight, Z. 2005 (Fulham) 2
Knowles, C. 1968 (Tottenham H) 4
Konchesky, P. M. 2003 (Charlton Ath, West Ham U) 2

Labone, B. L. 1963 (Everton) 26
Lampard, F. J. 2000 (West Ham U, Chelsea) 90
Lampard, F. R. G. 1973 (West Ham U) 2
Langley, E. J. 1958 (Fulham) 3
Langton, R. 1947 (Blackburn R, Preston NE, Bolton W) 11
Latchford, R. D. 1978 (Everton) 12
Latheron, E. G. 1913 (Blackburn R) 2
Lawler, C. 1971 (Liverpool) 4
Lawton, T. 1939 (Everton, Chelsea, Notts Co) 23
Leach, T. 1931 (Sheffield W) 2
Leake, A. 1904 (Aston Villa) 5
Lee, E. A. 1904 (Southampton) 1
Lee, F. H. 1969 (Manchester C) 27
Lee, J. 1951 (Derby Co) 1
Lee, R. M. 1995 (Newcastle U) 21
Lee, S. 1983 (Liverpool) 14
Leighton, J. E. 1886 (Nottingham F) 1
Lennon, A. J. 2006 (Tottenham H) 19
Lescott, J. P. 2008 (Everton, Manchester C) 20
Le Saux, G. P. 1994 (Blackburn R, Chelsea) 36
Le Tissier, M. P. 1994 (Southampton) 8
Lilley, H. E. 1892 (Sheffield U) 1
Linacre, H. J. 1905 (Nottingham F) 2
Lindley, T. 1886 (Cambridge University, Nottingham F) 13
Lindsay, A. 1974 (Liverpool) 4
Lindsay, W. 1877 (Wanderers) 1
Lineker, G. 1984 (Leicester C, Everton, Barcelona, Tottenham H) 80
Lintott, E. H. 1908 (QPR, Bradford C) 7
Lipsham, H. B. 1902 (Sheffield U) 1
Little, B. 1975 (Aston Villa) 1
Lloyd, L. V. 1971 (Liverpool, Nottingham F) 4
Lockett, A. 1903 (Stoke) 1
Lodge, L. V. 1894 (Cambridge University, Corinthians) 5
Lofthouse, J. M. 1885 (Blackburn R, Accrington, Blackburn R) 7
Lofthouse, N. 1951 (Bolton W) 33
Longworth, E. 1920 (Liverpool) 5
Lowder, A. 1889 (Wolverhampton W) 1
Lowe, E. 1947 (Aston Villa) 3
Lucas, T. 1922 (Liverpool) 3
Luntley, E. 1880 (Nottingham F) 2
Lyttelton, Hon. A. 1877 (Cambridge University) 1
Lyttelton, Hon. E. 1878 (Cambridge University) 1

Mabbutt, G. 1983 (Tottenham H) 16
Macaulay, R. H. 1881 (Cambridge University) 1
McCall, J. 1913 (Preston NE) 5
McCann, G. P. 2001 (Sunderland) 1
McDermott, T. 1978 (Liverpool) 25
McDonald, C. A. 1958 (Burnley) 8
Macdonald, M. 1972 (Newcastle U) 14
McFarland, R. L. 1971 (Derby Co) 28
McGarry, W. H. 1954 (Huddersfield T) 4
McGuinness, W. 1959 (Manchester U) 2
McInroy, A. 1927 (Sunderland) 1
McMahon, S. 1988 (Liverpool) 17
McManaman, S. 1995 (Liverpool, Real Madrid) 37
McNab, R. 1969 (Arsenal) 4
McNeal, R. 1914 (WBA) 2
McNeil, M. 1961 (Middlesbrough) 9
Macrae, S. 1883 (Notts Co) 5
Maddison, F. B. 1872 (Oxford University) 1
Madeley, P. E. 1971 (Leeds U) 24
Magee, T. P. 1923 (WBA) 5
Makepeace, H. 1906 (Everton) 4
Male, C. G. 1935 (Arsenal) 19
Mannion, W. J. 1947 (Middlesbrough) 26
Mariner, P. 1977 (Ipswich T, Arsenal) 35
Marsden, J. T. 1891 (Darwen) 1
Marsden, W. 1930 (Sheffield W) 3
Marsh, R. W. 1972 (QPR, Manchester C) 9
Marshall, T. 1880 (Darwen) 2
Martin, A. 1981 (West Ham U) 17
Martin, H. 1914 (Sunderland) 1
Martyn, A. N. 1992 (Crystal Palace, Leeds U) 23
Marwood, B. 1989 (Arsenal) 1
Maskrey, H. M. 1908 (Derby Co) 1
Mason, C. 1887 (Wolverhampton W) 3
Matthews, R. D. 1956 (Coventry C) 5
Matthews, S. 1935 (Stoke C, Blackpool) 54
Matthews, V. 1928 (Sheffield U) 2
Maynard, W. J. 1872 (1st Surrey Rifles) 2
Meadows, J. 1955 (Manchester C) 1
Medley, L. D. 1951 (Tottenham H) 6
Meehan, T. 1924 (Chelsea) 1
Melia, J. 1963 (Liverpool) 2
Mercer, D. W. 1923 (Sheffield U) 2
Mercer, J. 1939 (Everton) 5
Merrick, G. H. 1952 (Birmingham C) 23
Merson, P. C. 1992 (Arsenal, Middlesbrough, Aston Villa) 21
Metcalfe, V. 1951 (Huddersfield T) 2
Mew, J. W. 1921 (Manchester U) 1
Middleditch, B. 1897 (Corinthians) 1
Milburn, J. E. T. 1949 (Newcastle U) 13
Miller, B. G. 1961 (Burnley) 1
Miller, H. S. 1923 (Charlton Ath) 1
Mills, D. J. 2001 (Leeds U) 19
Mills, G. R. 1938 (Chelsea) 3
Mills, M. D. 1973 (Ipswich T) 42
Milne, G. 1963 (Liverpool) 14
Milner, J. P. 2010 (Aston Villa, Manchester C) 30
Milton, C. A. 1952 (Arsenal) 1
Milward, A. 1891 (Everton) 4
Mitchell, C. 1880 (Upton Park) 5
Mitchell, J. F. 1925 (Manchester C) 1
Moffat, H. 1913 (Oldham Ath) 1
Molyneux, G. 1902 (Southampton) 4
Moon, W. R. 1888 (Old Westminsters) 7
Moore, H. T. 1883 (Notts Co) 2
Moore, J. 1923 (Derby Co) 1
Moore, R. F. 1962 (West Ham U) 108
Moore, W. G. B. 1923 (West Ham U) 1
Mordue, J. 1912 (Sunderland) 2
Morice, C. J. 1872 (Barnes) 1
Morley, A. 1982 (Aston Villa) 6
Morley, H. 1910 (Notts Co) 1
Morren, T. 1898 (Sheffield U) 1
Morris, F. 1920 (WBA) 2
Morris, J. 1949 (Derby Co) 3
Morris, W. W. 1939 (Wolverhampton W) 3
Morse, H. 1879 (Notts Co) 1
Mort, T. 1924 (Aston Villa) 3
Morten, A. 1873 (Crystal Palace) 1
Mortensen, S. H. 1947 (Blackpool) 25
Morton, J. R. 1938 (West Ham U) 1
Mosforth, W. 1877 (Sheffield W, Sheffield Alb, Sheffield W) 9
Moss, F. 1922 (Aston Villa) 5
Moss, F. 1934 (Arsenal) 4
Mosscrop, E. 1914 (Burnley) 2
Mozley, B. 1950 (Derby Co) 3
Mullen, J. 1947 (Wolverhampton W) 12
Mullery, A. P. 1965 (Tottenham H) 35
Murphy, D. B. 2002 (Liverpool) 9

Neal, P. G. 1976 (Liverpool) 50
Needham, E. 1894 (Sheffield U) 16
Neville, G. A. 1995 (Manchester U) 85
Neville, P. J. 1996 (Manchester U, Everton) 59
Newton, K. R. 1966 (Blackburn R, Everton) 27
Nicholls, J. 1954 (WBA) 2
Nicholson, W. E. 1951 (Tottenham H) 1
Nish, D. J. 1973 (Derby Co) 5
Norman, M. 1962 (Tottenham H) 23
Nugent, D. J. 2007 (Preston NE) 1
Nuttall, H. 1928 (Bolton W) 3

Oakley, W. J. 1895 (Oxford University, Corinthians) 16
O'Dowd, J. P. 1932 (Chelsea) 3
O'Grady, M. 1963 (Huddersfield T, Leeds U) 2
Ogilvie, R. A. M. M. 1874 (Clapham R) 1
Oliver, L. F. 1929 (Fulham) 1
Olney, B. A. 1928 (Aston Villa) 2
Osborne, F. R. 1923 (Fulham, Tottenham H) 4
Osborne, R. 1928 (Leicester C) 1
Osgood, P. L. 1970 (Chelsea) 4
Osman, R. 1980 (Ipswich T) 11
Ottaway, C. J. 1872 (Oxford University) 2
Owen, J. R. B. 1874 (Sheffield) 1
Owen, M. J. 1998 (Liverpool, Real Madrid, NewcastleU) 89
Owen, S. W. 1954 (Luton T) 3
Oxlade-Chamberlain, A. M. D. 2012 (Arsenal) 5

Page, L. A. 1927 (Burnley) 7
Paine, T. L. 1963 (Southampton) 19
Pallister, G. A. 1988 (Middlesbrough, Manchester U) 22
Palmer, C. L. 1992 (Sheffield W) 18
Pantling, H. H. 1924 (Sheffield U) 1
Paravicini, P. J. de 1883 (Cambridge University) 3
Parker, P. A. 1989 (QPR, Manchester U) 19
Parker, S. M. 2004 (Charlton Ath, Chelsea, Newcastle U, West Ham U, Tottenham H) 17
Parker, T. R. 1925 (Southampton) 1
Parkes, P. B. 1974 (QPR) 1
Parkinson, J. 1910 (Liverpool) 2
Parlour, R. 1999 (Arsenal) 10
Parr, P. C. 1882 (Oxford University) 1
Parry, E. H. 1879 (Old Carthusians) 3
Parry, R. A. 1960 (Bolton W) 2
Patchitt, B. C. A. 1923 (Corinthians) 2
Pawson, F. W. 1883 (Cambridge University, Swifts) 2
Payne, J. 1937 (Luton T) 1
Peacock, A. 1962 (Middlesbrough, Leeds U) 6
Peacock, J. 1929 (Middlesbrough) 3
Pearce, S. 1987 (Nottingham F, West Ham U) 78
Pearson, H. F. 1932 (WBA) 1
Pearson, J. H. 1892 (Crewe Alex) 1
Pearson, J. S. 1976 (Manchester U) 15
Pearson, S. C. 1948 (Manchester U) 8
Pease, W. H. 1927 (Middlesbrough) 1
Pegg, D. 1957 (Manchester U) 1
Pejic, M. 1974 (Stoke C) 4
Pelly, F. R. 1893 (Old Foresters) 3
Pennington, J. 1907 (WBA) 25
Pentland, F. B. 1909 (Middlesbrough) 5
Perry, C. 1890 (WBA) 3
Perry, T. 1898 (WBA) 1
Perry, W. 1956 (Blackpool) 3
Perryman, S. 1982 (Tottenham H) 1
Peters, M. 1966 (West Ham U, Tottenham H) 67
Phelan, M. C. 1990 (Manchester U) 1
Phillips, K. 1999 (Sunderland) 8
Phillips, L. H. 1952 (Portsmouth) 3
Pickering, F. 1964 (Everton) 3
Pickering, J. 1933 (Sheffield U) 1
Pickering, N. 1983 (Sunderland) 1
Pike, T. M. 1886 (Cambridge University) 1
Pilkington, B. 1955 (Burnley) 1
Plant, J. 1900 (Bury) 1
Platt, D. 1990 (Aston Villa, Bari, Juventus, Sampdoria, Arsenal) 62
Plum, S. L. 1923 (Charlton Ath) 1
Pointer, R. 1962 (Burnley) 3
Porteous, T. S. 1891 (Sunderland) 1
Powell, C. G. 2001 (Charlton Ath) 5
Priest, A. E. 1900 (Sheffield U) 1
Prinsep, J. F. M. 1879 (Clapham R) 1
Puddefoot, S. C. 1926 (Blackburn R) 2
Pye, J. 1950 (Wolverhampton W) 1
Pym, R. H. 1925 (Bolton W) 3

Quantrill, A. 1920 (Derby Co) 4
Quixall, A. 1954 (Sheffield W) 5

Radford, J. 1969 (Arsenal) 2
Raikes, G. B. 1895 (Oxford University) 4
Ramsey, A. E. 1949 (Southampton, Tottenham H) 32
Rawlings, A. 1921 (Preston NE) 1
Rawlings, W. E. 1922 (Southampton) 2
Rawlinson, J. F. P. 1882 (Cambridge University) 1
Rawson, H. E. 1875 (Royal Engineers) 1
Rawson, W. S. 1875 (Oxford University) 2
Read, A. 1921 (Tufnell Park) 1
Reader, J. 1894 (WBA) 1
Reaney, P. 1969 (Leeds U) 3
Redknapp, J. F. 1996 (Liverpool) 17
Reeves, K. P. 1980 (Norwich C, Manchester C) 2
Regis, C. 1982 (WBA, Coventry C) 5
Reid, P. 1985 (Everton) 13
Revie, D. G. 1955 (Manchester C) 6
Reynolds, J. 1892 (WBA, Aston Villa) 8
Richards, C. H. 1898 (Nottingham F) 1
Richards, G. H. 1909 (Derby Co) 1
Richards, J. P. 1973 (Wolverhampton W) 1
Richards, M. 2007 (Manchester C) 13
Richardson, J. R. 1933 (Newcastle U) 2
Richardson, K. 1994 (Aston Villa) 1
Richardson, K. E. 2005 (Manchester U) 8
Richardson, W. G. 1935 (WBA) 1
Rickaby, S. 1954 (WBA) 1
Ricketts, M. B. 2002 (Bolton W) 1
Rigby, A. 1927 (Blackburn R) 5
Rimmer, E. J. 1930 (Sheffield W) 4
Rimmer, J. J. 1976 (Arsenal) 1
Ripley, S. E. 1994 (Blackburn R) 2
Rix, G. 1981 (Arsenal) 17
Robb, G. 1954 (Tottenham H) 1
Roberts, C. 1905 (Manchester U) 3
Roberts, F. 1925 (Manchester C) 4
Roberts, G. 1983 (Tottenham H) 6
Roberts, H. 1931 (Arsenal) 1
Roberts, H. 1931 (Millwall) 1
Roberts, R. 1887 (WBA) 3
Roberts, W. T. 1924 (Preston NE) 2
Robinson, J. 1937 (Sheffield W) 4
Robinson, J. W. 1897 (Derby Co, New Brighton Tower, Southampton) 11
Robinson, P. W. 2003 (Leeds U, Tottenham H, Blackburn R) 41
Robson, B. 1980 (WBA, Manchester U) 90
Robson, R. 1958 (WBA) 20
Rocastle, D. 1989 (Arsenal) 14
Rodwell, J. 2012 (Everton) 2
Rooney, W. 2003 (Everton, Manchester U) 76
Rose, W. C. 1884 (Swifts, Preston NE, Wolverhampton W) 5
Rostron, T. 1881 (Darwen) 2
Rowe, A. 1934 (Tottenham H) 1
Rowley, J. F. 1949 (Manchester U) 6
Rowley, W. 1889 (Stoke) 2
Royle, J. 1971 (Everton, Manchester C) 6
Ruddlesdin, H. 1904 (Sheffield W) 3
Ruddock, N. 1995 (Liverpool) 1
Ruffell, J. W. 1926 (West Ham U) 6
Russell, B. B. 1883 (Royal Engineers) 1
Rutherford, J. 1904 (Newcastle U) 11

Sadler, D. 1968 (Manchester U) 4
Sagar, C. 1900 (Bury) 2
Sagar, E. 1936 (Everton) 4
Salako, J. A. 1991 (Crystal Palace) 5
Sandford, E. A. 1933 (WBA) 1
Sandilands, R. R. 1892 (Old Westminsters) 5
Sands, J. 1880 (Nottingham F) 1
Sansom, K. G. 1979 (Crystal Palace, Arsenal) 86
Saunders, F. E. 1888 (Swifts) 1
Savage, A. H. 1876 (Crystal Palace) 1
Sayer, J. 1887 (Stoke) 1

Scales, J. R. 1995 (Liverpool) 3
Scattergood, E. 1913 (Derby Co) 1
Schofield, J. 1892 (Stoke) 3
Scholes, P. 1997 (Manchester U) 66
Scott, L. 1947 (Arsenal) 17
Scott, W. R. 1937 (Brentford) 1
Seaman, D. A. 1989 (QPR, Arsenal) 75
Seddon, J. 1923 (Bolton W) 6
Seed, J. M. 1921 (Tottenham H) 5
Settle, J. 1899 (Bury, Everton) 6
Sewell, J. 1952 (Sheffield W) 6
Sewell, W. R. 1924 (Blackburn R) 1
Shackleton, L. F. 1949 (Sunderland) 5
Sharp, J. 1903 (Everton) 2
Sharpe, L. S. 1991 (Manchester U) 8
Shaw, G. E. 1932 (WBA) 1
Shaw, G. L. 1959 (Sheffield U) 5
Shea, D. 1914 (Blackburn R) 2
Shearer, A. 1992 (Southampton, Blackburn R, Newcastle U) 63
Shellito, K. J. 1963 (Chelsea) 1
Shelton A. 1889 (Notts Co) 6
Shelton, C. 1888 (Notts Rangers) 1
Shepherd, A. 1906 (Bolton W, Newcastle U) 2
Sheringham, E. P. 1993 (Tottenham H, Manchester U, Tottenham H) 51
Sherwood, T. A. 1999 (Tottenham H) 3
Shilton, P. L. 1971 (Leicester C, Stoke C, Nottingham F, Southampton, Derby Co) 125
Shimwell, E. 1949 (Blackpool) 1
Shorey, N. 2007 (Reading) 2
Shutt, G. 1886 (Stoke) 1
Silcock, J. 1921 (Manchester U) 3
Sillett, R. P. 1955 (Chelsea) 3
Simms, E. 1922 (Luton T) 1
Simpson, J. 1911 (Blackburn R) 8
Sinclair, T. 2002 (West Ham U, Manchester C) 12
Sinton, A. 1992 (QPR, Sheffield W) 12
Slater, W. J. 1955 (Wolverhampton W) 12
Smalley, T. 1937 (Wolverhampton W) 1
Smalling, C. 2012 (Manchester U) 3
Smart, T. 1921 (Aston Villa) 5
Smith, A. 1891 (Nottingham F) 3
Smith, A. 2001 (Leeds U, Manchester U, Newcastle U) 19
Smith, A. K. 1872 (Oxford University) 1
Smith, A. M. 1989 (Arsenal) 13
Smith, B. 1921 (Tottenham H) 2
Smith, C. E. 1876 (Crystal Palace) 1
Smith, G. O. 1893 (Oxford University, Old Carthusians, Corinthians) 20
Smith, H. 1905 (Reading) 4
Smith, J. 1920 (WBA) 2
Smith, Joe 1913 (Bolton W) 5
Smith, J. C. R. 1939 (Millwall) 2
Smith, J. W. 1932 (Portsmouth) 3
Smith, Leslie 1939 (Brentford) 1
Smith, Lionel 1951 (Arsenal) 6
Smith, R. A. 1961 (Tottenham H) 15
Smith, S. 1895 (Aston Villa) 1
Smith, S. C. 1936 (Leicester C) 1
Smith, T. 1960 (Birmingham C) 2
Smith, T. 1971 (Liverpool) 1
Smith, W. H. 1922 (Huddersfield T) 3
Sorby, T. H. 1879 (Thursday Wanderers, Sheffield) 1
Southgate, G. 1996 (Aston Villa, Middlesbrough) 57
Southworth, J. 1889 (Blackburn R) 3
Sparks, F. J. 1879 (Herts Rangers, Clapham R) 3
Spence, J. W. 1926 (Manchester U) 2
Spence, R. 1936 (Chelsea) 2
Spencer, C. W. 1924 (Newcastle U) 2
Spencer, H. 1897 (Aston Villa) 6
Spiksley, F. 1893 (Sheffield W) 7
Spilsbury, B. W. 1885 (Cambridge University) 3
Spink, N. 1983 (Aston Villa) 1
Spouncer, W. A. 1900 (Nottingham F) 1
Springett, R. D. G. 1960 (Sheffield W) 33
Sproston, B. 1937 (Leeds U, Tottenham H, Manchester C) 11
Squire, R. T. 1886 (Cambridge University) 3
Stanbrough, M. H. 1895 (Old Carthusians) 1
Staniforth, R. 1954 (Huddersfield T) 8
Starling, R. W. 1933 (Sheffield W, Aston Villa) 2
Statham, D. J. 1983 (WBA) 3
Steele, F. C. 1937 (Stoke C) 6
Stein, B. 1984 (Luton T) 1
Stephenson, C. 1924 (Huddersfield T) 1
Stephenson, G. T. 1928 (Derby Co, Sheffield W) 3
Stephenson, J. E. 1938 (Leeds U) 2
Stepney, A. C. 1968 (Manchester U) 1
Sterland, M. 1989 (Sheffield W) 1
Steven, T. M. 1985 (Everton, Rangers, Marseille) 36
Stevens, G. A. 1985 (Tottenham H) 7
Stevens, M. G. 1985 (Everton, Rangers) 46
Stewart, J. 1907 (Sheffield W, Newcastle U) 3
Stewart, P. A. 1992 (Tottenham H) 3
Stiles, N. P. 1965 (Manchester U) 28
Stoker, J. 1933 (Birmingham) 3
Stone, S. B. 1996 (Nottingham F) 9
Storer, H. 1924 (Derby Co) 2
Storey, P. E. 1971 (Arsenal) 19
Storey-Moore, I. 1970 (Nottingham F) 1
Strange, A. H. 1930 (Sheffield W) 20
Stratford, A. H. 1874 (Wanderers) 1
Streten, B. 1950 (Luton T) 1
Sturgess, A. 1911 (Sheffield U) 2
Sturridge, D. 2012 (Chelsea) 2
Summerbee, M. G. 1968 (Manchester C) 8
Sunderland, A. 1980 (Arsenal) 1
Sutcliffe, J. W. 1893 (Bolton W, Millwall) 5
Sutton, C. R. 1998 (Blackburn R) 1
Swan, P. 1960 (Sheffield W) 19
Swepstone, H. A. 1880 (Pilgrims) 6
Swift, F. V. 1947 (Manchester C) 19

Tait, G. 1881 (Birmingham Excelsior) 1
Talbot, B. 1977 (Ipswich T, Arsenal) 6
Tambling, R. V. 1963 (Chelsea) 3
Tate, J. T. 1931 (Aston Villa) 3
Taylor, E. 1954 (Blackpool) 1
Taylor, E. H. 1923 (Huddersfield T) 8
Taylor, J. G. 1951 (Fulham) 2
Taylor, P. H. 1948 (Liverpool) 3
Taylor, P. J. 1976 (Crystal Palace) 4
Taylor, T. 1953 (Manchester U) 19
Temple, D. W. 1965 (Everton) 1
Terry, J. G. 2003 (Chelsea) 77
Thickett, H. 1899 (Sheffield U) 2
Thomas, D. 1975 (QPR) 8
Thomas, D. 1983 (Coventry C) 2
Thomas, G. R. 1991 (Crystal Palace) 9
Thomas, M. L. 1989 (Arsenal) 2
Thompson, A. 2004 (Celtic) 1
Thompson, P. 1964 (Liverpool) 16
Thompson, P. B. 1976 (Liverpool) 42
Thompson T. 1952 (Aston Villa, Preston NE) 2
Thomson, R. A. 1964 (Wolverhampton W) 8
Thornewell, G. 1923 (Derby Co) 4
Thornley, I. 1907 (Manchester C) 1
Tilson, S. F. 1934 (Manchester C) 4
Titmuss, F. 1922 (Southampton) 2
Todd, C. 1972 (Derby Co) 27
Toone, G. 1892 (Notts Co) 2
Topham, A. G. 1894 (Casuals) 1
Topham, R. 1893 (Wolverhampton W, Casuals) 2
Towers, M. A. 1976 (Sunderland) 3
Townley, W. J. 1889 (Blackburn R) 2
Townrow, J. E. 1925 (Clapton Orient) 2
Tremelling, D. R. 1928 (Birmingham) 1
Tresadern, J. 1923 (West Ham U) 2
Tueart, D. 1975 (Manchester C) 6
Tunstall, F. E. 1923 (Sheffield U) 7
Turnbull, R. J. 1920 (Bradford) 1
Turner, A. 1900 (Southampton) 2
Turner, H. 1931 (Huddersfield T) 2
Turner, J. A. 1893 (Bolton W, Stoke, Derby Co) 3
Tweedy, G. J. 1937 (Grimsby T) 1

Ufton, D. G. 1954 (Charlton Ath) 1
Underwood, A. 1891 (Stoke C) 2
Unsworth, D. G. 1995 (Everton) 1
Upson, M. J. 2003 (Birmingham C, West Ham U) 21
Urwin, T. 1923 (Middlesbrough, Newcastle U) 4
Utley, G. 1913 (Barnsley) 1

Vassell, D. 2002 (Aston Villa) 22
Vaughton, O. H. 1882 (Aston Villa) 5
Veitch, C. C. M. 1906 (Newcastle U) 6
Veitch, J. G. 1894 (Old Westminsters) 1
Venables, T. F. 1965 (Chelsea) 2
Venison, B. 1995 (Newcastle U) 2
Vidal, R. W. S. 1873 (Oxford University) 1
Viljoen, C. 1975 (Ipswich T) 2
Viollet, D. S. 1960 (Manchester U) 2
Von Donop 1873 (Royal Engineers) 2

Wace, H. 1878 (Wanderers) 3
Waddle, C. R. 1985 (Newcastle U, Tottenham H, Marseille) 62
Wadsworth, S. J. 1922 (Huddersfield T) 9
Wainscoat, W. R. 1929 (Leeds U) 1
Waiters, A. K. 1964 (Blackpool) 5
Walcott, T. J. 2006 (Arsenal) 28
Walden, F. I. 1914 (Tottenham H) 2
Walker, D. S. 1989 (Nottingham F, Sampdoria, Sheffield W) 59
Walker, I. M. 1996 (Tottenham H, Leicester C) 4
Walker, K. A. 2012 (Tottenham H) 2
Walker, W. H. 1921 (Aston Villa) 18
Wall, G. 1907 (Manchester U) 7
Wallace, C. W. 1913 (Aston Villa) 3
Wallace, D. L. 1986 (Southampton) 1
Walsh, P. A. 1983 (Luton T) 5
Walters, A. M. 1885 (Cambridge University, Old Carthusians) 9
Walters, K. M. 1991 (Rangers) 1
Walters, P. M. 1885 (Oxford University, Old Carthusians) 13
Walton, N. 1890 (Blackburn R) 1
Ward, J. T. 1885 (Blackburn Olympic) 1
Ward, P. 1980 (Brighton & HA) 1
Ward, T. V. 1948 (Derby Co) 2
Waring, T. 1931 (Aston Villa) 5
Warner, C. 1878 (Upton Park) 1
Warnock, S. 2008 (Blackburn R, Aston Villa) 2
Warren, B. 1906 (Derby Co, Chelsea) 22
Waterfield, G. S. 1927 (Burnley) 1
Watson, D. 1984 (Norwich C, Everton) 12
Watson, D. V. 1974 (Sunderland, Manchester C, Werder Bremen, Southampton, Stoke C) 65
Watson, V. M. 1923 (West Ham U) 5
Watson, W. 1913 (Burnley) 3
Watson, W. 1950 (Sunderland) 4
Weaver, S. 1932 (Newcastle U) 3
Webb, G. W. 1911 (West Ham U) 2
Webb, N. J. 1988 (Nottingham F, Manchester U) 26
Webster, M. 1930 (Middlesbrough) 3
Wedlock, W. J. 1907 (Bristol C) 26
Weir, D. 1889 (Bolton W) 2
Welbeck, D. 2011 (Manchester U) 9
Welch, R. de C. 1872 (Wanderers, Harrow Chequers) 2
Weller, K. 1974 (Leicester C) 4
Welsh, D. 1938 (Charlton Ath) 3
West, G. 1969 (Everton) 3
Westwood, R. W. 1935 (Bolton W) 6
Whateley, O. 1883 (Aston Villa) 2
Wheeler, J. E. 1955 (Bolton W) 1
Wheldon, G. F. 1897 (Aston Villa) 4
White, D. 1993 (Manchester C) 1
White, T. A. 1933 (Everton) 1
Whitehead, J. 1893 (Accrington, Blackburn R) 2
Whitfeld, H. 1879 (Old Etonians) 1
Whitham, M. 1892 (Sheffield U) 1
Whitworth, S. 1975 (Leicester C) 7
Whymark, T. J. 1978 (Ipswich T) 1
Widdowson, S. W. 1880 (Nottingham F) 1
Wignall, F. 1965 (Nottingham F) 2
Wilcox, J. M. 1996 (Blackburn R, Leeds U) 3
Wilkes, A. 1901 (Aston Villa) 5
Wilkins, R. C. 1976 (Chelsea, Manchester U, AC Milan) 84
Wilkinson, B. 1904 (Sheffield U) 1
Wilkinson, L. R. 1891 (Oxford University) 1
Williams, B. F. 1949 (Wolverhampton W) 24
Williams, O. 1923 (Clapton Orient) 2
Williams, S. 1983 (Southampton) 6
Williams, W. 1897 (WBA) 6
Williamson, E. C. 1923 (Arsenal) 2
Williamson, R. G. 1905 (Middlesbrough) 7
Willingham, C. K. 1937 (Huddersfield T) 12
Willis, A. 1952 (Tottenham H) 1
Wilshaw, D. J. 1954 (Wolverhampton W) 12
Wilshere, J. A. 2011 (Arsenal) 5
Wilson, C. P. 1884 (Hendon) 2
Wilson, C. W. 1879 (Oxford University) 2
Wilson, G. 1921 (Sheffield W) 12
Wilson, G. P. 1900 (Corinthians) 2
Wilson, R. 1960 (Huddersfield T, Everton) 63
Wilson, T. 1928 (Huddersfield T) 1
Winckworth, W. N. 1892 (Old Westminsters) 2
Windridge, J. E. 1908 (Chelsea) 8
Wingfield-Stratford, C. V. 1877 (Royal Engineers) 1
Winterburn, N. 1990 (Arsenal) 2
Wise, D. F. 1991 (Chelsea) 21
Withe, P. 1981 (Aston Villa) 11
Wollaston, C. H. R. 1874 (Wanderers) 4
Wolstenholme, S. 1904 (Everton, Blackburn R) 3
Wood, H. 1890 (Wolverhampton W) 3
Wood, R. E. 1955 (Manchester U) 3
Woodcock, A. S. 1978 (Nottingham F, Cologne, Arsenal) 42
Woodgate, J. S. 1999 (Leeds U, Newcastle U, Real Madrid, Tottenham H) 8
Woodger, G. 1911 (Oldham Ath) 1
Woodhall, G. 1888 (WBA) 2
Woodley, V. R. 1937 (Chelsea) 19
Woods, C. C. E. 1985 (Norwich C, Rangers, Sheffield W) 43
Woodward, V. J. 1903 (Tottenham H, Chelsea) 23
Woosnam, M. 1922 (Manchester C) 1
Worrall, F. 1935 (Portsmouth) 2
Worthington, F. S. 1974 (Leicester C) 8
Wreford-Brown, C. 1889 (Oxford University, Old Carthusians) 4
Wright, E. G. D. 1906 (Cambridge University) 1
Wright, I. E. 1991 (Crystal Palace, Arsenal, West Ham U) 33
Wright, J. D. 1939 (Newcastle U) 1
Wright, M. 1984 (Southampton, Derby Co, Liverpool) 45
Wright, R. I. 2000 (Ipswich T, Arsenal) 2
Wright, T. J. 1968 (Everton) 11
Wright, W. A. 1947 (Wolverhampton W) 105
Wright-Phillips, S. C. 2005 (Manchester C, Chelsea, Manchester C) 36
Wylie, J. G. 1878 (Wanderers) 1

Yates, J. 1889 (Burnley) 1
York, R. E. 1922 (Aston Villa) 2
Young, A. 1933 (Huddersfield T) 9
Young, A. S. 2008 (Aston Villa, Manchester U) 25
Young, G. M. 1965 (Sheffield W) 1
Young, L. P. 2005 (Charlton Ath) 7

Zamora, R. L. 2011 (Fulham) 2

NORTHERN IRELAND

Addis, D. J. 1922 (Cliftonville) 1
Aherne, T. 1947 (Belfast Celtic, Luton T) 4
Alexander, T. E. 1895 (Cliftonville) 1
Allan, C. 1936 (Cliftonville) 1
Allen, J. 1887 (Limavady) 1
Anderson, J. 1925 (Distillery) 1
Anderson, T. 1973 (Manchester U, Swindon T, Peterborough U) 22
Anderson, W. 1898 (Linfield, Cliftonville) 4
Andrews, W. 1908 (Glentoran, Grimsby T) 3
Armstrong, G. J. 1977 (Tottenham H, Watford, Real Mallorca, WBA, Chesterfield) 63

Baird, C. P. 2003 (Southampton, Fulham) 56
Baird, G. 1896 (Distillery) 3
Baird, H. C. 1939 (Huddersfield T) 1
Balfe, J. 1909 (Shelbourne) 2
Bambrick, J. 1929 (Linfield, Chelsea) 11
Banks, S. J. 1937 (Cliftonville) 1
Barr, H. H. 1962 (Linfield, Coventry C) 3
Barron, J. H. 1894 (Cliftonville) 7
Barry, J. 1888 (Cliftonville) 3
Barry, J. 1900 (Bohemians) 1
Barton, A. J. 2011 (Preston NE) 1
Baxter, R. A. 1887 (Distillery) 1
Baxter, S. N. 1887 (Cliftonville) 1
Bennett, L. V. 1889 (Dublin University) 1
Best, G. 1964 (Manchester U, Fulham) 37
Bingham, W. L. 1951 (Sunderland, Luton T, Everton, Port Vale) 56
Black, K. T. 1988 (Luton T, Nottingham F) 30
Black, T. 1901 (Glentoran) 1
Blair, H. 1928 (Portadown, Swansea T) 4
Blair, J. 1907 (Cliftonville) 5
Blair, R. V. 1975 (Oldham Ath) 5
Blanchflower, J. 1954 (Manchester U) 12
Blanchflower, R. D. 1950 (Barnsley, Aston Villa, Tottenham H) 56
Blayney, A. 2006 (Doncaster R, Linfield) 5
Bookman, L. J. O. 1914 (Bradford C, Luton T) 4
Bothwell, A. W. 1926 (Ards) 5
Bowler, G. C. 1950 (Hull C) 3
Boyce, L. 2011 (Werder Bremen) 4
Boyle, P. 1901 (Sheffield U) 5
Braithwaite, R. M. 1962 (Linfield, Middlesbrough) 10
Braniff, K. R. 2010 (Portadown) 2
Breen, T. 1935 (Belfast Celtic, Manchester U) 9
Brennan, B. 1912 (Bohemians) 1
Brennan, R. A. 1949 (Luton T, Birmingham C, Fulham) 5
Briggs, W. R. 1962 (Manchester U, Swansea T) 2
Brisby, D. 1891 (Distillery) 1
Brolly, T. H. 1937 (Millwall) 4
Brookes, E. A. 1920 (Shelbourne) 1
Brotherston, N. 1980 (Blackburn R) 27
Brown, J. 1921 (Glenavon, Tranmere R) 3
Brown, J. 1935 (Wolverhampton W, Coventry C, Birmingham C) 10
Brown, N. M. 1887 (Limavady) 1
Brown, W. G. 1926 (Glenavon) 1
Browne, F. 1887 (Cliftonville) 5
Browne, R. J. 1936 (Leeds U) 6
Bruce, A. 1925 (Belfast Celtic) 1
Bruce, W. 1961 (Glentoran) 2
Brunt, C. 2005 (Sheffield W, WBA) 36
Bryan, M. A. 2010 (Watford) 2
Buckle, H. R. 1903 (Cliftonville, Sunderland, Bristol R) 3
Buckle, J. 1882 (Cliftonville) 1
Burnett, J. 1894 (Distillery, Glentoran) 5
Burnison, J. 1901 (Distillery) 2
Burnison, S. 1908 (Distillery, Bradford, Distillery) 8
Burns, J. 1923 (Glenavon) 1
Burns, W. 1925 (Glentoran) 1
Butler, M. P. 1939 (Blackpool) 1

Camp, L. M. J. 2011 (Nottingham F) 8
Campbell, A. C. 1963 (Crusaders) 2
Campbell, D. A. 1986 (Nottingham F, Charlton Ath) 10
Campbell, James 1897 (Cliftonville) 14
Campbell, John 1896 (Cliftonville) 1
Campbell, J. P. 1951 (Fulham) 2
Campbell, R. M. 1982 (Bradford C) 2
Campbell, W. G. 1968 (Dundee) 6
Capaldi, A. C. 2004 (Plymouth Arg, Cardiff C) 22
Carey, J. J. 1947 (Manchester U) 7
Carroll, E. 1925 (Glenavon) 1
Carroll, R. E. 1997 (Wigan Ath, Manchester U, West Ham U, Olympiakos) 20
Carson, J. G. 2011 (Ipswich T) 3
Carson, S. 2009 (Coleraine) 1
Casement, C. 2009 (Ipswich T) 1
Casey, T. 1955 (Newcastle U, Portsmouth) 12
Caskey, W. 1979 (Derby Co, Tulsa Roughnecks) 8
Cassidy, T. 1971 (Newcastle U, Burnley) 24
Cathcart, C. G. 2011 (Blackpool) 9
Caughey, M. 1986 (Linfield) 2
Chambers, R. J. 1921 (Distillery, Bury, Nottingham F) 12
Chatton, H. A. 1925 (Partick Th) 3
Christian, J. 1889 (Linfield) 1
Clarke, C. J. 1986 (Bournemouth, Southampton, QPR, Portsmouth) 38
Clarke, R. 1901 (Belfast Celtic) 2
Cleary, J. 1982 (Glentoran) 5
Clements, D. 1965 (Coventry C, Sheffield W, Everton, New York Cosmos) 48
Clingan, S. G. 2006 (Nottingham F, Norwich C, Coventry C) 33
Clugston, J. 1888 (Cliftonville) 14
Clyde, M. G. 2005 (Wolverhampton W) 3
Coates, C. 2009 (Crusaders) 6
Cochrane, D. 1939 (Leeds U) 12
Cochrane, G. 1903 (Cliftonville) 1
Cochrane, G. T. 1976 (Coleraine, Burnley, Middlesbrough, Gillingham) 26
Cochrane, M. 1898 (Distillery, Leicester Fosse) 8
Collins, F. 1922 (Celtic) 1
Collins, R. 1922 (Cliftonville) 1
Condy, J. 1882 (Distillery) 3
Connell, T. E. 1978 (Coleraine) 1
Connor, J. 1901 (Glentoran, Belfast Celtic) 13
Connor, M. J. 1903 (Brentford, Fulham) 3
Cook, W. 1933 (Celtic, Everton) 15
Cooke, S. 1889 (Belfast YMCA, Cliftonville) 3
Coote, A. 1999 (Norwich C) 6
Coulter, J. 1934 (Belfast Celtic, Everton, Grimsby T, Chelmsford C) 11
Cowan, J. 1970 (Newcastle U) 1
Cowan, T. S. 1925 (Queen's Island) 1
Coyle, F. 1956 (Coleraine, Nottingham F) 4
Coyle, L. 1989 (Derry C) 1
Coyle, R. I. 1973 (Sheffield W) 5
Craig, A. B. 1908 (Rangers, Morton) 9
Craig, D. J. 1967 (Newcastle U) 25
Craigan, S. J. 2003 (Partick Th, Motherwell) 54
Crawford, A. 1889 (Distillery, Cliftonville) 7
Croft, T. 1922 (Queen's Island) 3
Crone, R. 1889 (Distillery) 4
Crone, W. 1882 (Distillery) 12
Crooks, W. J. 1922 (Manchester U) 1
Crossan, E. 1950 (Blackburn R) 3
Crossan, J. A. 1960 (Sparta-Rotterdam, Sunderland, Manchester C, Middlesbrough) 24
Crothers, C. 1907 (Distillery) 1
Cumming, L. 1929 (Huddersfield T, Oldham Ath) 3
Cunningham, W. 1892 (Ulster) 4
Cunningham, W. E. 1951 (St Mirren, Leicester C, Dunfermline Ath) 30
Curran, S. 1926 (Belfast Celtic) 4
Curran, J. J. 1922 (Glenavon, Pontypridd, Glenavon) 5
Cush, W. W. 1951 (Glenavon, Leeds U, Portadown) 26

Dallas, S. 2011 (Crusaders) 1
Dalrymple, J. 1922 (Distillery) 1
Dalton, W. 1888 (YMCA, Linfield) 11
D'Arcy, S. D. 1952 (Chelsea, Brentford) 5
Darling, J. 1897 (Linfield) 22
Davey, H. H. 1926 (Reading, Portsmouth) 5
Davis, S. 2005 (Aston Villa, Fulham, Rangers) 52
Davis, T. L. 1937 (Oldham Ath) 1
Davison, A. J. 1996 (Bolton W, Bradford C, Grimsby T) 3
Davison, J. R. 1882 (Cliftonville) 8
Dennison, R. 1988 (Wolverhampton W) 18
Devine, A. O. 1886 (Limavady) 4

Devine, J. 1990 (Glentoran) 1
Dickson, D. 1970 (Coleraine) 4
Dickson, T. A. 1957 (Linfield) 1
Dickson, W. 1951 (Chelsea, Arsenal) 12
Diffin, W. J. 1931 (Belfast Celtic) 1
Dill, A. H. 1882 (Knock, Down Ath, Cliftonville) 9
Doherty, I. 1901 (Belfast Celtic) 1
Doherty, J. 1928 (Portadown) 1
Doherty, J. 1933 (Cliftonville) 2
Doherty, L. 1985 (Linfield) 2
Doherty, M. 1938 (Derry C) 1
Doherty, P. D. 1935 (Blackpool, Manchester C, Derby Co, Huddersfield T, Doncaster R) 16
Doherty, T. E. 2003 (Bristol C) 9
Donaghey, B. 1903 (Belfast Celtic) 1
Donaghy, M. M. 1980 (Luton T, Manchester U, Chelsea) 91
Donnelly, L. 1913 (Distillery) 1
Donnelly, M. 2009 (Crusaders) 1
Doran, J. F. 1921 (Brighton) 3
Dougan, A. D. 1958 (Portsmouth, Blackburn R, Aston Villa, Leicester C, Wolverhampton W) 43
Douglas, J. P. 1947 (Belfast Celtic) 1
Dowd, H. O. 1974 (Glenavon, Sheffield W) 3
Dowie, I. 1990 (Luton T, West Ham U, Southampton, C Palace, West Ham U, QPR) 59
Duff, M. J. 2002 (Cheltenham T, Burnley) 24
Duggan, H. A. 1930 (Leeds U) 8
Dunlop, G. 1985 (Linfield) 4
Dunne, J. 1928 (Sheffield U) 7

Eames, W. L. E. 1885 (Dublin University) 3
Eglington, T. J. 1947 (Everton) 6
Elder, A. R. 1960 (Burnley, Stoke C) 40
Elleman, A. R. 1889 (Cliftonville) 2
Elliott, S. 2001 (Motherwell, Hull C) 39
Elwood, J. H. 1929 (Bradford) 2
Emerson, W. 1920 (Glentoran, Burnley) 11
English, S. 1933 (Rangers) 2
Enright, J. 1912 (Leeds C) 1
Evans, C. J. 2009 (Manchester U, Hull C) 16
Evans, J. G. 2007 (Manchester U) 29

Falloon, E. 1931 (Aberdeen) 2
Farquharson, T. G. 1923 (Cardiff C) 7
Farrell, P. 1901 (Distillery) 2
Farrell, P. 1938 (Hibernian) 1
Farrell, P. D. 1947 (Everton) 7
Feeney, J. M. 1947 (Linfield, Swansea T) 2
Feeney, W. 1976 (Glentoran) 1
Feeney, W. J. 2002 (Bournemouth, Luton T, Cardiff C, Oldham Ath, Plymouth Arg) 46
Ferguson, G. 1999 (Linfield) 5
Ferguson, S. 2009 (Newcastle U) 3
Ferguson, W. 1966 (Linfield) 2
Ferris, J. 1920 (Belfast Celtic, Chelsea, Belfast Celtic) 6
Ferris, R. O. 1950 (Birmingham C) 3
Fettis, A. W. 1992 (Hull C, Nottingham F, Blackburn R) 25
Finney, T. 1975 (Sunderland, Cambridge U) 14
Fitzpatrick, J. C. 1896 (Bohemians) 2
Flack, H. 1929 (Burnley) 1
Fleming, J. G. 1987 (Nottingham F, Manchester C, Barnsley) 31
Forbes, G. 1888 (Limavady, Distillery) 3
Forde, J. T. 1959 (Ards) 4
Foreman, T. A. 1899 (Cliftonville) 1
Forsythe, J. 1888 (YMCA) 2
Fox, W. T. 1887 (Ulster) 2
Frame, T. 1925 (Linfield) 1
Fulton, R. P. 1928 (Larne, Belfast Celtic) 21

Gaffikin, G. 1890 (Linfield Ath) 15
Galbraith, W. 1890 (Distillery) 1
Gallagher, P. 1920 (Celtic, Falkirk) 11
Gallogly, C. 1951 (Huddersfield T) 2
Gara, A. 1902 (Preston NE) 3
Gardiner, A. 1930 (Cliftonville) 5
Garrett, J. 1925 (Distillery) 1
Garrett, R. 2009 (Linfield) 5
Gaston, R. 1969 (Oxford U) 1
Gaukrodger, G. 1895 (Linfield) 1
Gault, M. 2008 (Linfield) 1
Gaussen, A. D. 1884 (Moyola Park, Magherafelt) 6
Geary, J. 1931 (Glentoran) 2
Gibb, J. T. 1884 (Wellington Park, Cliftonville) 10
Gibb, T. J. 1936 (Cliftonville) 1
Gibson W. K. 1894 (Cliftonville) 14
Gillespie, K. R. 1995 (Manchester U, Newcastle U, Blackburn R, Leicester C, Sheffield U) 86
Gillespie, S. 1886 (Hertford) 6
Gillespie, W. 1889 (West Down) 1
Gillespie, W. 1913 (Sheffield U) 25
Goodall, A. L. 1899 (Derby Co, Glossop) 10
Goodbody, M. F. 1889 (Dublin University) 2
Gordon, H. 1895 (Linfield) 3
Gordon R. W. 1891 (Linfield) 7
Gordon, T. 1894 (Linfield) 2
Gorman, R. J. 2010 (Wolverhampton W) 9
Gorman, W. C. 1947 (Brentford) 4
Gough, J. 1925 (Queen's Island) 1
Gowdy, J. 1920 (Glentoran, Queen's Island, Falkirk) 6
Gowdy, W. A. 1932 (Hull C, Sheffield W, Linfield, Hibernian) 6
Graham, W. G. L. 1951 (Doncaster R) 14
Gray, P. 1993 (Luton T, Sunderland, Nancy, Luton T, Burnley, Oxford U) 26
Greer, W. 1909 (QPR) 3
Gregg, H. 1954 (Doncaster R, Manchester U) 25
Griffin, D. J. 1996 (St Johnstone, Dundee U, Stockport Co) 29
Grigg, W. D. 2012 (Walsall) 1

Hall, G. 1897 (Distillery) 1
Halligan, W. 1911 (Derby Co, Wolverhampton W) 2
Hamill, M. 1912 (Manchester U, Belfast Celtic, Manchester C) 7
Hamill, R. 1999 (Glentoran) 1
Hamilton, B. 1969 (Linfield, Ipswich T, Everton, Millwall, Swindon T) 50
Hamilton, G. 2003 (Portadown) 5
Hamilton, J. 1882 (Knock) 2
Hamilton, R. 1928 (Rangers) 5
Hamilton, W. D. 1885 (Dublin Association) 1
Hamilton, W. J. 1885 (Dublin Association) 1
Hamilton, W. J. 1908 (Distillery) 1
Hamilton, W. R. 1978 (QPR, Burnley, Oxford U) 41
Hampton, H. 1911 (Bradford C) 9
Hanna, J. 1912 (Nottingham F) 2
Hanna, J. D. 1899 (Royal Artillery, Portsmouth) 1
Hannon, D. J. 1908 (Bohemians) 6
Harkin, J. T. 1968 (Southport, Shrewsbury T) 5
Harland, A. I. 1922 (Linfield) 2
Harris, J. 1921 (Cliftonville, Glenavon) 2
Harris, V. 1906 (Shelbourne, Everton) 20
Harvey, M. 1961 (Sunderland) 34
Hastings, J. 1882 (Knock, Ulster) 7
Hatton, S. 1963 (Linfield) 2
Hayes, W. E. 1938 (Huddersfield T) 4
Healy, D. J. 2000 (Manchester U, Preston NE, Leeds U, Fulham, Sunderland, Rangers) 93
Healy, P. J. 1982 (Coleraine, Glentoran) 4
Hegan, D. 1970 (WBA, Wolverhampton W) 7
Henderson, J. 1885 (Ulster) 3
Hewison, G. 1885 (Moyola Park) 2
Hill, C. F. 1990 (Sheffield U, Leicester C, Trelleborg, Northampton T) 27
Hill, M. J. 1959 (Norwich C, Everton) 7
Hinton, E. 1947 (Fulham, Millwall) 7
Hodson, L. J. S. 2011 (Watford) 8
Holmes, S. P. 2002 (Wrexham) 1
Hopkins, J. 1926 (Brighton) 1
Horlock, K. 1995 (Swindon T, Manchester C) 32
Houston, J. 1912 (Linfield, Everton) 6
Houston, W. 1933 (Linfield) 1
Houston, W. J. 1885 (Moyola Park) 2
Hughes, A. W. 1998 (Newcastle U, Aston Villa, Fulham) 80
Hughes, J. 2006 (Lincoln C) 2
Hughes, M.A. 2006 (Oldham Ath) 2
Hughes, M. E. 1992 (Manchester C, Strasbourg, West Ham U, Wimbledon, Crystal Palace) 71
Hughes, P. A. 1987 (Bury) 3
Hughes, W. 1951 (Bolton W) 1

Humphries, W. M. 1962 (Ards, Coventry C, Swansea T) 14
Hunter, A. 1905 (Distillery, Belfast Celtic) 8
Hunter, A. 1970 (Blackburn R, Ipswich T) 53
Hunter, B. V. 1995 (Wrexham, Reading) 15
Hunter, R. J. 1884 (Cliftonville) 3
Hunter, V. 1962 (Coleraine) 2

Ingham, M. G. 2005 (Sunderland, Wrexham) 3
Irvine, R. J. 1962 (Linfield, Stoke C) 8
Irvine, R. W. 1922 (Everton, Portsmouth, Connah's Quay, Derry C) 15
Irvine, W. J. 1963 (Burnley, Preston NE, Brighton & HA) 23
Irving, S. J. 1923 (Dundee, Cardiff C, Chelsea) 18

Jackson, T. A. 1969 (Everton, Nottingham F, Manchester U) 35
Jamison, J. 1976 (Glentoran) 1
Jenkins, I. 1997 (Chester C, Dundee U) 6
Jennings, P. A. 1964 (Watford, Tottenham H, Arsenal, Tottenham H) 119
Johnson, D. M. 1999 (Blackburn R, Birmingham C) 56
Johnston, H. 1927 (Portadown) 1
Johnston, R. S. 1882 (Distillery) 5
Johnston, R. S. 1905 (Distillery) 1
Johnston, S. 1890 (Linfield) 4
Johnston, W. 1885 (Oldpark) 2
Johnston, W. C. 1962 (Glenavon, Oldham Ath) 2
Jones, J. 1930 (Linfield, Hibernian, Glenavon) 23
Jones, J. 1956 (Glenavon) 3
Jones, S. 1934 (Distillery, Blackpool) 2
Jones, S. G. 2003 (Crewe Alex, Burnley) 29
Jordan, T. 1895 (Linfield) 2

Kavanagh, P. J. 1930 (Celtic) 1
Keane, T. R. 1949 (Swansea T) 1
Kearns, A. 1900 (Distillery) 6
Kee, P. V. 1990 (Oxford U, Ards) 9
Keith, R. M. 1958 (Newcastle U) 23
Kelly, H. R. 1950 (Fulham, Southampton) 4
Kelly, J. 1896 (Glentoran) 1
Kelly, J. 1932 (Derry C) 11
Kelly, P. J. 1921 (Manchester C) 1
Kelly, P. M. 1950 (Barnsley) 1
Kennedy, A. L. 1923 (Arsenal) 2
Kennedy, P. H. 1999 (Watford, Wigan Ath) 20
Kernaghan, N. 1936 (Belfast Celtic) 3
Kirk, A. R. 2000 (Hearts, Boston U, Northampton T, Dunfermline Ath) 11
Kirkwood, H. 1904 (Cliftonville) 1
Kirwan, J. 1900 (Tottenham H, Chelsea, Clyde) 17

Lacey, W. 1909 (Everton, Liverpool, New Brighton) 23
Lafferty, D. P. 2012 (Burnley) 1
Lafferty, K. 2006 (Burnley, Rangers) 30
Lawrie, J. 2009 (Port Vale) 3
Lawther, R. 1888 (Glentoran) 2
Lawther, W. I. 1960 (Sunderland, Blackburn R) 4
Leatham, J. 1939 (Belfast Celtic) 1
Ledwidge, J. J. 1906 (Shelbourne) 2
Lemon, J. 1886 (Glentoran, Belfast YMCA) 3
Lennon, N. F. 1994 (Crewe Alex, Leicester C, Celtic) 40
Leslie, W. 1887 (YMCA) 1
Lewis, J. 1899 (Glentoran, Distillery) 4
Little, A. 2009 (Rangers) 8
Lockhart, H. 1884 (Rossall School) 1
Lockhart, N. H. 1947 (Linfield, Coventry C, Aston Villa) 8
Lomas, S. M. 1994 (Manchester C, West Ham U) 45
Loyal, J. 1891 (Clarence) 1
Lutton, R. J. 1970 (Wolverhampton W, West Ham U) 6
Lynas, R. 1925 (Cliftonville) 1
Lyner, D. R. 1920 (Glentoran, Manchester U, Kilmarnock) 6
Lytle, J. 1898 (Glentoran) 1

McAdams, W. J. 1954 (Manchester C, Bolton W, Leeds U) 15
McAlery, J. M. 1882 (Cliftonville) 2
McAlinden, J. 1938 (Belfast Celtic, Portsmouth, Southend U) 4
McAllen, J. 1898 (Linfield) 9
McAlpine, S. 1901 (Cliftonville) 1
McArdle, R. A. 2010 (Rochdale, Aberdeen) 5
McArthur, A. 1886 (Distillery) 1
McAuley, G. 2005 (Lincoln C, Leicester C, Ipswich T, WBA) 36
McAuley, J. L. 1911 (Huddersfield T) 6
McAuley, P. 1900 (Belfast Celtic) 1
McBride, S. D. 1991 (Glenavon) 4
McCabe, J. J. 1949 (Leeds U) 6
McCabe, W. 1891 (Ulster) 1
McCambridge, J. 1930 (Ballymena, Cardiff C) 4
McCandless, J. 1912 (Bradford) 5
McCandless, W. 1920 (Linfield, Rangers) 9
McCann, G. S. 2002 (West Ham U, Cheltenham T, Barnsley, Scunthorpe U, Peterborough U) 39
McCann, P. 1910 (Belfast Celtic, Glentoran) 7
McCarthy, J. D. 1996 (Port Vale, Birmingham C) 18
McCartney, A. 1903 (Ulster, Linfield, Everton, Belfast Celtic, Glentoran) 15
McCartney, G. 2002 (Sunderland, West Ham U, Sunderland) 34
McCashin, J. W. 1896 (Cliftonville) 5
McCavana, W. T. 1955 (Coleraine) 3
McCaw, J. H. 1927 (Linfield) 6
McClatchey, J. 1886 (Distillery) 3
McClatchey, T. 1895 (Distillery) 1
McCleary, J. W. 1955 (Cliftonville) 1
McCleery, W. 1922 (Cliftonville, Linfield) 10
McClelland, J. 1980 (Mansfield T, Rangers, Watford, Leeds U) 53
McClelland, J. T. 1961 (Arsenal, Fulham) 6
McCluggage, A. 1922 (Cliftonville, Bradford, Burnley) 13
McClure, G. 1907 (Cliftonville, Distillery) 4
McConnell, E. 1904 (Cliftonville, Glentoran, Sunderland, Sheffield W) 12
McConnell, P. 1928 (Doncaster R, Southport) 2
McConnell, W. G. 1912 (Bohemians) 6
McConnell, W. H. 1925 (Reading) 8
McCourt, F. J. 1952 (Manchester C) 6
McCourt, P. J. 2002 (Rochdale, Celtic) 10
McCoy, R. K. 1987 (Coleraine) 1
McCoy, S. 1896 (Distillery) 1
McCracken, E. 1928 (Barking) 1
McCracken, R. 1921 (Crystal Palace) 4
McCracken, R. 1922 (Linfield) 1
McCracken, W. R. 1902 (Distillery, Newcastle U, Hull C) 16
McCreery, D. 1976 (Manchester U, QPR, Tulsa Roughnecks, Newcastle U, Hearts) 67
McCrory, S. 1958 (Southend U) 1
McCullough, K. 1935 (Belfast Celtic, Manchester C) 5
McCullough, W. J. 1961 (Arsenal, Millwall) 10
McCurdy, C. 1980 (Linfield) 1
McDonald, A. 1986 (QPR) 52
McDonald, R. 1930 (Rangers) 2
McDonnell, J. 1911 (Bohemians) 4
McElhinney, G. M. A. 1984 (Bolton W) 6
McEvilly, L. R. 2002 (Rochdale) 1
McFaul, W. S. 1967 (Linfield, Newcastle U) 6
McGarry, J. K. 1951 (Cliftonville) 3
McGaughey, M. 1985 (Linfield) 1
McGibbon, P. C. G. 1995 (Manchester U, Wigan Ath) 7
McGinn, N. 2009 (Celtic) 18
McGivern, R. 2009 (Manchester C) 16
McGovern, M. 2010 (Ross Co) 1
McGrath, R. C. 1974 (Tottenham H, Manchester U) 21
McGregor, S. 1921 (Glentoran) 1
McGrillen, J. 1924 (Clyde, Belfast Celtic) 2
McGuire, E. 1907 (Distillery) 1
McGuire, J. 1928 (Linfield) 1
McIlroy, H. 1906 (Cliftonville) 1
McIlroy, J. 1952 (Burnley, Stoke C) 55
McIlroy, S. B. 1972 (Manchester U, Stoke C, Manchester C) 88
McIlvenny, P. 1924 (Distillery) 1
McIlvenny, R. 1890 (Distillery, Ulster) 2
McKeag, W. 1968 (Glentoran) 2
McKeague, T. 1925 (Glentoran) 1
McKee, F. W. 1906 (Cliftonville, Belfast Celtic) 5
McKelvey, H. 1901 (Glentoran) 2
McKenna, J. 1950 (Huddersfield T) 7

McKenzie, H. 1922 (Distillery) 2
McKenzie, R. 1967 (Airdrieonians) 1
McKeown, N. 1892 (Linfield) 7
McKie, H. 1895 (Cliftonville) 3
Mackie, J. A. 1923 (Arsenal, Portsmouth) 3
McKinney, D. 1921 (Hull C, Bradford C) 2
McKinney, V. J. 1966 (Falkirk) 1
McKnight, A. D. 1988 (Celtic, West Ham U) 10
McKnight, J. 1912 (Preston NE, Glentoran) 2
McLaughlin, C. G. 2012 (Preston NE) 1
McLaughlin, J. C. 1962 (Shrewsbury T, Swansea T) 12
McLean, B. S. 2006 (Rangers) 1
McLean, T. 1885 (Limavady) 1
McMahon, G. J. 1995 (Tottenham H, Stoke C) 17
McMahon, J. 1934 (Bohemians) 1
McMaster, G. 1897 (Glentoran) 3
McMichael, A. 1950 (Newcastle U) 40
McMillan, G. 1903 (Distillery) 2
McMillan, S. T. 1963 (Manchester U) 2
McMillen, W. S. 1934 (Manchester U, Chesterfield) 7
McMordie, A. S. 1969 (Middlesbrough) 21
McMorran, E. J. 1947 (Belfast Celtic, Barnsley, Doncaster R) 15
McMullan, D. 1926 (Liverpool) 3
McNally, B. A. 1986 (Shrewsbury T) 5
McNinch, J. 1931 (Ballymena) 3
McPake, J. 2012 (Coventry C) 1
McParland, P. J. 1954 (Aston Villa, Wolverhampton W) 34
McQuoid, J. J. B. 2011 (Millwall) 5
McShane, J. 1899 (Cliftonville) 4
McVeigh, P. M. 1999 (Tottenham H, Norwich C) 20
McVicker, J. 1888 (Linfield, Glentoran) 2
McWha, W. B. R. 1882 (Knock, Cliftonville) 7
Madden, O. 1938 (Norwich C) 1
Magee, G. 1885 (Wellington Park) 3
Magennis, J. B. D. 2010 (Cardiff C, Aberdeen) 3
Magill, E. J. 1962 (Arsenal, Brighton & HA) 26
Magilton, J. 1991 (Oxford U, Southampton, Sheffield W, Ipswich T) 52
Maginnis, H. 1900 (Linfield) 8
Mahood, J. 1926 (Belfast Celtic, Ballymena) 9
Mannus, A. 2004 (Linfield) 4
Manderson, R. 1920 (Rangers) 5
Mansfield, J. 1901 (Dublin Freebooters) 1
Martin, C. 1882 (Cliftonville) 3
Martin, C. 1925 (Bo'ness) 1
Martin, C. J. 1947 (Glentoran, Leeds U, Aston Villa) 6
Martin, D. K. 1934 (Belfast Celtic, Wolverhampton W, Nottingham F) 10
Mathieson, A. 1921 (Luton T) 2
Maxwell, J. 1902 (Linfield, Glentoran, Belfast Celtic) 7
Meek, H. L. 1925 (Glentoran) 1
Mehaffy, J. A. C. 1922 (Queen's Island) 1
Meldon, P. A. 1899 (Dublin Freebooters) 2
Mercer, H. V. A. 1908 (Linfield) 1
Mercer, J. T. 1898 (Distillery, Linfield, Distillery, Derby Co) 12
Millar, W. 1932 (Barrow) 2
Miller, J. 1929 (Middlesbrough) 3
Milligan, D. 1939 (Chesterfield) 1
Milne, R. G. 1894 (Linfield) 28
Mitchell, E. J. 1933 (Cliftonville, Glentoran) 2
Mitchell, W. 1932 (Distillery, Chelsea) 15
Molyneux, T. B. 1883 (Ligoniel, Cliftonville) 11
Montgomery, F. J. 1955 (Coleraine) 1
Moore, C. 1949 (Glentoran) 1
Moore, P. 1933 (Aberdeen) 1
Moore, R. 1891 (Linfield Ath) 3
Moore, R. L. 1887 (Ulster) 2
Moore, W. 1923 (Falkirk) 1
Moorhead, F. W. 1885 (Dublin University) 1
Moorhead, G. 1923 (Linfield) 4
Moran, J. 1912 (Leeds C) 1
Moreland, V. 1979 (Derby Co) 6
Morgan, G. F. 1922 (Linfield, Nottingham F) 8
Morgan, S. 1972 (Port Vale, Aston Villa, Brighton & HA, Sparta Rotterdam) 18
Morrison, R. 1891 (Linfield Ath) 2
Morrison, T. 1895 (Glentoran, Burnley) 7
Morrogh, D. 1896 (Bohemians) 1
Morrow, S. J. 1990 (Arsenal, QPR) 39
Morrow, W. J. 1883 (Moyola Park) 3
Muir, R. 1885 (Oldpark) 2
Mulgrew, J. 2010 (Linfield) 2
Mulholland, T. S. 1906 (Belfast Celtic) 2
Mullan, G. 1983 (Glentoran) 4
Mulligan, J. 1921 (Manchester C) 1
Mulryne, P. P. 1997 (Manchester U, Norwich C, Cardiff C) 27
Murdock, C. J. 2000 (Preston NE, Hibernian, Crewe Alex, Rotherham U) 34
Murphy, J. 1910 (Bradford C) 3
Murphy, N. 1905 (QPR) 3
Murray, J. M. 1910 (Motherwell, Sheffield W) 3

Napier, R. J. 1966 (Bolton W) 1
Neill, W. J. T. 1961 (Arsenal, Hull C) 59
Nelis, P. 1923 (Nottingham F) 1
Nelson, S. 1970 (Arsenal, Brighton & HA) 51
Nicholl, C. J. 1975 (Aston Villa, Southampton, Grimsby T) 51
Nicholl, H. 1902 (Belfast Celtic) 3
Nicholl, J. M. 1976 (Manchester U, Toronto Blizzard, Sunderland, Toronto Blizzard, Rangers, Toronto Blizzard, WBA) 73
Nicholson, J. J. 1961 (Manchester U, Huddersfield T) 41
Nixon, R. 1914 (Linfield) 1
Nolan, I. R. 1997 (Sheffield W, Bradford C, Wigan Ath) 18
Nolan-Whelan, J. V. 1901 (Dublin Freebooters) 5
Norwood, O. J. 2011 (Manchester U) 6

O'Boyle, G. 1994 (Dunfermline Ath, St Johnstone) 13
O'Brien, M. T. 1921 (QPR, Leicester C, Hull C, Derby Co) 10
O'Connell, P. 1912 (Sheffield W, Hull C) 5
O'Connor, M. J. 2008 (Crewe Alex, Scunthorpe U) 10
O'Doherty, A. 1970 (Coleraine) 2
O'Driscoll, J. F. 1949 (Swansea T) 3
O'Hagan, C. 1905 (Tottenham H, Aberdeen) 11
O'Hagan, W. 1920 (St Mirren) 2
O'Hehir, J. C. 1910 (Bohemians) 1
O'Kane, W. J. 1970 (Nottingham F) 20
O'Mahoney, M. T. 1939 (Bristol R) 1
O'Neill, C. 1989 (Motherwell) 3
O'Neill, J. 1962 (Sunderland) 1
O'Neill, J. P. 1980 (Leicester C) 39
O'Neill, M. A. M. 1988 (Newcastle U, Dundee U, Hibernian, Coventry C) 31
O'Neill, M. H. M. 1972 (Distillery, Nottingham F, Norwich C, Manchester C, Norwich C, Notts Co) 64
O'Reilly, H. 1901 (Dublin Freebooters) 3
Owens, J. 2011 (Crusaders) 1

Parke, J. 1964 (Linfield, Hibernian, Sunderland) 14
Paterson, M. A. 2008 (Scunthorpe U, Burnley) 13
Patterson, D. J. 1994 (Crystal Palace, Luton T, Dundee U) 17
Patterson, R. 2010 (Coleraine, Plymouth Arg) 5
Peacock, R. 1952 (Celtic, Coleraine) 31
Peden, J. 1887 (Linfield, Distillery) 24
Penney, S. 1985 (Brighton & HA) 17
Percy, J. C. 1889 (Belfast YMCA) 1
Platt, J. A. 1976 (Middlesbrough, Ballymena U, Coleraine) 23
Pollock, W. 1928 (Belfast Celtic) 1
Ponsonby, J. 1895 (Distillery) 9
Potts, R. M. C. 1883 (Cliftonville) 2
Priestley, T. J. M. 1933 (Coleraine, Chelsea) 2
Pyper, Jas. 1897 (Cliftonville) 7
Pyper, John 1897 (Cliftonville) 9
Pyper, M. 1932 (Linfield) 1

Quinn, J. M. 1985 (Blackburn R, Swindon T, Leicester C, Bradford C, West Ham U, Bournemouth, Reading) 46
Quinn, S. J. 1996 (Blackpool, WBA, Willem II, Sheffield W, Peterborough U, Northampton T) 50

Rafferty, P. 1980 (Linfield) 1
Ramsey, P. C. 1984 (Leicester C) 14
Rankine, J. 1883 (Alexander) 2
Rattray, D. 1882 (Avoniel) 3
Rea, R. 1901 (Glentoran) 1

Redmond, R. 1884 (Cliftonville) 1
Reid, G. H. 1923 (Cardiff C) 1
Reid, J. 1883 (Ulster) 6
Reid, S. E. 1934 (Derby Co) 3
Reid, W. 1931 (Hearts) 1
Reilly, M. M. 1900 (Portsmouth) 2
Renneville, W. T. J. 1910 (Leyton, Aston Villa) 4
Reynolds, J. 1890 (Distillery, Ulster) 5
Reynolds, R. 1905 (Bohemians) 1
Rice, P. J. 1969 (Arsenal) 49
Roberts, F. C. 1931 (Glentoran) 1
Robinson, P. 1920 (Distillery, Blackburn R) 2
Robinson, S. 1997 (Bournemouth, Luton T) 7
Rogan, A. 1988 (Celtic, Sunderland, Millwall) 18
Rollo, D. 1912 (Linfield, Blackburn R) 16
Roper, E. O. 1886 (Dublin University) 1
Rosbotham, A. 1887 (Cliftonville) 7
Ross, W. E. 1969 (Newcastle U) 1
Rowland, K. 1994 (West Ham U, QPR) 19
Rowley, R. W. M. 1929 (Southampton, Tottenham H) 6
Rushe, F. 1925 (Distillery) 1
Russell, A. 1947 (Linfield) 1
Russell, S. R. 1930 (Bradford C, Derry C) 3
Ryan, R. A. 1950 (WBA) 1

Sanchez, L. P. 1987 (Wimbledon) 3
Scott, E. 1920 (Liverpool, Belfast Celtic) 31
Scott, J. 1958 (Grimsby) 2
Scott, J. E. 1901 (Cliftonville) 1
Scott, L. J. 1895 (Dublin University) 2
Scott, P. W. 1975 (Everton, York C, Aldershot) 10
Scott, T. 1894 (Cliftonville) 13
Scott, W. 1903 (Linfield, Everton, Leeds C) 25
Scraggs, M. J. 1921 (Glentoran) 2
Seymour, H. C. 1914 (Bohemians) 1
Seymour, J. 1907 (Cliftonville) 2
Shanks, T. 1903 (Woolwich Arsenal, Brentford) 3
Sharkey, P. G. 1976 (Ipswich T) 1
Sheehan, Dr G. 1899 (Bohemians) 3
Sheridan, J. 1903 (Everton, Stoke C) 6
Sherrard, J. 1885 (Limavady) 3
Sherrard, W. C. 1895 (Cliftonville) 3
Sherry, J. J. 1906 (Bohemians) 2
Shields, R. J. 1957 (Southampton) 1
Shiels, D. 2006 (Hibernian, Doncaster R, Kilmarnock) 10
Silo, M. 1888 (Belfast YMCA) 1
Simpson, W. J. 1951 (Rangers) 12
Sinclair, J. 1882 (Knock) 2
Slemin, J. C. 1909 (Bohemians) 1
Sloan, A. S. 1925 (London Caledonians) 1
Sloan, D. 1969 (Oxford U) 2
Sloan, H. A. de B. 1903 (Bohemians) 8
Sloan, J. W. 1947 (Arsenal) 1
Sloan, T. 1926 (Cardiff C, Linfield) 11
Sloan, T. 1979 (Manchester U) 3
Small, J. M. 1887 (Clarence, Cliftonville) 4
Smith, A. W. 2003 (Glentoran, Preston NE) 18
Smith, E. E. 1921 (Cardiff C) 4
Smith, J. E. 1901 (Distillery) 2
Smyth, R. H. 1886 (Dublin University) 1
Smyth, S. 1948 (Wolverhampton W, Stoke C) 9
Smyth, W. 1949 (Distillery) 4
Snape, A. 1920 (Airdrieonians) 1
Sonner, D. J. 1998 (Ipswich T, Sheffield W, Birmingham C, Nottingham F, Peterborough U) 13
Spence, D. W. 1975 (Bury, Blackpool, Southend U) 29
Spencer, S. 1890 (Distillery) 6
Spiller, E. A. 1883 (Cliftonville) 5
Sproule, I. 2006 (Hibernian, Bristol C) 11
Stanfield, O. M. 1887 (Distillery) 30
Steele, A. 1926 (Charlton Ath, Fulham) 4
Stevenson, A. E. 1934 (Rangers, Everton) 17
Stewart, A. 1967 (Glentoran, Derby Co) 7
Stewart, D. C. 1978 (Hull C) 1
Stewart, I. 1982 (QPR, Newcastle U) 31
Stewart, R. K. 1890 (St Columb's Court, Cliftonville) 11
Stewart, T. C. 1961 (Linfield) 1
Swan, S. 1899 (Linfield) 1

Taggart, G. P. 1990 (Barnsley, Bolton W, Leicester C) 51
Taggart, J. 1899 (Walsall) 1
Taylor, M. S. 1999 (Fulham, Birmingham C, unattached) 88
Thompson, A. L. 2011 (Watford) 2
Thompson, F. W. 1910 (Cliftonville, Linfield, Bradford C, Clyde) 12
Thompson, J. 1897 (Distillery) 1
Thompson, P. 2006 (Linfield, Stockport Co) 8
Thompson, R. 1928 (Queen's Island) 1
Thompson, W. 1889 (Belfast Ath) 1
Thunder, P. J. 1911 (Bohemians) 1
Todd, S. J. 1966 (Burnley, Sheffield W) 11
Toner, C. 2003 (Leyton Orient) 2
Toner, J. 1922 (Arsenal, St Johnstone) 8
Torrans, R. 1893 (Linfield) 1
Torrans, S. 1889 (Linfield) 26
Trainor, D. 1967 (Crusaders) 1
Tuffey, J. 2009 (Partick T, Inverness CT) 8
Tully, C. P. 1949 (Celtic) 10
Turner, A. 1896 (Cliftonville) 1
Turner, E. 1896 (Cliftonville) 1
Turner, W. 1886 (Cliftonville) 3
Twomey, J. F. 1938 (Leeds U) 2

Uprichard, W. N. M. C. 1952 (Swindon T, Portsmouth) 18

Vernon, J. 1947 (Belfast Celtic, WBA) 17

Waddell, T. M. R. 1906 (Cliftonville) 1
Walker, J. 1955 (Doncaster R) 1
Walker, T. 1911 (Bury) 1
Walsh, D. J. 1947 (WBA) 9
Walsh, W. 1948 (Manchester C) 5
Ward, J. J. 2012 (Derby Co) 1
Waring, J. 1899 (Cliftonville) 1
Warren, P. 1913 (Shelbourne) 2
Watson, J. 1883 (Ulster) 9
Watson, P. 1971 (Distillery) 1
Watson, T. 1926 (Cardiff C) 1
Wattie, J. 1899 (Distillery) 1
Webb, C. G. 1909 (Brighton & HA) 3
Webb, S. M. 2006 (Ross Co) 4
Weir, E. 1939 (Clyde) 1
Welsh, E. 1966 (Carlisle U) 4
Whiteside, N. 1982 (Manchester U, Everton) 38
Whiteside, T. 1891 (Distillery) 1
Whitfield, E. R. 1886 (Dublin University) 1
Whitley, Jeff 1997 (Manchester C, Sunderland, Cardiff C) 20
Whitley, Jim 1998 (Manchester C) 3
Williams, J. R. 1886 (Ulster) 2
Williams, M. S. 1999 (Chesterfield, Watford, Wimbledon, Stoke C, Wimbledon, Milton Keynes D) 36
Williams, P. A. 1991 (WBA) 1
Williamson, J. 1890 (Cliftonville) 3
Willighan, T. 1933 (Burnley) 2
Willis, G. 1906 (Linfield) 4
Wilson, D. J. 1987 (Brighton & HA, Luton T, Sheffield W) 24
Wilson, H. 1925 (Linfield) 2
Wilson, K. J. 1987 (Ipswich T, Chelsea, Notts Co, Walsall) 42
Wilson, M. 1884 (Distillery) 3
Wilson, R. 1888 (Cliftonville) 1
Wilson, S. J. 1962 (Glenavon, Falkirk, Dundee) 12
Wilton, J. M. 1888 (St Columb's Court, Cliftonville, St Columb's Court) 7
Winchester, C. 2011 (Oldham Ath) 1
Wood, T. J. 1996 (Walsall) 1
Worthington, N. 1984 (Sheffield W, Leeds U, Stoke C) 66
Wright, J. 1906 (Cliftonville) 6
Wright, T. J. 1989 (Newcastle U, Nottingham F, Manchester C) 31

Young, S. 1907 (Linfield, Airdrieonians, Linfield) 9

SCOTLAND

Adam, C. G. 2007 (Rangers, Blackpool, Liverpool) 16
Adams, J. 1889 (Hearts) 3
Agnew, W. B. 1907 (Kilmarnock) 3
Aird, J. 1954 (Burnley) 4
Aitken, A. 1901 (Newcastle U, Middlesbrough, Leicester Fosse) 14
Aitken, G. G. 1949 (East Fife, Sunderland) 8
Aitken, R. 1886 (Dumbarton) 2
Aitken, R. 1980 (Celtic, Newcastle U, St Mirren) 57
Aitkenhead, W. A. C. 1912 (Blackburn R) 1
Albiston, A. 1982 (Manchester U) 14
Alexander, D. 1894 (East Stirlingshire) 2
Alexander, G. 2002 (Preston NE, Burnley) 40
Alexander, N. 2006 (Cardiff C) 3
Allan, D. S. 1885 (Queen's Park) 3
Allan, G. 1897 (Liverpool) 1
Allan, H. 1902 (Hearts) 1
Allan, J. 1887 (Queen's Park) 2
Allan, T. 1974 (Dundee) 2
Ancell, R. F. D. 1937 (Newcastle U) 2
Anderson, A. 1933 (Hearts) 23
Anderson, F. 1874 (Clydesdale) 1
Anderson, G. 1901 (Kilmarnock) 1
Anderson, H. A. 1914 (Raith R) 1
Anderson, J. 1954 (Leicester C) 1
Anderson, K. 1896 (Queen's Park) 3
Anderson, R. 2003 (Aberdeen, Sunderland) 11
Anderson, W. 1882 (Queen's Park) 6
Andrews, P. 1875 (Eastern) 1
Archibald, A. 1921 (Rangers) 8
Archibald, S. 1980 (Aberdeen, Tottenham H, Barcelona) 27
Armstrong, M. W. 1936 (Aberdeen) 3
Arnott, W. 1883 (Queen's Park) 14
Auld, J. R. 1887 (Third Lanark) 3
Auld, R. 1959 (Celtic) 3

Baird, A. 1892 (Queen's Park) 2
Baird, D. 1890 (Hearts) 3
Baird, H. 1956 (Airdrieonians) 1
Baird, J. C. 1876 (Vale of Leven) 3
Baird, S. 1957 (Rangers) 7
Baird, W. U. 1897 (St Bernard) 1
Bannan, B. 2011 (Aston Villa) 11
Bannon, E. J. 1980 (Dundee U) 11
Barbour, A. 1885 (Renton) 1
Bardsley, P. A. 2011 (Sunderland) 12
Barker, J. B. 1893 (Rangers) 2
Barr, D. 2009 (Falkirk) 1
Barrett, F. 1894 (Dundee) 2
Battles, B. 1901 (Celtic) 3
Battles, B. jun. 1931 (Hearts) 1
Bauld, W. 1950 (Hearts) 3
Baxter, J. C. 1961 (Rangers, Sunderland) 34
Baxter, R. D. 1939 (Middlesbrough) 3
Beattie, A. 1937 (Preston NE) 7
Beattie, C. 2006 (Celtic, WBA) 7
Beattie, R. 1939 (Preston NE) 1
Begbie, I. 1890 (Hearts) 4
Bell, A. 1912 (Manchester U) 1
Bell, C. 2011 (Kilmarnock) 1
Bell, J. 1890 (Dumbarton, Everton, Celtic) 10
Bell, M. 1901 (Hearts) 1
Bell, W. J. 1966 (Leeds U) 2
Bennett, A. 1904 (Celtic, Rangers) 11
Bennie, R. 1925 (Airdrieonians) 3
Bernard, P. R. J. 1995 (Oldham Ath) 2
Berra, C. 2008 (Hearts, Wolverhampton W) 20
Berry, D. 1894 (Queen's Park) 3
Berry, W. H. 1888 (Queen's Park) 4
Bett, J. 1982 (Rangers, Lokeren, Aberdeen) 25
Beveridge, W. W. 1879 (Glasgow University) 3
Black, A. 1938 (Hearts) 3
Black, D. 1889 (Hurlford) 1
Black, E. 1988 (Metz) 2
Black, I. H. 1948 (Southampton) 1
Blackburn, J. E. 1873 (Royal Engineers) 1
Blacklaw, A. S. 1963 (Burnley) 3
Blackley, J. 1974 (Hibernian) 7
Blair, D. 1929 (Clyde, Aston Villa) 8
Blair, J. 1920 (Sheffield W, Cardiff C) 8
Blair, J. 1934 (Motherwell) 1
Blair, J. A. 1947 (Blackpool) 1
Blair, W. 1896 (Third Lanark) 1
Blessington, J. 1894 (Celtic) 4
Blyth, J. A. 1978 (Coventry C) 2
Bone, J. 1972 (Norwich C) 2
Booth, S. 1993 (Aberdeen, Borussia Dortmund, Twente) 21
Bowie, J. 1920 (Rangers) 2
Bowie, W. 1891 (Linthouse) 1
Bowman, D. 1992 (Dundee U) 6
Bowman, G. A. 1892 (Montrose) 1
Boyd, J. M. 1934 (Newcastle U) 1
Boyd, K. 2006 (Rangers, Middlesbrough) 18
Boyd, R. 1889 (Mossend Swifts) 2
Boyd, T. 1991 (Motherwell, Chelsea, Celtic) 72
Boyd, W. G. 1931 (Clyde) 2
Bradshaw, T. 1928 (Bury) 1
Brand, R. 1961 (Rangers) 8
Brandon, T. 1896 (Blackburn R) 1
Brazil, A. 1980 (Ipswich T, Tottenham H) 13
Breckenridge, T. 1888 (Hearts) 1
Bremner, D. 1976 (Hibernian) 1
Bremner, W. J. 1965 (Leeds U) 54
Brennan, F. 1947 (Newcastle U) 7
Breslin, B. 1897 (Hibernian) 1
Brewster, G. 1921 (Everton) 1
Broadfoot, K. 2009 (Rangers) 4
Brogan, J. 1971 (Celtic) 4
Brown, A. 1890 (St Mirren) 2
Brown, A. 1904 (Middlesbrough) 1
Brown, A. D. 1950 (East Fife, Blackpool) 14
Brown, G. C. P. 1931 (Rangers) 19
Brown, H. 1947 (Partick Th) 3
Brown, J. B. 1939 (Clyde) 1
Brown, J. G. 1975 (Sheffield U) 1
Brown, R. 1884 (Dumbarton) 2
Brown, R. 1890 (Cambuslang) 1
Brown, R. 1947 (Rangers) 3
Brown, R. jun. 1885 (Dumbarton) 1
Brown, S. 2006 (Hibernian, Celtic) 28
Brown, W. D. F. 1958 (Dundee, Tottenham H) 28
Browning, J. 1914 (Celtic) 1
Brownlie, J. 1909 (Third Lanark) 16
Brownlie, J. 1971 (Hibernian) 7
Bruce, D. 1890 (Vale of Leven) 1
Bruce, R. F. 1934 (Middlesbrough) 1
Bryson, C. 2011 (Kilmarnock) 1
Buchan, M. M. 1972 (Aberdeen, Manchester U) 34
Buchanan, J. 1889 (Cambuslang) 1
Buchanan, J. 1929 (Rangers) 2
Buchanan, P. S. 1938 (Chelsea) 1
Buchanan, R. 1891 (Abercorn) 1
Buckley, P. 1954 (Aberdeen) 3
Buick, A. 1902 (Hearts) 2
Burchill, M. J. 2000 (Celtic) 6
Burke, C. 2006 (Rangers) 2
Burley, C. W. 1995 (Chelsea, Celtic, Derby Co) 46
Burley, G. E. 1979 (Ipswich T) 11
Burns, F. 1970 (Manchester U) 1
Burns, K. 1974 (Birmingham C, Nottingham F) 20
Burns, T. 1981 (Celtic) 8
Busby, M. W. 1934 (Manchester C) 1

Cairns, T. 1920 (Rangers) 8
Calderhead, D. 1889 (Q of S Wanderers) 1
Calderwood, C. 1995 (Tottenham H) 36
Calderwood, R. 1885 (Cartvale) 3
Caldow, E. 1957 (Rangers) 40
Caldwell, G. 2002 (Newcastle U, Hibernian, Celtic, Wigan Ath) 48
Caldwell, S. 2001 (Newcastle U, Sunderland, Burnley,Wigan Ath) 12
Callaghan, P. 1900 (Hibernian) 1
Callaghan, W. 1970 (Dunfermline Ath) 2
Cameron, C. 1999 (Hearts, Wolverhampton W) 28
Cameron, J. 1886 (Rangers) 1
Cameron, J. 1896 (Queen's Park) 1
Cameron, J. 1904 (St Mirren, Chelsea) 2

Campbell, C. 1874 (Queen's Park) 13
Campbell, H. 1889 (Renton) 1
Campbell, Jas 1913 (Sheffield W) 1
Campbell, J. 1880 (South Western) 1
Campbell, J. 1891 (Kilmarnock) 2
Campbell, John 1893 (Celtic) 12
Campbell, John 1899 (Rangers) 4
Campbell, K. 1920 (Liverpool, Partick Th) 8
Campbell, P. 1878 (Rangers) 2
Campbell, P. 1898 (Morton) 1
Campbell, R. 1947 (Falkirk, Chelsea) 5
Campbell, W. 1947 (Morton) 5
Canero, P. 2004 (Leicester C) 1
Carabine, J. 1938 (Third Lanark) 3
Carr, W. M. 1970 (Coventry C) 6
Cassidy, J. 1921 (Celtic) 4
Chalmers, S. 1965 (Celtic) 5
Chalmers, W. 1885 (Rangers) 1
Chalmers, W. S. 1929 (Queen's Park) 1
Chambers, T. 1894 (Hearts) 1
Chaplin, G. D. 1908 (Dundee) 1
Cheyne, A. G. 1929 (Aberdeen) 5
Christie, A. J. 1898 (Queen's Park) 3
Christie, R. M. 1884 (Queen's Park) 1
Clark, J. 1966 (Celtic) 4
Clark, R. B. 1968 (Aberdeen) 17
Clarke, S. 1988 (Chelsea) 6
Clarkson, D. 2008 (Motherwell) 2
Cleland, J. 1891 (Royal Albert) 1
Clements, R. 1891 (Leith Ath) 1
Clunas, W. L. 1924 (Sunderland) 2
Collier, W. 1922 (Raith R) 1
Collins, J. 1988 (Hibernian, Celtic, Monaco, Everton) 58
Collins, R. Y. 1951 (Celtic, Everton, Leeds U) 31
Collins, T. 1909 (Hearts) 1
Colman, D. 1911 (Aberdeen) 4
Colquhoun, E. P. 1972 (Sheffield U) 9
Colquhoun, J. 1988 (Hearts) 2
Combe, J. R. 1948 (Hibernian) 3
Commons, K. 2009 (Derby Co, Celtic) 9
Conn, A. 1956 (Hearts) 1
Conn, A. 1975 (Tottenham H) 2
Connachan, E. D. 1962 (Dunfermline Ath) 2
Connelly, G. 1974 (Celtic) 2
Connolly, J. 1973 (Everton) 1
Connor, J. 1886 (Airdrieonians) 1
Connor, J. 1930 (Sunderland) 4
Connor, R. 1986 (Dundee, Aberdeen) 4
Conway, C. 2010 (Dundee U, Cardiff C) 3
Cook, W. L. 1934 (Bolton W) 3
Cooke, C. 1966 (Dundee, Chelsea) 16
Cooper, D. 1980 (Rangers, Motherwell) 22
Cormack, P. B. 1966 (Hibernian, Nottingham F) 9
Cowan, J. 1896 (Aston Villa) 3
Cowan, J. 1948 (Morton) 25
Cowan, W, D. 1924 (Newcastle U) 1
Cowie, D. 1953 (Dundee) 20
Cowie, D. M. 2010 (Watford, Cardiff C) 10
Cox, C. J. 1948 (Hearts) 1
Cox, S. 1949 (Rangers) 24
Craig, A. 1929 (Motherwell) 3
Craig, J. 1977 (Celtic) 1
Craig, J. P. 1968 (Celtic) 1
Craig, T. 1927 (Rangers) 8
Craig, T. B. 1976 (Newcastle U) 1
Crainey, S. D. 2002 (Celtic, Southampton, Blackpool) 12
Crapnell, J. 1929 (Airdrieonians) 9
Crawford, D. 1894 (St Mirren, Rangers) 3
Crawford, J. 1932 (Queen's Park) 5
Crawford, S. 1995 (Raith R, Dunfermline Ath, Plymouth Arg) 25
Crerand, P. T. 1961 (Celtic, Manchester U) 16
Cringan, W. 1920 (Celtic) 5
Crosbie, J. A. 1920 (Ayr U, Birmingham) 2
Croal, J. A. 1913 (Falkirk) 3
Cropley, A. J. 1972 (Hibernian) 2
Cross, J. H. 1903 (Third Lanark) 1
Cruickshank, J. 1964 (Hearts) 6
Crum, J. 1936 (Celtic) 2
Cullen, M. J. 1956 (Luton T) 1
Cumming, D. S. 1938 (Middlesbrough) 1
Cumming, J. 1955 (Hearts) 9
Cummings, G. 1935 (Partick Th, Aston Villa) 9
Cummings, W. 2002 (Chelsea) 1
Cunningham, A. N. 1920 (Rangers) 12
Cunningham, W. C. 1954 (Preston NE) 8
Curran, H. P. 1970 (Wolverhampton W) 5

Dailly, C. 1997 (Derby Co, Blackburn R, West Ham U, Rangers) 67
Dalglish, K. 1972 (Celtic, Liverpool) 102
Davidson, C. I. 1999 (Blackburn R, Leicester C, Preston NE) 19
Davidson, D. 1878 (Queen's Park) 5
Davidson, J. A. 1954 (Partick Th) 8
Davidson, S. 1921 (Middlesbrough) 1
Dawson, A. 1980 (Rangers) 5
Dawson, J. 1935 (Rangers) 14
Deans, J. 1975 (Celtic) 2
Delaney, J. 1936 (Celtic, Manchester U) 13
Devine, A. 1910 (Falkirk) 1
Devlin, P. J. 2003 (Birmingham C) 10
Dewar, G. 1888 (Dumbarton) 2
Dewar, N. 1932 (Third Lanark) 3
Dick, J. 1959 (West Ham U) 1
Dickie, M. 1897 (Rangers) 3
Dickov, P. 2001 (Manchester C, Leicester C, Blackburn R) 10
Dickson, W. 1888 (Dundee Strathmore) 1
Dickson, W. 1970 (Kilmarnock) 5
Divers, J. 1895 (Celtic) 1
Divers, J. 1939 (Celtic) 1
Dobie, R. S. 2002 (WBA) 6
Docherty, T. H. 1952 (Preston NE, Arsenal) 25
Dodds, D. 1984 (Dundee U) 2
Dodds, J. 1914 (Celtic) 3
Dodds, W. 1997 (Aberdeen, Dundee U, Rangers) 26
Doig, J. E. 1887 (Arbroath, Sunderland) 5
Donachie, W. 1972 (Manchester C) 35
Donaldson, A. 1914 (Bolton W) 6
Donnachie, J. 1913 (Oldham Ath) 3
Donnelly, S. 1997 (Celtic) 10
Dorrans, G. 2010 (WBA) 8
Dougal, J. 1939 (Preston NE) 1
Dougall, C. 1947 (Birmingham C) 1
Dougan, R. 1950 (Hearts) 1
Douglas, A. 1911 (Chelsea) 1
Douglas, J. 1880 (Renfrew) 1
Douglas, R. 2002 (Celtic, Leicester C) 19
Dowds, P. 1892 (Celtic) 1
Downie, R. 1892 (Third Lanark) 1
Doyle, D. 1892 (Celtic) 8
Doyle, J. 1976 (Ayr U) 1
Drummond, J. 1892 (Falkirk, Rangers) 14
Dunbar, M. 1886 (Cartvale) 1
Duncan, A. 1975 (Hibernian) 6
Duncan, D. 1933 (Derby Co) 14
Duncan, D. M. 1948 (East Fife) 3
Duncan, J. 1878 (Alexandra Ath) 2
Duncan, J. 1926 (Leicester C) 1
Duncanson, J. 1947 (Rangers) 1
Dunlop, J. 1890 (St Mirren) 1
Dunlop, W. 1906 (Liverpool) 1
Dunn, J. 1925 (Hibernian, Everton) 6
Durie, G. S. 1988 (Chelsea, Tottenham H, Rangers) 43
Durrant, I. 1988 (Rangers, Kilmarnock) 20
Dykes, J. 1938 (Hearts) 2

Easson, J. F. 1931 (Portsmouth) 3
Elliott, M. S. 1998 (Leicester C) 18
Ellis, J. 1892 (Mossend Swifts) 1
Evans, A. 1982 (Aston Villa) 4
Evans, R. 1949 (Celtic, Chelsea) 48
Ewart, J. 1921 (Bradford C) 1
Ewing, T. 1958 (Partick Th) 2

Farm, G. N. 1953 (Blackpool) 10
Ferguson, B. 1999 (Rangers, Blackburn R, Rangers) 45
Ferguson, D. 1988 (Rangers) 2
Ferguson, D. 1992 (Dundee U, Everton) 7
Ferguson, I. 1989 (Rangers) 9
Ferguson, J. 1874 (Vale of Leven) 6
Ferguson, R. 1966 (Kilmarnock) 7
Fernie, W. 1954 (Celtic) 12

Findlay, R. 1898 (Kilmarnock) 1
Fitchie, T. T. 1905 (Woolwich Arsenal, Queen's Park) 4
Flavell, R. 1947 (Airdrieonians) 2
Fleck, R. 1990 (Norwich C) 4
Fleming, C. 1954 (East Fife) 1
Fleming, J. W. 1929 (Rangers) 3
Fleming, R. 1886 (Morton) 1
Fletcher, D. B. 2004 (Manchester U) 58
Fletcher, S. 2008 (Hibernian, Burnley, Wolverhampton W) 8
Forbes, A. R. 1947 (Sheffield U, Arsenal) 14
Forbes, J. 1884 (Vale of Leven) 5
Ford, D. 1974 (Hearts) 3
Forrest, J. 1958 (Motherwell) 1
Forrest, J. 1966 (Rangers, Aberdeen) 5
Forrest, J. 2011 (Celtic) 5
Forsyth, A. 1972 (Partick Th, Manchester U) 10
Forsyth, C. 1964 (Kilmarnock) 4
Forsyth, T. 1971 (Motherwell, Rangers) 22
Fox, D. J. 2010 (Burnley) 1
Foyers, R. 1893 (St Bernards) 2
Fraser, D. M. 1968 (WBA) 2
Fraser, J. 1891 (Moffat) 1
Fraser, M. J. E. 1880 (Queen's Park) 5
Fraser, J. 1907 (Dundee) 1
Fraser, W. 1955 (Sunderland) 2
Freedman, D. A. 2002 (Crystal Palace) 2
Fulton, W. 1884 (Abercorn) 1
Fyfe, J. H. 1895 (Third Lanark) 1

Gabriel, J. 1961 (Everton) 2
Gallacher, H. K. 1924 (Airdrieonians, Newcastle U, Chelsea, Derby Co) 20
Gallacher, K. W. 1988 (Dundee U, Coventry C, Blackburn R, Newcastle U) 53
Gallacher, P. 1935 (Sunderland) 1
Gallacher, P. 2002 (Dundee U) 8
Gallagher, P. 2004 (Blackburn R) 1
Galloway, M. 1992 (Celtic) 1
Galt, J. H. 1908 (Rangers) 2
Gardiner, I. 1958 (Motherwell) 1
Gardner, D. R. 1897 (Third Lanark) 1
Gardner, R. 1872 (Queen's Park, Clydesdale) 5
Gemmell, T. 1955 (St Mirren) 2
Gemmell, T. 1966 (Celtic) 18
Gemmill, A. 1971 (Derby Co, Nottingham F, Birmingham C) 43
Gemmill, S. 1995 (Nottingham F, Everton) 26
Gibb, W. 1873 (Clydesdale) 1
Gibson, D. W. 1963 (Leicester C) 7
Gibson, J. D. 1926 (Partick Th, Aston Villa) 8
Gibson, N. 1895 (Rangers, Partick Th) 14
Gilchrist, J. E. 1922 (Celtic) 1
Gilhooley, M. 1922 (Hull C) 1
Gillespie, G. 1880 (Rangers, Queen's Park) 7
Gillespie, G. T. 1988 (Liverpool) 13
Gillespie, Jas 1898 (Third Lanark) 1
Gillespie, John 1896 (Queen's Park) 1
Gillespie, R. 1927 (Queen's Park) 4
Gillick, T. 1937 (Everton) 5
Gilmour, J. 1931 (Dundee) 1
Gilzean, A. J. 1964 (Dundee, Tottenham H) 22
Glass, S. 1999 (Newcastle U) 1
Glavin, R. 1977 (Celtic) 1
Glen, A. 1956 (Aberdeen) 2
Glen, R. 1895 (Renton, Hibernian) 3
Goodwillie, D. 2011 (Dundee U, Blackburn R) 3
Goram, A. L. 1986 (Oldham Ath, Hibernian, Rangers) 43
Gordon, C. S. 2004 (Hearts, Sunderland) 40
Gordon, J. E. 1912 (Rangers) 10
Gossland, J. 1884 (Rangers) 1
Goudle, J. 1884 (Abercorn) 1
Gough, C. R. 1983 (Dundee U, Tottenham H, Rangers) 61
Gould, J. 2000 (Celtic) 2
Gourlay, J. 1886 (Cambuslang) 2
Govan, J. 1948 (Hibernian) 6
Gow, D. R. 1888 (Rangers) 1
Gow, J. J. 1885 (Queen's Park) 1
Gow, J. R. 1888 (Rangers) 1
Graham, A. 1978 (Leeds U) 11
Graham, G. 1972 (Arsenal, Manchester U) 12
Graham, J. 1884 (Annbank) 1
Graham, J. A. 1921 (Arsenal) 1
Grant, J. 1959 (Hibernian) 2
Grant, P. 1989 (Celtic) 2
Gray, A. 1903 (Hibernian) 1
Gray, A. D. 2003 (Bradford C) 2
Gray, A. M. 1976 (Aston Villa, Wolverhampton W, Everton) 20
Gray, D. 1929 (Rangers) 10
Gray, E. 1969 (Leeds U) 12
Gray, F. T. 1976 (Leeds U, Nottingham F, Leeds U) 32
Gray, W. 1886 (Pollokshields Ath) 1
Green, A. 1971 (Blackpool, Newcastle U) 6
Greig, J. 1964 (Rangers) 44
Groves, W. 1888 (Hibernian, Celtic) 3
Gulliland, W. 1891 (Queen's Park) 4
Gunn, B. 1990 (Norwich C) 6

Haddock, H. 1955 (Clyde) 6
Haddow, D. 1894 (Rangers) 1
Haffey, F. 1960 (Celtic) 2
Hamilton, A. 1885 (Queen's Park) 4
Hamilton, A. W. 1962 (Dundee) 24
Hamilton, G. 1906 (Port Glasgow Ath) 1
Hamilton, G. 1947 (Aberdeen) 5
Hamilton, J. 1892 (Queen's Park) 3
Hamilton, J. 1924 (St Mirren) 1
Hamilton, R. C. 1899 (Rangers, Dundee) 11
Hamilton, T. 1891 (Hurlford) 1
Hamilton, T. 1932 (Rangers) 1
Hamilton, W. M. 1965 (Hibernian) 1
Hammell, S. 2005 (Motherwell) 1
Hanley, G. 2011 (Blackburn R) 3
Hannah, A. B. 1888 (Renton) 1
Hannah, J. 1889 (Third Lanark) 1
Hansen, A. D. 1979 (Liverpool) 26
Hansen, J. 1972 (Partick Th) 2
Harkness, J. D. 1927 (Queen's Park, Hearts) 12
Harper, J. M. 1973 (Aberdeen, Hibernian, Aberdeen) 4
Harper, W. 1923 (Hibernian, Arsenal) 11
Harris, J. 1921 (Partick Th) 2
Harris, N. 1924 (Newcastle U) 1
Harrower, W. 1882 (Queen's Park) 3
Hartford, R. A. 1972 (WBA, Manchester C, Everton, Manchester C) 50
Hartley, P. J. 2005 (Hearts, Celtic, Bristol C) 25
Harvey, D. 1973 (Leeds U) 16
Hastings, A. C. 1936 (Sunderland) 2
Haughney, M. 1954 (Celtic) 1
Hay, D. 1970 (Celtic) 27
Hay, J. 1905 (Celtic, Newcastle U) 11
Hegarty, P. 1979 (Dundee U) 8
Heggie, C. 1886 (Rangers) 1
Henderson, G. H. 1904 (Rangers) 1
Henderson, J. G. 1953 (Portsmouth, Arsenal) 7
Henderson, W. 1963 (Rangers) 29
Hendry, E. C. J. 1993 (Blackburn R, Rangers, Coventry C, Bolton W) 51
Hepburn, J. 1891 (Alloa Ath) 1
Hepburn, R. 1932 (Ayr U) 1
Herd, A. C. 1935 (Hearts) 1
Herd, D. G. 1959 (Arsenal) 5
Herd, G. 1958 (Clyde) 5
Herriot, J. 1969 (Birmingham C) 8
Hewie, J. D. 1956 (Charlton Ath) 19
Higgins, A. 1885 (Kilmarnock) 1
Higgins, A. 1910 (Newcastle U) 4
Highet, T. C. 1875 (Queen's Park) 4
Hill, D. 1881 (Rangers) 3
Hill, D. A. 1906 (Third Lanark) 1
Hill, F. R. 1930 (Aberdeen) 3
Hill, J. 1891 (Hearts) 2
Hogg, G. 1896 (Hearts) 2
Hogg, J. 1922 (Ayr U) 1
Hogg, R. M. 1937 (Celtic) 1
Holm, A. H. 1882 (Queen's Park) 3
Holt, D. D. 1963 (Hearts) 5
Holt, G. J. 2001 (Kilmarnock, Norwich C) 10
Holton, J. A. 1973 (Manchester U) 15
Hope, R. 1968 (WBA) 2
Hopkin, D. 1997 (Crystal Palace, Leeds U) 7
Houliston, W. 1949 (Queen of the South) 3

Houston, S. M. 1976 (Manchester U) 1
Howden, W. 1905 (Partick Th) 1
Howe, R. 1929 (Hamilton A) 2
Howie, H. 1949 (Hibernian) 1
Howie, J. 1905 (Newcastle U) 3
Howieson, J. 1927 (St Mirren) 1
Hughes, J. 1965 (Celtic) 8
Hughes, R. D. 2004 (Portsmouth) 5
Hughes, S. R. 2010 (Norwich C) 1
Hughes, W. 1975 (Sunderland) 1
Humphries, W. 1952 (Motherwell) 1
Hunter, A. 1972 (Kilmarnock, Celtic) 4
Hunter, J. 1909 (Dundee) 1
Hunter, J. 1874 (Third Lanark, Eastern, Third Lanark) 4
Hunter, W. 1960 (Motherwell) 3
Hunter, R. 1890 (St Mirren) 1
Husband, J. 1947 (Partick Th) 1
Hutchison, D. 1999 (Everton, Sunderland, West Ham U) 26
Hutchison, T. 1974 (Coventry C) 17
Hutton, A. 2007 (Rangers, Tottenham H) 23
Hutton, J. 1887 (St Bernards) 1
Hutton, J. 1923 (Aberdeen, Blackburn R) 10
Hyslop, T. 1896 (Stoke, Rangers) 2

Imlach, J. J. S. 1958 (Nottingham F) 4
Imrie, W. N. 1929 (St Johnstone) 2
Inglis, J. 1883 (Rangers) 2
Inglis, J. 1884 (Kilmarnock Ath) 1
Irons, J. H. 1900 (Queen's Park) 1
Irvine, B. 1991 (Aberdeen) 9
Iwelumo, C.R. 2009 (Wolverhampton W, Burnley) 4

Jackson, A. 1886 (Cambuslang) 2
Jackson, A. 1925 (Aberdeen, Huddersfield T) 17
Jackson, C. 1975 (Rangers) 8
Jackson, D. 1995 (Hibernian, Celtic) 28
Jackson, J. 1931 (Partick Th, Chelsea) 8
Jackson, T. A. 1904 (St Mirren) 6
James, A. W. 1926 (Preston NE, Arsenal) 8
Jardine, A. 1971 (Rangers) 38
Jarvie, A. 1971 (Airdrieonians) 3
Jenkinson, T. 1887 (Hearts) 1
Jess, E. 1993 (Aberdeen, Coventry C, Aberdeen) 18
Johnston, A. 1999 (Sunderland, Rangers, Middlesbrough) 18
Johnston, L. H. 1948 (Clyde) 2
Johnston, M. 1984 (Watford, Celtic, Nantes, Rangers) 38
Johnston, R. 1938 (Sunderland) 1
Johnston, W. 1966 (Rangers, WBA) 22
Johnstone, D. 1973 (Rangers) 14
Johnstone, J. 1888 (Abercorn) 1
Johnstone, J. 1965 (Celtic) 23
Johnstone, Jas 1894 (Kilmarnock) 1
Johnstone, J. A. 1930 (Hearts) 3
Johnstone, R. 1951 (Hibernian, Manchester C) 17
Johnstone, W. 1887 (Third Lanark) 3
Jordan, J. 1973 (Leeds U, Manchester U, AC Milan) 52

Kay, J. L. 1880 (Queen's Park) 6
Keillor, A. 1891 (Montrose, Dundee) 6
Keir, L. 1885 (Dumbarton) 5
Kelly, H. T. 1952 (Blackpool) 1
Kelly, J. 1888 (Renton, Celtic) 8
Kelly, J. C. 1949 (Barnsley) 2
Kelso, R. 1885 (Renton, Dundee) 7
Kelso, T. 1914 (Dundee) 1
Kennaway, J. 1934 (Celtic) 1
Kennedy, A. 1875 (Eastern, Third Lanark) 6
Kennedy, J. 1897 (Hibernian) 1
Kennedy, J. 1964 (Celtic) 6
Kennedy, J. 2004 (Celtic) 1
Kennedy, S. 1905 (Partick Th) 1
Kennedy, S. 1975 (Rangers) 5
Kennedy, S. 1978 (Aberdeen) 8
Kenneth, G. 2011 (Dundee U) 2
Ker, G. 1880 (Queen's Park) 5
Ker, W. 1872 (Queen's Park) 2
Kerr, A. 1955 (Partick Th) 2
Kerr, B. 2003 (Newcastle U) 3
Kerr, P. 1924 (Hibernian) 1
Key, G. 1902 (Hearts) 1
Key, W. 1907 (Queen's Park) 1
King, A. 1896 (Hearts, Celtic) 6
King, J. 1933 (Hamilton A) 2
King, W. S. 1929 (Queen's Park) 1
Kinloch, J. D. 1922 (Partick Th) 1
Kinnaird, A. F. 1873 (Wanderers) 1
Kinnear, D. 1938 (Rangers) 1
Kyle, K. 2002 (Sunderland, Kilmarnock) 10

Lambert, P. 1995 (Motherwell, Borussia Dortmund, Celtic) 40
Lambie, J. A. 1886 (Queen's Park) 3
Lambie, W. A. 1892 (Queen's Park) 9
Lamont, W. 1885 (Pilgrims) 1
Lang, A. 1880 (Dumbarton) 1
Lang, J. J. 1876 (Clydesdale, Third Lanark) 2
Latta, A. 1888 (Dumbarton) 2
Law, D. 1959 (Huddersfield T, Manchester C, Torino, Manchester U, Manchester C) 55
Law, G. 1910 (Rangers) 3
Law, T. 1928 (Chelsea) 2
Lawrence, J. 1911 (Newcastle U) 1
Lawrence, T. 1963 (Liverpool) 3
Lawson, D. 1923 (St Mirren) 1
Leckie, R. 1872 (Queen's Park) 1
Leggat, G. 1956 (Aberdeen, Fulham) 18
Leighton, J. 1983 (Aberdeen, Manchester U, Hibernian, Aberdeen) 91
Lennie, W. 1908 (Aberdeen) 2
Lennox, R. 1967 (Celtic) 10
Leslie, L. G. 1961 (Airdrieonians) 5
Levein, C. 1990 (Hearts) 16
Liddell, W. 1947 (Liverpool) 28
Liddle, D. 1931 (East Fife) 3
Lindsay, D. 1903 (St Mirren) 1
Lindsay, J. 1880 (Dumbarton) 8
Lindsay, J. 1888 (Renton) 3
Linwood, A. B. 1950 (Clyde) 1
Little, R. J. 1953 (Rangers) 1
Livingstone, G. T. 1906 (Manchester C, Rangers) 2
Lochhead, A. 1889 (Third Lanark) 1
Logan, J. 1891 (Ayr) 1
Logan, T. 1913 (Falkirk) 1
Logie, J. T. 1953 (Arsenal) 1
Loney, W. 1910 (Celtic) 2
Long, H. 1947 (Clyde) 1
Longair, W. 1894 (Dundee) 1
Lorimer, P. 1970 (Leeds U) 21
Love, A. 1931 (Aberdeen) 3
Low, A. 1934 (Falkirk) 1
Low, J. 1891 (Cambuslang) 1
Low, T. P. 1897 (Rangers) 1
Low, W. L. 1911 (Newcastle U) 5
Lowe, J. 1887 (St Bernards) 1
Lundie, J. 1886 (Hibernian) 1
Lyall, J. 1905 (Sheffield W) 1

McAdam, J. 1880 (Third Lanark) 1
McAllister, B. 1997 (Wimbledon) 3
McAllister, G. 1990 (Leicester C, Leeds U, Coventry C) 57
McAllister, J. R. 2004 (Livingston) 1
Macari, L. 1972 (Celtic, Manchester U) 24
McArthur, D. 1895 (Celtic) 3
McArthur, J. 2011 (Wigan Ath) 7
McAtee, A. 1913 (Celtic) 1
McAulay, J. 1884 (Arthurlie) 1
McAulay, J. D. 1882 (Dumbarton) 9
McAulay, R. 1932 (Rangers) 2
Macauley, A. R. 1947 (Brentford, Arsenal) 7
McAvennie, F. 1986 (West Ham U, Celtic) 5
McBain, E. 1894 (St Mirren) 1
McBain, N. 1922 (Manchester U, Everton) 3
McBride, J. 1967 (Celtic) 2
McBride, P. 1904 (Preston NE) 6
McCall, A. 1888 (Renton) 1
McCall, A. S. M. 1990 (Everton, Rangers) 40
McCall, J. 1886 (Renton) 5
McCalliog, J. 1967 (Sheffield W, Wolverhampton W) 5
McCallum, N. 1888 (Renton) 1
McCann, N. 1999 (Hearts, Rangers, Southampton) 26
McCann, R. J. 1959 (Motherwell) 5

McCartney, W. 1902 (Hibernian) 1
McClair, B. 1987 (Celtic, Manchester U) 30
McClory, A. 1927 (Motherwell) 3
McCloy, P. 1924 (Ayr U) 2
McCloy, P. 1973 (Rangers) 4
McCoist, A. 1986 (Rangers, Kilmarnock) 61
McColl, I. M. 1950 (Rangers) 14
McColl, R. S. 1896 (Queen's Park, Newcastle U, Queen's Park) 13
McColl, W. 1895 (Renton) 1
McCombie, A. 1903 (Sunderland, Newcastle U) 4
McCorkindale, J. 1891 (Partick Th) 1
McCormack, R. 2008 (Motherwell, Cardiff C, Leeds U) 7
McCormick, R. 1886 (Abercorn) 1
McCrae, D. 1929 (St Mirren) 2
McCreadie, A. 1893 (Rangers) 2
McCreadie, E. G. 1965 (Chelsea) 23
McCulloch, D. 1935 (Hearts, Brentford, Derby Co) 7
McCulloch, L. 2005 (Wigan Ath, Rangers) 18
MacDonald, A. 1976 (Rangers) 1
McDonald, J. 1886 (Edinburgh University) 1
McDonald, J. 1956 (Sunderland) 2
MacDougall, E. J. 1975 (Norwich C) 7
McDougall, J. 1877 (Vale of Leven) 5
McDougall, J. 1926 (Airdrieonians) 1
McDougall, J. 1931 (Liverpool) 2
McEveley, J. 2008 (Derby Co) 3
McFadden, J. 2002 (Motherwell, Everton, Birmingham C) 48
McFadyen, W. 1934 (Motherwell) 2
Macfarlane, A. 1904 (Dundee) 5
Macfarlane, W. 1947 (Hearts) 1
McFarlane, R. 1896 (Greenock Morton) 1
McGarr, E. 1970 (Aberdeen) 2
McGarvey, F. P. 1979 (Liverpool, Celtic) 7
McGeoch, A. 1876 (Dumbreck) 4
McGhee, J. 1886 (Hibernian) 1
McGhee, M. 1983 (Aberdeen) 4
McGinlay, J. 1994 (Bolton W) 13
McGonagle, W. 1933 (Celtic) 6
McGrain, D. 1973 (Celtic) 62
McGregor, A. 2007 (Rangers) 21
McGregor, J. C. 1877 (Vale of Leven) 4
McGrory, J. 1928 (Celtic) 7
McGrory, J. E. 1965 (Kilmarnock) 3
McGuire, W. 1881 (Beith) 2
McGurk, F. 1934 (Birmingham) 1
McHardy, H. 1885 (Rangers) 1
McInally, A. 1989 (Aston Villa, Bayern Munich) 8
McInally, J. 1987 (Dundee U) 10
McInally, T. B. 1926 (Celtic) 2
McInnes, D. 2003 (WBA) 2
McInnes, T. 1889 (Cowlairs) 1
McIntosh, W. 1905 (Third Lanark) 1
McIntyre, A. 1878 (Vale of Leven) 2
McIntyre, H. 1880 (Rangers) 1
McIntyre, J. 1884 (Rangers) 1
MacKay, D. 1959 (Celtic) 14
Mackay, D. C. 1957 (Hearts, Tottenham H) 22
Mackay, G. 1988 (Hearts) 4
Mackay, M. 2004 (Norwich C) 5
McKay, J. 1924 (Blackburn R) 1
McKay, R. 1928 (Newcastle U) 1
McKean, R. 1976 (Rangers) 1
McKenzie, D. 1938 (Brentford) 1
Mackenzie, J. A. 1954 (Partick Th) 9
McKeown, M. 1889 (Celtic) 2
McKie, J. 1898 (East Stirling) 1
McKillop, T. R. 1938 (Rangers) 1
McKimmie, S. 1989 (Aberdeen) 40
McKinlay, D. 1922 (Liverpool) 2
McKinlay, T. 1996 (Celtic) 22
McKinlay, W. 1994 (Dundee U, Blackburn R) 29
McKinnon, A. 1874 (Queen's Park) 1
McKinnon, R. 1966 (Rangers) 28
McKinnon, R. 1994 (Motherwell) 3
MacKinnon, W. 1883 (Dumbarton) 4
MacKinnon, W. W. 1872 (Queen's Park) 9
McLaren, A. 1929 (St Johnstone) 5
McLaren, A. 1947 (Preston NE) 4
McLaren, A. 1992 (Hearts, Rangers) 24
McLaren, A. 2001 (Kilmarnock) 1
McLaren, J. 1888 (Hibernian, Celtic) 3
McLean, A. 1926 (Celtic) 4
McLean, D. 1896 (St Bernards) 2
McLean, D. 1912 (Sheffield W) 1
McLean, G. 1968 (Dundee) 1
McLean, T. 1969 (Kilmarnock) 6
McLeish, A. 1980 (Aberdeen) 77
McLeod, D. 1905 (Celtic) 4
McLeod, J. 1888 (Dumbarton) 5
MacLeod, J. M. 1961 (Hibernian) 4
MacLeod, M. 1985 (Celtic, Borussia Dortmund, Hibernian) 20
McLeod, W. 1886 (Cowlairs) 1
McLintock, A. 1875 (Vale of Leven) 3
McLintock, F. 1963 (Leicester C, Arsenal) 9
McLuckie, J. S. 1934 (Manchester C) 1
McMahon, A. 1892 (Celtic) 6
McManus, S. 2007 (Celtic, Middlesbrough) 26
McMenemy, J. 1905 (Celtic) 12
McMenemy, J. 1934 (Motherwell) 1
McMillan, I. L. 1952 (Airdrieonians, Rangers) 6
McMillan, J. 1897 (St Bernards) 1
McMillan, T. 1887 (Dumbarton) 1
McMullan, J. 1920 (Partick Th, Manchester C) 16
McNab, A. 1921 (Morton) 2
McNab, A. 1937 (Sunderland, WBA) 2
McNab, C. D. 1931 (Dundee) 6
McNab, J. S. 1923 (Liverpool) 1
McNair, A. 1906 (Celtic) 15
McNamara, J. 1997 (Celtic, Wolverhampton W) 33
McNamee, D. 2004 (Livingston) 4
McNaught, W. 1951 (Raith R) 5
McNaughton, K. 2002 (Aberdeen, Cardiff C) 4
McNeill, W. 1961 (Celtic) 29
McNiel, H. 1874 (Queen's Park) 10
McNiel, M. 1876 (Rangers) 2
McPhail, J. 1950 (Celtic) 5
McPhail, R. 1927 (Airdrieonians, Rangers) 17
McPherson, D. 1892 (Kilmarnock) 1
McPherson, D. 1989 (Hearts, Rangers) 27
McPherson, J. 1875 (Clydesdale) 1
McPherson, J. 1879 (Vale of Leven) 8
McPherson, J. 1888 (Kilmarnock, Cowlairs, Rangers) 9
McPherson, J. 1891 (Hearts) 1
McPherson, R. 1882 (Arthurlie) 1
McQueen, G. 1974 (Leeds U, Manchester U) 30
McQueen, M. 1890 (Leith Ath) 2
McRorie, D. M. 1931 (Morton) 1
McSpadyen, A. 1939 (Partick Th) 2
McStay, P. 1984 (Celtic) 76
McStay, W. 1921 (Celtic) 13
McSwegan, G. 2000 (Hearts) 2
McTavish, J. 1910 (Falkirk) 1
McWattie, G. C. 1901 (Queen's Park) 2
McWilliam, P. 1905 (Newcastle U) 8
Mackail-Smith, C. 2011 (Peterborough U, Brighton & HA) 7
Mackie, J. C. 2011 (QPR) 5
Madden, J. 1893 (Celtic) 2
Maguire, C. 2011 (Aberdeen) 2
Main, F. R. 1938 (Rangers) 1
Main, J. 1909 (Hibernian) 1
Maley, W. 1893 (Celtic) 2
Maloney, S. R. 2006 (Celtic, Aston Villa, Celtic, Wigan Ath) 20
Malpas, M. 1984 (Dundee U) 55
Marshall, D. J. 2005 (Celtic, Cardiff C) 5
Marshall, G. 1992 (Celtic) 1
Marshall, H. 1899 (Celtic) 2
Marshall, J. 1885 (Third Lanark) 4
Marshall, J. 1921 (Middlesbrough, Llanelly) 7
Marshall, J. 1932 (Rangers) 3
Marshall, R. W. 1892 (Rangers) 2
Martin, B. 1995 (Motherwell) 2
Martin, F. 1954 (Aberdeen) 6
Martin, N. 1965 (Hibernian, Sunderland) 3
Martin, R. K. A. 2011 (Norwich C) 3
Martis, J. 1961 (Motherwell) 1
Mason, J. 1949 (Third Lanark) 7
Massie, A. 1932 (Hearts, Aston Villa) 18
Masson, D. S. 1976 (QPR, Derby Co) 17
Mathers, D. 1954 (Partick Th) 1

Matteo, D. 2001 (Leeds U) 6
Maxwell, W. S. 1898 (Stoke C) 1
May, J. 1906 (Rangers) 5
Meechan, P. 1896 (Celtic) 1
Meiklejohn, D. D. 1922 (Rangers) 15
Menzies, A. 1906 (Hearts) 1
Mercer, R. 1912 (Hearts) 2
Middleton, R. 1930 (Cowdenbeath) 1
Millar, J. 1897 (Rangers) 3
Millar, J. 1963 (Rangers) 2
Miller, A. 1939 (Hearts) 1
Miller, C. 2001 (Dundee U) 1
Miller, J. 1931 (St Mirren) 5
Miller, K. 2001 (Rangers, Wolverhampton W, Celtic, Derby Co, Rangers, Bursa, Cardiff C) 60
Miller, L. 2006 (Dundee U, Aberdeen) 3
Miller, P. 1882 (Dumbarton) 3
Miller, T. 1920 (Liverpool, Manchester U) 3
Miller, W. 1876 (Third Lanark) 1
Miller, W. 1947 (Celtic) 6
Miller, W. 1975 (Aberdeen) 65
Mills, W. 1936 (Aberdeen) 3
Milne, J. V. 1938 (Middlesbrough) 2
Mitchell, D. 1890 (Rangers) 5
Mitchell, J. 1908 (Kilmarnock) 3
Mitchell, R. C. 1951 (Newcastle U) 2
Mochan, N. 1954 (Celtic) 3
Moir, W. 1950 (Bolton W) 1
Moncur, R. 1968 (Newcastle U) 16
Morgan, H. 1898 (St Mirren, Liverpool) 2
Morgan, W. 1968 (Burnley, Manchester U) 21
Morris, D. 1923 (Raith R) 6
Morris, H. 1950 (East Fife) 1
Morrison, J. C. 2008 (WBA) 20
Morrison, T. 1927 (St Mirren) 1
Morton, A. L. 1920 (Queen's Park, Rangers) 31
Morton, H. A. 1929 (Kilmarnock) 2
Mudie, J. K. 1957 (Blackpool) 17
Muir, W. 1907 (Dundee) 1
Muirhead, T. A. 1922 (Rangers) 8
Mulgrew, C. 2012 (Celtic) 2
Mulhall, G. 1960 (Aberdeen, Sunderland) 3
Munro, A. D. 1937 (Hearts, Blackpool) 3
Munro, F. M. 1971 (Wolverhampton W) 9
Munro, I. 1979 (St Mirren) 7
Munro, N. 1888 (Abercorn) 2
Murdoch, J. 1931 (Motherwell) 1
Murdoch, R. 1966 (Celtic) 12
Murphy, F. 1938 (Celtic) 1
Murray, I. 2003 (Hibernian, Rangers) 6
Murray, J. 1895 (Renton) 1
Murray, J. 1958 (Hearts) 5
Murray, J. W. 1890 (Vale of Leven) 1
Murray, P. 1896 (Hibernian) 2
Murray, S. 1972 (Aberdeen) 1
Murty, G. S. 2004 (Reading) 4
Mutch, G. 1938 (Preston NE) 1

Naismith, S. J. 2007 (Kilmarnock, Rangers) 15
Napier, C. E. 1932 (Celtic, Derby Co) 5
Narey, D. 1977 (Dundee U) 35
Naysmith, G. A. 2000 (Hearts, Everton, Sheffield U) 46
Neil, R. G. 1896 (Hibernian, Rangers) 2
Neill, R. W. 1876 (Queen's Park) 5
Neilson, R. 2007 (Hearts) 1
Nellies, P. 1913 (Hearts) 2
Nelson, J. 1925 (Cardiff C) 4
Nevin, P. K. F. 1986 (Chelsea, Everton, Tranmere R) 28
Niblo, T. D. 1904 (Aston Villa) 1
Nibloe, J. 1929 (Kilmarnock) 11
Nicholas, C. 1983 (Celtic, Arsenal, Aberdeen) 20
Nicholson, B. 2001 (Dunfermline Ath) 3
Nicol, S. 1985 (Liverpool) 27
Nisbet, J. 1929 (Ayr U) 3
Niven, J. B. 1885 (Moffat) 1

O'Connor, G. 2002 (Hibernian, Lokomotiv Moscow, Birmingham C) 16
O'Donnell, F. 1937 (Preston NE, Blackpool) 6
O'Donnell, P. 1994 (Motherwell) 1
Ogilvie, D. H. 1934 (Motherwell) 1
O'Hare, J. 1970 (Derby Co) 13
O'Neil, B. 1996 (Celtic, Wolfsburg, Derby Co, Preston NE) 7
O'Neil, J. 2001 (Hibernian) 1
Ormond, W. E. 1954 (Hibernian) 6
O'Rourke, F. 1907 (Airdrieonians) 1
Orr, J. 1892 (Kilmarnock) 1
Orr, R. 1902 (Newcastle U) 2
Orr, T. 1952 (Morton) 2
Orr, W. 1900 (Celtic) 3
Orrock, R. 1913 (Falkirk) 1
Oswald, J. 1889 (Third Lanark, St Bernards, Rangers) 3

Parker, A. H. 1955 (Falkirk, Everton) 15
Parlane, D. 1973 (Rangers) 12
Parlane, R. 1878 (Vale of Leven) 3
Paterson, G. D. 1939 (Celtic) 1
Paterson, J. 1920 (Leicester C) 1
Paterson, J. 1931 (Cowdenbeath) 3
Paton, A. 1952 (Motherwell) 2
Paton, D. 1896 (St Bernards) 1
Paton, M. 1883 (Dumbarton) 5
Paton, R. 1879 (Vale of Leven) 2
Patrick, J. 1897 (St Mirren) 2
Paul, H. McD. 1909 (Queen's Park) 3
Paul, W. 1888 (Partick Th) 3
Paul, W. 1891 (Dykebar) 1
Pearson, S. P. 2004 (Motherwell, Celtic, Derby Co) 10
Pearson, T. 1947 (Newcastle U) 2
Penman, A. 1966 (Dundee) 1
Pettigrew, W. 1976 (Motherwell) 5
Phillips, J. 1877 (Queen's Park) 3
Phillips, M. 2012 (Blackpool) 1
Plenderleith, J. B. 1961 (Manchester C) 1
Porteous, W. 1903 (Hearts) 1
Pressley, S. J. 2000 (Hearts) 32
Pringle, C. 1921 (St Mirren) 1
Provan, D. 1964 (Rangers) 5
Provan, D. 1980 (Celtic) 10
Pursell, P. 1914 (Queen's Park) 1

Quashie, N. F. 2004 (Portsmouth, Southampton, WBA) 14
Quinn, J. 1905 (Celtic) 11
Quinn, P. 1961 (Motherwell) 4

Rae, G. 2001 (Dundee, Rangers, Cardiff C) 14
Rae, J. 1889 (Third Lanark) 2
Raeside, J. S. 1906 (Third Lanark) 1
Raisbeck, A. G. 1900 (Liverpool) 8
Rankin, G. 1890 (Vale of Leven) 2
Rankin, R. 1929 (St Mirren) 3
Redpath, W. 1949 (Motherwell) 9
Reid, J. G. 1914 (Airdrieonians) 3
Reid, R. 1938 (Brentford) 2
Reid, W. 1911 (Rangers) 9
Reilly, L. 1949 (Hibernian) 38
Rennie, H. G. 1900 (Hearts, Hibernian) 13
Renny-Tailyour, H. W. 1873 (Royal Engineers) 1
Rhind, A. 1872 (Queen's Park) 1
Rhodes, J. L. 2012 (Huddersfield T) 1
Richmond, A. 1906 (Queen's Park) 1
Richmond, J. T. 1877 (Clydesdale, Queen's Park) 3
Ring, T. 1953 (Clyde) 12
Rioch, B. D. 1975 (Derby Co, Everton, Derby Co) 24
Riordan, D. G. 2006 (Hibernian) 3
Ritchie, A. 1891 (East Stirlingshire) 1
Ritchie, H. 1923 (Hibernian) 2
Ritchie, J. 1897 (Queen's Park) 1
Ritchie, P. S. 1999 (Hearts, Bolton W, Walsall) 7
Ritchie, W. 1962 (Rangers) 1
Robb, D. T. 1971 (Aberdeen) 5
Robb, W. 1926 (Rangers, Hibernian) 2
Robertson, A. 1955 (Clyde) 5
Robertson, D. 1992 (Rangers) 3
Robertson, G. 1910 (Motherwell, Sheffield W) 4
Robertson, G. 1938 (Kilmarnock) 1
Robertson, H. 1962 (Dundee) 1
Robertson, J. 1931 (Dundee) 2
Robertson, J. 1991 (Hearts) 16
Robertson, J. N. 1978 (Nottingham F, Derby Co) 28
Robertson, J. G. 1965 (Tottenham H) 1

Robertson, J. T. 1898 (Everton, Southampton, Rangers) 16
Robertson, P. 1903 (Dundee) 1
Robertson, S. 2009 (Dundee U) 2
Robertson, T. 1889 (Queen's Park) 4
Robertson, T. 1898 (Hearts) 1
Robertson, W. 1887 (Dumbarton) 2
Robinson, R. 1974 (Dundee) 4
Robson, B. G. G. 2008 (Dundee U, Celtic, Middlesbrough) 17
Ross, M. 2002 (Rangers) 13
Rough, A. 1976 (Partick Th, Hibernian) 53
Rougvie, D. 1984 (Aberdeen) 1
Rowan, A. 1880 (Caledonian, Queen's Park) 2
Russell, D. 1895 (Hearts, Celtic) 6
Russell, J. 1890 (Cambuslang) 1
Russell, W. F. 1924 (Airdrieonians) 2
Rutherford, E. 1948 (Rangers) 1

St John, I. 1959 (Motherwell, Liverpool) 21
Saunders, S. 2011 (Motherwell) 1
Sawers, W. 1895 (Dundee) 1
Scarff, P. 1931 (Celtic) 1
Schaedler, E. 1974 (Hibernian) 1
Scott, A. S. 1957 (Rangers, Everton) 16
Scott, J. 1966 (Hibernian) 1
Scott, J. 1971 (Dundee) 2
Scott, M. 1898 (Airdrieonians) 1
Scott, R. 1894 (Airdrieonians) 1
Scoular, J. 1951 (Portsmouth) 9
Sellar, W. 1885 (Battlefield, Queen's Park) 9
Semple, W. 1886 (Cambuslang) 1
Severin, S. D. 2002 (Hearts, Aberdeen) 15
Shankly, W. 1938 (Preston NE) 5
Sharp, G. M. 1985 (Everton) 12
Sharp, J. 1904 (Dundee, Woolwich Arsenal, Fulham) 5
Shaw, D. 1947 (Hibernian) 8
Shaw, F. W. 1884 (Pollokshields Ath) 2
Shaw, J. 1947 (Rangers) 4
Shearer, D. 1994 (Aberdeen) 7
Shearer, R. 1961 (Rangers) 4
Sillars, D. C. 1891 (Queen's Park) 5
Simpson, J. 1895 (Third Lanark) 3
Simpson, J. 1935 (Rangers) 14
Simpson, N. 1983 (Aberdeen) 5
Simpson, R. C. 1967 (Celtic) 5
Sinclair, G. L. 1910 (Hearts) 3
Sinclair, J. W. E. 1966 (Leicester C) 1
Skene, L. H. 1904 (Queen's Park) 1
Sloan, T. 1904 (Third Lanark) 1
Smellie, R. 1887 (Queen's Park) 6
Smith, A. 1898 (Rangers) 20
Smith, D. 1966 (Aberdeen, Rangers) 2
Smith, G. 1947 (Hibernian) 18
Smith, H. G. 1988 (Hearts) 3
Smith, J. 1924 (Ayr U) 1
Smith, J. 1935 (Rangers) 2
Smith, J. 1968 (Aberdeen, Newcastle U) 4
Smith, J. 2003 (Celtic) 2
Smith, J. E. 1959 (Celtic) 2
Smith, Jas 1872 (Queen's Park) 1
Smith, John 1877 (Mauchline, Edinburgh University, Queen's Park) 10
Smith, N. 1897 (Rangers) 12
Smith, R. 1872 (Queen's Park) 2
Smith, T. M. 1934 (Kilmarnock, Preston NE) 2
Snodgrass, R. 2011 (Leeds U) 5
Somers, P. 1905 (Celtic) 4
Somers, W. S. 1879 (Third Lanark, Queen's Park) 3
Somerville, G. 1886 (Queen's Park) 1
Souness, G. J. 1975 (Middlesbrough, Liverpool, Sampdoria) 54
Speedie, D. R. 1985 (Chelsea, Coventry C) 10
Speedie, F. 1903 (Rangers) 3
Speirs, J. H. 1908 (Rangers) 1
Spencer, J. 1995 (Chelsea, QPR) 14
Stanton, P. 1966 (Hibernian) 16
Stark, J. 1909 (Rangers) 2
Steel, W. 1947 (Morton, Derby Co, Dundee) 30
Steele, D. M. 1923 (Huddersfield) 3
Stein, C. 1969 (Rangers, Coventry C) 21
Stephen, J. F. 1947 (Bradford) 2
Stevenson, G. 1928 (Motherwell) 12
Stewart, A. 1888 (Queen's Park) 2
Stewart, A. 1894 (Third Lanark) 1
Stewart, D. 1888 (Dumbarton) 1
Stewart, D. 1893 (Queen's Park) 3
Stewart, D. S. 1978 (Leeds U) 1
Stewart, G. 1906 (Hibernian, Manchester C) 4
Stewart, J. 1977 (Kilmarnock, Middlesbrough) 2
Stewart, M. J. 2002 (Manchester U, Hearts) 4
Stewart, R. 1981 (West Ham U) 10
Stewart, W. G. 1898 (Queen's Park) 2
Stockdale, R. K. 2002 (Middlesbrough) 5
Storrier, D. 1899 (Celtic) 3
Strachan, G. D. 1980 (Aberdeen, Manchester U, Leeds U) 50
Sturrock, P. 1981 (Dundee U) 20
Sullivan, N. 1997 (Wimbledon, Tottenham H) 28
Summers, W. 1926 (St Mirren) 1
Symon, J. S. 1939 (Rangers) 1

Tait, T. S. 1911 (Sunderland) 1
Taylor, J. 1872 (Queen's Park) 6
Taylor, J. D. 1892 (Dumbarton, St Mirren) 4
Taylor, W. 1892 (Hearts) 1
Teale, G. 2006 (Wigan Ath, Derby Co) 13
Telfer, P. N. 2000 (Coventry C) 1
Telfer, W. 1933 (Motherwell) 2
Telfer, W. D. 1954 (St Mirren) 1
Templeton, R. 1902 (Aston Villa, Newcastle U, Woolwich Arsenal, Kilmarnock) 11
Thompson, S. 2002 (Dundee U, Rangers) 16
Thomson, A. 1886 (Arthurlie) 1
Thomson, A. 1889 (Third Lanark) 1
Thomson, A. 1909 (Airdrieonians) 1
Thomson, A. 1926 (Celtic) 3
Thomson, C. 1904 (Hearts, Sunderland) 21
Thomson, C. 1937 (Sunderland) 1
Thomson, D. 1920 (Dundee) 1
Thomson, J. 1930 (Celtic) 4
Thomson, J. J. 1872 (Queen's Park) 3
Thomson, J. R. 1933 (Everton) 1
Thomson, K. 2009 (Rangers, Middlesbrough) 3
Thomson, R. 1932 (Celtic) 1
Thomson, R. W. 1927 (Falkirk) 1
Thomson, S. 1884 (Rangers) 2
Thomson, W. 1892 (Dumbarton) 4
Thomson, W. 1896 (Dundee) 1
Thomson, W. 1980 (St Mirren) 7
Thornton, W. 1947 (Rangers) 7
Toner, W. 1959 (Kilmarnock) 2
Townsley, T. 1926 (Falkirk) 1
Troup, A. 1920 (Dundee, Everton) 5
Turnbull, E. 1948 (Hibernian) 8
Turner, T. 1884 (Arthurlie) 1
Turner, W. 1885 (Pollokshields Ath) 2

Ure, J. F. 1962 (Dundee, Arsenal) 11
Urquhart, D. 1934 (Hibernian) 1

Vallance, T. 1877 (Rangers) 7
Venters, A. 1934 (Cowdenbeath, Rangers) 3

Waddell, T. S. 1891 (Queen's Park) 6
Waddell, W. 1947 (Rangers) 17
Wales, H. M. 1933 (Motherwell) 1
Walker, A. 1988 (Celtic) 3
Walker, F. 1922 (Third Lanark) 1
Walker, G. 1930 (St Mirren) 4
Walker, J. 1895 (Hearts, Rangers) 5
Walker, J. 1911 (Swindon T) 9
Walker, J. N. 1993 (Hearts, Partick Th) 2
Walker, R. 1900 (Hearts) 29
Walker, T. 1935 (Hearts) 20
Walker, W. 1909 (Clyde) 2
Wallace, I. A. 1978 (Coventry C) 3
Wallace, L. 2010 (Hearts) 6
Wallace, R. 2010 (Preston NE) 1
Wallace, W. S. B. 1965 (Hearts, Celtic) 7
Wardhaugh, J. 1955 (Hearts) 2
Wark, J. 1979 (Ipswich T, Liverpool) 29
Watson, A. 1881 (Queen's Park) 3
Watson, J. 1903 (Sunderland, Middlesbrough) 6

Watson, J. 1948 (Motherwell, Huddersfield T) 2
Watson, J. A. K. 1878 (Rangers) 1
Watson, P. R. 1934 (Blackpool) 1
Watson, R. 1971 (Motherwell) 1
Watson, W. 1898 (Falkirk) 1
Watt, F. 1889 (Kilbirnie) 4
Watt, W. W. 1887 (Queen's Park) 1
Waugh, W. 1938 (Hearts) 1
Webster, A. 2003 (Hearts, Dundee U) 24
Weir, A. 1959 (Motherwell) 6
Weir, D. G. 1997 (Hearts, Everton, Rangers) 69
Weir, J. 1887 (Third Lanark) 1
Weir, J. B. 1872 (Queen's Park) 4
Weir, P. 1980 (St Mirren, Aberdeen) 6
White, John 1922 (Albion R, Hearts) 2
White, J. A. 1959 (Falkirk, Tottenham H) 22
White, W. 1907 (Bolton W) 2
Whitelaw, A. 1887 (Vale of Leven) 2
Whittaker, S. G. 2010 (Rangers) 15
Whyte, D. 1988 (Celtic, Middlesbrough, Aberdeen) 12
Wilkie, L. 2002 (Dundee) 11
Williams, G. 2002 (Nottingham F) 5
Wilson, A. 1907 (Sheffield W) 6
Wilson, A. 1954 (Portsmouth) 1
Wilson, A. N. 1920 (Dunfermline, Middlesbrough) 12
Wilson, D. 1900 (Queen's Park) 1
Wilson, D. 1913 (Oldham Ath) 1
Wilson, D. 1961 (Rangers) 22
Wilson, D. 2011 (Liverpool) 5
Wilson, G. W. 1904 (Hearts, Everton, Newcastle U) 6
Wilson, Hugh 1890 (Newmilns, Sunderland, Third Lanark) 4
Wilson, I. A. 1987 (Leicester C, Everton) 5
Wilson, J. 1888 (Vale of Leven) 4
Wilson, M. 2011 (Celtic) 1
Wilson, P. 1926 (Celtic) 4
Wilson, P. 1975 (Celtic) 1
Wilson, R. P. 1972 (Arsenal) 2
Winters, R. 1999 (Aberdeen) 1
Wiseman, W. 1927 (Queen's Park) 2
Wood, G. 1979 (Everton, Arsenal) 4
Woodburn, W. A. 1947 (Rangers) 24
Wotherspoon, D. N. 1872 (Queen's Park) 2
Wright, K. 1992 (Hibernian) 1
Wright, S. 1993 (Aberdeen) 2
Wright, T. 1953 (Sunderland) 3
Wylie, T. G. 1890 (Rangers) 1

Yeats, R. 1965 (Liverpool) 2
Yorston, B. C. 1931 (Aberdeen) 1
Yorston, H. 1955 (Aberdeen) 1
Young, A. 1905 (Everton) 2
Young, A. 1960 (Hearts, Everton) 8
Young, G. L. 1947 (Rangers) 53
Young, J. 1906 (Celtic) 1
Younger, T. 1955 (Hibernian, Liverpool) 24

WALES

Adams, H. 1882 (Berwyn R, Druids) 4
Aizlewood, M. 1986 (Charlton Ath, Leeds U, Bradford C, Bristol C, Cardiff C) 39
Allchurch, I. J. 1951 (Swansea T, Newcastle U, Cardiff C, Swansea T) 68
Allchurch, L. 1955 (Swansea T, Sheffield U) 11
Allen, B. W. 1951 (Coventry C) 2
Allen, J. M. 2009 (Swansea C) 8
Allen, M. 1986 (Watford, Norwich C, Millwall, Newcastle U) 14
Arridge, S. 1892 (Bootle, Everton, New Brighton Tower) 8
Astley, D. J. 1931 (Charlton Ath, Aston Villa, Derby Co, Blackpool) 13
Atherton, R. W. 1899 (Hibernian, Middlesbrough) 9

Bailiff, W. E. 1913 (Llanelly) 4
Baker, C. W. 1958 (Cardiff C) 7
Baker, W. G. 1948 (Cardiff C) 1
Bale, G. 2006 (Southampton, Tottenham H) 33
Bamford, T. 1931 (Wrexham) 5
Barnard, D. S. 1998 (Barnsley, Grimsby T) 22
Barnes, W. 1948 (Arsenal) 22
Bartley, T. 1898 (Glossop NE) 1
Bastock, A. M. 1892 (Shrewsbury T) 1
Beadles, G. H. 1925 (Cardiff C) 2
Bell, W. S. 1881 (Shrewsbury Engineers, Crewe Alex) 5
Bellamy, C. D. 1998 (Norwich C, Coventry C, Newcastle U, Blackburn R, Liverpool, West Ham U, Manchester C, Liverpool) 69
Bennion, S. R. 1926 (Manchester U) 10
Berry, G. F. 1979 (Wolverhampton W, Stoke C) 5
Blackmore, C. G. 1985 (Manchester U, Middlesbrough) 39
Blake, D. J. 2011 (Cardiff C) 9
Blake, N. A. 1994 (Sheffield U, Bolton W, Blackburn R, Wolverhampton W) 29
Blew, H. 1899 (Wrexham) 22
Boden, T. 1880 (Wrexham) 1
Bodin, P. J. 1990 (Swindon T, Crystal Palace, Swindon T) 23
Boulter, L. M. 1939 (Brentford) 1
Bowdler, H. E. 1893 (Shrewsbury T) 1
Bowdler, J. C. H. 1890 (Shrewsbury T, Wolverhampton W, Shrewsbury T) 4
Bowen, D. L. 1955 (Arsenal) 19
Bowen, E. 1880 (Druids) 2
Bowen, J. P. 1994 (Swansea C, Birmingham C) 2
Bowen, M. R. 1986 (Tottenham H, Norwich C, West Ham U) 41
Bowsher, S. J. 1929 (Burnley) 1
Boyle, T. 1981 (Crystal Palace) 2
Bradley, M. S. 2010 (Walsall) 1
Britten, T. J. 1878 (Parkgrove, Presteigne) 2
Brookes, S. J. 1900 (Llandudno) 2
Brown, A. I. 1926 (Aberdare Ath) 1
Brown, J. R. 2006 (Gillingham, Blackburn R, Aberdeen) 3
Browning, M. T. 1996 (Bristol R, Huddersfield T) 5
Bryan, T. 1886 (Oswestry) 2
Buckland, T. 1899 (Bangor) 1
Burgess, W. A. R. 1947 (Tottenham H) 32
Burke, T. 1883 (Wrexham, Newton Heath) 8
Burnett, T. B. 1877 (Ruabon) 1
Burton, A. D. 1963 (Norwich C, Newcastle U) 9
Butler, J. 1893 (Chirk) 3
Butler, W. T. 1900 (Druids) 2

Cartwright, L. 1974 (Coventry C, Wrexham) 7
Carty, T. See McCarthy (Wrexham).
Challen, J. B. 1887 (Corinthians, Wellingborough GS) 4
Chapman, T. 1894 (Newtown, Manchester C, Grimsby T) 7
Charles, J. M. 1981 (Swansea C, QPR, Oxford U) 19
Charles, M. 1955 (Swansea T, Arsenal, Cardiff C) 31
Charles, W. J. 1950 (Leeds U, Juventus, Leeds U, Cardiff C) 38
Church, S. R. 2009 (Reading) 15
Clarke, R. J. 1949 (Manchester C) 22
Coleman, C. 1992 (Crystal Palace, Blackburn R, Fulham) 32
Collier, D. J. 1921 (Grimsby T) 1
Collins, D. L. 2005 (Sunderland, Stoke C) 12
Collins, J. M. 2004 (Cardiff C, West Ham U, Aston Villa) 39
Collins, W. S. 1931 (Llanelly) 1
Collison, J. D. 2008 (West Ham U) 11
Conde, C. 1884 (Chirk) 3
Cook, F. C. 1925 (Newport Co, Portsmouth) 8
Cornforth, J. M. 1995 (Swansea C) 2
Cotterill, D. R. G. B. 2006 (Bristol C, Wigan Ath, Sheffield U, Swansea C) 19
Coyne, D. 1996 (Tranmere R, Grimsby T, Leicester C, Burnley, Tranmere R) 16
Crofts, A. L. 2006 (Gillingham, Brighton & HA, Norwich C) 23
Crompton, W. 1931 (Wrexham) 3
Cross, E. A. 1876 (Wrexham) 2
Crosse, K. 1879 (Druids) 3

Crossley, M. G. 1997 (Nottingham F, Middlesbrough, Fulham) 8
Crowe, V. H. 1959 (Aston Villa) 16
Cumner, R. H. 1939 (Arsenal) 3
Curtis, A. T. 1976 (Swansea C, Leeds U, Swansea C, Southampton, Cardiff C) 35
Curtis, E. R. 1928 (Cardiff C, Birmingham) 3

Daniel, R. W. 1951 (Arsenal, Sunderland) 21
Darvell, S. 1897 (Oxford University) 2
Davies, A. 1876 (Wrexham) 2
Davies, A. 1904 (Druids, Middlesbrough) 2
Davies, A. 1983 (Manchester U, Newcastle U, Swansea C, Bradford C) 13
Davies, A. O. 1885 (Barmouth, Swifts, Wrexham, Crewe Alex) 9
Davies, A. R. 2006 (Yeovil T) 1
Davies, A. T. 1891 (Shrewsbury T) 1
Davies, C. 1972 (Charlton Ath) 1
Davies, C. M. 2006 (Oxford U, Verona, Oldham Ath) 5
Davies, D. 1904 (Bolton W) 3
Davies, D. C. 1899 (Brecon, Hereford) 2
Davies, D. W. 1912 (Treharris, Oldham Ath) 2
Davies, E. Lloyd 1904 (Stoke, Northampton T) 16
Davies, E. R. 1953 (Newcastle U) 6
Davies, G. 1980 (Fulham, Manchester C) 16
Davies, Rev. H. 1928 (Wrexham) 1
Davies, Idwal 1923 (Liverpool Marine) 1
Davies, J. E. 1885 (Oswestry) 1
Davies, Jas 1878 (Wrexham) 1
Davies, John 1879 (Wrexham) 1
Davies, Jos 1888 (Newton Heath, Wolverhampton W) 7
Davies, Jos 1889 (Everton, Chirk, Ardwick, Sheffield U, Manchester C, Millwall, Reading) 11
Davies, J. P. 1883 (Druids) 2
Davies, Ll. 1907 (Wrexham, Everton, Wrexham) 13
Davies, L. S. 1922 (Cardiff C) 23
Davies, O. 1890 (Wrexham) 1
Davies, R. 1883 (Wrexham) 3
Davies, R. 1885 (Druids) 1
Davies, R. O. 1892 (Wrexham) 2
Davies, R. T. 1964 (Norwich C, Southampton, Portsmouth) 29
Davies, R. W. 1964 (Bolton W, Newcastle U, Manchester C, Manchester U, Blackpool) 34
Davies, S. 2001 (Tottenham H, Everton, Fulham) 58
Davies, S. I. 1996 (Manchester U) 1
Davies, Stanley 1920 (Preston NE, Everton, WBA, Rotherham U) 18
Davies, T. 1886 (Oswestry) 1
Davies, T. 1903 (Druids) 4
Davies, W. 1884 (Wrexham) 1
Davies, W. 1924 (Swansea T, Cardiff C, Notts Co) 17
Davies, William 1903 (Wrexham, Blackburn R) 11
Davies, W. C. 1908 (Crystal Palace, WBA, Crystal Palace) 4
Davies, W. D. 1975 (Everton, Wrexham, Swansea C) 52
Davies, W. H. 1876 (Oswestry) 4
Davis, G. 1978 (Wrexham) 3
Davis, W. O. 1913 (Millwall Ath) 5
Day, A. 1934 (Tottenham H) 1
Deacy, N. 1977 (PSV Eindhoven, Beringen) 12
Dearson, D. J. 1939 (Birmingham) 3
Delaney, M. A. 2000 (Aston Villa) 36
Derrett, S. C. 1969 (Cardiff C) 4
Dewey, F. T. 1931 (Cardiff Corinthians) 2
Dibble, A. 1986 (Luton T, Manchester C) 3
Dorman, A. 2010 (St Mirren, Crystal Palace) 3
Doughty, J. 1886 (Druids, Newton Heath) 8
Doughty, R. 1888 (Newton Heath) 2
Duffy, R. M. 2006 (Portsmouth) 13
Durban, A. 1966 (Derby Co) 27
Dwyer, P. J. 1978 (Cardiff C) 10

Eardley, N. 2008 (Oldham Ath, Blackpool) 16
Earnshaw, R. 2002 (Cardiff C, WBA, Norwich C, Derby Co, Nottingham F, Cardiff C) 58
Easter, J. M. 2007 (Wycombe W, Plymouth Arg, Milton Keynes D, Crystal Palace) 10
Eastwood, F. 2008 (Wolverhampton W, Coventry C) 11
Edwards, C. 1878 (Wrexham) 1
Edwards, C. N. H. 1996 (Swansea C) 1
Edwards, D. 2008 (Luton T, Wolverhampton W) 24
Edwards, G. 1947 (Birmingham C, Cardiff C) 12
Edwards, H. 1878 (Wrexham Civil Service, Wrexham) 8
Edwards, J. H. 1876 (Wanderers) 1
Edwards, J. H. 1895 (Oswestry) 3
Edwards, J. H. 1898 (Aberystwyth) 1
Edwards, L. T. 1957 (Charlton Ath) 2
Edwards, R. I. 1978 (Chester, Wrexham) 4
Edwards, R. O. 2003 (Aston Villa, Wolverhampton W) 15
Edwards, R. W. 1998 (Bristol C) 4
Edwards, T. 1932 (Linfield) 1
Egan, W. 1892 (Chirk) 1
Ellis, B. 1932 (Motherwell) 6
Ellis, E. 1931 (Nunhead, Oswestry) 3
Emanuel, W. J. 1973 (Bristol C) 2
England, H. M. 1962 (Blackburn R, Tottenham H) 44
Evans, B. C. 1972 (Swansea C, Hereford U) 7
Evans, C. M. 2008 (Manchester C, Sheffield U) 13
Evans, D. G. 1926 (Reading, Huddersfield T) 4
Evans, H. P. 1922 (Cardiff C) 6
Evans, I. 1976 (Crystal Palace) 13
Evans, J. 1893 (Oswestry) 3
Evans, J. 1912 (Cardiff C) 8
Evans, J. H. 1922 (Southend U) 4
Evans, Len 1927 (Aberdare Ath, Cardiff C, Birmingham) 4
Evans, M. 1884 (Oswestry) 1
Evans, P. S. 2002 (Brentford, Bradford C) 2
Evans, R. 1902 (Clapton) 1
Evans, R. E. 1906 (Wrexham, Aston Villa, Sheffield U) 10
Evans, R. O. 1902 (Wrexham, Blackburn R, Coventry C) 10
Evans, R. S. 1964 (Swansea T) 1
Evans, S. J. 2007 (Wrexham) 7
Evans, T. J. 1927 (Clapton Orient, Newcastle U) 4
Evans, W. 1933 (Tottenham H) 6
Evans, W. A. W. 1876 (Oxford University) 2
Evans, W. G. 1890 (Bootle, Aston Villa) 3
Evelyn, E. C. 1887 (Crusaders) 1
Eyton-Jones, J. A. 1883 (Wrexham) 4

Farmer, G. 1885 (Oswestry) 2
Felgate, D. 1984 (Lincoln C) 1
Finnigan, R. J. 1930 (Wrexham) 1
Fletcher, C. N. 2004 (Bournemouth, West Ham U, Crystal Palace) 36
Flynn, B. 1975 (Burnley, Leeds U, Burnley) 66
Ford, T. 1947 (Swansea T, Aston Villa, Sunderland, Cardiff C) 38
Foulkes, H. E. 1932 (WBA) 1
Foulkes, W. I. 1952 (Newcastle U) 11
Foulkes, W. T. 1884 (Oswestry) 2
Fowler, J. 1925 (Swansea T) 6
Freestone, R. 2000 (Swansea C) 1

Gabbidon, D. L. 2002 (Cardiff C, West Ham U, QPR) 46
Garner, G. 2006 (Leyton Orient) 1
Garner, J. 1896 (Aberystwyth) 1
Giggs, R. J. 1992 (Manchester U) 64
Giles, D. C. 1980 (Swansea C, Crystal Palace) 12
Gillam, S. G. 1889 (Wrexham, Shrewsbury, Clapton) 5
Glascodine, G. 1879 (Wrexham) 1
Glover, E. M. 1932 (Grimsby T) 7
Godding, G. 1923 (Wrexham) 2
Godfrey, B. C. 1964 (Preston NE) 3
Goodwin, U. 1881 (Ruthin) 1
Goss, J. 1991 (Norwich C) 9
Gough, R. T. 1883 (Oswestry White Star) 1
Gray, A. 1924 (Oldham Ath, Manchester C, Manchester Central, Tranmere R, Chester) 24
Green, A. W. 1901 (Aston Villa, Notts Co, Nottingham F) 8
Green, C. R. 1965 (Birmingham C) 15
Green, G. H. 1938 (Charlton Ath) 4
Green, R. M. 1998 (Wolverhampton W) 2
Grey, Dr W. 1876 (Druids) 2
Griffiths, A. T. 1971 (Wrexham) 17
Griffiths, F. J. 1900 (Blackpool) 2
Griffiths, G. 1887 (Chirk) 1
Griffiths, J. H. 1953 (Swansea T) 1
Griffiths, L. 1902 (Wrexham) 1

Griffiths, M. W. 1947 (Leicester C) 11
Griffiths, P. 1884 (Chirk) 6
Griffiths, P. H. 1932 (Everton) 1
Griffiths, T. P. 1927 (Everton, Bolton W, Middlesbrough, Aston Villa) 21
Gunter, C. R. 2007 (Cardiff C, Tottenham H, Nottingham F) 37

Hall, G. D. 1988 (Chelsea) 9
Hallam, J. 1889 (Oswestry) 1
Hanford, H. 1934 (Swansea T, Sheffield W) 7
Harrington, A. C. 1956 (Cardiff C) 11
Harris, C. S. 1976 (Leeds U) 24
Harris, W. C. 1954 (Middlesbrough) 6
Harrison, W. C. 1899 (Wrexham) 5
Hartson, J. 1995 (Arsenal, West Ham U, Wimbledon, Coventry C, Celtic) 51
Haworth, S. O. 1997 (Cardiff C, Coventry C) 5
Hayes, A. 1890 (Wrexham) 2
Hennessey, W. R. 2007 (Wolverhampton W) 38
Hennessey, W. T. 1962 (Birmingham C, Nottingham F, Derby Co) 39
Hersee, A. M. 1886 (Bangor) 2
Hersee, R. 1886 (Llandudno) 1
Hewitt, R. 1958 (Cardiff C) 5
Hewitt, T. J. 1911 (Wrexham, Chelsea, South Liverpool) 8
Heywood, D. 1879 (Druids) 1
Hibbott, H. 1880 (Newtown Excelsior, Newtown) 3
Higham, G. G. 1878 (Oswestry) 2
Hill, M. R. 1972 (Ipswich T) 2
Hockey, T. 1972 (Sheffield U, Norwich C, Aston Villa) 9
Hoddinott, T. F. 1921 (Watford) 2
Hodges, G. 1984 (Wimbledon, Newcastle U, Watford, Sheffield U) 18
Hodgkinson, A. V. 1908 (Southampton) 1
Holden, A. 1984 (Chester C) 1
Hole, B. G. 1963 (Cardiff C, Blackburn R, Aston Villa, Swansea C) 30
Hole, W. J. 1921 (Swansea T) 9
Hollins, D. M. 1962 (Newcastle U) 11
Hopkins, I. J. 1935 (Brentford) 12
Hopkins, J. 1983 (Fulham, Crystal Palace) 16
Hopkins, M. 1956 (Tottenham H) 34
Horne, B. 1988 (Portsmouth, Southampton, Everton, Birmingham C) 59
Howell, E. G. 1888 (Builth) 3
Howells, R. G. 1954 (Cardiff C) 2
Hugh, A. R. 1930 (Newport Co) 1
Hughes, A. 1894 (Rhos) 2
Hughes, A. 1907 (Chirk) 1
Hughes, C. M. 1992 (Luton T, Wimbledon) 8
Hughes, E. 1899 (Everton, Tottenham H) 14
Hughes, E. 1906 (Wrexham, Nottingham F, Wrexham, Manchester C) 16
Hughes, F. W. 1882 (Northwich Victoria) 6
Hughes, I. 1951 (Luton T) 4
Hughes, J. 1877 (Cambridge University, Aberystwyth) 2
Hughes, J. 1905 (Liverpool) 3
Hughes, J. I. 1935 (Blackburn R) 1
Hughes, L. M. 1984 (Manchester U, Barcelona, Manchester U, Chelsea, Southampton) 72
Hughes, P. W. 1887 (Bangor) 3
Hughes, W. 1891 (Bootle) 3
Hughes, W. A. 1949 (Blackburn R) 5
Hughes, W. M. 1938 (Birmingham) 10
Humphreys, J. V. 1947 (Everton) 1
Humphreys, R. 1888 (Druids) 1
Hunter, A. H. 1887 (FA of Wales Secretary) 1

Jackett, K. 1983 (Watford) 31
Jackson, W. 1899 (St Helens Rec) 1
James, E. 1893 (Chirk) 8
James, E. G. 1966 (Blackpool) 9
James, L. 1972 (Burnley, Derby Co, QPR, Burnley, Swansea C, Sunderland) 54
James, R. M. 1979 (Swansea C, Stoke C, QPR, Leicester C, Swansea C) 47
James, W. 1931 (West Ham U) 2
Jarrett, R. H. 1889 (Ruthin) 2
Jarvis, A. L. 1967 (Hull C) 3
Jenkins, E. 1925 (Lovell's Ath) 1
Jenkins, J. 1924 (Brighton & HA) 8
Jenkins, R. W. 1902 (Rhyl) 1
Jenkins, S. R. 1996 (Swansea C, Huddersfield T) 16
Jenkyns, C. A. L. 1892 (Small Heath, Woolwich Arsenal, Newton Heath, Walsall) 8
Jennings, W. 1914 (Bolton W) 11
John, R. F. 1923 (Arsenal) 15
John, W. R. 1931 (Walsall, Stoke C, Preston NE, Sheffield U, Swansea T) 14
Johnson, A. J. 1999 (Nottingham F, WBA) 15
Johnson, M. G. 1964 (Swansea T) 1
Jones, A. 1987 (Port Vale, Charlton Ath) 6
Jones, A. F. 1877 (Oxford University) 1
Jones, A. T. 1905 (Nottingham F, Notts Co) 2
Jones, Bryn 1935 (Wolverhampton W, Arsenal) 17
Jones, B. S. 1963 (Swansea T, Plymouth Arg, Cardiff C) 15
Jones, Charlie 1926 (Nottingham F, Arsenal) 8
Jones, Cliff 1954 (Swansea T, Tottenham H, Fulham) 59
Jones, C. W. 1935 (Birmingham) 2
Jones, D. 1888 (Chirk, Bolton W, Manchester C) 14
Jones, D. E. 1976 (Norwich C) 8
Jones, D. O. 1934 (Leicester C) 7
Jones, Evan 1910 (Chelsea, Oldham Ath, Bolton W) 7
Jones, F. R. 1885 (Bangor) 3
Jones, F. W. 1893 (Small Heath) 1
Jones, G. P. 1907 (Wrexham) 2
Jones, H. 1902 (Aberaman) 1
Jones, Humphrey 1885 (Bangor, Queen's Park, East Stirlingshire, Queen's Park) 14
Jones, Ivor 1920 (Swansea T, WBA) 10
Jones, Jeffrey 1908 (Llandrindod Wells) 3
Jones, J. 1876 (Druids) 1
Jones, J. 1883 (Berwyn Rangers) 3
Jones, J. 1925 (Wrexham) 1
Jones, J. L. 1895 (Sheffield U, Tottenham H) 21
Jones, J. Love 1906 (Stoke, Middlesbrough) 2
Jones, J. O. 1901 (Bangor) 2
Jones, J. P. 1976 (Liverpool, Wrexham, Chelsea, Huddersfield T) 72
Jones, J. T. 1912 (Stoke, Crystal Palace) 15
Jones, K. 1950 (Aston Villa) 1
Jones, Leslie J. 1933 (Cardiff C, Coventry C, Arsenal 11
Jones, M. A. 2007 (Wrexham) 2
Jones, M. G. 2000 (Leeds U, Leicester C) 13
Jones, P. L. 1997 (Liverpool, Tranmere R) 2
Jones, P. S. 1997 (Stockport Co, Southampton, Wolverhampton W, QPR) 50
Jones, P. W. 1971 (Bristol R) 1
Jones, R. 1887 (Bangor, Crewe Alex) 3
Jones, R. 1898 (Leicester Fosse) 1
Jones, R. 1899 (Druids) 1
Jones, R. 1900 (Bangor) 2
Jones, R. 1906 (Millwall) 2
Jones, R. A. 1884 (Druids) 4
Jones, R. A. 1994 (Sheffield W) 1
Jones, R. S. 1894 (Everton) 1
Jones, S. 1887 (Wrexham, Chester) 2
Jones, S. 1893 (Wrexham, Burton Swifts, Druids) 6
Jones, T. 1926 (Manchester U) 4
Jones, T. D. 1908 (Aberdare) 1
Jones, T. G. 1938 (Everton) 17
Jones, T. J. 1932 (Sheffield W) 2
Jones, V. P. 1995 (Wimbledon) 9
Jones, W. E. A. 1947 (Swansea T, Tottenham H) 4
Jones, W. J. 1901 (Aberdare, West Ham U) 4
Jones, W. Lot 1905 (Manchester C, Southend U) 20
Jones, W. P. 1889 (Druids, Wynnstay) 4
Jones, W. R. 1897 (Aberystwyth) 1

Keenor, F. C. 1920 (Cardiff C, Crewe Alex) 32
Kelly, F. C. 1899 (Wrexham, Druids) 3
Kelsey, A. J. 1954 (Arsenal) 41
Kenrick, S. L. 1876 (Druids, Oswestry, Shropshire Wanderers) 5
Ketley, C. F. 1882 (Druids) 1
King, A. 2009 (Leicester C) 12
King, J. 1955 (Swansea T) 1
Kinsey, N. 1951 (Norwich C, Birmingham C) 7
Knill, A. R. 1989 (Swansea C) 1
Koumas, J. 2001 (Tranmere R, WBA, Wigan Ath) 34
Krzywicki, R. L. 1970 (WBA, Huddersfield T) 8

Lambert, R. 1947 (Liverpool) 5
Latham, G. 1905 (Liverpool, Southport Central, Cardiff C) 10
Law, B. J. 1990 (QPR) 1
Lawrence, E. 1930 (Clapton Orient, Notts Co) 2
Lawrence, S. 1932 (Swansea T) 8
Lea, A. 1889 (Wrexham) 4
Lea, C. 1965 (Ipswich T) 2
Leary, P. 1889 (Bangor) 1
Ledley, J. C. 2006 (Cardiff C, Celtic) 41
Leek, K. 1961 (Leicester C, Newcastle U, Birmingham C, Northampton T) 13
Legg, A. 1996 (Birmingham C, Cardiff C) 6
Lever, A. R. 1953 (Leicester C) 1
Lewis, B. 1891 (Chester, Wrexham, Middlesbrough, Wrexham) 10
Lewis, D. 1927 (Arsenal) 3
Lewis, D. 1983 (Swansea C) 1
Lewis, D. J. 1933 (Swansea T) 2
Lewis, D. M. 1890 (Bangor) 2
Lewis, J. 1906 (Bristol R) 1
Lewis, J. 1926 (Cardiff C) 1
Lewis, T. 1881 (Wrexham) 2
Lewis, W. 1885 (Bangor, Crewe Alex, Chester, Manchester C, Chester) 27
Lewis, W. L. 1927 (Swansea T, Huddersfield T) 6
Llewellyn, C. M. 1998 (Norwich C, Wrexham) 6
Lloyd, B. W. 1976 (Wrexham) 3
Lloyd, J. W. 1879 (Wrexham, Newtown) 2
Lloyd, R. A. 1891 (Ruthin) 2
Lockley, A. 1898 (Chirk) 1
Lovell, S. 1982 (Crystal Palace, Millwall) 6
Lowndes, S. R. 1983 (Newport Co, Millwall, Barnsley) 10
Lowrie, G. 1948 (Coventry C, Newcastle U) 4
Lucas, P. M. 1962 (Leyton Orient) 4
Lucas, W. H. 1949 (Swansea T) 7
Lumberg, A. 1929 (Wrexham, Wolverhampton W) 4

MacDonald, S. B. 2011 (Swansea C) 1
McCarthy, T. P. 1889 (Wrexham) 1
McMillan, R. 1881 (Shrewsbury Engineers) 2
Maguire, G. T. 1990 (Portsmouth) 7
Mahoney, J. F. 1968 (Stoke C, Middlesbrough, Swansea C) 51
Mardon, P. J. 1996 (WBA) 1
Margetson, M. W. 2004 (Cardiff C) 1
Marriott, A. 1996 (Wrexham) 5
Martin, T. J. 1930 (Newport Co) 1
Marustik, C. 1982 (Swansea C) 6
Mates, J. 1891 (Chirk) 3
Matthews, A. J. 2011 (Cardiff C, Celtic) 7
Matthews, R. W. 1921 (Liverpool, Bristol C, Bradford) 3
Matthews, W. 1905 (Chester) 2
Matthias, J. S. 1896 (Brymbo, Shrewsbury T, Wolverhampton W) 5
Matthias, T. J. 1914 (Wrexham) 12
Mays, A. W. 1929 (Wrexham) 1
Medwin, T. C. 1953 (Swansea T, Tottenham H) 30
Melville, A. K. 1990 (Swansea C, Oxford U, Sunderland, Fulham, West Ham U) 65
Meredith, S. 1900 (Chirk, Stoke, Leyton) 8
Meredith, W. H. 1895 (Manchester C, Manchester U) 48
Mielczarek, R. 1971 (Rotherham U) 1
Millership, H. 1920 (Rotherham Co) 6
Millington, A. H. 1963 (WBA, Crystal Palace, Peterborough U, Swansea C) 21
Mills, T. J. 1934 (Clapton Orient, Leicester C) 4
Mills-Roberts, R. H. 1885 (St Thomas' Hospital, Preston NE, Llanberis) 8
Moore, G. 1960 (Cardiff C, Chelsea, Manchester U, Northampton T, Charlton Ath) 21
Morgan, C. 2007 (Milton Keynes D, Peterborough U, Preston NE) 23
Morgan, J. R. 1877 (Cambridge University, Derby School Staff) 10
Morgan, J. T. 1905 (Wrexham) 1
Morgan-Owen, H. 1902 (Oxford University, Corinthians) 4
Morgan-Owen, M. M. 1897 (Oxford University, Corinthians) 13
Morison, S. W. 2011 (Millwall, Norwich C) 15
Morley, E. J. 1925 (Swansea T, Clapton Orient) 4
Morris, A. G. 1896 (Aberystwyth, Swindon T, Nottingham F) 21
Morris, C. 1900 (Chirk, Derby Co, Huddersfield T) 27
Morris, E. 1893 (Chirk) 3
Morris, H. 1894 (Sheffield U, Manchester C, Grimsby T) 3
Morris, J. 1887 (Oswestry) 1
Morris, J. 1898 (Chirk) 1
Morris, R. 1900 (Chirk, Shrewsbury T) 6
Morris, R. 1902 (Newtown, Druids, Liverpool, Leeds C, Grimsby T, Plymouth Arg) 11
Morris, S. 1937 (Birmingham) 5
Morris, W. 1947 (Burnley) 5
Moulsdale, J. R. B. 1925 (Corinthians) 1
Murphy, J. P. 1933 (WBA) 15
Myhill, G. O. 2008 (Hull C, WBA) 10

Nardiello, D. 1978 (Coventry C) 2
Nardiello, D. A. 2007 (Barnsley, QPR) 3
Neal, J. E. 1931 (Colwyn Bay) 2
Neilson, A. B. 1992 (Newcastle U, Southampton) 5
Newnes, J. 1926 (Nelson) 1
Newton, L. F. 1912 (Cardiff Corinthians) 1
Nicholas, D. S. 1923 (Stoke, Swansea T) 3
Nicholas, P. 1979 (Crystal Palace, Arsenal, Crystal Palace, Luton T, Aberdeen, Chelsea, Watford) 73
Nicholls, J. 1924 (Newport Co, Cardiff C) 4
Niedzwiecki, E. A. 1985 (Chelsea) 2
Nock, W. 1897 (Newtown) 1
Nogan, L. M. 1992 (Watford, Reading) 2
Norman, A. J. 1986 (Hull C) 5
Nurse, M. T. G. 1960 (Swansea T, Middlesbrough) 12
Nyatanga, L. J. 2006 (Derby Co, Bristol C) 34

O'Callaghan, E. 1929 (Tottenham H) 11
Oliver, A. 1905 (Bangor, Blackburn R) 2
Oster, J. M. 1998 (Everton, Sunderland) 13
O'Sullivan, P. A. 1973 (Brighton & HA) 3
Owen, D. 1879 (Oswestry) 1
Owen, E. 1884 (Ruthin Grammar School) 3
Owen, G. 1888 (Chirk, Newton Heath, Chirk) 4
Owen, J. 1892 (Newton Heath) 1
Owen, T. 1879 (Oswestry) 1
Owen, Trevor 1899 (Crewe Alex) 2
Owen, W. 1884 (Chirk) 16
Owen, W. P. 1880 (Ruthin) 12
Owens, J. 1902 (Wrexham) 1

Page, M. E. 1971 (Birmingham C) 28
Page, R. J. 1997 (Watford, Sheffield U, Cardiff C, Coventry C) 41
Palmer, D. 1957 (Swansea T) 3
Parris, J. E. 1932 (Bradford) 1
Parry, B. J. 1951 (Swansea T) 1
Parry, C. 1891 (Everton, Newtown) 13
Parry, E. 1922 (Liverpool) 5
Parry, M. 1901 (Liverpool) 16
Parry, P. I. 2004 (Cardiff C) 12
Parry, T. D. 1900 (Oswestry) 7
Parry, W. 1895 (Newtown) 1
Partridge, D. W. 2005 (Motherwell, Bristol C) 7
Pascoe, C. 1984 (Swansea C, Sunderland) 10
Paul, R. 1949 (Swansea T, Manchester C) 33
Peake, E. 1908 (Aberystwyth, Liverpool) 11
Peers, E. J. 1914 (Wolverhampton W, Port Vale) 12
Pembridge, M. A. 1992 (Luton T, Derby Co, Sheffield W, Benfica, Everton, Fulham) 54
Perry, E. 1938 (Doncaster R) 3
Perry, J. 1994 (Cardiff C) 1
Phennah, E. 1878 (Civil Service) 1
Phillips, C. 1931 (Wolverhampton W, Aston Villa) 13
Phillips, D. 1984 (Plymouth Arg, Manchester C, Coventry C, Norwich C, Nottingham F) 62
Phillips, L. 1971 (Cardiff C, Aston Villa, Swansea C, Charlton Ath) 58
Phillips, T. J. S. 1973 (Chelsea) 4
Phoenix, H. 1882 (Wrexham) 1
Pipe, D. R. 2003 (Coventry C) 1
Poland, G. 1939 (Wrexham) 2
Pontin, K. 1980 (Cardiff C) 2
Powell, A. 1947 (Leeds U, Everton, Birmingham C) 8
Powell, D. 1968 (Wrexham, Sheffield U) 11

Powell, I. V. 1947 (QPR, Aston Villa) 8
Powell, J. 1878 (Druids, Bolton W, Newton Heath) 15
Powell, Seth 1885 (Oswestry, WBA) 7
Price, H. 1907 (Aston Villa, Burton U, Wrexham) 5
Price, J. 1877 (Wrexham) 12
Price, L. P. 2006 (Ipswich T, Derby Co, Crystal Palace) 9
Price, P. 1980 (Luton T, Tottenham H) 25
Pring, K. D. 1966 (Rotherham U) 3
Pritchard, H. K. 1985 (Bristol C) 1
Pryce-Jones, A. W. 1895 (Newtown) 1
Pryce-Jones, W. E. 1887 (Cambridge University) 5
Pugh, A. 1889 (Rhostyllen) 1
Pugh, D. H. 1896 (Wrexham, Lincoln C) 7
Pugsley, J. 1930 (Charlton Ath) 1
Pullen, W. J. 1926 (Plymouth Arg) 1

Ramsey, A. 2009 (Arsenal) 21
Rankmore, F. E. J. 1966 (Peterborough U) 1
Ratcliffe, K. 1981 (Everton, Cardiff C) 59
Rea, J. C. 1894 (Aberystwyth) 9
Ready, K. 1997 (QPR) 5
Reece, G. I. 1966 (Sheffield U, Cardiff C) 29
Reed, W. G. 1955 (Ipswich T) 2
Rees, A. 1984 (Birmingham C) 1
Rees, J. M. 1992 (Luton T) 1
Rees, R. R. 1965 (Coventry C, WBA, Nottingham F) 39
Rees, W. 1949 (Cardiff C, Tottenham H) 4
Ribeiro, C. M. 2010 (Bristol C) 2
Richards, A. 1932 (Barnsley) 1
Richards, A. D. J. 2012 (Swansea C) 1
Richards, D. 1931 (Wolverhampton W, Brentford, Birmingham) 21
Richards, G. 1899 (Druids, Oswestry, Shrewsbury T) 6
Richards, R. W. 1920 (Wolverhampton W, West Ham U, Mold) 9
Richards, S. V. 1947 (Cardiff C) 1
Richards, W. E. 1933 (Fulham) 1
Ricketts, S. D. 2005 (Swansea C, Hull C, Bolton W) 44
Roach, J. 1885 (Oswestry) 1
Robbins, W. W. 1931 (Cardiff C, WBA) 11
Roberts, A. M. 1993 (QPR) 2
Roberts, D. F. 1973 (Oxford U, Hull C) 17
Roberts, G. W. 2000 (Tranmere R) 9
Roberts, I. W. 1990 (Watford, Huddersfield T, Leicester C, Norwich C) 15
Roberts, Jas 1913 (Wrexham) 2
Roberts, J. 1879 (Corwen, Berwyn R) 7
Roberts, J. 1881 (Ruthin) 2
Roberts, J. 1906 (Bradford C) 2
Roberts, J. G. 1971 (Arsenal, Birmingham C) 22
Roberts, J. H. 1949 (Bolton W) 1
Roberts, N. W. 2000 (Wrexham, Wigan Ath) 4
Roberts, P. S. 1974 (Portsmouth) 4
Roberts, R. 1884 (Druids, Bolton W, Preston NE) 9
Roberts, R. 1886 (Wrexham) 3
Roberts, R. 1891 (Rhos, Crewe Alex) 2
Roberts, R. L. 1890 (Chester) 1
Roberts, S. W. 2005 (Wrexham) 1
Roberts, W. 1879 (Llangollen, Berwyn R) 6
Roberts, W. 1883 (Rhyl) 1
Roberts, W. 1886 (Wrexham) 4
Roberts, W. H. 1882 (Ruthin, Rhyl) 6
Robinson, C. P. 2000 (Wolverhampton W, Portsmouth, Sunderland, Norwich C, Toronto Lynx) 52
Robinson, J. R. C. 1996 (Charlton Ath) 30
Robson-Kanu, T. H, 2010 (Reading) 7
Rodrigues, P. J. 1965 (Cardiff C, Leicester C, Sheffield W) 40
Rogers, J. P. 1896 (Wrexham) 3
Rogers, W. 1931 (Wrexham) 2
Roose, L. R. 1900 (Aberystwyth, London Welsh, Stoke, Everton, Stoke, Sunderland) 24
Rouse, R. V. 1959 (Crystal Palace) 1
Rowlands, A. C. 1914 (Tranmere R) 1
Rowley, T. 1959 (Tranmere R) 1
Rush, I. 1980 (Liverpool, Juventus, Liverpool) 73
Russell, M. R. 1912 (Merthyr T, Plymouth Arg) 23

Sabine, H. W. 1887 (Oswestry) 1
Saunders, D. 1986 (Brighton & HA, Oxford U, Derby Co, Liverpool, Aston Villa, Galatasaray, Nottingham F, Sheffield U, Benfica, Bradford C) 75
Savage, R. W. 1996 (Crewe Alex, Leicester C, Birmingham C) 39
Savin, G. 1878 (Oswestry) 1
Sayer, P. A. 1977 (Cardiff C) 7
Scrine, F. H. 1950 (Swansea T) 2
Sear, C. R. 1963 (Manchester C) 1
Shaw, E. G. 1882 (Oswestry) 3
Sherwood, A. T. 1947 (Cardiff C, Newport Co) 41
Shone, W. W. 1879 (Oswestry) 1
Shortt, W. W. 1947 (Plymouth Arg) 12
Showers, D. 1975 (Cardiff C) 2
Sidlow, C. 1947 (Liverpool) 7
Sisson, H. 1885 (Wrexham Olympic) 3
Slatter, N. 1983 (Bristol R, Oxford U) 22
Smallman, D. P. 1974 (Wrexham, Everton) 7
Southall, N. 1982 (Everton) 92
Speed, G. A. 1990 (Leeds U, Everton, Newcastle U, Bolton W) 85
Sprake, G. 1964 (Leeds U, Birmingham C) 37
Stansfield, F. 1949 (Cardiff C) 1
Stevenson, B. 1978 (Leeds U, Birmingham C) 15
Stevenson, N. 1982 (Swansea C) 4
Stitfall, R. F. 1953 (Cardiff C) 2
Stock, B. B. 2010 (Doncaster R) 3
Sullivan, D. 1953 (Cardiff C) 17
Symons, C. J. 1992 (Portsmouth, Manchester C, Fulham, Crystal Palace) 37

Tapscott, D. R. 1954 (Arsenal, Cardiff C) 14
Taylor, G. K. 1996 (Crystal Palace, Sheffield U, Burnley, Nottingham F) 15
Taylor, J. 1898 (Wrexham) 1
Taylor, N. J. 2010 (Wrexham, Swansea C) 9
Taylor, O. D. S. 1893 (Newtown) 4
Thatcher, B. D. 2004 (Leicester C, Manchester C) 7
Thomas, C. 1899 (Druids) 2
Thomas, D. A. 1957 (Swansea T) 2
Thomas, D. S. 1948 (Fulham) 4
Thomas, E. 1925 (Cardiff Corinthians) 1
Thomas, G. 1885 (Wrexham) 2
Thomas, H. 1927 (Manchester U) 1
Thomas, Martin R. 1987 (Newcastle U) 1
Thomas, Mickey 1977 (Wrexham, Manchester U, Everton, Brighton & HA, Stoke C, Chelsea, WBA) 51
Thomas, R. J. 1967 (Swindon T, Derby Co, Cardiff C) 50
Thomas, T. 1898 (Bangor) 2
Thomas, W. R. 1931 (Newport Co) 2
Thomson, D. 1876 (Druids) 1
Thomson, G. F. 1876 (Druids) 2
Toshack, J. B. 1969 (Cardiff C, Liverpool, Swansea C) 40
Townsend, W. 1887 (Newtown) 2
Trainer, H. 1895 (Wrexham) 3
Trainer, J. 1887 (Bolton W, Preston NE) 20
Trollope, P. J. 1997 (Derby Co, Fulham, Coventry C, Northampton T) 9
Tudur-Jones, O. 2008 (Swansea C, Norwich C) 6
Turner, H. G. 1937 (Charlton Ath) 8
Turner, J. 1892 (Wrexham) 1
Turner, R. E. 1891 (Wrexham) 2
Turner, W. H. 1887 (Wrexham) 5

Van Den Hauwe, P. W. R. 1985 (Everton) 13
Vaughan, D. O. 2003 (Crewe Alex, Real Sociedad, Blackpool, Sunderland) 29
Vaughan, Jas 1893 (Druids) 4
Vaughan, John 1879 (Oswestry, Druids, Bolton W) 11
Vaughan, J. O. 1885 (Rhyl) 4
Vaughan, N. 1983 (Newport Co, Cardiff C) 10
Vaughan, T. 1885 (Rhyl) 1
Vearncombe, G. 1958 (Cardiff C) 2
Vernon, T. R. 1957 (Blackburn R, Everton, Stoke C) 32
Villars, A. K. 1974 (Cardiff C) 3
Vizard, E. T. 1911 (Bolton W) 22
Vokes, S. M. 2008 (Bournemouth, Wolverhampton W) 21

Walley, J. T. 1971 (Watford) 1
Walsh, I. P. 1980 (Crystal Palace, Swansea C) 18
Ward, D. 1959 (Bristol R, Cardiff C) 2
Ward, D. 2000 (Notts Co, Nottingham F) 5
Warner, J. 1937 (Swansea T, Manchester U) 2
Warren, F. W. 1929 (Cardiff C, Middlesbrough, Hearts) 6

Watkins, A. E. 1898 (Leicester Fosse, Aston Villa, Millwall) 5
Watkins, W. M. 1902 (Stoke, Aston Villa, Sunderland, Stoke) 10
Webster, C. 1957 (Manchester U) 4
Weston, R. D. 2000 (Arsenal, Cardiff C) 7
Whatley, W. J. 1939 (Tottenham H) 2
White, P. F. 1896 (London Welsh) 1
Wilcock, A. R. 1890 (Oswestry) 1
Wilding, J. 1885 (Wrexham Olympians, Bootle, Wrexham) 9
Williams, A. 1994 (Reading, Wolverhampton W, Reading) 13
Williams, A. E. 2008 (Stockport Co, Swansea C) 33
Williams, A. L. 1931 (Wrexham) 1
Williams, A. P. 1998 (Southampton) 2
Williams, B. 1930 (Bristol C) 1
Williams, B. D. 1928 (Swansea T, Everton) 10
Williams, D. G. 1988 (Derby Co, Ipswich T) 13
Williams, D. M. 1986 (Norwich C) 5
Williams, D. R. 1921 (Merthyr T, Sheffield W, Manchester U) 8
Williams, E. 1893 (Crewe Alex) 2
Williams, E. 1901 (Druids) 5
Williams, G. 1893 (Chirk) 6
Williams, G. E. 1960 (WBA) 26
Williams, G. G. 1961 (Swansea T) 5
Williams, G. J. 2006 (West Ham U, Ipswich T) 2
Williams, G. J. J. 1951 (Cardiff C) 1
Williams, G. O. 1907 (Wrexham) 1
Williams, H. J. 1965 (Swansea T) 3
Williams, H. T. 1949 (Newport Co, Leeds U) 4
Williams, J. H. 1884 (Oswestry) 1
Williams, J. J. 1939 (Wrexham) 1
Williams, J. T. 1925 (Middlesbrough) 1
Williams, J. W. 1912 (Crystal Palace) 2
Williams, R. 1935 (Newcastle U) 2
Williams, R. P. 1886 (Caernarvon) 1
Williams, S. G. 1954 (WBA, Southampton) 43
Williams, W. 1876 (Druids, Oswestry, Druids) 11
Williams, W. 1925 (Northampton T) 1
Witcomb, D. F. 1947 (WBA, Sheffield W) 3
Woosnam, A. P. 1959 (Leyton Orient, West Ham U, Aston Villa) 17
Woosnam, G. 1879 (Newtown Excelsior) 1
Worthington, T. 1894 (Newtown) 1
Wynn, G. A. 1909 (Wrexham, Manchester C) 11
Wynn, W. 1903 (Chirk) 1

Yorath, T. C. 1970 (Leeds U, Coventry C, Tottenham H, Vancouver Whitecaps) 59
Young, E. 1990 (Wimbledon, Crystal Palace, Wolverhampton W) 21

REPUBLIC OF IRELAND

Aherne, T. 1946 (Belfast Celtic, Luton T) 16
Aldridge, J. W. 1986 (Oxford U, Liverpool, Real Sociedad, Tranmere R) 69
Ambrose, P. 1955 (Shamrock R) 5
Anderson, J. 1980 (Preston NE, Newcastle U) 16
Andrews, K. J. 2009 (Blackburn R, WBA) 32
Andrews, P. 1936 (Bohemians) 1
Arrigan, T. 1938 (Waterford) 1

Babb, P. A. 1994 (Coventry C, Liverpool, Sunderland) 35
Bailham, E. 1964 (Shamrock R) 1
Barber, E. 1966 (Shelbourne, Birmingham C) 2
Barrett, G. 2003 (Arsenal, Coventry C) 6
Barry, P. 1928 (Fordsons) 2
Beglin, J. 1984 (Liverpool) 15
Bennett, A. J. 2007 (Reading) 2
Bermingham, J. 1929 (Bohemians) 1
Bermingham, P. 1935 (St James' Gate) 1
Best, L. J. B. 2009 (Coventry C, Newcastle U) 7
Bonner, P. 1981 (Celtic) 80
Braddish, S. 1978 (Dundalk) 2
Bradshaw, P. 1939 (St James' Gate) 5
Brady, F. 1926 (Fordsons) 2
Brady, T. R. 1964 (QPR) 6
Brady, W. L. 1975 (Arsenal, Juventus, Sampdoria, Internazionale, Ascoli, West Ham U) 72
Branagan, K. G. 1997 (Bolton W) 1
Breen, G. 1996 (Birmingham C, Coventry C, West Ham U, Sunderland) 63
Breen, T. 1937 (Manchester U, Shamrock R) 5
Brennan, F. 1965 (Drumcondra) 1
Brennan, S. A. 1965 (Manchester U, Waterford) 19
Brown, J. 1937 (Coventry C) 2
Browne, W. 1964 (Bohemians) 3
Bruce, A. S. 2007 (Ipswich T) 2
Buckley, L. 1984 (Shamrock R, Waregem) 2
Burke, F. 1952 (Cork Ath) 1
Burke, J. 1929 (Shamrock R) 1
Burke, J. 1934 (Cork) 1
Butler, P. J. 2000 (Sunderland) 1
Butler, T. 2003 (Sunderland) 2
Byrne, A. B. 1970 (Southampton) 14
Byrne, D. 1929 (Shelbourne, Shamrock R, Coleraine) 3
Byrne, J. 1928 (Bray Unknowns) 1
Byrne, J. 1985 (QPR, Le Havre, Brighton & HA, Sunderland, Millwall) 23
Byrne, J. 2004 (Shelbourne) 2
Byrne, P. 1931 (Dolphin, Shelbourne, Drumcondra) 3
Byrne, P. 1984 (Shamrock R) 8
Byrne, S. 1931 (Bohemians) 1
Campbell, A. 1985 (Santander) 3
Campbell, N. 1971 (St Patrick's Ath, Fortuna Cologne) 11
Cannon, H. 1926 (Bohemians) 2
Cantwell, N. 1954 (West Ham U, Manchester U) 36
Carey, B. P. 1992 (Manchester U, Leicester C) 3
Carey, J. J. 1938 (Manchester U) 29
Carolan, J. 1960 (Manchester U) 2
Carr, S. 1999 (Tottenham H, Newcastle U) 44
Carroll, B. 1949 (Shelbourne) 2
Carroll, T. R. 1968 (Ipswich T, Birmingham C) 17
Carsley, L. K. 1998 (Derby Co, Blackburn R, Coventry C, Everton) 39
Cascarino, A. G. 1986 (Gillingham, Millwall, Aston Villa, Celtic, Chelsea, Marseille, Nancy) 88
Chandler, J. 1980 (Leeds U) 2
Chatton, H. A. 1931 (Shelbourne, Dumbarton, Cork) 3
Clark, C. 2011 (Aston Villa) 2
Clarke; C. R. 2004 (Stoke C) 2
Clarke, J. 1978 (Drogheda U) 1
Clarke, K. 1948 (Drumcondra) 2
Clarke, M. 1950 (Shamrock R) 1
Clinton, T. J. 1951 (Everton) 3
Coad, P. 1947 (Shamrock R) 11
Coffey, T. 1950 (Drumcondra) 1
Coleman, S. 2011 (Everton) 4
Colfer, M. D. 1950 (Shelbourne) 2
Colgan, N. 2002 (Hibernian, Barnsley) 9
Collins, F. 1927 (Jacobs) 1
Conmy, O. M. 1965 (Peterborough U) 5
Connolly, D. J. 1996 (Watford, Feyenoord, Wolverhampton W, Excelsior, Feyenoord, Wimbledon, West Ham U, Wigan Ath) 41
Connolly, H. 1937 (Cork) 1
Connolly, J. 1926 (Fordsons) 1
Conroy, G. A. 1970 (Stoke C) 27
Conway, J. P. 1967 (Fulham, Manchester C) 20
Corr, P. J. 1949 (Everton) 4
Courtney, E. 1946 (Cork U) 1
Cox, S. R. 2011 (WBA) 15
Coyle, O. C. 1994 (Bolton W) 1
Coyne, T. 1992 (Celtic, Tranmere R, Motherwell) 22
Crowe, G. 2003 (Bohemians) 2
Cummins, G. P. 1954 (Luton T) 19
Cuneen, T. 1951 (Limerick) 1
Cunningham, G. R. 2010 (Manchester C) 3
Cunningham, K. 1996 (Wimbledon, Birmingham C) 72
Curtis, D. P. 1957 (Shelbourne, Bristol C, Ipswich T, Exeter C) 17
Cusack, S. 1953 (Limerick) 1

Daish, L. S. 1992 (Cambridge U, Coventry C) 5
Daly, G. A. 1973 (Manchester U, Derby Co, Coventry C, Birmingham C, Shrewsbury T) 48
Daly, J. 1932 (Shamrock R) 2
Daly, M. 1978 (Wolverhampton W) 2
Daly, P. 1950 (Shamrock R) 1
Davis, T. L. 1937 (Oldham Ath, Tranmere R) 4
Deacy, E. 1982 (Aston Villa) 4
Delaney, D. F. 2008 (QPR, Ipswich T) 5
Delap, R. J. 1998 (Derby Co, Southampton) 11
De Mange, K. J. P. P. 1987 (Liverpool, Hull C) 2
Dempsey, J. T. 1967 (Fulham, Chelsea) 19
Dennehy, J. 1972 (Cork Hibernians, Nottingham F, Walsall) 11
Desmond, P. 1950 (Middlesbrough) 4
Devine, J. 1980 (Arsenal, Norwich C) 13
Doherty, G. M. T. 2000 (Luton T, Tottenham H, Norwich C) 34
Donnelly, J. 1935 (Dundalk) 10
Donnelly, T. 1938 (Drumcondra, Shamrock R) 2
Donovan, D. C. 1955 (Everton) 5
Donovan, T. 1980 (Aston Villa) 2
Douglas, J. 2004 (Blackburn R, Leeds U) 8
Dowdall, C. 1928 (Fordsons, Barnsley, Cork) 3
Doyle, C. 1959 (Shelbourne) 1
Doyle, Colin 2007 (Birmingham C) 1
Doyle, D. 1926 (Shamrock R) 1
Doyle, K. E. 2006 (Reading, Wolverhampton W) 50
Doyle, L. 1932 (Dolphin) 1
Doyle, M. P. 2004 (Coventry C) 1
Duff, D. A. 1998 (Blackburn R, Chelsea, Newcastle U, Fulham) 100
Duffy, B. 1950 (Shamrock R) 1
Duggan, H. A. 1927 (Leeds U, Newport Co) 5
Dunne, A. P. 1962 (Manchester U, Bolton W) 33
Dunne, J. 1930 (Sheffield U, Arsenal, Southampton, Shamrock R) 15
Dunne, J. C. 1971 (Fulham) 1
Dunne, L. 1935 (Manchester C) 2
Dunne, P. A. J. 1965 (Manchester U) 5
Dunne, R. P. 2000 (Everton, Manchester C, Aston Villa) 76
Dunne, S. 1953 (Luton T) 15
Dunne, T. 1956 (St Patrick's Ath) 3
Dunning, P. 1971 (Shelbourne) 2
Dunphy, E. M. 1966 (York C, Millwall) 23
Dwyer, N. M. 1960 (West Ham U, Swansea T) 14

Eccles, P. 1986 (Shamrock R) 1
Egan, R. 1929 (Dundalk) 1
Eglington, T. J. 1946 (Shamrock R, Everton) 24
Elliott, S. W. 2005 (Sunderland) 9
Ellis, P. 1935 (Bohemians) 7
Evans, M. J. 1998 (Southampton) 1

Fagan, E. 1973 (Shamrock R) 1
Fagan, F. 1955 (Manchester C, Derby Co) 8
Fagan, J. 1926 (Shamrock R) 1
Fahey, K. D. 2010 (Birmingham C) 15
Fairclough, M. 1982 (Dundalk) 2
Fallon, S. 1951 (Celtic) 8
Fallon, W. J. 1935 (Notts Co, Sheffield W) 9
Farquharson, T. G. 1929 (Cardiff C) 4
Farrell, P. 1937 (Hibernian) 2
Farrell, P. D. 1946 (Shamrock R, Everton) 28
Farrelly, G. 1996 (Aston Villa, Everton, Bolton W) 6
Feenan, J. J. 1937 (Sunderland) 2
Finnan, S. 2000 (Fulham, Liverpool, Espanyol) 53
Finucane, A. 1967 (Limerick) 11
Fitzgerald, F. J. 1955 (Waterford) 2
Fitzgerald, P. J. 1961 (Leeds U, Chester) 5
Fitzpatrick, K. 1970 (Limerick) 1
Fitzsimons, A. G. 1950 (Middlesbrough, Lincoln C) 26
Fleming, C. 1996 (Middlesbrough) 10
Flood, J. J. 1926 (Shamrock R) 5
Fogarty, A. 1960 (Sunderland, Hartlepools U) 11
Folan, C. C. 2009 (Hull C) 7
Foley, D. J. 2000 (Watford) 6
Foley, J. 1934 (Cork, Celtic) 7
Foley, K. P. 2009 (Wolverhampton W) 8
Foley, M. 1926 (Shelbourne) 1
Foley, T. C. 1964 (Northampton T) 9
Forde, D. 2011 (Millwall) 2
Foy, T. 1938 (Shamrock R) 2
Fullam, J. 1961 (Preston NE, Shamrock R) 11
Fullam, R. 1926 (Shamrock R) 2

Gallagher, C. 1967 (Celtic) 2
Gallagher, M. 1954 (Hibernian) 1
Gallagher, P. 1932 (Falkirk) 1
Galvin, A. 1983 (Tottenham H, Sheffield W, Swindon T) 29
Gamble, J. 2007 (Cork C) 2
Gannon, E. 1949 (Notts Co, Sheffield W, Shelbourne) 14
Gannon, M. 1972 (Shelbourne) 1
Gaskins, P. 1934 (Shamrock R, St James' Gate) 7
Gavin, J. T. 1950 (Norwich C, Tottenham H, Norwich C) 7
Geoghegan, M. 1937 (St James' Gate) 2
Gibbons, A. 1952 (St Patrick's Ath) 4
Gibson, D. T. D. 2008 (Manchester U, Everton) 19
Gilbert, R. 1966 (Shamrock R) 1
Giles, C. 1951 (Doncaster R) 1
Giles, M. J. 1960 (Manchester U, Leeds U, WBA, Shamrock R) 59
Given, S. J. J. 1996 (Blackburn R, Newcastle U, Manchester C, Aston Villa) 125
Givens, D. J. 1969 (Manchester U, Luton T, QPR, Birmingham C, Neuchatel X) 56
Gleeson, S. M. 2007 (Wolverhampton W) 2
Glen, W. 1927 (Shamrock R) 8
Glynn, D. 1952 (Drumcondra) 2
Godwin, T. F. 1949 (Shamrock R, Leicester C, Bournemouth) 13
Golding, J. 1928 (Shamrock R) 2
Goodman, J. 1997 (Wimbledon) 4
Goodwin, J. 2003 (Stockport Co) 1
Gorman, W. C. 1936 (Bury, Brentford) 13
Grace, J. 1926 (Drumcondra) 1
Grealish, A. 1976 (Orient, Luton T, Brighton & HA, WBA) 45
Green, P. J. 2010 (Derby Co) 12
Gregg, E. 1978 (Bohemians) 8
Griffith, R. 1935 (Walsall) 1
Grimes, A. A. 1978 (Manchester U, Coventry C, Luton T) 18

Hale, A. 1962 (Aston Villa, Doncaster R, Waterford) 14
Hamilton, T. 1959 (Shamrock R) 2
Hand, E. K. 1969 (Portsmouth) 20
Harrington, W. 1936 (Cork) 5
Harte, I. P. 1996 (Leeds U, Levante) 64
Hartnett, J. B. 1949 (Middlesbrough) 2
Haverty, J. 1956 (Arsenal, Blackburn R, Millwall, Celtic, Bristol R, Shelbourne) 32
Hayes, A. W. P. 1979 (Southampton) 1
Hayes, W. E. 1947 (Huddersfield T) 2
Hayes, W. J. 1949 (Limerick) 1
Healey, R. 1977 (Cardiff C) 2
Healy, C. 2002 (Celtic, Sunderland) 13
Heighway, S. D. 1971 (Liverpool, Minnesota K) 34
Henderson, B. 1948 (Drumcondra) 2
Henderson, W. C. P. 2006 (Brighton & HA, Preston NE) 6
Hennessy, J. 1965 (Shelbourne, St Patrick's Ath) 5
Herrick, J. 1972 (Cork Hibernians, Shamrock R) 3
Higgins, J. 1951 (Birmingham C) 1
Holland, M. R. 2000 (Ipswich T, Charlton Ath) 49
Holmes, J. 1971 (Coventry C, Tottenham H, Vancouver Whitecaps) 30
Hoolahan, W. 2008 (Blackpool) 1
Horlacher, A. F. 1930 (Bohemians) 7
Houghton, R. J. 1986 (Oxford U, Liverpool, Aston Villa, Crystal Palace, Reading) 73
Howlett, G. 1984 (Brighton & HA) 1
Hoy, M. 1938 (Dundalk) 6
Hughton, C. 1980 (Tottenham H, West Ham U) 53
Hunt, N. 2009 (Reading) 3

Hunt, S. P. 2007 (Reading, Hull C, Wolverhampton W) 39
Hurley, C. J. 1957 (Millwall, Sunderland, Bolton W) 40
Hutchinson, F. 1935 (Drumcondra) 2

Ireland S .J. 2006 (Manchester C) 6
Irwin, D. J. 1991 (Manchester U) 56

Jordan, D. 1937 (Wolverhampton W) 2
Jordan, W. 1934 (Bohemians) 2

Kavanagh, G. A. 1998 (Stoke C, Cardiff C, Wigan Ath) 16
Kavanagh, P. J. 1931 (Celtic) 2
Keane, R. D. 1998 (Wolverhampton W, Coventry C, Internazionale, Leeds U, Tottenham H, Liverpool, Tottenham H, LA Galaxy) 120
Keane, R. M. 1991 (Nottingham F, Manchester U) 67
Keane, T. R. 1949 (Swansea T) 4
Kearin, M. 1972 (Shamrock R) 1
Kearns, F. T. 1954 (West Ham U) 1
Kearns, M. 1971 (Oxford U, Walsall, Wolverhampton W) 18
Kelly, A. T. 1993 (Sheffield U, Blackburn R) 34
Kelly, D. T. 1988 (Walsall, West Ham U, Leicester C, Newcastle U, Wolverhampton W, Sunderland, Tranmere R) 26
Kelly, G. 1994 (Leeds U) 52
Kelly, J. 1932 (Derry C) 4
Kelly, J. A. 1957 (Drumcondra, Preston NE) 47
Kelly, J. P. V. 1961 (Wolverhampton W) 5
Kelly, M. J. 1988 (Portsmouth) 4
Kelly, N. 1954 (Nottingham F) 1
Kelly, S. M. 2006 (Tottenham H, Birmingham C, Fulham) 29
Kendrick, J. 1927 (Everton, Dolphin) 4
Kenna, J. J. 1995 (Blackburn R) 27
Kennedy, M. F. 1986 (Portsmouth) 2
Kennedy, M. J. 1996 (Liverpool, Wimbledon, Manchester C, Wolverhampton W) 34
Kennedy, W. 1932 (St James' Gate) 3
Kenny, P. 2004 (Sheffield U) 7
Keogh, A. D. 2007 (Wolverhampton W) 22
Keogh, J. 1966 (Shamrock R) 1
Keogh, S. 1959 (Shamrock R) 1
Kernaghan, A. N. 1993 (Middlesbrough, Manchester C) 22
Kiely, D. L. 2000 (Charlton Ath, WBA) 11
Kiernan, F. W. 1951 (Shamrock R, Southampton) 5
Kilbane, K. D. 1998 (WBA, Sunderland, Everton, Wigan Ath, Hull C) 110
Kinnear, J. P. 1967 (Tottenham H, Brighton & HA) 26
Kinsella, J. 1928 (Shelbourne) 1
Kinsella, M. A. 1998 (Charlton Ath, Aston Villa, WBA) 48
Kinsella, O. 1932 (Shamrock R) 2
Kirkland, A. 1927 (Shamrock R) 1

Lacey, W. 1927 (Shelbourne) 3
Langan, D. 1978 (Derby Co, Birmingham C, Oxford U) 26
Lapira, J. 2007 (Notre Dame) 1
Lawler, J. F. 1953 (Fulham) 8
Lawlor, J. C. 1949 (Drumcondra, Doncaster R) 3
Lawlor, M. 1971 (Shamrock R) 5
Lawrence, L. 2009 (Stoke C, Portsmouth) 15
Lawrenson, M. 1977 (Preston NE, Brighton & HA, Liverpool) 39
Lee, A. D. 2003 (Rotherham U, Cardiff C, Ipswich T) 10
Leech, M. 1969 (Shamrock R) 8
Lennon, C. 1935 (St James' Gate) 3
Lennox, G. 1931 (Dolphin) 2
Long, S. P. 2007 (Reading, WBA) 27
Lowry, D. 1962 (St Patrick's Ath) 1
Lunn, R. 1939 (Dundalk) 2
Lynch, J. 1934 (Cork Bohemians) 1

McAlinden, J. 1946 (Portsmouth) 2
McAteer, J. W. 1994 (Bolton W, Liverpool, Blackburn R, Sunderland) 52
McCann, J. 1957 (Shamrock R) 1
McCarthy, J. 1926 (Bohemians) 3
McCarthy, J. 2010 (Wigan Ath) 3
McCarthy, M. 1932 (Shamrock R) 1
McCarthy, M. 1984 (Manchester C, Celtic, Lyon, Millwall) 57
McClean, J. 2012 (Sunderland) 3
McConville, T. 1972 (Dundalk, Waterford) 6
McDonagh, Jacko 1984 (Shamrock R) 3
McDonagh, J. 1981 (Everton, Bolton W, Notts Co, Wichita Wings) 25
McEvoy, M. A. 1961 (Blackburn R) 17
McGeady, A. 2004 (Celtic, Spartak Moscow) 52
McGee, P. 1978 (QPR, Preston NE) 15
McGoldrick, E. J. 1992 (Crystal Palace, Arsenal) 15
McGowan, D. 1949 (West Ham U) 3
McGowan, J. 1947 (Cork U) 1
McGrath, M. 1958 (Blackburn R, Bradford) 22
McGrath, P. 1985 (Manchester U, Aston Villa, Derby Co) 83
McGuire, W. 1936 (Bohemians) 1
Macken, A. 1977 (Derby Co) 1
Macken J. P. 2005 (Manchester C) 1
McKenzie, G. 1938 (Southend U) 9
Mackey, G. 1957 (Shamrock R) 3
McLoughlin, A. F. 1990 (Swindon T, Southampton, Portsmouth) 42
McLoughlin, F. 1930 (Fordsons, Cork) 2
McMillan, W. 1946 (Belfast Celtic) 2
McNally, J. B. 1959 (Luton T) 3
McPhail, S. 2000 (Leeds U) 10
McShane, P. D. 2007 (WBA, Sunderland, Hull C) 27
Madden, O. 1936 (Cork) 1
Maguire, J. 1929 (Shamrock R) 1
Mahon, A. J. 2000 (Tranmere R) 2
Malone, G. 1949 (Shelbourne) 1
Mancini, T. J. 1974 (QPR, Arsenal) 5
Martin, C. 1927 (Bo'ness) 1
Martin, C. J. 1946 (Glentoran, Leeds U, Aston Villa) 30
Martin, M. P. 1972 (Bohemians, Manchester U, WBA, Newcastle U) 52
Maybury, A. 1998 (Leeds U, Hearts, Leicester C) 10
Meagan, M. K. 1961 (Everton, Huddersfield T, Drogheda) 17
Meehan, P. 1934 (Drumcondra) 1
Miller, L. W. P. 2004 (Celtic, Manchester U, Sunderland, Hibernian) 21
Milligan, M. J. 1992 (Oldham Ath) 1
Monahan, P. 1935 (Sligo R) 2
Mooney, J. 1965 (Shamrock R) 2
Moore, A. 1996 (Middlesbrough) 8
Moore, P. 1931 (Shamrock R, Aberdeen, Shamrock R) 9
Moran, K. 1980 (Manchester U, Sporting Gijon, Blackburn R) 71
Moroney, T. 1948 (West Ham U, Evergreen U) 12
Morris, C. B. 1988 (Celtic, Middlesbrough) 35
Morrison, C. H. 2002 (Crystal Palace, Birmingham C, Crystal Palace) 36
Moulson, C. 1936 (Lincoln C, Notts Co) 5
Moulson, G. B. 1948 (Lincoln C) 3
Muckian, C. 1978 (Drogheda U) 1
Muldoon, T. 1927 (Aston Villa) 1
Mulligan, P. M. 1969 (Shamrock R, Chelsea, Crystal Palace, WBA, Shamrock R) 50
Munroe, L. 1954 (Shamrock R) 1
Murphy, A. 1956 (Clyde) 1
Murphy, B. 1986 (Bohemians) 1
Murphy, D. 2007 (Sunderland) 9
Murphy, J. 1980 (Crystal Palace) 3
Murphy, J. 2004 (WBA, Scunthorpe U) 2
Murphy, P. M. 2007 (Carlisle U) 1
Murray, T. 1950 (Dundalk) 1

Newman, W. 1969 (Shelbourne) 1
Nolan. E. W. 2009 (Preston NE) 3
Nolan, R. 1957 (Shamrock R) 10

O'Brien, A. 2007 (Newcastle U) 5
O'Brien, A. J. 2001 (Newcastle U, Portsmouth) 26
O'Brien, F. 1980 (Philadelphia F) 3
O'Brien J. M. 2006 (Bolton W) 3
O'Brien, L. 1986 (Shamrock R, Manchester U, Newcastle U, Tranmere R) 16
O'Brien, M. T. 1927 (Derby Co, Walsall, Norwich C, Watford) 4
O'Brien, R. 1976 (Notts Co) 5
O'Byrne, L. B. 1949 (Shamrock R) 1
O'Callaghan, B. R. 1979 (Stoke C) 6
O'Callaghan, K. 1981 (Ipswich T, Portsmouth) 21
O'Cearuill, J. 2007 (Arsenal) 2
O'Connell, A. 1967 (Dundalk, Bohemians) 2
O'Connor, T. 1950 (Shamrock R) 4
O'Connor, T. 1968 (Fulham, Dundalk, Bohemians) 7
O'Dea, D. 2010 (Celtic) 14
O'Driscoll, J. F. 1949 (Swansea T) 3
O'Driscoll, S. 1982 (Fulham) 3
O'Farrell, F. 1952 (West Ham U, Preston NE) 9
O'Flanagan, K. P. 1938 (Bohemians, Arsenal) 10
O'Flanagan, M. 1947 (Bohemians) 1
O'Halloran, S. E. 2007 (Aston Villa) 2
O'Hanlon, K. G. 1988 (Rotherham U) 1
O'Kane, P. 1935 (Bohemians) 3
O'Keefe, E. 1981 (Everton, Port Vale) 5
O'Keefe, T. 1934 (Cork, Waterford) 3
O'Leary, D. 1977 (Arsenal) 68
O'Leary, P. 1980 (Shamrock R) 7
O'Mahoney, M. T. 1938 (Bristol R) 6
O'Neill, F. S. 1962 (Shamrock R) 20
O'Neill, J. 1952 (Everton) 17
O'Neill, J. 1961 (Preston NE) 1
O'Neill, K. P. 1996 (Norwich C, Middlesbrough) 13
O'Neill, W. 1936 (Dundalk) 11
O'Regan, K. 1984 (Brighton & HA) 4
O'Reilly, J. 1932 (Brideville, Aberdeen, Brideville, St James' Gate) 20
O'Reilly, J. 1946 (Cork U) 2
O'Shea, J. F. 2002 (Manchester U, Sunderland) 79

Peyton, G. 1977 (Fulham, Bournemouth, Everton) 33
Peyton, N. 1957 (Shamrock R, Leeds U) 6
Phelan, T. 1992 (Wimbledon, Manchester C, Chelsea, Everton, Fulham) 42
Potter, D. M. 2007 (Wolverhampton W) 5

Quinn, A. 2003 (Sheffield W, Sheffield U) 8
Quinn, B. S. 2000 (Coventry C) 4
Quinn, N. J. 1986 (Arsenal, Manchester C, Sunderland) 91

Reid, A. M. 2004 (Nottingham F, Tottenham H, Charlton Ath, Sunderland) 27
Reid, C. 1931 (Brideville) 1
Reid, S. J. 2002 (Millwall, Blackburn R) 23
Richardson, D. J. 1972 (Shamrock R, Gillingham) 3
Rigby, A. 1935 (St James' Gate) 3
Ringstead, A. 1951 (Sheffield U) 20
Robinson, J. 1928 (Bohemians, Dolphin) 2
Robinson, M. 1981 (Brighton & HA, Liverpool, QPR) 24
Roche, P. J. 1972 (Shelbourne, Manchester U) 8
Rogers, E. 1968 (Blackburn R, Charlton Ath) 19
Rowlands, M. C. 2004 (QPR) 5
Ryan, G. 1978 (Derby Co, Brighton & HA) 18
Ryan, R. A. 1950 (WBA, Derby Co) 16

Sadlier, R. T. 2002 (Millwall) 1
Savage, D. P. T. 1996 (Millwall) 5
Saward, P. 1954 (Millwall, Aston Villa, Huddersfield T) 18
Scannell, T. 1954 (Southend U) 1
Scully, P. J. 1989 (Arsenal) 1
Sheedy, K. 1984 (Everton, Newcastle U) 46
Sheridan, C. 2010 (Celtic, CSKA Sofia) 3
Sheridan, J. J. 1988 (Leeds U, Sheffield W) 34
Slaven, B. 1990 (Middlesbrough) 7
Sloan, J. W. 1946 (Arsenal) 2
Smyth, M. 1969 (Shamrock R) 1
Squires, J. 1934 (Shelbourne) 1
Stapleton, F. 1977 (Arsenal, Manchester U, Ajax, Le Havre, Blackburn R) 71
Staunton, S. 1989 (Liverpool, Aston Villa, Liverpool, Aston Villa) 102
St Ledger-Hall, S. P. 2009 (Preston NE, Leicester C) 30
Stevenson, A. E. 1932 (Dolphin, Everton) 7
Stokes, A. 2007 (Sunderland, Celtic) 4
Strahan, F. 1964 (Shelbourne) 5
Sullivan, J. 1928 (Fordsons) 1
Swan, M. M. G. 1960 (Drumcondra) 1
Synnott, N. 1978 (Shamrock R) 3

Taylor, T. 1959 (Waterford) 1
Thomas, P. 1974 (Waterford) 2
Thompson, J. 2004 (Nottingham F) 1
Townsend, A. D. 1989 (Norwich C, Chelsea, Aston Villa, Middlesbrough) 70
Traynor, T. J. 1954 (Southampton) 8
Treacy, K. 2011 (Preston NE, Burnley) 6
Treacy, R. C. P. 1966 (WBA, Charlton Ath, Swindon T, Preston NE, WBA, Shamrock R) 42
Tuohy, L. 1956 (Shamrock R, Newcastle U, Shamrock R) 8
Turner, C. J. 1936 (Southend U, West Ham U) 10
Turner, P. 1963 (Celtic) 2

Vernon, J. 1946 (Belfast Celtic) 2

Waddock, G. 1980 (QPR, Millwall) 21
Walsh, D. J. 1946 (Linfield, WBA, Aston Villa) 20
Walsh, J. 1982 (Limerick) 1
Walsh, M. 1976 (Blackpool, Everton, QPR, Porto) 21
Walsh, M. 1982 (Everton) 4
Walsh, W. 1947 (Manchester C) 9
Walters, J. R. 2011 (Stoke C) 10
Ward, S. R. 2011 (Wolverhampton W) 15
Waters, J. 1977 (Grimsby T) 2
Watters, F. 1926 (Shelbourne) 1
Weir, E. 1939 (Clyde) 3
Westwood, K. 2009 (Coventry C, Sunderland) 10
Whelan, G. D. 2008 (Stoke C) 42
Whelan, R. 1964 (St Patrick's Ath) 2
Whelan, R. 1981 (Liverpool, Southend U) 53
Whelan, W. 1956 (Manchester U) 4
White, J. J. 1928 (Bohemians) 1
Whittaker, R. 1959 (Chelsea) 1
Williams, J. 1938 (Shamrock R) 1
Wilson, M. D. 2011 (Stoke C) 1

BRITISH AND IRISH INTERNATIONAL GOALSCORERS SINCE 1872

Where two players with the same surname and initials have appeared for the same country, and one or both have scored, they have been distinguished by reference to the club which appears *first* against their name in the international appearances section.
Bold type indicates players who have scored international goals in season 2011–12.

ENGLAND

Player	Goals
A'Court, A.	1
Adams, T. A.	5
Adcock, H.	1
Alcock, C. W.	1
Allen, A.	3
Allen, R.	2
Amos, A.	1
Anderson, V.	2
Anderton, D. R.	7
Astall, G.	1
Athersmith, W. C.	3
Atyeo, P. J. W.	5
Bache, J. W.	4
Bailey, N. C.	2
Baily, E. F.	5
Baker, J. H.	3
Ball, A. J.	8
Bambridge, A. L.	1
Bambridge, E. C.	11
Barclay, R.	2
Barmby, N. J.	4
Barnes, J.	11
Barnes, P. S.	4
Barry, G.	**3**
Barton, J.	1
Bassett, W. I.	8
Bastin, C. S.	12
Beardsley, P. A.	9
Beasley, A.	1
Beattie, T. K.	1
Beckham, D. R. J.	17
Becton, F.	2
Bedford, H.	1
Bell, C.	9
Bent, D. A.	**4**
Bentley, R. T. F.	9
Bishop, S. M.	1
Blackburn, F.	1
Blissett, L.	3
Bloomer, S.	28
Bond, R.	2
Bonsor, A. G.	1
Bowden, E. R.	1
Bowers, J. W.	2
Bowles, S.	1
Bradford, G. R. W.	1
Bradford, J.	7
Bradley, W.	2
Bradshaw, F.	3
Brann, G.	1
Bridge, W. M.	1
Bridges, B. J.	1
Bridgett, A.	3
Brindle, T.	1
Britton, C. S.	1
Broadbent, P. F.	2
Broadis, I. A.	8
Brodie, J. B.	1
Bromley-Davenport, W.	2
Brook, E. F.	10
Brooking, T. D.	5
Brooks, J.	2
Broome, F. H.	3
Brown, A.	4
Brown, A. S.	1
Brown, G.	5
Brown, J.	3
Brown, W.	1
Brown, W. M.	1
Buchan, C. M.	4
Bull, S. G.	4
Bullock, N.	2
Burgess, H.	4
Butcher, T.	3
Byrne, J. J.	8
Cahill, G.	**2**
Campbell, S. J.	1
Camsell, G. H.	18
Carroll, A. T.	**2**
Carter, H. S.	7
Carter, J. H.	4
Chadwick, E.	3
Chamberlain, M.	1
Chambers, H.	5
Channon, M. R.	21
Charlton, J.	6
Charlton, R.	49
Chenery, C. J.	1
Chivers, M.	13
Clarke, A. J.	10
Cobbold, W. N.	6
Cock, J. G.	2
Cole, A.	1
Cole, J. J.	10
Common, A.	2
Connelly, J. M.	7
Coppell, S. J.	7
Cotterill, G. H.	2
Cowans, G.	2
Crawford, R.	1
Crawshaw, T. H.	1
Crayston, W. J.	1
Creek, F. N. S.	1
Crooks, S. D.	7
Crouch, P. J.	22
Currey, E. S.	2
Currie, A. W.	3
Cursham, A. W.	2
Cursham, H. A.	5
Daft, H. B.	3
Davenport, J. K.	2
Davis, G.	1
Davis, H.	1
Day, S. H.	2
Dean, W. R.	18
Defoe, J. C.	15
Devey, J. H. G.	1
Dewhurst, F.	11
Dix, W. R.	1
Dixon, K. M.	4
Dixon, L. M.	1
Dorrell, A. R.	1
Douglas, B.	11
Drake, E. J.	6
Ducat, A.	1
Dunn, A. T. B.	2
Eastham, G.	2
Edwards, D.	5
Ehiogu, U.	1
Elliott, W. H.	3
Evans, R. E.	1
Ferdinand, L.	5
Ferdinand, R. G.	3
Finney, T.	30
Fleming, H. J.	9
Flowers, R.	10
Forman, Frank	1
Forman, Fred	3
Foster, R. E.	3
Fowler, R. B.	7
Francis, G. C. J.	3
Francis, T.	12
Freeman, B. C.	3
Froggatt, J.	2
Froggatt, R.	2
Galley, T.	1
Gascoigne, P. J.	10
Geary, F.	3
Gerrard, S. G.	19
Gibbins, W. V. T.	3
Gilliatt, W. E.	3
Goddard, P.	1
Goodall, J.	12
Goodyer, A. C.	1
Gosling, R. C.	2
Goulden, L. A.	4
Grainger, C.	3
Greaves, J.	44
Grovesnor, A. T.	2
Gunn, W.	1
Haines, J. T. W.	2
Hall, G. W.	9
Halse, H. J.	2
Hampson, J.	5
Hampton, H.	2
Hancocks, J.	2
Hardman, H. P.	1
Harris, S. S.	2
Hassall, H. W.	4
Hateley, M.	9
Haynes, J. N.	18
Hegan, K. E.	4
Henfrey, A. G.	2
Heskey, E. W.	7
Hilsdon, G. R.	14
Hine, E. W.	4
Hinton, A. T.	1
Hirst, D. E.	1
Hitchens, G. A.	5
Hobbis, H. H. F.	1
Hoddle, G.	8
Hodgetts, D.	1
Hodgson, G.	1
Holley, G. H.	8
Houghton, W. E.	5
Howell, R.	1
Hughes, E. W.	1
Hulme, J. H. A.	4
Hunt, G. S.	1
Hunt, R.	18
Hunter, N.	2
Hurst, G. C.	24
Ince, P. E. C.	2
Jack, D. N. B.	3
Jeffers, F.	1
Jenas, J. A.	1
Johnson, A.	2
Johnson, D. E.	6
Johnson, E.	2
Johnson, G. M. C.	1
Johnson, J. A.	2
Johnson, T. C. F.	5
Johnson, W. H.	1
Kail, E. I. L.	2
Kay, A. H.	1
Keegan, J. K.	21
Kelly, R.	8
Kennedy, R.	3
Kenyon-Slaney, W. S.	2
Keown, M. R.	2
Kevan, D. T.	8
Kidd, B.	1
King, L. B.	2
Kingsford, R. K.	1
Kirchen, A. J.	2
Kirton, W. J.	1
Lampard, F. J.	**23**
Langton, R.	1
Latchford, R. D.	5
Latheron, E. G.	1
Lawler, C.	1
Lawton, T.	22
Lee, F.	10
Lee, J.	1
Lee, R. M.	2
Lee, S.	2
Lescott, J.	**1**
Le Saux, G. P.	1
Lindley, T.	14
Lineker, G.	48
Lofthouse, J. M.	3
Lofthouse, N.	30
Hon. A. Lyttelton	1
Mabbutt, G.	1
Macdonald, M.	6
Mannion, W. J.	11
Mariner, P.	13
Marsh, R. W.	1
Matthews, S.	11
Matthews, V.	1
McCall, J.	1
McDermott, T.	3
McManaman, S.	3
Medley, L. D.	1
Melia, J.	1
Mercer, D. W.	1
Merson, P. C.	3
Milburn, J. E. T.	10
Miller, H. S.	1
Mills, G. R.	3
Milward, A.	3
Mitchell, C.	5
Moore, J.	1
Moore, R. F.	2
Moore, W. G. B.	2
Morren, T.	1
Morris, F.	1
Morris, J.	3
Mortensen, S. H.	23
Morton, J. R.	1
Mosforth, W.	3
Mullen, J.	6
Mullery, A. P.	1
Murphy, D. B	1
Neal, P. G.	5
Needham, E.	3
Nicholls, J.	1
Nicholson, W. E.	1
Nugent, D. J.	1
O'Grady, M.	3

Osborne, F. R. 3
Owen, M. J. 40
Own goals 31

Page, L. A. 1
Paine, T. L. 7
Palmer, C. L. 1
Parry, E. H. 1
Parry, R. A. 1
Pawson, F. W. 1
Payne, J. 2
Peacock, A. 3
Pearce, S. 5
Pearson, J. S. 5
Pearson, S. C. 5
Perry, W. 2
Peters, M. 20
Pickering, F. 5
Platt, D. 27
Pointer, R. 2

Quantrill, A. 1

Ramsay, A. E. 3
Revie, D. G. 4
Redknapp, J. F. 1
Reynolds, J. 3
Richards, M. 1
Richardson, K. E. 2
Richardson, J. R. 2
Rigby, A. 3
Rimmer, E. J. 2
Roberts, F. 2
Roberts, H. 1
Roberts, W. T. 2
Robinson, J. 3
Robson, B. 26
Robson, R. 4
Rooney, W. 29
Rowley, J. F. 6
Royle, J. 2
Rutherford, J. 3

Sagar, C. 1
Sandilands, R. R. 3
Sansom, K. 1
Schofield, J. 1
Scholes, P. 14
Seed, J. M. 1
Settle, J. 6
Sewell, J. 3
Shackleton, L. F. 1
Sharp, J. 1
Shearer, A. 30
Shelton, A. 1
Shepherd, A. 2
Sheringham, E. P. 11
Simpson, J. 1
Smith, A. 1
Smith, A. M. 2
Smith, G. O. 11
Smith, Joe 1
Smith, J. R. 2
Smith, J. W. 4
Smith, R. 13
Smith, S. 1
Sorby, T. H. 1
Southgate, G. 2
Southworth, J. 3
Sparks, F. J. 3
Spence, J. W. 1
Spiksley, F. 5
Spilsbury, B. W. 5
Steele, F. C. 8
Stephenson, G. T. 2
Steven, T. M. 4
Stewart, J. 2
Stiles, N. P. 1
Storer, H. 1
Stone, S. B. 2
Summerbee, M. G. 1

Tambling, R. V. 1
Taylor, P. J. 2
Taylor, T. 16
Terry, J. G. 6
Thompson, P. B. 1
Thornewell, G. 1
Tilson, S. F. 6
Townley, W. J. 2
Tueart, D. 2

Upson, M. J. 2

Vassell, D. 6
Vaughton, O. H. 6
Veitch, J. G. 3
Viollet, D. S. 1

Waddle, C. R. 6
Walcott, T. J. 4
Walker, W. H. 9
Wall, G. 2
Wallace, D. 1
Walsh, P. 1
Waring, T. 4
Warren, B. 2
Watson, D. V. 4
Watson, V. M. 4
Webb, G. W. 1
Webb, N. 4
Wedlock, W. J. 2
Welbeck, D. 2
Weller, K. 1
Welsh, D. 1
Whateley, O. 2
Wheldon, G. F. 6
Whitfield, H. 1
Wignall, F. 2
Wilkes, A. 1
Wilkins, R. G. 3
Willingham, C. K. 1
Wilshaw, D. J. 10
Wilson, G. P. 1
Winckworth, W. N. 1
Windridge, J. E. 7
Wise, D. F. 1
Withe, P. 1
Wollaston, C. H. R. 1
Wood, H. 1
Woodcock, T. 16
Woodhall, G. 1
Woodward, V. J. 29
Worrall, F. 2
Worthington, F. S. 2
Wright, I. E. 9
Wright, M. 1
Wright, W. A. 3
Wright-Phillips, S. C. 6
Wylie, J. G. 1

Yates, J. 3
Young, A. S. 6

NORTHERN IRELAND

Anderson, T. 4
Armstrong, G. 12

Bambrick, J. 12
Barr, H. H. 1
Barron, H. 3
Best, G. 9
Bingham, W. L. 10
Black, K. 1
Blanchflower, D. 2
Blanchflower, J. 1
Brennan, B. 1
Brennan, R. A. 1
Brotherston, N. 3
Brown, J. 1
Browne, F. 2
Brunt, C. 1

Campbell, J. 1
Campbell, W. G. 1
Casey, T. 2
Caskey, W. 1
Cassidy, T. 1
Chambers, J. 3
Clarke, C. J. 13
Clements, D. 2
Cochrane, T. 1
Condy, J. 1
Connor, M. J. 1
Coulter, J. 1
Croft, T. 1
Crone, W. 1
Crossan, E. 1
Crossan, J. A. 10
Curran, S. 2
Cush, W. W. 5

Dalton, W. 4
D'Arcy, S. D. 1
Darling, J. 1
Davey, H. H. 1
Davis S. 4
Davis, T. L. 1
Dill, A. H. 1
Doherty, L. 1
Doherty, P. D. 3
Dougan, A. D. 8
Dowie, I. 12
Dunne, J. 4

Elder, A. R. 1
Elliott, S. 4
Emerson, W. 1
English, S. 1
Evans, C. 1
Evans, J. G. 1

Feeney, W. 1
Feeney, W. J. 5
Ferguson, W. 1
Ferris, J. 1
Ferris, R. O. 1
Finney, T. 2

Gaffkin, J. 4
Gara, A. 3
Gaukrodger, G. 1
Gibb, J. T. 2
Gibb, T. J. 1
Gibson, W. 1
Gillespie, K. R. 2
Gillespie, W. 13
Goodall, A. L. 2
Griffin, D. J. 1
Gray, P. 6

Halligan, W. 1
Hamill, M. 1
Hamilton, B. 4
Hamilton, W. R. 5
Hannon, D. J. 1
Harkin, J. T. 2
Harvey, M. 3
Healy, D. J. 35
Hill, C. F. 1
Hughes, A. 1
Hughes, M. E. 5
Humphries, W. 1
Hunter, A. *(Distillery)* 1
Hunter, A. *(Blackburn R)* 1
Hunter, B. V. 1

Irvine, R. W. 3
Irvine, W. J. 8

Johnston, H. 2
Johnston, S. 2
Johnston, W. C. 1
Jones, S. *(Distillery)* 1
Jones, S. *(Crewe Alex)* 1
Jones, J. 1

Kelly, J. 4
Kernaghan, N. 2
Kirwan, J. 2

Lacey, W. 3
Lafferty, K. 8
Lemon, J. 2
Lennon, N. F. 2
Lockhart, N. 3
Lomas, S. M. 3

Magilton, J. 5
Mahood, J. 2
Martin, D. K. 3
Maxwell, J. 2
McAdams, W. J. 7
McAllen, J. 1
McAuley, G. 2
Mcauley, J. L. 1
McCann, G. S. 4
McCartney, G. 1
McCandless, J. 2
McCandless, W. 1
McCaw, J. H. 1
McClelland, J. 1
McCluggage, A. 2
McCourt, P. 2
McCracken, W. 1
McCrory, S. 1
McCurdy, C. 1
McDonald, A. 3
McGarry, J. K. 1
McGrath, R. C. 4
McIlroy, J. 10
McIlroy, S. B. 5
McKenzie, H 1
McKnight, J. 2
McLaughlin, J. C. 6
McMahon, G. J. 2
McMordie, A. S. 3
McMorran, E. J. 4
McParland, P. J. 10
McWha, W. B. R. 1
Meldon, P. A 1
Mercer, J. T. 1
Millar, W. 1
Milligan, D. 1
Milne, R. G. 2
Molyneux, T. B. 1
Moreland, V. 1
Morgan, S. 3
Morrow, S. J. 1
Morrow, W. J. 1
Mulryne, P. P. 3
Murdock, C. J. 1
Murphy, N. 1

Neill, W. J. T. 2
Nelson, S. 1
Nicholl, C. J. 3
Nicholl, J. M. 1
Nicholson, J. J. 6

O'Boyle, G. 1
O'Hagan, C. 2
O'Kane, W. J. 1
O'Neill, J. 2
O'Neill, M. A. 4
O'Neill, M. H. 8
Own goals 10

Patterson, D. J. 1
Patterson, R. 1
Peacock, R. 2
Peden, J. 7
Penney, S. 2
Pyper, James 2
Pyper, John 1

Quinn, J. M. 12
Quinn, S. J. 4

Reynolds, J. 1
Rowland, K. 1
Rowley, R. W. M. 2
Rushe, F. 1
Sheridan, J. 2
Sherrard, J. 1
Sherrard, W. C. 2

Simpson, W. J. 5
Sloan, H. A. de B. 4
Smyth, S. 5
Spence, D. W. 3
Sproule, I. 1
Stanfield, O. M. 11
Stevenson, A. E. 5
Stewart, I. 2

Taggart, G. P. 7
Thompson, F. W. 2
Torrans, S. 1
Tully, C. P. 3
Turner, A. 1

Walker, J. 1
Walsh, D. J. 5
Welsh, E. 1
Whiteside, N. 9
Whiteside, T. 1
Whitley, Jeff 2
Williams, J. R. 1
Williams, M. S. 1
Williamson, J. 1
Wilson, D. J. 1
Wilson, K. J. 6
Wilson, S. J. 7
Wilton, J. M. 2

Young, S. 1
N.B. In 1914 Young goal should be credited to Gillespie W v Wales

SCOTLAND
Aitken, R. *(Celtic)* 1
Aitken, R. *(Dumbarton)* 1
Aitkenhead, W. A. C. 2
Alexander, D. 1
Allan, D. S. 4
Allan, J. 2
Anderson, F. 1
Anderson, W. 4
Andrews, P. 1
Archibald, A. 1
Archibald, S. 4

Baird, D. 2
Baird, J. C. 2
Baird, S. 2
Bannon, E. 1
Barbour, A. 1
Barker, J. B. 4
Battles, B. Jr 1
Bauld, W. 2
Baxter, J. C. 3
Beattie, C. 1
Bell, J. 5
Bennett, A. 2
Berra, C. 2
Berry, D. 1
Bett, J. 1
Beveridge, W. W. 1
Black, A. 3
Black, D. 1
Bone, J. 1
Booth, S. 6
Boyd, K 7
Boyd, R. 2
Boyd, T. 1
Boyd, W. G. 1
Brackenridge, T. 1
Brand, R. 8
Brazil, A. 1
Bremner, W. J. 3
Broadfoot, K. 1
Brown, A. D. 6
Brown, S. 2
Buchanan, P. S. 1
Buchanan, R. 1
Buckley, P. 1
Buick, A. 2

Burke, C. 2
Burley, C. W. 3
Burns, K. 1

Cairns, T. 1
Caldwell, G. 2
Calderwood, C. 1
Calderwood, R. 2
Caldow, E. 4
Cameron, C. 2
Campbell, C. 1
Campbell, John *(Celtic)* 5
Campbell, John *(Rangers)* 4
Campbell, J. *(South Western)* 1
Campbell, P. 2
Campbell, R. 1
Cassidy, J. 1
Chalmers, S. 3
Chambers, T. 1
Cheyne, A. G. 4
Christie, A. J. 1
Clarkson, D. 1
Clunas, W. L. 1
Collins, J. 12
Collins, R. Y. 10
Combe, J. R. 1
Commons, K. 2
Conn, A. 1
Cooper, D. 6
Craig, J. 1
Craig, T. 1
Crawford, S. 4
Cunningham, A. N. 5
Curran, H. P. 1

Dailly, C. 6
Dalglish, K. 30
Davidson, D. 1
Davidson, J. A. 1
Delaney, J. 3
Devine, A. 1
Dewar, G. 1
Dewar, N. 4
Dickov, P. 1
Dickson, W. 4
Divers, J. 1
Dobie, R. S. 1
Docherty, T. H. 1
Dodds, D. 1
Dodds, W. 7
Donaldson, A. 1
Donnachie, J. 1
Dougall, J. 1
Drummond, J. 2
Dunbar, M. 1
Duncan, D. 7
Duncan, D. M. 1
Duncan, J. 1
Dunn, J. 2
Durie, G. S. 7

Easson, J. F. 1
Elliott, M. S. 1
Ellis, J. 1

Ferguson, B. 3
Ferguson, J. 6
Fernie, W. 1
Fitchie, T. T. 1
Flavell, R. 2
Fleming, C. 2
Fleming, J. W. 3
Fletcher, D. 5
Fletcher, S. 1
Fraser, M. J. E. 3
Freedman, D. A. 1

Gallacher, H. K. 23
Gallacher, K. W. 9
Gallacher, P. 1
Galt, J. H. 1
Gemmell, T. *(St Mirren)* 1
Gemmell, T. *(Celtic)* 1
Gemmill, A. 8
Gemmill, S. 1
Gibb, W. 1
Gibson, D. W. 3
Gibson, J. D. 1
Gibson, N. 1
Gillespie, Jas. 3
Gillick, T. 3
Gilzean, A. J. 12
Goodwillie, D. 1
Gossland, J. 2
Goudie, J. 1
Gough, C. R. 6
Gourlay, J. 1
Graham, A. 2
Graham, G. 3
Gray, A. 7
Gray, E. 3
Gray, F. 1
Greig, J. 3
Groves, W. 4

Hamilton, G. 4
Hamilton, J. *(Queen's Park)* 3
Hamilton, R. C. 15
Harper, J. M. 2
Hartley, P. J. 1
Harrower, W. 5
Hartford, R. A. 4
Heggie, C. W 4
Henderson, J. G. 1
Henderson, W. 5
Hendry, E. C. J. 3
Herd, D. G. 3
Herd, G. 1
Hewie, J. D. 2
Higgins, A. *(Newcastle U)* 1
Higgins, A. *(Kilmarnock)* 4
Highet, T. C. 1
Holt, G.J. 1
Holton, J. A. 2
Hopkin, D. 2
Houliston, W. 2
Howie, H. 1
Howie, J. 2
Hughes, J. 1
Hunter, W. 1
Hutchison, D. 6
Hutchison, T. 1
Hutton, J. 1
Hyslop, T. 1

Imrie, W. N. 1

Jackson, A. 8
Jackson, C. 1
Jackson, D. 4
James, A. W. 4
Jardine, A. 1
Jenkinson, T. 1
Jess, E. 2
Johnston, A. 2
Johnston, L. H. 1
Johnston, M. 14
Johnstone, D. 2
Johnstone, J. 4
Johnstone, Jas. 1
Johnstone, R. 10
Johnstone, W. 1
Jordan, J. 11
Kay, J. L. 5
Keillor, A. 3
Kelly, J. 1
Kelso, R. 1
Ker, G. 10
King, A. 1

King, J. 1
Kinnear, D. 1
Kyle, K. 1

Lambert, P. 1
Lambie, J. 1
Lambie, W. A. 5
Lang, J. J. 2
Latta, A. 2
Law, D. 30
Leggat, G. 8
Lennie, W. 1
Lennox, R. 3
Liddell, W. 6
Lindsay, J. 6
Linwood, A. B. 1
Logan, J. 1
Lorimer, P. 4
Love, A. 1
Low, J. *(Cambuslang)* 1
Lowe, J. *(St Bernards)* 1

Macari, L. 5
MacDougall, E. J. 3
MacFarlane, A. 1
MacLeod, M. 1
Mackay, D. C. 4
Mackay, G. 1
MacKenzie, J. A. 1
Mackail-Smith, C. 1
Mackie, J. C. 2
MacKinnon, W. W. 5
Madden, J. 5
Maloney, S. 1
Marshall, H. 1
Marshall, J. 1
Mason, J. 4
Massie, A. 1
Masson, D. S. 5
McAdam, J. 1
McAllister, G. 5
McArthur, J. 1
McAulay, J. D. 1
McAvennie, F. 1
McCall, J. 1
McCall, S. M. 1
McCalliog, J. 1
McCallum, N. 1
McCann, N. 3
McClair, B. J. 2
McCoist, A. 19
McColl, R. S. 13
McCormack, R. 1
McCulloch, D. 3
McCulloch, L. 1
McDougall, J. 4
McFadden, J. 15*
McFadyen, W. 2
McGhee, M. 2
McGinlay, J. 4
McGregor, J. 1
McGrory, J. 6
McGuire, W. 1
McInally, A. 3
McInnes, T. 2
McKie, J. 2
McKimmie, S. 1
McKinlay, W. 4
McKinnon, A. 1
McKinnon, R. 1
McLaren, A. 4
McLaren, J. 1
McLean, A. 1
McLean, T. 1
McLintock, F. 1
McMahon, A. 6
McManus, S. 2
McMenemy, J. 5
McMillan, I. L. 2
McNeill, W. 3
McNiel, H. 5
McPhail, J. 3

** The Scottish FA officially changed Robsons's goal against Iceland on 10 September 2008 to McFadden.*

McPhail, R. 7
McPherson, J. *(Kilmarnock)* 7
McPherson, J. *(Vale of Leven)* 1
McPherson, R. 1
McQueen, G. 5
McStay, P. 9
McSwegan, G. 1
Meiklejohn, D. D. 3
Millar, J. 2
Miller, K. 16
Miller, T. 2
Miller, W. 1
Mitchell, R. C. 1
Morgan, W. 1
Morris, D. 1
Morris, H. 3
Morrison, J. C. 1
Morton, A. L. 5
Mudie, J. K. 9
Mulhall, G. 1
Munro, A. D. 1
Munro, N. 2
Murdoch, R. 5
Murphy, F. 1
Murray, J. 1

Napier, C. E. 3
Narey, D. 1
Naismith, S. 2
Naysmith, G. A. 1
Neil, R. G. 2
Nevin, P. K. F. 5
Nicholas, C. 5
Nisbet, J. 2

O'Connor, G. 4
O'Donnell, F. 2
O'Hare, J. 5
Ormond, W. E. 2
O'Rourke, F. 1
Orr, R. 1
Orr, T. 1
Oswald, J. 1
Own goals 19

Parlane, D. 1
Paul, H. McD. 2
Paul, W. 5
Pettigrew, W. 2
Provan, D. 1

Quashie, N. F. 1
Quinn, J. 7
Quinn, P. 1

Rankin, G. 2
Rankin, R. 2
Reid, W. 4
Reilly, L. 22
Renny-Tailyour, H. W. 1
Richmond, J. T. 1
Ring, T. 2
Rioch, B. D. 6
Ritchie, J. 1
Ritchie, P. S. 1
Robertson, A. 2
Robertson, J. 3
Robertson, J. N. 8
Robertson, J. T. 2
Robertson, T. 1
Robertson, W. 1
Russell, D. 1

Scott, A. S. 5
Sellar, W. 4
Sharp, G. 1
Shaw, F. W. 1
Shearer, D. 2
Simpson, J. 1
Smith, A. 5
Smith, G. 4
Smith, J. 1
Smith, John 13
Snodgrass, R. 1
Somerville, G. 1
Souness, G. J. 4
Speedie, F. 2
St John, I. 9
Steel, W. 12
Stein, C. 10
Stevenson, G. 4
Stewart, A. 1
Stewart, R. 1
Stewart, W. E. 1
Strachan, G. 5
Sturrock, P. 3

Taylor, J. D. 1
Templeton, R. 1
Thompson, S. 3
Thomson, A. 1
Thomson, C. 4
Thomson, R. 1
Thomson, W. 1
Thornton, W. 1

Waddell, T. S. 1
Waddell, W. 6
Walker, J. 2
Walker, R. 7
Walker, T. 9
Wallace, I. A. 1
Wark, J. 7
Watson, J. A. K. 1
Watt, F. 2
Watt, W. W. 1
Webster, A. 1
Weir, A. 1
Weir, D. 1
Weir, J. B. 2
White, J. A. 3
Wilkie, L. 1
Wilson, A. *(Sheffield W)* 2
Wilson, A. N. *(Dunfermline Ath)* 13
Wilson, D. *(Liverpool)* 1
Wilson, D. *(Queen's Park)* 2
Wilson, D. *(Rangers)* 9
Wilson, H. 1
Wylie, T. G. 1

Young, A. 5

WALES

Allchurch, I. J. 23
Allen, M. 3
Astley, D. J. 12
Atherton, R. W. 2

Bale, G. 6
Bamford, T. 1
Barnes, W. 1
Bellamy, C. D. 19
Blackmore, C. G. 1
Blake, D. 1
Blake, N. A. 4
Bodin, P. J. 3
Boulter, L. M. 1
Bowdler, J. C. H. 3
Bowen, D. L. 1
Bowen, M. 3
Boyle, T. 1
Bryan, T. 1
Burgess, W. A. R. 1
Burke, T. 1
Butler, W. T. 1

Chapman, T. 2
Charles, J. 1
Charles, M. 6
Charles, W. J. 15
Church, S. R. 1
Clarke, R. J. 5
Coleman, C. 4
Collier, D. J. 1
Collins, J. 2
Cotterill, D. 1
Crosse, K. 1
Cumner, R. H. 1
Curtis, A. 6
Curtis, E. R. 3

Davies, D. W. 1
Davies, E. Lloyd 1
Davies, G. 2
Davies, L. S. 6
Davies, R. T. 9
Davies, R. W. 6
Davies, Simon 6
Davies, Stanley 5
Davies, W. 6
Davies, W. H. 1
Davies, William 5
Davis, W. O. 1
Deacy, N. 4
Doughty, J. 6
Doughty, R. 2
Durban, A. 2
Dwyer, P. 2

Earnshaw, R. 16
Eastwood, F. 4
Edwards, D. 3
Edwards, G. 2
Edwards, R. I. 4
England, H. M. 4
Evans, C. 2
Evans, I. 1
Evans, J. 1
Evans, R. E. 2
Evans, W. 1
Eyton-Jones, J. A. 1

Fletcher, C. 1
Flynn, B. 7
Ford, T. 23
Foulkes, W. I. 1
Fowler, J. 3

Giles, D. 2
Giggs, R. J. 12
Glover, E. M. 7
Godfrey, B. C. 2
Green, A. W. 3
Griffiths, A. T. 6
Griffiths, M. W. 2
Griffiths, T. P. 3

Harris, C. S. 1
Hartson, J. 14
Hersee, R. 1
Hewitt, R. 1
Hockey, T. 1
Hodges, G. 2
Hole, W. J. 1
Hopkins, I. J. 2
Horne, B. 2
Howell, E. G. 3
Hughes, L. M. 16

James, E. 2
James, L. 10
James, R. 7
Jarrett, R. H. 3
Jenkyns, C. A. 1
Jones, A. 1
Jones, Bryn 6
Jones, B. S. 2
Jones, Cliff 16
Jones, C. W. 1
Jones, D. E. 1
Jones, Evan 1
Jones, H. 1
Jones, I. 1
Jones, J. L. 1
Jones, J. O. 1
Jones, J. P. 1
Jones, Leslie J. 1
Jones, R. A. 2
Jones, W. L. 6

Keenor, F. C. 2
King, A. 1
Koumas, J. 10
Krzywicki, R. L. 1

Ledley, J. 3
Leek, K. 5
Lewis, B. 4
Lewis, D. M. 2
Lewis, W. 8
Lewis, W. L. 3
Llewelyn, C. M 1
Lovell, S. 1
Lowrie, G. 2

Mahoney, J. F. 1
Mays, A. W. 1
Medwin, T. C. 6
Melville, A. K 3
Meredith, W. H. 11
Mills, T. J. 1
Moore, G. 1
Morgan, J. R. 2
Morgan-Owen, H. 1
Morgan-Owen, M. M. 2
Morison, S. 1
Morris, A. G. 9
Morris, H. 2
Morris, R. 1
Morris, S. 2

Nicholas, P. 2

O'Callaghan, E. 3
O'Sullivan, P. A. 1
Owen, G. 2
Owen, W. 4
Owen, W. P. 6
Own goals 14

Palmer, D. 3
Parry, P. I. 1
Parry, T. D. 3
Paul, R. 1
Peake, E. 1
Pembridge, M. 6
Perry, E. 1
Phillips, C. 5
Phillips, D. 2
Powell, A. 1
Powell, D. 1
Price, J. 4
Price, P. 1
Pryce-Jones, W. E. 3
Pugh, D. H. 2

Ramsay, A. 5
Reece, G. I. 2
Rees, R. R. 3
Richards, R. W. 1
Roach, J. 2
Robbins, W. W. 4
Roberts, J. *(Corwen)* 1
Roberts, Jas. 1
Roberts, P. S. 1
Roberts, R. *(Druids)* 1
Roberts, W. *(Llangollen)* 2
Roberts, W. *(Wrexham)* 1
Roberts, W. H. 1
Robinson, C. P. 1
Robinson, J. R. C. 3
Rush, I. 28
Russell, M. R. 1

Sabine, H. W. 1
Saunders, D. 22
Savage, R. W. 2
Shaw, E. G. 2
Sisson, H. 4
Slatter, N. 2
Smallman, D. P. 1

Speed, G. A.	7
Symons, C. J.	2
Tapscott, D. R.	4
Taylor, G. K.	1
Thomas, M.	4
Thomas, T.	1
Toshack, J. B.	12
Trainer, H.	2
Vaughan, D. O.	1
Vaughan, John	2
Vernon, T. R.	8
Vizard, E. T.	1
Vokes, S. M.	**4**
Walsh, I.	7
Warren, F. W.	3
Watkins, W. M.	4
Wilding, J.	4
Williams, A.	2
Williams, D. R.	2
Williams, G. E.	1
Williams, G. G.	1
Williams, W.	1
Woosnam, A. P.	3
Wynn, G. A.	1
Yorath, T. C.	2
Young, E.	1

REPUBLIC OF IRELAND

Aldridge, J.	19
Ambrose, P.	1
Anderson, J.	1
Andrews, K.	**3**
Barrett, G.	2
Bermingham, P.	1
Bradshaw, P.	4
Brady, L.	9
Breen, G.	7
Brown, J.	1
Byrne, D.	1
Byrne, J.	4
Cantwell, J.	14
Carey, J.	3
Carroll, T.	1
Cascarino, A.	19
Coad, P.	3
Connolly, D. J.	9
Conroy, T.	2
Conway, J.	3
Cox, S. R.	**3**
Coyne, T.	6
Cummins, G.	5
Curtis, D.	8
Daly, G.	13
Davis, T.	4
Dempsey, J.	1
Dennehy, M.	2
Doherty, G. M. T.	4
Donnelly, J.	4
Donnelly, T.	1
Doyle, K. E.	**10**
Duff, D. A.	8
Duffy, B.	1
Duggan, H.	1
Dunne, J.	13
Dunne, L.	1
Dunne, R. P.	**8**
Eglington, T.	2
Elliott, S. W.	1
Ellis, P.	1
Fagan, F.	5
Fahey, K.	3
Fallon, S.	2
Fallon, W.	2
Farrell, P.	3
Finnan, S.	2
Fitzgerald, P.	2
Fitzgerald, J.	1
Fitzsimons, A.	7
Flood, J. J.	4
Fogarty, A.	3
Foley, D.	2
Fullam, J.	1
Fullam, R.	1
Galvin, A.	1
Gavin, J.	2
Geoghegan, M.	2
Gibson, D.	1
Giles, J.	5
Givens, D.	19
Glynn, D.	1
Grealish, T.	8
Green, P. J.	1
Grimes, A. A.	1
Hale, A.	2
Hand, E.	2
Harte, I. P.	11
Haverty, J.	3
Healy, C.	1
Holland, M. R.	5
Holmes, J.	1
Horlacher, A.	2
Houghton, R.	6
Hughton, C.	1
Hunt, S. P.	1
Hurley, C.	2
Ireland, S. J.	4
Irwin, D.	4
Jordan, D.	1
Kavanagh, G. A.	1
Keane, R. D.	**53**
Keane, R. M.	9
Kelly, D.	9
Kelly, G.	2
Kelly, J.	2
Kennedy, M.	4
Keogh, A.	1
Kernaghan, A. N.	1
Kilbane, K. D.	8
Kinsella, M. A.	3
Lacey, W.	1
Lawrence, L.	2
Lawrenson, M.	5
Leech, M.	2
Long, S. P.	**7**
McAteer, J. W.	3
McCann, J.	1
McCarthy, M.	2
McEvoy, A.	6
McGeady, A.	**2**
McGee, P.	4
McGrath, P.	8
McLoughlin, A. F.	2
McPhail, S. J. P.	1
Mancini, T.	1
Martin, C.	6
Martin, M.	4
Miller, L. W. P.	1
Mooney, J.	1
Moore, P.	7
Moran, K.	6
Morrison, C. H.	9
Moroney, T.	1
Mulligan, P.	1
O'Brien, A. J.	1
O'Callaghan, K.	1
O'Connor, T.	2
O'Farrell, F.	2
O'Flanagan, K.	3
O'Keefe, E.	1
O'Leary, D. A.	1
O'Neill, F.	1
O'Neill, K. P.	4
O'Reilly, J. *(Brideville)*	2
O'Reilly, J. *(Cork)*	1
O'Shea, J. F.	1
Own goals	**12**
Quinn, N.	21
Reid, A. M.	4
Reid, S. J.	2
Ringstead, A.	7
Robinson, M.	4
Rogers, E.	5
Ryan, G.	1
Ryan, R.	3
St Ledger-Hall, S.	**3**
Sheedy, K.	9
Sheridan, J.	5
Slaven, B.	1
Sloan, J.	1
Squires, J.	1
Stapleton, F.	20
Staunton, S.	7
Strahan, J.	1
Sullivan, J.	1
Townsend, A. D.	7
Treacy, R.	5
Touhy, L.	4
Waddock, G.	3
Walsh, D.	5
Walsh, M.	3
Walters, J.	**1**
Ward, S.	**2**
Waters, J.	1
White, J. J.	2
Whelan, G. D.	2
Whelan, R.	3

BRITISH & IRISH INTERNATIONAL MANAGERS

England
Walter Winterbottom 1946–1962 (after period as coach); Alf Ramsey 1963–1974; Joe Mercer (caretaker) 1974; Don Revie 1974–1977; Ron Greenwood 1977–1982; Bobby Robson 1982–1990; Graham Taylor 1990–1993; Terry Venables (coach) 1994–1996; Glenn Hoddle 1996–1999; Kevin Keegan 1999–2000; Sven-Goran Eriksson 2001–2006; Steve McClaren 2006–07; Fabio Capello 2008–2012; Roy Hodgson from May 2012.

Northern Ireland
Peter Doherty 1951–1952; Bertie Peacock 1962–1967; Billy Bingham 1967–1971; Terry Neill 1971–1975; Dave Clements (player-manager) 1975–1976; Danny Blanchflower 1976–1979; Billy Bingham 1980–1994; Bryan Hamilton 1994–1998; Lawrie McMenemy 1998–1999; Sammy McIlroy 2000–2003; Lawrie Sanchez 2004–2007; Nigel Worthington 2007–2011; Michael O'Neill from December 2011.

Scotland (since 1967)
Bobby Brown 1967–1971; Tommy Docherty 1971–1972; Willie Ormond 1973–1977; Ally MacLeod 1977–1978; Jock Stein 1978–1985; Alex Ferguson (caretaker) 1985–1986 Andy Roxburgh (coach) 1986–1993; Craig Brown 1993–2001; Berti Vogts 2002–2004; Walter Smith 2004–2007; Alex McLeish 2007; George Burley 2008–2009; Craig Levein from December 2009.

Wales (since 1974)
Mike Smith 1974–1979; Mike England 1980–1988; David Williams (caretaker) 1988; Terry Yorath 1988–1993; John Toshack 1994 for one match; Mike Smith 1994–1995; Bobby Gould 1995–1999; Mark Hughes 1999–2004; John Toshack 2004–2010; Gary Speed 2010–2011; Chris Coleman from January 2012.

Republic of Ireland
Liam Tuohy 1971–1972; Johnny Giles 1973–1980 (after period as player-manager); Eoin Hand 1980–1985; Jack Charlton 1986–1996; Mick McCarthy 1996–2002; Brian Kerr 2003–2006; Steve Staunton 2006–2007; Giovanni Trapattoni from February 2008.

SOUTH AMERICA

COPA SUDAMERICANA 2011

FIRST ROUND FIRST LEG
Bella Vista 1, Univ Catolica 1
Univ Cesar Vallejo 1, Santa Fe 1
Dep Quito 1, Anzoategui 0
San Jose 0, Nacional (Par) 0
Olimpia 2, The Strongest 0
Yaracuyanos 1, LDU Quito 1
Univ de Chile 1, Fenix 0
La Equidad 2, Juan Aurich 0

FIRST ROUND SECOND LEG
Univ Catolica 3, Bella Vista 0
Santa Fe 2, Univ Cesar Vallejo 0
Anzoategui 2, Dep Quito 0
Nacional (Par) 1, San Jose 0
The Strongest 2, Olimpia 1
LDU Quito 1, Yaracuyanos 0
Fenix 0, Univ de Chile 0
Juan Aurich 1, La Equidad 2

SECOND ROUND FIRST LEG
Ceara 2, Sao Paulo 1
Atletico Mineiro 1, Botafogo 2
Flamengo 1, Atletico PR 0
Vasco da Gama 2, Palmeiras 0
Nacional (Par) 1, Aurora 1
Arsenal 2, Estudiantes 0
Lanus 2, Godoy Cruz 2
Argentinos Juniors 0, Velez Sarsfield 0
Anzoategui 1, Universitario 2
Univ Catolica 2, Dep Iquique 1
LDU Quito 4, Trujillanos 1
Univ de Chile 1, Nacional (Uru) 0
La Equidad 0, Libertad 1
Olimpia 2, Emelec 1
Santa Fe 1, Dep Cali 1

SECOND ROUND SECOND LEG
Sao Paulo 3, Ceara 0
Botafogo 1, Atletico Mineiro 0
Atletico PR 0, Flamengo 1
Palmeiras 3, Vasco da Gama 1
Aurora 5, Nacional (Par) 2
Estudiantes 1, Arsenal 0
Godoy Cruz 0, Lanus 0
Velez Sarsfield 4, Argentinos Juniors 0
Universitario 2, Anzoategui 0
Dep Iquique 0, Univ Catolica 0
Trujillanos 0, LDU Quito 1
Nacional (Uru) 0, Univ de Chile 2
Libertad 1, La Equidad 0
Emelec 1, Olimpia 2
Dep Cali 1, Santa Fe 1
Santa Fe won 5-6 on penalties.

THIRD ROUND FIRST LEG
LDU Quito 2, Independiente 0
Olimpia 0, Arsenal 0
Godoy Cruz 1, Universitario 1
Botafogo 1, Santa Fe 1
Univ Catolica 0, Velez Sarsfield 2
Aurora 3, Vasco da Gama 1
Sao Paulo 1, Libertad 0
Flamengo 0, Univ de Chile 4

THIRD ROUND SECOND LEG
Independiente 1, LDU Quito 0
Arsenal 3, Olimpia 2
Universitario 1, Godoy Cruz 1
Universitario won 3-2 on penalties.
Santa Fe 4, Botafogo 1
Velez Sarsfield 1, Univ Catolica 1
Vasco da Gama 8, Aurora 3
Libertad 2, Sao Paulo 0
Univ de Chile 1, Flamengo 0

QUARTER-FINALS FIRST LEG
Santa Fe 1, Velez Sarsfield 1
Universitario 2, Vasco da Gama 0
Arsenal 1, Univ de Chile 2
LDU Quito 1, Libertad 0

QUARTER-FINALS SECOND LEG
Velez Sarsfield 3, Santa Fe 2
Vasco da Gama 5, Universitario 2
Univ de Chile 3, Arsenal 0
Libertad 1, LDU Quito 0
LDU Quito won 5-4 on penalties.

SEMI-FINALS FIRST LEG
Vasco da Gama 1, Univ de Chile 1
LDU Quito 2, Velez Sarsfield 0

SEMI-FINALS SECOND LEG
Univ de Chile 2, Vasco da Gama 0
Velez Sarsfield 0, LDU Quito 1

FINAL FIRST LEG
LDU Quito 0, Univ de Chile 1

FINAL SECOND LEG
Univ de Chile 3, LDU Quito 0

COPA AMERICA 2011
(Finals in Argentina)

GROUP A	*P*	*W*	*D*	*L*	*F*	*A*	*Pts*
Colombia	3	2	1	0	3	0	7
Argentina	3	1	2	0	4	1	5
Costa Rica	3	1	0	2	2	4	3
Bolivia	3	0	1	2	1	5	1

GROUP B	*P*	*W*	*D*	*L*	*F*	*A*	*Pts*
Brazil	3	1	2	0	6	4	5
Venezuela	3	1	2	0	4	3	5
Paraguay	3	0	3	0	5	5	3
Ecuador	3	0	1	2	2	5	1

GROUP C	*P*	*W*	*D*	*L*	*F*	*A*	*Pts*
Chile	3	2	1	0	4	2	7
Uruguay	3	1	2	0	3	2	5
Peru	3	1	1	1	2	2	4
Mexico	3	0	0	3	1	4	0

QUARTER-FINALS
Colombia 0, Peru 2
Argentina 1, Uruguay 1
Uruguay won 5-4 on penalties.
Brazil 0, Paraguay 0
Paraguay won 2-0 on penalties.
Chile 1, Venezuela 2

SEMI-FINALS
Peru 0, Uruguay 2
Paraguay 0, Venezuela 0
Paraguay won 5-3 on penalties.

MATCH FOR THIRD PLACE
Peru 4, Venezuela 1

FINAL
Uruguay (2) 3 *(Suarez 11, Forlan 41, 89)*

Paraguay (0) 0

(at River Plate Stadium, Buenos Aires)
Uruguay: Muslera; Pereira M, Lugano, Coates, Caceres (Godin 88), Gonzalez, Perez (Eguren 69), Rios, Pereira A (Cavani 63), Forlan, Suarez.
Paraguay: Villar; Piris, Da Silva, Veron, Marecos, Vera (Estigarribia 64), Ortigoza, Caceres (Perez 64), Riveros, Valdez, Zeballos (Barrios 76).

COPA SANTANDER LIBERTADORES 2012

FIRST STAGE FIRST LEG
Sport Huancayo 0, Arsenal 3
Flamengo 1, Real Potosi 2
Caracas 0, Penarol 4
Libertad 0, El Nacional 1
Once Caldas 0, Internacional 1
UANL 0, Union Espanola 1

FIRST STAGE SECOND LEG
Arsenal 1, Sport Huancayo 1
Real Potosi 0, Flamengo 2
Penarol 1, Caracas 1
El Nacional 1, Libertad 4
Internacional 2, Once Caldas 2
Union Espanola 2, UANL 2

GROUP 1	P	W	D	L	F	A	Pts
Santos	6	4	1	1	12	5	13
Internacional	6	2	2	2	0	6	8
The Strongest	6	2	1	3	5	11	7
Juan Aurich	6	2	0	4	4	9	6

GROUP 2	P	W	D	L	F	A	Pts
Lanus	6	3	1	2	11	6	10
Emelec	6	3	0	3	7	8	9
Flamengo	6	2	2	2	12	10	8
Olimpia	6	2	1	3	10	16	7

GROUP 3	P	W	D	L	F	A	Pts
Union Espanola	6	3	1	2	10	7	10
Bolivar	6	3	1	2	9	7	10
Junior	6	2	1	3	8	8	7
Univ Catolica	6	1	3	2	6	11	6

GROUP 4	P	W	D	L	F	A	Pts
Fluminense	6	5	0	1	7	4	15
Boca Juniors	6	4	1	1	9	3	13
Arsenal	6	2	0	4	6	7	6
Zamora	6	0	1	5	0	8	1

GROUP 5	P	W	D	L	F	A	Pts
Libertad	6	4	1	1	11	7	13
Vasco da Gama	6	4	1	1	10	6	13
Nacional (Uru)	6	2	0	4	5	7	6
Alianza	6	1	0	5	6	12	3

GROUP 6	P	W	D	L	F	A	Pts
Corinthians	6	4	2	0	13	2	14
Cruz Azul	6	3	2	1	11	4	11
Nacional (Par)	6	1	1	4	6	13	4
Dep Tachira	6	0	3	3	4	17	3

GROUP 7	P	W	D	L	F	A	Pts
Velez Sarsfield	6	4	0	2	10	6	12
Dep Quito	6	3	1	2	11	4	10
Defensor	6	3	0	3	6	7	9
Guadalajara	6	1	1	4	2	12	4

GROUP 8	P	W	D	L	F	A	Pts
Univ de Chile	6	4	1	1	11	6	13
Atletico Nacional (Col)	6	3	2	1	16	8	11
Godoy Cruz	6	1	2	3	10	16	5
Penarol	6	1	1	4	6	13	4

FIRST ROUND FIRST LEG
Fluminense 0, Internacional 0
Union Espanola 1, Boca Juniors 2
Univ de Chile 1, Dep Quito 4
Libertad 1, Cruz Azul 1
Corinthians 0, Emelec 0
Lanus 1, Vasco da Gama 2
Santos 1, Bolivar 2
Velez Sarsfield 1, Atletico Nacional (Col) 0

FIRST ROUND SECOND LEG
Internacional 1, Fluminense 2
Boca Juniors 3, Union Espanola 2
Dep Quito 0, Univ de Chile 6
Cruz Azul 0, Libertad 2
Emelec 0, Corinthians 3
Vasco da Gama 1, Lanus 2
Vasco da Gama won 5-4 on penalties.
Bolivar 0, Santos 8
Atletico Nacional (Col) 1, Velez Sarsfield 1

QUARTER-FINALS FIRST LEG
Fluminense 0, Boca Juniors 1
Univ de Chile 1, Libertad 1
Corinthians 0, Vasco da Gama 0
Santos 0, Velez Sarsfield 1

QUARTER-FINALS SECOND LEG
Boca Juniors 1, Fluminense 1
Libertad 1, Univ de Chile 1
Univ de Chile won 5-3 on penalties.
Vasco da Gama 0, Corinthians 1
Velez Sarsfield 0, Santos 1
Santos won 4-2 on penalties.

SEMI-FINALS FIRST LEG
Univ de Chile 0, Boca Juniors 2
Corinthians 1, Santos 0

SEMI-FINALS SECOND LEG
Boca Juniors 0, Univ de Chile 0
Santos 1, Corinthians 1

FINAL FIRST LEG
Boca Juniors 1, Corinthians 1

FINAL SECOND LEG
Corinthians 2, Boca Juniors 0

The competition included a system of points awarded. If teams were tied on points and goal difference, extra time would be played and then decided by penalties. Corinthians were declared winners on points 4-1.

AFRICA

AFRICA CUP OF NATIONS

Finals in Gabon and Equatorial Guinea.

GROUP A

Equatorial Guinea v Libya	1-0
Senegal v Zambia	1-2
Libya v Zambia	2-2
Equatorial Guinea v Senegal	2-1
Equatorial Guinea v Zambia	0-1
Libya v Senegal	2-1

GROUP B

Ivory Coast v Sudan	1-0
Burkina Faso v Angola	1-2
Sudan v Angola	2-2
Ivory Coast v Burkina Faso	2-0
Sudan v Burkina Faso	2-1
Ivory Coast v Angola	2-0

GROUP C

Gabon v Niger	2-0
Morocco v Tunisia	1-2
Niger v Tunisia	1-2
Gabon v Morocco	3-2
Gabon v Tunisia	1-0
Niger v Morocco	0-1

GROUP D

Ghana v Botswana	1-0
Mali v Guinea	1-0
Botswana v Guinea	1-6
Ghana v Mali	2-0
Botswana v Mali	1-2
Ghana v Guinea	1-1

QUARTER-FINALS

Zambia v Sudan	3-0
Ivory Coast v Equatorial Guinea	3-0
Gabon v Mali	1-1
Mali won 5-4 on penalties.	
Ghana v Tunisia	2-1

SEMI-FINALS

Zambia v Ghana	1-0
Mali v Ivory Coast	0-1

MATCH FOR THIRD PLACE

Ghana v Mali	0-2

FINAL

Zambia 0 Ivory Coast 0

(in Libreville)

Zambia: Mweene; Himoonde, Musonda (Mulenga 12) (Katongo F 74), Sunzu, Nkausu, Chansa, Kalaba, Sinkala, Katongo C, Mayuka, Lungu.

Ivory Coast: Barry; Toure K, Tiene, Bamba, Zokora (Ya Konan 75), Toure Y (Bony 86), Tiote, Gosso, Drogba, Kalou (Gradel 63), Gervinho.

aet; Zambia won 8-7 on penalties.

Referee: B. Diatta (Senegal).

NORTH AMERICA

MAJOR LEAGUE SOCCER 2011

EASTERN CONFERENCE

	P	W	D	L	F	A	Pts
Sporting KC	34	13	12	9	50	40	51
Houston Dynamo	34	12	13	9	45	41	49
Philadelphia Union	34	11	15	8	44	36	48
Columbus Crew	34	13	8	13	43	44	47
New York Red Bulls	34	10	16	8	50	44	46
Chicago Fire	34	9	16	9	46	45	43
DC United	34	9	12	13	49	52	39
Toronto	34	6	15	13	36	59	33
New England Rev	34	5	13	16	38	58	28

WESTERN CONFERENCE

	P	W	D	L	F	A	Pts
Los Angeles Galaxy	34	19	10	5	48	28	67
Seattle Sounders	34	18	9	7	56	37	63
Real Salt Lake	34	15	8	11	44	36	53
Dallas	34	15	7	12	42	39	52
Colorado Rapids	34	12	13	9	44	41	49
Portland Timbers	34	11	9	14	40	48	42
San Jose Earthquakes	34	8	14	12	40	45	38
Chivas USA	34	8	12	14	41	43	36
Vancouver Whitecaps	34	6	10	18	35	55	28

PLAY-IN ROUND FINALS

Dallas v New York Red Bulls	0-2
Colorado Rapids v Columbus Crew	1-0

EASTERN SEMI-FINALS FIRST LEG

Philadelphia Union v Houston Dynamo	1-2
Colorado Rapids v Sporting KC	0-2

EASTERN SEMI-FINALS SECOND LEG

Houston Dynamo v Philadelphian Union	1-0
Sporting KC v Colorado Rapids	2-0

WESTERN SEMI-FINALS FIRST LEG

Real Salt Lake v Seattle Sounders	3-0
New York Red Bulls v Los Angeles Galaxy	0-1

WESTERN SEMI-FINALS SECOND LEG

Seattle Sounders v Real Salt Lake	2-0
Los Angeles Galaxy v New York Red Bulls	2-1

EASTERN FINAL

Sporting KC v Houston Dynamo	0-2

WESTERN FINAL

Los Angeles Galaxy v Real Salt Lake	3-1

MLS CUP 2011

Los Angeles Galaxy v Houston Dynamo	1-0

UEFA UNDER-21 CHAMPIONSHIP 2011–13

QUALIFYING ROUND

GROUP 1
Cyprus 6, San Marino 0
San Marino 0, Bosnia 3
Germany 4, Cyprus 1
Greece 2, Belarus 3
Germany 7, San Marino 0
Belarus 1, Bosnia 1
Cyprus 0, Greece 2
Belarus 0, Germany 1
Greece 2, San Marino 0
Germany 3, Bosnia 0
Cyprus 1, Belarus 3
San Marino 0, Germany 8
Bosnia 5, Cyprus 1
Belarus 1, Greece 3
Cyprus 2, Bosnia 1
Greece 0, Bosnia 1
San Marino 0, Belarus 2
Greece 4, Germany 5
Cyprus 0, Germany 3
Germany 1, Greece 0
San Marino 1, Cyprus 2
Bosnia 3, Belarus 0
San Marino 0, Greece 0
Bosnia 3, San Marino 1

GROUP 2
Lithuania 0, Slovenia 1
Finland 0, Malta 0
Lithuania 1, Malta 2
Finland 1, Slovenia 0
Lithuania 0, Sweden 1
Malta 1, Slovenia 4
Sweden 4, Lithuania 0
Malta 1, Finland 2
Slovenia 2, Ukraine 0
Sweden 1, Slovenia 1
Malta 2, Ukraine 2
Finland 0, Sweden 1
Malta 0, Lithuania 2
Slovenia 2, Lithuania 0
Ukraine 1, Finland 1
Ukraine 2, Lithuania 0
Malta 0, Sweden 1
Ukraine 6, Sweden 0
Slovenia 2, Malta 1
Lithuania 1, Ukraine 0
Slovenia 1, Finland 1
Sweden 4, Malta 0
Finland 1, Ukraine 2
Sweden 3, Finland 0

GROUP 3
Andorra 0, Wales 1
Andorra 0, Montenegro 5
Armenia 4, Montenegro 1
Czech Republic 8, Andorra 0
Andorra 0, Armenia 1
Czech Republic 1, Armenia 1
Montenegro 3, Wales 1
Wales 1, Montenegro 0
Wales 0, Czech Republic 1
Montenegro 4, Andorra 0
Armenia 0, Czech Republic 2
Armenia 0, Wales 0
Wales 4, Andorra 0
Czech Republic 2, Montenegro 1
Andorra 1, Czech Republic 5
Armenia 4, Andorra 1

GROUP 4
Faeroes 0, Northern Ireland 0
Northern Ireland 4, Faeroes 0
Serbia 1, Northern Ireland 0
Northern Ireland 0, Denmark 3
Serbia 5, Faeroes 1
Macedonia 1, Serbia 1
Denmark 4, Faeroes 0
Serbia 0, Denmark 0
Macedonia 1, Faeroes 0
Macedonia 1, Denmark 1
Northern Ireland 0, Serbia 2
Macedonia 1, Northern Ireland 0
Faeroes 1, Macedonia 1
Denmark 6, Macedonia 5
Faeroes 0, Serbia 2

GROUP 5
Croatia 0, Georgia 1
Georgia 2, Spain 7
Switzerland 4, Croatia 0
Spain 2, Georgia 0
Croatia 0, Spain 2
Georgia 0, Switzerland 1
Estonia 0, Croatia 1
Switzerland 5, Georgia 0
Spain 6, Estonia 0
Croatia 4, Estonia 0
Spain 3, Switzerland 0
Estonia 0, Spain 1
Croatia 1, Switzerland 2
Estonia 1, Georgia 2

GROUP 6
Moldova 0, Portugal 2
Albania 0, Poland 3
Poland 0, Russia 2
Albania 4, Moldova 3
Portugal 1, Poland 1
Moldova 0, Russia 6
Poland 4, Albania 3
Russia 2, Portugal 1
Albania 0, Russia 1
Portugal 5, Moldova 0
Poland 0, Moldova 1
Albania 2, Portugal 2
Moldova 2, Poland 4
Portugal 1, Russia 0
Portugal 3, Albania 1
Russia 0, Albania 0

GROUP 7
Turkey 6, Liechtenstein 1
Republic of Ireland 2, Hungary 1
Liechtenstein 0, Turkey 3
Hungary 0, Italy 3
Turkey 1, Republic of Ireland 0
Liechtenstein 2, Italy 7
Turkey 2, Hungary 1
Italy 2, Turkey 0
Liechtenstein 1, Republic of Ireland 4
Turkey 0, Italy 2
Republic of Ireland 2, Liechtenstein 0
Italy 2, Hungary 0
Hungary 1, Turkey 0
Republic of Ireland 2, Italy 2
Liechtenstein 0, Hungary 4

GROUP 8
Iceland 2, Belgium 1
England 6, Azerbaijan 0
Belgium 4, Azerbaijan 1
Iceland 0, Norway 2
Azerbaijan 0, Norway 1
Azerbaijan 0, Norway 2
Iceland 0, England 3
Azerbaijan 2, Belgium 2
Norway 1, England 2
Norway 2, Belgium 2
England 5, Iceland 0
Belgium 2, England 1
Azerbaijan 1, Iceland 0
England 4, Belgium 0
Norway 1, Azerbaijan 0
Iceland 1, Azerbaijan 2
Norway 2, Iceland 1

GROUP 9
Romania 0, Kazakhstan 0
Slovakia 2, Latvia 0
Latvia 0, France 3
Kazakhstan 1, Romania 1
Kazakhstan 0, Slovakia 1
Romania 2, Latvia 0
France 2, Kazakhstan 0
Latvia 0, Slovakia 6
Romania 0, France 2
France 3, Romania 0
France 2, Slovakia 0
Slovakia 0, Romania 2
France 3, Latvia 0
Romania 2, Slovakia 0
Kazakhstan 0, France 3
Kazakhstan 0, Latvia 0

GROUP 10
Luxembourg 1, Austria 4
Bulgaria 0, Holland 1
Scotland 0, Bulgaria 0
Holland 4, Luxembourg 0
Austria 0, Holland 1
Luxembourg 1, Scotland 5
Scotland 2, Austria 2
Bulgaria 3, Luxembourg 2
Austria 0, Bulgaria 2
Holland 1, Scotland 2
Bulgaria 1, Austria 1
Scotland 0, Holland 0
Bulgaria 2, Scotland 2
Luxembourg 0, Holland 5
Austria 4, Luxembourg 1
Holland 5, Bulgaria 0

Competition still being played.

FIFA UNDER-20 WORLD CUP

GROUP A
Mali v South Korea 0-2
Colombia v France 4-1
France v South Korea 3-1
Colombia v Mali 2-0
France v Mali 2-0
Colombia v South Korea 1-0

GROUP B
Cameroon v New Zealand 1-1
Portugal v Uruguay 0-0
Uruguay v New Zealand 1-1
Portugal v Cameroon 1-0
Portugal v New Zealand 1-0
Uruguay v Cameroon 0-1

GROUP C
Costa Rica v Spain 1-4
Australia v Ecuador 1-1
Ecuador v Spain 0-2
Australia v Costa Rica 2-3
Ecuador v Costa Rica 3-0
Australia v Spain 1-5

GROUP D
Nigeria v Guatemala 5-0
Croatia v Saudi Arabia 0-2
Saudi Arabia v Guatemala 6-0
Croatia v Nigeria 2-5
Saudi Arabia v Nigeria 0-2
Croatia v Guatemala 0-1

GROUP E
Brazil v Egypt 1-1
Austria v Panama 0-0
Egypt v Panama 1-0
Brazil v Austria 3-0
Brazil v Panama 4-0
Egypt v Austria 4-0

GROUP F
England v North Korea 0-0
Argentina v Mexico 1-0
Mexico v North Korea 3-0
Argentina v England 0-0
Mexico v England 0-0
Argentina v North Korea 3-0

FIRST ROUND
Portugal v Guatemala 1-0
Argentina v Egypt 2-1
Cameroon v Mexico 1-1
Mexico won 3-0 on penalties.
Colombia v Costa Rica 3-2
Nigeria v England 1-0
Spain v South Korea 0-0
Spain won 7-6 on penalties.
Brazil v Saudi Arabia 3-0
France v Ecuador 1-0

QUARTER-FINALS
Portugal v Argentina 0-0
Portugal won 5-4 on penalties.
Mexico v Colombia 3-1
France v Nigeria 3-2
Brazil v Spain 2-2
Brazil won 4-2 on penalties.

SEMI-FINALS
France v Portugal 0-2
Brazil v Mexico 2-0

MATCH FOR THIRD PLACE
Mexico v France 3-1

FINAL

Brazil (1) 3 *(Oscar 5, 78, 111)*

Portugal (1) 2 *(Alex 9, Nelson Oliveira 59)* 36,058

(in Bogota)

Brazil: Gabriel; Danilo, Bruno Uvini, Juan Jesus, Fernando, Casemiro, Willian (Allan 46), Philippe Coutinho (Dudu 62), Oscar, Gabriel Silva (Negueba 46), Henrique.
Portugal: Mika; Pele, Nuno Reis, Roderick, Nelson Oliveira, Cedric (Julio Alves 57), Sana (Ricardo Dias 100), Alex (Caetano 82), Danilo, Sergio Oliveira, Mario Rui.
aet.
Referee: M. Geiger (USA).

THE NEXTGEN SERIES TROPHY

(UNDER 19 TEAMS)

GROUP 1	P	W	D	L	F	A	Pts
Barcelona	6	5	0	1	20	9	15
Marseille	6	4	0	2	11	10	12
Celtic	6	3	0	3	11	12	9
Manchester C	6	0	0	6	6	17	0

GROUP 2	P	W	D	L	F	A	Pts
Sporting Lisbon	6	5	1	0	20	6	10
Liverpool	6	2	1	3	9	11	7
Wolfsburg	6	1	3	2	8	9	6
Molde	6	1	1	4	10	21	4

GROUP 3	P	W	D	L	F	A	Pts
Aston Villa	6	4	0	2	15	7	12
Ajax	6	3	1	2	9	7	10
Rosenborg	6	3	0	3	11	11	9
Fenerbahce	6	1	1	4	5	15	4

GROUP 4	P	W	D	L	F	A	Pts
Tottenham H	6	4	2	0	17	6	14
Internazionale	6	3	2	1	8	11	11
Basle	6	1	2	3	4	8	5
PSV Eindhoven	6	1	0	5	9	13	3

QUARTER-FINALS
Aston Villa 1, Marseille 2
Sporting Lisbon 0, Internazionale 1
Tottenham H 1, Liverpool 0
Tottenham H withdrew after breach of rule.
Barcelona 0, Ajax 3

SEMI-FINALS
Liverpool 0, Ajax 6
Internazionale 2, Marseille 0

MATCH FOR THIRD PLACE
Liverpool 2, Marseille 0

FINAL

25 March 2012
(at Leyton Orient)

Ajax (0) 1 *(Denswil 48)*

Internazionale (1) 1 *(Longo 44)* 2500

Ajax: Van Der Hart; Nieuwpoort, Veltman, Denswil, Dijks, Sparkslede, Klassen, Rits (El Hasnaoui 105), De Sa (De Bondt 75), Schoop (Gravenbergh 58), Fischer.
Internazionale: Di Gennaro; Pecorini, Kysela, Spendhofer, M'Baye, Romano, Crisetig, Bessa, Duncan, Longo, Livaja (Alborno 75).
aet; Internazionale won 5-3 on penalties.
Referee: L. Collins (England).

UEFA UNDER-19 CHAMPIONSHIP 2011–12

FINAL TOURNAMENT IN ROMANIA

GROUP A

Romania v Czech Republic	1-3
Greece v Republic of Ireland	1-2
Czech Republic v Republic of Ireland	2-1
Romania v Greece	0-1
Republic of Ireland v Romania	0-0
Czech Republic v Greece	1-0

GROUP B

Serbia v Turkey	2-0
Spain v Belgium	4-1
Turkey v Belgium	1-1
Serbia v Spain	0-4
Belgium v Serbia	1-1
Turkey v Spain	3-0

SEMI-FINALS

Czech Republic v Serbia	4-2
Spain v Republic of Ireland	5-0

FINAL

1 August 2011

Czech Republic (0) 2 *(Krejci 52, Lacha 97)*

Spain (0) 3 *(Aurtenetxe 85, Paco Alcacer 108, 115)* 3700

Czech Republic: Koubek; Brabec, Janos, Kalas, Kaderabek, Skalak (Lacha 79), Jelecek, Krejci, Prikryl (Fantis 102), Hala, Polom (Sladky 36).
Spain: Edgar Badia; Sergi Gomez, Ignasi Miquel, Aurtenetxe, Ruben Pardo, Morata, Alex Fernandez (Campana 55), Sarabia (Juan Muniz 78), Blazquez, Juanmi (Paco Alcacer 54), Deulofeu.
aet.
Referee: S. Attwell (England).

EUROPEAN CHAMPIONSHIP

3 July (in Tallinn)

Croatia 1 *(Pavicic 56)* **England 1** *(Chalobah 60)*

England: Johnstone; Dier, Coady (Robinson 64), Keane M, Thorpe, Barkley (Redmond 84), Chalobah, Kane H (Hall 77), Thorne, Garbutt, Afobe.

6 July (in Rakvere)

Serbia 1 *(Ninkovic 70)* **England 2** *(Afobe 6, Redmond 63)*

England: Johnstone; Robinson, Coady, Thorpe, Barkley (Lundstram 63), Chalobah, Kane H (Hope 79), Redmond, Thorne, Garbutt, Afobe (Berahino 71).

9 July (in Tallinn)

France 1 *(Veretout 31)*

England 2 *(Lundstram 16, Kane H 39)*

England: Johnstone; Dier, Robinson, Thorpe, Chalobah, Berahino, Kane H (Coady 84), Redmond (Hope 77), Hall (Garbutt 69), Thorne, Lundstram.

UEFA UNDER-17 CHAMPIONSHIP 2011–12

ELITE ROUND

GROUP 1
France 1, Italy 0
Sweden 2, Switzerland 0
Italy 0, Sweden 0
France 2, Switzerland 1
Sweden 1, France 3
Switzerland 1, Italy 2

GROUP 2
Czech Republic 0, Poland 2
Belarus 1, Luxembourg 1
Poland 2, Belarus 0
Czech Republic 2, Luxembourg 1
Belarus 0, Czech Republic 0
Luxembourg 1, Poland 3

GROUP 3
Spain 1, Georgia 1
England 1, Ukraine 0
Georgia 1, England 0
Spain 2, Ukraine 2
England 0, Spain 4
Ukraine 0, Georgia 1

GROUP 4
Germany 4, Turkey 0
Portugal 0, Bulgaria 0
Germany 2, Bulgaria 1
Turkey 0, Portugal 3
Portugal 0, Germany 0
Bulgaria 2, Turkey 0

GROUP 5
Serbia 1, Republic of Ireland 0
Holland 4, Albania 0
Serbia 3, Albania 0
Republic of Ireland 1, Holland 2
Holland 1, Serbia 1
Albania 2, Republic of Ireland 1

GROUP 6
Denmark 2, Iceland 2
Scotland 1, Lithuania 0
Denmark 3, Lithuania 1
Iceland 1, Scotland 0
Scotland 2, Denmark 3
Lithuania 0, Iceland 4

GROUP 7
Hungary 2, Belgium 2
Russia 2, Wales 1
Hungary 5, Wales 1
Belgium 3, Russia 0
Scoreline was 1-0 before default victory was awarded.
Russia 2, Hungary 3
Wales 0, Belgium 3

FINAL TOURNAMENT IN SLOVENIA

GROUP A
Georgia 0, Germany 1
France 2, Iceland 2
France 1, Georgia 1
Iceland 0, Germany 1
Germany 3, France 0
Iceland 0, Georgia 1

GROUP B
Poland 1, Belgium 0
Slovenia 1, Holland 3
Holland 0, Belgium 0
Slovenia 1, Poland 1
Belgium 3, Slovenia 1
Holland 0, Poland 0

SEMI-FINALS
Germany 1, Poland 0
Holland 2, Georgia 0

FINAL

16 May

Germany (0) 1 *(Goretzka 45)*

Holland (0) 1 *(Acolatse 80)* 11,674

Germany: Schnitzler; Dudziak, Sarr, Sule, Itter, Goretzka (Akpoguma 80), Dittgen (Stendera 41), Meyer, Brandenburger, Brandt (Kempf 73), Werner.
Holland: Olij; Ake, Haye, Hendrix, Bazoer, Anderson (Van den Boomen 71), Voest, Trindade de Vilhena, Vloet (Huser 64), Lumu (Acolatse 57), Menig.
aet; Holland won 5-4 on penalties.

ENGLAND UNDER-21 RESULTS 1976–2012

EC *UEFA Competition for Under-21 Teams*

Year	*Date*		*Venue*		
			v ALBANIA	Eng	Alb
EC1989	Mar	7	Shkroda	2	1
EC1989	April	25	Ipswich	2	0
EC2001	Mar	27	Tirana	1	0
EC2001	Sept	4	Middlesbrough	5	0
			v ANGOLA	Eng	Ang
1995	June	10	Toulon	1	0
1996	May	28	Toulon	0	2
			v ARGENTINA	Eng	Arg
1998	May	18	Toulon	0	2
2000	Feb	22	Fulham	1	0
			v AUSTRIA	Eng	Aus
1994	Oct	11	Kapfenberg	3	1
1995	Nov	14	Middlesbrough	2	1
EC2004	Sept	3	Krems	2	0
EC2005	Oct	7	Leeds	1	2
			v AZERBAIJAN	Eng	Az
EC2004	Oct	12	Baku	0	0
EC2005	Mar	29	Middlesbrough	2	0
2009	June	8	Milton Keynes	7	0
EC2011	Sept	1	Watford	6	0
			v BELGIUM	Eng	Bel
1994	June	5	Marseille	2	1
1996	May	24	Toulon	1	0
EC2011	Nov	14	Mons	1	2
EC2012	Feb	29	Middlesbrough	4	0
			v BRAZIL	Eng	B
1993	June	11	Toulon	0	0
1995	June	6	Toulon	0	2
1996	June	1	Toulon	1	2
			v BULGARIA	Eng	Bul
EC1979	June	5	Pernik	3	1
EC1979	Nov	20	Leicester	5	0
1989	June	5	Toulon	2	3
EC1998	Oct	9	West Ham	1	0
EC1999	June	8	Vratsa	1	0
EC2007	Sept	11	Sofia	2	0
EC2007	Nov	16	Milton Keynes	2	0
			v CROATIA	Eng	Cro
1996	Apr	23	Sunderland	0	1
2003	Aug	19	West Ham	0	3
			v CZECHOSLOVAKIA	Eng	Cz
1990	May	28	Toulon	2	1
1992	May	26	Toulon	1	2
1993	June	9	Toulon	1	1
			v CZECH REPUBLIC	Eng	CzR
1998	Nov	17	Ipswich	0	1
EC2007	June	11	Arnhem	0	0
2008	Nov	18	Bramall Lane	2	0
EC2011	June	19	Viborg	1	2
			v DENMARK	Eng	Den
EC1978	Sept	19	Hvidovre	2	1
EC1979	Sept	11	Watford	1	0
EC1982	Sept	21	Hvidovre	4	1
EC1983	Sept	20	Norwich	4	1
EC1986	Mar	12	Copenhagen	1	0
EC1986	Mar	26	Manchester	1	1
1988	Sept	13	Watford	0	0
1994	Mar	8	Brentford	1	0
1999	Oct	8	Bradford	4	1
2005	Aug	16	Herning	1	0
2011	Mar	24	Viborg	4	0
			v EQUADOR	Eng	E
2009	Feb	10	Malaga	2	3
			v FINLAND	Eng	Fin
EC1977	May	26	Helsinki	1	0
EC1977	Oct	12	Hull	8	1
EC1984	Oct	16	Southampton	2	0
EC1985	May	21	Mikkeli	1	3
EC2000	Oct	10	Valkeakoski	2	2
EC2001	Mar	23	Barnsley	4	0
EC2009	June	15	Halmstad	2	1
			v FRANCE	Eng	Fra
EC1984	Feb	28	Sheffield	6	1
EC1984	Mar	28	Rouen	1	0
1987	June	11	Toulon	0	2
EC1988	April	13	Besancon	2	4
EC1988	April	27	Highbury	2	2
1988	June	12	Toulon	2	4
1990	May	23	Toulon	7	3
1991	June	3	Toulon	1	0
1992	May	28	Toulon	0	0
1993	June	15	Toulon	1	0
1994	May	31	Aubagne	0	3
1995	June	10	Toulon	0	2
1998	May	14	Toulon	1	1
1999	Feb	9	Derby	2	1
EC2005	Nov	11	Tottenham	1	1
EC2005	Nov	15	Nancy	1	2
2009	Mar	31	Nottingham	0	2
			v GEORGIA	Eng	Geo
EC1996	Nov	8	Batumi	1	0
EC1997	April	29	Charlton	0	0
2000	Aug	31	Middlesbrough	6	1
			v GERMANY	Eng	Ger
1991	Sept	10	Scunthorpe	2	1
EC2000	Oct	6	Derby	1	1
EC2001	Aug	31	Frieburg	2	1
2005	Mar	25	Hull	2	2
2005	Sept	6	Mainz	1	1
EC2006	Oct	6	Coventry	1	0
EC2006	Oct	10	Leverkusen	2	0
EC2009	June	22	Halmstad	1	1
EC2009	June	29	Malmo	0	4
2010	Nov	16	Wiesbaden	0	2
			v EAST GERMANY	Eng	EG
EC1980	April	16	Sheffield	1	2
EC1980	April	23	Jena	0	1
			v WEST GERMANY	Eng	WG
EC1982	Sept	21	Sheffield	3	1
EC1982	Oct	12	Bremen	2	3
1987	Sept	8	Ludenscheid	0	2
			v GREECE	Eng	Gre
EC1982	Nov	16	Piraeus	0	1
EC1983	Mar	29	Portsmouth	2	1
1989	Feb	7	Patras	0	1
EC1997	Nov	13	Heraklion	0	2
EC1997	Dec	17	Norwich	4	2
EC2001	June	5	Athens	1	3
EC2001	Oct	5	Ewood Park	2	1
EC2009	Sept	8	Tripoli	1	1
EC2010	Mar	3	Doncaster	1	2
			v HOLLAND	Eng	H
EC1993	April	27	Portsmouth	3	0
EC1993	Oct	12	Utrecht	1	1
2001	Aug	14	Reading	4	0
EC2001	Nov	9	Utrecht	2	2
EC2001	Nov	13	Derby	1	0
2004	Feb	17	Hull	3	2
2005	Feb	8	Derby	1	2

				Eng	H
2006	Nov	14	Alkmaar	1	0
EC2007	June	20	Heerenveen	1	1
2009	Aug	11	Groningen	0	0

			v HUNGARY	Eng	Hun
EC1981	June	5	Keszthely	2	1
EC1981	Nov	17	Nottingham	2	0
EC1983	April	26	Newcastle	1	0
EC1983	Oct	11	Nyiregyhaza	2	0
1990	Sept	11	Southampton	3	1
1992	May	12	Budapest	2	2
1999	April	27	Budapest	2	2

			v ICELAND	Eng	Ice
2011	Mar	28	Preston	1	2
EC2011	Oct	6	Reykjavik	3	0
EC2011	Nov	10	Colchester	5	0

			v REPUBLIC OF IRELAND	Eng	RoI
1981	Feb	25	Liverpool	1	0
1985	Mar	25	Portsmouth	3	2
1989	June	9	Toulon	0	0
EC1990	Nov	13	Cork	3	0
EC1991	Mar	26	Brentford	3	0
1994	Nov	15	Newcastle	1	0
1995	Mar	27	Dublin	2	0
EC2007	Oct	16	Cork	3	0
EC2008	Feb	5	Southampton	3	0

			v ISRAEL	Eng	Isr
1985	Feb	27	Tel Aviv	2	1
2011	Sept	5	Barnsley	4	1

			v ITALY	Eng	Italy
EC1978	Mar	8	Manchester	2	1
EC1978	April	5	Rome	0	0
EC1984	April	18	Manchester	3	1
EC1984	May	2	Florence	0	1
EC1986	April	9	Pisa	0	2
EC1986	April	23	Swindon	1	1
EC1997	Feb	12	Bristol	1	0
EC1997	Oct	10	Rieti	1	0
EC2000	May	27	Bratislava	0	2
2000	Nov	14	Monza*	0	0
2002	Mar	26	Valley Parade	1	1
EC2002	May	20	Basle	1	2
2003	Feb	11	Pisa	0	1
2007	Mar	24	Wembley	3	3
EC2007	June	14	Arnhem	2	2
2011	Feb	8	Empoli	0	1

**Abandoned 11 mins; fog.*

			v LATVIA	Eng	Lat
1995	April	25	Riga	1	0
1995	June	7	Burnley	4	0

			v LITHUANIA	Eng	Lith
EC2009	Nov	17	Vilnius	0	0
EC2010	Sept	7	Colchester	3	0

			v LUXEMBOURG	Eng	Lux
EC1998	Oct	13	Greven Macher	5	0
EC1999	Sept	3	Reading	5	0

			v MACEDONIA	Eng	M
EC2002	Oct	15	Reading	3	1
EC2003	Sept	5	Skopje	1	1
EC2009	Sept	4	Prilep	2	1
EC2009	Oct	9	Coventry	6	3

			v MALAYSIA	Eng	Mal
1995	June	8	Toulon	2	0

			v MEXICO	Eng	Mex
1988	June	5	Toulon	2	1
1991	May	29	Toulon	6	0
1992	May	25	Toulon	1	1
2001	May	24	Leicester	3	0

			v MOLDOVA	Eng	Mol
EC1996	Aug	31	Chisinau	2	0
EC1997	Sept	9	Wycombe	1	0
EC2006	Aug	15	Ipswich	2	2

			v MONTENEGRO	Eng	M
EC2007	Sept	7	Podgorica	3	0
EC2007	Oct	12	Leicester	1	0

			v MOROCCO	Eng	Mor
1987	June	7	Toulon	2	0
1988	June	9	Toulon	1	0

			v NORWAY	Eng	Nor
EC1977	June	1	Bergen	2	1
EC1977	Sept	6	Brighton	6	0
1980	Sept	9	Southampton	3	0
1981	Sept	8	Drammen	0	0
EC1992	Oct	13	Peterborough	0	2
EC1993	June	1	Stavanger	1	1
1995	Oct	10	Stavanger	2	2
2006	Feb	28	Reading	3	1
2009	Mar	27	Sandefjord	5	0
2011	June	5	Southampton	2	0
EC2011	Oct	10	Drammen	2	1

			v POLAND	Eng	Pol
EC1982	Mar	17	Warsaw	2	1
EC1982	April	7	West Ham	2	2
EC1989	June	2	Plymouth	2	1
EC1989	Oct	10	Jastrzebie	3	1
EC1990	Oct	16	Tottenham	0	1
EC1991	Nov	12	Pila	1	2
EC1993	May	28	Zdroj	4	1
EC1993	Sept	7	Millwall	1	2
EC1996	Oct	8	Wolverhampton	0	0
EC1997	May	30	Katowice	1	1
EC1999	Mar	26	Southampton	5	0
EC1999	Sept	7	Plock	1	3
EC2004	Sept	7	Rybnik	3	1
EC2005	Oct	11	Hillsborough	4	1
2008	Mar	25	Wolverhampton	0	0

			v PORTUGAL	Eng	Por
1987	June	13	Toulon	0	0
1990	May	21	Toulon	0	1
1993	June	7	Toulon	2	0
1994	June	7	Toulon	2	0
EC1994	Sept	6	Leicester	0	0
1995	Sept	2	Lisbon	0	2
1996	May	30	Toulon	1	3
2000	Apr	16	Stoke	0	1
EC2002	May	22	Zurich	1	3
EC2003	Mar	28	Rio Major	2	4
EC2003	Sept	9	Everton	1	2
EC2008	Nov	20	Agueda	1	1
2008	Sept	5	Wembley	2	0
EC2009	Nov	14	Wembley	1	0
EC2010	Sept	3	Barcelos	1	0

			v ROMANIA	Eng	Rom
EC1980	Oct	14	Ploesti	0	4
EC1981	April	28	Swindon	3	0
EC1985	April	30	Brasov	0	0
EC1985	Sept	10	Ipswich	3	0
2007	Aug	21	Bristol	1	1
EC2010	Oct	8	Norwich	2	1
EC2010	Oct	12	Botosani	0	0

			v RUSSIA	Eng	Rus
1994	May	30	Bandol	2	0

			v SAN MARINO	Eng	SM
EC1993	Feb	16	Luton	6	0
EC1993	Nov	17	San Marino	4	0

			v SCOTLAND	Eng	Sco
1977	April	27	Sheffield	1	0
EC1980	Feb	12	Coventry	2	1
EC1980	Mar	4	Aberdeen	0	0
EC1982	April	19	Glasgow	1	0

				Eng	Sco
EC1982	April	28	Manchester	1	1
EC1988	Feb	16	Aberdeen	1	0
EC1988	Mar	22	Nottingham	1	0
1993	June	13	Toulon	1	0

			v SENEGAL	Eng	Sen
1989	June	7	Toulon	6	1
1991	May	27	Toulon	2	1

			v SERBIA	Eng	Ser
EC2007	June	17	Nijmegen	2	0

			v SERBIA-MONTENEGRO	Eng	S-M
2003	June	2	Hull	3	2

			v SLOVAKIA	Eng	Slo
EC2002	June	1	Bratislava	0	2
EC2002	Oct	11	Trnava	4	0
EC2003	June	10	Sunderland	2	0
2007	June	5	Norwich	5	0

			v SLOVENIA	Eng	Slo
2000	Feb	12	Nova Gorica	1	0
2008	Aug	19	Hull	2	1

			v SOUTH AFRICA	Eng	SA
1998	May	16	Toulon	3	1

			v SPAIN	Eng	Spa
EC1984	May	17	Seville	1	0
EC1984	May	24	Sheffield	2	0
1987	Feb	18	Burgos	2	1
1992	Sept	8	Burgos	1	0
2001	Feb	27	Birmingham	0	4
2004	Nov	16	Alcala	0	1
2007	Feb	6	Derby	2	2
EC2009	June	18	Gothenburg	2	0
EC2011	June	12	Herning	1	1

			v SWEDEN	Eng	Swe
1979	June	9	Vasteras	2	1
1986	Sept	9	Ostersund	1	1
EC1988	Oct	18	Coventry	1	1
EC1989	Sept	5	Uppsala	0	1
EC1998	Sept	4	Sundvall	2	0
EC1999	June	4	Huddersfield	3	0
2004	Mar	30	Kristiansund	2	2
EC2009	June	26	Gothenburg	3	3

			v SWITZERLAND	Eng	Swit
EC1980	Nov	18	Ipswich	5	0
EC1981	May	31	Neuenburg	0	0
1988	May	28	Lausanne	1	1
1996	April	1	Swindon	0	0
1998	Mar	24	Brugglifeld	0	2
EC2002	May	17	Zurich	2	1
EC2006	Sept	6	Lucerne	3	2

			v TURKEY	Eng	Tur
EC1984	Nov	13	Bursa	0	0
EC1985	Oct	15	Bristol	3	0
EC1987	April	28	Izmir	0	0
EC1987	Oct	13	Sheffield	1	1
EC1991	April	30	Izmir	2	2
1991	Oct	15	Reading	2	0
EC1992	Nov	17	Orient	0	1
EC1993	Mar	30	Izmir	0	0
EC2000	May	29	Bratislava	6	0
EC2003	April	1	Newcastle	1	1
EC2003	Oct	10	Istanbul	0	1

			v UKRAINE	Eng	Uk
2004	Aug	17	Middlesbrough	3	1
EC2011	June	15	Herning	0	0

			v USA	Eng	USA
1989	June	11	Toulon	0	2
1994	June	2	Toulon	3	0

			v UZBEKISTAN	Eng	Uzb
2010	Aug	10	Bristol	2	0

			v USSR	Eng	USSR
1987	June	9	Toulon	0	0
1988	June	7	Toulon	1	0
1990	May	25	Toulon	2	1
1991	May	31	Toulon	2	1

			v WALES	Eng	Wales
1976	Dec	15	Wolverhampton	0	0
1979	Feb	6	Swansea	1	0
1990	Dec	5	Tranmere	0	0
EC2004	Oct	8	Blackburn	2	0
EC2005	Sept	2	Wrexham	4	0
2008	May	5	Wrexham	2	0
EC2008	Oct	10	Cardiff	3	2
EC2008	Oct	14	Villa Park	2	2

			v YUGOSLAVIA	Eng	Yugo
EC1978	April	19	Novi Sad	1	2
EC1978	May	2	Manchester	1	1
EC1986	Nov	11	Peterborough	1	1
EC1987	Nov	10	Zemun	5	1
EC2000	Mar	29	Barcelona	3	0
2002	Sept	6	Bolton	1	1

ENGLAND C 2011–12

FRIENDLY

15 Nov

Gibraltar (1) 3 *(Casciaro 42, Perez 46 (pen), Guilling 54)*

England (0) 1 *(Jennings 80)* 1850

(in Victoria Stadium).
England: Hedge (Edwards 46); Beeley (Killock 46), Newton, Turley, McAuley (Watkins 46), Meikle, Reason, Rose (Davis 46), Willmott (Chambers 46), Boyes (Jennings 46), Kissock (West 46).

INTERNATIONAL CHALLENGE TROPHY

28 Feb

England (0) 1 *(Watkins 90)*

Italy (0) 1 *(Angiulli 48)* 4628

(at Fleetwood).
England: Hedge; Roberts, Brown, Turley, Davis, Oshodi, Coulson, Forbes (Watkins 75), Spencer (Boyes 69), Rose (Chambers 69), Blair (Owens 75).

5 June

Russia Under-23 (2) 4 *(Delkin 27, 55, Bibilov 42, Smolov 81 (pen))*

England (0) 0

(in Moscow).
England: Hedge (McDonald 77); Ainge, Garner, McAuley, Brown, Meikle (Owens 77), Forbes (Davis 73), Vincent, Johnson (Coulson 59), Wilson (Brogan 46), Gray.

BRITISH AND IRISH UNDER-21 TEAMS 2011–12

■ *Denotes player sent off.*

ENGLAND

Watford, 1 September 2011, 7738

England (3) 6 *(Dawson 4, 89, Lansbury 21, 73, Henderson 45, Waghorn 79)*

Azerbaijan (0) 0

England: Butland; Flanagan, Briggs, Rodwell, Caulker, Dawson, Oxlade-Chamberlain (Shelvey 77), Henderson, Wickham (Sordell 67), Lansbury, Delfouneso (Waghorn 67).

Barnsley, 5 September 2011, 9152

England (0) 4 *(Waghorn 58, Sordell 60, Delfouneso 82 (pen), Lansbury 90)*

Israel (1) 1 *(Klibat 25)*

England: Amos; Wisdom (Smith 46), Bennett J, Rodwell (Oxlade-Chamberlain 46), Dawson, Baker (Caulker 45), Gosling (Gardner 62), Barkley (Wickham 73), Sordell, Shelvey (Lansbury 46), Waghorn (Delfouneso 62).

Reykjavik, 6 October 2011, 2599

Iceland (0) 0

England (2) 3 *(Oxlade-Chamberlain 12, 14, 49)*

England: Butland; Flanagan, Briggs, Rodwell, Kelly, Dawson, Oxlade-Chamberlain (Barkley 83), Henderson, Sordell, Lansbury, Delfouneso (Waghorn 24) (McEachran 63).

Drammen, 10 October 2011, 2323

Norway (1) 1 *(Berisha 23)*

England (2) 2 *(Dawson 3, Henderson 7)*

England: Butland; Smith, Lowe, Bennett R, Dawson, Oxlade-Chamberlain, Henderson, Sordell (Shelvey 81), Lansbury, Barkley (Gardner 55), Baker (Flanagan 71).

Colchester, 10 November 2011, 10,051

England (1) 5 *(Sordell 39, Kelly 57, Dawson 86, Gardner 89, 90)*

Iceland (0) 0

England: Butland; Smith, Clyne, Lowe (Gardner 62), Kelly, Dawson, Oxlade-Chamberlain, Henderson, Sordell, McEachran (Keane W 78), Delfouneso (Sammy Ameobi 11).

Mons, 14 November 2011, 3519

Belgium (0) 2 *(Naessens 72, El Kaddouri 90)*

England (1) 1 *(Kelly 14)*

England: Butland; Kelly, Clyne, Smith, Dawson, Henderson, Oxlade-Chamberlain, McEachran, Lowe (Barkley 90), Sordell (Keane W 78), Sammy Ameobi (Gardner 63).

Middlesbrough, 29 February 2012, 22,647

England (2) 4 *(Lansbury 9, 53, Caulker 36, Oxlade-Chamberlain 90 (pen))*

Belgium (0) 0

England: Butland; Kelly, Rose, McEachran, Caulker, Dawson, Oxlade-Chamberlain, Henderson, Sordell (Keane W 82), Lansbury (Gardner 74), Zaha.

SCOTLAND

Paisley, 10 August 2011, 1654

Scotland (1) 3 *(Cairney 20, Jack 72, Armstrong 75)*

Norway (0) 0

Scotland: Adam; Jack, Booth, Saunders (Perry 4), Hanlon, Kelly, Russell (MacDonald 58), Allan (Cole 68), Rhodes (Griffiths 46), Cairney (Armstrong 46), Wylde (Ross 58).

Paisley, 5 September 2011, 2769

Scotland (0) 0

Bulgaria (0) 0

Scotland: Adam; Wotherspoon, Booth, Perry, Hanlon, Kelly, Russell, Allan (Pawlett 75), Rhodes (Griffiths 61), Cairney, Armstrong (Palmer 61).

Luxembourg, 6 October 2011, 320

Luxembourg (0) 1 *(Almeida 82)*

Scotland (3) 5 *(MacDonald 29, Rhodes 34, 44, 64, Hanlon 88)*

Scotland: Adam; Jack, Hanlon, Perry, Wilson D, Wotherspoon, MacDonald, Palmer, Allan (Russell 79), Rhodes (Griffiths 75), Wylde (Pawlett 66).

Paisley, 10 October 2011, 3058

Scotland (1) 2 *(Rhodes 38, 64)*

Austria (2) 2 *(Weimann 16, Alar 42)*

Scotland: Adam; Jack, Hanlon, Perry, Wilson D, Palmer, Wotherspoon, Russell (Pawlett 61), Rhodes, Allan (MacDonald 45), Wylde (Griffiths 75).

Nijmegen, 14 November 2011, 7500

Holland (1) 1 *(Maher 12)*

Scotland (1) 2 *(Rhodes 2, Wotherspoon 55)*

Scotland: Ridgers; Perry, Hanlon, Wilson D, Jack, Wotherspoon, Cairney (Palmer 71), Wylde (Griffiths 90), Forrest (Pawlett 84), Kelly, Rhodes.

Paisley, 29 February 2012, 6607

Scotland (0) 0

Holland (0) 0

Scotland: Ridgers; Jack, Hanlon, Wilson D, Perry, Kelly, Russell, Cairney (Allan 68), Rhodes (O'Halloran 86), Wotherspoon, Mackay-Steven.

Easter Road, 25 April 2012, 7541

Scotland (1) 1 *(Mackay-Steven 33)*

Italy (1) 4 *(Florenzi 8, Immobile 55, Insigne 75, Longo 89)*

Scotland: Ridgers (Adam 46) (Edwards 48); Jack (Toshney 80), Hanlon (Shinnie G 80), Wilson D, Perry, Kelly (McCabe 46), Russell (McGeouch 46), Wotherspoon (Palmer 76), MacDonald (Feruz 61), Allan (McLean 65), Mackay-Steven (Armstrong 76).

Lovech, 31 May 2012, 1200

Bulgaria (1) 2 *(Milanov 33, Kostadinov 90)*

Scotland (0) 2 *(Rhodes 69, 89)*

Scotland: Ridgers; Jack (Toshney 81), Hanlon, Wilson D, Perry, Kelly, Russell (Palmer 83), Wotherspoon (Armstrong 67), Rhodes, Allan, Mackay-Steven.

WALES

Haverfordwest, 10 August 2011

Wales (1) 1 *(Lucas 37)*

Hungary (1) 2 *(Balazs 6, Haraszti 90)*

Wales: Maxwell (Taylor R 46); Alfei, Freeman (Bender 74), Lucas, Stephens (Hewitt 46), Brown (Walsh 61), Taylor J, Howells, Peniket (Ogleby 46), Bodin (Thomas 78), Williams J.

Podgorica, 6 September 2011, 2650

Montenegro (0) 3 *(Golubovic 65, Mugosa 77, Nikolic 88)*

Wales (0) 1 *(Bradshaw 55)*

Wales: Maxwell; Freeman, Brown, Alfei, Richards, Doble, Lucas, Bodin (Chamberlain 71), Williams J (Taylor J 62), Hewitt (Meades 74), Bradshaw.

Wrexham, 8 October 2011, 525

Wales (0) 1 *(Alfei 58 (pen))*

Montenegro (0) 0

Wales: Maxwell; Howells, Brown, Alfei, Hewitt, Richards, Doble, Taylor J (Bodin 79), Lucas, Freeman, Bradshaw.

Wrexham, 11 October 2011, 595

Wales (0) 0

Czech Republic (1) 1 *(Kadlec 5)*

Wales: Maxwell; Freeman, Richards, Lucas, Brown, Alfei, Taylor J (Bodin 46), Hewitt, Bradshaw (Ogleby 74), Doble (Chamberlain 49), Howells.

Erevan, 15 November 2011, 750

Armenia (0) 0

Wales (0) 0

Wales: Maxwell; Stephens, Alfei (Brown 59), Hewitt, Richards, Taylor J, Lucas, Bodin, Freeman (Ogleby 83), Williams J (Chamberlain 72), Bradshaw.

Wrexham, 29 February 2012, 2213

Wales (3) 4 *(Bodin 22, 33, Vieira 44 (og), Doble 59)*

Andorra (0) 0

Wales: Maxwell; Henley, Freeman (Dummett 61), Richards, Stephens, Brown (Taylor A 57), Bodin, Howells, Cassidy (Bradshaw 69), Taylor J, Doble.

NORTHERN IRELAND

Belfast, 10 August 2011, 800

Northern Ireland (3) 4 *(Kee 25, 29, 75, Magennis 32)*

Faeroes (0) 0

Northern Ireland: Devlin; Knowles, Dudgeon, McLaughlin P, Hegarty, McKeown, Lund (Breeze 62), Norwood, Kee, Magennis (Boyce 67), Carson (Grigg 70).

Karadjordje, 2 September 2011, 2250

Serbia (1) 1 *(Milivojevic 17)*

Northern Ireland (0) 0

Northern Ireland: Devlin; McLaughlin C■, McKeown, McLaughlin P, McCashin (Clucas 64), Ramsey, Grigg (Magennis 64), Norwood, Kee, Ferguson (Breeze 77).

Belfast, 6 September 2011, 172

Northern Ireland (0) 0

Denmark (1) 3 *(Helenius 6, Laudrup 81, Larsen 89)*

Northern Ireland: Devlin; Winchester, McKeown, Breeze (Ball 65), Hegarty, Ramsey, Dallas (Grigg 65), Norwood, Boyce (McLellan 80), Magennis, Ferguson.
Denmark: Jorgensen■

Coleraine, 15 November 2011, 175

Northern Ireland (0) 0

Serbia (2) 2 *(Markovic 80, Gudelj 83 (pen))*

Northern Ireland: Devlin; Thompson, Hodson, Ferguson (Lavery 79), McLaughlin C, Dudgeon, Gorman (Winchester 79), Carson, Clucas, Grigg (Knowles 46), Magennis.

Kumanovo, 10 May 2012, 1200

Macedonia (0) 1 *(Urdinov 83 (pen))*

Northern Ireland (0) 0

Northern Ireland: Devlin; Thompson, McGivern, Hodson, Ferguson■, McLaughlin C, McLaughlin R (Lavery 77), Lund (McClure 86), Norwood, Clucas, Grigg.

REPUBLIC OF IRELAND

Sligo, 9 August 2011, 1800

Republic of Ireland (0) 2 *(Brady 71, 90)*

Austria (0) 1 *(Holzhauser 68)*

Republic of Ireland: McLoughlin (McCarey 46), Connolly, Kiernan, Canavan (Oyebanjo 46), Gunning (Stevens 46), Clifford (Mason 46), Towell, Hendrick (Duffy 46), Brady, Doran (Kearns 80), White (Greene 80).

Sligo, 1 September 2011, 2500

Republic of Ireland (1) 2 *(Brady 15, Murphy 69)*

Hungary (1) 1 *(Futacs 38)*

Republic of Ireland: McLoughlin; White, Kiernan, Canavan, Gunning, Towell, Connolly, McCarthy, Barton, Brady, Murphy.
Hungary: Iszlai■

Denizli, 6 September 2011, 2712

Turkey (1) 1 *(Sahin 10)*

Republic of Ireland (0) 0

Republic of Ireland: McLoughlin; White, Oyebanjo (Duffy 76), Kiernan, Canavan, Gunning, Towell (Hourihane 80), Connolly, Clifford, Brady, Hendrick (Collins 67).

Eschen, 11 October 2011, 293

Liechtenstein (1) 1 *(Pirker 14)*

Republic of Ireland (4) 4 *(Collins 25, 29, Clifford 33, Duffy 39)*

Republic of Ireland: McLoughlin; Connolly, Canavan, Kiernan, Cunningham (Stevens 69), Brady (Greene 79), Towell, Clifford (Hourihane 66), White, Barton, Collins.

Sligo,14 November 2011, 2108

Republic of Ireland (2) 2 *(Brady 13 (pen), White 37)*

Liechtenstein (0) 0

Republic of Ireland: McLoughlin; White, Kiernan, Duffy, Cunningham, Towell, Connolly, Barton (Hendrick 81), Clifford (Greene 86), Brady, Collins (Sheppard 72).

Dublin, 28 May 2012, 500

Republic of Ireland (0) 1 *(Brady 54)*

Denmark (0) 2 *(Albaek 57, 74 (pen))*

Republic of Ireland: McLoughlin; Egan, Duffy, Cunningham, Canavan, White, Towell, Hendrick (Clifford 55), Brady (Murray 77), O'Kane (Hourihane 54), Murphy (Collins 54).

Sligo, 4 June 2012, 2600

Republic of Ireland (0) 2 *(Brady 67 (pen), Cunningham 71)*

Italy (1) 2 *(Duffy 3 (og), Immobile 55)*

Republic of Ireland: McLoughlin (McCarey 59); Egan, Duffy, Canavan, Cunningham, Hendrick, Towell, O'Kane, Brady, Murphy (Collins 89), White.
Italy: Verratti■

BRITISH UNDER-21 APPEARANCES 1976–2012

Bold type indicates players who made an international appearance in season 2011–12.

ENGLAND

Ablett, G. 1988 (Liverpool) 1
Adams, N. 1987 (Everton) 1
Adams, T. A. 1985 (Arsenal) 5
Addison, M. 2010 (Derby Co) 1
Agbonlahor, G. 2007 (Aston Villa) 16
Albrighton, M. K. 2011 (Aston Villa) 8
Allen, B. 1992 (QPR) 8
Allen, C. 1980 (QPR, Crystal Palace) 3
Allen, C. A. 1995 (Oxford U) 2
Allen, M. 1987 (QPR) 2
Allen, P. 1985 (West Ham U, Tottenham H) 3
Allen, R. W. 1998 (Tottenham H) 3
Alnwick, B. R. 2008 (Tottenham H) 1
Ambrose, D. P. F. 2003 (Ipswich T, Newcastle U, Charlton Ath) 10
Ameobi, F. 2001 (Newcastle U) 19
Ameobi, S. 2012 (Newcastle U) 2
Amos, B. P. 2012 (Manchester U) 1
Anderson, V. A. 1978 (Nottingham F) 1
Anderton, D. R. 1993 (Tottenham H) 12
Andrews, I. 1987 (Leicester C) 1
Ardley, N. C. 1993 (Wimbledon) 10
Ashcroft, L. 1992 (Preston NE) 1
Ashton, D. 2004 (Crewe Alex, Norwich C) 9
Atherton, P. 1992 (Coventry C) 1
Atkinson, B. 1991 (Sunderland) 6
Awford, A. T. 1993 (Portsmouth) 9

Bailey, G. R. 1979 (Manchester U) 14
Baines, L. J. 2005 (Wigan Ath) 16
Baker, G. E. 1981 (Southampton) 2
Baker, N. L. 2011 (Aston Villa) 3
Ball, M. J. 1999 (Everton) 7
Barker, S. 1985 (Blackburn R) 4
Barmby, N. J. 1994 (Tottenham H, Everton) 4
Bannister, G. 1982 (Sheffield W) 1
Barkley, R. 2012 (Everton) 4
Barnes, J. 1983 (Watford) 2
Barnes, P. S. 1977 (Manchester C) 9
Barrett, E. D. 1990 (Oldham Ath) 4
Barry, G. 1999 (Aston Villa) 27
Barton, J. 2004 (Manchester C) 2
Bart-Williams, C. G. 1993 (Sheffield W) 16
Batty, D. 1988 (Leeds U) 7
Bazeley, D. S. 1992 (Watford) 1
Beagrie, P. 1988 (Sheffield U) 2
Beardsmore, R. 1989 (Manchester U) 5
Beattie, J. S. 1999 (Southampton) 5
Beckham, D. R. J. 1995 (Manchester U) 9
Bennett, J. 2011 (Middlesbrough) 3
Bennett, R. 2012 (Norwich C) 1
Bent, D. A. 2003 (Ipswich T, Charlton Ath) 14
Bent, M. N. 1998 (Crystal Palace) 2
Bentley, D. M. 2004 (Arsenal, Blackburn R) 8
Beeston, C 1988 (Stoke C) 1
Benjamin, T. J. 2001 (Leicester C) 1
Bertrand, R. 2009 (Chelsea) 16
Bertschin, K. E. 1977 (Birmingham C) 3
Birtles, G. 1980 (Nottingham F) 2
Blackstock, D. A. 2008 (QPR) 2
Blackwell, D. R. 1991 (Wimbledon) 6
Blake, M. A. 1990 (Aston Villa) 8
Blissett, L. L. 1979 (Watford) 4
Booth, A. D. 1995 (Huddersfield T) 3
Bothroyd, J. 2001 (Coventry C) 1
Bowyer, L. D. 1996 (Charlton Ath, Leeds U) 13
Bracewell, P. 1983 (Stoke C) 13
Bradbury, L. M. 1997 (Portsmouth, Manchester C) 3
Bramble, T. M. 2001 (Ipswich T, Newcastle U) 10
Branch, P. M. 1997 (Everton) 1
Bradshaw, P. W. 1977 (Wolverhampton W) 4
Breacker, T. 1986 (Luton T) 2
Brennan, M. 1987 (Ipswich T) 5
Bridge, W. M. 1999 (Southampton) 8
Bridges, M. 1997 (Sunderland, Leeds U) 3
Briggs, M. 2012 (Fulham) 2
Brightwell, I. 1989 (Manchester C) 4
Briscoe, L. S. 1996 (Sheffield W) 5
Brock, K. 1984 (Oxford U) 4
Broomes, M. C. 1997 (Blackburn R) 2
Brown, M. R. 1996 (Manchester C) 4
Brown, W. M. 1999 (Manchester U) 8
Bull, S. G. 1989 (Wolverhampton W) 5
Bullock, M. J. 1998 (Barnsley) 1
Burrows, D. 1989 (WBA, Liverpool) 7
Butcher, T. I. 1979 (Ipswich T) 7
Butland, J. 2012 (Birmingham C) 6
Butt, N. 1995 (Manchester U) 7
Butters, G. 1989 (Tottenham H) 3
Butterworth, I. 1985 (Coventry C, Nottingham F) 8
Bywater, S. 2001 (West Ham U) 6

Cadamarteri, D. L. 1999 (Everton) 3
Caesar, G. 1987 (Arsenal) 3
Cahill, G. J. 2007 (Aston Villa) 3
Callaghan, N. 1983 (Watford) 9
Camp, L. M. J. 2005 (Derby Co) 5
Campbell, A. P. 2000 (Middlesbrough) 4
Campbell, F. L. 2008 (Manchester U) 14
Campbell, K. J. 1991 (Arsenal) 4
Campbell, S. 1994 (Tottenham) 11
Carbon, M. P. 1996 (Derby Co) 4
Carr, C. 1985 (Fulham) 1
Carr, F. 1987 (Nottingham F) 9
Carragher, J. L. 1997 (Liverpool) 27
Carroll, A. T. 2010 (Newcastle U) 5
Carlisle, C. J. 2001 (QPR) 3
Carrick, M. 2001 (West Ham U) 14
Carson, S. P. 2004 (Leeds U, Liverpool) 29
Casper, C. M. 1995 (Manchester U) 1
Caton, T. 1982 (Manchester C) 14
Cattermole, L. B. 2008 (Middlesbrough, Wigan Ath, Sunderland) 16
Caulker, S. R. 2011 (Tottenham H) 4
Chadwick, L. H. 2000 (Manchester U) 13
Challis, T. M. 1996 (QPR) 2
Chamberlain, M. 1983 (Stoke C) 4
Chaplow, R. D. 2004 (Burnley) 1
Chapman, L. 1981 (Stoke C) 1
Charles, G. A. 1991 (Nottingham F) 4
Chettle, S. 1988 (Nottingham F) 12
Chopra, R. M. 2004 (Newcastle U) 1
Clark, L. R. 1992 (Newcastle U) 11
Clarke, P. M. 2003 (Everton) 8
Christie, M. N. 2001 (Derby Co) 11
Clegg, M. J. 1998 (Manchester U) 2
Clemence, S. N. 1999 (Tottenham H) 1
Cleverley, T. W. 2010 (Manchester U) 16
Clough, N. H. 1986 (Nottingham F) 15
Clyne, N. E. 2012 (Crystal Palace) 2
Cole, A. 2001 (Arsenal) 4
Cole, A. A. 1992 (Arsenal, Bristol C, Newcastle U) 8
Cole, C. 2003 (Chelsea) 19
Cole, J. J. 2000 (West Ham U) 8
Coney, D. 1985 (Fulham) 4
Connor, T. 1987 (Brighton & HA) 1
Cooke, R. 1986 (Tottenham H) 1
Cooke, T. J. 1996 (Manchester U) 4
Cooper, C. T. 1988 (Middlesbrough) 8
Cork, J. F. P. 2009 (Chelsea) 13
Corrigan, J. T. 1978 (Manchester C) 3
Cort, C. E. R. 1999 (Wimbledon) 12
Cottee, A. R. 1985 (West Ham U) 8
Couzens, A. J. 1995 (Leeds U) 3

Cowans, G. S. 1979 (Aston Villa) 5
Cox, N. J. 1993 (Aston Villa) 6
Cranie, M. J. 2008 (Portsmouth) 16
Cranson, I. 1985 (Ipswich T) 5
Cresswell, R. P. W. 1999 (York C, Sheffield W) 4
Croft, G. 1995 (Grimsby T) 4
Crooks, G. 1980 (Stoke C) 4
Crossley, M. G. 1990 (Nottingham F) 3
Crouch, P. J. 2002 (Portsmouth, Aston Villa) 5
Cundy, J. V. 1991 (Chelsea) 3
Cunningham, L. 1977 (WBA) 6
Curbishley, L. C. 1981 (Birmingham C) 1
Curtis, J. C. K. 1998 (Manchester U) 16

Daniel, P. W. 1977 (Hull C) 7
Dann, S. 2008 (Coventry C) 2
Davenport, C. R. P. 2005 (Tottenham H) 8
Davies, A. J. 2004 (Middlesbrough) 1
Davies, C. E. 2006 (WBA) 3
Davies, K. C. 1998 (Southampton, Blackburn R, Southampton) 3
Davis, K. G. 1995 (Luton T) 3
Davis, P. 1982 (Arsenal) 11
Davis, S. 2001 (Fulham) 11
Dawson, C. 2012 (WBA) 7
Dawson, M. R. 2003 (Nottingham F, Tottenham H) 13
Day, C. N. 1996 (Tottenham H, Crystal Palace) 6
D'Avray, M. 1984 (Ipswich T) 2
Deehan, J. M. 1977 (Aston Villa) 7
Defoe, J. C. 2001 (West Ham U) 23
Delfouneso, N. 2010 (Aston Villa) 12
Delph, F. 2009 (Leeds U, Aston Villa) 4
Dennis, M. E. 1980 (Birmingham C) 3
Derbyshire, M. A. 2007 (Blackburn R) 14
Dichio, D. S. E. 1996 (QPR) 1
Dickens, A. 1985 (West Ham U) 1
Dicks, J. 1988 (West Ham U) 4
Digby, F. 1987 (Swindon T) 5
Dillon, K. P. 1981 (Birmingham C) 1
Dixon, K. M. 1985 (Chelsea) 1
Dobson, A. 1989 (Coventry C) 4
Dodd, J. R. 1991 (Southampton) 8
Donowa, L. 1985 (Norwich C) 3
Dorigo, A. R. 1987 (Aston Villa) 11
Downing, S. 2004 (Middlesbrough) 8
Dozzell, J. 1987 (Ipswich T) 9
Draper, M. A. 1991 (Notts Co) 3
Driver, A. 2009 (Hearts) 1
Duberry, M. W. 1997 (Chelsea) 5
Dunn, D. J. I. 1999 (Blackburn R) 20
Duxbury, M. 1981 (Manchester U) 7
Dyer, B. A. 1994 (Crystal Palace) 10
Dyer, K. C. 1998 (Ipswich T, Newcastle U) 11
Dyson, P. I. 1981 (Coventry C) 4

Eadie, D. M. 1994 (Norwich C) 7
Ebanks-Blake, S. 2009 (Wolverhampton W) 1
Ebbrell, J. 1989 (Everton) 14
Edghill, R. A. 1994 (Manchester C) 3
Ehiogu, U. 1992 (Aston Villa) 15
Elliott, P. 1985 (Luton T) 3
Elliott, R. J. 1996 (Newcastle U) 2
Elliott, S. W. 1998 (Derby Co) 3
Etherington, N, 2002 (Tottenham H) 3
Euell, J. J. 1998 (Wimbledon) 6
Evans, R. 2003 (Chelsea) 2

Fairclough, C. 1985 (Nottingham F, Tottenham H) 7
Fairclough, D. 1977 (Liverpool) 1
Fashanu, J. 1980 (Norwich C, Nottingham F) 11
Fear, P. 1994 (Wimbledon) 3
Fenton, G. A. 1995 (Aston Villa) 1
Fenwick, T. W. 1981 (Crystal Palace, QPR) 11
Ferdinand, A. J. 2005 (West Ham U) 17
Ferdinand, R. G. 1997 (West Ham U) 5
Fereday, W. 1985 (QPR) 5
Fielding, F. D. 2009 (Blackburn R) 12
Flanagan, J. 2012 (Liverpool) 3
Flitcroft, G. W. 1993 (Manchester C) 10
Flowers, T. D. 1987 (Southampton) 3
Ford, M. 1996 (Leeds U) 2
Forster, N. M. 1995 (Brentford) 4
Forsyth, M. 1988 (Derby Co) 1
Foster, S. 1980 (Brighton & HA) 1
Fowler, R. B. 1994 (Liverpool) 8
Fox, D. J. 2008 (Coventry C) 1
Froggatt, S. J. 1993 (Aston Villa) 2
Futcher, P. 1977 (Luton T, Manchester C) 11

Gabbiadini, M. 1989 (Sunderland) 2
Gale, A. 1982 (Fulham) 1
Gallen, K. A. 1995 (QPR) 4
Gardner, A. 2002 (Tottenham H) 1
Gardner, C. 2008 (Aston Villa) 14
Gardner, G. 2012 (Aston Villa) 5
Gascoigne, P. J. 1987 (Newcastle U) 13
Gayle, H. 1984 (Birmingham C) 3
Gernon, T. 1983 (Ipswich T) 1
Gerrard, P. W. 1993 (Oldham Ath) 18
Gerrard, S. G. 2000 (Liverpool) 4
Gibbs, K. J. R. 2009 (Arsenal) 15
Gibbs, N. 1987 (Watford) 5
Gibson, C. 1982 (Aston Villa) 1
Gilbert, W. A. 1979 (Crystal Palace) 11
Goddard, P. 1981 (West Ham U) 8
Gordon, D. 1987 (Norwich C) 4
Gordon, D. D. 1994 (Crystal Palace) 13
Gosling, D. 2010 (Everton, Newcastle U) 3
Grant, A. J. 1996 (Everton) 1
Grant, L. A. 2003 (Derby Co) 4
Granville, D. P. 1997 (Chelsea) 3
Gray, A. 1988 (Aston Villa) 2
Greening, J. 1999 (Manchester U, Middlesbrough) 18
Griffin, A. 1999 (Newcastle U) 3
Guppy, S. A. 1998 (Leicester C) 1

Haigh, P. 1977 (Hull C) 1
Hall, M. T. J. 1997 (Coventry C) 8
Hall, R. A. 1992 (Southampton) 11
Hamilton, D. V. 1997 (Newcastle U) 1
Hammill, A. 2010 (Wolverhampton W) 1
Harding, D. A. 2005 (Brighton & HA) 4
Hardyman, P. 1985 (Portsmouth) 2
Hargreaves, O. 2001 (Bayern Munich) 3
Harley, J. 2000 (Chelsea) 3
Hart, C. 2007 (Manchester C) 21
Hateley, M. 1982 (Coventry C, Portsmouth) 10
Hayes, M. 1987 (Arsenal) 3
Hazell, R. J. 1979 (Wolverhampton W) 1
Heaney, N. A. 1992 (Arsenal) 6
Heath, A. 1981 (Stoke C, Everton) 8
Heaton, T. D. 2008 (Manchester U) 3
Henderson, J. B. 2011 (Sunderland, Liverpool) 16
Hendon, I. M. 1992 (Tottenham H) 7
Hendrie, L. A. 1996 (Aston Villa) 13
Hesford, I. 1981 (Blackpool) 7
Heskey, E. W. I. 1997 (Leicester C, Liverpool) 16
Hilaire, V. 1980 (Crystal Palace) 9
Hill, D. R. L. 1995 (Tottenham H) 4
Hillier, D. 1991 (Arsenal) 1
Hinchcliffe, A. 1989 (Manchester C) 1
Hines, Z. 2010 (West Ham U) 2
Hinshelwood, P. A. 1978 (Crystal Palace) 2
Hirst, D. E. 1988 (Sheffield W) 7
Hislop, N. S. 1998 (Newcastle U) 1
Hoddle, G. 1977 (Tottenham H) 12
Hodge, S. B. 1983 (Nottingham F, Aston Villa) 8
Hodgson, D. J. 1981 (Middlesbrough) 6
Holdsworth, D. 1989 (Watford) 1
Holland, C. J. 1995 (Newcastle U) 10
Holland, P. 1995 (Mansfield T) 4
Holloway, D. 1998 (Sunderland) 1
Horne, B. 1989 (Millwall) 5
Howe, E. J. F. 1998 (Bournemouth) 2
Howson, J. M. 2011 (Leeds U) 1
Hoyte, J. R. 2004 (Arsenal) 18
Hucker, P. 1984 (QPR) 2
Huckerby, D. 1997 (Coventry C) 4

Huddlestone, T. A. 2005 (Derby Co, Tottenham H) 33
Hughes, S. J. 1997 (Arsenal) 8
Humphreys, R. J. 1997 (Sheffield W) 3
Hunt, N. B. 2004 (Bolton W) 10

Impey, A. R. 1993 (QPR) 1
Ince, P. E. C. 1989 (West Ham U) 2
Jackson, M. A. 1992 (Everton) 10
Jagielka, P. N. 2003 (Sheffield U) 6
James, D. B. 1991 (Watford) 10
James, J. C. 1990 (Luton T) 2
Jansen, M. B. 1999 (Crystal Palace, Blackburn R) 6
Jeffers, F. 2000 (Everton, Arsenal) 16
Jemson, N. B. 1991 (Nottingham F) 1
Jenas, J. A. 2002 (Newcastle U) 9
Jerome, C. 2006 (Cardiff C, Birmingham C) 10
Joachim, J. K. 1994 (Leicester C) 9
Johnson, A. 2008 (Middlesbrough) 19
Johnson, G. M. C. 2003 (West Ham U, Chelsea) 14
Johnson, M. 2008 (Manchester C) 2
Johnson, S. A. M. 1999 (Crewe Alex, Derby Co, Leeds U) 15
Johnson, T. 1991 (Notts Co, Derby Co) 7
Johnston, C. P. 1981 (Middlesbrough) 2
Jones, D. R. 1977 (Everton) 1
Jones, C. H. 1978 (Tottenham H) 1
Jones, D. F. L. 2004 (Manchester U) 1
Jones, P. A. 2011 (Blackburn R) 9
Jones, R. 1993 (Liverpool) 2

Keane, W. D. 2012 (Manchester U) 3
Keegan, G. A. 1977 (Manchester C) 1
Kelly, M. R. 2011 (Liverpool) 6
Kenny, W. 1993 (Everton) 1
Keown, M. R. 1987 (Aston Villa) 8
Kerslake, D. 1986 (QPR) 1
Kightly, M. J. 2008 (Wolverhampton W) 7
Kilcline, B. 1983 (Notts C) 2
Kilgallon, M. 2004 (Leeds U) 5
King, A. E. 1977 (Everton) 2
King, L. B. 2000 (Tottenham H) 12
Kirkland, C. E. 2001 (Coventry C, Liverpool) 8
Kitson, P. 1991 (Leicester C, Derby Co) 7
Knight, A. 1983 (Portsmouth) 2
Knight, I. 1987 (Sheffield W) 2
Knight, Z. 2002 (Fulham) 4
Konchesky, P. M. 2002 (Charlton Ath) 15
Kozluk, R. 1998 (Derby Co) 2

Lake, P. 1989 (Manchester C) 5
Lallana, A. D. 2009 (Southampton) 1
Lampard, F. J. 1998 (West Ham U) 19
Langley, T. W. 1978 (Chelsea) 1
Lansbury, H. G. 2010 (Arsenal) 14
Leadbitter, G. 2008 (Sunderland) 3
Lee, D. J. 1990 (Chelsea) 10
Lee, R. M. 1986 (Charlton Ath) 2
Lee, S. 1981 (Liverpool) 6
Lennon, A. J. 2006 (Tottenham H) 5
Le Saux, G. P. 1990 (Chelsea) 4
Lescott, J. P. 2003 (Wolverhampton W) 2
Lewis, J. P. 2008 (Peterborough U) 5
Lita, L. H. 2005 (Bristol C, Reading) 9
Loach, S. J. 2009 (Watford) 14
Lowe, D. 1988 (Ipswich T) 2
Lowe, J. J. 2012 (Blackburn R) 3
Lukic, J. 1981 (Leeds U) 7
Lund, G. 1985 (Grimsby T) 3

McCall, S. H. 1981 (Ipswich T) 6
McCarthy, A. S. 2011 (Reading) 3
McDonald, N. 1987 (Newcastle U) 5
McEachran, J. M. 2011 (Chelsea) 8
McEveley, J. 2003 (Blackburn R) 1
McGrath, L. 1986 (Coventry C) 1
MacKenzie, S. 1982 (WBA) 3
McLeary, A. 1988 (Millwall) 1
McLeod, I. M. 2006 (Milton Keynes D) 1
McMahon, S. 1981 (Everton, Aston Villa) 6
McManaman, S. 1991 (Liverpool) 7
Mabbutt, G. 1982 (Bristol R, Tottenham H) 7
Makin, C. 1994 (Oldham Ath) 5
Mancienne, M. I. 2008 (Chelsea) 30
Marney, D. E. 2005 (Tottenham H) 1
Marriott, A. 1992 (Nottingham F) 1
Marsh, S. T. 1998 (Oxford U) 1
Marshall, A. J. 1995 (Norwich C) 4
Marshall, L. K. 1999 (Norwich C) 1
Martin, L. 1989 (Manchester U) 2
Martyn, A. N. 1988 (Bristol R) 11
Matteo, D. 1994 (Liverpool) 4
Mattock, J. W. 2008 (Leicester C) 5
Matthew, D. 1990 (Chelsea) 9
May, A. 1986 (Manchester C) 1
Mee, B. 2011 (Manchester C) 2
Merson, P. C. 1989 (Arsenal) 4
Middleton, J. 1977 (Nottingham F, Derby Co) 3
Miller, A. 1988 (Arsenal) 4
Mills, D. J. 1999 (Charlton Ath, Leeds U) 14
Mills, G. R. 1981 (Nottingham F) 2
Milner, J. P. 2004 (Leeds U, Newcastle U, Aston Villa) 46
Mimms, R. 1985 (Rotherham U, Everton) 3
Minto, S. C. 1991 (Charlton Ath) 6
Moore, I. 1996 (Tranmere R, Nottingham F) 7
Moore, L. I. 2006 (Aston Villa) 5
Moran, S. 1982 (Southampton) 2
Morgan, S. 1987 (Leicester C) 2
Morris, J. 1997 (Chelsea) 7
Mortimer, P. 1989 (Charlton Ath) 2
Moses, A. P. 1997 (Barnsley) 2
Moses, R. M. 1981 (WBA, Manchester U) 8
Moses, V. 2011 (Wigan Ath) 1
Mountfield, D. 1984 (Everton) 1
Muamba, F. N. 2008 (Birmingham C, Bolton W) 33
Muggleton, C. D. 1990 (Leicester C) 1
Mullins, H. I. 1999 (Crystal Palace) 3
Murphy, D. B. 1998 (Liverpool) 4
Murray, P. 1997 (QPR) 4
Murray, M. W. 2003 (Wolverhampton W) 5
Mutch, A. 1989 (Wolverhampton W) 1
Mutch, J. J. E. S. 2011 (Birmingham C) 1
Myers. A. 1995 (Chelsea) 4

Naughton, K. 2009 (Sheffield U, Tottenham H) 9
Naylor, L. M. 2000 (Wolverhampton W) 3
Nethercott, S. H. 1994 (Tottenham H) 8
Neville, P. J. 1995 (Manchester U) 7
Newell, M. 1986 (Luton T) 4
Newton, A. L. 2001 (West Ham U) 1
Newton, E. J. I. 1993 (Chelsea) 2
Newton, S. O. 1997 (Charlton Ath) 3
Nicholls, A. 1994 (Plymouth Arg) 1
Noble, M. J. 2007 (West Ham U) 20
Nolan, K. A. J. 2003 (Bolton W) 1
Nugent, D. J. 2006 (Preston NE) 14

Oakes, M. C. 1994 (Aston Villa) 6
Oakes, S. J. 1993 (Luton T) 1
Oakley, M. 1997 (Southampton) 4
O'Brien, A. J. 1999 (Bradford C) 1
O'Connor, J. 1996 (Everton) 3
O'Hara, J. D. 2008 (Tottenham H) 7
Oldfield, D. 1989 (Luton T) 1
Olney, I. A. 1990 (Aston Villa) 10
O'Neil, G. P. 2005 (Portsmouth) 9
Onuoha, C. 2006 (Manchester C) 21
Ord, R. J. 1991 (Sunderland) 3
Osman, R. C. 1979 (Ipswich T) 7
Owen, G. A. 1977 (Manchester C, WBA) 22
Owen, M. J. 1998 (Liverpool) 1
Oxlade-Chamberlain, A. M. D. 2011 (Southampton, Arsenal) 8

Painter, I. 1986 (Stoke C) 1
Palmer, C. L. 1989 (Sheffield W) 4
Parker, G. 1986 (Hull C, Nottingham F) 6
Parker, P. A. 1985 (Fulham) 8
Parker, S. M. 2001 (Charlton Ath) 12

Parkes, P. B. F. 1979 (QPR) 1
Parkin, S. 1987 (Stoke C) 5
Parlour, R. 1992 (Arsenal) 12
Parnaby, S. 2003 (Middlesbrough) 4
Peach, D. S. 1977 (Southampton) 6
Peake, A. 1982 (Leicester C) 1
Pearce, I. A. 1995 (Blackburn R) 3
Pearce, S. 1987 (Nottingham F) 1
Pennant, J. 2001 (Arsenal) 24
Pickering N. 1983 (Sunderland, Coventry C) 15
Platt, D. 1988 (Aston Villa) 3
Plummer, C. S. 1996 (QPR) 5
Pollock, J. 1995 (Middlesbrough) 3
Porter, G. 1987 (Watford) 12
Potter, G. S. 1997 (Southampton) 1
Pressman, K. 1989 (Sheffield W) 1
Proctor, M. 1981 (Middlesbrough, Nottingham F) 4
Prutton, D. T. 2001 (Nottingham F, Southampton) 25
Purse, D. J. 1998 (Birmingham C) 2

Quashie, N. F. 1997 (QPR) 4
Quinn, W. R. 1998 (Sheffield U) 2

Ramage, C. D. 1991 (Derby Co) 3
Ranson, R. 1980 (Manchester C) 10
Redknapp, J. F. 1993 (Liverpool) 19
Redmond, S. 1988 (Manchester C) 14
Reeves, K. P. 1978 (Norwich C, Manchester C) 10
Regis, C. 1979 (WBA) 6
Reid, N. S. 1981 (Manchester C) 6
Reid, P. 1977 (Bolton W) 6
Reo-Coker, N. S. A. 2004 (Wimbledon, West Ham U) 23
Richards, D. I. 1995 (Wolverhampton W) 4
Richards, J. P. 1977 (Wolverhampton W) 2
Richards, M. 2007 (Manchester C) 15
Richards, M. L. 2005 (Ipswich T) 1
Richardson, K. E. 2005 (Manchester U) 8
Rideout, P. 1985 (Aston Villa, Bari) 5
Ridgewell, L. M. 2004 (Aston Villa) 8
Riggott, C. M. 2001 (Derby Co) 8
Ripley, S. E. 1988 (Middlesbrough) 8
Ritchie, A. 1982 (Brighton & HA) 1
Rix, G. 1978 (Arsenal) 7
Roberts, A. J. 1995 (Millwall, Crystal Palace) 5
Roberts, B. J. 1997 (Middlesbrough) 1
Robins, M. G. 1990 (Manchester U) 6
Robinson, P. P. 1999 (Watford) 3
Robinson, P. W. 2000 (Leeds U) 11
Robson, B. 1979 (WBA) 7
Robson, S. 1984 (Arsenal, West Ham U) 8
Rocastle, D. 1987 (Arsenal) 14
Roche, L. P. 2001 (Manchester U) 1
Rodger, G. 1987 (Coventry C) 4
Rodriguez, J. E. 2011 (Burnley) 1
Rodwell, J. 2009 (Everton) 20
Rogers, A. 1998 (Nottingham F) 3
Rosario, R. 1987 (Norwich C) 4
Rose, D. L. 2009 (Tottenham H) 21
Rose, M. 1997 (Arsenal) 2
Rosenior, L. J. 2005 (Fulham) 7
Routledge, W. 2005 (Crystal Palace, Tottenham H) 12
Rowell, G. 1977 (Sunderland) 1
Ruddock, N. 1989 (Southampton) 4
Rufus, R. R. 1996 (Charlton Ath) 6
Ryan, J. 1983 (Oldham Ath) 1
Ryder, S. H. 1995 (Walsall) 3

Samuel, J. 2002 (Aston Villa) 7
Samways, V. 1988 (Tottenham H) 5
Sansom, K. G. 1979 (Crystal Palace) 8
Scimeca, R. 1996 (Aston Villa) 9
Scowcroft, J. B. 1997 (Ipswich T) 5
Seaman, D. A. 1985 (Birmingham C) 10
Sears, F. D. 2010 (West Ham U) 3
Sedgley, S. 1987 (Coventry C, Tottenham H) 11
Sellars, S. 1988 (Blackburn R) 3
Selley, I. 1994 (Arsenal) 3
Serrant, C. 1998 (Oldham Ath) 2
Sharpe, L. S. 1989 (Manchester U) 8
Shaw, G. R. 1981 (Aston Villa) 7
Shawcross, R. J. 2008 (Stoke C) 2
Shearer, A. 1991 (Southampton) 11
Shelton, G. 1985 (Sheffield W) 1
Shelvey, J. 2012 (Liverpool) 4
Sheringham, E. P. 1988 (Millwall) 1
Sheron, M. N. 1992 (Manchester C) 16
Sherwood, T. A. 1990 (Norwich C) 4
Shipperley, N. J. 1994 (Chelsea, Southampton) 7
Sidwell, S. J. 2003 (Reading) 5
Simonsen, S. P. A. 1998 (Tranmere R, Everton) 4
Simpson, P. 1986 (Manchester C) 5
Sims, S. 1977 (Leicester C) 10
Sinclair, S. A. 2011 (Swansea C) 7
Sinclair, T. 1994 (QPR, West Ham U) 5
Sinnott, L. 1985 (Watford) 1
Slade, S. A. 1996 (Tottenham H) 4
Slater, S. I. 1990 (West Ham U) 3
Small, B. 1993 (Aston Villa) 12
Smalling, C. L. 2010 (Fulham, Manchester U) 14
Smith, A. 2000 (Leeds U) 10
Smith, A. J. 2012 (Tottenham H) 4
Smith, D. 1988 (Coventry C) 10
Smith, M. 1981 (Sheffield W) 5
Smith, M. 1995 (Sunderland) 1
Smith, T. W. 2001 (Watford) 1
Snodin, I. 1985 (Doncaster R) 4
Soares, T. J. 2006 (Crystal Palace) 4
Sordell, M. A. 2012 (Watford, Bolton W) 7
Spence, J. 2011 (West Ham U) 1
Stanislaus, F. J. 2010 (West Ham U) 2
Statham, B. 1988 (Tottenham H) 3
Statham, D. J. 1978 (WBA) 6
Stead, J. G. 2004 (Blackburn R, Sunderland) 11
Stearman, R. J. 2009 (Wolverhampton W) 4
Steele, J. 2011 (Middlesbrough) 1
Stein, B. 1984 (Luton T) 3
Sterland, M. 1984 (Sheffield W) 7
Steven, T. M. 1985 (Everton) 2
Stevens, G. A. 1983 (Brighton & HA, Tottenham H) 8
Stewart, J. 2003 (Leicester C) 1
Stewart, P. 1988 (Manchester C) 1
Stockdale, R. K. 2001 (Middlesbrough) 1
Stuart, G. C. 1990 (Chelsea) 5
Stuart, J. C. 1996 (Charlton Ath) 4
Sturridge, D. A. 2010 (Chelsea) 15
Suckling, P. 1986 (Coventry C, Manchester C, Crystal Palace) 10
Summerbee, N. J. 1993 (Swindon T) 3
Sunderland, A. 1977 (Wolverhampton W) 1
Surman, A. R. E. 2008 (Southampton) 4
Sutch, D. 1992 (Norwich C) 4
Sutton, C. R. 1993 (Norwich C) 13
Swindlehurst, D. 1977 (Crystal Palace) 1

Talbot, B. 1977 (Ipswich T) 1
Taylor, A. D. 2007 (Middlesbrough) 13
Taylor, M. 2001 (Blackburn R) 1
Taylor, M. S. 2003 (Portsmouth) 3
Taylor, R. A. 2006 (Wigan Ath) 4
Taylor, S. J. 2002 (Arsenal) 3
Taylor, S. V. 2004 (Newcastle U) 29
Terry, J. G. 2001 (Chelsea) 9
Thatcher, B. D. 1996 (Millwall, Wimbledon) 4
Thelwell, A. A. 2001 (Tottenham H) 1
Thirlwell, P. 2001 (Sunderland) 1
Thomas, D. 1981 (Coventry C, Tottenham H) 7
Thomas, J. W. 2006 (Charlton Ath) 2
Thomas, M. 1986 (Luton T) 3
Thomas, M. L. 1988 (Arsenal) 12
Thomas, R. E. 1990 (Watford) 1
Thompson, A. 1995 (Bolton W) 2
Thompson, D. A. 1997 (Liverpool) 7
Thompson, G. L. 1981 (Coventry C) 6
Thorn, A. 1988 (Wimbledon) 5
Thornley, B. L. 1996 (Manchester U) 3
Tiler, C. 1990 (Barnsley, Nottingham F) 13
Tomkins, J. O. C. 2009 (West Ham U) 10
Tonge, M. W. E. 2004 (Sheffield U) 2

Trippier, K. J. 2011 (Manchester C) 2

Unsworth, D. G. 1995 (Everton) 6
Upson, M. J. 1999 (Arsenal) 11

Vassell, D. 1999 (Aston Villa) 11
Vaughan, J. O. 2007 (Everton) 4
Venison, B. 1983 (Sunderland) 10
Vernazza, P. A. P. 2001 (Arsenal, Watford) 2
Vinnicombe, C. 1991 (Rangers) 12

Waddle, C. R. 1985 (Newcastle U) 1
Waghorn, M. T. 2012 (Leicester C) 3
Walcott, T. J. 2007 (Arsenal) 21
Wallace, D. L. 1983 (Southampton) 14
Wallace, Ray 1989 (Southampton) 4
Wallace, Rod 1989 (Southampton) 11
Walker, D. 1985 (Nottingham F) 7
Walker, I. M. 1991 (Tottenham H) 9
Walker, K. 2010 (Tottenham H) 7
Walsh, G. 1988 (Manchester U) 2
Walsh, P. A. 1983 (Luton T) 4
Walters, K. 1984 (Aston Villa) 9
Ward, P. 1978 (Brighton & HA) 2
Warhurst, P. 1991 (Oldham Ath, Sheffield W) 8
Watson, B. 2007 (Crystal Palace) 1
Watson, D. 1984 (Norwich C) 7
Watson, D. N. 1994 (Barnsley) 5
Watson, G. 1991 (Sheffield W) 2
Watson, S. C. 1993 (Newcastle U) 12
Weaver, N. J. 2000 (Manchester C) 10
Webb, N. J. 1985 (Portsmouth, Nottingham F) 3
Welbeck, D. 2009 (Manchester U) 14
Welsh, J. J. 2004 (Liverpool, Hull C) 8
Wheater, D. J. 2008 (Middlesbrough) 11
Whelan, P. J. 1993 (Ipswich T) 3
Whelan, N. 1995 (Leeds U) 2
Whittingham, P. 2004 (Aston Villa, Cardiff C) 17
White, D. 1988 (Manchester C) 6
Whyte, C. 1982 (Arsenal) 4
Wickham, C. N. R. 2011 (Ipswich T, Sunderland) 5
Wicks, S. 1982 (QPR) 1
Wilkins, R. C. 1977 (Chelsea) 1
Wilkinson, P. 1985 (Grimsby T, Everton) 4
Williams, D. 1998 (Sunderland) 2
Williams, P. 1989 (Charlton Ath) 4
Williams, P. D. 1991 (Derby Co) 6
Williams, S. C. 1977 (Southampton) 14
Wilshere, J. A. 2010 (Arsenal) 7
Wilson, M. A. 2001 (Manchester U, Middlesbrough) 6
Winterburn, N. 1986 (Wimbledon) 1
Wisdom, A. 2012 (Liverpool) 1
Wise, D. F. 1988 (Wimbledon) 1
Woodcook, A. S. 1978 (Nottingham F) 2
Woodgate, J. S. 2000 (Leeds U) 1
Woodhouse, C. 1999 (Sheffield U) 4
Woods, C. C. E. 1979 (Nottingham F, QPR, Norwich C) 6
Wright, A. G. 1993 (Blackburn R) 2
Wright, M. 1983 (Southampton) 4
Wright, R. I. 1997 (Ipswich T) 15
Wright, S. J. 2001 (Liverpool) 10
Wright, W. 1979 (Everton) 6
Wright-Phillips, S. C. 2002 (Manchester C) 6

Yates, D. 1989 (Notts Co) 5
Young, A. S. 2007 (Watford, Aston Villa) 10
Young, L. P. 1999 (Tottenham H, Charlton Ath) 12

Zaha, D. W. A. 2012 (Crystal Palace) 1
Zamora, R. L. 2002 (Brighton & HA) 6

NORTHERN IRELAND

Allen, C. 2009 (Lisburn Distillery) 1
Armstrong, D. T. 2007 (Hearts) 1

Bagnall, L. 2011 (Sunderland) 1
Bailie, N. 1990 (Linfield) 2
Baird, C. P. 2002 (Southampton) 6
Ball, M. 2011 (Norwich C) 2
Beatty, S. 1990 (Chelsea, Linfield) 2
Black, J. 2003 (Tottenham H) 1
Black, K. T. 1990 (Luton T) 1
Black, R. Z. 2002 (Morecambe) 1
Blackledge, G. 1978 (Portadown) 1
Blake, R. G. 2011 (Brentford) 2
Blayney, A. 2003 (Southampton) 4
Boyce, L. 2010 (Cliftonville, Werder Bremen) 7
Boyle, W. S. 1998 (Leeds U) 7
Braniff, K. R. 2002 (Millwall) 11
Breeze, J. 2011 (Wigan Ath) 4
Brotherston, N. 1978 (Blackburn R) 1
Browne, G. 2003 (Manchester C) 5
Brunt, C. 2005 (Sheffield W) 2
Bryan, M. A. 2010 (Watford) 4
Buchanan, D. T. H. 2006 (Bury) 15
Buchanan, W. B. 2002 (Bolton W, Lisburn Distillery) 5
Burns, L. 1998 (Port Vale) 13

Callaghan, A. 2006 (Limavady U, Ballymena U, Derry C) 15
Campbell, S. 2003 (Ballymena U) 1
Capaldi, A. C. 2002 (Birmingham C, Plymouth Arg) 14
Carlisle, W. T. 2000 (Crystal Palace) 9
Carroll, R. E. 1998 (Wigan Ath) 11
Carson, J. G. 2011 (Ipswich T) 6
Carson, S. 2000 (Rangers, Dundee U) 2
Carson, T. 2007 (Sunderland) 15
Carvill, M. D. 2008 (Wrexham, Linfield) 8
Casement, C. 2007 (Ipswich T, Dundee) 18
Cathcart, C. 2007 (Manchester U) 15
Catney, R. 2007 (Lisburn Distillery) 1
Chapman, A. 2008 (Sheffield U, Oxford U) 7
Clarke, L. 2003 (Peterborough U) 4
Clarke, R. 2006 (Newry C) 7
Clarke, R. D. J. 1999 (Portadown) 5
Clingan, S. G. 2003 (Wolverhampton W, Nottingham F) 11
Close, B. 2002 (Middlesbrough) 10
Clucas, M. S. 2011 (Preston NE) 6
Clyde, M. G. 2002 (Wolverhampton W) 5
Colligan, L. 2009 (Ballymena U) 1
Connell, T. E. 1978 (Coleraine) 1
Coote, A. 1998 (Norwich C) 12
Convery, J. 2000 (Celtic) 4

Dallas, S. 2012 (Crusaders) 1
Davey, H. 2004 (UCD) 3
Davis, S. 2004 (Aston Villa) 3
Devine, D. 1994 (Omagh T) 1
Devine, D. G. 2011 (Preston NE) 2
Devine, J. 1990 (Glentoran) 1
Devlin, C. 2011 (Manchester U, unattached) 8
Dickson, H. 2002 (Wigan Ath) 1
Doherty, M. 2007 (Hearts) 2
Dolan, J. 2000 (Millwall) 6
Donaghy, M. M. 1978 (Larne) 1
Donnelly, M. 2007 (Sheffield U, Crusaders) 5
Dowie, I. 1990 (Luton T) 1
Drummond, W. 2011 (Rangers) 2
Dudgeon, J. P. 2010 (Manchester U) 4
Duff, S. 2003 (Cheltenham T) 1
Duffy, S. P. M. 2010 (Everton) 3

Elliott, S. 1999 (Glentoran) 3
Ervin, J. 2005 (Linfield) 2
Evans, C. J. 2009 (Manchester U) 10
Evans, J. 2006 (Manchester U) 3

Feeney, L. 1998 (Linfield, Rangers) 8
Feeney, W. 2002 (Bournemouth) 8
Ferguson, M. 2000 (Glentoran) 2
Ferguson, S. 2009 (Newcastle U) 11
Fitzgerald, D. 1998 (Rangers) 4
Flynn, J. J. 2009 (Blackburn R, Ross Co) 11

Fordyce, D. T. 2007 (Portsmouth, Glentoran) 12
Friars, E. C. 2005 (Notts Co) 7
Friars, S. M. 1998 (Liverpool, Ipswich T) 21

Garrett, R. 2007 (Stoke C, Linfield) 14
Gault, M. 2005 (Linfield) 2
Gibb, S. 2009 (Falkirk, Drogheda U) 2
Gilfillan, B. J. 2005 (Gretna, Peterhead) 9
Gillespie, K. R. 1994 (Manchester U) 1
Glendinning, M. 1994 (Bangor) 1
Gorman, R. J. 2012 (Wolverhampton W) 1
Graham, G. L. 1999 (Crystal Palace) 5
Graham, R. S. 1999 (QPR) 15
Gray, P. 1990 (Luton T) 1
Griffin, D. J. 1998 (St Johnstone) 10
Grigg, W. D. 2011 (Walsall) 10

Hamilton, G. 2000 (Blackburn R, Portadown) 12
Hamilton, W. R. 1978 (Linfield) 1
Hanley, N. 2011 (Linfield) 1
Harkin, M. P. 2000 (Wycombe W) 9
Harvey, J. 1978 (Arsenal) 1
Hawe, S. 2001 (Blackburn R) 2
Hayes, T. 1978 (Luton T) 1
Hazley, M. 2007 (Stoke C) 3
Healy, D. J. 1999 (Manchester U) 8
Hegarty, C. 2011 (Rangers) 4
Herron, C. J. 2003 (QPR) 2
Higgins, R. 2006 (Derry C) 1
Hodson, L. J. S. 2010 (Watford) 9
Holmes, S. 2000 (Manchester C, Wrexham) 13
Howland, D. 2007 (Birmingham C) 4
Hughes, J. 2006 (Lincoln C) 7
Hughes, M. A. 2003 (Tottenham H, Oldham Ath) 12
Hughes, M. E. 1990 (Manchester C) 1
Hunter, M. 2002 (Glentoran) 1

Ingham, M. G. 2001 (Sunderland) 4

Jarvis, D. 2010 (Aberdeen) 2
Johnson, D. M. 1998 (Blackburn R) 11
Johnston, B. 1978 (Cliftonville) 1
Julian, A. A. 2005 (Brentford) 1

Kane, A. M. 2008 (Blackburn R) 5
Kee, B. R. 2010 (Leicester C, Torquay U, Burton Alb) 8
Kee, P. V. 1990 (Oxford U) 1
Kelly, D. 2000 (Derry C) 11
Kelly, N. 1990 (Oldham Ath) 1
Kirk, A. R. 1999 (Hearts) 9
Knowles, J. 2012 (Blackburn R) 2

Lafferty, D. 2009 (Celtic) 6
Lafferty, K. 2006 (Burnley) 2
Lavery, C. 2011 (Ipswich T, unattached) 3
Lawrie, J. 2009 (Port Vale, AFC Telford U) 9
Lennon, N. F. 1990 (Manchester C, Crewe Alex) 2
Lindsay, K. 2006 (Larne) 1
Little, A. 2009 (Rangers) 6
Lowry, P. 2009 (Institute, Linfield) 6
Lund, M. 2011 (Stoke C) 4
Lyttle, G. 1998 (Celtic, Peterborough U) 8

Magee, J. 1994 (Bangor) 1
Magee, J. 2009 (Lisburn Distillery) 1
Magennis, J. B. D. 2010 (Cardiff C, Aberdeen) 13
Magilton, J. 1990 (Liverpool) 1
Magnay, C. 2010 (Chelsea) 1
Matthews, N. P. 1990 (Blackpool) 1
McAllister, M. 2007 (Dungannon Swifts) 4
McArdle, R. A. 2006 (Sheffield W, Rochdale) 19
McAreavey, P. 2000 (Swindon T) 7
McBride, J. 1994 (Glentoran) 1
McCaffrey, D. 2006 (Hibernian) 8
McCallion, E. 1998 (Coleraine) 1
McCann, G. S. 2000 (West Ham U) 11
McCann, P. 2003 (Portadown) 1
McCann, R. 2002 (Rangers, Linfield) 2
McCartney, G. 2001 (Sunderland) 5
McCashin, S. 2011 (Jerez Industrial, unattached) 2
McChrystal, M. 2005 (Derry C) 9
McClean, J. 2010 (Derry C) 3
McClure, M. 2012 (Wycombe W) 1
McCourt, P. J. 2002 (Rochdale, Derry C) 8
McCoy, R. K. 1990 (Coleraine) 1
McCreery, D. 1978 (Manchester U) 1
McEvilly, L. R. 2003 (Rochdale) 9
McFlynn, T. M. 2000 (QPR, Woking, Margate) 19
McGibbon, P. C. G. 1994 (Manchester U) 1
McGivern, R. 2010 (Manchester C) 6
McGlinchey, B. 1998 (Manchester C, Port Vale, Gillingham) 14
McGovern, M. 2005 (Celtic) 10
McGowan, M. V. 2006 (Clyde) 2
McGurk, A. 2010 (Aston Villa) 1
McIlroy, T. 1994 (Linfield) 1
McKay, W. 2009 (Leicester C, Northampton T) 7
McKenna, K. 2007 (Tottenham H) 6
McKeown, R. 2012 (Kilmarnock) 3
McKnight, P. 1998 (Rangers) 3
McLaughlin, C. G. 2010 (Preston NE) 5
McLaughlin, P. 2010 (Newcastle U, York C) 7
McLaughlin, R. 2012 (Liverpool) 1
McLean, B. S. 2006 (Rangers) 1
McLean, J. 2009 (Derry C) 4
McLellan, M. 2012 (Preston NE) 1
McMahon, G. J. 2002 (Tottenham H) 1
McMenamin, L. A. 2009 (Sheffield W) 4
McQuilken, J. 2009 (Tescoma Zlin) 1
McQuoid, J. J. B. 2009 (Bournemouth) 8
McVeigh, A. 2002 (Ayr U) 1
McVeigh, P. M. 1998 (Tottenham H) 11
McVey, K. 2006 (Coleraine) 8
Meenan, D. 2007 (Finn Harps, Monaghan U) 3
Melaugh, G. M. 2002 (Aston Villa, Glentoran) 11
Millar, K. S. 2011 (Oldham Ath) 2
Millar, W. P. 1990 (Port Vale) 1
Miskelly, D. T. 2000 (Oldham Ath) 10
Moreland, V. 1978 (Glentoran) 1
Morgan, M. P. T. 1999 (Preston NE) 1
Morris, E. J. 2002 (WBA, Glentoran) 8
Morrison, O. 2001 (Sheffield W, Sheffield U) 7
Morrow, A. 2001 (Northampton T) 1
Morrow, S. 2005 (Hibernian) 4
Mulgrew, J. 2007 (Linfield) 10
Mulryne, P. P. 1999 (Manchester U, Norwich C) 5
Murray, W. 1978 (Linfield) 1
Murtagh, C. 2005 (Hearts) 1

Nicholl, J. M. 1978 (Manchester U) 1
Nixon, C. 2000 (Glentoran) 1
Norwood, O. J. 2010 (Manchester U) 11

O'Connor, M. J. 2008 (Crewe Alex) 3
O'Hara, G. 1994 (Leeds U) 1
O'Kane, E. 2009 (Everton, Torquay U) 4
O'Neill, J. P. 1978 (Leicester C) 1
O'Neill, M. A. M. 1994 (Hibernian) 1
O'Neill, S. 2009 (Ballymena U) 4

Paterson, M. A. 2007 (Stoke C) 2
Patterson, D. J. 1994 (Crystal Palace) 1

Quinn, S. J. 1994 (Blackpool) 1

Ramsey, C. 2011 (Portadown) 3
Ramsey, K. 2006 (Institute) 1
Robinson, S. 1994 (Tottenham H) 1

Scullion, D. 2006 (Dungannon Swifts) 8
Shiels, D. 2005 (Hibernian) 6
Shroot, R. 2009 (Harrow B, Birmingham C) 4
Simms, G. 2001 (Hartlepool U) 14
Skates, G. 2000 (Blackburn R) 4
Sloan, T. 1978 (Ballymena U) 1
Smylie, D. 2006 (Newcastle U, Livingston) 6
Stewart, S. 2009 (Aberdeen) 1
Stewart, T. 2006 (Wolverhampton W, Linfield) 19

Taylor, J. 2007 (Hearts, Glentoran) 10
Taylor, M. S. 1998 (Fulham) 1
Teggart, N. 2005 (Sunderland) 2
Thompson, A. L. 2011 (Watford) 4
Thompson, P. 2006 (Linfield) 4
Toner, C. 2000 (Tottenham H, Leyton Orient) 17
Tuffey, J. 2007 (Partick Th) 13
Turner, C. 2007 (Sligo R, Bohemians) 12

Ward, J. J. 2006 (Aston Villa, Chesterfield) 7
Ward, M. 2006 (Dungannon Swifts) 1
Ward, S. 2005 (Glentoran) 10
Waterman, D. G. 1998 (Portsmouth) 14
Waterworth, A. 2008 (Lisburn Distillery, Hamilton A) 7
Webb, S. M. 2004 (Ross Co, St Johnstone, Ross Co) 6
Weir, R. J. 2009 (Sunderland) 8
Wells, D. P. 1999 (Barry T) 1
Whitley, J. 1998 (Manchester C) 17
Willis, P. 2006 (Liverpool) 1
Winchester, C. 2011 (Oldham Ath) 4

SCOTLAND

Adam, C. G. 2006 (Rangers) 5
Adam, G. 2011 (Rangers) 6
Adams, J. 2007 (Kilmarnock) 1
Aitken, R. 1977 (Celtic) 16
Albiston, A. 1977 (Manchester U) 5
Alexander, N. 1997 (Stenhousemuir, Livingston) 10
Allan, S. 2012 (WBA) 7
Anderson, I. 1997 (Dundee, Toulouse) 15
Anderson, R. 1997 (Aberdeen) 15
Andrews, M. 2011 (East Stirling) 1
Anthony, M. 1997 (Celtic) 3
Archdeacon, O. 1987 (Celtic) 1
Archibald, A. 1998 (Partick Th) 5
Archibald, S. 1980 (Aberdeen, Tottenham H) 5
Arfield, S. 2008 (Falkirk, Huddersfield T) 17
Armstrong, S. 2011 (Dundee U) 6

Bagen, D. 1997 (Kilmarnock) 4
Bain, K. 1993 (Dundee) 4
Baker, M. 1993 (St Mirren) 10
Baltacha, S. S. 2000 (St Mirren) 3
Bannan, B. 2009 (Aston Villa) 10
Bannon, E. J. 1979 (Hearts, Chelsea, Dundee U) 7
Barclay, J. 2011 (Falkirk) 1
Beattie, C. 2004 (Celtic) 7
Beattie, J. 1992 (St Mirren) 4
Beaumont, D. 1985 (Dundee U) 1
Bell, D. 1981 (Aberdeen) 2
Bernard, P. R. J. 1992 (Oldham Ath) 15
Berra, C. 2005 (Hearts) 6
Bett, J. 1981 (Rangers) 7
Black, E. 1983 (Aberdeen) 8
Blair, A. 1980 (Coventry C, Aston Villa) 5
Bollan, G. 1992 (Dundee U, Rangers) 17
Bonar, P. 1997 (Raith R) 4
Booth, C. 2011 (Hibernian) 4
Booth, S. 1991 (Aberdeen) 14
Bowes, M. J. 1992 (Dunfermline Ath) 1
Bowman, D. 1985 (Hearts) 1
Boyack, S. 1997 (Rangers) 1
Boyd, K. 2003 (Kilmarnock) 8
Boyd, T. 1987 (Motherwell) 5
Brazil, A. 1978 (Hibernian) 1
Brazil, A. 1979 (Ipswich T) 8
Brebner, G. I. 1997 (Manchester U, Reading, Hibernian) 18
Brighton, T. 2005 (Rangers, Clyde) 7
Broadfoot, K. 2005 (St Mirren) 5
Brough, J. 1981 (Hearts) 1
Brown, A. H. 2004 (Hibernian) 1
Brown, S. 2005 (Hibernian) 10
Browne, P. 1997 (Raith R) 1
Bryson, C. 2006 (Clyde) 1
Buchan, J. 1997 (Aberdeen) 13
Burchill, M. J. 1998 (Celtic) 15
Burke, A. 1997 (Kilmarnock) 4
Burke, C. 2004 (Rangers) 3
Burley, C. W. 1992 (Chelsea) 7
Burley, G. E. 1977 (Ipswich T) 5
Burns, H. 1985 (Rangers) 2
Burns, T. 1977 (Celtic) 5

Caddis, P. 2008 (Celtic, Dundee U, Celtic, Swindon T) 13
Cairney, T. 2011 (Hull C) 6
Caldwell, G. 2000 (Newcastle U) 19
Caldwell, S. 2001 (Newcastle U) 4
Cameron, G. 2008 (Dundee U) 3
Campbell, R. 2008 (Hibernian) 6
Campbell, S. 1989 (Dundee) 3
Campbell, S. P. 1998 (Leicester C) 15
Canero, P. 2000 (Kilmarnock) 17
Carey, L. A. 1998 (Bristol C) 1
Casey, J. 1978 (Celtic) 1
Christie, M. 1992 (Dundee) 3
Clark, R. B. 1977 (Aberdeen) 3
Clarke, S. 1984 (St Mirren) 8
Clarkson, D. 2004 (Motherwell) 13
Cleland, A. 1990 (Dundee U) 11
Cole, D. 2011 (Rangers) 2
Collins, J. 1988 (Hibernian) 8
Collins, N. 2005 (Sunderland) 7
Connolly, P. 1991 (Dundee U) 3
Connor, R. 1981 (Ayr U) 2
Conroy, R. 2007 (Celtic) 4
Considine, A. 2007 (Aberdeen) 5
Cooper, D. 1977 (Clydebank, Rangers) 6
Cooper, N. 1982 (Aberdeen) 13
Coutts, P. A. 2009 (Peterborough U, Preston NE) 7
Crabbe, S. 1990 (Hearts) 2
Craig, M. 1998 (Aberdeen) 2
Craig, T. 1977 (Newcastle U) 1
Crainey, S. D. 2000 (Celtic) 7
Crainie, D. 1983 (Celtic) 1
Crawford, S. 1994 (Raith R) 19
Creaney, G. 1991 (Celtic) 11
Cummings, W. 2000 (Chelsea) 8
Cuthbert, S. 2007 (Celtic, St Mirren) 13

Dailly, C. 1991 (Dundee U) 34
Dalglish, P. 1999 (Newcastle U, Norwich C) 6
Dargo, C. 1998 (Raith R) 10
Davidson, C. I. 1997 (St Johnstone) 2
Davidson, H. N. 2000 (Dundee U) 3
Davidson, M. 2011 (St Johnstone) 1
Dawson, A. 1979 (Rangers) 8
Deas, P. A. 1992 (St Johnstone) 2
Dempster, J. 2004 (Rushden & D) 1
Dennis, S. 1992 (Raith R) 1
Diamond, A. 2004 (Aberdeen) 12
Dickov, P. 1992 (Arsenal) 4
Dixon, P. 2008 (Dundee) 2
Dodds, D. 1978 (Dundee U) 1
Dods, D. 1997 (Hibernian) 5
Doig, C. R. 2000 (Nottingham F) 13
Donald, G. S. 1992 (Hibernian) 3
Donnelly, S. 1994 (Celtic) 11
Dorrans, G. 2007 (Livingston) 6
Dow, A. 1993 (Dundee, Chelsea) 3
Dowie, A. J. 2003 (Rangers, Partick Th) 14
Duff, J. 2009 (Inverness CT) 1
Duff, S. 2003 (Dundee U) 9
Duffie, K. 2011 (Falkirk) 1
Duffy, D. A. 2005 (Falkirk, Hull C) 8
Duffy, J. 1987 (Dundee) 1
Durie, G. S. 1987 (Chelsea) 4
Durrant, I. 1987 (Rangers) 4
Doyle, J. 1981 (Partick Th) 2

Easton, B. 2009 (Hamilton A) 3
Easton, C. 1997 (Dundee U) 21
Edwards, M. 2012 (Rochdale) 1
Elliot, B. 1998 (Celtic) 2

Elliot, C. 2006 (Hearts) 9
Esson, R. 2000 (Aberdeen) 7

Fagan, S. M. 2005 (Motherwell) 1
Ferguson, B. 1997 (Rangers) 12
Ferguson, D. 1987 (Rangers) 5
Ferguson, D. 1992 (Dundee U) 7
Ferguson, D. 1992 (Manchester U) 5
Ferguson, I. 1983 (Dundee) 4
Ferguson, I. 1987 (Clyde, St Mirren, Rangers) 6
Ferguson, R. 1977 (Hamilton A) 1
Feruz, I. 2012 (Chelsea) 1
Findlay, W. 1991 (Hibernian) 5
Fitzpatrick, A. 1977 (St Mirren) 5
Fitzpatrick, M. 2007 (Motherwell) 4
Flannigan, C. 1993 (Clydebank) 1
Fleck, J. 2009 (Rangers) 4
Fleck, R. 1987 (Rangers, Norwich C) 6
Fleming, G. 2008 (Gretna) 1
Fletcher, D. B. 2003 (Manchester U) 2
Fletcher, S. 2007 (Hibernian) 7
Forrest, J. 2011 (Celtic) 4
Foster, R. M. 2005 (Aberdeen) 5
Fotheringham, M. M. 2004 (Dundee) 3
Fowler, J. 2002 (Kilmarnock) 3
Foy, R. A. 2004 (Liverpool) 5
Fraser, S. T. 2000 (Luton T) 4
Freedman, D. A. 1995 (Barnet, Crystal Palace) 8
Fridge, L. 1989 (St Mirren) 2
Fullarton, J. 1993 (St Mirren) 17
Fulton, M. 1980 (St Mirren) 5
Fulton, S. 1991 (Celtic) 7

Gallacher, K. W. 1987 (Dundee U) 7
Gallacher, P. 1999 (Dundee U) 7
Gallacher, S. 2009 (Rangers) 2
Gallagher, P. 2003 (Blackburn R) 11
Galloway, M. 1989 (Hearts, Celtic) 2
Gardiner, J. 1993 (Hibernian) 1
Geddes, R. 1982 (Dundee) 5
Gemmill, S. 1992 (Nottingham F) 4
Germaine, G. 1997 (WBA) 1
Gilles, R. 1997 (St Mirren) 7
Gillespie, G. T. 1979 (Coventry C) 8
Glass, S. 1995 (Aberdeen) 11
Glover, L. 1988 (Nottingham F) 3
Goodwillie, D. 2009 (Dundee U) 9
Goram, A. L. 1987 (Oldham Ath) 1
Gordon, C. S. 2003 (Hearts) 5
Gough, C. R. 1983 (Dundee U) 5
Graham, D. 1998 (Rangers) 8
Grant, P. 1985 (Celtic) 10
Gray, D. P. 2009 (Manchester U) 2
Gray, S. 1987 (Aberdeen) 1
Gray S. 1995 (Celtic) 7
Griffiths, L. 2010 (Dundee, Wolverhampton W) 10
Gunn, B. 1984 (Aberdeen) 9

Hagen, D. 1992 (Rangers) 8
Hamill, J. 2008 (Kilmarnock) 11
Hamilton, B. 1989 (St Mirren) 4
Hamilton, J. 1995 (Dundee, Hearts) 14
Hammell, S. 2001 (Motherwell) 11
Handyside, P. 1993 (Grimsby T) 7
Hanley, G. 2011 (Blackburn R) 1
Hanlon, P. 2009 (Hibernian) 20
Hannah, D. 1993 (Dundee U) 16
Harper, K. 1995 (Hibernian) 7
Hartford, R. A. 1977 (Manchester C) 1
Hartley, P. J. 1997 (Millwall) 1
Hegarty, P. 1987 (Dundee U) 6
Hendry, J. 1992 (Tottenham H) 1
Hetherston, B. 1997 (St Mirren) 1
Hewitt, J. 1982 (Aberdeen) 6
Hogg, G. 1984 (Manchester U) 4
Hood, G. 1993 (Ayr U) 3
Horn, R. 1997 (Hearts) 6
Howie, S. 1993 (Cowdenbeath) 5
Hughes, R. D. 1999 (Bournemouth) 9
Hughes, S. 2002 (Rangers) 12
Hunter, G. 1987 (Hibernian) 3
Hunter, P. 1989 (East Fife) 3
Hutton, A. 2004 (Rangers) 7
Hutton, K. 2011 (Rangers) 1

Inman, B. 2011 (Newcastle U) 2
Irvine, G. 2006 (Celtic) 2

Jack, R. 2012 (Aberdeen) 7
James, K. F. 1997 (Falkirk) 1
Jardine, I. 1979 (Kilmarnock) 1
Jess, E. 1990 (Aberdeen) 14
Johnson, G. I. 1992 (Dundee U) 6
Johnston, A. 1994 (Hearts) 3
Johnston, F. 1993 (Falkirk) 1
Johnston, M. 1984 (Partick Th, Watford) 3
Jordan, A. J. 2000 (Bristol C) 3
Jupp, D. A. 1995 (Fulham) 9

Kelly, L. 2012 (Kilmarnock) 6
Kennedy, J. 2003 (Celtic) 15
Kenneth, G. 2008 (Dundee U) 8
Kerr, B. 2003 (Newcastle U) 14
Kerr, M. 2001 (Kilmarnock) 1
Kerr, S. 1993 (Celtic) 10
Kinniburgh, W. D. 2004 (Motherwell) 3
Kirkwood, D. 1990 (Hearts) 1
Kyle, K. 2001 (Sunderland) 12

Lambert, P. 1991 (St Mirren) 11
Langfield, J. 2000 (Dundee) 2
Lappin, S. 2004 (St Mirren) 10
Lauchlan, J. 1998 (Kilmarnock) 11
Lavety, B. 1993 (St Mirren) 9
Lavin, G. 1993 (Watford) 7
Lawson, P. 2004 (Celtic) 10
Leighton, J. 1982 (Aberdeen) 1
Lennon, S. 2008 (Rangers) 6
Levein, C. 1985 (Hearts) 2
Leven, P. 2005 (Kilmarnock) 2
Liddell, A. M. 1994 (Barnsley) 12
Lindsey, J. 1979 (Motherwell) 1
Locke, G. 1994 (Hearts) 10
Love, G. 1995 (Hibernian) 1
Loy, R. 2009 (Dunfermline Ath, Rangers) 5
Lynch, S. 2003 (Celtic, Preston NE) 13

McAllister, G. 1990 (Leicester C) 1
McAllister, R. 2008 (Inverness CT) 2
McAlpine, H. 1983 (Dundee U) 5
McAnespie, K. 1998 (St Johnstone) 4
McArthur, J. 2008 (Hamilton A) 2
McAuley, S. 1993 (St Johnstone) 1
McAvennie, F. 1982 (St Mirren) 5
McBride, J. 1981 (Everton) 1
McBride, J. P. 1998 (Celtic) 2
McCabe, R. 2012 (Rangers) 1
McCall, A. S. M. 1988 (Bradford C, Everton) 2
McCann, K. 2008 (Hibernian) 4
McCann, N. 1994 (Dundee) 9
McClair, B. 1984 (Celtic) 8
McCluskey, G. 1979 (Celtic) 6
McCluskey, S. 1997 (St Johnstone) 14
McCoist, A. 1984 (Rangers) 1
McConnell, I. 1997 (Clyde) 1
McCormack, D. 2008 (Hibernian) 1
McCormack, R. 2006 (Rangers, Motherwell, Cardiff C) 13
McCracken, D. 2002 (Dundee U) 5
McCulloch, A. 1981 (Kilmarnock) 1
McCulloch, I. 1982 (Notts Co) 2
McCulloch, L. 1997 (Motherwell) 14
McCunnie, J. 2001 (Dundee U, Ross Co, Dunfermline Ath) 20
MacDonald, A. 2011 (Burnley) 6
MacDonald, J. 1980 (Rangers) 8
MacDonald, J. 2007 (Hearts) 11
McDonald, C. 1995 (Falkirk) 5
McDonald, K. 2008 (Dundee, Burnley) 14

McEwan, C. 1997 (Clyde, Raith R) 17
McEwan, D. 2003 (Livingston) 2
McFadden, J. 2003 (Motherwell) 7
McFarlane, D. 1997 (Hamilton A) 3
McGarry, S. 1997 (St Mirren) 3
McGarvey, F. P. 1977 (St Mirren, Celtic) 3
McGarvey, S. 1982 (Manchester U) 4
McGeough, D. 2012 (Celtic) 1
McGhee, M. 1981 (Aberdeen) 1
McGinn, S. 2009 (St Mirren, Watford) 8
McGinnis, G. 1985 (Dundee U) 1
McGlinchey, M. R. 2007 (Celtic) 1
McGregor, A. 2003 (Rangers) 6
McGrillen, P. 1994 (Motherwell) 2
McGuire, D. 2002 (Aberdeen) 2
McInally, J. 1989 (Dundee U) 1
McKean, K. 2011 (St Mirren) 1
McKenzie, R. 1997 (Hearts) 2
McKimmie, S. 1985 (Aberdeen) 3
McKinlay, T. 1984 (Dundee) 6
McKinlay, W. 1989 (Dundee U) 6
McKinnon, R. 1991 (Dundee U) 6
McLaren, A, 1989 (Hearts) 11
McLaren, A. 1993 (Dundee U) 4
McLaughlin, B. 1995 (Celtic) 8
McLaughlin, J. 1981 (Morton) 10
McLean, E. 2008 (Dundee U, St Johnstone) 2
McLean, S. 2003 (Rangers) 4
McLeish, A. 1978 (Aberdeen) 6
MacLeod, A. 1979 (Hibernian) 3
McLean, K. 2012 (St Mirren) 1
McLeod, J. 1989 (Dundee U) 2
MacLeod, M. 1979 (Dumbarton, Celtic) 5
McManus, T. 2001 (Hibernian) 14
McMillan, S. 1997 (Motherwell) 4
McNab, N. 1978 (Tottenham H) 1
McNally, M. 1991 (Celtic) 2
McNamara, J. 1994 (Dunfermline Ath, Celtic) 12
McNaughton, K. 2002 (Aberdeen) 1
McNeil, A. 2007 (Hibernian) 1
McNichol, J. 1979 (Brentford) 7
McNiven, D. 1977 (Leeds U) 3
McNiven, S. A. 1996 (Oldham Ath) 1
McParland, A. 2003 (Celtic) 1
McPhee, S. 2002 (Port Vale) 1
McPherson, D. 1984 (Rangers, Hearts) 4
McQuilken, J. 1993 (Celtic) 2
McStay, P. 1983 (Celtic) 5
McWhirter, N. 1991 (St Mirren) 1
Mackay-Steven, G. 2012 (Dundee U) 3
Maguire, C. 2009 (Aberdeen) 12
Main, A. 1988 (Dundee U) 3
Malcolm, R. 2001 (Rangers) 1
Maloney, S. 2002 (Celtic) 21
Malpas, M. 1983 (Dundee U) 8
Marr, B. 2011 (Ross Co) 1
Marshall, D. J. 2004 (Celtic) 10
Marshall, S. R. 1995 (Arsenal) 5
Martin, A. 2009 (Leeds U, Ayr U) 12
Mason, G. R. 1999 (Manchester C, Dunfermline Ath) 2
Mathieson, D. 1997 (Queen of the South) 3
May, E. 1989 (Hibernian) 2
Meldrum, C. 1996 (Kilmarnock) 6
Melrose, J. 1977 (Partick Th) 8
Millar, M, 2009 (Celtic) 1
Miller, C. 1995 (Rangers) 8
Miller, J. 1987 (Aberdeen, Celtic) 7
Miller, K. 2000 (Hibernian, Rangers) 7
Miller, W. 1978 (Aberdeen) 2
Miller, W. 1991 (Hibernian) 7
Milne, K. 2000 (Hearts) 1
Milne, R. 1982 (Dundee U) 3
Mitchell, C. 2008 (Falkirk) 7
Money, I. C. 1987 (St Mirren) 3
Montgomery, N. A. 2003 (Sheffield U) 2
Morrison, S. A. 2004 (Aberdeen, Dunfermline Ath) 12
Muir, L. 1977 (Hibernian) 1
Mulgrew, C. P. 2006 (Celtic, Wolverhampton W, Aberdeen) 14
Murphy J. 2009 (Motherwell) 13
Murray, H. 2000 (St Mirren) 3
Murray, I. 2001 (Hibernian) 15
Murray, N. 1993 (Rangers) 16
Murray, R. 1993 (Bournemouth) 1
Murray, S. 2004 (Kilmarnock) 2

Narey, D. 1977 (Dundee U) 4
Naismith, S. J. 2006 (Kilmarnock, Rangers) 15
Naysmith, G. A. 1997 (Hearts) 22
Neilson, R. 2000 (Hearts) 1
Ness, J, 2011 (Rangers) 1
Nevin, P. 1985 (Chelsea) 5
Nicholas, C. 1981 (Celtic, Arsenal) 6
Nicholson, B. 1999 (Rangers) 7
Nicol, S. 1981 (Ayr U, Liverpool) 14
Nisbet, S. 1989 (Rangers) 5
Noble, D. J. 2003 (West Ham U) 2
Notman, A. M. 1999 (Manchester U) 10

O'Brien, B. 1999 (Blackburn R, Livingston) 6
O'Connor, G. 2003 (Hibernian) 8
O'Donnell, P. 1992 (Motherwell) 8
O'Halloran, M. 2012 (Bolton W) 1
O'Leary, R. 2008 (Kilmarnock) 2
O'Neil, B. 1992 (Celtic) 7
O'Neil, J. 1991 (Dundee U) 1
O'Neill, M. 1995 (Clyde) 6
Orr, N. 1978 (Morton) 7

Palmer, L. J. 2011 (Sheffield W) 8
Parker, K. 2001 (St Johnstone) 1
Parlane, D. 1977 (Rangers) 1
Paterson, C. 1981 (Hibernian) 2
Paterson, J. 1997 (Dundee U) 9
Pawlett, P. 2012 (Aberdeen) 4
Payne, G. 1978 (Dundee U) 3
Peacock, L. A. 1997 (Carlisle U) 1
Pearce, A. J. 2008 (Reading) 2
Pearson, S. P. 2003 (Motherwell) 8
Perry, R. 2010 (Rangers, Falkirk, Rangers) 14
Pressley, S. J. 1993 (Rangers, Coventry C, Dundee U) 26
Provan, D. 1977 (Kilmarnock) 1
Prunty, B. 2004 (Aberdeen) 6

Quinn, P. C. 2004 (Motherwell) 3
Quinn, R. 2006 (Celtic) 9

Rae, A. 1991 (Millwall) 8
Rae, G. 1999 (Dundee) 6
Redford, I. 1981 (Rangers) 6
Reid, B. 1991 (Rangers) 4
Reid, C. 1993 (Hibernian) 3
Reid, M. 1982 (Celtic) 2
Reid, R. 1977 (St Mirren) 3
Reilly, A. 2004 (Wycombe W) 1
Renicks, S. 1997 (Hamilton A) 1
Reynolds, M. 2007 (Motherwell) 9
Rhodes, J. L. 2011 (Huddersfield T) 8
Rice, B. 1985 (Hibernian) 1
Richardson, L. 1980 (St Mirren) 2
Ridgers, M. 2012 (Hearts) 4
Riordan, D. G. 2004 (Hibernian) 5
Ritchie, A. 1980 (Morton) 1
Ritchie, P. S. 1996 (Hearts) 7
Robertson, A. 1991 (Rangers) 1
Robertson, C. 1977 (Rangers) 1
Robertson, D. 1987 (Aberdeen) 7
Robertson, D. 2007 (Dundee U) 4
Robertson, G. A. 2004 (Nottingham F, Rotherham U) 15
Robertson, H. 1994 (Aberdeen) 2
Robertson, J. 1985 (Hearts) 2
Robertson, L. 1993 (Rangers) 3
Robertson, S. 1998 (St Johnstone) 2
Roddie, A. 1992 (Aberdeen) 5
Ross, G. 2007 (Dunfermline Ath) 1
Ross, N. 2011 (Inverness CT) 2
Ross, T. W. 1977 (Arsenal) 1
Rowson, D. 1997 (Aberdeen) 5

Russell, J. 2011 (Dundee U) **9**
Russell, R. 1978 (Rangers) 3

Salton, D. B. 1992 (Luton T) 6
Samson, C. I. 2004 (Kilmarnock) 6
Saunders, S. 2011 (Motherwell) **2**
Scobbie, T. 2008 (Falkirk) 12
Scott, M. 2006 (Livingston) 1
Scott, P. 1994 (St Johnstone) 4
Scrimgour, D. 1997 (St Mirren) 3
Seaton, A. 1998 (Falkirk) 1
Severin, S. D. 2000 (Hearts) 10
Shannon, R. 1987 (Dundee) 7
Sharp, G. M. 1982 (Everton) 1
Sharp, R. 1990 (Dunfermline Ath) 4
Sheerin, P. 1996 (Southampton) 1
Shields, G. 1997 (Rangers) 2
Shinnie, A. 2009 (Dundee, Rangers) 3
Shinnie, G. 2012 (Inverness CT) **1**
Simmons, S. 2003 (Hearts) 1
Simpson, N. 1982 (Aberdeen) 11
Sinclair, G. 1977 (Dumbarton) 1
Skilling, M. 1993 (Kilmarnock) 2
Smith, B. M. 1992 (Celtic) 5
Smith, C. 2008 (St Mirren) 2
Smith, D. L. 2006 (Motherwell) 2
Smith, G. 1978 (Rangers) 1
Smith, G. 2004 (Rangers) 8
Smith, H. G. 1987 (Hearts) 2
Smith, S. 2007 (Rangers) 1
Sneddon, A. 1979 (Celtic) 1
Snodgrass, R. 2008 (Livingston) 2
Soutar, D. 2003 (Dundee) 11
Speedie, D. R. 1985 (Chelsea) 1
Spencer, J. 1991 (Rangers) 3
Stanton, P. 1977 (Hibernian) 1
Stark, W. 1985 (Aberdeen) 1
Stephen, R. 1983 (Dundee) 1
Stevens, G. 1977 (Motherwell) 1
Stevenson, L. 2008 (Hibernian) 8
Stewart, C. 2002 (Kilmarnock) 1
Stewart, J. 1978 (Kilmarnock, Middlesbrough) 3
Stewart, M. J. 2000 (Manchester U) 17
Stewart, R. 1979 (Dundee U, West Ham U) 12
Stillie, D. 1995 (Aberdeen) 14
Strachan, G. D. 1998 (Coventry C) 7
Sturrock, P. 1977 (Dundee U) 9
Sweeney, P. H. 2004 (Millwall) 8
Sweeney, S. 1991 (Clydebank) 7

Tarrant, N. K. 1999 (Aston Villa) 5
Teale, G. 1997 (Clydebank, Ayr U) 6
Telfer, P. N. 1993 (Luton T) 3
Templeton, D. 2011 (Hearts) 2
Thomas, K. 1993 (Hearts) 8
Thompson, S. 1997 (Dundee U) 12
Thomson, C. 2011 (Hearts) 2
Thomson, K. 2005 (Hibernian) 6
Thomson, W. 1977 (Partick Th, St Mirren) 10
Tolmie, J. 1980 (Morton) 1
Tortolano, J. 1987 (Hibernian) 2
Toshney, L. 2012 (Kilmarnock) **2**
Turner, I. 2005 (Everton) 6
Tweed, S. 1993 (Hibernian) 3

Wales, G. 2000 (Hearts) 1
Walker, A. 1988 (Celtic) 1
Wallace, I. A. 1978 (Coventry C) 1
Wallace, L. 2007 (Hearts) 10
Wallace, R. 2004 (Celtic, Sunderland) 4
Walsh, C. 1984 (Nottingham F) 5
Wark, J. 1977 (Ipswich T) 8
Watson, A. 1981 (Aberdeen) 4
Watson, K. 1977 (Rangers) 2
Watt, M. 1991 (Aberdeen) 12
Watt. S. M. 2005 (Chelsea) 5
Webster, A. 2003 (Hearts) 2
Whiteford, A. 1997 (St Johnstone) 1
Whittaker, S. G. 2005 (Hibernian) 18
Whyte, D. 1987 (Celtic) 9
Wilkie, L. 2000 (Dundee) 6
Will, J. A. 1992 (Arsenal) 3
Williams, G. 2002 (Nottingham F) 9
Wilson, D. 2011 (Liverpool) **11**
Wilson, M. 2004 (Dundee U, Celtic) 19
Wilson, S. 1999 (Rangers) 7
Wilson, T. 1983 (St Mirren) 1
Wilson, T. 1988 (Nottingham F) 4
Winnie, D. 1988 (St Mirren) 1
Woods, M. 2006 (Sunderland) 2
Wotherspoon, D. 2011 (Hibernian) **13**
Wright, P. 1989 (Aberdeen, QPR) 3
Wright, S. 1991 (Aberdeen) 14
Wright, T. 1987 (Oldham Ath) 1
Wylde, G. 2011 (Rangers) **5**

Young, Darren 1997 (Aberdeen) 8
Young, Derek 2000 (Aberdeen) 5

WALES

Adams, N. W. 2008 (Bury, Leicester C) 5
Alfei, D. M. 2010 (Swansea C) **10**
Aizlewood, M. 1979 (Luton T) 2
Allen, J. M. 2008 (Swansea C) 13
Anthony, B. 2005 (Cardiff C) 8

Baddeley, L. M. 1996 (Cardiff C) 2
Balcombe, S. 1982 (Leeds U) 1
Bale, G. 2006 (Southampton, Tottenham H) 4
Barnhouse, D. J. 1995 (Swansea C) 3
Basey, G. W. 2009 (Charlton Ath) 1
Bater, P. T. 1977 (Bristol R) 2
Beevers, L. J. 2005 (Boston U, Lincoln C) 7
Bellamy, C. D. 1996 (Norwich C) 8
Bender, T. J. 2011 (Colchester U) **4**
Birchall, A. S. 2003 (Arsenal, Mansfield T) 12
Bird, A. 1993 (Cardiff C) 6
Blackmore, C. 1984 (Manchester U) 3
Blake, D. J. 2007 (Cardiff C) 14
Blake, N. A. 1991 (Cardiff C) 5
Blaney, S. D. 1997 (West Ham U) 3
Bloom, J. 2011 (Falkirk) 1
Bodin, B. P. 2010 (Swindon T) **12**
Bodin, P. J. 1983 (Cardiff C) 1
Bond, J. H. 2011 (Watford) 1

Bowen, J. P. 1993 (Swansea C) 5
Bowen, M. R. 1983 (Tottenham H) 3
Boyle, T. 1982 (Crystal Palace) 1
Brace, D. P. 1995 (Wrexham) 6
Bradley, M. S. 2007 (Walsall) 17
Bradshaw, T. 2012 (Shrewsbury T) **5**
Brough, M. 2003 (Notts Co) 3
Brown, J. D. 2008 (Cardiff C) 6
Brown, J. R. 2003 (Gillingham) 7
Brown, T. A. F. 2011 (Ipswich T, Rotherham U) **9**
Byrne, M. T. 2003 (Bolton W) 1
Calliste, R. T. 2005 (Manchester U, Liverpool) 15
Carpenter, R. E. 2005 (Burnley) 1
Cassidy, J. A. 2011 (Wolverhampton W) **2**
Cegielski, W. 1977 (Wrexham) 2
Chamberlain, E. C. 2010 (Leicester C) **9**
Chapple, S. R. 1992 (Swansea C) 8
Charles, J. M. 1979 (Swansea C) 2
Church, S. R. 2008 (Reading) 15
Clark, J. 1978 (Manchester U, Derby Co) 2
Coates, J. S. 1996 (Swansea C) 5
Coleman, C. 1990 (Swansea C) 3
Collins, J. M. 2003 (Cardiff C) 7
Collins, M. J. 2007 (Fulham, Swansea C) 2
Collison, J. D. 2008 (West Ham U) 7

Cornell, D. J. 2010 (Swansea C) 3
Cotterill, D. R. G. B. 2005 (Bristol C, Wigan Ath) 11
Coyne, D. 1992 (Tranmere R) 7
Craig, N. L. 2009 (Everton) 4
Critchell, K. A. R. 2005 (Southampton) 3
Crofts, A. L. 2005 (Gillingham) 10
Crowell, M. T. 2004 (Wrexham) 7
Curtis, A. T. 1977 (Swansea C) 1

Davies, A. 1982 (Manchester U) 6
Davies, A. G. 2006 (Cambridge U) 6
Davies, A. R. 2005 (Southampton, Yeovil T) 14
Davies, C. M. 2005 (Oxford U, Verona, Oldham Ath) 9
Davies, D. 1999 (Barry T) 1
Davies, G. M. 1993 (Hereford U, Crystal Palace) 7
Davies, I. C. 1978 (Norwich C) 1
Davies, L. 2005 (Bangor C) 1
Davies, R. J. 2006 (WBA) 4
Davies, S. 1999 (Peterborough U, Tottenham H) 10
Day, R. 2000 (Manchester C, Mansfield T) 11
Deacy, N. 1977 (PSV Eindhoven) 1
De-Vulgt, L. S. 2002 (Swansea C) 2
Dibble, A. 1983 (Cardiff C) 3
Doble, R. A. 2010 (Southampton) 10
Doyle, S. C. 1979 (Preston NE, Huddersfield T) 2
Duffy, R. M. 2005 (Portsmouth) 7
Dummett, P. 2011 (Newcastle U) 3
Dwyer, P. J. 1979 (Cardiff C) 1

Eardley, N. 2007 (Oldham Ath, Blackpool) 11
Earnshaw, R. 1999 (Cardiff C) 10
Easter, D. J. 2006 (Cardiff C) 1
Ebdon, M. 1990 (Everton) 2
Edwards, C. N. H. 1996 (Swansea C) 7
Edwards, D. A. 2006 (Shrewsbury T, Luton T, Wolverhampton W) 9
Edwards, R. I. 1977 (Chester) 2
Edwards, R. W. 1991 (Bristol C) 13
Evans, A. 1977 (Bristol R) 1
Evans, C. 2007 (Manchester C, Sheffield U) 13
Evans, K. 1999 (Leeds U, Cardiff C) 4
Evans, P. S. 1996 (Shrewsbury T) 1
Evans, S. J. 2001 (Crystal Palace) 2
Evans, T. 1995 (Cardiff C) 3

Fish, N. 2005 (Cardiff C) 2
Fleetwood, S. 2005 (Cardiff C) 5
Flynn, C. P. 2007 (Crewe Alex) 1
Folland, R. W. 2000 (Oxford U) 1
Foster, M. G. 1993 (Tranmere R) 1
Fowler, L. A. 2003 (Coventry C, Huddersfield T) 9
Freeman, K. 2012 (Nottingham F) 6
Freestone, R. 1990 (Chelsea) 1

Gabbidon, D. L. 1999 (WBA, Cardiff C) 17
Gale, D. 1983 (Swansea C) 2
Gall, K. A. 2002 (Bristol R, Yeovil T) 8
Gibson, N. D. 1999 (Tranmere R, Sheffield W) 11
Giggs, R. J. 1991 (Manchester U) 1
Gilbert, P. 2005 (Plymouth Arg) 12
Giles, D. C. 1977 (Cardiff C, Swansea C, Crystal Palace) 4
Giles, P. 1982 (Cardiff C) 3
Graham, D. 1991 (Manchester U) 1
Green, R. M. 1998 (Wolverhampton W) 16
Griffith, C. 1990 (Cardiff C) 1
Griffiths, C. 1991 (Shrewsbury T) 1
Grubb, D. 2007 (Bristol C) 1
Gunter, C. 2006 (Cardiff C, Tottenham H) 8

Haldane, L. O. 2007 (Bristol R) 1
Hall, G. D. 1990 (Chelsea) 1
Hartson, J. 1994 (Luton T, Arsenal) 9
Haworth, S. O. 1997 (Cardiff C, Coventry C, Wigan Ath) 12
Henley, A. 2012 (Blackburn R) 1
Hennessey, W. R. 2006 (Wolverhampton W) 6
Hewitt, E. 2012 (Macclesfield T) 5
Hillier, I. M. 2001 (Tottenham H, Luton T) 5
Hodges, G. 1983 (Wimbledon) 5
Holden, A. 1984 (Chester C) 1
Holloway, C. D. 1999 (Exeter C) 2
Hopkins, J. 1982 (Fulham) 5
Hopkins, S. A. 1999 (Wrexham) 1
Howells, J. 2012 (Luton T) 4
Huggins, D. S. 1996 (Bristol C) 1
Hughes, D. 2005 (Kaiserslautern, Regensburg) 2
Hughes, D. R. 1994 (Southampton) 1
Hughes, I. 1992 (Bury) 11
Hughes, L. M. 1983 (Manchester U) 5
Hughes, R. D. 1996 (Aston Villa, Shrewsbury T) 13
Hughes, W. 1977 (WBA) 3

Jackett, K. 1981 (Watford) 2
Jacobson, J. M. 2006 (Cardiff C, Bristol R) 15
James, L. R. S. 2006 (Southampton) 10
James, R. M. 1977 (Swansea C) 3
Jarman, L. 1996 (Cardiff C) 10
Jeanne, L. C. 1999 (QPR) 8
Jelleyman, G. A. 1999 (Peterborough U) 1
Jenkins, L. D. 1998 (Swansea C) 9
Jenkins, S. R. 1993 (Swansea C) 2
Jones, C. T. 2007 (Swansea C) 1
Jones, E. P. 2000 (Blackpool) 1
Jones, F. 1981 (Wrexham) 1
Jones, J. A. 2001 (Swansea C) 3
Jones, L. 1982 (Cardiff C) 3
Jones, M. A. 2004 (Wrexham) 4
Jones, M. G. 1998 (Leeds U) 7
Jones, P. L. 1992 (Liverpool) 12
Jones, R. 2011 (AFC Wimbledon) 1
Jones, R. A. 1994 (Sheffield W) 3
Jones, S. J. 2005 (Swansea C) 1
Jones, V. 1979 (Bristol R) 2

Kendall, L. M. 2001 (Crystal Palace) 2
Kendall, M. 1978 (Tottenham H) 1
Kenworthy, J. R. 1994 (Tranmere R) 3
King, A. 2008 (Leicester C) 11
Knott, G. R. 1996 (Tottenham H) 1

Law, B. J. 1990 (QPR) 2
Lawless, A. 2006 (Torquay U) 1
Ledley, J. C. 2005 (Cardiff C) 5
Letheran, G. 1977 (Leeds U) 2
Letheran, K. C. 2006 (Swansea C) 1
Lewis, D. 1982 (Swansea C) 9
Lewis, J. 1983 (Cardiff C) 1
Llewellyn, C. M. 1998 (Norwich C) 14
Loveridge, J. 1982 (Swansea C) 3
Low, J. D. 1999 (Bristol R, Cardiff C) 1
Lowndes, S. R. 1979 (Newport Co, Millwall) 4
Lucas, L. P. 2011 (Swansea C) 9

MacDonald, S. B. 2006 (Swansea C) 25
McCarthy, A. J. 1994 (QPR) 3
McDonald, C. 2006 (Cardiff C) 3
Mackin, L. 2006 (Wrexham) 1
Maddy, P. 1982 (Cardiff C) 2
Margetson, M. W. 1992 (Manchester C) 7
Martin, A. P. 1999 (Crystal Palace) 1
Martin, D. A. 2006 (Notts Co) 1
Marustik, C. 1982 (Swansea C) 7
Matthews, A. J. 2010 (Cardiff C) 5
Maxwell, C. 2009 (Wrexham) 15
Maxwell, L. J. 1999 (Liverpool, Cardiff C) 14
Meades, J. 2012 (Cardiff C) 1
Meaker, M. J. 1994 (QPR) 2
Melville, A. K. 1990 (Swansea C, Oxford U) 2
Micallef, C. 1982 (Cardiff C) 3
Morgan, A. M. 1995 (Tranmere R) 4
Morgan, C. 2004 (Wrexham, Milton Keynes D) 12
Morris, A. J. 2009 (Cardiff C, Aldershot T) 8
Moss, D. M. 2003 (Shrewsbury T) 6
Mountain, P. D. 1997 (Cardiff C) 2
Mumford, A. O. 2003 (Swansea C) 4

Nardiello, D. 1978 (Coventry C) 1
Neilson, A. B. 1993 (Newcastle U) 7

Nicholas, P. 1978 (Crystal Palace, Arsenal) 3
Nogan, K. 1990 (Luton T) 2
Nogan, L. M. 1991 (Oxford U) 1
Nyatanga, L. J. 2005 (Derby Co) 10

Ogleby, R. 2011 (Hearts, Wrexham) 6
Oster, J. M. 1997 (Grimsby T, Everton) 9
Owen, G. 1991 (Wrexham) 8

Page, R. J. 1995 (Watford) 4
Parslow, D. 2005 (Cardiff C) 4
Partington, J. M. 2009 (Bournemouth) 8
Partridge, D. W. 1997 (West Ham U) 1
Pascoe, C. 1983 (Swansea C) 4
Pearce, S. 2006 (Bristol C) 3
Pejic, S. M. 2003 (Wrexham) 6
Pembridge, M. A. 1991 (Luton T) 1
Peniket, R. 2012 (Fulham) 1
Perry, J. 1990 (Cardiff C) 3
Peters, M. 1992 (Manchester C, Norwich C) 3
Phillips, D. 1984 (Plymouth Arg) 3
Phillips, G. R. 2001 (Swansea C) 3
Phillips, L. 1979 (Swansea C, Charlton Ath) 2
Pipe, D. R. 2003 (Coventry C, Notts Co) 12
Pontin, K. 1978 (Cardiff C) 1
Powell, L. 1991 (Southampton) 4
Powell, L. 2004 (Leicester C) 3
Powell, R. 2006 (Bolton W) 1
Price, J. J. 1998 (Swansea C) 7
Price, L. P. 2005 (Ipswich T) 10
Price, M. D. 2001 (Everton, Hull C, Scarborough) 13
Price, P. 1981 (Luton T) 1
Pritchard, M. O. 2006 (Swansea C) 4
Pugh, D. 1982 (Doncaster R) 2
Pugh, S. 1993 (Wrexham) 2
Pulis, A. J. 2006 (Stoke C) 5

Ramasut, M. W. T. 1997 (Bristol R) 4
Ramsey, A. J. 2008, (Cardiff C, Arsenal) 12
Ratcliffe, K. 1981 (Everton) 2
Ready, K. 1992 (QPR) 5
Rees, A. 1984 (Birmingham C) 1
Rees, J. M. 1990 (Luton T) 3
Rees, M. R. 2003 (Millwall) 4
Ribeiro, C. M. 2008 (Bristol C) 8
Richards, A. D. J. 2010 (Swansea C) 15
Roberts, A. M. 1991 (QPR) 2
Roberts, C. J. 1999 (Cardiff C) 1
Roberts, G. 1983 (Hull C) 1
Roberts, G. W. 1997 (Liverpool, Panionios, Tranmere R) 11
Roberts, J. G. 1977 (Wrexham) 1
Roberts, N. W. 1999 (Wrexham) 3
Roberts, P. 1997 (Porthmadog) 1
Roberts, S. I. 1999 (Swansea C) 13
Roberts, S. W. 2000 (Wrexham) 3
Robinson, C. P. 1996 (Wolverhampton W) 6
Robinson, J. R. C. 1992 (Brighton & HA, Charlton Ath) 5
Robson-Kanu, K. H. 2010 (Reading) 4
Rowlands, A. J. R. 1996 (Manchester C) 5
Rush, I. 1981 (Liverpool) 2

Savage, R. W. 1995 (Crewe Alex) 3
Sayer, P. A. 1977 (Cardiff C) 2
Searle, D. 1991 (Cardiff C) 6
Slatter, D. 2000 (Chelsea) 6
Slatter, N. 1983 (Bristol R) 6
Somner, M. J. 2004 (Brentford) 2
Speed, G. A. 1990 (Leeds U) 3
Spender, S. 2005 (Wrexham) 6
Stephens, D. 2011 (Hibernian) 6
Stevenson, N. 1982 (Swansea C) 2
Stevenson, W. B. 1977 (Leeds U) 3
Stock, B. B. 2003 (Bournemouth) 4
Symons, C. J. 1991 (Portsmouth) 2

Taylor, A. 2012 (Tranmere R) 1
Taylor, G. K. 1995 (Bristol R) 4
Taylor, J. W. T. 2010 (Reading) 10
Taylor, N. J. 2008 (Wrexham, Swansea C) 13
Taylor, R. F. 2008 (Chelsea) 5
Thomas, C. E. 2010 (Swansea C) 3
Thomas, D. G. 1977 (Leeds U) 3
Thomas, D. J. 1998 (Watford) 2
Thomas, J. A. 1996 (Blackburn R) 21
Thomas, Martin R. 1979 (Bristol R) 2
Thomas, Mickey R. 1977 (Wrexham) 2
Thomas, S. 2001 (Wrexham) 5
Tibbott, L. 1977 (Ipswich T) 2
Tipton, M. J. 1998 (Oldham Ath) 6
Tolley, J. C. 2001 (Shrewsbury T) 12
Tudur-Jones, O. 2006 (Swansea C) 3
Twiddy, C. 1995 (Plymouth Arg) 3

Valentine, R. D. 2001 (Everton, Darlington) 8
Vaughan, D. O. 2003 (Crewe Alex) 8
Vaughan, N. 1982 (Newport Co) 2
Vokes, S. M. 2007 (Bournemouth, Wolverhampton W) 14

Walsh, D. 2000 (Wrexham) 8
Walsh, I. P. 1979 (Crystal Palace, Swansea C) 2
Walsh, J. 2012 (Swansea C) 1
Walton, M. 1991 (Norwich C.) 1
Ward, D. 1996 (Notts Co) 2
Warlow, O. J. 2007 (Lincoln C) 2
Weston, R. D. 2001 (Arsenal, Cardiff C) 4
Whitfield, P. M. 2003 (Wrexham) 1
Wiggins, R. 2006 (Crystal Palace) 9
Williams, A. P. 1998 (Southampton) 9
Williams, A. S. 1996 (Blackburn R) 16
Williams, D. 1983 (Bristol R) 1
Williams, D. I. L. 1998 (Liverpool, Wrexham) 9
Williams, D. T. 2006 (Yeovil T) 1
Williams, E. 1997 (Caernarfon T) 2
Williams, G. 1983 (Bristol R) 2
Williams, G. A. 2003 (Crystal Palace) 5
Williams, J. P. 2011 (Crystal Palace) 7
Williams, M. 2001 (Manchester U) 10
Williams, M. P. 2006 (Wrexham) 14
Williams, M. R. 2006 (Wrexham) 6
Williams, O. fon 2007 (Crewe Alex, Stockport Co) 11
Williams, R. 2007 (Middlesbrough) 10
Williams, S. J. 1995 (Wrexham) 4
Wilmot, R. 1982 (Arsenal) 6
Wilson, J. S. 2009 (Bristol C) 3
Worgan, L. J. 2005 (Milton Keynes D, Rushden & D) 5
Wright, A. A. 1998 (Oxford U) 3

Young, S. 1996 (Cardiff C) 5

FA SCHOOLS & YOUTH GAMES 2011–12

ENGLAND UNDER-16

VICTORY SHIELD

30 September 2011

Wales 0

Scotland 0

12 October 2011 *(at Chesterfield)*

England 3 *(Hunte 17, Bennett 44, 47)*

Northern Ireland 1 *(McDonagh 40)* 4126

(at Chesterfield).
England: Gunn; Aina, Smith-Brown (O'Hanlon 52), Hayden (Birch 41), Ogilvie, Cook, Loftus-Cheek, Bennett, Sonupe (Crowley 58), Hunte (Ojo 46), Marsh (Brown J 41).
Northern Ireland: Mitchell; Gray, Stewart, Harney (Gorman 25), Dummigan, McCawl (Toland 63), McDonagh, Donnelly (Gardner 71), Mullan (Teague 58), Doherty, Hale (Croskry 39).

27 October 2011 *(at Cheltenham)*

England 4 *(Loftus-Cheek 3, Sinclair 14, Kiwomya 67, Alassani 77)*

Wales 0 3477

England: Palmer; Birch (Allassani 41), O'Hanlon, Cullen (Rossiter 66), Morris, Clarke, Crowley (Lyons-Foster 41), Loftus-Cheek, Sinclair (Gilliead 54), Kiwomya, Ojo (Iwobi 54).
Wales: Owen; Jones J (Clarke), Harries, Atyeo, White, Morrell (Walsh 73), Noor (Wilson 78), Francis, Penny, Copp (Charles 59), Smith.

25 November 2011 *(at Inverness)*

Scotland 2 *(McMullan 20, Storie 60 (pen))*

England 4 *(Brown J 7, 31, Iwobi 14, Bennett 59)* 1454

Scotland: Fulton; Hogg (Dykes 76), Sinammon, McGhee, Pascazio, Henderson, McMullan, Walsh (Beaton 76), Stoney, Storie, Waters (McManus 41).
England: Gunn; Aina, Smith-Brown, Morris, Lyons-Foster (Clarke 41), Heaton (Hunte 55), Allassani (Crowley 50), Colkett (Brown R 68), Bennett, Brown J (Kiwomya 41), Iwobi.

FRIENDLY

15 February 2012 *(in Madrid)*

Spain 0

England 1 *(Green 80)*

England: Palmer (Burton 41); Aina (Birch 41), Smith-Brown (Ogilvie 56), Morris, Jones, Clarke, Fewster, Colkett (Ojo 56), Brown J (Brown R 64), Allassani (Green 41), Hunte (Iwobi 64).

THE MONTAIGU TOURNAMENT

3 April 2012 *(in St Laurent)*

Japan 1 *(Sugimoto 79)*

England 1 *(Jones 80)*

England: Atkinson; Birch, Smith-Brown, Morris, Jones, Clarke, Green, Sinclair (Iwobi 61), Brown J (Colkett 48), Hunte, Brown R (Bryan 72).

5 April 2012 *(in St Laurent)*

Morocco 0

England 1 *(Sinclair 8)*

England: Palmer; Morris, Jones (Smith-Brown 61), Clarke, Iwobi (Green 54), Sinclair (Brown J 68), Aina, Crowley, Colkett (Hunte 65), Bryan, Gilliead (Birch 75).

7 April 2012 *(in Montaigu)*

Russia 2

England 2 *(Brown J 49, Bryan 70 (pen))*

Russia won 4-3 on penalties.
England: Atkinson; Smith-Brown, Morris, Clarke, Brown J (Iwobi 66), Hunte, Aina, Colkett (Crowley 57), Brown R (Sinclair 66), Bryan, Gilliead.

9 April 2012 *(in Montaigu)*

France 0

England 1 *(Sinclair 35)*

England: Palmer; Birch, Smith-Brown, Morris, Jones, Iwobi (Gilliead 70), Sinclair (Brown J 73), Hunte, Aina (Clarke 60), Crowley (Brown R 73), Colkett (Bryan 56).

ENGLAND UNDER-17

NORDIC TOURNAMENT

2 August 2011 *(in Akureyri)*

Faeroes 0

England 4 *(Jacobsen 12 (og), Long 28, 47, Akporn42)*

England: McGee; Johns, Facey (Woodland 53), Gordon, Gorman, Randall (Hayden 53), Baker (Glendon 53), Akporn (Bennett 53), Long, Denton (Thomas 16), Smith (Smith-Brown 53).

3 August 2011 *(in Saudarkrokur)*

Norway 1 *(Stengel 67)*

England 1 *(Bennett 38)*

England: Gunn; Facey, Gordon (Gorman 79), Woodland, Hayden, Baker (Long 52), Akporn (Johns 52), Thomas (Smith 64), Smith-Brown (Randall 70), Glendon, Bennett.

5 August 2011 *(in Dalvik)*

Iceland 2 *(Johannesson 46, Palsson 48)*

England 1 *(Akporn 68)*

England: McGee; Woodland (Gordon 69), Gorman, Hayden, Randall (Baker 58), Long, Smith-Brown (Facey 60), Smith, Glendon (Akporn 58), Bennett (Thomas 80), Johns.

7 August 2011 *(in Akureyrarvollur)*

Finland 2 *(Jokinen 15, Hambo 62)*

England 3 *(Baker 13, Akporn 36, Randall 51)*

England: Gunn; Facey (Woodland 57), Gordon, Hayden, Randall, Baker (Bennett 57), Akporn (Johns 57), Long (Gorman 70), Glendon (Smith 70).

FRIENDLIES

24 August 2011 *(in Cambridge)*

England 1 *(Cole 78)*

Italy 0 1092

England: Willis; Shaw, Chambers L, Jebb (Swift 60), Cole, Graham (Wallace 60), Facey, Houghton, Rothwell (Pearson 71), Akporn (Robinson 65), Lipman (Dabo 71).

26 August 2011 *(in Bishop's Stortford)*

England 0

Czech Republic 1 *(Kurusta 52)* 1321

England: King; Dabo (Jebb 62), Shaw (Cole 41), Swift, Inniss (Facey 62), Chambers L, Robinson, Pearson (Houghton 41), Graham (Rothwell 57), Wallace, Lipman (Akporn 41).

28 August 2011 *(in Northampton)*

England 1 *(Jebb 42)*

Portugal 0 803

(in Northampton).
England: Willis; Shaw, Chambers L, Robinson, Jebb (Swift 62), Cole (Lipman 54), Facey, Houghton, Rothwell, Wallace (Graham 61), Akporn (Dabo 74).

EUROPEAN CHAMPIONSHIP

26 October 2011 *(in Sarajevo)*

England 4 *(Robinson 3, Shaw 15, Akporn 36, Cole 58)*

Latvia 0

England: Willis; Webb, Shaw, Poyet, Houghton, Robinson, Cole, Akporn (Graham 53), Inniss, Pearson (Rothwell 64), Lipman (Baker 53).

28 October 2011 *(in Sarajevo)*

England 2 *(Hayden 46, Akporn 68)*

Bosnia 0

England: Willis; Shaw, Poyet, Houghton (Inniss 74), Hayden, Robinson, Rothwell (Cole 56), Akporn, Dabo, Lipman (Baker 62), Swift.

31 October 2011 *(in Sarajevo)*

England 1 *(Cole 21)*

Holland 0

England: Coddington; Webb, Poyet, Hayden, Cole, Akporn (Swift 50), Graham (Robinson 73), Inniss, Pearson (Rothwell 64), Baker, Dabo.

26 March 2012 *(in Tbilisi)*

England 1 *(Chambers C 56)*

Ukraine 0

England: Willis; Shaw, Hayden, Chambers C (Woodland 75), Swift, Robinson (Jebb 66), Akporn, Hughes (Bennett 66), Inniss, Graham, Gordon.

28 March 2012 *(in Tbilisi)*

England 0

Georgia 1 *(Papunashvili 80)*

England: Willis; Webb, Shaw, Hayden, Chambers C, Swift, Robinson, Akporn, Jebb (Hughes 74), Graham (Bennett 41), Inniss (Chambers L 75).

31 March 2012 *(in Tbilisi)*

Spain 4 *(Calero 45, Grimaldi 47, Samper 57, Gaya 80)*

England 0

England: Willis; Shaw, Woodland, Chambers L, Hayden, Chambers C (Graham 51), Swift (Wallace 52), Robinson (Bennett 64), Akporn, Hughes, Gordon.

ALGARVE TOURNAMENT

2 February 2012 *(in Parchal)*

Portugal 1 *(Cristian 53)*

England 2 *(Campbell 5, Chambers L 80)*

England: Coddington; Webb, Chambers L, Houghton (Gordon 66), Campbell (Poyet 75), Wallace (Hughes 51), Bennett (Chambers C 51), Inniss, Swift (Woodland 66), Graham, Robinson (Cole 75).

4 February 2012 *(in Parchal)*

Holland 2 *(Vloet 18 (pen), Becker 39)*

England 2 *(Hughes 13, Chambers C 24)*

England: Willis; Gordon, Poyet, Houghton!, Wallace, Cole (Campbell 61), Hughes (Bennett 72), Inniss (Chambers L 5), Chambers C, Graham (Robinson 56), Woodland.

6 February 2012 *(in Lagoa)*

France 1 *(Martial 36)*

England 2 *(Chambers C 21, Robinson 80)*

(in Lagoa).
England: Coddington; Webb, Gordon, Houghton, Campbell (Cole 41), Hughes (Poyet 70), Bennett (Graham 70), Chambers C (Chambers L 75), Swift (Wallace 79), Robinson, Woodland.

ENGLAND UNDER-18

O'Connell, Pearson, Ramm (Blackburn R); Forster-Caskey (Brighton & HA); Cousins (Charlton Ath); Thomas, Willis (Coventry C); Clayton, Garratt, Powell (Crewe Alex); Hope (Everton); Hopper, Taft (Leicester C); Lussey (Liverpool); Hiwula, Meppen-Walters (Manchester C); Barmby, Blackett, Sutherland (Manchester U); Fowler, Gibson, Jackson (Middlesbrough); Alnwick (Newcastle U); Osborn (Nottingham F); Lecointe, Nelson (Plymouth Arg); Magri (Portsmouth), Long (Sheffield U); Stephens (Southampton); Agbaje (Stoke C); Pickford (Sunderland); Fanimo, Moncur, Morrison*, Potts, Turgott (West Ham U).

**Previously Manchester U.*

16 November 2011 *(in Nitra)*

Slovakia 1 *(Rusnak 90)*

England 1 *(Hope 48)*

England: Pickford (Sutherland 65); Cousins, Blackett (Walters 65), Lundstram, Dier, Jackson (Turgott 46), Clayton (Lussey 46), Caskey (Magri 46), Hope (Fanimo 65), Agbaje, Redmond (Hiwula 71).

2 March 2012 *(at Haverfordwest)*

Wales 1 *(Samuel 37)*

England 0

7 March 2012 *(at Crewe)*

England 3 *(Hiwula 36, Hope 60, Lecointe 65)*

Poland 0 6112

England: Pickford (Blackett 46); Stephens (Garratt 46), Potts (Barmby 46), Lundstram, Jackson, O'Connell, Powell (Lecointe 61), Lussey (Dunn 61), Hope (Osborn 69), Hiwula (Willis 46), Clayton.

23 March 2012 *(at Windsor Park)*

Northern Ireland 0

England 4 *(Glen-Ravenhill 5, Sweet 23, 57, Mooney 62)*

12 April 2012 *(at Newcastle)*

England 2 *(Sweet 61, Glen-Ravenhill 80)*

Scotland 0

26 April 2012 *(at Brighton)*

England 2

Republic of Ireland 1

Scotland 4, Northern Ireland 0
Scotland 1, Wales 2
Republic of Ireland 1, Northern Ireland 0
Republic of Ireland 1, Scotland 1
Wales 2, Republic of Ireland 2
Northern Ireland 2, Wales 1

	P	*W*	*D*	*L*	*F*	*A*	*Pts*
Northern Ireland	4	2	2	0	6	2	8
England	4	3	0	1	8	2	9
Wales	4	2	1	1	6	5	7
Republic of Ireland	4	1	2	1	5	5	5
Scotland	4	1	1	2	6	5	4
Northern Ireland	4	1	0	3	2	10	3

ENGLAND UNDER-19

Aneke, Yennaris (Arsenal); Redmond (Birmingham C); Sampson (Bolton W); Ralls (Cardiff C); Bamford*, Blackman, Chalobah, Deen-Conteh, Kane T (Chelsea); Barkley, Bidwell, Dier, Garbutt, Lundstram (Everton); Taylor (Leeds U); Coady, Dunn, Flanagan, Morgan, Robinson, Wisdom (Liverpool); Kennedy (Manchester C); Cole, Johnstone, Keane M, Keane W, Thorpe (Manchester U); Pilatos, Reach, Ripley, Williams (Middlesbrough); Lascelles (Nottingham F); Obita, Samuel (Reading); Laing (Sunderland); Kane H (Tottenham H); Berahino, Thorne (WBA); Hall (West Ham U).
**Previously Nottingham F.*

1 September 2011 *(in Maaseikerweg)*

Holland 0

England 0

England: Johnstone; Kennedy (Cole 46), Deen-Conteh (Obita 80), Thorne (Laing 46), Lascelles, Chalobah, Yennaris, Aneke (Reach 65), Keane W, Kane H (Sampson 65), Williams (Pilatos 46).

5 October 2011 *(in Limoges)*

France 2 *(Sanogo 42, Bahebeck 88)*

England 2 *(Keane W 22, Robinson 77)*

England: Blackman; Kane T, Robinson (Kennedy 90), Coady, Lascelles, Chalobah, Cole, Yennaris, Keane W (Laing 81), Thorne (Morgan 63), Berahino (Reach 63).

7 October 2011 *(in Limoges)*

Portugal 0

England 1 *(Morgan 65)*

England: Ripley; Kane T, Robinson (Taylor 46), Coady, Chalobah, Cole, Yennaris (Samuel 64), Morgan (Berahino 84), Keane W (Kennedy 66), Reach (Thorne 46), Laing.

9 October 2011 *(in Limoges)*

England 3 *(Berahino 27, 64, Samuel 45)*

Ukraine 1 *(Trubochkin 60)*

England: Blackman (Ripley 46); Lascelles, Yennaris (Kane T 72), Morgan (Chalobah 57), Reach (Coady 72), Taylor, Thorne, Laing, Berahino, Samuel (Keane W 63), Kennedy.

10 November 2011 *(at Brighton)*

England 1 *(Hall 80)*

Denmark 0 16,923

England: Ripley (Blackman 59); Flanagan, Bidwell (Kane T 46), Coady (Thorne 46), Wisdom, Chalobah, Barkley, Yennaris (Lascelles 89), Morgan (Deen-Conteh 72), Kane H (Hall 60), Cole (Williams 60).

28 February 2012 *(at Leyton Orient)*

England 2 *(Kane H 16, Bamford 65)*

Czech Republic 1 *(Twardzik 73)* 2270

(at Leyton Orient).
England: Johnstone (Ripley 46); Kane T, Garbutt (Bamford 46), Coady (Ralls 57), Chalobah (Lascelles 46), Wisdom, Yennaris, Barkley, Berahino (Redmond 57), Kane H (Bidwell 46), Williams (Thorne 71).

EUROPEAN CHAMPIONSHIP

25 May 2012 *(at Preston)*

England 5 *(Chalobah 48, Thorpe 53, Keane W 83, 90, Kane T 88)*

Slovenia 0 3816

England: Johnstone; Robinson, Chalobah, Keane M, Thorpe, Keane W, Barkley (Thorne 80), Kane H (Afobe 89), Dier, Berahino (Kane T 71), Lundstram.

27 May 2012 *(at Rochdale)*

England 1 *(Afobe 85)*

Montenegro 1 *(Vukcevic 25)* 1217

England: Johnstone; Kane T, Robinson, Chalobah, Keane M, Thorpe, Barkley (Keane W 46), Afobe, Thorne (Kane H 60), Dier, Bamford (Dunn 46).

30 May 2012 *(at Preston)*

England 1 *(Berahino 90)*

Switzerland 0 3266

England: Johnstone; Kane T, Keane M, Thorpe, Keane W (Berahino 62), Barkley, Afobe (Dunn 85), Kane H (Thorne 90), Bidwell, Dier, Lundstram.

ENGLAND UNDER-20

Baker (Aston Villa); Butland (Birmingham C); Lowe, Morris (Blackburn R); Phillips (Blackpool); Gordon (Chelsa); Wallace (Everton); Ngoo (Liverpool); Wabara (Manchester C); Brown (Manchester U); Adams, Knott (Sunderland); Parrett, Smith A (Tottenham H); Berahino, Hurst (WBA); McManaman (Wigan Ath).

FIFA UNDER-20 WORLD CUP

29 July 2011 *(in Medellin)*

North Korea 0

England 0 21,860

England: Butland; Adams, Baker, Berahino, Brown, Knott (Parrett 74), Lowe, McManaman (Morris 60), Phillips, Smith A, Wabara.

2 August 2011 *(in Medellin)*

Argentina 0

England 0 40,093

England: Butland; Adams, Baker (Wallace 31), Berahino (Hurst 82), Brown, Knott, Lowe, McManaman (Ngoo 72), Phillips, Smith A, Wabara.

4 August 2011 *(in Cartagena)*

Mexico 0

England 0 15,360

England: Butland; Baker, Berahino (Ngoo 63), Brown, Gordon, Knott (Parrett 46), Lowe, McManaman (Wallace 89), Phillips, Smith A, Wabara.

10 August 2011 *(in Armenia)*

Nigeria 1 *(Egbedi 52)*

England 0 18,187

England: Butland; Baker, Brown, Gordon, Knott, Lowe, McManaman (Morris 78), Ngoo (Berahino 59), Phillips, Smith A, Wabara (Wallace 22).

SCHOOLS FOOTBALL 2011–12

BOODLES INDEPENDENT SCHOOLS FA CUP 2011–12

FIRST ROUND
Ackworth 0 Tonbridge 8
ACS Cobham 0 Chigwell 0
(aet; Chigwell won 6-5 on penalties)
Alleyn's 5 Bury GS 3
Birkdale 4 Bolton 0
Bristol GS 0 Charterhouse 6
City of London 2 Ibstock Place 1
Colfe's 0 Bedales 1
Dulwich College 4 Worth 1
Forest 1 Ardingly 2
Frensham Heights 0 Eton 10
Grammar School at Leeds 5 Aldenham 1
Grange 1 Shrewsbury 2
Haileybury 8 Royal Russell 1
Harrodian 0 Repton 4
KES Witley 0 Hampton 8
King's School, Chester 4 Bradfield 2
Licensed Victuallers 1 Bedford Modern 8
Malvern 1 Cheadle Hulme 2
Norwich 0 Westminster 5
RGS Newcastle 1 Lancing 2
QEGS Blackburn 1 Brentwood 2
(aet)
Queen Ethelburga's College, York 3 Box Hill 2
(aet)
St Bede's College, Manchester 0 Millfield 3
St Bede's School 8 Highgate 0
Winchester 4 John Lyon 2
Wolverhampton GS 1 Kimbolton 3

SECOND ROUND
Bedales 1 Eton 8
Brentwood 3 St Columba's College 0
Charterhouse 5 Queen Ethelburga's Col, York 0
Cheadle Hulme 1 Grammar School at Leeds 0
Chigwell 0 Westminster 1
City of London 1 Birkdale 4
Haberdashers' Aske's 1 Bedford Modern 0
(aet; Haberdashers' won 4-3 on penalties)
Haileybury 1 Millfield 6
Kimbolton 0 Hampton 4
King's School, Chester 1 Ardingly 0
Lancing 1 Alleyn's 2
Oldham Hulme GS 0 Manchester GS 1
Repton 1 St Edmund's, Canterbury 0
St Bede's School 9 Dulwich College 2
Tonbridge 5 Latymer Upper 1
Winchester 2 Shrewsbury 1
(aet)

THIRD ROUND
Alleyn's 3 Birkdale 0
Brentwood 5 Manchester GS 1
Charterhouse 3 Hampton 3
(aet; Hampton won 4-3 on penalties)
Haberdashers' Aske's 1 Eton 5
King's School, Chester 1 Repton 3
Millfield 3 Cheadle Hulme 2
Tonbridge 2 Winchester 1
Westminster 1 St Bede's School 1
(aet; St Bede's won 5-4 on penalties)

FOURTH ROUND
Alleyn's 3 Eton 0
Brentwood 0 Tonbridge 1
Repton 1 Hampton 2
St Bede's School 0 Millfield 2

SEMI-FINALS
Alleyn's 1 Millfield 2
Hampton 2 Tonbridge 0

FINAL

Hampton 2
Millfield 1
(at Milton Keynes Dons FC)

Hampton: W. Legg, M. Roche, J. Williamson, J. Brown (C. Clark), B. Lewis-Clare, D. Ryan, A. Zubaidi (C. Murphy), F. Woodward-Gentle, M. Parsons, J. Dolman, C. Gerson (M. Lane).
Millfield: W. Godmon, L. Downing, J. Robertson, M. Mollloy, D. Webb (M. Berrow), A. Gibbs (A. Stewart), J. Parsons (H. Meneem), J. Golby, J. Radford, D. Williams, W. Oswin.
Referee: Mr. H. Webb (Yorkshire).

INVESTEC ISFA U15 CUP FINAL
Whitgift 2 Brentwood 1
(at Burton Albion FC)

INVESTEC ISFA U13 CUP FINAL
Hampton 1 Bolton 1
(aet; Hampton won 4-2 on penalties)
(at Burton Albion FC)

UNIVERSITY FOOTBALL 2012

128th UNIVERSITY MATCH

(Tuesday 13 March, at Cambridge City's Pro-Edge Stadium)

Oxford (0) 2 **Cambridge (2) 2**

(Cambridge won 4-3 on penalties)

Cambridge: Stefan Karakashian; Anthony Childs, Jamie Rutt, James May, Chris Peacock, James Day, Rick Totten, Paul Hartley (c), Haitham Sherif, Danny Kerrigan (Daniel Forde), Rory Griffiths (Mark Johnson).
Scorers: Kerrigan, Hartley.
Unused substitutes: Fergus Kent. Joe Huxley. Harry Dempsey.

Oxford: Tom Haigh; Robert Price, Dan Bassett, Anthony Beddows, Adam Fellows, Ezra Rubenstein (Ejike Onuchukwu), Luke Devereux (Alex Biggs), Alec Ward, Tom Castro (Sam Donald), Julian Austin (c), Adam Healy.
Scorers: Totten (own goal), Donald.
Unused substitutes: Mauro Pereira, Jack Fletcher.

Referee: Kevin Friend.

Oxford have won 51 games, Cambridge 49 and 28 drawn. *Oxford have scored 203 goals, Cambridge 201 goals.*

WOMEN'S FOOTBALL 2011–12

These days fans of women's football can double their chances of enjoyment. This is because the women's game is now an all-year-round entertainment thanks to the funding of the Football Association. In the traditional winter period it is the FA Women's Premier League and in the summer the professional Women's Super League (WSL) takes over. The Women's FA Cup is a cross-over between the two as it is an open competition and the 2011–12 Cup was won by WSL side Birmingham City Ladies who defeated fellow WSL Chelsea in the final held on the 26 May 2012 at Ashton Gate, Bristol. It was the first of these finals ever to go to a penalty shoot-out after the sides had drawn 2-2 following extra time. The scorers were Helen Lander (70 mins) and Kate Longhurst (101 mins) for Chelsea and Rachel Williams (91 mins) and Karen Carney (112 mins) for City; and when the inevitable penalties were taken Birmingham triumphed by three strikes to two, to win the FA Cup for the first time in their history.

There was no change in the pecking order for the inaugural season of the WSL with Arsenal Ladies (the most successful club ever in women's football) annexing the title in 2011. But it was a close run thing with victory only assured on the last day of the season. Arsenal beat Liverpool by 3-1 while Birmingham could only draw. This gave the Gunners the championship by 3 points over long-time leaders Birmingham with Everton finishing third. Arsenal went on to also win the first cup for teams in the WSL – the "Continental Cup" sponsored by Continental – again coming out the better of their nearest rivals Birmingham Ladies by 4-1 on Burton Albion's ground. The concluding WSL competition was the Reserve Subsidiary Cup in which Chelsea beat West Ham by 4-2.

The season itself was split in two because of England's participation in the Women's World Cup and the current season is likewise divided the same way to accommodate the Olympics. However, the FA's Kelly Simmons, who had done so much to get the League up and running, professed herself delighted that it had proved to be a "competitive achievement" and was further happy that "so many families, especially young girls, came to the matches making it a fun day out and more than just a game". In addition each of the eight clubs has a "Digital Ambassador" which has proved a very successful way to build a following on both the social media sites Facebook and Twitter.

The Women's Premier League competition saw the National Division won by Sunderland one point ahead of Leeds United with Reading and Nottingham Forest relegated. In the Northern Division just like their men's counterparts Manchester City were the champions five points clear of Sheffield United with Rotherham and Leeds City Vixens relegated, the latter both extraordinarily and sadly losing all their 18 matches. The Southern title went to Portsmouth who were 4 points beyond the reach of Colchester United with Plymouth Argyle and Keynsham Town taking the drop. In the several Divisions of the Reserve Leagues, Mid/North (1) was won by Everton; Mid/North (2) had Nottingham Forest the winners; Southern (1) was another success for Arsenal Ladies and Southern (2) became Cardiff City's honour .

The FA Women's Premier League Cup saw Sunderland Ladies complete a Cup and League "double" when they defeated Leeds United Ladies 2-1 in a match held on 6 May 2012 at Sixfields Stadium, Northampton. Two Natalie Gutteridge headers saw them home although Leeds did score a late consolation by virtue of a Carey Huegett penalty. The Wearsiders failed to pull off a "treble" when In the Premier League Reserve Cup Final they were defeated 3-0 by Everton.

The much anticipated Olympics will play a very big part in women's football in 2012 when for the first time a Great Britain side will take part. Led by Head Coach Hope Powell of England, a squad of 16 English and 2 Scottish women will have the honour of kicking off their campaign against New Zealand at the Millennium Stadium, Cardiff on 25 July 2012, two days before the Opening Ceremony. Their remaining qualifying games are against Cameroon and 2008 silver medallists Brazil. Domestically Powell oversaw her 150th match as England National Coach in June 2012 and England are currently one win away from qualification for the 2013 European Championships.

Individual items of merit to note include Amy Fearn being selected to referee the UEFA Women's Under 17 Championship final between France and Germany in Switzerland; Arsenal's Rachel Yankey equalling Doncaster Belles' Gillian Coultard's England international appearances record with her 119th cap against Slovenia in June 2012; and Leanne Hall, the ex-England 'keeper who has completed her FA Goalkeeper's A Licence which has made her the first female to attain both that and the outfield UEFA A Licence.

KEN GOLDMAN

Birmingham City's Ladies' Karen Carney goes close with a header against Chelsea Ladies' goalkeeper Carly Telford in the FA Women's Cup Final at Ashton Gate. The game finished 2-2 after extra time, Birmingham winning 3-2 on penalties. (PA)

WOMEN'S LEAGUE TABLES 2011–12

WOMEN'S SUPER LEAGUE 2011

			Home					*Away*					*Total*						
		P	*W*	*D*	*L*	*F*	*A*	*W*	*D*	*L*	*F*	*A*	*W*	*D*	*L*	*F*	*A*	*GD*	*Pts*
1	Arsenal Ladies	14	6	0	1	16	2	4	2	1	13	7	10	2	2	29	9	20	32
2	Birmingham City Ladies	14	4	2	1	14	6	4	3	0	15	7	8	5	1	29	13	16	29
3	Everton Ladies	14	3	2	2	7	6	4	2	1	12	7	7	4	3	19	13	6	25
4	Lincoln Ladies	14	2	2	3	8	8	4	1	2	10	8	6	3	5	18	16	2	21
5	Bristol Academy Women	14	1	3	3	8	11	3	1	3	6	9	4	4	6	14	20	–6	16
6	Chelsea Ladies	14	1	2	4	5	9	3	1	3	9	10	4	3	7	14	19	–5	15
7	Doncaster Rovers Belles	14	1	1	5	5	15	1	2	4	4	11	2	3	9	9	26	–17	9
8	Liverpool Ladies	14	0	2	5	6	16	1	2	4	4	10	1	4	9	10	26	–16	7

FA WOMEN'S PREMIER LEAGUE 2011–12

NATIONAL DIVISION	*P*	*W*	*D*	*L*	*GD*	*Pts*
1 Sunderland	18	13	3	2	31	42
2 Leeds U	18	13	2	3	26	41
3 Aston Villa	18	7	6	5	3	27
4 Barnet	18	7	5	6	9	26
5 Charlton Ath	18	7	5	6	1	26
6 Coventry C	18	7	5	6	0	26
7 Watford	18	5	2	11	–23	17
8 Cardiff C	18	4	4	10	–8	16
9 Reading	18	5	1	12	–18	16
10 Nottingham F	18	4	3	11	–21	15

NORTHERN DIVISION	*P*	*W*	*D*	*L*	*GD*	*Pts*
1 Manchester C	18	13	1	4	39	40
2 Sheffield	18	11	2	5	18	35
3 Leicester C	18	10	4	4	22	34
4 Blackburn R	18	9	5	4	20	32
5 Derby Co	18	9	5	4	14	32
6 Sporting Club Alb	18	8	5	5	13	29
7 Preston NE	18	7	3	8	0	24
8 Rochdale	18	4	3	11	–14	15
9 Rotherham U	18	3	4	11	–19	13
10 Leeds C Vixens	18	0	0	18	–93	0

SOUTHERN DIVISION	*P*	*W*	*D*	*L*	*GD*	*Pts*
1 Portsmouth	18	12	3	3	27	39
2 Colchester U	18	10	5	3	16	35
3 West Ham U	18	10	4	4	14	34
4 Brighton & HA	18	8	3	7	0	27
5 Gillingham	18	6	5	7	–7	23
6 Tottenham H	18	6	4	8	–1	22
7 QPR	18	5	5	8	–9	20
8 Millwall Lionesses	18	4	5	9	–13	17
9 Plymouth Arg	18	5	2	11	–19	17
10 Keynsham T	18	3	6	9	–8	15

FA WOMEN'S PREMIER RESERVE LEAGUES 2011–12

SOUTHERN DIVISION ONE (RESERVES)

		P	*W*	*D*	*L*	*GD*	*Pts*
1	Arsenal	14	12	2	0	45	38
2	Bristol Academy	14	9	4	1	16	31
3	Chelsea	14	7	1	6	11	22
4	Charlton Ath	14	4	5	5	–2	17
5	Gillingham	14	3	6	5	–14	15
6	West Ham U	14	4	2	8	–14	14
7	Watford	14	3	3	8	–18	12
8	Brighton & HA	14	2	1	11	–24	7

SOUTHERN DIVISION TWO (RESERVES)

		P	*W*	*D*	*L*	*GD*	*Pts*
1	Cardiff C	14	13	1	0	45	40
2	Colchester U	14	8	4	2	28	28
3	QPR	14	8	2	4	6	26
4	Reading	14	6	2	6	–2	20
5	Portsmouth	14	5	3	6	2	18
6	Millwall Lionesses	14	5	1	8	–10	16
7	Plymouth Arg	14	2	2	10	–28	8
8	Yeovil T	14	0	3	11	–41	3

MID/NORTH DIVISION ONE (RESERVES)

		P	*W*	*D*	*L*	*GD*	*Pts*
1	Everton	15	12	2	1	46	38
2	Liverpool	15	7	3	5	5	24
3	Sunderland	15	5	4	6	–7	19
4	Blackburn R	15	5	3	7	–23	18
5	Coventry C	15	4	3	8	–12	15
6	Manchester C	15	4	1	10	–9	13

MID/NORTH DIVISION TWO (RESERVES)

		P	*W*	*D*	*L*	*GD*	*Pts*
1	Nottingham F	18	13	3	2	35	42
2	Leicester C	18	12	3	3	21	39
3	Lincoln	18	9	2	7	8	29
4	Sheffield	18	8	3	7	–1	27
5	Derby Co	18	5	2	11	–16	17
6	Newcastle U	18	4	2	12	–22	14
7	Stoke C	18	3	3	12	–25	12

THE FA TESCO WOMEN'S PREMIER LEAGUE CUP 2011–12

FA WOMEN'S LEAGUE CUP FINAL

Sunday, 6 May 2012

(at Northampton, attendance 641)

Leeds U (0) 1 Sunderland (1) 2

Leeds U: Draycott; Emmonds (Johnson), Sharp, Birkby (Lipman), Sykes, Huegett, Rich (Danby), Galton, Holmes, Turner, Holbrook.

Scorer: Huegett 90 (pen).

Sunderland: Laws; Holmes (Salicki), Greenwell, Furness, Wilson, McDougall, Mead (Ramshaw), Gutteridge, Williams, Devine, Lee.

Scorer: Gutteridge 9, 66.

Referee: P. Forrester.

THE FA WOMEN'S CUP 2011–12

SPONSORED BY E.ON

FIRST QUALIFYING ROUND

Lowick U v Cramlington Jun	7-2
Lumley v Consett	2-1
Teesside Sp v California Ladies	0-4
Redcar Ath v Percy Main	4-0
Abbeytown v Forest H Women's	3-1
St Francis 2000 v Peterlee T	6-3
Ashington v Prudhoe T	3-2
Whitley Bay v Kendal T	8-1
Tyneside w.o. v Whitehaven withdrew	
Tynedale v Birtley T	3-2
Sheffield U Community v Hull C	3-0
Scunthorpe U v Rothwell	2-3
Bradford PA v Keighley Oaks	1-6
North Ferriby U v Appleby Frodingham	4-0
Barnsley v Ossett Alb	9-0
Sheffield U Jun Blades v Steel C W	1-2
Brighouse v Padiham	0-2
Blackpool G&L v Southport Birkdale	13-0
Kirklees v Crewe Alex	0-3
Chester C v Birkenhead Y	4-6
Bolton W v Tranmere R	2-5
Lancaster C v Warrington T	2-4
Accrington G&L v Blackpool Wren R	0-4
Morecambe v Middleton Ath	4-2
Arnold T v Oadby & Wigston Dyn	2-0
Retford U v Dronfield T	2-1
Mansfield T v Nettleham	7-5
Long Eaton U v Asfordby Amat	8-0
Lichfield D v Walsall	2-0
Southam U withdrew v Coventry Sphinx w.o.	
Bilbrook v Rugby T	7-0
Crusaders v Malvern T	3-2
Stafford T v Wyrley	4-0
Hereford Peg v Stratford T	1-5
Kettering T v Peterborough H	10-0
Corby S&L withdrew v Cogenhoe & K w.o.	
Moulton v Rothwell T	3-1
Huntingdon T v AFC Trinity	0-2
Peterborough N Star v Brackley Sp	2-1
Brantham Ath v Bungay T	5-3
Hethersett Ath v Haverhill R	3-1
Copleston v C&K Basildon	0-10
Braintree T v Billericay T	2-3
Wymondham T v Chelmsford C	0-8
Fakenham T v East Thurrock U	2-1
Hannakins v Thorpe U	4-2
Brandon withdrew v Woodbridge T w.o.	
Sawbridgeworth T v Arlesey T	1-6
Leyton Ladies v Harringey Bor	3-1
Leighton U Vixens v Tring Ath	2-1
Kikk U v Leverstock Green	7-2
MSA v Stevenage Bor	2-0
Hoddesdon Owls v Hemel Hempstead T	1-5
Oxford C v Banbury U	4-2
Colne Valley w.o. v Henley T withdrew	
Oxford U v Maidenhead U	5-2
Bracknell T v Beaconsfied SYCOB	7-0
Denham U v Marlow	3-0
Aylesbury U v Newbury	1-5
Reading T v Brentford	3-4
Headington v Launton	1-3
Bexhill U v Knaphill	2-1
Crawley Wasps v Meridian	5-0
Abbey R v Haywards Heath T	1-5
Eastbourne v South Park	1-1
South Park won 5-4 on penalties.	
London Cor v Rottingdean Vill	3-2
Ashford Girls v Chichester C	0-4
Ramsgate v Eastbourne T	2-9
AFC Wimbledon v East Preston	3-1
Malgo v Westfield	1-2
Parkwood R v Rusthall	3-3
Rusthall won 4-2 on penalties.	
New Forest v Boscombe Alb	1-13
Salisbury C v Weymouth	0-1
Aldershot T v Poole T	2-0
Purbeck v Andover New Street	0-4
Swindon Spitfires v Bridgwater T	0-1
Stoke Lane Ath v Frome T	2-4
Swindon Supermarine v Forest of Dean	3-1
Bitton v AEK-BOCO	4-1
Pen Mill v St Nicholas	1-2
Downend Flyers v Bristol Ladies U	3-5
Cheltenham T v Ilminster T	4-2
Shepton Mallet v Larkhall Ath	0-8
Marine Acad Plymouth withdrew v Exeter C w.o.	
AFC Telford U v Allscott	0-3
Peterborough Sp v Daventry T	5-2
Durham Wildcats v Penrith	4-0
Shanklin v Broadstone	12-0
Victoire v Maidstone T	1-7

SECOND QUALIFYING ROUND

St Francis 2000 v Lumley	13-2
California Ladies v Tyneside	3-1
Tynedale v Durham Wildcats	1-6
Lowick U v Norton & Stockton A	4-2
Abbeytown v Whitley Bay	1-3
Ashington v Redcar Ath	4-3
Barnsley v Keighley Oaks	5-3
North Ferriby U v Rothwell	0-15
Sheffield U Community v Steel C W	6-0
Warrington T v Crewe Alex	0-7
Tranmere R v Blackpool G&L	3-2
Blackpool Wren R v Padiham	2-1
Birkenhead Y v Morecambe	0-3
Sandiacre T v Mansfield T	1-3
Long Eaton U v Retford U	8-1
Arnold T v West Bridgford	9-0
Stratford T v FC Reedswood	4-3
Stafford T v Bilbrook	1-4
Crusaders v Cottage Farm R	2-2
Crusaders won 3-1 on penalties.	
Coventry Sphinx v Kenilworth T	4-1
Lichfield D v Allscott	6-1
Peterborough N Star v Moulton	8-1
AFC Trinity v Cogenhoe & K	5-3
Kettering T v Peterborough Sp	0-5
Fakenham T v C&K Basildon	1-4
Chelmsford C v Hethersett Ath	0-7
Hannakins v Brantham Ath	3-1
Billericay T w.o. v Woodbridge T failed to fulfil fixture.	
Hemel Hempstead T v Leighton U Vixens	3-1
MSA v Leyton	3-1
Barking v Arlesey T	5-1
Kikk U v Hampstead	0-3
Newbury v Oxford U	0-12
Denham U v Colne Valley	8-1
Brentford v Oxford C	1-2
Bracknell T v Launton	5-0
Eastbourne T v Crawley Wasps	2-3
South Park v Westfield	1-4
Rusthall v Panthers	2-2
Rusthall won 4-2 on penalties.	
Bexhill U v Haywards Heath T	4-2
Chichester C v Maidstone T	4-1
AFC Wimbledon v London Cor	3-4
Christchurch v Shanklin	0-6
Andover New Street v Weymouth	0-3
Locks Heath v Boscombe Alb	0-3
Aldershot T v Southampton W	0-2
Bristol Ladies U v Swindon Supermarine	3-2
St Nicholas v Frome T	1-3
Cheltenham T v Bridgwater T	0-3
Bitton v Larkhall Ath	0-4
Morley R v Exeter C	0-9
Falmouth T v Launceston	0-1

THIRD QUALIFYING ROUND

Mossley Hill v Curzon Ashton	6-0
Ashington v California Ladies	2-3
Rothwell v Newcastle U	0-4
Stockport Co v St Francis 2000	8-0
South Durham & C v Wakefield	9-0
Tranmere R v Sheffield W	0-4
Morecambe v Sheffield U Community	2-3
Liverpool Feds v Salford	1-0
Blackpool Wren R v Lowick U	4-2
Durham Wildcats v Barnsley	3-0
Whitley Bay v Middlesbrough	2-3
Huddersfield T v Bradford C	1-2
Arnold T v Coventry Sphinx	0-1
Lichfield D v Stoke C	1-5

Leicester C v Northampton T	4-0
Wolverhampton W v Leafield Ath	3-2
Loughborough S v Bilbrook	14-0
Stratford T v Loughborough F	3-6
Crewe Alex v Crusaders	2-3
Mansfield T v Copswood	3-4
AFC Trinity w.o. v Dudley U failed to fulfil fixture.	
Radcliffe Olym v Long Eaton U	3-1
C&K Basildon v Hemel Hempstead T	3-1
MSA v MK Dons	4-3
Ebbsfleet U v Barking	3-0
Norwich C v Chesham U	4-3
Ipswich T w.o. v Hannakins withdrew	
Hethersett Ath v Enfield T	0-5
Old Actonians v Billericay T	2-6
Peterborough N Star v Brentwood T	4-3
Hampstead v Cambridge W	1-2
Luton T v Peterborough Sp	0-1
London Cor v Oxford U	0-5
Bexhill U v Bracknell T	1-6
Chichester C v Rusthall	7-0
Crystal Palace v Crawley Wasps	1-2
Westfield v Oxford C	3-0
Lewes v Univ of Portsmouth	4-1
Denham U v Southampton Saints	1-1
Denham U won 3-2 on penalties.	
Yeovil T v Shanklin	1-2
Southampton W v Weymouth	2-3
Exeter C v Keynsham T Dev	4-0
Newquay v Frome T	3-2
Bristol Ladies U v Forest Green R	2-6
Larkhall Ath v Gloucester C	5-2
Bridgwater T v Swindon T	1-5
Boscombe Alb v Launceston	3-1

FIRST ROUND

Sheffield U Community v Middlesbrough	0-1
Stockport Co v South Durham & C	2-3
California Ladies v Durham Wildcats	0-8
Bradford C v Newcastle U	3-2
Liverpool Feds v Sheffield W	1-3
Blackpool Wren R v Mossley Hill	3-2
Crusaders v Coventry Sphinx	0-3
Loughborough F v Radcliffe Olym	3-0
AFC Trinity v Leicester C	2-5
Loughborough S v Wolverhampton W	5-3
Copswood v Stoke C	3-6
MSA v Westfield	2-1
Norwich C v Denham U	0-3
C&K Basildon v Lewes	0-3
Ebbsfleet U v Havant & Waterlooville	1-5
Crawley Wasps w.o. v Ipswich T failed to fulfil fixture.	
Cambridge W v Oxford U	2-5
Bracknell T v Enfield T	0-5
Chichester C v Peterborough Sp	5-2
Billericay T v Peterborough N Star	3-6
Shanklin v Boscombe Alb	3-1
Newquay v Larkhall Ath	2-2
Larkhall Ath won 7-6 on penalties.	
Forest Green R v Weymouth	5-1
Swindon T v Exeter C	2-1

SECOND ROUND

Manchester C v Leeds C Vixens	9-1
Sheffield W v Durham Wildcats	1-4
Preston NE v Stoke C	7-3
Sheffield Ladies v Middlesbrough	10-0
South Durham & C v Bradford C	0-3
Rochdale v Blackburn R	1-2
Blackpool Wren R v Rotherham U	3-4
Leicester C v Loughborough S	2-1
Derby Co v Loughborough F	3-1
Leicester C W v Sp Club Alb	0-1
Coventry Sphinx v Peterborough N Star	0-1
Crawley Wasps v MSA	0-0
MSA won 3-0 on penalties.	
Oxford U v Lewes	2-0
Enfield T v QPR	1-1
Enfield T won 4-3 on penalties.	
Gillingham v Colchester U	3-0
Brighton & HA v Millwall Lionesses	2-1
Tottenham H v Denham U	7-0
Chichester C v West Ham U	0-3
Havant & Waterlooville v Plymouth Arg	3-2
Keynsham T v Swindon T	7-1
Larkhall Ath v Shanklin	2-1
Portsmouth v Forest Green R	4-1

THIRD ROUND

Larkhall Ath v Tottenham H	1-1
Larkhall Ath won 4-3 on penalties.	
Brighton & HA v Havant & Waterlooville	4-2
Charlton Ath v Bradford C	3-1
Enfield T v MSA	2-0
Portsmouth v Sheffield Ladies	1-3
Watford v Leeds U	1-6
Keynsham T v Gillingham	4-1
Aston Villa v Coventry C	0-2
Derby Co v West Ham U	4-2
Leicester C v Cardiff C	1-2
Sunderland v Rotherham U	8-0
Nottingham F v Blackburn R	0-3
Barnet Ladies v Peterborough N Star	8-0
Manchester C v Oxford U	4-1
Durham Wildcats v Preston NE	0-2
Sp Club Albion v Reading Women	3-0

FOURTH ROUND

Cardiff C v Sunderland	0-7
Barnet Ladies v Sp Club Albion	3-0
Brighton & HA v Larkhall Ath	3-0
Charlton Ath v Derby Co	2-0
Coventry C v Leeds U	1-2
Preston NE v Blackburn R	0-2
Enfield T v Manchester C	0-2
Keynsham T v Sheffield Ladies	5-2

FIFTH ROUND

Bristol Acad v Leeds U	3-0
Barnet Ladies v Doncaster R Belles	1-2
Charlton Ath v Blackburn R	1-5
Lincoln v Arsenal	0-1
Birmingham C v Liverpool	3-0
Manchester C v Everton	1-5
Chelsea v Brighton & HA	3-0
Keynsham T v Sunderland	1-5

SIXTH ROUND

Doncaster R Belles v Chelsea	0-2
Arsenal v Everton	2-1
Birmingham C v Sunderland	4-0
Bristol Acad v Blackburn R	3-0

SEMI-FINALS

Birmingham C v Bristol Acad	4-1
Chelsea v Arsenal	2-0

WOMEN'S FA CUP FINAL

Saturday, 26 May 2012

(at Ashton Gate, attendance 8723)

Birmingham C (0) 2 Chelsea (0) 2

Birmingham C: Spencer; Weston, Harrop (Aluko), Bassett, Williams R, Carney, Potter, Moore, Taylor, Unitt, Westwood.
Scorers: Williams R 90, Carney 111.

Chelsea: Telford; Fay (Perry), Bonner, Sherwood, Buet, Lander (Longhurst), Rafferty, Bleazard, Ingle, Susi, Coombs (Spence).
Scorers: Lander 70, Longhurst 101.

aet; Birmingham C won 3-2 on penalties.

Referee: N. Walker.

UEFA WOMEN'S CHAMPIONS LEAGUE 2011–12

QUALIFYING ROUND
GROUP 1
PAOK 3, CS Goliador 0
Young Boys 3, ZFK Nase 1
PAOK 0, ZFK Nase 1
CS Goliador 0, Young Boys 7
Young Boys 1, PAOK 1
ZFK Nase 6, CS Goliador 0

GROUP 2
MTK 12, Liepajas 0
1st Dezembro 1, ASA Tel Aviv 1
ASA Tel Aviv 1, MTK 0
1st Dezembro 4, Liepajas 0
MTK 0, 1 Dezembro 0
Liepajas 1, ASA Tel Aviv 4

GROUP 3
Rayo Vallecano 1, Peamount 0
Krka 1, Parnu 2
Rayo Vallecano 4, Parnu 1
Peamount 7, Krka 0
Krka 0, Rayo Vallecano 4
Parnu 1, Peamount 5

GROUP 4
Gintra 1, Atasehir 1
Sarajevo 1, Olimpia Cluj 3
Olimpia Cluj 5, Gintra 0
Sarajevo 4, Atasehir 1
Gintra 1, Sarajevo 2
Atasehir 1, Olimpia Cluj 4

GROUP 5
Klaksvik 1, Mosta 0
Glasgow City 4, Spartak 0
Glasgow City 8, Mosta 0
Spartak 4, Klaksvik 2
Klaksvik 0, Glasgow City 5
Mosta 0, Spartak 11

GROUP 6
Unia Raciborz 0, Slovan Bratislava 1
PK-35 10, Ada 0
Slovan Bratislava 0, PK-35 1
Unia Raciborz 8, Ada 0
PK-35 1, Unia Raciborz 1
Ada 0, Slovan Bratislava 16

GROUP 7
Legenda Chernigiv 2, Swansea 0
Apollon 14, Progres 0
Legenda Chernigiv 8, Progres 0
Swansea 0, Apollon 8
Apollon 2, Legenda Chernigiv 1
Progres 0, Swansea 4

GROUP 8
Bobruichanka 7, Crusaders 0
NSA Sofia 1, Osijek 1
NSA Sofia 1, Crusaders 0
Osijek 1, Bobruichanka 0
Bobruichanka 3, NSA Sofia 0
Crusaders 1, Osijek 5

FIRST ROUND FIRST LEG
Standard 0, Brondby 2
ASA Tel Aviv 0, Torres 2
CSHVSM 2, Neulengbach 1
Olimpia Cluj 0, Lyon 9
Apollon 2, Sparta Prague 2
PK-35 1, Rayo Vallecano 4
Osijek 0, Gothenburg 4
Thor 0, Potsdam 6
Twente 0, Rossiyanka 2
Stabaek 1, Frankfurt 0
Young Boys 0, Fortuna 3
Peamount 0, Paris St Germain 2
Bobruichanka 0, Arsenal 4
Bristol Academy 1, Voronezh 1
Glasgow City 1, Valur 1
Tavagnacco 2, Malmo 1

FIRST ROUND SECOND LEG
Torres 3, ASA Tel Aviv 2
Frankfurt 4, Stabaek 1
Sparta Prague 2, Apollon 1
Paris St Germain 3, Peamount 0
Voronezh 4, Bristol Academy 2
Arsenal 6, Bobruichanka 0
Lyon 3, Olimpia Cluj 0
Fortuna 2, Young Boys 1
Potsdam 8, Thor 2
Neulengbach 5, CSHVSM 0
Rossiyanka 1, Twente 0
Valur 0, Glasgow City 3
Brondby 3, Standard 4
Rayo Vallecano 3, PK-35 0
Malmo 5, Tavagnacco 0
Gothenburg 7, Osijek 0

SECOND ROUND FIRST LEG
Frankfurt 3, Paris St Germain 0
Potsdam 10, Glasgow City 0
Brondby 2, Torres 1
Neulengbach 1, Malmo 3
Fortuna 0, Gothenburg 1
Sparta Prague 0, Lyon 6
Voronezh 0, Rossiyanka 4
Rayo Vallecano 1, Arsenal 1

SECOND ROUND SECOND LEG
Malmo 1, Neulengbach 0
Gothenburg 3, Fortuna 2
Glasgow City 0, Potsdam 7
Arsenal 5, Rayo Vallecano 1
Rossiyanka 3, Voronezh 3
Lyon 6, Sparta Prague 0
Torres 1, Brondby 3
Paris St Germain 2, Frankfurt 1

QUARTER-FINALS FIRST LEG
Arsenal 3, Gothenburg 1
Potsdam 2, Rossiyanka 0
Lyon 4, Brondby 0
Malmo 1, Frankfurt 0

QUARTER-FINALS SECOND LEG
Gothenburg 1, Arsenal 0
Rossiyanka 0, Potsdam 3
Brondby 0, Lyon 4
Frankurt 3, Malmo 0

SEMI-FINALS FIRST LEG
Arsenal 1, Frankfurt 2
Lyon 5, Potsdam 1

SEMI-FINALS SECOND LEG
Frankfurt 2, Arsenal 0
Potsdam 0, Lyon 0

FINAL
17 May (in Munich).

Lyon (2) 2 *(Le Sommer 15 (pen), Abily 28)*

Frankfurt (0) 0 50,212

Lyon: Bouhaddi; Renard, Henry, Schelin (Otaki 88), Le Sommer (Rosana 65), Necib (Dickenmann 49), Cruz Trana, Franco, Bompastor, Viguier, Abily.
Frankfurt: Schumann; Lewandowski, Kumagai, Thunebro, Behringer, Marozsan, Weber (Percival 61), Huth (Crnogorcevic 64), Garefrekas, Bartusiak, Simsek (Landstrom 83).
Referee: Palmqvist (Sweden).

WOMEN'S WORLD CUP 2011

FINALS IN GERMANY

Competition completed from last year.

QUARTER-FINALS
England 1, France 1
France won 4-3 on penalties.
Germany 0, Japan 1
Sweden 3, Australia 1
Brazil 2, USA 2
USA won 5-3 on penalties.

SEMI-FINALS
France 1, USA 3
Japan 3, Sweden 1

MATCH FOR THIRD PLACE
Sweden 2, France 1

FINAL
Japan 2, USA 2
Japan won 3-1 on penalties.

WOMEN'S EURO 2011–13

PRELIMINARY ROUND

GROUP 1
Lithuania 1, Macedonia 1
Luxembourg 2, Latvia 0
Luxembourg 1, Macedonia 5
Latvia 1, Lithuania 0
Lithuania 4, Luxembourg 1
Macedonia 1, Latvia 0

GROUP 2
Georgia 0, Malta 1
Faeroes 0, Armenia 1
Armenia 0, Georgia 0
Faeroes 2, Malta 0
Malta 1, Armenia 1
Georgia 1, Faeroes 0

GROUP STAGE

GROUP 1
Bosnia 0, Italy 1
Poland 0, Russia 2
Russia awarded 3-0 victory by default.
Russia 4, Bosnia 1
Macedonia 0, Italy 9
Poland 2, Greece 0
Macedonia 1, Greece 1
Italy 2, Russia 0
Poland 4, Bosnia 0
Macedonia 2, Bosnia 6
Greece 0, Russia 4
Poland 0, Italy 5
Macedonia 0, Poland 3
Italy 2, Greece 0
Greece 2, Bosnia 3
Russia 8, Macedonia 0
Greece 1, Poland 1
Italy 4,Bosnia 0
Russia 0, Italy 2
Greece 2, Macedonia 2
Italy 9, Macedonia 0
Russia 4, Greece 0
Bosnia 0, Poland 2
Poland 4, Macedonia 0
Bosnia 0, Russia 1

GROUP 2
Kazakhstan 0, Romania 3
Germany 4, Switzerland 1
Turkey 1, Spain 10
Switzerland 4, Romania 1
Kazakhstan 2, Turkey 0
Turkey 0, Kazakhstan 0
Romania 0, Germany 3
Spain 3, Switzerland 2
Kazakhstan 0, Spain 4
Romania 7, Turkey 1
Germany 17, Kazakhstan 0
Romania 0, Spain 4
Turkey 1, Romania 2
Switzerland 8, Kazakhstan 1
Spain 2, Germany 2
Turkey 0, Germany 5
Romania 3, Kazakhstan 0
Germany 5, Spain 0
Switzerland 5, Turkey 0
Spain 13, Kazakhstan 0
Switzerland 0, Germany 6
Germany 5, Romania 0
Switzerland 4, Spain 3
Spain 4, Turkey 0
Romania 4, Switzerland 2

GROUP 3
Iceland 6, Bulgaria 0
Belgium 2, Hungary 1
Iceland 3, Norway 1
Norway 6, Hungary 0
Iceland 0, Belgium 0
Hungary 0, Iceland 1
Bulgaria 0, Northern Ireland 1
Belgium 1, Norway 1
Northern Ireland 0, Iceland 2
Bulgaria 0, Hungary 4
Belgium 5, Bulgaria 0
Northern Ireland 3, Norway 1
Bulgaria 0, Belgium 1
Hungary 2, Northern Ireland 2
Belgium 2, Northern Ireland 2
Bulgaria 0, Norway 3
Hungary 0, Norway 5
Belgium 1, Iceland 0
Northern Ireland 0, Hungary 1
Northern Ireland 4, Bulgaria 1
Norway 11, Bulgaria 0
Iceland 3, Hungary 0
Hungary 1, Belgium 3
Norway 2, Northern Ireland 0
Bulgaria 0, Iceland 10

GROUP 4
Israel 0, France 5
Wales 0, Republic of Ireland 2
Republic of Ireland 1, France 3
Israel 1, Scotland 6
Republic of Ireland 2, Israel 0
Wales 1, France 4
France 5, Israel 0
Scotland 2, Wales 2
Israel 0, Wales 2
France 2, Scotland 0
France 4, Wales 0
Scotland 2, Republic of Ireland 1
Scotland 8, Israel 0
Republic of Ireland 0, Wales 1
Wales 5, Israel 0
Republic of Ireland 0, Scotland 1

GROUP 5
Belarus 2, Estonia 1
Estonia 1, Ukraine 4
Ukraine 0, Slovakia 0
Finland 6, Estonia 0
Slovakia 3, Estonia 1
Belarus 2, Finland 2

Slovakia 3, Belarus 0
Ukraine 0, Belarus 1
Slovakia 0, Finland 1
Ukraine 5, Estonia 0
Finland 2, Slovakia 0
Estonia 2, Belarus 4
Ukraine 1, Finland 2
Finland 4, Belarus 0
Slovakia 0, Ukraine 2

GROUP 6
Serbia 2, England 2
Holland 6, Serbia 0
England 4, Slovenia 0
Croatia 0, Holland 3
Slovenia 1, Serbia 2
Croatia 3, Slovenia 3
Holland 0, England 0
Serbia 4, Croatia 2
Slovenia 0, Holland 2
England 2, Serbia 0
Holland 2, Croatia 0
Croatia 0, England 6
Holland 3, Slovenia 1
Croatia 1, Serbia 4
England 1, Holland 0
Serbia 0, Holland 4
Slovenia 0, England 4

GROUP 7
Armenia 0, Portugal 8
Austria 1, Czech Republic 1
Armenia 0, Denmark 5
Czech Republic 1, Portugal 0
Denmark 3, Austria 0
Austria 3, Armenia 0
Portugal 0, Denmark 3
Portugal 0, Austria 1
Czech Republic 5, Armenia 0
Denmark 11, Armenia 0
Portugal 6, Armenia 0
Portugal 2, Czech Republic 5
Armenia 2, Austria 4
Czech Republic 0, Denmark 2
Austria 1, Portugal 0
Czech Republic 2, Austria 3
Denmark 1, Czech Republic 0
Competition still being played.

ENGLAND WOMEN'S INTERNATIONALS 2011–12

EUROPEAN CHAMPIONSHIP

17 Sept

Serbia 2 *(Podovac 55, Smiljkovic 90)*

England 2 *(Yankey 6, Slovic 19 (og))*

(in Omladinski).
England: Brown; Susi, Unitt, Scott J, Bradley, Stoney, White E, Bassett, Dowie (Williams R 46), Carney, Yankey.

22 Sept

England 4 *(Yankey 1, White E 5, Houghton 56, Williams R 87)*

Slovenia 0 3878

(at Swindon).
England: Bardsley; Scott A, Unitt, Houghton, Bradley (Whelan 76), Stoney, Clarke (Buet 90), Williams F, White E, Carney, Yankey (Williams R 81).

27 Oct

Holland 0

England 0

(in Zwolle). 8850
England: Bardsley; Scott A, Unitt, Scott J, Bradley, Stoney, Clarke (Houghton 46), Williams F, White E, Carney, Yankey.

23 Nov

England 2 *(Clarke 41, White E 51)*

Serbia 0

(at Doncaster). 4112
England: Bardsley; Scott A, Unitt, Scott J, Bradley, Stoney, Clarke, Williams F (Houghton 77), White E (Williams R 87), Carney, Yankey (Smith K 70).

31 Mar

England 6 *(Williams R 4, Clarke 15, Unitt 18, White E 35, Houghton 45, 68)*

Croatia 0

(in Vrbovec).
England: Bardsley; Scott A, Unitt, Scott J, Bassett, Houghton, White E (Aluko 62), Williams F (Moore 46), Williams R, Carney (Asante 46), Clarke.

17 June

England 1 *(Yankey 67)*

Holland 0

(at Salford City Stadium). 5505
England: Brown; Scott A, Houghton, Scott J, Bradley, Stoney, Aluko, Williams F, Williams R (White E 46), Carney (Asante 72).

21 June

Slovenia 0

England 4 *(Scott J 29, 43, Carney 54, Williams R 85)*

(at Velenje). 200
England: Brown; Scott A, Bradley, Stoney, Houghton (Rafferty 61), Scott J, Asante, Aluko, Williams F (Williams R 70), Yankey, White E (Carney 46).

CYPRUS CUP

28 Feb

England 2 *(Smith K 35 (pen), 88 (pen), Carney 50)*

Finland 1 *(Kukkonen 7)*

(in Larnaca).
England: Chamberlain; Scott A, Stoney, Carney, Williams F, White E (Williams R 71), Smith K, Bassett, Houghton, Moore, Smith S (Clarke 83).

1 Mar

England 1 *(Williams F 75)*

Switzerland 0

(in Larnaca).
England: Brown (Chamberlain 64); Unitt, Scott J, Bradley (Houghton 32), Carney (White E 64), Williams F, Clarke, Williams R, Susi, Smith S (Moore 64), Whelan (Stoney 16).

4 Mar

France 3 *Necib 11, Delie 49, Thiney 80)*

England 0

(in Larnaca).
England: Bardsley; Scott A, Scott J, Stoney, Carney, White E, Smith K (Williams R 57), Clarke (Telford 72), Bassett, Houghton, Asante (Williams F 46).

6 Mar

Italy 3 *(Panico 59, Conti 64, Gabbiadini 86)*

England 1 *(Moore 25)*

(in Larnaca).
England: Brown (Chamberlain 60); Scott A, Unitt, Stoney, Williams F, Williams R (White E 59), Susi (Carney 69), Bassett, Houghton (Scott J 46), Moore, Smith S.

NON-LEAGUE TABLES 2011–12

EVO-STIK NORTHERN PREMIER LEAGUE 2011–12

		Total						Home					Away						
		P	W	D	L	F	A	W	D	L	F	A	W	D	L	F	A	GD	Pts
1	Chester	42	31	7	4	102	29	16	4	1	55	12	15	3	3	47	17	73	100
2	Northwich Victoria	42	26	8	8	73	43	13	4	4	35	19	13	4	4	38	24	30	83
3	Chorley	42	24	7	11	76	48	13	5	3	41	19	11	2	8	35	29	28	79
4	Bradford Park Avenue¶	42	24	6	12	77	49	15	1	5	43	20	9	5	7	34	29	28	78
5	Hednesford T	42	21	10	11	67	49	9	8	4	36	21	12	2	7	31	28	18	73
6	FC United	42	21	9	12	83	51	11	5	5	45	25	10	4	7	38	26	32	72
7	Marine	42	19	9	14	56	50	6	4	11	22	30	13	5	3	34	20	6	66
8	Rushall Olympic	42	17	10	15	52	51	11	5	5	27	21	6	5	10	25	30	1	61
9	North Ferriby U	42	16	10	16	56	70	10	5	6	35	28	6	5	10	21	42	–14	58
10	Nantwich T	42	15	13	14	65	61	10	7	4	33	21	5	6	10	32	40	4	57
11	Kendal T	42	15	8	19	78	83	8	5	8	41	39	7	3	11	37	44	–5	53
12	Ashton U	42	15	8	19	61	67	10	1	10	34	32	5	7	9	27	35	–6	53
13	Buxton	42	15	8	19	64	77	7	3	11	33	45	8	5	8	31	32	–13	53
14	Matlock T	42	12	14	16	52	54	10	5	6	33	21	2	9	10	19	33	–2	50
15	Worksop T	42	13	10	19	56	76	8	4	9	34	39	5	6	10	22	37	–20	49
16	Stafford Rangers (R)	42	12	12	18	60	65	5	9	7	30	29	7	3	11	30	36	–5	48
17	Whitby T	42	12	11	19	57	80	4	8	9	32	43	8	3	10	25	37	–23	46
18	Stocksbridge PS	42	10	12	20	57	75	6	7	8	34	31	4	5	12	23	44	–18	42
19	Frickley Ath	42	10	12	20	48	69	7	4	10	23	27	3	8	10	25	42	–21	42
20	Chasetown	42	10	11	21	50	75	4	6	11	23	36	6	5	10	27	39	–25	41
21	Mickleover Sports	42	11	10	21	67	85	6	4	11	37	42	5	6	10	30	43	–18	40
22	Burscough	42	5	11	26	54	104	1	4	16	27	58	4	7	10	27	46	–50	26

Northwich Victoria deducted 3 points and relegated to NPL Divsion 1 South. Nantwich T deducted 1 point. Mickleover Sports deducted 3 points. Whitby T deducted 1 point. ¶Bradford Park Avenue promoted via play-offs.

EVO-STIK SOUTHERN PREMIER LEAGUE 2011–12

		Total						Home					Away						
		P	W	D	L	F	A	W	D	L	F	A	W	D	L	F	A	GD	Pts
1	Brackley T	42	25	10	7	92	48	16	3	2	59	20	9	7	5	33	28	44	85
2	Oxford C¶	42	22	11	9	68	41	12	7	2	37	12	10	4	7	31	29	27	77
3	AFC Totton	42	21	11	10	81	43	13	6	2	46	13	8	5	8	35	30	38	74
4	Chesham U	42	21	10	11	76	53	15	3	3	42	22	6	7	8	34	31	23	73
5	Cambridge C	42	21	9	12	78	52	13	5	3	51	19	8	4	9	27	33	26	72
6	Stourbridge	42	20	12	10	67	45	14	6	1	43	13	6	6	9	24	32	22	72
7	Leamington	42	18	15	9	60	47	13	6	2	38	21	5	9	7	22	26	13	69
8	St Albans C (R)	42	17	11	14	72	77	11	6	4	45	36	6	5	10	27	41	–5	62
9	Barwell	42	17	10	15	70	61	10	6	5	40	31	7	4	10	30	30	9	61
10	Bedford T	42	15	10	17	60	69	7	4	10	30	33	8	6	7	30	36	–9	55
11	Chippenham T	42	14	11	17	55	53	8	4	9	28	23	6	7	8	27	30	2	53
12	Frome T	42	12	16	14	44	49	4	10	7	16	22	8	6	7	28	27	–5	52
13	Bashley	42	13	13	16	58	74	6	9	6	32	33	7	4	10	26	41	–16	52
14	Hitchin T	42	13	12	17	54	57	8	5	8	31	29	5	7	9	23	28	–3	51
15	Redditch U (R)	42	14	9	19	45	50	8	5	8	25	26	6	4	11	20	24	–5	51
16	Banbury U	42	13	10	19	54	61	7	7	7	30	25	6	3	12	24	36	–7	49
17	Weymouth	42	13	9	20	54	75	9	5	7	31	29	4	4	13	23	46	–21	48
18	Arlesey T	42	12	11	19	43	60	6	5	10	20	28	6	6	9	23	32	–17	47
19	Hemel Hempstead T	42	10	14	18	46	66	6	8	7	29	30	4	6	11	17	36	–20	44
20	Evesham U	42	12	8	22	49	71	6	3	12	25	35	6	5	10	24	36	–22	44
21	Swindon Supermarine	42	11	11	20	50	86	6	4	11	25	42	5	7	9	25	44	–36	44
22	Cirencester T	42	7	9	26	40	78	2	4	15	15	36	5	5	11	25	42	–38	30

¶Oxford C promoted via play-offs.

RYMAN ISTHMIAN PREMIER LEAGUE 2011–12

		Total						Home					Away						
		P	W	D	L	F	A	W	D	L	F	A	W	D	L	F	A	GD	Pts
1	Billericay T	42	24	13	5	82	38	13	6	2	44	21	11	7	3	38	17	44	85
2	AFC Hornchurch¶	42	26	4	12	68	35	11	4	6	29	13	15	0	6	39	22	33	82
3	Lowestoft T	42	25	7	10	80	53	14	5	2	41	23	11	2	8	39	30	27	82
4	Wealdstone	42	20	15	7	76	39	12	6	3	40	21	8	9	4	36	18	37	75
5	Bury T	42	22	9	11	85	55	12	6	3	42	21	10	3	8	43	34	30	75
6	Lewes (R)	42	21	10	11	55	47	12	6	3	34	23	9	4	8	21	24	8	73
7	Hendon	42	21	9	12	69	44	9	7	5	32	26	12	2	7	37	18	25	72
8	Canvey Island	42	22	5	15	66	55	10	1	10	34	29	12	4	5	32	26	11	71
9	Cray Wanderers	42	20	8	14	74	55	9	4	8	33	31	11	4	6	41	24	19	68
10	East Thurrock U	42	18	8	16	70	65	10	3	8	33	26	8	5	8	37	39	5	62
11	Kingstonian	42	18	7	17	58	64	9	3	9	29	34	9	4	8	29	30	–6	61
12	Metropolitan Police	42	18	6	18	63	46	11	2	8	33	18	7	4	10	30	28	17	60
13	Wingate & Finchley	42	16	11	15	63	79	9	4	8	35	44	7	7	7	28	35	–16	59
14	Concord Rangers	42	16	9	17	72	66	7	6	8	39	34	9	3	9	33	32	6	57
15	Margate	42	15	9	18	66	65	9	3	9	37	29	6	6	9	29	36	1	54
16	Carshalton Ath	42	14	10	18	48	55	7	3	11	22	26	7	7	7	26	29	–7	52
17	Harrow Borough	42	13	8	21	53	70	7	5	9	28	35	6	3	12	25	35	–17	47
18	Hastings U	42	13	8	21	43	61	6	5	10	21	24	7	3	11	22	37	–18	47
19	Leatherhead	42	11	8	23	46	62	6	3	12	21	33	5	5	11	25	29	–16	41
20	Aveley	42	5	12	25	41	88	2	6	13	20	49	3	6	12	21	39	–47	27
21	Tooting & Mitcham	42	7	6	29	47	116	3	4	14	23	58	4	2	15	24	58	–69	27
22	Horsham	42	3	6	33	38	105	1	2	18	18	57	2	4	15	20	48	–67	14

Horsham deducted 1 point. ¶AFC Hornchurch promoted via play-offs.

THE FA TROPHY 2011–12

IN PARTNERSHIP WITH CARLSBERG

PRELIMINARY ROUND

Garforth T v Lancaster C	5-1
Trafford v AFC Fylde	1-4
Prescot Cables v Durham C	1-2
Cammel Laird v Bamber Bridge	0-3
Ossett Alb v Lincoln U	1-3
Salford C v Clitheroe	2-2, 2-1
Ossett T v Wakefield	2-1
Brigg T v Mossley	2-1
Woodley Sp v Skelmersdale U	4-3
New Mills v Radcliffe Bor	2-3
Sheffield v Warrington T	2-2, 3-2
Kidsgrove Ath v Loughborough Dyn	2-1
Barton R v Shepshed Dyn	2-1
Rainworth MW v Hucknall T	1-2
Carlton T v Belper T	4-5
Newcastle T v Woodford U	1-0
Stamford v Coalville T	5-4
Quorn v Biggleswade T	0-5
Bedworth U v Market Drayton T	2-1
Rugby T v Sutton Coldfield T	1-1, 0-4
Halesowen T v Romulus	0-1
Stourport Swifts v Daventry T	1-1, 1-3
Bedfont T v Romford	4-1
Waltham Abbey v Grays Ath	1-1, 0-4
Ilford v Redbridge	2-3
Ashford T (Middlesex) v Maidstone U	3-1
Thamesmead T v Whitstable T	3-2
Whyteleafe v North Greenford U	4-3
Ramsgate v Needham Market	2-7
Burgess Hill T v Corinthian Cas	3-0
Potters Bar T v Heybridge Swifts	1-0
Soham T R v Whitehawk	1-7
Brentwood T v Leiston	1-0
Ware v Chipstead	0-1
Sittingbourne v Northwood	1-1, 4-3
AFC Hayes v Cheshunt	2-1
Eastbourne T v Chatham T	4-3
Walton Cas v Faversham T	2-2, 3-5
AFC Sudbury v Great Wakering R	6-1
Walton & Hersham v Enfield T	1-2
Bideford v Beaconsfield SYCOB	2-0
Bognor Regis T v Mangotsfield U	0-1
Didcot T v Clevedon T	3-1
Yate T v Hungerford T	2-1
Worthing v Crawley Down	3-3, 2-0
Bridgwater T v Tiverton T	1-3
Thatcham T v North Leigh	2-0
Chalfont St Peter v Abingdon U	4-3
Cinderford T v Poole T	0-3
Gosport Bor v Slough T	3-0
Fleet T v Burnham	0-0, 1-0
Wimborne T v Sholing	0-2
Bishop's Cleeve v Paulton R	0-1
Waltham Forest v Tilbury	2-1

FIRST QUALIFYING ROUND

Chester v Ashton U	2-1
Goole v Durham C	2-3
Bradford PA v Worksop T	1-1, 1-4
Marine v Chorley	1-0
Witton Alb v Brigg T	6-1
Radcliffe Bor v Harrogate Railway Ath	2-1
Farsley v Curzon Ashton	2-2, 0-2
Buxton v Garforth T	4-2
Frickley Ath v FC United of Manchester	0-4
Northwich Vic v AFC Fylde	4-2
Sheffield v Bamber Bridge	3-0
Kendal T v Nantwich T	1-0
Woodley Sp v Whitby T	3-1
North Ferriby U v Lincoln U	3-1
Burscough v Salford C	0-1
Stocksbridge P S v Ossett T	2-2, 2-3
St Neots T v Sutton Coldfield T	3-1
Chasetown v Grantham T	5-0
Leek T v Hucknall T	4-1
Ilkeston v Biggleswade T	2-0
Leighton T v Banbury U	0-1
Rushall Olym v Cambridge C	0-2
Daventry T v Kidsgrove Ath	4-3
Brackley T v Mickleover Sp	1-0
Romulus v Leamington	1-0
Barton R v Belper T	0-1
Matlock T v Stamford	3-0
Bedworth U v Hednesford T	0-1
Newcastle T v Stafford R	1-1, 2-5
Stourbridge v Redditch U	2-1
Arlesey T v AFC Sudbury	3-1
Whyteleafe v Grays Ath	0-3
Brentwood T v Lowestoft T	2-3
Potters Bar T v AFC Hayes	1-0
Lewes v Cray W	2-1
Dulwich Hamlet v Harrow Bor	0-2
Chipstead v Margate	1-3
Folkestone Invicta v Met Police	1-0
Aveley v Bury T	0-1
St Albans C v Ashford T (Middlesex)	1-3
Canvey Island v Hendon	4-0
Eastbourne T v Hitchin T	1-3
Merstham v Maldon & Tiptree	0-4
Billericay T v Whitehawk	1-0
Uxbridge v Sittingbourne	3-1
Redbridge v Needham Market	3-1
Concord R v Harlow T	2-3
Hemel Hempstead T v Croydon Ath	1-1, 2-0
Hythe T v Burgess Hill T	1-0
Wealdstone v Tooting & Mitcham U	3-0
Bedfont T v Hastings U	1-1, 2-0
East Thurrock U v Bedford T	1-1, 2-1
Waltham Forest v Faversham T	0-1
Thamesmead T v Enfield T	2-0
Wingate & Finchley v AFC Hornchurch	1-2
Kingstonian v Godalming T	0-1
Marlow v Didcot T	1-1, 0-4
Andover removed v Swindon Supermarine w.o.	
Cirencester T v Leatherhead	3-1
Chertsey T v Chalfont St Peter	2-0
Gosport Bor v Sholing	1-0
Taunton T v Paulton R	0-3
Carshalton Ath v Bideford	3-1
Chesham U v Horsham	5-0
Oxford C v Mangotsfield U	0-3
Fleet T v Yate T	0-5
Weymouth v AFC Totton	3-2
Poole T v Chippenham T	1-1, 1-2
Bashley v Worthing	2-2, 2-4
Aylesbury v Tiverton T	0-0, 1-2
Frome T v Thatcham T	0-1

SECOND QUALIFYING ROUND

Chester v Stafford R	2-0
Northwich Vic v Buxton	3-0
Hednesford T v Matlock T	0-0, 1-2
Stourbridge v Kendal T	3-3, 6-0
Radcliffe Bor v Worksop T	1-1, 0-2
North Ferriby U v Salford C	2-0
Curzon Ashton v Belper T	2-1
Marine v Chasetown	5-2
Ossett T v Barwell	4-2
Sheffield v Romulus	2-0
Ilkeston v Woodley Sp	2-1
Durham C v FC United of Manchester	1-1, 1-3
Leek T v Witton Alb	3-3, 1-4
Folkestone Invicta v Daventry T	4-2
Grays Ath v Canvey Island	2-3
Faversham T v East Thurrock U	2-4

Margate v Wealdstone	1-1, 1-2
Harrow Bor v AFC Hornchurch	1-1, 0-1
Maldon & Tiptree v Bedfont T	3-2
Harlow T v Lewes	3-2
Bury T v Hythe T	3-2
Uxbridge v Potters Bar T	5-2
Cambridge C v Redbridge	1-2
Hitchin T v Lowestoft T	1-3
Billericay T v St Neots T	2-0
Thamesmead T v Arlesey T	3-0
Hemel Hempstead T v Brackley T	2-3
Banbury U v Paulton R	3-1
Carshalton Ath v Cirencester T	3-1
Worthing v Didcot T	0-2
Chesham U v Tiverton T	2-2, 0-1
Gosport Bor v Godalming T	4-0
Chippenham T v Mangotsfield U	1-1, 2-0
Chertsey T v Ashford T (Middlesex)	6-5
Thatcham T v Weymouth	1-1, 1-6
Yate T v Swindon Supermarine	0-1

THIRD QUALIFYING ROUND

Corby T v North Ferriby U	1-1, 2-3
Blyth Spartans v Stalybridge C	1-3
Boston U v Workington	1-0
Sheffield v Nuneaton T	0-4
Gainsborough T v Hinckley U	0-1
Worcester C v Harrogate T	0-1
Colwyn Bay v FC Halifax T	0-0, 2-1
Worksop T v Curzon Ashton	3-2
Guiseley v Eastwood T	7-0
Stourbridge v Chester	0-2
Matlock T v Hyde	0-1
Solihull Moors v Ossett T	2-2, 1-0
Droylsden v Witton Alb	2-1
FC United of Manchester v Altrincham	2-1
Northwich Vic v Ilkeston	1-1, 5-1
Vauxhall Motors v Marine	3-2
Farnborough v Bury T	2-2, 2-0
Maldon & Tiptree v Carshalton Ath	0-1
Sutton U v Basingstoke T	1-2
Banbury U v Wealdstone	0-0, 0-4
Bishop's Stortford v Tonbridge Angels	1-1, 2-1
Thamesmead T v Welling U	2-2, 1-3
Chelmsford C v Woking	2-0
Bromley v Didcot T	1-3
Folkestone Invicta v Staines T	1-3
Redbridge v East Thurrock U	1-2
Eastbourne Bor v Dartford	0-0, 1-2
Thurrock v AFC Hornchurch	0-5
Uxbridge v Histon	2-1
Harlow T v Lowestoft T	1-2
Hampton & Richmond Bor v Canvey Island	4-2
Brackley T v Chertsey T	2-0
Maidenhead U v Billericay T	1-0
Boreham Wood v Dover Ath	1-0
Tiverton T v Swindon Supermarine	0-1
Gloucester C v Truro C	1-1, 2-3
Salisbury C v Weston Super M	2-0
Dorchester T v Gosport Bor	1-2
Chippenham T v Eastleigh	1-1, 1-1
Chippenham T won 8-7 on penalties.	
Weymouth v Havant & Waterlooville	0-0, 2-0

FIRST ROUND

Northwich Vic v Fleetwood T	3-1
Colwyn Bay v Lincoln C	1-3
Vauxhall Motors v Kidderminster H	4-4, 0-2
Stockport Co v Stalybridge C	2-2, 1-2
York C v Solihull Moors	2-2, 3-0
Barrow v Harrogate T	3-2
Nuneaton T v AFC Telford U	
Guiseley v FC United of Manchester	2-0
Wrexham v Hinckley U	1-2
Droylsden v Mansfield T	2-1
Grimsby T v Darlington	3-0
Gateshead v Kettering T	3-2
Worksop T v Tamworth	1-0
North Ferriby U v Chester	1-5
Alfreton T v Southport	4-0
Boston U v Hyde	2-1
Salisbury C v Lowestoft T	4-1
Luton T v Swindon Supermarine	2-0
Didcot T v Basingstoke T	0-1
Chelmsford C v Bath C	2-3
Wealdstone v Uxbridge	5-0
Truro C v Ebbsfleet U	2-5
Hampton & Richmond Bor v Hayes & Yeading U	2-0
Carshalton Ath v Bishop's Stortford	5-0
East Thurrock U v Welling U	2-1
Staines T v Maidenhead U	0-0, 2-1
Weymouth v Chippenham T	2-1
Boreham Wood v Cambridge U	0-1
Brackley T v Dartford	0-3
AFC Hornchurch v Farnborough	0-0, 3-2
Newport Co v Forest Green R	0-0, 2-0
Gosport Bor v Braintree T	0-1

SECOND ROUND

Ebbsfleet U v Chester	3-2
Wealdstone v Barrow	2-1
Weymouth v Alfreton T	0-6
Worksop T v Newport Co	1-3
Gateshead v Braintree T	2-2, 1-1
Gateshead won 4-3 on penalties.	
Lincoln C v Carshalton Ath	0-0, 1-3
Kidderminster H v Droylsden	5-1
Dartford v Boston U	4-2
East Thurrock U v Hampton & Richmond Bor	1-1, 1-4
Grimsby T v AFC Hornchurch	4-0
Cambridge U v AFC Telford U	4-1
Northwich Vic v Staines T	1-0
Hinckley U v Luton T	0-0, 0-3
Salisbury C v York C	2-6
Guiseley v Stalybridge C	2-0
Bath C v Basingstoke T	1-0

THIRD ROUND

Kidderminster H v Luton T	1-2
Northwich Vic v Hampton & Richmond Bor	4-1
Cambridge U v Guiseley	1-0
Dartford v Wealdstone	2-2, 0-1
Bath C v Grimsby T	1-2
York C v Ebbsfleet U	1-0
Gateshead v Alfreton T	2-1
Newport Co v Carshalton Ath	4-0

FOURTH ROUND

Cambridge U v Wealdstone	1-2
Luton T v Gateshead	2-0
Grimsby T v York C	0-1
Northwich Vic v Newport Co	2-3

SEMI-FINALS

York C v Luton T	1-0, 1-1
Newport Co v Wealdstone	3-1, 0-0

FINAL (at Wembley)

Saturday, 12 May 2012

Newport Co (0) 0

York C (0) 2 *(Blair 65, Oyebanjo 72)* 19,844

Newport Co: Thompson; Hughes, Pipe, Minshull, Warren, Yakubu, Foley, Jarvis (Harris), Evans, Porter (Knights), Rose R (Buchanan).

York C: Ingham; Oyebanjo, Meredith, Smith, Parslow, McLaughlin (Fyfield), Walker (Reed), Gibson, Blair, Chambers (Moke), Challinor.

Referee: G. Mills.

THE FA VASE 2011–12

IN PARTNERSHIP WITH CARLSBERG

FIRST QUALIFYING ROUND

London Lions v London APSA	1-2
Canning T v Eton Manor	1-1, 0-3
Hook Norton v Wokingham & Emmbrook	1-1, 0-2
Warlingham v Farnham T	2-3
Washington v Tow Law T	1-5
Newton Aycliffe v Shildon	0-0, 2-3
Esh Winning v Morpeth T	5-2
North Shields v Northallerton T	1-3
Chester-le-Street T v Bishop Auckland	3-5
Bedlington Ter v Stokesley	9-1
Whitehaven v Horden CW	2-0
Easington Coll v Prudhoe T	2-1
Guisborough T v West Allotment C	2-1
Hebbburn T v Thornaby	5-1
Crook T v Seaham Red Star	4-2
West Auckland T v Cleator Moor C	3-1
Armthorpe Wel v Appleby Frodingham	3-1
Maltby Main v Kinsley Boys	1-2
Hallam v Rossington Main	2-5
Silsden v Askern Villa	2-5
Brighouse T v Winterton R	1-4
Atherton LR v Ashton T	3-1
AFC Blackpool v AFC Darwen	3-4
Congleton T v Runcorn Linnets	1-2
Holker OB v Northwich Villa	4-2
Bacup Bor v Rochdale T	1-0
Oldham Boro v Daisy Hill	1-0
Chadderton v Alsager T	3-1
Barnoldswick T v Irlam	3-1
Heanor T v Dunkirk	1-2
Lough T v Borrowash Vic	1-2
Retford U v Arnold T	2-2, 1-3
Ollerton T v South Normanton Ath	3-2
Shirebrook T v Radcliffe Olym	3-0
Greenwood Meadows v Graham St Prims	1-0
Blackstones v Kimberley T	5-2
Gedling MW v Boston T	1-5
Wolverhampton Cas v Coventry Copswood	1-3
Walsall Wood v Pershore T 88	3-2
AFC Wulfrunians v Shifnal T	2-1
Sp Khalsa v Heath Hayes	0-4
Lye T v Bartley Green	0-1
Highgate U v Bewdley T	3-1
Dudley Sp v Pegasus Jun	2-1
Malvern T v Southam U	0-1
Castle Vale v Cradley T	3-2
Shawbury U v Bridgnorth T	1-0
Eccleshall v Racing Club Warwick	0-5
Westfields v Cadbury Ath	6-0
Dudley T v Causeway U	3-2
Tividale v Nuneaton Griff	3-0
Studley v Castle Vale JKS	3-2
Rocester v Ellesmere R	2-3
Pelsall Villa v Coleshill T	3-2
Stone Dominoes v Alvechurch	0-1
Goodrich v Stafford T	6-7
Leek CSOB v Gornal Ath	0-1
Blaby & W'stone Ath v Yaxley	3-4
Rothwell T v Bugbrooke St M	0-4
Stewarts & Lloyds C v Ibstock U	4-0
Cogenhoe U v Rothwell Cor	3-2
Barrow T v Saffron Dyn	4-0
Ellistown v Friar Lane & Ep	3-2
Thurnby Nirvana v Birstall U	1-3
Eynesbury R v Desborough T	3-4
Hadleigh U v Stowmarket T	1-3
Walsham-le-Willows v Fakenham	4-1
FC Clacton v Ely C	2-1
Brightlingsea R v Stanway R	0-2
Thetford T v Long Melford	2-0
Kirkley & Pakefield v Woodbridge T	0-3
Swaffham T v Felixstowe & Walton U	3-6
Saffron Walden T removed v Team Bury w.o.	
Mildenhall T v March T U	6-1
Wivenhoe T v Halstead T	2-6
Basildon U v Wootton Blue Cross	1-1, 3-1
Barking v Crawley Green	2-0
Takeley v Cockfosters	2-0
Broxbourne Bor V&E v Burnham R	2-3
Cranfield U v Haringey & Waltham Dev	2-6
Welwyn Garden C v Bedford	1-2
Hullbridge Sp v Colney Heath	2-1
Berkhamsted v Stotfold	1-0
London Colney v Codicote	0-2
St Margaretsbury v Langford	1-0
Sawbridgeworth T v Wodson Park	5-4
Bowers & Pitsea v Hertford T	4-3
Hoddesdon T v Kentish T	6-0
Hatfield T v Sp Bengal U	2-3
Hanworth Villa v Sandhurst T	8-3
Thame U v Staines Lammas	4-1
Windsor v Oxford C Nomads	3-0
Winslow U v Holyport	2-1
Holmer Green v Newbury	4-5
Kidlington v Buckingham Ath	3-1
Reading T v Harefield U	1-0
Hillingdon Bor v AFC Wallingford	7-0
Seaford T v Cobham	2-1
Ashford U v Shoreham	0-0, 2-3
Wick v Woodstock Sp	0-2
St Francis R v South Park	0-2
Croydon v Beckenham T	1-2
Lingfield v Ringmer	2-3
Fisher v Ash U	4-0
Chessington & Hook U v East Preston	1-3
Lordswood v Steyning T	1-0
Frimley Green v Raynes Park Vale	1-5
Hailsham T v Epsom & Ewell	1-3
Holmesdale v Erith T	0-1
Colliers Wood U v Dorking	5-2
Sidley U v AFC Uckfield	4-2
Saltdean U v Chichester C	1-2
Selsey v Redhill	1-2
Littlehampton T v Haywards Heath T	3-3, 2-0
Erith & Belvedere v Tunbridge Wells	2-3
Bookham v Westfield	1-3
Knaphill v Horley T	1-4
Arundel v Crowborough Ath	5-0
Swanage T & Herston v GE Hamble	0-3
Alton T v Hamworthy U	2-1
Horndean v Lymington T	2-1
Cove v Verwood T	2-1
Christchurch v Newport (IW)	4-1
Totton & Eling v Cowes Sp	2-3
Fleet Spurs v Blackfield & Langley	1-6
East Cowes Vic Ath v Hayling U	0-3
Hayling U expelled for fielding ineligible players.	
Cheltenham Saracens v Melksham T	1-4
Devizes T v Shepton Mallet	5-0
Street v Hallen	0-2
Corsham T v Pewsey Vale	0-0, 0-2
Slimbridge v Portishead T	1-0
Almondsbury UWE v Bishop Sutton	2-3
Merthyr T v Brislington	1-0
Shortwood U v Wootton Bassett T	4-0
Westbury U v Bradford T	0-2
Wells C v Welton R	2-0
Longwell Green Sp v Odd Down	0-0, 1-2
Radstock T v Fairford T	0-1
Budley Salterton v Barnstaple T	1-4
Cullompton R v Porthleven	6-3
Chard T v Plymouth Parkway	0-11
Whickham v Gilford Park	1-3
Warstones W v Norton U	2-5
Willenhall T v Brockton	2-3
Thrapston T v Wellingborough W	2-1
Daventry U v Wellingborough T	2-0

SECOND QUALIFYING ROUND

Ryton & Crawcrook Alb v Crook T	1-3
Penrith v Guisborough T	0-1
Billingham T v Whitehaven	4-2
Sunderland RCA v Bishop Auckland	5-3
Jarrow R Boldon CA v Easington Coll	2-0
Hebburn T v Brandon U	6-0
Tow Law T v Shildon	0-6
Marske U v West Auckland T	2-6
Esh Winning v Darlington Railway Ath	0-1
Northallerton T v Bedlington Ter	0-1

Gilford Park v Willington 1-0
South Shields v Birtley T 2-1
Liversedge v AFC Emley 2-3
Dinnington T v Grimsby Bor 2-0
Hemsworth MW v Barton T OB 1-3
Selby T v Winterton R 2-1
Glasshoughton Wel v Bottesford T 6-0
Scarborough Ath v Worsbrough Bridge Ath 5-1
Armthorpe Wel v Kinsley Boys 10-0
Yorkshire Amat w.o. v Brodsworth removed.
Rossington Main v Eccleshill U 1-2
Askern Villa v Hall Road R 1-0
Pickering T v Thackley 1-2
Pontefract Coll v Nostell MW 1-1, 3-2
Ashville v West Didsbury & Chorlton 2-0
Atherton LR v Atherton Coll 3-2
Bacup Bor v Ashton Ath 3-1
Formby v Chadderton 4-2
Holker OB v Colne 0-2
Squires Gate v St Helens T 1-0
AFC Darwen v AFC Liverpool 2-2, 3-1
Runcorn Linnets v Bootle 2-0
Maine Road v Cheadle T 1-2
Barnoldswick T v Abbey Hey 5-2
Long Eaton U v Lincoln Moorlands Rail 1-1, 4-1
Greenwood Meadows v Sleaford T 2-0
Dunkirk v Pinxton 1-4
Shirebrook T v Glossop NE 1-3
Holwell Sp v Blackstones 4-0
Ollerton T v Deeping R 0-3
Holbeach U v Newark T 4-0
Borrowash Vic v Blidworth Wel 1-3
Arnold T v Calverton MW 6-2
Teversal v Blackwell MW 1-3
Boston T v Radford 4-2
Stafford T v Pelsall Villa 5-0
Highgate U v Dudley Sp 3-2
Brocton v Earlswood T 0-0, 2-0
Alvechurch v Pillkington XXX 0-1
Bustleholme v Bartley Green 0-3
Coventry Sphinx v Norton U 0-3
Studley v Gornal Ath 0-2
Wolverhampton SC v Atherstone T 0-2
Walsall Wood v Ellesmere R 0-1
Coventry Copswood v Castle Vale 2-1
Wellington v Tividale 0-5
Racing Club Warwick v Bromyard T 2-1
Continental Star v Shawbury U 3-2
Westfields v Dudley T 3-1
Stratford T v Southam U 2-0
Heath Hayes v AFC Wulfrunians 5-1
Oadby T v Huntingdon T 3-2
Barrow T v Ellistown 1-2
Ashby Ivanhoe v St Andrews 2-4
Birstall U v Yaxley 0-1
Lutterworth Ath v Anstey Nomads 3-1
Godmanchester R v Northampton Spencer 6-3
Thrapston T v Bardon Hill Sp 1-3
Aylestone Park v Desborough T 1-4
Cogenhoe U v Kirby Muxloe 3-2
Stewarts & Lloyds C v Irchester U 3-0
Raunds T v Bugbrooke St M 0-3
Rushden & Higham U v Peterborough N Star 1-2
Framlingham T v Diss T 0-4
Gorleston v Mildenhall T 2-4
Great Yarmouth T v Felixstowe & Walton U 0-5
Ipswich W v Thetford T 2-5
Debenham LC v Team Bury 0-1
Daventry U v Harborough T 1-2
Cambridge Reg Coll v Brantham Ath 0-2
Stowmarket T v Walsham-le-Willows 1-2
Whitton U v Downham T 4-1
FC Clacton v Cornard U 1-0
Stanway R v Woodbridge T 1-2
Halstead T v Newmarket T 2-0
Haverhill R v Norwich U 5-1
Clapton v Southend Manor 1-3
Hullbridge Sp v Bowers & Pitsea 2-0
Burnham R v Takeley 5-2
Barking v Potton U 4-0
Eton Manor v London APSA 2-3
Oxhey Jets v AFC Dunstable 3-2
Hadley v AFC Kempston R 1-0
Codicote v Biggleswade U 0-3
Sawbridgeworth T v Sp Bengal U 1-3
Bedford v Basildon U 1-3
Hoddesdon T v Berkhamsted 3-2
Haringey Bor v St Margaretsbury 2-1
Barkingside v Ampthill T 0-0, 0-1
Old Woodstock T w.o. v Bicester T removed.
Reading T v Aylesbury U 2-1
Winslow U v Wokingham & Emmbrook 2-1
Thame U v Hanwell T 2-5
Flackwell Heath v Windsor 3-1
Henley T v Milton U 1-0
Carterton v Shrivenham 3-1
Abingdon T v Feltham 0-0, 4-2
Newbury v Clanfield 85 3-5
Ascot U v Buckingham T 0-1
Kidlington v Hanworth Villa 2-3
Bracknell T v Hillingdon Bor 0-1
Witney T v Amersham T 6-3
Wembley v Bedfont Sp 0-0, 0-1
Banstead Ath v Erith T 1-3
Hassocks v Farnham T 0-0, 1-1
Farnham T won 8-7 on penalties.
Egham T v Mole Valley SCR 3-2
Erith & Dartford T v Seaford T 0-2
Deal T v Shoreham 2-1
Tunbridge Wells v Mile Oak 5-1
Woodstock Sp v Westfield 2-1
Lordswood v Horley T 2-1
Redhill v Colliers Wood U 2-3
Corinthian v East Preston 1-2
Three Bridges v Stevenoaks T 3-0
Littlehampton T v Arundel 2-1
Raynes Park Vale v Newhaven 5-3
South Park v Bagshot Lea 3-0
Ringmer v Epsom & Ewell 2-0
Sidley U v Chichester C 2-3
Beckenham T v Fisher 5-1
Downton v Ringwood T 9-1
East Cowes Vic Ath v Alresford T 0-4
Christchurch v Horndean 2-1
Alton T v New Milton T 2-1
Brockenhurst v Cove 2-0
Whitchurch U v Fareham T 1-2
Romsey T v Fawley 1-3
Gillingham T v Moneyfields 3-1
Cowes Sp v US Portsmouth 1-0
AFC Portchester v Bournemouth 1-3
Blackfield & Langley v GE Hamble 4-1
Andover New Street v Bridport 3-6
Shrewton U v Sherborne T 3-2
Petersfield T v Hartley Wintney 1-5
Bristol Manor Farm v Wells C 1-2
Slimbridge v Merthyr T 3-2
Bristol Acad v Bradford T 0-2
Ashton & Backwell U v Fairford T 0-1
Pewsey Vale v Devizes T 0-0, 1-3
Keynsham T v Lydney T 1-2
Shortwood U v Hallen 3-2
Hengrove Ath v Winterbourne U 2-4
Melksham T v Odd Down 2-1
Calne T v Bishop Sutton 0-2
Barnstaple T v St Blazey 3-0
Penzance v Witheridge 2-3
Liskeard Ath v Wadebridge T 4-2
Tavistock v Crediton U 4-3
Dawlish T removed v Saltash U w.o.
Wellington v Cullompton R 0-3
Buckland Ath v Elmore 5-1
Plymouth Parkway v Bovey Tracey 1-0
Falmouth T v Minehead 7-3
Oldham Bor v Wigan Robin Park 3-2
Haringey & Waltham Dev v Kings Langley 4-3

FIRST ROUND

Newcastle Benfield v Hebburn T 2-1
Shildon v West Auckland T 2-3
Jarrow R Boldon CA v Crook T 2-3
Billingham T v South Shields 5-2
Guisborough T v Consett 3-3, 2-3
Bedlington Ter v Sunderland RCA 4-1
Darlington Railway Ath v Gilford Park 1-4
Parkgate v Scarborough Ath 2-0
Armthorpe Wel v Yorkshire Amat 3-0
Glasshoughton Wel v AFC Emley 2-0
Barton T OB v Pontefract Coll 1-0
Dinnington T v Bridlington T 0-2
Askern Villa v Selby T 3-1
Eccleshill U v Thackley 1-0

Ramsbottom U v Colne 4-0
Squires Gate v AFC Darwen 3-0
Formby v Ashville 0-1
Atherton LR v Winsford U 1-2
Oldham Bor v Padiham 1-3
Cheadle T v Bacup Bor 0-2
Runcorn Linnets v Barnoldswick T 2-3
Blackwell MW v Pinxton 1-0
Deeping R v Holbeach U 3-1
Arnold T v Long Eaton U 0-2
Boston T v Holwell Sp 3-1
Glossop NE v Blidworth Wel 5-0
Spalding U v Greenwood Meadows 2-1
Stafford T v Atherstone T 3-2
Norton U v Heath Hayes 4-0
Bartley Green v Ellesmere R 0-6
Stratford T v Racing Club Warwick 0-4
Continental Star v Gornal Ath 0-2
Tipton T v Highgate U 2-1
Tividale v Westfields 4-1
Brocton v Coventry Copswood 3-0
Pilkington XXX v Boldmere St M 2-5
Bardon Hill Sp v Desborough T 2-0
Lutterworth Ath v Oadby T 1-2
St Andrews v Bugbrooke St M 4-2
Ellistown v Peterborough N Star 0-2
Cogenhoe U v Yaxley 2-1
Harborough T v Stewarts & Lloyds C 2-2, 0-1
Wisbech T v Walsham-le-Willows 3-0
Woodbridge T v Witham T 0-0, 1-4
Felixstowe & Walton U v Haverhill R 1-0
Diss T v Brantham Ath 1-0
FC Clacton v Whitton U 2-4
Halstead T v Team Bury 0-1
Dereham T v Thetford T 0-3
Mildenhall T v Wroxham 1-0
Southend Manor v Biggleswade U 2-1
Oxhey Jets v Enfield 1893 1-6
London APSA v Haringey & Waltham Dev 0-3
Bethnal Green U v Hoddesdon T 3-1
Haringey Bor v Hadley 2-0
Tring Ath v Hullbridge Sp 3-2
Basildon U v Ampthill T 0-4
Burnham R v Sp Bengal U 1-3
Barking v Royston T 0-1
Old Woodstock T v Abingdon T 4-3
Henley T v Newport Pagnell T 0-1
Flackwell Heath v Clanfield 85 2-0
Binfield v Hillingdon Bor 3-2
Witney T v Carterton 2-1
Ardley U v Reading T 1-3
Hanworth Villa v Bedfont Sp 3-1
Winslow U v Buckingham T 2-5
Hanwell T v Wantage T 1-2
Camberley T v Littlehampton T 1-2
South Park v Colliers Wood U 1-0
Ringmer v Woodstock Sp 5-0
Horsham YMCA v Deal T 1-2
VCD Ath v Lordswood 5-0
Three Bridges v Beckenham T 3-0
Erith T v Farnham T 6-1
Peacehaven & Telscombe v Raynes Park Vale 3-1
Egham T v Greenwich Bor 3-0
Seaford T v Tunbridge Wells 1-2
East Preston v Pagham 3-4
Molesey v Chichester C 3-4
Shrewton U v Fawley 1-2
Bournemouth v Hartley Wintney 2-0
Christchurch v Bridport 2-1
Downton v Fareham T 3-0
Cowes Sp v Gillingham T 3-0
Blackfield & Langley v Brockenhurst 2-1
Brading T v Alton T 4-5
Alresford T v Winchester C 1-6
Bishop Sutton v Bradford T 2-1
Lydney T v Shortwood U 1-2
Melksham T v Wells C 2-1
Highworth T v Devizes T 2-1
Fairford T v Winterbourne U 0-1
Larkhall Ath v Slimbridge 4-0
Ilfracombe T v Plymouth Parkway 1-0
Falmouth T v Buckland Ath 5-2
Cullompton R v Tavistock 2-1
Saltash U v Witheridge 3-2
Liskeard Ath v Barnstaple T 1-2
Loughborough Univ v Godmanchester R 1-2

SECOND ROUND

Squires Gate v Winsford U 3-1
Glasshoughton Wel v Runcorn T 0-2
Dunston UTS v Blackwell MW 12-1
Bridlington T v Gilford Park 1-0
Ashville v Staveley MW 1-2
Billingham T v Glossop NE 2-4
Newcastle Benfield v Barton T OB 2-1
West Auckland T v Bacup Bor 3-1
Ashington v Norton & Stockton Ancients 1-0
Billingham Syn v Crook T 2-0
Eccleshill U v Armthorpe Wel 1-3
Parkgate v Bedlington Ter 4-3
Whitley Bay v Tadcaster Alb 4-1
Padiham v Askern Villa 2-5
Consett v Ramsbottom U 4-2
Barnoldswick T v Spennymoor T 0-5
Norton U v Ellesmere R 2-1
Stafford T v Brocton 1-2
Boston T v Gornal Ath 0-3
Godmanchester R v Bloxwich U 3-2
Gresley v King's Lynn T 2-0
Deeping R v Cogenhoe U 4-1
Tipton T v Bardon Hill Sp 5-1
Oadby T v St Andrews 1-0
Long Eaton U v St Ives T 0-3
Boldmere St M v Peterborough N Star 0-2
Stewarts & Lloyds C v Holbrook Sp 0-2
Racing Club Warwick v Wisbech T 0-1
Spalding U v Tividale 0-3
Mildenhall T v Sp Bengal U 0-2
Felixstowe & Walton U v Bethnal Green U 0-7
Ampthill T v Haringey & Waltham Dev 3-2
Long Buckby v Dunstable T 4-2
Newport Pagnell T v Stansted 5-0
Leverstock Green v Enfield 1893 0-0, 2-2
Enfield 1893 won 5-4 on penalties.
Tring Ath v Haringey Bor 2-3
Diss T v Buckingham T 1-0
Witham T v Team Bury 3-1
Royston T v Thetford T 3-1
Southend Manor v Whitton U 4-2
Blackfield & Langley v VCD Ath 2-3
Rye U v Three Bridges 1-2
Alton T v Wantage T 1-1, 1-4
Reading T v Erith T 2-1
Old Woodstock T v Witney T 4-3
Tunbridge Wells v Chichester C 4-1
Pagham v Peacehaven & Telscombe 2-4
Hanworth Villa v Deal T 3-1
Ringmer v Binfield 2-2, 0-0
Binfield won 5-4 on penalties.
South Park v Fawley 3-0
Herne Bay v Winchester C 3-1
Egham T v Cowes Sp 0-1
Littlehampton T v Flackwell Heath 0-2
Lancing v Guildford C 2-1
Ilfracombe T v Winterbourne U 1-0
Bemerton Heath Harl v Saltash U 3-1
Bishop Sutton v Shortwood U 2-4
Willand R v Highworth T 0-0, 1-0
Bodmin T v Larkhall Ath 1-1, 1-2
Bournemouth v Torpoint Ath 4-0
Cadbury Heath v Falmouth T 1-2
Bitton v Cullompton R 3-2
Christchurch v Melksham T 3-1
Barnstaple T v Downton 3-2

THIRD ROUND

Tividale v Brocton 3-3, 2-1
Glossop NE v Runcorn T 1-2
Billingham Syn v Consett 4-0
Holbrook Sp v Norton U 1-1, 0-2
Squires Gate v Staveley MW 0-4
Dunston UTS v Parkgate 3-1
Spennymoor T v Ashington 0-2
Newcastle Benfield v Deeping R 3-1
Askern Villa v West Auckland T 2-3
Peterborough N Star v Armthorpe Wel 2-0
Whitley Bay v Bridlington T 5-1
Gresley v Gornal Ath 4-2
Oadby T v Tipton T 1-1, 2-1
Hanworth Villa v Herne Bay 1-1, 1-3
Bethnal Green U v Sp Bengal U 5-2
Newport Pagnell T v Godmanchester R 3-1
Southend Manor v Three Bridges 0-0, 1-4

Haringey Bor v Royston T	1-2
Long Buckby v Enfield 1893	1-2
Binfield v Flackwell Heath	3-1
VCD Ath v Tunbridge Wells	3-3, 0-2
Witham T v Wisbech T	1-2
Lancing v Ampthill T	1-3
South Park v Diss T	2-1
Peacehaven & Telscombe v St Ives T	1-2
Willand R v Falmouth T	2-1
Bemerton Heath Harl v Shortwood U	0-4
Bournemouth v Barnstaple T	2-0
Old Woodstock T v Wantage T	1-0
Ilfracombe T v Larkhall Ath	0-0, 0-1
Bitton v Christchurch	3-0
Reading T v Cowes Sp	1-0

FOURTH ROUND

Whitley Bay v South Park	5-0
Tunbridge Wells v St Ives T	0-1
Willand R v Staveley MW	1-3
Shortwood U v Enfield 1893	1-0
Newcastle Benfield v Herne Bay	1-2
Bournemouth v Royston T	2-1
Old Woodstock T v Bethnal Green U	0-2
Newport Pagnell T v Ashington	2-3
Norton U v Peterborough N Star	1-2
Wisbech T v Dunston UTS	2-2, 1-3
Bitton v West Auckland T	1-3
Tividale v Binfield	7-1
Gresley v Three Bridges	1-1, 2-2
Gresley won 7-6 on penalties.	
Billingham Syn v Runcorn T	0-0, 2-1
Reading T v Larkhall Ath	2-3
Oadby T v Ampthill T	2-1

FIFTH ROUND

Tividale v Peterborough N Star	0-2
Shortwood U v Ashington	3-0
Staveley MW v Oadby T	2-0
Billingham Syn v Bournemouth	0-0, 1-2
Dunston UTS v Bethnal Green U	3-0
Whitley Bay v West Auckland T	1-2
St Ives T v Gresley	4-0
Herne Bay v Larkhall Ath	1-0

SIXTH ROUND

Shortwood U v Herne Bay	1-2
Staveley MW v St Ives T	3-0
Peterborough N Star v Dunston UTS	3-4
Bournemouth v West Auckland T	0-2

SEMI-FINALS

Herne Bay v West Auckland T	2-2, 1-2
Dunston UTS v Staveley MW	1-0, 2-2

FINAL (at Wembley)

Sunday, 13 May 2012

Dunston UTS (0) 2 *(Bulford 33, 79)*

West Auckland T (0) 0 5126

Dunston UTS: Connell; Cattanach, Galbraith, Robson, Swailes, Young, Shaw, Dixon, Goddard (Preen), Bulford (Craggs), McAndrew.
West Auckland T: Bell; Pattinson, Green, Gibson, Parker, Stephenson (Hindmarsh), Banks, Hudson, Moffat, Rae, Nicholls (Young).
Referee: P. Dixon.

THE FA COUNTY YOUTH CUP 2011–12

FIRST ROUND

Gloucestershire v Berks & Bucks	4-8
Lincolnshire v Northumberland	0-2
Lancashire v Cheshire	0-1
Durham v Liverpool	3-0
Surrey v Devon	1-3
Middlesex v Dorset	3-1
Westmoreland v East Riding	0-10
Wiltshire v Jersey	2-1
Manchester v Isle of Man	3-1
Kent v Guernsey	5-0
Sussex v London	5-1
Huntingdonshire v Suffolk	2-1

SECOND ROUND

West Riding v Manchester	1-0
Leicestershire & Rutland v Durham	2-4
East Riding v Shropshire	3-2
Sheffield & Hallamshire v North Riding	3-3
Sheffield & Hallamshire won 3-1 on penalties.	
Northumberland v Cumberland	0-0
Northumberland won 3-2 on penalties.	
Nottinghamshire v Staffordshire	1-0
Birmingham v Cheshire	3-2
Devon v Somerset	2-3
Hertfordshire v Wiltshire	1-4
Herefordshire v Sussex	2-3
Oxfordshire v Kent	1-5
Essex v Bedfordshire	5-1
Cornwall v Huntingdonshire	2-0
Middlesex v Berks & Bucks	7-0
Norfolk v Amateur Football Alliance	3-2
Northamptonshire v Worcestershire	2-3

THIRD ROUND

Wiltshire v Birmingham	2-1
Somerset v Kent	1-0
West Riding v East Riding	2-0
Sussex v Worcestershire	2-4
Sheffield & Hallamshire v Norfolk	5-2
Durham v Nottinghamshire	11-0
Northumberland v Essex	0-2
Middlesex v Cornwall	1-0

FOURTH ROUND

Middlesex v Essex	1-2
Wiltshire v Worcestershire	2-1
Sheffield & Hallamshire v West Riding	1-3
Durham v Somerset	0-1

SEMI-FINALS

Essex v Wiltshire	4-0
West Riding v Somerset	2-0

FINAL (at Colchester)

Sunday, 22 April 2012

Essex (2) 4 *(Sartain 3, Walshe 5, Ibe 93, 119)*

West Riding (1) 2 *(Eastwood 9, Jackson 61)* 586

Essex: Pitman; Shepherd, Hall, Bertram-Cooper, Vickers, Levett, Sartain (Miller 108), Richardson (Ibe 63), Jones, Walshe, Norris.
West Riding: Hagreen; Swales, Bolton, Eastwood (McGurk 98), Webster, Hall (McPhee 87), Robson, Robinson, Harris, Brownlee (Feather 63), Jackson.
aet.
Referee: T. Robinson (Sussex).

THE FA YOUTH CUP 2011–12

PRELIMINARY ROUND

Pewsey Vale v Salisbury C	0-5
Romulus v Rugby T	3-1
Barton R v St Ives T	1-2
Woodley Sp v AFC Blackpool	4-1
Salford C v Daisy Hill	0-2
Ossett Alb v Grimsby T	0-1
Coventry Copswood v Walsall Wood	2-1
Wolverhampton SC v Kidsgrove Ath	2-4
Ellesmere R v Nuneaton T	0-3
Kirkley & Pakefield v Diss T	9-1
Leiston v Hadleigh U	0-1
Daventry T v Leighton T	0-1
Brentwood T v Ilford	2-2
Brentwood T won 3-1 on penalties.	
Royston T v Bowers & Pitsea	4-1
Enfield T v North Greenford U	6-1
Crowborough Ath v VCD Ath	3-5
Colliers Wood U v Erith T	1-4
Hastings U v Tonbridge Angels	3-2
Horsham v Epsom & Ewell	1-2
Chalfont St Peter v Binfield	0-8
Kidlington v Banbury U	5-1
Newport Pagnell T v Ascot U	4-0
Aylesbury v Basingstoke T	0-1
AFC Porchester v Dorchester T	0-3
Elmore v Weston Super M	3-5
Ashton Ath v Ashton T	5-0
Bardon Hill Sp v Calverton MW	2-5
Hullbridge Sp v Maldon & Tiptree	0-1
Leverstock Green v Stansted	1-3
South Park v Horley T	5-1
St Francis R v Margate	3-0
Thame U v Oxford C	0-2
Forest Green R v Bath C	0-2
Tiverton T v Paulton R	4-1
Bishop Sutton v Newport Co	0-3
Wells C v Taunton T	3-0
Whitstable T v Erith & Belvedere	3-1
Congleton T v Stalybridge C	2-3
Nantwich T v Altrincham	1-5
Boston U v Lincoln U	3-0
Wolverhampton Cas v Boldmere St M	1-0
Redditch U v AFC Telford U	0-1
Brantham Ath v Fakenham T	3-2
Great Yarmouth T v Swaffham T	2-2
Great Yarmouth T won 4-3 on penalties.	
Hertford T v Witham T	1-3
Halstead T v Tilbury	1-7
Stanway R v Sawbridgeworth T	2-0
Bishop's Stortford v Berkhamsted	5-1
Uxbridge v Kentish T	3-0
Redhill v Welling U	0-1
Sutton U v Dulwich Hamlet	2-3
Chessington & Hook U v Whyteleafe	0-3
Alton v Marlow	5-0
Pegasus Jun v Leek T	7-0
Chasetown v Newcastle T	3-1
Stourport Swifts v Gornal Ath	4-2
Grays Ath v Thurrock	0-3
Romford v Cheshunt	2-0
Oxhey Jets v Hemel Hempstead T	2-4
Chipstead v Carshalton Ath	3-1
Cray W v Dartford	0-3
Yate T v Chard T	2-2
Chard T won 12-11 on penalties.	
Brislington v Bishop's Cleeve	2-5
Ashington withdrew v York C w.o.	
Holwell Sp v St Andrews	2-5
New Mills v Long Eaton U	3-3
New Mills won 5-3 on penalties.	
Malvern T v Coventry Sphinx	1-3
Basildon U v Ware	3-2
Sevenoaks T v Met Police	4-0
Boreham Wood v Hoddesdon T	8-0
Gloucester C v Merthyr T	3-4
Woking v Dorking	4-0
Pickering T v Ryton & Crawcrook Alb	6-0
Prescot Cables v Curzon Ashton	3-1
Silsden v Pontefract Coll	3-4
Arnold T v Carlton T	4-2
Stone Dominoes v Atherstone T	1-0
Bury T v Cornard U	5-0
Corby T v AFC Kempston R	4-0
Hitchin T v FC Clacton	0-3
Ashford T (Middlesex) v Cockfosters	2-1
Eastbourne T v Faversham T	3-1
Lewes v Saltdean U	10-0
Farnborough T v AFC Wallingford	15-0
Sandhurst T v Fleet T	3-1
Havant & Waterlooville v Petersfield T	4-0
East Thurrock U v Barking	4-1
Redbridge v Canvey Island	8-0
Staines T v Harrow Bor	3-2
Kingstonian v Eastbourne Bor	2-0
Corinthian v Dover Ath	4-2
Westfield v Mile Oak	6-0
Chichester C v Camberley T	0-6
Prudhoe T withdrew v Chester-le-Street T w.o.	
Wrexham v Stockport Co	1-4
Eccleshall withdrew v Nuneaton Griff w.o.	
Yaxley w.o. v Dunstable T withdrew	
Ramsgate w.o. v Ringmer withdrew	
Chatham T withdrew v Tunbridge Wells w.o.	
Witney T w.o. v Buckingham T withdrew	
Burnham w.o. v Bicester T removed	
Almondsbury UWE v Mangotsfield U	2-3
Glossop NE v Blaby & W Stone Ath	2-4

FIRST QUALIFYING ROUND

Kingstonian v South Park	6-1
Lingfield v Welling U	0-5
Newport Co v Bath C	6-0
Stockport Co v Southport	12-1
Woodley Sp v Daisy Hill	2-0
Dinnington T v North Ferriby U	0-5
Worksop T v Brighouse T	2-3
Mickleover Sports v Boston U	0-5
Calverton MW v Oadby T	2-2
Calverton MW won 5-4 on penalties.	
Kidsgrove Ath v Racing C Warwick	0-4
Woodbridge T v Bury T	1-0
Newmarket T v Walsham-le-Willows	0-1
St Neots T v Yaxley	3-1
Cogenhoe U v Kettering T	2-3
Stansted v AFC Hornchurch	1-5
Hemel Hempstead T v Romford	3-2
Brentwood T v Boreham Wood	0-2
Maidstone U v Tooting & Mitcham U	4-5
Eastbourne T v Dartford	0-4
Thamesmead T v Hastings U	3-2
Pagham v Whitehawk	1-2
Chesham U v Didcot T	0-1
Dorchester T v Salisbury C	2-5
Christchurch v Eastleigh	0-2
AFC Totton v Weymouth	7-0
Vauxhall Motors v Lancaster C	0-1
Ashton Ath v Warrington T	2-1
Runcorn Linnets v Altrincham	5-7
Grimsby T v Pontefract Coll	4-0
Nuneaton T v Chasetown	1-0
Thrapston T v Bedford T	0-2
Sevenoaks T v Lewes	2-6
Whyteleafe v Woking	3-1
Gillingham T v Bournemouth	8-1
Moneyfields v Sholing	2-0
Tiverton T v Wells C	4-2
Bootle v Prescot Cables	2-4
Northwich Vic v Formby	5-0
Burscough v Marine	1-6
Sheffield v FC Halifax T	3-1
Harrogate Railway Ath v Thackley	3-2
Deeping R v Blaby & W Stone Ath	4-1
St Andrews v Gresley	0-1
Hednesford T v Wolverhampton Cas	4-0
Coventry Copswood v Tamworth	1-2
Gorleston v Ipswich W	2-1
Needham Market v Great Yarmouth T	2-0
Cambridge U v Norwich U	9-1
Dereham T v Kirkley & Pakefield	5-0
Soham T R v Stowmarket T	2-1
Brantham Ath v Lowestoft T	2-1
Hadleigh U v Histon U	2-2
Hadleigh U won 4-3 on penalties.	
Thurrock v St Albans C	4-1
Uxbridge v Enfield T	3-2

Hampton & Richmond Bor v Wingate & Finchley 3-1
Welling U v Dulwich Hamlet 2-5
Chipstead v Kingstonian 1-3
Molesey v Dulwich Hamlet 0-4
Burnham v Maidenhead U 0-3
Reading T v Newport Pagnell T 4-2
Basingstoke T v Bracknell T 1-4
Thatcham T v Cove 7-0
Wimborne T v Gosport Bor 3-2
York C v Newton Aycliffe 5-0
Kirby Muxloe v Loughborough Dyn 0-1
Pinxton v Lutterworth Ath 0-0
Pinxton won 3-2 on penalties.
Kiddminster H v Nuneaton Griff 5-0
Solihull Moors v Highgate U 1-3
Stourport Swifts v Coventry Sphinx 1-0
Woodford U v Rushden & Higham U 2-0
Luton T v Rothwell Cor 11-1
Clapton v Redbridge 0-7
Chelmsford C v Southend Manor 3-0
Bishop's Stortford v Basildon U 2-1
Merthyr T v Cirencester T 0-5
Matlock T v Spalding U 5-0
Teversall v New Mills 2-0
Tilbury v Stanway R 5-1
Billericay T v Royston T 3-0
Witham T v Maldon & Tiptree 0-4
Tunbridge Wells v Ramsgate 2-3
Poole T v Havant & Waterlooville 4-1
Mossley v Stalybridge C 5-1
Corinthian v VCD Ath 1-0
Chard T v Bishop's Cleeve 0-7
Pickering T w.o. v Scarborough Ath withdrew
Yorkshire Amat v Liversedge 5-0
Staveley MW v Hallam 4-0
Arnold T v Hinckley U 1-1
Arnold T won 5-4 on penalties.
Lye T v Pegasus Jun 2-1
Thetford T v Felixstowe & Walton U 2-1
Corby T v St Ives T 3-0
Leighton T v Bugbrooke St M 4-0
FC Clacton v Waltham Abbey 3-2
Enfield 1893 v Hanwell T 1-2
Ashford T (Middlesex) v Harefield U 3-0
Worthing v Shoreham 1-0
Camberley T v Walton & Hersham 4-1
Leatherhead v Cobham 3-2
Alton T v Kidlington 3-6
Witney T v Wokingham & Emmbrook 3-4
Oxford C v Sandhurst T 10-0
Chippenham T v Ringwood T 1-3
Bitton v Cheltenham Sar 1-2
Weston Super M v Mangotsfield U 3-1
AFC Fylde v Fleetwood T 0-4
AFC Telford U v Halesowen T 0-1
Stourbridge v Stratford T 0-2
East Thurrock U v Kings Langley 7-3
Staines T v Wealdstone 4-2
Hayes & Yeading U v Northwood 5-0
Whitstable T v Chipstead 1-9
Bromley v Ebbsfleet U 1-2
Westfield v Folkestone Invicta 2-0
Erith T v St Francis R 4-0
Godalming T v Lancing 1-2
Burgess Hill T v Horsham YMCA 7-0
Fleet Spurs v Binfield 0-4
Lydney T v Portishead T 1-2
Portishead T removed; tie awarded to Lydney T.
Chester-le-Street w.o. v Sunderland RCA withdrew
Gateshead v Darlington 0-3
Bottisford T v Stocksbridge P S 2-0
Romulus v Bromyard T 1-2
Stone Dominoes w.o. v Bedworth U withdrew
Stotfold w.o. v Biggleswade withdrew
Three Bridges v Croydon Ath 3-1
Epsom & Ewell w.o. v Arundel withdrew
Farnborough T w.o. v Milton U withdrew
Radstock T v Larkhall Ath 2-2
Larkhall Ath won 4-2 on penalties.
Lincoln C v Retford U 8-0

SECOND QUALIFYING ROUND

Lincoln C v Gresley 7-0
Stockport Co v Prescot Cables 0-3
Chester-le-Street T v Darlington 0-4
Altrincham v Lancaster C 2-2
Altrincham won 4-3 on penalties.
Northwich Vic v Mossley 1-1
Mossley won 4-2 on penalties.
North Ferriby U v Harrogate Railway Ath 4-1
Loughborough Dyn v Arnold T 4-3
Calverton MW v Deeping R 5-0
Stratford T v Hednesford T 5-1
Thetford T v Cambridge U 0-2
Brantham Ath v Needham Market 1-2
Walsham-le-Willows v Hadleigh U 1-2
AFC Hornchurch v Tilbury 0-4
Boreham Wood v Bishop's Stortford 1-0
Redbridge v FC Clacton 7-1
Three Bridges v Ramsgate 1-4
Lewes v Thamesmead T 7-1
Camberley T v Whitehawk 3-2
Burgess Hill T v Whyteleafe 2-2
Whyteleafe won 11-10 on penalties.
Kidlington v Maidenhead U 0-4
Didcot T v Bracknell T 2-4
Cirencester T v Tiverton T 3-1
York C v Pickering T 2-0
Marine v Woodley Sp 3-0
Sheffield v Bottisford T 2-1
Brighouse T v Grimsby T 3-2
Boston U v Pinxton 3-0
Racing C Warwick v Halesowen T 1-2
Stourport Swifts v Lye T 3-0
Highgate U v Tamworth 0-5
Soham T R v Woodbridge T 2-1
Luton T v Leighton T 5-1
Woodford U v Stotfold 3-1
Thurrock v Maldon & Tiptree 4-1
Chelmsford C v Hemel Hempstead T 2-1
Billericay T v East Thurrock U 2-1
Dartford v Westfield 3-2
Tooting & Mitcham U v Ebbsfleet U 0-2
Lancing v Epsom & Ewell 0-9
Wokingham & Emmbrook v Binfield 3-3
Wokingham & Emmbrook won 12-11 on penalties.
Thatcham T v Oxford C 0-2
Ringwood T v AFC Totton 1-6
Matlock T v Teversall 4-3
Bromyard T v Nuneaton T 2-3
Kiddminster H v Stone Dominoes 3-2
Dereham T v Gorleston 3-1
Wimborne T v Gillingham T 4-2
Poole T v Moneyfields 3-1
Fleetwood T v Ashton Ath 0-3
Yorkshire Amat v Staveley MW 3-0
Corby T v Bedford T 8-3
Kettering T v St Neots T 0-2
Ashford T (Middlesex) v Uxbridge 2-3
Hanwell T v Staines T 0-3
Hayes & Yeading U v Hampton & Richmond Bor 2-0
Worthing v Leatherhead 0-1
Farnborough v Reading T 4-3
Eastleigh v Salisbury C 1-0
Larkhall Ath v Weston Super M 1-0
Newport Co v Lydney T 9-0
Cheltenham Sar v Bishop's Cleeve 1-5
Corinthian v Erith T 4-2

THIRD QUALIFYING ROUND

Yorkshire Amat v Marine 1-2
Leatherhead v Camberley T 2-3
Epsom & Ewell v Ebbsfleet U 2-3
Oxford C v Maidenhead U 4-5
Eastleigh v AFC Totton 0-2
Corby T v Redbridge 3-0
Staines T v Hayes & Yeading U 2-4
Bishop's Cleeve v Poole T 7-2
Larkhall Ath v Cirencester T 0-4
Soham T R v St Neots T 2-1
Wokingham & Emmbrook v Farnborough 2-9
Tie ordered to be replayed: 0-5.
Altrincham v Darlington 0-3
Prescot Cables v York C 1-3
Dereham T v Luton T 2-1
Mossley v North Ferriby U 0-1
Boreham Wood v Billericay T 2-0
Sheffield v Ashton Ath 1-0
Boston U v Stourbridge Swifts 4-3
Kidderminster H v Matlock T 3-0
Brighouse T v Loughborough Dyn 2-1
Halesowen T v Calverton MW 2-1
Uxbridge v Needham Market 4-3
Hadleigh U v Thurrock 0-5
Bracknell T v Kingstonian 0-2
Nuneaton T v Stratford T 0-5

Woodford U v Cambridge U 0-4
Chelmsford C v Tilbury 2-2
Tilbury won 3-2 on penalties.
Dartford v Lewes 2-5
Wimbourne T v Newport Co 1-7
Tamworth v Lincoln C 2-0
Ramsgate v Corinthian 1-2
Whyteleafe v Dulwich Hamlet 1-3

FIRST ROUND

Scunthorpe U v Huddersfield T 1-2
Milton Keynes D v Walsall 0-1
Chesterfield v Tamworth 7-0
Burton Alb v Boston U 1-3
Corby T v Colchester U 2-0
Bishop's Cleeve v Torquay U 1-3
Hartlepool U v Bury 1-3
Rochdale v Oldham Ath 2-3
Carlisle U v Sheffield W 4-1
Shrewsbury T v Notts Co 2-0
Northampton T v Cambridge U 1-2
Leyton Orient v Dereham T 4-3
Dagenham & R v Barnet 3-2
AFC Bournemouth v Plymouth Arg 4-2
North Ferriby U v Crewe Alex 0-4
Bradford C v Marine 3-2
Gillingham v Hayes & Yeading U 0-1
Swindon T v Newport Co 2-0
Bristol R v Maidenhead U 4-1
Southend U v Corinthian 4-0
Rotherham U v Accrington S 0-1
Morecambe v Preston NE 0-3
Crawley T v Wycombe W 5-1
Cheltenham T v Oxford U 1-3
York C v Macclesfield T 1-3
Brentford v Lewes 3-0
Thurrock v Boreham Wood 2-0
AFC Totton v Exeter C 3-2
Darlington v Sheffield 7-1
Kidderminster H v Brighouse T 4-2
Uxbridge v AFC Wimbledon 1-3
Cirencester T v Camberley T 3-1
Tilbury v Stevenage 0-2
Hereford U v Halesowen T 5-3
Ebbsfleet U v Dulwich Hamlet 1-2
Soham T R v Charlton Ath 0-9
Aldershot T v Kingstonian 3-2
Tranmere R v Sheffield U 1-2
Stratford T v Port Vale 2-3
Farnborough v Yeovil T 1-3

SECOND ROUND

Corby T v Dagenham & R 2-2
Corby T won 3-2 on penalties.
Boston U v Bradford C 2-1
Bury v Accrington S 2-1
Darlington v Shrewsbury T 2-0
Hereford U v Chesterfield 2-0
AFC Bournemouth v Swindon T 1-3
Cambridge U v Crawley T 3-1
AFC Wimbledon v Bristol R 1-2
Southend U v Brentford 1-2
Torquay U v Cirencester T 1-1
Torquay U won 3-1 on penalties.
Stevenage v Leyton Orient 1-0
Kidderminster H v Carlisle U 0-1
Dulwich Hamlet v Oxford U 0-2
Sheffield U v Port Vale 2-2
Sheffield U won 8-7 on penalties.
Huddersfield T v Crewe Alex 2-1
Oldham Ath v Macclesfield T 1-1
Oldham Ath won 6-5 on penalties.
Charlton Ath v Yeovil T 3-0
Thurrock v Hayes & Yeading U 2-0
Preston NE v Walsall 1-1
Preston NE won 5-4 on penalties.
Aldershot T v AFC Totton 3-1

THIRD ROUND

Stevenage v Tottenham H 1-2
Swindon T v Birmingham C 3-2
Charlton Ath v Cambridge U 7-0
Ipswich T v Leeds U 2-0
Blackburn R v Thurrock 8-0
Manchester C v Corby T 4-1
Southampton v Sheffield U 7-0
Oxford U v Bolton W 1-2
Middlesbrough v Reading 1-2
Bury v Cardiff C 2-3
Leicester C v Aldershot T 5-0
Chelsea v Doncaster R 2-1
Hull C v Brentford 1-2
Portsmouth v Bristol C 5-1
Peterborough U v Blackpool 3-1
Swansea C v Liverpool 3-1
Wolverhampton W v West Ham U 2-3
Manchester U v Torquay U 4-0
Norwich C v Oldham Ath 5-0
Fulham v Carlisle U 3-1
Brighton & HA v Aston Villa 1-0
Millwall v Watford 1-2
Preston NE v Stoke C 1-2
Crystal Palace v Everton 1-2
Bristol R v Coventry C 2-3
Arsenal v Derby Co 0-1
Newcastle U v Darlington 3-0
QPR v Huddersfield T 2-1
Boston U v Burnley 0-7
Wigan Ath v Hereford U 4-0

FOURTH ROUND

Bolton W v Southampton 1-2
Charlton Ath v Leicester C 2-1
Cardiff C v Tottenham H 1-2
QPR v Everton 1-0
Reading v WBA 1-2
Stoke C v Brentford 2-1
Burnley v Ipswich T 3-1
Blackburn R v Coventry C 2-0
Swindon T v Manchester C 1-4
Nottingham F v Wigan Ath 9-1
Norwich C v Chelsea 0-0
Chelsea won 4-2 on penalties.
Portsmouth v Swansea C 1-2
Manchester U v Derby Co 2-1
Newcastle U v Watford 2-1
West Ham U v Brighton & HA 4-1
Peterborough U v Fulham 1-5

FIFTH ROUND

Swansea C v Manchester U 1-5
Manchester C v Fulham 1-2
Blackburn R v Stoke C 4-0
Charlton Ath v Tottenham H 1-0
WBA v Burnley 1-2
Chelsea v West Ham U 3-3
Chelsea won 5-4 on penalties.
Newcastle U v QPR 2-1
Southampton v Nottingham F 1-5

SIXTH ROUND

Newcastle U v Blackburn R 2-2
Blackburn R won 3-0 on penalties.
Manchester U v Charlton Ath 3-2
Fulham v Burnley 1-3
Nottingham F v Chelsea 3-4

SEMI-FINALS

Blackburn R v Burnley 1-0, 2-1
Manchester U v Chelsea 1-2, 1-1

FINAL FIRST LEG

Friday, 20 April 2012

Chelsea (2) 4 *(Chalobah 20, Baker 28, Feruz 60, 69)*

Blackburn R (0) 0 3142

Chelsea: Blackman; Kane, Davey, Ake, Nditi, Chalobah, Affane (Kiwomya 53), Swift, Feruz (Mitchell 78), Baker, Piazon.

Blackburn R: Unwin; Wylie (Lenihan 61), Beesley, Hands (Cotton 61), Edwards, O'Connell, Osaye, Hanley R, Haley (Payne 82), O'Sullivan, Fernandez.

FINAL SECOND LEG

Wednesday, 9 May 2012

Blackburn R (1) 1 *(Payne 25)*

Chelsea (0) 0 1490

Blackburn R: Urwin; Daly, Edwards, O'Connell, Wylie, Mason (Laverty), Cotton (Boland), Hanley R, Hernandez, Payne (Haley), O'Sullivan.

Chelsea: Blackman; Kane, Davey, Nkumu (Loftus-Cheek), Gordon (Nditi), Swift, Chalobah, Baker, Affane (Kiwomya), Feruz, Piazon.

THE FA INTER-LEAGUE CUP 2011–12

IN PARTNERSHIP WITH CARLSBERG

PRELIMINARY ROUND

Northern Football Alliance v Lancashire & Cheshire Amateur League	2-2
Northern Football Alliance won 3-1 on penalties.	
Lancashire Amateur League v Isle of Man League	1-3
Manchester League v Wearside League	2-1
Liverpool County FA Premier League v Teesside League	2-1
Peterborough & District League v Lincolnshire League	1-2
Northamptonshire Combination v Cambridgeshire County League	1-2
Birmingham & District AFA v West Riding County Amateur League	0-2
Anglian Combination w.o. v Nottinghamshire Senior League withdrew	
Worthing & District League v Somerset County League	3-4
Gloucestershire County League v Mid Sussex League	4-0
Dorset Premier League v Hampshire Premier League	2-2
Dorset Premier League won 5-4 on penalties.	
Sussex County League (Div 3) v Brighton Hove & District League	5-0
Suffolk & Ipswich League v Bedfordshire County League	4-0
Amateur Football Combination v Surrey Elite Intermediate League	1-2
Middlesex County League v Herts Senior County League	3-3
Herts Senior County League won 5-4 on penalties.	
Reading League v Kent County League	1-1
Reading League won 6-5 on penalties.	

West Riding County Amateur League, Gloucestershire County League and Dorset Premier League all removed for breaches of rules.

FIRST ROUND

Sussex County League (Div 3) w.o. v Wiltshire League withdrew	
Essex Olympian League v Herts Senior County League	1-4
Northampton Town League v Cambridgeshire County League	0-1
Lincolnshire League v Anglian Combination	3-2
Jersey Football Combination v Mid Sussex League	8-0
Birmingham & District AFA v Midland Football Combination (Div 1)	2-2
Birmingham & District AFA won 4-2 on penalties.	
Tie ordered to be replayed.	
Birmingham & District AFA v Midland Football Combination (Div 1)	0-1
Manchester League v Cheshire League	2-3
West Yorkshire League v Humber Premier League	3-0
Spartan South Midlands League (Div 2) v Southern Amateur League	0-1
West Cheshire League v Isle of Man League	0-5
Cumberland County League v Liverpool County FA Premier League	1-2
Suffolk & Ipswich League v Reading League	3-0
Suffolk & Ipswich League removed for fielding ineligible player.	
Surrey Elite Intermediate League v Essex & Suffolk Border League	1-2
Devon & Exeter League v Guernsey Senior County League	1-0
Northern Football Alliance v Yorkshire Amateur League	1-2
Somerset County League v Hampshire Premier League	5-1

SECOND ROUND

Somerset County League v Reading League	2-1
Isle of Man League v Yorkshire Amateur League	4-3
Herts Senior County League v Sussex County League (Div 3)	0-2
Cheshire League v Cambridgeshire County League	1-0
Southern Amateur League v Devon & Exeter League	6-1
Jersey Football Combination v Essex & Suffolk Border League	1-0
West Yorkshire League v Liverpool County FA Premier League	5-4
West Yorkshire League removed for fielding ineligible players.	
Midland Football Combination (Div 1) v Lincolnshire League	3-4

THIRD ROUND

Southern Amateur League v Sussex County League (Div 3)	5-2
Isle of Man League v Liverpool County FA Premier League	5-3
Lincolnshire League v Cheshire League	2-4
Jersey Football Combination v Somerset County League	4-0

SEMI-FINALS

Jersey Football Combination v Cheshire League	1-1
Jersey Football Combination won 4-3 on penalties.	
Isle of Man League v Southern Amateur League	2-1

FINAL

Isle of Man League v Jersey Football Combination	1-2

THE FA SUNDAY CUP 2011–12

IN PARTNERSHIP WITH CARLSBERG

FIRST ROUND

Sunderland RCA v Dawdon CW 2-5
South Bank 2006 v Hartlepool LH 3-5
Kelloe v Hartlepool RQ 1-0
St Bees v Stockton R N&SA 0-6
Burradown & NF v Hetton Lyons CC 0-1
Chapeltown FG v Dengo U 3-1
Lobster v Alder 6-4
Eagle Cons v Queens Park 1-0
Tie awarded to Queens Park; Eagle Cons removed.
Obiter v West Bowling 0-4
Nicosia v Derby Lane Gym 1-4
AFC Blackburn L v BRNESC 0-2
Sandstone v Eden Vale 3-5
Belt Road v Bolton Woods 3-0
Hessle R v Canada 1-2
Poulton Royal v Home & Bargain 1-3
Mariners v St Sebastians 4-3
Swanfield v Allerton 3-3
Allerton won 5-3 on penalties.
Brigg House withdrew v Britannia w.o.
JOB v Seymour 3-0
Salisbury Ath v Thirly 4-1
Hundred Acre v Advance Couriers 3-4
Wymeswold v Loughborough F 2-1
Loughborough S v Clumber 2-1
FC Hoskins v Lea Hall S&S 1-4
Whitwick C 2008 v Bartley Green S 4-2
Magnet Tavern v Plough Barfly's 2-1
The Dog v Hole in the Wall 4-0
Kingshurst P v Birstall Stamford 1-4
Travellers v RHP S&S 3-2
Seven Allstars v Hamstead 4-4
Seven Allstars won 4-3 on penalties.
St Joseph's (Luton) v Crawley G (Sunday) 3-2
Rumours v FC Houghton C 1-5
Club Lewsey v Duke of Rutland 4-1
AC Cadoza v Northampton D of Y 0-2
AC Sportsmen & R v Stanbridge & T 4-1
Highfield SC v Houghton T (Sunday) 7-0
St Margarets v Celtic SC (Luton) 2-0
Co-op SP v Britannia U 2-3
Belstone v Greengate 0-3
Gossams End v Torrun U 0-10
Gadeside R v FC Nirankari 2-5
Bari v New Salamis 1-3
Sungate v Hammer OGB 3-0
Royal Falcons v Comets SC 1-3
Falcons v London Maccabi L 12-1
FC Tripimeni v Upshire 4-1
Gym U w.o. v Offley Moat failed to fulfil fixture.
Elm Farm v North London Olym 7-4
CB Hounslow U (Sunday) v Wrightchoice 0-2
Barnes Alb v AFC Kumazi S 2-1
Bedfont Sunday v AFC Rayners Lane 5-2
Dee Road R v Broadfields U 5-3
AFC Donsville v Oak Park R 1-1
AFC Donsville won 3-1 on penalties.
Branksome Con v Goring R 2-0
The Lounge v Knighton Arms 3-1
Hazelhurst v Ajax LA 8-0
Nyetimber Pir v Fountain Court 4-2
CK v Kings Tamerton 5-2
SP Bristol v Lakeside Ath 1-2
Efford U B v All Saints 1-2
The Railway Inn v Wonford U 0-2
Lebeqs Tavern C v Windmill 3-2

SECOND ROUND

Home & Bargain v JOB 0-4
Allerton v Dawdon CW 0-3
Queens Park v Derby Lane Gym 3-0
West Bowling v Stockton R N&SA 3-4
Eden Vale v Kelloe 2-4
Hetton Lyons CC v Chapeltown FG 2-1
Oyster Martyrs v Belt Road 6-0
Paddock v Lobster 0-1
Britannia v Hartlepool LH 1-0
Salisbury Ath v BRNESC 4-0
Canada v Mariners 3-1
Loughborough S v St Joseph's (Luton) 5-0
AC Sportsmen & R v Northampton D of Y 1-6
Magnet Tavern v Wymeswold 2-0
FC Houghton C v Club Lewsey 2-5
The Dog v Whitwick C 2008 0-6
Travellers v Seven Allstars 6-3
Lea Hall S&S v St Margarets 5-0
Advance Couriers v Birstall Stamford 1-2
Highfield SC v Falcons 0-4
Greengate v Elm Farm 1-2
Gym U v FC Tripimeni 0-3
Comets SC v Britannia U 4-0
Sungate v Torrun U 4-3
FC Nirankari v New Salamis 0-5
AFC Donsville v Hazelhurst 1-1
Hazelhurst won 5-4 on penalties.
Barnes Alb v Nyetimber Pir 6-1
CK v Dee Road R 3-4
Wonford U v Lebeqs Tavern C 1-3
Bedfont Sunday v Branksome Con 0-1
All Saints v Lakeside Ath 0-3
Wrightchoice v The Lounge 2-0

THIRD ROUND

Canada v Queens Park 4-1
Lobster v Whitwick C 2008 2-3
Kelloe v JOB 5-2
Hetton Lyons CC v Britannia 4-1
Salisbury Ath v Oyster Martyrs 0-3
Dawdon CW v Stockton R N&SA 3-5
New Salamis v Lea Hall S&S 1-3
FC Tripimeni v Falcons 5-2
Club Lewsey v Magnet Tavern 1-0
Loughborough S v Comets SC 1-3
Sungate v Northampton D of Y 3-0
Travellers v Birstall Stamford 1-1
Birstall Stamford won 2-1 on penalties.
Barnes Alb v Wrightchoice 1-1
Barnes Alb won 5-4 on penalties.
Hazelhurst v Dee Road R 0-5
Lakeside Ath v Lebeqs Tavern C 4-2
Elm Farm v Branksome Con 2-1

FOURTH ROUND

Canada v Stockton R N&SA 2-0
Whitwick C 2008 v Lea Hall S&S 0-1
Hetton Lyons CC v Kelloe 3-1
Birstall Stamford v Oyster Martyrs 3-4
FC Tripimeni v Dee Road R 4-3
Club Lewsey v Lakeside Ath 2-2
Lakeside Ath won 4-3 on penalties.
Sungate v Comets SC 0-4
Elm Farm v Barnes Alb 3-1

FIFTH ROUND

Lakeside Ath v Comets SC 3-1
FC Tripimeni v Oyster Martyrs 1-0
Tie awarded to Oyster Martyrs; FC Tripimeni removed for several breaches of rule relating to an ineligible player.
Elm Farm v Canada 1-2
Lee Hall S&S v Hetton Lyons CC 0-5

SEMI-FINALS

Hetton Lyons CC v Oyster Martyrs 2-1
Lakeside Ath v Canada 0-1

FINAL (at Sunderland)

Sunday, 29 April 2012

Hetton Lyons CC (2) 5 *(Byrne 4, 19, Moore 52, Capper 60, Craggs 90)*

Canada (0) 1 *(Fargan 70)*

Hetton Lyons CC: Finch; Griffiths, Hunter, Price, Moore, Capper, Graydon (Ellison), Walton, Davison, Byrne (Davis), Watson (Craggs).

Canada: Brookfield; Wardle, O'Rourke, McNabb, Fargan, Downey (Hanley), O'Brien, Riley, Tames, Furlong (Williams A), Williams G (Davies).

FA PREMIER RESERVE LEAGUE 2011–12

BARCLAYS PREMIER RESERVE LEAGUE NORTH

		P	W	D	L	F	A	GD	Pts
1	Manchester U	22	15	4	3	58	23	35	49
2	Liverpool	22	9	8	5	44	30	14	35
3	Everton	22	9	8	5	38	29	9	35
4	Sunderland	22	9	5	8	38	36	2	32
5	Newcastle U	22	7	4	11	38	58	–20	25
6	Wigan Ath	22	5	9	8	27	37	–10	24
7	Blackburn R	22	4	10	8	18	22	–4	22
8	Bolton W	22	3	8	11	23	40	–17	17

BARCLAYS PREMIER RESERVE LEAGUE SOUTH

		P	W	D	L	F	A	GD	Pts
1	Aston Villa	22	13	4	5	45	22	23	43
2	Fulham	22	12	4	6	46	25	21	40
3	Arsenal	22	11	5	6	36	25	11	38
4	WBA	22	11	2	9	36	31	5	35
5	Chelsea	22	7	7	8	42	43	–1	28
6	Wolverhampton W	22	6	5	11	26	41	–15	23
7	Swansea C	22	4	8	10	21	38	–17	20
8	Norwich C	22	2	7	13	26	62	–36	13

MANCHESTER UNITED – APPEARANCES AND GOALS

Amos 10, Blackett 1+3, Brady 0+1, Brown 6, Cleverley 2, Cofie 0+5, Cole 15, Daehli 0+1, Da Silva F. 3, Da Silva R. 1, De Laet 10, Diouf 6, Drinkwater 1, Fletcher 2, Fornasier 8+6, Fryers 19, Gibson 3, Giverin 0+3, James 5+1, Johnstone 9, Jones 1, Keane M. 21+1, Keane W. 18+3, Kuszczak 2, Leao 0+1, Lindegaard 1, Lingard 15+4, McGinty 6+1, Macheda 4, Massacci 0+3, Morrison 1+2, Norwood 2, Petrucci 18+3, Pogba 16, Smalling 1, Thorpe 6+7, Tunnicliffe 8+2, van Velzen 0+3, Vermijl 17+3, Veseli 1+2, Wilson 0+1, Wootton 3+1.
Goals: Keane W. 15, Diouf 7, Petrucci 7, Lingard 6, Keane M. 4, Cole 3, Pogba 3, De Laet 2, Morrison 2, Brown 1, Fryers 1, Macheda 1, Massacci 1, Smalling 1, Tunnicliffe 1, Vermijl 1, own goals 2.

ASTON VILLA – APPEARANCES AND GOALS

Albrighton 4, Baker 8, Bannan 6, Barrett 4+2, Barton 1+3, Bryan 1, Burke 15, Caira 2+6, Cameron 17+4, Carruthers 15+2, Clark 5, Coleman +1, Cuellar 2, Darkin 1+2, Delfouneso 3, Devine +1, Donacien 10+1, Drennan 6+5, Gardner 9, Graham 2+5, Grealish 4+5, Guzan 2, Herd 5, Hogg 1, Johnson 21, Kinsella 2+2, Lichaj 7, Lowry 7, Melvin +1, Nelson-Addy 6+4, Robinson 8+5, Siegrist B 16, Stevens 10, Taylor 6+4, Ward C +1, Watkins M 1, Webb 10+1, Weimann 6, Williams 19.
Goals: Weimann 9, Drennan 5, Gardner 5, Johnson 5, Robinson 5, Burke 4, Carruthers 4, Bannan 3, Albrighton 1, Delfouneso 1, Lichaj 1, Taylor 1, own goal 1.

RESULTS 2011–12

	Ar	AV	BR	BW	Ch	Ev	Fu	Li	MU	NU	NC	Su	SC	WB	WA	WW
Arsenal	—	1-1	1-0		0-4	0-2	2-0		2-1		4-2	0-2	2-2	3-0		3-0
Aston Villa	2-0	—		3-1	1-0		3-0	1-4		4-0	2-0		2-1	4-1	1-1	7-1
Blackburn R		0-0	—	1-2		2-4	0-0	0-0	0-1	3-0		1-3	1-0		1-1	2-3
Bolton W	3-3		0-0	—	0-1	0-1		1-1	1-2	0-3	2-1	2-2		1-1	1-2	
Chelsea	0-2	2-0	1-1		—	3-3	3-2		1-4		3-0	3-2	1-1	2-3		2-3
Everton		2-1	2-0	2-2		—	0-2	0-0	1-4	6-3		2-0	1-1		1-2	1-1
Fulham	1-0	3-2		7-0	2-2		—	1-1		5-0	6-2		1-1	3-0	1-3	1-0
Liverpool	1-1		2-4	3-1	3-1	1-1		—	2-2	1-2	4-0	5-1		2-1	5-1	
Manchester U		3-1	0-0	2-1		2-0	2-1	4-0	—	6-0		0-0	6-0		4-1	2-0
Newcastle U	0-1		0-0	1-1	2-4	0-4		3-2	3-6		6-0	3-3		1-4	3-1	
Norwich C	0-5	1-1	0-0		3-3	2-1	1-5		2-4		—	1-1	1-1	2-4		3-2
Sunderland		0-2	2-0	1-0		0-1	1-2	3-3	6-3	3-0		—	2-0		3-1	3-1
Swansea C	0-2	0-2		2-1	2-2		1-0	2-1		3-5	0-0		—	1-0	0-2	2-3
WBA	3-1	0-3	0-2		4-0	2-2	1-2		1-0		3-1	3-0	2-0	—		0-1
Wigan Ath	1-3		0-0	1-1	2-2	1-1		0-2	0-0	0-2	2-2	3-0		0-2	—	
Wolverhampton W	0-0	1-2		0-2	3-2		0-1	0-1		1-1	3-2		1-1	0-1	2-2	—

LEADING GOALSCORERS

Keane, William David	15	Manchester U
Trotta, Marcello	15	Fulham
Noble, Ryan	10	Sunderland
Weimann, Andreas	9	Aston Villa
Eccleston, Nathan	8	Liverpool
Sawyers, Romaine Theodore	8	WBA
Watt, Herschel Oulio Sanchez	7	Arsenal
Lukaku, Romelu Menama	7	Chelsea
Vellios, Apostolos	7	Everton
Ngoo, Michael	7	Liverpool
Diouf, Mame Biram	7	Manchester U
Petrucci, Davide	7	Manchester U
Aneke, Chukwuemeka Ademola Amachi	6	Arsenal
Lalkovic, Milan	6	Chelsea
Baxter, Jose	6	Everton
Sterling, Raheem Shaquille	6	Liverpool
Lingard, Jesse Ellis	6	Manchester U
Ball, Matthew	6	Norwich C
Dobbie, Stephen	6	Swansea C
Berahino, Saido	6	WBA
Rugg, Jordan	6	Wigan Ath

PREMIER RESERVE LEAGUE FINAL

Manchester United 0 Aston Villa 0

(at Old Trafford, 10 May 2012, attendance 5130).

Manchester U: Johnstone; Fornasier (Vermijl), Fryers, Thorpe (Brady), Keane M, Wootton, Cole, Tunnicliffe, Keane W, Petrucci (King), Lingard.
Aston Villa: Siegrist; Webb, Stevens, Gardner, Williams, Baker, Carruthers, Grealish (Cameron), Drennan (Graham), Bannan, Johnson.
Manchester U won 3-1 on penalties: Bannan scored; King scored; Carruthers saved; Lingard scored; Johnson saved; Keane W scored; Cameron saved.

THE CENTRAL LEAGUE 2011–12

CENTRAL DIVISION	P	W	D	L	F	A	GD	Pts
Sheffield U	12	6	4	2	25	9	16	22
Derby Co	12	6	3	3	26	16	10	21
Nottingham F	12	5	3	4	24	20	4	18
Port Vale	12	4	3	5	12	21	–9	15
Walsall	12	4	3	5	17	27	–10	15
Burton Alb	12	4	1	7	24	27	–3	13
Stoke C	12	3	3	6	15	23	–8	12

WEST DIVISION	P	W	D	L	F	A	GD	Pts
Preston NE	12	8	1	3	25	12	13	25
Burnley	12	7	2	3	33	19	14	23
Tranmere R	12	6	1	5	27	17	10	19
Morecambe	12	5	2	5	21	26	–5	17
Wrexham	12	3	6	3	23	24	–1	15
Macclesfield T	12	3	1	8	20	40	–20	10
Oldham Ath	12	2	3	7	16	27	–11	9

EAST DIVISION	P	W	D	L	F	A	GD	Pts
Middlesbrough	12	9	1	2	32	15	17	28
Bradford C	12	7	2	3	24	20	4	23
Hull C	12	5	2	5	25	16	9	17
Hartlepool U	12	5	1	6	20	18	2	16
Rotherham U	12	4	2	6	13	20	–7	14
Gateshead	12	4	1	7	14	24	–10	13
Scunthorpe U	12	3	1	8	16	31	–15	10

THE CENTRAL LEAGUE CUP GROUPS

GROUP A	P	W	D	L	F	A	GD	Pts
Manchester C	3	2	0	1	12	4	8	6
Preston NE	3	2	0	1	7	5	2	6
Tranmere R	3	1	0	2	6	8	–2	3
Morecambe	3	1	0	2	5	13	–8	3

GROUP B	P	W	D	L	F	A	GD	Pts
Derby Co	4	3	1	0	10	3	7	10
Stoke C	4	2	2	0	11	4	7	8
Rotherham U	4	2	0	2	7	10	–3	6
Chesterfield	4	1	1	2	5	5	0	4
Port Vale	4	0	0	4	4	15	–11	0

GROUP C	P	W	D	L	F	A	GD	Pts
Sunderland	4	3	1	0	16	3	13	10
Hull C	4	2	1	1	15	9	6	7
Gateshead	4	2	0	2	5	7	–2	6
Hartlepool U	4	1	1	2	10	11	–1	4
Scunthorpe U	4	0	1	3	3	19	–16	1

SEMI-FINALS
Stoke C 1, Manchester C 4
Derby Co 3, Sunderland 2

FINAL
Manchester C v Derby Co
To be played in August.

TOTESPORT CUP FINAL 2010–11
Sunderland 3, Walsall 0

FA ACADEMY UNDER 18 LEAGUE 2011–12

GROUP A	P	W	D	L	F	A	GD	Pts
Fulham	28	18	0	10	73	48	25	54
Southampton	28	15	8	5	59	30	29	53
Arsenal	28	16	4	8	56	37	19	52
Charlton Ath	28	15	5	8	58	32	26	50
West Ham U	28	14	4	10	55	45	10	46
Crystal Palace	28	13	5	10	47	46	1	44
Chelsea	28	11	6	11	52	51	1	39
Norwich C	28	10	3	15	47	53	–6	33
Ipswich T	28	6	7	15	40	58	–18	25
Portsmouth	28	6	6	16	33	60	–27	24

GROUP B	P	W	D	L	F	A	GD	Pts
Leicester C	28	17	6	5	75	50	25	57
Coventry C	28	17	5	6	57	38	19	56
Reading	28	15	9	4	63	36	27	54
Tottenham H	28	13	8	7	71	53	18	47
Aston Villa	28	11	7	10	64	52	12	40
Cardiff C	28	7	6	15	37	52	–15	27
Watford	28	6	8	14	34	56	–22	26
Birmingham C	28	7	4	17	28	55	–27	25
Milton Keynes D	28	4	6	18	49	107	–58	18
Bristol C	28	4	5	19	28	55	–27	17

GROUP C	P	W	D	L	F	A	GD	Pts
Blackburn R	28	17	5	6	57	39	18	56
Manchester C	28	17	3	8	60	41	19	54
Liverpool	28	15	6	7	53	37	16	51
Wolverhampton W	28	15	3	10	60	50	10	48
Everton	28	13	4	11	60	45	15	43
Stoke C	28	12	7	9	45	41	4	43
Bolton W	28	9	5	14	41	48	–7	32
Manchester U	28	8	7	13	48	56	–8	31
Crewe Alex	28	8	5	15	40	60	–20	29
WBA	28	7	4	17	39	63	–24	25

GROUP D	P	W	D	L	F	A	GD	Pts
Newcastle U	28	17	4	7	59	39	20	55
Leeds U	28	16	5	7	60	31	29	53
Derby Co	28	12	6	10	54	45	9	42
Barnsley	28	12	5	11	44	36	8	41
Sheffield U	28	11	6	11	41	45	–4	39
Sunderland	28	11	5	12	50	51	–1	38
Middlesbrough	28	11	4	13	41	54	–13	37
Sheffield W	28	7	5	16	34	59	–25	26
Huddersfield T	28	5	8	15	35	65	–30	23
Nottingham F	28	5	5	18	36	64	–28	20

ACADEMY PLAY-OFF SEMI-FINALS
Fulham 2, Leicester C 1
Blackburn R 2, Newcastle U 0

ACADEMY FINAL
Fulham 2, Blackburn 0

THE FOOTBALL COMBINATION 2011–12

NORTHERN SECTION	P	W	D	L	GD	Pts
Colchester U	8	5	0	3	8	15
Southend U	8	5	0	3	7	15
Luton T	8	4	2	2	6	14
Stevenage	8	2	2	4	–13	8
Oxford U	8	1	2	5	–8	5

SOUTHERN SECTION	P	W	D	L	GD	Pts
Forest Green R	10	5	3	2	5	18
Brighton & HA	10	5	2	3	2	17
Cheltenham T	10	5	0	5	4	15
AFC Bournemouth	10	4	2	4	1	14
Crawley T	10	4	1	5	2	13
Torquay U	10	3	0	7	–14	9

IMPORTANT ADDRESSES

The Football Association: Wembley Stadium, P.O. Box 1966, London SW1P 9EQ. *0844 980 8200*

Scotland: David Taylor, Hampden Park, Glasgow G42 9AY. *0141 616 6000*

Northern Ireland (Irish FA): Chief Executive, 20 Windsor Avenue, Belfast BT9 6EE. *028 9066 9458*

Wales: 11/12 Neptune Court, Vanguard Way, Cardiff CF24 5PJ. *029 2043 5830*

Republic of Ireland National Sports Campus, Abbotstown, Dublin 15. *00 353 1 8999 500*

International Federation (FIFA): Strasse 20, P.O. Box 8044, Zurich, Switzerland. *00 41 43 222 7777. Fax: 00 411 384 9696*

Union of European Football Associations: Secretary, Route de Geneve 46, P.O. Box 1260, Nyon 2, Switzerland. *00 41 848 00 2727. Fax: 0041 22 994 44 88*

THE LEAGUES

The Premier League: M. Foster, 30 Gloucester Place, London W1U 8PL. *0207 864 9000*

The Football League: Andy Williamson, The Football League, Unit 5, Edward VII Quay, Navigation Way, Preston, Lancashire PR2 2YF. *0844 463 1888. Fax 0870 442 0 1188*

Scottish Premier League: R. Mitchell, Hampden Park, Somerville Drive, Glasgow G42 9BA. *0141 646 6962*

The Scottish League: Hampden Park, Glasgow G42 9EB. *0141 620 4160*

Football League of Ireland: D. Crowther, 80 Merrion Square, Dublin 2. *00353 16765120*

Football Conference: D. Strudwick, 3rd Floor, Wellington House, 31–34 Waterloo Street, Birmingham B2 5TJ. *0121 214 1950*

Southern League: J. Mills, Sansome Lodge, 4–6 Sansome Walk, Worcester WR1 1LH. *01905 330 444*

Northern Premier League: P. Bradley, 7 Guest Road, Prestwich, Manchester M25 3DJ. *0161 798 5198*

Isthmian League: B. Badcock, 14–15 Wisdom Facilities Centre, 42 Hollands Road, Haverhill, Suffolk CB9 8SA. *01440 768 840*

Eastern Counties League: N. Spurling, 16 Thanet Road, Ipswich, Suffolk IP4 5LB. *07855 279062*

Essex Senior League: Secretary: K. Wilmot, 35 Cecil Road, Walthamstow, London E17 5DH. *07540 441 829*

Hellenic League: B. King, 7 Stoneleigh Drive, Carterton, Oxon OX18 1EE. *0845 260 6644*

Kent League: A.R. Vinter, 4 Staple Court, Chilham Castle Estate, Chilham, Canterbury CT4 8DB. *01277 730457*

Midland Alliance: J. Shaw, 176 Springthorpe Road, Erdington, Birmingham B24 0SN. *0121 350 5869*

North West Counties League: J. Deal, 24 The Pastures, Crossens, Southport PR9 8RH. *07713 622210*

Northern Counties East: B. Gould, 42 Thirlmere Drive, Dronfield, Derbyshire S18 2HW. *07773 653 238*

Northern League: T. Golightly, 85 Park Road North, Chester-le-Street, Co. Durham DH3 3SA. *0191 388 2056*

Spartan South Midlands League: M. Mitchell, 26 Leighton Court, Dunstable, Beds LU6 1EW. *07710 455 409*

Sussex County League: P. Beard, 2 Van Gogh Place, North Bersted, Bognor Regis, West Sussex PO22 9BG. *07831 497 913*

United Counties League: N. Haycox, 12 Glenfield Drive, Great Doddington, Wellingborough NN29 7TE. *07879 036235*

Wessex League: J. Gorman, 6 Overton House, London Road, Overton, Hants RG25 3TP. *01256 770059*

Western League: K.A. Clarke, 32 Westmead Lane, Chippenham, Wilts SN15 3HZ. *07790 002279*

Suburban League (Formerly Combined Counties): M.J. Bidmead, 55 Grange Road, Chessington, Surrey KT9 1EZ. *0208 397 4834*

Midland Combination: N. Wood, 30 Glalsdale Road, Hall Green, Birmingham B28 8PX. *07967 440007*

West Midlands League: N.R. Juggins, 14 Badger Way, Blackwell, Bromsgrove, Worcs B60 1EX. *07977 422 362.*

South West Peninsula League: P. Hiscox, 45a Serge Court, The Quay, Exeter, Devon EX2 4EB. *07788 897706*

OTHER USEFUL ADDRESSES

Amateur Football Alliance: M. Brown, Unit 3, 7 Wenlock Road, London N1 7SL. *0844 980 8207*

English Schools FA: J. Read, 4 Parker Court, Staffordshire Technology Park, Stafford ST18 0WP. *01785 785 970*

British Universities Sports Association: G. Gregory-Jones, Chief Executive: BUSA, 20–24 King's Bench Street, London SE1 0QX. *0207 633 5050*

The Football Supporters Federation: The Fans Stadium, Kingsmeadow, Jack Goodchild Way, 422a Kingston Road, Kingston-upon-Thames KT1 3PB. *0330 44 000 44*

National Playing Fields Association: 25 Ovington Square, London SW3 1LQ. *0207 584 6445*

Professional Footballers' Association: G. Taylor, 2 Oxford Court, Bishopsgate, Off Lower Moseley Street, Manchester M2 3WQ. *0161 236 0575*

Referees' Association: A. Smith, Unit 12, Ensign Business Centre, Westwood Way, Westwood Business Park, Westwood Heath, Coventry CV4 8JA. *024 7642 0360*

Women's Football Alliance: Miss K. Doyle, The Football Association, 25 Soho Square, London W1D 4FA. *020 7745 4545*

Women's Football Conference: Mike Appleby, Wembley Stadium, PO Box 1966, London SW1P 9EQ. *0844 980 8200*

League Managers Association: The Camkin Suite, 1 Pegasus House, Tachbrook Park, Warwick CV34 6LW. *01926 831 556. Fax: 01926 429 781*

Institute of Football Management and Administration: Camkin House, 8 Charles Court, Budbrooke Road, Warwick CV34 5LZ. *01926 411 884.*

World Cup (1966) Association: Hon. Secretary, David Duncan, 96 Glenlea Road, Eltham, London SE9 1DZ.

The Ninety-Two Club: Mr M. Kimberley, The Ninety-Two Club, 153 Hayes Lane, Kenley, Surrey CR8 5HP.

Association of Provincial Football Supporters Clubs in London: Tina A. Robertson, 45 Durham Avenue, Heston, Middlesex TW5 0HG. *0208 843 9854*

World Association of Friends of English Football: Carlisle Hill, Gluck, Habichthof 2, D24939 Flensburg, Germany. *0049 461 4700222*

Football Postcard Collectors Club: PRO: Bryan Horsnell, 275 Overdown Road, Tilehurst, Reading RG31 6NX. *0118 942 4448 (and fax)*

UK Programme Collectors Club: PM Publications, 38 Lowther Road, Norwich NR4 6QW. *01603 449 237*

Programme Monthly & Football Collectable Magazine: 11 Tannington Terrace, London N5 1LE.

Scottish Football Historians Association: John Lister, 46 Milton Road, Kirkcaldy, Fife KY1 1TL. *01592 268718*

Phil Gould (Licensed Football Agent), c/o Whoppit Management Ltd, P. O. Box 27204, London N11 2WS. *07071 732 468. Fax: 07070 732 469*

The Scandinavian Union of Supporters of British Football: Postboks, 15 Stovner, N-0913 Oslo, Norway.

Programme Promotions: P.O. Box 209, Hounslow, Middlesex TW3 4QD. *01923 680 988* Web: www.footballprogrammes.com

Football Safety Officers Association: Chris Patzelt, P.O. Box 7482, Alfreton, Derbyshire. *0114 288 3366.*

Football Foundation: 30 Gloucester Place, London W1U 8FF. *0845 345 4555*

Football Licensing Authority: 27 Harcourt House, 19 Cavendish Square, London W1G 0PL. *0207 491 7191*

Sport England: 16 Upper Woburn Place, London WC1H 0QP. *0207 388 1277*

Association of Football Badge Collectors: K. Wilkinson, 18 Hinton St, Fairfield, Liverpool L6 3AR.

Soccer Nostalgia: G. Wallis, Albion Chambers, 1 Albion Road, Birchington, Kent CT7 9DN. *01303 275 432.*

Sir Norman Chester Centre for Football Research: Department of Sociology, University of Leicester LE1 7RH. *0116 252 2741/5.*

Sports Turf Research Unit: Bingley, West Yorkshire BD16 1AU. *01274 565 131*

FOOTBALL CLUB CHAPLAINCY

Younger or more recent readers of the *Sky Sports Football Yearbook* may perhaps not be aware that some thirty per cent of our current Premier and Football League clubs owe their very existence to a church or Sunday school, or an individual clergyman. That being so, at those clubs today the involvement of a chaplain is a perfectly natural expectation. Many other clubs involve a local clergyman when the need for him arises, so that a relationship grows up between them or circumstances encourage or permit.

Of course, the fact used to be that many clubs were decidedly reticent about their origins or links with a church or parson, but that has now changed, and whilst there remain a number of League clubs that have never had a chaplain (or have resolutely declared that they never will have one!), almost always today, a club that has experienced the benefits of such an appointment will testify to its value.

And don't forget that some clubs have had a chaplain (though the current one may not be the original one!), for nearly fifty years: that fact is beyond contradiction and speaks volumes about the value a clergyman is able to provide to a major football club.

THE REV

OFFICIAL CHAPLAINS TO FA PREMIERSHIP AND FOOTBALL LEAGUE CLUBS

Co-Chaplains Revs Mike Pusey and George Newton – Aldershot Town; Rev Ken Baker – Aston Villa; Rev Peter Amos – Barnsley; Rev Ken Howles – Blackburn R; Rev Michael Ward – Blackpool; Rev Phil Mason – Bolton W; Rev Andy Rimmer – Bournemouth; Rev Paul Deo – Bradford City Centre of Excellence; Rev Derek Cleave – Bristol C; Rev Dave Jeal – Bristol R; Rev Mark Hirst – Burnley; Rev David Ottley – Bury; Rev Dr John Weaver – Cardiff C; Rev Alun Jones – Carlisle U; Rev Matt Baker – Charlton Ath/Pastoral Supp. Direc.; Rev Malcolm Allen – Cheltenham T; Rev Jim McGlade – Chesterfield; Rev Steve Clapham – Crewe Alex; Rev Chris Roe – Crystal Palace; Rev Tony Luke – Derby Co; Rev Stephen Clark – Doncaster R; Co-Chaplains Henry Corbett and Harry Ross – Everton; Rev Gary Piper – Fulham; Rev Richard Hayton – Gillingham; Rev Allen Bagshawe – Hull C; Rev Kevan McCormack – Ipswich T; Rev Paul Welch – Leeds U; Rev Andrew Hulley – Leicester C; Rev Alan Comfort – Leyton Orient; Rev Bill Bygroves – Liverpool; Rev Howard Stringer – Macclesfield T; Rev Peter Horlock – Manchester C; Rev John Boyers – Manchester U; Rev Canon Owen Beament – Millwall; Rev Ron Smith – Milton Keynes D; Rev Glyn Evans – Newcastle United Academy; Co-Chaplains Revs Arthur Bowles and Albert Cadmore – Norwich C; Rev Steve Silvester – Nottingham F; Rev Canon Mark Tanner – Notts Co; Rev John Simmons – Oldham Ath; Rev Richard Longfoot – Peterborough U; Rev Arthur Goode – Plymouth Arg; Co-Chaplains Revs Jonathan Jeffrey and Mick Mellows – Portsmouth; Rev John Hibberts – Port Vale; Rev Chris Nelson – Preston NE; Co-Chaplains Revs Bob Mayo and Cameron Collington – QPR; Rev Steven Prince – Reading; Rev Alan Wright – Scunthorpe U; Rev Nigel Manges – Sheffield U; Rev Peter Allen – Sheffield W; Rev Christopher Deakin – Shrewsbury T; Rev Andy Bowerman – Southampton; Fr Marc Lyden-Smith – Sunderland; Rev Kevin Johns – Swansea C; Rev Simon Stevenette – Swindon T; Rev Tim Smith – Torquay U; Fr Gerald Courell – Tranmere R; Rev Martin Butt – Walsall; Rev Clive Ross – Watford; Rev Alan Bolding – West Ham U; Co-Chaplains Revs David Wright and Steve Davies – Wolverhampton W; Rev John Roberts – Wycombe W; Rev Jim Pearce – Yeovil T.

The chaplains hope that those who read this page will see the value and benefit of chaplaincy work in football and will take appropriate steps to spread the word where this is possible. They would also like to thank the editors of the Football Yearbook *for their continued support for this specialist and growing area of work.*

For further information, please contact: SCORE (Sports Chaplaincy Offering Resources and Encouragement), PO Box 123, Sale, Cheshire M33 4ZA). Telephone 0161 962 6068 or email admin@scorechaplaincy.org.uk.

OBITUARIES

Gary Ablett (Born Liverpool, 19 November 1965. Died 1 January 2012.) Gary Ablett was a versatile defender who made over 100 senior appearances for three clubs, Liverpool, Everton and Birmingham City, and won international honours for England at U21 level. He established a reputation as a solid and reliable defender at Anfield and was a member of the team defeated by Wimbledon in the 1988 FA Cup final. He returned to Wembley 12 months later and this time secured a winners' medal as the Reds defeated Merseyside rivals Everton after extra time. He later joined the Toffees, winning a second Cup winners' medal in 1995 before concluding his career with spells at Birmingham City, Blackpool and in the USA with Long Island Rough Riders. On retiring as a player he coached with both Everton and Liverpool, then had a spell as manager of Stockport County, before returning to coaching at Ipswich.

Jimmy Adamson (Born Ashington, Northumberland, 4 April 1929. Died 8 November 2011.) Jimmy Adamson developed in junior football in the North East before joining the Clarets as a professional in January 1947. He made his first-team debut in February 1951 and immediately established himself in the line-up, remaining as a regular for the next 11 seasons. An ever present in 1959–60 when he captained the team to the Football League title, he helped Burnley remain successful over the next few seasons and in 1961–62 they came close to achieving the coveted double, finishing runners-up in the League and going down 3-1 to Tottenham Hotspur in the FA Cup final. That season he received further recognition for his performances when he was awarded the Footballer of the Year title. After retiring as a player, Jimmy served Burnley as coach and then manager, later having spells in charge of Sparta Rotterdam, Sunderland and Leeds United before leaving football.

Jimmy Adamson

Flórián Albert (Born Hercegszántó, Hungary, 15 September 1941. Died Budapest, Hungary, 31 October 2011.) Florian Albert was a skilful and elegant striker who spent his entire playing career with Ferencvaros. He was one of the key figures for Hungary, winning 75 caps between 1959 and 1974, and in 1967 he was chosen as the European Footballer of the Year.

Dennis Alexander (Born Nottingham, 19 February 1935. Died 11 November 2011.) Dennis Alexander was on Nottingham Forest's books as a youngster, but although he broke into the first team he was never able to establish himself in the line-up. He then spent a short period on the books of Brighton without adding to his total of appearances, before adding a further 18 games for Gateshead in the 1958–59 season. Dennis subsequently returned to the East Midlands, signing for Ilkeston Town.

Ken Bainbridge (Born Barking, Essex, 15 January 1921. Died June 2011.) Ken Bainbridge was a pacy winger who made almost 100 wartime appearances for West Ham and continued to add to his total in the early post-war years. He is credited with scoring the fastest goal at the Boleyn Ground when he netted after 11 seconds against Barnsley in August 1949. Ken later played for Reading and Southend, taking his total of peacetime appearances beyond the 250-mark before joining Southern League club Chelmsford City.

Clive Baker (Born Adwick-le-Street, Doncaster, 5 July 1934. Died 20 February 2012.) Clive Baker made 58 League appearances as a player with Halifax Town in the late 1950s, but became much better known as a coach. He coached with Rotherham, Hartlepool and York and then spent 20 years on the backroom staff of Sheffield Wednesday where he went on to become director of the club's academy before retiring in November 1984.

Keith Bannister (Born Sheffield, 27 January 1923. Died Rotherham, 13 March 2012.) Keith Bannister was a right back who signed for Sheffield Wednesday in February 1945. He was mostly a reserve during his time with the Owls, but was a regular during the 1951–52 campaign when he captained the team to the Second Division title. He spent a season at Chesterfield but later returned to Hillsborough, serving the club for many years as a scout and then as manager of the club's recreation facilities.

Les Bardsley (Born Stockport, 18 August 1925. Died 30 January 2012.) Les Bardsley was on Manchester City's books as a youngster then played for Linfield before joining Bury towards the end of the 1947–48 season. He went on to make over 200 appearances for the Shakers over the next six seasons. Brief spells with Barrow and Mossley followed before he was appointed to the backroom staff at Bristol City. Les gave City 21 years of service as trainer and physio before eventually retiring.

Ray Barlow

Ray Barlow (Born Swindon, 17 August 1926. Died 13 March 2012.) Ray Barlow was one of the post-war greats for West Bromwich Albion. A tall, stylish wing half, he signed for the Baggies during the war and established himself in the line-up in the second half of the 1948–49 promotion campaign. He went on to become a key figure in the team throughout the 1950s, making over 400 Football League appearances and he was the last surviving member of the side that defeated Preston 3-2 to win the 1954 FA Cup final. Ray departed from The Hawthorns in August 1960 and spent a single season with Birmingham City before leaving senior football. He gained one full cap for England, featuring against Northern Ireland in October 1954.

George Beattie (Born Aberdeen, 16 June 1925. Died Newport, 10 March 2012.) George Beattie was a skilful inside forward who signed for Southampton in the summer of 1947. However, he made just one appearance for the Saints before moving on to Gloucester City. He subsequently returned to senior football with Newport County where he made over 100 Football League appearances then played for Bradford Park Avenue before returning to Gloucester where he was a member of the team that defeated Yeovil to win the Southern League Cup in 1955–56.

Frank Beaumont (Born Hoyland, Barnsley, 22 December 1939. Died 6 November 2011.) Frank Beaumont began his career as a young forward with Barnsley, making his first-team debut at the age of 17. In September 1961 he moved on to Bury and he was a member of the Shakers' team that reached the semi-finals of the League Cup in 1962–63. Frank subsequently spent two seasons with Fourth Division strugglers Stockport County, taking his total of Football League appearances past the 200 mark. He later became player-manager of then non-league club Macclesfield Town, guiding them to victory in the first-ever FA Trophy final against Telford at Wembley in 1970.

Alfie Biggs (Born Bristol, 8 February 1936. Died Poole, Dorset, 20 April 2012.) Alfie Biggs was a goalscoring centre forward who hit the net almost 200 times in a 15-year career with Bristol Rovers in between which was sandwiched a season with Preston. Brave and powerful, one of the highlights of his career came in January 1956 when he scored twice in a famous 4-0 FA Cup victory over Manchester United. Alfie later had spells with Walsall and Swansea before leaving senior football in the summer of 1970.

Bobby Black (Born Thornhill, Dumfriesshire, circa 1927. Died Bristol, 4 June 2012.) Bobby Black was a goalscoring right winger who began his career with East Fife in the closing seasons of wartime emergency football. He went on to become a member of the team that won the Scottish League Cup and reached the Scottish Cup final in 1949–50. After losing his place in the side he moved on to Queen of the South where he became something of a legendary figure, scoring 120 goals from 346 appearances to make him the Doonhamers' all-time second-top scorer. Bobby was released in 1961 and moved south to play for Bath City.

Jimmy Bloomer, Snr. (Born Rutherglen, Lanarkshire, 10 April 1926. Died 7 December 2011.) Jimmy Bloomer was a centre forward who joined Hull City from Strathclyde Juniors shortly after the war. Although he managed only a handful of appearances for the Tigers he went on to star for Grimsby Town, scoring regularly when making 109 appearances between 1949 and 1955. He later played for King's Lynn.

Arthur Bottom (Born Sheffield, 28 February 1930. Died Sheffield, 18 April 2012.) Centre forward Arthur Bottom is best known for a four-year spell with York City in the mid 1950s, where he scored 105 goals in 158 games and led the team to a place in the FA Cup semi-finals in 1954–55. He began his career at Sheffield United and also played for Newcastle and Chesterfield before leaving the senior game.

Harry Boyle (Born Glasgow, 22 April 1924. Died Southport, 9 April 2012.) Full back Harry Boyle was recruited by Southport from Murton Colliery Welfare in the 1947 close season and went on to make over 90 first-team appearances during a three-year stay at Haig Avenue. He added a further 150 outings for Rochdale and eventually moved into coaching, his career including a spell in charge of the Zambia national team.

Gerry Bridgwood (Born Stoke on Trent, 17 October 1944. Died 2 March 2012.) Gerry Bridgwood was a local lad who developed through the youth set-up at Stoke City, signing professional terms on reaching the age of 17. He made his first-team debut for the Potters as a teenager and was initially an understudy on the right wing for Stanley Matthews, although later in his career he became a versatile midfield player. He made over 100 senior appearances for Stoke, but never quite managed to establish himself in the line-up and in February 1969 he moved on to Shrewsbury Town. He remained with the Shrews until the summer of 1973, featuring regularly in the side before injuries brought his career to a premature end at the age of 28.

Brian Bromley (Born Burnley, 20 March 1946. Died Southampton, 9 March 2012.) Brian Bromley was an inside forward who gained England youth international honours and spent five years as a professional with Bolton Wanderers, making over 150 Football League appearances. He went on to play for Portsmouth, Brighton and Reading before leaving the senior game.

Peter Brown (Born Andover, Hampshire, 13 July 1934. Died Andover, Hampshire, 8 December 2011.) Peter Brown was a winger or inside forward who joined Southampton from local football in January 1952. He spent almost six years on the club's books but was mostly a reserve during his stay. He featured more regularly during a two-year spell with Wrexham before returning south to play for Poole Town.

Roger Brown (Born Tamworth, Staffs, 12 December 1952. Died 17 August 2011.) Roger Brown was a tall, commanding central defender, who drifted into non-league football after a period as an apprentice with Walsall. He resurrected his career at Bournemouth and went on to enjoy his best seasons at Fulham between 1980 and 1983. He was ever-present in the 1981–82 team when he scored 12 goals, including a vital equaliser to earn a 1-1 draw with Lincoln City to clinch promotion. He subsequently returned to Bournemouth and then Weymouth.

Phil Burn (Born 14 January 1969. Died March 2012.) Phil Burn was an attacking midfield player who made almost 70 first-team appearances for Raith Rovers between 1988 and 1992. He subsequently spent four seasons with Irish League club Ballymena United before returning to Scotland where he turned out in junior football for a number of clubs including Armadale Thistle.

Steve Buttle (Born Norwich, 1 January 1953. Died Norwich, 5 June 2012.) Steve Buttle was an apprentice with Ipswich Town, but it was only when he moved on to sign for Bournemouth in August 1973 that he played first-team football. He made over 130 appearances for the Cherries then joined the migration of players to the United States in the mid-1970s. Steve went on to become a legendary figure for the Seattle Sounders where he spent five years as a regular in the team, earning a reputation as a tenacious and hard working midfield player.

Larry Canning (Born Cowdenbeath, 1 November 1925. Died 4 April 2012.) Larry Canning was capped for Scotland Schoolboys before moving south. He signed for Aston Villa during the war but managed just 41 senior appearances in seven years as a professional before moving on to Kettering Town. He also had a very brief association with Northampton Town before retiring as a player. He became much better known as a reporter for BBC Radio, contributing to the Sports Report programme for many years.

David Cargill (Born Arbroath, 21 July 1936. Died 20 November 2011.) David Cargill was a speedy winger who spent his formative years with Burnley and Sheffield Wednesday, but is best known for the two years he spent as a regular with Derby County between 1958 and 1960, He then had a brief association with Lincoln City before he returned north where he made over 100 appearances for Arbroath before leaving at the end of the 1964–65 season.

Giorgio Chinaglia (Born Carrara, Italy, 24 January 1947. Died Naples, Florida, United States, 1 April 2012.) Giorgio Chinaglia made just a handful of senior appearances as a youngster for Swansea Town in the mid-1960s, but went on to become one of the all-time great strikers for Lazio and then New York Cosmos. He also won 14 caps for Italy.

Garry Church (Born Pontefract, 20 September 1944. Died Beverley, 24 December 2011.) Garry Church was a wing half who was on the books of Bradford PA in the early 1960s. His senior career consisted of a run of four games deputising at right half for Jimmy Scoular in September 1963.

Willie Corbett (Born Falkirk, 31 August 1922. Died Bonnybridge, Stirlingshire, 1 August 2011.) Willie Corbett was a determined centre half who joined Celtic in May 1941. He featured both for the Celts and as a guest for West Ham during the war years when he was also capped by Scotland. After the war he remained at Parkhead, making over 50 peacetime appearances before become something of a wanderer, spending time with Preston North End, Leicester City, Yeovil, Dunfermline and Morton before retiring at the end of the 1952–53 season.

George Crichton (Born Leslie, Fife, 11 December 1925. Died June 2011.) George Crichton was a defender who featured for Workington in their final season as a North Eastern League club and also in their inaugural Football League campaign. He remained with the club until the summer of 1954, but was mostly a reserve and only made four League appearances.

Peter Croker (Born Kingston upon Thames, 21 December 1921. Died 7 December 2011.) Peter Croker was a full back who was on the books of Charlton Athletic as an amateur during the war before turning professional in November 1945. He made over 60 appearances for the Addicks and gained an FA Cup winners' medal in 1947 as a member of the team that defeated Burnley 1-0. He later spent a season with Watford and also played for Gravesend & Northfleet before returning to The Valley as a scout.

Neil Davids (Born Bingley, Yorkshire, 22 September 1955. Died Poulton-le-Fylde, Lancashire, 23 December 2011.) Neil Davids was on the books of Leeds United and Norwich City as a youngster, winning England Youth international honours. He later played for Swansea City, but it was only when he joined Wigan Athletic in the 1978 close season that he gained regular first-team football. He played in the Latics' first-ever Football League fixture, against Hereford United, and went on to make over 60 appearances during his stay with the club.

Eamon Deacy (Born Galway, Republic of Ireland, 1 October 1958. Died Galway, Republic of Ireland, 13 February 2012.) Eamon Deacy was a left back who played League of Ireland football for Galway Rovers as a teenager before joining Aston Villa in March 1979. He featured for Villa in the team that won the Football League title in 1980–81 but made only 33 League appearances during his stay before returning to Ireland to play for Galway United. Eamon won four caps for the Republic of Ireland.

Malcolm Devitt (Born Bradford, 26 January 1937. Died Cyprus, 12 February 2012.) Malcolm Devitt was a wing half or inside forward who signed for Bradford City as an amateur, making his bow in League football before graduating to professional status in March 1959. He made over 100 competitive appearances during his time at Valley Parade before moving on to play for Wisbech Town.

Charlie Dore (Born Portsmouth, 22 January 1931. Died 3 November 2011.) Goalkeeper Charlie Dore signed for Portsmouth from local football in May 1950 and spent three seasons as a professional at Fratton Park. Although mostly a reserve, he made 18 Football League appearances during his stay before moving on to play for Worcester City and then Guildford City.

George Duncan (Born Glasgow, 16 January 1937. Died Chelmsford, 4 February 2012.) George Duncan was an outside right who won representative honours for Scotland Schoolboys before joining Rangers. However, he was mostly a reserve during his time at Ibrox and also in a season with Southend. He signed for Chesterfield in August 1961 and was a regular in four seasons with the Spireites, making over 150 appearances before moving on to Chelmsford City.

Gordon Dyas (Born Hednesford, Staffs, 17 May 1936. Died January 2012.) Gordon Dyas was a wing half who developed with Hednesford Town before signing for Walsall in the summer of 1955. He spent a season with the Saddlers, making 13 first-team appearances, before returning to the non-league game with Burton Albion.

Stan Earl (Born Alton, Hampshire, 9 July 1928. Died Yeovil, 26 February 2012.) Stan Earl was a full back who spent almost a decade in the game as a professional making some 64 Football League appearances. Stan began his career as a reserve with Portsmouth and later spent time with both Leyton Orient and Swindon. He left the senior game in the summer of 1958 and signed for Southern League club Yeovil Town.

Jack Evans (Born Coventry, 11 March 1926. Died 15 April 2012.) Jack Evans was a centre forward who signed for Coventry City during the war, but although he stayed on the club's books for a decade he was mostly a reserve and made just a handful of first-team appearances. He left Highfield Road in the summer of 1952 to join Nuneaton Borough. Jack was a part-time player who was also employed in the motor industry.

Harry Fearnley (Born Dewsbury, Yorkshire, 27 May 1923. Died Morley, Yorkshire, 6 January 2012.) Harry Fearnley was a goalkeeper who joined Leeds United during the 1944–45 season, but he was mostly a back-up at Elland Road and after a short spell with Halifax Town he signed for Newport County in July 1949. He spent four seasons on the books of the South Wales club and made over 100 first-team appearances before returning to Yorkshire to play for Selby Town, He later made a single appearance for Rochdale in the 1955–56 season.

Paul Feasey (Born Hull, 4 May 1933. Died Cottingham, East Yorkshire, 12 January 2012.) Paul Feasey spent 17 years on the books of Hull City after signing for the club as an amateur in August 1949. It was not until September 1956 that he established himself in the line-up and he retained the centre half position until April 1962, rarely missing a game. A member of the team that won promotion from Division Three in 1958–59, he went on to make a total of 304 competitive appearances for the Tigers. Paul left Boothferry Park in the summer of 1966 and took over as player-manager of Goole Town.

Willie Fernie (Born Kinglassie, Fife, 22 November 1928. Died Glasgow, 1 July 2011.) Willie Fernie was a very skilful inside forward who joined Celtic in October 1948 from Fife junior outfit Kinglassie Colliery. He was a regular at Parkhead from the 1952–53 season, assisting the team to a League and Scottish Cup double in 1953–54. Willie made almost 300 appearances before moving south to sign for Middlesbrough in December 1958. He was back with Celtic in October 1960 but just stayed for the season before seeing out his career with St Mirren and Alloa. Willie won 12 caps for Scotland and also won honours for the Scottish League representative side.

Jimmy Field (Died Doncaster, 27 May 2011.) Jimmy Field was capped for Scotland Amateurs against Wales in March 1960, turning out at left back in the 2-2 draw at Rugby Park. At the time he was playing for Methilhill Strollers, while he also turned out for Thornton Hibs and Blairgowrie. He later moved to South Yorkshire where he played in Yorkshire League football.

Alf Fields (Born Canning Town, London, 15 November 1918. Died 14 November 2011.) Centre half Alf Fields joined Arsenal in May 1937 and made his first-team debut for the Gunners shortly before war broke out. He added further appearances when peacetime football resumed in 1946–47 but then suffered a bad injury in September 1947. Once fit again he continued to play for the club's reserve team and eventually joined the backroom staff at Highbury, going on to serve as a coach, trainer and physio until his retirement in 1983.

Ken Fletcher (Born Liverpool, 31 December 1931. Died Corowa, New South Wales, Australia, 13 October 2011.) Full back Ken Fletcher represented Liverpool Schoolboys and then signed for Everton, but failed to make the first team at Goodison Park. In the summer of 1953 he joined Chester where he gained Football League experience, making 34 appearances in three seasons before moving on to non-league Prescot Cables. Ken later emigrated to Australia where he played for the Dandenong club of Victoria.

James Forshaw (Born Circa 1925. Died 3 November 2011.) James Forshaw was a wartime player for Tranmere Rovers. He made a total of 12 appearances for the Prenton Park club in 1944–45 and 1945–46.

Jock Forsyth (Born Circa 1940. Died Markinch, Glenrothes, Fife, 26 April 2012.) Jock Forsyth was a centre half who joined Raith Rovers from Newburgh juniors in the summer of 1961. He spent two seasons with the Kirkcaldy club and also turned out for Brechin City and Alloa before leaving the senior game. He subsequently gained a Scottish Junior Cup runners-up medal with Glenrothes and went on to serve the Fife club as manager, leading them to Junior Cup success in 1975.

Bernard Gallacher (Born Johnstone, Renfrewshire, 22 March 1967. Died Sutton Coldfield, 28 August 2011.) Bernard Gallacher was an attacking left back who spent six seasons on the books of Aston Villa. He joined the club from school and went on to become a near ever-present in the team that in the team that won promotion to the top flight in 1987–88. He later lost his place in the side and went on to play for Doncaster Rovers, Brighton and Northampton before leaving the senior game at the end of the 1993–94 season.

Eddie Gibbins (Born Shoreditch, London, 24 March 1926. Died Kingston St Mary, Somerset, 7 August 2011.) Eddie Gibbins was associated with Tottenham Hotspur for 15 years, joining the club as an amateur in April 1944. A regular in the club's 'A' and reserve teams in the immediate post-war years, he made four first-team appearances, all of which came in the early part of 1953. He later worked in the club ticket office and had spells as manager and coach of a number of non-league clubs in the London area.

Siggi Gíslason (Born Reykjavik, Iceland, 25 June 1968. Died Reykjavik, Iceland, 16 January 2012.) Siggi Gíslason was a neat midfield player who spent most of his career in his native Iceland, turning out for IA Akranes and KR Reykjavik. He spent four months on loan to Stoke City during the 1999–2000 season, making a total of 12 competitive appearances during his stay in the Potteries. Siggi won 22 caps for Iceland during his career, his early death being caused by cancer.

John Goodchild (Born Sherburn Hill, Co Durham, 2 January 1939. Died 25 August 2011.) John Goodchild was a versatile forward who joined Sunderland in September 1956 and spent five seasons on the books at Roker Park, making 45 competitive appearances. The best years of his career were spent at Brighton where he scored 44 goals in 163 Football League matches and he was a member of the team that won the Division Four title in 1964–65. He later played for York City and Darlington before leaving the senior game.

Jackie Gorman (Born Lurgan, Co Armagh, 6 January 1939. Died Portadown, Co Armagh, 7 April 2012.) Jackie Gorman was a pacy winger who won three amateur international caps for Northern Ireland in the early 1960s. He played his club football for RUC, Cliftonville, Newry Town, Glenavon and Portadown.

Russell Green (Born Donington, Lincs, 13 August 1933. Died Gainsborough, Lincs, 21 April 2012.) Russell Green was on Lincoln City's books as a youngster without making the grade but returned to Sincil Bank from Corby Town in May 1957 and went on to make over 100 Football League appearances for the Imps. A versatile player, he was mostly used in defence but could also play as an emergency centre forward and on one occasion he scored a hat-trick in that role. Russell moved on to become player-coach of Gainsborough Trinity in the summer of 1964, leading them to the Midland League title in 1966–67.

Roy Greenwood (Born Croydon, 22 May 1931. Died Caterham, Surrey, 31 December 2011.) Roy Greenwood was a solid and uncompromising left back who joined Crystal Palace from Beckenham Town in October 1954. Almost immediately he was called up into the Eagles' first team and for the next four seasons he was mostly a regular in the side, making over 100 senior appearances. He lost his place during the 1958–59 campaign and the following summer he moved on for a brief association with Bedford Town in the Southern League.

Ernie Gregory (Born Stratford, London, 10 November 1921. Died Basildon, Essex, 21 January 2012.) Ernie Gregory was a goalkeeper who progressed from the West Ham Schools' team to join the groundstaff at Upton Park in 1936. As a youngster he also played for Leytonstone, and it was not until the 1946–47 season that he made his Football League debut. Ernie was a regular in the Hammers' line-up for most of the 1950s, winning international honours for England B against France in May 1952. The club's regular 'keeper in the 1957–58 promotion team, he eventually lost his place in the side the following season, retiring as a player having made more than 400 first-team appearances. He remained at West Ham on the coaching staff and it was not until May 1987, some 51 years after arriving at Upton Park, that he eventually departed.

Derek Grierson (Born 5 October 1931. Died 7 September 2011.) Derek Grierson made his name as a goalscoring inside forward with Queen's Park, for whom he made his debut at the age of 16. He was honoured by Scotland Amateurs and also made the Great Britain squad for the 1952 Olympic Games. On his return from Helsinki he signed for Rangers and he was leading scorer for the Ibrox club in 1952–53 as they earned a League and Cup double. He suffered a bad injury at the beginning of 1955 which kept him out of action for many months and after recovering fitness moved on to Falkirk, gaining a second Scottish Cup winners' medal in 1957. Thereafter he did the rounds, turning out for Arbroath, Stirling Albion, Forfar, Coleraine and Cowdenbeath before leaving the senior game at the end of the 1961–62 season.

Ralph Gubbins (Born Ellesmere Port, 31 January 1932. Died 11 September 2011.) Ralph Gubbins was a centre forward who began his senior career with Bolton Wanderers. He spent seven years on the books at Burnden Park and although mostly serving as back-up to the legendary Nat Lofthouse he made over 100 first-team appearances. A highlight of his time at the club came when he appeared in the 1958 FA Cup semi-final with Blackburn at Maine Road, when he scored both goals as Wanderers progressed to the final with a 2-1 victory. Ralph later spent two seasons with Hull before concluding his senior career with a productive spell at Tranmere, which saw him score 37 goals in 107 games.

Gordon Haigh (Born Barnsley, 18 August 1921. Died 22 August 2011.) Gordon Haigh was an inside forward who joined Burnley from works' team Ransomes & Marles during the 1945–46 season. He spent seven years as a professional in the game, making just over 50 appearances for the Clarets, Bournemouth and Watford and later returned to Lancashire, turning out for Rossendale United and Nelson.

Tony Hapgood (Born Kettering, 13 June 1930. Died Blackburn, 1 September 2011.) Tony Hapgood was a winger who joined Burnley shortly after the war. The son of the legendary Eddie Hapgood, he made seven appearances for the Clarets and then had a season with Watford where he played once in the Football League. Thereafter he switched to the non-league game with Ashford Town and Chatham.

Harry Hart (Born Sheffield, 29 September 1926. Died Morecambe, 11 February 2012.) Harry Hart was an inside forward who joined Rotherham United from local football in the 1945–46 season. However, first-team opportunities were hard to come by at Millmoor, and in fact this proved to be the case for Harry throughout his career when he moved on to Coventry then Grimsby, with his final tally reaching a total of 33 Football League appearances. In the 1954 close season he joined Frickley Colliery.

James Henderson (Born 18 October 1976. Died Denny, Stirlingshire, 2 December 2011.) James Henderson was a left-sided midfield player who spent four seasons on the books of Stenhousemuir in the 1990s. Initially a reserve, he was a regular in the line-up during the 1996–97 season and went on to make over 80 senior appearances before leaving the senior game.

Brian Heward (Born Lincoln, 17 July 1935. Died South Hykeham, nr. Lincoln, 21 April 2012.) Brian Heward was an uncompromising centre half who began his career with Scunthorpe United with whom he made over 150 appearances, assisting them in their Second Division days. In the summer of 1961 he moved on to join Lincoln City and remained at Sincil Bank for six seasons, separated by a brief spell in Australia with Bankstown.

Adam Hodge (Born 1 December 1939. Died Ballingry, Fife, 30 September 2011.) Goalkeeper Adam Hodge joined Alloa Athletic from Fife junior outfit Blairhall Colliery in the summer of 1961 and went straight in the first team. He retained the 'keeper's jersey for the next eight seasons, making over 250 competitive appearances for the club. He is one of only 20 players to make more than 200 appearances for Alloa since the war.

Peter Hooper (Born Teignmouth, Devon, 2 February 1933. Died Barnstaple, Devon, 13 August 2011.) Peter Hooper was a winger with a powerful shot and good control on the ball. His best years were spent at Bristol Rovers, for whom he made over 300 appearances, scoring 107 goals, between 1953 and 1962. He also won representative honours for the Football League against the Irish League in October 1957. Peter later had spells with Cardiff and Bristol City before switching to non-league football with Worcester City.

Ron Howells (Born Llanelli, 18 September 1931. Died Myrtle Hill, Carmarthenshire, 29 December 2011.) Ron Howells was a goalkeeper who played for Swansea Town and Barry Town before signing for Cardiff City in the summer of 1950. He went straight into the first team at Ninian Park and was the club's regular 'keeper until January 1956, making over 150 appearances. After a season in the Southern League with Worcester City he returned to the Football League and made a further 80 appearances for Chester. Ron also won two caps for Wales.

Laurie Hughes (Born Liverpool, 2 March 1924. Died 9 September 2011.) Laurie Hughes played as a teenaged amateur for Tranmere Rovers during the war before signing for Liverpool in February 1943. A centre half, he was a mainstay of the Reds' defence in the early post-war years and went on to make over 300 appearances. He gained an FA Cup runners-up medal in 1950 and later that year featured for England in the 1950 World Cup finals, including an appearance in the sensational defeat by the United States. Laurie was capped three times for England.

Ron Humpston (Born Derby, 14 December 1923. Died Cheltenham, 4 January 2012.) Ron Humpston was a goalkeeper who signed for Portsmouth in January 1946 whilst stationed with the Royal Navy nearby. For the next five seasons he provided back-up for the 'keeper's jersey, making nine first-team appearances. Ron later played for Huddersfield Town and Headington United. He went on to manage Gravesend & Northfleet and also had a spell as trainer of the Czech national team.

Albert Johnson (Born Weaverham, Cheshire, 15 July 1920. Died 22 June 2011.) Albert Johnson was a winger who signed for Everton shortly before the outbreak of war. He went on to make nine League appearances for the Toffees in the seasons just after the war, then played fairly regularly for Chesterfield in the 1948–49 season before joining Witton Albion

Ken Johnson (Born Hartlepool, 15 February 1931. Died 29 December 2011.) Ken Johnson joined Hartlepools United from Seaton Holy Trinity Juniors in May 1949, but it was not until the 1953–54 season that he established himself as a first-team regular at the Victoria Ground. He stayed with the club for 15 seasons, making over 400 competitive appearances and establishing a club record of 98 Football League goals.

David Keddie (Born 30 April 1945. Died Sydney, Australia, 12 August 2011.) David Keddie was a forward who made over 50 appearances in two seasons for Alloa Athletic and then spent the 1967–68 season with Forfar where he added further appearances. He subsequently moved to Australia where he continued his playing career and won representative honours including a single cap for his adopted country in October 1970.

Harry Keough (Born St Louis, Missouri, United States, 15 November 1927. Died St Louis, Missouri, United States, 7 February 2012.) Harry Keough was a defender who played for the United States in their famous World Cup victory over England in June 1950. He had captained the team in an earlier World Cup encounter with Spain and in total won 19 caps for his country, also featuring in the 1952 and 1956 Olympic Games. A postman in St Louis, he was a member of the St Louis Kutis team that won the US Open Cup in 1957 and the National Amateur Cup six seasons in a row.

Peter King (Born Liverpool, 5 July 1964. Died 23 February 2012.) Peter King was on Liverpool's books as a youngster but never made it to the first team before moving on to Crewe Alexandra in the 1983 close season. He made over 50 League appearances during two seasons with the Railwaymen and then switched to non-league football, firstly with Southport and then with a string of clubs in the North West.

Barry Kitchener (Born Dagenham, 11 December 1947. Died 30 March 2012.) Barry Kitchener was a legendary figure in the history of Millwall FC. He made a club record total of 523 Football League appearances for the Lions between 1967 and 1982 and was a key figure in the team during his stay at The Den. A powerful, charismatic centre half with great leadership skills, he captained the side. At one point he was ever-present for five seasons in a row and led the team to promotion from Division Three in 1975–76. After retiring as a player Barry later coached the Lions' reserve and youth teams.

George Knight (Born Bolton, 12 May 1921. Died Birmingham, 24 August 2011.) George Knight was an inside forward who made his debut for Burnley in February 1939. He added further appearances that season and was a regular in the side in the early years of wartime football. However, when football resumed normal business in the 1946–47 season he played just one further game before injury brought his career to a close. He later scouted for the Clarets.

Jimmy Lawlor (Born Finglas Bridge, Dublin, Irish Free State, 10 May 1933. Died Bradford, 5 April 2012.) Jimmy Lawlor was a defender who joined Doncaster Rovers from League of Ireland club Drumcondra in the summer of 1952 but in three years at Belle Vue he found it difficult to establish himself in the side. After a spell in the Irish League with Coleraine he returned to Yorkshire, signing for Bradford City. He went on to make over 150 appearances for City before a fractured leg suffered in March 1962 effectively ended his career. Jimmy was capped for the Irish League representative side during his time with Coleraine.

Norman Lawson (Born Hetton-le-Hole, Co Durham, 6 April 1935. Died Sketty, Swansea, 25 September 2011.) Norman Lawson was an outside left or full back who spent six years as a professional in the late 1950s. His best years were spent with Bury, although he also played for Swansea Town and Watford before switching to non-league football with Kettering Town. Norman was also a talented cricketer and later played for the Wales Over 50's team.

Jim Lewis (Born Hackney, London, 26 June 1927. Died Kelvedon Hatch, Essex, 21 November 2011.) Jim Lewis was a tall, pacy winger, who could play across the forward line and who was an amateur throughout his career. He enjoyed a lengthy association with Walthamstow Amateurs but is best known for the six years he spent with Chelsea in the mid-1950s. He was a member of the team that won the club's first-ever League title in 1954–55 and altogether scored 38 goals from 90 Football League appearances during his time at Stamford Bridge. Jim was capped 49 times by England Amateurs and also won representative honours for the Great Britain Olympic squad.

Stan Lloyd (Born West Auckland, 1 October 1924. Died Cleethorpes, 6 July 2011.) Stan Lloyd was a winger who won representative honours for England Schoolboys before joining Sunderland during the war. He featured for the Black Cats in the immediate post-war period before becoming Grimsby Town's record signing in August 1948. Stan went on to play more than 150 games for the Mariners and also had a brief association with Scunthorpe United before leaving the game.

Harry Logan (Born Dundee, circa 1929. Died February 2012.) Harry Logan was best known for his time in junior football in the Dundee area and was centre half for the Lochee Harp team that lost out to Sunnybank in the 1954 Scottish Junior Cup final at Hampden. Earlier in his career he had played senior football in the Scottish League for Arbroath and Brechin City.

Barry Lowes (Born Barrow-in-Furness, 16 March 1939. Died 8 May 2012.) Barry Lowes was a flying winger who came to prominence with Barrow in the early 1960s. He enjoyed success at Workington, where he was a member of the team that won promotion from the Fourth Division in 1963–64 and made over 100 appearances. He later played for Bury, Coventry City and Swindon before injury curtailed his career.

Tommy McAnearney (Born Dundee, 6 January 1933. Died 14 February 2012.) Tommy McAnearney was an intelligent wing half who made over 350 appearances for Sheffield Wednesday. Signed from Dundee junior club St Joseph's in 1950, he spent some 15 years as a player at Hillsborough and featured in two Second Division title-winning sides (1955–56 and 1958–59). He eventually moved on to Peterborough in November 1965, then to Aldershot just four months later. Initially player-coach for the Shots, he enjoyed two spells in charge at the Recreation Ground and was widely regarded as the club's most successful manager having led the team to their first-ever Football League promotion in 1972–73. He also had a spell as manager of Bury.

Tommy McAnearney

Ronnie McCluskey (Born Johnstone, Renfrewshire, 3 November 1936. Died Lochgelly, Fife, 23 June 2011.) Goalkeeper Ronnie McCluskey joined East Fife from Rosyth Recreation in June 1955 and went on to become the club's first choice 'keeper in the

1959–60 season. He spent the 1960–61 campaign with Accrington Stanley, for whom he made four Football League appearances, before moving into non-league football with Gravesend & Northfleet and Gloucester City.

Alan McDonald (Born Belfast, 12 October 1963. Died Lisburn, Co Down, 23 June 2012.) Alan McDonald was a tall and powerful central defender who graduated from the trainee ranks at Queens Park Rangers and went on to spend 16 years as a professional at Loftus Road. He captained the side and made over 450 senior appearances during his stay, also featuring regularly for Northern Ireland, for whom he won 52 caps and appeared in the 1986 World Cup finals. When he eventually left Rangers he spent a season with Swindon Town as a player then remained for a further five years on the backroom staff. He later had spells coaching Northern Ireland U21s and Queens Park Rangers before spending three years as manager of Glentoran. Alan died suddenly after collapsing whilst playing golf.

Willie McDonald (Born Dundee, circa 1934. Died Dundee, 23 March 2012.) Willie McDonald was a winger who joined Dundee United from local junior outfit St Joseph's and went on to make almost 100 appearances during his stay at Tannadice. He subsequently turned out for Stirling Albion and Montrose before returning to St Joseph's as a player and then committee member.

John McLaughlin (Died August 2011.) John McLaughlin signed for Queen's Park from Bonar Bridge in December 1960 and spent 14 years on the club's books, making 182 senior appearances.

Stewart McLean (Born Neilston, Glasgow, 30 August 1923. Died Banff, 11 September 2011.) Stewart McLean signed for Partick Thistle in 1941, but it was not until the 1943–44 season that he played for the Jags in the wartime Southern League. He later became a Bevin Boy and worked at Hickleton Main Colliery in Yorkshire, during which time he turned out with some success for Rotherham United. He eventually returned to Scotland and after unproductive spells with East Fife and Dumbarton he featured for Forfar Athletic and Stenhousemuir.

Jim Malloy (Born Brechin. Died Cranbourne, Melbourne, Australia, 8 April 2012.) Jim Malloy was a centre forward who appeared in Scottish League football towards the end of the 1950s for Brechin City, Cowdenbeath and Forfar Athletic. He subsequently emigrated to Australia where he continued to play in the Victoria State League through until the mid-1960s.

Maurice Masters (Born Circa 1927. Died 10 April 2012.) Maurice Masters was a wing half or inside forward whose career in the Irish League spanned some 23 years. He played for Coleraine, Bangor, Glenavon and Cliftonville, winning three League titles and an Irish Cup winners' medal with the Glens in 1959. He also won eight caps for Northern Ireland amateurs.

Eddie May (Born Epping, Essex, 19 May 1943. Died 14 April 2012.) As a youngster Eddie May played at centre forward for Dagenham before joining Southend in January 1965 where he was converted to centre half. He made over 100 appearances for the Shrimpers then moved on to Wrexham where he played over 300 games, captaining the team that reached the quarter-finals of the European Cup Winners' Cup in 1975–76. After spells with Chicago Sting and Swansea City he switched to coaching and management and he spent time in charge of a number of clubs including Newport County, Cardiff City, Torquay and Brentford.

Frank Munro (Born Broughty Ferry, 25 October 1947. Died Wolverhampton, 16 August 2011.) Frank Munro was one of the stars of the successful Wolves team of the early 1970s, featuring in the 1972 UEFA Cup final and also gaining a League Cup winners' medal in 1974. Frank began his career as a midfielder with Dundee United, later moving on to Aberdeen by which time he had developed into a hard, uncompromising defender. He eventually returned to Scotland in October 1977 and spent a brief period with Celtic before continuing his career in Australia. He won nine full caps for Scotland.

George Nelson (Born Mexborough, Yorkshire, 5 February 1925. Died 8 September 2011.) George Nelson made 24 appearances for Sheffield United during the 1944–45 season and also appeared for the Blades' reserves before joining Lincoln City at the start of the 1946–47 season. His only peacetime appearance came for the Imps at New Brighton in November 1946 when he turned out at left half.

Ollie Norris (Born Londonderry, 1 April 1929. Died Melbourne, Australia, 13 June 2011.) Ollie Norris was a powerful centre forward best known for his time at Bournemouth in the mid 1950s when he scored 34 goals from 96 Football League appearances. He was one of the stars of the Cherries' team that reached the FA Cup quarter-finals in 1956–57, defeating Wolves and Tottenham Hotspur before going down to a narrow defeat to Manchester United. Ollie began his career with Middlesbrough and also played for Northampton Town and Rochdale before leaving senior football.

Ralph O'Donnell (Born Cudworth, Yorkshire, 17 October 1931. Died May 2011.) Ralph O'Donnell was a centre half who spent some 15 years on the books of Sheffield Wednesday, making almost 200 first-team appearances. He featured in the teams that won the Division Two title in 1951–52 and 1955–56 and later played for Buxton before becoming involved in coaching schools' teams in the Sheffield area.

Sid Ottewell (Born Horsley, Derbyshire, 23 October 1919. Died Eastwood, Notts, 31 January 2012.) Sid Ottewell was an inside forward who made his debut for Chesterfield in April 1937. During the war he served in the RAF and was a member of the professional soccer teams that toured the Indian Subcontinent. He went on to make over 200 senior appearances in a career that also included spells with Birmingham City, Luton, Nottingham Forest, Mansfield and Scunthorpe. He was later manager of several non-league clubs including Spalding United, Bourne Town and Lockheed Leamington.

Mark Ovendale (Born Leicester, 22 November 1973. Died 29 August 2011.) Mark Ovendale was a goalkeeper who was second choice for Northampton Town in the 1994–95 season before joining Barry Town. He enjoyed a successful three-year period with the League of Wales club, featuring in both Champions' League and UEFA Cup action before returning to the Football League with Bournemouth. Mark went on to make over 200 senior appearances for the Cherries, Luton Town and York City before switching to non-league football. His untimely death was a result of cancer.

Len Phillips

John Parke (Born Bangor, Co Down, 6 August 1937. Died 27 August 2011.) John Parke was a full back who spent his formative years with Linfield where he was a member of the famous 'seven-trophy team' of 1961–62. He then spent a season with Hibernian before joining Sunderland where he made over 90 appearances in four seasons. John concluded his career in Belgium with KV Mechelen. He won 14 caps for Northern Ireland and also won representative honours for the Irish League.

Derrick Parker (Born Wivenhoe, Essex, 23 June 1926. Died 8 April 2011.) Derrick Parker signed for West Ham as an inside forward during the war years, later converting to play at half back. He made over 200 first-team appearances for the Hammers and also went on the FA tour of United States and Australia in the summer of 1951. He later spent four seasons with Colchester United, making a further 137 appearances, before becoming player-manager of Stowmarket Town.

Bob Paterson (Born Circa 1931. Died 27 August 2011.) Bob Paterson was a defender who was on the books of Queen's Park where he won representative honours for Scotland Amateurs before moving on to Aberdeen in the summer of 1952. He was mostly a reserve during his stay at Pittodrie before concluding his senior career at Dumbarton.

Mike Pentecost (Born Hounslow, Middlesex, 13 April 1948. Died Durban, South Africa, 7 May 2011.) Mike Pentecost signed for Fulham from Sutton United in the summer of 1966. The Cottagers soon fell from the top flight to Division Three and he was a regular in the side that gained promotion from that division in 1970–71, mostly playing at right back. In January 1973 he moved to South Africa where he played for Durban City and African Wanderers. In his younger days he had represented the England Grammar Schools team.

Jens Petersen (Born Esbjerg, Denmark, 22 December 1941. Died 8 March 2012.) Jens Petersen was a midfield player and sweeper who began his career in his native Denmark with Esbjerg before joining the 'Scandinavian Invasion' of players to Scotland when he signed for Aberdeen at the beginning of 1965. Jens went on to spend the next five years at Pittodrie, making over 200 appearances and gaining a Scottish Cup runners-up medal as a member of the team that lost out to Celtic in the 1967 final. He later had spells in Austria with SK Rapid Vienna and in Belgium with Racing Mechelen. He won 22 caps for Denmark before switching to professional status.

Brian Phillips (Born Cadishead, Salford, 9 November 1931. Died Sutton-in-Ashfield, Notts, 28 March 2012.) Brian Phillips was a powerful stopper centre half who made over 200 senior appearances for Middlesbrough and Mansfield Town in the period from 1954 to 1963. His career was ended due to involvement in the match fixing scandal of the early 1960s and he later worked as an insurance agent. When the ban was lifted he returned to the game as manager of local clubs in Nottinghamshire, taking Rainworth MW to the final of the FA Vase in 1982.

Len Phillips (Born Shoreditch, London, 11 September 1922. Died Portsmouth, 9 December 2011.) Len Phillips was a talented midfield schemer who was one of the stars of the Portsmouth team that won consecutive Football League titles in 1948–49 and 1949–50. After wartime service in the Royal Marines, Len signed for Pompey in January 1946 and remained at Fratton Park for a decade, making over 250 first-team appearances before an injury brought his senior career to an end. He won three full caps for England and also appeared for the Football League representative side.

Cliff Portwood (Born Salford, 17 October 1937. Died Basingstoke, Hampshire, 10 January 2012.) Cliff Portwood was an attacking player who began his career with Preston North End. However, he was unable to break into the first team at Deepdale and moved on to Port Vale in the summer of 1959. He led the scoring charts for Vale in 1960–61 before moving on to Grimsby, helping the Mariners win promotion to Division Two in 1961–62. Cliff finished his senior career at Portsmouth before moving to South Africa to play for Durban United. He went on to become a well-known singer and television personality in Australia in the 1970s.

Graham Rathbone (Born, Newport, Monmouthshire, 22 August 1942. Died Newport, Monmouthshire, 8 January 2012.) Graham Rathbone was a tough centre half who had a no-nonsense approach to his game. He made over 500 senior appearances in a career which saw him play for Newport County, Grimsby Town and Cambridge United. He was a regular for the Mariners for most of the 1971–72 promotion campaign before losing his place to Clive Wigginton.

Ian Reid (Born Marsden, South Shields, Circa 1942. Died 25 July 2011.) Ian Reid was a full back who gained three FA Amateur Cup medals, finishing on the winning side with Crook Town (1964) and Enfield (1967) and as a runner-up with Slough Town (1973). He won 28 caps for the England Amateur team and also featured for Great Britain in the qualifying rounds for the 1968 Olympic Games. Ian, who also played for Hitchin Town, worked as a schoolteacher.

John Ritchie (Born Ashington, Northumberland, 10 April 1944. Died 16 February 2012.) John Ritchie was a quick, hard tackling full back who developed in the North East with Whitley Bay, with whom he won England Amateur international honours. In December 1965 he joined the professional ranks, signing for Port Vale. He quickly won a regular place in the line-up at Vale Park and in April 1967 he was sold to Preston North End. John made over 100 appearances during a five-year stay at Deepdale, although he was affected by injuries, and he then spent a short period with Bradford City. After leaving senior football he played for Stafford Rangers.

George Robb (Born Finsbury Park, London, 1 June 1926. Died 25 December 2011.) George Robb was a direct winger who made 200 competitive appearances for Tottenham Hotspur in the 1950s. A talented amateur with Finchley in his younger days he arrived at White Hart Lane in December 1951 but it was another 18 months before he switched to professional status. George was one of the few players to represent England at both amateur and senior levels in the post-war period, winning his only full cap in the catastrophic defeat to Hungary at Wembley in November 1953. He also represented Great Britain at the 1952 Olympic Games. A serious injury suffered during the 1957–58 campaign eventually led to his retirement.

Jimmy Rodger (Born, New Stevenston, Lanarkshire,1924. Died 5 June 2011.) Jimmy Rodger was a powerful centre half who gained representative honours for Scotland Schools before signing for Hearts in the summer of 1947. However, he found it difficult to establish himself in the side at Tynecastle and after a spell on loan with Stirling Albion he moved on to Third Lanark.

Ronnie Rooke (Born Carlisle, 12 December 1926. Died Kendal, 24 November 2011.) Ronnie Rooke was a winger who made a solitary Football League appearance for Carlisle United, lining up against Darlington at Brunton Park in October 1949. He later played in the Lancashire Combination for Netherfield.

Miki Roque (Born, Tremp, Catalonia, Spain, 8 July 1988. Died 24 June 2012.) Miki Roque joined Liverpool as a teenager making his only first-team appearance for the Reds as a substitute in a Champions' League game with Galatasaray in December 2006. He gained further experience in loan spells with Oldham Athletic and also in Spain before he returned there at the end of his contract in July 2009. He signed for Real Betis and was promoted from the B team to the senior squad for 2010–11. However, in March 2011 he was diagnosed with pelvic cancer and this eventually led to his death at a tragically early age. Miki represented Spain at U19 level.

Terry Ryder (Born Norwich, 3 June 1928. Died Norwich, 24 January 2012.) Terry Ryder was a busy and rather diminutive forward who had a good scoring record with the Norwich junior teams but never really established himself for the Canaries. Nevertheless he won a transfer to higher grade football with Pompey where he found himself well down the pecking order for a first-team place. He was a regular on the right wing in his season at Swindon, finishing as second-top scorer, but then returned to East Anglia to sign for King's Lynn.

Teddy Scott (Born Ellon, Aberdeenshire,1929. Died 20 June 2012.) Teddy Scott was a centre half who gained a Scottish Junior Cup winners' medal with Sunnybank before joining Aberdeen. He made just a solitary first-team appearance for the Dons, against Stirling Albion in February 1956, and also featured in a loan spell with Brechin City. Teddy later returned to Pittodrie where he became a legendary member of the backroom staff, serving the club for almost 50 years.

Alf Setchell (Born Coventry, 1924. Died 26 November 2011.) Alf Setchell was a winger who made 18 appearances for Coventry City during World War Two, when he also featured as a guest for Southport and Morton, but made no peacetime appearances before signing for Kidderminster Harriers.

Jim Shanks (Born Barrow, 31 October 1918. Died Barrow, 10 April 2011.) Jim Shanks joined Barrow from local football and featured in the 1945–46 and 1946–47 seasons for the Bluebirds.

Willie Smith (Died October 2011.) Goalkeeper Willie Smith joined Partick Thistle from junior outfit Linlithgow Rose in 1953. He later spent two seasons with Queen of the South before moving on to Berwick Rangers where he concluded his senior career.

Harry Smyth (Born Belfast, April 1928. Died Londonderry, November 2011.) Harry Smyth was a powerful wing half who signed for Linfield as a teenager in the 1947–48 season. He gained an Irish Cup winners' medal with the Blues in 1950 then transferred to Derry City where he was a member of the team that defeated Glentoran over three matches in 1954 to gain a second winners' medal. He remained with the Candystripes for nine seasons before leaving senior football.

Socrates (Born Belém do Pará, Brazil, 19 February 1954. Died São Paulo, Brazil, 4 December 2011.) Socrates was a tall and elegant midfield general who was one of the iconic players in the Brazil team in the early 1980s. He captained the team at the 1982 World Cup finals and won a total of 60 caps for his country between 1979 and 1986. At club level he principally played for Corinthians and also had a spell in Italy with Fiorentina. He was South American Footballer of the Year in 1983. A qualified medical doctor, he was, as befits his name, a great philosopher who was active in democracy and political campaigns in Brazil.

John Souza (Born Fall River, Massachusetts, United States, 12 July 1920. Died Dover, Pennsylvania, 11 March 2012.) John Souza appeared at inside right in the United States team that sensationally defeated England 1-0 in the 1950 World Cup finals in Brazil. John also played for his country in the 1948 and 1952 Olympic Games matches, while at club level he represented Fall River Ponta Delgada and New York German Hungarians.

Gary Speed

Gary Speed (Born Mancot, Flintshire, 8 September 1969. Died Huntington, Cheshire, 27 November 2011.) Gary Speed was a consummate professional, who spent over 20 seasons as a player in senior football and was both the first player to make 500 Premier League appearances and the most capped outfield player for Wales. A talented left-sided player, mostly used in midfield, he showed excellent leadership skills on the pitch. He began his professional career as an apprentice with Leeds United and went on to help the Elland Road club win the Football League title in 1991–92, the last season before the advent of the Premier League. He moved on to Everton, the club he had supported as a boy, and was appointed captain at Goodison and then Newcastle, where he gained two FA Cup runners-up medals. Spells with Bolton and Sheffield United followed before he was appointed as manager of the Blades in August 2010. However, his stay in the post was to be brief, for the following December he took over as manager of the Wales national team. He was still in post at the time of his tragic death. As a player he had earlier won 47 caps for his country.

Les Speed (Born Caergwrle, Denbighshire, 3 October 1923. Died Ruabon, 5 June 2012.) Les Speed was a wing half who made close on 250 appearances for Wrexham in the period immediately after World War Two. He later had spells as player-manager of Stafford Rangers and Holywell Town.

Tam Spence (Born Airdrie, 4 January 1962. Died 28 April 2012.) Tam Spence was a hard tackling full back who signed for Stirling Albion from Glenboig Juniors shortly after the start of the 1982–83 season. He made over 150 appearances during his stay at Annfield and captained the team that defeated Selkirk 20-0 in a Scottish Cup tie in December 1984. Tam went on to play for Clydebank, Clyde, Kilmarnock, East Fife and Albion Rovers, also having a spell as manager of Albion.

Les Spencer (Born Manchester, 16 September 1936. Died Sale, 4 April 2012.) Les Spencer was a versatile forward who enjoyed two seasons as a regular for Rochdale, finishing as the team's joint-top scorer in 1958–59. His form attracted attention from Luton Town and he moved south in the summer of 1960 only to suffer an injury just a few games into his time at Kenilworth Road, effectively bringing his career to a close.

Bill Spurdle (Born St Peter Port, Guernsey, 28 January 1926. Died St Peter Port, Guernsey, 16 June 2011.) Bill Spurdle was a wing half who made over 350 Football League appearances in a career that spanned the period from 1948 until the summer of 1963. One of the few professional footballers to hail from Guernsey, he began his senior career with Oldham before being sold to Manchester City in January 1950. The six years he spent at Maine Road proved to be the best of his career, with the highlight coming when he lined up on the right wing for the 1955 FA Cup final defeat by Newcastle. He later spent two seasons with Port Vale before returning to Boundary Park to conclude his career with the Latics.

George Stewart (Born Buckie, Banffshire, 17 February 1927. Died Buckie, Banffshire, 4 June 2011.) George Stewart developed a reputation for scoring goals with Buckie Thistle as a teenager, scoring seven times in a match on two consecutive occasions. He went on to play for Dundee and St Mirren, where he topped the goalscoring charts two seasons in a row. Later he scored 136 goals for Accrington at a rate of almost one every game but although he continued to score goals in spells with Coventry and Carlisle he was hampered by injuries. George represented Division Three North against their Southern counterparts in October 1957.

Keith Stott (Born Atherton, Lancashire, 12 March 1944. Died Holme Hall, Chesterfield, 6 March 2012.) Keith Stott was a no-nonsense centre half who was on the books of Manchester City as a youngster. He joined the professional ranks with Crewe in October 1964 and went on to play in over 200 first-team games for the Railwaymen before moving on to Chesterfield where he added a further 150 appearances. Keith later played for Matlock Town.

Bob Swankie (Born Arbroath, 25 February 1931. Died Gloucester, 28 June 2011.) Bob Swankie was a wing half who moved south from Scotland to sign for Burnley. However, he failed to make the first team at Turf Moor and after a spell with Gloucester City he returned to the Football League with Darlington. Bob managed a single senior appearance for the Quakers in the 1953–54 season. He later returned to Gloucester and also played for Kidderminster Harriers and Cinderford Town.

Syd Thomas (Born Machynlleth, Montgomeryshire, 12 November 1919. Died 19 January 2012.) Syd Thomas was a skilful winger who signed for Fulham shortly before the outbreak of war, although it was not until the 1946–47 season that he made his full debut for the club. He assisted the Cottagers when they won the Division Two title in 1948–49 but then moved on to Bristol City where his career was terminated when he contracted tuberculosis. Syd subsequently returned to live in Machynlleth and worked in the family bakery. He was capped four times for Wales.

Chris Thompson (Born Walsall, 24 January 1960. Died 5 June 2012.) Chris Thompson was a hard working attacking midfield player who won England Youth honours. He spent his formative years with Bolton Wanderers before going on to play for Blackburn, Wigan, Blackpool, Cardiff and Walsall. He made over 250 Football League appearances in a career that continued up to the early 1990s.

Lawrie Tierney (Born Leith, 4 April 1959. Died Phoenix, Arizona, United States, 6 December 2011.) Lawrie Tierney was a skilful midfield player who helped Hearts win promotion back to the Premier Division of the Scottish League in 1977–78. He later had brief spells with Hibernian and Wigan before moving to the United States where he played in indoor football for a number of teams including Phoenix Inferno and Golden Bay Earthquakes.

Don Walker (Born Edinburgh, 10 September 1935. Died 21 December 2011.) Don Walker joined Leicester from Tranent Juniors and enjoyed a decent run in the side at left half in the 1957–58 season. Thereafter he struggled to create an impact both at Filbert Street and later at Middlesbrough. He was briefly a regular at Grimsby before a broken leg put him on the sidelines, although he recovered to spend a lengthy spell in the Southern League with Rugby Town.

Derrick Ward (Born Stoke-on-Trent, 23 December 1934. Died Stoke-on-Trent, 6 October 2011.) Derrick Ward was a winger who spent a total of 11 seasons on the books of Stoke City but he was mostly a reserve, his best run in the line-up coming during the 1958–59 season. He fared better at Stockport, where he was ever-present in the 1961–62 season and made close on 100 appearances in a three-year stay.

Allan Watkins (Born Usk, Monmouthshire, 21 April 1922. Died Kidderminster, 3 August 2011.) Allan Watkins enjoyed a brief career in soccer as a wing half with Plymouth and then Cardiff City, where a cartilage injury effectively ended his involvement with the game before he had made his senior debut. An all-round sportsman who had played rugby union for Pontypool during the war, he is best known for his exploits as a cricketer. He made his debut for Glamorgan in 1939 and then returned to give the county 15 years' service from 1946 to 1961. He also won 15 caps for England.

Gordon West (Born Darfield, Yorkshire, 24 April 1943. Died 10 June 2012.) Goalkeeper Gordon West began his professional career with Blackpool, where he competed with Tony Waiters for the jersey. However, whilst still a teenager he was sold to Everton for what was then a British record fee for a 'keeper. At Goodison he was first choice for a decade at a time when the club was one of the most powerful in the land. He helped the Toffees win the Football League title in 1962–63 and again in 1969–70, while in 1966 he gained an FA Cup winners' medal after they came back from two down to beat Sheffield Wednesday in the final. Gordon won three full caps for England and after a brief period of retirement returned to assist Tranmere Rovers.

Gordon West

Harry Westwood (Born Rotherham, 11 October 1921. Died Bath, 1 February 2012.) Harry Westwood joined Rotherham United as a teenager and made 16 appearances scoring 10 goals in the 1940–41 season. He served with the Fleet Air Arm during the war, achieving the rank of Lieutenant Commander and later worked as an air traffic controller before returning to serve in the RAF.

Walter Whitehurst (Born Manchester, 7 June 1934. Died Blackpool, 20 January 2012.) Walter Whitehurst was an intelligent wing half for Manchester United reserves before switching to Chesterfield where he made close on 100 first-team appearances. After a brief spell at Crewe he then moved into non-league football with Macclesfield Town, Mossley and Ashton United,

Derrick Wilkie (Born Lanchester, Co Durham, 27 July 1939. Died Belmont, Durham, 3 February 2012.) Defender Derrick Wilkie joined the groundstaff at Middlesbrough on leaving school, but found opportunities few and far between at Ayresome Park. He moved on to Hartlepools where he was the regular centre half in the 1961–62 season after which he mostly featured at full back.

Bert Wilkinson (Born Sunderland, 2 August 1922. Died 9 July 2011.) Bert Wilkinson was a part-time player who featured both in defence and on the right wing for Lincoln City. Although mostly a reserve for the Imps, he enjoyed an extended run in the line-up at right back during the 1948–49 season. He later played for Frickley Colliery and Grantham Town.

Stan Willemse (Born Hove, Sussex, 23 August 1924. Died 5 August 2011.) Stan Willemse was a rugged defensive player who featured for Brighton as a teenager during the war before joining the Royal Marines. He is best known for his six-year spell at Chelsea, where he made over 200 first-team appearances and was a member of the team that won the Football League title in 1954–55. He won representative honours for the Football League against the Scottish League in April 1954 and also appeared for the London FA team that entered the first-ever Inter Cities Fairs Cup competition. He wound down his career with a couple of seasons with Leyton Orient.

Glyn Williams (Born Maesteg, 3 November 1918. Died Bridgend, 6 May 2011.) Glyn Williams came to prominence with the Caerau team that won the Welsh Amateur Cup in 1946 and joined Cardiff City for the first season of post-war football. Although a regular only in the 1950–51 season, he clocked up 150 senior appearances during his stay at Ninian Park, also winning a solitary Welsh cap before eventually moving on to play for Aberystwyth.

Johnny Williams (Born Bristol, 16 August 1935. Died Plymouth, 24 November 2011.) Johnny Williams was a physically strong wing half with a powerful long-range shot. He joined Plymouth as a youngster, having previously been an apprentice electrical fitter, and went on to become a stalwart of the Pilgrims' team for a decade. He featured in the sides that won the Division Three title in 1958–59 and reached the Football League Cup semi-finals in 1964–65 before concluding his career at Bristol Rovers.

Roy Williams (Born Hereford, 3 March 1932. Died Hereford, 25 October 2011.) Roy Williams was a short but stocky inside forward who was a legendary figure in the history of Hereford United, scoring over 150 goals in 357 appearances in the club's Southern League days. He played for the Bulls as a teenager but once he had completed a spell of National Service he was sold to Southampton where he gained Football League experience. He later returned to Edgar Street and eventually settled in Hereford.

Billy Windle (Born Maltby, nr. Rotherham, 9 July 1920. Died Chester, 4 November 2011.) Billy Windle was a diminutive outside left who joined Leeds United from Kilnhurst Colliery, but made little impact at Elland Road. In February 1948 he moved on to Lincoln City, and went on to score a vital goal in the 2-0 win over Rotherham to clinch the 1947–48 Division Three North title for the Imps. Billy later spent four seasons with Chester and remained in the North West, turning out for Caernarvon, New Brighton and Oswestry Town

Ron Windle (Born Circa 1922. Died Dinnington, nr. Rotherham, 22 August 2011.) Ron Windle made 5 appearances for Notts County, mostly at outside right, in the wartime emergency season of 1944–45. Away from football Ron worked as a coal miner and was an active member of the NUM, also serving as an elected member on Rotherham Council for almost 25 years. He was mayor of the Yorkshire town in 1998.

Cyril Wood (Born Great Harwood, Lancashire, circa 1926. Died Accrington, 6 June 2011.) Cyril Wood played for Accrington works' team Howard & Bullough during the war, making a solitary appearance for Accrington Stanley in the 1945–46 season, when football was still under its wartime structure.

Charlie Woollett (Born Dawdon, Co Durham, 25 November 1920. Died 16 July 2011.) Charlie Woollett was a pacy outside left who made 75 wartime appearances for Newcastle United, also guesting for Middlesbrough and Hartlepools. In peacetime he spent two seasons as a fairly regular player for Bradford City and also had a brief spell with York. He was a part-time player who also worked as a coal miner.

Monty Wright (Born Scarcliffe, nr. Bolsover, Derbyshire, 29 May 1931. Died Sutton-in-Ashfield, Notts, April 2012.) Monty Wright was on the books of Leeds United as a youngster without breaking into the first team. He later had spells with Stockport and Chester, where he featured regularly in the 1954–55 season before an eye injury brought his career to an end.

Willie Wyles (Born Kirkcaldy, Fife, 28 September 1940. Died Coaltown of Wemyss, Fife, 16 December 2011.) Willie Wyles was a pacy winger who joined Brechin City from Fife club Windygates Thistle and enjoyed an excellent first season at Glebe Park. He went on to play for Falkirk and East Fife before returning to Brechin. In later life he was a champion bowler, representing Scotland's Over 50's international team.

Ian Nannestad

Soccer History Magazine

www.soccer-history.co.uk

THE FOOTBALL RECORDS

BRITISH FOOTBALL RECORDS

ALL-TIME PREMIER LEAGUE CHAMPIONSHIP SEASONS ON POINTS AVERAGE

	Team	Season	P	W	D	L	F	A	Pts	Pts Av
1	Chelsea	2004–05	38	29	8	1	72	15	95	2.50
2	Manchester U	1999–2000	38	28	7	3	97	45	91	2.39
3	Chelsea	2005–06	38	29	4	5	72	22	91	2.39
4	Arsenal	2003–04	38	26	12	0	73	26	90	2.36
	Manchester U	2008–09	38	28	6	4	68	24	90	2.36
6	Manchester C	2011–12	38	28	5	5	93	29	89	2.34
	Manchester U	2006–07	38	28	5	5	83	27	89	2.34
8	Arsenal	2001–02	38	26	9	3	79	36	87	2.28
	Manchester U	2007–08	38	27	6	5	80	22	87	2.28
10	Chelsea	2009–10	38	27	5	6	103	32	86	2.26
11	Manchester U	1993–94	42	27	11	4	80	38	92	2.19
12	Manchester U	2002–03	38	25	8	5	74	34	83	2.18
13	Manchester U	1995–96	38	25	7	6	73	35	82	2.15
14	Blackburn R	1994–95	42	27	8	7	80	39	89	2.11
15	Manchester U	2000–01	38	24	8	6	79	31	80	2.10
	Manchester U	2010–11	38	23	11	4	78	37	80	2.10
17	Manchester U	1998–99	38	22	13	3	80	37	79	2.07
18	Arsenal	1997–98	38	23	9	6	68	33	78	2.05
19	Manchester U	1992–93	42	24	12	6	67	31	84	2.00
20	Manchester U	1996–97	38	21	12	5	76	44	75	1.97

PREMIER LEAGUE EVER-PRESENT CLUBS

	P	W	D	L	F	A	Pts
Manchester U	772	500	163	109	1541	661	1663
Arsenal	772	415	204	153	1345	718	1449
Chelsea	772	401	199	172	1282	743	1402
Liverpool	772	380	194	198	1236	753	1334
Aston Villa	772	283	240	249	973	923	1089
Tottenham H	772	294	204	274	1072	1020	1086
Everton	772	272	218	282	974	979	1034

TOP TEN PREMIERSHIP APPEARANCES

1	Giggs, Ryan	598	6	Campbell, Sol	503
2	James, David	572	7	Neville, Phil	487
3	Speed, Gary	535	8	Carragher, Jamie	484
4	Lampard, Frank	522	9	Scholes, Paul	483
5	Heskey, Emile	516	10	Schwarzer, Mark	468

TOP TEN PREMIERSHIP GOALSCORERS

1	Shearer, Alan	260	6	Ferdinand, Les	149
2	Cole, Andy	187	6	Owen, Michael	149
3	Henry, Thierry	175	8	Sheringham, Teddy	146
4	Fowler, Robbie	163	9	Rooney, Wayne	144
5	Lampard, Frank	150	10	Hasselbaink, Jimmy Floyd	127

SCOTTISH PREMIER LEAGUE EVER-PRESENT CLUBS

	P	W	D	L	F	A	Pts
Celtic	528	388	75	65	1212	418	1239
Rangers	528	364	93	71	1123	418	1175
Hearts	528	218	128	182	693	621	782
Kilmarnock	528	178	133	217	633	758	667
Aberdeen	528	177	128	223	610	742	659
Motherwell	528	177	123	228	641	788	654
Dundee U	528	162	148	218	623	783	634

DOMESTIC LANDMARKS

July 14 – Sheffield FC rule book (actually a pamphlet) sells for £881,250 at Sotherby's.
October 22 – Stranraer equal club record score by beating Wigtown & Bladnoch 9-0 in the William Hill Scottish Cup.
September 11 – The Tottenham Hotspur v West Bromwich Albion match features players from seventeen different countries.
November 5 – Macclesfield Town substitute Vinny Mukendi is sent off after seven seconds against Burton Albion.
November 12 – Two MK Dons players become the youngest players to score and appear in the FA Cup competition proper (from First Round onwards). Firstly George Williams made his debut at 16 years two months and five days in the 76th minute against Nantwich Town, becoming the youngest to score in the competition proper in the 89th minute and also getting a yellow card! Within three minutes of his appearance, Brendon Galloway came on at 15 years seven months and 26 days to become the youngest player to appear in the competition proper.
November 15 – England's 2,000th goal is registered in a full international as Sweden is beaten for the first time in 43 years.
November 18 – Manchester City announce a record loss of £197.5m.
November 19 – Huddersfield Town overhaul Nottingham Forest's long-standing record of unbeaten Football League matches with their 43rd game undefeated in a 2-1 win against Notts County.
November 19 – Airdrie United hit a club record 11 goals against Gala Fairydean in a William Hill Scottish Cup tie.
November 26 – Arsenal field players representing 14 different nationalities against Fulham.
December 3 – Ayegbeni Yakubu scores all four goals for Blackburn Rovers against Swansea City to become the fifth player to score a hat-trick for three different Premier League clubs. He had previously achieved a three-goal feat with Everton and Portsmouth. The other four players were: Nicolas Anelka, Kevin Campbell, Les Ferdinand and Teddy Sheringham.
December 17 – James Morrison of West Bromwich Albion hits the 1,000th Premier League goal of the 2011 calendar year.
December 21 – Marc Albrighton (Aston Villa) scores the 20,000th Premier League goal. In the same match Robin Van Persie equals Thierry Henry's record of 34 calendar goals.
December 21 – Ryan Giggs of Manchester United scores for the 20th Premier League season.
December 31 – Van Persie breaks Henry's year record with his 35th goal for Arsenal.
January 1 – Everton reach 1,002 Premier League points to become the last of the seven all-time Premier League clubs to top the thousand.
February 18 – Charlton Athletic equal the oft-forgotten Football League record for a fifth consecutive draw against the same team when they hold Tranmere Rovers to a 1-1 draw.
February 26 – Giggs completes his 900th outing for Manchester United in a Premier League match at Norwich City.
March 10 – Didier Drogba of Chelsea becomes the first African to score 100 Premier League goals.
March 10 – David James the Bristol City goalkeeper makes his 900th overall career appearance.
March 24 – Jordan Rhodes breaks the post-war Huddersfield Town record with his 35th goal.
April 6 – Crawley Town break their club record with an attendance of 4,723 for the visit of Crewe Alexandra.
April 9 – Charlton Athletic equal their club record of points with a 1-0 win over Walsall.
April 9 – MK Dons score their 100th goal in League and Cup matches during the season.
April 28 – Graham Alexander (Preston North End) makes his 1,023rd and last League and Cup appearance before retiring, but not before he scores from a free-kick!
May 5 – Chelsea make FA Cup history. Drogba scores his fourth goal in four finals (eight in eight Wembley games). Ashley Cole achieves his seventh winner's medal. John Terry is the first to captain the same club to four trophies. Manager Robert Di Matteo is the first twice-scoring cup winner in 1997 and 2000, then be in charge of the winning team. He is also the third Italian to win the trophy in the last three years.
May 13 – With the relegation of Bolton Wanderers, it is the first time three founder members of the Football League have been relegated at the same time. Wolverhampton Wanderers and Blackburn Rovers had previously been demoted.
May 13 – Manchester United become the first top flight team to achieve 89 points and only finish as runners-up.
May 13 – The average number of goals scored in the Premier League is a record 2.81 from a total of 1,066.
May 19 – Chelsea beat Bayern Munich on penalties to win the Champions League, the first London team to take the European Cup. They were also the first team to win the Champions League after ending their domestic season outside the top five places.
May 26 – Record number of penalties in a Play-off shoot-out as Huddersfield Town beats Sheffield United 8-7. Twenty-two kicks were taken including 12 successful in succession and ended with one goalkeeper scoring the winning goal, his opposite number missing his subsequent chance.

PREMIERSHIP GOAL MILESTONES

Goal	Date	Scorer	Match
1	15.8.92	Brian Deane	Sheffield U v Manchester U
100	25.8.92	Mark Walters	Liverpool v Ipswich T
1000	7.4.93	Mike Newell	Blackburn R v Nottingham F
5000	7.12.96	Andy Townsend	Aston Villa v Southampton
10,000	15.12.01	Les Ferdinand	Tottenham H v Fulham
11,000	7.12.02	Jay-Jay Okocha	Bolton W v Blackburn R
12,000	13.12.03	Alan Shearer	Newcastle U v Tottenham H
13,000	28.11.04	Frederic Kanoute	Tottenham H v Middlesbrough
14,000	26.12.05	Jermain Defoe	Tottenham H v Birmingham C
15,000	30.12.06	Moritz Volz	Fulham v Chelsea
20,000	21.12.11	Marc Albrighton	Aston Villa v Arsenal

EUROPEAN CUP AND CHAMPIONS LEAGUE RECORDS

CHAMPIONS LEAGUE ATTENDANCES AND GOALS FROM GROUP STAGES ONWARDS

Season	*Attendances*	*Average*	*Goals*	*Games*
1992–93	873,251	34,930	56	25
1993–94	1,202,289	44,529	71	27
1994–95	2,328,515	38,172	140	61
1995–96	1,874,316	30,726	159	61
1996–97	2,093,228	34,315	161	61
1997–98	2,868,271	33,744	239	85
1998–99	3,608,331	42,451	238	85
1999–2000	5,490,709	34,973	442	157
2000–01	5,773,486	36,774	449	157
2001–02	5,417,716	34,508	393	157
2002–03	6,461,112	41,154	431	157
2003–04	4,611,214	36,890	309	125
2004–05	4,946,820	39,575	331	125
2005–06	5,291,187	42,330	285	125
2006–07	5,591,463	44,732	309	125
2007–08	5,454,718	43,638	330	125
2008–09	5,003,754	40,030	329	125
2009–10	5,295,708	42,366	320	125
2010–11	5,474,654	43,797	355	125
2011–12	5,225,363	41,803	345	125

HIGHEST AVERAGE ATTENDANCE IN ONE EUROPEAN CUP SEASON

1959–60 50,545 from a total attendance of 2,780,000.

HIGHEST SCORE IN A EUROPEAN CUP MATCH

Feyenoord (Holland) 12, KR Reykjavik (Iceland) 0
(First Round First Leg 1969–70)

HIGHEST AGGREGATE

Benfica (Portugal) 18, Dudelange (Luxembourg) 0
(Preliminary Round 1965–66)

MOST GOALS OVERALL

71 Raul (Real Madrid, Schalke).
60 Ruud Van Nistelrooy (PSV Eindhoven, Manchester U, Real Madrid).
58 Andriy Shevchenko (Dynamo Kiev, AC Milan, Chelsea, Dynamo Kiev).
51 Lionel Messi (Barcelona)
51 Thierry Henry (Monaco, Arsenal, Barcelona)
50 Filippo Inzaghi (Juventus, AC Milan)
49 Alfredo Di Stefano (Real Madrid)
47 Eusebio (Benfica)
44 Alessandro Del Piero (Juventus)
39 Fernando Morientes (Real Madrid, Monaco, Liverpool, Valencia)
39 Cristiano Ronaldo (Manchester U, Real Madrid)
39 Didier Drogba (Marseille, Chelsea)

CHAMPIONS LEAGUE BIGGEST WINS

HJK Helsinki 10, Bangor C 0 19.7.2011.
Liverpool 8 Besiktas 0 6.11.2007
Juventus 7, Olympiakos 0 10.12.2003
Marseille 6, CKSA Moscow 0 17.3.93

FIRST TEAM TO SCORE SEVEN GOALS

Paris St Germain 7, Rosenborg 2 24.10.2000

HIGHEST AGGREGATE OF GOALS

Monaco 8, La Coruna 3 5.11.2003

HIGHEST SCORING DRAW

Hamburg 4, Juventus 4 13.9.2000; Chelsea 4, Liverpool 4 14.4.2009

GREATEST COMEBACKS

Werder Bremen beat Anderlecht 5-3 after being three goals down in 33 minutes on 8.12.1993. They scored five goals in 23 second-half minutes.
La Coruna beat Paris St Germain 4-3 after being three goals down in 55 minutes on 7.3.2001. They scored four goals in 27 second-half minutes.
Liverpool after being three goals down in the first half on 25.5.2005 in the Champions League Final. They scored three goals in five second-half minutes and won the penalty shoot-out after extra time 3-2.
Liverpool 3 goals down to Basle in 29 minutes on 12.11.2002. They scored three second half goals in 24 minutes to draw 3-3.

MOST GOALS IN CHAMPIONS LEAGUE MATCH

5, Lionel Messi Barcelona v Leverkusen 7.3.2012.
4, Marco Van Basten, AC Milan v IFK Gothenburg (33, 53 (pen), 61, 62 mins) 4-0 25.11.1992.
4, Simone Inzaghi, Lazio v Marseille (17, 37, 38, 71 mins) 5-1 14.3.2000.
4, Ruud Van Nistelrooy, Manchester U v Sparta Prague (14, 25 (pen), 60, 90 mins) 4-1 3.11.2004.
4, Dado Prso, Monaco v La Coruna (26, 30, 45, 49, 23 mins) 8-3 5.11.2003.
4, Andriy Shevchenko, AC Milan at Fenerbahce (16, 52, 70, 76 mins) 4-0 23.11.2005.

MOST GOALS IN ONE SEASON

14 Jose Altafini 1962–63
14 Ruud Van Nistelrooy 2002–03
14 Lionel Messi 2011–12

MOST WINS WITH DIFFERENT CLUBS

Clarence Seedorf (Ajax) 1995; (Real Madrid) 1998; (AC Milan) 2003, 2007.

MOST WINNERS MEDALS

6 Francisco Gento (Real Madrid) 1956, 1957, 1958, 1959, 1960, 1966.
5 Alfredo Di Stefano (Real Madrid) 1956, 1957, 1958, 1959, 1960.
5 Jose Maria Zarraga (Real Madrid) 1956, 1957, 1958, 1959, 1960.
4 Jose-Hector Rial (Real Madrid) 1956, 1957, 1958, 1959.
4 Marquitos (Real Madrid) 1956, 1957, 1959, 1960.
4 Phil Neal (Liverpool) 1977, 1978, 1981, 1984.

MOST GOALS SCORED IN FINALS

7 Alfredo Di Stefano (Real Madrid), 1956 (1), 1957 (1 pen), 1958 (1), 1959 (1), 1960 (3).
7 Ferenc Puskas (Real Madrid), 1960 (4), 1962 (3).

MOST FINAL APPEARANCES PER COUNTRY

Italy 26 (12 wins, 14 defeats).
Spain 22 (13 wins, 9 defeats)
England 19 (12 wins, 7 defeats)
Germany 15 (6 wins, 9 defeats).

MOST CLUB FINAL WINNERS

Real Madrid (Spain)	9	1956, 1957, 1958, 1959, 1960, 1966, 1998, 2000, 2002.
AC Milan (Italy)	7	1963, 1969, 1989, 1990, 1994, 2003, 2007.

MOST APPEARANCES IN FINAL

Real Madrid 12; AC Milan 11.

MOST EUROPEAN CUP APPEARANCES

Raul (Real Madrid, Schalke)

Season	*European Cup*		*CWC Cup*		*Super Cup*		*WCC*	
	A	*G*	*A*	*G*	*A*	*G*	*A*	*G*
1995–96	8	6	0	0	0	0	0	0
1997–98	11	2	0	0	0	0	0	0
1998–99	8	3	0	0	1	0	1	1
1999–2000	15	10	0	0	0	0	0	0
2000–01	12	7	4	2	1	1	1	0
2001–02	12	6	0	0	0	0	0	0
2002–03	12	9	0	0	1	0	1	0
2003–04	9	2	0	0	0	0	0	0
2004–05	10	4	0	0	0	0	0	0
2005–06	6	2	0	0	0	0	0	0
2006–07	7	5	0	0	0	0	0	0
2007–08	8	5	0	0	0	0	0	0
2008–09	7	3	0	0	0	0	0	0
2009–10	7	2	0	0	0	0	0	0
2010-11*	12	5	0	0	0	0	0	0
Total	144	71	4	2	3	1	3	1

*Schalke; *A* = Appearances, *G* = Goals

139 Ryan Giggs (Manchester U)
139 Paolo Maldini (AC Milan)
130 Clarence Seedorf (Ajax, Real Madrid, Internazionale, AC Milan)
128 Roberto Carlos (Internazionale, Real Madrid, Fenerbahce)
128 Paul Scholes (Manchester U)
126 Xavi (Barcelona)
124 Iker Casillas (Real Madrid)
116 Andriy Shevchenko (Dynamo Kiev, AC Milan, Chelsea)
115 Carles Puyol (Barcelona)

EUROPEAN CUP AND CHAMPIONS LEAGUE RECORDS – continued

MOST SUCCESSFUL MANAGER
Bob Paisley (Liverpool) 1977, 1978, 1981.

FASTEST GOALS SCORED IN CHAMPIONS LEAGUE

10.2 sec	Roy Makaay for Bayern Munich v Real Madrid 7 March 2007.
20.07 sec	Gilberto Silva for Arsenal at PSV Eindhoven 25 September 2002.
20.12 sec	Alessandro Del Piero for Juventus at Manchester United 1 October 1997.

YOUNGEST CHAMPIONS LEAGUE GOALSCORER
Peter Ofori-Quaye for Olympiakos v Rosenborg at 17 years 195 days in 1997–98.

FASTEST HAT-TRICK SCORED IN CHAMPIONS LEAGUE
Mike Newell, 9 mins for Blackburn R v Rosenborg (4-1) 6.12.95.

MOST SUCCESSIVE CHAMPIONS LEAGUE APPEARANCES
Manchester U (England) 16 1996–97 – 2011–12.

MOST SUCCESSIVE EUROPEAN CUP APPEARANCES
Real Madrid (Spain) 15 1955–56 – 1969–70.

MOST SUCCESSIVE WINS IN THE CHAMPIONS LEAGUE
Barcelona (Spain) 11 2002–03.

LONGEST UNBEATEN RUN IN THE CHAMPIONS LEAGUE
Manchester U (England) 25 2007–08 – 2009 (Final).

REINSTATED WINNERS EXCLUDED FROM NEXT COMPETITION
1993 Marseille originally stripped of title. This was rescinded but they were not allowed to compete the following season.

LANDMARK GOALS CHAMPIONS LEAGUE
1st Daniel Amokachi, Club Brugge v CSKA Moscow 17 minutes 25.11.992
1000th Dmitri Khokhlov, PSV Eindhoven v Benfica 41 minutes 9.12.1998
5000th Luisao, Benfica v Hapoel Tel Aviv 21 minutes 14.9.2010.

MOST CLEAN SHEETS
10 Arsenal 2005–06 (995 minutes with two goalkeepers Manuel Almunia 347 minutes and Jens Lehmann 648 minutes).

MOST GOALS BY A GOALKEEPER
Hans-Jorg Butt (for three different clubs)
Hamburg 13.9.2000, Leverkusen 12.5.2002, Bayern Munich 8.12.2009 – all achieved against Juventus.

FOREIGN LANDMARKS

July 19 – First recorded example of a back-heeled penalty kick in a full international by Theyab Awana for the United Arab Emirates v Lebanon.

July 24 – Uruguay win the Copa America for a record 15th time.

August 1 – Spain win the European Under-19 title.

August 26 – European Super Cup final sees Barcelona beat Porto.

November 5 – Iker Casillas wins a record 127th cap for Spain v Costa Rica.

November 22 – Six-goal Real Madrid against Dinamo Zagreb become the first team in the Champions League to score four goals in 20 minutes and also three in the opening nine minutes.

November 23 – American Samoa celebrates their first ever international victory defeating Tonga 2-1 after a run of thirty defeats in 17 years.

January 9 – Lionel Messi becomes Player of the Year for the third successive time.

February 12 – African Nations Cup final: Zambia beat Ivory Coast on penalties.

March 7 – Messi sets individual Champions League record with five goals for Barcelona against Bayer Leverkusen.

March 7 – Apoel become the first Cypriot team to reach the last eight of the Champions League (and with only two native players).

March 20 – Messi hat-trick for Barcelona takes his total for the club to 234 beating the 232 record of Cesar Rodriquez.

March 24 – Messi scores his 35th La Liga goal for Barcelona to overhaul the Brazilian Ronaldo's total in 1996–97.

April 3 – Messi equals Jose Altafini's record of 14 European Cup goals achieved in 1962–63 and Ruud Van Nistelrooy with the same total in 2002–03.

April 7 – Yet another milestone for Messi with his 60th senior goal in 50 games.

April 14 – Real Madrid equal their club record 107 goals and both Messi (Barcelona) and Cristiano Ronaldo (Real) have 41 La Liga goals in the season.

April 21 – Cristiano Ronaldo hits his 42nd La Liga goal (54th overall of the season).

May 5 – With all four goals for Barcelona, Messi reaches his 50th La Liga strike and 72 in all for the team. Barcelona had lost only seven of 118 home matches under the coaching of Pep Guardiola. Cristiano Ronaldo scores his 45th La Liga goal.

May 16 – Holland beat Germany on penalties in the European Under-17 final.

July 1 – Spain win the Euro 2012 title beating Italy 4-0 to become the first international team to win three major trophies in succession: Euro 2008, World Cup 2010 and Euro 2012. Fernando Torres whose goal won the 2008 title, becomes Golden Boot winner. Spain equalled the European Championship record of ten games unbeaten. Iker Casillas keeps their eighth clean sheet in major tournaments.

July 15 – Spain win the latest European Under-19 title beating Greece, their second such triumph in a year. winning goal, his opposite number missing his subsequent chance.

TOP TEN PREMIER LEAGUE AVERAGE ATTENDANCES 2011–12

1	Manchester U	75,387
2	Arsenal	60,000
3	Newcastle U	49,935
4	Manchester C	47,044
5	Liverpool	44,253
6	Chelsea	41,478
7	Sunderland	39,095
8	Tottenham H	36,026
9	Aston Villa	33,873
10	Everton	33,228

TOP TEN FOOTBALL LEAGUE AVERAGE ATTENDANCES 2011–12

1	West Ham U	30,923
2	Southampton	26,419
3	Derby Co	26,020
4	Leeds U	23,283
5	Leicester C	23,036
6	Cardiff C	22,100
7	Nottingham F	21,578
8	Sheffield W	21,336
9	Brighton & HA	20,027
10	Reading	19,219

TOP TEN AVERAGE ATTENDANCES

1	Manchester United	2006–07	75,826
2	Manchester United	2007–08	75,691
3	Manchester United	2011–12	75,387
4	Manchester United	2008–09	75,308
5	Manchester United	2010–11	75,109
6	Manchester United	2009–10	74,863
7	Manchester United	2005–06	68,765
8	Manchester United	2004–05	67,871
9	Manchester United	2003–04	67,641
10	Manchester United	2002–03	67,630

TOP TEN AVERAGE WORLD CUP FINAL CROWDS

1	In USA	1994	68,604
2	In Brazil	1950	60,772
3	In Germany	2006	52,416
4	In Mexico	1970	52,311
5	In England	1966	50,458
6	In South Africa	2010	49,670
7	In Italy	1990	48,368
8	In Mexico	1986	46,956
9	In West Germany	1974	46,684
10	In France	1998	43,366

TOP TEN ALL-TIME ENGLAND CAPS

1	Peter Shilton	125
2	David Beckham	115
3	Bobby Moore	108
4	Bobby Charlton	106
5	Billy Wright	105
6	Ashley Cole	98
7	Steven Gerrard	96
8	Bryan Robson	90
	Frank Lampard	90
10	Michael Owen	89

TOP TEN ALL-TIME ENGLAND GOALSCORERS

1	Bobby Charlton	49
2	Gary Lineker	48
3	Jimmy Greaves	44
4	Michael Owen	40
	Tom Finney	30
5	Nat Lofthouse	30
	Alan Shearer	30
8	Vivian Woodward	29
	Wayne Rooney	29
10	Steve Bloomer	28

GOALKEEPING RECORDS

(without conceding a goal)

BRITISH RECORD (all competitive games)
Chris Woods, Rangers, in 1196 minutes from 26 November 1986 to 31 January 1987.

FA PREMIER LEAGUE
Edwin Van der Sar (Manchester U) in 1311 minutes during the 2008–09 season.

FOOTBALL LEAGUE
Steve Death, Reading, 1103 minutes from 24 March to 18 August 1979.

MOST CLEAN SHEETS IN A SEASON

Petr Cech (Chelsea) 24 2004–05

MOST CLEAN SHEETS OVERALL IN PREMIER LEAGUE

David James (Liverpool, Aston Villa, West Ham U, Manchester C, Portsmouth and Bristol C) 173 games.

MOST GOALS FOR IN A SEASON

FA PREMIER LEAGUE		*Goals*	*Games*
2009–10	Chelsea	103	38
FOOTBALL LEAGUE			
Division 4			
1960–61	Peterborough U	134	46
SCOTTISH PREMIER LEAGUE			
2003–04	Celtic	105	38
SCOTTISH LEAGUE			
Division 2			
1937–38	Raith R	142	34

MOST GOALS AGAINST IN A SEASON

FA PREMIER LEAGUE		*Goals*	*Games*
1993–94	Swindon T	100	42
FOOTBALL LEAGUE			
Division 2			
1898–99	Darwen	141	34
SCOTTISH PREMIER LEAGUE			
1999–2000	Aberdeen	83	36
SCOTTISH LEAGUE			
Division 2			
1931–32	Edinburgh C	146	38

MOST LEAGUE GOALS IN A SEASON

FA PREMIER LEAGUE		*Goals*	*Games*
1993–94	Andy Cole (Newcastle U)	34	40
1994–95	Alan Shearer (Blackburn R)	34	42
FOOTBALL LEAGUE			
Division 1			
1927–28	Dixie Dean (Everton)	60	39
Division 2			
1926–27	George Camsell (Middlesbrough)	59	37
Division 3(S)			
1936–37	Joe Payne (Luton T)	55	39
Division 3(N)			
1936–37	Ted Harston (Mansfield T)	55	41
Division 3			
1959–60	Derek Reeves (Southampton)	39	46
Division 4			
1960–61	Terry Bly (Peterborough U)	52	46
FA CUP			
1887–88	Jimmy Ross (Preston NE)	20	8
LEAGUE CUP			
1986–87	Clive Allen (Tottenham H)	12	9
SCOTTISH PREMIER LEAGUE			
2000–01	Henrik Larsson (Celtic)	35	37
SCOTTISH LEAGUE			
Division 1			
1931–32	William McFadyen (Motherwell)	52	34
Division 2			
1927–28	Jim Smith (Ayr U)	66	38

MOST FA CUP FINAL GOALS

Ian Rush (Liverpool) 5: 1986(2), 1989(2), 1992(1)

SCORED IN EVERY PREMIERSHIP GAME

Arsenal 2001–02 38 matches

FEWEST GOALS FOR IN A SEASON

FA PREMIER LEAGUE		*Goals*	*Games*
2007–08	Derby Co	20	38
FOOTBALL LEAGUE			
Division 2			
1899–1900	Loughborough T	18	34
SCOTTISH PREMIER LEAGUE			
2010–11	St Johnstone	23	38
SCOTTISH LEAGUE			
New Division 1			
1980–81	Stirling Alb	18	39

FEWEST GOALS AGAINST IN A SEASON

FA PREMIER LEAGUE		*Goals*	*Games*
2004–05	Chelsea	15	38
FOOTBALL LEAGUE			
Division 1			
1978–79	Liverpool	16	42
SCOTTISH PREMIER LEAGUE			
2001–02	Celtic	18	38
SCOTTISH LEAGUE			
Division 1			
1913–14	Celtic	14	38

MOST LEAGUE GOALS IN A CAREER

FOOTBALL LEAGUE **Arthur Rowley**	*Goals*	*Games*	*Season*
WBA	4	24	1946–48
Fulham	27	56	1948–50
Leicester C	251	303	1950–58
Shrewsbury T	152	236	1958–65
	434	619	
SCOTTISH LEAGUE			
Jimmy McGrory			
Celtic	1	3	1922–23
Clydebank	13	30	1923–24
Celtic	396	375	1924–38
	410	408	

MOST HAT-TRICKS

Career
34 Dixie Dean (Tranmere R, Everton, Notts Co, England)

Division 1 (one season post-war)
6 Jimmy Greaves (Chelsea), 1960–61

Three for one team one match
West, Spouncer, Hooper, Nottingham F v Leicester Fosse, Division 1, 21 April 1909
Loasby, Smith, Wells, Northampton T v Walsall, Division 3S, 5 Nov 1927
Bowater, Hoyland, Readman, Mansfield T v Rotherham U, Division 3N, 27 Dec 1932
Barnes, Ambler, Davies, Wrexham v Hartlepools U, Division 4, 3 March 1962
Adcock, Stewart, White, Manchester C v Huddersfield T, Division 2, 7 Nov 1987

MOST CUP GOALS IN A CAREER

FA CUP (Pre-Second World war)
Henry Cursham 48 (Notts Co)

FA CUP (post-war)
Ian Rush 43 (Chester, Liverpool)

LEAGUE CUP
Geoff Hurst 49 (West Ham U, Stoke C)
Ian Rush 49 (Chester, Liverpool, Newcastle U)

GOALS PER GAME (Football League to 1991–92)

Goals per game	Division 1		Division 2		Division 3		Division 4		Division 3(S)		Division 3(N)	
	Games	Goals	Games	Goals	Games	Goals	Games	Goals	Games	Goals	Games	Goals
0	2465	0	2665	0	1446	0	1438	0	997	0	803	0
1	5606	5606	5836	5836	3225	3225	3106	3106	2073	2073	1914	1914
2	8275	16550	8609	17218	4569	9138	4441	8882	3314	6628	2939	5878
3	7731	23193	7842	23526	3784	11352	4041	12123	2996	8988	2922	8766
4	6229	24920	5897	23588	2837	11348	2784	11136	2445	9780	2410	9640
5	3752	18755	3634	18170	1566	7830	1506	7530	1554	7770	1599	7995
6	2137	12822	2007	12042	769	4614	786	4716	870	5220	930	5580
7	1092	7644	1001	7007	357	2499	336	2352	451	3157	461	3227
8	542	4336	376	3008	135	1080	143	1144	209	1672	221	1768
9	197	1773	164	1476	64	576	35	315	76	684	102	918
10	83	830	68	680	13	130	8	80	33	330	45	450
11	37	407	19	209	2	22	7	77	15	165	15	165
12	12	144	17	204	1	12	0	0	7	84	8	96
13	4	52	4	52	0	0	0	0	2	26	4	52
14	2	28	1	14	0	0	0	0	0	0	0	0
17	0	0	0	0	0	0	0	0	0	0	1	17
	38164	**117061**	**38140**	**113030**	**18768**	**51826**	**18631**	**51461**	**15042**	**46577**	**14374**	**46466**

New Overall Totals (since 1992)		Totals (up to 1991–92)		Complete Overall Totals (since 1888–89)	
Games	40696	Games	143119	Games	183815
Goals	105305	Goals	426421	Goals	531726

Extensive research by statisticians has unearthed seven results from early years of the Football League which differ from the original scores. These are 26 January 1889 Wolverhampton W 5 Everton 0 (not 4-0), 16 March 1889 Notts Co 3 Derby Co 5 (not 2-5), 4 January 1896 Arsenal 5 Loughborough 0 (not 6-0), 28 November 1896 Leicester Fosse 4 Walsall 2 (not 4-1), 21 April 1900 Burslem Port Vale 2 Lincoln City 1 (not 2-0), 25 December 1902 Glossop NE 3 Stockport Co 0 (not 3-1), 26 April 1913 Hull C 2 Leicester C 0 (not 2-1).

GOALS PER GAME (from 1992–93)

Goals per game	Premier		Championship/Div 1		League One/Div 2		League Two/Div 3	
	Games	Goals	Games	Goals	Games	Goals	Games	Goals
0	676	0	917	0	868	0	869	0
1	1440	1440	2059	2059	2054	2054	2078	2078
2	1944	3888	2825	5650	2820	5640	2754	5508
3	1640	4920	2344	7032	2407	7221	2363	7089
4	1126	4504	1528	6112	1540	6160	1445	5780
5	557	2785	832	4160	810	4050	728	3640
6	278	1668	365	2190	337	2022	332	1992
7	115	805	122	854	143	1001	135	945
8	56	448	36	288	42	336	41	328
9	10	90	5	45	16	144	17	153
10	3	30	5	50	3	30	5	50
11	1	11	2	22	0	0	3	33
	7846	**20589**	**11040**	**28462**	**11040**	**28658**	**10770**	**27596**

A CENTURY OF LEAGUE AND CUP GOALS IN CONSECUTIVE SEASONS

	League	*Cup*	*Season*
George Camsell			
Middlesbrough	59	5	1926–27
(101 goals)	33	4	1927–28

(Camsell's cup goals were all scored in the FA Cup.)

Steve Bull			
Wolverhampton W	34	18	1987–88
(102 goals)	37	13	1988–89

(Bull had 12 in the Sherpa Van Trophy, 3 Littlewoods Cup, 3 FA Cup in 1987–88; 11 Sherpa Van Trophy, 2 Littlewoods Cup in 1988–89.)

PENALTIES

Most in a Season (individual)

Division 1	*Goals*	*Season*
Francis Lee (Manchester C)	13	1971–72

Most awarded in one game

Five Crystal Palace (4 – 1 scored, 3 missed) v Brighton & HA (1 scored), Div 2 1988–89

Most saved in a Season

Division 1

Paul Cooper (Ipswich T) 8 (of 10) 1979–80

MOST GOALS IN A GAME

FA PREMIER LEAGUE

19 Sept 1999 Alan Shearer (Newcastle U) 5 goals v Sheffield W
4 Mar 1995 Andy Cole (Manchester U) 5 goals v Ipswich T
22 Nov 2009 Jermain Defoe (Tottenham H) 5 goals v Wigan Ath
27 Nov 2010 Dimitar Berbatov (Manchester U) 5 goals v Blackburn R

FOOTBALL LEAGUE

Division 1
14 Dec 1935 Ted Drake (Arsenal) 7 goals v Aston V

Division 2
5 Feb 1955 Tommy Briggs (Blackburn R) 7 goals v Bristol R
23 Feb 1957 Neville Coleman (Stoke C) 7 goals v Lincoln C

Division 3(S)
13 April 1936 Joe Payne (Luton T) 10 goals v Bristol R

Division 3(N)
26 Dec 1935 Bunny Bell (Tranmere R) 9 goals v Oldham Ath

Division 3
16 Sept 1969 Steve Earle (Fulham) 5 goals v Halifax T
24 April 1965 Barrie Thomas (Scunthorpe U) 5 goals v Luton T
20 Nov 1965 Keith East (Swindon T) 5 goals v Mansfield T
2 Oct 1971 Alf Wood (Shrewsbury T) 5 goals v Blackburn R
10 Sept 1983 Tony Caldwell (Bolton W) 5 goals v Walsall
4 May 1987 Andy Jones (Port Vale) 5 goals v Newport Co
3 April 1990 Steve Wilkinson (Mansfield T) 5 goals v Birmingham C
5 Sept 1998 Giuliano Grazioli (Peterborough U) 5 goals v Barnet
6 April 2002 Lee Jones (Wrexham) 5 goals v Cambridge U

Division 4
26 Dec 1962 Bert Lister (Oldham Ath) 6 goals v Southport

FA CUP

20 Nov 1971 Ted MacDougall (Bournemouth) 9 goals v Margate (*1st Round*)

LEAGUE CUP

25 Oct 1989 Frankie Bunn (Oldham Ath) 6 goals v Scarborough

SCOTTISH LEAGUE

Premier Division
17 Nov 1984 Paul Sturrock (Dundee U) 5 goals v Morton

Premier League
23 Aug 1996 Marco Negri (Rangers) 5 goals v Dundee U
4 Nov 2000 Kenny Miller (Rangers) 5 goals v St Mirren
25 Sept 2004 Kris Boyd (Kilmarnock) 5 goals v Dundee U
30 Dec 2009 Kris Boyd (Rangers) 5 goals v Dundee U
13 May 2012 Gary Hooper (Celtic) 5 goals v Hearts

Division 1
14 Sept 1928 Jimmy McGrory (Celtic) 8 goals v Dunfermline Ath

Division 2
1 Oct 1927 Owen McNally (Arthurlie) 8 goals v Armadale
2 Jan 1930 Jim Dyet (King's Park) 8 goals v Forfar Ath
18 April 1936 John Calder (Morton) 8 goals v Raith R
20 Aug 1937 Norman Hayward (Raith R) 8 goals v Brechin C

SCOTTISH CUP

12 Sept 1885 John Petrie (Arbroath) 13 goals v Bon Accord (*1st Round*)

LONGEST SEQUENCE OF CONSECUTIVE DEFEATS

FOOTBALL LEAGUE Division 2	*Team*	*Games*
1898–99	Darwen	18

LONGEST UNBEATEN SEQUENCE

FA PREMIER LEAGUE	*Team*	*Games*
May 2003–October 2004	Arsenal	49
FOOTBALL LEAGUE – League 1		
Jan 2011–Nov 2011	Huddersfield T	43

LONGEST UNBEATEN CUP SEQUENCE

Liverpool 25 rounds League/Milk Cup 1980–84

LONGEST UNBEATEN SEQUENCE IN A SEASON

FA PREMIER LEAGUE	*Team*	*Games*
2003–04	Arsenal	38
FOOTBALL LEAGUE – Division 1		
1920–21	Burnley	30
SCOTTISH PREMIER LEAGUE		
2003–04	Celtic	32

LONGEST UNBEATEN START TO A SEASON

FA PREMIER LEAGUE	*Team*	*Games*
2003–04	Arsenal	38
FOOTBALL LEAGUE – Division 1		
1973–74	Leeds U	29
1987–88	Liverpool	29

LONGEST SEQUENCE WITHOUT A WIN IN A SEASON

FA PREMIER LEAGUE	*Team*	*Games*
2007–08	Derby Co	32
FOOTBALL LEAGUE Division 2	*Team*	*Games*
1983–84	Cambridge U	31

LONGEST SEQUENCE WITHOUT A WIN FROM SEASON'S START

FOOTBALL LEAGUE Division 4	*Team*	*Games*
1970–71	Newport Co	25

LONGEST SEQUENCE OF CONSECUTIVE SCORING (Individual)

FA PREMIER LEAGUE
Ruud Van Nistelrooy (Manchester U) 15 in 10 games 2003–04

FOOTBALL LEAGUE RECORD
Tom Phillipson (Wolverhampton W) 23 in 13 games 1926–27

LONGEST WINNING SEQUENCE

FA PREMIER LEAGUE	*Team*	*Games*
2001–02 and 2002–03	Arsenal	14
FOOTBALL LEAGUE – Division 2		
1904–05	Manchester U	14
1905–06	Bristol C	14
1950–51	Preston NE	14
FROM SEASON'S START – Division 3		
1985–86	Reading	13
SCOTTISH PREMIER LEAGUE		
2003–04	Celtic	25

HIGHEST WINS

Highest win in a First-Class Match
(Scottish Cup 1st Round)

Arbroath	36	Bon Accord	0	12 Sept 1885

Highest win in an International Match

England	13	Ireland	0	18 Feb 1882

Highest win in an FA Cup Match

Preston NE *(1st Round)*	26	Hyde U	0	15 Oct 1887

Highest win in a League Cup Match

West Ham U *(2nd Round, 2nd Leg)*	10	Bury	0	25 Oct 1983
Liverpool *(2nd Round, 1st Leg)*	10	Fulham	0	23 Sept 1986

Highest win in an FA Premier League Match

Manchester U	9	Ipswich T	0	4 Mar 1995
Nottingham F	1	Manchester U	8	6 Feb 1999

Highest win in a Football League Match

Division 2 – highest home win

Newcastle U	13	Newport Co	0	5 Oct 1946

Division 3(N) – highest home win

Stockport Co	13	Halifax T	0	6 Jan 1934

Division 2 – highest away win

Burslem Port Vale	0	Sheffield U	10	10 Dec 1892

Highest wins in a Scottish League Match

Scottish Premier League – highest home win

Celtic	9	Aberdeen	0	6 Nov 2010

Scottish Division 2 – highest home win

Airdrieonians	15	Dundee Wanderers	1	1 Dec 1894

Scottish Premier League – away win

Hamilton A	0	Celtic	8	5 Nov 1988

MOST HOME WINS IN A SEASON

Brentford won all 21 games in Division 3(S), 1929–30

RECORD AWAY WINS IN A SEASON

Doncaster R won 18 of 21 games in Division 3(N), 1946–47

CONSECUTIVE AWAY WINS

FA PREMIER LEAGUE
Chelsea 9 games 2004–05

FOOTBALL LEAGUE
Division 1
Tottenham H 10 games (1959–60 (2), 1960–61 (8))

MOST WINS IN A SEASON

		Wins	*Games*
FA PREMIER LEAGUE			
2004–05	Chelsea	29	38
2005–06	Chelsea	29	38
FOOTBALL LEAGUE			
Division 3(N)			
1946–47	Doncaster R	33	42
SCOTTISH PREMIER LEAGUE			
2001–02	Celtic	33	38
SCOTTISH LEAGUE			
Division 1			
1920–21	Rangers	35	42

MOST POINTS IN A SEASON

(under old system of two points for a win)

		Points	*Games*
FOOTBALL LEAGUE			
Division 4			
1975–76	Lincoln C	74	46
SCOTTISH LEAGUE			
Division 1			
1920–21	Rangers	76	42

FEWEST WINS IN A SEASON

		Wins	*Games*
FA PREMIER LEAGUE			
2007–08	Derby Co	1	38
FOOTBALL LEAGUE			
Division 2			
1899–1900	Loughborough T	1	34
SCOTTISH PREMIER LEAGUE			
1998–99	Dunfermline Ath	4	36
SCOTTISH LEAGUE			
Division 1			
1891–92	Vale of Leven	0	22

UNDEFEATED AT HOME OVERALL

Liverpool 85 games (63 League, 9 League Cup, 7 European, 6 FA Cup), Jan 1978–Jan 1981

UNDEFEATED AT HOME LEAGUE

Chelsea 86 games, March 2004–October 2008

UNDEFEATED IN A SEASON

FA PREMIER LEAGUE		
2003–04	Arsenal	38 games
FOOTBALL LEAGUE		
1889–90	Preston NE	22 games
Division 2		
1893–94	Liverpool	22 games

UNDEFEATED AWAY

Arsenal 19 games FA Premier League 2001–02 and 2003–04 (only Preston NE with 11 in 1888–89 had previously remained unbeaten away) in the top flight

HIGHEST AGGREGATE SCORES

FA PREMIER LEAGUE

Portsmouth	7	Reading	4	29 Sept 2007

Highest Aggregate Score England
Division 3(N)

Tranmere R	13	Oldham Ath	4	26 Dec 1935

Highest Aggregate Score Scotland
Division 2

Airdrieonians	15	Dundee Wanderers	1	1 Dec 1894

MOST POINTS IN A SEASON

(three points for a win)

		Points	*Games*
FA PREMIER LEAGUE			
2004–05	Chelsea	95	38
FOOTBALL LEAGUE			
Championship			
2005–06	Reading	106	46
SCOTTISH PREMIER LEAGUE			
2001–02	Celtic	103	38
SCOTTISH LEAGUE			
New Division 3			
2004–05	Gretna	98	36

FEWEST POINTS IN A SEASON

		Points	*Games*
FA PREMIER LEAGUE			
2007–08	Derby Co	11	38
FOOTBALL LEAGUE			
Division 2			
1904–05	Doncaster R	8	34
1899–1900	Loughborough T	8	34
SCOTTISH PREMIER LEAGUE			
2005–06	Livingston	18	38
SCOTTISH LEAGUE			
Division 1			
1954–55	Stirling Alb	6	30

ONE DEFEAT IN A SEASON

FA PREMIER LEAGUE		*Defeats*	*Games*
2004–05	Chelsea	1	38
FOOTBALL LEAGUE			
Division 1			
1990–91	Arsenal	1	38
SCOTTISH PREMIER LEAGUE			
2001–02	Celtic	1	38
SCOTTISH LEAGUE			
Premier Division			
Division 1			
1920–21	Rangers	1	42
Division 2			
1956–57	Clyde	1	36
1962–63	Morton	1	36
1967–68	St Mirren	1	36
New Division 1			
2011–12	Ross Co	1	36
New Division 2			
1975–76	Raith R	1	26

MOST DEFEATS IN A SEASON

FA PREMIER LEAGUE		*Defeats*	*Games*
1994–95	Ipswich T	29	42
2005–06	Sunderland	29	38
2007–08	Derby Co	29	38
FOOTBALL LEAGUE			
Division 3			
1997–98	Doncaster R	34	46
SCOTTISH PREMIER LEAGUE			
2005–06	Livingston	28	38
SCOTTISH LEAGUE			
New Division 1			
1992–93	Cowdenbeath	34	44

NO DEFEATS IN A SEASON

FA PREMIER LEAGUE		
2003–04	Arsenal	won 26, drew 12
FOOTBALL LEAGUE		
Division 1		
1888–89	Preston NE	won 18, drew 4
Division 2		
1893–94	Liverpool	won 22, drew 6
SCOTTISH LEAGUE DIVISION 1		
1898–99	Rangers	won 18

SENDINGS-OFF

SEASON
451 (League alone) 2003–04
(Before rescinded cards taken into account)

DAY
19 (League) 13 Dec 2003

FA CUP FINAL
Kevin Moran, Manchester U v Everton 1985
Jose Antonio Reyes, Arsenal v Manchester U 2005

QUICKEST
FA Premier League
Andreas Johansson Wigan Ath v Arsenal 7 May 2006 and Keith Gillespie Sheffield U v Reading 20 January 2007 both in 10 seconds
Football League
Walter Boyd, Swansea C v Darlington Div 3 as substitute in zero seconds 23 Nov 1999

MOST IN ONE GAME
Five: Chesterfield (2) v Plymouth Arg (3) 22 Feb 1997
Five: Wigan Ath (1) v Bristol R (4) 2 Dec 1997
Five: Exeter C (3) v Cambridge U (2) 23 Nov 2002

MOST IN ONE TEAM
Wigan Ath (1) v Bristol R (4) 2 Dec 1997
Hereford U (4) v Northampton T (0) 6 Sept 1992

MOST DRAWN GAMES IN A SEASON

FA PREMIER LEAGUE		*Draws*	*Games*
1993–94	Manchester C	18	42
1993–94	Sheffield U	18	42
1994–95	Southampton	18	42
FOOTBALL LEAGUE			
Division 1			
1978–79	Norwich C	23	42
Division 3			
1997–98	Cardiff C	23	46
1997–98	Hartlepool U	23	46
Division 4			
1986–87	Exeter C	23	46
SCOTTISH PREMIER LEAGUE			
1998–99	Dunfermline Ath	16	38
SCOTTISH LEAGUE			
Premier Division			
1993–94	Aberdeen	21	44
New Division 1			
1986–87	East Fife	21	44

MOST SUCCESSFUL MANAGERS

Sir Alex Ferguson CBE
Manchester U
24 major trophies in 24 seasons:
12 Premier League, 5 FA Cup, 4 League Cup, 2 European Cup, 1 Cup-Winners' Cup.

Aberdeen
1976–86 – 9 trophies:
3 League, 4 Scottish Cup, 1 League Cup, 1 Cup-Winners' Cup.

Bob Paisley – Liverpool
1974–83 – 13 trophies:
6 League, 3 European Cup, 3 League Cup, 1 UEFA Cup.

Bill Struth – Rangers
1920–54 – 30 trophies:
18 League, 10 Scottish Cup, 2 League Cup

LEAGUE CHAMPIONSHIP HAT-TRICKS

Huddersfield T	1923–24 to 1925–26
Arsenal	1932–33 to 1934–35
Liverpool	1981–82 to 1983–84
Manchester U	1998–99 to 2000–01
Manchester U	2006–07 to 2008–09

MOST FA CUP MEDALS

Ashley Cole 7 (Arsenal 2002, 2003, 2005, Chelsea 2007, 2009, 2010, 2012)

MOST LEAGUE MEDALS

Ryan Giggs (Manchester U) 12: 1993, 1994, 1996, 1997, 1999, 2000, 2001, 2003, 2007, 2008, 2009 and 2011

MOST SENIOR MATCHES

1,390 Peter Shilton (1,005 League, 86 FA Cup, 102 League Cup, 125 Internationals, 13 Under-23, 4 Football League XI, 20 European Cup, 7 Texaco Cup, 5 Simod Cup, 4 European Super Cup, 4 UEFA Cup, 3 Screen Sport Super Cup, 3 Zenith Data Systems Cup, 2 Autoglass Trophy, 2 Charity Shield, 2 Full Members Cup, 1 Anglo-Italian Cup, 1 Football League play-offs, 1 World Club Championship)

MOST LEAGUE APPEARANCES (750+ matches)

1,005 Peter Shilton (286 Leicester C, 110 Stoke C, 202 Nottingham F, 188 Southampton, 175 Derby Co, 34 Plymouth Arg, 1 Bolton W, 9 Leyton Orient) 1966–97

931 Tony Ford (355 Grimsby T, 9 Sunderland (loan), 112 Stoke C, 114 WBA, 68 Grimsby T, 5 Bradford C (loan), 76 Scunthorpe U, 103 Mansfield T, 89 Rochdale) 1975–2002

909 Graeme Armstrong (204 Stirling A, 83 Berwick R, 353 Meadowbank Th, 268 Stenhousemuir, 1 Alloa Ath) 1975–2001

863 Tommy Hutchison (165 Blackpool, 314 Coventry C, 46 Manchester C, 92 Burnley, 178 Swansea C, 68 Alloa Ath) 1965–91

833 Graham Alexander (Scunthorpe U, 159, Luton T 150, Preston NE 370, Burnley 154).

824 Terry Paine (713 Southampton, 111 Hereford U) 1957–77

790 Neil Redfearn (35 Bolton W, 10 Lincoln C (loan), 90 Lincoln C, 46 Doncaster R, 57 Crystal Palace, 24 Watford, 62 Oldham Ath, 292 Barnsley, 30 Charlton Ath, 17 Bradford C, 22 Wigan Ath, 42 Halifax T, 54 Boston U, 9 Rochdale) 1982–2004

782 Robbie James (484 Swansea C, 48 Stoke C, 87 QPR, 23 Leicester C, 89 Bradford C, 51 Cardiff C) 1973–94

777 Alan Oakes (565 Manchester C, 211 Chester C, 1 Port Vale) 1959–84

774 Dave Beasant (340 Wimbledon, 20 Newcastle U, 133 Chelsea, 6 Grimsby T (loan), 4 Wolverhampton W (loan), 88 Southampton, 139 Nottingham F, 27 Portsmouth, 1 Tottenham H (loan), 16 Brighton & HA) 1979–2003

771 John Burridge (27 Workington, 134 Blackpool, 65 Aston Villa, 6 Southend U (loan), 88 Crystal Palace, 39 QPR, 74 Wolverhampton W, 6 Derby Co (loan), 109 Sheffield U, 62 Southampton, 67 Newcastle U, 65 Hibernian, 3 Scarborough, 4 Lincoln C, 3 Aberdeen, 3 Dumbarton, 3 Falkirk, 4 Manchester C, 3 Darlington, 6 Queen of the S) 1968–96

770 John Trollope (all for Swindon T) 1960–80†

764 Jimmy Dickinson (all for Portsmouth) 1946–65

763 Stuart McCall (395 Bradford C, 103 Everton, 194 Rangers, 71 Sheffield U) 1982–2004

761 Roy Sproson (all for Port Vale) 1950–72

760 Mick Tait (64 Oxford U, 106 Carlisle U, 33 Hull C, 240 Portsmouth, 99 Reading, 79 Darlington, 139 Hartlepool U) 1975–97

758 Ray Clemence (48 Scunthorpe U, 470 Liverpool, 240 Tottenham H) 1966–87

758 Billy Bonds (95 Charlton Ath, 663 West Ham U) 1964–88

757 Pat Jennings (48 Watford, 472 Tottenham H, 237 Arsenal) 1963–86

757 Frank Worthington (171 Huddersfield T, 210 Leicester C, 84 Bolton W, 75 Birmingham C, 32 Leeds U, 19 Sunderland, 34 Southampton, 31 Brighton & HA, 59 Tranmere R, 23 Preston NE, 19 Stockport Co) 1966–88

752 Wayne Allison (84 Halifax T, 7 Watford, 195 Bristol C, 101 Swindon T, 74 Huddersfield T, 103 Tranmere R, 73 Sheffield U, 115 Chesterfield)

† record for one club

CONSECUTIVE

401 Harold Bell (401 Tranmere R; 459 in all games) 1946–55

YOUNGEST PLAYERS

FA Premier League appearance
Matthew Briggs, 16 years 65 days, Fulham v Middlesbrough, 13.5.2007.

FA Premier League scorer
James Vaughan, 16 years 271 days, Everton v Crystal Palace 10.4.2005

Football League appearance
Reuben Noble-Lazarus 15 years 45 days, Barnsley v Ipswich T, FL Championship 30.9.2008

Football League scorer
Ronnie Dix, 15 years 180 days, Bristol Rovers v Norwich City, Division 3S, 3.3.28.

Division 1 appearance
Derek Forster, 15 years 185 days, Sunderland v Leicester City, 22.8.64.

Division 1 scorer
Jason Dozzell, 16 years 57 days as substitute Ipswich Town v Coventry City, 4.2.84

Division 1 hat-tricks
Alan Shearer, 17 years 240 days, Southampton v Arsenal, 9.4.88
Jimmy Greaves, 17 years 10 months, Chelsea v Portsmouth, 25.12.57

FA Cup appearance (any round)
Andy Awford, 15 years 88 days as substitute Worcester City v Boreham Wood, 3rd Qual. rd, 10.10.87

FA Cup proper appearance
Brendon Galloway, 15 years 240 days, MK Dons v Nantwich T

FA Cup Final appearance
Curtis Weston, 17 years 119 days, Millwall v Manchester U, 2004

FA Cup Final scorer
Norman Whiteside, 18 years 18 days, Manchester United v Brighton & Hove Albion, 1983

FA Cup Final captain
David Nish, 21 years 212 days, Leicester City v Manchester City, 1969

League Cup appearance
Chris Coward, 16 years 30 days, Stockport Co v Sheffield W, 2005

League Cup Final scorer
Norman Whiteside, 17 years 324 days, Manchester United v Liverpool, 1983

League Cup Final captain
Barry Venison, 20 years 7 months 8 days, Sunderland v Norwich City, 1985

Scottish Premier League appearance
Scott Robinson, 16 years 45 days, Hearts v Inverness CT, 26.4.2008

Scottish Premier League scorer
Fraser Fyvie, 16 years 306 days, Aberdeen v Hearts, 27.1.2010

OLDEST PLAYERS

FA Premier League appearance
John Burridge, 43 years 5 months, Manchester C v QPR, 14.5.1995

Football League appearance
Neil McBain, 52 years 4 months, New Brighton v Hartlepools United, Div 3N, 15.3.47 (McBain was New Brighton's manager and had to play in an emergency)

Division 1 appearance
Stanley Matthews, 50 years 5 days, Stoke City v Fulham, 6.2.65

INTERNATIONAL RECORDS

MOST GOALS IN AN INTERNATIONAL

Record/World Cup	Archie Thompson (Australia) 13 goals v American Samoa	11.4.2001
England	Malcolm Macdonald (Newcastle U) 5 goals v Cyprus, at Wembley	16.4.1975
	Willie Hall (Tottenham H) 5 goals v Ireland, at Old Trafford	16.11.1938
	Steve Bloomer (Derby Co) 5 goals v Wales, at Cardiff	16.3.1896
	Howard Vaughton (Aston Villa) 5 goals v Ireland, at Belfast	18.2.1882
Northern Ireland	Joe Bambrick (Linfield) 6 goals v Wales, at Belfast	1.2.1930
Wales	John Price (Wrexham) 4 goals v Ireland, at Wrexham	25.2.1882
	Mel Charles (Cardiff C) 4 goals v Ireland, at Cardiff	11.4.1962
	Ian Edwards (Chester) 4 goals v Malta, at Wrexham	25.10.1978

MOST GOALS IN AN INTERNATIONAL CAREER

		Goals	*Games*
England	Bobby Charlton (Manchester U)	49	106
Scotland	Denis Law (Huddersfield T, Manchester C, Torino, Manchester U)	30	55
	Kenny Dalglish (Celtic, Liverpool)	30	102
Northern Ireland	David Healy (Manchester U, Preston NE, Leeds U, Fulham, Sunderland, Rangers)	35	93
Wales	Ian Rush (Liverpool, Juventus)	28	73
Republic of Ireland	Robbie Keane (Wolverhampton W, Coventry C, Internazionale, Leeds U, Tottenham H, Liverpool, Tottenham H, LA Galaxy)	54	120

HIGHEST SCORES

Record/World Cup Match	Australia	31	American Samoa	0	2001
European Championship	San Marino	0	Germany	13	2006
Olympic Games	Denmark	17	France	1	1908
	Germany	16	USSR	0	1912
Other International Match	Libya	21	Oman	0	1966
European Cup	Feyenoord	12	K R Reykjavik	2	1969
European Cup-Winners' Cup	Sporting Lisbon	16	Apoel Nicosia	1	1963
Fairs & UEFA Cups	Ajax	14	Red Boys	0	1984

GOALSCORING RECORDS

World Cup Final	Geoff Hurst (England) 3 goals v West Germany	1966
World Cup Final tournament	Just Fontaine (France) 13 goals	1958
Career	Artur Friedenreich (Brazil) 1,329 goals	1910–30
	Pele (Brazil) 1,281 goals	*1956–78
	Franz 'Bimbo' Binder (Austria, Germany) 1,006 goals	1930–50
World Cup Finals fastest	Hakan Sukur (Turkey) 10.8 secs v South Korea	2002

**Pele subsequently scored two goals in Testimonial matches making his total 1,283.*

MOST CAPPED INTERNATIONALS IN THE BRITISH ISLES

England	Peter Shilton	125 appearances	1970–90
Northern Ireland	Pat Jennings	119 appearances	1964–86
Scotland	Kenny Dalglish	102 appearances	1971–86
Wales	Neville Southall	92 appearances	1982–97
Republic of Ireland	Shay Given	125 appearances	1996–2012

LONDON INTERNATIONAL VENUES

Eleven different venues in the London area have staged full England international games: Kennington Oval, Richmond Athletic Ground, Queen's Club, Crystal Palace, Craven Cottage, The Den, Stamford Bridge, Highbury, Wembley, Selhurst Park, White Hart Lane and Upton Park.

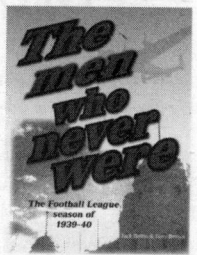

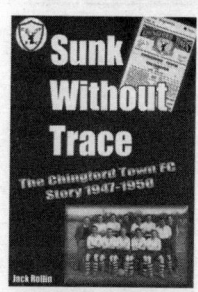

THE FA BARCLAYS PREMIERSHIP AND NPOWER FOOTBALL LEAGUE FIXTURES 2012–13

**Sky Sports* *All fixtures subject to change.*

Friday, 17 August 2012
npower Football League Championship
Cardiff C v Huddersfield T* (7.45)

Saturday, 18 August 2012
Barclays Premier League
Arsenal v Sunderland
Fulham v Norwich C
Newcastle U v Tottenham H
QPR v Swansea C
Reading v Stoke C
WBA v Liverpool
West Ham U v Aston Villa

npower Football League Championship
Barnsley v Middlesbrough
Birmingham C v Charlton Ath
Burnley v Bolton W
Crystal Palace v Watford
Derby Co v Sheffield W
Hull C v Brighton & HA
Ipswich T v Blackburn R
Leeds U v Wolverhampton W* (12.45)
Leicester C v Peterborough U
Millwall v Blackpool
Nottingham F v Bristol C

npower Football League One
Bury v Brentford
Crawley T v Scunthorpe U
Crewe Alex v Notts Co
Hartlepool U v Swindon T
Milton Keynes D v Oldham Ath
Portsmouth v Bournemouth
Preston NE v Colchester U
Sheffield U v Shrewsbury T
Stevenage v Carlisle U
Tranmere v Leyton Orient
Walsall v Doncaster R
Yeovil T v Coventry C

npower Football League Two
AFC Wimbledon v Chesterfield
Bristol R v Oxford U
Cheltenham T v Dagenham & R
Exeter C v Morecambe
Fleetwood T v Torquay U
Gillingham v Bradford C
Plymouth Arg v Aldershot T
Port Vale v Barnet
Rochdale v Northampton T
Rotherham U v Burton Alb
Southend U v Accrington S
York C v Wycombe W

Sunday, 19 August 2012
Barclays Premier League
Wigan Ath v Chelsea* (1.30)
Manchester C v Southampton* (4.00)

Monday, 20 August 2012
Barclays Premier League
Everton v Manchester U* (8.00)

Tuesday, 21 August 2012
npower Football League Championship
Blackpool v Leeds U
Bolton W v Derby Co
Brighton & HA v Cardiff C
Bristol C v Crystal Palace
Charlton Ath v Leicester C
Huddersfield T v Nottingham F
Middlesbrough v Burnley
Peterborough U v Millwall
Sheffield W v Birmingham C
Watford v Ipswich T
Wolverhampton W v Barnsley

npower Football League One
Bournemouth v Milton Keynes D
Brentford v Yeovil T
Carlisle U v Tranmere
Colchester U v Portsmouth
Coventry C v Sheffield U
Doncaster R v Bury
Leyton Orient v Stevenage
Notts Co v Hartlepool U
Oldham Ath v Walsall
Scunthorpe U v Crewe Alex
Shrewsbury T v Preston NE
Swindon T v Crawley T

npower Football League Two
Accrington S v Port Vale
Aldershot T v Exeter C
Barnet v Bristol R
Bradford C v Fleetwood T
Burton Alb v AFC Wimbledon
Chesterfield v Rochdale
Dagenham & R v Plymouth Arg
Morecambe v York C
Northampton T v Rotherham U
Oxford U v Southend U
Torquay U v Cheltenham T
Wycombe W v Gillingham

Wednesday, 22 August 2012
npower Football League Championship
Blackburn R v Hull C

Friday, 24 August 2012
npower Football League Championship
Bolton W v Nottingham F* (7.45)

Saturday, 25 August 2012
Barclays Premier League
Aston Villa v Everton
Chelsea v Newcastle U
Manchester U v Fulham
Norwich C v QPR
Southampton v Wigan Ath
Sunderland v Reading
Swansea C v West Ham U* (12.45)
Tottenham H v WBA

npower Football League Championship
Blackburn R v Leicester C
Blackpool v Ipswich T
Brighton & HA v Barnsley
Bristol C v Cardiff C
Charlton Ath v Hull C
Huddersfield T v Burnley
Middlesbrough v Crystal Palace
Peterborough U v Leeds U
Sheffield W v Millwall
Watford v Birmingham C
Wolverhampton W v Derby Co

npower Football League One
Bournemouth v Preston NE
Brentford v Crewe Alex
Carlisle U v Portsmouth
Colchester U v Sheffield U
Coventry C v Bury
Doncaster R v Crawley T
Leyton Orient v Hartlepool U
Notts Co v Walsall
Oldham Ath v Stevenage
Scunthorpe U v Yeovil T
Shrewsbury T v Tranmere
Swindon T v Milton Keynes D

npower Football League Two
Accrington S v Exeter C
Aldershot T v Cheltenham T
Barnet v York C
Bradford C v AFC Wimbledon
Burton Alb v Fleetwood T
Chesterfield v Rotherham U
Dagenham & R v Gillingham
Morecambe v Port Vale
Northampton T v Southend U
Oxford U v Plymouth Arg
Torquay U v Rochdale
Wycombe W v Bristol R

Sunday, 26 August 2012
Barclays Premier League
Stoke C v Arsenal* (1.30)
Liverpool v Manchester C* (4.00)

Saturday, 1 September 2012
Barclays Premier League
Chelsea v Reading
Manchester C v QPR
Newcastle U v Aston Villa
Swansea C v Sunderland
Tottenham H v Norwich C
WBA v Everton
West Ham U v Fulham* (12.45)
Wigan Ath v Stoke C

npower Football League Championship
Barnsley v Bristol C
Birmingham C v Peterborough U
Burnley v Brighton & HA
Cardiff C v Wolverhampton W
Crystal Palace v Sheffield W
Derby Co v Watford
Hull C v Bolton W
Ipswich T v Huddersfield T
Leeds U v Blackburn R
Leicester C v Blackpool
Millwall v Middlesbrough
Nottingham F v Charlton Ath

npower Football League One
Bury v Notts Co
Crawley T v Leyton Orient
Crewe Alex v Coventry C
Hartlepool U v Scunthorpe U
Milton Keynes D v Carlisle U
Portsmouth v Oldham Ath

Preston NE v Swindon T
Sheffield U v Bournemouth
Stevenage v Shrewsbury T
Tranmere v Colchester U
Walsall v Brentford
Yeovil T v Doncaster R

npower Football League Two
AFC Wimbledon v Dagenham & R
Bristol R v Morecambe
Cheltenham T v Accrington S
Exeter C v Burton Alb
Fleetwood T v Aldershot T
Gillingham v Chesterfield
Plymouth Arg v Northampton T
Port Vale v Torquay U
Rochdale v Barnet
Rotherham U v Bradford C
Southend U v Wycombe W
York C v Oxford U

Sunday, 2 September 2012
Barclays Premier League
Liverpool v Arsenal* (1.30)
Southampton v Manchester U* (4.00)

Saturday, 8 September 2012
npower Football League One
Brentford v Colchester U
Bury v Preston NE
Crewe Alex v Tranmere
Doncaster R v Oldham Ath
Hartlepool U v Carlisle U
Notts Co v Shrewsbury T
Scunthorpe U v Sheffield U
Swindon T v Leyton Orient
Walsall v Milton Keynes D
Yeovil T v Bournemouth

npower Football League Two
Accrington S v Bradford C
Barnet v Gillingham
Bristol R v Aldershot T
Morecambe v Fleetwood T
Northampton T v AFC Wimbledon
Oxford U v Exeter C
Port Vale v Rotherham U
Rochdale v Burton Alb
Southend U v Dagenham & R
Torquay U v Plymouth Arg
Wycombe W v Cheltenham T
York C v Chesterfield

Sunday, 9 September 2012
Barclays Premier League
Coventry C v Stevenage* (1.15)
Crawley T v Portsmouth* (3.30)

Friday, 14 September 2012
npower Football League Championship
Charlton Ath v Crystal Palace* (7.45)

Saturday, 15 September 2012
Barclays Premier League
Arsenal v Southampton
Aston Villa v Swansea C
Fulham v WBA
Manchester U v Wigan Ath
Norwich C v West Ham U* (12.45)
QPR v Chelsea
Stoke C v Manchester C
Sunderland v Liverpool

npower Football League Championship
Barnsley v Blackpool
Bolton W v Watford
Brighton & HA v Sheffield W
Bristol C v Blackburn R
Burnley v Peterborough U
Cardiff C v Leeds U
Huddersfield T v Derby Co
Hull C v Millwall
Middlesbrough v Ipswich T
Nottingham F v Birmingham C
Wolverhampton W v Leicester C

npower Football League One
Bournemouth v Hartlepool U
Carlisle U v Swindon T
Colchester U v Doncaster R
Leyton Orient v Brentford
Milton Keynes D v Yeovil T
Oldham Ath v Notts Co
Portsmouth v Walsall
Preston NE v Crawley T
Sheffield U v Bury
Shrewsbury T v Scunthorpe U
Stevenage v Crewe Alex
Tranmere v Coventry C

npower Football League Two
AFC Wimbledon v Rochdale
Aldershot T v Morecambe
Bradford C v Barnet
Burton Alb v Oxford U
Cheltenham T v Southend U
Chesterfield v Wycombe W
Dagenham & R v Accrington S
Exeter C v York C
Fleetwood T v Northampton T
Gillingham v Bristol R
Plymouth Arg v Port Vale
Rotherham U v Torquay U

Sunday, 16 September 2012
Barclays Premier League
Reading v Tottenham H* (4.00)

Monday, 17 September 2012
Barclays Premier League
Everton v Newcastle U* (8.00)

Tuesday, 18 September 2012
npower Football League Championship
Birmingham C v Bolton W
Blackpool v Middlesbrough
Crystal Palace v Nottingham F
Derby Co v Charlton Ath
Ipswich T v Wolverhampton W
Leeds U v Hull C
Leicester C v Burnley
Millwall v Cardiff C
Peterborough U v Bristol C
Sheffield W v Huddersfield T
Watford v Brighton & HA

npower Football League One
Bournemouth v Brentford
Carlisle U v Crewe Alex
Colchester U v Crawley T
Leyton Orient v Yeovil T
Milton Keynes D v Notts Co
Oldham Ath v Scunthorpe U
Portsmouth v Swindon T
Preston NE v Hartlepool U
Sheffield U v Doncaster R
Shrewsbury T v Coventry C
Stevenage v Walsall
Tranmere v Bury

npower Football League Two
AFC Wimbledon v Torquay U
Aldershot T v Barnet
Bradford C v Morecambe
Burton Alb v York C
Cheltenham T v Oxford U
Chesterfield v Accrington S
Dagenham & R v Northampton T
Exeter C v Wycombe W
Fleetwood T v Port Vale
Gillingham v Southend U
Plymouth Arg v Bristol R
Rotherham U v Rochdale

Wednesday, 19 September 2012
npower Football League Championship
Blackburn R v Barnsley

Friday, 21 September 2012
npower Football League Championship
Blackburn R v Middlesbrough* (7.45)

Saturday, 22 September 2012
Barclays Premier League
Chelsea v Stoke C
Newcastle U v Norwich C
Southampton v Aston Villa
Swansea C v Everton* (12.45)
Tottenham H v QPR
WBA v Reading
West Ham U v Sunderland
Wigan Ath v Fulham

npower Football League Championship
Birmingham C v Barnsley
Blackpool v Huddersfield T
Crystal Palace v Cardiff C
Derby Co v Burnley
Ipswich T v Charlton Ath
Leeds U v Nottingham F
Leicester C v Hull C
Millwall v Brighton & HA
Peterborough U v Wolverhampton W
Sheffield W v Bolton W
Watford v Bristol C

npower Football League One
Brentford v Oldham Ath
Bury v Milton Keynes D
Coventry C v Carlisle U
Crawley T v Tranmere
Crewe Alex v Leyton Orient
Doncaster R v Stevenage
Hartlepool U v Shrewsbury T
Notts Co v Portsmouth
Scunthorpe U v Colchester U
Swindon T v Bournemouth
Walsall v Preston NE
Yeovil T v Sheffield U

npower Football League Two
Accrington S v Aldershot T
Barnet v Rotherham U
Bristol R v Fleetwood T
Morecambe v Plymouth Arg
Northampton T v Chesterfield
Oxford U v Bradford C
Port Vale v Gillingham
Rochdale v Dagenham & R
Southend U v Exeter C
Torquay U v Burton Alb
Wycombe W v AFC Wimbledon
York C v Cheltenham T

Sunday, 23 September 2012
Barclays Premier League
Liverpool v Manchester U* (1.30)
Manchester C v Arsenal* (4.00)

Saturday, 29 September 2012
Barclays Premier League
Arsenal v Chelsea* (12.45)
Everton v Southampton
Fulham v Manchester C
Manchester U v Tottenham H
Norwich C v Liverpool
Reading v Newcastle U
Stoke C v Swansea C
Sunderland v Wigan Ath

npower Football League Championship
Barnsley v Ipswich T
Bolton W v Crystal Palace
Brighton & HA v Birmingham C
Bristol C v Leeds U
Burnley v Millwall
Cardiff C v Blackpool
Charlton Ath v Blackburn R
Huddersfield T v Watford
Hull C v Peterborough U
Middlesbrough v Leicester C
Nottingham F v Derby Co
Wolverhampton W v Sheffield W

npower Football League One
Bournemouth v Walsall
Carlisle U v Crawley T
Colchester U v Hartlepool U

Leyton Orient v Doncaster R
Milton Keynes D v Crewe Alex
Oldham Ath v Coventry C
Portsmouth v Scunthorpe U
Preston NE v Yeovil T
Sheffield U v Notts Co
Shrewsbury T v Swindon T
Stevenage v Bury
Tranmere v Brentford

npower Football League Two
AFC Wimbledon v Accrington S
Aldershot T v York C
Bradford C v Port Vale
Burton Alb v Northampton T
Cheltenham T v Morecambe
Chesterfield v Torquay U
Dagenham & R v Wycombe W
Exeter C v Bristol R
Fleetwood T v Barnet
Gillingham v Rochdale
Plymouth Arg v Southend U
Rotherham U v Oxford U

Sunday, 30 September 2012
Barclays Premier League
Aston Villa v WBA* (4.00)

Monday, 1 October 2012
Barclays Premier League
QPR v West Ham U* (8.00)

Tuesday, 2 October 2012
npower Football League Championship
Barnsley v Peterborough U
Bolton W v Leeds U
Brighton & HA v Ipswich T
Bristol C v Millwall
Burnley v Sheffield W
Cardiff C v Birmingham C
Charlton Ath v Watford
Huddersfield T v Leicester C
Hull C v Blackpool
Middlesbrough v Derby Co
Nottingham F v Blackburn R
Wolverhampton W v Crystal Palace

npower Football League One
Brentford v Shrewsbury T
Bury v Carlisle U
Coventry C v Milton Keynes D
Crawley T v Bournemouth
Crewe Alex v Oldham Ath
Doncaster R v Preston NE
Hartlepool U v Sheffield U
Notts Co v Stevenage
Scunthorpe U v Tranmere
Swindon T v Colchester U
Walsall v Leyton Orient
Yeovil T v Portsmouth

npower Football League Two
Accrington S v Rotherham U
Barnet v Exeter C
Bristol R v Cheltenham T
Morecambe v Chesterfield
Northampton T v Gillingham
Oxford U v AFC Wimbledon
Port Vale v Dagenham & R
Rochdale v Bradford C
Southend U v Burton Alb
Torquay U v Aldershot T
Wycombe W v Plymouth Arg
York C v Fleetwood T

Saturday, 6 October 2012
Barclays Premier League
Chelsea v Norwich C
Liverpool v Stoke C
Manchester C v Sunderland* (12.45)
Swansea C v Reading
Tottenham H v Aston Villa
WBA v QPR
West Ham U v Arsenal
Wigan Ath v Everton

npower Football League Championship
Birmingham C v Huddersfield T
Blackburn R v Wolverhampton W
Blackpool v Charlton Ath
Crystal Palace v Burnley
Derby Co v Brighton & HA
Ipswich T v Cardiff C
Leeds U v Barnsley
Leicester C v Bristol C
Millwall v Bolton W
Peterborough U v Nottingham F
Sheffield W v Hull C
Watford v Middlesbrough

npower Football League One
Brentford v Crawley T
Bury v Swindon T
Coventry C v Bournemouth
Crewe Alex v Hartlepool U
Doncaster R v Shrewsbury T
Leyton Orient v Sheffield U
Milton Keynes D v Portsmouth
Notts Co v Tranmere
Oldham Ath v Preston NE
Stevenage v Scunthorpe U
Walsall v Carlisle U
Yeovil T v Colchester U

npower Football League Two
Accrington S v Rochdale
Aldershot T v Chesterfield
Bristol R v Northampton T
Cheltenham T v Fleetwood T
Dagenham & R v Bradford C
Exeter C v Port Vale
Morecambe v Burton Alb
Oxford U v Gillingham
Plymouth Arg v AFC Wimbledon
Southend U v Barnet
Wycombe W v Torquay U
York C v Rotherham U

Sunday, 7 October 2012
Barclays Premier League
Southampton v Fulham* (1.30)
Newcastle U v Manchester U* (4.00)

Saturday, 13 October 2012
npower Football League One
Bournemouth v Leyton Orient
Carlisle U v Notts Co
Colchester U v Stevenage
Crawley T v Bury
Hartlepool U v Doncaster R
Portsmouth v Crewe Alex
Preston NE v Milton Keynes D
Scunthorpe U v Brentford
Sheffield U v Oldham Ath
Shrewsbury T v Walsall
Swindon T v Coventry C
Tranmere v Yeovil T

npower Football League Two
AFC Wimbledon v Cheltenham T
Barnet v Plymouth Arg
Bradford C v York C
Burton Alb v Bristol R
Chesterfield v Dagenham & R
Fleetwood T v Wycombe W
Gillingham v Aldershot T
Northampton T v Exeter C
Port Vale v Oxford U
Rochdale v Morecambe
Rotherham U v Southend U
Torquay U v Accrington S

Saturday, 20 October 2012
Barclays Premier League
Fulham v Aston Villa
Liverpool v Reading
Manchester U v Stoke C
Norwich C v Arsenal
Swansea C v Wigan Ath
Tottenham H v Chelsea* (12.45)
WBA v Manchester C
West Ham U v Southampton

npower Football League Championship
Birmingham C v Leicester C
Bolton W v Bristol C
Brighton & HA v Middlesbrough
Burnley v Blackpool
Charlton Ath v Barnsley
Crystal Palace v Millwall
Derby Co v Blackburn R
Huddersfield T v Wolverhampton W
Hull C v Ipswich T
Nottingham F v Cardiff C
Sheffield W v Leeds U
Watford v Peterborough U

npower Football League One
Bournemouth v Tranmere
Colchester U v Carlisle U
Coventry C v Notts Co
Doncaster R v Brentford
Hartlepool U v Crawley T
Milton Keynes D v Stevenage
Oldham Ath v Leyton Orient
Portsmouth v Shrewsbury T
Preston NE v Sheffield U
Swindon T v Scunthorpe U
Walsall v Crewe Alex
Yeovil T v Bury

npower Football League Two
Aldershot T v Rotherham U
Barnet v Northampton T
Bradford C v Cheltenham T
Bristol R v Torquay U
Exeter C v Chesterfield
Fleetwood T v AFC Wimbledon
Gillingham v Burton Alb
Morecambe v Southend U
Oxford U v Accrington S
Plymouth Arg v Rochdale
Port Vale v Wycombe W
York C v Dagenham & R

Sunday, 21 October 2012
Barclays Premier League
Sunderland v Newcastle U* (1.30)
QPR v Everton* (4.00)

Tuesday, 23 October 2012
npower Football League Championship
Barnsley v Crystal Palace
Blackpool v Nottingham F
Bristol C v Burnley
Cardiff C v Watford
Ipswich T v Derby Co
Leeds U v Charlton Ath
Leicester C v Brighton & HA
Middlesbrough v Hull C
Millwall v Birmingham C
Peterborough U v Huddersfield T
Wolverhampton W v Bolton W

npower Football League One
Brentford v Coventry C
Bury v Hartlepool U
Carlisle U v Oldham Ath
Crawley T v Milton Keynes D
Crewe Alex v Swindon T
Leyton Orient v Colchester U
Notts Co v Bournemouth
Scunthorpe U v Preston NE
Sheffield U v Walsall
Shrewsbury T v Yeovil T
Stevenage v Portsmouth
Tranmere v Doncaster R

npower Football League Two
AFC Wimbledon v Bristol R
Accrington S v York C
Burton Alb v Port Vale
Cheltenham T v Plymouth Arg
Chesterfield v Fleetwood T
Dagenham & R v Exeter C
Northampton T v Bradford C
Rochdale v Oxford U
Rotherham U v Morecambe
Southend U v Aldershot T

Torquay U v Gillingham
Wycombe W v Barnet

Wednesday, 24 October 2012

npower Football League Championship

Blackburn R v Sheffield W

Saturday, 27 October 2012

Barclays Premier League

Arsenal v QPR
Everton v Liverpool* (12.45)
Manchester C v Swansea C
Newcastle U v WBA
Reading v Fulham
Southampton v Tottenham H
Stoke C v Sunderland
Wigan Ath v West Ham U

npower Football League Championship

Barnsley v Nottingham F
Blackburn R v Watford
Blackpool v Brighton & HA
Bristol C v Hull C
Cardiff C v Burnley
Ipswich T v Sheffield W
Leeds U v Birmingham C
Leicester C v Crystal Palace
Middlesbrough v Bolton W
Millwall v Huddersfield T
Peterborough U v Derby Co
Wolverhampton W v Charlton Ath

npower Football League One

Brentford v Hartlepool U
Bury v Walsall
Carlisle U v Bournemouth
Crawley T v Oldham Ath
Crewe Alex v Yeovil T
Leyton Orient v Coventry C
Notts Co v Doncaster R
Scunthorpe U v Milton Keynes D
Sheffield U v Portsmouth
Shrewsbury T v Colchester U
Stevenage v Swindon T
Tranmere v Preston NE

npower Football League Two

AFC Wimbledon v Gillingham
Accrington S v Bristol R
Burton Alb v Bradford C
Cheltenham T v Exeter C
Chesterfield v Barnet
Dagenham & R v Aldershot T
Northampton T v Port Vale
Rochdale v Fleetwood T
Rotherham U v Plymouth Arg
Southend U v York C
Torquay U v Morecambe
Wycombe W v Oxford U

Sunday, 28 October 2012

Barclays Premier League

Aston Villa v Norwich C* (1.30)
Chelsea v Manchester U* (4.00)

Saturday, 3 November 2012

Barclays Premier League

Fulham v Everton
Manchester U v Arsenal* (12.45)
Norwich C v Stoke C
Sunderland v Aston Villa
Swansea C v Chelsea
Tottenham H v Wigan Ath
West Ham U v Manchester C

npower Football League Championship

Birmingham C v Ipswich T
Bolton W v Cardiff C
Brighton & HA v Leeds U
Burnley v Wolverhampton W
Charlton Ath v Middlesbrough
Crystal Palace v Blackburn R
Derby Co v Blackpool
Huddersfield T v Bristol C
Hull C v Barnsley
Nottingham F v Millwall
Sheffield W v Peterborough U
Watford v Leicester C

Sunday, 4 November 2012

Barclays Premier League

QPR v Reading* (1.30)
Liverpool v Newcastle U* (4.00)

Monday, 5 November 2012

Barclays Premier League

WBA v Southampton* (8.00)

Tuesday, 6 November 2012

npower Football League Championship

Birmingham C v Bristol C
Bolton W v Leicester C
Brighton & HA v Peterborough U
Burnley v Leeds U
Charlton Ath v Cardiff C
Crystal Palace v Ipswich T
Derby Co v Barnsley
Huddersfield T v Blackburn R
Hull C v Wolverhampton W
Nottingham F v Middlesbrough
Sheffield W v Blackpool
Watford v Millwall

npower Football League One

Bournemouth v Shrewsbury T
Colchester U v Notts Co
Coventry C v Crawley T
Doncaster R v Crewe Alex
Hartlepool U v Tranmere
Milton Keynes D v Leyton Orient
Oldham Ath v Bury
Portsmouth v Brentford
Preston NE v Carlisle U
Swindon T v Sheffield U
Walsall v Scunthorpe U
Yeovil T v Stevenage

npower Football League Two

Aldershot T v Wycombe W
Barnet v Torquay U
Bradford C v Chesterfield
Bristol R v Southend U
Exeter C v AFC Wimbledon
Fleetwood T v Rotherham U
Gillingham v Cheltenham T
Morecambe v Accrington S
Oxford U v Dagenham & R
Plymouth Arg v Burton Alb
Port Vale v Rochdale
York C v Northampton T

Saturday, 10 November 2012

Barclays Premier League

Arsenal v Fulham
Aston Villa v Manchester U* (5.30)
Everton v Sunderland
Newcastle U v West Ham U
Reading v Norwich C
Southampton v Swansea C
Stoke C v QPR
Wigan Ath v WBA

npower Football League Championship

Barnsley v Huddersfield T
Blackburn R v Birmingham C
Blackpool v Bolton W
Bristol C v Charlton Ath
Cardiff C v Hull C
Ipswich T v Burnley
Leeds U v Watford
Leicester C v Nottingham F
Middlesbrough v Sheffield W
Millwall v Derby Co
Peterborough U v Crystal Palace
Wolverhampton W v Brighton & HA

npower Football League One

Brentford v Carlisle U
Bury v Portsmouth
Coventry C v Scunthorpe U
Crewe Alex v Colchester U
Doncaster R v Bournemouth
Leyton Orient v Shrewsbury T
Milton Keynes D v Sheffield U
Notts Co v Crawley T
Oldham Ath v Tranmere
Stevenage v Preston NE
Walsall v Swindon T
Yeovil T v Hartlepool U

npower Football League Two

Accrington S v Northampton T
Aldershot T v Bradford C
Bristol R v Chesterfield
Cheltenham T v Burton Alb
Dagenham & R v Rotherham U
Exeter C v Fleetwood T
Morecambe v Barnet
Oxford U v Torquay U
Plymouth Arg v Gillingham
Southend U v Port Vale
Wycombe W v Rochdale
York C v AFC Wimbledon

Sunday, 11 November 2012

Barclays Premier League

Manchester C v Tottenham H* (1.30)
Chelsea v Liverpool* (4.00)

Saturday, 17 November 2012

Barclays Premier League

Arsenal v Tottenham H* (12.45)
Liverpool v Wigan Ath
Manchester C v Aston Villa
Newcastle U v Swansea C
Norwich C v Manchester U
QPR v Southampton
Reading v Everton
WBA v Chelsea

npower Football League Championship

Birmingham C v Hull C
Bolton W v Barnsley
Bristol C v Blackpool
Burnley v Charlton Ath
Cardiff C v Middlesbrough
Crystal Palace v Derby Co
Huddersfield T v Brighton & HA
Leicester C v Ipswich T
Millwall v Leeds U
Nottingham F v Sheffield W
Peterborough U v Blackburn R
Watford v Wolverhampton W

npower Football League One

Bournemouth v Oldham Ath
Carlisle U v Leyton Orient
Colchester U v Bury
Crawley T v Walsall
Hartlepool U v Coventry C
Portsmouth v Doncaster R
Preston NE v Brentford
Scunthorpe U v Notts Co
Sheffield U v Stevenage
Shrewsbury T v Crewe Alex
Swindon T v Yeovil T
Tranmere v Milton Keynes D

npower Football League Two

AFC Wimbledon v Aldershot T
Barnet v Accrington S
Bradford C v Exeter C
Burton Alb v Dagenham & R
Chesterfield v Oxford U
Fleetwood T v Plymouth Arg
Gillingham v Morecambe
Northampton T v Wycombe W
Port Vale v York C
Rochdale v Bristol R
Rotherham U v Cheltenham T
Torquay U v Southend U

Sunday, 18 November 2012

Barclays Premier League

Fulham v Sunderland* (4.00)

Monday, 19 November 2012

Barclays Premier League

West Ham U v Stoke C* (8.00)

Tuesday, 20 November 2012
npower Football League One
Bournemouth v Stevenage
Carlisle U v Doncaster R
Colchester U v Coventry C
Crawley T v Yeovil T
Hartlepool U v Oldham Ath
Portsmouth v Leyton Orient
Preston NE v Notts Co
Scunthorpe U v Bury
Sheffield U v Crewe Alex
Shrewsbury T v Milton Keynes D
Swindon T v Brentford
Tranmere v Walsall

npower Football League Two
AFC Wimbledon v Southend U
Barnet v Oxford U
Bradford C v Plymouth Arg
Burton Alb v Aldershot T
Chesterfield v Cheltenham T
Fleetwood T v Accrington S
Gillingham v Exeter C
Northampton T v Morecambe
Port Vale v Bristol R
Rochdale v York C
Rotherham U v Wycombe W
Torquay U v Dagenham & R

Saturday, 24 November 2012
Barclays Premier League
Aston Villa v Arsenal
Everton v Norwich C
Manchester U v QPR
Southampton v Newcastle U
Stoke C v Fulham
Swansea C v Liverpool* (12.45)
Tottenham H v West Ham U
Wigan Ath v Reading

npower Football League Championship
Barnsley v Cardiff C
Blackburn R v Millwall
Blackpool v Watford
Brighton & HA v Bolton W
Charlton Ath v Huddersfield T
Derby Co v Birmingham C
Hull C v Burnley
Ipswich T v Peterborough U
Leeds U v Crystal Palace
Middlesbrough v Bristol C
Sheffield W v Leicester C
Wolverhampton W v Nottingham F

npower Football League One
Brentford v Sheffield U
Bury v Bournemouth
Coventry C v Portsmouth
Crewe Alex v Crawley T
Doncaster R v Scunthorpe U
Leyton Orient v Preston NE
Milton Keynes D v Colchester U
Notts Co v Swindon T
Oldham Ath v Shrewsbury T
Stevenage v Tranmere
Walsall v Hartlepool U
Yeovil T v Carlisle U

npower Football League Two
Accrington S v Gillingham
Aldershot T v Port Vale
Bristol R v Bradford C
Cheltenham T v Barnet
Dagenham & R v Fleetwood T
Exeter C v Rotherham U
Morecambe v AFC Wimbledon
Oxford U v Northampton T
Plymouth Arg v Chesterfield
Southend U v Rochdale
Wycombe W v Burton Alb
York C v Torquay U

Sunday, 25 November 2012
Barclays Premier League
Sunderland v WBA* (1.30)
Chelsea v Manchester C* (4.00)

Tuesday, 27 November 2012
Barclays Premier League
Aston Villa v Reading* (8.00)
Manchester U v West Ham U
Southampton v Norwich C
Stoke C v Newcastle U
Sunderland v QPR
Swansea C v WBA
Tottenham H v Liverpool

npower Football League Championship
Barnsley v Burnley
Blackpool v Birmingham C
Brighton & HA v Bristol C
Charlton Ath v Peterborough U
Derby Co v Cardiff C
Hull C v Crystal Palace
Ipswich T v Nottingham F
Leeds U v Leicester C
Middlesbrough v Huddersfield T
Sheffield W v Watford
Wolverhampton W v Millwall

Wednesday, 28 November 2012
Barclays Premier League
Chelsea v Fulham
Everton v Arsenal
Wigan Ath v Manchester C* (8.00)

npower Football League Championship
Blackburn R v Bolton W

Saturday, 1 December 2012
Barclays Premier League
Arsenal v Swansea C
Fulham v Tottenham H
Liverpool v Southampton
Manchester C v Everton
Newcastle U v Wigan Ath
Norwich C v Sunderland
QPR v Aston Villa
Reading v Manchester U
WBA v Stoke C
West Ham U v Chelsea

npower Football League Championship
Birmingham C v Middlesbrough
Bolton W v Ipswich T
Bristol C v Wolverhampton W
Burnley v Blackburn R
Cardiff C v Sheffield W
Crystal Palace v Brighton & HA
Huddersfield T v Leeds U
Leicester C v Derby Co
Millwall v Charlton Ath
Nottingham F v Hull C
Peterborough U v Blackpool
Watford v Barnsley

Saturday, 8 December 2012
Barclays Premier League
Arsenal v WBA
Aston Villa v Stoke C
Everton v Tottenham H
Fulham v Newcastle U
Manchester C v Manchester U
Southampton v Reading
Sunderland v Chelsea
Swansea C v Norwich C
West Ham U v Liverpool
Wigan Ath v QPR

npower Football League Championship
Blackburn R v Cardiff C
Charlton Ath v Brighton & HA
Crystal Palace v Blackpool
Derby Co v Leeds U
Huddersfield T v Bolton W
Ipswich T v Millwall
Leicester C v Barnsley
Nottingham F v Burnley
Peterborough U v Middlesbrough
Sheffield W v Bristol C
Watford v Hull C
Wolverhampton W v Birmingham C

npower Football League One
Brentford v Milton Keynes D
Bury v Leyton Orient
Carlisle U v Sheffield U
Colchester U v Oldham Ath
Coventry C v Walsall
Crawley T v Shrewsbury T
Hartlepool U v Stevenage
Preston NE v Crewe Alex
Scunthorpe U v Bournemouth
Swindon T v Doncaster R
Tranmere v Portsmouth
Yeovil T v Notts Co

npower Football League Two
Barnet v AFC Wimbledon
Bradford C v Torquay U
Bristol R v Dagenham & R
Burton Alb v Accrington S
Fleetwood T v Southend U
Northampton T v Cheltenham T
Oxford U v Aldershot T
Plymouth Arg v York C
Port Vale v Chesterfield
Rochdale v Exeter C
Rotherham U v Gillingham
Wycombe W v Morecambe

Saturday, 15 December 2012
Barclays Premier League
Chelsea v Southampton
Liverpool v Aston Villa
Manchester U v Sunderland
Newcastle U v Manchester C
Norwich C v Wigan Ath
QPR v Fulham
Reading v Arsenal
Stoke C v Everton
Tottenham H v Swansea C
WBA v West Ham U

npower Football League Championship
Barnsley v Sheffield W
Birmingham C v Crystal Palace
Blackpool v Blackburn R
Bolton W v Charlton Ath
Brighton & HA v Nottingham F
Bristol C v Derby Co
Burnley v Watford
Cardiff C v Peterborough U
Hull C v Huddersfield T
Leeds U v Ipswich T
Middlesbrough v Wolverhampton W
Millwall v Leicester C

npower Football League One
Bournemouth v Colchester U
Crewe Alex v Bury
Doncaster R v Coventry C
Leyton Orient v Scunthorpe U
Milton Keynes D v Hartlepool U
Notts Co v Brentford
Oldham Ath v Swindon T
Portsmouth v Preston NE
Sheffield U v Tranmere
Shrewsbury T v Carlisle U
Stevenage v Crawley T
Walsall v Yeovil T

npower Football League Two
AFC Wimbledon v Rotherham U
Accrington S v Wycombe W
Aldershot T v Rochdale
Cheltenham T v Port Vale
Chesterfield v Burton Alb
Dagenham & R v Barnet
Exeter C v Plymouth Arg
Gillingham v Fleetwood T
Morecambe v Oxford U
Southend U v Bradford C
Torquay U v Northampton T
York C v Bristol R

Saturday, 22 December 2012

Barclays Premier League

Chelsea v Aston Villa
Liverpool v Fulham
Manchester C v Reading
Newcastle U v QPR
Southampton v Sunderland
Swansea C v Manchester U
Tottenham H v Stoke C
WBA v Norwich C
West Ham U v Everton
Wigan Ath v Arsenal

npower Football League Championship

Birmingham C v Burnley
Blackburn R v Brighton & HA
Blackpool v Wolverhampton W
Crystal Palace v Huddersfield T
Derby Co v Hull C
Ipswich T v Bristol C
Leeds U v Middlesbrough
Leicester C v Cardiff C
Millwall v Barnsley
Peterborough U v Bolton W
Sheffield W v Charlton Ath
Watford v Nottingham F

npower Football League One

Brentford v Stevenage
Bury v Shrewsbury T
Coventry C v Preston NE
Crawley T v Sheffield U
Crewe Alex v Bournemouth
Doncaster R v Milton Keynes D
Hartlepool U v Portsmouth
Notts Co v Leyton Orient
Scunthorpe U v Carlisle U
Swindon T v Tranmere
Walsall v Colchester U
Yeovil T v Oldham Ath

npower Football League Two

Accrington S v Plymouth Arg
Barnet v Burton Alb
Bristol R v Rotherham U
Morecambe v Dagenham & R
Northampton T v Aldershot T
Oxford U v Fleetwood T
Port Vale v AFC Wimbledon
Rochdale v Cheltenham T
Southend U v Chesterfield
Torquay U v Exeter C
Wycombe W v Bradford C
York C v Gillingham

Wednesday, 26 December 2012

Barclays Premier League

Arsenal v West Ham U
Aston Villa v Tottenham H
Everton v Wigan Ath
Fulham v Southampton
Manchester U v Newcastle U
Norwich C v Chelsea
QPR v WBA
Reading v Swansea C
Stoke C v Liverpool
Sunderland v Manchester C

npower Football League Championship

Barnsley v Birmingham C
Bolton W v Sheffield W
Brighton & HA v Millwall
Bristol C v Watford
Burnley v Derby Co
Cardiff C v Crystal Palace
Charlton Ath v Ipswich T
Huddersfield T v Blackpool
Hull C v Leicester C
Middlesbrough v Blackburn R
Nottingham F v Leeds U
Wolverhampton W v Peterborough U

npower Football League One

Bournemouth v Yeovil T
Carlisle U v Hartlepool U
Colchester U v Brentford
Leyton Orient v Swindon T
Milton Keynes D v Walsall
Oldham Ath v Doncaster R
Portsmouth v Crawley T
Preston NE v Bury
Sheffield U v Scunthorpe U
Shrewsbury T v Notts Co
Stevenage v Coventry C
Tranmere v Crewe Alex

npower Football League Two

AFC Wimbledon v Northampton T
Aldershot T v Bristol R
Bradford C v Accrington S
Burton Alb v Rochdale
Cheltenham T v Wycombe W
Chesterfield v York C
Dagenham & R v Southend U
Exeter C v Oxford U
Fleetwood T v Morecambe
Gillingham v Barnet
Plymouth Arg v Torquay U
Rotherham U v Port Vale

Saturday, 29 December 2012

Barclays Premier League

Arsenal v Newcastle U
Aston Villa v Wigan Ath
Everton v Chelsea
Fulham v Swansea C
Manchester U v WBA
Norwich C v Manchester C
QPR v Liverpool
Reading v West Ham U
Stoke C v Southampton
Sunderland v Tottenham H

npower Football League Championship

Barnsley v Blackburn R
Bolton W v Birmingham C
Brighton & HA v Watford
Bristol C v Peterborough U
Burnley v Leicester C
Cardiff C v Millwall
Charlton Ath v Derby Co
Huddersfield T v Sheffield W
Hull C v Leeds U
Middlesbrough v Blackpool
Nottingham F v Crystal Palace
Wolverhampton W v Ipswich T

npower Football League One

Bournemouth v Crawley T
Carlisle U v Bury
Colchester U v Swindon T
Leyton Orient v Walsall
Milton Keynes D v Coventry C
Oldham Ath v Crewe Alex
Portsmouth v Yeovil T
Preston NE v Doncaster R
Sheffield U v Hartlepool U
Shrewsbury T v Brentford
Stevenage v Notts Co
Tranmere v Scunthorpe U

npower Football League Two

AFC Wimbledon v Oxford U
Aldershot T v Torquay U
Bradford C v Rochdale
Burton Alb v Southend U
Cheltenham T v Bristol R
Chesterfield v Morecambe
Dagenham & R v Port Vale
Exeter C v Barnet
Fleetwood T v York C
Gillingham v Northampton T
Plymouth Arg v Wycombe W
Rotherham U v Accrington S

Tuesday, 1 January 2013

Barclays Premier League

Chelsea v QPR
Liverpool v Sunderland
Manchester C v Stoke C
Newcastle U v Everton
Southampton v Arsenal
Swansea C v Aston Villa
Tottenham H v Reading
WBA v Fulham
West Ham U v Norwich C
Wigan Ath v Manchester U

npower Football League Championship

Birmingham C v Cardiff C
Blackburn R v Nottingham F
Blackpool v Hull C
Crystal Palace v Wolverhampton W
Derby Co v Middlesbrough
Ipswich T v Brighton & HA
Leeds U v Bolton W
Leicester C v Huddersfield T
Millwall v Bristol C
Peterborough U v Barnsley
Sheffield W v Burnley
Watford v Charlton Ath

npower Football League One

Brentford v Bournemouth
Bury v Tranmere
Coventry C v Shrewsbury T
Crawley T v Colchester U
Crewe Alex v Carlisle U
Doncaster R v Sheffield U
Hartlepool U v Preston NE
Notts Co v Milton Keynes D
Scunthorpe U v Oldham Ath
Swindon T v Portsmouth
Walsall v Stevenage
Yeovil T v Leyton Orient

npower Football League Two

Accrington S v Chesterfield
Barnet v Aldershot T
Bristol R v Plymouth Arg
Morecambe v Bradford C
Northampton T v Dagenham & R
Oxford U v Cheltenham T
Port Vale v Fleetwood T
Rochdale v Rotherham U
Southend U v Gillingham
Torquay U v AFC Wimbledon
Wycombe W v Exeter C
York C v Burton Alb

Saturday, 5 January 2013

npower Football League One

Brentford v Leyton Orient
Bury v Sheffield U
Coventry C v Tranmere
Crawley T v Preston NE
Crewe Alex v Stevenage
Doncaster R v Colchester U
Hartlepool U v Bournemouth
Notts Co v Oldham Ath
Scunthorpe U v Shrewsbury T
Swindon T v Carlisle U
Walsall v Portsmouth
Yeovil T v Milton Keynes D

npower Football League Two

Accrington S v Dagenham & R
Barnet v Bradford C
Bristol R v Gillingham
Morecambe v Aldershot T
Northampton T v Fleetwood T
Oxford U v Burton Alb
Port Vale v Plymouth Arg
Rochdale v AFC Wimbledon
Southend U v Cheltenham T
Torquay U v Rotherham U
Wycombe W v Chesterfield
York C v Exeter C

Saturday, 12 January 2013

Barclays Premier League

Arsenal v Manchester C
Aston Villa v Southampton
Everton v Swansea C
Fulham v Wigan Ath
Manchester U v Liverpool
Norwich C v Newcastle U
QPR v Tottenham H
Reading v WBA

Stoke C v Chelsea
Sunderland v West Ham U

npower Football League Championship
Barnsley v Leeds U
Bolton W v Millwall
Brighton & HA v Derby Co
Bristol C v Leicester C
Burnley v Crystal Palace
Cardiff C v Ipswich T
Charlton Ath v Blackpool
Huddersfield T v Birmingham C
Hull C v Sheffield W
Middlesbrough v Watford
Nottingham F v Peterborough U
Wolverhampton W v Blackburn R

npower Football League One
Bournemouth v Swindon T
Carlisle U v Coventry C
Colchester U v Scunthorpe U
Leyton Orient v Crewe Alex
Milton Keynes D v Bury
Oldham Ath v Brentford
Portsmouth v Notts Co
Preston NE v Walsall
Sheffield U v Yeovil T
Shrewsbury T v Hartlepool U
Stevenage v Doncaster R
Tranmere v Crawley T

npower Football League Two
AFC Wimbledon v Wycombe W
Aldershot T v Accrington S
Bradford C v Oxford U
Burton Alb v Torquay U
Cheltenham T v York C
Chesterfield v Northampton T
Dagenham & R v Rochdale
Exeter C v Southend U
Fleetwood T v Bristol R
Gillingham v Port Vale
Plymouth Arg v Morecambe
Rotherham U v Barnet

Saturday, 19 January 2013

Barclays Premier League
Chelsea v Arsenal
Liverpool v Norwich C
Manchester C v Fulham
Newcastle U v Reading
Southampton v Everton
Swansea C v Stoke C
Tottenham H v Manchester U
WBA v Aston Villa
West Ham U v QPR
Wigan Ath v Sunderland

npower Football League Championship
Birmingham C v Brighton & HA
Blackburn R v Charlton Ath
Blackpool v Cardiff C
Crystal Palace v Bolton W
Derby Co v Nottingham F
Ipswich T v Barnsley
Leeds U v Bristol C
Leicester C v Middlesbrough
Millwall v Burnley
Peterborough U v Hull C
Sheffield W v Wolverhampton W
Watford v Huddersfield T

npower Football League One
Brentford v Tranmere
Bury v Stevenage
Coventry C v Oldham Ath
Crawley T v Carlisle U
Crewe Alex v Milton Keynes D
Doncaster R v Leyton Orient
Hartlepool U v Colchester U
Notts Co v Sheffield U
Scunthorpe U v Portsmouth
Swindon T v Shrewsbury T
Walsall v Bournemouth
Yeovil T v Preston NE

npower Football League Two
Accrington S v AFC Wimbledon
Barnet v Fleetwood T
Bristol R v Exeter C
Morecambe v Cheltenham T
Northampton T v Burton Alb
Oxford U v Rotherham U
Port Vale v Bradford C
Rochdale v Gillingham
Southend U v Plymouth Arg
Torquay U v Chesterfield
Wycombe W v Dagenham & R
York C v Aldershot T

Saturday, 26 January 2013

npower Football League Championship
Barnsley v Millwall
Bolton W v Peterborough U
Brighton & HA v Blackburn R
Bristol C v Ipswich T
Burnley v Birmingham C
Cardiff C v Leicester C
Charlton Ath v Sheffield W
Huddersfield T v Crystal Palace
Hull C v Derby Co
Middlesbrough v Leeds U
Nottingham F v Watford
Wolverhampton W v Blackpool

npower Football League One
Bournemouth v Crewe Alex
Carlisle U v Scunthorpe U
Colchester U v Walsall
Leyton Orient v Notts Co
Milton Keynes D v Doncaster R
Oldham Ath v Yeovil T
Portsmouth v Hartlepool U
Preston NE v Coventry C
Sheffield U v Crawley T
Shrewsbury T v Bury
Stevenage v Brentford
Tranmere v Swindon T

npower Football League Two
AFC Wimbledon v Port Vale
Aldershot T v Northampton T
Bradford C v Wycombe W
Burton Alb v Barnet
Cheltenham T v Rochdale
Chesterfield v Southend U
Dagenham & R v Morecambe
Exeter C v Torquay U
Fleetwood T v Oxford U
Gillingham v York C
Plymouth Arg v Accrington S
Rotherham U v Bristol R

Tuesday, 29 January 2013

Barclays Premier League
Arsenal v Liverpool
Aston Villa v Newcastle U
Manchester U v Southampton
Norwich C v Tottenham H
QPR v Manchester C
Reading v Chelsea
Stoke C v Wigan Ath
Sunderland v Swansea C

Wednesday, 30 January 2013

Barclays Premier League
Everton v WBA
Fulham v West Ham U

Saturday, 2 February 2013

Barclays Premier League
Arsenal v Stoke C
Everton v Aston Villa
Fulham v Manchester U
Manchester C v Liverpool
Newcastle U v Chelsea
QPR v Norwich C
Reading v Sunderland
WBA v Tottenham H
West Ham U v Swansea C
Wigan Ath v Southampton

npower Football League Championship
Birmingham C v Nottingham F
Blackburn R v Bristol C
Blackpool v Barnsley
Crystal Palace v Charlton Ath
Derby Co v Huddersfield T
Ipswich T v Middlesbrough
Leeds U v Cardiff C
Leicester C v Wolverhampton W
Millwall v Hull C
Peterborough U v Burnley
Sheffield W v Brighton & HA
Watford v Bolton W

npower Football League One
Bury v Doncaster R
Crawley T v Swindon T
Crewe Alex v Scunthorpe U
Hartlepool U v Notts Co
Milton Keynes D v Bournemouth
Portsmouth v Colchester U
Preston NE v Shrewsbury T
Sheffield U v Coventry C
Stevenage v Leyton Orient
Tranmere v Carlisle U
Walsall v Oldham Ath
Yeovil T v Brentford

npower Football League Two
AFC Wimbledon v Burton Alb
Bristol R v Barnet
Cheltenham T v Torquay U
Exeter C v Aldershot T
Fleetwood T v Bradford C
Gillingham v Wycombe W
Plymouth Arg v Dagenham & R
Port Vale v Accrington S
Rochdale v Chesterfield
Rotherham U v Northampton T
Southend U v Oxford U
York C v Morecambe

Saturday, 9 February 2013

Barclays Premier League
Aston Villa v West Ham U
Chelsea v Wigan Ath
Liverpool v WBA
Manchester U v Everton
Norwich C v Fulham
Southampton v Manchester C
Stoke C v Reading
Sunderland v Arsenal
Swansea C v QPR
Tottenham H v Newcastle U

npower Football League Championship
Blackburn R v Ipswich T
Blackpool v Millwall
Bolton W v Burnley
Brighton & HA v Hull C
Bristol C v Nottingham F
Charlton Ath v Birmingham C
Huddersfield T v Cardiff C
Middlesbrough v Barnsley
Peterborough U v Leicester C
Sheffield W v Derby Co
Watford v Crystal Palace
Wolverhampton W v Leeds U

npower Football League One
Bournemouth v Portsmouth
Brentford v Bury
Carlisle U v Stevenage
Colchester U v Preston NE
Coventry C v Yeovil T
Doncaster R v Walsall
Leyton Orient v Tranmere
Notts Co v Crewe Alex
Oldham Ath v Milton Keynes D
Scunthorpe U v Crawley T
Shrewsbury T v Sheffield U
Swindon T v Hartlepool U

npower Football League Two
Accrington S v Southend U
Aldershot T v Plymouth Arg

Barnet v Port Vale
Bradford C v Gillingham
Burton Alb v Rotherham U
Chesterfield v AFC Wimbledon
Dagenham & R v Cheltenham T
Morecambe v Exeter C
Northampton T v Rochdale
Oxford U v Bristol R
Torquay U v Fleetwood T
Wycombe W v York C

Saturday, 16 February 2013

npower Football League Championship

Barnsley v Brighton & HA
Birmingham C v Watford
Burnley v Huddersfield T
Cardiff C v Bristol C
Crystal Palace v Middlesbrough
Derby Co v Wolverhampton W
Hull C v Charlton Ath
Ipswich T v Blackpool
Leeds U v Peterborough U
Leicester C v Blackburn R
Millwall v Sheffield W
Nottingham F v Bolton W

npower Football League One

Bury v Coventry C
Crawley T v Doncaster R
Crewe Alex v Brentford
Hartlepool U v Leyton Orient
Milton Keynes D v Swindon T
Portsmouth v Carlisle U
Preston NE v Bournemouth
Sheffield U v Colchester U
Stevenage v Oldham Ath
Tranmere v Shrewsbury T
Walsall v Notts Co
Yeovil T v Scunthorpe U

npower Football League Two

AFC Wimbledon v Bradford C
Bristol R v Wycombe W
Cheltenham T v Aldershot T
Exeter C v Accrington S
Fleetwood T v Burton Alb
Gillingham v Dagenham & R
Plymouth Arg v Oxford U
Port Vale v Morecambe
Rochdale v Torquay U
Rotherham U v Chesterfield
Southend U v Northampton T
York C v Barnet

Tuesday, 19 February 2013

npower Football League Championship

Barnsley v Wolverhampton W
Birmingham C v Sheffield W
Burnley v Middlesbrough
Cardiff C v Brighton & HA
Crystal Palace v Bristol C
Derby Co v Bolton W
Hull C v Blackburn R
Ipswich T v Watford
Leeds U v Blackpool
Leicester C v Charlton Ath
Millwall v Peterborough U
Nottingham F v Huddersfield T

Saturday, 23 February 2013

Barclays Premier League

Arsenal v Aston Villa
Fulham v Stoke C
Liverpool v Swansea C
Manchester C v Chelsea
Newcastle U v Southampton
Norwich C v Everton
QPR v Manchester U
Reading v Wigan Ath
WBA v Sunderland
West Ham U v Tottenham H

npower Football League Championship

Blackburn R v Leeds U
Blackpool v Leicester C
Bolton W v Hull C
Brighton & HA v Burnley
Bristol C v Barnsley
Charlton Ath v Nottingham F
Huddersfield T v Ipswich T
Middlesbrough v Millwall
Peterborough U v Birmingham C
Sheffield W v Crystal Palace
Watford v Derby Co
Wolverhampton W v Cardiff C

npower Football League One

Bournemouth v Sheffield U
Brentford v Walsall
Carlisle U v Milton Keynes D
Colchester U v Tranmere
Coventry C v Crewe Alex
Doncaster R v Yeovil T
Leyton Orient v Crawley T
Notts Co v Bury
Oldham Ath v Portsmouth
Scunthorpe U v Hartlepool U
Shrewsbury T v Stevenage
Swindon T v Preston NE

npower Football League Two

Accrington S v Cheltenham T
Aldershot T v Fleetwood T
Barnet v Rochdale
Bradford C v Rotherham U
Burton Alb v Exeter C
Chesterfield v Gillingham
Dagenham & R v AFC Wimbledon
Morecambe v Bristol R
Northampton T v Plymouth Arg
Oxford U v York C
Torquay U v Port Vale
Wycombe W v Southend U

Tuesday, 26 February 2013

npower Football League One

Bournemouth v Coventry C
Carlisle U v Walsall
Colchester U v Yeovil T
Crawley T v Brentford
Hartlepool U v Crewe Alex
Portsmouth v Milton Keynes D
Preston NE v Oldham Ath
Scunthorpe U v Stevenage
Sheffield U v Leyton Orient
Shrewsbury T v Doncaster R
Swindon T v Bury
Tranmere v Notts Co

npower Football League Two

AFC Wimbledon v Plymouth Arg
Barnet v Southend U
Bradford C v Dagenham & R
Burton Alb v Morecambe
Chesterfield v Aldershot T
Fleetwood T v Cheltenham T
Gillingham v Oxford U
Northampton T v Bristol R
Port Vale v Exeter C
Rochdale v Accrington S
Rotherham U v York C
Torquay U v Wycombe W

Saturday, 2 March 2013

Barclays Premier League

Aston Villa v Manchester C
Chelsea v WBA
Everton v Reading
Manchester U v Norwich C
Southampton v QPR
Stoke C v West Ham U
Sunderland v Fulham
Swansea C v Newcastle U
Tottenham H v Arsenal
Wigan Ath v Liverpool

npower Football League Championship

Barnsley v Bolton W
Blackburn R v Peterborough U
Blackpool v Bristol C
Brighton & HA v Huddersfield T
Charlton Ath v Burnley
Derby Co v Crystal Palace
Hull C v Birmingham C
Ipswich T v Leicester C
Leeds U v Millwall
Middlesbrough v Cardiff C
Sheffield W v Nottingham F
Wolverhampton W v Watford

npower Football League One

Brentford v Scunthorpe U
Bury v Crawley T
Coventry C v Swindon T
Crewe Alex v Portsmouth
Doncaster R v Hartlepool U
Leyton Orient v Bournemouth
Milton Keynes D v Preston NE
Notts Co v Carlisle U
Oldham Ath v Sheffield U
Stevenage v Colchester U
Walsall v Shrewsbury T
Yeovil T v Tranmere

npower Football League Two

Accrington S v Torquay U
Aldershot T v Gillingham
Bristol R v Burton Alb
Cheltenham T v AFC Wimbledon
Dagenham & R v Chesterfield
Exeter C v Northampton T
Morecambe v Rochdale
Oxford U v Port Vale
Plymouth Arg v Barnet
Southend U v Rotherham U
Wycombe W v Fleetwood T
York C v Bradford C

Tuesday, 5 March 2013

npower Football League Championship

Birmingham C v Blackpool
Bolton W v Blackburn R
Bristol C v Brighton & HA
Burnley v Barnsley
Cardiff C v Derby Co
Crystal Palace v Hull C
Huddersfield T v Middlesbrough
Leicester C v Leeds U
Millwall v Wolverhampton W
Nottingham F v Ipswich T
Peterborough U v Charlton Ath
Watford v Sheffield W

Saturday, 9 March 2013

Barclays Premier League

Arsenal v Everton
Fulham v Chelsea
Liverpool v Tottenham H
Manchester C v Wigan Ath
Newcastle U v Stoke C
Norwich C v Southampton
QPR v Sunderland
Reading v Aston Villa
WBA v Swansea C
West Ham U v Manchester U

npower Football League Championship

Birmingham C v Derby Co
Bolton W v Brighton & HA
Bristol C v Middlesbrough
Burnley v Hull C
Cardiff C v Barnsley
Crystal Palace v Leeds U
Huddersfield T v Charlton Ath
Leicester C v Sheffield W
Millwall v Blackburn R
Nottingham F v Wolverhampton W
Peterborough U v Ipswich T
Watford v Blackpool

npower Football League One

Bournemouth v Doncaster R
Carlisle U v Brentford
Colchester U v Crewe Alex
Crawley T v Notts Co
Hartlepool U v Yeovil T
Portsmouth v Bury
Preston NE v Stevenage

Scunthorpe U v Coventry C
Sheffield U v Milton Keynes D
Shrewsbury T v Leyton Orient
Swindon T v Walsall
Tranmere v Oldham Ath

npower Football League Two
AFC Wimbledon v York C
Barnet v Morecambe
Bradford C v Aldershot T
Burton Alb v Cheltenham T
Chesterfield v Bristol R
Fleetwood T v Exeter C
Gillingham v Plymouth Arg
Northampton T v Accrington S
Port Vale v Southend U
Rochdale v Wycombe W
Rotherham U v Dagenham & R
Torquay U v Oxford U

Tuesday, 12 March 2013

npower Football League One
Brentford v Swindon T
Bury v Scunthorpe U
Coventry C v Colchester U
Crewe Alex v Sheffield U
Doncaster R v Carlisle U
Leyton Orient v Portsmouth
Milton Keynes D v Shrewsbury T
Notts Co v Preston NE
Oldham Ath v Hartlepool U
Stevenage v Bournemouth
Walsall v Tranmere
Yeovil T v Crawley T

npower Football League Two
Accrington S v Fleetwood T
Aldershot T v Burton Alb
Bristol R v Port Vale
Cheltenham T v Chesterfield
Dagenham & R v Torquay U
Exeter C v Gillingham
Morecambe v Northampton T
Oxford U v Barnet
Plymouth Arg v Bradford C
Southend U v AFC Wimbledon
Wycombe W v Rotherham U
York C v Rochdale

Saturday, 16 March 2013

Barclays Premier League
Aston Villa v QPR
Chelsea v West Ham U
Everton v Manchester C
Manchester U v Reading
Southampton v Liverpool
Stoke C v WBA
Sunderland v Norwich C
Swansea C v Arsenal
Tottenham H v Fulham
Wigan Ath v Newcastle U

npower Football League Championship
Barnsley v Watford
Blackburn R v Burnley
Blackpool v Peterborough U
Brighton & HA v Crystal Palace
Charlton Ath v Millwall
Derby Co v Leicester C
Hull C v Nottingham F
Ipswich T v Bolton W
Leeds U v Huddersfield T
Middlesbrough v Birmingham C
Sheffield W v Cardiff C
Wolverhampton W v Bristol C

npower Football League One
Brentford v Preston NE
Bury v Colchester U
Coventry C v Hartlepool U
Crewe Alex v Shrewsbury T
Doncaster R v Portsmouth
Leyton Orient v Carlisle U
Milton Keynes D v Tranmere
Notts Co v Scunthorpe U
Oldham Ath v Bournemouth
Stevenage v Sheffield U
Walsall v Crawley T
Yeovil T v Swindon T

npower Football League Two
Accrington S v Barnet
Aldershot T v AFC Wimbledon
Bristol R v Rochdale
Cheltenham T v Rotherham U
Dagenham & R v Burton Alb
Exeter C v Bradford C
Morecambe v Gillingham
Oxford U v Chesterfield
Plymouth Arg v Fleetwood T
Southend U v Torquay U
Wycombe W v Northampton T
York C v Port Vale

Saturday, 23 March 2013

npower Football League One
Bournemouth v Bury
Carlisle U v Yeovil T
Colchester U v Milton Keynes D
Crawley T v Crewe Alex
Hartlepool U v Walsall
Portsmouth v Coventry C
Preston NE v Leyton Orient
Scunthorpe U v Doncaster R
Sheffield U v Brentford
Shrewsbury T v Oldham Ath
Swindon T v Notts Co
Tranmere v Stevenage

npower Football League Two
AFC Wimbledon v Morecambe
Barnet v Cheltenham T
Bradford C v Bristol R
Burton Alb v Wycombe W
Chesterfield v Plymouth Arg
Fleetwood T v Dagenham & R
Gillingham v Accrington S
Northampton T v Oxford U
Port Vale v Aldershot T
Rochdale v Southend U
Rotherham U v Exeter C
Torquay U v York C

Saturday, 30 March 2013

Barclays Premier League
Arsenal v Reading
Aston Villa v Liverpool
Everton v Stoke C
Fulham v QPR
Manchester C v Newcastle U
Southampton v Chelsea
Sunderland v Manchester U
Swansea C v Tottenham H
West Ham U v WBA
Wigan Ath v Norwich C

npower Football League Championship
Blackburn R v Blackpool
Charlton Ath v Bolton W
Crystal Palace v Birmingham C
Derby Co v Bristol C
Huddersfield T v Hull C
Ipswich T v Leeds U
Leicester C v Millwall
Nottingham F v Brighton & HA
Peterborough U v Cardiff C
Sheffield W v Barnsley
Watford v Burnley
Wolverhampton W v Middlesbrough

npower Football League One
Brentford v Notts Co
Bury v Crewe Alex
Carlisle U v Shrewsbury T
Colchester U v Bournemouth
Coventry C v Doncaster R
Crawley T v Stevenage
Hartlepool U v Milton Keynes D
Preston NE v Portsmouth
Scunthorpe U v Leyton Orient
Swindon T v Oldham Ath
Tranmere v Sheffield U
Yeovil T v Walsall

npower Football League Two
Barnet v Dagenham & R
Bradford C v Southend U
Bristol R v York C
Burton Alb v Chesterfield
Fleetwood T v Gillingham
Northampton T v Torquay U
Oxford U v Morecambe
Plymouth Arg v Exeter C
Port Vale v Cheltenham T
Rochdale v Aldershot T
Rotherham U v AFC Wimbledon
Wycombe W v Accrington S

Monday, 1 April 2013

npower Football League Championship
Barnsley v Leicester C
Birmingham C v Wolverhampton W
Blackpool v Crystal Palace
Bolton W v Huddersfield T
Brighton & HA v Charlton Ath
Bristol C v Sheffield W
Burnley v Nottingham F
Cardiff C v Blackburn R
Hull C v Watford
Leeds U v Derby Co
Middlesbrough v Peterborough U
Millwall v Ipswich T

npower Football League One
Bournemouth v Scunthorpe U
Crewe Alex v Preston NE
Doncaster R v Swindon T
Leyton Orient v Bury
Milton Keynes D v Brentford
Notts Co v Yeovil T
Oldham Ath v Colchester U
Portsmouth v Tranmere
Sheffield U v Carlisle U
Shrewsbury T v Crawley T
Stevenage v Hartlepool U
Walsall v Coventry C

npower Football League Two
AFC Wimbledon v Barnet
Accrington S v Burton Alb
Aldershot T v Oxford U
Cheltenham T v Northampton T
Chesterfield v Port Vale
Dagenham & R v Bristol R
Exeter C v Rochdale
Gillingham v Rotherham U
Morecambe v Wycombe W
Southend U v Fleetwood T
Torquay U v Bradford C
York C v Plymouth Arg

Saturday, 6 April 2013

Barclays Premier League
Chelsea v Sunderland
Liverpool v West Ham U
Manchester U v Manchester C
Newcastle U v Fulham
Norwich C v Swansea C
QPR v Wigan Ath
Reading v Southampton
Stoke C v Aston Villa
Tottenham H v Everton
WBA v Arsenal

npower Football League Championship
Birmingham C v Millwall
Bolton W v Wolverhampton W
Brighton & HA v Leicester C
Burnley v Bristol C
Charlton Ath v Leeds U
Crystal Palace v Barnsley
Derby Co v Ipswich T
Huddersfield T v Peterborough U
Hull C v Middlesbrough
Nottingham F v Blackpool
Sheffield W v Blackburn R
Watford v Cardiff C

npower Football League One
Bournemouth v Notts Co

Colchester U v Leyton Orient
Coventry C v Brentford
Doncaster R v Tranmere
Hartlepool U v Bury
Milton Keynes D v Crawley T
Oldham Ath v Carlisle U
Portsmouth v Stevenage
Preston NE v Scunthorpe U
Swindon T v Crewe Alex
Walsall v Sheffield U
Yeovil T v Shrewsbury T

npower Football League Two
Aldershot T v Southend U
Barnet v Chesterfield
Bradford C v Northampton T
Bristol R v AFC Wimbledon
Exeter C v Dagenham & R
Fleetwood T v Rochdale
Gillingham v Torquay U
Morecambe v Rotherham U
Oxford U v Wycombe W
Plymouth Arg v Cheltenham T
Port Vale v Burton Alb
York C v Accrington S

Saturday, 13 April 2013
Barclays Premier League
Arsenal v Norwich C
Aston Villa v Fulham
Chelsea v Tottenham H
Everton v QPR
Manchester C v WBA
Newcastle U v Sunderland
Reading v Liverpool
Southampton v West Ham U
Stoke C v Manchester U
Wigan Ath v Swansea C

npower Football League Championship
Barnsley v Charlton Ath
Blackburn R v Derby Co
Blackpool v Burnley
Bristol C v Bolton W
Cardiff C v Nottingham F
Ipswich T v Hull C
Leeds U v Sheffield W
Leicester C v Birmingham C
Middlesbrough v Brighton & HA
Millwall v Crystal Palace
Peterborough U v Watford
Wolverhampton W v Huddersfield T

npower Football League One
Brentford v Portsmouth
Bury v Oldham Ath
Carlisle U v Preston NE
Crawley T v Coventry C
Crewe Alex v Doncaster R
Leyton Orient v Milton Keynes D
Notts Co v Colchester U
Scunthorpe U v Walsall
Sheffield U v Swindon T
Shrewsbury T v Bournemouth
Stevenage v Yeovil T
Tranmere v Hartlepool U

npower Football League Two
AFC Wimbledon v Exeter C
Accrington S v Morecambe
Burton Alb v Plymouth Arg
Cheltenham T v Gillingham
Chesterfield v Bradford C
Dagenham & R v Oxford U
Northampton T v York C
Rochdale v Port Vale
Rotherham U v Fleetwood T
Southend U v Bristol R
Torquay U v Barnet
Wycombe W v Aldershot T

Tuesday, 16 April 2013
npower Football League Championship
Barnsley v Derby Co
Blackpool v Sheffield W
Bristol C v Birmingham C
Cardiff C v Charlton Ath
Ipswich T v Crystal Palace
Leeds U v Burnley
Leicester C v Bolton W
Middlesbrough v Nottingham F
Millwall v Watford
Peterborough U v Brighton & HA
Wolverhampton W v Hull C

Wednesday, 17 April 2013
npower Football League Championship
Blackburn R v Huddersfield T

Saturday, 20 April 2013
Barclays Premier League
Fulham v Arsenal
Liverpool v Chelsea
Manchester U v Aston Villa
Norwich C v Reading
QPR v Stoke C
Sunderland v Everton
Swansea C v Southampton
Tottenham H v Manchester C
WBA v Newcastle U
West Ham U v Wigan Ath

npower Football League Championship
Birmingham C v Leeds U
Bolton W v Middlesbrough
Brighton & HA v Blackpool
Burnley v Cardiff C
Charlton Ath v Wolverhampton W
Crystal Palace v Leicester C
Derby Co v Peterborough U
Huddersfield T v Millwall
Hull C v Bristol C
Nottingham F v Barnsley
Sheffield W v Ipswich T
Watford v Blackburn R

npower Football League One
Bournemouth v Carlisle U
Colchester U v Shrewsbury T
Coventry C v Leyton Orient
Doncaster R v Notts Co
Hartlepool U v Brentford
Milton Keynes D v Scunthorpe U
Oldham Ath v Crawley T
Portsmouth v Sheffield U
Preston NE v Tranmere
Swindon T v Stevenage
Walsall v Bury
Yeovil T v Crewe Alex

npower Football League Two
Aldershot T v Dagenham & R
Barnet v Wycombe W
Bradford C v Burton Alb
Bristol R v Accrington S
Exeter C v Cheltenham T
Fleetwood T v Chesterfield
Gillingham v AFC Wimbledon
Morecambe v Torquay U
Oxford U v Rochdale
Plymouth Arg v Rotherham U
Port Vale v Northampton T
York C v Southend U

Saturday, 27 April 2013
Barclays Premier League
Arsenal v Manchester U
Aston Villa v Sunderland
Chelsea v Swansea C
Everton v Fulham
Manchester C v West Ham U
Newcastle U v Liverpool
Reading v QPR
Southampton v WBA
Stoke C v Norwich C
Wigan Ath v Tottenham H

npower Football League Championship
Barnsley v Hull C
Blackburn R v Crystal Palace
Blackpool v Derby Co
Bristol C v Huddersfield T
Cardiff C v Bolton W
Ipswich T v Birmingham C
Leeds U v Brighton & HA
Leicester C v Watford
Middlesbrough v Charlton Ath
Millwall v Nottingham F
Peterborough U v Sheffield W
Wolverhampton W v Burnley

npower Football League One
Brentford v Doncaster R
Bury v Yeovil T
Carlisle U v Colchester U
Crawley T v Hartlepool U
Crewe Alex v Walsall
Leyton Orient v Oldham Ath
Notts Co v Coventry C
Scunthorpe U v Swindon T
Sheffield U v Preston NE
Shrewsbury T v Portsmouth
Stevenage v Milton Keynes D
Tranmere v Bournemouth

npower Football League Two
AFC Wimbledon v Fleetwood T
Accrington S v Oxford U
Burton Alb v Gillingham
Cheltenham T v Bradford C
Chesterfield v Exeter C
Dagenham & R v York C
Northampton T v Barnet
Rochdale v Plymouth Arg
Rotherham U v Aldershot T
Southend U v Morecambe
Torquay U v Bristol R
Wycombe W v Port Vale

Saturday, 4 May 2013
Barclays Premier League
Fulham v Reading
Liverpool v Everton
Manchester U v Chelsea
Norwich C v Aston Villa
QPR v Arsenal
Sunderland v Stoke C
Swansea C v Manchester C
Tottenham H v Southampton
WBA v Wigan Ath
West Ham U v Newcastle U

npower Football League Championship
Birmingham C v Blackburn R
Bolton W v Blackpool
Brighton & HA v Wolverhampton W
Burnley v Ipswich T
Charlton Ath v Bristol C
Crystal Palace v Peterborough U
Derby Co v Millwall
Huddersfield T v Barnsley
Hull C v Cardiff C
Nottingham F v Leicester C
Sheffield W v Middlesbrough
Watford v Leeds U

Sunday, 12 May 2013
Barclays Premier League
Arsenal v Wigan Ath
Aston Villa v Chelsea
Everton v West Ham U
Fulham v Liverpool
Manchester U v Swansea C
Norwich C v WBA
QPR v Newcastle U
Reading v Manchester C
Stoke C v Tottenham H
Sunderland v Southampton

Sunday, 19 May 2013
Barclays Premier League
Chelsea v Everton
Liverpool v QPR
Manchester C v Norwich C
Newcastle U v Arsenal
Southampton v Stoke C
Swansea C v Fulham
Tottenham H v Sunderland
WBA v Manchester U
West Ham U v Reading
Wigan Ath v Aston Villa

BLUE SQUARE PREMIER FIXTURES 2012–13

Saturday, 11 August 2012
Barrow v AFC Telford
Braintree T v Hyde U
Dartford v Tamworth
Forest Green R v Cambridge U
Hereford U v Macclesfield T
Lincoln C v Kidderminster
Luton T v Gateshead
Mansfield T v Newport Co
Nuneaton T v Ebbsfleet U
Southport v Grimsby T
Stockport Co v Alfreton T
Wrexham v Woking

Tuesday, 14 August 2012
AFC Telford v Forest Green R
Alfreton T v Southport
Cambridge U v Lincoln C
Ebbsfleet U v Braintree T
Gateshead v Mansfield T
Grimsby T v Stockport Co
Hyde U v Barrow
Kidderminster v Luton T
Macclesfield T v Wrexham
Newport Co v Nuneaton T
Tamworth v Hereford U
Woking v Dartford

Saturday, 18 August 2012
AFC Telford v Braintree T
Alfreton T v Hereford U
Cambridge U v Southport
Ebbsfleet U v Wrexham
Gateshead v Forest Green R
Grimsby T v Nuneaton T
Hyde U v Luton T
Kidderminster v Mansfield T
Macclesfield T v Dartford
Newport Co v Lincoln C
Tamworth v Stockport Co
Woking v Barrow

Saturday, 25 August 2012
Barrow v Alfreton T
Braintree T v Newport Co
Dartford v Kidderminster
Forest Green R v Woking
Hereford U v Ebbsfleet U
Lincoln C v Macclesfield T
Luton T v AFC Telford
Mansfield T v Hyde U
Nuneaton T v Cambridge U
Southport v Tamworth
Stockport Co v Gateshead
Wrexham v Grimsby T

Monday, 27 August 2012
AFC Telford v Stockport Co
Alfreton T v Nuneaton T
Cambridge U v Dartford
Ebbsfleet U v Luton T
Gateshead v Lincoln C
Grimsby T v Mansfield T
Hyde U v Southport
Kidderminster v Forest Green R
Macclesfield T v Barrow
Newport Co v Hereford U
Tamworth v Wrexham

Tuesday, 28 August 2012
Woking v Braintree T
September Fixtures

Saturday, 1 September 2012
Barrow v Kidderminster
Braintree T v Tamworth
Dartford v Alfreton T
Forest Green R v Hyde U
Hereford U v Grimsby T
Lincoln C v Ebbsfleet U
Luton T v Macclesfield T
Mansfield T v Woking
Nuneaton T v Gateshead
Southport v AFC Telford
Stockport Co v Cambridge U
Wrexham v Newport Co

Tuesday, 4 September 2012
Barrow v Grimsby T
Braintree T v Kidderminster
Dartford v Newport Co
Forest Green R v Ebbsfleet U
Hereford U v Woking
Lincoln C v Alfreton T
Luton T v Cambridge U
Mansfield T v Tamworth
Nuneaton T v AFC Telford
Southport v Gateshead
Stockport Co v Macclesfield T
Wrexham v Hyde U

Saturday, 8 September 2012
AFC Telford v Lincoln C
Alfreton T v Luton T
Cambridge U v Wrexham
Ebbsfleet U v Mansfield T
Gateshead v Dartford
Grimsby T v Forest Green R
Hyde U v Hereford U
Kidderminster v Southport
Macclesfield T v Braintree T
Newport Co v Stockport Co
Tamworth v Barrow
Woking v Nuneaton T

Saturday, 15 September 2012
Barrow v Newport Co
Cambridge U v AFC Telford
Dartford v Hereford U
Forest Green R v Alfreton T
Gateshead v Tamworth
Kidderminster v Grimsby T
Lincoln C v Hyde U
Luton T v Wrexham
Mansfield T v Braintree T
Nuneaton T v Macclesfield T
Southport v Ebbsfleet U
Stockport Co v Woking

Saturday, 22 September 2012
AFC Telford v Mansfield T
Alfreton T v Kidderminster
Braintree T v Stockport Co
Ebbsfleet U v Barrow
Grimsby T v Luton T
Hereford U v Cambridge U
Hyde U v Nuneaton T
Macclesfield T v Forest Green R
Newport Co v Southport
Tamworth v Lincoln C
Woking v Gateshead
Wrexham v Dartford

Tuesday, 25 September 2012
AFC Telford v Newport Co
Braintree T v Dartford
Cambridge U v Kidderminster
Ebbsfleet U v Woking
Grimsby T v Gateshead
Hereford U v Forest Green R
Hyde U v Alfreton T
Lincoln C v Nuneaton T
Macclesfield T v Mansfield T
Southport v Stockport Co
Tamworth v Luton T
Wrexham v Barrow

Saturday, 29 September 2012
Alfreton T v Braintree T
Barrow v Cambridge U
Dartford v Hyde U
Forest Green R v Lincoln C
Gateshead v AFC Telford
Kidderminster v Macclesfield T
Luton T v Southport
Mansfield T v Hereford U
Newport Co v Grimsby T
Nuneaton T v Wrexham
Stockport Co v Ebbsfleet U
Woking v Tamworth
October Fixtures

Saturday, 6 October 2012
AFC Telford v Woking
Braintree T v Barrow
Cambridge U v Mansfield T
Ebbsfleet U v Kidderminster
Grimsby T v Dartford
Hereford U v Stockport Co
Hyde U v Gateshead
Lincoln C v Luton T
Macclesfield T v Alfreton T
Southport v Nuneaton T
Tamworth v Newport Co
Wrexham v Forest Green R

Tuesday, 9 October 2012
Alfreton T v Grimsby T
Barrow v Southport
Dartford v AFC Telford
Forest Green R v Tamworth
Gateshead v Macclesfield T
Kidderminster v Hyde U
Luton T v Braintree T
Mansfield T v Lincoln C
Newport Co v Ebbsfleet U
Nuneaton T v Hereford U
Stockport Co v Wrexham
Woking v Cambridge U

Saturday, 13 October 2012
AFC Telford v Grimsby T
Barrow v Dartford
Ebbsfleet U v Alfreton T
Gateshead v Cambridge U
Hereford U v Braintree T
Hyde U v Tamworth
Luton T v Nuneaton T
Macclesfield T v Newport Co
Mansfield T v Forest Green R
Stockport Co v Kidderminster
Woking v Southport
Wrexham v Lincoln C

Saturday, 27 October 2012
Alfreton T v AFC Telford
Braintree T v Wrexham
Cambridge U v Hyde U
Dartford v Mansfield T

Forest Green R v Luton T
Grimsby T v Macclesfield T
Kidderminster v Gateshead
Lincoln C v Stockport Co
Newport Co v Woking
Nuneaton T v Barrow
Southport v Hereford U
Tamworth v Ebbsfleet U
November Fixtures

Tuesday, 6 November 2012
AFC Telford v Ebbsfleet U
Dartford v Forest Green R
Gateshead v Alfreton T
Hereford U v Luton T
Hyde U v Grimsby T
Lincoln C v Braintree T
Macclesfield T v Tamworth
Newport Co v Cambridge U
Nuneaton T v Mansfield T
Southport v Wrexham
Stockport Co v Barrow
Woking v Kidderminster

Saturday, 10 November 2012
Alfreton T v Newport Co
Barrow v Lincoln C
Braintree T v Gateshead
Cambridge U v Macclesfield T
Ebbsfleet U v Hyde U
Forest Green R v Stockport Co
Grimsby T v Woking
Kidderminster v Nuneaton T
Luton T v Dartford
Mansfield T v Southport
Tamworth v AFC Telford
Wrexham v Hereford U

Saturday, 17 November 2012
AFC Telford v Kidderminster
Barrow v Forest Green R
Cambridge U v Tamworth
Dartford v Southport
Grimsby T v Braintree T
Lincoln C v Hereford U
Macclesfield T v Ebbsfleet U
Mansfield T v Luton T
Newport Co v Hyde U
Nuneaton T v Stockport Co
Woking v Alfreton T
Wrexham v Gateshead
December Fixtures

Saturday, 1 December 2012
Alfreton T v Cambridge U
Braintree T v Macclesfield T
Ebbsfleet U v Grimsby T
Forest Green R v Nuneaton T
Gateshead v Newport Co
Hereford U v AFC Telford
Hyde U v Woking
Kidderminster v Wrexham
Luton T v Barrow
Southport v Lincoln C
Stockport Co v Mansfield T
Tamworth v Dartford

Tuesday, 4 December 2012
AFC Telford v Barrow
Alfreton T v Wrexham
Braintree T v Forest Green R
Ebbsfleet U v Cambridge U
Gateshead v Grimsby T
Hereford U v Mansfield T
Lincoln C v Woking
Macclesfield T v Hyde U
Newport Co v Luton T
Nuneaton T v Dartford
Stockport Co v Southport
Tamworth v Kidderminster

Saturday, 8 December 2012
Barrow v Hereford U
Cambridge U v Gateshead
Dartford v Lincoln C
Forest Green R v Macclesfield T
Grimsby T v Tamworth
Hyde U v AFC Telford
Kidderminster v Newport Co
Luton T v Alfreton T
Mansfield T v Ebbsfleet U
Southport v Braintree T
Woking v Stockport Co
Wrexham v Nuneaton T

Saturday, 22 December 2012
AFC Telford v Luton T
Alfreton T v Barrow
Cambridge U v Nuneaton T
Ebbsfleet U v Hereford U
Gateshead v Stockport Co
Grimsby T v Wrexham
Hyde U v Mansfield T
Kidderminster v Dartford
Macclesfield T v Lincoln C
Newport Co v Braintree T
Tamworth v Southport
Woking v Forest Green R

Wednesday, 26 December 2012
Barrow v Gateshead
Braintree T v Cambridge U
Dartford v Ebbsfleet U
Forest Green R v Newport Co
Hereford U v Kidderminster
Lincoln C v Grimsby T
Luton T v Woking
Mansfield T v Alfreton T
Nuneaton T v Tamworth
Southport v Macclesfield T
Stockport Co v Hyde U
Wrexham v AFC Telford

Saturday, 29 December 2012
Barrow v Macclesfield T
Braintree T v Woking
Dartford v Cambridge U
Forest Green R v Kidderminster
Hereford U v Newport Co
Lincoln C v Gateshead
Luton T v Ebbsfleet U
Mansfield T v Grimsby T
Nuneaton T v Alfreton T
Southport v Hyde U
Stockport Co v AFC Telford
Wrexham v Tamworth
January Fixtures

Tuesday, 1 January 2013
AFC Telford v Wrexham
Alfreton T v Mansfield T
Cambridge U v Braintree T
Ebbsfleet U v Dartford
Gateshead v Barrow
Grimsby T v Lincoln C
Hyde U v Stockport Co
Kidderminster v Hereford U
Macclesfield T v Southport
Newport Co v Forest Green R
Woking v Luton T

Wednesday, 2 January 2013
Tamworth v Nuneaton T

Saturday, 5 January 2013
AFC Telford v Southport
Alfreton T v Dartford
Cambridge U v Stockport Co
Ebbsfleet U v Lincoln C
Gateshead v Nuneaton T
Grimsby T v Hereford U
Hyde U v Forest Green R
Kidderminster v Barrow
Macclesfield T v Luton T
Newport Co v Wrexham
Tamworth v Braintree T
Woking v Mansfield T

Saturday, 12 January 2013
Barrow v Woking
Braintree T v AFC Telford
Dartford v Macclesfield T
Forest Green R v Gateshead
Hereford U v Alfreton T
Lincoln C v Newport Co
Luton T v Hyde U
Mansfield T v Kidderminster
Nuneaton T v Grimsby T
Southport v Cambridge U
Stockport Co v Tamworth
Wrexham v Ebbsfleet U

Saturday, 19 January 2013
AFC Telford v Alfreton T
Braintree T v Grimsby T
Ebbsfleet U v Tamworth
Gateshead v Woking
Hereford U v Dartford
Hyde U v Cambridge U
Lincoln C v Wrexham
Macclesfield T v Kidderminster
Newport Co v Barrow
Nuneaton T v Luton T
Southport v Mansfield T
Stockport Co v Forest Green R

Tuesday, 22 January 2013
AFC Telford v Gateshead
Barrow v Stockport Co
Cambridge U v Ebbsfleet U
Dartford v Braintree T
Forest Green R v Hereford U
Grimsby T v Hyde U
Luton T v Lincoln C
Mansfield T v Nuneaton T
Tamworth v Macclesfield T
Woking v Newport Co
Wrexham v Southport

Saturday, 26 January 2013
Alfreton T v Tamworth
Cambridge U v Grimsby T
Dartford v Barrow
Gateshead v Hereford U
Hyde U v Ebbsfleet U
Kidderminster v Woking
Lincoln C v Forest Green R
Luton T v Stockport Co
Macclesfield T v AFC Telford
Nuneaton T v Braintree T
Southport v Newport Co
Wrexham v Mansfield T

Tuesday, 29 January 2013
Kidderminster v AFC Telford
February Fixtures

Saturday, 2 February 2013
AFC Telford v Cambridge U
Barrow v Luton T
Braintree T v Lincoln C

Ebbsfleet U v Macclesfield T
Forest Green R v Wrexham
Grimsby T v Alfreton T
Hereford U v Southport
Mansfield T v Dartford
Newport Co v Kidderminster
Stockport Co v Nuneaton T
Tamworth v Gateshead
Woking v Hyde U

Saturday, 9 February 2013
Alfreton T v Woking
Braintree T v Hereford U
Ebbsfleet U v Gateshead
Grimsby T v AFC Telford
Hyde U v Macclesfield T
Kidderminster v Cambridge U
Lincoln C v Dartford
Luton T v Forest Green R
Mansfield T v Barrow
Newport Co v Tamworth
Nuneaton T v Southport
Wrexham v Stockport Co

Tuesday, 12 February 2013
AFC Telford v Hyde U
Cambridge U v Alfreton T
Dartford v Luton T
Forest Green R v Braintree T
Gateshead v Kidderminster
Hereford U v Wrexham
Macclesfield T v Nuneaton T
Newport Co v Mansfield T
Southport v Barrow
Stockport Co v Lincoln C
Tamworth v Grimsby T
Woking v Ebbsfleet U

Saturday, 16 February 2013
AFC Telford v Tamworth
Alfreton T v Macclesfield T
Barrow v Nuneaton T
Braintree T v Southport
Ebbsfleet U v Stockport Co
Forest Green R v Dartford
Gateshead v Wrexham
Hereford U v Lincoln C
Hyde U v Kidderminster
Luton T v Newport Co
Mansfield T v Cambridge U
Woking v Grimsby T

Saturday, 23 February 2013
Cambridge U v Hereford U
Dartford v Stockport Co
Grimsby T v Ebbsfleet U
Kidderminster v Alfreton T
Lincoln C v Barrow
Luton T v Mansfield T
Macclesfield T v Gateshead
Newport Co v AFC Telford
Nuneaton T v Forest Green R
Southport v Woking
Tamworth v Hyde U
Wrexham v Braintree T

Tuesday, 26 February 2013
Alfreton T v Hyde U
Barrow v Wrexham
Braintree T v Luton T
Dartford v Grimsby T
Lincoln C v Mansfield T
Newport Co v Gateshead
Nuneaton T v Kidderminster
Stockport Co v Hereford U
Tamworth v Cambridge U
March Fixtures

Saturday, 2 March 2013
Barrow v Tamworth
Cambridge U v Forest Green R
Gateshead v Braintree T
Hereford U v Nuneaton T
Hyde U v Newport Co
Kidderminster v Ebbsfleet U
Macclesfield T v Grimsby T
Mansfield T v AFC Telford
Southport v Dartford
Stockport Co v Luton T
Woking v Lincoln C
Wrexham v Alfreton T

Saturday, 9 March 2013
AFC Telford v Macclesfield T
Braintree T v Nuneaton T
Cambridge U v Woking
Dartford v Wrexham
Ebbsfleet U v Newport Co
Forest Green R v Barrow
Gateshead v Hyde U
Grimsby T v Kidderminster
Lincoln C v Southport
Luton T v Hereford U
Mansfield T v Stockport Co
Tamworth v Alfreton T

Tuesday, 12 March 2013
Alfreton T v Ebbsfleet U
Macclesfield T v Woking
Southport v Forest Green R

Saturday, 16 March 2013
Alfreton T v Gateshead
Ebbsfleet U v Southport
Forest Green R v Mansfield T
Grimsby T v Cambridge U
Hereford U v Barrow
Hyde U v Dartford
Kidderminster v Tamworth
Newport Co v Macclesfield T
Nuneaton T v Lincoln C
Stockport Co v Braintree T
Woking v AFC Telford
Wrexham v Luton T

Saturday, 23 March 2013
Barrow v Ebbsfleet U
Braintree T v Alfreton T
Dartford v Gateshead
Forest Green R v Grimsby T
Hereford U v Hyde U
Lincoln C v AFC Telford
Luton T v Tamworth
Mansfield T v Macclesfield T
Nuneaton T v Woking
Southport v Kidderminster
Stockport Co v Newport Co
Wrexham v Cambridge U

Saturday, 30 March 2013
AFC Telford v Nuneaton T
Alfreton T v Lincoln C
Cambridge U v Luton T
Ebbsfleet U v Forest Green R
Gateshead v Southport
Grimsby T v Barrow
Hyde U v Wrexham
Kidderminster v Braintree T
Macclesfield T v Stockport Co
Newport Co v Dartford
Tamworth v Mansfield T
Woking v Hereford U
April Fixtures

Monday, 1 April 2013
Barrow v Hyde U
Braintree T v Ebbsfleet U
Dartford v Woking
Forest Green R v AFC Telford
Hereford U v Tamworth
Lincoln C v Cambridge U
Luton T v Kidderminster
Mansfield T v Gateshead
Nuneaton T v Newport Co
Southport v Alfreton T
Stockport Co v Grimsby T
Wrexham v Macclesfield T

Saturday, 6 April 2013
AFC Telford v Dartford
Alfreton T v Stockport Co
Barrow v Mansfield T
Cambridge U v Newport Co
Ebbsfleet U v Nuneaton T
Gateshead v Luton T
Grimsby T v Southport
Hyde U v Braintree T
Kidderminster v Lincoln C
Macclesfield T v Hereford U
Tamworth v Forest Green R
Woking v Wrexham

Saturday, 13 April 2013
Braintree T v Mansfield T
Cambridge U v Barrow
Ebbsfleet U v AFC Telford
Forest Green R v Southport
Hereford U v Gateshead
Lincoln C v Tamworth
Luton T v Grimsby T
Newport Co v Alfreton T
Nuneaton T v Hyde U
Stockport Co v Dartford
Woking v Macclesfield T
Wrexham v Kidderminster

Saturday, 20 April 2013
AFC Telford v Hereford U
Alfreton T v Forest Green R
Barrow v Braintree T
Dartford v Nuneaton T
Gateshead v Ebbsfleet U
Grimsby T v Newport Co
Hyde U v Lincoln C
Kidderminster v Stockport Co
Macclesfield T v Cambridge U
Mansfield T v Wrexham
Southport v Luton T
Tamworth v Woking

THE SCOTTISH PREMIER LEAGUE AND SCOTTISH LEAGUE FIXTURES 2012–13

All fixtures subject to change.

Saturday, 4 August 2012

Clydesdale Bank Premier League
Celtic v Aberdeen
Hearts v St Johnstone
Kilmarnock v Club 12
Ross Co v Motherwell
St Mirren v Inverness CT

Sunday, 5 August 2012

Clydesdale Bank Premier League
Dundee U v Hibernian

Saturday, 11 August 2012

Clydesdale Bank Premier League
Aberdeen v Ross Co
Celtic v Dundee U
Club 12 v St Mirren
Hibernian v Hearts
Inverness CT v Kilmarnock
Motherwell v St Johnstone

Irn-Bru First Division
Cowdenbeath v Dunfermline Ath
Dundee v Dumbarton
Morton v Livingston
Partick Th v Falkirk
Raith R v Hamilton A

Irn-Bru Second Division
Airdrie U v Arbroath
Alloa Ath v East Fife
Ayr U v Stenhousemuir
Brechin C v Albion R
Queen of the S v Forfar Ath

Irn-Bru Third Division
Berwick R v Elgin C
East Stirling v Queen's Park
Montrose v Clyde
Peterhead v Stranraer
Stirling Alb v Annan Ath

Saturday, 18 August 2012

Clydesdale Bank Premier League
Dundee U v Club 12
Hearts v Inverness CT
Kilmarnock v Motherwell
Ross Co v Celtic
St Johnstone v Aberdeen
St Mirren v Hibernian

Irn-Bru First Division
Dumbarton v Cowdenbeath
Dunfermline Ath v Partick Th
Falkirk v Raith R
Hamilton A v Morton
Livingston v Dundee

Irn-Bru Second Division
Albion R v Alloa Ath
Arbroath v Ayr U
East Fife v Queen of the S
Forfar Ath v Airdrie U
Stenhousemuir v Brechin C

Irn-Bru Third Division
Annan Ath v Berwick R
Clyde v Peterhead
Elgin C v Stirling Alb
Queen's Park v Montrose
Stranraer v East Stirling

Saturday, 25 August 2012

Clydesdale Bank Premier League
Club 12 v Ross Co
Hibernian v St Johnstone
Inverness CT v Celtic
Kilmarnock v Dundee U
Motherwell v St Mirren

Irn-Bru First Division
Cowdenbeath v Hamilton A
Dundee v Dunfermline Ath
Morton v Falkirk
Partick Th v Dumbarton
Raith R v Livingston

Irn-Bru Second Division
Airdrie U v Stenhousemuir
Alloa Ath v Arbroath
Ayr U v Forfar Ath
Brechin C v East Fife
Queen of the S v Albion R

Irn-Bru Third Division
Berwick R v Stranraer
East Stirling v Elgin C
Montrose v Annan Ath
Peterhead v Queen's Park
Stirling Alb v Clyde

Sunday, 26 August 2012

Clydesdale Bank Premier League
Aberdeen v Hearts

Saturday, 1 September 2012

Clydesdale Bank Premier League
Aberdeen v St Mirren
Celtic v Hibernian
Motherwell v Inverness CT
Ross Co v Kilmarnock
St Johnstone v Dundee U

Irn-Bru First Division
Dundee v Cowdenbeath
Dunfermline Ath v Raith R
Falkirk v Livingston
Morton v Dumbarton
Partick Th v Hamilton A

Irn-Bru Second Division
Airdrie U v Ayr U
Brechin C v Alloa Ath
East Fife v Albion R
Queen of the S v Arbroath
Stenhousemuir v Forfar Ath

Irn-Bru Third Division
Berwick R v East Stirling
Clyde v Annan Ath
Peterhead v Montrose
Stirling Alb v Queen's Park
Stranraer v Elgin C

Sunday, 2 September 2012

Clydesdale Bank Premier League
Hearts v Club 12

Saturday, 15 September 2012

Clydesdale Bank Premier League
Club 12 v Motherwell
Dundee U v Ross Co
Hibernian v Kilmarnock
Inverness CT v Aberdeen
St Johnstone v Celtic
St Mirren v Hearts

Irn-Bru First Division
Cowdenbeath v Morton
Dumbarton v Dunfermline Ath
Hamilton A v Falkirk
Livingston v Partick Th
Raith R v Dundee

Irn-Bru Second Division
Albion R v Airdrie U
Alloa Ath v Stenhousemuir
Arbroath v East Fife
Ayr U v Queen of the S
Forfar Ath v Brechin C

Irn-Bru Third Division
Annan Ath v Stranraer
East Stirling v Stirling Alb
Elgin C v Peterhead
Montrose v Berwick R
Queen's Park v Clyde

Saturday, 22 September 2012

Clydesdale Bank Premier League
Aberdeen v Motherwell
Celtic v Club 12
Dundee U v Hearts
Hibernian v Inverness CT
Kilmarnock v St Mirren
Ross Co v St Johnstone

Irn-Bru First Division
Dumbarton v Hamilton A
Dunfermline Ath v Livingston
Falkirk v Dundee
Morton v Raith R
Partick Th v Cowdenbeath

Irn-Bru Second Division
Albion R v Stenhousemuir
Alloa Ath v Airdrie U
Arbroath v Forfar Ath
Brechin C v Queen of the S
East Fife v Ayr U

Irn-Bru Third Division
Annan Ath v Peterhead
Berwick R v Stirling Alb
East Stirling v Clyde

Elgin C v Queen's Park
Stranraer v Montrose

Saturday, 29 September 2012
Clydesdale Bank Premier League
Aberdeen v Hibernian
Club 12 v St Johnstone
Hearts v Kilmarnock
Inverness CT v Dundee U
Motherwell v Celtic
St Mirren v Ross Co

Irn-Bru First Division
Cowdenbeath v Falkirk
Dundee v Morton
Hamilton A v Dunfermline Ath
Livingston v Dumbarton
Raith R v Partick Th

Irn-Bru Second Division
Airdrie U v East Fife
Ayr U v Brechin C
Forfar Ath v Albion R
Queen of the S v Alloa Ath
Stenhousemuir v Arbroath

Saturday, 6 October 2012
Clydesdale Bank Premier League
Celtic v Hearts
Hibernian v Club 12
Inverness CT v Ross Co
Kilmarnock v Aberdeen
Motherwell v Dundee U
St Johnstone v St Mirren

Irn-Bru First Division
Dundee v Hamilton A
Falkirk v Dunfermline Ath
Livingston v Cowdenbeath
Morton v Partick Th
Raith R v Dumbarton

Irn-Bru Second Division
Airdrie U v Queen of the S
Arbroath v Brechin C
Ayr U v Albion R
Forfar Ath v Alloa Ath
Stenhousemuir v East Fife

Irn-Bru Third Division
Clyde v Elgin C
Montrose v East Stirling
Peterhead v Berwick R
Queen's Park v Annan Ath
Stirling Alb v Stranraer

Saturday, 20 October 2012
Clydesdale Bank Premier League
Club 12 v Inverness CT
Dundee U v Aberdeen
Hearts v Motherwell
Ross Co v Hibernian
St Johnstone v Kilmarnock
St Mirren v Celtic

Irn-Bru First Division
Cowdenbeath v Raith R
Dumbarton v Falkirk
Dunfermline Ath v Morton
Hamilton A v Livingston
Partick Th v Dundee

Irn-Bru Second Division
Albion R v Arbroath
Alloa Ath v Ayr U
Brechin C v Airdrie U
East Fife v Forfar Ath
Queen of the S v Stenhousemuir

Irn-Bru Third Division
Berwick R v Clyde
East Stirling v Peterhead
Elgin C v Annan Ath
Stirling Alb v Montrose
Stranraer v Queen's Park

Saturday, 27 October 2012
Clydesdale Bank Premier League
Aberdeen v Club 12
Celtic v Kilmarnock
Hearts v Ross Co
Inverness CT v St Johnstone
Motherwell v Hibernian
St Mirren v Dundee U

Irn-Bru First Division
Dumbarton v Dundee
Dunfermline Ath v Cowdenbeath
Falkirk v Partick Th
Hamilton A v Raith R
Livingston v Morton

Irn-Bru Second Division
Airdrie U v Forfar Ath
Alloa Ath v Albion R
Ayr U v Arbroath
Brechin C v Stenhousemuir
Queen of the S v East Fife

Irn-Bru Third Division
Annan Ath v East Stirling
Clyde v Stranraer
Montrose v Elgin C
Peterhead v Stirling Alb
Queen's Park v Berwick R

Saturday, 3 November 2012
Clydesdale Bank Premier League
Club 12 v Hearts
Dundee U v Celtic
Hibernian v St Mirren
Kilmarnock v Inverness CT
Ross Co v Aberdeen
St Johnstone v Motherwell

Saturday, 10 November 2012
Clydesdale Bank Premier League
Celtic v St Johnstone
Hibernian v Dundee U
Inverness CT v Hearts
Kilmarnock v Ross Co
Motherwell v Club 12
St Mirren v Aberdeen

Irn-Bru First Division
Cowdenbeath v Dumbarton
Dundee v Livingston
Morton v Hamilton A
Partick Th v Dunfermline Ath
Raith R v Falkirk

Irn-Bru Second Division
Albion R v Brechin C
Arbroath v Airdrie U
East Fife v Alloa Ath
Forfar Ath v Queen of the S
Stenhousemuir v Ayr U

Irn-Bru Third Division
Annan Ath v Stirling Alb
Clyde v Montrose
Elgin C v Berwick R
Queen's Park v East Stirling
Stranraer v Peterhead

Saturday, 17 November 2012
Clydesdale Bank Premier League
Aberdeen v Celtic
Club 12 v Hibernian
Dundee U v Kilmarnock
Hearts v St Mirren
Inverness CT v Motherwell
St Johnstone v Ross Co

Irn-Bru First Division
Cowdenbeath v Dundee
Dumbarton v Morton
Hamilton A v Partick Th
Livingston v Falkirk
Raith R v Dunfermline Ath

Irn-Bru Second Division
Albion R v East Fife
Alloa Ath v Brechin C
Arbroath v Queen of the S
Ayr U v Airdrie U
Forfar Ath v Stenhousemuir

Irn-Bru Third Division
Berwick R v Annan Ath
East Stirling v Stranraer
Montrose v Queen's Park
Peterhead v Clyde
Stirling Alb v Elgin C

Saturday, 24 November 2012
Clydesdale Bank Premier League
Celtic v Inverness CT
Hibernian v Aberdeen
Kilmarnock v St Johnstone
Motherwell v Hearts
Ross Co v Dundee U
St Mirren v Club 12

Irn-Bru First Division
Dundee v Raith R
Dunfermline Ath v Dumbarton
Falkirk v Hamilton A
Morton v Cowdenbeath
Partick Th v Livingston

Irn-Bru Second Division
Airdrie U v Albion R
Brechin C v Forfar Ath
East Fife v Arbroath
Queen of the S v Ayr U
Stenhousemuir v Alloa Ath

Irn-Bru Third Division
Annan Ath v Clyde
Elgin C v Stranraer
Montrose v Peterhead
Queen's Park v Stirling Alb

Sunday, 25 November 2012
Irn-Bru Third Division
East Stirling v Berwick R

Wednesday, 28 November 2012
Clydesdale Bank Premier League
Aberdeen v Inverness CT
Club 12 v Kilmarnock
Dundee U v Motherwell
Hearts v Celtic
Ross Co v St Mirren
St Johnstone v Hibernian

Saturday, 1 December 2012
Irn-Bru Third Division
Berwick R v Montrose
Clyde v Queen's Park
Peterhead v Elgin C
Stirling Alb v East Stirling

Stranraer v Annan Ath

Saturday, 8 December 2012

Clydesdale Bank Premier League

Club 12 v Dundee U
Hearts v Aberdeen
Inverness CT v Hibernian
Kilmarnock v Celtic
Motherwell v Ross Co
St Mirren v St Johnstone

Irn-Bru First Division

Cowdenbeath v Partick Th
Dundee v Falkirk
Hamilton A v Dumbarton
Livingston v Dunfermline Ath
Raith R v Morton

Irn-Bru Second Division

Albion R v Forfar Ath
Alloa Ath v Queen of the S
Arbroath v Stenhousemuir
Brechin C v Ayr U
East Fife v Airdrie U

Irn-Bru Third Division

Annan Ath v Queen's Park
Berwick R v Peterhead
East Stirling v Montrose
Elgin C v Clyde
Stranraer v Stirling Alb

Saturday, 15 December 2012

Clydesdale Bank Premier League

Aberdeen v Kilmarnock
Celtic v St Mirren
Dundee U v Inverness CT
Hibernian v Motherwell
Ross Co v Club 12
St Johnstone v Hearts

Irn-Bru First Division

Dumbarton v Livingston
Dunfermline Ath v Hamilton A
Falkirk v Cowdenbeath
Morton v Dundee
Partick Th v Raith R

Irn-Bru Second Division

Airdrie U v Alloa Ath
Ayr U v East Fife
Forfar Ath v Arbroath
Queen of the S v Brechin C
Stenhousemuir v Albion R

Irn-Bru Third Division

Clyde v East Stirling
Montrose v Stranraer
Peterhead v Annan Ath
Queen's Park v Elgin C
Stirling Alb v Berwick R

Saturday, 22 December 2012

Clydesdale Bank Premier League

Aberdeen v St Johnstone
Celtic v Ross Co
Hearts v Dundee U
Inverness CT v Club 12
Kilmarnock v Hibernian
St Mirren v Motherwell

Wednesday, 26 December 2012

Clydesdale Bank Premier League

Club 12 v Celtic
Dundee U v St Johnstone
Hibernian v Ross Co
Inverness CT v St Mirren
Kilmarnock v Hearts
Motherwell v Aberdeen

Irn-Bru First Division

Cowdenbeath v Livingston
Dumbarton v Raith R
Dunfermline Ath v Falkirk
Hamilton A v Dundee
Partick Th v Morton

Irn-Bru Second Division

Albion R v Ayr U
Alloa Ath v Forfar Ath
Brechin C v Arbroath
East Fife v Stenhousemuir
Queen of the S v Airdrie U

Irn-Bru Third Division

Berwick R v Queen's Park
East Stirling v Annan Ath
Elgin C v Montrose
Stirling Alb v Peterhead
Stranraer v Clyde

Saturday, 29 December 2012

Clydesdale Bank Premier League

Club 12 v Aberdeen
Dundee U v St Mirren
Hibernian v Celtic
Motherwell v Kilmarnock
Ross Co v Hearts
St Johnstone v Inverness CT

Irn-Bru First Division

Dundee v Partick Th
Falkirk v Dumbarton
Livingston v Hamilton A
Morton v Dunfermline Ath
Raith R v Cowdenbeath

Irn-Bru Second Division

Airdrie U v Brechin C
Arbroath v Albion R
Ayr U v Alloa Ath
Forfar Ath v East Fife
Stenhousemuir v Queen of the S

Irn-Bru Third Division

Annan Ath v Elgin C
Clyde v Berwick R
Montrose v Stirling Alb
Peterhead v East Stirling
Queen's Park v Stranraer

Wednesday, 2 January 2013

Clydesdale Bank Premier League

Aberdeen v Dundee U
Celtic v Motherwell
Hearts v Hibernian
Ross Co v Inverness CT
St Johnstone v Club 12
St Mirren v Kilmarnock

Irn-Bru First Division

Dundee v Cowdenbeath
Dunfermline Ath v Raith R
Falkirk v Livingston
Morton v Dumbarton
Partick Th v Hamilton A

Irn-Bru Second Division

Albion R v Airdrie U
Alloa Ath v Stenhousemuir
Arbroath v East Fife
Ayr U v Queen of the S
Forfar Ath v Brechin C

Irn-Bru Third Division

Annan Ath v Stranraer
East Stirling v Stirling Alb
Elgin C v Peterhead
Montrose v Berwick R
Queen's Park v Clyde

Saturday, 5 January 2013

Irn-Bru First Division

Cowdenbeath v Morton
Dumbarton v Dunfermline Ath
Hamilton A v Falkirk
Livingston v Partick Th
Raith R v Dundee

Irn-Bru Second Division

Airdrie U v Ayr U
Brechin C v Alloa Ath
East Fife v Albion R
Queen of the S v Arbroath
Stenhousemuir v Forfar Ath

Irn-Bru Third Division

Berwick R v East Stirling
Clyde v Annan Ath
Peterhead v Montrose
Stirling Alb v Queen's Park
Stranraer v Elgin C

Saturday, 12 January 2013

Irn-Bru First Division

Dumbarton v Partick Th
Dunfermline Ath v Dundee
Falkirk v Morton
Hamilton A v Cowdenbeath
Livingston v Raith R

Irn-Bru Second Division

Albion R v Queen of the S
Arbroath v Alloa Ath
East Fife v Brechin C
Forfar Ath v Ayr U
Stenhousemuir v Airdrie U

Irn-Bru Third Division

Annan Ath v Montrose
Clyde v Stirling Alb
Elgin C v East Stirling
Queen's Park v Peterhead
Stranraer v Berwick R

Saturday, 19 January 2013

Clydesdale Bank Premier League

Celtic v Hearts
Hibernian v Club 12
Inverness CT v Aberdeen
Kilmarnock v Dundee U
Motherwell v St Johnstone
St Mirren v Ross Co

Irn-Bru First Division

Cowdenbeath v Dunfermline Ath
Dundee v Dumbarton
Morton v Livingston
Partick Th v Falkirk
Raith R v Hamilton A

Irn-Bru Second Division

Airdrie U v Arbroath
Alloa Ath v East Fife
Ayr U v Stenhousemuir
Brechin C v Albion R
Queen of the S v Forfar Ath

Irn-Bru Third Division

Berwick R v Elgin C
East Stirling v Queen's Park
Montrose v Clyde
Peterhead v Stranraer
Stirling Alb v Annan Ath

Saturday, 26 January 2013
Clydesdale Bank Premier League
Aberdeen v Hibernian
Club 12 v St Mirren
Dundee U v Ross Co
Hearts v Motherwell
Inverness CT v Kilmarnock
St Johnstone v Celtic

Irn-Bru First Division
Dumbarton v Hamilton A
Dunfermline Ath v Livingston
Falkirk v Dundee
Morton v Raith R
Partick Th v Cowdenbeath

Irn-Bru Second Division
Albion R v Stenhousemuir
Alloa Ath v Airdrie U
Arbroath v Forfar Ath
Brechin C v Queen of the S
East Fife v Ayr U

Irn-Bru Third Division
Annan Ath v Peterhead
Berwick R v Stirling Alb
East Stirling v Clyde
Elgin C v Queen's Park
Stranraer v Montrose

Wednesday, 30 January 2013
Clydesdale Bank Premier League
Celtic v Kilmarnock
Hearts v Club 12
Motherwell v Dundee U
Ross Co v Hibernian
St Johnstone v Aberdeen
St Mirren v Inverness CT

Saturday, 2 February 2013
Irn-Bru Second Division
Airdrie U v East Fife
Ayr U v Brechin C
Forfar Ath v Albion R
Queen of the S v Alloa Ath
Stenhousemuir v Arbroath

Irn-Bru Third Division
Clyde v Elgin C
Montrose v East Stirling
Peterhead v Berwick R
Queen's Park v Annan Ath
Stirling Alb v Stranraer

Saturday, 9 February 2013
Clydesdale Bank Premier League
Aberdeen v St Mirren
Club 12 v Ross Co
Dundee U v Hearts
Hibernian v St Johnstone
Inverness CT v Celtic
Kilmarnock v Motherwell

Irn-Bru First Division
Cowdenbeath v Falkirk
Dundee v Morton
Hamilton A v Dunfermline Ath
Livingston v Dumbarton
Raith R v Partick Th

Irn-Bru Second Division
Albion R v Arbroath
Alloa Ath v Ayr U
Brechin C v Airdrie U
East Fife v Forfar Ath
Queen of the S v Stenhousemuir

Irn-Bru Third Division
Berwick R v Clyde
East Stirling v Peterhead
Elgin C v Annan Ath
Stirling Alb v Montrose
Stranraer v Queen's Park

Saturday, 16 February 2013
Clydesdale Bank Premier League
Aberdeen v Club 12
Celtic v Dundee U
Hearts v Kilmarnock
Motherwell v Inverness CT
Ross Co v St Johnstone
St Mirren v Hibernian

Irn-Bru First Division
Dundee v Hamilton A
Falkirk v Dunfermline Ath
Livingston v Cowdenbeath
Morton v Partick Th
Raith R v Dumbarton

Irn-Bru Second Division
Airdrie U v Queen of the S
Arbroath v Brechin C
Ayr U v Albion R
Forfar Ath v Alloa Ath
Stenhousemuir v East Fife

Irn-Bru Third Division
Annan Ath v East Stirling
Clyde v Stranraer
Montrose v Elgin C
Peterhead v Stirling Alb
Queen's Park v Berwick R

Saturday, 23 February 2013
Clydesdale Bank Premier League
Celtic v Club 12
Dundee U v Hibernian
Hearts v Inverness CT
Kilmarnock v Aberdeen
Ross Co v Motherwell
St Johnstone v St Mirren

Irn-Bru First Division
Cowdenbeath v Raith R
Dumbarton v Falkirk
Dunfermline Ath v Morton
Hamilton A v Livingston
Partick Th v Dundee

Irn-Bru Second Division
Airdrie U v Stenhousemuir
Alloa Ath v Arbroath
Ayr U v Forfar Ath
Brechin C v East Fife
Queen of the S v Albion R

Irn-Bru Third Division
Berwick R v Stranraer
East Stirling v Elgin C
Montrose v Annan Ath
Peterhead v Queen's Park
Stirling Alb v Clyde

Wednesday, 27 February 2013
Clydesdale Bank Premier League
Aberdeen v Ross Co
Club 12 v St Johnstone
Hibernian v Kilmarnock
Inverness CT v Dundee U
Motherwell v Celtic
St Mirren v Hearts

Saturday, 2 March 2013
Irn-Bru First Division
Dumbarton v Cowdenbeath
Dunfermline Ath v Partick Th
Falkirk v Raith R
Hamilton A v Morton
Livingston v Dundee

Irn-Bru Second Division
Albion R v Alloa Ath
Arbroath v Ayr U
East Fife v Queen of the S
Forfar Ath v Airdrie U
Stenhousemuir v Brechin C

Irn-Bru Third Division
Annan Ath v Berwick R
Clyde v Peterhead
Elgin C v Stirling Alb
Queen's Park v Montrose
Stranraer v East Stirling

Saturday, 9 March 2013
Clydesdale Bank Premier League
Aberdeen v Motherwell
Club 12 v Inverness CT
Hibernian v Hearts
Ross Co v Celtic
St Johnstone v Kilmarnock
St Mirren v Dundee U

Irn-Bru First Division
Cowdenbeath v Hamilton A
Dundee v Dunfermline Ath
Morton v Falkirk
Partick Th v Dumbarton
Raith R v Livingston

Irn-Bru Second Division
Airdrie U v Albion R
Brechin C v Forfar Ath
East Fife v Arbroath
Queen of the S v Ayr U
Stenhousemuir v Alloa Ath

Irn-Bru Third Division
Berwick R v Montrose
Clyde v Queen's Park
Peterhead v Elgin C
Stirling Alb v East Stirling
Stranraer v Annan Ath

Saturday, 16 March 2013
Clydesdale Bank Premier League
Celtic v Aberdeen
Dundee U v Club 12
Hearts v St Johnstone
Inverness CT v Ross Co
Kilmarnock v St Mirren
Motherwell v Hibernian

Irn-Bru First Division
Cowdenbeath v Dundee
Dumbarton v Morton
Hamilton A v Partick Th
Livingston v Falkirk
Raith R v Dunfermline Ath

Irn-Bru Second Division
Albion R v East Fife
Alloa Ath v Brechin C
Arbroath v Queen of the S
Ayr U v Airdrie U
Forfar Ath v Stenhousemuir

Irn-Bru Third Division
Annan Ath v Clyde
East Stirling v Berwick R

Elgin C v Stranraer
Montrose v Peterhead

Saturday, 23 March 2013

Irn-Bru First Division
Dundee v Raith R
Dunfermline Ath v Dumbarton
Falkirk v Hamilton A
Morton v Cowdenbeath
Partick Th v Livingston

Irn-Bru Second Division
Albion R v Forfar Ath
Alloa Ath v Queen of the S
Arbroath v Stenhousemuir
Brechin C v Ayr U
East Fife v Airdrie U

Irn-Bru Third Division
Annan Ath v Queen's Park
Berwick R v Peterhead
East Stirling v Montrose
Elgin C v Clyde
Stranraer v Stirling Alb

Saturday, 30 March 2013

Clydesdale Bank Premier League
Aberdeen v Hearts
Club 12 v Motherwell
Hibernian v Inverness CT
Ross Co v Kilmarnock
St Johnstone v Dundee U
St Mirren v Celtic

Irn-Bru First Division
Cowdenbeath v Partick Th
Dundee v Falkirk
Hamilton A v Dumbarton
Livingston v Dunfermline Ath
Raith R v Morton

Irn-Bru Second Division
Airdrie U v Alloa Ath
Ayr U v East Fife
Forfar Ath v Arbroath
Queen of the S v Brechin C
Stenhousemuir v Albion R

Irn-Bru Third Division
Clyde v East Stirling
Montrose v Stranraer
Peterhead v Annan Ath
Queen's Park v Elgin C
Stirling Alb v Berwick R

Tuesday, 2 April 2013

Irn-Bru Third Division
Queen's Park v Stirling Alb

Saturday, 6 April 2013

Clydesdale Bank Premier League
Celtic v Hibernian
Dundee U v Aberdeen
Hearts v Ross Co
Inverness CT v St Johnstone
Kilmarnock v Club 12
Motherwell v St Mirren

Irn-Bru First Division
Dumbarton v Livingston
Dunfermline Ath v Hamilton A
Falkirk v Cowdenbeath
Morton v Dundee
Partick Th v Raith R

Irn-Bru Second Division
Airdrie U v Brechin C
Arbroath v Albion R
Ayr U v Alloa Ath
Forfar Ath v East Fife
Stenhousemuir v Queen of the S

Irn-Bru Third Division
Annan Ath v Elgin C
Clyde v Berwick R
Montrose v Stirling Alb
Peterhead v East Stirling
Queen's Park v Stranraer

Tuesday, 9 April 2013

Irn-Bru First Division
Cowdenbeath v Livingston
Dumbarton v Raith R
Dunfermline Ath v Falkirk
Hamilton A v Dundee
Partick Th v Morton

Saturday, 13 April 2013

Irn-Bru First Division
Dundee v Partick Th
Falkirk v Dumbarton
Livingston v Hamilton A
Morton v Dunfermline Ath
Raith R v Cowdenbeath

Irn-Bru Second Division
Albion R v Ayr U
Alloa Ath v Forfar Ath
Brechin C v Arbroath
East Fife v Stenhousemuir
Queen of the S v Airdrie U

Irn-Bru Third Division
Berwick R v Queen's Park
East Stirling v Annan Ath
Elgin C v Montrose
Stirling Alb v Peterhead
Stranraer v Clyde

Saturday, 20 April 2013

Irn-Bru First Division
Dumbarton v Dundee
Dunfermline Ath v Cowdenbeath
Falkirk v Partick Th
Hamilton A v Raith R
Livingston v Morton

Irn-Bru Second Division
Albion R v Brechin C
Arbroath v Airdrie U
East Fife v Alloa Ath
Forfar Ath v Queen of the S
Stenhousemuir v Ayr U

Irn-Bru Third Division
Annan Ath v Stirling Alb
Clyde v Montrose
Elgin C v Berwick R
Queen's Park v East Stirling
Stranraer v Peterhead

Saturday, 27 April 2013

Irn-Bru First Division
Cowdenbeath v Dumbarton
Dundee v Livingston
Morton v Hamilton A
Partick Th v Dunfermline Ath
Raith R v Falkirk

Irn-Bru Second Division
Airdrie U v Forfar Ath
Alloa Ath v Albion R
Ayr U v Arbroath
Brechin C v Stenhousemuir
Queen of the S v East Fife

Irn-Bru Third Division
Berwick R v Annan Ath
East Stirling v Stranraer
Montrose v Queen's Park
Peterhead v Clyde
Stirling Alb v Elgin C

Saturday, 4 May 2013

Irn-Bru First Division
Dumbarton v Partick Th
Dunfermline Ath v Dundee
Falkirk v Morton
Hamilton A v Cowdenbeath
Livingston v Raith R

Irn-Bru Second Division
Albion R v Queen of the S
Arbroath v Alloa Ath
East Fife v Brechin C
Forfar Ath v Ayr U
Stenhousemuir v Airdrie U

Irn-Bru Third Division
Annan Ath v Montrose
Clyde v Stirling Alb
Elgin C v East Stirling
Queen's Park v Peterhead
Stranraer v Berwick R

OTHER FIXTURES 2012–13

July 2012

05 Thur UEFA EL Q1 (1)
12 Thur UEFA EL Q1 (2)
17 Tue UEFA CL 2Q (1)
18 Wed UEFA CL 2Q (1)
19 Thur UEFA EL Q2 (1)
24 Tue UEFA CL 2Q (2)
25 Wed UEFA CL 2Q (2)
26 Thur UEFA EL Q2 (2)
31 Tue UEFA CL 3Q (1)

August 2012

01 Wed UEFA CL 3Q (1)
02 Thur UEFA EL Q3 (1)
07 Tue UEFA CL 3Q (2)
08 Wed UEFA CL 3Q (2)
09 Thur UEFA EL Q3 (2)
11 Sat Olympic Football Final (Wembley Stadium)
FA Cup with Budweiser EP
12 Sun FA Community Shield
15 Wed International (Friendly)
Football League Cup 1
18 Sat Premier and Football Leagues – Season Starts
21 Tue UEFA CL PO (1)
22 Wed UEFA CL PO (1)
23 Thurs UEFA EL PO (1)
25 Sat FA Cup with Budweiser P
28 Tue UEFA CL PO (2)
29 Wed UEFA CL PO (2)
Football League Cup 2
30 Thurs UEFA EL PO (2)
31 Fri UEFA Super Cup

September 2012

01 Sat FA Vase 1Q
03 Mon FA Youth Cup P+
05 Wed Football League Trophy 1
07 Fri Moldova v England – FIFA World Cup Qualifier
08 Sat FA Cup with Budweiser 1Q
11 Tue England v Ukraine – FIFA World Cup Qualifier
15 Sat FA Vase 2Q
17 Mon FA Youth Cup 1Q+
18 Tue UEFA CL MD1
19 Wed UEFA CL MD1
20 Thurs UEFA EL MD1
22 Sat FA Cup with Budweiser 2Q
26 Wed Football League Cup 3
29 Sat FA Trophy P

October 2012

01 Mon FA Youth Cup 2Q+
02 Tue UEFA CL MD2
03 Wed UEFA CL MD2
04 Thurs UEFA EL MD2
06 Sat FA Cup with Budweiser 3Q
10 Wed Football League Trophy 2
12 Fri England v San Marino – FIFA World Cup Qualifier
13 Sat FA Vase 1P
FA County Youth Cup 1*
15 Mon FA Youth Cup 3Q+
16 Tue Poland v England – FIFA World Cup Qualifier
20 Sat FA Cup with Budweiser 4Q
23 Tue UEFA CL MD3
24 Wed UEFA CL MD3
25 Thurs UEFA EL MD3
27 Sat FA Trophy 1Q
31 Wed Football League Cup 4

November 2012

03 Sat FA Cup with Budweiser 1P
FA Youth Cup 1P*
06 Tue UEFA CL MD4
07 Wed UEFA CL MD4
08 Thurs UEFA EL MD4
10 Sat FA Trophy 2Q
FA County Youth Cup 2*
14 Wed Sweden v England – FIFA World Cup Qualifier
FA Cup with Budweiser 1PR
17 Sat FA Vase 2P
FA Youth Cup 2P*
20 Tue UEFA CL MD5
21 Wed UEFA CL MD5
22 Thurs UEFA EL MD5
24 Sat FA Trophy 3Q

December 2012

01 Sat FA Cup with Budweiser 2P
04 Tue UEFA CL MD6
05 Wed UEFA CL MD6
Football League Trophy AQF
06 Thurs UEFA EL MD6
08 Sat FA Vase 3P
12 Wed FA Cup with Budweiser 2PR
Football League Cup 5
15 Sat FA Trophy 1P
FA Youth Cup 3P*
FA County Youth Cup 3*

January 2013

05 Sat FA Cup with Budweiser 3P
09 Wed Football League Cup SF1
Football League Trophy ASF
12 Sat FA Trophy 2P
16 Wed FA Cup with Budweiser 3PR

19 Sat FA Vase 4P
FA Youth Cup 4P*
23 Wed Football League Cup SF2
26 Sat FA Cup with Budweiser 4P
FA County Youth Cup 4*

February 2013

02 Sat FA Trophy 3P
06 Wed International (Friendly)
FA Cup with Budweiser 4PR
Football League Trophy AF1
09 Sat FA Vase 5P / FA Youth Cup 5P*
12 Tue UEFA CL 16 (1)
13 Wed UEFA CL 16 (1)
14 Thurs UEFA EL 32 (1)
16 Sat FA Cup with Budweiser 5P
19 Tue UEFA CL 16 (1)
20 Wed UEFA CL 16 (1)
21 Thurs UEFA EL 32 (2)
23 Sat FA Trophy 4P
FA Youth Cup 6P*
FA County Youth Cup SF*
24 Sun Football League Cup Final
27 Wed FA Cup with Budweiser 5PR
Football League Trophy AF2

March 2013

02 Sat FA Vase 6P
05 Tue UEFA CL 16 (2)
06 Wed UEFA CL 16 (2)
07 Thurs UEFA EL 16 (1)
09 Sat FA Cup with Budweiser 6P
FA Trophy SF1
12 Tue UEFA CL 16 (2)
13 Wed UEFA CL 16 (2)
14 Thurs UEFA EL 16 (2)
16 Sat FA Trophy SF2 / FA Youth Cup SF1*
20 Wed FA Cup with Budweiser 6PR
22 Fri San Marino v England – FIFA World Cup Qualifier
23 Sat FA Vase SF1
26 Tue Montenegro v England – FIFA World Cup Qualifier
30 Sat FA Vase SF2
FA Youth Cup SF2*

April 2013

03 Wed UEFA CL QF (1)
04 Thurs UEFA EL QF (1)
07 Sun Football League Trophy Final
09 Tue UEFA CL QF (1)
10 Wed UEFA CL QF (2)
11 Thurs UEFA EL QF (2)
13 Sat FA Cup with Budweiser SF
14 Sun FA Cup with Budweiser SF
20 Sat FA County Youth Cup Final (prov)
23 Tue UEFA CL SF (1)
24 Wed UEFA CL SF (1)
25 Thurs UEFA EL SF (1)
27 Sat Football League 1 and 2 – Season Ends
30 Tue UEFA CL SF (2)

May 2013

01 Wed UEFA CL SF (2)
02 Thurs UEFA EL SF (2)
04 Sat FA Trophy Final
Football League Championship – Season Ends
Football League 1 and 2 Play-off SF1
05 Sun FA Vase Final
08 Wed Football League 1 and 2 Play-off SF2
11 Sat FA Cup with Budweiser Final
Football League Championship Play-off SF1
15 Wed UEFA EL Final (at ArenaA, Amsterdam)
Football League Championship Play-off SF2
18 Sat Football League 2 Play-off Final
19 Sun Football League 1 Play-off Final
Premier League Season Ends
25 Sat UEFA CL Final (at Wembley)
27 Mon Football League Championship Play-off Final

June 2013

08 Sat International (Qualifier)
12 Wed International (Qualifier)

Friday 6 September 2013 – England v Moldova – FIFA World Cup Qualifier
Tuesday 10 September 2013 – Ukraine v England – FIFA World Cup Qualifier
Friday 11 October 2013 – England v Montenegro – FIFA World Cup Qualifier
Tuesday 15 October 2013 – England v Poland – FIFA World Cup Qualifier

* closing date of round
+ week commencing

STOP PRESS

SUMMER TRANSFER DIARY 2012

With Newco Rangers relegated to Scottish League Division 3, Stranraer are promoted to Division 2, Airdrie United to Division 1 and Dundee to the Scottish Premier League. The fixtures published in this edition do not reflect the changes caused by this situation.

Portsmouth deducted ten points ... Terry cleared in Court ... England Under-19s lose to Greece ... Capello for Russia ... Capital One League Cup.

April 30 Lukas Podolski, Cologne to Arsenal £11,900,000.

May 15 Ritchie De Laet, Manchester U to Leicester C; Matty James, Manchester U to Leicester C. **May 16** Garath McCleary, Nottingham F to Reading. **May 17** Jonathan Franks, Middlesbrough to Hartlepool U; James Severn, Derby Co to Scunthorpe U. **May 18** Jamie Vardy, Fleetwood T to Leicester C £1,000,000. **May 21** Harlee Dean, Southampton to Brentford; Adam Forshaw, Everton to Brentford; Stephen Henderson, Portsmouth to West Ham U. **May 22** Trevor Carson, Sunderland to Bury. **May 23** Romain Amalfitano, Reims to Newcastle U. **May 24** David Amoo, Liverpool to Preston NE; Fabio Aurelio, Liverpool to Gremio; Andrew Davies, Stoke C to Bradford C; Chris Kirkland, Wigan Ath to Sheffield W; Lomana LuaLua, Blackpool to Karabuk. **May 25** Joe Lewis, Peterborough U to Cardiff C. **May 26** Richard Wright, Ipswich T to Preston NE. **May 28** Paul Jones, Peterborough U to Crawley T; Kieran Lee, Oldham Ath to Sheffield W. **May 29** Lee Holmes, Southampton to Preston NE; Grant Leadbitter, Ipswich T to Middlesbrough; Jeffrey Monakana, Arsenal to Preston NE; Joel Ward, Portsmouth to Crystal Palace £400,000; Aaron Wildig, Cardiff C to Shrewsbury T. **May 30** Elliott Hewitt, Macclesfield T to Ipswich T; Scott Malone, Bournemouth to Millwall £750,000 + part exchange; Josh McQuoid, Millwall to Bournemouth part exchange.

June 3 Dirk Kuyt, Liverpool to Fenerbahce £1,000,000. **June 4** Eden Hazard, Lille to Chelsea £32,000,000. **June 6** Danny Swanson, Dundee U to Peterborough U. **June 7** Niko Kranjcar, Tottenham H to Dynamo Kiev £5,750,000; Ben Glasgow, Arsenal to Stoke C; Aaron Martin, Southampton to Crystal Palace (loan). **June 8** Kelvin Etuhu, Portsmouth to Barnsley; Joe Mattock, WBA to Sheffield W. **June 10** Jay Rodriguez, Burnley to Southampton £7,000,000. **June 11** Rhys Bennett, Bolton W to Rochdale; Louis Harris, Wolverhampton W to AFC Wimbledon. **June 12** Jody Morris, St Johnstone to Bristol C; Nick Powell, Crewe Alex to Manchester U. **June 13** Jussi Jaaskelainen, Bolton W to West Ham U; Jon Parkin, Cardiff C to Fleetwood T. **June 14** Sam Cowler, West Ham U to Barnet; George Williams, Milton Keynes D to Fulham; Dave Syers, Bradford C to Doncaster R. **June 15** Bartosz Bialkowski, Southampton to Notts Co; Luke O'Neill, Mansfield T to Burnley. **June 18** Sol Bamba, Leicester C to Trabzonspor; Andrew Johnson, Fulham to QPR; Ryan Nelsen, Tottenham H to QPR; Robert Olejnik, Torquay U to Peterborough U; Gary Roberts, Huddersfield T to Swindon T. **June 19** Adam Drury, Norwich C to Leeds U; Jacob Mellis, Chelsea to Barnsley; Bjorn Sigurdarson, Lillestrom to Wolverhampton W. **June 20** Mohamed Diame, Wigan Ath to West Ham U; Ryan Doble, Southampton to Shrewsbury T; Didier Drogba, Chelsea to Shanghai Shenhua; Paul Green, Derby Co to Leeds U; Tomasz Kuszczak, Manchester U to Brighton & HA. **June 21** Anthony Gardner, Crystal Palace to Sheffield W; Robert Green, West Ham U to QPR; Chris Maguire, Derby Co to Sheffield W; Jay McEveley, Barnsley to Swindon T; Mido, Zamalek to Barnsley; Tommy Miller, Huddersfield T to Swindon T; Alan Navarro, Brighton & HA to Swindon T. **June 22** Shinji Kagawa, Borussia Dortmund to Manchester U £17,000,000; Jordon Mutch, Birmingham C to Cardiff C; Frank Nouble, West Ham U to Wolverhampton W; Jamie Tank, Walsall to Wolverhampton W £20,000. **June 23** Sean Scannell, Crystal Palace to Huddersfield T. **June 25** Danny Murphy, Fulham to Blackburn R; Bruno Saltor, Valencia to Brighton & HA. **June 26** Olivier Giroud, Montpellier to Arsenal £13,000,000; Michael Jacobs, Northampton T to Derby Co; James Wallace, Everton to Tranmere R. **June 27** Robbie Blake, Bolton W to Doncaster R; Alban Bunjaku, Arsenal to Sevilla; Vedran Corluka, Tottenham H to Lokomotiv Moscow; Samba Diakite, Nancy to QPR; Paul Dixon, Dundee U to Huddersfield T; Joan Angel Roman, Manchester C to Barcelona. **June 28** Jordan Brown, West Ham U to Barnet; Thomas Cruise, Arsenal to Torquay U; Jamie McAllister, Bristol C to Yeovil T; Mladen Petric, Hamburg to Fulham; Michael Poke, Brighton & HA to Torquay U; Ayegbeni Yakubu, Blackburn R to Guangzhou. **June 29** Keith Andrews, WBA to Bolton W; Ben Foster, Birmingham C to WBA; Danny Guthrie, Newcastle U to Reading; Oliver Norwood, Manchester U to Huddersfield T. **June 30** Pavel Pogrebnyak, Fulham to Reading; Steven Whittaker, Rangers to Norwich C.

July 1 George McCartney, Sunderland to West Ham U. **July 2** Leon Best, Newcastle U to Blackburn R £3,000,000; Carlos Cuellar, Aston Villa to Sunderland; Fabio da Silva, Manchester U to QPR (loan); Ryan Edwards, Blackburn R to Rochdale (loan); Karim El Ahmadi, Feyenoord to Aston Villa; Jonathan Grounds, Middlesbrough to Oldham Ath; Brett Ormerod, Blackpool to Wrexham; Stuart Parnaby, unattached to Middlesbrough; Joe Rafferty, Liverpool to Rochdale; Nathan Ralph,

Peterborough U to Yeovil T. **July 3** Lee Angol, Tottenham H to Wycombe W; Will Atkinson, Hull C to Bradford C; Jacob Butterfield, Barnsley to Norwich C; Jamal Campbell-Ryce, Bristol C to Notts Co; Gary Doherty, Charlton Ath to Wycombe W; Nuno Gomes, Braga to Blackburn R; Chris Hackett, Millwall to Northampton T; Paul Pogba, Manchester U to Juventus; George Porter, Leyton Orient to Burnley; Daniel Waller, Fulham to Arsenal. **July 4** Christian Burgess, Arsenal to Middlesbrough; Lee Croft, Derby Co to Oldham Ath (loan); Lateef Elford-Alliyu, WBA to Bury; Rene Gilmartin, Watford to Plymouth Arg; Ashley Hemmings, Wolverhampton W to Walsall; Matt Mills, Leicester C to Bolton W; Steven Naismith, Rangers to Everton; Freddie Sears, West Ham U to Colchester U; Gylfi Sigurdsson, Hoffenheim to Tottenham H £8,000,000; Oliver Norburn, Leicester C to Bristol R; Aaron Wilbraham, Norwich C to Crystal Palace; Anthony Flood, Southend U to St Patrick's Ath. **July 5** Ben Alnwick, Tottenham H to Barnsley; Greg Cunningham, Manchester C to Bristol C; Stephen Darby, Liverpool to Bradford C; Fraser Forster, Newcastle U to Celtic £2,000,000; Kevin Kilbane, Hull C to Coventry C; Fabio Nunes, Portimonense to Blackburn R; Jon Otsemobor, Sheffield W to Milton Keynes D; Jason Shackell, Derby Co to Burnley £1,100,000; Joe McKee, Burnley to Bolton W; Sean Goss, Exeter C to Manchester U £100,000. **July 6** Gael Bigirimana, Coventry C to Newcastle U £1,000,000; Wayne Bridge, Manchester C to Brighton & HA (loan); Adam Clayton, Leeds U to Huddersfield T; Steven Davis, Rangers to Southampton; Denilson, Arsenal to Sao Paulo (loan); Jake Forster-Caskey, Brighton & HA to Oxford U (loan); Asamoah Gyan, Sunderland to Al Ain; Matthew Lowton, Sheffield U to Aston Villa £3,000,000; Nathaniel Mendez-Laing, Wolverhampton W to Peterborough U; Sascha Riether, Cologne to Fulham (loan); Pierce Sweeney, Bray W to Reading; Chris Weale, Leicester C to Shrewsbury T; Jonathan Woodgate, Stoke C to Middlesbrough. **July 7** Salomon Kalou, Chelsea to Lille. **July 9** Michael Bostwick, Stevenage to Peterborough U; Jake Caprice, Crystal Palace to Blackpool; Luke Chambers, Nottingham F to Ipswich T; Mark Connolly, Bolton W to Crawley T; Jordan Cook, Sunderland to Charlton Ath; Eldin Jakupovic, Aris to Hull C; Peter Lovenkrands, Newcastle U to Birmingham C; Park, Manchester U to QPR £2,000,000; Christian Ribeiro, Bristol C to Scunthorpe U; Lawrie Wilson, Stevenage to Charlton Ath. **July 10** Diogo Amado, Leiria to Sheffield W; Chico, Genoa to Swansea C £2,000,000; Jonathan de Guzman, Villarreal to Swansea C (loan); Gavin Hoyte, Arsenal to Dagenham & R; Emmanuel Ledesma, Walsall to Middlesbrough; David Lucas, Rochdale to Birmingham C; Nicky Shorey, WBA to Reading; Joao Silva, Everton to Levski; Alan Smith, Newcastle U to Milton Keynes D; Aaron Mokoena, Portsmouth to Bidvest Wits. **July 11** Yassine El Ghanassy, Gent to WBA (loan); Paddy Kenny, QPR to Leeds U; Joel Lynch, Nottingham F to Huddersfield T. **July 12** Miles Addison, Derby Co to Bournemouth; Yaser Kasim, Brighton & HA to Luton T (loan); Hayden Mullins, Portsmouth to Birmingham C; Etien Velikonja, Maribor to Cardiff C; Jan Vertonghen, Ajax to Tottenham H; Hugo Rodallega, Wigan Ath to Fulham. **July 13** Darren Ambrose, Crystal Palace to Birmingham C; Fabio Borini, Roma to Liverpool £10,500,000; John Cofie, Manchester U to Sheffield U (loan); Karleigh Osborne, Brentford to Millwall; Maxi Rodriguez, Liverpool to Newell's Old Boys. **July 14** Paul Coutts, Preston NE to Derby Co. **July 16** Florent Cuvelier, Stoke C to Walsall (loan); Fraser Fyvie, Aberdeen to Wigan Ath; Kenny Miller, Cardiff C to Vancouver Whitecaps; Clinton Morrison, Sheffield W to Colchester U; Nejc Pecnik, Nacional to Sheffield W. **July 17** Ryan Brunt, Stoke C to Leyton Orient (loan); Andrew Lonergan, Leeds U to Bolton W; Adrian Mariappa, Watford to Reading; Chris Gunter, Nottingham F to Reading; Bongani Khumalo, Tottenham H to PAOK Salonika (loan); Liam Palmer, Sheffield W to Tranmere R; Joe Mills, Reading to Burnley (loan). **July 18** Marko Futacs, Portsmouth to Leicester C; Nathan Clarke, Huddersfield T to Leyton Orient; Michael Liddle, Sunderland to Accrington S; Ryan Allsop, Millwall to Leyton Orient; Lee Hills, Crystal Palace to Stevenage; Modibo Maiga, Sochaux to West Ham U £4,700,000; Joseph Mills, Reading to Burnley (loan). **July 19** Nathaniel Clyne, Crystal Palace to Southampton; Callum Ball, Derby Co to Coventry C (loan); Richard Keogh, Coventry C to Derby Co; Scott Loach, Watford to Ipswich T; Nick Proschwitz, Paderborn to Hull C £2,600,000.

Johnstone's Paint Trophy
6 Sept 2011 Accrington amended goalscorer from Dunbavin to Amond.

FA Cup
28 Jan 2012 Swindon T substitute was Louis Thompson not Nathan Thompson.

Blackpool
Ground capacity is 16,220.

Crawley T
Director of Football: Steve Coppell.

Nottingham F
Manager: Sean O'Driscoll.

Watford
Additional appointments: Assistant Manager: Giancarlo Corradini; First Team Coach: Adolfo Sormani; Head of Medical: Marco Cesarini.